CASSELL'S

GERMAN–ENGLISH ENGLISH–GERMAN DICTIONARY

DEUTSCH–ENGLISCHES ENGLISCH–DEUTSCHES WÖRTERBUCH

Cassell's

German – English
English – German
Dictionary

Deutsch – Englisches
Englisch – Deutsches
Wörterbuch

Completely revised by

HAROLD T. BETTERIDGE,
M.A. (Birm.), Ph.D. (Lond.)
Formerly Senior Lecturer in German in the University of Glasgow

MACMILLAN PUBLISHING COMPANY
New York

Macmillan Publishing Company
866 Third Avenue, New York, N.Y. 10022

Completely revised and reset edition 1978

Library of Congress Cataloging in Publication Data
Betteridge, Harold T.
Cassell's German-English, English-German dictionary-Deutsch-englisches, englisch-deutsches
Wörterbuch.
1. German language–Dictionaries–English.
2. English language–Dictionaries–German.
I. Title. II. Title: Deutsch-englisches,
englisch-deutsches Wörterbuch.
PF3640.B453 1978 463'.21 77-18452

ISBN 0-02-522920-6 (standard)
ISBN 0-02-522930-3 (thumb-indexed)

15

Printed in the United States of America

Contents
Inhalt

Vorwort

Mit dieser umfassenden Bearbeitung des bewährten Nachschlagewerkes von Cassell liegt ein im wesentlichen neues Wörterbuch vor. Dieses Werk berücksichtigt die vielen, in den letzten Jahren neu aufgekommenen Wörter und Redewendungen. Jedem Stichwort ist eine phonetische Umschrift beigefügt worden, im englischen Teil auch in den Fällen, wo sich der Akzent verlagert.

Für jeden, der eine Fremdsprache lernt, sind zweisprachige Wörterbücher ein geradezu unentbehrliches Hilfsmittel, und um ihrem Zweck adäquat gerecht zu werden, müssen beide Teile in einem ausgewogenen Verhältnis zueinander stehen. Im deutsch-englischen Teil besteht die Hauptschwierigkeit in der Auswahl der nützlichsten Komposita aus den praktisch unbegrenzten Möglichkeiten, während es im englisch-deutschen Teil dagegen wichtiger ist, möglichst viele Beispiele idiomatischer Verwendung anzuführen.

Der Herausgeber schuldet Mr. A. E. Hammer, vormals Sedbergh School, besonderen Dank für eine Anzahl willkommener Hinweise und Anregungen. Auch möchte er den Kollegen an den Universitäten von Strathclyde und Heriot-Watt danken, sowie Miss Ingrid Paplavski, Bibliothekarin des Deutschen Instituts, London, die wertvolle Hilfe leisteten bei der Zusammenstellung der Listen vorhandener Spezialwörterbücher. H.T.B.

Preface

A virtually new dictionary has emerged from this comprehensive revision of Cassell's renowned German Dictionary. The present work takes account of the many new words and usages which have appeared in recent years. All head-words have been supplied with phonetic transcriptions and, in English, so have their derivatives whenever there is a change of stress.

For any foreign-language student bilingual dictionaries are an indispensable tool, and to serve their purpose properly the two halves of the dictionary must be equally balanced. In the German-English section the principal difficulty is the selection of the most useful compound forms from the virtually unlimited possibilities, while in the English-German half it is more important to give as many examples of idiomatic usage as possible.

The Editor owes a special debt of gratitude to Mr. A. E. Hammer, late of Sedbergh School, for his many welcome comments and suggestions. He would also like to thank his colleagues at the University of Strathclyde and Heriot-Watt University, and also Miss Ingrid Paplavski, Assistant Librarian at the German Institute, London, for their valuable help in compiling the list of available technical and specialist dictionaries. H.T.B.

Key to German Pronunciation

The standard description of German pronunciation is Siebs, *Deutsche Aussprache. Reine und gemäßigte Hochlautung mit Ausspracheworterbuch*, ed. H. de Boor, H. Moser and C. Winkler, Berlin, de Gruyter, 19th edition 1969 and, of course, as the invaluable arbiter in cases of doubt, *Duden: Ausspracheworterbuch*, Mannheim, Bibliographisches Institut, 1974. Among the most useful contributions in English are W. L. Wardale's brief and elementary *German Pronunciation*, Edinburgh University Press, 1955, J. Bithell's detailed and technical *German Pronunciation and Phonology*, Methuen, 1952 and, particularly in relation to American English, W. G. Moulton, *The Sounds of English and German*, Chicago University Press, 1962. No printed description of sounds, not even the above works, can teach pronunciation. All that can be attempted here is some explanation of the correspondence between German sounds and the orthographic conventions. Even those who are able, as it were, to 'play the notes' from phonetic notation cannot be sure that the result will appear satisfactory to a German. Not the eye, but the ear in league with the organs of speech can alone apprehend accent, pitch, rhythm, phrasing, intonation—and it is these subtler factors as much as the phonetic pronunciation of symbols that distinguish good speech from bad.

Where examples of a sound are given in both languages, it should not be assumed that the pronunciations are identical. In many cases the similarity is no more than approximate: notably, the lack of breath with German initial consonants is a point which cannot be treated briefly. In dealing with the letters *l* and *r* no attempt is made to distinguish between the characteristic English and German treatments of the sounds.

The first task is to distinguish long and short vowels. Briefly, a long vowel is one which could be prolonged indefinitely; a short vowel cannot be maintained without altering the quality of the sound. In phonetic transcription it is usual to indicate a vowel as long by following it with a colon [:]. German spelling goes some way, but not all the way, towards making this distinction apparent.

1. A vowel is short: (a) when followed by a double consonant, *e.g. lassen, schaffen, nennen, kommen, dumm, Wille*, or by *ck* (which has replaced *kk*), *e.g. hacken, Becken, dick, Rock, gucken*; (b) when followed by two or more consonants, *e.g. Abt, Amt, Land, sanft, Berg, Hilfe, Horn, Puls**; (c) when, contradicting 2 (c), it occurs in commonly used unstressed monosyllables, *e.g. man, das, bin, von, um*, and in some other words where it is followed by *ß*, *e.g. muß, Faß, Schloß***.

2. A vowel is long: (a) when doubled (*a, e, o* only), *e.g. Haar, Heer, Boot.* N.B. Instead of doubling, *i* becomes *ie*, *e.g. vier, studieren*; (b) when followed by mute *h*, *e.g. Bahn, Mehl, ihren, Bohne, Huhn, wählen, Söhne, führen.* N.B. In the case of *i*, there is even superfluous doubling when (b) is already satisfied,

e.g. sieht, Vieh; (c) usually when followed by a single consonant (including *ß*), *e.g. Tag, schwer, Lid, Hof, Ruf, Fuß*; (d) when in a stressed open syllable***, *e.g. ja, sagen, he!, geben, wider, wo, Ostern, Uhu, Muße*; (e) when among the exceptions mentioned in the footnote to 1 (b).

Further, it should be noted that the categoric distinction between long and short quantity in some vowels is not strictly scientific: emotive emphasis can apparently lengthen short vowels, the short, unemphatic forms of the definite article appear longer when used as demonstratives or relatives, and a following *r* or palatal consonant can have a lengthening effect. This applies especially to the *i* sounds. A more accurate account of the differences would indeed be that it is a change of quality between open and close vowels (*i.e.* more or less opening of the mouth) rather than change of quantity between long and short. Long vowels are normally close (*bieten*), and short vowels open (*bitten*), but the following consonant in *ich* makes the vowel more close than in *bin*. Similarly in the suffix *-lich* as compared with *Liste*, or the suffix *-ig*, as compared with *Ethik*.

* Compound consonants such as *ch, sch, tsch, ng* (that is, single consonantal sounds for which there exist no corresponding orthographic symbols) fail to give an unambiguous clue to the length of the preceding vowel, though this is in fact frequently short, *e.g. Bach, Wäsche, Fisch, singen, Frosch, Woche, Kutsche, Spruch.* See the tables below for examples of long vowels under this heading, as well as other exceptions from the general rule of following consonantal clusters as stated in 1 (b).

** For further examples of these exceptions to the general rule of 2 (c) see the tables below.

*** This must not be confused with an open vowel. An open syllable is one that is not closed by a terminal consonant. German syllable division is however different from English. Briefly, it may be said that, unless it is a monosyllabic word, a prefix such as *er-, emp-, ent-*, or a suffix such as *-ig, -isch, -ung*, a German syllable always has an initial consonant (here *ch, sch, st* are considered as single consonants.) Thus open syllables are illustrated in *tre/ten, nä/hen, fi/schen, Bü/cher, O/stern, Trau/ung, bö/ig.*

Vowels	**English**	**German**
[a:] long	father, half, harbour	Arzt, brach, Fraß, Gas, gehabt, Jagd, nach, Papst, sagt, saß
[a] short	(*Scots*) man	ab, ach, an, Bach, bald, Garten, hart, hast, Haß, Monat, naß, Walfisch, was
[ã] short, open, nasal	(*French*) en	(*only in loanwords*) arrangieren, Chance, Jean, Rouen
[ɛ:] long, open	—	Cäsar, Gemälde, Käse, Rätsel, Städte, Täler, Träne
[ɛ] short, open	—	Bett, brechen, hält, Härte, häßlich, heran, kräftig, Scherz
[ɛ̃] short, open, nasal	(*French*) vin	(*only in loanwords*) Bassin, Cousin, Teint
[e:] long, close	(*Scots*) say, cake, bait, Dane	bequem, Efeu, Ekel, er, Erde, ewig, Juwel, Pferd, stets, Dresden, Schleswig, Atelier
[e] short, close	very, head	(*in unstressed syllables*) genial, Medaille, Register, Theater; (*unemphatic*) der, den, dem, er
[ə] short, open	about, banana, bishop, collapse, common, honour, horror, mother, perhaps	Atem, Bauer, Handel, bekommen, Dame, Indien

Vowels	English	German *(cont.)*
[iː] long, close	be, see, beat, field	ihn, dir, Fiber, Nische, Stil, Medizin, Politik, naiv, Paris
[i] short, close	bit, hymn	*(in unstressed syllables)* Biologe, Idee, Kritik, Rivale, Spital, Tirol, zitieren
[ɪ] short, open	—	ich, Birke, Ethik, mischen, sitzen, selig
[ɔ] short, open	not, want	doch, floß, gehorchen, kosten, Bischof, Lexikon, Marmor, Pathos, Vorteil
[ɔ̃] short, open, nasal	*(French)* bon	*(only in loanwords)* Bonbon, Fasson, Salon
[oː] long, close	*(Scots)* hole, road	beobachten, Boden, Floß, hoch, Kloster, Mond, Obst, Ton, Atom, famos, Humor, Jod, Spion
[o] short, close	molest, obey	*(in unstressed syllables)* Auto, Photograph, Moral, sogleich; Fauteuil
[øː] long, close	*(more close than French)* émeute	böse, Goethe, Größe, höchst, öde, Öl, rösten, tödlich, graziös, Milieu, obszön, Redakteur
[ø] short, close	—	*(in unstressed syllables)* möblieren, Diözese
[œ] short, open	*(French)* œuf	Köche, löschen, Mönche, öfters, östlich, Wölfe
[uː] long, close	do, boot, soup, Luke	Buch, Geburt, genug, Gruß, Husten, nun, Ruß, Schuster, Tuch, Ursprung, Wuchs
[u] short, close	foot, pull, could	Busch, Druck, Genuß, Gurt, Spruch, Sturm, Urteil, Luther; Chirurg, Konsul, Purpur; Statue
[yː] long, close	*(French)* ruse	Bücher, düster, Füße, Kostüm, süß, Tür, Wüste; Asyl, Oxyd; Duisburg, Zypern
[y] short, open	—	Bürde, Büste, Küche, Küste, Mütze Budget, Mystik

Diphthongs	English	German
[aɪ]	my, wife, high	Bein, Seite; Kaiser, Mai, Saite
[au]	house, how, bough	Haus, Mauer, rauh
[ɔy]	boy, noise, royal	feudal, Leute, treu, Zeus; Häuser, läuten
[uɪ]	—	pfui!

Consonants

The sounds represented by the symbols [b], [d], [f], [g], [h], [k], [m], [n], [p], [s], [ʃ], [ʒ], [t], [tʃ] and [v] are more or less the same in both languages. Where these are cited below, it is merely to illustrate the variety of orthographic conventions which represent these sounds.

Consonants	English	German
[ç]	*as in whispered* 'huge', *or* 'yes' *in a prolonged forced whisper*	1. *ch* after *ä, e, i, ö, ü, ei, eu, äu*: Nächte, spreche, ich, Löcher, Bücher, Eiche, euch, räuchern 2. *ch* after consonants: manch, Milch, durch 3. in suffix *-chen*: bißchen, Mädchen 4. in suffix *-ig*: ewig, König 5. initially in some loanwords: Chemie, China
[x]	*(Scots)* loch	*ch* after *a, o, u, au*: Dach, Loch, Buch, auch
[f]	full, phone, rough	Feder, Philosophie, vier
[ʒ]	measure, garage	Genie, Loge, Regie; Giro
[dʒ]	just, German, ridge	Dschungel, Adagio
[ŋ]	hanging, thing	Angst, eng, England, Finger, hängen, langsam
[ŋg]	finger	Languste, Ungarn
[ŋk]	sink	Anker, Dank, links
[ʃ]	she, sugar, session, ration, special	Asche, schön, Spitze, stehen
[ts]	hats	trotz, Zaun, Nation
[tʃ]	chin, patch, mixture	deutsch, Patsche
[v]	van, vine, gravy, of	wann, ewig, zwei; nervös, Sklave, Venus
[j]	yes, battalion	ja, Jahr, Jesus; [lj] Bastille, Billard, Brillant
[z]	his, faces, zone	sehen, Soße, Wiese, Schicksal, Person, Salat, System; Gaze

In the phonetic transcription the stress-mark ['] precedes the syllable carrying the stress. The indication of the glottal stop in German [ˀ] is only used sparingly (far more sparingly than strict phonetic requirements would demand), but sufficiently, it is hoped, to avoid the worst examples of careless speech.

German Irregular Verbs

INCLUDING ALL VERBS OF THE STRONG CONJUGATION AS WELL AS THOSE OF THE WEAK WHICH ARE CONJUGATED IN ANY WAY IRREGULARLY.

* Plural imperative corresponds in form to the 3rd person present indicative unless otherwise stated.
† The past participle of the six modal auxiliaries is replaced by its infinitive in compound tenses when immediately preceded by an infinitive; this is also the case with *lassen* used as an auxiliary, as well as with *heißen, helfen, hören, lehren, lernen, sehen.*
Letters enclosed in parentheses may be included or omitted.
For compounds with *be-*, *ent-*, *er-*, *ge-*, *miß-*, *ver-*, *voll-*, *zer-*, and certain other prefixes see the simple verbs where not otherwise given.
For an explanation of the forms as they have been historically determined, cf. J. van Dam, *Handbuch der deutschen Sprache* (Groningen, 1951), II, 57–89.

Infinitive	Present Indicative	Imperfect Indicative	Imperfect Subjunctive	*Imperative	Past Participle
backen[1]	2 bäckst[2] 3 bäckt[2]	backte, buk[3]	backte, büke[3]	S backe! P backt!	gebacken[4]
befehlen	2 befiehlst 3 befiehlt	befahl	beföhle[5]	S befiehl! P befehlt!	befohlen
(sich) befleißen[6]	2 befleiß(es)t 3 befleißt	befliß	beflisse	S befleiß(e)! P befleißt!	beflissen
beginnen	2 beginnst 3 beginnt	begann	begönne[7]	beginn(e)!	begonnen
beißen	2 beiß(es)t 3 beißt	biß	bisse	beiß(e)!	gebissen
bellen[8]	1 billst 3 billt	boll	—	—	gebollen
bergen[9]	2 birgst 3 birgt	barg	bürge[10]	S birg! P bergt!	geborgen
bersten	2 birst, berstest 3 birst, berstet	barst[11]	börste[11]	S birst! P berstet!	geborsten
bewegen[12]	2 bewegst 3 bewegt	bewog	bewöge	beweg(e)!	bewogen
biegen	2 biegst 3 biegt	bog	böge	bieg(e)!	gebogen
bieten[13]	2 biet(e)st[14] 3 bietet[14]	bot	böte	biet(e)![14]	geboten
binden	2 bindest 3 bindet	band	bände	bind(e)!	gebunden
bitten	2 bittest 3 bittet	bat	bäte	bitte!	gebeten
blasen	2 bläs(es)t[15] 3 bläst[15]	blies	bliese	S blas(e)! P blast!	geblasen
bleiben	2 bleibst 3 bleibt	blieb	bliebe	bleib(e)!	geblieben
bleichen[16]	—	—	—	—	—
braten	2 brätst[17] 3 brät[17]	briet[18]	briete	S brat(e)! P bratet!	gebraten
brechen[19]	2 brichst[20] 3 bricht[20]	brach	bräche	S brich! P brecht!	gebrochen
brennen	2 brennst 3 brennt	brannte	brennte	brenne!	gebrannt
bringen	2 bringst 3 bringt	brachte	brächte	bring(e)!	gebracht
denken	2 denkst 3 denkt	dachte	dächte	denk(e)!	gedacht

1 Weak = 'clot', 'stick to', e.g. *festgebackt.*
2 Sometimes *backst, backt.*
3 Strong forms are Southern German or archaic.
4 But *altbacken, hausbacken.*
5 Less usual *befähle.*
6 Rare, now usually weak *sich befleißigen.* Strong past participle as adj. still used, as *dienstbeflissen.*
7 Less usual *begänne.*
8 Obsolete forms listed found till circa 1800.
9 Also *verbergen.*
10 Less usual *bärge.*
11 Less usual *borst, bärste*; weak forms are rare.
12 = 'induce someone to do something'. In the commoner meaning 'move', both physically and metaphorically, it is weak.
13 Also *gebieten, verbieten.*
14 Archaic *beutst, beut, beut!*
15 *blas(es)t, blast* also occur, but are rare.
16 Archaic = 'fade', 'grow pale'; see *erbleichen.* Transitive = 'bleach' is weak.
17 Occasionally *bratest, bratet.*
18 Occasionally weak *bratete.*
19 Weak as technical term with flax; *radebrechen* also weak; *ehebrechen* as compound verb only in infinitive and present participle; otherwise noun *Ehe* with normal verb *brechen.*
20 But *radebrechst, radebrecht.*

Infinitive	Present Indicative	Imperfect Indicative	Imperfect Subjunctive	*Imperative	Past Participle
dingen[21]	2 dingst 3 dingt	dang	dingte[22]	ding(e)!	gedungen, gedingt
dreschen	2 drisch(e)st 3 drischt	drosch[23]	drösche[24]	S drisch! P drescht!	gedroschen
dringen	2 dringst 3 dringt	drang	dränge	dring(e)!	gedrungen
dünken (*imp.*)	(mich *or* mir) dünkt	dünkte, deuchte	dünkte, deuchte	—	gedünkt, gedeucht
dürfen	S 1 & 3 darf 2 darfst	durfte	dürfte		†gedurft
erbleichen	2 erbleichst 3 erbleicht	erbleichte, erblich	erbleichte, erbliche	erbleiche!	erbleicht[25] erblichen[26]
erlöschen[27]	2 erlisch(e)st 3 erlischt	erlosch	erlösche	S erlisch! P erlöscht!	erloschen
erschrecken[28]	2 erschrickst 3 erschrickt	erschrak	erschräke	S erschrick! P erschrickt!	erschrocken
essen	2 ißt, issest 3 ißt	1, 3 aß 2 aßest	äße	S iß! P eßt!	gegessen[29]
fahren	2 fährst 3 fährt	fuhr	führe	S fahr(e)! P fahrt!	gefahren
fallen	2 fällst 3 fällt	fiel	fiele	S fall(e)! P fallt!	gefallen
falten[30]	—	—	—	—	—
fangen	2 fängst 3 fängt	fing	finge	S fang(e)! P fangt!	gefangen
fechten	2 ficht(e)st[31] 3 ficht[31]	focht	föchte	S ficht! P fechtet!	gefochten
finden	2 findest 3 findet	fand	fände	find(e)!	gefunden
flechten	2 flicht(e)st[32] 3 flicht[32]	flocht	flöchte	S flicht! P flechtet!	geflochten
fliegen	2 fliegst[33] 3 fliegt[33]	flog	flöge	flieg(e)![33]	geflogen
fliehen	2 fliehst[34] 3 flieht[34]	floh	flöhe	flieh(e)![34]	geflohen
fließen	2 fließ(es)t[35] 3 fließt[35]	floß	flösse	fließ(e)![35]	geflossen
fragen[36]	—	—	—	—	—
fressen	2 frißt, frissest 3 frißt	fraß	fräße	S friß! P freßt!	gefressen
frieren	2 frierst 3 friert	fror	fröre	frier(e)!	gefroren
gären[37]	2 gärst 3 gärt	gor[38]	göre[38]	gäre!	gegoren[38]
gebären	2 gebierst[39] 3 gebiert[39]	gebar	gebäre	S gebier! P gebärt!	geboren
geben	2 gibst[40] 3 gibt[40]	gab	gäbe	S gib! P gebt!	gegeben
gedeihen	2 gedeihst 3 gedeiht	gedieh	gediehe	gedeih(e)!	gediehen[41]
gehen[42]	2 gehst 3 geht	ging	ginge	geh(e)!	gegangen
gelingen (*imp.*)	3 (mir) gelingt	gelang	gelänge	geling(e)!	gelungen
gelten	2 giltst 3 gilt	galt	gölte[43]	S gilt! P geltet!	gegolten
genesen	2 genes(es)t 3 genest	genas	genäse	genese!	genesen

21 Also weak; *bedingen* = *dingen* is strong, but commoner meaning = 'condition' is weak.

22 Dialect also *dänge, dünge.*

23 This originally dialect form has, in spite of what Duden said earlier, now ousted the proper form *drasch* (with long *a*).

24 Dialect *dräsche* (with long *ä*).

25 = 'grown pale'.

26 = 'died'.

27 Intransitive = 'become extinguished'; similarly *auslöschen, verlöschen*; *(aus)löschen* as transitive is weak.

28 Intransitive = 'be afraid'. Transitive = 'frighten' is weak. N.B. *erschrecken* = 'frightened', 'afraid'; *erschreckt* = 'scared', 'startled'.

29 P.p. prefix originally elided with stem as *gessen*; prefix re-added subsequently.

30 Weak, except rarely in the past participle; *gefalten* particularly as adj.

31 Weak forms *fechtest, fechtet* rare.

32 Weak forms *flechtest, flechtet* rare.

33 Archaic *fleugst, fleugt, fleug!* still used in *was da kreucht und fleugt.*

34 Archaic *fleuchst, fleucht, fleuch!*

35 Archaic *fleußt, fleußt, fleuß!*

36 *frägst, frägt; frug; früge* are not properly speaking dialectal. Still used in North Germany due to misunderstanding of High German conjugation by Low German speakers.

37 Always weak when used figuratively, e.g. *es gärte im Volk.*

38 Weak forms *gärte, gärte, gegärt,* also sometimes used with literal meaning.

39 Weak forms *gebärst, gebärt* also found.

40 *ie* for *i* is archaic.

41 N.B. corresponding adj. *gediegen.*

42 Obsolete verb *gangen* survives in present and imperative in South German dialect, e.g. *jetzt gang i ans Brünnele.*

43 Less usual *gälte.*

Infinitive	Present Indicative	Imperfect Indicative	Imperfect Subjunctive	*Imperative	Past Participle
genießen	2 genieß(es)t 3 genießt	genoß	genösse	genieß(e)!	genossen
geschehen (*imp.*)	3 (mir) geschieht	geschah	geschähe	—	geschehen
gewinnen	2 gewinnst 3 gewinnt	gewann	gewönne[44]	gewinn(e)!	gewonnen
gießen	2 gieß(es)t[45] 3 gießt[45]	goß	gösse	gieß(e)![45]	gegossen
gleichen[46]	2 gleichst 3 gleicht	glich	gliche	gleich(e)!	geglichen
gleiten	2 gleit(e)st 3 gleitet	glitt[47]	glitte	gleit(e)!	geglitten[47]
glimmen	2 glimmst 3 glimmt	glomm[48]	glömme[48]	glimm(e)!	geglommen[48]
graben	2 gräbst 3 gräbt	grub	grübe	S grab(e)! P grabt!	gegraben
greifen	2 greifst 3 greift	griff	griffe	greif(e)!	gegriffen
haben	2 hast 3 hat	hatte	hätte	S hab(e)! P habt!	gehabt
halten	2 hältst 3 hält	hielt	hielte	S halt(e)! P haltet!	gehalten
hangen[49]	2 hängst 3 hängt	hing	hinge	häng(e)!	gehangen
hauen[50]	2 haust 3 haut	hieb[51]	hiebe	hau(e)!	gehauen[52]
heben	2 hebst 3 hebt	hob[53]	höbe[53]	hebe!	gehoben
heißen	2 heiß(es)t 3 heißt	hieß	hieße	heiß(e)!	†geheißen[54]
helfen	2 hilfst 3 hilft	half	hülfe[55]	S hilf! P helft!	†geholfen
keifen[56]	—	—	—	—	—
kennen	2 kennst 3 kennt	kannte	kennte	kenn(e)!	gekannt
kiesen[57] (*see* küren)	2 kies(es)t 3 kiest	kor	köre	kies(e)!	gekoren
klieben[58]	2 kliebst 3 kliebt	klob	klöbe	klieb(e)!	gekloben
klimmen[59]	2 klimmst 3 klimmt	klomm	klömme	klimm(e)!	geklommen
klingen	2 klingst 3 klingt	klang	klänge	kling(e)!	geklungen
kneifen[60]	2 kneifst 3 kneift	kniff[61]	kniffe[61]	kneif(e)!	gekniffen[61]
kommen	2 kommst[62] 3 kommt[62]	kam	käme	S komm(e)! P kommt!	gekommen
können	1 & 3 kann 2 kannst	konnte	könnte	—	†gekonnt

44 Less usual *gewänne.*
45 Archaic and poetic *geußest, geußt, geuß!*
46 Weak forms used until 18th century.
47 Weak forms are archaic. (N.B. *begleiten* is derived from *leiten*, and is weak.)
48 Also weak.
49 Properly speaking this is intransitive, but in the present indicative and imperative the forms of the weak transitive verb *hängen* have practically replaced the correct forms both in literal and figurative usage and also in compounds. The confusion goes even further in less educated speech: both infinitives *hangen* and *hängen* and imperfect *hing* are used transitively or intransitively; imperfect *hängte* only transitively, past participle *gehängt* only transitive; *gehangen* only intransitive, except in the proverb *mitgefangen, mitgehangen*; *abhängen* = 'be dependent on' is strong, weak when transitive and literal, and also when intransitive of telephone; *anhängen* strong as intransitive, weak as transitive*; einhängen* weak; *nachhangen* and *nachhängen* usually strong; *verhängen* usually weak; *zusammenhängen* weak in literal meaning, strong figuratively.
50 Colloquial *sich hauen, abhauen, sich verhauen,* always weak in imperfect.
51 Often *haute*; and always when = 'spank' or = 'chop' (wood).
52 Only in the North and South-West; *gehaut* always in Bavaria and Austria.
53 Poetic *hub, hübe*, especially in *anheben.*
54 *gehießen* in vulgar speech.
55 Less usual *hälfe.*
56 Normally weak, but strong forms *kiff, kiffe, gekiffen* in Bohemian dialect.
57 Archaic and poetic. Past participle (*aus*)*erkoren* still used. Weak forms of *erkiesen* are found. Weak *kiesen* = 'strew pebbles'.
58 Elevated style; weak forms also found.
59 Weak forms also found. N.B. adjective *beklommen* derived from an obsolete verb.
60 Dialect form *kneipen* = 'pinch', and always with the meaning 'carouse' is weak.
61 Weak forms also occur.
62 Archaic and dialect *kömmst, kömmt.*

Infinitive	Present Indicative	Imperfect Indicative	Imperfect Subjunctive	*Imperative	Past Participle
kreischen[63]	—	—	—	—	—
kriechen	2 kriechst[64] 3 kriecht[64]	kroch	kröche	kriech(e)![64]	gekrochen
küren[65] (*see* kiesen)	2 kürst 3 kürt	kürte, kor	kür(e)te, köre	kür(e)!	gekoren
laden[66]	2 lädst 3 lädt	lud	lüde	S lad(e)! P ladet!	geladen
laden[67]	2 ladest, lädst 3 ladet, lädt	lud[68]	lüde[68]	lad(e)!	geladen
lassen[69]	2 läßt, lässest 3 läßt	ließ	ließe	S laß! lasse! P laßt!	†gelassen
laufen	2 läufst[70] 3 läuft[70]	lief	liefe	S lauf(e)! P lauft!	gelaufen
leiden[71]	2 leidest 3 leidet	litt	litte	leid(e)!	gelitten
leihen	2 leihst 3 leiht	lieh	liehe	leih(e)!	geliehen
lesen	2 lies(es)t 3 liest	las	läse	S lies! P lest!	gelesen
liegen	2 liegst 3 liegt	lag	läge	lieg(e)!	gelegen
löschen[72]	(*see* erlöschen)	—	—	—	—
lügen	2 lügst[73] 3 lügt[73]	log	löge	lüg(e)!	gelogen
mahlen[74]	—	—	—	—	gemahlen
meiden[75]	2 meidest 3 meidet	mied	miede	meid(e)!	gemieden
melken	2 melkst, milkst[76] 3 melkt, milkt[76]	melkte, molk[77]	melkte, mölke[77]	melk(e)! milk![76]	gemelkt, gemolken[77]
messen	2 mißt, missest 3 mißt	maß	mäße	S miß! P meßt!	gemessen
mißlingen (*imp.*)	3 (mir) mißlingt	mißlang	mißlänge	—	mißlungen
mögen	1 & 3 mag 2 magst	mochte	möchte	—	†gemocht
müssen	1 & 3 muß 2 mußt	mußte	müßte	—	†gemußt
nehmen	2 nimmst 3 nimmt	nahm	nähme	S nimm! P nehmt!	genommen
nennen	2 nennst 3 nennt	nannte	nennte	nenn(e)!	genannt
pfeifen	2 pfeifst 3 pfeift	pfiff	pfiffe	pfeif(e)!	gepfiffen
pflegen[78]	—	pflog	pflöge	—	gepflogen
preisen[79]	2 preis(es)t 3 preist	pries	priese	preis(e)!	gepriesen
quellen[80]	2 quillst[81] 3 quillt	quoll	quölle	S quill! P quellt!	gequollen
rächen	—	—	—	—	gerochen[82]
raten	2 rätst[83] 3 rät[83]	riet	riete	S rat(e)! P ratet!	geraten
reiben	2 reibst 3 reibt	rieb	riebe	reib(e)!	gerieben
reißen	2 reiß(es)t 3 reißt	riß	risse	reiß(e)!	gerissen
reiten	2 reit(e)st 3 reitet	ritt	ritte	reit(e)!	geritten
rennen	2 rennst 3 rennt	rannte	rennte	renn(e)!	gerannt

63 Normally weak; strong forms *krisch, krische, gekrischen* are rare.
64 Archaic *kreuchst, kreucht, kreuch!* See also Note 33.
65 Archaic and poetic. Originally weak, it has assimilated the forms of *kiesen*; *erküren* is commoner than *küren*.
66 = *aufladen* ('load').
67 = *einladen* ('invite'). Originally weak, it has assimilated the forms of the strong verb *laden*.
68 Rarely weak *ladete, ladete*.
69 N.B. *veranlassen* is weak.
70 *Laufst, lauft* Bavarian and Austrian dialect.
71 N.B. *verleiden* is weak.
72 Rare as intransitive. Transitive *löschen* ('quench') is weak.
73 Archaic *leugst, leugt* found till circa 1800.
74 Weak except past participle.
75 Poetic style; usually *vermeiden*.
76 *milkst, milkt, milk!* less usual.
77 Weak forms more usual than strong, though past participle as adj. always *gemolken*.
78 Normally weak. Archaic strong forms listed occur only in certain stock phrases: *Ruhe pflegen, Umgang pflegen* etc.
79 Uncertainty with *lobpreisen*: *lobpries* or *lobpreiste*; *gelobpreisen* or *lobgepriesen*.
80 Causative transitive verb is weak.
81 1st persons singular *quille*, and plural *quillen* of present tense occur sometimes as survivals of archaic intransitive *quillen*.
82 Poetic survival of obsolete strong form.
83 N.B. the following stock phrases: *du ratest und tatest*; *er ratet und tatet*; and *wer nicht mitratet, auch nicht mittatet*; *wer will mitraten, soll auch mittaten*.

Infinitive	Present Indicative	Imperfect Indicative	Imperfect Subjective	*Imperative	Past Participle
riechen	2 riechst 3 riecht	roch	röche	riech(e)!	gerochen
ringen[84]	2 ringst 3 ringt	rang	ränge	ring(e)!	gerungen
rinnen	2 rinnst 3 rinnt	rann	rönne[85]	rinn(e)!	geronnen
rufen	2 rufst 3 ruft	rief[86]	riefe[86]	ruf(e)!	gerufen[86]
salzen[87]	—	—	—	—	gesalzt *or* gesalzen
saufen	2 säufst[88] 3 säuft[88]	soff	söffe	sauf(e)!	gesoffen
saugen	2 saugst 3 saugt	sog[89]	söge	saug(e)!	gesogen[90]
schaffen[91]	2 schaffst 3 schafft	schuf	schüfe	schaff(e)!	geschaffen
schallen[92]	2 schallst 3 schallt	schallte, scholl	schallte, schölle	schall(e)!	geschallt[93]
scheiden	2 scheidest 3 scheidet	schied	schiede	scheid(e)!	geschieden
scheinen	2 scheinst 3 scheint	schien	schiene	schein(e)!	geschienen
scheißen	2 scheiß(es)t 3 scheißt	schiß	schisse	scheiß(e)!	geschissen
schelten	2 schiltst 3 schilt	schalt[94]	schölte[94]	S schilt![95] schelte! P scheltet!	gescholten
scheren[96]	2 schierst, scherst 3 schiert, schert	schor	schöre	schier! scher(e)!	geschoren
schieben	2 schiebst 3 schiebt	schob	schöbe	schieb(e)!	geschoben
schießen	2 schieß(es)t 3 schießt	schoß	schösse	schieß(e)!	geschossen
schinden	2 schind(e)st 3 schindet	schund[97]	schünde	schind(e)!	geschunden
schlafen	2 schläfst 3 schläft	schlief	schliefe	schlaf(e)!	geschlafen
schlagen	2 schlägst 3 schlägt	schlug	schlüge	schlag(e)!	geschlagen
schleichen	2 schleichst 3 schleicht	schlich	schliche	schleich(e)!	geschlichen
schleifen[98]	2 schleifst 3 schleift	schliff	schliffe	schleif(e)!	geschliffen
schleißen[99]	2 schleiß(es)t 3 schleißt	schliß	schlisse	schleiß(e)!	geschlissen
schliefen[100]	2 schliefst 3 schlieft	schloff	schlöffe	schlief(e)!	geschloffen
schließen	2 schließ(es)t[101] 3 schließt[101]	schloß	schlösse	schließ(e)![101]	geschlossen
schlingen	2 schlingst 3 schlingt	schlang	schlänge	schling(e)!	geschlungen
schmeißen	2 schmeiß(es)t 3 schmeißt	schmiß	schmisse	schmeiß(e)!	geschmissen
schmelzen[102]	2 schmilz(es)t 3 schmilzt	schmolz	schmölze	S schmilz! P schmelzt!	geschmolzen

84 = 'struggle'. Weak only when = 'wrestle'. Causative *ringen* (from *Ring*) is weak.
85 Less usual *ränne.*
86 Weak forms are archaic.
87 Weak except past participle; *gesalzen* always when figurative, e.g. *gesalzene Preise* or *Witze,* but also literally *versalzen.*
88 Sometimes also *saufst, sauft.*
89 Archaic also *saugte.*
90 Technical usage also *gesaugt.*
91 Strong only when = *erschaffen* ('create'); weak when = 'do', 'be busy', and in compounds, as *wegschaffen.*
92 *schallen* rare, usually *erschallen.* Weak forms commoner in imperfect.
93 *erschollen* in elevated style, normal word would be *verklungen*; *verschollen* as adj.
94 Austrian dialect *scholt, schölte.*
95 Weak imperative commoner.
96 Strong when = 'cut', but present and imperative even here often weak. Colloquial = 'bother about' and reflexive = 'clear off' imperfect and past participle always weak, though present and imperative often strong; *bescheren* strong = 'cut', weak = 'bestow'.
97 Imperfect generally weak *schindete*; rarely also *schand.*
98 Strong = 'grind', 'polish', and Austrian = 'slide'; weak = 'drag', 'dismantle'.
99 Rare. Originally two verbs: intransitive = 'wear out' always strong; transitive = 'slit' either strong or weak. From the latter the intransitive or reflexive *verschleißen* and intransitive *zerschleißen* are strong. Austrian *verschleißen* = 'retail' is weak.
100 South German dialect.
101 Archaic *schleußest, schleußt, schleuß!*
102 Intransitive. Causative transitive is properly weak, though strong forms sometimes in imperfect and past participle.

Infinitive	Present Indicative	Imperfect Indicative	Imperfect Subjective	*Imperative	Past Participle
schnauben[103]	2 schnaubst[104] 3 schnaubt[104]	—	—	—	—
schneiden	2 schneid(e)st 3 schneidet	schnitt	schnitte	schneid(e)!	geschnitten
schrauben[105]	—	—	—	—	—
schrecken[106]	2 schrickst 3 schrickt	schrak	schräke	S schrick! P schreckt!	geschrocken
schreiben	2 schreibst 3 schreibt	schrieb	schriebe	schreib(e)!	geschrieben
schreien	2 schrei(e)st 3 schreit	schrie	schriee	schrei(e)!	geschrie(e)n
schreiten	2 schreit(e)st 3 schreitet	schritt	schritte	schreit(e)!	geschritten
schrinden[107]	2 schrind(e)st 3 schrindet	schrund, schrand	schründe	schrind(e)!	geschrunden
schroten[108]	—	—	—	—	—
schwären[109]	3 schwärt[110]	schwor[111]	schwöre[111]	S schwär(e)![110] P schwär(e)t!	geschworen[111]
schweigen[112]	2 schweigst 3 schweigt	schwieg	schwiege	schweig(e)!	geschwiegen
schwellen[113]	2 schwillst 3 schwillt	schwoll	schwölle	S schwill! P schwellt!	geschwollen
schwimmen	2 schwimmst 3 schwimmt	schwamm	schwömme[114]	schwimm(e)!	geschwommen
schwinden	2 schwindest 3 schwindet	schwand[115]	schwände	schwind(e)!	geschwunden
schwingen[116]	2 schwingst 3 schwingt	schwang[117]	schwänge	schwing(e)!	geschwungen
schwören	2 schwörst 3 schwört	schwur[118]	schwüre	schwör(e)!	geschworen
sehen	2 siehst 3 sieht	sah	sähe	S sieh![119] P seht!	†gesehen
sein	S I bin 2 bist 3 ist P I sind 2 seid 3 sind	war	wäre	S sei! P seid!	gewesen
senden	2 sendest 3 sendet	sandte[120] sendete[120]	sendete	send(e)!	gesandt[120] gesendet[120]
sieden	2 siedest 3 siedet	sott[121]	sötte[121]	sied(e)!	gesotten[121]
singen	2 singst 3 singt	sang	sänge	sing(e)!	gesungen
sinken	2 sinkst 3 sinkt	sank	sänke	sink(e)!	gesunken
sinnen	2 sinnst 3 sinnt	sann	sönne[122]	sinn(e)!	gesonnen[123]
sitzen	2 sitz(es)t 3 sitzt	saß	säße	sitz(e)!	gesessen
sollen	I & 3 soll 2 sollst	sollte	sollte	—	†gesollt
spalten[124]	—	—	—	—	gespalten

103 Normally weak; strong forms *schnob, schnöbe, geschnoben* are rare.
104 Archaic *schneubst, schneubt* or *schnäubst, schnäubt.*
105 Normally weak; *schrob, schröbe, geschroben* are rare. Figuratively past participle (= 'stilted', 'affected') always *geschraubt,* but *verschraubt* (= 'tortuous'), *verschroben* (= 'crack-brained', 'eccentric').
106 Intransitive strong verb now rare, replaced by *erschrecken*; past participle used in compounds as *zusammengeschrocken.* Transitive *schrecken* is weak.
107 Rare. Still lives in past participle as adj.
108 Rare except in technical usage, and weak except when *geschroten* is used as adj.
109 Usually impersonal.
110 Archaic *schwiert, schwier!*
111 Sometimes weak when figurative.
112 Intransitive = 'be silent'. Causative transitive = 'silence' is weak.
113 Intransitive. Causative transitive is weak, though often the forms are confused.
114 Less usual *schwämme.*
115 Archaic *schwund.*
116 Causative *beschwingen* weak.
117 Archaic *schwung.*
118 Less usual *schwor*; but compound *beschwor.*
119 As exclamation (interjection) *siehe!* Also the author's *siehe Seite 20!*
120 Weak forms are less usual, except in technical sense (= 'broadcast', 'transmit') where they alone are correct. As adj. the past participle is always strong (N.B. *der Gesandte*); also compounds, as *einsenden, versenden,* are usually strong.
121 Also weak, particularly figuratively, e.g. *er siedete vor Wut.*
122 Sometimes *sänne.*
123 = 'have the intention'; participle as adj. *gesinnt* (from *Sinn*) = 'be of the opinion'.
124 Weak except past participle, where strong form is usual; as adj. always strong. Weak past participle particularly in technical usage.

Infinitive	Present Indicative	Imperfect Indicative	Imperfect Subjunctive	*Imperative	Past Participle
speien	2 speist 3 speit	spie	spie(e)	spei(e)!	gespie(e)n
spinnen	2 spinnst 3 spinnt	spann	spönne[125]	spinn(e)!	gesponnen
spleißen[126]	2 spleiß(es)t 3 spleißt	spliß	splisse	spleiß(e)!	gesplissen
sprechen	2 sprichst 3 spricht	sprach	spräche	S sprich! P sprecht!	gesprochen
sprießen	2 sprieß(es)t 3 sprießt	sproß[127]	sprösse[127]	sprieß(e)!	gesprossen[127]
springen	2 springst 3 springt	sprang	spränge	spring(e)!	gesprungen
stechen	2 stichst 3 sticht	stach	stäche	S stich! P stecht!	gestochen
stecken[128]	2 steckst 3 steckt	steckte, stak	steckte, stäke	steck(e)!	gesteckt
steh(e)n	2 stehst 3 steht	stand[129]	stünde[130] stände[130]	steh(e)!	gestanden
stehlen	2 stiehlst 3 stiehlt	stahl	stöhle[131]	S stiehl! P stehlt!	gestohlen
steigen	2 steigst 3 steigt	stieg	stiege	steig(e)!	gestiegen
sterben	2 stirbst 3 stirbt	starb	stürbe[132]	S stirb! P sterbt!	gestorben
stieben[133]	2 stiebst 3 stiebt	stob	stöbe	stieb(e)!	gestoben
stinken	2 stinkst 3 stinkt	stank	stänke	stink(e)!	gestunken
stoßen	2 stöß(es)t 3 stößt	stieß	stieße	S stoß(e)! P stoßt!	gestoßen
streichen	2 streichst 3 streicht	strich	striche	streich(e)!	gestrichen
streiten	2 streit(e)st 3 streitet	stritt	stritte	streit(e)!	gestritten
tragen	2 trägst 3 trägt	trug	trüge	S trag(e)! P tragt!	getragen
treffen	2 triffst 3 trifft	traf	träfe	S triff! P trefft!	getroffen
treiben	2 treibst 3 treibt	trieb	triebe	treib(e)!	getrieben
treten	2 trittst 3 tritt	trat	träte	S tritt![134] P tretet!	getreten
triefen[135]	2 triefst 3 trieft	troff	tröffe	trief(e)!	getroffen
trinken	2 trinkst 3 trinkt	trank	tränke	trink(e)!	getrunken[136]
trügen[137]	2 trügst 3 trügt	trog	tröge	trüg(e)!	getrogen
tun	S 1 tue, 2 tust, 3 tut P 1 & 3 tun 2 tut	tat P 1 & 3 taten[138]	täte	tu(e)!	getan
verderben[139]	2 verdirbst 3 verdirbt	verdarb	verdürbe	S verdirb! P verderbt!	verdorben
verdrießen	2 verdrieß(es)t 3 verdrießt	verdroß	verdrösse	verdrieß(e)!	verdrossen
vergessen	2 vergißt, vergissest 3 vergißt	vergaß	vergäße	S vergiß! P vergeßt!	vergessen
verhehlen[140]	—	—	—	—	—

125 *spänne* considered incorrect by grammarians, but found nevertheless.
126 Rare except nautically, where normally weak.
127 Weak forms are rare.
128 Intransitive = 'stick fast', and colloquially 'be in a place'; weak forms commoner; strong past participle completely dead. Transitive verb is weak.
129 Archaic and dialect *stund.*
130 *stünde* commoner.
131 Less usual *stähle.*
132 Archaic *stärbe.*
133 Rare except in compound *zerstieben.* Weak forms of simple verb also found.
134 Sometimes *trete!*
135 Weak forms found, mainly with past participle to avoid confusion with *treffen.*
136 Archaic *trunken* still used as adj.
137 Compound *betrügen* is commoner.
138 Archaic *täten* as auxiliary with infinitive.
139 Originally two verbs, strong intransitive (= 'become spoiled') and weak transitive (= 'spoil'). Latter is archaic except past participle *verderbt* (= 'depraved'). Strong form has taken over both functions.
140 Weak except *verhohlen* as (usually negative) adj.

Infinitive	Present Indicative	Imperfect Indicative	Imperfect Subjunctive	*Imperative	Past Participle
verlieren	2 verlierst 3 verliert	verlor	verlöre	verlier(e)!	verloren
verwirren[141]	—	—	—	—	verworren
wachsen[142]	2 wächs(es)t 3 wächst	wuchs[143]	wüchse[143]	S wachs(e)! P wachst!	gewachsen
wägen[144]	2 wägst 3 wägt	wog[145]	wöge[145]	wäg(e)!	gewogen
waschen	2 wäsch(es)t 3 wäscht	wusch[146]	wüsche[146]	S wasch(e)! P wascht!	gewaschen
weben[147]	2 webst 3 webt	webte, wob	webte, wöbe	web(e)!	gewebt, gewoben
weichen[148]	2 weichst 3 weicht	wich	wiche	weich(e)!	gewichen
weisen[149]	2 weis(es)t 3 weist	wies	wiese	weis(e)!	gewiesen
wenden	2 wendest 3 wendet	wandte,[150] wendete[150]	wendete	wend(e)!	gewandt,[150] gewendet[150]
werben	2 wirbst 3 wirbt	warb	würbe[151]	S wirb! P werbt!	geworben
werden	2 wirst 3 wird	wurde[152]	würde	S werde! P werdet!	geworden[153]
werfen	2 wirfst 3 wirft	warf	würfe	S wirf! P werf(e)t!	geworfen
wiegen[154]	2 wiegst 3 wiegt	wog	wöge	wieg(e)!	gewogen
winden[155]	2 windest 3 windet	wand	wände	wind(e)!	gewunden
wissen	1 & 3 weiß 2 weißt	wußte	wüßte	S wisse! P wißt! *or* wisset!	gewußt
wollen	1 & 3 will 2 willst	wollte	wollte	S wolle! P wollt!	†gewollt
wringen[156] (*see* ringen)	—	—	—	—	—
zeihen[157]	2 zeihst 3 zeiht	zieh	ziehe	zeih(e)!	geziehen
ziehen	2 ziehst[158] 3 zieht[158]	zog	zöge	zieh(e)![158]	gezogen
zwingen	2 zwingst 3 zwingt	zwang	zwänge	zwing(e)!	gezwungen

141 Weak except past participle as adj. (things) = 'confused'; *verwirrt* (persons) = 'perplexed'.
142 Intransitive = 'grow'. Transitive = '(smear with) wax' is weak.
143 Vowels are long.
144 Transitive, but rarely used except figuratively (= 'ponder'); commoner is *erwägen*.
145 Also weak forms.
146 Vowels are long.
147 Normally weak. Strong forms are poetic, usually intransitive and often figurative, except in South German dialects. In the meaning 'move', 'flutter', 'hover' always weak.
148 Intransitive = 'yield'. Transitive = 'soften' is weak.
149 Also *verweisen*.
150 Weak forms less usual, except in more or less technical senses, e.g. *er hat den Rock* or *das Heu gewendet*. As adj. only strong, e.g. *gewandt, bewandt, (un)verwandt*. With *einwenden, verwenden* weak past participle is commoner.
151 *wärbe* and *wörbe* are also found.
152 Poetic and elevated style *ward*.
153 *worden* after another past participle.
154 Transitive and intransitive = 'weigh' (of concrete objects). N.B. *gewiegt* = 'experienced', 'shrewd'. Transitive verb = 'rock' (from *Wiege*) is weak.
155 Transitive = 'wind', 'twist'. Intransitive = 'writhe', 'meander' is weak.
156 North German variant of *ringen*. In laundry-work often weak.
157 Poetic or elevated; lives in *verzeihen*.
158 Archaic *zeuchst, zeucht, zeuch!*

Abbreviations used in the Dictionary
Im Wörterbuch benutzte Abkürzungen

Abkürzung	*abbr.*	abbreviation
Akkusativ	*Acc.*	accusative
Akustik	*Acoust.*	acoustics
Adjektiv	*adj.*	adjective
Adverb	*adv.*	adverb
Landwirtschaft	*Agr.*	agriculture
amerikanisches Englisch	*Am.*	American
Anatomie	*Anat.*	anatomy
Anthropologie	*Anthr.*	anthropology
Architektur	*Archit.*	architecture
Archäologie	*Archaeol.*	archaeology
Arithmetik	*Arith.*	arithmetic
Artikel	*art.*	article
Artillerie	*Artil.*	artillery
Astronomie	*Astr.*	astronomy
Astrologie	*Astrol.*	astrology
attributiv	*attrib.*	attributive
österreichisches Deutsch	*Austr.*	Austrian
australisches Englisch	*Austral.*	Australian
Hilfszeitwort	*aux.*	auxiliary
Flugwesen	*Av.*	aviation
(aus der) Bibel	*B.*	Biblical
Bakterienkunde	*Bacter.*	bacteriology
Backen	*Bak.*	baking
bayrisches Deutsch	*Bav.*	Bavarian
Billardspiel	*Bill.*	billiards
Biologie	*Biol.*	biology
Buchbinderei	*Bookb.*	bookbinding
Botanik	*Bot.*	botany
Brauen	*Brew.*	brewing
Brückenbau	*Bridgeb.*	bridgebuilding
Bauwesen	*Build.*	building
Majuskel	*cap.*	capital
Tischlerei	*Carp.*	carpentry
Chemie	*Chem.*	chemistry
anglikanische Kirche	*C. of E.*	Church of England
umgangsprachlich	*coll.*	colloquial
Sammelwort	*collect.*	collective
Handelssprache	*Comm.*	commercial language
Komparative; Zusammensetzung	*Comp.*	comparative; compound
Muschelkunde	*Conch.*	conchology
Konjunktion	*conj.*	conjunction
Satzbau	*constr.*	construction
Kricket	*Crick.*	cricket
(aus der) Kochkunst	*Cul.*	culinary
Radfahren	*Cycl.*	cycling
Tanzkunst	*Danc.*	dancing
Dativ	*Dat.*	dative
bestimmt	*def.*	definite
hinweisend	*dem.*	demonstrative
Mundart	*dial.*	dialect
Diminutiv	*dim.*	diminutive
Zeichnen	*Draw.*	drawing
Damenschneiderei	*Dressm.*	dressmaking
Färbereigewerbe	*Dye.*	dyeing
kirchlich	*Eccl.*	ecclesiastical
Elektrizität	*Elec.*	electricity
elliptisch	*ellipt.*	elliptical
betont	*emph.*	emphatic
Ingenieurwesen	*Engin.*	engineering
England; englisch	*Engl.*	England; English
Gravierkunst	*Engr.*	engraving
Entomologie	*Ent.*	entomology
Reiten	*Equest.*	equestrian
besonders; hauptsächlich	*esp.*	especially
Ethnologie	*Ethn.*	ethnology
euphemistisch	*euphem.*	euphemistic
weiblich	*f.*	feminine
Fechtkunst	*Fenc.*	fencing
figürlich	*fig.*	figurative
Feuerwerk	*Firew.*	fireworks
Fußball	*Footb.*	football

Forstwesen	*For.*	forestry
Befestigungskunst	*Fort.*	fortification
Gießerei	*Found.*	foundry-work
Freimaurerei	*Freem.*	freemasonry
französische Revolution	*Fr. Rev.*	French Revolution
Pelzwerk	*Furr.*	furriery
Genitiv	*Gen.*	genitive
Erdkunde	*Geog.*	geography
Geologie	*Geol.*	geology
Geometrie	*Geom.*	geometry
Glaserzeugung	*Glassw.*	glasswork
Grammatik	*Gram.*	grammar
Turnen	*Gymn.*	gymnastics
haben	h.	*haben* (= to have)
Wappenkunde	*Her.*	heraldry
Geschichte	*Hist.*	history
Zeitmessung	*Horol.*	horology
Gärtnerei	*Hort.*	horticulture
humoristisch	*hum.*	humorous
Jagdwesen	*Hunt.*	hunting
Fischkunde	*Ichth.*	ichthyology
unpersönlich	*imp.*	impersonal
Imperativ	*imper.*	imperative
Imperfekt	*imperf.*	imperfect
unbestimmt	*ind.*	indefinite
undeklinierbar	*indecl.*	indeclinable
Indikativ	*indic.*	indicative
Infinitiv	*inf.*	infinitive
untrennbar	*insep.*	inseparable
Versicherungswesen	*Insur.*	insurance
Ausruf	*int.*	interjection
Fragewort	*inter.*	interrogative
unveränderlich	*inv.*	invariable
unregelmässig	*irr.*	irregular
ironisch	*iron.*	ironic
jüdisch	*Jew.*	Jewish
wörtlich	*lit.*	literal
Literatur	*Liter.*	literature
Logik	*Log.*	logic
männlich	*m.*	masculine
Maschinenbau	*Mach.*	machinery
Magnetismus	*Magnet.*	magnetism
Mathematik	*Math.*	mathematics
Technik	*Mech.*	mechanics
Medizin	*Med.*	medical
Hüttenwesen	*Metall.*	metallurgy
metaphorisch	*metaph.*	metaphorical
Meteorologie	*Meteor.*	meteorology
Verslehre	*Metr.*	metrics
militärisch	*Mil.*	military
Bergbau	*Min.*	mining
Münzen	*Mint.*	minting
Molluske	*Mollusc.*	Mollusca
Kraftfahrzeugwesen	*Motor.*	motoring
Bergsteigen	*Mount.*	mountaineering
Musik	*Mus.*	music
Mythologie	*Myth.*	mythology
sächlich	*n.*	neuter
Naturgeschichte	*Nat. Hist.*	natural history
Nationalsozialismus	*Nat. Soc.*	National Socialism
nautisch	*Naut.*	nautical
Kriegsmarine	*Nav.*	navy
Navigation	*Navig.*	navigation
Nominativ	*Nom.*	nominative
Zahlzeichen	*num.*	numeral
veraltet	*obs.*	obsolete
gelegentlich	*occ.*	occasionally
Behördensprache	*offic.*	officialese
häufig	*oft.*	often
entgegengesetzt	*opp.*	opposite to
Optik	*Opt.*	optics
Orgel	*Org.*	organ
ursprünglich	*orig.*	originally
Ornithologie	*Orn.*	ornithology
sich	*o.s.*	oneself
Person	P.	*Person* (= person)
Person	*p.*	person
Malerei	*Paint.*	painting
Papierfabrikation	*Pap.*	papermaking
Parlament	*Parl.*	Parliament
Partikel	*part.*	particle
Passiv	*pass.*	passive
Pathologie	*Path.*	pathology
herabsetzend	*pej.*	pejorative

Perfekt	*perf.*	perfect
persönlich	*pers.*	personal
Arzneimittellehre	*Pharm.*	pharmacy
Philosophie	*Phil.*	philosophy
Philologie	*Philol.*	philology
Phonetik	*Phonet.*	phonetics
Photographie	*Phot.*	photography
Physik	*Phys.*	physics
Physiologie	*Physiol.*	physiology
Mehrzahl	*pl.*	plural
Dichtkunst	*Poet.*	poetry
Politik	*Pol.*	politics
besitzanzeigend	*poss.*	possessive
Mittelwort der Vergangenheit	*p.p.*	past participle
prädikativ	*pred.*	predicative
Präfix	*pref.*	prefix
Präposition	*prep.*	preposition
Präsens	*pres.*	present
Buchdruckerkunst	*Print.*	printing
Pronomen	*pron.*	pronoun
Prosodie	*Pros.*	prosody
Protestant	*Prot.*	Protestant
Sprichwort	*Prov.*	proverb
Mittelwort der Gegenwart	*pr. p.*	present participle
Psychologie	*Psych.*	psychology
quod vide	*q.v.*	*quod vide* (which see)
Rundfunk	*Rad.*	radio
römisch-katholisch	*R.C.*	Roman Catholic
Eisenbahn	*Railw.*	railways
Hinweis	*ref.*	reference
reflexiv	*refl.*	reflexive
regelmässig	*reg.*	regular
Religion	*Rel.*	religion
relativ	*rel.*	relative
Rhetorik	*Rhet.*	rhetoric
Sache	S.	*Sache* (= thing)
Substantiv	*s.*	substantive
sein	s.	*sein* (= to be)
Bildhauerkunst	*Sculp.*	sculpture
trennbar	*sep.*	separable
Nähmaschine	*Sew.-mach.*	sewing machine
Schiffbau	*Shipb.*	shipbuilding
Einzahl	*sing.*	singular
Slang	*sl.*	slang
Schmiedehandwerk	*Smith.*	smith's work
jemand	*s.o.*	someone
Soziologie	*Soc.*	sociology
Sport	*Spt.*	sport
Statistik	*Stat.*	statistics
Börse	*St. Exch.*	Stock Exchange
etwas	*s.th.*	something
Studentenslang	*Studs. sl.*	students' slang
Konjunktiv	*subj.*	subjunctive
Suffix	*suff.*	suffix
Superlativ	*sup.*	superlative
Chirurgie	*Surg.*	surgery
Landvermessung	*Surv.*	surveying
Gerberei	*Tan.*	tanning
Technik	*Tech.*	technology
Telegraphie	*Tele.*	telegraphy
Tennis	*Tenn.*	tennis
Textilien	*Text.*	textiles
Ding, Sache	*th.*	thing
Theater	*Theat.*	theatre
Theologie	*Theol.*	theology
Topographie	*Top.*	topography
Fernsehen	*T.V.*	television
Universität	*Univ.*	university
gewöhnlich	*usu.*	usual(ly)
Verb	*v.*	verb
Hilfszeitwort	*v.aux.*	auxiliary verb
Tiermedizin	*Vet.*	veterinary medicine
intransitives Verb	*v.i.*	intransitive verb
reflexives Verb	*v.r.*	reflexive verb
transitives Verb	*v.t.*	transitive verb
vulgär	*vulg.*	vulgar
Weberei	*Weav.*	weaving
Zoologie	*Zool.*	zoology

A, a [a:], *n.* (-, *pl.* -) 1. the letter A; (*B.*) ***ich bin das A und das O,*** I am Alpha and Omega ; ***das A und (das) O,*** in its entirety, all in all; ***von A bis Z,*** from beginning to end, from first to last; (*Prov.*) ***wer A sagt, muß auch B sagen,*** in for a penny, in for a pound; 2. the note A; ***A-Dur,*** (the key of) A major; ***a-Moll,*** (the key of) A minor; ***A-Saite,*** the A-string (*violin etc.*).

Aachen ['a:xən], *n.* Aix-la-Chapelle.

Aal [a:l], *m.* **(-(e)s,** *pl.* **-e,** *dim.* **Älchen)** 1. eel; ***– blau (gekocht),*** stewed eel; ***er ist glatt wie ein –,*** he's as slippery as an eel; ***den – beim Schwanz fassen,*** begin a thing at the wrong end; 2. wrong crease, crumple; 3. (*sl.*) torpedo. **Aal|beere,** *f.* black currant. **-butte,** *f.* eel-pout, burbot.

aalen ['a:lən], **1.** *v.t., v.i.* fish for eels. **2.** *v.r.* (*coll.*) loaf about, laze, relax. **aal|förmig,** *adj.* eel-shaped, anguilliform. **-glatt,** *adj.* slippery as an eel, elusive. **Aal|mutter,** *f.* viviparous blenny. **-puppe,** *f.* bob for catching eels. **-quappe,** *f. See* **-butte. -quaste,** *f. See* **-puppe. -raupe,** *f. See* **-butte. -reuse,** *f.* eelpot, eel-basket. **-streif, -strich,** *m.* black streak on the back of a dun-coloured horse *or* cow.

Aap [a:p], *n.* **(-es,** *pl.* **-en)** mizzen-staysail.

Aar [a:r], *m.* **(-(e)s,** *pl.* **-e)** (*Poet.*) (*orig.*) any large bird of prey; (*usu.*) eagle.

Aargau ['a:rgau], *m.* Argau, Argovia. **Aargauer,** *m.* Argovian.

Aas [a:s], *n.* **(-es,** *pl.* **-e** *or* **Äser)** 1. carrion, (rotten) carcass, offal; (*B., Prov.*) ***wo ein – ist, da sammeln sich die Geier,*** wherever the carcass is, there will the eagles be gathered together; 2. bait; ***ein – legen,*** to lay a bait; 3. (*vulg.*) swine, blackguard; (*vulg.*) ***kein – ließ sich sehen,*** not a bloody soul was to be seen.

aasen ['a:zən], **1.** *v.i.* 1. feed on carrion; 2. (***mit etwas***) squander, play ducks and drakes (with); make a mess (of); (*vulg.*) ***sich voll –,*** get filthy dirty; 3. *See* **äsen. 2.** *v.t.* flesh, curry (*hides*).

Aas|fliege, *f.* dung-fly. **-geier,** *m.* 1. *See* **Schmutzgeier**; 2. (*sl.*) shark. **-geruch,** *m.* putrid stench. **aasig,** *adj.* abominable, beastly; (*sl.*) ***er hat – viel Geld,*** he is stinking rich *or* stiff with money *or* rolling in money. **Aasjäger,** *m.* tuft-hunter, pot-hunter.

ab [ap], **1.** *adv.* off; down; from, away from; ***auf und –,*** up and down, to and fro; ***ein Mark auf oder –,*** a mark more or less; ***– und an, – und zu,*** off and on, now and then, from time to time; ***Bajonett –!*** unfix bayonets! ***Gewehr –!*** order arms! ***Hut –!*** take off your hat! off with your hat! (*iron.*) I take my hat off (***vor*** (*Dat.*), to); ***Maria –,*** exit Mary (*stage direction*); ***von Bremen –,*** from Bremen (onwards); ***von nun –,*** from now (on(wards)), henceforth; ***vom Wege – sein,*** have lost the way, be off the track; ***weit –,*** far off. **2.** *prep.* (*Dat.*) ***– Bremen,*** from Bremen (onwards); (*Comm.*) ***– Werk,*** ex works; ***– heute,*** from today (onwards); ***– erstem*** (*coll.* ***ersten***) ***Mai,*** on and after May 1st. **3.** *ellipt.* ***der Knopf ist –,*** the button has come off; (*coll.*) ***der Bart ist –,*** that's put the seal on it, it's all up; ***ich bin (sehr) –,*** I'm finished, exhausted, (*coll.*) all in, played out, whacked. **4.** *sep.pref. Variety of meanings, e.g.* departure, deviation, separation, removal (***abreisen, abweichen, abtrennen, abbürsten***), downward motion (***abstürzen***), attrition (***abtragen***), negation (***ableben***), imitation (***abschreiben***), appropriation (***abschmeicheln***). *For a compound verb with* **ab** *not given below, look under the simple verb, modifying the meaning by one or other of the above qualifications.*

Ab, *n.* (-, *no pl.*) 1. ***das Auf und –,*** the ups and downs; 2. *ellipt.* (= **Abfahrt**) departure (*timetables*).

abänderlich ['apˀɛndərliç], *adj.* alterable; modifiable, variable; (*Gram.*) declinable. **abändern,** *v.i.* alter, change; (*Law*) amend, modify. **Abänderung,** *f.* alteration; variation; modification. **Abänderungsantrag,** *m.* motion for the amendment. **abänderungsfähig,** *adj.* capable of modification *or* amendment.

abängstigen ['apˀɛŋstɪgən], **1.** *v.t.* alarm, harass, torment. **2.** *v.r.* worry, fret, be uneasy.

abarbeiten ['apˀarbaɪtən], **1.** *v.t.* 1. work off (*debt*); 2. get (*ship*) afloat *or* off; 3. wear out (*tool, horse etc.*); ***sich (Dat.) die Finger –,*** work one's fingers to the bone; ***das Gröbste –,*** rough-hew; ***ein abgearbeiteter Gaul,*** a worn-out nag; ***abgearbeitete Hände,*** toil-worn hands. **2.** *v.r.* toil, wear o.s. out with work.

abärgern ['apˀɛrgərn], **1.** *v.t.* worry to death. **2.** *v.r.* be mortified *or* vexed, fret o.s.

Abart ['apˀa:rt], *f.* degenerate species, variety, variation. **abarten,** *v.i.* (*aux.* s.) degenerate; deviate from type. **Abartung,** *f.* degeneracy, deviation from type.

abästen ['apˀɛstən], *v.t.* cut off branches from, lop, trim (*a tree*); ***abgeästete Weide,*** pollard willow.

abätzen ['apˀɛtsən], *v.t.* corrode, eat away, cauterize.

Abbau ['apbau], *m.* **(-(e)s,** *pl.* **-ten)** 1. demolition, dismantling; working (*of a mine*); 2. retrenchment, 'axe' (*e.g.* reduction of staff); 3. (*Chem.*) catabolism, decomposition, distintegration.

abbauen ['apbauən], **1.** *v.t.* 1. demolish, dismantle; exploit, work (*a mine*); 2. retrench, economize; reduce (*prices*), discharge (*employees*); 3. (*Chem.*) decompose, disintegrate. **2.** *v.i.* (*coll.*) withdraw (*from a contest*), weaken, throw in the towel, (*sl.*) pack it in.

abbefehlen ['apbəfe:lən], *irr.v.t.* countermand, cancel, recall.

abbefördern ['apbəfœrdərn], *v.t.* evacuate (*people or stores*).

abbeißen ['apbaɪsən], *irr.v.t.* bite off; (*coll.*) ***er hat aller Scham*** (or ***Schande***) ***den Kopf abgebissen,*** he is past all shame; ***da beißt keine Maus einen*** (or ***die Maus keinen***) ***Faden ab,*** there's absolutely nothing that can be done.

abbeizen ['apbaɪtsən], *v.t.* remove by caustics; macerate, dress (*skins*); (*Metall.*) remove oxidization, dip, pickle, taw.

abbekommen ['apbəkɔmən], *irr.v.t.* 1. remove, get loose *or* off; 2. (*coll.*) get a share of, come in for one's share; ***eins –,*** stop a blow; ***etwas –,*** get hurt; ***er hat dabei gar nichts –,*** he got off without a scratch.

abberufen ['apbəru:fən], *irr.v.t.* call away *or* back, recall; ***er wurde –,*** he passed on (*i.e.* died).

abbestellen ['apbəʃtɛlən], *v.t.* countermand, cancel.

abbetteln ['apbɛtəln], *v.t.* ***ihm etwas –,*** wheedle s.th. out of him; ***die Straße –,*** beg at every house in the street; ***ich ließ mir jedes Wort –,*** every word had to be dragged out of me.

abbezahlen ['apbətsa:lən], *v.t.* pay off; discharge (*a debt*).

abbiegen ['apbi:gən], **1.** *irr.v.t.* bend *or* turn aside, deflect, avert, divert. **2.** *irr.v.i.* (*aux.* s.) branch off, turn off *or* aside, diverge, deviate.

Abbild ['apbɪlt], *n.* likeness, copy, image.

abbilden ['apbɪldən], **1.** *v.t.* portray, delineate, depict, illustrate. **2.** *v.r.* be reflected, form an image. **Abbildung,** *f.* illustration; picture; drawing, diagram, figure, image. **Abbildungsvermögen,** *n.* resolving power (*lens*).

abbinden ['apbɪndən], **1.** *irr.v.t.* 1. untie; detach by ligature, tie off (*warts etc.*); apply a tourniquet to (*arm, vein etc.*); 2. wean (*calf*); 3. hoop (*cask*). **2.** *irr.v.i.* set (*of cement etc.*). *See* **abgebunden.**

Abbitte ['apbɪtə], *f.* apology; – ***tun*** or ***leisten,*** beg forgiveness, apologize.

abbitten ['apbɪtən], **1.** *irr.v.t.* (***ihm etwas***) apologize (*to him*) for (*s.th.*), beg (*his*) forgiveness for (*s.th*). **2.** *irr.v.i.* apologize, ask for forgiveness.

abblasen ['apbla:zən], *irr.v.t.* 1. blow off (*as dust from books*); ***Dampf* –,** blow off steam; (*Mil.*) ***Gas* –,** release gas; 2. (*coll.*) call off (*meeting, strike etc.*). **Abblaseventil,** *n.* exhaust valve.

abblassen ['apblasən], *v.i.* (*aux.* s.) turn pale, fade; ***abgeblaßte Redensart,*** hackneyed expression.

abblättern ['apblɛtərn], **1.** *v.t.* defoliate. **2.** *v.i.* (*aux.* s.), *v.r.* shed leaves, exfoliate; peel off; scale *or* flake off; (*Med.*) desquamate. **Abblätterung,** *f.* defoliation, exfoliation, desquamation *etc.*

abbläuen ['apblɔyən], *v.t.* blue (*linen*); dye blue.

abbleichen ['apblaɪçən], **1.** *v.t.* bleach. **2.** *irr.v.i.* (*aux.* s.) lose colour, fade, grow pale.

abblenden ['apblɛndən], **1.** *v.t.* dim, screen, turn off (*lights*), black-out; ***abgeblendet fahren,*** drive with *or* on dipped headlights. **2.** *v.i.* stop-down (*camera*).

abblitzen ['apblɪtsən], *v.i.* (*aux.* s.) (*coll.*) be snubbed, meet with a rebuff; ***sie ließ ihn* –,** she snubbed him.

abblühen ['apbly:ən], *v.i.* cease blooming, shed (its) blossom (*of plants*); (*aux.* s.) droop, wither, fade, fall (*of flowers*); ***die Nelken haben*** (or ***sind***) ***abgeblüht,*** the carnations are over.

abborgen ['apbɔrgən], *v.t.* (***ihm etwas***) borrow (*s.th.*) from (him).

abböschen ['apbœʃən], *v.t.* slope, incline; embank (*a track*).

Abbrand ['apbrant], *m.* (*Metall.*) residual metallic oxides in heat processing, heating loss; slag.

abbrauchen ['apbrauxən], *v.t.* use up, wear out *or* away. *See* **abgebraucht.**

abbräunen ['apbrɔynən], *v.t.* brown thoroughly.

abbrausen ['apbrauzən], **1.** *v.i.* 1. cease fermenting; 2. (*aux.* s.) (*coll.*) rush off. **2.** *v.t.* douche, rinse. **3.** *v.r.* take a shower(-bath).

abbrechen ['apbrɛçən], **1.** *irr.v.t.* 1. break off; pluck, pick (*fruit, flowers*), (*fig.*) ***einer S. die Spitze* –,** take the sting out of a th.; ***sich*** (*Dat.*) ***etwas*** (***vom Munde***) **–,** deny o.s. s.th., deprive *or* stint o.s. of s.th.; (*coll.*) ***brich dir nur keine Verzierung*** or ***keinen Zacken ab!*** come off your high horse! ***einem Pferd die Hufeisen* –,** unshoe a horse; 2. dismantle, demolish, pull down; interrupt, discontinue, terminate; (*fig.*) ***alle Brücken hinter sich* –,** burn one's boats; (*Mil.*) ***das Gefecht* –,** break off the engagement; ***das Lager* –,** break camp; ***Schießen* –!** cease fire! ***Zelte* –,** strike tents. *See* **abgebrochen. 2.** *irr.v.i.* 1. (*aux.* s.) break *or* snap off; ***mit ihm* –,** break (it off) with him; 2. ***kurz* –,** stop short; 3. (*Mil.*) change from line into column formation; ***zu Vieren brecht ab!*** form fours! **Abbrechung,** *f.* cessation, discontinuance; demolition, dismantling.

abbremsen ['apbrɛmzən], **1.** *v.i.* (apply the) brake. **2.** *v.t.* slow down (*vehicle*), moderate (*atomic particles*).

abbrennen ['apbrɛnən], **1.** *irr.v.t.* burn off; burn down; cleanse by fire; temper, refine (*metal*); calcine; sear; (*Chem.*) deflagrate; ***Feuerwerk* –,** let off *or* set off fireworks. **2.** *irr.v.i.* (*aux.* s.) burn down; ***die Leute sind abgebrannt,*** the people have been burnt out (= lost everything in the fire); *see* **abgebrannt. Abbrenn|lampe,** *f.* (painter's) blow-lamp. **–löffel,** *m.* (*Chem.*) deflagrating spoon. **–schweißung,** *f.* arc-welding.

Abbreviatur [abrevia'tu:r], *f.* (-, *pl.* **-en**) abbreviation.

abbringen ['apbrɪŋən], *irr.v.t.* 1. remove; get off *or* out *or* away *or* afloat; 2. divert; dissuade; ***vom rechten Wege* –,** lead astray; ***nichts soll mich davon* –,** nothing will put me off doing it; ***ich lasse mich davon nicht* –,** I won't budge.

abbröckeln ['apbrœkəln], *v.i.* crumble away, peel off; (*Comm.*) ease off (*of prices*); fall *or* drop away (*of people*).

Abbruch ['apbrux], *m.* 1. demolition; ***auf – verkaufen,*** sell for scrap; 2. damage, injury, loss, detriment; – ***tun*** (*Dat.*), damage, be prejudicial to, injure, impair; ***sich*** (*Dat.*) ***selbst – tun,*** deprive o.s. of; 3. rupture, breaking off, discontinuance; 4. debris, remains, fragments; scrap, junk. **Abbruch|-arbeit,** *f.* demolition (work). **–holz,** *n.* scrap wood.

abbrüchig ['apbryçɪç], *adj.* 1. brittle, friable, crumbly; 2. (*Law*) derogatory; prejudicial; detrimental (*für*, to).

Abbruchlinie ['apbruxli:niə], *f.* line of cleavage.

abbruchtuend ['apbruxtu:ənt], *adj.* derogatory, prejudicial, injurious, damaging.

abbrühen ['apbry:ən], *v.t.* scald, parboil. *See* **abgebrüht.**

abbrummen ['apbrumən], *v.t.* (*coll.*) ***drei Jahre* –,** do (a stretch of) three years (*in prison*).

abbuchen ['apbu:xən], *v.t.* write off (*debt, loss etc.*), debit (*amount*). **Abbuchung,** *f.* debit-entry.

abbürsten ['apbyrstən], *v.t.* brush off; (*coll.*) ***ihn* –,** give him a dressing down.

abbüßen ['apby:sən], *v.t.* expiate, atone *or* pay for; ***mit Geld* –,** pay a fine; ***eine Strafe* –,** serve a sentence. **Abbüßung,** *f.* atonement, expiation.

Abc [a:be:'tse:], *n.* (-, *pl.* -) 1. abc, alphabet; ***nach dem* –,** alphabetically; 2. (*fig.*) rudiments.

abdachen ['apdaxən], **1.** *v.t.* 1. slope, slant (*like a roof*), incline; ***eine Mauer* –,** cope a wall; 2. unroof, remove the roof. **2.** *v.r.* incline, slope away, shelve. **abdachig,** *adj.* sloping, shelving. **Abdachung,** *f.* slope, declivity, gradient, incline, ramp; glacis, scarp, escarpment. **Abdachungswinkel,** *m.* angle of inclination.

abdämmen ['apdɛmən], *v.t.* dam up *or* off (*water*); embank (*river*).

Abdampf ['apdampf], *m.* exhaust steam.

abdampfen ['apdampfən], **1.** *v.i.* 1. (*aux.* s.) steam off *or* away (*train, ship*); (*coll.*) take o.s. off; 2. (*aux.* s. & h.) evaporate (*liquids*), volatilize (*solids*). **2.** *v.t.* evaporate (*liquids*), volatilize (*solids*).

abdämpfen ['apdɛmpfən], *v.t.* 1. (cause to) evaporate; 2. damp down, deaden, muffle, stifle (*fire, sound, enthusiasm etc.*).

Abdampfrückstand ['apdampfrykʃtant], *m.* residue after evaporation.

abdanken ['apdaŋkən], **1.** *v.t.* (*obs.*) dismiss, discharge; retire, pension off, superannuate; pay off (*crew*), lay up, put out of commission (*ship*); ***zur Strafe* –,** cashier (*officer*). **2.** *v.i.* abdicate (*ruler*), resign, quit the service, take one's discharge; (*Swiss*) ***bei einem Toten* –,** deliver the funeral oration. **Abdankung,** *f.* 1. resignation, abdication; 2. dismissal, discharge, disbanding; 3. (*Swiss*) funeral oration.

abdarben ['apdarbən], *v.t.* ***sich*** (*Dat.*) ***etwas*** (***am*** or ***vom Munde***) **–,** deny o.s. s.th., pinch and scrape for s.th.

abdecken ['apdɛkən], *v.t.* 1. uncover; unroof, strip the roof off (*house*); clear (*table*), remove the tablecloth; uncover, strip (*bed*), remove the bedspread; 2. flay (*beasts*); 3. screen, shield, enclose, conceal; (*Phot.*) mask; (*Mil.*) camouflage; 4. cover, meet, settle, make good (*debt, deficiency*); 5. (*Footb.*) cover (*player*).

Abdecker ['apdɛkər], *m.* knacker, flayer. **Abdeckerei** [–'raɪ], *f.* knacker's yard. **Abdeck|platte,** *f.* cover plate. **–stein,** *m.* coping stone. **Abdeckung,** *f.* 1. (*Archit.*) coping, covering; 2. settlement, repayment.

Abderit [apdɛ'ri:t], *m.* (**-en**, ***pl.*** **-en**) Abderite, Gothamite

abdichten ['apdɪçtən], *v.t.* make (water)tight *etc.*, block *or* stop up, seal (up), pack, lute, caulk. **Abdichtung,** *f.* packing, caulking.

abdienen ['apdi:nən], *v.t.* pay off by service; serve (one's time) (*in the army*).

abdingen ['apdɪŋən], *irr.v.t.* ***ihm etwas* –**, hire s.th. from him, do a deal with him for s.th.; ***ich habe mir nichts – lassen,*** I have agreed to no reduction.

Abdomen [ap'do:mən], *n.* (**-s**, *pl.* - *or* **-mina**) abdomen.

abdorren ['apdɔrən], *v.i.* (*aux.* s.) wither, dry up.

abdörren ['apdœrən], *v.t.* dry up, parch, desiccate.

Abdraht ['apdra:t], *m.* turnings, swarf.

abdrängen ['apdrɛŋən], *v.t.* thrust *or* shove aside; ***ihm etwas* –**, badger s.th. out of him.

abdrechseln ['apdrɛksəln], *v.t.* turn off, separate by turning; turn (*on a lathe*). *See* **abgedrechselt.**

abdrehen ['apdre:ən], **1.** *v.t.* twist off, unscrew; strip (*thread of screw*); wring (*neck of fowl*); turn off (*gas, water*); switch off (*light, radio*); ***sein Gesicht* –**, turn one's face away. **2.** *v.i.* (*Av.*) go into a nosedive; sheer off (*of ship*); (*coll.*) push *or* clear off.

abdreschen ['apdrɛʃən], *irr.v.t.* thresh. *See* **abgedroschen.**

Abdrift ['apdrɪft], *f. See* **Abtrift.**

abdringen ['apdrɪŋən], *irr.v.t.* ***ihm etwas* –**, extort *or* exact *or* wring a th. from him.

abdrosseln ['apdrɔsəln], *v.t.* 1. throttle down, stall (*an engine*); 2 .(*fig.*) cut back (*production*).

Abdruck ['apdruk], *m.* 1. (**-(e)s**, *pl.* **-e**) printing, printed text; reprint, impression; copy, offprint; proof, print; reproduction; – ***vor der Schrift,*** proof before letters; 2. (**-(e)s**, *pl.* **⸚e**) stamping; mark, imprint, impress(ion); (*fig.*) image; 3. (act of pulling the) trigger.

abdrucken ['apdrukən], *v.t.* print (off); reprint; reproduce.

abdrücken ['apdrykən], **1.** *v.t.* take a cast *or* impression of; squeeze *or* force off, release (*catch*), press, pull (*trigger*), discharge (*gun*); ***es drückt mir das Herz ab,*** it breaks *or* wrings my heart. **2.** *v.r.* leave its mark, be plainly imprinted.

Abdruckmasse, *f.* (-, *no pl.*) plaster of Paris, moulding compound.

abdunsten ['apdunstən], *v.i.* (*aux.* s.) evaporate.

abdünsten ['apdynstən], *v.t.* (cause to) evaporate. **Abdünstung,** *f.* evaporation.

abebben ['apˀɛbən], *v.i.* (*aux.* s.) ebb (*of tide*); (*fig.*) ebb *or* die away, die down, abate, slacken off.

Abece, *n. See* **Abc.**

Abend ['a:bənt], *m.* (**-s**, *pl.* **-e**) 1. evening, night; ***am* –**, in the evening; ***am – vorher,*** on the previous evening; ***des –s,*** *see* **abends**; ***diesen* –**, this evening; ***eines –s,*** one evening; ***gegen* –**, towards evening; ***guten – sagen,*** say good evening; – ***des Lebens,*** evening of life; (*Prov.*) ***es ist noch nicht aller Tage* –**, we're not out of the wood yet; (*Prov.*) ***man soll den Tag nicht vor dem – loben,*** don't count your chickens before they're hatched; ***es wird* –**, evening is drawing on; ***zu – essen,*** have supper, dine in the evening; 2. (social) evening, party, at-home; (*Theat. etc.*) ***bunter* –**, social evening, variety show; 3. eve, day preceding (*see* **Vorabend**); ***am Heiligen* –**, on Christmas Eve; ***der – vor der Schlacht,*** the eve of the battle; 4. (*B., Poet.*) west, Occident; ***gegen* –**, in the west.

abend, *adv.* ***Dienstag* –**, Tuesday evening; ***gestern* –**, yesterday evening, last night; ***heute* –**, this evening, tonight; ***morgen* –**, tomorrow night *or* evening.

Abend|andacht, *f. See* **–gottesdienst. –blatt,** *n.* evening paper. **–brot,** *n. See* **–essen. –dämmerung,** *f.* evening twilight, dusk.

Abendessen ['a:bəntˀɛsən], *n.* supper, dinner, evening meal; ***vor (nach) dem* –**, before (after) supper; ***zum – einladen,*** invite to supper.

Abend|falter, *m.* (*Ent.*) hawkmoth. **–gebet,** *n.* evening prayers. **–gottesdienst,** *m.* evening service, evensong, (*R.C.*) vespers.

Abendland ['a:bəntlant], *n.* (**-es,** *no pl.*) west, Occident. **abendländisch,** *adj.* western, Occidental.

abendlich ['a:bəntlɪç], *adj.* 1. evening, of the evening; 2. occidental, western, westerly.

Abendmahl ['a:bəntma:l], *n.* (**-s,** *pl.* **-e**) 1. the Last Supper; 2. the Lord's Supper, (Holy) Communion, the Sacrament; (***ihm***) ***das – reichen,*** administer the Sacrament (to him); ***das – darauf nehmen,*** swear to God it is true. **Abendmahls|gänger, –gast,** *m.* communicant. **–kelch,** *m.* communion cup, chalice.

Abend|punkt, *m.* (*Astr.*) true west. **–rot,** *n.*, **–röte,** *f.* sunset. **–schule,** *f.* evening classes, night school. **–sonne,** *f.* setting sun. **–ständchen,** *n.* serenade. **–stern,** *m.* evening star, Venus, Hesperus. **–tau,** *m.* night dew. **–thermik,** *f.* terrestrial radiation. **abendwärts,** *adv.* (*Poet.*) westerly, westwards. **Abendwind,** *m.* 1. evening breeze; 2. west wind, zephyr.

Abenteuer ['a:bəntɔyər], *n.* adventure; ***auf – ausgehen,*** go out in search of adventure; ***ein – erleben,*** meet with *or* have an adventure. **Abenteuerin,** *f.* adventuress. **abenteuerlich,** *adj.* 1. adventurous; venturesome; hazardous; 2. fantastic, quixotic. **Abenteuerlichkeit,** *f.* 1. adventurousness; venturesomeness; 2. quixotry; quixotism, strangeness; *pl.* strange adventures *or* happenings. **Abenteuerlust,** *f.* venturesomeness, spirit of adventure. **abenteuern,** *v.i.* seek adventure(s). **Abenteurer,** *m.* adventurer, knight-errant. **Abenteurerin,** *f. See* **Abenteuerin.**

aber ['a:bər], **1.** *conj.* 1. (*adversative*) but, however, yet; ***nun* –**, and now (that); ***oder* –**, otherwise, or else; 2. (*coordinative*) but, and; 3. (*emphasis*) indeed; (*coll.*) ***– –!*** really! come, come! now, now! now then! ***er kommt – doch?*** he will (in fact) come, won't he? ***er wird doch – kommen?*** he'll come (for sure) I hope? ***– ja!*** why, certainly! ***– nein!*** by no means! not at all! **2.** *adv.* again; ***– und abermals,*** over and over again; ***tausend und – tausend*** (*Austr.* ***abertausend***), thousands and *or* upon thousands.

Aber, *n.* objection; ***das Wenn und* –**, the ifs and buts; ***es ist ein – dabei,*** there's one objection to be made; ***hier gibt es kein* –**, don't argue! (*coll.*) but me no buts!

Aberglaube(n) ['a:bərglaubə(n)], *m.* superstition. **aber|gläubig** [–glɔybɪç], (*usu.*) **–gläubisch,** *adj.* superstitious.

aberkennen ['apˀɛrkɛnən], *irr.v.t.* ***ihm etwas* –**, deny *or* disallow his right to s.th., deprive *or* dispossess him of s.th. **Aberkennung,** *f.* dispossession (by judicial decree); – ***der bürgerlichen Ehrenrechte,*** deprivation of civil rights.

abermalig ['a:bərma:lɪç], *adj.* reiterated, repeated. **abermal(s),** *adv.* again, once more *or* again.

Aberwitz ['a:bərvɪts], *m.* (**-es,** *no pl.*) 1. craziness, foolishness; 2. frenzy. **aberwitzig,** *adj.* 1. crazy, foolish, senseless; 2. crazed, frenzied, frantic, out of one's mind.

abessen ['apˀɛsən], **1.** *irr.v.t.* eat up, eat (*a plate*) clean; ***einen Knochen* –**, pick a bone. **2.** *irr.v.i.* finish eating; (*coll.*) ***du hast bei mir abgegessen,*** you'll get nothing more from *or* out of me.

Abessinien [abɛ'si:njən], *n.* Abyssinia. **Abessinier,** *m.* Abyssinian. **abessinisch,** *adj.* Abyssinian.

abfachen ['apfaxən], *v.t.* partition, divide into compartments.

abfahren ['apfa:rən], **1.** *irr.v.i.* (*aux.* s.) set off, depart, leave; start (off), move off, drive *or* ride off *or* away; sail, put to sea; run downhill (*skiing*); (*coll.*) ***ihn – lassen,*** send him packing *or* about his business, show him the door; ***er fuhr übel ab,*** he fared badly. **2.** *irr.v.t.* 1. cart away; 2. travel all over *or* the length and breadth of (*a district*), traverse, patrol (*a road*); 3. ***ein Rad* –**, lose a wheel. **3.** *irr.v.r.* wear out (*of tyres etc.*); ***abgefahrener Wagen,*** worn out car.

Abfahrt ['apfa:rt], *f.* 1. start, departure; 2. descent (*lift, mountain railw. etc.*), downhill run(ning), slope (*skiing*). **Abfahrt(s)|zeichen,** *n.* starting signal. **–zeit,** *f.* time of departure.

Abfall ['apfal], *m.* 1. (**-s,** *no pl.*) falling off; drop, decrease, decline, diminution; deficiency, shortage (*an* (*Dat.*), in); defection, secession, (*coll.*) backsliding; revolt, rebellion; (*Naut.*) drift; – ***an Gewicht,*** short weight; – ***gegen,*** contrast with *or* to; – ***der Niederlande,*** revolt of the Netherlands; – ***von einem Glauben,*** apostasy; 2. (**-s,** *no pl.*) slope, incline, declivity; 3. (**-s,** *pl.* **⸚e**) waste, refuse, litter, rubbish, garbage, scraps, shreds, shavings, parings, cuttings, clippings, scrap, (*coll.*) junk; waste-products, by-products.

Abfall|eimer, *m.* dustbin, refuse-bin, (*Am.*) ashcan. **–eisen,** *n.* scrap iron.

abfallen ['apfalən], *irr.v.i.* (*aux.* s.) 1. fall *or* drop (off); fall *or* drop behind; (*Naut.*) fall to leeward; 2. fall *or* drop away, slope, shelve; 3. wane, decline, deteriorate, waste away, fall away *or* (*coll.*) off, (*coll.*) drop off; be wasted *or* discarded, go to waste; be yielded as a by-product; ***bei ihm –,*** be snubbed by him; ***gegen etwas –,*** compare badly with s.th.; ***ihn – lassen,*** drop his acquaintance, give him the cold shoulder, (*coll.*) drop him; – ***von,*** secede from, desert (from), forsake, fall away from, (*coll.*) throw over (*adv.*); rebel (against); ***vom Glauben –,*** renounce one's faith, become an apostate; ***es fällt dabei nichts ab,*** there's nothing to be gained from it; ***für dich fällt etwas ab,*** there'll be s.th. in it for you, you'll come in for your share. *See* **abgefallen, Abgefallene(r). abfallend,** *adj.* 1. sloping, shelving; 2. (*Bot.*) deciduous, (*Biol.*) caducous.

Abfall|erzeugnis, *n. See* **–produkt. –haufen,** *m.* scrap-heap, dump. **–holz,** *n.* dead wood, waste wood.

abfällig ['apfɛlɪç], *adj.* 1. ready to fall, (*Bot.*) deciduous, (*Biol.*) caducous; 2. sloping, inclined, shelving, precipitous; 3. unfavourable, adverse, derogatory, disparaging; (*obs.*) disloyal, rebellious; (*Eccl.*) apostate, renegade; (*Comm.*) rubbishy, trashy; (*obs.*) – ***werden,*** revolt, rebel; ***sich – über ihn äußern,*** speak disparagingly of him; ***etwas – beurteilen,*** pass an unfavourable *or* adverse judgement on s.th.; ***ihn – bescheiden,*** give him an unfavourable answer. **Abfälligkeit,** *f.* 1. slope, declivity; 2. derogatory nature (*of opinion etc.*); 3. (*obs.*) (*Eccl.*) desertion, apostasy.

Abfall|produkt, *n.* by-product. **–rohr,** *n.*, **–röhre,** *f.* waste-pipe. **–stoff,** *m.* waste material; *pl.* sewage. **–ware,** *f.* reject(s), (*coll.*) throw-out(s).

abfangen ['apfaŋən], *irr.v.t.* 1. catch, seize, intercept; collect (*water*), divert (*watercourse*); catch up with (*another runner*), catch (*runner*) up; ***ihm die Kunden –,*** entice away *or* steal his customers; 2. level out (*aircraft*), get under control, right (*vehicle*); 3. foil, thwart, parry (*a blow*); 4. dispatch (*wounded game*); 5. (*Archit.*) support, prop up. **Abfangjäger,** *m.* (*Av.*) interceptor (fighter). **Abfang(s)vorrichtung,** *f.* (*Av.*) braking device.

abfärben ['apfɛrbən], *v.i.* 1. (*also fig.*) rub off (*of colour*); – ***auf*** (*Acc.*), influence, colour, leave its mark on; 2. (*aux.* s.) lose colour, fade; ***es färbt nicht ab,*** the dye is fast *or* does not run. *See* **abgefärbt.**

abfasern ['apfa:zərn], **1.** *v.t.* unravel, fray out. **2.** *v.i.*, *v.r.* unravel, fray, become frayed *or* unravelled.

abfassen ['apfasən], *v.t.* 1. compose, write (out), draw up, word; ***in bündigen Ausdrücken abgefaßt,*** couched in concise terms; 2. catch red-handed *or* in the act; 3. measure off *or* out, weigh out. **Abfassung,** *f.* composition, wording, formulation, drawing up.

abfaulen ['apfaulən], *v.i.* (*aux.* s.) rot and fall off.

abfedern ['apfe:dərn], **1.** *v.t.* 1. pluck (*poultry*); 2. fit with springs. *See* **abgefedert. 2.** *v.i.* moult.

abfegen ['apfe:gən], *v.t.* sweep *or* wipe off; ***Staub –,*** dust.

Abfeilicht ['apfaɪlɪçt], *n.* (**-(e)s,** *pl.* **-er**) filings.

abfeilschen ['apfaɪlʃən], *v.t.* beat down; ***ihm etwas –,*** get s.th. from him by bargaining *or* haggling; ***vom Preise 2 Mark –,*** knock 2 marks off the price; ***ihm 2 Mark –,*** beat him down by 2 marks.

abfertigen ['apfɛrtɪgən], *v.t.* (get ready for) dispatch (*goods*); attend to, deal with (*business*); attend to, serve (*customers*); dismiss without ceremony, get rid of, get out of the way; ***kurz –,*** snub, send packing *or* about one's business, be off-hand *or* short with (*s.o.*); ***etwas eilig –,*** make short work of s.th. **Abfertigung,** *f.* 1. dispatch; clearance; 2. rebuff, snub, dismissal. **Abfertigungs|schein,** *m.* (*Comm.*) dispatch-note, waybill, customs declaration. **–stelle,** *f.* dispatch office.

Abfett ['apfɛt], *n.* fat skimmings. **abfetten,** *v.t.* skim the fat off; remove grease from.

abfeuern ['apfɔyərn], **1.** *v.t.* fire (off), let off, discharge. **2.** *v.i.* cease firing *or* heating (*a boiler*), draw the fire. **Abfeuerung,** *f.* discharge, firing. **Abfeuerungs|hebel,** *m.* (*Artil.*) firing lever. **–verbindung,** *f.* (*Artil.*) remote-control firing mechanism.

abfinden ['apfɪndən], **1.** *irr.v.t.* satisfy, pay off (*creditor*), compensate, indemnify (***für,*** for); (*Law*) make a settlement on, (*Hist.*) endow (*prince*) with an apanage. **2.** *irr.v.r.* compound, come to terms, come to an agreement *or* arrangement (***mit ihm,*** with him); (***mit einer S.***) acquiesce (in), reconcile *or* accommodate o.s. (to), make the best (of), put up (with); ***sich gütlich –,*** settle things amicably (***mit,*** with). **Abfindung,** *f.* settlement, agreement, arrangement, composition, compromise; indemnity, compensation, indemnification; (*Law*) separate portion, (*Hist.*) apanage. **Abfindungs|geld,** *n.*, **–summe,** *f.* (money paid as) indemnification *or* indemnity; sum in full settlement of all claims; compensation.

abfischen ['apfɪʃən], *v.t.* empty (*a pond*) by fishing; ***das Beste –,*** skim the cream (***von,*** off).

abflachen ['apflaxən], **1.** *v.t.* flatten (out *or* off) smooth, level (off). **2.** *v.r.* become flat *or* level *or* smooth, flatten *or* level out; shoal (*of water*). **3.** *v.i.* (*aux.* s.) shoal (*of water*).

abflauen ['apflauən], **1.** *v.i.* (*aux.* h. & s.) abate, slacken (off), die down, subside (*of wind, also fig.*); (*fig.*) fail, flag, ease off; fall off, slump (*of trade*), sag, become easier (*of prices*). **2.** *v.t.* wash, rinse.

Abfleisch|eisen, *n. See* **–messer.**

abfleischen ['apflaɪʃən], *v.t.* flesh (*hides*). **Abfleischmesser,** *n.* fleshing-knife.

abfliegen ['apfli:gən], *irr.v.i.* (*aux.* s.) 1. fly away *or* off; take flight *or* wing (*of birds*); (*Av.*) take off; 2. (*For.*) dry and drop off.

abfließen ['apfli:sən], *irr.v.i.* (*aux.* s.) run *or* flow away *or* off *or* down, drain away *or* off.

Abflug ['apflu:k], *m.* 1. flight, departure (*of migratory birds*); (*Av.*) take-off; (*Av.*) – ***mit Starthilfe,*** assisted take-off; 2. descent, alighting. **Abflugdeck,** *n.* (*Nav.*) flight deck.

Abfluß ['apflus], *m.* 1. flowing, discharge, outflow, efflux; drainage (*also Med.*); (*Av.*) airflow; – ***des Geldes,*** drain of money; 2. sink, gutter, drain, drain-pipe, waste-pipe. **Abfluß|gebiet,** *m.* catchment area. **–graben,** *m.* drain, gutter, drain-trench. **–rohr,** *n.*, **–röhre,** *f.* waste-pipe, drain-pipe.

Abfolge ['apfɔlgə], *f.* succession, sequence, series, order.

abfordern ['apfɔrdərn], *v.t.* 1. ***ihm etwas –,*** demand *or* require s.th. of *or* from him; ***ihm Rechenschaft –,*** call him to account; 2. recall. **Abforderung,** *f.* 1. demand, requirement; 2. recall.

abformen ['apfɔrmən], *v.t.* mould, form, fashion, shape. **Abformmasse,** *f.* modelling *or* moulding compound.

abforsten ['apfɔrstən], *v.t.* clear of trees, deforest.

abfragen ['apfra:gən], **1.** *v.t.* ***ihn*** *or* (*coll.*) ***ihm etwas –,*** question *or* examine him orally about s.th.; ***die Klasse –,*** ask questions round the class. **2.** *v.i.* (*Tele.*) 1. answer *or* accept the call; 2. test the line.

abfressen ['apfrɛsən], *irr.v.i.* 1. crop, browse on; eat up, consume; 2. corrode, erode; ***der Gram frißt ihm das Herz ab,*** grief gnaws at his heart.

abfrieren ['apfri:rən], *irr.v.i.* (*aux.* s.) be killed *or* nipped by frost, be frost-bitten.

Abfuhr ['apfu:r], *f.* (-, *pl.* **-en**) 1. removal, carriage, cartage, disposal; elimination; emptying, voidance; 2. (*coll.*) rebuff; (*Studs. sl.*) disabling wound (*in duelling*).

abführen ['apfy:rən], **1.** *v.t.* 1. lead away, carry off, take into custody; ***vom rechten Wege –,*** lead astray; 2. discharge, clear, pay off (*debt*); dissipate (*heat etc.*), evacuate, purge (*impurities*); ***Geld – an*** (*Acc.*), pay out *or* over to; 3. (*coll.*) snub. **2.** *v.i.* act as a laxative, open *or* loosen the bowels. **abführend,** *adj.* purgative, laxative, aperient.

Abfuhr|karren, *m.* dustcart. **–kosten,** *pl.*, **–lohn,** *m.* transport charges, cartage.

Abführmittel ['apfy:rmıtəl], *n.* purgative, purge, laxative, aperient, opening medicine. **Abführung,** *f.* 1. removal, arrest, (*also Med.*) evacuation; 2. discharge (*of debt*), dissipation (*of heat etc.*). **Abführungsgang,** *m.* (*Physiol.*) excretory *or* efferent duct.

abfüllen ['apfylən], *v.t.* draw off, rack (*wine*), decant; ***Wein auf Flaschen –,*** bottle wine. **Abfüll|maschine,** *f.* bottling *or* racking machine. **–trichter,** *m.* funnel (*for filling*).

abfurchen ['apfurçən], **1.** *v.t.* divide by furrows. **2.** *v.r.* (*Biol.*) undergo segmentation. **Abfurchung,** *f.* cleavage, segmentation.

abfüttern ['apfytərn], *v.t.* 1. feed (*cattle*), give (*cattle*) last feed of the day; (*coll.*) feed (*one's guests*) well; 2. line (*with cloth*). **Abfütterung,** *f.* 1. feeding, (*coll.*) feed, spread; mass feeding; 2. lining.

Abgabe ['apga:bə], *f.* 1. delivery; posting, mailing, handing in; discharge, emission, secretion, liberation, generation, output, yield; casting (*of vote*); payment (*of taxes*); delivery, pronouncement (*of opinion*); *pl.* (*Comm.*) selling, sales; disposal; 2. tax, duty, levy, contribution, *pl.* (*Law*) fees, (*Naut.*) dues; 3. (*Comm.*) draft, bill of exchange.

Abgabekurs ['apga:bəkurs], *m.* (*Comm.*) issue price. **abgabenfrei,** *adj.* exempt from *or* free of tax *or* duty, tax-free, duty-free. **abgabe(n)pflichtig,** *adj.* liable to tax *or* duty, taxable, dutiable, assessable. **Abgabe(n)wesen,** *n.* system of taxation. **Abgabe|preis,** *m.* selling price, tariff, charge (*electricity etc.*). **–spannung,** *f.* (*Elec.*) output voltage. **–wesen,** *n. See* **Abgabe(n)wesen.**

Abgang ['apgaŋ], *m.* 1. departure; exit (*from stage*), retirement, retiral (*from office*); ***nach – von der Schule,*** on leaving school; (*fig.*) ***sich einen guten – verschaffen,*** retire gracefully; 2. sale; ***guten – haben,*** have *or* find a ready sale; ***es findet keinen –,*** there is no sale for it; 3. loss, wastage, depreciation, *pl.* waste, refuse, spoilage, scraps, scrapings, filings; ***nach – der männlichen Linie,*** failing male issue *or* heirs; (*obs.*) ***in – kommen,*** fall into abeyance *or* disuse, go out of fashion; ***– an Gewicht,*** deficiency in weight, (*Am.*) wantage.

abgängig ['apgɛŋıç], *adj.* 1. lost, mislaid, missing (*of papers etc.*); 2. marketable, saleable; 3. deteriorating, going bad *or* off; worn-out, shabby.

Abgangs|dampf, *m.* dead steam, exhaust-steam. **–prüfung,** *f.* leaving (*Am.* final) examination. **–winkel,** *m.* (*Artil.*) angle of departure. **–zeugnis,** *n.* leaving certificate, (*Am.*) diploma.

Abgas ['apga:s], *n.* exhaust gas, waste gas.

abgeben ['apge:bən], **1.** *irr.v.t.* 1. deliver (up), hand in *or* over; give up, part with, relinquish, cede; (*Footb.*) pass (*the ball*); ***ihm etwas –,*** give him some of s.th., share s.th. with him; ***er hat diesen Brief für Sie abgegeben,*** he has left this letter for you; (*coll.*) ***ihm eins –,*** let him have it; ***einen Schuß –,*** fire a shot; 2. give off (*heat etc.*), give (*opinion*), pass (*judgement*), cast (*vote*); 3. supply, sell (*goods*); ***wir können es zu diesem Preis nicht –,*** we cannot supply it on these terms; 4. serve as, play the part of; ***er hätte einen guten Arzt abgegeben,*** he would have made a good doctor; ***einen Narren –,*** play the fool; 5. ***einen Wechsel auf ihn –,*** draw (a bill) on him. **2.** *irr.v.imp.* (*coll.*) ***paß auf, sonst gibt's heute noch was ab!*** you mind, or you'll be in for trouble! **3.** *irr.v.r.* engage (*mit*, in), occupy o.s. (with), meddle (in), bother (about *or* o.s. with); ***mit ihm gebe ich mich nicht ab,*** I won't have anything to do with him; ***sich gern mit Kindern –,*** be fond of (playing with) children; ***sich mit Kleinigkeiten –,*** bother about details.

abgebrannt ['apgəbrant], *adj.* 1. burnt-out; ***–es Streichholz,*** spent match; 2. (*coll.*) stony-broke, on one's beam-ends, on the rocks. *See* **abbrennen.**

abgebraten ['apgəbra:tən], *adj.* well-done (*roast*).

abgebraucht ['apgəbrauxt], *adj.* shabby, threadbare. *See* **abbrauchen.**

abgebrochen ['apgəbrɔxən], *adj.* abrupt, disconnected, disjointed, incoherent. *See* **abbrechen.**

abgebrüht ['apgəbry:t], *adj.* (*coll.*) hard, callous; ***er ist gegen Schande –,*** he is past shame *or* lost to all shame.

abgebunden ['apgəbundən], *adj.* (*Swiss*) ***kurz –,*** briefly, in short. *See* **abbinden.**

abgedrechselt ['apgədrɛksəlt], *adj.* stiff, affected (*of style*). *See* **abdrechseln.**

abgedroschen ['apgədrɔʃən], *adj.* trite, hackneyed. *See* **abdreschen.**

abgefallen ['apgəfalən], *adj.* haggard, emaciated. *See* **abfallen. Abgefallene(r),** *m., f.* deserter, renegade; (*Eccl.*) apostate.

abgefärbt ['apgəfɛrpt], *adj.* faded. *See* **abfärben.**

abgefeimt ['apgəfaımt], *adj.* crafty, cunning, knowing; ***–er Bösewicht,*** out-and-out *or* unmitigated scoundrel.

abgegriffen ['apgəgrıfən], *adj.* 1. (well-)worn, shabby; well-thumbed (*book*), dog-eared (*pages*); 2. trite, hackneyed (*phrases*). *See* **abgreifen.**

abgehackt ['apgəhakt], *adj.* disjointed, jerky. *See* **abhacken.**

abgehärmt ['apgəhɛrmt], *adj.* careworn.

abgehen ['apge:ən], **1.** *irr.v.i.* (*aux.* s.) 1. depart, leave, start, set out, go off; (*Theat.*) make one's exit; give up, retire from, resign (*post, office*); come off *or* loose; ***wann geht die Post ab?*** when does the post leave? ***Shylock geht ab,*** exit Shylock; ***von der Schule –,*** leave school; ***mit (dem) Tode –,*** depart this life; ***das Rad ging ab,*** the wheel came off; 2. depart, deviate, diverge; lack, be lost, be deducted; ***der Weg geht links ab,*** the path branches off to the left; ***davon kann ich nicht –,*** I must insist upon that; ***von meiner Meinung –,*** change *or* alter my opinion; ***von meinem Vorhaben nicht –,*** stick to *or* persist in *or* not budge from my plan; ***bei Barzahlung gehen 5% ab,*** reduction *or* discount of 5% for cash; ***er läßt sich nichts –,*** he denies himself nothing, he does himself well; ***die nötigen Kenntnisse gehen ihm ab,*** he lacks the necessary knowledge; ***ihr soll nichts –,*** she shall want for nothing, she will not go short; ***es ging ihm viel Blut ab,*** he lost much blood; 3. (*coll.*) pass off, go off, finish, end; ***das ging gut ab,*** that went off well; ***es wird übel –,*** it will turn out badly *or* end in trouble; ***reißend –,*** sell like hot cakes, be in great demand, go well. **2.** *irr. v.t.* pace out (*a distance*), walk round, inspect, patrol (*fields etc.*).

abgeizen ['apgaıtsən], *v.t.* wrest (*Dat.*, from); ***sich (Dat.) etwas –,*** pinch and scrape.

abgekämpft ['apgəkɛmpft], *adj.* battle-weary, (*fig.*) worn out, dead beat. *See* **abkämpfen.**

abgekartet ['apgəkartət], *adj.* prearranged, (*coll.*) rigged, put-up (*job*). *See* **abkarten.**

abgeklärt ['apgəklɛ:rt], *adj.* serene, tranquil (*of character*), limpid (*of style*). *See* **abklären. Abgeklärtheit,** *f.* serenity, tranquillity; clarity.

abgelagert ['apgəla:gərt], *see* **ablagern.**

abgelebt ['apgəle:pt], *adj.* deceased, passed away; decrepit. *See* **ableben.**

abgelegen ['apgəle:gən], *adj.* remote, secluded, sequestered, unfrequented, (*coll.*) out-of-the-way. *See* **ablegen. Abgelegenheit,** *f.* remoteness, seclusion.

abgeleitet ['apgəlaɪtət], *adj.* (*Mus., Gram.*) derived. *See* **ableiten.**

abgemacht ['apgəmaxt], *adj.* settled, arranged, agreed. *See* **abmachen.**

abgemessen ['apgəmɛsən], *adj.* measured; precise; formal, stiff, ceremonious. *See* **abmessen. Abgemessenheit,** *f.* precision, exactness; formality, ceremoniousness, reserve, stiffness.

abgeneigt ['apgənaɪkt], *adj.* unwilling; unfavourably disposed; averse (*zu tun*, to doing), disinclined, reluctant *or* loath (to do). **Abgeneigtheit,** *f.* (*gegen*) disinclination (to *or* for), dislike (of), distaste (for), aversion (to *or* for), reluctance (to do).

abgenutzt ['apgənutst], *adj.* worn, thread-bare, shabby; blunt (*as pencil*). *See* **abnutzen.**

Abgeordnetenhaus ['apgəˀɔrdnətənhaus], *n.* parliament; (*Engl.*) House of Commons, (*U.S.A.*) House of Representatives, (*France*) Chamber of Deputies. **Abgeordnete(r),** *m., f.* deputy, delegate, (parliamentary) representative; (*Engl.*) Member of Parliament, (*U.S.A.*) representative, congressman, (*France*) deputy.

abgerben ['apgɛrbən], *v.t.* tan (*leather*); (*coll.*) tan (*s.o.'s*) hide.

abgerundet ['apgərundət], *adj.* perfect, finished (*performance*). *See* **abrunden.**

abgesagt ['apgəza:kt], *adj.* declared, avowed, professed, sworn (*enemy etc.*). *See* **absagen.**

Abgesandte(r) ['apgəzantə(r)], *m., f.* delegate, envoy, emissary, ambassador.

Abgesang ['apgəzaŋ], *m. A technical term in mediaeval lyric verse and the poetry of the mastersingers denoting* the latter portion of a stanza. *See* **Aufgesang.**

abgeschieden ['apgəʃi:dən], *adj.* 1. isolated, remote, solitary, secluded, retired; 2. departed, defunct; *-e Seele*, departed spirit. *See* **abscheiden. Abgeschiedene,** *pl.* the departed. **Abgeschiedenheit,** *f.* remoteness, isolation, seclusion, solitude, privacy, retirement.

abgeschliffen ['apgəʃlɪfən], *adj.* polished, refined, polite. *See* **abschleifen. Abgeschliffenheit,** *f.* polish, refinement, urbanity, (good) breeding.

abgeschlossen ['apgəʃlɔsən], *adj.* concluded, settled, closed (*also Math.*), completed, complete (in itself), self-contained. *See* **abschließen. Abgeschlossenheit,** *f.* 1. seclusion, isolation; (*Math.*) closure; 2. compactness, completeness (within itself).

abgeschmackt ['apgəʃmakt], *adj.* tasteless, tactless, inept, in bad taste. **Abgeschmacktheit,** *f.* bad taste; ineptitude, tactlessness.

abgeschnitten ['apgəʃnɪtən], *adj.* (*Geom.*) truncated. *See* **abschneiden.**

abgesehen ['apgəze:ən], *p.p.* – *von,* without regard to; apart from, disregarding, leaving out of account, not counting, not to mention, irrespective of, (*Am.*) aside from. *See* **absehen.**

abgesessen ['apgəzɛsən], *see* **absitzen.**

abgespannt ['apgəʃpant], *adj.* tired (out), weary, exhausted, fatigued, enervated. *See* **abspannen. Abgespanntheit,** *f.* exhaustion, debility, languor, enervation.

abgestanden ['apgəʃtandən], *adj.* stale (*bread etc.*), stagnant (*water*), flat (*beer etc.*), perished (*rubber*); (*fig.*) outworn (*ideas*). *See* **abstehen.**

abgestorben ['apgəʃtɔrbən], *adj.* numb, dead; *der Gesellschaft* –, lost to society. *See* **absterben. Abgestorbenheit,** *f.* torpor, apathy, numbness; insensitivity (*für,* to).

abgestumpft ['apgəʃtumpft], *adj.* (*Geom.*) truncated; blunted, dull; indifferent (*gegen,* to); (*Chem.*) neutralized. *See* **abstumpfen. Abgestumpftheit,** *f.* dullness, apathy, indifference, insensitivity.

abgetan ['apgətan], *see* **abtun.**

abgetragen ['apgətra:gən], *adj.* worn out, thread-bare, decrepit; (*fig.*) stale, hackneyed (*jokes etc.*). *See* **abtragen.**

abgetrennt ['apgətrɛnt], *adj.* detached. *See* **abtrennen.**

abgewinnen ['apgəvɪnən], *irr.v.t.* win *or* gain (*Dat.* from); extract; *ihm den Vorteil* –, get the better of him; *ihm den Vorsprung* –, get the start of *or* steal a march on him; *einer S. Geschmack* – acquire a taste for a th.

abgewöhnen ['apgəvø:nən], *v.t. ihm etwas* –, disaccustom *or* cure *or* break him of s.th.; *sich* (*Dat.*) *das Rauchen* –, break o.s. of the habit of *or* give up smoking.

abgezogen ['apgətso:gən], *adj.* subtracted, deducted; (*Phil.*) *-er Begriff,* abstract idea. *See* **abziehen. Abgezogenheit,** *f.* isolation, seclusion; (*Phil.*) abstraction.

abgieren ['apgi:rən], *v.i.* (*Naut.*) sheer off (course).

abgießen ['apgi:sən], *irr.v.t.* 1. pour off; decant; 2. fill (*the mould with molten metal*), found, cast (*in a foundry*); 3. strain, drain (*water from vegetables*). **Abgießer,** *m.* foundry hand, caster, moulder.

Abglanz ['apglants], *m.* (**-es,** *no pl.*) reflected splendour, reflection.

abglätten ['apglɛtən], **1.** *v.t.* smooth, polish. **2.** *v.r.* acquire polish (*of a p.*).

abgleichen ['apglaɪçən], *irr.v.t.* equalize, balance (*also Rad.*); (*Typ.*) adjust, justify; level up *or* down, even up; make flush, level *or* even; smooth; *Rechnungen* –, square *or* balance accounts. **Abgleichkondensator,** *m.* (*Rad.*) trimming condenser. **Abgleichung,** *f.* levelling; equalization; adjustment. **Abgleichungswaage,** *f. See* **Justierwaage. Abgleichzirkel,** *m.* divider.

abgleiten ['apglaɪtən], *irr.v.i.* (*aux.* s.) 1. slip *or* slide *or* glance *or* glide off *or* down; *alles gleitet an ihm ab,* he is deaf *or* unresponsive to *or* proof against everything; 2. (*fig.*) decline, sag, slump (*of prices*).

abgliedern ['apgli:dərn], **1.** *v.t.* dismember. **2.** *v.i.* segment off. **Abgliederung,** *f.* 1. dismemberment, segmentation; 2. offshoot.

abglühen ['apgly:ən], *v.t.* make red-hot; anneal, temper.

Abgott ['apgɔt], *m.* idol; *zu seinem* – *machen,* idolize.

Abgötterei [apgœtə'raɪ], *f.* idolatry. **abgöttisch** ['apgœtɪʃ], *adj.* idolatrous; – *lieben,* idolize.

Abgottschlange ['apgɔtʃlaŋə], *f.* boa-constrictor, anaconda.

abgraben ['apgra:bən], *irr.v.t.* dig away; separate, mark off *or* surround with a ditch; drain (*marsh etc.*), cut *or* draw off (*water*) (*Dat.,* from); (*fig.*) *ihm das Wasser* –, cut the ground from under his feet.

abgrämen ['apgrɛ:mən], *v.r.* pine away, worry o.s. to death.

abgrasen ['apgra:zən], *v.t.* graze on, crop (*a field*); (*fig.*) *alle Läden* –, scour all the shops; *ein Gebiet* –, thoroughly work over a domain (*i.e.* exhaust all possibilities).

abgraten ['apgra:tən], *v.t.* remove the burr from, trim (*metal*).

abgreifen ['apgraɪfən], *irr.v.t.* 1. wear out by constant handling. *See* **abgegriffen**; 2. span; measure off (*with compasses*).

abgrenzbar ['apgrɛntsba:r], *adj.* definable, distinguishable.

abgrenzen ['apgrɛntsən], *v.t.* demarcate, delimit, mark off *or* out; define, circumscribe; distinguish, differentiate, keep distinct *or* separate. **Abgrenzung,** *f.* demarcation, delimitation; definition. **Abgrenzungslinie,** *f.* line of demarcation.

Abgrund ['apgrunt], *m.* pit, gulf, chasm, abyss; (*fig.*) *am Rande des -s,* on the brink *or* verge of disaster (ruin *etc.*); *in einem* – *des Elends,* in the depths of *or* engulfed in misery.

abgründig ['apgryndɪç], *adj.* unfathomable (*depths*); abysmal; *ein -er Charakter,* a dark horse.

abgrundtief ['apgruntti:f], *adj. See* **abgründig.**

abgucken ['apgukən], *v.t.* (*coll.*) (***ihm etwas***) learn (*s.th.*) by watching (*him*), copy *or* crib (*s.th. from him*).

abgünstig ['apgynstɪç], *adj. See* **mißgünstig.**

Abguß ['apgus], *m.* 1. cast(ing), mould(ing); (*Typ.*) stereotype; 2. drain, gutter, sink.

abhaaren ['apha:rən], **1.** *v.t.* remove hair from. **2.** *v.i.* lose *or* shed its hair; moult.

abhacken ['aphakən], *v.t.* chop *or* cut *or* hack off *or* down.

abhaken ['apha:kən], *v.t.* 1. unhook, unfasten; (*Railw.*) uncouple, disconnect; take *or* lift off the hook; 2. put a tick against, tick (off), (*Am.*) check (off).

abhalftern ['aphalftərn], *v.t.* unharness; remove the halter from; (*coll.*) sack, fire (*an official etc.*).

abhalten ['aphaltən], **1.** *irr.v.t.* 1. hold off *or* back; keep *or* keep away (*von*, from), restrain, prevent, deter, hinder; ***lassen Sie sich nicht –!*** don't let me hinder you, don't disturb yourself; 2. hold (*assizes, service, meeting, parade etc.*); 3. hold (*a child*) out. **2.** *irr.v.i.* (*Naut.*) bear away; ***vom Lande –***, bear off from the land. **Abhaltung,** *f.* (*usu. pl.*) another engagement, other engagements.

abhandeln ['aphandəln], *v.t.* 1. negotiate; transact, handle (*business*); ***ihm etwas –***, do a deal with him for s.th.; ***etwas vom Preise –***, knock s.th. off the price (by bargaining); ***er läßt sich nichts –***, he won't reduce his price, he won't be beaten down; **2.** handle, discuss, deal with, treat (of) (*a subject*).

abhanden [ap'handən], *adv.* – ***sein***, be lost, mislaid *or* missing; – ***kommen***, get lost, go astray, be mislaid.

Abhandlung ['aphandluŋ], *f.* 1. treatise, dissertation, paper, essay (***über*** (*Acc.*), on); *pl.* proceedings, transactions (*of a learned society*); 2. discussion, discourse (***über*** (*Acc.*), about *or* on).

Abhang ['aphaŋ], *m.* slope, declivity, incline, gradient. **abhangen,** *irr.v.i. now usu.* **abhängen, 1.** *q.v.*

abhängen ['aphɛŋən], **1.** *irr.v.i.* 1. hang down, be suspended; hang (*of meat, game*); 2. slope *or* fall away; 3. (*fig.*) – ***von***, depend on, be dependent on, hang *or* rest *or* turn *or* hinge on. **2.** *reg.v.t.* 1. unhang; take down; take off the hook; (*Tele.*) take off *or* lift (*the receiver*), (*usu.*) ring off, hang up; (*Railw.*) disconnect, uncouple; 2. hang (*meat, game till tender*).

abhängig ['aphɛŋɪç], *adj.* 1. sloping, inclined; 2. conditional *or* dependent (***von***, on), subordinate *or* subject (to); ***–e Rede***, indirect *or* reported speech. **Abhängigkeit,** *f.* 1. slope, declivity; 2. dependency, dependence (***von***, on), subjection, subordination (to); (*Math.*) ***in – von . . . auftragen***, plot as a function of.

abhärmen ['aphɛrmən], *v.r.* languish; pine away, grieve (***über*** (*Acc.*), ***wegen***, over).

abhärten ['aphɛrtən], **1.** *v.t.* harden, toughen, inure; (*Metall.*) temper. **2.** *v.r.* inure o.s. (*to fatigue etc.*); become hardened *or* toughened, keep (o.s.) fit.

abhaschen ['aphaʃən], *v.t.* (***ihm etwas***) snatch (*s.th. from him*).

abhaspeln ['aphaspəln], *v.t.* unwind, wind off; (*coll.*) reel *or* rattle off (*poem etc.*).

abhauen ['aphauən], **1.** *irr.v.t.* cut off; cut down, fell. **2.** *irr.v.i.* (*aux.* s.) (*sl.*) clear out, beat it, sling one's hook, scram.

abhäuten ['aphɔytən], **1.** *v.t.* flay (*large animals*), skin (*small creatures*), peel, excoriate. **2.** *v.r.* cast its skin *or* slough, slough its skin.

abheben ['aphe:bən], **1.** *irr.v.t.* take *or* lift off, remove; ***Geld –***, (with)draw money (*from bank*); ***eine Masche –***, slip a stitch (*knitting*); ***den Rahm –***, skim the cream off, skim the milk. **2.** *irr.v.i.* 1. cut (*cards*); ***wer hebt ab?*** whose turn is it to cut? 2. (*Av.*) take off. **3.** *irr.v.r.* stand out (in relief); ***die Wolken hoben sich vom Himmel*** or ***gegen den Himmel ab***, the clouds stood out against the sky.

abhebern ['aphe:bərn], *v.t.* siphon off.

Abhebung ['aphe:buŋ], *f.* withdrawal (*money*).

abheilen ['aphaɪlən], *v.i.* (*aux.* s.) heal completely.

abhelfen ['aphɛlfən], *irr.v.i.* (*Dat.*) remedy, redress; ***dem ist nicht abzuhelfen***, that is beyond remedy, that is past mending, nothing more can be done; ***einer Schwierigkeit –***, remove a difficulty; ***einem Fehler –***, correct *or* rectify an error; ***einem Unrecht –***, redress *or* right a wrong.

abherzen ['aphɛrtsən], *v.t.* hug and kiss, smother with kisses.

abhetzen ['aphɛtsən], **1.** *v.t.* tire out, harass. **2.** *v.r.* tire *or* wear o.s. out.

Abhilfe ['aphɪlfə], *f.* remedy, redress.

Abhitze ['aphɪtsə], *f.* (-, *no pl.*) *see* **Abwärme.**

abhobeln ['apho:bəln], *v.t.* smooth with a plane; plane off.

abhold ['aphɔlt], *adj.* averse (*Dat.*, to); disinclined (for); unfavourable (to).

abholen ['apho:lən], *v.t.* fetch, collect (*things*), call for, go to meet (*persons*); (*Naut.*) haul *or* get off; ***ihn – lassen***, send for him; ***ich will Sie bei Ihrem Vater –***, I will call for you at your father's; ***das Auto wird mich –***, the car will come for me.

Abholz ['aphɔlts], *n.* (**-es,** *no pl.*) waste wood. **abholzen,** *v.t.* fell, cut down (*trees*), clear of timber (*land*), deforest. **Abholzung,** *f.* deforestation.

abhorchen ['aphɔrçən], *v.t.* 1. overhear; ***ihm etwas –***, learn s.th. from him by eavesdropping; 2. (*Med.*) auscultate. **Abhorchgerät,** *n.* (*Nav.*) anti-submarine sound-detector (ASDIC).

Abhördienst ['aphø:rdi:nst], *m.* (*Tele., Mil.*) monitoring service.

abhören ['aphø:rən], *v.t.* overhear, eavesdrop on (*conversation*), pick up *or* learn (*s.th.*) by listening; hear (*s.o.*) recite; tap the (telephone) wire; (*Tele., Rad. etc.*) intercept, listen in to, monitor; ***einen Schüler –***, hear a pupil's lesson; ***Zeugen –***, question witnesses. **Abhör|raum,** *m.*, **–zelle,** *f.* control *or* monitoring room.

Abhub ['aphu:p], *m.* (**-(e)s,** *no pl.*) leavings, remains (*of a meal*); waste, scum, dross.

äbich, äbicht ['ɛbɪç(t)], *adj.* reverse *or* wrong (*side of cloth*); (*fig.*) awkward, prickly (*character*).

abirren ['apˀɪrən], *v.i.* (*aux.* s.) lose one's way; deviate, stray, wander, err. **abirrend,** *adj.* (*Opt.*) aberrant. **Abirrung,** *f.* deviation; (*Opt.*) aberration.

Abitur [abi'tu:r], *n.* (**-s,** *pl.* **-e**) school-leaving examination (qualifying for admission to a university). **Abiturient** [-ri'ɛnt], *m.* (**-en,** *pl.* **-en**) candidate for *or* one who has recently passed this examination (= sixth-former, school-leaver).

abjagen ['apja:gən], **1.** *v.t.* 1. override (*horse*), overwork (*dog*); 2. hunt over (*ground*); 3. ***ihm etwas –***, retrieve *or* recover s.th. from him. **2.** *v.r.* over-exert o.s.

abjäten ['apjɛ:tən], *v.t.* weed (*ground*).

abkälten ['apkɛltən], *v.t.* cool (down), chill (*wine etc.*).

abkämpfen ['apkɛmpfən], *v.t.* fight off, drive away; ***ihm etwas –***, wrest s.th. from him. *See* **abgekämpft.**

abkanten ['apkantən], **1.** *v.t.* 1. take off the selvedge; 2. chamfer; bevel. **2.** *v.i.* cast off (*knitting*).

abkanzeln ['apkantsəln], *v.t.* (*coll.*) give (*s.o.*) a good talking-to *or* a good scolding; (*sl.*) dress down, tick off, blow up.

abkappen ['apkapɛn], *v.t.* lop, pollard (*trees*).

abkarten ['apkartən], *v.t.* prearrange, concert; ***sie haben es unter sich*** or ***miteinander abgekartet***, they are acting in collusion. *See* **abgekartet.**

abkauen ['apkauən], *v.t.* chew *or* gnaw away *or* off; ***sich*** (*Dat.*) ***die Nägel –***, bite one's nails (to the quick).

Abkauf ['apkauf], *m.* purchase (= act of purchasing). **abkaufen,** *v.t.* ***ihm etwas –***, buy *or* purchase s.th. from him; ***sich*** (*Dat.*) ***jedes Wort – lassen***, have the words dragged out of one.

Abkäufer ['apkɔyfər], *m.* purchaser; (*Law*) vendee.

Abkehr ['apke:r], *f.* (-, *no pl.*) withdrawing, renunciation; – *von Gott,* estrangement from God.

[1]**abkehren** ['apke:rən], **1.** *v.t.* turn away, avert. **2.** *v.r.* (*fig.*) withdraw, stand aloof, disassociate o.s., become estranged (*von,* from), turn one's back (on).

[2]**abkehren,** *v.t.* clean *or* sweep out (*room*), brush (*carpet*).

abkeltern ['apkɛltərn], *v.t.* press (*grapes etc.*).

abkippen ['apkɪpən], *v.i.* (*aux.* s.) (*sl.*) dive (*of submarine*), pitch *or* topple over.

abklappern ['apklapərn], *v.t.* (*coll.*) traipse round.

abklären ['apklɛ:rən], **1.** *v.t.* clarify, filter, decant (*liquid*); (*fig.*) (*Swiss*) *see* **aufklären.** *See* **abgeklärt. 2.** *v.r.* become clear, clear, settle (*of liquid*); (*fig.*) clarify themselves (*of ideas*), gain serenity (*of a p.*). **Abklärflasche,** *f.* decanting vessel. **Abklärung,** *f.* decantation; clarification (*also fig.*). **Abklärungsflasche,** *f. See* **Abklärflasche.**

Abklatsch ['apklatʃ], *m.* 1. cast(ing), (brush-)proof, stereotype(-plate); 2. (*fig.*) poor imitation. **abklatschen,** *v.t.* 1. (*Found.*) cast; print off (*proof-sheet*), stereotype; 2. (*fig.*) plagiarize, copy.

abklemmen ['apklɛmən], *v.t.* pinch off.

abklingen ['apklɪŋən], *irr.v.i.* die away (*of sound etc.*); fade away, (*fig.*) die down, ease *or* wear off.

abklopfen ['apklɔpfən], **1.** *v.t.* 1. beat (*carpets etc.*); 2. knock off; 3. tap, test (*by knocking, as a wall*); (*Med.*) percuss; 4. (*coll.*) give (*s.o.*) a sound drubbing; 5. (*coll.*) *alle Läden* –, scour the shops; 6. *einen Probebogen* –, strike off a proof-sheet. **2.** *v.i.* stop the orchestra (*by the conductor with his baton*).

abknabbern ['apknabərn], *v.t.* nibble off *or* bare.

abknallen ['apknalən], **1.** *v.i.* (*aux.* s.) explode, go off. **2.** *v.t.* (*coll.*) shoot down.

abknapsen ['apknapsən], *v.t.* break *or* nip off (the end of); *sich* (*Dat.*) *etwas* –, stint o.s. of s.th.; (*coll.*) *ihm vom Lohn etwas* –, dock s.th. off his wages.

abkneifen ['apknaɪfən], *irr.v.t.* pinch *or* nip off; *den Wind* –, haul the wind; ply to windward; (*einem Schiffe*) *den Wind* –, luff a ship.

abknöpfen ['apknœpfən], *v.t.* unbutton; (*coll.*) *ihm 10 Mark* –, sting him for 10 marks.

abknüpfen ['apknypfən], *v.t.* loosen; untie; undo.

abknutschen ['apknu:tʃən], *v.t.* (*sl.*) smother with kisses.

abkochen ['apkɔxən], **1.** *v.t.* 1. boil, sterilize; *Milch* –, scald milk; 2. make a decoction of. **2.** *v.i.* cook over a camp-fire.

abkommandieren ['apkɔmandi:rən], *v.t.* order off, detail (*troops*), detach, second (*officer*).

Abkomme ['apkɔmə], *m.* (**-n,** *pl.* **-n**) *see* **Abkömmling.**

abkommen ['apkɔmən], *irr.v.i.* (*aux.* s.) 1. get away (from), get off; *können Sie wohl eine Viertelstunde* –? can you get away *or* be spared for a quarter of an hour? (*Spt.*) *gut* –, get a good start, get off the mark well; *ich bin davon abgekommen,* I have given it up *or* dropped it; *ich bin von meiner früheren Ansicht abgekommen,* I have abandoned *or* forsaken *or* dropped my former opinion; *vom Kurs* –, get off one's course; *vom Wege* –, lose one's way; (*Naut.*) *vom Winde* –, fall to leeward; 2. fall into disuse *or* abeyance, become obsolete, go out (of fashion); 3. aim (*of marksman*); *gut, schlecht, rechts, links, hoch* or *tief* –, aim well, badly, to the right, to the left, high *or* low.

Abkommen, *n.* 1. agreement, settlement; *ein* – *treffen,* enter *or* conclude *or* come to an agreement; *ein gütliches* –, an amicable settlement; *Genfer* –, Geneva Convention; 2. *See* **Abkunft;** 3. (*Spt.*) start.

Abkommenschaft ['apkɔmənʃaft], *f.* (-, *no pl.*) offspring, progeny, issue, descendants; posterity.

Abkommlauf ['apkɔmlauf], *m.* sub-calibre barrel, Morris tube (*small arms*).

abkömmlich ['apkœmlɪç], *adj.* dispensable, superfluous.

Abkömmling ['apkœmlɪŋ], *m.* (**-s,** *pl.* **-e**) descendant, offspring, scion; (*Chem.*) derivative; *pl.* progeny.

Abkomm|punkt, *m.* point of aim. **-rohr,** *n.* (*Artil.*) sub-calibre barrel. **-schießen,** *n.* (sub-calibre) practice fire *or* firing, target practice.

abkoppeln ['apkɔpəln], *v.t.* uncouple (*horses*), unleash (*dogs*), unbuckle (*sword*).

Abkratz|bürste, *f.* wire brush. **-eisen,** *n.* (shoe- *or* door-)scraper.

abkratzen ['apkratsən], **1.** *v.t.* scrape *or* scratch off; *sich* (*Dat.*) *die Schuhe* –, scrape one's shoes. **2.** *v.i.* (*aux.* s.) (*sl.*) peg out.

abkriegen ['apkri:gən], *v.t.* (*coll.*) *see* **abbekommen.**

abkühlen ['apky:lən], **1.** *v.t.* cool, chill, anneal (*glass*), quench (*oil*); (*fig.*) damp, dash (*enthusiasm*), calm, quiet (*anger*). **2.** *v.i.* (*aux.* s.), *v.r.* cool down *or* off (*also fig.*). **Abkühlofen,** *m.* annealing oven (*for glass*). **Abkühlung,** *f.* cooling, chilling, refrigeration. **Abkühlungs|fläche,** *f.* cooling *or* radiating surface. **-mittel,** *n.* cooling medicine *or* medium; (*Engin.*) coolant. **-verlust,** *m.* loss by cooling, cooling loss.

abkündigen ['apkyndɪgən], *v.t.* announce from the pulpit, proclaim; *ein Brautpaar* –, put up *or* publish the banns.

Abkunft ['apkunft], *f.* (-, *pl.* ⸚e) descent, origin, lineage; race, blood; (*von*) *niedriger* –, of low birth, of humble origin *or* parentage; *adliger* –, of noble descent *or* lineage; *germanischer* –, of Germanic stock.

abkuppeln ['apkupəln], *v.t.* uncouple, disengage.

abkürzen ['apkyrtsən], **1.** *v.t.* shorten, curtail, cut down *or* short; abridge, condense; abbreviate; *eine Silbe* –, shorten a syllable; *den Weg* –, take a short cut; *ein Wort* –, abbreviate *or* contract a word. **2.** *v.i.* shorten the distance, be a short cut. **Abkürzung,** *f.* contraction, abbreviation; abridgement. **Abkürzungszeichen,** *n.* (*Stenography*) grammalogue, short form.

abküssen ['apkysən], *v.t.* keep on kissing; kiss away (*tears etc.*).

abladen ['apla:dən], *irr.v.t.* 1. unload; unlade, discharge (*cargo*); *Schutt* –, tip *or* dump rubbish; *seine Sorgen bei ihm* –, unburden one's sorrows to him; *die Verantwortung auf ihn* –, shift the responsibility to him; 2. (*sl.*) fork out; *lad ab!* cough *or* stump up! **Ablade|ort, -platz,** *m.* port of discharge; wharf. **Ablader,** *m.* unloader; docker, dock-labourer, stevedore; lighterman.

Ablage ['apla:gə], *f.* depository, repository, depot, warehouse, yard, dump; (*Theat.*) cloakroom. *See* **ablegen.**

ablagern ['apla:gərn], **1.** *v.t.* 1. deposit; 2. season, age, mature (*wine, cigars etc.*); *abgelagerte Zigarren,* matured *or* well-seasoned cigars. **2.** *v.r.* settle, form a deposit *or* sediment, be deposited. **3.** *v.i.* (*aux.* s.) mature, age, grow mellow; – *lassen, see* **1. Ablagerung,** *f.* 1. deposit. sediment, sedimentation; 2. (*Geol.*) stratum, layer, bed.

Ablaß ['aplas], *m.* (**-(ss)es,** *pl.* ⸚**(ss)e**) **1.** drainage, outlet, drain, sluice; 2. (*Comm.*) reduction, allowance; 3. (*R.C.*) indulgence; *vollkommener* –, plenary indulgence. **Ablaßbrief,** *m.* letter of indulgence.

ablassen ['aplasən], **1.** *irr.v.t.* 1. drain (off), empty, draw *or* run *or* let off, blow *or* let off (*steam*), draw, let (*blood*), rack (*wine*); 2. start *or* send (off), set going, dispatch; launch (*ship*), start (*train*), release (*pigeons*); 3. reduce (*in price*), deduct; *zum Selbstkostenpreis* –, sell *or* let go at cost price. **2.** *irr.v.i.* stop, leave off, cease, desist.

Ablaß|geld, *n.* shrove-money. **-hahn,** *m.* drain-cock. **-handel,** *m.* (*Hist.*) sale of indulgences. **-jahr,** *n.* (*R.C.*) (year of) jubilee. **-krämer, -prediger,** *m.* (*Hist.*) seller of indulgences. **-rohr,** *n.* wastepipe. **-schraube,** *f.* drain-plug. **-woche,** *f.* (*R.C.*) Corpus Christi week. **-zettel,** *m. See* **-brief.**

Ablauf ['aplauf], *m.* 1. running off, draining, ebb, discharge; 2. outlet, drain, gutter; 3. termination, completion, issue (*of a matter*); 4. lapse, expiry, expiration (*time, a treaty etc.*); *bei* – *eines Wechsels,* at maturity of a bill, when a bill matures *or* falls due; ***vor – des Jahres,*** before the end *or* close of the year; 5. launch(ing) (*of a ship*); 6. (*Archit.*) apophyge.

ablaufen ['aplaufən], **1.** *irr.v.i.* (*aux.* s.) 1. flow *or* run off, drain away, ebb, recede (*of tide*); start (*racing*); (*Shipb.*) be launched, come off the stocks; unwind, run off (*of s.th. on a spool*); ***– lassen,*** let out (*water*); (*Fenc.*) parry a thrust from (*one's opponent*), (*fig.*) snub, rebuff; launch (*a ship*); run off *or* out, pay out (*s.th. on a spool*); (*coll.*) ***wie am Schnürchen –,*** go *or* pass off without a hitch; ***schief–,*** go wrong; 2. elapse (*of time*), (*Comm., Insur. etc.*), lapse, expire, terminate, become due; (*Poet.*) ***deine Uhr ist abgelaufen,*** your hour has come, your sands have run out; 3. run down (*of clocks*). **2.** *irr.v.t.* 1. ***die ganze Stadt –,*** scour the whole town (***nach,*** for); 2. ***sich*** (*Dat.*) ***die Beine –,*** run o.s. off one's feet; ***sich*** (*Dat.*) ***die Schuhe –,*** wear out one's shoes; ***sich die Hörner –,*** sow one's wild oats; ***das habe ich*** (***mir***) ***längst an den Schuhen abgelaufen,*** I know all about that, you can't tell me anything about that; 3. ***ihm den Rang –,*** get the better of him, outstrip *or* outdo him.

Abläufer ['aplɔyfər], *m.* 1. *See* **Ablaufspule**; 2. (*Weav.*) misplaced thread; 3. (*Naut.*) scupper.

Ablauf|frist, *f.* (date of) maturity, date of expiration, due date. **–gerüst,** *n.* (*Shipb.*) (launching) cradle. **–rinne,** *f.* gutter, drainage channel; (*Naut.*) scupper. **–rohr,** *n.*, **–röhre,** *f.* waste-pipe. **–schlitten,** *m. See* **–gerüst. –seite,** *f.* (*Engin., Av.*) trailing edge. **–spule,** *f.* winding-off spool. **–termin,** *m. See* **–frist.**

ablauschen ['aplauʃən], *v.t.* learn by watching *or* listening; watch for (*a chance*); (*Rad.*) pick up, intercept (*signal*).

Ablaut ['aplaut], *m.* (*Gram.*) vowel gradation, ablaut. **ablauten,** *v.i.* (*Gram.*) undergo change of vowel by ablaut.

abläuten ['aplɔytən], *v.t.* signal the departure of (*train etc.*).

abläutern ['aplɔytərn], *v.t.* clarify, strain, filter (*liquids*); purify; wash, buddle (*ore*).

ableben ['aple:bən], **1.** *v.i.* (*only in*) ***er ist abgelebt,*** he is deceased, he has departed (from) this life. **2.** *v.r.* become obsolete; become decrepit; burn the candle at both ends. *See* **abgelebt. Ableben,** *n.* decease, demise.

ablecken ['aplɛkən], *v.t.* lick off.

Ablege|fehler, *m.* printer's error, misprint. **–mappe,** *f.* (letter-)file, folder.

ablegen ['aple:gən], **1.** *v.t.* 1. put *or* lay down (*a load*); take off, lay aside (*clothes*), throw down (*one's arms*), come out of (*mourning*), file (*letters etc.*), distribute (*type*); ***wollen Sie nicht –?*** won't you take off your things *or* your hat and coat? ***die Kinderschuhe –,*** be a child no longer; 2. give up, get rid of, break o.s. of (*a habit*), rid o.s. of (*a fault*), cast off, discard (*old clothes*), cast, slough (*old skin*), discard, throw away (*cards*), give up using, drop (*a name*), overcome (*shyness*), discharge, pay off, lay off (*workers*); ***abgelegte Kleider,*** cast-off clothes; 3. perform, execute, do; make (*a confession*), pay (*a visit*), take (*a vow*), give, furnish (*proof*), take (*an examination*), give, render (*an account*), account for (***vor ihm,*** to him). **2.** *v.i.* get under way, put out to sea (*of a ship*).

Ableger ['aple:gər], *m.* (*Hort.*) layer, scion, runner, cutting, shoot, sprig; (*fig.*) branch, off-shoot, subsidiary.

Ablege|satz, *m.* (*Typ.*) dead matter. **–span,** *m.* (*Typ.*) distributing stick.

ablehnen ['aple:nən], *v.t.* 1. decline (*responsibility*), refuse (*invitation*), turn down (*offer, proposal*), reject, refuse to accept *or* acknowledge (*views etc.*); ***einen Antrag –,*** reject *or* throw out *or* vote down a motion; 2. (*Law*) challenge, object to (*a witness*), (*Law*) impugn (*evidence*). **ablehnend,** *adj.* 1. negative; 2. (*Law*) declinatory. **Ablehnung,** *f.* 1. refusal, rejection, refusal to acknowledge; 2. challenge (*Gen.*, of), objection (*Gen.*, to), (*Law*) impugnment.

ableiern ['aplaɪərn], *v.t.* recite mechanically *or* in a sing-song manner.

ableisten ['aplaɪstən], *v.t.* 1. take (*an oath*); 2. serve in (*the armed forces*), complete (*one's military service*). **Ableistung,** *f.* 1. swearing, taking (*of an oath*); 2. serving (*one's time*); completion (*of military service*).

ableitbar ['aplaɪtba:r], *adj.* 1. derivable, capable of being derived; 2. drainable, that can be diverted.

ableiten ['aplaɪtən], **1.** *v.t.* 1. turn away *or* aside, deflect, divert; 2. draw away *or* off, drain off, conduct (*heat etc.*); 3. trace back (***von,*** to), (*Math., Philol.*) derive, be derived (***von, aus,*** from); 4. infer, deduce (***von, aus,*** from). **2.** *v.r.* proceed, issue, derive (***von, aus,*** from). *See* **abgeleitet. ableitend,** *adj.* (*Med.*) counter-irritant. **Ableiter,** *m.* 1. (*Elec.*) conductor; 2. *See* **Ableitungswort. Ableitung,** *f.* 1. diversion, drainage (channel); 2. (*Elec., heat etc.*) leakage, conductor; 3. (*Elec.*) branch circuit, by-pass; 4. (*Philol.*) derivation, etymology; 5. (*Math.*) derivation, differential coefficient, deduction.

Ableitungs|mittel, *n.* (*Med.*) counter-irritant. **–rechnung,** *f.* (*Math.*) differential calculus. **–silbe,** *f.* (*Philol.*) derivative syllable, affix. **–stange,** *f.* lightning conductor. **–wort,** *n.* (*Philol.*) derivative.

ablenken ['aplɛŋkən], **1.** *v.t.* turn aside, deflect (*also Opt., Magnet.*), (*Opt.*) diffract; (*Fenc.*) avert, ward off, parry; divert, distract. **2.** *v.i.* digress, wander (from the subject); create a diversion; (*Opt.*) diverge. **Ablenker,** *m.* (*Engin.*) baffle(-plate), (*Elec.*) deflector. **Ablenkspannung,** *f.* deflector voltage. **Ablenkung,** *f.* 1. diversion (*also Mil.*), distraction; digression (*from the subject*); (*Elec., Opt.*) deflection, (*Opt.*) diffraction, divergence, (*Magnet.*) deviation, (*Fenc.*) parry; 2. (*coll.*) change; ***ich brauche –,*** I need a change.

Ablenkungs|angriff, *m.* (*Mil.*) diversion. **–manöver,** *n.* (*Mil.*) diversion, (*fig.*) red herring. **–winkel,** *m.* angle of deflection.

ablesbar ['aple:sba:r], *adj.* readable (*as markings on a dial*).

ablesen ['aple:zən], *irr.v.t.* 1. pick (off); 2. read (off), read out (*a list, speech*), read (*a meter*); (*fig.*) ***ihm an den Augen –,*** read it in his eyes, tell from his face; ***von den Lippen –,*** lip-read. **Ablesestrich,** *m.* mark(ing), graduation (*on a dial*). **Ablesung,** *f.* reading (*taken from a meter*).

ableugnen ['aplɔygnən], *v.t.* deny, disown, disclaim; ***eidlich –,*** forswear, abjure. **Ableugnung,** *f.* denial, disclaimer, disavowal.

abliefern ['apli:fərn], *v.t.* deliver, consign; hand in *or* over, surrender. **Ablieferung,** *f.* delivery. **Ablieferungs|schein,** *m.* delivery note, receipt of delivery. **–termin,** *m.*, **–zeit,** *f.* (*St. Exch.*) settling day.

abliegen ['apli:gən], *irr.v.t.* 1. (*aux.* s.) lie at a distance, be remote; 2. (*aux.* h.) lie until mellow, (grow) mature; improve with keeping.

ablisten ['aplɪstən], *v.t.* ***ihm etwas –,*** swindle *or* trick *or* (*coll.*) diddle *or* twist *or* do him out of a th.

ablocken ['aplɔkən], *v.t.* ***ihm etwas –,*** coax *or* wheedle s.th. out of him; ***ihn von etwas –,*** lure *or* entice him away from s.th.; ***ihm Tränen –,*** bring tears to his eyes.

ablohnen ['aplo:nən], *v.t.* pay off; discharge.

ablösbar ['aplø:zba:r], *adj.* 1. separable, removable, detachable; 2. (*Insur., St. Exch.*) redeemable.

ablöschen ['aplœʃən], *v.t.* 1. extinguish, quench; slake (*lime*); temper (*iron*); 2. wipe, blot out, (*fig.*) wipe out.

ablösen ['aplø:zən], **1.** *v.t.* 1. detach, separate, remove; loosen, unstick; 2. relieve (*sentry etc.*), take (*s.o.'s*) place, take over from (*s.o.*); ***sich*** or ***einander –,*** take (it in) turns, alternate (with one another), relieve one another; 3. pay, settle, discharge (*debts etc.*), redeem (*pledge, annuity*), withdraw (*capital*). **2.** *v.r.* be(come) detached, break *or* come away *or* loose *or* off. **Ablösung,** *f.* 1. detachment, separation; 2. relief (*sentries etc.*); ***mit – arbeiten,*** work in shifts; 3. withdrawal (*of capital*), redemption (*of annuities*), settlement, payment; ***frei durch –***, official paid; ***frei durch – Reich,*** *equivalent to* On Her Majesty's Service.

ablöten ['aplø:tən], *v.t.* unsolder.

abluchsen ['apluksən], *v.t.* (*coll.*) *see* **ablisten.**

Abluft ['apluft], *f.* foul air, spent air.

abmachen ['apmaxən], *v.t.* 1. (*coll.*) detach, remove, take off; 2. settle, arrange, conclude; ***gütlich –***, settle amicably; ***ein Geschäft –***, settle business, conclude a bargain. *See* **abgemacht. Abmachung,** *f.* arrangement, settlement, agreement; (*Law*) ***vertragsmäßige –***, stipulation; ***laut –***, according to agreement; ***–en treffen,*** come to an agreement *or* arrangement.

abmagern ['apma:gərn], *v.i.* (*aux.* s.) grow thin lose weight, waste away. **Abmagerung,** *f.* emaciation. **Abmagerungskur,** *f.* slimming treatment, dieting.

abmähen ['apmɛ:ən], *v.t.* mow, cut (down), reap.

abmahnen ['apma:nən], *v.t.* dissuade (***von,*** from), warn (against).

abmalen ['apma:lən], *v.t.* paint a portrait of, portray; copy, paint a copy of; (*fig.*) picture, depict, describe.

Abmarsch ['apmarʃ], *m.* marching *or* moving off. **abmarschbereit,** *adj.* ready to march *or* move off *or* (*coll. fig.*) to start. **abmarschieren** [–'ʃi:rən], *v.i.* (*aux.* s.) march *or* move off; ***einzeln –***, file off.

abmartern ['apmartərn], **1.** *v.r.* torture *or* torment o.s. **2.** *v.t.* ***sein Gehirn –***, rack *or* cudgel one's brains.

Abmaß ['apma:s], *n.* (*Engin.*) tolerance.

abmatten ['apmatən], *v.t.* fatigue, weary.

abmeiern ['apmaɪərn], *v.t.* turn out, evict, dispossess (*tenant farmer*).

abmeißeln ['apmaɪsəln], *v.t.* chisel off *or* out.

Abmeldeformular ['apmɛldefɔrmula:r], *n.* form for registration of change of address.

abmelden ['apmɛldən], *v.t., v.r.* announce withdrawal (*or* removal); ***ihn*** (or ***sich***) ***polizeilich –***, report his (*or* one's) change of address; ***einen Schüler beim Direktor –***, give notice to the headmaster of a boy's removal from school. **Abmeldung,** *f.* notice of withdrawal, notification of departure, cancellation.

abmeßbar ['apmɛsba:r], *adj.* 1. measurable, mensurable; ***in –er Zeit,*** within measurable time; 2. commensurable (***an*** (*Dat.*), with).

abmessen ['apmɛsən], *irr.v.t.* 1. measure off (*length: as cloth*) *or* out (*quantity: as corn*), measure up, mark (*ground etc.*); gauge; survey; ***die Zeit –***, apportion time, time; ***das ist nicht abzumessen,*** that is incalculable; ***seine Schritte –***, measure one's steps; ***seine Worte –***, weigh one's words; 2. adjust, adapt; 3. ***gegeneinander –***, compare (*for size etc.*); ***die Möglichkeiten gegeneinander –***, weigh *or* assess the various possibilities. *See* **abgemessen. Abmesser,** *m.* (quantity) surveyor. **Abmessung,** *f.* measurement; dimension, size.

abmieten ['apmi:tən], *v.t.* hire *or* rent from.

abmildern ['apmɪldərn], *v.t.* moderate, tone down.

abmontieren ['apmɔnti:rən], *v.t.* take to pieces strip, dismantle (*machinery etc.*).

abmühen ['apmy:ən], *v.r.* take pains *or* trouble (*to do*).

abmurksen ['apmurksən], *v.t.* (*sl.*) do for (*s.o.*), do (*s.o.*) in, knock (*s.o.*) off.

abmüßigen ['apmy:sɪgən], *v.t.* 1. ***ihm etwas –***, extort s.th. from him; 2. take time off; ***ich kann mir die Zeit nicht –***, I cannot spare the time.

abmustern ['apmustərn], **1.** *v.t.* pay off (*a crew*). **2.** *v.i.* sign off (*of a crew*).

abnagen ['apna:gən], *v.t.* gnaw (off *or* away); ***sein Verlust nagt ihm das Herz ab,*** his loss preys upon his mind; ***einen Knochen –***, pick a bone, (*as a dog*) gnaw a bone.

Abnäher ['apnɛ:ər], *m.* (*Dressm.*) dart.

Abnahme ['apna:mə], *f.* 1. taking off *or* away, removal; (*Med.*) amputation; ***die – vom Kreuz,*** the Descent from the Cross; 2. (*Gen.*, of; ***an*** (*Dat.*), in) reduction, decrease, decline, diminution, falling off, lowering, weakening, depreciation (*in value*), fall, drop (*in temperature etc.*), ebb, shrinkage; ***– des Mondes,*** waning of the moon; ***– der Tage,*** shortening of the days; 3. delivery, purchase, acceptance; ***bei – größerer Mengen,*** on taking *or* purchasing larger quantities; ***vor –***, before taking delivery; ***die Ware findet keine –***, there is no demand for the goods; (*Law*) ***– eines Eides,*** administering an oath; ***– der Parade,*** review of the troops; ***– einer Rechnung,*** auditing of an account.

Abnahme|pflicht, *f.* obligation to accept delivery. **–prüfung,** *f.* acceptance test (*of goods delivered*), inspection (*before taking over*). **–vorschrift,** *f.* specifications for acceptance.

abnehmbar ['apne:mba:r], *adj.* removable, detachable.

abnehmen ['apne:mən], **1.** *irr.v.t.* 1. remove, take off (*hat, lid etc.*); remove, take away (***ihm,*** from him); relieve (***ihm,*** him) of (*a burden, responsibility etc.*); gather, pick (*fruit etc.*); decrease (*knitting etc.*); ***den Bart –***, shave off one's beard; (*Tele.*) ***den Hörer –***, take off *or* pick up *or* lift the receiver; ***ihm die Maske –***, unmask *or* expose him; ***darf ich dir das Paket –?*** may I relieve you of your parcel? 2. buy, purchase, take delivery of (*goods etc.*); (*coll.*) ***das nimmt dir niemand ab!*** you can't pull that one! 3. ***ihm einen Eid –***, administer an oath to him; ***die Parade –***, inspect *or* review the troops; ***eine Rechnung –***, audit an account; ***ihm ein Versprechen –***, obtain a promise from him. **2.** *irr.v.i.* 1. (***an*** (*Dat.*), in) decrease, grow less, diminish, decline, subside, dwindle, abate, fall *or* drop off, go down, fail (*as health*), flag (*as strength*), drop (*as temperature etc.*), slacken (*of speed*), depreciate (*in value*), draw in (*as winter days*), wane (*of moon, fame etc.*); 2. lose weight. **Abnehmen,** *n.* ***im – (begriffen) sein,*** be decreasing, declining, waning *etc.*, be on the decrease, decline, wane *etc.* *See* **Abnahme.**

Abnehmer ['apne:mər], *m.* purchaser, buyer, customer; consumer; subscriber (*to a newspaper*); receiver (*of stolen goods*).

abneigen ['apnaɪgən], *v.t.* *See* **abgeneigt, abwenden.**

Abneigung ['apnaɪguŋ], *f.* 1. turning away, turning aside, deviation (***von,*** from), (*Magnet.*) declination; 2. (*fig.*) (***gegen***) aversion (to, for), distaste (for), dislike (of, for), disinclination (for), antipathy (to), reluctance (to do); ***eine – gegen etwas fassen,*** take a dislike to s.th.

abnieten ['apni:tən], *v.t.* unrivet.

abnorm [ap'nɔrm], *adj.* abnormal, irregular, anomalous. **Abnormität** [-i'tɛ:t], *f.* abnormality, irregularity; anomaly; (*Biol.*) sport, freak (*of nature*).

abnötigen ['apnø:tɪgən], *v.t.* extort (*usu. money*), force, wring (*promise, apology etc.*) (*Dat.*, from).

abnutzen ['apnutsən], (*sometimes* **abnützen**) **1.** *v.t.* use up; wear out *or* away; wear, abrade, erode. **2.** *v.i.* (*aux.* s.) wear (out), show signs of wear. *See* **abgenutzt. Abnutzung (Abnützung),** *f.* wear and tear; depreciation; abrasion, wear; erosion; (*Geol.*) detrition; (*Mil.*) attrition. **Abnutzungssatz,** *m.* rate of depreciation.

Abonnement [abɔnə'mã], *n.* (**-s,** *pl.* **-s**) subscription (*to journals, concerts etc.*). **Abonnement(s)-karte,** *f.* subscriber's ticket; season ticket. **Abonnent** [abɔ'nɛnt], *m.* (**-en,** *pl.* **-en**) subscriber. **abonnieren** [–'ni:rən], **1.** *v.t.* subscribe to (*a newspaper*). **2.** *v.i., v.r.* take out a subscription (***auf*** (*Acc.*), for); ***im Theater abonniert sein,*** hold a season-ticket for the theatre.

abordnen ['apˀɔrdnən], *v.t.* delegate, depute. **Abordnung,** *f.* delegation, deputation. *See* **Abgeordnete(r).**

Abort [a'bɔrt], *m.* (**-(e)s,** *pl.* **-e**) 1. lavatory, toilet, W.C.; 2. (*Med.*) abortion. **abortieren** [–'ti:rən], *v.i.* abort, miscarry. **Abortus** [a'bɔrtus], *m.* (-, *pl.* -) abortion, miscarriage.

abpachten ['appaxtən], *v.t.* rent (*a farm*). **Abpachter** (*or* **Abpächter**), *m.* tenant farmer, lessee of a farm.

abpacken ['appakən], *v.t.* packet, package (*groceries etc.*).

abpassen ['appasən], *v.t.* 1. adjust, fit, trim (to size); 2. watch for, be on the look-out for, lie in wait for; ***gut abgepaßt,*** neatly timed; ***eine Gelegenheit –,*** watch one's opportunity; ***die Zeit –,*** bide one's time.

abpfeifen ['appfaɪfən], *irr.v.i.* (*Footb.*) blow the whistle (*to stop play*).

abpflöcken ['appflœkən], *v.t.* 1. mark *or* lay *or* peg out; 2. unpeg and take down from the line (*clothes*).

abpflücken ['appflykən], *v.t.* pluck, pick, gather.

abplacken ['applakən], *v.r.* (*coll.*) *see* **abplagen.**

abplagen ['appla:gən], **1.** *v.t.* worry, torment. **2.** *v.r.* tire o.s. out (*mit*, with); be at great pains (*zu tun*, to do).

abplatten ['applatən], *v.t.* flatten (out); (*Geom.*) (***an den Polen***) ***abgeplattet,*** oblate.

abplätten ['applɛtən], *v.t.* transfer (*pattern*) with a hot iron. **Abplättmuster,** *m.* (embroidery) transfer.

Abplattung ['applatuŋ], *f.* flattening, oblateness.

abprägen ['apprɛ:gən], *v.r.* (*auf* (*Acc.*), on) make an impression; print, stamp *or* impress itself.

Abprall ['appral], *m.* rebound, reverberation, reflection, ricochet. **abprallen,** *v.i.* (*aux.* s.) rebound; reverberate (*as sound*), be reflected (*as light*), ricochet (*of missiles*), bounce (off) (*of ball*); (*fig.*) ***an ihm –,*** make no impression on him. **Abpraller,** *m.* (*Artil.*) ricochet. **Abprallwinkel,** *m.* angle of reflection (*of light*) *or* of richochet (*of missiles*) *or* of rebound.

abpressen ['apprɛsən], *v.t.* ***ihm etwas –,*** extort *or* force *or* wring s.th. from him.

abprotzen ['apprɔtsən], **1.** *v.t.* unlimber (*a gun*). **2.** *v.i.* 1. (*Artil.*) take up firing position; 2. (*vulg.*) shit.

Abputz ['apputs], *m.* (**-es,** *no pl.*) rough-cast, plaster. **abputzen,** *v.t.* 1. cleanse, clean (*s.th. dirty*); clean *or* wipe off (*dirt*); 2. plaster, rough-cast (*a wall*).

abquälen ['apkvɛ:lən], **1.** *v.t.* ***ihm etwas –,*** torment *or* pester him for s.th. **2.** *v.r.* 1. torment o.s.; 2. take great pains.

abquetschen ['apkvɛtʃən], *v.t.* crush, squeeze off.

abquicken ['apkvɪkən], *v.t.* extract, separate (*usu. gold from amalgam*).

abracken ['apʔrakərn], *v.r.* (*coll.*) work o.s. to death, drudge, slave.

abraffen ['apʔrafən], *v.t.* snatch away *or* up.

Abraham ['a:braham], *m.* Abraham; ***in -s Schoß sitzen,*** be in the lap of luxury.

abrahmen ['apʔra:mən], *v.t.* skim (*milk*).

abrainen ['apʔraɪnən], *v.t.* separate (*fields*) by ridges; balk off.

abranken ['apʔraŋkən], *v.t.* prune (*a vine*); thin out.

abraspeln ['apʔraspəln], *v.t.* smooth off (*with a rasp*), grate (*cheese, bread etc.*).

abraten ['apʔra:tən], **1.** *irr.v.t., v.i.* ***ihm*** (***von***) ***etwas –,*** dissuade him from s.th., advise him against s.th.; ***ich rate*** (***es***) ***dir ab, dies zu tun,*** I advise you not to do it. **2.** *irr.v.t.* guess; ***ihm seine Gedanken –,*** guess *or* divine his thoughts.

abrauchen ['apʔrauxən], *v.i.* (*aux.* s.) evaporate, vaporize, fume. **Abrauchschale,** *f.* evaporating dish.

Abraum ['apʔraum], *m.* (**-s,** *no pl.*) 1. rubbish, rubble; refuse, waste, (*For.*) waste wood, loppings; 2. *or* **Abraumdecke,** *f.* (*Min.*) overburden.

abräumen ['apʔrɔymən], *v.t.* clear (away), remove; ***räume*** (***den Tisch***) ***ab!*** (*usu. without the Acc.*), clear the table! **Abräumer,** *m.* cowcatcher.

Abraumsalze ['apʔraumzaltsə], *pl.* abraum-salts.

Abräumung ['apʔrɔymuŋ], *f.* removal, clearance.

abrechnen ['apʔrɛçnən], **1.** *v.t.* 1. deduct, subtract, take off; ***abgerechnet*** (*Acc.*), setting aside, making allowances for, not to speak of, with the exception of, leaving out of account *or* consideration, apart from, except for; 2. settle, square (*an account*). **2.** *v.i.* settle *or* square *or* balance accounts; (*coll.*) get even (with), get one's own back. **Abrechnung,** *f.* 1. deduction; 2. settlement (*of accounts*); (statement of) account; ***auf –,*** on account; ***in – bringen,*** deduct, debit, (*fig.*) take account of; ***– halten,*** settle accounts (***mit,*** with); (*fig.*) ***der Tag der –,*** the day of reckoning. **Abrechnungs|stelle,** *f.* clearing house. **–tag,** *m.* (*St. Exch.*) settling day.

Abrechte ['apʔrɛçtə], *f.* reverse *or* wrong side (*of cloth*).

Abrede ['apʔre:də], *f.* 1. denial; ***in – stellen,*** deny, dispute, contest; 2. agreement, understanding; ***eine – treffen,*** come to an agreement *or* understanding; ***eine stillschweigend getroffene –,*** a tacit agreement. **abreden, 1.** *v.t.* dissuade; ***er redete mich davon ab,*** he dissuaded me from (doing) it. **2.** *v.t., v.i.* come to an agreement; ***er redete*** (***etwas***) ***mit mir ab,*** he came to an understanding with me (about s.th.); ***ein abgeredetes Spiel,*** a prearranged affair, (*coll.*) a put-up job.

abreiben ['apʔraɪbən], *irr.v.t.* rub off, scour; chafe, abrade; rub down, grind, triturate; ***sich tüchtig –,*** rub o.s. down well, give o.s. a good rub-down; ***die Schuhe –,*** scrape *or* wipe one's shoes; ***Einband etwas abgerieben,*** binding rubbed *or* scuffed; ***einen Flecken vom Glas –,*** rub a mark off the glass; ***ein Glas von Flecken –,*** clean the glass of all marks. **Abreibung,** *f.* 1. rub-down; 2. (*coll.*) dressing-down.

Abreise ['apʔraɪzə], *f.* departure (***nach,*** for); ***vor der –,*** before leaving; ***fertig zur –,*** ready to leave. **abreisen,** *v.i.* (*aux.* s.) (***nach,*** for) set out, start, leave, depart, take one's departure.

abreißen ['apʔraɪsən], **1.** *irr.v.t.* 1. tear *or* pull *or* wrench off; demolish, pull down; 2. draw a plan of, sketch. **2.** *irr.v.i.* (*aux.* s.) break off (*also fig.*), break, come apart *or* (*coll.*) adrift; (*fig.*) come to an end, be cut short, give out; ***abgerissene Kleider,*** tattered clothes; ***abgerissene Sätze,*** disconnected *or* disjointed *or* incoherent phrases. **Abreißer,** *m.* scriber. **Abreiß|kalender,** *m.* tear-off calendar. **–schnur,** *f.* rip cord (*parachute*), fuse cord (*hand grenade*). **–zünder,** *m.* (*Mil.*) friction igniter.

abreiten ['apʔraɪtən], **1.** *irr.v.t.* ***die Front –,*** inspect (the troop) on horseback; (*Naut.*) ***den Sturm –,*** ride out the storm. **2.** *irr.v.i.* (*aux.* s.) ride away; rise, fly off (*from the nest*: *of large birds*).

abrennen ['apʔrɛnən], **1.** *irr.v.i.* (*aux.* s.) run off *or* away. **2.** *irr.v.t.* ***sich*** (*Dat.*) ***die Beine –,*** run o.s. off one's legs.

abrichten ['apʔrɪçtən], *v.t.* 1. (*Mech.*) adjust, fit, set, true up; 2. smooth, dress, face (*a surface*); 3. coach, drill (*a p.*) (***auf*** (*Acc.*), ***zu,*** in), train, teach tricks to (*an animal*), break in (*a horse*); ***er ist gut darauf abgerichtet,*** he has the knack of it, (*coll.*) he knows the drill. **Abrichter,** *m.* trainer; horse-breaker, rough-rider. **Abricht|hammer,** *m.* planishing hammer. **–hobel,** *m.* smoothing plane. **Abrichtung,** *f.* 1. adjustment; 2. drill, training, breaking-in.

Abrieb ['apʔri:p], *m.* (**-(e)s,** *no pl.*) 1. abrasion, wear, attrition; 2. grit, dust; breeze (*coal*).

abriegeln ['apʔri:gəln], *v.t.* bolt, bar (*a door*); shut *or* cut off, block, barricade (*a road*), seal off; isolate (*an area*), contain (*an attack*). **Abriegelungsfeuer,** *n.* (*Artil.*) box-barrage.

abrieseln ['apʔri:zəln], *v.i.* (*aux.* s.) trickle down.

abringen ['apʔrɪŋən], *irr.v.t.* wrest, wrench, force (*Dat.*, from), wring (*concessions, a confession etc.*).

abrinnen ['apʔrɪnən], *irr.v.i.* (*aux.* s.) run *or* flow down *or* off, trickle away.

Abriß ['apʔrɪs], *m.* 1. synopsis, epitome, précis, abstract, digest, compendium, summary; 2. sketch; draft; outline. **Abrißpunkt,** *m.* (*Surv.*) benchmark.

Abritt ['apʔrit], *m.* departure on horseback.

abrollen ['apʔrɔlən], **1.** *v.t.* 1. roll away *or* off; 2. transport, convey (*goods*); 3. unroll, unreel, uncoil, unwind (*rope, film etc.*); *ein Tau* –, pay out a cable. **2.** *v.r.* unroll, unwind, come unrolled *or* unwound; (*fig.*) unfold, develop (*as events*). **3.** *v.i.* (*aux.* s.) roll *or* run down, roll off; pull out (*of train*), taxi off (*of plane*), (*fig.*) roll on (*as time*).

abrücken ['apʔrykən], **1.** *v.t.* 1. move *or* push *or* pull away *or* back; 2. (*Typ.*) lead (*lines*). **2.** *v.i.* (*aux.* s.) 1. move *or* march off (*of troops*), (*coll.*) push off, clear out; 2. draw back (*von*, from), dissociate o.s. (from), disavow.

Abruf ['apʔru:f], *m.* recall; *auf* –, subject to recall (*of a p.*), at *or* on call (*of money, goods*). **abrufen,** *irr.v.t.* 1. call away; recall; call off (*dogs*); *ihn – lassen,* have him called away, send for him; 2. call in (*money*), demand delivery of (*goods*); 3. *einen Zug* –, announce a train's departure. **Abrufung,** *f.* 1. recall; 2. request for delivery (*of goods*); 3. announcement (*of trains etc.*). **Abrufungs|schreiben,** *n.* letters of recall. **–schuß,** *m.* (shot fired as) recall signal.

abrühren ['apʔry:rən], *v.t.* beat up, stir.

abrunden ['apʔrundən], *v.t.* round off (*also fig.*); *nach oben* (*unten*) –, bring up (down) to round figures; *abgerundete Zahlen,* round figures; *abgerundetes Gewicht,* rough weight. *See* **abgerundet.**

abrüsten ['apʔrystən], *v.t.* 1. disarm; demobilize (*troops*); 2. take down *or* dismantle (*scaffolding*); 3. lay up (*a ship*). **Abrüstung,** *f.* disarmament. **Abrüstwagen,** *m.* breakdown lorry.

abrutschen ['apʔrutʃən], *v.i.* (*aux.* s.) slip *or* slide down *or* off, (*Geol.*) slip; (*coll.*) slither down; (*Av.*) sideslip; skid.

Abruzzen [a'brutsən], *pl.* the Abruzzi Mountains.

absacken ['apzakən], **1.** *v.t.* pack in bags *or* sacks. **2.** *v.r.* (*Biol.*) become encysted. **3.** *v.i.* (*aux.* s.) 1. (*coll.*) subside, sink, sag; (*Naut.*) go down, (*Av.*) pancake; go under (*of a p.*); 2. (*Naut.*) drift with the stream *or* current *or* tide. **Absackung,** *f.* (*Biol.*) encystment, sacculation.

Absage ['apza:gə], *f.* 1. refusal, declining (*of an invitation*); cancellation; 2. (*obs.*) repudiation, renunciation (*an* (*Acc.*), of). **Absagebrief,** *m.* letter refusing *or* declining an invitation, letter of apology; letter cancelling an appointment. **absagen, 1.** *v.t.* cancel, (*coll.*) call off (*an appointment*); decline, refuse (*an invitation*). **2.** *v.i.* 1. cancel an appointment, decline *or* refuse an invitation, (*coll.*) cry off; *er hat mir – lassen,* he sent word that he couldn't come; 2. (*Dat.*) renounce, repudiate, abjure. *See* **abgesagt.**

absägen ['apzɛ:gən], *v.t.* 1. saw off; 2. (*coll.*) give (*s.o.*) the sack.

absatteln ['apzatəln], *v.t.* unsaddle (*a horse*).

absättigen ['apzɛtɪgən], *v.t.* (*Chem.*) saturate (*a solution*), neutralize (*an acid*).

Absatz ['apzats], *m.* 1. interruption, pause, break, intermission; (*Typ.*) paragraph; (*Geol.*) (natural) terrace, shelf; ledge, berm, offset; stairhead, landing; *mit* –, starting a new paragraph; *ohne* –, without pause *or* interruption, 'run on' (*in dictating*); 2. heel (*of shoe*); 3. sale, turnover; *guten – finden,* sell well; *schnellen – finden,* find ready sale *or* a ready market; *großer –, kleiner Nutzen,* quick sale, small returns; 4. sediment, deposit. **absatzfähig,** *adj.* marketable.

Absatz|gebiet, *n.* sales *or* trading area, market, outlet *or* market for exports. **–gestein,** *n.* sedimentary (stratified) rock.

absätzig ['apzɛtsɪç], *adj.* – *sein,* be faulty, peter out, (*Min.*) go dead (*of stratum*).

Absatz|kosten, *pl.* distribution costs. **–markt,** *m.* *See* **–gebiet. –möglichkeit,** *f.* opening for trade. **–quelle,** *f.* market, outlet for exports.

absatzweise ['apzatsvaɪzə], *adv.* step by step, at intervals, paragraph by paragraph, one paragraph at a time.

absäugeln ['apzɔygəln], *v.t.* (*Hort.*) inarch.

absaugen ['apzaugən], *irr.v.t.* suck off *or* dry; remove, extract *or* filter by suction *or* with a hydro-extractor. **Absaug(e)pumpe,** *f.* vacuum pump. **Absauger,** *m.* suction fan, hydro-extractor. **Absaugung,** *f.* suction, hydro-extraction.

abschaben ['apʃa:bən], *v.t.* scrape (off); wear threadbare; *abgeschabt,* shabby, threadbare. **Abschabsel,** *n.* parings, shavings, shreds.

abschachern ['apʃaxərn], *v.t.* *ihm etwas* –, buy s.th. from him for a mere song.

abschachten ['apʃaxtən], *v.t.* (*Min.*) line, timber (*shaft etc.*).

abschaffen ['apʃafən], *v.t.* abolish, repeal, annul, rescind, abrogate, (*coll.*) do away with (*laws etc.*); stop, put down, put a stop *or* an end to (*an abuse*); give up, get rid of, no longer keep (*a dog, car etc.*); (*obs.*) disband (*troops*). **Abschaffung,** *f.* abolition, repeal, annulment, recission, abrogation; suppression; relinquishment, discontinuance; (*obs.*) disbandment.

abschälen ['apʃɛ:lən], **1.** *v.t.* peel, pare (*fruit etc.*), shell (*nuts*), blanch (*almonds*); decorticate, exfoliate, excoriate. **2.** *v.i., v.r.* peel off; exfoliate; (*Med.*) desquamate. **Abschälung,** *f.* decortication, exfoliation, excoriation; (*Med.*) desquamation.

abschalten ['apʃaltən], *v.t.* disconnect, switch off (*lamp etc.*), cut off (*current*).

abschärfen ['apʃɛrfən], *v.t.* bevel, chamfer (*an edge*), taper, cut to a point, sharpen (*a point*), pare (*hides*), fair (*hull of a ship*). *See also* **schärfen.**

abschatten ['apʃatən], **1.** *v.t.* shade (*a drawing*). **2.** *v.r.* cast a shadow.

abschattieren ['apʃati:rən], *v.t.* shade off (*colours*); (*fig.*) express nuances in. **Abschattierung,** *f.* shading, gradation of tints; (*fig.*) nuance.

abschätzen ['apʃɛtsən], *v.t.* 1. estimate, assess, appraise, value (*auf* (*Acc.*), at); gauge, calculate (*the effect*); *ihn nach seiner Steuerkraft* –, assess his taxable income; *unter dem Wert* –, underestimate, underrate; 2. disparage, depreciate, belittle. **abschätzend,** *adj.* *See* **abschätzig. Abschätzer,** *m.* valuer, assessor, appraiser. **abschätzig,** *adj.* adverse, unfavourable (*views*), disparaging, derogatory, depreciatory (*remarks*). **Abschätzung,** *f.* estimate, assessment, appraisal, valuation.

Abschaum ['apʃaum], *m.* (**-(e)s,** *no pl.*) scum, dross; – *der Gesellschaft,* dregs of society, scum of the earth.

abschäumen ['apʃɔymən], *v.t.* skim off.

abscheiden ['apʃaɪdən], **1.** *irr.v.t.* 1. separate, isolate, segregate; 2. precipitate, deposit (*solids*); liberate (*gases*); refine (*precious metals*); (*Physiol.*) discharge, secrete, excrete, eliminate. **2.** *irr.v.r.* separate, divide, precipitate; be separated, divided, precipitated, isolated, segregated, deposited, liberated, given off, discharged, secreted, excreted *or* eliminated; form a precipitate *or* deposit. **3.** *irr.v.i.* (*aux.* s.) take one's departure; take one's leave (*von*, of) (*a p. or place*); *von* or *aus der Welt* –, depart this life. *See* **abgeschieden. Abscheider,** *m.* separator, extractor; refiner. **Abscheidung,** *f.* deposit; discharge, secretion, excrement. **Abscheidungsmittel,** *n.* precipitant.

abscheren ['apʃe:rən], *irr.v.t.* shear *or* shave *or* cut off. **Abscher(ungs)|festigkeit,** *f.* (*Metall.*) shearing strength. **–kraft,** *f.* shearing stress, shear.

Abscheu ['apʃɔy], *m.* (**-s,** *no pl.*) disgust, loathing (*vor* (*Dat.*), for), horror, abhorrence (of), repugnance (to); *ein – sein,* be held in abhorrence (*Dat.*, by); *er ist mir ein –, ich habe* (*einen*) – *vor ihm,* I loathe *or* abhor *or* detest the very sight of him.

abscheuern ['apʃɔyərn], **1.** *v.t.* scour (off) (*dirt etc.*); wear away; chafe (*rope etc.*). **2.** *v.r.* wear away, chafe.

abscheulich [ap'ʃɔylɪç], *adj.* horrible, (*coll.*) horrid; hateful, abominable, detestable, loathsome, disgusting, revolting, repulsive, execrable, odious, heinous. **Abscheulichkeit,** *f.* horrible *etc.* thing *or* deed, hatefulness, loathsomeness, repulsiveness.

abschichten [ˈapʃɪçtən], **1.** *v.t.* 1. arrange in layers; (*Geol.*) stratify; 2. (*Law*) buy off the claims of (*an heir*). **2.** *v.r.* separate into layers; (*Geol.*) stratify.

abschicken [ˈapʃɪkən], *v.t.* dispatch, despatch, send (off), consign.

abschieben [ˈapʃiːbən], **1.** *irr.v.t.* 1. push *or* shove away; ***von sich –,*** shift (*responsibility etc.*) (***auf*** (*Acc.*), on to); 2. expel, deport (*undesirables*). **2.** *irr.v.i.* (*aux.* s.) (*coll.*) push *or* shove *or* clear off. **Abschiebung,** *f.* 1. expulsion, deportation; 2. (*Geol.*) fault.

Abschied [ˈapʃiːt], *m.* **(-(e)s,** *pl.* **-e)** 1. departure, farewell, leave-taking, parting; ***beim –,*** on parting, on taking one's leave; ***ohne –,*** without saying good-bye; ***– nehmen von,*** take leave of, say good-bye *or* bid farewell to; ***– vom Leben,*** demise, decease; 2. retirement, resignation; discharge, dismissal; ***den – geben,*** discharge, dismiss; ***seinen – einreichen,*** tender one's resignation; ***den – erhalten,*** be discharged *or* dismissed; ***seinen – nehmen,*** resign (one's appointment *or* (*Mil.*) commission), (*Mil.*) take one's discharge, (*Mil.*) quit the service; 3. (*obs.*) (***gerichtlicher***) –, decree, ordinance. **Abschiednehmen,** *n.* **(-s,** *no pl.*) leave-taking; ***beim –,*** on taking one's leave.

Abschieds|besuch, *m.* farewell *or* parting visit. **-brief,** *m.* farewell letter. **-essen,** *n.* farewell dinner *or* banquet. **-feier,** *f.* farewell celebration, (*coll.*) send-off. **-geschenk,** *n.* parting gift. **-gesuch,** *n.* letter of resignation. **-kuß,** *m.* parting kiss. **-rede,** *f.* farewell speech, valedictory address. **-trunk,** *m.* stirrup-cup, (*coll.*) 'one for the road'.

abschießen [ˈapʃiːsən], **1.** *irr.v.t.* shoot off *or* away (*leg etc.*); fire (off), let off, shoot, discharge (*firearms*), shoot, let fly (*an arrow*); shoot *or* bring down (*game etc.*); ***den Vogel –,*** be by far the best; hit the nail on the head. **2.** *irr.v.i.* (*aux.* s.) 1. rush *or* shoot down, drop sheer; rush *or* shoot away, dart *or* shoot off; 2. fade (*of dyes*).

abschiffen [ˈapʃɪfən], **1.** *v.t.* ship (*goods*). **2.** *v.i.* (*aux.* s.) set sail.

abschilfern [ˈapʃɪlfərn], *v.i.*, *v.r.* flake *or* peel *or* scale off, come off in layers; desquamate.

abschinden [ˈapʃɪndən], **1.** *irr.v.t.* graze, bark (*shin etc.*). **2.** *v.r.* toil, slave, drudge, work one's fingers to the bone.

abschirmen [ˈapʃɪrmən], *v.t.* screen (off), shield. **Abschirmhaube,** *f.* (*Rad.*) screen, screening can. **Abschirmung,** *f.* screening device, shield. **Abschirmvorrichtung,** *f.* interference suppressor.

abschirren [ˈapʃɪrən], *v.t.* unharness.

abschlachten [ˈapʃlaxtən], *v.t.* slaughter (*beasts*), butcher, massacre (*men*).

Abschlag [ˈapʃlaːk], *m.* 1. reduction (in price), rebate, discount; drop *or* fall in price; ***mit – verkaufen,*** sell at a reduced price *or* at a discount; ***Preise sind in – geraten,*** prices have fallen *or* dropped; 2. part *or* down payment; payment on account; ***auf –,*** on account, in part payment; 3. refusal, rejection; 4. closet, compartment; 5. felling, clearing (*of trees*); cuttings, chips (*from felling*); 6. rebound; 7. opening stroke; (*Golf*) drive, (*Hockey*) bully, (*Footb.*) goal kick; 8. discharge- *or* waste-pipe, overflow (pipe). **Abschlagdividende,** *f. See* **Abschlag(s)dividende.**

abschlagen [ˈapʃlaːgən], **1.** *irr.v.t.* 1. strike *or* knock *or* hammer *or* chop off; knock *or* beat down; fell, cut down (*trees*), clear (*a forest*), strike (*a medal*); 2. repel, repulse, beat back (*an attack*), parry, ward off (*a blow*), reject (*an offer*), refuse (*a request*); ***ich lasse es mir nicht –,*** I won't take no for an answer; 3. drain off (*water*); ***sein Wasser –,*** urinate, make water; 4. dismantle, pull *or* take down; strike (*a tent*), break (*camp*), unfurl, unbend (*sails*). **2.** *irr.v.i.* 1. (*aux.* s. *&* h.) fall, come down (*of prices*), come down *or* fall in price (*of goods*), abate (*as cold*), give less milk (*of cow*); 2. (*aux.* s.) rebound (*of ball, usu. Bill.*); 3. make the opening stroke; (*Golf*) drive (off), (*Hockey*) bully (off).

abschlägig [ˈapʃlɛːgɪç], *adj.* negative, unfavourable; ***-e Antwort,*** refusal; ***-er Bescheid,*** rebuff.

abschläglich [ˈapʃlɛːklɪç], *adj.* in part-payment, on account.

Abschlag(s)|dividende, *f.* interim dividend. **-zahlung,** *f.* part-payment, payment on account, instalment.

abschlämmen [ˈapʃlɛmən], *v.t.* clear of mud, wash (out), sluice; decant (*liquid*), (*Chem.*) elutriate (*solid*).

abschleifen [ˈapʃlaɪfən], **1.** *irr.v.t.* grind *or* smooth off; wear *or* rub away; polish; grind, whet, sharpen. **2.** *irr.v.r.* 1. acquire polish, improve one's manners (*of a p.*); 2. lose its freshness (*of metaphor etc.*). **Abschleifer,** *m.* grinder, polisher. **Abschleifung,** *f.* abrasion, attrition; (*fig.*) refinement (*of manners*). *See* **abgeschliffen.**

Abschleppdienst [ˈapʃlɛpdiːnst], *m.* breakdown *or* (*Mil.*) recovery service.

abschleppen [ˈapʃlɛpən], *v.t.* tow away, drag off; (*coll.*) ***sich – mit,*** wear o.s. out carrying. **Abschleppwagen,** *m.* breakdown lorry.

Abschleudermaschine [ˈapʃlɔydərmaʃiːnə], *f.* centrifuge, hydro-extractor. **abschleudern,** *v.t.* 1. fling *or* hurl off, throw (*a rider*), (*Av.*) catapult; 2. centrifuge, hydro-extract.

abschlichten [ˈapʃlɪçtən], *v.t.* smooth, plane (*wood*), planish (*metal*).

abschließen [ˈapʃliːsən], **1.** *irr.v.t.* 1. lock (up); seal (up), shut *or* cut *or* seal *or* separate off, isolate; 2. end, finish (off), conclude, complete, bring to an end *or* close *or* conclusion, close (*discussion etc.*), wind up (*debate*), settle (*quarrel*), finalize (*agreement*), come to terms *or* an agreement about (*business*); ***die Bücher –,*** balance the books; ***einen Handel –,*** strike *or* clinch a bargain; ***einen Kauf –,*** effect a sale; ***einen Vergleich –,*** come to terms; ***einen Vertrag –,*** conclude a treaty, come to *or* enter into an agreement. **2.** *irr.v.r.* seclude o.s., keep o.s. to o.s.; cut o.s. off, hold o.s. aloof (***von,*** from). *See* **abgeschlossen. 3.** *irr.v.i.* 1. end, conclude, close, break off, come to an end; 2. come to terms *or* to an agreement; ***ich habe mit ihm abgeschlossen,*** I have reached an agreement with him; ***ich habe damit abgeschlossen,*** I have settled the matter once and for all, I have set the matter at rest. **abschließend, 1.** *adj.* definite, definitive, final, conclusive, positive. **2.** *adv.* in conclusion. **Abschließung,** *f.* conclusion, completion, closure (*of debate*), settlement (*of accounts etc.*).

Abschluß [ˈapʃlʊs], *m.* 1. closure, fastening, seal; 2. end, close, conclusion, termination; ***zum – bringen,*** bring to an end *or* close *or* conclusion; end, conclude, terminate, finish, complete; ***zum – kommen,*** come to an end, draw to a close, conclude, terminate; 3. transaction, contract, deal; ***einen – machen,*** strike *or* clinch a bargain, (*coll.*) do a deal; ***Abschlüsse machen,*** enter into commitments; 4. settlement (*of accounts*), balancing (*of books*); balance(-sheet); ***jährlicher –,*** annual balance.

Abschluß|blende, *f.* (*Phot.*) front diaphragm. **-borte,** *f.* frieze. **-hahn,** *m.* stopcock. **-prüfung,** *f.* leaving *or* final examination. **-rechnung,** *f.* balance of account. **-zettel,** *m.* broker's contract *or* note.

abschmecken [ˈapʃmɛkən], *v.t.* 1. know by tasting; 2. taste for seasoning (*soup etc.*).

Abschmelzdraht [ˈapʃmɛltsdraːt], *m.* fuse wire.

abschmelzen [ˈapʃmɛltsən], **1.** *irr.v.i.* melt (away), fuse. **2.** *reg.v.t.* melt away *or* off, melt (down), fuse. **Abschmelzsicherung,** *f.* fuse.

abschmieren [ˈapʃmiːrən], **1.** *v.t.* 1. grease, lubricate; 2. (*coll.*) copy carelessly, (*sl.*) copy, crib; 3. (*sl.*) write off (*a debt etc.*). **2.** *v.i.* 1. make a grease stain *or* greasy mark; 2. (*aux.* s.) (*sl.*) crash, (*Av.*) prang.

abschmirgeln [ˈapʃmɪrgəln], *v.t.* grind (*or* rub down) with emery.

abschnallen [ˈapʃnalən], *v.t.* unbuckle.

abschnappen [ˈapʃnapən], **1.** *v.t.* 1. release (*lock or catch*); 2. (*coll.*) catch (*a p.*) in the nick of time. **2.** *v.i.* (*aux.* s.) come unfastened (*of lock or catch*); (*sl.*) peg out.

abschneiden ['apʃnaɪdən], **1.** *irr.v.t.* cut off (*also fig.*); deprive of; ***die Zufuhr –,*** cut off supplies; ***den Weg –,*** take a shortcut; ***ihm den Weg –,*** bar his way, head him off; ***sich die Nägel –,*** cut one's nails; ***ihm das Wort –,*** cut him short; ***ihm die Ehre –,*** injure his reputation, ruin his good name; ***ihm jede Möglichkeit –,*** deprive him of any chance; ***ihm die Kehle –,*** cut his throat; (*coll.*) ***ihm den Hals –,*** strangle *or* smash him (*economically*); (*coll.*) ***er sieht aus wie vom Stricke abgeschnitten,*** he looks like death warmed-up. **2.** *irr.v.r.* stand out, show up (***gegen,*** against). **3.** *irr.v.i.* ***gut*** (***schlecht***) –, show up *or* come out well (badly) (*in examination etc.*). **Abschneider,** *m.* cutter.

abschnellen ['apʃnɛlən], **1.** *v.t.* shoot, let fly. **2.** *v.i.* (*aux.* s.) fly off with a jerk.

Abschnitt ['apʃnɪt], *m.* 1. cut; 2. coupon, counterfoil; 3. paragraph, section; 4. (*Geom.*) segment; – ***auf der x-Achse,*** x-intercept; 5. (*Mil.*) sector; 6. period, epoch; 7. (*fig.*) phase, stage (*of development*).

Abschnittsgrenze ['apʃnɪtsgrɛntsə], *f.* (*Mil.*) sector boundary. **abschnittsweise,** *adv.* in *or* by stages; by sections *or* paragraphs; (*Mil.*) in sectors. **Abschnittszeichen,** *n.* (*Typ.*) section mark.

abschnitze(l)n ['apʃnɪtsə(l)n], *v.t.* pare off, trim (off), whittle away.

abschnüren ['apʃny:rən], *v.t.* 1. mark out *or* measure off with a string; 2. (*Surg.*) ligature, apply a tourniquet to, tie off; 3. cut off, enclose (*an area*); 4. (*fig.*) strangle, throttle, constrict. **Abschnürung,** *f.* 1. (*Surg.*) ligation; 2. constriction (*of the breathing*).

abschöpfen ['apʃœpfən], *v.t.* scoop off, skim; ladle out; ***Profite –,*** siphon off excess profits.

Abschoß ['apʃɔs], *m.* (*Hist.*) legacy duty.

abschrägen ['apʃrɛ:gən], *v.t.* plane off; slope, slant, bevel, chamfer. **Abschrägung,** *f.* bevel, bevel(led) edge, chamfer.

abschrammen ['apʃramən], **1.** *v.t.* scratch off, scar. **2.** *v.i.* (*aux.* s.) (*coll.*) hop it, clear off.

abschrauben ['apʃraubən], *v.t.* unscrew, screw off.

Abschreckbad ['apʃrɛkba:t], *n.* (*Metall.*) quenching bath.

abschrecken ['apʃrɛkən], *v.t.* 1. frighten off, frighten *or* scare away, startle; intimidate, deter, discourage, dishearten, (*coll.*) put off; 2. chill, cool down, (*Metall.*) quench; ***abgeschrecktes Wasser,*** lukewarm water. **abschreckend,** *adj.* forbidding, intimidating, deterrent; (*coll.*) horrible, dreadful, frightful; ***–es Beispiel,*** deterrent example, (*coll.*) horrid warning. **Abschreckung,** *f.* intimidation. **Abschreckungsmittel,** *n.* 1. deterrent; 2. (*Metall.*) cooling *or* quenching agent.

Abschreibegebühr ['apʃraɪbəgəby:r], *f.* copying fee.

abschreiben ['apʃraɪbən], *irr.v.t.* 1. copy, transcribe; crib (*in school*), plagiarize; 2. revoke, countermand, cancel (in writing); write off (*bad debts*); write off (as lost) (*aircrew etc.*), (*coll.*) write off as a dead loss (*s.th unsatisfactory*); 3. deduct (*from an account*), deduct *or* allow for depreciation. **Abschreiber,** *m.* transcriber, copyist; plagiarist. **Abschreiberei** [–'raɪ], *f.* copying, cribbing. **Abschreibung,** *f.* 1. transcription; 2. amount written off; 3. (*Comm.*) depreciation, amortization.

abschreien ['apʃraɪən], *irr.v.r.* ***sich*** (*Dat.*) ***die Kehle –,*** scream o.s. hoarse.

abschreiten ['apʃraɪtən], *irr.v.t.* measure by steps, pace off; inspect (*a parade*).

Abschrift ['apʃrɪft], *f.* copy, transcript, transcription; ***beglaubigte –,*** attested copy, (*Law*) estreat.

Abschub ['apʃu:p], *m.* expulsion, deportation.

abschuppen ['apʃupən], **1.** *v.t.* scale, remove the scales from. **2.** *v.i.* scale *or* peel *or* flake off; (*Geol.*) laminate, desquamate.

abschürfen ['apʃy:rfən], *v.t.* scrape, scratch, graze (*skin*). **Abschürfung,** *f.* graze, abrasion.

Abschuß ['apʃus], *m.* 1. slope, descent; 2. firing (*a shot*), discharge (*of a gun*); (*Av. etc.*) shooting down; killing (off) (*of game*). **Abschußgerüst,** *n.* launching pad (*for rockets*).

abschüssig ['apʃysɪç], *adj.* sloping, shelving; precipitous, steep. **Abschüssigkeit,** *f.* declivity, steepness.

abschütteln ['apʃytəln], *v.t.* shake off; (*fig.*) throw off (*one's chains*), cast away (*care*), put aside (*doubts, fears*).

abschütten ['apʃytən], *v.t.* pour off; pour out (*corn etc. from a sack*).

abschützen ['apʃytsən], *v.t.* cut off by a floodgate; drain (*ponds etc.*); shut off (*steam etc.*).

abschwächen ['apʃvɛçən], **1.** *v.t.* weaken; lessen, reduce, diminish; attenuate, tone *or* soften down, mitigate. **2.** *v.i.* (*aux.* s.), *v.r.* weaken, ease off, sag (*of prices*). **Abschwächer,** *m.* (*Phot.*) reducing agent. **Abschwächung,** *f.* weakening, reduction; decrease, diminution, attenuation, mitigation.

abschwarten ['apʃvartən], *v.t.* remove the bark of, skin (*ham etc.*).

abschwefeln ['apʃve:fəln], *v.t.* 1. desulphurize; 2. impregnate with sulphur.

Abschweif ['apʃvaɪf], *m.* (*obs.*) digression. **abschweifen, 1.** *v.i.* (*aux.* s.) digress; deviate, stray, wander (away). **2.** *v.t.* scallop. **abschweifend, abschweifig,** *adj.* discursive, digressive. **Abschweifung,** *f.* digression, deviation; ***ohne –,*** directly, to the point.

abschwellen ['apʃvɛlən], *irr.v.i.* subside, go down (*of swelling*), (*fig.*) die down *or* away (*of sound*).

abschwemmen ['apʃvɛmən], *v.t.* 1. wash away *or* down; 2. flush, wash, rinse (*ore etc.*); 3. water (*horses*).

abschwenken ['apʃvɛŋkən], **1.** *v.t.* wash *or* rinse off *or* away (*dirt*). **2.** *v.i.* turn aside; (*Mil.*) wheel; ***rechts*** (***links***) ***abgeschwenkt!*** right (left) wheel! **Abschwenkung,** *f.* wheeling movement.

abschwindeln ['apʃvɪndəln], *v.t.* ***ihm etwas –,*** cheat *or* swindle him out of a th.

abschwingen ['apʃvɪŋən], **1.** *irr.v.t.* shake *or* swing down *or* off. **2.** *irr.v.r.* swing o.s. down.

abschwitzen ['apʃvɪtsən], *v.t.* sweat (off) (*a disease, fat*).

abschwören ['apʃvø:rən], **1.** *irr.v.t.* deny on oath; abjure; ***seinen Glauben –,*** renounce his faith. **2.** *irr.v.i.* renounce, forswear; (*coll.*) ***dem Branntwein –,*** swear off spirits, swear to abstain from spirits. **Abschwörung,** *f.* denial, renunciation, recantation, abjuration.

Abschwung ['apʃvuŋ], *m.* leaping down, (*Gymn.*) swinging down.

absegeln ['apze:gəln], *v.i.* (*aux.* s.) set sail, sail away; ***vom Winde –,*** bear off.

absehbar ['apze:ba:r], *adj.* within sight, (*fig.*) foreseeable, conceivable; ***in –er Zeit,*** in the not-too-distant future.

absehen ['apze:ən], **1.** *irr.v.i.* look away (***von,*** from), turn one's eyes (away) (from); ***von etwas –,*** refrain from; – ***von,*** leave out of account *or* consideration, take no account of, disregard; *see* **abgesehen. 2.** *irr.v.t.* 1. see in its entirety, see the whole extent of, foresee; 2. ***auf etwas*** (*Acc.*) –, aim at, intend *or* mean for; ***es auf etwas*** (*Acc.*) ***abgesehen haben,*** have one's eye *or* designs on a th.; ***es darauf abgesehen haben,*** be intent *or* bent on (***zu tun,*** doing), have made up one's mind (to do); 3. ***ihm etwas –,*** learn s.th. by watching him; ***ihm etwas an den Augen –,*** read s.th. in his eyes, anticipate his wishes. **Absehen,** *n.* ***da ist kein –,*** there is no end to it *or* no end in sight. **Absehlinie,** *f.* (*Opt.*) line of sight *or* (*Surv.*) of collimation.

Abseide ['apzaɪdə], *f.* (-, *no pl.*) floss (silk), silk waste.

abseifen ['apzaɪfən], *v.t.* clean with soap, soap well.

abseigern ['apzaɪgərn], *v.t.* (*Metall.*) liquate. **Abseigerung,** *f.* liquation.

abseihen ['apzaɪən], *v.t.* strain, filter, decant. **Abseihung,** *f.* percolation, filtration.

abseilen ['apzaɪlən], *v.i.* (*Mount.*) rope down, abseil. **Abseilen,** *n.* roping down, abseil, rappel.

absein ['apzaɪn], *irr.v.i.* (*aux.* s.) (*coll.*) ***ich bin ganz ab,*** I am quite exhausted *or* played out *or* knocked up.

Abseit ['apzaɪt], *n.* (**-s**, *pl.* -) (*Spt.*) offside.

Abseite ['apzaɪtə], *f.* 1. back, rear (*of an edifice*), side-aisle (*of a church*), sloping wall *or* side; 2. part further off; 3. reverse (*of a coin*).

Abseiter ['apzaɪtər], *m.* outsider.

abseitig ['apzaɪtɪç], *adj.* 1. apart, aloof, solitary; 2. off the point (*of a remark*).

abseits ['apzaɪts], **1.** *adv.* aside, on one side of; (*Spt.*) offside; – ***vom Weg,*** off the beaten track, **2.** *prep.* (*Gen.*) on one side of, off from; apart from.

absenden ['apzɛndən], *irr.v.t.* send away *or* off, dispatch, despatch, post, mail; remit (*money*). **Absender,** *m.* sender, addresser, originator (*of a message*), consigner, shipper (*of goods*); ***an den – zurück,*** return to sender. **Absendung,** *f.* forwarding, dispatch, despatch; consignment, shipment (*of goods*).

absengen ['apzɛŋən], *v.t.* singe (off), scorch.

absenken ['apzɛŋkən], **1.** *v.t.* 1. sink (*a shaft*); 2. (*Hort.*) set (*runners*), layer. **2.** *v.i.*, *v.r.* slope, shelve. **Absenker,** *m.* (*Hort.*) runner, layer; cutting.

abservieren ['apzɛrvi:rən], **1.** *v.i.* clear the table. **2.** *v.t.* (*coll.*) give (*s.o.*) the push.

absetzbar ['apzɛtsba:r], *adj.* 1. removable, (*official*) subject to dismissal; 2. (*Comm.*) saleable, marketable.

absetzen ['apzetsən], **1.** *v.t.* 1. put *or* set *or* lay down; land (*troops from aircraft*), drop (*parachutists, pilot*); ***er setzte mich am Bahnhof ab,*** he put me down *or* dropped me at the station; 2. dismiss, discharge (*from post*), depose, dethrone (*monarch*), deposit (*sediment*), remove, take (*von*, from) (*its usual place*), push off *or* away (*from shore etc.*); ***die Feder –,*** lift one's pen; ***das Gewehr –,*** bring the rifle down to the ready; ***den Hut –,*** remove *or* take off one's hat; (*Naut.*) ***Kurs –,*** allow for the side-wind; ***das Seitengewehr –,*** unfix bayonets; ***die Zeile –,*** begin a new line *or* paragraph; (*Mil.*) ***setzt ab!*** ground arms! 3. (*von*, from) strike *or* cut out, remove, delete, cancel; ***Spesen –,*** deduct expenses; ***von der Tagesordnung –,*** strike from the agenda; (*Theat.*) ***ein Stück –,*** withdraw *or* take off a play; 4. set off, pick out (*as one colour from another*); (*Mus.*) ***abgesetzt,*** staccato; 5. (*Comm.*) sell, dispose of, get rid of (*goods*); 6. set up (*in type*); 7. (*Naut.*) shape (*a course*). **2.** *v.r.* 1. settle, form a deposit; set (*as concrete*); 2. contrast (*von, gegen*, with), stand out (*in relief*) (against). **3.** *v.i.* pause, stop (short), break, come to an end; ***ohne abzusetzen,*** without pausing, without a break, at one go. **Absetzung,** *f.* dismissal, discharge; dethronement, deposition (*also of sediment*); removal (*from office*); withdrawal (*of play etc.*).

Absicht ['apzɪçt], *f.* intention, purpose, design, objective, motive, intent; end, aim, object, view; ***in der besten –,*** with the best intentions; ***mit –,*** on purpose, deliberately; ***mit böswilliger –,*** with malicious intent, with malice aforethought; ***mit redlicher –,*** with honourable intentions; ***ohne –,*** unintentionally, without motive. **absichtlich, 1.** *adj.* intentional, deliberate, wilful. **2.** *adv. See* ***mit Absicht.*** **Absichtlichkeit,** *f.* deliberateness, wilfulness, deliberate intention, premeditation. **absichtslos,** *adj.* unintentional, unpremeditated. **Absichtssatz,** *m.* (*Gram.*) final clause.

absickern ['apzɪkərn], *v.i* (*aux* s.) trickle *or* ooze *or* seep down.

absieben ['apzi:bən], *v.t.* sieve, riddle, sift out.

absieden ['apzi:dən], *irr.v.t.* boil; extract by boiling, decoct.

absingen ['apzɪŋən], *irr.v.t.* sing at sight; chant.

absinken ['apzɪŋkən], *irr.v.i.* (*aux.* s.) sink (down), drop (*as speed etc.*).

absitzen ['apzɪtsən], **1.** *irr.v.i.* (*aux* s.) 1. sit away (*von*, from); 2. (*Mil.*) dismount (*cavalry*); ***abgesessen!*** dismount! **2.** *irr.v.t.* sit out *or* through (*period of time*); ***eine Strafe –,*** serve a sentence.

absolut [apzo'lu:t], *adj.* absolute; unconditional; (*coll. adv.*) perfectly, utterly; ***–e Malerei (Musik),*** abstract painting (music); (*Av.*) ***–e Geschwindigkeit,*** ground speed.

Absolution [apzolutsi'o:n], *f.* absolution; remission of sins.

Absolutismus [apzolu'tɪsmus], *m.* (-, *no pl.*) absolutism. **absolutistisch,** *adj.* absolutist.

Absolutorium [apzolu'to:rium], *n.* (**-s**, *pl.* **-rien**) 1. (*obs.*) (*Law*) acquittal; 2. (*Austr.*) *See* **Reifeprüfung.**

Absolvent [apzɔl'vɛnt], *m.* (**-en**, *pl.* **-en**) school-leaver, (*Am.*) graduate. **absolvieren** [–'vi:rən], *v.t.* 1. absolve, acquit; 2. finish, complete (*one's studies at college*).

absonderbar ['apzɔndərba:r], *adj.* detachable, separable. **absonderlich,** *adj.* exceptional, unusual, uncommon, remarkable; curious, strange, peculiar, singular, bizarre, queer, quaint, odd. **Absonderlichkeit,** *f.* particularity; strangeness, uncommonness, peculiarity, singularity, oddness, oddity, queerness, quaintness.

absondern ['apzɔndərn], **1.** *v.t.* 1. separate, isolate, segregate, divide, detach; 2. (*Med.*) secrete; 3. abstract (*ideas*); 4. (*Law*) treat as preferential. **2.** *v.r.* 1. separate; 2. seclude o.s., dissociate o.s., withdraw, hold aloof; 3. (*Med.*) be discharged *or* secreted. **Absonderung,** *f.* 1. separation, division; seclusion, isolation, segregation; 2. abstract concept, abstraction; 3. (*Med.*) secretion. **Absonderungs|anspruch,** *m.* (*Law*) preferential claim. **–berechtigte(r),** *m.*, *f.* (*Law*) preferential *or* secured creditor. **–bläschen,** *n.* (*Biol.*) vacuole. **–drüse,** *f.* secretory gland. **–vermögen,** *n.* power of abstraction.

absorbieren [apzɔr'bi:rən], *v.t.* absorb (*also fig.*), (*fig.*) engross. **absorbierend,** *adj.* absorbent; ***–es Mittel,*** absorbent. **Absorbierung,** *f. See* **Absorption.**

Absorption [apzɔrptsi'o:n], *f.* absorption.

abspalten ['apʃpaltən], **1.** *v.t.* split (off), separate. **2.** *v.i.* (*aux.* s.), *v.r.* split (off *or* asunder), separate.

abspannen ['apʃpanən], *v.t.* 1. loosen, relax, slacken (*a drum etc.*); release (*a spring*), uncock (*a gun*); 2. unyoke, unharness. *See* **abgespannt. Abspannung,** *f.* (*fig.*) relaxation.

absparen ['apʃpa:rən], *v.t.* spare from; ***ich will es mir am Munde –,*** I will stint myself for it *or* go short for the sake of it.

abspeisen ['apʃpaɪzən], **1.** *v.i.* finish a meal. **2.** *v.t.* ***ihn mit leeren Worten –,*** put *or* fob him off with fair *or* fine words.

abspenstig ['apʃpɛnstɪç], *adj.* – ***machen,*** entice away (*Dat.*, from); – ***werden,*** desert (*Dat., a p. or th.*).

absperren ['apʃpɛrən], **1.** *v.t.* 1. close, stop, block (up), bar, obstruct, barricade; stop up (*a pipe*), shut *or* cut off (*gas, water*), shut *or* cut *or* cordon off (*an area*); 2. laminate (*wood*). **2.** *v.r.* shut o.s. off *or* away. **Absperr|hahn,** *m.* stopcock. **–klinke,** *f.* pawl. **–sicherung,** *f.* (*Elec.*) cut-out. **Absperrung,** *f.* stoppage, barrier, obstruction, (road) block, barricade, cordon. **Absperrungssystem,** *n.* prohibition (of imports).

abspiegeln ['apʃpi:gəln], *v.t.* reflect, mirror.

abspielen ['apʃpi:lən], **1.** *v.t.* 1. play (over) (*gramophone record*), play back (*tape-recording*); (*Mus.*) ***vom Blatt –,*** sight-read; 2. (*Footb.*) pass (*the ball*). **2.** *v.r.* occur, happen, take place, be enacted; ***die Szene spielt sich in B. ab,*** the scene is laid *or* set in B.

abspitzen ['apʃpɪtsən], *v.t.* 1. blunt, break the point off (*s.th. pointed*); 2. sharpen, put a point on (*pencil etc.*).

absplittern ['apʃplɪtərn], **1.** *v.i.* (*aux.* s.) splinter, come off in splinters. **2.** *v.t.* splinter *or* split off.

absprechen ['apʃprɛçən], **1.** *irr.v.t.* 1. deprive, dispossess (***ihm etwas,*** him of s.th.); ***ihm das Leben –,*** condemn him to death; 2. deny, refuse to admit, question, dispute (***ihm etwas,*** his s.th.); ***Talent kann man ihm nicht –,*** there is no denying that he has talent; ***ich spreche Ihnen das Recht nicht ab,*** I do not dispute your right. **2.** *irr.v.i.* speak unfavourably (*über* (*Acc.*), of). **absprechend, absprecherisch,** *adj.* 1. unfavourable, adverse, disparaging, derogatory; 2. dogmatic, peremptory.

abspreizen ['apʃpraɪtsən], *v.t.* prop *or* shore up (*wall etc.*).

absprengen ['apʃprɛŋən], **1.** *v.t.* 1. blow up (*with* (*explosives*), blast away; 2. chip *or* split off; 3. cut off (*troops*); 4. water (*lawn, flowers*). **2.** *v.i.* (*aux.* s.) gallop away *or* off. **Absprenger,** *m.* glass cutter.

abspringen ['apʃprɪŋən], *irr.v.i.* (*aux.* s.) 1. leap *or* jump off *or* down; jump, bale out (*from aircraft*), jump out (*from moving vehicle*); (*fig.*) ***vom Thema –,*** change the subject abruptly, shift one's ground suddenly; 2. come *or* fly off (*button etc.*), chip *or* crack *or* peel off *as paint*); 3. bounce, rebound.

abspritzen ['apʃprɪtsən], *v.t.* wash down (*with a hose*), hose down, spray.

Absprung ['apʃpruŋ], *m.* 1. jump, leap; ***Absprünge machen,*** dodge, double (*of hunted game*); 2. bounce, rebound; 3. (*Spt.*) take-off; 4. (*Hort.*) offshoot. **Absprung|hafen,** *m.* (*Mil*). *etc.*) operational base. **–tisch,** *m.* take-off platform (*skiing*).

abspulen ['apʃpu:lən], *v.t.* uncoil, unwind, wind *or* reel off.

abspülen ['apʃpy:lən], *v.t.* rinse, swill, flush (*lavatory*), wash off; wash up (*crockery*); wash away (*a cliff*). **Abspülung,** *f.* erosion. **Abspülwasser,** *n.* dish-water.

abstammen ['apʃtamən], *v.i.* (*aux.* s.) descend *or* be descended (***von,*** from), come (of); (*Gram.*) derive *or* be derived (from). **Abstammung,** *f.* descent, parentage, lineage, extraction, ancestry, origin; etymology, derivation. **Abstammungs|lehre,** *f.* doctrine *or* theory of evolution *or* the origin of species. **–tafel,** *f.* pedigree, family tree, genealogical table.

Abstand ['apʃtant], *m.* 1. distance (away); distance (apart), clearance, interval, gap, space, spacing; ***– halten*** or ***wahren,*** keep one's distance; ***in gehörigem –,*** at a proper distance; ***in gleichmäßigen Abständen,*** at regular intervals; ***mit*** (***weitem***) ***–,*** far and away, by far; ***– nehmen von,*** stand back *or* away from; (*fig.*) refrain *or* desist from; waive, forego, abandon, relinquish (*a claim*); 2. (*fig.*) discrepancy (***zwischen,*** between), disparity (of); 3. renunciation, abandonment, (*Law*) waiving.

abständig ['apʃtɛndɪç], *adj.* deteriorated, decayed; dried up, stale, musty, flat.

Abstandsgeld ['apʃtantsgɛlt], *n.* 1. compensation, indemnification; 2. option money; 3. penalty, forfeit (*for non-fulfilment*). **abstandsgleich,** *adj.* equidistant. **Abstandspunkt,** *m.* (*Astr.*) apsis.

abstatten ['apʃtatən], *v.t.* give, make, pay, render, discharge; ***einen Bericht –,*** send in *or* make *or* present a report; ***einen Besuch –,*** pay a visit, pay *or* make a call; ***seinen Dank –,*** return *or* express *or* offer *or* extend one's thanks; ***seine Schuldigkeit –,*** discharge one's obligations; ***Zeugnis –,*** bear witness. **Abstattung,** *f.* presentation (*of report*), payment (*of visit*), return, expression, offer, extension (*of thanks*), discharge (*of obligations*).

abstauben ['apʃtaubən], **abstäuben** ['apʃtɔybən], *v.t.* 1. wipe *or* brush the dust off, beat the dust from, dust; 2. (*sl.*) pinch, swipe, snaffle, lift. **Abstäuber,** *m.* duster, mop.

abstechen ['apʃtɛçən], **1.** *irr.v.t.* 1. cut (*as turf, peat etc.*); ***den Rasen –,*** trim (the edges of) the lawn; ***den Bauplatz –,*** mark out the building plot; 2. pierce, prick; stick (*a pig*); ***ein Muster –,*** prick out a pattern; ***ein Faß –,*** breach *or* tap a cask; 3. beat, take, trump (*opponent's card*). **2.** *irr.v.i.* 1. contrast (***gegen, von,*** with), stand out (against); ***grell –,*** clash, jar (with); 2. (*Naut.*) sheer off. **Abstecher,** *m.* detour; trip, excursion (*also fig.*); (*fig.*) digression.

Absteckeisen ['apʃtɛkˀaɪzən], *n.* iron stake, (*Surv.*) picket.

abstecken ['apʃtɛkən], *v.t.* 1. unpin, unpeg; undo, unfasten (*hair*); 2. mark out; lay out, trace, stake out; (*Naut.*) ***den Kurs –,*** plot the course; (*Dressm.*) ***den Saum –,*** pin up the hem; ***das Ziel –,*** pinpoint the target. **Absteck|kette,** *f.* (surveyor's) measuring chain. **–pfahl,** *m.* peg, stake, picket, surveying rod. **–schnur,** *f.* measuring *or* tracing line.

abstehen ['apʃte:ən], *irr.v.i.* 1. stand off *or* away *or* apart *or* aside, be at a distance (***von,*** from); protrude, stand *or* stick out (from); ***weit voneinander –,*** be far apart from one another; 2. (*aux.* s. *&* h.) (*fig.*) refrain, desist (***von,*** from), abandon, forego, relinquish, waive (*a claim*); 3. (*aux.* s.) go bad, become stale, go flat (*of beer*), become stagnant (*of water*), turn sour (*of milk*). *See* **abgestanden. abstehend,** *adj.* spreading, (*Bot.*) patulous, squarrose (*of scales*); ***–e Ohren,*** prominent ears.

absteifen ['apʃtaɪfən], *v.t.* stiffen; support; reinforce; prop (up), stay, brace, shore up, underpin. **Absteifung,** *f.* props, struts, reinforcement.

Absteige ['apʃtaɪgə], *f.* temporary lodging.

absteigen ['apʃtaɪgən], *irr.v.i.* (*aux.* s.) 1. descend, come *or* go down; (*coll.*) ***auf dem –den Ast sein,*** be on the downgrade, be going downhill; 2. alight, dismount, get off, get down; put up (***bei,*** with; ***in*** (*Dat.*), at) (*at an inn etc.*). **Absteigequartier,** *n.* over-night lodging, temporary quarters.

Abstellbahnhof ['apʃtɛlba:nho:f], *m.* shunting yards, sidings.

abstellen ['apʃtɛlən], *v.t.* 1. put away; put down (*a burden etc.*); park (*vehicle*); (*Railw.*) shunt; 2. stop, put out of action; disconnect, switch *or* cut off (*current etc.*), turn *or* shut off (*steam*); 3. abolish; remedy, redress; put down, put an end to (*nuisances etc.*). **Abstell|gleis,** *n.* (*Railw.*) siding. **–hahn,** *m.* stopcock. **–tisch,** *m.* side table; dumb waiter. **–vorrichtung,** *f.* stopping mechanism.

abstempeln ['apʃtɛmpəln], *v.t.* stamp, hall-mark (*silver etc.*), cancel (*by stamping*); (*fig.*) characterize (***als,*** as).

absterben ['apʃtɛrbən], *irr.v.i.* (*aux.* s.) wither (away), be dying (*of plants*), go numb (*of limb*), (*fig.*) die out; ***der Welt –,*** withdraw from the world.

Abstich ['apʃtɪç], *m.* 1. engraved copy, pattern pricked off; 2. racking (*of wine*), running off, run-off, tap(ping) (*of molten metal*).

Abstieg ['apʃti:k], *m.* (**-(e)s,** *pl.* **-e**) descent, downward climb; (*fig.*) decline (*social, economic etc.*), (*Footb.*) relegation.

abstimmen ['apʃtɪmən], **1.** *v.t.* tune (***auf*** (*Acc.*), to), harmonize (with); (*Rad.*) tune in (to), tune up (*an engine*); (*Rad.*) ***abgestimmter Kreis,*** tuned circuit; ***aufeinander –,*** collate, check against one another. **2.** *v.i.* vote, record one's vote; (*Parl.*) divide, proceed to a division; ***durch Handaufheben –,*** vote by a show of hands; ***über eine S. – lassen,*** put a th. to the vote. **Abstimm|kondensator,** *m.* (*Rad.*) tuning condenser. **–schärfe,** *f.* (*Rad.*) selectivity. **–spule,** *f.* (*Rad.*) tuning coil. **Abstimmung,** *f.* voting, vote, ballot, poll; (*Parl.*) division; ***zur – bringen,*** put to the vote; ***geheime –,*** secret ballot. **Abstimmungs|leiter,** *m.* polling clerk, returning officer. **–recht,** *n.* right to vote, franchise. **–zettel,** *m.* ballot paper.

Abstinenz [apsti'nɛnts], *f.* (**-,** *no pl.*) abstinence, abstemiousness; total abstinence, teetotalism. **Abstinenzler,** *m.* total abstainer, teetotaler, (*sl.*) pussyfoot.

abstoppen ['apʃtɔpən], **1.** *v.t.* 1. time, measure the time (*with a stop-watch*); 2. stop, halt, bring to a stop. **2.** *v.i.* stop, come to a stop *or* halt.

abstöpseln ['apʃtœpsəln], *v.t.* uncork, unstopper.

abstoßen ['apʃto:sən], **1.** *irr.v.t.* 1. knock off, thrust off, scrape, plane (***von,*** off); ***es wird ihm das Herz –,*** it will break his heart; ***sich*** (*Dat.*) ***die Hörner –,*** sow one's wild oats; 2. (*Mus.*) play staccato; 3. push *or* shove off *or* away; 4. repel; 5. get rid of, dispose of (*merchandise*); ***eine Schuld –,*** pay off a debt; ***Zähne –,*** shed one's teeth. **2.** *irr.v.i.* (*aux.* s. *&* h.) push off, (*Naut.*) shove off. **abstoßend,** *adj.* 1. repellent, repulsive, repugnant; 2. unprepossessing. **Abstoßung,** *f.* repulsion.

abstottern [ˈapʃtɔtərn], *v.t.* (*coll.*) pay for by instalments.

abstrafen [ˈapʃtra:fən], *v.t.* punish, chastise.

abstrahieren [apstraˈhi:rən], *v.t.* abstract.

Abstrahl [ˈapʃtra:l], *m.* reflected ray. **abstrahlen,** **1.** *v.t.* reflect; radiate. **2.** *v.i.* (*aux.* s.) be reflected; radiate. **Abstrahlung,** *f.* reflection; radiation. **Abstrahlungswinkel,** *m.* angle of reflection.

abstrakt [apˈstrakt], **1.** *adj.* abstract; *–er Begriff,* abstract idea, abstraction. **2.** *adv.* in the abstract.

abstrapazieren [ˈapʃtrapatsi:rən], **1.** *v.t.* wear (*a th.*) out. **2.** *v.r.* toil hard; work o.s. to death.

Abstrebekraft [ˈapʃtre:bəkraft], *f.* centrifugal force.

abstreben [ˈapʃtre:bən], **1.** *v.i.* strive to get loose *or* away, tend to diverge. **2.** *v.t.* brace. **Abstrebung,** *f.* struts, bracing.

Abstreicheisen [ˈapʃtraɪçʔaɪzən], *n.* scraper.

abstreichen [ˈapʃtraɪçən], **1.** *irr.v.t.* 1. wipe off; scrape off; strike out, cancel (*from books*); 2. strop, whet (*a razor*); 3. beat (*a field*) for game. **2.** *irr.v.i.* (*aux.* s.) slip away; take flight (*of large birds*). **Abstreicher,** *m.* scraper.

Abstreich|holz, *n.* strickle. **–löffel,** *m.* skimming ladle. **–maß,** *n.* corn measure. **–riemen,** *m.* razor strop.

abstreifen [ˈapʃtraɪfən], **1.** *v.t.* take *or* pull *or* strip off; *die Haut –,* cast its skin, slough (*of reptiles*); (*fig.*) *von sich –,* divest *or* rid o.s. of, get rid of. **2.** *v.i.* (*aux.* s.) wander, stray, deviate; glance off (*of shot*).

abstreiten [ˈapʃtraɪtən], *irr.v.t.* dispute; contest; deny; *ihm etwas –,* deny his right to a th.; *das lasse ich mir nicht –,* I won't be argued out of it, I'll stick to my point.

abstreuen [ˈapʃtrɔyən], *v.t.* spray, (*Artil.*) sweep with fire.

Abstrich [ˈapʃtrɪç], *m.* 1. skimming, scum, dross; (*Med.*) swab; smear (*microscopic slide*); 2. reduction, cut (*in price*); deduction, discount, rebate; 3. down-stroke (*writing*), down-bow (*violin etc.*).

abstriegeln [ˈapʃtri:gəln], *v.t.* curry, rub down (*a horse*).

abströmen [ˈapʃtrø:mən], **1.** *v.i.* (*aux.* s.) flow out *or* away, pour out, stream out *or* forth; drift (away), be carried *or* swept *or* borne along *or* away by the tide *or* current. **2.** *v.t.* wash *or* sweep *or* carry away (*river bank*).

abstrus [apˈstru:s], *adj.* abstruse, recondite.

abstufen [ˈapʃtu:fən], **1.** *v.t.* 1. arrange in steps *or* tiers, lay out in terraces; 2. grade, graduate; shade off. **2.** *v.r.* shade off (*of colours*); be graduated. **Abstufung,** *f.* gradation; shade (*of colour*); *geometrische –,* geometrical progression.

abstumpfen [ˈapʃtumpfən], **1.** *v.t.* 1. blunt, dull (*also fig.*); (*Chem.*) saturate, neutralize; (*Geom.*) truncate; *abgestumpfter Kegel,* truncated cone; 2. (*fig.*) make indifferent (*gegen,* to), deaden. **2.** *v.i.* (*only fig.*) become dull *or* deadened *etc.* **Abstumpfung,** *f.* 1. dullness, apathy, indifference; 2. neutralization; truncation.

Absturz [ˈapʃturts], *m.* 1. headlong fall; *– eines Flugzeuges,* aeroplane crash; 2. precipice.

abstürzen [ˈapʃtʏrtsən], **1.** *v.t.* hurl down. **2.** *v.i.* (*aux.* s.) 1. fall headlong; (*Mount.*) fall; (*Av.*) crash; 2. slope away suddenly.

abstutzen [ˈapʃtutsən], *v.t.* lop, clip, dock, cut short; *abgestutzt,* truncated, docked, trimmed.

abstützen [ˈapʃtʏtsən], *v.t.* prop (up), shore up, support, strut, brace, underpin.

absuchen [ˈapzu:xən], *v.t.* search thoroughly, ransack, go through; pick (*von,* off); comb, scour (*a field*).

Absud [ˈapzu:t], *m.* decoction; extract.

absurd [apˈzurt], *adj.* absurd, nonsensical, irrational. **Absurdes** [apˈzurdəs], *n.*, **Absurdität** [–ˈtɛ:t], *f.* nonsense, absurdity, unreasonableness, irrationality; *das Theater des Absurden,* the theatre of the absurd.

Abszeß [apsˈtsɛs], *m.* (**-(ss)es,** *pl.* **-(ss)e**) abscess.

Absziß [apsˈtsɪs], *m.* (**-(ss)es,** *pl.* **-(ss)e**) segment (*of a circle*).

Abszisse [apsˈtsɪsə], *f.* abscissa. **Abszissenachse,** *f.* (*Math.*) x-axis.

Abt [apt], *m.* (**-(e)s,** *pl.* **⸚e**) abbot; (*coll.*) *den – reiten lassen,* let o.s. go, (*sl.*) blow one's top.

abtakeln [ˈapta:kəln], *v.t.* unrig, dismantle; (*coll.*) put out of action; (*sl.*) *eine abgetakelte Diva,* a has-been film star.

Abtastdose [ˈaptastdo:zə], *f.* pick-up (*gramophone*).

abtasten [ˈaptasten], *v.t.* explore *or* test *or* try (with the fingers), feel all over; prod; (*Med.*) probe, palpate; (*T.V. etc.*) scan. **Abtaster,** *m.* (*T.V.*) scanner. **Abtastperiode,** *f.* (*T.V.*) time-base.

abtauen [ˈaptauən], **1.** *v.i.* (*aux.* s.) thaw (off). **2.** *v.t.* melt, thaw (out), de-frost.

Abtei [apˈtaɪ], *f.* (-, *pl.* **-en**) abbey (*building*); abbacy (*office*).

Abteil [ˈaptaɪl], *n.* (*Railw.*) compartment.

abteilbar [ˈaptaɪlba:r], *adj.* divisible (into compartments), (*fig.*) classifiable.

abteilen [ˈaptaɪlən], *v.t.* divide, separate (*in* (*Acc.*), into), parcel out (*goods*), divide *or* partition off (*a room etc.*), (*fig.*) classify; graduate, calibrate (*measuring instrument*). **Abteilung,** *f.* 1. division, separation; classification; 2. [–ˈtaɪluŋ], part, portion, section (*of the whole*); compartment (*of a drawer etc.*), department (*shops, offices, Univ.*), (*Mil.*) detachment, unit, (*hospital*) ward; 3. [–ˈtaɪluŋ], category, class, head, rubric. **Abteilungs|kommandeur,** *m.* (*Mil.*) unit commander. **–leiter,** *m.* departmental head, head of a department. **–schott,** *n.* (*Naut.*) athwartships bulkhead. **–schreiber,** *m.* (*Mil.*) orderly-room clerk. **–vorstand, –vorsteher,** *m.* *See* **–leiter. –zeichen,** *n.* hyphen.

abteufen [ˈaptɔyfən], *v.t.* sink, bore, deepen (*a shaft*).

Abtgraf [ˈaptgra:f], *m.* (*Hist.*) secular abbot.

Äbtin [ˈɛptɪn], *f.* *See* **Äbtissin.**

abtippen [ˈaptɪpən], *v.t.* type out.

Äbtissin [ɛpˈtɪsɪn], *f.* abbess.

äbtlich [ˈɛptlɪç], *adj.* abbatial.

abtönen [ˈaptø:nən], *v.t.* shade off, blend (*colours*), vignette; tone down. **Abtönung,** *f.* gradation; shade, tint; nuance.

abtöten [ˈaptø:tən], *v.t.* kill (off), destroy; deaden; (*B.*) mortify (*the flesh*); *den Nerv –,* kill the nerve. **Abtötung,** *f.* (*B.*) mortification.

Abtrab [ˈaptra:p], *m.* cavalry detachment.

Abtrag [ˈaptra:k], *m.* (**-(e)s,** *pl.* **⸚e**) 1. spoil (*earth*), scraps, leavings (*from the table*); 2. compensation, indemnification; *ihm – leisten,* compensate *or* indemnify him; *ihm – tun,* hurt *or* injure him, do him harm *or* an injury; 3. (*Swiss*) yield, proceeds, profits, earnings.

abtragen [ˈaptra:gən], *irr.v.t.* 1. remove, carry *or* take away *or* off; excavate; clear *or* dig away (*earth*), level (*ground*); dismantle, demolish (*structure*), raze (*fortifications*); clear away (*dishes*), clear (*the table*); 2. (*fig.*) discharge, settle, pay (*a debt*), pay *or* clear off, redeem, amortize (*a mortgage*), pay (*interest, taxes*); 3. (*Geom.*) mark *or* lay off (*a distance along a line*); 4. wear out (*clothes*); 5. (*Swiss*) produce, yield, bring in (*profit etc.*). *See* **abgetragen.**

abträglich [ˈaptrɛ:klɪç], *adj.* 1. harmful, detrimental, injurious, prejudicial; 2. (*Swiss*) paying, profitable, lucrative.

Abtragung [ˈaptra:guŋ], *f.* 1. removal, excavation, demolition; 2. payment, settlement, discharge, redemption, amortization; 3. (*Geol.*) erosion, detrition, denudation.

Abtransport [ˈaptranspɔrt], *m.* removal, (*Mil.*) evacuation. **abtransportieren,** *v.t.* carry *or* cart away; move, (*Mil.*) evacuate.

abträufeln [ˈaptrɔyfəln], *v.i.* (*aux.* s.) drip *or* trickle down.

Abtreibanker [ˈaptraɪpʔaŋkər], *m.* (*Naut.*) drag-anchor, (*Av.*) drogue.

abtreiben [ˈaptraɪbən], **1.** *irr.v.t.* 1. drive off *or* away; repel, repulse; avert; 2. drive out, expel; eject, evict, oust; *ein Kind* –, procure (an) abortion; 3. overwork, (over)drive, exploit; ***abgetriebener Gaul,*** jade; 4. refine (*metals*) by cupellation. **2.** *irr. v.i.* (*aux.* s.) drift, be driven off course. **abtreibend,** *adj.* (*Med.*) abortifacient. **Abtreibeofen,** *m.* refining *or* cupel furnace. **Abtreibung,** *f.* 1. expulsion, eviction, ejection; 2. (*Med.*) abortion; 3. (*Metall.*) cupellation. **Abtreibungsmittel,** *n.* abortifacient.

abtrennbar ['aptrɛnba:r], *adj.* detachable, separable. **abtrennen,** *v.t.* separate, detach, remove (***von,*** from), take (off). **abtrennlich,** *adj. See* **abtrennbar. Abtrennung,** *f.* separation, removal, detachment.

abtreten ['aptre:tən], **1.** *irr.v.t.* 1. tread off (*dirt from shoes*), tread down (*snow etc.*); wear out (by constant treading) (*as steps, carpet etc.*); 2. relinquish, surrender, yield, give up (*Dat.*, to); transfer, assign, cede, make over (***an*** (*Acc.*), to); ***abgetretene Gebiete,*** ceded territories. **2.** *irr.v.i.* (*aux.* s.) step *or* move aside, withdraw, retire, (*euphem.*) leave the room; – ***von,*** give up, renounce, relinquish; retire from, resign, quit, lay down, give up (*one's post*); ***tritt ab,*** exit; ***treten ab,*** exeunt (*stage directions*); (*Mil.*) ***abgetreten!*** dismiss! fall out! – ***lassen,*** dismiss (*a parade*). **Abtreter,** *m.* 1. assignor, transferrer; 2. scraper, doormat. **Abtretung,** *f.* transfer, assignment, conveyance, cession, abandonment, surrender. **Abtretungsurkunde,** *f.* deed of transfer, instrument of conveyance *or* assignment.

Abtrieb ['aptri:p], *m.* 1. (*dial.*) driving (*the cattle*) down from the Alps; 2. (*For.*) felling; felled timber; 3. (*Hist.*) eviction; 4. (*Av.*) negative lift. **Abtriebs|alter,** *n.* (*For.*) felling age. **–ertrag,** *m.* yield of timber. **–recht,** *n.* 1. right to fell; 2. (*Hist.*) right to evict.

abtriefen ['aptri:fən], *irr.v.i.* (*aux.* s.) trickle down, drip.

Abtrift ['aptrɪft], *f.* 1. right of pasturage *or* common; 2. (*Naut.*) leeway; (*Av.*) drift.

Abtritt ['aptrɪt], *m.* 1. lavatory, W.C., latrine; 2. abdication, withdrawal, renunciation; cession, abandonment; exit; – ***vom Leben,*** decease, demise.

abtrocknen ['aptrɔknən], **1.** *v.t.* wipe *or* rub dry; dry (out *or* off); ***sich*** (*Dat.*) ***die Tränen*** –, wipe away *or* dry one's tears. **2.** *v.i.* (*aux.* s.) dry up *or* out *or* off, shrivel, wilt, wither away. **3.** *v.r.* dry o.s., wipe o.s. dry.

abtrollen ['aptrɔlən], *v.i.* (*aux.* s.) (*coll.*) vamoose, clear out, push off.

abtrommeln ['aptrɔməln], **1.** *v.t.* beat out on the drum; hammer out; ***auf dem Klavier*** –, hammer (*or* bang) out on the piano. **2.** *v.i.* leave off drumming; beat the retreat.

Abtropf ['aptrɔpf], *m.*, **Abtropfbrett,** *n.* draining board.

abtröpfeln ['aptrœpfəln], *v.i.* (*aux.* s.) trickle down; drip off; ooze, seep, exude, sweat.

abtropfen ['aptrɔpfən], *v.i.* (*aux.* s.) drip, trickle; drain (*crockery*); – ***lassen,*** drain (*crockery*).

abtrotzen ['aptrɔtsən], *v.t.* ***ihm etwas*** –, bully s.th. out of him.

abtrudeln ['aptru:dəln], *v.i.* (*aux.* s.) (*Av.*) go into a (tail) spin; (*dial.*) (*coll.*) push off, clear out, sling one's hook.

abtrumpfen ['aptrumpfən], *v.t.* trump; ***ihn*** –, snap him up, silence him with a snub.

abtrünnig ['aptrynɪç], *adj.* faithless, disloyal, (*B.*) rebellious; – ***werden*** (*Dat.*), revolt against, desert; turn apostate; ***der Religion*** (*Dat.*) –, renegade, apostate. **Abtrünnige(r),** *m., f.* deserter, renegade; apostate; turncoat. **Abtrünnigkeit,** *f.* disloyalty; defection, desertion; apostasy.

abtun ['aptu:n], *irr.v.t.* take *or* put off, lay aside; abolish, do away with, get rid of, settle, dispose of; kill, execute; (*Poet.*) ***sich seines Glaubens*** –, renounce one's faith; ***die Hand von ihm*** –, abandon him, leave him in the lurch; ***etwas geschwind*** –, finish a th. off hurriedly and carelessly, skimp a th.; ***die S. ist abgetan*** the matter is closed.

abtupfen ['aptupfən], *v.t.* mop up; remove by dabbing (*liquid*); mop, dab (*surface*).

aburteilen ['apˀurtaɪlən], **1.** *v.t.* pass final judgement on. **2.** *v.i.* – ***über*** (*Acc.*), reject summarily, condemn out of hand.

abverdienen ['apfɛrdi:nən], *v.t.* earn (*Dat.*, from); ***eine Schuld*** –, work off a debt.

abverlangen ['apfɛrlaŋən], *v.t.* ***ihm etwas*** –, demand s.th. from *or* of him, require s.th. of him.

abvermieten ['apfɛrmi:tən], *v.t.* sublet, (*coll.*) let off (*a room*).

abvisieren ['apvizi:rən], *v.t.* measure by eye; sight out, survey, gauge.

abwägen ['apvɛ:gən], *irr.v.t.* (*occ. reg.*) weigh out; ***seine Worte*** –, weigh one's words, ponder, consider carefully, weigh (up) in one's mind; ***gegeneinander*** –, balance one against the other, weigh the pros and cons.

abwägsam ['apvɛ:kza:m], *adj.* circumspect, prudent.

Abwägung ['apvɛ:guŋ], *f.* weighing, balancing; adjustment, consideration. **Abwägungskunst,** *f.* (art of) levelling *or* surveying.

abwalken ['apvalkən], *v.t.* 1. full (*cloth*); 2. (*coll.*) give (*s.o.*) a sound thrashing.

abwalzen ['apvaltsən], *v.t.* roll (*lawn etc.*), roll flat *or* level (*surfacing*).

abwälzen ['apvɛltsən], *v.t.* roll off *or* away; ***mir einen Stein vom Herzen*** –, take a load off my mind; ***die Beschuldigung von sich*** –, shift the blame from one's own shoulders, exculpate *or* exonerate *or* clear o.s.

abwandelbar ['apvandəlba:r], *adj.* declinable, capable of inflexion *or* conjugation.

abwandeln ['apvandəln], **1.** *v.t.* change, vary, modify; inflect, decline (*nouns*), conjugate (*verbs*). **2.** *v.r.* (*Gram.*) modify, inflect, decline, conjugate, be modified *or* inflected *or* declined *or* conjugated. **Abwand(e)lung,** *f.* change, modification, variation, inflexion; conjugation (*verbs*); declension (*nouns*). **abwand(e)lungsfähig,** *adj. See* **abwandelbar.**

abwandern ['apvandərn], *v.i.* (*aux.* s.) move, wander *or* drift away; ***vom Lande in die Großstadt*** –, migrate from the country to the towns. **Abwanderung,** *f.* movement *or* drift (away), migration (*of population*).

Abwandlung ['apwandluŋ], *f. See* **Abwand(e)lung.**

Abwärme ['apvɛrmə], *f.* waste heat.

abwarten ['apvartən], *v.t.* wait for, await; watch for; ***die Zeit*** –, temporize, wait for the right moment; ***den Zeitpunkt*** or ***Augenblick*** or ***die Gelegenheit*** –, watch one's opportunity, bide one's time; ***den Regen*** –, wait till the rain is over. **abwartend,** *adj.* expectant; cautious, temporizing; ***–e Haltung,*** temporizing *or* (*coll.*) wait-and-see attitude.

abwärts ['apvɛrts], *prep., adv.* downward(s); downhill; (*dial.*) aside; ***mit ihm geht's*** –, he is on the decline, he is breaking up (*health*), his affairs are going from bad to worse. **Abwärts|bewegung,** *f.* downward movement (*esp. of prices*). **–transformator,** *m.* step-down transformer.

abwaschen ['apvaʃən], *irr.v.t.* wash away *or* off *or* out, cleanse, bathe (*a wound*); wash up, wash *or* do the dishes. **Abwasch|lappen,** *m.* dish-cloth. **–magd,** *f.* scullery maid. **–seife,** *f.* kitchen soap. **Abwaschung,** *f.* washing, ablution. **Abwaschwasser,** *n.* washing-up *or* dish water.

Abwasser ['apvasər], *n.* (**-s,** *pl.* ¨) waste water, dirty water, effluent, sewage. **Abwasseranlage,** *f.* sewage disposal plant.

abwassern ['apvasərn], *v.i.* (*aux.* s.) (*Av.*) take off from the water.

abwässern ['apvɛsərn], *v.t.* drain. **Abwässerungsanlage,** *f.* drainage system.

abwechseln ['apvɛksəln], **1.** *v.t.* 1. exchange; 2. change, vary; modulate (*the voice*). **2.** *v.i.* do alternately, take it in turns; alternate, succeed one another. **abswechselnd, 1.** *adj.* alternating, alternate. **2.** *adv.* by turns, in turn, turn and turn about, one after the other, alternately. **Abwechs(e)lung,** *f.* variety, diversity, change; *zur –,* for a change. **abwechs(e)lungsreich,** *adj.* varied, diversified, animated, lively. **abwechslungsweise,** *adv.* alternately.

Abweg ['apve:k], *m.* by-way; wrong way; (*usu. pl.*) ***auf –e führen,*** mislead, seduce; ***auf –e geraten,*** go astray. **abwegig** ['apve:gıç], *adj.* off the track *or* point, erroneous, mistaken, misguided. **abwegs,** *adv.* out of the way; off the track.

Abwehr ['apve:r], *f.* (-, *no pl.*) defence, resistance; averting, repelling, parrying, warding off. **Abwehrdienst,** *m.* counter-espionage, (*Mil.*) intelligence service.

abwehren ['apve:rən], *v.t.* ward off; avert, fend *or* stave off, parry (*a blow*). **Abwehr|ferment,** *n.* (*Biol.*) defensive enzyme. **–körper,** *m.* antibody. **–manöver,** *n.* (*Mil.*) avoiding action. **–mittel,** *n.* means of defence, preventive, prophylactic, protection. **–offizier,** *m.* security officer. **–schlacht,** *f.* defensive battle.

[1]**abweichen** ['apvaıçən], *v.t.* soften; soak (off), steep, macerate.

[2]**abweichen,** *irr.v.i.* (*aux.* s.) deviate, diverge; digress; depart (*von,* from); deflect (*as the magnetic needle*); ***von der Wahrheit –,*** deviate *or* stray from the truth; ***er weicht keinen Fingerbreit ab,*** he will not budge an inch; ***wir weichen sehr voneinander ab,*** we differ widely; ***vom Kurs –,*** go off course. **abweichend,** *adj.* divergent, different, differing, variant, varying; discrepant, dissentient, dissenting (*opinion etc.*); exceptional, anomalous (*also Gram.*), (*Gram.*) irregular. **Abweichung,** *f.* deviation, variation, divergence; (*Opt.*) deflection, (*Magnet.*) declination; exception, anomaly, discrepancy, (*Astr.*) aberration; ***erlaubte –,*** (*Artil.*) allowance (for drift), (*Mech.*) tolerance; ***mittlere –,*** mean deviation. **Abweichungs|kompaß,** *m.* azimuth compass. **–kreis,** *m.* (*Astr.*) declination circle. **–winkel,** *m.* angle of divergence *or* deviation *or* deflection.

abweiden ['apvaıdən], *v.t.* feed on, graze (*a meadow*); feed (*a flock*); ***die Alp ist abgeweidet,*** the mountain pastures are grazed quite bare.

abweinen ['apvaınən], *v.r.* cry one's eyes out.

abweisen ['apvaızən], *irr.v.t.* refuse *or* deny admittance to, send *or* turn away; set aside, dismiss (*claim*), decline (*offer*), reject, refuse, (*coll.*) turn down (*application, candidate*), repulse, repel, beat off *or* back (*attack*), (*Law*) dismiss (*a case*), deny (*accusation*); ***er läßt sich nicht –,*** he will not take no for an answer, (*coll.*) he'll not be put off; ***ihn kurz*** or ***schroff –,*** send him about his business; (*Comm.*) ***einen Wechsel –,*** dishonour *or* protest a bill. **abweisend,** *adj.* unfavourable, adverse (*judgement etc.*), unfriendly, brusque (*manner*). **Abweisung,** *f.* refusal (*of request etc.*), rejection (*of offer, claim*), (*Comm.*) non-acceptance (*of a bill*), (*Law*) dismissal (*of a suit*); snub, rebuff.

abwelken ['apvɛlkən], *v.i.* (*aux.* s.) wither, fade, wilt.

abwendbar ['apvɛntba:r], *adj.* preventable, preventible, avertable, avertible.

abwenden ['apvɛndən], **1.** *reg. & irr.v.t.* turn away *or* aside, divert, avert, prevent; ward *or* stave off, parry. **2.** *irr.v.r.* turn away *or* aside, become alienated; ***sich von der Welt –,*** turn one's back on the world. **abwendig,** *adj.* alienated, estranged, averse; ***– machen,*** alienate, divert from, seduce; ***ihm etwas – machen,*** deprive him of a th. **Abwendung,** *f.* 1. averting, prevention; 2. alienation.

abwerfen ['apvɛrfən], *irr.v.t.* 1. throw *or* cast *or* fling off; throw out *or* down, jettison; drop (*bombs*); throw (*a horseman*); 2. yield (*a profit*); 3. cast, shed (*feathers, skin etc.*); throw away, discard (*cards*); 4. ***Junge –,*** bring forth young.

Abwerg ['apvɛrk], *m. or n.* **(-(e)s,** *no pl.*) (waste) tow.

abwerten ['apvɛrtən], *v.t.* 1. devalue, devaluate, depreciate (*currency*); 2. estimate, appraise, value (*goods*). **Abwertung,** *f.* 1. devaluation, depreciation; 2. valuation, estimation (of the value).

abwesend ['apve:zənt], *adj.* 1. absent, away (***von,*** from); (*Law*) defaulting; (*Hist.*) ***–er Gutsherr,*** absentee landlord; (*Law*) ***vorsätzlich –,*** contumacious; 2. absent-minded.

Abwesenheit ['apve:zənhaıt], *f.* 1. absence; absenteeism (*from work*); (*Law*) default, non-appearance, alibi; (*coll.*) ***durch – glänzen,*** be conspicuous by one's absence; (*Law*) ***vorsätzliche –,*** contumacy; 2. absent-mindedness.

abwetzen ['apvɛtsən], *v.t.* grind off; whet; wear out by grinding; (*coll.*) ***abgewetzte Hosen,*** trousers with the seat worn shiny.

abwichsen ['apvıksən], *v.t.* polish (with wax).

abwickeln ['apvıkəln], **1.** *v.t.* 1. unwind, wind *or* reel off; 2. unravel, disentangle; 3. settle (*affairs*), clear (*a debt*), wind up, liquidate (*a business*); 4. disperse (*troops*), (*obs.*) demobilize (*troops*). **2.** *v.r.* run its course, develop; ***sich glatt*** or ***reibungslos –,*** go off smoothly. **Abwickelspule,** *f.* feed reel, delivery spool. **Abwick(e)lung,** *f.* settlement, liquidation, winding up, wind-up. **Abwicklungskurve,** *f.* (*Geom.*) evolvent.

abwiegeln ['apvi:gəln], *v.t.* pacify, appease.

abwiegen ['apvi:gən], *irr.v.t.* weigh out.

abwimmeln ['apvıməln], *v.t.* (*coll.*) get rid of (*a p.*); shake *or* (*sl.*) choke (*s.o.*) off; ***mit einer Ausrede –,*** put *or* fob (*s.o.*) off with an excuse.

Abwind ['apvınt], *m.* (*Meteor.*) down current, downdraught, katabatic wind.

abwinden ['apvındən], *irr.v.t.* unwind; wind *or* reel off; (*Naut.*) pay out (*cable*); let down by a pulley.

abwinken ['apvıŋkən], *v.i.* (*Dat.*) motion away; decline with a nod.

abwirtschaften ['apvırtʃaftən], **1.** *v.t.* 1. ruin by bad management, mismanage; 2. exhaust (*soil*). **2.** *v.i., v.r.* make a mess of one's affairs, be ruined by bad management; (*coll.*) ***er hat abgewirtschaftet,*** he's finished *or* done for.

abwischen ['apvıʃən], *v.t.* wipe off; ***den Staub –,*** dust; ***sich*** (*Dat.*) ***die Hände –,*** wipe one's hands; ***die Tafel –,*** clean the blackboard; ***sich*** (*Dat.*) ***die Tränen –,*** wipe away one's tears. **Abwischer, Abwisch|lappen,** *m.*, **–tuch,** *n.* duster, floorcloth.

Abwitterung ['apvıtəruŋ], *f.* (*Geol.*) weathering.

abwracken ['apvrakən], *v.t.* break up (*ship*).

abwuchern ['apvu:xərn], *v.t.* wring, extort (**Dat.,** from).

Abwurf ['apvurf], *m.* 1. throwing down *or* off *or* away; 2. refuse, rubbish; 3. yield, proceeds; 4. last throw (*at dice*); 5. (*Build.*) rough-cast. **Abwurf|gerät,** *n.* (*Av.*) bomb-release. **–meldung,** *f.* (*Av.*) dropped message. **–munition,** *f.* (*Av.*) bombs. **–vorrichtung,** *f.* (*Av.*) bomb-release mechanism, device for jettisoning (*fuel tanks etc.*).

abwürgen ['apvyrgən], *v.t.* throttle, strangle; butcher, slaughter (*a p.*), wring the neck of (*poultry*), stifle (*opposition*); stall (*an engine*).

abyssisch [a'bysıʃ], *adj.* 1. abysmal; 2. (*Geol.*) plutonic.

abzahlen ['aptsa:lən], *v.t.* pay off; pay in instalments.

abzählen ['aptsɛ:lən], *v.t.* count (up), enumerate; count out (*money*), count down (*rocket launching*); ***ich kann es mir an den Fingern –,*** that's not hard to guess; ***Geld abgezählt bereithalten,*** have the exact money ready.

Abzahlung ['aptsa:luŋ], *f.* part payment, payment on account, instalment; ***auf –,*** by instalment(s), on hire-purchase. **Abzahlungsgeschäft,** *n.* hire purchase business.

abzapfen ['aptsapfən], *v.t.* tap; draw off (*liquid*); broach (*a cask*); ***Blut –*** (*Dat.*), bleed (*a p.*), let (*a p.'s*) blood; (*coll.*) ***ihm Geld –,*** fleece *or* bleed him.

abzäumen ['aptsɔymən], *v.t.* unbridle.

abzäunen ['aptsɔynən], *v.t.* fence *or* rail off *or* in; hedge in. **Abzäunung,** *f.* fence, fencing, railing(s), enclosure.

abzausen ['aptsauzən], *v.t.* pull *or* snatch off

roughly, worry (*as a dog*), tousle, rumple, dishevel, crumple, (*coll.* handle roughly, knock or bash (*s.o.*) about.

abzehren ['aptse:rən], **1.** *v.t.* waste, consume, emaciate. **2.** *v.i.* (*aux.* s.), *v.r.* waste *or* pine away, become emaciated. **abzehrend,** *adj.* wasting; ***-e Krankheit,*** wasting disease; atrophy. **Abzehrung,** *f.* emaciation; consumption wasting away.

Abzeichen ['aptsaɪçən], *n.* distinguishing mark, distinctive label, mark of distinction; emblem, badge; badge of rank, (*Mil.*) stripe; (*Av.*) marking; *pl.* insignia.

abzeichnen ['aptsaɪçnən], **1.** *v.t.* sketch, draw; copy, reproduce; mark off. **2.** *v.r.* stand out clearly *or* sharply (***gegen,*** against), contrast, stand in contrast (with), be a contrast (to). **Abzeichnung,** *f.* reproduction, copy.

Abzieh|bild, *n.* (stick-on) transfer. **-blase,** *f.* still, retort.

abziehen ['aptsi:ən], **1.** *irr.v.t.* 1. draw *or* pull *or* take off, remove; skim off (*froth*), drain off, pour off, decant; distil, rectify (*spirits*); string (*beans*); strip (*a bed*); (***auf Flaschen***) **-,** bottle (*wine, beer*); (*Typ.*) ***den Satz* -,** take (off) proofs; 2. take *or* pull *or* draw out, withdraw (*money etc.*); ***die Hand* -,** draw one's hand away *or* back; (*fig.*) ***die Hand von ihm* -,** leave him to his own devices, withdraw one's support from him; 3. turn *or* draw *or* lead away; divert, distract (*attention*), avert (*gaze*); (*Math.*) subtract, deduct, take away; (*Phil.*) abstract, formulate; 4. sharpen, grind, whet, hone, strop, put an edge on (*knife*). **2.** *irr.v.i.* (*aux.* s.) go away *or* off, leave, depart; retire, withdraw (*of troops*), be relieved (*of guard*); ***mit leeren Händen* -, *unverrichteter Dinge*** or ***S.* -,** come away empty-handed, not achieve one's purpose; ***mit langer Nase* -,** go off with a flea in one's ear; ***wie ein begossener Pudel* -,** slink away with one's tail between one's legs; ***mit Schimpf und Schande* -,** leave under a cloud, go away in disgrace.

Abzieher ['aptsi:ər], *m.* abductor muscle. **Abzieh|-feile,** *f.* smoothing file. **-flasche,** *f.*, **-kolben,** *m.* retort. **-leder,** *n.* razor-strop. **-maschine,** *f.* bottling *or* racking machine. **-mittel,** *n.* stripping agent. **-muskel,** *m.* *See* **Abzieher. -papier,** *n.* transfer *or* proof paper. **-riemen,** *m.* *See* **-leder. -stein,** *m.* whetstone, hone.

Abziehung ['aptsi:uŋ], *f.* (-, *no pl.*) removal, withdrawal (*also money*), (*Math.*) subtraction, (*Comm.*) deduction, (*Med.*) abduction, (*Phil.*) abstraction, formulation; distillation, rectification (*of spirit*), transfer (*of design*). *See* **Abzug.**

Abzieh|zahl, *f.* (*Math.*) subtrahend. **-zünder,** *m.* friction fuse *or* igniter.

abzielen ['aptsi:lən], *v.i.* ***auf eine S.* -,** aim at s.th., have a th. in view; ***das zielt auf dich ab,*** that is aimed at *or* intended *or* meant for you.

abzirkeln ['aptsɪrkəln], *v.t.* measure with compasses *or* dividers, (*fig.*) be very particular *or* precise *or* punctilious; (*fig.*) ***abgezirkelt,*** measured, (over-) precise, over-exact, stiff, formal (*manner*), well-considered (*words*).

Abzucht ['aptsuxt], *f.* (-, *pl.* **¨-e**) ventilating *or* ventilation shaft; (*Swiss*) conduit, drain, sewer.

Abzug ['aptsu:k], *m.* 1. departure, withdrawal (*also of money*), retirement, retreat; ***zum* - *blasen,*** sound the retreat; 2. discharge, outflow, escape (*of steam etc.*); outlet, vent (*for steam etc.*); drain, drainage trench *or* ditch, channel, groove, conduit, gutter, culvert, sewer; ventilation *or* ventilating shaft; ***keinen* - *finden,*** find no outlet; 3. deduction, reduction, allowance, rebate, discount; ***unter* - *von,*** subject to the deduction of; ***in* - *bringen,*** deduct; ***einen* - *gewähren,*** make *or* allow a reduction, allow a discount *or* rebate; ***ohne* -,** strictly nett; - ***vom Gewicht,*** tare; 4. (*Typ.*) proof, (*Engr.*) offset, impression; (*Phot.*) print, positive; transfer; ***erster* -,** slip proof; - ***in Fahnen,*** galley proof; (*Typ.*) - ***vor der Schrift,*** proof before letters; 5. trigger, catch, pawl.

abzüglich ['aptsy:klɪç], *prep.* deducting, less; - ***Rabatt*** or ***des Rabatts,*** less discount; - ***der Unkosten,*** charges deducted, deducting all charges.

Abzugpapier ['aptsu:kpapi:r], *n.* duplicating *or* manifold paper.

Abzugs|bogen, *m.* proof-sheet. **-bügel,** *m.* trigger guard. **-feder,** *f.* sear-spring. **-flagge,** *f.* (*Naut.*) Blue Peter. **-graben,** *m.* drain, ditch, sewer. **-hebel,** *m.* (*Artil.*) firing lever. **-papier,** *n.* *See* **Abzugpapier. -rohr,** *n.* waste-pipe. **-schleuse,** *f.* outlet sluice, tail-lock. **-sicherung,** *f.* safety-catch.

abzupfen ['aptsupfən], *v.t.* pull off, pluck off.

abzwacken ['aptsvakən], *v.t.* *See* **abzwicken.**

abzwecken ['aptsvɛkən], *v.i.*, *v.t.* (***etwas*** or ***auf eine S.***) aim at (*a th.*), have (*s.th.*) in view.

abzweigen ['aptsvaɪgən], **1.** *v.t.* 1. lop the branches off; 2. tap (*current from a circuit etc.*), (*fig.*) transfer, divert, switch, turn to other uses. **2.** *v.i.*, *v.r.* branch off. **Abzweig|muffe,** *f.* (*Elec.*) junction box. **-strom,** *m.* (*Elec.*) shunt current. **Abzweigung,** *f.* branch, bifurcation; offshoot, ramification; road junction; branch road; (*Railw.*) branch line; (*Elec.*) branch circuit.

abzwicken ['aptsvɪkən], *v.t.* pinch off, nip off.

abzwingen ['aptsvɪŋən], *irr.v.t.* ***ihm etwas* -,** extort *or* wrest *or* wring *or* force s.th. from him.

Ac— . . . *see under* **Ak—** *or* **Az—.**

Acc— . . . *see under* **Akk—** *or* **Akz—.**

Acca ['aka], **Accon** ['akən], *n.* Acre.

ach! [ax], *int.* alas! oh! - ***wo!* - *was!*** by no means! certainly not! **Ach,** *n.* ***mit* - *und Krach,*** with the greatest difficulty; by the skin of one's teeth; ***mit* - *und Weh,*** with a doleful outcry.

Achäer [a'xɛ:ər], *m.* (*Hist.*) Achaean, Greek. **achäisch,** *adj.* Achaean, Greek.

Achat [a'xa:t], *m.* (**-s,** *pl.* **-e**) agate. **achaten,** *adj.* (of) agate.

Achill [a'xɪl], *m.* Achilles. **Achillesferse,** *f.* Achilles' heel.

Achs|abstand, *m.* *See* **-stand.**

Achse ['aksə], *f.* 1. axle(-tree), shaft; spindle; arbor (*clocks*); (*Comm.*) ***auf*** or ***mit*** or ***per* -,** by road *or* rail; (*coll.*) ***ständig auf der* - *sein,*** be always travelling; 2. (*Math.*) axis.

Achsel ['aksəl], *f.* (-, *pl.* **-n**) shoulder; ***die -n zucken,*** shrug one's shoulders; ***ihn über die* - *ansehen,*** look down (up)on him; ***etwas auf seine -(n) nehmen,*** take the responsibility for a th.; ***auf die leichte* - *nehmen,*** make light of *or* easy work of.

Achsel|band, *n.* shoulder strap *or* knot, aiguillette. **-bein,** *n.* (*Anat.*) shoulder blade. **-gelenk,** *n.* shoulder joint. **-grube,** *f.* armpit, (*Anat.*) axilla. **-hemd,** *n.* sleeveless shirt (*men*) *or* chemise (*women*). **-höhle,** *f.* *See* **-grube. -klappe,** *f.* shoulder strap. **-schnur,** *f.* shoulder knot, aiguillette; lanyard. **achselständig,** *adj.* (*Bot.*) axillary. **Achsel|troddel,** *f.* lanyard. **-zucken,** *n.* shrug (of the shoulders).

Achsen|abschnitt, *m.* (*Math.*) intercept on an axis of coordinates. **-bruch,** *m.* breakage of the axle. **-drehung,** *f.* revolution *or* rotation round the axis. **-geld,** *n.* transport charges; toll (*on bridge etc.*). **-kreuz,** *n.* (*Math.*) system of coordinates. **-neigung,** *f.* (*Astr.*) obliquity of the ecliptic, axial inclination.

Achs|federung, *f.* axle suspension. **-gehäuse,** *n.* axle housing.

-achsig ['aksɪç], *adj. suff.* -axial; -axled.

Achs|lager, *n.* axle- *or* journal-bearing. **-motor,** *m.* direct-drive motor. **-nagel,** *m.* axle-pin, linchpin. **-schenkelbolzen,** *m.* kingpin. **-schenkelträger,** *m.* steering head. **-stand,** *m.* wheel-base. **-zapfen,** *m.* *See* **-schenkelbolzen.**

acht [axt], *num. adj.* eight (*coll.* **achte** *when pred.* ***es sind ihrer -e,*** there are eight of them; ***eine Mutter von -en,*** a mother of eight); ***um halb* -,** at half past seven; - ***Tage,*** a week; ***heute vor* - *Tagen,*** a week ago today; ***Freitag vor* - *Tagen,*** last Friday week; ***gestern vor* - *Tagen,*** yesterday week; ***heute in – Tagen*** or ***über – Tage,*** today week, this day week, a week from now; ***morgen*** or ***Freitag über – Tage,*** tomorrow *or* Friday week; ***binnen – Tagen,*** within a *or* the week, in the course of the week; ***alle – Tage,*** once a week, every week.

[1]**Acht,** *f.* (-, *pl.* **-en**) figure eight; ***–en laufen,*** do figures of eight (*skating*); (*coll.*) ***eine – bauen,*** come a cropper; ***eine – im Rad haben,*** have a buckled wheel (*cycle*); ***mit der – fahren,*** take the No. 8 tram *or* bus.

[2]**Acht,** *f.* (-, *no pl.*) (*Hist.*) outlawry, ban, banishment, boycott, ostracism; ***ihn in die – erklären*** or ***tun*** or ***in – und Bann tun,*** banish *or* proscribe *or* outlaw him.

[3]**Acht,** *f.* (-, *no pl.*) (*without def. art. usu.* **acht**) attention, care; heed, consideration; ***außer acht*** or ***aus der Acht lassen,*** disregard, leave out of account *or* consideration; ***in acht nehmen,*** take care of, look after; ***sich in acht nehmen,*** take care, beware; be careful *or* wary *or* cautious, look out, be on one's guard.

achtbar ['axtba:r], *adj.* respectable; estimable, worthy of respect; reputable, of high standing. **Achtbarkeit,** *f.* respectability, (good) repute, (high) standing.

Achtbrief ['axtbri:f], *m.* (*Hist.*) writ of outlawry.

achte ['axtə], *adj.* 1. *See* **achte(r)**; 2. *See* **acht.** **Achte,** *f.* (*coll.*) *see* [2]**Acht.**

Achteck ['axtˀɛk], *n.* (*Geom.*) octagon. **achteckig,** *adj.* octagonal.

achtehalb [axtə'halp], *num. adj.* seven and a half. **achteinhalb** ['axtˀaınhalp], *num. adj.* eight and a half.

Achtel ['axtəl], *n.* 1. eighth (part); (*often used as num. adj. e.g.* ***ein achtel Kilo***); 2. *See* **Achtelnote.**

Achtel-, *pref.* (*Chem.*) octo-. **-band,** *m.* (*Typ.*) octavo. **-kilo,** *n.* 125 grams. **-kreis,** *m.* (*Geom., Astr.*) octant. **-liter,** *n. approx.* ¼ pint. **-note,** *f.* (*Mus.*) quaver, (*Am.*) eighth note. **-pause,** *f.* (*Mus.*) quaver *or* (*Am.*) eighth rest. **-schlag,** *m.* (*Build.*) angle of 45 degrees. **-zentner,** *m. approx.* one stone (14 lb.).

achten ['axtən], **1.** *v.t.* 1. consider, regard, hold, deem; 2. esteem, respect, value, set store by, have regard for, have a high opinion of; ***nicht*** or ***gering –,*** set little store by, set little value on, hold in contempt, despise, make light of. **2.** *v.i.* ***– auf*** (*Acc.*), pay attention *or* regard *or* heed to, take notice of, mind; ***nicht – auf,*** disregard; ***darauf – daß,*** mind, see to it that, take care (that), be careful (that), make sure (that).

ächten ['ɛçtən], *v.t.* (*Hist.*) outlaw, banish; ban *or* forbid the use of (*a th.*), boycott, proscribe (*a p.*).

Achtender ['axtˀɛndər], *m.* stag with eight tines, four-pronger.

achtens ['axtəns], *adv.* in the eighth place, eighthly.

achtenswert ['axtənzve:rt], *adj.* worthy of respect, estimable; considerable.

achte(r) ['axtə(r)], **achte, achte(s),** *adj.* eighth; ***es war der achte Mai,*** it was the eighth of May; (*on letters*) ***den 8.*** (= ***achten***) ***Mai,*** 8th May; ***am achten Mai,*** on the eighth of May.

Achter ['axtər], *m.* figure eight; figure of eight (*skating*); wine of the '08 vintage; soldier of the 8th Regiment; anything with eight parts *or* cylinders *or* lines *etc.*

achter, (*dial.*) **1.** *adv.* behind, at the rear; (*Naut.*) aft. **2.** *prep.* (*Dat.*) behind; (*Naut.*) abaft, aft of. **Achter-,** *pref.* mizzen (*of sails*), after- (*of other parts of ship*). **achteraus,** *adv.* (*Naut.*) astern. **Achterdeck,** *n.* (*Naut.*) afterdeck, quarter-deck.

Achtereinmaleins ['axtərˀaınma:lˀaıns], *n.* (-, *pl.* -) eight times table.

achterlastig ['axtərlastiç], *adj.* (*Naut.*) heavy *or* down by the stern, (*coll.*) tail-heavy.

achterlei ['axtərlaı], *inv. adj.* of eight kinds *or* sorts.

achterlich ['axtərlıç], *adj., adv.* aft, astern; ***ein –er Wind,*** wind astern *or* dead aft; ***–er als dwars,*** abaft the beam. **achtern,** *adv.* 1. aft, abaft; 2. astern; ***– von,*** aft of, abaft; astern of; ***von –,*** from astern.

Achterrennen ['axtərrɛnən], *n.* eights (*rowing*).

Achtersteven ['axtərste:vən], *m.* (*Naut.*) sternpost.

acht|fach, -fältig, *adj.* eightfold. **Acht|flach,** *n.* *See* **-flächner.** **achtflächig,** *adj.* octahedral. **Achtflächner,** *m.* octahedron.

achtgeben ['axtge:bən], *irr.v.i.* pay attention (***auf*** (*Acc.*), to), take care (of), be careful (of), beware (of), look *or* watch out (for).

Achtgroschenjunge [axt'grɔʃənjuŋə], *m.* (*sl.*) copper's nark.

acht|haben, *irr.v.i. See* **-geben.**

acht|hundert, *adj.* eight hundred. **-jährig,** *adj.* 1. eight-year-old; 2. octenniel. **-jährlich,** *pred. adj.* recurring every eight years, octenniel. **Achtkant,** *m.* (**-s,** *pl.* **-e**) (*Geom.*) octahedron. **achtkantig,** *adj.* octagonal.

achtlos ['axtlo:s], *adj.* inattentive, indifferent (***auf*** (*Acc.*), to), careless, heedless (***gegen, auf*** (*Acc.*), ***gegenüber*** (*Dat.*), of), negligent, nonchalant, casual. **Achtlosigkeit,** *f.* inattention, indifference (***auf*** (*Acc.*), to), carelessness, negligence (***auf, gegen*** (*Acc.*), ***gegenüber*** (*Dat.*), of), disregard (of *or* for), nonchalance, casualness.

acht|mal, *adv.* eight times. **-malig,** *adj.* occurring *or* repeated eight times. **-männig,** *adj.* (*Bot.*) octandrous. **Achtpolröhre,** *f.* (*Rad.*) octode.

achtsam ['axtza:m], *adj.* attentive (***auf*** (*Acc.*), to), mindful, heedful, careful (of), cautious, prudent, wary, circumspect. **Achtsamkeit,** *f.* attention (***auf*** (*Acc.*), to), care, carefulness, mindfulness, heedfulness (of), caution, prudence, circumspectness, circumspection, wariness.

Achtserklärung ['axtsˀɛrklɛ:ruŋ], *f.* (*Hist.*) sentence of outlawry *or* banishment, proscription.

acht|silbig, *adj.* octosyllabic. **-stellig,** *adj.* eight-figure (*number*), eight-place (*decimal*). **-tägig,** *adj.* lasting a week; ***–er Urlaub,*** a week's holiday. **-täglich,** *pred. adj.* weekly. **-tausend** [-'tauzənt], *num. adj.* eight thousand.

Achtundneunziger [axtˀunt'nɔyntsıgər], *m.* red admiral (*butterfly*).

Achtung ['axtuŋ], *f.* (-, *no pl.*) 1. attention, heed; ***– geben*** or ***haben,*** pay attention *or* heed (***auf*** (*Acc.*), to); ***–!*** look out! take care! beware! (*Mil.*) attention! ***–, Stufe!*** mind the step! ***–, Steinschlag!*** Beware of falling rock! 2. esteem, respect, regard; ***– erweisen*** or ***entgegenbringen*** (*Dat.*), show respect *or* regard for; ***– haben vor ihm,*** hold him in respect, have respect for him, think highly of him; (*coll.*) ***alle –,*** I take my hat off to him, you *etc.*; ***– genießen,*** be respected *or* esteemed.

Ächtung ['ɛçtuŋ], *f.* (*Hist.*) outlawry, banishment, proscription.

achtunggebietend ['axtuŋgəbi:tənt], *adj.* imposing, impressive, commanding. **Achtungs|bezeigung, -bezeugung,** *f.* mark *or* token of respect, tribute. **achtungslos,** *adj.* disrespectful. **achtungs|voll,** *adj.* respectful. **-wert, -würdig,** *adj.* worthy of respect, estimable.

achtzehn ['axtse:n], *num.adj.* eighteen. (*For phrases see* **acht.**) **Achtzehntel,** *n.* eighteenth part.

achtzeilig ['axttsaılıç], *adj.* eight-line (*stanza*).

ächzen ['ɛçtsən], *v.i.* groan, moan; creak (*of door*).

achtzig ['axtsıç], *num. adj.* eighty. **achtziger,** *inv. adj.* ***die – Jahre,*** the eighties. **Achtziger,** *m.,* **Achtzigerin,** *f.* octogenarian; ***in den Achtzigern,*** in one's eighties. **achtzigjährig,** *adj.* octogenarian. **Achtzigstel,** *n.* eightieth part.

Acker ['akər], *m.* 1. (**-s,** *pl.* ⸚) field (under cultivation), ploughed *or* arable land; ***fetter –,*** rich soil; ***den – bauen*** or ***bestellen,*** till the ground; 2. (**-s,** *pl.* -) acre (*old German measure of area; local variations between 2,500 and 5,500 sq. metres*).

Acker|bau, *m.* agriculture, farming. **-bauschule,** *f.* agricultural college. **-bestellung,** *f.* tillage, cultivation. **-gaul,** *m.* farmhorse. **-gesetz,** *n.* agrarian law. **-knecht,** *m.* farm labourer, ploughman. **-land,** *n.* arable land. **-lohn,** *m.* farm-labourer's wages. **-mann,** *m.* farmhand, ploughman.

ackern ['akərn], **1.** *v.t.* till, cultivate, plough. **2.** *v.i.* (*coll.*) toil, labour, drudge.

Ackerrain ['akərraɪn], *m.* ridge (between fields), ba(u)lk.

Ackersmann, *m. See* **Ackermann.**

Acker|vieh, *n.* draught cattle. **–winde,** *f.* (*Bot.*) bindweed. **–wirtschaft,** *f.* agriculture, farming. (*Before many botanical terms,* **Acker–** = field, wild *or* corn, *Latin*: . . . *arvensis.*)

à condition [akõdisi'õ], (*Comm.*) on sale or return.

a conto [a'kɔnto], (*Italian*) (*Comm.*) on account. *See* **Akonto.**

Adam ['a:dam], *m.* Adam; (*fig.*) ***den alten – ausziehen,*** mend one's ways, turn over a new leaf; ***nach – Riese,*** according to Cocker *or* the rules of arithmetic. **Adams|apfel, –biß,** *m.* Adam's apple. **–feige,** *f.* oriental *or* Egyptian sycamore.

addieren [a'di:rən], *v.t.* add (up). **Addiermaschine,** *f.* adding machine. **Addierung,** *f.* addition.

Ade [a'de:], *n.* (**-s,** *pl.* **-s**) farewell, adieu. **ade!** *int.* goodbye! farewell! adieu!

Adel ['a:dəl], *m.* nobility; aristocracy; (*fig.*) nobility, loftiness, dignity (*of mind etc.*); ***von –,*** titled, of noble birth; ***der niedere –,*** the gentry.

Adelheid ['a:dəlhaɪt], *f.* Adelaide.

ad(e)lig ['a:d(ə)lɪç], *adj.* noble, aristocratic, titled; (*fig.*) noble, lofty, high-minded. **Ad(e)lige(r),** *m., f.* noble(man), noblewoman, aristocrat, member of the nobility *or* aristocracy, peer, peeress; ***die Ad(e)ligen,*** nobles, nobility, aristocracy.

adeln ['a:dəln], *v.t.* ennoble, raise to the nobility *or* peerage; dignify, exalt.

Adels|brief, *m.* patent of nobility. **–buch,** *n.* peerage (*book*). **–stand,** *m.* nobility; ***in den – erheben,*** ennoble, confer a title on, raise to the peerage.

Ader ['a:dər], *f.* (-, *pl.* **-n**) 1. (*Med.*) vein, artery; ***zur – lassen,*** bleed; 2. (*Min.*) lode, seam, (*Bot.*) vein, rib; core, conductor (*in cable*), strand (*in rope*), grain (*in wood*), trait, streak (*in character*); ***dichterische –,*** poetic vein; ***es ist keine gute – an ihm,*** there is no good in him; ***eine leichte –,*** a frivolous streak.

Ader|entzündung, *f.* phlebitis. **–geflecht, –gewebe,** *n.* vascular plexus. **–haut,** *f.* choroid membrane. **–holz,** *n.* wood cut along the grain.

ad(e)rig ['a:d(ə)rɪç], **äd(e)rig** ['ɛ:d(ə)rɪç], *adj.* veined, full of veins, (*Bot.*) venose, (*Med.*) vascular; cloudy, flawed (*of gem*).

Ader|knoten, *m.* varicose vein. **–laß,** *m.* (**-(ss)es,** *pl.* **⸚(ss)e**) phlebotomy, blood-letting.

ädern ['ɛ:dərn], *v.t.* grain (*paintwork*).

Ader|netz, *n.* (*Anat.*) venous network. **–presse,** *f.* tourniquet. **aderrippig,** *adj.* (*Bot.*) nerved. **Aderschlag,** *m.* pulse-beat, pulsation. **Aderung,** *f.* graining; (*Bot.*) veining, venation. **Aderwasser,** *n.* blood-serum, lymph.

Adhäsion [adhɛzi'o:n], *f.* adhesion.

adieu! [adi'ø:], *int.* farewell! **Adieu,** *n.* (**-s,** *pl.* **-s**) farewell.

Adjunkt [ad'juŋkt], *m.* (**-en,** *pl.* **-en**) assistant.

Adler ['a:dlər], *m.* eagle; ***doppelter –,*** two-headed eagle. **Adler|bussard,** *m.* long-legged buzzard (*Butes rufinus*). **–holz,** *n.* aloeswood. **–horst,** *m.* aerie, eyrie. **–nase,** *f.* aquiline nose. **–orden,** *m.* Order of the Eagle; (*Hist.*) ***Ritter des schwarzen*** (or ***roten***) *–s,* Knight of the Black (*or* Red) Eagle.

adlig, *adj. See* **ad(e)lig. Adlige(r),** *m., f. See* **Ad(e)lige(r).**

Admiral [admi'ra:l], *m.* (**-s,** *pl.* **-e**) admiral. **Admiralität** [–i'tɛ:t], *f.* Admiralty, (*Am.*) Navy Department. **Admiralitätsinseln,** *pl.* Admiralty Islands. **Admiralschaft,** *f.* admiralship; ***– machen,*** sail under convoy. **Admiralsschiff,** *n.* flag-ship. **Admiralstab** [–ʃta:p], *m.* naval staff.

Adolf ['a:dɔlf], *m.* Adolphus.

adoptieren [adɔp'ti:rən], *v.t.* adopt. **adoptiv,** *adj.* adoptive; (*in compounds, e.g.* **Adoptivtochter** ,*f.* adopted daughter).

adoucieren [adu'si:rən], *v.t.* (*Metall.*) anneal, temper, soften, edulcorate; (*fig.*) soften, sweeten, tone down.

Adressant [adrɛ'sant], *m.* (**-en,** *pl.* **-en**) writer, sender. **Adressat,** *m.* (**-en,** *pl.* **-en**) addressee; (*Comm.*) consignee. **Adreßbuch,** *n.* directory. **Adresse** [a'drɛsə], *f.* address; direction; (*Comm.*) firm; ***an die – von, per –,*** care of; ***an die falsche – kommen,*** come to the wrong person *or* (*coll.*) shop. **adressieren** [–'si:rən], *v.t.* address; consign. **Adreßzettel,** *m.* label.

adrett [a'drɛt], *adj.* 1. deft, handy, adroit; 2. smart, spick and span, neat, spruce, trim, dapper.

Adria ['a:dria], *f.* Adriatic Sea.

Adrianopel [adria'no:pəl], *n.* Adrianople.

adrig, ädrig, *adj. See* **ad(e)rig, äd(e)rig.**

Advent [ad'vɛnt], *m.* (**-s,** *pl.* **-e**) Advent.

Adventiv– [advɛn'ti:f], (*in compounds only*) adventitious, accessory.

Advokat [advo'ka:t], *m.* (**-en,** *pl.* **-en**) lawyer, barrister (at law), counsel, advocate. **Advokaten|gebühr,** *f.* lawyer's fee. **–kniff,** *m.* legal quibble. **Advokatur** [–'tu:r], *f.* (-, *pl.* **-en**) advocacy; ***zur – zugelassen werden,*** be called to the bar.

Aero– [a'ɛro], *pref.* **–dynamik,** *f.* aerodynamics. **aerodynamisch,** *adj.* aerodynamic. **Aerolith** [–'li:t], *m.* aerolite. **Aerostatik,** *f.* aerostatics. **aerostatisch,** *adj.* aerostatic.

Affäre [a'fɛ:rə], *f.* job; matter, incident, occurrence; affair; ***sich aus der – ziehen,*** make the best of a bad job.

Affe ['afə], *m.* (**-n,** *pl.* **-n**) 1. ape, monkey; ***einen –n an ihm gefressen haben,*** be infatuated with him; (*coll.*) ***seinem –n Zucker geben,*** be beside o.s. with glee; (*sl.*) ***einen*** (***kleinen***) ***–n haben,*** be tipsy; 2. (*Mil. sl.*) knapsack.

Affekt [a'fɛkt], *m.* (**-s,** *pl.* **-e**) emotional disturbance, emotional state; ***im –,*** on the impulse *or* in the heat of the moment; ***mit –,*** with warmth (of feeling) *or* feeling *or* emotion *or* passion. **affektbeladen,** *adj.* charged with emotive associations.

affektieren [afɛk'ti:rən], *v.t.* affect, feign, pretend, simulate. **affektiert,** *adj.* affected; feigned, simulated. **Affektiertheit,** *f.* affectation.

Affektion [afɛktsi'o:n], *f.* (*obs.*) fondness, liking, attachment. **Affektions|preis,** *m.* fancy price. **–wert,** *m.* sentimental value.

affektlos [a'fɛktlo:s], *adj.* dispassionate. **Affektlosigkeit,** *f.* (*obs.*) dispassionateness.

äffen ['ɛfən], *v.t.* ape, mimic, (*coll.*) take (*s.o.*) off; mock, make fun of, hoax, (*coll.*) take (*s.o.*) in.

affenartig ['afənʔartɪç], **1.** *adj.* (*Zool.*) simian, apelike; apish, monkeyish. **2.** *adv.* monkey-fashion.

Affen|fratze, *f.* apish grimace. **–gesicht,** *n.* ape-like face, (*coll.*) monkey-face.

affenhaft ['afənhaft], *adj. See* **affenartig. affenjung,** *adj.* very young and inexperienced, (*coll.*) green.

Affen|liebe, *f.* (-, *no pl.*) blind attachment, doting affection. **–schande,** *f.* (*coll.*) crying shame. **–schwanz,** *m.* (*coll.*) rigmarole; tomfool; ***auf den – führen,*** bamboozle, lead a dance. **–tanz,** *m.,* **–theater,** *n.* utter *or* sheer farce. **–weibchen,** *n. See* **Äffin.**

Äfferei [ɛfə'raɪ], *f.* mimicry, aping; banter, chaff.

affig ['afɪç], *adj.* affected, foppish.

Äffin ['ɛfɪn], *f.* female monkey, she-ape.

Affinität [afini'tɛ:t], *f.* affinity (***mit,*** with *or* to).

äffisch ['ɛfɪʃ], *adj.* ape-like, apish.

affizierbar [afi'tsi:rba:r], *adj.* sensitive, susceptible, impressionable. **Affizierbarkeit,** *f.* sensitivity, susceptibility, impressionability. **affizieren,** *v.t.* affect (*also Med.*), move, touch. **Affizierung,** *f.* *Med.*) affection.

Affodill [afo'dɪl], *m.* (**-s,** *pl.* **-e**) asphodel.

Afghane [af'ga:nə], *m.* (**-n,** *pl.* **-n**), **Afghanin,** *f.* Afghan. **afghanisch,** *adj.* Afghan.

Afrika ['afrɪka], *n.* Africa. **Afrikaner** [–'ka:nər], *m.* African. **afrikanisch** [–'ka:niʃ], *adj.* African.

After ['aftər], *m.* anus; hind quarters, backside.

After—, *pref., four main meanings*: *anatomical* = anal; *botanical, biological etc.* = pseudo–; *in*

(*Comm.*) = secondary, subsequent; *and in more figurative extensions* = spurious. **-bildung,** *f.* 1. pseudo-education; 2. malformation; 3. new formation, secondary growth. **-blatt,** *n.* (*Bot.*) stipule. **-blattlaus,** *f.* (*Ent.*) phylloxera. **-flosse,** *f.* (*Ichth.*) anal fin. **-geburt,** *f.* afterbirth. **-gelehrsamkeit,** *f.* sham erudition. **-größe,** *f.* false grandeur. **-kind,** *n.* posthumous child. **-klaue,** *f.* (*Zool.*) dew-claw. **-kohle,** *f.* coaldust, slack, dross. **-kritik,** *f.* would-be criticism. **-kugel,** *f.* spheroid. **-lehre,** *f.* heterodoxy, false doctrine. **-miete,** *f.* subtenancy. **-muse,** *f.* false muse; spurious art. **-rede,** *f.* calumny, slander. **afterreden,** *v.i.* (*insep.*) (*Dat.*) slander, calumniate. **After|schließer,** *m.* (*Anat.*) anal sphincter. **-weisheit,** *f.* sophistry.

Ägäisches Meer [ɛ'gɛ:ɪʃəs], *n.* Aegean Sea.

Agamie [aga'mi:], *f.* (-, *no pl.*) (*Bot.*) cryptogamy. **agamisch** [a'ga:mɪʃ], *adj.* cryptogamic, cryptogamous.

Ägatische Inseln [ɛ'ga:tɪʃə], *pl.* Aegades.

Agenda [a'gɛnda], *f.* (-, *pl.* **-den**) memorandum, (*Comm.*) price-list.

Agende [a'gɛndə], *f.* liturgy, ritual. *See* **Agenda.**

Agens ['a:gɛns], *n.* (-, *pl.* **Agenzien** [a:'gɛntsɪən]), active *or* motive force, agency, agent.

Agent [a'gɛnt], *m.* (**-en,** *pl.* **-en**) representative, agent. **Agentengebühr,** *f.* commission. **Agentin,** *f. See* **Agent. Agentur** [-'tu:r], *f.* agency.

Agenzien, *pl. of* **Agens.**

Ägide [ɛ'gi:də], *f.* aegis; auspices.

Ägidius [ɛ'gi:dius], *m.* Giles.

agieren [a'gi:rən], *v.t., v.i.* act; play one's part.

Agio ['a:ʒio:], *n.* (**-s,** *pl.* **-s**) agio; premium. **Agiokonto,** *n.* agio account. **Agiotage** [-'ta:ʒə], *f.* stock-jobbing. **Agioteur** [-'tø:r], *m.* (**-s,** *pl.* **-e**) stock-jobber. **agiotieren** [-'ti:rən], *v.i.* speculate in stocks.

Agnat [a'gna:t], *m.* (**-en,** *pl.* **-en**) paternal relation.

Agnostiker [a'gnɔstɪkər], *m.* agnostic. **agnostisch,** *adj.* agnostic. **Agnostizismus** [-'tsɪsmus], *m.* agnosticism.

Agraffe [a'grafə], *f.* brooch, clasp; clamp, cleat.

Agrar- [a'gra:r], *pref.* agrarian. **-gesetz,** *n.* agrarian law, land act. **Agrarier,** *m.* farmer, landed proprietor. **agrarisch,** *adj.* agrarian, agricultural. **Agrar|kommunismus,** *m.* collective farming. **-staat,** *m.* agrarian state.

Agronom [agro'no:m], *m.* (**-en,** *pl.* **-en**) agriculturalist. **agronomisch,** *adj.* agricultural; ***-e Schrift,*** treatise on farming.

Ägypten [ɛ'gyptən], *n.* Egypt. **Ägypter,** *m.* Egyptian. **ägyptisch,** *adj.* Egyptian.

ah! [a:, a], *int.* ah! oh! (*pleasure or admiration*).

äh! [ɛ:, ɛ], *int.* ugh! pooh! (*contempt or disgust*), (oh) bother! (*annoyance*), h'm (*doubt*).

aha! [a'ha:, a'ha], *int.* aha! there, you see! I told you so!

Ahasver [ahas've:r], *m.* (*B.*) Ahasuerus.

Ahle ['a:lə], *f.* awl, pricker, bodkin, (brad)awl.

Ahm [a:m], *n.* (**-s,** *pl.* **-e**) 1. aam (*liquid measure*); 2. ship's draught. **Ahming, Ahmung,** *f.* ship's draught.

Ahn [a:n], *m.* (**-s** *or* **-en,** *pl.* **-en**) ancestor; (*obs.*) grandfather; *pl.* ancestors, forefathers; (*Her.*) ***von vierzehn -en,*** with fourteen quarterings.

ahnden ['a:ndən], *v.t.* 1. avenge, requite (*a wrong*); punish; 2. *Obs. for* **ahnen. Ahndung,** *f.* 1. vengeance, revenge; 2. *Obs. for* **Ahnung.**

ähneln ['ɛ:nəln], *v.i.* (*Dat.*) bear a likeness to, look like, resemble; ***sie ähnelt ihrer Mutter,*** she takes after her mother.

ahnen ['a:nən], **1.** *v.t.* have a presentiment *or* foreboding *or* premonition of; suspect, surmise; have an inkling *or* some idea of; ***– lassen,*** foreshadow, forebode, portend; (*coll.*) ***ich hab's geahnt,*** I knew it; (*coll.*) ***du ahnst es nicht!*** whoever would believe it! that's the giddy limit! **2.** *v.i.* (*imp. with Dat.*) ***es ahnt mir*** or ***mir ahnt nichts Gutes,*** I fear the worst I have a foreboding of evil.

Ahnen|dünkel, *m.* pride in one's ancestry. **-kult,** *m.* ancestor-worship. **-paß,** *m.* (*Nat. Soc.*) family tree of Aryan descent. **-reihe,** *f.* line of ancestors. **-saal,** *m.* ancestral hall. **-stolz,** *m.* pride of birth. **ahnenstolz,** *adj.* proud of one's ancestors.

Ahn|frau, *f.* (first) ancestress. **-herr,** *m.* (first) ancestor.

ähnlich ['ɛ:nlɪç], *adj.* (*Dat.*) (more or less) alike; (quite *or* more or less) like, having (a certain) similarity (to), bearing some resemblance (to); ***sehr – sein,*** resemble closely, be very like *or* similar; ***und -es,*** and so forth; (*Math.*) ***-e Glieder*** or ***Dreiecke,*** similar terms *or* triangles; ***ihm – sein*** or ***sehen,*** be *or* look like him, resemble him; ***ihm taüschend*** or ***sprechend*** or ***zum Sprechen*** or ***zum Verwechseln – sein,*** be the speaking likeness *or* the living *or* very image of him; (*coll.*) ***das sieht dir –!*** that's just like you! that's you all over! **Ähnlichkeit,** *f.* likeness, resemblance, similarity (***mit,*** to), affinity (to *or* with). **Ähnlichkeitsbeweis,** *m.* proof by analogy.

Ahnung ['a:nuŋ], *f.* misgiving, presentiment, forewarning, foreboding, premonition; idea, notion, suspicion, inkling, (*coll.*) hunch; (*coll.*) ***keine –!*** don't ask me, I've no idea; ***keine blasse – haben,*** not have the least idea *or* the remotest conception *or* the faintest notion (***von,*** of), not know a thing *or* the first thing (about). **ahnungslos, 1.** *adj.* unsuspecting. **2.** *adv.* without misgiving, (all) unawares. **ahnungsvoll,** *adj.* ominous; apprehensive, fearful, full of misgivings.

Ahorn ['a:hɔrn], *m.* (**-s,** *pl.* **-e**) (***Feld-***) maple; (***Berg-***) sycamore.

Ährchen ['ɛ:rçən], *n.* (*Bot.*) spicule, spikelet. **Ähre,** *f.* ear (*of corn*), head (*of grasses*); ***taube –,*** tare; ***-n lesen,*** glean.

Ähren|lesen, *n.* gleaning. **-leser,** *m.* gleaner. **ährenständig,** *adj.* (*Bot.*) spicate. **-ährig,** *adj. suff.* (*Bot.*) -eared.

ais [aɪs], *n.* (-, *pl.* -) (*Mus.*) A sharp.

Ajourfassung [a'ʒu:rfasuŋ], *f.* claw setting (*of jewel*).

Akademie [akade'mi:], *f.* 1. academy, college, institute; 2. academy, learned society. **Akademiker** [-'de:mɪkər], *m.* academically-trained person, university man. **akademisch** [-'de:mɪʃ], *adj.* academic; ***-e Bildung,*** academic training, university education.

Akazie [a'ka:tsiə], *f.* acacia; ***unechte –,*** locust-tree. **Akaziengummi,** *n.* gum arabic.

Akelei [akə'laɪ], *f.* 1. (*Bot.*) columbine; 2. (*Med.*) whitlow.

Akka ['aka], *n.* Acre.

akkommodieren [akomo'di:rən], *v.t.* adapt, accommodate (***an*** (*Acc.*), to).

Akkon ['akon], *n. See* **Akka.**

Akkord [a'kɔrt], *m.* (**-es,** *pl.* **-e**) 1. (*Mus.*) chord; 2. (*fig.*) harmony, accord, concord, agreement; 3. bargain, compact, settlement, composition; contract; (*Comm.*) ***auf –, in –*** by contract. **Akkordarbeit,** *f.* piecework.

akkordieren [akɔr'di:rən], *v.i.* (*Mus.*) accord; be correct; ***– über*** (*Acc.*), agree upon, come to terms *or* to an agreement about.

akkreditieren [akredi'ti:rən], *v.t.* open a credit for; provide with a letter of credit; accredit (*ambassador*). **Akkreditiv** [-'ti:f], *n.* (**-s,** *pl.* **-e**) letter of credit; credentials (*of ambassador*).

Akkumulator [akumu'la:tɔr], *m.* (**-s,** *pl.* **-en** [-'to:rən]) (*Elec.*) accumulator.

akkurat [aku'ra:t], *adj.* accurate, exact, precise, careful, painstaking, meticulous, punctilious. **Akkuratesse** [-'tɛsə], *f.* exactitude, precision, exactness, accuracy, punctilousness.

Akkusativ ['akuzati:f], *m.* (**-s,** *pl.* **-e**) accusative.

Akoluth [ako'lu:t], *m.* (**-s,** *pl.* **-en**) acolyte.

Akontozahlung [a'kɔntotsa:luŋ], *f.* payment on account, instalment.

Akribie [akri'bi:], *f.* (-, *no pl.*) extreme precision, (over-)exactness.

Akrobat [akro'ba:t], *m.* (**-en**, *pl.* **-en**) acrobat. **Akrobatik,** *f.* (-, *no pl.*) acrobatics. **akrobatisch,** *adj.* acrobatic.

Akrostichon [a'krɔstɪçɔn], *n.* (-, *pl.* **-chen** *or* **-cha**) acrostic.

Akt [akt], *m.* (**-es,** *pl.* **-e**) 1. life model, nude (model); (*Sculp., Paint.*) study from the nude; 2. act, action, deed; 3. act (*of a play*).

Akte ['aktə], *f.* deed, document, (legal) instrument; *pl.* (official) records, file, dossier; ***in die -n eintragen,*** put on the record; ***zu den -n legen,*** file (*a document*), (*coll.*) pigeonhole, shelve.

Akten|hefter, *m.* document file. **-mappe,** *f.* portfolio, folder. **aktenmäßig,** *adj,* authentic, documentary. **Akten|papier,** *n.* folio, foolscap paper. **-reiter,** *m.* pettifogging official. **-schrank,** *m.* filing cabinet. **-stoß,** *m.* pile of documents. **-stück,** *n.* (official) document; file copy. **-tasche,** *f.* dispatch case, briefcase.

Aktie ['aktsiə], *f.* share, stock. **Aktien|bank,** *f.* joint-stock bank. **-besitz,** *m.* shareholdings. **-börse,** *f.* stock-exchange. **-gesellschaft,** *f.* joint-stock company. **-händler,** *m.* stockjobber. **-inhaber,** *m.* shareholder. **-kapital,** *n.* share capital. **-kurs,** *m.* quotation of shares. **-makler,** *m.* stockbroker. **-markt,** *m.* stock-market. **-notierung,** *f.* *See* **-kurs. -schein,** *m.* share certificate, scrip. **-schwindel,** *m.* share-pushing, market-rigging. **-zeichnung,** *f.* subscription to a joint-stock undertaking.

Aktion [aktsi'o:n], *f.* 1. act, action, activity; ***in - treten,*** come into action; 2. (civil) action, lawsuit; 3. (military) action, engagement, (military) operation; 4. (*as suff.*) operation(s), drive, scheme campaign, plan.

Aktionär [aktsio'nɛ:r], *m.* (**-s,** *pl.* **-e**), **Aktionärin,** *f.* shareholder, stockholder. **Aktionärversammlung,** *f.* shareholders' meeting.

Aktions|art, *f.* aspect (*of verb*). **-bereich,** *m.* cruising radius; effective range; (*fig.*) range *or* sphere of action.

aktiv [ak'ti:f], *adj.* active; effective; serving with the colours, on the active list; ***-er Teilhaber,*** working partner; ***- sein,*** be an active member (***bei,*** of), belong to a student society; ***- werden,*** join a student society; ***-es Heer,*** regular *or* standing army; ***-er Soldat,*** regular (soldier); ***-er Offizier,*** regular officer.

Aktiva [ak'ti:va], *n.pl.* 1. accrued assets; 2. bankrupt's estate.

Aktivbilanz [ak'ti:fbilants], *f.* favourable balance of trade.

Aktiven [ak'ti:vən], *n.pl.* = **Aktiva.**

aktivieren [akti'vi:rən], *v.t.* put into action, activate, get going; expedite. **Aktivierung,** *f.* activation; expedition. **Aktivität** [-i'tɛ:t], *f.* activity.

Aktiv|kapital, *n.* assets, capital. **-masse,** *f.* (bankrupt's) estate. **-saldo,** *m.* credit balance. **-schulden,** *f.pl.* outstanding debts. **-stand,** *m.* (*Comm.*) assets, (*Mil.*) effective strength.

Aktualität [aktuali'tɛ:t], *f.* actuality, topicality, contemporary reality *or* importance, (*coll.*) up-to-dateness; question of the moment, *pl.* current events, items of topical interest. **Aktualitätenkino,** *n.* news theatre.

Aktuar [aktu'a:r], *m.* (**-s,** *pl.* **-e**) registrar, clerk (of the court).

aktuell [aktu'ɛl], *adj.* 1. actual, real; (*Mech.*) ***-e Energie,*** kinetic energy; 2. present-day, up-to-date; topical; ***-e Frage,*** present-day question, question of current interest, topic of the day.

Aktus ['aktus], *m.* (-, *pl.* -) celebration; formal meeting; School Speech Day.

Akt|zeichnen, *n.* drawing from the nude. **-zeichnung,** *f.* sketch from the nude.

Akustik [a'kustɪk], *f.* (-, *no pl.*) acoustics. **akustisch,** *adj.* acoustic.

akut [a'ku:t], *adj.* acute; (*coll.*) urgent.

Akzent [ak'tsɛnt], *m.* (**-s,** *pl.* **-e**) stress (*also fig.*), accent; accent, pronunciation, brogue. **akzentfrei,** *adj.* without a foreign accent. **akzentlos,** *adj.* unaccented, unstressed. **Akzentträger,** *m.* accented *or* stressed syllable. **akzentuieren** [-tu'i:rən], *v.t.* accentuate, stress (*also fig.*), (*fig.*) lay stress on, emphasize.

Akzept [ak'tsɛpt], *n.* (**-s,** *pl.* **-e**) acceptance (*of a bill*); accepted bill *or* draft. **Akzeptant** [-'tant], *m.* acceptor, drawee. **akzeptieren** [-'ti:rən], *v.t.* accept, honour (*a bill of exchange*), (*fig.*) acknowledge, agree to, acquiesce in. **Akzept|vermerk,** *m.* endorsement. **-verweigerung,** *f.* non-acceptance.

Akzidens [aktsi'dɛns], *n.* (-, *pl.* **-enzien**) 1. (*Mus.*) accidental; 2. (*usu. pl.*) additional profits, casual earnings, perquisites, (*coll.*) perks.

Akzidenz [aktsi'dɛnts] (-, *pl.* **-en**), **Akzidenzarbeit,** *f.* (*Typ.*) job(bing)-work.

Akzidenzien [aktsi'dɛntsiən], *pl. of* **Akzidens.**

akzisbar [ak'tsi:sba:r], *adj. See* **akzispflichtig.**

Akzise [ak'tsi:zə], *f.* excise; (*Hist.*) octroi. **akzisfrei,** *adj.* free of excise duty. **akzisieren** [-'zi:rən], *v.t.* levy excise duty on (*goods*). **Akzisor,** *m.* (**-s,** *pl.* **-en**) exciseman. **akzispflichtig,** *adj.* excisable, subject to excise duty.

Alabaster [ala'bastər], *m.* (**-s,** *no pl.*) alabaster. **alabastern,** *adj.* of alabaster.

Alad(d)in ['aladi:n], *m.* Aladdin; ***-s Wunderlampe,*** Aladdin's lamp.

Aland ['a:lant], *m.* (**-s,** *pl.* **-e**) (*Ichth.*) ide, orfe (*Leuciscus idus*).

Alant [a'lant], *m.* (**-s** *pl.* **-e**) 1. *See* **Aland**; 2. (*Bot.*) elecampane. **Alantbeere,** *f.* (*dial.*) blackcurrant.

Alarich ['a:larɪç], *m.* (*Hist.*) Alaric.

Alarm [a'larm], *m.* (**-s** *pl.* **-e**) alarm, warning, alert; warning signal *or* system; ***blinder -,*** false alarm; ***- blasen*** *or* ***geben*** or ***schlagen,*** sound the alarm; ***- aus!*** all clear! **alarmbereit,** *adj.* on the alert, standing by. **Alarmbereitschaft,** *f.* stand-by. **alarmieren** [-'mi:rən], *v.t.* give *or* raise the alarm, alert, turn *or* call out (*troops etc.*), (*coll.*) alarm, startle, frighten. **Alarm|platz,** *m.* alarm station. **-tauchen,** *n.* crash-dive (*of submarine*). **-zustand,** *m.* (*Mil.*) stand-to.

Alaun [a'laun], *n.* (**-s,** *pl.* **-e**) alum. **alaunartig,** *adj.* aluminous. **alaunen,** *v.t.* steep in *or* impregnate with alum. **Alaunerde,** *f.* alumina. **alaun|erdehaltig,** *adj.* aluminiferous. **-gar,** *adj.* steeped in *or* impregnated with alum, tawed (*of leather*). **-haltig,** *adj.* 1. *See* **-artig**; 2. *See* **-erdehaltig. alaunieren** ['ni:rən], *v.t. See* **alaunen. alaunig,** *adj. See* **alaunartig. alaunsauer,** *adj.* (*Chem.*) aluminate of. **Alaunstein,** *m.* styptic pencil (*for shaving*).

[1]**Alb** [alp], *m.* (**-(e)s,** *pl.* **-en**) 1. elf, goblin, sprite; 2. nightmare.

[2]**Alb,** *f.* (-, *pl.* **-en**) (*dial.*) alp(s), upland(s).

Albane [al'ba:nə], (**-n,** *pl.* **-n**), **Albaner,** *m.* Albanian. **Albanien,** *n.* Albania. **albanisch,** *adj.* Albanian.

Alb|druck, *m.*, **-drücken,** *n.* nightmare.

Alben ['albən], 1. *pl. of* **Alb**; 2. *pl. of* **Album.**

Alber ['albər], *f.* (-, *pl.* **-n**) (*Bot.*) white poplar.

Alberei [albə'raɪ], *f. See* **Albernheit.**

albern ['albərn], *adj.* silly, foolish, absurd; ***-es Geschwätz*** or ***Zeug,*** (stuff and) nonsense. **Albernheit,** *f.* silliness; absurdity; tomfoolery.

Albigenser [albi'gɛnzər], *m.pl.* (*Hist.*) Albigenses.

Albrecht ['albrɛçt], *m.* Albert.

Album ['album], *n.* (**-s,** *pl.* **Alben**) album; scrapbook.

Albumin [albu'mi:n], *n.* (**-s,** *pl.* **-e**) albumin. **albuminartig,** *adj.* albuminoid. **albuminös** [-i'nø:s], *adj.* albuminous. **Albuminstoff,** *m.* protein.

Alemannen [alə'manən], *m.pl.* (*Hist.*) Alemanni.

Alexandriner [alɛksan'dri:nər], *m.* Alexandrine (*verse*). **alexandrinisch,** *adj.* Alexandrian.

Alfa ['alfa], *f.* (-, *no pl.*) esparto grass.

Alfanz ['alfants], *m.* (**-en,** *pl.* **-en**) 1. (*obs.*) fool, jester, buffoon; 2. *See* **Alfanzerei. Alfanzerei** [–ə'raɪ], *f.* foolery, buffoonery, clowning.

Alfons ['alfɔns], *m.* Alfonso, Alphonso.

Alge ['algə], *f.* seaweed.

Algebra ['algebra], *f.* (-, *no pl.*) algebra. **algebraisch** [–'bra:ɪʃ], *adj.* algebraic(al).

algenartig ['algənʔartɪç], *adj.* algoid.

Algerien [al'ge:riən], *n.* Algeria. **Algerier,** *m.* Algerian. **Algier** ['alʒi:r], *n.* Algiers.

Alibi ['a:libi], *n.* (**-s,** *pl.* **-s**) alibi; ***ein – nachweisen,*** establish an alibi; ***ein – erbringen*** or ***beibringen,*** produce an alibi.

Aliment [ali'mɛnt], *n.* (**-s,** *pl.* **-e**) (*usu. pl.*) maintenance allowance (*for wife or child*), alimony. **Alimentation** [–tatsi'o:n], *f.* alimentation; (*Law*) maintenance. **alimentieren** [–'ti:rən], *v.t.* provide for, (*Law*) maintain.

Alk [alk], *m.* (**-s,** *pl.* **-e**) (*Orn.*) auk.

Alkaleszenz [alkalɛs'tsɛns], *f.* (-, *pl.* **-en**) (*Chem.*) alkalinity.

Alkali [al'ka:li], *n.* (**-s,** *pl.* **-en**) alkali. **alkalinisch, alkalisch,** *adj.* alkaline, (*Chem.*) basic. **alkaloidisch,** *adj.* (*Chem.*) alkaloid.

Alkohol ['alkoho:l], *m.* (**-s,** *pl.* **-e**) alcohol. **alkoholfrei,** *adj.* non-alcoholic; (*coll.*) soft (*drink*), temperance (*restaurant*). **Alkoholgehalt,** *m.* alcoholic content. **alkoholhaltig,** *adj.* alcoholic. **Alkoholiker,** *m.* drunkard, habitual drinker, (*coll.*) alcoholic. **alkoholisch,** *adj.* alcoholic. **Alkohol|nachweise,** *m.* blood-test (for alcohol). **-teströhrchen,** *n.* breathalizer. **-verbot,** *n.* prohibition. **-vergiftung,** *f.* alcoholism.

Alkoven [al'ko:vən], *m.* alcove, closet, bed-recess.

All [al], *n.* (**-s,** *no pl.*) the universe.

all (aller, alle, alles), 1. *adj.* 1.(*with sing. noun*) (*usu. inv. when preceding strong declension dem. or poss. adj.*) all, every, (*after* ***ohne***) any; ***-er Art,*** of every kind, of all sorts; ***in -er Eile,*** with all speed; ***mit -er Kraft*** or ***Gewalt,*** with all one's might; ***ohne -en Grund*** or ***Zweifel,*** without any reason *or* doubt; ***ohne -e Mühe*** or ***Ursache,*** without any effort *or* cause; ***trotz – seiner Mühe,*** despite all his efforts; ***-e Welt,*** everyone, everybody; (*coll.*) ***was in -er Welt,*** what on earth *or* in (all) the world; ***für -e Zeit,*** for all time; 2. (*with nouns adjs. or adj. forms*) everything; ***-es Gute,*** all good things, everything good, (*coll.*) all the best! ***-en Ernstes,*** in all seriousness; ***-es andere als,*** anything but; ***vor -em andern,*** above all (things), first and foremost; 3. (*with pl. noun*) (*a following adj. now preferred with weak declension*) all, all the; ***-e Menschen,*** all men *or* mankind; ***-e anderen Menschen,*** all (the) other men; ***-e Leute,*** all the people, everybody, everyone; ***auf -e Fälle,*** at all events, in any case; ***vor -en Dingen,*** above all, in the first place, especially; ***-e Tage,*** everyday, daily; 4. (*with num.*) ***-e beide,*** both; ***-e zwei Tage,*** every second *or* other day; ***-e drei,*** all three; ***-e drei Wochen,*** every third week, once every three weeks. **2.** *indef. pron.* 1. **all** (*inv.*) *or* **aller,** each (one), every one; 2. **alles** (*n. sing.*), all (things), everything; ***-es oder nichts,*** all or nothing; ***-es in -em,*** all in all, all told, by and large, on the whole, all things considered, when all is said and done; ***vor -em,*** most of all, above all, first and foremost; ***bei*** or ***trotz -em,*** with all that, despite everything, in spite of all; ***-es das, das -es, das . . . -es,*** all this *or* that; ***und wer*** or ***Gott weiß was -es,*** and Heaven knows what else; ***Mädchen für -es,*** maid of all work; 3. **alle** (*pl.*), everyone, everybody, all; ***wir -e,*** all of us; ***er liebt sie -e,*** he likes them all; ***er liebt sie -e nicht,*** he doesn't like any of them; ***er liebt sie nicht -e,*** he doesn't like them all *or* like all of them; ***-e die wir sahen,*** everyone we saw; ***vor -er Augen,*** in sight of everybody, before everyone's eyes.

All–, all–, *pref.* universal(ly), all–, omni–. (*Before adv.* **–da, –hier, –überall** *etc. it is obs. and does not affect the meaning.*) *For examples see below.*

allabendlich [al'a:bəntlɪç] *adj., adv.* (occurring) every evening.

allbekannt ['albəkant], *adj.* generally *or* universally known, notorious.

allbeliebt ['albəli:pt], *adj.* generally liked, universally popular.

allda [al'da:], *adv.* there, in *or* at that (very) spot.

alldeutsch ['aldɔytʃ], *adj.* (*Hist.*) pan-German. **Alldeutschtum,** *n.* (*Hist.*) pan-Germanism.

alldieweil ['aldi:vaɪl], *conj.* (*obs.*) inasmuch *or* forasmuch as.

alldort [al'dɔrt], *adv. See* **allda.**

alle ['alə], *see* **all.**

alledem [alə'de:m], *indef. pron.* ***trotz –,*** nevertheless, for all that.

Allee [a'le:], *f.* avenue, boulevard.

Allegorie [alego'ri:], *f.* allegory. **allegorisch** [–'go:rɪʃ], *adj.* allegorical.

allein [a'laɪn], **1.** *indecl. pred.adj., adv.* (all) alone, (all) on one's own, by o.s.; only, mere, very; ***ich esse –,*** I eat alone *or* on my own; ***ich –*** or ***– ich esse das Fleisch,*** I alone *or* only I eat the meat; ***der Gedanke –*** or ***– der Gedanke,*** the thought by itself, the mere *or* very thought; ***für sich –,*** apart, separately; ***– stehen,*** stand alone *or* apart *or* on its own (*of a building*), live alone, be alone in the world (*of a person*), be single *or* unmarried *or* without family ties *or* without dependants (*of man or woman*). **2.** *adv.* only, merely, solely; ***einzig und –,*** solely, entirely; ***nicht – . . . sondern auch,*** not only *or* merely . . . but also. **3.** *conj.* but, yet, however, nevertheless.

Allein–, allein–, *pref.* sole, exclusive; solo, single-handed. *For examples see below.* **Allein|berechtigung,** *f.* sole *or* exclusive right. **-besitz,** *m.* sole property; exclusive possession.

alleine [a'laɪnə], (*coll. emph.*) *see* **allein.**

Allein|flug, *m.* solo flight. **-gang,** *m.* single-handed *or* lone effort, solo attempt; ***im –,*** on one's own. **-handel,** *m.* monopoly. **-herrschaft,** *f.* autocracy, dictatorship; absolute monarchy. **-herrscher,** *m.* autocrat, dictator, absolute monarch, sole ruler.

alleinig [a'laɪnɪç], *adj.* sole, exclusive; only, single.

Alleinsein [a'laɪnzaɪn], *n.* (**-s,** *no pl.*) solitariness, loneliness, solitude. **alleinseligmachend,** *adj.* only true (*church, faith*). **Alleinspiel,** *n.* (*Mus.*) solo, (*Theat.*) one-man *or* solo act. **alleinstehend,** *adj.* living alone, alone in the world, without dependants *or* family ties; unmarried. **Allein|verkauf,** *m.* exclusive sale, sales monopoly. **-vertrieb,** *m.* sole agency *or* distributing rights.

Allel [a'le:l], *n.* (**-s,** *pl.* **-e**) allele, (*Biol.*) allelomorph.

allemal ['alə'ma:l], *adv.* 1. always; ***– wenn,*** whenever, everytime when, as often as; ***ein für –,*** once and for all; 2. indeed, of course, certainly.

allenfalls ['alənfals], *adv.* if need be, (*coll.*) if the worst comes to the worst; if really necessary, possibly.

allenthalben ['alənthalbən], *adv.* everywhere, on all sides; in every way *or* respect, in all respects.

aller, *see* **all.**

aller–, *pref.* (*with sup. adj.*) (*sup. adj.*) of all, most (*adj.*) of all, (*adj.*) most; *e.g.* ***–weitest,*** farthest of all, most distant of all, furthermost.

alleräußerst ['alər'ɔysərst], *adj.* (most) extreme, utmost, uttermost.

Allerbarmer ['alʔɛrbarmər], *m.* All-Merciful.

aller|best, *adj.* very best, best of all. **-christlichst,** *adj.* Most Christian (*Majesty*).

allerdings ['alərdiŋs], *adv.* 1. (*emph. affirmative*) certainly, of course, by all means, to be sure; **2.** (*concessive*) certainly, indeed; nevertheless, yet.

aller|durchlauchtigst, *adj.* Most Serene (*Highness*). **-enden,** *adv.* (*obs.*) everywhere. **-erst, 1.** *adj.* very first, foremost. **2.** *adv.* ***zu –,*** first of all, first and foremost, originally. **-gnädigst,** *adj.* most gracious.

allerhand ['alərhant], *indecl. adj.* all sorts *or* kinds *or* manner of, of all sorts *or* kinds; (*coll.*) a lot of, a good deal of; (*coll.*) ***–!*** that's something like!

(*coll.*) ***das ist ja –!*** that's really too much *or* too bad! that's the limit! (*coll.*) ***es gehört – dazu,*** it takes some doing, it takes a lot of (*courage, nerve etc.*) (***zu tun,*** to do).

Allerheiligen [alər'haɪlɪgən], *n.inv.* All Saints' Day, All Hallows' Day. **aller|heiligst,** *adj.* Holy (*Father*), Blessed (*Virgin Mary*); ***das Allerheiligste,*** Holy of Holies; Blessed Sacrament. **–höchst,** *adj.* highest (of all), topmost, supreme; ***der Allerhöchste,*** Almighty God, the Most High; ***auf Allerhöchsten Befehl,*** by royal command.

allerlei ['alərlaɪ], *indecl. adj.* all sorts *or* kinds *or* manner of, of all sorts *or* kinds. *See also* **allerhand. Allerlei,** *n.* (**-s,** *no pl.*) (*coll.*) hotchpotch; medley, miscellany, pot-pourri.

aller|letzt, *adj.* last (of all), very last, (very) latest, final. **–liebst,** *adj.* dearest of all; delightful, charming; ***am –en,*** for preference; (*coll. iron.*) ***das ist ja –,*** that's a fine state of affairs. **–meist,** *adj.* (very) most, utmost; ***die –en,*** the (great *or* vast) majority of; ***am –en,*** chiefly, principally, most of all. **–meistens,** *adv.* most often, more often than not. **–mindestens,** *adv.* at the very least, at the lowest estimate. **–nächst,** *adj.* (very) next *or* nearest. **–neu(e)st,** *adj.* (very) newest *or* latest, most recent. **–neu(e)stens,** *adv.* only *or* quite *or* very recently, only a short time ago. **–nötigst,** *adj.* indispensable; ***das Allernötigste,*** the bare necessities. **–orten** [–'ɔrtən], **–orts,** *adv.* everywhere.

Allerseelen [alər'zeːlən] (-, *no pl.*), **Allerseelen|fest,** *n.*, **–tag,** *m.* All Souls' Day.

aller|seits, *adv.* far and wide, on all sides; (*coll.*) to all (of you). **–untertänigst,** *adj.* most humble *or* obedient.

allerwärts ['alər'vɛrts], *adv.* everywhere. **–wege(n)** [–'veːgə(n)], *adv.* everywhere; (*dial.*) at all events, in any case.

Allerweltskerl [alər'vɛltskɛrl], *m.* (*coll.*) good chap *or* fellow; smart guy *or* aleck.

aller|wenigst, *adj.* only (a) very few; ***am –en,*** least of all; ***das –e,*** the very least. **–wenigstens,** *adv.* at the very least. **–wertest,** *adj.* dearest, most precious; (*coll.*) ***der Allerwerteste,*** bottom, behind, backside.

alles, *see* **all.**

allesamt ['aləzamt], *adv.* all together, one and all.

Alles|fresser, *m.* (*Zool.*) pantophagist, (*coll.*) greedy guts, guzzler. **–wisser,** *m.* (*coll.*) know-all, wise guy.

alle|wege, *see* **allerwege(n). –weil(e),** *adv.* always; (*obs.*) just now, a moment ago; at present *or* the moment. **–zeit,** *adv.* always, for ever (and ever), for ever more.

allfällig ['alfɛlɪç], *adj.* possible, eventual, contingent.

Allgegenwart ['algeːgənvart], *f.* (-, *no pl.*) omnipresence, ubiquity. **allgegenwärtig,** *adj.* omnipresent, ubiquitous.

allgemach [algə'maːx], *adv.* gradually, little by little, gently, by degrees.

allgemein ['algəmaɪn], **1.** *adj.* general, universal; ***–e Meinung,*** general *or* common *or* prevailing opinion; ***–e Wehrpflicht,*** universal military service, conscription; ***im –en,*** in general, generally, generally *or* broadly speaking, in general terms; as a general thing, for the most part, in the main, by and large. **2.** *adv.* generally, universally, commonly, widely.

Allgemein|begriff, *m.* general idea *or* notion; (*Phil.*) concept. **–bildung,** *f.* general *or* all-round education; general knowledge. **allgemeingültig,** *adj.* universally *or* generally valid. **Allgemein|gültigkeit,** *f.* universal *or* general validity. **–gut,** *n.* public *or* common property; common knowledge, open secret.

Allgemeinheit [algə'maɪnhaɪt], *f.* (-, *no pl.*) universality, generality; general public, public *or* people at large.

allgemeinverständlich [algə'maɪnfɛrʃtɛntlɪç], *adj.* generally intelligible, popular (*work*).

Allgemeinwohl [algə'maɪnvoːl], *n.* (**-(e)s,** *no pl.*) common good, public welfare.

Allgewalt ['algəvalt], *f.* (-, *no pl.*) omnipotence, almighty power. **allgewaltig,** *adj.* omnipotent, almighty, all-powerful.

allgütig [al'gyːtɪç], *adj.* all-bountiful, infinitely good.

Allheilmittel [al'haɪlmɪtəl], *n.* panacea, sovereign remedy; (*coll.*) cure-all.

Allianz [ali'ants], *f.* (-, *pl.* **-en**) alliance.

alliebend [al'liːbənt], *adj.* infinitely loving.

alliieren [ali'iːrən], *v.r.* ally o.s. (***mit,*** with *or* to); ***die Alliierten,*** the allies, the allied powers.

alljährlich [al'jɛːrlɪç], **1.** *adj.* yearly, annual. **2.** *adv.* yearly, annually, year by year, every year.

Allmacht ['almaxt], *f.* (-, *no pl.*) omnipotence, almighty power. **allmächtig** [–'mɛçtɪç], *adj.* omnipotent, almighty, all-powerful.

allmählich [al'mɛːlɪç], **1.** *adj.* gradual. **2.** *adv.* gradually, little by little, bit by bit, by degrees.

Allme(i)nde [al'mɛndə], *f.* common (land), common pasture.

all|monatlich, 1. *adj.* monthly. **2.** *adv.* month by month, every month, monthly. **–nächtlich,** *adj., adv.* nightly.

Allonge [a'lɔ̃ʒə], *f.* extension, lengthening-piece; (*Comm.*) allonge; (*Equest.*) longe, lunge. **Allongeperücke,** *f.* full-bottomed wig.

allseitig ['alzaɪtɪç], **1.** *adj.* all-round, comprehensive. **2.** *adv.* from every angle *or* every point of view. **Allseitigkeit,** *f.* all-round ability, versatility.

Allstrom– ['alʃtroːm], *pref.* (*Elec.*) for A.C. and D.C., (*Rad.*) all-mains.

Alltag ['altaːk], *m.* 1. weekday, working day; 2. (monotonous) daily round. **alltäglich** [–'tɛːklɪç], *adj.* 1. daily, everyday; 2. accustomed, customary, ordinary, trite, banal, commonplace, humdrum. **Alltäglichkeit,** *f.* dullness, triteness, banality; everyday occurrence. **alltags,** *adv.* every day, daily; on weekdays, on working *or* ordinary days. **Alltags|geschwätz,** *n.* empty chatter, commonplaces. **–mensch,** *m.* ordinary *or* common *or* average man.

allumfassend ['alˀumfasənt], *adj.* all-round, all-embracing, comprehensive, encyclopaedic.

Allüre [a'lyːrə], *f.* 1. gait, action (*of a horse*); 2. *pl.* mannerisms, grand airs.

allwissend [al'vɪsənt], *adj.* omniscient, all-knowing. **Allwissenheit,** *f.* omniscience.

allwöchentlich [al'vœçəntlɪç], *adj.* weekly, hebdomadal.

allzu ['altsuː], *adv.* much too, far too, only too, all too, altogether too, too . . . (*adj. or adv.*) by far. (*With commoner adjs. or advs. frequently used as a pref.*) **allzu|mal,** *adv.* one and all, all together. **–sehr,** *adv.* excessively, inordinately, overmuch. **–viel,** *adv.* overmuch, (far) too much.

Allzweck– ['altsvɛk], *pref.* all-purpose, general-purpose, universal.

Allotria [a'loːtria], *n.pl.* trivialities; ***– treiben,*** play the fool, fool around, trifle, waste time on trifles.

Alm [alm], *f.* (-, *pl.* **-en**) alpine pasture.

Almanach ['almanax], *m.* (**-s** *pl.* **-e**) almanac, calendar, year-book.

Almosen [al'moːzən], *n.* alms; ***um ein – bitten,*** ask for a charity. **Almosen|büchse,** *f.* poorbox. **–empfänger,** *m.* beggar, pauper. **Almosenier** [–'niːr], *m.* (**-s,** *pl.* **-e**) almoner.

Aloe ['aːloe], *f.* aloe; aloes.

[1]**Alp** [alp], *m.* (**-es,** *pl.* **-e**) *see* [1]**Alb.**

[2]**Alp,** *f.* (-, *pl.* **-en**) 1. mountain pasture, alpine meadow; 2. *pl.* Alps; ***jenseits der –en,*** transalpine; ***diesseits der –en,*** cisalpine.

Alpaka [al'paka], *n.* (**-s,** *no pl.*) alpaca (*wool*); plated German silver.

Alp|druck, *m.*, **–drücken,** *n.* nightmare.

Alpen– ['alpən], *pref.* alpine. **–birkenzeisig,** *m.*

(*Orn.*) lesser redpoll (*Carduelis flammea cabaret*). **-braunelle,** *f.* (*Orn.*) alpine accentor (*Prunella collaris*). **-dohle,** *f.* (*Orn.*) alpine chough (*Pyrrhocorax graculus*). **-jäger,** *pl.* chasseurs alpins, mountain troops. **-krähe,** *f.* (*Orn.*) chough (*Pyrrhocorax pyrrhocorax*). **-rose,** *f.* (*Bot.*) rhododendron, alpine rose. **-schneehuhn,** *n.* (*Orn.*) (*Am.* rock) ptarmigan (*Lagopus mutus*). **-stock,** *m.* alpenstock. **-veilchen,** *n.* cyclamen. **-verein,** *m.* Alpine Club. **-vorland,** *n.* foothills of the Alps.

Alphabet [alfa'be:t], *n.* (**-(e)s,** *pl.* **-e**) alphabet. **alphabetisch,** *adj.* alphabetical.

alpin [al'pi:n], **alpinisch,** *adj.* alpine. **Alpinismus** [-'nɪsmus], *m.* alpine climbing.

Älpler ['ɛlplər], *m.* native of the Alps; Swiss cowherd.

Alptraum ['alptraum], *m.* nightmare.

Alraun [al'raun], *m.* (**-(e)s,** *pl.* **-e**), **Alraunchen,** *n.*, **Alraune,** *f.* mandrake. **Alraunwurzel,** *f.* mandrake root (*Atropa mandragora*).

als [als], **1.** *conj.* 1. (*comparison of inequality*) than; ***größer – ich,*** bigger than I (*or coll.* me); ***zu jung, – daß sie heiraten könnte,*** too young to marry *or* for marriage; 2. (*after neg.*) but, except, apart from; ***nichts –,*** nothing but; ***kein anderer –,*** no one else apart from *or* except; 3. (*obs., occ. with comparison of equality*) ***sowohl er – auch ich,*** he as well as I; ***darüber schweigen ist nicht so leicht – wie ein dummer Junge reden,*** it's not so easy to keep silent as to chatter like a silly youngster; ***so viel – möglich,*** as much as possible; 4. (*with inverted order subj.*) *or* ***– ob, – wenn*** (*with dependent order subj.*) as if, as though; ***– wäre er stumm*** or ***– ob er stumm wäre,*** as if he were dumb; (*coll.*) ***tun – ob,*** pretend, put on an act; 5. (*temporal: past time only*) *imperf. tense*: when, as; *pluperf. tense*: when, after. **2.** *adv.* (*identity of predicated complement*) (considered *or* regarded) as, in the capacity *or* rôle *or* guise of; ***– Soldat dienen,*** serve as a soldier; ***– wahrer Freund erscheinen,*** appear as a true friend; ***große Komponisten, – da sind Bach und Haydn,*** great composers such as B. and H.

als|bald, *adv.* at once, immediately, forthwith. **-baldig,** *adj.* immediate. **-dann,** *adv.* then, thereupon, whereupon, after that.

also ['alzo:], **1.** *conj.* so, therefore, consequently, accordingly, hence; (*coll.*) (*less consequence than emotive particle*) well now *or* then; ***– los!*** come on, then! ***er ist – tot,*** he's dead then, then he's dead; ***da bin ich –,*** so here I am; ***na –!*** what did I tell you? I told you so! there you are! **2.** *adv.* (*obs.*) so, thus; ***– sprach Zarathustra,*** thus spake Z. **alsobald,** *adv.* (*Austr.*) *see* **alsbald.**

alt [alt], *adj.* (*comp.* **älter,** *sup.* **ältest**) old, aged; olden, ancient, old-established; stale; (*coll.*) ***–es Haus,*** old fellow *or* chap; ***–er Herr,*** former member (*of student society*); (*Min.*) ***–er Mann,*** old working; ***–e Sprachen,*** ancient languages, classics; ***er ist noch immer der –e,*** he is still the same; ***es bleibt beim –en,*** let bygones be bygones; ***das ist etwas –es,*** that is nothing new; ***– tun,*** assume a knowing air; ***– werden,*** grow old; ***ich bleibe beim –en,*** I stick to the old way; ***der Alte,*** the old man (*also coll. = father*), (*coll.*) the boss, guv'ner *or* skipper; ***die Alte,*** the old woman (*also coll. = mother*), (*coll.*) the mistress *or* proprietress; ***das Alte,*** the old (state of affairs); ***mein Alter,*** my old friend; (*coll.*) old chap; my old man (*my father*); ***die Alten,*** the Ancients, the old people.

Alt, *m.* (**-(e)s,** *pl.* **-e**) alto, counter-tenor (*man*), contralto (*woman*).

Altan [al'ta:n], *m.* (**-s,** *pl.* **-e**) balcony, gallery.

Altar [al'ta:r], *m.* (**-s,** *pl.* **¨-e,** *Austr.* **-e**) altar. **Altar|aufsatz,** *m.* altar-piece, retable. **-bild, -blatt,** *n.* altar-piece, altar panel. **-platz, -raum,** *m.* chancel. **-schranke,** *f.* altar rail.

altbekannt ['altbəkant], *adj.* well-known, familiar.

Altbesitz ['altbəzɪts], *m.* old holding (*pre-inflation shares etc.*).

alt|bewährt, *adj.* of long standing, well-tried, trusty, old, approved. **-christlich,** *adj.* early Christian. **-deutsch,** *adj.* mediaeval German.

Alte, *see* **alt.**

altehrwürdig ['alt'ʔe:rvyrdɪç], *adj.* time-honoured, venerable.

Alteisen ['altʔaɪzən], *n.* (**-s,** *no pl.*) scrap iron.

altenglisch ['altʔɛŋlɪʃ], *adj.* Old English, Anglo-Saxon.

Altenteil ['altəntaɪl], *n.*, *m.* (*Law*) part of estate reserved by parents for their use; (*fig.*) ***sich aufs – zurückziehen,*** retire from the business, withdraw from participation in affairs.

[1]**Alter** ['altər], *see* **alt.**

[2]**Alter,** *n.* (**-s,** *pl.* **-n**) 1. age, old age; seniority, length of service; antiquity; ***blühendes –,*** prime of life; ***man sieht ihm sein – nicht an,*** he does not look his age; ***bis in das späteste –,*** up to advanced old age; ***über das – hinaus sein,*** be too old, (*coll. of sexual decline*) be past it; ***– schützt vor Torheit nicht,*** there's no fool like an old fool; 2. epoch, age.

älter ['ɛltər], *adj.* (*comp. of* **alt**) older, elder; oldish, elderly; senior; ***mein –er Bruder,*** my elder brother; ***die –e Fassung,*** the earlier *or* older version; ***ein –er Herr,*** an elderly gentleman.

altern ['altərn], *v.i.* (*aux.* s. & h.) grow old, age; be getting old(er).

alters ['altərs], *adv.* ***vor –,*** in olden times, in the days of old; ***von – her, seit –,*** from time immemorial.

Alters|bestimmung, *f.* determination of age. **-blödsinn,** *m.* (*Med.*) senile dementia. **-entartung,** *f.* senile decay. **-erscheinung,** *f.* symptom of old age. **-folge,** *f.* seniority. **-fürsorge,** *f.* geriatrics. **-genosse,** *m.*, **-genossin,** *f.* person of the same age, contemporary. **-grenze,** *f.* age limit. **-heim,** *n.* home for old people. **-klasse,** *f.* age group. **-rente,** *f.* old-age pension. **altersschwach,** *adj.* decrepit. **Alters|schwäche,** *f.* infirmity of age, decrepitude, senility. **-stufe,** *f.* stage of life. **-versicherung, -versorgung,** *f.* old age pension scheme.

Altertum ['altərtu:m], *n.* (**-s,** *pl.* **¨-er**) antiquity. **Altertümelei** [–ty:mə'laɪ], *f.* (**-,** *no pl.*) antiquarianism. **Altertümler** [–ty:mlər], *m.* antiquary; dabbler in antiquities. **altertümlich,** *adj.* antique, archaic, old-fashioned, old-world, antiquated, ancient. **Altertums|forscher,** *m.* antiquary, archaeologist. **-kunde,** *f.* archaeology; study of classical antiquity.

Alterung ['altəruŋ], *f.* (**-,** *no pl.*) ageing.

ältest ['ɛltəst], *adj.* (*sup. of* **alt**), oldest, most ancient, eldest, senior; ***die Ältesten,*** the elders, seniors *or* syndics. **Ältesten|recht,** *n.* right of primogeniture. **-würde,** *f.* eldership.

Alt|flicker, *m.* job(bing)-cobbler. **-flöte,** *f.* bass flute.

alt|fränkisch, *adj.* Old Franconian; (*coll.*) antiquated, old-fashioned, old-world. **-französisch,** *adj.* Old French. **-gedient,** *adj.* veteran (*soldier*). **-gläubig,** *adj.* orthodox. **-griechisch,** *adj.* ancient Greek. **-hergebracht, -herkömmlich,** *adj.* traditional. **-hochdeutsch,** *adj.* Old High German.

Altist [al'tɪst], *m.* (**-en,** *pl.* **-en**) alto (*singer*). **Altistin,** *f.* contralto (*singer*).

alt|jüngferlich, *adj.* old-maidish, spinsterish. **-klug,** *adj.* precocious.

Altlatein ['altlataɪn], *n.* (**-s,** *no pl.*) early Latin. **altlateinisch,** *adj.* early *or* old Latin.

ältlich ['ɛltlɪç], *adj.* oldish, elderly.

Alt|material, *n.* (**-s,** *no pl.*) *see* **-stoff. -meister,** *m.* past-master; patriarch, doyen, grand old man, (*Spt.*) ex- *or* former champion. **-metall,** *n.* scrap(-metal).

alt|modisch, *adj.* old-fashioned, out of fashion *or* date, outmoded. **-nordisch,** *adj.* Old Norse.

Alt|papier, *n.* (**-(e)s,** *no pl.*) waste paper. **-philologe,** *m.* classical scholar. **-schlüssel,** *m.* (*Mus.*) alto clef. **-steinzeit,** *f.* Palaeolithic Age. **-stimme,** *f.* alto (*male*) *or* contralto (*female*) voice. **-stoff,** *m.* scrap, used material (*suitable for reconditioning*). **-vater,** *m.* progenitor, patriarch. **altväterisch**

[–fɛ:tərɪʃ], *adj.* old-fashioned, antiquated. **altväterlich,** *adj.* patriarchal, ancestral, dignified. **Alt|vordern,** *pl.* forefathers, forebears, progenitors, ancestors. **–warenhändler,** *m.* secondhand dealer.

Altweiber|geschichte ['altvaɪbər–], *f.* old wives' tale, idle gossip. **–knoten,** *m.* (*Naut.*) granny knot. **–märchen,** *n.* *See* **–geschichte. –sommer,** *m.* 1. gossamer; 2. Indian summer, St. Luke's *or* Martin's summer.

Alumnat [alum'na:t], *n.* (**-s,** *pl.* **-e**) boarding school. **Alumnus** [a'lumnus], *m.* (-, *pl.* **-nen**) boarder.

am [am] (= *an dem*) *see* **an.** (*Never contracted when antecedent to a rel. clause; never resolved before substantival inf., in sup. adv. phrase, or in place-names.*) – ***Sterben,*** on the point of death, at death's door; ***Bonn – Rhein,*** Bonn on the Rhine; – ***besten,*** best of all; – ***ehesten,*** soonest.

Amalgam [amal'ga:m], *n.* (**-s,** *pl.* **-e**) amalgam. **amalgamieren** [–'mi:rən], *v.t.* amalgamate.

Amarant [ama'rant], *m.* (**-(e)s,** *pl.* **-e**) (*Bot.*) amaranth, love-lies-bleeding. **amarant(en), amarantfarben,** *adj.* amaranthine.

Amateur [ama'tø:r], *m.* (**-s,** *pl.* **-e**) amateur.

Amazonas [ama'tso:nas], *m.* (-, *no pl.*) (River) Amazon.

Amazone [ama'tso:nə], *f.* Amazon; virago; horsewoman. **Amazonenfluß,** *m.* River Amazon. **amazonenhaft,** *adj.* Amazon-like. **Amazonen|kleid,** *n.* lady's riding-habit. **–strom,** *m.* *See* **–fluß.**

Ambe ['ambə], *f.* combination of two lucky numbers drawn in lottery.

Amber ['ambər], *m.* (**-s,** *pl.* **-(n)**) amber (*resinous gum*); ambergris. (*For compounds see* **Ambra.**)

Amboß ['ambɔs], *m.* (**-(ss)es,** *pl.* **-(ss)e**) 1. anvil; ***zwischen Hammer und – sein,*** be between the devil and the deep blue sea; 2. (*Anat.*) incus.

Ambra ['ambra], *f.* (-, *pl.* **-s**) *or m.* (**-s,** *pl.* **-s**) *see* **Amber. Ambra|baum,** *m.* sweetgum tree; amber-tree. **–fett, –harz,** *n.* ambreine.

Ambrosia [am'bro:zia], *f.* (-, *no pl.*) ambrosia. **ambrosisch,** *adj.* ambrosial; fragrant.

Ambrosius [am'bro:zius], *m.* Ambrose.

ambulant [ambu'lant], *adj.* ambulatory, peripatetic, itinerant; (*Med.*) ***–e Behandlung,*** out-patient treatment. **Ambulanz,** *f.* (-, *pl.* **-en**) 1. (*Med.*) outpatient treatment; 2. (*Mil. etc.*) ambulance.

Ameise ['amaɪzə], *f.* ant; ***weiße –,*** termite. **Ameisen|bär, –fresser,** *m.* anteater. **–haufen,** *m.* anthill. **–kriechen, –laufen,** *n.* formication, paraesthesia, (*coll.*) pins and needles. **–säure,** *f.* formic acid.

Amel|korn ['a:məl–], *m.* amelcorn, emmer. **–mehl,** *n.* (*dial.*) starch.

Ammann ['aman], *m.* (**-s,** *pl.* **¨-er**) magistrate; (*Swiss*) bailiff.

Amme ['amə], *f.* 1. (wet-)nurse; ***zur – tun,*** put (out) to nurse; 2. (*Biol.*) asexual organism. **Ammen|märchen,** *n.* fairy tale; cock-and-bull story. **–zeugung,** *f.* (*Biol.*) asexual reproduction.

Ammer ['amər], *f.* (-, *pl.* **-n**) (*Orn.*) bunting (*Emberiza*).

Ammoniak [amoni'ak], *n.* (**-s,** *no pl.*) ammonia (gas). **ammoniakalisch** [–'ka:lɪʃ], *adj.* ammoniacal. **Ammoniaklösung,** *f.* (solution of) ammonia.

Ammonpulver ['amɔnpulfər], *n.* ammonal. **Ammonshorn,** *n.* ammonite.

Amnestie [amnɛs'ti:], *f.* amnesty.

Amöbe [a'mø:bə], *f.* amoeba.

Amorette [amo'rɛtə], *f.* little Cupid; *pl.* amoretti.

amorph [a'mɔrf], *adj.* amorphous.

Amortisation [amɔrtizatsi'o:n], *f.* legal extinction (*of a bill*), liquidation (*of mortgage etc.*); redemption (*of capital of a loan*). **Amortisationsfonds,** *m.* sinking-fund.

amortisieren [amɔrti'zi:rən], *v.t.* amortize, redeem, liquidate, pay off (*debts*); buy up (*annuities*); allow for depreciation of, write off (*stock*).

Ampel ['ampəl], *f.* (-, *pl.* **-n**) hanging lamp *or* vase.

Ampfer ['ampfər], *m.* (*Bot.*) sorrel, dock. **Ampferklee,** *m.* (*Bot.*) wood-sorrel, oxalis.

Amphibie [am'fi:biə], *f.* amphibious animal. **amphibisch,** *adj.* amphibian, amphibious.

Amsel ['amzəl], *f.* (-, *pl.* **-n**) blackbird (*Turdus merula*). **Amselschlag,** *m.* blackbird's song.

Amt [amt], *n.* (**-(e)s,** *pl.* **¨-er**) 1. official position, (public) office, appointment, employment, function, post, place, situation; ***das – antreten,*** take office, enter on one's (official) duties; ***ein – bekleiden,*** hold an office, a position *or* an appointment; ***kraft meines –es,*** by virtue of my office; ***es ist nicht seines –es,*** it is not within his province *or* not his business; ***seines –es walten,*** perform the duties of one's office; (*coll.*) ***tu, was deines –es ist!*** do what you have to! ***von –s wegen,*** ex officio, officially, by virtue of one's office; 2. government office *or* department, (*Am.*) bureau; (telephone) exchange; (*Tele.*) – ***bitte!*** exchange, please! (*Tele.*) ***hier –!*** exchange calling! ***das Auswärtige –,*** Foreign Office; 3. board (of management), (magistrates') court, council, corporation; 4. (*Prot.*) Divine Service, (*R.C.*) sung mass; ***das – halten,*** take *or* conduct the service.

amtieren [am'ti:rən], *v.i.* be in *or* hold office; perform the duties of one's office, exercise one's official function, officiate.

amtlich ['amtlɪç], *adj.* official; – ***handeln,*** act in one's official capacity. **amtlos,** *adj.* without *or* out of office.

Amtmann ['amtman], *m.* (**-(e)s,** *pl.* **¨-er** *or* **-leute**) 1. district magistrate; 2. bailiff, steward.

Amts|alter, *n.* seniority (in office). **–anruf,** *m.* (*Tele.*) call to *or* from the exchange. **–befugnis,** *f.* authority, competence, competency. **–bezirk,** *m.* jurisdiction, administrative district. **–blatt,** *n.* official gazette. **–dauer,** *f.* tenure of office. **–diener,** *m.* court usher. **–eid,** *m.* oath of office. **–enthebung, –entsetzung,** *f.* dismissal from office. **–folge,** *f.* rotation in office. **–freizeichen,** *n.* (*Phone*) dialling tone. **–führung,** *f.* administration. **–gebühr,** *f.* (official) charge, fee. **–geheimnis,** *n.* official secret. **–gericht,** *n.* District (*Engl.* County) Court. **–geschäfte,** *pl.* official business *or* duties. **–handlung,** *f.* official act; religious ceremony. **–inhaber,** *m.* office-holder; (*Eccl.*) incumbent. **–person,** *f.* official. **–personal,** *n.* official staff. **–rat,** *m.* chief executive officer (*civil service*). **–richter,** *m.* district (*Engl.* county) court judge. **–schimmel,** *m.* officialism, bureaucracy, (*coll.*) red-tape. **–sitz,** *m.* official residence. **–sprache,** *f.* official language, (*coll.*) officialese. **–stube,** *f.* magistrate's office. **–stunden,** *pl.* office hours. **–träger,** *m.* office-bearer. **–untersagung,** *f.* suspension from duty. **–unterschlagung,** *f.* embezzlement, malversation. **–verlust,** *m.* loss of office. **–verrichtung,** *f.* exercise of one's official function. **–vertreter,** *m.* deputy, substitute. **–verwaltung,** *f.* administration. **–verweser,** *m.* *See* **–vertreter. –vogt,** *m.* (*Hist.*) bailiff. **–vogtei,** *f.* (*Hist.*) bailliwick. **–vorgänger,** *m.* precursor (in office), predecessor. **–vormund,** *m.* officially appointed guardian (*of orphan*). **–weg,** *m.* official channels. **–widrigkeit,** *f.* dereliction of duty. **–zeichen,** *n.* (*Tele.*) dialling tone.

amüsant [amy'zant], *adj.* amusing, diverting, funny. **amüsieren, 1.** *v.t.* amuse, divert, entertain. **2.** *v.r.* amuse *or* enjoy o.s., have a good time.

an [an], **1.** *prep.* **A.** (*with Dat.*) 1. *indicating rest or limited motion within a place* (*in answer to the question wo?* = *where?*) *particularly* **(a)** in contact with, (lying *or* leaning) against, on at; ***Rücken – Rücken,*** back to back; ***Seite – Seite,*** side to *or* by side; – ***der Wand,*** against *or* on the wall; **(b)** close *or* adjacent to, near, by; – ***Bord,*** aboard, on board; – ***der Tür,*** at the door; ***nicht am Platz,*** out of place; ***am Wege,*** at *or* by *or* on the roadside; ***am Ziel,*** at the goal; **(c)** (*suspension*) from, by, on; **(d)** (*attached to*) on; – ***der Wange,*** on one's cheek; – ***der Schule,*** at school; 2. *indicating a point in time* (*in* *answer to the question* ***wann?*** *=* *when?*) ***am 4. Juli,*** on July 4th; **– *einem schönen Abend,*** on a fine evening; ***es ist – der Zeit,*** it is (high) time; 3. in respect of, with regard *or* respect to, in the *or* by way of; ***es ist nichts – der Sache,*** there is no truth in it, there's nothing in *or* to it; **– *sich,*** in itself, as such; **– *und für sich,*** actually, basically, in the abstract, by itself alone, purely as such; ***jung – Jahren,*** young in years; ***vier – der Zahl,*** four in number; 4. falling to the responsibility of; ***es ist – mir,*** it is for me *or* up to me (to do), it is my place (to do); 5. engaged in, in the act of; **– *der Arbeit,*** at work. *For its use with many verbs expressing delight, doubt, want, anger etc. or with adjs. such as* ***arm, reich, stark, schwach, ähnlich, krank,*** *see the characteristic word.* **B.** (*with Acc.*) 1. *indicating direction, progression or motion towards s.th., especially* **(a)** on, on to; **– *Bord gehen,*** go on board; **– *die Tür klopfen,*** knock on *or* at the door; ***etwas – die Wand hängen,*** hang s.th. on the wall; **(b)** to; **– *die falsche Adresse gerichtet,*** sent to the wrong address; **– *die Arbeit gehen,*** go *or* set to work; ***der Brief ist – mich,*** the letter is (addressed) to me; 2. *after verbs expressing thinking, believing, remembering etc. see the verb in question*; 3. *approximation*: about, round, round about, something like, approximately; **– *die zehn Tage,*** some ten days or so. **2.** *adv.* 1. on (*clothes, light etc.*) ***sie hatte nichts –,*** she had nothing on; ***das Licht blieb die ganze Nacht –,*** the light stayed on all night; 2. on(wards) (*place and time*); ***von jetzt –,*** from now on, henceforth, henceforward, from this time forth, hereafter.

an– ['an–], *pref. denoting inter alia approach, e.g.* ***sich annähern,*** approach; *direction of activity towards, e.g.* ***anmelden,*** announce; *fixing or attaching, e.g.* ***anbinden,*** tie; *acquisition, attraction, e.g.* ***aneignen,*** acquire; ***anziehen,*** attract; *beginning of activity, e.g.* ***anzünden,*** ignite.

Anachoret [anaxo're:t], *m.* (**-en**, *pl.* **-en**) recluse, anchorite.

Anakreontiker [anakre'ɔntikər], *m.* anacreontic poet.

analog [ana'lo:k], *adj.* analogous (*Dat.*, to *or* with). **Analogie** [–'gi:], *f.* analogy (***zu,*** to *or* with). **Analogie|bildung,** *f.* formation on (the) analogy (of); analogical form. **–schluß,** *m.* argument by *or* from analogy. **analogisch,** *adv.* analogically; **– *nach,*** on the analogy of, by analogy with.

Analphabet [analfa'be:t], *m.* (**-en**, *pl.* **-en**) illiterate (person).

Analyse [ana'ly:zə], *f.* analysis. **analysieren** [–'zi:rən], *v.t.* analyse; (*Gram.*) parse. **Analytiker,** *m.* analyst. **analytisch,** *adj.* analytic(al).

Ananas ['ananas], *f.* (-, *pl.* - *or* **-se**, *Austr. pl.* **-se**) pineapple. **Ananas|erdbeere,** *f.* (*dial.*) large *or* pine-strawberry. **–kirsche,** *f.* Cape gooseberry. **–vogel,** *m.* humming bird, colibri.

anarbeiten ['anˀarbaɪtən], **1.** *v.t.* join on to. **2.** *v.i.* bear (***gegen,*** against *or* on).

Anarchie [anar'çi:], *f.* anarchy. **anarchisch** [–'narçɪʃ], *adj.* anarchic(al). **Anarchismus** [–'çɪsmus], *m.* anarchism. **Anarchist** [–'çɪst], *m.* anarchist.

Anathem [ana'te:m], *n.* (**-s**, *pl.* **-e**) anathema, ban. **Anathema** [a'na:tema], *n.* (**-s**, *pl.* **-ta** [-'te:mata]) anathema (*a p. or th.*).

Anatom [ana'to:m], *m.* (**-en**, *pl.* **-en**) anatomist. **Anatomie** [–'mi:], *f.* 1. anatomy; 2. anatomy theatre, dissecting room. **anatomisch,** *adj.* anatomical.

anbahnen ['anba:nən], *v.t.* open *or* pave *or* smooth *or* prepare the way for, prepare *or* clear the ground for.

anballen ['anbalən], *v.r.* roll itself up, form into a ball.

anbändeln ['anbɛndəln], (*dial.*) **anbandeln** [–bandəln], *v.i.* (***mit***) make up (to), make advances (to), (*sl.*) pick (*s.o.*) up.

Anbau ['anbau], *m.* 1. (**-s**, *no pl.*) cultivation, tillage; culture; settlement; 2. (*pl.* **-ten**) extension, addition (*to a building*), outhouse, outbuilding, annex(e), new wing. **anbauen, 1.** *v.t.* 1. till, cultivate, bring into cultivation (*land*); grow, raise, cultivate (*plants*); 2. add (*s.th.*) to (*a building*), build on (***an*** (*Acc.*), to). **2.** *v.r.* establish o.s.; become settled. **Anbauer,** *m.* 1. cultivator; 2. settler. **Anbaumöbel,** *pl.* unit furniture.

anbefehlen ['anbəfe:lən], *irr.v.t.* 1. ***ihm etwas –,*** (re)commend s.th. to him, enjoin s.th. on him; 2. (*Dat.*) command, order.

Anbeginn ['anbəgɪn], *m.* (**-(e)s**, *no pl.*) earliest beginning, outset.

anbei [an'baɪ], *adv.* (*Comm.*) herewith, enclosed; **– *folgt,*** herewith you receive; please find enclosed; ***Rechnung –,*** account enclosed.

anbeißen ['anbaɪsən], **1.** *irr.v.t.* bite into *or* at; take a bite of. **2.** *irr.v.i.* bite, nibble (at); take the bait; (*fig. coll.*) ***nicht –,*** not fall for it.

anbelangen ['anbəlaŋən], *v.imp.* relate to, concern; ***was mich anbelangt,*** as for me, for my part, as far as I am concerned.

anbequemen ['anbəkve:mən], *v.t., v.r.* accommodate *or* adapt (o.s.) (*Dat.*, to).

anberaumen ['anbəraumən], *v.t.* fix, appoint, settle (*a time, a date*).

anberegt ['anbəre:kt], *adj.* aforesaid, (*Law*) abovementioned.

anbeten ['anbe:tən], *v.t.* worship, adore; (*coll.*) idolize, dote upon. **Anbeter,** *m.* worshipper; (*coll.*) adorer, ardent admirer.

Anbetracht ['anbətraxt], *m.* (*only in*) **in** – (*Gen.*), in view *or* consideration of, on account of, considering.

Anbetreff ['anbətrɛf], *m.* (*only in*) **in** – (*Gen.*), with reference *or* respect *or* regard to. **anbetreffen,** *irr.v.imp. See* **anbelangen. anbetreffs,** *prep.* (*Gen.*) *see* ***in Anbetreff.***

Anbetung ['anbe:tuŋ], *f.* worship, adoration. **anbetungswürdig,** *adj.* adorable.

anbiedern ['anbi:dərn], *v.r.* behave in a free and easy manner, make o.s. at home; ***sich bei ihm –,*** chum up *or* get on good terms with him. **Anbiederung,** *f.* (tactless) familiarity.

anbiegen ['anbi:gən], *irr.v.t.* annex; enclose; subjoin; ***angebogen,*** enclosed, attached.

anbieten ['anbi:tən], **1.** *irr.v.t.* offer, proffer, tender; ***ihm eine Ohrfeige –,*** threaten to box his ears. **2.** *irr.v.r.* ***eine Gelegenheit bietet sich an,*** an opportunity presents itself. **3.** *irr.v.i.* make the first bid, start a price (*at auctions*). **Anbieter,** *m.* (*Comm.*) bidder (*at auction*). **Anbietung,** *f.* tender, proposal, offer.

anbinden ['anbɪndən], **1.** *irr.v.t.* fasten, tie on (***an*** (*Acc.*), to); tie up, tether; (*sl.*) ***einen Bären bei ihm –,*** contract a debt with him. **2.** *irr.v.i.* ***mit ihm –,*** pick a quarrel with him; ***kurz angebunden sein (gegen),*** be curt *or* brusque *or* abrupt (with). **Anbinde|zeit,** *f.* setting-time (*cement etc.*). **–zettel,** *m.* tie-on label.

anblasen ['anbla:zən], *irr.v.t.* blow at *or* upon; blow (up) (*fire*), (*fig.*) fan, stir up (*passions etc.*).

Anblick ['anblɪk], *m.* view, sight; look, appearance, aspect, spectacle; ***beim ersten –,*** at first sight. **anblicken,** *v.t.* look *or* gaze at, gaze (up)on, contemplate; ***finster –,*** look threateningly at, frown at; ***flüchtig –,*** glance at; ***mißtrauisch –,*** eye suspiciously; ***schief –,*** look askance at; ***starr –,*** stare at; ***zornig –,*** glare at.

anbohren ['anbo:rən], *v.t.* bore, pierce; broach, tap (*casks*), (*fig.*) tap, touch (*s.o. for money*), sound, pump (*s.o. for information*).

anbrechen ['anbrɛçən], **1.** *irr.v.i.* (*aux.* s.) start; break; dawn; ***der Tag brach an,*** the day dawned *or* broke; ***bei –dem Tage,*** at daybreak *or* break of day. **2.** *irr.v.t.* broach; open; start on, break into; cut (*a loaf etc.*).

anbrennen ['anbrɛnən], **1.** *irr.v.t.* kindle, set alight, ignite, light, set fire to, set on fire; scorch, calcine; **– *lassen,*** burn (*meat etc.*). **2.** *irr.v.i.* (*aux.* s.) (begin to) burn, catch (fire *or* alight), ignite; burn, stick to the pan (*of food*). **Anbrennholz,** *n.* kindling, firewood.

anbringen ['anbrɪŋən], *irr.v.t.* 1. fix (in position), install, mount, (*coll.*) rig up; 2. bring about *or* to bear, put into operation, put in (*a word*) (*für*, for), lodge (*a complaint*), put forward, make, prefer (*a request*), effect (*improvements etc.*); (*coll.*) ***es bei ihm*** –, put it over on him, try it on with him; 3. sell, dispose of (*goods*), invest (*money*); 4. find employment *or* a place for (*a p.*); ***seine Tochter*** –, marry off *or* find a husband for one's daughter; ***angebracht,*** (be)fitting, proper, suitable, appropriate; timely, well-timed, apt, opportune, seasonable; ***falsch*** or ***schlecht*** or ***übel angebracht,*** out of place, misplaced, uncalled for, undeserved, ill-timed. **Anbringer,** *m.* (*obs.*) informer, telltale.

Anbruch ['anbrux], *m.* 1. beginning; opening; – ***des Tages,*** daybreak; – ***der Nacht,*** nightfall; 2. decay.

anbrüchig ['anbryçɪç], *adj.* decaying, putrescent.

anbrummen ['anbrumən], *v.t.* growl *or* grumble at; scold.

anbrüten ['anbry:tən], *v.t.* begin to hatch; ***angebrütete Eier,*** addled eggs.

Anciennität [ãsiɛni'tɛ:t], *f.* seniority.

Andacht ['andaxt], *f.* (-, *pl.* **-en**) devotion; devotions, prayers; ***seine – verrichten,*** say one's prayers, be at one's devotions.

Andächtelei [andɛçtə'laɪ], *f.* (-, *pl.* **-en**) sanctimoniousness.

andächteln ['andɛçtəln], *v.i.* affect devotion; be over-pious. **andächtig,** *adj., adv.* devout, pious; rapt, attentive; ***sie hörte – zu,*** she listened with rapt attention. **Andächtler,** *m.* hypocrite, sanctimonious person.

andacht(s)los ['andaxt(s)lo:s], *adj.* irreverent. **andacht(s)voll,** *adj.* devout, reverent.

andauern ['andauərn], *v.i.* continue, last, endure, persist, (*coll.*) go *or* keep on. **andauernd,** *adj.* lasting, continuous, uninterrupted, sustained, constant, persistent, incessant.

Anden ['andən], *pl.* Andes.

Andenken ['andɛŋkən], *n.* memory, remembrance; keepsake, memento, souvenir; ***zum – an ihn,*** in memory of him; ***seligen –s,*** of blessed memory; ***im – behalten,*** keep in mind.

ander ['andər] **(anderer, andere, anderes**; (*coll.*) **andrer, andre, andres,** *but* **andern, anderm),** *adj., pron.* 1. other (*of two*); ***das –e Ufer,*** the other bank *or* farther shore; ***die –e Seite,*** the other side (*of road etc.*), wrong side (*of cloth*), reverse (*cloth, coins*); 2. next, following; second; ***zum –en,*** in the second place, secondly; ***am –en Morgen,*** the next *or* following morning; ***einen Tag um den –en,*** every other *or* second day; 3. other, further; ***und –es mehr,*** and so on *or* so forth; ***unter –em*** or ***–en,*** among(st) other things *or* others; ***einer um den –en,*** in turn, alternately; ***einer nach dem –en,*** one after another, one by one; ***eins kommt zum –en,*** one thing comes on top of another; ***eins zum –en*** or ***in das –e gerechnet,*** taking one thing with another; 4. another, different; ***das ist etwas –es,*** that's different; ***–e Kleider anziehen,*** change one's clothes; ***–er Ansicht*** or ***Meinung sein,*** be of a different opinion; ***etwas –es,*** something else; ***nichts –es als,*** nothing else but; ***alles –e,*** everything else; ***ein –er,*** someone else; ***kein –er als er,*** no one else but he, none but he; (*coll.*) ***das glaube ein –er!*** tell that to the marines! ***in –en Umständen sein,*** be in the family way, be expecting; ***–e Länder, –e Sitten,*** when in Rome do as the Romans do.

änderbar ['ɛndərba:r], *adj.* alterable, changeable, variable.

andererseits ['andərərzaɪts], *see* **andrerseits.**

anderlei ['andərlaɪ], *indecl.adj.* of a different *or* another kind.

andermal ['andərma:l], *adv.* ***ein*** –, another time. **andermalig,** *adj.* at some other time, on some other occasion.

ändern ['ɛndərn], **1.** *v.t.* alter (*zu*, into), change, modify, amend; ***das läßt sich nicht*** –, that cannot be helped. **2.** *v.i., v.r.* alter, change, vary.

andernfalls ['andərnfals], *adv.* otherwise, (or) else.

andernteils ['andərntaɪls], *adv.* on the other hand.

anders ['andərs], *adv.* 1. differently; in a different way (***als,*** from), otherwise (***als,*** than); ***ich kann nicht – als lachen,*** I cannot help laughing; ***es ist nun einmal nicht*** –, that's how *or* the way things are, that's how matters stand; – ***herum,*** the other way about *or* round; ***sich – besinnen,*** change one's mind, have second thoughts; (*obs.*) ***wenn*** – or ***wo*** –, if indeed, provided that; 2. else; ***jemand (niemand)*** –, someone *or* somebody (no one *or* nobody) else; ***irgendwo (nirgendwo)*** –, somewhere (nowhere) else; ***wer (wo)*** –, who (where) else; 3. (*translated as adj.*) different; ***nichts – als,*** nothing (else) but; – ***sein als,*** be different from; – ***werden,*** change.

andersartig ['andərsˀartɪç], *adj.* of another *or* a different kind, different.

andersdenkend ['andərsdɛŋkənt], *adj.* dissenting, dissentient, dissident. **Andersdenkende(r),** *m., f.* dissenter, non-conformist.

anderseitig ['andərzaɪtɪç], *adj.* divergent, different, contrary. **anderseits,** *adv. See* **andrerseits.**

andersgesinnt ['andərsgəzɪnt], *adj.* differently minded.

andersgläubig ['andərsglɔybɪç], *adj.* of different faith, dissenting, unorthodox, heterodox, heretical. **Andersgläubige(r),** *m., f.* dissenter, non-conformist; (*R.C.*) non-Catholic.

anders|wo, *adv.* elsewhere, somewhere else. **–woher,** *adv.* from elsewhere, from somewhere else. **–wohin,** *adv.* elsewhere, somewhere else, to another *or* some other place.

anderthalb [andərt'halp], *adj.* one and a half, sesqui– (*in compounds*); – ***Pfund,*** a pound and a half.

Änderung ['ɛndəruŋ], *f.* change, alteration, modification, variation, fluctuation. **Änderungs|-antrag,** *m.* amendment (*to a bill*). **–geschwindigkeit,** *f.* rate of change. **–sucht,** *f.* mania for change.

anderwärtig ['andərvɛrtɪç], *adj.* in *or* from another *or* some other place. **anderwärts,** *adv.* elsewhere.

anderweit ['andərvaɪt], *adv. See* **anderwärts;** otherwise. **anderweitig, 1.** *adj.* further; ***–e Hilfe,*** help from some other quarter. **2.** *adv.* elsewhere, otherwise; – ***verfügen über*** (*Acc.*), otherwise dispose of.

andeuten ['andɔytən], *v.t.* suggest, intimate, allude to, indicate; hint at, insinuate, imply, give to understand. **Andeutung,** *f.* indication, suggestion, intimation; hint, allusion. **andeutungsweise,** *adv.* by way of suggestion, allusively.

andichten ['andɪçtən], *v.t.* ***ihm etwas*** –, attribute (falsely) *or* impute s.th. to him.

andienen ['andi:nən], *v.t.* 1. (*Naut.*) make (*land*), put into (*a port*); 2. (*Comm.*) offer (*immediate delivery*), deliver (*goods etc.*), notify (*intentions*).

andonnern ['andɔnərn], *v.t.* thunder *or* roar at; ***er stand wie angedonnert,*** he stood as if thunderstruck.

Andrang ['andraŋ], *m.* **(-(e)s,** *no pl.*) crowd, throng, multitude, dense mass; rush (***zu,*** to; ***nach,*** for); – ***auf eine Bank,*** run on a bank; (*Med.*) – ***des Blutes,*** rush of blood, congestion.

andrängen ['andrɛŋən], *v.t., v.r.* crowd, press, push, thrust (*an* (*Acc.*), towards *or* against).

andre, *see* **ander.**

Andreas [an'dre:as], *m.* Andrew.

andrehen ['andre:ən], *v.t.* 1. turn *or* switch on (*gas, water, electricity etc.*); start (up), crank up (engine); 2. (*coll.*) contrive to do, bring about, wangle; 3. (*coll.*) ***ihm etwas*** –, palm *or* foist *or* fob s.th. off on him. **Andrehkurbel,** *f.* crankhandle.

andrer, *see* **ander. andrerseits,** *adv.* on the other hand. **andres,** *see* **ander.**

andringen ['andrɪŋən], *irr.v.i.* (*aux.* s.) press forward; rush (***gegen, auf*** (*Acc.*), at *or* upon).

androhen ['andro:ən], *v.t.* ***ihm etwas*** –, menace *or* threaten him with s.th. **Androhung,** *f.* threat, menace; ***bei*** or ***unter*** –, under penalty *or* on pain (*Gen.*, of).

Äneas [ɛ'ne:as], *m.* Aeneas. **Äneide** [–'i:də], *f.* Aenid.

aneifern ['an?aɪfərn], *v.t.* stimulate, rouse, incite, spur on.

aneignen ['an?aɪgnən], *v.t.* acquire, adopt; appropriate; seize, lay hands on; usurp, misappropriate, *(coll.)* pinch, swipe, lift; *(Med.)* assimilate; ***sich (Dat.) Gewohnheiten –,*** contract habits; ***sich (Dat.) die Meinungen anderer –,*** adopt the opinions of others. **Aneignung,** *f.* acquisition, adoption, seizure, appropriation, misappropriation, usurpation; *(Med.)* assimilation.

aneinander [an?aɪn'andər], *adv.* together; to *or* by *or* against one another; – ***vorbei,*** past one another; – ***vorbeireden,*** talk at cross purposes.

aneinander|fügen, *v.t.* join, fit together. **–geraten,** *irr.v.i.* *(aux.*s.) come to blows *or* grips. **–grenzen,** *v.i.* *(aux.* s.) adjoin, be adjacent *or* contiguous, border on one another. **–grenzend,** *adj.* adjoining, adjacent, contiguous. **–kleben,** *v.t., v.i.* stick together. **–legen,** *v.t.* bring in juxtaposition, place side by side; bring into apposition *(fractured bones).* **–liegen,** *irr.v.i.* lie side by side, be in juxtaposition. **–liegend,** *adj.* juxtaposed, side by side. **–prallen,** *v.i.* *(aux.* s.) collide, cannon, *(fig.)* clash. **–reihen,** *v.t.* range side by side, line up, connect up, string together. **–rücken,** *v.t.* move closer together. **–schließen,** *irr.v.t.* join, connect. **–wachsen,** *irr.v.i.* *(aux.* s.) grow together, coalesce; knit *(of bones).*

Äneise [ɛne'i:zə], *f. See* **Äneide.**

Anekdote [anɛk'do:tə], *f.* anecdote.

anekeln ['an?e:kəln], *v.t., v.imp.* disgust, be repugnant *or* loathsome *or* distasteful.

anempfehlen ['an?ɛmpfe:lən], *irr.v.t.* (re)commend, advise.

anempfinden ['an?ɛmpfɪndən], *irr.v.r.* appreciate *or* share the feelings of others. **anempfunden,** *adj.* spurious, simulated, factitious.

Anerbe ['an?ɛrbə], *m.* heir to entailed property; next heir. **anerben,** *v.t.* transmit by inheritance. **Anerbenrecht,** *n.* law of entail.

anerbieten ['an?ɛrbi:tən], *irr.v.t.* offer. **Anerbieten,** *n.,* **Anerbietung,** *f.* proposal, proposition, offer.

anerkannt ['an?ɛrkant], *adj.* acknowledged, admitted, recognized, established *(fact),* accepted *(usage),* received *(pronunciation).* **anerkanntermaßen,** *adv.* admittedly, by common consent.

anerkennen ['an?ɛrkɛnən], *irr.v.t.* *(sep. & insep.)* recognize, acknowledge, admit, approve of, give one's approval to, appreciate; *(Comm.)* honour *(a bill);* ***nicht –,*** disown, disavow *(a child etc.),* disallow *(a claim),* repudiate *(a debt etc.),* deny, disclaim *(responsibility).* **anerkennenswert,** *adj.* commendable, laudable, praiseworthy (***wegen,*** for). **Anerkenntnis,** *n. or f.* acknowledgement, *(Law)* recognizance. **Anerkennung,** *f.* acknowledgement; recognition; appreciation; approval, approbation.

anerschaffen ['an?ɛrʃafən], *adj.* innate, inborn.

anerziehen ['an?ɛrtsi:ən], *v.t.* instil *(Dat.,* into), inculcate *(Dat.,* in *or* upon). **anerzogen,** *adj.* acquired *(taste etc.).*

anfachen ['anfaxən], *v.t.* blow into a flame; fan; stimulate, excite, inflame, rouse, stir up, foment.

anfahrbar ['anfa:rba:r], *adj.* negotiable, passable *(road),* navigable *(channel),* approachable, accessible *(shore).*

anfahren ['anfa:rən], **1.** *irr.v.i.* *(aux.* s.) 1. drive up; start *(of a vehicle);* 2. run *or* drive (***an*** or ***auf*** *(Acc.),* into), collide (with). **2.** *irr.v.t.* 1. run *or* drive into, collide with; 2. drive up to *or* towards; ***einen Hafen –,*** put into *or* call at a port; 3. bring *or* carry *or* cart up *(materials);* 4. rush at, *(coll.)* go for, snap at; ***"was fällt dir ein?" fuhr sie ihn an,*** 'What's the idea?' she snapped at him. **Anfahrt,** *f.* 1. approach, arrival; 2. landing-place; 3. drive, approach (-road), entrance.

Anfall ['anfal], *m.* 1. attack, assault; onslaught; 2. bout; onset; fit, seizure, outburst, paroxysm; 3. *pl.* amount accruing, revenue; yield, supply; ***künftige Anfälle,*** inheritance in reversion; 4. – ***eines Gutes,*** accession to an inheritance. **anfallen, 1.** *irr.v.t.* fall on, assail, attack, assault. **2.** *irr.v.i.* *(aux.* s.)*(Dat.)* fall to one's share *or* lot, devolve upon *(of property);* accrue, become available, come to hand *(of materials).*

anfällig ['anfɛlɪç], *adj.* susceptible, prone (***gegen, für,*** to); *(coll.)* prone to sickness, ailing, sickly. **Anfälligkeit,** *f.* proneness, susceptibility (to disease).

Anfalls|recht, *n.* right of escheat, reversionary interest *(in an estate).* **–steuer,** *f.* probate *or* estate duty.

Anfang ['anfaŋ], *m.* start, beginning, commencement, outset; inception, opening, introduction; *pl.* rudiments, elements; – ***Mai,*** at the beginning of May, early in May; ***ich bin – fünfzig,*** I am in my early fifties; ***für den –,*** for a start; ***den – machen,*** make a start; ***am*** or ***im*** or ***zu –,*** at the start *or* outset, at first, in the beginning; ***gleich am –,*** at the very beginning, right at the start; (***gleich***) ***von – an,*** (right) from the very start *or* first *or* beginning *or* outset; ***von – bis Ende,*** from beginning to end, from start to finish, from first to last; *(Prov.)* ***aller – ist schwer,*** the first step is the hardest.

anfangen ['anfaŋən], **1.** *irr.v.t.* begin, start, commence; set about, set on foot *or* in train, open; *(coll.)* manage to do, do, deal; ***ein Geschäft –,*** set up in business, set up shop; ***was wollen Sie heute –?*** what are you going to do today? ***was soll ich damit –?*** what shall I do with it? ***mit ihm ist nichts anzufangen,*** there's no doing anything with him, it's impossible to deal with him. **2.** *irr.v.i.* begin, start, commence, open; ***von vorne –,*** begin at the beginning; ***wieder von vorne –,*** start again *or* afresh, make a fresh start; ***er fängt immer wieder damit*** or ***davon an,*** he keeps harping on it.

Anfänger ['anfɛŋər], *m.,* **Anfängerin,** *f.* beginner, novice, tyro. **Anfängerkurs,** *m.* elementary *or* beginners' course.

anfänglich ['anfɛŋlɪç], **1.** *adj.* initial, incipient, original. **2.** *adv. See* **anfangs.**

anfangs ['anfaŋs], *adv.* in the beginning, at first, at the start *or* outset, originally, initially, to start *or* begin with; ***gleich –,*** right at the *or* at the very beginning, start *or* outset.

Anfangs–, *pref.* first, initial, opening, early, elementary, introductory. **–buchstabe,** *m.* initial letter; ***großer –,*** capital letter. **–geschwindigkeit,** *f.* initial velocity, *(Artil.)* muzzle velocity. **–gründe,** *pl.* rudiments, first principles, elements. **–kurs,** *m.* opening price. **–stadium,** *n.* initial stage. **–zeile,** *f.* first line. **–zustand,** *m.* original state.

anfassen ['anfasən], **1.** *v.t.* take *or* lay *or* catch hold of, seize, grasp, grab; touch, handle; set about *(a task);* ***nicht –!*** don't touch! ***etwas richtig*** or ***beim rechten Ende*** or ***Zipfel –,*** set *or* go about s.th. in the right way; ***etwas verkehrt –,*** set *or* go about s.th. in the wrong way; *(fig.)* ***mit Glacéhandschuhen –,*** handle with kid gloves. **2.** *v.i.* grip, take hold; take root *(of plants);* ***faßt an!*** give *or* lend a hand! ***mit –,*** take a hand oneself (***bei,*** in). **Anfasser,** *m.* oven-cloth, pot *or* kettle holder.

anfauchen ['anfauxən], *v.t.* spit at.

anfaulen ['anfaulən], *v.i.* *(aux.* s.) begin to rot *or* decay, go bad; ***angefault,*** tainted.

anfechtbar ['anfɛçtba:r], *adj.* questionable, disputable, contestable, controversial; impeachable, impugnable; *(Law)* defeasible, voidable.

anfechten ['anfɛçtən], *irr.v.t.* dispute, contest, challenge, call in question, take exception to; attack, assail, impugn, impeach; *(B.)* tempt; ***was ficht dich an?*** what is the matter with you? ***was ficht mich das an?*** what is that to me?

Anfechtung ['anfɛçtuŋ], *f.* opposition, objection *(Gen.,* to); challenge (to), impeachment, impugnment (of); *(B.)* temptation.

anfeinden ['anfaɪndən], *v.t.* bear *(s.o.)* malice *or* ill-will, show enmity *or* hostility towards, be hostile to *or* at enmity with. **Anfeindung,** *f.* persecution; enmity, hostility, ill-will.

anfertigen ['anfɛrtɪgən], *v.t.* make, manufacture, produce; draw up, draft, prepare (*document*). **Anfertigung,** *f.* manufacture; production, preparation.

anfetten ['anfɛtən], *v.t.* grease, lubricate, oil.

anfeuchten ['anfɔyçtən], *v.t.* moisten, damp, wet; sprinkle, spray.

anfeuern ['anfɔyərn], *v.t.* fire, inflame, incite, excite, stimulate; prime.

anflehen ['anfle:ən], *v.t.* implore, beg, beseech, entreat, supplicate (*um*, for). **Anflehung,** *f.* supplication, entreaty.

anfliegen ['anfli:gən], **1.** *irr.v.i.* (*aux.* s.) *usu.* ***angeflogen kommen,*** come flying, fly up; be wind-borne (*as seeds*); (*Metall.*) effloresce; (*fig.*) spring up spontaneously; ***es fliegt ihm alles an,*** everything comes easily to him; ***die Krankheit kam ihm wie angeflogen,*** the illness attacked him without warning; ***angeflogen,*** (*Bot.*) wind-borne; (*Metall.*) encrusted. **2.** *irr.v.t.* 1. land at (*an aerodrome*), make *or* head for (*of aircraft*); 2. (*fig.*) suffuse (*of blushes etc.*), come over (*s.o.*) suddenly (*as weakness etc.*).

Anflug ['anflu:k], *m.* 1. (*Av.*) approach (flight); rising flight, soaring (*of birds*); 2. (*Metall. etc.*) efflorescence, incrustation, film, coating, bloom; (*fig.*) mere suggestion, trace, hint, suspicion, touch, tinge, shade, spasm; – ***von Röte,*** slight blush; – ***von Narrheit,*** fit of folly. **Anflugweg,** *m.* (*Av.*) approach path, air corridor.

Anfluß ['anflus], *m.* 1. onflow, afflux; rising (*of the tide*); 2. alluvial deposit, alluvium.

anfordern ['anfɔrdərn], *v.t.* demand (as due), require, claim, requisition (*goods*), request (delivery of), call (*or Mil.*) indent for (***bei,*** on). **Anforderung,** *f.* demand, requirement; claim, requisition, request (for delivery), (*Mil.*) indent; (***hohe***) ***–en stellen,*** make (great) demands (***an*** (*Acc.*), upon), expect great things (from).

Anfrage ['anfra:gə], *f.* inquiry; (*Parl.*) question (in the House); ***auf*** –, on inquiry *or* application. **anfragen,** *v.i.* inquire, make inquiries (***bei,*** of; ***über*** (*Acc.*), ***wegen, nach,*** about), ask.

anfressen ['anfrɛsən], *irr.v.t.* gnaw, nibble; corrode, eat away; ***angefressener Zahn,*** decayed tooth. **Anfressung,** *f.* corrosion, erosion; decay.

anfreunden ['anfrɔyndən], *v.r.* become friendly, make friends, strike up a friendship.

anfrischen ['anfrɪʃən], *v.t.* (*Metall.*) reduce, refine. *See also* **auffrischen. Anfrisch|herd, –ofen,** *m.* refining furnace. **Anfrischung,** *f.* refining, reduction (*of metals*).

anfügen ['anfy:gən], *v.t.* join, attach; affix, append, enclose.

anfühlen ['anfy:lən], **1.** *v.t.* touch, feel; know by the feel; (*fig.*) sense, have a feeling (that). **2.** *v.r.* feel; ***es fühlt sich weich an,*** it feels soft.

Anfuhr ['anfu:r], *f.* (-, *pl.* **-en**) conveying, carting, haulage, transport, delivery, carriage (*of goods*).

anführbar ['anfy:rba:r], *adj.* quotable, citable (*passage*), adducible (*example etc.*).

anführen ['anfy:rən], *v.t.* 1. lead, head, be at the head of, command, be in command of; 2. quote, cite; allege (*reason*), bring forward, advance, adduce (*argument*), offer (*excuse*); ***am angeführten Orte*** (abbr. ***a.a.O.***), loc. cit; 3. deceive, hoax, fool, dupe, trick, take in. **Anführer,** *m.* chief, chieftain (*of tribe*), leader, (*Pol.*) party boss, (*Mil.*) commander, (*Spt.*) captain, ringleader (*of plot*). **Anführung,** *f.* 1. lead, leadership, direction, (*Mil.*) command; 2. quotation, citation; adduction; *falsche* –, misquotation. **Anführungs|striche, –zeichen,** *pl.* quotation marks, inverted commas.

anfüllen ['anfylən], *v.t.* fill (up); cram; ***neu*** or ***wieder*** –, replenish, refill.

Angabe ['anga:bə], *f.* 1. indication; declaration, statement, assertion; (*Law*) evidence, testimony; *pl.* instructions, directions, specifications, (*Math.*) data; ***beglaubigte*** –, sworn statement; ***nach seiner*** –, according to him; ***nähere –n,*** full particulars, details; 2. down payment, deposit, earnest-money; 3. (*coll.*) boasting, bragging, showing off; 4. (*Tenn.*) service.

angaffen ['angafən], *v.t.* gape at, stare open-mouthed at.

Angang ['angaŋ], *m.* first meeting; ***feindlicher*** –, hostile encounter.

angängig ['angɛŋɪç], *pred.adj.* permissible; feasible, practicable; ***soweit*** –, as far as is possible *or* practicable.

angeben ['ange:bən], **1.** *irr.v.t.* 1. indicate, state name, fix, appoint (*time, date etc.*); give, state, assign (*reasons etc.*); quote (*prices*); (make a) return, declare (*for customs etc.*); ***näher*** –, give details, specify; (*Mus.*) ***den Ton*** –, sound *or* strike the (key-)note; (*fig.*) set the tone *or* fashion, give the lead; 2. declare, assert, state, allege, claim; 3. (*Law*) denounce, inform against, (*coll.*) give away, (*sl.*) tell on; 4. pay down (as a deposit); 5. ***sich – für*** or ***als,*** represent o.s. as, pretend to be. **2.** *irr.v.i.* 1. (*Cards*) deal first; (*Tenn.*) serve; 2. boast, brag (***mit,*** of), show off, give o.s. airs (with); 3. make a fuss. *See* **Angabe. Angeber,** *m.* 1. (*Law*) informer, (*coll.*) talebearer, tell-tale, sneak, (*sl.*) nark; 2. boaster, braggart, poseur, (*coll.*) swank, show-off. **Angeberei** [–'raɪ], *f.* 1. denunciation, (*coll.*) talebearing, sneaking; 2. boasting, bragging, showing off. **angeberisch,** *adj.* 1. denunciatory, (*coll.*) talebearing; 2. pretentious, (*coll.*) swanky, uppish.

Angebinde ['angəbɪndə], *n.* gift, (birthday) present.

angeblich ['ange:plɪç], *adj.* alleged, supposed, reputed, pretended, ostensible; (*Law*) putative; (*coll.*) so-called, would-be; (*Comm.*) ***–er Preis,*** price quoted; (*Comm.*) ***–er Wert,*** nominal *or* face value.

angeboren ['angəbo:rən], *adj.* inborn, innate, (*fig.*) inherent (*Dat.*, in); congenital, hereditary.

Angebot ['angəbo:t], *n.* offer; (opening *or* starting) bid, quotation, tender; – ***und Nachfrage,*** supply and demand.

angebracht ['angəbraxt], *see* **anbringen.**

angebunden ['angəbundən], *see* **anbinden.**

angedeihen ['angədaɪən], *irr.v.i.* ***ihm etwas – lassen,*** confer *or* bestow s.th. upon him, grant s.th. to him.

Angedenken ['angədɛŋkən], *n.* *See* **Andenken.**

angeduselt ['angədu:zəlt], *adj.* (*coll.*) fuddled.

angegriffen ['angəgrɪfən], *see* **angreifen.**

Angehänge ['angəhɛŋə], *n.* appendage; pendant, amulet.

angeheiratet ['angəhaɪra:tət], *adj.* (connected) by marriage; ***–er Vetter,*** cousin by marriage.

angeheitert ['angəhaɪtərt], *adj.* (*coll.*) merry, lit up, tipsy.

angehen ['ange:ən], **1.** *irr.v.i.* (*aux.* s.) 1. go *or* fit on (*as lid*), fit (*as clothes*), (*coll.*) be passable *or* tolerable; ***das geht schwer an,*** that is hard to get on; (*coll.*) ***das geht*** or ***so geht's nicht an,*** that won't do; ***soweit es angeht,*** as far as is possible; ***der Verlust wird wohl noch*** –, the loss won't be too bad after all; 2. light, catch (*fire*), start; (*Hort.*) take *or* strike root; ***der Motor will nicht*** –, the engine won't start; 3. (*coll.*) commence, begin, start, set in, get going; ***morgen geht das Schuljahr an,*** the school year begins tomorrow; 4. go bad *or* off (*as meat etc.*); ***angegangenes Fleisch,*** tainted meat; 5. rise, slope up(wards); ***der Weg ging sachte an,*** the path rose gently. **2.** *irr.v.t.* 1. rush *or* make a rush at, go at, (*coll.*) go for; tackle (*an obstacle, problem*); apply to (*um*, for); 2. concern, affect, bear upon, have to do with; ***das geht mich nichts an,*** that is none of my business, that is no business *or* concern of mine, it is nothing to do with me; ***was geht mich das an?*** what business *or* concern is it of mine? what has it to do with me? what is that to me? ***was mich angeht,*** as far as I am concerned, as for me, (speaking) for myself.

angehend ['ange:ənt], *adj.* in the early *or* initial stages, incipient, in embryo, (*coll.*) budding; ***bei***

–er Nacht, as night was falling; ***das –e 20. Jahrhundert,*** the early 20th century; ***eine –e Neigung,*** growing *or* dawning affection; ***ein –er Fünfziger,*** a man in his early fifties, a man verging on fifty.

angehören ['angəhø:rən], *v.i.* belong (*Dat.*, to). **angehörig,** *adj.* belonging (*Dat.*, to). **Angehörige(r),** *m., f.* member; relative, relation; ***die Angehörigen,*** next of kin, family. **Angehörigkeit,** *f.* membership (***zu,*** of); kinship, relationship.

Angeklagte(r) ['angəkla:ktə(r)], *m., f.* accused, defendant; *see* **anklagen.**

Angel ['aŋəl], *f.* (-, *pl.* **-n**) 1. fishing-tackle, fishing-rod; fish-hook; 2. door-hinge; pivot; axis; ***aus den –n heben,*** unhinge (*a door*), (*fig.*) turn upside down; ***zwischen Tür und –,*** just before leaving, hurriedly, in passing; (*rare*) ***zwischen Tür und – stecken,*** be in a cleft stick. **Angelblei,** *n.* sinker. **angelborstig,** *adj.* (*Bot.*) glochidiate.

Angeld ['angɛlt], *n.* deposit, earnest-money; first instalment, part-payment.

angelegen ['angəle:gən], *see* **anliegen. Angelegenheit,** *f.* concern, matter, affair, business; ***in welcher – ...?*** in what connexion ...? ***Minister der auswärtigen –en,*** Minister (*Am.* Secretary of State) for Foreign Affairs. **angelegentlich,** *adj.* 1. pressing, urgent, earnest; 2. cordial, fervent.

angel|fest, *adj.* securely *or* firmly fixed. **–förmig,** *adj.* (*Nat. Hist.*) unciform, uncinate. **Angel|gerät,** *n.* fishing-tackle. **–haken,** *m.* fish-hook.

angeln ['aŋəln], **1.** *v.i.* fish (with rod and line), angle (*also fig.*) (***nach,*** for). **2.** *v.t.* catch, hook (*a fish, also fig. a husband*).

angeloben ['angəlo:bən], *v.t.* vow; promise solemnly.

Angel|punkt, *m.* pivot; (*Astr.*) pole; (*fig.*) cardinal point, point on which everything turns, hub. **–rute,** *f.* fishing-rod.

Angel|sachse, *m.*, **–sächsin,** *f.* Anglo-Saxon. **angelsächsisch,** *adj.* Anglo-Saxon.

Angel|schnur, *f.* fishing-line. **–stern,** *m.* pole star, lodestar. **angelweit,** *adj.* wide (open). **Angelzapfen,** *m.* hinge-pin.

angemessen ['angəmɛsən], *adj.* suitable (*Dat.*, for *or* to), suited, adapted, adequate, proper, appropriate, proportionate (to); fit, fitting (for); consistent, compatible, consonant, in keeping (with), (be)fitting, becoming (*behaviour etc.*), apt (*word etc.*), fair, acceptable (*in price*). **Angemessenheit,** *f.* suitability, appropriateness, adequacy, compatibility, aptness, fitness, propriety.

angenehm ['angəne:m], *adj.* agreeable, pleasant.

angenommen ['angənɔmən], *see* **annehmen.**

Anger ['aŋər], *m.* (village) green; meadow, pasture, grazing land, greensward.

Angeschuldigte(r) ['angəʃuldɪçtə(r)], *m., f.* suspect.

angesehen ['angəse:ən], *adj.* esteemed, respected, reputable, of excellent reputation, of high standing; eminent, distinguished, notable, noted. *See* **ansehen.**

angesessen ['angəzɛsən], *adj.* settled; resident, domiciled.

Angesicht ['angəzɪçt], *n.* face; countenance; ***von – zu –,*** face to face; ***im Schweiße seines –s,*** by the sweat of his brow; ***im –,*** *see* **angesichts. angesichts,** *prep.* (*Gen.*) in view *or* consideration *or* (the) face of, faced with, considering.

angestammt ['angəʃtamt], *adj.* hereditary, inherited; ancestral (*castle etc.*); innate.

Angestellte(r) ['angəʃtɛltə(r)], *m., f.* employee; shop assistant, clerk.

angetan ['angəta:n], *see* **antun.**

angetrunken ['angətruŋkən], *see* **antrinken.**

angewandt ['angəvant], *see* **anwenden.**

angewiesen ['angəvi:zən], *see* **anweisen.**

angewöhnen ['angəvø:nən], *v.t.* accustom, habituate, inure (***ihm etwas,*** him to a th.); ***sich*** (*Dat.*) –, accustom o.s. to, become accustomed to, get into the habit of.

Angewohnheit ['angəvo:nhaɪt], *f.* habit; ***aus –,*** from habit, by force of habit.

Angewöhnung ['angəvø:nuŋ], *f.* habituation (*Gen.*, to).

angießen ['angi:sən], *irr.v.t.* 1. infuse (*tea etc.*), water (*plants*); 2. (*Metall.*) mould *or* cast on; ***das Kleid sitzt wie angegossen,*** the dress fits like a glove.

angleichen ['anglaɪçən], *irr.v.t.* assimilate (*Dat.*, ***an*** (*Acc.*), to *or* with), adapt (to). **Angleichung,** *f.* assimilation, adaptation, matching.

Angler ['aŋlər], *m.* angler, fisherman; *see* **angeln.**

angliedern ['angli:dərn], *v.t.* join (on), attach, annex, append, affiliate (*Dat.*, ***an*** (*Acc.*), to). **Angliederung,** *f.* annexation, affiliation.

anglisieren [aŋgli'zi:rən], *v.t.* anglicize. **Anglist** [–'glɪst], *m.* student *or* teacher of English. **Anglistik** [–'glɪstɪk], *f.* (-, *no pl.*) (study of) English language and literature.

Anglizismus [aŋgli'tsɪsmus], *n.* (-, *pl.* **-men**) anglicism.

Anglomane [aŋglo'ma:nə], *m.* (**-n**, *pl.* **-n**) Anglomaniac. **Anglomanie** [–'ni:], *f.* Anglomania.

anglotzen ['anglɔtsən], *v.t.* stare *or* goggle at.

anglühen ['angly:ən], **1.** *v.t.* 1. heat red-hot, bring to red-heat; ***angeglüht,*** heated to red-heat, red-hot; 2. mull (*wine*). **2.** *v.i.* (*aux.* s.) begin to glow, become red-hot.

angreifbar ['angraɪfba:r], *adj.* assailable, vulnerable, open to criticism.

angreifen ['angraɪfən], **1.** *irr.v.t.* 1. seize, grasp, lay *or* take *or* catch hold of; 2. (*fig.*) undertake, set about, set one's hand to, grapple with, (*coll.*) tackle; 3. attack, assault, assail, set upon; (*fig.*) attack, corrode, eat into (*as acid*), break into (*capital, savings etc.*), (*Med.*) attack, affect (*an organ*), strain (*nerves*), try (*the eyes*), shatter, sap (*vitality*). **2.** *irr.v.i.* attack, take the offensive, commit an act of aggression. **3.** *irr.v.r.* 1. exert *or* strain o.s.; 2. feel (to the touch) (*of texture*). *See* **Angriff. Angreifer,** *m.* aggressor, attacker, assailant.

angrenzen ['angrɛntsən], *v.i.* – ***an*** (*Acc.*), border on, adjoin, be adjacent *or* contiguous to, abut on; be in touch *or* contact with. **angrenzend,** *adj.* adjacent, adjoining; neighbouring; – ***an*** (*Acc.*), adjacent *or* contiguous to, bordering *or* abutting on. **Angrenzer,** *m.* immediate *or* next-door neighbour, (*Law*) abutter.

Angriff ['angrɪf], *m.* attack, assault (***auf*** (*Acc.*), against *or* upon); onslaught, charge; aggression, offensive; ***zum – blasen,*** sound the charge; ***dem ersten – standhalten,*** bear the brunt of the attack; ***einen erneuten – machen,*** return to the attack; ***zum – übergehen,*** go over to *or* take *or* assume the offensive; ***in – nehmen,*** set about, set one's hand to, take in hand (*a task*), put into action (*a plan*).

Angriffs|bündnis, *n.* offensive alliance. **–krieg,** *m.* war of aggression. **angriffslustig,** *adj.* aggressive. **Angriffs|punkt,** *m.* (*Mil.*) point of attack, objective; (*Mech.*) point of application (*of a force*). **–waffe,** *f.* (*Mil.*) offensive weapon *or* arm. **–zeit,** *f.* (*Mil.*) zero hour. **–ziel,** *n.* target, (*Mil.*) objective, goal.

Angst [aŋst], *f.* (-, *pl.* **¨-e**) fear, anxiety, anguish, dread; ***– bekommen, in – geraten,*** take alarm *or* fright, get scared *or* alarmed *or* frightened; ***ihm – machen*** or ***einjagen,*** give him a fright, frighten *or* scare *or* alarm him; ***– haben,*** be *or* feel frightened *or* afraid; be alarmed; ***aus – vor*** (*Dat.*), for fear of; ***– um etwas haben,*** be nervous *or* worried *or* anxious about s.th., fear for s.th.

angst, *indecl. adj.* frightened, alarmed, scared; uneasy, anxious, apprehensive; ***mir ist – vor*** (*Dat.*), I am frightened of; ***mir ist – um,*** I am anxious *or* worried *or* nervous about. **angst|beklommen,** *adj.* oppressed by fears, fearful. **–erfüllt,** *adj.* anxious, full of anxiety.

Angst|gefühl, *n.* anxiety, anguish, distress. **–geschrei,** *n.* cry *or* cries of alarm *or* terror. **–hase,** *m.* (*coll.*) funk.

ängstigen ['ɛŋstɪgən], **1.** *v.t.* frighten, alarm. **2.** *v.r. sich – vor* (*Dat.*), be frightened *or* afraid of; *sich – um*, worry *or* fret *or* be uneasy *or* anxious about.

ängstlich ['ɛŋstlɪç], *adj.* 1. anxious, worried; apprehensive, uneasy, nervous, afraid; fearful, timid; 2. (*of situation*) alarming, disquieting, disturbing; 3. (*of character*) (over-)scrupulous *or* particular, meticulous, (*coll.*) finicky. **Ängstlichkeit,** *f.* 1. anxiety, nervousness, uneasiness, fearfulness, timidity, timorousness; 2. (over-)scrupulousness, meticulousness, (*coll.*) finickiness.

Angst|meier, *m.* (*coll.*) *see* **–hase. –neurose,** *f.* anxiety neurosis. **–röhre,** *f.* (*coll.*) top hat, topper. **–schweiß,** *m.* cold sweat. **angstvoll,** *adj.* anxious, fearful.

anhaben ['anha:bən], *irr.v.t.* 1. be wearing, have on, be dressed in; 2. *ihm etwas –*, hold s.th. against him; *ihm nichts –*, be able to find no fault with him; not have anything *or* have nothing against *or* (*coll.*) on him.

anhaften ['anhaftən], *v.i.* adhere, stick, cling (*Dat.*, to); attach (to) (*a p.*); be inherent (in).

anhaken ['anha:kən], *v.t.* 1. hook on; 2. mark with a tick; tick (*Am.* check) (off).

Anhalt ['anhalt], *m.* 1. basis, support; *einen – gewähren* (*Dat.*), offer a clue to; 2. (foot)hold; 3. halt, stop; stopping-place.

anhalten ['anhaltən], **1.** *irr.v.t.* 1. stop, halt, bring to a standstill; 2. detain, hold up, impede, hinder, delay; 3. urge, constrain, oblige; *zum Zahlen –*, dun; *ihn um etwas –, see bei ihm um etwas –*; 4. (*Mus.*) hold, sustain (*a note*); *den Atem –*, hold one's breath. **2.** *irr.v.i.* 1. stop, halt, come to a stop *or* halt *or* standstill, pull *or* draw up; 2. last, continue, endure, persist; 3. *– um*, apply for; *um ein Mädchen* or *um die Hand eines Mädchens –*, sue for a girl, ask a girl's hand in marriage; *bei ihm um etwas –*, solicit him for s.th. **anhaltend, 1.** *adj.* continuous, continual, continued, uninterrupted, unceasing, unremitting, unbroken, constant, persistent, sustained, prolonged. **2.** *adv.* (*Mus.*) sostenuto. **Anhaltepunkt,** *m.* stopping-place; reference point; (*Mus.*) fermata. **Anhalter,** *m.* 1. stop, arrester (device), detent; 2. (*coll.*) hitch-hiker; *per – reisen*, hitch-hike, thumb a lift. **Anhalteweg,** *m.* (*Motor.*) stopping distance.

Anhalts|punkt, *m.* guiding principle, deciding factor, criterion; clue, lead, basis; *keine –e für eine Vermutung haben*, make a conjecture without anything to go by *or* on. **–wert,** *m.* approximate figure *or* value.

anhand [an'hant], *prep.* (*Gen.*) *see an Hand.*

Anhang ['anhaŋ], *m.* 1. appendix, supplement, addendum, codicil (*to a will*), (*Law*) rider, (*Comm.*) allonge; appendage, (*Anat.*) apophysis; 2. supporters, adherents, followers, following; 3. dependants, (family) encumbrances.

anhangen ['anhaŋən], *irr.v.i.* (*rare*) *see* **anhängen, 3.**

anhängen ['anhɛŋən], **1.** *reg.v.t.* 1. hand up; (*Tele.*) *den Hörer –*, replace the receiver, hang up, ring off; (*fig.*) *ihm etwas –*, cast aspersions *or* a slur on him, find fault with him; (*coll.*) burden, saddle *or* (*sl.*) land him with s.th., palm *or* fob off *or* unload s.th. on him; (*coll.*) *ihm eins –*, pull a fast one on him; 2. fasten, join (on), attach, append, affix, subjoin, add (*an* (*Acc.*), to); (*Railw.*) couple, hitch (*a wagon*) (on to). **2.** *reg.v.r.* attach o.s., adhere (*an* (*Acc.*), to), inflict o.s. (on), force *or* foist o.s. (upon). **3.** *irr.v.i.* 1. hang on (*Dat.*, *an* (*Dat.*), to), be suspended (from); be attached (to), stick, cling, adhere (to); 2. (*Dat.*) hold to, hold (*an opinion*); be an adherent of. **anhängend,** *adj.* adhering, adhesive; adherent. **Anhänger,** *m.* 1. partisan, adherent; disciple, supporter, follower; 2. trailer; 3. appendage; tag, locket, pendant. **Anhängerschaft,** *f.* following, adherents, followers; disciples.

Anhänge|schloß, *n.* padlock. **–silbe,** *f.* suffix. **–wagen,** *m.* trailer. **–wort,** *n.* enclitic. **–zettel,** *m.* tag, tie-on label.

anhängig ['anhɛŋɪç], *adj.* (*Law*) pending; *eine Klage* or *einen Prozeß – machen*, bring an action *or* institute proceedings against.

anhänglich ['anhɛŋlɪç], *adj.* attached, devoted. **Anhänglichkeit,** *f.* attachment, devotion, affection.

Anhängsel ['anhɛŋsəl], *n.* appendage (*Gen.*, to), adjunct, accessory; unimportant addition.

Anhauch ['anhaux], *m.* breath (*of wind*); afflation; slight tint; touch, trace, tinge. **anhauchen,** *v.t.* 1. breathe upon; 2. (*sl.*) blow up, tell *or* tick off.

anhauen ['anhauən], *irr.v.t.* 1. start cutting *or* felling; 2. (*sl.*) touch, tap, sting (*um*, for).

anhäufen ['anhɔyfən], **1.** *v.t.* heap *or* pile *or* stack up; accumulate, amass, stockpile (*supplies*); hoard (up); (*Philol.*) *angehäuft*, agglomerate, agglomerated. **2.** *v.r.* accumulate, gather (together), pile up, collect, mass (together), cluster. **Anhäufung,** *f.* accumulation, collection, pile, heap, clutter, cluster; mass; aggregation, agglomeration.

anheben ['anhe:bən], **1.** *irr.v.t.* 1. hoist, raise, lift; jack up (*vehicle*), prime (*a pump*); 2. begin, start, commence. **2.** *irr.v.i.* begin.

anheften ['anhɛftən], *v.t.* fasten, fix (on), attach, affix; sew on, tack *or* clip *or* pin (on) (*Dat.*, *an* (*Acc.*), to); *ihm etwas –*, cast a slur on him.

anheilen ['anhaɪlən], *v.i.* (*aux.* s.) heal up (*of wounds*), knit (*of bones*).

anheimeln ['anhaɪməln], *v.t.* remind (*a p.*) of home, make (*a p.*) feel at home. **anheimelnd,** *adj.* homely, cosy.

anheim|fallen [an'haɪm–], *irr.v.i.* (*aux* s.) 1. fall (*Dat.*, to), devolve (upon *or* to) (*of inheritance*); 2. fall (*Dat.*, into), fall a prey (to), be reduced (to). **–geben,** *irr.v.t.*, **–stellen,** *v.t. es ihm – zu tun*, leave it to him to do, rely on him to do; *dem Urteile eines andern anheimstellen*, submit to the judgement of another; *das Weitere ist ihm anheimgestellt*, the rest is in his hands *or* is up to him.

anheischig ['anhaɪʃɪç], *adj. sich – machen*, pledge o.s., promise, undertake.

anheizen ['anhaɪtsən], **1.** *v.t.* stoke up. **2.** *v.i.* start the fire *or* heating.

anher [an'he:r], *adv.* (*obs.*) hither; *bis –*, **anhero,** *adv.* (*obs.*) hitherto, up to now.

anherrschen ['anhɛrʃən], *v.t.* address imperiously; hector.

anhetzen ['anhɛtsən], *v.t. See* **aufhetzen.**

Anhieb ['anhi:p], *m.* first stroke *or* blow; (*coll.*) *auf –*, at the first attempt *or* shot *or* go.

anhimmeln ['anhɪməln], *v.t.* (*coll.*) go into raptures over (*a p.*).

Anhöhe ['anhø:ə], *f.* high ground, eminence, hillock, knoll, mound.

anhören ['anhø:rən], *v.t.* hear, listen to; *das läßt sich –*, that is worth listening to *or* considering; *das hört sich schlecht an*, that sounds bad; *man hört ihm den Ausländer an*, one can tell by his accent that he is a foreigner. **Anhörung,** *f.* hearing (*of witnesses etc.*).

Anilin [ani'li:n], *n.* (**-s**, *no pl.*) anilin. **Anilinfarben,** *pl.* aniline (*or* coal-tar) dyes.

animalisch [ani'ma:lɪʃ], *adj.* animal; brutish, sensual.

animieren [ani'mi:rən], *v.t.* stir *or* liven up, enliven, quicken, animate. **Animier|kneipe,** *f.* dubious night-club. **–mädchen,** *n.* girl (*barmaid or drinking partner employed for the purpose*) who incites the guests to drink. **animiert,** *adj.* animated, lively, (*coll.*) tipsy, merry.

Animus ['a:nimus], *m.* (-, *no pl.*) mind, notion, inkling.

Anis [a'ni:s], *m.* (**-(e)s**, *pl.* **-e**) aniseed.

anjetzo [an'jɛtso], **anjetzt,** *adv.* (*obs.*) *see* **jetzt.**

ankämpfen ['ankɛmpfən], *v.t.* fight, struggle, battle, contend (*gegen*, with *or* against).

Ankauf ['ankauf], *m.* purchase; acquisition (*by purchase*). **ankaufen, 1.** *v.t.* purchase, buy, buy up. **2.** *v.r.* buy land, settle (on one's own property).

Anken ['aŋkən], *m.* (-, *no pl.*) (*Swiss*) butter.

Anker ['aŋkər], *m.* 1. anchor; ***vor – gehen, den – werfen,*** cast anchor, anchor; ***vor – liegen,*** ride *or* lie at anchor; ***den – lichten,*** weigh anchor; 2. (*Elec.*) armature, rotor; keeper (*of magnet*); (*Horol.*) pallet.

Anker|boje, *f.* anchor-buoy. **–fliege,** *f. See* **–flügel. –flott,** *n. See* **–boje. –flügel,** *m.* fluke of an anchor. **–geld,** *n.* harbour-dues. **–grund,** *m.* anchorage. **–hemmung,** *f.* (*Horol.*) lever escapement. **–kern,** *m.* armature core. **–klüse,** *f.* (*Naut.*) hawse-pipe. **ankerlos,** *adj.* adrift (*of ship*).

ankern ['aŋkərn], *v.t., v.i.* anchor; moor, (*fig.*) anchor, brace, tie.

Anker|platz, *m.* anchorage, berth. **–spannung,** *f.* (*Elec.*) armature voltage. **–strom,** *m.* (*Elec.*) armature current. **–tau,** *n.* anchor-cable. **–uhr,** *f.* lever-watch. **–welle,** *f.* armature shaft, (*Horol.*) pallet staff. **–wicklung,** *f.* armature winding. **–winde,** *f.* windlass, capstan.

anketten ['ankɛtən], *v.t.* chain (up).

ankitten ['ankɪtən], *v.t.* cement, fasten with putty.

anklagbar ['ankla:kba:r], *adj.* indictable, actionable (*of a deed*), chargeable, impeachable (*of a p.*).

Anklage ['ankla:gə], *f.* charge, accusation, indictment, impeachment, arraignment; ***Vertreter der –,*** counsel for the prosecution. **Anklagebank,** *f.* (*Law*) dock.

anklagen ['ankla:gən], *v.t.* accuse (***wegen*** *or Gen.*, of), charge (with), indict, arraign, impeach (for).

Ankläger ['anklɛ:gər], *m.* accuser, (*Law*) plaintiff; ***öffentlicher –,*** Public Prosecutor.

Anklage|rede, *f.* (*Law*) speech for the prosecution. **–schrift,** *f.* (*Law*) indictment, (*Mil.*) charge-sheet; bill of indictment.

anklammern ['anklamərn], **1.** *v.t.* fasten *or* clip on (***an*** (*Acc.*), to). **2.** *v.r.* cling (on), hold *or* hang on (***an*** (*Acc.*), to), keep tight hold (of). **Anklammerungspunkt,** *m.* (*Mil.*) strong point, centre of resistance.

Anklang ['anklaŋ], *m.* 1. (*Mus.*) accord; 2. favour, approval, approbation (***bei,*** with); ***der Vorschlag fand keinen –,*** the proposal did not find favour *or* met with no approval; 3. reminiscence, echo (***an*** (*Acc.*), of).

ankleben ['ankle:bən], **1.** *v.i.* stick, adhere (***an*** (*Acc.*), to). **2.** *v.t.* stick *or* gum *or* glue *or* paste (on) (***an*** (*Acc.*), to). **anklebend,** *adj.* adhesive; adherent. **Ankleber,** *m.* bill-sticker, billposter.

ankleiden ['anklaɪdən], **1.** *v.t.* dress, clothe, attire, robe. **2.** *v.r.* dress (o.s.), get dressed. **Ankleidepuppe,** *f.* naked doll (*that can be dressed*). **Ankleider,** *m.* (*Theat.*) dresser. **Ankleideraum,** *m.* dressing-room, changing-room; (*Eccl.*) vestry. **Ankleiderin,** *f. See* **Ankleider. Ankleide|-zimmer,** *n. See* **–raum.**

anklingeln ['anklɪŋəln], **1.** *v.t.* ***ihn –,*** ring him up (*on the telephone*). **2.** *v.i.* 1. ring the bell; 2. (*coll.*) ***bei ihm –,*** sound him.

anklingen ['anklɪŋən], **1.** *irr.v.i.* remind slightly, awaken *or* stir up memories (***an*** (*Acc.*), of). **2.** *irr. v.t.* clink (*glasses*).

anklopfen ['anklɔpfən], *v.i.* knock, hammer, rap (***an*** (*Acc.*), on *or* at); ***bei ihm –,*** knock at his door, call on him, (*coll.*) sound him (***wegen,*** about). **Anklopfer,** *m.* (door-)knocker.

anknöpfen ['anknœpfən], *v.t.* button on (***an*** (*Acc.*), to).

anknüpfen ['anknypfən], **1.** *v.t.* 1. tie, fasten, knot (***an*** (*Acc.*), to), (*fig.*) attach (to), connect, link up (with); 2. initiate, start, begin, enter into; ***Verbindungen –,*** establish relations; ***ein Gespräch wieder –,*** resume a conversation; ***eine Bekanntschaft –,*** strike up an acquaintance. **2.** *v.i.* link up, be linked up *or* connected (***an*** (*Acc.*), with). **Anknüpfung,** *f.* connexion, link; ***in – an,*** with reference to, referring to. **Anknüpfungspunkt,** *m.* point of contact, starting-point.

ankommen ['ankɔmən], **1.** *irr.v.i.* (*aux.* s.) 1. arrive; ***zu Hause –,*** arrive *or* get home; ***–de Briefe,*** incoming letters; 2. ***– auf*** (*Acc.*), depend on, be a question *or* matter of; ***es kommt mir darauf an, zu*** (*inf.*), it is (a matter) of importance *or* is important to me to (*inf.*); ***darauf kommt es an,*** that is the main thing *or* the point; ***als es darauf ankam,*** when it came to the point; ***darauf soll es nicht –,*** never mind about that; ***es kommt auf die Sekunde an,*** every second counts; ***es kommt ihm nicht auf einen Tag an,*** one day makes no difference to him; ***es darauf – lassen,*** leave it to chance, trust to luck; ***ich lasse es darauf –,*** I'll chance *or* risk it; ***es auf ihn – lassen,*** leave it to him, rely on him; 3. (*coll.*) ***– bei,*** be received by, get a reception from; ***bei ihm gut –,*** be well received by *or* successful with him; ***gegen ihn nicht –,*** be powerless against him; ***übel –,*** be ill *or* not well received; ***bei dem Geschäft gut*** (***schlecht***) ***–,*** make a profitable (unprofitable) deal; ***bei der Firma –,*** get a job *or* find employment with the firm; (*iron.*) ***da kam sie schön an!*** she got more than she bargained for; 4. (*coll.*) register, get across (*as a play etc.*); ***bei kleinen Kindern kommt das nicht an,*** that won't get home to small children; ***bei mir kommt man damit nicht an,*** that will not do for me, that cuts no ice with me. **2.** *irr.v.t., v.i.* (*aux.* s.) come upon, overcome; ***es kommt mich*** or (*coll.*) ***mir schwer an,*** it comes hard on me; ***was kommt dich*** or (*coll.*) ***dir an?*** what is the matter with you? what has come over you? (*coll.*) what's up with you? ***es kam mich*** or (*coll.*) ***mir eine Furcht an,*** I was overcome with fear. *See* **Ankunft.**

Ankömmling ['ankœmlɪŋ], *m.* (**-s,** *pl.* **-e**) newcomer, recent arrival.

ankörnen ['ankœrnən], *v.t.* mark the centre (*with a punch*). **Ankörner,** *m.* centre-punch.

ankreiden ['ankraɪdən], *v.t.* chalk (up); (*sl.*) ***etwas – lassen,*** have it chalked up *or* put on the slate; get it on tick; (*sl.*) ***das werde ich ihm schön –,*** I won't forget this in a hurry.

ankünden ['ankyndən], *v.t.* (*obs.*) *see* **ankündigen.**

ankündigen ['ankyndɪgən], *v.t.* announce, make known, give notice of; declare, proclaim; publish, advertise; (*fig.*) promise, foretell, herald, augur, usher in. **Ankündigung,** *f.* declaration, proclamation, announcement; notification, prospectus. **Ankündigungsbefehl,** *m.* (*Mil.*) cautionary word of command.

Ankunft ['ankunft], *f.* (-, *pl.* **¨e**) arrival, coming, (*Theol.*) advent.

ankuppeln ['ankupəln], *v.t.* couple up *or* on, connect (***an*** (*Acc.*), to).

ankurbeln ['ankurbəln], *v.t.* wind *or* crank up; (*fig.*) stimulate, boost.

Anlage ['anla:gə], *f.* 1. (*verbal noun*) installation, establishment, construction, erection, building; *see* **anlegen**; 2. installation, establishment, factory, works, plant; equipment; 3. (*verbal noun*) arrangement, disposition, ordering, construction, composition; lay-out, structure; 4. (public) park *or* grounds *or* enclosure, pleasure-ground, (ornamental) garden, laid-out walk, promenade; 5. design, plan, (rough) draft *or* sketch, outline, skeleton; 6. (*Comm.*) investment, invested capital; 7. (*Comm.*) enclosure; ***in der –,*** enclosed, herewith (enclosed); 8. natural inclination *or* tendency, predisposition (***zu,*** to), (*Med.*) diathesis, (*Biol.*) anlage; (*fig.*) aptness, aptitude, (natural) gift *or* bent *or* turn (***zu,*** for).

Anlage|kapital, *n.* invested capital, capital invested *or* available for investment, fixed assets *or* capital. **–kosten,** *pl.* initial outlay, cost of construction *or* installation, promotion costs.

anlagern ['anla:gərn], *v.t., v.r.* accumulate. **Anlagerung,** *f.* accumulation, (*Geol.*) juxtaposition (*of strata*).

Anlage|vermögen, *n. See* **–kapital. –wert,** *m.* (*Comm.*) security, investment.

anlangen ['anlaŋən], **1.** *v.i.* (*aux.* s.) arrive at, reach. **2.** *v.imp.* concern, relate to; ***was mich anlangt,*** as regards me, as far as I am concerned. **anlangend,** *prep.* (*Acc.*) with *or* in regard to, with respect to, as far as . . . is concerned, as for.

Anlaß ['anlas], *m.* (-**(ss)es**, *pl.* **¨(ss)e**) cause, occasion, incentive, reason (*zu*, for, to (*do*)), grounds, motive (*zu*, for (*doing*)); ***auf* –** (*Gen.*), on orders *or* instructions from, by order of; at the instigation of; ***ohne jeden* –**, gratuitously, for no reason at all; ***zu einem Gerüchte* – *geben***, give rise to rumours *or* a report.

anlassen ['anlasən], **1.** *irr.v.t.* 1. leave on, leave running (*as an engine*); 2. set going, start (*an engine*), turn on (*water etc.*); 3. temper (*metals*); 4. set (*dogs*) (***auf*** (*Acc.*), on *or* at), (*fig.*) ***hart*** or ***scharf*** or ***übel* –**, be uncivil *or* sharp with, treat with scant courtesy. **2.** *irr.v.r.* make a start; ***sich gut*** (***schlecht***) –, make a good (bad) start, show (no) great promise, promise well (ill), (not) look (at all) promising, (*coll.*) come along nicely. **Anlasser,** *m.* (*Motor.*) (self-)starter.

Anlaß|farbe, *f.* oxidization tint (*tempering metals*). **–kraftstoff,** *m.* primer *or* priming fuel. **–kurbel,** *f.* (*Motor.*) starting-handle.

anläßlich ['anlɛslɪç], *prep.* (*Gen.*) apropos of; on the occasion of.

Anlaßofen ['anlasˀo:fən], *m.* annealing *or* tempering furnace.

Anlauf ['anlauf], *m.* 1. take-off, run (up), approach run, (*Av.*) take-off run; (*fig.*) start; 2. (*Mil.*) rush, charge; ***im ersten* –**, (*also fig.*) at the first attempt *or* (*coll.*) shot *or* go, right away, straight off; 3. rising, swelling (*of water*); 4. tarnish, film (*on metal*), mist (*on glass*), (*Metall.*) oxidization tint.

anlaufen ['anlaufən], **1.** *irr.v.i.* (*aux.* s.) 1. run up; 2. rush (***gegen***, at), run (into), collide (with), (*fig.*) run counter (to), be contrary (to), go (against); ***bei ihm übel* –**, come *or* run up against his opposition, be rebuffed by him; (*iron.*) ***da bin ich schön angelaufen!*** I've come up against it nicely! I'm in a nice mess! that's a fine to-do! (*coll.*) ***ihn* – *lassen***, let *or* make him put his foot in it; 3. start (up) (*of an engine*); **–** ***lassen***, start (up) (*an engine*); 4. rise, swell (*as water*), collect (*as puddles*), mount *or* add up (*as bills, debts*) (***auf*** (*Acc.*), to), swell up (*as a limb*); 5. become tarnished *or* discoloured, tarnish, discolour, mist *or* film over, go mouldy *or* mildewed; ***angelaufen***, swollen; tarnished; mildewed. **2.** *irr.v.t.* run *or* rush at; (*Naut.*) make *or* run for (*a harbour*), call *or* touch at, put in at (*a port*); (*coll.*) bother, pester, badger (*a p.*).

Anlauf|farbe, *f. See* **Anlaßfarbe. –hafen,** *m.* port of call. **–streifen,** *m.* (*Films*) leader. **–temperatur,** *f.* (*Metall.*) tempering temperature.

Anlaut ['anlaut], *m.* (*Phonet.*) initial sound. **anlauten,** *v.i.* begin (***mit***, with) (*of a word*), be in the initial position (*of a sound*).

anläuten ['anlɔytən], **1.** *v.i.* ring the bell. **2.** *v.t.* (*Tele.*) ring *or* (*Am.*) call up.

anlautend ['anlautənt], *adj.* initial.

Anlege|brücke, *f.* jetty, landing-stage. **–hafen,** *m.* port of call.

anlegen ['anle:gən], **1.** *v.t.* 1. lay *or* put on, apply; ***Feuer* –**, set fire (***an*** (*Acc.*), to), set on fire; ***das Gewehr* –**, bring the gun to the shoulder *or* the firing position, take aim; ***auf ihn* –**, point *or* level a gun at him, aim at him; (*fig.*) ***das war auf mich angelegt***, that was aimed at *or* meant *or* intended for me; ***es darauf* – *zu tun***, aim at doing, make it one's aim *or* object to do, make a point of doing, be set *or* bent *or* intent on doing, go out of one's way to do; ***Holz* –**, put wood on (the fire); ***ihm Fesseln*** or ***Ketten* –**, fetter him, put him in fetters *or* chains *or* irons; ***Trauer* –**, go into mourning; 2. invest (*capital*), spend (*one's money*) (***in*** (*Dat.*), on), use, make use of, employ (*one's time*); 3. set out, arrange, dispose; found, establish, construct, set up; put in, install, (*coll.*) fix up, lay on; lay *or* plan out, design, sketch out, draw up, work out; (*Hist.*) ***eine Kolonie* –**, found *or* establish a colony; ***groß angelegt***, on a grand scale. **2.** *v.i.* (*Naut.*) come *or* draw alongside; land, put ashore; moor, make fast. **3.** *v.r.* 1. press *or* flatten o.s. (***an*** (*Acc.*), against); attach o.s. (to); 2. (*Chem.*) form a deposit, settle.

Anlege|schloß, *n.* padlock. **–stelle,** *f. See* **–brücke.**

Anlegung ['anle:guŋ], *f.* 1. application (***an*** (*Acc.*), to); 2. disposition; 3. construction, installation; 4. investment (*of money*).

anlehnen ['anle:nən], **1.** *v.t.* lean, prop, rest, support (***an*** (*Acc.*), on *or* against); ***die Tür* –** or ***angelehnt lassen***, leave the door ajar *or* on the latch; (*Mil.*) ***angelehnt sein***, be supported *or* covered; ***beiderseits angelehnt***, covered *or* supported on both flanks. **2.** *v.r.* ***sich* – *an*** (*Acc.*), (*of a p.*) lean upon, base o.s. *or* rely on, follow (the example of), imitate; (*of a th.*) rest, be based *or* modelled *or* dependent on; (*Mil.*) be covered *or* supported by.

Anlehnung ['anle:nuŋ], *f.* dependence (***an*** (*Acc.*), on); (*Mil.*) support; ***in* – *an***, under the influence of, in imitation of (*an author*); referring back to (*s.th. mentioned earlier*). **Anlehnungsbedürfnis,** *n.* lack of self-assurance. **anlehnungsbedürftig,** *adj.* lacking self-assurance.

Anleihe ['anlaɪə], *f.* loan (*of money*), borrowing (*of ideas*); *pl.* government stock, bonds. **Anleihe|ablösung,** *f.* redemption of a loan, amortization. **–kapital,** *n.*, **–schuld,** *f.* bonded debt.

anleimen ['anlaɪmən], *v.t.* glue *or* stick on. **anleimend,** *adj.* (*Philol.*) agglutinative.

anleiten ['anlaɪtən], *v.t.* guide, lead, give a lead, give initial guidance, introduce (*to a study etc.*) (***zu***, to); (*Hort.*) train (*a plant*). **Anleitung,** *f.* 1. direction, guidance; 2. preliminary instruction; introduction; primer.

Anlernberuf ['anlɛrnbəru:f], *m.* occupation requiring training (*as clerks trained to become factory hands in war-time*).

anlernen ['anlɛrnən], *v.t.* acquire by study; ***angelernter Arbeiter***, worker on completion of transfer-training. **Anlernling,** *m.* (**-s**, *pl.* **-e**) trainee (*under emergency training scheme*).

anleuchten ['anlɔyçtən], *v.t.* direct light on to, spotlight; (*of searchlight*) pick up (*a target*).

anliefern ['anli:fərn], *v.t.* deliver, supply (*goods*).

anliegen ['anli:gən], *irr.v.i.* 1. lie close, be adjacent *or* contiguous (***an*** (*Dat.*), to); border *or* abut (on), adjoin; 2. fit, sit (*of clothes*); ***eng* –**, be a close *or* tight *or* snug fit; 3. (*Naut.*) steer a course to, head for *or* to, stand to; ***landwärts* –**, stand in to land; ***seewärts* –**, stand out to sea; 4. (*imp. with Dat.*) concern; ***es liegt ihm an***, it is a matter of concern *or* consequence to him; ***angelegen***, of importance *or* consequence, important; ***es sich*** (*Dat.*) ***angelegen sein lassen*** (***zu tun***), make it one's business *or* concern *or* duty (to do), make a point (of doing), make every endeavour (to do); ***ich habe nichts Angelegeneres zu tun als***, my only concern is, I am above all concerned to; 5. ***ihm* –**, importune *or* pester *or* bother him. **Anliegen,** *n.* 1. concern; 2. petition, entreaty, suit, request, desire, wish. **anliegend,** *adj.* adjoining, neighbouring, abutting, bordering, contiguous, adjacent (*also Geom.*); (*Comm.*) attached, enclosed, annexed; (*Bot.*) accumbent; ***eng –es Kleid***, close- *or* tight-fitting dress.

Anlieger ['anli:gər], *m.* (*Law*) abutter; ***Parkplatz nur für* –**, parking only for residents. **Anlieger|siedlung,** *f.* factory estate. **–verkehr,** *m.* access only for residents.

anlocken ['anlɔkən], *v.t.* lure, decoy; (*fig.*) allure, attract, entice. **Anlockung,** *f.* enticement, attraction, allurement. **Anlockungsmittel,** *n.* lure, decoy, bait.

anlöten ['anlø:tən], *v.t.* solder on (***an*** (*Acc.*), to).

anlügen ['anly:gən], *irr.v.t.* ***ihn* –**, lie to his face, lie brazenly to him.

anluven ['anlu:fən], *v.i.* go to windward, luff.

anmachen ['anmaxən], *v.t.* 1. fasten, fix, attach (***an*** (*Acc.*), to); 2. prepare, mix; light (*a fire*); mix, adulterate; ***einen Salat* –**, dress a salad; ***Beton* –**, mix concrete; ***Kalk* –**, slake lime.

anmalen ['anma:lən], *v.t.* paint (on); give (*s.th.*) a coat of paint.

Anmarsch ['anmarʃ], *m.* approach march, advance (*of troops*). **anmarschieren,** *v.i.* (*aux.* s.) advance, approach.

anmaßen ['anma:sən], *v.t. sich* (*Dat.*) *etwas* –, *sich* (*Dat.*) – *etwas zu* (*inf.*), presume, take it upon o.s., feel entitled *or* qualified to, lay claim to, pretend to, claim, pretend; assume, usurp, arrogate to o.s.; *was maßest du dir an?* what presumption! **anmaßend, anmaßlich,** *adj.* presumptuous, arrogant, insolent, overweening. **Anmaßung,** *f.* 1. presumption, presumptuousness, insolence, effrontery, arrogance; (*coll.*) cheek; 2. usurpation; assumption, arrogation (*of power etc.*).

Anmelde|frist, *f.* (interval before the) closing date; – *bis zum* . . ., closing date for applications . . . **-gebühr,** *f.* registration *or* entrance fee.

anmelden ['anmɛldən], *v.t.* announce, notify, give notice of; enrol(l), enter (*s.o.'s*) name, report, register; *ich bin angemeldet,* I have an appointment; *sich* –, announce o.s., report one's arrival; *sich* – *lassen,* have o.s. announced; *sich zu etwas* –, enter for, go in for a (*a competition*). **Anmelde|pflicht,** *f.* obligation to register (with the police). **-stelle,** *f.* registration office, registry (office). **Anmeldung,** *f.* announcement, notification, registration; *ohne* –, without (making) an appointment. **Anmeldungsformular,** *n.* registration form, application *or* entry form.

anmerken ['anmɛrkən], *v.t.* 1. make *or* take a note of, note *or* jot down; 2. mark, indicate (*with a mark*); 3. (*Dat.*) perceive, see, not fail to notice; *laß dir nichts* –*!* don't give yourself *or* (*coll.*) the show *or* game away, (*coll.*) don't let the cat out of the bag; 4. observe (*orally*), remark. **Anmerkung,** *f.* 1. (foot-)note, annotation; *Text mit -en,* annotated text; 2. observation (*oral*), remark.

anmessen ['anmɛsən], *irr.v.t.* measure, take measurements for; *ihm einen Anzug* –, measure him *or* take his measurements for a suit. *See* **angemessen.**

anmustern ['anmustərn], **1.** *v.t.* enlist (*soldiers*); sign on (*a crew*). **2.** *v.i.* sign on (*of seamen*).

Anmut ['anmu:t], *f.* (-, *no pl.*) grace, charm, attractiveness, pleasantness, sweetness; gracefulness, elegance, graciousness.

anmuten ['anmu:tən], *v.imp. es mutet mich fremd an,* it strikes me as strange.

anmutig ['anmu:tɪç], *adj.* graceful, charming, pleasant, agreeable, attractive. **Anmutigkeit,** *f. See* **Anmut. anmutlos,** *adj.* ungraceful, graceless, devoid of charm, unlovely, uncouth, awkward. **anmutsvoll,** *adj. See* **anmutig.**

Anmutung ['anmu:tuŋ], *f. See* **Zumutung.**

annähen ['annɛ:ən], *v.t.* sew on (*an* (*Acc.*), to).

annähern ['annɛ:ərn], **1.** *v.t.* approximate, bring nearer *or* closer (*Dat.*, *an* (*Acc.*), to). **2.** *v.r.* approach, draw *or* come near (*Dat.*, to), (*Math.*) approximate (to) (*of values*), converge, approach one another (*of lines*). **annähernd, 1.** *adj.* approximate (*value*), converging (*lines*). **2.** *adv.* approximately, roughly; (*coll.*) *nicht* –, nothing like, nowhere near. **Annäherung,** *f.* 1. approach, convergence (*of lines*), approximation (*of values*); 2. reconciliation, rapprochement, understanding. **Annäherungs|graben,** *m.* approach *or* (*Mil.*) communication trench. **-versuch,** *m.* attempted rapprochement, overture. **-wert,** *m.* approximate figure *or* value, approximation.

Annahme ['anna:mə], *f.* 1. acceptance, receipt; engagement (*of a servant*); adoption (*of opinions, of children*); (*Comm.*) – *eines Wechsels verweigern,* dishonour a bill; *einem Wechsel eine willige* – *bereiten,* meet *or* duly honour a bill; 2. supposition, assumption, postulation; hypothesis; *alles spricht für die* –, there is every reason to believe. **Annahme|pflicht,** *f.* obligation to accept (legal tender). **-stelle,** *f.* receiving office. **-vermerk,** *m.* (*Comm.*) endorsement. **-verweigerung,** *f.* (*Comm.*) non-acceptance; refusal to accept.

Annalen [a'na:lən], *pl.* annals, records.

Annamit [ana'mi:t], *m.* (**-en,** *pl.* **-en**) Annamese. **annamitisch,** *adj.* Annamese.

Annaten [a'na:tən], *pl.* annates, first fruits; (*R.C.*) annals.

annehmbar ['anne:mba:r], *adj.* 1. acceptable, admissible, allowable; reasonable, plausible, passable, tolerable; 2. assumable, supposable. **Annehmbarkeit,** *f.* acceptability, admissibility.

annehmen ['anne:mən], *irr.v.t.* 1. accept; take (*pupils etc., employment, advice, polish, colour etc.*), take on (*applicant, task, responsibility, appearance*), take up (*challenge*), receive (*visit*), adopt (*child, name, view,* (*Pol.*) *resolution*), assume (*character, appearance, attitude, form*), undertake (*commission*), agree to (*condition, proposal*), (*Comm.*) honour (*a bill*), embrace (*a faith*), contract (*a habit*), acquire (*accent*), develop (*taste for*), pick up (*the scent*); *einstimmig* –, carry unanimously; *nicht* –, (*Pol.*) reject (*resolution*); (*Comm.*) dishonour (*a bill*); *Vernunft* or *Verstand* –, listen to *or* see reason; *Waren* –, accept *or* take delivery of goods; (*Law*) *an Kindes Statt* –, adopt; *sich einer S.* (*Gen.*) –, take care of *or* attend to a th., take a th. under one's care, (*coll.*) look after *or* see to a th.; espouse, (*coll.*) take up (*a cause*); *angenommen,* adopted (*child*), assumed (*name*), received, accepted, recognized (*doctrines etc.*); 2. assume, suppose, presume, believe, understand, accept, (*coll.*) take it (that); *angenommen daß,* supposing *or* assuming *or* granting that, if we take it that, if we take that (to be). *See* **Annahme. annehmlich,** *adj. See* **annehmbar. Annehmlichkeit,** *f.* 1. convenience; attractiveness, pleasantness; charm; 2. *pl.* amenities, comforts.

annektieren [anɛk'ti:rən], *v.t.* annex. **Annektierung,** *f.* annexation.

annoch [an'nɔx], *adv.* (*obs.*) as yet, hitherto.

Annonce [a'nɔ̃sə], *f.* (small) advertisement. **Annoncenexpedition,** *f.* advertising agency. **annoncieren** [–'si:rən], **1.** *v.t.* announce; advertise. **2.** *v.i.* advertise, put in an advertisement.

Annuität [anui'tɛ:t], *f.* annuity; *aufgeschobene* –, deferred annuity.

annullierbar [anu'li:rba:r], *adj.* (*Law*) voidable, defeasible.

annullieren [anu'li:rən], *v.t.* annul, nullify; (*Law*) repeal, quash, rescind, render void, revoke, set aside; (*Comm.*) cancel, countermand. **Annullierung,** *f.* annulment, nullification; (*Law*) repeal, revocation, rescission; (*Comm.*) cancellation.

Anode [a'no:də], *f.* anode, (*Rad.*) plate.

anöden ['anˀø:dən], *v.t.* (*sl.*) bore, weary.

Anoden|batterie, *f.* high-tension battery. **-gleichrichter,** *m.* anode-bend rectifier. **-schutznetz,** *n.* anode screen. **-widerstand,** *m.* anode load *or* resistor.

anomal ['anoma:l], *adj.* anomalous. **Anomalie** [–'li:], *f.* anomaly.

anonym [ano'ny:m], *adj.* anonymous, unnamed. **Anonymität** [–i'tɛ:t], *f.* (-, *no pl.*) anonymity.

Anorak ['anorak], *m.* (**-s,** *pl.* **-s**) windcheater.

anordnen ['anˀɔrdnən], *v.t.* 1. order, command, decree, direct; 2. put *or* set in order, arrange, regulate; marshal, dispose, array (*troops for battle*). **Anordner,** *m.* director; p. in charge of arrangements. **Anordnung,** *f.* 1. arrangement, disposal, disposition; regulation, direction; order, lay-out, grouping, structure; 2. instruction, direction, command, order; *pl.* arrangements, provisions, dispositions; *-en treffen,* make arrangements; give orders *or* instructions; *auf* – *des Arztes,* on doctor's orders.

Anorganiker ['anˀɔrga:nɪkər], *m.* inorganic chemist. **anorganisch,** *adj.* inorganic.

anormal ['anɔrma:l], *adj.* (*very common faulty contamination of* **anomal** *and* **abnorm**) abnormal.

anpacken ['anpakən], *v.t.* lay *or* take *or* catch *or* grasp *or* grab hold of, seize, grasp, grip, grab, clutch; (*fig.*) tackle (*a problem*).

anpassen ['anpasən], **1.** *v.t.* 1. try *or* fit on (*garment*); 2. (make) fit, adapt, adjust, accommodate, suit

(*Dat.*, to), make suitable (for). **2.** *v.r.* adapt, accommodate *or* adjust o.s., conform (*Dat.*, to). **Anpassung,** *f.* 1. fitting, trying-on (*garment*); 2. (*Biol.*) adaptation; adjustment, accommodation; conformation (***an*** (*Acc.*), to), conformity (to *or* with); 3. (*Phonet.*) partial assimilation (*of consonant*). **Anpassungsbüchse,** *f.* (*Elec.*) (plug) adaptor. **anpassungsfähig,** *adj.* adaptable (*also Biol.*), adaptive (***an*** (*Acc.*), to); flexible; (*of a p.*) accommodating. **Anpassungsfähigkeit,** *f.* adaptability (*also Biol.*), adaptiveness; flexibility, suppleness (*of character etc.*).

anpeilen ['anpaılən], *v.t.* take a bearing on.

anpflanzen ['anpflantsən], *v.t.* plant, grow (*trees*); cultivate. **Anpflanzer,** *m.* planter, settler, colonist. **Anpflanzung,** *f.* planting, cultivation, plantation.

anpflöcken ['anpflœkən], *v.t.* fasten with pegs; stretch (*a canvas*), tether to a post.

anpinseln ['anpınzəln], *v.t.* daub, brush over; paint, varnish (*fingernails*).

anpirschen ['anpırʃən], *v.r.* stalk; (*fig.*) approach stealthily.

anpöbeln ['anpø:bəln], *v.t.* abuse, vilify.

anpochen ['anpɔxən], *v.i.* knock (***an*** (*Acc.*), on *or* at); ***bei ihm –,*** knock at his door.

Anprall ['anpral], *m.* 1. collision (***gegen, an*** (*Acc.*), with), crash (against), impact (on); 2. shock, brunt. **anprallen,** *v.i.* (*aux.* s.) knock *or* strike (***gegen, an*** (*Acc.*), against), collide (with), run (against *or* into), impinge (on).

anprangern ['anpraŋərn], *v.t.* pillory, denounce.

anpreisen ['anpraızən], *irr.v.t.* praise, extol, commend; (*coll.*) boost, crack up. **Anpreisung,** *f.* (high) praise, commendation.

Anprobe ['anpro:bə], *f.* fitting (on), trying-on. **anprobieren,** *v.t.* try on (*clothes*).

anpumpen ['anpumpən], *v.t.* (*sl.*) borrow money from; touch (***um,*** for).

Anputz ['anputs], *m.* 1. finery, fine clothes; 2. plaster(ing). **anputzen,** *v.t.* 1. dress up, decorate; (*coll.*) get (*s.o.*) up; ***sich –,*** adorn *or* bedeck o.s., dress up, get o.s. up, deck o.s. out; 2. plaster (*a wall*).

anquicken ['ankvıkən], *v.t.* amalgamate (*metals*).

anranken ['anraŋkən], *v.r.* cling with its tendrils, (***an*** (*Acc.*), to), twine itself (around).

anranzen ['anrantsən], *v.t.* (*coll.*) ***ihn –,*** give him a severe dressing-down, pitch into him, bite his head off.

anraten ['anra:tən], *irr.v.t.* ***ihm etwas –,*** advise him to do s.th., recommend s.th. to him. **Anraten,** *n.* advice, counsel; ***auf sein –,*** on his advice.

anrauchen ['anrauxən], *v.t.* begin to smoke; smoke for the first time (*a new pipe*); blacken with smoke; ***eine Pfeife –,*** season a pipe; ***eine Zigarre –,*** light (up) a cigar; ***angeraucht,*** smoke-blackened; seasoned (*of a pipe*), already started (*of a cigar*).

anräuchern ['anrɔyçərn], *v.t.* fumigate; burn incense over.

anrechnen ['anrɛçnən], *v.t.* debit, charge; credit, allow; take into account; count to (*s.o.'s*) credit, give credit for; ***ihm etwas –,*** charge s.th. to him *or* him with s.th.; ***er hat es mir billig angerechnet,*** he let me have it cheap; ***ich rechne ihm diesen Dienst hoch an,*** I value his service highly. **Anrechnung,** *f.* allowance (***auf*** (*Acc.*), on *or* for), deduction (from); ***in – bringen,*** take into account *or* consideration, make allowance(s) for, allow for; take in part exchange, make an allowance *or* allow something on *or* for.

Anrecht ['anrɛçt], *n.* claim, title, right; ***ein – auf eine S. haben,*** have a right *or* be entitled to a th.

Anrede ['anre:də], *f.* 1. speech, address, harangue; 2. form of address, salutation; 3. (*Gram.*) apostrophe. **Anredefall,** *m.* (*Gram.*) vocative case. **anreden,** *v.t.* speak to, address; accost; apostrophize.

anregen ['anre:gən], *v.t.* incite, instigate, give fresh impetus to, stimulate, encourage, prompt, (*coll.*) get going; initiate, originate (*scheme*), raise, bring up, suggest (*subject*), whet (*appetite*); act as a stimulant (*as tea*), be stimulating (*as a book*); ***angeregt,*** lively, animated, spirited. **anregend,** *adj.* stimulating, stirring; (*Med.*) ***–es Mittel,*** excitant, stimulant. **Anregung,** *f.* stimulation, incitement, instigation (***zu,*** to); (*Med.*) excitation, (*Chem. etc.*) actuation; initiation (*of a scheme etc.*); animation, excitement; stimulus, impulse, initial idea, suggestion.

anreiben ['anraıbən], *irr.v.t.* rub on, apply with a rag.

anreichern ['anraıçərn], *v.t.* enrich, strengthen, concentrate. **Anreicherung,** *f.* enrichment (*of soil*), concentration (*of solution*).

anreihen ['anraıən], **1.** *v.t.* attach, join, add (*Dat.*, ***an*** (*Acc.*), to); ***aneinander –,*** co-ordinate (*clauses*). **2.** *v.r.* follow on, line up; form a queue, queue up; (*Math.*) continue a series. **anreihend,** *adj.* (*Gram.*) copulative. **Anreihung,** *f.* sequence, series; chain (*of events*); (*Gram.*) co-ordination.

Anreim ['anraım], *m.* alliteration. **anreimen,** *v.i.* alliterate. **anreimend,** *adj.* alliterative.

anreißen ['anraısən], *irr.v.t.* 1. tear slightly *or* the edge of, make a small tear in; (*fig.*) break into (*savings etc.*); 2. trace, sketch, make a first sketch; 3. notch (*tree etc.*), make *or* scratch a line on, mark (out) a line on; 4. (*coll.*) press (*s.o.*) to buy, tout (*s.o.*) for custom. **Anreißer,** *m.* 1. scriber; 2. (*coll.*) barker, tout, cheap-jack.

Anreiz ['anraıts], *m.* 1. incitement, stimulus, incentive, inducement (***zu,*** to); 2. attraction, appeal. **anreizen,** *v.t.* incite, stimulate, instigate; tempt, prompt, (*coll.*) egg on (***zu,*** to). **anreizend,** *adj.* attractive, seductive, alluring, enticing, tempting, provocative. **Anreizung,** *f.* *See* **Anreiz.**

anrempeln ['anrɛmpəln], *v.t.* (*coll.*) jostle, barge into.

anrennen ['anrɛnən], **1.** *irr.v.t.* rush at *or* into. **2.** *irr. v.i.* (*aux.* s.) rush *or* charge (***gegen,*** at); run (into); ***übel angerannt sein,*** get more than one bargained for, catch a Tartar; ***angerannt kommen,*** come running up.

Anrichte ['anrıçtə], *f.* dresser, sideboard.

anrichten ['anrıçtən], *v.t.* 1. produce, cause, give rise to; ***was hast du angerichtet?*** what have you done? (*coll.*) ***da haben Sie was Schönes angerichtet,*** you have really put your foot in it; 2. prepare; serve (up) (*a meal*); dress (*timber, a salad*); ***es ist angerichtet,*** the meal is served. **Anrichte|tisch,** *m.* kitchen-table, dresser. **–zimmer,** *n.* pantry.

anriechen ['anri:çən], *irr.v.t.* smell (at); ***ich habe ihm den Tabak angerochen,*** I noticed that he smelt of tobacco.

Anriß ['anrıs], *m.* crack, flaw, scratch.

Anritt ['antrıt], *m.* approach on horseback; cavalry charge.

anrollen ['anrɔlən], *v.i.* (*aux.* s.) roll up, (*Av.*) taxi up, (*Mil.*) be brought up (*of supplies*).

anrosten ['anrɔstən], *v.i.* (*aux.* s.) rust, get rusty *or* rusted on (*as a nut*).

anrüchig ['anryçıç], *adj.* of bad reputation *or* ill repute; disreputable; (*coll.*) ***–es Wort,*** dirty word. **Anrüchigkeit,** *f.* 1. bad reputation, ill-repute, disrepute; 2. shadiness, (*coll.*) fishiness.

anrücken ['anrykən], **1.** *v.i.* (*aux.* s.) approach, draw near (*of troops*), move forward *or* up, advance. **2.** *v.t.* move *or* bring nearer (***an*** (*Acc.*), to).

Anruf ['anruf], *m.* call, appeal; (*Mil.*) challenge (*of a sentry*); telephone call; (*Rad.*) call signal. **anrufen,** *irr.v.t.* 1. call (to), hail (*ship, taxi*), challenge (*as a sentry*), (*Tele.*) phone to, phone (*s.o.*) (up), call *or* ring (*s.o.*) up; 2. appeal to, call upon, invoke (***um,*** for); (*Law*) ***zum Zeugen –,*** call (*s.o.*) as a witness *or* to witness; ***eine höhere Instanz –,*** appeal to a higher court. **Anrufer,** *m.* (*Law*) appellant. **Anrufung,** *f.* appeal, invocation (*Gen.*, to). **Anrufzeichen,** *n.* call(ing) signal.

anrühren ['anry:rən], *v.t.* 1. touch; touch on (*a subject*); ***nicht –,*** not touch, leave alone; ***nicht –!*** hands off! don't touch! 2. mix, stir.

ans [ans], *abbr. of* ***an das.***

ansäen ['anzɛ:ən], *v.t.* sow (*a field*).

Ansage ['anza:gə], *f.* 1. notification, announcement; 2. (*Cards*) declaration, (first) call. **ansagen, 1.** *v.t.* 1. announce; give notice of, intimate; 2. (*Cards*) declare; ***Sie sagen an,*** it is your call; ***kein Spiel –,*** pass. **2.** *v.r.* announce an intended visit; ***er sagte sich bei uns zum Abendessen an,*** he said he would come to dinner. **Ansager,** *m.* (*Rad.*) announcer, (*Theat.*) compère.

ansammeln ['anzaməln], **1.** *v.t.* collect, gather (together), amass, accumulate, (*Mil.*) concentrate, assemble. **2.** *v.r.* collect, gather (together); accumulate, pile up; (*Mil.*) concentrate, mass, assemble. **Ansammlung,** *f.* collection, accumulation; hoard; pile, heap; gathering, crowd, throng, concourse, assemblage, mass; concentration (*of troops*).

ansässig ['anzɛ:sɪç], *adj.* domiciled, resident; – ***werden, sich – machen,*** take up one's residence *or* abode, settle (down). **Ansässige(r),** *m., f.* resident. **Ansässigkeit,** *f.* (permanent) residence, domicile.

Ansatz ['anzats], *m.* 1. (*initial stages of action*) (*Spt.*) stance; take-off (*for jump*); (*fig., coll.*) attempted start; ***einen – zum Reden machen,*** be on the point of speaking, be (as if) about to speak; ***auf den ersten –,*** at the first attempt *or* (*coll.*) go *or* shot, straight *or* right away, straight off; 2. (*usu. pl.*) first beginnings, rudiments, initial steps; inception, onset; 3. (*Mus.*) attack (*strings etc.*), embouchure (*wind*); 4. (*Bot.*) spore, germ; young shoot; (*Biol.*) rudiment; 5. (*Math.*) statement (*of a problem*); 6. (*Comm.*) account; charge, rate; ***ihm etwas in – bringen,*** charge him for s.th. *or* s.th. to his account, debit his account *or* him with s.th; 7. deposit, crust, coating; sediment, incrustation; fur, scale (*in a boiler*); 8. extension (piece), leaf (*of a table*), mouthpiece (*of wind instrument*); beading, flange; point *or* line of attachment; – ***des Haares,*** hair-line; – ***des Ärmels,*** line of the sleeve.

Ansatz|punkt, *m.* 1. starting-point, point of departure, (*coll.*) jumping-off point; 2. point of attachment. **–rohr,** *n.* nozzle, extension tube. **–schraube,** *f.* set-screw. **–stelle.** *f.* place of attachment. **–stück,** *n.* extension *or* attachment (piece).

ansäuern ['anzɔyərn], *v.t.* acidify, leaven. **Ansäuerung,** *f.* acidification, acidulation.

Ansaugehub ['anzaugəhu:p], *m.* (*Motor.*) suction stroke.

ansaugen ['anzaugən], **1.** *irr.v.t.* suck in *or* up, adsorb. **2.** *irr. v.i.* suck. **3.** *irr. v.r.* adhere by suction; take (*of leeches*). **Ansaug|heber,** *m.* siphon. **–leitung,** *f.* intake, inlet port. **–pumpe,** *f.* suction pump.

ansäuseln ['anzɔyzəln], *v.t.* breathe gently on, fan (*of wind etc.*); (*sl.*) ***angesäuselt,*** slightly tipsy.

anschaffen ['anʃafən], *v.t.* get, obtain; acquire, purchase; procure (***ihm etwas,*** s.th. for him); provide, supply, furnish, equip (him with s.th.); (*Austr.*) push (him into s.th.), land (him with s.th.). **Anschaffung,** *f.* 1. purchase, acquirement, provision; 2. acquisition, goods purchased, purchase; 3. (*Comm.*) remittance (***bei,*** to). **Anschaffungs|-kosten,** *pl.* initial cost, outlay; (*Comm.*) price delivered. **–preis,** *m.* list price, full price.

anschalten ['anʃaltən], *v.t., v.i.* (*Elec.*) switch on, make connexion.

anschauen ['anʃauən], *v.t.* look at, view, regard, contemplate. **anschauend,** *adj.* intuitive; contemplative; ***–e Erkenntnis,*** intuitive knowledge. **anschaulich,** *adj.* visual, clear, vivid, graphic, concrete; (*Phil.*) intuitive, perceptual. **Anschaulichkeit,** *f.* visual *or* graphic quality, clearness, vividness, perspicuity.

Anschauung ['anʃauuŋ], *f.* visual perception; ***zur – bringen,*** demonstrate graphically, make clear by means of a concrete illustration; 2. mode of viewing, way of looking at *or* seeing, idea, conception, notion, opinion, (point of) view, outlook; 3. (*Phil.*) perception; (***intuitive***) –, intuition; 4. (*Theol.*) contemplation. **Anschauungs|begriff,** *m.* intuitive idea. **–bild,** *n.* (*Psych.*) eidetic image. **–erkenntnis,** *f.* intuitive knowledge. **–material,** *n.* illustrative material. **–unterricht,** *m.* visual instruction, (*coll.*) object lesson. **–vermögen,** *n.* power of intuition, intuitive faculty. **–weise,** *f.* way of viewing things, point of view, attitude of mind, mental outlook.

Anschein ['anʃaɪn], *m.* (**-(e)s,** *no pl.*) appearance, look, semblance; likelihood; ***dem*** or ***allem – nach,*** apparently, seemingly, to all appearances; ***den – haben*** or ***erwecken als*** (*subj.*), have an air *or* a look of, give the impression of (*being*), appear *or* look as if; ***sich*** (*Dat.*) ***den – geben,*** make believe, pretend, feign (*to be*), put on a pretence (*of*).

anscheinen ['anʃaɪnən], *irr.v.t.* shine upon.

anscheinend ['anʃaɪnənt], **1.** *adj.* apparent, seeming, ostensible. **2.** *adv.* apparently, seemingly, to all appearances.

anscheißen ['anʃaɪsən], *irr.v.t.* (*vulg.*) welsh, bilk, do brown, tear a strip off.

anschicken ['anʃɪkən], *v.r.* get *or* make ready, prepare (***zu,*** for *or* to do); set about (doing).

anschieben ['anʃi:bən], **1.** *irr.v.t.* shove *or* push up (***an*** (*Acc.*), against). **2.** *irr.v.i.* 1. give a shove; 2. have first bowl (*at skittles*). **Anschieber,** *m.* extension piece, leaf (*of a table*). **Anschiebetisch,** *m.* extending table. **Anschiebsel,** *n.* piece added, addition, extension.

anschielen ['anʃi:lən], *v.t.* 1. squint at; 2. look askance at; cast a sidelong glance at.

anschienen ['anʃi:nən], *v.t.* put in splints.

anschießen ['anʃi:sən], **1.** *irr.v.t.* 1. fire *or* shoot at; wound (*game*), wing (*bird*); ***angeschossen,*** wounded (*of game*), winged (*of bird*), (*sl.*) smitten; cracked, crazy; 2. test, try out, prove (*a gun*); 3. (*Typ.*) add (*extra pages*); tack *or* sew in (*a sleeve*). **2.** *irr.v.i.* 1. fire (the) first (shot); 2. (*aux.* s.) dart *or* rush up; – ***auf*** (*Acc.*), dart at, rush upon; ***angeschossen kommen,*** come darting *or* rushing up; 3. (*aux.* s.) crystallize; form (*of crystals*). **Anschießen,** *n.* 1. firing test *or* trials; 2. crystallization.

anschimmeln ['anʃɪməln], *v.i.* (*aux.* s.) (begin to) go mouldy.

anschirren ['anʃɪrən], *v.t.* harness (*horse*).

Anschlag ['anʃla:k], *m.* 1. stroke, striking (*also of clocks*), impact, breaking (*of waves*), bark, barking, baying (*of dogs*), (*Tenn.*) service, (*knitting*) casting on; 2. touch (*also Mus.*), (*Mus.*) attack, tension (*of typewriter keys*); ***Anschläge pro Minute,*** words per minute (*in typing*); 3. poster, placard, notice; 4. plan, project, design, scheme; plot, conspiracy (***gegen,*** against); (criminal) attack, attempt (***auf*** (*Acc.*), on) (*s.o.'s life*); 5. estimate, assessment, evaluation; valuation; (*Pol.*) – ***der Einnahmen und Ausgaben,*** estimates (of revenue and expenditure); ***in – bringen,*** take into consideration *or* account, allow for, make allowance(s) for; ***in – kommen,*** be taken into consideration *or* account; 6. (*Tech.*) stop, check, buffer, lug, boss stock, chock, butt (*of rifle*), rabbet (*of door etc.*); 7. aiming position (*of rifle*); ***in*** or ***im – sein, das Gewehr im – halten,*** be ready to fire; ***in – gehen,*** take aim (***auf*** (*Acc.*), at); (*fig.*) ***im – sein,*** be aiming (***auf*** (*Acc.*), at); 8. (*child's game*) tig, tag.

Anschlag|arten, *pl.* firing positions (*i.e.* ***stehend, knieend, liegend***). **–brett,** *n.* notice-board.

anschlagen ['anʃla:gən], **1.** *irr.v.t.* 1. strike, hit, knock (***an*** (*Dat. or Acc.*), on *or* against), sound (*a bell*); ***Feuer –,*** strike a light; ***die Stunden –,*** strike the hours; ***den richtigen Ton –,*** strike *or* hit the right note; (*coll.*) ***einen anderen Ton –,*** change one's tune; 2. make a break *or* breach in, broach (*a cask*), chip (*crockery*); (*fig.*) ***schwer angeschlagen,*** badly knocked about, (*sl.*) groggy; (*fig.*) ***ein Thema –,*** touch on *or* broach a subject; ***ein Thema wieder –,*** revert *or* return to a subject; 3. attach, fasten, fix (***an*** (*Acc.*), to), nail on (*a board*), post *or* stick up (*a notice*), tack on (*a sleeve etc.*); ***das Gewehr –,*** aim the rifle (***auf*** (*Acc.*), at); ***eine Masche –,*** cast on a stitch, make one (*knitting*); ***das Segel –,*** bend the sail; 4. estimate, assess value, set (*a price*); ***hoch –,*** set a high price or value on, set great store by, rate high; ***zu hoch* –,** overestimate, overrate; ***zu gering* –,** underestimate, underrate. *See* **veranschlagen. 2.** *irr.v.i.* 1. strike, knock, bump (***an*** (*Acc.*), against); break, beat (*of waves*); strike (*as a clock*); strike the first blow; (*Tenn.*) serve; bark, bay, give tongue (*as hounds*); strike up (*as a drummer*); 2. take effect, operate, work, take (*as a vaccine*); take root (*as plants*); (*fig.*) be a hit; ***nicht* –,** misfire (*as a joke*); ***bei ihm schlägt keine Nahrung an,*** no food agrees with him *or* does him any good.

Anschläger ['anʃlɛ:gər], *m.* striking device; jack (*of harpsichord*); hammer (*of a piano*).

Anschlagfaden ['anʃla:kfa:dən], *m.* tacking thread.

anschlägig ['anʃlɛ:gɪç], *adj.* 1. ingenious, inventive, resourceful; skilful, dexterous, handy; 2. (*of food*) body-building.

Anschlag|randsteller, *m.* margin-stop (*of typewriter*). **–säule,** *f.* advertising pillar. **–schiene,** *f.* T-square. **–schraube,** *f.* locking- *or* set-screw. **–tafel,** *f.* notice-board. **–wert,** *m.* 1. estimated value; 2. (*diet*) food-value. **–winkel,** *m.* try-square. **–zettel,** *m.* poster, placard. **–zünder,** *m.* percussion-fuse.

anschließen ['anʃli:sən], **1.** *irr.v.t.* 1. attach, join (up), connect (*Dat.*, to); link up (with), add on (to); enclose (with), append (to); (*Comm.*) ***hier angeschlossen,*** herewith enclosed *or* attached; 2. (*Tech., Elec.*) connect (up) (***an*** (*Acc.*), with *or* to); (*fig.*) affiliate (*a body*) (***an*** (*Acc.*), to); ***Köln und die angeschlossenen Sender,*** Cologne and transmitters in *or* linked to that network. **2.** *irr.v.r.* 1. join (company) (*Dat.*, with), attach o.s. (to); agree, comply, fall in (with), concur, acquiesce (in), subscribe (to) (*opinions, proposals etc.*); 2. be adjacent (***an*** (*Acc.*), to), adjoin; follow immediately; (*fig.*) follow closely (*as a model*); 3. (*Mil.*) close the ranks, close up; ***rechts angeschlossen!*** close to the right! ***bitte nach vorne –!*** pass along the car, please! **3.** *irr.v.i.* fit (well) (*of clothes*); ***es schließt eng an,*** it fits closely *or* tightly *or* (*coll.*) like a glove. **anschließend, 1.** *adj.* adjacent; following. **2.** *adv.* subsequently, (immediately) afterwards *or* following.

Anschluß ['anʃlus], *m.* (*Tele., Railw. etc.*) connexion; supply (*of gas etc.*); accession, attachment, addition, junction (***an*** (*Acc.*), to), contact (*of troops, Elec.*); union, annexation (*of Austria to Germany*); (*Tele.*) ***den – bekommen,*** get one's connexion, be put *or* get through; (*Railw.*) ***den – erreichen,*** get *or* catch one's connexion; (*Railw.*) ***den – versäumen*** or ***verfehlen*** or ***verpassen,*** miss one's connexion; ***– suchen,*** try and make contact with people; ***er findet keinen –,*** he can't make any friends *or* (*Comm.*) has not established any connexions.

Anschluß|dose, *f.* (*Elec.*) junction box. **–klemme,** *f.* (*Elec.*) terminal. **–klinke,** *f.* (*Tele.*) connecting jack. **–schema,** *n.* wiring diagram. **–schnur,** *f.* (*Tele.*) connecting line, cord, flex. **–station,** *f.* (*Railw.*) junction; station where one gets a connexion.

anschmachten ['anʃmaxtən], *v.t.* make sheep's eyes at.

anschmeicheln ['anʃmaɪçəln], *v.r.* curry favour (***bei***, with), ingratiate o.s. (with).

anschmelzen ['anʃmɛltsən], **1.** *reg.* & *irr.v.t.* solder, weld *or* braze on (***an*** (*Acc.*), to). **2.** *irr. v.i.* (*aux.* s.) melt, fuse on (***an*** (*Acc.*), to).

anschmieden ['anʃmi:dən], *v.t.* forge on (***an*** (*Acc.*), to); chain, fetter, put in irons.

anschmiegen ['anʃmi:gən], **1.** *v.t.* press close (*Dat. or* ***an*** (*Acc.*), against), fit closely *or* snugly (to), adapt (to), adapt to the shape *or* contours (of). **2.** *v.r.* snuggle up (***an*** (*Acc.*), to), nestle close (up) (to); cling to, hug; (*Dat.*) adapt o.s. (to), fit in *or* accommodate o.s. (with), conform (to). **anschmiegsam,** *adj.* cuddlesome (*as a pet*), accommodating, tractable, complaisant (*of a p.*).

anschmieren ['anʃmi:rən], *v.t.* 1. besmear; daub; 2. (*coll.*) diddle, bamboozle; ***angeschmiert werden,*** be had, be sold a pup; ***ihn mit etwas –, ihm etwas –,*** foist s.th. on him, land him with s.th., fob *or* palm s.th. off on him.

anschnallen ['anʃnalən], **1.** *v.t.* buckle on (*belt*), gird on (*sword*), fasten (*ski*). **2.** *v.r.* strap o.s. in, (*Av., Motor.*) fasten one's safety belt.

anschnauzen ['anʃnautsən], *v.t.* (*coll.*) snarl at, browbeat; snap at, snap (*s.o.'s*) head off, jump down (*s.o.'s*) throat, bawl (*s.o.*) out. **Anschnauzer,** *m.* (*coll.*) dressing-down, blowing-up, telling-off.

Anschneide|ergebnisse, *n.pl.* (*Navig.*) cross-bearings. **–messer,** *n.* carving-knife.

anschneiden ['anʃnaɪdən], *irr.v.t.* 1. cut into, cut the first piece from, start cutting; (*Dressm.*) cut together with the garment; ***angeschnittene Ärmel,*** dolman sleeves; ***ein Thema –,*** broach *or* raise a subject; 2. (*Navig.*) get a bearing on; 3. (*Spt.*) put a spin on (*the ball*).

Anschnitt ['anʃnɪt], *m.* 1. first cut, outside slice (*of loaf etc.*); ***im – verkaufen,*** sell by the piece; 2. (*usu. pl.*) (*Navig.*) bearing.

Anschove [an'ʃo:və], **An(s)chovis,** *f.* (-, *pl.* -) anchovy.

anschrauben ['anʃraubən], *v.t.* screw on (***an*** (*Acc.*), to), screw up.

Anschreibe|blatt, *n.* (*Spt.*) score-card. **–buch,** *n.* note-book, memorandum book, (*Comm.*) credit sales account-book, (*Spt.*) score-book.

anschreiben ['anʃraɪbən], *irr.v.t.* write down, put *or* set down in writing; (*Comm.*) ***ihm etwas –,*** debit a th. to him, put s.th. on *or* charge s.th. to his account, charge s.th. up to him; ***– lassen,*** have charged to one's account, buy on credit; (*fig.*) ***bei ihm gut*** (***schlecht***) ***angeschrieben sein,*** be (not) thought well of by him, be in his good (bad *or* black) books, (not) be in his good graces, stand in good (bad) repute with him; (*Spt.*) ***die Punkte –,*** score, keep the score. **Anschreiber,** *m.* marker; scorer (*in games*). **Anschreibetafel,** *f.* scoreboard.

anschreien ['anʃraɪən], *irr.v.t.* scream *or* shout at.

Anschrift ['anʃrɪft], *f.* (-, *pl.* **-en**) address.

Anschrot ['anʃro:t], *n.*, **Anschrote,** *f.* selvage, selvedge (*cloth*).

Anschub ['anʃu:p], *m.* first shove, push off.

anschuldigen ['anʃuldɪgən], *v.t.* accuse (*Gen.*, of); charge (with); indict (for). **Anschuldigung,** *f.* charge, accusation, indictment.

anschüren ['anʃy:rən], *v.t.* stir up, rake; tend (*a fire*); excite, inflame; foment (*a quarrel*).

Anschuß ['anʃus], *m.* 1. shot-wound; 2. crystallization.

anschütten ['anʃytən], *v.t.* pile *or* heap up (***an*** (*Acc.*), against); bank up, fill up (*a gap, hole*).

anschwängern ['anʃvɛŋərn], *v.t.* (*Chem.*) saturate, impregnate. **Anschwängerung,** *f.* saturation, impregnation.

anschwärmen ['anʃvɛrmən], **1.** *v.i.* start swarming (*of bees*); (*fig.*) ***angeschwärmt kommen,*** arrive in swarms, come swarming in **2.** *v.t.* idolize, adulate.

anschwärzen ['anʃvɛrtsən], *v.t.* 1. blacken; 2. blacken (*s.o.'s*) character, disparage, speak disparagingly about. **Anschwärzung,** *f.* 1. blackening; 2. disparagement, backbiting.

anschwatzen ['anʃvatsən], *v.t.* (*coll.*) ***ihm etwas –,*** talk him into (*doing, taking, buying etc.*) s.th.

Anschweif ['anʃvaɪf], *m.* end-selvedge (*of cloth*).

anschweißen ['anʃvaɪsən], *v.t.* weld on, braze on (***an*** (*Acc.*), to).

anschwellen ['anʃvɛlən], **1.** *irr.v.i.* (*aux.* s.) swell (up *or* out), become distended *or* inflated, (*Med.*) tumefy; fill, belly (out), bunt (*as sails*); (*fig.*) increase, swell (*also Med.*), (*Mus.*) rise to a crescendo; ***angeschwollen,*** swelled, swollen; swollen, in spate (*as river*). **2.** *reg.v.t.* (cause to) swell, distend, inflate; fill, swell out (*sails*). **anschwellend,** *adj.* swelling, (*Med.*) tumid, (in)tumescent, (*Mus.*) crescendo. **Anschwellung,** *f.* swelling, protuberance, (*Med.*) (in)tumescence.

anschwemmen ['anʃvɛmən], *v.t.* wash ashore, wash up; deposit (*alluvium*). **Anschwemmung,** *f.* silting; alluvial deposit, alluvium.

anschwimmen ['anʃvɪmən], **1.** *irr.v.t.* swim towards *or* for. **2.** *irr.v.i.* (*aux.* s.) ***ans Ufer* –**, swim ashore; ***gegen den Strom* –**, swim against the tide *or* current *or* (*fig.*) stream.

ansegeln ['anze:gəln], *v.t.* 1. make for (*port*); 2. run foul of (*a ship*); run on to (*a reef*).

ansehen ['anze:ən], *irr.v.t.* 1. look at, have *or* take a look at; ***argwöhnisch* –**, eye suspiciously; ***erstaunt*** or ***verwundert* –**, gaze in astonishment at; ***mit* –**, look on at, be a spectator *or* (eye-)witness of; ***näher* –**, inspect, look closely at; ***scharf* –**, look hard at; ***scheel*** or ***schief* –**, look askance at; ***starr* –**, stare at, gaze (fixedly) at; ***von oben bis unten* –**, look (*s.o.*) up and down; 2. see, detect, notice; ***ihm etwas* –**, see s.th. from his appearance, detect s.th. by looking at him; 3. look (up)on, view, regard, consider, take to be; ***anders* –**, take a different view of; ***mit anderen Augen* –**, regard in quite another light; ***es – als***, regard *or* consider *or* look (up)on it to be *or* as; take it to be *or* as *or* for; deem it to be; ***es ernst* –**, take a grave view of it; ***wie ich die S. ansehe***, as I see it, in my view, as it strikes me, to my mind *or* way of thinking. *See* **angesehen.**

Ansehen, *n.* 1. sight; look, appearance; semblance; ***dem – nach***, to all appearance; ***vom – kennen***, know by sight; 2. distinction, esteem, respect, reputation, prestige; repute, standing, consequence; ***Leute von* –**, notabilities, reputable *or* eminent persons, people of note; ***sich*** (*Dat.*) ***– verschaffen***, make *or* gain a reputation (for o.s.); ***sein – verlieren*** or ***einbüßen***, fall into discredit, lose face; ***sich*** (*Dat.*) ***ein – geben***, give o.s. airs; ***vor Gott gilt kein – der Person***, God is no respecter of persons.

ansehnlich ['anze:nlɪç], *adj.* 1. considerable, large, very respectable, handsome, goodly, (*coll.*) sizeable (*fortune etc.*); 2. stately, good-looking, handsome; 3. important, eminent, distinguished, notable, of standing *or* importance *or* reputation, conspicuous. **Ansehnlichkeit,** *f.* 1. importance; 2. considerable size; 3. eminence, repute, reputation; 4. handsomeness, dignity, stateliness.

Ansehung ['anze:uŋ], *f.* ***in –*** (*Gen.*), considering, in consideration *or* view of, with respect to, having regard to; ***ohne – der Person***, without respect of persons.

anseilen ['anzaɪlən], *v.i., v.r.* (*Mount.*) rope (o.s.).

Ansetzblatt ['anzɛtsblat], *n.* 1. (*Bot.*) sprouting leaf; 2. end-paper (*of book*).

ansetzen ['anzɛtsən], **1.** *v.t.* 1. apply, put on (***an*** (*Acc.*), to); join *or* fix *or* add on (to); 2. (*implying setting an action going, starting*) launch (*an attack*), state (*a problem*), apply (*knife, brush etc.*), put forth (*buds, blossoms, roots etc.*); ***Fett*** or ***Fleisch* –**, put on fat *or* flesh; ***die Feder* –**, put *or* set one's pen to paper, start writing; ***das Glas* –**, raise the glass to one's lips, start drinking; ***Rost* –**, get rusty; ***Schimmel* –**, become mildewed; 3. fix, settle, determine, appoint, assign (*time or place*); fix, settle, quote, name (*price etc.*). **2.** *v.r.* (*of p.*) settle (down) (***in*** (*Dat.*), in); (*of th.*) accumulate, settle (*as dust*), form a crust *or* deposit (***an*** (*Acc.*), on), (*Chem.*) crystallize, effloresce. **3.** *v.i.* 1. (make a) start, begin; ***noch einmal* –**, make a fresh start, start *or* begin afresh *or* all over again; 2. raise one's glass to one's lips; 3. (*Chess etc.*) make the first move; 4. put on weight, get stout. **Ansetzer,** *m.* (*Artil.*) rammer. **Ansetzkolben,** *m.* ramrod. **Ansetzung,** *f.* 1. application (***an*** (*Acc.*), to); 2. estimation, assessment (***auf*** (*Acc.*), at); 3. accumulation (*of dust etc.*), (*Chem.*) crystallization, efflorescence. *See* **Ansatz.**

Ansicht ['anzɪçt], *f.* 1. (point of) view, views, opinion (***über*** (*Acc.*), on *or* about); ***nach meiner* –**, ***meiner – nach***, in my opinion *or* view, to my way of thinking; 2. view, prospect; 3. (*Comm.*) ***zur* –**, on appro(val). **ansichtig,** *adj.* ***– werden*** (*Gen.*), catch sight of. **Ansichts|(post)karte,** *f.* picture postcard. **–sache,** *f.* matter of opinion. **–sendung,** *f.* consignment for inspection *or* approval.

ansiedeln ['anzi:dəln], **1.** *v.t.* settle (*population, colonists*). **2.** *v.r.* settle (down), take up one's abode, establish o.s. **Ansiedler,** *m.* settler, colonist **Ansiedlung,** *f.* colonization; colony, settlement.

ansinnen ['anzɪnən], *irr.v.t.* ***ihm etwas* –**, demand *or* expect *or* require s.th. of him. **Ansinnen,** *n.* (unreasonable) request, (unexpected *or* unjustified) demand.

ansintern ['anzɪntərn], *v.i.* (*aux.* s.) form stalactites *or* stalagmites *or* concretions.

Ansitz ['anzɪts], *m.* hide, hiding-place. **ansitzen,** *irr.v.i.* 1. lie in wait *or* ambush; 2. stick, cling, adhere (***an*** (*Dat.*), to), fit closely *or* tightly (*as clothes*).

ansonsten [an'zɔnstən], *adv.* *See* **sonst.**

anspannen ['anʃpanən], **1.** *v.t.* 1. yoke (*oxen*), harness (*horses*); harness horses *or* a horse to (*a coach*); (*fig., coll.*) rope (*a p.*) in (*to do*); 2. stretch, tighten; tense (*muscles*); (*fig.*) strain; exert; ***angespannt***, tight, taut, stretched, strained, (*fig.*) tense, rapt. **2.** *v.r.* exert o.s., make an effort.

Anspänner ['anʃpɛnər], *m.* small farmer, smallholder.

Anspannung ['anʃpanuŋ], *f.* tension, strain; exertion.

anspeien ['anʃpaɪən], *irr.v.t.* spit at *or* upon, spit in (*s.o.'s*) face.

Anspiel ['anʃpi:l], *n.* start of play; (*Footb.*) kick-off, (*Golf*) drive-off, (*Tenn.*) service, (*Cards*) lead. **anspielen,** *v.i.* 1. begin to play; play first; (*Footb.*) kick-off, (*Golf*) drive-off, (*Tenn.*) serve, (*Cards*) lead; 2. allude, refer (***auf*** (*Acc.*), to); hint (at). **Anspielung,** *f.* allusion, reference, hint, insinuation, innuendo.

anspießen ['anʃpi:sən], *v.t.* run through with a spear; impale; spit (*meat*).

anspinnen ['anʃpɪnən], **1.** *irr.v.t.* establish, engage in, enter into (*relations, conversation etc.*), hatch (*plot*); ***wieder* –**, pick up (*thread of story etc.*). **2.** *irr. v.r.* 1. (*of spider*) weave its web, (*of caterpillar*) weave its cocoon; 2. (*fig.*) begin to develop, come about, be afoot; spring up, develop, originate.

anspitzen ['anʃpɪtsən], *v.t.* put a point on, sharpen (*a pencil etc.*). **Anspitzer,** *m.* (pencil-)sharpener.

Ansporn ['anʃpɔrn], *m.* **(-(e)s,** *no pl.*) incentive, spur, stimulus. **anspornen,** *v.t.* spur (*horse*), (*fig.*) spur on, stimulate, incite.

Ansprache ['anʃpra:xə], *f.* 1. address, speech (***an*** (*Acc.*), to); 2. response (*also fig.*); ***keine – finden***, meet with no response.

ansprechen ['anʃprɛçən], **1.** *irr.v.t.* 1. speak to, accost, address; ***ihn um etwas* –**, approach him for s.th.; 2. appeal to, interest, touch (*the heart etc.*); take one's fancy; ***das spricht mich nicht an***, that does not appeal to me; 3. (*Spt.*) address (*the ball*). **2.** *irr.v.i.* 1. respond, react (***auf*** (*Acc.*), to); 2. meet with a good response, appeal, please. **ansprechend,** *adj.* pleasing, attractive, pleasant, appealing, engaging, prepossessing.

ansprengen ['anʃprɛŋən], **1.** *v.t.* 1. water (*lawn, plant*); 2. blast (*rock*). **2.** *v.i.* (*aux.* s.) gallop up; ***angesprengt kommen***, come at full gallop.

anspringen ['anʃprɪŋən], **1.** *irr.v.i.* (*aux.* s.) begin to crack; break into a gallop; start (up) (*of an engine*). **2.** *irr.v.t.* jump at, leap at; ***angesprungen kommen***, come running *or* jumping *or* skipping.

anspritzen ['anʃprɪtsən], *v.t.* splash, spray, besprinkle, (be)spatter.

Anspruch ['anʃprux], *m.* claim, title, right (***auf*** (*Acc.*), to); claim, demand (***an ihn***, upon him; ***auf etwas***, for s.th.); ***– haben auf eine S.***, have a right to *or* be entitled to a th.; ***– machen*** (or ***erheben***) ***auf eine S., eine S. in – nehmen***, claim a th., put in a claim for *or* lay claim to a th.; ***es nimmt meine Zeit in* –**, it makes demands on my time, it takes up my time; ***sehr in – genommen***, very busy; ***Ansprüche stellen an*** (*Acc.*), make demands on, tax. **anspruchslos,** *adj.* unassuming, unpretentious, modest. **Anspruchslosigkeit,** *f.* modesty, unpretentiousness. **anspruchsvoll,** *adj.* pretentious, exacting, demanding, hard to please; fastidious.

anspucken ['anʃpukən], *v.t.* spit at.

anspülen ['anʃpy:lən], **1.** *v.i.* flow, wash (*an* (*Acc.*), against). **2.** *v.t.* wash ashore *or* up (on the tide), deposit. **Anspülung,** *f.* alluvial deposit.

anstacheln ['anʃtaxəln], *v.t.* goad (*oxen etc.*), (*fig.*) goad *or* spur on (*zu*, (in)to), incite (to).

Anstalt ['anʃtalt], *f.* (-, *pl.* **-en**) 1. institution; institute; establishment; 2. *pl.* preparations, arrangements; *-en machen* (*zu*), *-en treffen* (*für*), make arrangements (for).

Anstand [anʃtant], *m.* 1. (*no pl.*) propriety, decency, seemliness, decorum, a becoming manner; a good grace, civility, politeness, courtesy; (good) behaviour *or* breeding, good manners, deportment, etiquette; 2. (*no pl.*) delay; hesitation, reluctance, demur; *– nehmen,* be reluctant, hesitate (*to do*), hold back (*from doing*); *ohne –,* without delay *or* hesitation, without further *or* (any) more ado, readily, unhesitatingly; 3. *pl.* difficulties, objections, trouble; 4. (*Hunt.*) stand, hide.

anständig ['anʃtɛndɪç], *adj.* decent, respectable, well-behaved, seemly, decorous; gentlemanlike, ladylike; (*coll.*) (*indicating approval*) decent, respectable, pretty good, not (at all) bad; (*coll.*) (*indicating emphasis*) decent, considerable, sizeable. **Anständigkeit,** *f.* decency, respectability, seemliness, decorum.

Anstands|besuch, *m.* duty visit, formal call. **-dame,** *f.* chaperon. **-gefühl,** *n.* sense of decency *or* propriety, decorum, delicacy, tact.

anstandshalber ['anʃtantshalbər], *adv.* for decency's sake, out of politeness, for the sake of appearances. **anstandslos, 1.** *adj.* unhesitating. **2.** *adv.* without hesitation, without further *or* (any) more ado, readily.

Anstands|regeln, *pl.* rules of deportment, etiquette; social conventions. **-rock,** *m.* (*obs.*) petticoat. **-wauwau,** *m.* (*coll.*) *see* **-dame.**

anstandswidrig ['anʃtantsvi:drɪç], *adj.* unseemly, unbecoming, indecorous, indecent, improper.

anstapeln ['anʃta:pəln], *v.t.* pile up, hoard up.

anstarren ['anʃtarən], *v.t.* stare at, gaze at fixedly.

anstatt ['anʃtat], **1.** *prep.* (*Gen.*) instead of, in place of, in lieu of (*s.th.*), in (*s.o.'s*) place *or* stead. **2.** *conj.* *– daß* or *– (zu tun)*, instead of (doing).

anstauen ['anʃtauən], **1.** *v.t.* dam (up). **2.** *v.r.* collect, pile up.

anstaunen ['anʃtaunən], *v.t.* gaze at in wonder *or* amazement *or* surprise *or* astonishment, stare open-mouthed at.

anstechen ['anʃtɛçən], *irr.v.t.* pierce, puncture, prick; broach, tap (*a cask*).

anstecken ['anʃtɛkən], *v.t.* 1. pin *or* fasten on (*an* (*Acc.*), to); 2. light (*a candle etc.*); set fire to, kindle; 3. infect; contaminate, pollute, taint; *Lachen steckt an,* laughter is catching. **ansteckend,** *adj.* infectious, contagious, (*coll.*) catching. **Ansteckung,** *f.* infection; contagion. **Ansteckungsstoff,** *m.* contagious matter, virus.

anstehen ['anʃte:ən], *irr.v.i.* (*aux.* h. *&* s.) 1. stand near *or* next (*an* (*Dat.*), to), be contiguous (to); 2. queue up (*nach,* for); *es steht zur Diskussion an,* it is down for discussion; 3. be fixed *or* settled (*date etc.*); 4. delay, hesitate, scruple; *ich stehe nicht an zu sagen,* I have no hesitation in saying; 5. be deferred *or* held over; *es kann vorläufig noch –,* it can wait for the time being; *– lassen,* defer, postpone, hold over, (*coll.*) put off; *eine Schuld – lassen,* defer the payment of a debt; 6. *ihm –,* be becoming *or* suit him (*as clothes*), become *or* befit him, be fitting, seemly *or* proper for him (*as behaviour etc.*), suit him, suit his requirements, be to his taste, be just right for him; 7. (*Geol.*) crop out. **anstehend,** *adj.* (*Geol.*) *-es Gestein,* rocky outcrop.

ansteigen ['anʃtaɪgən], *irr.v.i.* (*aux.* s.) climb (up), mount, ascend (*as a p.*), rise, climb ascend (*as a road*), rise (*as water*), rise, increase (*as prices*); (*fig.*) *jäh –,* rocket, soar.

anstellen ['anʃtɛlən], **1.** *v.t.* 1. place, stand, put (*an* (*Acc.*), against); 2. appoint, engage, employ, take *or* sign on; *angestellt sein,* be employed (*bei,* with), be in the employ (of); *angestellt werden,* be engaged *or* appointed, find employment; *fest angestellt,* on the permanent staff; *see* **Angestellte(r)**; 3. start (up) (*an engine*), switch *or* put on (*light, radio etc.*), turn on (*water, gas etc.*); 4. make, undertake, carry out (*experiment etc.*), make, draw (*comparison*), institute, initiate (*proceedings*), contrive, manage, set about; 5. (*coll.*) *etwas –,* do s.th. silly, make trouble; *du hast was Schönes angestellt,* now you've gone and done it, now you've put your foot in it; *mit mir darfst du nichts –,* you shouldn't try any of your tricks with me *or* try anything on with me. **2.** *v.r.* 1. take one's place, take up one's position, stand in line *or* in a queue, form *or* queue up (*nach,* for); 2. behave, act (*in a certain manner*); *sich geschickt (dumm) bei* or *zu etwas –,* set *or* go about s.th. skilfully (in a stupid manner); *sich – als ob,* act as if; *stell dich nicht so an,* don't make such a fuss; 3. (*obs.*) pretend (to be), feign.

Anstellerei [anʃtɛlə'raɪ], *f.* (-, *no pl.*) (*coll.*) 1. queueing (up); 2. shamming; fussing.

anstellig ['anʃtɛlɪç], *adj.* skilful, deft, adroit, handy. **Anstelligkeit,** *f.* skilfulness, dexterity, adroitness, deftness.

Anstellung ['anʃtɛluŋ], *f.* appointment, engagement, employment; situation, post, office, (*coll.*) job; *feste –,* permanent appointment, post on the establishment *or* the permanent staff.

anstemmen ['anʃtɛmən], **1.** *v.t.* push, press (*gegen,* against). **2.** *v.r.* brace o.s.

ansteuern ['anʃtɔyərn], *v.i.* (*Naut.*) steer towards, shape a course for, head *or* make for. **Ansteuerungsfeuer,** *n.* homing *or* approach *or* (*Av.*) landing beacon.

Anstich ['anʃtɪç], *m.* tapping, broaching (*of cask*) puncture, pitting; first thrust of the spade.

Anstieg ['anʃti:k], *m.* 1. ascent, (*also fig.*) rise, climb; rise, increase (*of prices*); *im –,* rising, on the rise; 2. (*Mount.*) ascent route.

anstiften ['anʃtɪftən], *v.t.* cause, bring about, set on foot; provoke, foster, foment, incite, instigate, abet, suborn. **Anstifter,** *m.* inciter, instigator, ringleader, abettor, (*Law*) accessory before the fact; *– falscher Zeugen,* suborner. **Anstiftung,** *f.* incitement, instigation, suborning.

anstimmen ['anʃtɪmən], *v.t.* begin to sing; strike up; give the lead; *einen anderen Ton –,* change one's tune. **Anstimmung,** *f.* striking up; intonation.

Anstoß ['anʃto:s], *m.* 1. shock, impact, collision; *Stein des -es,* stumbling-block; 2. impulse, impulsion, impetus; 3. difficulty, (*coll.*) hitch; *ohne –,* without hesitation *or* hesitancy; 4. (*Carp.*) butt-joint; 5. (*Footb.*) kick-off; 6. scandal, offence; *– geben* or *erregen,* give *or* cause offence; *– nehmen an* (*Dat.*), take offence at, be scandalized by.

anstoßen ['anʃto:sən], **1.** *irr.v.t.* 1. strike, knock, bump (*an* (*Acc.*), against); *angestoßen,* bruised (*fruit*), chipped (*crockery*); 2. join end to end, (*Carp.*) butt-joint, (*Dressm.*) fine-draw. **2.** *irr.v.t., v.i.* (*Footb.*) (*den Ball*) *–,* kick off; (*die Gläser*) *–,* clink *or* touch glasses; *auf sein Wohl –,* drink (to) his health. **3.** *irr.v.i.* 1. (*aux.* s.) strike, knock, bump (*an* (*Acc.*), against), collide (with); 2. stumble, falter; *mit der Zunge –,* lisp; 3. border, abut (*an* (*Acc.*), on), be adjacent *or* contiguous (to), adjoin; *es stößt nicht an,* it does not meet; 4. (*aux.* s. *&* h.) give *or* cause offence. **anstoßend,** *adj.* adjoining, adjacent, contiguous, abutting.

anstößig ['anʃtø:sɪç], *adj.* offensive, objectionable, obnoxious; shocking, scandalous, improper, unseemly, indecorous. **Anstößigkeit,** *f.* offensiveness, impropriety, unseemliness.

Anstoß|kruste, *f.* kissing-crust. **-naht,** *f.* fine-drawn seam.

anstrahlen ['anʃtra:lən], **1.** *v.t.* cast its beam on, shed its radiance on, shine (up)on; floodlight; (*coll.*) (*of a p.*) beam upon. **Anstrahlung,** *f.* illumination, floodlighting.

Anstrebekraft ['anʃtre:bəkraft], *f.* centripetal force.

anstreben ['anʃtre:bən], **1.** *v.i.* strive (***gegen,*** against). **2.** *v.t.* aspire to, strive for, be hoping to get.

anstreichen ['anʃtraɪçən], *irr.v.t.* 1. paint; ***mit Tünche –,*** whitewash, distemper; ***mit Firnis –,*** put a coat of varnish on, varnish; 2. mark, underline (*a passage in a book etc.*); (*coll.*) ***das werde ich ihm gehörig –,*** I shall make him pay for this. **Anstreicher,** *m.* (house-)painter, decorator. **Anstreichpistole,** *f.* spray-gun.

anstreifen ['anʃtraɪfən], *v.i.* (*aux.* s. *&* h.) graze, brush, touch lightly.

anstrengen ['anʃtrɛŋən], **1.** *v.t.* strain, exert; ***alle Kräfte –,*** make every effort, strain every nerve; ***eine Klage –,*** bring an action (against); ***der kleine Druck strengt die Augen sehr an,*** small print is very trying to the eyes; ***angestrengt,*** unremitting, persistent (*toil*), intense, intensive (*work*), strenuous, assiduous (*efforts*), sedulous (*attention*). **2.** *v.r.* exert o.s., strive, make every effort; ***sich über seine Kräfte*** or ***die Maßen –,*** over-exert o.s. **anstrengend,** *adj.* exacting, trying, arduous, strenuous, laborious. **Anstrengung,** *f.* exertion, effort, strain; ***ohne –,*** without effort, effortlessly; without exertion *or* strain.

Anstrich ['anʃtrɪç], *m.* 1. paint, coat of paint; ***einer S. einen guten – geben,*** gloss over a matter; ***erster –,*** undercoat, first coat; ***letzter –,*** final *or* top coat; 2. colour(ing), tinge, shade; air, appearance.

anströmen ['anʃtrø:mən], **1.** *v.i.* (*aux.* s.) come streaming *or* pouring up *or* in; stream *or* pour *or* flock up *or* in. **2.** *v.t.* wash (against).

anstückeln ['anʃtykəln], *v.t.* add a piece to; piece on (***an*** (*Acc.*), to).

Ansturm ['anʃturm], *m.* assault (***an*** (*Acc.*), on), onset, charge, rush (against *or* upon); run (*on a bank*).

anstürmen ['anʃtyrmən], *v.i.* (*aux.* s.) charge, attack; – ***auf*** (*Acc.*) or ***gegen,*** make a rush at, assault, assail, storm (*a position*).

Ansturz ['anʃturts], *m.* violent onset, onrush.

anstürzen ['anʃtyrtsən], *v.i.* (*aux.* s.) ***angestürzt kommen,*** come on with a rush, rush *or* dash up.

ansuchen ['anzu:xən], **1.** *v.i.* ***bei ihm –,*** ask *or* petition *or* solicit him, apply *or* sue to him, make application to him (***um etwas,*** for s.th.); request (s.th.) of him; ***bei ihm um Erlaubnis –,*** ask *or* beg his permission. **Ansuchen,** *n.* request, petition, entreaty, solicitation, suit, application; ***auf – von,*** at the request of, on the application of. **Ansucher,** *m.* petitioner. **Ansuch(ungs)schreiben,** *n.* letter of application, (written) petition.

Antarktik [ant'arktɪk], *f.* Antarctic Ocean.

Antarktis [ant'arktɪs], *f.* the Antarctic.

antasten ['antastən], *v.t.* 1. feel, finger, touch, handle; 2. question, impugn, cast aspersions on, detract from, hurt, injure (*a p.'s reputation etc.*); 3. encroach on (*a p.'s rights*); break into, touch (*funds etc.*). **Antastung,** *f.* encroachment (*Gen.*, upon), impugnment (of), damage (to).

Anteil ['antaɪl], *m.* portion, part, share, quota (***an*** (*Dat.*), of); sympathy (for *or* with), interest (in), concern (for); dividend; allotment; constituent, fraction; ***– haben an*** (*Dat.*), participate in; ***– nehmen an*** (*Dat.*), take an interest in, sympathize with. **Anteilhaber,** *m.* participator, partaker; shareholder. **anteillos,** *adj.* indifferent, neutral; unsympathetic. **anteilmäßig,** *adj.* proportionate, proportional, pro rata. **Anteil|nahme,** *f.* sympathy (***an*** (*Dat.*), for *or* with); concern (about); participation (in). **–schein,** *m.*, **Anteilsverschreibung,** *f.* share certificate, scrip. **Anteilzahl,** *f.* percentage, fraction quota.

antelephonieren ['antelefoni:rən], *v.t.* telephone (to), phone, ring (up).

Antenne [an'tɛnə], *f.* (*Rad.*) aerial, antenna (*also Zool.*), (*Zool. coll.*) feeler. **Antennen|ableitung,** *f.* (*Rad.*) (aerial) lead-in. **–kreis,** *m.* (*Rad.*) aerial circuit.

Anti|alkoholiker [anti–], *m.* teetotaller, (total) abstainer. **–biotikum,** *n.* (*Med.*) antibiotic.

antichambrieren [antiʃam'bri:rən], *v.i.* ***–bei,*** dance attendance on, lobby (*members of parliament etc.*).

antichristlich [anti'krɪstlɪç], *adj.* antichristian (*and many others with prefix corresponding to English* anti–).

antik [an'ti:k], *adj.* ancient, classical, Graeco-Roman; antique, old-fashioned, antiquated. **Antike,** *f.* (classical) antiquity; classical sculpture, antique (*work of art*). **Antikenhändler,** *m.* antique dealer. **antikisieren** [–i'zi:rən], *v.i.* imitate (the style of) classical antiquity.

Anti|klopfmittel, *n.* (*Motor.*) anti-knock agent. **–körper,** *m.* (*Physiol.*) antibody. **–kritik,** *f.* counter-criticism.

Antillen [an'tɪlən], *f.pl.* Antilles.

Antilogarithmus [antiloga'rɪtmus], *m.* (*Math.*) antilogarithm.

Antimon [anti'mo:n], *n.* (**-s,** *no* ***pl.***) antimony. **Antimonbutter,** *f.* (*Chem.*) anhydrous antimony chloride. **antimonsauer,** *adj.* antimoniate of.

Antiochien [anti'ɔxiən], *n.* Antioch.

Antiparallelogramm [antiparalelo'gram], *n.* (*Geom.*) isosceles trapezoid.

Antipathie [antipa'ti:], *f.* antipathy (***gegen,*** to, for *or* against). **antipathisch** [–'pa:tɪʃ], *adj.* antipathetic (***gegen,*** to).

[1]**Antiphon** [anti'fo:n], *n.* (**-s,** ***pl.*** **-e**) ear-plug.

[2]**Antiphon,** *f.* (-, ***pl.*** **-en**) (*Mus.*) antiphon. **antiphonisch,** *adj.* antiphonal.

Antipode [anti'po:də], *m.* (**-n,** ***pl.*** **-n**) dweller in the antipodes; *pl.* antipodes.

antippen ['antɪpən], *v.t.* touch lightly, tap.

Antiqua [an'ti:kva], *f.* (-, *no* ***pl.***) (*Typ.*) Roman type.

Antiquar [anti'kva:r], *m.* (**-s,** ***pl.*** **-e**) second-hand *or* antiquarian bookseller; (*obs.*) dealer in antiquities. **Antiquariat** [–ri'a:t], *n.* (**-s,** ***pl.*** **-e**) second-hand *or* antiquarian bookseller. **antiquarisch,** **1.** *adj.* second-hand, antiquarian. **2.** *adv.* second-hand.

Antiquaschrift [an'ti:kvaʃrɪft], *f.* (-, *no pl.*) Roman type *or* letters *or* characters.

antiquieren [anti'kvi:rən], *v.i.* (*aux.* s.) become antiquated *or* obsolete *or* out-of-date.

Antiquität [antikvi'tɛ:t], *f.* antique. **Antiquitäten|händler,** *m.* antique dealer. **–sammler,** *m.* antiquarian, collector of antiques.

Antithese [anti'te:zə], *f.* antithesis.

Antlitz ['antlɪts], *n.* (**-es,** ***pl.*** **-e**) (*elevated style*) countenance, visage.

Anton ['anto:n], *m.* Anthony.

Antrag ['antra:k], *m.* 1. proposition, proposal, (*Parl.*) motion, resolution; ***einen – stellen,*** propose a motion, move a resolution; ***einen – unterstützen,*** second a motion; ***einen – annehmen,*** carry a motion, adopt a resolution; ***der – wurde abgelehnt,*** the motion was lost, the resolution was rejected; 2. application, petition (***auf*** (*Acc.*), for); ***einen – stellen,*** make an application, (*Law*) file a petition; 3. offer *or* proposal (of marriage); ***einen – machen,*** propose (marriage) (*Dat.*, to).

antragen ['antra:gən], **1.** *irr.v.t.* 1. ***ihm etwas –,*** offer him s.th.; 2. apply (*veneer etc.*); 3. (*Hunt.*) retrieve (*game*). **2.** *irr.v.i.* ***– auf*** (*Acc.*), propose.

Antragsformular ['antra:ksfɔrmula:r], *n.* application form. **Antragsteller,** *m.* applicant, (*Parl.*) proposer (*of a motion*), (*Law*) petitioner.

antrauen ['antrauən], *v.t.* marry to; ***mein angetrauter Mann,*** my wedded husband.

antreffen ['antrɛfən], *irr.v.t.* meet with, fall in with; encounter, hit upon, come across; find (at home *or* in); ***ich traf ihn zufällig an,*** by chance I found *or* caught him in; ***ich traf ihn gesund an,*** I found him well.

antreiben ['antraɪbən], **1.** *irr.v.t.* drive *or* urge along; propel, drive (*a machine etc.*); wash ashore; impel, excite, actuate, prompt; force (***plants***); ***vom Hunger angetrieben,*** impelled by hunger. **2.** *irr.v.i.* 1. sprout (*of plants*); 2. (*aux.* s.) drift *or* be washed ashore. **Antreibung,** *f.* impulsion; incitement. *See* **Antrieb.**

antreten ['antre:tən], **1.** *irr.v.t.* 1. enter upon, begin, take up, assume, accede to (*office*), set out on (*a journey*); take possession of; 2. tread down (*earth*); 3. (*Poet.*) go up to, accost; 4. (*Law*) ***den Beweis –***, offer proof (***für***, of). **2.** *irr.v.i.* (*aux.* s.) 1. step up for; line up, station o.s.; take one's place; ***zum Dienst –***, report for duty; ***zum Tanze –***, take one's place among the dancers; 2. (*Mil.*) fall in, form up in ranks; ***angetreten!*** fall in! *See* **Antritt.**

Antrieb ['antri:p], *m.* 1. impulse, impulsion, impetus, motive, incentive, inducement, stimulus; ***aus natürlichem –***, instinctively; ***aus freiem –***, of one's own accord *or* own free will; ***aus eigenem –***, spontaneously, of one's own volition, on one's own initiative; 2. drive, driving gear; 3. propulsion, (propelling) force, (motive) power. **Antriebs|-achse,** *f.* driving axle. **-kasten,** *m.* gear-box. **-scheibe,** *f.* driving pulley. **-welle,** *f.* driving *or* engine *or* main shaft.

antrinken ['antrɪŋkən], *irr.v.i.* (*aux.* h.) drink first, begin to drink; ***sich*** (*Dat.*) ***einen Rausch –***, get tipsy; ***sich*** (*Dat.*) ***Mut –***, give o.s. Dutch courage; ***angetrunken,*** the worse for drink, tipsy, fuddled.

Antritt ['antrɪt], *m.* 1. entrance (*Gen.*, upon); start, beginning, commencement; accession (to) (*throne*); assumption (of); setting out (on); entering (into) *or* taking possession (of); 2. first *or* bottom step (*of a staircase*). **Antritts|audienz,** *f.* first audience *or* reception (*at court*). **-predigt,** *f.* inaugural sermon. **-rede,** *f.* inaugural address. **-schmaus,** *m.* installation banquet. **-vorlesung,** *f.* inaugural lecture.

antrocknen ['antrɔknən], *v.i.* (*aux.* s.) 1. begin to dry; 2. dry on (*an* (*Acc.*), to).

antun ['antu:n], *irr.v.t.* 1. put on (*clothes*), don; 2. do (*Dat.*, to); ***ihm Ehre –***, honour him, do him an honour; ***ihm Gutes*** (***Böses***) **–**, do him a kindness (harm); ***ihm Gewalt –***, do violence to him; ***einer Frau Gewalt –***, violate *or* rape *or* ravish a woman; ***ihm ein Leid*** (or ***Leids***) **–**, lay violent hands on him; ***ihm Schande –***, disgrace him, bring disgrace on him; ***ihm Schimpf –***, insult him, offer an affront to him; ***sich*** (*Dat.*) ***Zwang –***, restrain o.s., keep o.s. in check; overcome one's reluctance, force *or* constrain o.s. (to do); ***sich*** (*Dat.*) ***keinen Zwang –***, not restrain o.s., let o.s. go; ***es ihm –***, captivate *or* charm him, take his fancy; 3. ***angetan,*** clad, attired; adapted; ***dazu*** or ***danach angetan sein,*** be suitable for, be of a kind *or* nature to, be likely to; ***angetan sein von,*** have a high opinion of, have a liking *or* a fancy for, (*coll.*) be taken with, be smitten by.

Antwerpen ['antvɛrpən], *n.* Antwerp.

Antwort ['antvɔrt], *f.* (**-**, *pl.* **-en**) answer, reply, response; ***in – auf*** (*Acc.*), in answer to; ***er ist gleich mit einer – da,*** he is never at a loss for an answer; ***sie blieb ihm keine – schuldig,*** she had an answer to everything he said; ***ihm Rede und – stehen über*** (*Acc.*), account for *or* answer for (*s.th.*) to him; ***abschlägige –***, refusal; ***spitzige*** or ***schlagfertige –***, pat answer, retort; ***um – wird gebeten*** (***u.A.w.g.***), (the favour of) an answer is requested (R.S.V.P.); (*Prov.*) ***keine – ist auch eine –***, silence gives consent. **antworten,** *v.t., v.i.* answer, reply; ***ihm auf seine Frage –***, reply to *or* answer his question. **Antwort|gesang,** *m.* antiphonal chant, response. **-karte,** *f.* reply (post-)card. **antwortlich,** *prep.* (*Gen.*) (*Comm.*) **–** ***Ihres Briefes,*** in reply to your letter. **Antwort|schein,** *m.* international reply-coupon. **-schreiben,** *n.* (written) reply, answering letter, answer in writing.

anüben ['anʔy:bən], *v.t.* ***sich*** (*Dat.*) ***etwas –***, acquire s.th. by practice.

anulken ['anʔulkən], *v.t.* (*coll.*) make fun of, pull (*s.o.'s*) leg.

anvertrauen ['anfɛrtrauən], **1.** *v.t.* ***ihm etwas –***, entrust s.th. to him, (en)trust him with s.th.; confide s.th. to him, tell him s.th. in confidence, impart *or* disclose s.th. to him in confidence; ***anvertrautes Geld,*** money held in trust, trust money. **2.** *v.r.* ***sich ihm –***, confide in him, unbosom o.s. *or* open one's heart to him; ***sich etwas*** (*Dat.*) **–**, (put one's) trust in s.th.

anverwandt ['anfɛrvant], *adj.* related (*Dat.*, to), connected (by marriage) (with).

Anverwandte(r) ['anfɛrvantə(r)], *m., f.* relation, relative, kinsman, kinswoman. **Anverwandtschaft,** *f.* relationship, kinship, connexion (by marriage).

anvisieren ['anvizi:rən], *v.t.* (take) aim at, (***Surv., Navig.***) (take a) sight on.

Anwachs ['anvaks], *m.* (**-es,** *no pl.*) increase, growth, swelling, (*Law*) accretion, accumulation, accruing (*of interest*); accession, (amount of) increase, increment, accumulated *or* accrued interest, (*Geol.*) alluvion.

anwachsen ['anvaksən], *irr.v.i.* 1. take *or* strike root, begin to grow; 2. grow on, adhere (*an* (*Acc.*), to); ***wie angewachsen sitzen,*** sit stock still, sit tight; ***wie angewachsen stehen,*** stand rooted to the spot; ***ihm ist die Zunge wie angewachsen,*** he is tongue-tied *or* (as though) struck dumb; ***ihm ist die Zunge nicht angewachsen,*** he has a glib *or* ready tongue; 3. grow, increase, swell (*also of sound*), accumulate, accrue (*of interest*). **Anwachsen,** *n.* 1. growth, increase; ***im – sein,*** be on the increase; 2. accretion, accumulation; 3. adhesion (*an* (*Acc.*), to). *See* **Anwachs, Anwuchs. Anwachsstreifen,** *pl.* (*Zool.*) lines of growth.

Anwalt ['anvalt], *m.* (**-s,** *pl.* **¨-e**) lawyer; attorney, solicitor; counsel, barrister, advocate (*also fig.*) (*N.B. in German Law there is no difference between barrister and solicitor*); *see also* **Rechtsanwalt, Staatsanwalt. Anwaltschaft,** *f.* the legal profession, the bar; agency, attorneyship. **Anwalts|-gebühr,** *f.,* **-honorar,** *n.* lawyer's fee; agent's fee. **-kammer,** *f.* (German) Bar Association. **-vorschuß,** *m.* retaining fee, retainer.

anwandeln ['anvandəln], *v.imp.* befall, come over, come upon; attack, seize (*of illness etc.*); ***was wandelt dich an?*** what has come over you? ***es wandelte mich eine Ohnmacht an,*** I was overcome by a fainting fit. **Anwandlung,** *f.* fit (*of rage, generosity etc.*); touch (*of pity, fear etc.*); slight attack (*of illness*); impulse.

anwärmen ['anvɛrmən], *v.t.* heat *or* warm slightly; take the chill off; warm up (*also an engine*).

Anwärter ['anvɛrtər], *m.* 1. (*Law*) reversioner, expectant (heir), heir in expectancy; 2. candidate (***auf*** (*Acc.*), for), aspirant (to); probationer; (*Mil.*) (officer) cadet.

Anwartschaft ['anvartʃaft], *f.* 1. (*Law*) (right of) reversion; 2. expectancy; expectation (***auf*** (*Acc.*), of); 3. qualifying period (*insurance*). **anwartschaftlich,** *adj.* reversionary. **Anwartschaftsrente,** *f.* reversionary *or* deferred annuity.

anwedeln ['anve:dəln], *v.t.* greet *or* welcome (by wagging tail), (*fig.*) toady to, fawn upon.

anwehen ['anve:ən], **1.** *v.t.* blow *or* breathe on; come over; ***Entsetzen wehte ihn an,*** horror seized him; (*coll.*) ***ihm etwas –***, give him a gentle hint. **2.** *v.i.* (*aux.* s.) drift (*as snow*), be wafted along.

anweichen ['anvaɪçən], *v.t.* soften a little, steep, soak.

anweisbar ['anvaɪsba:r], *adj.* transferable, assignable.

anweisen ['anvaɪzən], *irr.v.t.* 1. direct, instruct, give directions *or* instructions; ***ihm etwas –***, assign *or* allot *or* allocate s.th. to him; remit (*money*) to him; ***sich – lassen,*** take directions *or* advice; ***angewiesen sein zu tun,*** have orders *or* instructions to do; 2. ***angewiesen sein auf*** (*Acc.*), be dependent on, have to rely on, be entirely reliant on; ***er war auf sich selbst angewiesen,*** he was left to his own resources. **Anweisung,** *f.* 1. order, instruction, direction, directive; 2. allocation, allotment, assignation, assignment; 3. remittance, draft, money-order.

anwendbar ['anvɛntba:r], *adj.* applicable (***auf*** (*Acc.*), to); usable, employable, practicable, feasible. **Anwendbarkeit,** *f.* applicability (***auf*** (*Acc.*), to); practical usefulness, practicability, feasibility.

anwenden ['anvɛndən], *reg. & irr.v.t.* 1. employ, use, make use of, put to use, turn *or* put to account; ***Fleiß – bei,*** take pains with *or* over; ***Gewalt –,*** resort to *or* use *or* employ force; ***alle Kräfte –,*** do one's utmost, use every effort; ***viele Mühe –,*** take great trouble; ***Vorsicht –,*** take precautions *or* care, use caution; 2. apply, be applicable (***auf*** *(Acc.)*, to); bring to bear (on); ***praktisch –,*** put *or* carry into practice; ***angewandt,*** applied; ***angewandte Wissenschaften,*** applied sciences. **Anwendung,** *f.* 1. application (***auf*** *(Acc.)*, to); ***– finden*** (***auf***), apply, be applicable, have application (to); ***entsprechende – finden,*** apply mutatis mutandis; 2. employment; use (***für, zu,*** for), utilization (of); ***in – bringen,*** use, employ; ***in der –,*** in practice; ***– finden, zur – kommen,*** be used. **Anwendungsbereich,** *m.* range of application, scope.

anwerben ['anvɛrbən], *irr.v.t.* recruit, enlist (*troops*); ***sich – lassen,*** enlist. **Anwerbung,** *f.* enlistment, recruitment.

anwerfen ['anvɛrfən], **1.** *irr.v.i.* have the first throw (*dice etc.*). **2.** *irr.v.t.* 1. crank (*an engine*); ***den Motor –,*** crank the engine, start the engine (by hand); 2. throw (***an*** *(Acc.)*, on to *or* against); ***Putz an eine Wand –,*** roughcast a wall.

Anwesen ['anve:zən], *n.* property; real estate, premises, (*Law*) messuage.

anwesend ['anve:zənt], *adj.* present; ***die Anwesenden,*** those present, the company, the spectators, the audience; ***hochgeehrte Anwesende!*** (ladies and) gentlemen! **Anwesenheit,** *f.* presence, attendance.

anwidern ['anvi:dərn], *v.t.* disgust. **anwidernd,** *adj.* disgusting, offensive; repulsive, repellent.

Anwohner ['anvo:nər], *m.* adjacent *or* nearby resident. **Anwohnerschaft,** *f.* neighbouring inhabitants, adjacent owners.

Anwuchs ['anvuks], *m.* growth; increase; accretion; ***junger –,*** young copse.

anwünschen ['anvynʃən], *v.t.* ***ihm etwas –,*** wish s.th. upon him; ***er wünschte mir viel Gutes an,*** he wished me the best of luck.

Anwurf ['anvurf], *m.* 1. first throw; 2. rough-cast; 3. deposit payment on account, earnest-money; 4. *pl.* reproaches, offensive remarks. **Anwurfmotor,** *m.* starting-motor.

anwurzeln ['anvurtsəln], *v.i.* (*aux.* s.), *v.r.* strike *or* take root; ***wie angewurzelt,*** rooted *or* nailed to the spot.

Anzahl ['antsa:l], *f.* number, quantity, multitude.

anzahlen ['antsa:lən], *v.t., v.i.* pay on account, pay a deposit, pay a first instalment (***auf*** *(Acc.)*, on). **Anzahlung,** *f.* payment on account, down payment, first instalment, deposit.

anzapfen ['antsapfən], *v.t.* broach, tap (*a cask*); tap (*a tree for resin, a supply, and (coll.) a p. for money*), (*coll.*) pump (*for news*).

anzaubern ['antsaubərn], *v.t.* cast a spell on, bewitch; ***angezaubert,*** spellbound, bewitched.

anzäumen ['antsɔymən], *v.t.* bridle, put a bridle on.

Anzeichen ['antsaɪçən], *n.* mark, indication, sign, symptom; token, omen, foreboding, augury; ***alle – deuten darauf hin daß,*** there is every indication that.

anzeichnen ['anzaɪçnən], *v.t.* mark, note; make *or* put a mark on.

Anzeige ['antsaɪgə], *f.* 1. notice, notification, intimation, (*Comm.*) advice-note; (*Law*) ***– erstatten gegen,*** report on; denounce, inform against; ***eine – machen bei,*** file a declaration with, report to, notify; 2. advertisement, announcement; ***kleine –n,*** small advertisements; 3. review (*of a book*); ***kurze –,*** short notice *or* review (*of a book*). **Anzeige|amt,** *n.* registry office. **–blatt,** *n.* advertisement sheet *or* journal. **–brief,** *m.* intimation (*of wedding etc.*). **–gerät,** *n.* indicator, indicating instrument. **–material,** *n.* (*Law*) information furnished by an informer. **–mittel,** *n.* (*Chem.*) indicator.

anzeigen ['antsaɪgən], **1.** *v.t.* 1. register, record, indicate, read (*as measuring instruments*); 2. show, indicate, mark, denote; ***–des Fürwort,*** demonstrative pronoun; 3. announce, give notice of, notice (*a book*), advertise (*in newspaper*); 4. inform, notify, intimate, report; advise *or* apprise of, acquaint with; inform against, denounce; ***den Empfang –,*** acknowledge receipt; ***Preise –,*** quote prices; ***eine Tratte –,*** advise a draft; 5. betoken, (fore)bode, augur, portend, presage; ***es für angezeigt halten,*** think *or* see fit, think *or* judge *or* deem it proper, regard it as advisable *or* desirable. **2.** *v.r.* show *or* manifest itself; ***sich selbst –,*** give o.s. up, make a voluntary admission.

Anzeigen|blatt, *n. See* **Anzeigeblatt. –teil,** *m.* advertisement section *or* pages. **–vermittler,** *m.* advertising agent. **–vermittlung,** *f.* advertising agency.

Anzeigepflicht ['antsaɪgəpflɪçt], *f.* obligation to notify the authorites *or* to report to the police. **anzeigepflichtig,** *adj.* notifiable (*disease*).

Anzeiger ['antsaɪgər], *m.* 1. indicator (*person or device*), pointer; informer; advertiser; 2. gazette, advertising journal. **Anzeige|vorrichtung,** *f. See* **–gerät. Anzeigung,** *f.* informing; denunciation.

Anzettel ['antsɛtəl], *m.* warp. **anzetteln,** *v.t.* 1. set up the warp on (*a loom*); 2. hatch, weave, concoct, contrive, plot, scheme; ***eine Verschwörung – gegen,*** plot against. **Anzettler,** *m.* plotter, intriguer, schemer.

anziehbar ['antsi:ba:r], *adj.* 1. attractable; 2. wearable.

anziehen ['antsi:ən], **1.** *irr.v.t.* 1. pull (at), pull (*a door*) to, draw up (*knees etc.*), (*Anat.*) adduct; 2. pull tight *or* taught, tighten, strain, stretch; ***die Bremse –,*** put on *or* apply the brake; ***eine Schraube –,*** drive a screw home; (*coll.*) ***die Schrauben –,*** put on the screw, apply pressure; ***die Zügel –,*** draw rein; (*coll.*) ***die Zügel straff –,*** keep a tight rein (***bei,*** on) *or* a tight hand (on *or* over); 3. draw, attract, have an attraction for; ***sich angezogen fühlen von,*** feel attracted to *or* drawn towards; 4. put *or* pull on (*clothes*), clothe, dress (*a p.*); (*B.*) ***den neuen Menschen –,*** put on the new man, (*coll.*) become a new man, turn over a new leaf, mend one's ways. **2.** *irr.v.r.* dress (o.s.), put one's clothes on, put on one's clothes. **3.** *irr.v.i.* 1. pull, start pulling; 2. (*aux.* s.) march (up), move in (***gegen,*** against) (*of troops*); ***angezogen kommen,*** arrive, approach, come up *or* along; 3. hold, grip, bite (*as a screw*), hold, take, stick (*as glue*), bind, set (*as cement*); 4. (*Comm.*) rise, move up, advance (*as prices*), improve, stiffen, harden (*as markets*); 5. turn cold, get *or* grow colder (*of weather*).

anziehend ['antsi:ənt], *adj.* attractive, engaging, prepossessing; inviting, alluring; (*Comm.*) ***–er Markt,*** rising *or* seller's market. **Anzieher,** *m.* 1. shoehorn; 2. (*Anat.*) adductor muscle. **Anziehmuskel,** *m.* adductor muscle.

Anziehung ['antsi:uŋ], *f.* 1. attraction, pull; ***– der Schwere,*** gravitational pull, force of gravity, gravitation; 2. quoting, citation; 3. tightening. **Anziehungs|bereich,** *m.* (*Magnet.*) field of attraction. **–kraft,** *f.* attraction, pull, force of attraction; attractiveness. **–punkt,** *m.* centre of attraction. **–vermögen,** *n.* (force of) attraction.

Anzucht ['antsuxt], *f.* raising, breeding, rearing (*animals*), cultivation (*plants*).

Anzug ['antsu:k], *m.* 1. suit of clothes; dress, costume; ***fertiger –,*** ready-made suit; 2. approach, advance, (*obs.*) entrance (*upon duties*), (*Chess etc.*) opening move; ***der Feind ist im –e,*** the enemy is on the march; ***es ist etwas im –,*** there is s.th. in the wind *or* s.th. afoot *or* brewing *or* (*coll.*) up; ***es ist ein Gewitter im –,*** a storm is brewing *or* threatening *or* imminent *or* coming up.

anzüglich ['antsy:klɪç], *adj.* suggestive; personal; offensive; abusive. **Anzüglichkeit,** *f.* personal remark; offensiveness; *pl.* personalities.

Anzugordnung ['antsu:kʔɔrtnuŋ], *f.* (*Mil.*) dress regulations.

Anzugs|drehmoment, *m.* (*Mech.*) starting torque. **–stoff,** *m.* (gentleman's) suiting. **–vermögen,** *n.* starting power; (*Motor.*) ***gutes –,*** fast get-away.

anzünden ['antsyndən], *v.t.* kindle, light (*a fire etc.*); set fire to, set on fire; ignite; inflame; excite (*passion etc.*); ***ein Streichholz –***, light *or* strike a match. **Anzünder,** *m.* fire-lighter; (lamp)-lighter.

anzweifeln ['antsvaɪfəln], *v.t.* question, call in question, have one's doubts about, cast doubts upon.

Äolsharfe ['ɛ:ɔlsharfə], *f.* Aeolian harp.

Aorta [a'ɔrta], *f.* (-, *pl.* **Aorten**) aorta. **Aortenkammer,** *f.* left ventricle.

apart [a'part], **1.** *adj.* uncommon, out of the ordinary, unusual, striking, distinctive, stylish, smart. **2.** *adv.* separately, apart; ***nicht – abgegeben,*** not sold separately. **Aparte,** *n.* (-, *pl.* **-s**) (*Theat.*) aside, stage-whisper.

Apathie [apa'ti:], *f.* apathy, listlessness. **apathisch** [a'pa:tɪʃ], *adj.* apathetic, listless.

Apfel ['apfəl], *m.* (**-s,** *pl.* **⸚**) 1. apple; (*Prov.*) ***in den sauren – beißen,*** swallow a bitter pill; (*Prov.*) ***für einen – und ein Ei,*** for a song; (*Prov.*) ***der – fällt nicht weit vom Stamm,*** like father like son; what's bred in the bone will come out in the flesh; 2. orb (*of regalia*); 3. dapple (*on horse*); 4. (horse-)dropping, (*vulg.*) turd. **Apfeläther,** *m.* malic ether. **apfelbraun,** *adj.* dappled bay (*horse*). **Apfel|brei,** *m.* apple purée. **-dorn,** *m.* crab-apple tree. **-garten,** *m.* orchard. **-gehäuse,** *n.* apple core. **apfelgrau,** *adj.* dapple-grey. **apfelig,** *adj.* dappled. **Apfel|kern,** *m.* (apple) pip. **-kompott,** *n.* stewed apple. **-kuchen,** *m.* apple-tart. **-most,** *m.* new cider. **-mus,** *n.* apple purée.

äpfeln ['ɛpfəln], *v.i.* drop dung (*of horse*).

Apfel|presse, *f.* cider-press. **-saft,** *m.* apple juice (*unfermented*). **-säure,** *f.* malic acid. **-schale,** *f.* apple-paring, apple-peel. **-schimmel,** *m.* dapple-grey horse. **-sine** [–'zi:nə], *f.* orange. **-stecher,** *m.* apple corer. **-torte,** *f.* apple-tart. **-wein,** *m.* cider.

Aphongetriebe [a'fo:ŋgətri:bə], *n.* (*Motor.*) synchromesh transmission.

Apokalypse [apoka'lypsə], *f.* apocalypse. **apokalyptisch,** *adj.* apocalyptic, (*fig.*) gloomy; ***die -en Reiter,*** the (four) Horsemen of the Apocalypse.

apokryph(isch) [apo'kry:f(ɪʃ)], *adj.* apocryphal.

Apoll [a'pɔl], *m.* Apollo.

Apolog [apɔ'lo:k], *m.* (**-s,** *pl.* **-e**) apologue. **Apologet** [–'ge:t], *m.* (**-en,** *pl.* **-en**) apologist.

Apostat [apɔs'ta:t], *m.* (**-en,** *pl.* **-en**) apostate.

Apostel [a'pɔstəl], *m.* apostle. **Apostel|brief,** *m.* (*B.*) epistle. **-geschichte,** *f.* Acts of the Apostles. **-kollegium,** *n.* the Twelve Apostles.

Apostem [apo'ste:m], *m.* (**-s,** *pl.* **-e**) aposteme, abscess.

Apotheke [apo'te:kə], *f.* (dispensing) chemist's shop, pharmacy, dispensary. **Apotheker,** *m.* (dispensing *or* pharmaceutical) chemist, pharmacist; apothecary. **Apotheker|buch,** *n.* pharmacopœia. **-gewicht,** *n.* apothecary's weight. **-kunst,** *f.* pharmaceutics. **-waren,** *pl.* drugs. **-wissenschaft,** *f.* pharmaceutics.

Apotheose [apote'o:zə], *f.* apotheosis, deification.

Appalachen [apa'laxən], *n.pl.* Appalachian Mountains.

Apparat [apa'ra:t], *m.* (**-(e)s,** *pl.* **-e**) 1. apparatus; equipment, appliance, device, contrivance; instrument, (*esp. coll.*) camera, (*coll.*) telephone, (*coll.*) safety razor, electric razor; (*Tele.*) ***am –!*** speaking! 2. (*obs.*) pomp, array, trappings; 3. research material, (reference) books in constant use (*in library*). **Apparatebrett,** *n.* instrument board *or* panel. **apparativ** [–ra'ti:f], *adj.* relating to the apparatus. **Apparatur** [–ra'tu:r], *f.* (-, *pl.* **-en**) equipment.

Appell [a'pɛl], *m.* (**-s,** *pl.* **-e**) roll-call; parade, inspection; ***– haben,*** be obedient *or* well-trained (*of dogs*); (*Mil.*) ***– abhalten,*** call the roll; ***zum – antreten,*** fall in for roll-call.

Appellant [apɛ'lant], *m.* (**-en,** *pl.* **-en**) appellant. **Appellat** [–'la:t], *m.* (**-en,** *pl.* **-en**) defendant, respondent. **Appellation** [–tsi'o:n], *f.* (*Law*) appeal. **Appellations|freiheit,** *f.* right of appeal. **-gericht,** *n.* court of appeal. **-klage,** *f.* action upon appeal. **appellieren** [–'li:rən], *v.i.* appeal (*also Law*), make an appeal (*an* (*Acc.*), to).

Appellstärke [a'pɛlʃtɛrkə], *f.* (*Mil.*) parade state.

Appetit [apə'ti:t], *m.* (**-(e)s,** *pl.* **-e**) appetite (***auf*** (*Acc.*), ***nach,*** for). **appetitanregend,** *adj.* appetizing. **Appetit|brötchen,** *n.* savoury snack. **-happen,** *m.* tasty morsel. **appetitlich,** *adj.* dainty; appetizing. **appetitlos,** *adj.* having no appetite. **Appetitlosigkeit,** *f.* loss *or* lack of appetite.

applaudieren [aplau'di:rən], *v.t., v.i.* applaud.

Applikation [aplikatsi'o:n], *f.* 1. application, diligence; 2. appliqué. **Applikationsarbeit,** *f.* appliqué work.

Applikatur [aplika'tu:r], *f.* (-, *pl.* **-en**) (*Mus.*) fingering.

applizieren [apli'tsi:rən], *v.t.* apply, administer.

apportieren [apɔr'ti:rən], *v.t.* retrieve, fetch (*of dogs*). **Apportierhund,** *m.* retriever.

Appret [a'pre:t], *m. or n.* (**-s,** *pl.* **-s**) stiffening (agent), dressing.

appretieren [apre'ti:rən], *v.t.* dress, finish (*fabrics*). **Appretur,** *f.* (-, *pl.* **-en**) dressing; finish.

approbiert [apro'bi:rt], *adj.* certified, state-registered.

Aprikose [apri'ko:zə], *f.* apricot.

April [a'prɪl], *m.* (**-s,** *pl.* **-e**) April; ***ihn in den – schicken,*** make an April fool of him. **April|blume,** *f.* anemone (*Anemone nemorosa*). **-glück,** *n.* fleeting good luck, short-lived happiness. **-scherz,** *m.* April-fool hoax. **April(s)|geck, -narr,** *m.* April fool.

Apside [ap'si:də], *f.* (*Astr.*) apsis, (*Archit.*) apse.

Apsis ['apsɪs], *f.* (-, *pl.* **Apsiden** [–'si:dən]) apse.

Apulien [a'pu:liən], *n.* Apulia. **apulisch,** *adj.* Apulian.

Aquarell [akva'rɛl], *n.* (**-s,** *pl.* **-e**) water-colour. **aquarellieren** [–'li:rən], *v.t., v.i.* paint in water-colours. **Aquarellist** [–'lɪst], *m.* (**-en,** *pl.* **-en**) water-colour painter.

Äquator [ɛ'kva:tɔr], *m.* (**-s,** *no pl.*) equator; ***unter dem –,*** at the equator.

Aquavit [akva'vi:t], *m.* (**-(e)s,** *no pl.*) aqua vitae, eau-de-vie.

Äquilibrist [ɛkvili'brɪst], *m.* (**-en,** *pl.* **-en**) tight-rope walker, trapeze artiste.

Aquitanien [akvi'ta:niən], *n.* Aquitaine.

Ar [a:r], *n. or* (*Bavaria & Austr.*) *m.* (**-es,** *pl.* **-e**) 100 square metres.

Ära ['ɛ:ra], *f.* (-, *pl.* **Ären**) era.

Araber ['arabər], *m.* 1. Arab; 2. Arab (horse). **Arabien** [a'ra:biən], *n.* Arabia. **arabisch** [a'ra:bɪʃ], *adj.* Arabic (*language etc.*), Arabian, Arab. **Arabisch,** *n.* Arabic (*language*).

Arachis ['araxɪs], *f.* (-, *pl.* -) (*Bot.*) peanut, groundnut.

Aragonien [ara'go:niən], *n.* Aragon. **aragonisch,** *adj.* Aragonese.

Ärar [ɛ'ra:r], *n.* (*Austr.*) (**-s,** *pl.* **-e, -ien**) (public) treasury, exchequer.

ärarial [ɛrari'a:l], *adj.* fiscal; ***-e Ausgaben,*** public expenditure. **Ärarial|schuld,** *f.* public debt. **-vermögen,** *n.* public *or* State funds. **ärarisch,** *adj. See* **ärarial.**

Arbeit ['arbaɪt], *f.* (-, *pl.* **-en**) 1. work, labour, toil (***an*** (*Dat.*), on); ***an die – gehen, sich an die – machen,*** set to work; ***an*** or ***bei der –,*** at work; ***ganze – machen,*** make a good job of it; ***Kapital und –,*** capital and labour; ***der Tag der –,*** Labour Day; ***verlorene –,*** wasted effort, a waste of time; 2. (*Phys.*) work; ***Einheit der –,*** unit of work; 3. work, occupation, employment; ***– haben,*** be in work *or* employment, have a job; ***keine – haben,*** be out of work *or* a job, be unemployed; ***ihn in – nehmen,*** give him employment *or* a job, take him on; ***– nehmen,*** take *or* accept employment; ***ohne – sein,*** see ***keine – haben;*** 4. task, job; ***in – sein,*** be in hand, be in the process of manufacture; ***in – geben,*** put in hand, have work started on; ***in – haben,*** have in hand, be working on; ***in – nehmen,*** take in hand, start work on; ***eine saure –,*** a gruelling task; ***seine – tun,*** do one's job; 5. piece of work, achievement, handiwork, workmanship; ***alles ist meine –,*** it is all my own work; ***deutsche –,*** German work(manship); 6. working, functioning, operation (*of a machine etc.*), fermentation; ***in – sein,*** be fermenting *or* working (*of wine*); 7. essay, exercise (*school*); paper, thesis, dissertation (*university*); ***schriftliche –en,*** written work.

arbeiten [ˈarbaɪtən], **1.** *v.t.* make (*clothes etc.*), shape, fashion (*wood etc.*), work (*metal, stone*); ***gearbeitet,*** executed, wrought; ***sich zu Tode –,*** work o.s. to death; ***es arbeitet sich schlecht,*** conditions are bad for work; ***sich hindurch –,*** work one's way through; ***sich krank –,*** knock o.s. up with work. **2.** *v.i.* 1. work, toil, labour (*an* (*Dat.*), at *or* on); ***mit Händen und Füßen –,*** struggle, exert o.s.; ***in die Hände –,*** play into the hands (*Dat.*, of); 2. work, function, operate (*as a machine*), be active (*of volcano*), ferment, work (*of wine, beer*), rise (*of dough*); (*Comm.*) ***– mit,*** transact business with; (*Comm.*) ***Geld – lassen,*** put money out at interest, employ capital to advantage. **Arbeiter,** *m.* worker, workman, working man; hand, operative (*in factory*), artisan, labourer.

Arbeiter|ausschließung, *f.* lock-out. **–ausschuß,** *m.* workers' committee. **–ausstand,** *m.* strike. **–bevölkerung,** *f.* working population. **–bewegung,** *f.* working-class *or* Labour movement. **–fahrkarte,** *f.* workman's ticket. **–familie,** *f.* working-class family. **–frage,** *f.* labour question.

Arbeiterin [ˈarbaɪtərɪn], *f.* 1. (female *or* woman) worker, working woman *or* girl, work-woman, factory-girl, (female) hand *or* operative; 2. worker bee *or* ant.

Arbeiter|klasse, *f.* working class. **–partei,** *f.* Labour Party. **–rat,** *m.* workers' council.

Arbeiterschaft [ˈarbaɪtərʃaft], *f.* the workers *or* working class(es), proletariat.

Arbeiter|schutz, *m.* protection of labour. **–stand,** *m.* working class, labouring classes. **–tum,** *n.* *See* **Arbeiterschaft. –versicherung,** *f.* industrial insurance. **–viertel,** *n.* working-class district. **–wohnung,** *f.* working-class house, worker's flat.

Arbeit|geber, *m.* employer. **–nehmer,** *m.* employee.

arbeitsam [ˈarbaɪtza:m], *adj.* hard-working, diligent, industrious. **Arbeitsamkeit,** *f.* industry, diligence.

Arbeits|amt, *n.* Labour Exchange. **–anzug,** *m.* working *or* everyday clothes; dungarees, overalls; (*Mil.*) fatigue dress. **–äquivalent,** *n.* (*Mech.*) mechanical equivalent. **–aufwand,** *m.* expenditure of work, work *or* effort involved. **–bank,** *f.* (work-) bench. **–basis,** *f.* working basis. **–bereich,** *m.* sphere of action *or* activity. **–beschaffung,** *f.* provision of work (for unemployed), works programme. **–beutel,** *m.* workbag, toolbag. **–dienst,** *m.* labour service. **–einheit,** *f.* (*Mech.*) unit of work, erg. **–einsatz,** *m.* allocation *or* deployment of labour; labour force *or* pool. **–einstellung,** *f.* stoppage *or* cessation of work. **–erlaubnis,** *f.* work *or* labour permit. **–ersparnis,** *f.* labour-saving.

arbeitsfähig [ˈarbaɪtsfɛ:ɪç], *adj.* able-bodied, fit for work; ***–e Mehrheit,*** working majority.

Arbeits|feld, *n.* field of activity, sphere (of action). **–flugzeug,** *n.* army-cooperation plane. **–freude,** *f.* pleasure in one's work. **arbeitsfreudig,** *adj.* happy in one's work. **Arbeits|gang,** *m.* operation, stage (of manufacture); series of operations, process. **–gemeinschaft,** *f.* study group, seminar; (working) team; combine, syndicate; copartnership (of employers and workers). **–genehmigung,** *f.* *See* **–erlaubnis. –gericht,** *n.* Industrial *or* Labour Court. **–gruppe,** *f.* working party. **–haus,** *n.* corrective institution; (*Am.*) penitentiary. **–hub,** *m.* (*Engin.*) power stroke. **–hypothese,** *f.* working hypothesis *or* theory. **–kammer,** *f.* laboratory. **–kästchen,** *n.* (ladies') work-box; tool-box. **–kommando,** *n.* (*Mil.*) fatigue party. **–kräfte,** *pl.* hands, manpower, labour. **–lager,** *n.* work *or* labour camp. **–leistung,** *f.* 1. rate of work, output; 2. achievement, efficiency, power, performance. **–lohn,** *m.* wages.

arbeitslos [ˈarbaɪtslo:s], *adj.* out of work. **Arbeitslosenunterstützung,** *f.* unemployment benefit *or* pay, (*coll.*) dole. **Arbeitslosigkeit,** *f.* unemployment.

Arbeits|mann, *m.* workman. **–markt,** *m.* labour-market. **–nachweis,** *m.*, **–nachweisstelle,** *f.* employment agency. **arbeitsparend,** *adj.* labour-saving. **Arbeits|pause,** *f.* break (from work). **–pferd,** *n.* cart-horse, draught-horse, (*fig.*) tireless worker. **–platz,** *m.* job, position; place of work *or* employment; place to work (*desk, bench*). **–psychologie,** *f.* industrial psychology. **–raum,** *m.* workroom. **–recht,** *n.* industrial *or* labour legislation.

arbeits|reich, *adj.* active, busy (*life etc.*). **–scheu,** *adj.* work-shy, lazy, idle. **Arbeits|scheu,** *f.* laziness, idleness, slacking. **–schiene,** *f.* (*Elec.*) conductor *or* live rail. **–sperre,** *f.* lockout. **–stelle,** *f.* job, position; place of work *or* employment. **–streckung,** *f.* short-time working. **–strom,** *m.* (*Elec.*) operating *or* open-circuit current. **–stunden,** *pl.* working hours; hours of work, man-hours. **–tag,** *m.* working-day. **–teilung,** *f.* division of labour. **arbeitsunfähig,** *adj.* unfit for work, disabled. **Arbeits|vermögen,** *n.* capacity for work, (*Mech.*) kinetic energy. **–weise,** *f.* method *or* manner of working, mode of operation. **–wille,** *m.* willingness to work. **arbeitswillig,** *adj.* willing to work. **Arbeits|zeit,** *f.* working hours, hours of work. **–zeug,** *n.* tools.

archaisch [arˈça:ɪʃ], *adj.* archaic.

archäisch [arˈçɛ:ɪʃ], *adj.* (*Geol.*) Archaean, Pre-Cambrian, Azoic.

Archäologe [arçɛoˈlo:gə], *m.* (**-n,** *pl.* **-n**) archaeologist. **Archäologie** [–ˈgi:], *f.* archaeology. **archäologisch,** *adj.* archaeological.

Arche [ˈarçə], *f.* 1. ark; ***– Noah(s)*** or ***Noä,*** Noah's ark; 2. wind-chest (*of an organ*); 3. dyke, groyne, breakwater; coffer-dam.

Archidiakon [arçidiaˈko:n] (**-s,** *pl.* **-e(n)**), **Archidiakonus,** *m.* (-, *pl.* **-kone(n)**) archdeacon.

Archigonie [arçigoˈni:], *f.* spontaneous generation, abiogenesis.

archimedisch [arçiˈme:dɪʃ], *adj.* Archimedean.

Archipel [arçiˈpe:l], *m.* (**-s,** *pl.* **-e**) archipelago.

Architekt [arçiˈtɛkt], *m.* (**-en,** *pl.* **-en**) architect. **Architektonik** [–ˈto:nɪk], *f.* (-, *no pl.*) (architectonics. **architektonisch,** *adj.* architectural.

Architrav [arçiˈtra:f], *m.* (**-s,** *pl.* **-e**) architrave.

Archiv [arˈçi:f], *n.* (**-s,** *pl.* **-e**) record office; (*also pl.*) archives, records. **Archivalien** [–ˈva:liən], *pl.* archives, records, documents. **archivalisch** [–ˈva:lɪʃ], *adj.* documentary. **Archivar** [–ˈva:r], *m.* (**-s,** *pl.* **-e**) keeper of the archives, archivist. **Archivexemplar,** *n.* file-copy.

arg [ark], **1.** *adj.* (*comp.* *ärger,* *sup.* *ärgst*) 1. (*B.*) wicked, evil; 2. malicious, mischievous, harmful; ***–e Gedanken,*** evil thoughts; ***ein –er Geselle,*** a bad character; ***sein ärgster Feind,*** his worst *or* bitterest enemy; ***nichts Arges,*** no harm; 3. bad, severe, distressing, painful; (*coll.*) terrible, awful, dreadful; ***im ärgsten Falle,*** if it *or* if the worst comes to the worst, at worst; ***immer ärger werden,*** be getting worse and worse; ***sehr im –en liegen,*** be in a bad way; ***–es Mißverständnis,*** serious misunderstanding; ***–er Verdruß,*** serious annoyance; ***–e Verlegenheit,*** grave *or* serious trouble; ***–es Versehen,*** bad *or* grave *or* serious mistake; 4. confirmed, inveterate (*of a p., smoker, drunkard etc.*); ***–er Sünder,*** hardened sinner. **2.** *adv.* badly, seriously, severely; ill; (*coll.*) dreadfully, awfully, terribly; ***ihm – mitspielen,*** treat him badly, use him ill; ***es zu – treiben,*** carry things *or* go too far. **Arg,** *n.* (**-s,** *no pl.*) guile, malice; ***es ist kein – an*** or ***in ihm,*** there is no harm in him, he is not malicious; ***ohne –,*** without malice.

Argentinien [argɛnˈti:niən], *n.* Argentine (Republic). **Argentinier,** *m.* Argentine. **argentinisch,** *adj.* Argentine.

ärger ['ɛrgər], *see* **arg.**

Ärger, *m.* (**-s,** *no pl.*) annoyance, vexation, irritation; anger, chagrin (*über* (*Acc.*), at *or* about); ***ihm zum* –,** to spite him; **– *haben mit,*** have trouble with, be worried *or* bothered by. **ärgerlich, 1.** *adj.* 1. troublesome, annoying, irritating, exasperating, vexing, vexatious, provoking, tiresome, trying (*of things*); 2. angry, annoyed, vexed, exasperated (*über* (*Acc.*), at *or* about (*a th.*), with (*a p.*)), irritated (at *or* by (*a p. or th.*), with (*a p.*), about (*a th.*)), cross (about (*a th.*), with (*a p.*)). **2.** *adv.* angrily, irritably, in exasperation, with annoyance. **Ärgerlichkeit,** *f.* 1. irritability, irascibility, petulance, testiness (*of a p.*); 2. *pl.* vexations, annoyances, troubles, worries.

ärgern ['ɛrgərn], *v.t.* annoy, exasperate, irritate; vex, provoke, get on (*s.o.'s*) nerves, worry, bother; ***sich krank*** (***tot*** or ***zu Tode***) **–,** worry o.s. sick (to death); ***sich* – *über*** (*Acc.*), be angry *or* annoyed *or* irritated with *or* at (*a p.*) *or* about *or* at (*a th.*); worry, be worried, grieve, fret about (*a p. or th.*), be bothered about (*a th.*). **Ärgernis,** *n.* (**-ses,** *pl.* **-se**) vexation, annoyance; scandal; nuisance, cause of annoyance; **– *nehmen an*** (*Dat.*), be scandalized *or* take offence at; **– *geben,*** cause annoyance, give offence.

Arglist ['arklɪst], *f.* (-, *no pl.*) 1. cunning, craftiness, guile; 2. malice, (*Law*) malicious intent. **arglistig,** *adj.* 1. cunning, crafty, wily; 2. malicious (*also Law*).

arglos ['arklo:s], *adj.* without malice *or* guile guileless, artless, innocent, ingenuous, naïve, unsuspecting. **Arglosigkeit,** *f.* guilelessness, artlessness, innocence, ingenuousness, naïvety.

ärgst [ɛrkst], *see* **arg.**

Argument [argu'mɛnt], *n.* (**-(e)s,** *pl.* **-e**) argument. **argumentieren** [–'ti:rən], *v.i.* argue.

Argwille ['arkvɪlə], *m.* (**-ns,** *no pl.*) ill-will, spite, malevolence.

Argwohn ['arkvo:n], *m.* (**-(e)s,** *no pl.*) mistrust, distrust (***gegen,*** of), suspicion (about). **argwöhnen** [–'vø:nən] (*occ.* **argwohnen**), *v.t.* mistrust, distrust, suspect, be suspicious of, have a suspicion (that). **argwöhnisch,** *adj.* mistrustful, distrustful, suspicious.

Arianer [ari'a:nər], *m.* Arian. **arianisch,** *adj.* Arian.

Arie ['a:riə], *f.* (*Mus.*) aria.

Arier ['a:riər], *m.* Aryan (*abandoned by scientists, but used by Nat. Soc. = non-Jew*). **Arier|nachweis,** *m.* proof of 'Aryan' descent. **–paragraph,** *m.* Nat. Soc. anti-Jewish legislation.

Ariost [ari'ɔst], *m.* Ariosto.

Ariovist [ario'vɪst], *m.* Ariovistus.

arisch ['a:rɪʃ], *adj.* Aryan (*Nat. Soc.* = non-Jewish).

Aristokrat [arɪsto'kra:t], *m.* (**-en,** *pl.* **-en**) aristocrat. **Aristokratie** [–'ti:], *f.* aristocracy. **aristokratisch,** *adj.* aristocratic.

Aristoteles [arɪs'to:tələs], *m.* Aristotle. **Aristoteliker** [–'te:lɪkər], *m.* Aristotelian. **aristotelisch** [–'te:lɪʃ], *adj.* Aristotelian.

Arithmetik [arɪt'me:tɪk], *f.* (-, *no pl.*) arithmetic. **Arithmetiker,** *m.* arithmetician. **arithmetisch,** *adj.* arithmetical.

Arkadien [ar'ka:dɪən], *n.* Arcadia. **Arkadier,** *m.* Arcadian. **arkadisch,** *adj.* Arcadian.

Arktis ['arktɪs], *f.* (-, *no pl.*) the Arctic. **arktisch,** *adj.* arctic.

arm [arm], **1.** *adj.* (*comp.* ***ärmer,*** *sup.* ***ärmst***) 1. poor, needy, penniless, in want, penurious, impecunious, indigent; ***die Armen,*** the poor; ***geistig* –,** lacking in wit; (*B.*) ***die Armen im Geist,*** the poor in spirit; 2. poor, mean, sorry, wretched; ***ein –er Sünder,*** a miserable sinner *or* wretch; ***ein –er Teufel,*** a poor devil *or* wretch; 3. poor, unfortunate; ***ich Armer!*** poor me! ***du Armer!*** poor you! 4. (of) poor (quality), low-grade, deficient, weak; **– *an*** (*Dat.*), poor *or* lacking *or* deficient in. **–arm,** *adj. suff.* (*Chem. etc.*) poor in . . ., with a low . . . content; ***nikotinarm,*** with a low nicotine content.

Arm, *m.* (**-es,** *pl.* **-e**) 1. arm; ***am* –,** on one's arm; ***am* – *führen,*** lead by the arm; ***auf den* – *nehmen,*** pick up in one's arms; ***im* –,** in one's arms; ***ihm in den* – *fallen,*** seize him by the arm; ***ihm in die* –*e laufen,*** run to *or* into his arms; ***sich in die* –*e schließen,*** embrace (each other); ***ihm unter die* –*e greifen,*** give him a leg up (*also fig.*), (*fig.*) help him out; (*coll.*) ***die Beine unter die* –*e nehmen,*** pick up one's heels; 2. foreleg (*of a beast*); 3. arm, tributary (*of a river*); 4. beam (*of scales*); branch (*of a candlestick or river*); shaft (*of a barrow, carriage etc.*); arm (*of a chair, of the sea*); jib (*of a crane*), cross-piece, bracket.

Armatur [arma'tu:r], *f.* (-, *pl.* **-en**) (*Mil.*) accoutrements; (*usu. pl.*) fittings, mountings. **Armaturenbrett,** *n.* instrument-board *or* panel, (*Motor.*) dash-board.

Arm|band, *n.* 1. bracelet, bangle; 2. armlet, armband, brassard. **–banduhr,** *f.* wrist(let) watch. **–bein,** *n.* armbone, humerus. **–beuge, –biege,** *f.* bend of the elbow. **–binde,** *f.* armband, brassard, armlet, (*Med.*) sling. **–blätter,** *n.pl.* dress protectors *or* shields. **–blutader,** *f.* brachial artery. **–bruch,** *m.* fracture of the arm, broken arm. **–brust,** *f.* crossbow.

Armee [ar'me:], *f.* army.

Ärmel ['ɛrməl], *m.* sleeve; ***etwas in den* –*n stecken,*** put s.th. up one's sleeve; ***etwas aus dem* – *schütteln,*** do a th. with the greatest (of) ease, (*coll.*) do s.th. off the cuff *or* straight off the bat. **Ärmelaufschlag,** *m.* cuff. **–ärm(e)lig,** *adj. suff.* –sleeved. **Ärmelkanal,** *m.* English Channel. **ärmellos,** *adj.* sleeveless.

Armen|anstalt, *f.* alms-house, workhouse, poor-law institution. **–haus,** *n.* alms-house, workhouse.

Armenien [ar'me:niən], *n.* Armenia. **Armenier,** *m.* Armenian. **armenisch,** *adj.* Armenian.

Armen|kasse, *f.* (-, *no pl.*) relief fund. **–pflege,** *f.* poor-relief; public assistance. **–pfleger,** *m.* relieving officer, almoner. **–recht,** *n.* (right of pauper to) legal aid, (*Law*) right to sue in forma pauperis. **–schule,** *f.* charity school. **–viertel,** *n.* slum. **–vorsteher,** *m.* poor-law guardian. **–wesen,** *n.* poor-law administration.

ärmer ['ɛrmər], *see* **arm.**

Armesünder– [armə'zyndər], *pref.* of a condemned criminal. **–glocke,** *f.* death-knell. **–miene,** *f.* (*coll.*) hang-dog look, look of abject misery. **–stuhl,** *m.* stool of repentance; (*coll.*) ***auf dem* – *sitzen,*** be on the carpet.

Arm|flor, *m.* mourning armband. **–flosser,** *pl.* (*Ichth.*) pediculates. **–füßer,** *m.* (*Mollusc.*) brachiopod. **–gelenk,** *n.* elbow joint. **–grube,** *f.* *See* **–höhle. –heber,** *m.* (*Anat.*) deltoid muscle. **–höhle,** *f.* armpit, (*Bot.*) axilla.

armieren [ar'mi:rən], *v.t.* 1. arm, equip (*with arms*); 2. strengthen, reinforce (*a girder*), armour, sheath (*a cable*). **Armierung,** *f.* 1. armament, equipment; 2. reinforcement (*of girder*), armouring, sheathing (*of cable*).

–armig ['armɪç], *adj. suff.* –armed.

Arm|kiemer, *m.* *See* **–füßer. –knochen,** *m.* armbone, (*Anat.*) humerus.

armlang ['armlaŋ], *adj.* as long as one's arm. **Armlänge,** *f.* length of arm; ***auf* –,** to within *or* at arm's length.

Arm|lehne, *f.* arm (*of chair*), arm-rest. **–leuchter,** *m.* 1. chandelier, candelabra; 2. (*Bot.*) stonewort (*Charophycese*).

ärmlich ['ɛrmlɪç], *adj.* poor, mean, miserable, frugal, scanty, sparse, meagre. **Ärmlichkeit,** *f.* poorness, misery, poor *or* miserable appearance, scantiness, meanness, shabbiness.

Arm|reif(en), –ring, *m.* bangle. **–schiene,** *f.* 1. (*Med.*) arm-splint; 2. arm-guard (*of armour*). **–schlagader,** *f.* (*Anat.*) brachial artery.

armselig ['armze:lɪç], *adj.* poor, wretched, miserable, pitiable, pitiful, piteous, sorry, paltry, mean.

Arm|sessel, *m.* armchair, easy-chair. **–spange,** *f.* *See* **–ring. –speiche,** *f.* (*Anat.*) radius. **–spiegel,** *m.* arm-badge.

ärmst [ɛ:rmst], *see* **arm.**

Arm|stuhl, *m. See* **–sessel.**

Armut ['armu:t], *f.* (-, *no pl.*) poverty, want, indigence, penury; *– **an*** (*Dat.*), poverty in, lack *or* want of. **Armutszeugnis,** *n.* evidence of one's incapacity; ***sich*** (*Dat.*) ***ein – ausstellen,*** give oneself away, betray one's ignorance *or* incompetence.

Armvoll ['armfɔl], *m.* (-, *pl.* -) armful. **armvollweise,** *adv.* by the armful.

Arrangement [arãʒə'mã], *n.* (**-s,** *pl.* **-s**) 1. arrangement, ordering; 2. arrangement, agreement, terms; 3. (*Mus.*) arrangement, setting; 4. (*Swiss*) 'en pension' terms (*in hotel*). **arrangieren** [–'ʒi:rən], **1.** *v.t.* 1. arrange, set *or* put in order; (*Mus.*) arrange, set (*a song for violin etc.*); 2. arrange (for), organize, contrive, (*coll.*) fix up. **2.** *v.i., v.r.* come to an arrangement *or* settlement (***mit,*** with).

Arrest [a'rɛst], *m.* (**-(e)s,** *pl.* **–e**) 1. seizure, impounding, attachment (*of goods*), distraint (*of debtor's property*), arrest, detention (*of a ship*), embargo (*on a ship*); ***– legen auf*** (*Acc.*), ***mit – belegen,*** seize, attach; ***unter – stellen,*** order the detention of, lay an embargo on (*a ship*); (*Law*) ***dinglicher –,*** attachment, distress; (*Law*) ***offener –,*** sequestration; 2. arrest, detention (*also at school*), confinement (*of a p.*); ***– haben, im – sein,*** be under arrest; ***in – schicken, mit – bestrafen,*** put under arrest; ***leichter –,*** open arrest; ***strenger –,*** close arrest. **Arrestanstalt,** *f.* (*Mil.*) detention barracks, military prison. **Arrestant** [–'tant], *m.* (**-en,** *pl.* **-en**) prisoner; (*Law*) distrainer. **Arrestat** [–'ta:t], *m.* (**-en,** *pl.* **-en**) (*Law*) distrainee. **Arrest|lokal,** *n.* (*Mil.*) guardroom. **–vollziehung,** *f.* (*Law*) distraint. **–zelle,** *f.* (*Mil.*) detention cell.

arretieren [arɛ'ti:rən], *v.t.* 1. arrest, place under arrest, seize, apprehend, detain (*a p.*); 2. seize, impound, attach (*goods*); 3. arrest, check, stop, clamp, lock (*machinery*). **Arretierhebel,** *m.* catch, locking-lever. **Arretierung,** *f.* 1. arrest, apprehension, detention (*of a p.*); 2. seizure, attachment, confiscation (*of goods*); 3. locking device, catch, stop, check, detent.

arrivieren [ari'vi:rən], *v.i.* (*aux.* s.) succeed, (*coll.*) get on (*in the world*).

Arsch [arʃ], *m.* (**-es,** *pl.* **¨-e**) (*vulg.*) arse, bum, backside; ***du kannst mich am – lecken!*** (*ellipt.*) ***du kannst mich mal!*** to hell with you! go and take a running jump (at yourself)! (*vulg.*) ***im – sein,*** be a dead loss, be down the drain, be up the spout (*of a th.*); (*vulg.*) ***in den – gehen,*** go to pot; (*vulg.*) ***über – gehen,*** go arse over tip.

Arsch|backe, *f.* buttock. **–kriechen,** *n.*, **–kriecher,** *m.*, **–kriecherei,** *f. See* **–lecken** *etc.* **–lecken,** *n.* (*vulg.*) arse-crawling. **–lecker,** *m.* lick-spittle, arse-crawler. **–leckerei,** *f. See* **–lecken. –leder,** *n.* breech leather (*patch on seat of trousers*). **ärschlings,** *adv.* (*vulg.*) on one's arse, arse first. **Arsch|-loch,** *n.* (*vulg.*) arsehole; shit (*said of a p.*). **–pauker,** *m.* (*vulg.*) schoolmaster. **–wisch,** *m.* (*vulg.*) bumph.

Arsen [ar'ze:n], *n.* (**-s,** *no pl.*) arsenic. **Arsen–,** *pref.* arsenide of. **arsenführend,** *adj.* arseniferous. **arsenhaltig,** *adj.* arsenical. **arsenig,** *adj.* arsenious; ***arsenigsaures Salz,*** arsenite. **Arsenigsaüre,** *f.* arsenious acid.

Arsenik [ar'ze:nɪk], *n.* (**-s,** *no pl.*) arsenious oxide, arsenic trioxide, (white) arsenic. **arsenikalisch** [–'ka:lɪʃ], **arsenikhaltig,** *adj.* arsenical. **Arsenik|-kalk,** *m.* arsenolite. **–kies,** *m. See* **Arsenkies. –mehl,** *n.* flowers of arsenic.

Arsenkies [ar'ze:nki:s], *m.* (**-es,** *no pl.*) arsenical pyrites. **arsensauer,** *adj.* arsenate of. **Arsensaüre,** *f.* arsenic acid.

Art [art], *f.* (-, *pl.* **-en**) 1. (*Nat. Hist.*) species; breed, race (*dogs, horses etc.*), variety (*plants*); (*B.*) generation; ***aus der – schlagen,*** deviate from type, degenerate, (*fig.*) develop unexpected potentialities; (*Prov.*) ***– läßt nicht von –,*** blood is thicker than water, birds of a feather flock together, like father like son, like will to like; ***Entstehung der –en,*** origin of species; ***von göttlicher –,*** of divine origin; 2. type, kind, sort, class; ***aller –,*** of all kinds *or* sorts *or* types; all kinds *or* sorts *or* manner of; (***von***) ***welcher –?*** of what kind? ***welche –*** (***von***)***?*** what kind *or* sort of? 3. ***–*** (***und Weise***), manner (*also Gram.*), mode, way, style; ***in ähnlicher*** or ***auf ähnliche –,*** in a similar way *or* manner *or* fashion; in like manner; ***in seiner –,*** in its (own) way, of its kind, after its (own) fashion; ***nach*** (***der***) ***–, in der –,*** in the style *or* manner; 4. (good) manners *or* behaviour; ***keine – haben,*** have no manners; ***das hat doch keine –,*** that's not the sort of th. one would expect; ***was ist das für eine –?*** where are your manners?

arteigen ['artˀaɪgən], *adj.* true to type, characteristic of the species. **arten,** *v.i.* (*aux.* s.) partake of *or* acquire *or* assume the quality *or* form (***nach,*** of), take (after), resemble; ***gut geartet,*** good-natured.

Arterie [ar'te:riə], *f.* artery. **Arterien|erweiterung,** *f.* (*Med.*) aneurysm. **–verkalkung,** *f.* (*Med.*) arteriosclerosis, (*coll.*) hardening of the arteries.

artesisch [ar'te:zɪʃ], *adj.* artesian.

art|fremd, *adj.* alien, foreign. **–gleich,** *adj.* of the same species, of identical type.

arthaft ['arthaft], *adj.* characteristic, individual.

artig ['artɪç], *adj.* good, well- *or* nicely-behaved; polite, courteous, civil, well-bred, amiable, kind(ly), friendly; agreeable, pleasant, pleasing, nice; ***sei –!*** be good!

–artig, *suff.* -like, resembling (*e.g.* ***balladen–,*** in ballad style; ***gleich–,*** of the same *or* similar kind; ***gut–,*** good-natured; ***bös–,*** malicious).

Artigkeit ['artɪçkaɪt], *f.* good behaviour; politeness, courtesy, courteousness, civility, kindliness, friendliness, niceness; *pl.* civilities, polite attentions, kind words, compliments.

Artikel [ar'ti:kəl], *m.* 1. article, commodity, *pl.* goods, wares; 2. clause, article (*in contract etc.*), article (of faith), (newspaper) article; 3. (*Gram.*) article.

Artikulation [artikulatsi'o:n], *f.* 1. (*Anat.*) joint, articulation (*also dentistry*); 2. articulation, utterance. **artikulieren** [–'li:rən], **1.** *v.t.* 1. articulate (*joints*); 2. pronounce distinctly, articulate. **2.** *v.i.* articulate (*of teeth*).

Artillerie [artɪlə'ri:], *f.* artillery. **Artillerie|flieger,** *m.*, **–flugzeug,** *n.* (*Mil.*) spotting plane. **–führer,** *m.* (*Mil.*) divisional artillery commander. **–kampf,** *m.* artillery duel. **–leitstand,** *m.* (*Mil.*) artillery command post, (*Nav.*) fire-control tower. **–schule,** *f.* school of gunnery.

Artillerist [artɪlə'rɪst], *m.* (**-en,** *pl.* **-en**) artilleryman, gunner.

Artischocke [arti'ʃɔkə], *f.* artichoke.

Artist [ar'tɪst], *m.* (**-en,** *pl.* **-en**) artiste. **artistisch,** *adj.* artistic.

Artkreuzung ['artkrɔytsuŋ], *f.* crossing of two species. **artrein,** *adj.* pure-bred.

Artur ['artur], *m.* Arthur.

Artus ['artus], *m.* (King) Arthur. **Artusrunde,** *f.* the Round Table.

artverwandt ['artfɛrvant], *adj.* kindred, akin (***mit,*** to), of the same origin and nature.

Arznei [arts'naɪ], *f.* (-, *pl.* **-en**) medicine, drug, medicament, physic. **Arznei|buch,** *n.* pharmacopœia. **–kraut,** *n.* medicinal *or* officinal plant *or* herb, *pl.* simples. **–kunde,** *f.* pharmaceutics. **–mittel,** *n.* remedy; medicine; ***Herstellung von –n,*** pharmaceutics, pharmacy. **–mittellehre,** *f.* pharmacology. **–pflanze,** *f. See* **–kraut. –schrank,** *m.* medicine-chest. **–trank,** *m.* potion, draught. **–verordnung, –vorschrift,** *f.* medical prescription.

Arzt [a:rtst], *m.* (**-es,** *pl.* **¨-e**) doctor, physician, medical man *or* practitioner; ***praktischer –,*** general practitioner.

Ärztekammer ['ɛ:rtstəkamər], *f.* = General Medical Council.

Ärztin ['ɛ:rtstɪn], *f.* woman *or* lady doctor.

ärztlich ['ɛ:rtstlɪç], *adj.* medical; ***–e Hilfe,*** medical attention *or* aid; ***– empfohlen,*** as recommended by

the medical profession; – *verordnet,* on a doctor's prescription, prescribed by a doctor.
Arztrechnung ['artstrɛçnuŋ], *f.* doctor's bill.
[1]**As** [as], *n.* (-, *pl.* -) (*Mus.*) A flat; *As-Dur,* A flat major; *as-Moll,* A flat minor.
[2]**As,** *n.* (**-ses,** *pl.* **-se**) (*Cards*) ace (*also Av., of a p.*).
Asant [a'zant], *m.* (**-s,** *no pl.*) *wohlriechender –,* benzoin; *stinkender –,* asafoetida.
Asbest [as'bɛst], *m.* (**-(e)s,** *pl.* **-e**) asbestos. **Asbest|pappe,** *f.* asbestos board. **–platte,** *f.* asbestic mat.
Aschanti [a'ʃanti], *n.* Ashanti.
asch|bleich ['aʃ–], *adj. See* **–fahl.**
Asche ['aʃə], *f.* ash, ashes; *glimmende –,* embers; *in (Schutt und) – legen,* burn down, reduce to ashes; *bis ich zu – werde,* till my body turns to dust; *Friede seiner –!* may his ashes rest in peace!
Ascheimer ['aʃˀaɪmər], *m.* ash-can, ash-bin, dustbin.
Aschen|bahn, *f.* cinder-track, dirt-track. **–becher,** *m.* ashtray. **–brödel,** *n.* Cinderella; (*coll.*) skivvy, scullion. **–gehalt,** *m.* ash content (*of fuel*). **–grube,** *f.* ash-pit. **–haufen,** *m.* ash-heap. **–kasten,** *m. See* **Aschkasten. –krug,** *m.* funeral urn. **–pflanze,** *f.* cineraria. **–puttel,** *n. See* **–brödel. –salz,** *n.* potash. **–urne,** *f.* (funeral) urn.
Äscher ['ɛʃər], *m.* lye ashes; slaked lime; lime-pit (*tanning*). **Äscherkalk,** *m.* slaked lime.
Aschermittwoch [aʃər'mɪtvɔx], *m.* Ash Wednesday.
äschern ['ɛʃərn], *v.t.* 1. strew with ashes; 2. wash in *or* treat with lye; lime (*hides*).
asch|fahl, *adj.* ashy (*pale*), ashen (*grey*). **–farben,** *adj.* ashy, ash-grey, ash-coloured, cinereous (*plumage*). **–grau,** *adj. See* **–farben**; (*coll.*) *bis ins Aschgraue,* till the cows come home.
aschig ['aʃɪç], *adj.* covered with ashes, ashy.
Aschkasten ['aʃkastən], *m.* 1. dust-bin, ash-bin, ash-can; 2. ash-pan, ash-box (*of stove, boiler*).
Aschkopfammer ['aʃkɔpfˀamər], *f.* (*Orn.*) masked bunting (*Emberiza spodocephala*).
Aschlauch ['aʃlaux], *m.* eschalot, shallot.
äsen ['ɛ:zən], *v.i.* graze (*of deer*), browse.
aseptisch [a'sɛptɪʃ], *adj.* aseptic.
Asiat [azi'a:t], *m.* (**-en,** *pl.* **-en**) Asian, Asiatic. **asiatisch,** *adj.* Asian, Asiatic. **Asien** ['a:ziən], *n.* Asia.
Askese [as'ke:zə], *f.* asceticism. **Asket** (**-en,** *pl.* **-en**), **Asketiker,** *m.* ascetic. **asketisch,** *adj.* ascetic.
Äskulap [ɛsku'la:p], *m.* Aesculapius.
Äsop [ɛ'zo:p], *m.* Aesop.
Asow [a'zɔf], *n.* Azov. **Asowsches Meer,** Sea of Azov.
asozial [azotsi'a:l], *adj.* anti-social.
Aspekt [as'pɛkt], *m.* (**-s,** *pl.* **-e**) (*Astr., Philol., fig.*) aspect.
Asphaltbeton [as'faltbeto:n], *m.* (**-s,** *no pl.*) asphalt, concrete. **asphaltieren** [–'ti:rən], *v.t.* asphalt. **Asphaltpresse,** *f.* (*coll.*) gutter press.
Aspirant [aspi'rant], *m.* (**-en,** *pl.* **-en**) aspirant, candidate (*for a post*).
Aspirata [aspi'ra:ta], *f.* (-, *pl.* **Aspiraten**) (*Phonet.*) aspirate. **Aspirateur** [–'tø:r], *m.* (**-s,** *pl.* **-e**) dust-extractor, suction fan. **Aspiration** [–tsi'o:n], *f.* 1. (*Phonet.*) aspiration, rough breathing; 2. suction, exhaustion; 3. (*fig.*) aspiration, yearning. **aspirieren** [–'ri:rən], *v.t.* 1. (*Phonet.*) aspirate; 2. suck *or* draw up, suck in; 3. (*fig.*) aspire to *or* after.
aß [a:s], *see* **essen.**
assamisch [a'sa:mɪʃ], *adj.* Assamese.
Assanierung [asa'ni:ruŋ], *f.* sanitation, cleansing, purification.
Assekuradeur [asekura'dø:r], **Assekurador** [–'ra:dɔr], *m.* (**-s,** *pl.* **-e**) (*obs.*) insurer, underwriter. **Assekurant** [–'rant], *m.* (**-en,** *pl.* **-en**) (*obs.*) insurer. **Assekuranz,** *f.* (-, *pl.* **-en**) (*obs.*) insurance (*fire etc.*), assurance (*life*). **Assekuranz|brief,** *m.*, **–police,** *f.* insurance policy. **Assekurat,** *m.* (**-en,** *pl.* **-en**) (*obs.*) insured person, policy holder. **assekurieren** [–'ri:rən], *v.t.* (*obs.*) insure.
Assel ['asəl], *f.* (-, *pl.* **-n**) 1. (*Ent.*) wood-louse, slater; 2. (*Zool.*) isopod.
assentieren [asɛn'ti:rən], **1.** *v.i.* agree, assent, give one's assent. **2.** *v.t.* (*Austr.*) declare fit for military service. **Assentierung,** *f.* 1. agreement, assent; 2. (*Austr.*) acceptance as A.1.
Assessor [a'sɛsɔr], *m.* (**-s,** *pl.* **-en** [–'so:rən]) professional man (*lawyer, teacher etc.*) during probationary period, assistant judge, assistant teacher *etc.*
Assignant [asɪg'nant], *m.* (**-en,** *pl.* **-en**) (*obs., Comm.*) drawer, giver (*of a draft*). **Assignat** [–'na:t], *m.* (**-en,** *pl.* **-en**) (*obs.*) payee, drawee. **Assignatar** [–'ta:r], *m.* (**-s,** *pl.* **-e**) (*obs.*) payee, assignee. **Assignate,** *f.* (*Hist.*) assignat (= *paper money issued by French revolutionary government*). **Assignation** [–tsi'o:n], *f.* (*obs.*) assignment, transfer (*an* (*Acc.*), to). **assignieren** [–'ni:rən], *v.t.* (*obs.*) assign, transfer (*Dat. or an* (*Acc.*), to).
Assisen [a'si:zən], *f.pl.* assizes. **Assisenhof,** *m.* court of assizes.
Assistent [asɪs'tɛnt], *m.* (**-en,** *pl.* **-en**) assistant.
Associé [asosi'e:], *m.* (**-s,** *pl.* **-s**) (*Comm.*) (*obs.*) partner.
assortieren [asɔr'ti:rən], *v.t.* sort, assort. **Assortiment** [–ti'mɛnt], *n.* (**-(e)s,** *pl.* **-e**) (*Comm.*) assortment, selection (*of wares*).
assoziieren [asotsi'i:rən], *v.t.* (*Comm.*) associate; *sich –,* enter into partnership (*mit,* with).
Assuan [asu'a:n], *n.* Aswan.
Assyrier [a'sy:riər], *m.* Assyrian. **assyrisch,** *adj.* Assyrian.
Ast [ast], *m.* (**-es,** *pl.* **¨-e**) 1. bough, branch, limb (*of tree*); 2. knot (*in wood*).
Ästchen ['ɛstçən], *n.* twig, small bough. **ästen, 1.** *v.i.* put forth twigs *or* branches. **2.** *v.t.* lop the branches of (*a tree*). **3.** *v.r.* branch out, ramify; *geästet,* branching, branchy; ramose.
Aster ['astər], *f.* (-, *pl.* **-n**) (*Bot.*) aster.
astfrei ['astfraɪ], *adj.* free of *or* from knots (*of timber*).
Ästhet [ɛs'te:t], *m.* (**-en,** *pl.* **-en**) aesthete. **Ästhetentum,** *n.* (**-s,** *no pl.*) aestheticism. **Ästhetik,** *f.* aesthetics. **Ästhetiker,** *m.* writer on aesthetics, aesthetician. **ästhetisch,** *adj.* aesthetic. **ästhetisieren** [–ti'zi:rən], **1.** *v.i.* discuss aesthetics. **2.** *v.t.* treat from the aesthetic point of view. **Ästhetizismus** [–'tsɪsmus], *m.* aestheticism.
Astholz ['asthɔlts], *n.* (**-es,** *no pl.*) branches, boughs, loppings.
astig ['astɪç], **ästig** ['ɛstɪç], *adj.* branchy, branching; ramose; gnarled, knotty (*of timber*).
Ästling ['ɛstlɪŋ], *m.* (**-s,** *pl.* **-e**) 1. *See* **Ästchen**; 2. fledgling.
Astloch ['astlɔx], *n.* knot-hole. **astlochfrei,** *adj.* free from knot-holes.
astlos ['astlo:s], *adj.* 1. branchless; 2. free from knots *or* knot-holes. **Ast|putzer,** *m. See* **–schere. astrein,** *adj.* 1. free from knots (*of timber*); 2. (*coll.*) not on the level, fishy.
Astrologe [astro'lo:gə], *m.* (**-n,** *pl.* **-n**) astrologer. **Astrologie** [–'gi:], *f.* astrology. **astrologisch,** *adj.* astrological.
Astronaut [astro'naut], *m.* (**-en,** *pl.* **-en**) astronaut. **Astronautik,** *f.* astronautics. **astronautisch,** *adj.* astronautical.
Astronom [astro'no:m], *m.* (**-en,** *pl.* **-en**) astronomer. **Astronomie** [–'mi:], *f.* astronomy. **astronomisch,** *adj.* astronomical.
Ast|schere, *f.* pruning-shears, secateurs. **–werk,** *n.* branches, foliage; (Gothic) branch-ornament.
Äsung ['ɛ:zuŋ], *f.* grazing, browsing; feed, fodder.
Asyl [a'zy:l], *n.* (**-s,** *pl.* **-e**) refuge, sanctuary; (political) asylum; *– für Obdachlose,* casual ward, night-shelter, (*sl.*) doss-house.
Aszese [as'tse:zə], **Aszetiker, aszetisch,** *see* **Askese** *etc.*
Atelier [atəli'e:], *n.* (**-s,** *pl.* **-s**) studio.

Atem ['a:təm], *m.* (**-s,** *no pl.*) breath, breathing; respiration; ***außer – sein,*** be out of *or* short of breath, be blown *or* winded *or* (*coll.*) puffed; ***ihn in – halten,*** hold him breathless (with attention), keep him in suspense; ***in einem – nennen,*** mention in the same breath; ***zu – kommen,*** get one's breath, (*fig.*) have time to breathe; ***wieder zu – kommen,*** recover one's breath, get one's second wind; ***den letzten – aushauchen,*** breathe one's last; ***der – geht mir schnell aus,*** I soon *or* quickly get out of breath, (*fig.*) I soon run dry (*i.e. have nothing more to say*); ***– holen*** or ***schöpfen,*** draw *or* take a breath, (*coll.*) take a breather; ***tief – holen,*** take a deep breath, breathe deeply; (*fig.*) ***laß ihn – holen,*** give him time to breathe; ***kaum – holen können,*** breathe with difficulty, have difficulty in breathing *or* in getting one's breath; ***ihm den – nehmen*** or ***rauben,*** take his breath away, make him gasp, (*coll.*) flabbergast him; ***langen – haben,*** have plenty of wind *or* (*coll.*) a good pair of lungs; ***kurzen – haben,*** be short-winded *or* (*of horse*) broken-winded; ***übelriechender –,*** halitosis, bad breath. **atembar,** *adj.* breathable.

Atem|beklemmung, *f.* shortness of breath, difficulty in breathing, breathlessness, (*Med.*) anhelation. **–gerät,** *n.* (oxygen) breathing apparatus, respirator. **–geräusch,** *n.* (*Med.*) vesicular murmur. **–gymnastik,** *f.* (deep-)breathing exercises. **–holen,** *n.* respiration. **–kanal,** *m.* respiratory tract.

atemlos ['a:təmlo:s], *adj.* breathless. **Atemlosigkeit,** *f.* breathlessness.

Atem|not, *f.* (-, *no pl.*) difficulty in breathing. **–organ,** *n.* respiratory organ. **–pause,** *f.* breathing-space, (*coll.*) breather.

atemraubend ['atəmraubənt], *adj.* breath-taking (*sight*), breathless (*suspense etc.*).

Atem|schutzgerät, *n. See* **–gerät. –übung,** *f. See* **–gymnastik. –zug,** *m.* breath; ***in einem –,*** in one and the same *or* all in one breath; ***bis zum letzten –,*** to one's last breath, to the last gasp; ***in den letzten ¨–en,*** at one's last gasp; ***mit dem letzten –,*** with one's dying breath. **–zunge,** *f.* uvula.

athanasianisch [atanazi'a:nɪʃ], *adj.* Athanasian (*creed*).

Atheismus [ate'ɪsmus], *m.* atheism. **Atheist,** *m.* atheist. **atheistisch,** *adj.* atheistic.

Athen [a'te:n], *n.* Athens. **Athener,** *m.* Athenian. **athenisch,** *adj.* Athenian.

Äther ['ɛ:tər], *m.* (**-s,** *no pl.*) ether. **ätherisch,** *adj.* ethereal, volatile; ***–e Öle,*** essential *or* volatile oils.

Äthiopien [ɛti'o:piən], *n.* Ethiopia. **Äthiopier,** *m.* Ethiopian. **äthiopisch,** *adj.* Ethiopian.

Athlet [at'le:t], *m.* (**-en,** *pl.* **-en**) athlete. **Athletik,** *f.* athletics. **athletisch,** *adj.* athletic.

[1]**Atlas** ['atlas], *m.* (**-ses,** *pl.* **-se, Atlanten**) atlas.

[2]**Atlas,** *m.* (**-ses,** *pl.* **-se**) satin. **atlasartig,** *adj.* satiny, satin-like. **Atlasband,** *n.* satin ribbon.

Atlasformat ['atlasfɔrma:t], *n.* atlas folio.

atmen ['a:tmən], *v.t., v.i.* breathe, respire; inhale, exhale; ***schwer –,*** breathe heavily, gasp.

Atmosphäre [atmo'sfɛ:rə], *f.* atmosphere (*also fig.*), (*fig.*) air, environment; (*Phys.*) atmosphere (*= pressure of 760 mm. of mercury: abbr.* Atm.); ***metrische*** or ***neue –,*** metric atmosphere (*= pressure of 1 km. per sq. cm. or 735 mm. of mercury*: *abbr.* at). **Atmosphären|druck,** *m.* atmospheric pressure. **–überdruck,** *m.* absolute pressure (*abbr.* atü). **atmosphärisch,** *adj.* atmospheric; (*Rad.*) ***–e Störungen,*** atmospherics.

Atmung ['a:tmuŋ], *f.* (-, *no pl.*) breathing, respiration. **Atmungs|apparat,** *m.* respirator, breathing apparatus. **–geräusch,** *n.* respiratory murmur. **–organ, –werkzeug,** *n.* respiratory organ.

Ätna ['ɛ:tna], *m.* (*Mount.*) Etna.

Atom [a'to:m], *n.* (**-s,** *pl.* **-e**) atom (*also fig.*), (*fig.*) particle, scrap, grain (*of truth etc.*); ***in –e auflösen*** or ***zerspalten,*** reduce to atoms.

Atom–, *pref.* atomic, nuclear. **–abfall,** *m.* atomic waste *or* fallout. **–antrieb,** *m.* nuclear propulsion.

atomar [ato'ma:r], *adj.* atomic.

Atom|batterie, *f.* atomic pile. **–bau,** *m.* atomic structure. **–bombe,** *f.* atom(ic) bomb. **–brenner,** *m. See* **–batterie. –energie,** *f.* nuclear energy, atomic power *or* energy. **–gewicht,** *n.* atomic weight.

atomisieren [atomi'zi:rən], *v.t.* reduce to atoms, atomize.

Atom|kern, *m.* atomic nucleus. **–kernforschung,** *f.* nuclear research. **–kraft,** *f. See* **–energie. –kraftanlage,** *f.*, **–kraftwerk,** *n.* nuclear power station. **–krieg,** *m.* atomic *or* nuclear war *or* warfare. **–lehre,** *f.* atomic theory. **–meiler,** *m.* reactor, atomic pile. **–müll,** *m. See* **–abfall. –physik,** *f.* atomic *or* nuclear physics. **–schutt,** *m. See* **–abfall. –spaltung,** *f. See* **–zerfall. –sprengkopf,** *m.* nuclear warhead. **–waffe,** *f.* atomic weapon, nuclear arm. **–zerfall,** *m.* nuclear fission, (natural) disintegration of the atom. **–zertrümmerung,** *f.* splitting of the atom, (*coll.*) atom-smashing.

ätsch! [ɛtʃ], *int.* (*of derision*) boo! yah! (*of disgust*) bah!

Attachement [ataʃə'mã], *n.* (**-s,** *pl.* **-s**) (*obs.*) attachment (***an*** (*Acc.*), to), affection (for). **attachieren** [–'ʃi:rən], *v.t., v.r.* attach (o.s.) (*Dat.*, to).

Attacke [a'takə], *f.* (cavalry) charge; (*fig., Med., Mus.*) attack. **attackieren** [–'ki:rən], *v.t.* 1. charge (*of cavalry*), attack; 2. spur, put spurs to (*a horse*).

Attentat [atɛn'ta:t], *n.* (**-(e)s,** *pl.* **-e**) (attempted) assassination, attempt (***auf*** (*Acc.*), on) s.o.'s life; (*coll.*) designs. **Attentäter** [–'tɛ:tər], *m.* (would-be) assassin, perpetrator of an outrage *or* a murderous attack, (*coll.*) perpetrator.

Attest [a'tɛst], *n.* (**-es,** *pl.* **-e**) certificate; attestation. **attestieren** [–'ti:rən], *v.t.* attest, certify.

Attich ['atɪç], *m.* (**-s,** *pl.* **-e**) dwarf elder (*Sambucus ebulus*).

Attrappe [a'trapə], *f.* 1. dummy, sham, (*coll.*) mock-up; 2. trap, catch, (*coll.*) do; 3. (*fig.*) window-dressing, (*coll.*) eyewash. **attrappieren** [–'pi:rən], *v.t.* take (*s.o.*) in, catch *or* (*coll.*) do (*s.o.*).

atypisch ['aty:pɪʃ], *adj.* non-typical.

Ätzbad ['ɛ:tsba:t], *n.* (*Engr.*) etching-bath. **ätzbar,** *adj.* 1. suitable for etching; liable to corrosion; 2. capable of being bleached.

Ätz|beize, *f.* mordant. **–druck,** *m.* etching.

ätzen ['ɛ:tsən], *v.t.* 1. corrode; etch; (*Med.*) cauterize; eat into, bite into (*as acid*); 2. discharge (colour from), bleach (*fabric*). **ätzend,** *adj.* corrosive, caustic (*also fig.*), (*fig.*) mordant, pungent, biting (*as wit*).

Ätz|kali, *n.* (**-s,** *no pl.*) caustic potash. **–kalk,** *m.* quicklime. **–kraft,** *f.* causticity, corrosive power. **–kunst,** *f.* art of etching. **–mittel,** *n.* corrosive, (*Med.*) caustic. **–nadel,** *f.* etching needle. **–natron,** *n.* caustic soda, sodium hydroxide, **–silber,** *n.* lunar caustic. **–stoff,** *m. See* **–mittel. –sublimat,** *n.* corrosive sublimate, mercuric chloride.

Ätzung ['ɛ:tsuŋ], *f.* 1. corrosion, (*Med.*) cautery. cauterizing; 2. etching; etched plate.

Ätz|wasser, *n.* nitric acid; aqua fortis. **–wirkung,** *f.* corrosive action.

au! [au], *int.* (*of pain*) ouch! ow! oh!

Au, *f.* (-, *pl.* **-en**) *see* **Aue.**

Aubo– ['aubo:], *abbr. of* **Außenbord–,** *e.g.* **–fähre,** *f.* outboard motor ferry.

auch [aux], **1.** *adv.* 1. also, too, as well; likewise; ***sowohl . . . als –,*** both . . . and, as well as; ***nicht nur . . . sondern –,*** not only . . . but also; 2. (*emph.*) even; ***– er,*** even he; ***– nicht einer,*** not even one, (*coll.*) never a one; ***ohne – nur,*** without even *or* so much as; 3. (*in response*) so; (*negative response*) nor, neither; ***ich –!*** so am I, can I, shall I *etc.*, (*coll.*) me too! same here!; ***du –!*** so are you! (*coll.*) (the) same to you! ***ich – nicht,*** nor *or* neither am I *etc.* **2.** *adv., conj.* (*concessive with subj.*) ***– wenn, wenn . . . –,*** even if *or* though; ***wenn er – noch so dumm ist, so dumm er – ist, sei er – noch so dumm,*** however stupid he is *or* may be, stupid as he is; ***was . . . – (immer)***, whatever; ***wer . . . – immer,*** whoever; ***wo . . . – immer,*** wherever; ***wann immer . . . –,*** whenever. **3.** *adv.* in addition, also; ***– müssen wir die ganze Zeit zuhause bleiben,*** in addition we must stay at home all the time. **4.** *part.* (*oft. not translated*) really; ***bist du – glücklich?*** are you really happy? ***du willst es – wirklich tun?*** you will be sure to do it? ***so dumm bist du – nicht,*** you're not (really) *or* surely you're not as stupid as all that; ***wozu denn –?*** what (on earth) for? what would be the use?

Audienz [audi'ɛnts], *f.* (-, *pl.* **-en**) interview, audience; hearing, reception; ***– beim König,*** audience with *or* (*obs.*) of the king. **Audienz|saal,** *m.*, **-zimmer,** *n.* reception-chamber.

Audion ['audiɔn], *n.* (**-s**, *pl.* **-s** *or* **-en**), **Audionröhre,** *f.* (*Rad.*) audion, vacuum tube.

Auditeur [audi'tø:r], *m.* (**-s**, *pl.* **-e**) (*Mil.*) representative of Advocate General's branch at courts martial.

Auditor [au'di:tɔr], *m.* (**-s**, *pl.* **-en**) 1. judge in ecclesiastical courts; 2. (*Austr.*) *See* **Auditeur.**

Auditorium [audi'to:rium], *n.* (**-s**, *pl.* **-rien**) lecture-room *or* -hall *or* theatre; assembly, audience.

Aue ['auə], *f.* water-meadow; (*Poet.*) pasture.

Auer ['auər], *m. See* **Auerochs. Auer|huhn,** *n.* (*Orn.*) capercaillie (*Tetrao urogallus*). **-ochs,** *m.* aurochs (*extinct European bison*).

auf [auf], **1.** *prep.* **A.** (*with Dat.*) 1. *signifying rest, or limited motion within a place*: on, upon, on top of; ***etwas – dem Schrank finden,*** find s.th. on top of the cupboard; 2. (*fig.*) **(a)** on; ***– der Hut,*** on one's guard; ***– der Bühne*** or ***Reise,*** on the stage *or* the journey; ***– Urlaub,*** on holiday; **(b)** at; ***– der Post, Schule, Universität, – dem Markt,*** at the post-office, at school, at (the) university, at market; **(c)** in; ***– dem Bild, Feld, Hof, Lande, Zimmer, – der Straße, Welt,*** in the picture, the field, the yard, the country, the room, the street, the world; (*coll.*) ***es hat etwas – sich,*** there's s.th. in it, it's important. *For other idiomatic usage see the significant word.* **B.** (*with Acc.*) 1. *when signifying motion to a place, or change of state*: on (to), on top of; ***– den Schrank stellen,*** put on top of the cupboard; 2. (*fig.*) **(a)** on (to); ***– die Bühne, – Reisen gehen,*** go on to the stage, on a journey; **(b)** to; ***– die Post, Schule, Universität, – den Markt, – sein Zimmer gehen,*** go to the post-office, to school, to the university, to market, to one's room; **(c)** in(to); ***– das Feld, Land, – den Hof, – die Straße gehen,*** go into the field, country, yard, street; ***– die Welt bringen,*** bring into the world; **(d)** up (to); ***– den Berg, – das Schloß gehen,*** go up the mountain, up to the castle; **(e)** (down) to; ***– die Hälfte reduzieren,*** reduce to a half; ***– Heller und Pfennig,*** down to the last penny; 3. *in idiomatic constructions between verb or adj. and its complement* (*e.g.* ***achten –,*** pay attention to; ***stolz –,*** proud of) *see the significant word*; 4. (*time*) **(a)** for; ***– einige Wochen,*** for some weeks; **(b)** till, until; ***– Wiedersehen,*** au revoir; ***– morgen,*** till tomorrow; **(c)** after, upon; ***Tasse – Tasse heißen Tees,*** cup upon cup of hot tea; 5. (*manner*) **(a)** at, in; ***– diese Weise,*** in this way; ***– jeden Fall, – alle Fälle,*** in any case *or* event, at all events; ***– Deutsch,*** in German; ***– einen Zug,*** at a *or* in one draught; **(b)** (*with sup. adv.*) (*usu.* ***aufs***) as . . . as possible; ***–s beste,*** as well as possible. **2.** *adv.* 1. on(wards), up(wards); ***–!*** get up! ***von klein*** or ***Kindheit –,*** from (one's) childhood (on *or* onwards); ***– und ab,*** up and down, to and fro, backwards and forwards; ***– und nieder,*** up and down; ***– und davon gehen,*** get up and go away, (*coll.*) be up and away; ***sich – und davon machen,*** make off; 2. (*as noun*) ***das Auf und Ab,*** the ups and downs; 3. (*ellipt. for* ***aufgehen, aufmachen*** *etc.*) open. **3.** *conj.* (*obs.*) ***auf daß,*** so that.

auf–, *sep. pref. with a wide range of meanings*: *position or placing on top* (***aufsitzen,*** be on top (of)); ***aufsetzen,*** put on); *upright position* (***aufragen,*** tower, jut up); *motion upwards* (***aufrichten,*** set up); *initial activity* (***aufwachen,*** wake up); *activity completed* (***aufessen,*** eat up); *open state or opening* (***aufbleiben,*** stay open; ***aufmachen,*** open); *separation* (***aufteilen,*** distribute); *joining on to* (***aufschweißen,*** weld on to) *etc. Only a selection of the possible compound verbs can be given below*:

Auf–, *pref.* (*to verbal nouns*) *sometimes literal*: ***Aufwind,*** up-current; ***Aufzug,*** hoist, elevator; ***Aufguß,*** infusion; ***Aufschlag,*** impact; ***Aufdruck,*** imprint; *more often figurative*: ***Aufenthalt,*** stop, stay; ***Aufnahme,*** adoption; ***Aufschluß,*** enlightenment; ***Aufschub,*** postponement; ***Aufsicht,*** supervision.

aufarbeiten ['auf?arbaɪtən], **1.** *v.t.* 1. work up, process (*material*) (*zu*, into), recondition, renovate; (*coll.*) do up; 2. work *or* finish off, get through (*a task*), clear off *or* up (*arrears*); use *or* finish up (*all one's material*); 3. work open (*a lock etc.*). **2.** *v.r.* work one's way up.

aufatmen ['auf?a:tmən], *v.i.* breathe freely, breathe a sigh of relief; breathe again.

aufbahren ['aufba:rən], *v.t.* lay out, put to lie in state (*a corpse*). **Aufbahrung,** *f.* lying in state.

Aufbau ['aufbau], *m.* 1. (**-(e)s**, *no pl.*) building (up), construction, erection; setting up, organization, arrangement, disposition; (*Chem.*) synthesis; 2. (**-(e)s**, *pl.* **-ten**) structure; construction, organization, composition, build-up; *pl.* superstructure; body, coachwork (*of a vehicle*). **Aufbauarbeit,** *f.* 1. construction work; 2. social improvement.

aufbauen ['aufbauən], **1.** *v.t.* 1. erect, construct, put *or* set up, build up, assemble; pile *or* stack (up); organize; 2. (*Chem.*) synthesize; 3. base, found (*a theory*) (***auf*** (*Acc.*), on). **2.** *v.r.* be based *or* founded (***auf*** (*Dat. or Acc.*), on). **aufbauend,** *adj.* 1. constructive (*as criticism*); 2. (*Chem.*) synthetic.

aufbäumen ['aufbɔymən], **1.** *v.t.* (*Weav.*) wind up (*on a spool*). **2.** *v.r.* 1. rear (up), prance; 2. rebel, protest (***gegen,*** against).

Aufbau|prinzip, *n.* structural principle. **-salze,** *pl.* (*Physiol.*) nutrient salts.

aufbauschen ['aufbauʃən], **1.** *v.t.* 1. swell, bulge *or* balloon out (*with wind*); 2. (*fig.*) magnify, exaggerate, inflate the importance of (*a p.*). **2.** *v.i.* (*aux.* s.), *v.r.* bulge, balloon *or* belly (out), swell out.

Aufbauschule ['aufbau?ʃu:lə], *f.* intermediate school.

Aufbauten ['aufbautən], *pl. See* **Aufbau.**

aufbegehren ['aufbəge:rən], *v.i.* bridle *or* bristle up (in protest), (*coll.*) get one's back up; rebel (***gegen,*** against) (*a p.*), revolt (at *or* against), be up in arms (against), (*coll.*) kick (against) (*a th.*).

aufbehalten ['aufbəhaltən], *irr.v.t.* keep on (*one's hat*); keep open (*one's eyes*).

aufbeißen ['aufbaɪsən], *irr.v.t.* bite open.

aufbekommen ['aufbəkɔmən], *irr.v.t.* 1. get open, manage to open; 2. get, receive (*a task to do*); have set (*as an exercise*).

aufbereiten ['aufbəraɪtən], *v.t.* prepare; process (*raw materials*); dress (*hides*); separate; wash (*ore*).

aufbessern ['aufbɛsərn], *v.t.* improve, ameliorate, recondition, renovate (*clothes*); increase, raise (*wages, prices*). **Aufbesserung,** *f.* amelioration, betterment, improvement, renovation; increase (*Gen.*, of *or* in) (*wages etc.*).

aufbewahren ['aufbəva:rən], *v.t.* put by, store (up); save; preserve, keep, have in one's keeping, have custody of, hold in trust. **Aufbewahrer,** *m.* custodian; trustee. **Aufbewahrung,** *f.* storage; preservation; (safe) custody, safe keeping; (*Railw.*) left-luggage office. **Aufbewahrungsort,** *m.* depository, repository; whereabouts (*of art treasures*).

aufbieten ['aufbi:tən], *irr.v.t.* 1. summon, call together, (*Mil.*) levy (*troops*), raise (*an army*), call to arms (*a nation*); 2. (*fig.*) summon up, call forth, muster (*courage etc.*), exert, bring to bear, bring into play (*influence etc.*); ***alles –,*** strain every nerve, leave no stone unturned, bring every influence to bear, put *or* set everything in motion, (*sl.*) do one's damnedest; 3. ***ein Brautpaar* –**, publish banns of marriage. **Aufbietung,** *f.* summoning, summons; proclamation (*of banns*); levy, call to arms; ***unter – aller Kräfte,*** with the utmost exertion.

aufbinden [ˈaufbɪndən], *irr.v.t.* 1. tie *or* fasten up (*hair, skirt etc.*); 2. untie, undo (*knot etc.*); 3. (*fig.*) ***ihm etwas* –**, burden him with s.th.; (*coll.*) impose on him, pull his leg, (*sl.*) pull a fast one on him, make a sucker out of him, take him for a ride.

aufblähen [ˈaufblɛːən], **1.** *v.t.* inflate, distend, blow up (*bladder*), bulge (*cheeks*); ***aufgebläht,*** bulging, blown up, full (*as sail*), (*fig.*) puffed up. **2.** *v.r.* become inflated *or* distended, distend, belly, balloon out, fill; (*fig.*) puff o.s. up, give o.s. airs. **Aufblähung,** *f.* inflation (*also of currency*), distension; flatulence.

aufblasen [ˈaufblaːzən], **1.** *irr.v.t.* blow up, inflate, pump up (*tyre*), distend, bulge, puff out (*one's cheeks*); blow up (*a fire*); (*fig.*) inflate (the importance of), magnify (*an incident*); ***aufgeblasen,*** inflated, turgid (*style*); ***aufgeblasen sein,*** be puffed up, suffer from a swelled *or* swollen head. **2.** *irr.v.r.* puff o.s. up, give o.s. airs.

aufbleiben [ˈaufblaɪbən], *irr.v.i.* (*aux.* s.) remain open *or* up; ***spät* –**, sit up *or* stay up late.

Aufblick [ˈaufblɪk], *m.* 1. upward glance; 2. fulguration, sudden brightening, (*Metall.*) gleam, shine. **aufblicken,** *v.i.* 1. look up (*zu*, at), raise one's eyes; (*fig.*) look up (to); 2. (*Metall.*) gleam, shine.

aufblitzen [ˈaufblɪtsən], *v.i.* (*aux.* h. & s.) flash, sparkle, flare up, gleam out.

aufblühen [ˈaufblyːən], *v.i.* (*aux.* s.) blossom, come into bloom, unfold; open; (*fig.*) thrive, flourish; ***–de Schönheit,*** budding beauty.

aufbrauchen [ˈaufbrauxən], *v.t.* use up, consume, exhaust.

aufbrausen [ˈaufbrauzən], *v.i.* 1. (*aux.* s. & h.) effervesce; boil, bubble *or* froth up, seethe; surge (*as sea*), rise to a roar (*as wind*); 2. (*aux.* s.) flare *or* blaze up, fly into a rage (*of a p.*).

aufbrechen [ˈaufbrɛçən], **1.** *irr.v.t.* break *or* prize open; plough *or* break up (*land*), open up (*a road*), break up (*a ship*), force (*a door, safe*), pick (*a lock*). **2.** *irr.v.i.* (*aux.* s.) 1. break *or* burst open; break up (*as ship, ice*), open, blossom (out) (*as flower*), burst (*as bud, abscess*), open (*as wound*), chap, crack (*as skin*); 2. make a start, set out, be *or* start on one's way, (*coll.*) be off; 3. rise from the table. *See* **Aufbruch.**

aufbrennen [ˈaufbrɛnən], **1.** *irr.v.t.* burn up, consume (by burning); refine (*metals*); ***ihm ein Zeichen* –**, brand him with a mark. **2.** *irr.v.i.* (*aux.* s.) 1. burn *or* flare up, burst into flames, go up in flames; become brighter (*as a fire*); 2. fly into a temper *or* rage, (*coll.*) flare up.

aufbringen [ˈaufbrɪŋən], *irr.v.t.* 1. raise, get up, lift (up), hoist; (*fig.*) bring up, rear (*a child*); bring up, raise (*a question*); bring in, introduce, start (*a fashion*); bring into vogue *or* fashion *or* favour *or* currency *or* circulation (*new ideas etc.*); 2. procure, raise, find, get together (*money etc.*), levy (*taxes*), raise, levy (*troops*); (*Naut.*) capture, take, seize (*enemy ship*); (*fig.*) summon *or* muster up (*courage, strength*), (*coll.*) pluck up (*courage*); 3. enrage, anger, infuriate, incense, provoke, exasperate, irritate, rouse (*s.o.'s*) indignation; ***aufgebracht werden,*** get angry, fly into a rage (***über*** (*Acc.*), at). **Aufbringer,** *m.* (*Naut.*) captor. **Aufbringung,** *f.* 1. raising, bringing up, rearing; 2. capture (*of a ship*).

Aufbruch [ˈaufbrux], *m.* 1. break-up; 2. start, starting (out), departure; 3. breaking up (*of land*), taking up (*of road*); 4. fundamental change, spiritual uprising, awakening (*to national or political consciousness*).

aufbürden [ˈaufbyːrdən], *v.t.* ***ihm etwas* –**, burden *or* saddle him with s.th., saddle *or* impose s.th. on him; impute (*guilt etc.*) to him, put *or* lay *or* cast the blame for s.th. on him.

aufdämmern [ˈaufdɛmərn], *v.i.* (*aux.* s.) dawn, (*fig.*) dawn (*Dat.*, upon).

aufdecken [ˈaufdɛkən], *v.t.* 1. uncover; disclose, reveal, expose; lay bare; (*Cards, fig.*) ***seine Karten* –**, show one's hand; (*Chess*) ***aufgedecktes Schach,*** discovered check; 2. lay, spread (*tablecloth*); turn down (*bed*). **Aufdeckung,** *f.* disclosure, revelation, exposure.

aufdonnern [ˈaufdɔnərn], *v.r.* (*coll.*) dress showily *or* vulgarly; ***aufgedonnert,*** dressed up (to kill), dolled up (to the nines).

aufdrängen [ˈaufdrɛŋən], **1.** *v.t.* 1. push *or* thrust *or* burst *or* force open; 2. force, thrust, foist (*Dat.*, (up)on). **2.** *v.r.* force *or* thrust *or* foist o.s., obtrude (o.s.) (*Dat.*, (up)on); (*of ideas*) intrude (***mir***, into my mind), be borne in (*Dat.*, upon).

aufdrehen [ˈaufdreːən], **1.** *v.t.* 1. screw on, screw (*s.th.*) on (*Dat. or* ***an*** (*Acc.*), to); wind up (*clock etc.*), turn on (*tap*); (*fig., coll.*) ***ihm etwas* –**, hoax him, have him on; (*coll.*) ***aufgedreht sein,*** be worked up, be full of go; 2. unscrew, screw out, loosen (*screw*); unravel, untwist, untwine, unlay (*rope etc.*); 3. turn up(wards); feather (*an oar*); 4. ***sich*** (*Dat.*) ***die Haare* –**, put one's hair in curlers. **2.** *v.r.* become unravelled *or* frayed, unravel, untwist. **3.** *v.i.* increase speed, put on a spurt, (*coll.*) step on the gas, get a move on; (*Naut.*) hug *or* haul the wind.

aufdringen [ˈaufdrɪŋən], **1.** *irr.v.t. See* **aufdrängen. 2.** *irr.v.i.* (*aux.* s.) force itself *or* rise up (***zu***, to).

aufdringlich [ˈaufdrɪŋlɪç], *adj.* importunate, obtrusive, officious, insistent, pushing, pushful; loud, gaudy, flashy (*colours*). **Aufdringlichkeit,** *f.* importunity, obtrusiveness, officiousness, insistence, pushfulness; gaudiness, flashiness (*of colour*).

Aufdruck [ˈaufdruk], *m.* **(-(e)s,** *pl.* **-e)** imprint, impress, impression, stamp; print, printing, printed words, legend (*on coin etc.*); over-print, surcharge (*on postage stamp*). **aufdrucken,** *v.t.* (im)print, stamp (***auf*** (*Acc.*), on).

aufdrücken [ˈaufdrykən], *v.t.* 1. press *or* push *or* squeeze open; 2. impress; imprint (***auf*** (*Acc.*), on); (*fig.*) ***sein Siegel* –**, set one's seal, leave one's mark (*Dat.*, (up)on).

aufdunsen [ˈaufdunzən], *v.i.* (*aux.* s.) swell up, get bloated *or* puffy *or* puffed. *See* **aufgedunsen.**

aufdunsten [ˈaufdunstən], *v.i.* evaporate.

aufeinander [aufaɪnˈandər], *adv.* one after another *or* the other; one on top of *or* above *or* upon another *or* the other; (*of actions*) (up)on each other, (up)on one another.

Aufeinanderfolge [aufaɪnˈanderfolgə], *f.* succession, sequence, series. **aufeinander|folgen,** *v.i.* (*aux.* s.) follow *or* succeed one another. **–folgend,** *adj.* consecutive, successive.

aufeinander|legen, *v.t.* lay one on top of the other *or* one upon another, superpose *or* superimpose one (up)on another *or* the other. **–liegen,** *irr.v.i.* lie on top of one another, be superposed *or* superimposed on one another. **–platzen,** *v.i.* (*aux.* s.) clash (with one another) (*as opinions*).

Aufeinanderprall [aufaɪnˈandərpral], **aufeinanderprallen,** *see* **Aufeinanderstoß, aufeinanderstoßen.**

Aufeinanderstoß [aufaɪnˈandərʃtoːs], *m.* impact, collision, (*fig.*) clash, clashing (*of opinions*). **aufeinanderstoßen,** *irr.v.i.* (*aux.* s.) collide *or* come into collision (with one another), (*fig.*) conflict, clash (with one another) (*as opinions*).

aufeinander|treffen, *irr.v.i.* (*aux.* s.) meet *or* encounter one another. *See* **–stoßen. –treiben,** *irr.v.i.* (*Naut.*) run foul of one another (*as ships*). **–wirken,** *v.i.* act upon one another, interact.

Aufenthalt [ˈaufˀɛnthalt], *m.* **(-(e)s,** *pl.* **-e)** 1. (place of) abode, residence, domicile; ***ohne festen* –**, without fixed abode; 2. stay, sojourn; 3. stop; halt; ***ohne* –**, without a stop *or* break. **Aufenthalts|dauer,** *f.* length of stay. **–genehmigung,** *f.* residence permit. **–ort,** *m.* present abode, whereabouts.

auferlegen [ˈaufˀɛrleːgən], *v.t.* impose, enjoin, lay (*Dat.*, (up)on), inflict (on), lay down, dictate (to);

sich (Dat.) ***Zwang* –**, force *or* restrain *or* control o.s., do violence to one's feelings. **Auferlegung,** *f.* imposition, infliction.

auferstehen ['aufˀɛrʃte:ən], *irr.v.i.* (*aux.* s.) rise (again) from the dead. **Auferstehung,** *f.* resurrection.

auferwecken ['aufˀɛrvɛkən], *v.t.* raise from the dead, restore to life; (*fig.*) bring life to, bring to life, resuscitate. **Auferweckung,** *f.* raising (from the dead), resurrection; (*fig.*) rebirth, resurgence, resuscitation.

aufessen ['aufˀɛsən], *irr.v.t.* eat up, consume; finish (*a meal*).

auffädeln ['auffɛ:dəln], *v.t.* 1. string (*beads*); 2. untwist, unravel.

auffahren ['auffa:rən], **1.** *irr.v.i.* 1. rise (up), mount, ascend; (*Min.*) come to the surface; 2. start (involuntarily), start *or* jump up, give a start; snap (in reply); ***aus dem Schlaf* –**, wake up with a start; 3. drive *or* draw up (*in a vehicle*); 4. (*Naut.*) run (aground) (***auf*** (*Acc.*), on); 5. burst *or* fly open (*as a door*). **2.** *irr.v.t.* 1. bring up, cart, deposit (*earth etc. in a vehicle*); 2. bring into position *or* action (*guns*); (*coll.*) bring on, serve up (*food*); 3. cut *or* churn *or* (*coll.*) plough up (*a road by driving*).

Auffahrt ['auffa:rt], *f.* 1. rising, ascent; ascension; 2. drive, approach (*to a house*); 3. ramp, slope, (*Naut.*) slipway. **Auffahrtstag,** *m.* (*Swiss*) Ascension Day.

auffallen ['auffalən], *irr.v.i.* (*aux.* s.) 1. attract notice *or* attention, be conspicuous *or* striking *or* (very) noticeable; ***ihm* –**, strike him, be noticed by him, catch his attention *or* notice; 2. strike; (*Opt.*) ***–des Licht,*** incident light; 3. fall (***auf*** (*Acc.*), upon). **auffallend,** *adj.* striking, conspicuous, remarkable; **–** ***gekleidet,*** showily dressed.

auffällig ['auffɛlıç], *adj.* 1. striking, conspicuous, remarkable, noteworthy; 2. ostentatious, blatant, showy; gaudy, garish (*colour*). **Auffälligkeit,** *f.* conspicuousness; ostentation, blatancy; strangeness, oddity; gaudiness, garishness.

auffangen ['auffaŋən], *irr.v.t.* catch (in mid-air); snap up, snatch up; pick up (*words, news*); collect, gather (*rainwater*); intercept (*letters*); head off, round up (*fugitives*); break (*a fall*); parry (*a blow*); ***wo haben Sie das aufgefangen?*** where did you pick that up? ***einen Blick* –**, catch his eye. **Auffang|glas,** *n.* (*Opt.*) objective, object lens. **–lager,** *n.* reception camp. **–schale,** *f.* collecting dish.

auffärben ['auffɛrbən], *v.t.* re-dye; fresh(en) *or* touch up (*colours*).

auffassen ['auffasən], *v.t.* apprehend, comprehend, understand, grasp, take in (*ideas etc.*); regard, consider, see, view, conceive of, interpret (*phenomena*); ***falsch* –**, misunderstand, misconstrue, misinterpret, (*coll.*) get wrong. **Auffassung,** *f.* comprehension, apprehension, understanding; reading, interpretation; conception, view. **Auffassungs|art,** *f.* way of looking at things. **–gabe, –kraft,** *f.*, **–vermögen,** *n.* power of comprehension, perceptive faculty, perceptiveness, understanding, intellectual grasp.

auffindbar ['auffıntba:r], *adj.* discoverable, traceable, detectable; ***nirgends* –**, not to be found anywhere.

auffinden ['auffındən], *irr.v.t.* find, discover, locate, unearth, detect, trace. **Auffindung,** *f.* discovery, detection.

aufflackern ['aufflakərn], *v.i.* (*aux.* s.) flare up; (*Chem.*) deflagrate.

aufflammen ['aufflamən], *v.i.* (*aux.* s.) flame up, blaze up, burst into flames, go up in flames.

auffliegen ['auffli:gən], *irr.v.t.* (*aux.* s.) 1. fly up; soar, rise, take wing (*as birds*), ascend; ***einen Drachen – lassen,*** fly a kite; 2. fly open (*of doors etc.*); 3. explode, blow up; 4. (*fig.*) fail, collapse, (*coll.*) go up in smoke.

Aufflug ['aufflu:k], *m.* (soaring) flight, (*Av.*) ascent.

auffordern ['auffɔrdərn], *v.t.* call upon, ask, request, demand, invite, bid, summon; ***zum Duell* –**, challenge to a duel; (*Law*) ***gerichtlich* –**, summon; (*Cards*) ***Trumpf* –**, call for trumps; ***man forderte ihn auf, ein Lied zu singen,*** he was called on for a song. **Aufforderung,** *f.* summons, request, demand, invitation (***an*** (*Acc.*), to); **–** ***zum Duell,*** challenge to a duel; **–** ***zum Tanz,*** invitation to dance; **–** ***zur Zahlung,*** demand for payment; (*Law*) ***gerichtliche* –**, summons. **Aufforderungs|befehl,** *m.* (*Law*) writ of summons. **–schreiben,** *n.* (formal *or* written) summons, demand-note, (letter of) invitation.

aufforsten ['auffɔrstən], *v.t.* afforest. **Aufforstung,** *f.* afforestation.

auffressen ['auffrɛsən], *irr.v.t.* (*of beasts*) eat up; devour (*prey*); (*of a p.*) (*coll.*) gobble up, wolf; (*of acid*) corrode.

auffrischen ['auffrıʃən], *v.t.* freshen up, renew, renovate, refurbish; (*Paint.*) touch up; refresh; (*coll.*) brush *or* rub up (*memory etc.*).

aufführbar ['auffy:rba:r], *adj.* performable, actable, playable; ***schwer* –**, difficult to stage (*a play*).

aufführen ['auffy:rən], **1.** *v.t.* 1. (*Theat.*) put on (the stage), stage, present, give (*a play etc.*); perform, play; 2. quote, cite (*s.o. as evidence*); enter, list, ennumerate, itemize, specify (*items in a register*); (*obs.*) (*Mil.*) post (*sentries etc.*); (*Law*) bring forward, produce (*witness*); 3. raise, erect; set *or* throw up (*rampart etc.*). **2.** *v.r.* act, behave, conduct o.s. **Aufführung,** *f.* 1. performance, presentation; ***zur – bringen,*** put on the stage, get *or* have performed; 2. erection; posting (*of a sentry*); 3. specification, enumeration, itemization, listing; adducing (*of reasons*); production (*of witnesses*); 4. conduct, behaviour. **Aufführungsrecht,** *n.* (*Theat.*) performing rights.

auffüllen ['auffylən], *v.t.* fill up; refill, replenish, top up.

auffüttern ['auffytərn], *v.t.* feed up, fatten, rear.

Aufgabe ['aufga:bə], *f.* 1. task, duty, mission, assignment; purpose, function, business, (*coll.*) job; ***es sich*** (*Dat.*) ***zur – machen,*** make it one's business (***zu tun,*** to do), make a point of (doing); ***die – meines Lebens,*** my mission in life; ***meiner – gewachsen sein,*** be equal to my task, be able to cope with my task; 2. (*Math.*) problem; *pl.* homework; 3. giving, placing (*of an order*), setting, posing, propounding (*of a problem*), posting, mailing, handing in (*of letters etc.*), registering, booking, registration (*of luggage*), sending (*luggage*) in advance, inserting, insertion (*of advertisements*); (*Comm.*) advice, instructions; quotation, indication (*of prices*); 4. giving up, abandoning, abandonment, relinquishing, relinquishment, surrendering, surrender, renouncing, renouncement, waiving, (*Law*) waiver; retiring, retirement, resigning, resignation.

Aufgaben|bereich, *m.*, **–gebiet,** *n.* scope, function, terms of reference. **–heft,** *n.* homework exercise book.

Aufgabe|ort, *m.* place of posting (*letters*) *or* handing in (*luggage*). **–schein,** *m.* receipt for registered luggage. **–stempel,** *m.* stamp of the office of dispatch. **–vorrichtung,** *f.* feeding *or* charging mechanism. **–zeit,** *f.* time of posting (*letters*) *or* handing in (*luggage*).

Aufgang ['aufgaŋ], *m.* **(-(e)s,** *pl.* **¨-e)** 1. rise, rising, ascent; upstroke (*of piston*); 2. (*Astr.*) ascension; Orient, east; 3. staircase, (flight of) stairs.

aufgären ['aufgɛ:rən], *v.i.* ferment, rise; seethe, froth up.

aufgeben ['aufge:bən], *irr.v.t.* 1. give, set, assign (*a task*) (*Dat.*, to), (*Comm.*) advise, inform *or* give notice of; give up, hand in, post (*letters*), register (*luggage*), send (*luggage*) in advance; give, place (*an order*), put in, insert (*an advertisement*), put on (*fuel*), feed, charge (*a furnace*), serve (*food*); ***ein Rätsel* –**, ask a riddle; 2. give up, leave off, abandon, relinquish, renounce, surrender, resign; retire from, (*coll.*) drop out of (*a race*), give *or* throw up (*a job*), (*coll.*) throw in the sponge, pack it in; ***den Geist* –**, give up the ghost; ***das Geschäft* –**, retire from *or* go out of business; ***das Spiel* –**, throw in one's cards *or* hand, give it up as a bad job; ***den Versuch*** (or ***jede Hoffnung***) **–**, abandon the attempt (*or* all hope); ***den Verkehr mit ihm* –**, drop his accquaintance.

aufgeblasen ['aufgəbla:zən], *adj.* inflated, turgid (*as style*), bumptious, self-important, puffed up, arrogant (*of a p.*). *See* **aufblasen. Aufgeblasenheit,** *f.* 1. (self-)conceit, arrogance, self-importance, bumptiousness; flatulence, turgidity (*of style*); 2. swollen state, puffiness.

Aufgebot ['aufgəbo:t], *n.* (**-(e)s**, *pl.* **-e**) 1. (*Law*) public notice to creditors; banns (of marriage); (*Mil.*) levy, call to arms, (*coll.*) call-up; ***das* – *bestellen,*** put up the banns; ***allgemeines* –**, universal conscription; 2. contingent, force, posse, body (*of police etc.*); 3. (*fig.*) ***unter*** or ***mit* – *aller Kräfte,*** by straining every nerve, summoning all one's strength, exerting o.s. to the utmost.

aufgebracht ['aufgəbraxt], *see* **aufbringen.**

aufgedonnert ['aufgədɔnərt], *see* **aufdonnern.**

aufgedunsen ['aufgədunzən], *adj.* swollen, puffed (up), puffy, bloated; turgid (*style*). **Aufgedunsenheit,** *f.* puffiness, bloated state; turgidity, flatulence (*of style*).

aufgehen ['aufge:ən], *irr.v.i.* (*aux.* s.) 1. rise (*of dough, of the sun etc.*); swell, expand (*also fig. of the heart*); come up, sprout, shoot (*as seeds*); go up (*in smoke, flames*); 2. open (*as eyes, a wound*), burst (*as bud, abscess*), come open *or* undone *or* apart (*as a seam*); (*fig.*) ***mir gingen die Augen auf,*** my eyes were opened; 3. become apparent *or* clear (*Dat.*, to); ***mir ging ein Licht auf,*** I realized *or* became aware *or* saw *or* understood; it dawned on me; 4. – ***in*** (*Dat.*), merge *or* become merged in(to); (*fig.*) be wholly given up *or* entirely *or* utterly devoted to; be utterly absorbed *or* engrossed in; live for nothing else but; (*Math.*) divide *or* go exactly into, go into with no remainder (*of numbers*), come *or* work out exactly (*of a sum*).

aufgeklärt ['aufgəklɛ:rt], *adj.* enlightened, broad- *or* liberal-minded, free from prejudice *or* superstition; ***–er Despotismus,*** enlightened despotism. *See* **aufklären. Aufgeklärtheit,** *f.* enlightenment, open-mindedness; acquaintance with the facts of life.

aufgeknöpft ['aufgəknœpft], *adj.* (*coll.*) free and easy, in an expansive mood, communicative.

Aufgeld ['aufgɛlt], *n.* (*Comm.*) deposit; advance; earnest money; agio, contango; premium, extra charge.

aufgelegt ['aufgəle:kt], *see* **auflegen.**

aufgeräumt ['aufgərɔymt], *adj.* in high spirits, gay, cheerful, good-humoured, merry. **Aufgeräumtheit,** *f.* cheerfulness, gaiety, good humour *or* spirits.

aufgeregt ['aufgəre:kt], *adj.* excited, agitated, flustered, flurried. **Aufgeregtheit,** *f.* excitement, agitation.

Aufgesang ['aufgəzaŋ], *n.* (*technical term in mediaeval lyric verse and the poetry of the Mastersingers denoting*) the first part of the stanza. *See* **Abgesang.**

aufgesessen! ['aufgəzɛsən], *see* **aufsitzen.**

aufgeweckt ['aufgəvɛkt], *adj.* smart, bright, clever, quick-witted.

aufgeworfen ['aufgəvɔrfən], *see* **aufwerfen.**

aufgießen ['aufgi:sən], *irr.v.t.* 1. pour (***auf*** (*Acc.*), upon); 2. infuse; brew, make (*tea, coffee*). *See* **Aufguß.**

aufgliedern ['aufgli:dərn], *v.t.* arrange in groups *or* under headings. **Aufgliederung,** *f.* arrangement, classification.

aufgreifen ['aufgraɪfən], *irr.v.t.* take *or* pick *or* snatch up; catch, seize (*a fugitive*); take up, adopt, (*coll.*) catch on to (*an idea*).

Aufguß ['aufgus], *m.* (**-(ss)es**, *pl.* **¨-(ss)e**) infusion. **Aufgußtierchen,** *pl.* infusoria.

aufhaben ['aufha:bən], *irr.v.t.* 1. have on, wear; 2. have open; 3. have to do (*homework*); ***hast du heute viel auf?*** have you got much homework today?

aufhaken ['aufha:kən], *v.t.* unhook, undo.

aufhalsen ['aufhalzen], *v.t.* (*coll.*) ***ihm etwas* –**, land *or* saddle him with s.th., saddle a th. on him.

Aufhaltekraft ['aufhaltəkraft], *f.* stopping power (*of bullet*).

aufhalten ['aufhaltən], **1.** *irr.v.t.* 1. stop, halt (*vehicle*); hold up, hinder, impede, retard (*progress*); arrest, check (*motion*); detain, delay (*a p.*), take up (*s.o.'s*) time; stay (the progress of); ***seinen Fall* –**, break his fall; ***den Feind* –**, hold the enemy in check; ***den Fortschritt* –**, retard *or* arrest *or* block progress; ***einen Schlag* –**, break the force of a blow; ***den Verkehr* –**, hold up *or* obstruct *or* block the traffic, (*of policeman*) stop *or* hold up the traffic; (*Mus.*) ***aufgehaltener Ton,*** suspended note; 2. keep *or* hold open (*eyes, hand, door, shop etc.*). **2.** *irr.v.r.* 1. stay, stop (***in*** or ***an*** (*Dat.*), in (*a place*); ***bei,*** with (*a p.*)); 2. ***sich mit*** or ***bei etwas* –**, dwell on *or* enlarge upon *or* linger over s.th., spend *or* waste time on a th.; 3. ***sich über etwas*** (*Acc.*) **–**, be irritated by a th., get worked up about *or* over a th. **Aufhalter,** *m.* stop, check, retainer, catch. **Aufhalte|riemen,** *m.* breech-band. **–wucht,** *f. See* **–kraft. Aufhaltung,** *f.* hindrance, delay; detention; stoppage, obstruction, check, retardation.

Aufhänge|achse, *f.* (*Motor.*) suspension shaft. **–band,** *n.* 1. (*Anat.*) suspensory ligament; 2. (*Med.*) suspensory bandage. **–boden,** *m.* drying-room. **–gestänge,** *n.* (*Motor.*) suspension rods. **–leine,** *f.* clothes-line. **–muskel,** *m.* levator (muscle).

aufhängen ['aufhɛŋən], *v.t.* 1. hang (up), suspend (***an*** (*Dat.*), on *or* from); hang (*a p.*); ***sich* –**, hang o.s.; 2. (*coll.*) ***ihm etwas* –**, saddle *or* land him with s.th., fob *or* palm off *or* foist *or* saddle s.th. on him; let him in for *or* involve him in s.th.; ***ihm eine Lüge* –**, tell him a thundering lie; ***sich*** (*Dat.*) ***etwas* – *lassen,*** be had, be taken for a ride. **Aufhänger,** *m.* loop; hanger. **Aufhängestange,** *f.* (*Motor.*) suspension rod. **Aufhängsel,** *n.* loop, hanger (*inside garment*). **Aufhängung,** *f.* suspension, mounting, springs, springing.

aufhaschen ['aufhaʃən], *v.t.* snatch up; ***Neuigkeiten* –**, pick up news.

aufhauen ['aufhauən], **1.** *v.t.* cut *or* chop open; re-cut (*a file*). **2.** *v.i.* (*coll.*) throw one's money about. **Aufhauer,** *m.* cold chisel.

aufhäufen ['aufhɔyfən], **1.** *v.t.* heap *or* pile up, gather in a heap; amass, accumulate; ***aufgehäuftes Maß,*** heaped measure. **2.** *v.r.* accumulate, pile up, collect, gather; drift (*of snow*). **Aufhäufung,** *f.* heap, pile, accumulation, hoard; drift (*of snow*).

aufheben ['aufhe:bən], *irr.v.t.* 1. lift *or* raise (up) (*as eyes, arm etc.*); ***die Tafel* –**, leave the table, rise from table (*of the host*); 2. pick *or* take up; 3. keep, save (***für,*** for); ***gut aufgehoben,*** in safe keeping (*of a th.*), in good hands, well looked after, well off (*of a p.*); 4. terminate, cancel; break up (*meeting*); break off (*an engagement*); dissolve (*marriage, partnership, assembly, monastery*); annul (*marriage, agreement*); raise (*siege*); break, invalidate, (*Law*) disaffirm (*contract*); set aside, rescind, (*Law*) quash, render void (*judgement*); repeal, abrogate, (*Law*) revoke (*decree*); remove, lift (*restrictions*); take off, lift (*embargo*); (*Law*) withdraw (*action*); (*coll.*) ***aufgeschoben ist nicht aufgehoben,*** there is always another day; 5. balance out, counterbalance, compensate for, offset, neutralize, (*Math.*) cancel; ***einander*** or ***sich*** (***gegenseitig***) **–**, balance out, counterbalance *or* neutralize one another, (*Math.*) cancel out, cancel one another. **Aufheben,** *n.* 1. lifting (up); ***beim* – *der Hände,*** on a show of hands; 2. fuss, bother; ***ein großes* –, *viel* –*s*** or ***großes* – *wegen nichts,*** much ado *or* a great fuss *or* bother *or* pother *or* to-do about nothing.

Aufhebung ['aufhe:buŋ], *f.* termination, suspension, cancellation (*also Math.*); dissolution (*of marriage, partnership, assembly, monastery*);

suppression (*of monastery*); annulment (*of marriage, agreement*); raising (*of siege*); nullification, invalidation, (*Law*) disaffirmation (*of contract*); reversal, rescission (*of judgement*); repeal, abolition, abrogation (*of law*); revocation (*of decree*); removal (*of restrictions*); lifting (*of embargo*); neutralization (*of results*); – ***der ehelichen Gemeinschaft,*** legal separation. **Aufhebungs|gericht,** *n.* court of appeal *or* cassation. **–zeichen,** *n.* (*Mus.*) natural.

aufheitern ['aufhaɪtərn], **1.** *v.t.* brighten, liven *or* cheer up, gladden. **2.** *v.r.* cheer *or* brighten up; become brighter, brighten (*sky*), become brighter, clear up (*weather*). **Aufheiterung,** *f.* diversion, distraction, s.th. to cheer (one) up; improvement in the weather, clearing up (*of weather*).

aufhelfen ['aufhɛlfən], *irr.v.t.* ***ihm*** **–,** help him up.

aufhellen ['aufhɛlən], **1.** *v.t.* 1. brighten up, lighten, heighten (*a tint*); 2. clarify; 3. (*fig.*) elucidate, throw light on, illuminate, clear up, clarify. **2.** *v.r.* 1. brighten, clear up (*of weather*); 2. settle, clarify (*of liquors*). **Aufhellung,** *f.* clarification; brightening; heightening (*of a tint*); elucidation, illumination (*of a problem*). **Aufhellungsmittel,** *n.* clearing agent.

aufhetzen ['aufhɛtsən], *v.t.* stir up, rouse, incite, instigate; start (*game etc.*). **aufhetzend,** *adj.* provocative, inflammatory (*speech etc.*). **Aufhetzer,** *m.* instigator. **aufhetzerisch,** *adj. See* **aufhetzend. Aufhetzung,** *f.* instigation, incitement.

aufholen ['aufho:lən], **1.** *v.t.* 1. (*Naut.*) haul up *or* in; hoist, run up (*flag*), trice (*sail*), bring (*a ship*) close to the wind; 2. (*fig.*) make up for (*a loss*). **2.** *v.i.* make up for lost time, make up leeway, catch up, (*Railw.*) make up time, (*Racing*) close the gap, draw level. **Aufholer,** *m.* tricing line, relieving tackle; halyard.

aufhorchen ['aufhɔrçən], *v.i.* prick up one's ears, listen attentively; keep one's ears open, be all ears.

aufhören ['aufhø:rən], *v.i.* stop, cease, end, come to a stop *or* end; finish, leave *or* break off, discontinue, desist (from); ***allmählich*** **–,** peter out; ***plötzlich*** **–,** stop short *or* dead, come to a dead stop *or* end; ***zu zahlen*** **–,** suspend payment; ***hört doch nur auf!*** for goodness sake stop! have done! (*coll.*) ***da hört doch alles auf!*** that beats everything! that's the limit! **Aufhören,** *n.* stoppage, discontinuation, cessation; ***ohne*** **–,** incessantly, unceasingly, ceaselessly, constantly, without intermission *or* a break.

aufjagen ['aufja:gən], *v.t.* start, raise (*game*), flush (*birds*), draw (*fox*), (*fig. coll.*) rout out (*a p.*).

aufjammern ['aufjamərn], *v.i.* (*aux.* h.) set up a lamentation *or* (*coll.*) wail.

aufjauchzen ['aufjauxtsən], **aufjubeln** [–ju:bəln], *v.i.* burst into jubilation, exult, shout for joy.

Aufkauf ['aufkauf], *m.* (**-s,** *pl.* **-̈e**) buying up, purchase in bulk, (*Comm.*) engrossment. **aufkaufen,** *v.t.* buy up, purchase in bulk, (*Comm.*) engross; forestall, corner (*the market*).

Aufkäufer ['aufkɔyfər], *m.* forestaller, engrosser; buying-agent, buying-speculator.

aufkeimen ['aufkaɪmən], *v.i.* (*aux.* s.) germinate, bud, sprout. **aufkeimend,** *adj.* budding, dawning.

aufkitten ['aufkɪtən], *v.t.* cement on (***auf*** (*Acc.*), to).

aufklaffen ['aufklafən], *v.i.* yawn, gape open.

aufklappen ['aufklapən], *v.t.* open (*something folded, like a penknife*), raise, put up (*flap, folding hood*), turn up (*hat brim*).

aufklaren ['aufkla:rən], **1.** *v.i.* clear (up) (*of weather*). **2.** *v.t.* (*Naut.*) tidy *or* clear up (*the deck*); ***aufgeklart,*** ship-shape.

aufklären ['aufklɛ:rən], **1.** *v.t.* 1. clear up; elucidate, clarify, illuminate; throw *or* shed light on (*a matter*), make clear, explain (*a matter*) (*Dat.*, to) (*a p.*); 2. enlighten (*a p.*) (***über*** (*Acc.*), on *or* as to), instruct, inform (*a p.*) (about); tell (*s.o.*) the facts of life; 3. (*Mil.*) reconnoitre, (*coll.*) recce. **2.** *v.r.* clear up (*as weather*), brighten, light up (*as countenance*). *See* **aufgeklärt. Aufklärer,** *m.* 1. enlightener; representative of Enlightenment, rationalist; 2. (*Mil.*) scout *or* reconnaissance *or* (*coll.*) recce ship *or* aircraft. **aufklärerisch,** *adj.* imbued with the strivings of Enlightenment. **Aufklärung,** *f.* 1. elucidation, illumination, clarification, enlightenment; instruction about the facts of life; ***Zeitalter der*** **–,** Age of Enlightenment (*18th century*); 2. (*Mil.*) reconnaissance.

Aufklärungs|abteilung, *f.* (*Mil.*) reconnaissance unit. **–buch,** *n.* textbook on sex education. **–fahrt,** *f.* (*Nav.*) reconnaissance patrol. **–fahrzeug,** *n.* (*Mil.*) scout car. **–flugzeug,** *n.* reconnaissance aircraft. **–spähtrupp,** *m.* (*Mil.*) reconnoitring party. **–streife,** *f.* (*Mil.*) reconnaissance patrol. **–zeitalter,** *n.* Age of Enlightenment.

aufklauben ['aufklaubən], *v.t.* pick up; glean, garner.

aufkleben ['aufkle:bən], *v.t.* stick on, paste *or* glue on (***auf*** (*Acc.*), to). **Aufklebezettel,** *m.* gummed *or* stick-on *or* sticky label, sticker.

aufklinken ['aufklɪŋkən], *v.t.* unlatch (*a door*).

aufknacken ['aufknakən], *v.t.* crack (open) (*nuts*).

aufknöpfen ['aufknœpfən], **1.** *v.t.* 1. unbutton (*garment*), unfasten, undo (*button*); 2. button on (***auf*** (*Acc.*), to). *See* **aufgeknöpft. 2.** *v.r.* come unbuttoned.

aufknoten ['aufkno:tən], *v.t.* untie, undo, unknot (*parcel etc.*).

aufknüpfen ['aufknypfən], *v.t.* 1. tie up; string up (*also coll. a p. on the gallows*); 2. *See* **aufknoten.**

aufkochen ['aufkɔxən], **1.** *v.t.* boil up, warm up, bring to the boil. **2.** *v.i.* (*aux.* s. *&* h.) come to the boil.

aufkommen ['aufkɔmən], *irr.v.i.* (*aux.* s.) 1. get up, get *or* rise to one's feet; (***wieder***) **–,** recover (*from illness*), get well again, (*coll.*) pull round; 2. come up, grow (*of plants*); get *or* spring up (*of wind*); arise, spring up (*of s.th. new*); appear, be introduced, come into being *or* existence; become established, come into fashion *or* vogue, become fashionable, (*coll.*) come in; – ***lassen,*** give rise to; 3. stand up, prevail, make headway (***gegen,*** against), cope (with), do anything (in the face of); ***nicht* – *gegen,*** be no match for; 4. accept responsibility, be held responsible, make o.s. responsible *or* answerable (***für,*** for (*s.th.*); *Dat.*, to (*s.o.*)); ***für den Verlust*** **–,** make good *or* (*coll.*) stand the loss; ***für die Unkosten*** **–,** pay *or* defray the expenses; 5. reduce the lead, gain, make headway (*of a runner*). **Aufkommen,** *n.* 1. recovery (*from sickness*); 2. emergence, rise (*of a fashion*); rise in the world; 3. yield (*of a tax*).

Aufkömmling ['aufkœmlɪŋ], *m.* (**-s,** *pl.* **-e**) upstart, parvenu, self-made man.

aufkorken ['aufkɔrkən], *v.t.* uncork, open (*bottle*).

aufkratzen ['aufkratsən], *v.t.* scratch up; raise the nap (*of cloth*); card (*wool*); (*coll.*) ***ihn*** **–,** cheer *or* back him up; (*coll.*) ***aufgekratzt,*** in high spirits, in fine fettle, cheery.

aufkräusen ['aufkrɔyzən], *v.i.* form a head (*of beer*).

aufkrempe(l)n ['aufkrɛmpə(l)n], *v.t.* bend back, turn *or* roll up, tuck up (*sleeves, hat brim etc.*).

aufkreuzen ['aufkrɔytsən], *v.i.* (*Naut.*) ply to windward; (*coll.*) heave in sight, show up (*of a p.*).

aufkriegen ['aufkri:gən], *v.t.* (*coll.*) *see* **aufbekommen.**

aufkrimpen ['aufkrɪmpən], *v.i.* (*Naut.*) back (*of wind*).

aufkündigen ['aufkyndɪgən], *v.t.* (give notice to) terminate, cancel, withdraw from (*contract etc.*); ***ihm die Freundschaft*** **–,** withdraw one's friendship from him, renounce his friendship; ***ihm den Gehorsam*** **–,** disown one's allegiance to him, refuse obedience to him. **Aufkündigung,** *f.* (notice of) termination, cancellation, withdrawal.

auflachen ['auflaxən], *v.i.* burst out laughing.

Auflade|gebläse, *n.* supercharger. **–kommando,** *n.* (*Mil.*) loading detachment *or* party. **–motor,** *m.* forced induction engine.

aufladen ['aufla:dən], *irr.v.t.* 1. load (*goods*); ***ihm etwas –,*** saddle *or* burden him with s.th.; ***sich*** (*Dat.*) –, take upon o.s., saddle o.s. with, shoulder (*responsibility*); 2. (*Elec.*) charge; 3. (*Mil.*) entrain (*troops*); 4. boost (*an engine*). **Auflader,** *m.* packer, loader.

Auflage ['aufla:gə], *f.* 1. edition, impression (*of book*); circulation (*of newspaper*); ***unveränderte –,*** reprint, new impression; ***verbesserte und vermehrte –,*** revised and enlarged edition; 2. (*obs.*) tax, duty, impost; contribution, collective fine, levy; 3. (*obs.*) judge's order, injunction; 4. superimposed layer; overlay (*mattress*); 5. rest, support (*for tools*); 6. (*Cul.*) garnish(ing); 7. (*For.*) animal growth.

Auflage|fläche, *f.* bearing *or* working surface. **–humus,** *m.* superficial layer of humus deposit.

Auflager ['aufla:gər], *m.* (*Engin.*) bearing; bearer support; (*Archit.*) springer. **Auflagerdruck,** *m.* bearing pressure.

auflagern ['aufla:gərn], *v.t.* 1. lay in a stock of, store up; 2. (*Geol.*) superpose. **Auflagerung,** *f.* stratification, deposition.

auflassen ['auflasən], *irr.v.t.* 1. leave open; 2. let (*a p.*) get up; 3. (*Law*) cede, convey, assign (***an*** (*Acc.*), to); 4. shut down, abandon (*works, mine etc.*). **Auflassung,** *f.* 1. transfer, conveyance, assignment; 2. abandonment.

Auflau(e)rer ['auflau(ə)rər], *m.* eavesdropper, watcher, lurker, spy.

auflauern ['auflauərn], *v.i.* be on the watch *or* (*coll.*) look-out, lie in wait (*Dat.*, for); ***ihm –,*** waylay him.

Auflauf ['auflauf], *m.* 1. crowd, gathering (*of people*), riot, (*Law*) unlawful assembly; 2. (*Cul.*) soufflé, light pudding; 3. accumulation, accruing (*of debts, interest etc.*). **auflaufen,** *irr.v.i.* (*aux.* s.) 1. run up, charge (*as hunted game*); 2. swell up, become distended; rise (*as dough*); run *or* mount up, accrue, accumulate (*as debts, interest etc.*) (***auf*** (*Acc.*), to); 3. ground, run aground (*as ship*), get stuck (*as car*); ***– lassen,*** run (*a ship*) aground, beach, strand (*a ship*); get (*a car*) stuck. **Auflaufform,** *f.* soufflé dish.

aufleben ['aufle:bən], *v.i.* (*aux.* s.) revive, be revived, (*coll.*) be looking up.

auflegen ['aufle:gən], *v.t.* 1. put *or* lay *or* put on, apply (***auf*** (*Acc.*), to), impose (*a fine, a tax etc.*) (*Dat.*, on); ***eine Anleihe –,*** float a loan; ***die Ellbogen auf den Tisch –,*** lean *or* rest one's elbows on the table; ***Fett –,*** put on fat, (*fig.*) grow fat, thrive; 2. publish, issue, print (an edition of); 3. lay *or* put *or* set out, display; ***seine Karten –,*** show one's hand, lay one's cards on the table; 4. lay up (*ship, car*); 5. ***aufgelegt,*** disposed, inclined *or* in the mood *or* humour (***zu,*** for); laid-up (*as ships*); ***aufgelegter Schwindel,*** obvious *or* (*coll.*) barefaced swindle; ***gut aufgelegt,*** in a good mood *or* humour; ***schlecht aufgelegt,*** in a bad mood *or* humour, out of humour. **Auflegung,** *f.* 1. application (*of a plaster etc.*); imposition (*of fines, taxes etc.*); infliction (*of punishment*); 2. laying up (*of a ship*).

auflehnen ['aufle:nən], **1.** *v.t.* lean (***auf*** (*Acc.*), against *or* on). **2.** *v.r.* rear (*of horse*); rebel, revolt, rise (in rebellion); protest (***gegen,*** against); offer resistance (to). **Auflehnung,** *f.* revolt, rebellion, insurrection (***gegen,*** against), resistance (to).

auflesen ['aufle:zən], *irr.v.t.* glean (*corn*), gather *or* pick up, collect (*sticks etc.*), (*fig.*) pick up.

aufleuchten ['auflɔyçtən], *v.i.* flare *or* blaze up, flash; light up, shine (out), brighten (up) (*as eyes*). **Aufleuchten,** *n.* flare, flash.

auflichten ['auflɪçtən], *v.r.* look (a little) brighter.

aufliefern ['aufli:fərn], *v.t.* send, consign, dispatch (*goods*). **Auflieferung,** *f.* consignment, dispatch.

aufliegen ['aufli:gən], **1.** *irr.v.i.* (*aux.* s.) 1. lie, rest, be supported (***auf*** (*Dat.*), on); be put *or* set *or* laid out (for inspection *or* perusal), be available, (*Comm.*) be exposed (for sale); 2. be incumbent (*Dat.*, on), weigh (upon) (*as responsibility*). **2.** *irr.v.r.* develop bedsores. **Aufliegen,** *n.* (*Med.*) bed-sores, decubitus.

auflockern ['auflɔkərn], **1.** *v.t.* loosen (up); shake up (*a pillow*), break up (*a tight mass*), open out (*ranks*), slacken, ease (*knot*), relax (*restrictions*), (*fig.*) break the monotony of; (*fig.*) ***aufgelockert,*** relaxed. **2.** *v.r.* get loose, come undone (*as knot*), loosen up (*as muscles*), open out (*as ranks*), (begin to) break up (*as crowd*) *or* disintegrate (*as a mass*), grow lax (*as morals*). **Auflockerung,** *f.* loosening, relaxation; disintegration, growing laxity.

auflodern ['auflo:dərn], *v.i.* (*aux.* s.) flare *or* blaze up, burst into flames.

auflösbar ['auflø:sba:r], *adj.* (*Chem.*) soluble (***in*** (*Dat.*), in), (*Math.*) soluble, solvable, resolvable; (*fig.*) dissolvable (*as assembly*), dissoluble (*as contract*); ***nicht –,*** (*Chem.*) insoluble, (*Math.*) insoluble, unsolvable, (*fig.*) indissoluble. **Auflösbarkeit,** *f.* (*Chem.*) solubility, (*Math.*) solvability, (*fig.*) dissolubility.

auflösen ['auflø:zən], **1.** *v.t.* 1. loosen, untie, undo (*knot*); disentangle, unravel; ***sein Haar –,*** let down one's hair; 2. break *or* split up, disintegrate, decompose, resolve (***in*** (*Acc.*), into); dissolve (***in*** (*Dat.*), in); (*Chem.*) analyse; disband (*troops*); (*Math.*) ***die Klammern –,*** get rid of the brackets; (*Mus.*) ***eine Dissonanz –,*** resolve a discord; (*Mus.*) ***ein Versetzungszeichen –,*** cancel an accidental; ***eine Verlobung –,*** break off an engagement. **2.** *v.r.* 1. come undone (*as knot*); break *or* split up, disperse (*as a crowd*), disintegrate, decompose (*as an organism*), (*Mil.*) go into open order; 2. dissolve (***in*** (*Dat.* or (*fig.*) *Acc.*), in, (*fig.*) into); ***Salz löst sich im Wasser auf,*** salt dissolves in water; ***sich in Tränen –,*** dissolve *or* melt into tears; ***auflösendes Mittel,*** solvent; (*Law*) ***auflösende Bedingung,*** condition subsequent; ***aufgelöst,*** dissolved; dishevelled; (*coll.*) upset, worked up; (*Mil.*) in open order.

Auflösung ['auflø:zuŋ], *f.* disentanglement, (*Theat.*) dénouement; dissolution, disintegration, decomposition, (*Chem.*) analysis; (*Chem., Math.*) solution; resolution (*of discord*); disbandment (*of troops*). **auflösungsfähig,** *adj. See* **auflösbar.** **Auflösungs|grenze,** *f.* limit of resolution (*of lens*). **–kraft,** *f. See* **–vermögen.** **–mittel,** *n.* solvent. **–vermögen,** *n.* (*Chem.*) dissolving power, (*Opt.*) resolving power. **–zeichen,** *n.* (*Mus.*) natural.

aufmachen ['aufmaxən], **1.** *v.t.* 1. open; undo untie, unfasten, unbutton; unpick (*a seam*), turn on (*a tap*), put up (*an umbrella*); 2. make up (*material*), (*fig.*) work *or* get *or* do up (for effect); ***eine Rechnung –,*** make *or* draw up, make out an account; ***eine Havarie –,*** adjust an average. **2.** *v.r.* 1. get *or* rise up; set out, start on one's way, (*coll.*) be off; 2. dress *or* get o.s. up; make o.s. up, put on one's make-up. **Aufmachung,** *f.* 1. statement (*of account*); 2. presentation, lay-out, get-up (*of book etc.*), packaging (*of goods*), (*coll.*) window-dressing, eyewash; make-up (*cosmetics*).

Aufmarsch ['aufmarʃ], *m.* parade; forming up for deployment, concentration (*of troops*). **Aufmarschgebiet,** *n.* assembly *or* deployment area. **aufmarschieren,** *v.i.* (*aux.* s.) assemble, deploy; parade, form up; ***– lassen,*** deploy, assemble, array; parade.

aufmerken ['aufmɛrkən], *v.i.* listen attentively; note down, take *or* make a note of; attend, pay attention, give *or* pay heed (***auf*** (*Acc.*), to), take careful notice (of); keep a sharp *or* watchful eye (*Dat.*, on). **aufmerksam,** **1.** *adj.* 1. attentive; ***– werden,*** become aware *or* conscious (***auf*** (*Acc.*), of); ***ihn auf eine S. – machen,*** call *or* draw *or* attract his attention to a th., bring a th. to his attention *or* notice, point a th. out to him; 2. attentive (***gegen,*** to), considerate (towards), full of attentions *or* consideration (for). **2.** *adv.* attentively, intently, closely, carefully. **Aufmerksamkeit,** *f.* 1. attention (*Dat.*, to (*a p.*); ***auf*** (*Acc.*), to (*a th.*)); 2. attentiveness (*pl.* attentions), consideration; 3. mark *or* token of (one's) regard.

aufmöbeln ['aufmø:bəln], **1.** *v.t.* (*coll.*) buck up. **2.** *v.r.* (*coll.*) put on one's glad rags, doll o.s. up.

aufmucken ['aufmukən], *v.i.* (*coll.*) get one's back up; be up in arms (*gegen*, against).

aufmuntern ['aufmuntərn], *v.t.* cheer (up), put new heart *or* life into, encourage; (a)rouse, enliven, liven up, animate, encourage, incite. **Aufmunterung,** *f.* encouragement, incitement; animation.

aufmutzen ['aufmutsən], *v.t.* ***ihm etwas* –**, tax *or* reproach him with s.th.

Aufnäharbeit ['aufnɛ:ʔarbaɪt], *f.* appliqué work.

aufnähen ['aufnɛ:ən], *v.t.* sew on (***auf*** (*Acc.*), to). **Aufnäher,** *m.* tuck, false hem.

Aufnahme ['aufna:mə], *f.* 1. taking up, adoption (*of plan*), raising (*of money*), entering (*into*), establishing (*of relations*); 2. taking in *or* upon, intake, (*Elec.*) input, assimilation (*of food etc.*), absorbing, absorption, accepting, acceptance, inclusion; reception, admission, enrolment, affiliation; ***in* – *kommen*,** come into fashion *or* favour; ***eine kühle* – *finden*,** meet with a cool reception; 3. recording (*in writing, of sound*), keeping (*of minutes*); photographing, shooting (*a film*); surveying (*of land*); (sound) recording, photograph, exposure (*on roll of film*), survey.

aufnahme|bereit, *adj.* receptive (*für*, to). **-fähig,** *adj.* capable of absorbing. *See also* **-bereit. Aufnahme|fähigkeit,** *f.* receptivity. **-prüfung,** *f.* entrance examination. **-stellung,** *f.* (*Mil.*) delaying *or* rallying position.

aufnehmen ['aufne:mən], *irr.v.t.* 1. take *or* pick up; ***die Fährte* –**, pick up *or* get on the scent; 2. (*fig.*) take up, adopt (*a plan*), establish (*contact*), enter into *or* upon (*relations*), start, begin (*work*), open (*business*); ***wieder* –**, reopen, restart, resume, return to, pick up the thread of; ***den Kampf* –**, take up the cudgels (***für***, on (*s.o.'s*) behalf; ***gegen***, against), give battle (***mit***, to); ***es mit ihm* – (*können*)**, be as good as *or* be a match for him; 3. take in, receive, accept, include; (*fig.*) conceive, (*coll.*) take in (*with the mind*); admit; ***gut aufgenommen werden*,** meet with a good reception; ***in sich*** (*Acc.*) **–**, absorb, assimilate; 4. record, take *or* write down; (*Rad.*) receive, pick up (*signal*); survey, make a survey of (*land*); record, make a recording of (*voice*); photograph, take a photograph of, shoot (*a film*); ***die Bevölkerung* –**, take a census; ***ein Diktat* –**, take down from dictation; 5. raise (*money*).

aufnotieren ['aufnoti:rən], *v.t.* note (down), take *or* make a note of.

aufnötigen ['aufnø:tɪgən], *v.t.* ***ihm etwas* –**, force him to take *or* accept s.th., force s.th. (up)on him. **Aufnötigung,** *f.* enforced acceptance, compulsion (*to do*).

aufoktroyieren ['aufʔɔktroaji:rən], *v.t. See* **aufnötigen.**

aufopfern ['aufʔɔpfərn], **1.** *v.t.* sacrifice, offer up, offer as a sacrifice; give up, devote (***für***, to). **2.** *v.r.* sacrifice o.s., devote o.s., dedicate o.s. (***für***, to). **aufopfernd,** *adj.* unselfish, devoted. **Aufopferung,** *f.* (self-)sacrifice; devotion.

aufpäppeln ['aufpɛpəln], *v.t.* (*coll.*) cosset back to health.

aufpassen ['aufpasən], **1.** *v.i.* pay attention, attend, be attentive; watch *or* look out, take care, beware, mind, be careful *or* on the alert, keep one's eyes open; **– *auf*** (*Acc.*), keep an eye on; take care of, look after; ***aufgepaßt! paß auf!*** be careful! take care! look out! mind! pay attention! listen (carefully)! look (here)! **2.** *v.t.* fit (*lid, hat etc.*) (***auf*** (*Acc.*), on). **Aufpasser,** *m.* watcher, spy; look-out (man); (*coll.*) busybody.

aufpeitschen ['aufpaɪtʃən], *v.t.* excite; stir *or* whip up.

aufpflanzen ['aufpflantsən], **1.** *v.t.* set up, erect; raise (*a standard*); mount (*guns*); fix (*bayonets*). **2.** *v.r.* plant o.s.

aufpfropfen ['aufpfrɔpfən], *v.t.* graft (on).

aufplustern ['aufplu:stərn], *v.r.* ruffle the feathers (*of birds*); (*fig.*) give o.s. airs.

aufprägen ['aufprɛ:gən], *v.t.* imprint, stamp impress (***auf*** (*Acc.*), on).

Aufprall ['aufpral], *m.* impact (*of missile*). **aufprallen,** *v.i.* strike (***auf*** (*Acc.*), on), rebound.

aufprobieren ['aufprobi:rən], *v.t.* try on (*a hat*).

aufprotzen ['aufprɔtsən], *v.t.* limber (*guns*).

aufpulvern ['aufpulvərn], *v.t.* (*coll.*) pick *or* buck up, pull together.

aufpumpen ['aufpumpən], *v.t.* inflate, pump *or* blow up.

aufputschen ['aufputʃən], *v.t.* (*coll.*) rouse, incite, stir up (*a mob*); buck *or* pep up (*a p.*).

Aufputz ['aufputs], *m.* (**-(e)s,** *no pl.*) finery. **aufputzen,** *v.t.* clean, polish, rub *or* brush up; brighten up, make smart; dress up, deck out.

aufquellen ['aufkvɛlən], *irr.v.i.* (*aux.* s.) 1. bubble *or* well up; 2. swell (up), expand; **– *lassen*,** soak (*dried peas etc.*).

aufquirlen ['aufkvɪrlən], *v.t.* beat (up), whisk (*eggs etc.*).

aufraffen ['aufrafən], **1.** *v.t.* gather *or* snatch up. **2.** *v.r.* struggle to one's feet, (*fig.*) pull o.s. together, collect o.s.; bring o.s. (*to do*), summon the energy (*to do*).

aufragen ['aufra:gən], *v.i.* jut up, tower (up), rise (on) high.

aufrappeln ['aufrapəln], *v.r.* (*coll.*) pull o.s. together, collect o.s.; bring o.s. (*to do*); summon the energy (*to do*); pull round, pick up (*after illness*).

aufrauchen ['aufrauxən], *v.t.* finish (smoking) (*a cigarette*), smoke all (*one's cigarettes*).

aufräumen ['aufrɔymən], *v.t.* 1. straighten *or* tidy (up), clear up (*a room etc.*), clear *or* tidy *or* put away (*objects*), clear (*a table*); (*Comm.*) clear (out), sell off (*stock*); ***mit etwas* –**, do away with *or* get rid of s.th., make a clean sweep of s.th., (*Mil., coll.*) mop up; 2. open *or* ream out, enlarge, broach (*a hole*). *See* **aufgeräumt. Aufräumer,** *m.* reamer, broach. **Aufräumerin,** *f.* charwoman, cleaning woman. **Aufräumung,** *f.* clearing *or* tidying up, (*Mil.*) mopping up. **Aufräumungsarbeit,** *f.* salvage *or* clearance work.

aufrechnen ['aufrɛçnən], *v.t.* 1. reckon up, count *or* add up; ***ihm etwas* –**, charge s.th. to his account, (*fig.*) blame him for s.th., put *or* lay the blame for s.th. on him; 2. balance, set off (***gegen***, against). **Aufrechnung,** *f.* settling of accounts; (*Law*) balancing, set-off (*of claims*).

aufrecht ['aufrɛçt], *adj.* 1. upright, erect, on end; ***den Kopf* – *halten*,** hold one's head erect *or* up, hold up one's head; 2. (*fig.*) upright, honest, honourable, (*coll.*) straight.

aufrechterhalten ['aufrɛçtʔɛrhaltən], *irr.v.t.* maintain, uphold, abide by (*a decision*), adhere *or* (*coll.*) stick to (*an opinion*), keep up (*relationship*), keep (*the peace*). **Aufrechterhaltung,** *f.* maintenance, preservation (*Gen.*, of), adherence (to).

aufreden ['aufre:dən], *v.t.* ***ihm etwas* –**, talk him into a th.

aufregen ['aufre:gən], **1.** *v.t.* excite; upset, agitate. **2.** *v.r.* get excited; get agitated *or* upset *or* flurried *or* flustered, fuss (***über*** (*Acc.*), about). *See* **aufgeregt. aufregend,** *adj.* exciting, thrilling; upsetting. **Aufregung,** *f.* excitement; agitation, upset, flurry, fluster.

aufreiben ['aufraɪbən], *irr.v.t.* 1. abrade, chafe, gall, graze, (*Med.*) excoriate (*skin*); 2. exhaust; wear out *or* down, (*coll.*) get down; irritate, fret; sap (*one's strength*), undermine (*health*), fray (*one's nerves*); 3. destroy, cut to pieces (*enemy*); 4. enlarge, ream (out), broach (*a hole*). **aufreibend,** *adj.* exhausting, wearing, tiring, gruelling, trying. **Aufreiber,** *m.* reamer, broach.

aufreihen ['aufraɪən], *v.t.* string, thread (*beads*).

aufreißen ['aufraɪsən], **1.** *irr.v.t.* tear *or* rip open; burst *or* fling *or* wrench *or* force open; slit, cut, crack, split; take *or* rip *or* tear up (*a pavement*); ***die Augen* –**, open one's eyes wide; ***den Mund* –**, open one's mouth wide, (*fig. coll.*) talk big, shoot off one's mouth. **2.** *irr.v.i.* (*aux.* s.) split *or* burst (open), crack, gape.

aufreizen ['aufraɪtsən], *v.t.* incite, rouse, stir up, madden, infuriate; inflame, fire (*passions*), excite (*the senses*); provoke, urge *or* (*coll.*) egg on (*a p.*). **aufreizend,** *adj.* provocative. **Aufreizung,** *f.* provocation; incitement, instigation.

aufrichten ['aufrɪçtən], **1.** *v.t.* set up, set *or* stand *or* put upright *or* on end, erect; raise, plant (*a standard*); right (*a ship*), step (*a mast*); (*fig.*) cheer up, hearten, put fresh heart into; *den Kopf* –, lift up *or* raise one's head. **2.** *v.r.* become erect (*of a th.*); raise o.s.; straighten (up) (*of a p.*), rear, stand on its hind legs (*of an animal*); *sich im Bett* –, sit up in bed; *sich* (*hoch*) –, draw o.s. up (to one's full height); *sich wieder* –, pick o.s. up, get to one's feet.

aufrichtig ['aufrɪçtɪç], *adj.* sincere, candid, frank, open, honest, upright, straightforward. **Aufrichtigkeit,** *f.* sincerity, candour, frankness, openness; honesty, uprightness, straightforwardness.

Aufrichtung ['aufrɪçtuŋ], *f.* erection; establishment.

aufriegeln ['aufri:gəln], *v.t.* unbolt.

Aufriß ['aufrɪs], *m.* (*Geom., Archit.*) vertical projection, elevation; (*fig.*) outline, summary; *perspektivischer* –, perspective view.

aufritzen ['aufrɪtsən], *v.t.* slit open, scratch.

aufrollen ['aufrɔlən], **1.** *v.t.* 1. roll up (*map etc.*), furl (*flag*); roll up (*the enemy front*), turn (*the enemy's flank*); 2. (*less usual*) unroll, unfurl; 3. bring up, broach, open, go into (*a question*). **2.** *v.r.* 1. unroll, come unrolled *or* unfurled; 2. (*less usual*) roll up, curl up.

aufrücken ['aufrykən], *v.i.* (*aux.* s.) move up; close up (*ranks*); rise, be promoted.

Aufruf ['aufru:f], *m.* exhortation, appeal, call-up (*for service*), calling-in (*of bank-notes*); *öffentlicher* –, proclamation. **aufrufen,** *irr.v.t.* call (up)on, summon, appeal to, exhort; call up (*recruits*), call in (*banknotes*); call over (*names*).

Aufruhr ['aufru:r], *m.* (**-s**, *pl.* **-e**) tumult, commotion, turmoil, disorder, uproar; riot, revolt, rebellion, (up)rising, insurrection, (*Mil.*) mutiny.

aufrühren ['aufry:rən], *v.t.* stir up, incite, rouse (*to rebellion*); bring up, (*coll.*) rake up. **Aufrührer,** *m.* agitator, incendiary; rebel, insurgent, rioter, (*Mil.*) mutineer. **aufrührerisch,** *adj.* rebellious, insurgent, rioting, (*Mil.*) mutinous; seditious, inflammatory (*speech etc.*).

Aufruhrstifter ['aufru:rʃtɪftər], *m.* (political) agitator.

aufrunden ['aufrundən], *v.t.* bring up to a round figure, round up.

aufrüsten ['aufrystən], *v.i., v.t.* arm, rearm. **Aufrüstung,** *f.* (re)armament.

aufrütteln ['aufrytəln], *v.t.* shake up, rouse.

aufs [aufs] = *auf das.*

Aufsage ['aufza:gə], *f.* cancellation, withdrawal. **aufsagen,** *v.t.* 1. say, repeat, recite; 2. cancel, withdraw; annul, rescind, countermand; give notice (*Dat.*, to).

aufsammeln ['aufzaməln], *v.t.* gather *or* collect up.

aufsässig ['aufzɛsɪç], *adj.* rebellious, refractory (*gegen*, against); (*obs.*) – *sein*, bear a grudge (*Dat.*, against). **Aufsässigkeit,** *f.* rebelliousness.

Aufsatz ['aufzats], *m.* 1. (*anything fixed on top of s.th. else*) top, head-piece; knob; head-dress; year's growth; piece sewed on; attachment, finish, ornament *etc.*; centre-piece; chuck (*of lathe*); (*Artil.*) tangent-sight; 2. essay, article (*in a newspaper*); treatise; *vermischte Aufsätze*, miscellaneous essays. **Aufsatz|farbe,** *f.* topping colour. **–höhe,** *f.* (*Artil.*) elevation. **–platte,** *f.* plinth. **–schlüssel,** *m.* box spanner. **–thema,** *n.* essay-subject. **–winkel,** *m.* angle of sight, (*Artil.*) tangent elevation.

aufsaugen ['aufzaugən], *reg. & irr.v.t.* absorb, imbibe, soak up. **aufsaugend,** *adj.* absorbent. **Aufsaugung,** *f.* absorption.

aufschauen ['aufʃauən], *v.i.* look *or* glance up.

aufscheuchen ['aufʃɔyçən], *v.t.* disturb, startle, start (*game*).

aufschichten ['aufʃɪçtən], **1.** *v.t.* pile up, stack (*timber etc.*); arrange in layers, stratify; *aufgeschichtet*, stratified. **2.** *v.r.* pile up (*in layers*), stratify. **Aufschichtung,** *f.* stratification.

aufschieben ['aufʃi:bən], *irr.v.t.* 1. shove *or* push open; 2. postpone, defer, delay, (*coll.*) hold over, put off, adjourn, prorogue; *einen Termin* –, fix a later date; (*Law*) *–de Bedingung*, condition precedent. **Aufschiebung,** *f.* delay, postponement, deferment, adjournment; respite.

aufschießen ['aufʃi:sən], *irr.v.i.* (*aux.* s.) shoot *or* jump *or* spring *or* leap up; gush forth (*as water*).

aufschirren ['aufʃɪrən], *v.t.* harness.

Aufschlag ['aufʃla:k], *m.* 1. striking, impact; crash (*on landing*), bounce (*of ball*); 2. facing (*on garment*), lapel, revers (*of jacket*), turn-up (*of trousers*), upturned cuff (*of sleeve*); 3. (*Mus.*) up-beat, (*Metr.*) arsis, (*Tenn.*) service; 4. (*Comm.*) surcharge, supplementary charge, supplement; additional tax *or* duty.

aufschlagen ['aufʃla:gən], **1.** *irr.v.t.* 1. break open; crack (*eggs*), cut open (*head etc.*), untwist, unlay (*rope*); 2. put up, erect (*scaffold*), pitch (*tent*), (*fig.*) take up (*one's abode*); 3. turn up (*a card, trousers etc.*), cast on (*stitch*); 4. open (*book, door, eyes*), look up (*zu*, at), turn *or* look up (*passage in book*); 5. (*Comm.*) raise (*price*), make an additional charge of, charge as a supplement; 6. (*Tenn.*) serve; 7. *einen Lärm* –, make a sudden noise; *ein Gelächter* –, burst out laughing. **2.** *irr.v.i.* 1. (*aux.* s.) fly *or* spring open; hit *or* strike (*auf* (*Acc.*), against); (*coll.*) rise, go up (*as price*); 2. (*aux.* s. & h.) fall violently, hit *or* strike the ground, strike (*as a missile*), bounce (*as a ball*).

Aufschlag|feld, *n.* (*Tenn.*) service court. **–geschwindigkeit,** *f.* (*Artil.*) impact velocity. **–zünder,** *m.* percussion-fuse.

aufschlämmen ['aufʃlɛmən], *v.t.* 1. make into paste; 2. (*Chem.*) suspend (*in liquid*).

aufschließen ['aufʃli:sən], **1.** *irr.v.t.* 1. unlock, open (up), (*fig.*) open up, develop (*mine, trade etc.*); 2. (*Chem. etc.*) decompose, break down *or* up, dissolve, reduce; (*Min.*) crush (*ore*); 3. (*fig.*) elucidate, throw light on. **2.** *irr.v.i.* (*Mil.*) close ranks. **3.** *irr.v.r.* open up, pour out one's heart, unbosom o.s. **Aufschließung,** *f.* 1. opening (up), development; 2. (*Chem.*) decomposition.

Aufschluß ['aufʃlus], *m.* disclosure, information (*über* (*Acc.*), about), explanation, elucidation (of). *See also* **Aufschließung.** **aufschlußreich,** *adj.* informative, illuminating, revealing, enlightening.

aufschminken ['aufʃmɪŋkən], *v.t.* (*fig.*) paint in false colours.

aufschnappen ['aufʃnapən], **1.** *v.t.* catch in mid air *or* as it falls; (*coll.*) pick up (*a word*). **2.** *v.i.* (*aux.* s.) spring *or* snap *or* fly open.

aufschneiden ['aufʃnaɪdən], **1.** *irr.v.t.* cut *or* slit open; carve; slice, cut up (*meat*); (*Surg.*) open, lance (*abscess*); *ein Buch* –, cut the pages of a book. **2.** *irr.v.i.* (*coll.*) brag, talk big, draw the long bow. **Aufschneider,** *m.* (*coll.*) braggart, show-off. **Aufschneiderei,** *f.* bragging, big talk.

aufschnellen ['aufʃnɛlən], *v.i.* (*aux.* s.) fly *or* spring up *or* open, bounce (*of a ball*), leap (*of fish*).

Aufschnitt ['aufʃnɪt], *m. kalter* –, cold meat.

aufschnüren ['aufʃny:rən], **1.** *v.t.* unlace, untie, uncord; thread (*beads etc.*). **2.** *v.r.* come undone (*of parcels*).

aufschrauben ['aufʃraubən], *v.t.* 1. screw on (*auf* (*Acc.*), to), screw up; (*fig.*) intensify (*interest etc.*); 2. screw open, unscrew.

aufschrecken ['aufʃrɛkən], **1.** *v.t.* startle. **2.** *irr.v.i.* (*aux.* s.) give a start *or* jump, be startled.

Aufschrei ['aufʃraɪ], *m.* 1. shriek, scream, yell, shout, cry; 2. clamour, outcry.

aufschreiben ['aufʃraɪbən], *irr.v.t.* write *or* take *or* note down, take *or* make a note of; enter, book; record; take (*s.o.'s*) name. **Aufschreiber,** *m.* scorer (*games*).

aufschreien ['aufʃraɪən], *irr.v.i.* cry out, give a cry *or* shout; scream, shriek.

Aufschrift ['aufʃrɪft], *f.* address; inscription, legend (*on coins etc.*), lettering (*on book-cover*).

Aufschub ['aufʃu:p], *m.* postponement, postponing, deferment, deferring, delay; extension (*of time limit*); ***ohne –***, without delay; ***Zahlung ohne –***, immediate payment; ***die S. leidet keinen –***, the matter is urgent.

aufschürzen ['aufʃyrtsən], *v.t.* tuck up (*a skirt etc.*); ***die Segel –***, furl the sails.

aufschütteln ['aufʃytəln], *v.t.* shake up.

aufschütten ['aufʃytən], *v.t.* heap *or* pile up; pour (***auf*** (*Acc.*), on to), deposit (on), fill *or* bank up with (*earth etc.*), scatter, strew (*straw*).

aufschwatzen ['aufʃvatsən], *v.t.* (*coll.*) ***ihm etwas –***, palm off a th. on to him, talk him into a th.

aufschweißen ['aufʃvaɪsən], *v.t.* weld on, fuse on (***auf*** (*Acc.*), to).

aufschwellen ['aufʃvɛlən], **1.** *v.t.* distend, inflate; fill (*sail*). **2.** *irr.v.i.* (*aux.* s.) swell (up), become distended *or* inflated; swell, rise (*as river*), (*Med.*) swell (up), tumefy.

aufschwemmen ['aufʃvɛmən], *v.t.* 1. wash up, deposit (*sand etc.*); 2. soak; ***aufgeschwemmt***, flabby, bloated. **Aufschwemmung,** *f.* 1. suspension; 2. (*Med.*) swelling.

aufschwingen ['aufʃvɪŋən], **1.** *irr.v.t.* brandish in the air. **2.** *irr.v.r.* swing o.s. up; soar, rise (*of bird*); (*fig. coll.*) rise (*to a position*), bring o.s. (*to do*).

Aufschwung ['aufʃvuŋ], *m.* 1. upward swing; 2. turn for the better, advance, rise, (*Comm.*) boom; stimulus, impetus; ***einen neuen – nehmen,*** receive fresh impetus, show renewed activity.

aufsehen ['aufze:ən], *irr.v.i.* look up (***zu,*** at). **Aufsehen,** *n.* stir, sensation; ***jedes – vermeiden,*** avoid attracting attention *or* notice; ***– erregen,*** cause a sensation; make *or* create a stir. **aufsehenerregend,** *adj.* sensational, stirring. **Aufseher,** *m.* overseer, foreman, supervisor (*industry*), (railway) inspector; (prison) warder *or* (*Am.*) guard, shop- *or* (*Am.*) floor-walker, store detective.

aufsetzen ['aufzɛtsən], **1.** *v.t.* 1. put *or* place on (***auf*** (*Acc.*), (to); *or Dat. of p. to which th. belongs, e.g. hat*); ***Wasser –***, put water on to boil; ***einen Dickkopf –***, be stubborn *or* obstinate; ***einem Ehemann Hörner –***, cuckold a husband; ***das setzt allem die Krone auf!*** that's the limit! that beats everything! that crowns it! 2. set *or* stand upright *or* on end (*as skittles*), (*Golf*) tee (*the ball*); ***ein Schiff –***, run a ship aground; 3. draw up (*contract*), draft, make a rough draft of (*letter*), make out (*bill*). **2.** *v.i.* (*Av.*) touch down, land; ***mit dem Fuß ungeschickt –***, come down awkwardly on one's foot. **3.** *v.r.* raise o.s. to a sitting position, sit up (*as in bed*).

aufseufzen ['aufzɔyftsən], *v.i.* heave a sigh.

Aufsicht ['aufzɪçt], *f.* 1. supervision, surveillance, care, charge, control (***über*** (*Acc.*), of); 2. supervisor, p. in charge, invigilator (*at examination*). **Aufsichts|beamte(r),** *m.*, superintendent, supervisor; inspector. **–behörde,** *f.* control board, board of control. **aufsicht(s)führend,** *adj.* supervisory. **Aufsichts|führung,** *f.* supervision. **–rat,** *m.* board of trustees *or* directors.

aufsitzen ['aufzɪtsən], *irr.v.i.* (*aux.* s.) sit *or* rest on; perch, roost (*of birds*); (*Naut.*) be aground; sit up (*at night or in bed*); mount horse; (*Mil.*) ***aufgesessen!*** to horse! mount! ***das Ziel – lassen,*** aim just below the mark; (*coll.*) ***– lassen,*** let down, leave in the lurch.

aufspalten ['aufʃpaltən], **1.** *v.t.* split (open); split *or* divide up (*a group*); (*Chem.*) break down *or* up (*a substance*). **2.** *v.r.* crack, split, burst (open); divide *or* split (up); (*Chem.*) be broken down *or* up.

aufspannen ['aufʃpanən], *v.t.* stretch, spread (***auf*** (*Acc.*), on); put up, open (*umbrella*); pitch (*a tent*); set, spread (*sail*); mount (*an artist's canvas*); string (*a musical instrument*). **Aufspanner,** *m.* (*Elec.*) step-up transformer.

aufsparen ['aufʃpa:rən], *v.t.* save (up), lay by; reserve, keep (in reserve).

aufspeichern ['aufʃpaɪçərn], *v.t.* store *or* hoard (up); lay in a stock of; accumulate (*electricity, heat etc.*). **Aufspeicherung,** *f.* storage, accumulation.

aufsperren ['aufʃpɛrən], *v.t.* unlock; open wide.

aufspielen ['aufʃpi:lən], **1.** *v.t., v.i.* strike up (*a tune or the music*), start playing. **2.** *v.r.* give o.s. *or* put on airs, (*coll.*) put on side; set o.s. up (***als,*** as); ***sich mit etwas –***, brag about a th.

aufspießen ['aufʃpi:sən], *v.t.* impale; spear *or* fork up; run through with a sword; gore.

aufsprießen ['aufʃpri:sən], *irr.v.i.* (*aux.* s.) sprout, spring up, germinate.

aufspringen ['aufʃprɪŋən], *irr.v.i.* (*aux.* s.) 1. leap *or* jump *or* bound *or* spring up *or* to one's feet; 2. fly *or* burst *or* crack open; burst (*of buds*); 3. become chapped, chap (*of hands with the cold*); 4. rebound, bounce (*as a ball*); 5. gush, shoot *or* spout forth (*as water*). **aufspringend,** *adj.* 1. (*Her.*) rampant; 2. (*Bot.*) dehiscent.

aufspritzen ['aufʃprɪtsən], *v.i.* (*aux.* s.) splash up; squirt up.

aufsprudeln ['aufʃpru:dəln], *v.i.* (*aux.* s.) bubble up, boil up.

Aufsprung ['aufʃpruŋ], *m.* bound, leap, spring, jump; (re)bound, bounce (*of ball*).

aufspulen ['aufʃpu:lən], *v.t.* wind on (*a reel etc.*).

aufspülen ['aufʃpy:lən], *v.t.* wash up (*wreckage etc.*), wash up *or* do (*the dishes*).

aufspüren ['aufʃpy:rən], *v.t.* nose *or* smell out (*game*), (*coll.*) track down, nose *or* ferret out, unearth.

aufstacheln ['aufʃtaxəln], *v.t.* incite, rouse (*a p.*), work *or* stir up (*feelings*); ***ihn zu etwas –***, goad him into (doing) s.th.; ***ihn*** (***dazu***) ***–, etwas zu tun,*** goad *or* egg him into doing s.th.

aufstampfen ['aufʃtampfən], **1.** *v.i.* stamp (***mit dem Fuß,*** one's foot). **2.** *v.t.* 1. stamp down (*earth*); 2. trample up (*the ground*).

Aufstand ['aufʃtant], *m.* revolt, rebellion, insurrection, (up)rising, mutiny, riot.

aufständisch ['aufʃtɛndɪʃ], *adj.* rebellious, mutinous, rioting, insurgent; ***die Aufständischen,*** the rebels, insurgents.

aufstapeln ['aufʃta:pəln], *v.t.* pile up, stack; store, lay up a stock of, accumulate.

aufstauen ['aufʃtauən], **1.** *v.t.* dam up (*water*). **2.** *v.r.* collect, pile up; (*fig.*) be bottled *or* pent up (*as feelings*).

aufstechen ['aufʃtɛçən], *irr.v.t.* prick open, puncture; (*Surg.*) lance.

Aufsteck- ['aufʃtɛk], *pref. having the meaning of 'extension piece', something fixed or slipped on, e.g.* **–blende,** *f.* slip-on lens cover.

aufstecken ['aufʃtɛkən], *v.t.* 1. pin up (*hair*), put up (*curtains*); 2. put, fix (***auf*** (*Acc.*), on); ***ein trauriges Gesicht –***, put on a melancholy air; (*Naut.*) ***die Wache –***, set the watch; 3. (*coll.*) give up (*a habit*); (*coll.*) ***die Sache –***, turn *or* pack it in.

Aufsteck|rohr, *n.* extension tube. **–schlüssel,** *m.* box-spanner, (*Am.*) wrench.

aufstehen ['aufʃte:ən], *irr.v.i.* 1. (*aux.* s.) stand up; rise, get up (from one's seat); rise to one's feet, get on one's feet; get up (in the morning); ***früh –***, get up *or* rise early; ***mit dem linken Fuß zuerst –***, get out of bed on the wrong side; 2. rise (in revolt); 3. break cover (*game*), rise (from cover) (*birds*), rise (*fish*); 4. (*aux.* h.) be *or* stand open (*as a door*).

aufsteigen ['aufʃtaɪgən], *irr.v.i.* (*aux.* s.) ascend, rise, climb (up) (*as a road*); go *or* move up (*in a hierarchy*); rise (from the ground) (*as smoke*); get *or* climb (up)on (***auf*** (*Acc.*), to), mount (*horse etc.*); ***ein Gedanke stieg mir auf,*** a thought struck me. **Aufsteigen,** *n.* ascent; (*fig.*) ***im – begriffen,*** be in the ascendant. **aufsteigend,** *adj.* ascending ((*Math.*) *power*; (*Mus.*) *scale*), rising (*star*). **Aufsteigung,** *f.* (*Astr.*) ascension; ***gerade –***, right ascension. **Aufsteigungsunterschied,** *m.* (*Astr.*) ascensional difference.

aufstellen ['aufʃtɛlən], **1.** *v.t.* 1. set *or* stand *or* put up(right); erect, fit up, assemble, install; stand, arrange, place, put; ***Truppen* –,** draw up *or* array troops; ***eine Wache* –,** post a sentry; ***ein Heer* –,** form *or* raise an army; ***eine Falle* –,** set a trap; 2. (*fig.*) put forward, nominate (*as a candidate*), advance (*theory, opinion*); lay down (*principles*); ***eine Behauptung* –,** make an assertion; ***eine Bilanz* –,** make up a balance-sheet; ***eine Rechnung* –,** make out a bill, draw up an account; ***einen Rekord* –,** set up *or* establish a record. **2.** *v.r.* 1. take up one's position; place *or* station o.s.; ***sich in eine Reihe* –,** stand in *or* form (o.s. into) a line, form into line, line *or* form up; 2. ***sich* – *lassen,*** offer o.s. *or* stand (as a candidate). **Aufstellgleis,** *n.* *See* **Aufstellungsgleis.**

Aufstellung ['aufʃtɛluŋ], *f.* 1. erection, assembly, arrangement, position, placing, (*Mil.*) formation, disposition; 2. statement, list, table, tabulation; schedule, inventory, itemization; – ***einer Bilanz,*** preparation of a balance-sheet; – ***eines Rekords,*** establishment of a record. **Aufstellungsgleis,** *n.* (*Railw.*) siding.

aufstemmen ['aufʃtɛmən], *v.t.* 1. prop up, support, lean, rest (***auf*** (*Acc.*), on); 2. force *or* prize open.

Aufstieg ['aufʃti:k], *m.* 1. ascent (*of mountain or in aeroplane*); 2. step (*of a cycle*); 3. rise, advancement, promotion; ***Preußens* –,** the rise of Prussia; ***im* – (*begriffen*),** on the up-grade (*of a p.*), gaining ground (*of views*).

aufstöbern ['aufʃtø:bərn], *v.t.* stir up, start (*game*); unearth, ferret out, turn up.

aufstören ['aufʃtø:rən], *v.t.* stir up, rouse, disturb.

Aufstoß ['aufʃto:s], *m.* impact. **aufstoßen, 1.** *irr. v.t.* knock *or* kick *or* push open. **2.** *irr.v.i.* 1. (*aux.* s. & h.) knock *or* bump (***auf*** (*Acc.*), against); (*Naut.*) run aground; 2. (*aux.* s.) ***ihm* –,** occur to *or* strike him, cross his mind; (*of food*) repeat on him, cause him to belch; ***sauer* –,** cause heartburn; 3. (*aux.* h.) belch, eruct(ate). **Aufstoßen,** *n.* belching, eructation.

aufstreben ['aufʃtre:bən], *v.i.* rise, aspire, strive, struggle upwards. **aufstrebend,** *adj.* soaring, aspiring.

aufstrecken ['aufʃtrɛkən], *v.t.* raise, stretch out (***zu,*** towards).

aufstreichen ['aufʃtraɪçən], *irr.v.t.* spread (*butter on bread etc.*) (***auf*** (*Acc.*), on).

aufstreifen ['aufʃtraɪfən], *v.t.* turn *or* tuck up (*one's cuffs etc.*).

aufstreuen ['aufʃtrɔyən], *v.t.* strew, sprinkle (***auf*** (*Acc.*), on).

Aufstrich ['aufʃtrɪç], *m.* 1. paste, spread; 2. upstroke (*of the pen*); (*Mus.*) up-bow.

aufstülpen ['aufʃtylpən], *v.t.* 1. turn up, tuck up (*hat brim etc.*); ***aufgestülpte Nase,*** turned-up *or* snub *or* retroussé nose; 2. clap on (*a hat*).

aufstützen ['aufʃtytsən], **1.** *v.t.* prop up, support. **2.** *v.r.* lean, prop o.s. (up).

aufsuchen ['aufzu:xən], *v.t.* seek out, search for, go in quest of; call on, visit, go to see, (*coll.*) look up (*a p.*); look up (*a passage in a book etc.*).

auftakeln ['aufta:kəln], **1.** *v.t.* rig (*a ship*). **2.** *v.r.* (*coll.*) tog o.s. up, rig o.s. out.

Auftakt ['auftakt], *m.* (*Mus.*) upbeat; (*Metr.*) unaccented *or* opening syllable(s), anacrusis; (*fig.*) opening phase, prelude, preliminaries.

auftanken ['auftaŋkən], *v.i.* (*Motor., Av.*) refuel, fill the tank, tank up.

auftauchen ['auftauxən], *v.i.* (*aux.* s.) arise, appear suddenly; rise to the surface, surface (*of submarines*), (*coll.*) come into view, loom up; turn *or* crop up.

auftauen ['auftauən], **1.** *v.i.* (*aux.* s.) thaw; (*fig.*) become talkative *or* sociable, unbend, thaw. **2.** *v.t.* thaw (out) (*pipes etc.*).

aufteilen ['auftaɪlən], *v.t.* partition *or* parcel (out), divide (up *or* out), share out, distribute, allot. **Aufteilung,** *f.* partition; division, distribution.

auftischen ['auftɪʃən], *v.t.* serve (up); ***ihm etwas* –,** serve *or* regale him with a th.

Auftrag ['auftra:k], *m.* 1. commission, order, instructions, directions; charge, assignment, mandate, (*Law*) brief; errand, message, task, mission; – ***auf*** (*Acc.*), order for; ***im* –*e von,*** by order of, on behalf of; ***einen* – *ausführen,*** execute *or* carry out an order; ***etwas bei ihm in* – *geben,*** place an order with him for s.th., order s.th. from him, commission him (*to do*) s.th.; (*Mil.*) – ***erfüllt,*** mission accomplished; 2. coat, coating, application (*of colour, paint etc.*).

auftragen ['auftra:gən], *irr.v.t.* 1. bring in (*meal*), serve up (*food*); 2. lay *or* spread *or* smear on, apply (*colour*); (*coll.*) ***dick*** or ***stark* –,** exaggerate, lay it on thick *or* with a trowel; 3. ***ihm* –,** commission him (*to do*), entrust *or* charge him with (*a duty*); ***er hat mir Grüße aufgetragen,*** he sent greetings; ***ihm eine Arbeit* –,** set him a task, entrust him with a job; 4. wear out (*clothes*).

Auftrag|geber, *m.* employer; patron (*of artist*), customer; (*Law*) principal. **–nehmer,** *m.* supplier, contractor, (*Law*) authorized agent.

Auftrags|bestand, *m.* (*Comm.*) unfilled orders. **–eingang,** *m.* (*Comm.*) receipt of an order. **auftrag(s)gemäß,** *adv.* according to instructions, (*Comm.*) as per order. **Auftrags|lenkung,** *f.* (government) allocation of contracts. **–überhang,** *m.* (*Comm.*) orders on hand. **auftrag(s)widrig,** *adv.* contrary to instructions.

auftreffen ['auftrɛfən], *irr.v.t.* strike, impinge on. **Auftreff|geschwindigkeit,** *f.* impact *or* striking velocity. **–punkt,** *m.* point of impact. **–winkel,** *m.* angle of incidence.

auftreiben ['auftraɪbən], **1.** *irr.v.t.* 1. drive (*cattle*) up to a mountain pasture; 2. blow up, distend, make (*dough*) rise; 3. raise, start (*game*); 4. (*coll.*) get (hold of). **2.** *irr.v.i.* (*aux.* s.) 1. sprout, come up (*as plants*); 2. swell, become swollen *or* distended *or* bloated; 3. (*Naut.*) run aground (***auf*** (*Acc.*), on). **Auftreiber,** *m.* (*Hunt.*) beater.

auftrennen ['auftrɛnən], *v.t.* undo, unpick (*seam*); rip apart.

auftreten ['auftre:tən], **1.** *irr.v.t.* kick open. **2.** *irr.v.i.* (*aux.* s.) 1. put one's foot *or* feet down, tread, stand, walk; ***fest* –,** walk with a firm step; ***leise* –,** tread softly, walk quietly; 2. appear (*on the stage*); ***zum ersten Mal* –,** make one's début *or* first appearance; ***öffentlich* –,** appear in public; ***als Zeuge* –,** appear as a witness; ***als Kandidat* –,** stand as a candidate; (*Theat.*) ***Othello tritt auf,*** enter Othello; 3. (*fig.*) appear, make one's appearance (*of a th.*); occur (*of events*); 4. behave, act, proceed; (*fig.*) ***leise* –,** act *or* proceed cautiously (*see under* 1.); ***energisch* –,** make a firm stand. **Auftreten,** *n.* 1. appearance; ***erstes* –,** début; 2. occurrence (*of events*); 3. manner, demeanour, air.

Auftrieb ['auftri:p], *m.* 1. buoyance; (*Av.*) lift; (*fig.*) impetus, stimulus, (*coll.*) drive; 2. (*dial.*) driving cattle to the alpine pasture *or* to market.

Auftritt ['auftrɪt], *m.* 1. tread (*of stair*), banquette, fire step (*of trench*); 2. appearance, entrance (*of actor*), scene (*in a play*); 3. (*coll.*) scene, row.

auftrocknen ['auftrɔknən], **1.** *v.i.* (*aux.* s. & h.) dry (up) (*as puddles*). **2.** *v.t.* dry *or* mop up (*floor*).

auftrumpfen ['auftrumpfən], *v.i.* 1. raise one's voice in protest; 2. gain the upper hand.

auftun ['auftu:n], **1.** *irr.v.t.* 1. open; 2. open (up), start. **2.** *irr.v.r.* 1. open (up *or* out), unfold; become visible; 2. open, get started.

auftupfen ['auftupfən], *v.t.* 1. mop *or* dab up (*with towel*); 2. dab on, press down gently (*gold leaf*).

auftürmen ['auftyrmən], **1.** *v.t.* heap *or* pile *or* stack up, pile high. **2.** *v.r.* 1. tower up; 2. pile up, gather, collect, accumulate.

aufwachen ['aufvaxən], *v.i.* (*aux.* s.) awake(n), wake (up).

aufwachsen ['aufvaksən], *irr.v.i.* (*aux.* s.) grow up.

aufwägen ['aufvɛ:gən], *irr.v.t.* *See* **aufwiegen.**

aufwallen ['aufvalən], *v.i.* (*aux.* s.) boil up; foam

or bubble up, seethe, (*fig.*) surge (up), rise (*as anger*), boil (*as blood*). **Aufwallung,** *f.* ebullition, swell, surge (*of emotion*), fit (*of anger*), transport (*of joy*).

Aufwand ['aufvant], *m.* (**-(e)s,** *no pl.*) expense, expenditure, cost; extravagance, luxury, display; *- **an Kraft,*** expenditure of energy; ***unnützer - an Zeit,*** waste of time. **Aufwandgesetz,** *n.* sumptuary law. **Aufwandsentschädigung,** *f.* representation allowance. **Aufwandsteuer,** *f.* luxury tax.

aufwärmen ['aufvɛrmən], *v.t.* warm *or* heat up, reheat (*food*), (*fig. coll.*) revive, rehash, drag up.

Aufwartefrau ['aufvartəfrau], *f.* charwoman, cleaner.

aufwarten ['aufvartən], *v.i.* 1. (*Dat.*) wait on, serve (*at meals*); attend ((up)on); call on, pay one's respects to; ***bei Tisch -,*** wait at table; ***mit etwas -,*** oblige with s.th.; ***kann ich damit -?*** may I offer you some? 2. sit up, beg (*of dogs*).

Aufwärter ['aufvɛrtər], *m.* attendant; steward. **Aufwärterin,** *f. See* **Aufwartefrau.**

aufwärts ['aufvɛrts], *adv.* upward, upwards; uphill; up-stream. **Aufwärtsbewegung,** *f.* upward movement (*also of prices*). **aufwärtsgehen,** *irr.v.i.* (*aux.* s.) improve, (*coll.*) be looking up. **Aufwärts|-haken,** *m.* (*Boxing*) uppercut. **-transformator,** *m.* (*Elec.*) step-up transformer.

Aufwartung ['aufvartuŋ], *f.* 1. service, attendance; ***ihm seine - machen,*** pay one's respects to him; 2. call, formal visit; 3. (*coll.*) charwoman, cleaner, daily help.

aufwaschen ['aufvaʃən], *irr.v.t.* wash up (*crockery*). **Aufwasch|lappen,** *m.* dish-cloth. **-schüssel,** *f.* washing-up bowl. **-wasser,** *n.* washing-up water, dish-water.

aufwecken ['aufvɛkən], *v.t.* rouse, wake(n); wake (*s.o.*) up. *See* **aufgeweckt.**

aufweichen ['aufvaɪçən], *v.t.* soften; soak; mollify; (*Med.*) open by fomentation. **aufweichend,** *adj.* emollient.

aufweisen ['aufvaɪzən], *irr.v.t.* show, exhibit, produce, have to show.

aufwenden ['aufvɛndən], *reg. & irr.v.t.* spend, expend, use, employ (***für,*** on), devote (to); ***Mühe -,*** take pains (***für,*** over *or* with).

aufwendig ['aufvɛndɪç], *adj.* expensive, extravagant, sumptuous, lavish; involving great expense (*of a project*). **Aufwendung,** *f.* expenditure, employment, use; *pl.* expenditure, expenses, outlay.

aufwerfen ['aufvɛrfən], **1.** *irr.v.t.* 1. throw *or* fling open; 2. throw, cast *or* toss up; ***den Kopf -,*** toss one's head; ***die Lippen -,*** purse *or* pout one's lips; ***aufgeworfene Lippen,*** protruding lips; ***aufgeworfene Naselöcher,*** distended nostrils; 3. excavate (*earth*), dig (*a trench*), build (*a bank of earth*); (*fig.*) bring up, raise (*doubts etc.*), throw out (*suggestion*). **2.** *irr.v.r.* 1. set o.s. up, appoint o.s. (***zu,*** as); 2. (*fig.*) behave arrogantly.

aufwerten ['aufve:rtən], *v.t.* raise the value of, revalue. **Aufwertung,** *f.* revaluation.

aufwickeln ['aufvɪkəln], **1.** *v.t.* 1. wind *or* roll *or* coil up; wind (*thread*) on a reel, put (*hair*) in curlers; 2. unroll, unwind; unwrap (*a parcel*). **2.** *v.r.* unroll, come unrolled *or* unwound.

Aufwiegelei [aufvi:gə'laɪ], *f.* (-, *pl.* **-en**) incitement, instigation.

aufwiegeln ['aufvi:gəln], *v.t.* stir up, incite, rouse, urge on (***zu,*** to). **Aufwiegelung,** *f. See* **Aufwiegelei.**

aufwiegen ['aufvi:gən], *irr.v.t.* (counter)balance; compensate for, make up for, offset, outweigh, cancel out; (*coll.*) ***sie ist nicht mit Gold aufzuwiegen,*** she is worth her weight in gold.

Aufwiegler ['aufvi:glər], *m.* instigator (*to revolt*), agitator, (*coll.*) rabble-rouser. **aufwieglerisch,** *adj.* inflammatory, seditious.

Aufwind ['aufvɪnt], *m.* (*Meteor.*) upcurrent, anabatic wind.

aufwinden ['aufvɪndən], *irr.v.t.* wind up; hoist (*with a windlass*), haul up; weigh (*anchor*).

aufwirbeln ['aufvɪrbəln], **1.** *v.t.* whirl up, send whirling upwards; (*fig. coll.*) ***Staub -,*** make *or* raise *or* cause a stir *or* sensation. **2.** *v.i.* (*aux.* s.) fly *or* whirl up(wards).

aufwischen ['aufvɪʃən], *v.t.* wipe *or* mop up; wipe away, clean (*a room*), (*Naut.*) swab (*deck*). **Aufwischlappen,** *m.* floor-cloth, swab.

Aufwuchs ['aufvu:ks], *m.* (**-es,** *no pl.*) (plant) growth.

aufwühlen ['aufvy:lən], *v.t.* 1. turn up *or* over (*soil*), churn up (*water*), churn *or* plough up (*the ground*); grub *or* root up (*like swine*); turn up (*as with a plough*); 2. (*fig.*) stir (up), upset, excite.

aufzählen ['auftsɛ:lən], *v.t.* count out (*money*); enumerate, detail, recite, (*coll.*) reel off; (*coll.*) ***aufgezählt bekommen,*** get (*lashes*) (meted out). **Aufzählung,** *f.* enumeration; series, list. **Aufzählungsreihe,** *f.* (*Stat.*) frequency distribution.

aufzäumen ['auftsɔymən], *v.t.* bridle (*a horse*); (*coll.*) ***ein Pferd beim Schwanze -,*** put the cart before the horse.

aufzehren ['auftse:rən], *v.t.* eat up, devour, consume; (*fig.*) sap, use *or* eat up, absorb.

aufzeichnen [auftsaɪçnən], *v.t.* draw, sketch, make a sketch *or* diagram of; note *or* write down, take *or* make a note of, record; catalogue, make an inventory of. **Aufzeichnung,** *f.* (*usu. pl.*) note, record; sketch, diagram. **Aufzeichnungsplatte,** *f.* (*gramophone*) recording disc, wax record.

aufzeigen ['auftsaɪgən], **1.** *v.t.* show, exhibit. **2.** *v.i.* put up one's hand (*in school*).

Aufziehbrücke ['auftsi:brykə], *f.* drawbridge.

aufziehen ['auftsi:ən], **1.** *irr.v.t.* 1. draw *or* pull up, raise; hoist (*sail, flag*), wind up (*clock*), mount (*a print*), stretch (*embroidery on a frame*), string (*violin*); raise, rear (*cattle*), cultivate (*plants*), bring up (*child*); ***gelindere Saiten -,*** draw in one's horns, come down a peg; ***strengere Saiten -,*** take a firmer *or* stronger line; ***andere Saiten -,*** adopt a different tone; 2. pull open (*drawer*), open, uncork (*bottle*), undo (*knot*); 3. (*coll.*) tease, poke fun at, make fun of, pull (*s.o.'s*) leg (***mit,*** about); 4. set about, arrange, get up; ***groß -,*** plan in grand style; ***falsch -,*** set *or* go about in the wrong way; ***politisch -,*** make a political issue of. **2.** *irr.v.i.* (*aux.* s.) draw, approach; march up, parade (*of troops*). **Aufzieherei,** *f.* chaff, banter, teasing. **Aufzieh|-fenster,** *n.* sash-window. **-karton,** *m.* mounting-board (*for prints*). **-leine,** *f.* release cord, rip cord (*of a parachute*). **-loch,** *n.* winding-hole, keyhole (*of a watch*).

Aufzucht ['auftsuxt], *f.* breeding, rearing (*of animals*).

aufzucken ['auftsukən], *v.i.* start (convulsively); leap *or* shoot up (*as a flame*).

Aufzug ['auftsu:k], *m.* 1. procession, parade; ***- der Wache,*** changing of the guard; 2. lift, elevator; hoist, windlass; 3. attire, (*coll.*) get-up; 4. act (*of a play*); 5. warp (*in weaving*).

aufzwängen ['auftsvɛŋən], *v.t. See* **aufzwingen.**

aufzwingen ['auftsvɪŋən], *irr.v.t.* 1. force on (***auf*** (*Acc.*), to); 2. force open; 3. force, urge, press (*Dat.*, (up)on) (*a p.*).

Aug|apfel ['auk-], *m.* eyeball; (*coll.*) apple of the eye. **-apfelhäutchen,** *n.* (*Anat.*) choroid. **-bolzen,** *m.* (*Naut.*) eye- *or* ring-bolt.

Auge ['augə], *n.* (**-s,** *pl.* **-n**) 1. eye; ***auf einem -,*** in one eye; ***aus den -n, aus dem Sinn,*** out of sight out of mind; ***ihm ins -*** or ***in die -n sehen,*** look him straight in the eye *or* (straight) in the face; ***den Tatsachen ins - sehen,*** look facts in the face, face the facts; ***- in -,*** face to face; ***große -n machen,*** open one's eyes wide, stare in astonishment; ***mit offenen -n,*** with one's eyes open; ***sehenden -s,*** with one's eyes open; ***sein - bricht,*** his eyes grow dim; ***ihm gingen die -n über,*** his eyes popped out of his head; ***das geht ins -,*** that really hurts, I take that to heart; ***seine -n überall haben,*** keep an eye on everything; *-n machen,* look longingly (***nach,*** at), cast longing eyes (at); make eyes (*Dat.*, at); ***ihm die -n öffnen,*** open his eyes (*über* (*Acc.*), to); ***mir liefen die -n über,*** I was speechless with rage, I saw red; ***seine -n verschließen,*** shut one's eyes (***gegen,*** to); ***ein - zudrücken,*** pretend not to notice, wink an eye at, stretch a point, let it go at that; ***beide -n zudrücken,*** turn a blind eye; ***kein - zumachen,*** not sleep a wink; 2. (eye)sight; ***ihm an den -n absehen,*** see by his face; ***geh mir aus den -n!*** get out of my sight! ***ihm wie aus den -n geschnitten,*** the living *or* very image of him; ***aus den -n verlieren,*** lose sight of, lose from sight; ***im - behalten,*** keep in mind *or* sight, have an eye to; keep in view, keep one's eye on; ***ins - fallen,*** be conspicuous, attract attention, catch the eye; ***ins - fassen,*** fix one's eyes on; contemplate (*doing*), have in view (*to do*); ***in die -n springen*** or ***stechen,*** leap to the eye; ***ihr zu tief ins - sehen,*** be smitten with her; ***mit anderen -n ansehen,*** see (*things*) differently, look upon with a different eye (***als,*** from), not see eye to eye (with); ***mit dem -*** or ***den -n messen,*** judge by the eye; ***unter vier -n,*** between ourselves (themselves), when (we are) alone *or* by ourselves *etc.*, tête-à-tête; ***ihm unter die -n kommen,*** come face to face with him; ***komm mir nicht wieder vor die -n!*** keep out of my sight! *or* my way! ***vor meinen -n,*** before *or* in front of my eyes, before my face, in my sight; ***vor dem - des Gesetzes,*** in the eye(s) of the law; ***ihm vor -n führen,*** demonstrate to him; ***ihm vor -n halten,*** impress upon his mind; ***vorn und hinten -n haben,*** have eyes in the back of one's head; ***seine -n richten auf*** (*Acc.*), turn one's eyes on, direct one's gaze towards; ***vier -n sehen besser als zwei,*** two heads are better than one; ***ganz - sein,*** be all eyes; 3. (*Hort.*) (shield-)bud, eye (*as in potato*); 4. lustre, sheen, gloss (*of precious stones, fabrics etc.*); 5. spot (*dice, domino*), pip (*cards*), speck of fat (*in soup*), hole (*in cheese*), bird's-eye (*on polished wood*), eye (*of cyclone*), eyelet, eyelet-hole, eye-splice (*in rope*), lug, lifting ring.

äugeln ['ɔygəln], **1.** *v.t.* (*Hort.*) graft, bud. **2.** *v.i.* ***- auf*** (*Acc.*), eye, look menacingly at; ***- mit,*** wink at, ogle.

äugen ['ɔygən], *v.i.* (*Hunt.*) look (*of wild animals*); ***- nach,*** look out for, keep one's eye open for.

Augen|arzt, *m.* oculist, ophthalmic surgeon. **-bad,** *n.* eye-douche. **-bader,** *m.* eye-cup. **-binde,** *f.* bandage over the eyes; ***ihm eine - anlegen,*** blindfold him. **-bindehaut,** *f.* (*Anat.*) conjunctiva. **-blende,** *f.* eyeshade; (*harness*) blinkers.

Augenblick ['augənblɪk], *m.* moment, instant; ***alle -e, jeden -,*** at any moment, any minute; continually, constantly, at every turn; ***für den -,*** for the moment *or* present *or* time being; ***im letzten -,*** in the nick of time; ***im richtigen -,*** at the right moment; ***im -,*** in a moment *or* instant, directly, immediately; at present *or* the moment, just now, for the time being; ***auf einen -,*** for a moment; ***lichte -e,*** lucid intervals, moments of consciousness. **augenblicklich, 1.** *adj.* 1. instantaneous; immediate; 2. momentary. **2.** *adv.* instantaneously, immediately, instantly, forthwith. **augenblicks,** *adv. See* **augenblicklich, 2.**

Augenblicks|erfolg, *m.* momentary *or* short-lived success. **-mensch,** *m.* creature of impulse, impulsive p.; one who lives entirely for the moment. **-stimmung,** *f.* fleeting *or* passing mood. **-wirkung,** *f.* instantaneous effect. **-ziel,** *n.* (*Mil.*) fleeting target. **-zünder,** *m.* instantaneous fuse.

Augen|bogen, *m.* (*Anat.*) iris. **-braue,** *f.* eyebrow; ***die -n zusammenziehen,*** knit one's eyebrows, scowl. **-brauenstift,** *m.* eyebrow-pencil. **-diener,** *m.* toady, lickspittle, sycophant. **-dienerei,** *f.*, **-dienst,** *m.* toadying, sycophancy. **-dusche,** *f. See* **-bad, -bader. -entzündung,** *f.* ophthalmia, inflammation of the eye. **augenfällig,** *adj.* evident, manifest, obvious, conspicuous. **Augen|fehler,** *m.* 1. defect of sight; 2. visual error. **-fleck,** *m.* eyespot (*butterfly's wing*), ocellus (*peacock's feathers*). **-flimmern,** *n.* flickering of the visual image, (*coll.*) specks before the eyes. **augenförmig,** *adj.* eye-shaped; ocellate. **Augen|glas,** *n.* eye-glass, monocle; eyepiece (*of optical instrument, mask etc.*), *pl.* (pair of) eyeglasses, pince-nez. **-heilanstalt,** *f. See* **-klinik, -heilkunde,** *f.* ophthalmology. **-höhe,** *f.* ***in -,*** at eye-level. **-höhle,** *f.* eye-socket, orbital cavity. **-hornhaut,** *f.* cornea. **-kammer,** *f.* chamber of the eye. **-kammerwasser,** *n.* aqueous humour. **-klappe,** *f.* blinkers; patch (*over the eye*). **-klinik,** *f.* eye *or* ophthalmic hospital. **-leder,** *n.* blinker (*harness*). **-lehre,** *f.* ophthalmology. **-leiden,** *n.* eye trouble. **-licht,** *n.* (eye)sight. **-lid,** *n.* eyelid. **-loch,** *n.* pupil. **-lust,** *f. See* **-weide.**

Augen|maß, *n.* judgement by eye; visual estimate; ***ein gutes - haben,*** have a sure eye *or* an eye for proportion; (*fig.*) have sound *or* good judgement (***für,*** of); ***ihm fehlt jedes -,*** he has no judgement *or* sense of proportion. **-mensch,** *m.* one who thinks in visual terms. **-merk,** *n.* ***sein - auf eine S. richten,*** have a th. in view, turn *or* direct one's attention to a th.; fix *or* focus one's attention on a th. **-nerv,** *m.* optic nerve. **-paar,** *n.* pair of eyes. **-pfropfen,** *n.* (*Hort.*) bud grafting. **-pulver,** *n.* (*coll.*) very small print *or* illegible handwriting. **-reizstoff,** *m.* (*Mil.*) tear-gas.

Augenschein ['augənʃaɪn], *m.* inspection, examination; ***in - nehmen,*** examine closely, inspect; (*coll.*) have a good look at; ***dem - nach,*** to all appearances. **augenscheinlich, 1.** *adj.* (self-)evident *or* apparent, manifest, obvious, unmistakable, clear, plain; seeming, apparent. **2.** *adv.* obviously, unmistakably; to all appearances. **Augenscheinseinnahme,** *f.* inquiry *or* investigation on the spot.

Augen|schirm, *m.* eye-shade. **-schmaus,** *m.* feast for the eyes, delightful sight. **-schützer,** *m.* eye-shade, goggles. **-spiegel,** *m.* ophthalmoscope. **-stechen,** *n.* shooting pains in the eye. **-stern,** *m.* 1. pupil (*of the eye*); 2. favourite, pet, darling. **-täuschung,** *f.* optical illusion. **-trost,** *m.* 1. eyebright (*Euphrasia officinalis*); 2. (*fig.*) *See* **-weide. -wasser,** *n.* eye-lotion. **-weide,** *f.* welcome sight, feast for the eyes, a pleasure to look at, s.th. to feast one's eyes on, (*coll.*) sight for sore eyes. **-weite,** *f.* range of vision. **-wimper,** *f.* eyelash. **-wurz,** *f.* wood anemone (*Anemone nemorosa*). **-zahn,** *m.* eye-tooth, canine tooth. **-zauber,** *m.* evil eye. **-zeuge,** *m.* eyewitness. **-zeugenbericht,** *m.* eyewitness account.

Augias [au'gi:as], *m.* Augeas. **Augiasstall,** *m.* the Augean stables.

-äugig ['ɔygɪç], *adj.suff.* -eyed.

Äuglein ['ɔyklaɪn], *n.* little eye; little bud.

Aug|spleiß, *m.*, **-splissung,** *f.* (*Naut.*) eye-splice.

[1]**August** ['august], *m.* Augustus.

[2]**August** [au'gust], *m.* (**-s,** *pl.* **-e**) August (*the month*).

Augustiner [augus'ti:nər], *m.* Augustinian (*monk*).

Auktion [auktsi'o:n], *f.* auction (sale), sale by auction, (*Scots*) roup; ***in die - geben,*** put up for auction. **Auktionator** [-'na:tɔr], **Auktionskommissar,** *m.* auctioneer.

Aula ['aula], *f.* (-, *pl.* **Aulen**) great hall, assembly hall, auditorium.

Aurel [au're:l], *m.* Aurelius.

Aureole [aure'o:lə], *f.* aureole, halo, nimbus.

Aurikel [au'ri:kəl], *f.* (-, *pl.* **-n**) (*Bot.*) auricula, bear's-ear (*Primula auricula*).

aus [aus], **1.** *prep.* (*Dat.*) 1. out of; from; **(a)** (*place*) ***- Paris kommen,*** come from Paris; **(b)** (*fig.*) ***Sie sprechen mir - der Seele,*** you express my feelings exactly; ***- sich*** (***heraus***), of its own accord, on its own initiative, all by itself; **(c)** (*source, origin*) ***er ist - London gebürtig,*** he is a native of London *or* a Londoner by birth; ***- unserer Mitte,*** from among us, one of our number; ***- guter Familie,*** of good family; ***- dem Volk,*** of the people; ***- erster Hand,*** at first hand; ***- zuverlässiger Quelle,*** from a dependable source; ***- Erfahrung lernen,*** learn by *or* from experience; ***- dem Englischen,*** (translated) from the English; 2. (*away from*) ***ihm - dem Wege gehen,*** get *or* keep out of his way; ***- den Augen lassen,*** let out of one's sight; ***- dem Gedächtnis***

entschwinden or ***entfliehen,*** go from *or* slip one's memory; – ***der Mode,*** out of fashion; 3. made of; ***bestehen –,*** consist of; – ***Silber gearbeitet,*** made of silver; (*fig.*) ***was wird – ihr werden?*** what will become of her? – ***diesem Plan wird nichts,*** nothing will come of this plan; 4. for, from, because of; – ***verschiedenen Gründen,*** for various reasons; – ***Haß,*** through hatred; – ***Liebe zu,*** for love of, out of love for; – ***Mangel an*** (*Dat.*), for want *or* lack of. **2.** *adv.* 1. – ***und ein,*** in and out; ***er weiß nicht wo – wo ein, er weiß weder – noch ein,*** he is at his wit's end, he doesn't know which way to turn; 2. ***von . . . –,*** from; ***von hier –,*** from here; (*fig.*) ***von Grund –,*** thoroughly, radically, inside out, from the beginning; ***von Haus –,*** originally, from the start; ***von Haus – reich sein,*** be born rich, have rich parents, be brought up in a wealthy family; ***von Haus – arbeitsam,*** industrious by nature *or* by training; ***von mir –,*** for my part, as far as I'm concerned; on my own accord *or* initiative, (*coll.*) off my own bat; 3. ***auf . . .*** (*Acc.*) – ***sein,*** be after *or* out for *or* out to get (*s.th.*); 4. over, finished; ***die Kirche ist –,*** church is over; ***es ist – mit der Herrlichkeit,*** all good things come to an end; (*coll.*) ***es ist – mit ihm,*** it is all up with him, he is done for, (*sl.*) he's had it.

Aus, *n.* (-, *pl.* -) (*Spt.*) out of play *or* bounds, outside.

aus–, *sep. pref.* out; thoroughly, sufficiently, to the end; stop, cease, finish. (*For compounds not found in the following lists, see the simple verbs and add the appropriate modifying idea.*)

ausarbeiten ['ausˀarbaɪtən], **1.** *v.t.* work out (in detail), complete, finish (off), perfect, elaborate, fill in the details of. **2.** *v.i.* cease working *or* fermenting. **Ausarbeitung,** *f.* completion, development, elaboration.

ausarten ['ausˀartən], *v.i.* (*aux.* s.) degenerate; deteriorate. **Ausartung,** *f.* degeneration; deterioration; degeneracy.

ausästen ['ausˀɛstən], *v.t.* prune, lop branches off (*a tree*).

ausatmen ['ausˀa:tmən], *v.t., v.i.* breathe out, exhale.

ausbaden ['ausba:dən]. *v.t.* (*coll.*) pay; suffer *or* pay the penalty for; (*sl.*) carry the can for.

ausbaggern ['ausbagərn], *v.t.* dredge (*watercourse*), excavate (*site, trench*).

Ausbau ['ausbau], *m.* (**-(e)s,** *no pl.*) completion of the interior (*of a building*); conversion (*of building for another purpose*); elaboration (*of theory*); improvement, strengthening, consolidation (*of position, power*); extension, expansion, enlargement, development (*of existing structure, plans, trade etc.*); seasoning (*of wine*); (*pl.* **-ten**) projecting part (*of building*), attached outbuilding.

ausbauchen ['ausbauxən], **1.** *v.t.* cause to bulge; swell, belly (out), hollow out. **2.** *v.r.* bulge, swell *or* belly out. **Ausbauchung,** *f.* bulge, (*Archit.*) entasis (*of a column*).

ausbauen ['ausbauən], *v.t.* finish *or* complete the interior (*of a building*); convert (*a building for another purpose*); enlarge, expand, extend, develop (*existing structure, plans, trade*); improve, strengthen, consolidate (*position, power*); elaborate (*theory*); season (*wine*).

ausbedingen ['ausbədɪŋən], *irr.v.t.* ***sich*** (*Dat.*) –, stipulate for, make (s.th.) a condition (*that*), reserve (for o.s.).

ausbeizen ['ausbaɪtsən], *v.t.* 1. remove by caustics; 2. (*Med.*) cauterize.

ausbessern ['ausbɛsərn], *v.t.* mend, repair; restore, touch up (*a painting*), darn (*socks*), correct, rectify, put right (*a mistake*); ***es wird ausgebessert,*** it is undergoing repair. **Ausbesserung,** *f.* repair; corrections. **ausbesserungs|bedürftig,** *adj.* in need of *or* needing repair. **–fähig,** *adj.* mendable, repairable.

ausbeugen ['ausbɔygən], *v.t., v.i. See* **ausbiegen.**

Ausbeute ['ausbɔytə], *f.* gain; (net) profit, proceeds, returns, yield, output, produce, product. **ausbeuten,** *v.t.* exploit, utilize, make use of; take full advantage of, make capital out of, turn to account, make the most of; exploit, trade on, take (unfair) advantage of (*ignorance*). **Ausbeuter,** *m.* exploiter. **Ausbeuterei** [–'raɪ], *f.* exploitation, (*coll.*) slave-driving (*of workers*). **Ausbeutung,** *f.* exploitation, utilization, working (*of a mine*).

ausbiegen ['ausbi:gən], **1.** *irr.v.i.* turn aside *or* off (*as a road*), make way, get out of the way (*of a p.*); ***ihm*** or ***vor ihm –,*** make way for him, get out of his way, swerve to avoid him. **2.** *irr.v.t.* bend outwards.

ausbieten ['ausbi:tən], *irr.v.t.* offer for sale; cry (*wares*).

ausbilden ['ausbɪldən], *v.t.* form, develop (*one's powers*); instruct, train, educate. **Ausbildung,** *f.* development; formation, education; instruction, training; – ***von Rekruten,*** drilling of recruits; ***körperliche –,*** physical training.

Ausbiß ['ausbɪs], *m.* (*Geol.*) outcrop.

ausbitten ['ausbɪtən], *irr.v.t.* 1. (***sich*** (*Dat.*) –,) beg *or* ask for; request, demand, insist on (*silence etc.*); ***sich*** (*Dat.*) ***etwas von ihm –,*** ask him to let one have s.th., ask him to let one have the loan of s.th., ask him if he will lend s.th., ask him if one might borrow *or* have s.th.; 2. ask (*s.o.*) out; ***wir sind heute abend ausgebeten,*** we are asked out *or* have received an invitation for tonight.

Ausblasehahn ['ausbla:zəha:n], *m.* blow-off cock.

ausblasen ['ausbla:zən], *irr.v.t.* blow out (*a light etc.*), blow *or* puff out (*smoke*); blow (*obstructed pipes, an egg*); (*Poet.*) ***ihm das Lebenslicht –,*** launch him into eternity.

Ausbläser ['ausblɛ:zər], *m.* (*Artil.*) dud (= *shell with weak charge*).

ausbleiben ['ausblaɪbən], *irr.v.i.* (*aux.* s.) (*of a p.*) stay out *or* away, fail to appear, not come *or* (*coll.*) turn up, be absent; (*of a th.*) not be forthcoming, not take place, not occur, not come; cease, stop (*breathing, pulse*); ***nicht – können,*** be inevitable *or* inescapable; ***eine Gelegenheit blieb nicht lange aus,*** an opportunity soon presented itself; ***deine Strafe soll nicht –,*** you shall not escape punishment. **Ausbleiben,** *n.* non-appearance, absence, non-attendance; non-arrival; cessation (*of breathing*) failure (*of pulse*); – ***der Zahlung,*** failure to pay.

Ausblick ['ausblɪk], *m.* outlook, prospect, view.

ausblühen ['ausbly:ən], *v.i.* cease flowering; wither, fade, (*Chem.*) effloresce; ***die Rosen haben ausgeblüht,*** the roses are over.

ausbluten ['ausblu:tən], **1.** *v.i.* 1. bleed to death; 2. stop bleeding (*of a wound*). **2.** *v.t.* (*Poet.*) ***sein Leben –,*** breathe one's last.

ausbohren ['ausbo:rən], *v.t.* bore (out), drill (*hole, tooth*), gouge out (*eyes*).

ausbooten ['ausbo:tən], *v.t.* 1. disembark, take off (*passengers*); 2. (*coll.*) chuck out, give (*s.o.*) the sack.

ausbrausen ['ausbrauzən], *v.i., v.r.* subside, abate, spend itself (*of storm*).

ausbrechen ['ausbrɛçən], **1.** *irr.v.t.* 1. break off (*branches*), break, knock out (*tooth*); 2. weigh, trip (*anchor*); 3. bring up (*one's food*). **2.** *irr.v.i.* (*aux.* s.) 1. (*of a th.*) break out (*war, fire etc.*), erupt (*volcano, fury*), break (*storm*); ***der Schweiß brach mir aus,*** I broke out into a sweat; ***Schweiß brach mir auf der Stirn aus,*** sweat broke out on my brow; 2. (*of a p.*) break (out), escape; ***aus dem Gefängnis –,*** escape from *or* break out of prison, break gaol; ***in Schweiß –,*** break out into a sweat; ***in Lachen*** or ***Gelächter*** (***Weinen*** or ***Tränen***) –, burst out laughing (crying), break (out) into *or* burst into a laugh (tears); ***in Wut –,*** fly into a rage; 3. (*of a horse*) refuse, run out (*at a fence*). **Ausbrechen,** *n.* 1. outbreak (*of war, fire etc.*), eruption (*of volcano*), outburst (*of anger etc.*); breaking out, escaping (***aus,*** from); 2. refusal (*of horse at a fence*). *See* **Ausbruch.**

ausbreiten ['ausbraɪtən], **1.** *v.t.* 1. spread *or* stretch (out) (*arms, wings*); open out, unfold (*newspaper*); set *or* lay out, display (*wares*); ***mit ausgebreiteten Flügeln,*** with outstretched wings, (*Her.*) displayed; 2. (*fig.*) spread (abroad) (*rumours*), diffuse, (*warmth*). **2.** *v.r.* (*of a th.*) stretch, extend, spread, lie spread out (*as a plain*); spread, grow (*as epidemic, developing town*); (*Phys.*) be propagated (*as sound, light*); (*coll. of a p.*) spread o.s. out, take up a lot of room. **Ausbreitung,** *f.* 1. propagation (*of waves*); 2. diffusion (*of knowledge etc.*). **Ausbreitungsgeschwindigkeit,** *f.* velocity of propagation.

ausbrennen ['ausbrɛnən], **1.** *irr.v.t.* burn out; remove by burning; cauterize; scorch, parch. **2.** *irr.v.i.* (*aux.* s.) burn out, go out (*as a fire*), be burnt out, be gutted (*as a building*).

ausbringen ['ausbrɪŋən], *irr.v.t.* hatch (out) (*chickens*), hoist out, launch (*lifeboat*), run *or* pay out (*cable*), break (*news*), spread (*rumour*), divulge (*secret*), extract (*metal from ore*); ***eine Gesundheit auf ihn –,*** propose his health, toast him.

Ausbruch ['ausbrux], *m.* 1. outbreak (*of war, epidemic*), eruption (*of a volcano*); outburst (*of temper etc.*), burst (*of laughter*); 2. escape (*from prison etc.*), (*fig.*) breakaway, attempted escape (*from prison*), sally, sortie; (*Mil.*) ***zum – kommen,*** break out, erupt, burst forth. **Ausbruchsversuch,** *m.* attempted escape (*from prison*).

ausbrühen ['ausbry:ən], *v.t.* scald (out) (*a vessel*).

ausbrüten ['ausbry:tən], *v.t.* hatch (out), incubate; (*coll.*) scheme, plot. **Ausbrütung,** *f.* incubation (*of eggs*), hatching (*of chicks*).

ausbuchten ['ausbuxtən], *v.t.* make indentations in; scallop. **Ausbuchtung,** *f.* indentation; salient, protrusion.

ausbuddeln ['ausbudəln], *v.t.* (*coll.*) dig out *or* up.

ausbügeln ['ausby:gəln], *v.t.* iron out.

Ausbund ['ausbunt], *m.* selected specimen, pick, embodiment, quintessence; paragon (*though usu. only of negative attributes*); ***sie ist ein – an Frechheit,*** her impudence knows no bounds, she is impudence personified; ***– aller Schelme,*** arrant knave; ***– an Bosheit,*** regular demon.

ausbündig ['ausbyndɪç], *adj.* excellent, exemplary, exceptional.

ausbürgern ['ausbyrgərn], *v.t.* expatriate, deprive of citizenship.

ausdampfen ['ausdampfən], *v.i.* 1. (*aux.* s.) be emitted as steam, evaporate; 2. (*aux.* h.) finish steaming. **Ausdampfung,** *f.* evaporation.

Ausdauer ['ausdauər], *f.* (-, *no pl.*) perseverance, persistence, tenacity, assiduity, staying power, endurance. **ausdauern, 1.** *v.t.* endure, bear, (*coll.*) put up with. **2.** *v.i.* hold out, stay, last; persevere, be steadfast; (*Hort.*) be perennial. **ausdauernd,** *adj.* persistent, persevering, steadfast, resolute tenacious; (*Hort.*) perennial.

ausdehnbar ['ausde:nba:r], *adj.* expansible, extensible, elastic; diffusible, dilatable; (*of metals*) ductile, tensile. **Ausdehnbarkeit,** *f.* elasticity, expansibility, extensibility; ductility, tensility (*of metals*).

ausdehnen ['ausde:nən], *v.t., v.r.* stretch, expand, dilate; extend (***auf*** (*Acc.*), to); ***ausgedehnt,*** (*time*) prolonged, (*space*) extensive; ***im ausgedehntesten Sinne,*** in the widest sense; ***weit ausgedehnt,*** widespread. **Ausdehnung,** *f.* 1. expansion, extension, dilation, distension, elongation; ***– des Herzens,*** diastole; 2. compass, range, extent, expanse, size; 3. (*Math.*) dimension; ***ein Körper hat drei –en,*** a solid body has three dimensions. **ausdehnungsfähig,** *adj. See* **ausdehnbar. Ausdehnungs|kraft,** *f.*, **–vermögen,** *n.* expansive force, elasticity. **–zahl,** *f.* coefficient of expansion.

ausdenkbar ['ausdɛŋkba:r], *adj.* imaginable, conceivable.

ausdenken ['ausdɛŋkən], *irr.v.t.* think *or* work out (*a plan*), plan (in detail), contrive, devise; ***sich*** (*Dat.*) ***etwas –,*** imagine *or* invent *or* (*coll.*) make up s.th.; ***ich kann mir kein passendes Geschenk für ihn –,*** I cannot think of a suitable present for him; ***nicht auszudenken sein, sich nicht – lassen,*** be unimaginable, not bear thinking about.

ausdeuten ['ausdɔytən], *v.t.* interpret, explain; ***falsch –,*** misinterpret, misconstrue. **Ausdeutung,** *f.* construction, interpretation.

ausdienen ['ausdi:nən], *v.i.* serve (out) one's time; become superannuated; ***ausgedienter Soldat,*** time-expired soldier; (*coll.*) ***ausgedient haben,*** have had its day.

ausdörren ['ausdœrən], *v.t.* dry up, parch, wither; (*fig.*) (***wie***) ***ausgedörrt,*** a complete blank (*of mind*).

ausdrechseln ['ausdrɛksəln], *v.t.* turn (*on a lathe*); mould (*pottery*) (*on the wheel*); (*fig.*) polish, elaborate (*a speech etc.*).

ausdrehen ['ausdre:ən], *v.t.* turn out, turn off, switch off, put out (*a lamp, gas*).

Ausdruck ['ausdruk], *m.* (**-(e)s,** *pl.* **¨-e**) expression (*also Math.*); phrase, term; ***vulgärer –,*** vulgarism; ***veralteter –,*** archaism; ***bildlicher –,*** figure of speech, figurative expression; ***verblümter –,*** allusion; (*Mus.*) ***mit –,*** with expression; ***zum – kommen, – finden,*** find expression, be expressed *or* revealed; ***zum – bringen,*** express, give expression to, voice.

ausdrucken ['ausdrukən], *v.t.* 1. print (*text*) in full; 2. print off, machine (*a book*).

ausdrücken ['ausdrykən], **1.** *v.t.* 1. press *or* squeeze out (***aus,*** from); stub out (*a cigarette*); 2. express, utter, voice, put into words; show, reveal, give evidence of. **2.** *v.r.* (*of a p.*) express o.s., speak; (*of feelings etc.*) be expressed *or* shown. **ausdrücklich,** *adj.* express, explicit, clear, distinct, emphatic, intentional. **Ausdrücklichkeit,** *f.* distinctness, explicitness.

Ausdrucks|fülle, *f.* (-, *no pl.*) expressiveness (*of face etc.*). **–kraft,** *f.* expressiveness (*of language etc.*). **ausdrucksleer,** *adj.*, **ausdruckslos, 1.** *adj.* expressionless, devoid of expression, vacant, blank. **2.** *adv.* vacantly, blankly (*look*), without expression (*also Mus.*). **Ausdruckslosigkeit,** *f.* lack of expression, expressionlessness, blankness, vacancy. **ausdrucksvoll, 1.** *adj.* expressive, full of expression. **2.** *adv.* expressively (*look*), with expression (*also Mus.*). **Ausdrucksweise,** *f.* way of speaking, manner of speech; mode *or* manner of expression, choice of words.

Ausdunst ['ausdunst], *m.* evaporation, exhalation; perspiration. **ausdunsten,** *v.i.* (*aux.* s.) evaporate, pass off in vapour.

ausdünsten ['ausdynstən], **1.** *v.t.* exhale (*vapour*). **2.** *v.i. See* **ausdunsten. Ausdünstung,** *f. See* **Ausdunstung.**

Ausdunstung ['ausdunstuŋ], *f.* perspiration, evaporation, exhalation.

auseinander [ausaɪn'andər], *adv.* apart; asunder; separately.

auseinander–, *sep.pref.* **–breiten,** *v.t.* spread out, unfold. **–bringen,** *irr.v.t.* separate, part. **–fahren,** *irr.v.i.* (*aux.* s.) scatter (*of crowds*); diverge; ***–de Strahlen,*** divergent rays. **–fallen,** *irr.v.i.* (*aux.* s.) fall apart *or* to pieces, disintegrate, break up; diverge. **–fliegen,** *irr.v.i.* fly apart, scatter. **–gehen,** *irr.v.i.* (*aux.* s.) 1. separate, part (*as individuals*), disperse, scatter, break up (*as crowd*); come *or* fall apart, come unstuck, fall to pieces (*of a th.*); diverge (*as roads*), diverge, differ (*as opinions*); be broken off (*as an engagement*); 2. stretch (*as woollens*), (*coll.*) get fat (*of a p.*). **–halten,** *irr.v.t.* 1. distinguish between, tell apart; 2. keep apart. **–jagen,** *v.t.* scatter, disperse, break up. **–kommen,** *irr.v.i.* (*aux.* s.) separate, be *or* get *or* become separated; drift apart, become estranged. **–laufen,** *irr.v.i.* (*aux.* s.) 1. separate, part (*as individuals*), disperse, scatter, break up (*as crowd*), (*Math.*) diverge (*as lines*); 2. be too liquid (*of a mixture*). **–legen,** *v.t.* 1. spread *or* open out, unfold; 2. take apart *or* to pieces; *see also* **–setzen. –liegen,** *irr.v.i.* be *or* lie far apart, be *or* lie at a distance from one another; be widely divergent (*as opinions*). **–nehmen,** *irr.v.t.* dismantle, take apart *or* to pieces, (*coll.*) strip. **–setzen, 1.** *v.t.* explain, expound, set forth, make plain *or* clear, unfold (*Dat.*, to). **2.** *v.r.* come to terms *or* to an agreement *or* understanding, (*coll.*) have it out (***mit,*** with); face up (***mit,*** to), come to terms *or* grips (with) (*a situation*), grapple (with) (*a problem*). **Auseinandersetzung,** *f.* 1. explanation, exposition, elucidation; 2. settlement (*with creditors etc.*); 3.

discussion, argument, altercation, exchange *or* difference of opinion, (*coll.*) words; ***blutige –,*** blows.

auserkoren ['aus?ɛrko:rən], *adj.* (*Poet.*) chosen, (pre)ordained.

auserlesen ['aus?ɛrle:zən], *adj.* picked, selected, select, choice, exquisite.

ausersehen ['aus?ɛrze:ən], *irr.v.t.* choose, select, pick out; single out, destine.

auserwählen ['aus?ɛrvɛ:lən], *v.t.* select, choose; predestine; ***die Auserwählten,*** the elect *or* chosen, (*coll.*) the favoured few.

ausfahren ['ausfa:rən], **1.** *irr.v.t.* 1. take (out) for a drive *or* ride, take *or* push (*baby*) out; 2. (*Naut.*) run *or* lay *or* pay out (*cable*); 3. (*Av.*) lower (*undercarriage*); 4. ***ausgefahrener Weg,*** bad *or* bumpy road; (*fig.*) ***sich in ausgefahrenen Gleisen bewegen,*** keep to the beaten track. **2.** *irr.v.i.* (*aux.* s.) 1. drive out, go for a drive; (*of a baby*) be taken *or* pushed out (in the perambulator); (*of a ship*) put (out) to sea; (*of a train*) draw out (***aus,*** of); 2. (*of miners*) leave the pit, come up (to the surface); 3. (*B.*) (*of evil spirits*) go forth, come *or* go out. **Ausfahrt,** *f.* 1. drive, gateway; exit, exit road (*from motorway*); 2. excursion, trip, outing, drive; 3. departure (***aus,*** from), ascent (*from mine*). **Ausfahrtschacht,** *m.* (*Min.*) ascent shaft.

Ausfall ['ausfal], *m.* 1. falling out (*of hair, teeth, radioactive dust etc.*); loss (*of revenue*), deficiency, deficit, shortage, *pl.* (*Mil.*) casualties, losses; (*Chem.*) precipitation; precipitate, waste, scrap, (radioactive) fallout; 2. result, outcome, issue; dropping *or* falling out (*of competitors*), dropping *or* falling away *or* off (*of competition*); stoppage, breakdown, failure (*of machine*), (*Med.*) non-functioning, collapse, failure (*of organ*), non-payment (*of salary etc.*), cancellation (*of performance*), omission (*of letter, word etc.*); 3. (*Mil.*) sally, sortie, (*Fenc.*) lunge, thrust, pass, (*fig.*) (abusive) attack, invective, abuse. **ausfallen,** *irr.v.i.* (*aux.* s.) 1. fall *or* drop out (*as hair, teeth*), fall out (*of radioactive dust*); (*Chem.*) precipitate; 2. (*of a p.*) be unavailable; drop out (*as competitor*), (*Mil.*) become a casualty; become unserviceable, be out of action, fail (*as machine*), (*Med.*) collapse, fail (*as an organ*), not be paid (*as salary*), be cancelled, not take place (*of a performance*), be left out *or* omitted, drop out (*as letter, word etc.*), be elided (*as vowel*); 3. (*Mil.*) make a sally *or* sortie, sally (out), (*Fenc.*) lunge, thrust, make a thrust *or* pass, (*fig.*) make an (abusive) attack (***gegen,*** on), become abusive *or* offensive (towards); 4. turn out (*well, badly etc.*). *See* **ausgefallen.**

ausfällen ['ausfɛlən], *v.t.* (*Chem.*) separate out, precipitate.

ausfallend ['ausfalənt], **ausfällig** [–fɛlɪç], *adj.* offensive, insulting, abusive, rude.

Ausfällmittel ['ausfɛlmɪtəl], *n.* (*Chem.*) precipitant.

Ausfallschwung ['ausfalʃvuŋ], *m.* telemark (*skiing*). **Ausfall(s)erscheinung,** *f.* symptom of deficiency. **Ausfallstraße,** *f.* exit road. **Ausfall(s)winkel,** *m.* (*Opt.*) angle of reflection. **Ausfalltor,** *n.* sally-port.

Ausfällung ['ausfɛluŋ], *f.* (*Chem.*) precipitation.

ausfasern ['ausfa:zərn], **1.** *v.t.* unravel; tease *or* fray out. **2.** *v.i., v.r.* unravel, become unravelled *or* frayed, fray (out) (at the edges).

ausfechten ['ausfɛçtən], *irr.v.t.* fight out, settle by fighting; (*fig.*) ***die S. –,*** fight *or* have it out (*in words*).

ausfertigen ['ausfɛrtɪgən], *v.t.* draw up (*a deed, report etc.*), (*Law*) engross; write *or* make out (*bills etc.*); ***einen Paß –,*** issue *or* make out a passport. **Ausfertigung,** *f.* drawing up, (*Law*) engrossment; copy, draft; ***in dreifacher –,*** in triplicate.

ausfinden ['ausfɪndən], **1.** *irr.v.t.* (*usu.* ***ausfindig machen***) *see under* **ausfindig. 2.** *irr.v.r.* find one's way, know one's way about; (*fig. coll.*) make it out, be at home (***in*** (*Dat.*), in), (*neg. only*) not make head or tail of it.

ausfindig ['ausfɪndɪç], *adj.* (*only in*) – ***machen,*** find (out), trace, try to find.

ausflicken ['ausflɪkən], *v.t.* patch up, repair, mend.

ausfliegen ['ausfli:gən], **1.** *irr.v.i.* (*aux.* s.) (*coll.*) fly out *or* away, leave the nest; (*coll.*) ***der Vogel ist ausgeflogen,*** the bird has flown. **2.** *irr.v.t.* evacuate by air.

ausfließen ['ausfli:sən], *irr.v.i.* (*aux.* s.) flow *or* run out (***aus,*** of), discharge, be discharged (from), issue (out of); (*fig.*) issue forth, emanate (from).

Ausflucht ['ausfluxt], *f.* excuse, pretext, evasion, shift, subterfuge, loophole; ***Ausflüchte machen*** or ***suchen,*** look for *or* seek *or* make excuses, prevaricate, hedge, shuffle.

Ausflug ['ausflu:k], *m.* 1. ramble, trip, excursion, outing; ***einen – machen,*** go for an outing *or* trip *or* on an excursion; 2. first flight (*of young birds*); 3. entrance (*to a beehive*).

Ausflügler ['ausfly:klər], *m.* tourist, excursionist, tripper.

Ausfluß ['ausflus], *m.* 1. outflow, discharge, efflux; (*Med.*) discharge, secretion, flux; 2. (*fig.*) product, effluence, emanation; 3. outlet, opening, mouth (*of a river*).

ausfolgen ['ausfɔlgən], *v.t.* ***ihm etwas –,*** deliver up a th. to him, hand s.th. over to him.

ausforschen ['ausfɔrʃən], *v.t.* find out, inquire after (*a th.*): question, sound, (*coll.*) pump (*a p.*) (***über*** (*Acc.*), about).

ausfragen ['ausfra:gən], *v.t.* question, interrogate, sound, (*coll.*) pump (*a p.*) (***über*** (*Acc.*), about).

ausfransen ['ausfranzən], **1.** *v.t.* fray (out). **2.** *v.i.* (*aux.* s.), *v.r.* fray, become frayed.

ausfressen ['ausfrɛsən], *irr.v.t.* 1. corrode, eat into (*metal, as acid*), erode, wear away, hollow out (*rock, as water*); 2. eat up (*of animals*); (*coll.*) – ***müssen,*** have to pay for, take the consequences for; (*coll.*) ***etwas ausgefressen haben,*** get into mischief; (*coll.*) ***was hat er ausgefressen?*** what has he been up to?

ausfrieren ['ausfri:rən], *irr.v.i.* (*aux.* s.) freeze up thoroughly (*as a pond*), (*coll. of a p.*) be perished with cold.

Ausfuhr ['ausfu:r], *f.* (-, *pl.* **-en**) export; exportation; ***zur – geeignet,*** exportable. **Ausfuhrartikel,** *pl.* exports; export goods.

ausführbar ['ausfy:rba:r], *adj.* 1. exportable (*goods*); 2. practicable, feasible, workable (*as a plan*). **Ausführbarkeit,** *f.* practicability, feasibility.

Ausfuhr|bestimmungen, *pl.* export regulations. **–bewilligung,** *f.* export permit.

ausführen ['ausfy:rən], *v.t.* 1. carry out, execute, carry into execution, carry into effect, act upon (*plan, instructions*), realize, put into action, follow up (*idea*), perform (*action*), fulfil (*promise*), play (*trick*); ***weiter –,*** elaborate, enlarge upon, deal with at length; ***–de Gewalt,*** executive power; ***–der Künstler,*** performer, executant; 2. (*Comm.*) export (*goods*); 3. lead out; take for a walk, exercise (*a dog*); take out (*one's girl*).

Ausführer ['ausfy:rər], *m.* exporter.

Ausführgang ['ausfy:rgaŋ], *m.* excretory duct.

Ausfuhr|genehmigung, *f.* export permit *or* licence. **–gut,** *n.* export. **–handel,** *m.* export trade. **–kontingent,** *n.* export quota. **–land,** *n.* exporting country.

ausführlich ['ausfy:rlɪç], **1.** *adj.* detailed, circumstantial, full. **2.** *adv.* in detail, circumstantially, fully, in full, at length. **Ausführlichkeit,** *f.* fullness; ***mit großer –,*** in great detail, at great length.

Ausfuhr|prämie, *f.* export bounty, drawback. **–tarif,** *m.* reduced (transport) rates for export goods. **–taxe,** *f.* export duty. **–überschuß,** *m.* export surplus, favourable trade balance.

Ausführung ['ausfy:ruŋ], *f.* 1. execution, fulfilment (*of an order*); realization (*of a plan*); construction, erection (*of a building etc.*); ***zur – kommen,*** be carried into effect *or* execution, be put into execution; be constructed *or* erected (*of a building*); ***zur – bringen,*** carry into effect; 2. workmanship, finish; (*Comm.*) type, style, model (*of manufactured goods*);

3. *pl.* comments, remarks, discourse; 4. exportation; 5. ***in doppelter* –,** in duplicate. **Ausführungsorgan,** *n.* executive (authority).

Ausfuhr|verbot, *n.* ban on exports. **–ware,** *f.* export(ed commodity). **–zuschuß,** *m.* export subsidy.

ausfüllen ['ausfylən], *v.t.* 1. fill (up *or* in) (*a hole*); fill, occupy (*a position, one's thoughts etc.*), fill, take up (*time*); 2. fill in *or* out *or* up (*a form*).

ausfüttern ['ausfytərn], *v.t.* line (*a coat etc.*). **Ausfütterung,** *f.* lining (*of a coat*), liner (*of a cylinder*).

Ausgabe ['ausga:bə], *f.* 1. giving *or* handing out, distribution; delivery (*of post*), issue, issuing (*of tickets or (Mil.) of equipment*), emission (*of currency*); 2. issuing office, distribution centre; counter (*for issue of luggage*), hatch (*for issue of food*), window (*for issue of tickets etc.*); 3. expense, expenditure, outlay, outgoings; 4. edition (*of a book*). **Ausgabestelle,** *f. See* **Ausgabe,** 2.

Ausgang ['ausgaŋ], *m.* 1. exit, way out, outlet, egress; (*fig.*) (point of) departure, starting point; 2. end (*of line*), ending, termination (*of word*), end, close (*of epoch*); result, outcome, issue, upshot; 3. time *or* day *or* afternoon *or* evening off (*for a servant*), free time; (*Mil.*) **–** ***haben,*** be on pass; 4. *pl.* (*Comm.*) outgoings.

Ausgangs|kreis, *m.* (*Rad.*) output circuit. **–leistung,** *f.* (*Rad.*) (power) output. **–punkt,** *m.* starting point, point of departure (*also fig.*); (*Av.*) base. **–sperre,** *f.* (*Mil.*) confinement to barracks. **–stellung,** *f.* initial position. **–zoll,** *m.* export duty.

ausgären ['ausgɛ:rən], *v.i.* (*aux.* s.) finish fermenting.

ausgeben ['ausge:bən], **1.** *irr.v.t.* 1. give *or* hand out, distribute, issue, deal (*cards*); emit (*currency*); 2. spend, expend, lay out, disburse (*money*); 3. yield; 4. claim, declare (*für*, to be). **2.** *irr.v.r.* claim, pretend, give o.s. out (*für*, to be), pose, pass o.s. off (as). **3.** *irr.v.i.* 1. give tongue (*as hounds*); 2. ***gut* –,** yield a lot, have a good yield. **Ausgeber,** *m.* distributor, issuer; dealer (*of cards*), dispenser (*of drugs*).

Ausgebot ['ausgəbo:t], *n.* putting up for sale; first *or* opening bid (*at an auction*).

Ausgeburt ['ausgəburt], *f.* offspring, product, creature, creation; abortion, monstrous creation; **–** ***der Hölle,*** spawn of hell, fiend; diabolical scheme.

Ausgedinge ['ausgədɪŋə], *n.* reservation, rights reserved.

ausgefallen ['ausgəfalən], *adj.* strange, queer, curious, unusual, extraordinary, striking, out of the way *or* the ordinary. *See* **ausfallen.**

ausgeglichen ['ausgəglɪçən], *adj.* (well-)balanced, equable. *See* **ausgleichen. Ausgeglichenheit,** *f.* evenness (of temper); (good) balance, uniformity.

Ausgehanzug ['ausge:ˀantsu:k], *m.* lounge suit; best suit. *See also* **Ausgehuniform.**

ausgehechelt [ausgəhɛçəlt], *adj.* subtly contrived. *See* **aushecheln.**

ausgehen ['ausge:ən], *irr.v.i.* (*aux.* s.) 1. go out (*for a walk, to the cinema etc.*), leave the house; ***er geht jeden Abend aus,*** he goes out every evening; 2. go out (*as a fire*); give *or* run out, come to an end, run short, fail (*as provisions*); end, terminate (***auf*** or ***in*** (*Acc.*), in) (*as a word*); ***schief* –,** end badly; 3. come out (*as hair, colour etc.*); 4. **–** ***auf*** (*Acc.*), go *or* set out in search of; (*of a p.*) aim at, be bent on (*doing*), set out *or* aim (*to do*); (*of a th.*) be calculated (*to do*); ***der Plan geht darauf aus*** (***zu tun***), the aim *or* purpose of the plan is (to do); 4. **–** ***von,*** come from, start at (*place*); emanate *or* proceed from; start *or* originate with; 5. ***leer* –,** get nothing, be left out, come away empty-handed. **ausgehend,** *adj.* 1. outgoing (*mail etc.*); ***–e Waren,*** exports; 2. closing (*years*); 3. (*Geol.*) outcropping (*seam*); 4. salient (*angle*). **Ausgehendes,** *n.* (*Geol.*) outcrop.

Ausgeh|tag, *m.* (servant's) day off. **–uniform,** *f.* (*Mil.*) walking-out dress, (*Nav.*) shore kit. **–verbot,** *n.* curfew, (*Mil.*) confinement to barracks.

ausgekocht ['ausgəkɔxt], *adj.* (*coll.*) utter, out-and-out, unmitigated, arrant (*rogue*). *See* **auskochen.**

ausgelassen ['ausgəlasən], *adj.* wild, unruly, exuberant, boisterous, frolicsome; unrestrained, abandoned. *See* **auslassen. Ausgelassenheit,** *f.* wildness, unruliness, exuberance, boisterousness; lack of restraint, abandon.

ausgeleiert ['ausgəlaɪərt], *adj.* hackneyed, trite. *See* **ausleiern.**

ausgemacht ['ausgəmaxt], *adj.* complete, absolute, utter, out-and-out, downright, thorough(-paced) (*rogue, fool, swindle etc.*). *See* **ausmachen.**

ausgenommen ['ausgənɔmən], *prep.* (*with preceding Acc., occ. Nom.*) except, excepting, with the exception of, but (*sl.* but for), save, (*coll.*) bar, barring; ***nicht* –,** not excepting; ***Anwesende* –,** present company excepted; **–** ***daß,*** except that; **–** ***wenn,*** except when *or* if; ***überall* – *da wo,*** everywhere except *or* but where. *See* **ausnehmen.**

ausgepicht ['ausgəpɪçt], *adj.* (*coll.*) difficult, unmanageable (*of a p.*); ***–er Kerl,*** awkward customer; ***eine –e Kehle haben,*** be a hard drinker. *See* **auspichen.**

ausgeprägt ['ausgəprɛ:kt], *adj.* pronounced, (strongly) marked, (well) defined, prominent, decided, distinct. *See* **ausprägen. Ausgeprägtheit,** *f.* distinctness, marked *or* pronounced nature, prominence.

ausgerechnet ['ausgərɛçnət], *adv.* just, of all . . .; **–** ***heute,*** today of all days; **–** ***hier,*** here of all places, just here; **–** ***ich,*** me of all people; **–** ***als,*** just at the moment when, of all times when, just as. *See* **ausrechnen.**

ausgereift ['ausgəraɪft], *adj.* fully ripe, mature. *See* **ausreifen. Ausgereiftheit,** *f.* ripeness, (full) maturity.

ausgeschlossen ['ausgəʃlɔsən], *adj.* impossible, out of the question; ***nicht ganz* –,** just possible. *See* **ausschließen.**

ausgesprochen ['ausgeʃprɔxən], *adj.* pronounced, distinct, decided, marked, unqualified, unmistakable; outspoken, avowed, declared (*opponent etc.*); (*coll.*) absolute, utter (*fool etc.*). *See* **aussprechen.**

ausgestalten ['ausgəʃtaltən], *v.t.* 1. arrange, make the arrangements for; 2. develop, turn (***zu***, into). **Ausgestaltung,** *f.* arrangements; development (***zu***, into).

ausgesucht ['ausgəzu:xt], *adj.* choice, selected (*fruit etc.*); extreme (*cruelty*), exquisite (*politeness*). *See* **aussuchen.**

ausgewachsen ['ausgəvaksən], *adj.* full-grown, (*coll.*) fully-fledged; (*coll.*) complete, utter (*fool*); full-scale. *See* **auswachsen.**

ausgewogen ['ausgəvo:gən], *adj.* (well-)balanced (*character*). *See* **auswiegen. Ausgewogenheit,** *f.* balance.

ausgezeichnet ['ausgətsaɪçnət], **1.** *adj.* excellent, capital; (*coll.*) first-rate. **2.** *adv.* excellently, admirably, extremely well, (*coll.*) fine.

ausgiebig ['ausgi:bɪç], **1.** *adj.* extensive, exhaustive, thorough. *See also* **ergiebig. 2.** *adv.* **–** ***benutzen,*** make full *or* abundant use of; **–** ***frühstücken,*** have an ample breakfast. **Ausgiebigkeit,** *f.* thoroughness, extensiveness, exhaustiveness. *See also* **Ergiebigkeit.**

ausgießen ['ausgi:sən], *irr.v.t.* 1. pour *or* throw out (*water etc.*), empty (*water*) (***aus***, out of), empty (*bucket*); 2. pour over; (*fig.*) shed (*light*), shower (*presents*), vent (*one's rage*). **Ausgießung,** *f.* (*B.*) effusion (*of the Holy Ghost*).

Ausgleich ['ausglaɪç], *m.* **(-(e)s,** *pl.* **-e)** 1. balance, equilibrium, (*Footb.*) equalizing goal, equalizer; 2. offset, adjustment, compensation; ***ihm einen* – *schaffen,*** compensate him, make *or* pay compensation to him; 3. (*Comm.*) settlement (of account), (*Austr.*) legal settlement, composition; ***in* – *gehen,*** make a composition with one's creditors; 4. (*fig.*) settlement, compromise; ***zu einem* – *kommen,*** come to *or* reach a compromise, settle one's differences.

ausgleichen ['ausglaɪçən], **1.** *irr.v.t.* 1. smooth *or* level out (*irregularities*); bring to the same level (*surfaces*); adjust (*levels, sizes*); equalize, balance (*weights, values etc.*); 2. level *or* even up, adjust, balance (*differences*); compensate for, make good, offset (*loss etc.*), make amends for (*error*), (*coll.*) make up for; 3. settle, compose (*quarrel etc.*); ***die -de Gerechtigkeit,*** poetic justice. **2.** *irr.v.r.* balance, be balanced, be levelled up *or* adjusted; cancel one another out, (*Math.*) cancel out. **3.** *irr.v.i.* (*Footb.*) score the equalizing goal, equalize.

Ausgleichs|düse, *f.* compensator (jet) (*on carburettor*). **-getriebe,** *n.* differential gear. **-kapazität,** *f.* (*Elec.*) neutrodyne capacitance. **-kasse,** *f.* equalization fund. **-konto,** *n.* suspense account. **-rennen,** *n.* handicap race. **-verfahren,** *n.* (*Comm.*) partial satisfaction of creditors, (*Pol.*) procedure for settling international debts.

Ausgleichung ['ausglaɪçuŋ], *f.* settlement; equalization, adjustment; compensation; equilibrium, balance; (*Philol.*) assimilative analogy; (*Law*) hotchpot. **Ausgleichungshaus,** *n.* clearing house.

ausgleiten ['ausglaɪtən], *irr.v.i.* (*aux.* s.) slip, slide.

ausglühen ['ausgly:ən], *v.t.* (*Metall.*) temper, anneal.

ausgraben ['ausgra:bən], *irr.v.t.* dig up, uproot; disinter, exhume (*body*), excavate (*ruins*), (*fig. coll.*) unearth (*secret*), dig *or* rake up (*grievance*). **Ausgrabung,** *f.* excavation (*of ruins*), exhumation (*of body*).

ausgreifen ['ausgraɪfən], *irr.v.i.* step out; (*coll.*) step on it, (*Motor. coll.*) step on the gas; ***weit -de Schritte,*** long strides; (*fig.*) ***weit -d,*** far-reaching, comprehensive.

Ausguck ['ausguk], *m.* (*Naut., Mil.*) look-out. **ausgucken,** *v.i.* look out (***nach,*** for), keep *or* be on the look-out (for).

Ausguß ['ausgus], *m.* 1. effusion, outpouring; 2. sink, gutter, drain; 3. spout (*of a vessel*). **Ausguß|-leitung,** *f.* discharge pipe. **-masse,** *f.* (semi-) liquid compound. **-rinnen, -röhren,** *pl.* drain-pipes. **-wasser,** *n.* waste water.

aushacken ['aushakən], *v.t.* 1. rough-hew; 2. hoe up (*potatoes etc.*); pick out (*eyes from potatoes etc.*), (*coll.*) scratch out (*s.o.'s eyes*).

aushalten ['aushaltən], **1.** *irr.v.t.* 1. endure, bear, support, suffer, stand, (*coll.*) stick (*pain etc.*); sustain, stand up to (*a siege*); weather, ride out (*a storm*); sustain, suspend (*a note*); bear, stand (up to) (*comparison*); 2. keep (*a mistress*). **2.** *irr.v.i.* hold out, (*coll.*) hang on, stick it out; ***es ist nicht zum Aushalten,*** it is not to be borne, it is unendurable, it is beyond endurance.

aushändigen ['aushɛndɪgən], *v.t.* hand over, deliver up, surrender (*prisoner*), hand out (*leaflets etc.*).

Aushang ['aushaŋ], *m.* placard, notice.

Aushängebogen ['aushɛŋəbo:gən], *m.* (*Typ.*) advance-proof.

aushängen ['aushɛŋən], **1.** *v.t.* 1. hang *or* put out (*a sign, a flag etc.*); put *or* post up (*a bill*); 2. unhinge, take off its hinges (*a door*); unship (*a rudder*); remove (*telephone receiver*). **2.** *irr.v.i.* (*occ.* **aushangen**) 1. have been hung *or* put out (*flags*); 2. be announced *or* advertised. **Aushängeschild,** *n.* sign-board, sign; (*fig.*) ***unter dem - freisinniger Gedanken,*** under the pretence of liberal ideas.

ausharren ['ausharən], *v.i.* persevere, persist; stand fast, stand one's ground, hold out.

aushauchen ['aushauxən], *v.t.* exhale (*breath, perfume*); (*fig.*) ***seine Seele -, den Geist -,*** breathe one's last, expire.

aushauen ['aushauən], *irr.v.t.* 1. lop off *or* away (*branches*), lop, prune (*trees*), clear, thin (out) (*a forest*); 2. hew out.

aushäuten ['aushɔytən], **1.** *v.t.* skin, flay. **2.** *v.r.* cast its slough *or* skin.

ausheben ['aushe:bən], *irr.v.t.* 1. dig up (*a plant etc.*), lift (*potatoes*); dig (*a trench*); take off the hinges (*a door etc.*); lift (*opponent*) off his feet (*wrestling*); rob (*a nest*), take (*eggs*) from the nest; clean out (*a gang's hide-out*); 2. recruit, conscript, enrol, enlist, levy (*soldiers*), (*obs.*) pick out, select. **Ausheber,** *m.* 1. garden trowel; 2. recruiting officer.

aushebern ['aushe:bərn], *v.t.* siphon off.

Aushebung ['aushe:buŋ], *f.* levy, enlistment, enrolment, conscription, recruitment.

aushecheln ['aushɛçəln], *v.t.* hackle (*hemp*).

aushecken ['aushɛkən], *v.t.* hatch (*plot*), think up *or* out (*scheme*), be up to (*prank*); (*Prov.*) ***eine Taube heckt keinen Adler aus,*** you can't make a silk purse out of a sow's ear.

ausheilen ['aushaɪlən], *v.i.* (*aux.* s.) heal up, be (completely) cured.

aushelfen ['aushɛlfən], *irr.v.i.* (*Dat.*) help out, lend a hand. **Aushelfer,** *m.* temporary assistant.

Aushilfe ['aushɪlfə], *f.* (temporary *or* improvised) aid *or* assistance; temporary helper *or* assistant, substitute, (*coll.*) stop-gap, makeshift.

Aushilfs|arbeit, *f.* temporary work, casual labour, odd-jobs. **-arbeiter,** *m.* temporary worker, casual labourer. **-kraft,** *f.* temporary assistant. **aushilfsweise,** *adv.* temporarily, as a substitute *or* (*coll.*) stop-gap *or* makeshift.

aushöhlen ['aushø:lən], *v.t.* hollow out; wear away, erode, undermine (*river bank etc., also fig.*), (*fig.*) sap. **Aushöhlung,** *f.* erosion; hollow, cavity.

ausholen ['ausho:lən], **1.** *v.t.* (*coll.*) ***ihn -,*** question *or* sound *or* (*coll.*) pump him, draw him out (***über*** (*Acc.*), about). **2.** *v.i.* lift, swing (*the arm*) (*for throwing, striking etc.*); ***zu einem Sprunge -,*** take a run before jumping; (*fig.*) ***weit -,*** begin right at the beginning.

ausholzen ['aushɔltsən], *v.t.* thin (*a forest*).

aushorchen ['aushɔrçən], *v.t. See* **ausholen, 1.**

aushören ['aushø:rən], *v.t.* hear out, hear to the end.

Aushub ['aushu:p], *m.* (building) excavation; excavated material.

aushülsen ['aushylzən], *v.t.* shell (*peas etc.*); husk, peel.

aushungern ['aushuŋərn], *v.t.* starve out (*a town*), starve (*a p.*); (*coll.*) ***ausgehungert,*** famished, ravenous, starved.

ausjäten ['ausjɛ:tən], *v.t.* pull up, remove (*weeds*).

auskämmen ['auskɛmən], *v.t.* comb out (*hair*), comb, card (*wool*); (*fig. coll.*) comb, mop up (*an area*).

auskämpfen ['auskɛmpfən], **1.** *v.t.* fight out (to the end). **2.** *v.i.* 1. stop fighting; 2. (*fig.*) pass away.

auskaufen ['auskaufən], *v.t.* buy up (*shop*), buy out (*partner*), buy (*s.o.*) off; ***die Zeit -,*** make the most of one's time; ***die Gelegenheit -,*** improve the occasion.

auskehlen ['auske:lən], *v.t.* channel, groove, flute. **Auskehlung,** *f.* fluting, grooving, channel.

auskehren ['auske:rən], *v.t.* sweep (out), sweep clean, (*coll.*) clean up (*organization*), make a clean sweep of. **Auskehricht,** *m. or n.* sweepings.

auskeilen ['auskaɪlən], *v.i.* peter out, (*Geol.*) crop out, pinch.

auskeimen ['auskaɪmən], *v.i.* germinate, sprout.

auskennen ['auskɛnən], *irr.v.r.* (***in*** (*Dat.*)) know one's way about; know about, understand, be well versed in, know what's what; (*coll.*) ***ich kenne mich nicht mehr aus,*** I am stumped *or* at a loss.

auskerben ['auskɛrbən], *v.t.* notch, indent; mill (*the edge of a coin*); ***ausgekerbt,*** serrated; (*Her.*) engrailed; (*Bot.*) crenated.

auskernen ['auskɛrnən], *v.t.* stone (*fruit*); take out the kernel; shell (*nuts*).

ausklagen ['auskla:gən], **1.** *v.t.* sue *or* prosecute for. **2.** *v.r.* relate all one's grievances.

ausklammern ['ausklamərn], *v.t.* 1. (*Math.*) remove the brackets from; 2. (*fig.*) ignore, push on one side (*a p.*).

Ausklang ['ausklaŋ], *m.* final sound; (*coll.*) epilogue, end.

ausklauben ['ausklaubən], *v.t.* 1. pick out *or* over; sort, separate (*ore*); 2. (*fig.*) think out in detail, puzzle out, contrive, devise.

auskleiden ['ausklaɪdən], **1.** *v.t.* 1. undress; 2. line, panel (*a room*). **2.** *v.r.* undress o.s., take off one's clothes. **Auskleidung,** *f.* 1. act of undressing; 2. lining, panelling.

ausklingen ['ausklɪŋən], *irr.v.i.* (*aux.* s.) die away, fade (*as an echo*); (*fig.*) end, culminate.

ausklinken ['ausklɪŋkən], *v.i.* unlatch (*door*), disengage, release (*a catch*).

ausklopfen ['ausklɔpfən], *v.t.* beat out (*dust*), beat (*carpet*); knock out (*pipe, ashes from pipe*); (*coll.*) give (*a p.*) a dusting (down). **Ausklopfer,** *m.* carpet-beater.

ausklügeln ['auskly:gəln], *v.t.* think *or* work *or* worry *or* puzzle out.

auskneifen ['ausknaɪfən], *irr.v.i.* (*sl.*) do a bunk, hook it, make o.s. scarce, make off.

ausknobeln ['auskno:bəln], *v.t.* settle by dicing; toss for; (*coll.*) *see* **ausklügeln.**

auskochen ['auskɔxən], *v.t.* 1. extract by boiling; decoct; 2. scald, sterilize (*a vessel*); boil thoroughly. *See also* **ausgekocht.**

auskommen ['auskɔmən], *irr.v.i.* (*aux.* s.) 1. get out (of doors); hatch out (*of chicken*); 2. get out *or* away, escape; 3. hit it off, get on (well) (*mit*, with) (*a p.*); make do, manage, get along *or* by (with); ***ich kann unmöglich damit –***, I can't possibly manage (with so little); ***mit ihm nicht –***, not get on with him, not hit it off with him; ***mit dem Gehalt –***, make ends meet; ***ohne etwas –***, manage *or* do without s.th. **Auskommen,** *n.* 1. peaceable intercourse; ***es ist kein – mit ihm,*** it's impossible to hit it off *or* to get on with him; 2. (means of) livelihood *or* subsistence, living, competency, competence; ***ein gutes – haben,*** be well off.

auskömmlich ['auskœmlɪç], *adj.* adequate, sufficient; ***-es Gehalt,*** living wage, enough to live on.

auskoppeln ['auskɔpəln], *v.t.* slip, unleash (*hounds*).

auskosten ['auskɔstən], *v.t.* enjoy to the full; (*fig.*) ***bis zur Neige –***, drain the cup (*of sorrow etc.*).

auskramen ['auskra:mən], *v.t.* 1. display, make a parade of (*knowledge etc.*); 2. unearth, dig up (*information*), rummage through, turn out (*a drawer*); take *or* pull out (*contents of a drawer*).

auskratzen ['auskratsən], **1.** *v.t.* scratch *or* scrape out. **2.** *v.i.* (*aux.* s.) (*sl.*) sling one's hook, hook it.

auskühlen ['ausky:lən], *v.i.* (*aux.* s.), *v.t.* cool thoroughly.

Auskultant [auskul'tant], *m.* (**-en,** *pl.* **-en**) (*obs.*) 1. (*Med.*) auscultator; 2. member without voting powers. **Auskultation** [–tatsi'o:n], *f.* auscultation. **Auskultator** [–'ta:tɔr], *m.* (**-s,** *pl.* **-en**) (*obs.*) (*Law*) *see* **Auskultant,** 1. **auskultieren,** *v.t.* (*obs.*) 1. (*Med.*) auscultate, use the stethoscope, examine by auscultation; 2. listen, attend, sit in (*at a meeting*).

auskundschaften ['auskuntʃaftən], *v.t.* explore, reconnoitre, spy out, trace, locate, discover the whereabouts of; try to find *or* trace; (*coll.*) ferret out.

Auskunft ['auskunft], *f.* (-, *pl.* **⸚e**) information, intelligence; particulars; ***nähere –***, further *or* fuller particulars; – or ***Auskünfte einholen,*** make inquiries (*über* (*Acc.*), about). **Auskunftei,** *f.* (-, *pl.* **-en**), **Auskunfts|büro,** *n.*, **–stelle,** *f.* information bureau, inquiry office.

auskünsteln ['auskynstəln], *v.t.* contrive, work out in detail.

auskuppeln ['auskupəln], **1.** *v.t.* uncouple, disengage, disconnect. **2.** *v.i.* (*Motor.*) declutch, put into neutral gear.

auslachen ['auslaxən], **1.** *v.t.* laugh at, make fun of, poke fun at; jeer at, deride, laugh to scorn. **2.** *v.i.*, *v.r.* laugh one's fill.

Ausladebrücke ['ausla:dəbrykə], *f.* jetty, pier.

ausladen ['ausla:dən], **1.** *irr.v.t.* unload (*goods, vehicle*), unlade, discharge (*cargo, ship*); (*coll.*) put off (*invited guests*). **2.** *irr.v.i.* (*Archit.*) project, jut out, overhang; ***-de Gesten,*** expansive *or* sweeping gestures. **Ausladeort,** *m.* port of discharge. **Auslader,** *m.* 1. lighterman, stevedore; unloader, dock-hand; 2. (*Phys.*) discharging rod. **Ausladung,** *f.* 1. unloading, discharge (*of ship or cargo*); 2. (*Archit.*) projection, overhang; reach, (operating) radius (*of a crane*).

Auslage ['ausla:gə], *f.* 1. outlay, expenditure, expense; ***die -n ersetzen*** or ***erstatten,*** reimburse; ***persönliche -n,*** out-of-pocket expenses; 2. display (*of goods*); ***in der –***, in the window *or* showcase; 3. (*Fenc.*) guard. **Auslagekasten,** *m.* show-case.

Ausland ['auslant], *n.* foreign country, foreign parts; ***im -e,*** abroad; ***In- und –***, at home and abroad; ***Waren vom -e,*** foreign goods.

Ausländer ['auslɛndər], *m.* foreigner, alien. **ausländisch,** *adj.* foreign, alien.

Auslands|deutsche(r), *m., f.* German national living abroad. **–deutschtum,** *n.* those of German extraction living abroad. **–korrespondent,** *m.* (*Comm.*) foreign correspondent. **–paß,** *m.* passport. **–stimme,** *f.* voice *or* opinion of the foreign press.

auslangen ['auslaŋən], *v.i.* 1. be sufficient *or* adequate, suffice, do; ***mit etwas –***, make shift with s.th.; 2. – ***mit,*** raise (*one's hand or arm*); ***zum Streiche –***, raise the arm to strike.

Auslaß ['auslas], *m.* (**-(ss)es,** *pl.* **⸚(ss)e**) outlet.

auslassen ['auslasən], **1.** *irr.v.t.* 1. let out, release (*air*), let *or* run off (*water*), let *or* blow off (*steam*), (*fig.*) vent, give vent to (*one's rage etc.*); 2. leave *or* miss out, omit; miss *or* cut out (*intentionally*); 3. let out (*garment, seam*), let down (*hem*), render down (*fat*); ***ausgelassene Butter,*** melted butter. *See* **ausgelassen. 2.** *irr.v.r.* express one's opinion (*über* (*Acc.*), about). **Auslassung,** *f.* 1. omission; (*Phonet.*) ellipsis, elision; 2. (*usu. pl.*) expression of opinion, utterance, statement, remark(s). **Auslassungszeichen,** *n.* apostrophe; (*Typ.*) caret.

auslasten ['auslastən], *v.t.* 1. balance, equalize (*loads*); 2. (*Comm.*) employ (*s.o.*) fully, make (*a firm, a p.*) work to capacity; ***ausgelastet sein,*** (*of a p.*) be fully employed *or* occupied, (*of a firm*) be working at full capacity.

Auslauf ['auslauf], *m.* 1. outlet, outflow; 2. sailing, departure (*of ship*), (*Av.*) landing run, (*Spt.*) run-out past the tape; ***zum – bereit,*** ready to sail; 3. room to move about; ***der – für die Hühner,*** hen-run. **Auslaufbefehl,** *m.* (*Naut.*) sailing orders.

auslaufen ['auslaufən], **1.** *irr.v.i.* (*aux.* s.) 1. run *or* flow *or* leak *or* spill out (*aus*, of), leak (*as pen, bottle*), run (*as colour*); 2. (set) sail, put (out) to sea, clear the harbour, leave port (*of a ship*), leave (the station) (*of a train*); ***drei Straßen laufen vom Marktplatz aus,*** three roads start at *or* from *or* radiate from the square; 3. stop running, run down (*as a machine*), slow down (*as runner, horse when past the winning post*), (*fig.*) be discontinued (*as production*); 4. – ***in*** (*Acc.*), end in; ***spitz –***, taper off to a point; ***in Streit –***, end in a quarrel. **2.** *irr.v.t.* 1. (*Min.*) haul, truck (*coal*); 2. run to the end; ***die Bahn –***, run *or* stay the (whole) course. **3.** *irr.v.r.* exercise one's legs, get exercise.

Ausläufer ['auslɔyfər], *m.* 1. offshoot, branch; (*Bot.*) sucker, runner, stolon; spur, buttress (*of a mountain-chain*); *pl.* foot-hills; 2. (*Min.*) haulage-man; (*Swiss*) errand-boy.

Auslauf|hahn, *m.* drain-cock. **–modell,** *n.* (*Comm.*) discontinued model *or* line.

auslaugen ['auslaugən], *v.t.* 1. wash *or* steep in lye; 2. leach, lixiviate, clear of lye.

Auslaut ['auslaut], *m.* final sound (*at end of word or syllable*); ***im –***, when final, at the end (*of word or syllable*). **auslauten,** *v.i.* end, terminate (*of word or syllable*). **auslautend,** *adj.* final.

ausleben ['ausle:bən], **1.** *v.t.* live to the end of. **2.** *v.r.* enjoy life to the full, live a full life, make the most of one's life. **3.** *v.i.* depart this life, come to the end of one's days.

ausleeren ['ausle:rən], **1.** *v.t.* empty; drain (*a glass*), clear out (*a room etc.*); (*Med.*) evacuate, purge;

sich (*Dat.*) *das Herz* –, pour out one's heart. **2.** *v.r.* (*of a room etc.*) empty. **Ausleerung,** *f.* (*Med.*) motion *or* action of the bowels, evacuation; excretion.

auslegen ['ausle:gən], **1.** *v.t.* 1. lay out (*money etc.*), spend; 2. set *or* lay *or* spread out, display, expose for sale; inlay, veneer; lay (*tiles etc.*); 3. explain, expound, interpret, construe; ***falsch* –,** misinterpret, miscontrue, put a false construction *or* wrong interpretation on. **2.** *v.r.* (*Fenc.*) stand on guard. **Ausleger,** *m.* 1. expositor, interpreter, commentator, (*B.*) exegetist; 2. arm, bracket, (*Archit.*) cantilever; jib, beam (*of a crane*); outrigger (*of boat*). **Ausleger|brücke,** *f.* cantilever bridge. **–kran,** *m.* jib crane. **Auslegung,** *f.* exposition, construction, interpretation, explanation, exegesis.

ausleiern ['auslaɪərn], **1.** *v.t.* repeat (*song etc.*) till it is hackneyed. **2.** *v.i.* (*aux.* s.) (*coll.*) lose its stretch (*of elastic*). *See* **ausgeleiert.**

Ausleih|bibliothek ['auslaɪ–], *f.* lending library. **–bücherei,** *f.* circulating library. **Ausleihe,** *f.* lending (out) (*of books*); issue, distribution (*in library*). **ausleihen,** *irr.v.t.* lend (out), hire out; ***sich*** (*Dat.*) ***etwas* –,** borrow s.th. (***von,*** from).

auslernen ['auslɛrnən], **1.** *v.i.* finish one's apprenticeship; ***man lernt nie aus,*** one is never too old to learn, one lives and learns; ***ausgelernt,*** trained, qualified, experienced. **2.** *v.t.* 1. learn all about; 2. finish, get through (*a textbook*).

Auslese ['ausle:zə], *f.* selection, assortment, choice; élite, flower, cream, the pick; the choicest wine (= *from selected grapes*); ***natürliche* –,** natural selection. **auslesen,** *irr.v.t.* 1. select, choose, pick out; 2. read to the end, finish reading.

auslichten ['auslɪçtən], *v.t.* clear, thin (*a wood*); prune (*trees*).

ausliefern ['ausli:fərn], *v.t.* deliver (*goods*), hand over, deliver up (*Dat.*, to), deliver (into the hands of), (*Law*) extradite (*criminal*); ***ausgeliefert sein*** (*Dat.*), be at the mercy of. **Auslieferung,** *f.* surrender, extradition (*of a criminal*); delivery. **Auslieferungsschein,** *m.* delivery note.

ausliegen ['ausli:gən], *irr.v.i.* be displayed for inspection *or* sale; be exhibited; be on display *or* show; be available.

auslöschen ['auslœʃən], *v.t.* put out, extinguish, quench; efface; wipe *or* rub off (*writing from blackboard*); efface, obliterate, erase (*memories etc.*); annihilate, wipe out, blot out.

auslosen ['auslo:zən], *v.t.* draw (lots) for; raffle; toss (up) for.

auslösen ['auslø:zən], *v.t.* 1. remove, take out (*as bones from meat*); (*Chem.*) dissolve out (*solids*), release, liberate, set free (*gas*); (*Mech.*) release, disconnect; throw *or* put out of gear *or* action; ransom (*prisoner*); redeem (*pledge*); 2. cause, bring about, induce; set up *or* going, call forth, give rise to, elicit (*reaction*), start (off) (*series of events*), evoke, provoke, excite, arouse, awaken, kindle, stir up, (*coll.*) spark off (*interest etc.*). **Auslöser,** *m.* release mechanism, (*Phot.*) shutter release. **Auslösung,** *f.* 1. release; liberation (*of gas*), redemption (*of pledge*), ransom (*of prisoner*); 2. ratchet, escapement.

auslüften ['auslyftən], *v.t.* air, ventilate.

Auslug ['auslu:k], *m.* (*Naut.*) look-out.

ausmachen ['ausmaxən], *v.t.* 1. make up; amount *or* add up *or* come to; constitute, form; ***etwas* –,** matter, make a difference; ***nichts* –,** not matter at all, make no difference *or* odds; ***viel* –,** matter a lot; ***wenig* –,** not matter much; ***was macht das aus?*** what does it matter? what difference does it make? what's the odds? what of it? 2. decide, settle, determine; arrange, agree on, come to an agreement on; ***eine ausgemachte S.,*** a (dead) certainty, (*coll.*) a sure thing; *see also* **ausgemacht**; 3. put out (*fire, light etc.*), turn out (*light*), turn off (*gas, water etc.*), stub out (*cigarette*); 4. make out, discern, discover, trace.

ausmalen ['ausma:lən], *v.t.* 1. paint (*room, wall etc.*) (in fresco); 2. ***sich*** (*Dat.*) ***etwas* –,** picture s.th. (to o.s.), imagine s.th.; think *or* work s.th. out.

Ausmarsch ['ausmarʃ], *m.* marching out, departure (*of troops*). **ausmarschieren,** *v.i.* (*aux.* s.) march out.

Ausmaß ['ausma:s], *n.* measure; degree, extent; scale, scope, proportion; ***in großem –e,*** to a great *or* large extent, in large measure, on a large scale; ***das – des Erträglichen,*** the bounds of endurance.

ausmauern ['ausmauərn], *v.t.* line with bricks *or* masonry.

ausmergeln ['ausmɛrgəln], *v.t.* enervate; exhaust; wear *or* tire out, drain of all strength *or* energy; impoverish (*land*); ***ausgemergelt aussehen,*** look haggard *or* emaciated.

ausmerzen ['ausmɛrtsən], *v.t.* destroy, wipe out, suppress, eliminate, cut out; expurgate.

ausmessen ['ausmɛsən], *irr.v.t.* measure out; take the dimensions of; survey; gauge.

ausmieten ['ausmi:tən], *v.t.* let out on hire.

ausmisten ['ausmɪstən], *v.t.* cast out the dung *or* remove the manure from, cleanse (*a stable*); (*fig.*) clean up (*as government*).

ausmittig ['ausmɪtɪç], *adj.* (*Tech.*) eccentric.

ausmöblieren ['ausmøbli:rən], *v.t.* fit up, furnish.

ausmünden ['ausmyndən], *v.i.* empty, discharge itself, flow, open (***in*** (*Acc.*), into).

ausmustern ['ausmustərn], *v.t.* discharge, reject (*soldiers*); discard, scrap. **Ausmusterung,** *f.* (*Mil.*) rejection (of) (*as unsuitable*); discharge, exemption (from).

Ausnahme ['ausna:mə], *f.* exception; ***ohne* –,** without exception, absolutely; ***mit – von,*** with the exception of, except. **Ausnahme|erscheinung,** *f.*, **–fall,** *m.* special *or* exceptional case, exception. **–zustand,** *m.* (*Pol.*) state of emergency *or* (*Mil.*) of martial law. **ausnahmslos,** *adj.* without exception, invariable, admitting of no exception. **ausnahmsweise,** *adv.* by way of exception, exceptionally, for once in a while *or* way.

ausnehmen ['ausne:mən], **1.** *irr.v.t.* 1. take out, remove (***aus,*** from); take (*bird's eggs*), rob (*a nest*); 2. disembowel, eviscerate; draw (*a fowl*), gut, clean (*fish*); (*fig. coll.*) clean (*s.o.*) out, fleece; 3. make an exception of. *See* **ausgenommen. 2.** *irr.v.r.* look, appear, cut a . . . figure; ***sich schlecht* –,** look bad, cut a poor figure. **ausnehmend, 1.** *adj.* exceptional, outstanding, extraordinary, uncommon, exceeding. **2.** *adv.* exceedingly (well).

ausnutzen ['ausnutsən], *v.t.* 1. use, utilize, make (good *or* the best) use of, make the most of, take advantage of, turn to (good) account, follow up (*a success*), exploit (*resources*); 2. take (unfair) advantage of, exploit (*a weakness*). **Ausnutzung,** *f.* utilization, exploitation.

ausnützen ['ausnytsən], *v.t. See* **ausnutzen,** 1.

auspacken ['auspakən], *v.t.* unpack; (*coll.*) ***gründlich* –,** have one's say, speak one's mind.

auspeitschen ['auspaɪtʃən], *v.t.* whip, flog.

auspfänden ['auspfɛndən], *v.t.* seize for debt, destrain upon.

auspfeifen ['auspfaɪfən], *irr.v.t.* hiss (*a play*) off the stage; hiss *or* boo (at) (*an actor*).

auspflanzen ['auspflantsən], *v.t.* plant out, bed out, transplant.

auspichen ['auspɪçən], *v.t.* coat with pitch. *See* **ausgepicht.**

Auspizien [aus'pi:tsiən], *n.pl.* auspices.

ausplappern ['ausplapərn], *v.t.* blurt *or* blab out.

ausplaudern ['ausplaudərn], **1.** *v.t.* let out, give away (*secrets etc.*), (*coll.*) blab out, let on about. **2.** *v.r.* have a good long chat.

ausplündern ['ausplyndərn], *v.t.* pillage, plunder (*country, town*), ransack, strip (*building*), (*coll.*) fleece, clean out (*a p.*). **Ausplünderung,** *f.* pillage, plunder.

auspolstern ['auspɔlstərn], *v.t.* pad (out), line; upholster; (*coll.*) (*of a p.*) ***gut ausgepolstert,*** well padded, chubby, podgy.

ausposaunen ['auspozaunən], *v.t.* trumpet forth, blazon forth *or* abroad, (*coll.*) proclaim from the

housetops, broadcast; ***seinen eignen Ruhm –,*** blow one's own trumpet.
ausprägen ['ausprɛ:gən], **1.** *v.t. usually only p.p.* ***ausgeprägt sein*** = **2.** *v.r.* be stamped *or* impressed *or* clearly marked (*in* (*Dat.*), on). *See* **ausgeprägt.**
auspressen ['ausprɛsən], *v.t.* press *or* squeeze (*liquid*) out (***aus,*** from *or* of), squeeze out (*sponge etc.*); (*coll.*) bleed, milk (*a people, a p.*).
ausprobieren ['ausprobi:rən], *v.t.* test, try out.
Auspuff ['auspuf], *m.* (*Engin.*) exhaust. **Auspuff|-kanal,** *m.* exhaust port. **–klappe,** *f.* exhaust valve. **–krümmer,** *m.* exhaust manifold. **–rohr,** *n.* exhaust-pipe. **–topf,** *m.* silencer.
auspumpen ['auspumpən], *v.t.* pump out; (*coll.*) pump, pump (*a secret*) out of (*a p.*); (*coll.*) ***ausgepumpt,*** dead beat, all in.
auspusten ['auspustən], *v.t.* blow out (*candle etc.*).
Ausputz ['ausputs], *m.* ornamentation, adornment, decoration; finish (*of shoes*). **ausputzen, 1.** *v.t.* 1. adorn, decorate; 2. cleanse, clean (out), tidy up; (*coll.*) polish up (*one's plate*); clear dead wood from (*trees*). **2.** *v.r.* deck o.s. out, dress up.
ausquartieren ['auskvarti:rən], **1.** *v.t.* billet out (*soldiers*), put (*s.o.*) up elsewhere. **2.** *v.r.* find another lodging.
ausradieren ['ausradi:rən], *v.t.* erase, rub out; (*coll.*) wipe out, raze to the ground.
ausrangieren ['ausrãʒi:rən], *v.t.* (*coll.*) discard, cast off, throw out (*useless th.*), sack (*employee*), give (*s.o.*) the boot.
ausräuchern ['ausrɔyçərn], *v.t.* fumigate (*a room*), smoke out (*a fox etc.*).
ausraufen ['ausraufən], *v.t.* pull *or* pluck *or* tear up; ***sich*** (*Dat.*) ***die Haare –,*** tear one's hair.
ausräumen ['ausrɔymən], *v.t.* clear (*contents*) out of (*room, cupboard*), clear *or* empty (*room, cupboard*) of (*contents*), clean out (*ditch etc.*), (*fig.*) clear away (*difficulties, misunderstanding*).
ausrechnen ['ausrɛçnən], *v.t.* reckon (up), work *or* figure out, calculate, compute; (*Math.*) evaluate (*expression*). *See* **ausgerechnet. Ausrechnung,** *f.* computation, calculation; (*Math.*) evaluation.
ausrecken ['ausrɛkən], **1.** *v.r.* stretch *or* reach out (***nach,*** for). **2.** *v.t.* ***sich*** (*Dat.*) ***den Hals –,*** crane one's neck (***nach,*** to see).
Ausrede ['ausre:də], *f.* excuse, pretext; evasion, subterfuge, pretence; ***faule –,*** poor *or* feeble *or* lame excuse; ***gerichtliche –,*** legal quibble.
ausreden ['ausre:dən], **1.** *v.i.* finish speaking, finish what one has to say; ***laß mich –,*** let me finish. **2.** *v.t.* ***ihm etwas –,*** dissuade him from doing a th., talk him out of s.th. **3.** *v.r.* excuse o.s., make excuses.
ausreichen ['ausraıçən], *v.i.* suffice, be enough *or* adequate *or* sufficient (***für,*** for), (*coll.*) do (for), run (to). **ausreichend,** *adj.* adequate, sufficient, enough, (*on school report*) fairly good.
ausreifen ['ausraıfən], *v.t.* ripen, mature. *See* **ausgereift.**
Ausreise ['ausraızə], *f.* outward journey, departure. **Ausreisegenehmigung,** *f.* exit permit. **ausreisen,** *v.i.* (*aux.* s.) – ***aus,*** leave (*a country*).
ausreißen ['ausraısən], **1.** *irr.v.t.* pluck *or* tear *or* pull out; pull up; (*fig.*) ***er reißt sich kein Bein dabei aus,*** he does not strain himself over the job. **2.** *irr. v.i.* (*aux.* s.) 1. run off *or* away, decamp, abscond; bolt; (*Mil.*) desert; (*Spt.*) run away from the field; 2. split, pull away *or* apart. **Ausreißer,** *m.* 1. deserter; runaway; fugitive; 2. stray shot, wide (*in shooting*).
ausreiten ['ausraıtən], **1.** *irr.v.i.* (*aux.* s.) take a ride, go for a ride; ride out (***aus,*** of *or* from) (*as cavalry*). **2.** *irr.v.t.* take (*a horse*) out, ride (*a horse*) full out.
ausrenken ['ausrɛŋkən], *v.t.* dislocate, sprain. **Ausrenkung,** *f.* dislocation, sprain.
ausreuten ['ausrɔytən], *v.t. See* **ausrotten.**
ausrichten ['ausrıçtən], *v.t.* 1. straighten, align, bring into line *or* alignment (***nach,*** with), adjust (to); centre, true up (*work on a machine*); (*Mil.*) dress (*ranks*); 2. do, accomplish, get done; ***nichts –,*** have no success, fail to get *or* not manage to get anything done; ***damit ist nichts ausgerichtet,*** that is no use *or* good, (*coll.*) that's not getting us anywhere, that's getting us nowhere; ***eine Botschaft –,*** pass on *or* give *or* convey a message (*Dat.*, to); ***richten Sie ihm meinen Gruß aus,*** give him my kind regards, present my compliments to him. **Ausrichtung,** *f.* adjustment, alignment.
[1]**ausringen** ['ausrıŋən], *irr.v.t.* wring out (*washing etc.*).
[2]**ausringen,** *irr.v.i.* finish struggling; ***er hat ausgerungen,*** his struggles are over.
Ausritt ['ausrıt], *m.* ride, excursion on horseback; departure (*on horseback*).
ausroden ['ausro:dən], *v.t.* root *or* grub up, uproot, tear up by the roots.
ausrollen ['ausrɔlən], **1.** *v.t.* roll out (*dough*); unroll; run *or* pay out (*cable*). **2.** *v.i.* roll *or* (*Av.*) taxi to a standstill. **Ausroll|grenze,** *f.* plastic limit. **–strecke,** *f.* (*Av.*) landing run.
ausrotten ['ausrɔtən], *v.t.* 1. exterminate, extirpate, destroy, (*coll.*) wipe out; (*fig.*) eradicate, stamp out; 2. (*obs.*) *See* **ausroden. Ausrottung,** *f.* destruction, extermination, extirpation; eradication.
ausrücken ['ausrykən], **1.** *v.i.* (*aux.* s.) march out (*of troops*), set out; (*coll.*) make off, abscond, decamp. **2.** *v.t.* disconnect, release, disengage, uncouple.
Ausruf ['ausru:f], *m.* 1. cry, shout, exclamation; ejaculation; 2. proclamation. **ausrufen, 1.** *irr.v.t.* call out (*names etc.*), (*in hotel*) page (*a p.*); proclaim; call (*a strike*); cry (*one's wares*). **2.** *irr.v.i.* cry out, call out, ejaculate, exclaim. **Ausrufer,** *m.* town-crier, herald. **Ausrufewort,** *n.* (*Gram.*) interjection. **Ausrufung,** *f.* proclamation. **Ausrufungszeichen,** *n.* exclamation mark.
ausruhen ['ausru:ən], **1.** *v.i., v.r.* rest (o.s.), take a rest. **2.** *v.t.* rest (*one's eyes etc.*); ***ausgeruht sein,*** be rested.
ausrupfen ['ausrupfən], *v.t.* pluck *or* pull out.
ausrüsten ['ausrystən], *v.t.* 1. arm, equip, provide, furnish, fit out; 2. stiffen, finish, dress (*fabrics*). **Ausrüstung,** *f.* 1. equipment, outfit, (*Mil.*) accoutrements; (*coll.*) fittings, gear, tackle; (*Mil.*) ***in feldmarchmäßiger –,*** in full marching order; 2. stiffening, dressing, finish (*of fabrics*). **Ausrüstungsgegenstand,** *m.* piece *or* (*Mil.*) article of equipment.
ausrutschen ['ausrutʃən], *v.i.* (*aux.* s.) slip, lose one's footing, skid; (*coll.*) make a bloomer, drop a brick.
Aussaat ['ausza:t], *f.* 1. sowing; dissemination of seed; ***die Zeit der –,*** seed-time; 2. (*Med.*) metastasis.
aussäen ['auszɛ:ən], *v.t.* sow (*seed*); (*fig.*) spread, disseminate.
aussagbar ['ausza:kba:r], *adj.* (*Log.*) predicable.
Aussage ['ausza:gə], *f.* 1. declaration, assertion, statement; deposition, testimony; ***eine gerichtliche – machen,*** give evidence, make a deposition; ***eidliche –,*** deposition on oath; ***seine – beweisen,*** prove one's statement; ***nach aller –,*** by all accounts; ***auf seine – hin,*** from what he says, on his own showing; 2. (*Gram.*) predicate; (*Log., Geom.*) proposition. **aussagen, 1.** *v.t.* state, express, declare, (*Law*) say in evidence, give evidence, testify, assert, affirm. **2.** *v.i.* make a statement (*also Law*). **Aussage|satz,** *m.* affirmative proposition. **–weise,** *f.* (*Gram.*) mood.
Aussatz ['auszats], *m.* (**-es,** *no pl.*) 1. leprosy; scab, mange, itch (*in sheep*); tetter (*in horses*); 2. (*Bill.*) lead.
aussätzig ['auszɛtsıç], *adj.* leprous. **Aussätzige(r),** *m., f.* leper.
aussaugen ['auszaugən], *reg.v.t.* suck out (***aus,*** of *or* from), suck dry; (*usu. reg.*) exhaust, impoverish (*land*); (*coll.*) bleed, milk. **Aussauger,** *m.* (*coll.*) blood-sucker, leech, extortioner.

ausschaben ['ausʃa:bən], *v.t.* scrape out; (*Med.*) curette.

ausschachten ['ausʃaxtən], *v.t.* excavate, dig (*foundations*), dig *or* throw out (*earth*). **Ausschachtung,** *f.* excavation work.

ausschalten ['ausʃaltən], *v.t.* 1. (*Elec.*) switch off (*current*), cut out, disconnect (*part of circuit*); 2. (*fig.*) exclude, eliminate, dismiss, set aside, rule out (*possibility etc.*). **Ausschalter,** *m.* cut-out (switch), circuit-breaker.

Ausschank ['ausʃaŋk], *m.* 1. sale of alcohol (*Am.* liquor); 2. bar, counter (*where liquor is served*); 3. tavern.

ausscharren ['ausʃarən], *v.t.* rake *or* scratch up.

Ausschau ['ausʃau], *f.* (*only in the phrase*) – ***halten*** (***nach***), look out *or* watch (for), be on the *or* keep a look-out (for). **ausschauen,** *v.i.* 1. be on the look-out *or* watch, keep a look-out *or* watch, watch, look out (***nach***, for); ***weit ausschauend,*** far-sighted; 2. look, seem; ***traurig*** –, look sad.

ausscheiden ['ausʃaɪdən], **1.** *irr.v.t.* exclude, eliminate; (*Med.*) excrete, expel, exude, extrude; (*Chem.*) deposit, precipitate. **2.** *irr.v.r.* be excreted *or* expelled *or* eliminated. **3.** *irr.v.i.* (*aux.* s.) 1. retire, resign (***aus***, from) (*employment*), withdraw, secede (from) (*a group*); 2. (*fig.*) be ruled out, be left out of consideration, not be considered, be out of the question. **Ausscheidung,** *f.* 1. exclusion, elimination; 2. expulsion, extrusion, exudation, excretion; excrement, *pl.* excreta; 3. (*Chem.*) deposition, precipitation. **Ausscheidungs|-kampf,** *m.* (*Spt.*) eliminating bout *or* round, heat. **–organ,** *n.* (*Anat.*) excretory organ. **–runde,** *f.*, **–spiel,** *n.* *See* **–kampf.**

ausschelten ['ausʃɛltən], *irr.v.t.* reprimand, scold, rebuke (***wegen***, for).

ausschenken ['ausʃɛŋkən], *v.t.* 1. pour out; help (*Dat.*, *a p.*) to (*wine etc.*); 2. sell, retail (*liquor*). *See* **Ausschank.**

ausscheuern ['ausʃɔyərn], *v.t.* scour out, scrub out.

ausschicken ['ausʃɪkən], *v.t.* send out; send on an errand; dispatch.

ausschießen ['ausʃi:sən], **1.** *irr.v.t.* 1. shoot out; shoot for (*a prize*); ***ein Revier*** –, shoot all the game in a preserve; 2. wear, score (*a gun*); 3. cast *or* throw out, discard, reject, scrap (*inferior goods*); 4. discharge (*ballast etc.*). **2.** *irr.v.i.* (*aux.* s.) veer (*of wind*).

ausschiffen ['ausʃɪfən], **1.** *v.t.* put ashore, disembark, land (*passengers*), discharge, unload (*cargo*), (*coll.*) get rid of (*official etc.*). **2.** *v.i.* (*aux.* s.) (set) sail, put to sea. **Ausschiffung,** *f.* disembarkation.

ausschimpfen ['ausʃɪmpfən], *v.t.* give (*s.o.*) a good telling-off *or* ticking-off, tell *or* tick (*s.o.*) off, (*Am.*) bawl (*s.o.*) out.

ausschirren ['ausʃɪrən], *v.t.* unharness (*horse*), unyoke (*oxen*).

ausschlachten ['ausʃlaxtən], *v.t.* 1. cut up, dismember (*a carcass*); cannibalize (*a vehicle etc.*); 2. utilize, exploit; turn to account *or* advantage, make (full) use of; capitalize on, make capital out of. **Ausschlachter,** *m.* ship-breaker.

ausschlafen ['ausʃla:fən], **1.** *irr.v.i.*, *v.r.* sleep one's fill; have one's sleep out, (*coll.*) have a good lie in. **2.** *irr.v.t.* sleep off (*effects of drink etc.*); (*coll.*) ***seinen Rausch*** –, sleep it off; ***guten Morgen! Ausgeschlafen?*** Good morning! Did you sleep well?

Ausschlag ['ausʃla:k], *m.* 1. deflection; oscillation (*of pendulum*); (*fig.*) ***den – geben,*** tip *or* turn the scale *or* balance; be decisive, decide, settle, clinch; ***dies gab den –,*** this settled matters; ***die Stimme, die den – gibt,*** the casting vote; 2. (*Med.*) rash, eruption, (*coll.*) spots.

ausschlagen ['ausʃla:gən], **1.** *irr.v.t.* 1. knock out (*a tooth etc.*); stamp *or* punch out (*holes in material*); 2. line (*drawer or cupboard*), trim, face (*with fur etc.*); 3. refuse, decline, reject (*an offer*), renounce, relinquish, (*coll.*) give up (*an inheritance*); dismiss (*an idea*). **2.** *irr.v.i.* 1. kick *or* lash out (*as horses*); hit *or* lash out (*of a p.*); ***mit den Füßen –,*** kick; 2. (*aux.* s.) be deflected (*of pendulum, pointer etc.*); 3. (*aux.* s. & h.) sprout, bud, burgeon (*of plants*); 4. (*aux.* s.) turn out (***zu***, to); ***die S. schlägt gut aus,*** things will turn out all right. **ausschlaggebend,** *adj.* decisive, of prime importance; casting (*vote*).

Ausschlag|maschine, *f.* punching-machine. **–winkel,** *m.* angle of deflection.

ausschleifen ['ausʃlaɪfən], *irr.v.t.* grind (hollow), whet.

Ausschleudermaschine ['ausʃlɔydərmaʃi:nə], *f.* centrifuge. **ausschleudern,** *v.t.* fling *or* hurl out, vomit forth, eject.

ausschlichten ['ausʃlɪçtən], *v.t.* planish (*Metal*). **Ausschlichthammer,** *m.* planishing hammer.

ausschließen ['ausʃli:sən], *irr.v.t.* shut *or* lock out; exclude (***aus***, from), not admit, refuse admittance (to), debar (from); expel, dismiss, disqualify (from); (*fig.*) exclude, except, eliminate, preclude, rule out, make impossible. *See* **ausgeschlossen. ausschließlich, 1.** *adj.* exclusive. **2.** *prep.* (*Gen.*) exclusive of. **Ausschließlichkeit,** *f.* 1. exclusiveness; 2. exclusive interest, complete *or* utter dedication. **Ausschließung,** *f.* exclusion; expulsion.

ausschlüpfen ['ausʃlypfən], *v.i.* (*aux.* s.) slip *or* creep out; emerge, hatch out.

Ausschluß ['ausʃlus], *m.* exclusion, elimination; expulsion, dismissal, disqualification; ***mit – eines einzigen,*** with a single exception; ***unter – der Öffentlichkeit,*** behind closed doors, in camera.

ausschmälen ['ausʃmɛ:lən], *v.t.* rebuke, scold, chide, give (*s.o.*) a good scolding *or* dressing-down.

ausschmelzen ['ausʃmɛltsən], **1.** *v.t.* 1. extract by melting (***aus***, from), render (*fats*); 2. fuse (*metal etc.*). **2.** *irr.v.i.* (*aux.* s.) melt, be melted out (***aus***, from).

ausschmücken ['ausʃmykən], *v.t.* adorn, embellish, decorate, (*coll.*) deck out. **Ausschmückung,** *f.* adornment, embellishment, decoration, ornamentation.

ausschneiden ['ausʃnaɪdən], *irr.v.t.* cut out; excise; prune; ***tief –,*** cut (*a dress*) low; ***tief ausgeschnitten,*** low-cut, décolleté, low-necked (*dress*).

Ausschnitt ['ausʃnɪt], *m.* 1. piece cut out; (*Geom.*) sector; cutting (*from a newspaper*), extract, excerpt (*from a work*), detail (*from an illustration*), (*fig.*) facet, side (*of life etc.*); ***im – verkaufen,*** sell (*cloth*) retail *or* by the yard; 2. neck (*of dress*); ***spitzer –,*** V-neck. **Ausschnittarbeit,** *f.* fretwork.

ausschnüffeln ['ausʃnyfəln], *v.t.* (*coll.*) nose out (*secret etc.*).

ausschöpfen ['ausʃœpfən], *v.t.* 1. scoop *or* ladle *or* bail (*or less good* bale) out; empty, drain off; 2. (*fig.*) deal completely with, exhaust (*possibilities etc.*). **Ausschöpfkelle,** *f.* ladle, scoop, bailer (*or* baler).

ausschreiben ['ausʃraɪbən], **1.** *irr.v.t.* 1. write *or* make out (*cheque, bill*); write out (in full), finish (writing) (*a letter etc.*); finish, fill (*exercise book*); 2. write out, copy (out), plagiarize; 3. publish, announce, proclaim, advertise (*a vacant post*); invite (*tenders*); 4. ***ausgeschriebene Hand,*** fully developed handwriting. **2.** *irr.v.r.* exhaust one's powers as a writer; ***er hat sich ausgeschrieben,*** he has written himself out, he has nothing new to write about. **Ausschreibung,** *f.* announcement, advertisement, (*Comm.*) invitation of tenders.

ausschreien ['ausʃraɪən], *irr.v.t.* shout out; cry (*wares*); proclaim; ***sich*** (*Dat.*) ***die Lunge –,*** shout *or* scream one's head off.

ausschreiten ['ausʃraɪtən], **1.** *irr.v.t.* pace *or* step out (*a distance*), traverse. **2.** *irr.v.i.* (*aux.* s.) 1. go too far, commit excesses *or* outrages; 2. step out, (*coll.*) put one's best foot forward; get a move on; ***tüchtig –,*** take long strides. **Ausschreitung,** *f.* offence, outrage, excess.

Ausschuß ['ausʃus], *m.* 1. dross, refuse, rubbish, trash; damaged *or* sub-standard goods, spoilage, rejects, (*coll.*) throw-outs; ***– des Pöbels,*** the lowest rabble; 2. committee, board, panel, commission, (*Comm.*) board of directors; ***die größeren und***

engeren Ausschüsse, general committees and sub-committees; ***geschäftsleitender –,*** executive committee, board of management; ***allgemeiner –,*** general council; 3. exit wound (*of bullet*). **Ausschuß|korn,** *n.* tailings, tail-corn. **–papier,** *n.* retree, casse paper. **–ware,** *f.* sub-standard *or* defective goods, reject; rubbish, trash.

ausschütteln ['ausʃytəln], *v.t.* shake out.

ausschütten ['ausʃytən], **1.** *v.t.* 1. pour *or* empty (*water*) out (***aus,*** of), pour *or* empty out (*water*) (***aus,*** from); empty (out) (*a bucket*); spill (*water*) (***aus,*** out of); ***ihm sein Herz –,*** unburden *or* unbosom o.s., *or* pour out *or* open one's heart to him; ***das Kind mit dem Bade –,*** throw the baby out with the bathwater; 2. (*Comm.*) distribute (*dividends etc.*). **2.** *v.r.* ***sich vor Lachen –,*** be convulsed with *or* split one's sides with laughter. **Ausschüttung,** *f.* distribution (*of dividends*).

ausschwärmen ['ausʃvɛrmən], *v.i.* 1. (*aux.* s.) swarm (*as bees*); 2. (*Mil.*) proceed in extended line, deploy.

ausschweben ['ausʃve:bən], *v.i.* (*Av.*) flatten out.

ausschwefeln ['ausʃve:fəln], *v.t.* fumigate with sulphur.

ausschweifen ['ausʃvaɪfən], **1.** *v.t.* scallop, indent. **2.** *v.i.* (*aux. s. & h.*) 1. be prolix, digress; wander; 2. indulge in excess; lead a dissolute life. **ausschweifend,** *adj.* extravagant, unbridled, loose, debauched, dissolute, licentious. **Ausschweifung,** *f.* 1. excess, intemperance, debauchery, loose living; 2. digression (*in speech*), aberration (*of mind*).

ausschweigen ['ausʃvaɪgən], *irr.v.r.* (*coll.*) remain completely silent, not say a word.

ausschwemmen ['ausʃvɛmən], *v.t.* wash *or* rinse *or* flush *or* sluice out.

ausschwenken ['ausʃvɛŋkən], **1.** *v.t.* 1. rinse (out), wash *or* swill out (*a glass etc.*); 2. extract (*moisture*) with a spin-drier; 3. swivel *or* turn (outwards). **2.** *v.i.* (*aux.* s.) swivel, turn *or* be turned (outwards). **Ausschwenkmaschine,** *f.* centrifuge, hydro-extractor, spin-drier.

ausschwitzen ['ausʃvɪtsən], **1.** *v.t.* exude; sweat out. **2.** *v.i.* 1. (*aux.* s.) perspire; exude, ooze; 2. (*aux.* h.) stop perspiring. **Ausschwitzung,** *f.* exudation.

aussegnen ['ausze:gnən], *v.t.* bless, give benediction *or* absolution to (*at obsequies and churching of women*); ***ausgesegnet werden,*** be churched.

aussehen ['ausze:ən], *irr.v.i.* 1. look; ***gut –,*** be good-looking; 2. look well *or* healthy; ***wie sieht er aus?*** what does he look like? how does he look? ***wie sieht es bei*** or ***mit deinem Bruder aus?*** how is your brother (doing)? how are things with your brother? ***– wie, – als wenn, – als ob,*** look like, seem; ***es sieht aus, als ob es regnen wollte*** or ***es sieht nach Regen aus,*** it looks like rain; 3. ***– nach,*** be on the watch *or* look-out for, keep a look-out for, look *or* watch out for. **Aussehen,** *n.* appearance, look(s), air, exterior; ***nach dem – beurteilen,*** judge by appearances; ***er hat ganz das – danach,*** he quite looks it. **–aussehend,** *adj. suff.* -looking.

ausseigern ['auszaɪgərn], *v.t.* (*Metall.*) liquate.

außen ['ausən], *adj., adv.* outside; ***innen und –,*** inside and out(side); ***nach – aufgehen,*** open outwards; ***nach – hin,*** externally, outwardly; ***von –*** (***her***), from without, from the outside.

außen–, Außen–, *pref.* outer, external, outside; outdoor; foreign. **Außen|amt,** *n.* (*Austr.*) Foreign Office. **–aufnahme,** *f.* outdoor photograph, exterior. **–backenbremse,** *f.* external contraction brake. **–bezirk,** *m.* outlying suburb. **–bordmotor,** *m.* outboard motor. **außenbürtig,** *adj.* (*Geol.*) exogenous.

aussenden ['auszɛndən], *irr.v.t.* send out, dispatch (*messenger*), send out, issue (*order*), send out, emit, radiate (*rays*).

Außen|dienst, *m.* out-door work, outside duty (*i.e. outside the office or barracks*). **–front,** *f.* (*Archit.*) façade. **–gewinde,** *n.* male thread (*of screw*). **–handel,** *m.* foreign trade. **–haut,** *f.* (*Anat.*) epidermis; outer skin (*of fruit etc.*); skin, fabric (*of aeroplane etc.*); hull, shell (*of ship*).

aussenken ['auszɛŋkən], *v.t.* countersink, counterbore (*a hole*). **Aussenkung,** *f.* countersunk hole.

Außen|läufer, *m.* (*Footb.*) wing-half. **–linie,** *f.* (*Footb.*) touch-line. **–maße,** *pl.* external measurements. **–minister,** *m.* Secretary of State for Foreign Affairs. **–politik,** *f.* foreign policy. **–posten,** *m.* (*Mil.*) outpost. **–seite,** *f.* outside, exterior, surface, superficies. **–seiter,** *m.* outsider. **–stände,** *pl.* outstanding claims, liabilities. **–stehende(r),** *m., f.* outsider, non-participant, bystander, onlooker. **–stürmer,** *m.* (*Footb.*) wing-forward. **–taster,** *m.* outside callipers. **–welt,** *f.* world outside, outside world, environment. **–winkel,** *m.* external angle.

außer ['ausər], **1.** *prep.* **(a)** (*with Dat.*) 1. out of, outside; ***– Atem,*** out of breath; ***– Gefahr,*** out of danger; ***–*** (***dem***) ***Hause,*** out, not at home; ***– der Reihe,*** out of turn; 2. except, with the exception of, but, apart (*Am.* aside) from, besides, in addition to; ***überall – da wo,*** everywhere except *or* but where; **(b)** (*with Gen.*) *only in*: ***– Landes,*** abroad; **(c)** (*with Acc.*) ***– Betrieb setzen,*** put out of action (*machinery*); ***– Gefecht setzen,*** put out of action (*gun*); ***– den Schutz des Gesetzes stellen,*** place beyond the pale of the law. **2.** *conj.* ***– daß,*** except *or* save that; ***– wenn,*** except *or* save when, unless.

außer–, Außer–, *pref.* extra-.

äußer ['ɔysər], *attrib. adj.* outer, exterior, external, outside, outward; ***–e Bedeckung,*** outer covering; ***–e Einflüsse,*** outside influences; ***–e Erscheinung,*** exterior, appearance; ***–er Schein,*** (outward *or* external) appearance, externals; ***–e Umstände,*** outward circumstances; ***–e Verletzung,*** external injury; ***–er Winkel,*** exterior angle.

außeramtlich, *adj.* non-official, private.

außerdem ['ausərde:m], *adv.* besides, in addition, as well, into the bargain; moreover, furthermore, over and above; ***nichts –,*** nothing else *or* more.

außer|dienstlich, **1.** *adj.* unofficial, private. **2.** *adv.* (*coll.*) off the record. **–ehelich,** *adj.* extra-marital, illegitimate (*child*).

Äußere(s), ['ɔysərə(s)], *n.* outward appearance; externals, looks (*of a p.*); outside, exterior (*of a th.*); ***Minister des Äußeren,*** Minister of Foreign Affairs.

außer|etatmäßig, *adj.* extra-budgetary. **–fahrplanmäßig,** *adj.* unscheduled, extra, special (*train*). **–gerichtlich,** *adj., adv.* out of court. **–gesetzlich,** *adj.* outside the law. **–gewöhnlich,** *adj.* unusual, exceptional, remarkable, extraordinary.

außerhalb ['ausərhalp], **1.** *prep.* (*Gen.*) outside, beyond; (*Geom.*) exterior to. **2.** *adv.* outside (the town).

äußerlich ['ɔysərlɪç], **1.** *adj.* 1. external, outward; 2. superficial. **2.** *adv.* externally, outwardly, on the outside. **Äußerlichkeit,** *f.* 1. superficiality; matter of form, formality; 2. *pl.* externals, (outward) appearances.

außermittig ['ausərmɪtɪç], *adj.* (*Mech.*) eccentric.

äußern ['ɔysərn], **1.** *v.t.* 1. utter, express, give voice to; advance (*an opinion etc.*); 2. manifest. **2.** *v.r.* 1. express one's opinion *or* views (***über*** (*Acc.*), ***zu,*** about *or* on); 2. be shown *or* expressed (***in*** (*Dat.*), in), be *or* become apparent (in), find expression (in), make itself felt (in), be manifested *or* betrayed (in), manifest itself (in).

außer|ordentlich, *adj.* extraordinary, out of the ordinary, unusual, uncommon, exceptional; ***–er Professor,*** (*approx.*) university reader, (*Am.*) associate professor. **–planmäßig,** *adj.* unscheduled (*stop etc.*); supernumerary (*official, post*); extraordinary, extra-budgetary (*expenditure*).

äußerst ['ɔysərst], **1.** *attrib. adj.* farthest, furthermost, uttermost, utmost; extreme (maximum, minimum, latest possible *etc.*); ***die –e Belastung,*** the maximum load; ***der –e Preis,*** the maximum (*or* minimum) price; ***der –e Termin,*** the latest (possible) date; ***von –er Wichtigkeit,*** of extreme *or* utmost importance; ***im –en Fall,*** if the worse comes (*or* came *etc.*) to the worst. **2.** *adv.* extremely, exceedingly, immensely; ***aufs -e,*** extremely, exceedingly, excessively.

außerstand(e) ['ausərʃtant (-ʃtandə)], *adj.* – *sein,* be unable, not be in a position (*to do*); ***ihn – setzen,*** make it impossible for him (*to do*).

Äußerste ['ɔysərstə], *n.* (**-n**, *pl.* **-n**) the (extreme) limit, maximum; the last extremity; ***aufs – gefaßt sein,*** be prepared for the worst; ***bis zum -n gehen,*** go to the last extreme. **äußerstenfalls,** *adv.* if it *or* the worst comes to the worst, at the outside.

Äußerung ['ɔysəruŋ], *f.* 1. expression, manifestation; 2. utterance, remark, observation, saying.

aussetzen ['auszɛtsən], **1.** *v.t.* 1. expose (*Dat.*, to); plant out (*trees etc.*); launch (*a boat*); offer (*a prize*); abandon (*a new-born child*); maroon (*a sailor*); 2. suspend (*proceedings, payment etc.*); 3. ***etwas – an*** (*Dat.*), find fault with, object *or* make an objection to, take exception to; ***nichts daran auszusetzen haben,*** have no fault to find with it *or* no objection to make to it, find nothing in it to take exception to. **2.** *v.i.* be suspended, stop, fail; ***mit etwas –,*** interrupt *or* suspend s.th.; ***der Puls setzt häufig aus,*** the pulse is very irregular. **Aussetzung,** *f.* 1. settlement (*of a pension etc.*); abandonment, exposure (*of a child etc.*); exposition (*of goods*); 2. exception, objection; 3. interruption, intermission, suspension.

Aussicht ['auszɪçt], *f.* 1. view, outlook, prospect; ***das Haus hat eine – auf den Fluß,*** the house looks over the river; 2. expectation; likelihood; chance, prospect, outlook; ***ihm etwas in – stellen,*** hold out a prospect of s.th. to him; ***wir haben dies nicht in – genommen,*** we do not propose to do this, we do not contemplate doing this; ***er hat -(en) auf eine gute Stelle,*** he has a prospect *or* hopes of a good appointment; ***weitere -en,*** further outlook (*weather report*). **Aussichts|aufnahme,** *f.* (*Phot.*) distance *or* vista shot. **aussichtslos,** *adj.* hopeless, without prospects. **Aussichtslosigkeit,** *f.* absence of prospects, hopelessness. **Aussichtspunkt,** *m.* observation post; vantage point, view-point. **aussichts|-reich,** *adj.* *See* **-voll. Aussichtsturm,** *m.* observation tower, gazebo, belvedere. **aussichts-voll,** *adj.* offering good prospects, hopeful, promising, full of promise. **Aussichtswagen,** *m.* (*Railw.*) observation-car.

aussickern ['auszɪkərn], *v.i.* (*aux.* s.) trickle *or* seep *or* ooze (out).

aussiedeln ['auszi:dəln], *v.t.* evacuate (*population*). **Aussiedler,** *m.* evacuee. **Aussiedlung,** *f.* evacuation.

aussinnen ['auszɪnən], *irr.v.t.* contrive, devise (*plan*), think *or* work out carefully, plan (in detail).

aussöhnen ['auszø:nən], **1.** *v.t.* reconcile. **2.** *v.r.* ***sich mit ihm –,*** make one's peace *or* make it up with him, become reconciled. **Aussöhnung,** *f.* reconciliation.

aussondern ['auszɔndərn], *v.t.* 1. select; pick *or* single out, set aside *or* apart; 2. (*Physiol.*) eliminate, excrete. **Aussonderung,** *f.* 1. selection; 2. excretion.

aussortieren ['auszɔrti:rən], *v.t.* sort out.

ausspähen ['ausʃpɛ:ən], **1.** *v.t.* spy out. **2.** *v.i.* watch, keep a look-out (***nach,*** for).

Ausspann ['ausʃpan], *m.* (**-(e)s,** *pl.* **-e**) coaching inn, stage. **ausspannen, 1.** *v.t.* 1. spread *or* stretch out; 2. unharness, unyoke. **2.** *v.i.* relax, (*coll.*) take it easy. **Ausspannung,** *f.* relaxation, rest.

aussparen ['ausʃpa:rən], *v.t.* reserve, allow, leave (*a space*); (*Paint.*) leave uncoloured, reserve in the ground colour; (*Mil., Av.*) leave (*area*) unbombarded, unbombed *etc.*; (*Build.*) recess. **Aussparung,** *f.* recess.

ausspeien ['ausʃpaɪən], *irr.v.t.* spit *or* spew out; belch *or* vomit forth (*as volcano*).

aussperren ['ausʃpɛrən], *v.t.* shut out, bar (*a p.'s*) entry; lock out (*workmen*). **Aussperrung,** *f.* lock-out (*from work*).

ausspielen ['ausʃpi:lən], **1.** *v.t.* 1. play out; play to the end; (*coll.*) ***er hat seine Rolle ausgespielt,*** he's finished *or* done for; 2. play (*a card*); ***einen gegen den andern –,*** play off one p. against another; 3. raffle (*goods*). **2.** *v.i.* (*Cards*) 1. lead; 2. finish playing; (*coll.*) ***er hat ausgespielt,*** he's finished *or* done for. **Ausspielung,** *f.* raffle, lottery.

ausspinnen ['ausʃpɪnən], *irr.v.t.* spin out; prolong, elaborate, develop, enlarge upon (*a train of thought*).

Aussprache ['ausʃpra:xə], *f.* 1. pronunciation, articulation, enunciation, accent; ***falsche –,*** mispronunciation; 2. talk, conversation, discussion, exchange of views; ***öffentliche –,*** public discussion *or* debate. **Aussprache|bezeichnung,** *f.* phonetic representation. **-wörterbuch,** *n.* pronouncing dictionary.

aussprechbar ['ausʃprɛçba:r], *adj.* pronounceable.

aussprechen ['ausʃprɛçən], **1.** *irr.v.t.* 1. pronounce, articulate, enunciate (*words, sounds*); 2. utter, express, declare, state (*views*); 3. pronounce, pass (*sentence*) (***über*** (*Acc.*), on). **2.** *irr.v.r.* 1. (*of a p.*) speak one's mind, give *or* express one's opinion *or* views (***über*** (*Acc.*), about), declare o.s., speak (*for or against*); 2. (*of feelings etc.*) be expressed (*upon one's face*). *See* **ausgesprochen. 3.** *irr.v.i.* finish speaking; ***laß mich –!*** let me finish (what I have to say), hear me out.

ausspreizen ['ausʃpraɪtsən], *v.t.* extend, spread (out), stretch apart; ***mit ausgespreizten Armen,*** with arms akimbo; ***mit ausgespreizten Beinen,*** with straddling *or* widespread legs.

aussprengen ['ausʃprɛŋən], *v.t.* 1. spread (*a report or rumour*); 2. remove by blasting.

ausspringen ['ausʃprɪŋən], *irr.v.i.* (*aux.* s.) 1. jump *or* spring out of place, become dislodged, fly off; ***-de Winkel,*** salient angles; 2. (*of a p.*) turn renegade, withdraw (***aus,*** from).

ausspritzen ['ausʃprɪtsən], *v.t.* squirt *or* put out (*fire with a hose*); (*Med.*) syringe (*ear etc.*), eject (*secretion*). **Ausspritzung,** *f.* (*Anat.*) ejaculation.

Ausspruch ['ausʃprux], *m.* declaration, pronouncement, statement, utterance, saying, remark, dictum, maxim, (*Law*) decision, finding, verdict.

aussprühen ['ausʃpry:ən], *v.t.* emit (*sparks*), belch (out *or* forth) (*flames, smoke etc.*), eject, throw up.

ausspucken ['ausʃpukən], *v.t.* spit out; bring up (*food*); (*coll.*) cough up (*money*); give vent to (*anger*).

ausspülen ['ausʃpy:lən], *v.t.* rinse *or* wash out, flush (out) (*drain*); wash away, erode (*river bank*).

ausspüren ['ausʃpy:rən], *v.t.* track down (*game*).

ausstaffieren ['ausʃtafi:rən], *v.t.* equip, fit out, furnish *or* provide (with clothes). **Ausstaffierung,** *f.* outfit, set of clothes.

Ausstand ['ausʃtant], *m.* 1. strike; ***in den – treten,*** strike, go on *or* come out on strike (*of workers*); 2. *pl.* *See* **Außenstände**; 3. delay, extension (*for payment*).

ausständig ['ausʃtɛndɪç], *adj.* 1. on strike; 2. outstanding, in arrears.

ausstanzen ['ausʃtantsən], *v.t.* stamp *or* punch out (*material*).

ausstatten ['ausʃtatən], *v.t.* 1. provide, furnish, equip, fit out, endow, (*coll.*) set up; set up, establish (*son*) (*in business etc.*), give (*daughter*) her dowry; vest (*with authority etc.*); 2. produce, get up (*book etc.*). **Ausstattung,** *f.* 1. equipment, appointments, furnishings, fixtures and fittings (*of a building*), (*Theat.*) decor and costumes; outfit, kit, equipment (*of a p.*); dowry, marriage portion; (bride's) trousseau; provision made to set (*son*) up in life; 2. get-up (*of a book etc.*). **Ausstattungs-stück,** *n.* 1. piece of equipment; 2. (*Theat.*) spectacular (revue).

ausstauben ['ausʃtaubən], *v.t.* dust out (*drawer etc.*), wipe *or* brush *or* sweep the dust out of.

ausstäupen ['ausʃtɔypən], *v.t.* (*obs.*) flog soundly.

ausstechen ['ausʃtɛçən], *irr.v.t.* 1. dig, cut (*peat etc.*), core (*apples*), put out (*the eyes*), open (*oysters*); cut out (*pastry etc.*), prick out (*a pattern*); 2. (*coll.*) crack (*a bottle of wine with s.o.*); 3. (*Naut.*) let out (*a reef*); 4. (*fig.*) supplant, put in the shade, outshine; ***er will mich bei meinem Mädchen –,*** he's trying to cut me out with my girl. **Ausstecher,** *m.* 1. pastry-cutter; 2. apple-corer.

ausstecken ['ausʃtɛkən], *v.t.* put out, display (*a flag etc.*), pay out (*rope*), stake *or* mark out (*with pegs*); (*Austr.*) hang out (*vintner's sign*); ***ausgesteckt,*** new wine on tap (*vintner's notice*).

ausstehen ['ausʃte:ən], **1.** *irr.v.i.* 1. be outstanding *or* overdue (*of payment*), be owing (*of money*); not be forthcoming, be yet to come; ***–des Gehalt,*** arrears of salary; ***die Antwort steht noch aus,*** we are still waiting for the answer; ***die Entscheidung steht noch aus,*** no decision has been reached yet; 2. strike, come out on *or* go on strike (*of workers*). **2.** *irr.v.t.* endure, undergo, suffer, bear (*pain etc.*), come through (*danger*), (*coll.*) go through; tolerate, endure, abide (*also a p.*), (*coll.*) put up with, stand, stick (*a p., s.th. unpleasant*).

aussteigen ['ausʃtaɪgən], *irr.v.i.* (*aux.* s.) get out *or* off, alight (*from a carriage*); disembark (*from a ship*); (*Av.*) (*sl.*) bale out.

aussteinen ['ausʃtaɪnən], *v.t.* stone (*plums etc.*).

ausstellen ['ausʃtɛlən], *v.t.* exhibit, display, show (*paintings, goods*), lay (*a trap*), lay out (*a corpse in state*); post (*a sentry*); 2. make out, write out, issue (*a bill, cheque, receipt, testimonial etc.*); 3. ***etwas – an*** (*Dat.*), take exception to, find fault with. **Aussteller,** *m.* 1. exhibitor; 2. drawer (*of a bill*), issuing authority.

Ausstellung ['ausʃtɛluŋ], *f.* 1. exhibition, show, display; ***– auf dem Paradebette,*** lying in state; 2. issue (*of passport etc.*); 3. (*usu. pl.*) objection, fault; ***–en machen*** (***an*** (*Dat.*)), find fault (with), raise *or* make objections (to). **Ausstellungs|datum,** *n.* date of issue. **–gegenstand,** *m.* exhibit. **–gelände,** *n.* exhibition grounds *or* site. **–kasten,** *m.* showcase. **–ort,** *m.* place of issue. **–raum,** *m.* showroom (*of a firm*), exhibition hall. **–stück,** *n.* (*coll.*) ***kein –,*** not much to look at, no show-piece.

Aussterbeetat ['ausʃtɛrbəˀeta:], *m.* (*coll.*) ***auf den – setzen,*** decide to do away with, plan *or* propose to scrap; ***auf dem – stehen,*** be ready for scrapping, be destined for abolition.

aussterben ['ausʃtɛrbən], *irr.v.i.* (*aux.* s.) die out; become extinct (*of a family or prehistoric animal*); ***ausgestorben,*** died out, extinct; (*fig.*) totally deserted; ***die Stadt ist wie ausgestorben,*** the town is like a morgue. **Aussterbestand,** *m.* (state of) threatened extinction.

Aussteuer ['ausʃtɔyər], *f.* dowry, marriage portion, (bride's) trousseau, (*coll.*) bottom drawer. **aussteuern,** *v.t.* 1. portion, endow, provide (*daughter*) with a dowry *or* trousseau; 2. terminate (*s.o.'s*) entitlement to social security benefits; ***Ausgesteuerte(r),*** one no longer eligible (*for dole etc.*); 3. (*Rad.*) modulate (*carrier wave*), adjust *or* set *or* control (recording *or* reproduction) level (*of tape recorder*). **Aussteuerung,** *f.* (*Rad.*) modulation; (*of tape-recorder*) level control.

Ausstich ['ausʃtɪç], *m.* choice wine. **Ausstichware,** *f.* choicest brand, prime quality.

Ausstieg ['ausʃti:k], *m.* 1. disembarkation, alighting; 2. way out, exit; trap-door. **Ausstiegluke,** *f.* escape hatch.

ausstöbern ['ausʃtø:bərn], *v.t.* rummage out (*drawer etc.*); ferret out, unearth (*s.th.*).

ausstopfen ['ausʃtɔpfən], *v.t.* stuff (*birds, chairs*), pad out (*shoulders etc.*). **Ausstopfen,** *n.* stuffing (of animals), taxidermy. **Ausstopfer,** *m.* taxidermist.

Ausstoß ['ausʃto:s], *m.* 1. ejection (*of a th.*), expulsion (*of a p.*); tapping (*of a barrel*); launching, discharging (*of a torpedo*); 2. torpedo-tube; 3. production, output (*of industry*). **ausstoßen, 1.** *irr.v.t.* 1. knock out; 2. eject, expel, eliminate; discharge, emit, (*coll.*) give off (*gas, bubbles etc.*), throw out, belch forth (*smoke*); utter (*a cry*); give, heave (*a sigh*); launch, discharge (*a torpedo*); 3. expel, (*coll.*) turn *or* throw out (*a p.*), cashier (*an officer*); 4. (*Phonet.*) elide (*a vowel*), suppress (*a syllable*). **2.** *irr.v.i.* 1. (*Fenc.*) thrust, lunge, make a pass; (*Swimming*) strike out; 2. bubble *or* froth over (*of liquid*). **Ausstoßer,** *m.* ejector (device). **Ausstoß|produkt,** *n.* waste product. **–rohr,** *n.* torpedo-tube. **Ausstoßung,** *f.* ejection, emission, elimination, expulsion, (*Eccl.*) excommunication; (*Phonet.*) elision (*of vowel*), suppression (*of syllable*). **Ausstoßzahlen,** *pl.* output *or* production figures.

ausstrahlen ['ausʃtra:lən], **1.** *v.t.* emit, radiate (*rays*), (*Rad.*) transmit (*signal*). **2.** *v.i.* radiate. **Ausstrahlung,** *f.* radiation, emission; radiance.

ausstrecken ['ausʃtrɛkən], **1.** *v.t.* 1. stretch (out), extend (*one's arms, legs*), crane (*one's neck*); ***ausgestreckte Arme,*** outstretched arms; 2. stretch, reach, hold *or* put out (*one's hand*) (***nach,*** for). **2.** *v.r.* 1. stretch o.s. out (*of a p.*); 2. stretch (out), extend (*of land etc.*).

ausstreichen ['ausʃtraɪçən], **1.** *irr.v.t.* 1. delete, erase; strike *or* score *or* cross out (*a word*); 2. smooth out (*creases*); 3. fill up *or* in (*cracks*); 4. grease (*a cake tin etc.*). **2.** *irr.v.i.* (*Geol.*) outcrop, crop out.

ausstreuen ['ausʃtrɔyən], *v.t.* scatter (*seed etc.*), spread, strew (*straw etc.*), diffuse (*light*), (*fig.*) circulate, spread abroad, disseminate (*rumours*); ***den Samen der Zwietracht –,*** sow the seeds of discord. **Ausstreuung,** *f.* dissemination (*of news*), circulation (*of rumours*), diffusion (*of light*).

Ausstrich ['ausʃtrɪç], *m.* 1. (*Geol.*) outcrop; 2. smear (*microscopic preparation*).

ausströmen ['ausʃtrø:mən], **1.** *v.t.* pour (forth), emit, discharge, (*fig.*) shower, shed, radiate (*peace, blessings etc.*). **2.** *v.i.* (*aux.* s.) stream *or* issue forth, pour *or* run out, gush forth (*of water*), escape (*of steam etc.*), be radiated (*of rays, also fig. of happiness, contentment etc.*), emanate (*of grace*). **Ausströmung,** *f.* discharge, efflux, effusion, emission, emanation; radiation; escape (*of gas*).

ausstudieren ['ausʃtudi:rən], **1.** *v.i.* finish one's studies. **2.** *v.t.* study thoroughly. **ausstudiert,** *adj.* having completed a university course, graduate, qualified.

ausstülpen ['ausʃtylpən], *v.t.* (*Med.*) evaginate, evert. **Ausstülpung,** *f.* protrusion, eversion.

aussuchen ['auszu:xən], *v.t.* search (*pocket etc.*); choose, select; single *or* pick out. *See* **ausgesucht.**

aussüßen ['auszy:sən], *v.t.* sweeten, dulcify, (*Chem.*) edulcorate.

austäfeln ['austɛ:fəln], *v.t.* panel (*a room*).

austapezieren ['austapetsi:rən], *v.t.* paper (*a wall*), line (*a box etc.*).

Austausch ['austauʃ], *m.* exchange; (*Comm.*) barter, (*Chem.*) substitution (***gegen,*** for), interchange (***gegen, mit,*** with). **austauschbar,** *adj.* interchangeable (***gegen, mit,*** with), exchangeable (***gegen,*** for). **austauschen,** *v.t.* exchange (***gegen,*** for), interchange (***gegen, mit,*** with), (*Comm.*) barter; change, substitute (*one for another*), replace (*one by another*). **Austausch|offizier,** *m.* (*Mil.*) relief officer. **–stoff,** *m.* substitute. **–student,** *m.* exchange student.

austeilen ['austaɪlən], *v.t.* distribute; dispense, hand *or* deal out (***an*** or ***unter*** (*Acc.*), to); share out, divide, allot, apportion (among); deal (*cards*); issue (*orders*); administer (*the Sacraments*); deal out (*blows*); serve out (*meat etc.*).

Auster ['austər], *f.* (-, *pl.* **-n**) oyster. **Austern|bank,** *f.* oyster-bed. **–fischer,** *m.* (*Orn.*) (*Am.* European) oystercatcher (*Haemotopus ostralegus*). **–laich,** *m.* spat. **–schale,** *f.* oyster-shell.

austiefen ['austi:fən], *v.t.* deepen, hollow (out).

austilgen ['austɪlgən], *v.t.* destroy utterly, exterminate, extirpate, eradicate, (*coll.*) wipe *or* blot out; efface, obliterate, (*coll.*) blot out. **Austilgung,** *f.* extermination, extinction, extirpation; destruction, eradication.

austoben ['austo:bən], **1.** *v.i.* cease raging, abate, spend itself (*of storms*). **2.** *v.r.* romp, let off steam; have one's fling, sow one's wild oats.

Austrag ['austra:k], *m.* (*Law*) settlement, issue; ***eine S. zum – bringen,*** settle a matter; ***vor – der S.,***

while the case is pending, pending settlement of the matter; *gütlicher* –, amicable settlement. **austragen,** *irr.v.t.* 1. deliver (*letters*); spread, retail (*gossip*); 2. carry (*child*) for full time; wear out (*clothes etc.*); endure, bear, (*coll.*) put up with (*s.th.*) to the end; 3. (*Spt.*) decide, hold (*a contest*), play (*a match*), (*fig.*) settle (*a quarrel*), (*coll.*) have it out.

Austräger ['austrɛ:gər], *m.* 1. roundsman, delivery-boy; 2. (*coll.*) gossip, tale-bearer.

Australien [aus'tra:liən], *n.* Australia. **Australier,** *m.* Australian. **australisch,** *adj.* Australian.

austreiben ['austraɪbən], *irr.v.t.* drive out, eject, oust; expel (*air etc.*), evict (*tenant*), dislodge (*an enemy*); exorcise, drive *or* cast out (*devils*); (*coll.*) knock (*bad habits, silly ideas etc.*) out (*Dat.*, of) (*s.o. or s.o.'s head*); (*Prov.*) ***den Teufel durch*** or ***mit Beelzebub*** –, out of the frying-pan into the fire. **Austreibung,** *f.* ejection, eviction, expulsion; exorcism.

austreten ['austre:tən], **1.** *irr.v.t.* tread *or* stamp *or* kick out; tread (out) (*grapes etc.*); wear down (*steps*); stretch (*shoes*) in wear, break in (*new shoes*); (*coll.*) ***die Kinderschuhe ausgetreten haben,*** have outgrown *or* have put away childish things. **2.** *irr.v.i.* (*aux.* s.) 1. step out; (*coll.*) leave the room, be excused (*euphemism for 'go to the lavatory'*); (*Mil.*) ***aus dem Glied*** –, leave the ranks, fall out; 2. come *or* pass out, emerge (***aus***, from); 3. leave; resign, withdraw, secede (***aus***, from); 4. (*of a river*) overflow its banks; 5. (*Med.*) protrude (*as hernia*), be secreted (*as bile*), extravasate (*as blood*), be expelled (*of child from mother's body*). **austretend,** *adj.* (*Opt.*) emergent. *See* **Austritt.**

austrinken ['austrɪŋkən], **1.** *irr.v.t.* drink up (*wine etc.*), empty, drain (*a glass etc.*). **2.** *irr.v.i.* finish one's drink *or* glass, drain one's glass, drink up.

Austritt ['austrɪt], *m.* 1. leaving, withdrawal, resignation, retiral, retirement, secession; 2. passing *or* passage out, emergence, exit, egress, efflux, (*Med.*) protrusion (*of organ*), extravasation (*of blood*), expulsion (*of child*); 3. discharge, overflow; overflowing (*of river*); 4. outlet, vent, exhaust-port; 5. small balcony. **Austritts|erklärung,** *f.* notice of withdrawal *or* resignation. **–kanal,** *m.* exhaust-port. **–mechanismus,** *m.* (*Med.*) mechanism of labour. **–stufe,** *f.* top stair *or* step (*of staircase*).

austrocknen ['austrɔknən], **1.** *v.t.* dry (up), desiccate, parch; dry out, season (*timber*); drain (*a marsh*). **2.** *v.i.* (*aux.* s.) become dry *or* parched, dry up; dry out *or* off. **austrocknend,** *adj.* drying, desiccative. **Austrocknung,** *f.* drying, desiccation; drainage (*of land*).

auströpfeln ['austrœpfəln], **austropfen** [–trɔpfən], *v.t.* drip, ooze *or* trickle out.

austüfteln ['austyftəln], *v.t.* (*coll.*) puzzle out.

ausüben ['ausˀy:bən], *v.t.* 1. practise (*law, medicine etc.*), follow, pursue, carry on (*trade, profession*), ply (*a trade*); fulfil, perform, carry out (*a duty*); commit, perpetrate (*crimes*); 2. exercise (*authority, privilege*); exert, exercise, use, bring to bear (*influence*); ***Druck auf ihn*** –, bring pressure to bear on him, put pressure on him; ***Anziehungskraft auf mich*** –, have an attraction for me. **ausübend,** *adj.* practising; executive; ***–er Arzt,*** (general) practitioner; ***–er Künstler,*** executant. **Ausübung,** *f.* practice (*opp. to theory*); practice (*of one's profession*); exercise (*of privilege*); exertion (*of influence*), performance, execution (*of duty*); perpetration (*of crime*); ***in – des Dienstes,*** in the line of duty, in performance of one's duty.

Ausverkauf ['ausfɛrkauf], *m.* selling off (*goods*), selling out (*whole stock*); (clearance) sale. **ausverkaufen,** *v.t.* sell off, sell out; ***das Theater war ausverkauft,*** the house was sold out *or* filled to capacity.

auswachsen ['ausvaksən], **1.** *irr.v.i.* (*aux.* s.) sprout, germinate; attain full growth; ***ausgewachsen sein,*** be hump-backed; *see* **ausgewachsen. 2.** *irr.v.r.* 1. develop, grow (***zu***, into); 2. disappear in *or* with time, right itself eventually. **3.** *irr.v.t.* outgrow, grow out of (*a garment*); (*coll.*) ***das ist zum Auswachsen,*** that's really the limit.

Auswahl ['ausva:l], *f.* 1. choice, selection; assortment; ***eine – treffen,*** make a selection; ***– deutscher Lieder,*** selection *or* anthology of German songs; 2. choicest specimens, (*coll.*) pick (of the bunch).

auswählen ['ausvɛ:lən], *v.t.* choose, select, single *or* pick out, fix on; ***ausgewählt,*** selected, select, choice; ***ausgewählte Soldaten,*** picked soldiers; ***ausgewählte Gedichte,*** selected poems.

auswalzen ['ausvaltsən], *v.t.* roll out (thin); (*coll.*) labour, dwell on (*a point*).

Auswanderer ['ausvandərər], *m.* emigrant. **auswandern,** *v.i.* (*aux.* s.) migrate (*of birds etc.*), emigrate (*of a p.*). **Auswanderung,** *f.* 1. emigration, migration; 2. (*Artil.*) linear travel (*of anti-aircraft target*).

auswärtig ['ausvɛrtɪç], *adj.* foreign; from abroad; from outside, out-of-town, non-resident; ***das –e Amt, Ministerium des Auswärtigen,*** Foreign Office (*Am.* State Department), Foreign Ministry, Ministry for External Affairs; ***Minister der –en Angelegenheiten*** or ***des Auswärtigen,*** Foreign Secretary (*Am.* Secretary of State); ***–es Mitgleid,*** corresponding member.

auswärts ['ausvɛrts], *adv.* outwards; out of town, away from home; ***von*** –, from another town, from outside the town; ***nach*** –, to another town or place; ***– essen,*** go out to eat, eat out; ***die Fußspitzen – setzen,*** turn out the toes. **Auswärtsspiel,** *n.* (*Spt.*) away match *or* game.

auswaschen ['ausvaʃən], *irr.v.t.* 1. wash out; rinse; bathe (*a wound*); 2. wash away, erode (*river bank*). **Auswaschung,** *f.* erosion.

auswässern ['ausvɛsərn], *v.t.* soak, steep. **Auswässerung,** *f.* (*Naut.*) freeboard. **Auswässerungslinie,** *f.* load water-line.

auswechselbar ['ausvɛksəlba:r], *adj.* exchangeable (***gegen***, for), interchangeable (with), replaceable (by); removable, replaceable, renewable (*parts*).

auswechseln ['ausvɛksəln], *v.t.* exchange, change (***gegen***, for), interchange (with), replace (by), renew (*faulty parts*), change round (*tyres etc.*); (*coll.*) ***wie ausgewechselt sein, sich wie ausgewechselt fühlen,*** be *or* feel a new man. **Auswechs(e)lung,** *f.* change, exchange (***gegen***, for), interchange (*of two things*), replacement, renewal (by).

Ausweg ['ausve:k], *m.* **(-(e)s,** *pl.* **-e)** way out (***aus***, of), (way of) escape (from). **ausweglos,** *adj.* hopeless (*situation*). **Ausweglosigkeit,** *f.* hopelessness.

Ausweich– ['ausvaɪç], *pref.* 1. alternative; 2. evasive, avoiding. **–bewegung,** *f.* avoiding *or* evading *or* evasive movement.

ausweichen ['ausvaɪçən], *irr.v.i.* (*aux.* s.) 1. make way (***vor*** (*Dat.*), for), give way (to), get *or* keep out of (*s.o.'s*) way; turn *or* step aside, swerve; 2. (*Dat.*) avoid (*a p., temptation*), elude (*pursuers*), evade (*duty, a problem, a question*), shirk (*duty*), (*coll.*) side-step (*an issue*); ***einem Stoß*** –, avoid *or* evade *or* dodge a blow; 3. (*Mus.*) modulate (***in*** (*Acc.*), into). **Ausweichen,** *n.* avoidance, evasion (***vor*** (*Dat.*), of). **ausweichend,** *adj.* evasive, non-committal (*answer*), elusive.

Ausweich|gleis, *n.* (*Railw.*) passing-track, turn-out, loop(-line). **–hafen,** *m.* alternative base. **–klausel,** *f.* escape clause (*in contract*). **–lager,** *n.* emergency store. **–manöver,** *n.* evasive action. **–stelle,** *f.* passing-place, lay-by. **–straße,** *f.* by-pass.

Ausweichung ['ausvaɪçuŋ], *f.* 1. passing; 2. (*Mus.*) modulation.

Ausweich|welle, *f.* (*Rad.*) secondary *or* alternative frequency. **–ziel,** *n.* (*Av.*) alternative target.

ausweiden ['ausvaɪdən], *v.t.* eviscerate; gut, draw (*poultry etc.*).

ausweinen ['ausvaɪnən], **1.** *v.t.* weep; ***sich*** (*Dat.*) ***die Augen*** –, cry one's eyes out. **2.** *v.r.* cry one's heart out, have a good cry. **3.** *v.i.* stop weeping.

Ausweis ['ausvaɪs], *m.* **(-es,** *pl.* **-e)** 1. credentials, identification papers, identity card, passport; membership *or* admission card, ticket (*for library* *etc.*), (*Mil.*) pass; 2. documentary evidence, certificate, (bank) statement; (*fig.*) ***nach – von*** or *Gen.*, as proved by, on the evidence of. **ausweisen, 1.** *irr.v.t.* 1. turn out (*a p.*), expel, extradite; 2. prove, be proof of, testify, show. **2.** *irr.v.r.* prove one's identity; (*fig.*) prove *or* show o.s. (*als*, to be).

Ausweis|karte, *f.* membership *or* admission card, (*library etc.*) ticket. **-papiere,** *pl.* identification papers, identity card.

Ausweisung ['ausvaɪzuŋ], *f.* expulsion. **Ausweisungsbefehl,** *m.* extradition *or* expulsion order.

ausweiten ['ausvaɪtən], **1.** *v.t.* widen, broaden, enlarge, expand, dilate; stretch (*gloves etc.*). **2.** *v.r.* grow wider, widen; grow *or* become larger, expand, extend. **Ausweitung,** *f.* 1. expansion, extension, enlargement, dilation; 2. (*Carp.*) countersunk hole.

auswendig ['ausvɛndɪç], *adj.* 1. outer, outside, outward, external; 2. by heart, by rote, by memory; ***– lernen,*** commit to memory, memorize, learn by heart; ***– spielen,*** play from memory (*music*); ***– wissen,*** know by heart; ***etwas in- und – kennen,*** know a thing thoroughly *or* (*coll.*) inside out.

auswerfen ['ausvɛrfən], *irr.v.t.* 1. throw out; (*Naut.*) discharge (*ballast*), throw overboard, jettison (*cargo*), cast (*anchor, net, fishing line*), hoist out (*boat*); ***das Lot –,*** swing the lead, take soundings; 2. throw up (*earth etc.*), eject, vomit forth (*as volcano*); disgorge, vomit, expectorate, cough up; dig (*a trench*); 3. set aside *or* apart, allow (*sum of money*) (***für,*** for), allocate (to); distribute (*dividends*); offer (*prize*). *See* **Auswurf. Auswerfen,** *n.* 1. discharge, ejection; 2. vomiting, expectoration; 3. allocation, distribution. **Auswerfer,** *m.* ejector (*of a gun*).

auswerten ['ausve:rtən], *v.t.* 1. get the full value from, make full use of, exploit, utilize, turn to (good) account; 2. evaluate, interpret (*aerial photographs etc.*). **Auswertestelle,** *f.* (*Mil.*) plotting *or* computing centre. **Auswertung,** *f.* utilization, exploitation, evaluation, interpretation (*of evidence, photographs etc.*).

auswetzen ['ausvɛtsən], *v.t.* remove by grinding; (*fig.*) ***eine Scharte –,*** make amends, redeem o.s., wipe out a stain on one's character; avenge a defeat, (*coll.*) get even.

auswickeln ['ausvɪkəln], *v.t.* unwrap, undo (*a parcel*), disentangle, extricate.

auswiegen ['ausvi:gən], **1.** *irr.v.t.* weigh out. **2.** *irr. v.i.* (*Spt.*) weigh in. *See* **ausgewogen. Auswiegen,** *n.* (*Spt.*) weigh(ing)-in.

auswinden ['ausvɪndən], *irr.v.i.* wring out.

auswirken ['ausvɪrkən], **1.** *v.t.* 1. get, obtain, procure (***bei,*** from; *Dat.*, for); ***sich*** (*Dat.*) ***etwas –,*** obtain a th. for o.s.; 2. ***den Teig –,*** knead dough. **2.** *v.r.* 1. take effect, be effective, have its effects, bear (***auf*** (*Acc.*), on), have consequences (for); 2. turn *or* work out (***als,*** to be). **3.** *v.i.* (*partic. in perfect*) cease to operate, cease to have any effect. **Auswirkung,** *f.* effect, consequence, result.

auswischen ['ausvɪʃən], *v.t.* wipe *or* clean out, wipe clean, rub out (*from blackboard*); (*coll.*) ***ihm eins –,*** play a trick on him, do him one in the eye.

auswittern ['ausvɪtərn], **1.** *v.t.* 1. (*of dog*) scent, smell *or* nose out (*game*), (*coll.*) (*of a p.*) nose *or* ferret out (*a secret*); 2. cause (*material*) to effloresce; corrode away; season (*timber*). **2.** *v.i.* effloresce; weather (*of stone*), become weather-worn, suffer from exposure (to the weather); season, become seasoned (*of timber*). **Auswitterung,** *f.* efflorescence, exudation; weathering, seasoning.

auswringen ['ausvrɪŋən], *irr.v.t.* wring (out). **Auswringmaschine,** *f.* wringer.

Auswuchs ['ausvuks], *m.* excrescence, protuberance; (*Med.*) tumour; (*Bot.*) apophysis; (*fig. usu. pl.*) (unhealthy) product *or* creation, outgrowth, excess, aberration.

auswuchten ['ausvuxtən], *v.t.* (counter)balance, compensate.

auswühlen ['ausvy:lən], *v.t.* burrow (*a hole*), excavate, dig up, root up *or* out.

Auswurf ['ausvurf], *m.* 1. ejection, throwing up; 2. vomiting, expectoration; 3. (*Med.*) sputum; ***schleimiger –,*** phlegm; 4. *pl.* (*Geol.*) ejecta, ejectamenta (*of volcano*); 5. (*fig.*) scourings, scum, dregs; ***– der Menschheit,*** scum of the earth.

Auswürfling ['ausvyrflɪŋ], *m.* (**-s,** *pl.* **-e**) (*Geol.*) piece of ejected material.

auswüten ['ausvy:tən], *v.i.* spend itself *or* its force *or* fury (*of a storm*).

auszacken ['austsakən], *v.t.* notch, indent, scallop, jag; (*Her.*) engrail; ***ausgezackt,*** jagged, zig-zag; dentate, crenate, denticulate. **Auszackung,** *f.* indentation; denticulation.

auszahlen ['austsa:lən], **1.** *v.t.* pay (out, over *or* away); disburse (*sum of money*), cash (*postal order etc.*); pay off (*worker*); ***bar –,*** pay down in cash. **2.** *v.r.* (*coll.*) ***es zahlt sich nicht aus,*** it's not worth it.

auszählen ['austsɛ:lən], **1.** *v.t.* count out, count (*votes*). **2.** *v.i.* count to the end; count down (*rocketry*). **Auszählreim,** *m.* counting-out rhyme (*children's play*).

Auszahlung ['austsa:luŋ], *f.* payment, disbursement (*of money*); ***telegraphische –,*** telegraphic *or* cable transfer.

Auszählung [austsɛ:luŋ], *f.* counting (out); countdown (*rocketry*).

Auszahlungs|schein, *m.* payment slip. **-stelle,** *f.* office of payment, paying office.

auszanken ['austsaŋkən], **1.** *v.t.* give (*s.o.*) a good scolding. **2.** *v.i.* stop quarrelling *or* scolding.

auszehren ['austse:rən], *v.t.* consume, waste (away), emaciate (*body*); impoverish, lay waste, ravage (*a country*); ***-de Krankheit,*** consumptive disease. **Auszehrung,** *f.* wasting (away), (*Med.*) marasmus; wasting disease, consumption, tabes, phthisis.

auszeichnen ['austsaɪçnən], **1.** *v.t.* 1. mark out (for attention), distinguish, mark, emphasize; 2. honour, confer an honour upon, single out for distinction (*a p.*); ***– mit,*** award (*medal, prize*) to; 3. mark, price (*goods*); 4. (*Typ.*) display in bold type; *see* **ausgezeichnet. 2.** *v.r.* distinguish o.s. (***durch,*** by), be outstanding. **Auszeichnung,** *f.* (mark of) distinction; decoration, honour, award, prize, special mention. **Auszeichnungs|schrift,** *f.* (*Typ.*) bold type. **-zettel,** *m.* price tag *or* ticket.

ausziehen ['austsi:ən], **1.** *irr.v.t.* 1. pull *or* draw out; extract, remove (*a tooth*), pull up (*plants*), draw (*poultry*), take *or* make extracts *or* excerpts from (*a book*), make an abstract of (*an account*), draw (*wire*), extend (*telescope*); 2. take off, remove (*clothes*), (*coll.*) fleece (*a p.*); 3. ink in (*a sketch*); ***ausgezogene Linie,*** unbroken *or* continuous line. **2.** *irr.v.r.* undress (o.s.), get undressed. **3.** *irr.v.i.* (*aux.* s.) 1. set out *or* off, start out (***auf die Wanderschaft,*** on one's travels; ***zur Jagd,*** for the hunt); ***in den Krieg –,*** go off to war; 2. ***aus einer Wohnung –,*** move house, move from *or* leave a house. *See* **Auszug. Auszieher,** *m.* extractor.

Auszieh|leiter, *f.* extension *or* extending ladder. **-rohr,** *n.* telescopic tube. **-tisch,** *m.* pull-out *or* draw-leaf table. **-tusche,** *f.* Indian *or* drawing ink.

auszieren ['austsi:rən], *v.t.* adorn, decorate. **Auszierung,** *f.* decoration, adornment, ornamentation.

auszimmern ['austsɪmərn], *v.t.* line (*a shaft*) with timber, revet.

auszirkeln [austsɪrkəln], *v.t.* measure *or* mark out with compasses; (*fig.*) ***alles –,*** do everything by rule.

auszischen ['austsɪʃən], *v.t.* hiss off (*the stage*), hiss *or* boo (at) (*actor*).

Auszug ['austsu:k], *m.* 1. marching *or* going out *or* off; departure, emigration, exodus (***aus,*** from); removal, move (*from house*); ***– der Kinder Israels,*** Exodus; 2. extract, excerpt, abstract, gist; statement (of account); (*Mus.*) arrangement (for piano); 3. essence, extract, decoction, infusion; ***im – darstellen,*** epitomize; 4. leaf (*of table*), drawplate (*of oven*), number drawn (*in lottery*). **Auszugmehl,** *n.* superfine flour. **auszugsweise,** *adv.* in the form of an abstract *or* extracts.

auszupfen ['austsupfən], *v.t.* pluck out; unravel, disentangle; ***ausgezupfte Leinwand,*** lint.

Autarch [au'tarx], *m.* **(-en,** *pl.* **-en)** autocrat.

autark [au'tark], *adj.* economically self-sufficient. **Autarkie** [-'ki:], *f.* autarky, self-sufficiency.

authentisch [au'tɛntɪʃ], *adj.* authentic, genuine; authoritative (*text*). **authentisieren** [-'zi:rən], *v.t.* authenticate, certify. **Authentizität** [-itsi'tɛ:t], *f.* (*no pl.*) authenticity.

Auto ['auto], *n.* **(-s,** *pl.* **-s)** (motor-)car, (*Am.*) automobile; – ***fahren,*** drive a car; ***im – fahren,*** travel by car *or* by road. **Auto–,** *pref.* motor-, motoring.

auto–, *pref.* auto-.

Auto|ausstellung, *f.* motor show. **–bahn,** *f.* motorway, (*Am.*) freeway. **–besitzer,** *m.* car-owner.

Autobiograph [autobio'gra:f], *m.* autobiographer. **Autobiographie** [-'fi:], *f.* autobiography. **autobiographisch,** *adj.* autobiographical.

Auto|box [-bɔks], *f.* (-, *pl.* **-en**) lock-up (garage). **–brille,** *f.* (motoring) goggles. **–bus,** *m.* (motor-) bus.

autochthon [autox'to:n], *adj.* autochthonous, aboriginal.

Autodidakt [autodi'dakt], *m.* **(-en,** *pl.* **-en)** autodidact, self-educated man. **autodidaktisch,** *adj.* self-taught.

Auto|droschke, *f.* (taxi)cab. **–empfänger,** *m.* car-radio. **–fähre,** *f.* car-ferry. **–fahren,** *n.* driving, motoring. **–fahrer,** *m.* driver, motorist. **–fahrschule,** *f.* driving school, school of motoring. **–fahrt,** *f.* drive, trip by car. **–falle,** *f.* police trap, speed-trap. **–führer,** *m.* taxi-driver, bus-driver, chauffeur.

Autogamie [autoga'mi:], *f.* (-, *no pl.*) (*Bot., Biol.*) autogamy, self-fertilization. **autogamisch** [-'ga:miʃ], *adj.* self-fertilizing.

autogen [auto'ge:n], *adj.* autogenous; ***–e Schweißung,*** oxy-acetylene welding. **Autogenapparat,** *m.* oxy-acetylene welder. **Autogenese** [-gə'ne:zə], *f.* autogeny.

Autogramm [auto'gram], *n.* **(-(e)s,** *pl.* **-e)** autograph (*signature*).

[1]**Autograph** [auto'gra:f], *m.* **(-en,** *pl.* **-en)** copying machine.

[2]**Autograph,** *m.* **(-(e)s,** *pl.* **-e(n))** autograph (*manuscript*). **Autographie** [-'fi:], *f.* 1. autolithography; 2. (*Med.*) dermographia.

Auto|haltestelle, *f.* taxi-rank, (*Am.*) cabstand. **–karte,** *f.* road map.

Autokrat [auto'kra:t], *m.* **(-en,** *pl.* **-en)** autocrat. **Autokratie** [-'ti:], *f.* autocracy. **autokratisch,** *adj.* autocratic.

Automat [auto'ma:t], *m.* **(-en,** *pl.* **-en)** automaton, robot; automatic *or* self-acting device *or* mechanism; slot machine, vending machine. **Automatenrestaurant,** *n.* self-service restaurant (*from slot machines*), (*Am.*) automat. **Automatik,** *f.* (-, *no pl.*) automatic mechanism, automatic working. **automatisch,** *adj.* automatic, self-acting. **automatisieren** [-mati'zi:rən], *v.t.* mechanize. **Automatisierung,** *f.* automation, mechanization.

Automechaniker ['automeça:nikər], *m.* motor mechanic.

Automobil [automo'bi:l], *m.* **(-(e)s,** *pl.* **-e)** *see* **Auto.**

autonom [auto'no:m], *adj.* autonomous, independent, self-governing. **Autonomie** [-'mi:], *f.* autonomy, independence, self-government.

Autor ['autɔr], *m.* **(-s,** *pl.* **-en** [-'to:rən]) author, writer. **Autorenhonorar,** *n.* author's royalties.

Auto|rennbahn, *f.* (motor-)racing track. **–rennen,** *n.* motor-racing; motor-race.

Autorisation [autorizatsi'o:n], *f.* authorization. **autorisieren** [-'zi:rən], *v.t.* authorize. **Autorisierung,** *f.* *See* **Autorisation.**

autoritär [autori'tɛ:r], *adj.* authoritarian. **Autorität,** *f.* authority.

Autorschaft ['autɔrʃaft], *f.* authorship.

Auto|schlepp, *m.* **(-s,** *pl.* -) auto-tow (*for gliders*). **–schlosser,** *m.* motor-mechanic. **–sport,** *m.* car-racing, (participation in) speed trials, car rallies *etc.* **–stopp,** *m.* hitch-hiking; ***mit*** or ***per – fahren,*** hitch-hike. **–stunde,** *f.* hour's drive, hour by car. **–taxe,** *f.* taxi. **–technik,** *f.* motor *or* automobile engineering.

Autotypie [autoty'pi:], *f.* autotype, half-tone reproduction.

Auto|unfall, *m.* motor *or* road accident, car smash. **–vermietung,** *f.* car-hire.

autsch! [autʃ], *int.* ouch! ow! (*of pain*).

Aval [a'val], *n.* **(-s,** *pl.* **-e)** (written) security, surety, guarantee; – ***geben,*** stand surety *or* security. **avalieren** [-'li:rən], *v.t.* stand security, back, guarantee (*a bill of exchange*). **Avalist** [-'lɪst], *m.* **(-en,** *pl.* **-en)** guarantor, backer, acceptor.

Avance [a'vã:sə], *f.* (*Comm.*) advance, money advanced; profit differential; (*coll.*) ***–n machen,*** make advances, make up (*Dat.*, to). **Avancement** [-'mã], *n.* **(-s,** *pl.* **-s)** preferment, promotion, advancement. **avancieren** [-'si:rən], **1.** *v.i.* be promoted; ***im Dienste –,*** rise in the service. **2.** *v.t.* put on *or* forward (*clocks*).

Avantageur [avãta'ʒø:r], *m.* **(-s,** *pl.* **-s** *or* **-e)** (*Mil.*) ensign.

Avantgarde [a'vãgardə], *f.* vanguard (*of a movement*). **Avantgardist** [-'dɪst], *m.* **(-en,** *pl.* **-en)** avant-garde artist, writer *etc.* **avantgardistisch,** *adj.* avant-garde.

Ave-Maria, *n.* **(-(s),** *pl.* **-(s))** Ave Maria, Hail Mary; ***– –Läuten,*** Angelus (*bell*).

Avers [a'vɛrs], *m.* **(-es,** *pl.* **-e)** 1. obverse, head (*of a coin*); 2. (*Comm.*) settlement (*of a claim*). **Aversalsumme** [-'za:lzumə], *f.* sum (paid) in settlement.

Aversionalsumme [a'vɛrzio'na:lzumə], *f.* **Aversum,** *n.* **(-sums,** *pl.* **-sa)** *see* **Aversalsumme.**

avertieren [avɛr'ti:rən], *v.t.* warn, notify, advise. **Avertissement** [-'tis(ə)mã], *n.* **(-s,** *pl.* **-s)** warning, notification, advice.

Aviatik [avi'a:tɪk], *f.* (-, *no pl.*) aviation. **Aviatiker,** *m.* aviator.

Avis [a'vi:(s)], *m. or n.* **(-es,** *pl.* **-e)** (*Comm.*) advice, notice. **Avisbrief,** *m.* advice-note, letter of advice. **avisieren** [-'zi:rən], *v.t.* (*Comm.*) advise, notify, give notice of.

[1]**Aviso** [a'vi:zo], *n.* **(-s,** *pl.* **-s)** (*Austr.*) *see* **Avis.**

[2]**Aviso,** *m.* **(-s,** *pl.* **-s)** (*Nav.*) dispatch-boat, advice boat, aviso.

a vista [a'vɪsta], *adv.* (*Comm.*) at sight. **Avistawechsel,** *m.* sight-bill.

Awaren [a'va:rən], *pl.* (*Hist.*) Avars.

Awesta [a'vɛsta], *n.* Avesta.

axial [aksi'a:l], *adj.*, **Axial–,** *pref.* axial.

axillar [aksɪ'la:r], *adj.*, **Axillar–,** *pref.* (*Bot., Biol.*) axillary.

Axt [akst], *f.* (-, *pl.* **⸚e**) axe, hatchet. **Axt|eisen,** *n.* axe-head. **–stiel,** *m.* handle of an axe.

Azetat [atse'ta:t], *n.* **(-(e)s,** *pl.* **-e)** acetate. **Azetatlack,** *m.* cellulose varnish. **Azet(yl)säure,** *f.* acetic acid.

Azoikum [a'tso:ikum], *n.* **(-s,** *no pl.*) (*Geol.*) Azoic period. **azoisch,** *adj.* azoic.

Azoren [a'tso:rən], *pl.* Azores.

Azur [a'tsu:r], *m.* **(-s,** *pl.* **-e)** azure, sky blue. **azurblau,** *adj.* azure, sky blue. **azur(e)n,** *adj.* azure. **Azurit** [-'ri:t], **Azurstein,** *m.* **(-s,** *no pl.*) lapis lazuli.

B

B, b [be:], *n.* B, b; (*Mus.*) 1. *B* (= *B-Dur*), B flat major; *b* (= *b-Moll*), B flat minor; 2. flat, ♭; *ein ♭ vorzeichnen* or *vorschreiben*, flatten (*a note*).

Baal [ba:l], *m.* (**-s**, *pl.* **-im**) (*B.*) Baal. **Baalspriester,** *m.* (*coll.*) false priest.

babbeln ['babəln], *v.i.* (*coll.*) babble, chatter, prattle.

Babuin [babu'i:n], *m.* (**-s**, *pl.* **-e**) yellow *or* dog-faced baboon (*Papio cynocephalus*).

Baby ['be:bi], *n.* (**-s**, *pl.* **-s**) babe, infant. **Babyausstattung,** *f.* layette.

Bacchant [ba'xant], *m.* (**-en**, *pl.* **-en**) worshipper of Bacchus. **Bacchantentanz,** *m.* Bacchanal. **Bacchantin,** *f.* Bacchante, maenad. **bacchantisch,** *adj.* Bacchic, Bacchanalian.

Bach [bax], *m.* (**-(e)s**, *pl.* **⸚e**) brook, stream, rivulet, (*dial.*) beck, burn; (*sl.*) the drink (*i.e. the sea*); (*coll.*) *den – hinunter*, down the drain; (*coll.*) *einen – machen*, make a puddle, wee-wee (*of a child*); *viele Bäche machen einen Strom*, little streams make great rivers. **Bachamsel,** *f.* *See* **Wasseramsel.**

Bache ['baxə], *f.* wild sow. **Bacher,** *m.* young (wild) boar.

Bächlein ['bɛçlaɪn], *n.* (**-s**, *pl.* **-**) brooklet, rill.

Bach|mücke, *f.* crane-fly, daddy-longlegs (*Tipulidae*). **-stelze,** *f.* white wagtail (*Motacilla alba alba*); *gelbe –*, *see* **Schaftstelze**; *graue –*, *see* **Gebirgstelze.**

Back [bak], *f.* (-, *pl.* **-en**), *n.* (**-es**, *pl.* **-e**) (*Naut.*) 1. forecastle; 2. mess tin; mess table, mess.

back, *adv.* (*Naut.*) aback (*of sail*). **Backbord,** *n. or m.* (**-(e)s**, *pl.* **-e**) port (side), (*obs.*) larboard. **backbord,** *adv.* (*Naut.*) *– das Ruder!* port the helm!

Backe ['bakə], *f.* (*occ.* **Backen,** *m.*) 1. cheek; *dicke –*, swollen face; *die -n vollnehmen*, talk big; 2. wing (*of chair*); 3. (*usu. Backen, m.*) jaw (*of vice etc.*), shoe (*of brake*); 4. *pl.* haunches, buttocks (*of animal*), side-pieces, (*Naut.*) hounds (*of mast*).

backen ['bakən], **1.** *reg. & irr.v.t.* 1. bake (*bread etc.*), fry (*fish etc.*); burn, fire (*pottery, tiles*); (*coll.*) *sein Brot ist ihm gebacken*, there is a rod in pickle for him; 2. (*only reg.*) (*coll.*) cake (*as snow on shoes*).

Backen|bart, *m.* side-burns *or* -whiskers. **-bremse,** *f.* shoe brake. **-knochen,** *m.* cheek-bone. **-sessel,** *m.* wing-chair. **-streich,** *m.* box on the ear, slap in the face. **-zahn,** *m.* molar (tooth).

Bäcker ['bɛkər], *m.* baker. **Bäckerbeine,** *pl.* knock-knees. **Bäckerei** [–'raɪ], *f.* bakery; bakehouse; baker's shop; baking (trade); (*usu. pl.*) cakes and biscuits. **Bäcker|junge,** *m.* baker's boy. **-meister,** *m.* master baker.

Back|fett, *n.* cooking fat. **-fisch,** *m.* girl in her teens, (*coll.*) teenager. **-form,** *f.* cake-tin, baking-tin. **-hähnchen,** *n.* fried chicken. **-haube,** *f.* Dutch oven. **-haus,** *n.* bakehouse. **-hendel,** *n.* (*Austr.*) *see* **-hähnchen.**

-backig ['bakɪç], **-bäckig** ['bɛkɪç], *adj. suff.* -cheeked.

Backmannschaft ['bakmanʃaft], *f.* (*Naut.*) mess (*men who eat together*).

Back|mulde, *f.* kneading-trough. **-obst,** *n.* dried fruit. **-ofen,** *m.* oven.

Backpfeife ['bakpfaɪfə], *f.* slap in the face.

Back|pflaume, *f.* prune. **-pulver,** *n.* baking-powder. **-rädchen,** *n.* pastry cutter. **-röhre,** *f.* kitchen oven.

Backschaft ['bakʃaft], *f.* *See* **Backmannschaft.** **Backschafter,** *m.* (*Naut.*) ship's cook.

Backs|gast, *m.* (*Naut.*) forecastle hand. **-maat,** *m.* (*Naut.*) messmate.

Backstag ['bakʃta:k], *n.* (*Naut.*) (back-)stay. **Backstags|brise,** *f.*, **-wind,** *m.* wind on the quarter.

Back|stein, *m.* brick. **-steinbau,** *m.* 1. brickwork; 2. (*pl.* **-ten**) brick building. **-trog,** *m.* *See* **-mulde.** **-waren,** *pl.*, **-werk,** *n.* pastries, cakes and biscuits.

Bad [ba:t], *n.* (**-es**, *pl.* **⸚er**) 1. bath; 2. bathe (*in the open air*); 3. bathroom; bath(-tub); 4. bathing establishment, (public) baths, swimming pool; spa, watering-place; *ins – reisen*, go to a watering-place; go the seaside; *die Bäder brauchen*, take the waters.

Bade|anstalt, *f.* (public) baths, swimming bath. **-anzug,** *m.* bathing-costume, swim-suit. **-diener,** *m.* bath attendant. **-gast,** *m.* visitor at a watering-place. **-hose,** *f.* bathing-trunks. **-kappe,** *f.* bathing-cap. **-karren,** *m.* bathing-machine. **-kur,** *f.* treatment at a spa, taking the waters. **-laken,** *n.* *See* **-tuch.** **-mantel,** *m.* bathing-wrap; bath-wrap *or* -robe. **-meister,** *m.* bath attendant. **-mütze,** *f.* *See* **-kappe.**

baden ['ba:dən], **1.** *v.t.* 1. bath (*Am.* bathe) (*a child etc.*); 2. bathe (*eyes, feet, wounds etc.*); *in Blut* (*Schweiß*) *gebadet*, bathed in blood (perspiration). **2.** *v.i.* 1. bath, have *or* take a bath; *kalt –*, have *or* take a cold bath; 2. (*out of doors*) bathe; *– gehen*, go bathing *or* swimming, go for a bathe *or* swim. **3.** *v.r.* *See v.i.* 1.

Bade|nixe, *f.* bathing-beauty. **-ofen,** *m.* geyser, water-heater. **-ort,** *m.* watering-place, bathing resort, spa.

Bader ['ba:dər], *m.* (*obs.*) barber-surgeon.

Bade|salz, *n.* bath-salts. **-strand,** *m.* bathing beach. **-tuch,** *n.* bath towel. **-wanne,** *f.* bath(-tub), (*coll. Naut.*) old tub. **-zelle,** *f.* cubicle. **-zimmer,** *n.* bathroom.

bäen ['bɛ:ən], *v.i.* bleat, baa (*of sheep*).

Bafel ['ba:fəl], *m.* 1. silk waste; 2. (*sl.*) hot air.

baff [baf], *attrib.adj.* (*coll.*) dumbfounded, flabbergasted, speechless.

Bäffchen, *n.* *See* **Beffchen.**

Bagage [ba'ga:ʒə], *f.* luggage, baggage; (*coll.*) rabble, rag-tag and bobtail.

Bagatelle [baga'tɛlə], *f.* trifle, (*also Mus.*) bagatelle. **Bagatelle|sache,** *f.* petty lawsuit. **-schulden,** *pl.* trifling debts. **bagatellisieren** [–i'zi:rən], *v.t.* dismiss as trifling, make light of.

Bagdad [bag'da:t], *n.* Baghdad.

Bagger ['bagər], *m.* dredger, excavator. **Baggermaschine,** *f.* dredger. **baggern,** *v.t.* dredge. **Bagger|netz,** *n.* dredging net. **-prahm,** *m.* dredging float, mud-barge.

[1]**bähen** ['bɛ:ən], *v.i.* *See* **bäen.**

[2]**bähen,** *v.t.* bathe, (*Med.*) foment. **Bähung,** *f.* fomentation.

Bahn [ba:n], *f.* (-, *pl.* **-en**) 1. path, road, way; course (*of a star*), orbit (*of planet*), path, track, orbit (*of comet*), path, trajectory (*of missile*); 2. (*Spt. etc.*) arena, (running- *or* race-)track, (race-)course, lane (*of running-track*), (bowling) alley, slide (*on ice*), toboggan-run, (traffic-)lane (*on motorway*); (*golf*) *Platz mit 18 -en*, 18-hole course; *sich* (*Dat.*) *– brechen*, force *or* push one's way; *– brechen*, blaze a trail, pave the way (*Dat.*, for); *auf die schiefe – geraten*, get into evil ways, (*coll.*) go off the rails; *in die richtige – lenken*, put on the right track *or* right lines; *in ähnlichen -en*, on *or* along similar lines; 3. (*coll.*) railway (*Am.* railroad) (line); tram(way) (*Am.* streetcar) (line); (railway) station; *mit der –*, by rail *or* train; *ihn zur – or an die – bringen*, see him to the station *or* the tram. *See* **Eisenbahn, Straßenbahn**; 4. width, breadth (*of bricks*), face (*of hammer, plane, anvil*), edge (*of chisel*), groove, band (*of pulley*).

Bahn|anlagen, *pl.* railway installations. **-beamte(r),** *m.* railway official. **bahnbrechend,** *adj.* pioneering, epoch-making; *-e Arbeit*, pioneer work. **Bahn|brecher,** *m.* pioneer. **-breite,** *f.* (*Railw.*) gauge; (*Weav.*) width of the piece. **-bus,** *m.* bus operated by the railways. **-damm,** *m.* 1. railway embankment; 2. permanent way. **-ebene,** *f.* plane of motion, orbital plane.

bahnen ['ba:nən], *v.t.* *ihm den Weg – zu*, put him

on the right way for, clear *or* prepare *or* pave the way for him to; ***sich*** (*Dat.*) ***einen Weg –,*** make a way for o.s., make *or* push *or* force one's way.

Bahnfahrt ['ba:nfa:rt], *f.* railway journey. **bahnfrei,** *adj.* (*Comm.*) free on rail (*Am.* on board). **Bahn|-gelände,** *n.* railway property. **–geleise, –gleis,** *n.* railway track.

Bahnhof ['ba:nho:f], *m.* railway (*Am.* railroad) station; (*sl.*) ***mit großem – empfangen,*** put out the red carpet for (*a p.*). **Bahnhofs–,** *pref.* station. **Bahnhofs|kommandant,** *m.* (*Mil.*) Railway Transport Officer. **–mission,** *f.* Traveller's Aid Society. **–vorstand, –vorsteher,** *m.* station-master.

Bahn|knoten(punkt), *m.* railway junction. **–kör-per,** *m.* permanent way. **–kreuzung,** *f.* railway crossing, level-crossing. **bahnlagernd,** *adj.* to be collected (*at railw. station*). **Bahn|meister,** *m.* permanent way inspector. **–reiten,** *n.* show-jumping. **–rennen,** *n.* (*Cycl.*) track racing.

Bahnsteig ['ba:nʃtaɪk], *m.* platform. **Bahnsteig|-sperre,** *f.* ticket barrier. **–überführung,** *f.* foot-bridge (*between platforms*). **–unterführung,** *f.* subway (*between platforms*).

Bahn|überführung, *f.* railway bridge. **–übergang,** *m.* level crossing. **–unterführung,** *f.* railway tunnel. **–wärter,** *m.* linesman; level-crossing keeper.

Bahre ['ba:rə], *f.* stretcher, litter; bier (*for corpse*); ***von der Wiege bis zur –,*** from (the) cradle to (the) grave. **Bahrtuch,** *n.* pall.

Bähung ['bɛ:uŋ], *f.* fomentation.

Bai [baɪ], *f.* (-, *pl.* **-en**) bay, bight; ***kleine –,*** creek, cove.

Baiser [bɛ'ze:], *m. or n.* (**-s,** *pl.* **-s**) (*Cul.*) meringue.

Baisse ['bɛ:sə], *f.* (*Comm.*) (sudden) decline, fall, drop, slump (*in prices*), depression (*of market*); ***auf – spekulieren,*** sell short, sell *or* go a bear, speculate for a fall. **Baisse|geschäft,** *n.* bear transaction. **–spekulant,** *m.* bear. **–stimmung, –strömung, –tendenz,** *f.* downward tendency, bear tone. **Baissier** [–i'e:], *m.* (**-s,** *pl.* **-s**) *see* **Baissespeku-lant. baissieren** [–'si:rən], **1.** *v.t.* lower, depress (*prices*). **2.** *v.i.* decline *or* drop *or* fall (suddenly), slump (*of prices*).

Bajonett [bajon'ɛt], *n.* (**-s,** *pl.* **-e**) bayonet; (***das***) ***– ab!*** unfix bayonets! ***das – aufsetzen,*** fix bayonets; ***mit aufgepflanztem –,*** with fixed bayonets; ***mit gefälltem –,*** at the point of the bayonet. **bajo-nettieren** [–'ti:rən], *v.t.* bayonet.

Bajuware [baju'va:rə], *m.* (**-n,** *pl.* **-n**) (*obs.*) Bavarian. **bajuwarisch,** *adj.* Bavarian.

Bake ['ba:kə], *f.* beacon, landmark; (*Surv.*) range-pole; (*Railw.*) warning notice.

Bakel ['ba:kəl], *m.* schoolmaster's cane.

Bakelit [bakə'li:t], *n.* (**-s,** *no pl.*) bakelite.

Bakkalaureat [bakalaure'a:t], *n.* (**-(e)s,** *pl.* **-e**) bachelor's degree. **Bakkalaureus,** *m.* (-, *pl.* **-rei**) bachelor (*of arts etc.*).

Bakterie [bak'te:riə], *f.* bacterium (*usu.* bacillus). **bakteriell** [–i'ɛl], *adj.* bacterial. **Bakterien|-forschung,–kunde,** *f.* bacteriology. **Bakteriologe** [–'lo:gə], *m.* (**-n,** *pl.* **-n**) bacteriologist. **Bakterio-logie** [–olo'gi:], *f.* bacteriology. **bakteriologisch,** *adj.* bacteriological.

Balance [ba'lãsə], *f.* balance, equilibrium. **Balance-ment,** *n.* (**-s,** *pl.* **-s**) (*Mus.*) tremolo.

Balancier [balãsi'e:], *m.* (**-s,** *pl.* **-s**) beam (*of a balance or engine*); balance-wheel. **balancieren** [–'si:rən], *v.t., v.i.* balance. **Balancier|maschine** [–'si:r-], *f.* beam engine. **–presse,** *f.* screw-press, fly-press. **–stange,** *f.* balancing-pole (*of a tightrope walker*).

balbieren [bal'bi:rən], *v.t.* (*coll.*) *see* **barbieren.**

bald [balt], *adv.* (*comp.* ***eher,*** *sup.* ***am ehesten***) soon, shortly; easily, quickly; (*coll.*) almost, nearly; – . . . – . . ., now . . . now . . ., sometimes . . . sometimes . . .; ***er kam –,*** it was not long before he came; ***ich wäre – gestorben,*** I nearly died; ***das ist – gesagt,*** that's easy to explain; ***– gesagt, schwer getan,*** easier said than done; ***– so, – so,*** now one way, now another.

Baldachin ['baldaxi:n], *m.* (-, *pl.* **-e**) canopy.

Bälde ['bɛldə], *f.* ***in –,*** soon, in the near future.

balde ['baldə], *adv.* (*Poet.*) *see* **bald. balder, bälder,** *comp. adv. occ. for* ***eher.*** **baldest, bäldest,** *sup. adv. occ. for* ***ehest.*** *See* **bald.**

baldig ['baldɪç], *adj.* early; speedy. **baldigst, baldmöglichst,** *adv.* as soon as possible, at the earliest possible moment.

Baldrian ['baldri:an], *m.* (**-s,** *pl.* **-e**) valerian. **Baldrian|säure,** *f.* valeric acid. **–tropfen,** *pl.* valerian essence.

Balduin ['baldui:n], *m.* Baldwin.

Baldur ['baldur], *m.* Balder.

Balearen [balɛ'a:rən], *n.pl.* Balearic Islands.

[1]**Balg** [balk], *m.* (**-(e)s,** *pl.* **⸚e**) **1.** coat, fur (*of live animal*); skin, pelt (*of dead animal*); slough (*of snake*); (*dial.*) pod, shell (*of peas*); husk (*of corn*); skin (*of grapes*); (*Bot.*) glume (*of grasses*); **2.** bag (*of bagpipes*); *pl.* bellows (*of forge, organ, camera*); (*sl.*) ***dicker –,*** paunch, fat belly.

[2]**Balg,** *m. or n.* (**-(e)s,** *pl.* **⸚e(r)**) (*coll.*) urchin, brat, kid; ***süßes –,*** sweet little imp; ***freche Bälger,*** cheeky blighters.

Balgdrüse, *f.* (*Anat.*) follicular gland, lymph-node.

Balge ['balgə], *f.* (*dial.*) wash-tub.

[1]**balgen** ['balgən], **bälgen** ['bɛlgən], **1.** *v.t.* skin, flay (*animals*). **2.** *v.r.* (*of snake*) slough (its skin), cast its slough.

[2]**balgen,** *v.r.* wrestle, struggle, tussle, scuffle, squabble.

Balgen ['balgən], *m.* bellows (*of camera*). **Balgen-auszug,** *m.* bellows extension.

Balgerei [balgə'raɪ], *f.* tussle, scuffle, fisticuffs.

Bälgetreter [bɛlgətre:tər], *m.* organ-blower.

Balg|frucht, *f.* (*Bot.*) follicle. **–gebläse,** *n.* bellows (*of forge*). **–geschwulst,** *n.* (*Med.*) cyst, wen. **–kapsel,** *f. See* **–frucht. –kropf,** *m.* (*Med.*) cystic goitre. **–treter,** *m. See* **Bälgetreter.**

balhornisieren ['balhornizi:rən], *v.t.* corrupt (*text*) (*after the printer Balhorn*). *See* **verbalhornen.**

Balkan ['balka:n], *m.* Balkan Peninsula; Balkan states, Balkans.

Balken ['balkən], *m.* beam, rafter, joist, girder; ba(u)lk; beam, arm (*of balance*); (*Mus.*) bass-bar (*of violin*); land (*of rifle-bore*); (*Her.*) bar, fesse; (*Prov.*) ***Wasser hat keine –,*** don't trust yourself to the water; (*Anat.*) ***– des Gehirns,*** corpus callosum cerebri; ***den – im eigenen Auge nicht sehen,*** not see the beam in one's own eye.

Balken|anker, *m.* (*Build.*) cramp-iron, tie-bar, wall-plate. **–decke,** *f.* raftered ceiling. **–gerüst,** *n.* scaffolding, timberwork. **–kopf,** *m.* projecting beam-end. **–stein,** *m.* corbel. **–überschrift,** *f.* (*Typ.*) banner headline. **–waage,** *f.* steelyard, beam balance. **–werk,** *n.* timberwork, timbers, beams and joists (*of a building*).

Balkon [bal'ko:n], *m.* (**-s,** *pl.* **-e**) balcony; (*Theat.*) (dress-)circle.

[1]**Ball** [bal], *m.* (**-(e)s,** *pl.* **⸚e**) ball; globe, sphere; (*fig.*) ***den – ins Rollen bringen,*** start *or* set the ball rolling; (*Bill.*) ***einen – machen,*** pocket a ball.

[2]**Ball,** *m.* (**-(e)s,** *pl.* **⸚e**) ball, dance; ***auf einen*** or ***zu einem – gehen,*** go to a dance.

Ballade [ba'la:də], *f.* ballad. **Balladendichter,** *m.* ballad-writer.

Ballarbeit ['balˀarbaɪt], *f.* (*Boxing*) punch-ball practice.

Ballast ['balast], *m.* (**-es,** *pl.* **-e**) ballast; (*coll.*) bulk, (unnecessary) padding (*as in a book*).

Ballbehandlung, *f.* (*Footb.*) ball control.

Ballei [ba'laɪ], *f.* (-, *pl.* **-en**) (*Hist.*) bailiwick.

Ballen ['balən], *m.* 1. bale, ten reams (*of paper*); 2. ball (*of thumb, foot*), (*Anat.*) thenar; button (*of a foil*); (*Med.*) bunion. **Ballen|binder,** *m.* packer. **–entzündung,** *f.* bunion. **–schnur,** *f.* packing-cord. **–waren,** *pl.* bale-goods. **ballenweise,** *adv.* in bales, by the bale.

ballen ['balən], **1.** *v.t.* form *or* shape into a ball, clench (*fist etc.*). **2.** *v.r.* form into a ball *or* clump, conglomerate, cluster.
Ballerbüchse ['balərbyksə], *f.* pop-gun.
Ballerina [bale'ri:na] (-, *pl.* **-rinen**), **Ballerine,** *f.* ballerina, ballet-dancer.
ballern [balərn], *v.i.* (*coll.*) bang, shoot.
Ballett [ba'lɛt], *n.* (**-s,** *pl.* **-e**) ballet. **Ballettänzer,** *m.* ballet-dancer. **Ballettänzerin, Balletteuse** [–'tø:zə], *f.* ballet-dancer, ballerina.
ballförmig ['balfœrmɪç], *adj.* ball-shaped, spherical, globular.
ballig ['balɪç], *adj.* (slightly) convex.
Ballistik [ba'lɪstɪk], *f.* (-, *pl.* -) ballistics. **ballistisch,** *adj.* ballistic.
Ball|junge, *m.* (*Tenn.*) ball-boy. **-kleid,** *n.* (lady's) evening dress, dance dress.
Ballon [ba'lɔn], *m.* (**-s,** *pl.* **-e** *or* **-s**) balloon; (*Chem.*) flask, carboy. **Ballon|reifen,** *m.* balloon tyre. **-segel,** *n.* (*Naut.*) spinnaker. **-sperre,** *f.* balloon-barrage.
Ballotage [balo'ta:ʒə], *f.* balloting; (ball-)ballot. **ballotieren,** *v.i.* vote by (ball-)ballot.
Ball|schläger, *m.* 1. bat; 2. batsman. **-schuh,** *m.* evening shoe, dancing-slipper. **-spiel,** *n.* ball-game.
Ballung ['baluŋ], *f.* cluster, clump. *See* **ballen.**
Balsam ['balza:m], *m.* (**-s,** *pl.* **-e**) balsam, balm, salve. **balsamieren** [–'mi:rən], *v.t.* embalm, anoint. **Balsamine** [–'mi:nə], *f.* balsamine (*Impatiens balsamina*). **balsamisch** [–'za:mɪʃ], *adj.* balmy, fragrant, soothing. **Balsamkraut,** *n.* balsam herb (*Dianthera repens*), moschatel (*Adoxa moschatellina*).
Balthasar ['baltazar], *m.* (*B.*) Belshazzar.
Baltikum ['baltɪkum], *n.* Baltic states. **baltisch,** *adj.* Baltic.
Balz [balts], *f.* (-, *pl.* **-en**), *occ. m.* (**-es,** *pl.* **-e**) pairing, coupling, mating, treading (*of birds*); pairing *or* mating season; display, courtship play (*of cock*). **balzen,** *v.i.* pair, couple, mate, tread (*of birds*); court, woo, display (*of cock*). **Balzflug,** *m.* display flight.
Bambus ['bambus], *m.* (- *or* **-ses,** *pl.* - *or* **-se**) bamboo. **Bambus|bär,** *m.* (*Zool.*) giant panda. **-rohr,** *n.* bamboo cane.
Bammel ['baməl], *m.* (*coll.*) funk.
bammeln ['baməln], *v.i.* (*coll.*) dangle, hang down.
bamsen ['bamzən], *v.t.* (*coll.*) give (*s.o.*) a hiding.
banal [ba'na:l], *adj.* commonplace, trite, banal. **Banalität** [–i'tɛ:t], *f.* banality.
Banane [ba'na:nə], *f.* banana. **Bananen|faser,** *f.* manila hemp, abaca fibre. **-stecher,** *m.* (*Rad.*) banana plug.
Banause [ba'nauzə], *m.* (**-n,** *pl.* **-n**) lowbrow, philistine. **Banausentum,** *n.* narrow-mindedness, philistinism. **banausisch,** *adj.* narrow-minded, low-brow.
[1]**Band** [bant], *n.* (**-(e)s,** *pl.* **⸚er**) 1. ribbon (*decorative, also fig.*), tape (*for utility; also Spt.*), webbing (*heavy gauge*); band (*on hat*), string (*of apron*), (recording-)tape (*for tape-recorder*); ***das Blaue –,*** the Blue Riband; ***auf – sprechen,*** record one's voice, record (*speech etc.*); ***endloses –,*** (transmission) belt (*on pulleys*); ***laufendes –,*** conveyor(-belt) (*in industry*); ***Produktion am laufenden –,*** production on the assembly line, mass-production; (*fig. coll.*) ***am laufenden –,*** without respite *or* intermission, one after the other; ***das – zerschneiden,*** cut the tape (*at opening ceremony*); 2. (metal) strap; hoop (*on cask etc.*); fish (*on mast*); (*Build.*) brace, strut, tie(-piece), hinge (*also of mollusc*); (*Anat.*) ligament; (*Geol.*) seam, streak (*of ore*); (*Archit.*) fascia; (*Opt.*) spectrum band; (*Rad.*) frequency band; (*fig.*) ***außer Rand und – sein,*** be out of hand.
[2]**Band,** *n.* (**-(e)s,** *pl.* **-e**) 1. tie, bond, link; ***– der Freundschaft,*** bond of friendship; ***eheliches –,*** marriage tie, bond of matrimony; 2. *pl.* shackles, chains, irons, fetters, bonds, (*fig.*) trammels.
[3]**Band,** *m.* (**-es,** *pl.* **⸚e**) volume, tome; binding (*of a book*).

band, *see* **binden.**
Bandage [ban'da:ʒə], *f.* bandage, truss. **bandagieren** [–'ʒi:rən], *v.t.* bandage.
Bandantrieb ['bantˀantri:p], *m.* belt-drive. **bandartig,** *adj.* ribbon-like. **Band|aufnahme,** *f.* tape-recording. **-blitz,** *m.* ribbon lightning. **-breite,** *f.* (*Rad.*) band-width.
[1]**Bande** ['bandə], *f.* band, gang; (*coll.*) crowd, bunch (*of people*).
[2]**Bande,** *f.* border, edge, rim; (*Bill.*) cushion; ***den Ball an die – spielen,*** cushion the ball.
[3]**Bande,** *f.* (*Opt.*) (spectrum-)band.
bände ['bɛndə], *see* **binden.**
Bandeisen ['bantˀaɪzən], *n.* hoop-iron.
Bändel ['bɛndəl], *n.* apron-string; shoe-lace; (*fig. coll.*) ***ihn am – haben,*** keep him dangling, keep him on a string.
Bandenkrieg ['bandənkri:k], *m.* guerilla warfare.
bändern ['bɛndərn], *v.t.* mark with bands *or* stripes.
Banderole [bandə'ro:le], *f.* streamer, banderole, (*Mil.*) pennon; (*Art*) scroll; band (*on cigar*).
Bänderriß ['bɛndərrɪs], *m.* (*Med.*) torn ligament.
Bänderung ['bɛndəruŋ], *f.* stripes, bands; fasciation; (*Geol.*) lamination, foliation.
Band|feder, *f.* (flat) coil spring. **-filter,** *m.* (*Rad.*) band-pass filter. **-förderung,** *f.* *See* **-transport. -führung,** *f.* ribbon guide (*typewriter*). **-gerät,** *n.* tape-recorder. **-gesims,** *n.* (*Archit.*) string-course. **-haken,** *m.* hinge-pin.
-bändig ['bɛndɪç], *adj. suff.* -volume(d), in . . . volumes.
bändigen [bɛndɪgən], *v.t.* tame, subdue, reduce to obedience; break in (*a horse*); overcome, master, keep under control, discipline.
Bandit [ban'di:t], *m.* (**-en,** *pl.* **-en**) bandit, brigand, (*coll.*) ruffian, gangster.
Band|kegel, *m.* *See* **-haken. -kupplung,** *f.* (*Motor.*) rim clutch. **-maß,** *n.* tape-measure. **-montage,** *f.* assembly line. **-nudeln,** *pl.* ribbon vermicelli. **-rolle,** *f.* (*Art*) banderole, scroll. **-säge,** *f.* band-saw. **-scheibe,** *f.* (*Anat.*) intervertebral disc. **-scheibenvorfall,** *m.* (*coll.*) slipped disc. **-seeadler,** *m.* *See* **Weißbindenseeadler.**
Bändsel ['bɛntsəl], *n.* (*Naut.*) lashing, seizing.
Band|stahl, *m.* steel strip. **-transport,** *m.* (belt-) conveyor, assembly line. **-waren,** *pl.* haberdashery. **-wurm,** *m.* tapeworm. **-wurmrede,** *f.* (*coll.*) interminable speech.
Bang [baŋ], *m.* (*Bot.*) Indian hemp, bhang.
bang(e) ['baŋ(ə)], *adj.* (*comp.* ***banger, bänger;*** *sup.* ***bangst, bängst***) afraid, alarmed, scared, frightened; timid, anxious; ***–e machen,*** frighten, scare, alarm, terrify; (*coll.*) ***–e machen gilt nicht,*** you can't scare me; ***es ist mir –e um ihn,*** I am anxious, worried, uneasy, concerned *or* nervous about him; ***es ist mir –e vor ihm,*** I am afraid of him; ***uns war angst und –e,*** we were frightened to death; ***voll –er Ahnung,*** with a premonition of evil, full of *or* filled with apprehension. **Bange,** *f.* (*coll.*) fear, worry, anxiety; (*coll.*) ***haben Sie keine –!*** don't worry!
bangen [baŋən], **1.** *v.i., v.r.* worry, be uneasy *or* anxious *or* concerned (***um,*** about); long, yearn (***nach,*** for). **2.** *v.imp.* (*Dat.*) be nervous *or* fearful (***vor,*** of); be afraid, fear (***um, für,*** for).
Bangigkeit ['baŋɪçkait], *f.* anxiety, uneasiness, apprehension, fear, dread.
bänglich ['bɛŋlɪç], *adj.* (somewhat) anxious *or* uneasy *or* apprehensive *or* fearful.
Baniane [bani'a:nə], *f.* (*Bot.*) banyan(-tree).
[1]**Bank** [baŋk], *f.* (-, *pl.* **⸚e**) bench, seat, form (*at school*), pew (*in church*); (carpenter's) bench, (butcher's) block, bed (*of lathe*); (*Geol.*) mud-bank, sand-bank, reef, shoal; bed, layer, seam; (*Mil.*) fire-step, parapet, banquette, barbette; ***auf die lange – schieben,*** put aside, defer, postpone, keep putting off; ***durch die –,*** without exception, taking all in all, one and all.
[2]**Bank,** *f.* (-, *pl.* **-en**) bank, banking house *or* establishment; (gambling-)bank; ***Geld bei*** or ***auf***

der – haben, have money in the bank; ***ein Scheck auf die – von England,*** a cheque on the Bank of England; (*Cards*) ***die – sprengen,*** break the bank; (*Cards*) ***die – halten,*** (***die***) ***– machen,*** hold bank.

Bank|aktien, *pl.* bank-shares. **–angestellte(r),** *m., f. See* **–beamte(r). –ausweis,** *m.* bank statement. **–beamte(r),** *m., f.* bank clerk. **–bruch,** *m. See* **Bank(e)rott. –buch,** *n.* bank book, pass book. **–diskont,** *m.* bank rate.

Bänkel|kind ['bɛŋkəl–], *n. See* **Bankert. –lied,** *n.* popular ballad, street-ballad. **–sänger,** *m.* itinerant singer, ballad-monger.

Bank(e)rott [baŋk(ə)'rɔt], *m.* **(-(e)s,** *pl.* **-e)** bankruptcy, insolvency; ***– machen,*** go bankrupt; ***mit 50% – machen,*** pay 50p in the £; ***betrügerischer –,*** fraudulent bankruptcy; ***moralischer –,*** moral bankruptcy. **bank(e)rott,** *adj.* bankrupt, insolvent; (*coll.*) broke; ***sich für – erklären,*** file a petition in bankrupty. **Bank(e)rotterklärung,** *f.* petition in bankruptcy. **Bank(e)rotteur** [–'tø:r] **(-s,** *pl.* **-e), Bank(e)rottier** [–ti'e:] **(-s,** *pl.* **-s), Bank(e)rottierer** [–'ti:rər], *m.* bankrupt. **Bank(e)rott(s)masse,** *f.* (bankrupt's) estate *or* total assets.

Bankert ['baŋkərt], *m.* **(-s,** *pl.* **-e)** bastard, natural *or* illegitimate child; (*coll.*) brat.

[1]**Bankett** [baŋ'kɛt], *n.* **(-(e)s,** *pl.* -e) banquet, feast.

[2]**Bankett,** *n.* **(-(e)s,** *pl.* **-e), Bankette,** *f.* 1. (*Mil.*) banquette, fire-step; 2. (*Build.*) base-course, footing (*of wall*), berm, side-path.

Bankfach, *n.* 1. banking (business); 2. (customer's) strong box. **bankfähig,** *adj.* negotiable, bankable. **Bank|filiale,** *f.* branch bank. **–gebühren,** *pl.* bank charges, banker's commission. **–geschäft,** *n.* bank(ing) transaction. **–gewölbe,** *n.* strong-room, bullion-vault, safe-deposit. **–halter,** *m.* casino manager, holder of the bank.

Bankier [baŋki'e:], *m.* **(-s,** *pl.* **-s)** banker, financier.

Bank|konto, *n.* bank(ing) (*Am.* checking) account. **–note,** *f.* bank-note, (*Am.*) bill. **–notenausgabe,** *f.* note-issue. **–notenumlauf,** *m.* notes in circulation, paper currency. **–provision,** *f. See* **–gebühren. –rott,** *m. See* **Bank(e)rott. –satz,** *m. See* **–diskont. –spesen,** *pl. See* **–gebühren. –tratte,** *f.*, **–wechsel,** *m.* banker's draft. **–werte,** *pl.* bank shares, (*Am.*) stock. **–wesen,** *n.* banking (system).

Bann [ban], *m.* **(-(e)s,** *pl.* **-e)** 1. (*Hist.*) soke, jurisdiction; 2. (*Hist.*) proclamation, edict; 3. banishment, ban, proscription, interdict, (*Eccl.*) anathema, excommunication; ***in den –*** or ***in Acht und – tun,*** banish, proscribe, (*Eccl.*) excommunicate; 4. spell, charm; ***in seinen – geraten,*** come under his influence; ***in*** or ***im – halten, in – schlagen,*** hold spellbound; ***den – brechen,*** break the spell. **Bann|bezirk,** *m. See* **Bann,** 1. **–brief,** *m.*, **–bulle,** *f.* edict *or* bull of excommunication, anathema.

bannen ['banən], *v.t.* 1. (*Hist.*) banish, proscribe, (*Eccl.*) excommunicate; 2. (*Hist.*) ban *or* prohibit (the use of); 3. (*fig.*) banish (*want, fear etc.*), dispel, cast out (*fear*), exorcise, lay (*ghosts*); 4. charm, bewitch, put *or* cast a spell on; capture (*as a painter on canvas*); ***gebannt,*** spellbound.

Banner ['banər], *n.* banner, standard, flag. **Bannerträger,** *m.* standard-bearer.

Bann|fluch, *m.* (*Eccl.*) anathema, ban. **–forst,** *m.* royal forest. **–gerechtigkeit,** *f. See* **–recht. –gewalt,** *f. See* **Bann,** 1. **–herr,** *m.* feudal landlord.

bannig ['banɪç], *adv.* (*dial.*) terribly, terrifically, very.

Bann|kreis, *m.* 1. *See* **Bann,** 1; 2. (*fig.*) (sphere of) influence, spell. **–meile,** *f.* (*Hist.*) town precincts; (*Law*) prohibited area. **–recht,** *n.* feudal rights. **–spruch,** *m.* curse, ban; *see* **–fluch. –strahl,** *m. See* **–fluch. –vogt,** *m.* (*Hist.*) reeve of the soke. **–wald,** *m.* (*Swiss*) forest preserve (*as protection against avalanches*). **–waren,** *pl.* contraband goods. **–wart,** *m.* (*Swiss*) forester, forest-ranger *or* -warden.

Banse ['banzə], *f.* (*dial.*) barn. **bansen,** *v.t.* (*dial.*) stack (*sheaves*).

[1]**Bar** [ba:r], *m.* **(-(e)s,** *pl.* **-e)** strophe (*in mediaeval lyric and poetry of the Mastersingers*).

[2]**Bar,** *f.* (-, *pl.* **-s)** 1. public house; drinking and dancing saloon, night club; 2. cocktail-cabinet.

[3]**Bar,** *n.* **(-s,** *pl.* **-s)** (*Meteor.*) bar (= 750 *mm. mercury*).

bar, 1. *adj.* 1. bare, naked; 2. pure, sheer, unmixed (*also fig.*); ***für -e Münze nehmen,*** take for gospel truth *or* at face value; ***für -en Ernst nehmen,*** believe implicitly; ***-es Gold,*** pure gold; ***-er Unsinn,*** downright *or* sheer nonsense; ***die -e Wahrheit,*** the plain *or* unadulterated truth; 3. ready, spot (*cash*); (***in***) ***– bezahlen,*** pay (in) cash; ***-es Geld,*** ready money, spot cash. **2.** *pred. adj.* (*Gen. either preceding or following*) lacking, devoid of, without.

Bar–, *pref.* cash (*e.g.* ***–geschäft,*** cash transaction).

–bar, *adj. suff.* 1. (*to verb stem*) –able, –ible (*e.g.* ***lesbar,*** readable; ***erreichbar,*** accessible); 2. (*to nouns*) –ful (*e.g.* ***wunderbar,*** wonderful).

Bär [bɛ:r], *m.* **(-en,** *pl.* **-en)** 1. bear; ***junger –,*** bear's cub; ***der Große*** (***Kleine***) ***–,*** the Great (Lesser) Bear, Ursa major (minor); ***ihm einen -en aufbinden,*** hoax him, play him a practical joke, pull his leg; (*coll.*) ***ungeleckter –,*** unlicked cub; 2. (*Ent.*) tiger-moth; 3. rammer, pile-driver.

Baracke [ba'rakə], *f.* hut, barrack, shanty; ***elende –,*** hovel. **Barackenlager,** *n.* hutments.

Barratteur [bara'tø:r], *m.* **(-s,** *pl.* **-s** *or* **-e)** (*Comm.*) cheat, swindler, defrauder. **Barratthandel** [–'rathandəl], *m.* (*Comm.*) barter. **barrattieren** [–'ti:rən], *v.i.* (*Comm.*) barter, exchange goods.

Barauslagen ['ba:rʔausla:gən], *f.pl.* cash outlay, (out-of-pocket) expenses.

Barbar [bar'ba:r], *m.* **(-en,** *pl.* **-en)** barbarian. **Barbarei** [–'raɪ], *f.* barbarism; barbarity; 2. Barbary States. **barbarisch,** *adj.* barbaric, primitive (*people*); barbarous, brutal, inhuman (*behaviour*); (*coll.*) frightful, fearful, dreadful. **Barbarismus** [–'rɪsmus], *m.* (-, *pl.* **-men)** barbarism (*in language*), crudeness, uncouthness.

Barbe ['barbə], *f.* (*Ichth.*) barbel (*Barbus vulgaris*).

bärbeißig ['bɛ:rbaɪsɪç], *adj.* surly, grumpy, bearish, (*coll.*) like a bear with a sore head. **Bärbeißigkeit,** *f.* surliness, grumpiness.

Barbestand ['ba:rbəʃtant], *m.* cash reserve, cash in hand.

Barbier [bar'bi:r], *m.* **(-s,** *pl.* **-e)** barber. **barbieren,** *v.t.* shave; (*coll.*) ***ihn über den Löffel –,*** swindle *or* cheat *or* fleece him. **Barbier|messer,** *n.* open razor, (*coll.*) cut-throat (razor). **–schild,** *n.* (*English*) barber's pole, (*German*) barber's bowl.

Barbitursäure [barbi'tu:rzɔyrə], *f.* (*Chem.*) barbituric acid.

Barch [barç], *m.* **(-es,** *pl.* **¨-e)** (*dial.*) castrated boar.

barchen ['barçən], *adj.* fustian. **Barchent,** *m.* **(-s,** *pl.* **-e)** fustian.

Bardame ['ba:rda:mə], *f.* barmaid.

Barde ['bardə], *m.* **(-n,** *pl.* **-n)** bard, (Celtic) minstrel. **Bardendichtung,** *f.* bardic poetry *or* lays.

Bareme [ba'rɛ:mə], *m.* (-, *pl.* **-n)** ready-reckoner; price-schedule.

Bären|beißer, *m.* bear-hound. **–dienst,** *m.* (*coll.*) ***ihm einen – leisten,*** do him a disservice. **–dreck,** *m.* (*coll.*) liquorice. **–fell,** *n.* bearskin. **–fellmütze,** *f. See* **–mütze. –hatz,** *f. See* **–hetze. –haut,** *f.* bearskin; (*coll.*) ***auf der – liegen,*** lounge about. **–häuter,** *m.* (*coll.*) idler, lay-about, lazy-bones. **–hetze,** *f.* bearbaiting. **–hunger,** *m.* (*coll.*) ***einen – haben,*** be as hungry as a wolf. **–hüter,** *m.* (*Astr.*) Boötes. **–junge(r),** *m., f.* bear-cub. **–klau,** *m. or f.* (*Bot.*) hog-weed, cow-parsnip (*Heracleum sphondylium*); (*Bot.*) acanthus, bear's breech (*Acanthus mollis*). **–klee,** *m.* (*Bot.*) kidney-vetch (*Anthyllis vulneraria*); (*Bot.*) sweet clover (*Melilotus*). **–mütze,** *f.* (*Mil.*) bearskin (*headgear*). **–raupe,** *f.* (*Ent.*) (*coll.*) woolly bear. **–spinner,** *m.* (*Ent.*) tigermoth. **bärenstark,** *adj.* strong as an ox. **Bären|wurz(el),** *f.* (*Bot.*) spignel (*Meum athamanticum*). **–zwinger,** *m.* bear-pit.

Barett [ba'rɛt], *n.* (**-s,** *pl.* **-e**) biretta; cardinal's hat; academic hat, (*coll.*) mortar-board.
Barfreimachung ['ba:rfraımaxuŋ], *f.* bulk franking (*post*).
barfuß ['ba:rfus], **1.** *adj.* barefooted. **2.** *pred.adj., adv.* barefoot. **Barfüßer(mönch),** *m.* barefooted *or* discalced friar.
barg [bark], **bärge** ['bɛrgə], *see* **bergen.**
Bargeld ['ba:rgɛlt], *n.* cash, ready money. **bargeldlos,** *adj.* by cheque.
bar|haupt, *pred.adj., adv.,* **-häuptig,** *adj.* bareheaded.
Barhocker ['barhɔkər], *m.* bar-stool.
Bärin ['bɛ:rın], *f.* she-bear.
Bariton ['ba:ritɔn], *m.* (**-s,** *pl.* **-e**) baritone (*voice, clef*). **Bariton|horn,** *n.* euphonium. **-klarinette,** *f.* alto clarinet.
Bark [bark], *f.* (-, *pl.* **-en**) (*Naut.*) barque. **Barkasse,** *f.* longboat, launch. **Barke,** *f.* Mediterranean fishing craft.
Bärlapp ['bɛ:rlap], *m.* (**-s,** *no pl.*) (*Bot.*) club moss, lycopodium.
Barlauf ['ba:rlauf], *m.* prisoner's-base (*a game*).
Bärme ['bɛrmə], *f.* barm, yeast, leaven.
barmherzig ['barmhɛrtsıç], *adj.* compassionate, merciful; kind(-hearted); ***-er Bruder,*** monk-hospitaller; ***-e Schwester,*** sister of mercy; ***-er Samariter,*** good Samaritan. **Barmherzigkeit,** *f.* compassion, mercy; kind-heartedness.
Bar|mittel, *n. See* **-geld.**
Barock [ba'rɔk], *m. or n.* (**-s,** *no pl.*) Baroque, baroque style. **barock,** *adj.* baroque; quaint, grotesque.
Barometer [baro'me:tər], *n.* barometer. **Barometerstand,** *m.* barometer reading. **barometrisch,** *adj.* barometric(al).
Baron [ba'ro:n], *m.* (**-s,** *pl.* **-e**) baron. **Baronat** [–'na:t], *n.* (**-(e)s,** *pl.* **-e**) barony. **Baronesse** [–'nɛsə], *f.* titled lady (*i.e. baron's unmarried daughter*). **Baronin,** *f.* baroness (*i.e. baron's wife*). **baronisieren** [–i'zi:rən], *v.i.* (*coll.*) be a gentleman of leisure.
Barras ['baras], *m.* 1. army; ***beim –,*** in the forces; 2. army bread.
Barre ['barə], *f.* 1. bar (*at river's mouth*); barrier, rail(ing); 2. rail, metal bar.
Barren ['barən], *m.* 1. bar, ingot, bullion; 2. (*Gymn.*) parallel bars. **Barren|beißer,** *m.* crib-biter (*horse*). **-form,** *f.* ingot-mould; ***in –,*** in bars. **-gold,** *n.* (gold) bullion. **-turnen,** *n.* (*Gymn.*) parallel-bar exercises.
Barriere [bari'ɛ:rə], *f.* (*Railw.*) (ticket-)barrier; level-crossing gate; toll-bar; frontier post.
Barsch [ba:rʃ], *m.* (**-es,** *pl.* **-e**) (*Ichth.*) perch.
barsch [barʃ], *adj.* rough, curt, surly, uncivil, brusque, gruff.
Barschaft ['ba:rʃaft], *f. See* **Bargeld**; (*coll.*) ***meine ganze –,*** all I have to my name, all I have on me.
Barscheck ['ba:rʃɛk], *m.* (**-s,** *pl.* **-s**) open *or* uncrossed cheque.
Barschheit ['barʃhaıt], *f.* rudeness, roughness, curtness, brusqueness.
barst [barst], **bärste** ['bɛrstə], *see* **bersten.**
Bart [ba:rt], *m.* (**-es,** *pl.* **⸚e**) beard; wattles, gills (*of a bird*); whiskers (*of a cat*); wattles, barbels, barb (*of fish*); gills, beard (*of oysters*); web, vane, vexillum (*of feather*); beard, awns, barb, aristae (*of barley*); bit, web (*of key*); beard (*of type*); tail (*of comet*); ***ihn um den – gehen,*** flatter *or* coax *or* cajole him; ***in den – brummen,*** mutter to o.s.; ***in den – lachen,*** laugh up one's sleeve; ***sich um des Kaisers – streiten,*** quarrel about trifles; fight for a shadow; (*coll.*) ***der – ist ab,*** you've had it, that's torn it; you've given yourself away.
Barte ['bartə], *f.* 1. broad-axe, battle axe; 2. upper jaw of a whale; whalebone.
Bart|faden, *m. See* **Bart-flechte,** *f.* 1. (*Bot.*) greybeard lichen; 2. (*Med.*) sycosis, (*coll.*) barber's itch *or* rash. **-geier,** *m.* (*Orn.*) bearded vulture, lammergeier (*Gypaetus barbatus*). **-grasmücke,** *f.* (*Orn.*) subalpine warbler (*Sylvia cantilans*). **-grind,** *m. See* **-flechte,** 2. **-haar,** *n.* beard and moustache. **-hafer,** *m.* wild oats.
Barthel ['bartəl], *m.* (*dim. of*) Bartholomew; (*coll.*) ***wissen wo – den Most holt,*** know one's onions, know what's what.
Bartholomäus [bartolo'mɛ:us], *m.* Bartholomew. **Bartholomäusnacht,** *f.* Massacre of St. Bartholomew.
bärtig ['bɛ:rtıç], *adj.* bearded.
Bart|kauz, *m.* (*Orn.*) great grey owl (*Strix nebulosa*). **-kluppe,** *f.* hand-vice. **-lappen,** *pl.* wattles, gills (*of fowl etc.*). **-laubsänger,** *m.* (*Orn.*) Radde's bush warbler (*Phylloscopus schwarzi*).
bartlos ['ba:rtlos], *adj.* beardless, clean-shaven.
Bart|meise, *f.* (*Orn.*) bearded titmouse (*Panurus biarmicus*). **-moos,** *n. See* **-flechte,** 1. **-nelke,** *f.* (*Bot.*) sweet william (*Dianthus barbatus*). **-robbe,** *f.* (*Zool.*) bearded seal. **-stoppeln,** *pl.* stubble (*on the chin*). **-tasse,** *f.* moustache-cup. **-tracht,** *f.* style of beard. **-wichse,** *f.* wax for the moustache. **-wuchs,** *m.* growth of beard.
Baryt [ba'ry:t], *m.* (**-s,** *pl.* **-e**) 1. barytes, heavy spar; 2. (*Chem.*) barium oxide. **barythaltig,** *adj.* barytic. **Barytsalz,** *n.* barium salt.
Barzahlung ['ba:rtsa:luŋ], *f.* cash payment, cash down.
Basalt [ba'zalt], *m.* (**-(e)s,** *pl.* **-e**) basalt. **basalten, basaltig, basaltisch,** *adj.* basaltic.
Basar [ba'za:r], *m.* (**-s,** *pl.* **-e**) (Oriental) bazaar; (charity) bazaar; (cheap) stores, emporium.
[1]**Base** ['ba:zə], *f.* (female) cousin; (*Swiss obs.*) aunt.
[2]**Base,** *f.* 1. (*Chem.*) base, alkali; 2. *See* **Basis.**
basieren [ba'zi:rən], **1.** *v.t.* establish, base, ground, found (***auf*** (*Acc.*), on). **2.** *v.i.* be based *or* grounded *or* founded (***auf*** (*Dat.*), on). **3.** *v.r. See* 2.
Basilie [ba'zi:liə], *f.*, **Basilienkraut, Basilikum,** *n.* (-s, *pl.* **-s** *or* **-ken**) (*Bot.*) common *or* sweet basil.
Basilisk [bazi'lısk], *m.* (**-en,** *pl.* **-en**) basilisk; cockatrice. **Basiliskenbrut,** *f.* (*coll.*) viper's brood.
Basilius [ba'zi:lius], *m.* Basil.
Basis ['ba:zıs], *f.* (-, *pl.* **Basen**) foundation, basis; (*Archit.*) pedestal, foot, base; (*Geom.*) base (*of triangle*), (*Surv.*) ground-line, base(-line); (*Mil.*) base (of operations); (*Math.*) radix, root, base; basal plane (*of crystals*). **Basisbruch,** *m.* (*Med.*) fracture of the base of the skull. **basisch,** *adj.* basic. **Basiswinkel,** *m.* base angle (*of isosceles triangle*).
Baske ['baskə], *m.* (**-n,** *pl.* **-n**) Basque. **Baskenmütze,** *f.* beret. **baskisch,** *adj.* Basque. **Baskisch,** *n.* Basque (language).
Basküle [bas'ky:lə], *f.* fastening, catch, (*Scots*) snib (*of window etc.*).
Baß [bas], *m.* (**-(ss)es,** *pl.* **⸚(ss)e**) 1. bass, bass part; ***begleitender*** or ***gebundener*** or ***obligater –,*** thorough-bass; ***figurierter*** or ***bezifferter –,*** figured bass; 2. bass singer; ***hoher –,*** bass baritone (*voice*); 3. contrabass, double bass.
baß, *adv.* (*Poet.*) very, (very) much, highly, in a high degree.
Basset [ba'sɛt], *m.* (**-s,** *pl.* **-s**) basset hound.
Bassett [ba'sɛt], *n.* (**-(e)s,** *pl.* **-e**) bass viol. **Bassetthorn,** *n.* tenor clarinet, basset-horn.
Baßgeige ['basgaıgə], *f.* double-bass.
Bassin [ba'sɛ̃], *n.* (**-s,** *pl.* **-s**) receptacle, tank, cistern, reservoir; wash-basin, hand-basin; basin (*of fountain*); (*Naut.*) basin dock.
Bassist [ba'sıst], *m.* (**-en,** *pl.* **-en**) 1. bass singer; 2. double-bass player.
Baß|pfeife, *f.* bass-pipe (*of organ*), drone (*of a bagpipe*). **-posaune,** *f.* bass trombone. **-saite,** *f.* bass string. **-schlüssel,** *m.* bass clef, bass key. **-stimme,** *f.* bass voice; bass part. **-tölpel,** *m.* (*Orn.*) gannet (*Morus bassanus*).
Bast [bast], *m.* (**-(e)s,** *pl.* **-e**) 1. inner bark, phloem (*of trees etc.*), velvet (*of a stag's antler*); 2. bast, raffia.

basta! ['basta], *int.* enough; ***und damit –!*** and there's an end of it! and that's that! so there!
Bastard ['bastart], *m.* (**-s,** *pl.* **-e**) bastard, illegitimate *or* natural child; hybrid (*animal or plant*), cross-breed (*animal*), mongrel (*dog*), half-breed *or* -caste, mestizo (*a p.*). **Bastard|balken,** *m.* 1. (*Naut.*) half- *or* cross-beam; 2. (*Her.*) bend sinister. **–faden,** *m.* (*Her.*) scarp. **–feile,** *f.* bastard file. **–fenster,** *n.* mezzanine window. **–format,** *n.* bastard size (*of book*).
bastardieren [bastar'di:rən], *v.i.* hybridize. **Bastardierung,** *f.* hybridization.
Bastard|nachtigall, *f. See* **Gelbspötter. –pflanze,** *f.* hybrid. **–wechsel,** *m.* (*Comm.*) dummy bill.
Bastei [bas'taɪ], *f.* (-, *pl.* **-en**) bastion.
Bastelarbeit ['bastəlˀarbaɪt], **Bastelei,** *f.* handicraft (as a hobby); (piece of) handwork. **basteln, 1.** *v.t.* build, put together, rig *or* fix up (*models etc.*). **2.** *v.i.* occupy o.s. with handwork, do handicrafts. **Basteln,** *n.* handicrafts, handwork.
basten ['bastən], *adj.* (made of) bast *or* raffia.
Bastion [basti'o:n], *f. See* **Bastei.**
Bastler ['bastlər], *m.* home *or* amateur constructor.
Bastonade [basto'na:də], (*Austr.*) **Bastonnade,** *f.* bastinado; ***die – erhalten,*** be bastinadoed.
bat [ba:t], *see* **bitten.**
Bataillon [batal'jo:n], *n.* (**-s,** *pl.* **-e**) battalion. (*In Germany approx. English regiment.*)
bäte ['bɛ:tə], *see* **bitten.**
Bathseba ['batseba], *f.* (*B.*) Bathsheba.
Batist [ba'tɪst], *m.* (**-es,** *pl.* **-e**) cambric, batiste. **batisten,** *adj.* (made of) cambric.
Batterie [batə'ri:], *f.* 1. battery; turret of (*naval*) guns; ***reitende –,*** troop of horse artillery; 2. battery (*of electric cells*); 3. set (*of cooking utensils etc.*). **Batteriehahn,** *m.* combination tap.
Batzen ['batsən], *m.* 1. batz (*small silver coin*); 2. lump, clod; (*coll.*) ***er hat einen schönen – Geld,*** he has made a nice pile; ***das kostet einen ganzen –,*** that cost a pretty penny.
Bau [bau], *m.* 1. (**-(e)s,** *no pl.*) building, construction, erection; (method of) construction, structure, composition; build (*of a p.*); building-trade; ***im –,*** being built, under construction; ***beim –,*** in the building-trade; (*coll.*) ***er ist vom –,*** he is one of us, he's in the racket; 2. (**-(e)s,** *pl.* **-ten**) building, structure, edifice; (*Mil. sl.*) ***eine Woche –,*** one week confined to barracks; 3. (**-(e)s,** *pl.* **-e**) den; burrow, hole (*of rabbit*), form (*of a hare*), kennel, earth (*of a fox*), earth, sett (*of a badger*), lodge (*of a beaver*), couch (*of an otter*); mine, underground working.
-bau, *m.suff.* 1. -construction; -building; 2. -culture; 3. -mining.
Bau|akademie, *f.* school of architecture. **–amt,** *n.* (local government) surveyor's office. **–anschlag,** *m.* builder's estimate. **–arbeiten,** *f.pl.* construction works, building operations; road-works *or* -repairs. **–arbeiter,** *m.* builder's labourer. **–art,** *f.* type (of construction), model, design. **–aufseher,** *m.* inspector of buildings; district surveyor.
Bauch [baux], *m.* (**-es,** *pl.* **⸗e**) (*Anat.*) belly; abdomen; paunch; (*coll.*) stomach; (*fig.*) bowels (*of the earth*); belly (*of ship, of violin*); bulge (*of cask etc*); entasis (*of a pillar*); bunt (*of a sail*); ***sich*** (*Dat.*) ***den – halten,*** hold *or* split one's sides (*with laughing*); ***auf dem –e liegen,*** lie flat on one's stomach; ***seinem –e frönen*** or ***dienen, sich*** (*Dat.*) ***den – pflegen,*** make a god of one's belly; ***fauler –,*** sluggard.
Bauch|binde, *f.* 1. abdominal bandage, body-belt; 2. band (*on book or cigar*). **–bruch,** *m.* ventral *or* abdominal rupture. **–decke,** *f.* abdominal wall. **–decken-,** *pref.* epigastric. **–diener,** *m.* glutton, gormandizer. **–dienerei,** *f.* gluttony.
Bäuche, *f. See* **Beuche.**
bauchen ['bauxən], *v.t., v.r. See* **ausbauchen.**
bäuchen ['bɔyçən], *v.t. See* **beuchen.**
Bauch|fell, *n.* peritoneum. **–fellentzündung,** *f.* peritonitis. **–finne, –flosse,** *f.* ventral fin; (*Ichth.*) ***ohne –,*** apodal. **–freiheit,** *f.* ground clearance (*of vehicle*). **–gegend,** *f.* abdominal region; ***obere –,*** epigastrum; ***mittlere –,*** mesogastrium; ***untere –,*** hypogastrium. **–grimmen,** *n.* gripes, colic. **–gurt,** *m.* belly-band, girth. **–höhle,** *f.* abdominal cavity. **–höhlenschwangerschaft,** *f.* extra-uterine pregnancy.
bauchig ['bauxɪç], **bäuchig** ['bɔyçɪç], *adj.* bulging, convex, bellied; (*Bot.*) ventricose.
Bauch|klatscher, *m.* (*Swim. coll.*) belly-flop. **–kneifen, –kneipen,** *n.* gripes. **–lage,** *f.* prone position. **–landung,** *f.* (*Av.*) belly landing.
Bäuchlein ['bɔyçlaɪn], *n.* (**-s,** *pl.* -) (*coll.*) tummy.
bäuchlings ['bɔyçlɪŋs], *adv.* (flat) on one's stomach, prone.
Bauch|redner, *m.* ventriloquist. **–riemen,** *m. See* **–gurt. –schmerzen,** *m.pl. See* **–weh. –schnitt,** *m.* laparotomy. **–speichel,** *m.* pancreatic juice. **–speicheldrüse,** *f.* pancreas. **–stich,** *m.* tapping the abdomen (*for dropsy*).
Bauchung ['bauxuŋ], *f.* protuberance, bulge, convexity; (*Archit.*) entasis (*of a column*).
Bauch|wand, *f.* abdominal wall. **–weh,** *n.* stomach-ache. **–zange,** *f.* crucible tongs. **–zirkel,** *m.* callipers.
bauen ['bauən], **1.** *v.t.* 1. build; construct; erect; (*coll.*) ***Luftschlösser –,*** build castles in the air; (*coll.*) ***ein Examen –,*** sit (for) *or* take an examination; (*coll.*) ***seinen Doktor –,*** work for one's degree; 2. till, cultivate (*see* **bebauen**); grow, raise (*flowers etc.*) (*see* **anbauen**); (*fig.*) ***seinen Kohl –,*** cultivate one's garden. **2.** *v.i.* 1. build; ***auf Sand –,*** build on sand; ***– an*** (*Acc.*), build near; ***– an*** (*Dat.*), work on *or* for; 2. count, depend, rely (***auf*** (*Acc.*), on), trust; ***Leute, auf die man – kann,*** people on whom one can depend; 3. ***auf Gold –,*** mine for gold.
Bauentwurf ['bauˀɛntvurf], *m.* architect's plan (*of a building*).
[1]**Bauer** ['bauər], *m.* builder, constructor (*especially as second part of compound, e.g.* ***Orgelbauer, Schiffsbauer***).
[2]**Bauer,** *m.* (**-s** *or* **-n,** *pl.* **-n**) farmer, smallholder, husbandman; peasant, rustic, countryman; (*Cards*) knave, jack; (*Chess*) pawn.
[3]**Bauer,** *n. or m.* (bird)cage; aviary.
Bäu(e)rin ['bɔy(ə)rɪn], *f.* peasant woman; farmer's wife. **bäu(e)risch,** *adj.* rustic; boorish. **bäuerlich,** *adj.* rural, rustic, country.
Bauern|adel ['bauərn–], *m.* yeomanry. **–aufstand,** *m.* Peasants' Revolt. **–brot,** *n.* farm-house bread. **–bursche,** *m.* country lad, yokel. **–dirne,** *f.* country lass. **–fänger,** *m.* (*Cards*) sharper, swindler, trickster, confidence man. **–fängerkniff,** *m.* confidence trick. **–frau,** *f.* farmer's wife. **–frühstück,** *n.* bacon and potato omelet. **–gut,** *n.* farm, smallholding. **–haus,** *n.* farmhouse. **–hof,** *m.* farm, farmstead. **–junge,** *m. See* **–bursche. –kittel,** *m.* peasant's smock. **–knecht,** *m.* farm labourer, farm-hand. **–krieg,** *m.* Peasants' War (*1525 in Germany*). **–schaft,** *f.*, **–stand,** *m.* peasant class, peasantry. **–tölpel,** *m.* yokel, country bumpkin. **–tracht,** *f.* peasant dress *or* costume.
Bauerntum ['bauərntu:m], *n. See* **Bauernstand. Bauernvolk,** *n.* 1. *See* **Bauersleute**; 2. nation of farmers.
Bauers|frau, *f. See* **Bauernfrau. –leute,** *pl.* peasants, country-folk. **–mann,** *m.* (*pl.* **-leute**) peasant, countryman.
Baufach ['baufax], *n.* building trade. **bau|fähig,** *adj.* arable (*land*); (*Min.*) workable (*seam*). **–fällig,** *adj.* dilapidated, ramshackle, (*coll.*) tumble-down. **Bau|fälligkeit,** *f.* dilapidation, state of decay, ramshackle *or* tumble-down state. **–fehler,** *m.* structural fault. **–fluchtlinie,** *f.* building line (*of street*). **–führer,** *m.* building overseer *or* foreman. **–gelände,** *n.* building land *or* site. **–genehmigung,** *f.* building licence. **–genossenschaft,** *f.* building society, housing association. **–gerüst,** *n.* scaffold(ing); frame (*of a ship*). **–gesellschaft,** *f. See* **–genossenschaft. –grundstück,** *n.* building plot. **–handwerk,** *n.*

See **–fach. –herr,** *m.* assignor of a building contract. **–ingenieur,** *m.* structural engineer. **–kasten,** *m.* (children's) box of bricks. **–kastensystem,** *n.* manufacture of standardized units, unit construction. **–klotz,** *m.* (children's) building brick *or* block.

Baukosten|anschlag, *m.* builders' (detailed) estimate, building-tender. **–überschlag,** *m.* provisional estimate. **–zuschuß,** *m.* (tenants') contribution to the building costs.

Bau|kunst, *f.* architecture. **–leiter,** *m. See* **–führer. –leute,** *pl.* builders' labourers.

baulich ['baulıç], *adj.* structural, architectural; ***in –er Hinsicht,*** from an architectural point of view; ***–e Änderung,*** structural alteration.

Baum [baum], *m.* (**-es,** *pl.* **¨-e**) 1. tree; ***– der Erkenntnis,*** tree of knowledge; ***– des Lebens,*** tree of life; (*Prov.*) ***er sieht den Wald vor (lauter) Bäumen nicht,*** he does not see the wood for the trees; ***er wird keine Bäume ausreißen,*** he won't set the Thames on fire; (*Prov.*) ***an der Frucht erkennt man den Baum,*** the tree is known by its fruit; (*Prov.*) ***auf einen Hieb fällt kein –,*** Rome was not built in a day; ***es ist dafür gesorgt, daß die Bäume nicht in den Himmel wachsen,*** there is a limit to everything; (*coll.*) ***das ist um auf die Bäume zu klettern,*** it's enough to drive you up the wall; 2. shaft, axle, spindle; pole, beam; (*Naut.*) boom. **baumartig,** *adj.* tree-like, dendroid, arborescent.

Baumaterial ['baumateri'a:l], *n.* building material.

Baum|axt, *f.* felling axe. **–bestand,** *m.* plantation.

Baumeister ['baumaıstər], *m.* building contractor, (master)builder.

baumeln ['bauməln], *v.i.* dangle, hang, swing; (*sl.*) be hanged.

bäumen ['bɔymən], **1.** *v.t.* (*Weav.*) beam (*the warp*). **2.** *v.i.* rear, prance, stand on hind legs.

Baum|falke, *m.* (*Orn.*) hobby (*Falco subbuteo*). **–farn,** *m.* tree-fern. **–fraß,** *m.* tree-blight. **–gang,** *m.* avenue (of trees); shady walk. **–garten,** *m.* orchard. **–grassteppe,** *f.* savanna. **–grenze,** *f.* timber line, tree limit. **–gruppe,** *f.* clump of trees. **–harz,** *n.* resin. **–heide,** *f.* brier (*Erica arborea*). **–kahn,** *m.* dugout canoe. **–läufer,** *m. See* **Gartenbaumläufer. –krätze,** *f.* tree-lichen. **–krone,** *f.* tree top. **–kunde,** *f.* dendrology. **baumlang,** *adj.* tall as a lamp-post, strapping, lanky. **baumlos,** *adj.* treeless. **Baum|marder,** *m.* (*Zool.*) pine- *or* tree-marten. **–messer, 1.** *n.* pruning-knife. **2.** *m.* dendrometer. **–nymphe,** *f.* wood nymph, (hama-)dryad. **–öl,** *n.* olive oil, sweet oil. **–pflanzung,** *f.* (tree-)nursery, plantation. **–pieper,** *m.*(*Orn.*) tree-pipit (*Anthus trivialis*). **–rose,** *f.* hollyhock. **–schere,** *f.* garden shears. **–schlag,** *m.* (*Paint.*) foliage. **–schröter,** *m.* stag-beetle. **–schule,** *f. See* **–pflanzung. –stamm,** *m.* tree-trunk. **–stammwerfen,** *n.* tossing the caber. **baumstark,** *adj.* (as) strong as a horse. **Baum|stein,** *m.* dendrolite; tree- *or* dendritic *or* arborescent agate. **–stumpf,** *m.* tree-stump.

Baumuster ['baumustər], *n.* (production) model.

Baumvogel ['baumfo:gəl], *m.* passerine, percher.

Baumwollbaum ['baumvɔlbaum], *m.* kapok tree. **Baumwolle,** *f.* cotton. **baumwollen,** *adj.* (made of) cotton.

Baumwoll|garn, *n.* cotton yarn. **–kapsel,** *f.* cotton-boll. **–kapselkäfer,** *m.* boll-weevil. **–spinnerei,** *f.* cotton spinning; cotton-mill. **–samt,** *m.* velveteen. **–staude,** *f.* cotton plant. **–stoff,** *m.* cotton (cloth). **–watte,** *f.* cotton-wool, cotton wadding. **–zeug,** *n. See* **–stoff. –zwirn,** *m.* sewing cotton.

Baumzucht ['baumtsuxt], *f.* arboriculture.

Bau|ordnung, *f.* building regulations *or* by-laws. **–plan,** *m.* architect's drawing; (*coll.*) blue-print. **–platte,** *f.* blockboard; synthetic building material. **–platz,** *m.* building site *or* plot. **–polizei,** *f.* (local government) Surveyor's Office. **–rat,** *m.* (local government) planning officer.

Bäurin, *see* **Bäu(e)rin. bäurisch,** *see* **bäu(e)risch.**

Bau|riß, *m. See* **–plan.**

Bausch [bauʃ], *m.* (**-es,** *pl.* **¨-e**) pad, wad, lump; plug, roll; (*Surg.*) compress; bulge, hanging fold, belly (*of a sail*); ***in – und Bogen,*** in the lump, in bulk, en gros, wholesale (*also fig.*), (*fig.*) without distinction. **Bauschärmel,** *m.* puffed sleeve. **bauschen, 1.** *v.i., v.r.* bulge, bag, swell, billow (out), belly (*of sail*). **2.** *v.t.* puff *or* bulge out, make bulge *or* swell. **bauschig,** *adj.* bulging, bulgy, puffed (out), full, baggy.

Bau|schule, *f.* (technical) school for building trades. **–sparkasse,** *f.* building society. **–spekulant,** *m.* speculative builder. **–stahl,** *m.* structural steel. **–stein,** *m.* 1. building stone, brick; 2. (*fig.*) (integral) component, important element, significant contribution. **–stelle,** *f.* site of road-works; building site. **–stil,** *m.* (architectural) style. **–stoff,** *m.* building material.

Baute ['bautə], *f.* (*usu. pl.*) building, structure.

Bau|technik, *f.* constructional engineering. **–techniker,** *m.* constructional engineer. **–teil,** *m.* (structural) member. **–unternehmer,** *m.* building contractor, builder. **–unternehmung,** *f.* (firm of) building contractors. **–vergebung,** *f.* allocation of building contracts. **–vertrag,** *m.* building contract. **–weise,** *f.* method *or* style of building. **–werk,** *m.* building, structure, edifice. **–wesen,** *n.* building (industry). **bauwürdig,** *adj.* arable (*land*), (*Min.*) workable (*seam*).

Bauxit [bau'ksi:t], *m.* bauxite.

bauz! [bauts], *int.* bump, bang; ***– machen,*** tumble down (*as a child*).

Bau|zaun, *m.* hoarding. **–zeichner,** *m.* structural draughtsman. **–zeichnung,** *f. See* **–plan.**

Bayer ['baıər], *m.* (**-n,** *pl.* **-n**) Bavarian. **bayerisch,** *see* **bayrisch. Bayern,** *n.* Bavaria. **bayrisch,** *adj.* Bavarian. **Bayrisch,** *n.* Bavarian (dialect).

Bazille [ba'tsılə], *f.* bacillus. **Bazillen|ausscheider,** *m.* chronic carrier. **–krieg,** *m.* bacterial *or* germ warfare. **–lehre,** *f.* bacteriology. **–träger,** *m.* carrier. **Bazillus,** *m.* (**-s,** *pl.* **-len**) *see* **Bazille.**

be–, *insep.pref.* **1.** *Turns v.t. into v.i., e.g.* ***auf eine Frage antworten, eine Frage beantworten.*** **2.** *Among many subtle shifts in meaning it commonly has sense of* all over, all round, *e.g.* ***bespritzen,*** bespatter. **3.** *Prefixed to nouns* = providing with, *e.g.* ***benebeln,*** befog; ***bemuttern,*** mother. **4.** *Prefixed to adj.* = supplying that quality, *e.g.* ***bereichern,*** enrich; ***befähigen,*** enable. *For possible compounds not found in the following lists see the simple verbs.*

beabsichtigen [bə'apzıçtıgən], *v.t.* intend, have in view, aim, propose, mean; ***der beabsichtigte Zweck,*** the end in view.

beachten [bə'axtən], *v.t.* notice, heed, regard, take note *or* notice of, give *or* pay heed to, observe (*regulations*), follow (*advice*), attend *or* pay attention to, regard, have *or* pay regard to; ***nicht –,*** disregard, ignore, take no notice of, pay no heed *or* attention *or* regard to. **beachtenswert,** *adj.* noteworthy, remarkable. **beachtlich,** *adj.* notable, considerable. **Beachtung,** *f.* attention, notice; regard; ***zur gefälligen –,*** for your kind attention, kindly notice.

beackern [bə'akərn], *v.t.* plough, till, cultivate; (*fig.*) work over thoroughly.

Beamtenherrschaft [bə'amtənhɛrʃaft], *f.* bureaucracy. **Beamtenschaft,** *f.* civil service. **Beamtentum, Beamten|wesen,** *n.* officialdom. **–wirtschaft,** *f.* red tape; officialism.

Beamte(r) [bə'amtə(r)], *m., f.* official; civil servant, (government *etc.*) officer.

beängstigen [bə'ɛŋstıgən], *v.t.* alarm, make uneasy *or* anxious, fill with *or* cause anxiety. **beängstigend,** *adj.* alarming, disquieting, terrifying; uneasy (*feeling*). **Beängstigung,** *f.* anxiety, uneasiness, alarm.

beanlagt [bə'anla:kt], *adj. See* **begabt. Beanlagung,** *f. See* **Anlage.**

beanspruchen [bə'anʃpruxən], *v.t.* claim, have a *or* lay claim to; demand, call for (*attention etc.*), require, need (*time etc.*), make use of, avail o.s. of, have recourse to; ***zu sehr* –,** take (up) too much of, encroach upon, trespass on (*s.o.'s time*), make too great demands on, put a strain on, tax, try (*s.o.'s patience*); ***beansprucht werden,*** be subjected to stress *or* strain. **Beanspruchung,** *f.* 1. claim (*Gen.*, on), demands (upon); recourse (to), use (of); 2. (*Mech.*) stress, strain; ***zulässige* –,** working stress, safe load.

beanstanden [bəˈanʃtandən], *v.t.* 1. object to; raise objections to, find fault with, take exception to, demur at; ***die Entscheidung*** or ***etwas an der Entscheidung* –,** take exception to the decision, have some fault to find with the decision; 2. make a complaint about, reject as unsatisfactory (*goods etc.*), contest, challenge, query, question, appeal against (*a decision*). **Beanstandung,** *f.* objection (*Gen. or* ***an*** (*Dat.*), to), exception (to), complaint (about), rejection (of); protest, appeal (against).

beantragen [bəˈantra:gən], *v.t.* 1. apply for, put in *or* make an application *or* a claim for (***bei,*** to); 2. (*Parl.*) move; bring forward *or* put a motion for; propose, demand, ask for. **Beantragung,** *f.* application, request. *See* **Antrag.**

beantworten [bəˈantvɔrtən], *v.t.* answer, reply to. **Beantwortung,** *f.* answer, reply.

bearbeiten [bəˈarbaɪtən], *v.t.* 1. till, work, cultivate (*land*); process (*raw materials*), dress (*hides, timber*), work (*wood, iron etc.*), hew (*stone*), machine, tool (*castings*), face (*a surface*), shape, form, fashion (*soft materials*), treat (*with acid etc.*); 2. (*fig.*) work on, deal with, treat, handle (*a subject*); prepare, compile, edit, process; adapt (*for the stage etc.*), arrange (*for another musical instrument*); ***neu* –,** revise; 3. try to persuade, (seek to) influence (*a p.*), (*coll.*) work on (*a p.*); 4. (*coll.*) belabour, thrash, trounce (*a p.*), (*sl.*) beat (*a p.*) up; 5. ***einen Wahlbezirk* –,** canvass a constituency. **Bearbeiter,** *m.* person responsible (*for dealing with applications etc.*), official in charge; editor (*of text*), compiler (*of index etc.*), arranger (*of music*), adapter (*for the stage etc.*). **Bearbeitung,** *f.* cultivation (*of soil*), treatment, preparation, compilation, adaptation, revision, (*Mus.*) arrangement; ***freie* –,** free adaptation; ***neue* –,** revised edition.

beargwohnen [bəˈarkvo:nən], **beargwöhnen** [bəˈarkvø:nən], *v.t.* suspect, be *or* feel suspicious of *or* about.

Beata [beˈa:ta], **Beate,** *f.* Beatrice.

beatmen [bəˈa:tmən], *v.t.* apply artificial respiration to (*a p.*).

beaufsichtigen [bəˈaufzɪçtɪgən], *v.t.* superintend, supervise, be in *or* take charge of, keep an eye on, look after; invigilate (an examination). **Beaufsichtigung,** *f.* supervision, invigilation, surveillance. *See* **Aufsicht.**

beauftragen [bəˈauftra:gən], *v.t.* 1. instruct, charge, direct, commission, order, empower, authorize (***zu tun,*** to do), brief (*a lawyer*); 2. entrust (***mit,*** with). **Beauftragte(r),** *m., f.* deputy, delegate, agent, representative.

beäugeln [bəˈɔygəln], *v.t.* eye, watch closely.

beaugenscheinigen [bəˈaugənʃaɪnɪgən], *v.t.* inspect, examine closely, view, look closely at, take a good look at.

bebauen [bəˈbauən], *v.t.* build on; cultivate, till, work (*land*); ***bebaute Fläche,*** built-up area.

beben [ˈbe:bən], **1.** *v.i.* shake, tremble, quake; vibrate, palpitate, quiver; ***vor Angst* –,** tremble *or* shake *or* quake with fear; ***vor Frost* –,** shake *or* shiver with cold; ***für*** or ***um ihn* –,** be anxious about him, tremble for him; ***vor ihm* –,** be frightened of him. **Beben,** *n.* tremor, vibration; earthquake. **Beber,** *m.* tremolo-stop (*in organs*). **Bebereschen,** *f.* (*Bot.*) aspen.

bebildern [bəˈbɪldərn], *v.t.* illustrate (*a book*).

beblättern [bəˈblɛtərn], *v.t.* cover with leaves; ***beblättert,*** in leaf, leafy; foliate.

beblümt [bəˈbly:mt], *adj.* covered with flowers, flowery.

bebrillt [bəˈbrɪlt], *adj.* bespectacled.

bebrüten [bəˈbry:tən], *v.t.* incubate, hatch out; (*coll.*) brood over *or* on.

Bebung [ˈbe:buŋ], *f.* vibration; (*Mus.*) tremolo, vibrato. *See* **beben.**

Becher [ˈbɛçər], *m.* 1. cup, beaker, goblet, mug; ***die* – *kreisen lassen,*** keep the wine flowing; ***der* – *der Freude,*** the cup that cheers; 2. (*Astr.*) crater; 3. (*Anat.*) calix, cupule; 4. (*Bot.*) calyx; 5. bucket (*of conveyor*). **Becher|flechte,** *f.* cup- *or* reindeer moss. **–früchtler,** *m.pl.* (*Bot.*) cupuliferae. **–förmig,** *adj.* cup-shaped. **–glas,** *n.* beaker. **–held,** *m.* hard drinker, toper. **bechern,** *v.i.* booze, tipple, carouse. **Becherwerk,** *n.* bucket-conveyor, paternoster(-lift).

Becken [ˈbekən], *n.* 1. basin (*of a port*); bowl, hand- *or* wash-basin, (lavatory) pan, bed-pan, (*Eccl.*) font; (*Geog.*) catchment (area), (drainage) basin; 2. (*Anat.*) pelvis; 3. (*Mus.*) cymbal; 4. vortex (*of a whirlpool*). **Becken|abweichung,** *f.* malformation of the pelvis. **–endlage,** *f.* *See* **Steißlage.** **–schlag,** *m.* clash of cymbals.

bedachen [bəˈdaxən], *v.t.* roof (*a house*).

Bedacht [bəˈdaxt], *m.* consideration, deliberation, reflection, forethought, circumspection, caution, wariness; ***– nehmen auf eine S.,*** take s.th. into consideration; bear *or* keep s.th. in mind; ***mit* –,** advisedly, carefully, after mature reflection, deliberately, with care, circumspectly, cautiously, warily; ***ohne* –,** without thinking *or* forethought *or* consideration, carelessly, inconsiderately, heedlessly, incautiously. **bedacht,** *adj.* 1. thoughtful, careful, circumspect; ***– sein auf*** (*Acc.*), be concerned about *or* careful *or* mindful of, have a care for *or* an eye to, care for, look after; ***darauf – zu tun,*** careful *or* anxious to do; 2. endowed, provided, favoured. **Bedachte(r),** *m., f.* recipient, beneficiary, (*Law*) legatee.

bedächtig [bəˈdɛçtɪç], *adj.* 1. circumspect, careful, cautious; 2. deliberate. **Bedächtigkeit,** *f.* caution; care, circumspection.

bedachtlos [bəˈdaxtlos], *adj.* thoughtless, careless, rash, without consideration *or* deliberation **Bedachtlosigkeit,** *f.* thoughtlessness, carelessness, rashness, lack of consideration.

bedachtsam [bəˈdaxtza:m], *adj.* careful, thoughtful, circumspect. **Bedachtsamkeit,** *f.* *See* **Bedacht.**

Bedachung [bəˈdaxuŋ], *f.* roofing. *See* **bedachen.**

bedanken [bəˈdaŋkən], **1.** *v.t.* (*pass. only*) ***bedankt sein,*** be thanked, accept thanks. **2.** *v.r.* (***bei ihm***) thank (*him*), give *or* express one's thanks (*to him*), return thanks; (*iron.*) ***ich werde mich schön dafür* –,** I wouldn't say thank you for it.

Bedarf [bəˈdarf], *m.* **(-(e)s,** *no pl.*) need, want, requirement(s); supply; (*Comm.*) demand; ***– an einer S.,*** need of a th., demand *or* want for a th.; ***mein* –,** all I need; ***nach* –,** as occasion demands, as may be required; ***bei* –,** in case of need, if *or* when needed; (*coll.*) ***mein – ist gedeckt,*** I've had just about enough.

bedarf, *see* **bedürfen.**

Bedarfs|artikel, *pl.* requisites, necessaries, essential commodities. **–deckung,** *f.* supply covering all requirements, provision for needs. **–fall,** *m.* case of need. **–gegenstände, -güter,** *pl.* *See* **–artikel.** **–haltestelle,** *f.* request stop (*bus etc.*). **–wagen, –zug,** *m.* relief train.

bedauerlich [bəˈdauərlɪç], *adj.* regrettable, deplorable, lamentable, unfortunate. **bedauerlicherweise,** *adv.* unfortunately. **bedauern,** *v.t.* 1. regret, deplore (*a th., a fact*); 2. pity, feel pity for, feel *or* be sorry for; ***bedaure sehr!*** I very much regret, I'm sorry I can't. **Bedauern,** *n.* sorrow, pity; regret. **bedauerns|wert, –würdig,** *adj.* pitiable, pitiful, piteous; *see also* **bedauerlich.**

bedecken [bəˈdɛkən], **1.** *v.t.* 1. cover; (*Astr.*) occult; 2. (*Mil.*) escort; (*Naut.*) convoy. **2.** *v.r.* put on one's hat. **bedeckt,** *adj.* overcast (*sky, weather*); ***–e Stimme,*** husky voice. **Bedeckung,** *f.* covering; cover; escort, convoy; (*Astr.*) occultation. **Bedeckungs|schiff,** *n.* escort vessel. **–truppen,** *pl.* covering force.

bedenken [bə'dɛŋkən], **1.** *irr.v.t.* 1. consider, weigh, ponder (over), think over, reflect on, turn over in one's mind, bear in mind; 2. give a present to; remember in one's will, leave s.th. in one's will for, provide for (*in one's will etc.*); ***ihn mit etwas –***, bestow *or* confer s.th. upon him. *See also* **bedacht. 2.** *irr.v.r.* think about *or* consider the matter, weigh *or* ponder the consequences; ***sich eines anderen*** or ***Besseren –***, think better of it, change one's mind, have second thoughts on the matter. **Bedenken,** *n.* thought, reflection, deliberation; (*usu. pl.*) misgivings, hesitation, scruples, doubts; ***– tragen,*** have mental reservations; ***ohne –***, unhesitatingly, without giving a second thought. **bedenkenlos, 1.** *pred.adj.* unscrupulous. **2.** *adv.* without thinking, without another thought, without scruple.

bedenklich [bə'dɛŋklıç], **1.** *pred.adj.* thoughtful, pensive. **2.** *adj.* (*of action, character*) doubtful, questionable, dubious; (*of situation*) critical, serious, delicate, precarious, hazardous, risky. **Bedenklichkeit,** *f.* 1. scruple, hesitation; indecision, irresolution; 2. doubtfulness, dubiousness (*of character etc.*); seriousness, precariousness, critical state, riskiness (*of situation*).

Bedenkzeit [bə'dɛŋktsaıt], *f.* time for reflection, time to think it over.

bedeppert [bə'dɛpərt], *adj.* (*coll.*) crestfallen, abashed, in a maze.

bedeuten [bə'dɔytən], *v.t.* 1. mean, signify; 2. mean, matter; be of importance; ***nichts zu – haben,*** be of no importance *or* significance; 3. bode, portend, presage; 4. (*obs.*) notify, inform, advise, point out, intimate, give to understand.

bedeutend [bə'dɔytənt], **1.** *adj.* 1. significant, meaningful (*glance etc.*); 2. important, distinguished, eminent, outstanding, prominent (*a p., position etc.*); considerable, remarkable (*achievement*). **2.** *adv.* (*with comp.*) considerably, much. **bedeutsam,** *adj. See* **bedeutend,** 1. **Bedeutsamkeit,** *f.* significance; importance.

Bedeutung [bə'dɔytuŋ], *f.* 1. meaning, significance, import; 2. importance, eminence, prominence, consequence; ***ohne –***, of no importance *or* consequence; 3. sense, acceptation (*of a word*).

Bedeutungs|entwicklung, *f.* (*Philol.*) semantic development. **–gehalt,** *m.* (*Philol.*) lexical content. **bedeutungs|gleich,** *adj.* synonymous. **–leer,** *adj.* devoid of meaning, meaningless, trivial, shallow, empty. **Bedeutungslehre,** *f.* semantics, semasiology. **bedeutungslos,** *adj.* meaningless; insignificant; unimportant, of no importance *or* consequence. **Bedeutungslosigkeit,** *f.* insignificance. **bedeutungs|schwanger, –schwer,** *adj.* full of *or* pregnant with meaning *or* significance; momentous. **–voll,** *adj.* meaningful, significant.

bedienen [bə'di:nən], **1.** *v.t.* 1. wait *or* attend on (*a p.*); wait on (*at table*); attend to, serve (*a customer*); ***sich von vorne und hinten – lassen,*** be waited on hand and foot; 2. (*of stallion*) serve (*mare*); (*vulg.*) sleep with (*a woman*); 3. work, operate (*a machine*), serve (*a gun*), stoke (*a boiler*), (*coll.*) look after. **2.** *v.r.* 1. help *or* serve o.s. (*at table*); 2. (*with Gen.*) use, make use of, employ; avail o.s. of (*opportunity*). **3.** *v.i.* 1. serve, wait (*at table*), serve (*in a shop*); 2. (*Cards*) follow suit. **Bedienerin,** *f.* (*Austr.*) charwoman. **bedienstet,** *adj.* in service (*bei*, with). **Bedienstete,** *pl.* servants, domestic staff. **bedient,** *adj.* ***mit etwas gut*** (***schlecht***) ***– sein,*** get s.th. that is useful (no use) *or* that is more (less) than one deserves *or* that is good (poor) value. **bedientenhaft,** *adj.* servile, cringing. **Bedienten|kleidung,** *f.* livery. **–seele,** *f.* servile *or* cringing nature. **Bediente(r),** *m.* servant.

Bedienung [bə'di:nuŋ], *f.* 1. service, attendance; attention; 2. servants, (domestic) staff (*in hotel etc.*), shop-assistants; gun-crew; 3. operation (*of a machine*). **Bedienungs|mannschaft,** *f.* operating personnel, gun-crew. **–vorschriften,** *f. pl.* working *or* operating instructions.

Beding [bə'dıŋ], *m. or n.* **(-(e)s,** *pl.* **-e)** *see* **Bedingung.**

bedingen [bə'dıŋən], *v.t.* (*usu. pass.*) cause, determine, condition; ***bedingt sein durch,*** be determined *or* conditioned by, depend on; ***sich gegenseitig*** or ***einander –***, condition each other, be mutually dependent. *See also* **ausbedingen. bedingt,** *adj.* 1. contingent, conditional (*also Gram.*) (***durch***, upon); 2. restricted, limited, qualified, relative, (*Log.*) conditioned, modal. **Bedingtheit,** *f.* 1. dependence (on); relativity; 2. limitation, restrictedness.

Bedingung [bə'dıŋuŋ], *f.* (pre-)requisite, condition, stipulation, proviso; restriction, reservation, qualification; (*Comm.*) (*usu. pl.*) conditions, terms; ***unter der –***, on condition, provided, providing, with the proviso; ***auf diese –en eingehen,*** accept these terms *or* conditions; ***unter keiner –***, on no account, in no circumstances, in no case; ***unter jeder –***, in any case, under any condition, without reservation. **bedingungslos,** *adj.* unconditional, unreserved, without qualification *or* reservation; unquestioning (*loyalty etc.*). **Bedingungssatz,** *m.* conditional clause. **bedingungsweise,** *adv.* conditionally, on certain conditions.

bedrängen [bə'drɛŋən], *v.t.* press hard, beset, harry, (*coll.*) plague, pester, badger; ***bedrängte Verhältnisse,*** cramped conditions, (*fig.*) straitened circumstances, financial difficulties. **Bedrängnis,** *f.* affliction; distress; tribulation; financial embarrassment; ***in ärgster –***, in dire straits.

bedrohen [bə'dro:ən], *v.t.* threaten, menace. **bedrohlich,** *adj.* threatening, menacing, ominous. **Bedrohung,** *f.* menace, threat (*Gen.*, to); (*Eccl.*) commination, (*Law*) intimidation.

bedrucken [bə'drukən], *v.t.* print (on), imprint (with).

bedrücken [bə'drykən], *v.t.* press; oppress; depress; ***–des Wetter,*** depressing weather; ***–de Hitze,*** oppressive heat; ***die Armen –***, grind (the faces of) the poor. **Bedrücker,** *m.* oppressor. **bedrückt,** *adj.* oppressed, downtrodden (*people*); depressed, dejected (*mood*). **Bedrücktheit,** *f.* depression, dejection. **Bedrückung,** *f.* oppression.

Beduine [bedu'i:nə], *m.* **(-n,** *pl.* **-n)** Bedouin. **beduinisch,** *adj.* Bedouin.

bedungen [bə'duŋən], *see* **bedingen** = **ausbedingen.**

bedünken [bə'dyŋkən], *v.t. imp.* seem; ***mich bedünkt,*** I think, it seems to me, (*obs.*) methinks. **Bedünken,** *n.* opinion, view; ***meines –s,*** in my opinion, to my way of thinking.

bedürfen [bə'dyrfən], *irr.v.i., imp.* (*Gen.*) be *or* stand in need of, need, want, have need of, require; ***es bedarf keines Beweises,*** no proof is required; ***der Ruhe –***, need rest; ***es bedarf keiner weiteren Worte,*** no more need be said, that goes without saying. **Bedürfnis,** *n.* **(-ses,** *pl.* **-se)** 1. need, want, requirement; (strong) desire, urge; ***sein – verrichten,*** relieve o.s.; 2. (*obs., also f.*) poverty, want, necessity; 3. *pl.* necessities. **Bedürfnisanstalt,** *f.* public lavatory. **bedürfnislos,** *adj.* undemanding, unassuming, frugal, of few wants, of modest requirements. **Bedürfnislosigkeit,** *f.* frugality, modesty of (*one's*) requirements.

bedürftig [bə'dyrftıç], **1.** *adj.* poor, needy; ***– sein,*** be poor, needy, in need *or* want. **2.** *pred.adj.* ***– sein*** (*Gen.*), be *or* stand in need of, need, want. **Bedürftigkeit,** *f.* need, want, neediness, straitened circumstances, straits. **Bedürftigkeitsprüfung,** *f.* means test.

beduseln [bə'du:zəln], *v.r.* (*sl.*) get tipsy. **beduselt,** *adj.* (*sl.*) fuddled, tipsy; confused, muddled.

beehren [bə'e:rən], *v.t.* honour, do honour to; ***mit seiner Gegenwart –***, honour *or* favour with one's presence; ***ich beehre mich Ihnen anzuzeigen,*** I have the honour to inform you.

beeid(ig)en [bə'aıd(ıg)ən], *v.t.* 1. take one's oath on, declare on oath, swear to (*s.th.*); 2. administer an oath to, swear in (*a p.*); ***beeidigte Aussage,*** sworn disposition, affidavit.

beeilen [bə'aılən], *v.t.* hasten, hurry on, speed up (*a* *th.*), quicken (*one's steps*). **2.** *v.r.* hurry (up), hasten, make haste, be quick.

beeindrucken [bə'aɪndrukən], *v.t.* impress, make an impression (up)on.

beeinflussen [bə'aɪnflusən], *v.t.* influence, exercise *or* have an influence on *or* over, have an effect (up)on; (*of a th.*) effect; (*of a p.*) bring pressure to bear *or* put pressure (up)on, (*Law*) suborn (*witness*). **Beeinflussung,** *f.* influence.

beeinträchtigen [bə'aɪntrɛçtɪgən], *v.t.* hurt, injure, damage, be injurious *or* harmful to (*reputation etc.*), be detrimental *or* prejudicial to (*health etc.*), prejudice; detract *or* derogate from. **Beeinträchtigung,** *f.* prejudice, detriment, damage, injury (*Gen.*, to), detraction, derogation (from), impairment (of).

beend(ig)en [bə'ɛnd(ɪg)ən], *v.t.* finish, end, conclude, complete; close, terminate, bring to an end *or* close; put a stop to; ***beendet werden*** or ***sein,*** come to a close *or* an end. **Beend(ig)ung,** *f.* finish, end, conclusion, termination, completion, close; ***kurz vor Beendigung,*** near(ing) completion.

beengen [bə'ɛŋən], *v.t.* restrict, confine (*movement*), constrict, cramp, (*fig.*) oppress; ***–de Luft,*** oppressive *or* close atmosphere; ***beengt sein,*** be cramped *or* crowded; ***beengter Raum,*** confined *or* narrow space; ***beengte Verhältnisse,*** cramped conditions; ***sich beengt fühlen,*** feel oppressed *or* hemmed in, (*fig.*) feel constrained *or* uneasy. **Beengtheit, Beengung,** *f.* tightness, constriction, cramped state; ***Gefühl der Beengtheit,*** feeling of oppression.

beerben [bə'ɛrbən], *v.t.* be *or* become (*a p.'s*) heir, inherit from.

beerdigen [bə'e:rdɪgən], *v.t.* bury (*only of human beings*), inter. **Beerdigung,** *f.* burial, interment, funeral. **Beerdigungs|anstalt,** *f.*, **–institut,** *n.* (funeral) undertakers.

Beere ['be:rə], *f.* berry. **beeren|ähnlich, –artig,** *adj. See* **–förmig. Beerenauslese,** *f.* choice *or* select wine. **beeren|förmig,** *adj.* berry-like; (*Bot.*) bacciform. **–fressend,** *adj.* baccivorous. **–tragend,** *adj.* bacciferous. **Beerenwein,** *m.* home-made wine. **Beeresche,** *f.* mountain-ash (*Pirus aucuparia*).

Beet [be:t], *n.* (**-es,** *pl.* **-e**) bed, patch (*of land*).

Beete, *f. See* **Bete.**

befähigen [bə'fɛ:ɪgən], *v.t.* fit, qualify (***zu,*** for), enable, put in a position (to do). **befähigt,** *adj.* able (*to do*), capable (***zu,*** of), fit, qualified (for), talented, gifted, apt. **Befähigung,** *f.* qualification; ability, fitness, competence, capability. **Befähigungsnachweis,** *m.* certificate of competency.

befahl [bə'fa:l], *see* **befehlen.**

befahrbar [bə'fa:rba:r], *adj.* passable; practicable (for vehicles), navigable.

befahren [bə'fa:rən], *irr.v.t.* **1.** travel *or* drive over *or* on; cover (*a route*); navigate (*a river*); ***stark –er Weg,*** much frequented road; ***wenig –er Weg,*** little used road; ***Küsten –,*** sail along the coasts; ***–e Leute,*** old salts, old tars; ***eine Grube –,*** descend a pit; 2. spread *or* cover with (*gravel, dung etc.*).

Befall [bə'fal], *m.* attack, infection. **befallen,** *irr. v.t.* befall, come over; assail, attack, seize, strike, smite (*as disease, fear etc.*); ***von einer Krankheit – werden,*** be stricken with an illness.

befangen [bə'faŋən], **1.** *adj.* 1. embarrassed, self-conscious, ill at ease, disconcerted, (*coll.*) put out; shy, bashful; 2. partial, prejudiced, biased (in favour of); (*Law*) ***sich für – erklären,*** plead partiality. **2.** *pred.adj.* (*fig.*) enmeshed, entangled, caught up (in) (*error, prejudice etc.*); ***in einem Irrtum – sein,*** labour under a misapprehension *or* a delusion. **Befangenheit,** *f.* 1. constraint, self-consciousness, bashfulness, shyness, embarrassment; 2. prejudice, bias, partiality (*also Law*).

befassen [bə'fasən], *v.r.* ***sich – mit,*** occupy *or* concern o.s. with, enter into, engage in (*a problem*); be occupied with, attend *or* see to (*a p.*), deal with (*as a book or author*); ***– Sie sich mit Ihren eigenen Sachen!*** mind your own business!

befehden [bə'fe:dən], *v.t.* be at war with, make war upon; fight *or* war *or* battle *or* contend against, attack.

Befehl [bə'fe:l], *m.* (**-(e)s,** *pl.* **-e**) order, (word of) command, instruction, mandate; (position of) command (*also Mil.*); ***auf – des Königs,*** by order of the king; ***auf – handeln,*** act under orders, act on *or* according to instructions; ***zu –,*** yes, sir; very good, sir; (*Naut.*) aye, aye, sir; ***ich stehe Ihnen zu –,*** I am at your service; (*Mil.*) ***den – übernehmen,*** take *or* assume command; ***einen – überschreiten,*** exceed one's orders; ***bis auf weiteren –,*** till further orders; ***gerichtlicher –,*** warrant, writ; ***mündlicher*** (***schriftlicher***) ***–,*** verbal (written) order.

befehlen [bə'fe:lən], *irr.v.t.* **1.** (*Dat.*) order, command (*of a p.*), direct, dictate, bid (*of duty, the law etc.*); ***wie Sie –,*** as you wish; ***– Sie sonst noch etwas?*** do you wish for anything else? have you any further orders? 2. ***ihm etwas –,*** entrust s.th. to him *or* him with s.th., put *or* place s.th. in his care; ***sich Gott –,*** commend *or* commit o.s. to God; ***Gott befohlen!*** good-bye! God be with you! **befehlend,** *adj.* peremptory, imperious, commanding (*tone*), (*Gram.*) imperative; ***–er Ton,*** tone of authority. **befehlerisch,** *adj.* overbearing, imperious, peremptory.

befehligen [bə'fe:lɪgən], *v.t.* command (*a regiment, an army*); have under one's command; be in command of.

Befehls|ausgabe, *f.* issue of orders, briefing. **–empfang,** *m.* (*Mil.*) receipt of orders. **befehlsgemäß,** *adj., adv.* according to instructions. **Befehlshaber,** *m.* (*Mil.*) commander, (*Navy*) commander-in-chief. **befehlshaberisch,** *adj.* authoritative; imperious, dictatorial. **Befehls|satz,** *m.* (*Gram.*) imperative clause. **–stand,** *m.*, **–stelle,** *f.* (*Mil.*) command post. **–übermittlung,** *f.* transmission of orders. **befehlswidrig,** *adj.* contrary to orders.

befestigen [bə'fɛstɪgən], *v.t.* **1.** fasten, fix, attach (***auf*** or ***an*** (*Dat.*), on *or* to), make fast, fasten, secure, fix (*s.th. loose*); 2. fortify (*town*), entrench (*position*), (*fig.*) consolidate, establish, strengthen; (*Comm.*) stabilize (*prices*); fix (*dye etc.*); (*B.*) ***da wurden die Gemeinden im Glauben befestigt,*** so were the churches established in the faith. **Befestigung,** *f.* fastening; consolidation, stabilization (*of prices*), (*Mil.*) entrenchment, fortification. **Befestigungs|anlagen, –bauten,** *f.pl.* defences, fortifications. **–kunst,** *f.* science of fortification. **–mittel,** *n.* (*Chem.*) fixing agent; fastening(s). **–schraube,** *f.* set-screw, fixing screw.

befeuchten [bə'fɔyçtən], *v.t.* moisten, damp, dampen.

befeuern [bə'fɔyərn], *v.t.* **1.** fire, excite (*enthusiasm etc.*), stimulate, stir up; 2. (*Naut. etc.*) mark with lights (*coast etc.*). **Befeuerung,** *f.* lights, markers, beacons.

Beffchen ['bɛfçən], *n.pl.* bands (*of a Protestant clergyman, proctor etc.*).

befiedert [bə'fi:dərt], *adj.* feathered, fledged. **Befiederung,** *f.* plumage, feathers; feathering.

befiehl [bə'fi:l], *see* **befehlen.**

befiel [bə'fi:l], *see* **befallen.**

befinden [bə'fɪndən], **1.** *irr.v.t.* find, deem, consider, judge (to be), think (it) necessary *or* proper. **2.** *irr. v.r.* ***sich in Verlegenheit –,*** be embarrassed; ***wie – Sie sich?*** how are you? ***der Ausgang befindet sich unten,*** the exit is downstairs. **Befinden,** *n.* 1. (state of) health, condition; 2. judgement, view, opinion; ***je nach –,*** as you may think fit, according to taste; ***nach meinem –,*** in my judgement, view *or* opinion. **befindlich, 1.** *attrib.adj.* being, existing, lying, present, situated. **2.** *pred.adj.* ***– sein,*** (happen to) be.

befingern [bə'fɪŋərn], *v.t.* finger, feel, touch, handle.

beflaggen [bə'flagən], *v.t.* deck with flags, (*Naut.*) dress (*ship*). **Beflaggung,** *f.* flags, bunting.

beflecken [bə'flɛkən], *v.t.* **1.** spot, stain, soil, contaminate; defile, pollute, profane (*s.th. sacred*); ***seinen guten Namen –,*** sully his reputation; 2.

patch, heel (*shoes etc.*). **Befleckung,** *f.* stain, taint, blemish; defilement, profanation, pollution.

befleißen [bəˈflaɪsən], *irr.v.r.* (*rare*) *see* **befleißigen, beflissen.**

befleißigen [bəˈflaɪsɪgən], *v.r.* (*Gen.*) apply o.s. *or* one's mind to, strive for *or* after, take great pains with, devote o.s. to; strive, endeavour, be eager, set o.s., put *or* lay o.s. out, take *or* be at (great) pains (*zu tun*, to do); ***er befleißigt sich der Höflichkeit,*** he is at pains *or* he takes pains to be polite.

befliß [bəˈflɪs], *see* **befleißen.**

beflissen [bəˈflɪsən], **1.** *p.p. of* **befleißen. 2.** *attrib. adj.* intent (*Gen.*, upon), keenly interested (in), devoted (to); zealous in the pursuit (of); **3.** *pred. adj.* ***– sein*** (*Gen.*), *see* **befleißigen. Beflissene(r),** *m., f.* (eager) student, votary (*Gen.*, of). **Beflissenheit,** *f.* eagerness, intentness, studiousness, assiduity. **beflissentlich,** *adv.* sedulously.

beflügeln [bəˈfly:gəln], *v.t.* accelerate, quicken; ***die Angst beflügelt den eilenden Fuß,*** fear lends wings to hurrying feet.

beföhle [bəˈfø:lə], **befohlen** [bəˈfo:lən], *see* **befehlen.**

befolgen [bəˈfɔlgən], *v.t.* obey, follow, observe, act upon (*instructions*), comply with, abide by, adhere to (*a custom, a principle*).

Beförderer [bəˈfœrdərər], *m.* 1. forwarder, forwarding-agent; 2. promoter, instigator, patron. **beförderlich,** *adj.* 1. (*obs.*) *see* **förderlich**; 2. (*Swiss*) express (*delivery*). **befördern,** *v.t.* 1. forward, transport, dispatch, convey, carry, send (*goods etc.*); 2. stimulate, aid; (*obs.*) hasten, accelerate, promote, further; *see* **fördern**; 3. promote (*a p. in rank*). **Beförderung,** *f.* 1. forwarding, dispatch, transport, carriage, conveyance (*of goods etc.*); 2. promotion; advancement (*in rank*). **Beförderungs|anweisungen,** *f.pl.* *See* **–vorschriften. –mittel,** *n.* means of transport. **–vorschriften,** *f.pl.* forwarding instructions.

befrachten [bəˈfraxtən], *v.t.* freight; charter (*a vessel*); load. **Befrachtung,** *f.* freighting, loading.

befragen [bəˈfra:gən], **1.** *reg. & irr.v.t.* interrogate, question, ask (*a p.*), consult (*oracle, stars, one's conscience*). **2.** *reg. & irr.v.r.* (*obs.*) ***sich bei ihm –*** (***um*** or ***über eine S.*** or ***wegen einer S.***), consult with him (about a th.). **Befragung,** *f.* questioning, interrogation; consultation.

befranst [bəˈfranst], *adj.* fringed.

befreien [bəˈfraɪən], *v.t.* free, set free, liberate; deliver, rescue, release; exempt, dispense, excuse (*from obligations*), rid, clear (*of s.th.*), extricate, disentangle (*from s.th.*); ***befreit aufatmen,*** heave a sigh of relief; ***ein befreites Gefühl,*** a feeling of release; ***ein –des Lachen,*** laughter that breaks the tension. **Befreier,** *m.* liberator, deliverer, rescuer. **Befreiung,** *f.* liberation, deliverance, release; exemption, dispensation; riddance; extrication. **Befreiungskrieg,** *m.* war of independence *or* liberation.

befremden [bəˈfrɛmdən], *v.t., v.imp.* appear strange *or* odd to, strike as odd, astonish, surprise; create an unfavourable impression with. **Befremden,** *n.* consternation, surprise, amazement, astonishment. **befremdend, befremdlich,** *adj.* odd, strange, surprising.

befreunden [bəˈfrɔyndən], *v.r.* become friends, make friends (***mit***, with) (*a p.*), bring o.s. to like, get used *or* accustomed (to), reconcile o.s. (to) (*a th.*). **befreundet, 1.** *attrib.adj.* friendly; ***–e Macht,*** friendly power; ***ein mir –er Lehrer,*** a teacher friend of mine. **2.** *pred.adj.* ***– sein*** (***mit***), be on terms of friendship, be on friendly *or* intimate terms, be friends (with).

befrieden [beˈfri:dən], *v.t.* 1. pacify, restore peace to; 2. (*obs.*) fence in (*ground*). **Befriedung,** *f.* pacification.

befriedigen [bəˈfri:dɪgən], *v.t.* satisfy, gratify; please, comply with (*request*), meet, suit (*need, taste etc.*), give satisfaction to (*of a th.*); ***schwer zu –***, fastidious, hard to please. **befriedigend,** *adj.* satisfactory, satisfying, gratifying. **Befriedigung,** *f.* satisfaction; gratification; contentment.

befristen [bəˈfrɪstən], *v.t.* fix a time, limit; ***befristete Einreiseerlaubnis,*** entry permit for a stipulated period; ***befristete Forderung,*** deferred claim.

befruchten [bəˈfruxtən], *v.t.* fertilize (*egg*), impregnate (*female*); make fertile, inseminate, fructify; (*fig.*) stimulate, have a productive influence on. **Befruchtung,** *f.* fertilization, insemination, impregnation, fecundation, fructification; ***künstliche –***, artificial insemination; ***verborgene*** or ***unmerkliche –***, cryptogamy.

befugen [bəˈfu:gən], *v.t.* empower, authorize, give authority to. **Befugnis,** *f.* (-, *pl.* **-se**) authorization; authority, right, warrant; powers (*of an envoy etc.*); ***seine Befugnisse überschreiten,*** exceed one's powers *or* authority *or* competence, (*Law*) act ultra vires.

befühlen [bəˈfy:lən], *v.t.* feel (*the pulse etc.*); examine by feeling; handle; touch.

befummeln [bəˈfuməln], *v.t.* (*sl.*) handle (clumsily); (*fig.*) give (*s.th.*) the once over.

Befund [bəˈfunt], *m.* finding; report, result (*of an inquiry*), diagnosis; (scientifically attested) fact(s); ***nach ärztlichem –***, according to the medical evidence. **Befundbericht,** *m.* (expert's) report; doctor's certificate.

befürchten [bəˈfyrçtən], *v.t.* fear, be afraid of *or* that, apprehend; suspect. **Befürchtung,** *f.* (*usu. pl.*) fear, apprehension.

befürsorgen [bəˈfy:rzɔrgən], *v.t.* (*Austr.*) have care of, look after.

befürworten [bəˈfyrvɔrtən], *v.t.* support, advocate. **Befürwortung,** *f.* recommendation, reference; support.

Beg [be:k], *m.* (**-s,** *pl.* **-s**) bey (*Turkish official*).

begaben [bəˈga:bən], *v.t.* endow (***mit***, with), bestow *or* confer upon; give presents to. **begabt,** *adj.* gifted, talented, able, intelligent. **Begabung,** *f.* (natural) gift, talent, ability, aptitude, endowment.

begaffen [bəˈgafən], *v.t.* stare (open-mouthed) at, gape at.

Begängnis [bəˈgɛŋnɪs], *n.* (**-ses,** *pl.* **-se**) (*obs.*) solemn act, (act of) celebration (*esp.* funeral service).

begann [bəˈgan], **begänne** [bəˈgɛnə], *see* **beginnen.**

begatten [bəˈgatən], *v.r.* pair, mate; copulate. **Begattung,** *f.* pairing, mating, copulation (*of animals*), coitus, coition, sexual union (*of persons*). **Begattungs|akt,** *m.* sexual act. **–trieb,** *m.* sexual instinct. **–zeit,** *f.* mating season, pairing time.

begaukeln [bəˈgaukəln], *v.t.* charm, bewitch.

begaunern [bəˈgaunərn], *v.t.* swindle, cheat.

begebbar [bəˈgə:pba:r], *adj.* (*Comm.*) negotiable, transferable.

begeben [bəˈge:bən], **1.** *irr.v.t.* (*Comm.*) negotiate, transfer, dispose of, sell; float, issue (*loan*). **2.** *irr. v.r.* 1. go, proceed, repair, betake o.s., make one's way (to), make, set out (for); ***sich an die Arbeit –***, set to *or* begin work; ***sich zur Ruhe –***, go to bed, retire to rest; ***sich auf die Flucht –***, take to flight; ***sich auf den Weg –***, set out (*on one's journey*); ***sich in Gefahr –***, venture into *or* court danger; 2. (*with Gen.*) ***sich einer S. –***, give up, relinquish, renounce *or* forgo a th. **3.** *irr.v.r. imp.* ***es begab sich, daß,*** it so happened that, it came about *or* (*B.*) it came to pass that. **Begebenheit,** *f.*, **Begebnis,** *n.* (**-ses,** *pl.* **-se**) event, occurrence, happening, incident. **Begebung,** *f.* (*Comm.*) disposal, sale (*of securities etc.*), issue, negotiation (*of a bill*), floating (*of a loan*). **Begebungsvertrag,** *m.* deed *or* instrument of transfer.

begegnen [bəˈge:gnən], **1.** *v.i.* (*aux.* s.) (*Dat.*) 1. meet, meet with, come across *or* upon, run across *or* into, light upon, encounter; ***zufällig –***, chance *or* stumble upon; 2. (*of a th.*) be met with *or* found (***bei***, in); occur, happen, befall (*Dat.*, to); 3. receive, treat (*a p. well, badly etc.*); ***ihm grob –***, treat him rudely; 4. obviate, counter, provide against *or* take action *or* steps *or* precautions against (*dangers, difficulties etc.*). **2.** *v.r.* 1. meet;

unsere Blicke – sich, our eyes meet; 2. concur; *unsere Wünsche – sich,* we concur in the desire. **Begegnis,** *n.* (**-ses,** *pl.* **-se**) *or f.* (-, *pl.* **-se**) (*obs.*) *see* **Begegnung. Begegnung,** *f.* meeting, encounter; (*obs.*) treatment, reception.

begehen [bə'ge:ən], *irr.v.t.* 1. traverse, pace off; walk *or* go along, frequent (*a road*); 2. celebrate (*a festival*); 3. commit (*an error etc.*).

Begehr [bə'ge:r], *m. or n.* (**-(e)s,** *pl.* **-e**) desire, wish; (*Comm.*) *in –,* in demand; *was ist Ihr –?* what do you want?

begehren [bə'ge:rən], *v.t., v.i.* (*nach or obs. Gen.*) desire, want, wish for, covet (*a th.*); desire, lust after (*a p.*); be in rut *or* on heat (*of animals*); *heftig –,* long *or* yearn *or* crave for; (*B.*) *du sollst nicht – deines Nächsten Weib,* thou shalt not covet thy neighbour's wife. **Begehren,** *n.* desire, wish (*nach,* for); *see also* **Begier(d)e. begehrenswert,** *adj.* desirable, in demand, sought-after. **begehrlich,** *adj.* longing, wistful, covetous, lustful. **Begehrlichkeit,** *f,* wistfulness, longing, covetousness; desire.

Begehung [bə'ge:uŋ], *f.* traversing, inspection (on foot) (*of fields*), procession round the fields. **Begehungssünde,** *f.* sin of commission.

begeifern [bə'gaɪfərn], *v.t.* 1. dribble on *or* over; 2. (*fig.*) slander; cast aspersions *or* a slur on.

begeistern [bə'gaɪstərn], **1.** *v.t.* inspire; fill *or* fire with *or* rouse to enthusiasm; make enthusiastic, enrapture. **2.** *v.r. sich für eine S. –,* be enthusiastic about *or* go into raptures over *or* (*coll.*) enthuse over a th.; *sich an einer S. –,* be moved to enthusiasm by s.th. **begeistert,** *adj.* delighted, enraptured, in raptures (*über* (*Acc.*), with), enthusiastic (*für,* about). **Begeisterung,** *f.* enthusiasm, rapture; inspiration.

Begier(de) [bə'gi:r(də)], *f.* desire, wish, longing, eagerness, craving, hunger (*nach,* for); (carnal) desire, appetite, concupiscence, lust. **begierig,** *adj.* (*auf* (*Acc.*), *nach or* (*obs.*) *Gen.*) desirous (of), eager, anxious, hungry, greedy (for), (*coll.*) keen (on).

begießen [bə'gi:sən], *irr.v.t.* water (*plants etc.*); wet, pour on *or* over; baste (*meat*); (*coll.*) celebrate with a drink; *das müssen wir –,* that calls for a drink.

Beginn [bə'gɪn], *m.* beginning, start, commencement, outset; *zu –,* at the start *or* beginning; to start with, at first.

beginnen ['bəgɪnən], *irr.v.i., v.t.* begin, start, commence; open (*conversation etc.*); set about, undertake; take in hand (*a task*); *was wollen Sie –?* what do you want to do? **Beginnen,** *n.* undertaking, enterprise, activity, doings, effort(s), (*coll.*) goings-on.

begipsen [bə'gɪpsən], *v.t.* plaster (over).

beglaubigen [bə'glaubɪgən], *v.t.* attest, certify, authenticate, verify; accredit (*an ambassador*); *beglaubigte Abschrift,* certified copy. **Beglaubigung,** *f.* attestation, verification, authentication. **Beglaubigungsschreiben,** *n.* credentials.

begleichen [bə'glaɪçən], *irr.v.t.* (*Comm.*) discharge, pay, settle. **Begleichung,** *f.* settlement, payment.

begleiten [bə'glaɪtən], *v.t.* accompany (*also Mus.*), come *or* go with; escort, attend (on); *eine Dame nach Hause –,* see a lady home; *Schwächen – das Alter,* infirmities attend old age. **Begleiter,** *m.* attendant, escort, guide; companion; (*Mus.*) accompanist.

Begleit|erscheinung, *f.* accompanying *or* attendant phenomenon, concomitant (symptom). **-kommando,** *n.,* **-mannschaft,** *f.* (*Mil.*) escort. **-musik,** *f.* incidental music. **-schein,** *m.* (*Comm.*) way-bill. **-schiff,** *n.* escort vessel. **-schreiben,** *n.* letter of advice, advice note, covering letter; permit. **-stimme,** *f.* (*Mus.*) second *or* supporting voice. **-umstand,** *m.* (*usu. pl.*) accompanying *or* attendant *or* concomitant circumstance.

Begleitung [bə'glaɪtuŋ], *f.* 1. company, escort; attendants, train, retinue, suite; *in –* (*Gen.*), accompanied *or* attended by; 2. (*Mus.*) accompaniment; *ohne –,* unaccompanied.

beglücken [bə'glykən], *v.t.* make happy, bless. **Beglücker,** *m.* benefactor. **Beglücktheit, Beglückung,** *f.* happiness, felicity.

beglückwünschen [bə'glykvynʃən], *v.t.* congratulate. **Beglückwünschung,** *f.* congratulation (*zu,* on).

begnaden [bə'gna:dən], *v.t.* bless (*mit,* with); favour.

begnadigen [bə'gna:dɪgən], *v.t.* pardon, reprieve. **Begnadigung,** *f.* (free) pardon, reprieve; *allgemeine –,* amnesty. **Begnadigungs|gesuch,** *n.* petition for reprieve, appeal for mercy. **-recht,** *n.* right of pardon, prerogative of mercy.

begnügen [bə'gny:gən], *v.r.* be satisfied *or* content, content o.s. (*mit,* with); make do *or* shift (with), acquiesce (in).

begönne [bə'gœnə], **begonnen** [bə'gɔnən], *see* **beginnen.**

begönnern [bə'gœnərn], *v.t.* patronize, treat condescendingly *or* in a patronizing manner.

begoß [bə'gɔs], **begösse** [bə'gœsə], *see* **begießen;** *wie ein begossener Pudel,* shamefaced, with one's tail between one's legs.

begraben [bə'g:rabən], *irr.v.t.* bury, inter; entomb; (*fig.*) conceal; (*coll.*) *da liegt der Hund –!* there's the rub!

Begräbnis [bə'grɛ:pnɪs], *n.* (**-ses,** *pl.* **-se**) burial, funeral; burial-place, grave. **Begräbnis|feier,** *f.* funeral (ceremony), obsequies. **-platz,** *m.* cemetery, burial ground. **-stätte,** *f.* burial-place, last resting place.

begradigen [bə'gra:dɪgən], *v.t.* straighten (*road*), (*Mil.*) shorten (*front*).

begrannt [bə'grant], *adj.* (*Bot.*) bearded, awned, aristate.

begreifen [bə'graɪfən], *irr.v.t.* 1. understand, comprehend, (*coll.*) grasp; 2. *in sich –,* include, comprise, contain, cover, embrace, (*coll.*) sum up in a nutshell; *dieses Wort begreift mehrere Bedeutungen in sich,* this word has several meanings; 3. *begriffen sein in* (*Dat.*), (*of a p.*) be in the act of, be engaged in, be busy (*doing*); (*of a th.*) be in the process of; *im Aufbruch begriffen,* on the point of leaving; *im Bau begriffen,* being built, under construction; *in fortwährender Aufregung begriffen,* in a state of constant excitement; *mitten in der Arbeit begriffen sein,* be at work; *im Anmarsch begriffen sein,* be approaching, be on the way; *in Reparatur begriffen,* under repair; 4. (*obs.*) touch, feel, handle.

begreiflich [bə'graɪflɪç], *adj.* understandable, comprehensive, conceivable, intelligible; *ihm etwas – machen,* make him understand *or* see a th., make s.th. clear to him, bring s.th. home to him. **begreiflicherweise,** *adv.* understandably, naturally, of course.

begrenzen [bə'grentsən], *v.t.* form the boundary of, bound (*also Math.*); (*Math.*) intercept, circumscribe; define, confine. **begrenzt,** *adj.* restricted, limited, circumscribed. **Begrenztheit,** *f.* narrowness, limitation; finiteness. **Begrenzung,** *f.* limit, bounds; boundary, (*Math.*) surface, face, side (*of a solid body*); *see also* **Begrenztheit. Begrenzungs|fläche,** *f. See* **Begrenzung** (*Math.*). **-licht,** *n.* side-light (*on vehicle*). **-linie,** *f.* line of demarcation, boundary (line), (*Math.*) periphery.

Begriff [bə'grɪf], *m.* 1. idea, notion, conception; *sich* (*Dat.*) *einen – machen von,* conceive of, imagine; *sich* (*Dat.*) *keinen – machen von,* have no idea of; *über alle –e,* inconceivably, indescribably; 2. (*Phil. etc.*) concept, term; *ist dir das ein –?* does that mean *or* convey anything to you? (*Gram.*) *bedeutungsgleicher –,* synonym; (*Gram.*) *entgegengesetzter –,* antonym; *grammatikalischer –,* grammatical term; 3. understanding, comprehension, apprehension; *das geht über meine –e,* that passes *or* is beyond my comprehension, (*coll.*) that's beyond *or* above me; *schwer von – sein,* be slow *or* dull of comprehension, (*coll.*) be slow on the uptake; 4. *im – sein* or *stehen* (*zu*

tun), be on the point (of doing), be about *or* be going (to do).

begriffen [bə'grɪfən], *see* **begreifen.**

begrifflich [bə'grɪflɪç], *adj.* abstract; conceptual; ***– bestimmen,*** define.

Begriffs|bestimmung, *f.* definition. **–bildung,** *f.* abstraction, concept. **–form,** *f.* (conceptual) category. **–inhalt,** *m.* connotation. **begriffsstutzig,** *adj.* dense, obtuse, dull(-witted), slow(-witted), (*coll.*) thick-headed. **Begriffs|vermögen,** *n. See* **Begriff,** 3. **–verwirrung,** *f.* confusion of ideas.

begründen [bə'gryndən], *v.t.* 1. found, establish, set up; float, start (*a company*); 2. substantiate, make good (*an assertion etc.*), give *or* state the reasons *or* grounds for, supply evidence *or* arguments in support of. **Begründer,** *m.* founder. **begründet,** *adj.* well-founded, reasonable, (fully) justified. **Begründung,** *f.* 1. foundation, establishment; 2. substantiation, grounds, reasons.

begrüßen [bə'gry:sən], *v.t.* greet, welcome, salute, hail. **Begrüßung,** *f.* greeting, welcome, salutation; reception.

begucken [bə'gukən], *v.t.* (*coll.*) look *or* peep at.

begünstigen [bə'gynstɪgən], *v.t.* 1. favour, show favour towards *or* partiality for (*a p.*); 2. be in favour of *or* favourable to, to promote, foster, facilitate, encourage (*a project etc.*); (*Law*) aid and abet, be accessory after the fact. **Begünstiger,** *m.* (*Law*) accessory after the fact. **Begünstigung,** *f.* encouragement (for), promotion, facilitation (of); favour.

Beguß [bə'gus], *m.* icing (*of a cake*); slip (*pottery*).

begutachten [bə'gu:tˀaxtən], *v.t.* give *or* pass an opinion on; pass (expert) judgement on; appraise, evaluate. **Begutachtung,** *f.* expert opinion; judgement, appraisal.

begütert [bə'gy:tərt], *adj.* rich, wealthy, well-to-do, (*only pred.*) well-off.

begütigen [bə'gy:tɪgən], *v.t.* appease, soothe, calm, pacify, propitiate, placate.

behaart [bə'ha:rt], *adj.* hairy, hirsute, pilous, pilose, crinite, villous, villose.

behäbig [bə'hɛ:bɪç], *adj.* easy-going, unworried, placid, unperturbed, comfortable.

behaftet [bə'haftət], *adj.* subject (***mit***, to) (*fainting, fits etc.*); afflicted, burdened, cursed, saddled (with) (*debts etc.*).

behagen [bə'ha:gən], *v.i.* (*Dat.*) please, suit, be to one's taste; ***sie ließen es sich –,*** they made themselves comfortable. **Behagen,** *n.* comfort, ease, contentedness, contentment, enjoyment, pleasure; ***– an einer S. finden,*** take delight in a th. **behaglich,** *adj.* comfortable, agreeable, cosy, snug, peaceful, tranquil. **Behaglichkeit,** *f.* comfort, ease, well-being; cosiness.

behalten [bə'haltən], *irr.v.t.* keep, retain; maintain; remember; (*Math.*) carry; ***im Auge –,*** keep in view *or* in mind, not lose sight of; ***seine Fassung –,*** keep cool, keep one's composure *or* temper; ***bei sich –,*** hold one's tongue, keep secret, keep to o.s.; ***für sich –,*** keep for o.s.; *see also* ***bei sich –***; ***in Erinnerung –,*** remember, retain a memory of; ***im Gedächtnis*** or ***Kopf –,*** keep in mind *or* in one's head; ***die Oberhand –,*** maintain the upper hand; ***recht –,*** be right in the end, carry *or* gain one's point; ***übrig –,*** have (*s.th.*) left over.

Behälter [bə'hɛltər], *m.*, **Behältnis,** *n.* (**-ses,** *pl.* **-se**) container, receptacle; reservoir, tank (*for liquids*); vessel, holder, chamber, (*Chem.*) receiver; bin, bunker (*for coal etc.*); shrine (*for relics*); cage (*for wild beasts*).

behandeln [bə'handəln], *v.t.* 1. treat, deal with, handle; ***ihn wie ein Kind –,*** treat him like a child; ***sie versteht es, Kinder vernünftig zu –,*** she understands how to handle *or* manage children sensibly; ***mit Vorsicht*** or ***Sorgfalt –,*** handle with care; ***etwas leichtfertig –,*** make light of a th.; ***stiefmütterlich behandelt werden,*** be treated unkindly, (*coll.*) get a raw deal; ***von oben herab –,*** behave patronizingly to, put on airs with; ***sein Buch behandelt den Gegenstand ausführlich,*** his book deals with, treats (of), discusses, covers *or* handles the subject fully; 2. (*Med.*) treat (*a patient, a disease*), attend (*a patient*); ***sich ärztlich – lassen,*** receive medical attention; ***auf*** or ***wegen Krebs behandelt werden,*** be treated *or* undergo treatment for cancer.

Behandlung [be'handluŋ], *f.* 1. treatment; ***schlechte –,*** ill-treatment; 2. (medical) attention *or* treatment; ***in –,*** under treatment. **Behandlungs|art, –methode, –weise,** *f.* (mode *or* method of) treatment.

Behang [bə'haŋ], *m.* 1. hanging(s); tapestry; tassels, fringe, drapery; 2. fetlock (*of horse*), lop-ears (*of hound*); 3. crop (*of fruit*).

behängen [bə'hɛŋən], **1.** *irr. & reg. v.t.* hang (*walls etc.*); cover, drape, adorn, garland, festoon (***mit***, with); ***behangen mit,*** hung with (*medals etc.*), laden with (*fruit*). **2.** *v.r.* ***sich mit Schmuck –,*** adorn *or* cover *or* load o.s. with jewellery.

beharren [bə'harən], **1.** *v.i.* 1. (*of a p.*) continue, endure, persevere, be steadfast *or* firm (***in*** (*Dat.*), in); persist (***auf*** (*Dat.*), in), adhere (to), (*coll.*) stand (by), stick (to); 2. (*of a th.*) remain (constant *or* unchanged), persist, (*Phys.*) remain motionless, remain inert *or* in a state of inertia. **beharrend,** *adj.* unaltered, unchanged, permanent, persistent. **beharrlich,** *adj.* (*of a p.*) steadfast, persevering, tenacious, firm, assiduous; constant, unceasing, untiring, dogged (*effort etc.*). **Beharrlichkeit,** *f.* perseverance, persistence, steadfastness, determination, assiduity, tenacity; constancy. **Beharrung,** *f.* 1. perseverance, persistence (in), adherence (to); 2. permanence, permanency, constancy; (*Phys.*) inertness, inertia. **Beharrungs|gesetz,** *n.* law of inertia. **–moment,** *n.* moment of inertia. **–vermögen,** *n.* inertia.

behauen [bə'hauən], *irr.v.t.* hew; trim, dress, square (*timber, stone*); lop, poll (*trees*).

behaupten [bə'hauptən], **1.** *v.t.* 1. maintain, retain (*position etc.*), retain *or* keep possession of, (*coll.*) hold on to; keep; ***seine Rechte –,*** assert one's rights; 2. maintain, assert, affirm, contend, declare, avouch; ***das will ich –,*** I'll maintain that; ***es wird behauptet, man behauptet,*** it is said *or* claimed *or* reported *or* asserted; ***zu viel –,*** overstate one's case, go too far. **2.** *v.r.* hold one's own, stand one's ground, hold out, make good one's position; (*Comm.*) be maintained, remain steady *or* firm (*of prices etc.*). **Behauptung,** *f.* declaration, allegation, affirmation, assertion, statement, contention; maintenance (*of one's dignity, position etc.*); (*Geom.*) proposition; ***das ist eine bloße –,*** that is mere conjecture.

Behausung [bə'hausuŋ], *f.* accommodation, lodging; dwelling (place), home, abode, habitation.

beheben [bə'he:bən], *irr.v.t.* 1. remedy, rectify, redress (*faults etc.*), put an end to, remove (*difficulties etc.*), mend, repair (*damage*); 2. (*Austr.*) withdraw (*money from bank*).

beheimatet [bə'haɪma:tət], *adj.* resident, domiciled (***in*** (*Dat.*), in); (*Naut.*) whose home port (is), hailing (from).

beheizen [bə'haɪtsən], *v.t.* heat. **Beheizung,** *f.* heating.

Behelf [bə'hɛlf], *m.* 1. makeshift; 2. excuse, subterfuge; 3. (*Law*) corroboratory evidence; 4. (*Austr.*) remedy, expedient; 5. (*obs.*) help, resource. **behelfen,** *irr.v.r.* 1. make do *or* shift, improvise, manage (***mit***, with), resort, have recourse (to); 2. (*obs.*) make use (***mit***, of), help o.s. (with). **Behelfsbrücke,** *f.* emergency *or* improvised bridge. **behelfsmäßig,** *adj.* temporary, improvised, makeshift, (*coll.*) rough and ready. **Behelfsmittel,** *n.* expedient.

behelligen [bə'hɛlɪgən], *v.t.* importune, bother, worry, trouble, disturb, (*coll.*) pester. **Behelligung,** *f.* trouble, disturbance, bother.

behend(e) [bə'hɛnt (-ndə)], **behendig,** *adj.* agile, nimble, adroit, dexterous; light, quick, smart. **Behendigkeit,** *f.* agility, quickness, adroitness; dexterity.

beherbergen [bəˈhɛrbɛrgən], **1.** *v.t.* lodge, take in, put up, give hospitality *or* shelter to; harbour (*a criminal*). **Beherbergung,** *f.* lodging, accommodation.

beherrschen [bəˈhɛrʃən], **1.** *v.t.* 1. rule (over), have *or* hold dominion *or* sway over (*territory, people*); hold in one's power, dominate (*a p.*), (*Spt.*) have the mastery over (*opponent*), (*Mil. etc.*) have (*air etc.*) supremacy; 2. control, have control over, have under control, contain, keep in check (*o.s., feelings etc.*), be master *or* in control of (*a situation*), have a command of (*a language etc.*); 3. dominate, command, tower over, overlook (*of mountains, high buildings etc.*). **2.** *v.r.* control o.s., restrain o.s.; control one's feelings, keep one's temper, exercise self-control. **Beherrscher,** *m.* ruler, master, sovereign. **Beherrschung,** *f.* command, mastery, control; rule, domination, sway; self-control.

beherzen [bəˈhɛrtsən], *v.t.* instil courage into, encourage. *See* **beherzt.**

beherzigen [bəˈhɛrtsɪgən], *v.t.* 1. take to heart; 2. consider well, weigh, ponder, take heed of. **beherzigenswert,** *adj.* worthy of consideration, worth heeding. **Beherzigung,** *f.* taking heed (*of s.th.*), taking (*s.th.*) to heart; *zur –!* take good heed! mark well!

beherzt [bəˈhɛrtst], *adj.* brave, spirited, courageous, stout-hearted, valiant. **Beherztheit,** *f.* valiance, bravery, courage, daring.

behexen [bəˈhɛksən], *v.t.* bewitch (*also fig.*), put *or* cast a spell on; (*fig.*) turn (*s.o.'s*) head.

behielt [bəˈhiːlt], *see* **behalten.**

behilflich [bəˈhɪlflɪç], *pred.adj.* helpful; ***ihm – sein,*** help *or* assist him, lend him a helping hand.

behindern [bəˈhɪndərn], *v.t.* hinder, hamper, impede, obstruct; ***körperlich behindert,*** physically handicapped *or* disabled, with a physical disability. **Behinderung,** *f.* hindrance, restriction, impediment, encumbrance, obstacle, obstruction; (physical) disability.

behobeln [bəˈhoːbəln], *v.t.* (*Carp.*) plane.

behorchen [bəˈhɔrçən], *v.t.* overhear; eavesdrop on, listen to (secretly).

Behörde [bəˈhøːrdə], *f.* (public) authority; the authorities; governing body; (local) council. **behördlich,** *adj.* official.

Behuf [bəˈhuːf], *m.* purpose, object, aim, end; (*obs.*) behalf; ***zum –*** (*Gen.*), for the purpose of; ***zum –(e) der Armen,*** for the benefit of the poor. **behufs,** *prep.* (*Gen.*) *see* ***zum Behuf.***

behülflich [bəˈhylflɪç], *adj.* (*Poet.*) *see* **behilflich.**

behüten [bəˈhyːtən], *v.t.* guard, shield, protect, keep (safe) (*vor* (*Dat.*), from); watch over; (***Gott***) ***behüte! behüte Gott!*** certainly not! far from it! God forbid! ***Gott behüte euch! behüt' dich Gott!*** God bless you! good-bye! **Behüter,** *m.* guardian; protector.

behutsam [bəˈhuːtzaːm], *adj.* careful, cautious, wary, circumspect. **Behutsamkeit,** *f.* care, caution, wariness, circumspection.

bei [baɪ], **1.** *prep.* (*Dat.*) N.B. *– **dem** frequently contracted to **beim,** q.v. Only a sample from typical examples of the main usages can be given. Idiomatic expressions, esp. where prep. serves to link verb or adj. with its complement, should be sought under the characteristic word.* 1. (*proximity in place*) by, near, next to; ***Potsdam – Berlin,*** Potsdam by *or* near Berlin; ***die Schlacht – Sedan,*** the Battle of Sedan; ***Seite – Seite,*** side by side; 2. at, with; ***Herr Braun – Herrn Schmidt,*** Mr. Braun care of (c/o) Mr. Schmidt; ***er wohnt – seiner Mutter,*** he lives with his mother *or* at his mother's; ***– uns*** (***zu Hause***), at our house, at home; in our country; ***ich habe kein Geld – mir,*** I have no money with *or* about *or* (*coll.*) on me; ***– der Marine,*** with *or* in the navy; ***– Hofe,*** at court; ***es steht – Goethe,*** it occurs in Goethe; ***– der S. sein,*** give one's mind to it, concentrate; (*coll.*) ***– der Stange bleiben,*** keep to the point; ***– der Hand sein,*** (*of a p.*) be at hand, (*of a th.*) be handy *or* to hand; 3. (*coincidence in time*) at, while, during; ***– Nacht und Nebel,*** under cover of night; ***– Tisch*** or ***–m Essen,*** at table, at one's meal; ***– Gelegenheit,*** when(ever) convenient; (*Comm.*) ***– Sicht,*** at *or* on sight; ***– Tag,*** by day, in the day-time; 4. (*concomitant circumstances*) ***– Geld sein,*** be in funds; ***– einem Glas Wein,*** over a glass of wine; (*coll.*) ***knapp – Kasse sein,*** be short of funds, be hard-up; (*coll.*) ***nicht ganz – sich,*** not all there; ***– Sinnen,*** in one's right mind; ***nicht – Trost,*** off one's head, not in one's right mind; 5. (*contingent circumstances*) ***– günstigem Wetter,*** weather permitting; ***– alledem,*** notwithstanding, for all that; ***– Todesstrafe,*** on pain of death; ***–m besten Willen,*** with the best will in the world; 6. (*means, agency*) ***– der Hand nehmen,*** take by the hand; ***– den Haaren fassen,*** seize by the hair; ***–m Namen nennen,*** call by name; ***– Gott*** (***schwören***), (swear) by God; 7. (*approximation*) (*obs. or dial.*) ***– Heller und Pfennig,*** to the last farthing; ***– 1000 Mann,*** about 1,000 men; ***– weitem,*** by far. **2.** *adv.* 1. (*emphatic addition to other adv. of proximity*) *e.g.* ***nahe –,*** near by; (*Naut.*) ***alles –,*** under full sail; (*coll. ellipt. for dabei*) ***er will – sein,*** he wants to be there.

bei–, *pref.* 1. (*with v.i. indicating* side by side with) *e.g.* ***beiliegen,*** be enclosed with; ***beistehen,*** assist, support, stand by; 2. (*with v.t. indicating* in addition to) *e.g.* ***beilegen,*** enclose, add; ***beisteuern,*** contribute; 3. (*with adj. or adv. indicating proximity*) *e.g.* ***beieinander,*** side by side, together. *For other examples see below.*

Bei–, *pref.* 1. (*denoting equivalence*) co–, joint; *e.g.* ***Beileid,*** sympathy, condolence; **2.** (*denoting s.th. ancillary*), subordinate, secondary, subsidiary; supplementary, auxiliary, extra; *e.g.* ***Beiwagen,*** side-car; ***Beiklang,*** overtone. *For further examples see below.*

Beianker [ˈbaɪˀaŋkər], *m.* (*Naut.*) kedge.

beibehalten [ˈbaɪbəhaltən], *irr.v.t.* keep (up *or* on), maintain, retain, continue, adhere, keep *or* (*coll.*) stick to. **Beibehaltung,** *f.* retention, continuance (*Gen.*, of), adherence (to).

beibiegen [ˈbaɪbiːgən], *irr.v.t.* (*Comm.*) enclose; (*sl.*) ***das werde ich dir schon –!*** I'll learn you!

Beiblatt [ˈbaɪblat], *n.* supplement (*to a periodical*).

Beiboot [ˈbaɪboːt], *n.* long-boat, jolly-boat, cockboat, pinnace.

beibringen [ˈbaɪbrɪŋən], *irr.v.t.* 1. bring *or* put forward, provide, furnish, produce (*witnesses etc.*), cite (*authorities*), adduce (*reasons etc.*); 2. impose, inflict (*Dat.*, on), administer, apply, give (to) (*a p.*); ***ihm Trost –,*** comfort him; 3. teach, impart (*knowledge*) (*Dat.*, to); (*coll.*) ***dir werde ich's schon –!*** I'll teach you! **Beibringung,** *f.* infliction (*of wound*); production (*of evidence etc.*).

Beichte [ˈbaɪçtə], *f.* confession; ***– ablegen,*** confess, make one's confession. **beichten,** *v.t., v.i.* confess (*Dat. or bei*, to), go to confession. **Beicht|gänger,** *m. See* **–kind. Beichtiger,** *m. See* **Beichtvater. Beicht|kind,** *n.* penitant. **–stuhl,** *m.* confessional (-box). **–vater,** *m.* (father) confessor.

beidäugig [ˈbaɪtˀɔygɪç], *adj.* binocular.

beide [ˈbaɪdə], **1.** *adj.* (*stressed*) both, (*unstressed*) two; either, (*neg.*) neither; ***– Söhne,*** both sons; ***meine –n Söhne,*** both my sons, my two sons; ***in – Fällen,*** in both cases, in either case; ***in keiner der –n Fällen,*** in neither case. **2.** *pron.* both, two; either, (*neg.*) neither; ***die –n,*** both *or* the two of them; ***wir –,*** both of us; ***alle –,*** both of them; ***keiner von –n,*** neither of them; ***welcher von –n?*** which of the two? ***es ist mir –s recht,*** it's all one *or* all the same to me; ***–s ist ausgeschlossen,*** both are *or* either is out of the question; (*Tenn.*) ***dreißig –,*** thirty all.

beidemal [ˈbaɪdəmaːl], *adv.* both times, in both cases.

beiderlei [ˈbaɪdərlaɪ], *indecl.adj.* both kinds, both sorts, either sort; ***– Geschlechts,*** of either sex; of common gender.

beiderseitig [ˈbaɪdərzaɪtɪç], *adj.* on both sides, mutual, reciprocal; ***–e Lähmung,*** paraplegia. **beiderseits, 1.** *adv.* reciprocally, mutually; on both sides, at both ends. **2.** *prep.* (*Gen.*) on both sides (of).

beidhändig ['baɪthɛndɪç], *adj.* ambidextrous.
beidlebig ['baɪtle:bɪç], *adj.* amphibious.
beidrehen ['baɪdre:ən], *v.t., v.i.* (*Naut.*) heave to.
beieinander [baɪaɪn'andər], *adv.* together, next to each other.
Beierbe ['baɪˀɛrbə], *m.* coheir, joint-heir.
Beifahrer ['baɪfa:rər], *m.* driver's mate; side-car passenger; pillion-rider.
Beifall ['baɪfal], *m.* approval, approbation, commendation; applause, acclamation, cheering, clapping; *ihm – zollen* or *spenden,* applaud him; *– finden* or *ernten,* meet with approval, be applauded; *– klatschen,* clap; *– rufen,* cheer.
beifallen ['baɪfalən], *irr.v.i.* (*aux.* s.) (*Dat.*) 1. *imp.* come to mind; *jetzt fällt es mir bei,* now it strikes me *or* occurs to me; 2. (*obs.*) support, approve of; *einer Meinung –,* agree with an opinion.
beifällig ['baɪfɛlɪç], *adj.* approving; favourable; *– aufnehmen,* receive with approval.
Beifalls|äußerung, *f.* applause, acclamation. **–bezeugung,** *f.* mark *or* sign of approval. **–ruf,** *m.* cheer, shout of acclamation. **–sturm,** *m.* storm *or* thunder of applause.
Beifilm ['baɪfɪlm], *m.* supporting film, second feature.
beifolgend ['baɪfɔlgənt], *adj.* (*Comm.*) enclosed, herewith.
beifügen ['baɪfy:gən], *v.t.* add, enclose, subjoin, append, attach, annex. **beifügend,** *adj.* (*Gram.*) attributive. **Beifügung,** *f.* addition, enclosure; (*Gram.*) adjunct, attribute.
Beifuß [baɪfu:s], *m.* 1. (*Bot.*) mugwort (*Artemisia vulgaris*); 2. (*Naut.*) truss (*of a sail*).
Beigabe ['baɪga:bə], *f.* supplement, addition, free gift.
beigeben ['baɪge:bən], *irr.v.t.* (*Dat.*) add, attach; allot, assign, delegate (*as an assistant*); (*coll.*) *klein –,* give in, climb down, knuckle under.
Beigeordnete(r) ['baɪgəɔrdnətə(r)], *m., f.* assistant, second-in-command, second-in-charge, deputy; *see* **beiordnen.**
Beigericht ['baɪgərɪçt], *n.* hors d'œuvre; side-dish, entremets.
beigeschlossen ['baɪgəʃlɔsən], *see* **beischließen.**
Beigeschmack ['baɪgəʃmak], *m.* after-taste, smack, tang, flavour, savour.
beigesellen [baɪ'gəzɛlən], *v.t., v.r.* associate (*Dat.,* with), attach (to).
Beiheft ['baɪhɛft], *n.* supplement (*of a periodical*). **beiheften,** *v.t.* attach, affix, fasten *or* fix on (*Dat.,* to); pin *or* clip on (to).
beiher [baɪ'he:r], *adv.* (*obs.*) beside, alongside.
Beihilfe ['baɪhɪlfe], *f.* 1. help, aid, assistance; (*Law*) aiding and abetting; 2. grant (in aid), subvention, subsidy, allowance; *staatliche –,* state subsidy, government grant.
beiholen ['baɪho:lən], *v.t.* (*Naut.*) haul in (*the sheets*).
beikommen ['baɪkɔmən], *irr.v.i.* (*aux.* s.) (*Dat.*) 1. get at, get near, reach, make an impression on (*a p.*); *ihm ist nicht beizukommen,* you can't do anything *or* get anywhere with him; *ihm ist mit Argumenten nicht beizukommen,* arguments make no impression on him, he doesn't respond to argument; 2. overcome, get the better of (*a th.*); *der Festung ist nicht beizukommen,* the fortress is inaccessible; *mit dieser Behandlung kommt man der Krankheit nicht bei,* the illness won't respond to this treatment; 3. (*obs.*) come near to, be comparable with; *nicht –,* fall short of; 4. (*obs.*) (*imp.*) occur to, come into (*one's*) mind; *laß dir nicht –,* don't take it into your head. **beikommend,** *adj.* (*Comm. obs.*) *see* **beiliegend.**
Beil [baɪl], *n.* **(-s,** *pl.* **-e)** hatchet, chopper, axe.
Beiladung ['baɪla:duŋ], *f.* 1. extra freight *or* cargo; 2. (*Artil.*).) priming charge.
Beilage ['baɪla:gə], *f.* addition, enclosure; supplement; appendix; vegetables, garnishing; (*Mech.*) packing, shim.
Beilager ['baɪla:gər], *n.* (*obs.*) nuptials; *das – vollziehen,* consummate the marriage (*only used of persons of high estate*).
beiläufig ['baɪlɔyfɪç], **1.** *adj.* 1. incidental, casual, parenthetic; *–e Bemerkung,* incidental remark; 2. (*dial.*) approximate; *–e Berechnung,* rough calculation. **2.** *adv.* 1. incidentally, by the way, in passing; 2. (*dial.*) roughly, approximately, about.
Beilbrief ['baɪlbri:f], *m.* 1. (*Naut.*) ship's register; 2. (*Swiss*) title deeds (*of property*).
beilegen ['baɪle:gən], **1.** *v.t.* (*Dat.*) 1. add, join, annex (*a document etc.*) (to); enclose (in); *Geld einem Briefe –,* enclose money in a letter; 2. attribute, ascribe, assign (*quality etc.*) (to), attach (*importance*) (to); confer, bestow (*title*) (on); *sich* (*Dat.*) *einen Namen –,* claim *or* lay claim to *or* assume a name; 3. settle, compose, (*coll.*) make up (*a quarrel*), reconcile (*conflicting opinions*); 4. (*obs.*) lay *or* set *or* put aside, put by, lay in store. **2.** *v.i.* (*obs.*) *see* **beidrehen. Beilegung,** *f.* attribution, assignment; conferment, bestowal; adjustment, settlement, reconciliation.
beileibe [baɪ'laɪbə], *adv.* (*only in*) *– nicht,* by no means, on no account, not at all, not in the least; (*coll. int.*) not on your life!
Beileid ['baɪlaɪt], *n.* sympathy, condolence; *ihm sein – aussprechen* or *bezeigen,* express one's sympathy with him, offer him one's condolences. **Beileids|bezeugung,** *f.* expression of sympathy. **–brief,** *m.,* **–schreiben,** *n.* letter of condolence.
beilfertig ['baɪlfɛrtɪç], *adj.* (*Shipb.*) work on the hull completed.
beiliegen ['baɪli:gən], *irr.v.i.* 1. (*obs.*) (*Dat.*) lie with; sleep with; 2. be enclosed; *–der Brief,* the enclosed letter; 3. (*Naut.*) lie to, be hove to.
Beilke ['baɪlkə], *f.* shovelboard, shuffleboard; shove-halfpenny.
Beil|stein, *m.* jade, greenstone, nephrite. **–stiel,** *m.* hatchet-helve. **–träger,** *m.* lictor; halberdier.
beim [baɪm] = *bei dem wherever art. has little or no dem. force, e.g.* ***bei dem König.*** *Resolution rare with sup., e.g.* ***– besten Willen.*** *Resolution impossible with n. verbal nouns, e.g.* ***– Schlafengehen.***
beimengen ['baɪmɛŋən], *v.t. See* **beimischen.**
beimessen ['baɪmɛsən], *irr.v.t.* attribute, ascribe, attach (*Dat.,* to); *einer S. Glauben –* believe *or* credit s.th., give credence to s.th.
beimischen ['baɪmɪʃən], *v.t.* mix, admix, mingle (*Dat.* with), add (to). **Beimischung,** *f.* admixture; (*Cul.*) *geringe – von,* sprinkling *or* dash of.
Bein [baɪn], *n.* **(-(e)s,** *pl.* **-e)** leg, (*obs., B.*) bone; *ein Klotz am –,* a millstone round one's neck; *auf den –en sein,* (*of a p.*) be on the go, be on one's feet *or* legs, be up and about; (*of a group*) be afoot *or* astir; *früh auf den –en sein,* be up early; *auf die –e bringen,* raise (*an army*), launch, start (*s.th.*), set *or* get (*s.th.*) going; *ihm auf die –e helfen,* help him to his feet, give him a helping hand; *wieder auf die –e kommen,* get well again; *sich auf die –e machen,* set out, be off, (*coll.*) get moving, get a move on; *sich* (*Dat.*) *kein – ausreißen,* take one's time, take it easy, not break one's neck; *es ging* or *fuhr mir durch Mark und –,* it sent a shudder through me; *der Schreck ist mir in die –e gefahren,* the fright turned my legs to water; (*coll.*) *alles was –e hat,* all the world and his wife; (*sl.*) *kein –!* not a living soul; by no means, certainly not; *ich will dir –e machen,* I'll make you run; *Stein und – schwören,* swear till one is blue in the face; *mit einem – im Grabe stehen,* have one foot in the grave; *ihm ein – stellen,* trip him up; *die –e unter den Arm nehmen,* pick up one's heels.
beinah(e) ['baɪna:(ə)], *adv.* almost, nearly, all but, well-nigh; *es ist – einerlei* or *– dasselbe,* it is much the same thing; *ich wäre – gestorben,* I was on the point of dying; *– hätte ich es ihr gesagt,* I all but told her.
beinähnlich ['baɪnˀɛ:nlɪç], *adj.* osseous, bony, bone-like.
Beiname 'baɪna:mə], *m.* designation; nickname,

sobriquet; (*occ.*) surname; ***Friedrich II. mit dem –n der Große,*** Frederick II known as the Great.

Beinbruch, *m.* fracture of the leg. **beindürr,** *adj.* spindly. **beinern,** *adj.* of bone. **Bein|fäule,** *f.* caries. **–fügung,** *f.* articulation (*of joints*). **–geschwulst,** *f.* (*Med.*) osseous tumour. **–geschwür,** *n.* (*Med.*) varicose ulcer. **–gewächs,** *n.* (*Med.*) exostosis. **–harnisch,** *m.* greaves, cuisses. **–haus,** *n.* charnel-house. **–haut,** *f.* periosteum. **–hebel, –heber,** *m.* (*Surg.*) elevator. **–höhle,** *f.* bone-socket.

beinig ['baınıç], *adj.* (*suff.*) = –legged, *e.g.* ***krummbeinig,*** bandy-legged.

Bein|kehle, *f.* hollow of the knee. **–kleid,** *n.* (*usu. pl.*) trousers; knickers. **–leder,** *n.* leg (*of a riding-boot*); leather gaiter.

Beinling ['baınlıŋ], *m.* leg (*of stocking*).

Bein|prothese, *f.* artificial leg. **–röhre,** *f.* (*Anat.*) tibia. **–schellen,** *f.pl.* shackles, fetters. **–schere,** *f.* scissors hold (*wrestling*). **–schiene,** *f.* leg splint; *see also* **–schützer**; *pl.* greaves. **–schlag,** *m.* (*swimming*) leg stroke. **–schraube,** *f.* the boot (*torture*). **–schützer,** *m.* (*Spt.*) leg-pad, shin-guard. **–schwarz,** *n.* bone-black, ivory black.

beiordnen ['baiˀɔrdnən], *v.t.* set *or* place on a level (*Dat.*, with) *or* at the side (of); (*Gram.*) ***–d*** or ***beigeordnet,*** coordinating (*conjunction*), coordinate, paratactic (*clause*). **Beiordnung,** *f.* (*Gram.*) parataxis, coordination.

beipflichten ['baıpflıçtən], *v.i.* 1. ***ihm –,*** agree *or* concur with him (***in einer S.***, in, on *or* about a th.); 2. (*Dat.*) agree *or* consent to (*s.th.*), approve of (*s.th.*). **Beipflichtung,** *f.* consent, assent, agreement (to), approval (of).

Beirat ['baıra:t], *m.* adviser, counsellor; advisory body, board, commission; (*obs.*) counsel.

beirren [bəˈırən], *v.t. usu. neg.* ***sich nicht – lassen,*** not be dissuaded *or* diverted *or* (*coll.*) put off (***in*** (*Dat.*), from).

beisammen [baıˈzamən], *adv.* (gathered) together; ***seine Gedanken – haben,*** have one's wits about one; ***er hatte seine Gedanken nicht –,*** his mind was wandering, (*coll.*) he wasn't all there. **Beisammensein,** *n.* reunion, gathering; ***geselliges –,*** social (gathering), informal reception.

Beisatz ['baızats], *m.* 1. addition; admixture, alloy; ***ohne –,*** unalloyed; 2. (*Gram.*) apposition, adjunct.

beischießen ['baıʃi:sən], *irr.v.t.* contribute, advance (*money*).

Beischiff ['baıʃıf], *n.* cock-boat, tender, pinnace.

Beischlaf ['baıʃla:f], *m.* cohabitation, coition; ***außerehelicher –,*** extramarital relations, adultery. **beischlafen,** *irr.v.i.* (*Dat.*) sleep *or* lie with, have intercourse with.

Beischläfer ['baıʃlɛ:fər], *m.* lover, paramour, (*obs.*) bedfellow. **Beischläferin,** *f.* mistress, concubine.

beischließen ['baıʃli:sən], *irr.v.t.* enclose.

Beischluß ['baıʃlus], *m.* enclosure.

beischreiben ['baıʃraıbən], *irr.v.t.* write in the margin; add (*notes, comments etc.*). **Beischreiben,** *n.* appended *or* enclosed note *or* letter.

Beischrift ['baıʃrıft], *f.* annotation, marginal note; postscript; caption, legend, inscription (*to illustration etc.*).

Beisegel ['baıze:gəl], *m.* (*Naut.*) staysail, studding sail. **beisegeln,** *v.i.* (*aux.* s.) sail close-hauled.

Beisein ['baızaın], *n.* presence; ***ohne mein –,*** without my being present.

beiseite [baıˈzaıtə], *adv.* aside (*also Theat.*), on one side, apart; in an undertone *or* stage-whisper; ***Scherz –!*** joking apart!

beiseite–, *pref.* to the *or* one side, aside. **–bringen,** *irr.v.t. See* **–schaffen. –legen,** *v.t.* lay *or* put aside. **–schaffen,** *reg.v.t.* move aside *or* to one side; get rid of, put away; put aside *or* on one side (*for one's own use*). **–setzen,** *v.t.* put *or* set aside (*a th.*), neglect, pay no attention to (*a p.*). **–stehen,** *irr.v.i.* stand aside *or* back *or* in the background. **–stellen,** *v.t. See* **–legen**; shelve, defer consideration of.

Beisel ['baızəl], *n.* (*Austr.*) tavern.

beisetzen ['baızɛtsən], *v.t.* (*Dat.*) 1. place *or* set *or* put beside *or* by; add to; ***alle Segel –,*** set the sails, crowd all sails; 2. lay to rest, bury, inter. **Beisetzung,** *f.* burial, interment, funeral.

beisitzen ['baızıtsən], *irr.v.i.* sit in (*i.e. attend but take no part in*); have a seat on (*a committee etc.*). **Beisitzer,** *m.* assessor (*i.e. junior lawyer attending courts*); member of a committee *or* syndicate.

Beispiel ['baıʃpi:l], *n.* example, instance, illustration; precedent; ***ein – geben,*** set an example; ***als – anführen,*** quote as an illustration, hold up as an example; ***zum –*** (abbr. ***z.B.***), for example, for instance, such as, viz., e.g.; ***sich*** (*Dat.*) ***ein – nehmen an ihm,*** take an example from him; ***ein – aufstellen,*** set up as an example; ***abschreckendes –,*** awful warning, deterrent; ***warnendes –,*** warning, caution. **beispielhaft,** *adj.* exemplary. **beispiellos,** *adj.* unprecedented, unexampled, unparalleled, without equal *or* parallel, unheard of. **beispielshalber, beispielsweise,** *adv.* by way of example, for instance *or* example.

beispringen ['baıʃprıŋən], *irr.v.t.* (*aux.* s.) (*Dat.*) come to (*a p.'s*) aid *or* assistance, help (*a p.*) out.

Beißbeere ['baısbe:rə], *f.* (*Bot.*) capsicum, chilli, Guinea *or* Cayenne pepper.

Beißel ['baısəl], *m.* (*dial.*) *see* **Beitel.**

beißen, *irr.v.t., irr.v.i.* bite; sting, burn; smart; ***in eine S. –,*** take a bite out of s.th.; ***nicht viel zu – haben,*** be badly off; ***in die Angel –,*** take the bait; (*coll.*) ***in den sauren Apfel –,*** take one's medicine, swallow a bitter pill; (*coll.*) ***ins Gras –,*** bite the dust; ***auf die Stange –,*** champ the bit; ***es beißt in die Augen,*** it makes one's eyes smart; ***auf der Zunge –,*** bite one's tongue. **beißend,** *adj.* biting, pungent, caustic; mordant, sarcastic, cutting, bitter, stinging; sharp. **Beißer,** *m.* incisor (tooth). **Beißerchen,** *n.* (*nursery talk*) toothy-peg.

Beiß|kohl, *m.* mangelwurzel. **–korb,** *m.* muzzle. **–ring,** *m.* teething-ring. **–rübe,** *f. See* **–kohl. –zahn,** *m. See* **Beißer. –zange,** *f.* pincers, nippers.

Beistand ['baıʃtant], *m.* 1. help, aid, support, assistance; ***ihm – leisten,*** lend him a helping hand, give *or* render him assistance; 2. assistant, helper, support; counsel; ***ärztlicher –,*** medical adviser. **Beistandsvertrag,** *m.* mutual-aid pact.

beistechen ['baıʃtɛçən], *irr.v.i.* (*Naut.*) sail close-hauled.

beistehen ['baıʃte:ən], *irr.v.i.* (*Dat.*) help, aid, assist, support, succour; (*coll.*) stand by, back up; ***mit Trost –,*** comfort; ***Gott stehe mir bei!*** God help me! ***die Beistehenden,*** the bystanders, onlookers. **Beisteher,** *m.* assistant, helper; (*Naut.*) consort (vessel).

Beisteuer ['baıʃtɔyər], *f.* contribution, subvention, monetary aid. **beisteuern,** *v.t., v.i.* contribute (***zu,*** to).

beistimmen ['baıʃtımən], *v.i.* (*Dat.*) assent, consent, agree (to), approve (*a proposal*); agree, concur (with) (*a p.*) (***in*** (*Dat.*), in *or* about (*a th.*)), (*coll.*) fall in (with) (*a p. or a proposal*). **Beistimmung,** *f.* assent, consent, agreement (to) (*a proposal*); agreement, concurrence (with) (*a p.*).

Beistrich ['baıʃtrıç], *m.* comma.

Beitel ['baıtəl], *m.* chisel.

Beitöne ['baıtø:nə], *m.pl.* (*Mus.*) overtones.

Beitrag ['baıtra:k], *m.* contribution, quota, share; premium (*of insurance etc.*); (membership) subscription, (*Am.*) dues; ***Beiträge liefern,*** contribute (*to a journal*). **beitragen,** *irr.v.t.* contribute (***zu,*** to(wards)), bear a share (of); be conducive (to), assist, help (towards *or* in); ***es hat zu meinem Glücke beigetragen,*** it has increased my happiness; ***das trägt nur dazu bei, ihn zu erbittern,*** that will only serve to embitter him.

Beiträger ['baıtrɛ:gər], *m.* contributor.

beitreiben ['baıtraıbən], *irr.v.t.* collect, recover, (*debts*), (*Mil.*) requisition, commandeer. **Beitreibung,** *f.* requisition; collection, recovery.

beitreten ['baıtre:tən], *irr.v.i.* (*aux.* s.) (*Dat.*) agree to, assent to, accede to, concur in, adopt (*an* *opinion*), (*coll.*) fall in with, come round to; accede to, enter into (*a treaty etc.*); join, become a member of (*a party, a club etc.*).

Beitritt ['baɪtrɪt], *m.* accession (*zu*, to); enrolment (in), admission, admittance (to), joining (*a society*); concurrence (in), assent (to).

Beiwache ['baɪvaxə], *f.* *See* **Biwak.**

Beiwagen ['baɪva:gən], *m.* side-car.

Beiwerk ['baɪvɛrk], *n.* accessories, trimming, decoration, (*coll.*) frills, padding.

beiwohnen ['baɪvo:nən], *v.i.* (*Dat.*) 1. be present at, attend (*a meeting, lecture etc.*), witness (*an event*); 2. cohabit with, sleep with; 3. (*obs.*) ***einer S. –,*** be inherent in *or* be peculiar to a th. **Beiwohnung,** *f.* 1. presence, attendance; 2. cohabitation.

Beiwort ['baɪvɔrt], *n.* (*Gram.*) adjective; epithet.

Beiwurzel ['baɪvurtsəl], *f.* (*Bot.*) adventitious root.

Beizahl ['baɪtsa:l], *f.* (*Math.*) (numerical) coefficient.

beizählen ['baɪtsɛ:lən], *v.t.* reckon, count, number, include (*Dat.*, with *or* among).

Beiz|brühe, *f.* *See* **–flüssigkeit. –bütte,** *f.* *See* **–kufe.**

Beize ['baɪtsə], *f.* 1. corrosive, mordant, (etching) acid, tanning liquor, pickle, sauce (*in tobacco preparation*), (wood) stain, (*Med.*) caustic; (*Cul.*) pickle, marinade; 2. hawking, falconry.

Beizeichen ['baɪtsaɪçən], *n.* attribute; symbol; ***ein Wappen ohne –,*** a plain coat of arms.

beizeiten ['baɪtsaɪtən], *adv.* (*Poet.*) betimes, early, in (good) time, in good season.

beizen ['baɪtsən], *v.t.* 1. (*of acid etc.*) corrode, eat into; (*of a p.*) scour, pickle (*metals*), (*Engr.*) etch, soak, macerate, mordant (*fabrics etc.*), stain (*wood*), (*Med.*) cauterize, (*Cul.*) pickle, marinade; 2. go hawking. **beizend,** *adj.* corrosive, caustic, mordant, (*fig.*) pungent, stinging. **Beizenfarbe,** *f.* mordant *or* acid dye.

Beiz|falke, *m.* falcon. **–flüssigkeit,** *f.* corrosive, mordant, pickling liquor, pickle. **–jagd,** *f.* hawking, falconry. **–kraft,** *f.* corrosive power, causticity. **–kufe,** *f.* pickling tank *or* vat. **–mittel,** *n.* 1. corrosive, caustic, mordant; 2. (wood) stain.

bejahen [bə'ja:ən], *v.t.* answer in the affirmative, assent to, affirm, give consent (to); (*Prov.*) ***wer schweigt, bejaht,*** silence gives consent *or* means assent; ***–der Satz,*** affirmative sentence.

bejahrt [bə'ja:rt], *adj.* aged, venerable. **Bejahrtheit,** *f.* old age.

Bejahung [bə'ja:uŋ], *f.* affirmative answer, affirmation, assertion, assurance. **Bejahungssatz,** *m.* affirmative sentence.

bejammern [bə'jamərn], *v.t.* bewail, lament, deplore, bemoan. **bejammerns|wert, –würdig,** *adj.* lamentable, deplorable, pitiable, wretched.

bejubeln [bə'ju:bəln], *v.t.* cheer loudly, shout for joy about, give an ovation to, rejoice *or* exult at, be jubilant over.

bekämpfen [bə'kɛmpfən], *v.t.* fight (against), oppose, resist; (do) battle *or* contend with, combat, stand up *or* make a stand against. **Bekämpfung,** *f.* fight, battle (*Gen.*, against), opposition (to), control (*of pests*).

bekannt [bə'kant], *adj.* known, well- *or* generally known, of common knowledge; noted, of note, renowned, notorious; (*of a th.*) familiar; ***ich mache Sie mit ihm –,*** I will introduce you to him; ***ich mache Sie mit der S. –,*** I will acquaint you with the matter *or* of the fact; ***sich mit einer S. – machen,*** acquaint *or* familiarize o.s. *or* make o.s. acquainted *or* familiar with a matter (*see also* **bekanntmachen**); ***mit ihm – werden,*** become acquainted with him, get to know him (*see also* **bekanntwerden**); ***sie sind miteinander –,*** they are acquainted, they know each other; ***es kommt mir – vor,*** it strikes me as familiar; (*coll.*) ***– tun,*** be overfamiliar; ***– werden, sich – machen,*** become well-known, make a name for o.s.; ***als – annehmen*** or ***voraussetzen,*** take for granted; (*coll.*) ***ich bin in Hamburg –,*** I know Hamburg well, I am no stranger to Hamburg; ***ich bin hier selbst nicht –,*** I'm a stranger here myself. **Bekannte(r),** *m.,f.* acquaintance, friend. **bekanntermaßen,** *adv.* *See* **bekanntlich.**

Bekanntgabe [bə'kantga:bə], *f.* (public) announcement, publication, proclamation, promulgation. **bekanntgeben,** *irr.v.t.* make known *or* public, announce, publish; give notice of, notify; ***feierlich –,*** proclaim, promulgate (*laws etc.*).

bekanntlich [bə'kantlɪç], *adv.* as is well *or* generally known, as everyone knows.

bekannt|machen, *v.t.* *See* **–geben. Bekannt|machung,** *f.* *See* **–gabe.**

Bekanntschaft [bə'kantʃaft], *f.* 1. (circle of) acquaintances; connexions; 2 acquaintance, familiarity (***mit***, with), knowledge (of).

bekanntwerden [bə'kantve:rdən], *irr.v.i.* (*aux.* s.) become (well) known, become public (knowledge), come to (*s.o.'s*) knowledge *or* notice; get abroad, (*coll.*) come out, transpire (*of news*).

Bekassine [beka'si:nə], *f.* Common *or* (*Am.*) European snipe (*Gallinago gallinago*).

bekehrbar [bə'kɛ:rba:r], *adj.* convertible.

bekehren [bə'kɛ:rən], **1.** *v.t.* convert. **2.** *v.r.* be(come) converted. **Bekehrer,** *m.* proselytizer, converter; evangelist, missionary. **Bekehrte(r),** *m.,f.* convert, proselyte. **Bekehrung,** *f.* conversion. **Bekehrungseifer,** *m.* missionary zeal, proselytism. **bekehrungs|eifrig, –lustig,** *adj.* eager to convert, propagandist, proselytizing. **Bekehrungs|sucht,** *f.*, **–wut,** *f.* *See* **–eifer.**

bekennen [bə'kɛnnən], **1.** *irr.v.t.* confess, own (up to), admit, acknowledge, avow (*guilt etc.*), profess (*one's faith*); ***Farbe –,*** (*Cards*) follow suit, (*fig.*) show one's colours, be frank or candid. **2.** *irr.v.r.* ***sich zu einer S. –,*** *see* **1**; ***sich*** (***für***) (*adj.*) ***–,*** *see* **1**; ***sich zu ihm –,*** believe in *or* stand up for *or* declare one's allegiance *or* proclaim one's loyalty to him; ***sich zu einem Kind –,*** own *or* acknowledge a child (as one's own). **Bekenner,** *m.* confessor; ***Eduard der –,*** Edward the Confessor. **Bekennermut,** *m.* courage of one's convictions, unshakable faith.

Bekenntnis [bə'kɛntnɪs], *n.* (**-ses,** *pl.* **-se**) confession; profession, avowal (*of faith*); acknowledgement, declaration, affirmation (***zu***, of); confession (of faith), creed; (religious) denomination *or* persuasion. **bekenntnisfrei,** *adj.* non-denominational. **Bekenntnis|freiheit,** *f.* religious freedom. **–kirche,** *f.* (Lutheran) Confessional Church. **–schrift,** *f.* confession of faith, creed; *pl.* (Lutheran) symbolic books. **–schule,** *f.* denominational school.

beklagen [bə'kla:gən], **1.** *v.t.* 1. grieve over, mourn (for), lament (*death, loss etc.*), bewail, deplore (*fate, misfortune*); ***es ist zu –,*** it is regrettable *or* to be regretted; 2. (*Law*) ***beklagte Partei,*** *see* **Beklagte(r). 2.** *v.r.* protest, complain, make a complaint (***über*** (*Acc.*), about; ***bei***, to). **beklagens|wert, –würdig,** *adj.* lamentable, deplorable (*a th.*), pitiable (*a p.*). **Beklagte(r),** *m.,f.* (*Law*) defendant (*in civil action*).

beklatschen [bə'klatʃən], *v.t.* clap, applaud.

bekleben [bə'kle:bən], *v.t.* paste on, stick on, label, placard, cover; line (*with paper*).

bekleckern [bə'klɛkərn], *v.t.*, *v.r.* (*coll.*) soil, spot, (be)spatter (*o.s., one's clothes*).

beklecksen [bə'klɛksən], *v.t.* (*coll.*) blot, daub, smear.

bekleiden [bə'klaɪdən], *v.t.* 1. clothe, dress, attire, array (*a p.*), invest (*with insignia, office etc.*); 2. (*Build.*) line, face, revet; 3. occupy, fill (*position*), hold (*office*). **Bekleidung,** *f.* 1. clothing, clothes, dress; 2. revetment, casing, sheathing, lining, facing, hangings, tapestry; 3. investiture; tenure, exercise (*of an office*). **Bekleidungs|gegenstände,** *m.pl.* wearing apparel, articles of clothing. **–mauer,** *f.* revetment. **–stück,** *n.* article of clothing.

bekleistern [bə'klaɪstərn], *v.t.* daub *or* (be)smear with paste), paste (over).

beklemmen [bə'klɛmən], *v.t.* (*p.p. oft.* **beklommen**) stifle, oppress; ***Angst beklemmte mich*** or ***mir das Herz,*** fear gripped me *or* my heart; ***–de Luft,*** oppressive *or* stifling *or* suffocating atmosphere. **Beklemmtheit, Beklemmung,** *f.* oppression, constriction, tightness.

beklommen [bə'klɔmən], *adj.* uneasy, anxious. *See* **beklemmen. Beklommenheit,** *f.* uneasiness, anxiety, apprehension.

beklopfen [bə'klɔpfən], *v.t.* tap, knock (on); sound, test by knocking; (*Med.*) percuss.

bekohlen [bə'ko:lən], *v.t.* 1. bunker, coal (*ship etc.*), feed (*furnace*); 2. (*coll.*) tell a lie to, pull the wool over (*s.o.'s*) eyes. **Bekohlungsanlage,** *f.* coaling plant.

bekommen [bə'kɔmən], **1.** *irr.v.t.* 1. (*with nouns*) get, obtain; receive; develop (*holes, cracks, spots etc.*), get, become (*full of holes, cracked, spotted etc.*); ***Angst –,*** take fright, get frightened; ***Bescheid –,*** be notified *or* informed; ***Hunger –,*** get hungry; ***ein Kind –,*** have a baby; ***einen Korb –,*** be snubbed *or* rebuffed *or* rejected, meet with a refusal *or* rebuff; ***Lust –,*** take a fancy (***zu,*** to); ***Mut –,*** pluck up courage; ***einen Schnupfen –,*** catch (a) cold; ***Zähne –,*** teethe, cut one's teeth; 2. (*with adjs.*) ***fertig –,*** get finished *or* done, succeed in doing, manage *or* contrive to do; ***es satt –,*** get fed up (***zu tun,*** with doing); 3. (*with verbs*) ***zu sehen –,*** get a glimpse of, catch sight of; (*coll.*) ***zu tun –,*** have to deal with; (*coll.*) ***es mit der Angst zu tun –,*** get the wind up; 4. (*with p.p. = pass. constr.*) ***vorgesetzt –,*** be served with; ***geschenkt –,*** get *or* have as a present; ***geliehen –,*** have on loan. **2.** *irr.v.i.* (*aux.* s.) (*of food etc.*) (*Dat.*) agree (with), suit, do (*a p.*) good; ***wohl bekomm's (Ihnen)!*** your good health! (***iron.***) much good may it do you! ***diese Speise bekommt mir,*** this food agrees with me; ***es wird ihm übel*** or ***schlecht –,*** he will regret it *or* have to pay for it.

bekömmlich [bə'kœmlɪç], *adj.* digestible, nourishing, wholesome (*of foods*); beneficial (*climate etc.*).

beköstigen [bə'kœstɪgən], *v.t.* feed, board, provide meals for. **Beköstigung,** *f.* boarding, catering; board, food; ***Wohnung und –,*** board and lodging.

bekräftigen [bə'krɛftɪgən], *v.t.* strengthen, confirm (***in*** (*Dat.*), in); reinforce, reaffirm; support (*statement*), seal (*promise*). **Bekräftigung,** *f.* confirmation; reaffirmation, reinforcement; ***zur –,*** in support *or* confirmation.

bekränzen [bə'krɛntsən], *v.t.* wreathe, garland, bedeck, crown (*with laurels etc.*).

bekreuzen [bə'krɔytsən], *v.t. See* **bekreuzigen, 1.**

bekreuzigen [bə'krɔytsɪgən], **1.** *v.t.* make the sign of the cross over. **2.** *v.r.* cross o.s.

bekriegen [bə'kri:gən], **1.** *v.t.* fight (against), battle against, combat. **2.** *v.r.* (*coll.*) collect *or* compose o.s., sober down *or* up.

bekritteln [bə'krɪtəln], *v.t.* criticize, find fault with, cavil *or* carp at; (*coll.*) pick holes in.

bekritzeln [bə'krɪtsəln], *v.t.* scribble *or* scrawl on.

bekrönen [bə'krø:nən], *v.t.* crown, (*usu. p.p.*) ***bekrönt,*** crowned (*with glory etc.*), surmounted *or* capped (***von, mit,*** with), with a coping (of) (*as a wall, pillar etc.*).

bekrusten [bə'krustən], **1.** *v.t.* encrust, crust over, cover with a crust. **2.** *v.r.* become crusted over *or* encrusted.

bekümmern [bə'kymərn], **1.** *v.t.* trouble, worry, disturb; ***bekümmert sein,*** worry, be worried *or* anxious *or* troubled *or* concerned (***über eine S., um ihn,*** about a th. *or* him). **2.** *v.r.* concern *or* trouble o.s., bother (o.s.) (***um,*** about). **Bekümmernis,** *f.* (-, *pl.* **-se**) grief, sorrow, worry, trouble.

bekunden [bə'kundən], **1.** *v.t.* declare, state, depose, testify to; evince, (make) manifest, show openly, display, reveal, betray, give evidence of, demonstrate. **2.** *v.r.* (*of a th.*) become evident *or* apparent, reveal itself. **Bekundung,** *f.* manifestation, revelation, display; sign, evidence, testimony.

belächeln [bə'lɛçəln], *v.t.* smile (pityingly) at; (*fig.*) make light of.

beladen [bə'la:dən], **1.** *irr.v.t.* load (*goods*), load (up) (*vehicle*). **2.** *irr.v.r.* burden o.s. **3.** *adj.* loaded, laden.

Belag [bə'la:k], *m.* (**-(e)s,** *pl.* **¨-e**) coat, coating, layer (*of dust etc.*); deposit, film (*also on teeth*), bloom, (*Med.*) fur (*on tongue*); (*Chem.*) incrustation, efflorescence; (*floor*) covering, flooring; surface (*of road*), paving, planking (*of bridge*), plating (*of silver etc.*), foil (*of mirror*), lining (*of brake*); filling, spread (*of sandwich*).

Belagerer [bə'la:gərər], *m.* besieger, beleaguerer.

belagern [bə'la:gərn], *v.t.* besiege, lay siege to, invest (*a fortress*); beleaguer (*a garrison*); (*fig.*) beset; crowd *or* throng (round), besiege. **Belagerung,** *f.* siege. **Belagerungs|artillerie,** *f.* siege artillery. **–heer,** *n.* besieging army. **–zustand,** *m.* state of siege *or* (*fig.*) of emergency.

Belang [bə'laŋ], *m.* (**-(e)s,** *pl.* **-e**) 1. ***von –,*** of importance *or* consequence *or* moment; ***ohne –,*** of no importance *or* consequence *or* account; 2. *pl.* interests, affairs; spheres of interest.

belangbar [bə'laŋba:r], *adj.* (*Law*) indictable, actionable. **belangen, 1.** *v.t.* (*Law*) (***gerichtlich***) **–,** prosecute, sue, indict, arraign, take (legal) proceedings *or* action against, bring an action against (***wegen,*** for). **2.** *imp.v.t.* concern; ***was mich belangt,*** as far as I am concerned, as far as it concerns me, as for me. **belanglos,** *adj.* unimportant, insignificant, of no importance *or* consequence; ***es ist völlig –,*** it does not matter at all. **Belanglosigkeit,** *f.* unimportance, insignificance; matter of no importance, trifling matter, trifle. **Belangung,** *f.* (*Law*) prosecution, indictment, suit at law (***wegen,*** for). **belangvoll,** *adj.* important, significant, of consequence.

belassen [bə'lasən], *irr.v.t.* 1. leave (*it*), let (*it*) rest (***bei,*** at), leave (*it*) alone; 2. keep, retain (*a p.*) (*in office etc.*).

belasten [bə'lastən], *v.t.* 1. (*a th.*) load, put a load *or* weight on, make heavy, weigh down; ***zu stark*** or ***zu sehr –,*** overload; (*fig.*) put under load (*a motor*), subject to strain, make (heavy) demands on (*supply, services etc.*); 2. (*a p.*) weigh down, weigh (heavily) (up)on, burden, encumber; ***erblich belastet,*** with a hereditary taint *or* disease; with a hereditary disposition (towards); 3. (*Comm.*) charge, debit (*an account*); ***ein belastetes Grundstück,*** an encumbered estate; 4. (*Law*) incriminate; ***belastende Zeugenaussage,*** incriminating evidence.

belästigen [bə'lɛstɪgən], *v.t.* trouble, disturb, inconvenience, incommode, (*coll.*) bother; annoy, obtrude o.s. on, importune, molest, (*coll.*) pester, badger. **Belästigung,** *f.* disturbance, inconvenience, annoyance; obtrusion (on), molestation.

Belastung [bə'lastuŋ], *f.* 1. load, weight, burden (*also fig.*); (*fig.*) encumbrance, strain, (heavy) demand; ***erbliche –,*** hereditary taint *or* disease; ***steuerliche –,*** burden *or* incidence of taxation; ***die Stunden größter –,*** peak-hours; ***die Stunden geringer –,*** off-peak hours; ***zulässige –,*** safe *or* working load; 2. (*Comm.*) debit (*of account*), encumbrance (*of estate*); 3. (*Law*) incrimination; 4. head of water. **Belastungs|anzeige,** *f.* (*Comm.*) debit note. **–fähigkeit,** *f.* load *or* carrying capacity. **–raum,** *m.* (*Naut.*) hold. **–spitze,** *f.* peak-load. **–tal,** *n.* (*Elec.*) minimum load. **–zeuge,** *m.* (*Law*) witness for the prosecution.

belauben [bə'laubən], **1.** *v.t.* cover in leaves; (*Archit.*) foliate. **2.** *v.r.* burst into leaf. **belaubt,** *adj.* in leaf, covered with foliage. **Belaubtheit,** *f.* leafiness. **Belaubung,** *f.* foliage.

belauern [bə'lauərn], *v.t.* lie in wait *or* watch for, observe (secretly), spy on.

Belauf [bə'lauf], *m.* (*Comm.*) amount, sum; ***der ganze –,*** the sum total. **belaufen, 1.** *irr.v.t.* (*obs.*) traverse, cover; inspect. **2.** *irr.v.r.* 1. steam *or* cloud *or* mist over (*as window*); 2. ***sich – auf*** (*Acc.*), amount to; (*coll.*) come *or* run to.

belauschen [bə'lauʃən], *v.t.* listen (secretly) to, overhear, eavesdrop on.

beleben [bə'le:bən], **1.** *v.t.* animate, give life to; (*fig.*)

revive, enliven, invigorate, stimulate, quicken, brighten, cheer; *wieder* –, restore to life, resuscitate, revive. **2.** *v.r.* come to life, revive; come alive, become busy (*as a road*). **belebend,** *adj.* life-giving, (*fig.*) invigorating, stimulating, restorative. **belebt,** *adj.* animate; animated, lively, brisk, busy. **Belebtheit,** *f.* animation, liveliness, briskness, bustle. **Belebung,** *f.* resurrection, resuscitation, revival, animation, stimulation, invigoration. **Belebungs|mittel,** *n.* restorative, stimulant. **–versuch,** *m.* attempted resuscitation.

belecken [bəˈlɛkən], *v.t.* lick; (*coll.*) *von der Kultur beleckt,* with a trace *or* veneer of civilized manners.

Beleg [bəˈleːk], *m.* (**-(e)s,** *pl.* **-e**) **1.** (documentary) proof *or* evidence, voucher, receipt, document, record; 2. evidence, verification, instance, example, illustration (*of the use of a word etc.*), authority, (supporting) reference (*for the use of a word etc.*). **Belegbuch,** *n.* (student's) record book (*of classes attended*).

belegen [bəˈleːgən], *v.t.* 1. cover; (*Law*) *mit Arrest* or *Beschlag* –, seize, attach (*a th.*); *mit Bomben* –, bomb, plaster with bombs; *mit Brettern* –, board *or* plank (over); *ein Brötchen* –, fill *or* spread a roll; *mit Eiern* –, lay eggs in (*the nest*); *mit Fliesen* –, tile (*a floor*); *einen Spiegel* –, silver a mirror; *mit Steuern* –, impose taxes on, levy taxes from; *mit Strafe* –, inflict punishment on; *die Stute* –, cover the mare; *mit einem Teppich* –, carpet (*a floor*); *belegtes Butterbrot,* sandwich; *belegte Stimme,* thick *or* husky *or* strained voice; *belegte Zunge,* coated *or* furred tongue; (*Her.*) *belegt,* charged (*mit,* with); 2. reserve, occupy (*a seat etc.*); *der Platz ist belegt,* the seat is taken; (*Mil.*) *einen Posten* –, man a post; *eine Vorlesung* –, register *or* enrol for a course of lectures; 3. furnish evidence for *or* of (*expenses etc.*), give an example *or* instance of the occurrence of (*a word etc.*), prove, substantiate, document (*a statement*); *mit Beispielen* –, illustrate with examples.

Beleg|exemplar, *n.* author's copy. **–holz,** *n.* 1. veneer; 2. *pl.* (*Naut.*) bitts. **–nagel,** *m.* (*Naut.*) belaying pin.

Belegschaft [bəˈleːkʃaft], *f.* staff (*of employees*), personnel; gang, shift (*of workmen*), crew.

Beleg|schein, *m. See* **–stück. –stelle,** *f.* illustration, (illustrative) quotation, instance, example; reference, evidence, authority. **–stück,** *n.* voucher, receipt, record, copy.

Belegung [bəˈleːguŋ], *f.* (*Elec.*) condenser plate.

belehnen [bəˈleːnən], *v.t.* invest with (*a fief*), enfeoff. **Belehnte(r),** *m., f.* vassal. **Belehnung,** *f.* enfeoffment, investiture, investment.

belehren [bəˈleːrən], *v.t.* instruct, teach (*a p.*), inform, apprise (*über* (*Acc.*), of), advise (on), warn (about); *sich – lassen,* take advice, listen to reason, be willing to listen; *ihn eines Besseren* or *anderen* –, correct his misconception, undeceive him, set him right. **belehrend,** *adj.* instructive, informative; didactic (*poem etc.*). **Belehrung,** *f.* instruction; information.

beleibt [bəˈlaɪpt], *adj.* stout, portly, corpulent. **Beleibtheit,** *f.* corpulence, stoutness.

beleidigen [bəˈlaɪdɪgən], *v.t.* offend, give offence to, insult, abuse, affront; *gröblich* –, outrage, grossly insult; *schriftlich* –, libel; *tätlich* –, assault. **beleidigend,** *adj.* offensive, insulting, abusive. **Beleidigung,** *f.* offence (to *or* against), insult, affront. **Beleidigungsklage,** *f.* libel action.

beleihbar [bəˈlaɪbaːr], *adj.* acceptable for a mortgage (*as property*), pledgeable (*securities*).

beleihen [bəˈlaɪən], *irr.v.t.* (*Comm.*) grant a loan on (*securities*); raise a mortgage on (*property*).

belemmern [bəˈlɛmərn], *v.t.* (*coll.*) confuse; cheat, take in. **belemmert,** *adj.* cheated; silly, sheepish; *er ist meist der Belemmerte,* he is always getting his leg pulled.

belesen [bəˈleːzən], *adj.* well-read; *ein –er Mann,* a man of wide reading.

beleuchten [bəˈlɔʏçtən], *v.t.* 1. light (*mit,* by); *das Zimmer* (*Auto*) –, switch on the lights in the room (the car's lights); *eine* (*schlecht*) *beleuchtete Straße,* a lighted (badly lit) road; 2. illuminate, give light to, light up, shine on; (*Theat.*) throw a spotlight on, spotlight (*an actor etc.*); *eine dunkle Ecke* –, light up *or* give light to a dark corner; *eine rosa Lampe beleuchtet das Bild,* a pink lamp illuminates *or* shines on the picture; 3. (*fig.*) throw *or* shed light on, illuminate, elucidate; *näher* –, examine closely.

Beleuchtung [bəˈlɔʏçtuŋ], *f.* 1. illumination, exposure to light; light, lighting; – *der Bühne,* stage lighting; 2. (*fig.*) elucidation; *einer S. die rechte – geben,* show a th. in its true light; *bei näherer* –, on close examination. **Beleuchtungs|anlage, –einrichtung,** *f.* lighting installation, lighting *or* light-fitting. **–körper,** *m.* light, lamp, lighting appliance, light-fitting, lamp socket. **–messer,** *m.* (*Opt.*) lux-meter. **–schirm,** *m.* reflector. **–spiegel,** *m.* illuminating mirror (*on microscope*). **–stärke,** *f.* intensity of light. **–trupp,** *m.* (*Mil.*) searchlight squad.

beleum(un)det [bəˈlɔym(un)dət], *adj. gut* (*übel*) – held in good (bad) repute.

belfern [ˈbɛlfərn], *v.i.* yap, yelp; (*coll. of a p.*) rail, nag.

Belgien [ˈbɛlgiən], *n.* Belgium. **Belgier,** *m.* Belgian. **belgisch,** *adj.* Belgian.

belichten [bəˈlɪçtən], *v.t.* (*Phot.*) expose. **Belichtung,** *f.* exposure. **Belichtungsmesser,** *m.* exposure meter.

beliebäugeln [bəˈliːpˀɔygəln], *v.t.* cast a covetous eye on, (*coll.*) have an eye on, give (*s.o.*) the eye.

belieben [bəˈliːbən], **1.** *v.t.* wish; *gnädige Frau –?* is there anything further that madam wishes? *wie Sie* –, as you wish *or* please; (*with zu and inf.*) – *Sie einzutreten,* please walk in. **2.** *imp.v.i.* (*Dat. of p.*) please, be agreeable to; *wie es Ihnen beliebt,* as you please *or* like *or* choose; *wie beliebt?* I beg your pardon; *wenn's beliebt,* if you please; time, gentlemen, please! **Belieben,** *n.* choice, discretion, convenience, liking, (*obs.*) pleasure; *nach* –, as much as you like, (*Mus.*) ad libitum, (*coll.*) ad lib.; (*Cul.*) *Gewürz nach* –, seasoning to taste; *ganz nach Ihrem* –, exactly as you wish *or* please.

beliebig [bəˈliːbɪç], **1.** *adj.* optional, arbitrary, any . . . (you please), any . . . whatever, (*coll.*) ad lib.; *eine –e Zahl,* an arbitrary number, any number you like; *jede –e Menge,* any quantity (whatever); *jede –e Person,* anyone you please, any person whatever, no matter who. **2.** *adv.* – *viel(e),* as much (many) as you like.

beliebt [bəˈliːpt], *adj.* popular, (well) liked, (*Comm.*) in demand; *sich – machen,* curry favour, ingratiate o.s. (*bei,* with). **Beliebtheit,** *f.* popularity.

beliefern [bəˈliːfərn], *v.t.* furnish, supply. **Belieferung,** *f.* regular supply.

bellen [ˈbɛlən], *v.i.* bark, bay; (*of hounds*) give tongue *or* voice; *eine –de Stimme,* a yapping voice; *ein –der Husten,* a hacking cough.

Belletristik [bɛleˈtrɪstɪk], *f.* fiction, light literature, (*obs.*) belles-lettres. **belletristisch,** *adj.* fictional, belletristic.

beloben [bəˈloːbən], *v.t.* (*obs.*) *see* **belobigen.**

belobigen [bəˈloːbɪgən], *v.t.* praise, commend, (*Mil.*) cite. **Belobigung,** *f.* praise, commendation.

Belobung [bəˈloːbuŋ], *f.* praise; (*Mil.*) *eine – erhalten,* be mentioned in dispatches, (*Am.*) receive a citation.

belohnen [bəˈloːnən], *v.t.* reward; *mit Undank* –, repay with ingratitude; *schlecht belohnt,* ill requited. **Belohnung,** *f.* reward; *eine – aussetzen* (*Dat.*), offer (*s.o.*) a reward.

Belsazar [bɛlˈzaːtsar], **Belsazer,** *m.* (*B.*) Belshazzar.

belüften [bəˈlyftən], *v.t.* ventilate, air. **Belüftung,** *f.* ventilation. **Belüftungsanlage,** *f.* ventilation system, air-conditioning (plant).

belügen [bəˈlyːgən], *irr.v.t.* lie to, tell lies to, deceive by lying; *sich selbst* –, deceive o.s.

belustigen [bəˈlustɪgən], **1.** *v.t.* amuse, entertain, divert. **2.** *v.r.* amuse *or* enjoy o.s. **Belustigung,** *f.* amusement, entertainment, diversion. **Belustigungsort,** *m.* place of amusement, amusement ground *or* park.

bemächtigen [bə'mɛçtɪgən], *v.r.* (*Gen.*) 1. seize (upon), lay *or* take hold of, secure, take possession of, possess o.s. of (*a th.*); ***sich des Thrones –,*** seize *or* usurp the throne; 2. seize, lay hands on (*a p.*); (*of emotion*) overcome, take possession of (*a p.*); ***welche Wut bemächtigte sich deiner?*** what rage possessed you?

bemähnt [bə'mɛ:nt], *adj.* maned, (*Her.*) crined.

bemäkeln [bə'mɛ:kəln], *v.t.* find fault with.

bemalen [bə'ma:lən], *v.t.* paint (over), colour, stain; (be)daub, cover with paint. **Bemalung,** *f.* (coat of) paint; daubing.

bemängeln [bə'mɛŋəln], *v.t.* criticize (adversely), find fault with, cavil at. **Bemängelung,** *f.* adverse criticism, fault-finding.

bemannen [bə'manən], *v.t.* man (*a ship, fortress etc.*). **Bemannung,** *f.* crew (*of a ship*), ship's company; manning.

bemänteln [bə'mɛntəln], *v.t.* cover (over), cloak, disguise (*faults etc.*), palliate, gloss over, (*coll.*) varnish over (*facts etc.*). **Bemäntelung,** *f.* cover, cloak, disguise, gloss.

bemeistern [bə'maɪstərn], **1.** *v.t.* 1. (*of a p.*) control, subdue, master, overcome, curb, bridle (*emotions etc.*); 2. (*of emotions*) seize, take possession of (*a p.*). **2.** *v.r.* (*Gen.*) (*obs.*) seize, lay hands on (*a p.*). *See* **bemächtigen.**

bemerkbar [bə'mɛrkba:r], *adj.* perceptible, noticeable, apparent; ***sich – machen,*** (*of a p.*) draw attention to o.s.; (*of a th.*) become noticeable *or* apparent, make itself felt; ***sich unangenehm – machen,*** (*of a p.*) make one's presence unpleasantly felt; (*of a th.*) become painfully apparent.

bemerken [bə'mɛrkən], *v.t.* 1. notice, observe, become aware of; note (*a fact*), (*coll.*) spot; 2. mention, remark, observe, comment; ***wie unten bemerkt,*** as noted *or* stated below; ***nebenbei bemerkt,*** by the way, incidentally, in parentheses. **bemerkenswert,** *adj.* (*of a th.*) noteworthy, worthy of note, deserving notice, notable, remarkable; (*of a p.*) striking, remarkable. **bemerklich,** *adj. See* **bemerkbar. Bemerkung,** *f.* observation, remark, comment; ***–en am Rande,*** marginal notes.

bemessen [bə'mɛsən], **1.** *irr.v.t.* 1. evaluate, rate, measure, determine (***nach,*** by *or* according to); 2. adjust, adapt, apportion (***nach,*** to), regulate, (according to). **2.** *adj.* restricted, limited (*as time etc.*); (*Mech., Elec.*) ***–e Leistung,*** rated load. **Bemessung,** *f.* rating (*of a motor etc.*).

bemitleiden [bə'mɪtlaɪdən], *v.t.* pity, take pity on, commiserate with, be sorry for; ***zu –,*** to be pitied. **bemitleidens|wert, -würdig,** *adj.* pitiable, (*pred.*) to be pitied.

bemittelt [bə'mɪtəlt], *adj.* wealthy, in easy circumstances, well off, well-to-do.

Bemme ['bɛmə], *f.* (*Saxon dial.*) slice of bread and butter, (*coll.*) doorstep.

bemogeln [bə'mo:gəln], *v.t.* (*coll.*) swindle, cheat, diddle, do.

bemoost [bə'mo:st], *adj.* mossy; (*coll.*) ***–es Haupt, –er Bursche,*** student with many sessions *or* semesters *or* terms behind him.

bemopsen [bə'mɔpsən], *v.t.* (*coll.*) *see* **bemogeln.**

bemühen [bə'my:ən], **1.** *v.t.* trouble; ***darf ich Sie darum –?*** may I trouble you for it? ***bemüht sein,*** endeavour, be eager *or* at pains (***zu tun,*** to do); ***um ihn bemüht sein, see*** **2,** 3. **2.** *v.r.* 1. trouble o.s., (*coll.*) bother (***in*** (*Dat.*) *or* ***wegen,*** about) (*a th.*); ***Sie – sich umsonst,*** it's a waste of time *or* effort; ***sich bei ihm –,*** use one's influence with him, put in a good word (***für ihn,*** for him; ***um etwas,*** for s.th.); 2. take trouble, go to great pains, make every *or* an effort (***um etwas,*** to obtain s.th.), strive (***um,*** after); ***sich um Kundschaft –,*** solicit custom; ***sich um Gunst –,*** court favour; 3. concern *or* busy o.s. (***um,*** about (*a p.*)); ***sich um ihn –,*** try to help him. **Bemühen,** *n.* effort, endeavour. **Bemühung,** *f. See* **Bemühen**; pains, trouble; ***ärztliche –en,*** medical attention.

bemüßigt [bə'my:sɪçt], *p.p.* ***sich*** (*Acc.*) ***– sehen*** or ***finden*** or ***fühlen,*** find it necessary, feel bound *or* obliged (to).

bemustern [bə'mustərn], *v.t.* supply with a sample.

bemuttern [bə'mutərn], *v.t.* mother, act as *or* be a mother to.

benachbart [bə'naxba:rt], *adj.* neighbouring, adjoining, adjacent; ***das –e Haus,*** the house next-door.

benachrichtigen [bə'naxrɪçtɪgən], *v.t.* inform, notify (***von,*** of *or* about), give notice (of), (*Comm.*) advise, apprise (of). **Benachrichtigung,** *f.* information, advice; notice; notification, intimation. **Benachrichtigungsschreiben,** *n.* (*Comm.*) advice note, letter of advice.

benachteiligen [bə'naxtaɪlɪgən], *v.t.* (*of a p.*) discriminate against, deal unfairly with, place at a disadvantage; (*of a th.*) affect unfavourably, handicap; ***benachteiligt sein,*** be at a disadvantage (***durch,*** owing to), (*coll.*) come off badly; ***sich benachteiligt fühlen,*** feel at a disadvantage, feel (o.s.) handicapped *or* unfairly treated. **Benachteiligung,** *f.* discrimination; disadvantage, handicap.

benageln [bə'na:gəln], *v.t.* stud with nails.

benagen [bə'na:gən], *v.t.* gnaw *or* nibble at.

benamsen [bə'na:mzən], *v.t.* (*coll.*) name, give a name to.

benannt [bə'nant], *adj.* named, called; (*Math.*) ***–e Zahl,*** concrete number. *See* **bennenen.**

benarbt [bə'narpt], *adj.* scarred, marked with scars.

benässen [bə'nɛsən], *v.t.* wet, moisten, make wet.

bene ['be:nə], *adv.* (*coll.*) well. **Bene,** *n.* (**-s,** *no pl.*) (*coll.*) good turn.

benebeln [bə'ne:bəln], *v.t.* befog, cloud, obscure, dim. **benebelt,** *adj.* 1. clouded over, covered in mist, fogged; 2. (*sl.*) tipsy, fuddled.

benedeien [bene'daɪən], *v.t.* (*B.*) bless; glorify. **Benedeiung,** *f.* benediction; glorification.

Benediktiner [be:nedɪk'ti:nər], *m.* 1. Benedictine (monk); 2. Benedictine (*liqueur*).

Benefiz [bene'fi:ts], *n.* 1. (**-es,** *pl.* **-e**) benefit (performance); 2. (*pl.* **-ien**) benefice, living, prebend. **Benefiziant** [–fitsi'ant], *m.* (**-en,** *pl.* **-en**) beneficiary. **Benefiziar** [–fitsi'a:r], *m.* (**-s,** *pl.* **-e**) beneficiary (*i.e. holder of a benefice*), prebendary. **Benefiziat,** *s. See* **Benefiziant. Benefizvorstellung,** *f.* benefit performance.

benehmen [bə'ne:mən], **1.** *irr.v.t.* (*obs.*) ***ihm etwas*** or ***ihn etwas*** (*Gen.*) **–,** take s.th. away from him, remove s.th. from him, deprive him of s.th., dispel his (*doubt etc.*); ***ihm die Sprache –,*** strike him dumb; ***das benimmt mir den Atem,*** that takes my breath away. **2.** *irr.v.r.* behave (o.s.); ***benimm dich anständig!*** behave yourself properly! ***sich – mit,*** see ***sich ins Benehmen setzen.*** **Benehmen,** *n.* 1. conduct, behaviour, manners; ***das ist kein –,*** that is no way to behave; 2. agreement, understanding; ***sich mit ihm ins – setzen,*** get in touch with *or* seek an agreement with him; try to come to terms with *or* reach an understanding with him; ***im – mit Preußen,*** in agreement with Prussia.

beneiden [bə'naɪdən], *v.t.* ***ihn um etwas*** or (*obs.*) ***ihm etwas –,*** envy s.o. (for) s.th.; ***ihn um sein Glück –,*** envy him for his good fortune, envy (him) his good fortune; ***sie – ihn,*** they are envious of him. **beneidenswert,** *adj.* enviable, much to be envied.

benennen [bə'nɛnən], *irr.v.t.* name, give a name to; call, designate (***mit,*** by); (*Math.*) denominate; (*obs.*) appoint, fix, set, (*coll.*) name (*a date etc.*), nominate (*a p.*); ***etwas mit dem rechten Namen –,*** designate s.th. correctly, give a th. its proper name; (*coll.*) call a spade a spade. *See* **benannt. Benennung,** *f.* naming; designation; nomenclature, appellation; denomination; (*Math.*) ***Brüche unter einerlei – bringen,*** reduce fractions to a common denominator; ***falsche –,*** misnomer.

benetzen [bə'nɛtsən], *v.t.* dampen, moisten; sprinkle; humidify; ***vom Tau benetzt,*** wet with dew.

Bengale [bɛŋ'ɡa:lə], **Bengalese** [–'le:zə], *m.* (**-n**, *pl.* **-n**) Bengali, Bengalese. **bengalisch,** *adj.* Bengali, Bengalese; Bengal (*tiger, lights*).

Bengel ['bɛŋəl], *m.* 1. club, cudgel, bludgeon; clapper (*of a bell*); 2. (*coll.*) lad; urchin, scamp, rogue; lout; ***ungeschliffener –,*** boor; ***fauler*** (***frecher***) **–,** lazy (cheeky) blighter; ***süßer kleiner –,*** dear little rascal. **Bengelei** [–'laɪ], *f.* churlishness, boorishness. **bengelhaft,** *adj.* churlish, boorish, rude.

Benimm [bə'nɪm], *m.* (**-s,** *no pl.*) (*hum.*) manners; ***er hat keinen –,*** he has no manners *or* polish.

Benitzucker [be'nittsukər], *m.* barley sugar.

benommen [bə'nɔmən], *adj.* confused, distraught, dazed, bemused, stupefied. *See* **benehmen. Benommenheit,** *f.* day-dreaming, wool-gathering, absent-mindedness, distraction, confusion, stupefaction; giddiness.

benötigen [bə'nø:tɪɡən], *v.t.* require, need, be *or* stand in need of, want, be in want of; ***das benötigte Geld,*** the necessary money.

benutzbar [bə'nutsba:r], *adj.* usable; ***leicht –,*** easy to use.

benutzen [bə'nutsən], *v.t.* use, employ, make use of, utilize; avail o.s. of, take advantage of; ***mit Vorteil –,*** profit by *or* from; ***benutzte Bücher,*** books consulted. **Benutzer,** *m.* user; reader, borrower (*of a library*). **Benutzerkarte,** *f.* library ticket. **Benutzung,** *f.* use; ***freie – eines Gartens haben,*** have the use *or* (*coll.*) run of a garden. **Benutzungsgebühr,** *f.* fee *or* charge (for the use of), toll (*of road, bridge etc.*).

Benzin [bɛn'tsi:n], *n.* (**-s,** *pl.* **-e**) petrol, (*Am.*) gasoline; (*Chem.*) benzine. **Benzin|behälter,** *m.* petrol tank. **–motor,** *m.* petrol engine. **–standmesser,** *m.*, **–uhr,** *f.* petrol *or* fuel gauge. **–verbrauch,** *m.* petrol *or* fuel consumption.

Benzoe ['bɛntsoə], *n. or f.*, **Benzoe|harz,** *n.* (gum-) benzoin. **–salz,** *n.* (*Chem.*) benzoate. **benzoesauer,** *adj.* (*Chem.*) benzoate of. **Benzoesäure,** *f.* benzoic acid.

Benzol [bɛn'tso:l], *n.* (**-s,** *pl.* **-e**) benzole, benzene.

beobachten [bə'o:baxtən], *v.t.* 1. observe, watch, keep watch on, keep under observation, keep one's eye on; study; 2. comply with, adhere to, observe (*rules etc.*); ***eine strenge Diät –,*** keep to *or* follow a strict diet; ***Stillschweigen –,*** keep *or* preserve *or* observe silence. **Beobachter,** *m.* observer (*also Mil.*); onlooker, spectator. **Beobachterdelegation,** *f.* team of observers.

Beobachtung [bə'o:baxtuŋ], *f.* 1. observation; 2. (*fig.*) observance (of), adherence (to), compliance (with) (*rules etc.*). **Beobachtungs|gabe,** *f.* power of observation. **–stand,** *m.* (*Mil.*) observation post. **–station,** *f.* (*Med.*) observation ward, (*Astr.*) observatory. **–wagen,** *m.* (*Mil.*) reconnaissance car, (*Railw.*) observation car. **–warte,** *f.* (*Mil.*) observation tower.

beordern [bə'ɔrdərn], *v.t.* order, command, direct (*to a place*).

bepacken [bə'pakən], *v.t.* load, burden; ***schwer bepackt,*** heavily laden.

bepanzern [bə'pantsərn], *v.t.* (*obs.*) arm with a cuirass; armour-plate (*ship etc.*). **bepanzert,** *adj.* (*obs.*) wearing a cuirass; armoured (*vehicle*), armour-plated (*ship*); (*Zool.*) loricate.

bepflanzen [bə'pflantsən], *v.t.* plant (*a field etc.*).

bepflastern [bə'pflastərn], *v.t.* pave (*a yard etc.*); (*Med.*) put a plaster on (*a wound*). **Bepflasterung,** *f.* paving, pavement.

bepflügen [bə'pfly:ɡən], *v.t.* plough (up), till (*land*).

bepudern [bə'pu:dərn], *v.t.* powder, sprinkle with powder.

bequem [bə'kve:m], *adj.* 1. (*of a th.*) comfortable; easy, convenient, (*coll.*) handy; (*obs.*) apt, fitting, suitable; ***–e Gelegenheit,*** good opportunity; (*Comm.*) ***–e Raten,*** easy terms; (*Naut.*) ***–er Wind,*** fair wind; 2. (*of a p.*) good-natured, easy-going; lazy, indolent; ***machen Sie es sich –,*** make yourself comfortable *or* at home; ***er ist ein sehr –er Mensch,*** he likes to take it easy. **bequemen,** *v.r.* adapt *or* accommodate o.s. (***zu,*** to), conform (with *or* to), comply (with), submit (to), (*coll.*) put up (with); condescend, consent, bring o.s. (***zu tun,*** to do). **bequemlich,** *adj.* easy-going; indolent, lazy. **Bequemlichkeit,** *f.* indolence, laziness; ease, comfort; convenience.

Berapp [bə'rap], *m.* (**-(e)s,** *no pl.*) coat of plaster, rough-cast. **berappen,** *v.t.* 1. rough-cast, plaster (*a wall*); 2. (*sl.*) fork out, stump up (*money*).

beraten [bə'ra:tən], **1.** *irr.v.t.* 1. advise, give advice to (*a p.*); 2. *See* **2,** 2; 3. (*obs.*) furnish, provide, endow (*a p.*). **2.** *irr.v.i.* 1. confer, sit *or* be in conference; 2. ***über eine S. –,*** consider *or* discuss *or* debate a matter. **3.** *irr.v.i., v.r.* confer, deliberate, consult (***mit ihm,*** with him; ***über eine S.,*** on *or* about s.th.). **beratend,** *adj.* consultative, advisory; ***–er Ausschuß,*** advisory committee; ***eine –e Stimme haben,*** be present in an advisory capacity; ***–er Ingenieur,*** consulting engineer. **Berater,** *m.* adviser, counsellor, consultant.

beratschlagen [bə'ra:tʃla:ɡən], *v.i., v.r. See* **beraten, 3. Beratschlagung,** *f.* reflection, consideration, deliberation; discussion, consultation, conference.

Beratung [bə'ra:tuŋ], *f.* 1. advice; 2. consideration, deliberation, debate; consultation, (*coll.*) talks; ***in – sein,*** be in conference (*of a p.*), be under discussion *or* consideration (*of a th.*). **Beratungs|saal,** *m.* conference room, council chamber. **–stelle,** *f.* advice bureau, (*Med.*) medical health centre.

berauben [bə'raubən], *v.t.* ***ihn –*** (*Gen.*), rob him of; relieve *or* deprive him of; divest him of. **Beraubung,** *f*, robbery, theft; deprival, dispossession, divestment.

beräuchern [bə'rɔyçərn], *v.t.* adulate, fawn upon, (*coll.*) lay it on thick, lay it on with a trowel. **Beräucherung,** *f.* adulation, blandishment, oily *or* unctuous *or* mealy-mouthed flattery.

berauschen [bə'rauʃən], **1.** *v.t.* intoxicate, make drunk. **2.** *v.r.* become drunk *or* intoxicated *or* inebriated; (*fig.*) get carried away *or* become enraptured (***an*** (*Dat.*), with). **berauschend,** *adj.* intoxicating, heady; enthralling.

Berberei [bɛrbə'raɪ], *f.* Barbary States.

Berberis ['bɛrbərɪs], *f.* barberry.

berberisch ['bɛrbərɪʃ], *adj.* Berber.

Berberitze [bɛrbə'rɪtsə], *f. See* **Berberis.**

berechenbar [bə'rɛçənba:r], *adj.* calculable, assessable, computable.

berechnen [bə'rɛçnən], *v.t.* 1. calculate, work out, (*Math.*) find the value of, evaluate; reckon (*cost etc.*), estimate, assess, compute, appraise (*loss, damage etc.*) (***auf*** (*Acc.*), at); (*fig.*) estimate, assess *or* gauge the effect of (*one's words etc.*); ***alles auf Effekt berechnet,*** everything (designed) for show *or* effect *or* aimed at effect; ***alles berechnet,*** taking everything into account *or* consideration, all things considered; 2. mean, intend, design (***für,*** for); ***meine Rede ist nur für Kinder berechnet,*** my speech is only intended for children; 3. (*Comm.*) charge (*Dat.*, (up) to); ***Porto und Verpackung wird berechnet,*** postage and packing will be charged extra; ***er hat mir däfur zuviel berechnet,*** he has overcharged me for it; ***ich habe mir 50 Pfund für die Ferien berechnet,*** I have allowed myself £50 for my holidays. **berechnend,** *adj.* (coolly) calculating (*of a p.*). **Berechner,** *m.* calculator, computer. **berechnet,** *adj.* calculated, theoretical (*as an estimate*); (*Mech.*) rated (*engine, load etc.*).

Berechnung [bə'rɛçnuŋ], *f.* 1. calculation, computation, estimate; (*Comm.*) price, charge; ***falsche –,*** miscalculation; ***annähernde*** or ***ungefähre –,*** approximation, rough estimate; ***– des Wertes,*** valuation; 2. calculation, deliberation; ***aus –,*** from motives of self-interest; ***mit –,*** in a (coolly) calculating *or* calculated manner.

berechtigen [bə'rɛçtɪɡən], *v.t.* give (*a p.*) the right (***zu,*** to); (*of a p.*) entitle, authorize, empower (***zu,*** to); (*of a th.*) warrant, justify (*his doing*); ***sich für berechtigt halten,*** hold *or* consider o.s. justified *or* qualified *or* competent (*to do*); ***berechtigt sein,***

have the right, be authorized *or* entitled (*to do*), be justified (*in doing*). **berechtigt,** *adj.* authorized; just, justifiable, legitimate. **Berechtigung,** *f.* title, right(s), qualification; authorization, authority, warrant, competence; right, justification; justness, rightness, correctness, validity. **Berechtigungs|-nachweis, -schein,** *m.* (written) authority *or* authorization, permit, voucher, licence.

bereden [bə're:dən], **1.** *v.t.* 1. discuss, talk (*s.th.*) over, talk over (*s.th.*); (*coll.*) criticize, find fault with; 2. persuade, induce, prevail upon (*s.o.*) ((*dazu*) *zu tun,* to do), (*coll.*) talk (*s.o.*) (into doing); (*coll.*) ***ich bin nicht dazu zu –,*** I'm not going to be talked into it. **2.** *v.r.* ***sich mit ihm über eine S. –,*** confer with him about s.th., talk s.th. over with him.

beredsam [bə're:tza:m], *adj.* eloquent, fluent. **Beredsamkeit,** *f.* eloquence, persuasiveness; oratory, rhetoric.

beredt [bə're:t], *adj.* eloquent; fluent, talkative; ***–e Zunge,*** glib tongue; ***–es Schweigen,*** eloquent *or* expressive *or* meaningful silence.

Bereich [bə'raıç], *m. or n.* (**-s,** *pl.* **-e**) district, region, domain (*also fig.*); (*Mil.*) area, zone, range; (*Tele.*) band (*of frequencies*); (*fig.*) field (*of inquiry*), province (*of science, an expert's knowledge*), scope (*of activity, work*), compass, range, extent (*of knowledge*); ***im – des menschlichen Verstandes,*** within the compass of the human mind; ***in seinen – gehören,*** be his province, (*coll.*) be right up his street; ***außer meinem –e,*** beyond my reach, scope *or* ken, outside my province; ***im – des Möglichen*** or ***der Möglichkeit,*** within the bounds *or* realm of possibility; ***im – des Unmöglichen*** or ***der Unmöglichkeit,*** beyond the bounds *or* realm of possibility; ***im – der Wirklichkeit,*** in the world of reality; ***im – der Phantasie,*** in the realm of fancy; ***im – der Wirtschaft,*** in the economic sphere; ***im – der Industrie,*** in the industrial sector.

bereichern [bə'raıçərn], **1.** *v.t.* enrich; enlarge, extend. **2.** *v.r.* enrich o.s., acquire wealth *or* riches, make money, (*coll.*) make one's pile, line one's pockets, feather one's nest. **Bereicherung,** *f.* enrichment; enlargement, extension; acquisition, gain; (*Law*) ***ungerechtfertigte –,*** misappropriation of funds.

[1]**bereifen** [bə'raıfən], *v.t.* hoop (*casks*); fit with tyres (*vehicle*).

[2]**bereifen,** *v.t.* cover with hoar-frost. **bereift,** *adj.* covered *or* white with frost, frost-covered.

Bereifung [bə'raıfuŋ], *f.* set of tyres.

bereinigen [bə'raınıgən], *v.t.* settle (*a dispute, an account*), resolve, clear up, (*coll.*) straighten *or* iron out (*a misunderstanding*), adjust, correct (*marks, a boundary etc.*), (*Comm.*) validate, reassess (*securities*). **Bereinigung,** *f.* settlement; resolution; adjustment, correction; (*Comm.*) validation, reassessment.

bereisen [bə'raızən], *v.t.* travel (in *or* over), tour, visit (*a country*); (*of commercial traveller*) travel in, cover, work (*a district*); ***– lassen,*** send a (commercial) traveller to (*an area*); ***ein viel bereistes Land,*** a much-visited country, a country popular with tourists *or* travellers; ***ein bereister Mann,*** a much- *or* widely-travelled man.

bereit [bə'raıt], *adj.* 1. (*of a p.*) willing, prepared, ready; ***zu allem –,*** willing to agree to anything, (*coll.*) game for anything; ***sich – erklären,*** express o.s. willing *or* prepared, express one's willingness *or* readiness; ***sich – finden,*** be prepared *or* ready; ***sich – halten,*** hold o.s. ready *or* in readiness, stand by; 2. (*of a th.*) ready; ***– halten,*** hold ready *or* in readiness (*see also* **bereithalten**); ***– machen,*** make *or* get ready, prepare (*see also* **bereitmachen**).

[1]**bereiten** [bə'raıtən], *v.t.* 1. make *or* get ready, prepare; make, brew (*tea, coffee*); make up (*a bed*), mix (*concrete etc.*); ***ihm ein Bad –,*** run a bath for him; (*coll.*) put a rod in pickle for him; ***den Boden –,*** prepare the soil *or* ground, (*fig.*) prepare the ground *or* way; 2. (*Dat. of p.*) give (*reception, pleasure, surprise etc.*), offer (*competition*), cause (*trouble, pain, disappointment, embarrassment etc.*), bring (*disgrace etc.*) on.

[2]**bereiten,** *irr.v.t.* ride over (*an area*), ride through (*a territory*), patrol (*on horseback*), break in (*a horse*). *See* **beritten. Bereiter,** *m.* horse-trainer, rough-rider.

bereit|halten, *irr.v.t.* keep *or* hold in readiness, keep on *or* at hand. **–machen, 1.** *v.t.* get *or* make ready, prepare. **2.** *v.r.* get (o.s.) ready.

bereits [bə'raıts], *adv.* already; (*Swiss; dial.*) nearly, almost, practically.

Bereitschaft [bə'raıtʃaft], *f.* 1. (*of a th.*) readiness, preparedness; (*Mil.*) stand-to, alert, stand-by; (*of a p.*) willingness, readiness; 2. squad, team, *pl.* (*Mil.*) reserves, supporting troops. **Bereitschafts|-dienst,** *m.* (*Mil.*) stand-by duty; emergency service; ***– haben,*** be on call (*of a doctor*). **–graben,** *m.* (*Mil.*) support trench. **–polizei,** *f.* mobile police. **–raum,** *m.* (*Mil. etc.*) operations *or* briefing room. **–tasche,** *f.* (ever-ready) carrying case (*for camera etc.*).

bereitstehen [bə'raıtʃte:ən], *irr.v.i.* (*of a p.*) be ready; (*Mil. etc.*) stand-to, stand by; (*of a th.*) be ready *or* available, be to hand, be ready waiting.

bereitstellen [bə'raıtʃtεlən], *v.t.* 1. place ready, put out, arrange, (*Mil.*) assemble (*troops*); 2. provide, allocate, make available. **Bereitstellung,** *f.* 1. provision, allocation, allotment, appropriation, (*coll.*) earmarking, (*Mil.*) assembly (*of troops*); 2. (*Mil.*) action *or* battle stations. **Bereitstellungs|fonds,** *m.* appropriation (*of funds*). **–raum,** *m.* (*Mil.*) assembly area.

Bereitung [bə'raıtuŋ], *f.* preparation.

bereitwillig [bə'raıtvılıç], **1.** *adj.* ready, willing, obliging. **2.** *adv.* readily, willingly. **Bereitwilligkeit,** *f.* readiness, willingness, alacrity; ***allzu große –,*** over-eagerness, officiousness.

berennen [bə'rεnən], *irr.v.t.* attack, assault, storm, charge, rush (*a defended position*). **Berennung,** *f.* assault (*of a fortress*).

bereuen [bə'rɔyən], *v.t.* repent (of), regret, be sorry for, (*obs.*) rue; ***nichts zu –,*** no regrets.

Berg [bεrk], *m.* (**-es,** *pl.* **-e**) mountain; hill; peak (*also of a curve*); (*coll.*) ***am*** or ***vor einem –e stehen,*** encounter a difficulty, reach an impasse; ***wie der Ochs vorm*** or ***am –e stehen,*** be nonplussed *or* at a loss, not know which way to turn; (***mit einer S.***) ***hinterm –e halten,*** hold back (one's opinions of a th.), keep (a th.) dark; ***eine Geschichte, die einem die Haare zu –e stehen läßt,*** a tale to make one's hair stand on end, a hair-raising story; (*coll.*) ***die Haare standen mir zu –e,*** my hair stood on end; ***den – hinauf,*** uphill; ***den – hinunter*** or ***hinab,*** downhill; ***über – und Tal,*** over hill and dale; ***jetzt ist er über alle –e,*** he is miles away by now; ***wir sind noch nicht über den –,*** we are not yet over the worst (of our difficulties) *or* out of the wood *or* round the corner; ***unten am –e,*** at the foot of the mountain; (*B.*) ***–e versetzen,*** move mountains; ***goldene –e versprechen,*** promise the moon, make extravagant promises; ***zu – fahren,*** travel up-stream.

bergab [bεrk'ap], *adv.* downhill (*also fig.*); (*fig.*) on the down-grade. **bergabwärts,** *adv.* downhill.

Berg|ahorn, *m.* sycamore (*Acer pseudoplatanus*). **–akademie,** *f.* school of mining. **–alaun,** *m.* rock-alum.

Bergamotte [bεrga'mɔtə], *f.* bergamot.

Bergamt ['bεrkʔamt], *n.* mining office.

bergan [bεrk'an], *adv. See* **bergauf.**

Berg|arbeiter, *m.* miner, mine-worker. **–bahn,** *f.* mountain *or* alpine railway.

bergauf ['bεrkauf], *adv.* uphill.

Bergbau [bεrk'bau], *m.* (**-(e)s,** *pl.* **-ten**) mining (industry). **Bergbau|ingenieur,** *m.* mining engineer. **–schule,** *f. See* **Bergakademie.**

Berg|beamte(r), *m.* mining official. **–bewohner,** *m.* mountain-dweller, highlander. **–bock,** *m. See* **Steinbock. –braunelle,** *f.* (*Orn.*) mountain accentor (*Prunella montanella*). **–distel,** *f.* spear thistle (*Cirsium lanceolatum*).

bergehoch ['bεrgəho:x], *adj. See* **berghoch.**

bergen ['bɛrgən], **1.** *irr.v.t.* 1. recover (*corpse, wreck, cargo*), salvage, salve (*wreck, cargo*), save, rescue (*shipwrecked p.*), recover, rescue (*wounded*), bring to safety (*trapped p.*), get *or* bring in (*crops*); 2. (*fig.*) secure, protect, shelter, shield (***vor*** (*Dat.*), from); ***geborgen sein,*** be safe *or* in safety; 3. (***in sich***) –, hold, hide, conceal (*secrets, dangers etc.*); (*fig.*) contain, involve (*problems, difficulties etc.*); ***das Gesicht in den Händen –,*** hide *or* bury one's face in one's hands; 4. (*Naut.*) strike, lower, take in, shorten (*sail*). **2.** *irr.v.r.* take shelter, withdraw *or* retire to a place of safety, get under cover (***vor*** (*Dat.*), from).

Berg|enge, *f.* gorge, defile. **–ente,** *f.* (*Orn.*) (*Am.* greater) scaup (*Aythya marila*).

Berge|recht, *n.* right to salvage. **–schlämme,** *m.pl.* (*Min.*) tailings.

Bergeshöhe ['bɛrgəshø:ə], *f.* height of a mountain; (*Poet.*) mountain top, peak.

Berg|fach, *n.* mining profession. **–fahrt,** *f.* excursion into the mountains; voyage up-stream; uphill journey (*on mountain railway*); (*Motor.*) hill-climb.

bergfertig ['bɛrkfɛrtɪç], *adj.* unfit for work (*of miners, usu. as result of miners' phthisis*).

Berg|feuer, *n.* signal fire, (*coll.*) beacon. **–fex,** *m.* enthusiastic alpinist. **–fink,** *m.* (*Orn.*) brambling (*Fringilla montifringilla*). **–freiheit,** *f.* mining rights. **–fried,** *m.* watch-tower, donjon, keep. **–führer,** *m.* mountain *or* alpine guide. **–geist,** *m.* mountain sprite, goblin, gnome. **–gelb,** *n.* yellow ochre. **–gipfel,** *m.* mountain top, summit. **–glas,** *n.* rock-crystal. **–grat,** *m.* mountain ridge, crest. **–grün,** *n.* malachite. **–halde,** *f.* mountain slope, hillside; (*Min.*) spoil bank, slag heap. **–hänfling,** *m.* (*Orn.*) twite (*Carduelis flavirostris*). **–hang,** *m.* mountain slope, hillside. **–haue,** *f.* miner's pick, pickaxe. **–hauer, –häuer,** *m.* (*Min.*) hewer, cutter.

berghoch ['bɛrkho:x], *adj.* mountain-high (*as waves*), in great piles (*as rubbish*).

Berg|höhe, *f.* height of a mountain. **–holz,** *n.* rock-wood, ligniform asbestos.

bergicht ['bɛrgɪçt] (*obs.*), **bergig,** *adj.* mountainous, hilly.

Berg|ingenieur, *m.* *See* **Bergbauingenieur. –inspektor,** *m.* mine-surveyor *or* inspector. **–kamm,** *m.* crest, ridge. **–kegel,** *m.* sugar-loaf mountain. **–kessel,** *m.* deep valley, corrie. **–kette,** *f.* mountain chain, range of mountains. **–kiesel,** *m.* rock flint. **–knappe,** *m.* miner, pitman. **–knappschaft,** *f.* miners' guild *or* union.

berg|krank, *adj.* 1. *See* **–fertig**; 2. suffering from mountain sickness. **Bergkrankheit,** *f.* mountain sickness.

Berg|kristall, *m.* rock-crystal. **–kunde,** *f.* orology. **–kundige(r),** *m.* orologist; mining expert. **–land,** *n.* hill-country, upland, highland. **–laubsänger,** *m.* (*Orn.*) Bonelli's warbler (*Phylloscopus bonelli*). **–lehne,** *f.* mountain slope. **–leute,** *pl.* miners. **–mann,** *m.* miner, mine-worker; – ***vom Leder,*** pitman, underground worker; – ***von der Feder,*** surface worker, clerical worker at a mine.

bergmännisch ['bɛrkmɛnɪʃ], *adj.* mining; relating to miners.

Berg|not, *f.* (*of a climber*) ***in –,*** in difficulties. **–nymphe,** *f.* oread, mountain sprite *or* nymph. **–öl,** *n.* petroleum, mineral *or* rock-oil. **–ordnung,** *f.* mining regulations. **–partie,** *f.* climbing expedition. **–pech,** *n.* mineral pitch, asphalt. **–pecherde,** *f.* bituminous earth. **–predigt,** *f.* Sermon on the Mount. **–recht,** *n.* right to work a mine; mining law. **bergrechtlich,** *adj.* according to mining law. **Berg|rücken,** *m.* ridge, crest. **–rüster,** *f.* *See* **–ulme. –rutsch,** *m.* landslide. **–sattel,** *m.* col, saddle. **–schlucht,** *f.* ravine, gorge, glen. **–schotten,** *m.pl.* Scottish Highlanders. **–schuh,** *m.* climbing boot. **–schule,** *f.* *See* **–akademie. –schwaden,** *m.pl.* fire damp. **–schwefel,** *m.* rock *or* native sulphur. **–see,** *m.* mountain lake, tarn. **–start,** *m.* (*Motor.*) hill-start. **–steigen,** *n.* mountaineering, climbing. **–steiger,** *m.* climber, mountaineer, alpinist. **–stiefel,** *m.* *See* **–schuh. –stock,** *m.* massif, mountain mass. **–striche,** *m.pl.* hachures (*on maps*). **–sucht,** *f.* miner's phthisis. **berg|süchtig,** *adj.* *See* **–fertig. Berg|teer,** *m.* mineral tar, bitumen. **–tour,** *f.* *See* **–partie. –ulme,** *f.* wych-elm (*Ulmus montana*).

Bergung ['bɛrguŋ], *f.* salvage, recovery, rescue. **Bergungsarbeit(en),** *f.*(*pl.*) salvage operations, rescue work.

Berg|verwaltung, *f.* administration of mines (*cp.* Coal Board). **–volk,** *n.* highlanders; mountain tribes, hill-people. **–wacht,** *f.* mountain rescue service. **–wand,** *f.* rock face, cliff face, escarpment, bluff.

Bergwerk ['bɛrkvɛrk], *n.* mine; pit. **Bergwerks|aktie,** *f.*, **–anteil,** *m.* mining shares. **–aufseher,** *m.* superintendent of mines, viewer. **–eigentümer,** *m.* mine-owner. **–unglück,** *n.* pit accident.

Berg|wicht, *m.*, **–wichtel,** *n.* *See* **–geist.**

Bericht [bə'rɪçt], *m.* **(-(e)s,** *pl.* **-e)** report (***über*** (*Acc.*) *or* ***von,*** on *or* of), statement (on *or* about), account, record, survey, summary (of), dispatch, bulletin (about), commentary (on), minutes (*of a meeting*), (*Comm.*) advice. **berichten,** *v.t.*, *v.i.* report (*also of journalist*), make a report (***über*** (*Acc.*) *or* ***von,*** on); give an account *or* particulars (of), record; inform, advise, apprise (of), tell (about *or* of), relate. **Bericht|erstatter,** *m.* reporter, (newspaper) correspondent; (radio) commentator. **–erstattung,** *f.* reporting; report, commentary; account.

berichtigen [bə'rɪçtɪgən], *v.t.* correct, (set *or* put) right, rectify, amend, revise; adjust; (*Comm.*) pay, settle (*a bill etc.*). **Berichtigung,** *f.* correction, emendation, amendment, rectification; adjustment; (*Comm.*) settlement, payment. **Berichtigungskonto,** *n.* suspense account.

beriechen [bə'ri:çən], *irr.v.t.* smell, sniff at, (*coll.*) poke one's nose into (*a th.*); size (*s.o.*) up, give (*s.o.*) the once-over.

berieseln [bə'ri:zəln], *v.t.* trickle over; water, irrigate (*a field with spraying apparatus*), water, spray (*a road etc.*), scrub (*gas*). **Berieselung,** *f.* (overhead) irrigation, spraying. **Berieselungs|feld,** *n.* sewage farm. **–turm,** *m.* scrubbing plant, scrubber.

berindet [bə'rɪndət], *adj.* covered with bark, encrusted.

Beritt [bə'rɪt], *m.* area covered by mounted patrol; (*Mil.*) cavalry section. **beritten,** *adj.* mounted, on horseback; ***–e Garde,*** horseguards; ***–e Polizei,*** mounted police. *See* [2]**bereiten.**

Berliner [bɛr'li:nər], *m.* 1. doughnut; 2. inhabitant of Berlin. **Berliner|blau,** *n.* Prussian blue. **–säure,** *f.* Prussic acid.

Berlocke [bɛr'lɔkə], *f.* pendant, trinket, charm.

Berme ['bɛrmə], *f.* (*Mil.*) berm, fire (*or* firing) step.

Bernhard ['bɛrnhart], *m.* Bernard.

Bernickelgans ['bɛrnikəlgans], *f.* *See* **Ringelgans.**

Bernstein ['bɛrnʃtaɪn], *m.* amber; ***grauer –,*** ambergris; ***schwarzer –,*** jet. **bernsteine(r)n,** *adj.* (made of) amber. **Bernsteinsäure,** *f.* succinic acid.

berotzt [bə'rɔtst], *adj.* (*sl.*) drunk, sozzled.

bersten ['bɛrstən], *irr.v.i.* (*though often reg. in pres. and imperf.*) (*aux.* s.) burst, crack, split. **Bersten,** *n.* ***zum – voll,*** full to bursting (point), ready to burst.

berüchtigt [bə'ryçtɪçt], *adj.* infamous, ill-famed, notorious.

berücken [bə'rykən], *v.t.* ensnare, inveigle; impose upon, cheat, (*coll.*) take in; beguile, fascinate, captivate, enthrall, charm, enchant. **berückend,** *adj.* enchanting, captivating, enthralling, entrancing, beguiling, bewitching.

berücksichtigen [bə'rykzɪçtɪgən], *v.t.* consider, bear in mind (*a th. or a p.*), have *or* pay regard to, take into consideration, allow for, make allowance(s) for (*a th.*); have consideration for (*a p.*). **Berücksichtigung,** *f.* consideration, regard; ***unter –*** (*Gen.*), in consideration *or* view (of), taking . . . into account, allowing (for).

Berückung [bə'rykuŋ], *f.* charm, spell, enchantment.

Beruf [bə'ru:f], *m.* vocation, call, calling; profession, occupation, trade, work, (*coll.*) job; ***die freien –e,*** the professions; ***in den freien – gehen,*** go into private practice (*of doctor, lawyer*), take up freelance work (*of journalist*); ***der innere –,*** the inner voice, the divine call; ***kaufmännischer –,*** career in commerce; ***technischer –,*** skilled trade; ***ohne –,*** without occupation; ***im – stehen,*** be in work, have a job; ***seinen – verfehlt haben,*** to have missed one's vocation.

berufen [bə'ru:fən], **1.** *irr.v.t.* 1. summon, call together; call, convene (*a meeting*), convoke (*an assembly*); ***zu sich –,*** summon *or* send for (*a p.*); ***(dazu) – sein, sich (dazu) – fühlen,*** feel a vocation (for), feel a call (to *or* to do), be destined (for *or* to do); 2. appoint (*to a committee, professorship etc.*); ***auf den Lehrstuhl – werden,*** be offered the chair *or* professorship; ***an der Universität – werden,*** be appointed to a professorship at the university; 3. (*obs.*) blame, reproach (*a p.*); 4. tempt (*providence*); (*coll.*) ***unberufen,*** touch wood. **2.** *irr.v.r.* 1. ***sich – auf*** (*Acc.*), quote *or* cite (as one's authority), refer (to), rely (on); ***sich auf seine Unwissenheit –,*** plead ignorance; ***Sie können sich auf mich –,*** you can quote *or* mention *or* use me *or* my name (as a reference); 2. (*Law*) appeal (***auf*** or ***an*** (*Acc.*), to). **3.** *adj.* competent, qualified; in a position (*to judge etc.*); (*Law*) legally qualified, entitled; ***mehr*** or ***eher –, –er,*** in a better position, better qualified, more competent.

beruflich [bə'ru:flɪç], *adj.* professional; vocational; ***– zu tun haben,*** be on business; ***– verhindert sein,*** be detained by work.

Berufs|ausbildung, *f.* professional *or* vocational training. **–beamte(r),** *m.,f.* permanent official, civil servant. **–beratung,** *f.* vocational guidance. **–genosse,** *m. See* **–kamerad. –gruppe,** *f.* occupational group, type of occupation. **–heer,** *n.* regular *or* professional army. **–kamerad,** *m.* colleague. **–kleidung,** *f.* work(ing) clothes. **–krankheit,** *f.* occupational disease. **berufsmäßig,** *adj.* professional. **Berufs|offizier,** *m.* regular officer. **–organisation,** *f.* professional association. **–risiko,** *n.* occupational hazard. **–schule,** *f.* trade school, vocational training establishment. **–soldat** *m.* regular *or* professional soldier. **–sportler,** *m.* professional (player). **–stand,** *m.* profession, trade.

berufstätig [bə'rufstɛ:tɪç], *adj.* working, employed, in a job; *– sein,* have a job; *–e Frauen,* women who go out to work, working women, women who follow a career; ***die Berufstätigen,*** the working population. **Berufstätigkeit,** *f.* occupation, work, job.

Berufs|umschulung, *f.* transfer training. **–unfähigkeit,** *f.* disablement. **–verband,** *m. See* **–organisation. –verbrecher,** *m.* professional criminal. **–wahl,** *f.* choice of career *or* occupation. **berufswidrig,** *adj.* unprofessional.

Berufung [bə'ru:fuŋ], *f.* 1. vocation (***zu,*** for), call, summons (to), calling, mission; 2. convocation (*of assembly*); 3. nomination, (offer of) appointment (***auf*** (*Acc.*), to; ***an*** (*Acc.*), at); 4. reference; ***unter – auf*** (*Acc.*), with reference to, referring to, on the authority of; 5. (*Law*) entitlement (***zu,*** to); 6. (*Law*) appeal (***gegen,*** against; ***an*** (*Acc.*) *or* ***bei,*** to); (*Law*) ***– einlegen,*** (lodge an) appeal, give notice of appeal. **Berufungs|beklagte(r),** *m.,f.* defendant, respondent (*before appeal court*). **–gericht,** *n.,* **–instanz,** *f.* higher court, court of appeal. **–klage,** *f.* (action of) appeal.

beruhen [bə'ru:ən], *v.i.* be based *or* founded (***auf*** or ***in*** (*Dat.*), on), have its cause *or* root (in), be caused (by), be due (to), rest (in *or* on); ***etwas auf sich – lassen,*** not proceed (further) with s.th., let a th. pass *or* rest *or* (*coll.*) drop, (*coll.*) take a th. lying down (*insult etc.*); ***ich will es dabei*** or ***darauf – lassen,*** I will be satisfied with that, I will let it pass.

beruhigen [bə'ru:ɪgən], **1.** *v.t.* quiet(en), calm (down), soothe, pacify, appease, reassure, set (*s.o.'s*) mind at rest; calm, compose, allay (*fears etc.*). **2.** *v.r.* (*of a p.*) calm down, set one's mind at rest, compose o.s. *or* one's mind, recover one's composure, (*coll.*) pull o.s. together; feel reassured, stop worrying; become appeased *or* pacified, be contented *or* satisfied, console *or* comfort o.s. (***bei,*** with). **beruhigend,** *adj.* calming, soothing; reassuring, heartening; sedative (*drugs*). **Beruhigung,** *f.* pacification, appeasement; comfort, reassurance; calm, peace. **Beruhigungsmittel,** *n.* sedative, anodyne.

berühmt [bə'ry:mt], *adj.* famous, celebrated, renowned; famed, illustrious; well-known, noted; ***sich – machen,*** make a name for o.s., distinguish o.s.; (*coll.*) ***nicht –,*** not up to much, nothing to write home about. **Berühmtheit,** *f.* 1. fame, renown, distinction; 2. celebrity, famous person, person of note.

berühren [bə'ry:rən], **1.** *v.t.* 1. touch, border on; 2. touch (up)on, allude *or* refer (briefly) to, mention; 3. concern, affect (*a p.'s interests*); make an impression *or* have an effect on; ***peinlich –,*** cause embarrassment to; ***seltsam –,*** strike as odd; strangely affect *or* impress; ***schmerzlich –,*** give pain to, pain; ***unangenehm –,*** make an unpleasant impression on. **2.** *v.r.* 1. touch (one another), be in *or* come into contact; 2. (*fig.*) have s.th. in common, be in accord *or* in harmony (***mit,*** with). **Berührung,** *f.* touch, contact; contiguity; (*Geom.*) tangency; reference (*to a subject*); ***in – kommen,*** come in *or* into contact. **Berührungs|ebene,** *f.* tangential plane. **–elektrizität,** *f.* voltaic *or* contact electricity. **–fläche,** *f.* surface of contact. **–linie,** *f.* tangent. **–punkt,** *m.* point of contact (*also fig.*). **–reiz,** *m.* contact stimulus. **–winkel,** *m.* angle of contingence.

berußen [bə'ru:sən], *v.t.* cover *or* blacken with soot. **berußt,** *adj.* sooty, black with soot.

Beryll [bə'ryl], *m.* (**-s,** *pl.* **-e**) beryl; ***edler –,*** aquamarine.

besabbern [bə'zabərn], *v.t., v.r.* (*coll.*) dribble *or* slobber over (o.s.).

besäen [bə'zɛ:ən], *v.t.* sow (*a field etc.*).

besagen [bə'za:gən], *v.t.* say (*as text*); signify, mean; ***das hat nichts zu –, das will gar nichts –,*** that does not amount to *or* mean *or* signify anything at all. **besagt,** *adj.* (afore)said, above(mentioned).

besaiten [bə'zaɪtən], *v.t.* string (*an instrument*); ***zart besaitet,*** sensitive, touchy (*of a p.*).

besamen [bə'za:mən], *v.t.* impregnate, inseminate (*animal*), pollinate (*plant*). **Besamung,** *f.* impregnation, insemination; pollination.

Besan [be'za:n], *m.* (**-s,** *pl.* **-e**) (*Naut.*) mizzen, spanker.

besänftigen [bə'zɛnftɪgən], **1.** *v.t.* appease, soothe, pacify, calm, soften, allay, assuage. **2.** *v.r.* calm down; abate, subside.

besaß [bə'za:s], **besäße** [bə'zɛsə], *see* **besitzen.**

besät [bə'zɛ:t], *adj.* sowed; studded, strewn, covered; ***mit Sternen –,*** star-spangled.

Besatz [bə'zats], *m.* trimming, edging. **Besatz|litze,** *f.* braid, braiding. **–streifen,** *m.* (*Mil.*) cap band.

Besatzung [bə'zatsuŋ], *f.* (*Mil.*) garrison; (*Naut., Av.*) crew; occupation. **Besatzungsheer,** *n.* army of occupation.

besaufen [bə'zaufən], *v.r.* (*sl.*) get drunk; ***total besoffen,*** dead *or* blind drunk.

besäumen [bə'zɔymən], *v.t.* border, edge, fringe (*a road etc.*).

beschädigen [bə'ʃɛ:dɪgən], *v.t.* injure, damage, do injury *or* damage to; ***beschädigt werden,*** be harmed *or* damaged, suffer injury *or* damage. **Beschädigung,** *f.* damage, injury.

1**beschaffen** [bə'ʃafən], *reg.v.t.* procure, supply, provide, find, get, raise (*money*).

2**beschaffen,** *adj.* ***– sein,*** be in a (. . .) state *or* condition; ***so ist er –,*** that is his nature; ***gut –,*** in good condition, in good circumstances; ***so ist die Welt –,*** that is the way of the world; ***die S. ist so –,*** the matter stands thus. **Beschaffenheit,** *f.* nature, state, condition, quality, property; *– der Körper*, properties of matter; *nach – der Umstände*, according to circumstances.

Beschaffung [bəˈʃafuŋ], *f.* procurement, provision; raising (*of funds*); (*Comm.*) *wir bitten um gütige –*, please procure for us. **Beschaffungsstelle,** *f.* supply centre.

beschäftigen [bəˈʃɛftɪgən], **1.** *v.t.* occupy, keep occupied *or* busy; employ, engage. **2.** *v.r.* (*of a p.*) occupy *or* concern o.s., be occupied *or* concerned (*mit*, with), put one's mind (to); (*of a th.*) occupy *or* fill one's mind. **beschäftigt,** *pred.adj.* busy; occupied; *bei ihm – sein*, be in the employ of *or* be employed by him; *sehr – sein*, be fully occupied *or* very busy. **Beschäftigung,** *f.* employment, occupation, pursuit. **Beschäftigungs|behandlung,** *f.* occupational therapy. **–genehmigung,** *f.* labour permit. **beschäftigungslos,** *adj.* unemployed. **Beschäftigungsspiele,** *n.pl.* creative *or* active play (*in kindergarten*).

[1]**beschälen** [bəˈʃɛːlən], *v.t.* peel, strip the bark from (*trees*).

[2]**beschälen,** *v.t.* cover (*of horses*). **Beschäler,** *m.* stallion, stud-horse. **Beschälstation,** *f.* stud-farm.

beschämen [bəˈʃɛːmən], *v.t.* shame, put to shame, make ashamed; humiliate, disconcert, abash. **beschämend,** *adj.* humiliating, shameful. **beschämt,** *adj.* ashamed, shamefaced, abashed. **Beschämung,** *f.* shame, humiliation.

beschatten [bəˈʃatən], *v.t.* overshadow; shade; shadow (*as a detective*).

Beschau [bəˈʃau], *f.* examination, inspection (*of goods, meat*), assaying (*of metals*). **beschauen,** *v.t.* look at, contemplate, view, behold; inspect, examine (*goods, meat*). **Beschauer,** *m.* beholder, onlooker, looker-on; (official) inspector. **beschaulich,** *adj.* contemplative, meditative, introspective. **Beschaulichkeit,** *f.* contemplation, meditation, introspection, introversion. **Beschauung,** *f.* viewing, examination, inspection; *see also* **Beschaulichkeit.**

Bescheid [bəˈʃaɪt], *m.* (**-(e)s,** *pl.* **-e**) information, instruction(s), direction(s); answer, decision; (*Law*) ruling, judgment, award; *abschlägiger –*, refusal, rebuff; *– bekommen*, be notified *or* informed; *– geben* or *sagen* (*Dat.*), inform, instruct, give information to; tell, let (*s.o.*) know; (*coll.*) *ihm gehörig – sagen*, give him *or* let him have a piece of one's mind; *– trinken* or *tun*, reply to a toast; *– wissen*, know, be acquainted (*mit*, with), be well informed (about); *ich weiß genau –*, I know all about it, (*coll.*) I'm well up in it, I know my stuff; *in einem Hause – wissen*, know one's way about a house.

[1]**bescheiden** [bəˈʃaɪdən], **1.** *irr.v.t.* 1. inform (*über* (*Acc.*), of); 2. (*obs.*) summon, send for; 3. (*Dat.*) ordain, grant; *genieße was dir Gott beschieden!* enjoy what God has granted you. **2.** *irr.v.r.* be satisfied *or* contented (*mit*, with), resign o.s. (to), acquiesce (in); *er weiß sich zu –*, he knows his place.

[2]**bescheiden,** *adj.* 1. modest, unassuming; *in meiner -en Meinung*, in my humble opinion; 2. modest, reasonable, moderate; *ein -es Vermögen*, a modest fortune; *in -em Maße*, in a small way; 3. simple, humble (*dwelling*), frugal (*meal*). **Bescheidenheit,** *f.* modesty; moderation; simplicity, unpretentiousness.

bescheinen [bəˈʃaɪnən], *irr.v.t.* shine upon, irradiate; illuminate.

bescheinigen [bəˈʃaɪnɪgən], *v.t.* confirm in writing, certify; give a receipt for, acknowledge (receipt of); issue a certificate for. **Bescheinigung,** *f.* certificate, voucher; receipt, certification, acknowledgement (of receipt).

bescheißen [bəˈʃaɪsən], *irr.v.t.* foul with excrement, (*vulg.*) shit on; (*coll. fig.*) do the dirty on.

beschenken [bəˈʃɛŋkən], *v.t.* give a present to, give *or* make (*s.o.*) a present; present (*mit*, with), make (*s.o.*) a present (of); *mit einem Töchterchen –*, present with a baby daughter.

[1]**bescheren** [bəˈʃeːrən], *irr.v.t.* shave; clip, trim.

[2]**bescheren,** *reg.v.t. ihm etwas –*, bestow s.th. upon him, bless him with s.th.; *die Kinder zu Weihnachten –*, give the children Christmas presents. **Bescherung,** *f.* distribution of (Christmas) presents; (*coll.*) *eine schöne –!* a nice mess! a pretty kettle of fish! a fine business! (*coll.*) *da haben wir die –!* now we're (in) for it!

beschicken [bəˈʃɪkən], *v.t.* put in order, attend *or* see to, look after, take care of; stoke, make up (*a fire*); till (*the soil*); feed, charge (*a furnace*); alloy, mix; *eine Ausstellung –*, exhibit, submit for exhibition; *den Reichstag –*, send *or* return a member to parliament; (*coll.*) *sein Haus –*, put one's house *or* affairs in order. **Beschickung,** *f.* deputation; alloying, alloy; preparation; *– des Landes*, tillage.

beschieden [bəˈʃiːdən], *see* [1]**bescheiden.**

beschienen [bəˈʃiːnən], *v.t.* fix with splints; fit with bands of iron; shoe (*a wheel*); (*Railw.*) lay rails on.

beschießen [bəˈʃiːsən], *irr.v.t.* fire *or* shoot at *or* on; (*Mil.*) bombard, shell. **Beschießung,** *f.* bombardment, shelling, cannonading.

beschiffen [bəˈʃɪfən], *v.t.* 1. sail, plough (*the seas*); 2. make water on, (*coll.*) piddle on.

beschildern [bəˈʃɪldərn], *v.t.* label (*luggage*), signpost (*a road*), mark (*streets*) with street-names.

beschilft [bəˈʃɪlft], *adj.* reedy, sedgy.

beschimmeln [bəˈʃɪməln], *v.i.* (*aux.* s.) go mouldy.

beschimpfen [bəˈʃɪmpfən], *v.t.* insult, abuse, revile, vilify, slander; use abusive language to, call (*a p.*) names; cast aspersions *or* a slur on (*s.o.'s good name*), drag (*s.o.'s name*) in the mud. **Beschimpfung,** *f.* insult, affront, abuse; aspersion; slander.

beschirmen [bəˈʃɪrmən], *v.t.* screen, shield, guard, protect, shelter (*vor* (*Dat.*), from).

beschirren [bəˈʃɪrən], *v.t.* harness. **Beschirrung,** *f.* harness.

Beschiß [bəˈʃɪs], *m.* (**-(ss)es,** *no pl.*) (*coll.*) swindle, dirty trick. **beschissen,** *adj.* (*sl.*) lousy, stinking.

beschlabbern [bəˈʃlabərn], *v.t.* slobber *or* dribble on *or* over.

beschlafen [bəˈʃlaːfən], *irr.v.t.* (*obs.*) sleep *or* lie with (*a p.*); *etwas –*, sleep on *or* over s.th.

Beschlag [bəˈʃlaːk], *m.* 1. metal fitting(s), mountings, furnishings; sheathing; (metal) hoop *or* band *or* rim; (metal) tyre, shoe (*of wheel*), (metal) cap, ferrule; horse-shoe; ward(s) (*of lock*); studs, nails (*of climbing boots*); clasp, fastener, catch, hasp; 2. thin coating, surface layer; mist, vapour, moisture, steam (*on glass*); film, bloom, (*Chem.*) incrustation, efflorescence; lining, jacket, lagging, luting; 3. seizure, confiscation, sequestration, distraint, attachment, embargo; *in – nehmen, mit – belegen*, seize, confiscate, distrain upon, attach, lay an embargo on; (*fig.*) engross (*attention*).

beschlagen [bəˈʃlaːgən], **1.** *irr.v.t.* 1. hew (*stone*), square (*timber*); *grob –*, rough-hew; 2. fit *or* mount with metal; line, cover (*a roof etc.*), shoe (*a horse*); hoop (*a cask*), fit (*boot*) with (hob)nails, (*Shipb.*) sheathe (*a hull*); *scharf –*, rough-shoe (*a horse*); 3. cover, hang (*wall etc. with drapings*), lag (*a boiler*), lute (*a retort*); (*fig.*) (*of vapour*) steam, mist, cloud (*glass*); 4. (*of stag*) cover, serve (*female*); 5. (*Naut.*) furl (*sail*). **2.** *irr.v.i.* (*aux.* s.), *v.r.* (*of glass*) steam up, mist *or* cloud over. **3.** *adj.* 1. studded, nailed (*as boots*); *scharf –*, rough-shod (*horse*); 2. misted over, steamed up (*as window*); 3. in fawn (*of deer*); 4. *grob –*, rough-hewn (*timber*); 5. (*of a p.*) proficient, well-informed, well-versed, knowledgeable (*in* (*Dat.*), in), (*coll.*) at home (with), well up (in). **Beschlagenheit,** *f.* (sound *or* thorough) knowledge (*in* (*Dat.*), in).

Beschlag|hammer, *m.* shoeing- *or* shoesmith's hammer. **–leine,** *f.* (*Naut.*) furling-line. **–metall,** *n.* (*Shipb. etc.*) sheathing metal, metal lining.

Beschlagnahme [bəˈʃlaːknaːmə], *f.* seizure, confiscation, (*Law*) attachment, sequestration, (*Naut.*)

detention, embargo (*of ship*); commandeering, requisition, impounding, expropriation; ***unter* –,** requisitioned; confiscated; (*Naut.*) under embargo. **beschlagnahmen,** *v.t.* seize, confiscate, impound, distrain upon (*goods*), requisition (*houses*), (*Law*) attach, sequester, sequestrate, (*Naut.*) lay an embargo on (*a ship*); commandeer, expropriate.

beschleichen [bə'ʃlaɪçən], *irr.v.t.* creep up on *or* to (*a p.*) (stealthily), stalk, steal upon, take hold of, overcome, seize (*as fear etc.*).

beschleunigen [bə'ʃlɔynɪgən], **1.** *v.t.* accelerate, hasten, expedite; speed, quicken, force; precipitate. **2.** *v.r.* become faster, quicken. **Beschleuniger,** *m.* (*Phys.*) accelerator. **Beschleunigung,** *f.* acceleration; quickening (*of pulse etc.*). **Beschleunigungsabnahme,** *f.* retardation, deceleration, negative acceleration.

beschließen [bə'ʃli:sən], *irr.v.t.* 1. close, conclude, end, (*coll.*) end up, wind up; bring up the rear; 2. resolve, determine on, decide; come to the conclusion, make up one's mind; ***einstimmig* –,** decide *or* resolve unanimously; 3. (*obs.*) shut in, enclose; ***in sich* –,** contain, comprise, include, embrace, sum up (in a nutshell). **Beschließer,** *m.* custodian, caretaker, keeper; warder, (*obs.*) turnkey.

beschlossen [bə'ʃlɔsən], *adj.* 1. sheltered, shut in, enclosed; 2. settled, decided, resolved; ***es wurde* –,** it was agreed *or* resolved. *See* **beschließen. beschlossenermaßen,** *adv.* as agreed (upon).

Beschluß [bə'ʃlus], *m.* 1. close, end, termination, conclusion; ***als*** or ***zum* –,** finally, in conclusion, in short; 2. decision, determination; resolve, resolution; (*Law*) order, act (of parliament), decree; ***laut* –,** in accordance with the resolution; 3. custody; ***unter* –,** in custody, under lock and key. **beschlußfähig,** *adj.* competent to pass resolutions; ***–e Anzahl,*** quorum; ***– sein, in –er Anzahl sein,*** be *or* constitute a quorum. **Beschlußfassung,** *f.* passing of a resolution.

beschmieren [bə'ʃmi:rən], *v.t.* (be)smear; cover, coat; scribble on, scrawl on; grease; ***mit Butter* –,** butter; ***mit Öl* –,** oil, grease, lubricate; ***mit Dreck* –,** plaster with mud.

beschmutzen [bə'ʃmutsən], **1.** *v.t.* soil, dirty, bespatter; ***sich*** (*Dat.*) ***die Hände* –,** get one's hands dirty, soil one's hands (*also fig.*). **2.** *v.r.* get dirty; (*fig.*) soil one's hands, lower o.s.

beschnarchen [bə'ʃnarçən], *v.t.* (*coll.*) sleep on *or* over (*before deciding*); (*sl.*) poke one's nose into.

Beschneidemaschine [bə'ʃnaɪdəmaʃi:nə], *f.* guillotine, cutting *or* trimming press, clipper.

beschneiden [bə'ʃnaɪdən], *irr.v.t.* cut, clip, trim, lop, prune, pare, crop, dock; circumcise; curtail, reduce, (*coll.*) cut down; restrict, limit; ***ihm die Krallen*** or ***Flügel* –,** clip his wings. *See* **beschnitten. Beschneidung,** *f.* cutting, clipping; circumcision; curtailment, reduction, restriction, limitation. **Beschneidungsfest,** *n.* (*Eccl.*) the Circumcision.

beschneit [bə'ʃnaɪt], *adj.* snow-covered, snow-capped.

beschnitten [bə'ʃnɪtən], *adj.* ***–e Bäume,*** pollards; ***–es Papier,*** cut paper; ***die Beschnittenen,*** the circumcised. *See* **beschneiden.**

beschnüffeln [bə'ʃnyfəln], **beschnuppern** [bə'ʃnupərn], *v.t.* sniff at; (*coll.*) ***er beschnüffelt alles,*** he pokes his nose into everything.

bescholten [bə'ʃɔltən], *adj.* (*of a p.*) ill-famed, of ill-repute; (*of reputation etc.*) tarnished, sullied. **Bescholtenheit,** *f.* evil repute.

beschön(ig)en [bə'ʃø:n(ɪg)ən], *v.t.* varnish over, gloss over, cover up, disguise, camouflage, put in a favourable light, put a good face on, explain away; ***beschönigende Ausdrücke,*** extenuating phrases, euphemistic terms.

beschottern [bə'ʃɔtərn], *v.t.* metal, surface, macadamize (*a road*). **Beschotterung,** *f.* macadam, (road) metal, (*Railw.*) ballast.

beschränken [bə'ʃrɛŋkən], *v.t.* limit, restrict, confine, set limits *or* bounds (***auf*** (*Acc.*), to). **beschränkt,** *adj.* 1. limited, restricted; (*Comm.*) ***–e Haftung,*** limited liability; ***–e Verhältnisse,*** straitened circumstances; 2. of limited intelligence, of limited views *or* restricted outlook, narrow-minded. **Beschränktheit,** *f.* limited intelligence, obtuseness; stupidity; narrow-mindedness. **Beschränkung,** *f.* restriction, limitation.

beschreiben [bə'ʃraɪbən], *irr.v.t.* write on (*paper*); (*Geom.*) describe (*a circle etc.*); describe, give an account *or* description of; ***nicht zu* –,** indescribable. **beschreibend,** *adj.* descriptive. **Beschreibung,** *f.* description, account. (*In compounds often* = -logy *or* -graphy.)

beschreien [bə'ʃraɪən], *irr.v.t.* 1. (*obs.*) decry, disparage; 2. tempt providence by praising; ***– Sie es mir nicht!*** don't crow over it! ***man soll es nicht –!*** touch wood!

beschreiten [bə'ʃraɪtən], *irr.v.t.* walk on, go along; cross (*a threshold etc.*); bestride (*a horse*); ***ein viel beschrittener Weg,*** a well-trodden path; ***ein kaum beschrittener Weg,*** a little-used path; ***den Rechtsweg* –,** go to law *or* court, take legal proceedings; ***das Ehebett* –,** consummate one's marriage.

beschrieben [bə'ʃri:bən], *see* **beschreiben. beschriebenermaßen,** *adv.* as described.

beschriften [bə'ʃrɪftən], *v.t.* letter, inscribe, write captions for; (*Comm.*) classify (under letter-heads). **Beschriftung,** *f.* lettering, labelling; inscription, legend, caption; classification (under letter-heads).

beschuhen [bə'ʃu:ən], *v.t.* provide with shoes, shoe.

beschuldigen [bə'ʃuldɪgən], *v.t.* accuse (*Gen.*, of), charge (with), indict (for), impute (to), tax (with); incriminate. **Beschuldiger,** *m.* accuser; plaintiff. **Beschuldigte(r),** *m.,f.* the accused, defendant. **Beschuldigung,** *f.* charge, accusation, indictment, impeachment; incrimination, imputation.

beschummeln [bə'ʃuməln], *v.t.* (*coll.*) diddle, bamboozle.

beschuppt [bə'ʃupt], *adj.* covered with scales, scaly.

Beschuß [bə'ʃus], *m.* fire, shelling, bombardment, cannonade.

beschütten [bə'ʃytən], *v.t.* throw *or* cast on; pour over; cover with.

beschützen [bə'ʃytsən], *v.t.* protect, guard, shelter, shield, defend (***vor*** (*Dat.*), from *or* against). **Beschützer,** *m.* protector, defender, shield, guardian; patron.

beschwatzen [bə'ʃvatsən], **beschwätzen** [bə'ʃvɛtsən], *v.t.* persuade, wheedle, talk (*s.o.*) into *or* round to (*doing*).

Beschwer [bə'ʃve:r], *n.* (*only in the expression ohne* –) *see* **Beschwerde,** 1.

Beschwerde [bə'ʃve:rdə], *f.* 1. difficulty; burden, inconvenience; (*Med.*) complaint; ***körperliche –n,*** bodily ailments; ***die –n des Alters,*** the infirmities of old age; 2. complaint, (*Law*) objection; ***– führen,*** complain (***über*** (*Dat.*), of *or* about), make *or* lodge a complaint (against *or* about). **Beschwerde|-buch,** *n.* complaints book. **–führer,** *m.* complainant. **–punkt,** *m.* matter for *or* of complaint, grievance. **–schrift,** *f.* written complaint.

beschweren [bə'ʃve:rən], **1.** *v.t.* load, weight, make heavy; weight *or* anchor down (*loose papers etc.*); (*fig.*) burden, encumber; clog (*one's memory*); lie heavy on (*the stomach*); weigh on, be a load *or* a weight on (*one's conscience*). **2.** *v.r.* complain (***bei ihm,*** to him; ***über*** (*Acc.*), of *or* about), make *or* lodge a complaint (about *or* against), grumble (over *or* about), protest (against). **Beschwerer,** *m.* paper-weight; weight, sinker.

beschwerlich [bə'ʃve:rlɪç], *adj.* troublesome; wearisome, tiresome, tedious, trying; tiring, arduous, fatiguing; ***ihm – sein*** or ***fallen,*** inconvenience him, be a burden *or* inconvenience *or* nuisance *or* trouble to him; ***das Gehen fällt ihm* –,** he finds walking tiring. **Beschwerlichkeit,** *f.* tediousness, tiresomeness, wearisomeness; inconvenience, trouble, difficulty, nuisance. **Beschwernis,** *f.* (-, *pl.* **-se**) *see* **Beschwerde,** 1.

beschwert [bəˈʃveːrt], *adj.* loaded; encumbered, mortgaged; *–er Brief,* letter containing valuables; *–es Papier,* loaded *or* weighted paper. **Beschwerte(r),** *m., f.* (*Law*) trustee. **Beschwerung,** *f.* lead (*of plumb-line etc.*), weight, sinker; ballast. *See also* **Beschwerde.**

beschwichtigen [bəˈʃvɪçtɪgən], **1.** *v.t.* appease, allay, quiet(en), calm, still, soothe, pacify. **2.** *v.r.* calm down, abate (*as storm*). **Beschwichtigung,** *f.* appeasement, pacification; consolation, solace. **Beschwichtigungspolitik,** *f.* appeasement policy.

beschwindeln [bəˈʃvɪndəln], *v.t.* swindle, cheat.

beschwingen [bəˈʃvɪŋən], *v.t.* quicken, exhilarate, elevate, elate.

beschwipst [bəˈʃvɪpst], *adj.* (*coll.*) tipsy, fuddled.

beschwören [bəˈʃvøːrən], *irr.v.t.* 1. swear to, affirm *or* testify on oath, take one's oath on; 2. conjure *or* call up, exorcize, summon, raise (*spirits*), charm (*snakes*); beseech, entreat, implore, adjure. **Beschwörer,** *m.* conjurer, exorcist, magician; snake-charmer. **Beschwörung,** *f.* exorcism, incantation, magic formula; (*usu. pl.*) entreaty, adjuration. **Beschwörungs|formel,** *f.* incantation, charm. **–kunst,** *f.* exorcism, magic.

beseelen [bəˈzeːlən], *v.t.* breathe life into, endow with a living spirit, animate, inspire, quicken. **beseelend,** *adj.* animating, life-giving. **beseelt,** *adj.* inspired, animated; sentient, animate. **Beseeltheit,** *f.* animate *or* sentient quality, inspired feeling. **Beseelung,** *f.* animation, inspiration.

besegeln [bəˈzeːgəln], *v.t.* navigate, sail (*the ocean etc.*); *die Küste –,* coast, sail along the coast; *ein Schiff –,* fit a ship with sails. **Besegelung,** *f.* (suit of) sails.

besehen [bəˈzeːən], *irr.v.t.* look at; inspect, examine, (*coll.*) *eine Tracht Prügel –,* come in for *or* get a sound thrashing; *sich* (*Dat.*) *etwas –,* have a look at s.th., view s.th.; *zu –,* on view, for inspection.

beseitigen [bəˈzaɪtɪgən], *v.t.* remove, clear away (*debris etc.*), get rid of, destroy (*vermin etc.*), dispatch, get rid of, account for, liquidate (*a p.*), do away with, put an end to (*restrictions, abuses etc.*), eliminate, correct, put right (*mistakes etc.*). **Beseitigung,** *f.* removal, clearance; destruction, dispatch, liquidation; elimination, correction, rectification.

beseligen [bəˈzeːlɪgən], *v.t.* make happy. **beseligt,** *adj.* blissful, overjoyed. **Beseligung,** *f.* bliss, rapture.

Besen [ˈbeːzən], *m.* 1. broom; *mit eisernem – kehren,* rule with a rod of iron; (*coll.*) *ich fresse einen –,* I'll eat my hat; (*Prov.*) *neue – kehren gut,* a new broom sweeps clean; 2. egg-whisk; 3. (*sl.*) charwoman; (*sl.*) hag, battle-axe. **Besen|ginster,** *m.* (*Bot.*) broom (*Cytisus scoparius*). **–putz,** *m.* rough coat (of plaster). **besenrein,** *adj.* well-swept, swept clean. **Besen|reis,** *n.* birch-twig. **–stiel,** *m.* broomstick; *steif wie ein –,* stiff as a ram-rod *or* poker.

besessen [bəˈzɛsən], *adj.* possessed; frenzied; obsessed; *er lief wie –,* he ran like mad. *See* **besitzen. Besessene(r),** *m., f.* demoniac, fanatic; *wie ein Besessener,* like one possessed. **Besessenheit,** *f.* frenzy, madness, demoniacal possession; obsession.

besetzen [bəˈzɛtsən], *v.t.* 1. occupy, take (*seat etc.*), fill (*post, part in a play*), man (*guns, defence*), (*Mil.*) take possession of, occupy (*territory, town etc.*), stock (*pond with fish*), charge (*furnace*); 2. trim, decorate (*hat etc.*), set, stud (*with jewels*); ram down (*paving*), tamp (*blasting charge*).

Besetz|platte, *f.* paving stone, flagstone. **–ramme,** *f.*, **–schlegel,** *m.* (paving-)beetle, rammer.

besetzt [bəˈzɛtst], *adj.* taken, occupied (*as seat*), engaged (*as lavatory, table, telephone line*), full (up) (*as hotel, bus etc.*), (already) filled (*as appointment*); *vom Feinde –,* enemy-occupied; (*Theat.*) *gut –,* with a good cast.

Besetzteich [bəˈzɛtstaɪç], *m.* breeding pond.

Besetztzeichen [bəˈzɛtsttsaɪçən], *n.* (*Phone*) engaged signal.

Besetzung [bəˈzɛtsuŋ], *f.* (military) occupation; filling (*of a vacancy*); casting (*of actors*), cast (*of a play*), players (*of orchestra*). *See* **Besatz, Besatzung.**

besichtigen [bəˈzɪçtɪgən], *v.t.* inspect, review (*troops*), inspect, examine (*goods*), go sight-seeing in, see the sights in (*a place*), visit, look *or* go round (*ruins etc.*), look over (*house for sale*), survey (*ship*). **Besichtiger,** *m.* inspector; surveyor (*of ship*). **Besichtigung,** *f.* inspection, examination, survey; sightseeing; *zur –,* on view, open to inspection. **Besichtigungs|bericht,** *m.* inspector's report. **–fahrt,** *f. See* **–tour. –offizier,** *m.* inspecting officer. **–reise, –runde,** *f.* tour of inspection. **–tour,** *f.* sight-seeing tour.

besiedeln [bəˈziːdəln], *v.t.* colonize, settle; *ein Land –,* settle in a country; *dicht besiedelt,* thickly *or* densely populated. **Besied(e)lung,** *f.* colonization, settlement. **Besied(e)lungsdichte,** *f.* density of population.

besiegeln [bəˈziːgəln], *v.t.* seal, put one's seal to; (*fig.*) seal, confirm. **Besiegelung,** *f.* sealing, confirmation.

besiegen [bəˈziːgən], *v.t.* defeat, conquer, beat, vanquish, overthrow, overcome, subdue. **Besieger,** *m.* conqueror, victor, (*Spt.*) winner. **Besiegung,** *f.* defeat, conquest.

Besing [ˈbeːzɪŋ], *m.* (**-s,** *pl.* **-e**), **Besinge,** *f. schwarze Besinge,* bilberry, myrtle whortleberry; *rote Besinge,* red whortleberry.

besingen [bəˈzɪŋən], *irr.v.t.* sing, celebrate (in song), praise, extol, laud.

besinnen [bəˈzɪnən], *irr.v.r.* 1. think about, consider, give (some) thought to; *sich eines Besseren –,* think better of a th.; *sich anders* or *eines anderen –,* change one's mind; *ohne sich zu –,* without thinking *or* considering; *ohne sich lange zu –,* without a moment's thought, without stopping to think; *see* **besonnen**; 2. *sich – auf* (*Acc.*), think of, remember, recollect, recall, call to mind; *besinne dich doch!* try and think, try to remember; *wenn ich mich recht besinne,* if I remember correctly; *jetzt besinne ich mich,* now I recollect, it's coming back to me now; *ich besinne mich nicht auf seinen Namen,* I can't recall his name. **Besinnen,** *n.* reflection, consideration; *ohne –,* without (a moment's) hesitation. **besinnlich,** *adj.* thoughtful, reflective, meditative, contemplative (*of a p., moods etc.*); thought-provoking (*book, speech etc.*). **Besinnlichkeit,** *f,* thoughtfulness, meditation, contemplation.

Besinnung [bəˈzɪnuŋ], *f.* 1. consciousness; *die – wiedererlangen,* regain *or* recover consciousness; *die – wiedererlangen,* regain *or* recover consciousness; *bei – bleiben,* not lose consciousness, remain fully conscious; (*coll.*) *er ist ja nicht ganz bei –,* he must be out of his mind; (*coll.*) *ihn zur – bringen,* bring him to his senses; 2. meditation, contemplation, deliberation. **besinnungslos,** *adj.* 1. unconscious, insensible; 2. thoughtless, inconsiderate, rash. **Besinnungslosigkeit,** *f.* 1. unconsciousness, loss of consciousness, insensibility; 2. thoughtlessness.

Besitz [bəˈzɪts], *m.* 1. possession, ownership, (*Law*) occupancy; *juristischer –,* possession in law; *– von Aktien,* holding of shares; *in den – kommen* (*Gen.*), get possession of; *in – nehmen,* take possession of; *den – entziehen* (*Dat.*), expropriate, dispossess; *sei im –, und du wohnst im Recht,* possession is nine points of the law; 2. possessions, belongings, property, (*Comm.*) holdings (*of shares*); *in privatem –,* privately owned; 3. (landed) property, estate. **besitzanzeigend,** *adj.* (*Gram.*) possessive.

besitzen [bəˈzɪtsən], *irr.v.t.* possess, be in possession of, own, have; *er besitzt mein Vertrauen,* he has my confidence. *See* **besessen. besitzend,** *adj. die –en Klassen,* the moneyed *or* propertied classes. **Besitzentziehung,** *f.* dispossession, expropriation. **Besitzer,** *m.* owner, possessor; proprietor (*of a business*); occupant, occupier (*of house or land*); *den – wechseln,* change ownership *or* hands.

Besitzergreifung [bəˈzɪtsˀɛrgraɪfuŋ], *f.* occupancy,

seizure, (*Law*) entry; ***widerrechtliche –,*** usurpation.
Besitzerrecht [bəˈzɪtsərrɛçt], *n.* owner's right(s).
besitzlos [bəˈzɪtslo:s], *adj.* unpropertied; ***die –e Klasse,*** the 'have-nots'.
Besitz|nahme, *f.* taking possession, occupation, seizure. **–recht,** *n.* right of possession, legal ownership, (*Law*) title. **–steuer,** *f.* property tax. **–störung,** *f.* (*Law*) trespass. **–titel,** *m.* (*Law*) title-deed.
Besitztum [bəˈzɪtstu:m], *n.* (**-s,** *pl.* **¨-er**) 1. possession; 2. (landed) property.
Besitzung [bəˈzɪtsuŋ], *f.* (landed) property, estate; *pl.* dominions, dependencies. *See* **Besitz.**
Besitz|urkunde, *f.* (*Law*) *see* **–titel. –veränderung,** *f.*, **–wechsel,** *m.* transfer (of property).
besoffen [bəˈzɔfən], *see* **besaufen.**
besohlen [bəˈso:lən], *v.t.* sole (*shoes etc.*).
besolden [bəˈzɔldən], *v.t.* pay (*officials, soldiers etc.*); ***besoldete Stelle,*** paid post. **Besoldung,** *f.* payment (*of officials, soldiers etc.*); pay, salary, stipend. **Besoldungs|gruppe,** *f.* salary grade. **–ordnung,** *f.* scales of pay, (*Mil.*) pay regulations. **–stufe,** *f. See* **–gruppe.**
besonder [bəˈzɔndər], *attrib. adj.* 1. separate; ***ein –es Zimmer für die Kinder,*** a separate room for the children; 2. (e)special, particular, (*coll.*) extra-special; ***die –en Umstände,*** the special *or* particular circumstances; ***im –en,*** especially, particularly, in particular; 3. peculiar, unusual; ***nichts Besonderes,*** nothing out of the ordinary, nothing special *or* unusual. *See* **besonders. Besonderheit,** *f.* special *or* peculiar feature, characteristic, special nature, peculiarity, individuality.
besonders [bəˈzɔndərs], *adv.* 1. especially, particularly, in particular; ***ganz –,*** above all; (*coll.*) ***nicht –,*** not up to much; 2. separately; ***– gerechnet,*** charged separately, not included in the bill.
besonnen [bəˈzɔnən], *adj.* prudent, circumspect, discreet; ***ruhig und –,*** calm and collected. *See* **besinnen. Besonnenheit,** *f.* prudence, discretion, circumspection, presence of mind, self-possession.
besorgen [bəˈzɔrgən], *v.t.* 1. take care of, care *or* provide for, look after (*a p. etc.*); carry out, see to, attend to, do (*s.th.*); ***ich werde es –,*** I shall see to it; ***den Haushalt –,*** keep house (*Dat.*, for); 2. get, procure, buy; ***– Sie mir drei Plätze,*** get three seats for me; 3. (*obs.*) fear, be afraid; (*now imp.*) ***es ist zu – daß,*** it is to be feared that.
besorglich [bəˈzɔrklɪç], *adj.* disturbing, alarming, perturbing, disquieting (*news etc.*), apprehensive, anxious (*of a p.*).
Besorgnis [bəˈzɔrknɪs], *f.* (-, *pl.* **-se**) fear, anxiety, alarm, worry, concern, apprehension. **besorgniserregend,** *adj.* disquieting, worrying, alarming.
besorgt [bəˈzɔrkt], *adj.* anxious, worried, uneasy, apprehensive, concerned (***um,*** about), solicitous (for). **Besorgtheit,** *f.* anxiety, uneasiness, worry, alarm; concern, solicitude.
Besorgung [bəˈzɔrguŋ], *f.* 1. care, attention; 2. execution (*of orders etc.*), procurement, purchase; errand, shopping; ***eine – machen,*** go on an errand; ***–en machen,*** do the shopping. **Besorgungszettel,** *m.* shopping list.
bespannen [bəˈʃpanən], *v.t.* stretch over, cover; string (*an instrument*), hair (*a bow*), warp (*a loom*), harness (*vehicle*); ***mit Ochsen bespannt,*** ox-drawn. **Bespannung,** *f.* covering *or* lining fabric; strings, stringing (*of instrument*), warp (*of loom*); team (*of horses etc.*).
bespeien [bəˈʃpaɪən], *irr.v.t.* spit on *or* at; (*coll.*) abuse.
bespiegeln [bəˈʃpi:gəln], *v.r.* 1. be reflected *or* mirrored; 2. look at o.s. in a mirror; (*coll.*) admire *or* preen o.s., be self-complacent.
besponnen [bəˈʃpɔnən], *adj.* covered; (*Mus.*) ***–e Saiten,*** covered strings; ***–er Knopf,*** covered button.
bespötteln [bəˈʃpœtəln], *v.t.* jeer *or* scoff at, ridicule, deride, mock, make fun of. **Bespöttelung,** *f.* mockery, ridicule, derision.
besprechen [bəˈʃprɛçən], **1.** *irr.v.t.* 1. discuss, talk over, debate; (*coll.*) ***besprich es nicht,*** keep your fingers crossed; 2. review (*a book etc.*); 3. (*obs.*) cure by incantation *or* magic spell. **2.** *irr.v.r.* confer, consult (***mit,*** with; ***über*** (*Acc.*), about). **Besprechung,** *f.* discussion, talk(s), conference, consultation; criticism, review (*of a book*).
besprengen [bəˈʃprɛŋən], *v.t.* sprinkle (with water), spray, water (*streets, plants*).
bespringen [bəˈʃprɪŋən], *irr.v.t.* cover (*a mare*).
bespritzen [bəˈʃprɪtsən], *v.t.* spray, splash; bespatter.
bespülen [bəˈʃpy:lən], *v.t.* wash (against); ***von der See bespült,*** washed by the sea.
besser [ˈbɛsər], *adj., adv.* 1. (*comp. of* ***gut***) better; ***ich habe Besseres zu tun,*** I have something better *or* more important to do; ***– ist –,*** it is best to be on the safe side; ***– werden,*** improve, get better; change for the better, clear up (*of weather*); ***jetzt steht es – mit ihm*** or ***geht es ihm –,*** his affairs are looking up, he is getting along better; ***eine Wendung zum Besseren,*** an improvement, a change *or* turn for the better; ***sich eines Besseren besinnen,*** think better of a th.; ***ihn eines Besseren belehren,*** set *or* put him right, enlighten *or* disabuse him; (*coll.*) ***ich werde dich eines Besseren belehren, als so mit deinem Vater zu sprechen,*** I'll teach you to speak to your father like that; ***immer –,*** better and better; ***noch –,*** better still; ***oder – . . .,*** or perhaps I should say . . ., or rather . . .; ***desto*** or ***um so –,*** so much the better; 2. better-class, superior; ***ein –er Herr,*** a gentleman, a man in easy circumstances; ***aus –er Familie,*** from a better-class family; ***er ist nur ein –er Knecht,*** he is merely a superior sort of labourer, he is not much better than a labourer.
bessern [ˈbɛsərn], **1.** *v.t.* (make) better, improve. **2.** *v.r.* (*of a th.*) improve, get better, change for the better, (be on the) mend; (*of a p.*) reform, mend one's ways, (*coll.*) turn over a new leaf; (*Comm.*) rise, advance (*of prices*). **Besserung,** *f.* improvement, amelioration, betterment; change for the better; reform; recovery (*in health*); ***gute –!*** I wish you a speedy recovery! I hope you will soon be better *or* well; ***es ist eine – eingetreten,*** there is a change for the better. **Besserungsanstalt,** *f.* reformatory, approved school, remand home. **besserungsfähig,** *adj.* capable of improvement, remediable.
Besserwisser [ˈbɛsərvɪsər], *m.* wiseacre, pompous ass, (*coll.*) know-all, (*Am.*) know-it-all.
best [bɛst], *adj.* 1. best; (*before names: patronizingly*) ***mein –er Herr Schmidt,*** my dear Mr. Smith; ***der erste*** or ***nächste –e,*** the first (available); ***in –er*** or ***der –en Absicht,*** with the best (of) intentions; ***im –en Alter,*** in the prime of life; ***–en Dank,*** many thanks; ***im –en Einvernehmen,*** on the best of terms, in complete agreement; ***im –en Fall,*** at (the) best; ***aus –er Familie,*** of a very good family; ***nach –en Kräften,*** to the best of one's ability; ***bei –er Gesundheit,*** in excellent *or* in the best of health; ***mit –em Gruß*** or ***–en Grüßen,*** with kindest regards; ***auf dem –en Wege,*** well on the way, in a fair way; ***beim –en Willen,*** with the best will in the world; ***nach –em Wissen (und Gewissen),*** to the best of one's knowledge, in all good faith; ***im –en Zuge,*** in the middle *or* midst (of doing), in full swing; ***in –em Zustand,*** in excellent *or* first-class condition; 2. ***das Beste,*** the best (thing *or* plan); ***das Beste was man tun kann,*** the best (thing) one can do; ***das Beste daran ist,*** the best (part) of it is; ***das Beste hoffen,*** hope for the best; ***das Beste vom Besten,*** the very best, (*coll.*) the pick of the bunch; ***zum Besten der Armen,*** for the benefit of the poor; ***sein Bestes tun,*** do one's best; ***sein Bestes geben,*** give of one's best; 3. *sup.adv.* ***am –en,*** best (of all); ***am –en abschneiden,*** come off best, get *or* have the best of it *or* of the bargain; ***auf das*** or ***aufs –e,*** in the best possible way, most satisfactorily; ***zum –en,*** (*usu. neg.*) ***nicht zum –en,*** not too *or* very well *or* promising; ***zum –en geben,*** recite (*poem*), tell (*story*), sing (*song*), oblige with; ***ihn zum –en haben*** or ***halten,*** make a fool of him, (*coll.*) pull his leg.

best–, *pref.* (*forming sup. of pres.p. or p.p. used as adj.*) best-, best, most.

bestallen [bəˈʃtalən], *v.t.* appoint (*in* (*Dat.*), to), invest (with) (*an office*). **Bestallung,** *f.* appointment; installation, investiture. **Bestallungsurkunde,** *f.* (letters) patent, diploma, commission.

Bestand [bəˈʃtant], *m.* 1. (continued) existence, permanence, continuance, stability, duration; – *haben, von – sein,* be lasting, permanent *or* enduring; *von kurzem –,* of short duration, short-lived; 2. stock(s), store, supply, holdings, (*Comm.*) stock-in-trade, stock (in hand), (*Mil.*) effectives, effective strength; – *aufnehmen,* take stock *or* (*Am.*) inventory; *unverkäufliche Bestände,* dead stock; (*Mil.*) *eiserner –,* emergency *or* iron rations, (*fig.*) basic requirements, the minimum necessary; (*Theat.*) *eiserner – des Spielplans,* permanent item of the repertoire; – (*an Geld*), (cash) reserves, cash-balance, assets; – (*an Effekten*), holdings, securities in hand; – *der Kasse,* takings, cash in hand, (*coll.*) resources, funds; 3. (*Austr.*) lease, tenure; *in – geben,* let on lease. **Bestand|buch,** *n.* inventory, stock-book. **–geber,** *m.* (*Austr.*) landlord, lessor. **–liste,** *f.* *See* **Bestandsliste.** **–nachweis,** *m.* *See* **Bestandsnachweis.**

beständig [bəˈʃtɛndɪç], **1.** *adj.* (*of states, conditions*) constant, invariable, unchanging, enduring, lasting, permanent, settled, stable; (*of activities*) constant, continual, persistent, perpetual; (*of a p.*) constant, steadfast, unwavering; *–er Regen,* persistent *or* continual rain; *–es Wetter,* settled weather; (*Naut.*) *–er Wind,* steady wind; (*Comm.*) *–e Nachfrage,* steady *or* brisk demand. **2.** *adv.* continually, persistently, perpetually, constantly; permanently. **Beständigkeit,** *f.* constancy; invariability, uniformity, permanence, stability; continuance, persistence; steadfastness, persistency.

Bestandnehmer [bəˈʃtantnɛːmər], *m.* (*Austr.*) tenant, lease-holder, lessee.

Bestands|aufnahme, *f.* stock-taking; – *machen,* take stock *or* (*Am.*) inventory. **–dichte,** *f.* crop density. **–liste,** *f.*, **–nachweis,** *m.* inventory, stock-list.

Bestand|teil, *m.* (component *or* constituent) part, component; (*Chem. etc.*) constituent, ingredient, element; *fremder –,* foreign body *or* matter, impurity. **–verzeichnis,** *n.* *See* **Bestandsliste.**

bestärken [bəˈʃtɛrkən], *v.t.* confirm, strengthen, fortify. **Bestärkung,** *f.* confirmation; strengthening.

bestätigen [bəˈʃtɛːtɪgən], **1.** *v.t.* confirm, corroborate, verify, endorse, prove, bear out (*a statement etc.*); (*Law*) approve, ratify, sanction, validate, (*Scots*) homologate (*contract etc.*); (*Comm.*) acknowledge (receipt of); *im Amt –,* re-appoint. **2.** *v.r.* be confirmed, prove (to be) true *or* correct, turn out to be true, come true, hold good. **bestätigend,** *adj.* confirmative, confirmatory, corroborative. **Bestätigung,** *f.* confirmation, corroboration, verification, approval; ratification, validation, (*Scots*) homologation; acknowledgement (of receipt); receipt; *zur –,* in confirmation *or* corroboration (*Gen.*, of); *– finden,* be confirmed, prove (to be) true *or* correct, turn out to be true, come true.

bestatten [bəˈʃtatən], *v.t.* bury, inter. **Bestatter,** *m.* undertaker.

Bestätterei [bəʃtɛtəˈraɪ], *f.* (*dial.*) conveyance, forwarding, carriage (*of goods*). **Bestätter(er)** [bəˈʃtɛtər(ər)], *m.* (*dial.*) conveyor, forwarder, forwarding agent, carrier.

Bestattung [bəˈʃtatuŋ], *f.* burial, funeral, interment.

bestauben [bəˈʃtaubən], *v.i.* (*aux.* s.) gather dust, get dusty.

bestäuben [bəˈʃtɔybən], *v.t.* dust, sprinkle (*with flour, sugar etc.*), spray (*plants*); (*Bot.*) pollinate. **Bestäubung,** *f.* pollination.

bestaunen [bəˈʃtaunən], *v.t.* look at in surprise *or* amazement *or* wonder *or* astonishment; admire, marvel at. **bestaunenswert,** *adj.* amazing, astonishing.

beste, *see* **best.**

bestechen [bəˈʃtɛçən], *irr.v.t.* 1. bribe, offer bribes to, (*Law*) suborn (*witness*), (*coll.*) grease *or* oil (*s.o.'s*) palm, (*sl.*) square (*a p.*); *sich – lassen,* take *or* accept bribes *or* a bribe; 2. (*fig.*) fascinate, charm, captivate, (*coll.*) take (*s.o.*) in; 3. oversew, stitch. **bestechend,** *adj.* fascinating, attractive, (*coll.*) fetching; charming, captivating, seductive, engaging, winning (*manner etc.*); attractive, tempting (*offer, prospects etc.*), **bestechlich,** *adj.* corrupt, corruptible, bribable, open to bribery, venal. **Bestechlichkeit,** *f.* corruptibility, venality, corruption. **Bestechung,** *f.* bribery, corruption, (*Law*) subornation (*of witness*), (*sl.*) graft; bribe(s); (*Law*) *aktive –,* bribery; (*Law*) *passive –,* acceptance of bribes *or* a bribe.

Besteck [bəˈʃtɛk], *n.* **(-(e)s,** *pl.* **-e)** 1. knife, fork and spoon; (set of) cutlery; set of (*medical*) instruments; instrument case; place (at table); 2. (*Naut.*) (ship's) position *or* reckoning; *das – (auf)nehmen,* fix (a ship's) position, work out the reckoning, (*coll.*) take a fix; *gegißtes –,* dead reckoning, estimated position. **Besteckbreite,** *f.* latitude of fix; *gegißte –,* latitude by dead reckoning.

bestecken [bəˈʃtɛkən], *v.t.* stake (*peas etc.*); mark *or* stake out (*ground*); *mit Blumen –,* stick flowers in (*one's hat etc.*), decorate (*one's hat etc.*) with flowers.

Besteck|kasten, *m.* canteen of cutlery. **–länge,** *f.* (*Naut.*) longitude of fix. **–nahme,** *f.* determination of (*ship's*) position, (*coll.*) fix. **–rechnung,** *f.* (*Naut.*) reckoning; *gegißte –,* dead reckoning. **–schrank,** *m.* *See* **–kasten.** **–versetzung,** *f.* (*Naut.*) difference between dead and observed reckoning.

Besteder [bəˈʃteːdər], *m.* ship-broker; ship-wright.

bestehen [bəˈʃteːən], **1.** *irr.v.t.* have, meet, encounter (*adventures*), undergo, endure, (*coll.*) go through (*trials*), fight (*battles*), pass (*examination*); *glücklich –,* come (safely) through, come out victorious from, survive, surmount, overcome (*danger etc.*). **2.** *irr.v.i.* 1. be (in existence *or* in being), exist, subsist, endure, persist, continue, last; *zu Recht –,* be justified; *am Bestehenden festhalten,* adhere to tradition; 2. hold one's own (*gegen,* against *or* with), stand *or* hold one's ground, stand firm, hold out (against), (*coll.*) stand up (to), withstand; *vor Gott –,* be justified in the sight of God *or* before God; *in einer Prüfung –,* pass (in) an examination; 3. – *auf* (*usu. Dat.*), persist in, insist on; (*occ. Acc.*) insist on; *darauf – zu tun,* insist on doing; *darauf – daß er etwas tut,* insist (on it) that he shall do s.th., insist on his doing s.th.; *auf seiner Meinung –,* persist in *or* (*coll.*) stick to one's opinion; 4. – *aus,* consist *or* be composed of; (*of manufactured article*) be made of; 5. (*fig.*) – *in* (*Dat.*), consist *or* lie in (the fact); *die Schwierigkeiten – darin daß,* the difficulties are that *or* consist *or* lie in the fact that. **Bestehen,** *n.* 1. existence; *seit dem –,* since the beginning; *das 20-jährige –,* the twentieth anniversary; *das 100-jährige –,* the centenary; 2. insistence (*auf* (*Acc.*), upon), persistence (in); 3. pass (*Gen.*, in) (*an examination*).

bestehlen [bəˈʃteːlən], *irr.v.t.* *ihn um 10 Mark –,* rob him of 10 marks, steal 10 marks from him.

besteigen [bəˈʃtaɪgən], *irr.v.t.* climb, ascend (*mountain*), climb (up) (*ladder, tree*), mount (*a horse, pulpit, scaffold etc.*); board (*a train, ship*); ascend, succeed to (*throne*). **Besteigung,** *f.* ascent (*of mountain*), accession (*to throne*).

Bestellbuch [bəˈʃtɛlbuːx], *n.* order-book.

bestellen [bəˈʃtɛlən], *v.t.* 1. order, give *or* place an order for (*goods*), book, reserve (*seats, a room*), commission (*work of art*), make *or* fix an appointment with (*a p.*); *ihn zu sich –,* send for *or* summon him; *ich bin bestellt,* I have an appointment; (*coll.*) *wie bestellt und nicht abgeholt,* all dressed up and nowhere to go; 2. arrange, prepare; cultivate, till (*soil*), deliver (*message, greetings, post etc.*) (*Dat.*, to); – *Sie ihm einen Gruß von mir,* give him my kind regards; *haben Sie etwas zu –?* have you any message? can I take any message from you?

sein Haus –, set *or* put one's affairs in order, settle one's affairs; ***mit ihm*** or ***um ihn ist es schlecht bestellt,*** he is in a bad way; 3. appoint (*zu*, as); ***ihn zu seinem Erben*** –, appoint him as one's heir.

Bestell|gebühr, *f.*, **–geld,** *n.* charge for delivery. **–schein,** *m.* order-form.

Bestellung [bə'ʃtɛlʊŋ], *f.* 1. order, booking, reservation; ***auf*** –, to order; 2. appointment (***von***, of; ***zu***, as); 3. (postal) delivery; message; – ***ins Haus,*** delivery to the door; ***sonntags gibt es keine*** –, there is no post on Sundays; 4. cultivation (*of soil*). **Bestellungs|brief,** *m.* letter of appointment. **–zeiten,** *f.pl.* times of delivery.

Bestellzettel [bə'ʃtɛltsɛtəl], *m.* order-form.

bestenfalls ['bɛstənfals], *adv.* at (the) best.

bestens ['bɛstəns], *adv.* very *or* extremely well, most satisfactorily, (*Comm.*) at the most favourable rate, at best.

besternt [bə'ʃtɛrnt], *adj.* starry, star-lit (*sky*); star-spangled (*flag etc.*); (*coll.*) bemedalled; marked with an asterisk.

besteuern [bə'ʃtɔyərn], *v.t.* tax, impose a tax on (*goods*), rate, assess for rates (*buildings, land*). **Besteuerung,** *f.* taxation, rating assessment.

bestialisch [bɛsti'a:lɪʃ], *adj.* bestial, brutal, (*coll.*) beastly (*weather etc.*). **Bestialität** [–li'tɛ:t], *f.* brutality, bestiality; (*Law*) sodomy.

besticken [bə'ʃtɪkən], *v.t.* embroider.

Bestie ['bɛstiə], *f.* (wild) beast, brute; inhuman *or* brutal p., brute, (*coll.*) beast.

bestielt [bə'ʃti:lt], *adj.* furnished with a handle *or* stalk; (*Bot.*) pedunculate, petiolate.

bestimmbar [bə'ʃtɪmba:r], *adj.* determinable, definable.

bestimmen [bə'ʃtɪmən], **1.** *v.t.* 1. determine, settle, ordain, appoint, arrange, decide (up)on, fix (*time, place etc.*), be decisive for, decide (*s.o.'s*) fate, dispose (*as God*), lay down (*conditions*); ***Sie haben nichts zu*** –, you have no say *or* voice; 2. (*usu. pass.*) (*Dat.*) destine, grant (to); ***es war ihm nur Unglück bestimmt*** or ***es war ihm bestimmt, nur unglücklich zu sein,*** he was destined *or* doomed *or* fated to nothing but misfortune, nothing but misfortune was granted to him; 3. designate, nominate, appoint (*a p.*) (*zu*, as); ***ihn zu meinem Erben*** –, appoint him (as) my heir; ***wir – unseren Sohn zum Mediziner,*** we intend our son for the medical profession; 4. (*usu. pass.*) allocate (*a th.*) (*für or occ. Dat.*, to), appropriate, set apart, (*coll.*) earmark (for); intend, mean (for); ***nicht für Kinder bestimmt,*** not (intended *or* meant) for children; ***das Geld ist für ein neues Auto bestimmt,*** the money is earmarked for a new car; ***die Kugel war mir*** or ***für mich bestimmt,*** the bullet was intended for me; 5. determine (*also Math.*), define, specify, give a definition of, (*Math.*) find, work out (*answer to a problem*), (*Gram.*) parse (*a word*), qualify, define (*as an adj.*), modify (*as an adv.*); ***näher*** or ***genauer*** –, specify; 6. – ***zu,*** move, impel, induce (*a p.*) (***zu tun***, to do); ***kannst du ihn dazu –, fleißiger zu sein?*** can you induce him to work harder? **2.** *v.i.* 1. – ***über*** (*Acc.*), dispose of, have at (one's) disposal; ***nach Belieben darüber*** –, be able to do what one likes with it; 2. decree, ordain; ***wenn ich zu – hätte,*** if I had my way, if it were for me to decide; ***das Gesetz bestimmt daß*** . . ., the law says *or* provides that . . .; ***das Gericht bestimmt daß*** . . ., the court rules *or* directs that . . . **bestimmend,** *adj.* determining, deciding, decisive; ***das Bestimmende dabei war,*** what decided the matter was.

bestimmt [bə'ʃtɪmt], **1.** *adj.* decided, determined, resolute, firm (*of a p.*); definite, positive, firm (*of attitudes, statements etc.*); definite, well-defined, precise, specific, distinct, special, particular, certain, fixed, given; certain, (*Math.*) finite, determinate; (*Gram.*) ***-er Artikel,*** definite article; ***-e Antwort,*** definite *or* positive *or* firm answer; ***bis zu einem -en Grade,*** to a certain degree; ***-e Gleichung,*** determinate equation; ***zu -en Zwecken,*** for special purposes. **2.** *adv.* certainly, for sure, for certain, for a certainty, definitely, firmly; certainly, surely, assuredly, without doubt; ***ganz –!*** certainly! most assuredly! I'm quite sure (of it)! ***ganz –?*** are you quite sure? are you really? surely not? **Bestimmtheit,** *f.* certainty, definiteness; determination, resolution, firmness; ***mit*** –, definitely, certainly, for certain, positively, categorically.

Bestimmung [bə'ʃtɪmʊŋ], *f.* determination; appointment, settlement (*of time, place etc.*), arrangement, fixing (of), decision (about *or* as to); (*of a p.*) designation, nomination, appointment (***zu***, as); (*of a th.*) allocation, appropriation, (*coll.*) earmarking (***für***, for); definition, determination, (*Gram.*) qualification, modification; (*Gram.*) modifier; destination (*of journey*), intended purpose (*of means*); fate, destiny; decree, order, regulation, rule, provision, ordinance, enactment. **bestimmungsgemäß,** *adj., adv.* according to the rules, in accordance with regulations. **Bestimmungs|hafen,** *m.* port of destination. **–mensur,** *f.* students' duel in which combatants represent their 'corps'. **–methode,** *f.* (*Chem.*) method of identification *or* determination. **–ort,** *m.* destination. **–satz,** *m.* (*Gram.*) defining *or* limiting clause. **bestimmungswidrig,** *adj., adv.* against the rules, contrary to *or* in contravention of regulations. **Bestimmungswort,** *n.* determinative element *or* component (*of compound word*).

Bestleistung ['bɛstlaɪstʊŋ], *f.* (*Spt.*) record (performance).

bestochen [bə'ʃtɔxən], *see* **bestechen.**

bestohlen [bə'ʃto:lən], *see* **bestehlen.**

bestoßen [bə'ʃto:sən], **1.** *irr.v.t.* 1. knock, chip; damage; 2. smooth, trim, plane down, rough-file, (*Typ.*) ***Lettern*** –, dress the type. **2.** *adj.* worn, rubbed, damaged (*of binding or corners of books*). **Bestoß|feile,** *f.* rasp. **–hobel,** *m.* jack-plane; (*Typ.*) dresser.

bestrafen [bə'ʃtra:fən], *v.t.* punish; (*of actions*) ***sich bestraft machen,*** be punished. **Bestrafung,** *f.* punishing; punishment (***von***, of *or* for), penalty.

bestrahlen [bə'ʃtra:lən], *v.t.* shine upon, illuminate, irradiate; (*Med.*) give (sun-)ray treatment, treat with ray-therapy. **Bestrahlung,** *f.* irradiation, illumination; ray-therapy, sun-ray treatment, radiotherapy.

bestreben [bə'ʃtre:bən], *v.r.* exert o.s., strive, endeavour, be anxious *or* eager (*to do*). **Bestreben,** *n.*, **Bestrebung,** *f.* effort, attempt, endeavour, aim, desire, aspiration, striving.

bestreichen [bə'ʃtraɪçən], *irr.v.t.* 1. pass one's hand over, stroke; 2. cover, coat (*with paint etc.*), give a coat of paint to, paint (*door, wall etc.*); spread (*bread etc.*); cover, smear (*with ointment*); 3. (*Artil.*) rake *or* sweep (with fire); ***der Länge nach*** –, enfilade; ***bestrichener Raum,*** area under fire, danger-zone.

bestreitbar [bə'ʃtraɪtba:r], *adj.* disputable, challengeable, contravertible, deniable, contestable, controversial (*facts, statements*); defrayable (*costs*).

bestreiten [bə'ʃtraɪtən], *irr.v.t.* 1. dispute, challenge, question, contest, deny; ***er bestritt mir das Recht,*** he disputed my right; 2. defray, pay, bear, meet (*expenses*), pay, settle (*debt*); ***die Kosten*** –, defray *or* meet *or* cover the cost, (*coll.*) foot the bill; ***seine Ausgaben*** –, pay one's way, meet one's expenses; ***er bestritt die Hälfte des Programms,*** he filled *or* contributed half the programme. **Bestreitung,** *f.* 1. denial; combating; 2. defrayal (*of cost*).

bestreuen [bə'ʃtrɔyən], *v.t.* strew, sprinkle, dust, powder. **Bestreuung,** *f.* sand, gravel (*for paths*).

bestricken [bə'ʃtrɪkən], *v.t.* captivate; charm, fascinate; ***-des Lächeln,*** captivating *or* winning smile.

bestücken [bə'ʃtykən], *v.t.* arm (*a ship*) with guns; ***bestückt mit,*** mounted with (*guns*). **Bestückung,** *f.* armament (*of a ship*), naval guns, ordnance.

bestürmen [bə'ʃtyrmən], *v.t.* charge, storm, assault, make an assault on, attack, assail, (*coll.*) rush, make a rush on (*a shop etc.*); (*fig.*) worry, pester, plague, (*coll.*) badger (*a p.*). **Bestürmung,** *f.* attack, assault, charge; rush (*on a shop etc.*); (*fig.*) persistent requests, badgering.

bestürzen [bə'ʃtyrtsən], *v.t.* confound, dismay, strike with dismay *or* consternation; ***bestürzt machen,*** startle, surprise; confound, throw into confusion; dismay; ***ein bestürztes Gesicht machen,*** look aghast, be taken aback, show blank dismay. **Bestürztheit, Bestürzung,** *f.* consternation, dismay.

Besuch [bə'zu:x], *m.* (**-(e)s,** *pl.* **-e**) 1. visit (*Gen.*, to), attendance (at); (social) visit, call (*Gen.*, from); visit (***in***, to), stay, sojourn (in); ***ihm einen – machen*** or ***abstatten,*** visit him, call on him, pay him a call *or* visit; ***auf*** or ***zu – sein,*** be on a visit (***bei***, to); 2. visitor(s), caller(s), company; ***– haben,*** have visitors *or* a visitor, have company. **besuchen,** *v.t.* visit, call on (*a p.*), pay (*s.o.*) a call *or* visit; visit (*place, museum etc.*), attend (*lecture, school, church etc.*), frequent, patronize (*place of entertainment*); ***das Theater ist schlecht*** or ***schwach besucht,*** the theatre is poorly attended; ***ein wenig besuchter Ort,*** an unfrequented spot. **Besucher,** *m.* visitor, caller, guest.

Besuchs|karte, *f.* visiting-card. **–tag,** *m.* visiting day. **–zeit,** *f.* visiting hours. **–zimmer,** *n.* guest room, spare room; (*in prisons etc.*) visiting *or* visitors' room.

besudeln [bə'zu:dəln], *v.t.* defile, befoul; (*fig.*) stain, soil (*one's hands*), sully, besmirch, tarnish, cast aspersions on, drag in the mud (*s.o.'s good name*).

betagt [bə'ta:kt], *adj.* aged; advanced *or* stricken in years; (*Comm.*) due (*of a bill*).

betakeln [bə'ta:keln], *v.t.* rig (*a ship*). **Betakelung,** *f.* rigging.

betasten [bə'tastən], *v.t.* handle, touch, finger, feel, (*Med.*) palpate. **Betastung,** *f.* (*Med.*) palpation.

betätigen [bə'tɛ:tɪgən], **1.** *v.t.* set in motion *or* action *or* operation, operate, work (*a machine*), apply, put on (*brake*); ***den Hebel –,*** work the handle; ***den Knopf –,*** press the button. **2.** *v.r.* take an active part, participate, be active (***an*** (*Dat.*), *or* ***bei***, in); ***er betätigt sich politisch,*** he is active politically; ***sich nützlich –,*** make o.s. useful, do s.th. to help. **Betätigung,** *f.* operation; application (*of brake*); participation (in); occupation, job.

betäuben [bə'tɔybən], *v.t.* stun, knock senseless; deafen, stupefy; daze; numb, kill, deaden (*pain*); (*Med.*) anaesthetize. **betäubend,** *adj.* stunning (*blow*), deafening (*noise*). **Betäubung,** *f.* daze, stupor; (*Med.*) anaesthetization (*of a p.*); anaesthesia; ***– des Bewußtseins,*** general anaesthesia, narcosis; ***örtliche –,*** local anaesthesia. **Betäubungsmittel,** *n.* anaesthetic, narcotic, drug; pain-killer, analgesic, anodyne.

betaut [bə'taut], *adj.* dewy, bedewed.

Betbruder ['be:tbru:dər], *m.* religious bigot; devout churchgoer.

[1]**Bete** ['be:tə], *f.* stake lost (*at cards*); ***er ist –,*** he has lost the game; he must pay the forfeit.

[2]**Bete,** *f.* beet, beetroot.

beteiligen [bə'taɪlɪgən], **1.** *v.t.* give a share *or* interest (***an*** (*Dat.*), in); make a party (to); ***an einer S. beteiligt sein,*** have a share *or* interest in, share *or* participate in a th.; ***an der S. nicht beteiligt sein,*** have no share *or* part in the matter, have nothing to do with it; ***die beteiligten Parteien,*** the parties concerned *or* involved, the interested parties. **2.** *v.r.* take part (***an*** (*Dat.*), in); share *or* participate (in), join (in), take an interest *or* be interested (in), be concerned *or* involved (with), take a hand (in), be *or* become a party (to). **Beteiligung,** *f.* share, interest; participation, support; ***aus Mangel an –,*** from lack of support; (*Comm.*) ***stille –,*** sleeping (*Am.* silent) partnership. **Beteiligungsgesellschaft,** *f.* (*Comm.*) holding company.

beten ['be:tən], **1.** *v.t.* say, recite (*a prayer*); ***den Rosenkranz –,*** tell one's beads; ***das Vaterunser –,*** say the Lord's Prayer. **2.** *v.i.* pray, say one's prayers; ***vor*** (or ***nach***) ***Tische –,*** say grace; ***– um eine S.,*** pray for a th. **Beter,** *m.* man at his prayers, worshipper.

beteuern [bə'tɔyərn], *v.t.* assert, aver, protest, asseverate; declare solemnly, vow, swear (to). **Beteuerung,** *f.* protestation, assertion; asseveration, solemn declaration; ***eidesgleiche –,*** solemn affirmation in lieu of oath.

Betfahrt ['be:tfa:rt], *f.* pilgrimage.

bethlehemitisch [betlehe'mi:tɪʃ], *adj.* of Bethlehem; (*B.*) ***Bethlehemitischer Kindermord,*** Massacre of the Innocents.

Beting ['be:tiŋ], *m.* (**-s,** *pl.* **-e**) *or f.* (-, *pl.* **-e**) (*Naut.*) bitts; ***das Ankertau um die -e schlagen,*** bitt the cable.

Betise [be'ti:zə], *f.* stupidity, folly, silliness.

betiteln [bə'ti:təln], **1.** *v.t.* entitle, give a title to (*book*); head, give a heading to (*chapter, paragraph*); address as, call (*a p.*). **2.** *v.r.* (*of a book etc.*) be entitled.

Beton [be'to:n], *m.* (**-s,** *pl.* **-s**) concrete; ***armierter*** or ***bewehrter –,*** reinforced concrete, ferro-concrete. **Beton|automat,** *m.* concrete mixer. **–bereitung,** *f.* concrete mixing.

betonen [bə'to:nən], *v.t.* stress, lay stress on, accentuate (*also Mus.*); emphasize, lay emphasis on.

betonieren [beto'ni:rən], *v.t.* concrete (*road etc.*).

Beton|mischer, *m. See* **–automat. –stein,** *m.* pre-cast concrete block.

betont [bə'to:nt], *adj.* 1. accentuated; ***-e Silbe,*** stressed *or* accented syllable; 2. (*fig.*) emphatic, marked, striking.

Betonung [bə'to:nuŋ], *f.* accentuation (*also Mus.*), stress, accent; emphasis; ***zur –,*** for emphasis; ***fallende –,*** falling stress. **Betonungszeichen,** *n.* (*Phonet.*) stress-mark, (*Mus.*) accent (mark).

betören [bə'tø:rən], *v.t.* delude, turn (*s.o.'s*) head, infatuate, (*coll.*) dazzle, take (*s.o.*) in. **Betörung,** *f.* delusion, infatuation, bemused state; blandishments.

Betracht [bə'traxt], *m.* 1. (*only in the following phrases*) ***außer – bleiben,*** be left out of account *or* consideration; ***in – kommen,*** (*of a th.*) be possible, be a possibility; (*of a p.*) be suitable; ***nicht in – kommen,*** (*of a th.*) be out of the question, (*of a p.*) be unsuitable, have to be ruled out; ***außer – lassen,*** disregard, leave aside *or* out of account *or* consideration, rule out; ***in – ziehen,*** take into account *or* consideration, consider, bear in mind, contemplate; allow for, make allowance for; ***nicht in – ziehen,*** leave out of *or* not take into account *or* consideration, not consider, disregard; make no allowance for; 2. *adv. phrase* (*obs.*) ***in jedem*** (***keinem***) ***–,*** in every (no) respect; ***in gewissem –,*** in certain respects; 3. *prep. phrase* ***in –*** (*Gen.*), *see* **Anbetracht.**

betrachten [bə'traxtən], *v.t.* 1. look (closely) at, inspect; 2. (*fig.*) consider, contemplate, regard, look upon *or* at, see, take a (*wrong, different etc.*) view of, be (*favourably etc.*) disposed towards; ***etwas als . . . –,*** look upon *or* regard s.th. as . . ., take s.th. for . . . *or* to be . . .; ***es als meine Pflicht –,*** look upon *or* regard *or* see it as my duty, consider *or* count *or* deem it (to be) my duty; ***wie ich die S. betrachte,*** as I see the matter, in my view, to my mind *or* my way of thinking; 3. examine (*in one's mind*), meditate *or* reflect (up)on. **Betrachter,** *m.* observer, beholder; onlooker, spectator.

beträchtlich [bə'trɛçtlɪç], *adj.* considerable, important; substantial, extensive, (*coll.*) sizeable. **Beträchtlichkeit,** *f.* importance; extent, size.

Betrachtung [bə'traxtuŋ], *f.* inspection, examination (of); consideration, contemplation (of); reflection, meditation (***über*** (*Acc.*), upon *or* on); ***-en anstellen,*** reflect, meditate (***über*** (*Acc.*), (up)on).

Betrag [bə'tra:k], *m.* (**-es,** *pl.* **⸚e**) amount, sum, total; ***eine Rechnung im – von DM. 10,*** a bill amounting to 10 marks.

betragen [bə'tra:gən], **1.** *irr.v.t.* come to, amount to, (*coll.*) run to; ***wieviel beträgt meine Rechnung?*** what does my bill come to? how much is my bill? **2.** *irr.v.r.* behave, conduct *or* deport o.s.; ***sich schlecht –,*** misbehave. **Betragen,** *n.* behaviour, conduct.

betrauen [bəˈtrauən], *v.t.* entrust (*a p.*) (*mit,* with); ***betraut sein mit,*** be in charge of, have the care of.

betrauern [bəˈtrauərn], *v.t.* mourn (for *or* over).

Betreff [bəˈtrɛf], *m.* reference; ***in – einer S.,*** with regard to, as to *or* in respect of a matter; ***in dem –,*** in that respect, as for that. *See* **betreffs.**

betreffen [bəˈtrɛfən], *irr.v.t.* 1. concern, affect, (*coll.*) hit; ***vom Krieg schwer*** or ***hart betroffen,*** badly hit by the war; 2. have to do with, be relevant to, (*coll.*) touch; ***was mich betrifft,*** as far as I am concerned, as regards me, as for me, as to me, for my part; 3. (*of misfortune etc.*) befall. *See* **betroffen. betreffend,** *adj.* concerned, in question, referred to; concerned with, relating to, with reference to; concerning, regarding; pertaining *or* relevant to; ***das –e Wort,*** the word in question; ***jeder in seiner –en Abteilung,*** each in his own respective department; ***eine Frage diese S. –, eine Frage – diese S., eine diese S. –e Frage,*** a question concerning *or* regarding this matter.

betreffs [bəˈtrɛfs], *prep.* (*Gen.*) concerning, respecting, regarding, with respect *or* regard to, as to, as regards, about.

betreiben [bəˈtraɪbən], *irr.v.t.* follow, carry on (*trade etc.*), pursue (*studies etc.*); push *or* hurry on, urge forward, push *or* press on with (*piece of work*); operate, work, run (*machine etc.*) (*mit,* on). **Betreiben,** *n.* ***auf –*** (*Gen.*) or ***von,*** at the instigation *or* prompting of. **Betreibung,** *f.* operation, working, running (*of machine etc.*); exercise (*of a profession*); prosecution, pursuit (*of a task*).

betreten [bəˈtreːtən], **1.** *irr.v.t.* 1. walk *or* step on (*path etc.*), set foot in, go *or* step into, enter (*house etc.*); set foot into (*territory*), step over, cross (*threshold*), enter on (*career*), mount (*pulpit*); ***unbefugt –,*** trespass on; ***das Betreten des Rasens ist verboten,*** keep off the grass; 2. (*of cock*) tread (*a hen*). **2.** *adj.* trodden; embarrassed, abashed, disconcerted.

betreuen [bəˈtrɔyən], *v.t.* take care of, have (the) care of, have under one's care, look after, tend. **Betreuung,** *f.* care, control, welfare.

Betrieb [bəˈtriːp], *m.* 1. operation, management, running, working (*of machine, mine etc.*); ***aus dem – ziehen,*** take out of service; ***außer –,*** out of action *or* order, not working; ***außer – setzen,*** put out of action; ***in – sein,*** be in operation, (be) working; ***im – sein,*** be in service; ***in – halten,*** keep (*machine*) working *or* running *or* going; ***in – setzen,*** set (*machine*) going *or* in operation, start (*machine*) working; ***in – genommen werden,*** go into operation (*of machine etc.*), be open *or* opened to *or* for traffic (*of road, railway*), be brought *or* put into service (*of vehicle*); 2. activity (*of an institution*), traffic, bustle, commotion, rush (*in streets, shops etc.*); (*coll.*) high jinks; ***an dieser Ecke ist immer viel –,*** this corner is always very busy; ***– machen,*** make merry; 3. business, firm, concern, undertaking; (work)shop, works. **betriebsam,** *adj.* bustling, busy, energetic, active, industrious. **Betriebsamkeit,** *f.* bustle, activity, industry.

Betriebs|anlage, *f.* (industrial) plant. **–anleitung, –anweisung,** *f.* operating instructions. **–arzt,** *m.* factory doctor. **–ausflug,** *m.* works *or* firm's outing. **–ausgaben,** *f.pl.* working expenses. **–einnahmen,** *f.pl.* (*Railw.*) traffic receipts. **betriebs|fähig,** *adj.* in working order, in running order. **–fertig,** *adj.* ready for use *or* service. **Betriebs|führer,** *m.* (works) manager, managing director. **–führung,** *f.* (works) management. **–geheimnis,** *n.* trade secret. **–ingenieur,** *m.* operating *or* production engineer. **–kapital,** *n.* working capital. **–kosten,** *pl.* operating *or* maintenance *or* running costs, working *or* overhead expenses, overheads. **–leiter,** *m.* *See* **–führer. –material,** *n.* (*Railw.*) rolling stock. **–mittel,** *n.pl.* *See* **–kapital. –ordnung,** *f.* regulations governing conditions of work. **–personal,** *n.* operating staff. **–rat,** *m.* works council; shop steward. **–ruhe,** *f.* closed for business (*notice in shops etc.*). **betriebssicher,** *adj.* safe to operate, dependable *or* reliable in operation, foolproof. **Betriebs|stockung,** *f.* interruption of work, dislocation (*of service*), hold-up. **–stoff,** *m.* fuel, petrol. **–stoffwechsel,** *m.* (*Physiol.*) basal metabolism. **–störung,** *f.* break-down; *see* **–stockung. –unfall,** *m.* industrial injury. **–unfallversicherung,** *f.* workmen's compensation. **–unkosten,** *pl.* *See* **–kosten. –wirtschaft(slehre),** *f.* (science of) business administration *or* industrial management. **–zustand,** *m.* working *or* operating condition. **–zweig,** *m.* branch of industry.

betrinken [bəˈtrɪŋkən], *irr.v.r.* get drunk.

betroffen [bəˈtrɔfən], *adj.* disconcerted, bewildered, taken aback, dismayed, in dismay. *See* **betreffen. Betroffenheit,** *f.* bewilderment, dismay, perplexity.

betrog [bəˈtroːk], **betröge** [bəˈtrøːgə], **betrogen** [bəˈtroːgən], *see* **betrügen. Betrogene(r),** *m., f.* dupe.

betrüben [bəˈtryːbən], *v.t.* sadden, make sad, grieve, distress. **betrüblich,** *adj.* (*of news etc.*) sad, distressing, grievous. **Betrübnis,** *f.* grief, sorrow, sadness; misery, distress. **betrübt,** *adj.* sad, grieved, distressed; dejected, depressed, melancholy; sorrowful, miserable, woebegone (*appearance*). **Betrübtheit,** *f.* sadness, distress; dejection, depression, melancholy; misery.

Betrug [bəˈtruːk], *m.* (**-s,** *pl.* **Betrügereien**) fraud, deceit, deception, cheating, trickery; swindle, trick, imposture, humbug; deceit(fulness), guile, fraudulence; ***frommer –,*** white lie.

betrügen [bəˈtryːgən], *irr.v.t.* deceive; defraud (*um,* of), cheat (of *or* out of), swindle *or* trick (out of). *See* **Betrug. Betrüger,** *m.* deceiver, swindler, cheat, imposter, trickster. **Betrügerei** [–ˈraɪ], *f.* cheating, trickery, deceit, deception, swindling; trick, fraud, swindle. **betrügerisch,** *adj.* deceitful, fraudulent; deceptive; ***in –er Absicht,*** with fraudulent intent, with intent to defraud. **betrüglich,** *adj.* false, deceptive, illusory, fallacious.

betrunken [bəˈtruŋkən], *adj.* intoxicated, drunk, inebriated. *See* **betrinken. Betrunkenheit,** *f.* drunkenness, intoxication, inebriation.

Betstuhl [ˈbeːtʃtuːl], *m.* kneeling-chair, prie-dieu.

Bett [bɛt], *n.* (**-es,** *pl.* **-en**) bed, (*Naut., Railw.*) berth, bunk, bedstead; (feather) bed; bed (*of a river*); lair (*of stag*); (*Bot., Anat.*) thalamus; foundation, seating, bed, cradle (*of machines*), base-plate, bed-plate (*of a motor*); (*Geol.*) stratum, layer, deposit, bed; ***ins – gehen, zu – gehen, sich ins – legen,*** go to bed; ***zu*** or ***ins – bringen,*** put to bed; ***zu*** or ***ins – schicken,*** send to bed; ***sich aufs – legen,*** lie down on the bed; ***das – hüten,*** be confined to bed, (*coll.*) be laid up; ***ans – gefesselt sein,*** be bed-ridden; ***das – aufschlagen,*** turn back the bed-clothes; ***die –en lüften,*** air the beds *or* bedding *or* bed-clothes; ***das – überziehen,*** change the bed; ***zweischläfriges –,*** double bed; ***Zimmer mit zwei –en,*** double(-bedded) room.

Bett|becken, *n.* bed-pan. **–behang,** *m.* valance. **–bezug,** *m.* bed-linen. **–decke,** *f.* counterpane, quilt, bedspread, coverlet; blanket; ***wollene –,*** blanket; ***gesteppte –,*** quilt.

Bettel [ˈbɛtəl], *m.* 1. beggary, begging, mendicancy; 2. (*fig.*) trash, trumpery; ***der ganze –,*** the whole (paltry) show; ***ist das der ganze –?*** is that all it amounts to? **bettelarm,** *adj.* (wholly) destitute, desperately poor. **Bettel|brief,** *m.* begging-letter; licence to beg. **–bruder,** *m.* professional beggar; mendicant (friar).

Bettelei [bɛtəˈlaɪ], *f.* (-, *pl.* **-en**) begging, mendicancy; (*coll.*) pestering, pleading, begging.

Bettel|frau, *f.* beggar-woman. **–geld,** *n.* alms; (*coll.*) ***für ein –,*** for next to nothing, for a song. **bettelhaft,** *adj.* beggarly. **Bettel|handwerk,** *n.* professional begging. **–kram,** *m.* trumpery, trash. **–mann,** *m.* (*Cards*) beggar-my-neighbour, strip-jack-naked. **–mönch,** *m.* mendicant friar.

betteln [ˈbɛtəln], *v.t.* beg (*um,* for); (*fig.*) plead, entreat, beg (*um,* for); ***– gehen, sich aufs – legen,*** live by begging, go begging; ***die Kunst geht –,*** there's no money to be made with art. **Betteln,** *n.*

See **Bettelei**; – ***und Hausieren verboten,*** no beggars no hawkers.

Bettel|orden, *m.* order of mendicant friars. **-pack,** *n. See* **-volk. -stab,** *m.* beggar's staff; ***an den – bringen,*** reduce to beggary; ***an den – kommen,*** be reduced to beggary. **-vogt,** *m.* (*obs.*) beadle. **-volk,** *n.* beggars; paupers. **-weib,** *n. See* **-frau.**

betten ['bɛtən], **1.** *v.t.* bed, lay, rest; (*Mech.*) seat (*valves*); ***auf Stroh gebettet,*** bedded *or* lying in straw; (*coll.*) ***ihn weich –,*** find him a cushy job. **2.** *v.r.* make a bed for o.s., find somewhere to lie down; (*coll.*) ***sich weich –,*** marry money; do well for o.s., feather one's nest; ***wie man sich bettet so liegt man,*** as you make your bed so you must lie in it.

Bett|flasche, *f.* hot-water bottle. **-genosse,** *m.* bedfellow. **-geschirr,** *n.* bed-pan. **-geselle,** *m. See* **-genosse. -gestell,** *n.* bedstead. **-häschen,** *n.* (*coll.*) dolly-bird. **-himmel,** *m.* canopy, tester. **-jacke,** *f.* bed-jacket. **-lade,** *f.* (wooden) bedstead. **bettlägerig,** *adj.* bed-ridden, (*Am.*) bedfast; confined to bed, (*coll.*) laid up. **Bett|laken,** *n.* (bed-)sheet. **-lektüre,** *f.* bedside reading.

Bettler ['bɛtlər], *m.* beggar, mendicant; ***zum – machen,*** reduce to beggary, (*fig.*) reduce to poverty, ruin. **Bettlergesindel,** *n. See* **Bettelvolk. bettlerhaft,** *adj. See* **bettelhaft. Bettlerin,** *f.* beggar-woman. **Bettleroper,** *f.* (*Mus.*) Beggar's Opera.

Bett|nässen, *n.* bed-wetting. **-nische,** *f.* bed-recess, alcove. **-pfanne,** *f.* warming-pan. **-rolle,** *f.* (*Mil.*) bedding roll. **-ruhe,** *f.* (*Med.*) confinement to bed; – ***verordnen,*** order (*s.o.*) to stay in bed. **-schieber,** *m. See* **-becken. -schuh,** *m.* bed-sock. **-schüssel,** *f. See* **-becken. -schwere,** *f.* (*coll.*) – ***haben,*** be ready for bed, be hardly able to keep one's eyes open, be (practically) asleep on one's feet. **-sessel,** *m.* chair-bed. **-sofa,** *n.* settee-bed. **-stelle,** *f.* bedstead. **Bettuch,** *n. See* **Bettlaken.**

Bettung ['bɛtuŋ], *f.* bed, foundation, layer (*of concrete etc.*); (*Railw.*) ballast; base-plate, bed-plate, seating (*of machine*); mounting, platform (*of gun*).

Bett|vorhang, *m.* bed-curtain. **-vorleger,** *m.* bedside rug. **-wäsche,** *f.* bed-linen. **-zeug,** *n.* bedding, bed-clothes.

betulich [bə'tu:lıç], *adj.* (over-)attentive, solicitous, fussing. **Betulichkeit,** *f.* (over-)attentiveness, solicitude, fussing.

betun [bə'tu:n], *irr.v.r.* (make a) fuss.

betupfen [bə'tupfən], *v.t.* 1. dot, speckle, fleck, mark with dots *or* spots; 2. dab, mop, touch lightly.

betüpfeln ['bə'typfəln], *v.t. See* **betupfen,** 1.

Beuche ['bɔyçə], *f.* (*Dye.*) kier-boiling, bucking (*linen*); (bucking) lye. **beuchen,** *v.t.* steep (*in lye*), buck, kier-boil. **Beuch|faß,** *n.,* **-kessel,** *m.* (bucking *or* bleaching) kier.

Beuge ['bɔygə], *f.* bent position, (*Gymn.*) knees-bend; bend (*of knee*), crook (*of arm*); (*occ.*) bend, curve (*of road etc.*); (*Gymn.*) ***in die – gehen!*** knees bend! ***in der – bleiben!*** keep your knees bent! **Beugemuskel,** *m.* (*Anat.*) flexor (muscle). **beugen, 1.** *v.t.* 1. bend (*knee, arm etc.*), bow (*head*); (*fig.*) humble (*pride*), twist (*the law*), pervert (*justice*); ***den Nacken unter das Joch –,*** bend one's neck under the yoke; ***vom Alter gebeugt,*** bowed down *or* bent with age; ***von Sorgen gebeugt,*** bowed down with care; ***gebeugt gehen,*** walk with a stoop; 2. (*Opt.*) deflect, diffract (*rays*). **2.** *v.r.* bend, lean; (*fig.*) bow (down), submit, humble o.s. **Beuger,** *m.* (*Anat.*) flexor (muscle *or* tendon). **Beugestellung,** *f.* (*Anat.*) position of flexion. **beugsam,** *adj. See* **biegsam.**

Beugung ['bɔyguŋ], *f.* bending; (*Anat.*) flexion, flexure; warping (*of justice etc.*); (*Opt.*) deflection, diffraction (*of light*); (*Gram.*) inflexion, declension. **Beugungs|bild,** *n.* (*Opt.*) diffraction image. **-endung,** *f.* (*Gram.*) flexional ending. **beugungsfähig,** *adj.* (*Gram.*) declinable. **Beugungs|fall,** *m.* (*Gram.*) oblique case. **-gitter,** *n.* (*Opt.*) diffraction grating.

Beule ['bɔylə], *f.* bulge, bump; (*Med.*) boil, tumour, lump, swelling; bruise; (*in metal etc.*) dent, dint; (*Archit.*) boss. **beulen,** *v.r.* (*of metal*) buckle. **Beulenpest,** *f.* bubonic plague. **beulig,** *adj.* bruised, dented, battered.

beunruhigen [bə'unru:ıgən], **1.** *v.t.* disturb, upset, make uneasy *or* anxious, disquiet, trouble, worry, harass (*the enemy*); ***beunruhigt sein,*** *see* **2. 2.** *v.r.* be anxious *or* worried *or* concerned (***über*** (*Acc.*), about). **Beunruhigung,** *f.* disturbance, uneasiness, anxiety, misgivings. **Beunruhigungsfeuer,** *n.* (*Mil.*) harassing fire.

beurkunden [bə'urkunden], *v.t.* attest, authenticate, certify; register (*birth, death etc.*). **Beurkundung,** *f.* attestation, certification, authentication; registration (*of births etc.*); documentary proof, documentation.

beurlauben [bə'urlaubən], **1.** *v.t.* grant *or* give leave (of absence); suspend (*an official*), discharge (*troops*). **2.** *v.r.* take one's leave (***bei,*** of); ***sich – lassen,*** ask *or* apply for leave (of absence) *or* for suspension. **Beurlaubtenstand,** *m.* (*Mil.*) reserve status.

Beurlaubung [bə'urlaubuŋ], *f.* leave (of absence); suspension (*of official*), (conditional) discharge (*of troops*).

beurteilen [bə'urtaılən], *v.t.* judge, pass judgement on, give one's opinion on; ***anders –,*** take a different view of, see *or* view differently, look upon in a different light *or* from a different angle. **Beurteiler,** *m.* judge. **Beurteilung,** *f.* judgement, view (of), opinion (on *or* of), views (on).

Beuschel ['bɔyʃəl], *n.* (*Austr.*) (*Cul.*) lights.

[1]**Beute** ['bɔytə], *f.* (*Mil.*) booty, spoil, captured material, (*Nav.*) prize; loot, plunder; (*coll.*) haul (*of thieves*), (*sl.*) swag; (*Hunt.*) game, bag, quarry, prey; – ***der Angst,*** prey to terror; ***eine – des Todes sein,*** be doomed, (*sl.*) be a goner; – ***machen,*** plunder, pillage, loot; ***zur – fallen,*** fall prey (*Dat.*, to); (***eine***) ***leichte –,*** fair game (***für,*** for); ***auf – ausgehen,*** go marauding *or* plundering; (*of animals*) go in search of prey.

[2]**Beute,** *f.* 1. kneading-trough; 2. wooden beehive.

beutegierig ['bɔytəgi:rıç], *adj.* eager for plunder.

Beutel ['bɔytəl], *m.* bag, pouch (*also Zool.*), purse, satchel; (*Anat.*) bursa, sac, cyst; (*Bill.*) pocket; bolter *or* boulter (sieve) (*for flour*); – ***werfen,*** bag, pucker; (*coll.*) ***seinen – spicken,*** line one's pocket; ***tief in den – greifen,*** dip deep into one's pocket; (*coll.*) ***das geht an den –,*** that touches my (his *etc.*) pocket, that costs a lot. **Beutelbär,** *m.* koala (bear). **beutelförmig,** *adj.* bag- *or* pouch-like. **Beutelhase,** *m.* hare-wallaby. **beutelig,** *adj.* baggy, bagged, puckered. **Beutel|kasten,** *m.* bolting-hutch, bolter(sieve); flour bin. **-krabbe,** *f.,* **-krebs,** *m.* purse-crab. **-maus,** *f.* wombat. **-meise,** *f.* (*Orn.*) penduline tit (*Remiz pendulinus*). **-melone,** *f.* cantaloup.

beuteln ['bɔytəln], **1.** *v.t.* bolt, sift, sieve; ***man hat ihn ordentlich gebeutelt,*** he's been properly cleaned out *or* fleeced. **2.** *v.i., v.r.* bag, be baggy; bulge.

Beutel|nager, *m. See* **-maus. -perücke,** *f.* bag-wig. **-ratte,** *f.* opossum. **-schneider,** *m.* pickpocket, cutpurse; swindler. **-schneiderei,** *f.* pilfering, purse-snatching. **-star,** *m.* mocking bird. **-tier,** *n.* marsupial.

beute|lustig, *adj. See* **-gierig. Beute|stück,** *n.* prize, trophy. **-zug,** *m.* marauding *or* plundering expedition.

Beutler ['bɔytlər], *m. See* **Beuteltier.**

bevölkern [bə'fœlkərn], *v.t.* people, populate; ***dicht*** (***spärlich***) ***bevölkert,*** thickly (sparsely) populated. **Bevölkerung,** *f.* population, inhabitants. **Bevölkerungs|dichte,** *f.* (density of) population. **-schutz,** *m.* civil defence.

bevollmächtigen [bə'fɔlmɛçtıgən], *v.t.* authorize, give authority to, empower; (*Law*) confer power of attorney on, invest with full powers. **bevollmächtigt,** *adj.* authorized. **Bevollmächtigte(r),** *m., f.* authorized agent *or* representative, (*Law*) attorney, (*Pol.*) (minister) plenipotentiary. **Bevoll-**

mächtigung, *f.* authority, authorization; power of attorney; warrant; mandate. **Bevollmächtigungs|schreiben,** *n.*, **–urkunde,** *f.*, **–vertrag,** *m.* (*Law*) letter *or* power of attorney.

bevor [bəˈfoːr], **1.** *conj.* before; (*with neg. in principal clause*) until; ***– ich dies tue, muß ich . . .,*** before doing this, I must . . .; ***keinen Schritt weiter – ich gegessen habe,*** not a step further until I've had s.th. to eat. **2.** *verb. pref. either adverbial and sep.* (= **1,** *e.g.* **–stehen,** *or factitive,* **be–** *preceding a compound verb in* **vor–**, *the whole pref. then being insep., e.g.* **–zugen.**

bevormunden [bəˈfoːrmundən], *v.t.* (*insep.*) keep *or* hold in tutelage; (*fig.*) patronize, treat patronizingly *or* in a patronizing manner; ***ich lasse mich nicht –,*** I won't be treated like a child. **Bevormundung,** *f.* tutelage, patronizing treatment.

bevorraten [bəˈfoːrraːtən], *v.t.* (*insep.*) stock up (***mit,*** with), pile up reserves (*of a th.*) for (*s.o.*).

bevorrechten [bəˈfoːrrɛçtən], *v.t.* (*insep.*) (*usu. pass.*) ***bevorrechtet sein,*** be privileged. **Bevorrechtung,** *f.* privilege.

bevorrechtigen [bəˈfoːrrɛçtɪgən], *v.t.* (*insep.*) (*Law*) give a prior claim to. **bevorrechtigt,** *adj.* preferred, privileged, preferential. **Bevorrechtigung,** *f.* preference, preferential right.

bevorstehen [bəˈfoːrʃteːən], *irr.v.i.* (*sep.*) 1. be approaching *or* impending *or* close *or* near *or* imminent (*of events*); impend, approach, be (close *or* near) at hand, be forthcoming; 2. (*Dat.*) be in store for, await, hang over (*s.o.'s*) head, be threatening; ***eine Enttäuschung steht ihm bevor,*** he is faced with a disappointment; ***eine –de Enttäuschung,*** a disappointment yet to come; ***mir steht*** (***etwas***) ***Schlimmes bevor,*** there's s.th. unpleasant in store for me; ***die –de Woche,*** the next *or* coming *or* ensuing week; ***das –de Gewitter*** the impending storm.

bevorworten [bəˈfoːrvɔrtən], *v.t.* (*insep.*) preface, supply with a foreword.

bevorzugen [bəˈfoːrtzuːgən], *v.t.* (*insep.*) prefer (***vor*** (*Dat.*) *or* ***gegenüber,*** to); favour, show partiality to, grant (special) privilege to; ***bevorzugt werden,*** get favours *or* privileges (***von,*** from), be favoured (by), be the favourite (of). **bevorzugt, 1.** *adj.* favourite, preferred; privileged (*position etc.*), preferential (*treatment etc.*). **2.** *adv.* ***– behandeln,*** give preferential treatment to, give priority to; ***– abgefertigt werden,*** have *or* receive priority, be given priority. **Bevorzugung,** *f.* preference, partiality, favour, preferential treatment.

bewachen [bəˈvaxən], *v.t.* (keep) watch over, guard, set a guard on; watch, keep a watch on; ***bewachter Parkplatz,*** car-park with an attendant.

bewachsen [bəˈvaksən], *adj.* overgrown; covered, carpeted (***mit,*** with). **Bewachsung,** *f.* ground vegetation (*of woodland*), flora.

Bewachung [bəˈvaxuŋ], *f.* guard; ***unter –,*** under guard *or* escort.

bewaffnen [bəˈvafnən], *v.t.* arm, provide *or* equip with arms. **bewaffnet,** *adj.* armed; ***bis an die Zähne –,*** armed to the teeth; ***mit –er Hand,*** by force of arms; ***mit bewaffnetem Auge,*** with artificial aid to vision, with spectacles (telescope, microscope, magnifying glass *etc.*). **Bewaffnung,** *f.* armament, arms; ***mit schwerer –,*** heavily armed.

Bewahranstalt [bəˈvaːrˀanʃtalt], *f.* day-nursery.

bewahren [bəˈvaːrən], *v.t.* 1. guard, keep, look after, mind; ***im Gedächtnis –,*** keep *or* bear in mind; ***ein Geheimnis –,*** keep *or* guard a secret; ***seine Zunge –,*** keep a watch *or* rein on one's tongue, guard one's tongue; 2. keep up, preserve, maintain (*tradition, appearances etc.*); ***ruhig Blut –,*** keep cool, keep one's head *or* temper, keep calm *or* cool and collected; ***den Ernst –,*** keep a straight face; ***die Fassung –,*** maintain *or* preserve one's composure, keep one's countenance; ***sein Gesicht –,*** save one's face; ***im Herzen –,*** treasure *or* cherish (in one's heart); 3. ***– vor*** (*Dat.*), keep, save, preserve, spare (from), protect (from *or* against); ***Gott bewahre!*** God forbid!

bewähren [bəˈvɛːrən], **1.** *v.t.* (*obs.*) establish as true; prove. **2.** *v.r.* 1. (*of a p.*) prove o.s. (***als,*** to be), prove one's ability *or* worth *or* mettle, give a good account of o.s.; (*Law*) maintain good conduct (during probation); 2. (*of a th.*) prove effective, prove a success (*as a remedy*), prove its worth, stand the test, work well (*as ideas*), hold good (*as principles*); ***sich nicht –,*** (*of a p. or th.*) fail, prove a failure; (*of a th.*) not stand up to the test, turn out not to be true.

bewährt [bəˈvɛːrt], *adj.* proved, proven, well-tried, established, approved (*as a remedy etc.*), trustworthy, old and trusted, trusty, tried (*friend etc.*), well-established, of long standing (*as friendship etc.*), experienced (*exponent*).

bewahrheiten [bəˈvaːrhaɪtən], *v.r.* prove (to be) true, come true; ***sich nicht –,*** prove (to be) false.

Bewahrung [bəˈvaːruŋ], *f.* preservation, conservation.

Bewährung [bəˈvɛːruŋ], *f.* trial, testing; rehabilitation; (*Law*) probation. **Bewährungs|einheit,** *f.* (*Mil.*) rehabilitation unit. **–frist,** *f.* (*Law*) probation (under suspended sentence). **–helfer,** *m.* probation officer. **–probe,** *f.* test; ***die – der Zeit bestehen,*** stand the test of time.

bewaldet [bəˈvaldət], *adj.* woody, wooded. **Bewaldung,** *f.* afforestation; forests, woods.

bewältigen [bəˈvɛltɪgən], *v.t.* conquer, master (*difficulties*), overcome, surmount (*obstacles*), accomplish, manage (*a task*); (*of a horse etc.*) clear (*a fence*), (*of a climber*) reach the top of (*a mountain*).

bewandern [bəˈvandərn], *v.t.* walk *or* hike through (*a district*), travel over *or* cover (*on foot*). **bewandert,** *adj.* (*fig.*) well-informed, well-versed, proficient, (*coll.*) well up (***in*** (*Dat.*), in), knowledgeable (about), with a thorough knowledge (of), conversant, (*coll.*) perfectly at home (with).

bewandt [bəˈvant], *adj.* (*in phrase*) ***wie es damit*** or ***darum – ist,*** how the matter stands, what the real case is, what the facts of the case are. **Bewandtnis,** *f.* (-, *pl.* **-se**) (special) circumstances, peculiarity; ***was es auch damit für eine – hat,*** be the case as it may, however matters really stand; ***es hat damit eine ganz andere –,*** that's quite another story, that's s.th. quite different; ***es hat damit folgende –,*** the matter is as follows, it has this peculiarity; ***damit hat es seine eigene*** or ***besondere –,*** the circumstances of the case are peculiar, thereby hangs a tale.

bewarb [bəˈvarp], *see* **bewerben.**

bewarf [bəˈvarf], *see* **bewerfen.**

bewässern [bəˈvɛsərn], *v.t.* water, irrigate. **Bewässerung,** *f.* irrigation; water supply. **Bewässerungsanlage,** *f.* irrigation works *or* system.

bewegbar [bəˈveːkbaːr], *adj.* movable. *See* **beweglich,** 2.

[1]**bewegen** [bəˈveːgən], **1.** *v.t.* move; stir, agitate, move, affect (*feelings*); stir, occupy (*one's mind*); ***sich zum Mitleid – lassen,*** be moved to pity; ***–de Geschichte,*** pathetic *or* moving *or* touching story; ***–de Kraft,*** motive power. **2.** *v.r.* move (about), stir, be in motion; take exercise; ***sich auf und nieder*** or ***ab –,*** work up and down (*as a piston*); ***sich in gebildeten Kreisen –,*** move in good society; ***die Erde bewegt sich um die Sonne,*** the earth revolves around the sun.

[2]**bewegen,** *irr.v.t.* induce, persuade, prevail upon; get, bring, prompt, move (*s.o.*) (***zu etwas*** or ***dazu etwas zu tun,*** to do s.th.), make (*s.o.*) (do s.th.); ***sich bewogen fühlen,*** feel inclined (***zu etwas*** or ***etwas zu tun,*** to do s.th.), feel like (doing s.th.).

Beweg|grund, *m.* motive (*Gen. or* ***für,*** for). **–kraft,** *f. See* **Bewegungskraft.**

beweglich [bəˈveːklɪç], *adj.* 1. (*able to move*) movable, mobile, (*Biol.*) motile; (*Eccl.*) ***–es Fest,*** movable feast; (*Mil.*) ***–e Kolonne,*** mobile column; (*Mil.*) ***–es Feuer,*** shifting fire; ***–e Sandbank,*** shifting sands; 2. (*able to be moved*) movable, moving; portable; ***–e Teile,*** moving parts (*of machine*); ***–e Typen,*** movable type; (*Law*) ***–es Eigentum*** or ***Gut, –e Habe, –e Güter*** or ***Effekten,*** movables, movable property *or* effects, personal estate; ***frei – sein,*** be free to move; 3. (*fig.*) mobile (*features*), flexible, pliable, pliant (*attitudes*), active, nimble, versatile (*mind*); manœuvrable (*vehicle*); ***geistig –,*** with an active mind; ***–e Preise,*** flexible prices; 4. moving, touching (*entreaties etc.*). **Beweglichkeit,** *f.* ability to move, power of movement, mobility, flexibility, agility, sprightliness, nimbleness, versatility, manœuvrability.

bewegt [bəˈveːkt], *adj.* agitated, moved; lively, animated (*as conversation etc.*); adventurous, eventful, colourful (*life*); stirring, exciting, stormy, troubled (*times*); ***–e See,*** heavy seas, rough sea.

Bewegung [bəˈveːɡuŋ], *f.* 1. movement (*also of stars etc.*), motion; ***in – sein,*** (*of a th.*) be moving *or* in motion; (*of a p.*) be on the move *or* the go, be in a state of activity; ***in – setzen,*** (*a th.*) set in action, set going, start, actuate; (*coll.*) get (*a p.*) moving, make (*a p.*) get a move on; ***alles*** or ***Himmel und Erde in – setzen,*** move heaven and earth, leave no stone unturned; ***alle Hebel in – setzen,*** pull every string, set every spring into motion; ***sich in – setzen,*** (*of a th.*) start moving, start to move, start off, begin working, come into action; (*of a p.*) move *or* set off, start to move, (*coll.*) make a move; ***rückläufige –,*** retrogression, (*Astr.*) retrogradation; ***dauernde –,*** perpetual motion; 2. (physical) exercise; ***sich*** (*Dat.*) ***– verschaffen,*** take exercise; 3. movement, move, action, gesture; ***sie machte eine – zum Fenster,*** she made a move towards the window; ***eine – der Ungeduld,*** a gesture of impatience; (*fig.*) ***eine politische –,*** a political movement; (*fig.*) ***dramatische –,*** dramatic action; 4. emotion, feelings; ***ihre Stimme zitterte vor –,*** her voice trembled with emotion; ***er konnte seine innere – nicht verbergen,*** he couldn't hide his agitation.

Bewegungs|achse, *f.* axis of rotation. **–antrieb,** *m.* impulse, impulsion, impelling force, propulsion, propelling force. **–aufnahme,** *f.* (*Phot.*) action shot. **–ebene,** *f.* plane of motion. **–empfindung,** *f.* (*Physiol.*) kinesthesia. **–energie,** *f.* kinetic energy. **–fähigkeit,** *f.* mobility, (*Biol.*) motility, ability to move, power of locomotion. **–freiheit,** *f.* freedom of movement, room to move; (*fig.*) liberty of action; (*Mil.*) freedom of manœuvre. **–kraft,** *f.* motive power *or* force. **–krieg,** *m.* mobile *or* open warfare, war of movement *or* manœuvre. **–lehre,** *f.* theory of motion, kinetics. **bewegungslos,** *adj.* still, motionless, immobile. **Bewegungs|möglichkeit,** *f.* possibility of movement; room *or* scope for action. **–nerv,** *m.* motor nerve. **–organ,** *n.* motory organ. **–spiel,** *n.* athletic *or* active games. **–störung,** *f.* (*Med.*) ataxia. **–studien,** *f.pl.* motion study.

bewehren [bəˈveːrən], *v.t.* arm (*a p.*), fortify (*a place*); reinforce (*concrete*); armour (*a cable*). **bewehrt,** *adj.* armed; armoured (*cable*), reinforced (*concrete*); (*Her.*) armed, with claws, horned, attired. **Bewehrung,** *f.* arming, fortification; reinforcement (*of concrete*), armouring (*on cables*).

beweibt [bəˈvaɪpt], *adj.* wedded, married (*of men*).

beweihräuchern [bəˈvaɪrɔyçərn], *v.t.* (*Eccl.*) cense (*altar etc.*); (*coll.*) lay it on thick *or* on with a trowel, butter (*a p.*) up. **Beweihräucherung,** *f.* (*coll.*) fawning, back-scratching, honeyed words, soft soap.

beweinen [bəˈvaɪnən], *v.t.* mourn *or* lament (for *or* over); bewail, bemoan (*loss, one's lot etc.*); shed tears over, cry *or* weep over. **beweinenswert,** *adj.* deplorable, pitiable, lamentable.

Beweis [bəˈvaɪs], *m.* (**-es,** ***pl.*** **-e**) 1. proof (***für,*** of); ***den – antreten*** or ***erbringen*** or ***führen*** or ***liefern,*** offer proof, prove; ***unter – stellen,*** provide proof of; ***eindeutiger*** or ***schlagender*** or ***schlüssiger*** or ***stichhaltiger –,*** conclusive *or* irrefutable *or* (*coll.*) cast-iron proof; 2. substantiation, demonstration (*Gen.*, of); ***zum –*** (*Gen.*), to prove, in proof of, by way of proof; 3. (*oft. pl.*) (piece of) evidence, argument, proof; ***ein schlüssiger*** or ***zwingender –,*** a conclusive argument; ***ein hinkender –,*** a lame argument; ***schriftliche*** or ***urkundliche –e,*** written *or* documentary evidence, documentary proof; ***zulässiger –,*** admissible evidence; ***–e*** or ***einen – anführen*** or ***beibringen*** or ***liefern,*** adduce *or* furnish *or* produce *or* submit *or* supply evidence; (*Law*) ***– des ersten Anscheins,*** prima facie evidence; ***aus Mangel an –en,*** on grounds of insufficient evidence; 4. proof, sign, mark, token (*of friendship, good-will etc.*).

Beweisaufnahme [bəˈvaɪsˀaufnaːmə], *f.* hearing of evidence. **beweisbar,** *adj.* demonstrable, provable.

beweisen [bəˈvaɪzən], **1.** *irr.v.t.* prove, show, demonstrate (the truth of), substantiate (*a statement etc.*), make good (*a claim*); (*of a p.*) prove, show, demonstrate, show *or* give proof *or* evidence of (*some quality*); (*of a th. or action*) prove, show, be a mark *or* sign of, give evidence of (*some quality in the doer*). **2.** *irr.v.r.* prove *or* show o.s. (***als,*** to be).

Beweis|erhebung, *f. See* **–aufnahme. –fähigkeit,** *f.* (*Law*) validity (as evidence). **–führung,** *f.* (line of) argument, argumentation, (line of) reasoning, (*Law*) marshalling of evidence. **–grund,** *m.* argument, reason(s). **–kraft,** *f.* cogency, conviction, (*Law*) probative weight; ***der Zeuge hat hier keine –,*** witness's evidence is inconclusive. **beweiskräftig,** *adj.* conclusive, convincing, cogent. **Beweis|last,** *f.* burden *or* onus of proof. **–material,** *n.* (*Law*) (probative) evidence. **–mittel,** *n.* (*Law*) (piece of) evidence. **–nachholung,** *f.* (*Law*) introduction of new evidence. **–stelle,** *f.* illustrative quotation, quotation *or* illustration in establishment of proof. **–stück,** *n.* (piece of) evidence, (*Law*) exhibit.

bewenden [bəˈvɛndən], *v.i.* (*used only in inf. with* ***lassen***) ***es dabei*** or ***damit – lassen,*** let it rest at that, leave it as it is, leave it at that, let it be, let it take its course; rest satisfied with it as it is. **Bewenden,** *n.* ***dabei*** or ***damit hatte es sein –,*** there the matter rested.

bewerben [bəˈvɛrbən], *irr.v.r.* apply (***um,*** for; ***bei,*** to); compete (for) (*a prize*); ask (for) (*girl's hand*), propose (to) (*a girl*). **Bewerber,** *m.* applicant, candidate (for), aspirant (to); competitor (for); suitor, wooer. **Bewerbung,** *f.* application, candidature; competition. **Bewerbungs|formular,** *n.* application form. **–schreiben,** *n.* (letter of) application.

bewerfen [bəˈvɛrfən], *irr.v.t.* 1. ***ihn mit etwas –,*** throw *or* fling s.th. at him, pelt him with s.th.; 2. rough-cast, parget, plaster (*a wall*).

bewerkstelligen [bəˈvɛrkʃtɛlɪɡən], *v.t.* manage, effect, accomplish, bring about, achieve, contrive.

bewerten [bəˈveːrtən], *v.t.* value, estimate, assess; rate, appraise; ***zu hoch –,*** overrate, overestimate; ***zu niedrig –,*** underrate, underestimate. **Bewertung,** *f.* valuation, estimation, appraisal, assessment.

Bewetterung [bəˈvɛtəruŋ], *f.* air conditioning, forced ventilation.

bewickeln [bəˈvɪkəln], *v.t.* wrap, envelop (***mit,*** with).

bewilligen [bəˈvɪlɪɡən], *v.t.* grant, concede, agree *or* consent to, allow, permit, sanction; ***bewilligt werden,*** be granted *or* sanctioned *or* carried. **Bewilligung,** *f.* grant, allowance; permit; permission, consent, sanction.

bewillkommnen [bəˈvɪlkɔmnən], *v.t.* welcome, greet. **Bewillkommnung,** *f.* welcome; reception.

bewimpert [bəˈvɪmpərt], *adj.* (*Bot., Physiol.*) ciliate.

bewinden [bəˈvɪndən], *irr.v.t.* entwine.

bewirken [bəˈvɪrkən], *v.t.* effect, cause, occasion, bring about, produce.

bewirten [bəˈvɪrtən], *v.t.* entertain, give hospitality to, regale.

bewirtschaften [bəˈvɪrtʃaftən], *v.t.* manage, work (*a farm*), run (*a hotel etc.*), cultivate (*a field*), farm (*land*); control (*currency, goods etc.*), ration (*food*). **Bewirtschaftung,** *f.* cultivation (*of land*), management (*of farm etc.*); control, rationing (*of goods, food etc.*).

Bewirtung [bəˈvɪrtuŋ], *f.* hospitality, entertainment; service (*in hotel etc.*).

Bewitterung [bəˈvɪtəruŋ], *f.* weathering, exposure.

bewitzeln [bəˈvɪtsəln], *v.t.* ridicule, hold up to

ridicule; deride, make derisive remarks about; mock, scoff *or* jeer at; make fun of.

bewog [bəˈvoːk], **bewöge** [bəˈvøːgə], **bewogen** [bəˈvoːgən], *see* ²**bewegen.**

bewohnbar [bəˈvoːnbaːr], *adj.* (in)habitable, fit to live in, fit for habitation; ***nicht –,*** uninhabitable. **Bewohnbarkeit,** *f.* fitness for habitation, habitable condition.

bewohnen [bəˈvoːnən], *v.t.* (*of a group*) inhabit, live in (*a country, a house etc.*); (*of a p.*) live in, occupy (*house etc.*). **Bewohner,** *m.* inhabitant; occupant, occupier (*of house*); resident (*of district*); (*Poet.*) denizen (*of the air etc.*). **–bewohner,** *m.* (*suff.*) inhabitant of, –dweller; (*Nat. Hist.*) (*animal*) that lives in, (*plant*) that grows in.

bewölken [bəˈvœlkən], **1.** *v.t.* cloud, darken. **2.** *v.r.* become cloudy *or* overcast, cloud over; (*fig.*) become clouded (*of the mind*). **bewölkt,** *adj.* clouded, cloudy, overcast. **Bewölkung,** *f.* clouds; clouding, cloudiness.

beworben [bəˈvɔrbən], *see* **bewerben.**

Bewunderer [bəˈvundərə], *m.* admirer. **bewundern,** *v.t.* admire. **bewunderns|wert, –würdig,** *adj.* admirable. **Bewunderung,** *f.* admiration.

Bewurf [bəˈvurf], *m.* plastering; plaster, rough-cast, stucco.

bewürfe [bəˈvyːrfə], *see* **bewerfen.**

bewurzeln [bəˈvurtsəln], *v.r.* strike *or* take root.

bewußt [bəˈvust], *adj.* 1. conscious, intentional, deliberate; 2. agreed, fixed, afore-mentioned, in question; ***die –en Leute,*** the people in question; 3. ***sich*** (*Dat.*) ***etwas*** (*Gen.*) ***– sein*** (***werden***), be (become) aware *or* conscious of a th.; ***es*** or ***ich wurde mir –,*** it occurred to me, it dawned on me, it came to my mind. **Bewußtheit,** *f.* consciousness, awareness.

bewußtlos [bəˈvustlos], *adj.* unconscious, insensible, senseless. **Bewußtlosigkeit,** *f.* unconsciousness, insensibility.

Bewußtsein [bəˈvustzaɪn], *n.* (state of) consciousness; awareness; ***bei – sein,*** be conscious; ***zu – kommen,*** become conscious; ***wieder zu – kommen,*** recover *or* regain consciousness, (*coll.*) come to *or* round; ***ihm zum – kommen,*** occur to him, come to his mind, dawn on him; ***ihm etwas zum – bringen,*** make him aware *or* conscious of s.th.; ***ihn wieder zum – bringen,*** bring him round. **Bewußtseins|inhalt,** *m.* conscious experience. **–kunst,** *f.* stream-of-consciousness technique (*in writing*).

bezahlbar [bəˈtsaːlbaːr], *adj.* payable.

bezahlen [bəˈtsaːlən], *v.t.* pay (*money*), pay off, repay (*a debt*), settle, discharge, pay (*a debt, bill etc.*), honour, cash (*a bill of exchange*); pay for (*goods*); pay, remunerate (*a p.*); ***bar –,*** pay cash *or* ready money; ***auf Heller und Pfennig –,*** pay to the last penny; ***die Zeche –,*** pay the bill, (*coll. fig.*) foot the bill, take the consequences; ***eine Runde –,*** pay for *or* (*coll.*) stand a round of drinks; ***im voraus –,*** pay for in advance, prepay; ***bezahlte Arbeit,*** paid work; ***das ist teuer bezahlt,*** that is expensive *or* (*coll.*) a stiff price; (*fig.*) (I've, he's *etc.*) paid dearly; (*of a th.*) ***sich bezahlt machen,*** pay; ***Ehrlichkeit macht sich bezahlt,*** honesty pays (in the end); ***die Arbeit wird sich mir bezahlt machen,*** the work will pay for itself. **Bezahlung,** *f.* payment (*of money, of a debt, of a p.*), settlement, discharge (*of a debt*), pay, remuneration (*of a p.*); ***gegen –,*** against *or* on payment.

bezähmen [bəˈtsɛːmən], **1.** *v.t.* tame; curb, check, control, master, restrain, subdue, overcome, suppress; ***seine Zunge –,*** put a curb *or* bridle on *or* curb *or* bridle one's tongue. **2.** *v.r.* control *or* restrain o.s.

bezahnt [bəˈtsaːnt], *adj.* toothed, indented.

bezaubern [bəˈtsaubərn], *v.t.* bewitch, enchant; fascinate. **Bezauberung,** *f.* fascination, charm; enchantment, spell.

bezeichnen [bəˈtsaɪçnən], *v.t.* 1. (put a) mark (on); signpost (*a path*), notch, blaze (*trees*); mark, indicate, (*fig.*) be indicative of; (*fig.*) appoint, fix (*time, place etc.*); ***an dem bezeichneten Tag,*** on the appointed day; 2. designate, name, refer to, describe (***mit,*** by); indicate, represent (***durch,*** by); ***die unbekannte Größe mit x –,*** designate the unknown quantity by (the letter) x, call the unknown quantity x; ***Zahlen durch Buchstaben –,*** represent *or* indicate numbers by letters; 3. denote, signify, mean; ***x bezeichnet eine unbekannte Größe,*** x denotes *or* signifies an unknown quantity; ***genau –,*** specify, give precise details of. **bezeichnend,** *adj.* indicative, significant; characteristic, typical (***für,*** of). **Bezeichnung,** *f.* 1. indication, representation; ***genaue*** or ***nähere –,*** detailed description, specification; 2. mark, sign, symbol; name, designation, term, expression; description, title (*of a p. etc.*); ***falsche –,*** wrong term, misnomer; ***treffende –,*** apt description. **Bezeichnungsweise,** *f.* nomenclature, (*Math., Mus.*) notation.

bezeigen [bəˈtsaɪgən], *v.t.* show, exhibit, give signs of, manifest, display, express, profess; ***ihm Ehre –,*** honour him, do *or* pay honour to him. **Bezeigung,** *f.* manifestation, display, exhibition, demonstration, expression.

bezeugen [bəˈtsɔygən], *v.t.* attest, testify (to), bear witness *or* testimony to, provide evidence *or* proof of. **Bezeugung,** *f.* testimony; attestation. *See also* **Bezeigung.**

bezichtigen [bəˈtsɪçtɪgən], *v.t.* accuse (*Gen.,* of), charge (with).

beziehen [bəˈtsiːən], **1.** *irr.v.t.* 1. cover (*furniture, cushions etc.*); string (*a violin etc.*); ***die Betten –,*** change the bed-linen; ***einen Knopf –,*** cover a button; ***bezogener Knopf,*** covered button; ***bezogener Himmel,*** overcast *or* cloudy sky; 2. go to, enter (*a university*), take up (*a position*); move into, occupy (*a house*); ***sofort zu –,*** vacant possession, ready for immediate occupation; ***die Wache –,*** mount guard; 3. get (supplies), buy (***bei*** or ***von,*** from), be supplied with (by), subscribe to (*a newspaper etc.*); draw (*rations, income etc.*); (*Comm.*) draw (a bill) on (*a p.*), draw on (*an account*); ***zu – durch,*** obtainable from, stocked by; ***die Waren aus Birmingham –,*** procure *or* obtain the goods from Birmingham; ***er bezog eine Ohrfeige,*** he got a box on the ears; *see* **bezogen**; 4. ***– auf*** (*Acc.*), relate *or* refer to, connect *or* link up with, take in relation to *or* connection with; assign to, intend *or* mean for, aim at; ***falsch –,*** draw the wrong inference; (*of two things*) ***aufeinander –,*** relate with one another, bring into relationship (with one another), correlate. **2.** *irr.v.r.* 1. become cloudy *or* overcast, cloud over; 2. (*of a p.*) refer (***auf*** (*Acc.*), to); (*of a th.*) refer, have reference, be relevant, be related, bear a relation, relate (to); be aimed (at) *or* meant *or* intended (for). **Bezieher,** *m.* drawer (*of a bill*); buyer, importer (*of goods*); subscriber, customer.

Beziehung [bəˈtsiːuŋ], *f.* 1. relation(ship), connection; ***– haben*** or ***in – stehen,*** be related, bear a relation, have reference (***zu,*** to); ***keine – haben*** or ***in keiner – stehen,*** bear no relation, be out of all relation (***zu,*** to); ***in enge – zueinander bringen*** or ***setzen,*** bring into close relationship; ***in – zueinander stehen,*** be connected, be bound up with one another; ***ohne – zu,*** without any bearing *or* having no bearing on, without reference to, irrelevant to; ***wechselseitige –,*** interrelation, correlation; 2. regard, respect; ***in – auf*** (*Dat.*), with regard *or* respect to; ***in jeder –,*** in every way *or* respect, in all respects; ***in anderer –,*** in other respects, otherwise; ***in dramatischer –,*** from a dramatic point of view, dramatically; *see* **Bezug**; 3. *pl.* connection, relations, intercourse (*between persons*); similarities, affinities, correspondences, connections (*between things*); ***–en aufnehmen*** or ***in –en treten,*** enter into *or* establish relations (***zu,*** with); ***–en haben*** or ***unterhalten,*** have relations *or* dealings (***zu,*** with); ***in guten –en stehen,*** be on good terms (***zu,*** with); ***geschäftliche –en,*** business relations; ***gespannte –en,*** strained relations; (***gute***) ***–en haben,*** have good connections *or* influential friends *or* influence; ***mit –en erreicht man alles,*** you can do anything by pulling strings *or* with a little string-pulling. **Beziehungsfürwort,** *n.* (*Gram.*) relative pronoun. **beziehungslos,** *adj.* unconnected, unrelated, irrelevant. **Beziehungssatz,** *m.* relative clause. **beziehungsweise** (*abbr.* **bzw.**), *adv.* respectively, or, or . . . as the case may be; in certain respects, relatively. **Beziehungswort,** *n.* (*Gram.*) antecedent.

beziffern [bə'tsɪfərn], **1.** *v.t.* 1. number, mark with figures; (*Mus.*) ***bezifferter Baß,*** figured bass; 2. assess, estimate, (*coll.*) put (***auf*** (*Acc.*), at). **2.** *v.r.* amount (***auf*** (*Acc.*), to). **Bezifferung,** *f.* numbering, numbers.

Bezirk [bə'tsɪrk], *m.* (**-(e)s,** *pl.* **-e**) 1. (administrative) district (*approx.* = *Engl.* county), region; (postal) district (*of large towns, esp. Vienna*); (electoral) constituency; 2. (*fig.*) sphere, province, field, domain (*of knowledge etc.*). **Bezirks|amt,** *n.* local government offices; local authority. **-gericht,** *n.* county court. **-kommando,** *n.* (*Mil.*) district command. **-postamt,** *n.* district head (post-)office. **-regierung,** *f.* local government authority, county council, borough council.

bezog [bə'tso:k], **bezöge** [bə'tsø:gə], *see* **beziehen.** **bezogen,** *adj.* related, relative; ***wechselseitig*** or ***aufeinander* –,** interrelated, correlative. **Bezogene(r),** *m., f.* (*Comm.*) drawee, acceptor (*of a bill*). **Bezogenheit,** *f.* relativity, relatedness.

Bezug [bə'tsu:k], *m.* 1. occupation (*of house or* (*Mil.*) *of position*); ***fertig zum* –,** ready for occupation; 2. (loose) cover, covering (*for furniture, cushions etc.*), (pillow-*etc.*)case, pillow-slip; (set of) strings (*for violin etc.*); 3. purchase (*of goods*), subscription (*to newspaper*), drawing (*of salary, rations etc.*); ***bei* – *von,*** with order for *or* of; 4. reference; **–** ***haben*** or ***nehmen auf*** (*Acc.*), (*of a p.*) refer to; (*of a th.*) relate *or* refer to; bear a relation, be related *or* have reference to; ***in bezug auf*** (*Acc.*), with respect *or* regard *or* reference to, in respect of, respecting, regarding, concerning, as regards *or* concerns, as to, relative to, in connection with, as far as . . . (is, was *etc.*) concerned; *see* **beziehen**; 5. *pl.* earnings, emoluments; (*Comm.*) orders, purchases.

bezüglich [bə'tsy:klɪç], **1.** *adj.* relating, relative, relevant, referring (***auf*** (*Acc.*), to); ***–es Fürwort,*** relative pronoun. **2.** *prep.* (*Gen.*) with respect *or* regard to, respecting, regarding, concerning, as to, about, in connection with, relative to, as far as . . . (is, was *etc.*) concerned.

Bezugnahme [bə'tsu:kna:mə], *f.* (*Comm.*) ***unter* – *auf*** (*Acc.*), with reference to, respecting.

Bezugs|anweisung, *f.* order to deliver; authorization to collect. **-bedingungen,** *f.pl.* terms *or* conditions of supply *or* delivery. **-dauer,** *f.* delivery time. **-ebene,** *f.* datum level. **-linie,** *f.* reference *or* datum line. **-marke,** *f.* ration coupon. **-preis,** *m.* subscription price (*of newspaper etc.*). **-punkt,** *m.* point of reference, datum point. **-quelle,** *f.* source of supply, supplier. **Bezug(s)-schein,** *m.* permit; licence (*for raw materials*), ration card *or* coupon, priority voucher (*for controlled goods, petrol etc.*), (*Mil.*) indent form.

bezwecken [bə'tsvɛkən], *v.t.* (*of a p.*) aim at, have in view *or* mind, intend; (*of a th.*) aim at, have as *or* for an object.

bezweifeln [bə'tsvaɪfəln], *v.t.* doubt, have one's doubts about, be doubtful of *or* about *or* as to, question, call in question; ***nicht zu* –,** beyond doubt, beyond all question, indubitable, unquestionable.

bezwingbar [bə'tsvɪŋba:r], *adj.* conquerable; controllable.

bezwingen [bə'tsvɪŋən], **1.** *irr.v.t.* overcome, conquer, vanquish, subdue; master, control, get the better of. **2.** *irr.v.r.* restrain *or* control o.s. *or* one's feelings, keep o.s. *or* one's feelings under control. **Bezwinger,** *m.* conqueror, subduer, vanquisher. **Bezwingung,** *f.* conquest.

Bibel ['bi:bəl], *f.* (-, *pl.* **-n**) Bible; Holy Scriptures. **Bibel|auslegung,** *f.* exegesis *or* interpretation of the Bible. **bibelfest,** *adj.* versed in the Scriptures. **Bibel|forscher,** *m.* Jehovah's Witness. **-kritik,** *f.* biblical criticism. **-kunde,** *f.* biblical research. **-lehre,** *f.* scriptural doctrine. **-sprache,** *f.* scriptural language. **-spruch,** *m.* (biblical) text. **-stelle,** *f.* biblical passage; text; lesson (*read in church*). **-stunde,** *f.* Bible class; scripture lesson.

Biber ['bi:bər], *m.* beaver, castor. **Biber|bau,** *m.* beaver's lodge. **-baum,** *m.* magnolia. **-fell,** *n.* beaver skin. **-geil,** *n.* castor(eum). **-hut,** *m.* beaver (hat). **-nell(e),** *f.* (*Bot.*) burnet saxifrage (*Pimpinella*). **-ratte,** *f.* coyp(o)u (*rat*); nutria (*fur*). **-schwanz,** *m.* 1. beaver's tail; 2. flat roofing tile. **-wehr,** *f.* beaver dam. **-zahn,** *m.* projecting tooth.

Bibliograph [biblio'gra:f], *m.* (**-en,** *pl.* **-en**) bibliographer. **Bibliographie** [–'fi:], *f.* bibliography. **bibliographisch,** *adj.* bibliographic(al).

Bibliothek [biblio'te:k], *f.* (-, *pl.* **-en**) library. **Bibliothekar** [–'ka:r], *m.* (**-s,** *pl.* **-e**) librarian. **bibliothekarisch,** *adj.* library, librarian's. **Bibliotheks|wesen,** *n.* librarianship. **-wissenschaft,** *f.* (study of) librarianship.

biblisch ['bi:blɪʃ], *adj.* biblical, scriptural; ***–e Geschichte,*** scripture; ***–e Geschichten,*** Bible stories.

Bickbeere ['bɪkbe:rə], *f.* (*dial.*) bilberry, whortleberry (*Vaccinium myrtillus*).

bieder ['bi:dər], *adj.* 1. upright, honest, trustworthy; staunch, worthy, trusty; 2. simple-minded, gullible, ingenuous. **Biederkeit,** *f.* 1. uprightness, trustworthiness, honesty, integrity; staunchness, worthiness, trustiness; 2. simple-mindedness, gullibility, ingenuousness. **Bieder|mann,** *m.* man of worth *or* integrity; man of honour; *pl.* (*iron.*) worthies, philistines. **-meier,** *n.* homely *or* Early Victorian style. **-meierzeit,** *f.* Early Victorian period (*in Germany* 1820–48).

biegbar [bi:k'ba:r], *adj.* pliable, flexible; ductile, malleable (*metal*); (*Gram.*) declinable. **Biegbarkeit,** *f.* pliability, flexibility; ductility, malleability (*of metal*); (*Gram.*) ability to decline *or* inflect.

Biege ['bi:gə], *f.* curve, curvature, bend. *See* **biegen.** **Biege|eisen,** *n.* tyre-lever. **-festigkeit,** *f.* bending strength.

biegen ['bi:gən], **1.** *irr.v.t.* bend, curve, crook (*finger*), flex (*limb*); (*Gram.*) decline, inflect; ***das Recht* –,** misrepresent the law, pervert justice; ***die Wahrheit* –,** twist *or* distort the truth. *See* **gebogen.** **2.** *irr.v.i.* (*aux.* s.), *v.r.* bend, curve, wind; be curved *or* bent, warp (*as wood*), bulge, buckle; turn (***um,*** round); incline, sag, bend, (*coll.*) give (*under strain*); ***sich vor Lachen* –,** double up with laughter; ***sich vor Höflichkeit* –, *sich schmiegen und* –,** cringe, bow and scrape; ***lügen daß sich die Balken* –,** lie like a trooper; (*coll.*) ***auf Biegen oder Brechen,*** by hook or by crook, willy-nilly. **Biegespannung,** *f.* bending stress.

biegsam ['bi:kza:m], *adj.* flexible, pliant, pliable; supple; lithe (*limbs*); ductile (*metal*); limp (*binding of books*); (*fig.*) yielding, docile, tractable (*character*). **Biegsamkeit,** *f.* pliancy, pliability, flexibility; ductility; suppleness, litheness; docility.

Biegung ['bi:gʊŋ], *f.* curve, curvature; bend, wind, turn, turning; (*Geol.*) flexure, (*Gram.*) inflexion, declension. **Biegungsbeanspruchung,** *f.* *See* **Biegespannung.** **biegungsfähig,** *adj.* (*Gram.*) declinable. **Biegungsfestigkeit,** *f.* *See* **Biegefestigkeit.**

Biene ['bi:nə], *f.* bee; (*Astr.*) Apis, the Bee (*a southern constellation*); ***faule*** or ***männliche* –,** drone.

Bienen|brut, *f.* larvae of bees. **-fang,** *m.* *See* **-saug.** **-fresser,** *m.* (*Orn.*) bee-eater (*Merops apiaster*). **-harz,** *n.*, **-kitt,** *m.* bee-glue, hive dross, propolis. **-königin,** *f.* queen-bee. **-korb,** *m.* beehive. **-kraut,** *n.* thyme. **-pest,** *f.* foul brood. **-raubwespe,** *f.* *See* **-wespe.** **-saug,** *m.* (*Bot.*) white dead-nettle (*Lamium*). **-schwarm,** *m.* swarm of bees. **-stachel,** *m.* bee's sting (*organ*). **-stand,** *m.* apiary. **-stich,** *m.* 1. bee-sting; 2. (kind of) cake. **-stock,** *m.* beehive. **-vater,** *m.* bee-keeper. **-wabe,** *f.* honeycomb. **-wachs,** *n.* beeswax. **-weisel,** *m.* queen-bee. **-wespe,** *f.* robber wasp. **-zelle,** *f.* cell (*in honeycomb*), alveole. **bienenzellig,** *adj.* honeycombed, alveolar, alveolate. **Bienen|zucht,** *f.* bee-keeping, bee-farming, apiculture. **-züchter,** *m.* bee-keeper, apiarist.

Bier [bi:r], *n.* **(-(e)s,** *pl.* **-e)** beer; ale; ***helles –,*** light *or* pale ale; ***dunkles –,*** dark *or* brown ale; ***beim – sitzen,*** sit over one's beer; ***etwas wie saures – ausbieten,*** get rid of s.th. with difficulty, have s.th. hanging on one's hands; ***– vom Faß,*** beer on tap *or* on draught.

Bier|bauch, *m.* pot-belly, paunch. **–brauer,** *m.* brewer. **–brauerei,** *f.* brewery. **–bruder,** *m.* heavy drinker, toper. **–eifer,** *m.* (*coll.*) excessive zeal. **biereifrig,** *adj.* over-zealous, most studious. **Bier|essig,** *m.* malt vinegar. **–faß,** *n.* beer-barrel. **–filz,** *m.* table mat. **–garten,** *m.* beer-garden, open-air restaurant. **–hahn,** *m.* tap, spigot. **–heber,** *m.* beer-engine, beer-pump. **–hefe,** *f.* barm, brewers' yeast. **–idee,** *f.* (*coll.*) crazy idea. **–kanne,** *f.* tankard. **–karren,** *m.* (brewers') dray. **–kneipe,** *f.* ale-house, (*coll.*) pub. **–komment,** *m.* students' drinking ritual. **–krug,** *m.* mug, pot. **–kutscher,** *m.* (brewers') drayman. **–lokal,** *n.* *See* **–stube.** **–reise,** *f.* (*sl.*) pub-crawl. **–schwengel,** *m.* *See* **–heber.** **–seidel,** *n.* beer-glass, beer-mug. **–stube,** *f.* tap-room, bar. **–tonne,** *f.* beer-barrel; (*coll.*) pot-bellied fellow. **–wirtschaft,** *f.* public house, alehouse. **–zapfer,** *m.* tapster. **–zeitung,** *f.* comic (and crude) programme at students' smoking concert. **–zipfel,** *m.* pendant (on a watch chain).

Biese ['bi:zə], *f.* braid, piping.

Biesfliege ['bi:sfli:gə], *f.* gad-fly, bot-fly, horse-fly.

[1]**Biest** [bi:st], *m.* *See* **Biestmilch.**

[2]**Biest,** *n.* **(-es,** *pl.* **-er)** beast, creature; (*fig. coll.*) brute (*used partic. of annoying insects, but also, as vulgar abuse, of people*); (*of women*) bitch.

Biestmilch ['bi:stmılç], *f.* beestings.

bieten ['bi:tən], **1.** *irr.v.t.* 1. offer, proffer, tender, give; ***ihm die Hand –,*** hold out one's hand to him; ***ihm einen guten Morgen –,*** wish him a good morning; ***ihm die Stirn –,*** stand up to *or* hold one's own against him; ***dem König Schach –,*** check the king (*chess*); ***ihm Trotz –,*** defy him, bid defiance to him; ***sich*** (*Dat.*) ***alles – lassen,*** submit *or* give way to *or* (*coll.*) put up with everything; ***das lasse ich mir nicht –,*** I won't stand (for) *or* put up with this; ***ein Unglück bietet dem andern die Hand,*** misfortunes never come singly, it never rains but it pours; 2. bid (***auf*** (*Acc.*), for) (*at auctions*); 3. (*fig.*) offer, present, provide, furnish, afford; display, show (*examples, difficulties, opportunities etc.*). **2.** *irr.v.r.* offer *or* present itself; ***wenn sich eine Gelegenheit bietet,*** when an opportunity presents itself *or* arises *or* offers *or* occurs; ***ein wunderschöner Anblick bietet sich dem Augen,*** a splendid view meets one's eyes *or* gaze. **Bieten,** *n.* bidding (*at auctions*). **Bieter,** *m.* bidder.

Bigamie [biga'mi:], *f.* bigamy. **bigamisch** [–'ga:mıʃ], *adj.* bigamous.

Bigarade [biga'ra:də], *f.* bitter *or* Seville orange.

bigott [bi'gɔt], *adj.* bigoted; sanctimonious. **Bigotterie** [–ə'ri:], *f.* bigotry.

Bijouterie [biʒutə'ri:], *f.* (costume) jewellery, trinkets.

Bilanz [bi'lants], *f.* **(-,** *pl.* **-en)** balance; ***die – ziehen,*** strike the balance, balance the books, (*coll., fig.*) take stock; ***eine – aufstellen,*** draw up a balance-sheet. **Bilanz|bogen,** *m.* cash-ruled paper. **–buch,** *n.* balance ledger. **–buchhalter,** *m.* accountant. **bilanzieren** [–'tsi:rən], *v.t.* balance (*an account*). **Bilanz|jahr,** *n.* financial year. **–konto,** *n.* balance-sheet. **–prüfer,** *m.* auditor.

Bild [bılt], *n.* **(-es,** *pl.* **-er)** 1. picture, image, likeness; representation, effigy; ***das gegossene –,*** the cast; graven image; (*Phot.*) ***negatives –,*** negative; ***im –e verbrannt,*** burnt in effigy; ***Gott schuf den Menschen ihm zum –e,*** God created man in His own image; ***anschauliches –,*** graphic description, vivid picture; ***ein sprechend ähnliches –,*** a speaking likeness; 2. portrait; painting, drawing, print; illustration, figure (*in books*); head (*on coin*); (*Math.*) graph; *pl.* (*Cards*) court *or* picture-cards, (*Am.*) face cards; ***zu einem –e sitzen,*** sit for a portrait; ***– oder Wappen,*** heads or tails; ***Karten ohne –er,*** low cards; 3. (*Phot.*) photograph, exposure (*on roll of film*); (*T.V.*) image, picture (*result on the screen*), (*Films, T.V.*) frame (*constituent element producing the result*); (*Theat.*) scene, spectacle; (*Phot.*) ***25 –er in der Sekunde,*** 25 frames per second; ***lebende –er,*** tableaux vivants; (***es bietet sich***) ***ein anderes –,*** the scene changes; 4. image, imagery, metaphor, simile; ***in –ern reden,*** speak figuratively *or* metaphorically; 5. (*fig.*) conception, notion, idea; ***machen Sie sich einmal ein – davon!*** just picture it to yourself! just fancy! (*coll.*) ***ich bin im –e,*** I see, I understand, I am clear about it, I'm in the picture.

Bild|abtaster, *m.* (*T.V.*) scanner. **–abzug,** *m.* (photographic) copy, photostat. **–achat,** *m.* *See* **Bilderachat.** **–anbetung,** *f.* *See* **Bilderanbetung.** **–aufklärung,** *f.* (*Av.*) photographic reconnaissance. **–auflösung,** *f.* definition, resolution. **–ausschnitt,** *m.* detail. **–auswertung,** *f.* interpretation of aerial photographs. **–band,** *n.* 1. book of illustrations, volume of plates; 2. (*T.V.*) video tape. **–bericht,** *m.* documentary film. **–berichterstatter,** *m.* press photographer; news cameraman. **–beschreibung,** *f.* iconography. **–betrachter,** *m.* (slide) viewer (*for colour films*). **–ebene,** *f.* (*Phot.*) focal plane. **–einstellung,** *f.* focusing.

bilden ['bıldən], **1.** *v.t.* 1. form, fashion, shape, mould, model (***aus,*** from *or* out of), construct (*a sentence, examples*), coin (*new words*); ***eine Figur aus Wachs –,*** shape a model in wax; ***die Kinder – einen Kreis,*** the children form a circle; 2. constitute, compose, make (up) (*whole from parts*), set up, form (*committee, government, alliance etc.*), bring up (*rearguard*); 3. educate, train (*a p.*), cultivate, improve, develop (*the mind*). *See* **gebildet. 2.** *v.r.* 1. form, be formed (*as crystals, bubbles etc.*), be produced *or* generated *or* given off (*as steam etc.*); 2. (*fig.*) arise, develop, be created (*as qualities*); ***es bildet ein Talent sich in der Stille,*** talent develops in solitude; 3. educate o.s.; cultivate *or* develop *or* improve one's mind. **bildend,** *adj.* plastic; graphic; ***–e Künste,*** plastic and graphic arts, fine arts (*architecture, sculpture, painting*); ***–er Künstler,*** sculptor, painter, architect.

Bilder|achat, *m.* figured agate. **–anbetung,** *f.* image-worship, idolatry. **–bogen,** *m.* pictorial broadsheet. **–buch,** *n.* picture-book. **–dienst,** *m.* idolatry; photo service. **–fibel,** *f.* illustrated primer. **–galerie,** *f.* picture *or* art gallery. **–geräusch,** *n.* 1. (*Films*) frame noise; 2. (*T.V.*) sound on vision. **–glaser,** *m.* picture-framer.

Bild|erkundung, *f.* *See* **–aufklärung.**

Bilder|leiste, *f.* picture-moulding, picture-rail. **–rätsel,** *n.* picture-puzzle, rebus. **bilderreich,** *adj.* copiously illustrated; figurative, abounding in metaphors, flowery, florid, ornate (*language*). **Bilder|schrift,** *f.* hieroglyphics, picture-language. **–sprache,** *f.* metaphorical language, imagery. **–stürmer,** *m.* iconoclast. **–stürmerei,** *f.* iconoclasm.

Bild|feld, *n.* (*Phot.*) field of view *or* vision. **–fenster,** *n.* (*Films*) picture gate. **–fläche,** *f.* surface of the picture; perspective plane; (*coll.*) ***auf der – erscheinen,*** appear upon the scene; enter the field; come into existence; (*coll.*) ***von der – verschwinden,*** disappear (from sight *or* view), disappear from the scene. **–frequenz,** *f.* (*Films*) camera speed; (*T.V.*) frame *or* picture speed. **–funk,** *m.* phototelegraphy; television. **–gießer,** *m.* bronze-founder. **–hauer,** *m.* sculptor. **–hauerkunst,** *f.* sculpture. **bildhübsch,** *adj.* as pretty as a picture, charming, lovely. **bildlich,** *adj.* pictorial, graphic; figurative, metaphorical. **bildlos,** *adj.* (*Chem.*) amorphous.

Bildner ['bıltnər], *m.* modeller, sculptor; (*fig.*) shaper, moulder, organizer, maker; (*Chem.*) component. **bildnerisch,** *adj.* sculptural.

Bildnis ['bıltnıs], *n.* **(-ses,** *pl.* **-se)** portrait, likeness; image; effigy; head (*on coins*). **Bildnismalerei,** *f.* portraiture.

Bild|plan, *m.* photographic map. **–raum,** *m.* field of vision. **–röhre,** *f.* television *or* cathode-ray tube.

bildsam ['bıltza:m], *adj.* plastic, ductile, flexible,

easy to shape; (*fig.*) educable, adaptive. **Bildsamkeit,** *f.* plasticity, ductility, flexibility; educability, capacity for improvement, adaptiveness.

Bild|säule, *f.* statue; – ***zu Pferde,*** equestrian statue. **–schärfe,** *f.* (*Opt.*) definition, focus. **–schirm,** *m.* (*T.V.*) (television) screen. **–schnitt,** *m.* cutting, editing (*of film*). **–schnitzer,** *m.* (wood-)carver. **–schnitzerei,** *f.* (wood-)carving. **bild|schön,** *adj. See* **–hübsch. Bild|seite,** *f.* face, obverse, head (*of coin*). **–stecher,** *m.* engraver. **–stein,** *m.* figured stone. **–stock,** *m.*, **–stöckel** (*dial.*), *n.* wayside shrine. **–streifen,** *m.* 1. reel of film, film strip; 2. strip cartoon, comic strip. **–strich,** *m.* (*Films*) frame line. **–sucher,** *m.* (*Phot.*) view finder. **–telegraphie,** *f.* photo-telegraphy. **–teppich,** *m.* (figured) tapestry. **–tonkamera,** *f.* sound-film camera. **–tonmaschine,** *f.* sound projector. **–treiben,** *n.* embossing. **–übertragung,** *f. See* **–telegraphie.**

Bildung ['bɪldʊŋ], *f.* 1. formation, forming, creation, production, growth (*of crystals etc.*), generation (*of steam etc.*), coining, coinage (*of new words*); 2. (*of a th.*) form, shape, structure, organization, constitution, (*Geol.*) formation; (*of a p.*) demeanour, features, stature; 3. education, culture; (good) breeding; ***akademische –,*** university education; ***allgemeine –,*** liberal education; ***höhere –,*** secondary education; ***humanistische –,*** classical education.

Bildungs|anstalt, *f.* educational establishment; school. **–arbeit,** *f.* educational work. **–drang,** *m.* desire for self-improvement. **–element,** *n.* constituent, (*Gram.*) formative element. **bildungs|fähig,** *adj.* educable; capable of development. **–feindlich,** *adj.* hostile to culture. **Bildungs|gang,** *m.* course of instruction. **–gewebe,** *n.* (*Bot.*) meristem. **–ideal,** *n.* educational ideal. **–philister,** *m.* narrow-minded intellectual. **–prozeß,** *m.* formative process. **–roman,** *m.* psychological novel. **–silbe,** *f.* (*Gram.*) affix. **–trieb,** *m. See* **–drang. –wesen,** *n.* educational and cultural matters.

Bild|unterschrift, *f.* caption, legend. **–verzerrung,** *f.* distortion (of the image). **–wand,** *f.* (projection) screen. **–wechselfrequenz, –wechselzahl,** *f.* (*T.V.*) picture-frequency. **–weite,** *f.* focal length *or* distance. **–werfer,** *m.* projector, epidiascope, (*obs.*) magic lantern. **–werk,** *n.* 1. picture-book; 2. carvings, sculpture; tapestry-work, embroidery. **–wirker,** *m.* tapestry-weaver. **bildwirksam,** *adj.* photogenic. **Bild|wirkung,** *f.* visual effect. **–zeichen,** *n.* (picture) symbol; (*T.V.*) picture signal. **–zeile,** *f.* (*T.V.*) (scanning) line. **–zeitung,** *f.* illustrated (news)paper. **–zerleger,** *m.* (*T.V.*) scanner. **–zerrung,** *f. See* **–verzerrung. –zuschrift,** *f.* letter (of application) enclosing a photograph.

Billard ['bɪljart], *n.* **(-s,** *pl.* **-s)** billiards; billiard-table. **Billard|kugel,** *f.* billiard-ball. **–kellner,** *m.* marker. **–spiel,** *n.* game of billiards. **–stock,** *m.* cue.

Billett [bɪl'jɛt], *n.* **(-(e)s,** *pl.* **-e)** (*Austr., Swiss*) (railway) ticket.

Billiarde [bɪl'jardə], *f.* a thousand billions, (*Am.*) quadrillion.

billig ['bɪlɪç], *adj.* 1. just, fair, equitable; ***recht und –,*** right and proper; (*Prov.*) ***was dem einen recht ist, ist dem andern –,*** what is sauce for the goose is sauce for the gander; ***das ist nicht mehr als –,*** that is only fair; (*Law*) ***–es Ermessen,*** discretion; 2. cheap, inexpensive, low-priced (*goods*), reasonable, moderate, low (*prices*); ***–e Ausrede,*** weak *or* feeble *or* paltry excuse; ***–es Mädchen,*** cheap *or* common girl; ***– davonkommen,*** get off cheaply *or* lightly.

billigen ['bɪlɪgən], *v.t.* approve (*deed*), approve of (*doing*), sanction, countenance, admit *or* acknowledge the justice of; (*Comm.*) pass (*an account etc.*).

billiger|maßen, –weise, *adv.* fairly, in fairness, justly, with justice.

Billigkeit ['bɪlɪçkaɪt], *f.* 1. justice, equity; fairness; ***der – gemäß,*** in equity; 2. cheapness, reasonableness. **Billigkeits|gericht,** *n.* court of equity. **–gründe,** *m.pl.* reasons of fairness. **–recht,** *n.* equity.

Billigung ['bɪlɪgʊŋ], *f.* approval, consent, sanction, approbation.

Billion [bɪl'jo:n], *f.* billion (= 10^{12}); (*Am.*) trillion.

Bilse ['bɪlsə], *f.* (*Bot.*) bullace (*Prunus insititia*). **Bilsenkraut,** *n.* (*Bot.*) henbane (*Hyoscyamus niger*).

bimbam [bɪm'bam], *int.* ding-dong! (*coll.*) ***heiliger Bimbam!*** dear me! goodness gracious!

Bimmel ['bɪməl], *f.* (-, *pl.* **-n)** little tinkling bell. **Bimmelbahn,** *f.* (*coll.*) (slow) local train. **bimmeln,** *v.i.* tinkle.

Bims [bɪms], *m.* **(-es,** *pl.* **-e)** pumice (stone); (*sl.*) army bread; *pl.* (*Mil. sl.*) square-bashing, (*coll.*) beating, hiding. **bimsen,** *v.t.* rub with pumice-stone; (*Mil. sl.*) drill (*soldiers*) hard; (*coll.*) give (*s.o.*) a good hiding; tan, leather, lay into (*s.o.*); (*coll.*) swot. **Bimsstein,** *m.* pumice-stone; (*Build.*) breeze-block.

bin [bɪn], *see* **sein.**

binär [bi'nɛ:r], *adj.* (*Mus., Chem., Math., Astr.* binary.

Binde ['bɪndə], *f.* 1. band; arm-band, armlet; head-band, fillet; bow-tie; *pl.* wrappings, (*Mil.*) gaiters; ***eine – vor den Augen,*** a bandage over one's eyes; (*coll.*) ***eins hinter die – gießen,*** wet one's whistle; ***die – fiel mir von den Augen,*** the scales fell from my eyes; 2. (roller) bandage; (arm) sling; sanitary towel *or* (*Am.*) napkin; 3. (*Archit.*) fascia (*of architrave*); (*Anat.*) fascia, facial band, aponeurosis (*of muscle*); (*Her.*) fesse.

Binde|balken, *m.* tie beam. **–bogen,** *m.* (*Mus.*) slur, tie. **–festigkeit,** *f.* adhesion. **–garn,** *n.* thread, twine. **–gewebe,** *n.* (*Anat.*) connective tissue. **–glied,** *n.* connecting link. **–haut,** *f.* (*Anat.*) conjunctiva. **–hautentzündung,** *f.* conjunctivitis. **–kalk,** *m.* cement. **–klammer,** *f.* (joiner's) cramp. **–kraft,** *f.* binding *or* bonding power. **–mittel,** *n.* adhesive (cement), binding *or* bonding agent, agglutinant; (*Cul.*) thickening.

binden ['bɪndən], **1.** *irr.v.t.* 1. bind (*also books*), tie up, fasten (up), moor (*boat*), tether (*horse*); ***ihm etwas auf die Seele –,*** impress s.th. on him, beg *or* urge him to do s.th.; (*coll.*) ***ihm etwas auf die Nase –,*** make sure that he gets to know s.th., rub his nose into s.th.; (*coll.*) ***ihm etwas unter die Nase –,*** pull his leg about s.th.; 2. tie (together), join (up), (*Mus.*) tie, slur (*notes*), (*Phonet.*) sound the liaison, (*Chem.*) combine, enter into combination with, absorb (*heat*), (*Build.*) bond, (*Cul.*) thicken (*with flour etc.*); ***sich – lassen,*** thicken (*as soup*); ***eine glückliche Ehe bindet die verschiedensten Menschen,*** a happy marriage unites the most unlike people; 3. (*fig.*) compel, oblige; ***mein mündliches Wort bindet mich auch,*** my verbal promise is also binding. **2.** *irr.v.r.* bind *or* pledge *or* commit o.s. (***an*** (*Acc.*), to); ***sich an etwas binden,*** hold *or* keep o.s. to s.th., pledge one's word to s.th.; ***sich an die Regel –,*** keep *or* stick to the rules. **3.** *irr.v.i.* have power to bind *or* unite; be binding (***für,*** on); harden, set (*as cement*). **bindend,** *adj.* binding (*agreement*); (*quick etc.*) -setting (*cement*). **–bindend,** *adj.suff.* (*Chem.*) combining with.

Binden|kreuzschnabel, *m.* (*Orn.*) two-barred *or* (*Am.* white-winged) crossbill (*Loxia leucoptera*). **–laubsänger,** *m. See* ***grüner Laubsänger.*** **–sandlerche,** *f.* (*Orn.*) bar-tailed desert lark (*Ammomanes phoenicura*).

Binder ['bɪndər], *m.* binder; reaper and binder, combine harvester; (*Build.*) binder, bonder, bond-stone; truss (*of roof*); (*coll.*) (neck-)tie.

Binder|balken, *m.* (*Build.*) main beam *or* girder. **–schicht,** *f.* (*Build.*) course of headers. **–sparren,** *m.* (*Build.*) main rafter.

Binde|strich, *m.* hyphen; (*Mus.*) legato sign. **–wort,** *n.* **(-s,** *pl.* **⸚er)** conjunction; copula. **–zeichen,** *n. See* **–strich. –zeit,** *f.* setting time (*of cement*).

Bindfaden ['bɪntfa:dən], *m.* string, twine, pack-thread; ***es regnet Bindfäden,*** it is raining cats and dogs.

bindig ['bındıç], *adj.* cohesive, binding, heavy (*of soil*); (*Build.*) bonded in. **Bindigkeit,** *f.* cohesiveness, binding power, consistency.

Bindung ['bınduŋ], *f.* 1. binding, tying, fastening; tie, binding (*also books, skis*), (*Mus.*) slur, tie, ligature; (*Phonet.*) liaison, (*Chem.*) linkage (*of atoms etc.*), (*Weav.*) weave (*of fabric*); 2. (*fig.*) obligation, commitment; (*social etc.*) tie(s), attachment(s), (*coll.*) roots; limitation, restriction; subjection, subordination (*an* (*Acc.*), to).

Binge ['bıŋə], *f.* (*Min.*) surface depression, crater. **Bingenbau,** *m.* (*Min.*) open-cast working.

binnen ['bınən], *prep.* (*Gen., Dat.*) within; – ***weniger Stunden,*** in a few hours; – ***acht Tagen,*** in the course of a week; – ***kurzem,*** before *or* ere long, within a short time, shortly.

Binnen–, *pref.* inner, internal; inland, home, domestic. **–deich,** *m.* inner dam *or* dyke. **–fischerei,** *f.* freshwater fishing. **–gewässer,** *n.* inland water(s). **–hafen,** *m.* inland *or* river port; inner basin (*of a harbour*). **–handel,** *m.* home *or* domestic trade. **–klima,** *n.* continental climate. **–land,** *n.* inland; interior (*of a country*). **–mauer,** *f.* party wall. **–meer,** *n.* inland *or* land-locked sea. **–raum,** *m.* inner *or* interior space. **–reim,** *m.* internal rhyme. **–schiffahrt,** *f.* inland navigation. **–see,** *m.* inland lake. **–verkehr,** *m.* overland traffic, inland trade. **–vordersteven,** *m.* (*Naut.*) apron.

Binom [bi'no:m], *n.* (**-s,** *pl.* **-e**) binomial. **binomial** [–i'a:l], *adj. See* **binomisch. Binomialsatz,** *m.* binomial theorem. **binomisch,** *adj.* binomial.

Binse ['bınzə], *f.* (*Bot.*) rush (*Juncus*); sedge; bent-grass; ***glatte –,*** bulrush; (*coll.*) ***in die –n gehen,*** go to rack and ruin. **Binsen|blume,** *f.* flowering rush. **–gras,** *n.* club-rush; sedge. **–korb,** *m.* frail; plaited *or* rush basket. **–rohrsänger,** *m. See* **Seggenrohrsänger. –wahrheit,** *f.* platitude, truism.

Biochemie [bioçe'mi:], *f.* biochemistry. **Biochemiker** [–'çe:mıkər], *m.* biochemist.

Biograph [bio'gra:f], *m.* (**-en,** *pl.* **-en**) biographer. **Biographie** [–'fi:], *f.* biography. **biographisch,** *adj.* biographical.

Biologe [bio'lo:gə], *m.* (**-n,** *pl.* **-n**) biologist. **Biologie** [–'gi:], *f.* biology. **biologisch,** *adj.* biological.

Biquadrat [bi:kva'dra:t], *n.* (*Math.*) fourth power.

Bircht [bırçt], *m. or n.* (**-s,** *no pl.*) (*Swiss*) hoar-frost.

birg [bırk], **birgst, birgt,** *see* **bergen.**

Birke ['bırkə], *f.* birch-tree (*Betula*). **birken,** *adj.* of birch. **Birken|baum,** *m. See* **Birke. –reis,** *n.* birch rod. **–zeisig,** *m.* (*Orn.*) mealy (*or Am.* common) redpoll (*Acanthis flammea*); ***grönländischer –,*** Coues's (*or Am.* hoary) redpoll (*Carduelis hornemanni exilipes*); ***heller –,*** Hollböll's redpoll (*Carduelis flammea holboelli*); ***kleiner –,*** *see* **Alpenbirkenzeisig.**

Birkhuhn ['bırkhu:n], *n.* (*Orn.*) black grouse (*Lyrurus tetrix*).

Birma ['bırma:], *n.* Burma. **Birmane** [–'ma:nə], *m.* (**-n,** *pl.* **-n**) Burmese. **birmanisch,** *adj.* Burmese.

Birnbaum ['bırnbaum], *m.* pear-tree (*Pyrus communis*). **Birne,** *f.* pear; (electric) bulb; (Bessemer) converter; (*sl.*) nut, loaf, bean; ***eine weiche – haben,*** be cracked *or* touched. **Birnenessenz,** *f.* (*Chem.*) amyl acetate. **birnenförmig,** *adj.* pear-shaped; pyriform. **Birn|most, –wein,** *m.* perry.

Birsch [bırʃ], *see* **Pirsch.**

birst [bırst], *see* **bersten.**

bis [bıs], **1.** *prep.* 1. (*Acc.*) (*space*) as far as, (up)to; – ***dahin,*** that far; – ***wohin?*** how far? ***von Kopf – Fuß,*** from head to foot; – ***hierher und nicht weiter,*** thus far and no farther; (*duration*) until, till, to; ***von Mittwoch – Freitag,*** from Wednesday to (*Am.* through) Friday; – ***jetzt,*** until *or* till now, hitherto, so far; (*time limit*) – ***morgen kommt er bestimmt,*** he will certainly be here by tomorrow; – ***wann?*** by what time? (*approximation: between numerals*) ***10 – 12,*** 10 or *or* to 12; 2. (*with another prep.*) (*space*) – ***an*** (*Acc.*), – ***nach*** (*Dat.*), – ***vor*** (*Dat.*), – ***zu*** (*Dat.*), *see* 1; – ***in*** (*Acc.*), right into; (*duration*) – ***auf weiteres,*** for the meantime; – ***in*** (*Acc.*), till well into; – ***gegen*** (*Acc.*), till nearly *or* about; – ***zu*** (*Dat.*), till, to; – ***zum Ende,*** to the end; (*time limit*) – ***in*** (*Dat.*), within, at the latest in; – ***zu*** (*Dat.*), *see* 1; (*limited number or degree*); – ***an den Tod,*** even unto death; – ***an die Ohren,*** up to one's ears (*in work*); – ***auf*** (*Acc.*), up to but excluding; up to and including; – ***auf den letzten Mann,*** to a man; – ***auf die Haut naß,*** wet to the skin; – ***in den Tod,*** till *or* unto death; – (***und***) ***mit,*** up to . . . inclusive; – ***über die Ohren,*** up to one's eyes *or* ears (*in debt*); – ***über beide Ohren verliebt,*** head over heels in love; ***Kampf – zum Tode,*** fight to the death; – ***zum Sterben müde,*** dead tired; (*approximation*) – ***an 5000 Mann,*** close on 5,000 men. **2.** *conj.* until, till; ***nicht eher . . . als –,*** not . . . until; ***komm nicht wieder, – du nicht vernünftig reden kannst,*** don't come back unless you can talk sense.

Bisam ['bi:zam], *m.* (**-s,** *pl.* **-e**) (*Bot., Zool.*) musk; musquash (*fur*). **Bisam|fell,** *n.* musk-rat skin, musquash (*fur*). **–hirsch,** *m.* (male) musk-deer. **–katze,** *f.* civet(-cat). **–körner,** *n.pl.* musk-seed. **–kraut,** *n.* (*Bot.*) musk crowfoot, moschatel. **–ratte,** *f.* musk-rat. **–schwein,** *n.* (*Zool.*) peccary. **–stier,** *m.* (*Zool.*) musk-ox. **–tier,** *n.* musk-deer.

Bischof ['bıʃɔf], *m.* (**-s,** *pl.* **⸚e**) bishop.

bischöflich ['bıʃø:flıç], *adj.* episcopal; (*R.C.*) pontifical; ***Seine –e Gnaden,*** His Lordship the Bishop.

Bischofs|amt, *n.* episcopate. **–hut,** *m.*, **–mütze,** *f.* 1. mitre; 2. (*Bot.*) mitre-wort; bishop's cap; alpine barrenwort. **–ornat,** *m.* pontificals. **–sitz,** *m.* (bishop's) see; bishop's palace; cathedral town. **–stab,** *m.* crosier. **–würde,** *f.* episcopal dignity; episcopate, bishopric.

Bise ['bi:zə], *f.* cutting (north-easterly) wind (*esp. in Switzerland*).

bisher [bıs'he:r], *adv.* hitherto, up to now, so far. **bisherig,** *adj.* as up to the present; former, previous; retiring, outgoing (*official*); (*rendered as adv.*) to date, so far, hitherto.

Biskotte [bıs'kɔtə], *f.* sponge finger.

Biskuit [bıs'kvi:t], *m.* (**-s,** *pl.* **-e**) rusk, biscuit. **Biskuitporzellan,** *n.* biscuit *or* bisque ware.

bislang ['bıslaŋ], *adv. See* **bisher.**

Bison ['bi:zɔn], *m.* (**-s,** *pl.* **-s**) bison.

biß [bıs], *see* **beißen.**

Biß, *m.* (**-es,** *pl.* **-e**) bite; sting.

Bißchen ['bısçən], *n.*, (*now usu.*) **bißchen,** *indecl. adj.* little bit, morsel; a little; (*used adverbially*) somewhat, slightly, rather; ***ein – Brot,*** a little (bit of) bread; ***kein – Brot,*** not a scrap of bread, no bread at all; ***kein – müde,*** not in the least *or* not a bit *or* not at all tired; ***sein – Vermögen,*** his little bit of a fortune; ***das ist ein – zuviel verlangt!*** that's asking a bit too much, (*sl.*) that's going *or* coming it a bit strong; ***ein – früh,*** rather early; ***ein – bange,*** somewhat uneasy, rather frightened.

bisse ['bısə], *see* **beißen.**

Bissel ['bısəl], *n.*, **bissel,** *indecl. adj.* (*dial.*) *see* **bißchen.**

Bissen ['bısən], *m.* bite; mouthful; snack; (*coll.*) ***ein fetter –,*** a piece of good luck. **bissenweise,** *adv.* in mouthfuls; bit by bit.

bissig [bısıç], *adj.* biting.

bist [bıst], *see* **sein.**

Bister ['bi:stεr], *m. or n.* bistre.

Bistum ['bıstu:m], *n.* (**-s,** *pl.* **⸚er**) bishopric; episcopate; diocese, see.

bisweilen [bıs'vaılən], *adv.* sometimes, at times, occasionally, now and then, off and on.

bisyllabisch [bizy'la:bıʃ], *adj.* disyllabic.

Bittage ['bıtta:gə], *m.pl.* (*Eccl.*) Rogation days.

Bitte ['bıtə], *f.* request, petition, wish; (*Eccl.*) prayer, supplication; ***demütige –,*** supplication; ***dringende –,*** entreaty; ***die sieben –n des Vaterunsers,*** the seven petitions of the Lord's Prayer; ***eine – an ihn richten*** or ***tun,*** ask a favour of him; ***auf seine –,*** at his request.

bitte, *int.* please; (*replying to knock on door*) come in! (*replying to request*) with pleasure! certainly! (*replying to thanks*) don't mention it! (*coll.*) you're welcome! (*when offering s.th.*) help yourself! (*polite request for repetition*) (*wie*) *–?* I beg your pardon? pardon? (*indignation*) *wie –!* I beg your pardon!

bitten ['bɪtən], *irr.v.t.* 1. ask, request, beg (*um*, for); ***um Entschuldigung –***, beg (*s.o.'s*) pardon; ***um Gnade –***, beg for mercy; ***um Gehör –***, request a hearing, ask to be heard; ***um seinen Namen –***, ask his name; ***um Verzeihung –***, ask *or* beg forgiveness; 2. ask, invite (***zu***, to); ***zu Tisch –***, invite to a meal; ask (*guests*) to come to table; ***ihn zu sich –***, invite him home, (*coll.*) ask him round; 3. plead, intercede (***für***, for; ***bei ihm***, with him); ***wenn ich – darf!*** if you would be so kind! (*expressing surprise*) ***ich bitte Sie!*** you don't say so! I ask you! would you believe it! (*expressing indignation*) ***ich muß doch –!*** I really must protest! how can you say such a thing! **Bitten,** *n.* prayers, entreaties, solicitation. **bittend,** *adj.* pleading, beseeching. **Bittende(r),** *m., f.* suppliant, supplicant, petitioner.

bitter ['bɪtər], *adj.* bitter (*also fig. of cold, wind, disappointment, remorse etc.*); (*fig.*) sharp (*frost*), grievous (*pain, wrong*), abject (*poverty*), dire (*need*); ***Sparsamkeit ist – nötig,*** economy is urgently necessary. **bitterböse,** *adj.* furious with rage; very wicked. **Bitter|erde,** *f.* magnesia. **–kalk,** *m.* magnesium limestone.

Bitterkeit ['bɪtərkaɪt], *f.* bitterness; sharpness, grievousness.

Bitter|klee, *m.* (*Bot.*) marsh trefoil, buckbean (*Menyanthes trifoliata*). **–kleesalz,** *n.* oxalic acid. **bitterlich,** 1. *adj.* rather bitter. 2. *adv.* bitterly.

Bitterling ['bɪtərlɪŋ], *m.* (**-s,** *pl.* **-e**) 1. (*Ichth.*) bitterling; 2. (*Bot.*) yellow-wort (*Chlora perfoliata*).

Bitter|mandelöl, *n.* oil of bitter almonds, benzaldehyde. **–mittel,** *n.* bitters.

Bitternis ['bɪtərnɪs], *f.* *See* **Bitterkeit.**

Bitter|salz, *n.* Epsom salts; sulphate of magnesia. **–spat,** *m.* magnesite. **–stein,** *m.* jade, nephrite. **–stoff,** *m.* (*Chem.*) bitter principle. **bittersüß,** *adj.* bittersweet. **Bitter|süß,** *n.* (*Bot.*) bittersweet, woody nightshade (*Solanum dulcamara*). **–wasser,** *n.* bitter mineral water, magnesium sulphate water. **–wurz(el),** *f.* yellow gentian.

Bitt|fahrt, *f.* pilgrimage. **–gang,** *m.* procession (of pilgrims); (*coll.*) ***ihn – tun*** or ***machen,*** approach him with a request. **–gebet,** *n.,* **–gesang,** *m.* rogation, litany. **–gesuch,** *n.* petition, suit, request (*um*, for). **–gottesdienst,** *m.* Rogation service. **–schreiben,** *n.,* **–schrift,** *f.* written petition; begging letter; ***eine – richten*** (***an*** (*Acc.*)) *or* ***einreichen*** (***bei***), petition. **–steller,** *m.* petitioner, supplicant. **bittweise,** *adv.* by means of prayer *or* entreaty, by way of request. **Bittwoche,** *f.* (*Eccl.*) Rogation week.

Bitumen [bi'tu:mən], *n.* bitumen. **bituminös** [–'nø:s], *adj.* bituminous.

Biwak ['bi:vak], *n.* (**-s,** *pl.* **-s**) bivouac. **biwakieren** [–'ki:rən], *v.i.* bivouac, camp out.

bizarr [bi'tsar], *adj.* eccentric, bizarre, strange, odd. **Bizarrerie** [–ə'ri:], *f.* eccentricity, strangeness, oddity.

Blachfeld ['blaxfɛlt], *n.* (*obs.*) open field, open country.

Blackfisch ['blakfɪʃ], *m.* cuttle-fish.

blaffen ['blafən], **bläffen** ['blɛfən], *v.i.* bark, yelp.

Blage ['bla:gə], *f.* (*dial.*) noisy child, urchin, brat.

blähen ['blɛ:ən], 1. *v.t.* inflate, distend, swell (out); bulge (*cheeks*), distend (*nostrils*). 2. *v.r.* become inflated *or* distended; belly, balloon (out); (*fig.*) give o.s. airs; ***er bläht sich wie der Frosch in der Fabel,*** he puffs himself up like the frog in the fable. **Bläh|hals,** *m.* (*Med.*) goitre. **–sucht, Blähung,** *f.* flatulence, (*coll.*) wind.

Blak [bla:k], *m.* (*dial.*) smoky flame, soot. **blaken,** *v.i.* smoke (*of a lamp*).

Blamage [bla'ma:ʒə], *f.* humiliation; disgrace. **blamieren,** 1. *v.t.* expose to ridicule; make a fool of; disgrace, compromise, (*coll.*) let (*s.o.*) down. 2. *v.r.* disgrace o.s.; make o.s. ridiculous, make a fool of o.s., lose face, (*coll.*) put one's foot in it.

blanchieren [blã'ʃi:rən], *v.t.* blanch, whiten; flesh (*hides*). **Blanchissure** [–'sy:r], *f.* light spot (*in dyeing*).

blank [blaŋk], *adj.* shining; shiny, bright, polished; sleek (*of animal's coat*); bare, naked; (*Elec.*) ***–er Draht,*** bare wire, uncovered wire; ***–e Lüge,*** barefaced lie; (*Mil.*) ***–e Waffe,*** cold steel; ***die –e Wahrheit,*** the naked truth; ***–e Worte,*** mere words; ***mit ihm – stehen,*** be at open enmity with him; (*Metall.*) ***– beizen,*** pickle, dip; ***– putzen, – reiben,*** scour, polish; ***– ziehen,*** draw one's sword; (*sl.*) ***ich bin –,*** I'm cleaned out, I'm broke.

Blankett [blaŋ'kɛt], *n.* (**-(e)s,** *pl.* **-e**) blank (form *or* cheque).

Blankleder ['blaŋkle:dər], *n.* sleek *or* shiny leather.

blanko ['blaŋko], *adj.* (*Comm.*) blank (*form, cheque etc.*), unsecured, uncovered; ***– abgeben,*** sell short; ***in – trassieren,*** draw in blank; ***Giro in –,*** blank endorsement. **Blanko|akzept,** *n.* acceptance in blank. **–kredit,** *m.* open credit, unlimited credit. **–scheck,** *m.* blank cheque. **–verkauf,** *m.* short sale. **–vollmacht,** *f.* carte-blanche, (*Law*) full power of attorney.

Blankvers ['blaŋkfɛrs], *m.* blank verse.

Bläschen ['blɛ:sçən], *n.* bubble; pustule, pimple, vesicle, small blister; (*Bot.*) utricle. **Bläschen|-ausschlag,** *m.,* **–flechte,** *f.* (*Med.*) shingles, herpes. **bläschenförmig,** *adj.* vesicular.

Blase ['bla:zə], *f.* bubble; blister; bladder (*also Anat.*); flaw, bleb (*in metal, glass etc.*); still, alembic; ***–n ziehen,*** blister, raise blisters; ***–n werfen,*** blister, become blistered; (*sl.*) ***die ganze –,*** the whole shoot, the whole boiling. **Blase|balg,** *m.*(pair of) bellows. **–balgtreter,** *m.* organ-blower.

blasen ['bla:zən], *irr.v.t.,* & *irr.v.i.* blow; blow, sound, play (*trumpets etc.*); blow (*glass*); ***zum Angriffe*** or ***zum Rückzuge –,*** sound the charge *or* the retreat; ***einen Stein –,*** huff (*at draughts*); ***ihm ins Ohr*** or ***in die Ohren –,*** whisper in his ear; (*coll.*) ***sie – in dasselbe*** or ***ein Horn,*** there is a secret understanding between them, they play into one another's hands; (*Prov.*) ***was dich nicht brennt, das blase nicht!*** let sleeping dogs lie; (*coll.*) ***Trübsal –,*** whine, be a jeremiah; (*sl.*) ***du kannst mir eins –,*** go chase yourself!

Blasen|bruch, *m.* (*Med.*) cystocele, hernia (of the bladder). **–entzündung,** *f.* cystitis, inflammation of the bladder. **–farn,** *m.* bladder fern (*Cystopteris*). **–fuß,** *m.* (*Ent.*) thrips. **–galle** *f.* cystic bile. **–gang,** *m.* vesicular *or* cystic duct. **–grieß,** *m.* (*Med.*) gravel. **–grind,** *m.* (*Med.*) impetigo. **–grün,** *n.* sap-green (*artist's colour*). **–höhle,** *f.* vesicular cavity. **–käfer,** *m.* cantharis (*pl.* cantharides), Spanish fly. **–katarrh,** *m.* cystic catarrh, blennorrhoea. **–keim,** *m.* blastula. **–kraut,** *n.* bladderwort. **–leiden,** *n.* bladder trouble. **–pflaster,** *n.* vesicant, vesicatory, blistering plaster. **–rohr,** *n.* cystoscope. **–schlagader,** *f.* cystic artery. **–schnitt,** *m.* lithotomy, cystotomy. **–sonde,** *f.* catheter. **–stein,** *m.* (*Med.*) (vesicle) calculus. **–steinschnitt,** *m.* lithotomy. **–tang,** *m.* bladder-wrack (*Fucus vesiculosus*). **blasenziehend,** *adj.* blistering, vesicatory.

Blaseofen ['bla:zəˀo:fən], *m.* blast-furnace.

Bläser ['blɛ:zər], *m.* (*Mus.*) wind-player; *pl.* the wind(-instruments).

Blasewerk ['bla:zəvɛrk], *n.* bellows (of an organ).

blasiert [bla'zi:rt], *adj.* blasé. **Blasiertheit,** *f.* blasé attitude.

blasig ['bla:zɪç], *adj.* blistered, vesicular.

Blas|instrument, *n.* wind-instrument. **–kapelle,** *f.* brass *or* silver band. **–loch,** *n.* blow-hole (*of flute*). **–musik,** *f.* music for *or* of wind instruments. **–ofen,** *m.* blast-furnace.

blasonieren [blazo'ni:rən], *v.t.* emblazon.

Blasphemie [blasfe'mi:], *f.* blasphemy. **blasphemieren,** *v.i.* blaspheme. **blasphemisch** [–'fe:mɪʃ], *adj.* blasphemous.

Blasrohr ['bla:sro:r], *n.* blow-pipe; pea-shooter.

blaß [blas], *adj.* (*comp. blasser* or *blässer*; *sup. blassest* or *blässest*) pale, pallid; colourless, wan; (*coll.*) *keine blasse Ahnung,* not the faintest notion, not the foggiest idea. **blaßblau,** *adj.*, **Blaßblau,** *n.* pale blue.

Blässe ['blɛsə], *f.* paleness, pallor; blaze (*on face of horse, cow etc.*); (*Poet.*) *von des Gedankens – angekränkelt,* sicklied o'er with the pale cast of thought.

blaßfarbig ['blasfarbɪç], *adj.* light-coloured, pale.

Bläß|gans, *f.* (*Orn.*) white-fronted goose (*Anser albifrons*); *kleine –, see* **Zwerggans. –huhn,** *n.* (*Orn.*) (*Am.* European) coot (*Fulica atra*).

bläßlich ['blɛslɪç], *adj.* rather pale, palish.

Blaß|segler, *m. See* **Fahlsegler. –spötter,** *m.* (*Orn.*) olivaceous warbler (*Hippolais pallida*).

Blatt [blat], *n.* (**-s,** *pl.* **⸚er**) 1. leaf (*of plant*), petal (*of flower*); *kein – vor den Mund nehmen,* be plain spoken, not mince matters, speak one's mind; 2. leaf, page (*of book*), folio (*of manuscript*), leaf, sheet, piece (*of paper*); (*fig.*) *ein unbeschriebenes –,* (*of a p.*) an unknown quantity, a dark horse; a novice, a greenhorn; a nobody, a nonentity; (*coll.*) *das steht auf einem anderen –,* that's quite another *or* a different matter altogether; *das – hat sich gewendet,* the tables are turned; the tide has turned; (*Mus.*) *vom – spielen* or *singen,* play *or* sing from sight, sight-read; 3. (news)paper; 4. plate, layer, lamina, flake (*of metal*), blade (*of grass, oar, propellor, saw, axe etc.*), reed (*of clarinet etc.*); 5. hand (*of cards*); 6. (*Geom.*) folium.

Blattachsel ['blatˀaksəl], *f.* (leaf) axil. **blattachselständig,** *adj.* (*Bot.*) axillary. **Blatt|anordnung,** *f.* phyllotaxis. **–ansatz,** *m.* stipule. **–auge,** *n.* leaf-bud. **–bildung,** *f.* (*Metall.*) scaling; (*Bot.*) foliation. **–bleiche,** *f.* chlorosis. **–brand,** *m.* leaf blight.

Blättchen ['blɛtçən], *n.* leaflet, foliole; lamella (*of fungus*); (*Metall., Geol.*) lamina.

blatten ['blatən], **1.** *v.t.* strip *or* clear of leaves. **2.** *v.i.* (*Hunt.*) imitate call of doe (*as decoy*).

Blatter ['blatər], *f.* (-, *pl.* **-n**) (*Med.*) pustule, pock; *pl.* smallpox.

blätterabwerfend ['blɛtərˀapvɛrfənt], *adj.* deciduous. **Blättererz,** *n.* black *or* foliated tellurium, nagyagite. **blätter|förmig,** *adj.* leaf-shaped, foliated, laminated. **–fressend,** *adj.* phyllophagous.

blatt(e)rig ['blat(ə)rɪç], *adj. See* **blatternarbig.**

blätt(e)rig [blɛt(ə)rɪç], *adj.* foliated; laminated, lamellar; flaky. **–blätt(e)rig,** *adj.suff.* -leaved; *vier–er Klee,* four-leaved clover.

Blätter|kern, *m.* (*Elec.*) laminated core. **–kohle,** *f.* slaty coal. **–magen,** *m.* third stomach of ruminants, omasum.

blättern ['blɛtərn], **1.** *v.i.* turn over the pages, leaf, glance, skim, (*Am.*) page (*in* (*Dat.*), through). **2.** *v.i., v.r.* flake (off).

Blatternarbe ['blatərnarbə], *f.* pock-mark. **blatternarbig,** *adj.* pock-marked.

Blätter|pilz, *m. See* **–schwamm. blätterreich,** *adj.* leafy. **Blätter|schwamm,** *m.* agaric. **–stand,** *m.* foliation. **–teig,** *m.* puff pastry.

Blätterung ['blɛtərʊŋ], *f.* foliation, lamination.

Blatt|erz, *n. See* **Blättererz. –feder,** *f.* leaf- *or* laminated spring. **–füßer,** *m.* phyllopod. **–gelb,** *n.* xanthophyll. **–gold,** *n.* gold-leaf *or* -foil. **–grün,** *n.* chlorophyll. **–kapitell,** *n.* (*Archit.*) foliated capital. **–keim,** *m.* (*Bot.*) plumule. **–keimer,** *m.* (*Bot.*) dicotyledon. **–knospe,** *f.* leaf-bud. **–kohl,** *m.* kale. **–laus,** *f.* aphis, green-fly. **–lauskäfer,** *m.* (*Ent.*) ladybird, (*Am.*) lady-bug. **blattlos,** *adj.* leafless, aphyllous. **Blatt|metall,** *n.* metal foil. **–narbe,** *f.* leaf-scar. **–pflanze,** *f.* foliage plant.

blattrig, *see* **blatt(e)rig.**

blättrig, –blättrig, *see* **blätt(e)rig, –blätt(e)rig.**

Blatt|rot, *n.* (*Bot.*) carotin. **–säge,** *f.* pad-saw. **–silber,** *n.* silver-foil. **–stellung,** *f.* (*Bot.*) phyllotaxis. **–stiel,** *m.* leaf-stalk, petiole. **–stoß,** *m.* (*Carp.*) scarf(-joint).

Blattung ['blatʊŋ], *f.* (*Carp.*) scarfing.

Blatt|vergoldung, *f.* gilding (with gold leaf). **–werk,** *n.* (*Archit. etc.*) (ornamental) foliage. **–zeit,** *f.* rutting season (*of deer*). **–zinn,** *n.* tinfoil.

blau [blau], *adj.* blue; (*Her.*) azure; *–es Auge,* black eye; *mit einem –en Auge davonkommen,* have a narrow escape, get off lightly; *das –e Band,* the Blue Riband; *–es Blut,* blue blood; (*Mil. sl.*) *–e Bohne,* bullet; *–er Brief,* official letter of dismissal (*in envelope*); (*coll.*) *ihm* (*einen*) *–en Dunst vormachen,* throw dust in *or* pull the wool over his eyes; *–e Flecke,* bruises; *die –en Jungen(s)* or *Jungs,* the boys in blue (*sailors*); *–e Märchen erzählen,* tell tall stories; (*obs.*) *der –e Montag,* Saint Monday, (*school sl.*) black Monday (= first day of term); (*coll.*) *sein –es Wunder erleben,* get the surprise of one's life; *– kochen,* boil (*fish*); (*sl.*) *– machen,* take the day off; (*coll.*) *– sein,* be blotto *or* sozzled; *es wurde mir – und grün vor den Augen,* I turned giddy; *ihn braun und – schlagen,* beat him black and blue.

Blau, *n.* (**-s,** *pl.* **-(s)**) blue (*colour*), blueness, azure; *Berliner –,* Prussian blue. **blauäugig,** *adj.* blue-eyed. **Blau|bart,** *m.* Bluebeard. **–beere,** *f.* bilberry, whortleberry (*Vaccinium myrtillus*). **blau|blütig,** *adj.* aristocratic. **–brüchig,** *adj.* (*Metall.*) blue-short. **Blau|drossel,** *f. See* **–merle.**

Blaue ['blauə], *n.* (*as adj.*) *ins – hinein,* haphazard, thoughtlessly, at random; *Fahrt ins –,* mystery trip; (*coll.*) *das – vom Himmel herunterschwatzen,* talk the hind legs off a donkey; *ins – hineinreden,* talk wildly; (*coll.*) *die –n,* the Prussians; the Protestants.

Bläue ['blɔyə], *f.* blueness; blue; azure (*of sky*). **Bläuel,** *n.* blue-bag.

Blauelster ['blauˀɛlstər], *f.* (*Orn.*) azure-winged magpie (*Cyanopica cyanus*).

blauen ['blauən], **1.** *v.t.* blue (*laundry*). **2.** *v.i.* (*Liter.*) be blue; *der Himmel blaut,* the sky is blue; *soweit die Berge –,* so far as the blue peaks are seen.

bläuen ['blɔyən], *v.t.* blue (*laundry*).

Blau|felche, *f.*, **–felch(en),** *m.* (*Ichth.*) blue char. **–flügelente,** *f.* (*Orn.*) blue-winged teal (*Anus discors*). **–fuchs,** *m.* arctic fox. **–holz,** *n.* logwood, campeachy wood. **–jacke,** *f.* (*coll.*) bluejacket. **–kehlchen,** *n.* (*Orn.*) bluethroat (*Luscinia svecica*). **–kohl,** *m.* red cabbage. **–kreuz,** *n.* (*Mil.*) poison gas (diphanyl-arsin).

bläulich ['blɔylɪç], *adj.* bluish. **Bläuling,** *m.* large blue (butterfly) (*Lycoenidae*).

Blau|meise, *f.* (*Orn.*) blue tit(-mouse) (*Parus caeruleus*). **–merle,** *f.* (*Orn.*) blue rock-thrush (*Monticola solitarius*). **–papier,** *n.* carbon paper, blueprint paper. **–pause,** *f.* blueprint. **–racke,** *f.* (*Orn.*) roller (*Coracias garrulus*). **–säure,** *f.* prussic *or* hydrocyanic acid. **–schimmel,** *m.* dapple-grey (horse). **–schwanz,** *m.* (*Orn.*) red-flanked bluetail (*Tarsiger cyanurus*). **–spat,** *m.* lazulite. **–stern,** *m.* bluebell (*Scilla*). **–stift,** *m.* blue pencil; indelible pencil. **–strumpf,** *m.* bluestocking. **–sucht,** *f.* cyanosis. **–wangenbienenfresser,** *m.* (*Orn.*) blue-cheeked bee-eater (*Merops superciliosus*). **–zwecke,** *f.* tintack.

Blech [blɛç], *n.* (**-(e)s,** *pl.* **-e**) 1. sheet metal; tinplate, (metal) sheet *or* plate; (*sl.*) (*money*) dough, brass; 2. (*sl.*) rubbish, balderdash, piffle, bosh, tripe; (*coll.*) *rede doch kein –!* don't talk such rubbish! **Blech|büchse, –dose,** *f.* tin can *or* box. **–eisen,** *n.* sheet iron.

blechen ['blɛçən], *v.i.* (*coll.*) fork out, stump *or* cough up (*money*).

blechern ['blɛçərn], *adj.* metal, tinplate; (*fig.*) tinny, brassy (*sound*).

Blech|geschirr, *n.* (*Mil.*) mess-tin. **–instrument,** *n.* (*Mus.*) brass instrument. **–musik,** *f.* brass-band music. **–schere,** *f.* shears, tin-snips. **–schmied,** *m.* tinsmith, sheet-metal worker.

blecken ['blɛkən], *v.t. die Zähne –,* show *or* bare one's teeth (*auf* (*Acc.*) *or gegen,* at).

[1]**Blei** [blaɪ], *m.* (**-s,** *pl.* **-e**) (*Ichth.*) bream.

[2]**Blei,** *n.* (**-s,** *pl.* **-e**) lead; (*Naut.*) plummet; (*coll.*)

pencil; ***Pulver und –,*** powder and shot. **Bleiader,** *f.* lode *or* vein of lead.

Bleibe ['blaɪbə], *f.* home, accommodation, shelter; (*sl.*) digs; ***keine – haben,*** have nowhere to live *or* stay.

bleiben ['blaɪbən], *irr.v.i.* (*aux.* s.) 1. remain, stay; continue; (*Tele.*) ***am Apparat –,*** hold the line; ***es bleibt unter uns,*** it's strictly between ourselves *or* between you and me; ***an Ort und Stelle –,*** remain *or* stay where one is, (*coll.*) stay put; ***auf dem Schlachtfelde*** or ***Platze –,*** fall *or* be killed on the battlefield; 2. be left over; *see* **übrigbleiben**; ***nichts bleibt mir als . . .*** (*inf.*), nothing remains *or* is left for me but (*to do*); ***mir bleibt keine Wahl,*** I have no choice; ***2 von 9 bleibt 7,*** 2 from 9 leaves 7; 3. ***– bei,*** keep *or* adhere *or* stick to, abide by; ***es bleibt dabei!*** agreed! ***es bleibt beim alten,*** things go on just as before *or* as they were, no change will be made; ***er bleibt bei seiner Meinung,*** he persists in his opinion; ***bei der S.*** or ***Stange –,*** keep *or* stick to the point; ***bei der Wahrheit –,*** stick to the truth; ***der Schuster bleibt bei seinem Leisten,*** the cobbler sticks to his last; (*fig.*) ***er blieb dabei,*** he insisted; 4. (*with other preps.*) ***am Leben –,*** survive; ***aus dem Spiel –,*** not meddle, not get involved; ***in Bewegung*** or ***im Gange –,*** keep going; ***in der Schwebe –,*** be still in the balance; ***ohne Wirkung –,*** be to *or* have no effect, be without result; ***bleib mir vom Leibe!*** don't touch me! keep off! keep your distance! keep away from me! ***davon –,*** don't touch (it), keep away (from it), keep clear (of it); 5. (*with adjs.*) ***ernst –,*** be serious, keep a straight face; ***gesund –,*** keep well *or* fit; ***sich*** (*Dat.*) ***gleich –,*** not change, remain *or* stay the same as one is; ***ledig –,*** stay single; ***nüchtern –,*** stay sober; go without food; ***ruhig –,*** keep calm; ***unbeachtet*** (***unbestraft***) ***–,*** go unnoticed (unpunished); 6. be late, fail to arrive; ***wo ist er geblieben?*** what has happened to him? where has he got to? ***er bleibt ja lange,*** he is a long time coming, he has been gone a long time; ***wo bleibt denn das Geld?*** what have you done with the money? where has the money gone? **Bleiben,** *n.* stay; ***hier ist meines –s nicht,*** here is no place for me, I can stay here no longer. **bleibend,** *adj.* lasting, permanent, abiding, fixed; ***–e Eindrücke,*** lasting impressions. **bleibenlassen,** *irr.v.t.* let *or* leave alone, have nothing to do with.

Bleiblech ['blaɪblɛç], *n.* lead sheet, lead foil.

bleich [blaɪç], *adj.* pale, wan, pallid; light, pale (*of colour*). **Bleiche,** *f.* pallor, paleness; bleaching-ground. **bleichen, 1.** *v.t.* bleach; blanch, whiten; ***der Ernst, den keine Mühe bleichet,*** that earnestness (of purpose) which is not afraid of any toil; ***einen Mohren – wollen,*** attempt the impossible. **2.** (*occ. irr.*) *v.i.* (*aux.* h. & s.) grow *or* turn pale *or* white; fade; blanch. **Bleich|erde,** *f.* fuller's earth. **–kalk,** *m.* chloride of lime. **–mittel,** *n.* bleach, bleaching agent. **–sucht,** *f.* anaemia; chlorosis, green-sickness. **bleichsüchtig,** *adj.* anaemic.

Bleie ['blaɪə], *f. See* [2]**Blei.**

Bleier ['blaɪər], *m.* (*Ichth.*) roach.

bleiern ['blaɪərn], *adj.* lead, leaden; ***wie eine –e Ente,*** clumsily, awkwardly.

blei|farben, –farbig, *adj.* leaden, livid. **Blei|gelb,** *n.* chromate of lead. **–glanz,** *m.* sulphide of lead, galena. **–glätte,** *f.* yellow lead oxide, litharge. **bleihaltig,** *adj.* plumbiferous, lead-bearing.

Bleihe ['blaɪə], *f. See* [1]**Blei.**

Blei|kolik, *f.* (*Med.*) painter's colic. **–lot,** *n.* plumb-line, plummet, (*Naut.*) lead-line. **–mennige,** *f.* red (oxide of) lead, minium. **–mulde,** *f.* pig-lead. **bleirecht,** *adj.* perpendicular. **Blei|rot,** *n. See* **–mennige. –schrot,** *n.* lead-shot. **–soldat,** *m.* lead *or* tin solder. **–stift,** *m.* (lead) pencil. **–stift-spitzer,** *m.* pencil sharpener. **–waage,** *f.* plumb-line. **–wasser,** *n.* Goulard water, lead wash. **–weiß,** *n.* lead carbonate. **–zinn,** *n.* pewter. **–zinnober,** *m. See* **–mennige. –zucker,** *m.* lead acetate, sugar of lead.

Blend|anstrich ['blɛnt–], *m.* (*Mil. etc.*) dazzle-paint. **–bogen,** *m.* (*Archit.*) blind arcade *or* arch.

Blende ['blɛndə], *f.* 1. shutter, (window-)blind; blind *or* sham window *or* door; blind niche (*in a wall*); 2. (*Min.*) blende; 3. diaphragm, stop (*of camera*); 4. *pl.* (*Naut.*) dead-lights; 5. (*Dressm.*) facing. **blenden,** *v.t.* (*fig.*) blind, dazzle; deceive, hoodwink; blindfold; hood (*a falcon*). **blendend,** *adj.* dazzling, brilliant, radiant, resplendent; (*coll.*) brilliant, wonderful, marvellous.

Blenden|einstellung, *f.* (*Phot.*) stop. **–öffnung,** *f.* (*Phot.*) aperture.

Blend|glas, *n.* dark *or* smoked glass. **–laterne,** *f.* dark lantern, bull's-eye lantern. **–leder,** *n.* blinkers.

Blendling ['blɛntlɪŋ], *m.* (**-s,** *pl.* **-e**) (*of animals*) mongrel, cross-breed; (*of plants*) hybrid; (*of persons*) half-breed.

Blend|mauer, *f.* blind wall. **–rahmen,** *m.* (*Archit.*) casing, (outer) frame (*of window, door etc.*). **–scheibe,** *f.* eye-shade, eyeshield; (*Motor.*) anti-dazzle shield. **–stein,** *m.* facing stone *or* brick.

Blendung ['blɛnduŋ], *f.* blinding, dazzling; (*obs.*) deception, delusion.

Blend|werk, *n.* deception, delusion, snare(s), (*coll.*) eye-wash; illusion, mirage. **–ziegel,** *m.* facing brick.

Blesse ['blɛsə], *f.* blaze (*on face of animal*); animal with a blaze on its face.

blessieren [blɛ'si:rən], *v.t.* wound. **Blessur,** *f.* (-, *pl.* **-en**) wound.

Bleuel ['blɔyəl], *m.* beater; rolling-pin; mallet. **bleuen,** *v.t.* beat black and blue.

Blick [blɪk], *m.* (**-es,** *pl.* **-e**) 1. look, glance, view; ***der böse –,*** the evil eye; ***auf den ersten –,*** at first sight; ***finstere –e,*** black looks; ***flüchtiger –,*** glimpse, cursory glance; ***neidischer –,*** covetous eye; ***scharfer –,*** penetrating glance; ***schräger –,*** side-long glance; ***sicherer –,*** sure eye; ***sprechender –,*** telling glance; ***verstohlener –,*** furtive glance; ***keinen – für etwas haben,*** have no eye *or* understanding for a th.; ***er wandte keinen – von ihr,*** his eyes never left her, he did not take his eyes off her; ***mit dem –e verfolgen,*** follow with one's eyes; ***einen – auf eine S. werfen,*** glance at *or* take a look at a th., run *or* cast one's eyes over a th.; ***mit einem – auf den See,*** with a view of *or* over *or* across the lake, overlooking the lake; 2. fulguration (*of silver*).

blicken ['blɪkən], *v.i.* look (***auf*** (*Acc.*) *or* ***nach,*** at); ***zur Seite –,*** look away; ***sich – lassen,*** show o.s. *or* itself, (let o.s. *or* itself) be seen, show one's face; ***tief – lassen,*** be revealing, (*coll.*) be an eye-opener.

Blick|fang, *m.* stunt, (*coll.*) eye-catcher. **–feld,** *n.* field of view *or* vision. **–feuer,** *n.* signal fire; flashing light (*of lighthouse*). **–linie,** *f.* line of sight. **–punkt,** *m.* visual *or* focal point; ***im – sein,*** be in the limelight. **–richtung,** *f.* line of sight. **–silber,** *n.* refined silver. **–winkel,** *m.* visual angle.

blieb [bli:p], **bliebe** ['bli:bə], *see* **bleiben.**

blies [bli:s], **bliese** ['bli:zə], *see* **blasen.**

blind [blɪnt], **1.** *adj.* blind; dim, clouded, tarnished, dull, mat(t), opaque; dead, blank; (*fig.*) blind, implicit; ***–er Alarm,*** *see* ***–er Lärm***; (*Typ.*) ***–er Bogen,*** blank sheet; ***–er Eifer,*** blind enthusiasm; (*Prov.*) ***–er Eifer schadet nur,*** zeal without knowledge is frenzy; ***–es Gefecht,*** sham fight; ***–er Gehorsam,*** blind *or* implicit obedience; ***–er Kauf,*** fictitious purchase; ***–e Klippen,*** sunken rocks; ***–er Lärm,*** false alarm; ***–er Passagier,*** stowaway, deadhead; ***–e Patrone,*** blank cartridge; ***–e Versteigerung,*** sham auction; ***–er Zufall,*** pure chance; ***– auf einem Auge,*** blind in one eye; ***– geboren,*** blind from birth. **2.** *adv.* blindly, implicitly; (*Av.*) ***– fliegen,*** fly blind; ***– laden,*** load with blank (cartridges); ***– schießen,*** fire blanks; fire at random *or* blindly; ***– schreiben,*** touch-type; ***– zugreifen,*** make a wild grab, grab wildly.

Blind|boden, *m.* under-flooring. **–darm,** *m.* appendix, caecum. **–darmentzündung,** *f.* appendicitis. **–druck,** *m.* (*Typ.*) blind tooling *or* blocking.

Blindekuh ['blɪndəku:], *f.* blind-man's buff.

Blinden|anstalt, *f.* blind institution. **–druck,** *m.*

braille. **–(führer)hund,** *m.* guide dog (for the blind), (*Am.*) seeing-eye dog. **–schrift,** *f. See* **–druck.**

Blinde(r) ['blɪndə(r)], *m., f.* blind man (*or* woman).

Blind|flug, *m.* (*Av.*) blind flight; blind flying. **–gänger,** *m.* (*Artil.*) misfire, blind, dud. **–geborene(r),** *m., f.* one born blind. **Blindheit,** *f.* blindness. **Blind|holz,** *n.* wood to be veneered. **–leitwert,** *m.* (*Elec.*) susceptance. **blindlings,** *adv.* (*fig.*) blindly, wildly, headlong, at random. **Blind|-material,** *n.* (*Typ.*) spacing material. **–muster,** *n.* (showcase) dummy. **–prägung, –pressung,** *f. See* **–druck. blindschlagen,** *irr.v.t.* (*Typ.*) leave blank. **Blind|schleiche,** *f.* slow-worm, blind-worm; (*fig.*) snake in the grass. **–schloß,** *n.* mortise lock. **–strom,** *m.* (*Elec.*) wattless *or* idle current. **–wert,** *m.* (*Elec.*) wattless *or* imaginary component. **–widerstand,** *m.* (*Elec.*) reactance.

Blink [blɪŋk], *m.* **(-(e)s,** *pl.* **-e)** flash.

blinken ['blɪŋkən], *v.i.* 1. glitter, gleam, shine; flash, blink, twinkle, sparkle; 2. signal (*with lamps*). **Blinker,** *m.* 1. lamp-signaller; 2. (*Motor.*) direction indicator, flasher; 3. (*fishing*) spoon-bait. **Blinkfeuer,** *n.* flashing *or* occulting light.

blinzeln ['blɪntsəln], *v.i.* blink, wink.

Blitz [blɪts], *m.* **(-es,** *pl.* **-e)** lightning (flash), (*fig.*) flash (*of wit etc.*); ***vom –e berührt*** or ***getroffen,*** struck by lightning; ***wie vom –e gerührt*** or ***getroffen,*** thunderstruck; ***–e zucken,*** the lightning flashes; ***– aus heiterm Himmel,*** bolt from the blue; ***Potz –!*** ye gods! ***wie der –*** or ***wie ein geölter –,*** like a shot, like a streak of lightning, like greased lightning. **Blitzableiter,** *m.* lightning conductor. **blitz|-artig,** *adj.* like lightning, in a flash. **–blank,** *adj.* bright and shiny, spick and span; black and blue.

blitzen ['blɪtsən], **1.** *v.imp.* ***es blitzt,*** the lightning flashes. **2.** *v.i.* flash, sparkle; (*coll.*) ***es blitzt bei dir,*** your slip is showing.

Blitzesschnelle ['blɪtsəzʃnɛlə], *f.* lightning speed.

Blitz|krieg, *m.* lightning war *or* warfare. **–licht,** *n.* flash-light. **–lichtaufnahme,** *f.* flash(-light) photograph. **–mädel,** *n.* (*Mil. coll.*) woman auxiliary telegraphist. **–pulver,** *n.* lycopodium. **blitz|sauber,** *adj. See* **–blank. Blitzschlag,** *m.* flash of lightning. **blitzschnell,** *adj.* quick as lightning, like a flash. **Blitz|strahl,** *m. See* **–schlag.**

Block [blɔk], *m.* **(-(e)s,** *pl.* **⸚e)** block, log; boulder; pad (*of paper*); stocks; block of houses *or* flats, (*Pol.*) coalition, bloc; (***Verbrecher***) ***in den – legen,*** put (criminal) in the stocks.

Blockade [blɔ'ka:də], *f.* blockade. **Blockadenbrecher,** *m.* blockade-runner.

blocken ['blɔkən], *v.t.* block (*railway line etc.*).

blöcken ['blœkən], *v.t.* block (*hat etc.*).

Block|flöte, *f.* (*Mus.*) recorder. **–form,** *f.* ingot mould. **–haus,** *n.* log hut; (*Mil.*) blockhouse, pill-box.

blockieren [blɔ'ki:rən], *v.t.* block up, obstruct; (*Mil.*) blockade; (*sl.*) stymie; (*Bill.*) ***einen Ball –,*** send a ball into a corner-pocket, make a coup. **Blockierung,** *f.* blockage, blockade.

Block|kondensator, *m.* (*Rad.*) blocking condenser. **–lehm,** *m.* boulder clay. **–mehrheit,** *f.* coalition majority. **–schiff,** *n.* raft; blockship, hulk. **–schrift,** *f.* block letters. **–stelle,** *f.* (*Railw.*) signalbox. **–strecke,** *f.* (*Railw.*) block. **–verschluß,** *m.* (*Artil.*) breech-block mechanism. **–wagen,** *m.* truck. **–wart,** *m.* block warden (*Nat. Soc.: combining duties of air-raid warden, public relations man and general informer*).

blöd(e) ['blø:d(ə)], *adj.* 1. *See* **blödsinnig**; 2. bashful, timid, shy; 3. (*coll.*) stupid, idiotic, foolish, silly, daft. **Blödheit, Blödigkeit,** *f.* 1. bashfulness, timidity, shyness; 2. stupidity, foolishness, silliness; (*obs.*) ***– der Augen,*** weak eyesight. **blödsichtig,** *adj.* (*obs.*) weak-sighted.

Blödsinn ['blø:dzɪn], *m.* imbecility, idiocy, feeble-mindedness, mental deficiency; (*coll.*) nonsense, rubbish, fooling. **blödsinnig,** *adj.* imbecile, mentally defective *or* deficient; (*coll.*) *See* **blöd(e),** 3.

blöken ['blø:kən], *v.t.* bleat (*sheep*); low (*cattle*).

blond [blɔnt], *adj.* blond (*masc.*), blonde (*fem.*), fair(-haired). **Blonde** [–ndə], *f.* (*coll.*) (glass of) light ale. **blondieren** [–'di:rən], *v.t.* bleach (*hair*). **Blondine** [–'di:nə], *f.* blonde. **Blondkopf,** *m.* fair-haired person. **blondlockig,** *adj.* fair-haired.

bloß [blo:s], **1.** *adj.* bare, naked; uncovered, deprived (of); destitute; mere; ***–er Argwohn*** or ***Verdacht,*** mere suspicion; ***mit –em Auge,*** with the naked eye; ***der –e Gedanke,*** the mere idea, the very thought; ***auf –er Haut,*** next to the skin; ***im –en Hemd,*** wearing nothing but a shirt; ***mit –em Kopfe,*** bare-headed; ***auf einem –en Pferde reiten,*** ride barebacked; ***mit –em Schwert,*** with naked *or* drawn sword; ***–e Worte,*** empty *or* mere words. **2.** *adv.* merely, only, solely, simply; ***– um Ihnen zu gefallen,*** simply to please you; ***es kostet – eine Mark,*** it costs only one mark.

Blöße ['blø:sə], *f.* nakedness; clearing (*in a wood*); weakness, weak spot; ***sich*** (*Dat.*) ***eine – geben,*** expose o.s., lay o.s. open (*to attack, ridicule etc.*); compromise o.s., give o.s. away; ***sich*** (*Dat.*) ***keine – geben,*** be invulnerable *or* infallible, have no chinks in one's armour.

bloß|geben, *irr.v.r.* expose o.s., betray o.s.; (*Fenc., fig.*) lay o.s. open (to). **–legen,** *v.t.* lay bare; (*fig.*) expose, uncover. **Bloßlegung,** *f.* exposure. **bloßstellen,** *v.t.* expose, unmask; compromise. **Bloßstellung,** *f.* exposure, compromise.

Bluff [bluf], *m.* **(-s,** *pl.* **-s)** bluff, deception, trick. **bluffen,** *v.t., v.i.* bluff.

blühen ['bly:ən], *v.i.* flower, bloom, blossom; be in flower *or* bloom *or* blossom; (*fig.*) prosper, thrive, flourish; boom (*of business*); be rosy (*as cheeks*); (*coll.*) ***mir blüht noch eine Prüfung,*** there is still an examination in store for me; ***es blüht sein Glück,*** fortune smiles on him; ***das Geschäft blüht,*** business prospers; ***sein Weizen blüht,*** he is in luck('s way) *or* in clover. **blühend,** *adj.* in blossom, blooming; flourishing, prosperous, radiant; ***im –sten Alter,*** in the prime of life; ***–er Blödsinn,*** arrant nonsense; ***–es Mädchen,*** radiant young girl, girl in the full bloom of youth.

Blümchen ['bly:mçən], *n.* 1. floweret; 2. scut (*of hare etc.*). **Blümchenkaffee,** *m.* (*coll.*) very weak coffee.

Blume ['blu:mə], *f.* 1. flower, blossom; aroma; bouquet (*of wine*); froth, head (*on beer*); gloss (*on linen etc.*); ***man streut ihr –n auf den Weg,*** her path is strewn with roses; 3. (*Hunt.*) tip of the tail, scut; 3. (*Chem.*) efflorescence; 4. (*fig.*) figure of speech, metaphor; ***durch die – sprechen,*** speak in riddles; 5. choice, pick, élite. **blumenartig,** *adj.* flowerlike.

Blumen|becher, *m.* calyx. **–beet,** *n.* flower-bed. **–blatt,** *n.* petal. **–deckblatt,** *n.* sepal. **–decke,** *f.* perianth. **–duft,** *m.* fragrance, perfume. **–erde,** *f.* garden-mould. **–flor,** *m.* show of flowers. **–gärtner,** *m.* florist. **–gehänge, –gewinde,** *n.* festoon, garland. **–göttin,** *f.* Flora, goddess of flowers. **–händler,** *m.* florist, nursery-gardener. **–honig,** *m.* nectar. **–hülle,** *f. See* **–decke. –kelch,** *m.* calyx. **–kohl,** *m.* cauliflower. **–korb,** *m.* flower-basket; (*Archit.*) corbel. **–korso,** *m.* battle of flowers. **–krone,** *f.* corolla. **–laden,** *m.* flower shop, florist's. **–lese,** *f.* anthology, selection. **–mädchen,** *n.* flower girl. **–muster,** *n.* floral pattern. **–rohr,** *n.* arrowroot (*Canna tulema*). **–sauger,** *m.* humming bird. **–scherbe,** *f.* (*dial.*) flower-pot. **–schmuck,** *m.* floral decoration. **–seite,** *f.* hairy side (*of leather*). **–staub,** *m.* pollen. **–stengel,** *m.* flower stem *or* stalk. **–stiel,** *m.* peduncle. **blumenstielständig,** *adj.* pedunculate, peduncular. **Blumen|strauß,** *m.* bunch of flowers, bouquet. **–stück,** *n.* 1. flower-painting; 2. (*Cul.*) silverside. **–topf,** *m.* flower-pot. **–werk,** *n.* festoons, garlands, floral work. **–zucht,** *f.* floriculture. **–züchter,** *m.* florist, nursery-gardener. **–zwiebel,** *f.* (flower-)bulb.

blümerant [bly:mə'rant], *adj.* pale-blue (***bleu mourant***); (*coll.*) ***mir wird ganz –,*** I feel quite dizzy *or* giddy, my head reels.

blumig ['blu:mɪç], *adj.* flowering, flower-covered; flowered (*fabric*); (*fig.*) flowery, florid; (*of wine*) with bouquet.

-blumig, *adj.suff.* -flowered.

Bluse ['blu:zə], *f.* blouse; smock; ***gestrickte* –,** jumper.

Blut [blu:t], *n.* (**-(e)s,** *no pl.*) blood; race; lineage; sap, juice (*of plants etc.*); ***ihn bis aufs – aussaugen,*** bleed him white; ***ihn bis aufs – hassen,*** hate him like poison *or* like the plague; ***ihn bis aufs – quälen*** or ***peinigen,*** torment him, (*coll.*) give him hell; ***blaues – in den Adern haben,*** have blue blood in one's veins; ***– und Boden,*** blood and soil (*Nat. Soc. catchword*); ***böses – machen*** or ***geben*** or ***setzen,*** cause bad blood, arouse ill feeling; ***der Schreck ließ mir das – gerinnen,*** fear turned my blood to water; ***geronnenes –,*** clotted blood; ***junges –,*** young thing *or* creature; ***mit kaltem –e,*** in cold blood; ***ihm – lassen,*** bleed him; ***es liegt im –e,*** it runs in the blood; ***Gesicht wie Milch und –,*** complexion like peaches and cream; ***(nur) ruhig –!*** calm yourself! steady! – ***stillen,*** stop the bleeding; ***der Schreck ließ mir das – stocken*** or ***erstarren,*** fear made my blood run cold; ***Menschen unseres –s,*** people of our race.

Blut|ader, *f.* blood-vessel. **-andrang,** *m.* congestion (*of blood*). **-apfelsine,** *f.* blood orange. **blutarm,** *adj.* 1. ['blu:tˀarm] anaemic; 2. [-'arm] poor as a churchmouse. **Blut|armut,** *f.* anaemia. **-auge,** *n.* 1. bloodshot eye; 2. (*Bot.*) finger fern (*Comarum palustre*). **-auswurf,** *m.* bloody sputum. **-bad,** *n.* blood-bath, slaughter, massacre, carnage, butchery. **-bahn,** *f.* blood-stream. **-bank,** *f.* blood bank. **-bann,** *m.* (*Hist.*) jurisdiction with capital powers. **blutbefleckt,** *adj.* blood-stained. **Blut|blase,** *f.* blood blister. **-blume,** *f.* (*Bot.*) blood-flower, arnica (*Haemanthus*). **-brechen,** *n.* vomiting of blood, haemetemesis. **-buche,** *f.* copper beech (*Fagus*). **-druck,** *m.* blood pressure. **-druckmesser,** *m.* sphygmomanometer. **-durst,** *m.* bloodthirstiness, blood-lust. **blutdürstig,** *adj.* bloodthirsty.

Blüte ['bly:tə], *f.* blossom, flower, bloom; flowering, (in)florescence; (*fig.*) prime; cream, flower; ***in voller –,*** in full bloom, in blossom; (*fig.*) ***seine – haben,*** flourish.

Blutegel ['blu:tˀe:gəl], *m.* leech.

bluten ['blu:tən], *v.i.* bleed; shed one's blood; (*coll.*) cough *or* stump up, fork out (*money*), pay through the nose; ***mir blutet das Herz,*** my heart bleeds; ***fürs Vaterland –,*** die for one's country.

Blüten|art, *f.* flower family. **-auge,** *n.* flower-bud. **-bestäubung,** *f.* pollin(iz)ation. **-blatt,** *n.* petal. **blütenblattlos,** *adj.* apetalous. **Blüten|büschel,** *n.* (*Bot.*) fascicle. **-decke,** *f.* (*Bot.*) perianth. **-dolde,** *f.* (*Bot.*) umbel. **-hülle,** *f.* perianth. **-hüllenblatt,** *n.* sepal. **-kätzchen,** *n.* catkin. **-kelch,** *m.* calyx. **-knäuel,** *m.* glomerule. **-knospe,** *f.* flower-bud. **-krone,** *f.* corolla. **-lese,** *f.* anthology. **blütenlos,** *adj.* cryptogamous. **Blüten|pflanze,** *f.* flowering plant, phanerogam. **-scheibe,** *f.* thalamus. **-scheide,** *f.* spathe. **-spelze,** *f.* glume. **-stand,** *m.* inflorescence. **-staub,** *m.* pollen. **-stiel,** *m.* pedicle.

Blutentnahme ['blu:tˀɛntna:mə], *f.* blood-sample.

blütentragend ['bly:təntra:gənt], *adj.* flower-bearing, floriferous. **Blütentraube,** *f.* raceme.

Blutentziehung ['blu:tˀɛnttsi:uŋ], *f.* blood-letting, venesection.

blütenweiß ['bly:tənvaɪs], *adj.* snow-white. **Blütenzweig,** *m.* spray of flowers.

Bluter ['blu:tər], *m.* haemophiliac, (*coll.*) bleeder.

Blut|erbrechen, *n. See* **-brechen. -erguß,** *m.* haemorrhage, effusion, extravasation.

Bluterkrankheit ['blu:tərkraŋkaɪt], *f.* haemophilia.

Blütezeit ['bly:tətsaɪt], *f.* blossom-time, flowering period; (*fig.*) prime, heyday; golden age.

blutfarbig ['blu:tfarbɪç], *adj.* crimson. **Blut|farbstoff,** *m.* haemoglobin, blood pigment. **-faserstoff,** *m.* fibrin. **-fleck(en),** *m.* blood-stain. **-fleckenkrankheit,** *f.* (*Med.*) purpura, (*coll.*) the purples. **-fluß,** *m.* haemorrhage, bleeding; menorrhagia. **-flüssigkeit,** *f.* blood plasma. **-führung,** *f.* pedigree. **-gefäß,** *n.* blood-vessel. **-geräusch,** *n.* (*Med.*) haemic murmurs. **-gericht,** *n.* (*Hist.*) assize. **-gerinnsel,** *n.* blood clot. **-gerinnung,** *f.* coagulation, clotting. **-gerüst,** *n.* scaffold. **-geschwulst,** *f.* (*Med.*) haemotoma. **-geschwür,** *n.* boil, furuncle, phlegmon. **-gier,** *f.* bloodthirstiness, blood-lust. **blutgierig,** *adj.* bloodthirsty. **Blut|gruppe,** *f.* blood group. **-hänfling,** *n. See* **Hänfling. -harnen,** *n.* (*Med.*) haematuria. **-hochzeit,** *f.* bloodbath, massacre. **-hund,** *m.* bloodhound. **-husten,** *n.* (*Med.*) haemoptysis.

blutig ['blu:tɪç], *adj.* blood-stained, bloody, gory, sanguinary; ***–er Anfänger,*** utter novice; ***–er Ernst,*** deadly earnest(ness); ***–e Hände,*** blood-stained hands; ***–e Nase,*** bloody nose; ***–e Schlacht,*** bloody battle; ***–e Tat,*** bloody deed; ***–e Tränen,*** bitter tears; ***–e Zwischenfälle,*** incidents involving bloodshed.

-blutig, *adj.suff.* -blooded; *e.g.* ***voll–,*** full-blooded.

-blütig ['bly:tɪç], *adj. suff.* with . . . blossoms, -flowered.

blutjung [blu:t'juŋ], *adj.* very young.

Blut|körperchen, *n.* blood corpuscle. **-körperchenzählung,** *f.* blood count. **-kreislauf,** *m.* circulation of the blood. **-kuchen,** *m.* clotted fibrin. **-lassen,** *n.* bloodletting. **-lauf,** *m. See* **-kreislauf. blutleer,** *adj.* (*usu. fig.*) bloodless. **Blut|leere,** *f.* (*Med.*) anaemia. **-leiter,** *m.* (*Anat.*) sinus. **-linie,** *f.* pedigree. **blutlos,** *adj.* bloodless. **Blut|mangel,** *m.* anaemia. **-nachweis,** *m.* blood-test. **-netzen,** *n.* (*Vet.*) red-water disease. **-pfropf,** *m.* (*Med.*) thrombus. **-probe,** *f.* blood test. **-rache,** *f.* vendetta. **blutrünstig,** *adj.* bloody, bloodthirsty. **Blut|sauger,** *m.* blood-sucker (*also fig.*). **-schande,** *f.* incest. **-scheibe,** *f.* corpuscle. **-schuld,** *f.* capital crime; murder; incest. **-schwär(e),** *m.* (*f.*) *See* **-geschwür. -specht,** *m.* (*Orn.*) Syrian woodpecker (*Dendrocopus syriacus*). **-spender,** *m.* blood-donor. **-spucken,** *n. See* **-husten. -stein,** *m.* haematite. **-blutstillend,** *adj.* haemostatic, styptic. **Blut|stockung,** *f.* haemostasia. **-sturz,** *m.* violent haemorrhage; bursting of a blood-vessel. **-sucht,** *f.* haemophilia.

blutsverwandt ['blu:tsfɛrvant], *adj.* related by blood (*mit,* to). **Blutsverwandte(r),** *m., f.* blood relation. **Blutsverwandtschaft,** *f.* consanguinity, blood relationship.

Blut|tat, *f.* bloody deed, murder. **-übertragung,** *f.* blood transfusion. **-umlauf,** *m.* circulation of the blood.

Blutung ['blu:tuŋ], *f.* bleeding, haemorrhage.

blutunterlaufen ['blu:tˀuntərlaufən], *adj.* bloodshot. **Blut|unterlaufung,** *f.* effusion of blood. **-unterschung,** *f.* blood-test. **-vergießen,** *n.* bloodshed, slaughter. **-vergiftung,** *f.* blood poisoning, toxaemia, sepsis, septicaemia. **blutvoll,** *adj.* (*fig.*) vivid, lively, racy. **Blut|wallung,** *f. See* **-andrang. blutwarm,** *adj.* at blood-heat. **Blut|wärme,** *f.* blood heat. **-wasser,** *n.* lymph; serum. **-wassergefäß,** *n.* lymphatic vessel. **blutwenig** [-'ve:nɪç], *adj.* very little, next to nothing. **Blut|wurst,** *f.* black pudding. **-zeuge,** *m.* martyr. **-zufuhr,** *f.* supply of blood.

Bö [bø:], *f.* (-, *pl.* **-en**) gust, squall.

Bob [bɔb], *m.* (**-s,** *pl.* **-s**) bob-sleigh. **Bob(fahr)bahn,** *f.* bob-sleigh run. **bobfahren,** *irr.v.i.* bob-sleigh.

Bock [bɔk], *m.* (**-(e)s,** *pl.* **⸚e**) 1. ram; buck; he-goat, (*coll.*) billy-goat; (*coll.*) pigheaded person, awkward customer *or* (*sl.*) bugger; (*coll.*) rake, lecher, whoremonger, (*sl.*) ram; ***den – zum Gärtner machen*** or ***setzen,*** set the fox to keep the geese; ***die Schafe von den Böcken scheiden,*** separate the sheep from the goats; ***einen – schießen,*** commit a blunder *or* (*coll.*) bloomer; 2. lifting jack; derrick, gin, sheer-legs; 3. stand, rest, rack, trestle; stool; strut, stay, prop, support, bearer, bracket; truss (*of a bridge*); (*Bill.*) bridge, cue-rest; (*Gymn.*)

vaulting-horse; – *springen,* play at leap-frog; *über den – springen,* jump over the vaulting-horse; 4. (coachman's) box; 5. (*Hist.*) battering ram; 6. *See* **Bockbier.**

bockbeinig [ˈbɔkbaɪnɪç], *adj.* 1. bowlegged; 2. stubborn, obstinate, mulish; awkward, clumsy. **Bock|bier,** *n.* strong *or* double beer. **–brücke,** *f.* trestle bridge.

bocken [ˈbɔkən], *v.i.* 1. be on heat (*of goat, sheep etc.*); 2. plunge, rear (*as a horse*); kick (*as a gun*), misfire, backfire (*as an engine*), pitch (and toss) (*as a ship*); 3. be obstinate; sulk.

bockfüßig, *adj. See* **bock(s)füßig.**

bockig [ˈbɔkɪç], *adj.* 1. obstinate, mulish, pig-headed; sulky, refractory; 2. rutting (*of male deer*), on heat (*of female animals*); stinking; 3. (*Av.*) bumpy.

Bock|käfer, *m.* (*Ent.*) capricorn beetle (*Cerambycidae*). **–kasten,** *m.* boot (*of a coach*). **–kran,** *m.* gantry. **–leder,** *n.* buckskin. **–leiter,** *f.* step-ladder, pair of steps. **–motor,** *m.* underslung vertical engine. **–pfeife,** *f.* bagpipe(s).

Bocks|bart, *m.* (*Bot.*) goat's beard (*Tragapogon*), (*coll.*) goatee (*beard*). **–beutel,** *m.* squat wine bottle.

Bock|schnurbund, *m.* (*Naut.*) square lashing. **–setzen,** *n.* pile-driving.

Bocks|fuß [ˈbɔksfus], *m.* cloven hoof. **bocks|füßig,** *adj.* cloven-hoofed, cloven-footed. **Bocks|horn,** *n.* hartshorn; *ihn ins – jagen,* intimidate *or* browbeat him, bully him, frighten him out of his wits. **–hornkraut,** *n.* (*Bot.*) fenugreek (*Trigonella*).

Bock|sitz, *m.* driver's seat. **–spiel, –springen,** *n.* leapfrog. **–sprung,** *m.* caper, gambol; *Bocksprünge machen,* caper, gambol; frisk. **bocksteif,** *adj.* mulish, stubborn; awkward, clumsy. **Bock|-winde,** *f.* winch, windlass. **–wurst,** *f.* sausage (*for boiling*).

Boden [ˈbo:dən], *m.* (**-s,** *pl.* *- or* ̈–) 1. ground, soil, earth, land; *ihm – abgewinnen,* gain (ground) on him; *den – ebnen,* prepare *or* clear the ground; *ihm den – entziehen,* cut the ground from under his feet; *– fassen,* (*of ideas*) take root, (*of a p.*) settle down, establish o.s.; *festen – finden,* find one's feet; *gemeinsamen – finden,* find common ground *or* a basis; *festen – gewinnen,* gain *or* get a footing *or* foothold; *den – (unter den Füßen) verlieren,* lose one's footing, be carried *or* swept off one's feet, be *or* get out of one's depth (*in water, also fig.*); *an – gewinnen,* gain ground (*of ideas etc.*); *auf deutschem –,* on German soil; *auf festem – stehen,* be on dry land, (*fig.*) be on sure *or* firm ground, be sure of one's ground; *auf festen – stellen,* place on a firm footing *or* foundation; *sich auf schwankendem – bewegen,* get out of one's element *or* depth; *auf dem – der Tatsachen,* on a factual basis, on the basis of facts; *zu – fallen,* fall down, fall to the ground; *zu – schlagen,* strike *or* knock down, knock to the ground, (*fig.*) shatter, dash (*hopes etc.*), cast down *or* to the ground (*one's eyes*); *zu – werfen,* fling *or* throw down *or* to the ground, (*fig.*) crush (*enemy*); 2. bottom, bed (*of sea*), bottom, floor (*of valley*), floor (*of room*), bottom (*of box etc.*), seat (*of trousers*), back (*of violin, watch etc.*), base(-board); *das schlägt dem Faß den – aus,* that's the limit *or* the last straw, that puts the lid on it; 3. loft, attic, garret.

Boden|abstand, *m.* (ground) clearance (*of vehicle*). **–abwehr,** *f.* (*Mil.*) ground defences. **–bearbeitung,** *f.* cultivation of the soil. **–belag,** *m.* floor covering, flooring. **–beschaffenheit,** *f.* condition *or* nature of the soil, state of the ground; (*Geog.*) topographical features. **–besitz,** *m.* landed property. **–bildung,** *f.* soil formation. **–brett,** *n.* base-board; *pl.* heading (*of casks*). **–entwässerung,** *f.* land drainage. **–fenster,** *n.* attic window. **–fläche,** *f.* floor space (*of room*), ground space (*of building*), acreage (*of land*). **–freiheit,** *f. See* **–abstand. –fund,** *m.* archaeological find. **–geschoß,** *n.* attic storey *or* floor. **–gestaltung,** *f.* topography. **–kammer,** *f.* garret, attic. **–kennung,** *f.* (*Av.*) ground markers. **–kredit,** *m.* loan on landed property, land credit. **–kreditanstalt,** *f.* land(-mortgage) bank. **–kunde,** *f.* science of soils.

bodenlos [ˈbo:dənlo:s], **1.** *adj.* bottomless, fathomless; (*fig.*) abysmal, unbounded, colossal, unheard of. **2.** *adv.* exceedingly, excessively, abysmally (*stupid etc.*).

Boden|luke, *f.* attic window, sky-light; escape hatch (*of tank etc.*). **–mannschaft,** *f.* (*Av.*) ground crew. **–markierung,** *f.* (*Artil.*) target indicator. **–müdigkeit,** *f.* soil exhaustion. **–nebel,** *m.* ground mist. **–nutzung,** *f.* land utilization. **–personal,** *n. See* **–mannschaft. –planke,** *f.* (*Naut.*) garboard strake. **–punkt,** *m.* (*Surv.*) bench mark. **–raum,** *m.* attic, box-room. **–reform,** *f.* agrarian reform. **–satz,** *m.* dregs, grounds, deposit, sediment, (*Chem.*) residuum, precipitate; sludge, foot (*of oil*), lees (*of wine*). **–schätze,** *m.pl.* mineral resources. **–schicht,** *f.* layer of soil *or* earth; (*Geol.*) formation, stratum. **–schnelle,** *f.* (*Gymn.*) push-up. **–schwankung,** *f.* (*Astr.*) nutation. **–see,** *m.* Lake (of) Constance. **–senke,** *f.* depression, dip *or* hollow (in the ground). **–senkung,** *f.* subsidence. **–sicht,** *f.* (*Av.*) ground visibility. **–speicher,** *m.* granary, (grain) elevator. **–spekulation,** *f.* land speculation, land-jobbing.

bodenständig [ˈbo:dənʃtɛndɪç], *adj.* indigenous; autochthonous, native (*population*); (*Bot.*) radical; (*fig.*) settled, firmly established, permanent; *–e Familien,* families of old standing.

Boden|stein, *m.* nether millstone. **–stück,** *n.* breechplate (*of a gun*); heading (*of a cask*). **–waage,** *f.* weigh-bridge. **–welle,** *f.* (*Rad.*) ground wave. **–wuchs,** *m.* undergrowth. **–zins,** *m.* ground-rent. **–zünder,** *m.* base percussion fuse.

bodmen [ˈbo:dmən], *v.t.* 1. (*Naut.*) raise money on bottomry; 2. (*obs.*) floor, plank (*a room*); head (*a cask*). **Bodmerei** [–ˈraɪ], *f.* (-, *pl.* **-en**) (*Naut.*) bottomry; *– auf die Schiffsladung,* respondentia. **Bodmerei|brief,** *m.* bottomry bond, respondentia bond. **–nehmer,** *m.* raiser of money on bottomry bonds. **Bodmerist** [–ˈrɪst], *m.* (**-en,** *pl.* **-en**) lender on bottomry.

Böe [ˈbø:ə], *f. See* **Bö. Böenlinie,** *f.* (*Meteor.*) cold front.

Bofist [ˈbo:fɪst, boˈfɪst], *m.* (**-s,** *pl.* **-e**) (*Bot.*) puff-ball.

bog [bo:k], **böge** [ˈbø:gə], *see* **biegen.**

Bogen [ˈbo:gən], *m.* (**-s,** *pl.* *- or* ̈–) 1. bend, curve, arc (*also Geom.*); (*coll.*) *den – heraus haben,* get the hang of s.th., know what one is about; *den Fluß macht einen –,* the river makes a bend; (*fig.*) *einen großen – um etwas machen,* give s.th. a wide berth; *einen – schlagen,* describe a curve *or* an arc; 2. (*Archit.*) arch; (*Mus.*) slur; bridge (*of spectacles*); (*Archit.*) *äußerer –,* extrados; *gedrückter –,* elliptical arch; *gestelzter –,* stilted arch; *innerer –,* intrados, soffit, archivolt; *runder –,* semicircular arch; *scheitrechter –,* flat arch; 3. bow (*violin, archery*); *einen – spannen,* bend *or* draw a bow; (*fig.*) *den – überspannen,* carry things too far, overdo it; 4. sheet (*of paper*); *in Bausch und –,* in the lump; *bedruckter –,* printed sheet; *in rohen –,* in quires; 5. (*Elec.*) (electric) arc.

Bogen|achter, *m.* figure of eight (*skating*). **–anfänger,** *m.* (*Archit.*) springer. **–blende,** *f.* (*Archit.*) blind arch. **–brücke,** *f.* arched bridge. **–feld,** *n.* (*Archit.*) tympanum. **–fenster,** *n.* bay-window, oriel. **bogenförmig,** *adj.* curved, arched. **Bogen|führung,** *f.* (*Mus.*) bowing (technique). **–gang,** *m.* arcade, colonnade. **–größe,** *f.* folio size. **–lampe,** *f.* arc-lamp. **–laufen,** *n.* figure-skating. **–linie,** *f.* curve. **–maß,** *n.* (*Math.*) radian measure. **–rücken,** *m.* (*Archit.*) extrados. **–säge,** *f.* bow-saw. **–schießen,** *n.* archery. **–schluß,** *m.* keystone. **–schuß,** *m.* bow-shot; (*Artil.*) high-angle fire; *einen – weit,* within bowshot. **–schütze,** *m.* archer, bowman. **–sehne,** *f.* bowstring; (*Math.*) chord of a segment. **–spitze,** *f.* (*Archit.*) ogive. **–stirn,** *f.* intrados, soffit, archivolt. **–strich,** *m. See* **–führung**; *mit ganzem –,* with the full bow. **bogenweise,** *adv.* in sheets, by the sheet. **Bogen|weite,** *f.* span of an arch. **–zeichen,** *n.* (folio) signature. **–zirkel,** *m.* bow-compasses, callipers.

–bogig [ˈbo:gɪç], *adj.suff.* -arched.

Bogner [ˈbo:gnər], *m.* (*obs.*) bow-maker; archer, crossbowman.

Bohle [ˈbo:lə], *f.* plank, thick board. **bohlen,** *v.t.* board *or* plank (over). **Bohlen|bahn,** *f.* log *or* corduroy road. **–säge,** *f.* rip-saw.

Böhme [ˈbø:mə], *m.* **(-n,** *pl.* **-n)** Bohemian. **Böhmen,** *n.* Bohemia. **Böhmer Wald,** *m.* Bohemian Forest. **böhmisch,** *adj.* Bohemian, (*coll.*) queer, strange, odd.

Bohne [ˈbo:nə], *f.* bean; (*sl.*) ***blaue –,*** bullet; ***dicke –n,*** broad beans; ***grüne –n,*** French *or* runner beans; ***türkische –n,*** scarlet runners; ***keine – wert,*** not worth a fig *or* straw; ***weiße –n,*** haricot beans.

bohnen [ˈbo:nən], *v.t. See* **bohne(r)n.**

Bohnen|baum, *m.* laburnum. **–fest,** *n.* Twelfth-night. **–kaffee,** *m.* pure coffee. **–ranke,** *f.* beanstalk. **–stange,** *f.* bean-pole; ***sie ist die reine –,*** she is as tall as a lamp-post.

Bohner|(besen), *m.* floor-polisher. **–bürste,** *f.* polishing brush. **–masse,** *f.* (floor) polish. **bohne(r)n,** *v.t.* wax, polish (*a floor*).

Bohreisen [ˈbo:rˀaɪzən], *n.* bit, drill.

bohren [ˈbo:rən], **1.** *v.t.* bore, drill; ***ein Schiff in den Grund –,*** sink *or* scuttle a vessel, send a ship to the bottom; ***das Brett –, wo es am dünnsten ist,*** take the easiest way out, shun trouble; ***hartes Holz –,*** have a tough *or* up-hill job, be up against it; ***ihm das Schwert durch den Leib –,*** run one's sword through him, run him through with one's sword. **2.** *v.r.* bore one's way (*in* (*Acc.*), into; ***durch,*** through) (*as grubs etc.*). **3.** *v.i.* drill, bore (***auf*** (*Dat.*) *or* ***nach,*** for); ***sich*** (*Dat.*) ***in der Nase –,*** pick one's nose; ***sich*** (*Dat.*) ***in den Ohren –,*** poke one's ears; ***an ihm –,*** pester *or* worry *or* harass him. **Bohrer,** *m.* drill, borer, auger, gimlet, awl, bit.

Bohr|futter, *n.* drill-chuck. **–käfer,** *m.* death-watch beetle (*Anobiidae*). **–knarre,** *f.* ratchet drill. **–kurbel,** *f.* brace. **–ladung,** *f.* blasting charge. **–loch,** *n.* bore-hole, drill-hole; (*Min.*) blast- *or* shot-hole; burrow (*of grub*). **–maschine,** *f.* drilling machine, hand-drill; (dentist's) drill. **–patrone,** *f.* blasting charge. **–ratsche,** *f. See* **–knarre. –schlamm, –schmant,** *m.* (*Min.*) sludge. **–schuß,** *m. See* **patrone. –späne,** *m.pl.* borings. **–turm,** *m.* (*Min.*) drilling derrick.

Bohrung [ˈbo:ruŋ], *f.* bore (*of cylinder*); boring; borehole.

Bohr|winde, *f. See* **–kurbel. –wurm,** *m.* ship worm, teredo.

böig [ˈbø:ɪç], *adj.* gusty, squally.

Boje [ˈbo:jə], *f.* buoy; ***stumpfe –,*** can-buoy; ***spitze –,*** conical buoy; ***die – steht blind,*** the buoy is not visible; ***die – wacht,*** the buoy is floating. **Bojereep,** *n.* buoy-line.

Bolle [ˈbɔlə], *f.* (*dial.*) bulb; onion.

Boller [ˈbɔlər], *m.* (*Naut.*) bollard, bitt.

Böller [ˈbœlər], *m.* small cannon, mortar. **Böllerschuß,** *m.* gun-salute; mortar shot.

Bollwerk [ˈbɔlvɛrk], *n.* bulwark, bastion, rampart, stronghold.

Bolschewik [bɔlʃəˈvɪk], *m.* **(-en,** *pl.* **-en)** Bolshevik, Bolshevist. **Bolschewismus,** *m.* Bolshevism. **Bolschewist,** *m.* **(-en** *pl.* **-en)** *see* **Bolschewik. bolschewistisch,** *adj.* Bolshevist.

Bolus [ˈbo:lus], *m.* bole; ***roter –,*** reddle; ***weißer –,*** kaolin.

Bolz [bɔlts] **(-es,** *pl.* **-e), Bolzen,** *m.* bolt; (*Carp.*) dowel, peg, plug; (*Engin.*) gudgeon, chock, quoin, key; pin, pintle (*of a hinge*); soldering iron; bolt, quarrel (*of a crossbow*), dart (*of an airgun*); (*Min.*) prop, stay, post, shore. **Bolzen|büchse,** *f.* air-gun. **–eisen,** *n.* box-iron. **bolzengerade,** *adv.* bolt upright. **Bolzen|gewinde,** *n.* male thread. **–mutter,** *f.* (*Engin.*) nut. **–ring,** *m.* shackle. **–scheibe,** *f.* (*Engin.*) washer. **–schloß,** *n.* cylindrical padlock.

Bombage [bɔmˈba:ʒə], *f.* dishing, flanging (*o sheet-metal etc.*).

Bombardement [bɔmbardəˈmã], *n.* **(-s,** *pl.* **-s)** bombardment, shelling, bombing. **bombardieren** [–ˈdi:rən], *v.t.* bombard, shell, bomb. **Bombardierung,** *f.* bombardment, shelling.

Bombast [bɔmˈbast], *m.* (**-s,** *no pl.*) bombast, pomposity, grandiloquence. **bombastisch,** *adj.* bombastic, pompous, inflated, high-flown, highfalutin(g).

Bombe [ˈbɔmbə], *f.* 1. bomb, (*fig.*) bomb-shell; gas-cylinder, oxygen bottle; ***mit –n belegen,*** bomb; ***wie eine – hereinplatzen,*** burst in like a bomb-shell; (*coll.*) ***die – ist geplatzt,*** the balloon has gone up; 2. (*sl.*) (*of a performance or performer*) smash-hit, (*of article*) snip, (*of a shot at goal*) sizzler.

Bomben– [ˈbɔmbən], *pref.* 1. bomb, bombing; 2. (*coll.*) colossal, enormous. **–abwurf,** *m.* bombing **–abwurfgerät,** *n.* bomb-release mechanism. **–abwurfzielgerät,** *n.* bomb-sight. **–angriff,** *m.* bomb attack, air *or* bombing raid. **–anschlag,** *m.,* **–attentat,** *n.* bomb outrage. **–attraktion,** *f.* (*Theat. etc.*) big draw. **–einschlag,** *m.* bomb explosion; bomb crater. **–erfolg,** *m.* (*coll.*) huge success, smash hit. **bombenfest,** *adj.* bomb-proof, shell-proof; (*coll.*) *sda steht –,* that's a daed –cert. **flugzeug,** *n.* bomber. **–klappe,** *f.* bomb-door. **–last,** *f.* bomb-load. **–punktzielwurf,** *m.* pinpoint bombing. **–räumtrupp,** *m.* bomb-disposal squad. **–reihenwurf,** *m.* carpet bombing. **–schütze,** *m.* bomb aimer, (*Am.*) bombardier. **bomben|sicher,** *adj. See* **–fest. Bomben|-sprengkommando,** *n. See* **–räumtrupp. –treffer,** *m.* bomb hit. **–trichter,** *m.* bomb crater. **–zielgerät,** *n.* bomb-sight.

Bomber [ˈbɔmbər], *m. See* **Bombenflugzeug. Bomber|geschwader,** *n.* bomber group *or* (*Am.*) wing. **–gruppe,** *f.* bomber wing *or* (*Am.*) group. **–staffel,** *f.* bomber squadron. **–verband,** *m.* bomber formation.

Bombierung [bɔmˈbi:ruŋ], *f.* camber.

Bon [bɔ̃], *m.* **(-s,** *pl.* **-s)** (*Comm.*) credit note, voucher, chit, ticket, receipt, bill.

Bonbon [bɔ̃ˈbɔ̃], *m. or n.* **(-s,** *pl.* **-s)** sweet, bonbon, (*Am.*) candy.

Bönhase [ˈbø:nha:zə], *m.* bungler, botcher; blackleg.

Bonifatius [boniˈfa:tsius], **Bonifaz,** *m.* Boniface.

bonifizieren [bonifɪˈtsi:rən], *v.t.* (*Comm.*) make good, compensate, indemnify, reimburse; allow a rebate, make an allowance.

Bonität [boniˈtɛ:t], *f.* (-, *pl.* **-en**) (*Comm.*) (good) quality (*of an article*); solvency, credit, reliability (*of a firm*), soundness, validity (*of a claim*). **bonitieren,** *v.t.* value, assess, estimate, appraise.

Bonne [ˈbɔnə], *f.* nurse; nursery governess.

Bonze [ˈbɔntsə], *m.* **(-n,** *pl.* **-n)** (*coll.*) bigwig, party boss. **Bonzentum,** *n.* **(-s,** *no pl.*) political favouritism.

Boot [bo:t], *n.* **(-es,** *pl.* **-e)** boat; body, hull (*of an aircraft*); ***das – aussetzen,*** lower *or* launch the boat. **Boot|fahren,** *n.* boating. **–führer,** *m.* boatman, waterman.

Boots|anker, *m.* kedge, grapnel. **–breite,** *f.* beam. **–deck,** *n.* boat-deck. **–fahrt,** *f.* boat(ing) trip. **–führer,** *m.* coxswain, (*coll.*) cox (*rowing*). **–gast,** *m.* sailor, seaman. **–haken,** *m.* boat-hook. **–haus,** *n.* boathouse. **–leine,** *f. See* **–tau. –mann,** *m.* (*pl.* **-leute**) boatswain, (*coll.*) bosun. **–mannschaft,** *f.* boat's crew. **–tau,** *n.* painter.

Bor [bo:r], *n.* **(-s,** *no pl.*) (*Chem.*) boron. **borartig,** *adj.* boric, (*coll.*) boracic. **Borat** [–ˈra:t], *n.* **(-s,** *pl.* **-e)** borate. **Borax,** *m.* (-, *no pl.*) borax. **Borax|-blei,** *n.* lead borate. **–seife,** *f.* boracic soap.

[1]**Bord** [bɔrt], *n.* **(-es,** *pl.* **-e)** board, shelf.

[2]**Bord,** *m.* **(-es,** *pl.* **-e)** (ship)board; edge, border, rim; shore (*of the sea*); ***an –,*** aboard, on board; ***– an –,*** alongside; ***über –,*** overboard; (*coll.*) ***über – werfen,*** throw overboard, throw to the winds; (*Comm.*) ***frei an –,*** free on board. **Bord|anker,** *m.* bower (anchor). **–buch,** *n.* (*Naut., Av.*) log-book.

Bordell [bor'dɛl], *n.* (**-s,** *pl.* **-e**) brothel, disorderly house.
bördeln ['bœrdəln], *v.t.* flange. **Bördelung,** *f.* flange.
Bord|flugzeug, *n.* carrier-borne aircraft. **–funker,** *m.* (*Naut., Av.*) wireless operator.
bordieren [bor'di:rən], *v.t.* trim, edge, border. **Bordierung,** *f.* border, edging.
Bord|kante, *f.* edge of the kerb. **–küche,** *f.* galley. **–mechaniker,** *m.* flight engineer. **–monteur,** *m.* flight mechanic. **–schütze,** *m.* air gunner. **–schwelle,** *f.* kerb. **–sprechanlage, –verständigungsanlage,** *f.* intercommunication equipment (*on aircraft*), (*sl.*) intercom.
Bordüre [bɔr'dy:rə], *f.* border, edging.
Bord|wache, *f.* (*Naut.*) watch on deck. **–wand,** *f.* ship's side. **–zulage,** *f.* (*Naut.*) hard-lying allowance.
Borg [bɔrk], *m.* (*coll.*) borrowing; ***auf –,*** on credit, (*sl.*) on tick.
borgen ['bɔrgən], *v.t.* 1. borrow (***von*** or ***bei,*** from); 2. lend; ***hier wird nicht geborgt,*** no credit given, terms cash; (*Prov.*) ***Borgen macht Sorgen,*** borrowing brings sorrowing. **Borger,** *m.* borrower; lender.
Borke ['bɔrkə], *f.* bark, rind; crust, cortex, scab (*on a wound*). **Borkenkäfer,** *m.* bark-beetle. **borkig,** *adj.* covered with bark; scabby.
Born [bɔrn], *m.* (**-es,** *pl.* **-e**) (*Poet.*) spring, well, fountain, source, fount.
borniert [bɔr'ni:rt], *adj.* narrow-minded, limited, ignorant. **Borniertheit,** *f.* narrow-mindedness.
Bor|pulver, *n.* boracic powder. **–salbe,** *f.* boracic ointment. **borsauer,** *adj.* borate of. **Borsäure,** *f.* boric *or* (*coll.*) boracic acid.
Börse ['bœrzə], *f.* 1. purse (*also Spt.*); 2. (*Comm.*) stock exchange, bourse; money *or* stock *or* commodity market; ***an der –,*** on the stock exchange. **Börsen|bericht,** *m.* market report. **–blatt,** *n.* exchange list; commercial newspaper; (German) book-trade journal. **börsenfähig,** *adj.* negotiable. **Börsen|geschäft,** *n.* stock-exchange transaction. **–kommissionsgeschäft,** *n.* stockbroking (business). **–kurs,** *m.* quotation, market price *or* rate. **–makler,** *m.* stockbroker. **–notierung,** *f. See* **–kurs. –papiere,** *n.pl.* stocks. **–spekulant,** *m.* stock-jobber, dabbler on the stock exchange. **–spekulation,** *f.* deal *or* speculation on the stock exchange, jobbery. **–termingeschäft,** *n.* trading in futures, forward dealing. **–zeitung,** *f.* financial *or* commercial paper. **–zettel,** *m.* official stock-list, list of quotations.
börste ['bœrstə], *see* **bersten.**
Borste ['bɔrstə], *f.* bristle; (*Bot.*) seta. **borstenartig,** *adj.* bristly; (*Bot.*) setaceous. **Borsten|besen,** *m.* hard *or* stiff broom. **–fäule,** *f.* swine scurvy. **borstig,** *adj.* bristly; (*Bot.*) setaceous, setiform, strigose, hispid; (*fig.*) irritable, crusty, crotchety; (*coll.*) ***– werden,*** fly off the handle.
Bort, *n. See* [1]**Bord.**
Borte ['bɔrtə], *f.* border, frieze; edging, trimming, braid, braiding.
bös [bø:s], *adj. See* **böse. bösartig,** *adj.* malicious, ill-natured; vicious (*of an animal*); (*Med.*) virulent, malignant. **Bösartigkeit,** *f.* ill-nature, spitefulness; viciousness; (*Med.*) virulence, malignancy.
böschen ['bœʃən], *v.t.* slope; escarp, embank. **Böschung,** *f.* slope; scarp. **Böschungswinkel,** *m.* gradient, angle of inclination.
böse ['bø:zə], *adj.* bad, evil, wicked; malicious, malevolent, vicious, pernicious; angry, annoyed, offended, displeased, (*coll.*) cross; malignant (*tumour*), virulent (*fever*), inflamed, sore (*finger etc.*), bad, nasty (*cough etc.*); ***er war sehr – auf mich (über eine S.),*** he was very angry with me (over *or* about a th.); ***damit sieht es – aus,*** things look bad *or* black, it is in a bad way; ***er ist – dran,*** he's in a bad way; ***er meinte es nicht –,*** he meant no harm; ***es wurde ihm – mitgespielt,*** he was treated shabbily; ***ihm – sein,*** be cross *or* annoyed with him; (*Law*) ***in –r Absicht,*** with malice aforethought; ***–s Blut,*** bad blood, ill-feeling, ill-will; ***–r Engel*** or ***Geist,*** evil genius; ***der – Feind,*** the Devil, the Evil One, the foul fiend; ***– Gesellschaft,*** bad *or* evil company; ***ein –r Hund,*** a vicious dog; ***gute Miene zum –n Spiel machen,*** make the best of a bad job, put a good *or* brave face on the matter; (*Min.*) ***–s Wetter,*** fire-damp; ***–r Wille,*** malice, evil intent; ***ein –s Wort,*** an angry *or* a cross word; ***– Zeiten,*** hard times; ***ein –r Zufall,*** an unlucky coincidence; ***eine – Zunge,*** an evil *or* malicious *or* spiteful tongue.
Böse(s), *n.* evil, ill, harm.
Bösewicht ['bø:zəvɪçt], *m.* (**-s,** *pl.* **-e(r)**) villain (*also Theat.*), evil-doer, rogue, scoundrel, (*coll.*) scamp, rascal.
boshaft ['bo:shaft], *adj., adv.* malicious, spiteful, unkind, ill-natured; malignant, wicked, evil. **Boshaftigkeit,** *f.* malice, spitefulness, unkindness, spite. **Bosheit,** *f.* wickedness, evil, depravity; *see also* **Boshaftigkeit**; naughtiness; ***aus reiner –,*** from sheer spite *or* malice.
Boskett [bɔs'kɛt], *n.* (**-(e)s,** *pl.* **-e**) shrubbery, grove, thicket, bosket.
böslich ['bø:zlɪç], *adj.* (*obs.*) *see* **böse**; (*Law*) ***–es Verlassen,*** wilful desertion.
Bosse ['bɔsə], *f.* boss, umbo; (*Sculp.*) roughly blocked-out figure.
Bossel ['bɔsəl], *f.* (-, *pl.* **-n**) skittle-ball.
bosselieren [bɔsə'li:rən], *v.t. See* **bossieren.**
bosseln ['bɔsəln], *v.i.* play at skittles *or* curling (*on ice*).
bossieren [bɔ'si:rən], *v.t.* emboss, mould, model. **Bossierwachs,** *n.* modelling-wax.
böswillig ['bø:svɪlɪç], *adj.* malicious, malevolent; (*Law*) ***–e Beschädigung,*** malicious *or* wilful damage. **Böswilligkeit,** *f.* ill-will, malice, maliciousness, malevolence.
bot [bo:t], *see* **bieten.**
Botanik [bo'ta:nik], *f.* (-, *no pl.*) botany. **Botaniker,** *m.* botanist. **botanisch,** *adj.* botanical. **botanisieren** [–'zi:rən], *v.i.* botanize. **Botanisiertrommel,** *f.* specimen box, vasculum.
Bote ['bo:tə], *m.* (**-n,** *pl.* **-n**) messenger, courier; bearer (*of a letter*), postman; carter, carrier (*of goods*); (*Poet.*) emissary, ambassador, (*fig.*) herald; (*B.*) apostle; ***der hinkende – kommt nach,*** the bad news will follow; ***reitender –,*** mounted courier, estafette; ***die –n des Frühlings,*** the heralds of spring; ***die –n Christi,*** Christ's Apostles.
böte ['bø:tə], *see* **bieten.**
Boten|dienst, *m.* messenger service. **–gang,** *m.* errand, message. **–lohn,** *m.* porterage, tip, carrier's fee.
botmäßig ['bo:tmɛ:sɪç], *adj.* subject, in subjection (*Dat.,* to). **Botmäßigkeit,** *f.* dominion, sway, power, jurisdiction.
Botschaft ['bo:tʃaft], *f.* 1. message; news, tidings, intelligence; ***frohe –,*** joyful tidings; ***eine – ausrichten*** or ***bestellen,*** take *or* deliver a message; 2. legation, embassy; ***Deutsche –,*** German Embassy. **Botschafter,** *m.* ambassador; ***der päpstliche –,*** nuncio, (papal) legate; ***britischer – in Kanada,*** British High Commissioner in Canada.
Böttcher ['bœtçər], *m.* cooper. **Böttcherei** [–'raɪ], *f.* cooper's trade *or* workshop.
Botten ['bɔtən], *n.* Bothnia.
Bottich ['bɔtɪç], *m.* (**-es,** *pl.* **-e**) tub; vat, tun; cistern, tank.
bottnisch ['bɔtnɪʃ], *adj.* Bothnian.
Bouillon [bu'ljɔ̃], *f.* (-, *pl.* **-s**) clear soup, broth; beef-tea.
Boulevard [bulə'va:r], *m.* (**-s,** *pl.* **-s**) boulevard. **Boulevard|presse,** *f.* gutter press. **–stück,** *n.* kitchen-sink drama.
Bovist, *m. See* **Bofist.**
Bowle ['bo:lə], *f.* prepared cold drink; jorum, bowl (*for such a drink*).
Box(e) ['bɔks(ə)], *f.* (-, *pl.* **-n**) lock-up (garage); (submarine) pen; pit (*motor-racing*); loose box (*in stable*).

boxen ['bɔksən], **1.** *v.i., v.r.* box. **2.** *v.t.* punch. **Boxer,** *m.* 1. boxer, pugilist; 2. boxer(dog).
Boxer|motor, *m.* horizontally-opposed engine. **–ohr,** *n.* cauliflower ear.
Box|handschuh, *m.* boxing-glove. **–kampf,** *m.* boxing-match, bout, contest. **–sport,** *n.* boxing.
Boy [bɔy], *m.* **(-s,** *pl.* **-s)** 1. page-boy, bellboy, *(coll.)* bellhop; 2. dumb waiter, tea-trolley.
boykottieren [bɔykɔ'ti:rən], *v.t.* boycott. **Boykottierung,** *f.* boycott.
Bozen ['bo:tsən], *n.* *(Geog.)* Bolzano.
[1]**brach** [bra:x], *see* **brechen.**
[2]**brach,** *adj.* fallow, unploughed, untilled, uncultivated. **Brach|acker,** *m. See* **–feld. Brache,** *f.* fallow (ground).
bräche ['brɛçə], *see* **brechen.**
brachen ['bra:xən], *v.t.* 1. plough *or* break up fallow land; fallow; 2. leave uncropped, let lie fallow.
Brachet ['bra:xət], *m.* *(obs., Poet.)* June.
Brach|feld, *n.* fallow (land). **–flur,** *f.* tract of fallow land. **–jahr,** *n.* (Jewish) sabbatical year; year of fallow. **brachliegen,** *irr.v.i.* lie fallow; *(fig.)* be unexploited *(as potentialities),* be tied up *(as money).* **Brach|monat,** *m. See* **Brachet. –pieper,** *m.* *(Orn.)* tawny pipit *(Anthus compestris).* **–schwalbe,** *f.* *(Orn.)* collared pratincole *(Glareola pratincola).*
Brachse ['braksə], *f.,* **Brachsen,** *m.* *(Ichth.)* bream *(Ambrames)*; sea-bream, chad *(Pagellus).*
brachte ['braxtə], **brächte** ['brɛçtə], *see* **bringen.**
Brachvogel ['bra:xfo:gəl], *m.* *(Orn.)* ***dünnschnäbliger –,*** *see* **Dünnschnabel-Brachvogel;** ***großer –,*** curlew, *(Am.)* Eurasian curlew *(Numenius arquata)*; ***kleiner –,*** *see* **Regenbrachvogel.**
[1]**Brack** [brak], *n.* **(-s,** *pl.* **-e)** refuse, waste.
[2]**Brack,** *m.* **(-s,** *pl.* **-e)** young (animal).
Bracke ['brakə], *m.* **(-n,** *pl.* **-n)** spaniel.
bracken ['brakən], *v.t.* sort (out) *(refuse)*; beat *(flax).* **Bracker,** *m.* sorter. **Brack|gut,** *n. See* [1]**Brack. –holz,** *n.* rotten wood.
brackig ['brakıç], **brackisch,** *adj.* brackish. **Brackwasser,** *n.* brackish water.
Brägen, *m. See* **Bregen.**
Braktee [brak'te:ə], *f.* *(Bot.)* bract.
Bram [bra:m], *m.* **(-es,** *pl.* **-e)** *(Bot.)* broom *(Cytisus scoparius).*
bramarbasieren [bramarba'zi:rən], *v.i.* swagger, brag.
Bräme ['brɛ:mə], *f.* edge, border; (fur) trimming; undergrowth *(at edge of wood),* hedge.
Bramsegel ['bra:mze:gəl], *n.* *(Naut.)* topgallant sail.
Branche ['brãʃə], *f.* *(Comm.)* branch, department *(of a firm),* line *(of business).* **Branchenverzeichnis,** *n.* *(Tele.)* classified directory.
Brand [brant], *m.* **(-es,** *pl.* **⸚e)** 1. burning, combustion; fire, blaze, conflagration; firebrand; ***in – geraten*** or ***kommen,*** catch fire; ***in – setzen*** or ***stecken*** or ***legen,*** set fire to, set on fire; ***in – stehen*** or ***sein,*** be ablaze, be on fire; ***das Haus steht in –,*** the house is in flames; ***mit – und Mord,*** with fire and sword; 2. *(Med.)* gangrene, mortification, necrosis; *(Bot.)* mildew, blight; brand (mark) *(on cattle etc.)*; 3. firing, baking *(of bricks etc.),* refining *(of metals),* distillation; 4. *(Poet.)* flame, fervour, passion, ardour; 5. *(sl.)* raging thirst.
Brand|binde, *f.* burn-dressing. **–bombe,** *f.* incendiary bomb. **–brief,** *m.* threatening letter. **–direktor,** *m.* superintendent of the fire-brigade, *(coll.)* fire-chief. **–eisen,** *n.* branding iron.
branden ['brandən], *v.i.* break, surge *(of waves).*
Brandente ['brantˀɛntə], *f.* *(Orn.)* shelduck *(Tadorna tadorna).*
Brander ['brandər], *m.* 1. fire-ship; 2. *(Elec.)* fuse.
Brand|fackel, *f.* torch, firebrand; ***– des Krieges,*** torch of war. **–fleck,** *m.* barren patch of land; burn, scald, burn mark; flaw *(in porcelain).* **–gans,** *f. See* **–ente. –gasse,** *f.* space between houses. **–geschwür,** *n.* *(Med.)* gangrenous ulcer. **–glocke,** *f.* *(Hist.)* tocsin. **–gold,** *n.* refined gold. **–herd,** *m.* source of a fire, *(fig.)* storm-centre.
brandig ['brandıç], *adj.* blighted; gangrenous; ***– riechen*** or ***schmecken,*** smell *or* taste of burning.
Brand|kasse, *f.* fire-insurance office. **–legung,** *f. See* **–stiftung. –mal,** *n.* scar from burning; brand; *(fig.)* stigma. **–malerei,** *f.* poker-work. **brandmarken,** *v.t.* *(insep.)* brand, stigmatize. **Brand|mauer,** *f.* fireproof wall. **–opfer,** *n.* burnt offering; holocaust. **–ordnung,** *f.* fire-regulations. **–probe,** *f.* fire-test, assay. **–rede,** *f.* inflammatory address. **brandrot,** *adj.* fiery red. **Brand|satz,** *m.* powder train *(fuse).* **–schaden,** *m.* damage by fire. **brandschatzen,** *v.t.* *(insep.)* 1. levy contribution from; 2. ravage, plunder, pillage. **Brand|schatzung,** *f.* levy; war-contribution. **–schiefer,** *m.* bituminous shale. **–schott,** *m.* fireproof bulkhead. **–seeschwalbe,** *f.* *(Orn.)* Sandwich tern *(Thallaseus sandvicensis).* **–silber,** *n.* refined silver. **–sohle,** *f.* insole *(of shoe).* **–stätte, –stelle,** *f.* scene of a fire. **–stifter,** *m.* incendiary, fire-raiser. **–stiftung,** *f.* arson, incendiarism. **–tür,** *f.* fireproof door.
Brandung ['brandʊŋ], *f.* surf, breakers.
Brand|versicherung, *f.* fire-insurance. **–wache,** *f.* fire-guard, fire-watcher *(civil defence).* **–wunde,** *f.* burn; scald.
brannte ['brantə], *see* **brennen.**
Branntwein ['brantvaın], *m.* spirits, brandy. **Branntwein|brenner,** *m.* distiller. **–brennerei,** *f.* distillery.
Brasilianer [brazili'a:nər], *m.* Brazilian. **brasilianisch,** *adj.* Brazilian. **Brasilien** [–'zi:liən], *n.* Brazil.
[1]**Brasse** ['brasə] **(-n,** *pl.* **-n), Brassen,** *m. See* **Brachse.**
[2]**Brasse,** *f.* *(Naut.)* brace; ***die großen –n,*** the main braces. **brassen,** *v.t.* brace; trim *(the sails)*; ***dicht beim Winde gebraßt,*** close-hauled.
Bratapfel ['bra:tˀapfəl], *m.* baked apple.
braten ['bra:tən], **1.** *reg. & irr.v.t.* roast, bake; ***(auf dem Roste)*** grill, broil; ***(in der Pfanne)*** fry; ***(am Spieße)*** roast on a spit; ***gar gebraten,*** well done; ***(zu) wenig gebraten,*** underdone. **2.** *reg. & irr.v.i., v.r.* roast, be roasted; ***sich in der Sonne –,*** get sunburnt, sunbathe. **Braten,** *m.* roast (meat), joint; ***den – begießen,*** baste the meat; *(coll.)* ***den – riechen,*** get wind of a th., smell a rat.
Braten|brühe, *f.* gravy. **–fett,** *n.* dripping. **–kleid,** *n.* *(coll.)* evening dress. **–rock,** *m.* *(coll.)* best coat, dress-coat. **–soße,** *f.* gravy. **–wender,** *m.* turnspit, roasting-jack.
Brat|fett, *n.* cooking fat. **–fisch,** *m.* fried fish. **–hering,** *m.* grilled herring. **–huhn,** *n.* roast chicken. **–kartoffeln,** *f.pl.* fried potatoes, chips.
Brätling ['brɛ:tlıŋ], *m.* **(-s,** *pl.* **-e)** 1. *(Ichth.)* sprat *(Clupea sprattus)*; 2. *(Bot.)* agaric, edible fungus *(Lactarius volemus).*
Brat|ofen, *m.* (kitchen) oven. **–pfanne,** *f.* frying-pan. **–rost,** *m.* gridiron, grill.
Bratsche ['bra:tʃə], *f.* *(Mus.)* viola. **Bratschenschlüssel,** *m.* alto clef.
Brat|spieß, *m.* spit. **–wurst,** *f.* frying sausage; fried sausage.
Bräu [brɔy], *n. or m.* **(-es,** *pl.* **-e)** brew; brewery.
Brauch [braux], *m.* **(-es,** *pl.* **⸚e)** usage, custom, practice; *(obs.)* use. **brauchbar,** *adj.* useful; serviceable. **Brauchbarkeit,** *f.* utility, usefulness fitness.
brauchen ['brauxən], **1.** *v.t.* 1. need, want, require; 2. *(with inf. with zu)* need, have *(to do)*; ***Sie – es nur zu sagen,*** you only need mention it, you only have to say so; 3. *(with inf. with um zu) (of time)* need, take; ***Sie – nur wenig Zeit um mir zu schreiben,*** you only need *or* it only takes a short time to write to me; ***wie lange braucht man um zu . . . ?*** how long does it take to . . . ? 4. *(as negation of müssen)* ***Sie – mich nicht daran zu erinnern,*** you don't have to remind me of that; ***man braucht sich nicht zu wundern,*** it is not to be wondered at; 5. *See* **gebrauchen**; *(coll.)* ***das könnt, ich gerade –,***

that is just my luck; (*coll.*) ***das kann ich nicht –,*** that is no use to me. **2.** *imp.v.* (*Gen.*) ***es braucht keines Beweises,*** no proof is required *or* needed.

brauen ['brauən], *v.t.* brew. **Brauer,** *m.* brewer. **Brauerei** [–'raɪ], *f.* brewery; brewing. **Brauhaus,** *n.* brewery.

braun [braun], *adj.* brown; ***–es Pferd,*** bay horse; ***ein Brauner,*** a bay (horse). **Braun,** *n.* (the colour) brown; (*Liter.*) Bruin. **Braun|bär,** *m.* (*Zool.*) brown bear (*Ursus arctos*). **–bleierz,** *n.* brown phosphate of lead, pyromorphite.

Bräune ['brɔynə], *f.* 1. brown colour, brownness; (sun-)tan; 2. (*Med.*) angina; ***entzündliche –,*** quinsy; ***häutige –,*** croup; 3. (*Vet.*) strangles.

Brauneisen|erz, *n.*, **–stein,** *m.* brown iron-ore, limonite.

Braunelle [brau'nɛlə], *f.* 1. (*Orn.*) *See* **Heckenbraunelle**; 2. (*Bot.*) common bugle.

bräunen ['brɔynən], **1.** *v.t.* dye *or* make brown; (*Cul.*) brown (*gravy etc.*); (*of the sun*) tan. **2.** *v.i.* become brown *or* tanned.

Braun|kehlammer, *f.* (*Orn.*) *see* **–kopfammer. –kehlchen,** *n.* (*Orn.*) whinchat (*Saxicola rubetra*). **–kohl,** *m.* (*Bot.*) broccoli (*Brassica oleracea*). **–kohle,** *f.* brown coal, lignite. **–kopfammer,** *f.* (*Orn.*) red-headed bunting (*Emberiza bruniceps*).

bräunlich ['brɔynlɪç], *adj.* brownish.

braun|rot, *adj.* brownish red, russet. **–scheckig,** *adj.* skewbald (*of horse*).

Braunschnäpper ['braunʃnɛpər], *m.* (*Orn.*) brown flycatcher (*Muscicapa latirostris*).

Braunschweig ['braunʃvaɪk], *n.* Brunswick.

Braun|stein, *m.* manganese dioxide, pyrolusite. **–wurz,** *f.* (*Bot.*) figwort.

Braus [braus], *m.* (**-es,** *no pl.*) tumult, bustle, uproar; ***in Saus und – leben,*** live riotously, lead a gay life.

Brausche ['brauʃə], *f.* bruise; bump (*on the head*); swelling.

Brause ['brauzə], *f.* shower (bath), douche, spray; rose (*of watering can*); aerated *or* mineral water, (*coll.*) pop. **Brause|aufsatz,** *m.* rose (*of a watering can*). **–bad,** *n.* shower-bath, douche. **–kopf,** *m.* (*coll.*) hothead. **–limonade,** *f.* aerated water, (*coll.*) fizzy drink, pop.

brausen ['brauzən], **1.** *v.i.* 1. storm, rage, thunder, roar; effervesce; ***die Ohren – mir,*** I have a singing in my ears; ***vor Zorn –,*** storm with rage; 2. (*aux.* s.) rush. **2.** *v.t.* water, sprinkle, spray.

Braut [braut], *f.* (-, *pl.* **⸚e**) fiancée, betrothed, bride-to-be, (*coll.*) intended; bride (*on wedding-day*); ***sie ist –,*** she is engaged *or* betrothed; ***sie ist meine –,*** she is my fiancée; ***bitte grüßen Sie Ihr Fräulein –,*** please remember me to your fiancée; (*Bot.*) – ***in Haaren,*** fennel-flower. **Braut|ausstattung,** *f.* trousseau. **–bett,** *n.* marriage *or* wedding *or* bridal bed. **–führer,** *m.* *See* **vater. –gemach,** *n.* bridal chamber. **–geschenk,** *n.* wedding present.

Bräutigam ['brɔytɪgam], *m.* (**-s,** *pl.* **-e**) fiancé; bridegroom (*on the wedding-day*); (*coll.*) intended.

Braut|jungfer, *f.* bridesmaid. **–kind,** *n.* legitimized child. **–kleid,** *n.* wedding-dress. **–kranz,** *m.* bridal wreath. **–leute,** *pl.* engaged couple.

bräutlich ['brɔytlɪç], *adj.* bridal.

Braut|nacht, *f.* wedding-night. **–paar,** *n.* newly married couple, (*at wedding*) bridal pair, bride and bridegroom. **–schatz,** *m.* dowry. **–schmuck, –staat,** *m.* bridal attire. **–stand,** *m.* engagement, betrothal. **–vater,** *m.* bride's father; ***den – machen,*** give the bride away. **–zug,** *m.* bridal procession.

brav [bra:f], **1.** *adj.* honest, upright; worthy, fine; good, well-behaved; brave; ***es ist sehr – von dir,*** it is very good of you; – ***gemacht!*** well done! ***–es Kind,*** good *or* well-behaved child. **2.** *adv.* bravely; like a good child; – ***ins Bett gehen,*** be good and go to bed, go to bed like a good child.

Bravo ['bra:vo], *n.* (**-s,** *pl.* **-s**) bravo. **bravo!** *int.* bravo! cheers! fine! well done! splendid! **Bravoruf,** *m.* cheer.

Bravour [bra'vu:r], *f.* bravado, gusto. **Bravourstück,** *n.* act of daring.

Brecharznei ['brɛçˀartsnaɪ], *f.* emetic.

brechbar ['brɛçba:r], *adj.* breakable, fragile; (*Opt.*) refrangible.

Brech|bohne, *f.* (young) kidney bean. **–eisen,** *n.* crowbar, handspike, jemmy.

brechen ['brɛçən], **1.** *irr.v.t.* break, crush; break *or* turn (up) (*soil*), quarry (*stone*), cut (*coal*), break (through), breach (*obstacle*), break (down) (*resistance*), break, fracture (*a bone*); pluck, pick, gather (*flowers etc.*); fold (*letters*); (*Opt.*) bend, refract; (*Med.*) vomit; ***Bahn –,*** force a passage; (*fig.*) be first in the field, be a pioneer; ***die Ehe –,*** commit adultery; (*Prov.*) ***Not bricht Eisen,*** needs must when the devil drives, necessity knows no law; ***Flachs –,*** (*not irr.*) beat *or* hackle flax; ***sich*** (*Dat.*) ***das Genick –,*** break one's neck; ***etwas übers Knie –,*** do a th. hurriedly *or* sketchily, rush a th.; ***für etwas eine Lanze –,*** champion the cause of s.th., defend a th.; ***den Rekord –,*** break *or* beat the record; ***das Schweigen –,*** break (the) silence; ***den Stab über ihn –,*** (*Hist.*) sentence him to death; (*fig.*) condemn him out of hand; ***einen Streit vom Zaun –,*** pick a quarrel; ***gebrochen,*** broken; fractional (*number, distillation*), (*Geol.*) faulted (*seam*); (*fig.*) stricken; ***gebrochenen Herzens,*** broken-hearted, heartbroken; ***gebrochener Akkord,*** arpeggio; ***gebrochenes Deutsch sprechen,*** speak broken German; ***gebrochene Schreibart,*** abrupt style; ***gebrochene Schrift,*** Old English type; ***gebrochene Treppe,*** staircase with a landing. **2.** *irr.v.r.* break (*as waves*); be interrupted; (*Opt.*) be refracted; (*coll.*) vomit, be sick. **3.** *irr.v.i.* (*aux.* s.) break, get *or* be broken, split, crack, come apart; rupture; break forth, dawn (*as the day*); ***die Augen brachen ihm,*** his eyes became glazed (in death) *or* grew dim; ***das Eis brach,*** the ice cracked; ***die Geduld bricht ihm,*** his patience is exhausted; ***das Herz bricht mir,*** my heart is breaking; ***in den Jahren, wo die Stimme bricht,*** at the age when the voice breaks; ***er brach mit mir,*** he broke (off relations) with me, he fell out with me.

brechend ['brɛçənt], *adj.* bursting; – ***voll,*** full to bursting.

Brecher ['brɛçər], *m.* (**-s,** *pl.* **-**) 1. crusher, crushing machine; 2. (*Naut.*) breaker, heavy sea.

Brech|mittel, *n.* emetic. **–nuß,** *f.* nux vomica. **–reiz,** *m.* nausea. **–stange,** *f.* *See* **–eisen.**

Brechung ['brɛçuŋ], *f.* (-, *pl.* **-en**) breaking; refraction; (*Mus.*) arpeggio; (*Gram.*) modification, aberration. **Brechungszahl,** *f.* (*Opt.*) refractive index.

Brech|weinstein, *m.* tartar emetic. **–wurz, –wurzel,** *f.* ipecacuanha. **–zahl,** *f.* *See* **Brechungszahl.**

Bregen ['bre:gən], *m.* brain(s).

Brei [braɪ], *m.* (**-(e)s,** *pl.* **-e**) paste, pulp, mash; purée; gruel, (*for infants*) pap; ***wie die Katze um den heißen – herumgehen,*** beat about the bush; (*Prov.*) ***viele Köche verderben den –,*** too many cooks spoil the broth. **breiartig, breiig,** *adj.* pappy, pulpy, pasty; slushy (*of snow*).

breit [braɪt], *adj.* broad, wide; (*fig.*) long-winded, prolix; (*fig.*) ***einen –en Buckel haben,*** have broad shoulders, be able to take it; ***sie erzählte mir ein langes und –es darüber,*** she spun me a long yarn about it; ***einen Finger –,*** a finger's breadth; ***die –e Masse Volkes,*** the broad masses; – ***schlagen,*** flatten (*metal*) (*see also* **breitschlagen**); – ***treten,*** tread out of shape (*as shoes*) (*see also* **breittreten**); ***weit und –,*** far and wide.

Breitbeil ['braɪtbaɪl], *n.* broad-axe. **breit|beinig,** *adj.* straddle-legged; straddling. **–blättrig,** *adj.* broad-leaved, (*Bot.*) latifoliate. **–brüstig,** *adj.* broad-chested.

Breite ['braɪtə], *f.* breadth, width, broadness; gauge (*of a railway line*); beam (*of a ship*); (*Geog.*) latitude; (*fig.*) long-windedness, verbosity, prolixity; (*coll.*) ***in die – gehen,*** put on weight, get stout; ***der – nach,*** broadwise, breadthwise.

Breiteisen ['braɪtˀaɪzən], *n.* mason's *or* sculptor's chisel.

Breiten|grad, *m.* degree of latitude. **-kreis,** *m.* parallel of latitude.

breitgetakelt ['braɪtɡəta:kəlt], *adj.* (*Naut.*) square-rigged.

Breithalter ['braɪthaltər], *m.* stretcher, tension-piece, tenter. **breit|köpfig,** *adj.* broad-headed; platycephalous, brachycephalic. **-krempig,** *adj.* broad-brimmed. **-machen,** *v.r.* spread o.s. (out), take up (a lot of) room; (*fig.*) give o.s. airs, swagger, boast. **-nasig,** *adj.* broad- *or* flat-nosed. **-schlagen,** *irr.v.t.* (*coll.*) ***ihn zu einer S. –,*** persuade him to (do) a th., talk him into (doing) s.th. **-schultrig,** *adj.* broad-shouldered. **Breitseite,** *f.* (*Naut.*) broadside. **breit|spurig,** *adj.* (*Railw.*) wide-gauge; (*fig.*) pompous, bombastic, imperious. **-treten,** *irr.v.t.* dilate upon, dwell on, labour (*a point*). **-zehig,** *adj.* (*Zool.*) platydactylous.

Breiumschlag ['braɪˀumʃla:k], *m.* poultice.

Brems|backe, *f.* brake-shoe. **-belag,** *m.* brake-lining.

[1]**Bremse** ['brɛmzə], *f.* brake; ***die – anziehen,*** apply *or* put on the brake; ***die – lösen,*** take off the brake.

[2]**Bremse,** *f.* horsefly, gadfly, cleg (*Tabanidae*).

bremsen ['brɛmzən], **1.** *v.i.* brake, put on the brake(s). **2.** *v.t.* slow down, stop, halt (*vehicle*); slow down, moderate (*atomic particles*); (*fig.*) curb, restrain.

Bremsenschwindel ['brɛmzənʃvɪndəl], *m.* (*Vet.*) staggers.

Bremser ['brɛmzər], *m.* (*Railw.*) brake(s)man.

Bremsfliege ['brɛmsfli:ɡə], *f. See* [2]**Bremse.**

Brems|flüssigkeit, *f.* brake fluid. **-gitter,** *n.* (*Rad.*) suppressor grid. **-gitterröhre,** *f.* (*Rad.*) pentode. **-hebel,** *m.* brake lever. **-klappe,** *f.* (*Av.*) wing-flap. **-klotz,** *m.* brake-block; chock. **-länge,** *f.* breaking distance. **-leistung,** *f.* braking efficiency, brake horse-power. **-mittel,** *n.* moderator (*atomic physics*). **-rakete,** *f.* retro-rocket. **-schuh,** *m. See* **-backe. bremssicher,** *adj.* skid-proof (*tyres*), with reliable brakes (*vehicle*). **Brems|spur,** *f.* skid mark (*on road*). **-träger,** *m.* back-plate of brake. **-trommel,** *f.* brake-drum. **-wagen,** *m.* (*Railw.*) brake-van, guard's van. **-weg,** *m. See* **-länge. -wirkung,** *f.* retarding effect.

brennbar ['brɛnba:r], *adj.* burnable, combustible, inflammable. **Brennbarkeit,** *f.* combustibility, inflammability.

Brenn|blase, *f.* still, alembic. **-ebene,** *f.* (*Opt.*) focal plane. **-eisen,** *n.* branding iron; curling tongs *or* irons; (*Med.*) cautery.

brennen ['brɛnən], **1.** *irr.v.t.* burn; brand; (*Med.*) cauterize; calcine, carbonize (*ore*); char (*wood*); distil (*spirits*); bake (*bricks*); fire (*pottery*); roast (*coffee*); (*fig.*) rankle with (*a p.*), rankle in (*s.o.'s*) mind; (*coll.*) ***ihn rein*** (or ***weiß***) ***–,*** exculpate him, clear him of suspicion. **2.** *irr.v.i.* burn, be on fire; be alight *or* burning; (*fig.*) be aglow *or* aflame; be all agog; sting, smart; ***mir – die Augen,*** my eyes smart; ***vor Ungeduld –,*** be consumed with impatience; (*coll.*) ***wo brennt's denn,*** what's the hurry; ***es brennt mir auf den Nägeln,*** I can hardly contain myself; **brennend,** *adj.* burning; caustic; smarting; pungent; ardent, fervent, eager, fiery; ***-e Frage,*** burning *or* vital question. **Brenner,** *m.* distiller; brickmaker; burner. **Brennerei** [–'raɪ], distillery, kiln.

Brennessel ['brɛnnɛsəl], *f.* (*Bot.*) stinging nettle (*Urtica*).

Brenn|gemisch, *n.* (combustible) mixture (*petrol engine*). **-glas,** *n.* burning-glass. **-holz,** *n.* firewood. **-linse,** *f. See* **-glas. -material,** *n.* fuel. **-mittel,** *n.* corrosive, caustic. **-ofen,** *m.* kiln. **-öl,** *n.* lamp-oil. **-punkt,** *m.* focus; focal point; (*Av.*) aerodynamic centre; (*fig.*) ***im – des Interesses,*** in the limelight. **-schere,** *f.* curling-tongs. **-schneiden,** *n.* flame-cutting. **-spiegel,** *m.* burning- *or* concave mirror. **-spiritus,** *m.* methylated spirits. **-stahl,** *m.* blister steel. **-stoff,** *m.* fuel; inflammable matter. **-weite,** *f.* focal length *or* distance. **-wert** *m.* calorific value. **-ziegel,** *m.* fire-brick.

brenzeln ['brɛntsəln], *v.i.* smell *or* taste of burning.

Brenz|essiggeist, *m.* (*Chem.*) acetone. **-gallussäure,** *f.* (*Chem.*) pyrogallic acid, (*Phot. coll.*) pyro.

brenzlich, brenzlig ['brɛntslɪç], *adj.* smelling *or* tasting of burning; (*fig.*) dangerous, precarious, risky, (*coll.*) tricky.

Bresche ['brɛʃə], *f.* gap, breach; ***eine – schlagen*** or ***legen*** or ***schießen in*** (*Acc.*), make a breach in; ***in die – treten*** or ***springen,*** step into the breach.

Brestling ['brɛstlɪŋ], *m.* (**-s,** *pl.* **-e**) (*dial.*) strawberry.

Brett [brɛt], *n.* (**-(e)s,** *pl.* **-er**) board; plank; shelf; *pl.* the stage, (*coll.*) the boards; *pl.* skis; ***schwarzes –,*** noticeboard; ***bis acht auf die -er,*** down for a count of eight (*boxing*); ***das – bohren, wo es am dünnsten ist,*** take the line of least resistance; ***ein – vor dem Kopf haben,*** be stupid, be a blockhead; ***ein Stück geht über die -er,*** a play is put on the stage; (*coll.*) ***da ist die Welt mit -ern vernagelt,*** there is the end of it, there no headway can be made.

Bretter|bude, *f.* shed, hut, shack; (market) stall. **-(ver)schalung,** *f.* boarding, wooden lining *or* casing. **-verschlag,** *m.* wooden shed; wooden partition; crate. **-wand,** *f.* (*indoors*) wooden partition, (*outdoors*) hoarding. **-zaun,** *m.* wooden fence, palisade; hoarding.

Brettl ['brɛtəl], *n. See* **Überbrettl;** (*dial.*) ski.

Brett|mühle, *f.* saw-mill. **-schuppen,** *m.* wooden shed. **-spiel,** *n.* game played on a board (*chess, draughts etc.*).

Breve ['bre:və], *n.* (**-s,** *pl.* **-n** *or* **-s**) (papal) brief.

Brevier [bre'vi:r], *n.* (**-s,** *pl.* **-e**) breviary.

Brevis ['bre:vɪs], *f.* (**-,** *pl.* **-ves**) (*Mus.*) breve.

Brezel ['bre:tsəl], *f.* (**-,** *pl.* **-n**) cracknel, crusty type of roll, pretzel.

brich [brɪç], **brichst, bricht,** *see* **brechen.**

Brief [bri:f], *m.* (**-(e)s,** *pl.* **-e**) 1. letter; epistle, document; ***eingeschriebener –,*** registered letter; ***frankierter –,*** prepaid letter; ***postlagernder –,*** letter to be called for, 'poste restante' letter; ***unter – und Siegel,*** under hand and seal; ***– und Siegel darauf geben,*** give one's word on it; ***unbestellbarer –,*** dead letter; ***-e wechseln,*** correspond; (*Comm.*) ***Ihr werter –,*** your favour; 2. packet *or* paper (*of pins*), book (*of matches*); 3. (*St. Exch. jargon*) sellers only, offered at.

Brief|ablage, *f.* letter file. **-adel,** *m.* patent of nobility. **-aufgabe,** *f.* posting *or* mailing (of) a letter. **-aufgabestempel,** *m.* postmark. **-aufschrift,** *f.* address. **-ausgabe,** *f.* issue of letters (*at the counter*). **-beschwerer,** *m.* paper-weight. **-bestellung,** *f.* delivery of letters. **-block,** *m.* writing-pad. **-bogen,** *m.* sheet of note-paper. **-bote,** *m.* postman, (*Am.*) mailman. **-einwurf,** *m.* letter-box. **-fach,** *n.* 'pigeon-hole', letter-rack. **-geheimnis,** *n.* privacy of letters; ***das – verletzen,*** disclose the contents of a private letter. **-karte,** *f.* letter-card. **-kasten,** *m.* letter-box, post-box, pillar-box, (*Am.*) mailbox. **-klammer,** *f.* paper-clip. **-kopf,** *m.* letter-head. **-kurs,** *m.* (*St. Exch.*) selling-price. **-kuvert,** *n.* envelope.

brieflich ['bri:flɪç], *adj.* in writing, by letter; ***-er Verkehr,*** correspondence.

Briefmappe ['bri:fmapə], *f.* portfolio, writing-case.

Briefmarke ['bri:fmarkə], *f.* postage stamp. **Briefmarken|album,** *n.* stamp album. **-automat,** *m.* stamp-machine. **-kunde,** *f.* philately. **-sammler,** *m.* philatelist, stamp-collector. **-sammlung,** *f.* stamp collection.

Brief|öffner, *m.* paper-knife. **-ordner,** *m.* letter-file. **-papier,** *n.* notepaper, stationery. **-porto,** *n.* postage. **-post,** *f.* letter post, mail. **-presse,** *f.* copying press, letter press. **-schaften,** *f.pl.* letters, papers, documents, correspondence. **-schreiber,** *m.* letter-writer, correspondent. **-schulden,** *f.pl.* arrears of correspondence. **-sendung,** *f.* (small) postal package. **-steller,** *m.*

1. letter-writer; drawer of a bill; 2. letter writer's guide *or* handbook. **-stempel,** *m.* postmark. **-tasche,** *f.* pocket-book, wallet, (*Am.*) billfold. **-taube,** *f.* carrier-pigeon, homing pigeon. **-träger,** *m.* postman, (*Am.*) mailman. **-umschlag,** *m.* envelope. **-verkehr,** *m.* postal service. **-waage,** *f.* letter balance *or* scales. **-wahl,** *f.* postal vote. **-wechsel,** *m.* correspondence. **-zensur,** *f.* postal censorship.

Bries [bri:s], *n.* (**-es,** *pl.* **-e**) (*Anat.*) thymus; *see* **Bröschen. Brieseldrüse,** *f.* (*Anat.*) thymus gland.

briet [bri:t], **briete,** *see* **braten.**

Brigade [bri'ga:də], *f.* brigade (*German army* = *two regiments*). **Brigadegeneral, Brigadier** [–'di:r], *m.* (**-s,** *pl.* **-s**) brigadier.

Brigg [brɪk], *f.* (-, *pl.* **-s**) (*Naut.*) brig.

Brikett [bri'kɛt], *n.* (**-(e)s,** *pl.* **-e**) briquette, pressed coal.

Brikole [bri'ko:lə], *f.* (*Bill., Artil.*) rebound.

brillant [brɪl'jant], *adj.* brilliant, (*fig.*) excellent, superlative.

Brillant, *m.* (**-en,** *pl.* **-en**) brilliant, cut diamond.

Brillantine [brɪljan'ti:nə], *f.* brilliantine, hair-oil.

Brille ['brɪlə], *f.* (pair of) spectacles, (eye)glasses; ***durch die rechte – sehen,*** see things in the right light; ***durch eine rosige – betrachten,*** see through rose-tinted spectacles; ***durch eine schwarze – sehen,*** take a gloomy view of everything; ***durch eine fremde – sehen,*** see with another p.'s eyes.

Brillen|einfassung, *f.* spectacle frame. **-ente,** *f.* (*Orn.*) surf-scoter (*Melanitta perspicillata*). **-etui,** *n.* spectacle case. **-fassung,** *f. See* **-einfassung. -futteral,** *n. See* **-etui. -gestell,** *n. See* **-einfassung. -glas,** *n.* spectacle lens. **-grasmücke,** *f.* (*Orn.*) spectacled warbler (*Sylvia conspicillata*). **-schlange,** *f.* (*Zool.*) cobra (de capello) (*Naja tripudians*). **-stärling,** *m. See* **Gelbkopfstärling. -träger,** *m.* one who wears spectacles.

brillieren [brɪl'ji:rən], *v.i.* shine, sparkle (*of a p.*).

Brimborium [brɪm'bo:rium], *n.* (**-s,** *no pl.*) fuss, bother, (*coll.*) to-do.

bringen ['brɪŋən], *irr.v.t.* 1. (*viewed from standpoint of subject*) take; ***er brachte sie nach Hause,*** he took her home; ***er brachte ihr ein Glas Wasser,*** he took her a glass of water; (*viewed from standpoint of dative object or of the destination*) bring; ***er brachte mich nach Hause,*** he brought me home; ***er brachte mir ein Glas Wasser,*** he brought me a glass of water; 2. bring forth, produce, yield, bear (*crops etc.*); ***Zinsen –,*** yield *or* produce interest; ***das Geschäft bringt wenig,*** the business yields little profit; 3. (*of newspapers*) print, bring (*news*), (*of theatres etc.*) present, put on (*play*).
a) (*with nouns*) ***Ärger –,*** cause annoyance (*Dat.,* to); ***eine Gesundheit –,*** drink a toast (*Dat.,* to); ***(ein) Opfer –,*** sacrifice, make sacrifices *or* a sacrifice; ***zum Opfer –,*** offer (up) as a sacrifice; ***ihr ein Ständchen –,*** serenade her.
b) (*with adv.*) ***es dahin – daß . . .,*** carry things so far that . . .; ***keine zehn Pferde würden mich dahin –,*** wild horses wouldn't drag me there; ***es fertig –,*** manage (to do); ***es hoch –,*** make a success of, bring (it) off, (*sl.*) make the grade; ***soweit –,*** see ***dazu –***; ***es weit –,*** get on well, make a go of it.
c) (*with prep.*) ***ihn an die Bahn –,*** see him to the station, come *or* go to the station with him; ***an den Bettelstab –,*** reduce to beggary; ***ans Licht –,*** bring to light; ***an den Mann –,*** dispose of (*goods*), find a husband for, marry off; ***an die Öffentlichkeit –,*** make public; ***an sich –,*** acquire, get possession of; ***an den Tag –,*** expose, lay bare; ***ihn aufs äußerste –,*** provoke him greatly; ***auf die Beine –,*** set up, raise (*an army etc.*); ***ihn auf eine S. –,*** put him on to s.th., put s.th. in his mind, suggest s.th. to him; ***ihn darauf – (zu tun),*** bring *or* lead *or* influence him (to do); ***ihn auf dumme Gedanken –,*** put silly ideas into his head; ***auf die Post –,*** take to the post; ***auf die Seite –,*** embezzle, appropriate; ***etwas aufs Tapet –,*** raise a matter, discuss s.th.; ***auf den rechten Weg –,*** put on the right path *or* track; ***aus der Fassung –,*** disconcert; ***ihn außer sich –,*** enrage him; ***etwas hinter sich –,*** get s.th. over and done with; ***ins Bett –,*** put to bed; ***in Erfahrung –,*** get to know, find out, discover, ascertain; ***in Gang –,*** start, get going; ***in Gefahr –,*** lead into danger; ***ins Haus –,*** deliver (to the door); ***in eine Lage –,*** put in a position; ***in Ordnung –,*** arrange, put in order, tidy up; ***in Rechnung –,*** take into account; ***in schlechten Ruf –,*** bring into bad repute; ***in Sicherheit –,*** remove to safety; ***in Umlauf –,*** bring into circulation; ***ins Unglück –,*** ruin; ***in Verdacht –,*** throw suspicion on; ***ins Verderben –,*** bring about (*s.o.'s*) downfall; ***in Verlegenheit –,*** embarrass; ***mit sich –,*** involve, entail, bring about, be followed *or* attended by, have the *or* produce as a consequence; ***übers Herz*** or ***über sich –,*** be able to bear; ***ich kann es nicht über die Lippen –,*** I cannot bear to say it; (*sl.*) ***ihn um die Ecke –,*** do him in; ***ihn um etwas –,*** deprive him of a th., do him out of s.th.; ***ihn ums Leben –,*** kill him, cause his death; ***sich ums Leben –,*** kill o.s., commit suicide; ***um den Verstand –,*** drive (*s.o.*) mad; ***seine Tochter unter die Haube –,*** find a husband for one's daughter, get one's daughter married off; ***verschiedene Sachen unter einen Hut –,*** bring various things under one heading; ***eine Nachricht unter die Leute –,*** make the news widely known, spread the news abroad; (*coll.*) ***vom Fleck –,*** see ***zustande –***; ***zum Ausdruck –,*** express, give expression to; ***zur Bahn –,*** see ***an die Bahn –***; ***zu Bett –,*** put to bed; ***ihn wieder zum Bewußtsein –,*** bring him round; ***ihm etwas zum Bewußtsein –,*** make s.th. clear to him, put him in mind of a th.; ***ihn dazu –,*** get *or* induce him (to do), make him (do); ***sich dazu –,*** bring o.s. (to do); ***zu Ende –,*** finish, complete, bring to a conclusion; ***es zu etwas –,*** achieve s.th.; ***ihn zu Fall –,*** cause his downfall; ***ihn zum Fallen –,*** make him fall down *or* over; ***ihm etwas zur Kenntnis –,*** bring s.th. to his knowledge; ***es bis zum Major –,*** rise to be a major, rise to the rank of major; ***zu Papier –,*** write down, put in writing, get down (on paper), set down in black and white; ***zur Ruhe –,*** quieten, pacify, calm down; ***ihn wieder zu sich –,*** bring him round; ***zum Schweigen –,*** put to silence; ***zur Sprache –,*** start *or* broach (*a subject*); ***etwas zustande –,*** get s.th. done, achieve *or* accomplish s.th.; ***ihn zur Vernunft –,*** bring him to his senses; ***etwas zuwege –,*** see ***zustande –***; ***ihn zum Wahnsinn –,*** drive him mad; ***ein Kind zur Welt –,*** give birth to a child, bring a child into the world.
d) (*Periphrastic phrases with* **bringen** *and prep. governing verbal noun, e.g.* **zur Durchführung bringen** *are common, though stylistically poor equivalents of the verb, e.g.* **durchführen.** *See under the relevant verb.*)

Brisanz [bri'zants], *f.* (-, *pl.* **-en**) explosive power; high explosive. **Brisanzgranate,** *f.* high explosive shell.

Brise ['bri:zə], *f.* breeze, light wind.

Britannien [bri'tanjən], *n.* Britain. **Brite** ['brɪtə], *m.* (**-n,** *pl.* **-n**) Briton. **Britin,** *f.* Briton.

bröckelig ['brœkəlɪç], *adj.* crumbly, crumbling, brittle, friable. **bröckeln, 1.** *v.t.* crumble, break into small pieces. **2.** *v.i.* crumble, become brittle *or* friable.

Brocken ['brɔkən], *m.* crumb, morsel, mouthful; fragment, bit, piece, lump; *pl.* scraps, odds and ends, bits and pieces. **Brockensammlung,** *f.* collection of old clothes. **brockenweise,** *adv.* bit by bit, little by little, piecemeal.

brodeln ['bro:dəln], *v.i.* bubble, boil up fiercely, seethe, effervesce.

Brodem ['bro:dəm], *m.* (**-s,** *pl.* -) steam, vapour; (*Min.*) fumes, foul air.

Broderie [brodə'ri:], *f.* embroidery. **brodieren** [–'di:rən], *v.t.* embroider.

Brokat [bro'ka:t], *m.* (**-(e)s,** *pl.* **-e**) brocade.

Brom [bro:m], *n.* (**-s,** *no pl.*) bromine. **Bromäther,** *m.* (*Chem.*) ethyl bromide.

Brombeere ['brɔmbe:rə], *f.* (*Bot.*) blackberry, bramble (*Rubus*). **Brombeerstrauch,** *m.* bramble, blackberry-bush.

Bromid [bro'mi:t], *n.* (**-s,** *pl.* **-e**) bromide. **Brom|-kalium,** *n.* bromide of potassium. **–silber,** *n.* silver bromide.

bronchial [brɔnçi'a:l], *adj.* bronchial. **Bronchial-katarrh,** *m.* bronchial catarrh. **Bronchien** ['brɔnçiən], *f.pl.* bronchia. **Bronchitis,** *f.* bronchitis.

Bronn [brɔn], (**-(e)s,** *pl.* **-en**), **Bronnen,** *m.* (*Poet.*) spring, well, fountain.

Bronze ['brɔ̃sə], *f.* bronze. **bronzen,** *adj.* bronze (-coloured). **Bronzezeit,** *f.* Bronze Age. **bron-zieren** [–'si:rən], *v.t.* bronze, braze.

Brosam ['bro:za:m], *m.* (**-(e)s,** *pl.* **-e**), **Brosame** [–'za:mə], *f.* (*usu. pl.*) crumb, scrap.

Brosche ['brɔʃə], *f.* brooch.

Bröschen, *n.* (*calf's*) sweetbread.

broschieren [brɔ'ʃi:rən], *v.t.* stitch (together), sew (*as a pamphlet*); figure, brocade (*fabric*). **bro-schiert,** *adj.* paper-bound, paper-backed (*book*). **Broschierung, Broschur,** *f.* stitching, sewing (*of books*), binding in paper covers; paper cover. **Broschüre,** *f.* pamphlet, booklet, brochure.

Brösel ['brø:zəl], *m.* (*usu. pl.*) (bread-)crumb; (*Cul.*) ***mit –,*** au gratin.

Brossage [brɔ'sa:ʒə], *f.* carding (*textiles*). **brossie-ren,** *v.t.* card.

Brot [bro:t], *n.* (**-es,** *pl.* **-e**) bread; loaf; (*fig.*) support, sustenance, livelihood; ***ein – anschneiden,*** cut a loaf; ***sein eignes – essen,*** be one's own master; (*Prov.*) ***wes – ich esse, des Lied ich singe,*** he who pays the piper calls the tune; ***die Kunst geht nach –,*** art must pay its way; ***gesäuertes –,*** leavened bread; ***ein halbes –,*** half a loaf; ***ein hartes – haben,*** work hard for one's living; ***Kampf ums liebe –,*** struggle for a livelihood; ***– schneiden,*** cut (the) bread; ***in – bei ihm stehen,*** be in his service; ***sein – verdienen,*** earn one's living.

Brot|aufstrich, *m.* jam, meat-paste (*or anything to spread on bread*). **–beruf,** *m.* livelihood, (*coll.*) bread-and-butter job. **–beutel,** *m.* haversack. **–bohrer,** *m.* (*Ent.*) meal beetle.

Brötchen ['brø:tçən], *n.* roll (*of bread*); breakfast-roll; French *or* Vienna roll; ***belegtes –,*** open sandwich.

Brot|erwerb, *m.* livelihood. **–fruchtbaum,** *m.* (*Bot.*) bread-fruit tree (*Artocarpus*). **–herr,** *m.* master; employer. **–käfer,** *m.* biscuit weevil, bread mite. **–kammer,** *f.* pantry. **–karte,** *f.* ration card. **–kasten,** *m.* bread-bin. **–korb,** *m.* bread-basket; ***ihm den – höher hängen,*** keep him on short rations; underpay *or* take unfair advantage of him. **–laib,** *m.* loaf.

brotlos ['bro:tlo:s], *adj.* unemployed. ***–e Künste,*** unprofitable *or* unremunerative arts.

Brot|marke, *f.* bread-coupon. **–maschine,** *f.* bread-slicer. **–neid,** *m.* professional jealousy. **–rinde,** *f.* crust. **–röster,** *m.* toaster. **–schaufel,** *f.* baker's peel. **–scheibe,** *f. See* **–schnitte. –schie-ber,** *m. See* **–schaufel. –schnitte,** *f.* slice of bread. **–studium,** *n.* professional *or* utilitarian studies. **–verdiener,** *m.* bread-winner. **–ver-wandlung,** *f.* (*Eccl.*) transubstantiation. **–wurzel,** *f.* (*Bot.*) yam; cassava, tapioca *or* manioc (plant) (*Dioscorea*). **–zucker,** *m.* loaf-sugar.

[1]**Bruch** [brux], *m.* (**-(e)s,** *pl.* **⸚e**) 1. breaking (*also of voice*), bursting, rupture, breakage; (*fig.*) breach, rupture, violation, infringement; ***es kam zum –,*** relations were broken off; ***– des Friedens,*** breach of the peace; 2. break, crack, fissure, flaw; burst, leak (*in a pipe*), breach (*of a dam*), fold (*in paper*), (*Geol.*) fault, (*Med.*) fracture, (*Med.*) hernia, rupture, (*Av.*) crash, (*fig.*) break, interruption; (*coll.*) ***in die Brüche gehen,*** break, get broken; (*of a p.*) fail, (*sl.*) come unstuck; (*of friendship*) break up; (*Av.*) ***– machen,*** crash; (*Med.*) ***eingeklemmter –,*** strangulated hernia; (*Med.*) ***einen – einrichten,*** set a fracture; (*Med.*) ***einen – einbringen,*** reduce a hernia; 3. (*Math.*) fraction; ***einen – kürzen,*** reduce a fraction; ***einen – erweitern,*** reduce a fraction to higher terms; ***echter –,*** proper fraction; 4. broken fragments; scrap (metal *etc.*); 5. (stone-)quarry.

[2]**Bruch,** *m.* (**-es,** *pl.* **⸚e**) *or n.* (**-es,** *pl.* **⸚e(r)**) bog, marsh, swamp, morass.

Bruch|band, *n.* truss. **–beanspruchung,** *f.* (*Metall.*) breaking-stress. **–belastung,** *f.* (*Metall.*) breaking-load. **–bildung,** *f.* (*Med.*) herniation. **–blei,** *n.* scrap lead. **–boden,** *m.* boggy *or* marshy ground. **–bude,** *f.* (*coll.*) tumble-down *or* ramshackle building; ramshackle *or* shaky concern *or* business. **–dehnung,** *f.* (*Metall.*) elongation at break. **–ebene,** *f.* (*Geol.*) fault-plane. **–einklemmung,** *f.* strangulation of a hernia. **bruch|fällig,** *adj.* dilapidated, ramshackle. **–fest,** *adj.* unbreakable, crash-proof, elastic. **Bruch|festigkeit,** *f.* (*Metall.*) tensile strength. **–glas,** *n.* broken glass.

bruchig ['bruxıç], *adj.* boggy, marshy, swampy.

brüchig ['bryçıç], *adj.* brittle, friable; full of cracks *or* breaks *or* flaws; short (*as metal*); (*fig.*) weak. **Brüchigkeit,** *f.* brittleness, friability; liability to crack, (*Metall.*) shortness.

bruchlanden ['bruxlandən], *v.i.* (*aux.* s.) (*Av.*) crash-land, make a crash-landing. **Bruch|-landung,** *f.* (*Av.*) crash-landing. **–last,** *f.* breaking load. **–linie,** *f.* split, fracture, (line of the) crack, (*Geol.*) fault-line. **–metall,** *n.* scrap metal. **–probe,** *f.* breaking-test. **–rechnung,** *f.* (*Arith.*) fractions. **–schaden,** *m.* (damage by) breakage. **–schiene,** *f.* splint. **–schlange, –schleiche,** *f.* blind- *or* slow-worm. **–schrift,** *f.* Gothic *or* black-letter type. **bruchsicher,** *adj.* unbreakable. **Bruch|span-nung,** *f.* breaking-stress *or* -strain *or* -load. **–stein,** *m.* (rough) quarry stone; rubble. **–strich,** *m.* (*Math.*) division sign, fraction stroke; shilling stroke, solidus.

Bruchstück ['bruxʃtyk], *n.* fragment, splinter, chip; (*fig.*) scrap. **bruchstückhaft,** 1. *adj.* fragmentary. 2. *adv.* in fragmentary form, as fragments *or* a fragment. **bruchstückweise,** *adv.* in fragments.

Bruch|teil, *m.* fraction. **–wasserlaüfer,** *m.* (*Orn.*) wood-sandpiper (*Tringa glareola*). **–weide,** *f.* (*Bot.*) crack willow (*Salix fragilis*). **–weißkehl-chen,** *n.* (*Orn.*) *see* **Schilfrohrsänger. –wurz,** *f.* (*Bot.*) agrimony. **–zahl,** *f.* fractional number.

Brücke ['brykə], *f.* bridge, viaduct; (*Naut.*) (captain's) bridge; jetty, pier, landing-stage; (landing) gangway, gangplank; (floor-)rug; dental arch *or* bridge; (*fig.*) bridge, link; ***alle –n hinter sich abbrechen,*** burn one's boats; ***eine – über einen Fluß schlagen,*** throw a bridge across a river; ***hängende –,*** suspension bridge.

Brücken|arbeit, *f.* (dental) bridgework. **–bau,** *m.* bridge-building. **–bogen,** *m.* arch of a bridge. **–boot,** *n.* pontoon. **–geld,** *n.* bridge-toll. **–kopf,** *m.* bridgehead. **–pfeiler,** *m.* pier, pile. **–stütz-weite,** *f.* span (*of bridge*). **–waage,** *f.* weigh-bridge. **–zoll,** *m.* bridge-toll.

Bruder ['bru:dər], *m.* (**-s,** *pl.* **⸚**) brother; friar, lay brother; (*coll.*) fellow, chap; (*Prov.*) ***gleiche Brüder, gleiche Kappen,*** share and share alike, we're all in the same boat; ***lustiger –,*** boon companion; ***Barmherzige Brüder,*** Brothers Hospitallers; ***Böhmische Brüder,*** Moravian Brethren; (*Eccl.*) ***meine lieben Brüder,*** dearly beloved brethren; ***nasser –,*** toper; ***willst du nicht mein – sein, so schlag ich dir den Schädel ein,*** if you're not with me you're against me, (*sl.*) be my buddy or I'll bash your head in; ***warmer –,*** homosexual; ***das ist unter Brüdern DM. 50 wert,*** 50 marks between friends, that's cheap at 50 marks.

Bruder|bund, *m.* fraternity, brotherhood. **–fehde,** *f.* fraternal strife.

Brüdergemeine ['bry:dərgəmaınə], *f.* fraternity; Moravian Brethren. **brüderlich,** *adj.* brotherly, fraternal, (*fig.*) friendly.

Bruder|liebe, *f.* brotherly love; ***christliche –,*** love of one's fellow men. **–mord,** *m.* fratricide.

Bruderschaft ['bru:dərʃaft], *f.* (*Eccl.*) brotherhood, (con)fraternity.

Brüderschaft ['bry:dərʃaft], *f.* ***– trinken,*** pledge close friendship (change from '***Sie***' form of address to '***Du***'). *See also* **Bruderschaft.**

Bruders|frau, *f.* (*obs.*) sister-in-law. **–kind,** *n.* brother's child, nephew *or* niece.

Bruder|volk, *n.* kindred nation. **–zwist,** *m.* *See* **–fehde.**

Brühe ['bry:ə], *f.* broth, clear soup; stock, vegetable water; sauce, gravy; extract, solution, (*sl.*) dishwater, hogwash (*of a drink*); (dyeing) liquor, sauce (*in tobacco preparation*); (*coll.*) ***in der – sitzen*** or ***stecken,*** be in a fine mess; ***ihn in der – sitzen*** or ***stecken lassen,*** leave him in the lurch, (*sl.*) leave him to stew in his own juice. **brühen,** *v.t.* scald; soak in boiling water. **brühheiß,** *adj.* scalding *or* piping hot.

Brühl [bry:l], *m.* (**-es,** *pl.* **-e**) swampy meadow, marshy ground.

brüh|warm, *adj.* *See* **–heiß**; (*fig.*) red-hot; (*coll.*) ***eine –e Neuigkeit,*** hot news; ***etwas – erzählen,*** retail news while it's red-hot.

brüllen ['brylən], *v.t., v.i.* roar, bellow, howl, low (*as cattle*), shout, (*coll.*) bawl, holler; ***vor Lachen –,*** roar with laughter. **Brüll|frosch,** *m.* (*Zool.*) bullfrog (*Rana catesbyana*). **–husten,** *n.* hacking *or* barking cough. **–stimme,** *f.* stentorian voice.

Brumm|bär, –bart, *m.* grumbler, (*coll.*) bear (with a sore head). **–baß,** *m.* bourdon (*of an organ*); (*coll.*) deep *or* gruff voice; (*Mus.*) double bass. **–eisen,** *n.* Jew's harp.

brummen ['brumən], *v.t., v.i.* 1. growl, grumble; buzz, drone (*of insects*); boom, hum; mutter, mumble; ***in den Bart –,*** mutter to o.s.; grumble to o.s.; ***ein Lied vor sich hin –,*** hum a tune to o.s. 2. (*coll.*) do time (*in prison*), stay in (*at school*). **Brummer,** *m.* grumbler, growler; (*Elec. etc.*) buzzer; (*Ent.*) bluebottle. **Brummfliege,** *f.* (*Ent.*) bluebottle, meat fly (*Musca comitoria*). **brummig,** *adj.* grumbling, grumpy, surly, bad-tempered. **Brumm|kreisel,** *m.* humming-top, musical top. **–ochse,** *m.* blockhead, dunderhead. **–schädel,** *m.* (*coll.*) hangover.

brünett [bry'nɛt], *adj.* dark-haired, dark-complexioned. **Brünette,** *f.* brunette.

Brunft [brunft], *f.* (-, *pl.* **⸚e**) rut, heat (*of animals*). **brunftig, brünftig,** *adj.* rutting. **Brunftzeit,** *f.* rutting season.

brünieren [bry'ni:rən], *v.t.* blue (*metals*); brown (*metals*); burnish. **Brünier|eisen,** *n.,* **–stahl,** *m.* burnisher, burnishing tool. **–stein,** *m.* burnishing stone, bloodstone.

Brunn [brun], *m.* (**-(e)s,** *pl.* **-e(n)**) (*Poet.*) *see* **Brunnen.**

Brunnen ['brunən], *m.* spring, well, fountain, (*Liter.*) fount; (medicinal) waters, mineral spring; ***meine Pläne sind in den – gefallen,*** my plans have miscarried *or* have come to nothing *or* have gone up in smoke; (*Prov.*) ***den – zudecken, wenn das Kind hineingefallen ist,*** shut the stable-door after the horse has bolted *or* is stolen; ***– trinken,*** take the waters; (*coll.*) ***einen – machen,*** pass water.

Brunnen|arzt, *m.* spa doctor. **–becken,** *n.* basin of a fountain. **–bohrer,** *m.* sinking auger. **–eimer,** *m.* well-bucket. **–geist,** *m.* spirit (*or* nymph) of a well. **–haus,** *n.,* **–kammer,** *f.* pump-room (*of a spa*). **–kresse,** *f.* (*Bot.*) watercress (*Nasturtium officinale*). **–kur,** *f.* treatment at a spa. **–lattich,** *m.* (*Bot.*) coltsfoot. **–mantel,** *m.* lining of a well. **–schacht,** *f.* shaft of a well. **–schwengel,** *m.* beam, lift (*for the well-bucket*). **–stock,** *m.* (*Bot.*) great bindweed. **–stube,** *f.* *See* **–haus**; (*fig.*) well-spring(s). **–vergiftung,** *f.* (*fig.*) defamation, calumny. **–wasser,** *n.* spring *or* well-water.

Brunnquell ['brunkvɛl], *m.* (*Poet.*) fount, well-spring.

Brunst [brunst], *f.* (-, *pl.* **⸚e**) sexual desire; heat (*of animals*); (*Poet.*) fervour, ardour, passion. **brunsten,** *v.i.* be in *or* on heat (*of animals*).

brünstig ['brynstɪç], *adj.* in *or* on heat; (*Poet.*) fervent, ardent.

Brunst|zeit, *f.* season of heat. **–zyklus,** *m.* oestrous cycle.

brunzen ['bruntsən], *v.i.* (*vulg.*) piss.

brüsk [brysk], *adj.* brusque, curt, blunt, abrupt, off-hand, short.

Brust [brust], *f.* (-, *pl.* **⸚e**) breast; chest; (woman's) breast; thorax (*of insect*); breast, front (*of shirt*); breast, (working-)face (*of quarry*); ***an die – drücken,*** press to one's heart, clasp to one's breast; ***ihm die Pistole auf die – setzen,*** stick a gun in his ribs, (*fig.*) hold a pistol to his head; ***– an – stehen,*** stand shoulder to shoulder; ***es auf der – haben,*** be short of breath, have difficulty in breathing; ***schwach auf der – sein,*** have a weak chest, have bronchial trouble; (*coll.*) be short of money, be hard-up; ***sich an die – schlagen, an seine – klopfen,*** beat one's breast; be sorry, blame o.s.; ***ein Kind an der – haben,*** have a child at the breast; ***einem Kind die – geben,*** give a child the breast, suckle a child, (*coll.*) give a child suck; ***aus voller –,*** at the top of one's voice.

Brust–, *pref.* breast-, of the chest, thoracic, pectoral, mammary; of the lungs. **–atmung,** *f.* deep *or* costal breathing. **–band-Sturmschwalbe,** *f.* (*Orn.*) white-winged petrel (*Pterodroma leucoptera*). **–bein,** *n.* breastbone, sternum. **–beklemmung,** *f.* tightness of the chest. **–beschwerde,** *f.* chest-complaint. **–bild,** *n.* half-length portrait; bust. **–bräune,** *f.* (*Med.*) angina pectoris. **–drüse,** *f.* mammary gland. **–drüsenentzündung,** *f.* (*Med.*) mastitis. **–drüsenkrebs,** *m.* cancer of the breast.

brüsten ['brystən], *v.r.* give o.s. airs, boast, brag (*über* (*Acc.*), about), plume o.s. (on); ***der Schwan brüstet sich,*** the swan stands with outspread wings.

Brust|entzündung, *f.* pleurisy; mastitis. **–fell,** *n.* pleura. **–fellentzündung,** *f.* pleurisy. **–fleisch,** *n.* breast, white meat (*of poultry*). **–flosse,** *f.* (*Ichth.*) pectoral fin. **–flosser,** *m.pl.* (*Ichth.*) thoracici. **–gang,** *m.* thoracic duct. **–glas,** *n.* breast-pump; nipple glass. **–harnisch,** *m.* corselet, cuirass. **–höhle,** *f.* thoracic cavity. **–kasten,** *m.* (*Anat.*) thorax, thoracic cage. **–korb,** *m.* *See* **–kasten. brustkrank,** *adj.* consumptive, suffering from a chest complaint. **Brust|krause,** *f.* frill, ruffle, jabot. **–krebs,** *m.* *See* **–drüsenkrebs. –lattich,** *m.* (*Bot.*) coltsfoot. **–latz,** *m.* stomacher; (*Hist., Fenc.*) plastron; modesty vest. **–lehne,** *f.* *See* **–mauer. –leiden,** *n.* *See* **–beschwerde. –leier,** *f.* brace and bit. **–mauer,** *f.* breastwork, balustrade, parapet, railing. **–messer,** *m.* (*Med.*) stethometer. **–muskel,** *f.* pectoral muscle. **–panzer,** *m.* (*Hist.*) cuirass, (*Zool.*) plastron (*of tortoise*). **–schutz,** *m.* chest-protector, (*Fenc.*) plastron. **–schwimmen,** *n.* breast-stroke. **–stärker,** *m.* chest expander. **–stimme,** *f.* chest-voice. **–stück,** *n.* 1. breast, brisket (*of meat*); 2. (*Ent.*) thorax. **–tasche,** *f.* breast-pocket. **–ton,** *m.* chest-note; ***– der Überzeugung,*** true ring of conviction. **–tuch,** *n.* kerchief, jabot. **–umfang,** *m.* chest measurement (*of man*), bust measurement (*of woman*).

Brüstung ['brystuŋ], *f.* balustrade, parapet.

Brust|wams, *n.* (*Hist.*) doublet. **–warze,** *f.* nipple. **–wassersucht,** *f.* hydrothorax, dropsy of the chest. **–wehr,** *f.* breastwork, rampart, parapet. **–wirbel,** *m.* (*Anat.*) dorsal vertebra.

Brut [bru:t], *f.* (-, *pl.* **-en**) (*Orn.*) brood, hatch, (*Ichth.*) fry, spawn, (*Bot.*) shoot, gemma; young, progeny; (*fig.*) brood, rabble, pack, brats; brooding, hatching; ***die Henne ist in der –,*** the hen is sitting; ***– setzen,*** spawn, stock with spawn; ***die ganze – taugt nichts,*** they are a worthless set.

brutal [bru'ta:l], *adj.* brutal, cruel; ***–e Gewalt,*** brute force; ***– machen,*** brutalize; ***– werden,*** become brutalized. **Brutalität** [–i'tɛ:t], *f.* brutality, cruelty.

Brut|apparat, *m.* incubator. **–ei,** *n.* egg for hatching; addled egg.

brüten ['bry:tən], **1.** *v.i.* sit (*of hen*) (***auf*** (*Dat.*), on), incubate, brood; (*fig.*) brood (***auf*** (*Dat.*), over; ***über*** (*Acc.*), over *or* about), meditate, ponder, reflect (about); ***–de Sonnenhitze,*** stifling *or* oppressive heat of the sun. **2.** *v.t.* *See* **ausbrüten**; (*usu. fig.*) brood over, hatch, plan, be intent on (*mischief, revenge etc.*). **Brüten,** *n.* incubation. **Brüter,** *m.* 1. brooder, broody hen; 2. incubator, (*Am.*) brooder.

Brut|henne, *f.* brood-hen, sitting hen. **-hitze,** *f.* incubation heat, (*coll.*) scorching heat.

brütig ['bry:tɪç], *adj.* broody (*hen*), addled (*egg*).

Brut|kasten, *m.* incubator. **-knolle,** *f.* (*Bot.*) tuber. **-knospe,** *f.*, **-korn,** *n.* (*Bot., Biol.*) gemma, germ. **-ofen,** *m.* incubator. **-pest,** *f.* foul brood (*bees*). **-platz,** *m.* (*Orn.*) breeding place *or* ground. **-rahmen,** *m.* brood comb (*bees*). **-sack,** *m.* (*Zool.*) marsupial pouch. **-scheibe,** *f.* brood comb (*bees*). **-schrank,** *m.* incubator. **-stätte,** *f.* (*fig.*) breeding-place *or* -ground, hot-bed. **-tasche,** *f.* *See* **-sack. -teich,** *m.* spawning pond.

brutto ['bruto], *adv.* gross. **Brutto|gewicht,** *n.* gross weight. **-registertonnen,** *f.pl.* (*Naut.*) register tons.

Brut|vogel, *m.* nester. **-wabe,** *f.* brood-comb. **-wärme,** *f.* incubation temperature. **-zeit,** *f.* breeding season, sitting *or* breeding time (*of birds*), spawning time (*of fish*).

brutzeln ['brutsəln], *v.i.* splutter, sizzle.

Bub [bu:p] **(-en,** *pl.* **-en)** (*dial.*), **Bube** ['bu:bə], *m.* **(-n,** *pl.* **-n)** boy, lad; (*dial.*) rogue, scamp, knave, scoundrel; (*Cards*) knave, jack. **buben,** *v.i.* (*obs.*) ***huren und* –,** whore and fornicate. **Buben|streich,** *m.* prank, lark. **-stück,** *n.*, **Büberei** [by:bə'raɪ], *f.* knavish *or* rascally trick.

Bubikopf ['bu:bikɔpf], *m.* bobbed *or* shingled hair, Eton crop.

bübisch ['by:bɪʃ], *adj.* rascally, treacherous, knavish, villainous.

Buch [bu:x], *n.* **(-es,** *pl.* **⸚er)** 1. book; (*fig.*) ***ein – mit sieben Siegeln,*** a sealed book, a complete mystery; (*coll.*) ***gelehrt wie ein –,*** a mine of information, a walking encyclopaedia; ***wie es im – steht,*** such as might have come straight out of a book; 2. quire (*of paper*); 3. full suit (*of cards*); six tricks (*at whist*); 4. (*oft. pl.*) (*Comm.*) accounts, books; ***die Bücher abschließen,*** close *or* balance the accounts; ***zu – bringen, in die Bücher*** or ***ins – eintragen,*** enter in the books, book; ***ihm die Bücher führen,*** keep the books for him; (*fig.*) ***über eine S. – und Rechnung führen,*** keep a detailed account *or* make a careful note of everything concerning a th.

Buch|adel, *m.* patent of nobility. **-ampfer,** *m.* (*Bot.*) wood-sorrel. **-ausstattung,** *f.* get-up of a book. **-besprechung,** *f.* book review. **-binder,** *m.* bookbinder. **-bindergold,** *n.* gold leaf. **-binderwerkstatt,** *f.* binding-shop, bindery. **-deckel,** *m.* binding, cover. **-druck,** *m.* 1. (letterpress) printing; 2. typography. **-drucker,** *m.* (letterpress) printer. **-druckerei,** *f.* printing works, printing-press; printing-office. **-druckfarbe,** *f.* printers' ink. **-druckerstock,** *m.* (*Typ.*) vignette, tailpiece.

Buche ['bu:xə], *f.* beech(tree) (*Fagus*). **Buch|ecker, -eichel, Buchel, Büchel** ['by:çəl], *f.* (-, *pl.* **-n)** beech-nut, *pl.* beech-mast.

[1]**buchen** ['bu:xən], *adj.* beech(-wood).

[2]**buchen,** *v.t.* 1. book, enter (in the books); put down, place *or* charge (to an account); (*fig.*) ***das wäre als ein Fortschritt zu –,*** that should be counted *or* reckoned as a step forward; 2. book, reserve (*flight etc.*).

büchen ['by:çən], *adj.* *See* [1]**buchen.**

Bücher|abschluß ['by:çər–], *m.* closing *or* balancing the books. **-bord, -brett,** *n.* bookshelf.

Bücherei [by:çə'raɪ], *f.* library.

Bücher|folge, *f.* series of books. **-freund,** *m.* book-lover, bibliophile. **-gestell,** *n.* bookcase, bookshelves. **-halle,** *f.* public library, reading-room. **-kunde,** *f.* book-lore, bibliography. **-mappe,** *f.* brief case, (school) satchel. **-mensch,** *m.* bookish person. **-milde,** *f.* book-worm. **-narr,** *m.* bibliomaniac. **-regal,** *n.* book-shelf; book-stack (*in a library*). **-revisor,** *m.* accountant, auditor. **-sammlung,** *f.* (private) library, collection of books. **-schatz,** *m.* collection of rare books. **-schau,** *f.* book reviews. **-schrank,** *m.* bookcase. **-staffel,** *f.* showcase for books. **-ständer,** *m.* book-stand, bookcase. **-stütze,** *f.* book-end, book-rest. **-tasche,** *f.* satchel, brief-case. **-verzeichnis,** *n.* list *or* catalogue of books, bibliography. **-wurm,** *m.* *See* **-milde**; (*fig.*) bookworm, (*school sl.*) swot. **-wut,** *f.* bookishness, bibliomania. **-zensur,** *f.* censorship of the press; (*R.C.*) Index (*librorum prohibitorum*).

Buch|esche, *f.* (*Bot.*) hornbeam (*Carpinus betulus*). **-fink,** *m.* (*Orn.*) chaffinch (*Fringilla coelebs*).

Buch|format, *n.* size (of book), format. **-führer,** *m.* *See* **-halter. -führung,** *f.* *See* **-haltung. -gelehrsamkeit,** *f.* book-learning. **-gemeinschaft,** *f.* book-club. **-halter,** *m.* book-keeper, accountant. **-haltung,** *f.* book-keeping, accountancy; ***einfache (doppelte) –,*** single (double) entry book-keeping. **-handel,** *m.* book trade. **-händler,** *m.* bookseller. **-handlung,** *f.* bookshop.

Büchlein ['by:çlaɪn], *n.* booklet, little book.

Buch|macher, *m.* bookmaker, (*coll.*) bookie. **-macherei,** *f.* bookmaking.

Buchs [buks] **(-es,** *pl.* **-e), Buchsbaum,** *m.* (*Bot.*) box-tree (*Buxus sempervirens*).

Buchse ['buksə], *f.* (*Tech.*) bush, bushing; liner (*of cylinder*), sleeve (*of shaft*); (*Elec.*) socket.

Büchse ['byksə], *f.* 1. box; case; tin, can, tin-can, canister; (*Bot.*) pyxidium; ***mit der – herumgehen,*** go round with the collecting box; 2. sporting gun, (*obs.*) musket, firearm; 3. *See* **Buxe, Büx(e).**

Büchsen|fleisch, *n.* tinned *or* canned meat, (*sl.*) bully beef. **-macher,** *m.* gunsmith, armourer. **-meister,** *m.* (*obs.*) musketeer. **-metal,** *n.* gun metal. **-milch,** *f.* tinned milk. **-öffner,** *m.* tin- *or* can-opener. **-schütze,** *m.* (*Hist.*) arquebusier. **-stein,** *m.* iron pyrites.

Buchstabe ['buxʃta:bə], *m.* **(-ns,** *pl.* **-n)** (*Typ.*) letter, character; type; ***großer –,*** capital letter; ***– für –,*** letter by letter, literatim; ***bis auf den letzten –n, auf den –n genau,*** to the last letter; (*vulg.*) ***setz dich auf deine vier –n!*** find somewhere to put your backside.

Buchstaben|bild, *n.* (*Typ.*) typeface. **-glaube,** *m.* literalism, strict adherence to the letter. **-gleichklang,** *m.* alliteration. **-gleichung,** *f.* algebraic equation. **-klauber, -krämer, -mensch,** *m.* pedant, quibbler, literal-minded p. **-rätsel,** *n.* anagram. **-rechnen,** *n.* algebra. **-schloß,** *n.* combination lock. **-tafel,** *f.* phonetic alphabet (*signalling*). **-versetzung,** *f.* (*Gram.*) transposition of letters, metathesis. **buchstabenweise,** *adv.* letter by letter, literatim.

buchstabieren [bu:xʃta'bi:rən], *v.t.* spell; ***falsch –,*** misspell. **Buchstabierung,** *f.* spelling.

buchstäblich ['bu:xʃtɛ:plɪç], *adj.* literal, verbal, exact; ***er nimmt alles –,*** he takes everything literally.

Buchstütze ['bu:xʃtytsə], *f.* book-end.

Bucht [buxt], *f.* (-, *pl.* **-en)** (*Geog.*) bay, bight; creek, cove, inlet, (*Naut.*) camber; bight (*of rope*); (*Anat. etc.*) sinus; ***die deutsche –,*** Bay of Heligoland. **buchtig,** *adj.* indented; (*Bot.*) sinuate. **Buchtung,** *f.* indentation.

Buchumschlag ['bu:xˀumʃla:k], *m.* (book) jacket.

Buchung ['bu:xuŋ], *f.* 1. entry; 2. booking, reservation. **Buchungs|fehler,** *m.* error in the books. **-maschine,** *f.* book-keeping machine. **-stelle,** *f.* auditing *or* accountancy department.

Buch|verleih, *m.* lending *or* circulating library; lending of books. **-weizen,** *m.* (*Bot.*) buckwheat (*Fagopyrum*). **-zeichen,** *n.* book-mark(er).

Buckel ['bukəl], **1.** *m.* hump, humpback; bump (*phrenology*); protuberance, bulge, curb; mound, knoll, hummock (*of ground*); (*coll.*) back; (*vulg.*) ***du kannst mir den – runter rutschen,*** go and chase yourself! nothing doing! (*vulg.*) ***steig mir den – hinauf!*** you get my back up; (*coll.*) ***einen breiten – haben,*** be able to take it; ***die Katze macht einen –,*** the cat arches its back. **2.** *f.* (-, *pl.* **-n)** *or* *m.* boss, stud, knob; umbo (*of a shield*). **buck(e)lig,** *adj.* humpbacked, hunchbacked, (*of moon*) gibbous, gibbose; ***sich – lachen,*** be doubled up with laughter.

buckeln ['bukəln], **1.** *v.t.* (em)boss (*metal*). **2.** *v.i.* hump *or* arch one's back; (*coll.*) bow and scrape, cringe (**vor** (*Dat.*), to).

Buckel|ochs(e), *m.*, **–rind,** *n.* (*Zool.*) zebu. **–schild,** *m.* (*Hist.*) buckler. **–tier,** *n.* (*coll.*) camel. **–wal,** *m.* (*Zool.*) humpback whale.

bücken ['bykən], **1.** *v.t.* bow, bend (*one's head etc.*); ***gebückt gehen,*** walk with a stoop; ***gebückt sein,*** be bent *or* bowed. **2.** *v.r.* stoop, bend down.

Buckerl ['bukərl], *n.* (*coll.*) bow.

Bücking ['bykɪŋ], *m.* **(-s,** *pl.* **-e)** *see* ^{2}**Bückling.**

bucklig ['buklɪç], *adj. See* **buck(e)lig.**

^{1}**Bückling** ['byklɪŋ], *m.* **(-s,** *pl.* **-e)** (*coll.*) bow, obeisance.

^{2}**Bückling,** *m.* **(-s,** *pl.* **-e)** kipper, bloater, smoked herring.

Buckram ['bukram], *m.* **(-s,** *no pl.***)** buckram.

Buddel ['budəl], *f.* **(-,** *pl.* **-n)** (*dial.*) bottle.

buddeln ['budəln], *v.t., v.i.* (*dial., coll.*) dig.

Bude ['bu:də], *f.* cabin, hut, shack; stand, stall; (*Studs. sl.*) digs, rooms, lodgings, den; (*coll.*) ***sturmfreie –,*** lodging with a private entrance; (*coll.*) ***die – auf den Kopf stellen,*** turn the place upside down, make an unholy mess of the place; (*coll.*) ***ihm auf die – rücken*** or ***steigen,*** drop in (*or sl.* blow in) on him; (*coll.*) ***Leben in die – bringen,*** make things lively, ginger things up. **Buden|angst,** *f.* (*coll.*) claustrophobia. **–geld,** *n.* standing-rent (*for a stall*). **–zauber,** *m.* hectic party.

Budget [by'dʒe:], *n.* **(-s,** *pl.* **-s)** budget.

Büdner ['by:tnər], *m.* (*dial.*) stall-keeper; cottager, crofter.

Büfett [by'fe:, –'fɛt], *n.* **(-s,** *pl.* **-s** [–'fe:s] *or* **-e** [–'fɛtə]) sideboard, dresser, buffet; refreshment *or* snack bar; ***kaltes –,*** cold buffet. **Büfett|fräulein,** *n.* waitress, barmaid. **–kellner,** *m.* barman, bartender.

Büffel ['byfəl], *m.* 1. buffalo; ***amerikanischer –,*** bison; 2. coarse tufted cloth; 3. (*coll.*) lout, clod; blockhead. **Büffelei** [–'laɪ], *f.* **(-,** *pl.* **-en)** (*coll.*) swotting, grind; sweat. **Büffelkopfente,** *f.* (*Orn.*) buffle-headed duck, (*Am.*) bufflehead (*Bucephala albeola*). **büffeln,** *v.t.* (*coll.*) work hard at, slog away at, swot, mug up (*a subject*). **Büffler,** *m.* (*coll.*) hard worker, plodder; swot.

Bug [bu:k], *m.* **(-(e)s,** *pl.* **¨e)** 1. shoulder joint (*of animal*); ***das Pferd ist am – wund,*** the horse is collar-galled; 2. bow (*of a ship*), nose (*of aircraft*). **Buganker,** *m.* bower(-anchor).

Bügel ['by:gəl], *m.* hoop, bow; guard (*of trigger, sword-hilt etc.*); stirrup; coat-hanger, dress-hanger; (*Naut.*) gimbals. **Bügel|brett,** *n.* ironing-board. **–eisen,** *n.* (flat-)iron. **–falte,** *f.* crease (*in trousers*). **bügelfest,** *adj.* 1. not damaged by ironing; 2. firm in one's stirrups.

bügeln ['by:gəln], *v.t.* iron, press (*with an iron*).

Bügel|pumpe, *f.* stirrup-pump. **–riemen,** *m.* stirrup-leather.

Bug|figur, *f.* (*Naut.*) figurehead. **–flagge,** *f.* (*Naut.*) jack. **–flaggenstock,** *m.* jack-staff. **–geschütz,** *n.* (*Naut.*) bow-chaser. **–holzmöbel,** *n.* bentwood furniture. **bug|lahm,** *adj.* splay-shouldered, shoulder-shot. **–lastig,** *adj.* (*Av.*) nose-heavy. **Bug|leine,** *f.* (*Naut.*) bowline. **–mann,** *m.* (*pl.* **¨er**) bow (oar), **–rad,** *n.* (*Av.*) nose-wheel. **–radfahrgestell,** *n.* (*Av.*) tricycle undercarriage. **–säge,** *f.* bow saw. **–schütze,** *m.* (*Av.*) forward gunner. **–schutzgerät,** *n.* (*Nav.*) paravane.

Bugsier|anker [buk'si:r–], *m.* kedge(-anchor). **–boot,** *n.*, **–dampfer,** *m.* tugboat.

bugsieren [buk'si:rən], *v.t.* tow, take in tow, (*coll.*) drag, trail, pull. **Bugsierer,** *m.* tugboat; tugboatman.

Bugsier|tau, *n.*, **–trosse,** *f.* (*Naut.*) tow-rope, towing line.

Bug|spriet, *n.* (*Naut.*) bowsprit. **–stand,** *m.* (*Av.*) forward gun position. **–stange,** *f.* foremast. **–stück,** *n.* brisket (*of beef*); shoulder (*of veal, pork or mutton*). **–welle,** *f.* (*Naut.*) bow-wave.

Büh(e)l [by:l], *m.* (*Swiss*) hillock.

Buhle ['bu:lə], **1.** *m.* **(-n,** *pl.* **-n)** (*obs., Poet.*) lover, swain, gallant. **2.** *f.* (*obs., Poet.*) lady(-love), sweetheart; mistress, paramour. **buhlen,** *v.i.* (*obs.*) make love (***mit,*** to), have illicit intercourse (with); (*Poet.*) toy (with), caress (*as the wind*); ***– um,*** court, woo; (*fig., Poet.*) strive for, court (*favour etc.*). **Buhlerei** [–'raɪ], *f.* coquetry; lovemaking; wooing; illicit intercourse, fornication, lechery. **Buhlerin,** *f. See* **Buhle, 2. buhlerisch,** *adj.* (*obs.*) lecherous, lascivious, wanton; (*Poet.*) amorous, playful, caressing (*as wind*). **Buhlschaft,** *f. See* **Buhlerei.**

Buhne ['bu:nə], *f.* dam, breakwater; dike, groyne, mole, jetty.

Bühne ['by:nə], *f.* stage, platform, dais; theatre; (*fig.*) scene (of action), arena.

Bühnen|anweisung, *f.* stage-direction. **–arbeiter,** *m.* stage-hand. **–ausgabe,** *f.* acting edition. **–aussprache,** *f.* standard pronunciation. **–ausstattung,** *f.* scenery, décor, stage properties. **–bearbeitung,** *f.* adaptation for the stage, dramatization. **–bild,** *n.* décor, setting, scenery. **–bildner,** *m.* stage designer. **–dichter,** *m.* dramatist, playwright. **–deutsch,** *n.* standard German. **bühnen|-gerecht,** *adj.* suitable for *or* adapted for the stage. **–kundig,** *adj.* having theatrical experience. **Bühnen|künstler,** *m.* actor, stage-performer. **–maler,** *m.* scene-painter. **–manuskript,** *n.* acting copy. **bühnen|mäßig,** *adj. See* **–gerecht;** scenic, theatrical. **Bühnen|musik,** *f.* incidental music. **–öffnung,** *f.* proscenium. **–schriftsteller,** *m. See* **–dichter. –sprache,** *f. See* **–deutsch. –stück,** *n.* stage play. **–vertrieb,** *m.* theatrical agency. **–werk,** *n.* dramatic work, drama, play. **–wirkung,** *f.* stage-effect. **–zubehör,** *n.* stage properties.

buk [bu:k], **büke** ['by:kə], *see* **backen.**

Bukett [bu'kɛt], *n.* **(-(e)s,** *pl.* **-e)** 1. bunch *or* bouquet (*of flowers*); 2. bouquet (*of wine*).

Bulette [bu'lɛtə], *f.* meat-ball, rissole.

Bulgare [bul'ga:rə], *m.* **(-n,** *pl.* **-n)** Bulgarian. **Bulgarien,** *n.* Bulgaria. **bulgarisch,** *adj.* Bulgarian.

Bulin(e) [bu'li:n(ə)], *f.* **(-,** *pl.* **Bulinen), Bulinstich,** *m.* (*Naut.*) bowline.

Bull|auge ['bul–], *n.* (*Naut.*) porthole. **–dogge,** *f.* bulldog.

^{1}**Bulle** ['bulə], *m.* **(-n,** *pl.* **-n)** bull, bullock; (*sl.*) tough guy; copper, fuzz (= policeman).

^{2}**Bulle,** *f.* seal (*on a deed*); edict, papal bull.

bullen ['bulən], *v.i.* be in *or* on heat (*of a cow*), take the bull.

Bullen|beißer, *m.* bulldog. **–hetze,** *f.* bull-baiting. **–hitze,** *f.* (*coll.*) sweltering heat. **–kalb,** *n.* bull-calf.

bullern ['bulərn], *v.i.* seethe, boil vigorously; (*coll.*) rage, storm, thunder.

Bult [bult], *m.* **(-(e)s,** *pl.* **¨e), Bülte** ['byltə], *f.*, **Bulten,** *m.* (*dial.*) hillock, grassy mound *or* hummock.

bum [bum], *int. See* **bums;** ***bim, bam, –,*** ding-dong (*bell*).

Bummel ['buməl], *m.* stroll; ***einen – machen,*** go for a stroll; ***auf den – gehen,*** go out on the spree. **Bummelant** [–'lant], *m.* **(-en,** *pl.* **-en)** *see* **Bummler. Bummelei** [–'laɪ], *f.* **(-,** *no pl.***)** dawdling, loitering; laziness; negligence, slovenliness, slackness. **Bummelfritz,** *m.* (*coll.*) *see* **Bummler. bummelig,** *adj.* unpunctual; lackadaisical, slovenly, slack. **Bummelleben,** *n.* dissipated life; ***ein – führen,*** gad about. **bummeln,** *v.i.* 1. waste one's time, loaf about, loiter; dawdle, take it easy, slack; gad about; ***– gehen,*** go on the spree; 2. (*aux.* s.) saunter, stroll. **Bummel|streik,** *m.* go-slow strike, working to rule. **–zug,** *m.* (*coll.*) slow train, local train. **Bummler,** *m.* idler, loafer, lounger, gadabout; dawdler, slowcoach.

bums! [bums], *int.* bump! crash! bang! **bumsen,** *v.i.* bang, bump, thump. **Bums|landung,** *f.* (*Av. coll.*) crash *or* pancake landing. **–lokal,** *n.* (*sl.*) low dance-hall, dive.

Buna ['bu:na], *n. or m.* (**-s**, *no pl.*) synthetic rubber.

[1]**Bund** [bunt], *n.* (**-(e)s**, *pl.* **-e**) bundle; bunch (*of keys etc.*); truss (*of hay*); knot, skein, hank (*of silk*); hank (*of flax*); ***vier – Radieschen,*** four bunches of radishes.

[2]**Bund,** *m.* (**-(e)s,** *pl.* **⸚e**) 1. band, neckband (*of shirt*), waistband (*of skirt etc.*), (*Mech.*) collar, flange, (*Build.*) (roof-)truss, (*Naut.*) lashing, tie, (*Mus.*) fret (*of guitar etc.*); 2. (*fig.*) agreement, bond, compact, covenant; (*Pol.*) alliance, league, coalition, confederacy, (con)federation; (*Comm.*) union, association; ***der –,*** the Federal Government (*of Germany today*); ***der Alte –,*** the Old Testament; ***der Deutsche –,*** the German Confederation (1815–66); ***der – der Ehe,*** the bond of marriage; ***der Hanseatische –,*** the Hanseatic League. **Bundbruch,** *m.* breach of an alliance *or* (*B.*) of a covenant. **bundbrüchig,** *adj.* faithless, treacherous; ***– werden,*** violate an agreement, break a contract; turn traitor, perjure o.s.

Bündel ['byndəl], *n.* bundle, packet, package, parcel, bale; beam (*of rays*); (*coll.*) ***sein – schnüren,*** pack up one's traps; (*sl.*) sling one's hook, hook it; ***ein – Knochen,*** a bag of bones; ***ein – Nerven,*** a bundle of nerves. **bündelförmig,** *adj.* (*Bot. etc.*) fasciculate, fascicular. **bündeln,** *v.t.* bundle (up), make a bundle of, make up into bundles; bunch, cluster, concentrate into a beam, focus (*rays*). **Bündelpresse,** *f.* baling-press. **bündelweise,** *adv.* in bundles.

Bundes– ['bundəs], *pref.* federal. **–arbeitsgericht,** *n.* Federal Labour Court. **–bahn,** *f.* Federal Railway. **–bruder,** *m.* fellow-member of students' society. **–finanzhof,** *m.* Federal Fiscal Court. **–fürst,** *m.* (*Hist.*) ruler of a member-state in the German Confederation. **–genosse,** *m.* confederate, ally. **–gerichtshof,** *m.* Federal High Court. **–haus,** *n.* Federal parliament buildings (*in Bonn*). **–hymne,** *f.* Austrian national anthem. **–kanzler,** *m.* Federal Chancellor. **–lade,** *f.* (*B.*) Ark of the Covenant. **–land,** *n.* province (*in Austria*). **–präsident,** *m.* President of the Federal Republic (*Germany*) *or* of the Republic (*Austria*) *or* of the Confederation (*Switzerland*). **–rat,** *m.* Federal Council. **–sozialgericht,** *n.* Federal Social Court. **–staat,** *m.* federal state, centralized Confederacy. **–tag,** *m.* Lower House of the German Federal Republic; (*Hist.*) Diet of the German Confederation. **–verfassungsgericht,** *n.* Federal Constitutional Court. **–verwaltungsgericht,** *n.* Federal Administrative Court. **–wehr,** *f.* German Federal Armed Forces.

Bund|garn, *n.* thread in hanks *or* skeins. **–holz,** *n.* faggots, bundles of wood.

bündig ['byndɪç], *adj.* 1. binding, valid (*agreement*), conclusive (*argument*), concise, succinct, to the point (*statement*); ***kurz und –,*** short and to the point; 2. (*Build. etc.*) flush, level. **Bündigkeit,** *f.* validity, conclusiveness; conciseness, brevity.

bündisch ['byndɪʃ], *adj.* (organized) in a league *or* union *or* association.

Bündnis ['byntnɪs], *n.* (**-ses,** *pl.* **-se**) agreement, alliance, compact, league.

Bund|ring, *m.* (*Mech.*) collar. **–schuh,** *m.* sandal; clog; symbol of German Peasants' Confederation (1525). **–weite,** *f.* 1. waist measurement (*of trousers*); 2. (*Build.*) distance between roof-trusses.

Bunker ['buŋkər], *m.* (coal) bunker; bin, hopper, (grain-)silo; (*Mil.*) dugout, pill-box, bunker; air-raid shelter; (submarine) pen; (*Golf*) bunker. **bunkern,** *v.t.* (*Naut. etc.*) bunker (*coal*), coal (*a ship*).

bunt [bunt], *adj.* coloured; bright, gay, colourful; motley, multi- *or* many-coloured, variegated; mottled, spotted, speckled, dappled, pied, parti-coloured, stained (*glass*); (*fig.*) varied, motley, full of variety; (*coll.*) confused, muddled, topsy-turvy, higgledy-piggledy, upside down; ***–er Abend,*** variety show *or* entertainment; ***ein –es Durcheinander,*** utter confusion, a complete muddle; (*coll.*) ***bekannt wie ein –er Hund,*** known to everyone; ***–e Kuh,*** skewbald cow; ***–e Karte,*** court-card; ***–es Musikprogramm,*** musical medley; ***–e Platte,*** dish of various cold meats; ***–e Reihe machen,*** pair off ladies and gentlemen, mix the sexes; (*obs.*) ***den –en Rock anziehen,*** put on uniform, join the red-coats; (*coll.*) ***hier sieht es – aus,*** the place is in an awful mess, everything is upside down; (*coll.*) ***es – treiben,*** go the pace; ***das wird mir zu –,*** that is really carrying it *or* going too far; ***etwas – durcheinander werfen,*** get s.th. in a terrible muddle.

Bunt|druck, *m.* colour-printing. **–falke,** *m.* (*Orn.*) American sparrow hawk, (*Am.*) sparrow hawk (*Falco sparverius*). **–farbenanstrich,** *m.* (*Mil.*) protective colouring, camouflage. **buntfarbig,** *adj.* brightly coloured, gay. **Buntfeuer,** *n.* (distress) flare, light-signal, Bengal light. **bunt|fleckig, –gesprenkelt,** *adj.* spotted, speckled, mottled, dappled. **Buntheit,** *f.* brightness, vividness, colourfulness, (*fig.*) variety, diversity. **buntkariert,** *adj.* chequered, tartan. **Bunt|metall,** *n.* non-ferrous metal. **–papier,** *n.* coloured paper. **bunt|scheckig,** *adj.* skewbald (*of a cow*), (*fig.*) motley (*as a crowd*). **–schillernd,** *adj.* iridescent, opalescent. **Bunt|specht,** *m.* (*Orn.*) greater spotted woodpecker (*Dendrocopus major*); ***kleiner –,*** *see* **Kleinspecht**; ***mittlerer –,*** *see* **Mittelspecht.** **–stift,** *m.* coloured pencil, crayon. **–waren,** *f.pl.* printed cottons. **–wäsche,** *f.* coloured washing, (*coll.*) coloureds.

Bürde ['byrdə], *f.* burden, load; ***Würde bringt –,*** responsibility brings responsibilities.

Bure ['bu:rə], *m.* (**-n,** *pl.* **-n**) Boer.

Bureau, *n. See* **Büro.**

Burenkrieg ['bu:rənkri:k], *m.* Boer War.

Burg [burk], *f.* (-, *pl.* **-en**) castle, citadel; stronghold, fortress, fort, (place of) refuge, (*beaver's*) lodge; ***eine feste – ist unser Gott*** (Luther), God is our refuge (and our strength); ***mein Haus: meine –*** (an Englishman's) home is (his) castle.

Burg|bann, *m.* castle precincts; jurisdiction of a castellan. **–besatzung,** *f.* castle garrison. **–ding,** *n. See* **–bann.**

bürge ['byrgə], *see* **bürgen, bergen.**

Bürge, *m.* (**-n,** *pl.* **-n**) surety, security, guarantor; sponsor; ***als – haften,*** guarantee, vouch, answer (***für,*** for), stand security; go *or* stand bail (*for a prisoner*); ***einen –n stellen,*** find security, surety *or* bail. **bürgen,** *v.i.* go *or* stand bail (***für,*** for); stand security *or* surety (for), vouch (for), answer (for), guarantee.

Bürger ['byrgər], *m.* citizen, townsman, burgess, burgher; member of the middle classes, bourgeois, commoner; ***– und Studenten,*** town and gown.

Bürger|adel, *m.* patriciate. **–garde,** *f.* town militia, civic guard, city volunteers. **–krieg,** *m.* civil war. **–kunde,** *f.* civics.

bürgerlich ['byrgərlɪç], *adj.* 1. civic, civil; ***–e (Ehren)rechte,*** civil *or* civic rights; ***–es Recht,*** civil law; ***–es Gesetzbuch,*** code of Civil Law; ***–er Tod,*** outlawry, loss of civil rights; 2. middle-class, bourgeois; ***–es Drama,*** domestic drama, drama of middle-class life; ***–e Partei,*** non-socialist party; 3. simple, plain, homely; ***sie kann – kochen,*** she understands plain cooking; ***–er Mittagstisch,*** plain lunches. **Bürgerliche(r),** *m., f.* commoner. **Bürgerlichkeit,** *f.* homeliness, plainness, conventionality.

Bürger|mädchen, *n.* middle-class girl. **–meister,** *m.* mayor, (*Scots*) provost, (*foreign*) burgomaster. **–meistermöwe,** *f. See* **Eismöwe.** **–pflicht,** *f.* civic duties, duties as a citizen. **–recht,** *n.* civil rights. **–schaft,** *f.* citizens, townspeople. **–sinn,** *m.* public spirit.

Bürgersmann ['byrgərsman], *m.* (**-(e)s,** *pl.* **-leute**) member of the middle classes; *pl.* middle-class people.

Bürger|stand, *m.* the middle classes, bourgeoisie. **–steig,** *m.* pavement, (*Am.*) sidewalk. **–steuer,** *f.* poll-tax. **–stolz,** *m.* civic pride.

Bürgertum, *n.* (**-s,** *no pl.*) middle class.

Bürger|wache, –wehr, *f. See* **–garde.**

Burg|frau, *f.* chatelaine, lady of the castle. **–fräu-**

lein, *n.* high-born young lady. **–friede,** *m.* (*Hist.*) jurisdiction of a castellan; (*coll.*) truce. **–graf,** *m.* feudal lord, baron, castellan. **–gräfin,** *f.* chatelaine. **–herr,** *m.* knight of the castle, castellan. **–hof,** *m.* bailey, courtyard.

Bürgschaft ['byrkʃaft], *f.* security, guarantee, sponsorship, surety; – ***leisten,*** stand security; ***die – übernehmen,*** go bail. **Bürgschaftsschein,** *m.* surety-bond.

Burgund [bur'gunt], *n.* (*Geog.*) Burgundy. **Burgunder** [–'gundər], *m.* burgundy (*wine*).

Burg|verlies, –verließ, *n.* dungeon, oubliette. **–vogt,** *m.* castellan. **–wache,** *f. See* **–besatzung. –warte,** *f.* watch-tower.

burlesk [bur'lɛsk], *adj.* burlesque, farcical. **Burleske,** *f.* burlesque, farce.

Büro [by'ro:], *n.* (**-s,** *pl.* **-s**) office, bureau; (*Mil.*) orderly room. **Büro|beamte(r),** *m., f.* clerk. **–chef,** *m.* head *or* chief clerk. **–haus,** *n.* office-block, block of offices. **–klammer,** *f.* paper-fastener *or* clip. **–kraft,** *f.* office worker; *pl.* office personnel.

Bürokrat [byro'kra:t], *m.* (**-en,** *pl.* **-en**) bureaucrat. **Bürokratie** [–'ti:], *f.* bureaucracy. **bürokratisch,** *adj.* bureaucratic.

Büro|vorsteher, *m. See* **–chef. –zeit,** *f.* office-hours.

Bursch(e) ['burʃ(ə)], *m.* (**-en,** *pl.* **-en**) youth, boy, lad; fellow, (*obs.*) apprentice, journeyman; student (*usu. a German student after the first year*); (*Mil.*) batman, orderly. **Burschen|herrlichkeit,** *f.* the good old student days. **–lied,** *n.* students' song.

Burschenschaft ['burʃənʃaft], *f.* (*German*) Students' Association. **Burschenschaft(l)er,** *m.* member of a Burschenschaft.

burschikos [burʃi'ko:s], *adj.* free and easy, hail-fellow-well-met, hearty; (*of girls*) tomboyish, hoydenish.

Burse ['burzə], *f.* 1. grant, scholarship; 2. students' hostel, (*obs.*) college.

Bürste ['byrstə], *f.* brush (*also Elec.*); (*coll.*) crew-cut. **bürsten,** *v.t., v.i.* brush. **Bürsten|abzug,** *m.* (*Typ.*) galley-proof. **–binder,** *m.* brush maker; ***laufen wie ein –,*** run like a hare; ***trinken wie ein –,*** drink like a fish. **–entladung,** *f.,* **–feuer,** *n.* (*Elec.*) brush discharge *or* sparking. **–schnitt,** *m.* crew-cut.

–bürtig ['byrtıç], *suff. See* **–gebürtig.**

Bürzel ['byrtsəl], *m.* rump; uropygium (*of a bird*); (*coll.*) parson's nose. **Bürzeldrüse,** *f.* preen *or* uropygial gland.

Burzelkraut ['burtsəlkraut], *n.* (*Bot.*) purslane.

burzeln ['burtsəln], *v.i. See* **purzeln.**

Bus [bus], *m.* (**-ses,** *pl.* **-se**) bus.

Busch [buʃ], *m.* (**-es,** *pl.* **-̈e**) bush, shrub; (*sing. only*) thicket, copse, covert, scrub, undergrowth; brushwood; tuft, plume, crest (*of a bird*), plume (*of a helmet*), bunch (*of flowers*), shock (of hair); ***auf den – klopfen,*** fish for information, pump *or* sound (*a p.*) for information.

Busch|affe, *m.* (*Zool.*) oran(g)utang. **–baum,** *m.* dwarf tree. **–egge,** *f.* brush-harrow.

Büschel ['byʃəl], *n.* tuft, clump, cluster, bunch, wisp; bundle, sheaf, (*Bot.*) fascicle; pencil (*of rays*). **Büschelentladung,** *f.* (*Elec.*) brush-discharge. **büschel|förmig,** *adj.* tufted, bunched, clustered. **–kiemig,** *adj.* (*Ichth.*) lophobranch(iate). **Büschelnelke,** *f.* (*Bot.*) sweetwilliam.

Busch|hemd, *n.* bush-shirt; sport shirt. **–holz,** *n.* undergrowth, scrub, brushwood. **buschig,** *adj.* bushy; shaggy; tufted, dendroid; covered with scrub *or* undergrowth. **Busch|klepper,** *m.* highwayman, (*obs.*) footpad, cutpurse. **–mann,** *m.* (*pl.* **-̈er**) bushman. **–neger,** *m.* Negro slave, maroon. **–rohrsänger,** *m.* (*Orn.*) Blythe's reed-warbler (*Acrocephalus dumentorum*). **–spötter,** *m.* (*Orn.*) booted warbler (*Hippolais caligata*). **–werk,** *n.* bushes, shrubbery, undergrowth. **–windröschen,** *n.* (*Bot.*) wood-anemone (*Anemone nemorosa*).

Büse ['by:zə], *f.* small fishing-boat.

Busen ['bu:zən], *m.* 1. bosom; breast; heart; ***eine Schlange am – nähren,*** cherish a viper in one's bosom; ***im – verschließen,*** keep locked in one's heart; 2. (*Geog.*) gulf, bay; 3. (chimney-)breast. **Busen|freund,** *m.* bosom friend. **–krause,** *f.* frill, ruffle. **–nadel,** *f.* scarf- *or* tie-pin.

Buße ['bu:sə], *f.* repentance, penitence; expiation, penance, atonement; fine; – ***tun,*** do penance.

büßen ['by:sən], *v.t., v.i.* make amends (***für,*** for), atone (for), pay the penalty (of), expiate. **Büßer,** *m.* penitent. **Büßerhemd,** *n.* penitential robe, hair-shirt.

Busserl ['busərl], *n.* (**-s,** *pl.* **-(n)**) (*dial.*) kiss. **busserln,** *v.t.* (*dial.*) kiss.

buß|fällig, *adj.* liable to punishment, punishable. **–fertig,** *adj.* penitent, repentant, contrite. **Buß|fertigkeit,** *f.* penitence, repentance, contrition. **–hemd,** *n.* hair-shirt.

Bussole [bu'so:lə], *f.* magnetic compass.

Buß|prediger, *m.* Lenten preacher. **–predigt,** *f.* Lenten sermon. **–tag,** *m.* day of repentance. **–übung,** *f.* penance.

Büßung ['by:suŋ], *f.* expiation, atonement.

Büste ['bystə], *f.* bust. **Büstenhalter,** *m.* brassière.

Butt [but], *m.* (**-(e)s,** *pl.* **-e**) (*Ichth.*) butt, flounder (*Pleuronectidae*).

Butte ['butə], *f.* 1. rose hip; 2. *See* **Butt**; 3. *See* **Bütte.**

Bütte ['bytə], *f.* butt, tub, vat; basket for carrying on the back; (*coll.*) ***Hand von der –,*** hands off! let well alone!

Büttel ['bytəl], *m.* beadle; bailiff.

Bütten|papier, *n.* hand-made paper. **–rand,** *m.* deckle-edge (*paper*).

Butter ['butər], *f.* (-, *no pl.*) butter; (*coll.*) ***es ist alles in –,*** everything is ship-shape *or* fine and dandy; (*coll.*) ***ihm war die – vom Brote gefallen,*** you could have knocked him down with a feather; (*coll.*) ***sich*** (*Dat.*) ***die – vom Brot nehmen lassen,*** let o.s. be done down; ***gesalzene –,*** salt(ed) butter; – ***schlagen,*** churn butter.

Butter|blume, *f.* buttercup, ranunculus; marigold. **–brot,** *n.* (slice of) bread and butter; ***belegtes –,*** open sandwich; – ***mit Schinken,*** ham-sandwich. **–brotpapier,** *n.* grease-proof paper. **–dose,** *f.* butterdish. **–faß,** *n.* churn. **butterhaltig, butterig,** *adj.* buttery, containing butter; butyrous, butyraceous. **Buttermilch,** *f.* buttermilk.

buttern ['butərn], **1.** *v.t.* butter, spread with butter. **2.** *v.i.* make butter, churn; (*of cream*) turn to butter.

Butter|napf, *m. See* **–dose. –säure,** *f.* butyric acid. **–stulle,** *f.* slice of bread and butter. **–teig,** *m.* short pastry. **butterweich,** *adj.* as soft as butter.

Büttner ['bytnər], *m.* cooper.

[1]Butz [buts], *m.* (**-en,** *pl.* **-en**) *see* **Butzen.**

[2]Butz, *m.* (**-en,** *pl.* **-en**) *see* **[1]Butze.**

[1]Butze ['butsə], *m.* (**-n,** *pl.* **-n**) dwarf, gnome.

[2]Butze, *f.* (*dial.*) 1. partition; bed-recess; 2. lump (*see* **Butzen**).

Butzemann ['butsəman], *s. See* **Butzenmann.**

Butzen ['butsən], *m.* 1. (apple *etc.*) core; 2. flaw (*in casting*); 3. lump; head of pus; (*vulg.*) snot.

Butzen|mann, *m.* (*pl.* **-̈er**) bogey(-man). **–scheibe,** *f.* bull's-eye glass, glass-roundel. **–scheibenromantik,** *f.* pseudo-Gothic.

Butzkopf ['butskɔpf], *m.* (*Zool.*) grampus (*Orcinus orca*).

Buxe ['buksə], **Büx(e)** ['by:ks(ə)], *f.* (-, *pl.* **-en**) (*dial., coll.*) trousers. **buxen,** *v.t.* (*coll.*) pinch, swipe, pilfer.

C

*Except in the ligatures ch and ck and sch this is not a genuine German letter, and occurs only in foreign borrowings. Before the vowels **a**, **o**, and **u** it was formerly replaced by **k** and before the vowels **ä**, **e**, **i**, and **y** by **z** (though less so nowadays). Words not found below should be sought under **K**, **Sch**, or **Z**.*

C, c [tse:], *n.* C, c; (*Mus.*) key of C; do (*first note of octave*); ***C-Dur*** (***c-moll***), (the key of) C major (minor); ***C-Schlüssel***, C clef, bass clef.

Cäcilia [tsɛ'tsi:lia], **Cäcilie,** *f.* Cecilia, Cicely.

Caesur [tsɛ'zu:r], *f.* (-, *pl.* **-en**) (*Mus.*, *Pros.*) caesura.

Cafe [ka'fe:], *n.* (**-s**, *pl.* **-s**) café, coffee house, tea-room; *see* **Kaffee.**

Canaille [ka'na:ljə], *f.* blackguard(s).

Caritas ['ka:ritas], *f.* (-, *no pl.*) (Roman Catholic) charitable organisation. **caritativ** [-'ti:v], *adj.* charitable.

Cäsar ['tsɛ:zar], *m.* Caesar. **cäsarisch** [-'za:rɪʃ], *adj.* Caesarian.

Cäsur, *f. See* **Caesur.**

Causerie [kozə'ri:], *f.* discussion, chat.

Cecilie, *f. See* **Cäcilia.**

Celesta [tʃe'lɛsta], *f.* (-, *pl.* **-s** *or* **-en**) (*Mus.*) celeste.

Cellist [tʃɛ'lɪst], *m.* (**-en**, *pl.* **-en**) violoncello player, (violon)cellist.

Cello ['tʃɛlo], *n.* (**-s**, *pl.* **-s** *or* **Celli**) violoncello.

Cembalo ['tʃɛmbalo], *n.* (**-s**, *pl.* **-s**) harpsichord.

Ces [tsɛs], *n.* (*Mus.*) C flat.

Cettisänger ['tsɛtizɛŋər], *m.* (*Orn.*) *see* **Seidensänger.**

Chagrin [ʃa'grɛ̃], **1.** *m.* (**-s**, *pl.* **-s**) chagrin, mortification. **2.** *n.* (**-s**, *no pl.*) shagreen.

Chaiselongue [ʃɛz(ə)'lɔ̃g], *f.* (-, *pl.* **-s** *or* **-n**) couch, lounge-chair.

Chamäleon [ka'mɛ:leɔn], *n.* (**-s**, *pl.* **-s**) chameleon.

Champagner [ʃam'panjər], *m.* champagne (*wine*); ***deutscher*** –, sparkling hock *or* moselle.

Champignon ['ʃampɪnjɔ̃], *m.* (**-s**, *pl.* **-s**) (common *or* field) mushroom (*Psalliota*).

Chance ['ʃɑ̃sə], *f.* (*coll.*) prospect, chance; opportunity.

changeant [ʃɑ̃:'ʒɑ̃], *adj.* shot (*fabric*), shimmering.

Chaos ['ka:ɔs], *n.* (-, *no pl.*) chaos. **chaotisch** [-'o:tɪʃ], *adj.* chaotic.

Charakter [ka'raktər], *m.* (**-s**, *pl.* **-e** [-'te:rə]) 1. character, personality, disposition, nature, quality; 2. (*Typ.*) character, status; 3. (*Mil.*) honorary *or* brevet rank; 4. (*Theat.*) character, part. **Charakter|anlage,** *f.* disposition, natural tendency. **–bild,** *n.* character sketch. **–bildung,** *f.* character building. **charakterfest,** *adj.* of strong character; steadfast, reliable.

charakterisieren [karakteri'zi:rən], *v.t.* 1. characterize, be characteristic of, distinguish; 2. characterize, give a character-sketch of; 3. (*Mil.*) grant honorary *or* brevet rank to. **Charakterisierung,** *f.* characterization; portrayal *or* depiction *or* delineation of character. **Charakteristik** [-'rɪstɪk], *f.* (-, *pl.* **-en**) characteristic; *see also* **Charakterisierung. Charakteristikum,** *n.* (**-s**, *pl.* **-ka**) characteristic. **charakteristisch,** *adj.* characteristic, typical.

charakterlich [ka'raktərlɪç], *adj.* concerning *or* of character *or* the personality. **charakterlos,** *adj.* (*of a th.*) characterless, lacking (in) *or* without character, nondescript, insipid, colourless, (*coll.*) wishy-washy; (*of a p.*) characterless, without (strength of) character *or* (strong) personality, (*coll.*) spineless. **Charakterlosigkeit,** *f.* characterlessness, lack of (strength of) character, lack of personality.

Charakter|schilderung, *f. See* **Charakterisierung**; character-study. **–schulung,** *f.* character-building *or* -training. **charakter|voll,** *adj. See* **–fest. Charakterzug,** *m.* characteristic, distinguishing feature, trait.

Charge ['ʃarʒə], *f.* 1. office, rank; 2. officer-bearer, official; (*Mil.*) noncommissioned officer; 3. (*Theat.*) (minor) character-role; 4. (*Tech.*) charge (*of a furnace*). **Chargen|pferd,** *n.* charger. **–spieler,** *m.* character-actor.

chargieren [ʃar'ʒi:rən], **1.** *v.i.* be represented, send representatives (*of student bodies*). **2.** *v.t.* 1. (*Theat.*) overact (*a part*); 2. (*Tech.*) charge, stoke (*a furnace*), (*obs.*) load (*fire-arms*). **Chargierte(r),** *m.*, *f.* office bearer (*of student's corporation*).

Charivari [ʃari'va:ri], *m. or n.* (**-s**, *pl.* **-s**) din, caterwauling.

Charta ['karta], *f.* (-, *pl.* **-s**) charter.

Chassis [ʃa'si:], *n.* (- [-'si:s], *pl.* - [-'si:s]) chassis.

Chauffeur [ʃɔ'fø:r], *m.* (**-s**, *pl.* **-e**) chauffeur, driver. **chauffieren,** *v.i.* drive (*a car*).

Chaussee [ʃo'se], *f.* (-, *pl.* **-n** [ʃɔ'se:ən]) main road, thoroughfare, highway. **chaussieren,** *v.t.* (*obs.*) macadamize (*road*).

Chef [ʃɛf], *m.* (**-s**, *pl.* **-s**) principal, head, director, manager, (*coll.*) chief, boss; (*Mil.*, *Naut.*) commander; – ***des Generalstabs,*** Chief of General Staff. **Chef|arzt,** *m.* medical superintendent (*in hospital*), (*Mil.*) senior medical officer. **–redakteur,** *m.* editor-in-chief.

Chemie [çe'mi:] (*in South Germany and Austria* [ke'mi:]), *f.* chemistry; ***angewandte*** –, applied chemistry; ***gerichtliche*** –, forensic chemistry. **Chemiefaser,** *f.* man-made fibre. **Chemikalien** [-'ka:liən], *n.pl.* chemicals. **chemikalisch,** *adj.* chemical. **Chemiker** ['çe:mɪkər], *m.* chemist; student *or* teacher of chemistry. **chemisch,** *adj.* chemical; ***–e Präparate,*** chemicals; ***–e Reinigung*** or ***Wäsche,*** dry-cleaning. **chemisch–,** *pref.* chemico-.

Cherub ['çe:rup], *m.* (**-s**, *pl.* **-inen** [-'bi:nən] *or* **-im** [-'bɪm]) cherub. **cherubinisch** [-'bi:nɪʃ], *adj.* cherubic.

Chiffre ['ʃɪfər], *f.* cipher, code; box number (*of advertisement*). **chiffrieren** [-'fri:rən], *v.t.* code, (en)cipher.

Chignon [ʃin'jɔ̃], *m.* (**-s**, *pl.* **-s**) knot *or* coil of hair, chignon, (*coll.*) bun.

Chimäre [çi'mɛ:rə], *f.* chimera, fantasy, bogey. **chimärisch,** *adj.* chimerical, imaginary, fanciful.

China ['çi:na], **1.** *n.* China. **2.** *f.* cinchona. **China|krepp,** *m.* crêpe de chine. **–rinde,** *f.* Peruvian bark, cinchona bark.

Chinese [çi'ne:zə], *m.* (**-n**, *pl.* **-n**) Chinaman. **Chinesin,** *f.* Chinese woman. **chinesisch,** *adj.* Chinese; ***–es Feuer,*** Bengal lights; ***–e Mauer,*** Great Wall of China; ***–es Meer,*** China Sea; ***–e Tusche,*** Indian *or* Chinese ink.

Chinin [çi'ni:n], *n.* (**-s**, *no pl.*) quinine.

Chiromant [çiro'mant], *m.* (**-en**, *pl.* **-en**) palmist, hand-reader. **Chiromantie** [-'ti:], *f.* palmistry, chiromancy.

Chirurg [çi'rurk], *m.* (**-en**, *pl.* **-en**) surgeon. **Chirurgie** [-'gi:], *f.* surgery. **chirurgisch,** *adj.* surgical.

Chlor [klo:r], *n.* (**-s**, *no pl.*) chlorine. **Chlorammonium,** *n.* salammoniac, ammonium chloride. **Chlorat** [-'ra:t], *n.* (**-s**, *pl.* **-e**) chlorate. **Chlorbrom(silber)papier,** *n.* (*Phot.*) chlorobromide *or* (*coll.*) gas-light paper. **chloren,** *v.t.* chlorinate. **chlorhaltig,** *adj.* containing chlorine. **Chlorid** [-'ri:t], *n.* (**-(e)s**, *pl.* **-e**) chloride. **chlorieren** [-'ri:rən], *v.t. See* **chloren. chlorigsauer,** *adj.* chlorite of; ***–es Salz,*** chlorite. **Chlorigsäure,** *f.* chlorous acid. **Chlor|kali(um),** *n.* potassium chloride. **–kalk,** *m.* chloride of lime, bleaching powder. **–kalzium,** *n.* calcium chloride, chloride of lime. **–kohlenoxyd,** *n.* (*Mil.*) phosgene gas, carbonyl chloride. **–natrium,** *n.* sodium chloride, common salt.

Chloroform [kloro'fɔrm], *n.* (**-s**, *no pl.*) chloroform. **chloroformieren** [-'mi:rən], *v.t.* (give) chloroform (to).

Chlorophyll [kloro'fyl], *n.* (**-s**, *no pl.*) (*Bot.*) chlorophyll.

chlorsauer ['klorzauər], *adj.* chlorate of; *–es Salz,* chlorate. **Chlorsäure,** *f.* chloric acid. **Chlorür** [–'ry:r], *n.* (**-s,** *pl.* **-e**) chloride. **Chlor|wasser,** *n.* chlorine water. **–wasserstoff,** *m.* hydrochloric acid, hydrogen chloride.

chokant [ʃɔ'kant], *adj.* shocking. **chokieren,** *v.t.* *See* **schockieren.**

Cholera ['ko:lera], *f.* cholera. **Choleriker** [ko'le:rɪker], *m.* choleric *or* (*coll.*) irascible p. **cholerisch** [–'le:rɪʃ], *adj.* choleric, (*coll.*) irascible, hot-tempered.

Cholesterin [koleste'ri:n], *n.* (**-s,** *no pl.*) cholesterol.

Chor [ko:r], **1.** *m.* (**-s,** *pl.* **⸚e**) choir; chorus, section (*of orchestra*). **2.** *n. or m.* (**-s,** *pl.* **-e** *or* **⸚e**) 1. (*obs.*) choir, chancel; ***im – singen,*** sing in chorus; 2. organ loft; 3. (*coll.*) pack, tribe (*esp. of rowdy children*).

Choral [ko'ra:l], *m.* (**-s,** *p.* **⸚e**) chorale, anthem, hymn, plainsong, (Gregorian) chant.

Chor|bischof, *m.* suffragan bishop. **–direktor,** *m.* choir-master. **–führer,** *m.* (*Eccl.*) first chorister; choragus (*in Greek drama*). **–gesang,** *m.* chorus; choral singing; *see* **Choral. –hemd,** *n.* surplice. **–herr,** *m.* canon, prebendary.

Chorist [ko'rɪst], *m.* (**-en,** *pl.* **-en**) member of a choir.

Chor|knabe, *m.* choir-boy, chorister. **–leiter,** *m.* *See* **–direktor. –mantel,** *m.* cope. **–nische,** *f.* apse. **–regent,** *m.* *See* **–direktor. –rock,** *m.* *See* **–hemd. –sänger,** *m.* chorister. **–stuhl,** *m.* choir-stall.

Chrie ['çri:(ə)], *f.* 1. (school) theme; 2. (*Rhet.*) essay composed according to definite rules.

Christ [krɪst], *m.* (**-en,** *pl.* **-en**) Christian; ***der Heilige –,*** Christmas. **Christ|abend,** *n.* Christmas Eve. **–baum,** *m.* Christmas tree. **–dorn,** *m.* (*Bot.*) holly (*Ilex aquafolium*).

Christenheit ['krɪstənhaɪt], *f.* Christendom. **Christentum,** *n.* Christianity.

Christ|fest, *n.* Christmas. **–kind,** *n.* Christ child, (*obs., Poet.*) Jesus. **christlich,** *adj.* Christian; (*sl.*) honest-to-God. **Christ|mette,** *f.* carol service, Christmas matins *or* mass, midnight mass. **–monat, –mond,** *m.* (*obs., Poet.*) December. **–nacht,** *f.* night before Christmas.

Christoph ['krɪstɔf], *m.* Christopher.

Christus ['krɪstus], *m.* Christ; ***nach –, nach Christi Geburt,*** after Christ (*abbr.* A.D.); ***vor –, vor Christi Geburt,*** before Christ (*abbr.* B.C.).

Chrom [kro:m], *n.* (**-s,** *no pl.*) chromium, chrome.

Chromatik [kro'ma:tik], *f.* (-, *pl.* **-en**) chromatics, science of colours. **chromatisch,** *adj.* chromatic; ***–e Tonleiter,*** chromatic scale.

chromgelb, *adj.* chrome-yellow. **Chrom|kali,** *n.* potassium bichromate. **–oxyd,** *n.* chromium oxide. **chromsauer,** *adj.* chromate of; ***–es Salz,*** chromate.

Chronik ['kro:nɪk], *f.* (-, *pl.* **-en**) chronicle. **Chronika,** *f.pl.* (*B.*) Chronicles.

chronisch ['kro:nɪʃ], *adj.* chronic.

Chronist [kro'nɪst], *m.* (**-en,** *pl.* **-en**) chronicler.

Chronologie [kronolo'gi:], *f.* chronology. **chronologisch** [–'lo:gɪʃ], *adj.* chronological.

Chronometer [krono'me:tər], *n.* chronometer.

Chrysalide [çryza'li:də], *f.* (*Ent.*) chrysalis, pupa.

Cilli ['tsɪli], *f.* (*dim. of* **Cäcilie**) Cissie.

Cis [tsɪs], *n.* (-, *pl.* -) (*Mus.*) C sharp. **Cisis,** *n.* (-, *pl.* -) C double sharp.

Cistensänger ['tsɪstənzɛŋər], *m.* (*Orn.*) fan-tailed warbler (*Cisticola juncidis*).

Clique ['klɪkə], *f.* clique, set, coterie.

Comment [ko'mã], *m.* (**-s,** *pl.* -) students' drinking ritual.

Cord [kɔrt] (**-(e)s,** *pl.* **-e**), **Cordsamt,** *m.* corduroy.

Cosinus ['ko:zinus], *m.* (-, *pl.* -) (*Math.*) cosine.

Cotangens ['ko:taŋgɛns], *m.* (-, *pl.* -) (*Math.*) cotangent.

coulant [ku'lant], *adj.* obliging.

Couleur [ku'lø:r], *f.* (-, *pl.* **-en**) 1. (shade of) colour; (*coll.*) ***das ist dieselbe – in Grün,*** that is as near as makes no difference; 2. a uniformed students' association. **Couleurstudent,** *m.* student belonging to a uniformed association.

Coupage [ku'pa:ʒə], *f.* blending, mixing (*wine etc.*).

Coupé [ku'pe:], *n.* (**-s,** *pl.* **-s**) (railway) compartment; carriage.

Cour [ku:r], *f.* (-, *no pl.*) ***einem Mädchen die – machen*** or ***schneiden,*** pay court to a girl; ***eine – halten,*** hold a levée.

Courage [ku'ra:ʒə], *f.* pluck, spirit; (*coll.*) ***Angst vor der eignen – kriegen,*** be afraid one has stuck one's neck out.

Cour|macher, –schneider, *m.* suitor, admirer, beau; ladies' man, (*coll.*) lady-killer.

Courtage [kur'ta:ʒə], *f.* (*Comm.*) brokerage.

Cousin [ku'zɛ̃:], *m.* (**-s,** *pl.* **-s**) (male) cousin. **Cousine** [–'zi:nə], *f.* (female) cousin; *see* **Kusine.**

Crackanlage ['krakˀanla:gə], *f.* cracking plant (*for oil*).

Creme [krɛ:m], *f.* 1. custard; cream (*as in cream chocolates*); 2. cream, paste (*as shoe-cream, hair-cream, tooth-paste etc.*); *see* **Krem.**

Crin [krɛ̃], *m.* (-, *pl.* **-s**) horsehair.

Croisé [kroa'ze:], *n.* (**-s,** *pl.* **-s**) (*Weav.*) twill. **croisiert** [–'zi:rt], *adj.* twilled.

Curette [ky'rɛtə], *f.* (*Surg.*) curette, scraper. **curettieren** [–'ti:rən], *v.t.* curette (*womb*).

D

D, d [de:], *n.* D, d; (*Mus.*) D; ***D-Dur,*** D major; ***D-moll,*** D minor; ***D-Schieber,*** D-valve (*in steam-engines*); ***D-Zug,*** through *or* express train.

da [da:], **1.** *adv.* **(a)** (*place*) 1. (*emph. dem.*) there; ***hier und –, – und dort,*** here and there; ***– ist sein Zimmer,*** there is his room; (*Mil.*) ***wer –?*** who goes there? ***–draußen,*** out there; ***– droben*** (or ***drunten***), up (*or* down) there; ***– herum,*** round there; ***von – ging er nach Hause,*** from there he went home; ***bleib –!*** stay where you are! don't move! ***wieder –,*** here again, back once more; 2. (*less emph. dem. of existence*) here, there, present; ***– bin ich,*** here I am; ***wozu ist es –?*** what's it here for? ***du –!*** you there! ***der –,*** the one here *or* there; ***ist schon Post für mich –?*** are there any letters for me yet? (*coll.*) ***wenn noch etwas – ist,*** if there is anything left *or* over; ***für mich ist das gar nicht –,*** for me it is non-existent; 3. (*unemphatic dem. introductory part.*) there, that; ***– hast du's!*** there you are! ***– hast du mein letztes Wort,*** that is my final word; ***– hast du eine Dummheit gemacht,*** that was a stupid thing to do; 4. (*emph. rel.*) (*Poet.*) where; ***ein Ort, – mich niemand kennt,*** a place where I am unknown; 5. (*unemphatic after rel.*) (*not translated*) ***alle die – kamen,*** all who came; ***es lache wer – will,*** whoever likes may laugh; ***was – kommt,*** whatever comes.

(b) (*time*) 1. (*emph. dem.*) then, at that time; ***– lachte er,*** then he laughed; ***wenn ich – noch lebe,*** if I am still alive then; ***– war es zu spät,*** by that time it was too late; ***von – an*** or ***ab war er ganz anders,*** thenceforth *or* from that time *or* from then onwards he was quite different; 2. (*unemphatic dem. introductory part.*) and, (and) then, (and) so, and so then; ***ja, – wird man aber fragen,*** true, but then people will ask; ***ich wollte weggehen, – fing sie an zu weinen,*** I was about to leave, and so then she started to cry; 3. (*emph. rel.*) (*Poet.*) when, that;

zu einer Zeit, – alles sich regte, at a time when all were stirring; *in dem Augenblick, – . . .,* the moment that, at the moment when . . .; *das erste Mal, – . . .,* the first time (that). . ..
(c) (*consequence*) so, then, in that *or* which case, for which reason; ***wenn ich schon gehen muß, – gehe ich lieber gleich,*** if it's time for me to go, then I'll go right away; ***ich muß also gehen, – gehe ich sofort,*** and so I must go, in which case I'll go immediately.
2. *conj.* 1. (*causal*) since, because, (inasmuch) as; – ***sie eine Engländerin ist, muß sie die englische Sprache verstehen,*** as she is an Englishwoman, she must understand English; 2. (*concessive*) – . . . ***doch,*** although, since, when; 3. (*time*) (*Poet.*) – ***ich ein Kind war, – redete ich wie ein Kind,*** when I was a child I spoke as a child; ***nun da . . ., da . . . nun,*** now that. . . .

da–, *pref.* 1. (*to preps.*) *referring to things, but not to persons,* ***da–*** *may replace Acc. or Dat. sing. or pl. of pers. or dem. pron. object of the prep.* = it, that, them *or* those. *When the prep. begins with a vowel, the older form* ***dar–*** *is used. See below the combined forms,* **dabei, dafür, daran, darauf** *etc.*; 2. (*to advs. and preps.*) = there. *See below* **daher, dahin, damit**; 3. (*to verbs*) = here, there. *See below* **dastehen** *etc.*

dabei [da'baɪ], *adv.* 1. by *or* near (*etc.*) it *or* them, with . . . attached (to it *or* them); – ***bleiben,*** stick to one's point; ***es bleibt –,*** that's settled *or* final, that's that; 2. at the same time; ***er redete fortwährend und aß –,*** he talked on and on and kept *or* went on eating *or* and didn't stop eating; – ***darfst du dich anziehen,*** you can be getting yourself dressed at the same time; 3. in addition, moreover, withal, besides, yet (at the same time), into the bargain; ***er ist gescheit und – fleißig,*** he is clever and hardworking into the bargain, he is clever and moreover hardworking; – ***sagte er,*** yet at the same time he said, in this connexion he said; 4. in the act (***zu tun,*** of doing), (*coll.*) red-handed; – ***erwischen*** or ***ertappen,*** catch in the act; – ***sein*** (***zu tun***), be (in the act of) doing; ***nahe – sein*** (***zu tun***), be on the point *or* verge (of doing); ***gerade – sein*** (***zu tun***), be just (on the point of) doing; 5. (*coll.*) on one's person; ***ich habe kein Geld –,*** I haven't any money with *or* on me; 6. ***was ist schon –?*** what does it matter? what harm can it do? ***es ist nichts –,*** there's nothing to it.

Dach [dax], *n.* (**-es,** *pl.* **¨-er**) roof; (*fig.*) shelter, house; (*Av.*) ceiling; (*coll.*) ***eins aufs – bekommen*** or ***kriegen,*** get a dressing down *or* ticking off; get a clip over the ear; (*coll.*) ***ihm aufs – steigen,*** blow him up, come down upon him, haul him over the coals, give him a piece of one's mind; (*Prov.*) ***ein Sperling in der Hand ist besser als eine Taube auf dem –,*** a bird in the hand is worth two in the bush; ***bei ihm ist gleich Feuer im –,*** he is very hot-headed, he goes off the deep end, he flies off the handle; ***unter – und Fach,*** safely under cover, in safety; (*of a project*) well under way, with the necessary backing secured.

Dach|boden, *m.* loft, attic. **–decker,** *m.* roofer, slater, tiler, thatcher. **dachen,** *v.t.* roof. **Dach|-fahne,** *f.* weather-vane *or* -cock. **–fenster,** *n.* garret window, attic window, dormer window, skylight. **–first,** *m.* roof-ridge. **–gesellschaft,** *f.* holding company. **–gespärre,** *n.* rafters. **–haut,** *f.* roofing, roof covering. **–kammer,** *f.* garret, attic. **–luke,** *f.* skylight, (*Av. coll.*) turret. **–pappe,** *f.* roofing felt. **–reiter,** *m.* ridge turret. **–rinne,** *f.* gutter. **–röhre,** *f.* gutter-pipe, down-pipe.

Dachs [daks], *m.* (**-es,** *pl.* **-e**) badger; (*coll.*) ***frecher –,*** whipper-snapper, cheeky puppy. **Dachbau,** *m.* badger's sett *or* earth.

Dachschiefer ['daxʃi:fər], *m.* (roofing) slate.

Dachshund ['dakshunt], *m.* dachshund.

Dach|sparren, *m.* rafter. **–stroh,** *n.* thatch. **–stube,** *f. See* **–kammer. –stuhl,** *m.* woodwork *or* framework of a roof, roof timbers; rafters.

dachte ['daxtə], **dächte** ['dɛçtə], *see* **denken.**

Dachtel ['daxtəl], *f.* (**-,** *pl.* **-n**) (*coll.*) box on the ears.

Dachtraufe ['daxtraufə], *f.* eaves. **Dachung,** *f.* roofing. **Dach|werk,** *n.* roofing. **–ziegel,** *m.* tile.

Dackel ['dakəl], *m.* (*coll.*) *see* **Dachshund.**

dadurch [da'durç], *adv.* thereby, by this means, in that way, for this reason, thus; – ***daß er es tat,*** by doing so, because he did it.

dafern [da'fɛrn], *conj.* (*Poet.*) inasmuch as.

dafür [da'fy:r], *adv.* for it *or* them; for that reason, on behalf of it, (*coll.*) that's why; in favour of it; in return for it, instead (of it); in its place; (but) on the other hand; ***ich verlange 10 DM. –,*** I'm asking 10 marks for it; ***ich kann nichts –,*** I can't help it, it's not my fault; – ***sein*** (***daß man es tut***), be in favour (of doing it), (*coll.*) be all for it, be for (doing) it; – ***läßt sich sagen daß, – spricht daß,*** a point in (its) favour is; – ***läßt sich vieles sagen,*** there's a lot to be said for it; ***teurer, – aber auch besser,*** dearer, but correspondingly better; – ***daß er es tut,*** for doing it, for the fact that he does it; (*Austr.*) ***es steht nicht –,*** it's not worth it.

dafürhalten [da'fy:rhaltən], *irr.v.i.* (*sep.*) be of the opinion. **Dafürhalten,** *n.* opinion, estimation, judgement.

dagegen [da'ge:gən], **1.** *adv.* against it *or* them; (*fig.*) against it, opposed *or* in opposition to it; in contradiction to it, to the contrary; instead (of), in exchange (for); by comparison; ***haben Sie etwas –?*** have you any objection? **2.** *conj.* on the contrary, on the other hand, however, nevertheless. **dagegenhalten,** *irr.v.t.* hold *or* set against it *or* them; ***etwas*** (***nichts***) –, raise an (no) objection to it.

daheim [da'haɪm], *adv.* at home; in one's own (part of the) country. **Daheim,** *n.* (**-s,** *no pl.*) home.

daher [da'he:r], **1.** *adv.* from that place, from there, (*Poet.*) (from) thence. **2.** *adv., conj.* hence, thence, for this *or* that reason, therefore, accordingly, (*coll.*) that's why.

daher–, *sep.pref.* (*with verbs of motion*) along; (*with other activities*) on and on.

daherum [dahɛ'rum], *adv.* thereabouts, approximately.

dahin [da'hɪn], *adv.* there, to that place, (*Poet.*) thither; along, past, by; (*Poet.*) away; (*fig.*) as far, to that point, to that effect, to that end; ***bis –,*** as far as *or* up to there, that far; until *or* till that time *or* moment, until *or* till then; by that time, by then ; ***er äußerte sich –,*** he spoke to this effect; ***sein Bestreben geht – daß . . .,*** his efforts are bent *or* directed on . . .; ***diese Dinge gehören nicht –,*** these things have no bearing on the subject; ***meine Meinung geht –,*** my opinion is; (*Poet.*) ***mein Glück ist –,*** my good fortune is past *or* over; (*Poet.*) ***seine Seele ist –,*** his soul has departed.

dahin–, *sep.pref.* 1. (*to prep. to form adv. indicating aim of motion*) there, *e.g.* ***–ab,*** down there; ***–auf,*** up there; 2. (*to verbs indicating aim of motion, motion along, past or by, or* (*Poet.*) *motion away. See below*). **–aus,** *adv.* out there; ***bis –,*** completely, utterly, to the last degree. **–gegen,** *adv.* on the other hand, on the contrary.

dahin|gehen [dahɪn'ge:ən], *irr.v.i.* (*sep.*) (*aux.* s.) move along *or* on, go by, pass, (*Poet.*) die, pass away *or* on. **–gehend,** *adv.* to the effect (that), in the following terms; thus.

dahingestellt [da'hɪŋgəʃtɛlt], *adj.* ***es bleibt –,*** it is impossible to say, it remains to be seen; ***es – sein lassen,*** leave the question aside, form no opinion as to, leave it undecided (***ob,*** whether).

dahin|leben, *v.i.* (*sep.*) live (on) *or* exist from day to day. **–scheiden,** *irr.v.i.* (*sep.*) (*aux.* s.) depart this life, pass away. **–siechen,** *v.i.* (*sep.*) (*aux.* s.) waste away. **–stehen,** *irr.v.i.* (*sep.*) be uncertain *or* undecided, be a matter of doubt (***ob,*** whether).

dahinten [da'hɪntən], *adv.* back there.

dahinter [da'hɪntər], *adv.* behind it *or* them, beyond. **dahinter|her,** *adv.* – ***sein*** (***zu tun***), be very keen *or* (*coll.*) dead set on (doing). **–kommen,** *irr.v.i.* (*sep.*) (*aux.* s.) find out *or* get at the truth about. **–machen,** *v.r.* (*sep.*) (*coll.*) go all out. **–sein,** *irr.v.i.* (*sep.*) (*aux. s.*) (*Dat.*) urge (*s.o.*) on, pester, (*coll.*) chivvy. **–setzen, 1.** *v.t.* (*sep.*) put (*a p.*) on to it. **2.** *v.r.* put one's back into it, (*coll.*) pull up one's socks. **–stecken,** *v.i.* (*sep.*) be behind it, be at the back of it; ***es steckt etwas dahinter,*** there's more to it than meets the eye.

Dalles ['daləs], *m.* (*sl.*) ***den – haben, an – leiden, im – sein,*** be on the rocks *or* on one's beam-ends.

dalli! ['dali], *int.* (*sl.*) get cracking! get a move on! step on it!

Dam [da:m], *m.* (**-(e)s,** *pl.* **-e**) fallow-deer.

damalig ['da:ma:lɪç], *adj.* of that time, then; ***in der –en Zeit,*** at that time, in those days; ***der –e König,*** the then king, the king at that time. **damals,** *adv.* then, in those days, at that time; ***erst –,*** only *or* not till then; ***schon –,*** even then, even at that time, even in those days; ***seit –,*** since then *or* that time.

Damast [da'mast], *m.* (**-es,** *pl.* **-e**) damask. **damasten,** *adj.* damask.

Damaszener [damas'tse:nər], **1.** *indecl.adj.* Damascene. **2.** *m.* inhabitant of Damascus. **Damaszener|rose,** *f.* damask rose. **–klinge,** *f.* Damascus blade. **–pflaume,** *f.* damson. **damaszieren,** *v.t.* damask; damascene (*steel etc.*).

Dambock ['da:mbɔk], *m. See* **Dam.**

[1]**Dame** ['da:mə], *f.* 1. lady; partner (*at a dance*); (*coll.*) ***seine alte –,*** his old woman; 2. queen (*at cards, chess*); ***sich*** (*Dat.*) ***eine – machen, in die – gehen, die – ziehen,*** queen a pawn; ***zur – gehen,*** queen (*of pawn*).

[2]**Dame,** *f.* draughts, (*Am.*) checkers; king (*at draughts*). **Damebrett,** *n.* draught- *or* (*Am.*) checker-board.

Dämel ['dɛ:məl], **Däm(e)lack (-s,** *pl.* **-e** *or* **-s),** *m.* blockhead, fathead, ass. **Dämelei** [–'laɪ], *f.* (-, *pl.* **-en**) (tom)foolery.

Damen|abteil, *n.* ladies' compartment, '(for) ladies only'. **–binde,** *f.* sanitary towel. **–friede,** *m.* treaty of Cambray (1529). **damenhaft,** *adj.* ladylike; (*of small girl*) grown-up. **Damen|held,** *m.* lady-killer; ladies' man. **–hose,** *f.* slacks. **–pferd,** *n.* lady's horse, palfrey. **–sattel,** *m.* side-saddle. **–wahl,** *f.* ladies' choice (*at a dance*). **–wäsche,** *f.* lingerie. **–welt,** *f.* the ladies, the fair sex.

Dame|spiel, *n.* (the game of) draughts *or* (*Am.*) checkers; draught-board and pieces, (*Am.*) checker-board and checkers. **–stein,** *m.* draughtsman, piece.

Dam|geiß, *f.* fallow-doe. **–hirsch,** *m. See* **Dam.**

damit [da'mɪt], **1.** *adv.* with it *or* them; by it *or* that, thereby; thereupon, (and) with that; ***– daß er es tut,*** by doing it (he); ***es ist aus –,*** there's an end of *or* to it; ***heraus –!*** (*news*) out with it! (*money*) (*coll.*) fork out! ***es ist nichts –,*** that is no use, (*coll.*) that's no go; ***was soll ich –?*** what use is that to me? what good is that? ***– einverstanden sein,*** be agreeable *or* agree (***daß er tut,*** to his doing). **2.** *conj.* in order that, so that; ***– nicht,*** lest, in order that . . . not, for fear that.

Dam|kalb, –kitz, *n.* fawn (of fallow-deer).

Dämlack, *m. See* **Däm(e)lack.**

damledern ['da:mle:dərn], *adj.* buckskin.

dämlich ['dɛ:mlɪç], *adj.* foolish, silly, stupid, (*coll.*) barmy, daft.

Damm [dam], *m.* (**-es,** *pl.* **¨-e**) dam; dike, dyke; embankment, barrage; jetty, mole, pier, causeway; (*fig.*) barrier, check; (*Anat.*) perineum; (*coll.*) ***auf den – bringen,*** set *or* put (*s.o.*) on his feet; (*coll.*) ***auf dem – sein,*** be on one's toes, be alert; (*coll.*) ***nicht recht auf dem –,*** out of sorts, under the weather, not up to the mark. **Dammbruch,** *m.* breach in a dyke; (*Med.*) rupture of the perineum.

dämmen ['dɛmən], *v.t.* dam (up *or* off); embank (*river*), dike (*land*), (*fig.*) restrain, check, stop, curb.

Dämmer ['dɛmər], *m.* (*Poet.*) dusk, twilight, gloaming.

Dammerde ['damʔe:rdə], *f.* (vegetable-)mould, humus, surface soil.

dämmerhaft ['dɛmərhaft], *adj.* dim, dusky, rather dark; shadowy, vague, indefinite, uncertain. **dämm(e)rig,** *adj. See* **dämmerhaft**; ***noch –,*** not yet light; ***– werden,*** get dark. **Dämmerlicht,** *n.* twilight, half-light, dusk, (*Poet.*) gloaming. **dämmern,** *v.i.* 1. dawn, grow light; ***es dämmert,*** day is dawning *or* breaking; ***mir dämmert's,*** it dawns on me, I have a faint *or* hazy recollection, I have a vague idea (that); 2. get *or* grow dark; ***es*** or ***der Abend dämmert,*** dusk *or* twilight is falling. **dämmernd,** *adj.* (*of a light*) faint, feeble, glimmering.

Dämmer|schein, *m. See* **–licht**; faint *or* feeble *or* glimmering light (*of a candle etc.*). **–schlaf,** *m.* dozing, half-sleep; (*Med.*) twilight sleep. **Dämmerung,** *f.* twilight, half-light; dawn (*in morning*); (evening) dusk, (*Poet.*) gloaming (*in evening*). **Dämmerzustand,** *m.* dazed condition; (*Med.*) twilight state.

Dammriff ['damrɪf], *n.* (*Geog.*) barrier reef.

dämmrig, *adj. See* **dämm(e)rig.**

Dämmstoff ['dɛmʃtɔf], *n.* insulation material.

Dammweg ['damve:k], *m.* causeway.

Dämon ['dɛ:mɔn], *m.* (**-s,** *pl.* **-en** [–'mo:nən]) demon, spirit; evil genius, fiend. **Dämonenglaube,** *m.* demonism. **Dämonie** [–'ni:], *f.* demonic element *or* spirit. **dämonisch** [–'mo:nɪʃ], *adj.* demonic, diabolical, demoniac(al); possessed (of a devil). **Dämonische,** *n. See* **Dämonie.**

Dampf [dampf], *m.* (**-es,** *pl.* **¨-e**) steam; mist, haze, smoke; *pl.* fumes; ***– aufhaben,*** have steam up; ***– aufmachen,*** raise *or* get up steam; ***mit vollem –,*** at full steam; (*fig.*) with a will; (*coll.*) ***– geben,*** step on the gas; ***Hans –,*** busybody, jack-of-all-trades; (*coll.*) ***– haben*** or ***kriegen,*** get the wind up; ***den – haben,*** be broken-winded (*of a horse*).

Dampf|bad, *n.* sauna bath, Turkish bath. **–boot,** *n.* steamer, steamboat. **–druck,** *m.* steam pressure.

dampfen ['dampfən], *v.i.* 1. steam, smoke, give off smoke *or* steam *or* fumes; 2. (*aux.* s.) (*of a ship etc.*) steam (along *or* away).

dämpfen ['dɛmpfən], *v.t.* 1. damp, muffle, deaden (*sound*), mute (*violin etc.*), damp (down), bank (*a furnace*); damp (out), (*Rad., Elec.*) attenuate; soften (*colour*); shade, subdue (*light*); stabilize (*aircraft*); suppress, curb (*feelings etc.*); ***mit gedämpfter Stimme,*** with muffled *or* hushed *or* lowered voice, under one's breath, in an undertone; 2. (*Cul.*) stew, braise (*meat*), stew (*fruit*), steam (*potatoes, fish etc.*).

Dampfer ['dampfər], *m. See* **Dampfboot.**

Dämpfer ['dɛmpfər], *m.* damper; mute (*of violin*); (*fig.*) curb (*on enthusiasm etc.*).

dampfig ['dampfɪç], *adj.* steamy.

dämpfig ['dɛmpfɪç], *adj.* broken-winded (*horse*).

Dampf|kessel, *m.* (*Mech.*) boiler; (*Cul.*) steam-kettle, steamer. **–kocher, –kochtopf,** *m.* pressure-cooker. **–kompresse,** *f.* (*Med.*) fomentation. **–kraft,** *f.* steam-power. **–maschine,** *f.* steam-engine. **–nudel,** *f.* dumpling. **–roß,** *n.* iron horse. **–schiff,** *n.* steamboat, steamer. **–schiffahrt,** *f.* steam navigation. **–schiffahrtsgesellschaft,** *f.* steamship line. **–topf,** *m.* digester, pressure cooker, autoclave.

Dämpfung ['dɛmpfuŋ], *f.* damping, deadening (*of sound*), attenuation, damping (*of waves*); stabilization (*of aircraft*). **Dämpfungs|fläche,** *f.* (*Av.*) stabilizer. **–flosse,** *f.* (*Av.*) tailplane.

Dampf|walze, *f.* steam-roller. **–wärme,** *f.* heat of vaporization. **–wäscherei,** *f.* steam-laundry.

Dam|tier, *n. See* **–geiß. –wild,** *n.* fallow-deer.

danach [da'na:x], *adv.* behind *or* after it *or* that; after that, afterwards, thereupon, thereafter; according to *or* in accordance with it *or* that, accordingly, correspondingly; to *or* for *or* about this *or* that; ***–, daß***; ***–, ob***; ***–*** (*inf.*), whether (***–*** *untranslated*); ***es sieht ganz – aus,*** it looks very much like it; ***seine Kräfte sind nicht –,*** his strength is not equal to it; ***sehen Sie –!*** look to it! ***dies ist billig und ist auch –,*** the price is low and the quality correspondingly poor; ***er wird – handeln,*** he will act accordingly; ***bald –,*** soon after(wards).

Däne ['dɛ:nə], *m.* (**-n,** *pl.* **-n**) Dane.

daneben [da'ne:bən], *adv.* next to *or* beside it *or* that; close by, alongside; in addition, besides, as well; *das Haus* –, (the house) next door. **daneben|gehen,** *irr.v.i.* (*sep.*) go wide of *or* miss the mark; (*fig.*) go wrong, misfire. **–hauen,** *v.i.* (*sep.*) miss (*as a nail*), hit the wrong note (*on the piano*), (*coll.*) bungle, make a hash of.

Dänemark ['dɛ:nəmark], *n.* Denmark.

dang [daŋ], **dänge** ['dɛŋə], *see* **dingen.**

danieder [da'ni:dər], *adv.* (*Poet.*) down, on the ground. **daniederliegen,** *irr.v.i.* (*sep.*) 1. (*Poet.*) be lying down; ***krank*** –, be ill, be laid up, be confined to one's bed (*an* (*Dat.*), with); 2. (*Comm.*) be depressed, stagnate (*trade*).

Dänin ['dɛ:nɪn], *f.* Danish woman. **dänisch,** *adj.* Danish.

Dank [daŋk], *m.* (**-s,** *no pl.*) thanks, gratitude, reward; recompense; prize; *– **abstatten,*** see *– **sagen;*** ***mit – annehmen,*** accept with gratitude; ***das ist der – dafür,*** that is all the thanks one gets; ***– ernten,*** earn gratitude, be thanked; ***Gott sei –!*** thank God! ***– vom Haus Österreich,*** ingratitude (*i.e. a Hapsburg's gratitude*); ***ihm seinen – sagen,*** give, offer, express, extend, render *or* return one's thanks to him, thank him (***für,*** for); ***schönen –!*** many thanks! ***ihm – schulden,*** be indebted to him, owe him gratitude *or* thanks; ***schlechten – mit etwas verdienen,*** be paid with ingratitude for a th.; ***Sie würden mich zu – verpflichten, wenn Sie*** . . ., you would much oblige me by . . .; ***vielen –!*** see ***schönen –! ihm für eine S. – wissen,*** be thankful (grateful, obliged) to him for a th.

dank, *prep.* (*with Gen. or Dat.*) thanks to, owing to.

dankbar ['daŋkba:r], *adj.* 1. grateful, thankful, obliged (*Dat.*, to); 2. profitable, rewarding, worthwhile; 3. appreciative (*audience*); 4. hard-wearing (*material*). **Dankbarkeit,** *f.* gratitude; thankfulness.

danken ['daŋkən], **1.** *v.i.* 1. (*Dat.*) thank, return *or* give thanks to (***für,*** for); ***er läßt –,*** he sends his thanks; (*Comm.*) ***–d erhalten,*** received with thanks; paid, settled; ***danke!*** thanks! thank you! no thank you! 2. refuse (*with thanks*), decline (*an offer*); ***danke sagen,*** refuse with thanks. **2.** *v.t.* owe (*s.th.*) (*Dat.*, to); ***dir danke ich mein Leben,*** to you I owe my life. **dankenswert,** *adj.* deserving of thanks; rewarding, profitable, worthwhile.

Dankes|bezeigung, *f.* (expression of) thanks. **–brief,** *m.* letter of thanks, (*coll.*) thank-you letter.

Dank|gottesdienst, *m.* thanksgiving service. **–opfer,** *n.* thank-offering. **–sagung,** *f.* thanksgiving.

dann [dan], *adv.* then, at that time; then, after that, next, thereupon; then, furthermore, besides; *– **und wann,*** (every) now and then, from time to time; ***erst wägen, – wagen,*** look before you leap; *– **erst*** or ***erst*** –, only then, not till then; ***selbst –, wenn er käme,*** even in case *or* even if he should come. **dannen,** *adv.* (*Poet.*) ***von*** –, (from) hence *or* thence.

dar [da:r], *pref.* 1. (*to prep. with initial vowel*) *see* **da–**; 2. (*to other prep., e.g.* **darnach, darzu**) *see below*; 3. (*to verbs*) = *display or presentation. See examples below.*

daran [da'ran], *adv.* 1. on it *or* them, on to it *or* them; (on) to it *or* them; against it *or* them; at it *or* them; 2. (*as object of v.i. taking **an**, used either as connective with dependent clause or absolutely. Translation depends on use of prep. appropriate to v.i. in question. See under the verbs below, e.g.* **denken** (***an*** = of), **glauben** (***an*** = in), **leiden** (***an*** = from), **zweifeln** (***an*** = about); ***was liegt –?*** what does it matter? ***es liegt viel –,*** a great deal depends on it; ***denk –!*** don't forget! ***ich denke nicht –,*** I wouldn't think of it; ***nahe –,*** close to it *or* them; ***nahe – sein,*** be on the point *or* verge (***zu tun,*** of doing); ***er war nahe –, sein Leben zu verlieren,*** he very nearly lost his life; ***es ist nichts –,*** there is nothing in it (*or coll.* to it); ***übel*** (***schlimm***) ***– sein,*** be badly off, be in a bad position; ***er tut gut –, das Haus zu verkaufen,*** he does well *or* he is wise to sell the house; ***er will nicht gern –,*** he does not like the business, he doesn't want to have anything to do with it; *see* **dran.**

daran|geben, 1. *irr.v.t.* (*sep.*) *see* **–setzen, 1. 2.** *irr.v.r. See* **–gehen. –gehen,** *irr.v.i.* (*aux.* s.), **–machen,** *v.r.* (*sep.*) set to work, set about. **–setzen, 1.** *v.t.* (*sep.*) ***alles*** –, do one's utmost *or* (*coll.*) one's level best; ***eine ganze Woche –,*** give up *or* devote a whole week to it. **2.** *v.r. See* **–gehen.**

darauf [da'rauf], *adv.* 1. (up)on it *or* them; 2. (*See general note under* **daran, 2.** *Translation of* **darauf** *similarly depends on meaning of* **auf** *appropriate to the v.i. in question, e.g.* **hinweisen** (***auf*** = to), **bestehen** (***auf*** = on) *etc.*); 3. after that, later, next; thereupon; ***– kommt es an,*** that's the main point; ***sein ganzes Geld geht –,*** he spends all his money on it, it takes all his money; ***bald*** *or* ***kurz*** or ***gleich –,*** directly, immediately *or* shortly afterwards, thereupon; ***er hält sehr –,*** he lays stress upon that; ***– will er eben hinaus,*** that's just what he's aiming at; ***wie kommen Sie –?*** what put that idea into your head? how did you hit on that? ***– losgehen*** or ***zugehen,*** go *or* make straight for; ***es steht der Kopf –,*** it is a capital offence; ***im Sommer –,*** the next summer; ***am Tage –,*** on the following day; ***eine Woche –,*** a week later. **daraufhin,** *adv.* on the strength of it, as a result, consequently.

daraus [da'raus], *adv.* out of *or* from it *or* them; ***– folgt,*** hence it follows; ***ich mache mir nichts –,*** I do not care for it much, I'm not particularly keen on it; it means nothing to me; ***was wird*** (***am Ende***) ***–?*** what will come of it (in the end)? ***– kann ich nicht klug werden,*** I cannot make it out, I can't make head or tail of it.

darben ['darbən], *v.i.* famish; be in want, live in want *or* poverty, want, go short *or* without.

darbieten ['da:rbi:tən], *irr.v.t.* (*sep.*) offer, present, hold out, (*Poet.*) tender. **Darbietung,** *f.* (*Theat.*) presentation, recital, performance.

darbringen ['da:rbrɪŋən], *irr.v.t.* (*sep.*) offer, make (*a sacrifice etc.*), give (*ovation*), pay (*homage*).

darein [da'raɪn], *adv.* in(to) it *or* them, *see* **drein;** ***sich – ergeben,*** resign o.s. (to it), become resigned (to it); ***sich – finden,*** get used to it, put up with it; ***sich – fügen,*** accommodate o.s. to it, fit in (with it). **darein|geben,** *irr.v.t.* (*sep.*) ***seinen Willen –,*** *see* **–willigen. –mengen, –mischen,** *v.r.* (*sep.*) interfere (in it). **–willigen,** *v.i.* (*sep.*) consent, agree (to it).

darf [darf], **darfst,** *see* **dürfen.**

Darg [dark], *m.* (**-es,** *pl.* **-e**) peat.

darin [da'rɪn], *adv.* in it *or* them, there; –, ***daß er es tut,*** in *or* by doing it (he), in that he does it, in doing it; *see* **drin. darinnen,** *see* **drinnen.**

darlegen ['da:rle:gən], *v.t.* (*sep.*) state, declare, set forth, explain, expound, unfold. **Darlegung,** *f.* statement, explanation, exposition; exposé, argument.

Darleh(e)n ['da:rle:ən], *n.* loan. **Darleh(e)nskasse,** *f.* loan-bank.

Darleihen ['da:rlaɪən], *n.* (*Swiss*) loan. **Darleiher,** *m.* loaner, lender.

Darm [darm], *m.* (**-(e)s,** *pl.* **¨-e**) gut, intestine, bowel; skin (*of a sausage*). **Darm|bein,** *n.* haunchbone; (*Anat.*) ilium. **–bewegung,** *f.* peristaltic movement. **–bruch,** *m.* enterocele. **–entleerung,** *f.* evacuation of the bowels. **–entzündung,** *f.* enteritis. **–fäule,** *f.* dysentery. **–fell,** *n.* peritoneum. **–gang,** *m.* intestinal tract. **–grimmen,** *n.* colic, (*coll.*) gripes. **–kanal,** *m. See* **–gang. –knochen,** *m. See* **–bein. –kot,** *m.* faeces. **–saite,** *f.* catgut. **–schnitt,** *m.* enterotomy. **–spritze,** *f.* clyster-pipe. **–spülung,** *f.* enema. **–verschließung,** *f. See* **–verchluß. –verschlingung,** *f.* volvulus. **–verschluß,** *m.* intestinal stoppage. **–verstopfung,** *f.* constipation. **–würmer,** *m.pl.* ascarides, tapeworms.

darnach [dar'na:x], *adv.* (*obs.*) *see* **danach.**

darneben [dar'ne:bən], *adv.* (*obs.*) *see* **daneben.**

darnieder [dar'ni:dər], *adv. See* **danieder.**

darob [da'rɔp], *adv.* on that account.

Darre ['darə], *f.* 1. kiln-drying; desiccation; liquation (*of metals*); *see* **Darrofen**; 2. (*Vet.*) phthisis; roup (*in birds*).

darreichen ['da:rraɪçən], *v.t.* (*sep.*) offer, proffer, hold out (*hand etc.*), give, hand (*a th.*), administer (*sacrament*).

darren ['darən], *v.t.* kiln-dry; desiccate; liquate (*metals*). **Darr|ofen,** *m.* (drying-)kiln; (*for hops*) oast; liquation hearth. **–sucht,** *f.* (*Vet.*) consumption.

darstellbar ['da:rʃtɛlba:r], *adj.* portrayable, representable, educible, capable of graphic representation.

darstellen ['da:rʃtɛlən], **1.** *v.t.* (*sep.*) 1. represent, depict, portray; present, describe; (*Theat.*) represent, interpret (*character, part*); (*Math.*) plot, graph (*a curve*), draw a diagram of; (*of a th.*) represent, constitute, be; 2. (*obs.*) bring forth, produce; (*Chem.*) prepare, disengage; (*coll.*) afford, manage (to provide). **2.** *v.r.* appear, show itself to be, be (apparent *or* obvious). **darstellend,** *adj.* representational, interpretative (*arts*), descriptive (*geometry*). **Darsteller,** *m.* interpreter, portrayer, (*Theat.*) actor. **Darstellerin,** *f.* actress. **darstellerisch,** *adj.* as regards the acting.

Darstellung ['da:rʃtɛluŋ], *f.* representation, depiction, portrayal, description, delineation; (*Theat.*) (re)presentation, interpretation (*of part*), performance (*of play*); (*Math.*) graphical illustration; (*Chem.*) preparation; statement, version, account; ***Christi – im Tempel,*** presentation of Christ; ***falsche –,*** misrepresentation. **Darstellungs|gabe,** *f.* gift of graphic representation *or* (*Theat.*) of dramatic presentation. **–weise,** *f.* (*Chem.*) method of preparation; manner *or* style of representation.

dartun ['da:rtun], *irr.v.t.* (*sep.*) *see* **darlegen.**

darüber [da'ry:bər], *adv.* over *or* across it *or* them, over *or* across there; over *or* above it *or* them; over and above; more, besides; in the meantime *or* process. *As clausal connective with verbs, see general note under* **daran,** *e.g.* ***sich freuen*** (*über* = about); ***– ist er gestorben,*** he died in the meantime *or* while engaged on it; ***– geht nichts,*** nothing surpasses that, there's nothing better *or* (*coll.*) nothing to beat it; ***es geht ihm nichts –,*** there's nothing he likes better; ***– hinaus,*** beyond that, moreover, in addition; ***– hinaus sein,*** be beyond *or* past it, be beyond *or* have passed that stage. **darübermachen,** *v.r.* (*sep.*) attack, fall upon, set to work on, (*coll.*) go for, pitch into.

darum [da'rum], **1.** *adv.* (a)round it *or* them; ***– herumkommen,*** get out of it. *As clausal connective with verbs, see general note under* **daran,** *e.g.* ***bitten*** (*um* = for), ***wissen*** (*um* = about); ***es sei –!*** so be it! for all I care! ***es ist mir nur – zu tun,*** all that I ask *or* my only object is to *or* I am only concerned to; ***es handelt sich –,*** it is a question *or* matter (of). **2.** *conj.* therefore, for this *or* that reason, that is (the reason) why. **darum|bringen,** *irr.v.i.* (*sep.*) deprive *or* rob (*s.o.*) of it, do (*s.o.*) out of it. **–kommen,** *irr.v.i.* (*sep.*) (*aux.* s.) lose it.

darunter [da'runtər], *adv.* beneath *or* under(neath) it *or* them, underneath; under, less; in it, among(st) them; ***10 DM. eher – als darüber,*** 10 marks, less rather than more; ***– leiden,*** suffer from it *or* them; ***– verstehen, sich*** (*Dat.*) ***– vorstellen,*** understand by it *or* them.

das [das], **1.** *Nom. and Acc. n. sing. def. art.* the (*for usage see* **der**). **2.** *Nom. and Acc. n. sing. dem. pron. and adj.* this, that, it; ***– und –,*** such and such a thing. **3.** *Nom. and Acc. n. sing. rel. pron.* that, which (*often omitted*).

Dasein ['da:zaɪn], *n.* (**-s,** *no pl.*) presence; existence, life, being; ***im – der Königin,*** in the presence of the queen; ***der Kampf ums –,*** the struggle for existence. **Daseinsberechtigung,** *f.* right to exist; raison d'être. **daseins|hungrig,** *adj.* hungry for life. **–müde,** *adj.* weary *or* tired of life.

daselbst [da'zɛlpst], *adv.* (just) there, in that (very) place.

dasjenige, *see* **derjenige.**

daß [das], *conj.* that (*oft. omitted*); (***an***)***statt – er es tut,*** instead of doing it (he), instead of his doing it; ***außer***(***dem***) **–**, except that, apart from the fact that, besides (the fact) that; ***bis –,*** till *or* until (such time as); ***für den Fall – ich komme,*** in case I come, in the case of my coming; ***ohne – er es tut,*** without doing it (he), without his doing it; (*coll.*) ***– ich es nicht vergesse,*** lest *or* in case I should forget.

dasselbe, *see* **derselbe.**

dastehen ['da:ʃte:ən], *irr.v.i.* (*sep.*) stand (there), be; ***so steht er nun da!*** so he has landed himself in this awkward position! what a fool he has made of himself *or* he has been made to look! ***gut –,*** be in a good position; ***einmalig –,*** be unrivalled.

Daten, *pl. See* **Datum.**

Datenverarbeitung ['da:tənfɛrˀarbaɪtuŋ], *f.* data processing (*computers*).

datieren [da'ti:rən], **1.** *v.t.* date (*a letter*), date, assign a date to (*work of art*); ***falsch –,*** misdate. **2.** *v.i.* date (***von, aus,*** from).

Dativ ['da:ti:f], *m.* (**-s,** *pl.* **-e** [-ti:və]) dative (case).

dato ['da:to], *adv.* (*Comm.*) of the date; ***bis –,*** (up) to date, till now; ***de*** or ***a –,*** from today, after *or* from date. **Datowechsel,** *m.* time-bill.

Dattel ['datəl], *f.* (-, *pl.* **-n**) date (*fruit*). **Dattel|baum,** *m.*, **–palme,** *f.* date-palm.

Datum ['da:tum], *n.* (**-s,** *pl.* **Daten**) 1. date (*of time*); ***welches – haben wir heute?*** what is today's date? ***ohne –,*** undated; ***jungen*** or ***neuesten -s sein,*** be new *or* recent *or* up-to-date; 2. *pl.* facts, particulars, data. **Datumgrenze,** *f.* date line.

Daube ['daubə], *f.* (barrel-)stave.

Dauer ['dauər], *f.* (-, *no pl.*) length, duration, continuance; (*Phys.*) time, period (*of oscillations*); permanence, durability; ***von kurzer –,*** of short duration, short-lived, ephemeral; ***auf die –,*** for a length of time, permanently; with time, in (the course of) time, in the long run; ***auf – gemacht,*** made to last; ***keine – haben, nicht von – sein,*** not last (long), have no permanence.

Dauer|apfel, *m.* winter apple. **–auftrag,** *m.* (*Comm.*) standing order. **–ausscheider,** *m.* (*Med.*) chronic carrier. **–befehl,** *m.* (*Mil.*) standing order. **–betrieb,** *m.* continuous operation *or* working. **–brandofen,** *m.* slow combustion stove. **–brenner,** *m.* slow combustion burner; (*coll.*) long drawn-out kiss. **–farbe,** *f.* fast colour. **–festigkeit,** *f.* (*Mech.*) fatigue limit. **–flamme,** *f.* pilot light. **–flug,** *m.* long-distance flight. **–gast,** *m.* permanent resident (*in hotel*); guest who will not leave.

dauerhaft ['dauərhaft], *adj.* durable, hard-wearing; lasting, enduring; fast (*of colours*); sound, solid (*construction*). **Dauerhaftigkeit,** *f.* durability; stability, permanence; fastness (*of dye*).

Dauer|karte, *f.* season-ticket. **–lauf,** *m.* long-distance race. **–laut,** *m.* (*Phonet.*) continuant. **–lutscher,** *m.* (*coll.*) gob-stopper. **–marsch,** *m.* forced march. **–miete,** *f.* permanent *or* long-term tenancy. **–milch,** *f.* sterilized milk.

1**dauern** ['dauərn], **1.** *v.i.* last, continue, endure, (*coll.*) go on; take (*of time*); hold out; keep (*of meat, fruit*); ***lange –,*** take a long time; ***es dauerte über eine Stunde,*** it lasted *or* took more than an hour; ***es dauert nicht lange,*** it won't be long. **2.** *v.t.* (*obs.*) endure, bear, tolerate.

2**dauern,** *v.t.* make sorry; be sorry for, regret; ***der arme Kerl dauert mich,*** I am sorry for the poor fellow; ***es dauert mich, dies getan zu haben,*** I regret having done it; ***mich dauert mein Geld nicht,*** I do not begrudge the money.

dauernd ['dauərnd], *adj.* permanent, enduring, lasting, abiding; continual, constant, perpetual, unremitting; ***ewig –,*** everlasting, perennial.

Dauer|pflanze, *f.* perennial plant. **–strom,** *m.* (*Elec.*) closed-circuit *or* constant current. **–versuch,** *m.* (*Mech.*) endurance test, fatigue test. **–welle,** *f.* permanent wave (*in hair*). **–wurst,** *f.* smoked sausage.

Daumen ['daumən], *m.* 1. thumb; ***ihm den – aufs Auge halten*** or ***setzen*** or ***drücken,*** put the screw on him, put on the screw, keep a tight rein on him, keep him under one's thumb; ***ihm*** (or ***für ihn***) ***den – halten,*** keep one's fingers crossed for him; ***die – drehen,*** twiddle one's thumbs; ***über den – peilen*** or ***schätzen,*** make a rough estimate; 2. (*Mech.*) tappet, cam.

Daumen|abdruck, *m.* thumb-print. **–beuger,** *m.* (*Anat.*) flexor of thumb. **–drücker,** *m.* 1. handle, thumb-latch; 2. (*coll.*) protector, patron. **–kappe,** *f.* thumb-stall. **–rad,** *n.* sprocket-wheel. **–schraube,** *f.* 1. thumb-screw, wing-bolt; 2. *See* **Daumschrauben. –steuerung,** *f.* (*Mech.*) cam gear. **–welle,** *f.* camshaft.

Däumling ['dɔymlɪŋ], *m.* (**-s,** *pl.* **-e**) 1. thumb-stall, finger-stall, thumb (*of glove*); 2. (*Mech.*) tappet, cam; 3. Tom Thumb.

Daumschrauben ['daumʃraubən], *f.pl.* (*Hist.*) thumb-screws.

Daune ['daunə], *f.* down, feather; *pl.* down. **Daunen|bett,** *n.* feather-bed. **–(stepp)decke,** *f.* eiderdown (quilt).

Daus [daus], **1.** *n.* (**-es,** *pl.* **-e** *or* **⸗er**) deuce (*dice*); ace (*cards*). **2.** *m.* (**-es,** *pl.* **-e**) (*coll.*) ***ei der –! potz –!*** Good Lord! Great Scott! What the deuce *or* devil! ***geputzt wie ein –,*** dressed up to the nines; ***ich bin ein – (im Zeichnen),*** I'm a wizard (at sketching).

davon [da'fɔn], *adv.* from it *or* them; off it *or* them; of it *or* them; away, off; ***bleibt –!*** keep off! ***was habe ich –?*** what do I get from it *or* out of it? ***das kommt –,*** that's what you might expect; ***das kommt – daß,*** that's because; ***drei – weg*** or ***ab bleibt sechs,*** take away three leaves six.

davon–, *pref.* away, off. **–kommen,** *irr.v.i.* (*sep.*) (*aux.* s.) get off, escape; ***er kam mit dem bloßen Schrecken davon,*** he got off with no more than a fright; ***mit knapper Not –,*** have a narrow escape; ***billig*** or ***glimpflich –,*** get off lightly *or* easily. **–laufen,** *irr.v.i.* (*sep.*) (*aux.* s.) run away; (*coll.*) ***es ist zum Davonlaufen,*** it is unbearable *or* intolerable; ***auf und –,*** take to one's heels. **–machen,** *v.r.* (*sep.*) make off, run away, take to one's heels. **–tragen,** *irr.v.t.* (*sep.*) carry off, win (*a prize*), suffer (*damage*), receive (*injuries*).

davor [da'fo:r], *adv.* (*of place*) before *or* in front of it *or* them; (*of time*) before that, first, beforehand; of *or* from it *or* them; ***– fürchte ich mich nicht,*** I am not afraid of it; ***hüte dich –,*** beware of it; ***– behüte uns Gott!*** God forbid!

dawider [da'vi:dər], *adv. See* **dagegen**; to the contrary; ***dafür und –,*** for and against (it), the pros and cons. **dawiderreden,** *v.i.* (*sep.*) contradict, raise objections, make objections (to it *or* them).

dazu [da'tsu:], *adv.* for it *or* them, for that purpose, to that end; with it *or* them, besides, into the bargain; to it *or* them, as well, in addition. *As connective between verb and clause dependent on it, see general note under* **daran**; ***– ist er da,*** it is for that purpose that he is there, (*coll.*) that's what he's there for; ***noch –,*** besides, moreover; ***was sagen Sie –?*** what have you to say (about it)?

dazu|gehören, *v.i.* (*sep.*) belong to; ***dazu gehört Mut,*** that takes courage; ***dazu gehört Zeit,*** that requires time; ***alles was dazugehört,*** (*of a th.*) everything that goes with it; (*of a p., sl.*) what it takes; (*coll.*) ***es gehört mit dazu,*** it's all in a day's work. **–gehörig,** *adj.* proper, appropriate. **–kommen,** *irr.v.i.* (*sep.*) (*aux.* s.) 1. (*of a th.*) be added, supervene; ***es kommt noch dazu,*** added to which, (and) moreover; 2. (*of a p.*) appear (on the scene), join (the group).

dazumal ['da:tsu:ma:l], *adv.* then, at that time; ***von anno –,*** once upon a time, from time immemorial, (*obs.*) erstwhile, in days of yore.

dazu|schreiben, *irr.v.t.* (*sep.*) add (as) a postscript. **–setzen, 1.** *v.t.* (*sep.*) add, append. **2.** *v.r.* sit down with, join (*those already seated*). **–tun,** *irr.v.t.* (*sep.*) add (to); ***das Seine –,*** do one's share *or* (*coll.*) bit, pull one's weight.

dazwischen [da'tsvɪʃən], *adv.* between them, (in) between; among(st) them, in their midst; between times. **dazwischen|fahren,** *irr.v.i.* (*sep.*) (*aux.* s.) intervene (*in a quarrel etc.*). **–funken,** *v.i.* (*sep.*) (*coll.*) butt in. **–kommen,** *irr.v.i.* (*sep.*) (*aux.* s.) intervene, interfere, interpose; ***wenn nichts dazwischenkommt,*** if nothing interferes (with the plans), if nothing happens to stop (me *etc.*) *or* to prevent (it *etc.*). **Dazwischenkunft,** *f.* intervention, interference. **dazwischen|rufen, 1.** *irr. v.i.* (*sep.*) interrupt, shout interruptions. **2.** *irr.v.t.* interrupt with (*catcalls etc.*). **–treten,** *irr.v.i.* (*sep.*) (*aux.* s.) intervene. **–werfen,** *irr.v.t.* (*sep.*) interject, interpose.

Debatte [de'batə], *f.* debate, discussion. **debattieren** [–'ti:rən], *v.t., v.i.* debate, discuss. **Debattierklub,** *m.* debating society, discussion group.

Debent [də'bɛnt], *m.* (**-en,** *pl.* **-en**) debtor.

Debet ['de:bɛt], *n.* (**-s,** *pl.* **-s**) debit; ***im – stehen,*** be on the debit side. **Debet|posten,** *m.* debit (entry). **–saldo,** *m.* debit-balance. **–seite,** *f.* debit side.

Debit [de'bi:t], *m.* (**-s,** *no pl.*) (retail) sale. **debitieren** [–'ti:rən], *v.t.* 1. ***ihn mit einer Summe –, ihm eine Summe –,*** debit him with an amount, charge a sum to his account; 2. ***Waren –,*** dispose of *or* sell goods. **Debit|kommission,** *f.* commission of bankruptcy. **–masse,** *f.* bankrupt's estate. **Debitor** ['de:bitɔr], *m.* (**-s,** *pl.* **-en** [–'to:rən]) debtor. **Debitverfahren,** *n.* legal proceedings in bankruptcy.

Debüt [de'by:], *n.* (**-s,** *pl.* **-s**) first appearance, début. **debütieren** [–'ti:rən], *v.i.* make one's début.

Dechanat [deça'na:t], *n.* (**-s,** *pl.* **-e**) *see* **Dekanat**; deanery. **Dechant** [dɛ'çant], *m.* (**-en,** *pl.* **-en**) (*Eccl.*) dean.

Decher ['dɛçər], *m.* bale *or* set of ten (*esp. of hides*).

dechiffrieren [deʃɪ'fri:rən], *v.t.* decode, decipher.

Deck [dɛk], *n.* (**-(e)s,** *pl.* **-e**) (*Naut.*) deck; (*coll.*) ***nicht ganz auf –,*** off colour, out of sorts.

Deck|adresse, *f.* accommodation address. **–anstrich,** *m.* top *or* finishing coat (*of paint*). **–bett,** *n.* coverlet, feather-bed (*covering, not mattress*). **–blatt,** *n.* 1. outer leaf (*of cigar*), (*Bot.*) bract; 2. (*Mil.*) amendment.

Decke ['dɛkə], *f.* 1. cover, coverlet, blanket, quilt, bedspread, (travelling-)rug, covering; tablecloth; ***mit ihm unter einer – stecken,*** conspire with him, be in league *or* in collusion with him, be hand in glove with him; ***sich nach der – strecken,*** cut one's coat according to one's cloth; 2. cover, binding (*of book*); outer cover (*of tyre*), outer tyre; 3. (*Geol.*) layer, stratum; surface (*of road*); 4. ceiling (*of room*), roof (*of cave etc.*); 5. belly (*of violin*).

Deckel ['dɛkəl], *m.* lid, cover (*of a box etc.*); (*Typ.*) tympan; (*Bot.*) operculum; (*Archit.*) cornice; (*Artil.*) apron; (*coll.*) hat, (*sl.*) lid; (*sl.*) ***eins auf den – kriegen,*** get a crack on the nut. **Deckel|becher,** *m.*, **–kanne,** *f.* tankard with lid. **–korb,** *m.* basket with lid, hamper. **–krug,** *m.* tankard. **deckeln,** *v.t.* cover with a lid. **Deckeluhr,** *f.* hunter watch.

decken ['dɛkən], **1.** *v.t.* 1. cover; roof (*a building*); ***mit Stroh –,*** thatch (*a roof*); ***mit Ziegeln –,*** tile (*a roof*); ***den Tisch –,*** lay the table; 2. cover, guard, protect, shelter, screen; (*Spt.*) cover, mark (*an opponent*); 3. (*Comm.*) cover, meet (*needs*), defray (*expenses*), make good *or* up (*deficit*); stand surety *or* security for (*a debt*); 4. (*of male animal*) cover, serve (*female*); ***eine Stute – lassen,*** have a mare mated. **2.** *v.r.* 1. (*Poet.*) become covered; deck *or* adorn o.s. *or* itself; 2. take cover, guard *or* shield o.s., hide *or* conceal o.s.; (*fig.*) take precautions, cover o.s. (*against loss etc.*); 3. (*of two things*) coincide with one another, (*Geom.*) be congruent *or* coincident; (*fig.*) be identical, coincide; ***sich teilweise –,*** overlap (one another).

Decken|beleuchtung, *f.* ceiling lighting. **–bild, –gemälde,** *n.*, **–malerei,** *f.* ceiling fresco, painted ceiling. **–vorgelege,** *n.* overhead transmission gear.

Decker ['dɛkər], *m.* roofer, slater, thatcher. **–decker,** *suff.* -decker, *e.g.* (*Naut.*) ***Dreidecker,*** three-decker.

deckfähig ['dɛkfɛ:ɪç], *adj.* with good covering qualities, opaque (*of paint*). **Deck|farbe,** *f.* body colour, opaque *or* poster paint; top *or* final coat (*of paint*).

–**flügel,** *m.* (*Ent.*) wing-sheath, elytron. –**flügler,** *m.* (*Ent.*) coleopter; *pl.* coleoptera. –**geld,** *n.* stud-fee. –**glas,** *n.* cover-glass. –**haut,** *f.* (in)tegument. –**hengst,** *m.* stallion. **deck|kräftig,** *adj. See* –**fähig. Deck|ladung,** *f.* (*Naut.*) deck cargo. –**lage,** *f.* surface, top layer. –**mantel,** *m.* (*fig.*) pretext, pretence, mask, guise, cloak. –**name,** *m.* pseudonym, nom-de-plume, assumed name, alias, code-name. –**offizier,** *m.* (*Naut.*) warrant officer. –**papp,** *m.*, –**pappe,** *f.* (*Weav.*) resist. –**plane,** *f.* tarpaulin, awning. –**platte,** *f.* cover-plate; (*Build.*) coping stone. –**rohr,** –**stroh,** *n.* thatch. –**stütze,** *f.* stanchion.

Deckung [ˈdɛkuŋ], *f.* 1. cover, covering; protection, shelter, guard (*also boxing etc.*), (*Footb.*) defence; *in – gehen,* take cover; 2. (*Comm.*) cover, security, surety, guarantee; funds, resources, reserve; 3. (*Build.*) roofing; 4. (*by male animals*) service; 5. (*Math.*) congruence, coincidence. **Deckungs|-bestände,** *m.pl.* cover of notes in circulation. –**forderungen,** *f.pl.* assets. –**graben,** *m.* slit-trench. –**klausel,** *f.* cover clause. –**linie,** *f.* line of defence. –**truppen,** *f.pl.* covering party.

Deck|wort, *n.* (**-s,** *pl.* –**wörter**) codeword. –**ziegel,** *m.* roofing tile.

dedizieren [dedɪˈtsiːrən], *v.t.* dedicate, (*coll.*) make a present (of).

deduzieren [deduˈtsiːrən], *v.t.* deduce, infer.

Defekt [deˈfɛkt], *m.* (**-es,** *pl.* **-e**) defect, flaw, imperfection, fault; deficiency; (*Comm.*) deficit; (*Typ.*) broken letter. **defekt,** *adj.* defective, imperfect, faulty, damaged; *geistig –,* mentally deficient. **Defektenprotokoll,** *n.* statement of deficit. **defektiv** [–ˈtiːf], *adj. See* **defekt**; (*Gram.*) defective (*verb*). **Defektivkirche,** *f.* schismatic church.

defensiv [defɛnˈziːf], *adj.* defensive. **Defensive,** *f.* defence, defensive.

defilieren [defiˈliːrən], *v.i.* defile, march past.

definierbar [defiˈniːrbaːr], *adj.* definable. **definieren,** *v.t.* define. **definitiv** [–niˈtiːf], *adj.* definite, final, definitive; permanent (*post*).

Defizit [ˈdeːfɪtsiːt], *n.* (**-s,** *pl.* **-e**) deficit.

Defraudant [defrauˈdant], *m.* (**-en,** *pl.* **-en**) cheat, swindler, defrauder. **defraudieren,** *v.t.* cheat, defraud.

deftig [ˈdɛftɪç], *adj.* capable, able, efficient; solid, strong, sound; suitable, apt, thorough; nimble, agile.

Degen [ˈdeːgən], *m.* 1. sword; (*Fenc.*) épée; 2. (*Poet.*) warrior, soldier, fighter; thane.

Degeneration [degeneratsiˈoːn], *f.* 1. (*Med. etc.*) degeneration; 2. (*Rad.*) negative feedback. **degenerieren** [–ˈriːrən], *v.i.* (*aux.* s.) degenerate.

degen|fähig, *adj.* (*obs.*) with the right to appear at court. –**fest,** *adj.* proof against swordthrusts, invulnerable. **Degen|gehänge,** –**gehenk,** *n.* sword-belt, baldric. –**griff,** *m.* hilt. –**klinge,** *f.* sword-blade. –**knopf,** *m.* pommel. –**koppel,** *f. See* –**gehenk.** –**scheide,** *f.* scabbard. –**stich,** –**stoß,** *m.* sword-thrust.

degradieren [degraˈdiːrən], *v.t.* degrade (*from office*), reduce to the ranks, demote.

degraissieren [degrɛˈsiːrən], *v.t.* remove fat from.

dehnbar [ˈdeːnbaːr], *adj.* extensible, extensile, elastic, tensile, ductile, (*fig.*) vague, loose, adaptable (*of ideas*). **Dehnbarkeit,** *f.* extensibility, elasticity; ductility; looseness, vagueness.

dehnen [ˈdeːnən], **1.** *v.t.* stretch, extend, lengthen, elongate, expand; (*Phonet.*) lengthen, pronounce long (*a vowel*), (*Mus.*) sustain, hold (on) (*a note*); linger on, hold on to (*a word*), drawl (*one's words*); (*fig.*) extend, spin out (*a discussion etc.*); *gedehnte Silbe,* long syllable. **2.** *v.r.* (*of a p.*) stretch (o.s.), stretch one's limbs; (*of a th.*) stretch, be *or* become stretched; (*of materials*) expand, swell, dilate; (*of scenery*) extend, stretch *or* spread (out); (*in time*) last a long time.

Dehn|holz, *n.* stretcher (*for gloves*). –**kraft,** *f.* tensile strength. –**länge,** *f.* linear expansion. –**strich,** *m. See* **Dehnungszeichen.**

Dehnung [ˈdeːnuŋ], *f.* extension, lengthening, elongation, expansion, stretching, dilation; (*Metall.*) stretch, creep. **Dehnungs|grenze,** *f.* elastic limit. –**kraft,** *f. See* **Dehnkraft.** –**muskel,** *m.* extensor (muscle). –**zeichen,** *n.* sign indicating long vowel.

Deich [daɪç], *m.* (**-(e)s,** *pl.* **-e**) dike, dam; embankment. **Deichanker,** *m.* foundation of a dike. **deichen,** *v.t.* dike; embank, dam up. **Deich|graf,** –**hauptmann,** *m.* dike-reeve.

Deichsel [ˈdaɪksəl], *f.* (-, *pl.* **-n**) pole, shaft (*of wagon*), thill. **Deichsel|gabel,** *f.* shafts (*of a cart etc.*). –**nagel,** *m.* thill-pin. –**riemen,** *m.* trace.

deichseln [ˈdaɪksəln], *v.t.* (*coll.*) manage, wangle.

dein [daɪn], **1.** *m. or n. poss. adj.* (*f. & pl.* **-e**) your; (*B., Poet.*) thy, (*before vowel*) thine. **2.** (*poss. pron. declined as adj.*) yours, (*B., Poet.*) thine; *das Deine,* your possessions *or* property, your affair, your share; *die Deinen,* your family, your people.

deinerseits [ˈdaɪnərˈzaɪts], *adv.* on your side, for your part, as concerns you. **deinesgleichen,** *indecl. pron.* of your own kind, the likes of you, such as you; your equal(s). **deinethalben, deinetwegen, deinetwillen,** *adv.* on your account *or* behalf, for your sake, because of you.

deinige [ˈdaɪnɪgə], *poss. pron. der, das* or *die* – (*declined as adj.*) *see* **dein, 2.**

Deining [ˈdaɪnɪŋ], *f.* (-, *pl.* **-en**) breakers, high seas, swell.

deinsen [ˈdaɪnsən], *v.i.* (*Naut.*) make stern way; drop *or* fall astern.

Deismus [deˈɪsmus], *m.* deism. **deistisch,** *adj.* deistic.

Deka [ˈdɛka], *n.* (**-s,** *pl.* -) (*Austr.*) *abbr. of* **Dekagramm.**

Dekade [deˈkaːdə], *f.* 1. decade; 2. period of ten days. **dekadisch,** *adj.* decadal; decimal (*system*).

Dekaeder [dekaˈeːdər], *n.* (*Geom.*) decahedron.

Deka|gramm [deka–], *n.* 10 grammes. –**liter,** *n.* 10 litres.

Dekan [deˈkaːn], *m.* (**-s,** *pl.* **-e**) (*Eccl., Univ.*) dean. **Dekanat** [–ˈnaːt], *n.* (**-s,** *pl.* **-e**) (*Univ.*) dean's office, (*Eccl.*) deanery; deanship.

dekatieren [dekaˈtiːrən], *v.t.* hot-press, steam (*cloth*).

Deklamation [deklamatsiˈoːn], *f.* declamation, recitation. **Deklamator** [–ˈmaːtɔr], *m.* (**-s,** *pl.* **-en** [–ˈtoːrən]) reciter, declaimer; ranter. **deklamieren** [–ˈmiːrən], *v.t., v.i.* declaim, recite; harangue, hold forth.

deklarieren [deklaˈriːrən], *v.t.* declare; make a declaration; *deklarierter Wert,* registered value (*of a postal packet*).

Deklination [deklinatsiˈoːn], *f.* 1. (*Gram.*) declension; 2. (*Astr.*) declination, variation (*of compass*). **deklinierbar** [–ˈniːrbaːr], *adj.* (*Gram.*) declinable. **deklinieren, 1.** *v.t.* (*Gram.*) decline. **2.** *v.i.* diverge, deviate.

Dekokt [deˈkɔkt], *n.* (**-es,** *pl.* **-e**) decoction, infusion.

dekolletieren [dekɔlˈtiːrən], **1.** *v.i.* cut a dress low, (leave) bare the neck and shoulders. **2.** *v.r.* wear a low-necked dress; go open-necked; *sie dekolletiert sich zu sehr,* she wears her dresses too low. **dekolletiert,** *adj.* low(-necked), open-necked.

Dekor [deˈkoːr], *m.* (**-s,** *pl.* **-s**) decoration, ornamentation; (*Theat.*) décor, set(ting), scenery.

Dekorateur [dekoraˈtøːr], *m.* (**-s,** *pl.* **-e**) painter and decorator, interior decorator, (*Theat.*) scene-painter; window-dresser. **Dekoration** [–tsiˈoːn], *f.* adornment, embellishment, ornamentation, decoration; window-dressing; scene-painting; (window) display; furnishings; *pl.* decorations (*at a party*); (*Theat.*) décor, scenery, setting. **Dekorations|etikett,** *n.*, –**karte,** *f.* display label *or* card. –**maler,** *m.* (*Theat.*) scene-painter; house-painter. –**stoff,** *m.* furnishing fabric. **dekorativ** [–ˈtiːf], *adj.* decorative, ornamental. **dekorieren** [–ˈriːrən], *v.t.* decorate (*a room*), dress (*a window*).

Dekort [deˈkɔrt], *m.* (**-(e)s,** *pl.* **-e**) (*Comm.*) deduction, discount, allowance. **dekortieren** [–ˈtiːrən], *v.t.* make an allowance of, discount, deduct.

Dekret [de'kre:t], *n.* (**-(e)s,** *pl.* **-e**) decree, edict, ordinance. **Dekretale** [–'ta:lə], *n.* (*pl.* **-n, -lien**) decretal; Papal decree. **dekretieren** [–'ti:rən], *v.t.* decree, ordain by decree.

Dekupiersäge [deku'pi:rzɛ:gə], *f.* fret-saw machine.

delegieren [dele'gi:rən], *v.t.* delegate, depute, assign. **Delegierte(r),** *m. f.* delegate, deputy.

delikat [deli'ka:t], *adj.* 1. delicate, delicious, exquisite; 2. tactful; 3. critical, difficult, (*coll.*) ticklish. **Delikatesse** [–'tɛsə], *f.* 1. (*sing. only*) delicacy; tactfulness, tact; 2. (*with pl.*) delicacy, dainty. **Delikatessen(handlung),** *f.* delicatessen (shop).

Delikt [de'lɪkt], *n.* (**-s,** *pl.* **-e**) crime, (indictable) offence. **deliktsfähig,** *adj.* responsible before the law.

Delinquent [delɪŋ'kvɛnt], *m.* (**-en,** *pl.* **-en**) delinquent.

delirieren [deli'ri:rən], *v.i.* be delirious, rave.

Delkredere [dɛl'kre:dərə], *n.* (**-,** *pl.* **-n**) (*Comm.*) guarantee, security; (*as pref.*) contingent.

Delle ['dɛlə], *f.* dent, depression.

Delphin [dɛl'fi:n], *m.* (**-(e)s,** *pl.* **-e**) dolphin. **delphisch** ['dɛlfɪʃ], *adj.* Delphian, Delphic; obscure, ambiguous.

Delta ['dɛlta], *n.* (**-s,** *pl.* **-s**) delta. **deltaförmig,** *adj.* deltoid, triangular.

dem [de:m], **1.** *Dat. m. and n. sing. def. art.* (*of a p.*) (to) him, (*of a th.*) (to) it. **2.** *Dat. m. and n. sing. dem. pron.* (*of a p.*) (to) him, (*of a th.*) (to) that one. **3.** *Dat. m. and n. sing. dem. adj.* (to) this *or* that. **4.** *Dat. m. and n. sing. rel. pron.* (*of a p.*) (to) whom, (*of a th.*) (to) which.

Demagoge [dema'go:gə], *m.* (**-n,** *pl.* **-n**) demagogue. **Demagogentum,** *n.,* **Demagogie** [–'gi:], *f.* demagogy. **demagogisch,** *adj.* demagogic.

Demant ['de:mant], *m.* (*Poet.*) *see* **Diamant. demanten** [–'mantən], *adj. See* **diamanten.**

Demarche [de'marʃ], *f.* diplomatic step, démarche.

demarkieren [demar'ki:rən], *v.t.* demarcate. delimit; mark the boundaries of.

demaskieren [demas'ki:rən], *v.t., v.r.* unmask.

Dementi [de'mɛnti], *n.* (**-s,** *pl.* **-s**) (formal) denial, contradiction. **dementieren** [–'ti:rən], *v.t.* contradict, deny.

dementsprechend ['de:mʔɛntʃprɛçənt], **1.** *adj.* corresponding. **2.** *adv.* correspondingly, accordingly.

Demerit [deme'ri:t], *m.* (**-en,** *pl.* **-en**) delinquent priest.

demgegenüber ['de:mge:gənʔy:bər], *adv.* on the contrary, in opposition *or* as opposed to this; on the other hand.

demgemäß ['de:mgəmɛ:s], *see* **dementsprechend.**

Demission [demɪsi'o:n], *f.* resignation; dismissal. **demissionieren** [–'ni:rən], *v.i.* resign, hand *or* send in *or* tender one's resignation.

demnach ['de:mna:x], *adv., conj.* accordingly, consequently, according to that *or* this, according to which.

demnächst ['de:mnɛ:çst], *adv.* before long, in the near future, shortly, soon.

demobilisieren [demobili'zi:rən], *v.t., v.i.* demobilize. **Demobilmachung** [–'bi:lmaxuŋ], *f.* demobilization.

Demokrat [demo'kra:t], *m.* (**-en,** *pl.* **-en**) democrat. **Demokratie** [–'ti:], democracy. **demokratisch, 1.** *adj.* democratic. **2.** *adv.* democratically.

demolieren [demo'li:rən], *v.t.* demolish.

Demonstrant [demɔn'strant], *m.* (**-en,** *pl.* **-en**) demonstrator. **Demonstration** [–tsi'o:n], *f.* (practical) demonstration, (*Mil.*) show of force. **Demonstrationszug,** *m.* (*Pol.*) protest march. **demonstrativ** [–'ti:f], *adj.* demonstrative, ostentatious, emphatic, (*Gram.*) demonstrative. **demonstrieren, 1.** *v.t.* demonstrate, show, illustrate, prove. **2.** *v.i.* (*Pol.*) make *or* take part in a demonstration, demonstrate.

demontieren [demɔn'ti:rən], *v.t.* dismantle, take apart *or* to pieces, strip.

demoralisieren [demɔrali'zi:rən], *v.t.* demoralize.

demselben, *see* **derselbe.**

demungeachtet [de:m'ungəaxtət], *see* **dessenungeachtet.**

Demut ['de:mu:t], *f.* humility, meekness, lowliness.

demütig ['de:my:tɪç], *adj.* humble, submissive, meek. **demütigen, 1.** *v.t.* humble; humiliate, abase, bring low. **2.** *v.r.* submit; stoop, abase o.s., eat humble pie. **demütigend,** *adj.* humiliating, mortifying. **Demütigung,** *f.* humiliation, abasement, mortification.

demutsvoll ['de:mu:tsfɔl], *adj.* humble, meek.

demzufolge ['de:mtsufɔlgə], **1.** *adv.* accordingly, consequently. **2.** *rel.pron.* according to which.

den [de:n], **1.** *Acc. m. sing. def. art.* the. **2.** *Dat. pl. def. art.* (to) the. **3.** *Acc. m. sing. dem. pron.* (*of a p.*) him, (*of a th.*) that. **4.** *Acc. m. sing. dem. adj.* this, that. **5.** *Acc. m. sing. rel. pron.* (*of a p.*) whom, that, (*of a th.*) which, that.

denen ['de:nən], **1.** *Dat. pl. dem. pron.* (*of a p.*) (to) them *or* those, (*of th.*) (to) those. **2.** *Dat. pl. rel. pron.* (*of p.*) (to) whom, (*of th.*) (to) which.

dengeln ['dɛŋəln], *v.t.* whet (*a scythe*).

Denk|arbeit, *f.* mental effort. **–art,** *f.* way of thinking; turn of mind; mental attitude; ***er hat eine edle –,*** he is high-minded. **–aufgabe,** *f.* brain-twister.

denkbar ['dɛŋkba:r], **1.** *adj.* imaginable, conceivable, thinkable, possible. **2.** *adv.* ***die – größte Mühe,*** the greatest possible care, the utmost pains; ***das – schönste Verhältnis,*** the most harmonious relationship imaginable *or* conceivable.

denken ['dɛŋkən], **1.** *irr.v.t., irr.v.i.* 1. think; ***bei*** or ***für sich –,*** think to o.s.; ***selbständig –,*** think for o.s.; 2. think of, conceive of, have the idea of; ***denke eine beliebige Zahl,*** think of any number; ***das war groß gedacht,*** that was splendidly conceived, it was a splendid idea; 3. think, consider, bear in mind; ***ihm zu – geben,*** set him thinking, give him food for thought; 4. think, believe, suppose, be of the opinion; ***ich denke ja,*** I think so; ***ich denke nicht,*** I don't think so, I think not; ***das dachte ich doch,*** I thought so, I thought as much; 5. think, imagine; ***das läßt sich –,*** I should think so, that's quite understandable; 6. mean, intend; (*Prov.*) ***der Mensch denkt, Gott lenkt,*** man proposes, God disposes; ***gedacht, getan,*** no sooner said than done; ***zur gedachten Zeit,*** at the agreed time *or* the time agreed upon; (*with inf. clause*) ***ich denke, nächste Woche abzufahren,*** I intend to leave *or* I'm thinking of *or* I contemplate leaving next week; (*perf. tense+für*) ***ich habe es für ihn gedacht,*** it was meant for him; 7. ***sich*** (*Dat.*) ***–,*** think, imagine, believe, picture to o.s.; ***das habe ich mir gleich gedacht,*** I thought as much; ***das hätte ich mir gleich – können,*** I might have known (that); ***– Sie sich nur!*** just imagine! 8. recall, remember; ***solange ich – kann,*** as far back *or* as long as I can remember; (*Poet.*) (*with Gen.*) ***ich denke dein, wenn mir der Sonne Schimmer,*** I think of you when the sun shines.
2. *irr.v.i.* (*with preps.*) ***– an*** (*Acc.*) 1. think of *or* about, have in (one's) mind; ***nur an sich selbst –,*** think only of o.s.; 2. remember, not forget, think of, bear in mind; ***denke daran, das Wasser abzudrehen,*** don't forget to turn off the water; 3. (***zu tun***) consider, intend, think *or* dream of (doing); ***es ist nicht daran zu –,*** it's out of the question. ***– auf*** (*Acc.*), be concerned with, concern o.s. with *or* about; ***wir – nur darauf, dich glücklich zu machen,*** our only thought *or* concern is to make you happy. ***– über*** (*Acc.*), 1. ponder, think about (*a th.*), think (*s.th.*) over; ***– Sie bitte darüber!*** please think it over; 2. have an opinion on *or* about; ***was – Sie darüber?*** what do you think about it? what is your view on *or* opinion of it? ***– von,*** have an opinion of (*a p.*); ***von dir hätte ich das nie gedacht,*** I should never have thought *or* expected that of you; ***er denkt nur Schlechtes von mir,*** he only thinks the

worst of me, he has a very low opinion of me. **Denken,** *n.* thinking, thought; *pl.* (*Poet.*) thoughts. **Denker,** *m.* thinker. **denkerisch,** *adj.* intellectual.

denk|fähig, *adj.* capable of thought. **–faul,** *adj.* mentally lazy. **Denk|fehler,** *m.* faulty reasoning, flaw in (*his*) reasoning, error in (*his*) logic. **–form,** *f.* mode of thought. **–freiheit,** *f.* freedom of thought *or* opinion. **–kraft,** *f.* intellect, mental ability, brain power. **–lehre,** *f.* logic.

Denkmal [′dɛŋkma:l], *n.* (**-s,** *pl.* **¨-er**) monument, memorial; (historic) relic. **Denkmal|pflege,** *f.*, **–schutz,** *m.* preservation of ancient monuments; ***unter Denkmalschutz stellen,*** schedule as an ancient monument.

Denk|münze, *f.* commemorative medal. **–schrift,** *f.* written petition; report, statement, memorandum; in memoriam, memorial, inscription. **–spruch,** *m.* motto, maxim.

Denkungs|art, –weise, *f. See* **Denkart.**

Denk|vermögen, *n.* faculty of thought, reasoning power. **–weise,** *f. See* **–art. denkwürdig,** *adj.* memorable, noteworthy, notable. **Denk|würdigkeit,** *f.* memorable occurrence; a th. to be remembered; *pl.* memoirs. **–zettel,** *m.* note, memorandum, reminder; reprimand, reproof, (*coll.*) box on the ear.

denn [dɛn], **1.** *conj.* 1. for, because; ***er ißt nichts, – er ist krank,*** he eats nothing, for he is ill; 2. ***es sei –, daß,*** unless, except; 3. (*in comparison, usu. to avoid repetition of als*) than; ***er ist größer als Feldherr – als Mensch,*** he is greater as a general than as a man; ***mehr – je,*** more than ever. **2.** *part.* (*oft. untranslated*) (*usu. in inter.*) ***wo ist er –?*** where can he be? I wonder where he is? ***wieso –?*** how so? ***was –?*** what is it then? ***was ist – los?*** what's the matter?

dennoch [′dɛnɔx], *conj.* yet, (but) still, however, nevertheless, all the same, for all that.

denselben, *see* **derselbe.**

Denunziant [denuntsi′ant], *m.* (**-en,** *pl.* **-en**) informer. **denunzieren** [–′tsi:rən], *v.t.* denounce, inform against.

Dependance [depɑ̃′dɑ̃s], *f.* annex(e) (*of hotel etc.*).

Depesche [de′pɛʃə], *f.* telegram, (*coll.*) wire, (*obs.*) rider. **depeschieren** [–′ʃi:rən], *v.t., v.i.* telegraph, wire.

Deplacement [deplas(e)′mɑ̃], *n.* (**-s,** *pl.* **-s**) (*Naut.*) displacement. **deplacieren** [–′si:rən], *v.t.* displace (*water*); displace, shift, change the position of (*a th.*). **deplaciert,** *adj.* out of place (*of a p.*), out of place, misplaced (*as a remark*).

Deponent [depo′nɛnt], *m.* (**-en,** *pl.* **-en**) (*Comm.*) depositor, (*Law*) deponent. **deponieren,** *v.t.* 1. leave, deposit (***bei,*** with); 2. (*Law*) depose, give evidence. **Deponierung,** *f.* deposition.

Deportation [depɔrtatsi′o:n], *f.* deportation, (*Hist.*) transportation. **deportieren** [–′ti:rən], *v.t.* deport, transport.

Depositar [depozi′ta:r], **Depositär,** *m.* (**-s,** *pl.* **-e**) (*Law*) depository. **Depositen** [–′zi:tən], *n.pl.*, **Depositen|gelder,** *n.pl.* deposits. **–kasse,** *f.* branch office *or* sub-branch of a bank. **–konto,** *n.* deposit account. **–schein,** *m.* safe-custody *or* safe-deposit receipt.

depossedieren [depɔse′di:rən], *v.t.* dispossess; depose, dethrone (*a monarch*).

Depot [de′po:], *n.* (**-s,** *pl.* **-s**) storehouse, warehouse, repository, depository (*for goods*), depot (*for goods, vehicles and Mil.*), (ammunition) dump; safe custody *or* keeping, (*Am.*) safe deposit; ***in – geben,*** place (*securities*) on deposit; ***ins – geben,*** place (*furniture etc.*) in store. **Depot|quittung,** *f.*, **–schein,** *m.* safe deposit receipt.

Depp [dɛp], *m.* (**-s,** *pl.* **-e**) (*coll.*) blockhead, nincompoop, ass.

deprimieren [depri′mi:rən], *v.t.* depress, discourage.

Deputat [depu′ta:t], *n.* (**-s,** *pl.* **-e**) (extra) allowance, perquisites, free coal (*for miners*), free produce (*for farmworkers*).

Deputation [deputatsi′o:n], *f.* deputation, delegation; committee. **Deputierte(r),** *m., f.* deputy, delegate, representative, member of a deputation *or* delegation.

der [de:r], **1.** *nom. sing. m. of def. art.* the; (*with parts of one's body and one's clothes*) one's, my, his *etc.*; ***die Augen tun mir weh,*** my eyes ache; ***sie zogen die Schuhe aus,*** they took off their shoes; (*distributive*) ***£10 der Zentner,*** £10 a cwt; ***4 DM. das halbe Dutzend,*** 4 marks a half-dozen; (*with abstracts often not translated*) ***die Natur,*** nature; ***die englische Literatur,*** English literature; (*with proper names: indicating familiarity*) ***wo ist der Heinz?*** where is Heinz? (*suggesting a spurious familiarity*) ***der alte Fritz,*** Frederick the Great; ***die Bardot ist meine Lieblingsschauspielerin,*** Bardot is my favourite actress; (*with names of authors, meaning their works*) ***wer hat den ganzen Shakespeare gelesen?*** who has read the whole of Shakespeare? (*with names of dramatic works, rôles, streets, mountains, days, months*) ***wer spielt den Hamlet?*** who is playing Hamlet? ***auf dem Trafalgarplatz,*** in Trafalgar Square; ***der Everest,*** (Mount) Everest; ***auch der Sonntag bringt mir keine Ruhe,*** even Sunday doesn't bring me any rest; ***im Juni fahren wir aufs Land,*** in June we leave for the country; (*with verbal nouns*) ***das Schwimmen ist sehr gesund,*** swimming is very healthy. **2.** *Gen. f. sing. and Gen. pl. def. art.* of the. **3.** *Dat. f. sing. def. art.* to the. **4.** *Nom. m. sing. dem. pron.* (*of a p.*) he, the one; (*of a th.*) that, the one; ***– und –,*** such and such a man *or* one. **5.** *Dat. f. sing. dem. pron.* (*of a p.*) (to) her; (*of a th.*) (to) it. **6.** *Nom. m. sing. dem. adj.* this, that. **7.** *Gen. f. sing. dem. adj.* (of) this *or* that. **8.** *Dat. f. sing. dem. adj.* (to) this *or* that. **9.** *Gen. pl. dem. adj.* (of) these *or* those. **10.** *Nom. m. sing. rel. pron.* (*oft. omitted*) (*of a p.*) who, that; (*of a th.*) which, that. **11.** *Dat. f. sing. rel. pron.* (*of a p.*) (to) whom; (*of a th.*) (to) which.

derart [′de:rʔa:rt], *adv.* in such a way *or* manner, to such an extent, so (much). **derartig, 1.** *adj.* of this *or* that kind, such; ***nichts –es,*** nothing of the kind. **2.** *adv. See* **derart.**

derb [dɛrp], *adj.* (*of a p.*) rough, strong, sturdy, robust, (*coll.*) tough; (*of materials*) coarse, rough, strong, hard-wearing, tough; sound, stout (*boots etc.*); (*of manners*) rough, coarse, unrefined, uncouth, unpolished, crude, plain(-spoken), blunt, rude; ***–e Gesundheit,*** rude health; ***–er Humor,*** broad humour; ***–er Junge,*** tough youngster; ***–er Spaß*** or ***Witz,*** crude *or* coarse joke. **Derbgehalt,** *m.* solid *or* cubic content. **Derbheit,** *f.* (*of a p.*) roughness, sturdiness, robustness, toughness; (*of materials*) coarseness, roughness, strength, toughness, soundness, stoutness; (*of manners*) roughness, coarseness, uncouthness, crudity, bluntness, rudeness; *pl.* crudities, harsh words, home truths.

dereinst [de:r′aɪnst], *adv.* some *or* one day, at some future time, in days to come. **dereinstig,** *adj.* future.

deren [′de:rən], **1.** *Gen. f. sing. dem. pron.* (*of a p.*) of her, (*of a th.*) of that. **2.** *Gen. pl. dem. pron.* (*of p.*) of them *or* those, (*of th.*) of those. **3.** *Gen. f. sing. and Gen. pl. rel. pron.* (*of p.*) whose, (*of th.*) of which. **4.** *Gen. f. sing. and Gen. pl. of poss. adj.* ***ihr*** (*when this does not refer to the subject of the sentence*); ***sie traf ihre Freundin und – Mann,*** she met her friend and her (*i.e. the friend's*) husband; ***sie trafen ihre Freundinnen und – Männer,*** they met their friends and their (*i.e. the friends'*) husbands; ***kaufe keine Blumen, ich habe – genug,*** buy no flowers, I have enough of them; ***ich sah zwei Mädchen, – Gesichter mir bekannt waren,*** I saw two girls whose faces were familiar. **derenthalben, derentwegen, derentwillen,** *adv.* because of her *or* them, for her *or* their sake, on her *or* their account; (*of th.*) because of this, that, them *or* those; (*used as rel.*) for whose sake, on whose account, (*of th.*) for the sake *or* on account of which.

derer [′de:rər], **1.** *Gen. f. sing. dem. pron.* (*when followed by rel. pron.*) (*of a p.*) of her, (*of a th.*)

of that. **2.** *Gen. pl. dem. pron.* (*when followed by rel. pron.*) (*of p.*) of them *or* those, (*of th.*) of those; ***das Geschlecht – von Bismarck,*** the family of the Bismarcks; ***die Freunde –, die . . .,*** the friends of those who . . ..

dergestalt ['de:rgəʃtalt], *adv.* in this *or* that *or* in such a manner, thus; – . . . ***daß,*** so . . . that. **dergestaltig,** *adj.* (*Poet.*) of such a kind, such.

dergleichen ['de:rglaɪçən], **1.** *inv. dem. pron.* a thing *or* things like that, such a thing, such things; ***nichts –,*** no such thing, nothing of the kind; – ***habe ich nie gesehen,*** I never saw the like; – ***mehr,*** more (of) such (things); ***und – mehr,*** and so on and so forth. **2.** *inv. dem. adj.* of this *or* that kind, similar, such, like that *or* those, (*coll.*) suchlike. **3.** *inv. rel. pron.* such as, the like of which.

Derivat [deri'va:t], *n.* (**-(e)s,** *pl.* **-e**) (*Chem.*) derivative. **Derivation** [–tsi'o:n], *f.* derivation. **Derivations|rechnung,** *f.* differential calculus. **–winkel,** *m.* (*Naut.*) angle of drift. **Derivativ** [–'ti:f], *n.* (**-s,** *pl.* **-e**) (*Gram.*) derivative. **derivativ,** *adj.* derivative. **derivieren,** *v.t.* derive.

derjenige ['de:rje:nɪgə] (**diejenige, dasjenige, diejenigen**), **1.** *dem. adj.* that, *pl.* those. **2.** *dem. pron.* (*of p.*) he, she, it *etc.*; (*of th.*) that (one), the one; *pl.* (*p. and th.*) those, the ones.

derlei ['de:rlaɪ], *inv. adj.* of that kind, like that, such.

dermaßen ['de:rma:sən], *adv.* to such an extent *or* degree.

dero ['de:ro], *inv. poss. adj.* (*obs.*) your (*3rd pers. address to superior*).

derselbe [de:r'zɛlbə] (**dieselbe, dasselbe, dieselben**), **1.** *dem.adj. and pron.* the same; ***ein und –,*** one and the same, the very same; ***zu –n Zeit,*** at the same time; ***auf dasselbe herauskommen,*** come *or* amount to the same (thing). **2.** *dem. pron.* he, she, it *etc.*, the same, the aforesaid; ***er sprach von seinen Söhnen und rühmte die Talente –n,*** he spoke of his sons and praised their talents.

derweil [de:r'vaɪl], **derweilen, 1.** *conj.* while. **2.** *adv.* (in the) meantime, meanwhile.

Derwisch ['dɛrvɪʃ], *m.* (**-(e)s,** *pl.* **-e**) dervish.

derzeit ['de:rtsaɪt], *adv.* at present, at this time; then, at that time. **derzeitig,** *adj.* present; at that time.

Des [dɛs], *n.* (*Mus.*) D flat; – ***Dur,*** D flat major; – ***moll,*** D flat minor.

des, *Gen. m. and n. sing.* 1. *of def. art.* of the; 2. (*Poet.*) *of dem. pron.* (*See* **dessen**); (*of a p.*) of him, (*of a th.*) of it, of the one; (*Prov.*) ***wes Brot ich eß', – Lied ich sing',*** he who pays the piper calls the tune.

desfalls ['dɛsfals], *adv.* (*obs.*) in that case; on that account.

desgleichen ['dɛsglaɪçən], **1.** *inv. dem. pron.* a thing like that, such a thing; the same, likewise. **2.** *inv. rel. pron.* (*of a p.*) the like of whom; (*of a th.*) the like of which, such as. **3.** *conj.* in the same way, similarly, likewise, also.

deshalb ['dɛshalp], **1.** *adv.* on this account, for this reason (*usu. omitted in English*); ***ich habe es – gesagt, weil*** . . . (***damit*** . . .), I said it (just) because . . . (so that . . .). **2.** *conj.* therefore, on this *or* that account, for this *or* that reason, because of this *or* that, that is (the reason) why; – . . . ***doch,*** nevertheless, but . . ., all the same, just the same.

designieren [dezɪg'ni:rən], *v.t.* designate.

Desinfektion [dɛzɪnfɛktsi'o:n], *f.* disinfection. **Desinfektionsmittel,** *n.* disinfectant, antiseptic. **desinfizieren** [–fi'tsi:rən], *v.t.* disinfect.

despektierlich [despɛk'ti:rlɪç], *adj.* disrespectful, irreverent.

Despot [dɛs'po:t], *m.* (**-en,** *pl.* **-en**) despot, tyrant. **Despotie** [–'ti:], *f.* despotism, despotic rule, tyranny. **despotisch,** *adj.* despotic, tyrannical. **Despotismus** [–'tɪsmus], *m. See* **Despotie.**

deß [dɛs], (*obs.*) *see* **dessen.**

dessen ['dɛsən], **1.** *Gen. m. and n. sing. dem. pron.* (*of a p.*) of him, (*of a th.*) of it. **2.** *Gen. m. and n. sing. rel. pron.* (*of a p.*) whose, (*of a th.*) of which. **3.** *Gen. m. and n. sing. of poss. adj.* ***sein,*** (*when this does not refer to subject of sentence*) ***er traf seinen Freund und – Sohn,*** he met his friend and his (the latter's) son. **dessenthalben, dessentwegen,** *adv.* (*Poet.*) *see* **deshalb**; (*used as rel.*) (*of a p.*) because of whom, on whose account; (*of a th.*) because of which, on account of which. **dessentwillen,** *adv.* (*Poet.*) for his (*etc.*) sake; (*used as rel.*) (*of a p.*) for whose sake; (*of a th.*) for the sake of which. **dessenungeachtet,** *conj.* nevertheless, for all that, notwithstanding that, in spite of that.

Destillat [dɛstɪ'la:t], *n.* (**-s,** *pl.* **-e**) distillate. **Destillateur** [–'tø:r], *m.* (**-s,** *pl.* **-e**) distiller. **Destillation** [–tsi'o:n], *f. See* **Destillierung. Destillier|apparat,** *m.*, **–blase,** *f.* retort, still. **destillieren,** *v.t.* distil. **Destillier|gefäß,** *n.* **–kolben,** *m. See* **–apparat. Destillierung,** *f.* distilling, distillation.

Destinatar [dɛstina'ta:r], **Destinatär,** *m.* (**-s,** *pl.* **-e**) (*coll.*) consignee.

desto ['dɛsto], *adv.* (*used before comp.*) all the (more), so much; ***je mehr man eine fremde Sprache hört, – besser versteht man sie,*** the more one hears a foreign language, the better one understands it; – ***besser,*** all the better, so much the better; – ***eher,*** all the sooner; all the more reason; – ***mehr,*** so much the more.

desungeachtet [dɛsˀungə'axtət], *conj. See* **dessenungeachtet.**

deswegen ['dɛsve:gən], *see* **deshalb.**

Deszendenz [dɛstsɛn'dɛnts], *f.* descent, lineage. **Deszendenztheorie,** *f.* theory of heredity *or* evolution, origin of species.

Detachiermittel [deta'ʃi:rmɪtəl], *n.* stain remover.

Detail [de'ta:j], *n.* (**-s,** *pl.* **-s**) 1. detail, particular; ***ins*** – or ***aufs*** – (***ein***)***gehen,*** particularize; ***bis ins kleinste –,*** (down) to the last detail; 2. (*Comm.*) retail. **Detail|geschäft,** *n.* retail business. **–handel,** *m.* retail trade. **–handlung,** *f. See* **–geschäft. detaillieren** [–'ji:rən], *v.t.* detail, specify, enumerate. **Detaillist** [–'jɪst], *m.* (**-en,** *pl.* **-en**) retailer.

Detektor [de'tɛktɔr], *m.* (**-s,** *pl.* **-en**) (*Rad.*) detector; (*obs.*) crystal set.

detonieren [deto'ni:rən], *v.i.* (*aux.* s.) detonate.

deucht [dɔyçt], **deuchte,** (*obs., Poet.*) *see* **dünken.**

Deut [dɔyt], *m.* (**-(e)s,** *pl.* **-e**) jot, whit, grain, atom, (*obs.*) doit; ***keinen – wert,*** not worth a farthing.

deutbar ['dɔytba:r], *adj.* explainable, explicable.

Deutelei [dɔytə'laɪ], *f.* (-, *pl.* **-en**) pedantic interpretation, hair-splitting, splitting hairs, quibbling. **deuteln** ['dɔytəln], *v.i.* interpret pedantically, split hairs, quibble, cavil (***an*** (*Dat.*), about); twist the meaning.

deuten ['dɔytən], **1.** *v.t.* explain, expound, interpret. **2.** *v.i.* point (***auf*** (*Acc.*), to *or* at), indicate, signify; bode, augur; – ***auf ihn,*** point to *or* refer to him; ***auf gutes Wetter –,*** be a sign of good weather. **Deuter,** *m.* 1. explainer, interpreter; 2. forefinger, index-finger. **–deutig,** *adj.suff.* with . . . meaning(s).

deutlich ['dɔytlɪç], *adj.* distinct, clear, plain, evident; intelligible, articulate. **Deutlichkeit,** *f.* distinctness, clearness.

deutsch [dɔytʃ], **1.** *adj.* German; ***der Deutsche Krieg,*** the Prusso-Austrian War (1866); ***das Heilige Römische Reich Deutscher Nation,*** the Holy Roman Empire; ***der Deutsche Orden,*** the Teutonic Order; ***Deutscher Ritter,*** Teutonic Knight. **2.** *adv.* (in) German; – ***schreiben,*** write (in) German; ***auf gut –,*** in good German, (*coll.*) in plain language, bluntly. **Deutsch,** *n.* German (*language*); – ***können,*** know German; ***kein Wort –,*** not a word of German. **Deutsche(r),** *m., f.* German; ***die Deutschen,*** the Germans.

deutsch|feindlich, *adj.* anti-German. **–freundlich,** *adj.* pro-German. **Deutsch|herr,** *m.* Teutonic Knight. **–kunde,** *f.* German history and affairs. **–land,** *n.* Germany. **–landlied,** *n.* German national anthem ("Deutschland, Deutschland über alles"). **–lehrer,** *m.* German master *or* teacher. **–meister,** *m.* Master of the Teutonic Order. **–ordensritter,** *m. See* **–herr. –ritterorden,** *m.* Teutonic Order. **–schweizer,** *m.* German Swiss. **deutschsprachlich,** *adj.* German-speaking (*peoples*), German-language (*newspaper etc.*). **Deutschstunde,** *f.* German lesson. **Deutschtum,** *n.* (**-s,** *no pl.*) German culture *or* customs, German language and way of life. **Deutschtümelei,** *f.* (-, *no pl.*) Germanomania, Teutomania. **Deutschunterricht,** *m.* German lessons, (teaching of) German.

Deutung ['dɔytuŋ], *f.* interpretation, explanation; (*obs.*) *see* **Bedeutung**; ***falsche* –,** misinterpretation, misconstruction.

Devise [de'vi:zə], *f.* 1. device, motto; 2. *pl.* foreign currency *or* exchange. **Devisen|bilanz,** *f.* balance of payments. **–kurs,** *m.* rate of exchange, exchange rate. **–schiebung,** *f.* currency smuggling, evasion of currency regulations.

devot [de'vo:t], *adj.* 1. devout, pious; 2. submissive, servile, cringing, abject.

Dezember [de'tsɛmbər], *m.* December.

Dezennium [de'tsɛnium], *n.* (**-s,** *pl.* **-nien**) decade.

dezent [de'tsɛnt], *adj.* seemly, proper, modest, restrained, subdued. **Dezenz,** *f.* seemliness, modesty, restraint.

Dezernat [detsɛr'na:t], *n.* (administrative) department. **Dezernent,** *m.* (**-en,** *pl.* **-en**) departmental head *or* chief; (cultural *etc.*) adviser, official responsible (for cultural activities *etc.*).

dezimal [detsi'ma:l], *adj.* decimal. **Dezimalbruch,** *m.* decimal (fraction). **Dezimale,** *f.* decimal place. **Dezimal|klassifikation,** *f.* Dewey decimal system (*in libraries*). **–rechnung,** *f.* decimal arithmetic, (*coll.*) decimals. **–stelle,** *f.* decimal place.

dezimieren [detsi'mi:rən], *v.t.* decimate.

Dia ['di:a], *n.* (**-s,** *pl.* **-s**) (*coll.*) *see* **Diapositiv.**

Diabetiker [dia'be:tikər], *m.* diabetic (patient).

diabolisch [dia'bo:lɪʃ], *adj.* diabolic(al).

Diademrotschwanz [dia'de:mro:tʃvants], *m.* (*Orn.*) Moussier's redstart (*Diplootocus moussieri*).

Diagnose [dia'gno:zə], *f.* diagnosis; diagnostics. **diagnosieren** [–'zi:rən], *v.t. See* **diagnostizieren. Diagnostik,** *f.* diagnostics. **Diagnostiker,** *m.* diagnostician. **diagnostisch,** *adj.* diagnostic. **diagnostizieren** [–'tsi:rən], *v.t.* diagnose.

Diagonale [diago'na:lə], *f.* diagonal.

Diagonalkraft [diago'na:lkraft], *f.* resultant (force).

Diagramm [dia'gram], *n.* (**-s,** *pl.* **-e**) diagram; (schematic) lay-out; graph; chart. **Diagrammpapier,** *n.* graph-paper.

Diakon [dia'ko:n], *m.* (**-s** *or* **-en,** *pl.* **-e** *or* **-en**) deacon. **Diakonat** [–'na:t], *n.* (**-(e)s,** *pl.* **-e**) diaconate. **Diakonissin,** *f.* sister of a Protestant nursing order.

Dialekt [dia'lɛkt], *m.* (**-s,** *pl.* **-e**) dialect. **dialektfrei,** *adj.* free from dialectical peculiarities, pure, standard (*of speech*).

Dialektik [dia'lɛktɪk], *f.* dialectics. **Dialektiker,** *m.* dialectician. **dialektisch,** *adj.* (*Phonet.*) dialectal, (*Phil.*) dialectic.

Dialog [dia'lo:k], *m.* (**-s,** *pl.* **-e**) dialogue. **dialogisch,** *adj.* in dialogue form.

1**Diamant** [dia'mant], *m.* (**-en,** *pl.* **-en**) diamond.

2**Diamant,** *f.* (*Typ.*) diamond (type).

diamanten [dia'mantən], *adj.* (of) diamond, set with diamonds; (*fig.*) adamantine. **Diamant|glanz,** *m.* adamantine lustre. **–schleifer,** *m.* diamond cutter. **–schliff,** *m.* diamond cutting. **–schrift,** *f. See* 2**Diamant. –stahl,** *m.* hard steel, tool steel.

diametral [diame'tra:l], *adj.* diametric(al).

diaphan [dia'fa:n], *adj.* transparent, diaphanous.

Diapositiv [diapozi'ti:f], *n.* lantern slide, transparency.

Diät [di'e:t], *f.* (-, *pl.* **-en**) 1. diet, regimen; 2. *pl.* daily allowance, attendance money (*to deputies*). **diät,** *adv.* – ***leben,*** keep to a diet, be strict in one's diet. **Diätetik** [–'tɛ:tɪk], *f.* dietetics. **Diätetiker,** *m.* dietician. **diätetisch,** *adj.* dietary, (*Am.*) dietetic.

diatherm [dia'tɛrm], **diatherman** [–'ma:n], *adj.* diathermic, diathermal, permeable to heat.

diatonisch [dia'to:nɪʃ], *adj.* (*Mus.*) diatonic.

dich [dɪç], **1.** *pers. pron. Acc. of* **du. 2.** *Acc. refl. pron.* yourself.

dicht [dɪçt], **1.** *adj.* dense, compact, tight; thick (*woods, fog, snow etc.*), close-grained (*texture*), close-woven (*fabric*), close-set (*hedge*); waterproof, watertight, leak-proof, (*coll.*) sound; (*fig.*) concise (*as style*); (*coll.*) ***den Laden – machen,*** shut up shop, close down; pack up; (*Stat.*) ***–ester Wert,*** mode. **2.** *adv.* 1. densely, thickly, closely; – ***halten,*** be watertight; *see also* **dichthalten**; – ***schließen,*** close tightly; – ***verhängte Fenster,*** heavily curtained windows; 2. close, near (***an*** (*Dat.*), ***bei,*** to); – ***an* –,** – ***bei* –,** close together, cheek by jowl; – ***daneben,*** close *or* hard by; (*Naut.*) – ***am Winde halten*** or ***beim Winde laufen,*** sail close to the wind, hug the wind; – ***am Ziel,*** near the end *or* goal; – ***vorm Examen,*** about to take an examination. **dichtbesiedelt,** *adj.* thickly *or* densely populated. **Dichte,** *f.* 1. (*Chem. etc.*) density, specific gravity *or* weight; 2. (*fig.*) density, thickness, denseness; closeness (*of weave*). **Dichteisen,** *n.* (*Naut.*) caulking-iron. **Dichtemesser,** *m.* hydrometer, aerometer.

1**dichten** ['dɪçtən], *v.t.* make tight; stop up, pack, lute, seal, caulk (*a ship*).

2**dichten,** *v.t.* 1. write, compose (*a literary work*); 2. (*obs.*) meditate *or* reflect on, think of *or* about. **Dichten,** *n.* ***all sein – und Trachten,*** his whole mind, all his thoughts *or* efforts. **Dichter,** *m.* poet, author, writer. **dichterisch,** *adj.* poetic, literary; ***–e Freiheit,*** poetic licence. **Dichterling,** *m.* (**-s,** *pl.* **-e**) would-be poet, poetaster.

dicht|gedrängt, *adj., adv.* closely packed (*as a crowd*). **–halten,** *irr.v.i.* (*sep.*) (*coll.*) keep one's mouth shut, not breathe a word, not say anything, hold one's tongue, keep mum.

Dichtheit ['dɪçthaɪt], *f.* density, denseness, compactness; (water)tightness. **Dichtigkeit,** *f.* density, imperviousness, (*fig.*) conciseness, compactness. **Dichtigkeitsmesser,** *m. See* **Dichtemesser.**

Dichtkunst ['dɪçtkunst], *f.* poetry, creative writing.

1**Dichtung** ['dɪçtuŋ], *f.* caulking, packing, seal, joint, gasket.

2**Dichtung,** *f.* 1. poetry; (creative) literature, literary works; work of literature, poetic work, poem; 2. imagination, fiction. **Dichtungsart,** *f.* style (*of poetry*), poetic genre.

Dichtungs|material, *n.* packing *or* sealing material, luting, caulking. **–muffe,** *f.* sleeve-joint. **–ring,** *m.*, **–scheibe,** *f.* expanding washer, gasket.

Dichtwerg ['dɪçtvɛrk], *n.* luting, oakum.

Dichtwerk ['dɪçtvɛrk], *n.* poetic work, poem; literary work.

dick [dɪk], **1.** *adj.* thick; (*of a p.*) fat, stout, corpulent; (*of a th.*) big, bulky, large; (*of liquid*) thick, muddy, syrupy; ***–e Backe,*** swollen cheek; ***–e Backen,*** fat *or* chubby cheeks; (*coll.*) ***das –e Ende,*** the worst, the snag; (*fig.*) ***ein –es Fell haben,*** have a thick skin, be thick-skinned; ***–e Freunde,*** close friends; ***einen –en Kopf haben,*** have a thick head (*after drinking*), (*fig.*) be pig-headed; ***–e Luft,*** stale air, thick atmosphere, (*coll.*) fug; (*fig.*) trouble, tense atmosphere; ***–e Milch,*** sour *or* curdled milk; (*coll.*) ***–e Töne reden,*** talk big; (*Naut.*) ***–es Wetter,*** poor visibility. **2.** *adv.* thickly, (*coll.*) thick; (*coll.*) – ***auftragen,*** lay it on thick, lay it on with a trowel, pile it on; ***es – einkochen lassen,*** boil it till it thickens; ***es – haben,*** live on the fat of the land; (*coll.*) be fed up (to the teeth); (*coll.*) ***es – hinter den Ohren haben,*** know what's what; (*coll.*) ***sich –(e) tun,*** give o.s. airs, talk big.

dickbäuchig ['dɪkbɔyçɪç], *adj.* paunchy, big-bellied, pot-bellied. **Dick|darm,** *m.* colon, large intestine. **–darmentzündung,** *f.* (*Med.*) colitis. **Dicke,** *f.* thickness; diameter; bulkiness, size; (*of a p.*) stoutness, fatness, corpulence; denseness (*of fog* *etc.*), density, consistency, viscosity, body (*of liquid*). **Dickenmesser,** *m.* callipers; micrometer; feeler-gauge.

dicketun ['dɪkətu:n], *irr.v.r. See dick(e) tun, under* **dick.**

dick|fellig, *adj.* (*Zool.*) with a thick skin, (*fig.*) thick-skinned, phlegmatic. **-flüssig,** *adj.* viscid, viscous, (*coll.*) thick, syrupy, treacly. **Dick|-flüssigkeit,** *f.* viscosity, viscidity. **-haüter,** *m.* (*Zool.*) pachyderm, (*coll.*) thick-skinned *or* phlegmatic *or* insensitive p.

Dickicht ['dɪkɪçt], *n.* (**-(e)s,** *pl.* **-e**) thicket.

Dickkopf ['dɪkkɔpf], *m.* 1. (*Ichth.*) chub; 2. (*coll.*) pig-headed p. **dickköpfig,** *adj.* (*coll.*) pig-headed.

dickleibig ['dɪklaɪbɪç], *adj.* stout, corpulent, (*fig.*) bulky. **Dickleibigkeit,** *f.* stoutness, corpulence, (*fig.*) bulkiness.

Dick|milch, *f.* sour milk, curds. **-schädel,** *m. See* **-kopf,** 2. **-schnabellumme,** *f.* (*Orn.*) Brunnich's guillemot, (*Am.*) thick-billed murre (*Uria lomvia*).

Dickte ['dɪktə], *f.* 1. *See* **Dicke**; (*Typ.*) width (of letter); 2. (*Carp.*) veneer. **Dicktenschablone,** *f.* feeler-gauge.

Dicktuer ['dɪktu:ər], *m.* boaster, braggart. **Dick-tuerei,** *f.* bragging, boasting (*mit,* of). **dick-tuerisch,** *adj.* bragging, boasting, self-important.

Dick|wanst, *m.* paunch, pot-belly. **-zirkel,** *m.* outside callipers.

Didaktik [di'daktɪk], *f.* didactics; didacticism. **Didaktiker,** *m.* didactic person; teacher of didactics. **didaktisch,** *adj.* didactic, instructional.

die [di:], **1.** *Nom. f. sing. def. art.* (*of a p.*) she, (*of a th.*) it. **2.** *Acc. f. sing. def. art.* (*of a p.*) her, (*of a th.*) it. **3.** *Nom. pl. def. art.* they. **4.** *Acc. pl. def. art.* them. **5.** *Nom. f. sing. dem. pron.* (*of a p.*) she, (*of a th.*) that. **6.** *Acc. f. sing. dem. pron.* (*of a p.*) her, (*of a th.*) that. **7.** *Nom. pl. dem. pron.* (*of p.*) they, (*of th.*) those. **8.** *Acc. pl. dem. pron.* (*of p.*) them, (*of th.*) those. **9.** *Nom. and Acc. f. sing. dem. adj.* this, that. **10.** *Nom. and Acc. pl. dem. adj.* those. **11.** *Nom. f. sing. rel. pron.* (*of a p.*) who, that, (*of a th.*) which, that. **12.** *Acc. f. sing. rel. pron.* (*of a p.*) whom, that, (*of a th.*) which, that. **13.** *Nom. pl. rel. pron.* (*of p.*) who, that, (*of th.*) which, that. **14.** *Acc. pl. rel. pron.* (*of p.*) whom, that, (*of th.*) which, that.

Dieb [di:p], *m.* (**-(e)s,** *pl.* **-e**) thief, burglar; ***haltet den -!*** stop thief! **Dieberei** [-bə'raɪ], *f.* (petty) theft, thieving, pilfering, stealing. **Dieb(e)sehre,** *f.* honour among thieves. **Diebesfalle,** *f.* burglar alarm. **Dieb(e)s|finger,** *m.pl.* ***- haben,*** be light-fingered. **-gut,** *n.* stolen property, (*coll.*) loot, swag. **-schlüssel,** *m.* picklock, skeleton key. **diebessicher,** *adj.* burglar-proof. **Dieb(e)s-volk,** *n.* pack of thieves. **diebisch, 1.** *adj.* thieving, pilfering; (*coll.*) ***-e Freude,*** gloating *or* malicious pleasure. **2.** *adv.* ***sich - freuen,*** gloat.

Diebstahl ['di:pʃta:l], *m.* (**-(e)s,** *pl.* **⸚e**) theft, robbery, burglary; (*Law*) larceny; ***bewaffneter -,*** armed robbery; ***gering(fügig)er -,*** petty theft *or* larceny; ***räuberischer -,*** robbery with violence.

Diebel ['di:bəl], *m.* dowel (pin), peg.

diejenige, *see* **derjenige.**

Diele ['di:lə], *f.* 1. board, plank; floor; 2. (entrance) hall, vestibule; (ice-cream *etc.*) parlour.

Dielektrikum [die'lɛktrɪkum], *n.* (**-s,** *pl.* **-ken**) (*Elec.*) dielectric. **Dielektrizitätskonstante,** *f.* (*Elec.*) permittivity.

dielen ['di:lən], *v.t.* floor (*a room*), board *or* plank over. **Dielen|balken,** *m.* joist. **-brett,** *n.* floor-board. **-fußboden,** *m.* wooden floor(ing).

dienen ['di:nən], *v.i.* (*with Dat.*) 1. serve; be in service (***bei,*** with), be a servant (of); serve, do military service (***bei,*** in); (*Mil.*) ***von der Pike auf -,*** rise from the ranks; (*coll.*) (start at the bottom and) work one's way up; 2. (*of a p.*) serve, be of use *or* help *or* service to; ***damit kann ich (Ihnen) nicht -,*** sorry I can't help you; ***womit kann ich Ihnen -?*** can I help you? what can I do for you? ***damit ist mir nicht gedient,*** that is of no use to me; 3. (*of a th.*) serve, be useful to, stand (*s.o.*) in good stead; ***- zu,*** be useful *or* fit for, serve as; ***das dient zu nichts,*** that serves no purpose, that is no use; ***es soll mir zur Warnung -,*** it will serve as *or* be a warning to me; ***wozu dient es?*** what is it used for? what is the use of it? ***- als,*** serve as, be useful as, do duty as.

Diener ['di:nər], *m.* 1. (man-)servant, attendant, footman, lackey; ***gehorsamer -!*** your obedient servant; no, thank you! ***stummer -,*** dumb-waiter; serving table; cake-stand; (*Prov.*) ***wie der Herr, so der -,*** like master like man; 2. curtsy, bow; ***er machte mir einen -,*** he bowed to me. **Dienerin,** *f.* maidservant, maid, (*fig.*) handmaid. **dienern,** *v.i.* bow and scrape. **Dienerschaft,** *f.* servants, domestics, attendants. **Dienertracht,** *f.* livery.

dienlich ['di:nlɪç], *adj.* appropriate, convenient, useful, of use (*Dat.,* for); opportune, advisable. **Dienlichkeit,** *f.* convenience, usefulness, appropriateness.

Dienst ['di:nst], *m.* (**-es,** *pl.* **-e**) service (*an* (*Dat.*), to *or* of); post, employment, office, situation; duty; ***- am Kunden,*** service to (one's) customers, after-sale service; ***außer -,*** off duty; (*Mil.*) (*abbr.* ***a. D.***), retired; ***Major a. D.,*** retired major, ex-major; ***- annehmen, in - gehen,*** go into (domestic) service; ***gute -e,*** kind offices; ***er hatte -,*** he was on duty; ***aktiver -,*** service with the colours; ***ihm einen - tun*** or ***erweisen*** or ***leisten,*** render him a service, help *or* oblige him; (*of a th.*) ***-*** or ***-e tun*** or ***leisten,*** do (good) service, stand in good stead; ***bei ihm im - stehen,*** be in his service; ***es steht Ihnen zu -en,*** you are welcome to it, it is at your disposal; ***was steht Ihnen zu -en?*** what can I do for you? ***ein - ist des andern wert,*** one good turn deserves another.

Dienstag ['di:nsta:k], *m.* Tuesday. **dienstags,** *adv.* on Tuesday(s); every Tuesday.

Dienst|alter, *n.* seniority (in office), length of service. **-antritt,** *m.* accession to *or* assumption of office, commencement of duties. **-anweisung,** *f.* official instructions. **-anzug,** *m.* uniform, livery.

dienstbar ['di:nstba:r], *adj.* liable to serve; subservient, subject; ***er macht sich alle Welt -,*** he makes use of everybody; (*B.*) ***-e Geister,*** ministering spirits, (*hum.*) domestic servants. **Dienstbarkeit,** *f.* servitude, bondage, subjection; power, sway, clutches; (*Hist.*) bond service; (*Law*) easement.

dienstbeflissen ['di:nstbəflɪsən], *adj.* officious, zealous, (over-)eager, (over-)attentive. **Dienstbereich,** *m.* competence, competency (*of official*), sphere (*of duty*). **dienstbereit,** *adj.* (*of a p.*) helpful, obliging, assiduous; (*of a th.*) available, in readiness. **Dienst|bote,** *m.* domestic servant. **-eid,** *m.* oath of allegiance. **-eifer,** *m.* devotion to duty, zealousness. **diensteifrig,** *adj.* zealous (in service), eager to serve. **Dienst|einteilung,** *f.* work schedule; (*Mil.*) duty roster. **-enthebung,** *f.* suspension (from duty). **-entlassung,** *f.* dismissal, discharge (from office). **dienst|fertig,** *adj.* eager, zealous, obliging. **-frei,** *adj.* exempt from service; (*of a p.*) off duty; leisure (*time*). **Dienst|geheimnis,** *n.* official secret. **-gewalt,** *f.* (official) authority. **-grad,** *m.* (military) rank, (civil-service) grade. **-habende(r),** *m., f.* official on duty. **-herr,** *m.* master, lord; employer. **-kleidung,** *f.* uniform, livery. **-lehen,** *n.* (*Hist.*) soc(c)age. **-leistung,** *f.* service (rendered). **-leute,** *pl.* servants, (*Hist.*) retainers, vassals.

dienstlich ['di:nstlɪç], **1.** *adj.* 1. official, (*Mil.*) service; 2. (*obs.*) *see* **dienstbereit, dienlich. 2.** *adv.* officially, in an official capacity, on official business.

Dienst|mädchen, *n.* domestic servant, maid, servant girl. **-mann,** *m.* 1. (*pl.* **⸚er**) out-porter, town porter; 2. (*Hist.*) (*pl.* **-en** *or* **-leute**) vassal. **-personal,** *n.* servants; officials. **-pflicht,** *f.* (*Hist.*) statute labour; (*Mil.*) liability to *or* for service, compulsory military service. **dienst-pflichtig,** *adj.* liable for duty *or* service; ***im -en Alter,*** of military age. **Dienst|prämie,** *f.* (*Mil.*) gratuity. **-reise,** *f.* duty journey. **-sache,** *f.* official communication *or* business. **-stelle,** *f.* government office *or* department *or* headquarters, centre *or* depot; (*Mil.*) duty station. **–stunden,** *f.pl.* office hours. **dienst|tauglich,** *adj.* fit for (military) service. **–tuend,** *adj.* on duty. **–untauglich,** *adj.* unfit for (military) service. **Dienst|verhältnis,** *n.* contract of employment. **–verweigerung,** *f.* refusal to obey orders, recalcitrance. **–vorschrift,** *f.* official *or* (*Mil.*) service regulations, military manual. **–weg,** *m.* official channels. **dienstwidrig,** *adj.* contrary to official regulations. **Dienst|wohnung,** *f.* official residence. **–zweig,** *m.* branch of the civil service.

dies [di:s], *contraction of* **dieses** (*as n. Nom. or Acc., but not as m. and n. Gen.*). *See under* **dieser. diesbezüglich,** *adj., adv.* in respect of *or* with respect to this *or* that *or* these *or* those; relating to, respecting, regarding *or* concerning it *or* this *or* that *or* these *or* those; in this connection, relevant.

diese ['di:zə], *see under* **dieser. dieselbe,** *see* **derselbe.**

dieser [di:zər], *m.*, **diese,** *f.*, **dieses,** *n.* (*declined as adj.*) **1.** *dem. adj.* this, *pl.* these; (*Comm.*) ***am*** or ***den vierten dieses,*** on the fourth instant; ***einer dieser Tage,*** one of these days, in a day or so; (*Law*) ***zur Bewahrheitung dieses,*** in faith whereof. **2.** *dem. pron.* this (one), *pl.* these; he, she, it, *pl.* they; the latter; (*obs., Lit.*) ***nach diesem,*** hereafter, thereafter; ***vor diesem,*** ere now; ***mit diesem,*** thereupon, whereupon.

diesig ['di:zıç], *adj.* misty, hazy.

dies|jährig, *adj.* of this year, this year's. **–mal,** *adv.* this time, now. **–malig,** *adj.* this, present, in this instance. **–seitig,** *adj.* on this side, on our side; of this world. **–seits, 1.** *prep.* (*Gen.*) on this side of. **2.** *adv.* on this *or* our side; here below, in this life, on earth. **Diesseits,** *n.* the real *or* this world, this life.

Dietrich ['di:trıç], *m.* 1. Dietrich; 2. (**-s,** *pl.* **-e**) picklock, skeleton key.

dieweil ['di:vaıl], **1.** *adv.* meanwhile, in the meantime. **2.** *conj.* as long as, whilst, while.

Diffamation [dıfamatsi'o:n], *f.* defamation, denigration; calumny. **diffamatorisch** [–'to:rıʃ], *adj.* defamatory, libellous, slanderous. **diffamieren** [–'mi:rən], *v.t.* defame, bring into disrepute, speak ill of.

Differential [dıferɛntsi'a:l], *n.* (**-s,** *pl.* **-e**) (*Motor.*) differential (gear); (*Math.*) differential. **differential,** *adj.* differential. **Differential|getriebe,** *n.* differential gear. **–rechnung,** *f.* differential calculus. **differentiell,** *adj. See* **differential.**

Differenz [dıfe'rɛnts], *f.* (-, *pl.* **-en**) difference, discrepancy; (*usu. pl.*) disagreement, misunderstanding. **Differenz|geschäft,** *n.*, **–handel,** *m.* (*Comm.*) speculation in futures. **differenzieren** [–'tsi:rən], *v.t., v.i.* differentiate (*also Math.*), distinguish, make distinctions (between). **Differenziertheit,** *f.* distinctiveness.

differieren [dıfe'ri:rən], *v.i.* differ, be different, diverge.

diffizil [dıfi'tsi:l], *adj.* difficult, delicate, awkward, (*coll.*) ticklish; (*of a p.*) hard to please.

diffundieren [dıfun'di:rən], **1.** *v.i.* diffuse, mix. **2.** *v.t.* diffuse, scatter, spread (*rays etc.*).

diffus [dı'fu:s], *adj.* (*Opt.*) diffuse(d), (*Med.*) diffuse.

digen [di:'ge:n], *adj.* (*Biol.*) digenous.

Dignitar [dıgni'ta:r], *m.* (**-s,** *pl.* **-e**) dignitary. **Dignität,** *f.* dignity.

Dikotyle [diko'ty:lə], *f.* (*Bot.*) dicotyledon.

Diktat [dık'ta:t], *n.* (**-s,** *pl.* **-e**) 1. dictation; ***nach – schreiben,*** write from dictation; 2. dictate; ***Versailler –,*** (dictated) Treaty of Versailles. **diktatorisch** [–'to:rıʃ], *adj.* dictatorial. **Diktatur** [–'tu:r], *f.* (-, *pl.* **-en**) dictatorship. **diktieren,** *v.t.* dictate; ***ich lasse mich nicht –,*** I will not be dictated to. **Diktiermaschine,** *f.* dictaphone, dictagraph.

dilatorisch [dila'to:rıʃ], *adj.* dilatory.

Dilemma [di'lɛma], *n.* (**-s,** *pl.* **-s** *or* **-ta**) dilemma.

Dilettant [dilɛ'tant], *m.* (**-en,** *pl.* **-en**) dilettante, amateur. **dilettantisch,** *adj.* amateurish. **dilettieren,** *v.i.* dabble (***in*** (*Dat.*), in), toy (with).

Dill [dıl], *m.* (**-s,** *pl.* **-e**), (*dial.*) **Dille,** *f.* (*Bot.*) anet, dill (*Anethum graveolens*).

Dimission [dimısi'o:n], *f. See* **Demission. dimissionieren,** *v.i. See* **demissionieren.**

dimorph [di'mɔrf], *adj.* dimorphous, dimorphic.

Diner [di'ne], *n.* (**-s,** *pl.* **-s**) dinner-party, banquet.

[1]**Ding** [dıŋ], *n.* 1. (**-(e)s,** *pl.* **-e**) object, thing, matter; ***vor allen –en,*** in the first place, above all (things), chiefly, primarily; (*Prov.*) ***aller guten –e sind drei,*** all blessings come in threes; ***guter –e sein,*** be in good *or* high spirits, be of good cheer *or* heart; ***den –en ihren Lauf lassen,*** let things run their course; ***das geht mir nicht mit rechten –en zu,*** there is s.th. uncanny *or* deceptive; (*Phil.*) ***das – an sich,*** the noumenon, the thing in itself; 2. (**-es,** *pl.* **-er**) (*contemptuously or pityingly*) creature (*usu. refers to a girl*); ***ihr dummen –er,*** you silly creatures.

[2]**Ding,** *n.* (**-(e)s,** *pl.* **-e**) (*Hist.*) t(h)ing.

dingen ['dıŋən], **1.** *reg. & irr.v.t.* hire, engage. **2.** *irr. v.i.* (*obs.*) bargain, haggle.

dingfest ['dıŋfɛst], *adj.* ***ihn – machen,*** apprehend *or* arrest him. **dinglich,** *adj.* real; (*Law*) ***–e Klage,*** real action.

Dings [dıŋs], **1.** *n.* (*inv.*) (*coll.*) thingamy(bob), what's-its-name. **2.** *m., f.* (*inv.*) (*coll.*) what's-his- (*or* her-)name. **Dingsda, 1.** *n.* (*inv.*) you know where. **2.** *m., f.* (*inv.*) *see* **Dings,** *m., f.* **Dingskirchen,** *n.* (*coll.*) *see* **Dingsda, 1.**

dinieren [di'ni:rən], *v.i.* (*obs.*) dine, attend a dinner-party.

Dinkel ['dıŋkəl], *m.* spelt, German wheat.

Dionys [dio'ny:s], **Dionysios,** *m.* Dionysius. **dionysisch,** *adj.* Dionysian.

Diopter [di'ɔptər], *n.* sight (*of optical instrument*), view-finder (*of camera*).

Dioxyd [diɔ'ksy:t], *n.* (**-(e)s,** *pl.* **-e**) (*Chem.*) dioxide.

Diözese [diø'tse:zə], *f.* diocese.

Diphtherie [dıfte'ri:], **Diphtheritis,** *f.* diphtheria.

diphthongieren [dıftɔŋ'gi:rən], *v.t.* (*Phonet.*) diphthongize. **diphthongisch** [–'tɔŋıʃ], *adj.* diphthongal.

Diplom [di'plo:m], *n.* (**-s,** *pl.* **-e**) diploma, certificate, patent.

Diplomat [diplo'ma:t], *m.* (**-en,** *pl.* **-en**) diplomat; diplomatist, (*coll.*) diplomat. **Diplomatie** [–'ti:], *f.* diplomacy; diplomatic corps. **Diplomatik** [–'ma:tık], *f.* diplomatics. **Diplomatiker,** *m.* expert in diplomatics. **diplomatisch,** *adj.* diplomatic; ***– getreue Abschrift,*** exact copy.

Diplom|ingenieur, *m.* certified engineer. **–prüfung,** *f.* examination for a diploma.

dir [di:r], **1.** *Dat. sing. of pers. pron.* **du,** to you. **2.** *Dat. sing. refl. pron.* yourself.

direkt [di'rɛkt], **1.** *adj.* direct, immediate; ***in –er Beziehung zu,*** in close connection with, closely related to; ***–e Fahrkarte,*** through ticket; ***–e Verbindung,*** through train *or* connection. **2.** *adv.* direct(ly), straight; at first hand; (*coll.*) directly, straight away; (*coll.*) really.

Direktion [dirɛktsi'o:n], *f.* 1. way, direction; 2. direction, management, control, administration; 3. (board of) management, (board of) directors; 4. (manager's *or* director's) office, office of the board of management.

Direktive [dirɛk'ti:və], *f.* (general) instructions, directive.

Direktor [di'rɛktɔr], *m.* (**-s,** *pl.* **-en** [–'to:rən]) manager, (managing) director; principal, head, headmaster. **Direktorat** [–'ra:t], *n.* (**-(e)s,** *pl.* **-e**) 1. directorship, directorate, management; headship, headmastership; 2. office (of the director *etc.*). **Direktorenversammlung,** *f.* headmasters' conference. **Direktorialversammlung,** *f.* directors' *or* board meeting. **Direktorin,** *f.* headmistress. **Direktorium** [–'to:rium], *m.* (**-s,** *pl.* **-rien**) directorate, board (of directors *or* managers), executive *or* governing body.

Dirigent [diri'gɛnt], *m.* (**-en,** *pl.* **-en**) conductor (*of an orchestra*). **dirigieren,** *v.t.* direct, control, manage, (*coll.*) run (*a business*); (*Mus.*) conduct.

Dirk [dɪrk], *m.* (**-s,** *pl.* **-e**) (*Naut.*) topping-lift. **dirken,** *v.t.* (*Naut.*) peak, top (*the boom*).

Dirndl [dɪrndəl], *n.* (**-s,** *pl.* **-**) (*dial.*) young girl. **Dirndl(kleid),** *n.* Austrian *or* Bavarian costume, peasant dress (*for girls*).

Dirne ['dɪrnə], *f.* prostitute; (*Lit., obs.*) damsel, lass, wench.

Dis [dɪs], *n.* (*Mus.*) D sharp.

Disharmonie [dɪsharmo'ni:], *f.* discord, disharmony. **disharmonisch** [–'mo:nɪʃ], *adj.* discordant, dissonant.

Diskant [dɪs'kant], *m.* (**-s,** *pl.* **-e**) treble, soprano. **Diskantschlüssel,** *m.* C *or* treble clef.

Diskont [dɪs'kɔnt], *m.* (**-(e)s,** *pl.* **-e**) discount; bank-rate; rebate. **diskontieren** [–'ti:rən], *v.t.* discount.

diskontinuierlich [dɪskɔntinu'i:rlɪç], *adj.* discontinuous, intermittent. **Diskontinuität** [–i'tɛ:t], *f.* discontinuity.

Diskont|makler, *m.* bill-broker. **–satz,** *m.* discount-rate, bank-rate. **–wechsel,** discounted bill.

Diskordanz [dɪskɔr'dants], *f.* (-, *pl.* **-en**) discordance.

Diskrepanz [dɪskre'pants], *f.* (-, *pl.* **-en**) discrepancy.

diskret [dɪs'kre:t], *adj.* 1. discreet, tactful; ***–e Farbe,*** quiet *or* unobtrusive colour; ***in –en Verhältnissen sein,*** be in trouble (*of unmarried expectant mothers*); 2. (*Math.*) discrete. **Diskretion** [–tsi'o:n], *f.* ***sich auf – ergeben,*** surrender unconditionally *or* at discretion. **Diskretionstage,** ***m.pl.*** days of grace.

diskriminieren [dɪskrimi'ni:rən], **1.** *v.t.* discriminate against, treat unfairly. **2.** *v.i.* discriminate, differentiate (***zwischen,*** between). **Diskriminierung,** *f.* discrimination (*Gen.*, against).

Diskurs [dɪs'kurs], *m.* (**-es,** *pl.* **-e**) discourse. **diskursiv** [–'si:f], *adj.* discursive.

Diskussion [dɪskusi'o:n], *f.* discussion; ***die Frage steht*** or ***kommt zur –,*** the question is up for discussion.

Diskus|werfen ['dɪskus–], *n.*, **–wurf,** *m.* throwing the discus.

diskutabel [dɪsku'ta:bəl], **diskutierbar,** *adj.* debatable, worth talking about *or* considering. **diskutieren,** *v.t., v.i.* discuss, debate.

Dispens [dɪs'pɛns], *m.* (**-es,** *pl.* **-e**) *or f.* (-, *pl.* **-en**) dispensation, exemption. **dispensieren** [–'si:rən], *v.t.* exempt, dispense, excuse (***von,*** from).

Disponenden [dɪspo'nɛndən], *n.pl.* wares taken 'on sale or return'. **Disponent,** *m.* (**-en,** *pl.* **-en**) manager; authorized agent. **disponieren, 1.** *v.i.* make arrangements, arrange matters, plan; ***– über*** (*Acc.*), have at one's disposal; ***er kann über mich –,*** I am at his disposal; ***ich kann über meine Zeit –,*** my time is my own. **2.** *v.t.* dispose of, make arrangements for, arrange, plan. **disponiert,** *adj.* in (*good etc.*) form; ***nicht –,*** indisposed; ***– sein,*** feel disposed *or* inclined; (*Med.*) have a predisposition *or* tendency (***für,*** to); ***gut –,*** in a good humour *or* mood.

Disposition [dɪspozitsi'o:r.], *f.* 1. disposition, arrangement, lay-out; 2. disposal; ***zur – stehen,*** be at one's disposal; ***ihm etwas zur – stellen,*** place s.th. at his disposal; (*Mil.*) ***zur –,*** with the reserve; 3. (pre)disposition, tendency, frame *or* state of mind.

Disputation [dɪsputatsi'o:n], *f.* debate. **disputieren** [–'ti:rən], *v.i.* dispute; debate; quarrel, argue, wrangle.

Dissertation [dɪsɛrtatsi'o:n], *f.* dissertation, thesis.

Dissident [dɪsi'dɛnt], *m.* (**-en,** *pl.* **-en**) dissenter, dissentient.

dissolut [dɪso'lu:t], *adj.* dissolute (*behaviour*); disjointed, disconnected, unconnected, incoherent.

Dissonanz [dɪso'nants], *f.* (-, *pl.* **-en**) dissonance, discord.

Distanz [dɪs'tants], *f.* (-, *pl.* **-en**) distance; interval; detachment, aloofness; ***– halten,*** keep one's distance; remain aloof. **Distanzgeschäft,** *n.* (*Comm.*) business for future delivery, forward contract. **distanzieren** [–'tsi:rən], **1.** *v.t.* (*Spt.*) outdistance, outpace, outrun, outstrip. **2.** *v.r.* place o.s. at a distance; (*fig.*) dis(as)sociate o.s., hold aloof; (*fig.*) ***sich – von,*** view dispassionately *or* with detachment.

Distel ['dɪstəl], *f.* (-, *pl.* **-n**) thistle. **Distelfink,** *m.* *See* **Stieglitz.**

Distichon ['dɪstɪçɔn], *n.* (**-s,** *pl.* **-chen**) distich.

Disziplin [dɪstsi'pli:n], *f.* (-, *pl.* **-en**) 1. discipline; 2. branch of knowledge, system. **disziplinarisch** [–'na:rɪʃ], *adj.* disciplinary. **Disziplinarverfahren,** *n.* disciplinary measure. **disziplinieren** [–'ni:rən], *v.t.* discipline.

Diva ['di:va], *f.* (-, *pl.* **-s** *or* **Diven**) prima donna.

Divan, *m.* *See* **Diwan.**

divers [di'vɛrs], *adj.* (*Comm.*) sundry.

Dividend [divi'dɛnt], *m.* (**-en,** *pl.* **-en**) (*Math.*) dividend, numerator. **Dividende,** *f.* (*Comm.*) dividend, share. **dividieren,** *v.t.* (*Math.*) divide (***durch,*** by).

Divis [di'vi:s], *n.* (**-es,** *pl.* **-e**) (*Typ.*) hyphen.

Division [divizi'o:n], *f.* (*Math., Mil.*) division.

Divisor [di'vi:zɔr], *m.* (**-s,** *pl.* **-en** [–'zo:rən]) (*Math.*) divisor, denominator.

Diwan ['di:van], *m.* (**-s,** *pl.* **-s** *or* **-e**) 1. divan, sofa, couch, ottoman; 2. (Sultan's) council; 3. (*rare*) collection of Oriental poems.

[1]**Döbel** ['dø:bəl], *m.* peg, plug, pin, dowel.

[2]**Döbel,** *m.* (**-s,** *pl.* **-**) (*Ichth.*) chub (*Squalius cephalus*).

döbeln ['dø:bəln], *v.t.* peg, fasten with dowels; plug (*a wall*).

doch [dɔx], **1.** *conj.* but, though, yet, however, nevertheless; for all that, all the same. **2.** *adv.* (*repudiating a negative question*) yes; oh! yes; of course. **3.** *part.* **(a)** (*unaccented*) 1. (*expressing encouragement or urgency*) just, (*oft. untranslated, the verb being stressed*) ***hilf mir –!*** help me! ***hättest du das – gesagt!*** if you had just said so! ***seien Sie – ruhig,*** do be quiet! 2. (*expressing uncertainty*) surely, (*oft. untranslated, the verbal statement being repeated interrogatively*) ***du siehst es –?*** you can surely see it? you can see it, I suppose? you can see it, can't you? ***er ist – hier?*** he is here, isn't he? 3. (*optative*) ***wenn . . . –,*** if only. **(b)** (*accented*) (*contradiction*) ***leugne nicht, du siehst es –!*** do not deny it, you cannot help but see it *or* after all you must be able to see it; ***sie ist häßlich, aber er liebt sie –,*** she is ugly, yet he loves her all the same; ***ja –,*** yes indeed; but of course; certainly; ***nein –,*** certainly not, of course not; ***also –!*** what did I tell you? there you are! that's what I said!

Docht [dɔxt], *m.* (**-s,** *pl.* **-e**) wick.

Dock [dɔk], *n.* (**-s,** *pl.* **-s** *or* **-e**) dock, dockyard. **Dockarbeiter,** *m.* docker, dock labourer, (*Am.*) longshoreman.

Docke ['dɔkə], *f.* 1. skein, hank (*of wool etc.*), shock, stook (*of corn*); 2. (*dial.*) doll; 3. baluster; 4. spindle (*of a lathe*).

[1]**docken** ['dɔkən], *v.t.* roll together; wind into skeins; shock, stook (*sheaves*).

[2]**docken,** *v.t.* dock (*ships*).

Docken|spindel, *f.* mandrel. **–stock,** *m.* stock (*of lathe*).

Dockgebühren ['dɔkgəby:rən], *f.pl.* dockage, dock-dues.

dodekadisch [dode'ka:dɪʃ], *adj.* dodecahedral; ***–es System,*** duodecimal system. **Dodekaeder** [–'e:dər], *n.* (*Geom.*) dodecahedron.

Dodekanes [dodeka'ne:s], *m.* (*Geog.*) the Dodecanese.

Dogge ['dɔgə], *f.* a breed of large dog; ***englische –,*** mastiff; ***dänische –,*** Great Dane.

Dogger ['dɔgər], *m.* (*Geol.*) Brown Jura, dogger; Lower Oolite.

Dogma ['dɔgma], *n.* (**-s,** *pl.* **-men**) dogma, article of faith. **Dogmatik** [–'ma:tɪk], *f.* (*Eccl.*) dogmatics, (*coll.*) dogmatism. **Dogmatiker,** *m.* (*Eccl.*) dogmatician, (*coll.*) dogmatist. **dogmatisch,** *adj.* dogmatic. **dogmatisieren** [–'zi:rən], *v.i.* dogmatize. **Dogmatismus** [–'tɪsmus], *m.* dogmatism.

Dohle ['do:lə], *f.* (*Orn.*) jackdaw (*Coloeus monedula*).

Dohne ['do:nə], *f.* bird-snare, springe. **Dohnen|-stieg, –strich,** *m.* springe-line.

Doktor ['dɔktɔr], *m.* (**-s,** *pl.* **-en** [–to:rən]) (*Univ.*) doctor; (*coll.*) doctor, physician, medical practitioner *or* adviser; ***den – machen*** or (*coll.*) ***bauen,*** take the degree of doctor; ***er hat seinen – in Berlin gemacht,*** he took his doctorate at Berlin. **Doktorand** [–'rant], *m.* (**-en,** *pl.* **-en**) candidate for a doctor's degree. **Doktorarbeit,** *f.* doctoral dissertation. **Doktorat,** *n.* (**-s,** *pl.* **-e**), **Doktor|grad,** *m.* degree of doctor, doctorate. **–hut,** *m.* academic head-dress; ***sich*** (*Dat.*) ***den – holen*** or ***erwerben,*** obtain the doctor's degree. **–vater,** *m.* academic supervisor. **–würde,** *f. See* **Doktorat.**

Dokument [doku'mɛnt], *n.* (**-s,** *pl.* **-e**) document, paper, (*Law*) instrument. **Dokumentarfilm** [–'ta:rfɪlm], *m.* documentary (film). **dokumentarisch,** *adj.* documentary. **dokumentieren** [–'ti:rən], *v.t.* prove (by documents), testify.

Dolch [dɔlç], *m.* (**-es,** *pl.* **-e**) dagger, poniard, dirk. **Dolchstoß,** *m.* stab with a dagger; (*coll.*) stab in the back.

Dolde ['dɔldə], *f.* (*Bot.*) umbel. **dolden|blütig,** *adj. See* **–tragend. Dolden|blütler,** *m.pl.* (*Bot.*) umbelliferae. **–rebe,** *f.* Virginia creeper (*Ampelopsis quinquefolia*). **doldentragend,** *adj.* umbelliferous. **doldig,** *adj.* umbellate.

doll [dɔl], *adj.* (*dial.*) *see* **toll.**

Dollbord ['dɔlbɔrt], *n.* (*Naut.*) gunwale. **Dolle,** *f.* (*Naut.*) rowlock, thole-pin.

dolmetschen ['dɔlmɛtʃən], **1.** *v.t.* interpret, translate. **2.** *v.i.* interpret, act as interpreter. **Dolmetscher,** *m.* interpreter.

Dom [do:m], *m* (**-(e)s,** *pl.* **-e**) 1. cathedral; 2. (*Archit.*) dome, cupola; (*fig.*) vault, canopy.

Domäne [do'mɛ:nə], *f.* domain, demesne; (*fig.*) sphere, province, field. **Domänen|pächter,** *m.* crown-land lessee. **–wald,** *m.* state forest.

Dom|freiheit, *f.* cathedral close. **–herr,** *m.* prebendary, canon. **domherrlich,** *adj.* canonical.

Dominante [dɔmi'nantə], *f.* (*Mus.*) dominant. **Dominanz,** *f.* (-, *pl.* **-en**) dominance, preponderance. **dominieren,** *v.i.* (pre)dominate, be dominant.

Dominikaner [domini'ka:nər], *m.* (*Eccl.*) Dominican (friar), Black Friar. **dominikanisch,** *adj.* Dominican.

[1]**Domino** ['do:mino], *m.* (**-s,** *pl.* **-s**) domino (*cloak*).

[2]**Domino,** *n.* (**-s,** *pl.* **-s**) (game of) dominoes; ***– spielen,*** play at dominoes. **Dominosteine,** *m.pl.* dominoes.

Domizil [domi'tsi:l], *n.* (**-s,** *pl.* **-e**) domicile, residence; (*Comm.*) address for payment. **Domizilwechsel,** *m.* (*Comm.*) addressed *or* domiciled bill.

Dom|kapital, *n.* (cathedral) chapter; dean and chapter. **–pfaff,** *m. See* **Gimpel.**

Dompteur [dɔmp'tø:r], *m.* (**-s,** *pl.* **-e**), **Dompteuse,** *f.* animal trainer *or* tamer.

Dom|sänger, *m.* cathedral chorister. **–schule,** *f.* cathedral-school.

Donau ['do:nau], *f.* (*Geog.*) the (river) Danube. **Donau–,** *pref.* Danubian.

Donner ['dɔnər], *m.* thunder; Thor; thunderbolt; (*fig.*) thunder, roar, din; ***wie vom – gerührt,*** thunderstruck. **Donner|büchse,** *f.* blunderbuss. **–keil,** *m.* belemnite, (*coll.*) thunderbolt. **donnern,** *v.i.* thunder, roar. **donnernd,** *adj.* thunderous. **Donnerschlag,** *m.* thunder-clap, peal of thunder, thunderbolt (*also fig.*).

Donnerstag ['dɔnərsta:k], *m.* Thursday; ***grüner –,*** Maundy Thursday. **donnerstags,** *adv.* on Thursdays, each *or* every Thursday.

Donnerwetter ['dɔnərvɛtər], **1.** *n.* thunderstorm, (*fig. coll.*) blowing-up, dressing down, (*sl.*) rocket, stink. **2.** *int.* (*surprise*) good Lord! heavens above! (*oath*) ***zum –,*** damn it all! blast!

doof [do:f], *adj.* (*coll.*) stupid, simple; tiresome, boring.

Doppel ['dɔpəl], *n.* duplicate; (*Tenn.*) doubles. **Doppel–, doppel–,** *pref.* double, twin, di-, bi-, dual, duplex.

Doppel|adler, *m.* (*Her.*) two-headed eagle. **–bahn,** *f.* double-track railway. **–bereifung,** *f.* twin tyres. **–bett,** *n.* double bed. **–bier,** *n.* strong ale. **–bild,** *n.* (*Opt.*) double image. **–boden,** *m.* false bottom. **–boot,** *n.* catamaran. **–brechung,** *f.* (*Opt.*) double refraction. **–bruch,** *m.* (*Surg.*) compound fracture. **–büchse,** *f.* double-barrelled gun. **–buchstabe,** *m.* ligature, digraph. **–decker,** *m.* (*Av.*) biplane; double-decker (bus). **doppeldeutig,** *adj.* equivocal, ambiguous. **Doppel|druck,** *m.* (*Typ.*) mackle. **–ehe,** *f.* bigamy; bigamous marriage. **doppelfarbig,** *adj.* dichromatic. **Doppel|fenster,** *n.* double-glazed window. **–fernglas,** *n.* binoculars. **–flinte,** *f. See* **–büchse. –form,** *f.* doublet, alternative. **–gänger,** *m.* double (*a p.*). **–gespann,** *n.* four-in-hand. **–gestaltung,** *f.* dimorphism. **–gestirn,** *n.* binary star. **doppelgleisig,** *adj.* (*Railw.*) double-track. **Doppel|griff,** *m.* (*Mus.*) double stop. **–haus,** *n.* (pair of) semi-detached house(s). **–hub,** *m.* (*Engin.*) up-and-down stroke. **doppelkohlensauer,** *adj.* bicarbonate of. **Doppel|kreuz,** *n.* (*Mus.*) double sharp; (*Her.*) double cross, cross of Lorraine, (*Typ.*) double dagger. **–lafette,** f. twin mounting (*of guns*). **doppelläufig,** *adj.* double-barrelled. **Doppellaut,** *m.* diphthong. **doppellebig,** *adj.* amphibious. **Doppel|meister,** *m.* (*Tenn.*) doubles champion. **–monarchie,** *f.* Dual Monarchy (*Austria-Hungary* 1867–1918).

doppeln ['dɔpəln], **1.** *v.t.* double; line, sheath; sole (*shoes*). **2.** *v.i.* double one's stakes; (*Theat. & fig.*) double, stand in (*für*, for).

Doppel|naht, *f.* French seam; double stitching. **–name,** *m.* hyphenated *or* (*coll.*) double-barrelled name. **–punkt,** *m.* colon. **doppelreihig,** *adj.* double-breasted (*of jacket*). **Doppel|schalter,** *m.* (*Elec.*) two-way switch **–schlußmotor,** *m.* (*Elec.*) compound-wound motor. **–schnepfe,** *f.* (*Orn.*) great snipe (*Gallinago media*). **doppelseitig,** *adj.* bilateral, double-sided; double-page; (*fig.*) mutual, reciprocal; ***–e Lähmung,*** diplegia; ***–e Lungenentzündung,*** double pneumonia. **Doppelsinn,** *m.* double meaning, ambiguity. **doppelsinnig,** *adj.* equivocal, ambiguous. **Doppel|sitzer,** *m.* two-seater (*vehicle*). **–spat,** *m.* Iceland spar. **–spiel,** *n.* 1. (*Tenn.*) doubles; 2. double-dealing, trickery. **–stecher,** *m.* (*Elec.*) two-way adaptor. **–steppnaht,** *f. See* **–naht. –steppstich,** *m.* lock-stitch. **–stern,** *m. See* **–gestirn. –steuer,** *n.*, **–steuerung,** *f.* (*Av., Motor.*) dual control.

doppelt ['dɔpəlt], *adj.* double, twofold, twin; twice; ***in –er Abschrift*** or ***Ausführung,*** in duplicate; ***–e Buchführung,*** double entry (*book-keeping*); ***um das –e größer,*** double the size, twice as big. **doppelt|-hochrund,** *adj.* biconvex, convexo-concave. **–hohl,** *adj.* biconcave. **–kohlensauer,** *adj. See* **doppelkohlensauer.**

Doppel|tür, *f.* double door. **–verhältnis,** *n.* (*Math.*) cross *or* duplicate ratio. **–verkehr,** *m.* two-way communication. **–vers,** *m.* distich, couplet. **–vierer,** *m.* sculling-four. **–währung,** *f.* double standard of currency, bimetallism. **–weggleichrichtung,** *f.* (*Rad.*) full-wave rectification. **–zentner,** *m.* 100 kilograms. **–zünder,** *m.* combination fuse (*time, percussion*). **doppelzüngig,** *adj.* two-faced, double-dealing, disingenuous. **Doppel|zweier,** *m.* double-sculler. **–zylinder,** *m.* (*Motor.*) twin cylinder.

Dorf [dɔrf], *n.* (**-es,** *pl.* **⸗er**) village; ***das sind ihm böhmische*** or ***spanische Dörfer,*** that's all Greek *or* double Dutch to him; (*coll.*) ***auf die Dörfer gehen,*** lower one's standards *or* sights, be forced to come down a peg; (*Cards*) discard. **Dorf|bengel,** *m.*

country bumpkin. **-bewohner,** *m.* villager, countryman, country-dweller.

Dörfchen ['dœrfçən], *n.* hamlet.

Dorf|gemeinde, *f.* rural *or* village community, country parish. **-krug,** *m.* village inn.

Dörflein ['dœrflaın], *n. See* **Dörfchen. Dörfler,** *m.* p. from the back of beyond. **dörflich,** *adj.* village, rural, rustic.

Dorf|pfarrer, *m.* country parson, (*R.C.*) village priest. **-schenke,** *f.* village inn. **-schulze,** *m.* chairman of the rural council.

dorisch ['dɔrıʃ], *adj.* (*Archit.*) Doric, (*Mus.*) Dorian.

[1]**Dorn** [dɔrn], *m.* (**-es,** *pl.* **-en**) (*Bot.*) thorn, prickle, spine; hawthorn; *see also* **Dornrose**; ***ein – im Auge sein,*** be a thorn in one's flesh *or* side; ***keine Rose ohne -en,*** no rose without a thorn; ***-en ernten,*** get nothing for one's pains; ***auf -en gebettet sein,*** have a hard time.

[2]**Dorn,** *m.* (**-(e)s,** *pl.* **-e** *or* **¨-er**) spike, prong; tongue (*of a buckle*), arbor, mandrel (*of lathe*), pin, pintle (*of hinge*), tang, tongue, shank (*of blade*), web, bit (*of key*), awl, punch.

Dorn|busch, *m.* brier, briar, bramble. **-dreher,** *m.* (*Orn.*) *see* **Neuntöter.**

Dornen|balken, *m.* (*Her.*) engrailment. **-hecke,** *f.* thorn hedge. **-krone,** *f.* (*Eccl.*) crown of thorns. **dornen|tragend,** *adj.* (*Bot.*) spinous, spinose, spiny, thorny. **-voll,** *adj.* (*fig.*) hard, difficult.

Dorn|fortsatz, *m.* (*Anat.*) spinous process. **-grasmücke,** *f.* (*Orn.*) whitethroat (*Sylvia communis*). **dornig,** *adj.* (*Bot.*) *see* **dornentragend**; (*fig.*) *see* **dornenvoll.**

Dorn|röschen, *n.* Sleeping Beauty. **-röschenschlaf,** *m.* ***aus dem – erwachen,*** wake up to reality, come out of one's dream world, wake up from a long sleep, wake up like Rip van Winkle. **-rose,** *f.* (*Bot.*) wild rose, dog-rose, briar. **-schuhe,** *m.pl.* spiked *or* track *or* running shoes, (*coll.*) spikes. **-strauch,** *m. See* **-busch.**

dorren ['dɔrən], *v.i.* (*aux.* s.) become dry; dry up, wither, shrivel.

dörren ['dœrən], *v.t.* dry, desiccate, dehydrate; kiln-dry. **Dörrobst,** *n.* dried fruit.

Dorsch [dɔrʃ], *m.* (**-es,** *pl.* **-e**) (*Ichth.*) cod (*Gadus morrhua*). **Dorschlebertran,** *m.* cod-liver oil.

dort [dɔrt], (*Poet.* **dorten**) *adv.* there, over there, (*Poet.*) yonder; (*Comm.*) ***franko –,*** carriage paid; ***franko Bahnhof –,*** carriage paid to the nearest railway station. **dorther,** *adv.* from there, (*Poet.*) thence. **dortherum,** *adv.* thereabouts. **dorthin,** *adv.* (to) there, to that place, that way, (*Poet.*) thither. **dorthinaus,** *adv.* ***bis –,*** ad nauseam, (*coll.*) till the cows come home. **dortig,** *adj.* in *or* of that place, there. **dortselbst,** *adv.* right there.

Dose ['do:zə], *f.* 1. box, tin, can, tin-can; pot, jar; 2. *See* **Dosis.**

dösen ['dø:zən], *v.i.* (*coll.*) doze, be drowsy; day-dream, let one's thoughts wander.

Dosen|entwicklung, *f.* (*Phot.*) tank development. **-öffner,** *m.* tin-opener, can-opener.

dosieren [do'zi:rən], *v.t.* prescribe *or* administer *or* measure out a dose of.

dösig ['dø:zıç], *adj.* dozy, drowsy, sleepy; absent-minded; stupid, (*coll.*) dopey; tedious, boring, dull.

Dosis ['do:zıs], *f.* (-, *pl.* **Dosen**) dose; ***zu starke*** or ***große –,*** overdose; ***zu geringe*** or ***kleine –,*** under-dose.

dossieren [dɔ'si:rən], *v.t.* slope (*an embankment*); grind (*glass*). **Dossierung,** *f.* slope; taper (*of chimney*).

Dost [do:st], *m.* (**-s,** *pl.* **-e**) (*Bot.*) origan (*Origanum*); ***gemeiner –,*** wild marjoram.

dotal [do'ta:l], *adj.* pertaining to a dower *or* dowry. **Dotalgüter,** *n.pl.* glebe lands. **Dotation** [-tsi'o:n], *f.* dowry, portion; endowment, bequest, donation; grant, allocation (*of state funds*). **dotieren,** *v.t.* endow. **Dotierung,** *f. See* **Dotation.**

Dotter ['dɔtər], *m. or n.* yolk (*of egg*). **Dotterblume,** *f.* (*Bot.*) marsh-marigold (*Caltha palustris*).

doublieren [du'bli:rən], *v.t.* plate (*metal*).

Dozent [do'tsɛnt], *m.* (**-en,** *pl.* **-en**) university lecturer, (*Am.*) assistant professor. **Dozentenschaft,** *f.* academic staff, university teachers. **Dozentenzimmer,** *n.* staff *or* senior common-room. **Dozentur** [-'tu:r], *f.* (-, *pl.* **-en**) university lectureship. **dozieren,** *v.i., v.t.* give lectures, lecture, teach; (*coll.*) hold forth, pontificate.

Drache ['draxə], *m.* (**-n,** *pl.* **-n**) dragon; (*Her.*) wyvern; (*coll.*) virago, termagant, shrew; *see also* **Drachen.**

Drachen ['draxən], *m.* kite; ***einen – steigen lassen,*** fly a kite.

Drachen|ampfer, *m.* (*Bot.*) dock. **-anker,** *m.* (*Naut.*) grapnel, grappling anchor. **-kraut,** *n.* (*Bot.*) dragon's-wort (*Dracontium*). **-theorie,** *f.* (*Av.*) theory of dynamic lift. **-wurz,** *f. See* **-kraut.**

Drachme ['draxmə], *f.* 1. (*Pharm.*) drachm, dram; 2. drachma (*coin*).

Dragee [dra'ʒe:], *f. or n.* (**-s,** *pl.* **-s**) sugar-coated sweetmeat *or* pill.

Dragganker ['dragˀaŋkər], *m.*, **Dragge,** *f.* (*Naut.*) *see* **Drachenanker.**

Dragoner [dra'go:nər], *m.* dragoon; (*coll.*) masterful female.

Draht [dra:t], *m.* (**-es,** *pl.* **¨-e**) 1. wire, cable; (*Tele.*) line; (*coll.*) ***auf – sein,*** be all there, know one's stuff; ***blanker –,*** bare wire; ***besponnener –,*** covered wire; 2. (*sl.*) dough, brass (*i.e. money*).

Draht|abschneider, *m.* wire-cutter(s). **-adresse, -anschrift,** *f.* telegraphic address. **-antwort,** *f.* telegraphic reply. **-anweisung,** *f.* telegraphic money-order. **-arbeit,** *f.* wire-work; filigree. **-auslöser,** *m.* (*Phot.*) cable-release. **-bauer,** *n.* wire cage. **-bürste,** *f.* wire- *or* scratch-brush.

[1]**drahten** ['dra:tən], *adj.* (made) of wire.

[2]**drahten,** *v.t.* wire, telegraph.

Draht|funk, *m.* carrier current telegraphy; wired radio. **-geflecht,** *n.* wire netting *or* mesh. **-gewebe,** *n.* wire gauze. **-gitter,** *n. See* **-geflecht. drahthaarig,** *adj.* wire-haired (*of dogs*). **-heftung,** *f.* stapling, wire stitching (*of books*). **-hindernis,** *n.* wire entanglement.

drahtig ['dra:tıç], *adj.* (*fig.*) wiry.

-drähtig ['drɛ:tıç], *adj.suff.* -wired, with . . .wire(s); -stranded, with . . . strand(s).

Draht|klemme, *f.* (*Elec.*) terminal. **-lehre,** *f.* wire-gauge. **drahtlich,** *adj.* telegraphic. **Drahtlitze,** *f.* strand (*of wire*). **drahtlos,** *adj.* wireless, radio. **Draht|meldung, -nachricht,** *f.* telegram. **-netz,** *n.* wire netting. **-puppe,** *f.* puppet, marionette. **-saite,** *f.* metal string (*on violin etc.*). **-schere,** *f.* wire cutter. **-seil,** *n.* wire rope, cable. **-seilbahn,** *f.* cable *or* funicular railway. **-seilbrücke,** *f.* suspension bridge. **-sieb,** *n.* wire sieve. **-stift,** *m.* wire-nail, brad. **-verhau,** *m.* wire entanglement. **-wort,** *n.* telegraphic address. **-wurm,** *m.* wire-worm. **-zange,** *f.* cutting pliers, nippers. **-zecher,** *m.* wiredrawer; (*fig. of p.*) wirepuller.

drähtern ['drɛ:tərn], *adj.* (*obs.*) *See* [1]**drahten.**

drainieren, *v.t. See* **dränieren.**

drakonisch [dra'ko:nıʃ], *adj.* rigorous, harsh, Draconic, Draconian.

drall [dral], *adj.* tight, tightly twisted; (*fig.*) strapping, sturdy, buxom; ***-e Dirne,*** buxom lass. **Drall,** *m.* (**-s,** *pl.* **-e**) rifling (*of a gun*); twist, torque, torsion, angular momentum. **Drallabweichung,** *f.* (*Artil.*) drift. **drallieren** [-'li:rən], *v.t.* twist tightly.

Drama ['dra:ma], *n.* (**-s,** *pl.* **-men**) drama, dramatic play. **Dramatik** [-'ma:tık], *f.* drama, dramatic art. **Dramatiker,** *m.* dramatist, playwright. **dramatisch,** *adj.* dramatic. **dramatisieren** [-ti'zi:rən], *v.t.* dramatize, adapt for the stage. **Dramaturg** [-'tu:rk], *m.* (**-en,** *pl.* **-en**) dramatic producer *or* adviser. **Dramaturgie** [-'gi:], *f.* dramatic theory *or* technique, stagecraft.

dran [dran], *adv.* (*coll.*) *see* **daran**; – *sein,* have one's turn; be blamed; ***gut – sein,*** be on top of the world; ***übel – sein,*** be in a bad way.

Drän [drɛ:n], *m.* (**-s,** *pl.* **-s**) (*Med.*) drain tube; drain(age) pipe. **Dränage** [–'na:ʒə], *f.* drainage, draining; drainage system.

drang [draŋ], *see* **dringen.**

Drang, *m.* (**-(e)s,** *pl.* **⸚e**) pressure; urge, impulse, longing, craving; (*Poet.*) throng, press; ***Sturm und –,*** Storm and Stress; ***ich habe den – zu,*** I feel a craving for; ***einen heftigen – verspüren,*** need the lavatory badly; (*coll.*) have a sudden call, be taken short; ***– nach Osten,*** eastward expansion.

dränge ['drɛŋə], *see* **dringen.**

Drängelei [drɛŋə'laɪ], *f.* (-, *pl.* **-en**) jostling, shoving; scuffle. **drängeln,** *v.i., v.t.* jostle, shove; (*fig.*) pester, badger.

drängen ['drɛŋən], **1.** *v.t.* push, shove, thrust, press; urge; (*obs.*) *see* **bedrängen**; ***er drängt auf Zahlung,*** he presses for payment; ***gedrängt,*** crowded, thronged; succinct, terse (*of style*); ***sich zu etwas gedrängt fühlen,*** feel moved *or* prompted *or* obliged *or* impelled to do s.th.; ***gedrängt voll,*** crammed full, closely packed. **2.** *v.r.* crowd (together), throng; push (one's way). **3.** *v.i.* be in a hurry; press (on); ***die Zeit drängt,*** time is running short, time presses; ***es drängt nicht,*** it is not urgent.

Drangsal ['draŋza:l], *f.* (-, *pl.* **-e**) (*occ. n.* (**-s,** *pl.* **-e**)) anguish, distress, affliction; hardship, suffering, tribulation, oppression. **drangsalieren** [–'li:rən], *v.t.* plague, harass, torment.

drangvoll ['draŋfɔl], *adj.* crowded, thronged; intense, ardent.

dränieren [drɛ'ni:rən], *v.t., v.i.* drain.

drapieren [dra'pi:rən], *v.t.* drape, hang with drapery.

drasch [draʃ], **dräsche** ['drɛʃə], *see* **dreschen.**

drastisch ['drastɪʃ], *adj.* drastic.

dräuen ['drɔyən], *v.i.* (*Poet.*) *see* **drohen.**

drauf [drauf], *adv. See* **darauf**; ***– und dran sein,*** be on the point *or* verge (***zu tun,*** of doing).

Draufgänger ['draufgɛŋər], *m.* daredevil. **Draufgängertum,** *n.* recklessness, foolhardiness.

draufgehen ['draufge:ən], *irr.v.i.* (*sep.*) (*aux.* s.) be spent *or* wasted *or* lost, perish, (*coll.*) die.

Draufgeld ['draufgɛlt], *n.* deposit, earnest-money.

drauflegen ['draufle:gən], *v.t.* (*sep.*) add (*usu. money*), put . . . to, pay *or* give in addition.

drauflos [drauf'lo:s], *adv.,* **drauflos–,** *sep. pref.* straight on *or* ahead; recklessly. **drauflos|gehen,** *irr.v.i.* (*sep.*) (*aux.* s.) rush at, go straight for. **–wirtschaften,** *v.i.* (*sep.*) spend recklessly, (*coll.*) muddle along.

draus [draus], *adv. See* **daraus.**

draußen ['drausən], *adv.* outside, out of doors, (*Poet.*) without; abroad; ***von –,*** from (the) outside; ***nach –,*** outside; outward.

Drawida [dra'vi:da], *m.* Dravidian. **drawidisch,** *adj.* Dravidian.

Drechselbank ['drɛksəlbaŋk], *f. See* **Drehbank.**

drechseln ['drɛksəln], *v.t., v.i.* turn (*on a lathe*); (*fig.*) elaborate; ***Komplimente –,*** bandy compliments; (*fig.*) ***gedrechselt,*** elaborate; affected, prettily turned (*phrases*). **Drechsler,** *m.* turner. **Drechslerarbeit,** *f.* turnery; turning, lathe-work. **Drechslerei** [–'raɪ], *f.* turner's workshops; *See also* **Drechslerarbeit.**

Dreck [drɛk], *m.* mud, dirt, mire, filth, (*coll.*) muck; dung, droppings, excrement, faeces; dross, scum; ***– am Stecken haben,*** be not without a blemish; ***bis über die Ohren im – stecken,*** be up to the eyes in mud; (*coll.*) ***im – sitzen,*** be down and out, be on one's uppers; ***mach deinen – alleine!*** do your own dirty work! **Dreckfink,** *m.* (*coll.*) guttersnipe, dirty pig. **dreckig,** *adj.* muddy, dirty, soiled, filthy; foul, nasty. **Dreck|käfer,** *m.* dung-beetle. **–karren,** *m.* muck cart. **–spatz, –vogel,** *m. See* **–fink. –wetter,** *n.* foul *or* filthy weather.

dreesch [dre:ʃ], *adj.* fallow, uncultivated. **Dreesch,** *m.* (**-es,** *pl.* **-e**) green fallow. **Dreeschling,** *m. See* **Dreischling.**

Dreh [dre:], *m.* (*coll.*) ***den – heraushaben,*** have got the knack; ***im – sein,*** be in the swing. **Dreh–,** *pref.* rotary, rotational; revolving, swivel-; (*of lathe*) turning; torsional.

Dreh|achse, *f.* axis of rotation. **–bank,** *f.* (turning) lathe. **drehbar,** *adj.* revolving, rotary, rotating, swivelling; ***– gelagert,*** pivoted. **Dreh|beanspruchung,** *f.* torsional stress. **–bewegung,** *f.* rotary motion, rotation. **–bleistift,** *m.* propelling pencil. **–bohrer,** *m.* brace and bit. **–bolzen,** *m.* swivel-pin. **–brücke,** *f.* swing-bridge. **–buch,** *n.* scenario, film-script. **–bühne,** *f.* (*Theat.*) revolving stage. **–eisen,** *n.* lathe-tool, turning chisel. **–eiseninstrument,** *n.* (*Elec.*) moving-iron instrument.

drehen ['dre:ən], **1.** *v.t.* turn, twist, rotate; turn (on a lathe); ***ihm eine Nase –,*** cock a snook at him; ***einen Film –,*** make *or* shoot a film; ***ihm den Rücken –,*** turn one's back on him; (*fig.*) give him the cold shoulder; ***seinen Mantel nach dem Winde –,*** trim one's sails to the wind; ***etwas – und wenden wie man will,*** look at s.th. from whatever angle one will; ***die Daumen –,*** twiddle one's thumbs; ***eine Zigarette –,*** roll a cigarette; (*coll.*) ***das Ding –,*** do the job, manage it (all right). *See also* **drechseln. 2.** *v.r.* turn, rotate, revolve, go round; swivel, spin, swing; (*of wind*) veer; ***es dreht sich um,*** it is a question of *or* whether, the question hinges on; ***mir dreht sich alles im Kopfe,*** my head is going round *or* spinning; ***sich – und winden,*** squirm, writhe. **Dreher,** *m.* turner, lathe hand; winch, winder, crank-handle, knob; rotator (muscle); slow waltz.

Dreh|feld, *n.* (*Elec.*) rotating field. **–festigkeit,** *f.* torsional strength. **–flügel,** *m.* rotor. **–gestell,** *n.* pivot mounting. **–grill,** *m.* rotisserie. **–knopf,** *m.* control knob (*of radio set*). **–kondensator,** *m.* (*Rad.*) variable condenser. **–kopf,** *m.* capstan, turret *of lathe*). **–kran,** *m.* derrick, revolving crane. **–krankheit,** *f.* giddiness; staggers (*of sheep*). **–kranz,** *m.* turntable. **–kreis,** *m.* (*Motor.*) turning-circle. **–kreuz,** *n.* turnstile. **–moment,** *n.* torque. **–muskel,** *m.* rotator (muscle). **–orgel,** *f.* barrel-organ. **–punkt,** *m.* pivot, fulcrum. **–scheibe,** *f.* potter's wheel; turnplate, turntable; disk. **–seide,** *f.* silk twist. **–späne,** *m.pl.* turnings, shavings, swarf. **–spiegel,** *m.* cheval-glass. **–spulinstrument,** *n.* (*Elec.*) moving-coil instrument. **–stab,** *m.* (*Motor.*) torsion bar. **–stahl,** *m.* lathe-tool. **–stift,** *m.* mandrel (*of a lathe*), arbor (*of clock*); *see also* **–bleistift. –strom,** *m.* (*Elec.*) three-phase current. **–stuhl,** *m.* revolving chair; music-stool. **–tisch,** *m.* dumb-waiter, revolving table. **–tür,** *f.* revolving door. **–turm,** *m.* revolving turret (*of a tank*).

Drehung ['dre:uŋ], *f.* turn, rotation, revolution; turning, twist, torsion, torque; ***eine – nach links,*** a turn to the left; ***halbe – der Kurbel,*** half-stroke of the crank. **Drehungs|achse,** *f.* axis of rotation. **–ellipsoid,** *n.* spheroid. **–versuch,** *m.* (*Metall.*) torsion test. **–winkel,** *m.* (*Math.*) co-ordinate, angle of rotation.

Dreh|waage, *f.* torsion balance. **–wuchs,** *m.* spiral grain (*in wood*). **–zahl,** *f.* speed of rotation, (number of) revolutions (*usu.* per minute). **–zähler, –zahlmesser,** *m.* tachometer, revolution counter. **–zapfen,** *m.* pivot, swivel-pin, gudgeon(-pin), journal.

drei [draɪ], **1.** *num.adj.* three; ***ehe man – zählen kann,*** in a trice; ***zu –en,*** in threes, three by three. **Drei,** *f.* (-, *pl.* **-en**) (figure) three. **Drei–, drei–,** *pref.* three-, tri-, triple. **Drei|achsenwagen,** *m.* six-wheeler. **–achtel,** *n.pl.* three-eighths. **–bein,** *n.* tripod. **–blatt,** *n.* (*Bot.*) trefoil (*Trillium*). **dreiblätterig,** *adj.* (*Bot.*) three-leaved, trifoliate. **Dreibund,** *m.* Triple Alliance. **drei|dimensional,** *adj.* three-dimensional. **–drähtig,** *adj.* three-ply (*wool etc.*), three-lead (*cable*).

Dreieck ['draɪʔɛk], *n.* triangle, (*Archit.*) spandrel. **dreieckig,** *adj.* triangular, three-cornered; (*Bot., Anat.*) deltoid. **Dreieckpunkt,** *m.* (*Surv.*) triangulation point. **Dreiecksaufnahme,** *f.* (*Surv.*) triangulation. **Dreischaltung,** *f.* (*Elec.*) delta connection.

dreieinhalb ['draɪˀaɪn'halp], *inv. num.adj.* three and a half. **Dreieinheit,** *f.* triad; trinity. **dreieinig,** *adj.* three in one, triune. **Drei|einigkeit,** *f.* Trinity. **-elektrodenröhre,** *f.* (*Rad.*) triode.

dreier ['draɪər], *Gen. of* **drei**; ***Tagebuch – Kinder,*** diary kept by 3 children. **Dreier,** *m.* 1. number three (*tram etc.*); 2. (*obs.*) 3-pfennig piece (*now fig.*); ***spar deine –!*** save your money; ***dafür kriegst du keinen –,*** you won't get a penny for it. **Dreier|-einmaleins,** *n.* three-times table. **-gruppe,** *f.* group of three, trio, triad. **dreierlei,** *indecl. adj.* of 3 kinds, threefold.

dreifach ['draɪfax], *adj.* threefold; triple, treble, tri-; ***in -er Ausfertigung,*** in triplicate; ***-e Größe,*** trinomial; ***-e Krone,*** triple crown, tiara (*of the Pope*). **Dreifachstecker,** *m.* (*Elec.*) three-way (plug) adaptor.

dreifältig ['draɪfɛltɪç], *adj. See* **dreifach.**

dreifaltig [draɪ'faltɪç], *adj.* (*Eccl.*) threefold, triune. **Dreifaltigkeit,** *f.* Trinity. **Dreifaltigkeits|-blume,** *f.* (*Bot.*) wild pansy, heartsease. **-fest,** *n.* (*Eccl.*) Trinity Sunday. **-kirche,** *f.* Holy Trinity Church.

Drei|farbendruck, *m.* three-colour print(ing). **-felderwirtschaft,** *f.* three-field system. **-finger-regel,** *f.* (*Elec.*) Fleming's rule. **-firner,** *m.* wine 3 years old. **-fuß,** *m.* tripod. **-gangge-triebe,** *n.* three-speed gear(ing). **-gespann,** *n.* troika, (*fig.*) trio, threesome (*of friends*). **-gitterröhre,** *f.* (*Rad.*) pentode. **dreigliedrig,** *adj.* three-membered, in 3 sections; (*Math.*) trinomial. **Dreiheit,** *f.* triad; group of 3; threefold nature (*of God*). **Dreiherrschaft,** *f.* triumvirate.

dreihundert ['draɪhundərt], *num.adj.* three hundred. **Dreihundertjahrfeier,** *f.* tercentenary (celebration). **dreihundertst,** *num.adj.* three-hundredth.

dreijährig ['draɪjɛ:rɪç], *adj.* 3-year-old, lasting 3 years, triennial. **dreijährlich, 1.** *adj.* triennial, (occurring once) every 3 years. **2.** *adv.* every 3 years, triennally.

Drei|kaiserschlacht, *f.* battle of Austerlitz (1805). **-kant,** *m.* (**-es,** *pl.* **-e**) (*Geom.*) trihedron; *see also* **-kantfeile. -kantfeile,** *f.* triangular *or* three-cornered *or* three-square file. **dreikantig,** *adj.* (*Geom.*) trihedral; three-cornered, three-edged. **Drei|käsehoch,** *m.* (**-s,** *pl.* **-**) (*coll.*) whippersnapper, nipper, (little-)titch. **-klang,** *m.* (*Mus.*) triad. **-königsabend,** *m.* Twelfth Night. **-königsfest,** *n.* (feast of the) Epiphany. **dreiköpfig,** *adj.* three-headed, tricephalous, tricephalic (*monster*); (*Anat.*) triceps; ***-e Familie,*** family of three. **Dreimächteabkommen,** *n.* three-power agreement, tripartite pact. **dreimal,** *adv.* 3 times, (*Poet.*) thrice. **dreimalig,** *adj.* occurring *or* repeated 3 times, triple. **Dreimannhochspiel,** *n.* odd-man-out. **dreimännig,** *adj.* (*Bot.*) triandrian. **Dreimaster,** *m.* three-master; three-cornered hat. **dreimonatlich,** *adj.* quarterly.

drein [draɪn], *adv., pref.* (*coll.*) = **darein.**

Drei|paß, *m.* (**-(ss)es,** *pl.* **-(ss)e**) (*Archit.*) trefoil. **-phasen-,** *pref.* (*Elec.*) three-phase. **-phasen-(wechsel)strom,** *m.* three-phase current. **-polröhre,** *f.* (*Rad.*) triode. **dreiprozentig,** *adj.* (at) 3 per cent. **Drei|rad,** *n.* tricycle. **-satz,** *m.* rule of three.

Dreisch [draɪʃ], *m. See* **Dreesch.**

Drei|schlag, *m.* 1. ambling pace, uneven trot (*of a horse*); 2. (*Mus.*) triple time. **-schlitz,** *m.* (*Archit.*) triglyph. **drei|schürig,** *adj.* producing 3 crops a year. **-seitig,** *adj.* trilateral, three-sided; tripartite (*agreement*). **-silbig,** *adj.* of 3 syllables, trisyllabic. **-spaltig,** *adj.* (*Bot. etc.*) trifid; three-column(ed) (*page*). **Drei|spänner,** *m.* three-horse carriage. **-spitz,** *m.* three-cornered hat, tricorn. **dreisprachig,** *adj.* trilingual. **Dreisprung,** *m.* hop-step- (*Am.* skip-)and-jump, triple jump.

dreißig ['draɪsɪç], *num.adj.* thirty. **Dreißig,** *f.* (-, *pl.* **-en**) (number) thirty; ***in den -en sein,*** be in one's thirties. **dreißiger,** *inv.adj.*; ***die – Jahre,*** the thirties (*of the century and of age*). **Dreißiger,** *m.* man in his thirties; wine of 1930; soldier of the 30th regiment; ***in den -n sein,*** be in one's thirties. **dreißigjährig,** *adj.* 30 years old, lasting 30 years; ***der -e Krieg,*** the Thirty Years War (1618–48); ***ein -er Mann,*** a man of 30, a 30-year-old man. **dreißigst,** *num.adj.* thirtieth. **Dreißigstel,** *n.* thirtieth (part). **dreißigstens,** *adv.* in the thirtieth place.

dreist [draɪst], *adj.* bold, daring (*action*); audacious, impudent, pert, cheeky, forward, brazen (*person*); barefaced (*lie*); ***– wie ein Elster,*** as bold as brass.

dreistellig ['draɪʃtɛlɪç], *adj.* (*Math.*) three-figure (*number*), with 3 places (of decimals).

Dreistigkeit ['draɪstɪçkaɪt], *f.* boldness, daring; audacity, impudence, pertness, cheek, cheekiness, forwardness, brazenness.

drei|stimmig, *adj.* (*Mus.*) for 3 voices, in 3 parts. **-stöckig,** *adj.* three-storied. **-stündig,** *adj.* *adj.* lasting 3 hours. **-stündlich,** *adv.* (occurring) every 3 hours, at 3-hour(ly) intervals. **-tägig,** *adj.* lasting 3 days; ***-es Fieber,*** tertian fever. **-teilig,** *adj.* in 3 parts, tripartite, three-piece (*suit*); ***-er Altar, -es Altarbild,*** triptych; (*Mus.*) ***-er Takt,*** triple time. **Dreiteilung,** *f.* division into 3 parts, trisection. **dreiundeinhalb,** *inv. num.adj.* three and a half. **Dreiverband,** *m.* Triple Entente.

dreiviertel ['draɪfɪrtəl], *inv. attrib. adj.* three-quarter; ***um – vier,*** at a quarter to four. **Dreiviertel,** *n.* three quarters. **dreiviertel-,** *pref.* three-quarter. **Dreiviertel|ärmel,** *m.* three-quarter (length) sleeve. **-stunde,** *f.* three quarters of an hour. **-takt,** *m.* (*Mus.*) three-four time.

Dreiwegschalter ['draɪve:kʃaltər], *m.* (*Elec.*) three-way switch. **drei|wertig,** *adj.* trivalent. **-wink(e)-lig,** *adj.* triangular. **-wöchentlich, 1.** *adj.* three-weekly. **2.** *adv.* every three weeks. **-wöchig,** *adj.* lasting (for) 3 weeks. **Dreizack,** *m.* trident; (*Bot.*) arrowgrass. **dreizackig,** *adj.* three-pronged.

Dreizehen|möwe, *f.* (*Orn.*) kittiwake (*Rissa tridactyla*). **-specht,** *m.* (*Orn.*) three-toed woodpecker (*Picoïdes tridactylus*). **dreizehig,** *adj.* tridactylous.

dreizehn ['draɪtse:n], *num.adj.* thirteen; (*coll.*) ***jetzt schlägt's aber –,*** that's really too much, that's the limit, that's finished it. **dreizehnjährig,** *adj.* thirteen-year-old. **dreizehnt,** *num.adj.* thirteenth. **Dreizehntel,** *n.* thirteenth (part).

Drell [drɛl], *m.* (**-s,** *pl.* **-e**) *see* **Drillich.**

Dreschdiele ['drɛʃdi:lə], *f.* threshing-floor. **Dresche,** *f.* (*coll.*) thrashing. **dreschen,** *irr.v.t.* thresh; (*coll.*) thrash; ***leeres Stroh –,*** beat the air. **Dresch|flegel,** *m.* flail. **-maschine,** *f.* threshing machine, thresher. **-tenne,** *f. See* **-diele.**

Dresseur [drɛ'sø:r], *m.* (**-s,** *pl.* **-e**) animal trainer. **dressieren,** *v.t.* 1. train; break in (*animals*); 2. comb (*silk*). **Dressur,** *f.* breaking in, training. **Dressurreiten,** *n.* dressage.

driesch [dri:ʃ], *adj. See* **dreesch. Drieschling,** *m.* (**-s,** *pl.* **-e**) (common) mushroom.

Drilch [drɪlç], *m.*(**-(e)s,** *pl.* **-e**) *see* **Drillich.**

¹**Drill** [drɪl], *m.* (**-s,** *pl.* **-e**) *see* **Drillich.**

²**Drill,** *m.* (**-es,** *pl.* **-e**) drill, drilling. **Drill|bohrer,** *m.* drill, borer. **-egge,** *f.* drill-harrow.

drillen ['drɪlən], *v.t.* 1. drill, train, school, exercise; 2. drill, bore.

Drillich ['drɪlɪç], *m.* (**-s,** *pl.* **-e**) coarse canvas, drill, ticking. **Drillichanzug,** *m.* overalls, dungarees, (*Mil.*) fatigue dress, denims.

Drilling ['drɪlɪŋ], *m.* (**-s,** *pl.* **-e**) 1. triplet, one of triplets; 2. three-barrelled gun; 3. tripling (*crystal*). **Drillingsbalken,** *m.* (*Her.*) tierce.

Drill|kultur, *f.* drill-husbandry. **-maschine,** *f.* ridge-drill. **-saat,** *f* drill-sowing.

Drillung ['drɪluŋ], *f.* torsion, twist.

drin [drɪn], *adv. See* **darin.**

dringen ['drɪŋən], *irr.v.i.* 1. (*aux.* s.) – ***in*** (*Acc.*), penetrate, enter, make one's way *or* get into, surge *or* throng into; – (*bis*) *an* (*Acc.*) or *zu*, reach, get as far as; *an die Öffentlichkeit* –, become known *or* public, get abroad; *zum Herzen* –, stir the soul; 2. (*aux.* h.) – *in* (*Acc.*), beseech, entreat, beg, plead with, try to persuade, press, urge (*a. p*); – *auf* (*Acc.*), press for, insist on; *darauf – daß es getan wird*, press for it to be done, insist on its being done. *See* **gedrungen. dringend,** *adj.* pressing, urgent, (*Tele. etc.*) priority; *–er Fall*, urgent case, (case of) emergency; *–e Gründe*, compelling *or* cogent reasons; *–er Verdacht*, strong suspicion; *– ersucht*, earnestly *or* urgently requested. **dringlich,** *adj. See* **dringend. Dringlichkeit,** *f.* urgency, priority. **Dringlichkeits|antrag,** *m.* (*Parl.*) vote of urgency. **–liste,** *f.* priority schedule, list of priorities.

drinnen ['drɪnən], *adv.* within, indoors.

drisch [drɪʃ], **drischst, drischt,** *see* **dreschen.**

dritt [drɪt], **1.** *adv. zu* –, the three of us *or* you *or* them. **2.** *num.adj.* third; *aus –er Hand*, indirectly; at third hand; *der –e Stand*, the third estate, the lower classes; *zum ersten! zum zweiten! zum –en und letzen!* going, going, gone! *eine Zahl in die –e Potenz erheben*, cube a number; *den –en abschlagen*, play two and threes (*a game*); come in third, take third place (*in a race or competition*); (*Gram.*) *–e Person*, third person; *eine –e Person, ein Dritter*, a third *or* disinterested person, someone *or* anyone else, an outsider, any other person, (*Law*) a third party. **dritt–, Dritt–,** *pref.* third, (*Law*) third-party. **dritt(e)halb,** *inv. adj.* two and a half. **Dritteil,** *n. See* **Drittel. dritteilen,** *v.t. See* **dritteln. Drittel,** *n.* (**-s,** *pl.* -) third (part). **dritteln,** *v.t.* divide into thirds *or* three parts. **drittens,** *adv.* thirdly, in the third place. **dritt|klassig,** *adj.* third-class; inferior. **–letzt,** *adj.* last but two; third from last, antepenultimate. **–rangig,** *adj.* third-rate, inferior, mediocre.

drob [drɔp], *adv. See* **darob.**

droben ['dro:bən], *adv.* above, up there.

Drogen ['dro:gən], *f.pl.* drugs, medicine(s). **Drogenhändler,** *m. See* **Drogist. Drogenhandlung, Drogerie** [–'ri:], *f.* drug-store, chemist's shop. **Drogeriewaren,** *f.pl.* pharmaceutical products. **Drogist** [–'gɪst], *m.* (**-en,** *pl.* **-en**) druggist, chemist.

Drohbrief ['dro:bri:f], *m.* threatening letter.

drohen ['dro:ən] *v.i.* (*occ. v.t.*) 1. (*ihm mit einer S. occ. ihm eine S.*) threaten (him with s.th.); *ihm mit der Faust* –, shake one's fist at him; *ihm mit dem Finger* –, wag one's finger at him; 2. (*of a th.*) be in danger (*zu fallen*, of falling). **drohend,** *adj.* threatening, menacing; impending, imminent (*danger etc.*).

Drohne ['dro:nə], *f.* drone; (*fig.*) parasite, wastrel, good-for-nothing.

dröhnen ['drø:nən], *v.i.* roar, boom; resound; *ihm in die Ohren* –, din in his ears. **Dröhnen,** *n.* boom, roar, din.

Drohung ['dro:uŋ], *f.* threat, menace, (*Law*) intimidation.

drollig ['drɔlɪç], *adj.* droll, amusing, funny, comical, quaint, (*Am.*) cute.

Dromedar [drome'da:r], *n.* (**-s,** *pl.* **-e**) dromedary.

Drommete [drɔ'me:tə], *f.* (*obs.*) *see* **Trompete.**

Dronte ['drɔntə], *f.* (*Orn.*) dodo.

Drops [drɔps], *m.* (-, *pl.* -) boiled sweet(s).

drosch [drɔʃ], **drösche** ['drœʃə], *see* **dreschen.**

Droschke ['drɔʃkə], *f.* cab, hackney-carriage; taxi(-cab). **Droschkenhalteplatz,** *m.* cab-stand, taxi-rank.

dröseln ['drø:zəln], *v.t.* (*dial.*) twist (*thread*).

1**Drossel** ['drɔsəl], *f.* (-, *pl.* **-n**) (*Orn.*) *bunte* –, *see* **Erddrossel**; *sibirische* –, Siberian thrush (*Turdus sibiricus*).

2**Drossel,** *f.* (-, *pl.* **-n**) 1. (*Hunt.*) windpipe; throat, gullet, (*coll.*) throttle; 2. (*Motor.*) throttle; (*Rad.*) *see* **Drosselspule.**

Drossel|ader, *f.* jugular vein. **–klappe,** *f.* throttle-valve, butterfly valve, damper. **–kreis,** *m.* (*Rad.*) rejector circuit. **drosseln,** *v.t.* throttle, strangle; (*Rad.*) choke; throttle (back) (*steam etc.*), (*fig.*) curb, check, limit. **Drossel|rohrsänger,** *m.* (*Orn.*) great reed-warbler (*Acrocephalus arundinaceus*). **–spule,** *f.* (*Rad.*) choke, inductance *or* impedance (coil). **–ventil,** *n. See* **–klappe.**

Drost [drɔst], *m.* (**-es,** *pl.* **-e**) (*Hist.*) bailiff. **Drostei** [–'taɪ], *f.* (-, *pl.* **-en**) (*Hist.*) bailiwick.

drüben ['dry:bən], *adv.* over there, on the other side, across; across the sea (*esp.* the Atlantic); in the other world *or* the hereafter; yonder, opposite; *hüben und* or *wie* –, everywhere, on all sides.

1**Druck** [druk], *m.* (**-(e)s,** *pl.* **⸚e**) pressure, squeeze (*of the hand*); (*Mech.*) compression, thrust; oppressive feeling, weight, burden; (*fig.*) pressure.

2**Druck,** *m.* (**-(e)s,** *pl.* **-e**) print, printing; impression; type; *im* –, in print, in printed form; *im – erscheinen*, be printed *or* published, appear in print; *in – geben*, have printed, publish; *in – gehen*, go to press.

Druck|akzent, *m.* (*Phonet.*) stress. **–anzug,** *m.* (*Av.*) pressurized *or* space suit. **–arbeit,** *f.* (*Typ.*) presswork, printing. **–ausgleichskabine,** *f.* (*Av.*) pressurized cabin. **–beanspruchung,** *f.* (*Metall.*) compression, stress. **–bogen,** *m.* printed sheet. **–brand,** *m.* (*Med.*) bed-sore, decubitus. **–buchstabe,** *m.* type; block letter *or* capital. **druckdicht,** *adj.* (*Av.*) pressurized.

Drückeberger ['drykəbɛrgər], *m.* slacker, shirker, (*Mil.*) malingerer; (*sl.*) skiver.

drucken ['drukən], *v.t.* print; – *lassen*, have printed *or* published; *lügen wie gedruckt*, lie like a trooper.

drücken ['drykən], (*obs. and dial. also* **drucken**) **1.** *v.t.* 1. press, squeeze, clasp (*s.o.'s hand*); *ihm die Hand* –, shake hands with him, shake his hand; 2. (im)press, (im)print, stamp (*auf* (*Acc.*), (up)on); 3. push, force (*nach unten*, down; *nach oben*, upwards; *zur Seite*, to one side); *zu Boden* –, force *or* weigh to the ground, (*fig.*) force down (*prices etc.*); *die Stimmung* –, cast a gloom on (the party *etc.*), be a wet blanket; (*Spt.*) *den Rekord* –, lower the record; *an die Wand* –, press against the wall, (*fig.*) push to the wall, push aside; *ihm etwas in die Hand* –, thrust *or* slip s.th. into his hand. **2.** *v.t., v.i.* – or – *auf* (*Acc.*), press, push (*knob etc.*); *der Schuh drückt*, the shoe pinches *or* is too tight; (*fig.*) *es drückt mich* or *mein Gewissen*, it weighs on my conscience; *der Gedanke drückt mich*, the thought weighs on my mind *or* oppresses me; *das Wetter drückt* (*auf*) *mich*, the weather is getting me down; *gedrückt*, depressed, dejected; *gedrückt voll*, crammed full. **3.** *v.r.* 1. (*of a p.*) press *or* squeeze *or* flatten o.s., huddle, crouch (*against a wall, into a corner etc.*); (*of a th.*) force itself, be forced *or* pressed *or* pushed; 2. (*coll.*) (*of a p.*) slip *or* steal away, make o.s. scarce; – *vor* (*Dat.*), evade, shirk, dodge, back out of.

drückend ['drykənt], *adj.* heavy, pressing; (*of weather*) heavy, close, oppressive; grievous, dire (*poverty etc.*).

Drucker ['drukər], *m.* printer.

Drücker ['drykər], *m.* latch (*on door*), thumb-release; (*Elec.*) push-button.

Druckerei [drukə'raɪ], *f.* press, printing-press, printing-works.

Druckerlaubnis ['drukˀɛrlaupnɪs], *f.* imprimatur.

Druckerschwärze ['drukərʃvɛrtsə], *f.* printer's *or* printing ink.

Druck|feder, *f.* compression spring. **–fehler,** *m.* misprint, printer's error, typographical error. **–fehlerverzeichnis,** *n.* (list of) errata. **druck|-fertig,** *adj.* ready for press. **–fest,** *adj.* resistant to compression, (*Av.*) pressurized. **Druck|-festigkeit,** *f.* compression strength, resistance to pressure. **–flasche,** *f.* siphon. **–förderung,** *f.* (*Mech.*) pressure feed. **–form,** *f.* (*Typ.*) forme. **–freiheit,** *f.* liberty of the press. **–gefälle,** *n.* pressure gradient. **–höhe,** *f.* head of water, height of fall. **–hub,** *m.* (*Motor.*) compression stroke. **–jahr,** *n.* date of publication. **–kabine,** *f.* (*Av.*) pressurized cabin. **–kammer,** *f.* caisson; air-lock.

-**kessel,** *m.* autoclave. -**knopf,** *m.* press-button, push-button; bell-push; press-stud, patent fastener. -**kosten,** *pl.* printing costs. -**kraft,** *f.* pressure, force of compression. -**kugelschreiber,** *m.* retractable ball-point pen. -**lager,** *n.* thrust bearing. -**legung,** *f.* printing. -**linie,** *f.* axis of thrust *or* compression. -**luft,** *f.* compressed air; (*as pref.*) pneumatic. -**luftkrankheit,** *f.* caisson disease, (*coll.*) the bends. -**messer,** *m.* pressure gauge, manometer. -**ölung,** *f.* forced *or* pressure oil feed. -**ort,** *m.* place of publication. -**platte,** *f.* engraving *or* stereotype plate, electrotype. -**posten,** *m.* (*coll.*) soft *or* cushy job. -**probe,** *f.* proof. -**pumpe,** *f.* force-pump, compression *or* pressure pump. -**punkt,** *m.* (*Med.*) pressure point; (*Av.*) aerodynamic centre; – ***nehmen,*** take the first pressure (*firing a rifle*), (*sl.*) shirk one's duty, scrimshank. **druckreif,** *adj.* ready for publication. **Druck|sache,** *f.* printed matter, printed papers; (by) book post. -**schmierpresse,** *f.* grease-gun. -**schmierung,** *f. See* -**ölung.** -**schraube,** *f.* (*Av.*) pusher propeller. -**schrift,** *f.* type; block letters *or* capitals; printed work, publication; pamphlet, prospectus, leaflet. -**seite,** *f.* printed page.

drucksen ['druksən], *v.i.* (*coll.*) hesitate, waver, hold back, shilly-shally, hum and haw (***an*** (*Dat.*), over).

Druck|stock, *m.* (*Typ.*) block, electrotype. -**taster,** *m.* signalling key. -**tiegel,** *m.* (*Typ.*) platen. -**topf,** *m.* pressure-cooker. -**verband,** *m.* compression bandage, compress. -**vermerk,** *m.* printer's imprint; colophon. -**vorlage,** *f.* (printer's) copy, manuscript (ready for press). -**vorschrift,** *f.* (*Mil.*) training manual. -**walze,** *f.* impression roller. -**wasser**-, *pref.* hydraulic. -**welle,** *f.* blast, pressure wave. -**zerstäuber,** *m.* spray gun. -**zugdämpfer,** *m.* (*Rad.*) quiescent push-pull. -**zwang,** *m.* obligation to print (a thesis).

Drude ['dru:də], *f.* witch. **Druden|beutel,** *m.* (*Bot.*) puff-ball. -**fuß,** *m.* 1. (*Bot.*) club moss (*Lycopodium clavatum*), drude's foot; 2. pentagram (*symbol ☆ against witches and evil spirits*).

Druide [dru'i:də], *m.* (-**n,** *pl.* -**n**) druid.

drum [drum], *adv. See* **darum**; ***mit allem Drum und Dran,*** with everything that goes with it, with all the paraphernalia, (*coll.*) lock, stock and barrel, with all the trimmings.

drunten ['druntən], *adv.* down there, (down) below. **drunter,** *adv. See* **darunter**; – ***und drüber,*** higgledy-piggledy, upside down, at sixes and sevens.

Druse ['dru:zə], *f.* 1. (*Geol.*) druse, geode; 2. strangles, glanders (*in horses etc.*); 3. (*dial.*) (*usu. pl.*) sediment, dregs, lees.

Drüse ['dry:zə], *f.* gland. **Drüsen|entzündung,** *f.* adenitis. -**gang,** *m.* glandular duct. -**geschwulst,** *f.* glandular swelling, struma. **drüsenkrank,** *adj.* suffering from a glandular disease, (*obs.*) scrofulous.

drusenkrank ['dru:zənkraŋk], *adj.* suffering from strangles.

Drüsen|krankheit, *f.,* -**leiden,** *n.* glandular disease; (*obs.*) scrofula. -**verhärtung,** *f.* bubo.

drusig ['dru:zıç], *adj.* 1. suffering from strangles; 2. (*Geol.*) containing druses.

drüsig ['dry:zıç], *adj.* glandular.

Dschungel ['dʒuŋəl], *m.* or *n.* or *f.* (-, *pl.* -**n**) jungle.

du [du:], *pers. pron.* you, (*B., Poet.*) thou; ***mit ihm auf – und – stehen,*** be on intimate terms with him. **Du,** *n.* (*Phil.*) non-ego; ***dein anderes*** or ***zweites*** –, your other self.

Dual ['du:a:l], *m.* (-**s,** *pl.* -**e**) dual (number). **Dualismus** [dualısmus], *m.* dualism. **dualistisch,** *adj.* dualistic. **Dualität** [-i'tɛ:t], *f.* duality.

Dübel ['dy:bəl], *m. See* [1]**Döbel.**

Dublee [du'ble:], *n.* (-**s,** *pl.* -**s**) 1. rolled gold, gold-plate; 2. (*Bill.*) stroke off the cushion.

Dublette [du'blɛtə], *f.* duplicate, double, doublet.

dublieren [du'bli:rən], *v.t.* 1. plate (*metal*), line (*a garment*); 2. (*Bill.*) play off the cushion; 3. (*Theat.*) double (*an actor*); 4. (*Typ.*) mackle, stur.

Dublone [du'blo:nə], *f.* doubloon.

ducken ['dukən], **1.** *v.t.* duck (*one's head*); humble, humiliate, bring low, break (*s.o.'s*) spirit, (*coll.*) take (*s.o.*) down a peg (or two). **2.** *v.i., v.r.* duck, stoop, bend down, crouch (down); submit, humble o.s., knuckle under. **Duckmäuser,** *m.* (-**s,** *pl.* -) yes-man, toady, lickspittle, (*sl.*) arse-crawler. **duckmäuserig, duckmäuserisch,** *adj.* servile, fawning, grovelling, cringing.

Dudelei [du:də'laı], *f.* toot(l)ing; droning. **dudeln** ['du:dəln], **1.** *v.i.* play the bagpipes; toot(le), drone. **2.** *v.t.* hum, drool (*a tune*). **Dudelsack,** *m.* bagpipes. **Dudelsackpfeifer,** *m.* bagpiper, piper.

Duell [du'ɛl], *n.* (-**s,** *pl.* -**e**) duel; – ***auf Degen*** or ***Pistolen,*** duel with swords *or* pistols. **Duellant** [-'lant], *m.* (-**en,** *pl.* -**en**) duellist. **duellieren,** *v.r.* fight a duel.

Duett [du'ɛt], *n.* (-**s,** *pl.* -**e**) duet.

Duft [duft], *m.* (-**es,** *pl.* ⸚**e**) scent, perfume, (agreeable) odour, sweet smell, aroma, fragrance; (*Poet.*) vapour.

duft(e) ['duft(ə)], *adj.* (*coll.*) fine, splendid, grand; (*sl.*) ***eine dufte Nummer,*** a smashing bit of stuff.

duften ['duftən], *v.i.* be fragrant, smell sweet, (*Poet.*) be misty *or* vaporous. **duftend,** *adj.* fragrant, scented, sweet-smelling. **duftig,** *adj.* light, filmy, delicate, gossamer (*as clouds*), hazy; fragrant. **Duft|stoff,** *m.* aromatic substance *or* oil. -**wasser,** *n.* perfume, scent.

Dukaten [du'ka:tən], *m.* (-**s,** *pl.* -) ducat.

Duktus ['duktus], *m.* lines (*of a building*), flow (*of handwriting*).

dulden ['duldən], *v.t.* suffer, endure, bear (patiently); tolerate; (*coll.*) put up with, stand, allow; permit (*s.th. to be done*). **Dulder,** *m.* long-suffering p., patient sufferer. **Duldermiene,** *f.* martyred expression. **duldsam,** *adj.* tolerant, long-suffering, (*obs.*) patient. **Duldsamkeit,** *f.* tolerance, (spirit of) toleration. **Duldung,** *f.* toleration, endurance; tolerance; ***stillschweigende*** –, tacit permission, connivance.

Dult [dult], *f.* (-, *pl.* -**en**) (*Austr. and Bav. dial.*) fair.

dumm [dum], *adj.* dull, stupid, slow, (*coll.*) dense, (*Am.*) dumb; foolish, silly, ridiculous; (*coll.*) ***das ist*** –, that is a nuisance *or* awkward; ***der -e August,*** circus clown; ***ein -es Gesicht machen,*** look innocent, pretend not to know; ***-er Junge*** (*if said to an adult*), fool (*the acknowledged word of challenge to a duel*); (*coll.*) ***der Dumme sein, den Dummen machen,*** be the loser *or* the one who pays, (*sl.*) be the sucker; (*coll.*) ***-es Zeug!*** rubbish, piffle, (stuff and) nonsense! **dummdreist,** *adj.* impudent, impertinent. **Dummdreistigkeit,** *f.* impertinence. **Dummerchen,** *n.,* **Dummerjan,** *m.* (-**s,** *pl.* -**e**), **Dummerling,** *m.* (-**s,** *pl.* -**e**) silly child. **dummerweise,** *adv.* foolishly, stupidly. **Dummheit,** *f.* stupidity, folly; foolishness, silliness; foolish *or* stupid action; blunder, mistake; tomfoolery, foolish prank. **Dummkopf,** *m.* blockhead, simpleton. **Dummrian,** *m.* (-**s,** *pl.* -**e**) *see* **Dummerjan.**

dumpf [dumpf], *adj.* 1. (*of sound*) dull, muffled, hollow; ***-er Schlag,*** thud; 2. (*of feeling*) dull, numb, torpid, heavy; 3. (*of atmosphere*) heavy, sultry, close, stifling, oppressive; stuffy, stale, musty, fusty, muggy. **Dumpfheit,** *f.* 1. dullness, hollowness; 2. numbness, heaviness, torpidity, apathy; 3. sultriness, closeness, oppressiveness, stuffiness, staleness, mustiness, fustiness. **dumpfig,** *adj. See* **dumpf,** 3. **Dumpfigkeit,** *f. See* **Dumpfheit,** 3.

dun [du:n], *adj.* (*dial.*) tipsy.

Dune ['du:nə], *f. See* **Daune.**

Düne ['dy:nə], *f.* (sand-)dune, sandhill.

Dung [duŋ], *m.* (-**(e)s,** *no pl.*) dung, manure.

Düngemittel ['dyŋəmıtəl], *n.* fertilizer, artificial manure. **düngen,** *v.t.* fertilize, manure. **Dünger,** *m.* fertilizer, manure, dung. **Düngerhaufen,** *m.* dunghill. **Düngung,** *f.* manuring, fertilization.

dunkel ['duŋkəl], *adj.* dark, in darkness; (*fig.*) cloudy, dim, faint, vague (*as memories*); gloomy, sombre, black (*as moods*); mysterious; sinister, obscure, unknown, doubtful, hidden (*as meaning*); deep, dark (*colour*); ***der –ste Tag meines Lebens,*** the blackest day of my life; ***von dunkler Herkunft,*** of doubtful antecedents; ***eine dunkle Existenz,*** a shady existence; ***ein Sprung ins Dunkle,*** a leap in the dark; ***im Dunkeln sitzen,*** sit in the dark *or* in darkness; (*fig.*) ***im –n sitzen,*** be *or* remain in the dark; (*Prov.*) ***im Dunkeln ist gut munkeln,*** it's easy to talk, those are empty words. **Dunkel,** *n.* dark(ness), obscurity, ambiguity.

Dünkel ['dyŋkəl], *m.* conceit, vanity; presumption; ***– haben,*** be conceited.

Dunkelheit ['duŋkəlhaɪt], *f.* dark(ness); obscurity. **Dunkel|kammer,** *f.* (*Phot.*) dark room. **–mann,** *m.* (*pl.* **-männer**) obscurantist. **dunkeln, 1.** *v.i.* grow dark *or* dim. **2.** *v.t.* darken, deepen, dim (*colour*).

dünken ['dyŋkən], **1.** *reg. & irr.v.i. imp.* seem, look, appear; ***es dünkt mich*** (or ***mir***), ***mich*** (or ***mir***) ***dünkt,*** it seems to me, I fancy, (*Poet.*) methinks; ***es dünkte*** (*Poet.* ***deuchte***) ***ihn*** (or ***ihm***), it seemed to him, he thought; ***tue, was dir gut dünkt,*** do what you think proper. **2.** *v.r.* imagine *or* fancy o.s. (to be); ***er dünkt sich was*** (***Rechtes***), he has a high opinion of himself, he thinks a great deal of himself.

Dünkirchen ['dy:nkɪrçən], *n.* Dunkirk.

dünn [dyn], *adj.* thin; (*of a p.*) thin, lean, spare; slender, fine (*thread*); thin, scanty, sparse (*growth*); thin, watery (*liquid*); rare, rarefied, attenuated (*atmosphere*); thin, reedy (*voice*); (*fig.*) faint, half-hearted (*as praise etc.*); ***das Brett bohren wo es am –sten ist,*** take the easy *or* easiest way out; (*coll.*) ***sich – machen,*** make o.s. scarce. **Dünn|bier,** *n.* small *or* weak beer. **–darm,** *m.* small intestine. **–druckausgabe,** *f.* India paper edition. **Dünne,** *f.* thinness; leanness, spareness; slenderness, fineness; scantiness, spareness; wateriness; reediness; faintness, half-heartedness. **dünnen,** *v.t. See* **verdünnen. dünnflüssig,** *adj.* fluid, watery. **Dünnflüssigkeit,** *f.* low viscosity. **dünn|gesät,** *adj.* sparsely sown, thinly scattered; (*fig.*) scarce. **–häutig,** *adj.* filmy; thin-skinned. **Dünnheit,** *f. See* **Dünne. dünnleibig,** *adj.* lank, slender. **Dünn|pfiff,** *m.* (*coll.*) diarrhœa. **–schliff,** *m.* thin *or* microscopic section. **–schnabel-Brachvogel,** *m.* (*Orn.*) slender-billed curlew (*Numenius tenuirostris*). **Dünnung,** *f.* flank.

Dunst [dunst], *m.* (**-es,** *pl.* **⸚e**) vapour, haze, mist; fume, exhalation; ***übler –,*** miasma; (*coll.*) ***ihm einen blauen – vormachen,*** humbug him; ***keinen blassen – davon haben,*** not have the haziest *or* foggiest notion of; (*fig.*) ***in – und Rauch aufgehen,*** go up in smoke, vanish into thin air.

dunsten ['dunstən], *v.i.* exhale vapour, give off fumes, steam, smoke.

dünsten ['dynstən], *v.t.* steam, stew.

dunstig ['dunstɪç], *adj.* misty, hazy, steamy. **Dunst|kreis,** *m.* (*obs.*) atmosphere; (*fig.*) atmosphere, aura. **–obst,** *n.* stewed fruit. **–schleier,** *m.* haze.

Dünung ['dy:nuŋ], *f.* (*Naut.*) (ground-)swell, surf.

Duo ['du:o], *n.* (**-s,** *pl.* **-s**) (*Mus.*) duet. **Duodez** [–'de:ts], *n.* (*Typ.*) duodecimo. **Duodezfürst,** *m.* petty prince.

duplieren [du'pli:rən], *v.t.* 1. plate (*metal*), line (*a garment*); *see* **dublieren**; 2. (*obs.*) (*Law*) make a rejoinder. **Duplik,** *f.* (-, *pl.* **-en**) (*Law*) rejoinder. **Duplikat** [–'ka:t], *n.* (**-(e)s,** *pl.* **-e**) duplicate. **duplizieren** [–'tsi:rən], *v.t.* (make a) duplicate. **Duplizität** [–i'tɛ:t], *f.* 1. duplexity, doubleness; identical pair; 2. (*fig.*) duplicity, double-dealing.

Dupont-Lerche [dy'pɔ̃], *f.* (*Orn.*) Dupont's lark (*Chersophilus duponti*).

Dur [du:r], *n.* (*Mus.*) major (key). **Durakkord,** *m.* major chord.

durch [durç], **1.** *prep.* (*Acc.*) 1. (*place*) through; 2. (*time*) all through, throughout, for (*oft. with verb pref.* ***hindurch***); ***– viele Jahre*** (***hindurch***), for many years; ***– den ganzen Monat Mai*** all through the month of May; ***– viele Jahrhunderte*** (***hindurch***), throughout *or* down the centuries; 3. (*instrumental*) by (means of), as a result of, by the agency of; because of, thanks to, through; ***– die Post,*** by post, through the post; ***Tod – Vergiftung,*** death as a result of *or* death by poisoning; ***– seine Hilfe,*** thanks to his help. **2.** *adv.* 1. (*place*) (*emph. following* **durch,** *prep.* 1); ***durch den dichtesten Wald –,*** right through the thickest wood; (*Poet.*) (*without the prep.*) ***die Wolken –,*** through the clouds; 2. (*fig.*) thoroughly; ***– und –,*** through and through, utterly; ***– und – naß,*** wet through (and through), wet to the skin; 3. (*time*) ***die ganze Nacht –,*** all (through) the night, the whole night (*see* **durch,** *prep.* 2); ***fünf Uhr –,*** past five o'clock; 4. (*elliptical verb pref. with verb understood*) ***ich muß –,*** I must get through; ***der Zug ist schon –,*** the train has passed through; ***hast du das Buch schon –?*** have you finished the book? ***er ist –,*** he has got through *or* passed (his examination); ***die Hose ist –,*** the trousers are (worn) through *or* worn out; ***bei uns ist er unten –,*** we have finished *or* done *or* we are through with him; ***der Käse ist –,*** the cheese is ripe *or* is in prime condition.

durch–, *verb pref.* (*v.i. sep., v.t. sep. and insep.*) 1. (*passage through*) *e.g.* ***durchdringen,*** penetrate; 2. (*from beginning to end*) *e.g.* ***durchlesen,*** read (through); 3. (*through penetration*) *e.g.* ***durchdringen,*** permeate, pervade; 4. (*thoroughness*) *e.g.* ***durchlüften,*** air *or* ventilate thoroughly. *See examples below.*

Durch–, *pref.* (*usu. to verbal derivatives*) *e.g.* ***Durchreise,*** journey (passing) through. *See examples below.*

durcharbeiten [durç'ʔarbaɪtən], **1.** *v.t.* (*sep.*) work through; work thoroughly, exercise; study thoroughly, make a study of; complete, finish, work out, elaborate, perfect; knead (*dough*). **2.** *v.i.* (*insep.*) work through (*period of time*); (*sep.*) work (through) without stopping *or* without a break. **3.** *v.r.* (*sep.*) work *or* push *or* elbow *or* make one's way through (*a crowd*), work *or* get through (*a task, a book*).

durchaus [durç'aus], *adv.* throughout, thoroughly, quite, altogether, entirely, completely, absolutely, certainly, positively, by all means; ***– nicht,*** by no means, not at all, not in the least; ***weil Sie es – wollen,*** since you insist upon it.

durchbacken ['durçbakən], *irr.v.t.* (*sep.*) bake thoroughly *or* through.

durchbeben [durç'be:bən], *v.t.* (*insep.*) thrill *or* pulsate *or* vibrate through.

durchbeißen [durçbaɪsən], **1.** *irr.v.t.* (*sep.*) bite through (*a rope etc.*); (*insep.*) bite (*a hole etc.*) through. **2.** *irr.v.r.* (*sep.*) fight it out; struggle through.

durchbetteln [durçbɛtəln], **1.** *v.r.* (*sep.*) beg one's way, live by begging. **2.** *v.t.* (*insep.*) wander through (*a place*) begging.

durchbiegen ['durçbi:gən], **1.** *irr.v.t.* (*sep.*) break by bending, bend (*s.th.*) till (it) breaks; bend (*s.th.*) to the limit, bend (*s.th.*) as far as (it) will go. **2.** *irr.v.i.* (*sep.*) (*aux.* s.), *v.r.* (*sep.*) deflect, sag.

Durchbiegung ['durçbi:guŋ], *f.* sag, deflection; curvature (*of lens*).

Durchbinder ['durçbɪndər], *m.* (*Build.*) bond- *or* through-stone, parpen, (*Am.*) perpend.

durchblättern [durçblɛtərn], *v.t.* (*sep. and insep.*) turn the pages of, dip into, glance *or* skim *or* leaf *or* (*Am.*) page through (*a book*).

Durchblick ['durçblɪk], *m.* (**-(e)s,** *pl.* **-e**) view, prospect, vista; glimpse. **durchblicken, 1.** *v.i.* (*sep.*) 1. ***– durch,*** peer *or* look *or* see through (*a gap etc.*); 2. shine *or* peep through, show itself, be apparent; ***– lassen,*** let (*s.th.*) be seen; hint at, intimate, give a hint of. **2.** *v.t.* (*insep.*) penetrate *or* pierce with a look, see through.

durchbohren [durçbo:rən], **1.** *v.t.* (*insep.*) bore *or* pierce through, penetrate; (*sep.*) bore (right) through. **2.** *v.i.* (*sep.*) ***– durch,*** *see v.t.* (*sep.*). **3.** *v.r.* (*sep.*) bore *or* burrow *or* wriggle through.

durchbrechen [durçbrɛçən], **1.** *irr.v.t.* (*sep.*) break (*s.th.*) in two, break (*a hole etc.*) through (*a wall etc.*); (*insep.*) break *or* pierce through, perforate, breach; (*fig.*) violate, infringe. **2.** *irr.v.i.* (*sep.*) (*aux.* s.) break in two *or* apart *or* asunder, break, burst; – ***durch,*** break through *or* out of *or* forth from; break through, appear, come to light, (*of teeth*) erupt, come through; ***durchgebrochene Blinddarmentzündung,*** peritonitis. **Durchbrechung,** *f.* breakthrough; breach, violation, infringement. *See* **Durchbruch, durchbrochen.**

durchbrennen ['durçbrɛnən], **1.** *irr.v.t.* (*sep.*) burn through. **2.** *irr.v.i.* (*sep.*) 1. – ***durch,*** *see* **1**; 2. stay alight, keep burning; 3. (*aux.* s.) burn through; (*Elec.*) burn out (*of a lamp*), blow (*of a fuse*); (*Elec.*) ***durchgebrannt,*** burnt-out (*lamp, coil*), blown (*fuse*); 4. (*aux.* s.) (*fig.*) (*coll.*) abscond, decamp, vamose; elope (*with a lover*).

durchbringen ['durçbrɪŋən], *irr.v.t.* (*sep.*) 1. bring *or* get *or* take *or* carry through; ***die Ärzte hoffen ihn durchzubringen,*** the doctors hope to pull him through; ***eine Gesetzesvorlage* –,** get a bill passed *or* carried; 2. get through, squander, dissipate.

durchbrochen ['durçbrɔxən], *adj.* open-work, filigree, pierced, perforated; *see* **durchbrechen.**

Durchbruch ['durçbrux], *m.* breaking through, opening up (*of passage*), breach, bursting (*of dike etc.*), breakthrough (*of enemy lines, in knowledge etc.*), perforation, rupture (*of ulcer*); gap, opening, aperture; eruption; cutting (*of teeth*); (religious) awakening, revival, change for the better; ***zum – kommen,*** burst forth, break through; ***der – durch die Schallmauer,*** breaking the sound-barrier. **Durchbrucharbeit,** *f.* drawn-thread work; filigree; (*Archit.*) openwork.

durchdacht [durç'daxt], *adj.* carefully thought out; studied, planned; *see* **durchdenken.**

durchdenken [durçdɛŋkən], *irr.v.t.* (*sep.*) think over carefully, reflect on, ponder over; (*insep.*) think out, plan.

durchdrängen ['durçdrɛŋən], *v.r.* (*sep.*) force *or* push (one's way) through.

durchdrehen ['durçdre:ən], **1.** *v.t.* (*sep.*) wring, mangle (*washing*), put through the mangle; mince (*meat etc.*), put through the mincer; grind (*coffee etc.*); (*Av.*) swing (*propeller*), rev up (*the engine*). **2.** *v.i.* (*sep.*) 1. spin (*as wheels*); – ***lassen,*** rev up (*the engine*); 2. have a mental *or* nervous breakdown; (*coll.*) ***vollständig durchgedreht sein,*** be at one's last gasp, be on one's last legs, be on the point of a breakdown; be quite crazy.

durchdringen [durçdrɪŋən], **1.** *irr.v.i.* (*aux.* s.) (*sep.*) force one's way; penetrate; win acceptance (***mit,*** for) (*one's views*); ***diese Meinung ist durchgedrungen,*** this view has prevailed. **2.** *irr.v.t.* (*insep.*) penetrate, pierce; permeate, pervade; ***er ist von Eifersucht durchdrungen,*** he is filled with jealousy. **durchdringend,** *adj.* penetrating, piercing, shrill (*cry*), penetrating, acute, keen, incisive, trenchant (*mind, judgement*). **Durchdringung,** *f.* penetration, permeation, pervasion.

durchdrücken ['durçdrykən], *v.t.* (*sep.*) push *or* squeeze *or* press *or* force through; straighten (the knees) (*in drill*); ***ein Gesetz* –,** carry a bill with difficulty, force a bill through; ***durchgedrückte Hosenbeine,*** baggy trouser legs.

durchdrungen [durç'druŋən], *adj.* filled, pervaded, imbued (***von,*** with), convinced (of).

durcheilen [durç'ʔaɪlən], **1.** *v.i.* (*aux.* s.) (*sep.*) – ***durch,*** hurry through. **2.** *v.t.* (*insep.*) hurry through, pass through in haste.

durcheinander [durçʔaɪn'andər], *adv.* at random, indiscriminately, promiscuously; in confusion *or* disorder, pell-mell; confused, muddled, upside down, topsy-turvy, higgledy-piggledy, at sixes and sevens. **Durcheinander,** *n.* muddle, confusion, disorder, mess(-up), mix-up, (*coll.*) chaos.

durcheinander|bringen, *irr.v.t.* (*sep.*) confuse, make confused, get (*a th.*) into a muddle. **–gehen,** *irr.v.i.* (*aux.* s.) (*sep.*) get (all) mixed up. **–laufen,** *irr.v.i.* (*aux.* s.) (*sep.*) run about in confusion; run (*of colours*). **–schreien,** *irr.v.i.* (*sep.*) (all) be shouting at once. **–trinken,** *irr.v.i.* (*sep.*) mix one's drinks. **–werfen,** *irr.v.t.* (*sep.*) throw into disorder *or* confusion, turn upside down.

durchfahren [durçfa:rən], **1.** *irr.v.i.* (*aux.* s.) (*sep.*) drive *or* go *or* travel *or* pass (straight) through. **2.** *irr.v.t.* (*insep.*) go *or* drive *or* pass *or* travel through *or* across, traverse; (*fig.*) go *or* pass through *or* over (*as emotion*); ***es durchfuhr mich wie ein Blitz,*** it came over me in a flash.

Durchfahrt ['durçfa:rt], *f.* passage *or* journey through; gateway, passage; way through; ***auf der* –,** on the way through; – ***verboten!*** no thoroughfare! **Durchfahrts|höhe,** *f.* headroom (*under bridges*). **–recht,** *n.* right of way.

Durchfall ['durçfal], *m.* 1. falling through; 2. (*Med.*) diarrhoea; 3. failure, (*sl.*) flop (*at examination or theatre*); 4. throughs (*of flour*). **durchfallen,** *irr.v.i.* (*aux.* s.) (*sep.*) fall through; fail, be unsuccessful *or* a failure *or* (*sl.*) a flop, be rejected; (*sl.*) be ploughed (*at examination*).

durchfechten ['durçfɛçtən], **1.** *irr.v.t.* (*sep.*) carry one's point; fight it out *or* it to the end. **2.** *irr.v.r.* (*sep.*) fight one's way through.

durchfeuchten [durç'fɔyçtən], *v.t.* (*insep.*) wet thoroughly, soak, steep.

durchfinden ['durçfɪndən], *irr.v.r.* (*sep.*) find one's way (through); ***sich – durch,*** master (*a problem*).

durchflammen [durç'flamən], *v.t.* (*insep.*) flash through; (*fig.*) inflame, animate, fire.

durchfliegen [durçfli:gən], **1.** *irr.v.i.* (*aux.* s.) (*sep.*) fly (straight) through (*to a place*); (*coll.*) fail, plough (*an examination*). **2.** *irr.v.t.* (*insep.*) fly through *or* across (*a region*), fly *or* race *or* tear *or* rush through; skim through (*a book*); ***ich habe den Brief nur eben durchflogen,*** I have only just glanced through the letter.

durchfließen [durçfli:sən], **1.** *irr.v.i.* (*aux.* s.) (*sep.*) – ***durch,*** flow (right) through. **2.** *irr.v.t.* (*insep.*) (*of river*) flow through. **Durchflußgeschwindigkeit,** *f.* velocity of flow.

durchfluten [durçflu:tən], **1.** *v.t.* (*insep.*) pour *or* flow *or* stream through, flood, inundate. **2.** *v.i.* (*aux.* s.) (*sep.*) flow *or* pour *or* stream *or* flood through.

durchformen ['durçfɔrmən], *v.t.* (*sep.*) develop fully, work out thoroughly; ***durchgeformt,*** fully worked out *or* developed, mature. **Durchformung,** *f.* development.

durchforschen [durçfɔrʃən], *v.t.* 1. (*sep.*) examine thoroughly, investigate, make a thorough inquiry into *or* study of; 2. (*insep.*) search, explore, carry out research into; ***sich*** or ***sein Gewissen* –,** search one's conscience *or* heart. **Durchforschung,** *f.* search, inquiry, exploration, research.

durchforsten [durç'fɔrstən], *v.t.* (*insep.*) thin (out) (*a forest*).

durchfressen [durçfrɛsən], **1.** *irr.v.t.* (*sep.*) eat *or* gnaw through; (*insep.*) corrode. **2.** *irr.v.r.* (*sep.*) (*coll.*) manage on what one can pick up; (*coll.*) ***sich – durch,*** work *or* plod one's way through (*a task*), wade *or* plough through (*a book*).

durchfrieren [durçfri:rən], *irr.v.t.* (*insep.*) & *v.i.* (*aux.* s.) (*sep.*) (*usu. p.p.*) ***durchfroren*** or ***durchgefroren,*** frozen stiff, chilled to the marrow, perished with cold.

Durchfuhr ['durçfu:r], *f.* (-, *pl.* **-en**) transit (*of goods*).

durchführbar ['durçfy:rba:r], *adj.* practicable, feasible, workable, possible. **Durchführbarkeit,** *f.* practicability, feasibility.

durchführen ['durçfy:rən], *v.t.* (*sep.*) convey, bring *or* take *or* lead through; accomplish, realize, carry out *or* through, execute; enforce (*a law*), follow through (*train of thought*), act out (*a part*); (*Mus.*) develop (*a theme*).

Durchfuhrhandel ['durçfu:rhandəl], *m.* transit trade.

Durchführung ['durçfy:ruŋ], *f.* conveyance (*of goods*) through; laying, extension (*of lines, pipes, wires etc.*); accomplishment; execution, performance, realization; enforcement (*of law*), (*Mus.*) development.

Durchfuhrzoll ['durçfu:rtsɔl], *m.* transit tariff *or* duty.

durchfurcht [durç'furçt], *adj.* furrowed, wrinkled.

Durchgabe ['durçga:bə], *f.* 1. transmission, broadcast (*of radio programme*), announcement, release, circulation (*of news*), dictation, delivery by telephone (*of a telegram*); 2. (service) hatch.

Durchgang ['durçgaŋ], *m.* passage through, transit (*of goods*), thoroughfare, way through, gangway, aisle, passage, passage-way, opening; (*Railw.*) corridor; (*Mus.*) passing note; (*Astr.*) transit; (*fig.*) transition; ***freier* –,** open thoroughfare; ***– verboten!*** no through road!

Durchgänger ['durçgɛŋər], *m.* runaway horse, horse liable to bolt; runaway, absconder; (*fig.*) hothead. **durchgängig, 1.** *adj.* general, universal; prevailing, constant, continual. **2.** *adv.* generally, universally, without exception, at all points.

Durchgangs|handel, *m.* transit trade. **–lager,** *n.* transit camp. **–stadium,** *n.* transition stage *or* period. **–station,** *f.* (*Rail v.*) through station; intermediate station. *See also* **–stadium. –straße,** *f.* through road, thoroughfare. **–ton,** *m.* (*Mus.*) passing note. **–verkehr,** *m.* transit(-trade), through traffic. **–wagen,** *m.* through carriage, (*Am.*) vestibule car. **–zimmer,** *n.* anteroom, vestibule. **–zug** (*abbr.* **D-Zug**), *m.* through *or* express train; corridor *or* (*Am.*) vestibule train.

durchgeben ['durçge:bən], *irr.v.t.* (*sep.*) pass *or* hand on, circulate (*message*), make (*an announcement*), transmit, broadcast (*radio programme*); ***telephonisch* –,** (send by) telephone, dictate over the phone (*a message, telegram*), (*of the operator*) deliver (*telegram*) over the phone.

durchgehen [durçge:ən], **1.** *irr.v.i.* (*aux.* s.) (*sep.*) 1. go *or* walk *or* pass through, go across, cross, (*of goods*) be transported through, be in transit, (*Astr.*) transit, (*of water*) come *or* soak through, penetrate, (*of trains*) go right *or* straight through, (*Parl. etc.*) go through, be passed *or* adopted *or* accepted; ***– lassen,*** let pass, overlook, shut one's eyes to, (*coll.*) let (*s.o.*) get away with; 2. run away, elope, (*of a husband or wife*) go *or* run off; get out of control; ***ihm geht alles durch,*** he carries everything off, he is always lucky *or* successful; ***das geht (mit) durch, das mag so mit* –,** that may pass. **2.** *irr.v.t.* (*sep.*) (*aux.* h. *&* s.) look *or* run *or* go *or* read over *or* through, examine, peruse, check; (*aux.* h.) wear out (*shoes etc.*); (*sep.* (*aux.* s.) *and insep.* (*aux.* h.)) go *or* walk (right) through. **durchgehend,** *adj.* continuous, uninterrupted, (*goods*) in transit, (*train, ticket etc.*) through. **durchgehends,** *adv.* all *or* right through, from beginning to end, from start to finish; without exception, universally, generally, altogether.

durchglühen [durçgly:ən], **1.** *v.i.* (*aux.* s.) (*sep.*) burn out (*of electric lamp*). **2.** *v.t.* (*sep.*) make red-hot, heat thoroughly *or* through; (*insep.*) (*fig.*) make glow, fire, enthuse, inflame, inspire.

durchgreifen ['durçgraɪfən], *irr.v.i.* (*sep.*) 1. proceed without ceremony, take (decisive *or* vigorous) action, take drastic steps, take drastic *or* strong measures, act effectively; 2. put *or* reach one's hand through, reach through. **durchgreifend,** *adj.* vigorous, strong, energetic, drastic, decisive, effective, far-reaching, sweeping.

durchhalten ['durçhaltən], **1.** *irr.v.t.* (*sep.*) keep up, maintain. **2.** *irr.v.i.* (*sep.*) carry on to the end, hold out, (*coll.*) stick it out.

Durchhang ['durçhaŋ], *m.* dip, sag (*of a wire*).

durchhängen ['durçhɛŋən], *v.t.* (*sep.*) sag, dip.

durchhauen ['durçhauən], **1.** *irr.v.t.* (*sep.*) hew *or* cut through; knock a hole through; (*coll.*) ***ihn* –,** give him a sound thrashing. **2.** *irr.v.r.* (*sep.*) hack one's way through. **3.** *irr.v.i.* (*aux.* s.) (*sep.*) (*coll.*) blow (*of a fuse*).

durchhecheln ['durçhɛçəln], *v.t.* (*sep.*) hackle, heckle (*flax*), (*fig.*) pick *or* pull to pieces.

durchhelfen ['durçhɛlfən], *irr.v.i.* (*sep.*) (*Dat.*) help (out of a difficulty), help through (*a difficulty, a window*); ***sich* (*Dat.*) –,** manage, get by (***mit,*** on).

Durchhieb ['durçhi:p], *m.* cutting, clearing, passage (*in a wood*).

durchirren [durç'ɪrən], *v.t.* (*insep.*) wander through *or* over.

durchkämmen ['durçkɛmən], *v.t.* (*sep.*) comb (*hair*), comb, search (***nach,*** for).

durchkämpfen [durçkɛmpfən], **1.** *v.t.* (*sep.*) fight out (*a battle*) (to the end), come through (victorious); (*insep.*) continue fighting *or* struggling for (*a period*), fight *or* struggle through. **2.** *v.r.* (*sep.*) fight one's way, struggle *or* battle through, overcome; ***eine Idee muß sich erst* –,** an idea must first get itself established *or* accepted.

durchkauen ['durçkauən], *v.t.* (*sep.*) chew thoroughly; (*coll.*) chew over (*a problem, a book*).

durchkommen ['durçkɔmən], *irr.v.i.* (*aux.* s.) (*sep.*) come *or* pass *or* get through; pass, get through (*examinations*); come *or* pull through (*illness*), come *or* soak through (*as damp*), (*fig.*) appear, show *or* reveal itself, be apparent; ***mit seiner Einnahme* –,** make both ends meet, get by *or* manage on one's income; ***mit Lügen kommt man nicht durch,*** lies won't get you anywhere, you won't get away with lying; ***mit diesen Ausflüchten kommst du bei mir nicht durch,*** these excuses cut no ice with me; ***mit ihm* –,** achieve one's ends with him.

durchkosten ['durçkɔstən], *v.t.* (*sep.*) taste, savour, enjoy, run the gamut of.

durchkreuzen [durç'krɔytsən], *v.t.* (*insep.*) travel across *or* over, cross, traverse; (*fig.*) foil, frustrate, cross, thwart; ***sich*** or ***einander* –,** cross (one another), intersect.

Durchlaß ['durçlas], *m.* **(-(ss)es,** *pl.* **¨(ss)e)** 1. passage, way through, gap, opening, inlet, outlet; 2. check-point, control post; 3. culvert; 4. sieve, filter. **durchlassen,** *irr.v.t.* (*sep.*) let through, permit *or* allow to pass; let through (*as a sieve*), transmit (*light etc.*). **durchlässig,** *adj.* pervious, porous, permeable (***für,*** to). **Durchlaßkreis,** *m.* (*Rad.*) acceptor circuit.

Durchlaucht ['durçlauxt], *f.* (-, *pl.* **-en**) (Serene) Highness; ***Ew.*** (= ***Euer***) – (*m.*), ***Ihre*** – (*f.*), Your Highness. **durchlaucht(ig),** *adj.* serene, illustrious, august.

durchlaufen [durçlaufən], **1.** *irr.v.i.* (*aux.* s.) (*sep.*) run *or* pass through *or* across, traverse, (*of a road*) run right *or* straight through; (*of water*) filter *or* seep *or* percolate *or* run through. **2.** *irr.v.t.* **(a)** (*sep.*) 1. wear out (*shoes etc.*); ***durchgelaufene Schuhe,*** shoes worn into holes; 2. (*aux.* s.) run through (*streets etc.*); **(b)** (*insep.*) 1. go *or* run *or* pass *or* travel through *or* across (*an area*), cover, traverse (*a distance*); ***es durchläuft mich kalt,*** a cold shudder goes through me; ***ein Gerücht durchläuft die Stadt,*** a report is going about the town; ***alle Läden* –,** hunt through all the shops; (*Naut.*) ***–e Strecke,*** ship's run; 2. run *or* go *or* look over *or* through hurriedly, examine *or* peruse hastily, skim over. **durchlaufend,** *adj.* continuous.

durchlesen ['durçle:zən], *irr.v.t.* (*sep.*) read through *or* over, peruse.

durchleuchten [durçlɔyçtən], **1.** *v.i.* (*sep.*) shine through, (*fig.*) be apparent. **2.** *v.t.* (*insep.*) fill *or* flood with light, light (up), illuminate, irradiate; test (*eggs etc.*) with a strong light, (*Med.*) X-ray, (*fig.*) probe into, investigate. **Durchleuchtung,** *f.* illumination; X-ray examination; (*fig.*) investigation (of), examination (of *or* into). **Durchleuchtungs|schirm,** *m.* fluorescent screen. **–verfahren,** *n.* radioscopy.

durchliegen ['durçli:gən], *irr.v.r.* (*sep.*) get bedsores.

durchlochen [durç'lɔxən], *v.t.* (*insep.*) punch (*tickets*).

durchlöchern [durç'lœçərn], *v.t.* (*insep.*) perforate, pierce, puncture; (*coll.*) render meaningless (*laws etc.*).

durchlüften [durçlyftən], *v.i.* (*sep.*), *v.t.* (*insep.*) ventilate, air.

durchmachen ['durçmaxən], *v.t.* (*sep.*) 1. finish, accomplish; 2. go *or* pass through, experience, undergo, suffer; ***er hat viel durchgemacht,*** he has been through a good deal, he has had a hard time.
Durchmarsch ['durçmarʃ], *m.* 1. passage of troops; 2. getting all the tricks (*at cards*); 3. (*coll.*) diarrhoea. **durchmarschieren,** *v.i.* (*aux.* s.) (*sep.*) march through. (*N.B. p.p.* ***durchmarschiert.***)
durchmessen [durçmɛsən], *irr.v.t.* 1. (*insep.*) traverse, travel through *or* over *or* across, cover (*distance*), pass from end to end of; ***die Lebensbahn ist bald –,*** life's measure is soon run; 2. (*sep.*) measure in all directions, take the dimension of. **Durchmesser,** *m.* diameter; (*Artil.*) calibre.
durchmustern [durçmustərn], *v.t.* (*insep. & sep.*) pass in review, inspect, examine, scrutinize, scan.
durchnässen [durçnɛsən], **1.** *v.i.* (*sep.*) let the wet soak through. **2.** *v.t.* (*insep.*) wet thoroughly, drench, soak, steep, saturate; ***wir kamen ganz durchnäßt heim,*** we got home soaked *or* wet through *or* absolutely drenched.
durchnehmen ['durçne:mən], *irr.v.t.* (*sep.*) examine, analyse, go through, do (*s.th. with a p.*); discuss.
durchpausen ['durçpauzən], *v.t.* (*sep.*) trace, copy, transfer.
durchprügeln ['durçpry:gəln], *v.t.* (*sep.*) beat *or* thrash (soundly).
durchqueren [durç'kve:rən], *v.t* (*insep.*) traverse, cross, travel across, (*fig.*) frustrate, thwart.
durchrasen [durçra:zən], *v.i.* (*aux.* s.) (*sep.*), *v.t.* (*insep.*) rush, dash, tear *or* race furiously through *or* over.
durchrasseln ['durchrasəln], *v.i.* (*aux.* s.) (*sep.*) (*sl.*) fail in an examination.
durchregnen [durçre:gnən], **1.** *v.imp.* (*sep.*) rain through *or* in; ***es regnet hier durch,*** it rains in here; ***es regnete die ganzen Ferien durch,*** it rained all (through) the holidays. **2.** *occ. v.t.* (*insep.*) ***wir waren alle völlig durchregnet,*** we were all drenched to the skin.
Durchreiche ['durçraiçə], *f.* (service) hatch. **durchreichen,** *v.t.* (*sep.*) hand round; pass through.
Durchreise ['durçraizə], *f.* journey through *or* across, passage, transit; ***ich bin nur auf der –,*** I am merely passing through *or* on the way through. **durchreisen, 1.** *v.i.* (*aux.* s.) (*sep.*) travel *or* go *or* drive *or* pass through. **2.** *v.t.* (*insep.*) travel over *or* through *or* across *or* from end to end, traverse. **Durchreisende(r),** *m., f.* traveller, p. travelling *or* passing through, (*Am.*) transient; through passenger (*on train*). **Durchreisevisum,** *n.* transit visa.
durchreißen [durçraisən], **1.** *irr.v.t.* (*insep. and sep.*) tear up *or* in two, jerk (*the trigger*). **2.** *irr.v.i.* (*aux.* s.) (*sep.*) break, tear, get torn.
durchrieseln [durçri:zəln], **1.** *v.t.* (*insep.*) trickle through; (*fig.*) pervade. **2.** *v.i.* (*sep.*) trickle through.
durchringen ['durçrɪŋən], *irr.v.t.* (*sep.*) fight one's way *or* struggle through; ***er ringt sich zu der Überzeugung durch,*** he reaches conviction after a struggle.
durchrühren ['durçry:rən], *v.t.* (*sep.*) stir up well, agitate; strain.
durchs [durçs] = ***durch das.***
durchsacken ['durçzakən], *v.i.* (*sep.*) (*aux.* s.) sag, (*Av.*) pancake.
Durchsage ['durçza:gə], *f.* (*Rad. etc.*) announcement, message. **durchsagen,** *v.t.* (*sep.*) (*Rad.*) announce, broadcast (*on the radio*), make (*an announcement on the radio*), say (*over the phone, on the radio*), dictate (*a telegram*) over the phone; ***die Nachrichten –,*** read the news (*on the radio*).
durchschaubar ['durçʃauba:r], *adj.* obvious, easily discoverable *or* detectable; transparent (*trick*); ***schwer –,*** puzzling, enigmatic.
durchschauen [durçʃauən], **1.** *v.i., v.t.* (*sep.*) see through, look through. *See* **durchsehen. 2.** *v.t.* (*insep.*) (*fig.*) see through, detect (*motives etc.*), penetrate, understand, grasp, see into the heart of, know the secret behind; know where one is with (*a p.*), know what (*s.o.*) is up to; ***ich durchschaue seine Kniffe,*** I see through his game, I am wise to his tricks.
durchscheinen [durçʃainən], **1.** *irr.v.i.* (*sep.*) shine through; show through, be visible through, (*fig.*) be seen, become apparent *or* evident. **2.** *irr.v.t.* (*insep.*) shine through, light up, illuminate, fill *or* flood with light. **durchscheinend,** *adj.* transparent, translucent, diaphanous.
durchschießen ['durçʃi:sən], **1.** *irr.v.i.* (*sep.*) shoot *or* fire through (*a window etc.*); (*aux.* s.) dash *or* race *or* shoot *or* fly through. **2.** *irr.v.t.* (*insep.*) riddle with bullets; (*of ideas*) flash through (*the mind*); (*Typ.*) space (out), set out, lead (*lines*), interleave (*book*); (*Weav.*) interweave; ***durchschossen,*** riddled with bullets; leaded (*type*), interleaved (*book*), (*fabric*) interwoven ***(mit,*** with), (*fig.*) shot through (with) (*light etc.*).
durchschimmern [durçʃɪmərn], *v.i.* (*sep.*), *v.t.* (*insep.*) glitter *or* glisten *or* glimmer *or* shimmer *or* gleam *or* shine through, be dimly visible through.
durchschlafen [durçʃla:fən], **1.** *irr.v.t.* (*insep.*) sleep through (*the night*), sleep (*the night*) through. **2.** *irr.v.i.* (*sep.*) sleep right through *or* without waking *or* without interruption.
Durchschlag ['durçʃla:k], *m.* 1. strainer, colander; 2. carbon copy; 3. driving-punch; 4. (*Min.*) cutting, driving (*a tunnel*). **durchschlagen, 1.** *irr.v.t.* (*insep.*) make *or* knock a hole through, break through, penetrate; break down (*door*), smash (*window*); (*sep.*) make an opening in, knock a hole through; knock (*a bolt etc.*) right through; break through (*opponent's guard*); strain, sieve, pass *or* rub through a sieve; make a carbon copy of (*on typewriter*). **2.** *irr.v.i.* (*sep.*) come *or* go through, penetrate; (*fig.*) prove convincing, (*coll.*) tell; be successful *or* effective; have a telling effect, take effect (*of medicines*); (*of characteristics*) come *or* show through, appear, be apparent; ***der eine Typus schlägt im Mischling durch,*** in the hybrid one type is dominant. **3.** *irr.v.r.* (*sep.*) fight one's way through (*an enemy*); struggle through; fend for o.s., manage, (*coll.*) get by *or* along; ***sich kümmerlich –,*** live from hand to mouth, manage to make ends meet; ***–der Erfolg,*** signal *or* outstanding success. **Durchschläger,** *m.* driving-punch. **Durchschlagpapier,** *n.* 1. carbon paper; 2. copy paper.
Durchschlags|festigkeit, *f.* (*Elec.*) dielectric strength. **–kraft,** *f.* 1. (*Artil.*) penetration, penetrating power; 2. force (*of an argument*). **–spannung,** *f.* (*Elec.*) breakdown voltage. **–vermögen,** *n. See* **–kraft,** 1.
durchschleichen ['durçʃlaiçən], *irr.v.i.* (*aux.* s.), *v.r.* (*sep.*) sneak *or* creep *or* slip *or* steal through.
durchschleusen ['durçʃlɔyzən], *v.t.* (*sep.*) pass (*ship*) through a lock, (*coll.*) pass (*people*) through (*control point etc.*), pour (*troops etc.*) through a gap.
Durchschlupf ['durçʃlupf], *m.* way through, (*coll.*) bolt-hole; (*fig.*) way out (*of difficulties*).
durchschlüpfen ['durçʃlypfən], *v.i.* (*aux.* s.) (*sep.*) slip through; escape *or* pass unnoticed.
durchschneiden [durçʃnaidən], *irr.v.t.* 1. (*sep.*) cut through *or* across; ***man kann die Luft mit einem Messer –,*** you can cut the air with a knife; 2. (*insep.*) cut through *or* in two; divide in(to) two, bisect, intersect; cut (through) (*a knot*), (*fig.*) pierce (*Dat.*, s.o.'s) (*heart*), pierce (*Dat.*, s.o.) (*to the heart*); ***sich*** or ***einander –,*** intersect, cross. **Durchschneidung,** *f.* bisection, intersection.
Durchschnitt ['durçʃnɪt], *m.* 1. cut, section; cross-section, profile; (*Railw.*) cutting; ***– eines Gebäudes,*** section of a building; 2. average, mean; ***im –,*** on the average. **durchschnittlich, 1.** *adj.* average, normal, ordinary. **2.** *adv.* on an average. **Durchschnitts–,** *pref.* average, mean. **Durchschnitts|leistung,** *f.* mediocre achievement. **–mensch,** *m.* ordinary person, common man, man in the street.

durchschossen [durç'ʃɔsən], *see* **durchschießen.**
durchschreiben ['durçʃraɪbən], *irr.v.t.* (*sep.*) make a (carbon) copy of.
durchschreiten [durçʃraɪtən], **1.** *irr.v.i.* (*aux.* s.) (*sep.*) stride through. **2.** *irr.v.t.* (*insep.*) cross, traverse, walk *or* pace *or* stride across, (*fig.*) cover (*a whole range of knowledge*).
Durchschrift ['durçʃrɪft], *f.* carbon copy.
Durchschuß ['durçʃus], *m.* 1. gunshot wound that passes right through; 2. (*Weav.*) woof, weft; 3. (*Typ.*) interleaved sheet; spacing, setting out (*of type*), leading out (*of lines*). **Durchschußmaterial,** *n.* (*Typ.*) leads.
durchschweifen [durç'ʃvaɪfən], *v.t.* (*insep.*) wander through *or* across *or* over, range *or* rove *or* roam over *or* across.
durchsegeln [durçze:gəln], **1.** *v.i.* (*aux.* s.) (*sep.*) sail *or* navigate through; (*coll.*) fail, be ploughed (*in an examination*). **2.** *v.t.* (*insep.*) sail over *or* across (*the sea*).
durchsehen ['durçze:ən], **1.** *irr.v.i.* (*sep.*) see *or* look through; (*of a th.*) show *or* peep through, be able to be seen through; (*fig.*) – ***durch,*** see clearly, make head or tail of, grasp the meaning of *or* the reason for (*s.th.*), see through (*a p.*), read (*a p.*) like a book. **2.** *irr.v.t.* (*sep.*) look *or* search through; look *or* go through *or* over, examine, scrutinize, revise, correct (*exercises etc.*).
durchseihen ['durçzaɪən], *v.t.* (*sep.*) strain, filter, percolate. **Durchseihung,** *f.* filtration.
durchsetzen [durçzɛtsən], **1.** *v.t.* 1. (*sep.*) sift, sieve, screen, riddle, size (*ore*); accomplish, carry *or* put through, carry out, achieve, bring about, succeed with *or* in; get accepted *or* adopted; ***bei ihm –,*** succeed in persuading him, prevail upon *or* induce him; 2. (*insep.*) intersperse; penetrate, permeate, pervade; ***durchsetzt sein mit,*** be mixed *or* interspersed with, be full of. **2.** *v.r.* (*sep.*) (*of a p.*) make one's way, be successful; get one's (own) way; hold one's own; (*of a th.*) be *or* become (generally) accepted *or* adopted, gain acceptance.
Durchsicht ['durçzɪçt], *f.* 1. perusal, examination, inspection, correction (*of exercises etc.*); 2. vista, view. **durchsichtig,** *adj.* clear, transparent, pellucid, diaphanous, (*fig.*) clear, lucid (*style*), transparent (*intentions*). **Durchsichtigkeit,** *f.* transparency; transparence, clearness; (*fig.*) clarity, lucidity, perspicuity. **Durchsichtssucher,** *m.* (*Phot.*) direct (vision) view-finder.
durchsickern ['durçzɪkərn], *v.i.* (*aux.* s.) (*sep.*) leak *or* drip *or* filter *or* seep *or* ooze, percolate *or* trickle through; (*fig.*) leak out, (*coll.*) trickle through (*as news etc.*).
durchsieben ['durçzi:bən], *v.t.* (*sep.*) sift, sieve, pass through a sieve; screen, riddle (*ore*), garble, bolt (*flour*).
durchsitzen ['durçzɪtsən], *irr.v.t.* (*sep.*) 1. wear out (*trousers etc.*) by sitting, wear through; 2. sit through (*a lecture*), sit (*a lecture*) out *or* through; ***die Nacht –,*** sit up all night, (*Parl.*) sit all night.
durchspielen ['durçʃpi:lən], *v.t.* (*sep.*) play through *or* over (*music, part in a play etc.*); spend (*all the time*) playing.
durchsprechen ['durçʃprɛçən], *irr.v.t.* (*sep.*) talk over, discuss thoroughly.
durchstechen [durçʃtɛçən], **1.** *irr.v.i.* (*sep.*) 1. (*of needle etc.*) stick *or* be sticking through; 2. (*obs.*) be in league *or* collusion. **2.** *irr.v.t.* (*sep.*) stick (*needle etc.*) through, pierce, perforate, prick, stab; pounce (*a pattern of perforations*); (*insep.*) transfix, pierce (through), run through (*with spear etc.*); puncture, prick holes in; cut *or* dig through (*a bank of earth etc.*); ***durchstochen,*** perforated, rouletted (*of postage stamps*). **Durchstecherei** [–'raɪ], *f.* (*obs.*) plotting, intrigue; – ***treiben,*** play into each other's hands. **Durchstechung,** *f.* piercing, perforation; perforation (*of postage stamps*).
durchstehen ['durçʃte:ən], **1.** *irr.v.i.* (*sep.*) continue standing, have to stand all the time, *or* all the journey *etc.* **2.** *irr.v.t.* (*sep.*) go *or* come through (*danger, difficulties*).
Durchstich ['durçʃtɪç], *m.* cutting, driving (*tunnel etc.*); (railway) cutting, tunnel; canal, ditch, (*coll.*) cut; perforation, roulette (*of postage stamps*).
durchstöbern [durç'ʃtø:bərn], *v.t.* (*insep.*) ransack; search *or* hunt *or* rummage through.
Durchstoß ['durçʃto:s], *m.* 1. (*Mil.*) breakthrough; 2. (*Mech.*) mechanical punch, punching machine. **durchstoßen, 1.** *irr.v.i.* (*sep.*) – ***durch,*** knock a hole through, (*Mil.*) break through, pierce, penetrate (*enemy's lines*). **2.** *irr.v.t.* (*sep.*) push *or* thrust through, wear a hole in (*socks etc.*), knock a hole in, knock in two, (*insep.*) transfix, pierce through (*with sword etc.*), stab; knock *or* make a hole in *or* through.
durchstreichen [durçʃtraɪçən], **1.** *irr.v.t.* 1. (*sep.*) strike *or* cross out, delete, cancel; 2. (*insep.*) roam *or* rove *or* wander through *or* over *or* across. **2.** *irr.v.i.* (*aux.* s.) (*sep.*) pass through (*as migratory birds*); ***–de Linie,*** trajectory (*of a comet*).
durchstreifen [durç'ʃtraɪfən], *v.t.* (*insep.*) roam *or* rove *or* wander *or* range through *or* all over.
durchströmen [durçʃtrø:mən], **1.** *v.t.* (*insep.*) flow *or* run through; (*fig.*) ***mich durchströmte ein freudiges Gefühl,*** a feeling of delight flooded through me. **2.** *v.i.* (*aux.* s.) (*sep.*) stream *or* pour through.
durchsuchen [durçzu:xən], *v.t.* (*sep. and insep.*) search *or* (*coll.*) go through (*a drawer, papers etc.*), search, scour (*an area*) (***nach,*** for); ***gerichtlich –,*** search under warrant. **Durchsuchung,** *f.* search, examination (*baggage etc.*); (police) raid.
durchtränken [durç'trɛŋkən], *v.t.* (*insep.*) impregnate, saturate, soak (***mit,*** with); (*fig.*) ***durchtränkt von*** or ***mit,*** filled with, steeped in.
durchtreiben ['durçtraɪbən], *irr.v.t.* (*sep.*) drive through (*a peg, cattle etc.*); (*fig.*) push *or* force through (*a plan*).
durchtrennen ['durçtrɛnən], *v.t.* (*sep.*) split, divide, cut in half *or* two.
durchtreten ['durçtre:tən], **1.** *irr.v.t.* (*sep.*) tread through, put one's foot through, wear out (*shoes etc.*); tread (*grapes*); ***sich*** (*Dat.*) ***die Füße –,*** develop fallen arches. **2.** *irr.v.i.* (*sep.*) (*aux.* s.) (*of a p.*) go *or* walk *or* step through, (*of water*) pass through, (*of a th.*) come *or* stick through, protrude; (*aux.* h.) pedal hard, stand on the pedals. *See* **Durchtritt.**
durchtrieben [durç'tri:bən], *adj.* sly, artful, cunning, crafty, wily. **Durchtriebenheit,** *f.* artfulness, cunning, craftiness, slyness, guile.
Durchtritt ['durçtrɪt], *m.* passage.
durchwachen [durç'vaxən], **1.** *v.t.* (*insep.*) stay awake *or* keep watch through (*the night*); ***durchwachte Nächte,*** sleepless nights. **2.** *v.i.* (*sep.*) lie awake, sit *or* stay up (*all night*).
durchwachsen [durçvaxsən], **1.** *irr.v.i.* (*aux.* s.) (*sep.*), *irr.v.t.* (*insep.*) grow through. **2.** *adj.* (*Bot.*) perfoliate; marbled, streaky (*of meat*). **Durchwachsung,** *f.* (*Bot.*) diaphysis.
durchwandern [durçvandərn], *v.i.* (*aux.* s.) (*sep.*) – ***durch*** & *v.t.* (*insep.*) wander *or* walk *or* hike *or* go *or* pass *or* travel through.
durchwärmen [durçvɛrmən], *v.t.* (*sep. and insep.*) warm through *or* thoroughly.
durchwaten [durçva:tən], *v.i.* (*aux.* s.) (*sep.*), *v.t.* (*insep.*) wade through, ford.
Durchweg ['durçve:k, –'vɛk], *m.* thoroughfare, way through, passage (through).
durchweg ['durçvɛk], *adv.* from beginning to end, all through, throughout, altogether; without exception, consistently, always, ordinarily. **durchwegs** [–'ve:ks], *adv.* (*dial.*) *see* **durchweg.**
durchwetzen ['durçvɛtsən], *v.t.* (*sep.*) wear through, wear a hole in (*trousers etc.*).
durchwirken [durçvɪrkən], *v.t.* (*insep.*) interweave, weave in with; (*sep.*) knead *or* work (*dough*) thoroughly.
durchwühlen [durçvy:lən], **1.** *v.t.* (*sep. and insep.*) root *or* burrow through; rummage through *or* among, ransack, turn over; (*insep.*) (*fig.*) (*of emotions etc.*) upset, convulse; ***durchwühlt,*** torn, in a

turmoil. **2.** *v.r.* (*sep.*) work *or* burrow one's way through.

Durchwurf ['durçvurf], *m.* screen, sieve, riddle.

durchzählen ['durçtsɛ:lən], **1.** *v.t.* (*sep.*) count (over *or* up). **2.** *v.i.* (*Mil.*) number (off).

durchzechen [durçtsɛçən], *v.t.* (*insep.*), *v.i.* (*sep.*) drink *or* carouse (*the night etc.*) through; pass in carousing; ***eine durch(ge)zechte Nacht,*** a night spent in carousal.

durchzeichnen ['durçtsaıçnən], *v.t.* (*sep.*) trace, make a tracing of.

durchziehen [durçtsi:ən], **1.** *irr.v.t.* 1. (*sep.*) draw *or* drag *or* pull through; (*Av.*) pull out of a dive; pass through (*a hole*), thread (*needles*); 2. (*insep.*) go *or* travel through, pass *or* run *or* flow through, traverse, cross, penetrate, intersect; (*fig.*) run through, fill, pervade, permeate, intersperse (***mit,*** with); interweave, interlace; ***mit Gräben –,*** cover with trenches. **2.** *irr.v.i.* 1. (*aux.* s.) (*sep.*) go *or* come *or* pass *or* march through; 2. (*aux.* h.) (*sep.*) be absorbed, soak well in, (*of tea etc.*) draw; ***– lassen,*** simmer till cooked. **3.** *irr.v.r.* (*sep.*) *see* **1,** 1. **Durchzieher(hieb),** *m.* (*Fenc.*) hit. **Durchziehglas,** *n.* slide (*in microscopes*).

durchzittern [durç'tsıtərn], *v.t.* (*insep.*) 1. spend (*night etc.*) shivering; 2. tremble through, vibrate through, (*fig.*) thrill (through).

durchzogen [durçtso:gən], *adj.* *See* **durchziehen.**

durchzucken [durç'tsukən], *v.t.* (*insep.*) give a sudden shock to, vibrate, thrill, convulse; flash through.

Durchzug ['durçtsu:k], *m.* 1. march *or* passage through; way *or* journey through; 2. circulation, through draught; 3. passage, (*Archit.*) architrave; 4. hem for elastic; 5. (*rowing*) stroke (*of oar*).

durchzwängen ['durçtsvɛŋən], *v.t.*, *v.r.* (*sep.*) force *or* squeeze through.

Durdreiklang ['durdraıklaŋ], *m.* (*Mus.*) major triad.

dürfen ['dyrfən], *irr.v. aux.* **(a)** 1. *pres. tense* (*permissive*) may, might; (*possibility dependent on external factors*) be allowed *or* permitted to; ***wenn ich bitten darf,*** if you please; ***darf ich rauchen? Ja, das dürfen Sie,*** may *or* might I smoke? Yes, you may; 2. *past tense* be allowed *or* permitted to; ***früher durfte ich es nicht*** or ***früher habe ich es nicht gedurft,*** previously I have not been *or* I was not permitted to; (N.B. might *is rarely used as past tense of* may; *it is unambiguous in indirect speech, e.g.* ***er sagte, daß ich rauchen durfte,*** he said I might smoke; *and in conjectures, cf.* **(c)** *below*); **(b)** ***nicht –,*** must not (*all tenses*), not be allowed *or* permitted to (*necessary if defective* must *does not sufficiently render past tense*; (N.B. *simple negation of permission* may not *rarely used to negate the situation permitted by* may, *except in contrasted phrases, e.g.* ***du darfst mich mit Wilhelm aber du darfst mich nicht mit Willi anreden,*** you may call me William but you may not call me Willy; ***darf ich dich küssen? Nein, das darfst du nicht!*** may I kiss you? No, you may not!) **(c)** *imperf. subj.* ***dürfte*** 1. *indicating conjecture,* might, could; ***ich meine, auch ich dürfte mich einmal freuen,*** I think that even I might *or* could enjoy myself for once; ***wenn ich immer solche Gnade genießen dürfte!*** if I might *or* could only enjoy such favour. *Also with compound tense of predicated inf.* ***er dürfte kaum daran gedacht haben,*** he would scarcely have thought of that; (N.B. *compound tense of aux. with simple inf. has to be rendered simply by aux. with perf. inf., e.g.* ***hätte ich das nicht erwarten –?*** might I not have *or* ought I not to have expected that?) 2. *frequently as polite or hesitant affection*; ***es dürfte sich erübrigen,*** it would seem to be superfluous, it is probably not necessary; ***jetzt dürfte es zu spät sein,*** now it will probably be too late; **(d)** *p.p.* ***gedurft*** (*only used when there is no predicated inf.*) been allowed *or* permitted to (*cf. example of perf. tense under* **(a)** *above*).

dürftig ['dyrftıç], *adj.* (*of a th.*) poor, miserable, wretched, mean, bare, shabby, sorry; paltry, meagre, barren, scanty, (*coll.*) sketchy; (*of a p.*) (*obs., Poet.*) *see* **bedürftig. Dürftigkeit,** *f.* poverty, wretchedness, meanness, shabbiness, bareness; paltriness, meagreness, scantiness, barrenness.

dürr [dyr], *adj.* (*of land*) barren, arid, parched; (*of a p.*) lean, thin, skinny, gaunt, spare, emaciated, (*coll.*) scraggy; (*of leaves*) dry, dead, withered; ***–e Worte,*** straightforward *or* stark *or* plain *or* blunt language. **Dürre,** *f.* drought; dryness, barrenness, infertility, sterility; thinness, leanness, gauntness. **Dürr|futter,** *n.* dry fodder, hay. **–kraut,** *n.*, **–wurz,** *f.* (*Bot.*) fleabane.

Durst [durst], *m.* 1. thirst; ***– bekommen,*** get thirsty; ***– haben,*** be *or* feel thirsty *or* (*coll.*) dry; (***an***) ***– leiden,*** be thirsty, suffer (from) thirst; ***diese Arbeit macht –,*** this work makes you thirsty, (*coll.*) this is thirsty work; ***an – sterben,*** die of thirst; (*fig.*) ***vor – sterben,*** be dying of thirst, be very thirsty; 2. (*fig.*) thirst, craving, burning desire (***nach,*** for). **dursten** (*occ.* **dürsten**), *v.i.* go thirsty, (*Poet.*) thirst. **dürsten** (*occ.* **dursten**), *v.i.*, *v.imp.* ***mich dürstet,*** I am thirsty; (*fig.*) ***– nach,*** thirst, crave, be thirsting *or* (*Poet.*) athirst for. **durstig,** *adj.* thirsty; (*fig.*) thirsting, craving, eager (***nach,*** for). **Durstigkeit,** *f.* thirstiness. **durst|löschend, –stillend,** *adj.* thirst-quenching.

Durtonart ['durto:na:rt], *f.* (*Mus.*) major key.

Dusche ['duʃə], *f.* shower-bath, (*coll.*) shower; douche; ***ihm eine kalte – geben,*** pour cold water on his enthusiasm. **duschen, 1.** *v.t.* douche, swill, (*coll.*) douse. **2.** *v.i.* have *or* take a shower (-bath).

Düse ['dy:zə], *f.* nozzle; jet; fuel injector.

Dusel ['du:zəl], *m.* (*coll.*) 1. stupor; sleepiness, drowsiness, dreamy state; inebriation, tipsiness; ***im*** (***holden***) ***– sein,*** be day-dreaming; be half-seas-over; 2. fluke; (***einen***) ***– haben,*** be a lucky dog, escape by the skin of one's teeth. **Duselei** [–'laı], *f.* (*coll.*) day-dream(ing), absent-mindedness, drowsiness; fuddled state. **duselig,** *adj.* dizzy, (*coll.*) dopey; sleepy, drowsy; (be)fuddled, tipsy. **duseln,** *v.i.* be drowsy *or* half asleep *or* day-dreaming, doze.

Düsen|antrieb, *m.* (*Av.*) jet-propulsion. **–flugzeug,** *n.* jet(-propelled) aircraft, (*coll.*) jet.

Dussel ['dusəl], *m.* (*coll.*) imbecile, idiot. **dusselig,** *adj.* idiotic, fatuous.

düster ['dy:stər], *adj.* dark, gloomy, sombre, overcast; mournful, melancholy, dismal; dire, ominous, sepulchral, funereal. **Düster,** *n.*, **Düsterheit, Düsterkeit,** *f.* darkness, obscurity, gloom; (*fig.*) gloom(iness), melancholy. **düstern, 1.** *v.t.*, *v.i.* (*Poet.*) darken, spread darkness *or* cast shadows (over). **2.** *v.imp.* (*Poet.*) ***es düstert,*** it grows dark, darkness is falling.

Düte ['dy:tə], *f.* *See* **Tüte.**

Dutt [dut], *m.* **(-(e)s,** *pl.* **-e)** bun (*of hair*).

Dutzend ['dutsənt], *n.* **(-s,** *pl.* **-(e))** dozen; ***ein halbes –,*** half a dozen, a half-dozen; ***ein großes –,*** a gross; ***im –,*** by the dozen; ***zu –en,*** in their dozens. **dutzendemal,** *adv.* dozens (and dozens) of times. **dutzendmal,** *adv.* a dozen times. **Dutzend|mensch,** *m.* commonplace *or* average fellow. **–ware,** *f.* cheap *or* mass-produced article. **dutzendweise,** *adv.* by the dozen, in dozens.

Duz|bruder ['du:ts–], *m.* *See* **–freund. duzen,** *v.t.*, *v.r.* be on 'Christian name' terms with. **Duz|-freund,** *m.* intimate companion, crony. **–fuß,** *m.* ***auf*** (***dem***) ***– stehen,*** be on familiar *or* intimate terms.

dwars [dvars], *adv.* (*Naut.*) athwart. **dwarsab,** *adv.* (*Naut.*) abeam. **Dwars|linie,** *f.* line abreast. **–saling,** *f.* cross-trees. **dwarsschlagen,** *irr.v.i.* (*aux.* s.) (*sep.*) (*Naut.*) broach to. **Dwars|-schlingen,** *f.pl.* *See* **–saling. –see,** *f.* beam sea.

Dweil [dvaıl], *m.* **(-s,** *pl.* **-e)** (*Naut.*) mop, swab, scrubber.

Dynamik [dy'na:mık], *f.* dynamics, (*coll.*) vitality, dynamic force (*of personality etc.*). **dynamisch,** *adj.* dynamic (*also Mus., Phonet., Med., fig.*), (*fig.*) forceful (*of personality*), full of movement (*of artistic work*).

Dynamit [dyna'mi:t], *n. or m.* dynamite.
Dynamo [dy'na:mo, 'dy:namo], *m.* (**-s**, *pl.* **-s**), **Dynamomaschine,** *f.* (*Elec.*) dynamo, generator.
Dynast [dy'nast], *m.* (**-en**, *pl.* **-en**) feudal lord, ruler, dynast. **Dynastie** [–'ti:], *f.* dynasty. **dynastisch,** *adj.* dynastic.

E

E, e [e:], *n.* (the letter) E, e; (*Mus.*) (the note) E; ***E-dur*** (***-moll***), E major (minor).
ebauchieren [ebo'ʃi:rən], *v.t.* outline, sketch, make a rough draft *or* skeleton of.
Ebbe ['ɛbə], *f.* ebb-tide, low water *or* tide; ***– und Flut,*** low and high tide *or* water; ebb and flow; ***niedrige –,*** neap-tide; ***die – tritt ein,*** the tide is going out; (*fig.*) ***– sein,*** be at a low ebb. **ebben,** *v.i.* (*aux.* h. *&* s.) ebb; (*fig.*) subside, abate; ***das Meer ebbt,*** the tide is going out.
eben ['e:bən], **1.** *adj.* even, level, flat, smooth; (*Math.*) plane, two-dimensional; open (*country*); ***zu –er Erde,*** on the ground floor; ***–e Geometrie,*** plane geometry. **2.** *adv.* 1. just, precisely, exactly; (*ja*) ***–!*** quite so! exactly! precisely! ***– nicht!*** quite the contrary! not exactly! ***es geschieht dir – recht,*** it just serves you right; ***das wäre mir – recht,*** that's precisely what I want; 2. (*of time*) just (now), this (very) moment; (just) a moment ago, only just; ***– danach,*** a moment *or* a short time *or* just after; just (then), at that moment; ***– erst,*** only just, just now; ***an – dem Tag,*** on that very day; 3. (*unemphatic*) just, simply; ***das wollte ich – sagen,*** that is just what I was going to say, I was about to say simply *or* just that.
eben–, *pref.* (the) said *or* same *or* very. **Ebenbild,** *n.* image, likeness; ***das – des Schöpfers,*** God's image. **ebenbürtig,** *adj.* of equally high birth *or* rank, equal. **Ebenbürtigkeit,** *f.* equality (of birth *or* rank). **eben|da(selbst),** *adv.* in that very *or* the same place, just there; ibidem. **–derjenige, –derselbe,** *dem.adj., pron.* the *or* that same *or* very, the very same, the aforesaid. **–deshalb,** *adv.* for that very reason.
Ebene ['e:bənə], *f.* (*Geog.*) plain; (*Math.*) plane; (*fig.*) plane, level; ***geneigte*** or ***schiefe –,*** gradient, inclined plane; (*fig.*) ***auf die schiefe – kommen*** or ***geraten,*** get into evil ways; ***auf hoher –,*** high-level (*talks etc.*); ***auf höchster –,*** at the highest level; ***in gleicher – mit,*** flush with.
ebenen ['e:bənən], *v.t. See* **ebnen. eben|erdig,** *adj. adv.* on the ground floor, at street level. **–falls,** *adv.* likewise, also, too; ***er tat es –,*** so did he; ***danke –!*** thank you! the same to you! **Ebenheit,** *f.* evenness, levelness, flatness, smoothness.
Ebenholz ['e:bənhɔlts], *n.* ebony.
Ebenmaß ['e:bənma:s], *n.* symmetry, proportion, harmony, regularity. **ebenmäßig,** *adj.* symmetrical, harmonious, regular, even.
ebenso ['e:bənzo:], *adv.* likewise, in the same way; just as; ***er hat – große Kinder wie wir,*** he has quite *or* just as big children as we have, he has children just *or* quite as big as ours (N.B. *never prefixed to declined adj.*). **ebenso–,** *pref.* just as (N.B. *formation of compounds with adv. or undeclined adj. is optional*). **ebenso|gern,** *adv.* just as well *or* soon. **–gut,** *adv.* just as well. **–häufig, –oft,** *adv.* just as frequently *or* often. **–sehr,** *adv.* just as much. **–viel,** *adv.* just as much *or* many; ***– wie . . .,*** tantamount to . . . . **–wenig,** *adv.* just as little *or* few, as infrequently. **–wohl,** *adv. See* **–gut.**

Eber ['e:bər], *m.* (wild) boar. **Eber|esche,** *f.* (*Bot.*) rowan, mountain ash (*Sorbus aucuparia*). **–wurz(el),** *f.* (*Bot.*) carline thistle (*Carlina vulgaris*).
ebnen ['e:bnən], *v.t.* level, smooth, even up, flatten; (*fig.*) remove, smooth away (*difficulties*); ***ihm die Bahn –,*** pave *or* clear the way for him.
E-Boot, *n.* motor torpedo boat.
Ebräer [ɛ'brɛ:ər], *m.* Hebrew. *See also* **Hebräer, ebräisch,** *adj.* Hebrew. *See also* **Hebräisch.**
Echo ['ɛço:], *n.* (**-s,** *pl.* **-s**) echo; ***ein – geben,*** echo, resound; (*fig.*) ***ein – finden,*** meet with response *or* approval. **echoen,** *v.i.* echo, re-echo, resound. **Echolot,** *n.* (*Naut.*) echo-sounder, sonic depth-finder.
echt [ɛçt], *adj.* genuine, authentic, true, real; sincere, unaffected (*of a p.*), unmixed, unalloyed (*feelings etc.*); fast (*of colours*); natural (*hair*); (*Math.*) ***–e Brüche,*** proper fractions. **Echtheit,** *f.* genuineness, authenticity; sincerity (*of a p.*); fastness (*of colours*).
Eck [ɛk], *n.* (**-s,** *pl.* **-e**) (*dial.*) corner, angle; ***über –,*** crosswise, diagonally; ***das Deutsche –,*** Rhine elbow (*at Coblenz*). **Eck|ball,** *m.* (*Spt.*) corner(-kick). **–beschläge,** *m.pl.* (metal) corner pieces. **–brett,** *n.* bracket, corner shelf. **Eckchen,** *n.* (*coll.*) short distance; ***ich will dich ein – auf den Weg bringen,*** I will go a little way with you.
Ecke ['ɛkə], *f.* edge; corner, angle; (*coll.*) ***eine ganze –,*** a considerable distance; ***in die – stellen,*** stand *or* place in the corner; (*fig.*) lay aside, hold over, shelve, pigeon-hole; (*coll.*) ***um die – bringen,*** dispose of, take for a ride, bump off; ***an allen –n brennen,*** burn from end to end; ***an allen –n und Enden,*** (here there and) everywhere, at every turn; ***von allen –n und Enden,*** from everywhere under the sun. **Eckeisen,** *n.* gusset *or* corner plate, angle iron. **Eckensteher,** *m.* loiterer, loafer.
Ecker ['ɛkər], *f.* (-, *pl.* **-n**) acorn; mast; beechnut.
Eckholz ['ɛkhɔlts], *n.* squared timber. **eckig,** *adj.* 1. angular; square; 2. (*fig.*) awkward, wooden. **–eckig,** *adj.suff.* -cornered, -angular. **Eck|punkt,** *m.* vertex, corner (*of a triangle*). **–stein,** *m.* corner-stone (*also fig.*); curb-stone; (*Cards*) diamonds. **–stoß,** *m.* (*Footb.*) corner(-kick). **–zahn,** *m.* eye-tooth, canine-tooth.
edel ['e:dəl], *adj.* 1. noble; of noble birth *or* blood *or* descent, high-born, well-born; high-minded, lofty; exalted, stately; precious (*stone, metal*), superior, excellent, high-class (*wine etc.*), dessert (*fruit*); ***Edle(r),*** person of noble *or* high birth, noble(man), noblewoman; peer, peeress (*in England*); ***das Edle,*** nobility (*of mind etc.*), that which is noble; ***edler Gang,*** rich vein (*of ore*); ***edle Teile,*** vital parts; 2. (*Chem.*) inert (*gas*), (*Elec.*) electro-positive.
Edel|auge, *n.* grafting *or* shield-bud. **–beere,** *f.* choice grape. **–beerenauslese,** *f.* (superior) wine from choice grape. **–dame,** *f.* titled lady, noblewoman, gentlewoman. **–erz,** *n.* rich ore. **–falke,** *m.* (trained) falcon. **–fink,** *m.* (*Orn.*) *see* **Buchfink. –fräulein,** *n.* titled (unmarried) lady, nobleman's daughter.
Edeling ['e:dəlɪŋ], *m.* (**-s,** *pl.* **-e**) 1. (*early Germanic*) chieftain, aetheling; 2. (*Bot.*) graft, scion.
Edel|kastanie, *f.* (*Bot.*) sweet *or* Spanish chestnut, edible chestnut (*Castanea sativa*). **–knabe,** *m.* page. **–leute,** *pl.* nobles, noblemen. **–mann,** *m.* (*pl.* **-leute**) nobleman, noble. **–marder,** *m.* (*Zool.*) pinemarten (*Martes*). **–metall,** *n.* precious metal. **–mist,** *m.* farmyard manure. **–mut,** *m.* high-mindedness, generosity, magnanimity. **edelmütig,** *adj.* high-minded, noble, magnanimous, generous. **Edel|pilz,** *m.* field mushroom. **–reiher,** *m.* (*Orn.*) *see* **Silberreiher. –reis,** *n.* scion, graft. **–rost,** *m.* patina. **–sinn,** *m.* high-mindedness. **–stahl,** *m.* high-grade *or* high-tensile steel. **–stein,** *m.* precious stone, gem, jewel. **–steinschleifer,** *m.* gem-cutter, lapidary. **–tanne,** *f.* (*Bot.*) silver fir (*Abies picea*). **–valuta,** *f.* hard currency. **–weiß,** *n.* (*Bot.*) edelweiss, lion's foot (*Gnaphalium leontopodium*). **–wild,** *n.* red deer. **–zinn,** *m.* pewter.

edieren [e'di:rən], *v.t.* edit.

Edikt [e'dɪkt], *n.* (**-(e)s,** *pl.* **-e**) edict.

Edition [edɪtsi'o:n], *f.* 1. edition; 2. editing.

Edle(r) ['e:dlə(r)], *m., f. See* **edel.**

Eduard ['e:duart], *m.* Edward.

Efeu ['e:fɔy], *m.* (*Bot.*) ivy (*Hedera helix*).

Effekt [e'fɛkt], *m.* (**-(e)s,** *pl.* **-e**) effect, result; end, purpose, object; (*Mech.*) performance, efficiency; – ***machen,*** have *or* produce an effect, be effective; ***ohne –,*** ineffective, without avail.

Effekten [e'fɛktən], *pl.* 1. (personal) effects, personal belongings, goods and chattels; 2. (*Comm.*) securities, stocks, bonds. **Effekten|bestand,** *m.* holdings. **–börse,** *f.* Stock Exchange. **–handel,** *m.* stock-exchange business. **–händler,** *m.* stock-broker, stockjobber. **–kurs,** *m.* quotation, market price.

Effekthascherei [e'fɛkthaʃəraɪ], *f.* straining for effect, sensationalism, showing off, clap-trap.

effektiv [efɛk'ti:f], **1.** *adj.* effective, efficacious; effective, real, actual; (*Comm.*) ***–er Bestand,*** realizable assets; (*Mil.*) effective strength, effectives; (*Elec.*) ***–e Spannung,*** root-mean-square voltage. **2.** *adv.* (*coll.*) definitely, distinctly, really. **Effektivbestand,** *m. See* ***effektiver Bestand.*** **Effektiven,** *pl.* (*Comm.*) realizable assets. **Effektiv|geschäft,** *n.* spot-market transaction. **–lohn,** *m.* net wages *or* earnings. **–preis,** *m.* cash price. **–stand,** *m. See* ***effektiver Bestand*** (*Mil.*).

effektvoll [e'fɛktfɔl], *adj.* effective, striking.

Effet [ɛ'fe:], *n.* (**-s,** *pl.* **-s**) break, spin, screw, twist (*on a ball*), (*Bill.*) side(-screw); – ***geben,*** put spin *etc. or* a break (*Dat.,* on).

effloreszieren [eflorɛs'tsi:rən], *v.i.* effloresce.

egal [e'ga:l], *adj.* equal, alike; even, level; (*coll.*) all one, all the same; (*coll.*) ***das ist mir ganz –,*** I don't mind *or* care, it's all one *or* all the same to me, it doesn't matter to me. **egalisieren** [–i'zi:rən], *v.t.* equalize, adjust. **Egalität** [–i'tɛ:t], *f.* equality, evenness, uniformity.

Egel ['e:gəl], *m.* leech.

Egge ['ɛgə], *f.* 1. harrow; 2. selvage. **eggen,** *v.t.* harrow.

Egoismus [ego'ɪsmus], *m.* egoism, selfishness. **Egoist,** *m.* (**-en,** *pl.* **-en**) egoist. **egoistisch,** *adj.* selfish, egoistic(al).

egrenieren [egre'ni:rən], *v.t.* gin, clean (*cotton*).

eh [e:], **1.** *int.* eh! hullo! **2.** *conj. See* **ehe. 3.** *adv.* (*Austr.*) anyhow, anyway.

ehe ['e:ə], *conj.* before, prior *or* previous to, (*Poet.*) ere; (*with neg. in principal clause*) until; (*with reference to future*) – (***daß***), rather than; ***ich gehe nicht zu Bett, – du nach Hause kommst,*** I shall not go to bed until *or* before you get home; ***– du bei dem Wetter zu Fuß gehst, hole ich ein Taxi,*** I'll call a taxi rather than that you should walk in this weather.

Ehe, *f.* marriage; matrimony, (*Poet., Law*) wedlock; ***außer der – geboren,*** illegitimate; ***aus erster –,*** by his *or* her first marriage; ***eine zweite – eingehen,*** re-marry, marry again *or* a second time; ***– zur linken Hand,*** morganatic marriage; ***eine – schließen,*** contract a marriage, be joined in marriage (***mit,*** with), get married (to); (*Prov.*) ***–n werden im Himmel geschlossen,*** marriages are made in heaven; ***eine – vollziehen,*** consummate a marriage; ***wilde –,*** concubinage; ***in wilder – leben,*** live in sin, live together; ***zerrüttete –,*** broken marriage. **Ehe|anbahnung,** *f.* (introduction by) marriage bureau. **–aufhebung,** *f.* annulment of a marriage, declaration *or* decree of nullity. **–auflösung,** *f.* divorce, dissolution of a marriage.

ehebaldigst ['e:əbaldɪçst], *adv.* (*obs.*) as soon as possible.

Ehe|band, *n.* (**-(e)s,** *pl.* **-e**) matrimonial *or* marriage tie, bond of wedlock. **–beratung,** *f.* marriage guidance (bureau). **–bett,** *n.* marriage bed; double bed. **ehebrechen,** *irr.v.i.* (*inf. only*) commit adultery. **Ehe|brecher,** *m.* adulterer. **–brecherin,** *f.* adulteress. **ehebrecherisch,** *adj.* adulterous. **Ehebruch,** *m.* adultery. **ehebrüchig,** *adj.* adulterous (*of a p.*). **Ehe|bund,** *m.,* **–bündis,** *n.* matrimony, marriage tie.

ehedem ['e:əde:m], *adv.* formerly, in former times.

ehefähig ['e:əfɛ:ɪç], *adj.* marriageable, nubile; fit *or* free to marry. **Ehe|frau,** *f.* wife. **–gatte,** *m.* husband, (lawful) spouse. **–gattin,** *f.* wife, (lawful) spouse. **–gelübde,** *n.* marriage vows. **–gemahl,** *m.* (*Poet.*) husband, (*hum.*) spouse. **–gemahlin,** *f.* (*Poet.*) wife, (*hum.*) spouse. **–gesetz,** *n.* marriage law.

ehegestern ['e:əgɛstərn], *adv.* (*obs.*) the day before yesterday.

Ehe|glück, *n.* conjugal bliss. **–hälfte,** *f.* (*coll., hum.*) better half. **–hindernis,** *n.* impediment to marriage. **–leben,** *n.* married life. **eheleiblich,** *adj.* (*obs.*) legitimate, born in wedlock. **Eheleute,** *pl.* married people; married couple.

ehelich ['e:əlɪç], *adj.* matrimonial, marital, conjugal; ***–e Gemeinschaft,*** marital relations; (*Law*) ***Aufhebung der –en Gemeinschaft,*** judicial separation; (*Law*) ***Wiederherstellung der –en Gemeinschaft,*** restitution of conjugal rights; ***–e Treue,*** conjugal fidelity; ***–e Kinder,*** legitimate offspring, children born in wedlock; ***für – erklären,*** legitimatize. **ehelichen,** *v.t.* (*of the man*) take in marriage, marry. **ehelos,** *adj.* unmarried, single, (*of a monk*) celibate. **Ehelosigkeit,** *f.* celibacy; single state. **Ehemakler,** *m.* marriage broker.

ehemalig ['e:əma:lɪç], *attrib. adj.* former, ex-, old, (*obs.*) quondam. **ehemals,** *adv.* formerly, (*obs.*) ere now, (*Law*) heretofore.

Ehemann ['e:əman], *m.* (*pl.* **-männer**) husband. **ehemündig,** *adj.* of marriageable age, nubile; (*coll.*) of an age *or* old enough to marry. **Ehe|nichtigkeit,** *f.* nullity of marriage. **–paar,** *n.* married couple. **–pfand,** *n.* issue, child.

eher ['e:ər], *adv.* 1. sooner, earlier, before; ***nicht – als,*** not until; ***je – desto besser,*** the sooner the better; 2. more likely; (***schon***) ***– möglich,*** more likely; ***schon – danach,*** more like it; ***um so – als,*** the more so as, all the more as, more especially as; 3. preferably, rather; – . . . ***als,*** rather . . . than, . . . rather than; ***– Tod als Schande,*** death before dishonour.

Ehe|recht, *n.* marriage law. **–ring,** *m.* wedding ring.

ehern ['e:ərn], *adj.* (of) brass, bronze, brazen; (*fig.*) iron (*as will*), pitiless (*as fate*); ***mit –er Stirn,*** boldly, brazen-faced.

Ehe|schänder, *m.* adulterer. **–schändung,** *f.* adultery. **–scheidung,** *f.* divorce. **–scheidungsklage,** *f.* petition for divorce. **–scheidungsprozeß,** *m.* divorce suit. **–schließung,** *f.* marriage (ceremony). **–segen,** *m.* issue, children.

ehest ['e:əst], **1.** *adj.* earliest. **2.** *adv.* soonest; as soon as possible, at the earliest opportunity; ***am ehesten,*** (the) earliest; most likely, most easily, best of all.

Ehestand ['e:əʃtant], *m.* married state, matrimony.

ehestens ['e:əstəns], *adv.* as soon as possible; at the (very) earliest.

Ehestifter ['e:əʃtɪftər], *m.* matchmaker. **ehetauglich,** *adj.* fit to marry. **Ehe|trennung,** *f.* judicial separation. **–verlöbnis, –versprechen,** *n.* betrothal, engagement. **–vertrag,** *m.* marriage settlement.

Ehrabschneidung ['e:rˀapʃnaɪduŋ], *f.* slander, vilification, calumniation, denigration.

ehrbar ['e:rba:r], *adj.* honourable, respected, esteemed, worthy; respectable. **Ehrbarkeit,** *f.* worthiness; respectability.

Ehrbegier(de) ['e:rbəgi:r(də)], *f.* ambition. **ehrbegierig,** *adj.* ambitious.

Ehre ['e:rə], *f.* 1. honour; ***ihm bei der – packen,*** put him on his honour, appeal to his honour; ***seine – darin setzen,*** make it a point *or* matter of honour; ***bei meiner –,*** on my (word of) honour; ***in allen –n,*** in all good faith; 2. honour, credit; ***die – einer Frau,*** a woman's honour; ***er raubte ihr die –,*** he seduced her; (***alle***) ***– machen,*** do credit, be a credit (*Dat.,* to), reflect credit (on), redound to s.o.'s credit; ***eine Prüfung mit –n bestehen,*** acquit o.s. creditably in an examination; 3. honour, glory; esteem, renown; ***in –n halten,*** honour, hold in high esteem; ***seine grauen Haare in –n,*** with all due respect to his grey hairs; ***mit*** (***allen***) ***–n,*** with (all due) honour, with full honours; ***zu –n,*** in honour (*Gen.*, of); ***zur – Gottes,*** to the glory of God; (*coll.*) ***alle – antun,*** do justice (*Dat.*, to); 4. honour, privilege; ***mit wem habe ich die –?*** whom have I the honour of speaking to? ***darf ich um die – bitten?*** may I have the honour (*of dancing with you etc.*)? ***ich betrachte es als eine –*** or ***ich halte es für eine –*** or ***ich rechne es mir zur –*** (***an***), ***Ihnen zu dienen,*** I consider *or* deem *or* esteem it an honour *or* privilege to serve you; (*Austr.*) ***hab' die –,*** (*servile form of greeting*).

ehren ['e:rən], *v.t.* honour, esteem, revere; (*of actions etc.*) reflect honour on, do honour *or* credit to; ***ich fühle mich geehrt,*** I am honoured; ***meine geehrten Kollegen,*** my respected colleagues; (***sehr***) ***geehrter Herr,*** Sir; dear Sir.

Ehren|abzeichen, *n.* medal, decoration. **–akzept,** *n.* (*Comm.*) acceptance supra protest. **–amt,** *n.* honorary *or* titular office. **ehrenamtlich,** *adj.* honorary. **Ehren|beleidigung,** *f.* insult; ***mündliche –,*** slander. **–bezeigung, –bezeugung,** *f.* mark of esteem *or* respect; ovation; (military) salute. **–bürger,** *m.* freeman (*of a city*). **–dame,** *f.* lady-in-waiting. **–doktor,** *m.* honorary doctor (*of a university*). **–erklärung,** *f.* (full) apology. **–gast,** *m.* guest of honour. **–gefolge,** *n.* retinue, escort, suite. **–geleit,** *n.* escort. **–gericht,** *n.* court of honour, disciplinary court. **ehrengerichtlich,** *adj.* disciplinary.

ehrenhaft ['e:rənhaft], **1.** *adj.* honourable, of honour, worthy, respectable. **2.** *adv.* honourably, worthily, with honour. **Ehrenhaftigkeit,** *f.* honourableness, worthiness, respectability. **ehrenhalber,** *adv.* for honour's sake; honoris causa.

Ehren|handel, *m.* affair of honour, duel. **–jungfer,** *f.* maid of honour. **–klage,** *f.* action for libel *or* slander. **–kodex,** *m.* duelling code, code of honour. **–kränkung,** *f.* insult, (*Law*) defamation. **–legion,** *f.* Legion of Honour. **–mahl,** *n.* dinner *or* banquet in a p.'s honour. **–mal,** *n.* war memorial, cenotaph. **–mann,** *m.* (*pl.* **–männer**) man of honour; gentleman. **–mitglied,** *n.* honorary member. **–pforte,** *f.* triumphal arch. **–platz,** *m.* seat *or* place of honour. **–preis,** *m.* **1.** (first) prize, trophy; 2. (*Bot.*) speedwell (*Veronica*). **–rechte,** *n.pl.* ***bürgerliche –,*** civil rights. **ehrenrührig,** *adj.* slanderous, libellous, defamatory. **Ehren|sache,** *f.* **1.** affair of honour, duel; 2. point of honour; 3. (*Law*) action for libel *or* slander. **–salve,** *f.*, **–schießen,** *n.* (gun) salute. **–schuld,** *f.* debt of honour, gambling debt. **–schutz,** *m.* (*Austr.*) patronage. **–sold,** *m.* honorarium *or* gratuity (for holders of gallantry medals). **–stelle,** *f.* **1.** honorary post; 2. post of honour; 3. (*Her.*) honour point. **–tafel,** *f.* roll of honour. **–titel,** *m.* honorary title. **–tod,** *m.* ***den – sterben,*** die for one's country, die on the field of honour.

ehrenvoll ['e:rənfɔl], *adj.* honourable, creditable; ***er wurde – erwähnt,*** he received honourable mention. **Ehrenwache,** *f.* guard of honour. **ehrenwert,** *adj.* respectable, reputable; respected, esteemed, worthy, honourable. **Ehrenwort,** *n.* word of honour; ***auf –,*** on parole. **ehrenwörtlich, 1.** *adj.* solemn (*promise*). **2.** *adv.* on one's word of honour, on parole. **Ehrenzeichen,** *n.* medal, decoration; (*Her.*) augmentation.

ehrerbietig ['e:rʔɛrbi:tɪç], *adj.* respectful, deferential. **Ehr|erbietigkeit, –erbietung,** *f.* deference, respect, respectfulness. **–furcht,** *f.* respect, reverence, awe. **ehr|fürchtig,** *adj.* reverential, reverent, respectful. **–furchtslos,** *adj.* disrespectful, irreverent. **–furchtsvoll,** *adj.* *See* **–fürchtig. Ehr|gefühl,** *n.* self-respect, sense of honour. **–geiz,** *m.* ambition. **ehrgeizig,** *adj.* ambitious.

ehrlich ['e:rlɪç], *adj.* (*of a p.*) honest; sincere, frank, open; (*of dealings*) honest, fair, square; ***–e Absichten,*** honourable intentions (*esp. with a girl*); (*coll.*) ***er ist eine –e Haut,*** he is as honest as the day is long; ***–es Begräbnis,*** honourable *or* Christian *or* decent burial; (*Prov.*) ***– währt am längsten,*** honesty is the best policy. **Ehrlichkeit,** *f.* honesty, frankness, truthfulness; sincerity, integrity; fairness. **ehrlos,** *adj.* dishonourable, disreputable, infamous; ***–es Weib,*** woman of easy virtue. **Ehrlosigkeit,** *f.* infamy, disrepute; dishonesty. **ehrsam,** *adj.* decent, respectable. **Ehrsamkeit,** *f.* decency, respectability. **Ehrsucht,** *f.* overweening ambition. **ehrsüchtig,** *adj.* very ambitious. **Ehrung,** *f.* distinction, honour; token of esteem. **ehrvergessen,** *adj.* unprincipled, dishonourable, despicable, vile. **Ehrwürden,** *f.* Reverence; ***Ew.*** (***Euer***) ***–,*** your Reverence, Reverend Sir. **ehrwürdig,** *adj.* venerable; (*Eccl.*) reverend. **Ehrwürdigkeit,** *f.* venerableness, venerability.

ei! [aɪ], *int.* indeed! oh! ah! – ***was!*** nonsense! rubbish! –, *–!* (*mild annoyance*) aha! oho! dear me!

Ei [aɪ], *n.* (**-(e)s,** *pl.* **-er**) egg; (*Biol.*) ovum, spawn (*of fish*); (*sl.*) (*Av.*) bomb; *pl.* (*vulg.*) balls; ***frisches –,*** new-laid egg; ***faules –,*** bad *or* addled egg; ***verlorene –er,*** poached eggs; ***aussehen wie aus dem – geschält*** or ***gepellt,*** be spick and span, look as if one had just stepped out of a bandbox; ***sie gleichen sich wie ein – dem andern,*** they are as like as two peas *or* pins; (*Prov.*) ***das – will klüger sein als die Henne,*** don't teach your grandmother to suck eggs; (*coll.*) ***er ist eben erst aus dem – gekrochen,*** he is a greenhorn; he is wet behind the ears; ***man muß ihn anfassen*** or ***behandeln wie ein rohes –,*** you must deal gently *or* tactfully with him; ***kümmre dich nicht um ungelegte –er!*** don't cross your bridges before you come to them.

Ei|ablage, *f.* laying *or* depositing of eggs, oviposition. **–abstoßung,** *f.* ovulation.

eiapopeia! [aɪapo'paɪa], *int.* hushaby baby!

Eibe ['aɪbə], *f.* yew-tree. **eiben,** *adj.* (of) yew(-wood).

Eibisch ['aɪbɪʃ], *m.* (**-es,** *pl.* **-e**) (*Bot.*) marshmallow (*Althea officinalis*).

Eichamt ['aɪçʔamt], *n.* Office of Weights and Measures, (*Am.*) Bureau of Standards.

Eich|apfel, *m.* oak-apple. **–baum,** *m.* *See* **Eiche. Eiche,** *f.* (*Bot.*) oak(-tree).

Eichel ['aɪçəl], *f.* (-, *pl.* **-n**) **1.** acorn; 2. (*Anat.*) glans penis; 3. (*Cards*) club. **eichelförmig,** *adj.* acorn-shaped, glandiform. **Eichelhäher,** *m.* (*Orn.*) jay (*Gerrulus glandarius*).

[1]**eichen** ['aɪçən], *v.t.* gauge, standardize, graduate, calibrate; (*fig. of a p.*) ***geeicht,*** qualified (***auf*** (*Acc.*), for), versed (in).

[2]**eichen,** *adj.* oaken, (made of) oak(-wood).

Eichen|baum, *m.* *See* **Eiche. –blatt,** *n.* oakleaf. **–galle,** *f.* oak gall, oak apple. **–laub,** *n.* oak leaves.

Eich|horn, –hörnchen, –kätzchen, *n.*, **–katze,** *f.* squirrel.

Eich|maß, *n.* gauge, standard. **–ordnung,** *f.* regulations for the standardization of weights and measures. **–pfahl,** *m.* calibration mark. **Eichung,** *f.* standardization; calibration, graduation, gauging, rating; verification, marking. **Eichungsamt,** *n.* *See* **Eichamt. Eichzeichen,** *n.* official stamp (after standardization, calibration *etc.*).

Eid [aɪt], *m.* (**-es,** *pl.* **-e**) (solemn) oath; ***einen – ablegen*** or ***leisten*** or ***schwören,*** take an oath, swear, attest; (***ihm***) ***einen – abnehmen*** (***lassen***), put (him) on his oath, swear him in, administer an oath to him; ***unter –,*** (up)on *or* under oath; ***an –es Statt,*** in lieu of an oath; ***eine Erklärung an –es Statt ablegen,*** make a statutory declaration, make an affirmation.

Eidam ['aɪdam], *m.* (**-s,** *pl.* **-e**) (*obs.*) son-in-law.

Eid|brecher, *m.* perjurer. **–bruch,** *m.* perjury, breach of oath. **eidbrüchig,** *adj.* perjured, forsworn; ***– werden,*** perjure o.s.

Eidechse ['aɪdɛksə], *f.* lizard, (*Astr.*) Lacerta.

Eider|(ente) ['aɪdər–], **–gans,** *f.* (*Orn.*) eider-duck, (*Am.*) eider (*Somateria mollissima*).

Eides|belehrung, *f.* caution (*before administering oath*). **–brecher, –bruch, eidesbrüchig,** *see* **Eid|brecher, –bruch, eidbrüchig. Eides-**

formel, *f.* form *or* wording of an oath. **eides|-gleich,** *adj. See an Eides Statt under* **Eid. -kräftig,** *adj.* upon oath, sworn, attested. **Eidesleistung,** *f.* taking an oath, act of swearing. **eidesstattlich,** *adj. See an Eides Statt under* **Eid.**

Eides|versicherung, *f.* affidavit, sworn statement, statement on oath. **-verwarnung,** *f. See* **-belehrung. -verweigerung,** *f.* objection to an oath, refusal to submit to an oath.

Eid|genosse, *m.* 1. confederate; 2. Swiss subject. **-genossenschaft,** *f.* (Swiss) Confederation, Switzerland. **eidgenössisch,** *adj.* 1. federal; 2. Swiss.

eidlich ['aɪtlɪç], *adj.* sworn, under *or* (up)on oath; ***-e Aussage,*** affidavit, sworn deposition.

Eidotter ['aɪdɔtər], *m. or n.* yolk of egg, (*Biol.*) vitellus.

Eidschwur ['aɪtʃvu:r], *m.* (solemn) oath. **eidvergessen,** *adj.* perjured, forsworn.

Eier|apfel, *m.* aubergine, egg-fruit. **-becher,** *m.* egg-cup. **eierförmig,** *adj.* egg-shaped, ovoid. **Eier|frucht,** *f. See* **-apfel. -kuchen,** *m.* omelet, pancake. **-laufen,** *n.* egg-and-spoon race. **eierlegend,** *adj.* oviparous. **Eier|-leger,** *m.pl.* ovipara; ***diese Hühner sind gute -,*** these hens are good layers. **-likör,** *m.* egg-flip. **-löffel,** *m.* egg-spoon. **-mehl,** *n.* egg-powder. **-pflanze,** *f. See* **-apfel. -pflaume,** *f.* Victoria plum. **-pulver,** *n.* dried egg. **-sack,** *m.* (*Anat.*) ovary. **-schale,** *f.* eggshell. **-schläger,** *m.* egg-whisk, egg-beater. **-schnee,** *m.* whisked *or* beaten white of egg. **-schwamm,** *m.* chanterelle. **-speise,** *f.* egg-dish, (*Austr.*) scrambled eggs. **-spiegel,** *m.* ooscope. **-stein,** *m.* (*Geol.*) oolite. **-stock,** *m.* ovary.

Eifer ['aɪfər], *m.* eagerness, enthusiasm, zeal; fervour, ardour, passion; (*Prov.*) ***blinder - schadet nur,*** more haste, less speed. **Eiferer,** *m.* fanatic, zealot. **eifern,** *v.i.* act *or* advocate with zeal; agitate, campaign (***für,*** for), devote o.s. (to); strive, vie, compete (for); ***- gegen,*** agitate *or* campaign against. **Eifersucht,** *f.* jealousy. **Eifersüchtelei** [-'zyçtəlaɪ], *f.* petty jealousy. **eifersüchtig,** *adj.* jealous, envious (***auf*** (*Acc.*), of).

Eiform ['aɪfɔrm], *f.* egg-shape. **eiförmig,** *adj.* egg-shaped, ovoid.

eifrig ['aɪfrɪç], *adj.* eager, enthusiastic, keen, zealous; ***- bei einer S. sein,*** be busy at *or* with *or* over s.th., be busily occupied with s.th.; show a keen interest in s.th. **Eifrigkeit,** *f.* eagerness, enthusiasm, zeal, keenness.

Ei|gang, *m.* oviduct. **-gelb,** *n.* yolk of egg.

eigen ['aɪgən], *adj.* 1. own; ***aus -em Antrieb,*** of one's own free will, on one's own accord; ***mit -em Antrieb,*** self-propelled (*vehicle*), self-driven (*machine*); ***für den -en Bedarf*** or ***Gebrauch,*** for personal use *or* requirements *or* consumption; ***es ihm zu -en Händen abgeben,*** deliver it to him in person; (*Prov.*) ***-er Herd ist Goldes wert,*** there's no place like home; (*Hist.*) ***-e Leute,*** serfs, thralls, bond(s)-men; ***in -er Person erscheinen,*** appear personally *or* in person; (*Comm.*) ***-er Wechsel,*** note of hand, promissory note; ***sein -es Wort nicht hören können,*** not be able to hear one's own voice; ***eine -e Wohnung,*** a home of one's own; 2. (*inv.*) ***mein -,*** my own; ***ihm etwas zu - geben,*** give him s.th. for himself *or* for his (very) own; ***sich ihm zu - geben,*** give *or* devote o.s. to him, devote one's life to him; ***etwas zu - haben,*** own *or* possess s.th., have s.th. for one's own; ***sich*** (*Dat.*) ***etwas zu - machen,*** acquire s.th., take s.th. into one's possesison, make s.th. one's own; adopt, agree with (*opinion etc.*); 3. (*with Dat.*) peculiar, characteristic; ***die Grobheit die ihm - ist, die ihm -e Grobheit,*** the rudeness that is characteristic of him, his characteristic rudeness; 4. peculiar, strange, queer, odd; ***es ist mir - (zu Mute),*** I feel queer, I have a strange *or* peculiar feeling; 5. (*coll.*) particular, careful, tidy, fussy, finicky; ***im Essen - sein,*** be fussy *or* finicky about one's food; ***in der Kleidung - sein,*** be particular *or* careful *or* tidy in one's dress.

-eigen, *adj.suff.* property of, belonging to; (*e.g.* ***staatseigen,*** state-owned; ***bahneigenes Gelände,*** railway property).

Eigenantrieb ['aɪgənˀantri:p], *m.* ***mit -,*** self-propelling, self-propelled (*vehicle*), self-powered, self-driven (*machine*).

Eigenart ['aɪgənˀa:rt], *f.* peculiarity, individuality, singularity, peculiar nature *or* character. **eigenartig,** *adj.* peculiar, strange, odd, queer, singular. **eigenartigerweise,** *adv.* strange to say, strangely *or* oddly (enough). **Eigenartigkeit,** *f.* peculiarity, strangeness, oddness, queerness.

Eigen|bedarf, *m.* personal requirements. **-bericht,** *m.* (*Press*) from our own correspondent. **-besitz,** *m.* personal property; personal ownership, proprietorship. **-besitzer,** *m.* proprietor, owner. **-bewegung,** *f.* (*Astr.*) proper motion. **-brödler,** *m.* crank, eccentric, oddity; recluse. **eigenbrödlerisch,** *adj.* eccentric, cranky, queer; solitary. **Eigen|brötler,** *m. See* **-brödler. eigen|brötlerisch,** *adj. See* **-brödlerisch.**

Eigen|dünkel, *m.* self-conceit, self-importance, (*coll.*) bumptiousness. **-frequenz,** *f.* fundamental *or* natural *or* resonant frequency. **-geräusch,** *n.* needle scratch, surface noise (*gramophone*). **-geschwindigkeit,** *f.* (*Phys.*) initial velocity; (*Av.*) air speed. **-gesetzlichkeit,** *f.* determination by inner laws, uninhibited individuality (*of the mind*). **-gewässer,** *n.pl.* territorial waters. **-gewicht,** *n.* dead weight, tare weight.

eigenhändig ['aɪgənhɛndɪç], *adj.* with one's own hand(s), personally, in one's own handwriting; ***-es Manuskript,*** autograph; ***-er Brief,*** holograph letter; ***einen Brief - abgeben,*** deliver a letter to the addressee in person *or* into the addressee's hands.

Eigenheit ['aɪgənhaɪt], *f.* peculiarity, singularity, oddity, idiosyncrasy, peculiar nature; peculiarity, strangeness, queerness, oddness, odd manner (*of a p.*).

Eigen|hilfe, *f.* self-help. **-hörigkeit,** *f.* (*Hist.*) serfdom, bondage. **-leute,** *pl.* (*Hist.*) serfs, bond(s)men, thralls, vassals. **-liebe,** *f.* egoism; self-love, narcissism. **-lob,** *n.* self-praise, (*coll.*) blowing one's own trumpet; (*Prov.*) ***- stinkt,*** self-praise is no recommendation.

Eigenmacht ['aɪgənmaxt], *f.* (assumed) authority, (*Law*) trespass, unlawful interference. **eigenmächtig,** *adj.* arbitrary, unauthorized, unsanctioned, on (*one's*) own authority, (*coll.*) off (*one's*) own bat, without authority *or* permission *or* consent; high-handed. **Eigenmächtigkeit,** *f.* unauthorized step *or* action; highhandedness.

Eigen|mann, *m.* (*pl.* **-leute**) (*Hist.*) serf, bond(s)-man, thrall, vassal. **-name,** *m.* proper name; (*Gram.*) proper noun. **-nutz,** *m.* self-interest, selfishness; (*Nat. Soc. slogan*) ***Gemeinnutz geht vor -,*** the state's needs override personal profit. **eigennützig,** *adj.* selfish, self-seeking. **Eigennützigkeit,** *f.* selfishness.

eigens ['aɪgəns], *adv.* expressly, on purpose, especially, particularly.

Eigenschaft ['aɪgənʃaft], *f.* quality (*of a p.*), property (*of a th.*), attribute (*of a p. or th.*); capacity; ***Farbe ist eine - des Lichtes,*** colour is a property of light; ***göttliche -,*** divine attribute; ***in seiner - als,*** in his capacity as *or* of; ***gute -en,*** good points *or* qualities. **Eigenschafts|verkettung,** *f.* correlation. **-wort,** *n.* adjective. **eigenschaftswörtlich,** *adj.* adjectival.

Eigen|schwingung, *f.* natural *or* free oscillation. **-sinn,** *m.* self-will, obstinacy; caprice, wilfulness. **eigen|sinnig,** *adj.* self-willed, headstrong, stubborn, obstinate; capricious. **-ständig,** *adj.* self-reliant, independent. **Eigensucht,** *f.* egoism; selfishness. **eigensüchtig,** *adj.* selfish, egoistic(al).

eigentlich ['aɪgəntlɪç], **1.** *adj.* proper, true, real, actual; ***die -en Umstände,*** the circumstances as such *or* (in) themselves. **2.** *adv.* properly *or* strictly speaking, in reality, in actual fact, actually, really; ***was soll das - bedeuten?*** what does that really mean? ***- habe ich es nicht erwartet,*** to tell the truth I did not expect it; ***was willst du -?*** what in fact do you want?

Eigenton [ˈaɪɡənto:n], *m.* characteristic sound.

Eigentum [ˈaɪɡəntu:m], *n.* (**-s,** *pl.* **⸚er**) **1.** property, belongings, possessions; ***bewegliches –,*** movable property *or* effects, personal estate, (goods and) chattels; ***unbewegliches –,*** real property; 2. ownership, proprietorship. **Eigentümer,** *m.* owner, proprietor. **eigentümlich,** *adj.* 1. (*Dat.*) belonging exclusively (to), proper (to), peculiar (to), characteristic (of), specific; 2. peculiar, singular, strange, queer, odd. **Eigentümlichkeit,** *f.* peculiarity, characteristic. **Eigentums|recht,** *n.* right of possession *or* ownership, proprietory right, title. **–titel,** *m.*, **–urkunde,** *f.* title-deed. **–verletzung,** *f.* damage to property, trespass.

Eigen|wärme, *f.* body-heat (*of animal etc.*), (*Geol.*) interior heat (*of earth*), (*Chem. etc.*) specific heat. **–wechsel,** *m.* (*Comm.*) note of hand, promissory note. **–wert,** *m.* actual *or* intrinsic value, value in itself; (*Math.*) eigenvalue. **–wille,** *m.* self-will, wilfulness. **eigenwillig,** *adj.* self-willed, with a will of (*one's*) own; highly individual, independent. **Eigenwilligkeit,** *f.* individuality, independence of mind. **Eigenwohnung,** *f.* owner-occupied dwelling. **eigenwüchsig,** *adj.* indigenous.

eignen [ˈaɪɡnən], **1.** *v.r.* be suitable *or* adapted *or* suited *or* qualified *or* (*coll.*) cut out (*für* or *zu*, for). **2.** *v.i.* (*Dat.*) be peculiar to *or* characteristic of; (*obs.*) belong to; *– **für** or **zu, geeignet sein für** or **zu,*** *see* **1. Eigner,** *m.* owner, proprietor. **Eignung,** *f.* suitability. **Eignungsprüfung,** *f.* aptitude test.

Ei|haut, –hülle, *f.* chorion. **–klar,** *n.* (*Austr.*) white of egg.

Eiland [ˈaɪlant], *n.* (**-es,** *pl.* **-e**) (*Poet.*) island, isle.

Eil|bestellung [ˈaɪl–], *f.* express *or* special delivery. **–bote,** *m.* special delivery *or* express messenger. **–botschaft,** *f.* express letter *or* telegram. **–brief,** *m.* express letter, (*Am.*) special delivery letter.

Eile [ˈaɪlə], *f.* haste, hurry; ***in*** (***der***) **–**, in haste, in a hurry; ***es hat keine –,*** there is no hurry, there is plenty of time.

Eileiter [ˈaɪlaɪtər], *m.* (*Anat.*) Fallopian tube; (*Orn.*) oviduct. **Eileiterschwangerschaft,** *f.* ectopic pregnancy.

eilen [ˈaɪlən], *v.i.* (*aux.* s.), *v.r.* (*of a p.*) make haste, lose no time, hasten, hurry (up), (*coll.*) rush, dash; (*of a th.*) be urgent *or* pressing; ***Eilt!*** urgent! (*on letters*); ***das eilt ja nicht,*** that is not by any means urgent; ***was eilen Sie so?*** why are you in such a hurry? ***sie eilen nicht sehr damit,*** they take their time over it; (*Prov.*) ***eile mit Weile,*** more haste less speed, slow and steady wins the race. **eilends,** *adv.* hurriedly, quickly. **eilfertig,** *adj.* hasty, rash. **Eil|fertigkeit,** *f.* overhaste; hastiness, rashness. **–fracht,** *f.*, **–gut,** *n.* express goods *or* freight.

eilig [ˈaɪlɪç], *adj.* quick, speedy, hurried; ***es – haben,*** be in a hurry; ***die S. ist nicht so –,*** the matter is not so urgent; ***–e Drucksache,*** urgent printed matter; ***nicht so –!*** don't be in such a hurry! ***sie hatte nichts Eiligeres zu tun, als die ganze Geschichte zu erzählen,*** she could not rest until she had told the whole story. **Eiligkeit,** *f.* urgency.

Eil|marsch, *m.* forced march. **–post,** *f.* express *or* (*Am.*) special delivery. **–schritt,** *m.* ***im –,*** at a fast walk *or* pace. **–sendung,** *f.* letter *or* parcel *etc.* by express *or* special delivery. **–tempo,** *n.* (*coll.*) ***im –,*** at high speed, quickly, hurriedly. **–zug,** *m.* limited stop *or* semi-fast train. **–zustellung,** *f. See* **–post.**

Eimer [ˈaɪmər], *m.* pail, bucket; hod, scuttle (*for coal*), can, bin (*for ashes etc.*). **Eimerkette,** *f.* bucket-chain. **eimerweise,** *adv.* in bucketfuls.

[1]**ein** [aɪn], *m.*, **eine,** *f.*, **ein,** *n.* **1.** *num.adj.* one (single), a single; the same; ***– Herz und –e Seele sein,*** be hand in glove, be the best of friends; ***–er Meinung sein mit,*** be of the same opinion as; (*coll.*) ***in –er Tour,*** in *or* at one go, without a break; ***–e um die andere Woche,*** one week in two *or* out of two, every other *or* second week; ***– für allemal,*** once and for all. **2.** *indef.adj.* 1. (*Acc. for specific time*) ***–en Herbst vor einigen Jahren,*** one autumn some years ago; ***kommen Sie –en Abend nächste Woche,*** come one *or* some evening next week; 2. (*Gen. for indefinite time*) ***–es Abends im vorigen Winter,*** one evening last winter; ***–es Tages werde ich reich sein,*** one *or* some day I will be rich. **3.** *indef.art.* (*before consonant*) a, (*before vowel*) an; ***so*** or ***solch –e*** or ***–e solche unruhige Nacht,*** such a disturbed night; ***was für – Mann?*** what sort *or* kind of a man? (*exclamation*) what a man! (*as emph. individualization usu. untranslated*) ***das war –e Kälte!*** it was exceptionally cold, the cold was quite unusual; ***– Schreien und Lärmen sondergleichen,*** screaming and shouting such as you never heard. **4.** *pron.* (*einer, m., eine, f., ein(e)s, n.*) ***ich hatte zwei Brüder, –er starb,*** I had two brothers, one died; ***–er meiner Brüder,*** one of my brothers; ***–er für alle und alle für –en,*** one for all and all for one; ***nicht –er meiner Freunde besucht mich,*** not (a single) one of my friends visits me; ***–s nach dem anderen,*** one thing after the other; ***ich habe einen Hund bekommen. Was für –en? So –en, wie ich ihn mir gewünscht habe,*** I have got a dog. What sort of one? One just like I wanted; ***ich bin nicht –er, der . . .,*** I am not (the) one to . . .; ***nicht das –e ohne das andere,*** not the one without the other; (*indefinite*) ***es ist leicht wenn –er so viel Geld hat,*** it is easy if one has *or* you have so much money; ***das tut –em ganz gut,*** that does one *or* you good.

[2]**ein–,** *pref.* 1. (*forming numerals*) –one; *e.g.* ***–unddreißig,*** thirty-one, (*obs.*) one and thirty; ***–hundert,*** one hundred; 2. (*forming adjs.*) one-, single; uni-, mono-; *e.g.* ***–achsig,*** uniaxial; ***–äugig,*** one-eyed; ***–gleisig,*** single-rail; ***–silbig,*** monosyllabic. **Ein–,** *pref.* (*forming nouns*) *e.g.* ***–bahnstraße,*** one-way street; ***–klang,*** unison; ***–sitzer,*** single-seater; ***–tönigkeit,*** monotony.

[3]**ein,** *adv.* ***– und aus,*** in and out; ***nicht*** or ***weder – noch aus*** or ***weder aus noch – wissen,*** be at one's wits' end, not know which way to turn, have no idea what to do: ***Jahr aus Jahr –,*** year in year out.

[4]**ein–,** *sep. pref. forms v.t. and less usu. v.i. indicating among other notions*: motion into, *e.g.* ***einmarschieren in,*** march in(to); insertion, *e.g.* ***einfügen,*** fit into; inclusion, *e.g.* ***einmischen in,*** mix in with; enclosure, *e.g.* ***einwickeln,*** wrap up; increasing familiarity, *oft. v.r., e.g.* ***sich einleben,*** acclimatize o.s.; diminution, *e.g.* ***eingehen,*** shrink; addition of the notion of the simplex, *e.g.* ***einsalzen,*** add salt to. *For further examples see below.*

einachsig [ˈaɪnˀaksɪç], *adj.* two-wheeled, uniaxial.

einackern [ˈaɪnˀakərn], *v.t.* plough in.

Einakter [ˈaɪnˀaktər], *m.* one-act play. **einaktig,** *adj.* one-act.

einander [aɪnˈandər], *indecl.pron.* one another, each other. **–einander,** *adv.suff.* each other, one another; *see* **aneinander, auseinander, beieinander, durcheinander, füreinander, hintereinander, ineinander, miteinander, nacheinander, nebeneinander, voneinander** *etc.*

Einankerumformer [ˈaɪnˀaŋkərˀumfɔrmər], *m.* (*Elec.*) rotary convertor.

einarbeiten [ˈaɪnˀarbaɪtən], **1.** *v.t.* train, break in; ***– in*** (*Acc.*), work into (*as flour into a mixture*), (*fig.*) work into, incorporate in (*as incidents into a story*). **2.** *v.r.* ***sich – in*** (*Acc. or Dat.*), make o.s. thoroughly acquainted with, get used to, get into the way of (*doing*), familiarize o.s. with; (*coll.*) work *or* break o.s. in, get the hang of.

einarmig [ˈaɪnˀarmɪç], *adj.* one-armed.

einäschern [ˈaɪnˀɛʃərn], *v.t.* burn *or* reduce to ashes; incinerate; cremate (*a corpse*). **Einäscherung,** *f.* incineration, cremation. **Einäscherungshalle,** *f.* crematorium.

einatmen [ˈaɪnˀa:tmən], *v.t.*, *v.i.* inhale, breathe in. **Einatmung,** *f.* inhalation, inhaling, breathing in.

einätzen [ˈaɪnˀɛtsən], *v.t.* etch into.

einäugeln [ˈaɪnˀɔyɡəln], *v.t.* graft into.

einäugig [ˈaɪnˀɔyɡɪç], *adj.* one-eyed.

einbahnig [ˈaɪnba:nɪç], *adj.* single-line *or* lane (*traffic*), one-way (*street*). **Einbahnstraße,** *f.* one-way street.

einbalsamieren [ˈaɪnbalzami:rən], *v.t.* embalm. **Einbalsamierung,** *f.* embalming; embalmment.

Einband ['aɪnbant], *m.* (**-s**, *pl.* **¨e**) binding, cover (*of a book*). **Einbanddecke,** *f.* book-cover.

einbändig ['aɪnbɛndɪç], *adj.* in one volume, one-volume.

einbasisch ['aɪnba:zɪʃ], *adj.* (*Chem.*) monobasic (*acid*).

Einbau ['aɪnbau], *m.* fitting (in), installation; (*pl.* **-ten**) (internal) fitting, built-in element, addition (built in). **Einbauantenne,** *f.* (*Rad.*) built-in aerial. **einbauen,** *v.t.* (*in* (*Acc.*)) install, fit (in), build (into), mount (permanently) (on); (*fig.*) work (into), incorporate (in); ***eingebaute Schränke,*** built-in cupboards. **einbaufertig,** *adj.* ready for fitting. **Einbauküche,** *f.* ready-fitted kitchen.

Einbaum ['aɪnbaum], *m.* dug-out canoe, primitive boat.

Einbau|möbel, *n.pl.* unit furniture. **-schrank,** *m.* built-in cupboard.

einbegreifen ['aɪnbəgraɪfən], *irr.v.t.* comprise, contain, embrace; sum up (*in* (*Acc. or Dat.*), in); ***mit einbegriffen,*** included in, inclusive of.

einbehalten ['aɪnbəhaltən], *irr.v.t.* keep back, withhold (*Dat.*, from), retain; deduct (*taxes*). **Einbehaltung,** *f.* retention, deduction.

einbekennen ['aɪnbəkɛnən], *irr.v.t.* admit, acknowledge; (*Austr.*) declare *or* return one's income. **Einbekennung,** *f.* (*Austr.*) income-tax return.

einberufen ['aɪnbəru:fən], *irr.v.t.* call together, summon, convene, convoke, (*coll.*) call (*a meeting*); (*Mil.*) call up, draft, conscript (*zu*, for *or* into), call out (*reserves*). **Einberufung,** *f.* convocation, summoning (*of a meeting*), call-up, conscription, draft (*of troops*). **Einberufungsbefehl,** *m.* call-up order *or* papers.

einbetonieren ['aɪnbeto:ni:rən], *v.t.* set in concrete.

einbetten ['aɪnbɛtən], *v.t.* (em)bed, bury (*in* (*Acc.*), in); ***eingebettet sein*** or ***liegen,*** nestle.

einbeziehen ['aɪnbətsi:ən], *irr.v.t.* (*in* (*Acc.*)) include (in), incorporate (into); (*in* (*Acc. or Dat.*)) ***einbezogen sein,*** be included (in). **Einbeziehung,** *f.* inclusion, incorporation.

einbiegen ['aɪnbi:gən], **1.** *irr.v.t.* bend inwards *or* downwards *or* back. **2.** *irr.v.i.* (*aux.* s.) turn, take a turning (*in* (*Acc.*), into *or* down). **Einbiegung,** *f.* inward bend *or* curve.

einbilden ['aɪnbɪldən], *v.t.* (*with Dat. refl. pron.*) 1. fancy, suppose, imagine, think, believe, (*sl.*) kid o.s.; 2. be conceited, give o.s. airs, (*coll.*) think a lot of o.s., be stuck up; ***sich*** (*Dat.*) ***– auf*** (*Acc.*), flatter *or* pride o.s. on, be conceited *or* (*coll.*) stuck up about; ***eingebildet,*** imaginary; vain, conceited, (*coll.*) stuck up. **Einbildung,** *f.* imagination, fancy, the mind's eye; ***er leidet an -en,*** he suffers from delusions *or* hallucinations. **Einbildungs|-kraft,** *f.*, **-vermögen,** *n.* imagination, fantasy.

einbinden ['aɪnbɪndən], *irr.v.t.* bind (*a book*); furl (*sails*); take in (*a reef*); hoop (*a barrel*), tyre, shoe (*a wheel*); ***– in*** (*Acc.*), tie into, tie up (together) with, tie on to.

einblasen ['aɪnbla:zən], *irr.v.t.* 1. blow *or* breathe (*in* (*Acc.*), into); inject (*steam etc.*), insufflate; (*fig.*) whisper, suggest, insinuate (*Dat.*, to); ***seinem Nachbarn die Antwort –,*** prompt one's neighbour with the answer (*in school*); 2. (*of the wind*) blow down (*walls*), blow in (*windows etc.*). **Einblasung,** *f.* (*Med.*) insufflation, resuscitation *or* artificial respiration by expired air method, (*coll.*) kiss of life. **Einbläser,** *m.* prompter; insinuator; (*Med.*) insufflator.

Einblattdruck ['aɪnblatdruk], *m.* broadsheet.

einblättrig ['aɪnblɛtrɪç], *adj.* monophyllous, unifoliate.

einblenden ['aɪnblɛndən], *v.t.* focus, concentrate (*rays*); ***– in*** (*Acc.*), blend with (*colours*), (*Rad., Films*) fade in.

einbleuen ['aɪnblɔyən], *v.t.* (*coll.*) knock, hammer, drive, ram, drum (*Dat.*, into).

Einblick ['aɪnblɪk], *m.* insight (*in* (*Acc.*), into). **Einblickfenster,** *n.* eyepiece.

einbrechen ['aɪnbrɛçən], **1.** *irr.v.t.* break *or* smash in *or* down *or* open; break in (*a horse*). **2.** *irr.v.i.* (*aux.* s.) (*of a th.*) fall in, collapse, give way, (*coll.*) cave in; (*of a p.*) break through (*ice etc.*); ***– in*** (*Acc.*), (*of troops*) march into, invade; (*of burglar*) break in(to); (*fig.*) (*of night*) close in, fall; (*of winter*) set in; ***bei –der Nacht,*** at nightfall; ***bei –der Dunkelheit,*** when darkness falls *or* fell. **Einbrecher,** *m.* burglar, housebreaker.

einbrennen ['aɪnbrɛnən], *irr.v.t.* brand (*animal*); stove (*enamel*), fix by firing; (*Cul.*) brown (*flour*). **Einbrenn|lack,** *m.* stove enamel. **-soße,** *f.* brown sauce.

einbringen ['aɪnbrɪŋən], *irr.v.t.* 1. bring *or* get in (*crops*); bring in *or* back (*prisoner*), send in, submit (*application*), bring, lodge (*complaint*), make, propose (*suggestion*), put, introduce, bring forward (*motion*); ***– in*** (*Acc.*), get *or* put into; ***wieder –,*** make up for (*lost time*), retrieve, make good (*loss*); (*Typ.*) ***Raum –,*** make room (*for insertion*); 2. bring in, yield, bear, produce (*profit*), win, gain (*approbation, friends*); ***Ehre –,*** bring *or* do credit (*Dat.*, to); ***das Eingebrachte,*** dowry. **einbringlich,** *adj.* profitable, lucrative, paying (*business etc.*).

einbröckeln ['aɪnbrœkəln], *v.i.* (*aux.* s.) crumble (to pieces).

einbrocken ['aɪnbrɔkən], *v.t.* crumble, break into small pieces; ***sich*** (*Dat.*) ***etwas –,*** get into trouble, (*coll.*) land o.s. in a nice mess *or* fix *or* pickle, let o.s. in for s.th., put one's foot in it; ***er muß nun auslöffeln, was er sich eingebrockt hat,*** now he's made his bed he must lie on it.

Einbruch ['aɪnbrux], *m.* 1. collapse, breaking down, falling *or* (*coll.*) caving in, (*Min.*) fall (*of roof*), (*Geol.*) subsidence, sinking, down-faulting; (*Comm.*) fall, drop, decline, slump (*in prices*); 2. incursion (*also Mil.*), encroachment, ingress (*of sea*); (*Law*) breaking and entering, (*by day*) housebreaking, (*by night*) burglary; 3. onset; ***– der Nacht,*** nightfall; 4. (*Her.*) bar sinister.

Einbruchs|becken, *n.* (*Geol.*) syncline. **-diebstahl,** *m.* (*Law*) (*by day*) theft by breaking and entering, (*coll.*) daylight robbery, (*by night*) burglary. **-flieger,** *m.* (*Av.*) intruder, (*coll.*) tip-and-run raider. **-front,** *f.* (*Meteor.*) cold front. **einbruchssicher,** *adj.* burglar-proof. **Einbruchstal,** *m.* (*Geol.*) rift valley.

einbuchten ['aɪnbuxtən], *v.t.* 1. indent, hollow out; 2. (*coll.*) put in jug. **Einbuchtung,** *f.* indentation, hollow, recess; (*Geog.*) bay.

einbürgern ['aɪnbyːrgərn], **1.** *v.t.* naturalize (*alien*), acclimatize (*plant, animal*); ***eingebürgerte Lehnwörter,*** naturalized loanwords. **2.** *v.r.* become naturalized *or* acclimatized *or* established *or* adopted, take root, come into use, gain vogue; settle, establish o.s.; ***dieses Wort hat sich eingebürgert,*** this word has come to stay. **Einbürgerung,** *f.* naturalization.

Einbuße ['aɪnbu:sə], *f.* loss, forfeiture. **einbüßen,** *v.t.* suffer loss (*bei*, from), lose (on *or* by), forfeit.

eindämmen ['aɪndɛmən], *v.t.* dam up (*water*), embank (*land*); (*fig.*) check, stem, stay, limit, control.

eindampfen ['aɪndampfən], *v.i.* (*aux.* s.) 1. boil down *or* away, thicken (*through boiling*), evaporate; 2. steam *or* come steaming in (*as a train*).

eindämpfen ['aɪndɛmpfən], *v.t.* boil down *or* away, evaporate, thicken (by boiling), inspissate.

eindecken ['aɪndɛkən], **1.** *v.t.* 1. cover (up *or* over); roof (*a building*); provide (*a trench etc.*) with a cover *or* roof; ***mit Stroh –,*** thatch; ***mit Ziegeln –,*** tile; 2. (*fig.*) provide, stock up (*mit*, with), lay in a supply *or* stock *or* store (of).

Eindecker ['aɪndɛkər], *m.* (*Av.*) monoplane; single-decker (*bus etc.*).

Eindeckung ['aɪndɛkuŋ], *f.* 1. overhead cover, roof; covering, roofing; 2. (*fig.*) sufficient supply, provision (*of stores*).

eindeutig ['aɪndɔytɪç], *adj.* clear, plain, unequivocal, unambiguous, unmistakable. **Eindeutigkeit,** *f.* unequivocalness, singleness of meaning.

eindeutschen [ˈaındɔytʃən], *v.t.* Germanize, translate into German.
eindicken [ˈaındıkən], **1.** *v.t.* boil down, thicken, condense, inspissate, concentrate. **2.** *v.i.* (*aux.* s.) thicken, get *or* become thick, coagulate.
eindorren [ˈaındɔrən], *v.t.* dry up, shrink.
eindrängen [ˈaındrɛŋən], *v.t.* force *or* push o.s. in, squeeze (o.s.) in, crowd in; intrude *or* force o.s. (*bei*, on); (*of water*) come *or* run *or* seep *or* pour *or* rush in.
eindrehen [ˈaındre:ən], *v.t.* screw in.
eindringen [ˈaındrıŋən], *irr.v.i.* (*aux.* s.) 1. (*in* (*Acc.*)) make *or* force one's way into, penetrate, enter, invade; (*of crowd*) throng *or* surge into; (*of water*) *see* **eindrängen**; (*fig.*) study closely, go deeply into; see into (*the future*); penetrate, fathom (*a secret*); move deeply, cut, wound; 2. (*auf* (*Acc.*)) attack, assault, storm, charge, rush (*the enemy*), (*of a crowd*) mob; (*fig.*) entreat, beseech; plead *or* reason with, beg, urge, press, ply (*with questions*).
eindringlich [ˈaındrıŋlıç], **1.** *adj.* forcible, urgent; moving, striking, vivid, impressive. **2.** *adv.* urgently; strongly, sternly, strictly. **Eindringlichkeit,** *f.* forcefulness, urgency. **Eindringling,** *m.* (**-s,** *pl.* **-e**) intruder, (*coll.*) gatecrasher. **Eindring(ungs)tiefe,** *f.* (*Mil.*) operational radius (*of raiding aircraft*), depth of penetration (*measured from coast or frontier, not from base*).
1 **Eindruck** [ˈaındruk], *m.* (**-(e)s,** *pl.* **-̈e**) impress(ion), imprint, mark, stamp; (mental) impression; – *machen*, produce an impression, be impressive.
2 **Eindruck,** *m.* (**-(e)s,** *pl.* **-e**) 1. printing, blocking *or* grounding in (*colour*); 2. (*Typ.*) insert. **eindrucken,** *v.t.* 1. print, block *or* ground in (*cloth*); 2. (*Typ.*) insert (*printed matter*); emboss.
eindrücken [ˈaındrykən], **1.** *v.t.* press *or* push *or* stave in; crush, flatten (down), squash, smash; – *in* (*Acc.*), press into, press down in; imprint, impress (on). **2.** *v.r.* (*of a th.*) be impressed *or* imprinted, leave an imprint *or* impress *or* impression, imprint, impress (*on the memory*). **eindrücklich,** *adj.* impressive, emphatic.
eindrucks|fähig, *adj.* impressionable, sensitive. **–voll,** *adj.* impressive.
eindunsten [ˈaındunstən], *see* **eindampfen.**
eindünsten [ˈaındynstən], *see* **eindämpfen.**
eine, *see* **ein.**
einebnen [ˈaınʔe:bnən], *v.t.* level, even up; flatten, demolish, raze to the ground.
Einehe [ˈaınʔe:ə], *f.* monogamy.
eineiig [ˈaınʔaııç], *adj.* uniovular, (*coll.*) identical (*twins*).
eineinhalb [ˈaınʔaınhalb], *num.adj.* one and a half.
einen [ˈaınən], **1.** *v.t.* unite, unify. **2.** *v.r.* unite, become united *or* unified.
einengen [ˈaınʔɛŋən], *v.t.* narrow (down), make narrower; restrict, confine, hem in, limit, set limits *or* bounds to, constrict. **Einengung,** *f.* limitation, restriction; narrowing, confining, limiting, restricting; constriction.
Einer [ˈaınər], *m.* 1. (*Math.*) unit; 2. (*Rowing*) single-sculler.
einer, *see* **ein.**
einerlei [ˈaınərlaı], *indecl.adj.* of one sort *or* kind; (*coll.*) ***es ist alles*** –, it's all one *or* all the same, it makes no difference, it doesn't matter; ***es ist ziemlich*** –, it matters little, it makes little difference. **Einerlei,** *n.* monotony, sameness; humdrum routine.
einernten [ˈaınʔɛrntən], *v.t.* harvest, gather in; (*fig.*) win, earn, gain, acquire.
einerseits [ˈaınərzaıts], **einesteils,** *adv.* on the one hand *or* side, in one respect.
einexerzieren [ˈaınʔɛksɛrtsi:rən], *v.t.* drill, train.
einfach [ˈaınfax], *adj.* 1. single; ***–e Farben,*** primary colours; (*Gram.*) ***–er Satz,*** simple sentence; (*Gram.*) ***–e Zeit,*** simple tense; (*Comm.*) ***–er Zins,*** simple interest; 2. simple, elementary, easy; (*Math.*) ***einen Bruch auf die –ste Form bringen,*** reduce a fraction to its lowest terms; (*fig.*) ***es auf den –sten Nenner bringen,*** put it in a nutshell; 3. simple, plain, ordinary, homely, frugal; ***der –e Mann,*** the common man, the man in the street; ***–er Soldat,*** common *or* ordinary soldier, private, *pl.* rank and file, other ranks. **Einfachheit,** *f.* simplicity; plainness; elementary nature, singleness. **Einfachleitung,** *f.* (*Elec.*) single conductor.
einfädeln [ˈaınfɛ:dəln], *v.t.* 1. thread (*a needle*); ***soll ich Ihnen –?*** shall I thread the needle for you? 2. (*also v.r.*) filter (*traffic*); 3. (*coll.*) get *or* set going, set on foot, set the ball rolling.
einfahren [ˈaınfa:rən], **1.** *irr.v.t.* bring *or* fetch *or* get *or* take *or* carry in (*on wheels*); (*Av.*) retract (*undercarriage*); break in (*horse*), run in (*a new engine*); smash (*gate, etc. in collision*). **2.** *irr.v.r.* (*of new car*) (be) run in, (*of a p.*) get used to driving. **3.** *irr.v.i.* (*aux.* s.) (*in* (*Acc.*)) drive into, enter; (*of train*) come in(to), enter; (*of ship*) enter (*port*); descend (*a mine*). **Einfahr|gleis,** *n.* (*Railw.*) arrival line. **–signal,** *n.* (*Railw.*) home signal.
Einfahrt [ˈaınfa:rt], *f.* entrance, gateway; access road; pit-head; way in; harbour mouth; entry, arrival; descent (*of a mine*). **Einfahrtssignal,** *n.* *See* **Einfahrsignal.**
Einfall [ˈaınfal], *m.* 1. falling in, falling down, fall, collapse; 2. (*Mil.*) invasion (*in* (*Acc.*), of), incursion, raid, sally (into); 3. incidence (*of light*); 4. sudden idea, brainwave, fancy, notion; ***witziger*** –, flash of wit; ***wunderlicher*** –, whim, conceit; ***ich geriet auf den*** –, it struck me, the idea occurred to me, it came into my head. **einfallen, 1.** *irr.v.i.* (*aux.* s.) 1. fall in *or* down, collapse, give way, cave in; (*of features*) become hollow *or* gaunt *or* haggard *or* wasted *or* sunken; ***eingefallene Augen,*** sunken *or* hollow eyes; ***eingefallene Wangen,*** gaunt *or* hollow *or* sunken *or* pinched cheeks; 2. (*in* (*Acc.*)) invade, make an inroad *or* raid *or* incursion into, overrun; interrupt, break in (on), come *or* join in, (*coll.*) chime *or* butt in; 3. (*Dat.*) occur (to), strike (*s.o.*); ***das hätte ich mir nie – lassen,*** I should never have dreamt of such a thing, it would never have entered my head; ***wie es ihm gerade einfiel,*** as the humour seized him; ***es will mir nicht*** –, I cannot remember it; ***was fällt dir ein?*** what are you thinking of? what do you mean by it? ***es fällt mir nicht ein, das zu tun,*** I have not the least intention of doing so, (*coll.*) catch me doing that; 4. alight, come down to roost (*of birds*); enter (from above), fall, be incident (*as light*); 5. engage, snap *or* click to (*as a lock*); 6. fall (*as night*), set in (*as winter*). **2.** *irr.v.t.* ***sich*** (*Dat.*) ***den Schädel*** –, crack one's skull by a fall. **einfallend,** *adj.* incident (*ray*); (*Min.*) ***–er Schacht,*** incline; (*Min.*) ***–es Wetter,*** intake air. **Einfallklinke,** *f.* pawl, catch. **Einfallslot,** *n.* perpendicular. **Einfall(s)winkel,** *m.* angle of incidence.
Einfalt [ˈaınfalt], *f.* simplicity, artlessness, naïveté; simpleness, simple-mindedness, stupidity.
einfalten [ˈaınfaltən], *v.t.* turn *or* fold in *or* down.
einfältig [ˈaınfɛltıç], *adj.* simple, single; simple (-hearted), artless, naïve; simple(-minded), stupid. **Einfältigkeit,** *f.* singleness, simplicity; simplicity, artlessness, naïveté; simpleness, simple-mindedness, stupidity.
Einfaltspinsel [ˈaınfaltspınsəl], *m.* (*coll.*) simpleton.
Einfamilienhaus [ˈaınfami:liənhaus], *n.* villa, self-contained house.
einfangen [ˈaınfaŋən], **1.** *irr.v.t.* seize, catch, capture, apprehend, (*fig.*) catch, capture (*a mood*). **2.** *irr.v.i.* catch (on).
Einfarbdrossel [ˈaınfarpdrɔsəl], *f.* (*Orn.*) Tickell's thrush (*Turdus unicolor*).
einfärben [ˈaınfɛrbən], *v.t.* dye (*fabric*), (*Typ.*) ink (*type*).
einfarbig [ˈaınfarbıç], *adj.* plain, of one colour, self-coloured, monochrome.
Einfarbstar [ˈaınfarpʃta:r], *m.* (*Orn.*) spotless starling (*Sturnus unicolor*).
einfassen [ˈaınfasən], *v.t.* surround, enclose, encompass; bound, close in; fence *or* hedge *or* wall in;

border, line, edge; bind, hem, braid, pipe, trim (*fabric*); set, mount (*jewels*). **Einfassung,** *f.* border, edge, frame; mount(ing), setting, bezel (*of jewel*); curb(-stone), lip (*of well*). **Einfassungs|band,** *n.* (bias) binding. **–mauer,** *f.* surrounding *or* retaining wall.

einfetten ['aɪnfɛtən], *v.t.* grease, oil, lubricate; rub in (*grease etc.*).

einfeuchten ['aɪnfɔyçtən], *v.t.* wet, moisten, damp, sprinkle.

einfinden ['aɪnfɪndən], *irr.v.r.* 1. appear, make one's appearance, present o.s., arrive, (*coll.*) turn up (*an* (*Dat.*), at; *zu*, for); 2. familiarize o.s. (*in* (*Dat.*), with).

einflechten ['aɪnflɛçtən], *v.t.* plait, interlace, interweave (*in* (*Acc.*), into); adorn with; insert, include, mention casually, put in (*a word*), interlard (*with oaths etc.*).

einflicken ['aɪnflɪkən], *irr.v.t.* insert, sew on (*a patch*); (*fig.*) interpolate.

einfliegen ['aɪnfli:gən], **1.** *irr.v.t.* 1. test (*a plane*), carry out test flight on *or* with; 2. fly in (*troops, supplies*). **2.** *irr.v.i.* (*aux.* s.) fly in; – *in* (*Acc.*), fly into. **Einflieger,** *m.* test pilot.

einfließen ['aɪnfli:sən], *irr.v.i.* (*aux.* s.) flow in; come in (*of money*); – *in* (*Acc.*), flow into; (*mit*) – *lassen,* throw out *or* let fall *or* drop a hint; slip *or* throw in a word, let (*it*) be understood, mention casually.

einflößen ['aɪnflø:sən], *v.t.* (*Dat.*) feed with (*patients' food*), administer (*medicine*) to; impart (*s.th.*) to, instil (*s.th.*) into, imbue *or* infuse *or* inspire with (*s.th.*); *ihm Mut* –, inspire him with courage; *ihm Mitleid* –, enlist *or* arouse his sympathy.

Einflug ['aɪnflu:k], *m.* 1. test flight; 2. arrival (*at airport*); 3, penetration by enemy aircraft, attack from the air. **Einflugschneise,** *f.* (*Av.*) approach lane, air corridor.

Einfluß ['aɪnflus], *m.* 1. inflow, influx; inlet, entrance (*for water etc.*); 2. influence (*auf* (*Acc.*), (up)on *or* over; *bei*, with), effect, bearing ((up)on), power, sway (over), weight (with); – *haben auf* (*Acc.*), (*of a p.*) have influence over, have *or* exercise an influence over, influence; (*of a th.*) have an effect on, affect; – *bei Hofe,* influence *or* credit at court; *ein Name von* –, a name of consequence. **Einflußnahme,** *f.* exercise of influence. **einflußreich,** *adj.* influential. **Einfluß|röhre,** *f.* feed-pipe, inlet-pipe. **–sphäre,** *f.* sphere of influence.

einflüstern ['aɪnflystərn], *v.t.* (*Dat.*) whisper to, prompt. **Einflüsterung,** *f.* prompting(s), insinuation, innuendo.

einfordern ['aɪnfɔrdərn], *v.t.* call in, demand payment of (*debt*).

einförmig ['aɪnfœrmɪç], *adj.* uniform, unvaried, monotonous. **Einförmigkeit,** *f.* uniformity, monotony, (*coll.*) sameness.

einfressen ['aɪnfrɛsən], **1.** *irr.v.t.* 1. swallow; 2. eat into (*as acid*); *eingefressen,* corroded, pitted. **2.** *irr.v.r.* (*in* (*Acc.*)) eat into, corrode, erode.

einfried(ig)en ['aɪnfri:d(ɪg)ən], *v.t.* enclose, fence in. **Einfried(ig)ung,** *f.* enclosure; enclosed ground; fencing, fence.

einfrieren ['aɪnfri:rən], **1.** *irr.v.i.* (*aux.* s.) freeze in *or* up; be *or* become ice-bound. **2.** *irr.v.t.* freeze (*foodstuffs, also* (*fig.*) *capital*); *eingefrorene Kredite,* frozen assets.

einfügen ['aɪnfy:gən], **1.** *v.t.* (*in* (*Acc.*)) fit *or* set into, insert in, interpolate (*word etc.*); (*Carp.*) dovetail, rabbet. **2.** *v.r.* (*fig.*) (*in* (*Acc.*)) fit in (with), adapt o.s. (to). **Einfügung,** *f.* insertion; interpolation, interpolated word (*etc.*), parenthesis.

einfühlen ['aɪnfy:lən], *v.r.* (*in* (*Acc.*)) have a sympathetic understanding (of), project o.s. into the mind (of) (*a p.*), get into the spirit (of) (*ideas, author's work etc.*). **Einfühlung,** *f.* sympathetic understanding; empathy.

Einfuhr ['aɪnfu:r], *f.* (-, *pl.* **-en**) imports, imported goods; import(ation).

einführbar ['aɪnfy:rba:r], *adj.* (*Comm.*) importable.

Einfuhr|beschränkung, *f.* import restriction. **–bewilligung,** *f. See* **–erlaubnis.**

einführen ['aɪnfy:rən], *v.t.* 1. introduce, initiate, institute, inaugurate, establish, (*coll.*) bring in, set up; set, start (*a fashion*); 2. introduce (*a p.*) (*in* (*Acc.*), into (*a family*)), present (*a p.*) (*bei*, to (*a p.*), at (*court etc.*)); install (*a p. in an office*), induct (*a clergyman in a living*); 3. (*Comm.*) import (*goods*) (*in* (*Acc.*), into); 4. insert (*in* (*Acc.*), into), feed (in(to)), introduce (into), lead (*cable, pipes etc.*) (into).

Einfuhr|erlaubnis, –genehmigung, *f.* import permit *or* licence. **–handel,** *m.* import trade. **–prämie,** *f.* import bounty. **–schein,** *m.* (preferential) import licence.

Einführung ['aɪnfy:ruŋ], *f.* introduction, initiation, inauguration, establishment, institution; introduction, presentation (*of a p.*), installation, induction; introduction, insertion (*of a th.*); (*Comm.*) importation. **Einführungs|kabel,** *n.* lead-in (cable). **–schreiben,** *n.* letter of introduction. **–unterricht,** *m.* preliminary instruction, introductory tuition. **–walze,** *f.* feed-roll (*typewriter etc.*).

Einfuhr|verbot, *n.* import embargo. **–zoll,** *m.* import duty. **–zuschuß,** *m.* import subsidy.

einfüllen ['aɪnfylən], *v t.* put *or* pour in; put, pour (*in* (*Acc.*), into), fill, charge (*a container*); *in Flaschen* –, bottle (*wine etc.*); *in Säcke* –, sack (*corn etc.*). **Einfülltrichter,** *m.* funnel, hopper.

Eingabe ['aɪnga:bə], *f.* petition, application (*für, um*, for; *bei*, to).

eingabeln ['aɪnga:bəln], *v.t.* (*Artil.*) bracket; straddle.

Eingang ['aɪngaŋ], *m.* entering, entry; arrival, receipt (*of goods etc.*); entrance, gateway, doorway, way in; inlet (*of a bay etc.*), mouth (*of a cave etc.*), (*Min.*) pithead, adit, (*fig.*) introduction, beginning, preamble, prelude; *pl.* (*Comm.*) receipts; deliveries, incoming mail; – *von Geld,* receipt of payment; *nach* –, on receipt *or* payment; *verbotener* –, *kein* –, no admittance, no entry; – *der Messe,* introit; – *finden bei,* be (well) received by, find favour *or* acceptance with; – *finden in* (*Acc.*), gain access *or* entry to; – *verschaffen* (*Dat.*), obtain access for, open the door to, clear a path *or* way for; *sich* (*Dat.*) – *verschaffen,* manage to get in, force one's way in.

eingängig ['aɪngɛŋɪç], **eingänglich,** *adj* comprehensible.

eingangs ['aɪngaŋs], *adv.* at the beginning *or* outset.

Eingangs|anzeige, –bestätigung, *f.* acknowledgement of receipt. **–buch,** *n.* register of deliveries *or* incoming mail. **–energie,** *f.* (*Elec.*) input. **–lied,** *n.* (*Eccl.*) introit. **–rede,** *f.* inaugural *or* opening speech. **–spannung,** *f.* (*Elec.*) input voltage. **–tor,** *n.* gate, gateway, portal. **–zoll,** *m. See* **Einfuhrzoll.**

eingeben ['aɪnge:bən], *irr.v.t.* 1. hand in, present (*application etc.*), put forward (*s.o.'s name*); – *um,* apply for, make application for; 2. (*Dat.*) administer to, feed with; (*fig.*) *ihm etwas* –, inspire him with s.th., suggest s.th. to him, (*coll.*) put s.th. into his head.

eingebildet ['aɪngəbɪldət], *adj. See* **einbilden.**

Eingebinde ['aɪngəbɪndə], *n.* (**-s,** *pl.* -) (*Poet.*) christening present.

eingeboren ['aɪngəbo:rən], *adj.* 1. native, indigenous (*population*); inborn, innate, inherent (*quality*); 2. (*B.*) only-begotten. **Eingeborene(r),** *m., f.* 1. native; 2. (*B.*) *der Eingeborene,* the only-begotten Son.

Eingebung ['aɪnge:buŋ], *f.* inspiration, suggestion.

eingedenk ['aɪngədɛŋk], *pred.adj.* (*Gen.*) mindful of, remembering; – *sein* (*Gen.*), bear *or* keep in mind.

eingefallen ['aɪngəfalən], *see* **einfallen.**

eingefleischt ['aɪngəflaɪʃt], *adj.* incarnate; (*fig.*) (*of a p.*) inveterate, confirmed, (*coll.*) die-hard, dyed-in-the-wool; (*of habits etc.*) confirmed, ingrained.

eingegossen ['aɪngəgɔsən], *see* **eingießen.**

eingehen ['aɪnge:ən], **1.** *irr.v.i.* (*aux.* s.) 1. come in, arrive, be received (*as goods*), come in, come to hand, be paid (*as funds*); (*Poet.*) – *in* (*Acc.*), come *or* enter in; 2. die, perish, cease to exist; (*of periodical*) cease publication; (*of fabric*) shrink; – *lassen,* close down (*business, publication etc.*); 3. (*Dat.*) be credible to; *das geht mir ein,* I realize *or* grasp *or* can see that; *es geht mir schwer* or *hart ein,* I find it hard to understand; 4. – *auf* (*Acc.*), go *or* enter into *or* consider carefully the details of; agree, consent, accede *or* submit to; comply *or* (*coll.*) fall in with, accept (*condition, request etc.*); *auf den Scherz* –, enter into (the spirit of) the joke. **2.** *irr.v.t.* enter into, (*coll.*) strike, clinch (*a bargain*), contract, conclude (*an agreement*), assume (*obligation*), incur, (*coll.*) run, take (*risk*), make, lay, take up (*wager*); *einen Vergleich* –, reach (an) agreement, come to terms. **eingehend,** *adj.* thorough, searching, exhaustive (*inquiry*), careful, close (*consideration*), detailed, circumstantial (*account*).

eingemacht ['aɪngəmaxt], *see* **einmachen.**

eingemeinden ['aɪngəmaɪndən], *v.t.* incorporate (*a suburb, village etc.*) (*Dat. or in* (*Acc.*), into).

eingenommen ['aɪngənɔmən], *adj.* – *von,* taken with, intrigued by; biased *or* prejudiced in favour of; *von sich* –, taken up with o.s., full of self-conceit *or* one's own importance, conceited; – *für,* well-disposed *or* biased towards, predisposed *or* prepossessed in favour of; – *gegen,* ill-disposed towards; biased *or* prejudiced *or* predisposed *or* prepossessed against; *see* **einnehmen. Eingenommenheit,** *f.* predilection, partiality (*für,* for), bias (*für,* towards *or* in favour of; *gegen,* against), prejudice (*für,* in favour of; *gegen,* against).

Eingerichte ['aɪngərɪçtə], *n.* (**-s,** *pl.* -) ward (*of lock*).

eingeschlechtig ['aɪngəʃlɛçtɪç], *adj.* (*Biol.*) unisexual; *-e Fortpflanzung,* parthenogenesis.

eingeschrieben ['aɪngəʃri:bən], *see* **einschreiben.**

eingesessen ['aɪngəzɛsən], *adj.* old-established.

eingestanden ['aɪngəʃtandən], *see* **eingestehen. eingestandenermaßen,** *adv.* on (*s.o.'s*) own admission. **Eingeständnis,** *n.* admission; acknowledgement (*of mistake*).

eingestehen ['aɪngəʃte:ən], *irr.v.t.* confess, admit, acknowledge, own (up) to. **Eingestehung,** *f. See* **Eingeständnis.**

eingestrichen ['aɪngəʃtrɪçən], *adj.* (*Mus.*) once-accented; *-es C,* middle C.

Eingeweide ['aɪngəvaɪdə], *n.* (**-s,** *pl.* -) (*usu. pl.*) viscera, (*coll.*) innards, guts; entrails (*of game*), guts (*of fish*); (*inaccurate use*) intestines, bowels; (*fig.*) bowels (*of the earth*). **Eingeweide|lehre,** *f.* (*Med.*) splanchnology. **-schau,** *f.* haruspicy, extispicy. **-vorfall,** *m.* (*Med.*) prolapsus. **-wurm,** *m.* intestinal worm.

Eingeweihte(r) ['aɪngəvaɪtə(r)], *m., f. See* **einweihen.**

eingewöhnen ['aɪngəvø:nən], **1.** *v.t.* accustom to new surroundings, make (*s.o.*) feel at home. **2.** *v.r.* get accustomed *or* used to new surroundings, become acclimatized, settle down.

eingezogen ['aɪngətso:gən], *adj.* retired, secluded; *see* **einziehen. Eingezogenheit,** *f.* seclusion.

eingießen ['aɪngi:sən], *irr.v.t.* 1. pour out (*tea etc.*); – *in* (*Acc.*), pour *or* run into (*a vessel*); 2. set *or* fix *or* cast in (*with cement etc.*); *eingegossen,* cast-in. **Eingießung,** *f.* (*Med.*) infusion; *see* **Einguß.**

eingittern ['aɪngɪtərn], *v.t.* fence off, rail in.

Eingitterröhre ['aɪngɪtərrø:rə], *f.* (*Rad.*) triode.

Einglas ['aɪnglas], *n.* monocle.

einglasen ['aɪngla:zən], *v.t.* glaze, put new glass in.

eingleisen ['aɪnglaɪzən], **1.** *v.t.* (*Railw.*) put on the rails (again), (*fig., coll.*) put right. **2.** *v.r.* (*coll.*) come (out all) right.

eingleisig ['aɪnglaɪzɪç], *adj.* single-track.

eingliedern ['aɪngli:dərn], **1.** *v.t.* incorporate insert, fit (*in* (*Acc.*), into). **2.** *v.r.* fit in; *sich* – *in* (*Acc.*), fit into. **Eingliederung,** *f.* incorporation, insertion.

eingraben ['aɪngra:bən], **1.** *irr.v.t.* bury; (*Build.*) drive, ram, sink (*in* (*Acc.*), into); carve, cut, incise, engrave, chase (*inscription*). **2.** *irr.v.r.* (*of animal*) dig itself in; (*fig.*) bury o.s. (*in* (*Acc.*), in) (*one's work etc.*); (*Mil.*) entrench o.s.; (*coll.*) dig in; *das Ereignis hat sich tief in mein Gedächtnis eingegraben,* the event is engraved *or* has impressed itself deeply in my memory.

eingravieren ['aɪngravi:rən], *v.t.* engrave.

eingreifen ['aɪngraɪfən], *irr.v.t.* 1. catch, hold, grip, bite (*as anchor etc.*); be in gear *or* mesh (*in* (*Acc.*), with), engage, mesh (*as cogs*); *ineinander* –, fit into *or* engage one another, interlock, (*fig.*) be interdependent; 2. take energetic action *or* drastic measures; – *in* (*Acc.*), influence decisively; intervene *or* interfere in, intrude *or* infringe *or* encroach on. **Eingreifen,** *n.* engagement, meshing; intervention, interference; *see* **Eingriff. eingreifend,** *adj.* radical, effective, energetic, drastic.

eingrenzen ['aɪngrɛntsən], *v.t.* enclose (*ground etc.*); localize (*epidemic etc.*), define, delimit, narrow down (*sphere of activity, powers etc.*).

Eingriff ['aɪngrɪf], *m.* 1. engagement, meshing (*of cogs*); *in* – *bringen,* put *or* throw into gear; *außer* – *bringen,* throw out of gear, disengage; 2. interference, intervention (*in* (*Dat.*), in), intrusion, encroachment, trespass (on), disruption, infringement (of); chemical action; *chirurgischer* –, surgical operation; *unerlaubter* –, illegal operation; *see* **eingreifen.**

Einguß ['aɪngus], *m.* pouring *or* running in (*of fluid*); (*Med.*) infusion; fixing, setting *or* casting in (*with cement etc.*); (*Metall.*) ingot mould. **Einguß|-kanal,** *m.,* **-röhre,** *f.,* **-trichter,** *m.* sprue (-gate).

einhaken ['aɪnhakən], **1.** *v.t.* fasten (*with a hook*), hook on. **2.** *v.i., v.r.* (*coll.*) go arm in arm, link arms, take (*s.o.'s*) arm; *sie gingen eingehakt,* they walked arm in arm; *sie hakte* (*sich*) *bei mir ein,* she took my arm. **3.** *v.i.* (*coll.*) cut *or* break in (*conversation*), seize (*bei,* on) (*s.th. said by s.o.*).

Einhalt ['aɪnhalt], *m.* stop, check, restraint; prohibition; impediment; interruption; – *tun* or *gebieten* (*Dat.*), stop, check, put a stop to. **einhalten, 1.** *irr.v.t.* 1. follow, observe, keep *or* adhere to, abide by, (*coll.*) stick to; hold (*a course*), keep up (*payments*); retain, hold (*one's water*); 2. take in, gather, pucker (*a seam etc.*). **2.** *irr.v.i.* stop, leave off, pause, desist. **Einhaltung,** *f.* observance (of), adherence (to).

einhämmern ['aɪnhɛmərn], *v.t.* drive *or* hammer in; – *in* (*Acc.*), drive *or* hammer into; (*coll.*) *ihm etwas* –, drum *or* hammer s.th. into him.

einhändig ['aɪnhɛndɪç], **1.** *adj.* one-handed. **2.** *adv.* single-handed, with one hand. **einhändigen,** *v.t.* hand in; deliver, hand over (*Dat.,* to).

einhängen ['aɪnhɛŋən], **1.** *v.t.* hang, suspend; put (*a door*) on its hinges; ship (*a rudder*); (*Tele.*) *den Hörer* –, replace the receiver, (*coll.*) hang up, ring off. **2.** *v.r.* (*coll.*) *see* **einhaken, 2.**

einhauchen ['aɪnhauxən], *v.t. ihm etwas* –, inspire him with s.th., breathe *or* inculcate *or* instil s.th. into him.

einhauen ['aɪnhauən], **1.** *irr.v.t.* – *in* (*Acc.*), hew *or* cut in(to); break open. **2.** *irr.v.i.* – *auf* (*Acc.*), attack, fall upon; (*coll.*) *tüchtig* –, fall to, tuck in.

einheben ['aɪnhe:bən], *irr.v.t.* lift into place.

einheften ['aɪnhɛftən], *v.t.* – *in* (*Acc.*), sew *or* tack *or* stitch in; file (*papers etc.*).

einhegen ['aɪnhe:gən], *v.t.* fence in, enclose.

einheimisch ['aɪnhaɪmɪʃ], *adj.* native, indigenous, local, (*Nat. Hist.*) endemic; home-bred, home-grown, home-produced, home-made, home; *die Einheimischen,* the locals, the natives.

einheimsen ['aɪnhaɪmzən], *v.t.* bring home *or* in, garner, gather, reap, (*coll.*) pocket, rake in.

einheiraten ['aɪnhaɪra:tən], *v.i.* (*sometimes v.r.*) (*sich*) *in ein Geschäft* –, marry into a business.

Einheit ['aɪnhaɪt], *f.* unity, oneness, uniformity; (*Math., Mil.*) unit; (*Golf*) bogey; *eine* – *bilden,* be as one; ***zu einer – zusammenschließen,*** unify, unite; ***– von Zeit und Ort,*** unities of time and place. **einheitlich,** *adj.* uniform, homogeneous, integrated, coherent, consistent; standardized, standard (*prices, quality etc.*); united, centralized (*government etc.*), concerted (*action*). **Einheitlichkeit,** *f.* uniformity, homogeneity, coherence, consistency.

Einheits– ['aɪnhaɪts], *pref.* 1. united, unitary; 2. uniform, standardized, standard; 3. (*Math.*) unit. **–bewegung,** *f.* movement towards unity. **–boot,** *n.* one-design (racing) boat. **–front,** *f.* (*Pol.*) united front, bloc. **–gewicht,** *n.* unit weight; (*Motor., Av.*) power-weight ratio. **–kurs,** *m.* (*Comm.*) adjusted rate. **–kurzschrift,** *f.* standard shorthand (*approved by German civil service*). **–länge,** *f.* (*Math.*) unit length. **–preis,** *m.* uniform *or* standard *or* fixed price; (*auctions*) reserve price. **–schule,** *f.* comprehensive school. **–spiel,** *n.* (*Golf*) bogey play. **–staat,** *m.* centralized state. **–strecke,** *f.* (*Math.*) unit of distance. **–versicherung,** *f.* all-risks *or* comprehensive insurance. **–wert,** *m.* rateable value (*of property*).

einheizen ['aɪnhaɪtsən], *v.t., v.i.* light a fire; heat (*a room*); (*coll.*) ***ihm –,*** make it hot for him; (*sl.*) ***er hat tüchtig eingeheizt,*** he's had a few, he's well lit up.

einhellig ['aɪnhɛlɪç], *adj., adv.* unanimous(ly), with one accord, by common consent. **Einhelligkeit,** *f.* unanimity.

einher– [aɪn'he:r], *sep.pref.* along (*oft. implying stateliness*). **–gehen, –schreiten,** *irr.v.i.* move along, proceed. **–stolzieren,** *v.i.* strut, stalk along. **–ziehen,** *irr.v.i.* move on, go one's way.

einholen ['aɪnho:lən], *v.t.* 1. get *or* take *or* bring in; haul in *or* home (*a rope*); strike, lower, haul down (*sail*); receive (*a p.*) with ceremony; ask *or* apply for, seek, get, obtain (*permission etc.*); ***Auskunft –,*** make inquiries; ***– gehen,*** go shopping; 2. draw level with, catch up with; make up for (*lost time*). **Einholer,** *m.* (*Naut.*) inhaul. **Einholtasche,** *f.* shopping bag *or* basket.

Einhorn ['aɪnhɔrn], *n.* unicorn.

Einhufer ['aɪnhu:fər], *m.* (*Zool.*) soliped(e). **einhufig,** *adj.* (*Zool.*) soliped, solidungulate, whole-hoofed.

einhüllen ['aɪnhylən], *v.t.* wrap *or* muffle (up) (***in*** (*Acc.*), in); enclose, encase, envelop, swathe (in), (*fig.*) shroud (in) (*mist etc.*).

einig ['aɪnɪç], *adj.* united, at one; (***sich*** (*Dat.*)) ***– sein,*** agree, be in agreement; be of one mind, be of the same opinion; (***sich*** (*Dat.*)) ***– werden,*** come to *or* reach an agreement; ***mit sich – werden,*** make up one's mind.

einige, *see* **einiger.**

einigeln ['aɪnˀi:gəln], *v.r.* (*Mil.*) take up an all-round defensive position, 'hedgehog'.

einigemal ['aɪnɪgəma:l], *adv.* a few times, once or twice.

einigen ['aɪnɪgən], 1. *v.t.* unite, unify. 2. *v.r.* agree, come to *or* reach an agreement.

einiger ['aɪnɪgər], *m.*, **einige,** *f.*, **einiges,** *n.* 1. *indef.adj.* some, a certain; *pl.* some, several, a few. 2. *indef.pron.* ***einiges,*** something, some things, (quite) a few things, quite a lot; *pl.* ***einige,*** some, a few.

einigermaßen ['aɪnɪgərma:sən], *adv.* to some *or* to a certain extent, in some *or* in a certain degree, in some measure, somewhat, rather, quite, (*coll.*) fairly, pretty.

einiges, *see* **einiger.**

Einigkeit ['aɪnɪçkaɪt], *f.* unity, union; agreement, unanimity; harmony, concord.

Einigung ['aɪnɪguŋ], *f.* unification; agreement, understanding. **Einigungsamt,** *n.* arbitration tribunal, conciliation board.

einimpfen ['aɪnˀɪmpfən], *v.t.* ***ihm etwas –,*** inoculate him with s.th.; (*fig.*) implant s.th. in him, instil s.th. into him. **Einimpfung,** *f.* inoculation.

einjagen ['aɪnja:gən], 1. *v.t.* ***ihm Schrecken –,*** give him a fright, strike terror into him; ***einen Hund –,*** train a dog for shooting.

einjährig ['aɪnjɛ:rɪç], *adj.* lasting a year; year-old; ***–e Pflanze,*** annual; ***–es Fohlen,*** yearling. **Einjährige,** *n.* (*coll.*) lower school-leaving certificate (*two years before* Reifezeugnis) (*orig. the educational standard required for one-year volunteers; now required for minor civil service and similar non-academic employment*). **Einjährig-(Freiwillig)e(r),** *m.* (*before* 1919) German one-year volunteer.

einkalken ['aɪnkalkən], *v.t.* lime, lay in *or* dress with lime, lime-wash.

einkapseln ['aɪnkapsəln], 1. *v.t.* incapsulate. 2. *v.r.* become incapsulated *or* encysted, encyst, (*coll. of a p.*) retire into one's shell. **Einkapselung,** *f.* encystment, incapsulation.

einkassieren ['aɪnkasi:rən], *v.t.* collect (*money*), recover, call in (*debts*).

Einkauf ['aɪnkauf], *m.* purchase; buying, purchasing; ***Einkäufe machen,*** do one's shopping. **einkaufen,** *v.t.* buy, purchase, shop for; ***– gehen,*** go shopping. **Einkäufer,** *m.* buyer (*for a firm*). **Einkaufs|netz,** *n.* string (shopping-)bag. **–preis,** *m.* purchase price, (*Comm.*) prime cost. **–rechnung,** *f.* buyer's invoice. **–tasche,** *f.* shopping-bag. **–wägelchen,** *n.* trolley (*in supermarket etc.*).

einkehlen ['aɪnke:lən], *v.t.* groove, channel, provide with a gutter. **Einkehlung,** *f.* groove, channel, hollow moulding.

Einkehr ['aɪnke:r], *f.* 1. stop (at an inn) for refreshment; overnight stay (at an inn); 2. (*fig.*) (*of moods etc.*) ***– halten bei,*** come to (*a p.*); ***– halten in*** (*Dat.*), enter, come into; ***innere –,*** self-communion; ***bei*** or ***in sich – halten,*** search one's heart. **einkehren,** *v.i.* (*aux.* s.) 1. call (***bei,*** on) for refreshment; stay overnight (***bei,*** at), (*coll.*) put up (***bei,*** at); 2. (*fig.*) *see* ***Einkehr halten bei.***

einkeilen ['aɪnkaɪlən], *v.t.* wedge (***in*** (*Acc.*), in); fasten with wedges; (*fig.*) hem in; (*Surg.*) ***eingekeilt,*** impacted.

einkellern ['aɪnkɛlərn], *v.t.* lay *or* store *or* deposit in a cellar; lay in *or* up.

einkerben ['aɪnkɛrbən], *v.t.* notch, nick, indent, score.

einkerkern ['aɪnkɛrkərn], *v.t.* imprison, incarcerate.

einkesseln ['aɪnkɛsəln], *v.t.* encircle, hem in.

einklagen ['aɪnkla:gən], *v.t.* sue for; ***ihn Schuld –,*** sue for debt.

einklammern ['aɪnklamərn], *v.t.* bracket, enclose in brackets, put in parentheses.

Einklang ['aɪnklaŋ], *m.* unison; accord, accordance, agreement, harmony, concord; ***in – bringen,*** harmonize, bring into harmony, reconcile, (*coll.*) square; ***im – stehen,*** agree, be in agreement; accord, be in keeping, be compatible.

einkleben ['aɪnkle:bən], *v.t.* stick *or* glue *or* paste in; ***– in*** (*Acc.*), stick *or* glue *or* paste into.

einkleiden ['aɪnklaɪdən], *v.t.* clothe, fit out (*with clothes*), invest with (*a uniform etc.*), robe; (*fig.*) put, couch, clothe, wrap up (*one's meaning*). **Einkleidung,** *f.* robing ceremony, investiture; (*Mil.*) fitting out; (*fig.*) wording, form (*of words*). **Einkleidungsgeld,** *n.* (*Mil.*) uniform allowance.

einklemmen ['aɪnklɛmən], *v.t.* squeeze, force, clamp, grip, jam, pinch (***in*** (*Acc. or Dat.*), in(to)); ***eingeklemmt,*** jammed, stuck; (*Med.*) strangulated.

einklinken ['aɪnklɪŋkən], 1. *v.t.* latch (*a door*), engage (*a catch*); ***eingeklinkt,*** on the latch. 2. *v.i.* (*aux.* s.) click *or* snap to, engage.

einkneifen ['aɪnknaɪfən], *irr.v.t.* set (*one's lips*), half close (*one's eyes*); ***mit eingekniffenem Schwanz,*** with its tail between its legs.

einknicken ['aɪnknɪkən], 1. *v.t.* make a bend in, bend, kink; snap, partially break (*twig etc.*); fold down, dog-ear (*a page*); buckle (*wheel*). 2. *v.i.* (*aux.* s.) break, snap, buckle; bend, kink, become bent *or* kinked.

einkochen ['aɪnkɔxən], 1. *v.t.* boil down, evaporate (down) (*liquid*); preserve, bottle, can (*fruit etc.*); make jam *or* preserve. 2. *v.i.* (*aux.* s.) evaporate, boil away (*of liquid*), boil dry (*of s.th. boiling*). **Einkochen,** *n.* evaporation; preservation. **Einkoch|glas,** *n.* preserving jar. **–ring,** *m.* sealing ring (*for preserving jar*).

einkommen ['aɪnkɔmən], *irr.v.i.* (*aux.* s.) 1. come forward (*with a complaint etc.*); **– *gegen,*** protest against; 2. apply, make application (***bei,*** to); ***er ist um seinen Abschied eingekommen,*** he has sent in his resignation; 3. come in, arrive (*as mail etc.*); ***die eingekommenen Zinsen,*** the interest received. **Einkommen,** *n.* income, earnings, revenue. **Einkommen|steuer,** *f.* income-tax. **–steuer-erklärung,** *f.* income-tax return.

einkreisen ['aɪnkraɪzən], *v.t.* encircle, surround. **Einkreisung,** *f.* encirclement. **Einkreisungs-politik,** *f.* policy of encirclement.

einkrimpen ['aɪnkrɪmpən], *v.i.* slacken (*of the wind*); (*Naut.*) ***gegen den Wind –,*** sail too close to the wind, pinch up to windward.

Einkünfte ['aɪnkynftə], *f.pl.* income, earnings, revenue; proceeds, takings, receipts.

einkuppeln ['aɪnkupəln], *v.i.* (*Motor.*) let in the clutch.

einkuscheln ['aɪnkuʃəln], *v.r.* (*coll.*) snuggle up.

einladen ['aɪnla:dən], *irr.v.t.* 1. invite (***zu,*** to); 2. load, lade, ship (*goods*). **einladend,** *adj.* inviting, attractive, tempting. **Einladung,** *f.* 1. invitation; 2. lading, shipment.

Einlage ['aɪnla:gə], *f.* 1. enclosure (*in a letter etc.*), insertion; loose leaves (*for ring-book*); (*Mus. etc.*) interlude, intermezzo; (*Dentistry*) temporary filling; 2. deposit, investment; (*Gambling*) stake; 3. filler, stiffening, padding, lining, reinforcement, arch-support (*for fallen insteps*). **Einlage|buch,** *n.* bank-book, pass-book. **–kapital,** *n.* capital invested.

einlagern ['aɪnla:gərn], **1.** *v.t.* store, lay in (*stores*). **2.** *v.r.* (*Geol. etc.*) form a deposit; ***eingelagert,*** embedded, intercalated. **Einlagerung,** *f.* deposit; intercalation; storage.

einlangen ['aɪnlaŋən], (*Austr.*) **1.** *v.t.* submit, hand in (*application*). **2.** *v.i.* apply, make application, submit *or* hand in an application (***um,*** for). **3.** *v.i.* (*aux.* s.) *see* **eintreffen.**

Einlaß ['aɪnlas], *m.* (**-(ss)es,** ***pl.*** **¨-(ss)e**) admission (***in*** (*Acc.*), to), admittance, access (***bei,*** to); entrance, wicket-gate; (*Mech.*) inlet; ***ihm – gewähren,*** let him in; ***ihm – verschaffen,*** gain admittance for him.

einlassen ['aɪnlasən], **1.** *irr.v.t.* 1. let in, admit; **– *in*** (*Acc.*), let into, admit to; 2. set *or* fit *or* fix in, insert; set, mount (*gems etc.*); sink, embed (*in the ground etc.*). **2.** *irr.v.r.* 1. (*with a th.*) (let o.s.) get involved *or* get mixed up (***auf*** (*Acc.*) or ***in*** (*Acc.*), in), (*coll.*) let o.s. in (for), go (into); ***auf diese Frage lasse ich mich nicht ein,*** I won't go into this matter; (*Law*) ***auf eine Klage –,*** enter an appearance; 2. (*with a p.*) enter into relations, be *or* get involved, have to do (***mit,*** with), (*coll.*) get mixed up (with); (*with the opposite sex*) have an affair (with), (*coll.*) get entangled (with).

Einlaß|grund, *m.* primer (paint). **–hub,** *m.* (*Motor.*) induction stroke. **–karte,** *f.* ticket of admission. **–klappe,** *f.* induction *or* inlet *or* intake valve.

einläßlich ['aɪnlɛslɪç], *adj.* (*Swiss*) detailed, thorough.

Einlassung ['aɪnlasuŋ], *f.* (*Law*) (entering of an) appearance.

Einlaß|ventil, *n. See* **–klappe.**

Einlauf ['aɪnlauf], *m.* 1. (*Comm.*) arrival, delivery (*of goods, mail etc.*); goods *etc.* received, incoming goods *etc.*; 2. (*Med.*) enema; 3. (*Cul.*) thickening.

einlaufecht ['aɪnlaufˀɛçt], *adj.* unshrinkable, pre-shrunk.

einlaufen ['aɪnlaufən], **1.** *irr.v.i.* (*aux.* s.) 1. come in, arrive, (*coll. of train*) pull in; (*of water*) run *or* flow in; (*of money*) come in, come to hand, be paid *or* received, (*of mail*) come in, arrive, be received; **– *in*** (*Acc.*), come into, enter, arrive at *or* in, reach (*a place*); (*of a street*) lead *or* run into; (*of water*) run *or* flow into; ***ins Ziel –,*** reach *or* pass the winning post; ***das Bad(ewasser) – lassen,*** run the bath; 2. (*of fabric*) shrink. **2.** *irr.v.t.* 1. break in (*new shoes*); 2. (*coll.*) ***ihm das Haus*** or ***die Tür –,*** be constantly calling at his house, pester him with unwanted visits. **3.** *irr.v.r.* (*of new engine*) (be) run in; (*fig. of plan etc.*) get going, get running smoothly; (*of athlete*) warm up, get warmed up.

Einläufer ['aɪnlɔyfər], *m.* single-barrelled gun. **einläufig,** *adj.* single-barrelled.

einleben ['aɪnle:bən], *v.r.* grow *or* get accustomed *or* used to new conditions, become *or* get acclimatized (to new conditions), settle (***in*** (*Acc.*), into), settle down (in), familiarize o.s., begin to feel at home (with); ***sich in eine S. –,*** get familiar with *or* enter into the spirit of a th.

Einlege|arbeit, *f.* inlaid work. **–lauf,** *m.* Morris tube (*for rifle*), (*Artil.*) liner, sub-calibre barrel.

einlegen ['aɪnle:gən], *v.t.* 1. lay *or* place *or* put in, insert; enclose (*with letter*); 2. steep, pickle, souse, marinade, put in brine *or* pickle, preserve; 3. lay in *or* by, store, stock up with (*provisions etc.*); 4. inlay; ***einen Tisch mit Elfenbein –, Elfenbein in einen Tisch –,*** inlay a table with ivory; ***eingelegte Arbeit,*** inlaid work; 5. make, lay, lodge (*complaint*), make, enter (*protest*); ***ein (gutes) Wort für ihn –,*** put in a good word for him (***bei,*** with); ***Berufung –,*** appeal (***bei,*** to), lodge an appeal (with); ***sein Veto – gegen,*** veto, put *or* place one's veto on; ***mit etwas Ehre –,*** bring honour upon o.s. with s.th.

Einlegeplatte ['aɪnle:gəplatə], *f.* extension leaf (*of table*). **Einleger,** *m.* inlayer; depositor. **Einlege|-rohr,** *n. See* **–lauf. –sohle,** *f.* (cork) sock, insole. **–stück,** *n.* inset, lining, reinforcement. **Einlegung,** *f.* laying in, storage; insertion; *see* **Einlage.**

einleiten ['aɪnlaɪtən], *v.t.* begin, start, commence, (*coll.*) usher in; institute, set up, initiate, open; introduce, preface, write an introduction *or* preface to (*a book*); **– *in*** (*Acc.*), inject *or* lead *or* feed into. **einleitend,** *adj.* introductory, preliminary. **Einleitung,** *f.* introduction, initiation; introduction, preamble, prelude; preface; *pl.* preliminary arrangements; preparations.

einlenken ['aɪnlɛŋkən], **1.** *v.t.* turn (*vehicle*) (***in*** (*Acc.*), into). **2.** *v.i.* turn (***in*** (*Acc.*), into); (*fig.*) come round, give in, become more reasonable *or* conciliatory.

einlernen ['aɪnlɛrnən], *v.t. See* **einstudieren.**

einleuchten ['aɪnlɔyçtən], *v.i.* be clear *or* intelligible *or* comprehensible *or* obvious; stand to reason, be plain *or* (clearly) evident; ***das will mir nicht –,*** I cannot see that, I don't see the point of that.

einliefern ['aɪnli:fərn], *v.t.* deliver up, hand over, take (***in*** (*Acc.*), to).

einliegen ['aɪnli:gən], *irr.v.i.* (*aux.* s.) be enclosed (*Dat.*, with); ***–d sende ich,*** enclosed please find.

einlochen ['aɪnlɔxən], *v.t.* (*Golf*) hole (*a ball*); (*sl.*) put in clink *or* in jug.

einlösen ['aɪnlø:zən], *v.t.* ransom (*prisoner*), redeem (*pledge*), take (*goods*) out of pawn, cash (*cheque*), honour (*a bill*), carry out, make good (*one's promise*). **Einlösung,** *f.* redemption; ransom; cashing, honouring.

einlullen ['aɪnlulən], *v.t.* lull to sleep, (*fig.*) lull (*suspicions*).

einmachen ['aɪnmaxən], *v.t.* preserve, bottle, can (*fruit etc.*); ***Marmalade –,*** make jam; ***eingemacht,*** preserved, tinned *or* (*Am.*) canned, bottled; ***Eingemachtes,*** preserves. **Einmachglas,** *n.* preserving jar.

einmal ['aɪn'ma:l], **1.** *adv.* (*stressed*) 1. once; **– *in der Woche,*** once a week; (*Prov.*) **– *ist keinmal,*** once won't matter; ***noch –,*** once again *or* more; ***noch – soviel,*** as much again, twice as much; **– *dies,* – *das,*** now this now *or* then that, sometimes this sometimes that, at one time this at another time that; **– *hier* – *dort,*** here one moment, there the next; **– *um das andere,*** again *or* time and again; 2. ***auf –,*** at once, at one time *or* one go, at the same time; all at once, all of a sudden, suddenly; 3. (*past*) once (upon a time), one day, at one time, (*Poet.*) time was when; (*future*) one *or* some day, some time; ***irgend –,*** some time or other; 4. (*unstressed*) ***nicht –,*** not even. **2.** *part.* (*unstressed, oft. not translated*) (***nun***) ***–,*** just; ***es ist*** (***nun***) ***– so,*** that's how it is *or* how things are, such is life; ***da es nun – so ist,*** things being so *or* being as they are, as matters stand; (*with imper.*) ***komm – her!*** just *or* now come here! ***hören Sie –!*** I say!

Einmaleins [aɪnma:l'aɪns], *n.* multiplication table(s); ***– mit der Sieben,*** seven-times table.

einmalig ['aɪnma:lɪç], *adj.* single, (*coll.*) solitary; non-recurring; unique. **Einmalpackung,** *f.* disposable wrapper *or* package.

einmännig ['aɪnmɛnɪç], *adj.* (*Bot.*) monandrous.

Einmarsch ['aɪnmarʃ], *m.* marching in, entry. **einmarschieren,** *v.i.* (*aux.* s.) march in, enter; *– **in*** (*Acc.*), march into, enter.

Einmaster ['aɪnmastər], *m.* single-masted ship.

einmauern ['aɪnmauərn], *v.t.* wall in *or* up, immure; enclose *or* embed in a wall.

einmengen ['aɪnmɛŋən], *v.t., v.r. See* **einmischen.**

einmieten ['aɪnmi:tən], *v.t., v.r.* get *or* take rooms (*bei,* with); clamp *or* store (*potatoes*). **Einmieter,** *m.* (*Nat. Hist.*) guest, commensal.

einmischen ['aɪnmɪʃən], **1.** *v.t.* mix in; *– **in*** (*Acc.*), mix in with, mix into. **2.** *v.r.* meddle (*in* (*Acc.*), in *or* with), interfere (in), involve o.s. (in), (*coll.*) poke one's nose (into); join (in), (*coll.*) butt (into), butt in (on) (*a conversation*). **Einmischung,** *f.* interference, intervention.

einmitten ['aɪnmɪtən], *v.t.* (*Opt.*) centre, adjust.

einmotorig ['aɪnmoto:rɪç], *adj.* single-engined.

einmotten ['aɪnmɔtən], *v.t.* put in mothballs; (*coll.*) mothball (*a ship*).

einmünden ['aɪnmyndən], *v.i.* (*of river*) flow *or* discharge (***in*** (*Acc.*), into), empty itself (into), enter; (*of road etc.*) run *or* lead (into), open (on to), join; (*Anat.*) (*of vein*) inosculate, anastomose (with). **Einmündung,** *f.* confluence, junction; (*Anat.*) inosculation, anastomosis.

einmütig ['aɪnmy:tɪç], *adj.* unanimous, with one voice, by common consent; harmonious, in harmony, united. **Einmütigkeit,** *f.* unanimity; harmony, unity, concord.

einnähen ['aɪnnɛ:ən], *v.t.* 1. sew in; sew up; *– **in*** (*Acc.*), sew into; sew up in; 2. make *or* take a tuck in (*a skirt etc.*), take (*a skirt*) in.

Einnahme ['aɪnna:mə], *f.* 1. taking (*of meal*), taking, receiving, receipt (*of money*), taking up (*of a position*), capture, seizure (*of a fortress etc.*); 2. (*usu. pl.*) takings, proceeds, receipts; earnings, income, revenue; ***–n und Ausgaben,*** income and expenditure. **Einnahmequelle,** *f.* source of revenue *or* income.

einnehmen ['aɪnne:mən], *irr.v.t.* 1. take in *or* on (*supplies*), take aboard *or* on board, ship, lade (*goods*); (*of a business*) take, make (*money*); get, receive, collect (*revenue*); partake of (*a meal*), take (*meal, medicine*); 2. take, seize, capture (*fortress*), take up, hold, assume (*position, rank*), take, occupy (*one's seat*), take up, fill, occupy (*space*); 3. (*of a p.*) ***für sich –,*** captivate, gain (*s.o.'s*) favour, prepossess (*s.o.*) in one's favour; ***gegen sich –,*** prejudice against; 4. (*Dressm.*) take in (*a tuck, a skirt*). **einnehmend,** *adj.* captivating, prepossessing, engaging, winning, charming, (*coll.*) fetching. *See* **eingenommen.**

einnicken ['aɪnnɪkən], *v.i.* (*aux.* s.) drop *or* fall asleep, (*coll.*) doze *or* drop off.

einnisten ['aɪnnɪstən], *v.r.* (build one's) nest; establish itself; (*coll. of a p.*) park o.s.

Einöde ['aɪnˀø:də], *f.* desert, wilderness.

einölen ['aɪnˀø:lən], *v.t.* oil, grease, lubricate.

einordnen ['aɪnˀɔrdnən], **1.** *v.t.* arrange (in order), put in (*its*) (proper) place, classify, file; ***falsch –,*** put in (*its*) wrong place, classify wrongly. **2.** *v.r.* (*of a th.*) fall *or* drop into place, fit in; (*of a p.*) take one's place, fall into line; (*of traffic*) get in the right lane.

einpacken ['aɪnpakən], *v.t.* pack *or* wrap (up); put up (*goods*); (*coll.*) pack up (and go); give (*it*) up (as a bad job).

einpassen ['aɪnpasən], *v.t.* fit (in); *– **in*** (*Acc.*), fit into.

einpauken ['aɪnpaukən], *v.t.* (*coll.*) ***ihn –,*** cram him (*for an examination*); ***ihm etwas –,*** cram *or* knock *or* hammer *or* drive s.th. into him; ***sich*** (*Dat.*) ***etwas –,*** swot up s.th. **Einpauker,** *m.* crammer, coach.

Einpeitscher ['aɪnpaɪtʃər], *m.* (*Parl.*) whip, (*Am.*) floor leader.

einpferchen ['aɪnpfɛrçən], *v.t.* pen (*sheep etc.*), (*coll.*) coop up, crowd *or* cram together.

einpflanzen ['aɪnpflantsən], *v.t.* plant; (*fig.*) implant (*Dat.*, in), instil (into), impart (to).

einpfropfen ['aɪnpfrɔpfən], *v.t.* graft (***in*** (*Acc.*), into).

einphasig ['aɪnfa:zɪç], *adj.* (*Elec.*) single-phase.

einpökeln ['aɪnpø:kəln], *v.t.* salt (down), cure, souse, pickle; ***eingepökeltes Fleisch,*** corned meat; (*vulg.*) ***du kannst dich – lassen,*** go and fry your face!

einprägen ['aɪnprɛ:gən], *v.t.* imprint, impress (***in*** (*Acc.*), on); (*fig.*) ***ihm etwas –,*** fix s.th. in his mind, impress s.th. upon him; ***sich*** (*Dat.*) ***etwas –,*** fix s.th. in *or* implant *or* impress s.th. on one's memory.

einprobieren ['aɪnprobi:rən], *v.t.* rehearse (*a play, a part*).

einpuppen ['aɪnpupən], *v.r.* (*Ent.*) change into a chrysalis, pupate.

einquartieren ['aɪnkvarti:rən], **1.** *v.t.* quarter, billet (*troops*) (***bei,*** on), find *or* get lodgings for (***bei,*** with). **2.** *v.r.* take lodgings *or* (*coll.*) take up one's quarters. **Einquartierung,** *f.* quartering, billeting; soldiers billeted, (*coll.*) unwelcome guest(s).

einrahmen ['aɪnra:mən], *v.t.* frame (*picture*), tenter (*cloth*), (*fig.*) surround (*with trees etc.*), put in a (*musical etc.*) setting.

einrammen ['aɪnramən], *v.t.* ram *or* sink *or* drive in *or* down.

einrangieren ['aɪnrãʒi:rən], *v.t.* fit in; *– **in*** (*Acc.*), fit into.

einrasten ['aɪnrastən], **1.** *v.t.* lock in position, engage (*a catch etc.*). **2.** *v.i.* (*aux.* s.) lock, catch, snap into position.

einräumen ['aɪnrɔymən], *v.t.* 1. clear *or* stow *or* put away, put in order *or* in its place; 2. ***ihm etwas –,*** concede *or* allow *or* admit *or* accord *or* grant s.th. to him; ***seinen Platz –,*** give up *or* yield one's place (*Dat.*, to); ***ihm ein Zimmer –,*** give up *or* vacate a room for him, let him have (the use of) a room. **einräumend,** *adj.* (*Gram.*) concessive. **Einräumung,** *f.* concession, admission; allowance (*in weighing*). **Einräumungssatz,** *m.* (*Gram.*) concessive clause.

einrechnen ['aɪnrɛçnən], *v.t.* reckon, count (***in*** (*Dat.*), in), include (in); allow for, take account of, take into account (in); ***alles eingerechnet,*** all things considered, taking everything into account.

Einrede ['aɪnre:də], *f.* objection, protest, remonstrance, contradiction, (*Law*) exception, plea; ***– erheben,*** protest, demur, raise an objection, take exception; ***keine –!*** don't contradict! ***ohne –,*** without demur. **einreden,** **1.** *v.t.* ***ihm etwas –,*** persuade him of a th., talk him into a th., put a th. into his head, make him believe s.th.; ***sich*** (*Dat.*) ***etwas –,*** persuade o.s. of s.th., make o.s. believe s.th., talk o.s. into s.th., imagine s.th. **2.** *v.i.* ***– auf*** (*Acc.*), try to convince *or* persuade, reason with, talk persuasively to, (*coll.*) keep on at.

Einreibemittel, *n. See* **Einreibungsmittel.**

einreiben ['aɪnraɪbən], **1.** *irr.v.t.* rub in (*oil etc.*), rub (*ointment etc.*) (***in*** (*Acc.*), into) (*part of body*), embrocate; ***sich*** (*Dat.*) ***den Fuß –,*** rub *or* massage one's foot with embrocation. **2.** *irr.v.r.* rub o.s. (down), rub embrocation in. **Einreibung,** *f.* application of ointment; massage with embrocation. **Einreibungsmittel,** *n.* liniment, embrocation.

einreichen ['aɪnraɪçən], *v.t.* hand in, deliver, submit, present; tender (*one's resignation*); *– um*, make application *or* apply for.

einreihen ['aɪnraɪən], **1.** *v.t.* (*a th.*) put in (*its*) proper place, arrange in correct order; (*a p.*) enrol, enlist; place, rank. **2.** *v.r.* fall in, fall into line; take one's place, fall *or* drop into place. **3.** *v.t.* (*Dressm.*) gather, lay in little pleats.

einreihig ['aɪnraɪɪç], *adj.* single-breasted.

Einreise ['aɪnraɪzə], *f.* journey, entry (*in* (*Acc.*), into). **Einreise|bewilligung, –erlaubnis,** *f.* entry permit.

einreißen ['aɪnraɪsən], **1.** *irr.v.t.* 1. tear, make a tear in; incise, slash, score; 2. break *or* tear *or* pull down, demolish. **2.** *irr.v.i.* (*aux.* s.) 1. tear, get torn; (*coll.*) ***es reißt in den Beutel ein,*** it makes a hole in your pocket; 2. spread, prevail, gain ground.

einrenken ['aɪnrɛŋkən], *v.t.* reduce, set (*fracture etc.*); (*fig.*) straighten out, (put *or* set) right. **Einrenker,** *m.* bone-setter.

einrennen ['aɪnrɛnən], **1.** *irr.v.t.* knock *or* charge down (*fence etc.*), run (*one's head etc.*) against; ***den Schädel an der Tür –,*** crack *or* bash one's head on the door; (*fig.*) ***sich*** (*Dat.*) ***den Schädel –,*** bang one's head against a brick wall; ***offene Türe –,*** flog a dead horse. **2.** *irr.v.i.* (*aux.* s.) ***– auf*** (*Acc.*), run at, charge up to.

einrichten ['aɪnrɪçtən], **1.** *v.t.* 1. arrange, adjust, dispose, organize, regulate, manage (***nach,*** according to); equip, fit up *or* out, furnish (*a house*); establish, institute, found, start, set up (*business, school etc.*); ***gut eingerichtet,*** well appointed; 2. (*Med.*) reduce, set (*fracture etc.*); 3. (*Math.*) reduce to an improper fraction; 4. (*Mus.*) arrange. **2.** *v.r.* settle down, establish o.s.; ***sich – auf*** (*Acc.*), prepare *or* make (one's) preparations for, make arrangements for; ***er weiß sich einzurichten,*** he makes ends meet, he knows how to manage; ***sich – nach,*** adapt *or* adjust *or* accommodate o.s. to; ***sich danach –,*** take measures accordingly, take the appropriate measures.

Einrichtung ['aɪnrɪçtuŋ], *f.* 1. arrangement, layout; 2. institution, establishment; 3. equipment; contrivance, device; fittings, furnishings, furniture, household appointments. **Einrichtungs|-gegenstand,** *m.*, **–stück,** *n.* piece of furniture *or* equipment.

Einriß ['aɪnrɪs], *m.* tear, rent, slit (*in fabric*), crack, split, cleft, fissure; *see* **einreißen.**

einritzen ['aɪnrɪtsən], *v.t.* scratch, score, incise, make an incision in.

einrollen ['aɪnrɔlən], **1.** *v.t.* roll (up). **2.** *v.r.* roll *or* curl (o.s.) up (into a ball); (*Bot.*) ***eingerollt,*** involute.

einrosten ['aɪnrɔstən], *v.i.* (*aux.* s.) rust, become rusty, get rusted up; (*coll.*) get rusty; ***eingerostetes Übel,*** deep(ly) rooted evil.

einrücken ['aɪnrykən], **1.** *v.i.* (*aux.* s.) 1. march in, enter; ***– in*** (*Acc.*), march into, enter; move *or* step into (*another's post*), succeed to, come into (*inheritance*); 2. (*Mil.*) report for duty; join up. **2.** *v.t.* insert, put in (*advertisement*); (*Typ.*) indent; (*Mech.*) engage (*gear*), put (*machine*) in gear, start, set in motion. **Einrücken,** *n.* indention, indentation; insertion; entry.

einrühren ['aɪnry:rən], *v.t.* stir *or* mix in; ***– in*** (*Acc.*), stir into; (*coll.*) ***ich habe mir etwas Nettes*** or ***eine schöne Suppe eingerührt,*** I have landed myself in the soup *or* in a nice mess *or* pickle.

[1]**eins** [aɪns], *cardinal num.* (number) one; (*coll.*) one (o'clock); ***sich*** (*Dat.*) ***– sein mit,*** be at one with; ***darin sind wir*** (***uns***) ***–,*** we are in complete agreement over it; (*coll.*) ***es ist alles –, es kommt auf – heraus,*** it's all one, it's all the same, it makes no difference (at all). **Eins,** *f.* (-, *pl.* **-en**) (figure) one; (*coll.*) number one bus *or* tram; (*School*) full marks, alpha, (*Univ.*) first (class).

[2]**eins,** *indef.pron. See* **ein.**

einsacken ['aɪnsakən], **1.** *v.t.* pack in(to) bags *or* sacks; (*coll.*) pocket, rake in (*sum of money*). **2.** *v.r.* (*Med.*) encyst, become encysted. **3.** *v.i.* (*aux.* s.) sag; ***in den Knien –,*** sag at the knees.

einsalben ['aɪnzalbən], *v.t., v.r. See* **einreiben.**

einsalzen ['aɪnzaltsən], *irr.v.t. See* **einpökeln.**

einsam ['aɪnza:m], *adj.* lonely, lonesome; solitary, alone. **Einsamkeit,** *f.* loneliness, solitude.

einsammeln ['aɪnzaməln], *v.t.* collect; gather, (*Poet.*) gather in (*harvest*).

einsargen ['aɪnzargən], *v.t.* put in a coffin, (*fig.*) bury, abandon (*hopes etc.*).

Einsatz ['aɪnzats], *m.* 1. insertion; insert, anything inserted, *e.g.* charge (*of furnace etc.*), extension leaf (*of table*), liner (*of cylinder*), extension (piece), interchangeable part; (*Dressm.*) inset, panel, gusset; shirt-front, (*coll.*) dicky, modesty-vest; 2. deposit (*on bottle, book etc.*), stake, pledge; pool (*at cards*); 3. use, employment, mustering (*of resources etc.*), (*Mil.*) operation, action, engagement, (*Av.*) sortie, mission; (*Mus.*) entry, (*Phonet.*) (initial) glide, (*Rowing or any such activity*) attack; quick response, willingness to obey; (*Mil.*) ***elastischer –,*** defence in depth; ***im –,*** (*of machines*) in action *or* operation, (*of personnel*) on operational duties, on active service; ***zum – bringen,*** bring into use, put into operation (*machines*), use, employ (*a p.*); bring into action (*troops, military equipment etc.*); ***zum – kommen,*** come into operation, be brought into use (*machines*), be brought into action (*personnel, military equipment*); ***mit vollem – arbeiten,*** work all out, give of one's best; ***unter – des Lebens,*** at the risk of one's life.

Einsatzbefehl ['aɪnzatsbəfe:l], *m.* (*Mil.*) operational order. **einsatzbereit,** *adj.* ready for use *or* service, (*Mil.*) ready for action, at the stand-by, (*Av.*) ready to take off. **Einsatz|bereitschaft,** *f.* readiness for use (*of equipment*), (*Mil.*) readiness for action, fighting efficiency; willingness (to be of service). **–besprechung,** *f.* (*Mil.*) briefing. **einsatzfähig,** *adj.* available, serviceable, fit for use, (*Mil.*) fit for operational use (*equipment*), fit for action (*personnel*). **Einsatz|fähigkeit,** *f.* availability, serviceability, fitness for use; fitness for action. **–gebiet,** *n.* operational area. **–hafen,** *m.* (*Nav., Av.*) operational base. **–härtung,** *f.* (*Metall.*) case-hardening. **–leiter,** *m.* (*Nav.*) gunnery control officer. **–ofen,** *m.* (*Metall.*) case-hardening *or* carburizing furnace. **–raum,** *m. See* **–gebiet. –stahl,** *m.* (*Metall.*) case-hardened steel; cutting tool (*of lathe*). **–stück,** *n.* insertion, insert. **–verpflegung,** *f.* (*Mil.*) iron rations.

einsäuern ['aɪnzɔyərn], *v.t.* 1. leaven (*bread*), pickle (*in vinegar*), acidify; 2. silo, ensile, ensilage (*fodder*).

einsaugen ['aɪnzaugən], **1.** *irr.v.t.* suck up *or* in; absorb, soak up; imbibe, drink in, take in **2.** *irr.v.r.* soak in (*of liquid*), cling, stick on (*as a leech*). **Einsaugungsmittel,** *n.* absorbent (material).

einschachteln ['aɪnʃaxtəln], *v.t.* put in a box; ***– in*** (*Acc.*), fit *or* insert into; (*Gram.*) ***eingeschachtelt,*** incapsulated.

einschalten ['aɪnʃaltən], **1.** *v.t.* insert, put in, fit in; interpolate, intercalate; (*Elec.*) switch on, connect, plug in; (*Motor.*) let in (*clutch*), engage, put *or* go into (*gear*); ***eingeschaltete Stelle,*** interpolation; ***eingeschalteter Tag,*** intercalary day. **2.** *v.r.* 1. (*of machine*) switch on automatically; 2. (*of a p.*) intervene, (*coll.*) step in; join in (*conversation*). **Einschalt|knopf,** *m.* push-button, switch. **–motor,** *m.* starting motor. **–stellung,** *f.* on-position (*of switch*). **Einschaltung,** *f.* insertion; interpolation; intercalation; parenthesis. **Einschaltungszeichen,** *n.* caret. **Einschaltvorrichtung,** *f.* switchgear.

einschanzen ['aɪnʃantsən], *v.t., v.r.* entrench.

einschärfen ['aɪnʃɛrfən], *v.t.* inculcate, enjoin; ***ihm etwas –,*** impress s.th. on him.

einscharren ['aɪnʃarən], *v.t.* bury hastily, cover lightly with earth.

einschätzen ['aɪnʃɛtsən], *v.t.* assess, estimate, evaluate, value, appraise, form an estimate of, have a (*high, poor etc.*) opinion of. **Einschätzung,** *f.* assessment, estimation, valuation, appraisal; opinion, estimate.

einschenken ['aɪnʃɛŋkən], *v.t.* pour out (*Dat.*, for); ***schenk ein!*** fill your glasses! ***ihm reinen Wein –,*** tell him the plain truth, come out into the open.

einschichten ['aɪnʃɪçtən], *v.t.* arrange in layers; ***eingeschichtet,*** stratified.

einschicken ['aɪnʃɪkən], *v.t.* send in, submit.

einschieben ['aɪnʃi:bən], *irr.v.t.* push *or* put *or* feed in; insert, introduce, interpolate, intercalate; – ***in*** (*Acc.*), push *etc.* into. **Einschieb(e)satz,** *m.* parenthetical clause. **Einschiebsel,** *n.*, **Einschiebung,** *f.* insertion; interpolation, intercalation.

einschießen ['aɪnʃi:sən], **1.** *irr.v.t.* 1. batter down, demolish, breach (*by artillery fire*); 2. donate, contribute (*money*); insert (*leaf in a book*), load *or* set (*bread*) in the oven, (*Weav.*) shoot (*the weft*); (*coll.*) ***auf eine S. eingeschossen sein,*** know all the tricks of the trade. **2.** *irr.v.r.* ***sich*** (***auf ein Ziel***) –, range (on a target), find the range (of a target). **3.** *irr.v.i.* (*aux.* s.) rush *or* come rushing in; – ***in*** (*Acc.*), rush into. **Einschießen,** *n.* (*Artil.*) ranging, adjustment fire.

einschiffen ['aɪnʃɪfən], **1.** *v.t.* embark (*people*), take *or* bring on board, ship (*goods*). **2.** *v.i.* (*aux.* s.), *v.r.* embark, go on board; take *or* board a ship (***nach,*** for). **Einschiffung,** *f.* embarkation; shipment.

einschirren ['aɪnʃɪrən], *v.t.* harness.

einschlachten ['aɪnʃlaxtən], *v.t.* slaughter (*esp. pig*) for household use.

einschlafen ['aɪnʃla:fən], *irr.v.i.* (*aux.* s.) go to sleep, fall asleep; (*Poet.*) pass away, die (peacefully); (*coll.*) die out, fall into disuse (*as customs*), die down, abate, slacken (*as wind*), flag, peter out, die a natural death (*as friendship etc.*); ***der Fuß ist mir eingeschlafen,*** my foot has gone to sleep.

einschläfern ['aɪnʃlɛ:fərn], *v.t.* lull *or* send to sleep; put (*animal*) to sleep; (*fig.*) lull into security, allay (*fears, suspicions etc.*), salve (*one's conscience*). **einschläfernd,** *adj.* narcotic, soporific; ***–es Mittel,*** opiate, sleeping draught. **einschläfrig,** *adj.* single (*bed*).

Einschlag ['aɪnʃla:k], *m.* 1. striking, hitting, impact; hole *or* damage (caused by impact), bomb crater; 2. felling (*of timber*); timber (to be) felled; young plantation (*of trees*); 3. handshake (to seal a bargain); 4. paper cover, wrapper; (*Weav.*) woof, weft; part turned down *or* in (*as a leaf of a book*); (*Dressm.*) tuck, fold, turn-up; ***Kette und –,*** warp and woof; 5. (*Golf*) putt; 6. (*fig.*) infusion, tinge, strain, hint, touch, admixture; ***Rede mit einem leisen – ins Ironische,*** speech with a slight touch *or* tinge of irony.

Einschlag(e)|garn, *n.* (*Weav.*) weft-yarn. **–messer,** *n.* clasp-knife.

einschlagen ['aɪnʃla:gən], **1.** *irr.v.t.* 1. drive *or* knock *or* hammer in, hammer home (*a nail*), stave in (*a cask*), break, smash (*window*), break *or* batter down, burst open (*door*), crack, bash in (*s.o.'s skull*); – ***in*** (*Acc.*), drive *or* knock *or* hammer into; 2. wrap (up); 3. fold *or* turn up *or* down, (*Dressm.*) turn up (*hem*); 4. fell (*timber*); 5. take, follow (*road, course*). **2.** *irr.v.i.* 1. shake hands (to seal an agreement), agree to a proposal; ***schlag ein!*** give me your hand on it! ***eingeschlagen!*** agreed! 2. – ***auf*** (*Acc.*), rain blows on, belabour; (*occ. aux.* s.) – ***in*** (*Acc.*), strike (*of lightning*), hit, land (*as a bomb*); (*fig.*) concern, be relevant to, have reference to; ***das schlägt nicht in mein Fach ein,*** that's not my province *or* not (in) my line; 3. (*aux.* s. *&* h.) be a success, (*coll.*) come off, catch *or* take on; 4. soak in (*as paint*).

Einschlag(e)tuch ['aɪnʃla:g(ə)tu:x], *n.* shawl; wrapper.

einschlägig ['aɪnʃlɛ:gɪç], *adj.* relevant, pertinent; competent, appropriate; ***–e Literatur,*** relevant literature, literature on *or* relevant to the subject; ***alle –en Artikel,*** the whole range of this (type of) article; ***alle –en Geschäfte,*** all the appropriate dealers *or* stockists.

Einschlag|papier, *n.* wrapping paper. **–punkt,** *m.* point of impact. **–winkel,** *m.* angle of impact; (*Motor.*) ***– der Lenkung,*** angle of lock.

einschlämmen ['aɪnʃlɛmən], *v.t.* soak, saturate, sluice (*the ground*) *or* the ground around (*a tree etc.*).

einschleichen ['aɪnʃlaɪçən], *irr.v.r.* creep, steal, (*coll.*) slip (*in* (*Acc.*), into); infiltrate, insinuate o.s. (into); ***sich bei ihm –,*** insinuate o.s. *or* (*coll.*) worm one's way into his confidence *or* affections *etc.*

einschleifen ['aɪnʃlaɪfən], *irr.v.t.* grind in, reseat (*a valve*).

einschleppen ['aɪnʃlɛpən], *v.t.* tow in (*boat*), (*fig.*) bring *or* carry in, introduce (*disease etc.*).

einschleusen ['aɪnʃlɔyzən], *v.t.* – ***in*** (*Acc.*), pass (*ship*) into (*a dock*); introduce (*s.o.*) through (*an airlock*); pass, feed, channel, infiltrate (*spies etc.*) into; feed, pump (*money*) into.

einschließen ['aɪnʃli:sən], *irr.v.t.* 1. lock in *or* up, shut in *or* up, imprison, put into prison; 2. enclose (***mit,*** in *or* with), encircle, surround (by *or* with), encompass (by), (*Poet.*) girdle (with), (*Mil.*) surround, encircle, invest, (*coll.*) bottle up; 3. include, comprise, contain, embrace, (*coll.*) sum up; – ***in*** (*Acc.*), include in; ***eingeschlossen in*** (*Dat.*), included in; 4. (*Chem.*) occlude.

einschließlich ['aɪnʃli:slɪç], **1.** *adv.* inclusive, inclusively, including; ***vom 3. bis zum 6. –,*** from the 3rd to the 6th inclusive, (*Am.*) from 3rd through 6th. **2.** *prep.* (*Gen.*) including, inclusive of. **Einschließen,** *n.* inclusion; enclosure; (*Chem.*) occlusion. **Einschließung,** *f.* locking in *or* up; imprisonment, confinement; blockade, siege, encirclement, investment; *see* **Einschluß.**

einschlucken ['aɪnʃlukən], *v.t.* swallow, gulp down; absorb, (*fig.*) swallow, stomach, put up with (*insult etc.*).

einschlummern ['aɪnʃlumərn], *v.i.* (*aux.* s.) fall into a slumber, fall asleep; pass quietly away (*i.e. die*).

einschlürfen ['aɪnʃlyrfən], *v.t.* sip; ***gierig –,*** gulp down.

Einschluß ['aɪnʃlus], *m.* 1. enclosure; (*obs.*) ***Brief mit –,*** letter with enclosure; 2. inclusion, comprisal; ***mit*** or ***unter – der Kinder,*** including the *or* inclusive of the children; 3. encirclement; parenthesis; 4. (*Geol.*) inlier, xenolith, enclosure; *see* **einschließen. Einschluß|gebiet,** *n.* enclave. **–klammer,** *f. See* **–zeichen. einschlußweise,** *adv.* parenthetically. **Einschlußzeichen,** *n.* bracket, parenthesis.

einschmeicheln ['aɪnʃmaɪçəln], *v.r.* ingratiate o.s., curry favour (*bei*, with). **einschmeichelnd,** *adj.* insinuating, ingratiating, (*coll.*) catchy (*of music*).

einschmelzen ['aɪnʃmɛltsən], **1.** *reg. & irr.v.t.* melt down. **2.** *irr.v.i.* (*aux.* s.) melt (away), fuse.

einschmieren ['aɪnʃmi:rən], *v.t.* grease, oil, lubricate, rub, smear (*grease, hair-oil, shoe-polish etc.*) on *or* in.

einschmuggeln ['aɪnʃmugəln], **1.** *v.t.* smuggle in. **2.** *v.r.* (*in* (*Acc.*)) enter illegally, (*coll.*) gate-crash.

einschnappen ['aɪnʃnapən], *v.i.* (*aux.* s.) 1. catch, engage, snap to, click *or* snap into place; 2. (*fig.*) be offended, take offence, (*coll.*) be touchy, have the sulks. **Einschnappfeder,** *f.* snap-spring.

einschneiden ['aɪnʃnaɪdən], **1.** *irr.v.t.* notch; make a cut *or* cuts *or* a notch *or* notches *or* an incision *or* incisions in; cut (up) (*timber etc.*); (*Artil.*) dig in (*guns*); – ***in*** (*Acc.*), cut *or* carve *or* engrave (*pattern etc.*) in. **2.** *irr.v.i.* 1. (*of events etc.*) have a profound effect on, have far-reaching consequences (for), cause *or* mean a great upheaval, make a decisive break (in), (*coll.*) cut right across; 2. (*of foetal head*) appear (through the vulva); 3. (*Navig.*) take cross-bearings. **3.** *irr.v.i.*, *v.r.* (***sich***) – ***in*** (*Acc.*), cut into (*as a garter, a river*). **Einschneiden,** *n.* 1. incision; 2. (*Navig.*) fixing position by cross-bearings; 3. crowning (*of foetal head*). *See* **Einschnitt. einschneidend,** *adj.* incisive, radical, fundamental, decisive, thorough.

einschneien ['aɪnʃnaɪən], *v.t.* (*usu. pass.*) ***eingeschneit,*** snowed up *or* (*Am.*) under, snowbound.

Einschnitt ['aɪnʃnɪt], *m.* incision, cut; notch, nick, slot (*of screw etc.*); (*Bot.*) serration, indentation;

(*Metr.*) caesura; (*Railw.*) cutting; (*Geog.*) gorge, ravine, cleft; (*fig.*) break, hiatus, upheaval, decisive turning-point.

einschnüren ['aɪnʃny:rən], **1.** *v.t.* lace up, tie up; constrict, (*Med.*) strangulate, (*Mil.*) hem in, encircle. **2.** *v.r.* corset o.s., lace one's stays; ***sich eng –,*** lace o.s. tightly; ***eingeschnürt,*** constricted, (*Biol.*) segmented, (*fig. of a p.*) straight-laced. **Einschnürung,** *f.* constriction, restriction, tight-lacing; (*Med.*) strangulation (*of organ*), (*Biol.*) segmentation, (*fig.*) neck (*in a pipe*), bottleneck (*in a street*).

einschränken ['aɪnʃrɛŋkən], **1.** *v.t.* keep *or* confine within limits; limit (***auf*** (*Acc.*), within *or* to), restrain, curb, check; retrench, curtail, restrict, reduce, (*coll.*) cut down (on); modify, qualify (*a statement etc.*); ***eingeschränkte Monarchie,*** limited monarchy. **2.** *v.r.* limit *or* confine *or* restrict o.s. (***auf*** (*Acc.*), to), economize, retrench, (*coll.*) tighten one's belt. **einschränkend,** *adj.* restrictive; modifying, qualifying (*clause etc.*). **Einschränkung,** *f.* limitation, restriction, reduction, curtailment (of), restriction, limit (on); modification, qualification; ***ohne –,*** unreservedly, without reservation(s).

einschrauben ['aɪnʃraubən], *v.t.* screw in *or* on; ***– in*** (*Acc.*), screw into. **Einschrauböse,** *f.* screw-eye.

Einschreib(e)|brief, *m.* registered letter. **–gebühr,** *f.* registration *or* (*Am.*) registry fee.

einschreiben ['aɪnʃraɪbən], **1.** *irr.v.t.* write in *or* down, inscribe; enter, put down (*one's name*), enrol, register; register (*a letter*); (*Geom.*) inscribe. **2.** *irr.v.r.* enrol, put one's name down (for), matriculate (*at a university*). **Einschreiben,** *n.* ***per –,*** by registered post. **Einschreiber,** *m.* registrar. **Einschreibung,** *f.* enrolment; registration.

einschreiten ['aɪnʃraɪtən], *irr.v.i.* (*aux.* s.) pace *or* stride in; (*fig.*) step in, interfere, interpose, intervene, take steps *or* action; ***gerichtlich –,*** take legal steps *or* measures *or* proceedings (***gegen,*** against).

Einschrieb ['aɪnʃri:p], *m.* (*Swiss*) registration (*of post*).

einschrumpfen ['aɪnʃrumpfən], *v.i.* (*aux.* s.) shrivel (up) (*as a leaf*); shrink, contract; dry up, become wrinkled *or* wizened, (*Med.*) atrophy; (*fig.*) shrink, become depleted (*of resources*). **Einschrumpfung,** *f.* shrivelling, shrinkage, (*Med.*) atrophy, contabescence.

Einschub ['aɪnʃu:p], *m.* insertion, interpolation (*of s.th.*); inserted passage, insertion, interpolation (in), addition (to); piece inserted, insert (between). **Einschubvokal,** *m.* (*Phonet.*) glide; parasitic *or* epenthetic vowel.

einschüchtern ['aɪnʃyçtərn], *v.t.* intimidate, overawe, daunt; ***nicht eingeschüchtert,*** undaunted, unabashed. **Einschüchterung,** *f.* intimidation, threat.

einschulen ['aɪnʃu:lən], *v.t.* 1. school, train (*in some activity*); 2. (*of school authority*) admit (*child*) to a school; (*of child*) ***eingeschult werden,*** start school; (*of parent*) ***– lassen,*** send (*child*) to school (for the first time).

Einschur ['aɪnʃu:r], *f.* annual shearing. **einschürig,** *adj.* (*sheep*) shorn once a year, (*field*) mown once a year.

Einschuß ['aɪnʃus], *m.* 1. money *or* funds *or* capital invested, investment, share; deposit; payment on account; (*St. Exch.*) ***– leisten,*** margin; 2. (*Weav.*) weft, woof; 3. bullet-hole, entry wound, point of entry (*of a bullet*); (*Footb.*) (shot into) goal; 4. (*Vet.*) phlegmon. *See* **einschießen.**

einschütten ['aɪnʃytən], *v.t.* pour in; ***– in*** (*Acc.*), pour into; charge *or* feed (*a furnace*) with.

einschwenken ['aɪnʃvɛŋkən], **1.** *v.i.* (*aux.* s. & h.) swing *or* swivel into position (*as gun*), (*Mil.*) wheel (*of a column*); ***nach rechts schwenkt ein!*** right wheel! (*of a p. etc.*) ***nach rechts –,*** turn to the right; ***– in*** (*Acc.*), turn into (*a side-street*). **2.** *v.t.* swing, swivel (*gun etc.*) (***in*** (*Acc.*), in (*the direction*), into (*the position*)).

einsegnen ['aɪnze:gnən], *v.t.* (*R.C.*) consecrate, bless, (*Prot.*) confirm. **Einsegnung,** *f.* (*R.C.*) consecration, benediction; (*Prot.*) confirmation.

einsehen ['aɪnze:ən], **1.** *irr.v.t.* 1. look at *or* over, inspect, examine, (*coll.*) have a look at; look through; consult, study, (*coll.*) get a look at; (*Mil.*) ***vom Feind eingesehen werden,*** be observed by the enemy, be open to enemy observation; 2. (*fig.*) see, realize, understand, (*Poet.*) perceive, (*coll.*) grasp. **2.** *irr.v.i.* ***mit ihm – in*** (*Acc.*), ***bei ihm –,*** look over (*s.th.*) with him, share (*his book*); ***bei ihm –,*** look *or* (*coll.*) drop in on him. **Einsehen,** *n.* 1. examination, inspection; 2. ***ein – haben,*** show consideration *or* understanding *or* sense, make allowances, be reasonable; (*coll.*) ***der Himmel hatte ein –,*** the weather was favourable *or* kind. **Einsehung,** *f.* examination, inspection.

einseifen ['aɪnzaɪfən], *v.t.* soap, rub soap into, rub with soap; lather (*a p., one's face etc.*); (*sl.*) take in, bamboozle, softsoap.

einseitig ['aɪnzaɪtɪç], **1.** *adj.* one-sided, unilateral; non-reversible (*fabric*); asymmetrical, one-sided, ill-balanced, partial, biased, prejudiced; (*Law*) ex parte, by one party; ***–e Lähmung,*** hemiplegia; (*Law*) ***–er Vertrag,*** nude contract. **2.** *adv.* unilaterally; on one side (only); to one side; one-sidedly, in a partial manner. **Einseitigkeit,** *f.* one-sidedness, partiality, narrow-mindedness, bias, prejudice.

einsenden ['aɪnzɛndən], *irr.v.t.* send in, submit; remit; ***eingesandte Rechnung,*** account rendered. **Einsendung,** *f.* submission (*of application etc.*); (*of money*) remittance, (*for charity etc.*) contribution, (*for competition*) entry; (*Comm.*) ***gegen –*** (*Gen.*), on receipt of.

einsenken ['aɪnzɛŋkən], **1.** *v.t.* sink (***in*** (*Acc.*), in, into), lower (*coffin*). **2.** *v.r.* subside, sag. **Einsenkung,** *f.* sagging, subsidence; hollow, trough, depression (*in ground*).

Einser ['aɪnzər], *m.* (figure) one. *See* **[1]eins.**

einsetzen ['aɪnzɛtsən], **1.** *v.t.* 1. insert; put *or* place *or* lay *or* set *or* fit *or* fix in; install (*engine*), step (*mast*), hang (*rudder*); (*Railw.*) ***der Speisewagen wird in Köln eingesetzt,*** the restaurant car is put on *or* starts at Cologne; ***– an Stelle*** (*Gen.*), ***– für,*** substitute for; ***– in*** (*Acc.*), insert *or* put *etc.* into; stock (*pond*) with (*fish*); plant out, put (*plants*) in (*the ground*); 2. call in *or* out (*troops, police*), send (*troops*) into action; bring (*machines etc.*) into action *or* use; use, make use of, bring to bear, muster (*resources*); ***seine besten Kräfte –,*** summon (up) all one's strength; 3. appoint, establish, set up, institute; ***– in*** (*Acc.*), appoint *or* nominate to, install in; 4. stake, wager, bet; ***als Pfand –,*** pledge as security, pawn; ***sein Leben –,*** risk one's life. **2.** *v.r.* ***sich – für,*** stand *or* speak *or* (*coll.*) stick up for, support, side with; ***sich voll –,*** pull one's weight. **3.** *v.i.* begin, open, start (off), (*Mus.*) enter, come in, (*of weather etc.*) set in, (*of storm*) break, blow up. **Einsetzen,** *n.* start, beginning, opening. **Einsetzung,** *f.* establishment, installation, appointment. **Einsetzungsworte,** *n.pl.* (Christ's) sacramental words.

Einsicht ['aɪnzɪçt], *f.* insight; understanding, discernment; inspection, examination, consultation (*in* (*Acc.*), of); ***– gewähren in*** (*Acc.*), give an insight into; ***mit –,*** judiciously; ***nach bester –,*** as one thinks best; ***– nehmen in*** (*Acc.*), look at *or* through, consult, examine, inspect. **einsichtig,** *adj.* discerning, understanding, sensible, judicious, prudent. **Einsichtigkeit,** *f.* discernment, understanding, good judgement. **Einsichtnahme,** *f.* examination, inspection, consultation; ***zur –,*** for your attention. **einsichtslos,** *adj.* lacking in insight *or* judgement, undiscerning. **Einsichtslosigkeit,** *f.* lack of insight *or* judgement *or* discernment. **einsichtsvoll,** *adj. See* **einsichtig.**

einsickern ['aɪnzɪkərn], *v.i.* (*aux.* s.) trickle *or* soak *or* seep in *or* away; ***– in*** (*Acc.*), trickle *or* soak *or* seep *or* infiltrate into. **Einsickerung,** *f.* infiltration, seepage.

Einsiedelei [aɪnzi:də'laɪ], *f.* hermitage. **Einsiedler**

['aɪnzi:dlər], *m.* hermit, recluse, anchorite. **Einsiedlerdrossel,** *m.* (*Orn.*) hermit thrush (*Hylocichla guttata*). **einsiedlerisch,** *adj.* secluded, solitary. **Einsiedlerkrebs,** *m.* hermit-crab.

einsilbig ['aɪnzɪlbɪç], *adj.* monosyllabic; (*of a p.*) taciturn, laconic; *-es Wort,* monosyllable. **Einsilbigkeit,** *f.* taciturnity.

einsingen ['aɪnzɪŋən], **1.** *irr.v.t.* sing to sleep. **2.** *irr. v.r.* get into voice; ***sich – in*** (*Acc.*), sing o.s. into, get warmed up to (*a part*).

einsinken ['aɪnzɪŋkən], *irr.v.i.* (*aux.* s.) sink in, subside, collapse, give way (under one's feet); (*coll.*) cave in; – ***in*** (*Acc.*), sink into.

Einsitzer ['aɪnzɪtsər], *m.* single-seater.

Einsonderungsdrüse ['aɪnzɔndəruŋsdry:zə], *f.* (*Anat.*) endocrine gland.

einspannen ['aɪnʃpanən], *v.t.* fasten *or* fix *or* clamp in position, harness (up) (*horse*), yoke (*oxen*); – ***in*** (*Acc.*), fasten *or* fix *or* clamp (*s.th.*) in (*vice etc.*). **Einspänner,** *m.* one-horse vehicle; (*coll.*) p. living alone, recluse; single man *or* woman. **einspännig,** *adj.* drawn by one horse, one-horse. **Einspannschraube,** *f.* clamping *or* locking *or* set screw.

einsparen ['aɪnʃpa:rən], *v.t.* save (*money, time etc.*). **Einsparung,** *f.* saving, economy.

einsperren ['aɪnʃpɛrən], *v.t.* shut *or* lock up; confine; imprison, jail; (*St. Exch.*) corner, make a corner in.

einspielen ['aɪnʃpi:lən], *v.r.* get going, get into full swing; (*of a p.*) get into practice; ***sich – in*** (*Acc.*), get the feel of (*a rôle*); ***sich – auf*** (*Acc.*), get the hang of; ***sich aufeinander –,*** become fully coordinated, learn to work *or* play *etc.* together as a team; ***das Quartett ist gut eingespielt,*** the ensemble of the quartet is admirable.

einspinnen ['aɪnʃpɪnən], **1.** *irr.v.t.* spin a web round; (*sl.*) ***ihn –,*** run him in, book him. **2.** *irr.v.r.* (*Zool.*) spin a cocoon; (*fig.*) seclude o.s., be wrapped up *or* absorbed (***in*** (*Acc. or Dat.*), in), shut *or* wrap o.s. up (in).

Einsprache ['aɪnʃpra:xə], *f.* 1. objection, protest; *see* **Einspruch**; 2. mouthpiece (*of a telephone*); 3. (*Swiss*) *see* **Einrede** (*Law*).

einsprechen ['aɪnʃprɛçən], **1.** *irr.v.t.* ***ihm etwas –,*** instil s.th. into him, inspire him with s.th. **2.** *irr.v.i.* – ***auf*** (*Acc.*), *see* **einreden**; (*obs.*) – ***gegen,*** *see* ***Einspruch erheben***; (*obs.*) – ***für,*** speak up *or* intercede for; (*obs.*) – ***bei,*** drop in *or* call on.

einsprengen ['aɪnʃprɛŋən], **1.** *v.t.* 1. sprinkle; intersperse, intermingle, admix; 2. burst open, blast open, blast an opening. **2.** *v.i.* (*aux.* s.) charge, rush (***auf*** (*Acc.*), upon). **Einsprengling,** *m.* **(-s,** *pl.* **-e), Einsprengung,** *f.* (*Geol.*) scattered deposit, xenolith.

einspringen ['aɪnʃprɪŋən], *irr.v.i.* (*aux.* s.) 1. spring *or* leap *or* jump in; catch, snap (*of locks*); (*Math.*) re-enter (*of angles*); – ***auf*** (*Acc.*), fall upon, spring *or* pounce (up)on; rush at; – ***in*** (*Acc.*), spring *or* jump *or* leap into; 2. shrink, contract; crack, chap (*as skin*); (*Archit.*) recede; 3. (*coll., fig.*) help out; step into the breach; – ***für,*** take (*s.o.'s*) place; step in (in place of). **einspringend,** *adj.* (*Math.*) re-entrant (*angle*), (*Archit.*) recessed, set back.

Einspritz– ['aɪnʃprɪts], *pref.* injection, jet-. **einspritzen,** *v.t.* 1. inject; – ***in*** (*Acc.*), inject *or* syringe *or* (*coll.*) squirt into; 2. damp, sprinkle (*ironing*); spatter (*with mud*). **Einspritzung,** *f.* injection.

Einspruch ['aɪnʃprux], *m.* protest, objection, (*Law*) appeal; – ***erheben*** (***gegen***), appeal *or* protest (against), object (to), make a protest *or* lodge an appeal (against), raise an objection (to).

einspurig ['aɪnʃpu:rɪç], *adj.* (*Railw.*) single-line, single-track.

einst [aɪnst], *adv.* 1. (*past*) in the past, formerly, at one time, once (upon a time), long ago, in past *or* olden times, (*Poet.*) in times past; – ***wie jetzt,*** (now) as ever; 2. (*future*) one *or* some day, in the future, in days *or* times to come.

einstampfen ['aɪnʃtampfən], *v.t.* press *or* ram down, tamp (*earth*), pulp (*paper*); – ***in*** (*Acc.*), ram *or* trample into.

Einstand ['aɪnʃtant], *m.* 1. entering upon *or* entry into (a new job); setting up house; ***seinen – feiern,*** give a house-warming party; 2. initiation *or* enrolment fee; (*obs.*) footing; – ***geben,*** pay one's footing; 3. (*Tenn.*) deuce. **Einstands|preis,** *m.* cost price, prime cost. **–recht,** *n.* (*obs.*) right of refusal, (right of) pre-emption.

einstanzen ['aɪnʃtantsən], *v.t.* emboss, stamp.

einstauben ['aɪnʃtaubən], *v.i.* (*aux.* s.) get dusty.

einstäuben ['aɪnʃtɔybən], *v.t.* dust, powder, sprinkle.

einstechen ['aɪnʃtɛçən], **1.** *irr.v.t.* prick (*pattern*) (***in*** (*Acc.*), in), stick (*needle*) (into). **2.** *irr.v.i.* stick *or* sink *or* go in. **Einstech|rahmen,** *m.* welt (*of shoe*). **–schloß,** *n.* mortise lock.

Einsteck– ['aɪnʃtɛk], *pref.* insertable, attachable. **einstecken,** *v.t.* put, stick, insert (***in*** (*Acc.*), into); sheathe (*sword*), post (*letter*), plug in (*lamp etc.*); put in one's pocket, pocket, make off with; (*fig.*) pocket, take; (*coll.*) swallow, take lying down (*insult etc.*); run (*a p.*) in, clap (*a p.*) in prison. **Einsteck|lauf,** *m.* (*Artil.*) liner, subcalibre barrel; (*of rifle*) Morris tube.

einstehen ['aɪnʃte:ən], *irr.v.i.* (*aux.* s.) – ***für,*** take *or* fill (*s.o.'s*) place, deputize for; answer *or* be answerable for, take *or* accept responsibility for, vouch for, guarantee; ***dafür – daß,*** guarantee *or* warrant that, vouch *or* answer for it that, pledge o.s. that; (*obs.*) – ***in*** (*Acc.*), take up (*a job*), go into (*service*). **Einsteher,** *m.* (*Mil. obs.*) substitute.

einstehlen ['aɪnʃte:lən], *irr.v.r.* ***sich – in*** (*Acc.*), steal *or* slip *or* creep *or* (*coll.*) sneak into; (*fig.*) insinuate o.s. into.

Einsteige|brücke, *f.* gangway (*of ship*), ramp. **–loch,** *n. See* **–schacht. –luke,** *f.* (access) hatch.

einsteigen ['aɪnʃtaɪgən], *irr.v.i.* (*aux.* s.) get *or* climb in; – ***in*** (*Acc.*), get *or* climb into; get on *or* in, board (*vehicle*), embark, go aboard *or* on board (*ship*); *–!* all aboard! take your seats! **Einsteigeschacht,** *m.* man-hole. **Einsteigluke,** *f. See* **Einsteigeluke.**

Einstell– ['aɪnʃtɛl], *pref.* adjusting, setting, focusing. **einstellbar,** *adj.* adjustable, variable.

einstellen ['aɪnʃtelən], **1.** *v.t.* 1. put *or* place in (the proper place), put back *or* away, garage (*car*), replace (*books*) on the shelves; – ***in*** (*Acc.*), put *or* place in(to); – ***bei,*** leave *or* deposit with; 2. engage, hire (*a p.*), (*coll.*) take on, (*Mil.*) enrol, enlist; – ***in*** (*Acc.*), give (*s.o.*) employment *or* a job in; 3. (***auf*** (*Acc.*)) adjust, set (*instruments etc.*) (to), (*Opt.*) focus (on), (*Rad.*) tune in (to); (*fig.*) centre, concentrate, direct (*effort, attention etc.*) (on), adapt (*endeavours*) (to); 4. stop, cease, discontinue, suspend, (*coll.*) leave off, (*Law*) stay, not proceed with. **2.** *v.r.* (*of a p.*) go, come (***bei,*** to (see)) (*a p. or th.*), appear, present o.s., (*coll.*) turn *or* show up; (*of a th.*) come to pass, arise, occur; come on (*as fits*); set in (*of winter etc.*); ***sich wieder –,*** return, reappear, recur; ***sich – auf*** (*Acc.*), adapt o.s. to, prepare o.s. *or* be prepared for, get in the right mood *or* right frame of mind for; ***eingestellt sein,*** be (*adv.*) minded, have (*adj.*) leanings; ***eingestellt sein gegen,*** be unfavourably disposed towards, be against. **Einsteller,** *m.* regulator, setting device.

einstellig ['aɪnʃtɛlɪç], *adj.* (*Math.*) of one digit, one-figure (*number*), one-place (*decimal*).

Einstellung ['aɪnʃtɛluŋ], *f.* 1. engagement, enrolment, enlistment; 2. adjustment, setting, focusing, focus; 3. stoppage, discontinuation, discontinuance, suspension; 4. (*fig.*) attitude, approach, outlook, view(s).

Einstich ['aɪnʃtɪç], *m.* sticking, insertion (*of needle etc.*) (into); prick, perforation, (*Surg.*) puncture.

Einstieg ['aɪnʃti:k], *m.* **(-(e)s,** *pl.* **-e)** entrance (*to vehicle*). **Einstiegluke,** *f. See* **Einsteigeluke.**

einstig ['aɪnstɪç], *adj.* 1. former, sometime, onetime, of old, (*Poet.*) erstwhile, of yore; 2. future, prospective. *See* **einst.**

einstimmen [ˈaɪnʃtɪmən], **1.** *v.i.* – *in* (*Acc.*), join in (*with the voice*), (*coll.*) chime in; (*fig.*) agree *or* consent to. **2.** *v.t.* *aufeinander* –, tune (*instruments*) to each other, (*of persons*) become attuned to one another.

einstimmig [ˈaɪnʃtɪmɪç], **1.** *adj.* unanimous; (*Mus.*) for one voice, unison. **2.** *adv.* unanimously, with one voice *or* accord, by common consent, (*Mus.*) in unison. **Einstimmigkeit,** *f.* agreement, unanimity, (*Mus.*) unison.

einstmalig [ˈaɪnstma:lɪç], *adj.* (*Poet.*) *see* **einstig. einstmals,** *adv.* (*Poet.*) *see* **einst.**

einstöckig [ˈaɪnʃtœkɪç], *adj.* one-storied (*of a house*).

einstoßen [ˈaɪnʃto:sən], *irr.v.t.* 1. – *in* (*Acc.*), push *or* drive *or* force *or* thrust into; 2. knock a hole in, smash *or* batter in *or* down (*door etc.*), stave in (*cask*).

einstreichen [ˈaɪnʃtraɪçən], **1.** *irr.v.t.* 1. – *in* (*Acc.*), rub *or* smear into; fill in, stop up, lute (*cracks*) (*Acc.*, with); 2. (*fig.*, *coll.*) rake in, pocket; 3. (*Tech.*) file a nick *or* notch in. **2.** *irr.v.i.* (*aux.* s.) (*Hunt.*) go to cover.

einstreuen [ˈaɪnʃtrɔyən], **1.** *v.t.* (*in* (*Acc.*)) strew, scatter (in), (*fig.*) insert (into), include (in) (*anecdotes etc.*), intersperse, interlard (*a speech etc.*) with; *eingestreute Bemerkungen,* occasional remarks. **2.** *v.i.* *dem Vieh* –, bed down cattle.

Einstrich [ˈaɪnʃtrɪç], *m.* slot, nick, notch (*of screw*); pointing (*of walls*).

einströmen [ˈaɪnʃtrø:mən], *v.i.* (*aux.* s.) flow *or* pour *or* stream in. **einströmend,** *adj.* inflowing, incoming. **Einströmperiode,** *f.* induction stroke. **Einströmung,** *f.* inflow, influx. **Einströmungsventil,** *n.* inlet *or* intake *or* induction valve.

einstücke(l)n [ˈaɪnʃtykə(l)n], *v.t.* piece in; patch.

einstudieren [ˈaɪnʃtudi:rən], *v.t.* learn thoroughly, study, rehearse, (*coll.*) get up (*a part etc.*). **Einstudierung,** *f.* study, rehearsal (*of a part*), (*Theat.*) production (*of a play*).

einstufen [ˈaɪnʃtu:fən], *v.t.* classify, grade. **Einstufung,** *f.* classification; class, grade.

einstülpen [ˈaɪnʃtylpən], *v.t.* turn *or* tuck in, turn inside out, (*Surg.*) invaginate.

einstürmen [ˈaɪnʃtyrmən], *v.i.* (*aux.* s.) – *in* (*Acc.*), rush *or* burst *or* storm into; – *auf* (*Acc.*), storm, charge, attack, make an assault on, rush at *or* on, bear down on; (*fig.*) assail, bombard (*with questions etc.*), crowd *or* swarm *or* press in upon (*as doubts, difficulties etc.*).

Einsturz [ˈaɪnʃturts], *m.* fall, collapse; subsidence.

einstürzen [ˈaɪnʃtyrtsən], **1.** *v.i.* (*aux.* s.) fall in, collapse, give way, cave in; – *auf* (*Acc.*), crowd in upon, assail. **2.** *v.t.* batter down, demolish.

einst|weilen, *adv.* meanwhile, in the meantime, for the time being, for the present, temporarily, provisionally. **–weilig,** *adj.* temporary, provisional, (*Law*) interim.

eintägig [ˈaɪntɛ:gɪç], *adj.* lasting one day, day-old, ephemeral.

Eintags|fieber [ˈaɪnta:gs–], *n.* ephemeral fever. **–fliege,** *f.* (*Ent.*) ephemeron, ephemera, may-fly.

Eintänzer [ˈaɪntɛntsər], *m.* gigolo.

eintauchen [ˈaɪntauxən], **1.** *v.t.* dip; – *in* (*Acc.*), dip *or* plunge into, immerse in. **2.** *v.i.* (*aux.* s.) dive, plunge (in); plunge, pitch (*as a ship*).

Eintausch [ˈaɪntauʃ], *m.* exchange, barter, (*obs.*) truck, (*coll.*) swap, swapping, trading. **eintauschen,** *v.t.* exchange, barter, (*coll.*) swap, trade (*gegen*, *für*, for).

einteilen [ˈaɪntaɪlən], *v.t.* divide up, classify, arrange; graduate, calibrate (*a scale*); plan (out), arrange, organize (*one's time, work etc.*); (*Mil.*) detail (off). **Einteilung,** *f.* distribution, division, arrangement, planning; classification; graduation, calibration. **Einteilungsgrund,** *m.* principle of classification.

eintönig [ˈaɪntø:nɪç], *adj.* monotonous, (*fig.*) tedious, humdrum, dull. **Eintönigkeit,** *f.* monotony, (*fig.*) dullness, sameness, tediousness.

Eintopf [ˈaɪntɔpf], *m.*, **Eintopfgericht,** *n.* hot-pot.

Eintracht [ˈaɪntraxt], *f.* concord, harmony, agreement, unity.

einträchtig [ˈaɪntrɛçtɪç], **1.** *adj.* harmonious, united. **2.** *adv.* harmoniously, in harmony *or* unity *or* concord.

Eintrag [ˈaɪntra:k], *m.* (**-(e)s,** *pl.* **¨-e**) 1. entry, item; 2. (*Weav.*) woof; 3. – *tun* (*Dat.*), harm, damage, wrong, (*coll.*) hurt (*a p.*); hurt, injure, impair, prejudice, detract from, be detrimental *or* prejudicial *or* injurious *or* hurtful to (*interests, reputation etc.*).

eintragen [ˈaɪntra:gən], **1.** *irr.v.t.* 1. carry *or* bring *or* gather in; yield, bring in, bear (*profit*); gain, earn, bring (*ihm*, him) (*praise, enmity etc.*); *das Geschäft trägt wenig ein,* the business is unremunerative *or* unprofitable *or* is not lucrative *or* is not a paying proposition *or* yields little profit *or* brings little in; 2. (*Math.*) plot (*curve etc.*); 3. (*Weav.*) work in, shoot (*weft*); 4. write *or* put down, enter, record, register (*in* (*Acc.*), in); (*Comm.*) enter (up), make an entry of, book, post (in); (*Law*) empanel (*jurors*); *eingetragenes Warenzeichen,* registered trade-mark. **2.** *irr.v.r.* sign the register, enter one's name.

einträglich [ˈaɪntrɛ:klɪç], *adj.* lucrative, profitable, remunerative, paying; (*coll*). *–e Pfründe,* fat living.

Eintragung [ˈaɪntra:guŋ], *f.* entry, registration, enrolment, (*Comm.*) entry (*in a ledger*).

eintränken [ˈaɪntrɛŋkən], *v.t.* steep, impregnate; (*coll.*) *ich werde es ihm* –, I'll pay him out *or* back for it, I'll make him smart *or* pay for it, I'll get even with him for that.

einträufeln [ˈaɪntrɔyfəln], *v.t.* drip (*in* (*Acc.*), into), add *or* administer drop by drop.

eintreffen [ˈaɪntrɛfən], *irr.v.i.* (*aux.* s.) 1. (*of a p., goods etc.*) arrive (*bei*, *in* or *an* (*Dat.*), at), reach; 2. (*of prophecy, dream etc.*) prove correct, be fulfilled, happen, come true, (*Poet.*) come to pass.

eintreiben [ˈaɪntraɪbən], *irr.v.t.* 1. drive *or* ram in *or* home (*peg, wedge etc.*), drive home (*cattle*); – *in* (*Acc.*), drive *or* ram into; 2. call in, recover, collect (*debts, taxes*), exact (*payment*).

eintreten [ˈaɪntre:tən], **1.** *irr.v.i.* (*aux.* s.) 1. come *or* go *or* step *or* walk in, enter; – *in* (*Acc.*), enter, step into; 2. – *in* (*Acc.*), join, enter (*army, club etc.*); 3. – *für*, take *or* fill (*s.o.'s*) place, deputize for, (*coll.*) stand in for; 4. – *für*, intercede *or* plead for (*a p.*), take (*s.o.'s*) part, champion (*s.o.'s*) cause; speak *or* stand *or* (*coll.*) stick up for, support (*a p. or cause*), champion, espouse (*a cause*); 5. occur, happen, take place, arise, ensue, (*coll.*) crop up; set in (*of weather, darkness etc.*), fall (*of silence*). **2.** *irr.v.t.* stamp *or* tread *or* trample down *or* in; kick open; *sich* (*Dat.*) *einen Dorn in den Fuß* –, run a thorn into one's foot. **Eintreten,** *n.* 1. entrance, entry; 2. intercession, championship, espousal; 3. occurrence. *See* **Eintritt. eintretendenfalls,** *adv.* in such an event, should the case arise, in case of need, if need(s) be.

eintrichtern [ˈaɪntrɪçtərn], *v.t.* (*coll.*) *ihm etwas* –, drum s.th. into his head.

Eintritt [ˈaɪntrɪt], *m.* 1. entering, entrance, entry; going *or* coming *or* passing in; 2. entry (*into war etc.*), entering (*upon career, negotiations etc.*), joining (*army, club etc.*); 3. beginning, onset; 4. entrance-fee, admission *or* gate-money; – *frei,* admission free. **Eintritts|geld,** *n.* charge for admission, entrance fee *or* money, admission fee. **–karte,** *f.* ticket of admission, admission ticket.

eintrocknen [ˈaɪntrɔknən], *v.i.* (*aux.* s.) dry in, dry up, go dry, shrivel.

einträpfeln [ˈaɪntrœpfəln], *v.t.* *See* **einträufeln.**

eintunken [ˈaɪntuŋkən], *v.t.* dip in; – *in* (*Acc.*), dip into.

einüben [ˈaɪnˀy:bən], *v.t.* practise (*activity*), exercise, train, coach (*executant*).

einverleiben [ˈaɪnfɛrlaɪbən], *v.t.* (*sep. and insep.*) incorporate, embody (*Dat.* or *in* (*Acc.*), in), annex (to); (*coll.*) *sich* (*Dat.*) –, put o.s. outside (*food*), knock back (*drink*). **Einverleibung,** *f.* incorporation, annexation.

Einvernahme ['aɪnfɛrna:mə], *f.* (*Austr., Swiss*) interrogation, questioning. **einvernehmen,** *irr.v.t.* (*Austr., Swiss*) interrogate, question.

Einvernehmen ['aɪnfɛrne:mən], *n.* consent, agreement; understanding; ***in gutem – (mit)***, on good *or* friendly terms, on the best of terms (with); ***sich mit ihm ins – setzen,*** come to an understanding *or* agreement *or* arrangement with him, come to terms with him.

einverstanden ['aɪnfɛrʃtandən], *pred.adj.* – ***sein (mit)***, consent, agree (to), approve (of) (*a th.*); agree, be in agreement (with) (*a p.*); ***nicht – sein (mit)***, disagree (with), disapprove (of) (*a th.*); disagree, be in disagreement, be at variance (with) (*a p.*); ***sich – erklären (mit)***, agree, consent, assent (to), approve, express one's approval (of); ***–!*** agreed! all right! very well! (*coll.*) right oh! O.K.!

Einverständnis ['aɪnfɛrʃtɛntnɪs], *n.* understanding, agreement; (*Law*) approval, assent, consent; ***stillschweigendes*** or ***geheimes –***, tacit agreement, secret understanding, connivance, collusion.

Einwand ['aɪnvant], *m.* **(-(e)s,** *pl.* **⸗e)** objection (*gegen,* to); *see* **einwenden.**

Einwanderer ['aɪnvandərər], *m.* immigrant. **einwandern,** *v.i.* (*aux.* s.) immigrate; ***– in*** (*Acc.*), enter (*a country*), migrate into, come and settle in. **Einwanderung,** *f.* immigration.

einwandfrei ['aɪnvantfraɪ], *adj.* unobjectionable, impeccable, unimpeachable, irreproachable (*behaviour etc.*), indubitable, incontestable (*evidence etc.*), faultless, perfect, satisfactory; ***– feststellen,*** establish beyond a ((*coll.*) shadow of) doubt *or* beyond question; ***nicht –***, doubtful, contestable; dubious, questionable, (*coll.*) shady; unreliable.

einwärts ['aɪnvɛrts], *adv.*, **einwärts–,** *pref.* inward(s). **–einwärts,** *suff.* into . . .

einweben ['aɪnve:bən], *reg. & irr.v.t.* weave *or* work in, interweave; ***– in*** (*Acc.*), weave *or* work into.

einwechseln ['aɪnvɛksəln], *v.t.* change (*money*); (ex)change (*gegen, für,* for); ***einen Scheck –***, cash a cheque.

einwecken ['aɪnvɛkən], *v.t.* bottle, preserve (*fruit etc.*).

Einweg– ['aɪnve:k], *pref.* one-way (*switch etc.*), non-returnable (*bottle etc.*).

einweibig ['aɪnvaɪbɪç], *adj.* (*Bot.*) monogynous. **Einweibigkeit,** *f.* monogyny.

einweichen ['aɪnvaɪçən], *v.t.* soak, steep, macerate; put (*dirty washing*) to soak; ***– in*** (*Acc.*), soak *etc.* in.

einweihen ['aɪnvaɪən], *v.t.* consecrate, dedicate; inaugurate, initiate, open (*ceremonially*); (*coll.*) wear *or* use for the first time; ***eine neue Wohnung –***, give a house-warming party; ***– in*** (*Acc.*), initiate in (*a mystery*), (*coll.*) let into (*a secret*); ***ein Eingeweihter,*** initiate, adept, (*coll.*) s.o. in the know; ***eingeweiht sein,*** be in (on) the secret *or* (*coll.*) in the know. **Einweihung,** *f.* consecration, dedication, initiation, inauguration, ceremonial opening. **Einweihungsfeier,** *f.* inaugural *or* dedication ceremony.

einweisen ['aɪnvaɪzən], *irr.v.t.* instruct (*in* (*Acc.*), in), introduce (to) (*duties*); install, (*Eccl.*) induct (in) (*office*); direct, assign, allocate, send (to) (*appropriate place*). **Einweisung,** *f.* instruction, introduction; installation, induction; direction, allocation.

einwenden ['aɪnvɛndən], *reg. & irr.v.t.* ***etwas – gegen,*** make *or* raise an objection to; ***– daß . . .***, object that . . .; ***dagegen läßt sich nichts –***, there can be no objection to that. **Einwendung,** *f.* objection; (*Law*) plea. *See* **Einwand.**

einwerfen ['aɪnvɛrfən], *irr.v.t.* **1.** insert, put *or* throw in; (*Footb.*) throw in; ***– in*** (*Acc.*), throw into; 2. smash; 3. interpose; object.

einwickeln ['aɪnvɪkəln], *v.t.* wrap (up); envelop, swathe; (*coll.*) get round, get the better of, twist round one's little finger (*a p.*).

einwiegen ['aɪnvi:gən], *v.t.* rock to sleep, (*fig.*) lull (*with promises etc.*).

einwilligen ['aɪnvɪlɪgən], *v.i.* consent, agree (*in* (*Acc.*), to), acquiesce (in); accept. **Einwilligung,** *f.* consent.

[1]**einwirken** ['aɪnvɪrkən], *v.t.* weave *or* work in, interweave.

[2]**einwirken,** *v.i.* ***– auf*** (*Acc.*), influence, affect; have *or* exert *or* exercise an influence on, have an effect on, act on. **Einwirkung,** *f.* influence, action, effect.

Einwohner ['aɪnvo:nər], *m.* inhabitant, resident. **Einwohnerschaft,** *f.* inhabitants, population. **Einwohnerzahl,** *f.* total population.

Einwurf ['aɪnvurf], *m.* **1.** throwing in, insertion, (*Footb.*) throw-in; 2. slot (*of slot-machine or pillar-box*); 3. interjection (*of remark*), objection.

einwurzeln ['aɪnvurtsəln], *v.i.* (*aux.* s.) take root (*in* (*Dat.*), in); ***tief eingewurzelt,*** settled, established; deep(ly)-rooted, inveterate.

Einzahl ['aɪntsa:l], *f.* (*Gram.*) singular (number).

einzahlen ['aɪntsa:lən], *v.t.* pay in, deposit (***bei,*** at). **Einzahlung,** *f.* payment, deposit.

einzäunen ['aɪntsɔynən], *v.t.* hedge *or* fence in, enclose. **Einzäunung,** *f.* fence, enclosure; fencing.

einzeichnen ['aɪntsaɪçnən], **1.** *v.t.* mark *or* draw in, (*Geom.*) inscribe; plot (*a curve*). **2.** *v.r.* enter one's name, put o.s. down.

Einzel ['aɪntsəl], *m.* (*Tenn.*) singles.

Einzel–, *pref.* single, individual. **–anfertigung,** *f.* job-work. **–aufhängung,** *f.* independent suspension. **–aufzählung,** *f.* detailed enumeration. **–ausgabe,** *f.* separate edition. **–bett,** *n.* single bed. **–erscheinung,** *f.* isolated phenomenon. **–exemplar,** *n.* unique specimen *or* copy (*of book*). **–fall,** *m.* individual *or* special *or* isolated *or* particular instance *or* case. **–gänger,** *m.* individualist, lone-wolf. **–haft,** *f.* solitary confinement. **–handel,** *m.* retail business. **–haus,** *n.* detached house.

Einzelheit ['aɪntsəlhaɪt], *f.* detail; *pl.* details, particulars.

Einzel|kampf, *m.* single *or* hand-to-hand combat. **–kind,** *n.* only child. **–mensch,** *m.* individual.

einzeln ['aɪntsəln], **1.** *adj.* single, individual, separate; isolated, solitary, (*Poet.*) lone. **2.** *adv.* singly, individually, separately, one by one, one at a time. **3.** *indef.pron.* ***der –e,*** the individual; ***jeder –e,*** each one, every single *or* individual one; ***das –e,*** detail(s); ***im –en,*** in detail; ***bis ins –e,*** to the last detail; ***–es,*** a few things, matters *or* points; ***–e pl.,*** a few, some. **einzelnstehend,** *adj.* isolated, solitary, lone.

Einzel|person, *f.* individual. **–spiel,** *n. See* **Einzel. –teil,** *n.* component (part). **–verkauf,** *m.* retail (sale). **–wesen,** *n.* individual. **–zimmer,** *n.* single (bed)room.

einziehen ['aɪntsi:ən], **1.** *irr.v.t.* **1.** draw *or* pull *or* haul *or* get *or* take in; retract; ***den Faden –***, thread a needle; ***eine Fahne –***, lower *or* furl a flag; ***die Hörner –***, draw in one's horns; ***den Schwanz –***, (*of animal*) put its tail between its legs, (*coll. of a p.*) climb down, slink off with one's tail between one's legs; 2. withdraw (from circulation), call in (*bank-notes etc.*); 3. collect, gather; ***Erkundigungen –***, seek *or* obtain information, make inquiries (***über*** (*Acc.*), about); 4. call up (*for military service*); 5. take *or* soak in, absorb (*moisture*), inhale (*air etc.*); 6. (*Law*) seize, confiscate (*goods, property*); 7. discontinue, abolish, suppress; 8. (*Typ.*) indent (*a line*). **2.** *irr. v.i.* (*aux.* s.) **1.** ***– in*** (*Acc.*), enter, march *or* move into, make one's entry into; move into (*new house*); ***bei ihm –***, take lodgings *or* take up residence with him; 2. (*of liquids*) seep *or* soak in, infiltrate; *see* **eingezogen. Einziehung,** *f.* drawing in, retraction; absorption, inhalation; withdrawal, abolition, discontinuation, suspension; collection; confiscation, seizure; (*Typ.*) indentation; (*Build.*) recess (*of a wall*).

einzig ['aɪntsɪç], **1.** *adj.* only, single, sole, unique; ***– (in seiner Art),*** unique, unrivalled, unparalleled, peerless; (*coll.*) ***er ist doch ganz –***, he is really the limit. **2.** *adv.* only; ***– und allein,*** (simply and) solely, purely and simply; ***mein – Geliebter,*** my own darling. **einzigartig,** *adj.* unique, unparalleled, outstanding, extraordinary, remarkable, uncommon, singular. **Einzigartigkeit,** *f.* uniqueness, singularity.

einzuckern ['aıntsukərn], *v.t.* sugar (over); cover with sugar.

Einzug ['aıntsu:k], *m.* entry, entrance; moving in (*into a new house etc.*); – ***halten,*** make one's entry *or* entrance *or* appearance.

Einzüger ['aıntsy:gər], *m.* (*Swiss*) (tax) collector.

Einzugs|gebiet, *n.* catchment *or* drainage area. **–schmaus,** *m.* house-warming.

einzwängen ['aıntsvɛŋən], *v.t.* force, squeeze, jam, wedge (*in* (*Acc.*), in(to)).

Eipulver ['aıpulvər], *n.* dried egg.

eirund ['aırunt], *adj.* oval, egg-shaped. **Eirund,** *n.* oval.

eis ['e:ıs], *n.* (*Mus.*) E-sharp.

Eis [aıs], *n.* (**-es,** *no pl.*) ice; ice-cream; ***aufs – führen,*** lead on to thin ice *or* on to dangerous ground; ***aufs – legen,*** put into cold storage (*also fig.*); ***zu – werden,*** freeze; ***vom –e besetzt,*** icebound; ***gehendes –,*** floating ice; ***mürbes –,*** unsound ice; ***der Fluß geht mit –,*** large blocks of ice are floating down the river. **Eis|bahn,** *f.* slide; skating-ice, ice-rink. **–bär,** *m.* polar bear. **–bein,** *n.* pig's trotters, knuckle of pork; (*Anat.*) aitch-bone; *pl.* (*sl.*) cold feet. **–berg,** *m.* iceberg. **–bock, –brecher,** *m.* ice-breaker.

Eischale ['aı'ʃa:lə], *f.* egg-shell.

Eis|decke, *f.* sheet of ice, coating of ice. **–diele,** *f.* ice-cream parlour.

Eisen ['aızən], *n.* iron; horseshoe; sword, dagger, blade, cutting-iron *or* tool; branding- *or* cauterizing iron, flat-iron, (*Hunt.*) trap; *pl.* irons, fetters, shackles, chains; ***heißes – anfassen,*** grasp the nettle; ***an kaltem – sterben,*** die by the sword; ***ihn in – legen,*** put him in irons; ***durch – und Blut,*** with blood and iron (*Bismarck*); (*Prov.*) ***Not bricht –,*** needs must when the devil drives, necessity knows no law; (*Prov.*) ***man muß das – schmieden, solange es heiß ist,*** make hay while the sun shines, strike while the iron is hot; (*coll.*) ***zum alten – werfen,*** throw on the scrap-heap; scrap, shelve (*a plan*), cast aside, discard (*a p.*). **Eisenabfall,** *m.* scrap-iron. **eisenartig,** *adj.* ferruginous.

Eisenbahn ['aızənba:n], *f.* railway, (*Am.*) railroad; (*sl.*) ***es ist*** (***die***) ***höchste –,*** it is high time, time presses, there's not a moment to lose. **Eisenbahn|damm,** *m.* railway embankment. **Eisenbahner,** *m.* (*coll.*) railwayman. **Eisenbahn|fähre,** *f.* train ferry. **–fahrt,** *f.* rail(way) *or* train journey. **–gesellschaft,** *f.* railway company. **–knotenpunkt,** *m.* railway junction. **–netz,** *n.* railway system *or* network. **–schwelle,** *f.* sleeper, (*Am.*) tie. **–schmöker,** *m.* (*coll.*) light reading for the train. **–strecke,** *f.* section *or* (*Am.*) division (of railway), (*coll.*) stretch of line. **–übergang,** *m.* level- *or* (*Am.*) grade crossing. **–unfall,** *m.*, **–unglück,** *n.* railway accident, (*coll.*) train crash. **–verband,** *m.* National Union of Railwaymen. **–verkehr,** *m.* rail(way) traffic. **–wagen,** *m.* railway carriage (*for passengers*), goods van, truck, wagon.

Eisen|bau, *m.* (*pl.* **-ten**) ironwork, iron structure. **–beißer,** *m.* (*coll.*) fire-eater, dare-devil, swashbuckler, braggart, bully. **–beton,** *m.* reinforced concrete, ferro-concrete. **–blau,** *n.* *See* **–blauspat. eisenblausauer,** *adj.* (*Chem.*) ferrocyanide of . . .. **Eisen|blausäure,** *f.* (*Chem.*) ferrocyanic acid. **–blauspat,** *m.* vivianite. **–blech,** *n.* sheet-iron, iron plate. **–chlorid,** *n.* (*Chem.*) iron *or* ferric chloride. **–chlorür,** *n.* (*Chem.*) ferrous chloride. **–erde,** *f.* iron-stone, ferruginous earth. **–erz,** *n.* iron-ore. **–feilicht,** *n.* iron-filings. **–fleck,** *m.* iron-mould. **–fresser,** *m.* (*coll.*) *see* **–beißer. –frischen,** *n.* refining. **–gehalt,** *m.* iron content. **–gießerei,** *f.* ironfoundry. **–glanz,** *m.* haematite. **–grube,** *f.* iron-mine. **–guß,** *m.* iron casting; cast-iron. **eisenhaltig,** *adj.* containing iron; ferruginous, chalybeate. **Eisenhändler,** *m.* ironmonger. **eisenhart,** *adj.* hard as iron.

Eisen|hut, *m.*, **–hütchen,** *n.* (*Bot.*) aconite, monkshood (*Aconitum napellus*). **–hütte,** *f.* iron-works. **–kernspule,** *f.* (*Elec.*) iron-cored inductance. **–kernverlust,** *m.* (*Elec.*) core losses. **–kies,** *m.* iron pyrites. **–kram,** *m.* (*coll.*) ironmongery, hardware. **–kraut,** *n.* (*Bot.*) verbena, vervain. **–nährpräparat,** *n.* (*Med.*) iron blood-tonic. **–oxyd,** *n.* ferric oxide. **–oxydul,** *n.* ferrous oxide. **–quelle,** *f.* chalybeate spring. **–rost,** *m.* 1. rust; 2. iron grate. **–säge,** *f.* hacksaw. **eisensauer,** *adj.* (*Chem.*) ferrate of . . . **Eisen|säuerling,** *m.* chalybeate water. **–säure,** *f.* ferric acid. **–schimmel,** *m.* iron-grey (horse). **–schlacke,** *f.* clinker, slag, iron-dross. **–schmied,** *m.* blacksmith. **–schmiede,** *f.* (blacksmith's) forge. **–schrott,** *m.* scrap-iron. **eisenschüssig,** *adj.* ferruginous. **Eisen|schwärze,** *f.* black-lead, graphite, plumbago. **–spat,** *m.* siderite. **–sulfat,** *n.* (*Chem.*) ferrous sulphate, copperas, green vitriol.

Eisente ['aıs'ɛntə], *f.* (*Orn.*) long-tailed duck, (*Am.*) oldsquaw (*Clangula hyemalis*).

Eisen|waren, *f.pl.* ironmongery, hardware. **–warenhändler,** *m.* ironmonger. **–wasser,** *n.* chalybeate water. **–werk,** *n.* ironworks. **–zeit,** *f.* Iron Age.

eisern ['aızərn], *adj.* iron; hard, strong, inflexible; unyielding, unrelenting, relentless, implacable; untiring, tireless, unwearing, indefatigable, unremitting, unflagging; inescapable, inevitable, iron (*necessity*), immutable (*law*), irrefutable (*logic*), stern, rigid (*discipline*); (*Law*) inalienable; ***–e Miene,*** stony look; ***–e Stirn,*** brazen effrontery; ***–es Vieh,*** permanent head of cattle; ***–er Bestand,*** emergency *or* reserve stock(s), reserve fund; (*Mil.*) emergency *or* iron rations; ***der –e Herzog,*** the Iron Duke (*Wellington*); ***der –e Kanzler,*** the Iron Chancellor (*Bismarck*); ***–es Kapital,*** tied-up capital; ***–es Kreuz,*** Iron Cross (*Prussian war medal*); ***das –e Tor,*** the Iron Gates (*of the Danube*); ***–er Vorhang,*** fire-curtain, safety curtain (*in theatres*); (*Pol.*) Iron Curtain.

Eis|essig, *m.* (*Chem.*) glacial acetic acid. **–figurenlaufen,** *n.* figure-skating. **–fisch,** *m.* (*Zool.*) arctic *or* Greenland whale. **–fuchs,** *m.* (*Zool.*) arctic fox. **–gang,** *m.* drift-ice, floating ice. **eis|gekühlt,** *adj.* iced, chilled, frappé. **–grau,** *adj.* hoary. **eisig,** *adj.* icy, ice-cold, cold as ice; (*fig.*) icy, frigid, chilling. **eiskalt,** *adj.* icy (cold), freezing; (*fig.*) like ice, (*coll.*) frozen (*as feet etc.*). **Eis|kunstlauf,** *m.* figure-skating. **–lauf,** *m.* skating. **–laufbahn,** *f.* skating *or* ice rink. **eislaufen,** *irr.v.i.* (*sep.*) (*aux.* s.) skate. **Eis|laüfer,** *m.* skater. **–masse,** *f.* ice-floe. **–meer,** *n.* (*Geog.*) polar sea; ***Nördliches –,*** Arctic Ocean; ***Südliches –,*** Antarctic Ocean. **–monat, –mond,** *m.* (*obs., Poet.*) January. **–möwe,** *f.* (*Orn.*) glaucous gull (*Larus hyperboreus*). **–nadel,** *f.*, **–pfeiler,** *m.* sérac. **–pickel,** *m.* ice-axe.

Eisprung ['aıʃpruŋ], *m.* (*Biol.*) ovulation.

Eis|regen, *m.* sleet. **–scheurung,** *f.*, **–schliff,** *m.* (*Geol.*) glacial scouring. **–schnellauf,** *m.* speed skating. **–scholle,** *f.* ice-floe. **–schrank,** *m.* refrigerator. **–seetaucher,** *m.* *See* **–taucher**; ***wießschnäbliger –,*** see ***gelbschnäbliger Eistaucher.*** **–segeln,** *n.* ice-yachting. **–sturmvogel,** *m.* (*Orn.*) fulmar petrel, (*Am.*) fulmar (*Fulmarus glacialis*). **–taucher,** *m.* (*Orn.*) Great Northern diver, (*Am.*) common loon (*Gavia immer*); ***gelbschnäbliger –,*** white-billed diver, (*Am.*) yellow-billed loon (*Gavia adamsii*). **–tüte,** *f.* ice-cream cornet. **–vogel,** *m.* (*Orn.*) kingfisher (*Alcedo atthis*). **–waffel,** *f.* ice-cream wafer. **–würfel,** *m.* ice-cube. **–wüste,** *f.* frozen waste. **–zacken,** *m.* icicle. **–zeit,** *f.* ice-age, glacial period. **eiszeitlich,** *adj.* glacial, of the ice age. **Eis|zone,** *f.* glacial *or* frigid zone. **–zucker,** *m.* sugar icing; icing sugar.

eitel ['aıtəl], **1.** *adj.* (*of a p.*) vain, conceited (***auf*** (*Acc.*), about), (*of words, pleasures etc.*) vain, frivolous, empty, idle, futile; (*Poet., usu. inv.*) sheer, pure. **2.** *adv.* (*Poet.*) nothing but, only, merely. **Eitelkeit,** *f.* vanity; emptiness, futility.

Eiter ['aıtər], *m.* matter, pus. **Eiter|abfluß,** *m.* (purulent) discharge. **–ansammlung,** *f.* gathering. **–beule,** *f.* abscess, (*fig.*) den of iniquity. **–bildung,** *f.* suppuration. **–bläschen,** *n.*, **–blase,** *f.* pustule. **–brust,** *f.* empyema. **–fieber,** *n.* pyaemia. **–fluß,** *m.* blennorrhoea. **–gang,** *m.* fistula. **–geschwulst,** *f.*, **–geschwür,** *n.* abscess. **eiterig,** *adj.* purulent. **eitern,** *v.i.* suppurate, fester; discharge (pus), (*coll.*) run. **eiternd,** *adj.* festering, suppurating, running. **Eitersack,** *m.* cyst (*of a tumour*). **Eiterung,** *f.* suppuration, festering; discharge, pus. **Eitervergiftung,** *f.* pyaemia.

eitrig ['aɪtrɪç], *adj. See* **eiterig.**

Eiweiß ['aɪvaɪs], *n.* egg-white, white of egg; (*Chem.*) protein; (*Biol.*) albumin, albumen. **eiweißartig,** *adj.* albuminous. **Eiweißbedarf,** *m.* protein requirement. **eiweiß|förmig,** *adj. See* **–artig. Eiweißgehalt,** *m.* protein *or* albumin content. **eiweiß|haltig,** *adj. See* **–artig. Eiweiß|haushalt,** *m.* protein metabolism. **–körper, –stoff,** *m.* protein. **–stoffwechsel, –umsatz,** *m. See* **–haushalt.**

Eizelle ['aɪtsɛlə], *f.* ovum.

Ekart [e'ka:r], *m.* (**-s,** *pl.* **-s**) (*Comm.*) margin of profit.

Ekel ['e:kəl], **1.** *m.* loathing (*vor* (*Dat.*), for), disgust (at, for), aversion (to, for), repugnance (to), repulsion (for), nausea; ***bis zum –,*** ad nauseam. **2.** *n.* (*coll. of a p.*) beast, horror.

ekel, *adj.* (*Poet.*) repulsive, repellent, repugnant, loathsome; (*obs. of a p.*) fastidious, squeamish. **ekelhaft,** *adj.* repulsive, repellent, revolting, repugnant, atrocious, disgusting, offensive; loathsome, (*coll.*) horrid, beastly, nasty. **Ekelhaftigkeit,** *f.* repulsiveness, atrociousness, loathsomeness, (*coll.*) beastliness, nastiness. **ekelig,** *adj. See* **ekelhaft. ekeln, 1.** *v.imp.* ***mir*** or ***mich ekelt davor, es ekelt mir*** or ***mich,*** I loathe it, it disgusts me. **2.** *v.r.* ***ich ekle mich davor,*** it nauseates *or* disgusts me, it fills me with horror *or* repulsion *or* loathing, I feel repulsion for *or* aversion to it, (*coll.*) it makes me feel sick.

Eklat [e:'kla:], *m.* (**-s,** *pl.* **-s**) stir, commotion; ***mit –,*** splendidly, (*coll.*) famously; (*iron.*) ***mit – durchfallen,*** fail dismally, be a resounding failure, (*coll.*) be an utter flop. **eklatant** [–'tant], *adj.* clear, striking, blatant.

eklig ['e:klɪç], *adj. See* **ekelhaft.**

Eklipse [ɛk'lɪpsə], *f.* eclipse. **Ekliptik,** *f.* (*Astr.*) ecliptic. **ekliptisch,** *adj.* ecliptic.

Ekloge [ɛk'lo:gə], *f.* eclogue.

Ekstase [ɛk'sta:zə], *f.* ecstasy, trance, rapture, transport, exaltation. **ekstatisch,** *adj.* ecstatic, rapturous; enraptured.

Ektoplasma [ɛkto'plasma], *n.* ectoplasm.

Ekuador [ekua'do:r], *n.* (*Geog.*) Ecuador. **Ekuadorianer** [–i'a:nər], *m.* Ecuadorian. **ekuadorianisch,** *adj.* Ecuadorian.

Ekzem [ɛk'tse:m], *n.* (**-es,** *pl.* **-e**) eczema.

Elan [e'lã, e'la:n], *m.* (**-s,** *no pl.*) dash, energy, vigour.

elastisch [e'lastɪʃ], *adj.* elastic, resilient, springy, pliant, supple, flexible; (*fig.*) elastic, buoyant (*step*), resiliant, adaptable (*mind*). **Elastizität** [–titsi'tɛ:t], *f.* elasticity, resilience, flexibility, suppleness. **Elastizitätsgrenze,** *f.* (*Metall.*) elastic limit.

Elbe ['ɛlbə], *f.*, **Elbstrom,** *m.* (*Geog.*) (River) Elbe.

Elch [ɛlç], *m.* (**-(e)s,** *pl.* **-e**) elk, moose.

Elefant [ele'fant], *m.* (**-en,** *pl.* **-en**) elephant; ***wie ein – im Porzellanladen,*** like a bull in a china-shop; ***aus einer Mücke einen –en machen,*** make a mountain out of a mole-hill. **Elefanten|bein,** *n.* (*Med.*) elephantiasis. **–führer,** *m.* mahout. **–haut,** *f.* ***eine – haben,*** have a hide like a rhinoceros. **–rüssel,** *m.* elephant's trunk. **–zahn,** *m.* tusk.

elegant [ele'gant], *adj.* elegant, smart; graceful. **Eleganz,** *f.* elegance; gracefulness.

Elegie [ele'gi:], *f.* elegy. **elegisch** [–'le:gɪʃ], *adj.* elegiac; melancholy, mournful; ***–e Verse,*** elegiacs; mournful verses, melancholy lines.

Elektor [elɛk'to:r], *m.* (**-s,** *pl.* **-en**) (*Hist.*) Elector.

Elektra [e'lɛktra], *f.* Electra.

elektrifizieren [elɛktrifi'tsi:rən], *v.t.* electrify (*railway etc.*). **Elektriker** [–'lɛktrɪkər], *m.* electrician. **elektrisch,** *adj.* electric(al); ***–es Feld,*** electrical field; (*Ichth.*) ***–er Fisch,*** electric eel; ***–e Ladung,*** electrical charge; ***–er Rasierapparat,*** electric razor; ***–er Schlag,*** electric shock. **Elektrische,** *f.* (*coll.*) (electric) tram(car). **elektrisieren** [–'zi:rən], *v.t.* electrify (*substance*), (*fig.*) electrify, galvanize (*audience*). **Elektrisiermaschine,** *f.* electrostatic machine.

Elektrizität [elɛktritsi'tɛ:t], *f.* electricity. **Elektrizitäts–,** *pref.* electricity, electric, electro-. **Elektrizitäts|leiter,** *m.* conductor (of electricity). **–leitung,** *f.* electric cable. **–messer,** *m.* electrometer. **–werk,** *n.* generating *or* power station. **–zähler,** *m.* electricity meter.

Elektro|antrieb [elɛktro–], *m.* electric traction. **–chemie,** *f.* electro-chemistry. **–dose,** *f.* electromagnetic pickup (*gramophone*). **–energie,** *f.* electrical energy. **–gerät,** *n.* electrical appliance. **–ingenieur,** *m.* electrical engineer. **–installateur,** *m.* electrical fitter. **–lot,** *n.* electrical depth sounder.

Elektrolyse [elɛktro'ly:zə], *f.* electrolysis.

Elektro|mechaniker, –monteur, *m. See* **–installateur. –motor,** *m.* electric motor. **elektromotorisch,** *adj.* electromotive.

Elektron [elɛk'tro:n], *n.* (**-s,** *pl.* **-en**) electron. **Elektronen–,** *pref.* electron(ic), thermionic. **Elektronen|fernrohr,** *n.* electron telescope. **–gehirn,** *n.* electronic brain. **–lehre,** *f.* electron theory; electronics. **–röhre,** *f.* thermionic valve *or* (*Am.*) tube. **–schleuder,** *m.* betatron. **–strahl,** *m.* electron beam, cathode ray.

Elecktro|technik, *f.* electrical engineering. **–techniker,** *m.* electrical engineer.

Element [ele'mɛnt], *n.* (**-(e)s,** *pl.* **-e**) element; component, member, (*Elec.*) cell; *pl.* elements, rudiments, first principles; ***in seinem –,*** in his element; ***chemische –e,*** chemical elements; ***–e der Mathematik,*** rudiments of mathematics; ***die üblen –e gewannen die Oberhand,*** the undesirable elements gained the upper hand; ***das Wüten der –e,*** the raging of the elements.

elementar [elemɛn'ta:r], *adj.* fundamental, basic; elementary, rudimentary; elemental; (*Chem.*) simple, uncompounded, uncombined. **Elementar|bildung,** *f.* primary *or* elementary education. **–buch,** *n.* primer. **–geist,** *m.* elemental spirit. **–gewalt,** *f.* force of nature, elemental power. **–schule,** *f.* primary *or* elementary school. **–stoff,** *m.* (*Chem.*) element. **–teilchen,** *n.* elementary particle.

Elen ['e:lɛn], *m. or n.* elk, moose.

Elend ['e:lɛnt], *n.* (**-s,** *no pl.*) 1. destitution, penury, poverty, want, squalor; 2. distress, misery, wretchedness; (*coll.*) ***das graue –,*** (fit of) the blues; (*coll.*) ***das heulende –,*** (fit of) the willies; (*coll.*) ***wie ein Häufchen –,*** (like) a picture of misery; (*coll.*) ***sieben Stunden hinterm –,*** at the back of (the) beyond; 3. (*obs.*) exile, banishment. **elend,** *adj.* 1. wretched, miserable, poverty-stricken, squalid; 2. (*of a p.*) wretched, miserable, distressed; (*of actor, performance etc.*) vile, deplorable, pitiful, (*coll.*) awful, rotten; ***Elender!*** you wretch! ***du Elender!*** you poor wretch! 3. (*of deeds*) mean, despicable, contemptible, shameful. **elendig,** *adj. See* **elend** (*esp.* 1). **elendiglich,** *adv.* miserably, wretchedly. **Elendsviertel,** *n.* slums.

Elentier ['e:lɛnti:r], *n. See* **Elen.**

Elephant, *m. See* **Elefant.**

Elevation [elevatsi'o:n], *f.* elevation; (*Astr.*) altitude (*of star*); (*psychic*) levitation. **Elevator** [–'va:tər], *m.* (**-s,** *pl.* **-en** [–'to:rən]) (grain) elevator, bucket conveyor, paternoster; (*Anat.*) elevator (muscle).

[1]**Elf** [ɛlf], *m.* (**-en,** *pl.* **-en**) elf; fairy; goblin; imp.

[2]**Elf,** *f.* (-, *pl.* **-en**) (*Footb.*) team, eleven.

elf, *num.adj.* eleven.

Elfe ['ɛlfə], *f.* elf, fairy, pixie, sprite.
Elfenbein ['ɛlfənbaɪn], *n.* ivory. **elfenbeine(r)n,** *adj.* ivory, (made) of ivory. **Elfenbein|küste,** *f.* (*Geog.*) Ivory Coast. **–möwe,** *f.* (*Orn.*) ivory gull (*Pagophila eburnea*).
elfenhaft ['ɛlfənhaft], *adj.* elfish, elfin, fairylike. **Elfen|könig,** *m.* fairy-king. **–reich,** *n.* fairyland. **–reigen,** *m.* fairy-dance. **–tanzplatz,** *m.* fairy-ring.
Elfer ['ɛlfər], *m.* (figure) eleven; wine of '11 vintage; soldier of 11th regiment; (*Footb.*) penalty (kick). **Elfereinmaleins,** *n.* eleven times table.
elffach ['ɛlffax], *adj.* elevenfold, eleven times. **Elfflach,** *n.* hendecahedron. **elfflächig,** *adj.* hendecahedral. **elfjährig,** *adj.* eleven-year-old; lasting eleven years. **elfmal,** *adv.* eleven times. **Elfmeter(stoß),** *m.* (*Footb.*) penalty (kick). **elfstellig,** *adj.* eleven-figure (*number*), eleven-place (*decimal*).
elft [ɛlft], **1.** *adv.* ***zu –,*** (the) eleven of us (you, them *etc.*). **2.** *num.adj.* eleventh; ***in –er Stunde,*** at the eleventh hour (*see also under* **acht**). **elft–, Elft–,** *pref.* eleventh. **Elftel,** *n.* eleventh (part). **elftel,** *inv.adj.* eleventh (part) of . . . . **elftens,** *adv.* in the eleventh place.
Elger ['ɛlɡər], *m.* harpoon; eel-dart.
Elias [e'li:as], *m.* (*B.*) Elijah.
elidieren [eli'di:rən], *v.t.* elide, suppress (*a vowel*).
eliminieren [elimi'ni:rən], *v.t.* eliminate.
Elite [e'li:tə], *f.* élite, pick, flower. **Elitetruppe,** *f.* crack regiment, *pl.* picked troops.
Ellbogen ['ɛlbo:ɡən], *m.* elbow; ***mit den – anstoßen,*** elbow, nudge; ***die – benutzen,*** be pushing; ***keine – haben,*** let o.s. be pushed around; ***die – frei haben,*** have elbow-room; (*fig.*) have free scope *or* a free hand. **Ellbogen|freiheit,** *f.* elbow-room. **–knochen,** *m.* (*Anat.*) ulna, cubitus. **–nerv,** *m.* ulnar nerve.
Elle ['ɛlə], *f.* 1. ell, yard, yardstick; ***als hätte er eine – verschluckt,*** he was as straight as a poker *or* ramrod; 2. (*Anat.*) ulna. **Ellenbogen,** *m.* *See* **Ellbogen. ellenlang,** *adj.* an ell long, (*coll.*) extremely long, endless, interminable. **Ellenmaß,** *n.* yardstick. **ellenweise,** *adv.* by the yard.
Eller ['ɛlər], *f.* (-, *pl.* **-n**) *see* **Erle.**
Ellipse [ɛ'lɪpsə], *f.* (*Geom.*) ellipse; (*Gram.*) ellipsis. **elliptisch,** *adj.* elliptical.
Elritze ['ɛlrɪtsə], *f.* (*Ichth.*) minnow (*Phoxinus laevis*).
Elsaß ['ɛlzas], *n.* (*Geog.*) Alsace. **Elsässer,** *m.* Alsatian. **elsässisch,** *adj.* Alsatian.
Elster ['ɛlstər], *f.* (-, *pl.* **-n**) (*Orn.*) magpie (*Pica pica*). **Elsterspecht,** *m.* *See* **Weißrückenspecht.**
elterlich ['ɛltərlɪç], *adj.* parental. **Eltern,** *pl.* parents; (*coll.*) ***nicht von schlechten –,*** not at all bad, (*sl.*) not to be sneezed at. **Eltern|haus,** *n.* house of one's parents, home. **–liebe,** *f.* parental love, filial love. **elternlos,** *adj.* orphan, orphaned.
Email [e'ma:j], *n.* (**-s,** *pl.* **-s**), **Emaille,** *f.* enamel. **emallieren** [–'ji:rən], *v.t.* enamel.
emanzipieren [emantsi'pi:rən], *v.t.* emancipate; (*Hist.*) manumit (*slave*).
Emballage [ãba'la:ʒə], *f.* (cost of) packing. **emballieren,** *v.t.* pack.
Embolie [ɛmbo'li:], *f.* embolism.
Emd [e:mt], **Emde** ['ɛmdə], *n.* (*Swiss*) aftermath.
emendieren [emɛn'di:rən], *v.t.* emend.
emeritieren [emeri'ti:rən], *v.t.* discharge, retire, relieve of duties.
Emetikum [e'me:tɪkum], *n.* (**-s,** *pl.* **-ka**) emetic.
Emigrant [emi'ɡrant], *m.* (**-en,** *pl.* **-en**) emigrant, emigré, (political) refugee. **Emigration** [–tsi'o:n], *f.* emigration, exile; ***innere –,*** passive resistance. **emigrieren,** *v.i.* (*aux.* s.) emigrate, seek political asylum, seek refuge.
eminent [emi'nɛnt], *adj.* eminent, prominent, distinguished. **Eminenz,** *f.* Eminence (*title*); ***die graue –,*** the power behind the throne.
Emissär [emɪ'sɛ:r], *m.* (**-s,** *pl.* **-e**) emissary.
Emission [emɪsi'o:n], *f.* emission, (*Comm.*) issue (*of shares*). **Emissionstheorie,** *f.* (*Opt.*) corpuscular theory.
Emittent [emɪ'tɛnt], *m.* (**-en,** *pl.* **-en**) (*Comm.*) issuing authority. **emittieren,** *v.t.* emit, send out *or* forth; (*Comm.*) issue (*shares*).
empfahl [ɛmp'fa:l], *see* **empfehlen.**
empfand [ɛmp'fant], **empfände,** *see* **empfinden.**
Empfang [ɛmp'faŋ], *m.* (**-s,** *pl.* **¨-e**) reception (*of guests, radio etc.*), receipt (*of a letter etc.*), reception, levee, at-home; ***in – nehmen,*** take delivery of; ***den – bestätigen,*** acknowledge receipt (*Gen.,* of). **empfangen, 1.** *irr.v.t.* take, receive, (*Comm.*) be in receipt of; (*Rad.*) receive; receive, greet, welcome (*guests*). **2.** *irr.v.i.* conceive, become pregnant.
Empfänger [ɛmp'fɛŋər], *m.* 1. recipient, addressee, consignee; acceptor (*of a bill*), payee; 2. (*Rad.*) receiving set, receiver.
empfänglich [ɛmp'fɛŋlɪç], *adj.* susceptible, receptive, responsive (***für,*** to); liable, prone (to), predisposed (towards). **Empfänglichkeit,** *f.* susceptibility, receptiveness, proneness, liability.
Empfangnahme [ɛmp'faŋna:mə], *f.* receipt (*of goods*).
Empfängnis [ɛmp'fɛŋnɪs], *f.* (-, *pl.* **-se**) conception; ***Unbefleckte –,*** Immaculate Conception. **empfängnisverhütend,** *adj.* contraceptive.
Empfangs|anzeige, *f.* acknowledgement of receipt. **–apparat,** *m.* (*Rad.*) receiving set, receiver. **empfangsberechtigt,** *adj.* authorized to take delivery. **Empfangs|bereich,** *m.* (*Rad.*) reception *or* service area. **–bescheinigung, –bestätigung,** *f.* (acknowledgement of) receipt. **–chef,** *m.* reception *or* (*Am.*) room clerk. **–dame,** *f.* receptionist. **–halle,** *f.* reception hall. **–schein,** *m.* receipt. **–störung,** *f.* (*Rad.*) interference. **–tag,** *m.* 1. reception *or* at-home day; 2. (*Comm.*) day of delivery. **–verstärker,** *f.* (*Rad.*) receiving amplifier.
empfehlen [ɛmp'fe:lən], **1.** *irr.v.t.* commend, recommend (*Dat.,* to); ***– Sie mich ihm bestens,*** give my kind regards to him, remember me to him most kindly. **2.** *irr.v.r.* 1. take one's leave (*Dat.,* of), bid farewell, say good-bye (to); 2. (*of a th.*) ***es empfiehlt sich,*** it is advisable. **empfehlens|wert, –würdig,** *adj.* (re)commendable, advisable. **Empfehlung,** *f.* recommendation, advice; (letter of) introduction, letter of recommendation, testimonial; compliments; (*in letters*) ***mit (den) besten –en,*** yours truly. **Empfehlungs|brief,** *m.,* **–schreiben,** *n.* letter of introduction; credentials.
empfiehlst [ɛmp'fi:lst], **empfiehlt,** *see* **empfehlen.**
empfindbar [ɛmp'fɪntba:r], *adj.* perceptible, sensible; (*obs.*) sensitive. **Empfindbarkeit,** *f.* sensibility, perceptibility.
Empfindelei [ɛmpfɪndə'laɪ], *f.* sentimentality. **empfindeln** [–'fɪndəln], *v.i.* be sentimental, sentimentalize, (*sl.*) gush.
empfinden [ɛmp'fɪndən], **1.** *irr.v.t.* feel, perceive, have a sensation of (*with the senses*); be aware *or* conscious *or* sensible of, sense (*with the mind*). **2.** *irr.v.i.* ***– für*** or ***mit,*** feel for, sympathize with. **empfindend,** *adj.* sentient; feeling, sensitive, perceptive.
empfindlich [ɛmp'fɪntlɪç], *adj.* 1. sensitive, susceptible (***für, gegen,*** to); ***gegen Kälte – sein,*** feel the cold; 2. delicate, tender (*as fabric or* (*fig.*) *susceptibilities*); (*coll.*) touchy (*of a p.*); sensitive, tender, sore (*to pain*); ***–e Stelle,*** sore *or* tender spot, (*fig.*) sore point, (*coll.*) the raw, pet corn; 3. palpable, perceptible, noticeable; serious, severe, heavy (*loss etc.*). **–empfindlich,** *adj.suff.* sensitive *or* susceptible to. **Empfindlichkeit,** *f.* susceptibility, sensitivity, sensitiveness (***für, gegen,*** to); sensitiveness, tenderness, soreness (*to pain*), touchiness (*of a p.*).
empfindsam [ɛmp'fɪntza:m], *adj.* sentimental. **Empfindsamkeit,** *f.* sentimentality, sentimentalism.
Empfindung [ɛmp'fɪnduŋ], *f.* sensation, feeling; sentiment, feeling; instinct. **empfindungsfähig,** *adj.* sensitive, susceptible; capable of feeling *or*

emotion. **Empfindungslaut,** *m.* interjection; exclamation. **empfindungslos,** *adj.* (*of a p.*) unfeeling, callous; (*as a limb*) devoid of feeling, numb. **Empfindungs|organ,** *n.* sense *or* sensory organ. **–vermögen,** *n.* faculty of perception. **–wort,** *n. See* **–laut.**

empfing [ɛmp'fɪŋ], *see* **empfangen.**

empföhle [ɛmp'fø:lə], **empfohlen** [ɛmp'fo:lən], *see* **empfehlen.**

empfunden [ɛmp'fundən], *see* **empfinden.**

Emphase [ɛm'fa:zə], *f.* emphasis. **emphatisch, 1.** *adj.* emphatic. **2.** *adv.* emphatically.

Empirie [ɛmpi'ri:], **Empirik** [–'pi:rɪk], *f.* empiricism.

empor [ɛm'po:r], *adv.*, **empor–,** *sep.pref.* up (above), upwards, on high, aloft. **empor|arbeiten,** *v.t., v.r.* work (one's way) up. **–dringen,** *irr.v.i.* (*aux.* s.) gush forth; rise.

Empore [ɛm'po:rə], *f.* choir loft, gallery.

empören [ɛm'pø:rən], **1.** *v.t.* fill with *or* rouse to indignation; ***empört sein,*** be indignant, be full of indignation (***über*** (*Acc.*), at *or* about). **2.** *v.r.* (rise in) revolt, rebel, (*Mil.*) mutiny. **empörend,** *adj.* disgraceful, shocking. **Empörer,** *m.* mutineer, insurgent, rebel. **empörerisch,** *adj.* mutinous, rebellious, insurgent.

empor|fahren, *irr.v.i.* (*aux.* s.) jump *or* start up, give a jump *or* sudden start. **–heben,** *irr.v.t.* lift up, raise, (*Poet.*) cast up (*eyes, hands etc.*).

Emporium [ɛm'po:rium], *n.* (**-s,** *pl.* **-rien**) mart, (*obs.*) emporium.

empor|keimen, *v.i.* (*aux.* s.) (*of plant*) sprout, shoot, spring up, (*fig.*) bud, dawn. **–kommen,** *irr.v.i.* (*aux.* s.) rise, come up; come up in the world, prosper, thrive, (*coll.*) get on. **Emporkömmling,** *m.* upstart, parvenu. **empor|ragen,** *v.i.* tower up. **–richten,** *v.r.* draw o.s. up, straighten up. **–schwingen,** *irr.v.r.* rise, soar. **–steigen,** *irr.v.i.* (*aux.* s.) rise, ascend. **–streben,** *v.i.* (*aux.* s.) rise *or* tower *or* soar up; (*aux.* h.) aspire, strive upwards.

Empörung [ɛm'pø:ruŋ], *f.* rebellion, revolt, insurrection, mutiny, rising; indignation (***über*** (*Acc.*), at).

emsig ['ɛmzɪç], *adj.* busy, active, industrious; assiduous, eager, diligent. **Emsigkeit,** *f.* industry, activity, assiduity; diligence.

Emu ['e:mu], *m.* (**-s,** *pl.* **-s**) (*Orn.*) emu.

emulgieren [emul'gi:rən], **emulsionieren** [–sio-'ni:rən], *v.t.* emulsify. **Emulsionsfarbe** [–i'o:ns-farbə], *f.* emulsion paint.

Enak ['e:nak], *m.* (*B.*) Anak.

Enarthrose [enar'tro:zə], *f.* (*Anat.*) enarthrosis, ball-and-socket joint.

End– [ɛnt], *pref.* final, ultimate; terminal; ***–fünfziger,*** man in his late fifties. **End|bahnhof,** *m.* terminal (station), terminus; rail-head. **–buchstabe,** *m.* final letter. **Endchen,** *n.* (*coll.*) scrap, bit, small piece; short *or* little way. **Enddarm,** *m.* (*Anat.*) rectum.

Ende ['ɛndə], *n.* (**-s,** *pl.* **-n**) end; conclusion, close, finish, ending, termination; aim, end, object, purpose; tine, point (*of antler*); (*coll.*) piece, fragment (*of fabric, string etc.*); (*coll.*) ***ein*** (***gutes***) ***–,*** some distance, a good way; ***am –,*** in the end *or* (*coll.*) upshot, finally, eventually, ultimately; ***an allen*** (***Ecken und***) ***–n,*** at every turn, (here, there and) everywhere; ***äußerstes –,*** extremity; ***bis ans –,*** to the last; ***bis ans – der Welt,*** to the ends of the earth; (*coll.*) ***am anderen – der Welt,*** in the middle of nowhere, at the back of beyond; ***das dicke – kommt noch nach,*** the worst has still to come; ***letzten –s,*** in the long run, after all (is said and done), in the final analysis; ***das – vom Liede,*** the upshot of it all; ***ein – machen*** (*Dat.*), put an end to (*a th.*); ***das nimmt kein –,*** there is no end to it, that goes on for ever; ***das obere –,*** the top; ***das untere –,*** the bottom; ***er faßte es am verkehrten – an,*** he set about it the wrong way; ***zu –,*** at *or* to an end, over; ***zu – führen*** or ***bringen,*** bring to an end *or* close, finish (off), complete, conclude; ***zu – gehen,*** draw *or* come to an end, near its end; run *or* give out, run short; ***zu dem –,*** to this end, with this end in view, for this purpose; ***zu dem –, daß,*** in order that.

Endel ['ɛndəl], *n.* (*Austr.*) selvedge. **endeln,** *v.t.* (*Austr.*) oversew.

endemisch [ɛn'de:mɪʃ], *adj.* endemic.

enden ['ɛndən], **1.** *v.t.* finish, (put an) end (to), terminate, conclude. **2.** *v.i.* end, finish, terminate, stop, cease, come to an end *or* a conclusion, be over; end one's days.

End|ergebnis, *n.* ultimate *or* final result, upshot. **–geschwindigkeit,** *f.* (*Artil.*) terminal velocity, striking velocity.

endgültig ['ɛntgyltɪç], *adj.* final, definitive, ultimate, conclusive. **Endgültigkeit,** *f.* definitiveness, finality.

endigen ['ɛndɪgən], *v.t., v.i. See* **enden.**

Endivie [ɛn'di:viə], *f.* endive.

endlich ['ɛntlɪç], **1.** *adj.* (*Phil., Math.*) finite; final, ultimate. **2.** *adv.* at last, at length, in the end, finally, ultimately. **Endlichkeit,** *f.* finiteness.

endlos ['ɛntlo:s], *adj.* endless, boundless, infinite; endless, unending, never-ending, interminable. **Endlosigkeit,** *f.* endlessness, boundlessness, infinity.

endo– ['ɛndo], **Endo–,** *pref.* endo-. **Endogamie** [–ga'mi:], *f.* in-breeding, endogamy. **endogen** [–'ge:n], *adj.* (*Bot., Med.*) endogenous, (*Geol., Biol.*) endogenetic. **endokrin** [–'kri:n], *adj.* ductless, endocrine. **endomorph** [–'mɔrf], *adj.* endomorphic, endomorphous. **Endothel** [–'te:l], *n.* (**-s,** *pl.* **-e**) endothelium.

End|produkt, *n.* end *or* final product. **–punkt,** *m.* end, extremity, terminal *or* farthest point, terminus, destination. **–reim,** *m.* end-rhyme. **–röhre,** *f.* (*Rad.*) output valve. **–runde,** *f.* final heat, final; final lap, final round. **–silbe,** *f.* end *or* last *or* final syllable. **–spiel,** *n.* final (*of a tournament*). **–station,** *f.* (*Railw.*) terminus, rail-head. **–stellung,** *f.* (*Gram.*) end *or* final position (*of verb etc.*). **–stufe,** *f.* final stage. **–termin,** *m.* final *or* closing date.

Endung ['ɛnduŋ], *f.* (*Gram.*) ending, termination (*of word*).

End|urteil, *n.* final judgement, verdict. **–verstärkerröhre,** *f.* (*Rad.*) output valve. **–zeit,** *f.* (*Theol.*) last days, last things. **endzeitlich,** *adj.* eschatalogical. **End|ziel,** *n.* final *or* ultimate object *or* purpose *or* aim, (ultimate) objective, ultimate goal; destination, end (*of journey*). **–zweck,** *m.* aim, goal, design, purpose.

Energie [enɛr'gi:], *f.* energy. **Energie|abgabe,** *f.* release of energy. **–aufwand,** *m.* expenditure of energy. **–einsparung,** *f.* shedding the load (*of electric consumption*). **energielos,** *adj.* lacking in *or* without energy. **Energielosigkeit,** *f.* lack of energy. **energisch** [–'nɛrgɪʃ], *adj.* energetic, vigorous, forceful, resolute, strong, firm, determined.

enfilieren [ãfi'li:rən], *v.t.* (*Mil.*) enfilade.

eng [ɛŋ], *adj.* narrow; tight; cramped, confined; close, intimate; ***–erer Ausschuß,*** select committee; ***–e Freundschaft,*** close *or* intimate friendship; ***in –en Grenzen,*** within narrow limits; (*coll.*) ***den Gürtel –er schnallen,*** tighten one's belt; ***im –en Kreis,*** in the immediate circle; (*B.*) ***die –e Pforte,*** the strait gate; ***im –eren Sinne,*** strictly speaking; ***–e Verhältnisse,*** straitened circumstances; (*of candidates*) ***in die –ere Wahl kommen,*** be put on the select *or* short list; ***–e Zusammenarbeit,*** close co-operation.

Engagement [ãgaʒə'mã], *n.* (**-s,** *pl.* **-s**) (*Theat.*) engagement; (*Comm.*) commitment. **engagieren** [–'ʒi:rən], *v.t.* engage, take on (*employee*). **engagiert,** *adj.* (*Comm.*) committed, tied-up, locked-up (*capital*).

eng|anliegend, *adj.* tight- *or* close-fitting, clinging (*garment*). **–anschließend,** *adj.* adjoining. **–befreundet,** *adj.* on terms of close friendship. **–begrenzt,** *adj.* limited, restricted. **–brüstig,** *adj.*

narrow-chested; asthmatic, short-winded, (*of horse*) broken-winded.

Enge ['ɛŋə], *f.* narrowness; tightness, constriction; restrictions; closeness (*of relations*); confines, narrow place *or* space, (*in mountains*) defile, (*in sea*) narrows, strait(s); difficulty, dilemma; ***ihn in die – treiben,*** drive him into a corner; corner him.

Engel ['ɛŋəl], *m.* angel; ***guter*** or ***rettender –,*** guardian angel; ***böser –,*** evil genius; (*coll.*) ***ein – flog durch das Zimmer,*** there was sudden hush. **Engelchen,** *n.* cherub. **Engelehe,** *f.* unconsummated marriage. **engelgleich, engelhaft,** *adj.* angelic. **Engel|macher,** *m.* baby-farmer. **–schar,** *f.* angelic host. **Engelsgeduld,** *f.* endless patience, the patience of Job. **Engelwurz,** *f.* (*Bot.*) angelica (*Angelica archangelica*).

engen ['ɛŋən], **1.** *v.t.* (*obs.*) *see* **beengen. 2.** *v.r.* narrow, become narrower.

Engerling ['ɛŋərlɪŋ], *m.* (**-s,** *pl.* **-e**) cockchafer larva.

Engführung ['ɛŋfy:ruŋ], *f.* (*Mus.*) stretto.

Engheit ['ɛŋhaɪt], *f.* narrowness (*of space*), tightness (*of dress*), closeness (*of relations*); (*fig.*) narrowness, narrow-mindedness.

engherzig ['ɛŋhɛrtsɪç], *adj.* ungenerous, illiberal, strait-laced, petty; unsympathetic. **Engherzigkeit,** *f.* illiberality, pettiness; lack of sympathy.

England ['ɛŋlant], *n.* (*Geog.*) England; (*used wrongly*) (Great) Britain, British Isles. **Engländer,** *m.* 1. Englishman, (*used wrongly*) Briton; 2. adjustable spanner, monkey-wrench. **Engländerei** [–də'raɪ], *f.* Anglomania. **Engländerin,** *f.* Englishwoman, (*used wrongly*) British woman. **england|feindlich,** *adj.* anti-British. **–freundlich,** *adj.* pro-British.

[1]**englisch** ['ɛŋlɪʃ], **1.** *adj.* English, (*used wrongly*) British; ***–er Garten,*** landscape garden; ***die –e Krankheit,*** rachitis, rickets; ***–es Pflaster,*** court-plaster. **2.** *adv.* in English. **Englisch,** *n.* English (language); ***auf englisch,*** in English.

[2]**englisch,** *adj.* (*Poet.*) angelic(al); (*Eccl.*) ***der –e Gruß,*** the Annunciation, Angelic Salutation, Ave Maria.

Englisch–, *pref.* English-, Anglo-. **Englisch|blau,** *n.* royal blue. **–horn,** *m.* (*Mus.*) cor anglais. **–leder,** *n.* moleskin.

engmaschig ['ɛŋmaʃɪç], *adj.* close-meshed.

Engpaß ['ɛŋpas], *m.* defile, narrow pass (*in mountains*); bottleneck (*in road, production*), (*fig.*) tight spot *or* corner.

en gros [ã'gro], *adv.* (*Comm.*) wholesale. **Engros|-handel,** *m.* wholesale trade. **–preis,** *m.* wholesale price.

engstirnig ['ɛŋʃtɪrnɪç], *adj.* narrow(-minded), hidebound. **Engstirnigkeit,** *f.* narrow-mindedness (*of a p.*), narrowness (*of views*).

Enjambement [ãʒãmbə'mã], *n.* (**-s,** *pl.* **-s**) (*Metr.*) overflow, enjambement.

[1]**Enkel** ['ɛŋkəl], *m.* ankle.

[2]**Enkel,** *m.* grandson, *pl.* grandchildren. **Enkelin,** *f.* granddaughter. **Enkelkind,** *n.* grandchild.

enorm [e'nɔrm], *adj.* huge, vast, immense, enormous, (*coll.*) tremendous.

Enquete [ã'kɛt], *f.* (official) inquiry *or* investigation.

ent– [ɛnt], *insep.pref.* 1. (*negation, reversal, removal*) im-, de-, dis-, *e.g.* ***enthüllen,*** unveil, disclose; ***entmenschen,*** dehumanize; 2. (*separation*) *v.i., e.g.* ***entkommen, entlaufen,*** run away, escape; *v.t., e.g.* ***entlassen,*** dismiss; 3. (*emergence*) *e.g.* ***entstammen,*** stem from; 4. (*initiation of a state*) *e.g.* ***entzünden,*** kindle, set alight; 5. (*intensification of simplex*) *e.g.* ***enthalten,*** contain. *For other meanings see examples below.*

entarten [ɛnt'artən], *v.i.* (*aux.* s.) degenerate, deteriorate. **Entartung,** *f.* degeneration, deterioration, degeneracy.

entäußern [ɛnt'ɔysərn], *v.r.* (*Gen.*) part with, give up, relinquish, renounce, forgo, divest o.s. of. **Entäußerung,** *f.* renunciation, giving up, parting with; alienation (*of property*).

entbehren [ɛnt'be:rən], **1.** *v.t.* 1. do without, dispense with; be *or* go without; ***ich kann dich nicht –,*** I cannot do without you, I cannot spare you; 2. miss, spare; ***ich kann noch etwas –,*** I have still s.th. to spare. **2.** *v.i.* (*Gen.*) be lacking in, be without, lack; ***jeglicher Grundlage –,*** be without *or* lack any foundation. **entbehrlich,** *adj.* dispensable, superfluous, spare, who *or* that can be dispensed with *or* spared. **Entbehrung,** *f.* want, privation.

entbieten [ɛnt'bi:tən], *irr.v.t.* send; present, offer (*Dat.,* to); (*obs.*) ***ihm etwas –,*** inform *or* notify *or* advise *or* apprise him of s.th., make s.th. known to him; ***zu sich –,*** send for, summon (to one's presence).

entbinden [ɛnt'bɪndən], *irr.v.t.* 1. release, absolve (*Gen. or* ***von,*** from), relieve (of); 2. release, liberate, set free (*gas, heat etc. also fig. the spirit etc.*); 3. (*Med.*) (*of a doctor*) deliver; ***entbunden werden von,*** be confined with, be delivered of, give birth to. **Entbindung,** *f.* release, liberation; (*Med.*) delivery, confinement, birth. **Entbindungsanstalt,** *f.* maternity hospital.

entblättern [ɛnt'blɛtərn], **1.** *v.t.* strip of leaves, defoliate. **2.** *v.r.* shed leaves.

entblöden [ɛnt'blø:dən], *v.r.* ***er entblödete sich nicht zu behaupten*** ((*obs.*) . . . ***sich zu behaupten***), he had the impudence to maintain.

entblößen [ɛnt'blø:sən], **1.** *v.t.* bare, uncover (*the head*); unsheath (*one's sword*); strip, divest, denude, deprive (*Gen. or* ***von,*** of). **2.** *v.r.* strip, take off one's clothes; take off one's hat, uncover one's head; (*fig.*) bare one's soul, lay o.s. bare.

entbrennen [ɛnt'brɛnən], *irr.v.i.* (*aux.* s.) (*of passions*) be aroused, become inflamed; (*as a quarrel*) flare up, break out; (*of a p.*) be seized (*in* (*Dat.*), ***von,*** with); fly into a rage; (*Poet.*) be kindled, burst into flame.

entbunden [ɛnt'bundən], *see* **entbinden.**

entdecken [ɛnt'dɛkən], **1.** *v.t.* discover, detect, find out, bring to light, expose (*plot*); discern, (*Poet.*) descry, (*coll.*) make out, spot; (*Poet.*) make known, reveal, discover (*Dat.,* to); ***sein Herz –,*** unbosom o.s. **2.** *v.r.* (*of a p.*) disclose one's identity *or* (*Poet.*) one's presence (*Dat.,* to); confide (in), open one's heart (to); (*of fact*) become known, reveal itself. **Entdecker,** *m.* explorer, discoverer. **Entdeckung,** *f.* discovery, detection, disclosure. **Entdeckungsreise,** *f.* voyage of discovery *or* exploration, expedition.

Ente ['ɛntə], *f.* 1. duck; (*sl.*) ***eine – machen,*** crash-dive (*of submarine*); 2. hoax, canard, false report.

entehren [ɛnt'e:rən], *v.t.* (*of a p.*) dishonour, disgrace, bring dishonour *or* disgrace upon; (*of actions*) degrade, debase; violate, ravish (*a woman*), deflower (*a virgin*), defile (*the marriage bed*). **entehrend,** *adj.* dishonourable, degrading, disgraceful. **Entehrung,** *f.* dishonour, disgrace, degradation; deprivation of civic rights; violation, defloration (*of a girl*).

enteignen [ɛnt'aɪgnən], *v.t.* expropriate, dispossess. **Enteignung,** *f.* dispossession, expropriation.

enteilen [ɛnt'aɪlən], *v.i.* (*aux.* s.) (*Poet.*) hurry *or* speed away, depart in haste, flee (*Dat.,* from).

enteisen [ɛnt'aɪzən], *v.t.* (*Av.*) de-ice, (*refrigerator*) de-frost.

Enten|beere, *f.* (*Swiss*) raspberry. **–beize,** *f.* duck-shooting. **–braten,** *m.* roast duck. **–dunst,** *m.* duck-shot. **–fall,** *m.* place where ducks roost. **–fang,** *m.* decoy for ducks. **–jagd,** *f. See* **–beize. –muschel,** *f.* (stalked) barnacle. **–pfuhl,** *m.,* **–pfütze,** *f. See* **–teich. –schrot,** *m. or n. See* **–dunst. –teich,** *m.* duck-pond.

enterben [ɛnt'ɛrbən], *v.t.* disinherit, (*coll.*) cut out of one's will, cut off; (*Poet.*) ***die Enterbten,*** the outcasts of fortune. **Enterbung,** *f.* disinheritance.

Enter|haken ['ɛntər–], *m.* grappling-iron, grapnel. **–mannschaft,** *f.* boarding party. **–messer,** *n.* (*obs.*) cutlass. **entern, 1.** *v.t.* board (*a ship*). **2.** *v.i.* (*aux.* s. & h.) (*Naut.*) climb the rigging, go aloft, (*Gymn.*) climb the rope.

entfachen [ɛnt'faxən], *v.t.* fan, kindle; excite, rouse, inflame, foment, stir up.

entfahren [ɛnt'fa:rən], *irr.v.i.* (*aux.* s.) escape, slip out (*Dat.*, from).

Entfall [ɛnt'fal], *m.* loss, waste.

entfallen [ɛnt'falən], *irr.v.i.* (*aux.* s.) 1. (*Dat.*) slip *or* fall out of *or* from; escape, slip (*the memory*); 2. be cancelled *or* (*coll.*) dropped; ***entfällt,*** not applicable (*official comment on a form*); 3. – ***auf*** (*Acc.*), fall to (the share of); ***auf jeden der Brüder entfiel ein Drittel,*** one third was allotted to each of the brothers.

entfalten [ɛnt'faltən], **1.** *v.t.* unfold, unfurl, spread (out), open out; (*fig.*) show, display; (*Mil.*) deploy. **2.** *v.r.* unfold, open, develop. **Entfaltung,** *f.* development; deployment.

entfärben [ɛnt'fɛrbən], **1.** *v.t.* remove the colour from, bleach. **2.** *v.r.* lose colour, grow pale.

entfasern [ɛnt'fa:zərn], *v.t.* string (*beans etc.*), remove the fibres from.

entfernen [ɛnt'fɛrnən], **1.** *v.t.* move away (***von,*** from); remove, take off *or* away; dismiss, discharge (*a p.*) (***aus,*** from). **2.** *v.r.* move away *or* off (***von,*** from); (*fig.*) depart, deviate, wander (from); (*of a p.*) go away, leave (the room), withdraw. **entfernt, 1.** *adj.* far off, far from; away, distant, removed (***von,*** from); remote, slight, faint; ***weit davon –, das zu tun,*** far from doing so. **2.** *adv.* remotely, vaguely; distantly; ***nicht im –esten,*** not in the least, not at all, in no way. **Entfernung,** *f.* 1. distance, range; ***auf kurze –,*** at close range; ***auf eine – von,*** at a *or* to within a distance of, at a range of; 2. deviation, divergence, departure (***von,*** from); (*Mil.*) ***unerlaubte –,*** absence without leave; 3. removal, dismissal (***aus,*** from). **Entfernungsmesser,** *m.* range-finder.

entfesseln [ɛnt'fɛsəln], *v.t.* unleash, let loose; ***entfesselte Elemente,*** raging elements; ***entfesselte Leidenschaften,*** uncontrolled passions.

entfetten [ɛnt'fɛtən], *v.t.* extract *or* remove the fat from, de-grease. **Entfettungs|kur,** *f.* slimming, reducing, treatment for obesity. **–mittel,** *n.* detergent, scouring agent; slimming agent.

entfeuchten [ɛnt'fɔyçtən], *v.t.* desiccate. **Entfeuchter,** *m.* desiccator.

entflammbar [ɛnt'flamba:r], *adj.* (in)flammable, easily ignitable; (*of a p.*) easily roused *or* fired, excitable.

entflammen [ɛnt'flamən], **1.** *v.t.* ignite; (*fig.*) inflame, kindle, rouse, excite, fire, stir up, foment. **2.** *v.i.* (*aux.* s.) flash, ignite; (*also v.r.*) (*of passions*) be aroused; (*of a p.*) be fired *or* inflamed *or* burning, burn (***von,*** with), be roused (to). **Entflammungspunkt,** *m.* flash-point.

entfleischt [ɛnt'flaɪʃt], *adj.* fleshless; lean; ***–e Hände,*** lean *or* (*coll.*) scraggy *or* scrawny hands.

entfliehen [ɛnt'fli:ən], *irr.v.i.* (*aux.* s.) (*Dat.*) run away *or* flee from, escape; pass quickly, slip by, fly (*of time*).

entfließen [ɛnt'fli:sən], *irr.v.i.* (*aux.* s.) flow, stream (*Dat.*, from).

entfremden [ɛnt'frɛmdən], *v.t.* ***ihm –,*** estrange *or* alienate him from. **Entfremdung,** *f.* estrangement, alienation.

entführen [ɛnt'fy:rən], *v.t.* (*a p.*) carry off *or* away (by force); run away *or* elope with; abduct (*a minor*), kidnap; (*aircraft etc.*) hijack; ***sie hat sich von ihm – lassen,*** she has eloped with him. **Entführung,** *f.* abduction; elopement; kidnapping; hijacking.

entgasen [ɛnt'ga:zən], *v.t.* remove *or* extract gas from, degas, decontaminate.

entgegen [ɛnt'ge:gən], *adv., prep.* (*with preceding Dat.*) 1. towards, -wards; 2. against, in face of; opposed to, contrary to; ***dem Wind –,*** into the wind, in the teeth of the wind; ***auf, ihm –!*** let us go to meet him!

entgegen–, *sep.pref., implying* 1. *approach*; 2. *opposition.* **–arbeiten,** *v.i.* (*Dat.*) work against, counter(act). **–bringen,** *irr.v.t.* ***ihm –,*** bring *or* carry (*s.th.*) to him, (*fig.*) show (*sympathy etc.*) towards him, have (*understanding etc.*) for him. **–gehen,** *irr.v.i.* (*aux.* s.) (*Dat.*) go to meet, go towards; be nearing, be heading for. **–gesetzt,** *adj.* contrary, opposite, opposed. **–halten,** *irr.v.t.* hold out (*Dat.*, to), stretch out (towards), (*fig.*) (say in) reply (to), point out in reply (to). **–kommen,** *irr.v.i.* (*aux.* s.) (*Dat.*) advance *or* come to meet; meet (*one's*) ear; oblige, make concessions to, meet (*s.o.'s*) wishes, meet half-way, cater for (*taste*). **Entgegenkommen,** *n.* kindness, willingness to oblige, co-operation. **entgegen|kommend,** *adj.* 1. oncoming (*traffic*); 2. accommodating, willing to oblige, helpful, obliging. **–laufen,** *irr.v.i.* (*aux.* s.) (*Dat.*) run to meet; run counter to, go against. **Entgegennahme,** *f.* acceptance. **entgegen|nehmen,** *irr.v.t.* accept, receive, take (*orders*). **–sehen,** *irr.v.i.* (*Dat.*) look forward to. **–setzen,** *v.t.* (*Dat.*) set against, oppose; put up *or* offer resistance to. **–stehen,** *irr.v.i.* (*aux.* s.) (*Dat.*) stand in the way of, oppose, be opposed to; confront, contrast with. **–stellen, 1.** *v.t.* set (*Dat.*, against), contrast (with). **2.** *v.r.* (*Dat.*) oppose; obstruct, stand in the way of, put up *or* offer resistance to. **–treten,** *irr.v.i.* (*aux.* s.) (*Dat.*) oppose, face, confront; stand up to, put up *or* offer resistance to, set o.s. *or* take steps against; advance towards, come to meet. **–wirken,** *v.i.* (*Dat.*) counteract; thwart, counter.

entgegnen [ɛnt'ge:gnən], *v.t., v.i.* 1. (*Dat.*) answer; ***ihm – auf*** (*Acc.*), give him an answer to, make him a reply to (*a statement*); ***ihm nichts –,*** give him no answer, make no reply to him; (***nichts***) ***darauf –,*** say (nothing) in reply to it; 2. (*v.i. only*) retort. **2.** *v.i.* (*aux.* s.) (*obs.*) (*Dat.*) approach; go *or* come towards; meet, face (*danger etc.*). **Entgegnung,** *f.* reply, answer, retort, rejoinder, response.

entgehen [ɛnt'ge:ən], *irr.v.i.* (*aux.* s.) (*Dat.*) get away from; escape, elude; avoid, evade; ***sich*** (*Dat.*) ***– lassen,*** let slip; ***es kann Ihnen nicht –,*** you cannot fail to notice it.

entgeistert [ɛnt'gaɪstərt], *adj.* flabbergasted, thunderstruck, dumbfounded.

Entgelt [ɛnt'gɛlt], *n.* remuneration, (monetary) reward, payment, fee, (*coll.*) consideration; ***ohne –,*** free of charge, gratis; ***gegen –,*** against payment, for a consideration. **entgelten,** *irr.v.t.* pay (the penalty) for, suffer for; ***ihn etwas – lassen,*** make him suffer *or* pay for a th. **entgeltlich,** *adj., adv.* against payment.

entgiften [ɛnt'gɪftən], *v.t.* decontaminate.

entging [ɛnt'gɪŋ], *see* **entgehen.**

entgleisen [ɛnt'glaɪzən], *v.i.* (*aux.* s.) be derailed, leave the rails; (*fig.*) slip up, make a slip, commit a faux pas, (*coll.*) go off the rails; ***– lassen,*** derail (*a train*). **Entgleisung,** *f.* derailment; (*fig.*) slip, blunder, gaffe, faux pas, (*Am.*) boner.

entgleiten [ɛnt'glaɪtən], *irr.v.i.* (*aux.* s.) (*Dat.*) slip from.

entgräten [ɛnt'grɛ:tən], *v.t.* bone, fillet (*fish*).

enthaaren [ɛnt'ha:rən], *v.t.* remove hair from, depilate; remove (*one's*) superfluous hair. **enthaarend,** *adj.* depilatory. **Enthaarung,** *f.* removal of superfluous hair.

enthalten [ɛnt'haltən], **1.** *irr.v.t.* hold, contain, comprise, embody, include; ***wie oft ist 2 in 10 –?*** how many twos are there in ten? how many times does 2 go into 10? **2.** *irr.v.r.* contain *or* restrain o.s.; refrain (*Gen. or von*, from); ***ich konnte mich des Lachens nicht –,*** I could dot refrain from *or* help laughing; ***sich der Stimme –,*** abstain from voting. **enthaltsam,** *adj.* abstemious, moderate, temperate; continent, chaste. **Enthaltsamkeit,** *f.* abstemiousness, abstention, temperance, moderation; continence, chastity. **Enthaltung,** *f.* abstention (***von,*** from) (*also from voting*).

enthärten [ɛnt'hɛrtən], *v.t.* anneal (*metals*), soften (*water*).

enthaupten [ɛnt'hauptən], *v.t.* behead, decapitate. **Enthauptung,** *f.* beheading, decapitation.

entheben [ɛnt'he:bən], *irr.v.t.* relieve (*Gen.*, of), free, release, absolve, exempt (from); ***ihn der Mühe –,*** save *or* spare him the trouble.

entheiligen [ɛntˈhaɪlɪɡən], *v.t.* profane, desecrate. **Entheiligung,** *f.* desecration, profanation.

enthüllen [ɛntˈhylən], *v.t.* unveil; expose, uncover; reveal, disclose, bring to light, divulge. **Enthüllung,** *f.* unveiling; exposure; revelation, disclosure.

enthülsen [ɛntˈhylzən], *v.t.* shell, husk (*peas etc.*).

Enthusiasmus [ɛntuziˈasmus], *m.* enthusiasm. **Enthusiast,** *m.* (**-en,** *pl.* **-en**) enthusiast. **enthusiastisch,** *adj.* enthusiastic.

entjungfern [ɛntˈjuŋfərn], *v.t.* ravish, rape, deflower (*a virgin*).

entkeimen [ɛntˈkaɪmən], **1.** *v.i.* (*aux.* s.) germinate, sprout; spring up. **2.** *v.t.* sterilize, pasteurize (*milk*).

entkernen [ɛntˈkɛrnən], *v.t.* stone, seed (*fruit*).

entkleiden [ɛntˈklaɪdən], **1.** *v.t.* undress, unclothe; strip, divest, bare, denude (*Gen. or* **von,** of). **2.** *v.r.* undress o.s., take one's clothes off, (*coll.*) strip. **Entkleidungsnummer,** *f.* strip-tease act.

entkohlen [ɛntˈkoːlən], *v.t.* decarbonize, decarburize.

entkommen [ɛntˈkɔmən], *irr.v.i.* (*aux.* s.) get away, escape (*Dat.*, from); ***aus dem Gefängnis –,*** escape from prison; ***den Verfolgern –,*** get away from *or* escape (from) the pursuers.

entkoppeln [ɛntˈkɔpəln], *v.t.* (*Rad.*) neutralize, decouple.

entkorken [ɛntˈkɔrkən], *v.t.* uncork.

entkörpern [ɛntˈkœrpərn], *v.t.* disembody.

entkräften [ɛntˈkrɛftən], *v.t.* enfeeble, enervate, weaken, sap, debilitate; invalidate, refute (*evidence etc.*). **entkräftigen,** *v.t.* (*obs.*) *see* **entkräften. Entkräftung,** *f.* weakening, enfeeblement, enervation; weakness, feebleness, physical exhaustion, collapse, debility, inanition; invalidation.

entkuppeln [ɛntˈkupəln], *v.t.* (*Mech.*) uncouple, disconnect, disengage.

entladen [ɛntˈlaːdən], **1.** *irr.v.t.* unload (*vehicle*), unlade, discharge (*boat*); (*obs.*) release, free (*Gen. or* **von,** from), relieve (of); discharge (*electricity etc.*), unload (*firearms*), discharge, (*coll.*) let off (*firearms*), vent, give vent to (*one's anger*). **2.** *irr.v.r.* discharge, (*coll.*) go off (*as a gun*), discharge, run down (*as a battery*), break (*as a storm*), break out, burst forth (*as anger*); (*obs.*) ***sich*** – (*Gen.*) or **von,** rid o.s. *or* get rid of, free o.s. from, lay down (*a burden*), carry out (*an order*). **Entlader,** *m.* unloader (*of goods*), (*Elec.*) discharger. **Entlade|-spannung,** *f.*, **–strom,** *m.* discharge voltage (current). **Entladung,** *f.* unloading; discharge.

entlang [ɛntˈlaŋ], *adv., prep.* (*usu. with* **an** *and following Dat.*; *oft. with preceding Acc.*; *occ. with preceding or following Dat.*; *occ. with following Gen.*) along; ***an dem Flusse –, den Fluß –,*** along the river.

entlang–, *sep.pref. with verbs of motion,* along. **–fahren,** *irr.v.t.* (*v.i.* – **an** (*Dat.*)) travel along. **–führen,** *v.i.* – **an** (*Dat.*), skirt, run along the edge of. **–gehen, 1.** *irr.v.t.* go *or* walk the length of. **2.** *irr.v.i.* – **an** (*Dat.*), run along(side).

entlarven [ɛntˈlarfən], *v.t.* unmask, expose.

entlassen [ɛntˈlasən], *irr.v.t.* dismiss, send away, let go; discharge, release; disband, pay off (*troops*), dismiss, (*coll.*) sack (*an employee*); (*obs.*) free, release, discharge (*Gen.*, from) (*obligation etc.*); ***mit Pension –,*** pension off. **Entlassung,** *f.* dismissal; disbanding; discharge; release; ***er bat um seine –,*** he applied for his discharge. **Entlassungs|-papiere,** *n.pl.* discharge papers. **–schein,** *m.* certificate of discharge. **–stelle,** *f.* (*Mil.*) demobilization centre.

entlasten [ɛntˈlastən], *v.t.* 1. lift *or* remove the burden from, (*Law*) exonerate, exculpate, (*coll.*) clear of suspicion; 2. (*of a meeting*) give formal approval to, accept the (*treasurer's etc.*) report; 3. ease *or* lighten (*s.o.'s*) burden, relieve (*s.o.*) of, ease the strain on, take the strain *or* weight off, ease the load *or* relieve the pressure on; 4. (*Comm.*) ***ihn für eine Summe*** or ***sein Konto um*** or ***für diese Summe –,*** credit him *or* his account with this sum. **Entlastung,** *f.* easing the burden, relief; exoneration, exculpation; (*Comm.*) credit (*to one's account*). **Entlastungs|angriff,** *m.* (*Mil.*) diversionary attack. **–anzeige,** *f.* (*Comm.*) credit note. **–straße,** *f.* by-pass (road). **–wehr,** *n.* spill-way. **–zeuge,** *m.* witness for the defence. **–zug,** *m.* relief train.

entlauben [ɛntˈlaubən], **1.** *v.t.* strip of foliage. **2.** *v.r.* (*of tree*) shed its leaves.

entlaufen [ɛntˈlaufən], *irr.v.i.* (*aux.* s.) run away, escape (*Dat.*, from); desert.

entlausen [ɛntˈlauzən], *v.t.* delouse. **Entlausung,** *f.* delousing.

entledigen [ɛntˈleːdɪɡən], *v.r.* (*Gen.*) get rid of, rid o.s. of, free o.s. from; acquit o.s. of, fulfil, discharge, (*coll.*) carry out (*one's duties etc.*).

entleeren [ɛntˈleːrən], **1.** *v.t.* empty (out), drain (off); empty (*bladder*), evacuate (*bowels*), clear (*letter box*); – ***in*** (*Acc.*), empty into. **2.** *v.r.* (become) empty, be cleared *or* evacuated. **Entleerung,** *f.* evacuation (*of bowels*), clearance (*of letter box*), collection (*of letters*).

entlegen [ɛntˈleːɡən], *adj.* remote, distant, far away; isolated, out-of-the-way, unfrequented, (*Poet.*) sequestered. **Entlegenheit,** *f.* remoteness, isolation, seclusion.

entlehnen [ɛntˈleːnən], *v.t.* (*of ideas etc.*) borrow, derive (*Dat.*, **von, aus,** from). **Entlehnung,** *f.* borrowing; loan(-word).

entleiben [ɛntˈlaɪbən], **1.** *v.t.* (*Poet.*) kill. **2.** *v.r.* commit suicide, take one's (own) life.

entleihen [ɛntˈlaɪən], *irr.v.t.* borrow ((**von,** from) (*a p.*); **aus,** from (*a library etc.*)).

Entlein [ˈɛntlaɪn], *n.* duckling.

entloben [ɛntˈloːbən], *v.r.* (*coll.*) break off one's engagement.

entlocken [ɛntˈlɔkən], *v.t.* elicit (*Dat.*, from), coax, wheedle, worm (out of); ***ihm Tränen –,*** bring tears to his eyes.

entlohnen [ɛntˈloːnən], *v.t.* pay (off). **Entlohnung,** *f.* payment, pay.

entlüften [ɛntˈlyftən], *v.t.* ventilate. **Entlüftung,** *f.* ventilation; (air-)vent.

entmagnetisieren [ɛntmaɡnɛtiˈziːrən], *v.t.* demagnetize, (*Nav.*) degauss (*a magnetic mine*).

entmannen [ɛntˈmanən], *v.t.* castrate; emasculate; (*fig.*) unnerve, unman. **Entmannung,** *f.* castration; emasculation.

entmenscht [ɛntˈmɛnʃt], *adj.* brutalized, inhuman, brutal, brutish.

entmilitarisieren [ɛntmilitariˈziːrən], *v.t.* demilitarize.

entmündigen [ɛntˈmyndɪɡən], *v.t.* (*Law*) put in the care of trustees, incapacitate. **Entmündigung,** *f.* incapacitation.

entmutigen [ɛntˈmuːtɪɡən], *v.t.* discourage, dishearten, demoralize. **entmutigend,** *adj.* discouraging, disheartening. **Entmutigung,** *f.* discouragement, despondency.

Entnahme [ɛntˈnaːmə], *f.* taking, drawing (out), withdrawal (*money*), use, using (*electricity etc.*); money withdrawn; borrowing (*from an author*). **Entnahme|kreis,** *m.* (*Elec.*) load circuit. **–punkt,** *m.* output terminals.

entnehmen [ɛntˈneːmən], *irr.v.t.* take *or* draw (*Dat. or* **aus,** from), take *or* draw out (of), withdraw (from), consume, use (*electricity etc.*), take, lift (from) (*passage from a book*); (*fig.*) understand, deduce, infer, conclude, gather (from); (*Comm.*) ***100 DM auf ihn –,*** draw (a bill) on him for 100 marks. **Entnehmer,** *m.* user, consumer (*of electricity*), (*Comm.*) drawer.

entnerven [ɛntˈnɛrfən], *v.t.* enervate, unnerve; drain *or* undermine (*s.o.'s*) strength. **entnervend,** *adj.* enervating, nerve-racking.

Entomologe [ɛntomoˈloːɡə], *m.* (**-n,** *pl.* **-n**) entomologist. **Entomologie** [–ˈɡiː], *f.* entomology. **entomologisch,** *adj.* entomological.

Entourage [ãtuːˈraːʒ(ə)], *f.* suite, entourage.

entpersönlichen [ɛntpɛrˈzøːnlɪçən], **1.** *v.t.* make impersonal, deprive of individuality. **2.** *v.r.* become impersonal, surrender one's individuality *or*

personality. **Entpersönlichung,** *f.* loss of individuality, surrender of personality.
entpesten [ɛnt'pɛstən], *v.t.* free from vermin, disinfect.
entpuppen [ɛnt'pupən], *v.r.* (*Ent.*) emerge from the cocoon; (*fig.*) reveal o.s. (*als*, as); show o.s., turn out (to be).
entquellen [ɛnt'kvɛlən], *irr.v.i.* (*aux.* s.) flow, pour, stream, spring, issue (*Dat.*, from), (*fig. as emotion*) well up (from).
entraffen [ɛnt'rafən], *v.t.* (*Poet.*) carry off, snatch away.
entrahmen [ɛnt'ra:mən], *v.t.* take the cream off, skim.
entraten [ɛnt'ra:tən], *irr.v.i.* (*Gen.*) dispense with, do without.
enträtseln [ɛnt'rɛ:tsəln], *v.t.* solve, (*coll.*) make *or* puzzle out; decipher.
entrechten [ɛnt'rɛçtən], *v.t.* deprive of rights. **Entrechtung,** *f.* deprivation of rights.
entreißen [ɛnt'raɪsən], *irr.v.t.* (*Dat.*) take away (from), tear *or* snatch (from).
Entrepot [ãtrə'po:], *n.* (-, *pl.* **-s**) store, bonded warehouse.
entrichten [ɛnt'rɪçtən], *v.t.* pay (*Dat. or an* (*Acc.*), to); offer, render, tender, extend (*thanks*) (to). **Entrichtung,** *f.* payment, due discharge (*of debts etc.*).
entringen [ɛnt'rɪŋən], **1.** *irr.v.t.* (*Poet.*) wrench *or* wrest (*Dat.*, from). **2.** *irr.v.r.* burst *or* break forth (*Dat.*, from).
entrinnen [ɛnt'rɪnən], *irr.v.i.* (*aux.* s.) (*Poet.*) (*of liquid*) run, flow (*Dat.*, from *or* out of); (*of time*) fly *or* slip by; (*of a p.*) escape (*Dat. or* ***aus***, from); ***dem Tode* –**, escape (from) death. **Entrinnen,** *n.* escape.
entrollen [ɛnt'rɔlən], **1.** *v.t.* unfurl, unroll. **2.** *v.r.* come unrolled, unroll; (*fig.*) unfold itself, stretch out. **3.** *v.i.* (*aux.* s.) roll away (*Dat.*, from); (*of time*) roll by; (*as tears*) roll down.
entrosten [ɛnt'rɔstən], *v.t.* remove rust from. **Entrostung,** *f.* removal of rust. **Entrostungsmittel,** *n.* rust remover.
entrücken [ɛnt'rykən], *v.t.* take away, carry off, remove (*Dat. or* ***von***, from); (*fig.*) enrapture, entrance, transport; ***sich*** (*Dat.*) ***selbst entrückt sein,*** be beside o.s.
entrümpeln [ɛnt'rympəln], *v.t.* clear out (*an attic etc.*). **Entrümpelung,** *f.* **1.** removal of lumber; **2.** collection of salvage.
entrüsten [ɛnt'rystən], **1.** *v.t.* fill with indignation, provoke, irritate, make indignant *or* angry. **2.** *v.r.* be full of indignation, be *or* get *or* feel indignant (*über* (*Acc.*), about, at). **Entrüstung,** *f.* indignation.
entsagen [ɛnt'za:gən], *v.i.* (*Dat.*) renounce, abjure, relinquish, forgo, (*coll.*) give up; waive (*a claim*); ***den Thron* –**, abdicate. **Entsagung,** *f.* renunciation, abjuration; self-denial. **entsagungsvoll,** *adj.* full of self-denial, resigned (*appearance*).
Entsatz [ɛnt'zats], *m.* (*Mil.*) relief (*of fortress etc.*). **Entsatztruppen,** *f.pl.* relief *or* relieving forces.
entschädigen [ɛnt'ʃɛ:dɪgən], **1.** *v.t.* indemnify, compensate, (*coll.*) make up; pay damages (***für***, for). **2.** *v.r.* recoup o.s. (***für***, for). **Entschädigung,** *f.* indemnity, compensation, damages, amends; indemnification, compensation. **Entschädigungs|anspruch, –antrag,** *m.* claim for damages.
Entschärfungskommando [ɛnt'ʃɛrfuŋskomando], *n.* bomb-disposal squad.
entschäumen [ɛnt'ʃɔymən], *v.t.* scum, skim, take the froth off.
Entscheid [ɛnt'ʃaɪt], *m.* (**-(e)s,** *pl.* **-e**) (*Law*) decision. **entscheiden** [–'ʃaɪdən], *irr.v.t., v.r., v.i.* decide, settle, determine, (*coll.*) fix; make up one's mind, resolve; ***das entschied,*** that clinched matters; ***er entschied*** (***sich***) ***für mich,*** he decided in my favvour, he decided *or* settled on me. **entscheidend,** *adj.* decisive, deciding, critical, crucial; ***–e Stimme,*** deciding *or* casting vote. **Entscheidung,** *f.* decision. **Entscheidungs|frage,** *f.* categorical question. **–grund,** *m.* decisive factor. **–runde,** *f.* final round (*tournament*). **–schlacht,** *f.* decisive battle. **–spiel,** *n.* deciding game, decider, final.
entschied [ɛnt'ʃi:t], *see* **entscheiden.**
entschieden [ɛnt'ʃi:dən], *adj.* decided, decisive, determined, resolute, firm, dogmatic, categorical, emphatic, peremptory; confirmed, declared, staunch (*adherent etc.*), marked, pronounced, positive, definite, undeniable. **Entschiedenheit,** *f.* firmness, determination, decisiveness; ***mit* –**, decidedly, emphatically, categorically.
entschlafen [ɛnt'ʃla:fən], *irr.v.i.* (*aux.* s.) (*obs.*) fall asleep; (*Poet.*) die, pass away; ***der*** (***die***) ***Entschlafene,*** the deceased; ***er ist sanft* –**, he has passed away peacefully.
entschlagen [ɛnt'ʃla:gən], *irr.v.r.* (*Poet.*) (*Gen.*) get rid of, rid o.s. of, free o.s. from, throw off, cast aside, give up, dismiss from one's mind; ***sich der Sorgen* –**, banish cares; ***sich aller Wünsche* –**, renounce all desires.
entschleiern [ɛnt'ʃlaɪərn], **1.** *v.t.* unveil. **2.** *v.r.* unveil, (*fig.*) be disclosed *or* revealed.
entschlichten [ɛnt'ʃlɪçtən], *v.t.* remove the size *or* dressing from (*linen etc.*).
entschließen [ɛnt'ʃli:sən], *irr.v.r.* make up one's mind, come to a decision; decide (***zu***, on), resolve (on). **Entschließung,** *f.* resolution. *See* **Entschluß.**
entschlossen [ɛnt'ʃlɔsən], *adj.* resolute, determined; **–** ***auftreten,*** take a firm stand; ***kurz* –**, without thinking, without a moment's thought *or* hesitation; **–** ***sein,*** be resolved *or* determined *or* decided (***zu***, on). **Entschlossenheit,** *f.* decision, determination, resolution.
entschlummern [ɛnt'ʃlumərn], *v.i.* *See* **entschlafen.**
entschlüpfen [ɛnt'ʃlypfən], *v.i.* (*aux.* s.) slip away, escape (*Dat.*, from); (*of a bird*) emerge (*from egg*); ***eine Gelegenheit – lassen,*** let an opportunity slip; ***das Wort entschlüpfte mir,*** the word slipped out.
Entschluß [ɛnt'ʃlus], *m.* resolve, decision, determination, resolution; ***einen – fassen,*** make a resolution *or* resolve, come to *or* make a decision.
entschlüsseln [ɛnt'ʃlysəln], *v.t.* decode.
Entschlußkraft [ɛnt'ʃluskraft], *f.* decision, resolution, determination (*of character*).
entschulden [ɛnt'ʃuldən], *v.t.* (*Law*) free from debts, disencumber.
entschuldigen [ɛnt'ʃuldɪgən], **1.** *v.t.* excuse, pardon, exonerate, exculpate; make excuses for, justify, defend. **2.** *v.r.* send *or* make one's excuses *or* apologies, apologize (***bei***, to; ***für, wegen,*** for); ***es läßt sich nicht* –**, it admits of no excuse; ***ich bitte mich zu* –**, I would rather be excused; ***ich muß mich bei ihm –, daß ich . . .,*** I must apologize to him for . . .; ***sie läßt sich wegen Unpäßlichkeit* –**, she begs to be excused on account of indisposition; **–** ***Sie,*** I beg your pardon. **Entschuldigung,** *f.* excuse; apology; ***ich bitte*** (***Sie***) ***um* –**, I beg (your) pardon. **Entschuldigungs|brief,** *m.*, **–schreiben,** *n.* written excuse *or* apology.
Entschuldung [ɛnt'ʃulduŋ], *f.* (*Law*) disencumberment. *See* **entschulden.**
entschwinden [ɛnt'ʃvɪndən], *irr.v.i.* (*aux.* s.) disappear, vanish (*Dat.*, from).
entseelen [ɛnt'ze:lən], *v.t.* make soulless. **entseelend,** *adj.* soul-destroying. **entseelt,** *adj.* (*Poet.*) dead, lifeless.
entsenden [ɛnt'zɛndən], *irr.v.t.* send out *or* forth, dispatch.
entsetzen [ɛnt'zɛtsən], **1.** *v.t.* **1.** relieve (*Gen.*, of), dismiss (from) (*office*); ***des Thrones* –**, dethrone, depose (*a king etc.*); **2.** relieve (*a garrison etc.*); **3.** horrify, appal, fill with horror. **2.** *v.r.* be horrified *or* appalled (***über*** (*Acc.*), at); have a *or* be seized with (a) horror (***vor*** (*Dat.*), of). **Entsetzen,** *n.* horror; ***voller* –**, horror-stricken. **entsetzlich,** *adj.* horrible, horrifying, gruesome, ghastly, terrible, (*coll.*) dreadful, frightful, awful, appalling, horrid,

shocking. **Entsetzlichkeit,** *f.* frightfulness, dreadfulness; atrocity. **entsetzt,** *adj.* horrified, appalled, horror-stricken, in horror. **Entsetzung,** *f.* 1. dismissal; 2. relief (*of a garrison*); *see* **Entsatz**; 3. (*obs.*) *see* **Entsetzen.**

entseuchen [ɛnt'zɔyçən], *v.t.* disinfect, sterilize.

entsichern [ɛnt'zɪçərn], *v.t.* release the safety catch of; arm (*a bomb*), cock (*firearm*).

entsinken [ɛnt'zɪŋkən], *irr.v.i.* (*aux.* s.) (*Poet.*) fall (*Dat.*, from); ***ihm entsinkt der Mut,*** his courage fails him.

entsinnen [ɛnt'zɪnən], *irr.v.r.* (*Gen.*) recollect, recall, remember; ***wenn ich mich recht entsinne,*** if I remember rightly, if my memory serves me right, to the best of my recollection.

entspannen [ɛnt'ʃpanən], **1.** *v.t.* relax, relieve, release, loosen, slacken (*tension*); uncock (*firearm*), relax (*the mind, nerves*), ease (*a tense situation*). **2.** *v.r.* slacken, become slack (*of a th.*); find relaxation, relax (*of a p.*); calm down, become easier (*of a situation*). **entspannend,** *adj.* relaxing. **Entspannung,** *f.* relaxation; (*Pol.*) relaxation of tension, détente. **Entspannungsübungen,** *f.pl.* (*Gymn.*) loosening-up exercises.

entspinnen [ɛnt'ʃpɪnən], *irr.v.r.* arise, spring up, come into being, start, ensue, develop.

entsprechen [ɛnt'ʃprɛçən], *irr.v.i.* (*Dat.*) agree, be in agreement, correspond, accord, be consistent *or* in accordance (with), (*coll.*) tally, square (with); answer, suit, satisfy, meet, be equal to, (*coll.*) come up to; comply *or* conform with, be adequate *or* adapted to, correspond to, (*coll.*) fall in with; ***es entsprach meinen Erwartungen nicht,*** it fell short of *or* did not come up to my expectations. **entsprechend, 1.** *adj.* according (*Dat.*, to); corresponding, appropriate, suitable; analogous, homologous. **2.** *adv.* accordingly, correspondingly; *see also* **dementsprechend. Entsprechung,** *f.* agreement, correspondence; analogy, parallel.

entspringen [ɛnt'ʃprɪŋən], *irr.v.i.* (*aux.* s.) rise, have its source (*of rivers*); arise, spring (*Dat. or* ***aus,*** from), originate (in *or* from); escape (***aus,*** from); (*Poet.*) spring, issue (*Dat.*, from) (*as a family*).

entstaatlichen [ɛnt'ʃta:tlɪçən], *v.t.* denationalize (*industry*), disestablish (*Church*).

entstammen [ɛnt'ʃtamən], *v.i.* (*aux.* s.) be descended *or* sprung, issue (*Dat. or* ***von,*** from), be born, come (of); (*of words*) derive, be derived (from).

entstauben [ɛnt'ʃtaubən], **entstäuben** [–'ʃtɔybən], *v.t.* remove dust from, dust.

entstehen [ɛnt'ʃte:ən], *irr.v.i.* (*aux.* s.) originate (***aus,*** from *or* in), result, spring, come, arise (from), grow (out of), follow (from), ensue, accrue; come into being, emerge, be made *or* created, be formed *or* produced *or* developed *or* generated; be caused; ***was ist daraus entstanden?*** what has come of it? what has been the upshot (of it)? ***entstehe was da wolle,*** come what may. **Entstehen,** *n.* ***im –,*** in embryo, in the process of creation. **Entstehung,** *f.* beginning, rise, origin, birth, genesis; emergence, generation, development, formation. **Entstehungs|art,** *f.* mode of origin *or* development *or* formation. **–geschichte,** *f.* history of the origin and rise (of), genesis. **–zustand,** *m.* nascent *or* embryonic state.

entsteigen [ɛnt'ʃtaɪgən], *irr.v.i.* (*aux.* s.) come up, rise (*Dat.*, from *or* out of).

entstellen [ɛnt'ʃtɛlən], *v.t.* deform, disfigure, deface, mutilate, mar, spoil; distort (*a meaning etc.*); garble (*an account*); misrepresent (*facts*). **Entstellung,** *f.* distortion, misrepresentation; disfigurement, deformation, defacement; deformity.

entstören [ɛnt'ʃtø:rən], *v.t.* (*Rad.*) suppress interference from, fit suppressors to. **Entstörung,** *f.* (*Rad.*) interference suppression.

entströmen [ɛnt'ʃtrø:mən], *v.i.* (*aux.* s.) flow, stream, pour, gush (*Dat.*, from).

entsühnen [ɛnt'zy:nən], *v.t.* absolve, purify (*from sin*).

enttäuschen [ɛnt'tɔyʃən], *v.t.* disappoint; disillusion. **Enttäuschung,** *f.* disappointment, disillusion(ment).

entthronen [ɛnt'tro:nən], *v.t.* dethrone. **Entthronung,** *f.* dethronement.

entvölkern [ɛnt'fœlkərn], *v.t.* depopulate. **Entvölkerung,** *f.* depopulation.

entwachsen [ɛnt'vaksən], *irr.v.i.* (*aux.* s.) (*Dat.*) grow from *or* out of; (*of a p.*) ***den Kinderschuhen – sein,*** be no longer a child, be grown up.

entwaffnen [ɛnt'vafnən], *v.t.* disarm. **Entwaffnung,** *f.* disarming.

entwalden [ɛnt'valdən], *v.t.* clear of trees, deforest. **Entwaldung,** *f.* deforestation.

Entwarnung [ɛnt'varnuŋ], *f.* 'all-clear' signal (*air-raids*).

entwässern [ɛnt'vɛsərn], *v.t.* drain, reclaim (*land*); concentrate (*solution*), rectify (*alcohol*), (*Chem.*) dehydrate, desiccate. **Entwässerung,** *f.* drainage, reclamation (of land), dehydration, desiccation, concentration (*of solution*), rectification (*of alcohol*). **Entwässerungs|gebiet,** *n.* catchment area. **–graben,** *m.* drain, drainage ditch.

entweder [ɛnt've:dər], *conj.* either; ***das Entweder Oder,*** the decision one way or the other.

Entwehrung [ɛnt've:ruŋ], *f.* (*Law*) eviction.

entweichen [ɛnt'vaɪçən], *irr.v.i.* (*aux.* s.) leak, escape (*as gas etc.*); escape, flee (***aus,*** from). **Entweichung,** *f.* escape; leakage. **Entweichungs|klappe,** *f.*, **–ventil,** *n.* escape valve.

entweihen [ɛnt'vaɪən], *v.t.* profane, desecrate. **Entweihung,** *f.* profanation, desecration.

entwenden [ɛnt'vɛndən], *reg.v.t., also irr.v.t.* misappropriate, embezzle, (*coll.*) steal, purloin, pilfer; make away *or* (*coll.*) off with (*Dat.*, from), (*sl.*) filch, swipe. **Entwendung,** *f.* misappropriation, embezzlement.

entwerfen [ɛnt'vɛrfən], *irr.v.t.* sketch, make a sketch for (*a picture*), (*coll.*) rough out; outline, draw up an outline *or* skeleton of (*novel etc.*); draw up, draft, make a draft of (*a document*); design (*clothes, machine etc.*), plan (*any project*); ***Pläne –,*** work out *or* make plans.

entwerten [ɛnt've:rtən], *v.t.* depreciate, debase (*in value*), lower the value of, devalu(at)e (*currency*), cancel (*stamps*); ***entwertet werden,*** depreciate, lose value, fall in value. **Entwertung,** *f.* depreciation; devaluation (*of currency*), cancellation (*of stamps*); decrease *or* loss *or* fall in value. **Entwertungsstempel,** *m.* cancellation stamp, postmark.

entwickeln [ɛnt'vɪkəln], **1.** *v.t.* 1. develop (*also Phot.*); expound, enlarge on (*subject*), evolve (*plan*), (*Mil.*) deploy; 2. show, display, give proof of (*a quality*). **2.** *v.r.* 1. evolve, develop (***aus,*** from), grow, develop (***zu,*** into); 2. (*Chem.*) be produced *or* developed, evolve, form (*as gas*). **Entwickler,** *m.* (*Phot.*) developer.

Entwicklung [ɛnt'vɪkluŋ], *f.* development; growth, evolution, expansion; (*Mil.*) deployment; (*Phot.*) development, developing; ***zur – kommen,*** develop. **Entwicklungs|ablauf,** *m.* course of development. **–dose,** *f.* (*Phot.*) developing tank. **entwicklungsfähig,** *adj.* capable of development, viable. **Entwicklungs|geschichte,** *f.* history of development, biogenetics. **–jahre,** *n.pl.* formative years. **–land,** *n.* underdeveloped country, development area. **–lehre,** *f.* theory of evolution. **–möglichkeit,** *f.* developmental possibility. **–roman,** *m.* novel dealing with a character's personal development. **–stufe,** *f.* stage of development, phase. **–zeit,** *f.* period of development; (*Phot.*) developing time.

entwinden [ɛnt'vɪndən], **1.** *irr.v.t.* wrest, wrench (*Dat.*, from). **2.** *irr.v.r.* wrench o.s. (free), extricate o.s. (*Dat.*, from).

entwirren [ɛnt'vɪrən], **1.** *v.t.* disentangle, unravel; (*fig.*) disentangle, (*coll.*) sort out, clear up (*confused situation*). **2.** *v.r.* unravel, become disentangled; (*fig.*) sort itself out, clear itself up.

entwischen [ɛnt'vɪʃən], *v.i.* (*aux.* s.) (*Dat.*) get *or* slip away from, give (*s.o.*) the slip, escape.

entwöhnen [ɛnt'vø:nən], **1.** *v.t.* disaccustom (*Gen., or* ***von,*** to), cure, break (of) (*a habit*); wean (*an infant*). **2.** *v.r.* (*Gen. or* ***von***) break *or* cure o.s. of, wean o.s. from, grow unused *or* become disaccustomed to, give up, leave off. **Entwöhnung,** *f.* weaning; breaking (*of a habit*).

entwürdigen [ɛnt'vyrdɪgən], *v.t.* degrade, debase. **Entwürdigung,** *f.* degradation, debasement.

Entwurf [ɛnt'vurf], *m.* 1. sketching, outlining, drafting, drawing up, designing, planning; 2. (preliminary) sketch, (rough *or* first) draft, outline, skeleton, plan, design. *See* **entwerfen.**

entwurzeln [ɛnt'vurtsəln], *v.t.* tear up by the roots, uproot; root out, eradicate. **Entwurzelung,** *f.* uprooting, eradication.

entzaubern [ɛnt'tsaubərn], *v.t.* (*of magician*) break the (magic) spell of, free from the charm *or* magic spell; ***entzaubert werden,*** lose its spell *or* magic.

entzerren [ɛnt'tsɛrən], *v.t.* rectify; compensate for, correct (*distortion*). **Entzerrung,** *f.* rectification; compensation, correction of distortion.

entziehen [ɛnt'tsi:ən], **1.** *irr.v.t.* take away, remove, withhold, withdraw (*Dat.*, from), deprive, (*coll.*) dock (of); (*Chem.*) extract (from); ***den Besitz –*** (*Dat.*), dispossess; (*coll.*) ***den Boden –*** (*Dat.*), knock the bottom out of (*rumour etc.*); ***der Strafe –***, protect *or* shield from *or* put out of reach of punishment; ***das Wort –*** (*Dat.*), withhold (*s.o.'s*) permission to speak, impose silence on. **2.** *irr.v.r.* (*Dat.*) avoid, elude, escape; evade, (*coll.*) dodge, shirk, back out of; ***sich der Strafe –,*** avoid *or* evade *or* keep out of reach of punishment. **Entziehung,** *f. See* **Entzug**; ***– des Gebrauches des Vermögens,*** sequestration of property. **Entziehungskur,** *f.* treatment for drug addicts.

entzifferbar [ɛnt'tsɪfərba:r], *adj.* decipherable.

entziffern [ɛnt'tsɪfərn], *v.t.* decipher, (*coll.*) make out. **Entzifferung,** *f.* deciphering.

entzücken [ɛnt'tsykən], *v.t.* charm, delight, enchant, enrapture. **Entzücken,** *n.* delight, joy, rapture; ***zum –,*** ravishing, charming. **entzückend,** *adj.* delightful, charming, enchanting, ravishing. **entzückt,** *adj.* charmed, delighted, enraptured, overjoyed. **Entzückung,** *f.* (*Poet.*) *see* **Entzücken.**

Entzug [ɛnt'tsu:k], *m.* withdrawal, cancellation; deprivation, stopping, (*coll.*) docking; (*Chem.*) extraction. *See* **entziehen.**

entzündbar [ɛnt'tsyntba:r], *adj.* (in)flammable, combustible.

entzünden [ɛnt'tsyndən], **1.** *v.t.* kindle, set fire *or* light to, set alight *or* on fire, ignite, light; (*fig.*) excite, (a)rouse, stir (up), kindle, inflame, fire, foment (*passions etc.*). **2.** *v.r.* catch fire *or* alight, kindle; (*fig.*) be aroused *or* stirred *or* kindled (*an* (*Dat.*), by); (*Med.*) become inflamed. **entzündet,** *adj.* inflamed. **entzündlich,** *adj. See* **entzündbar. Entzündung,** *f.* ignition; inflammation. **Entzündungs|herd,** *m.* centre of inflammation. **–probe,** *f.* ignition *or* flash test. **–punkt,** *m.* flash-point. **entzündungswidrig,** *adj.* (*Med.*) antiphlogistic.

entzwei [ɛnt'tsvaɪ], *adv.*, **entzwei–,** *sep.pref.* in two, in pieces, asunder, apart; broken. **entzweibrechen,** *irr.v.i.* (*aux.* s.), *irr.v.t.* break in two *or* into pieces.

entzweien [ɛnt'tsvaɪən], **1.** *v.t.* disunite, divide, bring discord *or* division into, set at variance. **2.** *v.r.* quarrel, (*coll.*) fall out.

entzwei|gehen, *irr.v.i.* (*aux.* s.) fall to pieces. **–schlagen,** *irr.v.t.* smash in two *or* to pieces. **–sein,** *irr.v.i.* be torn *or* broken. **–springen,** *irr.v.i.* (*aux.* s.) crack, split, burst *or* break in two.

entzweit [ɛnt'tsvaɪt], *adj.* estranged, divided, at variance. **Entzweiung,** *f.* dissension, division, disunity, discord; estrangement.

Enzian ['ɛntsia:n], *m.* (**-s,** *pl.* **-e**) (*Bot.*) gentian.

Enzyklika [ɛn'tsy:klɪka], *f.* (-, *pl.* **-ken**) encyclic(al).

Enzyklopädie [ɛntsyklopɛ:'di:], *f.* encyclopedia. **enzyklopädisch** [–'pɛ:dɪʃ], *adj.* encyclopedic.

Epakte [e'paktə], *f.* (*Astr.*) epact.

1**Ephemera** [e'fe:məra], *f.* (-, *pl.* **-ren**) 1. *See* **Ephemeride**; 2. (*Bot.*) diurnal flower.

2**Ephemera,** *n.pl.* (*Med.*) ephemeral fever.

Ephemeride [efeme'ri:də], *f.* 1. (*Ent.*) ephemera, may-fly; 2. (*Astr., Naut.*) ephemeris, astronomical *or* nautical almanac; 3. almanac, daily chronicle. **ephemerisch** [–'me:rɪʃ], *adj.* ephemeral.

Epheser ['e:fezər], *m.* (*B., Hist.*) Ephesian. **Epheserbrief,** *m.* (*B.*) Epistle to the Ephesians. **ephesisch** [e'fe:zɪʃ], *adj.* Ephesian.

Epheu, *see* **Efeu.**

Epidemie [epide'mi:], *f.* epidemic. **epidemisch** [–'de:mɪʃ], *adj.* epidemic(al).

Epidermis [epi'dɛrmɪs], *f.* (-, *pl.* **-men**) epidermis, cuticle. **epidermisch,** *adj.* epidermic. **Epidermistransplantation,** *f.* skin-grafting.

Epigone [epi'go:nə], *m.* (**-n,** *pl.* **-n**) undistinguished descendant *or* follower. **epigonenhaft,** *adj.* decadent, epigonous. **Epigonentum,** *n.* decadence (*in literature or art*).

Epigramm [epi'gram], *n.* (**-s,** *pl.* **-e**) epigram. **epigrammatisch** [–'ma:tɪʃ], *adj.* epigrammatic.

Epik ['e:pɪk], *f.* epic poetry. **Epiker,** *m.* epic poet.

Epiktet [epɪ'kte:t], *m.* (*Hist.*) Epictetus.

epikureisch [epiku're:ɪʃ], **epikurisch** [–'ku:rɪʃ], *adj.* epicurean.

Epilepsie [epilɛp'si:], *f.* epilepsy. **Epileptiker** [–'lɛptɪkər], *m.* epileptic. **epileptisch,** *adj.* epileptic.

Epilog [epi'lo:k], *m.* (**-s,** *pl.* **-e**) epilogue.

Epiphania(s) [epi'fa:nia(s)], *f.*, **Epiphaniasfest,** *n.* (*Eccl.*) Epiphany.

episch ['e:pɪʃ], *adj.* epic; narrative.

Episkopalkirche [epɪsko'pa:lkɪrçə], *f.* Anglican *or* (*Scots, Am.*) Episcopal Church.

Episode [epi'zo:də], *f.* episode, incident. **episodisch,** *adj.* episodic(al).

Epistel [e'pɪstəl], *f.* (-, *pl.* **-n**) epistle; ***ihm gehörig die – lesen,*** give him a good telling-off *or* dressing-down. **epistolisch** [–'sto:lɪʃ], *adj.* epistolary.

Epithel [epi'te:l], *n.* (**-s,** *pl.* **-e**) (*Anat.*) epithelium.

epithetisch [epi'te:tɪʃ], *adj.* epithetic(al).

epitomisieren [epitomi'zi:rən], *v.t.* epitomize, abridge.

Epizentrum [epi'tsɛntrum], *n.* (**-s,** *pl.* **-ren**) epicentre (*of earthquake*).

epizön [epi'tsø:n], *adj.* (*Biol.*) hermaphrodite; (*Gram.*) epicene.

epizyklisch [epi'tsy:klɪʃ], *adj.* epicyclic.

epochal [epɔ'xa:l], *adj.* epoch-making. **Epoche** [e'pɔxə], *f.* epoch, era; ***– machen,*** be epoch-making, mark an epoch. **epochemachend,** *adj.* epoch-making.

Eponym [epo'nym], *n.* (**-s,** *pl.* **-e**) appellation, surname. **eponymisch,** *adj.* eponymous.

Epopöe [epo'pø:ə], *f.*, **Epos** ['e:pɔs], *n.* (-, *pl.* **Epen**) epic (poem), epos, epopee.

Eppich ['ɛpɪç], *m.* (**-(e)s,** *pl.* **-e**) 1. (*Bot.*) celery (*Apium graveolens*); 2. (*Poet.*) ivy.

Eprouvette [epru'vɛt(ə)], *f.* (*Austr.*) test-tube.

Equipage [ekvi'pa:ʒə], *f.* 1. carriage *or* coach and horses, equipage; 2. equipment; 3. crew, ship's company; 4. suite, train, retinue. **equipieren,** *v.t.* fit out, equip; man (*a ship*).

Equitation [ekvita:tsi'o:n], *f.* horsemanship, riding, equitation. **Equitationschule,** *f.* riding-school.

er [e:r], **1.** *m. pers. pron.* it, he; ***– ist es,*** it is he; ***– selbst,*** he himself. **2.** (*obs. form of address to inferiors*) you; ***wie heißt Er?*** what is your name?

er– [ɛr], *forming v.t. and v.i. from simplex verbs and adjs. is insep. and unaccented; the p.p. loses the* ***ge–****, It indicates in the main: achievement of the aim set by the action, e.g.* ***erarbeiten, ermorden, erbleichen, erröten.*** *For examples see below.* **Er–,** *pref. forming verbal nouns corresponding in meaning to the verbs from which they are derived. See below.*

–er [ər], *adj. and adv. suff. forming comp.*; ***–er,*** more . . .

erachten [ɛr'axtən], *v.t.* think, consider, be of the opinion, (*Poet.*) deem, opine. **Erachten,** *n.*

opinion, judgement, estimation, view; ***meinem* – *nach, meines –s*** (*abbr.* ***m.E.***), in my opinion *or* view, to my mind.

erarbeiten [ɛr'arbaɪtən], *v.t.* gain *or* get by working for, work hard for, earn, acquire by one's own efforts, achieve by work.

Erb|abweichung ['ɛrp–], *f.* (*Biol.*) mutation. **–adel,** *m.* hereditary nobility, peers. **–anfall,** *m.* (*Law*) inheritance, reversion of an estate. **–anlage,** *f.* (*Biol.*) gene, (*Med.*) inherited disposition, hereditary inclination. **–anspruch,** *m.* (*Law*) claim *or* title to an inheritance. **–anteil,** *m.* *See* **–teil. –anwartschaft,** *f.* (*Law*) expectation (*of an inheritance*).

Erbarmedich [ɛr'barmədɪç], *n.* (-, *pl.* -) (*Eccl.*) kyrie eleison.

erbarmen [ɛr'barmən], **1.** *v.t.* 1. move to pity; ***daß Gott erbarme!*** God help us! 2. (*obs.*) *imp.* (*with Acc. or Gen.*) ***mich erbarmet des Armen,*** I pity the poor man. **2.** *v.r.* pity, have *or* take pity (*Gen. or über* (*Acc.*), on); ***Herr, erbarme dich unser!*** Lord have mercy upon us! **Erbarmen,** *n.* pity, compassion, mercy; ***zum* –,** pitiful, pitiable. **Erbarmer,** *m.* merciful God, God of Mercy.

erbärmlich [ɛr'bɛrmlɪç], *adj.* pitiful, pitiable, piteous, lamentable, miserable, wretched, (*Poet.*) sorry; abominable, contemptible, despicable, (*coll.*) shabby; (*coll.*) very poor, wretched, shoddy. **Erbärmlichkeit,** *f.* wretchedness, pitiableness, pitifulness, piteousness.

Erbarmung [ɛr'barmuŋ], *f.* *See* **Erbarmen. erbarmungslos,** *adj.* pitiless, merciless, cruel, hard-hearted, remorseless. **Erbarmungslosigkeit,** *f.* pitilessness, remorselessness, cruelty, hard-heartedness. **erbarmungs|voll,** *adj.* pitiful, merciful, compassionate. **–würdig,** *adj.* pitiable, pitiful, piteous, lamentable, (*Poet.*) sorry. **Erbarmungswürdigkeit,** *f.* *See* **Erbärmlichkeit.**

erbauen [ɛr'bauən], **1.** *v.t.* build, raise, erect, construct, set up; (*fig.*) edify; (*Prov.*) ***Rom ist nicht an einem Tage erbaut worden,*** Rome was not built in a day. **2.** *v.r.* be edified (***an*** (*Dat.*), by). **Erbauer,** *m.* builder; architect, constructor. **erbaulich,** *adj.* edifying, improving, uplifting; devotional; (*iron.*) ***das ist ja recht* –,** that's a fine state of affairs. **Erbauung,** *f.* erection, building, construction; edification, (moral) uplift. **Erbauungs|lektüre,** *f.* improving reading. **–schrift,** *f.* devotional book, religious tract. **–stunde,** *f.* hour of devotion.

Erb|begräbnis, *n.* family vault *or* grave. **–berechtigung,** *f.* (right of) succession. **–besitz,** *m.* heritable property, (family) inheritance. **–bild,** *n.* (*Biol.*) genotype. **–biologie,** *f.* genetics. **erbbiologisch,** *adj.* genetic.

Erbe ['ɛrbə], **1.** *m.* (**-n,** *pl.* **-n**) heir; successor; ***mutmaßlicher* –,** heir presumptive; ***ohne leibliche –n,*** without issue; ***gesetzlicher* –,** legal heir, heir at law; ***rechtmäßiger* –,** rightful heir; ***testamentarischer* –,** heir by devise. **2.** *n.* (**-s,** *pl.* **Erbschaften** *or* **Erbgüter**) heritage, inheritance; ***elterliches*** or ***väterliches* –,** patrimony; ***das – der Sünde,*** the fruits of sin. (*See N.B. under* [2]**erblich.**)

erbeben [ɛr'be:bən], *v.i.* (*aux.* s.) tremble, shudder (***vor*** (*Dat.*), at), shake, quiver, quake.

Erb|einheit, *f.* (*Biol.*) gene. **–einsetzung,** *f.* appointment of an heir.

erben ['ɛrbən], *v.t.* inherit, succeed to, (*coll.*) be left, come into; (*coll.*) ***hier ist nichts zu* –,** there's nothing to be got here. **Erbengemeinschaft,** *f.* joint heirs. **Erbeserbe,** *m.* reversionary heir.

erbeten [ɛr'be:tən], *v.t.* obtain by prayer; solicit, request.

erbetteln [ɛr'bɛtəln], *v.t.* obtain by begging, (*coll.*) wheedle (***von,*** out of).

erbeuten [ɛr'bɔytən], *v.t.* seize, carry off *or* take (as booty), capture.

Erb|faktor, *m.* (*Biol.*) gene. **–fall,** *m.* succession; fortune in reversion. **–fehler,** *m.* inherited *or* congenital defect; family failing. **–feind,** *m.* hereditary foe, (*fig.*) sworn *or* old enemy. **–folge,** *f.* succession (by inheritance); ***die – bestimmen,*** entail. **–folgekrieg,** *m.* ***Spanischer* –,** War of the Spanish Succession. **–gang,** *m.* inheritance; ***dominanter* –,** inheritance of dominant characteristics. **erb|gesessen,** *adj.* long-established (*family etc.*). **–gesund,** *adj.* free from heredity taint. **Erb|gut,** *n.* ancestral estate; inheritance, patrimony; (*Biol.*) genotype. **–hof,** *m.* entailed estate.

erbieten [ɛr'bi:tən], *irr.v.r.* offer; volunteer (to do). **Erbieten,** *n.* offer.

Erbin ['ɛrbɪn], *f.* heiress.

erbitten [ɛr'bɪtən], *irr.v.t.* ***sich*** (*Dat.*) ***etwas von ihm* –,** beg *or* ask him for s.th., request s.th. from him, prevail on him for s.th.; ***er läßt sich* –,** he is moved by entreaties; ***er läßt sich nicht* –,** he is inexorable.

erbittern [ɛr'bɪtərn], *v.t.* embitter, provoke, incense, exasperate. **erbittert,** *adj.* embittered, bitter, stubborn (*fight*). **Erbitterung,** *f.* bitterness, resentment.

erbkrank ['ɛrpkraŋk], *adj.* congenitally diseased. **Erb|krankheit,** *f.* congenital disease. **–lande,** *n.pl.* hereditary land; ***kaiserliche* –,** the emperor's patrimonial dominions.

erblassen [ɛr'blasən], *v.i.* (*aux.* s.) (*of a th.*) grow pale, fade; (*of a p.*) turn pale, go white (***vor*** (*Dat.*), with); (*fig.*) pale, be overshadowed (*as glory etc.*); (*Poet.*) die.

Erb|lasser, *m.* testator. **–lehen,** *n.* hereditary fief. **–lehre,** *f.* genetics.

erbleichen [ɛr'blaɪçən], *reg. & irr.v.i.* (*aux.* s.) (*of a p.*) turn pale, go white (*p.p.* ***erbleicht***); (*Poet.*) die (*p.p.* ***erblichen***).

[1]**erblich** [ɛr'blɪç], *see* **erbleichen.**

[2]**erblich** ['ɛrplɪç], *adj.* hereditary, (in)heritable. (N.B. *This word, with its derivatives and in particular its compounds, has suffered from the Nat. Soc. confusion of the legal concept of inheritance with the biological one of heredity. Pride in the national heritage and pride of race blended and supported each other so that it is nowadays often difficult to isolate and identify the connotations.*) – ***belastet,*** congenitally afflicted; ***–e Belastung,*** hereditary *or* congenital taint. **Erblichkeit,** *f.* heritability, hereditariness; (*Biol.*) hereditary character.

erblicken [ɛr'blɪkən], *v.t.* catch sight of, see, (*coll.*) set eyes on, (*Poet.*) behold; ***das Licht der Welt* –,** come into the world; be born.

erblinden [ɛr'blɪndən], *v.i.* (*aux.* s.) go *or* become blind, lose one's sight, be blinded (***an*** (*Dat.*), by). **Erblindung,** *f.* blindness.

Erblinie ['ɛrpli:njə], *f.* pedigree. **erblos,** *adj.* without heirs *or* an heir. **Erb|mangel,** *m.* congenital infirmity, inherited fault. **–masse,** *f.* (deceased p.'s) estate *or* assets; (*Biol.*) genotype.

erbosen [ɛr'bo:zən], **1.** *v.t.* make angry, annoy, infuriate, vex, provoke. **2.** *v.r.* get infuriated *or* furious *or* annoyed *or* angry *or* (*coll.*) cross.

erbötig [ɛr'bø:tɪç], *adj.* ready, willing.

erbrechen [ɛr'brɛçən], **1.** *irr.v.t.* 1. break open, force (open), break (*a seal*), unseal, (tear) open (*a letter*); 2. vomit, (*coll.*) bring up (*food*). **2.** *irr.v.r., v.i.* vomit, retch, be sick. **Erbrechen,** *n.* 1. breaking open, forcing; opening (*a letter etc.*); 2. vomiting, sickness.

Erbrecht ['ɛrprɛçt], *n.* law of inheritance; hereditary right, right of succession.

erbringen [ɛr'brɪŋən], *irr.v.t.* produce, furnish, adduce (*proof etc.*).

Erbschaft ['ɛrpʃaft], *f.* inheritance, legacy; ***eine – erwarten,*** have expectations (of a legacy). **Erbschafts|anwärter,** *m.* heir in expectancy. **–masse,** *f.* testator's estate. **–steuer,** *f.* death *or* estate duties, probate duty.

Erbschleicher ['ɛrpʃlaɪçər], *m.* legacy-hunter.

Erbse ['ɛrpsə], *f.* pea; ***–n für Bohnen,*** tit for tat. **Erbsenbrei,** *m.* pease-pudding. **erbsengroß,** *adj.* the size of a pea. **Erbsen|hülse, –schote** (*coll.*), *f.* pea-pod. **–suppe,** *f.* pea-soup.

Erb|staaten, *m.pl.* *See* **–lande. –stück,** *n.* heirloom. **–sünde,** *f.* original sin. **–teil,** *m.* (inherited) portion, share in an inheritance. **-übel,** *n.* deep-rooted *or* ingrained failing *or* weakness. **-untertänigkeit,** *f.* serfdom. **-zelle,** *f.* (*Biol.*) zygote.

Erchtag ['ɛrçta:k], *m.* (*dial.*) Tuesday.

Erd|ableitung ['e:rt–], *f.* (*Rad.*) earth *or* (*Am.*) ground connexion. **-abwehr,** *f.* ground defences. **-achse,** *f.* axis of the earth. **-alter,** *n.* 1. age of the earth; 2. geological era. **-anschluß,** *m. See* **-ableitung.** **-apfel,** *m.* potato. **-arbeiten,** *f.pl.* excavations, earthworks. **-arbeiter,** *m.* navvy. **-art,** *f.* type of soil. **-artischocke,** *f.* Jerusalem artichoke. **-aufklärung,** *f.* (*Mil.*) ground reconnaissance. **-bahn,** *f.* earth's orbit. **-ball,** *m.* terrestrial sphere, globe, world. **-bauten,** *m.pl.* 1. *See* **-arbeiten**; 2. mud huts.

Erdbeben ['e:rtbe:bən], *n.* earthquake. **Erdbeben|-flut,** *f.* seismic wave. **-forschung,** *f. See* **-kunde.** **-herd,** *m.* centre of an earthquake, seismic focus. **-kunde,** *f.* seismology. **-messer,** *m.* seismometer, seismograph. **-warte,** *f.* seismological station.

Erd|beere, *f.* strawberry. **-beschleunigung,** *f.* acceleration due to gravity. **-bestattung,** *f.* burial, interment, inhumation. **-boden,** *m.* earth, ground, soil; ***dem – gleichmachen,*** raze to the ground. **-drossel,** *f.* (*Orn.*) golden mountain-thrush (*Turdus dauma aureas*).

Erde ['e:rdə], *f.* earth, ground, soil; (the) earth, (the) world; ***auf -n,*** on earth, here below; ***zu ebener –,*** on the ground floor, at street-level; ***über die ganze –, überall auf der –,*** all over the world, all the world over; ***über der –,*** above ground; ***unter der –,*** underground; in the grave; (*coll.*) ***unter die – bringen,*** bring to the grave; ***der – gleichmachen,*** level to the ground; ***die – kauen,*** bite the dust; (*coll.*) ***aus der – stampfen,*** produce out of a hat; (*B.*) ***– zu –,*** ashes to ashes; (*B.*) ***zu – werden,*** return to dust.

Erd|eichel, *f.* (*Bot.*) peanut, earthnut (*Arachis hypogaea*). **-elektrizität,** *f.* terrestrial electricity.

erden ['e:rdən], *v.t.* (*Rad.*) earth, (*Am.*) ground, connect to earth.

erdenkbar [ɛr'dɛŋkba:r], *adj. See* **erdenklich.** **erdenken,** *irr.v.t.* invent, devise, concoct, think *or* make up.

Erdenkind ['e:rdənkɪnt], *n.* mortal.

erdenklich [ɛr'dɛŋklɪç], *adj.* imaginable, conceivable, thinkable, possible; ***alle -e Mühe,*** the utmost pains.

Erden|kloß, *m.* (*Poet.*) lump of mortal clay. **-leben,** *n.* mortal existence, life on earth. **-rund,** *n.* the wide world. **-sohn,** *m. See* **-kind.** **-wallen,** *n.* (*Poet.*) earthly pilgrimage. **-wurm,** *m.* (*Poet.*) (wretched) mortal.

Erder ['e:rdər], *m.* (*Rad.*) *see* **Erdanschluß.**

Erd|erschütterung, *f.* earth-tremor. **-fall,** *m.* subsidence, sink-hole. **-ferne,** *f.* (*Astr.*) apogee. **-feste,** *f.* land areas of the globe. **-gas,** *n.* natural gas. **erdgebunden,** *adj.* (*Poet.*) earth-bound, earthly. **Erd|geschichte,** *f.* geology. **-geschoß,** *n.* ground *or* (*Am.*) first floor. **-gürtel,** *m.* (*Geog.*) zone. **-hälfte,** *f.* hemisphere. **-harz,** *n.* bitumen; ***gelbes –,*** amber. **-haue,** *f.* mattock. **-haus,** *n.* mud hut. **-hülle,** *f.* earth's envelope.

erdichten [ɛr'dɪçtən], *v.t.* invent, imagine, fabricate, make up. **Erdichtung,** *f.* fabrication, fiction, invention.

erdig ['e:rdɪç], *adj.* earthy. **Erdigkeit,** *f.* earthiness.

Erd|innere(s), *n.* interior *or* (*Poet.*) bowels of the earth. **-kabel,** *n.* underground cable. **-kampf,** *m.* (*Mil.*) ground fighting, land operations. **-karte,** *f.* map of the world. **-klemme,** *f.* (*Rad.*) earth *or* (*Am.*) ground terminal. **-klumpen,** *m.* clod *or* lump of earth. **-kohle,** *f.* lignite, brown coal. **-kreis,** *m.* earth, world, globe. **-krume,** *f.* topsoil, surface soil. **-kruste,** *f.* earth's crust. **-kugel,** *f.* terrestrial sphere, globe. **-kunde,** *f.* geography. **erdkundlich,** *adj.* geographical. **Erd|leitung,** *f.* (*Tele.*) earth *or* (*Am.*) ground circuit; (*Rad.*) earth *or* (*Am.*) ground wire *or* lead *or* connexion. **-licht,** *n.* (*Astr.*) zodiacal light. **-loch,** *n.* (*Mil.*) dug-out, fox-hole. **-magnetismus,** *m.* terrestrial magnetism. **-männchen,** *n.* 1. gnome, dwarf; 2. mandrake. **-maus,** *f.* field-mouse. **-messung,** *f.* geodesy. **-mine,** *f.* (*Mil.*) land mine. **-mittelalter,** *n.* (*Geol.*) mesozoic age. **-nähe,** *f.* (*Astr.*) perigee. **-neuzeit,** *f.* (*Geol.*) neozoic age. **-nuß,** *f. See* **-eichel.** **-oberfläche,** *f.* surface of the earth. **-öl,** *n.* petroleum, mineral oil.

erdolchen [ɛr'dɔlçən], *v.t.* stab to death; (*fig.*) ***mit seinen Blicken –,*** look daggers at, give (*s.o.*) a withering look.

erdölführend ['e:rtˀø:lfy:rənt], *adj.* oil-bearing, petroliferous. **Erdölquelle,** *f.* oil-well; ***auf eine – stoßen,*** strike oil.

Erd|pech, *n.* bitumen, asphalt. **-periode,** *f.* age of the earth, geological era. **-pol,** *m.* (*Geog.*) pole. **-reich,** *n.* earth, soil, ground; (*B.*) Earthly Kingdom.

erdreisten [ɛr'draɪstən], *v.r.* dare, presume; ***darf ich mich –?*** may I be so bold? ***sie erdreistete sich, mir zu sagen,*** she had the impudence *or* audacity *or* (*coll.*) nerve *or* cheek to tell me.

Erdrinde ['e:rtrɪndə], *f.* earth's crust.

erdrosseln [ɛr'drɔsəln], *v.t.* throttle, strangle; garrotte. **Erdrosselung,** *f.* strangulation, strangling, throttling; garrotting.

erdrücken [ɛr'drykən], *v.t.* crush to death; stifle; smother; (*fig.*) crush, overwhelm, weigh *or* bear down on, bow down.

Erd|rutsch, *m.* landslide, landslip. **-schalter,** *m.* (*Elec.*) earthing switch. **-schein,** *m. See* **-licht.** **-schicht,** *f.* layer of earth, stratum; ***untere –,*** subsoil. **-schierling,** *m.* (*Bot.*) hemlock (*Conium maculatum*). **-schluß,** *m.* (accidental) earth *or* (*Am.*) ground connexion, short (circuit) to earth *or* ground. **-schnecke,** *f.* slug. **-scholle,** *f.* clod, glebe. **-schwalbe,** *f.* (*Orn.*) *see* **Uferschwalbe.** **-strich,** *m.* zone, region. **-teil,** *m.* continent.

erdulden [ɛr'duldən], *v.t.* endure, suffer, bear, (*coll.*) put up with.

Erd|umdrehung, *f.* rotation of the earth. **-umlauf,** *m.* revolution of the earth. **-umsegelung,** *f.* circumnavigation of the earth.

Erdung ['e:rduŋ], *f.* (*Rad.*) earth *or* (*Am.*) ground (wire, lead *or* connexion).

Erd|vermessung, *f.* geodesy. **-verwerfung,** *f.* (*Geol.*) fault. **-weg,** *m.* ***auf dem –,*** by surface route. **-weite,** *f.* mean distance of the earth from the sun. **-werke,** *n.pl.* earthworks, ramparts.

ereifern [ɛrˈˀaɪfərn], *v.r.* get excited *or* agitated *or* heated *or* (*coll.*) worked up (***über*** (*Acc.*), about), fly into a temper, lose one's temper.

ereignen [ɛrˈˀaɪgnən], *v.r.* occur, happen, take place, come about *or* to pass. **Ereignis,** *n.* (**-ses,** *pl.* **-se**) happening, event, occurrence, incident; ***sie sieht einem freudigen – entgegen,*** she is expecting a happy event. **ereignislos,** *adj.* uneventful. **ereignisreich,** *adj.* eventful.

ereilen [ɛrˈˀaɪlən], *v.t.* overtake (*as fate etc.*).

Eremit [ere'mi:t], *m.* (**-en,** *pl.* **-en**) hermit, recluse, anchorite. **Eremitage** [–'ta:ʒə], *f.* hermitage.

ererben [ɛrˈˀɛrbən], *v.t.* inherit; ***ererbte Krankheit,*** congenital disease.

erfahren [ɛr'fa:rən] 1. *irr.v.t.* come to know, learn, hear, be told, discover; experience, suffer, undergo; ***am eigenen Leibe –,*** learn from personal experience, experience personally. 2. *adj.* experienced, practised, proficient, versed, (*coll.*) well up (***in*** (*Dat.*), in), conversant (with). **Erfahrenheit,** *f.* experience, proficiency, skill.

Erfahrung [ɛr'fa:ruŋ], *f.* (practical) experience, (*Phil.*) empirical knowledge; ***in – bringen,*** learn, ascertain; ***aus –,*** from experience. **Erfahrungs|-beweis,** *m.* (*Phil.*) a posteriori proof. **erfahrungsgemäß,** *adv.* (*Phil.*) empirically; from previous experience. **Erfahrungskreis,** *m.* range of experience. **erfahrungslos,** *adj.* inexperienced. **erfahrungs|mäßig,** *adj.* empirical, from experience. **-reich,** *adj.* experienced. **Erfahrungswissenschaft,** *f.* (*Phil.*) empiricism.

erfassen [ɛr'fasən], *v.t.* 1. lay *or* take *or* catch hold of, seize, grasp; (*of emotions*) seize, overcome; 2. (*fig.*

of the mind) comprehend; understand, grasp, (*coll.*) take in; 3. (*of activities*) include, (*coll.*) take in; ***alle Staatsbürger werden von der Staatskrankenkasse erfaßt,*** all citizens are included in the National Health Insurance scheme; ***statistisch –,*** make a statistical survey of. **Erfassung,** *f.* inclusion.

erfinden [ɛr'fɪndən], *irr.v.t.* invent, devise, contrive; fabricate; make up (*a story*); (*Prov.*) ***das Pulver hat er nicht erfunden,*** he will never set the Thames on fire. **Erfinder,** *m.* inventor. **erfinderisch,** *adj.* resourceful, ingenious, inventive; (*Prov.*) ***Not macht –,*** necessity is the mother of invention. **Erfinderrecht,** *n.* patent rights. **Erfindung,** *f.* invention; fabrication. **Erfindungs|gabe,** *f.* inventiveness, ingenuity. **–patent,** *n.* (letters) patent. **erfindungs|reich, –voll,** *adj.* *See* **erfinderisch.**

erflehen [ɛr'fle:ən], *v.t.* beg for, implore (***von,*** from); ***laß dich –!*** be moved by my entreaties!

Erfolg [ɛr'fɔlk], *m.* (**-(e)s,** *pl.* **-e**) success; result, issue, outcome, effect; ***ohne –,*** unsuccessful, fruitless, unavailing; without (any) success, in vain, empty-handed; ***– haben,*** succeed, be successful, meet with *or* achieve success.

erfolgen [ɛr'fɔlgən], *v.i.* (*aux.* s.) 1. ***– auf*** (*Acc.*), be the result *or* consequence of, be due to, be caused by, ensue from *or* upon, follow from; 2. happen, occur, take place; ***was erfolgte darauf?*** what happened next *or* then *or* afterwards? what ensued? ***die Antwort ist noch nicht erfolgt,*** as yet there is no reply; no answer has been received yet; 3. (*of payment*) be effected *or* made; ***nach erfolgter Bezahlung,*** on payment.

erfolglos [ɛr'fɔlklo:s], **1.** *adj.* unsuccessful, ineffectual, unavailing, vain, fruitless, without effect *or* result. **2.** *adv.* without success *or* avail, in vain. **Erfolglosigkeit,** *f.* lack of success, failure, miscarriage. **erfolgreich,** *adj.* successful.

Erfolgs|anteilsystem, *n.* (*Comm.*) profit-sharing *or* bonus system. **–konto,** *n.* (*Comm.*) profit and loss account. **erfolgsversprechend,** *adj.* promising.

erforderlich [ɛr'fɔrdərlɪç], *adj.* necessary, requisite, needed, required.

erfordern [ɛr'fɔrdərn], *v.t.* require, need; necessitate, render necessary, call for, demand. **Erfordernis,** *n.* (**-ses,** *pl.* **-se**) requirement, requisite, demand, exigency; *pl.* necessaries (*of life*); ***nach – der Umstände,*** according to circumstances.

erforschen [ɛr'fɔrʃən], *v.t.* search for, try to discover *or* find out, investigate, inquire into, study, explore, fathom; ***sein Gewissen –,*** search *or* examine one's conscience. **Erforscher,** *m.* explorer. **Erforschung,** *f.* investigation, inquiry, examination, exploration.

erfragen [ɛr'fra:gən], *reg. & irr.v.t.* ascertain by questioning, ask for; ***den Weg –,*** ask the way; ***zu – bei . . .,*** inquire at. . . .

erfrechen [ɛr'frɛçən], *v.r.* dare, have the impudence *or* (*coll.*) the nerve *or* cheek, presume (to do).

erfreuen [ɛr'frɔyən], **1.** *v.t.* gladden, delight, please, give pleasure *or* joy to, cheer, comfort. **2.** *v.r.* 1. delight, take pleasure (***an*** (*Dat.*), in), be pleased *or* delighted (by); 2. (*Gen.*) enjoy (*good health etc.*). **erfreulich,** *adj.* pleasing, pleasant; gratifying, encouraging, welcome. **erfreulicherweise,** *adv.* fortunately, happily. **erfreut,** *adj.* glad, pleased, delighted (***über*** (*Acc.*), about).

erfrieren [ɛr'fri:rən], *irr.v.i.* (*aux.* s.) (*of a p.*) freeze to death, die from exposure *or* of cold, (*of plants*) be killed by the frost; ***erfroren,*** (*of a p.*) frozen to death, (*of a limb*) frostbitten; (*coll.*) ***halb*** or ***fast erfroren,*** frozen (to death), numb with cold, (*of plants*) killed by frost. **Erfrieren,** *n.* death by freezing *or* from exposure. **Erfrierung,** *f.* *See* **Erfrieren**; (*usu. pl.*) freezing; frostbite.

erfrischen [ɛr'frɪʃən], **1.** *v.t.* freshen, refresh, revive, reinvigorate. **2.** *v.r.* refresh o.s., be refreshed. **erfrischend,** *adj.* refreshing. **Erfrischung,** *f.* refreshment, (*esp.*) refreshing drink. **Erfrischungs|halle,** *f.*, **–raum,** *m.* refreshment room.

erfror [ɛr'fro:r], **erfroren,** *see* **erfrieren.**

erfüllbar [ɛr'fylba:r], *adj.* that can be fulfilled, realizable, reasonable.

erfüllen [ɛr'fylən], **1.** *v.t.* 1. fill; 2. fulfil, perform, discharge, implement, (*coll.*) carry out; conform *or* accede to, comply with (*request*), meet, satisfy (*demand*), fulfil, achieve, answer, serve (*a purpose*); ***seine Pflicht –,*** fulfil *or* perform *or* do one's duty; ***sein Versprechen –,*** fulfil *or* keep one's promise. **2.** *v.r.* be fulfilled, come to pass, come true, be realized, take place. **Erfüllung,** *f.* fulfilment (of), compliance (with), accomplishment, performance, discharge, satisfaction, implementation, execution, realization (of); ***in – gehen,*** come true, be fulfilled *or* realized, materialize, come to fruition. **Erfüllungs|ort,** *m.* (*Comm.*) place where a contract is to be fulfilled, place of payment *or* settlement, place of delivery. **–tag,** *m.* (*Comm.*) settlement day.

erfunden [ɛr'fundən], *see* **erfinden.**

ergänzen [ɛr'gɛntsən], *v.t.* complete (*s.th. incomplete*), restore (*s.th. mutilated*), replenish (*supplies*), complement, supplement, make up (*a deficiency*); ***sich*** or ***einander –,*** be complementary to one another; (*Geom.*) ***einander zu 90° –,*** be complementary; (*Geom.*) ***einander zu 180° –,*** be supplementary. **ergänzend, 1.** *adj.* supplementary; complementary. **2.** *adv.* in addition, as a rider. **Ergänzung,** *f.* completion; supplement; complement; replenishment, restoration. **Ergänzungs|band,** *m.* supplementary volume. **–farben,** *f.pl.* complementary colours. **–heft,** *n.* supplement. **–mannschaft,** *f.* (*Mil.*) replacements, reserves. **–nährstoff,** *m.* vitamin. **–satz,** *m.* (*Gram.*) complement. **–strich,** *m.* (*Typ.*) dash, ellipsis. **–wahl,** *f.* by-election. **–winkel,** *m.* (*Geom.*) complementary angle, supplemental *or* supplementary angle.

ergattern [ɛr'gatərn], *v.t.* (*coll.*) pick up, ferret out, unearth, manage to get, (contrive to) get hold of, (*of a woman*) hook *or* land (*a man*).

ergeben [ɛr'ge:bən], **1.** *irr.v.t.* produce, yield, show, establish, prove; amount *or* (*coll.*) come to (*an amount*). **2.** *irr.v.r.* 1. (*of a th.*) be the result *or* consequence (***aus,*** of), ensue, spring (from), arise (out of); ***die Untersuchungen – dieses Resultat,*** the tests establish this result; ***aus den Untersuchungen ergibt sich dieses Resultat,*** this is the result of the tests; ***hieraus ergibt sich,*** hence it follows; 2. (*of a p.*) surrender (o.s.), yield (*Dat.*, to); ***sich auf Gnade und Ungnade –,*** surrender unconditionally; ***sich der Sünde –,*** yield to sin; 3. resign o.s., submit (***in*** (*Acc.*), to); ***sich in das Unvermeidliche –,*** resign o.s. *or* submit to the inevitable; 4. become addicted, (*coll.*) take (*Dat.*, to); ***sich dem Trunk –,*** take to drink. **3.** *adj.* devoted, loyal, attached (*Dat.*, to); resigned, submissive (***in*** (*Acc.*), to); addicted (*Dat.*, to); (*Comm.*) (*in letters*) ***Ihr –(st)er,*** Yours faithfully, Yours truly. **Ergebenheit,** *f.* resignation, submissiveness (***in*** (*Acc.*), to); loyalty, devotion (*Dat.*, to). **ergebenst,** *sup. adj.* *See* **ergeben, 3.**

Ergebnis [ɛr'ge:pnɪs], *n.* (**-ses,** *pl.* **-se**) result, outcome, effect, consequence; (*Math.*) result, solution, answer; ***zu einem – kommen,*** come to *or* arrive at a conclusion; ***ein Mathematikbuch mit –sen,*** a mathematics book with answers. **ergebnislos,** *adj.* without result, unsuccessful, fruitless, ineffectual, vain. **ergebnisreich,** *adj.* successful, fruitful.

Ergebung [ɛr'ge:buŋ], *f.* submission, resignation, (*Mil.*) surrender.

ergehen [ɛr'ge:ən], **1.** *irr.v.i.* (*aux.* s.) 1. be issued *or* published *or* promulgated, (*coll.*) come out; ***– lassen,*** issue (*a decree*), make (*an appeal*), pass (*sentence*); ***Gnade für*** or ***vor Recht – lassen,*** be lenient, deal leniently, show leniency; 2. ***etwas über sich – lassen,*** submit to *or* bear *or* endure *or* suffer s.th. patiently; 3. *imp.* (*Dat.*) go *or* fare with; become of; ***es erging ihm schlecht,*** things went badly with him; ***möge es ihm wohl –!*** may he prosper! ***wie ist es Ihnen ergangen?*** how did you get on? **2.** *irr.v.r.* 1. (*Poet.*) walk, stroll; ***sich im Garten –,*** stroll in the garden; 2. ***sich in einer Rede –,*** break out *or* launch forth into a speech. **Ergehen,** *n.* condition, state (*health, prosperity etc.*).

ergiebig [ɛr'gi:bɪç], *adj.* productive, lucrative, fertile, rich, plentiful, abundant, (*Poet.*) bountiful, bounteous. **Ergiebigkeit,** *f.* productiveness, abundance, richness, fertility.

ergießen [ɛr'gi:sən], *irr.v.r.* pour *or* flow *or* gush forth; ***sich in Tränen –,*** burst into tears.

erglühen [ɛr'gly:ən], *v.i.* (*aux.* s.) (begin to) glow, light up.

ergötzen [ɛr'gœtsən], **1.** *v.t.* delight, please, amuse, divert, entertain, edify. **2.** *v.r.* take delight (***an*** (*Dat.*), in), be amused (at). **Ergötzen,** *n.* joy, delight, amusement. **ergötzend, ergötzlich,** *adj.* amusing, entertaining, diverting; delightful. **Ergötzung,** *f. See* **Ergötzen.**

ergrauen [ɛr'grauən], *v.i.* (*aux.* s.) turn *or* get grey (*of hair*); go grey (*of a p.*).

ergreifen [ɛr'graɪfən], *irr.v.t.* lay *or* catch *or* take hold of, seize, grasp (*a th.*), seize, capture, apprehend (*a p.*); (*of feelings*) seize, overcome; (*of a sight, speech etc.*) move (deeply), touch, affect; take *or* assume (*the offensive*), take up (*a trade etc.*); ***Besitz von einer S. –,*** take possession of a th.; ***die Feder –,*** take up the pen; ***die Flucht –,*** flee, take (to) flight; ***die Gelegenheit beim Schopfe –,*** seize *or* take the occasion by the forelock, seize the opportunity; ***strenge Maßregeln –,*** have recourse to stern measures; ***Partei –,*** take sides, side (*Gen. or* ***für,*** with), stand *or* (*coll.*) stick up (for); ***auf frischer Tat –,*** catch in the act; ***die Waffen –,*** take up arms; ***das Wort –,*** begin to speak. **ergreifend,** *adj.* moving, touching, affecting, stirring, impressive, gripping. **Ergreifung,** *f.* seizure, capture; adoption (*of measures*).

ergriffen [ɛr'grɪfən], *adj.* deeply moved, touched, stirred, affected. **Ergriffenheit,** *f.* emotion.

ergrimmen [ɛr'grɪmən], *v.i.* (*aux.* s.) (*Poet.*) become angry *or* furious.

ergründen [ɛr'gryndən], *v.t.* fathom, sound, probe into, examine *or* explore thoroughly, penetrate, (*coll.*) go deeply *or* thoroughly into, get to the bottom *or* the root of; ***nicht zu –,*** unfathomable, inexplicable. **ergründlich,** *adj.* fathomable, penetrable.

Erguß [ɛr'gus], *m.* (*Med.*) effusion, extravasation (*of blood*); ejaculation (*of semen*); (*fig.*) outpouring, outburst, effusion; flow, flood, torrent. **Ergußgestein,** *n.* eruptive rock.

erhaben [ɛr'ha:bən], *adj.* raised, elevated; embossed; (*fig.*) sublime, exalted, noble, lofty, illustrious, stately, magnificent; ***–e Arbeit,*** relief, embossed work; (*fig.*) ***– sein über*** (*Acc.*), be superior to, be above; ***über jede kritik*** (***jeden Verdacht***) ***– sein,*** be above all criticism (be above *or* beyond suspicion); ***über alles Lob*** (***allen Zweifel***) ***– sein,*** be beyond praise (doubt); ***das Erhabene,*** the Sublime; ***vom Erhabenen zum Lächerlichen,*** from the sublime to the ridiculous. **Erhabenheit,** *f.* sublimity, nobility, grandeur, loftiness; elevation, prominence, relief; superiority.

erhaltbar [ɛr'haltba:r], *adj.* 1. *See* **erhältlich**; 2. preservable.

Erhalt [ɛr'halt], *m.* (**-(e)s,** *no pl.*) (*Comm.*) receipt. **erhalten, 1.** *irr.v.t.* 1. get, receive, obtain; ***einen höheren Preis –,*** fetch a higher price; ***wenn Sie dieses –,*** when this reaches you; 2. save, conserve, preserve; keep, maintain, support (financially); ***in Gang –,*** keep going; ***sich selbst –,*** support o.s.; ***sich gut –,*** wear *or* last *or* keep well. **2.** *adj.* surviving, preserved; received; ***– bleiben,*** survive; ***schlecht*** (***gut***) ***–,*** in poor (good) repair *or* condition. **erhaltenswert,** *adj.* worthy of preservation. **Erhalter,** *m.* preserver, supporter; upholder.

erhältlich [ɛr'hɛltlɪç], *adj.* obtainable, suppliable; ***– bei allen Buchhändlern,*** obtainable at all booksellers.

Erhaltung [ɛr'haltuŋ], *f.* support, maintenance, preservation, conservation (*of energy etc.*). **Erhaltungs|mittel,** *n.* means of subsistence. **–trieb,** *m.* instinct of self-preservation. **–umsatz,** *m.* (*Physiol.*) basal metabolism. **–zustand,** *m.* condition, state of preservation.

erhängen [ɛr'hɛŋən], *v.t.* (*v.r.*) hang (o.s.). **Erhängen,** *n.*, **Erhängung,** *f.* execution by hanging.

erhärten [ɛr'hɛrtən], **1.** *v.t.* harden; (*fig.*) confirm, corroborate, substantiate; ***eidlich –,*** affirm upon oath. **2.** *v.i.* (*aux.* s.) harden, become hard, set. **Erhärtung,** *f.* corroboration, confirmation, proof; hardening; ***eidliche –,*** affidavit.

erhaschen [ɛr'haʃən], *v.t.* seize, catch (hold of); ***einen Blick – von,*** catch (*s.o.'s*) eye.

erheben [ɛr'he:bən], **1.** *irr.v.t.* raise, lift up, elevate; edify, exalt; set up (*a cry*), raise (*objection*), put forward, make (*claim*); charge (*a fee*), make (*a charge*); levy, impose (*taxes*); bring (*an action against*); ***ihn in den Adelstand –,*** raise *or* elevate him to the peerage; ***Anspruch – auf*** (*Acc.*), lay claim to; ***Einspruch –,*** object, raise an objection, protest, enter a protest; ***ein Geschrei –,*** set up an outcry; ***in den Himmel –,*** laud to the skies; ***seine Stimme –,*** raise one's voice, speak up; begin to speak; (*Math.*) ***zur zweiten Potenz*** or ***ins Quadrat –,*** square; ***zur dritten Potenz –,*** cube; ***zur vierten Potenz –,*** raise to the fourth power *or* to the power (of) four; ***auf den Thron –,*** put *or* install on the throne; ***Zweifel –,*** raise doubts. **2.** *irr.v.r.* (*of a p.*) rise (to one's feet), get up; (*Poet.*) rise (from one's bed); (*of a th.*) rise (up), (*as wind*) rise, spring up; (*fig.*) (*of a p.*) rise (in revolt), rebel, revolt, (*as difficulties*) arise, spring up. **erhebend,** *adj.* edifying, uplifting, elevating, solemn, impressive.

erheblich [ɛr'he:plɪç], *adj.* considerable, substantial, weighty, important, (*coll.*) sizeable. **Erheblichkeit,** *f.* importance, consequence; extensive nature, considerable extent.

Erhebung [ɛr'he:buŋ], *f.* elevation; promotion; imposition, collection, levy; elevation, uplift, exaltation; (*Math.*) involution; rising ground, eminence, elevation, high ground; rising, revolt, rebellion; ***nationale –,*** Nat. Soc. seizure of power (1933); ***–en anstellen,*** make inquiries, hold an (official) inquiry into. **Erhebungskosten,** *f.pl.* expenses of collection.

erheischen [ɛr'haɪʃən], *v.t.* require, demand, claim.

erheitern [ɛr'haɪtərn], **1.** *v.t.* cheer, amuse, entertain. **2.** *v.r.* become cheerful, cheer up. **Erheiterung,** *f.* entertainment, amusement, diversion.

erhellen [ɛr'hɛlən], **1.** *v.t.* light up, illuminate; (*fig.*) throw light on (*mystery*). **2.** *v.r.* brighten, clear up (*as weather*), light up (*as a face*). **3.** *imp. v.i.* become clear *or* apparent *or* evident; ***daraus erhellt, daß,*** from this it appears *or* would appear that.

erheucheln [ɛr'hɔyçəln], *v.t.* simulate, feign, (*coll.*) put on.

erhitzen [ɛr'hɪtsən], **1.** *v.t.* heat, raise the temperature of; excite, inflame. **2.** *v.r.* get hot, become heated; (*of a p.*) get (over)heated. **erhitzt,** *adj.* heated, hot, (*fig.*) heated, fierce (*as argument*), (*of a p.*) overheated, flushed, excited, hot-headed.

erhoffen [ɛr'hɔfən], *v.t.* hope *or* wish for, expect, anticipate.

erhöhen [ɛr'hø:ən], *v.t.* raise, make higher; raise, heighten, increase, (*Mus.*) sharpen (*a note*); enhance (*value etc.*); (*coll.*) put up (*price*), step up (*production*); extol, exalt. **erhöht,** *adj.* raised; increased, heightened, (*Mus.*) sharp(ened); enhanced, elevated; (*Mus.*) ***–es C,*** C sharp. **Erhöhung,** *f.* elevation; rise, advance, increase, enhancement; rising ground, eminence; exaltation. **Erhöhungs|winkel,** *m.* angle of elevation. **–zeichen,** *n.* (*Mus.*) sharp.

erholen [ɛr'ho:lən], *v.r.* recover, get well again, be restored to health, (*coll.*) pick up again; recuperate, convalesce; (have a) rest, relax; (*Comm.*) recover, rally, (*coll.*) look *or* pick up (*of prices*); ***sie erholt sich gut,*** she is making a good recovery. **erholsam,** *adj.* restful, refreshing. **Erholung,** *f.* recovery; recuperation, convalescence; rest, recreation, relaxation. **erholungsbedürftig,** *adj.* in need of a change *or* rest. **Erholungs|heim,** *n.* convalescent home. **–ort,** *m.* holiday resort.

erhören [ɛr'hø:rən], *v.t.* give a favourable hearing to, fulfil, grant (*request*), hear, answer (*prayer*).

Erika ['e:rika], *f.* (*Bot.*) heather (*Erica*).

erinnerlich [ɛr'ˀɪnərlɪç], *adj.* remembered (*Dat.*, by); ***es ist mir –,*** I remember; ***soviel mir – ist,*** so far as I remember, to the best of my recollection.

erinnern [ɛr'ˀɪnərn], **1.** *v.t.* 1. remind (*an* (*Acc.*), of); ***ihn daran –,*** recall it to his mind, draw his attention to it; ***das erinnert mich an meinen Vater,*** that puts me in mind of my father; 2. (*N.Germ. dial.*) *see* **2**; 3. (*obs.*) make *or* raise an objection. **2.** *v.r.* ***sich – an*** (*Acc.*), (*Poet.*) ***sich –*** (*Gen.*), recall, remember, recollect, call to mind; ***wenn ich mich recht erinnere,*** if my memory serves me right.

Erinnerung [ɛr'ˀɪnərʊŋ], *f.* remembrance, memory, recollection (*an* (*Acc.*), of); ***ihm etwas in – bringen,*** recall s.th. to his mind; ***zur – an*** (*Acc.*), in remembrance of, in memory of; as a souvenir of. **Erinnerungsbild,** *n.* visual memory. **Erinnerungslosigkeit,** *f.* amnesia, loss of memory. **Erinnerungs|tafel,** *f.* memorial plaque. **–verlust,** *m. See* **Erinnerungslosigkeit.**

erjagen [ɛr'ja:gən], *v.t.* hunt (down); (*fig. coll.*) gain, achieve; (*fig.*) ***zu – versuchen,*** chase after (*success, etc.*)

erkalten [ɛr'kaltən], *v.i.* (*aux.* s.) get cool *or* cold; cool (down); (*fig.*) cool off (*of zeal, friendship etc.*), grow cold (*of love*); ***– lassen,*** chill, damp (*enthusiasm etc.*).

erkälten [ɛr'kɛltən], **1.** *v.t.* cool, chill; ***ich bin erkältet,*** I have a chill *or* cold; ***er hat sich*** (*Dat.*) ***den Magen erkältet,*** he has a chill on the stomach. **2.** *v.r.* catch cold, catch a chill. **Erkältung,** *f.* cold, chill.

erkämpfen [ɛr'kɛmpfən], *v.t.* gain by fighting *or* by strenuous effort *or* with a struggle.

erkannt [ɛr'kant], *see* **erkennen.**

erkaufen [ər'kaufən], *v.t.* buy, purchase; bribe, corrupt; ***teuer –,*** pay a high price for, pay dearly for.

erkecken [ɛr'kɛkən], *v.r.* dare, make bold, be so bold as (to).

erkennbar [ɛr'kɛnba:r], *adj.* perceivable, perceptible, discernible, detectable, visible; distinguishable, recognizable, identifiable; (*Phil.*) knowable, cognizable. **Erkennbarkeit,** *f.* recognizability *etc.*

erkennen [ɛr'kɛnən], **1.** *irr.v.t.* 1. perceive, distinguish, discern, recognize, (*coll.*) make out; recognize, identify, know, (*coll.*) tell, spot (***an*** (*Dat.*), by); (*fig.*) realize, appreciate, detect, (*coll.*) be alive to; ***– lassen,*** show, make plain *or* clear, reveal; ***es läßt sich nicht –,*** one cannot tell; ***zu – geben,*** indicate; ***sich zu – geben,*** make o.s. known, disclose one's identity, (*Poet.*) disclose o.s.; 2. (*Phil.*) know, have cognition of, be cognizant of; 3. (*B.*) have carnal knowledge of; 4. (*Comm.*) credit (*an account*) (***mit,*** with). **2.** *irr.v.i.* (*Law*) ***– auf*** (*Acc.*), pass sentence of (*death etc.*); ***auf Freispruch –,*** dismiss the charge; ***auf eine Geldstrafe –,*** impose a fine; ***auf Schadenersatz –,*** award damages; ***zu seinem Gunsten –,*** give judgement in his favour; ***das Gericht erkannte zu*** or ***für Recht, daß . . .,*** the verdict of the court was that . . ., the court found that . . ..

Erkennen [ɛr'kɛnən], *n.* recognition; perception, realization, appreciation; (*Med.*) diagnosis; (*Phil.*) cognition.

erkenntlich [ɛr'kɛntlɪç], *adj.* grateful (*Dat.*, to), appreciative (of). *See also* **erkennbar. Erkenntlichkeit,** *f.* gratitude; appreciation; token of gratitude; (*obs.*) *see* **Erkennbarkeit.**

Erkenntnis [ɛr'kɛntnɪs], **1.** *f.* (-, *pl.* **-se**) (*Phil.*) knowledge, cognition; perception, recognition, realization, appreciation; ***zur – kommen,*** (come to) realize; (*B.*) ***der Baum der –,*** the tree of knowledge. **2.** *n.* (**-ses,** *pl.* **-se**) (*Law*) verdict, finding, decision, award, sentence, judgement. **erkenntnistheoretisch,** *adj.* (*Phil.*) epistomological. **Erkenntnis|drang,** *m.* thirst for knowledge. **–theorie,** *f.* theory of cognition, epistemology. **–vermögen,** *n.* cognition, cognitive faculty.

Erkennung [ɛr'kɛnʊŋ], *f. See* **Erkennen. Erkennungs|dienst,** *m.* (police) records department. **–karte,** *f.* label with name and address. **–marke,** *f.* identification marking, identity disc. **–merkmal,** *n.* distinguishing mark. **–signal,** *n.* (*Av.*) recognition signal. **–tuch,** *n.* (*Av.*) ground strip *or* panel. **–wort,** *n.* password, watchword. **–zahl,** *f.* index number. **–zeichen,** *n.* characteristic symptom, distinctive mark, distinguishing sign, (*Av.*) recognition marking.

Erker ['ɛrkər], *m.* bay (window). **Erkerfenster,** *n.* oriel, bow (*curved*) *or* bay (*angular*) window.

erkiesen [ɛr'ki:zən], *irr.v.t.* (*Poet.*) choose, elect.

erklärbar [ɛr'klɛ:rba:r], *adj. See* **erklärlich.**

erklären [ɛr'klɛ:rən], **1.** *v.t.* 1. explain, account for (*facts*), expound, interpret, comment on (*text, meaning etc.*), (*Gram.*) parse (*a word*), analyse (*a sentence*); ***sich – lassen,*** be explained *or* explicable; 2. declare, announce, state, affirm; ***eidesstattlich*** or ***an Eides Statt –,*** make a statutory declaration; ***– für,*** pronounce to be; ***in die Acht –,*** outlaw; ***den Krieg –,*** declare war (*Dat.*, on). **2.** *v.r.* explain o.s.; declare o.s. (*for or against*); make an offer of marriage, propose; ***daraus erklärt sich sein Benehmen,*** that accounts for his behaviour; ***sich für bankrott –,*** declare o.s. bankrupt; ***sich bereit –,*** declare one's willingness.

erklärlich [ɛr'klɛ:rlɪç], *adj.* explainable, explicable, accountable, understandable, obvious, evident. **erklärlicherweise,** *adv.* for obvious reasons, quite understandably. **erklärt,** *adj.* declared, avowed, acknowledged, professed, open; ***–er Feind,*** open *or* sworn enemy.

Erklärung [ɛr'klɛ:rʊŋ], *f.* explanation, interpretation, exposition, commentary, elucidation; (*Theol.*) exegesis, (*Gram.*) analysis; statement, announcement, declaration, affirmation, asseveration, manifesto, (*Law*) deposition. **Erklärungs|tag,** *m.* (*St. Exch.*) contango day. **–versuch,** *m.* attempted explanation.

erklecklich [ɛr'klɛklɪç], *adj.* considerable, (*coll.*) sizeable, tidy, handsome, goodly (*amount*).

erklettern [ɛr'klɛtərn], *v.t.* climb (up), scale.

erklimmen [ɛr'klɪmən], *irr.v.t. See* **erklettern**; (*fig.*) reach the summit of (*power etc.*).

erklingen [ɛr'klɪŋən], *irr.v.i.* (*aux.* s.) sound, resound, ring out.

erkor [ɛr'ko:r], **erkoren,** *see* **erkiesen.**

erkranken [ɛr'kraŋkən], *v.i.* (*aux.* s.) be taken *or* fall sick *or* ill, (*Am.*) take *or* get sick (***an*** (*Dat.*), with), (*of organ, plant or animal*) become diseased *or* affected. **erkrankt,** *adj.* sick, ill; affected, diseased. **Erkrankung,** *f.* illness, sickness, disease, affection.

erkühnen [ɛr'ky:nən], *v.r.* (*Poet.*) (*Gen.*) venture, dare, make bold (to).

erkunden [ɛr'kʊndən], *v.t.* (*Mil.*) reconnoitre; explore, investigate.

erkundigen [ɛr'kʊndɪgən], *v.r.* inquire, make inquiries (*bei,* of *or* from; ***über*** (*Acc.*) *or* ***nach,*** about). **Erkundigung,** *f.* inquiry; ***–en einziehen*** or ***einholen über*** (*Acc.*), collect information on *or* about; make inquiries about.

Erkundung [ɛr'kʊndʊŋ], *f.* (*Mil.*) reconnaissance; exploration, investigation. **Erkundungs|fahrzeug,** *n.* (*Mil.*) scout car. **–flugzeug,** *n.* (*Av.*) reconnaissance aircraft.

erkünsteln [ɛr'kynstəln], *v.t.* pretend, feign, affect. **erkünstelt,** *adj.* affected, pretended; constrained, forced.

Erlag [ɛr'la:k], *m.* (**-s,** *pl.* **¨-e**) (*Austr.*) payment, deposit. **Erlagschein,** *m.* (*Austr.*) money order, postal order.

erlahmen [ɛr'la:mən], *v.i.* (*aux.* s.) (become) weary, tire; slacken, fail, abate, grow weak, flag.

erlangbar [ɛr'laŋba:r], *adj.* obtainable, attainable.

erlangen [ɛr'laŋən], *v.t.* 1. attain (to), acquire, achieve, get; ***Gnade –,*** find favour (***bei,*** with); ***seinen Zweck –,*** attain one's end, achieve one's purpose; 2. (*obs.*) reach, grasp. **Erlangung,** *f.* attainment, achievement (*of a purpose etc.*).

Erlaß [ɛr'las], *m.* (**-(ss)es,** *pl.* **-(ss)e**) 1. edict, decree, ordinance, order, enactment, (official) regulation *or* announcement, (*Eccl.*) rescript; 2. issuing, enactment, enaction (*Gen.*, of); 3

(*Comm., Law*) remission; dispensation, exemption (*Gen.*, from), acquittal, acquittance (*of debt*), remission (*of sin*), (*R.C.*) indulgence. **erlaßbar,** *adj.* remissable (*debt, sin*), dispensable (*obligation*).

erlassen [ɛrˈlasən], *irr.v.t.* 1. issue (*order*), enact, proclaim (*law*), lay down (*regulations*); 2. release, absolve, exempt (*Dat.*, from), (*coll.*) let off (from), relieve, acquit (of), excuse, remit; ***eine Schuld –,*** forgo *or* excuse repayment of a debt; ***(ihm) die Strafe –,*** let (him) go unpunished; ***– Sie mir Antwort auf die Frage,*** do not ask me to answer this question, permit me to refrain from answering this question; 3. (*obs.*) release (*prisoner*).

Erlaßjahr [ɛrˈlasja:r], *n.* (*R.C.*) jubilee year.

erläßlich [ɛrˈlɛslɪç], *adj.* remissible, venial, pardonable.

Erlaßsünde [ɛrˈlaszyndə], *f.* (*Theol.*) venial sin.

Erlassung [ɛrˈlasuŋ], *f.* *See* **Erlaß,** 2, 3. **Erlassungs|jahr,** *n.* *See* **Erlaßjahr. –vergleich, –vertrag,** *m.* (*Law*) composition (between debtor and creditor).

erlauben [ɛrˈlaubən], *v.t.* (*ihm etwas*) allow, permit; ***– Sie!*** allow *or* permit me! (*coll.*) ***– Sie mal!*** what's the idea? what do you think you're up to? (*iron. expression of indignation*); ***ich erlaube mir zu sagen,*** I beg to say, I take the liberty of saying; ***sich*** (*Dat.*) ***–,*** permit *or* allow o.s., indulge in; ***sich Freiheiten –,*** take liberties; ***sich eine Meinungsäußerung –,*** venture an opinion, be so bold as to express an opinion; (*coll.*) ***das können Sie sich bei mir nicht –,*** you can't get away with it with me; ***was – Sie sich?*** how dare you! ***sich*** (*Dat.*) ***– können,*** be able to afford.

Erlaubnis [ɛrˈlaupnɪs], *f.* (-, *pl.* **-se**) leave, permission, consent; ***mit höherer – gedruckt,*** printed by authority. **Erlaubnisschein,** *m.* permit, (written) permission.

erlaubt [ɛrˈlaupt], *adj.* permitted, permissible, sanctioned, allowed; allowable, lawful, legitimate.

erlaucht [ɛrˈlauxt], *adj.* illustrious, noble; (*Hist. as address*) ***Erlaucht,*** your Lordship.

erlauschen [ɛrˈlauʃən], *v.t.* overhear; learn by eavesdropping.

erläutern [ɛrˈlɔytərn], *v.t.* explain, elucidate, commentate, comment on; ***durch Beispiele –,*** illustrate by examples, exemplify. **Erläuterung,** *f.* explanation, elucidation; illustration, exemplification; (*usu. pl.*) commentary, explanatory comments *or* notes; ***zur –,*** in illustration.

Erle [ˈɛrlə], *f.* (*Bot.*) alder (*Alnus glutinosa*).

erleben [ɛrˈle:bən], *v.t.* experience; live *or* pass *or* go through (*exciting times etc.*), know (from experience), live to see; ***wir werden nie den Tag –,*** we shall never (live to) see the day; ***ich habe einen glücklichen Tag erlebt,*** I have had *or* spent a happy day; ***hat einer so etwas je erlebt?*** did anyone ever see *or* hear the like? ***viele Auflagen –,*** go through *or* see many editions; (*coll.*) ***du wirst*** or ***kannst was –,*** you'll get into trouble, you'll be sorry you were ever born, you'll live to regret it; ***Freude – an*** (*Dat.*), take *or* find pleasure in.

Erlebnis [ɛrˈle:pnɪs], *n.* (**-ses,** *pl.* **-se**) (personal) experience, adventure; occurrence, event; ***widrige –se,*** adversities.

erledigen [ɛrˈle:dɪgən], **1.** *v.t.* 1. deal with, attend *or* (*coll.*) see to; arrange, adjust; put *or* set right; handle, manage (*a matter*); 2. settle, dispose of, dispatch, finish (off), get finished, clear up, do (*a job*), get through, clear off (*work*); 3. (*coll.*) settle, dispose of, finish off (*a p.*), settle (*s.o.'s*) hash, cook (*s.o.'s*) goose, put paid to (*s.o.'s*) account; 4. (*obs.*) (set) free, liberate (*Gen.*, from). **2.** *v.r.* 1. (*of a matter*) settle itself, be settled, be disposed of; 2. (*obs.*) (*of a p.*) free o.s., escape (*Gen.*, from); 3. (*of an office etc.*) fall vacant *or* (*obs.*) void. **erledigt,** *adj.* 1. settled, finished; ***und damit ist die Sache –,*** and that's (an *or* the end of) that; 2. (*coll.*) (*of a matter*) finished, (dead and) done for; (*of a p.*) played out, worn out, done in *or* up, all in, deadbeat, whacked; (*sl.*) ***er ist –,*** he's had it; ***er ist für mich –,*** I have done *or* am through with him; 3. ***–e Stelle (Pfründe),*** vacant position (living). **Erledigung,** *f.* 1. attention, arrangement, adjustment; settlement, disposal, dispatch, discharge (*of business*); ***zur –,*** for attention; 2. (*obs.*) voidance (*of a benefice*); 3. release, discharge (*of a prisoner*).

¹**erlegen** [ɛrˈle:gən], *v.t.* 1. (*Hunt.*) shoot, kill, bring down (*game*), (*Poet.*) slay, lay low (*opponent*); 2. pay (down), deposit.

²**erlegen,** *p.p.* *See* **erliegen.**

erleichtern [ɛrˈlaɪçtərn], **1.** *v.t.* ease, lighten, make easy *or* easier, assist, help, aid, facilitate; relieve, allay, alleviate, assuage (*suffering*). **2.** *v.r.* relieve one's feelings, unburden o.s.; (*coll.*) relieve nature. **erleichtert,** *adj.* relieved, easier in one's mind. **Erleichterung,** *f.* facilitation; (*usu. pl.*) facility; relief, mitigation, alleviation (*of suffering*).

erleiden [ɛrˈlaɪdən], *irr.v.t.* suffer, undergo, sustain, (*coll.*) meet with; ***Schiffbruch –,*** be shipwrecked, (*fig.*) come to grief; ***den Tod –,*** suffer death, meet one's death.

erlen [ˈɛrlən], *adj.* (made of) alderwood. **Erlenzeisig,** *m.* (*Orn.*) see **Zeisig.**

erlernen [ɛrˈlɛrnən], *v.t.* learn, acquire.

erlesen [ɛrˈle:zən], **1.** *irr.v.t.* (*obs.*) select, choose, elect. **2.** *adj.* select; selected; choice; ***–e Mannschaft,*** picked men.

erleuchten [ɛrˈlɔyçtən], *v.t.* illuminate, light (up); (*fig.*) illumine, enlighten; inspire; ***die Erleuchteten,*** the Illuminati. **Erleuchtung,** *f.* illumination; enlightenment, inspiration.

erliegen [ɛrˈli:gən], *irr.v.i.* (*aux.* s.) be overpowered *or* overcome *or* worsted *or* defeated (*Dat.*, by), succumb, give in, give way, yield (to); die (from), be killed (by), succumb (to) (*disease*). **Erliegen,** *n.* ***zum – kommen,*** close *or* shut down (*of business etc.*), be brought *or* come to a standstill (*of movement, traffic etc.*), give way, fail, flag (*of strength etc.*).

erlischt [ɛrˈlɪʃt], *see* **erlöschen.**

erlisten [ɛrˈlɪstən], *v.t.* obtain by cunning *or* trickery *or* stealth; (*sl.*) wangle.

Erlkönig [ˈɛrlkø:nɪç], *m.* elf-king.

erlogen [ɛrˈlo:gən], *adj.* false, untrue, fictitious, invented, trumped up; ***das ist erstunken und –,*** there's not a grain of truth in it, it's made up from beginning to end.

Erlös [ɛrˈlø:s], *m.* (**-es,** *pl.* **-e**) (net) proceeds.

erloschen [ɛrˈlɔʃən], *adj.* extinguished; expired (*policy etc.*), extinct (*volcano*), obliterated, effaced; ***das Licht ist –,*** the light is out; ***bei ihm ist alle Scham –,*** he is dead to all sense of shame. *See* **erlöschen.**

erlöschen [ɛrˈlœʃən], *irr.v.t.* (*aux.* s.) go out, (*Poet.*) expire (*of light, fire*); die down; (*fig.*) become extinct; die out; cease to exist, go out of existence; be cancelled *or* dissolved, expire, lapse; ***ein Recht – lassen,*** forfeit a right, allow a right to lapse. **Erlöschen,** *n.* extinction, expiration, lapse.

erlösen [ɛrˈlø:zən], *v.t.* 1. (*Theol.*) save, deliver, redeem; (set) free, release, liberate (***von,*** from); free, relieve (***von,*** of); 2. (*Comm.*) realize (*from a sale*). **Erlöser,** *m.* deliverer, liberator, (*Theol.*) Saviour, the Redeemer. **Erlösung,** *f.* release, deliverance, liberation; (*Theol.*) salvation, redemption.

ermächtigen [ɛrˈmɛçtɪgən], **1.** *v.t.* empower, authorize. **2.** *v.r.* (*Gen.*) lay *or* take hold of, take possession of, seize, usurp. **Ermächtigung,** *f.* authorization, authority, full powers. **Ermächtigungsgesetz,** *n.* enabling act.

ermahnen [ɛrˈma:nən], *v.t.* admonish, exhort, urge, warn. **ermahnend,** *adj.* (ad)monitory, hortatory. **Ermahnung,** *f.* admonition, exhortation; warning.

ermangeln [ɛrˈmaŋəln], *v.i.* 1. (*Gen.*) lack, be lacking, be short of, be in want *or* need of; 2. (*imp.*) ***es mangelt ihm an*** (*Dat.*), he lacks *or* is lacking in; 3. (*with inf. complement*) ***– zu tun,*** fail to do. **Ermangelung,** *f.* ***in –*** (*Gen.*), for want *or* lack of, in the absence of, in default of; ***in – dessen,*** failing which.

ermannen [ɛrˈmanən], *v.r.* pull o.s. together, brace o.s., take courage *or* heart.

ermäßigen [ɛrˈmɛːsɪɡən], *v.t.* lower, reduce, bring down, (*coll.*) cut, (*Am.*) cut down (*prices*). **Ermäßigung,** *f.* reduction, (*coll.*) cut; (*Comm.*) discount; (tax) allowance.

ermatten [ɛrˈmatən], **1.** *v.t.* (*obs.*) tire, exhaust, weary, weaken, wear down. **2.** *v.i.* (*aux.* s.) weary, tire, grow weary *or* tired *or* exhausted. **Ermattung,** *f.* exhaustion, weariness, tiredness, fatigue, lassitude.

ermessen [ɛrˈmɛsən], *irr.v.t.* judge, weigh, measure, calculate, assess, estimate; comprehend, realize, grasp, fathom; ***es ist nicht zu –,*** there is no way of knowing *or* telling. **Ermessen,** *n.* judgement, estimation, opinion; discretion; ***meines –s, nach meinem –,*** in my view *or* estimation *or* opinion, to my mind; ***nach eigenem (freien) – handeln,*** use one's own discretion, do as one thinks best; ***nach bestem*** or ***menschlichem –,*** as far as one can judge. **Ermessens|frage,** *f.* matter of discretion. **–recht,** *n.* discretionary power.

ermeßlich [ɛrˈmɛslɪç], *adj.* measurable, calculable, assessable, foreseeable.

ermitteln [ɛrˈmɪtəln], *v.t.* ascertain, discover, elicit, establish, (*coll.*) find out (*facts*), trace (*whereabouts*), (*Math.*) determine (*a value*). **Ermitt(e)lung,** *f.* ascertainment, establishment, discovery, determination (*of facts*); *pl.* inquiries, investigations. **Ermitt(e)lungsverfahren,** *n.* (*Law*) judicial inquiry.

ermöglichen [ɛrˈmøːɡlɪçən], *v.t.* render *or* make possible *or* feasible, enable, bring about.

ermorden [ɛrˈmɔrdən], **1.** *v.t.* murder, assassinate. **Ermordete(r),** *m., f.* murdered person, murder victim. **Ermordung,** *f.* murder, assassination.

ermüden [ɛrˈmyːdən], **1.** *v.t.* tire (out), weary, make tired *or* weary, fatigue, exhaust, wear out. **2.** *v.i.* (*aux.* s.) tire, weary, get tired, grow weary, become fatigued. **ermüdend,** *adj.* tiring, fatiguing, wearisome, irksome, tedious. **Ermüdung,** *f.* tiredness, fatigue, weariness. **Ermüdungs|festigkeit,** *f.* (*Metall.*) fatigue strength. **–grenze,** *f.* (*Metall.*) fatigue limit.

ermuntern [ɛrˈmuntərn], *v.t.* rouse (from lethargy), encourage, incite, urge on, prompt; cheer (up), (*coll.*) buck up; put new life *or* heart into. **Ermunterung,** *f.* encouragement.

ermutigen [ɛrˈmuːtɪɡən], *v.t.* encourage, hearten, inspire with courage. **ermutigend,** *adj.* encouraging, reassuring, heartening. **Ermutigung,** *f.* encouragement.

ernähren [ɛrˈnɛːrən], **1.** *v.t.* nourish, feed; support, maintain, keep (*a family etc.*); ***sich von ihm – lassen,*** depend on him for support. **2.** *v.r.* earn one's livelihood, support o.s., live (***von,*** by); (*of animal*) feed (***von,*** on), (*of a p.*) live *or* subsist (***von,*** on). **Ernährer,** *m.* provider, bread-winner. **Ernährung,** *f.* nourishment, food; feeding, nutrition, alimentation; support, maintenance (*of a family*); ***schlechte –,*** malnutrition; ***ungenügende –,*** underfeeding. **Ernährungs|amt,** *n.* Food Office, Ministry of Food. **–fachmann,** *m.* dietician. **–flüssigkeit,** *f.* lymph. **–kunde, –lehre,** *f.* dietetics. **–weise,** *f.* (*of a p.*) diet, (*of animals*) feeding habits.

ernannt [ɛrˈnant], *see* **ernennen**; ***der (die) Ernannte,*** the nominee.

ernennen [ɛrˈnɛnən], *irr.v.t.* nominate, appoint; designate; ***ihn zum Herzog –,*** create him a duke; ***Geschworene –,*** empanel a jury. **Ernennung,** *f.* nomination, appointment; designation. **Ernennungsurkunde,** *f.* letter of appointment.

erneuen [ɛrˈnɔyən], **1.** *v.t.* renew, resume, revive. **2.** *v.r.* be renewed, revive, be revived.

erneuern [ɛrˈnɔyərn], **1.** *v.t.* renew, replace (*damaged part*), mend, repair (*damaged article*), restore, renovate (*building, painting etc.*), touch up (*paintwork etc.*), resurface (*road*), recharge (*battery*), change (*oil in a car*), renew (*passport etc.*, (*Comm.*) *a bill,* (*fig.*) *old friendship, one's efforts*), resume (*friendship, efforts*). **2.** *v.r.* be renewed, revive, be revived. **Erneuerung,** *f.* renewal, replacement, repair, restoration, renovation, revival, resumption.

erneut [ɛrˈnɔyt], **1.** *adj.* renewed, new, fresh. **2.** *adv.* anew, afresh, (once) again, once more. *See* **erneuen.**

erniedrigen [ɛrˈniːdrɪɡən], **1.** *v.t.* 1. lower, reduce, bring down, (*coll.*) cut (*prices*); (*Mus.*) flatten (*a note*); 2. bring low, humble, humiliate, degrade, debase, abase (*a p.*). **2.** *v.r.* lower *or* demean *or* degrade *or* debase *or* abase o.s., (*coll.*) stoop. **erniedrigend,** *adj.* degrading, humiliating. **Erniedrigung,** *f.* lowering, reduction (*of price*); humiliation, degradation, abasement. **Erniedrigungszeichen,** *n.* (*Mus.*) flat (♭).

1**Ernst** [ɛrnst], *m.* Ernest.

2**Ernst,** *m.* earnestness, seriousness, serious-mindedness, gravity (*of a p.*); seriousness, gravity, importance, weightiness (*of a matter*); severity, gravity (*of illness etc.*); ***ist es Ihr –?*** are you serious *or* in earnest? ***im –, in allem*** or ***vollem –e, allen –es,*** in downright *or* sober earnest, in all seriousness, quite seriously; ***das ist nicht Ihr –?*** you don't (really) mean that? surely you are joking? ***mit etwas – machen,*** put s.th. into effect; ***jetzt wird es (blutiger) –,*** now matters are getting serious *or* critical.

ernst, *adj.* earnest, serious, serious-minded (*of a p.*); serious, grave, solemn (*mood etc.*); serious, grave, important, weighty (*matter*); serious, grave, severe, dangerous (*illness*); ***–e Absichten haben,*** have serious *or* (*with a woman*) honourable intentions; ***eine –e Mahnung,*** a solemn warning; ***mit –er Miene,*** with a straight face; ***–e Musik,*** serious music; ***–e Nachrichten,*** grave news.

Ernstfall [ˈɛrnstfal], *m.* ***im –,*** in case of emergency. **ernstgemeint,** *adj.* serious, earnest, sincerely meant, genuine. **ernsthaft, 1.** *adj.* serious (-minded), earnest, solemn, grave. **2.** *adv.* seriously, earnestly, solemnly, gravely, in earnest, in all seriousness. **Ernsthaftigkeit,** *f.* earnestness, seriousness, gravity, solemnity. **ernstlich, 1.** *adj.* serious, grave (*of a th.*). **2.** *adv.* seriously, in earnest.

Ernte [ˈɛrntə], *f.* harvest, crop(s); vintage; harvest time *or* season; ***– auf dem Halm,*** standing crop; (*coll.*) ***ihm ist die – verhagelt,*** his hopes are blighted; (*fig.*) ***eine reiche*** or ***fruchtbare –,*** a heavy toll; (*Prov.*) ***ohne Saat keine –,*** as ye have sown so shall ye reap. **Ernte|arbeit,** *f.* harvesting. **–(dank)-fest,** *n.* harvest thanksgiving (festival), harvest-home, (*Am.*) Thanksgiving Day. **–maschine,** *f.* harvester, reaping machine. **–monat, –mond,** *m.* (*Poet.*) August.

ernten [ˈɛrntən], *v.t.* harvest, gather (in), reap (*also fig.*), pick (*fruit*), (*fig.*) earn, gain, win.

Ernte|segen, *m.* (*Poet.*) rich harvest. **–urlaub,** *m.* (*Mil.*) agricultural leave. **–wetter,** *n.* good harvest-weather. **–zeit,** *f.* harvest-time.

Ernting [ˈɛrntɪŋ], *m.* (*Poet.*) August.

ernüchtern [ɛrˈnyçtərn], **1.** *v.t.* 1. sober (down), bring (*s.o.*) to his senses; 2. disillusion, disenchant. **2.** *v.r.* 1. become sober, sober up *or* down, come to one's senses; 2. be disillusioned *or* disenchanted. **Ernüchterung,** *f.* disillusionment, disenchantment.

Eroberer [ɛrˈʔoːbərər], *m.* conqueror. **erobern,** *v.t.* conquer; take, capture (*fortress*); (*coll.*) win, captivate (*hearts etc.*). **Eroberung,** *f.* conquest; capture (*of fortress*), (*coll.*) captivation (*of hearts*); (*coll.*) ***eine – machen,*** make a conquest.

eröffnen [ɛrˈʔœfnən], **1.** *v.t.* 1. (break) open, unseal (*tomb, letter etc.*); open (up), inaugurate (*new enterprise*), (*fig.*) open up (*prospects etc.*), open, start, begin (*activity*); 2. (*Dat.*) disclose *or* make known *or* reveal to, tell, inform, notify. **2.** *v.i.* open, start (*as theatre season*). **3.** *v.r.* open one's heart (*Dat.*, to). **Eröffnung,** *f.* 1. opening, inauguration; 2. disclosure, communication, announcement. **Eröffnungs|feier,** *f.* opening *or* inauguration ceremony. **–kurs,** *m.* (*St. Exch.*) opening price. **–periode,** *f.* (*Med.*) first stage of labour. **–rede,** *f.* opening address, inaugural speech.

erörtern [ɛrˈʔœrtərn], *v.t.* discuss, argue, consider, debate; treat, deal with. **Erörterung,** *f.* discussion, debate, consideration, examination, ventilation (*of views*); *zur – kommen,* come up for discussion.

Erotik [e'ro:tɪk], *f.* eroticism, (*coll.*) sexiness. **erotisch,** *adj.* erotic, (*coll.*) sexy.

Erpel ['ɛrpəl], *m.* (*Orn.*) drake.

erpicht [ɛr'pɪçt], *adj.* intent, bent, set, (*coll.*) keen (*auf* (*Acc.*), on), eager (for), looking forward (to).

erpressen [ɛr'prɛsən], *v.t.* blackmail (*a p.*); – *von ihm,* blackmail him for (*s.th.*), extort *or* exact (*s.th.*) from him. **Erpresser,** *m.* blackmailer, extortioner. **erpresserisch,** *adj.* extortionary (*methods*), (*fig.*) extortionate, exorbitant (*price*). **Erpressung,** *f.* blackmail, extortion; exaction.

erproben [ɛr'pro:bən], *v.t.* try, test, prove, put to the test, (*coll.*) try out. **erprobt,** *adj.* proved, proven, (well-)tried, approved; (old-)established, reliable. **Erprobtheit,** *f.* reliability. **Erprobung,** *f.* test, trial. **Erprobungs|flieger,** *m.* (*Av.*) test pilot. **-flug,** *m.* test *or* trial flight. **-gelände,** *n.* proving ground, test range.

erquicken [ɛr'kvɪkən], *v.t.* revive, refresh. **erquickend,** *adj.* refreshing. **erquicklich,** *adj.* refreshing, uplifting, edifying. **Erquickung,** *f.* refreshment.

erraffen [ɛr'rafən], *v.t.* snatch, grab, seize; *ein Vermögen –,* make money hand over fist, get rich quick.

erraten [ɛr'ra:tən], *irr.v.t.* solve (*a riddle*), guess, divine; *ich errate es nicht,* I give (it) up.

erratisch [ɛ'ra:tɪʃ], *adj.* (*Geol.*) erratic.

errechnen [ɛr'rɛçnən], *v.t.* work *or* find out, calculate, compute, (*coll.*) arrive at. **Errechnung,** *f.* calculation, computation.

erregbar [ɛr're:kba:r], *adj.* excitable, irritable. **Erregbarkeit,** *f.* excitability, irritability, (*Med.*) erethism.

erregen [ɛr're:gən], **1.** *v.t.* 1. excite, provoke, arouse, call forth, cause, create, produce, stir up (*emotional response*); 2. rouse, agitate, stir up (*a p.*); 3. (*Physiol.*) excite, stimulate (*nerve etc.*); 4. (*Elec.*) excite *magnetic field*), energize (*dynamo etc.*). **2.** *v.r.* get *or* grow *or* become excited *or* agitated (*über* (*Acc.*), about *or* over). **erregend,** *adj.* exciting, sensational; (*Med.*) *-es Mittel,* stimulant, excitant; *-es Moment,* starting point of the dramatic action. **-erregend,** *adj.suff.* causing, creating, arousing, provoking, *e.g. aufsehen–,* causing a stir; -ing, *e.g. furcht–,* terrifying; (*Med.*) -genic, *e.g. krankheits–,* pathogenic.

Erreger [ɛr're:gər], *m.* 1. instigator; 2. (*Elec.*) exciter; (*Med.*) causal *or* exciting *or* pathogenic agent, pathogenic organism, pathogen. **Erreger|feld,** *n.* (*Elec.*) exciter *or* exciting field. **-spule,** *f.* exciter *or* field coil. **-strom,** *m.* field *or* induction current. **-wicklung,** *f.* induction *or* field winding.

erregt [ɛr're:kt], *adj.* excited, agitated, heated. **Erregtheit,** *f.* excitement, agitation.

Erregung [ɛr're:guŋ], *f.* (state of) excitement *or* agitation, commotion; stimulation, excitation, provocation, generation (of). **Erregungs|mittel,** *n.* (*Med.*) stimulant, excitant. **-zustand,** *m.* state of (*esp.* sexual) excitement.

erreichbar [ɛr'raɪçba:r], *adj.* attainable, accessible, available, within reach *or* range *or* distance; *telephonisch – sein,* be on the telephone; *nicht –,* out of reach.

erreichen [ɛr'raɪçən], *v.t.* reach; attain, obtain, achieve, gain (*one's end*), succeed in getting; reach, arrive at, get to (*destination*); fetch (*a price, also* (*Naut.*) *the shore, a harbour*), catch (*bus, train*), get in touch with (*a p.*), equal (*a record*); (*bei ihm*) prevail upon, induce, succeed in persuading (him), (*coll.*) get somewhere with (him); *bei ihm ist alles zu –,* you can do anything with him, you can get anything out of him; *wie kann man Sie –?* how can I get in touch with you? how can you be reached *or* got at? *ich bin telephonisch zu –,* I am on the phone, you can get (in touch with) me on the phone; *nichts –,* have no success, achieve nothing, come away empty-handed. **Erreichung,** *f.* reaching; attainment, achievement.

erretten [ɛr'rɛtən], *v.t.* save, rescue, (*Theol.*) redeem' deliver. **Erretter,** *m.* (*Theol.*) Saviour, Redeemer. **Errettung,** *f.* rescue, (*Theol.*) salvation, redemption, deliverance.

errichten [ɛr'rɪçtən], *v.t.* put *or* set up, raise, erect (*mast etc.*); erect, build, construct (*a tower etc.*); found, establish, set up; (*Geom.*) *eine Senkrechte –,* erect a perpendicular. **Errichtung,** *f.* erection, construction, establishment, foundation.

erringen [ɛr'rɪŋən], *irr.v.t.* win, gain, attain, acquire, achieve. **Erringung,** *f.* attainment, acquisition, achievement.

erröten [ɛr'rø:tən], *v.i.* (*aux.* s.) blush, go red, redden; – *machen,* make (*s.o.*) blush. **Erröten,** *n.* blush, blushing.

Errungenschaft [ɛr'ruŋənʃaft], *f.* achievement, attainment, acquirement; acquisition, (*Law*) acquest. *See* **erringen.**

ersättigen [ɛr'zɛtɪgən], *v.t.* (*obs.*) *see* **sättigen. ersättlich,** *adj.* (*obs.*) satiable.

Ersatz [ɛr'zats], *m.* (**-es,** *no pl.*) 1. replacement, substitution; – *von B. durch M.,* replacement of B. by *or* with M., substitution of M. for B.; 2. compensation, indemnification (*for loss*), indemnity, damages, compensation, restitution; – *fordern,* claim damages; *ihm – geben,* indemnify him; – *leisten,* make restitution *or* amends; 3. (*a p.*) substitute, replacement, (*Spt.*) reserve, (*coll.*) stand-in; (*a th.*) replacement, spare, (*coll.*) stand-by; (*Mil.*) intake, draft, replacements.

Ersatz–, *pref.* alternative . . ., substitute . . ., replacement . . ., spare . . .; (*Mil.*) recruiting . . .. **-ersatz,** *m. suff.* -substitute. **Ersatz|anspruch,** *m.* claim for indemnity *or* damages. **-bataillon,** *n.* (*Mil.*) depot battalion. **-batterie,** *f.* spare battery, refill (*for torch*). **-behörde,** *f.* recruiting authority. **-berechtigung,** *f.* title to compensation. **-dienst,** *m.* alternative service (*for conscientious objectors*). **-freiheitsstrafe,** *f.* imprisonment in lieu of fine. **-geldstrafe,** *f.* fine in lieu of imprisonment. **-gewicht,** *n.* (*Chem.*) equivalent weight. **-glied,** *n.* artificial limb. **-heer,** *n.* army reserve. **-kasse,** *f.* recognized private sickness benefit. **-mann,** *m.* (*pl.* ⸚**er**) substitute, replacement, (*Spt.*) reserve. **-mannschaft,** *f.* reserve team; *pl.* (*Mil.*) replacements, reserves, drafts. **-mine,** *f.* spare lead, refill (*for pencil*). **-mittel,** *n.* substitute, surrogate, (*coll.*) makeshift. **-pferd,** *n.* remount. **-pflicht,** *f.* liability for damages, (manufacturer's) obligation to supply replacements. **-rad,** *n.* (*Motor.*) spare wheel. **-regiment,** *n.* training regiment. **-reifen,** *m.* (*Motor.*) spare tyre ((*Am.*) tire). **-reserve,** *f.* (*Mil.*) supplementary reserve. **-spieler,** *m.* (*Spt.*) reserve, (*Theat.*) understudy, (*Mus.*) substitute. **-stoff,** *m.* substitute, surrogate. **-stück, -teil,** *n.* spare (part), replacement. **-truppen,** *f.pl.* reserves, depot troops. **-truppenteil,** *m.* (*Mil.*) depot unit. **-wahl,** *f.* by-election. **-wesen,** *n.* (*Mil.*) recruitment. **-widerstand,** *m.* (*Elec.*) equivalent resistance. **-zahn,** *m.* second *or* permanent tooth.

ersaufen [ɛr'zaufən], *irr.v.i.* (*aux.* s.) (*of a p.*) be drowned, drown, (*of fields etc.*) be flooded *or* inundated *or* swamped *or* waterlogged.

ersäufen [ɛr'zɔyfən], *v.t.* drown; (*coll.*) *die Sorgen im Alkohol –,* drown one's sorrows in drink. **Ersäufung,** *f.* drowning.

erschaffen [ɛr'ʃafən], *irr.v.t.* (*of God*) create. **Erschaffer,** *m.* Creator. **Erschaffung,** *f.* creation.

erschallen [ɛr'ʃalən], *reg. & irr.v.i.* (*aux.* s.) resound, ring out, sound forth; – *lassen,* sound *or* spread abroad; sound (*trumpet*); *es erscholl ein Gerücht,* a rumour spread abroad.

erschaudern [ɛr'ʃaudərn], *v.i.* (*aux.* s.) tremble, shudder, be seized with horror.

erschauen [ɛr'ʃauən], *v.t.* (*Poet.*) see, behold.

erschauern [ɛr'ʃauərn], *v.i.* (*aux.* s.) vibrate, quiver, thrill (with emotion); – *lassen,* thrill, grip.

erscheinen [ɛr'ʃaɪnən], *irr.v.i.* (*aux.* s.) 1. appear, show itself, become visible; make (*its*) appearance, come out (*as flower, a rash*); be published, come out (*of a book*); appear, make (*one's*) appearance (*as an actor*); appear, occur (*of phenomena*); *– lassen*, bring out, publish; *soeben erschienen*, just published; 2. appear, seem. **Erscheinen,** *n.* appearance; publication, issue. **Erscheinung,** *f.* occurrence, manifestation, visitation; feature, symptom, (*Phil.*) phenomenon; apparition, vision, spectre, ghost; *in – treten*, appear, become visible *or* evident, (*coll.*) show up, (*of a p.*) show o.s., (*of effect etc.*) come to light, make (itself *etc.*) felt; *äußere –*, outward appearance, aspect, look, bearing, presence; *eine glänzende – sein*, cut a fine figure; *das Fest der – Christi*, Epiphany. **Erscheinungs|form,** *f.* outward manifestation; (*Phil.*) hypostasis; (*Biol.*) phenotype. **–lehre,** *f.* (*Phil.*) phenomenology. **–welt,** *f.* tangible *or* physical world.

erschießen [ɛr'ʃi:sən], *irr.v.t.* shoot (dead); *erschossen werden*, be shot; (*coll.*) *erschossen sein*, be done-up *or* dead-beat *or* whacked. **Erschießen,** *n. Tod durch –*, death by shooting; (*Artil.*) *– der Entfernung*, ranging fire. **Erschießung,** *f.* shooting, execution (by firing squad). **Erschießungskommando,** *n.* firing-squad.

erschlaffen [ɛr'ʃlafən], *v.i.* (*aux.* s.) become slack *or* relaxed, lose tone (*as muscle*), become tired *or* sluggish (*as a p.*), languish, flag, abate, (*coll.*) fall off (*as enthusiasm*). **Erschlaffer,** *m.* (*Anat.*) laxator (*muscle*). **Erschlaffung,** *f.* slackness, sluggishness, debility, (*Med.*) enervation, atony; (*coll.*) *bis zur –*, to the last gasp.

erschlagen [ɛr'ʃla:gən], **1.** *irr.v.t.* 1. kill, strike dead, slay; *vom Blitz –*, struck by lightning; 2. (*obs.*) beat down, flatten (*crops etc.*). **2.** *adj.* (*coll.*) dead-beat, done-up, worn out, dog-tired; thunderstruck, dumbfounded, struck dumb, bowled over.

erschleichen [ɛr'ʃlaɪçən], *irr.v.t.* obtain surreptitiously *or* by insidious means *or* by trickery *or* (*coll.*) by hook or by crook, obtain on the 'black market'.

erschließen [ɛr'ʃli:sən], *irr.v.t.* 1. open (*one's heart*), open up (*new markets*), make accessible, exploit, develop, work (*a mine etc.*); 2. conjecture, deduce, infer, conclude (*aus*, from). **Erschließung,** *f.* 1. opening up, exploitation, development; 2. deduction.

erschlug [ɛr'ʃlu:k], **erschlüge** [–'ʃly:gə], *see* **erschlagen.**

erschmeicheln [ɛr'ʃmaɪçəln], *v.t.* obtain by flattery, (*von*, from), wheedle, cajole (out of).

erscholl [ɛr'ʃɔl], **erschölle** [ɛr'ʃœlə], **erschollen,** *see* **erschallen.**

erschöpfen [ɛr'ʃœpfən], *v.t.* exhaust, deplete, consume, use up, (*coll.*) run out of (*supplies etc.*); exhaust, tire *or* wear out (*a p.*). **erschöpfend,** *adj.* exhaustive. **erschöpft,** *adj.* spent, exhausted, at an end, (*coll.*) run out (*of supplies etc.*); exhausted, tired *or* worn out. **Erschöpftheit,** *f.* (state of) exhaustion, prostration; lassitude. **Erschöpfung,** *f.* exhaustion, depletion; *see also* **Erschöpftheit.**

erschossen [ɛr'ʃɔsən], *see* **erschießen.**

erschrak [ɛr'ʃra:k], **erschräke** [–'ʃrɛ:kə], *see* **erschrecken, 1.**

erschrecken [ɛr'ʃrɛkən], **1.** *irr.v.i.* (*aux.* s.) be frightened *or* scared *or* alarmed *or* terrified *or* startled (*über* (*Acc.*), at *or* by), take fright (*über* (*Acc.*), at), be frightened *or* scared (*vor* (*Dat.*), by). **2.** *reg.v.t.* frighten, scare, startle, alarm, give (*s.o.*) a shock. **3.** *reg.v.r. See* **1. Erschrecken,** *n.* fright, alarm, terror, scare. **erschreckend,** *adj.* frightening, alarming, terrifying; dreadful, terrible, appalling, (*coll.*) awful. **erschrecklich,** *adj.* (*Poet.*) *see* **erschreckend. Erschrecknis,** *n.* **(-ses,** *pl.* **-se)** (*Poet.*) *see* **Erschrecken. erschreckt,** *adj.* terrified, startled.

erschrickst [ɛr'ʃrɪkst], **erschrickt,** *see* **erschrecken.**

erschrocken [ɛr'ʃrɔkən], *adj.* frightened, scared, alarmed, terrified; horrified, appalled; *see* **erschrecken, 1. Erschrockenheit,** *f.* terror, (state of) fright *or* alarm, frightened *or* terrified state; horrified state of mind.

erschüttern [ɛr'ʃytərn], *v.t.* shake, convulse, set quivering, make (*s.th.*) shake *or* shudder *or* tremble; (*fig.*) disturb, upset, unsettle, have a disturbing *or* unsettling effect on, shake (*one's faith etc.*); (*fig.*) shake (*a p.*) up, give (*a p.*) a shaking *or* a shock; unnerve, upset, disturb (*a p.*); (*coll.*) *er läßt sich durch nichts –*, nothing ever worries *or* ruffles him. **erschütternd,** *adj.* disturbing, deeply moving. **Erschütterung,** *f.* tremor, shock, vibration, jolt, (*Med.*) concussion; (*fig.*) shock, emotional upset. **erschütterungsfest,** *adj.* shock-proof. **Erschütterungs|gebiet,** *n.* area of seismic disturbance. **–messer,** *m. See* **–zeiger. –reiz,** *m.* contact stimulus. **–welle,** *f.* earth tremor. **–zeiger,** *m.* seismograph.

erschweren [ɛr'ʃve:rən], *v.t.* make (more) difficult, hinder, impede; aggravate (*crime*). **Erschwerung,** *f.* added difficulty, hindrance, impediment; aggravation.

erschwingen [ɛr'ʃvɪŋən], *irr.v.t.* 1. afford, manage (to pay); 2. (*Poet.*) rise to (*position etc.*), attain (*wealth etc.*). **erschwinglich,** *adj.* within one's means; reasonable (*price*).

ersehen [ɛr'ze:ən], *irr.v.t.* 1. learn, understand, gather, see (*aus*, from); *hieraus ist zu –, hieraus läßt sich –*, this indicates *or* shows (clearly), this makes clear; 2. *sich* (*Dat.*) *etwas –*, choose *or* select s.th. for o.s.; 3. (*obs.*) (*also v.i.*) perceive, behold, recognize, descry.

ersehnen [ɛr'zə:nən], *v.t.* long *or* yearn for, desire.

ersetzbar [ɛr'zɛtsba:r], *adj. See* **ersetzlich.**

ersetzen [ɛr'zɛtsən], *v.t.* replace, take *or* fill the place of, (serve as a) substitute for, do duty for; make up for, make good (*a loss*); compensate for, make amends for (*damage*); reimburse, refund (*expenses*); provide *or* supply a replacement for, replace (*s.th. lost or damaged*); *B. durch* (*occ. mit*) *M. –*, replace B. by M., substitute M. for B. **ersetzlich,** *adj.* replaceable; (*Poet.*) reparable. **Ersetzung,** *f. See* **Ersatz.**

ersichtlich [ɛr'zɪçtlɪç], *adj.* evident, apparent, obvious, manifest; *hieraus ist –*, this shows, this makes clear *or* obvious.

ersinnen [ɛr'zɪnən], *irr.v.t.* think out, conceive, devise, invent, (*coll.*) think up.

ersisch ['ɛrzɪʃ], *adj.* Erse.

ersitzen [ɛr'zɪtsən], *irr.v.t.* (*Law*) acquire by (positive) prescription *or* by usucaption; (*coll.*) *er hat sich die Beförderung einfach ersessen*, he obtained promotion solely by virtue of his long service. **Ersitzung,** *f.* (*Law*) (positive) prescriptive right, usucaption.

ersonnen [ɛr'zɔnən], *see* **ersinnen.**

erspähen [ɛr'ʃpɛ:ən], *v.t.* (*Poet.*) espy, descry.

ersparen [ɛr'ʃpa:rən], *v.t.* save (*time*), save (up) (*money*); *du hättest dir die Mühe – können*, you might have saved *or* spared yourself the trouble; you need not have bothered; *mir bleibt nichts erspart*, I am spared nothing; *das Weitere kannst du dir –*, that's enough, you need say no more. **Ersparnis,** *f.* (-, *pl.* **-se)** saving, (*usu. pl. except in compounds*) savings.

ersprießen [ɛr'ʃpri:sən], *irr.v.i.* (*aux.* s.) 1. (*obs.*) be profitable *or* fruitful *or* beneficial (*Dat.*, for); 2. (*coll.*) arise, follow, result (*aus*, from), come (of). **ersprießlich,** *adj.* fruitful, profitable, beneficial; salutary. **Ersprießlichkeit,** *f.* benefit, advantage, profitableness.

erst [e:rst], **1.** *adj. See* **erste(r), erste, erste(s). 2.** *adv.* 1. at first, first (of all); (*Prov.*) *– wägen dann wagen*, look before you leap; (*Prov.*) *– die Arbeit dann das Spiel*, business before pleasure; *es muß sich – noch zeigen*, it remains to be seen; 2. not until, only; *– als* or *wenn*, only when; *dann –*, only then; *eben –*, just now, only just; 3. (only) just; *wäre ich nur – da!* if only I were there! 4. (*emotive part.*) really, just; *wenn etwas verboten wird, geschieht es – recht*, if a thing is forbidden, it is done all the more; *nun – recht*, now more than ever (before); *– recht nicht*, less than ever, still *or* even less; *das macht es – recht schlimm*, that makes it all the worse.

erstarken [ɛr'ʃtarkən], *v.i.* (*aux.* s.) grow strong *or* stronger, gain *or* gather strength.

erstarren [ɛr'ʃtarən], **1.** *v.i.* (*aux.* s.) (*of fluid*) congeal, solidify, consolidate, become solid, set, harden; (*of a limb etc.*) go stiff, stiffen, become rigid; go numb; (*fig.*) freeze (*as blood, a smile*); ***vor Entsetzen –***, be petrified *or* paralysed with fear. **2.** *v.t.* (*obs.*) benumb. **erstarrt,** *adj.* stiff, rigid; (*fig.*) stiff, numb (***vor*** (*Dat.*), with); rigid, cast-iron, fossilized (*as traditions*). **Erstarrtheit,** *f.* stiffness, rigidity; numbness. **Erstarrung,** *f.* numbness, stiffness, rigidity; solidification, coagulation; rigid formalization. **Erstarrungs|gestein,** *n.* igneous *or* pyrogenic rock. **–punkt,** *m.* freezing *or* solidification point. **–wärme,** *f.* heat evolved by solidification. **–zustand,** *m.* congealed *or* solidified state; (state of) rigidity (*of a corpse*).

erstatten [ɛr'ʃtatən], *v.t.* 1. refund, reimburse, repay (*money*); (*obs.*) return, restore, make restitution of, make good (*s.th. taken*); 2. ***Bericht –***, report, give *or* make a report. **Erstattung,** *f.* 1. refunding, reimbursement, restitution; 2. delivery (*of a report*).

Erstaufführung ['e:rstˀauffy:ruŋ], *f.* (*Theat.*) first performance, première, first night.

erstaunen [ɛr'ʃtaunən], **1.** *v.i.* (*aux.* s.) (*occ. v.r.*) be astonished *or* surprised *or* amazed *or* astounded, marvel (***über*** (*Acc.*), at). **2.** *v.t.* astonish, surprise, amaze, astound. **Erstaunen,** *n.* astonishment, amazement, surprise; ***in – (ver)setzen,*** astonish, amaze, fill with amazement *or* surprise. **erstaunend,** *adj.* astonishing. **erstaunens|wert, –würdig,** *adj.* astounding, amazing, astonishing. **erstaunlich,** *adj.* surprising, astonishing, amazing, (*coll.*) remarkable, unbelievable, stupendous, prodigious.

Erst|ausgabe, *f.*, **–druck,** *m.* first edition.

erste ['e:rstə], *adj. See* **erste(r).**

erstechen [ɛr'ʃtɛçən], *irr.v.t.* stab to death.

erstehen [ɛr'ʃte:ən], **1.** *irr.v.i.* (*aux.* s.) 1. (*Poet.*) rise from the dead; ***Christ ist erstanden,*** Christ is arisen; 2. arise, spring up (*as towns etc.*); 3. arise, result (***aus,*** from); ***es – mir nichts als Unannehmlichkeiten daraus,*** it brings me nothing but unpleasantness. **2.** *irr.v.t.* 1. buy, acquire, pick up (*as at an auction*); 2. (*obs.*) suffer, endure, (*coll.*) go *or* get through. **Ersteher,** *m.* purchaser (*at an auction*).

ersteigbar [ɛr'ʃtaɪkba:r], *adj.* climbable.

ersteigen [ɛr'ʃtaɪgən], *v.t.* climb, scale, ascend (*mountain*), mount (*ladder*). **Ersteigung,** *f.* ascent.

erstellen [ɛr'ʃtɛlən], *v.t.* make available.

erstens ['e:rstəns], *adv.* first(ly), in the first place.

erste(r) ['e:rstə(r)], *m.*, **erste,** *f.*, **erste(s),** *n.*, *num.adj.* first; ***der, die*** or ***das –e beste,*** the first (that comes) to hand; ***fürs –e,*** for now, for the time being, for the moment; (*at auctions*) ***zum –en, zum zweiten, zum dritten,*** going, going, gone; ***–e Etage,*** first floor, (*Am.*) second storey; (*Comm.*) ***–e Güte,*** prime *or* top quality; ***–e Klasse,*** (*Railw.*) first class (*also of hotels*); (*elementary school*) first class *or* form *or* (*Am.*) grade; (*secondary school*) sixth form, (*Am.*) twelfth grade; (*Comm.*) ***–er Kurs,*** opening price; ***in –er Linie,*** above all, first and foremost, in the first place; ***–er Preis,*** see ***–er Kurs***; (*Geom.*) ***–e Projektion,*** horizontal projection; (*Theat.*) ***–er Rang,*** dress circle; ***–en Ranges,*** outstanding, first-rate, (*coll.*) top; ***an –er Stelle,*** as a first consideration, first and foremost; (*Comm.*) ***–e Wahl,*** see ***–e Güte***; ***in der –en Zeit,*** in the early days, at first.

ersterben [ɛr'ʃtɛrbən], *irr.v.i.* (*aux.* s.) 1. (*Poet.*) die (away), fade, vanish (*of sound, a smile, feelings*); ***das Wort erstarb auf seinen Lippen,*** the word died on his lips; 2. (*obs.*) expire, sink into death (*of a p.*), wither away (*of plants*), grow numb *or* insensible, mortify (*as limb etc.*); ***vor Ehrfurcht*** (*fast*) *–*, be awestruck, stand rooted to the spot in awe.

erstere(r) ['e:rstərə(r)], *m.*, **erstere,** *f.*, **erstere(s),** *n., adj.* (the) former.

erstgeboren ['e:rstgəbo:rən], *adj.* first-born.

Erstgeburt, *f.* 1. first-born (child); 2. primogeniture; birthright.

erstgenannt ['e:rstgənant], *adj.* first-mentioned *or* -named.

ersticken [ɛr'ʃtɪkən], **1.** *v.t.* suffocate, asphyxiate, choke, smother; stifle, suppress; ***im Keime –***, nip in the bud; ***ein ersticktes Lachen,*** strangled *or* smothered *or* suppressed laughter. **2.** *v.i.* (*aux.* s.) choke, suffocate, stifle (*of a p.*); be stifled *or* choked *or* suffocated (*of plants*); (*coll.*) ***in der Arbeit –***, be snowed under with work, be up to one's eyes in work. **Ersticken,** *n. See* **Erstickung**; ***zum – heiß,*** stiflingly hot; ***zum – voll,*** crammed to suffocation. **erstickend,** *adj.* stifling (*heat*); (*Min.*) ***–e Wetter*** (*pl.*), choke-damp; (*Mil.*) ***–er Kampfstoff,*** asphyxiating gas. **Erstickung,** *f.* suffocation, asphyxiation, asphyxia. **Erstickungstod,** *m.* death from suffocation, asphyxiation.

erstklassig ['e:rstklasɪç], *adj.* first-class, first-rate; (*Comm.*) prime, gilt-edged.

erstlich ['e:rstlɪç], *adv.* first(ly), in the first place.

Erstling ['e:rstlɪŋ], *m.* (**-(e)s,** *pl.* **-e**) (*Poet.*) first-born (child); first fruit; firstling; *pl.* (*Hist.*) annates. **Erstlings–,** *pref.* first, beginner's. **Erstlings|ausstattung,** *f.* layette. **–rede,** *f.* (*Parl.*) maiden speech.

erstmalig ['e:rstma:lɪç], **1.** *adj.* first. **2.** *or* **erstmals,** *adv.* (for) the first time.

Erst|meldung, *f.* exclusive news, (*coll.*) scoop. **–milch,** *f.* colostrum; beestings.

erstrahlen [ɛr'ʃtra:lən], *v.i.* shine forth, light up.

erst|rangig, *adj. See* **–klassig.**

erstreben [ɛr'ʃtre:bən], *v.t.* strive for *or* after, aspire to, seek *or* aim to bring about; ***so wird erstrebt,*** the aim is. **erstrebenswert,** *adj.* desirable, worth striving for.

erstrecken [ɛr'ʃtrɛkən], *v.r.* extend, stretch, run, reach (***auf*** (*Acc.*), ***bis an*** or ***auf*** (*Acc.*), ***bis zu etc.,*** to); (*fig.*) ***sich – auf*** (*Acc.*), extend *or* apply to, deal *or* be concerned with, comprise, include, embrace, cover. **Erstreckung,** *f.* extent, extension.

erstürmen [ɛr'ʃtyrmən], *v.t.* storm, take by storm *or* assault.

ersuchen [ɛr'zu:xən], *v.t.* ask, request. **Ersuchen,** *n.*, **Ersuchung,** *f.* request, entreaty.

ertappen [ɛr'tapən], *v.t.* catch (***bei,*** in the act of), catch unawares, surprise; ***auf frischer Tat –***, catch red-handed *or* in the act.

erteilen [ɛr'taɪlən], *v.t.* (***ihm etwas***) give, grant (*permission*), impart (*information*), give, issue (*orders*); ***Antwort –***, (give a) reply (to); ***Auskunft –***, inform (*a p.*), give information (to); ***Lob –***, praise (*a p.*), give praise (to); ***Unterricht –***, teach, instruct (*a p.*), give lessons (to); ***Vollmacht –***, authorize, empower (*a p.*), give authority (to); ***die Absolution*** (***Sakramente***) *–*, administer absolution (the sacrament) (to); ***ein Patent –***, grant a patent (to); ***Prokura –***, confer powers of attorney (on). **Erteilung,** *f.* bestowal, grant; publication (*of an order*); administration (*of sacrament etc.*).

ertönen [ɛr'tø:nən], *v.i.* (*aux.* s.) sound, resound, ring out, be heard; ***– lassen,*** sound; raise (*the voice*).

ertöten [ɛr'tø:tən], *v.t.* 1. deaden, extinguish, smother, stifle; 2. mortify (*the flesh*).

Ertrag [ɛr'tra:k], *m.* (**-(e)s,** *pl.* **⸚e**) produce, yield, fruits, output; proceeds, profit, return(s), revenue; ***einen – geben, – bringen,*** yield profit, bring in returns.

ertragen [ɛr'tra:gən], *irr.v.t.* bear, suffer, tolerate, endure, (*coll.*) stand, stick, put up with; ***nicht zu – sein, sich nicht – lassen,*** not to be borne *or* endured, be unbearable *or* unendurable *or* intolerable *or* insupportable *or* beyond endurance. **ertragfähig,** *adj.* capable of yielding profit. **Ertragfähigkeit,** *f.* earning capacity.

erträglich [ɛr'trɛ:klɪç], *adj.* bearable, tolerable, endurable, supportable; (*coll.*) tolerable, passable.

ertraglos [ɛr'tra:klo:s], *adj.* unprofitable, unproductive, non-productive.

Erträgnis [ɛr'trɛ:knɪs], *n.* (**-ses,** *pl.* **-se**) *see* **Ertrag. erträgnisreich,** *adj. See* **ertragreich.**

ertragreich [ɛr'tra:kraɪç], *adj.* profitable, productive, fruitful; lucrative, paying.

ertränken [ɛr'trɛŋkən], *v.t.* drown; ***den Kummer im Wein –,*** drown one's misery in wine.

erträumen [ɛr'trɔymən], *v.t.* dream of *or* about; imagine.

ertrinken [ɛr'trɪŋkən], *irr.v.i.* (*aux.* s.) drown, be drowned; ***der (die) Ertrinkende,*** drowning p.; ***der (die) Ertrunkene,*** drowned p.

ertrotzen [ɛr'trɔtsən], *v.t.* (***sich*** (*Dat.*)) ***etwas –,*** extort (*Dat.*, from), obtain by insolence *or* obstinacy *or* stubbornness *or* defiance *etc.*

ertüchtigen [ɛr'tyçtɪgən], **1.** *v.t.* make fit *or* tough *or* vigorous; train, harden, toughen. **2.** *v.r.* toughen *or* harden o.s., become tough *or* fit *or* hardened. **Ertüchtigung,** *f.* training, attainment of physical fitness; ***körperliche –,*** physical training.

erübrigen [ɛr'y:brɪgən], **1.** *v.t.* save, lay *or* put by; spare; ***für dich kann ich eine Stunde –,*** I can spare an hour for you. **2.** *v.i.* remain, be left over; ***es erübrigt nur noch, zu bemerken,*** it only remains for me to say *or* add. **3.** *v.r.* be superfluous *or* unnecessary, be useless *or* pointless; ***es dürfte sich –,*** it is hardly necessary.

eruieren [eru'i:rən], *v.t.* elicit (*facts*); (*Austr.*) establish the identity of.

erwachen [ɛr'vaxən], *v.i.* (*aux.* s.) awake, awaken, wake (up); (*fig.*) be roused *or* awakened, stir (*as memories, feelings etc.*). **Erwachen,** *n.* awakening; ***beim –,*** on waking.

erwachsen [ɛr'vaksən], **1.** *irr.v.i.* (*aux.* s.) 1. grow up (*of a p.*), develop, grow (***aus,*** out of, from; ***zu,*** into); 2. (*fig.*) result, arise, spring, proceed, accrue (***aus,*** from); (*of expenses etc.*) be incurred (*Dat.*, by), (*of advantages*) accrue (to). **2.** *adj.* grown up; ***der (die) Erwachsene,*** adult, grown-up. **Erwachsenenbildung,** *f.* adult education.

erwägen [ɛr'vɛ:gən], *irr.* (*occ. reg.*) *v.t.* consider, weigh, ponder, reflect *or* deliberate on, think over, turn over in one's mind. **erwägenswert,** *adj.* worth thinking about *or* considering *or* consideration, worthy of consideration. **Erwägung,** *f.* consideration, reflection, deliberation; ***wenn man alles in – zieht,*** taking all things into consideration *or* account, all things considered; ***in der –, daß,*** in consideration *or* view of the fact that.

erwählen [ɛr'vɛ:lən], *v.t.* choose (***zu,*** for), elect (as). **erwählt,** *adj.* chosen, elected; (*Theol.*) ***die Erwählten,*** the chosen *or* elect. **Erwählung,** *f.* choice, election.

erwähnen [ɛr'vɛ:nən], *v.t.* (*obs. v.i.* (*Gen.*)) mention, make mention of, refer to, make reference to; ***es möge hinreichen zu –,*** suffice it to say; ***oben erwähnt,*** mentioned above, aforesaid, aforementioned. **erwähnenswert,** *adj.* worth mentioning, worthy of mention. **Erwähnung,** *f.* mention; ***– tun*** (*Gen.*), make mention of, mention; (*Mil.*) ***– im Tagesbericht,*** mention in dispatches; ***ehrenvolle –,*** honourable mention.

erwärmen [ɛr'vɛrmən], **1.** *v.t.* 1. make warm, warm *or* heat (up), raise the temperature of (***auf*** (*Acc.*), to); 2. (*fig.*) arouse (*s.o.'s*) interest (***für,*** in) *or* sympathy *or* enthusiasm (for), get (*s.o.*) interested (in) *or* enthusiastic (for, about). **2.** *v.r.* 1. (*of a p.*) warm o.s. (*by the fire*), warm o.s. up (*with exercise*); (*of a th.*) warm up, get warm; 2. (*fig.*) take a lively interest (***für,*** in), become enthusiastic (over, about), (*coll.*) warm, take (to). **Erwärmung,** *f.* warming, rise in temperature. **Erwärmungskraft,** *f.* calorific power.

erwarten [ɛr'vartən], *v.t.* 1. expect, anticipate; ***ein Kind –,*** be expectant, be expecting a baby, (*coll.*) be expecting; ***das läßt sich kaum –,*** that is scarcely to be expected; 2. (*of a p.*) await, wait for; (*of a th.*) await, be waiting for, be in store for. **Erwarten,** *n.* ***über –,*** beyond (all) expectation; ***wider –,*** contrary to (all) expectation(s). **Erwartung,** *f.* expectation, anticipation; expectancy. **erwartungsvoll,** *adj.* expectant, full of hope.

erwecken [ɛr'vɛkən], *v.t.* 1. wake(n), awake(n), (a)rouse, wake up; ***vom Tode –,*** raise from the dead; 2. (*fig.*) arouse, awaken (*feelings, memories etc.*), stir up, excite (*feelings*), wake, call forth (*memories*); ***Hoffnung –,*** give rise to *or* raise hope; ***Vertrauen –,*** inspire confidence; ***den Anschein –,*** create the impression. **Erweckung,** *f.* awakening; ***religiöse –,*** religious awakening (*of a p.*), religious revival (*in a group*). **Erweckungs|bewegung,** *f.* (*Rel.*) revivalist movement. **-prediger,** *m.* revivalist.

erwehren [ɛr've:rən], *v.r.* (*Gen.*) 1. ward off, keep at bay, offer resistance to, resist; (*fig.*) put out of *or* banish from (*one's*) mind; ***sich nicht – können*** (*Gen.*), be helpless *or* defenceless against, not be able to resist; 2. refrain, keep (***des Lachens,*** from laughing); ***sie konnte sich der Tränen kaum –,*** she could scarcely hold *or* keep back *or* restrain her tears; ***sie konnte sich des Eindrucks nicht –,*** she couldn't help feeling, she couldn't avoid the impression.

erweichen [ɛr'vaɪçən], **1.** *v.t.* soften (*a th.*); (*fig.*) move, soften (*a p.*); ***sich – lassen,*** relent. **2.** *v.i.* soften, become *or* go soft. **erweichend,** *adj.* (*Med.*) emollient. **Erweichung,** *f.* softening. **Erweichungsmittel,** *n.* (*Med.*) emollient.

Erweis [ɛr'vaɪs], *m.* (**-es,** *pl.* **-e**) proof, demonstration.

erweisen [ɛr'vaɪzən], **1.** *irr.v.t.* 1. prove; establish *or* demonstrate (the proof of); 2. show, do, pay, render (*mercy, honour, favour etc.*) (*Dat.*, to); ***nur Gutes –,*** show nothing but kindness (*Dat.*, to). **2.** *irr.v.r.* show *or* prove o.s. (to be), turn out to be; ***er erwies sich als einen tüchtigen*** (or ***als ein tüchtiger) Geschäftsmann,*** he proved himself to be an excellent businessman; ***das Gerücht erwies sich als falsch,*** the report turned out to be false; ***sich dankbar –,*** show o.s. grateful, show one's gratitude; ***sich (als) nützlich –,*** prove to be useful. *See* **erwiesen.**

erweislich [ɛr'vaɪslɪç], *adj.* demonstrable, provable.

Erweisung [ɛr'vaɪzuŋ], *f.* establishment *or* demonstration (of the truth).

erweitern [ɛr'vaɪtərn], **1.** *v.t.* widen (*road etc.*), enlarge (*hole etc.*), expand, extend; dilate, distend; (*fig.*) broaden, amplify; ***seine Kenntnisse –,*** improve *or* extend *or* broaden one's knowledge; (*Math.*) ***einen Bruch –,*** reduce a fraction to higher terms. **2.** *v.r.* grow larger, enlarge, become enlarged; open out, become wider, widen; spread, expand; become dilated *or* distended. **Erweiterung,** *f.* widening, expansion, enlargement, extension; distension, dilation; (*Med.*) ***die – der Adern,*** aneurysm. **Erweiterungs|bau,** *m.* (*pl.* **-ten**) (building) extension. **-bohrer,** *m.* reamer, broaching bit. **-kleid,** *n.* maternity dress.

Erwerb [ɛr'vɛrp], *m.* (**-(e)s,** *pl.* **-e**) 1. acquisition, gain; 2. earnings, (earned) income; 3. livelihood, living. **erwerben,** *irr.v.t.* obtain, acquire; (*fig.*) gain, earn, win (*glory etc.*). **Erwerber,** *m.* acquirer, buyer, purchaser, (*Law*) transferee, vendee. **erwerbsam,** *adj.* industrious. **Erwerbsamkeit,** *f.* industry, industriousness. **erwerbsbeschränkt,** *adj.* partially disabled. **Erwerbsbeschränktheit,** *f.* partial disablement. **erwerbsfähig,** *adj.* capable of gainful employment. **Erwerbsfähigkeit,** *f.* earning capacity.

erwerbslos [ɛr'vɛrpslo:s], *adj.* unemployed, out of work, out of a job. **Erwerbslosen|fürsorge,** *f.* national assistance, unemployment relief. **-unterstützung,** *f.* unemployment benefit, (*coll.*) dole. **Erwerbslose(r),** *m., f.* unemployed p.; *pl.* the unemployed, the out of work.

Erwerbs|quelle, *f.* source of income, means of livelihood. **-sinn,** *m.* acquisitiveness; business acumen. **-steuer,** *f.* profit(s) tax. **erwerbstätig,** *adj.* gainfully employed. **Erwerbstätigkeit,** *f.* gainful employment. **erwerbsunfähig,** *adj.* disabled, unfit for work. **Erwerbs|unfähigkeit,** *f.* disablement. **-zweig,** *m.* line of business.

Erwerbung [ɛr'vɛrbuŋ], *f.* acquisition, obtainment; (*the th. obtained*) purchase, acquisition.

erwidern [ɛrˈviːdərn], *v.t.* (make a) reply, (give an) answer, say in reply (***auf*** (*Acc.*), to), retort, rejoin; (*fig.*) return, reciprocate (*feelings*), return, requite (*a service*), return (*greeting, visit, enemy fire etc.*). **Erwiderung,** *f.* reply, answer, retort, response, rejoinder; (*fig.*) return, reciprocation, response.

erwiesen [ɛrˈviːzən], *adj.* proved, (*Scots*) proven; established. **erwiesenermaßen,** *adv.* as has been proved *or* established *or* demonstrated.

erwirken [ɛrˈvɪrkən], *v.t.* bring about, procure, obtain, secure, succeed in getting.

erwischen [ɛrˈvɪʃən], *v.t.* (*coll.*) catch, get *or* catch hold of, lay hands on; (*sl.*) cop, nab; ***laß dich nicht –!*** mind you don't get caught!

erwog [ɛrˈvoːk], **erwöge** [ɛrˈvøːgə], **erwogen,** *see* **erwägen.**

erworben [ɛrˈvɔrbən], *see* **erwerben.**

erwünschen [ɛrˈvynʃən], *v.t.* wish for, desire. **erwünscht,** *adj.* desired; desirable; opportune, apropos; ***das ist mir sehr –,*** that suits me very well *or* perfectly, I shall be very pleased at that; ***persönliche Vorstellung –,*** personal application is desirable *or* requested; ***–e Wirkung,*** desired effect. **Erwünschtheit,** *f.* desirability; opportuneness.

erwürgen [ɛrˈvyːrgən], **1.** *v.t.* strangle, choke, throttle; (*Poet.*) slaughter, put to death. **2.** *v.i.* (*aux.* s.) choke (***an*** (*Dat.*), on). **Erwürgung,** *f.* strangling, strangulation; (*Poet.*) slaughter.

Erythräa [eryˈtrɛːa], *n.* (*Geog.*) Eritrea. **Erythräer,** *m.* Eritrean. **erythräisch,** *adj.* Eritrean.

Erz [eːrts], *n.* (**-es,** *pl.* **-e**) ore; (*Poet.*) brass, bronze; ***wie aus*** or ***in – gegossen dastehen,*** stand like a statue.

[1]**Erz-, erz-** [eːrts], *pref.* 1. (of) ore; 2. (*Poet.*) (of) bronze *or* brass, brazen.

[2]**Erz-, erz-** [ɛrts], *pref.* arch-, archi-; arrant, (*coll.*) extremely, utterly.

Erz|abfälle, *m.pl.* tailings. **-ader,** *f.* vein of ore, lode.

erzählbar [ɛrˈtsɛːlbaːr], *adj.* tellable, narratable, fit for recital, (*coll.*) 'drawing-room'.

erzählen [ɛrˈtsɛːlən], *v.t.* tell, relate, narrate, recount; ***man erzählt,*** they *or* people say, it is said, the story goes; (*coll.*) ***du kannst mir doch nichts –,*** tell me another! don't give me that! come off it! **Erzählen,** *n.* narration, recital, relation; ***beim –,*** in the course of the story, while talking. **erzählend,** *adj. See* **erzählerisch. erzählenswert,** *adj.* worth telling *or* relating *or* recounting. **Erzähler,** *m.* (story)teller, narrator; narrative writer. **erzählerisch,** *adj.* narrative. **Erzählkunst,** *f.* art of narrative. **Erzählung,** *f.* story, tale; (*written*) narrative, (*oral*) narration, (*written or oral*) account.

Erzaufbereitung [ˈeːrts-], *f.* ore dressing.

Erz|betrüger, *m.* arrant cheat. **-bischof,** *m.* archbishop. **erzbischöflich,** *adj.* archiepiscopal.

Erz|bistum, *n.* archbishopric. **-bösewicht,** *m.* arch-scoundrel, arrant rogue.

Erzbrecher [eːrts-], *m.* ore *or* rock crusher.

erzeigen [ɛrˈtsaɪgən], **1.** *v.t.* show, render, do (*kindness etc.*) (*Dat.*, to). **2.** *v.r.* show *or* prove o.s. (***als,*** to be).

erzen [ˈeːrtsən], *adj.* brazen, (made of) brass *or* bronze.

Erzengel [ˈɛrts-], *m.* archangel.

erzeugen [ɛrˈtsɔygən], *v.t.* produce, beget, procreate (*offspring*); make, produce, manufacture (*goods*), produce (*foodstuffs*), produce, generate (*electricity, heat, steam etc.*); (*fig.*) produce, bring forth, give rise to, generate, engender (*results*), breed (*hatred, contempt etc.*). **erzeugend,** *adj.* productive, producing, generative, generating. **Erzeuger,** *m.* begetter, procreator, father; (*Theol.*) Maker, Creator; (*Comm.*) producer; (*Engin.*) generator. **Erzeugnis,** *n.* (**-ses,** *pl.* **-se**) (*industrial*) product, (*agricultural*) produce. **Erzeugung,** *f.* procreation (*of offspring*), production, manufacture (*of goods*), generation, production (*of energy*).

Erzfeind [ˈɛrts-], *m.* arch-enemy, (*Eccl.*) arch-fiend.

Erzförderung [ˈeːrts-], *f.* output of ore. **erzführend,** *adj.* ore-bearing. **Erz|führung,** *f.* ore content. **-gang,** *m.* lode, vein of ore. **erzhaltig,** *adj.* ore-bearing.

Erz|herzog, *m.* archduke. **-herzogin,** *f.* archduchess. **erzherzoglich,** *adj.* archducal. **Erzherzogtum,** *n.* archduchy.

erziehbar [ɛrˈtsiːbaːr], *adj.* educable, trainable, teachable; ***schwer –e Kinder,*** problem children.

erziehen [ɛrˈtsiːən], *irr.v.t.* bring up, raise (*a child*), educate, train (*the young*). *See* **erzogen. Erzieher,** *m.* educator, instructor; (private) tutor. **Erziehergabe,** *f.* pedagogic gift. **Erzieherin,** *f.* instructress, governess. **erzieherisch,** *adj.* educative, instructive; educational, instructional, pedagogic. **erziehlich,** *adj.* educational; educative, instructive.

Erziehung [ɛrˈtsiːʊŋ], *f.* 1. upbringing (*of children*); education, training; 2. good breeding *or* manners. **Erziehungs|anstalt,** *f.* educational establishment. **-beihilfe,** *f.* educational allowance. **-minister,** *m.* Minister of Education. **-wesen,** *n.* educational matters *or* affairs, education. **-wissenschaft,** *f.* theory and practice of education.

erzielen [ɛrˈtsiːlən], *v.t.* obtain, achieve, attain, reach, arrive at; fetch, make, realize (*a price*); (*Spt.*) score (*goal, points etc.*). **Erzielung,** *f.* achievement, attainment, realization.

erzittern [ɛrˈtsɪtərn], *v.i.* (*aux.* s.) (begin to) tremble *or* shake *or* quiver *or* quake.

Erz|lager, *n.*, **-lagerstätte,** *f.* ore deposit.

erzogen [ɛrˈtsoːgən], *adj.* ***wohl*** or ***gut –,*** well brought up, well-bred, well-behaved, well-mannered; ***schlecht –,*** badly brought up, ill-bred, badly-behaved, ill-mannered. *See* **erziehen.**

Erz|probe, *f.* assay. **-scheidung,** *f.* separation of ore.

erzürnen [ɛrˈtsyːrnən], **1.** *v.t.* irritate, annoy, anger, make angry. **2.** *v.r.* get angry *or* annoyed *or* irritated, lose one's temper (***über*** (*Acc.*), with, about, at); quarrel, (*coll.*) fall out (***mit,*** with).

Erzvater [ˈɛrts-], *m.* (*B.*) patriarch. **erzväterlich,** *adj.* patriarchal.

erzwingen [ɛrˈtsvɪŋən], *irr.v.t.* force, wring, wrest, exact, extort (***von,*** from); gain *or* get *or* obtain by force. **erzwungen,** *adj.* forced; simulated, affected, artificial; ***erzwungenes Lächeln,*** forced smile.

es [ɛs], *pers. pron.* (*Nom. and Acc. of 3rd sing. neuter*) 1. (*Nom.*) he, she, it (*depending on the sex or sexlessness*), (*Acc.*) him, her, it; 2. *as imp. subject; sometimes* = there; ***– schneit,*** it is snowing, there is snow; ***– gibt Leute,*** there are people; ***– sagt sich schwer,*** it is difficult to say; it is hard to tell; ***– friert mich,*** I feel cold; ***– macht nichts,*** it doesn't matter; ***– stimmt,*** it is true; ***– geht ihm gut,*** all is well with him; ***wie geht – ihm?*** how is he? 3. *demonstratively* = he, she, it, they; ***– ist sein erster Versuch,*** it *or* this is his first attempt; ***– sind Männer von Ansehen,*** they are men of position *or* of consequence; ***wer ist der Mann? – ist mein Bruder,*** who is this man? he is my brother; ***wer ist diese Frau? – ist die Mutter,*** who is this woman? it is the mother; ***– ist eine Freundin von mir,*** she is a friend of mine; 4. *as dummy subject with the sole aim of supplying the expected word order, the true subject follows the verb* (*es always omitted if the sentence is rearranged so that the true subject precedes the verb*): *sometimes* = it, there *etc.*; *sometimes untranslatable*; ***– klopft jemand,*** somebody is knocking; ***– lebe der König!*** long live the king! (*Prov.*) ***– ist nicht alles Gold was glänzt,*** all is not gold that glitters; ***– waren ihrer drei,*** there were three of them; ***– ist ein Gott,*** there is a God; ***– spiele wer da will,*** let them play that wish to; ***– war einmal ein Mann,*** there was once a man; 5. *similarly, as functional subject anticipating a following noun clause, oft. untranslatable*: ***– tut mir leid, daß*** . . ., I am sorry that; ***– freut mich, daß*** . . ., I am glad that; ***– wundert mich, daß*** . . ., I am surprised that, it surprised me that; ***– ärgert mich daß*** . . ., I am annoyed that, it annoyed me that; ***– sei denn, daß*** . . ., unless, provided that; ***– fragt sich, ob*** . . ., it is a question of whether, the question is whether; 6. *to denote a subject that is deliberately vague*:

– ruft aus den Tiefen, a voice is heard from the deep; *– pocht an die Tür,* there is a knock at the door; *– spukt hier,* the place is haunted; *– riß mich blitzschnell hinunter,* I was carried down as quick as lightning; (*oft. as subj. of pass. verb*) *– wird getanzt,* there is dancing; *– wird erzählt,* it is said, people *or* they say, the story goes; 7. *as completion of predicate*; *ich bin –,* it is I; *sie sind –,* it is they; *wir sind –, die es getan haben,* it is we who did it; *keiner will – gewesen sein,* no one would admit to it, no one would acknowledge that it was he; 8. *as provisional functional object anticipating noun clause*: *ich bin – gewohnt, daß . . .,* I am used (to (*with gerund*)); *er hat – mit mir zu tun,* he has *or* will have me to deal with; *er hält – für unmöglich, daß . . .,* he considers it impossible that; 9. *as object recapitulating idea expressed or implied earlier*: = so; *er ist reich, ich bin – auch,* he is rich and so am I; *er sagt –,* he says so; *ich weiß –,* I know; *ich hoffe –,* I hope so; *ich glaube – nicht,* I don't think so; *ich selber bin – nicht mehr,* as for me I am no longer (*i.e. whatever had been referred to earlier*); *hast du – getan?* (*i.e. s.th. asked previously*) have you done so? *da haben wir's,* now we're getting at it, there's the rub, (*coll.*) that's the snag; 10. *as a deliberately unspecified object* (*usu. untranslated*): *– gut haben,* be well off; *– weit bringen,* make good progress, get on well; *er hat – mit ihr verdorben,* he has lost favour with her; *ich meine – gut mit dir,* I mean well towards *or* by you, I am well disposed towards you; *er treibt – zu bunt,* he goes too far; *er kann – nicht über sich gewinnen,* he can't bring himself to it.

[1]**Es,** *n.* (*Psych.*) id.

[2]**Es, es,** *n.* (-, *pl.* -) (*Mus.*) E flat; *es-Dur,* E-flat major; *es-moll,* E-flat minor; *es-es,* E double flat.

Esch [ɛʃ], *m.* (**-es,** *pl.* **-e**) arable (land).

Esche ['ɛʃə], *f.* (*Bot.*) ash, ash-tree (*Fraxinus excelsior*). **eschen,** *adj.* of ash, ashen.

Esdragon [ɛsdra'ɡo:n], *m.* (**-s,** *no pl.*) (*Bot.*) tarragon.

Esel ['e:zəl], *m.* ass, donkey; (silly) ass, fool, jackass; *hölzerner –,* easel; *wilder –,* onager; *gestreifter –,* zebra; *den – (einen) – nennen,* call a spade a spade; *dummer –!* duffer! dunce! *störrisch wie ein –,* stubborn as a mule; *bepackt* or *beladen wie ein –,* laden like a beast of burden; (*Prov.*) *ein – schilt den anderen Langohr,* the pot calling the kettle black; *den – zu Grabe läuten,* dangle one's feet; *vom Pferde auf den – kommen,* come down in the world; *den Sack schlagen und den – meinen,* say (*or* do) one thing and mean another; *wenn's dem – zu wohl wird, geht er aufs Eis,* pride will have a fall. **Eselei** [–'laɪ], *f.* stupid *or* idiotic th., piece of stupidity. **eselhaft,** *adj.* asinine, stupid, foolish, idiotic. **Eselin,** *f.* she-donkey, she-ass.

Esels|bank, *f.* dunce's seat. **–brücke,** *f.* (*school sl.*) crib, (*Am.*) pony. **–ohr,** *n.* dog's ear, dog-ear (= *turned down corner of page*). **–tritt,** *m.* kick of an ass; cowardly revenge. **–wiese,** *f.* (*sl.*) correspondence column (*in a newspaper*).

Eskadron [ɛska'dro:n], *f.* (-, *pl.* **-en**) troop (*of cavalry*).

Eskorte [ɛs'kɔrtə], *f.* escort, convoy. **eskortieren** [–'ti:rən], *v.t.* escort, convoy.

Esparsette [ɛspar'zɛtə], *f.* (*Bot.*) sainfoin.

Espe ['ɛspə], *f.* (*Bot.*) aspen(-tree) (*Populus tremula*). **espen,** *adj.* (made of) aspen-wood. **Espenlaub,** *n.* aspen leaves; *zittern wie –,* tremble like an aspen leaf.

Esra ['ɛsra], *m.* (*B.*) Ezra.

Essay [ɛ'sə, 'ɛse], *m.* (**-s,** *pl.* **-s**) essay. **Essayist** [–'ɪst], *m.* (**-en,** *pl.* **-en**) essayist. **essayistisch,** *adj.* unscholarly, unsystematic, dilettante, superficial, trivial.

eßbar ['ɛsba:r], *adj.* eatable, edible. **Eßbesteck,** *n.* knife fork and spoon; (*collect.*) cutlery.

Esse ['ɛsə], *f.* 1. chimney, chimney-pipe, funnel; 2. forge, smithy.

essen ['ɛsən], *irr.v.t., irr.v.i.* eat; take one's meals; have ((*for*) *dinner etc.*); (*Mil., Naut.*) mess; *zu Mittag –,* lunch, dine, have lunch *or* dinner; *zu Abend –,* dine, have dinner *or* supper; *wir haben zu Mittag Fisch gegessen,* we had fish for lunch; *auswärts –,* eat out; *zu – haben,* have *or* get enough to eat; *wenig zu – haben,* not get enough to eat; *nichts zu – haben,* have nothing to eat; *den Teller* or *die Schüssel leer –,* clear *or* (*coll.*) clean one's plate; *sich satt –,* eat one's fill (*an* (*Dat.*), of); *er ißt täglich dreimal,* he takes three meals a day. **Essen,** *n.* food; meal; eating, feeding; (*Mil.*) *– fassen,* draw rations; *ich kann das fette – nicht vertragen,* rich food does not agree with me; *das – abtragen,* clear the table; *beim –,* while eating, at meals, at meal-time; *nach dem –,* after the meal; after meals; *zum – bleiben,* stay for a *or* the meal; (*immer*) *spät zum – kommen,* (always) be late for one's meal(s).

Essen|aufsatz, *m.* chimney-pot. **–kehrer,** *m.* chimney-sweep.

Essenszeit ['ɛsənstsaɪt], *f.* meal-time.

Essenz [ɛ'sɛnts], *f.* (-, *pl.* **-en**) essence.

Esser ['ɛsər], *m.* eater. **Esserei** [–'raɪ], *f.* (*coll.*) guzzling.

Eß|gabel, *f.* table-fork. **–geschirr,** *n.* tableware, service; (*Mil. etc.*) mess-tin, billy-can. **–gier,** *f.* craving for food, ravenous hunger, gluttony.

Essig ['ɛsɪç], *m.* (**-s,** *pl.* **-e**) vinegar; (*coll.*) *damit ist es –!* it's all up with it! it's fallen through; it's a flop, it's no go. **Essig|äther,** *m.* acetic ether, ethyl acetate. **–bildung,** *f.* acetification. **–gärung,** *f.* acetic fermentation. **–gurke,** *f.* pickled cucumber *or* gherkin. **essigsauer,** *adj.* (*Chem.*) acetic, acetate of; *essigsaures Salz,* acetate; *essigsaure Tonerde,* aluminium acetate; (*coll.*) *essigsaure Miene,* sour face. **Essigsäure,** *f.* acetic acid.

Eß|kastanie, *f.* sweet *or* Spanish chestnut. **–korb,** *m.* picnic-basket, hamper. **–löffel,** *m.* tablespoon; *zwei – voll,* two tablespoonfuls. **–lust,** *f.* appetite. **–messer,** *n.* table-knife. **–napf,** *m.* (*child's*) bowl, (*dog's*) feeding bowl; (*Mil. etc.*) mess-tin. **–obst,** *n.* dessert fruit. **–saal,** *m.* dining-hall. **–tisch,** *m.* dining-table. **–unlust,** *f.* lack *or* loss of appetite. **–waren,** *f.pl.* provisions, victuals, (*coll.*) eatables. **–zimmer,** *n.* dining-room. **–zimmerschrank,** *m.* sideboard, dresser.

Estafette [ɛsta'fɛtə], *f.* dispatch-rider, mounted orderly.

Estampe [ɛs'tɑ̃p(ə)], *f.* print, engraving.

Este ['e:stə], *m.* (**-n,** *pl.* **-n**) Esthonian. **Estland,** *n.* Esthonia. **Estländer,** *m. See* **Este. estländisch.** *adj.* Esthonian. **estnisch,** *adj.* Esthonian (*language etc.*).

Estragon ['ɛstraɡɔn], *m. See* **Esdragon.**

Estrich ['ɛstrɪç], *m.* (**-s,** *pl.* **-e**) 1. earth *or* cement *or* stone floor; flagstones; 2. (*Swiss*) loft.

etablieren [eta'bli:rən], **1.** *v.t.* establish, set up. **2.** *v.r.* set up in business.

Etage [e'ta:ʒə], *f.* floor, stor(e)y, tier. **Etagen|heizung,** *f.* self-contained central heating. **–schlüssel,** *m.* latchkey (*of a flat*). **–wohnung,** *f.* self-contained flat, (*Am.*) apartment.

Etagere [eta'ʒɛ:rə], *f.* stand, rack, what-not.

Etappe [e'tapə], *f.* (*Mil.*) communications zone; (*fig.*) stage. **Etappen|anfangsort,** *m.* (*Mil.*) advanced base. **–gebiet,** *n.* (*Mil.*) lines of communication area. **–kommandantur,** *f.* L. of C. Commandant's headquarters. **–lazarett,** *n.* base hospital. **–ort,** *m.* post on L. of C., field base. **–schwein,** *n.* (*sl.*) base-wallah. **etappenweise,** *adv.* by stages, stage by stage.

Etat [e'ta:], *m.* (**-s,** *pl.* **-s**) 1. (*Parl.*) budget; *veranschlagter –,* estimates; 2. (*Mil.*) strength, establishment. **etatisieren** [–ti'zi:rən], *v.t.* (*Parl.*) budget for. **etatmäßig** [e'ta:mɛ:sɪç], *adj.* (*Parl.*) accounted for in the budget, (*Mil. etc.*) on the establishment. **Etatsjahr,** *n.* fiscal *or* financial year.

etepetete [e:təpe'te:tə], *adj.* (*coll.*) finicky, finicking, over-fastidious, over-refined; pernickerty, over-particular.

Ethik ['e:tɪk], *f.* ethics, moral philosophy. **Ethiker,**

m. moral philosopher. **ethisch,** *adj.* ethical, (*Gram.*) ethic.

ethnisch ['ɛtnɪʃ], *adj.* ethnic.

Ethnograph [ɛtno'gra:f], *m.* (**-en,** *pl.* **-en**) ethnographer. **Ethnographie** [–fi:], *f.* ethnography. **ethnographisch,** *adj.* ethnographic(al).

Ethnologe [ɛtno'lo:gə], *m.* (**-n,** *pl.* **-n**) ethnologist. **Ethnologie** [–'gi:], *f.* ethnology. **ethnologisch,** *adj.* ethnological, ethnic(al).

Ethos ['e:tɔs], *n.* ethos, ethical *or* moral sense *or* values *or* principles.

Etikett [eti'kɛt], *n.* (**-(e)s,** *pl.* **-e**) (price-)label *or* tag, price-ticket.

Etikette [eti'kɛtə], *f.* 1. etiquette; 2. *See* **Etikett. etikettieren** [–'ti:rən], *v.t.* label, ticket.

etlicher [ɛtlɪçər], *m.*, **etliche,** *f.*, **etliches,** *n.* **1.** *indef. adj.* some, a certain; *pl.* *etliche,* some, several, a few, a number of; ***etliche achtzig Jahre, achtzig Jahre und etliche,*** about *or* some eighty years, eighty years odd. **2.** *indef. pron.* (*n. and pl. only*) ***etliches,*** a few *or* a number of *or* some *or* several *or* sundry things; ***um etliches größer als,*** quite a bit bigger than; ***ich habe etliches hinzuzufügen,*** I have a thing or two to add; *pl.* ***etliche,*** a few, a number, some, several.

Etmal ['ɛtma:l], *n.* (**-(e)s,** *pl.* **-e**) (*Naut.*) (time *or* work done) round the clock; day's run.

Etrurien [e'tru:riən], *n.* (*Geog.*) Etruria. **Etrurier,** *m.* Etrurian, Etruscan. **etrurisch,** *adj.* Etrurian, Etruscan. **Etrusker,** *m.* Etruscan. **etruskisch,** *adj.* Etruscan (*language*).

Etsch [ɛtʃ], *f.* (*Geog.*) (River) Adige. **Etschland,** *n.* South Tyrol.

Etui [ɛt'vi:], *n.* (**-s,** *pl.* **-s**) case (*for small articles*), box.

etwa ['ɛtva], *adv.* 1. (*before numeral*) (round) about, around, approximately; 2. (*emotive part.*) perhaps, by (any) chance, (*Poet.*) perchance; ***ist's Ihnen – um 5 Uhr gefällig?*** shall we say 5 o'clock? ***was – vorkommen mag,*** whatever perchance may happen; ***wenn sie – hören,*** if you should hear by any chance; ***nicht –,*** surely not; ***er wird doch nicht – glauben,*** he surely won't believe; ***und nicht –,*** and not as one might expect *or* suppose. **etwaig,** *adj.* possible, eventual; ***–e Schwierigkeiten,*** contingent difficulties, difficulties that might *or* may arise.

etwas ['ɛtvas], **1.** *indef.pron.* (*indecl.*) something, anything; ***– Neues,*** s.th. new, news; ***– Neues?*** any news? anything fresh? ***– anderes,*** s.th. else *or* different; ***das ist – anderes,*** that is a different *or* another matter; ***irgend –,*** anything, something or other; ***in*** or ***um –,*** in some measure, in some respects; ***es hat – an*** or ***für sich,*** it has its points, there is s.th. about it *or* s.th. to be said for it; ***das will schon – sagen,*** that really is s.th., now we're getting somewhere, that's s.th. like; ***so –,*** such a th., a th. like that, s.th. of the kind *or* sort; ***so – Dummes!*** what a stupid thing! ***so – bedarf Zeit,*** such a matter requires time; ***nein, so –!*** you surprise me, I can't credit it, would you believe it? ***so – ist mir doch noch nie vorgekommen!*** well, nothing like that has ever happened to me before! **2.** *indef.adj.* some, a little; ***– Geld (Zeit),*** some *or* a little money (time). **3.** *adv.* somewhat; a little; rather; (*coll.*) a short time, a bit; ***vorm Schlafengehen – spazieren,*** go for a bit of a walk before going to bed; ***– weitschweifig,*** rather prolix. **Etwas,** *n.* something; ***ein gewisses –,*** a certain thing, an indefinable something, something unaccountable.

Etymologe [etymo'lo:gə], *m.* (**-n,** *pl.* **-n**) etymologist. **Etymologie** [–'gi:], *f.* etymology. **etymologisch,** *adj.* etymological.

Et-Zeichen [ɛt'tsaɪçən], *n.* (*Typ.*) ampersand.

Etzel ['ɛtsəl], *m.* (*Hist.*) Attila.

euch [ɔyç], **1.** *pers. pron.* (*Acc. and Dat. pl.*) (*in letters* ***Euch***) you, to you. **2.** *refl. pron.* yourself.

Eucharistie [ɔyçarɪs'ti:], *f.* (*Theol.*) eucharist. **eucharistisch** [–'rɪstɪʃ], *adj.* eucharistic.

euer ['ɔyər], **1.** *pers. pron.* (*Gen. pl.*) (of) you; ***– sind drei,*** there are three of you; ***ich erinnere mich –,*** I remember you. **2.** *poss.adj.* 1. (***euer,*** *m.*, ***eu(e)re,*** *f.*, ***euer,*** *n.*) (*cap. in correspondence*) your (*pl.*); ***euer Vater,*** your father; ***eu(e)re Mutter,*** your mother; ***euer Kind,*** your child; ***eu(e)re Kinder,*** your children; 2. (*obs., Poet.*) (*with cap.; abbr.* ***Ew.***) your (*sing.*) (*in titles and formal address*); ***Euer Exzellenz,*** Your Excellency; ***Euer Gnaden,*** Your Grace. **3.** *poss. pron.* (*declined as adj., viz. m.* ***euer*** or ***eu(e)rer, euer(e)n, eu(e)res, euer(e)m;*** *f.* ***eu(e)re, eu(e)rer;*** *n.* ***euer*** or ***eu(e)res, euer(e)m;*** *pl.* ***eu(e)re, eu(e)rer, euer(e)n; der, die*** or ***das eu(e)re*** *etc.*, ***die eu(e)ren***), yours; ***unsre Tochter ist etwas älter als eure*** or ***die eure,*** our daughter is a little older than yours; ***das Eu(e)re,*** your property, belongings *or* affairs; ***ihr müßt das Eure tun,*** you must do your share *or* play your part; ***die Eu(e)ren,*** your family *or* people *or* folks.

Eugen ['ɔyge:n, ɔy'ge:n], *m.* Eugene.

Euklid [ɔy'kli:t], *m.* Euclid. **euklidisch** [–'kli:dɪʃ], *adj.* Euclidian.

Eule ['ɔylə], *f.* 1. owl; ***Eulen nach Athen tragen,*** carry coals to Newcastle; (*Prov.*) ***des einen – ist des anderen Nachtigall,*** one man's meat is another man's poison; 2. owlet, moth; 3. (*coll.*) feather-brush. **eulenartig,** *adj.* owlish. **Eulenspiegel,** *m.* Owl-glass. **Eulenspiegelei,** *f.* practical joke, prank, tomfoolery.

Euphrat ['ɔyfrat], *m.* (*Geog.*) (River) Euphrates.

eure ['ɔyrə], *see* **euer. eurerseits,** *adv.* on your part *or* side. **euresgleichen,** *pron.* of your (own) kind. **eurethalben, euretwegen, euretwillen,** *adv.* on your account, for your sake; on your behalf. **eurige,** *poss.pron.* ***der, die, das –,*** see ***der, die, das eu(e)re*** *under* **euer, 3.**

Europa [ɔy'ro:pa], *n.* (*Geog.*) Europe; (*Myth.*) Europa. **Europäer** [–'pɛ:ər], *m.* European. **europäisch,** *adj.* European; ***–e Wirtschaftsgemeinschaft,*** European Common Market, European Economic Community. **Europa|rat,** *m.* Council of Europe. **–union,** *f.* European Union.

Euter ['ɔytər], *n.* udder.

Eva ['e:va], *f.* (*B.*) Eve.

evakuieren [evaku'i:rən], *v.t.* evacuate (*also Mil. etc.*). **Evakuierung,** *f.* evacuation.

Evangelienpult [evaŋ'ge:liənpult], *n.* lectern. **evangelisch,** *adj.* evangelic(al); Protestant. **Evangelium,** *n.* (**-s,** *pl.* **-lien**) gospel.

Eventualforderung [evɛntu'a:lfɔrdəruŋ], *f.* (*Comm.*) contingent claim. **Eventualität** [–ali'tɛ:t], *f.* possibility, eventuality, contingency. **eventualiter,** *adv.* (*Law*) alternatively, as an alternative; *see also* **eventuell. Eventualverbindlichkeit,** *f.* (*Comm.*) contingent liability.

eventuell [evɛntu'ɛl], **1.** *adj.* possible. **2.** *adv.* possibly, perhaps, if occasion should arise, if necessary.

evident [evi'dɛnt], *adj.* evident, manifest, obvious, clear, plain. **Evidenz,** *f.* manifestness, obviousness.

Evolutionismus [evolutsio'nɪsmus], *m.* evolutionism. **evolutionistisch,** *adj.* evolutionary.

Evolvente [evɔl'vɛntə], *f.* involute. **evolventisch,** *adj.* involute. **evolvieren,** *v.t.* evolve.

Ewe ['e:və], *f.* (*Poet.*) era, epoch.

Ewer ['e:vər], *m.* wherry, lighter, sailing-barge.

ewig ['e:vɪç], **1.** *adj.* everlasting, eternal; endless, unending, never-ending, perpetual (*as snow*); ***zum –en Andenken,*** to the everlasting *or* immortal memory; ***der Ewige Jude,*** the Wandering Jew. **2.** *adv.* always, for ever(more); for ever and ever; ***das dauert –,*** that will last ages; ***das ist – schade,*** that is a great pity; ***auf –,*** for ever, in perpetuity. **Ewigkeit,** *f.* eternity; perpetuity; age(s); ***von – zu –, in alle –,*** for ever and ever, without end, to all eternity. **Ewigkeitsblume,** *f.* (*Bot.*) immortelle. **ewiglich,** *adv.* *See* **ewig, 2.**

exakt [ɛ'ksakt], *adj.* exact, accurate; ***–e Wissenschaften,*** mathematical sciences. **Exaktheit,** *f.* exactness, exactitude, precision, punctiliousness.

exaltiert [ɛksal'ti:rt], *adj.* exalted, rapturous, (*coll.*) over-excited, highly strung.

Examen [ɛ'ksa:mən], *n.* (**-s,** *pl.* **-mina** *or* -) examination; *mündliches –,* oral *or* viva-voce examination, (*coll.*) viva; *ein – ablegen,* (*coll.*) *ins – steigen,* go in for *or* sit for an examination; *ein – bestehen,* pass an examination; *im – durchfallen,* (*coll.*) *durch das – fallen,* fail an examination.

Examinand [ɛksami'nant], *m.* (**-en,** *pl.* **-en**) examinee. **Examinator,** *m.* (**-s,** *pl.* **-en**) examiner. **examinieren,** *v.t.* examine.

Exegese [ɛksə'ɡe:zə], *f.* exegesis. **Exeget,** *m.* (**-en,** *pl.* **-en**) commentator. **Exegetik,** *f.* exegetics.

Exekution [ɛksekutsi'o:n], *f.* execution, carrying out (*of orders*), execution (*of criminal*), (*Law*) distraint, execution; (*St. Exch.*) buying-in, selling-out. **exekutionsfrei,** *adj.* (*Law*) immune from distraint. **Exekutions|kauf,** *m.* (*St. Exch.*) buying-in. **-verkauf,** *m.* (*St. Exch.*) selling-out.

Exempel [ɛ'ksɛmpəl], *n.* example, model, instance; (*Math.*) problem; *zum –* (*abbr. z. E.*), for instance; *ein – an ihm statuieren,* let him be a warning *or* an example; *ein – statuieren,* be a warning, set an example.

Exemplar [ɛksɛm'pla:r], *n.* (**-s,** *pl.* **-e**) copy (*of a book*); sample, specimen. **exemplarisch,** *adj.* exemplary.

Exequien [ɛ'kse:kviən], *n.pl.* obsequies; mass for the dead.

exerzieren [ɛksɛr'tsi:rən], *v.t., v.i.* exercise; drill. **Exerzieren,** *n.* drilling, drill. **Exerzier|meister,** *m.* drill-sergeant, drill-instructor. **-patrone,** *f.* dummy (cartridge), blank. **-platz,** *m.* parade ground, drill yard, barrack square.

Exerzitium [ɛksɛr'tsi:tsium], *n.* (**-s,** *pl.* **-tien**) written homework; *pl.* (*Eccl.*) devotions.

exigieren [ɛksi'ɡi:rən], *v.t.* demand (*payment etc.*).

Exil [ɛ'ksi:l], *n.* (**-(e)s,** *pl.* **-e**) exile, banishment.

Existenz [ɛksɪs'tɛnts], *f.* (-, *pl.* **-en**) 1. existence; being, life; *verfehlte* or *verkrachte –,* ne'er-do-well, failure; *dunkle –,* shady character; 2. (means of) existence, subsistence, livelihood, living; *eine sichere –,* a secure means of livelihood, an established position. **Existenzberechtigung,** *f.* right to exist, right to live. **existenzfähig,** *adj.* capable of existence, viable. **Existenzfrage,** *f.* matter of life and death.

existenzial [ɛksɪstɛntsi'a:l], *adj.* existentialist. **Existenzialismus** [–'lɪsmus], *m.* existentialism.

Existenz|kampf, *m.* struggle for existence. **-minimum,** *n.* living wage, subsistence level. **-mittel,** *n.pl.* means of subsistence, livelihood.

existieren [ɛksɪs'ti:rən], *v.i.* exist, live, subsist, survive, be viable, manage *or* be able to exist.

exklusiv [ɛksklu'zi:f], *adj.* exclusive, sole; *-e Gesellschaft,* exclusive society. **exklusive,** *adv.* exclusive of, excluding.

exkommunizieren [ɛkskɔmuni'tsi:rən], *v.t.* excommunicate.

Exkurs [ɛks'kurs], *m.* excursus. **Exkursion** [–si'o:n], *f.* excursion, outing, study-tour.

exmatrikulieren [ɛksmatrɪku'li:rən], *v.t. er läßt sich –,* he leaves the university, (*coll.*) he goes down.

Exmission [ɛksmɪsi'o:n], *f.* (*Law*) eviction; ejection. **exmittieren** [–'ti:rən], *v.t.* (*Law*) evict, eject.

exogam [ɛkso'ɡa:m], *adj.* exogamous.

exogen [ɛkso'ɡe:n], *adj.* exogenous.

exorzieren [ɛksɔr'tsi:rən], *v.t.* exorcise, expel, cast out.

Exot [ɛ'kso:t], *m.* (**-en,** *pl.* **-en**), **Exote,** *f.* exotic (*plant etc.*). **exotisch,** *adj.* exotic.

Expedient [ɛkspedi'ɛnt], *m.* (**-en,** *pl.* **-en**) forwarder, forwarding agent *or* clerk. **expedieren** [–'di:rən], *v.t.* dispatch, forward, send off (*a parcel etc.*). **Expedition** [–dɪtsi'o:n], *f.* 1. dispatch, forwarding, delivery; 2. (*Mil. etc.*) expedition; 3. (*obs.*) office (*of a journal etc.*). **Expeditionsgeschäft,** *n.* hauliers, delivery service.

Experiment [ɛksperi'mɛnt], *n.* (**-s,** *pl.* **-e**) experiment; *ein – machen* or *anstellen,* make *or* try an experiment. **experimentell** [–'tɛl], *adj.* experimental, empirical. **experimentieren** [–'ti:rən], *v.i.* experiment.

Expert [ɛks'pɛrt], *m.* (**-en,** *pl.* **-en**), **Experte,** *m.* (**-n,** *pl.* **-n**) expert.

explizieren [ɛksplɪ'tsi:rən], **1.** *v.t.* explain, interpret. **2.** *v.r.* make one's meaning clear. **explizite** [–'pli:tsitə], *adv.* explicitly, clearly, plainly.

explodieren [ɛksplo'di:rən], *v.i.* (*aux.* s.) explode, (*coll.*) blow up. **Explosion** [–zi'o:n], *f.* explosion, detonation. **Explosions|gemisch,** *n.* explosive mixture. **-motor,** *m.* internal combustion engine. **-raum,** *m.* combustion chamber. **Explosiv|kraft,** *f.* disruptive *or* explosive force. **-laut,** *m.* (*Phonet.*) plosive. **-stoff,** *m.* explosive.

Exponent [ɛkspo'nɛnt], *m.* (**-en,** *pl.* **-en**) exponent, representative; (*Math.*) exponent, index. **Exponentialgleichung,** *f.* exponential equation.

exponieren [ɛkspo'ni:rən], *v.t.* expound, explain, unfold, set out *or* forth; (*Phot.*) expose; (*fig.*) lay open to criticism.

Export [ɛks'pɔrt], *m.* (**-s,** *pl.* **-e**) export, exportation; *pl.* exports, articles of export. **Exporteur** [–'tø:r], *m.* (**-s,** *pl.* **-e**) exporter. **Export|geschäft,** *n.* export house; export trade; transaction on the export market. **-gut,** *n.* (goods for) export. **-hafen,** *m.* port of exportation. **-handel,** *m.* export trade. **exportieren** [–'ti:rən], *v.t.* export.

Exposition [ɛkspozitsi'o:n], *f.* (*Log., Mus. etc.*) exposition; (*Phot.*) exposure; (*obs.*) exhibition, show.

Expositur [ɛkspɔzi'tu:r], *f.* (-, *pl.* **-en**) 1. (*Eccl.*) chapel of ease *or* rest; 2. (*Austr.*) overflow premises.

expreß [ɛks'prɛs], **1.** *adj.* (*coll.*) express, explicit, distinct. **2.** *adv.* (*coll.*) specially, for the *or* on purpose. **Expreß,** *m.* (**-(ss)es,** *pl.* **-(ss)e**) (*Railw. etc.*) express. **Expreß|brief,** *m.* express letter. **-gut,** *n.* express parcel(s).

Expressionismus [ɛksprɛsio'nɪsmus], *m.* expressionism. **expressionistisch,** *adj.* expressionist.

Exspiration [ɛkspiratsi'o:n], *f.* exhalation. **Exspirationsluft,** *f.* exhaled air. **expirieren** [–'ri:rən], *v.i.* (*aux.* s.) be exhaled; (*of lease etc.*) expire.

Exspoliation [ɛkspoliatsi'o:n], *f.* spoliation. **exspoliieren** [–i'i:rən], *v.t.* despoil, plunder.

Exsudat [ɛkszu'da:t], *n.* (**-(e)s,** *pl.* **-e**) (*Med.*) exudation, exuded matter. **exsudieren,** *v.t.* exude.

Extemporale [ɛkstɛmpo'ra:lə], *n.* (**-s,** *pl.* **-lien**), **Extempore** [–'tɛmpore:], *n.* (**-s,** *pl.* **-(s)**) extemporization, improvisation; (*school*) class exercise, test. **extemporieren,** *v.t., v.i.* extemporize, improvise.

exterminieren [ɛkstɛrmi'ni:rən], *v.t.* exterminate, eradicate, extirpate, (*coll.*) root out.

extern [ɛks'tɛrn], *adj.* external; *-e Schüler,* day-pupils. **Externat** [–'na:t], *n.* (**-(e)s,** *pl.* **-e**) day school. **Externe(r),** *m., f.* lay-pupil; external candidate (*for examination*). **Externist** [–'nɪst], *m.* (**-en,** *pl.* **-en**) 1. (*Med.*) specialist for external diseases; 2. (*Austr.*) *see* **Externe(r).**

exterritorial [ɛkstɛritori'a:l], *adj.* extra-territorial.

extra ['ɛkstra], **1.** *adj.* (*coll.*) extra, additional; special. **2.** *adv.* apart, separately, extra, over and above, (*coll.*) into the bargain; (*coll.*) specially, on purpose; *– deswegen,* for that very purpose. **Extra|ausgabe,** *f.* 1. special edition; 2. extra expense. **-blatt,** *n.* special edition *or* issue (*of newspaper*).

extradieren [ɛkstra'di:rən], *v.t.* extradite.

Extradividende ['ɛkstradivi'dɛndə], *f.* bonus.

extrafein ['ɛkstrafaɪn], *adj.* superfine.

Extrahent [ɛkstra'hɛnt], *m.* (**-en,** *pl.* **-en**) (*Comm.*) p. making a statement *or* abstract of account; (*Law*) p. issuing a writ. **extrahieren,** *v.t.* extract (*passages etc.*), (*Chem. etc.*) extract; (*Comm.*) make an abstract from, draw up a statement of (*account*).

Extrakosten ['ɛkstrakɔstən], *pl.* extra *or* additional charges, extras.

Extrakt [ɛks'trakt], *m. or n.* (**-(e)s,** *pl.* **-e**) extract, excerpt (*from book*); (*Chem. etc.*) extract(ion).

extran [ɛks'tra:n], *adj.* extraneous, foreign, strange. **Extraneer** [–neər], **Extraner,** *m.* day-pupil.

extraordinär [ɛkstraʔɔrdi'nɛ:r], *adj* extraordinary. **Extraordinariat** [–na:ri'a:t], *n.* (supernumerary) professorship, (*Am.*) associate professorship. **Extraordinarium,** *n.* (*Parl.*) supplementary budget. **Extraordinarius,** *m.* (supernumerary) professor, (*Am.*) associate professor.

Extra|strom, *m.* (*Elec.*) self-induction current. **–wurst,** *f.* (*Austr.*) (type of) pork sausage; (*coll.*) s.th. extra-special *or* out of the ordinary. **–zug,** *m.* (*Railw.*) special train.

Extrem [ɛks'tre:m], *n.* (**-s,** *pl.* **-e**) extreme (limit) *or* (*Math.*) (value); ***die –e berühren sich,*** the extremes meet. **extrem,** *adj.* extreme, utmost, farthest; intense, drastic, exaggerated. **Extremität** [–i'tɛ:t], *f.* extremity. **Extremthermometer,** *n.* maximum and minimum thermometer.

Exulant [ɛksu'lant], *m.* (**-en,** *pl.* **-en**) exile.

Exzedent [ɛkstse'dɛnt], *m.* (**-en,** *pl.* **-en**) transgressor, evildoer, malefactor.

Exzellenz [ɛkstsɛ'lɛnts], *f.* (-, *pl.* **-en**) excellence; Excellency (*title*); ***Ew.*** **–,** Your Excellency.

Exzenter [ɛks'tsɛntər], *m.* eccentric, cam. **Exzenter|getriebe,** *n.* cam gear. **–hub,** *m.* throw of the eccentric. **–rolle,** *f.* cam follower. **exzentrisch,** *adj.* eccentric (*also fig.*). **Exzentrizität** [–tritsi'tɛ:t], *f.* eccentricity.

exzerpieren [ɛkstsɛr'pi:rən], *v.t.* extract, excerpt, make excerpts from, cull passages from. **Exzerpt** [–'tsɛrpt], *n.* (**-(e)s,** *pl.* **-e**) excerpt, extract.

Exzeß [ɛks'tsɛs], *m.* (**-(ss)es,** *pl.* **-(ss)e**) excess, outrage; excess, immoderation. **exzessiv** [–'si:f], *adj.* excessive, outrageous; excessive, immoderate; ***–es Klima,*** continental climate.

exzidieren [ɛkstsi'di:rən], *v.t.* (*Surg.*) excise.

exzipieren [ɛkstsi'pi:rən], *v.t.* except, make an exception of.

exzitieren [ɛkstsi'ti:rən], *v.t.* excite, stimulate.

F

F, f [ɛf], *n.* F, f; (*Mus.*) F; (*coll.*) ***nach Schema F gehen,*** be perfectly in order, (*coll.*) be under control. *See the Index of Abbreviations.*

Fabel ['fa:bəl], *f.* (-, *pl.* **-n**) fable, tale, story; plot (*of a drama*); tall *or* cock-and-bull story. **Fabelei** [–'laɪ], *f.* (-, *pl.* **-en**) fantastic tale, imagination gone *or* run wild. **fabelhaft,** *adj.* fabulous, amazing, phenomenal, incredible, marvellous, wonderful. **fabeln,** *v.i.* tell stories, spin yarns (***von,*** about). **Fabel|tier,** *n.* fabulous *or* mythical *or* legendary beast. **–welt,** *f.* fabulous *or* mythical world. **–wesen,** *n.* fabulous creature.

Fabrik [fa'bri:k], *f.* (-, *pl.* **-en**) factory, works, mill. **Fabrikanlage,** *f.* manufacturing plant, *pl.* works. **Fabrikant** [–'kant], *m.* (**-en,** *pl.* **-en**) manufacturer; factory owner. **Fabrik|arbeit,** *f.* factory work; factory-made articles. **–arbeiter,** *m.* factory hand *or* worker, operative. **Fabrikat** [–'ka:t], *n.* (**-(e)s,** *pl.* **-e**) manufacture; manufactured article, product, make, brand. **Fabrikation** [–tsi'o:n], *f.* production, manufacture. **Fabrikationsfehler,** *m.* flaw in manufacture. **Fabrikbesitzer,** *m.* factory owner. **fabrikfertig,** *adj.* factory-built, prefabricated. **Fabrik|marke,** *f. See* **–zeichen.** **fabrikmäßig,** *adj.* mass-produced; ***–e Herstellung,*** bulk processing, mass production. **fabrikneu,** *adj.* brand-new. **Fabrik|preis,** *m.* factory price, prime cost. **–stadt,** *f.* manufacturing town. **–waren,** *f.pl.* manufactures, factory- *or* machine-made goods. **–zeichen,** *n.* trade-mark.

fabrizieren [fabri'tsi:rən], *v.t.* manufacture, make, produce, (*fig.*) fabricate (*excuses etc.*).

fabulieren [fabu'li:rən], *v.i. See* **fabeln.**

Facette [fa'sɛtə], *f.* facet.

Fach [fax], *n.* (**-(e)s,** *pl.* **¨er**) compartment, division; (*Bot.*) cell; shelf, partition, pigeon-hole, drawer; panel (*of a door etc.*), (*Typ.*) case; (*fig.*) province, field, subject, branch, speciality, line, business, trade, department; ***das ist gerade sein –,*** that is just his speciality; ***von –,*** by profession; ***das ist nicht mein –*** or ***schlägt nicht in mein –,*** that is not within my province, that is not in my line; ***er versteht sein – vollkommen,*** he is an expert in his subject; ***unter Dach und – bringen,*** house, accommodate; put the finishing touches to, get finished; ***unter Dach und – kommen,*** find shelter *or* accommodation.

-fach, *adv.suff.* -fold (*e.g.* ***hundert–,*** hundredfold).

Fach|arbeiter, *m.* skilled worker, specialist. **–arzt,** *m.* (medical) specialist (***für,*** in). **–ausbildung,** *f.* professional *or* specialized training. **–ausdruck,** *m.* technical term. **–berater,** *m.* consultant.

fächeln ['fɛçəln], **1.** *v.t.* (*v.r.*) fan (o.s.). **2.** *v.i.* waft. **Fächer,** *m.* fan. **Fächerfenster,** *n.* fanlight. **fächerförmig,** *adj.* fan-shaped; ***sich – ausbreiten,*** fan out.

Fach|gebiet, *n.* speciality, special field *or* subject. **–gelehrte(r),** *m., f.* specialist. **–geschäft,** *n.* specialized dealer, stockist. **–kenntnis,** *f.* technical *or* specialist knowledge. **fachkundig,** *adj.* competent, expert; ***–e Leitung,*** expert guidance, expert opinion. **Fachlehrer,** *m.* teacher of a special subject, specialist. **fachlich,** *adj.* professional; technical; departmental; ***–e Vorbildung,*** professional training. **Fachmann,** *m.* (*pl.* **-leute**) expert, specialist. **fachmännisch,** *adj.* expert, specialist, professional; workmanlike, competent (*job*). **Fachschaft,** *f.* trade association, professional body *or* organization. **Fachschule,** *f.* trade *or* technical school.

fachsimpeln ['faxzɪmpəln], *v.i.* (*insep.*) (*coll.*) talk shop.

Fach|sprache, *f.* technical language *or* jargon. **–studium,** *n.* special study; professional training. **–werk,** *n.* panelling; framework. **–werkbau,** *m.* half-timbered building. **–wissen,** *n.,* **–wissenschaft,** *f.* special branch of science. **–wort,** *n.* technical term. **–zeitschrift,** *f.* technical *or* scientific periodical; trade journal.

Fackel ['fakəl], *f.* (-, *pl.* **-n**) torch, flare, flambeau. **fackeln,** *v.i.* flare, flicker; (*fig., coll.*) dither, shilly-shally, (dilly-)dally; ***hier wurde nicht lange gefackelt,*** not much time was lost, there was no beating about the bush. **Fackelzug,** *m.* torchlight procession.

Fädchen ['fɛ:dçən], *n.* small thread, filament.

fad(e) ['fa:d(ə)], *adj.* tasteless, insipid, flat; (*fig.*) vacuous, trite, jejune, dull, boring, stale.

Faden ['fa:dən], **1.** *m.* (**-s,** *pl.* **¨**) thread; string, twine, cord; fibre, filament; (*Opt.*) hairline; shred, particle; burr, feather-edge (*of a knife*); thread (*of a discourse, of life etc.*); (***ihn***) ***am – haben,*** have him under one's thumb; (*fig.*) ***alle Fäden in der Hand halten,*** hold all the strings in one's hand; ***an einem – hängen,*** hang by a thread; ***sie läßt keinen guten – an ihm,*** she hasn't a good word to say for him; ***ein – Seide,*** a bobbin of silk; ***er hat keinen trocknen – am Leibe,*** he is wet through, he hasn't a dry stitch on; (*fig.*) ***den – verlieren,*** lose the thread; (*fig.*) ***den – wiederaufnehmen,*** pick up the thread; (*coll.*) ***in einem – weg,*** without stopping for a breath. *See also under* **abbeißen. 2.** *m.* (**-s,** *pl.* **-**) 1. (*Naut.*) fathom; 2. cord (*128 cu. ft. of cut wood*). **fadenförmig,** *adj.* thread-like, filiform.

Faden|führer, *m.* (*Weav.*) thread guide. **–holz,** *n.*

cordwood. **-kreuz,** *n.* (*Opt.*) crosswires, reticule. **-nudeln,** *f.pl.* vermicelli. **-rolle,** *f.* reel of thread. **fadenscheinig,** *adj.* threadbare, sleazy; (*fig.*) thin, shabby (*of an excuse*). **fadenweise,** *adv.* thread by thread. **Fadenwurm,** *m.* worm of the phylum *nematoda.* **fadenziehend,** *adj.* stringy, ropy, viscous.

Fadheit ['fa:thaɪt], *f.* tastelessness, insipidity, flatness, staleness, dullness, boredom.

Fading ['fɛ:dɪŋ], **Fäding,** *n.* (*Rad.*) fading. **Fadingregler,** *m.* automatic gain control.

Fagott [fa'gɔt], *n.* (**-s,** *pl.* **-e**) bassoon. **Fagottist** [-'tɪst], *m.* (**-en,** *pl.* **-en**) bassoonist.

Fähe ['fɛ:ə], *f.* female (*of hounds, foxes and wolves*); bitch, vixen, she-wolf.

fähig ['fɛ:ɪç], *adj.* 1. (*Gen. or* ***zu***) able (to do), capable (of); apt, liable (to do); qualified, fit (for); – ***machen,*** enable (*zu,* to); ***sich – machen,*** qualify o.s. (*zu,* for); ***zu allem –,*** capable of anything; 2. competent, efficient, clever; ***-er Kopf,*** man of parts, clever fellow. **Fähigkeit,** *f.* capability, ability; competence, efficiency, qualification; faculty, talent, capacity; *pl.* abilities; ***das geht über meine -en,*** that is beyond my power(s), that beats me.

fahl [fa:l], *adj.* pale, sallow, fawn-coloured, dun; (*rare*) fallow (*as in fallow deer*). **fahl|grau,** *adj.* ashy grey, livid. **-rot,** *adj.* fawn. **Fahlsegler,** *m.* (*Orn.*) pallid swift (*Apus pallidus*).

Fahne ['fa:nə], *f.* 1. flag, standard, banner; (*Mil.*) colours; (*obs.*) company, troop, squadron; ***Dienst bei der –,*** service with the colours, active service; ***mit fliegenden -n,*** with flying colours; ***die – hochhalten,*** keep the flag flying; 2. feather, beard (*of a quill*); 3. vane, weather-cock; 4. trail (*of smoke*); 5. *See* **Fahnenabzug.**

Fahnen|abzug, *m.* (*Typ.*) galley proof. **-eid,** *m.* oath of allegiance *or* loyalty. **-flucht,** *f.* desertion. **-flüchtige(r),** *m., f.* deserter. **-junker,** *m.* (*Mil.*) officer cadet, ensign. **-stange,** *f.,* **-stock,** *m.* flagpole, flagstaff. **-träger,** *m.* standard-bearer. **-tuch,** *n.* bunting. **-weihe,** *f.* presentation of colours, consecration of the colours.

Fähnlein ['fɛ:nlaɪn], *n.* (*obs.*) (*Mil.*) troop, squad.

Fähnrich ['fɛ:nrɪç], *m.* (**-s,** *pl.* **-e**) (*Mil.*) officer cadet, ensign; (*Naut.*) midshipman.

Fahrbahn ['fa:rba:n], *f.* roadway, (*Am.*) pavement, driveway; (*on motorway*) (traffic) lane. **fahrbar,** *adj.* 1. passable, practicable (*road*), navigable (*waterway*); ***-es Eis,*** open ice; 2. portable, mobile, travelling (*equipment*); ***-e Feldküche,*** mobile kitchen. **Fahrbereich,** *m.* (*Mil.*) operational *or* cruising radius. **fahrbereit,** *adj.* in running order, ready to move off. **Fahr|damm,** *m.* roadway, (*Am.*) pavement, driveway. **-dienst,** *m.* train service. **-dienstleiter,** *m.* (*Railw.*) traffic superintendent.

Fähre ['fɛ:rə], *f.* ferry; ferry-boat; ***fliegende –,*** flying bridge; ***in einer – übersetzen,*** ferry across.

fahren ['fa:rən], **1.** *irr.v.i.* (*aux.* s.) 1. (*in any conveyance*) go, travel (*mit,* by); (*driving o.s. in any land vehicle*) drive; (*on animal, bicycle or driven in land vehicle*) ride, (*by water*) sail; (*of vehicle*) go, run; be moving; ***über einen Fluß –,*** cross a river; ***auf den Grund –,*** run aground; ***aus dem Hafen –,*** clear the port; ***mit dem Rad –,*** cycle; ***zur*** or ***in die Hölle*** or ***zum Teufel –,*** go to hell (*or* the devil); ***gen Himmel –,*** ascend into heaven; ***dieses Schiff fährt zweimal wöchentlich,*** this ship sails twice a week; ***spazieren –,*** go for a drive *or* ride; ***fahre wohl!*** farewell! ***rechts –,*** keep to the right; 2. (*fig.*) (*aux.* s. *&* h.) move hurriedly *or* violently, flash, shoot; start; ***aus dem Bette –,*** start up from one's bed, leap out of bed; ***ihm aus der Hand –,*** slip out of his hand; ***aus der Haut –,*** lose all patience, lose one's temper; ***gut (schlecht) – bei,*** fare well (ill) with, come off well (badly) in; ***es fuhr mir durch den Sinn,*** it flashed across my mind; ***in die Höhe –,*** start up, jump *or* leap up; ***in die Kleider –,*** fling *or* slip one's clothes on, slip into one's clothes; ***er fuhr in die Tasche,*** his hand went to his pocket; ***einander in die Haare –,*** come to blows; ***was ist in ihn gefahren?*** what has come over him? ***– lassen,*** let go *or* slip, (*fig.*) renounce, abandon, give *or* (*Am.*) pass up; ***die Sorge – lassen,*** banish care; ***eine Gelegenheit – lassen,*** let an opportunity slip; ***einen (Wind) – lassen,*** break wind; ***mit der Hand – über (Acc.),*** pass one's hand over; (*coll.*) ***ihm übers Maul –,*** reply rudely, snap *or* take him up; ***es fuhr mir kalt über den Rücken,*** a cold shudder passed through me *or* went down my back *or* spine. **2.** *irr.v.t.* drive; convey, take, carry, cart (*goods by vehicle*); sail (*a boat*); ride (*a cycle*); ***eine Strecke –,*** cover a distance; ***er fährt seine Mutter spazieren,*** he takes his mother for a drive; ***Sand –,*** cart sand; ***ihn über einen Fluß –,*** ferry him over a river; ***Karussell –,*** ride on the roundabout; ***welche Marke fährt er?*** what make of car does he drive? ***er fuhr die beste Zeit,*** he made *or* clocked the best time (*motor racing*). **3.** *irr.v.r.* ***es fährt sich gut auf dieser Straße,*** this is a good road for driving; ***in diesem Wagen fährt es sich angenehm,*** this car rides well.

Fahren, *n.* travelling, driving, riding, motoring *etc.* **fahrend,** *adj.* going, travelling; vagrant, itinerant, (*Mech.*) sliding; ***-er Ritter,*** knight errant; ***-e Habe,*** movable property, movables; ***-e Artillerie,*** mobile artillery; ***-e Post,*** stage-coach; ***-es Volk,*** gipsies; tramps, vagrants. **Fahrer,** *m.* driver, chauffeur; motorist, (*motorcycle etc.*) rider, (motor-) cyclist; ***rücksichtsloser –,*** dangerous *or* careless driver, road-hog; ***flüchtiger –,*** hit-and-run driver. **Fahrerflucht,** *f.* hit-and-run offence.

Fahr|gast, *m.* passenger. **-geld,** *n.* fare. **-gelegenheit,** *f.* conveyance. **-geschwindigkeit,** *f.* (driving) speed. **-gestell,** *n.* (*Motor.*) chassis, (*Av.*) under-carriage, landing gear. **-gleis,** *n.* rut; track.

fahrig ['fa:rɪç], *adj.* careless, inattentive; erratic, haphazard, happy-go-lucky, fickle, flighty; nervous, fidgety.

Fahrkarte ['fa:rkartə], *f.* ticket; ***eine – lösen,*** book *or* take a ticket (*nach,* for); ***einfache –,*** single ticket; ***– hin und zurück,*** return ticket. **Fahrkarten|ausgabe,** *f.,* **-schalter,** *m.* ticket office.

Fahrkolonne ['fa:rkɔlɔnə], *f.* supply train, (*Mil.*) transport column.

fahrlässig ['fa:rlɛsɪç], *adj.* negligent, reckless, careless; ***-e Tötung,*** accidental homicide. **Fahrlässigkeit,** *f.* negligence, recklessness, carelessness.

Fahr|lehrer, *m.* driving instructor. **-leistung,** *f.* (*vehicle*) performance, (*fuel*) miles per gallon.

Fährmann ['fɛ:rman], *m.* (*pl.* **¨er** *or* **-leute**) ferryman.

Fahrnis ['fa:rnɪs], *f.* (-, *pl.* **-se**) movable goods, goods and chattels.

Fahrplan ['fa:rpla:n], *m.* time-table, (*Am.*) schedule. **fahrplanmäßig,** **1.** *adj.* regular, (*Am.*) scheduled. **2.** *adv.* on *or* to time, (*Am.*) to schedule; ***der Zug kommt – in fünf Minuten an,*** the train is due *or* scheduled to arrive in five minutes.

Fahr|praxis, *f.* driving experience. **-preis,** *m.* fare. **-preisermäßigung,** *f.* reduction of fare, reduced fare. **-preiszone,** *f.* farestage. **-prüfung,** *f.* driving test. **-rad,** *n.* (bi)cycle. **-rinne,** *f.* (*on water*) fairway, shipping lane, (*on land*) rut, wheel-track. **-schein,** *m.* ticket. **-schule,** *f.* driving school. **-schüler,** *m.* learner (driver). **-straße,** *f.* highway. **-stuhl,** *m.* 1. lift, (*Am.*) elevator; (*for goods*) hoist; 2. bath-chair, wheelchair, invalid chair. **-stuhlführer,** *m.* lift attendant, lift-boy.

Fahrt ['fa:rt], *f.* (-, *pl.* **-en**) ride, drive; journey, voyage, (*by sea*) passage, cruise; excursion, outing, trip; run, course, rate of progress; (*Naut.*) ***– aufnehmen,*** get under way, gather speed; ***– ins Blaue,*** mystery trip; ***freie –!*** all clear (ahead)! ***freie – haben,*** have a clear course *or* road ahead, (*at traffic lights*) have the green light; (*Naut.*) ***große –,*** three-quarter speed; ***gute –!*** bon voyage! ***in –,*** (*Naut.*) under way, (*fig.*) under way, in full swing; (*Naut.*) ***kleine –,*** dead slow; (*Naut.*) ***– verlieren,*** lose way; (*Naut.*) ***volle –,*** full speed; (*Naut.*) ***wenig – machen,*** make little headway.

Fährte ['fɛ:rtə], *f.* track, trail, footprint(s); (*Hunt.*) scent; ***auf der falschen –,*** on the wrong scent *or* track, (*fig.*) barking up the wrong tree.

Fahrtenbuch ['fa:rtənbu:x], *n.* (driver's) logbook.

Fahrt|flagge, *f.* (*Naut.*) blue Peter. **-messer,** *m.* (*Av.*) air-speed indicator, (*Naut.*) log(line). **-richtung,** *f.* direction of traffic, (*Railw.*) facing the engine. **-signal,** *n.* (*Railw.*) clear signal. **-unterbrechung,** *f.* break in a journey, (*Am.*) stopover. **-wind,** *m.* (*Av.*) airstream.

Fahr|vorschrift, *f.* rule(s) of the road. **-wasser,** *n.* navigable water, shipping lane, fairway, channel; (*fig.*) tendency, direction; ***ins politische – geraten,*** take a political turn; ***in seinem*** or ***im richtigen – sein,*** be in his element. **-weg,** *m.* *See* **-bahn**; drive, carriage way, approach road, (*Am.*) driveway. **-werk,** *n.* (*Av.*) *see* **-gestell**; tracks (*of tanks etc.*). **-zeit,** *f.* running-time, hours of operation, engine mileage. **-zeug,** *n.* vehicle, (*Naut.*) vessel, craft.

Fäkalien [fɛ'ka:liən], *n.pl.* faeces, night-soil, sewage.

Fakir ['fa:kɪr], *m.* (**-s,** *pl.* **-e**) fakir.

Faksimile [fak'zi:mile], *n.* (**-s,** *pl.* **-s** *or* **-milia**) facsimile.

Faktion [faktsi'o:n], *f.* faction.

Faktis [faktɪs], *n.* (-, *no pl.*) synthetic rubber.

faktisch ['faktɪʃ], **1.** *adj.* real, actual; de facto; effective. **2.** *adv.* in fact, actually.

faktitiv [fakti'ti:f], *adj.* causative; (*Gram.*) factitive.

Faktor ['faktɔr], *m.* (**-s,** *pl.* **-en**) 1. fact, circumstance, factor; (*Arith.*) factor; 2. factor, agent, manager, foreman. **Faktorei** [-'raɪ], *f.* agency abroad, trading post.

Faktotum [fak'to:tum], *n.* (**-s,** *pl.* **-s**) factotum, jack-of-all-trades.

Faktum ['faktum], *n.* (**-s,** *pl.* **-ten**) fact; *pl.* data.

Faktur(a) [fak'tu:r(a)], *f.* (-, *pl.* **-ren**) invoice; ***laut –,*** as per invoice. **fakturieren** [-'ri:rən], *v.t.* invoice. **Fakturist** [-'rɪst], *m.* (**-en,** *pl.* **-en**) invoice clerk.

Fäkulenz [fɛku'lɛnts], *f.* sediment, dregs, feculence.

Fakultät [fakul'tɛ:t], *f.* (*Univ.*) faculty, (*Am.*) department.

fakultativ [fakulta'ti:f], *adj.* optional.

falb [falp], *adj.* pale yellow, dun, fallow.

Falbel ['falbəl], *f.* (-, *pl.* **-n**) flounce, furbelow.

Falke ['falkə], *m.* (**-n,** *pl.* **-n**) falcon, hawk. **Falken|-augen,** *n.pl.* (*fig.*) eyes of a hawk. **-beize,** *f.* falconry, hawking. **-bussard,** *m.* (*Orn.*) desert buzzard (*Buteo vulpinus*). **Falkenier** [-'ni:r], *m.* (**-s,** *pl.* **-e**) falconer. **Falkenraubmöwe,** *f.* *See* ***Kleine Raubmöwe.*** **Falkner,** *m.* *See* **Falkenier.**

¹**Fall** [fal], *m.* (**-(e)s,** *pl.* **¨-e**) 1. fall, drop, tumble; decay, decline, ruin, overthrow, downfall, failure; waterfall, cataract; (*Prov.*) ***Hochmut kommt vor dem –,*** pride goes before a fall; ***zu – bringen,*** bring to the ground, trip up; (*fig.*) ruin, bring about the downfall of, (*Parl.*) defeat; ***zu – kommen,*** have a fall, (*coll.*) come to grief, collapse, be ruined; (*coll.*) ***Knall und –,*** like a bolt from the blue; 2. case, instance, matter, affair; ***auf jeden –, auf alle Fälle,*** in any case, by all means, at all events; ***auf keinen –,*** on no account, by no means; ***im –e, daß,*** in case, in the event of; ***in dem –e,*** in that case; ***im besten –,*** at best; ***im schlimmsten –,*** at worst, if the worst comes to the worst, in the last resort; ***ich setze den –,*** I make the supposition, suppose; ***von – zu –,*** according to circumstances, each case on its merits, as the case may be; ***der vorliegende –,*** the case in point.

²**Fall,** *n.* (**-(e)s,** *pl.* **-en**) (*Naut.*) halyard.

fällbar ['fɛlba:r], *adj.* (*Chem.*) precipitable.

Fall|beil, *n.* guillotine. **-beschleunigung,** *f.* acceleration due to gravity. **-bö,** *f.* (*Av.*) air pocket. **-brücke,** *f.* drawbridge.

Falle ['falə], *f.* trap, snare; pitfall; latch (*of door*); ***eine – aufstellen,*** set a trap (***gegen,*** for); (*fig.*) ***eine – stellen,*** set a trap (*Dat.*, for); (*fig.*) ***in die – gehen,*** walk into the trap; (*sl.*) ***sich in die – hauen,*** doss down, hit the hay.

fallen ['falən], *irr.v.i.* (*aux.* s.) fall, drop, fall *or* tumble (down), have *or* take a tumble (*of a p.*); fall, be taken *or* captured (*of fortress*); fall *or* be killed (in action) (*of soldier*); subside (*as floods*); be falling (*of barometer etc.*); (*Mus.*) descend; (*fig.*) decline, abate, diminish; fall, drop, go down (*of prices*), (*St. Exch.*) slump, (*Am.*) tumble; ***es fällt mir schwer,*** it is difficult for me, I find it hard, it goes hard with me; ***es fiel die Bemerkung,*** the observation was made, it was observed; ***es fiel ein Schuß,*** a shot was fired; ***der Würfel ist gefallen,*** the die is cast; ***es fielen heftige Reden,*** violent language was used; ***– an*** (*Acc.*), devolve on, descend to; ***die Erbschaft fällt an seinen Vetter,*** the legacy falls to his cousin; ***– auf*** (*Acc.*), fall *or* light on, turn upon, fall upon; ***die Wahl fiel auf ihn,*** the choice fell on him; ***mein Geburtstag fällt auf einen Sonntag,*** my birthday falls on a Sunday; ***mein Auge fiel auf sie,*** my eye fell *or* lighted on her; ***er fällt mir auf die Nerven,*** he gets on my nerves; ***das Gespräch fiel auf . . .,*** the conversation turned upon . . .; ***er ist nicht auf den Kopf gefallen,*** he is no fool; ***es fällt mir schwer aufs Herz,*** it weighs upon my mind; ***das fällt völlig aus dem Rahmen,*** that does not fit at all into the picture; ***aus den*** or ***allen Wolken –,*** be thunderstruck; ***aus allen Himmeln –,*** become thoroughly disillusioned; ***aus der Rolle –,*** act out of part, be inconsistent; ***es fiel mir aus der Hand,*** it dropped out of my hand; ***es fällt in die Augen,*** it catches the eye, it strikes one; ***ihm in den Arm –,*** seize him by the arm, (*fig.*) restrain him; ***ihm in die Zügel –,*** seize the bridle of his horse; (*fig.*) restrain him; ***ihm in die Rede –,*** interrupt him, cut him short; ***ihm in die Hände –,*** fall into his power; ***in Ohnmacht –,*** faint, swoon; ***mit der Tür ins Haus –,*** blurt out, go at it like a bull at a gate; ***das fällt nicht ins Gewicht,*** that is of no importance *or* consequence, it is of no great weight; ***sein Zeugnis fällt schwer in die Waagschale,*** his evidence carries great weight; ***in den Rücken –,*** attack from behind, (*fig.*) stab in the back; ***er ist beim König in Ungnade gefallen,*** he has fallen into disfavour with the king, he has incurred the king's displeasure; ***– lassen,*** drop, let fall; discard, put aside; ***einige triftige Bemerkungen – lassen,*** put in *or* let drop a few pointed remarks; ***einen Freund – lassen,*** throw over *or* (*coll.*) drop a friend; ***Ansprüche – lassen,*** drop *or* waive claims; ***Bomben – lassen,*** drop *or* release bombs; ***einen Gedanken – lassen,*** dismiss *or* drop an idea; ***den Plan – lassen,*** abandon *or* give up *or* drop the plan; ***– über*** (*Acc.*), fall *or* stumble over, fall upon; ***über den Haufen –,*** fall headlong; ***– unter,*** fall under; fall among; (*fig.*) fall within (the scope of); ***unter den Tisch –,*** be shelved; (*coll.*) ***ich bin fast vom Stengel gefallen,*** I was thunderstruck *or* flabbergasted *or* struck all of a heap; ***es fiel mir wie Schuppen von den Augen,*** my eyes were suddenly opened, a light *or* the truth suddenly dawned (on me), the scales fell from my eyes; ***zu Boden –,*** fall to the ground; (*fig.*) come to nothing; ***ihm zur Last –,*** be a burden *or* troublesome to him; ***ihm zu Füßen –,*** throw o.s. at his feet; (*Prov.*) ***der Apfel fällt nicht weit vom Stamm,*** he's a chip of the old block; *see* **gefallen.**

Fallen ['falən], *n.* fall, falling, subsidence; descent, slope, dip, drop; decline, downward trend, decay, diminution.

fällen ['fɛlən], *v.t.* fell, cut, hew (*timber*), lay low, bring down (*adversary*); drop (*a perpendicular*); sink (*a shaft*); pass (*a sentence or judgement*); (*Chem.*) precipitate; ***mit gefälltem Bajonett angreifen,*** charge with fixed bayonets.

Fallen|leger, -steller, *m.* trapper.

Fall|gatter, *n.* portcullis. **-geschwindigkeit,** *f.* velocity of fall(ing bodies). **-gesetz,** *n.* law of gravity. **-grube,** *f.* trap, (*Am.*) deadfall; (*fig.*) pitfall. **-hammer,** *m.* drop hammer. **-höhe,** *f.* height of fall, (*coll.*) drop. **-holz,** *n.* fallen wood.

fallieren [fa'li:rən], *v.i.* (*Comm.*) fail, become bankrupt *or* insolvent.

fällig ['fɛlɪç], *adj.* payable, due (*of debt*), mature (*of bond*); ***längst –,*** overdue; ***wenn –,*** when due (*of payment*), at maturity (*of bond*); ***– werden,*** be payable; be *or* fall *or* become due (*of payment*), mature (*of bond*), expire (*of rights*). **Fälligkeit,** *f.* expiration, maturity. **Fälligkeits|tag, -termin,** *m.* due date, maturity.

Falliment [fali'mɛnt], *n.* (**-(e)s,** *pl.* **-e**), **Fallissement** [falɪs(ə)'mã], *n.* (**-s,** *pl.* **-s**) (*Comm.*) failure, bankruptcy. **fallit** [fa'li:t], *adj.* – *sein,* be bankrupt. **Fallit,** *m.* (**-en,** *pl.* **-en**) bankrupt (person).

Fall|klappe, *f.* drop (*on telephone switchboard*). **-obst,** *n.* fallen fruit, windfall. **-recht,** *n.* case law. **-reep,** *n.* (*Naut.*) gangway, companionway. **-rohr,** *n.* down pipe, waste pipe.

falls [fals], *conj.* in case, in the event of, if, providing *or* supposing (that), provided (that).

Fallschirm ['falʃɪrm], *m.* parachute; *mit – absetzen,* parachute (*a p. or th.*); *mit – abspringen,* parachute, (*coll.*) bale out. **Fallschirm|absprung,** *m.* parachute descent. **-jäger,** *m.* paratrooper. **-springen,** *n.* parachute jumping. **-truppen,** *f.pl.* paratroops.

Fall|strick, *m.* snare, noose, gin; (*fig.*) trick, catch, pitfall, ruse. **-sucht,** *f.* epilepsy. **fallsüchtig,** *adj.* epileptic. **Fall|tor,** *n.* portcullis. **-tür,** *f.* trap-door.

Fällung ['fɛluŋ], *f.* 1. felling, cutting (*of timber*); 2. (*Chem.*) precipitation. **Fällungsmittel,** *n.* precipitant.

fallweise ['falvaɪzə], *adv.* case by case, (taking) each case in turn.

Fall|werk, *n.* stamp, press, pile-driver. **-wild,** *n.* carrion. **-winkel,** *m.* gradient, dip; angle of fall *or* inclination *or* descent.

falsch [falʃ], **1.** *adj.* 1. wrong, false, incorrect, untrue, erroneous; imitated, artificial, counterfeit, spurious, bogus, (*coll.*) fake, phoney; pseudo-, adulterated, forged; insincere, deceitful, fraudulent; perfidious, treacherous; (*Archit.*) blank; *-e Ansicht,* erroneous view; *-e Anwendung,* misapplication; *-e Bezeichnung,* misnomer; *-e Darstellung,* misrepresentation; *-er Diskant,* falsetto; *unter -er Flagge,* under false colours; *-es Geld,* counterfeit *or* base money; *-er Hase,* rissole; *-er König,* usurper, pretender; *-er Mensch,* deceitful person, double-dealer; *-er Name,* false *or* fictitious name; *-es Pferd,* vicious horse; *-e Rippen,* floating ribs; *-e Schlange,* snake in the grass; *-es Spiel,* foul play, trickery, double dealing; *-er Stein,* spurious stone; *-er Wechsel,* forged bill; *-e Zähne,* false teeth, dentures; 2. (*obs.*) angry, (*Poet.*) wroth, (*coll.*) mad (*auf ihn,* with him). **2.** *adv.* – *anführen,* misquote; – *antworten,* give the wrong answer; – *auffassen,* misunderstand, misconceive, (*coll.*) get wrong; – *aussprechen,* pronounce incorrectly, mispronounce; – *darstellen,* misrepresent; *die Uhr geht –,* the clock is wrong; – *geraten!* (you've guessed) wrong! – *schreiben,* write incorrectly, misspell; – *schwören,* perjure o.s.; – *singen,* sing out of tune; – *spielen,* (*Mus.*) play out of tune; (*Spt. etc.*) play without regard for the rules (*see* **falschspielen**) – *unterrichten,* misinform; (*Tele.*) – *verbunden!* wrong number! – *verstehen,* misunderstand. **Falsch,** *m. ohne –,* guileless, without guile; (*B.*) *ohne – wie die Tauben,* harmless as doves; *es ist kein – an ihm,* he is quite open and above board.

fälschen ['fɛlʃən], *v.t.* falsify (*an entry*), forge (*a document*), counterfeit (*money*), adulterate (*foodstuffs*), fake (*a picture*), (*coll.*) tamper with, doctor, cook (*accounts etc.*). **Fälscher,** *m.* falsifier, forger, counterfeiter.

Falschgeld ['falʃgɛlt], *n.* counterfeit (money).

Falschheit ['falʃhaɪt], *f.* (*of a th.*) falsity, falseness; spuriousness; (*of a p.*) deceit, guile, perfidy, duplicity, insincerity; (*of statements*) untruth, falsehood; (*of actions*) treachery, double-dealing.

fälschlich ['fɛlʃlɪç], *adj., adv.*, **fälschlicherweise,** *adv.* false(ly), wrong(ly), fraudulent(ly), incorrect(ly), erroneous(ly), mistaken(ly), by mistake, in error.

Falsch|meldung, *f.* false report; hoax, canard. **-münzer,** *m.* counterfeiter, forger, coiner. **-münzerei,** *f.* counterfeiting, forgery. **falschspielen,** *v.i.* (*sep.*) (*cards etc.*) cheat. **Falschspieler,** *m.* cardsharper, cheat.

Fälschung ['fɛlʃuŋ], *f.* falsification, forgery; adulteration; (*the th.*) forgery, counterfeit, fake.

Falsett [fal'zɛt], *n.* (**-(e)s,** *pl.* **-e**) falsetto (voice).

Falt [falt], *m.* 1. (**-s,** *pl.* **⸚e**) (*Swiss*) *see* **Falte**; 2. (**-(e)s,** *pl.* **-e**) hinge. **Falt|blatt,** *n.* folder. **-boot,** *n.* collapsible boat. **-dach,** *n.* folding roof.

Falte ['faltə], *f.* fold, pleat; crease, wrinkle; furrow (*in brow*), fold (*in ground*); *in -n legen,* fold; *-n werfen* or *schlagen,* pucker, get creased; *diese Kleid wirft keine -n,* this dress does not crease; *die Stirn in -n ziehen,* wrinkle *or* furrow *or* pucker *or* knit the brow; *die geheimsten -n des Herzens,* the inmost recesses of the heart.

fälteln ['fɛltəln], **1.** *v.t.* pleat, gather, frill. **2.** *v.r.* gather, frill. **Fältelung,** *f.* gathering, pleats, frills.

falten ['faltən], *v.t.* fold; pleat; knit (*the brow*); crease, wrinkle, pucker; *mit gefalteten Händen,* with hands clasped (*as in prayer*). **faltenfrei, faltenlos,** *adj.* unwrinkled, smooth, without folds *or* creases. **Falten|magen,** *m.* third stomach of ruminants. **-näher,** *m.* pleater (*on sewing machines*). **-rock,** *m.* pleated skirt. **-wurf,** *m.* (*Paint., Sculp.*) drapery.

Falter ['faltər], *m.* 1. butterfly, moth, lepidopter; 2. third stomach of ruminants.

faltig ['faltɪç], *adj.* folded, pleated, puckered; wrinkled (*forehead*). **-faltig,** *suff. See* **-fältig. -faltig,** *suff.* -fold.

Faltung ['faltuŋ], *f.* fold, convolution. **Faltwerk,** *n.* (*Archit.*) fluting.

Falz [falts], *m.* (**-es,** *pl.* **-e**) fold, welt, folded joint, turned-over edge; groove, notch; (*Engin.*) slideway; rabbet, lap-joint. **Falz|amboß,** *m.* coppersmith's anvil. **-bein,** *n.* folder, paperknife. **falzen,** *v.t.* fold (*paper*); groove, flute; (*Carp.*) rabbet; lap, welt (*tin etc.*). **Falzhobel,** *m.* grooving plane. **falzig,** *adj.* folded; grooved, furrowed. **Falz|maschine,** *f.* seaming *or* welting machine; (*Bookb.*) folding machine. **-scheine,** *f.* slotted rail, tram-rail.

Fama ['fa:ma], *f.* fame, (good) repute.

familiär [famili'ɛ:r], *adj.* familiar, intimate; forward, importunate; *-er Ausdruck,* colloquialism; *im -en Kreise,* in the family circle. **Familiarität** [–liari'tɛ:t], *f.* familiarity, intimacy; forwardness, importunity.

Familie [fa'mi:liə], *f.* family; household; *eine – gründen,* (marry and) settle down; *es liegt in der –,* it runs in the family; – *haben,* have children; *von guter – sein,* be of *or* from a good family.

Familien|ähnlichkeit, *f.* family likeness. **-angelegenheiten,** *f.pl.* family affairs. **-anschluß,** *m. er wünscht –,* he wishes to be treated like one of the family. **-bad,** *n.* mixed bathing. **-beihilfe,** *f.* family allowance, dependants' benefits. **-forschung,** *f.* genealogical investigation. **-glück,** *n.* domestic happiness. **-kreis,** *m.* domestic *or* family circle. **-nachrichten,** *f.pl.* (announcement of) births, marriages and deaths. **-name,** *m.* surname. **-stand,** *m.* family *or* marital status (*single, married, widowed etc.*). **-vater,** *m.* head of a *or* the family, family man, paterfamilias. **-vermächtnis,** *n.* entail. **-wappen,** *n.* family coat of arms. **-zulage,** *f. See* **-beihilfe. -zuwachs,** *m.* addition to the family. **-zwist,** *m.* family squabble, domestic discord.

famos [fa'mo:s], *adj.* (*coll.*) spendid, capital, fine, grand, great; *-er Kerl,* great guy.

Famulus ['fa:mulus], *m.* (-, *pl.* **-li**) amanuensis.

Fanal [fa'na:l], *n.* (**-(e)s,** *pl.* **-e**) beacon, torch, signal.

Fanatiker [fa'na:tikər], *m.* fanatic. **fanatisch,** *adj.* fanatic(al). **Fanatismus** [–'tɪsmus], *m.* fanaticism.

fand [fant], **fände** ['fɛndə], *see* **finden.**

Fanfare [fan'fa:rə], *f.* fanfare, flourish of trumpets.

Fang [faŋ], *m.* (**-es,** *pl.* **⸚e**) 1. catch(ing), capture; booty; *einen guten – tun,* make a good catch; 2. prey; booty; (*of fish*) draught, (*also fig.*) catch, haul; 3. fang, talon, claw, tusk; *in den Fängen* *halten,* have *or* hold in one's clutches; 4. (*Hunt.*) coup de grâce. **Fang|arm,** *m.* tentacle. **-ball,** *m.* (*Spt.*) (game of) catching. **-eisen,** *n.* (spring) trap.

fangen ['faŋən], **1.** *irr.v.t.* catch, seize, capture; trap, hook, net, snare; take prisoner; ***Feuer* -,** catch fire; ***leicht Feuer* -,** be inflammable *or* (*fig.*) impetuous *or* impressionable *or* excitable; ***sich* - *lassen,*** get caught, (*fig.*) walk into the trap; (*Prov.*) ***mit gefangen, mit gehangen,*** rogues of a gang on one gibbet must hang. **2.** *irr.v.r.* be *or* get caught, become entangled; catch, take hold; ***sich wieder* -,** (*Av.*) straighten *or* flatten out, (*fig.*) regain one's composure.

Fänger ['fɛŋər], *m.* 1. catcher; 2. *See also* **Fangzahn.**

Fang|gitter, *n.* (*Rad.*) suppressor grid. **-korb,** *m.* cow-catcher. **-leine,** *f.* harpoon-line; painter (*of a boat*), ripcord (*of parachute*). **-messer,** *n.* hunting knife. **-netz,** *n.* landing *or* dip net. **-schnur,** *f.* aiguillette (*on uniforms*). **-schuß, -stoß,** *m.* coup de grâce. **-vogel,** *m.* decoy-bird. **-vorrichtung,** *f.* 1. safety-catch; 2. *See also* **-korb. -zahn,** *m.* fang, tusk.

Fant [fant], *m.* **(-(e)s,** ***pl.*** **-e)** coxcomb, fop.

Fantasie [fanta'zi:], *f.* (*Mus.*) fantasia. **fantasieren,** *v.i.* (*Mus.*) improvise.

Farb|band ['farp-], *n.* typewriter ribbon. **-brühe,** *f.* dye. **-druck,** *m.* colour print(ing).

Farbe ['farbə], *f.* colour, tint, hue, shade; stain, paint, dye, pigment; complexion; (*Cards*) suit; (*Typ.*) ink; (*fig.*) allegiance; **-** ***auftragen,*** apply paint; **-** ***bekennen,*** (*Cards*) follow suit, (*fig.*) lay one's cards on the table, show one's colours, declare o.s.; ***echte* -,** fast colour; **-** ***halten,*** keep its colour, not fade; (*fig.*) stick to one's guns; **-** ***wechseln,*** change colour, (*fig.*) change sides.

farbecht ['farpˀɛçt], *adj.* of fast colour, unfadeable, fadeless, (*Phot.*) orthochromatic.

Färbemittel ['fɛrbəmɪtəl], *n.* pigment, colouring matter.

färben ['fɛrbən], **1.** *v.t.* dye, colour, stain, tint, (*also fig.*) tinge; (*fig.*) ***in der Wolle gefärbt,*** dyed-in-the-wool, out-and-out, engrained; ***mit Humor gefärbt,*** tinged with humour; ***mit Blut gefärbt,*** blood-stained. **2.** *v.r.* get a colour (in one's cheeks); blush; apply rouge *or* make-up.

-farben [farbən], *adj.suff.* (*to names of substances* =) -coloured; *e.g.* ***goldfarben,*** golden-coloured.

Farben|abweichung, *f.* chromatic aberration. **-band, -bild,** *n.* spectrum. **farbenblind,** *adj.* colour-blind. **Farben|blindheit,** *f.* colour-blindness. **-brechung,** *f.* colour refraction. **-druck,** *m.* colour printing; colour print. **farben|empfindlich,** *adj.* (*Phot.*) colour-sensitive, orthochromatic. **-freudig, -froh,** *adj.* colourful, gaily coloured. **Farben|gebung,** *f.* colouring (*of a painting*). **-grund,** *m.* ground colour. **-kasten,** *m.* paint box. **-kleckser,** *m.* dauber. **-pracht,** *f.* gorgeous colours, colourful splendour. **farben|prächtig, -prangend, -reich,** *adj.* splendidly *or* gorgeously colourful, richly coloured. **-rein,** *adj.* in clear colours. **Farben|sehen,** *n.* colour vision. **-sinn,** *m.* (fine) sense of colour, eye for colour. **-skala,** *f.* colour chart. **-spiel,** *n.* opalescence, iridescence, play of colours.

Färber ['fɛrbər], *m.* dyer. **Färber|baum,** *m.* (*Bot.*) sumac(h). **-distel,** *f.* (*Bot.*) safflower (*Carthamus tinctorius*). **Färberei** [-'raɪ], *f.* dye-works; dyer's (trade). **Färber|ginster,** *m.* (*Bot.*) dyer's greenweed (*Genista tinctoria*). **-wurzel,** *f.* (*Bot.*) (dyer's) madder (*Rubia tinctorum*).

Farb|fernsehen, *n.* colour television. **-film,** *m.* colour film. **-gebung,** *f. See* **Farbengebung.**

farbig ['farbɪç], *adj.* coloured, stained; chromatic, (*fig.*) colourful; ***die Farbigen,*** the coloured races. **-farbig,** *adj.suff.* -coloured, -chrome. **Farbigkeit,** *f.* colourfulness.

färbig ['fɛrbɪç], **-färbig,** (*Austr.*) *see* **farbig, -farbig.**

Farbigkeit ['farbɪçkaɪt], *f.* colourfulness.

Farb|kasten, *m. See* **Farbenkasten. -kissen,** *n.* inking pad. **-körper,** *m.* pigment, colouring matter.

farblos ['farplo:s], *adj.* colourless, pale; achromatic. **Farblosigkeit,** *f.* pallor, paleness; colourlessness; achromatism.

Farb|photographie, *f.* colour photography. **-stift,** *m.* coloured pencil *or* crayon. **-stoff,** *m.* dye-stuff; stain, pigment. **-ton,** *m.* tint, shade, tone, hue. **farbtonrichtig,** *adj.* (*Phot.*) isochromatic.

Färbung ['fɛrbuŋ], *f.* colouring, pigmentation, coloration; tone, hue, tinge, shade.

Farb|walze, *f.* inking roller. **-zelle,** *f.* pigment cell.

Farce ['farsə], *f.* (*Cul.*) forcemeat, stuffing. **farcieren** [-'si:rən], *v.t.* stuff.

Farinade [fari'na:də], *f. See* **Farinzucker.**

Färinger ['fɛ:rɪŋər], *m.* (*Geog.*) Faroese (islander).

Farinzucker [fa'ri:ntsukər], *m.* powdered *or* castor sugar.

Farm [farm], *f.* **(-,** ***pl.*** **-en)** (colonial) settlement; (cattle) ranch, (sheep) farm, (chicken) farm. **Farmer,** *m.* (colonial) settler; ranch owner, (sheep *or* chicken) farmer.

Farn [farn], *m.* **(-es,** ***pl.*** **-e), Farnkraut,** *n.* fern.

Färöer [fɛ'rø:ər], *pl.* (*Geog.*) Faroe Islands. **färöisch,** *adj.* Faroese.

Farre ['farə], *m.* **(-n,** ***pl.*** **-n)** bullock, young bull, steer.

Färse ['fɛrzə], *f.* heifer.

Fasan [fa'za:n], *m.* **(-s,** ***pl.*** **-(e)n)** (*Orn.*) (*Am.* ring-necked) pheasant (*Phasianus colchicus*). **Fasanen|-garten,** *m.*, **-gehege,** *n.*, **Fasanerie** [-ə'ri:], *f.* pheasant-preserve.

Faschierte(s) [fa'ʃi:rtə(s)], *n.* (*Austr.*) minced meat.

Faschine [fa'ʃi:nə], *f.* (*Fort.*) fascine; hurdle, bundle of faggots. **Faschinenmesser,** *n.* matchet, machete.

Fasching ['faʃɪŋ], *m.* **(-s,** ***pl.*** **-e)** (*dial.*) carnival. **Faschingszeit,** *f.* Shrovetide.

Faschismus [fa'ʃɪsmus], *m.* fascism. **Faschist,** *m.* **(-en,** ***pl.*** **-en)** fascist. **faschistisch,** *adj.* fascist.

Fase ['fa:zə], *f.* bevel-edge, chamfer.

1**Fasel** ['fa:zəl], *f.* **(-,** ***pl.*** **-n)** (*Bot.*) runner bean (*Phaseolus vulgaris*).

2**Fasel,** *m.* (*dial.*) farrow (*of pigs*); brood, young (*of animals*).

Faselei [fa:zə'laɪ], *f.* (*coll.*) twaddle, drivel, balderdash. **Faselhans,** *m.* babbler, scatterbrain, drivelling fool. **faselig,** *adj.* scatterbrained, drivelling. **faseln,** *v.i.* drivel, babble, talk twaddle *or* drivel.

Fasen ['fa:zən], *m. See* **Faser. fasennackt,** *adj. See* **fasernackt.**

Faser ['fa:zər], *f.* **(-,** ***pl.*** **-n)** thread, fibre, (*in wood*) grain, (*on beans*) string; ***dünne* -,** filament; (*fig.*) ***mit jeder* -** ***seines Herzens,*** with every fibre of his being.

Fäserchen ['fɛ:zərçən], *n.* filament, fibril; fluff.

Faser|gewebe, *n.* fibrous tissue. **-haut,** *f.* fibrous membrane. **-holzplatte,** *f.* fibreboard. **faserig,** *adj.* fibrous, stringy, filaceous. **fasern, 1.** *v.t.* unravel, fray. **2.** *v.i., v.r.* unravel, become frayed.

fasernackt ['fa:zərnakt], *adj.* (*coll.*) stark naked.

Faserstoff ['fa:zərʃtɔf], *m.* man-made fibres; synthetic fabrics; fibrin, fibrous material. **Faserung,** *f.* texture; fibrillation, (*in wood*) grain; fraying, unravelling.

Faß [fas], *n.* **(-(ss)es,** ***pl.*** **¨(ss)er)** cask, barrel; tub, vat; tun, keg; ***drei* - *Bier,*** three casks of ale; ***Wein vom* -,** wine from the wood; ***Bier vom* -,** draught-ale; (*coll.*) ***das schlägt dem* - *den Boden aus,*** that is the last straw, that is the limit.

Fassade [fa'sa:də], *f.* façade, front. **Fassadenkletterer,** *m.* cat-burglar.

faßbar ['fasba:r], *adj.* tangible; comprehensible.

Faß|bier, *n.* draught beer. **-binder,** *m.* cooper. **-boden,** *m.* head of a cask.

fassen ['fasən], **1.** *v.t.* grasp, seize, take *or* lay hold of; apprehend (*fugitive*); hold, contain, accommodate, include, embrace, comprise; (*fig.*) grasp, understand, apprehend, comprehend, conceive, (*coll.*) take in; put (*in* (*Acc.*), in(to)), barrel (*beer*); sack (*corn*); hive (*bees*); set, mount (*gems*); clothe, express (*in a certain form*); form (*a resolve, a liking etc.*); *faß!* (*to a dog*) fetch it! ***Abneigung –***, take a dislike (*gegen*, to); ***Anschläge –***, form plans; ***ins Auge –***, fix one's eyes upon, take a good look at; (*fig.*) consider, envisage, keep in mind; ***einen Beschluß –***, pass a resolution; ***ihn bei der Ehre –***, appeal to his honour; ***einen Entschluß –***, reach a decision; (*sl.*) ***Essen –!*** come and get it! (*soldiers' sl.*); ***Fuß –***, gain a foothold, get a firm footing; ***festen Fuß –***, settle down, establish o.s.; ***einen Gedanken –***, form an idea; ***an*** or ***bei der Hand –***, take by the hand; ***sich*** (*Dat.*) ***ein Herz –, Mut –***, take courage; ***Neigung –***, take a liking (***für***, to); ***in einen Rahmen –***, frame; ***einen Vorsatz –***, make up one's mind, resolve; ***in Worte –***, put into *or* clothe *or* express in words, formulate; ***Wurzel –***, take *or* strike root. **2.** *v.r.* collect *or* contain *or* compose o.s., pull o.s. together; ***sich in Geduld –***, have patience, possess one's soul in patience; ***sich kurz –***, be brief, (*coll.*) make *or* cut it short; *see* **gefaßt.**

faßlich ['faslıç], *adj.* comprehensible, intelligible, conceivable; ***leicht –***, easily understood.

Fasson [fa'sɔ̃:], *f.* (-, *pl.* **-s**) fashion, style, design, cut, shape, form; (*Engin.*) section; ***nach – gearbeitet***, fully fashioned. **Fassonarbeit,** *f.* (*Engin.*) profiling, shaping. **fassonieren** [faso'ni:rən], *v.t.* (*Engin.*) profile, form, shape.

Fassung ['fasuŋ], *f.* **1.** setting, mounting, frame; socket, lampholder; **2.** draft, version, formulation, wording; diction, form, style; capacity; ***in dieser – ist es kaum verständlich***, it is scarcely intelligible as it stands; **3.** composure, poise, self-control; ***seine – bewahren, nicht aus der – kommen***, remain calm *or* collected *or* composed; ***ihn aus der – bringen***, disconcert *or* confuse *or* upset him, (*coll.*) rattle him; ***aus der – kommen***, lose one's self-control; ***ganz außer – sein***, be completely beside o.s. **Fassungs|gabe, -kraft,** *f.* (power of) comprehension, grasp, mental capacity. **fassungslos,** *adj.* aghast, perplexed, speechless, beside o.s. **Fassungslosigkeit,** *f.* perplexity, speechlessness. **Fassungs|raum,** *m.*, **-vermögen,** *n.* seating capacity, holding capacity, carrying capacity.

Faßwein ['fasvaın], *m.* wine from *or* in the wood. **faßweise,** *adv.* by the barrel.

fast [fast], *adv.* almost, nearly, (well)nigh, close upon; ***– nichts***, next to nothing; ***– nie***, hardly *or* scarcely ever.

fasten [fastən], *v.i.* fast. **Fasten,** *n.* fasting; *pl.* fast, time of fasting, Lent. **Fasten|sonntag,** *m.* Sunday in Lent. **-speise,** *f.* Lenten fare. **-zeit,** *f.* Lent.

Fastnacht ['fastnaxt], *f.* Shrove Tuesday. **Fastnachtsspiel,** *n.* shrovetide farce, carnival play.

Faszikel [fas'tsi:kəl], *m.* fascicle, file (*of papers*).

fatal [fa'ta:l], *adj.* disagreeable, annoying, awkward, unfortunate; ***das ist –***, that is a nuisance; ***eine -e Geschichte***, an awkward business.

Fatalismus [fata'lısmus], *m.* fatalism. **fatalistisch,** *adj.* fatalistic. **Fatalität** [-'tɛ:t], *f.* ill luck, misfortune, adversity.

Fatum ['fa:tum], *n.* (**-s,** *pl.* **-ta**) fate, destiny.

fatzen ['fatsən], *v.i.* (*dial.*) play the fool. **Fatzke,** *m.* (**-n,** *pl.* **-n**) dandy, fop, coxcomb.

fauchen ['fauxən], *v.i.* spit, hiss (*as cats*); puff (*as engine*).

faul [faul], *adj.* **1.** decayed, rotten, putrid, foul, stale, bad; (*fig.*) worthless, shady, (*coll.*) fishy; ***-e Ausrede***, lame *or* poor *or* thin excuse; ***-es Geschwätz***, idle talk, empty words; ***-es Fleisch***, proud flesh; (*Comm.*) ***-er Kunde***, bad *or* (*coll.*) shady customer; (*coll.*) ***-e Sache***, rotten state of affairs; ***-e Witze***, bad *or* poor *or* stale jokes; ***-er Zauber***, humbug; **2.** lazy, idle, indolent, (*of metal*) brittle; ***sich auf die -e Haut legen***, eat the bread of idleness; loll in the lap of indolence; ***-er Knecht***, ready reckoner; (*Naut.*) ***-e See***, calm.

Faul|baum, *m.* (*Bot.*) breaking buckthorn, berry-bearing alder (*Rhamnus frangula*). **-bett,** *n.* (*fig.*) lap of idleness, inactivity. **-brand,** *m.* smut. **-brut,** *f.* foul brood (*bees*). **-bütte,** *f.* fermenting trough.

Fäule ['fɔylə], *f.* (dry) rot, blight; *see also* **Fäulnis.**

faulen ['faulən], *v.i.* (*aux.* s.) rot, decay, decompose, putrefy.

faulenzen ['faulɛntsən], *v.i.* idle, lounge, loaf (about), laze, take it easy; be lazy, lead an idle life. **Faulenzer,** *m.* sluggard, idler, loafer, (*coll.*) lazybones; deckchair. **Faulenzerei** [-'raı], *f.* laziness, idleness, lounging, loafing (about), idling.

Faul|fieber, *n.* putrid fever; (*coll.*) fit of laziness. **-gas,** *n.* sewer gas. **Faulheit,** *f.* laziness, idleness, sloth. **faulig,** *adj.* putrescent, putrid, rotten, rotting, mouldy.

Fäulnis ['fɔylnıs], *f.* decay, putrefaction, putrescence, decomposition, (*Med.*) sepsis, (*of bone*) caries, (*fig.*) rottenness, corruption. **fäulniserregend,** *adj.* putrefactive, septic. **Fäulniserreger,** *m.* bacterium. **fäulnis|hemmend, -verhütend,** *adj.* antiseptic.

Faul|pelz, *m.* (*coll.*) lazybones, sluggard, idler. **-tier,** *n.* (*Zool.*) sloth (*Bradypus*); (*fig.*) sluggard.

Faun [faun], *m.* (**-en,** *pl.* **-en**) faun, satyr.

Fauna ['fauna], *f.* (-, *pl.* **-nen**) fauna.

1**Faust** [faust], *m.* Faustus.

2**Faust,** *f.* (-, *pl.* **¨-e**) (clenched) fist; (*coll.*) ***das paßt wie die – aufs Auge***, that's neither here nor there, that's beside the mark *or* point; ***auf eigene –***, on one's own (account *or* responsibility); (*coll.*) off one's own bat; ***mit eiserner*** or ***gepanzerter –***, with an iron hand *or* a mailed fist; ***geballte –***, clenched fist; ***schwer auf der – liegen***, be hard-mouthed (*of horses*); ***ihm eine – machen***, shake one's fist at him; ***mit der – auf den Tisch schlagen***, put one's foot down. **Faustball,** *m.* punch-ball (*game*).

Fäustchen ['fɔystçən], *n.* ***sich ins – lachen***, laugh up one's sleeve, gloat.

faustdick ['faustdık], *adj.* clumsy, awkward, lumbering, laboured; (*coll.*) ***er hat es – hinter den Ohren***, he is a sly dog; ***das ist – gelogen***, that's a thumping lie *or* (*coll.*) a whopper.

Fäustel ['fɔystəl], *m.* (miners') mallet; *see also* **Faustkeil.**

faustgroß ['faustgro:s], *adj.* as big as one's fist. **Faust|handschuh,** *m.* mitten; boxing glove. **-huhn,** *n. See* **Steppenhuhn. -kampf,** *m.* boxing, pugilism; boxing-match. **-keil,** *m.* (*Archaeol.*) flint (weapon *or* tool), stone implement.

Fäustling ['fɔystlıŋ], *m.* (**-s,** *pl.* **-e**) mitten; (early type of) pistol. **fäustlings,** *adv.* with the fist.

Faust|pfand, *n.* dead pledge. **-recht,** *n.* club-law. **-regel,** *f.* rule of thumb. **-schlag,** *m.* punch, blow with the fist; *pl.* fisticuffs. **-zeichnung,** *f.* rough sketch.

Fauteuil [fo'tø:j], *m.* (**-s,** *pl.* **-s**) armchair.

Favorit [favo'ri:t], *m.* (**-en,** *pl.* **-en**), **Favorite,** *f.*, **Favoritin,** *f.* favourite.

Faxen ['faksən], *pl.* (*coll.*) (tom)foolery, buffoonery, pranks, antics; (*coll.*) ***mach keine –!*** don't play the fool! **Faxenmacher,** *m.* fool, buffoon, wag.

Fazit ['fa:tsıt], *n.* (**-s,** *pl.* **-e** *or* **-s**) result, total, sum, product.

Feber ['fe:bər], *m.* (*Austr.*) *see* **Februar.**

febril [fe'bri:l], *adj.* feverish.

Februar ['fe:brua:r], *m.* (**-s,** *pl.* **-e**) February.

fechsen ['fɛksən], *v.t.* (*dial.*) gather in the vintage. **Fechser,** *m.* seedling, cutting (*of grape-vines*).

Fecht|bahn, *f.*, **-boden,** *m.* piste. **-bruder,** *m.* (*sl.*) beggar, tramp, mendicant. **-degen,** *m.* foil, rapier.

fechten ['fɛçtən], *irr.v.i.* fight; fence; (*coll.*) ***– gehen***, go begging; ***mit den Händen –***, gesticulate. **Fechten,** *n.* fencing; fighting. **Fechter,** *m.* fencer; gladiator. **Fechterstellung,** *f.* stance. **Fecht|handschuh,** *m.* fencing-glove. **-meister,** *m.* fencing master.

Feder ['fe:dər], *f.* (-, *pl.* **-n**) **1.** feather; plume; *pl.* (*coll.*) bed; ***er ist soeben aus den -n***, he is just out of bed; (*fig.*) ***sich mit fremden –n schmücken,*** deck o.s. out in borrowed plumes; 2. pen, (pen) nib; (*obs.*) quill (pen); ***in die – diktieren,*** dictate; ***aus meiner –,*** written by me; ***die – führen,*** act as secretary, do the clerical work; ***ein Werk unter der – haben,*** be engaged in writing a book; 3. spring; (*Mech.*) spline; (*Carp.*) tongue, slip-feather. **Federantrieb,** *m.* spring *or* clockwork mechanism. **federartig,** *adj.* feathery, plumose, plumaceous.

Feder|ball, *m.* shuttle-cock; (*game*) badminton. **–barometer,** *n.* aneroid barometer. **–bett,** *n.* feather-bed. **–blatt,** *n.* spring-plate (*of a lock*). **–brett,** *n.* (*Gymn.*) springboard. **–busch,** *m.* tuft *or* plume (of feathers); crest. **–decke,** *f.* eiderdown (quilt). **–fuchser,** *m.* (*coll.*) quill-driver, pen-pusher, scribbler. **federführend,** *adj.* competent, responsible, authorized (*authority*); responsible for (the) overall control. **Feder|führung,** *f.* competence, jurisdiction; centralized *or* overall control. **–gehäuse,** *n.* (*Mech.*) spring housing. **–gewicht,** *n.* (*Boxing*) feather-weight. **–gewichtler,** *m.* featherweight (*boxer*). **–halter,** *m.* penholder. **federhart,** *adj.* elastic, springy. **federig,** *adj.* feathery. **Feder|kasten,** *m.* pencil-case. **–kiel,** *m.* quill. **–kleid,** *n.* plumage. **–kraft,** *f.* elasticity, resilience, springiness. **–krieg,** *m.* literary feud. **federleicht,** *adj.* light as a feather, very light. **Feder|leinwand,** *f.* tick(ing). **–lesen,** *n.* ***ohne –,*** without ceremony; ***nicht viel –s machen mit,*** make short work of. **–matratze,** *f.* spring mattress. **–motor,** *m.* clockwork motor.

federn ['fe:dərn], **1.** *v.i.* 1. be elastic *or* springy; fly *or* spring back, jump up and down, bounce; 2. shed feathers, moult. **2.** *v.t.* 1. provide with springs; 2. pluck, feather (*a bird*); 3. (*Carp.*) tongue. **federnd,** *adj.* resilient, springy; moulting.

Feder|nelke, *f.* (*Bot.*) feathered pink. **–ring,** *m.* (*Mech*) spring-washer. **–schmuck,** *m.* plume(s); (*Indian's*) feathered head-dress. **–spannung,** *f.* spring tension; ***unter –,*** spring-loaded. **–spitze,** *f.* nib, penpoint. **–spule,** *f.* quill. **–stahl,** *m.* spring steel. **–strich,** *m.* stroke of the pen.

Federung ['fe:dəruŋ], *f.* spring-suspension, springing, springs; springiness, elasticity.

Feder|vieh, *n.* poultry. **–waage,** *f.* spring-balance. **–wechsel,** *m.* moulting. **–weiß,** *n.* French chalk, talc. **–werk,** *n.* spring drive, clockwork mechanism. **–wild,** *n.* wild fowl, winged game. **–wisch,** *m.* feather broom, feather duster. **–wischer,** *m.* pen-wiper. **–wolke,** *f.* cirrus (cloud). **–zange,** *f.* forceps. **–zeichnung,** *f.* 1. pen-and-ink drawing; 2. plumage markings. **–zug,** *m.* *See* **–strich.**

Fee [fe:], *f.* (-, *pl.* **-n**) fairy. **feenhaft,** *adj.* fairy-like, magical. **Feenreigen,** *m.* fairy-ring, fairy dance.

Fege ['fe:gə], *f.* riddle, screen, sieve.

Fegefeuer ['fe:gəfɔyər], *n.* purgatory.

fegen ['fe:gən], **1.** *v.t.* sweep, wipe, clean, cleanse, scour; winnow (*corn*); (*of a stag*) ***das Geweih –,*** fray its head; (*coll.*) ***ihm den Beutel –,*** clean him out. **2.** *v.i.* (*aux.* h. & s.) sweep, rush, race (*as wind*). **Feger,** *m.* broom, (*also the p.*) sweeper; (*coll.*) flibbertigibbet. **Fegesand,** *m.* scouring sand.

Feh [fe:], *n.* **(-(e)s,** *pl.* **-e)** Siberian squirrel; miniver.

Fehde ['fe:də], *f.* feud, quarrel; ***– ansagen*** (*Dat.*), challenge, throw down the gauntlet to; ***– bieten*** (*Dat.*), defy. **Fehde|brief,** *m.* (written) challenge. **–handschuh,** *m.* gauntlet; ***den – aufnehmen,*** accept *or* take up the challenge. **–recht,** *n.* right of self-defence.

Fehl [fe:l], *m.* **(-s,** *pl.* **-e)** (*B.*) fault, blemish, flaw; (*only in*) ***ohne –,*** without blemish, unblemished. **fehl,** *adv.* wrongly, amiss; ***– am Platz,*** be out of place *or* misplaced; ***der Schuß ging –,*** the shot went wide of the mark. **Fehl–, fehl–,** *pref.* mis-. **Fehl|anruf,** *m.* (*Tele.*) wrong number. **–anzeige,** *f.* nil return, negative report. **–ball,** *m.* (*Tenn.*) fault, (*Crick.*) no-ball. **fehlbar,** *adj.* fallible. **Fehlbarkeit,** *f.* fallibility. **Fehl|bestand,** *m.* deficiency, shortage. **–betrag,** *m.* deficit. **–bezeichnung,** *f.* misnomer. **–bitte,** *f.* vain request, fruitless appeal; ***eine – tun,*** meet with a refusal, be turned down. **–blatt,** *n.* missing leaf *or* card; (*Cards*) low *or* bad card. **–diagnose,** *f.* mistaken diagnosis. **–disposition,** *f.* blunder, (*coll.*) bloomer. **–druck,** *m.* (*Typ.*) foul impression.

fehlen ['fe:lən], **1.** *v.i.* do wrong, err, sin, blunder; ***– gegen,*** offend against, violate; 2. (*of a th.*) be missing *or* wanting, fail; (*of a p.*) be absent, fail to appear *or* attend; ***es fehlte nur, daß,*** all that was missing was; ***sie hat uns sehr gefehlt,*** we missed her badly *or* very much; ***es fehlt im ganzen 30,*** altogether there are 30 missing; ***es fehlt uns Geld,*** some of our money is missing; ***das fehlte gerade noch,*** what next? that's the last straw; 3. (*imp.*) (an (*Dat.*)) lack, be short of, be in need of; ***es fehlt uns an Geld,*** we are short of money; ***es fehlt ihm an Mut,*** he is wanting in courage; ***an mir soll es nicht –,*** it will not be my fault; ***es – lassen an*** (*Dat.*), be wanting in, lack; ***er ließ es an nichts –,*** he spared no pains, he left no stone unturned; 4. be the matter (*Dat.*, with), (*Poet.*) ail; ***wo fehlt's denn?*** what's the trouble? what's wrong? ***es fehlt ihm immer etwas,*** there is always something the matter with him; ***ihr fehlt nichts,*** she is quite well; she has all she wants; ***was fehlt Ihnen?*** what is the matter with you? **2.** *v.t.* miss (*target*); ***weit gefehlt,*** far from it, you are making a big mistake.

Fehlen, *n.* absence, lack, want; absence, non-appearance, non-attendance. **fehlend,** *adj.* erring; wanting, missing, deficient; ***das Fehlende,*** deficit, deficiency, that which is missing; ***der*** or ***die Fehlende,*** absentee.

Fehler ['fe:lər], *m.* fault, failing, weakness, imperfection, blemish, flaw, drawback, shortcoming, defect; mistake, error, blunder. **fehlerfrei,** *adj.* perfect, faultless, flawless, sound. **Fehlergrenze,** *f.* (*Engin.*) margin of error, tolerance. **fehlerhaft,** *adj.* faulty, defective, imperfect, deficient, incorrect. **fehlerlos,** *adj.* *See* **fehlerfrei. Fehler|-quelle,** *f.* source of error. **–verzeichnis,** *n.* (list of) errata.

Fehlfarbe ['fe:lfarbə], *f.* cigar of imperfect appearance. **fehlgebären,** *irr.v.i.* miscarry. **Fehlgeburt,** *f.* miscarriage, abortion. **fehlgehen,** *irr.v.i.* (*aux.* s.) go astray, miss *or* lose one's way; (*of bullet*) miss its mark; go wrong *or* amiss, not succeed; make a mistake, fail, err. **Fehlgewicht,** *n.* short weight, underweight. **fehlgreifen,** *irr.v.t.* miss one's hold; make a mistake, err. **Fehl|griff,** *m.* blunder, mistake. **–jahr,** *n.* year of a bad harvest; (*coll.*) off year. **–kauf,** *m.* bad bargain. **–landung,** *f.* (*Av.*) crash landing. **fehlleiten,** *v.t.* mislead, misguide. **Fehlrechnung,** *f.* miscalculation. **fehlschießen,** *irr.v.i.* miss one's aim *or* the mark, (*coll. fig.*) make a bad shot, be wildly out. **Fehlschlag,** *m.* failure; (*coll.*) wash-out; disappointment; wrong stroke. **fehl|schlagen,** *irr.v.i.* (*aux.* h. & s.) miss (one's blow); (*fig.*) miscarry, fail, come to nothing, be disappointed (*as hopes*). **–schließen,** *irr.v.i.* draw a wrong conclusion. **Fehl|schluß,** *m.* wrong inference, error of judgement, false conclusion, fallacy. **–schritt,** *m.* false step; error. **–schuß,** *m.* miss; unlucky *or* bad shot. **–spruch,** *m.* miscarriage of justice. **–start,** *m.* false start. **–treffer,** *m.* (*Artil.*) near miss. **fehltreten,** *irr.v.i.* make a false step, miss one's footing, trip, slip, stumble. **Fehl|tritt,** *m.* false step; slip, fault; moral lapse; ***einen – tun,*** miss one's footing, stumble; ***das Mädchen hat einen – begangen,*** the girl has gone astray, has lost her virtue *or* (*hum.*) has misbehaved. **–urteil,** *n.* misjudgement. **–zündung,** *f.* (*Motor.*) backfire; misfire (*gun*).

Fehwerk ['fe:vɛrk], *n.* furs, furriery.

feien ['faɪən], *v.t.* charm (*gegen,* against); make (*s.o.*) proof (against); *see* **gefeit.**

Feier ['faɪər], *f.* (-, *pl.* **-n**) 1. celebration, festival, fête, ceremony; 2. rest; holiday. **Feier|abend,** *m.* time for leaving off work; closing time, (*coll.*) knocking-off time; leisure after work, spare *or* free time; ***– machen,*** finish work; (*coll.*) knock off (work), (*fig., coll.*) call it a day. **–gesang,** *m.* solemn hymn. **–jahr,** *n.* sabbatical year. **–kleid,** *n.* festive raiment.

feierlich ['faɪərlɪç], *adj.* solemn; ceremonious; festive; – *begehen,* solemnize, celebrate; (*coll.*) *es war nicht mehr* –, it was rather awful. **Feierlichkeit,** *f.* solemnity, pomp, ceremony, ceremoniousness; ceremony, festivity.

feiern ['faɪərn], **1.** *v.i.* rest (from work), take a holiday, stop work, be idle, take it easy. **2.** *v.t,* celebrate; observe, keep, commemorate (*a holiday*). fête, extol, honour (*a p.*). **Feier|stunde,** *f.* time of solemn meditation; leisure hour, **–tag,** *m.* (public) holiday; day of rest; (*Eccl.*) feast-days.

feig [faɪk], *adj. See* **feige.**

Feig|blatter, *f.* tumour. **–bohne,** *f.* lupine, horse-bean.

feige ['faɪgə], *adj.* cowardly, timid, faint-hearted; (*coll.*) lily-livered, yellow; (*Min.*) crumbling, rotten; – *Memme,* arrant coward, poltroon; *sich – zeigen,* have cold feet, (*coll.*) funk it, quit.

Feige, *f.* fig; (*coll.*) *ihm die – weisen,* cock a snook at him. **Feigen|blatt,** *n.* fig-leaf; (*fig.*) shamefaced concealment. **–kaktus,** *m.* prickly pear.

Feigheit ['faɪkhaɪt], *f.* cowardice, cowardliness, (*coll.*) funk. **feigherzig,** *adj.* cowardly, faint-hearted, pusillanimous. **Feigherzigkeit,** *f.* cowardice, faint-heartedness, pusillanimity. **Feigling,** *m.* (**-s,** *pl.* **-e**) coward, poltroon, (*coll.*) funk.

Feigwurz ['faɪkvurts], *f.* (*Bot.*) lesser celandine, pilewort (*Ranunculus ficaria*).

feil [faɪl], *adj.* on *or* for sale, to be sold; (*fig.*) venal, corruptible, mercenary; *dieses Pferd ist mir um keinen Preis* –, I would not sell this horse at any price; *–er Mensch,* hireling; *–e Dirne,* prostitute. **feilbieten,** *irr.v.t.* offer *or* (*coll.*) put up for sale, (*fig.*) prostitute (*talent etc.*).

Feile ['faɪlə], *f.* file; *grobe* –, rasp; (*fig.*) *die letzte – legen an* (*Acc.*), put the finishing touches to. **feilen, 1.** *v.t.* file. **2.** *v.i.* – *an* (*Dat.*), file, finish, polish, put the finishing touches to.

feilhalten ['faɪlhaltən], *irr.v.t.* have for *or* on sale; (*coll.*) *Maulaffen* –, stand agape with astonishment.

Feilheit ['faɪlhaɪt], *f.* venality, corruptibility.

Feilicht ['faɪlɪçt], *n.* filings. **Feilkloben,** *m.* hand-vice.

feilschen ['faɪlʃən], *v.i.* bargain (*um,* for), haggle.

Feil|späne, *m.pl.* filings. **–stock,** *m. See* **–kloben.**

Feimen ['faɪmən], *m.* stack, rick (*of hay, corn*).

fein [faɪn], **1.** *adj.* 1. fine, delicate, minute, dainty, graceful; precise, accurate, fine (*adjustment etc.*); delicate, acute, subtle (*feelings etc.*); *–es Gebäck,* fancy pastries; *–e Nase,* sensitive nose; *–es Ohr,* sharp ear; *–er Regen,* drizzling rain; *–er Ton,* good form; *–er Unterschied,* nice *or* fine *or* subtle distinction; *–e Wäsche,* dainty underwear; 2. refined, polite, cultivated, distinguished, elegant, fashionable, (*coll.*) smart; *–e Sitten,* cultivated manners; *–e Welt,* fashionable *or* polite society, people of fashion; 3. exquisite, choice, splendid, excellent, capital, (*coll.*) fine, grand, great, swell; (*coll.*) *er ist – heraus,* he is a lucky fellow. **2.** *adv.* (*coll.*) *sei mir – klug,* for my sake mind what you're doing; *es ist – warm hier!* it's nice and warm here!

Fein|abstimmung, *f.* (*Rad.*) fine tuning. **–arbeit,** *f.* precision work. **–bäcker,** *m.* confectioner, pastry-cook. **–bäckerei,** *f.* confectioner's shop. **–blech,** *n.* thin sheet (metal). **–brenner,** *m.* refiner (*of metals*).

Feind [faɪnt], *m.* (**-(e)s,** *pl.* **-e**) enemy, foe; adversary, antagonist, opponent, rival; (*Eccl.*) *der böse* –, the Evil One, the Devil; *abgesagter* –, sworn enemy; *Freund und* –, friend and foe; *sich* (*Dat.*) *–e machen,* make enemies; *vor dem* –, in the face of the enemy. **feind,** *pred.adj.* – *sein* (*Dat.*), be an enemy of, be hostile to, loathe, hate.

Feind|berührung, *f.* contact with the enemy. **–beurteilung,** *f.* estimate of the enemy position. **Feindes|hand,** *f.* enemy hands, the enemy's hands, the hands of the enemy. **–land,** *n.* hostile territory. **–macht,** *f.* enemy forces. **Feindflug,** *m.* (*Av.*) sortie, operational flight, combat mission.

feindlich ['faɪntlɪç], *adj.* 1. (*Mil.*) enemy('s), hostile; *–er Ausländer,* enemy alien; *das –e Heer,* the enemy; 2. (*of p. or th.*) hostile, antagonistic, adverse, inimical (*Dat.*, to); opposed (*gegen,* to), unfriendly (towards). **Feindlichkeit,** *f.* hostility, animosity, enmity, antagonism; hatred, rancour, ill-will.

Feindschaft ['faɪntʃaft], *f. See* **Feindlichkeit;** feud, strife, discord, quarrel; *in – mit,* in enmity *or* at variance with, (*coll.*) at daggers drawn with. **feindschaftlich,** *adj. See* **feindlich.**

feindselig ['faɪntze:lɪç], *adj.* hostile, antagonistic (*gegen,* to), malevolent. **Feindseligkeit,** *f.* hostility, animosity, malevolence (*gegen,* towards); *pl.* hostilities.

Fein|einstellung, *f.* vernier adjustment. **–erde,** *f.* garden soil. **fein|fühlend, –fühlig,** *adj.* tactful, sensitive; thin-skinned. **Fein|fühligkeit,** *f.*, **–gefühl,** *n.* sensitiveness, delicacy, tact. **–gehalt,** *m.* fineness; standard (*gold etc.*). **–gehaltsstempel,** *m.* hall-mark. **feinglied(e)rig,** *adj.* finely *or* delicately proportioned. **Feingold,** *n.* fine *or* refined gold.

Feinheit ['faɪnhaɪt], *f.* fineness, delicacy; grace(fulness), daintiness; elegance, refinement, politeness, polish; delicacy, tact; subtlety, finesse; fine detail, sharpness (*of image*), purity, superior quality (*of substance*); *pl.* niceties, fine points. **Feinheitsgrad,** *m.* degree of fineness (*of metals*).

fein|hörig, *adj.* quick of hearing. **–körnig,** *adj.* fine grained. **Fein|kost(handlung),** *f.* delicatessen (shop). **–mechaniker,** *m.* precision tool maker, instrument maker. **–messer,** *m.* micrometer. **–probe,** *f.* assay. **–schliff,** *m.* final polish(ing), finish(ing). **–schmecker,** *m.* gourmet, epicure. **–schnitt,** *m.* fine cut (tobacco). **feinsinnig,** *adj.* sensitive, tasteful; subtle, delicate.

Feinsliebchen [faɪns'li:pçən], *n.* (*Poet.*) darling, sweetheart.

feinstellen ['faɪnʃtɛlən], *v.t.* make fine adjustments to, adjust, set exactly. **Fein|stellschraube,** *f.* vernier adjustment screw. **–struktur,** *f.* microstructure. **–waage,** *f.* precision balance. **–wäsche,** *f.* lingerie. **–zeug,** *n.* (paper) pulp. **–zucker,** *m.* refined sugar.

feist [faɪst], **1.** *adj.* fat, stout, corpulent, obese; chubby, plump (*of cheeks*); *–er Sonntag,* the last Sunday before Lent. **Feist,** *n.* (*Hunt.*) fat (*of deer etc.*). **Feiste, Feistheit, Feistigkeit,** *f.* obesity. **Feistzeit,** *f.* season of venison.

feixen ['faɪksən], *v.i.* (*coll.*) grin.

Felbe ['fɛlbə], *f.* (*Bot.*) white willow (*Salix alba*).

Felbel ['fɛlbəl], *m.* velveteen.

Felber, Felbinger, *m. See* **Felbe.**

Felchen ['fɛlçən], *m.* (*Ichth.*) whitefish (*Coregonus*).

Feld [fɛlt], *n.* (**-(e)s,** *pl.* **-er**) field, open country, plain, ground; (*fig.*) area, field (of action), sphere, domain, department, scope; battlefield; square (*of a chessboard*); panel; *pl.* lands (*of rifling on a barrel*); *abgenutztes* –, scoring of the bore; *elektrisches* –, electric field; *ein rotes Kreuz im weißen* –, a red cross on a white ground; *das – bebauen* or *bestellen,* till the ground; *das – behaupten,* hold *or* stand one's ground, win the day; (*fig.*) *freies* –, full *or* free scope; (*fig.*) *ins – führen,* advance (*arguments etc.*); *im freien –e liegen,* bivouac; *noch im weiten –e liegen,* be still very uncertain *or* quite unsettled, still have a long way to go, still be very remote; *das – räumen,* fall back, retreat; (*fig.*) make off, quit, (*coll.*) clear off; (*Mil.*) *ins – rücken, zu –e ziehen,* go to the front, take the field; *aus dem – schlagen,* drive from the field, (*fig.*) rout, outstrip, eliminate (*an opponent*).

Feld|ahorn, *m.* (*Bot.*) common maple (*Acer campestre*). **–arbeit,** *f.* agricultural labour. **–artillerie,** *f.* field artillery. **–arzt,** *m.* (*Mil.*) medical officer. **–bau,** *m.* agriculture, tillage. **–bett,** *n.* camp-bed. **–biene,** *f.* wild bee. **–blume,** *f.* wild flower. **–bluse,** *f.* battle-dress tunic.

Felddienst ['fɛltdi:nst], *m.* (*Mil.*) active service. **felddienstfähig,** *adj.* fit for active service. **Feld-dienst|ordnung,** *f.* field-service regulations. **–übung,** *f.* (*Mil.*) manœuvres, field-day.

Feld|eggsfalke, *m.* (*Orn.*) lanner falcon (*Falco biarmicus*). **–flasche,** *f.* waterbottle. **–flüchter,** *m.* stray pigeon. **–flur,** *f.* arable (land). **–früchte,** *f.pl.* farm produce; crops. **–geistliche(r),** *m.* chaplain to the forces, army chaplain. **–gendarmerie,** *f.* military police. **–gericht,** *n.* field court-martial. **–geschrei,** *n.* war-cry; password. **–geschütz,** *n.* field gun. **–gottesdienst,** *m.* drumhead service. **feldgrau,** *adj.* field grey (*uniform of German soldiers*). **Feldheer,** *n.* field force.

Feldherr ['fɛlthɛr], *m.* commander-in-chief; general, (*fig.*) strategist. **Feldherrn|kunst,** *f.* generalship; strategy. **–stab,** *m.* field-marshal's baton.

Feld|jäger, *m.* chasseur; (*Hist.*) courier, king's messenger. **–kessel,** *m.* camp kettle. **–koch,** *m.* army cook. **–küche,** *f.* field-kitchen. **–lager,** *n.* camp, bivouac. **–lazarett,** *n.* field hospital, casualty clearing station. **–lerche,** *f.* (*Orn.*) skylark (*Alauda arvensis*). **–mark,** *f.* boundary; (*Hist.*) arable. **–marschall,** *m.* field-marshal. **feldmarschmäßig,** *adj.* in full marching order. **Feld|maus,** *f.* fieldmouse. **–messer,** *m.* (land-)surveyor. **–meßkunst,** *f.* surveying. **–mütze,** *f.* field service cap, forage cap. **–post,** *f.* army postal service. **–postbrief,** *m.* letter on active service. **–posten,** *m.* outpost, picket. **–prediger,** *m. See* **–geistliche(r). –rohrsänger,** *m.* (*Orn.*) paddy-field warbler (*Acrocephalus agricola*). **–rübe,** *f.* (*Bot.*) rape. **–salat,** *m.* (*Bot.*) lamb's lettuce. **–schaden,** *m.* damage to crops.

Feldscher ['fɛltʃe:r], *m.* (*Hist.*) army surgeon.

Feld|schlacht, *f.* pitched battle. **–schlange,** *f.* (*Hist.*) culverin. **–schmiede,** *f.* mobile forge. **–schwirl,** *m.* (*Orn.*) grasshopper warbler (*Locustella naevia*). **–soldat,** *m.* soldier of the line, soldier on active service. **–spannung,** *f.* (*Elec.*) field voltage. **–spat,** *m.* feldspar. **–sperling,** *m.* (*Orn.*) (*Am.* European) tree sparrow (*Passer montanus*). **–stärke,** *f.* (*Elec.*) field strength. **–stecher,** *m.* field-glasses, binoculars. **–stein,** *m.* boulder; landmark. **–stiefel,** *m.* field-service boots. **–stück,** *n.* (*Hist.*) field-piece. **–stuhl,** *m.* camp-stool. **–verbandsplatz,** *m.* (*Mil.*) advanced dressing station. **–verpflegung,** *f.* commissariat. **–wache,** *f.* picket, outpost. **–webel,** *m.* sergeant. **–weg,** *m.* lane, field-path. **–werkstätte,** *f.* (*Mil.*) 1st echelon workshop. **–wicklung,** *f.* (*Elec.*) field coil. **–zeichen,** *n.* banner, ensign, standard. **–zeug,** *n.* munition; ordnance, stores. **–zeugmeister,** *m.* master of ordnance, quartermaster. **–zeugmeisterei,** *f.* ordnance depot. **–zug,** *m.* campaign (*also fig.*). **–zulage,** *f.* (*Mil.*) field allowance.

[1]**Felge** ['fɛlgə], *f.* felloe (*of a wheel*); (*Cycl.*) (wheel-) rim.

[2]**Felge,** *f.* ploughing of fallow land.

[1]**felgen,** *v.t.* provide (*a wheel*) with felloes.

[2]**felgen,** *v.i.* plough up fallow land.

Felgen|bremse, *f.* (*Cycl.*) calliper brake. **–hauer, Felgner,** *m.* wheelwright.

Fell [fɛl], *n.* **(-(e)s,** *pl.* **-e)** skin, hide, pelt, fur, coat (*of animals*); ***ihm das – über die Ohren ziehen,*** fleece him; (*coll.*) ***ihm das – gehörig gerben,*** tan the hide off him; ***er hat ein dickes –,*** he is very thick-skinned; ***ihm sind die –e weggeschwommen*** or ***fortgeschwommen*** or ***davongeschwommen,*** he has lost his chance, (*coll.*) he's had it; (*Prov.*) ***man soll das – nicht verkaufen, ehe man (nicht) den Bären hat,*** don't count your chickens before they're hatched.

Fellache [fɛ'laxə], *m.* **(-n,** *pl,* **-n)** fellah, *pl.* fellaheen.

Felleisen ['fɛlˀaɪzən], *n.* knapsack.

Fels [fɛls], *m.* **(-en,** *pl.* **-en)** *see* **Felsen. Fels|block,** *m.* boulder. **–boden,** *m.* rocky soil.

Felsen ['fɛlzən], *m.* rock. **felsenfest,** *adj.* firm as a rock, unwavering, unshakeable, adamant; ***das steht –,*** that is indisputable. **Felsen|gebirge,** *n.* (*Geog.*) Rocky Mountains. **–höhle,** *f.* grotto, rock-cave. **–huhn,** *n.* (*Orn.*) Barbary partridge (*Alectoris barbara*). **–kleiber,** *m.* (*Orn.*) rock nuthatch (*Sitta neumayer*). **–klippe,** *f.* cliff. **–küste,** *f.* rocky coast. **–nest,** *n.* (*fig.*) castle on a rock, rocky refuge. **–pieper,** *m.* (*Orn.*) Scandinavian rock pipit (*Anthus spinoletta littoralis*). **–riff,** *n.* reef. **–schicht,** *f.* layer of rock. **–schlucht,** *f.* rocky gorge. **–schwalbe,** *f.* (*Orn.*) crag martin (*Ptyonoprogne rupestris*). **–spitze,** *f.* peak, crag. **–taube,** *f.* (*Orn.*) rock dove (*Columba livia*).

Fels|geröll, *n.* scree, talus, detritus. **–glimmer,** *m.* mica. **–grat,** *m.* rocky ridge. **felsig,** *adj.* rocky, craggy, rock-like. **Fels|kluft, –spalte,** *f.* cleft, crevice, chasm. **–spitze,** *f.* crag, rocky peak *or* pinnacle. **–sturz,** *m.* fall of rock. **–wand,** *f.* wall of rock, rock face.

Feme ['fə:mə], *f.* Vehme. **Femgericht,** *n.* Vehmic court.

Femininum [fɛmi'ni:num], *n.* **(-s,** *pl.* **-na)** (*Gram.*) feminine (noun). **Feminismus,** *m.* femininity.

Fenchel ['fɛnçəl], *m.* (*Bot.*) fennel (*Foeniculum vulgare*). **Fenchelholz,** *n.* sassafras.

Fenn [fɛn], *n.* **(-s,** *pl.* **-e)** fen, swamp, marsh, bog.

Fenster ['fɛnstər], *n.* window; ***er wirft sein Geld zum – hinaus,*** he pours his money down the drain. **Fenster|bank,** *f.* window-ledge *or* sill; window seat. **–brett,** *n. See* **–brüstung. –brief,** *m.* window envelope. **–brüstung,** *f.* window-sill. **–flügel,** *m.* casement. **–geld,** *n.* window-tax. **–gewände,** *n.* (window) reveal. **–gitter,** *n.* lattice (*of a window*). **–haken,** *m.* window catch. **–jalousie,** *f.* Venetian blind. **–kitt,** *m.* putty. **–kreuz,** *n.* window bars. **–laden,** *m.* (window) shutter.

Fensterln ['fɛnstərln], *n.* (*dial.*) bundling.

Fenster|nische, *f.* embrasure. **–pfeiler,** *m.* pier. **–pfosten,** *m.* mullion. **–putzer,** *m.* window cleaner. **–rahmen,** *m.* window-frame. **–riegel,** *m.* sash-bolt, window fastener *or* catch. **–rose,** *f.* rose-window. **–scheibe,** *f.* window-pane. **–sims,** *m.* window-sill. **–steuer,** *f. See* **–geld. –sturz,** *m.* lintel. **–tür,** *f.* glass door, French window.

Ferch [fɛrç], *m.* (*Min.*) fire-damp.

Ferge ['fɛrgə], *m.* **(-n,** *pl.* **-n)** (*Poet.*) ferryman.

Fergger ['fɛrgər], *m.* (*Swiss*) carrier, haulage contractor, (forwarding) agent.

Ferialkurs [fɛri'a:lkurs], *m.* (*Austr.*) holiday course.

Ferien ['fe:riən], *pl.* vacation, holidays; (*Law, Parl.*) recess; ***die großen –,*** the long vacation, the summer holidays; ***– machen, in die – gehen,*** go away on holiday *or* for the vacation; ***– vom Ich,*** freedom from everyday cares. **Ferien|arbeit,** *f.* vacation employment. **–kolonie,** *f.* holiday camp. **–kurs(us),** *m.* holiday course, vacation course. **–lager,** *n. See* **–kolonie.**

Ferkel ['fɛrkəl], *n.* young pig, sucking pig; (*coll.*) dirty pig; ***eine Tracht –,*** a litter of pigs; ***– werfen,*** farrow. **Ferkelei** [–'laɪ], *f.* (*coll.*) dirty habit(s); dirty joke. **Ferkelmaus,** *f.* (*Zool.*) guinea pig (*Cavia cobaya*). **ferkeln,** *v.i.* farrow, (*coll.*) talk smut.

Fermate [fɛr'ma:tə], *f.* (*Mus.*) pause (*ad lib. lengthening of note or rest*); fine (*at conclusion of repeat*) 𝄐.

Ferment [fɛr'mɛnt], *n.* **(-(e)s,** *pl.* **-e)** ferment, enzyme. **fermentieren** [–'ti:rən], *v.i., v.t.* ferment.

fern [fɛrn], **1.** *adj.* (*Dat.*) far, distant, far off, remote; ***das sei mir –*** or ***– von mir,*** far be it from me; ***er steht mir –,*** he has no close connexion with me. **2.** *adv.* (*also* **-e**) ***von*** *–(e),* from afar, from *or* at a distance.

Fernambukholz [fɛrnam'bu:khɔlts], *n.* Brazil wood.

Fern|amt, *n.* (*Tele.*) trunk exchange. **–anruf,** *m.* long-distance *or* trunk call. **–antrieb,** *m.* remote drive. **–aufklärung,** *f.* (*Mil.*) strategical *or* long-range reconnaissance. **–aufklärungflugszeug,** *n.* long-range reconnaissance aircraft. **–aufnahme,** *f. See* **–bild. –bahn,** *f.* main line. **–bedienung,** *f. See* **–lenkung. –bild,** *n.* telephoto.

fernbleiben ['fɛrnblaɪbən], *irr.v.i.* absent o.s., keep *or* stay away (*Dat.,* from), not come *or* attend *or* appear. **Fernbleiben,** *n.* absence, non-appearance, non-attendance; ***– vom Arbeitsplatz,*** absenteeism.

Fern|blick, *m.* vista, distant view. **–drucker,** *m. See* **–schreiber.**

Ferne ['fɛrnə], *f.* remoteness, distance, distant place *or* time; ***aus der –,*** from a distance, from afar; ***in der –,*** in the distance, at a distance, far off; ***das liegt noch in weiter –,*** that is still a long way off, there's still a long way to go. **ferne,** *adv. See* **fern, 2.**

ferner ['fɛrnər], **1.** *comp.adj.* further, farther. **2.** *adv.* further, furthermore, moreover, besides, in addition, and then; ***– im Amte bleiben,*** continue in office; ***erstens . . . zweitens . . . –,*** first . . . second . . . and for the rest.

Ferner, *m.* (*Austr.*) *see* **Firn.**

fernerhin ['fɛrnərhɪn], *adv.* for the future, in future, henceforth, henceforward, furthermore.

Fern|fahrer, *m.* long-distance lorry driver. **–flug,** *m.* long-distance flight. **–geschütz,** *n.* long-range gun. **–gespräch,** *n.* trunk-call. **–glas,** *n.* telescope, binoculars, field-glass.

fernhalten ['fɛrnhaltən], **1.** *irr.v.t.* keep away *or* at a distance, hold *or* fend off. **2.** *irr.v.r.* keep away, keep *or* stand aloof (***von,*** from), (*coll.*) steer clear (of).

Fernheizung ['fɛrnhaɪtsuŋ], *f.* district heating. **fernher,** *adv.* from afar. **Fern|hörer,** *m.* telephone receiver. **–kurs(us),** *m.* correspondence course. **–laster,** *m.* (*coll.*) long-distance lorry. **–lastverkehr,** *m.* long-distance road haulage. **–leitung,** *f.* (*Tele.*) trunk-line; (*Elec.*) grid power-line; (oil) pipeline. **–lenkung,** *f.* remote control, radio control.

fernliegen ['fɛrnli:gən], *irr.v.i.* (*Dat.*) be remote from (one's desires) *or* far from (one's thoughts); ***es liegt mir fern (zu tun),*** far be it from me (to do), I am far from (doing).

Fern|meldedienst, *m.* telecommunications. **–meldetechnik,** *f.* telecommunication engineering. **fernmündlich,** *adj.* (by) telephone, telephonic. **Fernost,** *m.* Far East. **fernöstlich,** *adj.* Far-Eastern. **Fern|photographie,** *f.* radio photograph *or* photography, telephotography. **–rohr,** *n.* telescope. **–rohraufsatz,** *m.* telescopic sight. **–ruf,** *m.* telephone call; ***– 329,*** telephone number 329. **–schaltung,** *f. See* **–lenkung. –schnellzug,** *m.* de-luxe train. **–schreiber,** *m.* teletype apparatus, teleprinter. **–schuß,** *m.* long-range shot, (*Footb., fig.*) long shot.

Fernseh– ['fɛrnze:–], *pref.* television. **–apparat,** *m.* television set. **Fernsehen,** *n.* television; ***im –,*** on television.

Fernsicht ['fɛrnzɪçt], *f.* prospect, distant view, vista, perspective. **fernsichtig,** *adj.* far *or* long-sighted.

Fernsprech|amt ['fɛrnʃprɛç–], *m.* telephone exchange. **–anschluß,** *m.* telephone connexion. **–automat,** *m.* automatic telephone. **–buch,** *n.* telephone directory, (*coll.*) phone book. **Fernsprecher,** *m.* telephone. **Fernsprech|teilnehmer,** *m.* telephone subscriber. **–zelle,** *f.* public telephone, telephone kiosk, call box. **–zentrale,** *f. See* **–amt.**

Fernspruch ['fɛrnʃprux], *m.* telephone message.

fernstehen ['fɛrnʃte:ən], *irr.v.i.* (*Dat.*) have no contact(s) with, be a stranger to. **Fernstehende(r),** *m., f.* onlooker, outsider.

Fern|steuerung, *f. See* **–lenkung. –trauung,** *f.* marriage by proxy. **–unterricht,** *m.* correspondence course. **–verkehr,** *m.* long-distance traffic. **–weh,** *n.* wanderlust. **–wirkung,** *f.* long-range effect, telekinesis; radiation effect; ***seelische –,*** telepathy. **–ziel,** *n.* long-range objective. **–zug,** *m.* long-distance train, main-line train.

Ferrisalz ['fɛrizalts], *n.* (*Chem.*) ferric compound.

Ferrosalz ['fɛrozalts], *n.* (*Chem.*) ferrous compound.

Ferse ['fɛrzə], *f.* heel; ***die –n zeigen,*** take to *or* show one's heels, show a clean pair of heels; ***auf den –n sein*** (*Dat.*), be at *or* on (*a p.'s*) heels, follow (*s.o.*) closely, run (*a p.*) close; ***dicht auf den –n*** or ***der – folgen,*** follow hot *or* hard on the heels (*Dat.*, of); ***ihm auf die – treten,*** get under his feet; ***sich an seinen –n heften,*** dog his footsteps. **Fersen|bein,** *n.* heel-bone. **–flechse,** *f.* Achilles' tendon. **–geld,** *n.* (*coll.*) ***– geben,*** show a clean pair of heels, take to one's heels. **–sehne,** *f. See* **–flechse.**

fertig ['fɛrtɪç], *adj.* ready, prepared, ready to start; complete(d), finished, done; perfect, skilled, dexterous, accomplished, fluent; ready-made (*clothes*), ready-cooked (*food*), prefabricated (*buildings*); (*of a p.*) ruined, broken, at the end of one's tether, (*coll.*) done for; (*coll. of a p.*) dead beat, all in, played out; ***sich – halten,*** be in readiness, hold o.s. in readiness, be prepared; ***sich – machen,*** get o.s. ready; ***– sein,*** have finished *or* done (***mit,*** with), (*coll.*) be through (with); ***wir sind – miteinander,*** it is all over between us; (*Spt.*) ***–!*** ready! ***– werden,*** get ready; ***– werden mit,*** deal *or* cope with, manage, handle; get over (*affliction*); ***– werden ohne,*** manage *or* get along *or* do without.

fertigbringen ['fɛrtɪçbrɪŋən], *irr.v.t.* complete, finish; achieve, accomplish, bring about; ***es – zu tun,*** manage *or* contrive to do, succeed in doing; (*coll.*) ***er bringt es nicht fertig,*** he won't make it; (*coll.*) ***er bringt es glatt fertig,*** he is capable of it, I shouldn't put it past him.

fertigen ['fɛrtɪgən], *v.t.* make, manufacture, produce.

Fertig|erzeugnis, *n.* finished product. **–fabrikat,** *n.* ready-made article. **–haus,** *n.* prefabricated house, (*coll.*) prefab.

Fertigkeit ['fɛrtɪçkaɪt], *f.* skill, dexterity, proficiency, facility (***in*** (*Dat.*), in); fluency (*speech*), (*Mus.*) execution, (*coll.*) knack; *pl.* accomplishments. **Fertigkleidung,** *f.* ready-made *or* ready-to-wear clothes. **fertigmachen,** *v.t.* finish, complete, get ready; (*Typ.*) adjust; (*coll.*) dispose of, do for (*a p.*), settle (*s.o.'s*) hash. **fertigstellen,** *v.t.* finish, complete. **Fertigstellung,** *f.* completion.

Fertigung ['fɛrtɪguŋ], *f.* making, manufacture, fabrication, production. **Fertigungskapazität,** *f.* production capacity. **Fertigwaren,** *f.pl.* ready-made goods, finished products.

Fes [fɛs], *n.* (*Mus.*) F flat.

fesch [fɛʃ], *adj.* stylish, smart, chic; dashing (*fellow*), fetching (*girl*).

Fessel ['fɛsəl], *f.* (-, *pl.* **-n**) 1. fetter, chain, shackle; (*wrestling*) lock; (*fig.*) trammels; *pl.* irons, manacles, handcuffs; ***ihm –n anlegen, ihn in –n legen,*** put him in irons, handcuff him; 2. fetlock, pastern-joint (*of a horse*). **Fessel|ballon,** *m.* captive balloon. **–bein, –gelenk,** *n.* pastern.

fesseln ['fɛsəln], *v.t.* fetter, chain, shackle, put in chains; fasten, tether, bind; (*fig.*) contain, pin down (*enemy*); captivate, fascinate, absorb, arrest, enthrall (*attention*); ***ans Bett gefesselt,*** confined to bed, bed-ridden. **fesselnd,** *adj.* captivating, enthralling, fascinating, absorbing, gripping, thrilling, spell-binding.

fest [fɛst], *adj., adv.* firm, solid, hard, compact; strong, sturdy, stout, tight, fast, stable; fixed, stationary, immovable, rigid; (*fig.*) unshakeable, inflexible, durable, lasting, constant, permanent, enduring; sound (*sleep*), close (*weave*), fortified (*place*), regular (*customer*), robust (*health*); ***– abgemacht,*** definitely agreed; ***– angestellt,*** appointed to the permanent staff; ***–es Angebot,*** firm *or* binding offer; ***– beharren auf*** (*Dat.*), make a point of, insist on; ***– behaupten,*** assert *or* maintain positively; (*Comm.*) ***Weizen bleibt –,*** wheat remains firm *or* steady; ***–er Boden,*** firm ground; (*coll.*) ***nur – drauf los!*** give it all you've got! ***–es Einkommen,*** fixed income; ***–er Entschluß,*** firm resolve; ***–e Farben,*** fast colours; ***–en Fuß fassen,*** gain a (firm) footing; ***– gegen,*** proof against; ***–er Gewahrsam,*** safe custody; ***–er Glaube,*** firm belief, unshakeable faith; ***–e Grundlage haben,*** have a sound basis *or* foundation; ***–e Grundsätze,*** fixed principles; ***in –en Händen,*** in safe hands; (*Comm.*) not to be sold; ***–er Knoten,*** tight knot; ***–e Körper,*** solid bodies; ***das –e Land,*** terra firma; ***–e Masse,*** compact mass; ***–e Meinung,*** firm opinion; ***–e Nahrung,*** solid food; ***–er Ort,*** fortress, stronghold; ***–e Preise,*** fixed prices; ***so viel steht –,*** this (at least) is definite *or* certain; ***steif und –,*** categorically; ***–e Stellung,*** permanent post, (*Mil.*) secure position; ***–es Tuch,*** close-woven material; ***– davon überzeugt sein,*** be firmly *or* perfectly convinced; ***–er Wohnsitz,*** permanent home *or* address; (*Phys.*) ***–er Zustand,*** solid state.

–fest, *adj.suff.* firmly *or* well grounded in, well versed in, *e.g.* ***bibelfest,*** well versed in the Scriptures; ***sattelfest,*** firm in the saddle, (*fig.*) sure of one's subject.

fest–, *sep. pref.* firm(ly), fast. *See examples of verbs below.*

Fest, *n.* **(-es,** *pl.* **-e)** festival, fête, celebration, festivities, (*Eccl.*) feast; holiday; banquet, feast, party; ***bewegliches –,*** movable feast; (*Prov.*) ***man muß die –e feiern wie sie fallen,*** Christmas comes but once a year; ***ein – geben,*** give a banquet.

Fest–, *pref.* festival, festive. **–abend,** *m.* evening festivity. **–akt,** *m.* ceremony.

fest|backen, *v.i.* cake together. **–bannen,** *v.t.* fix *or* rivet to the spot. **–binden,** *irr.v.t.* tie up, fasten, make fast.

Feste ['fɛstə], *f.* (*Poet.*) firmness, solidity, density; (*Mil.*) stronghold, fortress, prison; (*B.*) ***– des Himmels,*** firmament of heaven.

Festessen ['fɛstˀɛsən], *n.* official banquet, (*coll.*) feast.

fest|fahren, *irr.v.t., v.r.* (*at sea*) run aground, (*on land*) get bogged down, stick fast; (*coll.*) ***festgefahren sein,*** be at a loss *or* in a quandary *or* in a jam, get stuck. **–frieren,** *irr.v.i.* freeze solid. **–halten, 1.** *irr.v.t.* hold tight *or* fast; detain, hold in custody; arrest, seize, take into custody; (*fig.*) seize, capture (*a likeness etc.*). **2.** *irr.v.i.* hold fast, cling, adhere (***an*** (*Dat.*), to).

festigen ['fɛstɪgən], *v.t.* secure, strengthen, consolidate, establish; stabilize (*currency*). **Festigkeit,** *f.* firmness, solidity; soundness, stability; strength, resistance, (*Metall.*) tensile strength; (*fig.*) firmness, steadiness, steadfastness, determination, tenacity. **Festigkeitsgrenze,** *f.* (*Metall.*) breaking strength. **Festigung,** *f.* strengthening, consolidation, establishment; stabilization.

festkleben ['fɛstkle:bən], **1.** *v.t.* fasten, stick, glue. **2.** *v.i.* adhere, stick (***an*** (*Dat.*), to).

Festkleid ['fɛstklaɪt], *n.* party dress; holiday dress.

Fest|körperphysik, *f.* solid state physics. **–kraftstoff,** *m.* solid fuel. **–land,** *n.* continent, mainland.

festlegen ['fɛstle:gən], **1.** *v.t.* lay down, fix, determine, establish; stipulate, define; tie up, sink, freeze (*capital*); plot (*a course*). **2.** *v.r.* (*fig.*) tie o.s. down, pledge *or* bind *or* commit o.s. (***an*** (*Acc.*), to). **Fest|legung,** *f. See* **–setzung.**

festlich ['fɛstlɪç], *adj.* festive, solemn, splendid; ***– begehen,*** celebrate, solemnize. **Festlichkeit,** *f.* festivity; splendour, solemnity.

festmachen ['fɛstmaxən], **1.** *v.t.* fasten, fix, attach (***an*** (*Dat.*), to), make fast, belay (*rope*), moor (*ship*); (*fig.*) fix, settle (*agreement*). **2.** *v.i.* (*of ship*) moor.

Festmahl ['fɛstma:l], *n.* banquet.

Festmeter ['fɛstmetər], *n.* cubic metre (*of timber*).

festnageln ['fɛstna:gəln], *v.t.* nail up *or* down; (*fig.*) pin (*a p.*) down (***auf*** (*Acc.*), to).

Festnahme ['fɛstna:mə], *f.* seizure, arrest, capture, apprehension. **festnehmen,** *irr.v.t.* seize, capture, arrest, put under arrest, take into custody, apprehend.

Feston [fɛ'stõ], *n.* **(-s,** *pl.* **-s)** festoon.

Fest|ordner, *m.* master of ceremonies, steward. **–ordnung,** *f.* programme of festivities.

Fest|preis, *m.* fixed price. **–punkt,** *m.* fixed *or* reference point, base.

Fest|rede, *f.* official speech, formal address. **–redner,** *m.* orator of the day, official speaker. **–saal,** *m.* banqueting hall.

fest|schnüren, *v.t.* tie *or* fasten securely, lace tightly. **–schrauben,** *v.t.* screw tight, screw up (tightly).

Festschrift ['fɛstʃrɪft], *f.* commemorative volume.

festsetzen ['fɛstzɛtsən], **1.** *v.t.* 1. arrange, settle, establish, fix, stipulate, appoint, prescribe, lay down; assess (*damages etc.*); ***die Abfahrt ist auf nächsten Dienstag festgesetzt,*** the departure is fixed *or* timed *or* scheduled for next Tuesday; 2. take into custody, arrest. **2.** *v.r.* (*of a p.*) settle, establish o.s.; (*of disease etc.*) gain a footing (***in*** (*Dat.*), in). **Festsetzung,** *f.* 1. arrangement, establishment, settling, fixing; appointment, stipulation, laying down (*of rules*), assessment (*of damages*); 2. arrest, imprisonment.

festsitzen ['fɛstzɪtsən], *irr.v.i.* be stuck *or* attached, sit fast, (*of clothes*) fit tightly, be tight, (*Naut.*) be aground.

Festspiel ['fɛstʃpi:l], *n.* festival performance, *pl.* festival; ***Salzburger –e,*** Salzburg Festival. **Festspielwoche,** *f.* festival.

feststehen ['fɛstʃte:ən], *irr.v.i.* stand fast *or* firm, be steady; (*fig.*) be certain *or* settled *or* (established as) a fact. **feststehend,** *adj.* fixed, stationary, (*fig.*) settled, well- *or* old-established (*habit, custom*), established, certain, positive (*fact*).

feststellbar ['fɛstʃtɛlba:r], *adj.* ascertainable, determinable, identifiable; noticeable, detectable. **Feststellbremse,** *f.* (*Motor.*) hand *or* parking brake. **feststellen,** *v.t.* 1. establish, ascertain, determine, find out; state, declare; observe, notice; locate (*whereabouts, error etc.*), identify (*a p.*), assess (*damage etc.*), (*Chem.*) determine; 2. (*Tech.*) set, lock, secure. **Feststeller,** *m.* (*typewriter*) shift lock. **Festellschraube,** *f.* set screw. **Feststellung,** *f.* 1. establishment, determination, location, identification; statement, observation, comment, assessment, *pl.* findings; 2. (*Tech.*) locking, securing, setting; stop, lock, detent, locking device. **Feststellungsurteil,** *n.* (*Law*) declaratory judgement.

Festtag ['fɛstta:k], *m.* festival, holiday, (*Eccl.*) feast (day), (*coll.*) red-letter day. **festtäglich,** *adj.* festive, holiday (*mood etc.*).

Festung [fɛstuŋ], *f.* fortress, stronghold, citadel, fort. **Festungs|anlage,** *f.*, **–bauten,** *m.pl.* fortifications. **–graben,** *m.* moat. **–haft,** *f.* confinement (in a fortress) (*more honourable punishment than imprisonment*). **–wall,** *m.* rampart.

festverzinslich ['fɛstfɛrtsɪnslɪç], *adj.* (*Comm.*) bearing fixed interest. **Festwert,** *m.* standard value, (*Phys.*) coefficient, constant.

Festwoche ['fɛstvɔxə], *f. See* **Festspielwoche.**

festwurzeln ['fɛstvurtsəln], *v.i.* (*aux.* s.) be firmly *or* deeply rooted.

Festzug ['fɛsttsu:k], *m.* procession, parade, pageant.

Fetisch ['fe:tɪʃ], *m.* **(-es,** *pl.* **-e)** fetish. **Fetischismus** [–'ʃɪsmus], *m.* idolatry, (*Psych.*) fetishism.

fett [fɛt], *adj.* fatty, greasy, oily; rich, fertile (*soil*), bituminous (*coal*), bold (*type*); (*of a p.*) fat, corpulent, obese; (*fig.*) lucrative; (*coll.*) ***–er Bissen,*** fat pickings, pretty penny; ***–e Pfründe,*** fat living; ***– machen,*** fatten; (*coll.*) ***das macht den Kohl nicht –,*** that won't make much difference, that won't help; ***– werden,*** run to *or* get fat, put on flesh; ***davon wird man nicht –,*** it doesn't pay.

Fett *n.* grease; lard, dripping, shortening; (*coll.*) ***er hat sein – weg,*** that will teach him; (*coll.*) ***ihm sein – geben,*** let him have it, settle his hash; ***im eigenen Fett schmoren,*** stew in one's own juice; ***– ansetzen,*** put on weight *or* flesh.

Fett|auge, *n.* blob of fat (*on soup etc.*). **–druck,** *m.* heavy *or* bold type. **–drüse,** *f.* sebaceous gland.

Fette ['fɛtə], *f. See* **Fettheit. fetten,** *v.t.* grease, oil, lubricate.

Fett|fang, *m.* grease trap. **–fleck(en),** *m.* grease spot. **fettgedruckt,** *adj.* in bold *or* heavy type. **Fett|gehalt,** *m.* fat-content. **–glanz,** *m.* greasy shine. **fett|glänzend,** *adj.* greasy, shiny. **–haltig,** *adj.* fatty, containing fat. **Fettheit,** *f.* fattiness, greasiness; fatness. **Fetthenne,** *f.* (*Bot.*) stonecrop (*Sedum*).

fettig ['fɛtɪç], *adj.* fatty, greasy; adipose (*tissue*). **Fettigkeit,** *f.* fattiness, greasiness, *pl.* fats, fatty foods.

Fett|kohle, *f.* bituminous coal, house coal (*as distinct from steam coal and gas coal*). **–körper,**

m.pl. fatty bodies. **-kügelchen,** *n.* fat globule. **fettleibig,** *adj.* obese, corpulent. **Fettleibigkeit,** *f.* obesity, corpulence. **fett|lösend,** *adj.* fat-dissolving. **-löslich,** *adj.* soluble in fat. **Fett|näpfchen,** *n.* (*sl.*) *da bin ich ins – getreten,* I dropped a brick, I put my foot in it, I made a mess of it. **-polster,** *n.* subcutaneous fatty layer. **-presse,** *f.* grease-gun. **-reihe,** *f.* fatty compounds, (*Chem.*) aliphatic series. **-säure,** *f.* fatty acid. **-spritze,** *f.* *See* **-presse. -stift,** *m.* wax crayon. **-sucht,** *f.* obesity, fatty degeneration. **fettsüchtig,** *adj.* obese. **Fettwanst,** *m.* (*coll.*) big belly, fat paunch. **fettwanstig,** *adj.* big-bellied, paunchy.

Fetzen [fɛtsən], *m.* rag, tatter, scrap, shred; ***in – gehen,*** fall *or* go to pieces; ***in – reißen,*** tear to shreds; (*coll.*) ***daß die – fliegen,*** like blazes, with a vengeance. **fetzen,** *v.t.* shred. **Fetzer,** *m.* shoddy-machine.

feucht [fɔyçt], *adj.* moist, damp, humid; clammy (*hands*), dank; ***-er Brand,*** gangrene. **Feuchte,** *f.* *See* **Feuchtigkeit. feuchten,** *v.t.* moisten, damp. **feuchtfröhlich,** *adj.* (*coll.*) hilarious, bibulous. **Feuchtigkeit,** *f.* moisture (content), dampness, humidity, humour (*of the body*). **Feuchtigkeitsmesser,** *m.* hygrometer. **feucht|kalt,** *adj.* clammy. **-warm,** *adj.* muggy.

feudal [fɔy'da:l], *adj.* feudal, aristocratic; (*coll.*) splendid, magnificent, sumptuous, tip-top, first-rate. **Feudal|recht,** *n.* feudal law. **-system,** *n.* feudal system, feudalism.

Feuer ['fɔyər], *n.* fire, conflagration; (*Mil.*) fire, firing, bombardment; (*fig.*) fervour, ardour, passion, fire, spirit, mettle; brilliance, sparkle, fire, lustre; ***– anmachen, – anzünden,*** light a fire; (*Mil.*) ***mit – bestreichen,*** rake with fire; ***darf ich Sie um – bitten?*** may I ask you for a light? ***das – einstellen,*** cease firing; ***das – eröffnen*** or ***einschalten,*** open fire; (*Mil.*) ***– erhalten,*** come *or* be under fire; ***– fangen,*** catch fire; ***ihm – geben,*** give him a light; ***durchs – gehen,*** go through fire and water; ***bei gelinden*** or ***auf schwachem – kochen,*** cook on *or* over a slow fire; ***in – und Flamme geraten,*** get excited *or* enthusiastic; ***– und Flamme speien,*** breathe fire; ***Öl ins – gießen,*** add fuel to the fire; ***dafür lege ich die Hand ins –,*** cross my heart; (*coll.*) ***ich mache ihm – unter den Hintern,*** I'll put my boot behind him; (*Mil.*) ***unter – nehmen,*** open fire upon; ***im – sein*** or ***liegen*** or ***stehen,*** be under fire; ***die Dinge sind wie – und Wasser,*** the things are as different as chalk from cheese; ***zwischen zwei – geraten,*** be caught between two fires *or* between the devil and the deep blue sea.

Feuer|abriegelung, *f.* box-barrage. **-alarm,** *m.* fire-alarm. **-alarmübung,** *f.* fire-drill. **-anbeter,** *m.* fire-worshipper. **-anzünder,** *m.* fire-lighter. **-bake,** *f.* beacon. **-becken,** *n.* brazier. **-befehl,** *m.* fire *or* firing order. **-bereich,** *m.* (*Mil.*) danger zone, field of fire. **feuer|bereit,** *adj.* ready to open fire. **-beständig,** *adj.* fire-proof, heat-resistant; (*Chem.*) incombustible, refractory. **Feuer|-bestattung,** *f.* cremation. **-bock,** *m.* fire-basket, fire-grate. **-bohne,** *f.* scarlet-runner. **-büchse,** *f.* (*Railw.*) fire-box. **-eifer,** *m.* ardent zeal, ardour. **-esse,** *f.* chimney (*of a forge*); furnace, forge. **feuer|farben, -farbig,** *adj.* flame-coloured, flaming red. **-fest,** *adj.* fire-proof; ***-er Ton,*** fire-clay; ***-er Ziegel,*** firebrick; *see* **-beständig. -flüssig,** *adj.* molten. **Feuerfresser,** *m.* fire-eater. **feuergefährlich,** *adj.* highly inflammable, combustible. **Feuer|geschwindigkeit,** *f.* (*Mil.*) rate of fire. **-glocke,** *f.* tocsin. **-hahn,** *m.* hydrant. **-haken,** *m.* poker. **feuerhemmend,** *adj.* flame-resistant. **Feuer|herd,** *m.* source of the fire. **-kasse,** *f.* fire-insurance office. **-kiste,** *f.* *See* **-büchse. -kitt,** *m.* fire-proof cement. **-kopf,** *m.* hothead, firebrand. **-kraft,** *f.* (*Mil.*) fire-power. **-land,** *n.* (*Geog.*) Tierra del Fuego. **-leiter,** *f.* fire-escape. **-leitung,** *f.* (*Artil.*) fire control. **-lilie,** *f.* tiger-lily. **-linie,** *f.* (*Mil.*) firing-line, front-line. **-löschboot,** *n.* fire-float. **-löscher,** *m.* fire-extinguisher. **-löschgerät,** *n.* fire-fighting equipment. **-löschteich,** *m.* static water tank. **-mal,** *n.* mole, birthmark. **-mauer,** *f.* chimney wall, party-wall, fire-proof wall. **-meer,** *n.* sheet of flames. **-melder,** *m.* fire-alarm.

feuern [fɔyərn], *v.t.* fire (*a boiler or firearms*); kindle; (*fig.*) hurl, fling.

Feuer|nelke, *f.* (*Bot.*) scarlet lychnis (*Lychnis chalcedonica*). **-ordnung,** *f.* fire regulations. **-pein,** *f.* perdition. **-pfanne,** *f.* chafing-dish; censer. **-pfuhl,** *m.* (*B.*) the fiery furnace. **-probe,** *f.* ordeal by fire; (*fig.*) crucial *or* acid test. **-rad,** *n.* Catherine-wheel. **-rohr,** *n.* (*Hist.*) firelock. **-rost,** *m.* *See* **-bock. feuerrot,** *adj.* red as fire, fiery *or* flaming red.

Feuersbrunst ['fɔyərsbrunst], *f.* fire, conflagration.

Feuer|schaden, *m.* fire damage. **-schein,** *m.* glare of fire, fire-light; gun flash. **-schiff,** *n.* lightship. **-schirm,** *m.* fire-screen. **-schlucker,** *m.* *See* **-fresser. -schutz,** *m.* 1. fire prevention; 2. (*Mil.*) covering fire, fire support. **-schwamm,** *m.* tinder, kindling.

Feuers|gefahr, *f.* danger of fire. **-glut,** *f.* blazing heat.

feuersicher ['fɔyərzıçər], *adj.* fireproof, non-inflammable, incombustible.

Feuersnot ['fɔyərsno:t], *f.* fire disaster.

feuerspeiend ['fɔyərʃpaıənt], *adj.* spouting fire; active (*of volcano*); volcanic. **Feuer|sperre,** *f.* (*Artil.*) barrage. **-spritze,** *f.* fire-engine. **-stätte,** *f.* hearth, fireplace. **-stein,** *m.* flint. **-stelle,** *f.* *See* **-stätte. -stellung,** *f.* firing position; (*Artil.*) emplacement. **-strafe,** *f.* death by burning *or* at the stake. **-taufe,** *f.* baptism of fire; ***die – erhalten,*** be under fire for the first time. **-tod,** *m.* death by (accidental) burning. **-ton,** *m.* fire-clay. **-turm,** *m.* lighthouse.

Feuerung ['fɔyəruŋ], *f.* fuel; firing, heating.

Feuer|versicherung, *f.* fire-insurance. **-versicherungspolice,** *f.* fire-policy. **-wache,** *f.* fire-station. **-waffe,** *f.* gun; *pl.* fire-arms. **-walze,** *f.* (*Artil.*) creeping barrage. **-wehr,** *f.* fire-brigade. **-wehrmann,** *m.* (*pl.* **-männer** *or* **-leute**) fireman. **-werk,** *n.* firework; firework display; pyrotechnics. **-werker,** *m.* (*Mil.*) sergeant-artificer (*guns*); (*Nav.*) gunner. **-werkerei,** *f.* pyrotechnics. **-zange,** *f.* (fire-)tongs. **-zeichen,** *n.* beacon, signal flash. **-zeug,** *n.* (petrol-)lighter. **-ziegel,** *m.* firebrick.

Feuilleton [fœjə'tõ], *n.* (**-s,** *pl.* **-s**) feuilleton, light literature. **feuilletonistisch** [-tɔ'nıstıʃ], *adj.* belletristic.

feurig ['fɔyrıç], *adj.* fiery, burning, blazing; sparkling, flashing; (*fig.*) fiery, impetuous, ardent, passionate, fervent, fervid; impassioned, glowing (*speech*), strong, heady (*wine*), mettlesome (*horse*).

Fex [fɛks], *m.* (**-es,** *pl.* **-e**) crank, faddist; (*usu. in compounds, e.g.* ***Bergfex,*** enthusiastic climber, mountaineering crank).

Fez [fe:ts], *m.* (*coll.*) lark, joke.

Fiaker [fi'akər], *m.* (*Austr.*) cab. **Fiakerkutscher,** *m.* cabman, cabby.

Fiasko [fi'asko], *n.* (**-s,** *pl.* **-s**) failure; fiasco, (*coll.*) flop; ***– machen,*** break down, fail utterly.

Fibel [fi:bəl], *f.* (**-,** *pl.* **-n**) 1. primer, spelling-book; 2. clasp, brooch.

Fiber ['fi:bər], *f.* (**-,** *pl.* **-n**) fibre; (*also fig.*) ***mit jeder – seines Herzens,*** with every fibre of his being.

Fibrille [fi'brılə], *f.* fibril. **Fibrin,** *n.* fibrin. **fibrös,** *adj.* fibrous.

ficht [fıçt], *see* **fechten.**

Fichte ['fıçtə], *f.* (*Bot.*) spruce, fir (*Picea excelsa*). **fichten,** *adj.* of spruce-wood, spruce. **Fichten|-ammer,** *f.* (*Orn.*) pine bunting (*Emberiza leucocephala*). **-baum,** *m.* *See* **Fichte. -gimpel,** *m.* (*Orn.*) *see* **Hakengimpel. -harz,** *n.* common resin. **-holz,** *n.* spruce(-wood). **-kreuzschnabel,** *m.* (*Orn.*) (*Am.* red) crossbill (*Loxia curvirostra*). **-zapfen,** *m.* spruce-cone.

fichtst [fıçtst], *see* **fechten.**

Ficke ['fıkə], *f.* (*dial.*) pocket.

ficken ['fıkən], **1.** *v.i.* move quickly to and fro. **2.** *v.t.* (*vulg.*) have sex with (*woman*). **fickerig,** *adj.* (*coll.*)

restless. **Fickfack,** *m.* (**-s,** *pl.* **-e**) (*coll.*) excuse, let-out. **Fickfacker,** *m.* shifty person. **fickfacke(r)n,** *v.i.* dither, vacillate; do evil, conspire.

Fideikommiß [ˈfiːdeikɔmɪs], *n.* (**-(ss)es,** *pl.* **-(ss)e**) (*Law*) entail.

fidel [fiˈdeːl], *adj.* merry, jolly.

Fidibus [ˈfidɪbus], *m.* (- *or* **-ses,** *pl.* - *or* **-se**) spill.

Fiduz [fiˈduts], *n.* (*Studs. sl.*) ***kein – zu einer S. haben,*** have no confidence in a th. **fiduzit!** *int.* (*Studs. sl.*) to your very good health!

Fieber [fiːbər], *n.* fever; ***kaltes –,*** ague; ***aussetzendes –,*** intermittent fever; ***auszehrendes –,*** hectic fever; ***– haben,*** have *or* run a temperature; ***– messen,*** take the temperature. **Fieberanfall,** *m.* attack of fever. **fieberartig,** *adj.* feverish, febrile. **Fieberfrost,** *m.* shivering fit; chill. **fieberhaft,** *adj.* (*fig.*) feverish. **Fieberhaftigkeit,** *f.* feverishness, feverish activity. **Fieberhitze,** *f.* feverishness, fever heat; (*Med.*) cauma. **fieb(e)rig,** *adj. See* **fieberartig. fieberkrank,** *adj.* feverish. **Fiebermittel,** *n.* ague powder, febrifuge. **fiebern,** *v.i.* have a temperature, be feverish; be delirious; (*fig.*) rave (*nach,* for). **Fieber|phantasie,** *f. See* **–wahn. –rinde,** *f.* cinchona bark, quinine. **–schauer,** *m. See* **–frost. –tabelle,** *f.* temperature chart. **–thermometer,** *n.* clinical thermometer. **–traum,** *m.* feverish dream; hallucination. **–wahn,** *m.* delirium.

Fiedel [ˈfiːdəl], *f.* (-, *pl.* **-n**) fiddle. **Fiedelbogen,** *m.* bow, fiddlestick. **fiedeln,** *v.t., v.i.* fiddle, scrape on the fiddle.

Fieder [fiːdər], *f.* (-, *pl.* **-n**) (*Bot.*) pinnule, leaflet. **fied(e)rig,** *adj.* (*Bot.*) feathered, plumed; pinnate. **fiedern,** *v.t.* (*Bot.*) feather; (*usu. p.p.*) ***gefiedert,*** plumed, feathered; pinnate.

Fiedler [ˈfiːdlər], *m.* fiddler.

fiedrig, *adj. See* **fied(e)rig.**

fiel [fiːl], **fiele,** *see* **fallen.**

fieng (*obs.*), *see* **fing.**

fieren [fiːrən], *v.t.* (*Naut.*) slack, slacken.

Figur [fiˈguːr], *f.* (-, *pl.* **-en**) 1. figure, statue, statuette; illustration, diagram; shape, form; 2. (*Dressm.*) waist-line; 3. trope, figure of speech; figurative *or* metaphorical expression, metaphor; 4. chessman; court-card. **figural** [figuˈraːl], *adj.* figured, ornate. **Figuralmusik,** *f.* florid counterpoint. **Figurant** [–ˈrant], *m.* (**-en,** *pl.* **-en**) (*Theat.*) walker-on, super. **Figurenlaufen,** *n.* figure skating. **figurieren** [–ˈriːrən], **1.** *v.i.* figure; cut a figure. **2.** *v.t.* pattern, ornament; ***figurierter Stoff,*** figured *or* patterned material.

figürlich [fiˈgyːrlɪç], *adj.* figurative, metaphorical.

Fiktion [fɪkstiˈoːn], *f.* invention, fabrication, pretence. **fiktiv** [–ˈtiːf], *adj.* fictitious, untrue, unreal, imaginary.

Filet [fiˈleː], *n.* (**-s,** *pl.* **-s**) 1. netting, net-work; 2. (*Cul.*) rump-steak, fillet (*beef*), loin (*mutton, veal, pork*); fillet (*of fish*).

Filete [fiˈleːtə], *f.* (*Bookb.*) tooling.

Filiale [filiˈaːlə], *f.* branch, subsidiary (*establishment or office*), affiliated institution. **Filialgeschäft,** *n.* chain-store.

Filigran [filiˈgraːn], *n.* (**-s,** *pl.* **-e**) filigree.

Film [fɪlm], *m.* (**-s,** *pl.* **-e**) (photographic) film, (roll of) film, cine film; film, motion picture, (*coll.*) movie; ***beim*** or ***im –,*** on the films *or* screen; ***zum – gehen,*** go on the films; ***einen – drehen,*** shoot a film; ***einen – vorführen,*** show a film.

Film|apparat, *m.* cine- *or* (*Am.*) movie camera. **–atelier,** *n.* film studio. **–bearbeitung,** *f.* screen adaptation. **–besucher,** *m.* cinema- *or* (*Am.*) movie-goer. **–diva,** *f.* film star.

filmen [ˈfɪlmən], *v.t., v.i.* film, make *or* shoot a film.

Film|größe, *f.* film star. **–kassette,** *f.* (*Phot.*) plate-holder, film-pack. **–regisseur,** *m.* film director. **–schauspieler,** *m.* film actor. **–streifen,** *m.* film strip. **–verleih, –vertrieb,** *m.* film distributors. **–vorführer,** *m.* projectionist. **–vorführgerät,** *n.* film projector. **–vorführung,** *f.* cinema performance. **–vorschau,** *f.* preview (*for critics*), trailer (*advertisement*). **–vorstellung,** *f. See* **–vorführung.**

Filter [ˈfɪltər], *m. or* (*Tech.*) *n.* filter, strainer. **Filter|anlage,** *f.* filtration plant. **–kanne,** *f.* coffee percolator. **–mundstück,** *n.* filter tip (*of cigarette*). **filtern,** *v.t.* filter, filtrate, strain. **Filter|rest, –rückstand,** *m.* residue, sludge. **–zigarette,** *f.* filter-tip cigarette.

Filtrat [fɪlˈtraːt], *n.* (**-s,** *pl.* **-e**) filtrate.

Filtrierapparat [fɪlˈtriːr–], *m.* filter, strainer, sieve, percolator. **filtrieren,** *v.t. See* **filtern. Filtrier|papier,** *n.* (*Chem.*) filter paper. **–trichter,** *m.* funnel. **Filtrierung,** *f.* filtration.

Filz [fɪlts], *m.* (**-es,** *pl.* **-e**) 1. felt; (*Typ.*) blanket; (*Bot.*) tomentum; (*coll.*) felt hat; 2. (*coll.*) miser, niggard, skinflint. **filzen, 1.** *adj.* of felt. **2.** *v.t.* 1. felt, line *or* cover with felt; 2. snub, scold; 3. (*sl.*) frisk. **3.** *v.i.* (*coll.*) be niggardly *or* stingy. **Filzhut,** *m.* felt hat. **filzig,** *adj.* 1. felt, felt-like, fluffy, downy, (*of hair*) matted; 2. (*coll.*) mean, stingy. **Filzunterlage,** *f.* (*Typ.*) blanket.

Fimmel [ˈfɪməl], *m.* iron wedge; sledge-hammer; (*sl.*) craze, fad; ***einen – haben,*** have a bee in one's bonnet.

final [fiˈnaːl], *adj.* final, concluding. **Finale,** *n.* (**-s,** *pl.* **-s**) (*Mus.*) finale, (*Spt.*) final(s). **Finalsatz,** *m.* (*Gram.*) consecutive clause of result.

Finanz [fiˈnants], *f.* (-, *pl.* **-en**) (*usu. pl.*) finance(s), money-matters. **Finanz|amt,** *n.* inland revenue office. **–ausgleich,** *m.* allocation of revenue between central and local authorities. **–behörde,** *f.* department of inland revenue. **–blatt,** *n.* financial newspaper. **Finanzer,** *m.* (*Austr.*) tax-collector. **Finanz|gebarung,** *f.* fiscal policy. **–gericht,** *n.* Fiscal Court. **finanziell** [–iˈɛl], *adj.* financial, pecuniary. **Finanzier** [–iˈeː], *m.* (**-s,** *pl.* **-s**) financier. **finanzieren** [–ˈtsiːrən], *v.t.* finance, subsidize, support. **Finanz|jahr,** *n.* fiscal year. **–kammer,** *f.* committee of the treasury. **–mann,** *m.* (*pl.* **-leute**) financier; financial expert. **–minister,** *m.* Chancellor of the Exchequer, (*Am.*) Secretary of the Treasury. **–ministerium,** *n.* Treasury. **–rat,** *m.* (Under-) Secretary to the Treasury, Treasury official. **–wechsel,** *m.* paper transaction; accommodation bill. **–wesen,** *n.* finance, financial matters.

Findel|haus [ˈfɪndəl–], *n.* foundling hospital. **–kind,** *n.* foundling.

finden [ˈfɪndən], **1.** *irr.v.t.* find, discover; meet with, come across, light *or* chance upon; think, consider, deem; ***wie – Sie diesen Wein?*** how do you like this wine? ***große Freude an einer S. –,*** take great delight in a th.; ***Geschmack an einer S. –,*** relish a th.; ***für gut –,*** think proper; ***den Tod –,*** meet one's death. **2.** *irr.v.r.* (*of a p.*) get into one's stride, find o.s., (*of a th.*) be found; ***sich – in*** (*Acc.*), accommodate *or* resign *or* reconcile o.s. to, comply *or* (*coll.*) put up with; ***es fand sich oft,*** it often happened, there were often; ***es wird sich –, daß . . .,*** it will be seen *or* found that . . .; ***es wird sich schon –,*** it will turn out all right, you wait and see. **Finder,** *m.* finder, discoverer. **Finderlohn,** *m.* finder's reward.

findig [fɪndɪç], *adj.* clever, resourceful; ingenious. **Findigkeit,** *f.* cleverness, resourcefulness, ingenuity.

Findling [ˈfɪntlɪŋ], *m.* (**-s,** *pl.* **-e**) 1. *See* **Findelkind**; 2. (*Geol.*) erratic block, drift block *or* boulder.

Finesse [fiˈnɛsə], *f.* finesse, *pl.* wiles, ruses, trickery, stratagem.

fing [fɪŋ], **finge,** *see* **fangen.**

Finger [ˈfɪŋər], *m.* finger; digit; ***an den (fünf) –n abzählen,*** count on the fingers (of one hand); (*fig.*) ***das kannst du dir an den –n abzählen,*** it's as clear as daylight; ***er faßt es mit spitzen –n an,*** he touches it very cautiously; ***sich die – wund arbeiten,*** work one's fingers to the bone; ***die – davonlassen,*** keep one's fingers *or* hands off, (*fig.*) leave alone, keep clear of; ***er hat überall die – im Spiel,*** he has a finger in every pie; ***an den –n***

hersagen, have at one's finger-tips; ***ihm auf die – klopfen,*** rap his knuckles, rap him over the knuckles; ***er macht lange –,*** he is light-fingered *or* is given to pilfering; ***du hast keinen – gerührt,*** you didn't raise a finger; ***aus den –n saugen,*** invent, (*coll.*) cook up; ***ihm auf die – sehen,*** keep a sharp eye on him; (*fig.*) ***durch die – sehen,*** close one's eyes to, turn a blind eye to, wink at; (*fig.*) ***sich*** (*Dat.*) ***die – verbrennen,*** burn one's fingers; ***ihn um den – wickeln,*** twist him round one's little finger; ***mit –n*** or ***dem – weisen*** or ***zeigen auf*** (*Acc.*), point at *or* to; point out; ***mir zerrinnt das Geld unter den –n,*** money runs through my fingers like water.

Finger|abdruck, *m.* finger-print. **–breit,** *m.* a finger's breadth. **fingerfertig,** *adj.* dexterous, deft, nimble-fingered. **Finger|fertigkeit,** *f.* manual skill, dexterity; (*Mus.*) execution. **–glied,** *n.* finger-joint. **–hut,** *m.* 1. thimble; 2. (*Bot.*) foxglove (*Digitalis*). **–kraut,** *n.* (*Bot.*) cinquefoil (*Potentilla*).

Fingerling ['fıŋərlıŋ], *m.* (**-s,** *pl.* **-e**) fingerstall.

fingern ['fıŋərn], **1.** *v.t.* finger, (*coll.*) wangle, manage. **2.** *v.i.* ***er –t nach dem Geld,*** his fingers are itching for the money.

Finger|nagel, *m.* fingernail. **–nerven,** *m.pl.* digital nerves. **–platte,** *f.* door-guard, finger-plate. **–satz,** *m.* (*Mus.*) fingering. **–spitze,** *f.* finger-tip, finger-end; (*fig.*) ***es juckt ihm in den –n,*** his fingers are itching. **–spitzengefühl,** *n.* instinct, intuition; flair. **–sprache,** *f.* deaf-and-dumb language. **–stock,** *m.* glove-stretcher. **–übung,** *f.* (*Mus.*) fingering, finger-exercises. **–zeig,** *m.* sign; indication, hint; cue, tip, pointer.

fingieren [fıŋ'gi:rən], *v.t.* simulate, pretend, feign, sham. **fingiert,** *adj.* assumed, fictitious, imaginary.

Fink [fıŋk], *m.* (**-en,** *pl.* **-en**) 1. (*Orn.*) finch (*Fringillidae*); 2. (*Studs. sl.*) student without affiliations (*i.e. belonging to no corporation*); 3. (*Swiss*) house-shoe, slipper; 4. (*coll.*) harum-scarum. **Finkler,** *m.* bird-catcher, fowler.

1**Finne** ['fınə], *m.* (**-n,** *pl.* **-n**) (*Geog.*) Finn.

2**Finne,** *f.* fin (*of whales*); pane (*of a hammer*); pimple, pustule; (*Med.*) bladder-worm. **finnig,** *adj.* pimply, pustular, measly (*of pigs*).

finnisch ['fınıʃ], *adj.* (*Geog.*) Finnish; ***Finnischer Meerbusen,*** Gulf of Finland. **Finnland,** *n.* Finland. **Finnländer,** *m.* Finlander.

Finnwal ['fınva:l], *m.* whale of the family *Balaenopteridae.*

finster ['fınstər], *adj.* dark, obscure; gloomy, dim; ominous, sinister, grim, threatening; ***– aussehen,*** look black; ***– ansehen,*** scowl at; ***–er Blick,*** scowl; ***das –e Mittelalter,*** the Dark Ages; ***im Finstern,*** in the dark(ness), (*fig.*) in the dark. **Finsterling,** *m.* (**-s,** *pl.* **-e**) obscurantist, bigot; ignoramus. **Finsternis,** *f.* (-, *pl.* **-se**) darkness; obscurity; gloom; (*Astr.*) eclipse; ***die Macht der –,*** the power of darkness.

Finte ['fıntə], *f.* feint; trick, wile, ruse, strategem.

Fips [fıps], *m.* (**-es,** *pl.* **-e**) 1. snap of the fingers; 2. fillip; 3. nickname for a tailor. **fipsig,** *adj.* (*coll.*) paltry, footling, fiddling.

Firlefanz [fırlə'fants], *m.* (**-es,** *pl.* **-e**) nonsense, foolery, hocus-pocus; frippery. **Firlefanzer,** *m.* buffoon, trifler. **Firlefanzerei** [–ə'raı], *f.* nonsense, fooling, trifling.

Firma ['fırma], *f.* (-, *pl.* **-men**) firm, business, (commercial) house *or* establishment; (*Comm.*) ***unter der –,*** under the style of; (*in letters*) ***an –,*** Messrs.

Firmament [fırma'mɛnt], *n.* (**-(e)s,** *pl.* **-e**) firmament, sky, vault of heaven.

firmeln ['fırməln], *v.t.* (*R.C.*) confirm. **Firmelung,** *f.* confirmation. **firmen,** *v.t.* (*Austr.*) *see* **firmeln.**

Firmen|inhaber, *m.* proprietor. **–schild,** *n.* sign-(board), name-plate. **–verzeichnis,** *n.* business *or* trade directory. **–wert,** *m.* intangible assets, good-will. **–zeichen,** *n.* trade-mark.

firmieren [fır'mi:rən], *v.t., v.i.* sign (in) the firm's name.

Firmling ['fırmlıŋ], *m.* candidate for confirmation. **Firmung,** *f.* (*Austr.*) *see* **Firmelung.**

Firn [fırn], *m.* (**-(e)s,** *pl.* **-e**) old snow, perpetual snow (*on mountains*), névé. **Firne,** *f.* 1. age, mellowness (*of wine*); 2. snow-covered mountain. **firnen,** *v.i.* age (*of wine*). **Firner,** *m.* (*Austr., Bav.*) *see* **Firn. Firn(e)wein,** *m.* old wine, matured wine. **Firngürtel,** *m.* region of perpetual snow.

Firnis ['fırnıs], *m.* (**-ses,** *pl.* **-se**) varnish, gloss; (*fig.*) ***Bildung als bloßer –,*** education that is a mere veneer. **Firnispapier,** *n.* glazed paper. **firnissen,** *v.t.* (***du firnissest*** or ***firnißt, gefirnißt***) varnish.

Firnwein, *m. See* **Firn(e)wein.**

First [fırst], *m.* (**-es,** *pl.* **-e**) ridge (*of a roof or hill*); coping (*of a wall*). **First|balken,** *m.* ridge-piece. **–ziegel,** *m.* ridge-tile.

Fis [fıs], *n.* (*Mus.*) F sharp.

Fisch [fıʃ], *m.* (**-es,** *pl.* **-e**) fish; *pl.* (*Astr.*) Pisces; ***gesund wie ein – im Wasser,*** as sound as a bell, fit as a fiddle; (*coll.*) ***faule –e,*** lame *or* paltry excuses; (*coll.*) ***kleine –e,*** small fry *or* (*Am.*) potatoes; ***stumm wie ein –,*** silent as the grave; ***nicht –, nicht Fleisch,*** neither fish nor flesh. **Fisch|adler,** *m.* (*Orn.*) osprey (*Pandion haliaetus*). **–angel,** *f.* fish(ing)-hook. **fischartig,** *adj.* fish-like. **Fisch|behälter,** *m.* fish tank, aquarium. **–bein,** *n.* whalebone; ***weißes –,*** bone of cuttle-fish. **–beinern,** *adj.* of whalebone. **Fischblut,** *n.* sluggishness, apathy; ***– in den Adern haben,*** be phlegmatic. **fischblütig,** *adj.* phlegmatic. **Fisch|brut,** *f.* fry. **–dampfer,** *m.* steam-trawler.

fischen ['fıʃən], *v.t., v.i.* fish (***nach,*** for) (*also fig.*); ***im Trüben –,*** fish in troubled waters; (*coll.*) ***dabei ist nichts zu –,*** no *or* nothing good will come of it, there's nothing doing there; ***die Brocken aus der Suppe –,*** pick and choose, pick out the plums. **Fischen,** *n.* fishing, angling.

Fischer ['fıʃər], *m.* fisherman, angler. **Fischer|-boot,** *n.* fishing-boat, fishing smack. **–dorf,** *n.* fishing village.

Fischerei [fıʃə'raı], *f.* fishing, fishery. **Fischerei-hafen,** *m.* fishing harbour.

Fischer|gerät, *n.* fishing tackle. **–gilde,** *f. See* **–innung. –hütte,** *f.* fisherman's cottage. **–innung,** *f.* fishmongers' company. **–netz,** *n.* fishing-net. **–ring,** *m.* (*R.C.*) (papal) Ring of the Fisherman.

Fisch|fang, *m.* fishing; fishery. **–geruch,** *m.* fishy smell. **–gräte,** *f.* fish-bone. **–gräten-muster,** *n.* herring-bone pattern. **–grätenstich,** *m.* herring-bone stitch. **–händler,** *m.* fishmonger. **fischig,** *adj.* fishy; tasting *or* smelling of fish. **Fisch|kelle,** *f.* (*Cul.*) fish-slice. **–köder,** *m.* bait. **–konserve,** *f.* pickled *or* canned fish. **–korb,** *m.* creel. **–kunde,** *f.* ichthyology. **–kutter,** *m.* fishing smack. **–laich,** *m.* spawn, hard roe. **–leim,** *m.* fish-glue, isinglass. **–mehl,** *n.* fish-meal. **–milch,** *f.* soft roe, milt. **–möwe,** *f.* (*Orn.*) great black-headed gull (*Larus ichthyaëtus*). **–netz,** *n.* fishing-net. **–otter,** *m.* otter. **–reiher,** *m.* (*Orn.*) heron, (*Am.*) gray heron (*Ardea cinerea*). **–reuse,** *f.* fish-trap, bow-net, weir-basket. **–rogen,** *m.* roe. **–satz,** *m.* fry, spawn. **–schuppe,** *f.* fish's scale. **–strich,** *m.* spawning; spawn (*of fish*). **–teich,** *m.* fish-pond. **–tran,** *m.* train-oil, fish-oil, whale-oil, cod-liver oil. **–wasser,** *n.* fishing-ground. **–weib,** *n.* fishwife. **–zucht,** *f.* pisciculture, fish breeding. **–zug,** *m.* catch, haul, draught (*of fish*).

Fisimatenten [fizima'tɛntən], *pl.* (*coll.*) excuses, humbug, fuss, shuffling.

fiskalisch [fıs'ka:lıʃ], *adj.* fiscal, treasury, state-owned; ***–es Eigentum,*** government property. **Fiskus** ['fıskus], *m.* exchequer, treasury.

Fisole [fi'zo:lə], *f.* (*Austr.*) runner *or* French bean.

Fistel ['fıstəl], *f.* (-, *pl.* **-n**) fistula; falsetto (*voice*). **fisteln,** *v.i.* sing falsetto. **Fistel|schnitt,** *m.* (*Surg.*) syringotomy. **–stimme,** *f.* falsetto.

fistulieren [fıstu'li:rən], *v.i. See* **fisteln. fistulös,** *adj.* fistular, fistulous.

Fitis ['fıtıs], *m.* (**-ses,** *pl.* **-se**), **Fitislaubsänger,** *m.* (*Orn.*) willow-warbler (*Phylloscopus trochilus*).

Fittich ['fıtıç], *m.* (**-(e)s,** *pl.* **-e**) (*Poet.*) wing, pinion; ***ihn unter seine −e nehmen,*** take him under one's wing.

Fitting ['fıtıŋ], *n.* (**-s,** *pl.* **-s**) union, joint (*for pipes etc.*).

Fitze ['fıtsə], *f.* skein; hank; (*coll.*) trifle, triviality; tangle, muddle; (*dial.*) wrinkle. **fitzen, 1.** *v.t.* tie up into skeins; string (*beans*); wrinkle, crumple; (*coll.*) whip, chastise, trounce. **2.** *v.i.* (*coll.*) work by fits and starts.

fix [fıks], *adj.* 1. fixed, firm, settled, (*coll.*) cut and dried; ***− und fertig,*** quite ready; (*coll.*) all in, dead beat; ***−e Idee,*** fixed idea, monomania; 2. (*of a p.*) quick, alert, smart, deft, adroit; ***mach −!*** be quick! get a move on! ***−er Kerl,*** smart fellow; (*Prov.*) ***außen −, innen nix,*** great show, but no substance. **Fixage** [−'sa:ʒə], *f.* (*Chem., Phot.*) fixing. **Fixativ** [−'ti:f], *n.* (**-s,** *pl.* **-e**) (*Chem.*) fixing agent, fixer, fixative.

fixen ['fıksən], *v.i.* (*Comm.*) sell short, bear, speculate for a fall. **Fixer,** *m.* bear.

Fixierbad [fık'si:rba:t], *n.* (*Phot.*) fixing bath *or* solution, (*coll.*) fixer. **fixieren,** *v.t.* 1. fix, settle, establish; 2. stare at, fix one's eyes on; 3. (*Phot.*) fix. **Fixiermittel,** *n.* fixing agent, fixative.

Fix|punkt, *m.* fixed point. **−stern,** *m.* fixed star. **Fixum,** *n.* (**-s,** *pl.* **-xa**) fixed sum; fixed stipend *or* salary.

flach [flax], *adj.* 1. flat, plain, level, even; ***die −e Hand,*** palm, flat of the hand; (*coll.*) ***das liegt auf der −en Hand,*** that's quite plain *or* evident; ***auf dem −en Lande,*** in the open country; ***mit der −en Klinge,*** with the flat of the blade; 2. shallow, shoal; (*fig.*) superficial; (*coll.*) ***da kennst du ihn −,*** in that respect you do not know him at all; (*Naut.*) ***−e Stelle,*** shoal, shallows. **Flach,** *n.* (**-(e)s,** *pl.* **-e**) (*Naut.*) shoal, shallows. **−flach,** *n.suff.* (*Geom.*) −hedron.

Flach|bahn, *f.* flat trajectory. **−boot,** *n.* flat-bottomed boat, punt. **−brenner,** *m.* flat *or* fish-tail burner. **−druck,** *m.* (**-(e)s,** *pl.* **-e**) lithograph (printing).

Fläche ['flɛçə], *f.* surface, area, expanse, space; (*Geom.*) plane; face, facet.

flachen ['flaxən], *v.t.* flatten, level, smooth.

Flächen|ausdehnung, *f.* square dimension. **−bedarf,** *m.* requisite floor-space. **−belastung,** *f.* (*Av.*) wing loading. **−blitz,** *m.* sheet-lightning. **−bombardierung,** *f.* (*Av.*) carpet bombing. **−brand,** *m.* extensive fire, widespread conflagration. **−druck,** *m.* surface pressure, pressure per unit area. **−einheit,** *f.* unit of area. **−inhalt,** *m.* (surface) area, superficies, acreage. **−maß,** *n.* square measure, surface measure(ment). **−raum,** *m.* area. **−umriß,** *m.* perimeter. **−winkel,** *m.* plane angle.

flach|fallen, *irr.v.i.* (*aux.* s.) (*coll.*) fall flat, be no go. **−gedrückt,** *adj.* flattened (out *or* down). **Flach|gewinde,** *n.* square thread (*of screw*). **−hang,** *m.* gentle slope. **Flachheit,** *f.* flatness, (*fig.*) shallowness, superficiality; platitude, triviality.

−flächig ['flɛçıç], *suff.* -faced, -hedral.

Flach|kopf, *m.* (*coll.*) blockhead, dunderhead. **−kopfschraube,** *f.* countersunk screw. **−küste,** *f.* low-lying coast. **−land,** *n.* flat country, lowland, plain. **−rennen,** *n.* flat racing.

Flachs [flaks], *m.* (**-es,** *no pl.*) flax; (*coll.*) teasing, mockery. **Flachsbau,** *m.* flax-growing. **flachsblond,** *adj.* flaxen-haired. **Flachs|breche,** *f.*, **−brecher,** *m.* flax-scutcher. **−darre,** *f.* flax-drying house. **flachsen,** *v.i.* (*coll.*) tease, mock.

flächse(r)n ['flɛksə(r)n], *adj.* flaxen.

flachs|farben, −farbig, *adj.* flaxen (coloured). **−haarig,** *adj.* flaxen-haired. **Flachs|hechel,** *f.* flax comb. **−kopf,** *m.* flaxen-haired person. **−seide,** *f.* (*Bot.*) dodder (*Cuscuta*).

Flach|zange, *f.* flat-nosed pliers. **−ziegel,** *m.* flat *or* plain tile.

Flackerfeuer ['flakərfɔyər], *n.* (*Naut.*) flashing light.

flackerig ['flakərıç], *adj.* flickering, uncertain. **flackern,** *v.i.* flicker, flare.

Fladdermine ['fladərmi:nə], *f. See* **Flattermine.**

Fladen ['fla:dən], *m.* flat cake; (*Swiss*) slice of bread and butter.

Flader ['fla:dər], *f.* (**-,** *pl.* **-n**) grain (*of wood*), annual ring. **fladerig,** *adj.* grained.

Flageolett [flaʒo'lɛt], *n.* (**-s,** *pl.* **-e**) flageolet.

Flagge ['flagə], *f.* 1. flag, colours; ***die − hissen,*** hoist the flag; ***seine − führen,*** show one's colours; ***die − streichen,*** strike the flag; (*fig.*) give in; ***die − halbstock setzen,*** fly the flag at half-mast; ***unter falscher −,*** under false colours; 2. defect in spinning. **flaggen,** *v.t., v.i.* fly *or* hoist *or* show one's flag; deck *or* dress with flags; signal with flags; ***halbstocks*** or ***halbmast −,*** hoist the flag at half-mast. **Flaggen|ehrung,** *f.* saluting the colours. **−gala,** *f.* ***− setzen,*** dress a ship. **−kopf,** *m.* (mast-head) truck. **−leine,** *f.* signal-halyard. **−stange,** *f.*, **−stock,** *m.* flag-staff, flag-pole. **−tuch,** *n.* bunting. **−zeichen,** *n.* flag signal. **Flaggschiff,** *n.* flag-ship.

Flak [flak], *f.* anti-aircraft artillery, (*coll.*) ack-ack. **Flakabwehr,** *f.* anti-aircraft defence(s).

Flakon [fla'ko:n], *n.* or *m.* (**-s,** *pl.* **-s**) phial, small bottle.

Flak|posten, *m.* anti-aircraft spotter. **−sperre,** *f.* anti-aircraft barrage.

Flamberg ['flambɛrk], *m.* (**-(e)s,** *pl.* **-e**) (*Poet.*) sword, brand.

Flame ['fla:mə], *m.* (**-n,** *pl.* **-n**) (*Geog.*) Fleming. **flämisch,** *adj.* Flemish.

Flamme ['flamə], *f.* flame (*also fig. coll.* = *sweetheart*); ***Feuer und − für eine S. sein,*** be wildly enthusiastic about a th.; ***−n schlagen,*** blaze up; ***in −n,*** in flames, ablaze. **flammen, 1.** *v.i.* flame, blaze, flare, glow. **2.** *v.t.* singe; water (*silks etc.*). **Flammen|blume,** *f.* (*Bot.*) phlox. **−bogen,** *m.* electric arc. **flammend,** *adj.* flaming, blazing, (*fig.*) burnning, glowing (*enthusiasm*), flashing, sparkling (*eyes*). **Flammen|meer,** *n.* sea of flames. **−säule,** *f.* fiery column. **−tod,** *m.* death by burning at the stake. **−werfer,** *m.* (*Mil.*) flame-thrower. **−zeichen,** *n.* beacon, signal fire.

Flammeri ['flaməri:], *m.* (**-(s),** *pl.* **-s**) blancmange.

flammig ['flamıç], *adj.* flame-like; watered (*of fabric*), veined, grained (*of wood*).

Flamm|kohle, *f.* steam coal. **−ofen,** *m.* smelting furnace. **−punkt,** *m.* flash point. **−rohr,** *n.* fire tube, flue.

Flandern ['flandərn], *n.* (*Geog.*) Flanders. **flandrisch,** *adj.* Flemish.

Flanell [fla'nɛl], *m.* (**-s,** *pl.* **-e**) flannel. **flanellen,** *adj.* of flannel.

Flaneur [fla'nø:r], *m.* (**-s,** *pl.* **-e**) idler, loiterer, loafer. **flanieren,** *v.i.* stroll about, saunter, dawdle, loaf about, loiter.

Flanke ['flaŋkə], *f.* flank, side; (*Gymn.*) side-vault; (*Footb.*) wing; (*Mil.*) ***− aufrollen,*** turn a flank; ***in die − fallen, in der − angreifen,*** attack in the flank. **Flanken|angriff,** *m.* flank attack. **−ball,** *m.* (*Footb.*) centre. **−bewegung,** *f.* (out)flanking movement. **−feuer,** *n.* enfilade fire, flanking fire.

flankieren [flaŋ'ki:rən], *v.t.* flank, enfilade, outflank. **Flankierung,** *f.* flanking position, flanking fire.

Flansch [flanʃ], *m.* (**-es,** *pl.* **-e**) flange. **Flanschendichtung,** *f.* gasket.

Flaps [flaps], *m.* (**-es,** *pl.* **-e**) (*coll.*) boor, lout. **flapsig,** *adj.* boorish, loutish, uncouth.

Flasche ['flaʃə], *f.* 1. bottle, flask, phial, cylinder; ***auf −n ziehen,*** bottle, put in bottles; ***einem Kind die − geben,*** give a child the (feeding) bottle, feed a child from the bottle; ***mit der − aufziehen,*** bring up on the bottle; 2. pulley block. **Flaschen|bier,** *n.* bottled beer. **−gas,** *n.* gas in cylinders. **−hals,** *m.* neck of bottle, (*coll.*) bottle-neck. **−kapsel,** *f.* bottle top *or* cap. **−kürbis,** *m.* gourd. **flaschenreif,** *adj.* matured in bottle. **Flaschen|spüler,** *m.* bottle-washer. **−verschluß,** *m.* stopper. **−zug,** *m.* pulley block, block-and-tackle.

Flaschner ['flaʃnər], *m.* (*dial.*) plumber.

Flaser ['fla:zər], *f.* (-, *pl.* **-n**) vein (*in rock*). **flas(e)rig,** *adj.* veined.

Flattergeist ['flatərgaɪst], *m.* flighty *or* fickle *or* unstable p., gad-about, flibbertigibbet. **flatterhaft,** *adj.* flighty, fickle. **Flatterhaftigkeit,** *f.* flightiness, fickleness, inconstancy. **flatterig,** *adj.* *See* **flatterhaft. Flattermine,** *f.* (*Mil.*) contact mine, land-mine, booby-trap.

flattern ['flatərn], *v.i.* (*aux.* h. & s.) flutter, flap, float in the wind, wave, stream (*of hair*); dangle; (*of wheels*) wobble.

flau [flau], *adj.* feeble, weak, faint; insipid, flat, stale, lifeless, vapid; dull, slack (*of trade*); indifferent, half-hearted, lukewarm; ***der Wind wird -er,*** the wind is dropping; **– *machen,*** depress (*the exchange*); ***die Geschäfte gehen –,*** business is dull, trade is slack; (*Phot.*) ***der Film ist –,*** the film is under-exposed. **Flauheit,** *f.* flatness; faintness; indifference; dullness, deadness (*of trade*).

Flaum [flaum], *m.* down, fluff; (*Bot., Anat.*) tomentum.

Flau|macher, *m.* defeatist, alarmist, (*coll.*) scaremonger. **–macherei,** *f.* defeatism.

Flaum|feder, *f.* down (feather), plumule. **–haar,** *n.* (*Bot.*) down, pubescence. **flaumig,** *adj.* fluffy, downy, soft as down; (*Bot.*) pubescent.

Flaus, Flausch [flaus, flauʃ], *m.* (**-es,** *pl.* **-e**) 1. tuft, bunch, wisp; 2. fleecy woollen material; pilot-cloth, coarse coating; greatcoat of coarse cloth, duffle-coat.

Flause ['flauzə], *f.* (*usu. pl.*) shift, evasion, humbug, shuffling, lie. **Flausenmacher,** *m.* liar, shuffler, humbug.

Flaute ['flautə], *f.* (dead) calm, doldrums (*at sea*); stagnation, recession, slackness (*of trade*).

Fläz [flɛ:ts], *m.* (**-es,** *pl.* **-e**) (*dial.*) lout, boor. **fläzen,** *v.r.* (*coll.*) loll *or* lounge about.

Flechse ['flɛksə], *f.* tendon, sinew. **Flechsenhaube,** *f.* (*Anat.*) caul, epicranium. **flechsig,** *adj.* sinewy.

Flechte ['flɛçtə], *f.* plait, tress (*of hair*); twist, braid; (*Med.*) tetter, herpes; (*Bot.*) lichen. **flechten, 1.** *irr.v.t.* plait, braid, twist; wreathe, intertwine, interweave, interlace; ***einen Korb –,*** weave a basket; ***aufs Rad –,*** break on the wheel (*torture*). **2.** *irr.v.r.* wind, twine. **flechtenartig,** *adj.* (*Med.*) herpetic; (*Bot.*) lichenous. **Flecht|korb,** *m.* wicker-basket. **–werk,** *n.* wickerwork; wattle; (*Archit.*) trellis pattern. **–zaun,** *m.* wattle fence.

Fleck [flɛk], *m.* (**-(e)s,** *pl.* **-e**) place, spot; plot, patch, piece (*of ground*); spot, blemish, flaw, blot, stain, smudge, mark, speck; patch; (*dial.*) tripe; ***auf dem -e,*** on the spot, without delay, at once, post-haste; ***blaue -e,*** bruises; **– *im Auge,*** speck in the eye, s.th. in one's eye; ***das Herz auf dem rechten – haben,*** have one's heart in the right place; ***den rechten – treffen,*** hit the nail on the head, strike home; **– *schießen,*** hit the bull's-eye; ***der schwarze –,*** bull's-eye; ***gehe nicht vom -e!*** don't budge *or* stir! ***wir kommen nicht vom –,*** we are not getting on *or* making headway; ***vom – weg,*** see ***auf dem -e.*** **Flecken,** *m.* 1. *See* **Fleck**; 2. market-town, country-town.

flecken ['flɛkən], **1.** *v.t.* spot, stain, mark, make *or* leave marks *or* stains on; patch (*shoe*). **2.** *v.i.* 1. mark, show marks *or* stains; ***der Stoff fleckt leicht,*** this material marks easily *or* shows marks readily; 2. (*coll.*) make progress, get on well; ***es fleckt mir nicht,*** I cannot get on with my work; ***heute hat es gefleckt,*** today I have got on well.

fleckenfrei ['flɛkənfraɪ], **fleckenlos,** *adj.* spotless, stainless, unblemished. **Fleckenwasser,** *n.* *See* **Fleckwasser.**

Fleck|fieber, *n.* *See* **–typhus. fleckig,** *adj.* spotted, stained, marked; mottled, speckled; freckled (*face*). **Fleck|schuß,** *m.* (shot in the) bull's-eye. **–schußweite,** *f.* point-blank range. **–seife,** *f.* scouring soap. **–typhus,** *m.* typhus, spotted fever. **–wasser,** *n.* stain remover.

fleddern ['flɛdərn], *v.t.* plunder, rob (*corpses etc.*).

Fledermaus ['fle:dərmaus], *f.* (*Zool.*) bat (*Chiroptera*). **Flederwisch,** *m.* feather-duster, (*coll.*) flighty *or* wanton creature (*of a woman*).

Fle(e)t [fle:t], *n.* (**-(e)s,** *pl.* **-e**) (*dial.*) canal, waterway (*in Hamburg*).

Flegel ['fle:gəl], *m.* 1. flail; 2. (*fig.*) lout, boor, hooligan. **Flegelei** [–'laɪ], *f.* boorishness, loutishness, rudeness, impudence. **flegelhaft,** *adj.* rude, unmannerly, boorish, loutish; tomboyish, hoydenish (*of girls only*). **Flegeljahre,** *n.pl.* teens, adolescence, the awkward age (*applied to boys only aged 13–17 yrs. approx.*). **flegeln, 1.** *v.t.* (*dial.*) (beat with a) flail, thresh. **2.** *v.r.* loll, lounge, sprawl.

flehen ['fle:ən], *v.i.* **– *zu,*** implore, entreat, beseech (***um,*** for). **Flehen,** *n.* entreaty, prayers; supplication. **flehentlich,** *adj.* suppliant, imploring, beseeching, urgent, fervent; **– *bitten,*** beseech; ***-e Bitte,*** earnest prayer, fervent supplication, entreaty.

Fleisch [flaɪʃ], *n.* flesh; meat; flesh *or* pulp (*of fruit*); cellular tissue (*in leaves*); the flesh (*physical and sensual part of man*); **– *ansetzen,*** put on flesh; ***ihm in – und Blut gehen,*** become second nature with him; ***das ist weder Fisch noch –,*** that is neither fish, flesh, fowl, nor good red herring; ***gehacktes –,*** minced meat; ***wildes –,*** proud flesh; (*fig.*) ***ins eigene – schneiden,*** cut one's own throat; (*B.*) ***das – kreuzigen,*** mortify the flesh.

Fleisch|bank, *f.* butcher's stall, meat counter. **–beschau,** *f.* meat inspection. **–brühe,** *f.* clear soup, broth, bouillon. **fleischen, 1.** *v.t.* strip of flesh. **2.** *v.i.* cut into the flesh, cut deep. **Fleischer,** *m.* butcher. **Fleischerei** [–ə'raɪ], *f.*, **Fleischerladen,** *m.* butcher('s) shop. **fleischern, 1.** *adj.* meaty, fleshy. **2.** *v.i.* work as a butcher. **Fleischeslust,** *f.* lust, carnal desire. **Fleischfarbe,** *f.* flesh-colour. **fleisch|farbig,** *adj.* flesh-coloured. **–fressend,** *adj.* carnivorous. **Fleischfresser,** *m.* carnivorous animal, carnivore. **fleischgeworden,** *adj.* incarnate. **Fleisch|hacker, –hauer,** *m.* butcher. **–halle,** *f.* meat-market. **fleischig,** *adj.* fleshy, meaty; plump, fat; pulpy. **Fleischigkeit,** *f.* fleshiness. **Fleisch|kammer,** *f.* larder. **–kloß,** *m.* meat-ball. **–konserve,** *f.* potted *or* tinned *or* canned meat. **fleischlich,** *adj.* carnal, sensual; fleshly. **Fleischlichkeit,** *f.* sensuality, carnal-mindedness. **fleischlos,** *adj.* fleshless; meatless, vegetarian. **Fleisch|made,** *f.* maggot. **–markt,** *m.* meat-market. **–mehl,** *n.* cattle fodder (*from meat refuse*). **–teile,** *m.pl.* fleshy parts. **–topf,** *m.* (*usu. pl.*) flesh-pot (*symbol of good living*). **–vergiftung,** *f.* ptomaine poisoning. **–werdung,** *f.* (*Theol.*) incarnation. **–wolf,** *m.* mincing machine, mincer. **–wunde,** *f.* flesh wound.

Fleiß [flaɪs], *m.* diligence, industry, hard work; application, assiduity, pains; ***mit –,*** intentionally, deliberately, purposely, on purpose; (*Prov.*) ***ohne – kein Preis,*** hard work brings its own reward. **fleißig,** *adj.* industrious, hardworking, diligent, assiduous; ***-er Besucher,*** frequent *or* regular visitor.

flektieren [flɛk'ti:rən], *v.t.* (*Gram.*) inflect.

flennen ['flɛnən], *v.i.* (*coll.*) whine, snivel, blubber.

Flet, *n.* *See* **Fle(e)t.**

fletschen ['flɛtʃən], *v.t.* ***die Zähne –,*** show one's teeth, snarl.

fleuch [flɔyç], **fleuchst, fleucht,** (*obs.*) *see* **fliehen.**

fleug [flɔyk], **fleugst, fleugt,** (*obs.*) *see* **fliegen.**

Flexion [flɛksi'o:n], *f.* (*Gram.*) inflexion. **Flexionslehre,** *f.* (*Gram.*) accidence.

Flibustier [flibus'ti:r], *m.* filibuster, buccaneer, freebooter, pirate.

flicht [flɪçt], **flichst, flicht,** (*obs.*) *see* **flechten.**

Flick [flɪk], *n.* (**-s,** *pl.* **-e**) patch (*of material for repairs*). **Flickarbeit,** *f.* patchwork. **flicken, 1.** *v.t.* patch (up), mend, repair; bungle, botch; ***ihm etwas am Zeuge –,*** pick holes in him; find fault with him; run him down. **Flicken,** *m.* patch. **Flickerei** [–ə'raɪ], *f.* patchwork, mending; bungling. **Flick|korb,** *m.* work-basket. **–reim,** *m.* makeshift rhyme. **–schneider,** *m.* jobbing tailor.

–schuster, *m.* jobbing cobbler. **–werk,** *n.* patchwork, patched-up job, botched job. **–wort,** *n.* expletive. **–zeug,** *n.* (puncture) repair outfit; mending things.

Flieder ['fli:dər], *m.* (*Bot.*) lilac (*Syringa vulgaris*); (*Bot.*) elder (*Sambucus nigra*).

Fliege ['fli:gə], *f.* 1. fly; (*Ent.*) ***spanische –n,*** Spanish fly, cantharides (*Lytta versicatoria*); ***von –n beschmissen,*** fly-blown; ***in der Not frißt der Teufel –n,*** beggars can't be choosers; ***zwei –n mit einer Klappe schlagen,*** kill two birds with one stone; 2. imperial (*beard*); 3. bow-tie; 4. (*coll.*) flibbertigibbet.

fliegen ['fli:gən], **1.** *irr.v.i.* (*aux.* s.) 1. fly, (*fig.*) rush, dash; (*coll.*) ***ich fliege gerade nach Hause,*** I am just rushing home; ***in die Höhe –,*** soar (up); ***in die Luft –,*** go up in the air, blow up, explode; ***in Stücke –,*** burst *or* fly in pieces; 2. (*coll.*) get the sack; (*coll.*) be thrown out, go out on one's ear; ***aus*** or ***von der Schule –,*** be expelled. **2.** *irr.v.t.* fly, pilot; ***er flog seine eigene Maschine,*** he piloted his own machine; ***einen Keil –,*** fly in V-formation; ***Einsatz –,*** fly a sortie. **Fliegen,** *n.* flight, flying, aviation; ***– im Verbande,*** formation flying. **fliegend,** *adj.* flying; ***–es Blatt,*** flysheet, broadsheet, pamphlet; ***–er Bote,*** express courier; ***–e Fahnen,*** flying colours; ***–er Fisch,*** flying-fish; ***–e Haare,*** loose *or* flowing hair; ***–er Händler,*** itinerant *or* door-to-door salesman, pedlar; ***–e Hitze,*** sudden flush; ***–e Kolonne,*** flying column; ***–es Personal,*** air crew.

Fliegen|dreck, *m.* fly-blow. **–falle,** *f.* (*Bot.*) Venus's fly-trap (*Dionaea muscipula*). **–fänger,** *m.* fly-paper. **–fürst,** *m.* Beelzebub. **–gewicht,** *n.* (*Boxing*) fly-weight (*under 8 st. or 50 kg.*). **–gott,** *m. See* **–fürst. –klappe, –klatsche,** *f.* fly swatter. **–kopf,** *m.* (*Typ.*) turned letter. **–pilz,** *m.* toadstool, fly agaric (*Amanita muscaria*). **–schimmel,** *m.* spotted grey (*horse*). **–schnäpper,** *m.* (*Orn.*) ***grauer –,*** *see* **Grauschnäpper. –schrank,** *m.* meat-safe. **–tod,** *m.* fly-killer.

Flieger ['fli:gər], *m.* 1. airman, aviator, pilot; aircraftman 2nd class, (*Am.*) airman basic; 2. aeroplane; 3. short-distance cycle racer, sprinter, flyer. **Flieger|abwehr,** *f.* anti-aircraft *or* air defence. **–abwehrkanone,** *f.* anti-aircraft gun. **–abzeichen,** *n.* (*coll.*) wings. **–alarm,** *m.* air-raid warning. **–angriff,** *m.* aerial attack, air raid. **–aufnahme,** *f.* aerial photograph. **–bombe,** *f.* (aerial) bomb.

Fliegerei [fli:gə'raı], *f.* aviation.

Flieger|geschädigte(r), *m., f.* bomb-damage victim. **–hauptmann,** *m.* flight lieutenant *or* (*Am.*) captain. **–horst,** *m.* air-station, air-base. **fliegerisch,** *adj.* flying, aeronautical. **Flieger|-kanone,** *f.* (*sl.*) air ace. **–karussell,** *n.* chairoplane. **–krankheit,** *f.* air sickness. **–leutnant,** *m.* pilot officer, (*Am.*) second lieutenant. **–offizier,** *m.* air-force officer. **–schule,** *f.* flying school. **–schütze,** *m.* air gunner. **–sicht,** *f.* visibility from the air. **–stützpunkt,** *m.* advance airfield, landing ground. **–tauglichkeit,** *f.* fitness for flying duties. **–truppe,** *f.* air force, flying corps. **–warnungsdienst,** *m.* air-warning system, observer corps.

Fliehburg ['fli:burk], *f.* (*obs.*) refuge tower, keep.

fliehen ['fli:ən], **1.** *irr.v.i.* (*aux.* s.) flee, run away, take to one's heels, turn tail, retreat, escape (***vor*** (*Dat.*), from); ***–de Stirn,*** receding forehead. **2.** *irr. v.t.* shun, avoid, get out of the way of, flee from. **Fliehkraft,** *f.* centrifugal force.

Fliese ['fli:zə], *f.* flagstone; paving stone, tile.

Fließ|arbeit ['fli:s–], *f.* conveyor-belt, assembly-line *or* serial production. **–band,** *n.* conveyor-belt, assembly-line.

fließen ['fli:sən], *irr.v.i.* (*aux.* s.) 1. flow, pour, stream, gush, run; flow smoothly *or* easily (*of words*); 2. blot (*of paper*); 3. (*fig.*) ***– aus,*** proceed *or* follow *or* result from. **fließend,** *adj.* flowing, running; (*fig.*) fluid; (*fig.*) fluent; smooth, easy; ***eine Sprache – sprechen,*** speak a language fluently; ***–es Wasser,*** running water.

Fließ|laut, *m.*(*Phonet.*) liquid. **–papier,** *n.* blotting-paper, (*Chem.*) filter paper. **–sand,** *m.* quicksand.

Flimmer ['flımər], *m.* glimmer, glitter, sparkle; tinsel, spangle; (*dial.*) mica. **Flimmerkiste,** *f.* (*sl.*) flicks. **flimmern, 1.** *v.i.* glitter, glisten, glimmer, shimmer, flicker, sparkle, scintillate; twinkle (*star*); ***es flimmert mir vor den Augen,*** my eyes are swimming. **2.** *v.t.* (*sl.*) polish.

flink [flıŋk], *adj.* quick, brisk, agile, nimble, light-footed; alert, lively; quick as a flash. **Flinkheit,** *f.* nimbleness, quickness, liveliness, agility.

Flinte ['flıntə], *f.* (shot-)gun, (*Hist.*) musket; (*coll.*) ***die – ins Korn werfen,*** throw up the sponge. **Flintenweib,** *n.* woman revolutionary, female partisan.

flirren ['flırən], *v.i.* flit about, flicker, whirr, vibrate (*of air*); glitter, sparkle.

Flirt [flœrt], *m.* (**-s,** *pl.* **-s**) flirtation. **flirten,** *v.i.* flirt.

Flitter ['flıtər], *m.* tinsel, spangle, (*fig.*) frippery. **Flitter|glanz,** *m.* false lustre, empty show, hollow pomp. **–gold,** *n.* tinsel. **–kram,** *m.* cheap trinkets, tawdry finery. **flittern,** *v.i. See* **flimmern. Flitter|staat,** *m.* tawdry finery. **–werk,** *n.* gewgaw. **–wochen,** *f.pl.* honeymoon.

Flitzbogen ['flıtsbo:gən], *m.* toy bow.

flitzen ['flıtsən], *v.i.* (*dial.*) flit, whiz, dash, scurry.

flocht [flɔxt], **flöchte** ['flœçtə], *see* **flechten.**

Flocke ['flɔkə], *f.* flake (*of snow, oats etc.*); flock, tuft (*of wool, hair etc.*). **flocken, 1.** *v.i., v.r.* flake, come down in flakes. **2.** *v.t.* beat into flocks, form into flakes. **Flocken|bildung,** *f.* flocculation. **–blume,** *f.* (*Bot.*) knapweed (*Centaurea*). **–stoff,** *m.,* **–tuch,** *n.* coarse tufted cloth. **flockig,** *adj.* flaky, fluffy, flocculent. **Flock|seide,** *f.* floss silk. **–wolle,** *f.* waste wool flock.

Flödel ['flø:dəl], *m.* (*Mus.*) purfling.

flog [flo:k], **flöge** ['flø:gə], *see* **fliegen.**

floh [flo:], *see* **fliehen.**

Floh [flo:], *m.* (**-s,** *pl.* **¨-e**) flea; ***ihm einen – ins Ohr setzen,*** put ideas into his head; ***lieber einen Sack Flöhe hüten, als . . .,*** eat one's hat rather than . . .; (*Prov.*) ***er hört die Flöhe husten,*** he can hear the grass growing.

flöhe ['flø:ə], *see* **fliehen.**

flöhen ['flø:ən], *v.t., v.r.* catch fleas; rid (*o.s. or s.o.*) of fleas.

Floh|kraut, *n.* (*Bot.*) fleabane (*Pulicaria*). **–krebs,** *m.* (*Ent.*) water flea (*Amphipoda*). **–stich,** *m.* fleabite.

Flor [flo:r], *m.* 1. (**-s,** *pl.* **-e** (*Austr.* **¨-e**)) gauze, crape; nap, pile; 2. riot of bloom; florescence; blossoming time, (*fig.*) prime; bevy (*of girls*); flourishing condition, prosperity. **Flora,** *f.* 1. Flora (*goddess of flowers*); 2. (*Bot.*) the vegetable kingdom, flora. **Flor|band,** *n.,* **–binde,** *f.* mourning *or* crape band.

Florentiner [flɔrɛn'ti:nər], *m.,* **florentinisch,** *adj.* Florentine. **Florenz** [–'rɛnts], *n.* (*Geog.*) Florence.

Floreszenz [flɔrɛs'tsɛnts], *f.* floresence.

[1]**Florett** [flɔ'rɛt], *n.* (**-(e)s,** *pl.* **-e**) (*Fenc.*) foil.

[2]**Florett,** *m.* (**-s,** *pl.* **-e** (*Austr.* **-s**)) coarse silk; silk refuse. **Florettseide,** *f.* sarsanet.

florieren [flɔ'ri:rən], *v.i.* flourish, prosper, thrive.

Flor|schleier, *m.* gauze veil. **–strumpf,** *m.* lisle stocking.

Floskel ['flɔskəl], *f.* (**-,** *pl.* **-n**) flourish, fine phrase; *pl.* empty words, flowery language.

floß [flɔs] *see* **fließen.**

Floß [flo:s], *n.* (*Austr. m.*) (**-es,** *pl.* **¨-e**) raft, float.

flößbar ['flø:sba:r], *adj.* navigable for rafts.

Floßbrücke ['flo:sbrykə], *f.* floating *or* pontoon bridge.

Flosse ['flɔsə], *f.* fin, flipper; (*sl.*) paw (= *hand*), plate (= *foot*); float (*on a fishing-net*); pig iron; stabilizer fin.

flösse ['flœsə], *see* **fließen.**

Flöße ['flø:sə], *f.* float (*on fishing-net*). **flößen,** *v.t.* float, cause to float; raft (*timber*); (*dial.*) fish with a floating net. **Flößer,** *m.* raftsman. **Flößerei** [–'raɪ], *f.* flotation, timber transportation (*by river*).

Floß|feder, *f.* fin. **–füßer,** *m.* (*Mollusc.*) pteropod, (*Zool.*) pinnipedia.

Flöte ['flø:tə], *f.* 1. flute; pipe; 2. (*Cards*) flush. **flöten,** *v.t., v.i.* play the flute; whistle, (*fig.*) speak sweetly. **Flötenbläser,** *m.* flute-player, flautist. **flötengehen,** *irr.v.i.* (*coll.*) be lost *or* squandered, crash, fail, go to pieces, go up in smoke, go to pot, go west. **Flöten|register,** *n. See* **–zug. –töne,** *m. pl.* (*fig.*) good manners *or* behaviour. **–zug,** *m.* flute-stop (*in organs*). **Flötist** [–'tɪst], *m.* (**-en,** *pl.* **-en**) flute-player, flautist.

flott [flɔt], *adj.* floating, afloat; lively, brisk, dashing, smooth; chic, smart, (*sl.*) snappy; ***es ging – her,*** there were fine goings-on; ***– leben,*** lead a fast life, (*sl.*) go the pace; ***das Geschäft geht –,*** business booms. **Flott,** *n.* (*dial.*) cream.

Flotte ['flɔtə], *f.* 1. fleet, navy; 2. dye liquor, dye-bath. **Flotten|abkommen,** *n.* naval agreement. **–basis,** *f. See* **–station. –begleitschiff,** *n.* escort vessel, corvette, (*Nav.*) sloop. **–chef,** *m.* commander-in-chief of the navy. **–etat,** *m.* naval estimates (*in Parl.*). **–parade, –schau,** *f.* naval review. **–station,** *f.* home naval base (*e.g. Portsmouth*). **–stützpunkt,** *m.* naval station.

Flotille [flɔ'tɪljə], *f.* flotilla, squadron. **Flotillen-admiral,** *m.* (*Nav.*) commodore, (*Am.*) rear admiral.

flott|machen, *v.t.* float, refloat, get afloat. **–weg,** *adv.* smartly, briskly, promptly, at one fell swoop, without a hitch.

Flöz [flø:ts], *n.* (**-es,** *pl.* **-e**) deposit, (workable) seam (*of coal etc.*), layer, stratum; ***in –en,*** stratified. **Flöz|gebirge,** *n.* stratified *or* sedimentary rocks. **–gebirgsarten,** *f.pl.* secondary rocks. **–sandstein,** *m.* new red sandstone.

Fluch [flu:x], *m.* (**-(e)s,** *pl.* **⸚e**) curse, imprecation, malediction, execration, (*Eccl.*) anathema; bane, plague; oath, profanity, swear-word; ***– über dich!*** curse you! damn you! **fluchbeladen,** *adj.* under a curse, accursed. **fluchen,** *v.i.* (*Dat.*) curse, swear; blaspheme; use bad language; ***ihm –,*** curse him; ***auf ihn –,*** swear at him.

Flucht [fluxt], *f.* (-, *pl.* **-en**) 1. flight, escape (***vor*** (*Dat.*), from); ***auf der –,*** on the run, in flight; ***die – ergreifen, sich auf die – begeben*** or ***machen,*** run away, take to flight, flee; ***in die – schlagen,*** put to flight, chase off; 2. covey (*of pigeons etc.*); 3. play, swing (*of a door, hammer etc.*); 4. row, series, range, suite (*of rooms*); flight (*of stairs*); 5. (*Build.*) alignment, straight line. **fluchtartig,** *adj.* in full flight, head over heels, in great haste, (*coll.*) like a shot. **Fluchtbild,** *n.* perspective. **fluchten,** *v.t.* align.

flüchten ['flyçtən], **1.** *v.t.* (*Poet.*) take *or* carry away *or* hide for safety, rescue, secure. **2.** *v.i.* (*aux.* s.) (*Swiss v.r.*) flee, take to flight, escape; take *or* seek refuge.

fluchtgerecht ['fluxtgərɛçt], *adj.* flush, (truly) aligned (*Dat.,* with). **fluchtig,** *adj.* (in) perspective.

flüchtig ['flyçtɪç], *adj.* fugitive, runaway, absconding; transient, transitory, short-lived, passing, fleeting, non-persistent; (*Chem.*) volatile; hasty, hurried, cursory, desultory, superficial, casual, careless, fickle, changeable, shifting; ***–es Gestein,*** brittle *or* friable rock; ***– werden,*** run away, abscond; ***–es Salz,*** sal volatile; ***– niederschreiben,*** jot down; ***ich habe das Buch nur – durchgeblättert,*** I have only just glanced at *or* skimmed through the book. **flüchtigen,** *v.t.* volatilize. **Flüchtigkeit,** *f.* hastiness, transitoriness; carelessness; volatility. **Flüchtigkeitsfehler,** *m.* mistake due to inadvertence, slip (of the pen), oversight.

Flüchtling ['flyçtlɪŋ], *m.* (**-s,** *pl.* **-e**) fugitive, refugee, deserter. **Flüchtlingslager,** *n.* refugee camp.

Flucht|linie, *f.* (*Build.*) alignment, building line; (*Opt.*) vanishing line. **–punkt,** *m.* vanishing point. **–verdacht,** *m.* suspicion of intended escape. **–versuch,** *m.* attempted escape.

fluchwürdig ['flu:xvyrdɪç], *adj.* accursed, damnable, execrable.

fludderig ['fludərɪç], *adj.* (*coll.*) disorderly, untidy.

Fluder ['flu:dər], *n.* mill race.

Flug [flu:k], *m.* (**-(e)s,** *pl.* **⸚e**) flying, soaring, flight, air travel; flock, swarm, covey; ***im –e,*** flying, in flight, on the wing; (*fig.*) in one's stride, in haste, in passing; ***einen Vogel im –e schießen,*** shoot a bird on the wing.

Flug|abkommen, *n.* air-agreement. **–abwehr,** *f.* anti-aircraft defence. **–asche,** *f.* flue ash. **–bahn,** *f.* line of flight, trajectory. **–ball,** *m.* (*Tenn.*) volley. **–bereich,** *m.* flying range, operational radius. **flugbereit,** *adj.* (*Av.*) ready to take off. **Flug|-besprechung,** *f.* briefing. **–blatt,** *n.* pamphlet, broadsheet; handbill. **–boot,** *n.* seaplane, flying boat. **–dauer,** *f.* duration of flight. **–deck,** *n.* flight deck (*aircraft carrier*).

Flügel ['fly:gəl], *m.* 1. wing; vane, fin, blade; sail (*of windmill*), casement (*of window*), leaf (*of double door*), aisle (*of church*), wing (*of building*), wing, mudguard, (*Am.*) fender (*of car*), side-piece (*of altar*), lobe (*of lungs*), fluke (*of anchor*); (*fig.*) ***die – hängen lassen,*** be despondent *or* crestfallen, lose heart; (*fig.*) ***sich*** (*Dat.*) ***die – verbrennen,*** burn one's fingers; 2. grand piano.

Flügel|adjutant, *m.* aide-de-camp. **–altar,** *m.* altar-(piece) with side wings, triptych. **–angriff,** *m.* flank attack. **–breite,** *f.* (*Av.*) wing-span. **–decke,** *f.* (*Ent.*) wing-case, elytron. **–fenster,** *n.* french *or* casement window. **–frucht,** *f.* winged seed.

–flügelig ['fly:gəlɪç], *adj.suff.* -winged. **flügellahm,** *adj.* broken-winged, (*Hunt.*) winged. **Flügel|-mann,** *m.* (*pl.* **-männer** *or* **-leute**) (*Mil.*) flank-man, marker, (*obs.*) fugleman, (*Footb.*) wing-forward. **–mutter,** *f.* butterfly- *or* wing- *or* thumb-nut. **flügeln,** *v.t.* (*Hunt.*) wing (*a bird*); *see* **geflügelt. flügeloffen,** *adj.* wide open. **Flügel|pferd,** *n.* (*Poet.*) winged steed, Pegasus. **–profil,** *n.* (*Av.*) airfoil. **–schlag,** *m.* beat *or* flapping of wings. **–schraube,** *f.* (*Tech.*) butterfly-screw. **–spannweite,** *f.* wing-span. **–spiegel,** *m.* (*Orn.*) speculum. **–streckung,** *f.* (*Av.*) aspect ratio. **–tür,** *f.* folding door. **–ventil,** *n.* butterfly valve.

Flug|figuren, *f.pl.* aerobatics. **–früchtler,** *m.* plant with winged seed. **–gast,** *m.* air-passenger.

flügge ['flygə], *adj.* fledged; ***noch nicht –,*** (still) unfledged.

Flug|hafen, *m.* aerodrome, airport, airfield. **–hafer,** *m.* (*Bot.*) wild oats (*Avena fatua*). **–halle,** *f.* hangar. **–höhe,** *f.* altitude. **–hörnchen,** *n.* (*Zool.*) flying squirrel (*Sciuropterus*). **–jahr,** *n.* swarm year. **–kapitän,** *m.* aeroplane pilot. **–karte,** *f.* plane *or* air-ticket. **–lehrer,** *m.* flying instructor. **–linie,** *f.* airline (route). **–loch,** *n.* entrance to a hive *or* dove-cote. **–meldezentrale,** *f.* air-raid warning headquarters. **–personal,** *n.* flight personnel. **–plan,** *m.* air service time-table. **–platz,** *m.* aerodrome, landing ground. **–post,** *f.* air mail.

flugs [flu:ks], *adv.* instantly, at once, immediately, without delay, swiftly, quickly.

Flug|sand, *m.* quicksand. **–schein,** *m. See* **–karte. –schiff,** *n.* airship. **–schrift,** *f.* pamphlet. **–schule,** *f.* flying school. **–schüler,** *m.* trainee pilot. **–strecke,** *f.* distance flown, flight, route. **–streitkräfte,** *f.pl.* air force *or* arm. **flugtechnisch,** *adj.* concerning aviation. **Flug|verkehr,** *m.* air traffic; air service; civil aviation. **–weite,** *f.* (*Av.*) wing-span. **–wesen,** *n.* aviation, aeronautics.

Flugzeug ['flu:ktsɔyk], *n.* aeroplane, (*Am.*) airplane, (*coll.*) plane; (*collect. pl.*) aircraft. **Flugzeug|-besatzung,** *f.* air-crew. **–führer,** *m.* pilot. **–halle,** *f. See* **–schuppen. –mutterschiff,** *n. See* **–träger. –personal,** *n.* aircraft maintenance personnel, ground staff. **–rumpf,** *m.* fuselage. **–schlosser,** *m.* aircraft fitter *or* mechanic. **–schuppen,** *m.* hangar. **–stewardeß,** *f.* air hostess. **–träger,** *m.* aircraft-carrier. **–wart,** *m. See* **–schlosser.**

[1]**Fluh** [flu:], *f.* (-, *pl.* **⸚e**) (*Swiss*) rock-face, precipice; concrete.

[2]**Fluh,** *n.* (**-s,** *pl.* **-**) fluke (*of anchor*).

Flühe ['fly:ə], *f. See* [1]**Fluh.**

Fluidum ['fluidum], *n.* **(-s,** *pl.* **-da)** fluid, liquid; (*fig.*) atmosphere, tone, influence, aura.

Flunder ['flundər], *m.* **(-s,** *pl.* -) *or f.* (-, *pl.* **-n**) (*Ichth.*) flounder (*Limanda flesus*).

Flunkerei [fluŋkə'raɪ], *f.* (*coll.*) fibbing, fibs, fairy-tale, sham; bragging. **flunkern,** *v.i.* (*coll.*) tell fibs *or* stories, spin yarns, brag, boast.

Flunsch [flunʃ], *m.* **(-s,** *pl.* **-e)** (*dial.*) pouting expression; ***einen – machen,*** pout.

Fluor ['flu:ɔr], *n.* fluorine. **Fluoreszenz** [–rɛs-'tsɛnts], *f.* fluorescence. **fluoreszieren,** *v.i.* fluoresce, be fluorescent.

[1]**Flur** [flu:r], *f.* (-, *pl.* **-en**) field, meadow, pasture, plain; (*Hist.*) common land; (*Poet.*) ***durch Feld und –,*** over hill and dale.

[2]**Flur,** *m.* **(-s,** *pl.* **-e)** vestibule, (entrance-)hall, corridor.

Flur|(be)gang, *m.* beating the bounds (of a parish). **–bereinigung,** *f.* enclosure of land. **–hüter,** *m.* keeper, ranger. **–schaden,** *m.* damage to crops. **–umgang,** *m. See* **–(be)gang.**

Fluse ['flu:zə], *f.* frayed edge *or* ends, loose ends (of thread). **flusig,** *adj.* frayed, fuzzy.

Fluß [flus], *m.* **(-(ss)es,** *pl.* **¨-(ss)e)** 1. river, stream; 2. flow, flux; ***im –,*** in a state of flux; (*fig.*) ***in – bringen,*** get *or* set going; (*fig.*) ***in – kommen,*** get going, get under way *or* into full swing; 3. melting, fusion; molten glass *or* metal; 4. catarrh, discharge, issue, running; 5. (*Geol.*) fluorspar, fluorite; 6. (*Med.*) menstruation; ***weißer –,*** leucorrhoea, (*coll.*) the whites; 7. fluency. **fluß|abwärts,** *adv.* down-stream. **–aufwärts,** *adv.* up-stream. **Fluß|bad,** *n.* river bathing *or* bathing-place. **–bett,** *n.* channel, river bed. **–eisen,** *n.* ingot steel. **–gebiet,** *n.* river basin.

flüssig ['flysɪç], *adj.* 1. fluid, liquid; melted, molten; ***– machen,*** melt, liquefy; convert into ready money; 2. rheumatic; 3. (*of cash*) ready; ***Geld – machen,*** make money available; ***–es Kapital,*** liquid assets; 4. (*of style*) flowing, fluent. **Flüssigkeit,** *f.* fluid, liquid, liquor; fluidity. **Flüssigkeits|aufnahme,** *f.* fluid intake. **–bremse,** *f.* hydraulic brake. **–druck,** *m.* hydraulic pressure. **–getriebe,** *n.* fluid transmission. **–grad,** *m.* viscosity. **–maß,** *n.* liquid measure.

Flüssig|machen, *n.* liquefaction. **–machung,** *f.* realization (*of money*). **flüssigwerdend,** *adj.* liquescent.

Fluß|krebs, *m.* river crayfish. **–lauf,** *m.* course of a river. **–mittel,** *n.* flux (*for soldering etc.*). **–mündung,** *f.* estuary. **–netz,** *n.* river network. **–pferd,** *n.* hippopotamus. **–regenpfeifer,** *m.* (*Orn.*) little ringed plover (*Charadrius dubius*). **–rohrsänger,** *m.* (*Orn.*) river warbler (*Locustella fluviatilis*). **flußsauer,** *adj.* fluorated. **Fluß|saüre,** *f.* hydrofluoric acid. **–schiffahrt,** *f.* river traffic. **–seeschwalbe,** *f.* (*Orn.*) common tern (*Sterna hirundo*). **–spat,** *m.* (*Min.*) fluorspar, fluorite. **–übergang,** *m.* river-crossing. **–uferläufer,** *m.* (*Orn.*) common sandpiper (*Tringa hypoleuca*). **–verkehr,** *m.* river traffic. **–wasser,** *n.* river-water.

flüstern ['flystərn], *v.t., v.i.* whisper. **Flüster|-propaganda,** *f.* whispering campaign. **–ton,** *m.* whisper, undertone. **–tüte,** *f.* (*sl.*) megaphone.

Flut [flu:t], *f.* (-, *pl.* **-en**) flood, deluge, inundation; torrent, stream; high-tide, high-water, flood-tide, incoming *or* rising tide; ***– von Worten,*** torrent of words. **fluten, 1.** *v.i.* flood, stream, flow; swell, surge, crowd; ***es flutet,*** the tide is coming in. **2.** *v.t.* flood (*tanks*). **Flutenzelle,** *f.* flooding tank (*of submarines*). **Flut|gang,** *m.,* **–gerinne,** *n.* channel; mill-race. **–grenze,** *f.* high-water mark. **–hafen,** *m.* tidal harbour. **–höhe,** *f.* height of the tide, high-water. **–karte,** *f.* tide-chart. **–licht,** *n.* floodlight(ing). **–tabellen,** *f.pl.* tide-tables. **–tor,** *n.* flood-gate. **–wasser,** *n.* tidal water; mill-race. **–wechsel,** *m.,* **–wende,** *f.* turn of the tide. **–welle,** *f.* tidal wave. **–zeit,** *f.* flood-tide, high-water.

focht [fɔxt], **föchte** ['fœçtə], *see* **fechten.**

Fockmast ['fɔkmast], *m.* foremast. **Focksegel,** *n.* foresail.

Föderalismus [fø:dəra'lɪsmus], *m.* federalism. **föderativ,** *adj.* federative, confederate.

Fohlen ['fo:lən], *n.* foal, filly, colt (*foal is newly born, colt and filly till 4–5 years;* ***Fohlen*** *till 3 years*). **fohlen,** *v.i.* foal.

Föhn [fø:n], *m.* **(-(e)s,** *pl.* **-e)** warm wind (*in Switzerland*), spring storm. **föhnig,** *adj.* sultry, stormy.

Föhre ['fø:rə], *f.* (*Bot.*) Scots pine (*Pinus sylvestris*).

Fokus ['fo:kus], *m.* (-, *pl.* -) focus. **Fokustiefe,** *f.* focal depth.

Folge ['fɔlgə], *f.* succession, sequence, series, order; set, suit, suite; sequel, continuation; result, issue, upshot, effect, consequence, aftermath; conclusion, inference; ***in der –,*** subsequently, afterwards, thereafter, in future; ***in bunter –,*** in random succession; ***– von Karten,*** sequence, flush; ***– leisten*** (*Dat.*), obey, comply with; accept (*invitation*), grant (*request*), follow (*advice*); ***die nächste – dieses Werkes,*** the next instalment *or* issue of this work; ***die – sein von,*** be due to; ***üble –n,*** evil results, dire consequences; ***zur – haben,*** entail, lead to, result in, bring about, bring in its wake. **Folge|erscheinung,** *f.* consequence, (after-)effect, result, sequel, corollary. **–leistung,** *f.* obedience.

folgen ['fɔlgən], *v.i.* (*Dat.*) 1. (*aux.* s.) follow (after); follow, ensue (***aus,*** from); succeed (***auf*** (*Acc.*), to); be derived; ***ich bin ihm gefolgt,*** I followed him; ***was folgt daraus?*** what will ensue? ***ihm auf Schritt und Tritt –,*** shadow *or* (*sl.*) tail him, dog his footsteps; ***er sprach wie folgt,*** he spoke as follows; ***Fortsetzung folgt,*** to be continued; 2. (*aux.* h.) obey, attend to, listen to, conform to; ***ich habe ihm gefolgt,*** I was guided by him (*his advice or wishes*), I obeyed him; ***dem Strom –,*** swim with the stream; ***seinem Kopfe –,*** act according to one's lights; persist in one's whim; ***– Sie mir,*** take my advice.

folgend ['fɔlgənt], *adj.* subsequent, next; following, ensuing; ***–e Woche,*** next week; ***–es,*** the following (words); ***aus*** (or ***im***) ***–en,*** from (*or* in) the following *or* what follows. **folgendermaßen, folgenderweise,** *adv.* as follows, in the following manner.

folgenschwer ['fɔlgənʃvər], *adj.* grave, momentous, portentous.

folgerichtig ['fɔlgərɪçtɪç], *adj.* logical, consistent. **Folgerichtigkeit,** *f.* (logical) consistency.

folgern ['fɔlgərn], *v.t.* infer, deduce, conclude, reason out, (*coll.*) gather (***aus,*** from); ***falsch –,*** draw wrong inferences. **Folgerung,** *f.* inference, deduction, conclusion, induction.

Folge|satz, *m.* (*Gram.*) consecutive clause, (*Geom.*) corollary. **–schluß,** *m.* logical consequence. **folgewidrig,** *adj.* inconsistent, illogical, inconsequential. **Folge|widrigkeit,** *f.* illogicality, inconsistency. **–zeit,** *f.* future, time to come, following period, sequel.

folglich ['fɔlklɪç], *adv., conj.* consequently, hence, therefore, so, thus, accordingly.

folgsam ['fɔlkza:m], *adj.* (*Dat.*) obedient, tractable, submissive, docile. **Folgsamkeit,** *f.* obedience, docility.

Foliant [foli'ant], *m.* **(-en,** *pl.* **-en)** folio volume, (*coll.*) tome.

Folie ['fo:liə], *f.* foil; thin leaf of metal; film, silvering (*of mirrors*); (*fig.*) background, framework, basis of comparison; ***mit – belegte Oberfläche,*** silvered surface; ***zur – dienen*** (*Dat.*), be a foil to, set off; ***einer S. eine – geben,*** set a th. off. **foliieren** [–li'i:rən], *v.t.* page (*a book*); silver (*a mirror*).

Folio ['fo:lio], *n.* **(-s,** *pl.* **-s** *or* **-lien)** folio; page (*of a ledger*). **Folioformat,** *n.* folio size.

Folter ['fɔltər], *f.* (-, *pl.* **-n**) torture; ***auf die – spannen,*** put to the rack; (*fig.*) tantalize, keep on tenterhooks. **Folter|bank,** *f.* rack. **–kammer,** *f.* torture-chamber. **–knecht,** *m.* torturer. **foltern,** *v.t.* torture, torment. **Folterqualen,** *f.pl.* torture, torment, (*fig.*) mental anguish. **Folterung,** *f.* torture.

Fond [fɔ̃], *m.* (**-s,** *pl.* **-s**) 1. ground; foundation, base, background; 2. (*Motor.*) back (seat).
Fonds [fɔ̃], *m.* (-, *pl.* - [fɔ̃s]) fund, capital; public funds, government securities. **Fonds|besitzer,** *m.* stockholder. **–börse,** *f.* stock-exchange. **–makler,** *m.* stockbroker.
Fontäne [fɔn'tɛ:nə], *f.* fountain.
Fontanelle [fɔnta'nɛlə], *f.* (*Anat.*) fontanel.
foppen ['fɔpən], *v.t.* fool, hoax; chaff, tease, (*coll.*) rag, pull (*a p.'s*) leg. **Fopperei** [–'raɪ], *f.* teasing, chaffing, (*coll.*) ragging, kidding, leg-pulling.
Force [fɔrs], *f.* strong point, strength, forte. **forcieren** [–'si:rən], *v.t.* take by assault, force; overtax. **forciert,** *adj.* forced, exaggerated, unnatural.
Förder|anlage ['fœrdər–], *f.* conveyor system, handling equipment. **–band,** *n.* conveyor belt. **Förderer,** *m.* sponsor, promoter, patron. **Förder|gerüst,** *n.* (*Min.*) pithead rig. **–gut,** *n.* output, goods delivered. **–korb,** *m.* pit-cage. **–leistung,** *f.* output, production; delivery (*of a pump*). **–leitung,** *f.* pipe-line, feed pipe.
förderlich ['fœrdərlɪç], *adj.* conducive (*Dat.*, to), promotive (of), in furtherance (of); effective, useful, beneficial, profitable; speedy.
Förder|maschine, *f.* (*Min.*) winding engine. **–menge,** *f.* *See* **–leistung.**
fordern ['fɔrdərn], *v.t.* demand, require (*von,* of), ask *or* call for, claim, exact; (*Law*) summon; challenge; ***wie viel – Sie dafür?*** what are you asking for it? how much do you want for it? ***vor Gericht –,*** summon before a court; ***Rechenschaft von ihm –,*** call him to account; ***ihn auf Pistolen –,*** challenge him to a duel with pistols; ***zuviel –,*** overcharge.
fördern ['fœrdərn], *v.t.* 1. further, promote, sponsor, support, patronize; benefit, aid, assist, stimulate, encourage, expedite, hasten, speed up; 2. (*Min. etc.*) convey; raise, haul, transport; (*fig.*) ***zutage –,*** unearth, bring to light.
Förder|schacht, *m.* (*Min.*) winding-shaft. **–seil,** *n.* (*Min.*) (haulage) rope.
Forderung ['fɔrdəruŋ], *f.* demand, claim, call (***an*** (*Acc.*), on (*a p.*); ***nach,*** for (*a th.*)), requisition; summons, challenge; ***–en ausstehen haben,*** have debts outstanding; ***–en an ihn stellen,*** make claims on him; ***–en geltend machen,*** make good one's claims.
Förderung ['fœrdəruŋ], *f.* 1. furtherance, promotion, advancement, support, encouragement, assistance; conveyance, transport, dispatch; 2. (*Min.*) hauling; 3. yield, output, production.
Forderungssatz ['fɔrdəruŋszats], *m.* postulate.
Förder|wagen, *m.* mine-tram *or* trolley. **–werk,** *n.* (*Min.*) hoisting machinery.
Forelle [fɔ'rɛlə], *f.* trout.
Forke ['fɔrkə], *f.* pitchfork, large fork.
Form [fɔrm], *f.* (-, *pl.* **-en**) form, figure, shape; make, fashion, style, type, design; manner, mode, usage, method of procedure, ceremony; model, pattern, cut, section, profile; block (*for hats*), last (*for shoes*); mould, die; (*Typ.*) frame, forme; (*Cul.*) tin (*for cakes*); (*Gram.*) voice; ***in gehöriger –,*** in due form, in proper shape; ***in – Rechtens,*** legally; ***in aller –,*** formally, in due form, with due ceremony; (*Spt.*) ***in – sein,*** be in *or* on form; (*Spt.*) ***nicht in – sein,*** be off form *or* out of form; (*Spt.*) ***in – kommen,*** get into form; (*Spt.*) ***in – bleiben,*** keep in form; (*Spt.*) ***gegen die –,*** contrary to form; ***der – wegen*** or ***halber,*** for the sake of appearances, for form's sake; ***über die – schlagen,*** block (*hats*); put on the last (*shoes*).
formal [fɔr'ma:l], *adj.* formal; ***–e Ausbildung,*** formal training, physical training, (*Mil.*) drill. **Formalien,** *pl.* formalities. **Formalismus** [–'lɪsmus], *m.* formalism. **Formalist,** *m.* (**-en,** *pl.* **-en**) formalist, pedantic person. **Formalität** [–i'tɛ:t], *f.* formality; *pl.* forms (*of courts etc.*).
Format [fɔr'ma:t], *n.* (**-(e)s,** *pl.* **-e**) size (*of book*), form, shape, format; (*fig.*) importance, weight.
Formation [fɔrmatsi'o:n], *f.* (*Mil.*) formation; unit.
formbar ['fɔrmba:r], *adj.* mouldable, malleable, workable, plastic.
Formel ['fɔrməl], *f.* formula, rule.
formell [fɔr'mɛl], *adj.* formal, ceremonious, stiff.
formen ['fɔrmən], *v.t.* form, mould, cast, model, shape, fashion; put on the block (*hats*).
Formen|lehre, *f.* (*Gram.*) accidence. **–mensch,** *m.* pedant, formalist.
Form|fehler, *m.* faux pas, breach of etiquette, social blunder; error in form; informality. **–gebung,** *f.* fashioning, shaping; moulding. **–gestaltung,** *f.* shape, form.
formieren [fɔr'mi:rən], **1.** *v.t.* form; arrange, line up; (*Typ.*) ***in Seiten –,*** make up into pages. **2.** *v.r.* (*Mil.*) fall in.
–förmig ['fœrmɪç], *adj.suff.* -formed, -shaped.
förmlich ['fœrmlɪç], **1.** *adj.* formal, ceremonious, (*coll.*) literal, veritable, downright, regular, real; ***–e Schlacht,*** pitched battle. **2.** *adv.* absolutely, literally, practically, almost, as it were. **Förmlichkeit,** *f.* formality, ceremony.
formlos ['fɔrmlo:s], *adj.* shapeless, formless; amorphous, amorphic; informal, unceremonious, impolite. **Formlosigkeit,** *f.* shapelessness, formlessness; amorphousness; unceremoniousness; rudeness.
Form|sache, *f.* matter of (outward) form, formality. **–stein,** *m.* moulded brick, shaped brick. **–trieb,** *m.* artistic impulse.
Formular [fɔrmu'la:r], *n.* (**-s,** *pl.* **-e**) 1. (printed) form, blank, schedule; 2. (*Law*) precedent.
formulieren [fɔrmu'li:rən], *v.t.* formulate, define, put into words. **Formulierung,** *f.* (precise) wording, formulation, definition.
Formung ['fɔrmuŋ], *f.* shaping, moulding, forming, formation. **form|vollendet,** *adj.* perfect in form; highly finished. **–widrig,** *adj.* diverging from pattern, contrary to usage, offending against good form, in bad taste, informal. **Formzahl,** *f.* form factor.
forsch [fɔrʃ], *adj.* (*coll.*) forthright, outspoken, enterprising, energetic, vigorous.
forschen ['fɔrʃən], *v.i.* search (***nach,*** for), inquire (after), seek; ***– in*** (*Dat.*), investigate, explore, examine; do research (work) on; ***einer, der nach Wahrheit forscht,*** a seeker after truth. **forschend,** *adj.* searching, inquiring. **Forscher,** *m.* investigator; inquirer; research worker; scholar; scientist; explorer. **Forscher|blick,** *m.* searching glance. **–drang, –geist, –sinn,** *m.* inquiring mind, scientific curiosity. **Forschung,** *f.* investigation, inquiry; research (work). **Forschungs|amt,** *n.* directorate of scientific research. **–anstalt,** *f.* *See* **–institut.** **–gebiet,** *n.* field of research. **–institut,** *n.* research institute *or* station, laboratory. **–reise,** *f.* voyage of discovery *or* exploration. **–reisende(r),** *m.,f.* explorer.
Forst [fɔrst], *m.* (**-es,** *pl.* **-e**) forest, wood. **Forst|akademie,** *f.* school of forestry. **–amt,** *n.* forestry superintendent's office. **–aufseher,** *m.* ranger. **–beamte(r),** *m.* forestry officer. **–bezirk,** *m.* forest range. **–direktion,** *f.* forestry commission.
Förster ['fœrstər], *m.* forester, game-keeper, forest ranger. **Försterei** [–'raɪ], *f.* forester's *etc.* house.
Forst|fach, *n.* forestry. **–frevel,** *m.* infringement of forest laws. **–gefälle,** *n.* revenue deriving from forests. **–gesetz,** *n.* forestry law. **–haus,** *n.* forester's *etc.* house. **–hüter,** *m.* forester's assistant, woodman. **–kunde,** *f.* forestry. **–lehrling,** *m.* forestry student. **–mann,** *m.* (*pl.* **-leute**) forester. ranger. **–meister,** *m.* head ranger, chief forester, forestry superintendent. **–revier,** *n.* forest range, **–verwaltung,** *f.* forest administration. **–wart,** *m.* forest warden. **–wesen,** *n.,* **–wirtschaft,** *f.* forestry. **–wissenschaft,** *f.* science of forestry.
Fort [fo:rt], *n.* (**-s,** *pl.* **-s**) fort, fortress, fortification.
fort [fɔrt], *adv.* away, off, gone, forth; forward, onward, on; ***– damit!*** away with it! ***er ist –,*** he is off *or* away; ***es will mit ihm nicht recht –,*** he does not get on; ***ich muß –,*** I must be off; ***mein Mantel ist –,*** my coat is gone *or* lost; ***all mein Geld ist –,*** all my money is gone *or* spent; ***– mit dir!*** get *or* clear out! be off! go to blazes! ***und so –,*** and so forth, and so

on; *in einem –*, ceaselessly, uninterruptedly, without stopping, (*coll.*) on and on.

fort–, *sep.pref.* 1. *removal in space, see also compounds with* **weg–**; 2. *continuation in time.*

fortan [fɔrt'an], *adv.* from this time on, from now on, henceforth, hereafter.

fortbegeben ['fɔrtbəge:bən], *irr.v.r.* withdraw, retire; depart.

Fortbestand ['fɔrtbəʃtant], *m.* continuation, continuance, permanence, duration.

fortbestehen ['fɔrtbəʃte:ən], *irr.v.i.* survive, continue, last, endure, persist.

fortbewegen ['fɔrtbəve:gən], **1.** *v.t.* propel, move along *or* on. **2.** *v.r.* continue moving, move on, progress; ***sich nicht –***, not move *or* budge *or* stir (from the spot). **Fortbewegung,** *f.* locomotion (*of animals*), progression.

fortbilden ['fɔrtbɪldən], *v.r.* continue one's studies. **Fortbildung,** *f.* further education, further development. **Fortbildungsschule,** *f.* continuation school; evening school.

fortbleiben ['fɔrtblaɪbən], *irr.v.i.* keep *or* stay away, fail to return.

fortbringen ['fɔrtbrɪŋən], **1.** *irr.v.t.* take *or* carry away, remove (*a th.*), see (*a p.*) off, see *or* bring (*a p.*) to the station *etc.*; ***er ist nicht fortzubringen,*** you can't get rid of him. **2.** *irr.v.r.* make one's way in the world, get on in life.

Fortdauer ['fɔrtdauər], *f.* continuance, permanence, duration; ***– nach dem Tode,*** existence after death. **fort|dauern,** *v.i.* continue, last, endure, persist. **–dauernd,** *adj.* lasting, permanent; constant, incessant, continuous; recurrent (*payment etc.*).

forterben ['fɔrtʔɛrbən], *v.r.* be inherited *or* transmitted, go down to posterity, descend (***auf*** (*Acc.*), to).

fortfahren ['fɔrtfa:rən], **1.** *irr.v.i.* 1. (*aux.* s.) drive off *or* away; depart, leave, start, set out *or* off; 2. (*aux.* h.) ***mit*** or ***in einer S. –***, continue, proceed, keep *or* go on with a th.; ***– zu tun,*** continue doing *or* to do, keep *or* (*coll.*) carry on doing. **2.** *irr.v.t.* carry away; remove (*in a vehicle*); drive away.

Fortfall ['fɔrtfal], *m.* discontinuing, cessation, abolition; *see* **Wegfall. fortfallen,** *irr.v.i.* (*aux.* s.) be omitted; *see* **ausfallen, wegfallen.**

fortführen ['fɔrtfy:rən], *v.t.* 1. march (*a p.*) off, remove, lead forth *or* away; 2. continue, pursue, carry on, keep *or* go on with. **Fortführung,** *f.* continuation; resumption; prosecution, pursuit.

Fortgang ['fɔrtgaŋ], *m.* 1. continuation, progress, advance; *see also* **Fortdauer, Fortschritt**; ***die S. wird ihren – nehmen,*** the matter will take its course; ***den – abwarten,*** await developments, see how things develop; 2. departure; *see also* **Weggang.**

fortgehen ['fɔrtge:ən], *irr.v.i.* (*aux.* s.) 1. go away, leave, depart; 2. go on, continue, proceed, progress.

fortgeschritten ['fɔrtgəʃrɪtən], *adj.* advanced, progressed; ***Kurs für Fortgeschrittene,*** advanced course.

fortgesetzt ['fɔrtgəzɛtst], *adj.* continual, constant, continuous, incessant.

forthelfen ['fɔrthɛlfən], *irr.v.t.* (*Dat.*) help to escape; help on; ***sich kümmerlich –***, make shift to live.

forthin [fɔrt'hɪn], *see* **fortan.**

fortjagen ['fɔrtja:gən], *v.t.* chase *or* drive off *or* away, expel (***aus,*** from) (*school etc.*); (*coll.*) kick out, turn out on one's ear.

fortkommen ['fɔrtkɔmən], *irr.v.i.* (*aux.* s.) 1. get away, escape; (*coll.*) ***mach, daß du fortkommst!*** be off! clear out! (*sl.*) get lost! beat it! 2. get on, prosper, thrive, make progress *or* headway. **Fortkommen,** *n.* 1. escape; 2. advancement, progress; prosperity, success; livelihood, living.

fortlassen ['fɔrtlasən], *irr.v.t.* (*ellipt.*; *a verb of motion understood*) (*a p.*) let go, allow to go; (*a th.*) omit, leave out, (*coll.*) drop.

fortlaufen ['fɔrtlaufən], *irr.v.i.* (*aux.* s.) 1. run away, escape (***vor*** (*Dat.*), from); 2. run on; continue, be continued. **fortlaufend,** *adj.* running, continuous, consecutive, successive, serial.

fortleben ['fɔrtle:bən], *v.i.* live on, survive. **Fortleben,** *n.* survival; after-life, life after death.

fortmachen ['fɔrtmaxən], *v.i.* 1. (*coll.*) carry on; 2. (*coll.*) make off, clear out.

fortpflanzen ['fɔrtpflantsən], **1.** *v.t.* propagate, spread, communicate, transmit, reproduce. **2.** *v.r.* be propagated *or* reproduced *or* transmitted; (*of disease*) spread, (*of animals etc.*) reproduce, multiply. **Fortpflanzung,** *f.* propagation; transmission, communication, reproduction (*of animals etc.*), spread (*of disease*). **fortpflanzungsfähig,** *adj.* generative, reproductive; transmissible, communicable. **Fortpflanzungs|geschwindigkeit,** *f.* velocity of propagation (*of waves etc.*). **–organe,** *n.pl.* sexual *or* reproductive organs. **–trieb,** *m.* reproductive *or* sexual instinct.

Fortreise ['fɔrtraɪzə], *f.* departure. **fortreisen,** *v.i.* (*aux.* s.) depart, set out *or* off (on a journey).

fortreißen ['fɔrtraɪsən], *irr.v.t.* carry away (*by passion etc.*); sweep away.

Fortsatz ['fɔrtzats], *m.* projection; (*Anat., Bot.*) appendix; process.

fortschaffen ['fɔrtʃafən], *reg.v.t.* get rid of, remove, discard; transport, carry away.

fortscheren ['fɔrtʃe:rən], *reg.v.r.* (*sl.*) beat it, sling one's hook.

fortschleichen ['fɔrtʃlaɪçən], *irr.v.r.* sneak off, steal away.

fortschreiten ['fɔrtʃraɪtən], *irr.v.i.* (*aux.* s.) move *or* go on, advance, proceed, (make) progress, improve; ***– mit,*** keep pace with, keep up with. **fortschreitend,** *adj.* progressive; ***mit –er Zeit,*** with the passage of time; (*Phys.*) ***–e Welle,*** travelling wave. **Fortschreitung,** *f.* (*Mus.*) progression, consecutive chords.

Fortschritt ['fɔrtʃrɪt], *m.* progress, advance, headway, development, improvement; ***–e machen,*** advance, make progress. **fortschrittlich,** *adj.* progressive; (*coll.*) go-ahead.

fortschwemmen ['fɔrtʃvɛmən], *v.t.* wash away (*of floods*).

fortsehnen ['fɔrtze:nən], *v.r.* wish o.s. away, wish to be elsewhere.

fortsetzen ['fɔrtzɛtsən], **1.** *v.t.* carry on, continue, pursue, proceed with; ***wieder –***, resume; ***nicht –***, discontinue. **2.** *v.r.* (*of a th.*) continue, be continued, carry on, proceed. **Fortsetzung,** *f.* continuation, sequel; pursuit, prosecution; resumption; ***– folgt,*** to be continued (in our next).

fort|stehlen, *irr.v.r. See* **–schleichen.**

forttreiben ['fɔrttraɪbən], **1.** *irr.v.t.* 1. drive away, force out; 2. continue, go on with, carry on; ***sie treiben es noch immer so fort,*** they go on in just the same way. **2.** *irr.v.i.* (*aux.* s.) drift away.

Fortuna [fɔr'tu:na], *f.* Fortune.

fortwähren ['fɔrtvɛ:rən], *v.i.* last, persist, continue, endure. **fortwährend,** **1.** *adj.* lasting, continuous, perpetual, continual, constant, incessant, permanent. **2.** *adv.* constantly, continually, incessantly, without stopping, all the time.

fortwursteln ['fɔrtvurstəln], *v.i.* (*coll.*) muddle on *or* along *or* through.

fortziehen ['fɔrttsi:ən], **1.** *irr.v.t.* draw *or* pull *or* drag away. **2.** *irr.v.i.* (*aux.* s.) (*Mil.*) move *or* march on *or* off; move (***aus,*** from), leave (*a house*); migrate (*of birds*).

Forum ['fo:rum], *n.* (**-s,** *pl.* **-s** *or* **Fora**) tribunal, forum; (*fig.*) judgement seat, bar.

Fossil [fɔ'si:l], *n.* (**-s,** *pl.* **-ien**) fossil. **fossil,** *adj.* fossil, fossilized. **Fossilienbildung,** *f.* fossilization. **fossilienhaltig,** *adj.* fossiliferous.

Foto, *n. See* **Photo.**

fötal [fø:ta:l], *adj.* foetal, intra-uterine. **Fötus** ['fø:tus], *m.* foetus.

Fourage, *f. See* **Furage.**

Fournier, *n. See* **Furnier.**

Foyer [fɔa'je:], *n.* (**-s,** *pl.* **-s**) foyer, lobby, lounge.

Fracht [fraxt], *f.* (-, *pl.* **-en**) freight, cargo, load; carriage (*by land*); ***in gewöhnlicher –,*** at the usual freight; ***ausgehende –,*** freight outwards; ***ein Schiff in – nehmen,*** charter a vessel.

Fracht|aufseher, *m.* supercargo. **–besorger,** *m.* shipping agent. **–brief,** *m.* bill of lading, consignment note, waybill. **–dampfer,** *m.* cargo boat, freighter. **–empfänger,** *m.* consignee.

frachten ['fraxtən], *v.t.* load; ship, consign; ***wohin habt ihr gefrachtet?*** where are you bound for? **Frachter,** *m.* 1. consigner, shipper; 2. *See* **Frachtdampfer.**

Frächter ['frɛçtər], *m. See* **Frachter,** 1.

Frachtflug ['fraxtflu:k], *m.* air transport. **frachtfrei,** *adj.* carriage paid. **Fracht|gebühr,** *f.*, **–geld,** *n.* freight, carriage, cartage. **–gut,** *n.* lading, cargo, freight, goods; (*Railw.*) ***als –,*** by goods (*Am.* freight) train. **–handel,** *m.* carrying-trade. **–liste,** *f.* consignment-sheet, waybill, freight-note. **–makler,** *m.* shipping *or* forwarding agent. **–raum,** *m.* hold (*of a ship*); freight capacity. **–raumnot,** *f.* lack of shipping space. **–satz,** *m.* freight tariff. **–schiff,** *n.* freighter, cargo-boat. **–stück,** *n.* package, bale. **–verkehr,** *m.* goods- (*Am.* freight-)traffic. **–versender,** *m.* consigner. **–wagen,** *m.* goods wagon *or* van. **–zettel,** *m. See* **–brief. –zoll,** *m.* tonnage-dues.

Frack [frak], *m.* (**-(e)s,** *pl.* **-s** *or* **⸚e**) dress-coat; (*coll.*) tail-coat; ***– und weiße Binde,*** evening dress, (*coll.*) tails. **Frack|anzug,** *m.* dress-suit. **–hemd,** *n.* dress-shirt. **–zwang,** *m.* obligation to wear evening dress.

Frage ['fra:gə], *f.* question, query, inquiry (***über*** (*Acc.*), about); questionable *or* uncertain th., point in question, problem; ***außer – stehen,*** be beyond question, be quite certain; ***eine – bejahen,*** answer in the affirmative; ***das ist eben die –,*** that is just the point *or* question; ***das kommt nicht in –,*** that does not come into consideration, that is out of the question; ***in – kommend,*** suitable (*of a th.*), eligible (*of a p.*); ***die – nahelegen,*** raise the question; ***ohne –,*** no doubt, doubtless, undoubtedly; beyond question; ***es ist gar keine –,*** there is no doubt; ***es ist sehr die –,*** it is very doubtful; ***eine – stellen*** (***an ihn***), put a question (to him), ask (him) a question; ***in – stellen,*** call in question, jeopardize; query, question, doubt; ***eine – tun,*** see ***eine – stellen***; ***um die – nicht herumkommen,*** not evade the point, (*coll.*) not dodge the issue; ***in – ziehen,*** (call in) question, query, challenge.

Frage|bogen, *m.* questionnaire. **–buch,** *n.* catechism. **–fürwort,** *n.* interrogative pronoun. **–kasten,** *m.* correspondence column (*in newspaper*).

fragen ['fra:gən], *v.t.* ask (***nach,*** for), inquire (about *or* after), interrogate, question, query; ***ihn um Rat –,*** ask his advice, consult him; (*Comm.*) ***Baumwolle wird*** or ***ist sehr gefragt,*** cotton is in great demand; ***ich fragte gar nicht danach,*** (*coll.*) ***ich fragte den Kuckuck*** or ***Henker*** or ***Teufel danach,*** I didn't care (a rap) *or* (*coll.*) a damn; ***hat jemand nach mir gefragt?*** has anyone asked for me? ***es fragte sich, ob,*** the question was whether, it was doubtful whether; ***ich fragte mich, ob . . .,*** I wondered whether . . .; ***um Erlaubnis –,*** ask permission; (*Prov.*) ***wer viel fragt, erhält viel Antwort,*** many questions, many answers. **fragend,** *adj.* interrogative; interrogatory; ***er sah sie – an,*** he looked at her inquiringly.

Frage|satz, *m.* (*Gram.*) interrogative sentence. **–steller,** *m.* interrogator, questioner. **–stellung,** *f.* formulation of a question, questioning; statement of a problem. **–wort,** *n.* (*Gram.*) interrogative. **–zeichen,** *n.* question mark, interrogation mark.

fraglich ['fra:klɪç], *adj.* questionable, doubtful, problematic(al), uncertain; under consideration *or* discussion, in question; ***es ist –,*** it is open to question, it is questionable. **fraglos, 1.** *adj.* unquestionable, indubitable, indisputable. **2.** *adv.* decidedly, unquestionably, undoubtedly, beyond (all) question.

Fragment [frak'mɛnt], *n.* (**-(e)s,** *pl.* **-e**) fragment. **fragmentarisch** [–'ta:rɪʃ], *adj.* fragmentary.

fragwürdig ['fra:kvyrdɪç], *adj.* questionable, doubtful, dubious, (*coll. of a p.*) shady.

Fraktion [fraktsi'o:n], *f.* parliamentary group *or* grouping, faction.

Fraktionierung [fraktsio:'ni:ruŋ], *f.* (*Chem.*) fractionation, fractional distillation.

Fraktions|beschluß, *m.* party resolution, factional motion. **–führer,** *m.* (*Parl.*) party whip, (*Am.*) floor leader. **fraktionslos,** *adj.* non-party. **Fraktionszwang,** *m.* party line *or* discipline; ***Abstimmung ohne –,*** non-party voting.

Fraktur [frak'tu:r], *f.* 1. black letter *or* Gothic type; (*fig.*) ***– sprechen,*** talk plain English, (*coll.*) talk turkey; 2. (*Surg.*) fracture.

frank [fraŋk], *adv.* frankly, openly, freely, without restraint; (*usu. in the phrase*) ***– und frei,*** quite frankly.

Frank, *m.* (**-en** (*Austr.* **-s**), *pl.* (*coins*) -, (*sum of money*) **-en**) (*Austr. pl. always* **-en**)) franc.

Frankatur [fraŋka'tu:r], *f.* pre-payment, postage paid.

Franke ['fraŋkə], *m.* (**-n,** *pl.* **-n**) (*Hist.*) Franconian, Frank.

[1]**Franken** ['fraŋkən], *n.* (*Hist.*) Franconia.

[2]**Franken,** *m.* (*Swiss*) *see* **Frank.**

frankieren [fraŋ'ki:rən], *v.t.* stamp (*a letter*), prepay (*a parcel*), pay the postage *or* carriage on. **franko** ['fraŋko:], *adv.* post-paid, prepaid; carriage-paid.

Frankreich ['fraŋkraɪç], *n.* France; ***wie der Herrgott in – leben,*** live like a fighting-cock.

Franse ['franzə], *f.* fringe; valance. **fransen,** *v.i.* fray, become frayed. **fransig,** *adj.* fringed; frayed.

Franz [frants], *m.* 1. Frank, Francis; ***– von Assisi,*** St. Francis of Assisi; 2. (*sl.*) air observer. **Franz|band,** *m.* calf-binding. **–branntwein,** *m.* surgical spirit. **franzen,** *v.i.* (*Av.*) (*sl.*) stooge around.

Franziskaner [frantsis'ka:nər], *m.* Franciscan (friar).

Franzose [fran'tso:zə], *m.* (**-n,** *pl.* **-n**) Frenchman; ***die –n,*** the French. **französeln,** *v.i.* ape French ways. **Franzosenfeind,** *m.* Francophobe. **franzosenfeindlich,** *adj.* anti-French. **Franzosenfreund,** *m.* Francophile. **franzosenfreundlich,** *adj.* pro-French. **französieren** [–tsø:'zi:rən], *v.t.* Frenchify. **Französin,** *f.* Frenchwoman. **französisch,** *adj.* French; ***sich – empfehlen,*** take French leave.

frappant [fra'pant], *adj.* striking, surprising, staggering. **frappieren,** *v.t.* 1. strike, astound; 2. chill, put on ice (*wine*).

Fräse ['frɛ:zə], *f.* 1. milling tool *or* machine; 2. Newgate fringe (*beard*); 3. rotary hoe. **fräsen,** *v.t., v.i.* mill (*metal*). **Fräser,** *m.* 1. *See* **Fräse,** 1.; 2. milling operative.

Fraß [fra:s], *m.* (**-es,** *pl.* **-e**) 1. feed, fodder (*for beasts*); (*sl.*) grub, prog; 2. (*dial.*) voracity, gluttony; 3. (*Med.*) caries; 4. (*Metall.*) corrosion; insect damage. **fraß, fräße** ['frɛ:sə], *see* **fressen.**

Fraß|mehl, *n.* (*Bot., Ent.*) frass, larval excrement. **–trog,** *m.* feeding-trough.

Fratz [frats], *m.* (**-es** (*Austr.* **-en**), *pl.* **-en**) little rascal, mischievous brat.

Fratze [fratsə], *f.* grimace; (*coll.*) phiz(og), mug; (*sl.*) clock, dial (*for face*); prank, antic; caricature; (*Archit.*) mask; ***–n schneiden,*** make *or* pull faces. **Fratzen|bild,** *n.* caricature. **–gesicht,** *n.* grotesque *or* distorted face; wry face; (*Archit.*) mask. **fratzenhaft,** *adj.* grotesque, distorted, contorted, whimsical, burlesque.

Frau [frau], *f.* (-, *pl.* **-en**) woman; wife; lady; madam; Mrs.; ***meine –,*** my wife; ***Herr und –,*** master and mistress; ***die – des Hauses,*** lady of the house, mistress; ***adlige –,*** (titled) lady; ***gnädige –,*** madam; ***Unsre*** (***liebe***) ***–,*** Our Lady, the Blessed Virgin; ***– Scherer*** or ***– Dr. Scherer,*** Mrs. Scherer; ***Herr und – Professor Scherer,*** Professor and Mrs. Scherer; ***wie geht es Ihrer – Gemahlin?*** how is your wife? *die – Doktor,* the doctor's wife; *die – Rat,* the councillor's lady; (*often untranslatable, e.g.*) *die – Gräfin,* the countess; her ladyship; *Ihre – Mutter,* your mother; *zur – geben* (*nehmen*), give (take) in marriage. **Frauchen,** *n.* 1. (*hum.*) little woman, wifey; 2. (*of dogs*) bitch (*after pupping*).

Frauen|abteil, *n.* (*also m.*) (*Railw.*) ladies' compartment. **–arzt,** *m.* specialist for women's diseases, gynaecologist. **–befreiung,** *f.*, **–bewegung,** *f.* feminist movement, (*coll.*) women's lib; **–dienst,** *m.* (*Nat. Soc.*) women's national service. **–distel,** *f.* (*Bot.*) Scotch thistle. **–feind,** *m.* woman-hater, misogynist. **–fest,** *n.* Lady Day. **–frage,** *f.* question of women's rights. **–gestalt,** *f.* female character (*in literary works*). **–haar,** *n.* 1. women's hair; 2. (*Bot.*) maidenhair (*Adiantum capillus-veneris*).

frauenhaft ['frauənhaft], *adj.* womanly.

Frauen|hemd, *n.* chemise. **–herrschaft,** *f.* matriarchy, (*coll.*) petticoat government. **–jäger,** *m.* gay Lothario. **–käfer,** *m.* ladybird. **–kirche,** *f.* Church of Our Lady. **–kloster,** *n.* nunnery. **–lyzeum,** *n.* high school for girls. **–mantel,** *m.* (*Bot.*) lady's mantle (*Alchemilla vulgaris*). **–raub,** *m.* abduction, (*Poet.*) rape. **–rechtlerin,** *f.* suffragette. **–rolle,** *f.* (*Theat.*) female role *or* part. **–sattel,** *m.* side-saddle. **Frauenschaft,** *f.* (*Nat. Soc.*) women's organization. **Frauenschuh,** *m.* (*Bot.*) lady's slipper (*Cypripedium calceolus*).

Frauens|leute, *pl.* women, womenfolk. **–person,** *f.* female.

Frauen|stand, *m.* wifehood, married state, womanhood; (*Law*) coverture. **–stift,** *n.* (religious) foundation for women; nunnery. **–stimme,** *f.* female voice. **–stimmrecht,** *n.* women's suffrage. **–tag,** *m.* (*Eccl.*) Lady Day. **–verein,** *m.* women's guild. **–welt,** *f.* womankind. **–werk,** *n.* women's welfare organization. **–zimmer,** *n.* female, wench; (*obs.*) lady, woman.

Fräulein ['frɔylaɪn], *n.* (*Swiss f.*) young lady; unmarried lady; Miss (*also to address shop-assistant, officials etc.*); home governess; shop-girl, shop-assistant; (*Tele.*) *– vom Amt,* operator; *meine –!* young ladies! *gnädiges –,* Miss, madam; Miss (*followed by surname*); *Ihr* or *Ihre – Braut,* your fiancée; *ich habe mit Ihrem* or *Ihrer – Tochter getanzt,* I have danced with your daughter; *liebes – Lieschen,* dear Miss Lizzie.

frech [frɛç], *adj.* insolent, impudent, (*coll.*) cheeky, (*sl.*) fresh; daring, bold, audacious; *–e Lüge,* brazen lie; *– wie Oskar,* bold as brass; *mit –er Stirn,* brazen-faced. **Frechdachs,** *m.* (*coll.*) cheeky young rascal. **Frechheit,** *f.* insolence, impudence, effrontery, audacity, (*coll.*) cheek; (*sl.*) nerve; insolent behaviour, piece of impudence.

Fregatte [fre'gatə], *f.* frigate. **Fregattenkapitän,** *m.* (*Nav.*) commander.

frei [fraɪ], *adj.* free, independent (*von,* of); unconfined, uncontrolled, unconstrained, unrestrained, unhampered, at liberty, at large; frank, outspoken, candid, open; voluntary, spontaneous; vacant, disengaged; exempt (*von,* from), clear (of); prepaid, carriage-paid, post-free; gratuitous, gratis, free of charge, for nothing; bold, free and easy, loose, licentious; (*Chem.*) uncombined; *– ausgehen,* get off scot-free; *–e Aussicht,* open view; *die –en Berufe,* the professions; *–e Bühne,* independent theatre; *–er Eintritt,* entrance free; (*Railw. etc.*) *–e Fahrt,* clear road ahead, all clear; *–es Feld,* open country; (*fig.*) full scope; *auf –en Fuß setzen,* set at liberty, set free, release; *–es Geleit,* safe conduct; *–e Gemeinde,* rationalistic religious community; *Passagiere haben 60 Pfund Gepäck –,* passengers are allowed 60 lb. of luggage free; *–e Hand,* free hand, free rein, full authority; *aus –er Hand,* freehand; off hand; *im –en Handel,* in the shops; *–er Handwerker,* artisan belonging to no guild; *– ins Haus liefern,* deliver free to the door; *unter –em Himmel,* in the open (air); *– von Kosten,* all charges paid; *die –en Künste,* the liberal arts; *–er Künstler,* freelance artist; *–en Lauf lassen* (*Dat.*), let (*a matter*) take its course; *–e Liebe,* free love; *–e Luft,* open air; *–er Nachmittag,* afternoon off, half holiday; *ist dieser Platz –?* is this seat taken? *dieser Platz ist –,* this seat is unoccupied; *– von Schulden,* clear of debt; (*coll.*) *ich bin so –,* I don't mind if I do; *darf ich so – sein?* may I take the liberty; *–es Spiel lassen, –en Spielraum gewähren,* leave *or* give full scope (*Dat.*, to); *– sprechen,* speak openly; (*of a speaker*) speak extempore *or* without notes *or* (*coll.*) off the cuff; *–e Station,* free board and lodging; *–e Stätte,* place of refuge, asylum; *–e Stelle,* vacancy; *Straße –!* make way, please! *aus –en Stücken,* voluntarily, of one's own accord; *–er Tag,* holiday, day off; *–er Teil,* commercial partnership free of all commitments; *–er Tisch,* free board; *–e Übersetzung,* free *or* loose translation; *zur –en Verfügung sein,* be freely at one's disposal; *aus –em Willen,* of one's own free will; *–e Zeit,* spare time, leisure.

Frei|bad, *n.* open-air baths, outdoor swimming pool. **–ballon,** *m.* free balloon. **freiberuflich,** *adj.* professional, (*coll.*) freelance. **Frei|besitz,** *m.* freehold. **–betrag,** *m.* sum (of money) exempt from tax. **–beuter,** *m.* freebooter. **freibeweglich,** *adj.* mobile, motile. **Freibillet,** *n.* complimentary ticket, pass. **freibleibend,** *adj., adv.* (*Comm.*) without prejudice, subject to alteration; if unsold, if still available. **Frei|bord,** *m.* (*Naut.*) freeboard. **–brief,** *m.* permit, licence, privilege, patent, charter, (*fig.*) carte-blanche (*für,* for), passport (to). **–denker,** *m.* freethinker. **–denkerei,** *f.* freethinking, latitudinarianism.

Freie ['fraɪə], *n.* open air; *im –n,* out of doors, outdoors, in the open air.

freien ['fraɪən], **1.** *v.t.* (*obs.*) marry; (*Prov.*) *jung gefreit hat niemand gereut,* happy the wooing that's not long in doing; (*Prov.*) *schnell gefreit, lange gereut,* marry in haste and repent at leisure. **2.** *v.i. – um,* court, woo. **Freien,** *n.* wooing, courting, courtship. **Freie(r),** *m., f.* freeman, free-born citizen. **Freier,** *m.* suitor, wooer. **Freiersfüße,** *m.pl. auf –n gehen,* be looking round for a wife.

Frei|exemplar, *n.* complimentary *or* presentation *or* specimen copy. **–frau,** *f.* baroness. **–gabe,** *f.* release (*of news etc.*), opening (*of new road, bridge etc.*), decontrol (*of rationed goods*).

freigeben ['fraɪge:bən], *irr.v.t.* set free, release; open (*new road, bridge etc.*), decontrol, derequisition (*goods*); give time off, give a holiday. **freigebig,** *adj.* liberal, generous. **Freigebigkeit,** *f.* liberality, generosity, open-handedness.

Frei|geist, *m.* freethinker; latitudinarian. **–geisterei,** *f.* freethinking. **–gepäck,** *n.* allowed luggage, luggage conveyed free. **–graben,** *m.* open drain. **–grenze,** *f.* allowance of tax-free income. **–gut,** *n.* duty-free goods; (*Hist.*) landed estate free from feudal dues.

freihaben ['fraiha:bən], *irr.v.i.* have time off, have a holiday.

Freihafen ['fraɪha:fən], *m.* free port (*outside the bond area*).

freihalten ['fraɪhaltən], *irr.v.t.* 1. keep free (*of time or place*); keep clear *or* open (*a passage*); 2. *ihn –,* treat him to *or* (*coll.*) stand him a drink *etc.*, pay his expenses.

Frei|hand, *f.* open access (*library*). **–handel,** *m.* free-trade. **freihändig,** *adj.* freehand; unsupported, unassisted; direct, by private treaty (*sale*); voluntary. **Frei|händler,** *m.* free-trader; believer in principles of free-trade. **–handzeichnen,** *n.* freehand drawing.

Freiheit ['fraɪhaɪt], *f.* freedom, liberty; franchise, privilege, exemption, immunity; (*Mil.*) tactical mobility; licence, charter; *in –,* at liberty, free, (*coll.*) at large (*of a fugitive*); *in – setzen,* set free, set at liberty, liberate, release; *dichterische –,* poetic licence; *– der Meere,* freedom of the seas; *er erlaubt sich viele –en,* he takes a lot upon himself *or* takes liberties. **freiheitlich,** *adj.* independent, liberal. **Freiheits|beraubung,** *f.* false imprisonment. **–brief,** *m.* charter. **–drang,** *m.* urge towards *or* desire for independence. **–kampf,**

-krieg, *m.* war of independence. **-strafe,** *f.* imprisonment.
freiheraus [fraɪhɛ'raus], *adv.* frankly. **Frei|herr,** *m.* baron. **-herrin,** *f. See* **-frau. frei|herrlich,** *adj.* baronial. **-herrschend,** *adj.* sovereign. **-herzig,** *adj.* open-hearted, frank. **Freiin,** *f. See* **-frau. Frei|karte,** *f.* complimentary ticket, free pass. **-knecht,** *m. See* **-mann.**
freikommen ['fraɪkɔmən], *irr.v.i.* (*aux.* s.) get free, be released.
Frei|korps, *n.* volunteer corps. **-lage,** *f.* exposed site, unsheltered position. **-lager,** *n.* bivouac.
freilassen ['fraɪlasən], *irr.v.t.* release, set at liberty, set free, liberate. **Freilassung,** *f.* emancipation, release, liberation.
Freilauf ['fraɪlauf], *m.* free-wheeling, (*coll.*) coasting.
freilegen ['fraɪle:gən], *v.t.* expose, uncover, lay bare, lay open.
Freileitung ['fraɪlaɪtuŋ], *f.* (*Elec.*) overhead cable *or* (*Tele.*) line.
freilich ['fraɪlɪç], *adv.* **1.** (*affirmative*) to be sure, of course, certainly, by all means; **2.** (*concessive*) indeed, quite so, though, I admit *or* confess.
Freilicht|bühne ['fraɪlɪçt–], *f.* open-air theatre. **-malerei,** *f.* plein-air painting.
freiliegen ['fraɪli:gən], *irr.v.i.* be open *or* exposed; be unencumbered.
freimachen ['fraɪmaxən], *v.t.* **1.** stamp (*letters*), prepay; **2.** clear (*a route*); disconnect, disengage, free, liberate, extricate, set free; (*fig.*) ***die Bahn –,*** clear *or* pave the way; ***sich von der Arbeit –,*** take time off from work. **Freimachung,** *f.* freeing, liberation, disengagement, extrication, release.
Frei|mann, *m.* (*pl.* **-männer**) (*Hist.*) hangman; knacker. **-marke,** *f.* postage stamp. **-maurer,** *m.* freemason. **-maurerei,** *f.* freemasonry. **freimaurerisch,** *adj.* masonic. **Frei|maurerloge,** *f.* masonic lodge. **-mut,** *m.* frankness, candour, sincerity. **freimütig,** *adj.* candid, frank. **Frei|mütigkeit,** *f. See* **-mut. -saß, -sasse,** *m.* yeoman.
freischaffend ['fraɪʃafənt], *adj.* freelance (*artist etc.*).
Frei|schar, *f.* irregular troops, guerrilla detachment, volunteer corps. **-schärler,** *m.* (*only applied in praise of Germans, never of the enemy*) volunteer; armed insurgent; guerrilla. **-schein,** *m.* licence. **-schüler,** *m.* public scholar, scholarship holder.
frei|schwebend, *adj. See* **-tragend.**
Freisinn ['fraɪzɪn], *m.* enlightenment, broadmindedness, liberalism. **freisinnig,** *adj.* broad-minded, enlightened, liberal (*views*) (*in Germany the implication has usu. been 'radical', 'left-wing'*).
freisprechen ['fraɪʃprɛçən], *irr.v.t.* acquit, exonerate, absolve. **Frei|sprechung,** *f.* acquittal, exoneration, absolution. **-spruch,** *m.* acquittal, verdict of not guilty.
Frei|staat, *m.* republic; free state; ***der irische –,*** the Irish Free State. **-statt, -stätte,** *f.* refuge, sanctuary, asylum.
frei|stehen, *irr.v.i.* be free *or* at liberty; ***es steht dir frei,*** you are at liberty, you may. **-stehend,** *adj.* detached, exposed, isolated, (*Spt.*) unmarked.
Freistelle ['fraɪʃtɛlə], *f.* scholarship, bursary, free place. **freistellen,** *v.t.* exempt (***von,*** from); ***ihm etwas –,*** leave s.th. to his discretion; ***freigestellt,*** optional. **Freistellung,** *f.* exemption (*esp. from military service*).
Frei|stoß, *m.* (*Footb.*) free kick. **-stunde,** *f.* leisure hour.
Freitag ['fraɪta:k], *m.* Friday; ***Stiller –,*** Good Friday.
Frei|tisch, *m.* free board. **-tod,** *m.* suicide. **freitragend,** *adj.* cantilever (*bridge*), floating (*axle*); ***-er Mast,*** pylon. **Frei|treppe,** *f.* outside staircase, front steps. **-truppe,** *f.* volunteer corps. **-übungen,** *f.pl.* physical exercises; callisthenics; (*coll.*) physical jerks, P.T. **-verkehr,** *m.* (*St. Exch.*) unofficial *or* kerb (*Am.* curb) market; ***im –,*** in *or* on the open market, (*coll.*) over the counter. **-wasser,** *n.* uncontrolled fishing area, water open to public fishing; superfluous water.
frei|werden, *irr.v.i.* become free *or* liberated, (*Mil., Chem.*) become disengaged. **-werdend,** *adj.* (*Chem.*) nascent.
Freiwild ['fraɪvɪlt], *n.* (*esp. fig.*) fair game.
freiwillig ['fraɪvɪlɪç], **1.** *adj.* voluntary, spontaneous. **2.** *adv.* voluntarily, of one's own free will. **Freiwillige(r),** *m., f.* volunteer. **Freiwilligkeit,** *f.* voluntariness, spontaneity.
Frei|zeichen, *n.* (*Tele.*) dialling tone. **-zeichnung,** *f.* (*Law*) exoneration, (*Comm.*) public subscription (*of shares*).
Freizeit ['fraɪtsaɪt], *f.* spare *or* free time, leisure. **Freizeit|gestaltung,** *f.* recreational activities, organized recreation. **-lager,** *n.* holiday camp.
freizügig ['fraɪtsy:gɪç], *adj.* free to move (about) *or* to live where one likes, unhampered. **Freizügigkeit,** *f.* freedom of movement, freedom to live *or* travel *or* study where one likes.
fremd [frɛmt], *adj.* strange; foreign, alien, unknown, unfamiliar, unaccustomed; unusual, peculiar, exotic; extraneous, heterogeneous; ***ich bin hier –,*** I am a stranger here; ***dies kommt mir sehr – vor,*** this seems very strange to me; ***es war mir –,*** I was not aware of it; ***unter -em Namen,*** under an assumed name; ***-es Gut,*** other people's property; ***-e Hilfe,*** outside help; ***gegen ihn – tun,*** be aloof *or* distant *or* (*coll.*) cool with him. **Fremdarbeiter,** *m.* (immigrant) foreign labourer. **fremdartig,** *adj.* strange, odd; unfamiliar; heterogeneous; (*Chem.*) extraneous. **Fremdartigkeit,** *f.* heterogeneity; oddness. **Fremd|befruchtung,** *f.* cross-fertilization. **-bestäubung,** *f.* cross-pollination, allogamy.
Fremde ['frɛmdə], *f.* foreign country *or* parts; ***in der –,*** abroad.
Fremden|buch, *n.* visitor's book, hotel register. **-führer,** *m.* guide; guide book. **-haß,** *m.* xenophobia. **-heim,** *n.* private hotel, boarding house. **-industrie,** *f.* tourist trade. **-legion,** *f.* foreign legion. **-verkehr,** *m.* tourist traffic. **-zimmer,** *n.* spare room, visitors' room.
Fremde(r) ['frɛmdə(r)], *m., f.* foreigner, alien; stranger, visitor, guest.
Fremdgeräusch ['frɛmtgərɔyʃ], *n.* (*Rad.*) parasitic noise.
Fremdheit ['frɛmthaɪt], *f.* strangeness, unfamiliarity; peculiarity.
Fremd|herrschaft, *f.* foreign rule. **-körper,** *m.* foreign body. **fremdländisch,** *adj.* foreign, exotic. **Fremdling,** *m.* (**-s,** *pl.* **-e**) stranger, foreigner, alien; *pl.* (*Geol.*) erratic blocks. **fremdrassig,** *adj.* of different race *or* stock, alien. **Fremdsprache,** *f.* foreign language. **fremd|sprachig,** *adj.* speaking a foreign language. **-sprachlich,** *adj.* foreign-language. **-stämmig,** *adj. See* **-rassig. Fremd|stoff,** *m.* impurity, foreign matter. **-wort,** *n.* foreign borrowing, foreign word. **-wörterbuch,** *n.* dictionary of foreign borrowings.
frenetisch [fre'ne:tɪʃ], *adj.* frenzied, frantic, demented, insensate.
frequentieren [frekvɛn'ti:rən], *v.t.* frequent, patronize.
Frequenz [fre'kvɛnts], *f.* (-, *pl.* **-en**) attendance; (*Railw.*) traffic, (*Phys.*) frequency. **Frequenz|-(abhängigkeits)kennlinie,** *f.* (*Rad.*) frequency characteristics response curve. **-wandler,** *m.* (*Rad.*) frequency changer.
Freske ['frɛskə], *f.* fresco.
Fressalien [frɛ'sa:liən], *pl.* (*sl.*) eatables. **Freßbeutel,** *m.* nose-bag. **Fresse,** *f.* (*sl.*) mug, trap, gob.
fressen ['frɛsən], *irr.v.t., v.i.* eat (*of beasts*); feed; (*vulg.*) gorge, guzzle, devour, (*fig.*) swallow, consume, (*Metall.*) pit, corrode; (*Prov.*) ***Vogel friß oder stirb,*** it is sink or swim; ***der Ärger frißt ihn,*** he is eaten up with annoyance; ***der Ärger frißt an ihm,*** the annoyance preys on his mind; ***seinen***

Ärger in sich* –**, swallow one's annoyance; ***sie hat einen Narren daran gefressen, she is infatuated with it *or* dotes upon it; ***–der Gram,*** gnawing *or* consuming anxiety. **Fressen,** *n.* feed, food, fodder (*for beasts*); (*sl.*) ***das war ein elendes –,*** that was a wretched meal; (*sl.*) ***ein gefundenes –,*** the very th., a godsend (*Dat.*, for), a gift from the gods, grist to (his) mill. **Fresser,** *m.* glutton, gormandizer, (*sl.*) guzzler. **Fresserei** [–'raɪ], *f.* gluttony, gormandizing, (*sl.*) guzzling; (*sl.*) feed, spread. **Freßgier,** *f.* voracity, gluttony. **freßgierig,** *adj.* gluttonous, voracious. **Freß|napf,** *m.* feeding bowl. **–trog,** *m.* feeding-trough, manger.

Frettchen ['frɛtçən], *n.* ferret.

Freude ['frɔydə], *f.* joy, gladness; delight, pleasure, satisfaction (*an* (*Dat.*), in; *in* (*Acc.*), at); ***mit –(n),*** gladly, joyfully, with pleasure; ***vor – außer sich sein,*** be overjoyed *or* beside o.s. with joy; ***– haben*** or ***finden an*** (*Dat.*), take pleasure *or* delight in; ***es macht*** or ***bereitet mir große –,*** it gives me great pleasure; (*Prov.*) ***geteilte – ist doppelte –,*** shared joys are doubled.

Freuden|botschaft, *f.* glad tidings. **–fest,** *n.* festival, festivity, feast, rejoicing. **–feuer,** *n.* bonfire. **–geschrei,** *n.* shouts of joy; cheers. **–haus,** *n.* disorderly house, brothel. **–mädchen,** *n.* prostitute. **–rausch,** *m.* rapture(s), transport of joy. **–ruf, –schrei,** *m.* cry *or* shout of joy, cheer. **–störer,** *m.* mischief-maker; kill-joy. **–tag,** *m.* day of rejoicing, red-letter day.

freude|strahlend, *adj.* beaming with joy, radiant. **–trunken,** *adj.* exultant, rapturous, in an ecstasy of delight, intoxicated with joy.

freudig ['frɔydɪç], *adj.* joyful, joyous, glad, cheerful; ***einem –en Ereignis entgegensehen,*** be expecting a happy event; ***– stimmen,*** gladden, cheer, elate. **Freudigkeit,** *f.* joyousness. **freudlos,** *adj.* cheerless, joyless.

freuen ['frɔyən], **1.** *v.t.* (*usu. imp.*) make glad, gladden, give pleasure to, delight; ***es freut mich,*** (***daß***), I am glad (that). **2.** *v.r.* 1. rejoice (***über*** (*Acc.*), over, at), be glad *or* happy (about), be pleased (with); ***wir – uns, zu erfahren,*** we are pleased to learn; ***freut euch des Lebens!*** let life be full of gladness; 2. (***an*** (*Dat.*)) enjoy, take pleasure in, delight in; ***sie freut sich am Glück ihrer Kinder,*** she takes delight in the happiness of her children; 3. (***auf*** (*Acc.*)) look forward to; ***wir – uns auf dein Kommen,*** we are looking forward to your visit.

Freund [frɔynt], *m.* **(-(e)s,** *pl.* **-e)** friend; boy friend, gentleman friend (*when used by women*); *pl.* Quakers, Friends; ***– der Wahrheit,*** lover of truth; ***–e im Glücke,*** fair-weather friends; (*Prov.*) ***–e erkennt man in der Not,*** a friend in need is a friend indeed; ***ein – von mir,*** a friend of mine; ***ein – sein von,*** be fond of, be partial to, like. **Freundeskreis,** *n.* (circle of) friends. **Freundin,** *f.* girl friend, lady friend (*when used by men*); friend (*when used by women*).

freundlich ['frɔyntlɪç], *adj.* friendly, kind, affable, amiable, genial, obliging; pleasant, cheerful; ***das ist sehr – von Ihnen,*** that is very kind of you; ***–es Wesen,*** obliging *or* affable *or* kindly manner; ***–es Wetter,*** pleasant *or* mild weather, favourable weather; ***–es Zimmer,*** cheerful *or* cosy room; ***bitte recht –!*** smile, please! (*photographer's injunction.*) **Freundlichkeit,** *f.* kindness, friendliness, amiability, affability, pleasantness.

Freundschaft ['frɔyntʃaft], *f.* friendship; ***– schließen,*** make friends. **freundschaftlich,** *adj.* friendly, amicable, cordial, well-disposed; ***auf –en Fuße,*** on friendly terms. **Freundschaftlichkeit,** *f.* friendly disposition, camaraderie. **Freundschafts|bande,** *pl.* ties *or* bond of friendship. **–bezeigung,** *f.* mark of friendship. **–botschaft,** *f.* goodwill mission. **–bund,** *m.* friendly alliance. **–dienst,** *m.* kind service, good offices, friendly turn. **–inseln,** *pl.* (*Geog.*) Friendly Islands. **–wechsel,** *m.* (*Comm.*) accommodation-bill.

Frevel ['fre:fəl], *m.* outrage (*an* (*Dat.*), ***gegen***, on), crime (against), misdeed; (*Eccl.*) sacrilege, wantonness, wickedness. **frevelhaft,** *adj.* sacrilegious, impious; wicked, criminal, wanton, malicious, outrageous. **Frevelmut,** *m.* malicious *or* wicked disposition; wantonness. **freveln,** *v.i.* commit an outrage (***an*** (*Dat.*), ***gegen, wider,*** against); blaspheme; outrage, transgress; trespass. **Freveltat,** *f.* outrage, crime. **freventlich,** *adj. See* **frevelhaft. Frevler,** *m.* evil-doer, offender, transgressor; blasphemer. **frevlerisch,** *adj. See* **frevelhaft.**

Friaul [fri'aul], *n.* (*Geog.*) Friuli.

friderizianisch [fri:dərɪtsi'a:nɪʃ], *adj.* of Frederick the Great.

Friedel ['fri:dəl], *m.* (*dim. of* **Gottfried**) Geoff, Jeff.

Friede(n) ['fri:də(n)], *m.* **(-(n)s,** *no pl.*) peace; tranquillity; harmony; ***den –n bewahren,*** keep the peace; ***–n machen*** or ***schließen,*** make peace; ***im –n,*** in peacetime; ***im –n mit,*** at peace with; ***in –n lassen,*** let alone, leave in peace; ***–n haben vor*** (*Dat.*), be safe from; ***–n halten,*** keep quiet; ***in Fried und Freud,*** in peace and amity; (*coll.*) ***dem –n ist nicht zu trauen,*** I smell a rat; (*Prov.*) ***– ernährt, Unfriede verzehrt,*** a bad peace is better than a good war; ***fauler –,*** hollow truce.

Friedens|angebot, *n.* overtures of peace, peace offer. **–bedingungen,** *f.pl.* condition of peace, peace terms. **–bruch,** *m.* breach *or* violation of the peace. **friedensbrüchig,** *adj.* guilty of a breach of the peace. **Friedens|diktat,** *n.* dictated peace (*referring to Versailles Treaty*). **–fest,** *n.* peace celebrations. **–fürst,** *m.* Prince of Peace; Christ. **–fuß,** *m.* peace-footing. **–güte,** *f.* pre-war quality. **friedensmäßig,** *adj.* as in peace-time, pre-war. **Friedens|pfeife,** *f.* pipe of peace. **–politik,** *f.* pacific policy. **–produktion,** *f.* peace-time production. **–richter,** *m.* justice of the peace (*in England*); arbitrator (*when applied to German conditions*). **–schluß,** *m.* conclusion of peace. **–spruch,** *m.* arbitrational award. **–stand,** *m.*, **–stärke,** *f.* (*Mil.*) peace-time strength, peace establishment.

Frieden(s)|stifter, *m.* mediator, peacemaker. **–störer,** *m.* disturber of the peace; rioter. **–störung,** *f.* (*Law*) disturbance *or* breach of the peace.

Friedens|verhandlungen, *f.pl.* peace negotiations. **–vermittler,** *m.* mediator. **–vertrag,** *m.* peace treaty.

Friederika [fri:də'ri:ka], *f.* Frederica, Freda.

friedfertig ['fri:tfɛrtɪç], *adj.* peaceable, (*B.*) peace-loving, pacific; (*B.*) ***selig sind die Friedfertigen,*** blessed are the peacemakers. **Friedfertigkeit,** *f.* peaceableness.

Friedhof ['fri:tho:f], *m.* churchyard, cemetery, graveyard, burial ground.

friedlich ['fri:tlɪç], *adj.* peaceable, pacific; peaceful, tranquil, untroubled, undisturbed. **Friedlichkeit,** *f.* peacefulness, peaceableness. **friedliebend,** *adj.* peace-loving. **friedlos,** *adj.* 1. quarrelsome; 2. (*obs.*) outlawed, outcast, proscribed.

Friedrich ['fri:trɪç], *m.* Frederic(k).

friedsam ['fri:tza:m], *adj.* (*Poet.*) *see* **friedlich.**

frieren ['fri:rən], *irr.v.i.* (*aux.* h. & s.), *v.t.*, *v.imp.* freeze, chill; ***hat es gefroren?*** did it freeze? ***es friert,*** it is freezing, there is a frost; ***mich friert,*** I am cold; ***mich friert an den Händen,*** my hands are numb with cold; ***die Finger sind mir steif gefroren,*** my fingers are stiff with cold; ***der Fluß ist gefroren,*** the river is frozen (over). **Frieren,** *n.* freezing, congelation; shivering, chill. **Frierpunkt,** *m.* freezing-point.

Fries [fri:s], *m.* **(-es,** *pl.* **-e)** 1. frieze, baize (*coarse woollen cloth*); 2. (*Archit.*) frieze.

Friese ['fri:zə], *m.* **(-n,** *pl.* **-n)** Frisian.

Friesel ['fri:zəl], *m. or n.* **(-s,** *pl.* **-n)** *or f.* (-, *pl.* **-n)** 1. pustule; 2. *pl.* (*Med.*) military fever, purples.

friesisch ['fri:zɪʃ], *adj.* (*Geog.*) Frisian.

Frikadelle [frika'dɛlə], *f.* meat ball, rissole.

Frikassee [frika'se:], *n.* **(-s,** *pl.* **-s)** fricassee. **frikassieren,** *v.t.* mince, make into fricassee.

Friktion [frɪkti'o:n], *f.* friction. **Friktionsantrieb,** *m.* friction drive.

frisch [frɪʃ], *adj.* fresh, cool, refreshing; new, unused, recent, raw, green; ruddy (*complexion*); sharp, brisk, vigorous, lively, sprightly, alert; – ***gestrichen,*** wet paint; – ***drauf los!*** courage! go to it! ***–es Brot,*** new bread; ***–e Eier,*** new-laid *or* fresh eggs; ***–e Farbe,*** bright colour; (*Prov.*) ***–e Fische, gute Fische,*** never put off till tomorrow what you can do today; – ***und froh,*** happily, joyfully; ***es geht ihm – von der Hand,*** he is a quick worker; ***–e Milch,*** fresh milk; – ***und munter,*** fresh as a daisy, (*coll.*) alive and kicking; ***–en Mut fassen,*** take fresh courage; ***–e Spur,*** hot scent; ***auf –er Tat,*** in the (very) act, red-handed; (*Prov.*) – ***gewagt ist halb gewonnen,*** well begun is half done, a good start is half the battle; ***–e Wäsche anziehen,*** put on clean underclothes; ***–er werden,*** freshen, stiffen (*of wind*).

Frisch|arbeit, *f.* (*Metall.*) fining. **–dampf,** *m.* live-steam. **Frische,** *f.* freshness; coolness; liveliness, briskness, brightness, vigour. **Frisch|ei,** *n.* new-laid *or* fresh egg. **–eisen,** *n.* (re)fined iron. **frischen,** *v.t.* 1. (*Metall.*) (re)fine, puddle; 2. (*Poet.*) cool, refresh; revive. **Frischerei** [–'raɪ], *f.* (re)finery. **Frisch|esse,** *f.* refining furnace, refinery. **–haltepackung,** *f.* sealed *or* vacuum-packed container. **–herd,** *m.* puddling-furnace. **Frischling,** *m.* (**-s,** *pl.* **-e**) young boar. **Frisch|ofen,** *m. See* **–herd. –stahl,** *m.* German steel, natural steel. **–wasser,** *n.* fresh water.

Friseur [fri'zø:r], *m.* (**-s,** *pl.* **-e**), **Friseurin,** *f.* (*Austr.*), **Friseuse,** *f.* hairdresser, (*also for men*) barber. **Frisiereisen,** *n.* curling-tongs. **frisieren,** *v.t.* dress *or* cut the hair; nap (*cloth*); trim; (*coll.*) cook, doctor (*accounts*); (*sl.*) hot up (*an engine*); ***sich – lassen,*** have one's hair done *or* cut. **Frisier|mantel,** *m.* dressing-jacket, peignoir. **–salon,** *m.* hairdresser's, barber's. **–tisch,** *m.* dressing-table, toilet-table. **Frisör** *etc. See* **Friseur** *etc.*

friß [frɪs], **frißt,** *see* **fressen.**

Frist [frɪst], *f.* (-, *pl.* **-en**) space of time, (prescribed) period, interval, time allowed; appointed time, time-limit, (set) term; respite, extension, days of grace; (*coll.*) deadline; ***zwei Tage –,*** two day's grace; ***innerhalb einer – von zwei Tagen,*** within a period *or* an interval of two days; ***in kürzester –,*** at very short notice, as soon as possible, without delay; ***die – ist abgelaufen,*** the time is up. **Frist|ablauf,** *m.* lapse of time; (*Comm.*) expiry, maturity.

fristen ['frɪstən], *v.t.* prolong, delay; (*coll.*) put off; ***ihm das Leben –,*** prolong *or* spare his life; ***sein Leben –,*** make a bare living, keep body and soul together, just manage to live. **fristgerecht,** *adv.* within the prescribed period, in time. **Fristgesuch,** *n.* (*Law*) motion in arrest of judgement. **fristlos,** *adv.* without notice; ***–e Entlassung,*** summary dismissal. **Fristung,** *f.* 1. fixing a term; 2. prolongation. **Frist|verlängerung,** *f.* extension (of time). **–versäumnis,** *n.* default.

Frisur [fri'zu:r], *f.* (-, *pl.* **-en**) 1. hairdressing; 2. hair-style, coiffure; (*coll.*) hair-do.

fritten ['frɪtən], *v.i.* cohere; frit, sinter (*pottery, glass-making etc.*). **Fritter,** *m.* (*Rad.*) coherer.

Fritz [frɪts], *m.* (*dim. of* **Friedrich**) Fred(dy); (*coll.*) ***der alte –,*** Frederick the Great.

frivol [fri'vo:l], *adj.* frivolous, flippant. **Frivolität** [–i'tɛ:t], *f.* frivolity, flippancy. **Frivolitätenarbeit,** *f.* tatting.

froh [fro:], *adj.* glad, joyful, gay, merry, cheerful, happy; (*Poet.*) blithe; – ***sein über*** (*Acc.*), rejoice at, be pleased with, be glad about; ***einer S.*** (*Gen.*) – ***werden,*** take pleasure in *or* enjoy a th.; ***–en Mutes*** or ***Herzens,*** cheerful, in good spirits; ***–e Botschaft,*** good news, good *or* glad tidings. **frohgemut,** *adj.* happy, cheerful, joyful.

fröhlich ['frø:lɪç], *adj.* cheerful, gay, happy, merry, joyous, joyful, (*Poet.*) blithe, gladsome. **Fröhlichkeit,** *f.* cheerfulness, high spirits, mirth, hilarity, gaiety; gladness, joyfulness.

frohlocken [fro'lɔkən], *v.i.* rejoice (***über*** (*Acc.*), at), triumph (over), gloat (over), be jubilant (over *or* about), exult (over), shout for joy (about); (*B.*) ***frohlocket dem Herrn!*** rejoice in the Lord!

Frohsinn ['fro:zɪn], *m.* cheerfulness, gaiety, happy disposition. **frohsinnig,** *adj.* cheerful, joyful, happy.

fromm [frɔm], *adj.* (*comp.* ***-er*** *or* ***¨-er,*** *sup.* ***-st*** *or* ***¨-st***) pious, religious, godly, devout; harmless, good, gentle, meek; ***–er Betrug,*** well-intentioned *or* pious deception; ***–e Lüge,*** white lie; ***–es Pferd,*** quiet horse; ***–er Wunsch,*** pious hope, wishful thinking; (*B.*) ***–er und getreuer Diener,*** good and faithful servant.

Frömmelei [frœmə'laɪ], *f.* hypocrisy; bigotry. **frömmeln,** *v.i.* be sanctimonious *or* bigoted, affect piety. **frömmelnd,** *adj.* canting, sanctimonious, hypocritical; ***–e Sprache,*** cant.

frommen ['frɔmən], *v.i.* (*Dat.*) avail, profit, benefit, be of use to. **Frommen,** *n.* ***zu Nutz und*** – (*Gen.*) *or* ***von,*** for the benefit *or* good *or* advantage of.

Frömmigkeit ['frœmɪçkaɪt], *f.* piety, devoutness, godliness; meekness. **Frömmler,** *m.* hypocrite; devotee.

Fron [fro:n], **Fron|arbeit,** *f.,* **–dienst,** *m.* compulsory *or* enforced *or* statute-labour; (*Hist.*) socage, villeinage; (*fig.*) drudgery. **fronen,** *v.i.* do compulsory labour; (*Hist.*) do socage-service, (*fig.*) slave, drudge.

frönen ['frø:nən], *v.i.* (*Dat.*) be a slave to, be addicted to; indulge in, pander to (*vice, weakness etc.*); ***seinen Launen –,*** humour his whims.

Fronfasten ['fro:nfastən], *pl.* ember-weeks; (*R.C.*) quarter-fastings. **fronfrei,** *adj.* exempt from compulsory service. **Fron|geld,** *n.* money paid in lieu of statute-labour. **–herr,** *m.* feudal overlord. **–knecht,** *m.* villein, serf. **–lehen,** *n.* socage-tenure. **–leichnam,** *m.* (*Eccl.*) Corpus Christi. **fronpflichtig,** *adj.* subject to socage.

Front [frɔnt], *f.* (-, *pl.* **-en**) front (*also Mil., Meteor.*), face, frontage, forepart (*the political use dates from before Nat. Soc., e.g.* ***Einheitsfront,*** united workers' block; ***Volksfront,*** popular front. *Nat. Soc. extended the meaning from 'political organization' or 'body' to include entire political activities of unorganized or quasi-organized sections of the community, e.g.* ***Arbeitsfront,*** labour front (*i.e. all the workers*), ***innere Front,*** domestic front (*i.e. propaganda fight against grumblers*)); (*fig.*) – ***machen gegen,*** set one's face against, turn against. **Frontabschnitt,** *m.* (*Mil.*) sector.

frontal [frɔn'ta:l], *adj.* frontal, direct, head-on (*collision*).

Front|angriff, *m.* frontal attack. **–antrieb,** *m.* (*Motor.*) front-wheel drive. **–arterie,** *f.* (*Anat.*) frontal artery. **–ausdehnung,** *f.* extent of front held. **–bericht,** *m.* (*Mil.*) front-line report, report from the front. **–einsatz,** *m.* (*Mil.*) combat duty, front-line service. **–kämpfer,** *m.* front-line fighter, combatant, combat veteran. **–länge,** *f.* frontage, front. **–linie,** *f.* (*Nav.*) ***in –,*** drawn up abreast. **–seite,** *f.* frontispiece. **–soldat,** *m. See* **–kämpfer. –wechsel,** *m.* change of front, (*esp. fig.*) about-face. **–zulage,** *f.* (*Mil.*) field allowance.

Fronvogt ['fro:nfo:kt], *m.* (*Hist.*) taskmaster, feudal overlord.

fror [fro:r], **fröre** ['frø:rə], *see* **frieren.**

Frosch [frɔʃ], *m.* (**-es,** *pl.* **¨-e**) 1. frog; (*coll.*) ***ich habe einen – im Halse,*** I have a frog in my throat, I am hoarse; (*coll.*) ***sei kein –!*** don't be a kill-joy *or* spoil-sport *or* wet-blanket! be a sport! 2. cracker, squib (*fireworks*); 3. (*Mech.*) cam; 4. nut, frog (*of the fiddle-bow*); 5. rammer, pile-driver. **Frosch|arten,** *f.pl.* batrachians, ranidae. **–biß,** *m.* (*Bot.*) frog-bit (*Hydrocharis*). **–gequake,** *n.* croaking of frogs. **–keule,** *f.* (*Cul.*) frog's leg. **–laich,** *m.* frog-spawn. **–perspektive,** *f.* 'worm's-eye view'. **–quappe,** *f.* tadpole. **–schenkel,** *m. See* **–keule.**

Frost [frɔst], *m.* (**-es,** *pl.* **¨-e**) frost; cold, chill, coldness; shivering, (*coll.*) shivers; ***vom –(e) beschädigt,*** frostbitten; ***vor – beben,*** shiver with cold. **Frostbeule,** *f.* chilblain.

frösteln ['frœstəln], *v.imp.* ***mich fröstelt,*** I feel chilly, I am shivering (with cold); a chill *or* shudder runs down my spine. **Frösteln,** *n.* (cold) shiver; chill.

Frostfieber ['frɔstfi:bər], *n.* ague. **frostig,** *adj.* frosty; cold, chilly; (*fig.*) cool, stand-offish, icy, frigid (*of behaviour*); *-er Empfang,* chilly reception; *-e Antwort,* icy rejoinder. **Frost|mittel,** *n.* frostbite remedy. **-salbe,** *f.* chilblain ointment. **-schaden,** *m.* frost damage. **-schutzmittel,** *n.* anti-freeze. **-wetter,** *n.* frosty weather.

Frottee [frɔ'te:], *n. or m.* (**-s,** *pl.* **-s**) terry towelling. **frottieren,** *v.t.* rub down. **Frottier(hand)tuch,** *n.* bath-towel, Turkish towel.

Frucht [fruxt], *f.* (-, *pl.* ⸗**e**) fruit, crop, harvest; corn, grain, (*fig.*) fruit, result, outcome, upshot, product, profit; (*Med.*) embryo, foetus; *eingemachte Früchte,* preserves; *– der Liebe,* love-child. **Frucht|abtreibungsmittel,** *n.* abortifacient. **-acker,** *m.* cornfield. **-auge,** *n.* bud, germ.

fruchtbar ['fruxtba:r], *adj.* fruitful, fecund, fertile, prolific, productive; *– machen,* fertilize. **Fruchtbarkeit,** *f.* fruitfulness, fertility, fecundity. **Fruchtbarmachung,** *f.* fertilization.

Frucht|beet, *n.* hotbed (*of manure*). **-boden,** *m.* (*Anat., Bot.*) placenta, thalamus; (*Bot.*) receptacle. **-bonbon,** *m.* fruit drop *or* pastille, boiled sweet. **-brand,** *m.* cornblight; ergot. **fruchtbringend,** *adj.* productive, fertile, fruitful.

Früchtchen ['fryçtçən], *n.* (*coll.*) scamp, rascal, scapegrace.

fruchten ['fruxtən], *v.i.* be of use *or* profit, have effect, avail; bear fruit; *nichts –,* be of no use *or* avail, be in vain.

Frucht|fleisch, *n.* fruit pulp. **-folge,** *f. See* **-wechsel. -göttin,** *f.* Pomona (*of trees*), Ceres (*of crops*). **-gülte,** *f.* rent to be paid in corn. **-halter,** *m.* matrix, uterus. **-häutchen,** *n.* (*Bot.*) epicarp. **-horn,** *n.* cornucopia. **-hülle,** *f.* (*Bot.*) husk, pericarp; (*Anat.*) foetal envelope. **-kelch,** *m.* (*Bot.*) calyx. **-kern,** *m.* kernel. **-knospe,** *f. See* **-auge. -knoten,** *m.* (*Bot.*) seed-vessel, ovary. **-korn,** *n.* seed-corn. **-kuchen,** *m.* (*Anat.*) foetal placenta.

fruchtlos ['fruxtlo:s], *adj.* fruitless (*also fig.*), (*fig.*) barren, useless, unavailing. **Fruchtlosigkeit,** *f.* fruitlessness.

Frucht|monat, *m.* (*obs.*) September. **-presse,** *f.* fruit squeezer *or* press. **-röhre,** *f.* (*Bot.*) pistil. **-saft,** *m.* fruit-juice. **fruchttragend,** *adj.* fruit-bearing, fructiferous.

Fruchtung ['fruxtuŋ], *f.* germination, fertilization. **Fruchtungs|kern,** *m.* fertilized egg. **-vermögen,** *n.* fertility.

Frucht|wasser, *n.* (*Anat.*) amnion fluid. **-wechsel,** *m.* rotation of crops. **-zehnte,** *m.* tithe in corn. **-zucker,** *m.* fructose, laevulose.

frug [fru:k], **früge** ['fry:gə], *see* **fragen.**

früh [fry:], **1.** *adj.* early; in the morning; untimely, premature; *– morgens, am -en Morgen,* early in the morning; *heute –,* (early) this morning; *morgen –,* tomorrow morning; *übermorgen –,* early the day after tomorrow; *-e Morgenstunden,* small hours (of the morning); *-er Tod,* early *or* untimely death; *– genug ankommen,* arrive in (good) time; *von – bis spät,* from morning till night, all day long; (*Prov.*) *– ins Bett und – heraus, frommt dem Leib, dem Geist, dem Haus,* early to bed and early to rise makes a man healthy, wealthy and wise. **2.** *adv.* early, in good time. **Früh|apfel,** *m.* summer apple. **-aufsteher,** *m.* early riser, (*coll.*) early bird. **-beet,** *n.* hotbed.

Frühe ['fry:ə], *f.* early hour; (early) morning; *in der –,* (early) in the morning; *in aller –,* very early, the first th. in the morning; *bis in die* or *der –,* till the early hours.

früher ['fry:ər], **1.** *adj.* (*comp. of früh*) earlier; previous, prior, former. **2.** *adv.* earlier, sooner; formerly, in former times, at one time; *– als,* previous *or* prior to; *in – als acht Tagen,* in less than 8 days; *– oder später,* sooner or later; *– habe ich viel geschwommen,* I used to do a lot of swimming.

frühestens ['fry:əstəns], *adv.* as early as possible; at the earliest; not before, not earlier than.

Früh|gebet, *n.* morning prayer, matins. **-geburt,** *f.* premature birth. **-gesang,** *m.* dawn chorus (*of birds*). **-gottesdienst,** *m.* morning service. **-jahr,** *n.* spring. **-jahrs(-Tagund)nachtgleiche,** *f.* vernal equinox.

Frühling ['fry:lɪŋ], *m.* (**-s,** *pl.* **-e**) **1.** spring, spring-time, (*fig.*) youth, early prime; 2. animal born in spring. **frühlingshaft,** *adj.* spring-like.

Frühmesse ['fry:mɛsə], *f.* early mass, matins. **früh|morgens,** *adv.* early in the morning. **-reif,** *adj.* precocious, forward, premature, early; *-e Früchte,* forced fruit. **Früh|reife,** *f.* precocity, forwardness, prematurity; earliness (*of ripening*). **-saat,** *f.* first sowing. **-schoppen,** *m.* morning pint. **-sprenger,** *m.* (*Artil.*) premature burst. **-stadium,** *n.* early stage. **-start,** *m.* (*Spt.*) false start. **frühsteinzeitlich,** *adj.* paleolithic.

Frühstück ['fry:ʃtyk], *n.* breakfast; *zweites –,* mid-morning snack, (*coll.*) brunch. **frühstücken,** *v.i.* breakfast, have *or* take breakfast. **Früh|treiberei,** *f.* forcing (*plants*). **-zeit,** *f.* early epoch, dawn (of history). **frühzeitig,** *adj.* early, in good time; premature, untimely. **Frühzeitigkeit,** *f.* earliness, prematurity, untimeliness. **Früh|zug,** *m.* early morning train. **-zündung,** *f.* (*Artil.*) premature ignition; (*Motor.*) pre-ignition.

Fuchs [fuks], *m.* (**-es,** *pl.* ⸗**e**) 1. fox; fox fur; (*coll.*) *alter –,* cunning old devil; (*coll.*) *wo sich – und Hase gute Nacht sagen,* in the back of beyond; (*Prov.*) *wer den – fangen will, muß früh aufstehen,* the early bird catches the worm; 2. chestnut, bay, sorrel (horse); 3. (*Ent.*) tortoise-shell butterfly (*Vanessa*); 4. (*Univ.*) freshman, (*coll.*) fresher; 5. (*Bill. etc.*) fluke. **Fuchs|affe,** *f.* (*Zool.*) lemur. **-balg,** *m.* fox-skin. **-bau,** *m.* fox-hole *or* -earth *or* -kennel.

fuchsen ['fuksən], **1.** *v.t.* (*coll.*) annoy, vex; play a trick on. **2.** *v.r.* fret, be annoyed *or* vexed *or* rattled (*über* (*Acc.*), at, about *or* over).

Fuchsia ['fuksia:] (-, *pl.* **-sien**), **Fuchsie** ['fuksiə], *f.* (*Bot.*) fuchsia (*Onagraceae*).

fuchsig ['fuksɪç], *adj.* foxy, (*coll.*) furious, mad.

Füchsin ['fyksɪn], *f.* vixen.

Fuchs|jagd, *f.* fox-hunt(ing). **-major,** *m.* older student who looks after the freshers (*in a students' club*). **-pelz,** *m.* fur of a fox; (*coll.*) *den – anziehen,* use a dodge *or* subterfuge. **fuchsrot,** *adj.* foxy-red, sorrel. **Fuchsschwanz,** *m.* 1. brush (*tail of a fox*); (*coll.*) *den – streichen, see* **fuchsschwänzen**; 2. (*Bot.*) love-lies-bleeding (*Amarantus caudatus*); (*Bot.*) fox-tail grass (*Alopecurus*); 3. padsaw. **fuchsschwänzen,** *v.i.* flatter, fawn, toady, wheedle. **Fuchsstute,** *f.* sorrel mare. **fuchs(teufels)wild,** *adj.* (*coll.*) mad *or* wild with rage, furious, mad.

Fuchtel ['fuxtəl], *f.* (-, *pl.* **-n**) rod; (*fig.*) strict discipline; *ihn unter der – haben* or *halten, ihn in die – bekommen,* keep him under one's thumb, keep a tight hand *or* rein over him. **fuchteln,** *v.i.* *– mit,* (*nervously*) fidget with, wave (*s.th.*) about; (*threateningly*) brandish; *mit den Händen –,* wave one's arms about, gesticulate.

Fuder ['fu:dər], *n.* load, cart-load; large measure for wine (*800–1,000 litres according to locality*). **fuderweise,** *adj.* by cart-loads.

Fug [fu:k], *m.* *mit –,* fittingly, justly; *mit – und Recht,* with full justification *or* authority; *mit gutem –,* with good reason.

[1]**Fuge** ['fu:gə], *f.* joint, seam; gap, groove, slit, space (*where bricks etc. should join*); (*Carp.*) mortise, rabbet; (*Anat., Bot.*) suture; *aus den -n bringen,* put out of joint, unhinge; *die Zeit ist aus den -n,* the times are out of joint; *aus den -n gehen,* come apart, fall apart *or* to pieces, (*coll.*) come off (*its*) hinges.

[2]**Fuge,** *f.* (*Mus.*) fugue.

fugen ['fu:gən], *v.t.* joint, fit together; groove, rabbet; point (*a wall*).

fügen ['fy:gən], **1.** *v.t.* 1. ordain, decree, will, direct, dispose; *wie Gott es fügt,* as God wills *or* ordains;

2. add. **2.** *v.r.* **1.** accommodate *or* reconcile o.s. (*Dat. or* ***in*** (*Acc.*), to); comply (with), acquiesce (in), resign o.s. *or* yield *or* submit (to); ***was sich fügt,*** what is fitting *or* seemly; 2. be fitted *or* suitable *or* proper; come to pass, happen, chance; ***wie es sich fügt,*** as it so happens, as occasion demands.

Fugenkelle ['fu:gənkɛlə], *f.* pointing trowel. **fugenlos,** *adj.* seamless, without joints.

Fügewort ['fy:gəvɔrt], *n.* conjunction.

füglich ['fy:klıç], *adv.* conveniently, appropriately, (very) well, properly, rightly, justly, suitably, reasonably; ***er hätte – schweigen können,*** he might well have held his tongue; ***er konnte es nicht – vermeiden,*** he could not very well avoid it. **Füglichkeit,** *f.* suitability, fitness; pertinence, justice.

fügsam ['fy:kza:m], *adj.* adaptive; pliant, supple, yielding, tractable, manageable, docile, obedient, submissive, agreeable. **Fügsamkeit,** *f.* pliancy, submissiveness, docility, tractability, obedience.

Fügung ['fy:guŋ], *f.* arrangement; dispensation (of providence), decree, providence, fate; coincidence, juncture; submission, resignation (***in*** (*Acc.*), to); ***durch eine – Gottes,*** providentially.

fühlbar ['fy:lba:r], *adj.* sensible, tangible, palpable, tactile; noticeable, perceptible, appreciable, considerable, distinct, marked; ***sich – machen,*** make itself felt, be (much) in evidence; ***–er Mangel,*** felt want; ***–er Verlust,*** appreciable *or* serious loss. **Fühlbarkeit,** *f.* sensibility; perceptibility; tangibility, palpability, distinctness.

fühlen ['fy:lən], **1.** *v.t.* feel, perceive, sense, have a sense of, be sensitive to; experience, be aware of; ***ihm den Puls –,*** feel his pulse; ***alles, was lebt, fühlt,*** every living creature has perceptions; ***Lust –,*** be inclined. **2.** *v.r.* ***sich glücklich –,*** feel happy; ***sich wohl –,*** feel content *or* comfortable *or* at ease. **3.** *v.i.* feel; ***mit ihm –,*** feel for him, sympathize with him; ***ihm auf den Zahn –,*** sound him *or* his opinion. **Fühlen,** *n.* feeling, perception, sensation. **Fühler,** *m.* (*Zool.*) feeler, antenna, tentacle; (*fig.*) ***die – ausstrecken,*** put out a feeler.

Fühl|faden, *m.,* **–horn,** *n.* feeler (*of insects*). **fühllos,** *adj.* unreceptive, insensitive (***gegen,*** to), unfeeling.

Fühlung ['fy:luŋ], *f.* (*Mil., fig.*) touch, contact; feel (*of cloth*); ***– mit dem Feinde,*** contact with the enemy; ***in enger – mit,*** in close touch with; ***– halten,*** keep in touch, maintain contact; ***– nehmen (mit),*** get in touch, establish contact (with), (*coll.*) contact. **Fühlungnahme,** *f.* close touch, contact.

fuhr [fu:r], **führe** ['fy:rə], *see* **fahren.**

Fuhre ['fu:rə], *f.* **1.** cart-load, wagon-load; cartful; 2. carrying, carriage, carting, transport, conveyance.

führen ['fy:rən], **1.** *v.t.* conduct, lead, guide, direct; take, convey, carry, bring; handle, manage, control, superintend, (*Mil.*) command; drive, steer (*a vehicle*), pilot (*a plane*); hold (*office*), strike, deal (*a blow etc.*); bear, go by *or* under (*a name*), bear, hold (*a title*); show (*proof*); ***den Artikel – wir nicht,*** we do not stock *or* keep that article; ***die Aufsicht –,*** superintend; invigilate (*at examinations*); ***einen Aufstand –,*** head *or* lead a revolt; ***bei sich –,*** carry about one; ***den Beweis –,*** prove, furnish proof; ***die Bücher –,*** keep the books *or* accounts; ***in den Büchern –,*** carry on the books; ***zu Ende –,*** carry through to the end; ***die Feder –,*** wield the pen, write; ***ihm zu Gemüte –,*** impress on his mind; ***ein Geschäft –,*** carry on *or* run a business; ***ein Gespräch –,*** hold a conversation, converse (***mit,*** with), talk (to); ***den Haushalt –,*** keep house, run the household (*Dat.,* for); ***Klage –,*** complain (***über,*** of), lodge a complaint (about); ***Krieg –,*** wage war (***mit,*** with), make war (on), be at war (with); ***ein Leben –,*** live *or* lead a life; ***hinters Licht –,*** deceive, dupe, hoodwink; ***mit*** or ***bei sich –,*** have with one, carry on one's person; ***zum Munde –,*** raise to one's lips; ***die Hand an die Mütze –,*** touch one's cap; ***zu nichts –,*** come *or* lead to nothing; ***Protokoll –,*** keep the minutes; ***einen Prozeß –,*** (*of litigant*) carry on a lawsuit, (*of lawyer*) conduct a case; ***sein Rad –,*** wheel one's bicycle; ***sonderbare Reden –,*** say strange things, be given to strange utterances; ***das Ruder*** or ***das Regiment*** or ***die Regierung –,*** sit at the helm, govern, rule; (*also fig.*) have the whip hand; ***ein Schiff –,*** navigate a ship; ***etwas im Schilde –,*** have s.th. up one's sleeve, be up to s.th.; ***das Schwert –,*** wear *or* wield the sword; ***den Vorsitz –,*** take the chair; ***ein Wappen –,*** bear *or* have a coat of arms; ***Waren –,*** have *or* carry goods in stock, keep goods, deal in *or* sell goods; ***auf den rechten Weg –,*** put on the right road; ***das Wort –,*** be the spokesman; ***das große Wort –,*** brag, boast; lay down the law. **2.** *v.r.* conduct *or* comport o.s., behave. **3.** *v.i.* lead, be ahead, hold the lead; lead (***nach*** *or* ***zu,*** to); (*fig.*) ***– zu,*** lead to, result in, end in, entail; ***zu nichts –,*** come to nothing, lead nowhere; ***zum Tode –,*** prove fatal.

führend ['fy:rənt], *adj.* leading, (*coll.*) top-ranking; prominent; ***– sein,*** be in the lead, hold the lead, be at the top *or* head; ***–e Stellung,*** position of authority.

Führer ['fy:rər], *m.* leader, chief, head; guide; guide-book; conductor; director, manager; driver; (*Av.*) pilot; (*Nav.*) commander; (*Spt.*) captain; (*Mus.*) fugue-theme. (*Nat. Soc. decree forbade use of the word except for Adolf Hitler unless in compounds. It was the usual way of referring to him, and had the same sort of aura as* 'His Majesty'.) **Führerhaus,** *n.* driver's cab. **führerlos,** *adj.* leaderless; (*Av.*) pilotless; abandoned (*car*). **Führer|prinzip,** *n.* authoritarian principle. **–raum,** *m.* (*Av.*) cockpit, pilot's cabin. **Führerschaft,** *f.* guidance, leadership, direction; the leaders. **Führer|schein,** *m.* driving-licence; pilot's certificate. **–sitz,** *m.* driving *or* driver's seat, cab; (*Av.*) cockpit. **–stand,** *m.* (*Railw. etc.*) driver's cab.

Fuhr|geld, *n.* (charge for) carriage, delivery *or* transport charge. **–geschäft,** *n. See* **–unternehmen. –lohn,** *m. See* **–geld. –mann,** *m.* (*pl.* **-leute**) carrier, carter, haulier; wagoner, driver. **–park,** *m.* (*Mil.*) transport park, vehicle pool; fleet of vehicles.

Führung ['fy:ruŋ], *f.* leading, conducting, guiding; leadership; direction, command, management; control; driving, steering (*a vehicle*), piloting (*a plane*); (*Spt.*) lead; guided tour, visit of inspection; guidance (*towards a goal*); (*Mech.*) guide, slide, (*Artil.*) driving band; conduct, demeanour, behaviour; ***– des Haushalts,*** housekeeping; ***unter der – von,*** under the guidance *or* direction *or* (*Mil.*) command of, headed by; ***die – übernehmen,*** take charge, (*Spt.*) take the lead; (*Spt.*) ***in – sein,*** be in the lead, be leading; ***persönliche –,*** personal record. **Führungs–,** *pref.* (*Mech.*) guide-. **Führungs|stab,** *m.* (*Mil.*) operations staff. **–zeugnis,** *n.* certificate of good conduct; character reference.

Fuhr|unternehmen, *n.* haulage contractors, (*Am.*) trucking company. **–unternehmer,** *m.* haulage contractor, haulier, (*Am.*) trucker, teamster. **–werk,** *n.* vehicle, conveyance; cart, wagon, carriage. **fuhrwerken,** *v.i.* (*coll.*) fidget, create a disturbance. **Fuhrwesen,** *n.* carrying (*Am.* trucking) trade, haulage business.

Fülle ['fylə], *f.* abundance, wealth, profusion, plenty, fullness; corpulence, stoutness, plumpness; intensity, body, richness, depth; ***Hülle und –,*** abundance, plenty (of).

Füllelement ['fylˀelemɛnt], *n.* (*Elec.*) dry-cell.

füllen ['fylən], **1.** *v.t.* fill (up); inflate (*with air etc.*), stuff, cram (*with feathers etc.*), load, charge (*battery etc.*), fill, stop (*teeth*), stuff (*a roast*); ***auf Flaschen –,*** bottle; ***in Säcke –,*** sack, put into bags; ***wieder –,*** replenish; ***gefüllte Nelke,*** double carnation. **2.** *v.r.* fill (up).

Füllen, *n.* foal (*new-born*), colt (*male*), filly (*female*). **Füllenstute,** *f.* brood mare.

Füller ['fylər], *m.* (*coll.*) *see* **Füllfeder. Füll|erde,** *f.* fuller's earth. **–feder,** *f.,* **–federhalter,** *m.* fountain-pen. **–horn,** *n.* horn of plenty, cornucopia. **füllig,** *adj.* plump. **Füll|kelle,** *f.* filling-trowel; ladle. **–masse,** *f.,* **–material, –mittel,** *n.* filling material *or* compound, filler, filling, packing. **–röhre,** *f.* feed-pipe. **–säure,** *f.* accumulator acid, electrolyte.

Füllsel ['fylzəl], *n.* (*Cul.*) stuffing, (*in text*) padding, (*fig.*) stopgap.

Füll|steine, *m.pl.* rubble. **–stoff,** *m. See* **–masse. –strich,** *m.* filling level *or* mark. **–trichter,** *m.* hopper, funnel. **Füllung,** *f.* filling, packing; (*Cul.*) stuffing; stopping, filling (*of teeth*), batch (*of oven*), (*Artil.*) charge; doubling (*of blossom*), panel (*of door etc.*). **Füllwort,** *n.* expletive.

fummeln ['fuməln], *v.i.* (*coll.*) fumble, grope about, fidget (*an* (*Dat.*), with).

Fund [funt], *m.* (**-(e)s,** *pl.* **-e**) finding, discovery; thing found, find; ***einen – tun,*** make a find *or* discovery.

Fundament [funda'mɛnt], *n.* (**-s,** *pl.* **-e**) foundation(s), basis, base(-plate), bed-plate; (*fig.*) foundation, basis, groundwork. **fundamental** [–'ta:l], *adj.* fundamental, basic. **fundamentieren,** *v.t.* lay the foundation(s) for *or* of.

Fund|büro, *n.* lost property office. **–grube,** *f.* fund, mine, storehouse, rich source (*of information etc.*).

fundieren [fun'di:rən], *v.t.* found, endow; establish, consolidate. **fundiert,** *adj.* well-founded, well-grounded, consolidated, (*Comm.*) funded. **Fundierung,** *f.* founding; foundation, establishment, funding.

fündig ['fyndıç], *adj.* ore- *or* oil-bearing, economically worthwhile (*of a mine etc.*).

Fund|ort, *m.* place of discovery *or* where a th. is found; (*Bot., Orn., Zool.*) locality, habitat. **–recht,** *n.* finder's rights. **–unterschlagung,** *f.* (*Law*) larceny by finder.

Fünen ['fy:nən], *n.* (*Geog.*) Fyen.

fünf [fynf], *num.adj.* five; ***– vom hundert,*** five per cent.; ***– gerade sein lassen,*** wink at a th., be not over-particular, stretch a point; (*fig.*) ***– Minuten vor zwölf,*** at the eleventh hour. (*For usage see* **acht.**) **Fünf,** *f.* (-, *pl.* **-en**) the number five; cinque (*at dice*); fives (*a game*); the lowest mark (*at school*), very poor. **Fünfeck,** *n.* pentagon. **fünfeckig,** *adj.* pentagonal. **Fünfelektrodenröhre,** *f.* (*Rad.*) pentode.

Fünfer ['fynfər], *m.* five; five-pfennig piece, coin *or* note of five (marks, pounds, francs, florins *etc.*). **Fünferausschuß,** *m.* committee of five. **fünferlei,** *indecl.adj.* of five (*sorts, ways etc.*); ***das Wort kann – bedeuten,*** the word can have five meanings.

fünf|fach, *adj.* quintuple, fivefold; ***Fünffache(s)***, fivefold *or* five times the amount. **–faltig,** *adj. See* **–fach.**

Fünf|gesang, *m.* quintet. **–gitterröhre,** *f.* (*Rad.*) pentagrid. **fünf|jährig,** *adj.* five-year(-old). **–jährlich,** *adj.* every five years, quinquennial. **–kantig,** *adj.* pentagonal.

Fünfling ['fynflıŋ], *m.* (**-s,** *pl.* **-e**) quintuplet.

fünf|mal, *adv.* five times. **–malig,** *adj.* occurring five times; ***nach –em Besuch,*** after five visits. **Fünfpolröhre,** *f.* (*Rad.*) pentode. **fünf|prozentig,** *adj.* of *or* at *or* yielding five per cent. **–seitig,** *adj.* pentahedral. **–silbig,** *adj.* pentasyllabic. **–stellig,** *adj.* of five digits. **–stimmig,** *adj.* (arranged) for five voices. **–stöckig,** *adj.* five-storeyed.

fünft [fynft], *num.adj.* fifth; ***das –e Rad am Wagen sein,*** be quite superfluous, be in the way, be not wanted. (*For other usages see* **acht.**) **fünfteilig,** *adj.* with *or* of five parts, five-part. **Fünftel,** *n.* fifth (part). **fünftens,** *adv.* fifthly, in the fifth place. **Fünfuhrtee,** *m.* afternoon tea.

fünfzehn ['fynftse:n], *num.adj.* fifteen. **Fünfzehntel,** *n.* fifteenth (part).

fünfzig ['fynftsıç], *num.adj.* fifty. **Fünfziger(in),** *m.* (*f.*) man (woman) in his (her) fifties, quinquagenarian. **fünfzigjährig,** *adj.* fifty-year-old (*person*), fiftieth (*anniversary*). **fünfzigst,** *num.adj.* fiftieth. **Fünfzigstel,** *n.* fiftieth (part).

fungieren [fuŋ'gi:rən], *v.i.* act, function; officiate.

fungös [fuŋ'gø:s], *adj.* fungous, spongy.

Funk [fuŋk, funk], *m.* (**-s,** *no pl.*) radio, wireless.

Funk|anlage, *f.* wireless installation. **–apparat,** *m.* wireless set. **–ausstellung,** *f.* radio exhibition. **–bake,** *f.* radio beacon. **–bastler,** *m.* radio amateur, (*sl.*) ham; home constructor (*of wireless set*). **–bearbeitung,** *f.* radio adaptation. **–bericht,** *m.* radio commentary. **–berichter,** *m.* radio commentator.

Fünkchen ['fynkçən], *n.* (*usu. fig.*) ray, gleam, flicker, grain, vestige (*of hope etc.*).

Funkdienst ['funkdi:nst], *m.* wireless telegraphic service.

Funke ['fuŋkə], *m.* (**-n,** *pl.* **-n**) spark; sparkle, flash, gleam, scintillation; *also fig., see* **Fünkchen. funkeln,** *v.i.* sparkle, glitter, glisten, glint, twinkle, scintillate, shine, flash. **Funkeln,** *n.* sparkle, sparkling; scintillation, glitter, twinkling, coruscation. **funkel(nagel)neu,** *adj.* brand-new.

funken ['fuŋkən], *v.t., v.i.* broadcast, transmit, radio.

Funken, *m. See* **Funke.**

Funken|bildung, *f.* sparking. **–entladung,** *f.* spark discharge. **–fänger,** *m.* spark-catcher (*on locomotives etc.*). **–garbe,** *f.* shower of sparks. **–induktor,** *m.* induction coil. **funkensprühend,** *adj.* sparkling, scintillating. **Funken|strecke,** *f.* spark gap. **–telegraphie,** *f.* wireless *or* radio telegraphy.

Funkentstörung ['funkʔɛntʃtø:ruŋ], *f.* (*Rad.*) interference suppression. **Funker,** *m.* radio-operator, wireless operator, telegraphist. **funkferngesteuert,** *adj.* radio *or* remote controlled. **Funk|fernpeilung,** *f.* (*Naut., Av.*) long-range navigation (LORAN). **–feuer,** *n.* radio beacon. **–frequenz,** *f.* radio-frequency. **–gerät,** *n. See* **–apparat. –haus,** *n.* broadcasting studios. **–ortung,** *f.* radiolocation. **–peilung,** *f.* radio direction finding. **–sender,** *m.* wireless transmitter. **–sendung,** *f.* transmission. **–spruch,** *m.* wireless message, radiogram. **–station, –stelle,** *f.* wireless *or* radio *or* broadcasting station. **–steuerung,** *f.* remote control. **–techniker,** *m.* radio engineer.

Funktion [fuŋktsi'o:n], *f.* function (*also Math.*); role, office; ***in – treten,*** (*of a th.*) act, serve, function, (*of a p.*) take charge *or* (*coll.*) over, officiate. **Funktionär** [–'nɛ:r], *m.* (**-s,** *pl.* **-e**) functionary, official. **funktionell,** *adj.* functional. **funktionieren,** *v.i.* act, function, operate; (*coll.*) work. **Funktions|bedingung,** *f.* conditions of operation. **–störung,** *f.* functional disturbance. **–zulage,** *f.* additional emolument, perquisite.

Funk|turm, *m.* wireless *or* radio mast. **–verbindung,** *f.* radio communication *or* contact. **–zeitung,** *f.* radio periodical, published radio programmes.

Funsel ['funsəl], **Funzel** ['funtsəl], *f.* (-, *no pl.*) (*coll.*) poor *or* dim *or* miserable lamp, guttering candle.

für [fy:r], **1.** *prep.* (*Acc.*) for; instead of, in place *or* lieu of, in exchange *or* return for; in favour of; for the sake *or* benefit of, on behalf of; ***ein – allemal,*** once and for all; ***–s erste,*** (in the) first (place), for a start, for the present; ***– Ernst halten,*** take seriously; ***es – gut halten,*** consider it (to be) a good thing, deem it advisable; ***ich habe es – mein Leben gern,*** I like it above all things; ***ich – meine Person,*** as for me, I for my part, I for one; ***– sich,*** in an undertone, under one's breath, (*Theat.*) aside; ***an und – sich,*** properly speaking, of *or* in itself; ***– sich arbeiten,*** work for o.s.; ***es hat etwas – sich,*** there is s.th. about *or* in it, there is s.th. *or* much to be said for it; ***sich – sich halten,*** keep o.s. to o.s., be *or* stand aloof; ***– sich leben,*** live alone *or* by o.s.; ***eine S. – sich,*** quite another matter, another matter altogether, a separate question, a matter apart; ***Stück – Stück,*** piece by piece, taken individually; ***Schritt – Schritt,*** step by step; ***Tag (Jahr) – Tag (Jahr),*** day (year) in day (year) out, day (year) by *or* after day (year); ***was waren das – Fragen?*** what kind of questions were those? ***was – ein Mann?*** what sort of a man? ***was – Leute auch da sein mögen,*** whatever kind of people may be there; ***er hat viele Bücher, aber was – welche!*** he has a lot of books, but what trash! ***Wort – Wort,*** word by word, one word at a time. **2.** *adv.* (*obs., Poet.*) =

vor; – *und* –, for ever and ever, for good. **Für,** *n. das* – *und Wider,* the pros and cons.

Furage [fu'ra:ʒə], *f.* (*Mil.*) forage; fodder. **furagieren** [–'ʒi:rən], *v.i.* go foraging, forage.

fürbaß ['fyrbas], *adv.* (*obs.*) further, forward, on.

Fürbitte ['fy:rbɪtə], *f.* intercession; *eine – einlegen,* intercede, plead (*bei,* with); *öffentliche* –, public prayers.

Furche ['furçə], *f.* furrow; wrinkle; groove, channel. **furchen,** *v.t.* furrow; groove; wrinkle, crease, knit (*the brow etc.*). **Furchen|bildung,** *f.* segmentation, furrowing, cleavage. **–rain,** *m.* ridge.

Furcht [furçt], *f.* fear, terror, dread, apprehension, awe (*vor* (*Dat.*), of), fright, anxiety; – *haben vor,* be afraid of, stand in fear of; *außer sich vor* –, frightened out of one's senses *or* wits; *aus – vor,* for fear of; *ihn in – setzen, ihm – einflößen,* intimidate *or* terrify *or* frighten him. **furchtbar,** *adj.* frightful, terrible, awful, dreadful; formidable, fearful; (*coll.*) *er ist – klug* (*freundlich*), he is awfully clever (kind).

fürchten ['fyrçtən], **1.** *v.t., v.i.* fear, be afraid *or* apprehensive of; be terrified of *or* by, dread, stand in dread *or* awe of; *es ist* or *steht zu* –, it is to be feared; – *für,* fear for, be anxious about. **2.** *v.r.* be afraid, stand in fear (*vor* (*Dat.*), of). **fürchterlich,** *adj.* fearful, frightful, horrible, terrible, dreadful, horrid, appalling.

furchterregend ['furçtˀɛrre:gənt], *adj.* frightening, terrifying, alarming, formidable. **furchtlos,** *adj.* fearless, intrepid, undaunted, unflinching. **Furchtlosigkeit,** *f.* fearlessness, intrepidity. **furchtsam,** *adj.* timid, timorous, faint-hearted, fearful. **Furchtsamkeit,** *f.* timidity, timorousness, faint-heartedness.

fürder(hin) ['fyrdər(hɪn)], *adv.* (*obs.*) *see* **ferner(hin).**

Furie ['fu:riə], *f.* fury, termagant, virago.

Furier [fu'ri:r], *m.* (**-s,** *pl.* **-e**) (*Mil.*) quartermaster-sergeant.

Furnier [fur'ni:r], *n.* (**-s,** *pl.* **-e**) veneer. **furnieren,** *v.t.* inlay, veneer. **Furnierholz,** *n.* wood for inlaying, veneer.

fürliebnehmen [fyr'li:pne:mən], *irr.v.i.* be content, (*coll.*) put up (*mit,* with).

Furore [fu'ro:rə], *n.* (**-s,** *no pl.*) sensation, furore, (*coll.*) noise, splash; *er hat – gemacht,* he has created (quite) a sensation.

Fürsorge ['fy:rzɔrgə], *f.* care, solicitude; *öffentliche* –, public relief *or* assistance; *soziale* –, social welfare. **Fürsorge|amt,** *n.* welfare centre. **–arbeit,** *f.* social *or* welfare work. **–erziehung,** *f.* education in a remand home. **Fürsorger(in),** *m.* (*f.*) social *or* welfare worker. **fürsorglich,** *adj.* careful, solicitous.

Fürsprache ['fy:rʃpra:xə], *f.* intercession, plea, advocacy; mediation, recommendation. **Fürsprech,** *m.* (*Swiss*), **Fürsprecher,** *m.* advocate, intercessor.

Fürst [fyrst], *m.* (**-en,** *pl.* **-en**) prince, sovereign. **Fürstbischof,** *m.* prince bishop (*with sovereign rights*). **Fürsten|geschlecht, –haus,** *n.* dynasty, royal line. **–stand,** *m.,* sovereign *or* princely rank. **Fürstentum,** *n.* principality. **Fürsten|würde,** *f. See* **–stand. Fürstin,** *f.* princess. **fürstlich,** *adj.* princely (*also fig.*), (*fig.*) grand, magnificent, sumptuous, generous, lavish; *–e Durchlaucht,* Serene Highness; *–es Trinkgeld,* (over-)generous tip. **Fürstlichkeit,** *f.* **1.** princeliness; magnificence; **2.** *pl.* princely personages.

Furt [furt], *f.* (-, *pl.* **-en**) ford.

Furunkel [fu'ruŋkəl], *m.* furuncle, boil. **furunkulös** [–'lø:s], *adj.* furuncular.

fürwahr [fyr'va:r], *adv.* indeed, in truth, truly, (*obs.*) forsooth, verily.

Fürwitz ['fy:rvɪts], *m.* (*obs.*) *see* **Vorwitz.**

Fürwort ['fy:rvɔrt], *n.* pronoun.

Furz [furts], *m.* (**-es,** *pl.* **¨-e**) (*vulg.*) fart. **furzen,** *v.i.* fart.

fusche(l)n ['fuʃə(l)n], *v.i.* **1.** handle dexterously, make rapid *or* cunning movements (*usu. with intent to deceive*); **2.** (*dial.*) *see* **pfuschen. Fuscherei** [–'raɪ], *f.* sleight-of-hand.

Fusel ['fu:zəl], *m.* fusel oil; (*coll.*) cheap spirits.

füsilieren [fyzi'li:rən], *v.t.* (*Mil.*) shoot, execute by firing squad.

Fusion [fuzi'o:n], *f.* (*Chem.*) fusion, (*fig., Comm.*) merger, amalgamation, consolidation. **fusionieren** [–'ni:rən], *v.t., v.r.* merge, amalgamate, consolidate.

Fuß [fu:s], *m.* (**-es,** *pl.* **¨-e**) foot, (*Anat.*) tarsus; footing, basis; foot, bottom, base; pedestal; leg (*of chair*); stem (*of a glass*); foot (*measure*); *auf den Füßen,* up, not in bed, on one's legs; *auf die Füße bringen,* raise (*troops etc.*); *sich die Füße abrennen,* run o.s. off one's feet; *sein Haus mit keinem – mehr betreten,* never set foot in his house again; *der Boden brennt mir unter den Füßen,* it's getting too hot for me; *ihm den Boden unter den Füßen entziehen,* cut the ground from under his feet; *den Boden unter den Füßen verlieren,* have the ground cut from under one's feet; *festen –es,* without stirring, unflinchingly; *fest auf den Füßen,* sure-footed; (*festen*) *– fassen,* gain a foothold, get a (firm) footing, establish o.s.; *ihm auf dem –e folgen,* follow close *or* hard on his heels; *auf freiem –e,* at liberty, at large; *auf freien – setzen,* release, set at liberty; *auf gleichem –e,* on the same footing, on equal terms; *auf großem – leben,* live in grand style; *auf gutem –e stehen,* be on good terms (*mit,* with); *die S. hat weder Hand noch* –, the th. is without rhyme or reason; *er wehrte sich* or *sträubte sich mit Händen und Füßen,* he defended himself tooth and nail; *ihm auf die Füße helfen,* help him up, assist him; (*coll.*) *er ist* (*heute*) *mit dem linken –e zuerst aufgestanden,* (today) he got out of bed on the wrong side, he is irritable *or* bad-tempered; *sich* (*Dat.*) *den – verstauchen,* sprain one's ankle; *auf eigenen Füßen stehen,* be self-supporting *or* independent, stand on one's own feet; *auf schwachen Füßen,* on a weak *or* unsound *or* shaky foundation; *auf gespanntem –e mit ihm,* on bad terms with him; *stehenden –es,* immediately; *mehrere – hoch,* several feet high; *mit dem –e stoßen,* kick; *ihm auf die Füße treten,* tread on his toes (*lit. or fig.*) *or* corns (*only fig.*); *mit Füßen treten,* trample *or* tread underfoot, (*coll.*) walk over, spurn; *trocknen –es,* dry-shod; *sich auf die Füße machen,* take to one's heels; *auf vertrautem –e,* on intimate terms; *vor die Füße werfen,* reject with disdain; *zu* –, on foot; *zu – gehen,* go on foot; walk; *zu – erreichbar,* within walking distance; *Soldat zu* –, foot-soldier; *schlecht zu –e sein,* be a poor walker, be bad on one's feet; *sich ihm zu Füßen werfen,* throw o.s. at his feet; *sich die Füße wund laufen,* get blisters on one's feet.

Fuß|abstreifer, *m.* door-mat, scraper. **–angel,** *f.* mantrap, (*Hist.*) caltrop. **–ball,** *m.* football. **–ballen,** *m.* ball of the foot. **–bänder,** *n.pl.* **1.** tarsal ligaments; **2.** (*Falconry*) jesses. **–bank,** *f.* footstool. **–bekleidung,** *f.* footwear. **–beuge, –biege,** *f.* instep. **–blatt,** *n.* flat *or* sole of the foot. **–blech,** *n.* snatch block. **–boden,** *m.* floor; ground; flooring. **–bodenbelag,** *m.* floor covering, flooring. **–bodenfläche,** *f.* floor space, floorage. **–brand,** *m.* (*Med.*) trench foot. **–breit,** *m. ein – Landes,* a foot of ground; *keinen – weichen,* not budge an inch. **–bremse,** *f.* (*Motor.*) foot-brake. **–brett,** *n.* pedal. **–decke,** *f.* coverlet (*for the feet*), travelling-rug; bedside rug, mat. **–eisen,** *n.* mantrap; fetters, shackles; shoe iron, calkin (*on shoes etc.*).

Fussel ['fusəl], *f.* (-, *pl.* **-n**) (*coll.*) fluff.

füßeln ['fysəln], *v.i.* (*coll.*) toddle, shuffle along; shuffle with one's feet; (*sl.*) play footsie (*under the table*).

fußen ['fu:sən], *v.i.* depend, rely, rest, be based (*auf* (*Dat.*), on).

Fuß|ende, *n.* foot (*of bed etc.*). **–fall,** *m.* prostration; *einen – tun vor ihm,* prostrate o.s. before him, throw o.s. at *or* fall prostrate at his feet. **fuß|fällig,** *adv.* prostrate, on one's knees; *– bitten,* beg on one's knees, plead humbly. **–frei,** *adj.* ankle-length (*skirt*). **Fuß|gänger,** *m.* pedestrian. **–garde,** *f.* (*Mil.*) footguards. **–gelenk,** *n.* ankle (joint), fetlock (*of horse*). **–gestell,** *n.* pedestal, base, foot; trestle. **–latscher,** *m.* (*coll.*) foot-slogger. **–leiste,** *f.* skirting board.

Füßling ['fyslɪŋ], *m.* (**-s,** *pl.* **-e**) foot (*of stocking*).

Fuß|note, *f.* footnote, annotation. **–pflege,** *f.* chiropody, pedicure. **–punkt,** *m.* (*Astr.*) nadir. **–register,** *n.* pedal-stop (*organ*). **–reiniger,** *m.* scraper, doormat. **–reise,** *f.* walking-tour. **–rücken,** *m.* instep. **–sack,** *m.* foot-muff. **–schemel,** *m.* footstool. **–sohle,** *f.* sole of the foot. **–spann,** *m.* instep. **–spitze,** *f.* tip-toe. **–spur,** *f.* footprint, footstep, footmark, track. **–standbild,** *n.* pedestrian statue. **–stapfe,** *f.* *See* **–spur.** **–steig,** *m.* pavement, footpath, (*Am.*) sidewalk. **–stütze,** *f.* foot-rest, (*Med.*) arch-support. **–taste,** *f.* organ-pedal. **–tritt,** *m.* 1. kick; (*coll.*) ***einen – bekommen,*** get kicked out, (*sl.*) get the boot; 2. (sound of a) footstep; 3. footboard (*of carriages*); 4. treadle. **–volk,** *n.* foot-soldiers, infantry. **–wanderung,** *f.* walking-tour, hike. **–wanne,** *f.* foot bath, slipper bath. **–weg,** *m.* footpath. **–wurzel,** *f.* (*Anat.*) tarsus.

Fustage [fus'ta:ʒə], *f.* casks, barrels.

futsch [futʃ], *int., pred.adj.* (*coll.*) gone, lost, ruined, broken, done for, (*sl.*) phut.

[1]**Futter** ['futər], *n.* (*of animals only except sl.*) food, fodder, feed; (*sl.*) grub; ***in gutem – stehen,*** be well fed; (*Mil.*) ***– fassen,*** go foraging.

[2]**Futter,** *n.* lining, casing; sheath; (*Mech.*) chuck; bushing.

Futteral [futə'ra:l], *n.* (**-(e)s,** *pl.* **-e**) case; box; sheath.

Futter|beutel, *m.* nose-bag. **–boden,** *m.* hay-loft. **–bohne,** *f.* horse bean. **–brei,** *m.* mash. **–gerste,** *f.* feed barley. **–hafer,** *m.* feed oats. **–kasten,** *m.* feed-box. **–kraut,** *n.* green fodder. **–krippe,** *f.* crib, manger; (*coll.*) remunerative post. **–krippenjäger,** *m.* (*coll.*) placeman, (*Am.*) spoilsman. **–krippensystem,** *n.* (*coll.*) spoils system.

futtern ['futərn], *v.i.* (*coll.*) eat heartily *or* ravenously; (*sl.*) tuck in, stuff o.s.

füttern ['fytərn], *v.t.* 1. feed; 2. line (*coat etc.*), pad, stuff; (*Mech.*) sheathe, case.

Futter|neid, *m.* professional jealousy. **–pflanze,** *f.* forage plant, green fodder. **–rübe,** *f.* (*Bot.*) turnip (*Brassica rapa*). **–sack,** *m.* *See* **–beutel.** **–saft,** *m.* royal jelly, brood food (*bees*). **–seide,** *f.* lining silk. **–stoff,** *m.* lining (material). **–stroh,** *n.* feeding straw. **–tisch,** *m.* bird-table. **–trog,** *m.* feeding-trough, manger.

Fütterung ['fytəruŋ], *f.* 1. feed, fodder, provender, forage; 2. lining, padding, sheathing, casing.

Futter|wicke, *f.* (*Bot.*) common vetch (*Vicia sativa*). **–wiese,** *f.* meadow cultivated for fodder. **–zeug,** *n.* *See* **–stoff.**

Futur [fu'tu:r], *n.* *See* **Futurum.** **Futurismus** [–'rɪsmus], *m.* futurism, modernism (*in art*). **futuristisch,** *adj.* futuristic, modernistic. **Futurum,** *n.* (**-s,** *pl.* **Futura**) (*Gram.*) future (tense).

G

G, g [ge:], *n.* letter G, (*Mus.*) G; ***der G-Schlüssel,*** the treble clef; ***G-Dur,*** G-major; ***G-moll,*** G-minor.

gab [ga:p], *see* **geben.**

Gabbro ['gabro], *m.* (*Geol.*) gabbro, igneous *or* plutonic rock. **Gabbrochaussierung,** *f.* macadamized surface (*of a road*).

Gabe ['ga:bə], *f.* gift, present, donation; offering, gratuity; (*Med.*) dose; gift, talent, endowment; ***milde –,*** alms, charity.

gäbe ['gɛ:bə], *see* **geben.**

Gabel ['ga:bəl], *f.* (-, *pl.* **-n**) fork, pitchfork; prong; (*Bot.*) tendril, (*Artil.*) bracket; (*Naut.*) crutch; *pl.* shafts (*of a cart etc.*); (front *or* rear) fork (*of a bicycle*); bifurcation.

Gabel|anker, *m.* grapnel, small bow-anchor; cramp-iron. **–bäume,** *m.pl.* *See* **–deichsel.** **–bein,** *n.* wish-bone, furcula. **–bildung,** *f.* forking, bifurcation, (*Artil.*) bracketing. **–bissen,** *m.* titbit. **–deichsel,** *f.* pair of shafts. **gabelförmig,** *adj.* forked, bifurcated, (*Bot.*) furcate, dichotomous. **Gabel|frühstück,** *n.* warm snack. **–geweih,** *n.* forked antlers. **–hirsch,** *m.* brocket. **gabelig,** *adj.* forked, branched, furcate, bifurcated, fork-like, pronged. **Gabel|knochen,** *m.* *See* **–bein.** **–kopf,** *m.* (*Cycl.*) crown. **–maß,** *n.* calliper. **–motor,** *m.* V-engine.

gabeln ['ga:bəln], **1.** *v.t.* fork; pitchfork; impale, gore. **2.** *v.r.* fork, branch *or* fork off, bifurcate. **3.** *v.i.* (*coll.*) ***tüchtig –,*** eat heartily.

Gabel|pferd, *n.* shaft-horse, wheeler. **–röhre,** *f.* branched *or* forked pipe. **–scheiden,** *f.pl.* (*Cycl.*) fork blades. **–schwanz,** *m.* (*Ent.*) puss moth (*Dicranura vinula*). **–spaltung,** *f.* *See* **–teilung.** **–stapler,** *m.* fork(-lift) truck. **–stütze,** *f.* forked support, bipod. **–teilung,** *f.* *See* **Gabelung.**

Gabelung ['ga:bəluŋ], *f.* forking, bifurcation, dichotomy.

Gabel|weihe, *m.* (*Orn.*) kite (*Milvus milvus*). **–zinke,** *f.* prong (*of a fork*).

Gabler ['ga:blər], *m.* *See* **Gabelhirsch.**

Gackelei [gakə'laɪ], *f.*, **Gackeln** ['gakəln], *n.* cackling, clucking; chatter. **gackeln, gackern, gacksen,** *v.i.* cackle, cluck; (*sl.*) chatter, prattle.

Gaden ['ga:dən], *m. or n.* (*dial.*) one-roomed house *or* hut; (*Scots*) single-end.

Gaffel ['gafəl], *f.* (-, *pl.* **-n**), **Gaffelbaum,** *m.* (*Naut.*) gaff.

gaffen ['gafən], *v.i.* gape, stare. **Gaffer,** *m.* gaper, idle onlooker *or* bystander.

Gagat [ga'ga:t], *m. or n.* (**-s,** *pl.* **-e**) jet, black amber.

Gage ['ga:ʒə], *f.* salary, fee, honorarium (*esp. of actors*).

Gagel ['ga:gəl], *m.* (*Bot.*) bog myrtle, sweet gale (*Myrica gale*).

gäh [gɛ:], *adj.* (*dial.*) *see* **jäh.**

gähnen ['gɛ:nən], *v.i.* yawn; (*coll.*) gape. **Gähnen,** *n.* yawning. **Gähnkrampf,** *m.* fit of yawning.

Gais, *f.* *See* **Geiß.**

Gala ['ga:la], *f.* court-, gala- *or* full-dress; (*coll.*) party clothes, evening dress; ***sich in – werfen,*** dress (*for a party*). **Gala|anzug,** *m.* *See* **Gala.** **–ball,** *m.* (full-)dress ball. **–kleid,** *n.* *See* **Gala**; *pl.* state robes.

Galan [ga'la:n], *m.* (**-s,** *pl.* **-e**) lover, beau, gallant, swain.

galant [ga'lant], *adj.* gallant, courteous; amorous, amatory; ***–es Abenteuer,*** affair of the heart; (*coll.*) ***–e Krankheit,*** syphilis. **Galanterie** [–tə'ri:], *f.* gallantry, courtesy. **Galanterie|arbeit,** *f.* *See* **–waren.** **–degen,** *m.* dress sword. **–waren,** *f.pl.* fancy goods, imitation *or* dress jewellery, trinkets, (*Am.*) notions.

Galater ['ga:latər], *pl.* (*B.*) Galatians.

Gala|uniform, *f.* full-dress uniform. **–vorstellung,** *f.* (*Theat.*) gala *or* special performance. **–wagen,** *m.* state coach. **–zimmer,** *n.* state room.

Gäle ['gɛ:lə], *m.* Gael.

Galeere [ga'le:rə], *f.* galley. **Galeeren|sklave, –sträfling,** *m.* galley-slave.

Galeone [gale'o:nə], *f.* galleon.

Galeote [gale'o:tə], *f.* galiot, small coasting-vessel.

Galerie [galə'ri:], *f.* (*Theat., Min., Mil.*) gallery; balcony (*cheapest theatre seats*); ***für die – spielen,*** play to the gallery *or* (*Am.*) grandstand. **Galeriewald,** *m.* (*Geog.*) galleria.

Galgen ['galgən], *m.* gallows, gibbet; cross-beam, horse; *geh' an den –!* be hanged to you! *dafür an den – kommen,* be hanged *or* (*coll.*) swing for it; *sein Bild ist an den – geschlagen,* he was executed in effigy; *es steht – und Rad darauf,* it is a capital crime. **Galgen|bube,** *m.* rascal, rogue, scoundrel, ne'er-do-well, good-for-nothing, scalliwag. **–frist,** *f.* short grace *or* delay, respite. **–gesicht,** *n.* hang-dog look. **–humor,** *m.* grim humour. **–männlein,** *n.* (*Bot.*) mandrake (*Mandragora*). **–strick, –vogel,** *m.* 1. gallows-bird; 2. *See* **–bube.**

Galiläa [gali'lɛ:a], *n.* (*B.*) Galilee. **Galiläer,** *m.*, **galiläisch,** *adj.* Galilean.

Galion [gali'o:n], *n.* (**-s,** *pl.* **-e** *or* **-s**) figurehead (*of a ship*). **Galione,** *f. See* **Galeone. Galionsfigur,** *f.* figurehead.

Galiote, *f. See* **Galeote.**

gälisch ['gɛ:liʃ], *adj.* Gaelic.

Galizien [ga'li:tsiən], *n.* (*Geog.*) Galicia.

Gallapfel ['gal?apfəl], *m.* gall-nut, oak-apple. **Gallapfelsäure,** *f.* gallic acid.

Galle ['galə], *f.* 1. gall, bile; bad temper, asperity, rancour, venom, spite, choler; *seine – ausschütten,* vent one's spleen; *Gift und – speien* or *spucken* or *sein,* give vent to one's rage; *die – läuft ihm über,* his blood is up *or* boils; 2. (*Metall.*) flaw (*in casting etc.*), blister, defect; 3. marshy *or* stony place (*in fields*); 4. (*Bot., horses*) protuberance, swelling. **galleführend,** *adj.* bilious.

Gallen, St. [zaŋkt 'galən], *n.* (*Geog.*) St. Gall.

Gallen|ader, *f.* (*Anat.*) cystic vein. **–anfall,** *m.* bilious attack. **gallenbitter,** *adj.* bitter as gall, acrid. **Gallen|blase,** *f.* gall-bladder. **–brechen,** *n.* bilious vomiting, cholemesis. **–fett,** *n.* cholesterin. **–fieber,** *n.* bilious fever. **–gang,** *m.* bile duct. **–krankheit,** *f.*, **–leiden,** *n.* bilious complaint. **–seife,** *f.* ox-gall soap. **–stein,** *m.* gallstone, biliary calculus. **–steinoperation,** *f.* cholecystotomy. **–sucht,** *f.* jaundice. **gallensüchtig,** *adj.* choleric; melancholic; bilious. **Gallenweg,** *m.* bile-duct.

Gallert ['galərt], *n.* (**-(e)s,** *pl.* **-e**) gelatine; jelly. **gallertartig,** *adj.* gelatinous, colloidal. **Gallerte,** *f. See* **Gallert.**

Gallien ['galiən], *n.* (*Hist.*) Gaul. **Gallier,** *m.* Gaul (*inhabitant*).

gallikanisch [gali'ka:niʃ], *adj.* French Catholic.

gallisch ['galɪʃ], *adj.* (*Hist.*) Gallic, Gaulish.

Gallizismus [gali'tsɪsmus], *m.* Gallicism.

Gallone [ga'lo:nə], *f.* gallon.

Gallsucht ['galzuxt], *f. See* **Gallensucht. gallsüchtig,** *adj. See* **gallensüchtig.**

Gallus ['galus], *m. der heilige –,* St. Gall (*saint*).

Galmei [gal'maɪ], *m.* (**-(e)s,** *pl.* **-e**) zinc ore, calamine.

Galon [ga'lɔ̃], *m.* (**-s,** *pl.* **-s**), **Galone** [–'lo:nə], *f.* (*Austr.*) gold *or* silver lace, braid; galloon. **galonieren** [–'ni:rən], *v.t.* trim with lace *or* braid; *galonierte Diener,* liveried servants.

Galopp [ga'lɔp], *m.* (**-s,** *pl.* **-s** *or* **-e**) gallop; galop (*dance*); *in – setzen,* put to a gallop; *im –,* at a gallop, galloping, (*fig.*) at full speed; *in gestrecktem –,* at full gallop; *er erledigte die Arbeit im –,* he raced through the work; *im kurzen – reiten,* canter. **galoppieren** [–'pi:rən], *v.i.* gallop; *–de Schwindsucht,* galloping consumption; phthisis florida.

Galosche [ga'lɔʃə], *f.* galosh, overshoe.

[1]**galt** [galt], *adj. See* **gelt.**

[2]**galt, gälte** ['gɛltə], *see* **gelten.**

galvanisch [gal'va:nɪʃ], *adj.* galvanic; *–e Kette,* voltaic couple *or* cell; *–e Plattierung,* electroplating. **galvanisieren** [–ni'zi:rən], *v.t.* galvanize, electroplate. **Galvanisierung,** *f.* galvanization, electroplating. **Galvanismus** [–'nɪsmus], *m.* galvanism. **Galvano,** *n.* (**-s,** *pl.* **-s**) (*Typ.*) electrotype, (*coll.*) electro. **Galvanoplastik,** *f.* electrodeposition, electrotyping.

Gamasche [ga'maʃə], *f.* gaiter, legging, spat; (*sl.*) *ich hatte höllische –n,* I was in an awful funk. **Gamaschendienst,** *m.* (*Mil. sl.*) square bashing.

Gambe ['gambə], *f.* bass-viol, viola da gamba.

Gamet [ga'me:t], *m.* (**-s,** *pl.* **-e**) (*Biol.*) gamete.

Gams [gams], *f.* (-, *pl.* **-en**) (*dial.*) *see* **Gemse.**

Ganerbe ['gan?ɛrbə], *m.* (*dial., obs.*) joint-heir; co-proprietor.

Gang [gaŋ], *m.* (**-(e)s,** *pl.* **⸚e**) 1. motion, movement, action, operation, running, working, process, procedure; course (*of disease, the planets, a lawsuit, dinner, a river*); progress; action (*of a drama*); flow, cadence (*of verse*); errand, commission, (*Scots*) message; carriage, gait, pace; stroll, walk; *im – bleiben,* keep going *or* moving; *in – bringen* or *setzen,* set going, set in motion, put into operation, (*fig.*) set on foot, launch, introduce; *– der Dinge,* way of the world; *– der Ereignisse,* course *or* march of events; *die S. muß nun ihren – gehen* or *nehmen,* the matter must now take its course; *gewohnheitsmäßiger –,* routine; *in vollem –e,* in full swing; *in – kommen,* get going *or* moving *or* into action; *man lauert auf alle seine Gänge,* his every movement is watched; *das Pferd hat einen guten –,* the horse has good action; *in – sein,* be in operation, be running *or* working, (*fig.*) be in progress, be under way, be afoot; *ruhiger –,* smooth running (*of an engine*); *in – setzen,* see *in – bringen*; *einen – tun,* go *or* run an errand; *vergeblicher –,* fool's errand; 2. path, alley, avenue, way, gangway, aisle; hall, passage, corridor, gallery, arcade, colonnade; (*Min.*) lode, vein; (*Anat.*) canal, duct; passage (*of music, of arms*); (*Fort.*) *bedeckter –,* sap, mine; covered way, (*Archit.*) portico; *unterirdischer –,* underground passage; 3. (*Spt.*) bout, round; 4. (*Motor.*) gear; stroke (*of an engine*); *außer –, sein,* be out of gear, idle; *erster* (*dritter*) *–,* bottom (top) gear; *toter –,* steering play, backlash; 5. worm, thread, pitch (*of a screw*); *Anzahl der Gänge auf den Zoll,* threads per inch (*of a screw*).

gang, *pred. adj. – und gäbe,* customary, usual, the usual thing; *durchaus – und gäbe,* nothing out of the ordinary.

Gangart ['gaŋ?art], *f.* 1. gait, walk, action, pace; 2. (*Geol.*) gange, matrix. **gangbar,** *adj.* (*of route*) practicable, passable; customary, usual, prevalent; (*of coin*) current; (*of goods*) marketable, saleable; *–e Artikel,* staple commodities; *Wasserröhren – erhalten,* keep water-pipes in order. **Gangbarkeit,** *f.* practicability; currency; saleability. **Gangbildung,** *f.* lode-formation.

Gängelband ['gɛŋəlbant], *n.* leading-strings. **gängeln,** *v.t.* (*fig.*) lead by the nose.

Gang|gewicht, *n.* weight (*driving a clock*). **–hebel,** *m. See* **–schalter. –höhe,** *f.* pitch (*of a screw*).

gängig ['gɛŋɪç], *adj.* saleable, in great demand (*goods*), common, current (*expression*), swift, quick, fleet (*as a horse*); *–er Hund,* well-trained dog.

Ganglien ['gaŋliən], *n.pl.* (*Anat.*) ganglia.

Gangrän [gaŋ'grɛ:n], *n.* (**-s,** *no pl.*) (*Med.*) gangrene.

Gang|schalter, *m.* gear lever. **–schaltung,** *f.* gear shift *or* change. **–spill,** *n.* capstan.

Gangster ['gɛŋstər], *m.* gangster. **Gangsterbande,** *f.* gang (*of criminals*).

Gang|unterschied, *m.* (*Elec.*) phase difference. **–werk,** *n.* driving-gear, machinery, machine; works, movement (*of a clock*). **–woche,** *f.* (*R.C.*) Rogation week.

Gans [gans], *f.* (-, *pl.* **⸚e**) goose (*in general, but properly female only*); *dumme –,* ninny, silly girl; *goldene –,* foolish young heiress; (*Prov.*) *die Gänse gehen überall barfuß,* human nature is always the same; *er ist so dumm, daß ihn die Gänse beißen,* he can't say bo to a goose; *aussehen wie eine –, wenn es blitzt* or *donnert,* look like a dying duck in a thunderstorm.

Gänschen ['gɛnsçən], *n.* 1. gosling; 2. silly young girl.

Gänse|adler, *m.* (*Orn.*) erne, sea-eagle (*Haliaetus albicilla*). **–blümchen,** *n.*, **–blume,** *f.* (*Bot.*) daisy (*Bellis perennis*). **–braten,** *m.* roast goose. **–feder,** *f.* goose-feather, quill. **–fett,** *n.* goose oil. **–füßchen,** *n.pl.* inverted commas, quotation marks. **–geier,** *m.* (*Orn.*) griffon-vulture (*Gyps fulvus*).

-haut, *f.* goose-pimples, goose-flesh, (*coll.*) the creeps. **-kiel,** *m.* goose-quill. **-klein,** *n.* giblets. **-küchlein, -küken,** *n.* gosling. **-leberpastete,** *f.* pâté de foie gras. **-marsch,** *m.* single file; follow-my-leader (*game*).

Gänserich ['gɛnsərɪç], *m.* (**-s,** *pl.* **-e**) gander.

Gänse|schmalz, *n.* goose oil. **-säger,** *m.* (*Orn.*) goosander, (*Am.*) merganser (*Mergus merganser*). **-spiel,** *n.* game of fox and geese. **-wein,** *m.* (*hum.*) Adam's ale (*water*).

Gant [gant], *f.* (-, *pl.* **-en**) (*dial.*) auction of bankrupt's property; ***auf die – kommen,*** go bankrupt. **Gant|anwalt,** *m.* trustee in bankruptcy. **-buch,** *n.* inventory of a (bankrupt) sale. **ganten,** *v.i.* institute a legal execution; ***um eine S. –,*** bid for a th. at an auction. **Gant|haus,** *n.* auction-mart. **-mann,** *m.* bankrupt. **-masse,** *f.* bankrupt's estate. **-recht,** *n.* law of bankruptcy; auction laws. **-schuldner,** *m. See* **-mann.**

Ganymed [gany'me:t], *m.* Ganymede.

ganz [gants], **1.** *adj.* whole, entire, undivided, complete, intact, full, total; ***-e zwanzig Sekunden,*** for fully twenty seconds *or* (*coll.*) all of twenty seconds; ***der -e Betrag,*** the full amount, the total; ***es ist mein -er Ernst,*** I am quite serious; I really mean it; ***in -er Figur,*** full length (*portrait etc.*); ***von -em Herzen,*** with all my heart; ***-e Länge,*** total *or* overall length; ***-er Mann,*** real man, downright good fellow; ***die -e Nacht hindurch,*** all through the night, all night long; (*Mus.*) ***-e Note,*** semibreve; ***die -e Welt,*** all the world, the whole world; ***in der -en Welt,*** all over the world; ***-e Zahl,*** whole number, integer; ***die -e Zeit,*** all the time. **2.** *adv.* quite, wholly, altogether, entirely, completely, perfectly, thoroughly, all; ***– anders,*** altogether *or* entirely *or* quite different, quite another thing; ***– besonders,*** all the more so, more especially; ***– bezahlen,*** pay in full; ***– fremd,*** an utter stranger; ***sie war – Freude,*** she was overjoyed *or* full of joy; ***– und gar,*** totally, wholly, absolutely; ***– und gar nicht,*** not at all, by no means, not in the least; ***– und gar nichts,*** nothing at all; ***– gewiß,*** most certainly *or* assuredly, absolutely; ***– gleich,*** all the same, quite immaterial, unimportant; ***– gut,*** quite good, (*coll.*) not (at all) bad; ***– der Ihrige,*** yours truly; ***im (großen und) -en,*** on the whole, generally speaking, taken all together, altogether; ***– der Mann dazu,*** quite the man for it, the right *or* proper man for it; ***– meiner Meinung,*** I quite agree; ***ich bin – Ohr,*** I am all attention *or* ears; ***– der Vater,*** the (very) image of his *etc.*) father; ***– wohl,*** very well.

Ganzaufnahme ['gants?aufna:mə], *f.* full-length portrait.

Ganze ['gantsə], *n.* whole, entirety, totality, total amount, (sum) total; (*Arith.*) integer; ***aufs – gehen,*** go *or* be all out (for), go to all lengths, (*sl.*) go the whole hog; (*coll.*) ***jetzt geht's aufs –,*** it's do or die, it's all or nothing; ***im -n genommen,*** taking everything into consideration, in general; ***im -n verkaufen,*** sell wholesale *or* in bulk.

Gänze ['gɛntsə], *f.* ***zur –,*** in its entirety, entirely.

Ganzfabrikat ['gantsfabrika:t], *n.* finished product *or* article. **Ganzheit,** *f.* entirety, totality. **Ganzholz,** *n.* logs, round timber. **ganzjährig,** *adj.* all the year round, all-season. **Ganz|lederband,** *m.* leather *or* calf binding. **-leinenband,** *m.* cloth binding.

gänzlich ['gɛntslɪç], **1.** *adj.* complete, full, total, entire, whole, thorough, utter. **2.** *adv.* completely, fully, wholly, entirely, totally, utterly, in every respect.

ganzrandig ['gantsrandɪç], *adj.* (*Bot.*) entire (*of leaves*). **Ganz|sachen,** *f.pl.* entires (*envelopes, postcards, wrappers*). **-seide,** *f.* pure silk, all silk. **ganztägig,** *adj.* all-day, full-time. **Ganz|wolle,** *f.* pure wool, all wool. **-zeug,** *n.* (paper) pulp.

gar [ga:r], **1.** *pred.adj.* (sufficiently) cooked, tender, well done, well roasted *or* boiled; purified, refined (*of metals*); tanned, dressed (*of skins*), (*dial.*) finished, all gone; ***nicht –,*** underdone (*meat*); ***mehr als –,*** overcooked. **2.** *adv.* entirely, fully, absolutely; very, quite, even, at all; perhaps; ***ist er krank oder – tot?*** is he ill or even *or* perhaps dead? ***das ist – wohl möglich,*** that is indeed quite possible; ***– kein Zweifel,*** not the least *or* slightest doubt; ***– keiner,*** not a single one, none whatever; ***– mancher,*** many a one (to be sure); ***– nicht,*** not at all, by no means; ***warum nicht –!*** you don't say so! ***das fällt mir – nicht ein,*** I wouldn't dream of it; ***– nichts,*** nothing at all; not a thing; ***– niemand,*** not a soul; ***– oft,*** very often; ***– selten,*** very rarely; ***vielleicht gefällt er mir –,*** perhaps I may even like him; ***– zu,*** much too, far too; ***– zu sehr,*** overmuch.

Garage [ga'ra:ʒə], *f.* garage. **garagieren** [-'ʒi:rən], *v.t.* (*Austr., Swiss*) garage.

Garant [ga'rant], *m.* (**-en,** *pl.* **-en**) guarantor.

Garantie [-'ti:], *f.* guarantee, warranty, surety. **garantieren,** *v.t.* (*or v.i.* ***– für***) guarantee, warrant.

Garaus ['ga:raus], *m.* finishing stroke; end; death; ***ihm den – machen,*** dispatch him, complete his ruin, finish him off, (*coll.*) do for him; ***einer S. den – machen,*** put an end *or* give the deathblow to a th.

Garbe ['garbə], *f.* sheaf; (*Bot.*) milfoil, yarrow (*Achillea millefolium*); (*Mil.*) burst, cone (*of fire*); beam, cone (*of light*); (*dial.*) neck of beef. **garben,** *v.t.* sheave, bundle.

gärben ['gɛrbən], *v.t.* (*Metall.*) weld.

Gärbottich ['gɛ:rbɔtɪç], *m.* fermenting vat.

Garde ['gardə], *f.* guards; Guards regiment; (*coll.*) ***die alte –,*** the old guard, the 'die-hards'; ***– zu Fuß,*** foot-guards. **Garde|regiment,** *n.* regiment of the Guards. **-reiterei,** *f.* Horse Guards.

Garderobe [gardə'ro:bə], *f.* clothes; wardrobe; cloakroom, (*Am.*) check-room; (*Theat.*) dressing room; (*periphrastic for*) closet; ***wo ist die –?*** where is the cloak-room? **Garderoben|frau,** *f.* cloak-room attendant. **-ständer,** *m.* hall-stand. **Garderobier** [-'bie:], *m.* (**-s,** *pl.* **-s**) cloak-room attendant; (*Theat.*) property-man. **Garderobiere** [-'biɛ:rə], *f.* cloak-room attendant; (*Theat.*) wardrobe mistress.

Gardine [gar'di:nə], *f.* curtain; (*coll.*) ***hinter schwedischen -n sitzen,*** be behind bars. **Gardinen|haken,** *m.* curtain-hook. **-predigt,** *f.* curtain-lecture; (*coll.*) telling-off from the wife. **-stange,** *f.* curtain rail *or* pole.

Gardist [gar'dɪst], *m.* (**-en,** *pl.* **-en**) guardsman.

Gare ['ga:rə], *f.* mellowness, friability (*of soil*).

Gäre ['gɛ:rə], *f.* fermentation; leaven, yeast; bouquet (*of wine*). **gären,** *irr.v.i.,* (*fig.*) *reg.v.i.* (*aux.* h. & s.) ferment; effervesce, work; ***es gärte in den Köpfen,*** (discontent *etc.*) was seething in their minds; ***es gärte im Volk,*** there was unrest among the people; ***der Wein ist*** (or ***hat sich***) ***zu Essig gegoren,*** the wine has turned to vinegar. **Gären,** *n.* fermentation; (*fig.*) unrest, agitation. **gärfähig,** *adj.* fermentable. **Gär|futter,** *n.* ensilage. **-futterbehälter,** *m.* silo.

Garküche ['ga:rkyçə], *f.* cook-shop, eating house.

Gärmittel ['gɛ:rmɪtəl], *n.* ferment, leaven(ing), yeast.

Garmond(schrift) [gar'mɔ̃:-], *f.* (*Typ.*) long primer.

Garn [garn], *n.* (**-s,** *pl.* **-e**) **1.** yarn, thread, twine; (*coll.*) (sewing) cotton; worsted; (*coll.*) ***ein – erzählen*** or ***spinnen,*** spin a yarn; 2. net, snare; decoy; ***ins – gehen,*** fall into the trap; ***ins – locken,*** ensnare, decoy.

Garnele [gar'ne:lə], *f.* prawn (*large*); shrimp (*small*).

Garnenden ['garn?ɛndən], *n.pl.* thrums.

garnieren [gar'ni:rən], *v.t.* trim (*a hat etc.*); (*Cul.*) garnish. **Garnierung,** *f.* trimming; garnish.

Garnison [garni'zo:n], *f.* (-, *pl.* **-en**) garrison, military post; ***mit einer – versehen,*** garrison (*a town*); ***in – liegen,*** be quartered (*in* (*Dat.*), at *or* in). **Garnisondienst,** *m.* garrison duty. **garnison|dienstfähig, -diensttauglich,** *adj.* fit for garrison duty. **Garnison|lazarett,** *n.* military hospital. **-stadt,** *f.* garrison town. **garnison|verwendungsfähig,** *adj. See* **-dienstfähig.**

Garnitur [garni'tu:r], *f.* (-, *pl.* **-en**) trimming; (*Cul.*) trimmings, garnish; outfit, equipment, set (*esp. of toilet articles & underwear*); mountings, fittings, accessories, furnishings; ***zweite* –**, (*Mil.*) second(-best) uniform; (*coll.*) of the second rank, second-rater(s); (*coll.*) ***die erste* –**, the élite, the very best.

Garn|knäuel, *n. or m.* ball of thread. **–rolle, –spule,** *f.* reel, spool, bobbin. **–strähne,** *f.* hank *or* skein of thread. **–winde,** *f. See* **–rolle.**

Garrotte [ga'rɔtə], *f.* gar(r)otte. **garrottieren** [–'ti:rən], *v.t.* strangle, throttle, gar(r)otte. **Garrottierung,** *f.* (Spanish method of) execution by strangulation.

garstig ['garstɪç], *adj.* nasty; ugly; horrid, loathsome, vile, detestable; filthy, foul. **Garstigkeit,** *f.* nastiness; vileness, loathsomeness; ugliness; filthiness.

Gär|stoff, –teig, *m. See* **–mittel.**

Garten ['gartən], *m.* (**-s,** *pl.* **⸚**) garden. **Garten|ammer,** *f.* (*Orn.*) Ortolan bunting (*Emberiza hortulana*). **–anlage,** *f.* public gardens, pleasure grounds. **–arbeit,** *f.* gardening. **–bau,** *m.* horticulture. **–bauausstellung,** *f.* horticultural show. **–bohne,** *f.* kidney bean. **–distel,** *f.* (*Bot.*) globe artichoke (*Cyanara scolymus*). **–erde,** *f.* garden-mould. **–fest,** *n.* garden *or* (*Am.* lawn) party. **–gerät,** *n.* gardening-tools. **–gestaltung,** *f.* landscape-gardening. **–gewächse,** *n.pl.* garden produce. **–grasmücke,** *f.* (*Orn.*) garden warbler (*Sylvia borum*). **–haus,** *n.* summer-house. **–kerbel,** *m.* (*Bot.*) chervil (*Scandix cerefolium*). **–kräuter,** *n.pl.* pot-herbs. **–kresse,** *f.* (*Bot.*) cress (*Lepidium sativum*). **–kunst,** *f.* horticulture. **–lattich,** *m.* (*Bot.*) lettuce (*Lactuca sativa*). **–laube,** *f.* arbour, summer-house. **–laubenroman,** *m.* (*coll.*) trashy sentimental novel (*reference to the* 'Gartenlaube', *a once popular family magazine*). **–lokal,** *n.* tea *or* beer garden, open-air restaurant. **–messer,** *n.* pruning-knife. **–raute,** *f.* (*Bot.*) common rue (*Ruta graveolens*). **–rotschwanz,** *m.* (*Orn.*) redstart (*Phoenicurus phoenicurus*). **–saal,** *m.* room (*of inn etc.*) overlooking the garden. **–schädling,** *m.* garden pest. **–schau,** *f.* flower *or* horticultural show. **–schere,** *f.* garden shears. **–schirm,** *m.* beach umbrella. **–spritze,** *f.* garden hose. **–stuhl,** *m.* deck chair. **–walze,** *f.* garden roller. **–wirtschaft,** *f. See* **–lokal.**

Gärtner ['gɛrtnər], *m.* gardener. **Gärtnerei** [–'raɪ], *f.* gardening, horticulture; nursery; market-garden, (*Am.*) truck farm. **gärtnerisch,** *adj.* horticultural. **gärtnern,** *v.i.* do gardening, work in the garden.

Gärung ['gɛ:ruŋ], *f.* fermentation, zymosis; (*fig.*) ferment, unrest, agitation, upheaval; ***in – kommen,*** begin to ferment *or* (*coll.*) rise; ***zur – bringen,*** ferment; (*fig.*) ***in – bringen,*** throw into a state of ferment. **Gärungs|lehre,** *f.* zymology. **–mittel,** *n.*, **–stoff,** *m. See* **Gärmittel.**

Gas [ga:s], *n.* (**-es,** *pl.* **-e**) gas; ***das – abdrehen,*** turn off the gas; (*coll.*) kill (*a p.*), ruin (*a p. economically*) (*with Dat.*); (*Mil.*) ***– ablassen*** or ***abblasen,*** release gas; (*coll.*) ***– geben,*** open the throttle, step on the gas.

Gas|abwehr, *f.* (*Mil.*) anti-gas defence. **–anstalt,** *f.* gas works. **–anzeiger,** *m.* (*Mil.*) gas detector. **–arbeiter,** *m.* gas-fitter. **gasartig,** *adj.* gaseous. **Gas|austritt,** *m.* escape of gas. **–behälter,** *m.* gasometer, gas-holder. **–beleuchtung,** *f.* gas lighting, gaslight. **–benzin,** *n.* natural gas(oline). **–bereitschaft,** *f.* (*Mil.*) gas alert. **–blase,** *f.* (*Metall.*) blow-hole. **–brenner,** *m.* gas-burner. **gasdicht,** *adj.* gas-tight, hermetically sealed. **Gas|dichte,** *f.* gas density. **–düse,** *f.* gas-jet.

gasen ['ga:zən], *v.i.* gas, develop gas.

Gas|entbindung, –entwicklung, –erzeugung, *f.* production *or* generation of gas. **–feuerung,** *f.* gas heating. **–flamme,** *f.* gas-jet. **–flasche,** *f.* gas cylinder. **gasförmig,** *adj.* gaseous. **Gas|gemenge, –gemisch,** *n.* gas *or* gaseous mixture. **–gewinnung,** *f.* gas production. **–glühlicht,** *n.* incandescent light. **–hahn,** *m.* gas-tap; (*coll.*) ***den – aufdrehen,*** put one's head in the gas-oven, commit suicide. **–hebel,** *m.* (*Motor.*) throttle, accelerator. **–herd,** *m.* gas-cooker, gas-stove. **–kammer,** *f.* gas chamber. **–kampfstoff,** *m.* (*Mil.*) poison gas. **–kocher,** *m. See* **–herd.**

Gaskogne [gas'kɔnjə], *f.* (*Geog.*) Gascony. **Gaskogner,** *m.* Gascon.

Gaskoks ['ga:sko:ks], *m.* gas coke.

Gaskonade [gasko'na:də], *f.* bragging, boasting.

gaskrank ['ga:skraŋk], *adj.* gassed. **Gas|krieg,** *m.* gas *or* chemical warfare. **–leitung,** *f.* gas-main *or* pipe. **–maske,** *f.* gas mask. **–messer,** *m.* gas-meter. **–ofen,** *m.* gas-stove, gas-furnace.

Gasolin [gazo'li:n], *n.* gasoline, petroleum spirit.

Gas|pedal, *n. See* **–hebel. –rest,** *m.* residual gas. **–schutz,** *m.* (*Mil.*) anti-gas protection. **–schwade,** *f.* gas fumes.

Gasse ['gasə], *f.* lane, alley; (*Austr.*) street; ***auf der* –**, in the street; ***auf allen –n,*** at every street-corner; ***Hans in allen –n,*** busybody; (*Austr.*) ***über die* –**, outdoor (*sale of liquor for consumption off the premises*). **Gassen|bube,** *m.* street-arab, urchin, guttersnipe. **–dieb,** *m.* pickpocket. **–dirne,** *f.* prostitute, street-walker. **–hauer,** *m.* popular song, street-ballad. **–junge,** *m. See* **–bube. –laufen,** *n.* (*Hist.*) running the gauntlet. **–treter,** *m.* street-corner lounger. **–wirt,** *m.* publican. **–witz,** *m.* vulgar joke.

Gasstrumpf ['ga:sʃtrumpf], *m.* gas-mantle.

Gast [gast], *m.* 1. (**-es,** *pl.* **⸚e**) guest, visitor; (*at an inn etc.*) customer; stranger; (*Theat.*) guest star; ***ihn zu –e bitten,*** invite him; ***Gäste haben,*** have company; (*iron.*) ***saubrer* –**, fine fellow; ***seltener* –**, queer fish, rara avis; ***bei ihm zu – sein,*** be his guest, stay with him; 2. (**-s,** *pl.* **-en**) sailor, seaman (*usu. in compounds, e.g.* **Boots–**). **Gast|bett,** *n.* spare bed. **–dirigent,** *m.* guest conductor.

Gästebuch ['gɛstəbu:x], *n.* visitors' book.

Gasterei [gastə'raɪ], *f.* feast, banquet; (*coll.*) bean-feast, bun-fight.

gastfrei ['gastfraɪ], *adj.* hospitable. **Gast|freiheit,** *f.* hospitality. **–freund,** *m.* guest; host. **gastfreundlich,** *adj.* hospitable. **Gast|freundschaft,** *f.* hospitality. **–geber,** *m.* host. **–geberin,** *f.* hostess. **–haus,** *n.*, **–hof,** *m.* restaurant; inn; tavern. **–hörer,** *m.* part-time student.

gastieren [gas'ti:rən], *v.i.* (*Theat.*) be a guest star.

gastlich ['gastlɪç], *adj.* hospitable. **Gastlichkeit,** *f.* hospitality. **Gast|mahl,** *n.* banquet, dinner party. **–pflanze,** *f.* (*Bot.*) parasite. **–predigt,** *f.* sermon by a visiting clergyman. **–professor,** *m.* visiting professor. **–recht,** *n.* 1. right to hospitality (*of a visitor in a foreign country*); 2. host's privilege; 3. law regulating relations between innkeeper and traveller.

gastrisch ['gastrɪʃ], *adj.* (*Med.*) gastric.

Gastrolle ['gastrɔlə], *f.* (*Theat.*) star part (*played by visiting actor*).

Gastronom [gastro'no:m], *m.* (**-en,** *pl.* **-en**) gourmet, epicure. **gastronomisch,** *adj.* gastronomic(al).

Gast|spiel, *n.* (*Theat.*) performance by visiting actors. **–stätte,** *f.* restaurant, café, teashop, public-house. **–stättengewerbe,** *n.* catering trade. **–stube,** *f.* general room (*in inn*), hotel lounge, bar parlour. **–tafel,** *f.*, **–tisch,** *m.* table-d'hôte. **–vorstellung,** *f.* (*Theat.*) performance of visiting star. **–wirt,** *m.* landlord, innkeeper, hotel-keeper. **–wirtschaft,** *f. See* **–haus. –zimmer,** *n.* spare bedroom; *see also* **–stube.**

Gas|uhr, *f.* gas-meter. **–vergiftung,** *f.* gas-poisoning, gassing. **–versorgung,** *f.* gas-supply. **–werk,** *n.* gasworks. **–zufuhr,** *f. See* **–versorgung.**

gäten ['gɛ:tən], *v.t. See* **jäten.**

gätlich ['gɛ:tlɪç], *adj.* (*dial.*) tolerable, middling; convenient; middle-sized.

Gatt [gat], *n.* (**-(e)s,** *pl.* **-s** *or* **-en**) (*dial.*) hole, narrow opening.

Gatte ['gatə], *m.* (**-n,** *pl.* **-n**) husband, (*Poet.*) consort, spouse; mate (*of animals*); *pl.* married couple. **gatten,** *v.t.*, *v.r.* match, pair, couple, copulate, unite; (*dial.*) sort. **Gatten|liebe,** *f.* conjugal love. **–rechte,** *n.pl.* marital rights. **–wahl,** *f.* (*Biol.*) assortative mating.

Gatter ['gatər], *n.* railing, fence; grating, lattice, trellis; enclosure. **gattern,** *v.t.* (*dial.*) 1. fence; 2. spy out. **Gatter|säge,** *f.* frame saw. **–tor,** *n.*, **–tür,** *f.* barred gate, grated door. **–werk,** *n.* lattice-work.

gattieren [ga'ti:rən], *v.t.* classify, sort; (*Min.*, textiles) mix.

Gattin ['gatɪn], *f.* wife, (*Poet.*) consort, spouse; mate (*of animals*).

Gattung ['gatuŋ], *f.* kind, class, type, sort; species; genus, race, breed, family (*of plants*), (*Gram.*) gender; (*Mil.*) arm of the service. **Gattungs|-bastard,** *m.* genus hybrid. **–begriff,** *m.* generic concept. **–maler,** *m.* genre-painter. **–name,** *m.* generic name; (*Gram.*) collective noun. **–verwandte(r),** *m., f.* allied species, congener.

Gau [gau], *m. or n.* (**-(e)s,** *pl.* **-e** (*Austr.* **-en**)) (*dial.* **Gäu**) district, region; province, administrative district.

Gauch [gaux], *m.* (**-(e)s,** *pl.* **-e** (*Austr.*) **⸚e**) fool, simpleton; oddity, odd fish; (*dial.*) cuckoo. **Gauch|bart,** *m.*, **–haar,** *n.* stripling's downy beard. **–heil,** *n.* (*dial. m.*) (*Bot.*) scarlet pimpernel (*Anagallis arvensis*).

Gaudi ['gaudi], *n.* (**-s,** *no pl.*) (*dial., coll.*) fun, spree.

Gaudieb ['gaudi:p], *m.* (*dial.*) professional thief.

gaufrieren [go'fri:rən], *v.t.* emboss, goffer (*paper*).

Gaukelbild ['gaukəlbɪlt], *n.* illusion, mirage; delusion, phantasm. **Gaukelei** [–'laɪ], *f.* (-, *pl.* **-en**) jugglery, sleight of hand, legerdemain; trick, illusion; trickery, deception, hocus-pocus. **gaukelhaft,** *adj.* delusive, deceptive. **gaukeln,** *v.i.* juggle, do tricks; flutter (about), flit about, rock (to and fro). **Gaukel|spiel, –werk,** *n. See* **Gaukelei. Gaukler,** *m.* juggler, conjurer, illusionist; clown, buffoon; charlatan, impostor, humbug. **gauklerisch,** *adj. See* **gaukelhaft.**

Gaul [gaul], *m.* (**-(e)s,** *pl.* **⸚e**) old horse, nag; (*dial.*) carthorse; ***elender –,*** (miserable) jade; (*Prov.*) ***einem geschenkten – sieht man nicht ins Maul,*** never look a gift horse in the mouth; beggars can't be choosers.

Gauleiter ['gaulaɪtər], *m.* (*Nat. Soc.*) area commander.

Gaumen ['gaumən], *m.* palate, roof of the mouth; ***harter –,*** hard palate; ***weicher –,*** soft palate, velum. **Gaumen|laut,** *m.* (*Phonet.*) palatal (sound). **–naht,** *f.* (*Anat.*) palatine suture. **–platte,** *f.* (dental) plate. **–segel,** *n.*, **–vorhang,** *m.* velum, soft palate. **–zäpfchen,** *n.* uvula.

Gauner ['gaunər], *m.* rogue, scoundrel; swindler, cheat, sharper, trickster, (*coll.*) scamp, scalliwag. **Gaunerei** [–'raɪ], *f.* swindling, swindle, trickery, sharp practice, (*coll.*) skulduggery. **gaunerhaft,** *adj.* thievish, knavish, (*coll.*) crooked. **gaunern,** *v.i.* swindle, cheat. **Gauner|sprache,** *f.* thieves' slang *or* Latin. **–streich,** *m.*, **–stück,** *n.* swindle, imposture, rascally trick. **–zinke,** *f.* beggars' *or* thieves' mark (*outside a house*).

Gaupe ['gaupə], *f.*, **Gauploch,** *n.* (*dial.*) dormer-window; attic.

Gautsche ['gautʃə], *f.* (*dial.*) swing. **gautschen,** *v.t.* couch (*paper*).

Gaze ['ga:zə], *f.* gauze; net, cheesecloth; ***feine –,*** gossamer.

Gdingen ['gdɪŋən], *n.* (*Geog.*) Gdynia.

Ge–, ge– [gə–], *unaccented pref.*: *forms* 1. Collective nouns *from substantives, nearly all neuter, root vowel, if possible, modified, e.g.* **Geäder, Geäst, Gebüsch, Gefilde, Gestein, Gesträuch, Gewässer, Gewölk**; 2. Verbal nouns *denoting repetition or continuation of the action, all neuter and without plural, e.g.* **Geächze, Gebalge, Geheul, Gerede, Geschwätz, Gestöhn(e), Gewinsel**; 3. Past participles, *e.g.* **geachtet,** *from* **achten, geächtet** *from* **ächten, geboren** *from* **gebären,** *and nouns from these, e.g.* **Geächtete(r), Erstgeborene(r).** *For any words not given below, partic. in the case of* 3, *see the simple words.*

Geächtete(r) [gə'ɛçtətə(r)], *m., f.* outlaw, proscript.

Geächze [gə'ɛçtsə], *n.* continual groaning, groans.

Geäder [gə'ɛ:dər], *n.* blood vessels, veins, arteries, arterial system; veined structure, marbling. **geädert,** *adj.* veined, grained, marbled.

geartet [gə'a:rtət], *adj., suff.* constituted, natured, disposed, conditioned; ***anders –,*** of a different nature. **Geartetheit,** *f.* nature, disposition, qualities, constitution, attributes, peculiarities.

Geäse [gə'ɛ:zə], *n.* (**-s,** *pl.* **-**) 1. pasture, fodder *or* feeding ground for deer; 2. deer's mouth.

Geäst [gə'ɛst], *n.* branches, branch-work.

Gebäck [gə'bɛk], *n.* (**-(e)s,** *pl.* **-e**) 1. pastry, fancy cakes, confectionery; (*Scots*) tea-bread; (*Am.*) cookies; 2. baking, batch.

Gebackene(s) [gə'bakənə(s)], *n.* pastry.

Gebalge [gə'balgə], *n.* tussle, scuffle.

Gebälk [gə'bɛlk], *n.* beams, framework, joists; timber-work; (*Archit.*) entablature (*of a column*). **Gebälkträger,** *m.* (*Archit.*) atlas, telamon.

geballt [gə'balt], *adj.* concentrated; ***–e Faust,*** clenched fist; (*Artil.*) ***–es Feuer,*** concentrated fire; ***–e Ladung,*** demolition charge.

gebannt [gə'bant], *adj.* fascinated, spellbound.

gebar [gə'ba:r], *see* **gebären.**

Gebärde [gə'bɛ:rdə], *f.* air, bearing, appearance, demeanour; gesture, gesticulation. **gebärden,** *v.r.* behave; conduct *or* deport o.s.; ***sich – als ob,*** act *or* do as if. **Gebärden|spiel,** *n.* pantomime, dumb show, miming, gesticulation. **–sprache,** *f.* gesture *or* sign language; miming.

gebäre [gə'bɛ:rə], *see* **gebären.**

gebaren [gə'ba:rən], *v.r.* (*rare*) behave; conduct *or* deport o.s. **Gebaren,** *n.* conduct, behaviour, demeanour, deportment.

gebären [gə'bɛ:rən], *irr.v.t.* bear, bring forth, give birth to; (*fig.*) bring forth, produce, beget; ***vorzeitig –,*** give premature birth to, miscarry; (***ein Kind***) ***geboren haben,*** be delivered (of a child); ***geboren werden,*** be born. *See* **geboren. Gebären,** *n.* parturition; child-bearing. **gebärend,** *adj.* ***–e Frau,*** woman in labour; ***lebendige Junge –,*** viviparous.

Gebärmutter [gə'bɛ:rmutər], *f.* womb, uterus. **Gebärmutter|bruch,** *m.* hysterocele. **–entfernung,** *f.* hysterectomy. **–schmerz,** *m.* hysteralgia. **–schnitt,** *m.* hysterotomy, Caesarian section.

Gebarung [gə'baruŋ], *f.* management, (*coll.*) running (*of a business*); policy.

Gebäude [gə'bɔydə], *n.* (**-s,** *pl.* **-**) building, structure, edifice; (*fig.*) framework, structure. **Gebäudesteuer,** *f.* property tax, rates.

gebefreudig ['ge:bəfrɔydɪç], *adj.* open-handed, generous, bountiful, munificent.

Gebein [gə'baɪn], *n.* (**-(e)s,** *pl.* **-e**) bones; frame, skeleton; *pl.* (mortal) remains.

Gebelfer [gə'bɛlfər], *n.* yelping, barking; (*fig.*) bawling, abusive language.

Gebell [gə'bɛl], *n.* barking, baying.

geben ['ge:bən], **1.** *irr.v.t.* give, hand (over), present, confer, bestow, impart; grant, allow, yield, furnish, produce, emit; (*Theat.*) perform, show, play, act; (*Tenn.*) serve; (*Cards*) deal; ***ihm den Abschied –,*** dismiss *or* discharge him; ***acht –,*** pay attention, give heed; ***Anlaß – zu,*** give rise *or* occasion to; ***sich*** (*Dat.*) ***ein Ansehen –,*** give o.s. airs; ***sich*** (*Dat.*) ***das Ansehen –,*** assume the appearance of; ***auf eine S. etwas –,*** set store by a th.; ***nichts auf eine S. –,*** think nothing of a th.; ***viel auf sich –,*** be particular about one's person; ***den Ausschlag –,*** be decisive *or* the decisive factor; ***ich gebe dir zu bedenken,*** I would have you consider; ***ein Beispiel –,*** set an example; ***Bescheid –,*** give notice, send *or* bring word; ***zum besten –,*** stand (*a drink etc.*), tell (*a story, joke etc.*), sing (*a song*), recite (*a poem*), play (*a piece*); ***Bewegung –,*** impart motion to; ***das gibt zu denken,*** that makes one think; ***in Druck –,*** have printed; ***sich*** (*Dat.*) ***die Ehre –,*** do o.s. the honour; ***Ertrag –,*** yield a return; (*Cards*) ***falsch –,*** misdeal,

deal wrongly; (*coll.*) ***Fersengeld* –**, run away, decamp; ***Feuer* –**, fire (*a rifle*); give *or* offer (*s.o.*) a light; ***ihm einen Freibrief* –**, give him carte-blanche; ***Frist* –**, allow time, grant a respite; ***Gewinn* –**, yield profit, turn out well; ***Gott gebe!*** God grant! ***ihm etwas in die Hand* –**, suggest s.th. to him; ***Hitze* –**, throw out *or* emit heat; ***ihm das Jawort* –**, accept his offer of marriage, consent to marry him; ***Karten* –**, deal; ***der Hund gab Laut,*** the dog gave tongue; ***in die Lehre* –**, apprentice; ***ans Licht* –**, see ***an den Tag* –**; ***sich* (*Dat.*) *Mühe* –**, take pains *or* trouble; ***Nachricht* –**, send word; ***Obacht* –**, pay attention (*Dat.*, to), take care (of); ***in Pension* –**, place at a boarding-school; put out to board; ***auf die Post* –**, post; ***Raum* –**, make room; ***ihm recht* –**, acknowledge that he is right; ***ihm das Recht* –**, empower *or* sanction him; ***das gibt keinen Sinn,*** that makes no sense; ***ihm gewonnenes Spiel* –**, acknowledge his victory; throw in one's hand; ***dem Pferde die Sporen* –**, set spurs to one's horse; ***ihm Schuld* –**, blame him, impute blame to *or* accuse him; ***an den Tag* –**, bring to light, publish; ***Unterricht* –**, teach, give instruction; ***verloren* –**, look upon as lost; renounce (one's claim to); ***ein Spiel verloren* –**, acknowledge defeat, throw up the sponge; ***ihm etwas in Verwahrung* –**, place s.th. in *or* give s.th. into his charge; ***von sich* –**, give out, emit (*a sound etc.*), utter; give off (*a smell*); deliver (*a speech*); bring up, vomit (*food*); ***ihm den Vorzug* –**, acknowledge his superiority *or* priority; show one's preference for him; ***sein Wort* (*auf eine S.*) –**, give *or* pledge one's word; ***gute Worte* –**, entreat, persuade; ***ein Wort gab das andere,*** one word led to another; ***die Zeit wird es* –**, time will tell *or* show; ***Zeugnis* –**, bear witness; ***auf Zinsen* –**, put out at interest; ***die Zusage* –**, accept (*an invitation etc.*), promise (*help etc.*). *See* **gegeben.**
2. *irr.v.r.* (*of a p.*) submit, yield, (*of feelings etc.*) settle (down), abate, (*of fabric*) stretch; (*of a p.*) ***sich* – *als,*** pretend to be, behave as if one were, give o.s. the air of, (try to) pass (o.s.) off as; ***das gibt sich,*** that will pass, that will not last long; ***es gibt sich von selbst,*** it is a matter of course; ***sein Eifer wird sich* –**, his zeal will cool; ***der Schmerz hat sich gegeben,*** the pain has abated; ***sich zu erkennen* –**, reveal one's identity, make o.s. known; ***sich gefangen* –**, surrender, give o.s. up; ***sich kund* –**, be revealed, make itself apparent; ***Erstaunen gab sich in aller Mienen kund,*** surprise manifested itself *or* was expressed on every face; ***sich verloren* –**, admit defeat; ***sich zufrieden* – *mit,*** put up with, submit to, be content with; ***sich* – *in*** (*Acc.*), resign o.s. to.
3. *irr.v.t. imp.* ***es gibt,*** there is, there are; ***der größte Prahler, den es gibt,*** the greatest braggart living; ***es gibt heute Regen,*** there will be rain today; ***es gab einen Zank,*** a quarrel arose; ***was gibt's?*** what is the matter? (*coll.*) what's up? what is it? ***was es nicht alles gibt!*** you surprise me! you'd hardly credit it! (*coll.*) ***es wird gleich* (*et*)*was* –!** there'll be trouble in a minute! you'll catch it! ***gibt es etwas Schöneres?*** what is more beautiful? ***was gibt's Neues?*** what's the news? (*coll.*) ***das gibt's nicht!*** there's no such thing! that's out of the question! that's impossible! nonsense! it just isn't done, it won't do, (*coll.*) that's out! nothing doing! (*coll.*) ***da gibt's nichts,*** one cannot deny it, one must admit that; ***es gibt nichts derartiges,*** there is nothing of the kind *or* like it; ***es gibt viel zu tun,*** there's a lot to do *or* to be done.

Geben, *n.* giving; ***das* – *hat kein Ende bei ihr,*** she never leaves off giving; (*Cards*) ***am* – *sein,*** have the deal; (*B.*) ***– ist seliger denn Nehmen,*** it is more blessed to give than to receive; ***ein* – *und Nehmen,*** a matter of give and take. **Geber,** *m.* giver, donor, dispenser, dealer (*at cards*), (*Comm.*) seller, (*Tele.*) transmitter. **Geberlaune,** *f.* fit of generosity.

Gebet [gə'be:t], *n.* **(-(e)s,** *pl.* **-e)** prayer; ***das* – *des Herrn,*** the Lord's Prayer; ***sein* – *verrichten,*** say one's prayers; ***ein* – *sprechen,*** offer prayers; ***ins* – *nehmen,*** question closely, catechize; take to task, (*coll.*) give a good talking-to *or* a dressing-down, have on the carpet. **Gebetbuch,** *n.* prayer-book, breviary; (*hum.*) ***des Teufels* –**, playing cards.

gebeten [gə'be:tən], *see* **bitten.**

Gebet|mühle, *f.* prayer-wheel. **–schnur,** *f.* phylactery.

Gebettel [gə'bɛtəl], *n.* importunity, continual begging.

gebier [gə'bi:r], **gebierst, gebiert,** *see* **gebären.**

Gebiet [gə'bi:t], *n.* **(-(e)s,** *pl.* **-e)** district, territory, region, zone, province; area, domain, department, branch, field, sphere, range, scope; ***auf deutschem* –**, on German territory.

gebieten [gə'bi:tən], **1.** *irr.v.t.* (***ihm etwas***) command, order, bid, enjoin, require, call for; ***Ruhe*** or ***Stillschweigen* –**, impose silence; ***Rücksicht scheint geboten,*** some consideration seems to be called for. **2.** *irr.v.i.* (***über*** (*Acc.*)) rule over, govern, have jurisdiction *or* control over; have at one's disposal. **Gebieter,** *m.* master, lord, commander, ruler, governor. **gebieterisch,** *adj.* domineering, dictatorial; imperious; categoric, peremptory, commanding, imperative. **Gebietshoheit,** *f.* territorial sovereignty.

Gebilde [gə'bɪldə], *n.* **(-s,** *pl.* **-)** creation; creature; product; structure, (*Geol.*) formation; (*Weav.*) pattern; form, figure, shape.

gebildet [gə'bɪldət], *adj.* educated, cultured, cultivated, well-bred, refined; shaped, fashioned; ***die Gebildeten,*** the intelligentsia, the educated classes. *See* **bilden.**

Gebimmel [gə'bɪməl], *n.* ringing *or* tinkling of bells.

Gebinde [gə'bɪndə], *n.* **(-s,** *pl.* **-)** bundle; (*of thread*) skein, hank; (*of corn*) sheaf; cask, barrel.

Gebirge [gə'bɪrgə], *n.* **(-s,** *pl.* **-)** mountain-chain *or* range, mountains, highlands; (*Min.*) rock. **gebirgig,** *adj.* mountainous. **Gebirgler,** *m.* mountain-dweller.

Gebirgs|art [gə'bɪrks–], *f.* species of rock. **–bewohner,** *m.* mountain dweller, highlander. **–joch,** *n.* saddle (*of a mountain*). **–kamm,** *m.* *See* **–rücken. –kunde,** *f.* orology. **–rücken,** *m.* mountain ridge. **–stock,** *m.* massif. **–volk,** *n.* mountain tribe, highlanders. **–vorsprung,** *m.* shoulder of a mountain. **–wand,** *f.* wall of rocks. **–zug,** *m.* mountain-chain, range of mountains.

Gebiß [gə'bɪs], *n.* **(-(ss)es,** *pl.* **-(ss)e)** set of teeth; denture, (set of) false *or* artificial teeth; bridle-bit. **gebissen,** *see* **beißen. Gebißkette,** *f.* curb (*of a bit*).

Gebläse [gə'blɛ:zə], *n.* **(-s,** *pl.* **-)** blast apparatus, blower, bellows; blowpipe; (*Motor.*) supercharger. **Gebläse|brenner,** *m.* blowlamp. **–luft,** *f.* forced air. **–ofen,** *m.* blast-furnace.

geblichen [gə'blɪçən], *see* **bleichen.**

geblieben [gə'bli:bən], *see* **bleiben**; ***die Gebliebenen,*** the killed, the (fatal) casualties (*in battle*).

Geblök [gə'blø:k], *n.* **(-(e)s,** *pl.* **-e)** bleating (*of sheep*); lowing (*of cattle*).

geblümt [gə'bly:mt], *adj.* flowered, figured, flowery, with floral design.

Geblüt [gə'bly:t], *n.* blood, blood system; line, lineage, family, descent, race; ***es steckt im* –**, it runs in the blood *or* in the family; ***Prinz von* –**, prince of the blood, prince of the royal line; ***zu nahe ins* – *heiraten,*** marry too near of kin.

gebogen [gə'bo:gən], *adj.* bent, curved, refracted; hooked; arched; vaulted; ***–e Nase,*** aquiline nose, Roman nose. *See* **biegen.**

geboren [gə'bo:rən], *adj.* (*abbr.* **geb.**) born; née; by birth, by nature; ***unehelich* –**, born out of wedlock, illegitimate; ***–er Deutscher,*** German by birth; ***–er Londoner,*** native of London; ***–er Dichter,*** born poet; ***eine –e N.,*** née N.; ***was für eine –e ist sie?*** what was her maiden name? *See* **gebären.**

geborgen [gə'bɔrgən], *adj.* ***– sein,*** be hidden *or* sheltered *or* safe (***vor*** (*Dat.*), from), be in safety *or* out of danger. *See* **bergen. Geborgenheit,** *f.* (place of) safety *or* security.

geborsten [gə'bɔrstən], *see* **bersten.**

Gebot [gə'bo:t], *n.* **(-(e)s,** *pl.* **-e)** **1.** command, order; precept; (*B.*) commandment; ***ihm zu –e stehen,***

be at his disposal; ***die zehn –e,*** the ten commandments; ***das – der Stunde,*** the need of the moment; ***das – der Vernunft,*** the dictates of reason; (*Prov.*) ***Not kennt kein –,*** necessity knows no law; 2. (*Comm.*) advance, bid, offer; ***das erste – tun,*** start a price, make the first bid.

geboten [gə'bo:tən], *adj.* necessary, requisite, required, indicated; ***dringend –,*** imperative, mandatory; ***es wird – sein,*** it seems advisable. *See* **bieten, gebieten.**

gebracht [gə'braxt], *see* **bringen.**

gebrannt [gə'brant], *adj.* (*Prov.*) ***ein –es Kind scheut das Feuer,*** a burnt child dreads the fire; once bit, twice shy; ***–er Kalk,*** quicklime. *See* **brennen.**

Gebräu [gə'brɔy], *n.* (**-(e)s,** *pl.* **-e**) brewing, brew, (*fig.*) mixture, concoction.

Gebrauch [gə'braux], *m.* (**-(e)s,** *pl.* **⸗e**) 1. employment, use, application; ***außer – kommen,*** go out of use, fall into disuse; ***falscher –,*** improper use *or* application, abuse (*of words etc.*); ***in – nehmen,*** take into use; ***nach – zurückzugeben,*** return after use; ***von einer S. – machen,*** make use of *or* avail o.s. of a.th.; ***zu eigenem –,*** for one's personal use; 2. usage, custom, practice, habit, fashion; ***alter –,*** ancient (well-established) custom; ***heiliger –,*** sacred rite; ***Sitten und Gebräuche,*** habits and customs.

gebrauchen [gə'brauxən], *v.t.* use, employ, make use of, avail o.s. of; ***dies ist nicht zu –,*** this is of no use (whatever); ***sich – lassen zu,*** lend o.s. to, be instrumental to; ***– Sie mein Wörterbuch noch?*** are you still using my dictionary? ***Gewalt –,*** employ *or* use force.

gebräuchlich [gə'brɔyçlıç], *adj.* usual, common, ordinary, in use, commonly used, customary, current; ***–e Orthographie,*** current spelling; ***nicht mehr –,*** no longer used, obsolete; ***– sein,*** be in use. **Gebräuchlichkeit,** *f.* usualness, customariness, commonness, frequency.

Gebrauchs|anweisung, *f.* directions (for use). **–artikel,** *m.* everyday commodity, article in common use. **–diebstahl,** *m.* (*of a car*) joy-riding. **–dosis,** *f.* usual dose, normal dose. **gebrauchsfähig,** *adj.* usable, serviceable. **Gebrauchsfahrzeug,** *n.* utility vehicle. **gebrauchsfertig,** *adj.* ready for use. **Gebrauchs|gegenstand,** *m.* commodity, household utensil. **–graphik,** *f.* commercial art. **–güter,** *n.pl.* necessaries. **–muster,** *n.* patent, registered design. **–musterschutz,** *m.* registered trade-mark. **–wasser,** *n.* fresh water, tap water. **–wert,** *m.* intrinsic value.

gebraucht [gə'brauxt], *adj.* used, second-hand; ***–es Bad,*** spent bath (*dyeing*). **Gebrauchtwagen,** *m.* used *or* second-hand car.

Gebrech [gə'brɛç], *n.* (**-s,** *pl.* **-e**) 1. boar's snout; 2. rooting place of wild boars; 3. friable *or* crumbling rock. **gebrech,** *pred.adj.* brittle, crumbling, friable (*of rocks*).

gebrechen [gə'brɛçən], *irr.v.i. imp.* (*rare*) (*pres. and imperf. tenses only*) (*Dat.*) lack, be in need of, be wanting; ***es soll Ihnen an nichts –,*** you shall want for nothing; ***es gebricht ihm an Geld,*** he is short *or* in need of money; ***wenn es dir an Mut gebricht,*** if you are lacking in courage.

Gebrechen, *n.* (physical *or* bodily) infirmity, malady, ailment, affliction, physical defect; defect; (*fig.*) handicap, shortcoming. **gebrechlich,** *adj.* (*of a th.*) brittle, fragile, (*coll.*) rickety; (*of a p.*) frail, feeble, infirm, decrepit. **Gebrechlichkeit,** *f.* fragility; frailty, feebleness, infirmity, decrepitude

Gebresten [gə'brɛstən], *n. See* **Gebrechen.**

gebrochen [gə'brɔxən], *adj.* broken; bent, deflected; halting, broken (*of speech*); broken in spirit, bowed down; dim, dull, subdued (*of colour, light etc.*); (*Mus.*) arpeggiando; ***–en Herzens,*** broken-hearted. *See* **brechen.**

Gebrüder [gə'bry:dər], *m.pl.* (*abbr.* **Gebr.**) brothers; ***die – Grimm,*** the brothers Grimm.

Gebrüll [gə'bryl], *n.* roaring; lowing (*of cattle*).

Gebühr [gə'by:r], *f.* (**-,** *pl.* **-en**) 1. fee, tax, rate, charge, toll, duty, due; *pl.* dues, money due, taxes; payment, commission, royalty *or* royalties; 2. propriety, seemliness, decency; ***seine – leisten,*** do one's duty; ***nach –,*** according to merit, duly, deservedly; ***über –,*** immoderately, excessively, unduly.

gebühren [gə'by:rən], **1.** *v.i.* (*Dat.*) be due to, belong of right to; appertain to; ***Ehre, dem Ehre gebühr(e)t,*** honour to whom honour is due; ***gib mir was mir gebührt,*** give me my due. **2.** *v.r., imp.* be fitting *or* proper *or* becoming; ***wie sich's gebührt,*** as it ought to be, in a becoming manner, properly. **gebührend,** *adj.* due, fit, fitting, proper, appropriate, meet, befitting; ***Ihre Tratte soll –en Schutz finden,*** your draft shall be duly honoured. **gebührendermaßen, gebührenderweise,** *adv.* properly, duly, in a fitting manner.

Gebühren|erlaß, *m.* remission of fees. **–ermäßigung,** *f.* reduction of fees. **gebührenfrei,** *adj.* tax-free, duty-free, post-free. **Gebührenordnung,** *f.* tariff, scale of charges. **gebührenpflichtig,** *adj.* liable *or* subject to tax, dutiable, postage due. **Gebührenvorschuß,** *m.* (*Law*) retainer.

gebührlich [gə'by:rlıç], *adj.* (*rare*) *see* **gebührend.**

Gebund [gə'bunt], *n.* (**-(e)s,** *pl.* **⸗e**) bunch, bundle, skein, truss.

gebunden [gə'bundən], *adj.* bound, obliged, constrained; (*Bookb.*) bound; (*Comm.*) tied, blocked, controlled, earmarked; metrical; combined (***an*** (*Acc.*), with), linked (to); ***–e Wärme,*** latent heat; (*Mus.*) ***–e Noten,*** tied notes; ***–e Rede,*** verse, poetry. *See* **binden. Gebundenheit,** *f.* constraint; subjection, dependence, affiliation.

Geburt [gə'bu:rt], *f.* (**-,** *pl.* **-en**) birth; labour, delivery, (*Med.*) parturition; (*Poet.*) offspring; origin, family, descent, extraction; ***unzeitige –,*** abortion; ***von –,*** by birth; of good birth; ***nach Christi –,*** anno Domini, A.D.; ***vor Christi –,*** before Christ, B.C.; ***in der – sterben,*** die in childbirth; ***die – abtreiben,*** bring about a miscarriage; ***von (seiner) – an,*** from (his) birth. **Geburten|beihilfe,** *f.* maternity benefit. **–beschränkung, –regelung,** *f.* birth-control, family planning. **–rückgang,** *m.* fall in the birth-rate. **–ziffer,** *f.* birth-rate.

gebürtig [gə'byrtıç], *adj.* native (***aus,*** of), born (in).

Geburts|anzeige, *f.* announcement of birth. **–fehler,** *m.* congenital defect. **–haus,** *n.* birthplace. **–helfer,** *m.* obstetrician, accoucheur. **–helferin,** *f.* midwife. **–hilfe,** *f.* midwifery, obstetrics. **–jahr,** *n.* year of birth. **–land,** *n.* native land. **–ort,** *m.* birthplace, place of birth, native place. **–schein,** *m.* birth certificate. **–stadt,** *f.* native town. **–tag,** *m.* birthday; ***ihm zum – Glück wünschen,*** wish him many happy returns of the day. **–vorgang,** *m.* (*Med.*) parturition. **–wehen,** *f.pl.* labour pains; ***in – liegen,*** be in labour.

Gebüsch [gə'byʃ], *n.* (**-es,** *pl.* **-e**) bushes, shrubs, shrubbery, thicket, copse, underwood, undergrowth.

Geck [gɛk], *m.* (**-en,** *pl.* **-en**) fop, dandy, coxcomb, conceited ass. **geckenhaft,** *adj.* foppish, dandified.

gedacht [gə'daxt], *adj.* ***der –e Herr,*** the aforesaid gentleman; ***–e Zahl,*** number thought of. *See* **denken**; *also see* **gedenken, dachen.**

Gedächtnis [gə'dɛçtnıs], *n.* (**-ses,** *pl.* **-se**) memory, recollection, remembrance; memorial, monument; ***aus dem –,*** from memory, by heart; ***im – behalten,*** remember, keep *or* bear in mind; ***ihm etwas ins – zurückrufen,*** remind him of a th.; ***sich etwas ins – zurückrufen,*** recall s.th., call a th. to mind; ***zum –*** (*Gen.*) *or* ***an*** (*Acc.*), in memory *or* remembrance *or* commemoration of; ***es ist meinem – entfallen,*** it has escaped *or* slipped my memory; ***wenn mein – mich nicht täuscht*** or ***trügt,*** if my memory serves me right, if I remember rightly.

Gedächtnis|fehler, *m.* slip of the memory. **–feier,** *f.* commemoration; ***kirchliche –,*** memorial service, **–hilfe,** *f.* mnemonic. **–kirche,** *f.* memorial church. **–rede,** *f.* speech in commemoration. **–schwäche,** *f.*, **–schwund,** *m.* amnesia, loss of memory. **–übung,** *f.* memory training.

gedämpft [gə'dɛmpft], *adj.* subdued, muffled; ***mit –er Stimme,*** in an undertone, in a hushed voice, under one's breath; (*Rad. etc.*) *-e Welle*, damped wave.

Gedanke [gə'daŋkə], *m.* (**-ns,** *pl.* **-n**) thought, conception, idea, notion (*an* (*Acc.*), of); design, purpose, plan; ***kein - daran!*** it's out of the question! ***ihn auf andere -n bringen,*** divert his thoughts, make him think of other things; ***ihn auf den -n bringen daß,*** make him think that; ***auf den -n kommen,*** hit upon the idea; ***ich kam auf den -n,*** the idea *or* thought occurred to *or* struck me; ***wie kam er auf den -n?*** what made him think of that? what gave him that idea? ***sich*** (*Dat.*) ***etwas aus den -n schlagen,*** banish a th. from one's mind; ***seine -n beisammen haben,*** have one's wits about one; ***seine -n nicht beisammen haben,*** be absent-minded *or* inattentive; ***den -n erwecken,*** give *or* create the impression; ***in -n beiwohnen,*** be present in spirit; ***in -n sah sie sich,*** in fancy she saw herself (*a queen etc.*); ***in -n vertieft*** or ***versunken,*** rapt *or* engrossed in thought, preoccupied, (*coll.*) in a brown study; ***seinen -n nachhängen,*** muse, daydream, be lost in thought; ***sich*** (*Dat.*) ***-n über eine S. machen,*** worry, be worried *or* uneasy *or* have misgivings about a th.; ***sich mit dem -n tragen zu tun,*** think of *or* consider doing, have in mind to do; ***-n sind zollfrei,*** opinions are free.

Gedanken|austausch, *m.* exchange of thoughts *or* ideas. **-blitz,** *m.* flash of thought *or* insight, brilliant idea, brainwave. **-folge,** *f.* train of thought, (chain of) reasoning. **-freiheit,** *f.* freedom of thought. **-gang,** *m. See* **-folge. -kreis,** *m.* range of ideas. **-lauf,** *m. See* **-folge. -lesen,** *n.* thought-reading. **gedankenlos,** *adj.* thoughtless, inconsiderate. **Gedankenlosigkeit,** *f.* thoughtlessness, lack of consideration. **Gedanken|lyrik,** *f.* philosophical *or* contemplative poetry. **-raub,** *m.* plagiarism. **gedankenreich,** *adj.* full of good ideas, fertile in ideas. **Gedanken|reichtum,** *m.* wealth of ideas, fertility of the mind. **-späne, -splitter,** *m.pl.* aphorisms, aperçus. **-strich,** *m.* (*Typ.*) dash, em rule. **-übertragung,** *f.* thought-transference, telepathy. **-verbindung,** *f.* association of ideas. **gedankenvoll,** *adj.* thoughtful, pensive; deep in thought. **Gedanken|vorbehalt,** *m.* mental reservation. **-welt,** *f.* world of ideas, ideal world.

gedanklich [gə'daŋklıç], *adj.* 1. mental, intellectual; 2. imaginary.

Gedärm [gə'dɛrm], *n.* (**-(e)s,** *pl.* **-e**) (*usu. pl.*), **Gedärme,** *n.* (**-s,** *pl.* -) intestines, entrails, bowels, guts, (*Cul.*) tripe.

Gedeck [gə'dɛk], *n.* (**-(e)s,** *pl.* **-e**) cover (*at table*); menu (*in restaurant*); ***ein - auflegen,*** lay a place; ***- für 20 Personen,*** covers for 20 persons, table laid for 20 persons.

Gedeih [gə'daı], *m.* (*only in*) ***auf - und Verderb,*** (*or rare*) ***auf - und Ungedeih,*** for better or for worse.

gedeihen [gə'daıən], *irr.v.i.* (*aux.* s.) increase, develop, grow, thrive, flourish, get on well, prosper, succeed; ***das Kind gedeiht prächtig,*** the child is developing splendidly; ***die Arbeit ist schon weit gediehen,*** the work has progressed well; ***die S. ist nun dahin gediehen, daß,*** the affair has now developed to the point that *or* now reached the stage where *or* when; ***unrecht Gut gedeiht nicht,*** ill-gotten gains never prosper. **Gedeihen,** *n.* growth, development, prosperity, success, increase, advantage. **gedeihlich,** *adj.* thriving, prosperous, successful; salutary, beneficial, profitable, favourable.

gedenken [gə'dɛŋkən], **1.** *irr.v.i.* (*with Gen.*) bear in mind, think of, be mindful of, remember, recollect; make mention of; mention (*esp. in one's will*); ***- zu tun,*** intend *or* propose *or* plan *or* have in mind to do, think of doing; ***einer S. nicht -,*** pass over a th. in silence; ***dessen nicht zu -, daß,*** not to mention that. **2.** *irr.v.t.* (***ihm etwas***) remember to the disadvantage of; ***ich will es ihm schon -,*** I'll make him pay for it yet, I'll hold that against him. **Gedenken,** *n.* memory; ***ihn in gutem - behalten,*** have pleasant *or* happy memories of him.

Gedenk|feier, *f.* commemoration. **-gottesdienst,** *m.* memorial service. **-münze,** *f.* commemorative medal. **-rede,** *f.* commemorative address. **-spruch,** *m.* motto, device. **-stein,** *m.* monument, memorial. **-tafel,** *f.* memorial tablet. **-tag,** *m.* commemoration day; anniversary. **-zettel,** *m.* memorandum.

gedeucht [gə'dɔyçt], *see* **dünken.**

Gedicht [gə'dıçt], *n.* (**-(e)s,** *pl.* **-e**) poem; (*also fig.*) gem, dream (*in extravagant praise of an omelette, a lady's hat etc.*). **Gedicht|form,** *f.* ***in -,*** in verse. **-sammlung,** *f.* anthology.

gediegen [gə'di:gən], *adj.* solid, compact, massive; (*Chem.*) unmixed, pure, native; true, genuine, thorough; sterling, upright, high-principled; (*coll.*) splendid, funny; ***-e Kenntnisse,*** profound *or* sound knowledge; ***-e Arbeit,*** sound *or* thorough piece of work; ***-es Gold,*** pure gold; ***-er Witz,*** capital joke; (*coll.*) ***du bist aber -,*** you're the limit. **Gediegenheit,** *f.* solidity, purity, genuineness; (*Chem.*) native state; reliability, thoroughness; sterling quality, intrinsic value.

gedieh [gə'di:], **gediehe, gediehen,** *see* **gedeihen.**

Gedinge [gə'dıŋə], *n.* (**-s,** *pl.* -) bargain, contract, agreement; piecework, contract job; (*dial.*) haggling, bargaining; ***in - arbeiten,*** do piecework, work by contract. **Gedinge|arbeit,** *f.* piecework, contract work. **-geld,** *n.*, **-preis,** *m.* contract price, piece rate.

Gedränge [gə'drɛŋə], *n.* crowd, crush, press, throng, (*coll.*) jam, squash; (*fig.*) embarrassment, distress, difficulty, dilemma, (*fig.*) fix, tight spot; crowding, pushing, thrusting; (*Footb.*) scrimmage. **gedrängt,** *adj.* crowded, dense, packed, crammed, thronged, serried; (*of style*) compact, terse, concise. **Gedrängtheit,** *f.* conciseness, terseness.

gedrechselt [gə'drɛksəlt], *adj.* pretentious, stilted, highfalutin(g) (*of speech*).

gedroschen [gə'drɔʃən], *see* **dreschen.**

gedruckt [gə'drukt], *adj.* printed; ***er lügt wie -,*** he lies like a gas-meter; ***Gedruckte(s),*** printed matter, printed papers, print.

gedrückt [gə'drykt], *adj.* depressed, dejected, in low spirits, down-hearted. **Gedrücktheit,** *f.* depression, dejection, low spirits.

gedrungen [gə'druŋən], *adj.* thick-set, stocky, squat; compact; (*of style*) terse, concise. *See* **dringen.**

Gedudel [gə'du:dəl], *n.* piping, toot(l)ing, tantara, taratantara.

Geduld [gə'dult], *f.* patience, forbearance, indulgence; ***seine - auf die Probe stellen,*** try his patience; ***seine - ermüden,*** wear out his patience; ***endlich war meine - erschöpft*** or ***ging mir die - aus,*** at last I lost all patience; ***fasse dich in -!*** have patience! be patient! possess your soul in patience! **gedulden,** *v.r.* have patience, wait patiently; ***wollen Sie sich einen Augenblick -,*** kindly wait a few moments. **geduldig,** *adj.* patient, forbearing, indulgent. **Geduldsfaden,** *m.* patience; ***der - reißt,*** patience is exhausted *or* at an end. **Geduldspiel,** *n.* puzzle, (*Cards*) patience. **Geduldsprobe,** *f.* nerve-racking ordeal.

gedungen [gə'duŋən], *see* **dingen.**

gedunsen [gə'dunzən], *adj.* bloated, puffy, puffed up; turgid.

gedurft [gə'durft], *see* **dürfen.**

geehrt [gə'e:rt], *adj.* honoured; ***-er Herr,*** Sir; ***Ihr Geehrtes vom 16. April,*** your favour of April 16.

geeicht [gə'aıçt], *p.p. See* **eichen**; (*coll.*) ***darauf - sein,*** be *au fait* with it; (*coll.*) ***darauf nicht - sein,*** not have a clue, be quite in the dark.

geeignet [gə'aıgnət], *adj.* suitable (***für*** *or* ***zu,*** for *or* to), qualified, fit (for), suited, adapted, appropriate (to).

Geest [ge:st], *f.* sandy uplands (*esp. North German coastal plain*).

Gefahr [gə'fa:r], *f.* (-, *pl.* **-en**) danger (***für,*** to), peril, hazard, risk, jeopardy; ***auf die - hin, ihn zu beleidigen*** or ***daß ich ihn beleidige,*** at the risk of insulting him; ***auf eigene -,*** at one's own risk; ***auf meine -,*** at my own risk; ***der - ins Auge sehen,*** look danger in the face; ***sich der - aussetzen,*** expose o.s. to danger, run great risk; ***die gelbe -,*** the yellow peril; ***in – bringen,*** endanger; ***es hat keine –,*** there is no danger; ***der – trotzen,*** brave the danger; (*Comm.*) ***für Rechnung und – von,*** for account and risk of. **gefahrbringend,** *adj.* dangerous, perilous, hazardous.

Gefährde [gə'fɛ:rdə], *f.* (*Poet.*) risk, danger. **gefährden,** *v.t.* endanger, imperil, expose to danger, jeopardize; risk, hazard. **Gefährdung,** *f.* endangering; danger, threat, menace (*Gen.*, to).

Gefahren|zone, *f.* (*Mil.*) danger zone, mined area. **–zulage,** *f.* danger money.

gefährlich [gə'fɛ:rlɪç], *adj.* dangerous, hazardous, perilous, risky; serious, grave, critical; ***ein –es Spiel treiben,*** ride for a fall, skate on thin ice; ***das –e Alter,*** climacteric, 'change of life'; (*coll.*) ***tun Sie doch nicht so –!*** don't make such a fuss! (*coll.*) ***das ist nicht –,*** that's not very serious, that's nothing much. **Gefährlichkeit,** *f.* danger, risk; insecurity.

gefahrlos [gə'fa:rlo:s], *adj.* without risk *or* danger, safe, harmless. **Gefahrlosigkeit,** *f.* safety, security, harmlessness.

Gefährt [gə'fɛ:rt], *n.* **(-(e)s,** *pl.* **-e)** vehicle, cart; ***vierspänniges –,*** coach and four, four-in-hand.

Gefährte [gə'fɛ:rtə], *m.* **(-n,** *pl.* **-n), Gefährtin,** *f.* companion, comrade, associate.

gefahrvoll [gə'fa:rfɔl], *adj.* dangerous, perilous, risky.

Gefäll [gə'fɛl], *n.* **(-(e)s,** *pl.* **-e), Gefälle,** *n.* **(-s,** *pl.* **-)** 1. fall, drop, descent, incline, slope, gradient, grade; ***elektrisches –,*** potential drop; ***die Mühle hat ein gutes –,*** the mill has a good head of water; 2. fallen trees, fallen timber; 3. *pl.* income, revenue. **Gefällemesser,** *m.* clinometer.

[1]**Gefallen** [gə'falən], *m.* favour, kindness; ***ihm einen – tun,*** do him a favour *or* good turn.

[2]**Gefallen,** *n.* pleasure; ***– finden an*** (*Dat.*), take (a) pleasure in, be pleased *or* delighted with, enjoy; take (a fancy) to; ***– haben an*** (*Dat.*), have a liking *or* fondness for; ***ihm zu –,*** to please *or* oblige him.

[1]**gefallen,** *irr.v.i.* (*Dat.*) please; ***wie es Ihnen gefällt,*** as you please; ***es gefällt ihm,*** he likes it, it is to his liking, he is pleased with it; ***er tut was ihm gefällt,*** he does as he pleases; ***das will mir nicht recht –,*** I have misgivings about it; ***sich*** (*Dat.*) ***etwas – lassen,*** put up with a th., submit to a th.; agree with, consent to *or* approve of a th.; ***das lasse ich mir nicht –,*** I will not stand for that; (*coll.*) ***das lasse ich mir –,*** that's nice, that's splendid; ***sich*** (*Dat.*) ***– in*** (*Dat.*), fancy *or* flatter o.s. with; ***er gefiel sich in dem Glauben, daß,*** he fondly imagined that.

[2]**gefallen,** *adj.* fallen; (*Mil.*) killed in action; ***das Los ist –,*** the die is cast, there is no going back. **Gefallene,** *f.* fallen woman. **Gefallenenfriedhof,** *m.* war cemetery. **Gefallene(r),** *m.* (*Mil.*) dead soldier; *pl.* the fallen, the dead.

gefällig [gə'fɛlɪç], *adj.* 1. pleasing, pleasant, agreeable, engaging, (*coll.*) winning, fetching; helpful, accommodating, obliging, kind, complaisant; ***–es Benehmen,*** pleasing *or* easy manners; ***was ist Ihnen –?*** what can I do for you *or* get you? ***Bier –?*** would you like some beer? (*said by waiters*); (*Comm.*) ***Ihr –es Schreiben,*** your favour; (*Comm.*) ***Ihrer –en Antwort entgegensehend,*** awaiting (the favour of) your reply; 2. (*dial. See* **fällig**) due, payable. **Gefälligkeit,** *f.* kindness, favour; complaisance; ***nur aus – für Sie,*** only to oblige you *or* as a favour. **Gefälligkeits|akzept,** *n.*, **–wechsel,** *m.* (*Comm.*) accommodation bill. **gefälligst,** *adv.* (*stiff and formal, often threatening*) if you please; ***nehmen Sie – Platz!*** will you please sit down; pray, be seated; ***schicken Sie mir –,*** kindly send me.

Gefallsucht [gə'falzuxt], *f.* desire to please, coquetry. **gefallsüchtig,** *adj.* coquettish.

Gefällwechsel [gə'fɛlvɛksəl], *m.* (*Railw.*) change in gradient.

Gefältel [gə'fɛltəl], *n.* gathers, folds, pleats. **gefältelt,** *adj.* folded, pleated.

gefangen [gə'faŋən], *adj.* captured, caught, captive, imprisoned; (*fig.*) captivated, enthralled; ***sich – geben,*** surrender, give o.s. up; ***– halten,*** hold captive, detain in custody. **Gefangenen|arbeit,** *f.* convict labour. **–lager,** *n.* prison camp. **Gefangene(r),** *m., f.* captive, prisoner. **gefangenhalten,** *irr.v.t. See* ***gefangen halten***; (*fig.*) hold under one's spell, captivate. **Gefangennahme,** *f.* arrest, capture, apprehension, seizure. **gefangennehmen,** *irr.v.t.* capture, seize, take prisoner; arrest, apprehend; (*fig.*) captivate, enthrall. **Gefangenschaft,** *f.* captivity, imprisonment, confinement, custody. **gefangensetzen,** *v.t.* arrest, take into custody.

gefänglich [gə'fɛŋlɪç], *adj.* (*obs.*) imprisoned, captive; ***– einziehen,*** imprison. **Gefängnis,** *n.* **(-ses,** *pl.* **-se)** prison, gaol, jail; ***zu zweijährigem – verurteilen,*** sentence to two years' imprisonment. **Gefängnis|strafe,** *f.* (term of) imprisonment. **–wärter,** *m.* gaoler, jailer, warder.

Gefasel [gə'fa:zəl], *n.* (*coll.*) twaddle, tosh, bosh.

gefasert [gə'fa:zərt], *adj.* fibrous; ***–es Papier,*** granite paper.

Gefäß [gə'fɛ:s], *n.* **(-es,** *pl.* **-e)** vessel, container, receptacle; hilt (*of sword*). **Gefäß|bildung,** *f.* vascular structure. **–bündel,** *n.* vascular tissue. **–haut,** *f.* vascular membrane. **–lehre,** *f.* angiology. **–system,** *n.* vascular system.

gefaßt [gə'fast], *adj.* 1. ready, prepared; ***sich*** (*Acc.*) ***auf eine S. – machen,*** be prepared for a th.; 2. composed, resigned, calm, collected; 3. written; 4. set (*of stones*). **Gefaßtheit,** *f.* composure, resignation, calmness, calm.

Gefecht [gə'fɛçt], *n.* **(-(e)s,** *pl.* **-e)** fight, fighting, battle, combat, encounter, action, engagement; ***außer – gesetzt werden,*** be put out of action, be knocked out; ***hinhaltendes –,*** containing *or* delaying action; ***örtliches –,*** local engagement; (*fig.*) ***ins – führen,*** advance (*arguments etc.*). **Gefechts|ausbildung,** *f.* battle *or* combat training. **–bereitschaft,** *f.* readiness for action, fighting trim. **–deck,** *n.* (*Nav.*) gun deck. **gefechtsklar,** *adj.* (*Nav.*) cleared for action. **Gefechts|kopf,** *m.* warhead (*of torpedo*). **–lage,** *f.* tactical situation. **–schießen,** *n.* field firing-exercise. **–stand,** *m.* battle headquarters, operation room, command post. **–stärke,** *f.* fighting strength. **–stellung,** *f.* battle station. **–übung,** *f.* mock battle, field exercise. **–ziel,** *n.* tactical objective.

gefeit [gə'faɪt], *adj.* proof (***gegen,*** against); immune (from), invulnerable (to).

gefertigt [gə'fɛrtɪçt], *adj.* made, manufactured, prepared.

Gefieder [gə'fi:dər], *n.* feathers, plumage. **gefiedert,** *adj.* feathered; (*Bot.*) pinnate.

gefiel [gə'fi:l], **gefiele,** *see* **gefallen.**

Gefilde [gə'fɪldə], *n.* **(-s,** *no pl.*) (*Poet.*) fields, open country, tract of land; domain; ***– der Seligen,*** Elysian Fields.

geflammt [gə'flamt], *adj.* mottled, wavy; watered (*silk*).

Geflatter [gə'flatər], *n.* fluttering.

Geflecht [gə'flɛçt], *n.* **(-(e)s,** *pl.* **-e)** wickerwork; mesh, netting, lattice, (*of fabric*) texture; (*Anat.*) plexus.

gefleckt [gə'flɛkt], *adj.* spotted, speckled, stained, freckled, maculose.

Geflimmer [gə'flɪmər], *n.* glittering, scintillation; (*Mil. sl.*) spit and polish.

Geflissenheit [gə'flɪsənhaɪt], *f.* diligence, assiduity. **geflissentlich,** 1. *adj.* wilful, intentional, deliberate, premeditated, (*Law*) with malice aforethought. 2. *adv.* assiduously, diligently, designedly, studiously, on purpose.

geflochten [gə'flɔxtən], *see* **flechten.**

geflogen [gə'flo:gən], *see* **fliegen.**

geflohen [gə'flo:ən], *see* **fliehen.**

geflossen [gə'flɔsən], *see* **fließen.**

Geflügel [gə'fly:gəl], *n.* poultry, fowl(s). **Geflügelhändler,** *m.* poulterer. **geflügelt,** *adj.* winged; ***–es Wort,*** familiar quotation, household word. **Geflügelzucht,** *f.* poultry-farming.

Geflunker [gə'fluŋkər], *n.* (*coll.*) fibbing, lies.

Geflüster [gə'flystər], *n.* whispering.
gefochten [gə'fɔxtən], *see* **fechten.**
Gefolge [gə'fɔlgə], *n.* train, attendants, suite, entourage, retinue; consequences; ***im – haben,*** be attended with, lead to, result in; (*fig.*) ***im – von,*** in the train *or* wake of. **Gefolgschaft,** *f.* 1. followers, adherents; – ***leisten,*** obey, be under the orders of, serve; 2. (*Nat. Soc.*) staff, personnel. **Gefolgschaftsgeist,** *m.* (*Nat. Soc.*) team spirit. **Gefolgsmann,** *m.* follower; vassal, thane; (*fig.*) supporter, henchman.
gefragt [gə'fra:kt], *adj.* in demand *or* request; asked for, sought after.
gefranst [gə'franst], *adj.* fringed.
Gefräß [gə'frɛ:s], *n.* (**-es,** *pl.* **-e**) (*vulg.*) *see* **Fraß. gefräßig,** *adj.* voracious, gluttonous, greedy. **Gefräßigkeit,** *f.* voracity, gluttony, greediness.
Gefreite(r) [gə'fraɪtə(r)], *m.* lance-corporal (*infantry*) *or* bombardier (*artillery*), able seaman, aircraftman 1st class.
Gefrier|anlage [gə'fri:r–], *f.* refrigeration plant. **–apparat,** *m.* ice-machine, freezer. **gefrieren,** *irr.v.i.* (*aux.* s.) freeze, congeal. **Gefrier|fleisch,** *n.* frozen meat. **–punkt,** *m.* freezing-point. **–schutzmittel,** *n.* (*Motor.*) anti-freeze solution.
gefroren [gə'fro:rən], *see* **frieren. Gefrorene(s),** *n.* ice(-cream).
Gefüge [gə'fy:gə], *n.* (**-s,** *no pl.*) construction, structure, system, framework; articulation, joints; texture; (*Geol.*) stratification.
gefügig [gə'fy:gɪç], *adj.* pliant, pliable, flexible; tractable, docile, pliant, submissive, accommodating. **Gefügigkeit,** *f.* pliancy, flexibility; docility, submissiveness, tractability.
Gefühl [gə'fy:l], *n.* (**-(e)s,** *pl.* **-e**) feeling, sentiment, emotion; sensation, touch, sense of feeling; sense, instinct, intuitive grasp. **gefühllos,** *adj.* unfeeling, hard(-hearted), heartless, callous; numb; – ***gegen,*** insensible to. **Gefühllosigkeit,** *f.* heartlessness; numbness. **Gefühlsausbruch,** *m.* outburst. **gefühlsbetont,** *adj.* sentimental, sensitive. **Gefühlsduselei,** *f.* sentimentalism, sentimentality, (*sl.*) mush. **gefühlsduselig,** *adj.* sentimental, (*sl.*) s(l)oppy, mushy. **gefühlsmäßig,** *adj.* intuitive. **Gefühls|mensch,** *m.* emotional character; sentimentalist. **–sinn,** *m.* sense of touch. **gefühlvoll,** *adj.* feeling, tender; affectionate, sensitive; full of expression; sentimental.
geführig [gə'fy:rɪç], *adj.* good for skiing (*of snow*).
gefüllt [gə'fylt], *adj.* 1. filled; 2. (*Bot.*) double.
gefunden [gə'fundən], *see* **finden.**
gefurcht [gə'furçt], *adj.* furrowed, channelled, grooved, (*Bot.*) sulcate.
gegabelt [gə'ga:bəlt], *adj.* forked, furcate, dichotomous.
Gegacker [gə'gakər], *n.* cackle, cackling (*of geese*).
gegangen [gə'gaŋən], *see* **gehen.**
gegeben [gə'ge:bən], *adj.* given, stated, specified, accepted, acknowledged; prevailing, traditional, inherited; ***als – voraussetzen,*** assume as a fact, take for granted; ***unter den –en Umständen,*** things being as they are; ***zu –er Zeit,*** when the occasion arises, at the proper time; ***das ist das Gegebene,*** that's the (obvious) thing, that suggests itself as obvious. **gegebenenfalls,** *adv.* if occasion arises, in that case, if need be, if necessary. **Gegebenheit,** *f.* reality, actuality, (conditioning) factor; *pl.* (given) facts, data.
gegen ['ge:gən], *prep.* (*Acc.*) 1. (*time or place*) – ***Osten,*** eastward, towards,the east, in the east; ***er hat etwas davon – mich erwähnt,*** he mentioned s.th. about it to me; 2. (*opposition*) against, opposed to, in the face of, contrary to, over against, opposite to; versus; – ***das Abkommen,*** in violation of the agreement; ***Heilmittel –,*** remedy for *or* against; – ***den Strom,*** against the current; – ***die Vernunft,*** in the face of reason; 3. (*comparison*) compared with *or* to, as against; ***die Mode ist so verschieden – früher,*** fashion is so different from what it was; ***eins – das andere halten,*** compare one th. with another; ***Sie sind jung – mich,*** you are young compared with me; 4. (in exchange *or* return) for; – ***bare Zahlung,*** for ready money, for cash; ***ich wette 10 – eins,*** I lay 10 to one; – ***Empfangsbescheinigung,*** against a receipt; ***Geld leihen – einen Wechsel,*** lend money on a bill; – ***Quittung,*** against a receipt; 5. (*approximation*) about, nearly, roughly, in the neighbourhood of, (*Am.*) around; – ***dreißig Jahre alt,*** about thirty years old, round thirty; ***es geht – Morgen,*** it is nearly morning; – ***diese Zeit,*** about this time.
Gegen|absicht, *f.* opposite intention, cross-purpose. **–angriff,** *m.* counter-attack. **–anklage,** *f.* counter-charge. **–antrag,** *m.* counter-motion. **–antwort,** *f.* rejoinder, (*Law*) replication. **–arznei,** *f.* antidote. **–bedingung,** *f.* ***wir haben zur – gemacht, daß,*** in return, we have stipulated that. **–befehl,** *m.* counter-order; – ***geben,*** countermand. **–bemerkung,** *f.* reply, criticism. **–beschuldigung,** *f.* recrimination. **–besuch,** *m.* return visit; ***einen – machen,*** return a visit. **–bewegung,** *f.* reaction, counter-movement. **–beweis,** *m.* counter-evidence; ***den – anbringen,*** rebut (*an assertion*). **–beziehung,** *f.*, **–bezug,** *m.* correlation. **–bild,** *n.* contrast; counterpart; antitype. **–böschung,** *f.* (*Fort.*) counterscarp. **–buchung,** *f.* (*Comm.*) cross-entry. **–bürgschaft,** *f.* collateral.
Gegend ['ge:gənt], *f.* (-, *pl.* **-en**) region, district; tract of country; area, locality, neighbourhood; part, quarter (*of the sky*); ***in unsrer –,*** in our parts; ***in der – von,*** in the neighbourhood of, close to, near; ***umliegende –,*** surroundings, environs, vicinity; ***die – um Potsdam,*** the environs of Potsdam; ***in welcher –?*** whereabouts?
Gegen|dienst, *m.* service in return. **–druck,** *m.* reaction, resistance; counter-pressure.
gegeneinander [ge:gənaɪn'andər], *adv.* towards *or* against each other, reciprocally, mutually; – ***versetzt,*** staggered; (*Math.*) – ***geneigt,*** converging. **gegeneinander|halten,** *irr.v.t.*, **–setzen,** *v.t.* compare, place side by side, bring face to face, confront. **–stoßen,** *irr.v.i.* (*aux.* s.) collide, run *or* bump into each other, crash (together).
Gegen|erklärung, *f.* counter-declaration; denial, protest. **–faktor,** *m.* opposing factor. **–farbe,** *f.* complementary colour, contrasting colour. **–forderung,** *f.* counter-claim, (*Comm.*) set-off. **–frage,** *f.* question in reply to a question. **–füßler,** *m.* dweller in the antipodes, antipode. **–gefühl,** *n.* opposite feeling; aversion. **–gerade,** *f.* (*Spt.*) back straight. **–gesang,** *m.* antiphony. **–getriebe,** *n.* (*Mech.*) differential (gear). **–gewicht,** *n.* counterpoise, counterweight; (*fig.*) compensating factor; ***als – zu,*** to set off *or* counterbalance. **–gift,** *n.* antidote; antitoxin. **–grund,** *m.* objection, counter-argument. **–gruß,** *m.* greeting in return. **–halt,** *m.* counter-pressure, resistance; holdfast, prop. **–halter,** *m.* (*Mech.*) back-stop, dolly. **–kandidat,** *m.* rival candidate; ***ohne –,*** unopposed. **–klage,** *f.* recrimination, counter-charge, (*Law*) cross-action. **–kopplung,** *f.* (*Rad.*) negative feedback. **–kraft,** *f.* reaction, opposing force. **–kurs,** *m.* reciprocal course. **gegenläufig,** *adj.* counter-rotating. **Gegen|leistung,** *f.* (service in) return, equivalent, (*Comm.*) consideration; ***als –,*** in return. **–licht,** *n.* light in one's eyes. **–lichtblende,** *f.* (*Phot.*) lens shade, (*Motor.*) anti-dazzle screen. **–liebe,** *f.* love in return; (*coll.*) ***er fand mit diesem Vorschlag keine –,*** his proposal met with no support *or* was not taken up.
Gegen|maßnahme, **–maßregel,** *f.* counter-measure, preventive measure; *pl.* retaliation, reprisals. **–mittel,** *n.* remedy, antidote. **–mutter,** *f.* (*Mech.*) check- *or* lock-nut. **–papst,** *m.* antipope. **–part,** *m.* 1. ***den – halten,*** maintain the contrary; *see* **–teil**; 2. adversary, antagonist. **–partei,** *f.* (party in) opposition, opponents. **–posten,** *m.* set-off. **–probe,** *f.* cross-check, check(-test), control test. **–propaganda,** *f.* counter-propaganda. **–rechnung,** *f.* check-account, control account; set-off, offset; ***in – stehen,*** have mutual accounts; ***durch – beglichen*** or ***saldiert,*** set off *or* offset *per contra.* **–rede,** *f.* contradiction; rejoinder, (*Law*) counter-plea, replication. **–reiz,** *m.* counter-

irritant. **–revolution,** *f.* counter-revolution. **–richtung,** *f.* reverse direction.

Gegensatz ['ge:gənzats], *m.* antithesis; contrast (*zu*, to), (the) opposite *or* contrary (*von*, of); antagonism, opposition (*zwischen*, between). **gegensätzlich,** *adj.* contrary, opposite; opposing, antagonistic. conflicting.

Gegen|schein, *m.* (*Phys.*) reflection; (*Astr.*) opposition. **–schiene,** *f.* guard-rail. **–schrift,** *f.* refutation; rejoinder. **–see,** *f.* head sea.

Gegenseite ['ge:gənzaɪtə], *f.* opposite *or* reverse side, reverse; opponent, the other party. **gegenseitig,** *adj.* reciprocal, mutual; *–e Beziehung,* correlation, interrelation; *–e Freundschaft,* mutual friendship. **Gegenseitigkeit,** *f.* reciprocity, mutuality; (*coll.*) *das beruht ganz auf –,* same here.

Gegen|signal, *n.* answering signal. **–sinn,** *m.* contrary sense. **–sonne,** *f.* parhelion, mock sun. **–spiel,** *n.* counterpart, reverse; opposition. **–spieler,** *m.* opponent, antagonist, adversary, (*coll.*) opposite number. **–spionage,** *f.* counter-espionage. **–sprechanlage,** *f.*, **–sprechen,** *n.* (*Tele.*) duplex *or* two-way communication system.

Gegenstand ['ge:gənʃtant], *m.* object, thing; subject (matter), theme, topic; item, matter, affair, issue; *zum – haben,* deal *or* be concerned with; *– des Spottes,* laughing-stock. **gegenständig,** *adj.* (*Bot.*) opposite. **gegenständlich,** *adj.* objective, concrete, perspicuous, graphic. **gegenstandslos,** *adj.* 1. superfluous, unnecessary; without object, meaningless, unfounded, invalid; irrelevant, immaterial, to no purpose; 2. abstract, non-representational (*art*). **Gegenstandswort,** *n.* concrete noun.

Gegen|stimme, *f.* (*Mus.*) counterpart; dissentient voice, adverse vote. **–stoff,** *m.* antidote, antibody. **–stoß,** *m.* counter-thrust, counter-attack; (*Phys.*) reaction. **–strahl,** *m.* (*Phys.*) reflection, reflected ray. **–strom,** *m.* (*Elec.*) reverse current. **–strömung,** *f.* eddy, counter-current. **–stück,** *n.* counterpart; antithesis; matching *or* companion picture *or* piece, the other one of a pair, fellow. **–takt,** *m.* (*Rad.*) push-pull. **–teil,** *n.* contrary (*von*, to), opposite, reverse, converse (of); *gerade das –,* just the opposite *or* contrary; *das – behaupten,* maintain the contrary; *im –,* on the contrary. **gegenteilig,** *adj.* contrary, to the contrary, opposite.

gegenüber [ge:gən'y:bər], **1.** *adv.* opposite, face to face, facing, vis-à-vis, abreast. **2.** *prep.* (*von* or *preceding Dat.*) opposite (to), vis-à-vis, face to face with, in front of; compared with *or* to, over *or* as against, contrary *or* opposed to; in relation to, in view of, in the face of, considering; *ihm freundlich etc. –,* kind *etc.* to him; *sich* (*einer Aufgabe etc.*) *– sehen,* be faced *or* confronted with *or* (*coll.*) be up against (a problem *etc.*). **Gegenüber,** *n.* that which is opposite; vis-à-vis (*p. at table, in railw. carriage etc.*), outlook (*from one's window etc.*).

gegenüber|liegend, *adj.* facing, opposite; *–e Winkel,* alternate angles. **–stehen,** *irr.v.i.* (*Dat.*) face, stand opposite, be face to face with; be opposed to. **–stellen,** *v.t.* (*Dat.*) set against, oppose to; confront with; contrast with. **Gegenüberstellung,** *f.* confrontation, opposition; comparison; contrast.

Gegen|unterschrift, –unterzeichnung, *f.* counter-signature. **–verhör,** *n.* cross-examination. **–verkehr,** *m.* oncoming traffic. **–verschreibung,** *f.* collateral (security), counter-bond. **–versicherung,** *f.* reinsurance. **–versuch,** *m.* control experiment. **–vorschlag,** *m.* counter-proposal. **–vorstellung,** *f.* remonstrance. **–vorwurf,** *m.* recrimination.

Gegenwart ['ge:gənvart], *f.* presence, the present (time); (*Gram.*) present tense. **gegenwärtig,** **1.** *adj.* present-day, today's; present, actual, current, prevailing, extant; *–e Preise,* current *or* today's prices; *ihm – sein,* be present in his mind; (*Comm.*) *–es Schreiben,* these presents, the present; (*Comm.*) *mit –em melde ich Ihnen,* I beg to inform you by the present. **2.** *adv.* at the moment, at present, for the time being, just now; nowadays, in our time. **gegenwartsnahe,** *adj.* up-to-date, topical.

Gegen|wehr, *f.* resistance, defence. **–wert,** *m.* equivalent, set-off; proceeds. **–wind,** *m.* head-wind. **–winkel,** *m.* alternate angle. **–wirkung,** *f.* reaction, counteraction, counter-effect. **gegenzeichnen,** *v.t.* countersign. **Gegen|zeichnung,** *f.* counter-signature. **–zeugnis,** *n.* counter-evidence, contradictory evidence. **–zug,** *m.* counter-move.

gegessen [gə'gɛsən], *see* **essen.**

Gegirre [gə'gɪrə], *n.* cooing (*of doves*).

geglichen [gə'glɪçən], *see* **gleichen.**

gegliedert [gə'gli:dərt], *adj.* jointed, articulate; constructed organically, organized.

geglitten [gə'glɪtən], *see* **gleiten.**

geglommen [gə'glɔmən], *see* **glimmen.**

Gegner ['ge:gnər], *m.* opponent, adversary, antagonist, rival, enemy, foe. **gegnerisch,** *adj.* hostile, antagonistic, opposing, opposed, adverse. **Gegnerschaft,** *f.* opponents, antagonists, adversaries; opposition, antagonism, hostility, enmity, rivalry.

gegolten [gə'gɔltən], *see* **gelten.**

gegoren [gə'go:rən], *see* **gären.**

gegossen [gə'gɔsən], *see* **gießen.**

gegriffen [gə'grɪfən], *see* **greifen.**

Gegrö(h)le [gə'grø:lə], *n.* (*coll.*) cacophony, clamour, catawauling, hullaballoo, hubbub.

Gehabe [gə'ha:bə], *n.* (*coll.*) fussy *or* affected *or* pretentious behaviour; mannerisms, affectation. **gehaben,** *irr.v.r.* (*pres. only*) conduct o.s., behave; *gehabt euch wohl!* farewell! **Gehaben,** *n.* behaviour.

Gehackte(s) [gə'haktə(s)], *n.* minced meat, mince.

Gehader [gə'ha:dər], *n.* brawling.

[1]**Gehalt** [gə'halt], *m.* (**-s,** *pl.* **-e**) contents; capacity; strength, body, concentration; content, substance, intrinsic value, merit; *– an Säure,* acid content, proportion *or* percentage of acid.

[2]**Gehalt,** *n.* (*Austr. and Bav. m.*) (**-(e)s,** *pl.* **¨-er** *or* **-e**) pay, wages, salary, stipend; allowance.

gehalten [gə'haltən], *adj.* bound, obliged; self-controlled, sober, steady; *gut –,* well kept; well treated. *See* **halten.**

gehaltlos [gə'haltlo:s], *adj.* lacking substance, insubstantial, (*fig.*) worthless, shallow, superficial, empty, hollow, trivial. **Gehaltlosigkeit,** *f.* lack of substance; worthlessness, superficiality, triviality, emptiness, hollowness, shallowness. **gehaltreich,** *adj.* nutritious, rich (*in content*), substantial, of value; full-bodied, racy (*of wine*); informative, profound (*as a book*).

Gehalts|abzug, *m.* deduction from salary. **–aufbesserung,** *f. See* **–erhöhung. –bestimmung,** *f.* (*Chem., Metall.*) analysis, assay. **–einstufung,** *f.* salary grade. **–empfänger,** *m.* salaried employee. **–erhöhung,** *f.* increase *or* rise in salary. **–forderung,** *f.* salary demand. **–gruppe,** *f. See* **–einstufung. –kürzung,** *f.* reduction *or* cut in salary. **–sätze,** *m.pl.* salary scale. **–vorschuß,** *m.* advance on salary. **–zulage,** *f.* increment; bonus, additional pay.

gehalt|voll, *adj. See* **–reich.**

Gehänge [gə'hɛŋə], *n.* (**-s,** *pl.* **-**) 1. slope, incline, declivity; 2. hangings, pendants, festoon; hanging ears (*of a dog*); sword-belt; (*Engin.*) suspension gear.

Gehänge|schutt, *m.* scree. **–ton,** *m.* residual clay.

geharnischt [gə'harnɪʃt], *adj.* (clad) in armour, armoured; (*of words*) withering, sharp, fiery, barbed, stinging.

gehässig [gə'hɛsɪç], *adj.* spiteful, hateful, vindictive, malicious, venomous, odious. **Gehässigkeit,** *f.* odiousness; spite, spitefulness, vindictiveness, animosity, malice, rancour, venom.

Gehau [gə'hau], *n.* (**-(e)s,** *pl.* **-e**) clearing; copse; wood where trees are being felled.

Gehäuse [gəˈhɔyzə], *n.* (**-s,** *pl.* -) box, case, cabinet, receptacle; shell, casing, housing, capsule, jacket; binnacle (*of compass*); shell (*of snail*); core (*of fruit*); *– einer Reliquie,* shrine.

Gehbahn [ˈge:ba:n], *f.* pavement, (*Am.*) sidewalk.

Geheck(e) [gəˈhɛk(ə)], *n.* (**-(e)s,** *pl.* **-e**) hatch, brood; covey.

Gehege [gəˈhe:gə], *n.* (**-s,** *pl.* -) enclosure, enclosed place; pen, paddock (*for animals*); precinct; preserve, reservation, plantation; (*fig.*) *ihm ins – kommen,* encroach on his preserves; (*coll.*) poke one's nose in his business.

geheim [gəˈhaɪm], *adj.* secret; private, confidential, (*coll.*) hush-hush; mysterious, occult, hidden, concealed, surreptitious, clandestine; underground; (*in titles*) confidential, privy; *im –en,* secretly, in secret, privately; *in –em Einvernehmen mit,* in collusion with; *–e Dienstsache,* classified *or* restricted material; (*B.*) *die –e Offenbarung,* Apocalypse; *–er Rat,* privy council; privy councillor (*see* **Geheimrat**); *–es Siegel,* privy seal; *streng –,* top secret; *–e Wissenschaft,* occult science; *mit einer S. – tun,* be secretive about what one is doing.

Geheim|agent, *m.* secret *or* confidential agent. **-bund,** *m.* secret society; underground organization; clandestine alliance. **-bündler,** *m.* member of a secret society. **-dienst,** *m.* secret service. **-fach,** *n.* secret drawer, private safe, safe-deposit. **geheimhalten,** *irr.v.t.* keep secret, conceal. **Geheim|haltung,** *f.* secrecy, concealment. **-lehre,** *f.* esoteric doctrine; *jüdische –,* cab(b)ala. **-mittel,** *n.* secret remedy, patent medicine, nostrum.

Geheimnis [gəˈhaɪmnɪs], *n.* (**-ses,** *pl.* **-se**) secret (*vor* (*Dat.*), from), mystery; secrecy; arcanum; *öffentliches –,* open secret; *ein – bewahren,* keep *or* guard a secret; (*coll.*) *das ganze –,* the whole story. **Geheimnis|krämer,** *m.* mystery-monger. **-krämerei,** *f. See* **Geheimtuerei. geheimnisvoll,** *adj.* mysterious, obscure; secretive; (*coll.*) *tu' nicht so –,* don't be so secretive *or* make such a mystery of it.

Geheim|polizei, *f.* secret police. **-rat,** *m.* privy councillor. **-ratsecken,** *f.pl.* (*coll.*) receding hair, frontal baldness. **-schloß,** *n.* letter-lock. **-schlüssel,** *m.* cipher key *or* code. **-schreibekunst,** *f.* cryptography. **-schreiber,** *m.* private *or* confidential secretary. **-schrift,** *f.* cipher, code, secret writing. **-sender,** *m.* clandestine *or* pirate radio transmitter. **-siegel,** *n.* privy seal. **-sprache,** *f.* secret language, code language. **-tinte,** *f.* invisible *or* sympathetic ink. **-treppe,** *f.* private staircase, backstairs. **-tuer,** *m. See* **Geheimniskrämer. -tuerei,** *f.* secretiveness. **geheimtuerisch,** *adj.* secretive. **Geheimwissenschaft,** *f.* occult science.

Geheiß [gəˈhaɪs], *n.* command, order, bidding, injunction; *auf mein –,* at my bidding *or* behest, by my order.

gehen [ˈge:ən], **1.** *irr.v.i.* (*aux.* s.) go, move, walk, proceed, pass; leave, go away, depart; run, work, function, operate (*of machinery*); sell (well) (*of goods*); blow (*of wind*); rise (*of dough*).
(a) (*with preps.*) *– bis* **an** (*Acc.*), go *or* come up to *or* as far as, extend to, reach; *an die Arbeit –,* set about *or* start working, set *or* begin to work; *geh nicht an meine Briefe!* do not touch my letters; *ihm an die Hand –,* assist him; give him a (helping) hand; *einer S.* **auf** *den Grund –,* get to the bottom of a th.; *auf die Jagd –,* go (a-)hunting; *das Fenster geht auf den Garten,* the window overlooks the garden *or* looks *or* opens *or* gives on to the garden; *ihm auf den Leim –,* fall into his trap, allow o.s. to be hoodwinked by him; *wie viel Pfennige – auf eine Mark?* how many pfennigs are there in a mark? *die Uhr* or *es geht auf Mittag,* it is going on *or* getting on for midday; *auf die Neige –,* come to an end, draw to a close; *das geht mir auf die Nerven,* that is getting on my nerves; *auf Reisen* or *auf die Reise –,* set out on a journey *or* one's travels; *diese Worte gingen auf mich,* these words were aimed *or* directed at *or* meant for me; *geh mir* **aus** *den Augen,* get out of my sight; *aus den Fugen –,* get out of joint, come to grief, come apart, come *or* fall to pieces; *aus dem Wege –,* step aside, get *or* stand out of the way; **durch** *den Kopf* or *Sinn –,* cross one's mind, strike one, occur to one; *sich* (*Dat.*) *etwas durch den Kopf – lassen,* think a th. over; *das geht mir durch Mark und Bein,* that goes through and through me *or* cuts me to the quick; (*mir etc.*) **gegen** *den Strich –,* go against the grain; upset (my *etc.*) plans; **in** *die Binsen –,* come to grief *or* naught; *in die Brüche* or *in Stücke* or *in Trümmer –,* go *or* fall to pieces, disintegrate, break down, come to grief, come to naught; *ins einzelne –,* go into details; *in Erfüllung –,* come true, be realized, come to pass; *die Preise – in die Höhe,* prices are rising *or* soaring *or* rocketing; *ihm ins Garn –,* fall into his trap, let o.s. be hoodwinked by him; *mit ihm streng ins Gericht –,* take him to task; *ins vierte Jahr –,* enter the fourth year; *das geht mit in den Kauf,* that is included *or* is part of the bargain; *in die Millionen –,* run into millions; *in See –,* put out to sea; *in Seide –,* wear silk; *in sich –,* commune with o.s., take stock of one's position; feel remorse, repent, turn over a new leaf; *er ist ins Wasser gegangen,* he has thrown himself into the water; *der Strom geht* **mit** *Eis,* the river is full of drift-ice; *sie geht mit ihm,* she is keeping company *or* going out with him; *mit der Zeit –,* march with the times; **nach** *Brot –,* go a-begging; seek a livelihood; *das geht nicht nach mir,* I have no say in the matter; *nach der Regel –,* follow the rule; *alles geht nach Wunsch,* everything is going according to plan *or* as well as we could wish; *die Zimmer – alle nach der Straße,* all the rooms face *or* overlook the street; *wann geht der Zug nach Hannover?* when does the train leave for Hanover? *das geht* **über** *alles,* there's nothing like it, that beats everything; *das geht mir über alles,* I prize it above everything *or* like it better than anything; (*coll.*) *das geht über alle Begriffe,* that beats everything, that is beyond belief; *das geht über meine Kraft,* that is beyond my powers; *über Land –,* go across country; *über Leichen –,* ride rough-shod; *ihm* **um** *den Bart –,* wheedle *or* coax *or* flatter him; *wie die Katze um den heißen Brei –,* be like a cat on hot bricks; **unter** *die Leute –,* go into society; *unter die Soldaten –,* enlist; *es geht ihm* **von** *der Hand,* he is a quick and successful worker; *von Hand zu Hand –,* pass from hand to hand; *ihm nicht von der Seite –,* not move *or* budge from his side; **vor** *Anker –,* cast anchor; *er ist vor die Hunde gegangen,* he has gone to the dogs; *vor sich –,* take place, happen, (*coll.*) go on, be up, proceed; **zu** *ihm –,* go to see him, call on him; go *or* step up to him, join him; *zum Abendmahl –,* take (the holy) communion; *zu Fuß –,* walk, go on foot; *ihm zur Hand –,* help him; *das geht mir zu Herzen,* that touches my heart, I am very sorry about it; *zur Industrie –,* go into industry; *ihm zu Leibe –,* lay a hand on him; *zur Neige –,* come to an end; *mit sich zu Rate –,* deliberate, consider; *behutsam zu Werke –,* set about cautiously.
(b) (*with advs.*) *seine Absicht geht dahin,* his intention *or* aim is; *sein ganzes Vermögen ging darauf,* it cost him his whole fortune; (*coll.*) *drunter und drüber –,* be topsy-turvy *or* higgledy-piggledy; *das Geschäft geht gut,* the business is doing well; (*coll.*) *kaputt –,* get broken; (*coll.*) *schief –,* go wrong; *schwanger –,* be pregnant *or* with child; *mit großen Ideen schwanger –,* be full of big ideas; *die Uhr geht richtig,* the clock is right; *verlustig –* (*Gen.*), be deprived of, forfeit, lose; *vonstatten –,* get on *or* proceed well, succeed; *zugrunde –,* be ruined *or* wrecked, break down, come to grief *or* to nothing.
(c) (*other idioms*) (*coll.*) *er kam gegangen,* he came on foot; *– lassen,* let go *or* free; let off (scot-free); leave alone *or* in place; *sich – lassen,* let o.s. go, lose control of o.s.; take it easy, indulge one's inclinations; speak freely; *sich gut – lassen,* take good care of o.s., look after o.s. well; have a good time; *schlafen –,* go to bed; *er ist von uns gegangen,* he has departed (this life), he has passed on *or* away; *geh deine Wege!* be off! *wie geht das Lied?* how does the song go *or* run? (*coll.*)

er wurde gegangen or *ist gegangen worden,* he was sacked *or* (*sl.*) given the boot.
2. *irr.v.imp. es geht,* it is possible, it can be done, it will be all right, it will do; (*as reply*) it could be worse, fairly well, not bad; (*as assurance*) I can manage (all right); *es geht nicht,* it can't be done, it doesn't *or* won't work, it's out of the question, it won't do, it's no go; *es geht mir schlecht,* (*health*) I'm not well, (*affairs*) I'm doing badly, things go badly with me; *es ging mir genau so,* it was exactly the same with me, the same th. happened to me; *es geht mir an den Kragen,* it touches me closely, things are getting warm *or* hot *or* critical for me; *wenn es nach mir ginge,* if I had my way; *es geht um Geld,* it's a question of money, money is at stake, it's a money matter; *es geht um die letzte Entscheidung,* the final decision must be made *or* reached; *es geht um Leben und Tod,* it's a matter of life and death; *um was geht es?* what's the (point at) issue? what's it all about? *es geht sich schlecht hier,* the going *or* way is difficult here, it's difficult to walk here.

Gehen, *n.* walking; *das – wird ihm sauer,* he has difficulty in walking; *des –s müde sein,* be tired of walking; *das Kommen und –,* coming and going.

Gehenk [gəˈhɛŋk], *n.* (**-(e)s,** *pl.* **-e**) sword-belt; strap (*for hanging s.th. up by*); loop.

Gehentfernung [ˈgeːɛntfɛrnuŋ], *f.* walking distance.

geheuer [gəˈhɔyər], *adj.* (*only neg.*) *nicht –,* uncanny, eerie, (*coll.*) fishy; haunted.

Geheul [gəˈhɔyl], *n.* howling, wailing.

gehfähig [ˈgeːfɛːɪç], *adj.* (*Med.*) ambulant, walking.

Gehilfe [gəˈhɪlfə], *m.* (**-n,** *pl.* **-n**) assistant, helper, helpmate.

Gehirn [gəˈhɪrn], *n.* (**-(e)s,** *pl.* **-e**) brain; brains, brain-power, sense; *das kleine –,* cerebellum; *ihm das – einschlagen,* knock his brains out.

Gehirn|blatt, *n.* fontanel. **–entzündung,** *f.* encephalitis, brain-fever. **–erschütterung,** *f.* concussion (of the brain). **–erweichung,** *f.* softening of the brain. **–haut,** *f.* cerebral membrane, meninges. **–hautentzündung,** *f.* meningitis. **–kasten,** *m.* (*coll.*) skull, brain-box. **–krankheit,** *f.* brain disorder. **–mark,** *n.* medulla. **–rinde,** *f.* cerebral cortex. **–schale,** *f.* skull, cranium. **–schlag,** *m.* cerebral apoplexy. **–substanz,** *f.* (*coll.*) *graue –,* grey matter. **–tätigkeit,** *f.* cerebration. **–wäsche,** *f.* brain-washing. **–wassersucht,** *f.* hydrocephalus.

gehoben [gəˈhoːbən], *adj. –e Sprache,* elevated speech, high style; *fünfmal –e Verse,* verses of five beats, pentameters; *–e Stellung,* senior *or* executive position; *–e Stimmung,* elation, high spirits. *See* **heben.**

Gehöft [gəˈhøːft], *n.* (**-(e)s,** *pl.* **-e**) (*dial.*) **Gehöfte,** *n.* (**-s,** *pl.* **-**) farm, farm buildings, farmstead.

geholfen [gəˈhɔlfən], *see* **helfen.**

Gehölz [gəˈhœlts], *n.* (**-es,** *pl.* **-e**) wood, woodland, copse, thicket.

Gehör [gəˈhøːr], *n.* (sense of) hearing; musical ear; *gutes* or *feines* or *scharfes –,* acute hearing, quick ear; *zu – kommen,* be heard; be performed (*of music*); *sich* (*Dat.*) *– verschaffen,* make o.s. heard, (*Law*) obtain a hearing; *nach dem – singen* (*spielen*), sing (play) by ear; *der Vernunft – geben,* listen to reason; *um – bitten,* crave a hearing; *– schenken* (*Dat.*), listen to, lend an ear *or* give a hearing to; *kein – schenken* (*Dat.*), turn a deaf ear to.

gehorchen [gəˈhɔrçən], *v.i.* (*Dat.*) obey; *der Vernunft –,* listen to reason; *das Schiff gehorcht dem Ruder,* the ship obeys *or* responds to the tiller.

gehören [gəˈhøːrən], **1.** *v.i.* (*Dat. or zu*) belong to, be owned by, form part of, appertain to; be classed with, rank among; *das gehört nicht hierher,* (*of a th.*) that does not belong here, (*of an argument*) that is beside the point *or* is irrelevant; *gehört das Ihnen?* is it yours? *dazu gehört Geld und Zeit,* that requires time and money; *dazu gehört Mut,* courage is needed for that; *er gehört in die Irrenanstalt,* he ought to be in a madhouse; *es gehört zum guten Ton,* it is the polite *or* proper thing to do; *diese – zu den besten,* these are among the best; (*coll.*) *es gehört schon etwas dazu,* that really takes some doing; *– unter* (*Acc.*), be subject to, come *or* fall under. **2.** *imp.v.r.* be suitable *or* right *or* proper *or* becoming; *wie sich's gehört,* as is right, as is seemly, as it should be, properly, duly; *das gehört sich nicht,* that isn't the way to behave, (*coll.*) it's not done.

Gehör|fehler, *m.* defective hearing. **–gang,** *m.* auditory canal.

gehörig [gəˈhøːrɪç], *adj.* **1.** (*Dat. or zu*) belonging to, owned by; forming part of, appertaining to; *nicht zur S. –,* beside the point, irrelevant; **2.** fitting, suitable; right, proper, fit, due, (*coll.*) thorough, sound, quite a . . .; *der –e Respekt,* the proper *or* due respect; (*coll.*) *ich hab's ihm – gegeben,* I have given him what for.

gehörleidend [gəˈhøːrlaɪdənt], *adj.* with defective hearing. **gehörlos,** *adj.* deaf.

Gehörn [gəˈhœrn], *n.* (**-(e)s,** *pl.* **-e**) horns, antlers.

Gehörnerv [gəˈhøːrnɛrf], *m.* auditory nerve.

gehörnt [gəˈhœrnt], *adj.* horned, antlered; *der –e Siegfried,* S. the invulnerable; (*coll.*) *der –e Ehemann,* cuckold.

Gehör|organ, *n.* organ of hearing. **–probe,** *f.* hearing test.

gehorsam [gəˈhɔrzaːm], *adj.* obedient (*gegen,* to), dutiful; submissive, docile; *Ihr –er Diener,* your obedient servant (*at the end of letters to newspapers etc.*). **Gehorsam,** *m.* obedience, dutifulness; *aus – gegen,* in obedience to; *– leisten* (*Dat.*), obey; *den – verweigern* (*Dat.*), refuse to obey, disobey. **gehorsamst,** *sup. adj.* obediently yours (*at the end of a letter, rather servile*); *–er Diener!* at your service; (*Mil.*) *melde –,* I beg to report. **Gehorsamsverweigerung,** *f.* insubordination.

Gehörsinn [gəˈhøːrzin], *m.* (sense of) hearing.

Gehre [ˈgeːrə], *f.*, (*dial.*) **Gehren,** *m.* wedge; gusset, gore, triangular field. **gehren,** *v.t.* bevel. **Gehr|hobel,** *m.* bevel-plane. **–holz, –maß,** *n.* bevel.

Gehrock [ˈgeːrɔk], *m.* frock coat.

Gehrung [ˈgeːruŋ], *f.* mitre, bevel.

Geh|steig, *m.* pavement, (*Am.*) sidewalk. **–störung,** *f.* locomotor disturbance.

Gehudel [gəˈhuːdəl], *n.* bungling, botched work.

gehüpft [gəˈhypft], *p.p.* (*coll.*) *das ist – wie gesprungen,* that's as broad as it's long, it's much of a muchness, six of one and half a dozen of the other.

Geh|versuch, *m.* attempt to walk. **–werk,** *n.* movement, works (*of clock*), clockwork mechanism.

Geier [ˈgaɪər], *m.* vulture, hawk; *hol' dich der –!* to hell with *or* confound you!

Geifer [ˈgaɪfər], *m.* drivel, spittle, slaver; (*fig.*) spite, spleen, venom; *seinen – auslassen,* vent one's spleen (*an* (*Acc.*), upon). **Geiferer,** *m.* vilifier, disparager, vituperator, carper, caviller, slanderer, traducer. **Geifer|läppchen,** *n. See* **–tuch. geifern,** *v.i.* drivel, slaver, foam at the mouth; (*fig.*) foam with rage. **Geifertuch,** *n.* bib.

Geige [ˈgaɪgə], *f.* violin, (*coll.*) fiddle; (*coll.*) *der Himmel hängt ihm voller –n,* he sees the bright side of things. **Geigen|bauer,** *m.* violin maker. **–bogen,** *m.* (violin-)bow; (*coll.*) fiddle-stick. **–harz,** *n.* rosin, colophony. **–steg,** *m.* violin bridge. **–stimme,** *f.* violin-part. **Geiger,** *m.* violinist, violin-player, fiddler.

geil [gaɪl], *adj.* (*of a plant*) luxuriant, rank, (*of a p.*) lewd, lecherous, lustful, lascivious, (*of animals*) in *or* on heat; *–es Fleisch,* proud flesh. **Geile,** *f.* **1.** *See* **Geilheit;** **2.** (*dial.*) manure; **3.** *pl.* testicles (*of animals*). **geilen,** *v.i.* lust (*nach,* after), be lascivious; ask for presents (in an importunate way). **Geilheit,** *f.* rankness, luxuriance (*of growth*), lasciviousness, lewdness, lechery, lust (*of a p.*), rut, heat (*of animals*).

Geisel [ˈgaɪzəl], *m.* (**-s,** *pl.* **-** (*Austr.* **-n**)), *f.* (**-,** *pl.* **-n**) hostage; *– stellen,* give *or* furnish hostages.

Geiser ['gaɪzər], *m.* geyser, hot spring.

Geiß [gaɪs], *f.* (-, *pl.* **-en**) (she- *or* nanny) goat, wild goat, doe. **Geiß|bart,** *m.* (*Bot.*) meadowsweet (*Filipendula ulmaria*); goatsbeard (*Spiraea aruncus*). **-blatt,** *n.* (*Bot.*) honeysuckle, woodbine (*Lonicera periclymenum*). **-bock,** *m.* he-goat, billy-goat.

Geißel ['gaɪsəl], *f.* (-, *pl.* **-n**) lash, whip; (*fig.*) scourge; (*Bot., Zool., Ent.*) flagellum, cilium; cutting reproach *or* sarcasm; ***Gottes –,*** the scourge of God (Attila). **Geißel|brüder,** *m.pl.* flagellants. **-faden,** *m.* (*Bot., Zool., Ent.*) flagellum, cilium. **geißeln,** *v.t.* scourge, lash, whip, flagellate; (*fig., Eccl.*) castigate, chastise; stigmatize, criticize, harshly censure, reprimand, condemn. **Geißel-tierchen,** *n.pl.* flagellata. **Geißelung,** *f.* scourging, lashing, flagellation; (*fig.*) condemnation, castigation, harsh criticism.

Geiß|fuß, *m.* 1. crow-bar, hand-spike; sculptor's veining tool; dentist's implement; 2. (*Bot.*) goatweed, bishop's weed *or* herb gerard (*Aegopodium podagraria*). **-klee,** *m.* (*Bot.*) broom (*Cytisus*).

Geist [gaɪst], *m.* (**-es,** *pl.* **-er** (*Bohemian* **-e**)) spirit; mind, intellect, brains, intelligence, wit, imagination; genius, soul; morale; essence; ghost, spirit, spectre, apparition, phantom, sprite; ***den – aufgeben,*** give up the ghost, breathe one's last; ***ein großer –,*** a master-mind, a genius; ***er war von allen guten -ern verlassen,*** he was out of his mind *or* had lost all sense of reason; ***im –,*** in spirit, in one's mind's eye; ***wir handeln in seinem –,*** we are acting as he would have wished; ***der heilige –,*** the Holy Ghost *or* Spirit; ***wes -es Kind ist er?*** what sort of a fellow is he? ***voll – und Leben,*** witty and vivacious; ***ein Mann von –,*** a brilliant *or* witty man; ***– und Materie,*** mind and matter; ***– einer Sprache,*** genius of a language; ***der –, der stets verneint,*** the spirit of negation.

Geister|banner, *m. See* **-beschwörer. -bannung,** *f. See* **-beschwörung. -beschwörer,** *m.* exorcist, necromancer. **-beschwörung,** *f.* exorcism, necromancy. **-erscheinung,** *f.* apparition, vision, phantom. **-geschichte,** *f.* ghost-story. **-glaube,** *m.* belief in ghosts, spiritism, superstition. **geisterhaft,** *adj.* supernatural, ghostly; ghostlike, spectral. **geistern,** *v.i.* haunt. **Geister|-seher,** *m.* visionary, seer. **-stunde,** *f.* witching hour. **-welt,** *f.* spirit-world.

geistesabwesend ['gaɪstəsˀapve:zənt], *adj.* absent-minded. **Geistes|abwesenheit,** *f.* absent-mindedness, absence of mind. **-anlagen,** *f.pl.* talents, mental faculties. **-anstrengung,** *f.* mental effort. **-arbeit,** *f.* brain work. **-art,** *f.* cast of mind. **-bildung,** *f.* cultivation of the mind. **-blitz,** *m.* brain-wave; stroke *or* flash of genius. **-flug,** *m.* flight of imagination. **-freiheit,** *f.* freedom of thought *or* conscience. **-frische,** *f.* mental vigour. **-frucht,** *f.* literary *or* artistic production. **-funke,** *m.* flash of wit. **-gabe,** *f.* talent, gift. **-gegenwart,** *f.* presence of mind. **geistesgegenwärtig,** *adj.* quick-witted, alert. **Geistesgeschichte,** *f.* history of ideas. **geistesgestört,** *adj.* deranged, unhinged. **Geistes|größe,** *f.* 1. intellectual greatness; 2. intellectual giant; 3. magnanimity. **-haltung,** *f.* mentality, attitude of mind. **-kraft,** *f.* mental power *or* vigour. **geisteskrank,** *adj.* of unsound mind, insane. **Geistes|kranke(r),** *m., f.* mental patient *or* case, lunatic. **-krankheit,** *f.* mental disorder, insanity. **-produkt,** *n.* literary *or* artistic production, (*coll.*) brain-child. **-richtung,** *f.* school *or* trend of thought; philosophy of life. **geistesschwach,** *adj.* feeble-minded, imbecile. **Geistes|schwäche,** *f.* imbecility. **-störung,** *f.* mental derangement; psychopathic disorder. **geistesträge,** *adj.* intellectually lazy. **Geistes|trägheit,** *f.* mental indolence. **-verfassung,** *f.* state *or* frame of mind, mentality. **geistesverwandt,** *adj.* congenial (**mit,** to). **Geistes|verwandtschaft,** *f.* congeniality, affinity of ideas. **-verwirrung,** *f.* mental disturbance *or* unbalance, derangement, delirium. **-wissenschaften,** *f.pl.* the Arts (*contrasted with 'the Sciences'*), humanities. **-zerrüttung,** *f.* mental disturbance. **-zustand,** *m.* mental condition, state of mind.

geistig ['gaɪstɪç], *adj.* 1. spiritual, immaterial; mental, intellectual; ***-e Arbeit,*** brain work; ***-es Auge,*** mind's eye; ***– beschränkt,*** stupid; ***-es Eigentum,*** intellectual property; ***-e Liebe,*** platonic love; ***-er Vorbehalt,*** mental reservation; 2. spirituous, volatile, alcoholic; ***-e Getränke,*** spirits, alcoholic beverages. **Geistigkeit,** *f.* 1. spirituality; intellectuality; 2. alcoholic content.

geistlich ['gaɪstlɪç], *adj.* spiritual, religious, sacred; clerical, ecclesiastic; ***-es Amt,*** ministry; (*B.*) ***selig sind, die da – arm sind,*** blessed are the poor in spirit; ***die -e Behörde,*** the ecclesiastical authorities; ***-e Güter,*** church lands; ***-er Herr,*** clerical gentleman; ***-e Kurfürsten,*** spiritual electors; ***-e Musik,*** sacred music; ***-er Orden,*** religious order; ***-es Recht,*** canon law; ***in den -en Stand treten,*** take (holy) orders, enter the Church. **Geistliche(r),** *m.* clergyman, minister, priest, pastor, (*Mil. etc.*) chaplain; ecclesiastic, divine. **Geistlichkeit,** *f.* 1. spirituality; 2. priesthood, clergy, the Church.

geistlos ['gaɪstlo:s], *adj,* dull, lifeless, spiritless; unintellectual; senseless, stupid, trivial, platitudinous, insipid. **Geistlosigkeit,** *f.* dullness, mental sluggishness, lifelessness, spiritlessness; lack of intellectual interests; platitude.

geist|reich, *adj.* ingenious, witty, clever, gifted. **-tötend,** *adj.* soul-destroying, monotonous, tedious. **-voll,** *adj. See* **-reich.**

Geitau ['gaɪtau], *n.* (**-(e)s,** *pl.* **-e**) (*Naut.*) brail, clew-line.

Geiz [gaɪts], *m.* 1. greediness, covetousness; parsimony, avarice, stinginess; 2. (*Bot.*) sucker. **geizen,** *v.i.* (**nach**) covet, be covetous of, be greedy for; be avaricious *or* niggardly *or* stingy, (**mit**) stint, economize, be economical with; ***nicht – mit,*** not stint, be lavish with; ***mit jeder Minute –,*** grudge every minute. **Geiz|hals, -hammel,** *m.* miser, niggard, skinflint. **geizig,** *adj.* avaricious, covetous; stingy, miserly, niggardly, tight- *or* close-fisted; ***– nach,*** covetous of, greedy for. **Geiz|-kragen,** *m. See* **-hals.**

Gejammer [gə'jamər], *n.* wailing, lamentation, complaints, (*sl.*) belly-aching.

Gejauchze [gə'jauxtsə], *n.* rejoicing, jubilation, exultation.

Gejohle [gə'jo:lə], *n.* hooting, yelling.

gekachelt [gə'kaxəlt], *adj.* tiled.

gekannt [gə'kant], *see* **kennen.**

Gekeife [gə'kaɪfə], *n.* scolding, nagging.

gekeimt [gə'kaɪmt], *adj.* germinated.

gekerbt [gə'kɛrpt], *adj.* crenate.

Gekicher [gə'kɪçər], *n.* tittering, giggling, sniggering.

gekielt [gə'ki:lt], *adj.* carinate, keeled.

Geklapper [gə'klapər], *n.* rattling, clatter.

Geklimper [gə'klɪmpər], *n.* jingling, jangling; strumming (*on a piano*).

Geklingel [gə'klɪŋəl], *n.* tinkling, jangling.

Geklirr(e) [gə'klɪr(ə)], *n.* clanking, clanging, clashing; clink(ing) (*of glasses*).

gekloben [gə'klo:bən], (*obs.*) *see* **klieben.**

geklommen [gə'klɔmən], *see* **klimmen.**

Geklöne [gə'klø:nə], *n.* (*coll.*) gossip, chat, tittle-tattle.

Geklopfe [gə'klɔpfə], *n.* knocking, banging.

geklungen [gə'kluŋən], *see* **klingen.**

Geknatter [gə'knatər], *n.* rattle, clatter; crackling.

geknäult [gə'knɔylt], *adj.* glomerate, coiled.

geknickt [gə'knɪkt], *adj.* bent *or* broken (down); geniculate; (*fig.*) cast down, subdued, disheartened, crestfallen, crushed.

gekniffen [gə'knɪfən], *see* **kneifen.**

Geknirsche [gə'knɪrʃə], *n.* grinding, gnashing (*of teeth*), crunching.

Geknister [gə'knɪstər], *n.* crackling, rustling, rustle, crepitation.

gekonnt [gə'kɔnt], *adj.* (*coll.*) well-versed, slick. *See* **können.**

geköpert [gəˈkø:pərt], *adj.* 1. (*Weav.*) twilled; 2. (*coll.*) stinking rich.
gekoren [gəˈko:rən], *see* **kiesen.**
gekörn(el)t [gəˈkœrn(əl)t], *adj.* grained, granular, granulated.
Gekose [gəˈko:zə], *n.* (*coll.*) billing and cooing.
Gekrächze [gəˈkrɛçtsə], *n.* croaking.
Gekrätz(e) [gəˈkrɛts(ə)], *n.* (*Min.*) waste, refuse, slag, dross, sweeps.
Gekreisch(e) [gəˈkraɪʃ(ə)], *n.* shrieking, shrieks, screaming, screams.
Gekritzel [gəˈkrɪtsəl], *n.* scrawling, scrawl, scribbling, scribble.
gekrochen [gəˈkrɔxən], *see* **kriechen.**
gekröpft [gəˈkrœpft], *adj.* off-set (*of tools etc.*), angulate (*as a cornice*).
Gekröse [gəˈkrø:zə], *n.* (*Anat.*) mesentery; pluck (*of a calf*), (*Cul.*) tripe, giblets.
gekünstelt [gəˈkynstəlt], *adj.* artificial, affected.
Gelächter [gəˈlɛçtər], *n.* laughing, laughter; laughing-stock; ***in ein schallendes – ausbrechen,*** burst out laughing; ***wieherndes –,*** guffaw, horse-laugh; ***ihn zum – machen,*** make him a laughing-stock, make sport of him; ***sich dem – aussetzen,*** expose o.s. to ridicule, make an exhibition of o.s.
geladen [gəˈla:dən], *adj.* 1. charged, loaded; (*Elec.*) charged (*battery*), live (*wire*); ***– mit,*** laden with, (*fig.*) full *or* brimming with; (*Mil.*) *–!* load! (*coll.*) ***schwer – haben,*** be tipsy; 2. invited; *see* **laden.**
Gelag(e) [gəˈla:g(ə)], *n.* (**-s,** *pl.* **-e**) drinking-bout, carouse; feast, banquet; revel.
Geläger [gəˈlɛ:gər], *n.* dregs, bottoms, deposit.
gelagert [gəˈla:gərt], *adj.* beaten down; stratified; mounted on bearings; (*fig.*) circumstanced; ***besonders –e Fälle,*** special cases, cases of a special nature.
Gelände [gəˈlɛndə], *n.* (**-s,** *pl.* **-**) (tract of) land, country, area, territory, region; ground, (*Mil.*) terrain; site, plot, lot; ***abfallendes*** (***aufsteigendes***) ***–,*** falling (rising) ground; (*Mil.*) ***bestrichenes –,*** beaten zone; ***freies –,*** open country; ***schwieriges –,*** difficult terrain.
Gelände|abschnitt, *m.* sector, area. **–antrieb,** *m.* (*Motor.*) four-wheel drive. **–aufnahme,** *f.* aerial photograph, ground survey. **–bö,** *f.* ground squall. **–erschließung,** *f.* land development. **gelände|-fähig, –gängig,** *adj.* suitable for *or* able to traverse rough country, *e.g.* ***geländegängiger Wagen,*** cross-country vehicle, jeep. **Gelände|hindernis,** *n.* natural obstacle. **–kunde,** *f.* topography. **–lauf,** *m.* cross-country run *or* race. **–punkt,** *m.* landmark.
Geländer [gəˈlɛndər], *n.* railing, rails; balustrade, parapet, handrail; trellis, espalier. **Geländer-fenster,** *n.* window with balcony.
Geländeritt [gəˈlɛndərɪt], *m.* cross-country race (*horses*).
Geländer|pfosten, *m.* banister. **–säule,** *f.* baluster.
Gelände|spiel, *n.* scoutcraft, scouting game. **–sport,** *m.* field-sports. **–übung,** *f.* (*Mil.*) field exercise. **–verhältnisse,** *n.pl.* terrain conditions. **–wagen,** *m.* (*Motor.*) cross-country vehicle.
gelang [gəˈlaŋ], **gelänge** [gəˈlɛŋə], *see* **gelingen.**
gelangen [gəˈlaŋən], *v.i.* (*aux. s.*) (*an* (*Acc.*), *nach* or *zu*) gain, acquire, reach, attain (to); arrive at, get *or* come to, get admitted to; ***in die richtigen Hände –,*** get into the right hands; ***ans*** or ***zum Ziel –,*** attain *or* gain one's end, accomplish one's purpose; ***zur Reife –,*** come to maturity; ***etwas an ihn – lassen,*** have a th. delivered, forward *or* transmit *or* address s.th. to him; ***zu einer Ansicht –,*** arrive at *or* reach a conclusion, form an opinion; (*Theat.*) ***zur Aufführung –,*** be put on the stage, be performed; ***auf die Nachwelt –,*** be handed down to posterity; ***zur Macht –,*** come into power; ***zu Macht und Ansehen –,*** reach a position of influence and esteem; ***zur Reichtum –,*** attain to prosperity, make a fortune.
Gelaß [gəˈlas], *n.* (**-(ss)es,** *pl.* **-(ss)e**) small room, lobby; space.
gelassen [gəˈlasən], *adj.* calm, cool, composed, collected; tranquil, imperturbable; passive; ***– bleiben,*** keep one's temper, remain calm, (*coll.*) keep cool. **Gelassenheit,** *f.* self-possession, calm(ness), composure, imperturbability, even temper.
Gelatine [ʒelaˈti:nə], *f.* gelatine. **gelatinös** [–ˈnø:s], *adj.* gelatinous.
Gelaufe [gəˈlaufə], *n.* running to and fro, bustle.
geläufig [gəˈlɔyfɪç], *adj.* fluent, easy; familiar, common, current; ***–e Hand,*** practised hand; ***–e Redensart,*** everyday remark, common saying; ***–e Zunge,*** ready tongue; ***er spricht – Deutsch,*** he speaks German fluently; ***das ist ihm –,*** he is familiar *or* conversant with it. **Geläufigkeit,** *f.* easiness, ease, facility; fluency.
gelaunt [gəˈlaunt], *adj.* disposed; humoured; ***gut –,*** in good humour, good-humoured, sweet-tempered; ***schlecht*** or ***übel –,*** cross, peevish, out of temper, bad-tempered, irritable.
Geläut(e) [gəˈlɔyt(ə)], *n.* ringing *or* peal (of bells), chime; baying (*of hounds*).
gelb [gɛlp], *adj.* yellow; sallow (*complexion*); ***die –e Gefahr,*** the yellow peril; ***– vor Neid,*** green with envy; ***–e Rübe,*** carrot; ***–er Verband,*** non-affiliated trade union. **Gelb,** *n. See* **Gelbe(s).**
Gelb|bleierz, *n.* wulfenite. **–brauenlaubsänger,** *m.* (*Orn.*) yellow-browed warbler (*Phylloscopus inornatus*). **gelbbrennen,** *irr.v.t.* dip, pickle. **Gelb|brennsäure,** *f.* (*Metall.*) pickling acid. **–eisenerz,** *n.* yellow ochre.
Gelbe(r) [ˈgɛlbə(r)], *m., f.* (*coll.*) member of a non-affiliated trade union.
Gelb|erde, *f. See* **–eisenerz.**
Gelbe(s) [ˈgɛlbə(s)], *n.* yellow colour; ***das Gelbe im Ei,*** egg-yolk.
Gelb|filter, *m.* (*Phot.*) light filter. **–fuchs,** *m.* sorrel horse. **–gießer,** *m.* brass-founder. **–guß,** *m.* brass-founding. **–kali,** *n.* (*Chem.*) potassium ferrocyanide. **–kopfstärling,** *m.* (*Orn.*) yellow-headed blackbird (*Xanthocephalus xanthocephalus*). **–kreuzgas,** *n.* mustard gas. **–kupfer,** *n.* yellow metal, brass.
gelblich [ˈgɛlplɪç], *adj.* yellowish. **Gelbling,** *m.* (**-s,** *pl.* **-e**) 1. (*Bot.*) chanterella (*Cantharellus cibarius*); 2. (*Colias*) species of butterfly.
Gelb|scheibe, *f. See* **–filter. –schenkel,** *m.* (*Orn.*) lesser yellowlegs (*Tringa flavipes*); ***großer –,*** greater yellowlegs (*Tringa melanoleuca*). **–schnabel,** *m.* fledgeling; (*fig.*) whipper-snapper; greenhorn. **–schnabelkuckuck,** *m.* (*Orn.*) yellow-billed cuckoo (*Coccyzus americanus*). **–schnabel-Sturmtaucher,** *m.* (*Orn.*) Mediterranean shearwater (*Puffinus diomedea*). **–spötter,** *m.* (*Orn.*) icterine warbler (*Hippolais icterina*). **–sucht,** *f.* jaundice. **gelbsüchtig,** *adj.* jaundiced.
Geld [gɛlt], *n.* (**-(e)s,** *pl.* **-er**) coin; money; cash, currency, capital; *pl.* funds, deposits; ***anvertrautes –,*** money in trust; ***ausstehendes –,*** money outstanding *or* due; ***bares –,*** ready money, cash, money in hand; ***bei –e sein,*** have plenty of money, be well off, (*coll.*) be flush; ***knapp bei –e sein,*** be short of money, be hard up; ***falsches –,*** base *or* counterfeit coin(s); ***– zum Fenster hinauswerfen,*** throw money down the drain; ***nicht für – und gute Worte,*** neither for love nor money; ***gemünztes –,*** coin; ***– und Gut,*** wealth and property; ***er hat – wie Heu,*** he is rolling in wealth; ***von seinem – leben,*** live on one's capital *or* money; ***nicht mit – zu bezahlen,*** invaluable; ***öffentliche –er,*** public funds; (*coll.*) ***das kostet ein schönes –,*** that will cost a packet; ***tägliches –,*** day-to-day *or* call money; ***ihn um sein – bringen,*** separate him from his money; ***zu – machen,*** turn into money *or* cash, realize.
Geld|abfindung, *f.* cash settlement; (*Mil.*) service gratuity. **–adel,** *m. See* **–aristokratie. –angelegenheit,** *f.* money matter. **–anlage,** *f.* investment. **–anleihe,** *f.* loan. **–anweisung,** *f.* money-order, postal-order, remittance. **–aristokratie,** *f.* plutocracy. **–aufnahme,** *f.* raising money, borrowing. **–aufwand,** *f.* expenditure. **–ausgabe,** *f.* disbursement, expenses, expenditure. **–ausleiher,** *m.* money lender. **–auszahler,** *m.* cashier,

teller. **–bestand,** *m.* monetary holdings. **–beutel,** *m.* purse. **–brief,** *m.* letter containing money, registered letter. **–büchse,** *f.* money-box. **–buße,** *f.* fine, penalty. **–einheit,** *f.* monetary unit. **–einlage,** *f.* deposit. **–einnahme,** *f.* receipts. **–einnehmer,** *m.* cashier, receiver. **–einwurf,** *m.* slot (*for coins*). **–entschädigung,** *f.* indemnity. **–entwertung,** *f.* inflation.

Geldeswert ['gɛldəsve:rt], *m.* money's worth; ***Geld und –,*** money and valuables, (*coll.*) the wherewithal.

Geld|flüssigkeit, *f.* money turnover. **–forderung,** *f.* outstanding debt, money due *or* owing. **–geber,** *m.* money lender, financial backer; mortgagee. **–geschäft,** *n.* money-transaction. **–gier,** *f.* avarice. **geldgierig,** *adj.* avaricious. **Geld|heirat,** *f.* marriage of convenience, money-match. **–herrschaft,** *f.* capitalism, plutocracy. **–hilfe,** *f.* financial aid; subsidy. **–kasse,** *f.* till; cash register; strong-box, cash-box. **–klemme,** *f.* financial straits. **–kurs,** *m.* rate of exchange. **–lade,** *f.* till. **–leihsatz,** *m.* bank rate. **–leistung,** *f.* payment.

geldlich ['gɛltlɪç], *adj.* monetary, financial, pecuniary.

Geld|makler, *m.* money-broker, bill-broker. **–mangel,** *m.* scarcity of money. **–mann,** *m.* (*pl.* **-leute**) financier. **–markt,** *m.* money market. **–mittel,** *n.pl.* funds, means, resources. **–münze,** *f.* coin. **–nehmer,** *m.* borrower, mortgagor. **–not,** *f.* financial straits, pecuniary embarrassment. **–posten,** *m.* sum of money; item (*in an account book*). **–preis,** *m.* cash prize, (*Spt.*) prize money. **–protz,** *m.* purse-proud man. **–quelle,** *f.* source of income. **–sache,** *f.* money-matter; (*Prov.*) ***in –n hört die Gemütlichkeit auf,*** business is business. **–schein,** *m.* paper-money, bank-note, (*Am.*) bill. **–schneiderei,** *f.* extortion, overcharging, usury. **–schrank,** *m.* safe, strong box. **–schwemme,** *f.* glut of money. **–schwierigkeit,** *f. See* **–verlegenheit.** **–sendung,** *f.* cash remittance. **–sorte,** *f.* (monetary) denomination. **–spende,** *f.* contribution, subscription. **–stand,** *m.* state of the money-market. **–strafe,** *f.* fine. **–stück,** *n.* coin. **–theorie,** *f.* monetary theory. **–überfluß,** *m. See* **–schwemme.** **–umlauf,** *m.* circulation of money. **–umsatz,** *m.* turnover of money. **–umtausch,** *m.* conversion *or* exchange of money. **–verlegenheit,** *f.* financial difficulty, pecuniary embarrassment. **–verlust,** *m.* pecuniary loss. **–vermögenswert,** *m.* monetary asset. **–vorrat,** *m.* cash reserve, cash in hand. **–vorschuß,** *m.* advance of money. **–währung,** *f.* currency. **–wechsel,** *m.* exchange of money. **–wechsler,** *m.* money-changer. **–wert,** *m.* value in money; value of currency. **–wesen,** *n.* money matters, finance, monetary system. **–wucher,** *m.* usury. **–wucherer,** *m.* usurer.

geleckt [gə'lɛkt], *adj.* (*coll.*) ***wie –,*** spick and span, spotless, immaculate.

Gelee [ʒe'le:], *n. or m.* (**-s,** *pl.* **-s**) jelly.

Gelege [gə'le:gə], *n.* nest of eggs, spawn.

gelegen [gə'le:gən], *adj.* 1. situated, located; 2. (*with Dat.*) convenient, suitable, opportune, apt, fit, proper; ***zu –er Zeit,*** opportunely, in due time; ***es kommt mir gerade –,*** it just suits me, it comes in handy; ***es ist mir wenig daran –,*** it is a matter of indifference to me; ***mir ist daran –,*** I am concerned *or* anxious; ***Sie kommen mir sehr –,*** you come very opportunely. *See* **liegen.**

Gelegenheit [gə'le:gənhaɪt], *f.* 1. occasion, opportunity; chance, favourable moment; ***bei –,*** on occasion, when the occasion arises, when (I *etc.*) have the chance, some time; ***bei dieser –,*** on this occasion; ***bei der ersten (besten) –,*** at the first opportunity; (*Prov.*) ***– macht Diebe,*** opportunity makes the thief; ***die – beim Schopfe packen,*** take the occasion by the forelock, not let the opportunity slip; jump at the chance; 2. (*coll.*) convenience (= W.C.); 3. *pl.* facilities.

Gelegenheits|arbeiter, *m.* casual labourer. **–gedicht,** *n.* occasional poem. **–kauf,** *m.* bargain. **–schrift,** *f.* work written for a particular occasion.

gelegentlich [gə'le:gəntlɪç], **1.** *adj.* 1. occasional; 2. incidental, accidental, casual, chance; opportune. **2.** *adv.* incidentally; occasionally, at times, on occasion, at some time or other, when there's a chance, at one's convenience *or* leisure, as occasion offers, now and then, by chance. **3.** *prep.* (*Gen.*) on the occasion of.

gelehrig [gə'le:rɪç], *adj.* docile, teachable; intelligent, (*coll.*) quick on the uptake.

Gelehrsamkeit [gə'le:rza:mkaɪt], *f.* learning, erudition, scholarship.

gelehrt [gə'le:rt], *adj.* learned, scholarly, erudite; (*coll.*) ***–es Haus,*** pundit, know-all. **Gelehrten|dünkel,** *m.* donnishness. **–kreise,** *m.pl.* scholars, the learned world. **–republik,** *f.* republic of letters. **–schule,** *f.* (*obs.*) grammar-school, classical school. **Gelehrte(r),** *m., f.* learned p., man *or* woman of learning, scholar, savant.

Geleier [gə'laɪər], *n.* drawling, sing-song delivery, monotonous discourse, speechifying.

geleimt [gə'laɪmt], *adj.* sized (*stiffened paper*). *See* **Leimen.**

Geleise [gə'laɪzə], *n.* (**-s,** *pl.* **-**) rut, track (*of a wheel*), (*Railw.*) rails, line, track, (*fig.*) beaten track; ***einfaches (doppeltes) –,*** single (double) track; (*fig.*) ***auf ein falsches*** or ***totes – geraten,*** get on the wrong track, reach a deadlock; ***aus dem –,*** off the rails (*also fig.*), derailed; ***im (alten) – bleiben, sich in ausgefahrenen –n bewegen,*** go on in the old way, be in a rut *or* groove, follow the beaten track. *See* **Gleis.**

Geleit [gə'laɪt], *n.* (**-(e)s,** *pl.* **-e**) *see* **Geleite.**

Geleit|boot, *n.* escort vessel. **–brief,** *m.* (letter of) safe-conduct; customs certificate; (*Comm.*) advice-note.

Geleite [gə'laɪtə], *n.* (**-s,** *pl.* **-**) retinue; (*Mil.*) guard, escort; (*Nav.*) convoy; ***ihm das – geben,*** accompany *or* escort him; ***ihm das letzte – geben,*** pay him the last honours; ***freies –,*** safe-conduct. **geleiten,** *v.t.* accompany, conduct, escort, convoy; ***an die Tür –,*** see to the door.

Geleit|flotille, *f.* convoy. **–schein,** *m.* safe-conduct; (*Nav.*) navicert. **–schiff,** *n. See* **–boot.** **–schutz,** *m.* escort, convoy. **–wort,** *n.* preface, foreword. **–zug,** *m.* (*Nav.*) convoy; ***im – fahren,*** sail in convoy. **–zugsicherung,** *f.* convoy escort.

Gelenk [gə'lɛŋk], *n.* (**-(e)s,** *pl.* **-e**) joint, articulation; wrist; ankle; link (*of a chain*); hinge; (*coll.*) ***keine –e haben,*** be stiff in the joints *or* awkward in movement. **Gelenk|band,** *n.* ligament. **–ende,** *n.* head (*of a bone*), articular extremity, condyle. **–entzündung,** *f.* arthritis.

gelenkig [gə'lɛŋkɪç], *adj.* flexible, pliable, pliant, supple; jointed, articulated; (*Bot.*) geniculate; agile, nimble. **Gelenkigkeit,** *f.* pliability, pliancy, flexibility; suppleness, agility, nimbleness.

Gelenk|kopf, *m.* (*Motor.*) cardan joint. **–kuppelung,** *f.* joint-coupling. **–pfanne,** *f.* (*Anat.*) socket (*of a joint*). **–puppe,** *f.* jointed doll. **–rheumatismus,** *m.* articular rheumatism, rheumatoid arthritis. **–schmiere,** *f.* joint-oil, synovia. **–welle,** *f.* cardan shaft.

gelernt [gə'lɛrnt], *adj.* skilled, trained, practised; ***–er Arbeiter,*** skilled worker.

Gelichter [gə'lɪçtər], *n.* gang, band, crew, riffraff, rabble.

Geliebte [gə'li:ptə], *f.* sweetheart, darling; mistress, kept woman. **Geliebte(r),** *m.* lover, beloved, sweetheart, love, darling; (*Eccl.*) ***meine Geliebten!*** dearly beloved brethren!

geliehen [gə'li:ən], *see* **leihen.**

gelind(e) [gə'lɪnt (–'lɪndə)], *adj.* soft, gentle, light, slight, lenient, mild; ***–e Strafe,*** lenient *or* light punishment; ***–e gesagt,*** putting it mildly, to say the least; ***–e Saiten aufziehen,*** relent, be mollified, become lenient.

gelingen [gə'lɪŋən], *irr.v.i., imp.* (*aux.* s.) (*Dat.*) succeed, be successful (*in doing*), manage, contrive (*to do*); ***sein Plan ist ihm nicht gelungen,*** his plan did not succeed; ***es gelang mir nicht, meinen Plan auszuführen,*** I was not able to carry out my plan; ***es gelingt mir,*** I succeed *or* prosper in; (*coll.*) ***es ist***

ihm übel (or *sl.* ***vorbei-)gelungen,*** he has had no success, he has failed. **Gelingen,** *n.* success.

Gelispel [gə'lɪspəl], *n.* lisping, whispering.

gelitten [gə'lɪtən], *see* **leiden.**

[1]**gell** [gɛl], *int.* *(dial.)* see [2]**gelt.**

[2]**gell,** *adj.* *See* **gellend.**

gellen ['gɛlən], *v.i.* sound shrill, jar, resound; sing *(of ears)*; call *(of the quail)*; ***das Schreien gellt mir in den Ohren,*** the screaming jars on my ears *or* makes my ears sing. **gellend,** *adj.* shrill, piercing.

geloben [gə'lo:bən], *v.t.* promise solemnly, vow, pledge; ***mit Hand und Mund*** or ***in die Hand –,*** take a solemn oath; ***das Gelobte Land,*** the Promised Land; ***sich etwas –,*** make a solemn resolve.

Gelöbnis [gə'lø:pnɪs], *n.* **(-ses,** *pl.* **-se)** solemn promise, vow, pledge.

gelogen [gə'lo:gən], *see* **lügen.**

gelöscht [gə'lœʃt], *adj.* quenched; ***–er Kalk,*** slaked lime.

Gelöstheit [gə'lø:sthaɪt], *f.* relaxed mood.

[1]**gelt** [gɛlt], *adj.* *(dial.)* not giving milk; barren.

[2]**gelt,** *int.* *(dial.)* isn't that so? isn't it? don't you think so? eh?

Gelte ['gɛltə], *f.* *(dial.)* pail, bucket, tub *(with one handle)*.

gelten ['gɛltən], **1.** *irr.v.i.* mean, matter, count, carry weight, be effective, be in force *or* operation, be current, be of *or* have value; be valid, hold good *or* true; *(with Dat.)* concern, apply to, be meant *or* intended for, be aimed at; ***– für*** or ***als,*** be looked upon *or* considered as, pass for; be thought *or* reputed *or* supposed to be; ***– für,*** apply to, be applicable to, be right *or* true for; ***diese Briefmarke gilt nicht mehr,*** this stamp is no longer valid; ***was er sagt, gilt,*** his word is (the) law, *(coll.)* what he says, goes; ***was gilt's? was gilt die Wette?*** what do you bet? ***es gilt!*** done! agreed! ***das gilt nicht,*** that is not allowed *or* does not count *or* is not fair (play); ***jetzt gilt's!*** now's the time! now for it! ***er war tapfer, wo es galt,*** he was brave when the moment came; ***jetzt gilt's, die Begeisterung zu entflammen,*** the main point is now to fire the enthusiasm; ***es galt mein Leben,*** my life was at stake; ***es gilt mir gleich,*** it is all the same to me; ***diese Bemerkung galt mir,*** this remark was aimed at *or* intended for me; ***sein Wort gilt viel bei mir,*** his word carries great weight with me; *(B.)* ***bei Gott gilt kein Ansehen der Person,*** God is no respecter of persons; ***es gilt für ausgemacht,*** it is taken for granted; ***er gilt für einen redlichen Mann,*** he passes for an honest man, he is supposed to be honest; ***das gilt für alle Zeiten,*** that always remains true; ***– lassen,*** let pass, not dispute, allow, admit; ***das will ich – lassen,*** granted! I don't dispute that; ***für voll – lassen,*** take (fully) seriously. **2.** *irr.v.t.* be worth; ***die Note gilt einen Takt,*** the note is equal to one beat; *(Prov.)* ***der Prophet gilt nichts in seinem Vaterland,*** a prophet is without honour in his own country; ***es gilt Sieg oder Tod,*** victory or death! ***es gilt einen Versuch,*** an attempt should be made, *(coll.)* let's have a shot *or* go.

geltend ['gɛltənt], *adj.* valid, effective, applicable, in force *or* operation; prevailing, accepted, current; ***– machen,*** maintain, assert, put forward, advance *(views)*, bring to bear *(influence)*; ***sich – machen,*** *(of a p.)* assert o.s., claim recognition, *(coll.)* throw one's weight about, make o.s. felt; *(of a th.)* make itself felt.

Geltling ['gɛltlɪŋ], *m.* **(-s,** *pl.* **-e)** 1. one-year-old calf, gelding; 2. eunuch.

Geltung ['gɛltuŋ], *f.* value, worth, validity, consequence, weight, importance; currency, acceptance, respect, recognition, authority, prestige; ***– haben,*** be valid; ***zur – bringen,*** bring to bear; ***sich*** *(Dat.)* ***– verschaffen,*** make o.s. felt *or* respected, bring one's influence to bear; ***ohne –,*** of no account; ***zur – kommen,*** take effect, make itself felt, begin to tell, become important, come into play. **Geltungs|bedürfnis,** *n.* desire for admiration, desire to show off. **–bereich,** *m.* jurisdiction *(of a law)*, range *or* scope of validity *(of a postulate)*, purview. **–dauer,** *f.* (period of) validity, term, life. **–trieb,** *m.* urge to dominate.

Gelübde [gə'lypdə], *n.* **(-s,** *pl.* **-)** vow.

gelungen [gə'luŋən], *adj.* successful, well done; *(coll.)* excellent, capital; funny; *(coll.)* ***das ist –!*** that is splendid! that beats everything! ***–er Kerl,*** quite a character. *See* **gelingen.**

Gelüst [gə'lyst], *n.* **(-s,** *pl.* **-e)** desire, longing, appetite, craving, lust (***nach,*** for). **gelüsten,** *v.i.imp.* (***nach***) desire, long for, hanker after; ***sich*** *(Acc.)* ***– lassen,*** covet, lust after; *(B.)* ***laß dich nicht – deines Nächsten Weib!*** thou shalt not covet thy neighbour's wife *(Gen. obs., now it would be* ***nach deines Nächsten Weib****)*.

Gelze ['gɛltsə], *f.* gelded sow. **gelzen,** *v.t.* geld, castrate.

gemach [gə'ma:x], *adv., int.* easy! softly! quietly! gently! slowly; *(Prov.)* ***– geht auch weit,*** slow and steady wins the race.

Gemach, *n.* **(-(e)s,** *pl.* **⸗er)** *(Poet.)* room, apartment, chamber.

gemächlich [gə'mɛ:çlɪç], *adj.* comfortable, easy; leisurely; ***–er Mensch,*** easy-going *or* lackadaisical person; ***– leben,*** live at ease *or* comfortably. **Gemächlichkeit,** *f.* comfort, ease, leisureliness.

gemacht [gə'maxt], *adj.* affected, simulated; *(Comm.)* ***–e Wechselbriefe,*** bills read for endorsement; ***–er Mann,*** a p. in an established position *or* whose fortune is assured.

Gemahl [gə'ma:l], *m.* **(-(e)s,** *pl.* **-e)** husband, consort. **Gemahlin,** *f.* wife, spouse; consort; ***wie geht es Ihrer Frau –, Herr Bolz?*** how is Mrs. Bolz?

gemahnen [gə'ma:nən], *v.t.* remind (***an*** *(Acc.)*, of), put in mind (of), be suggestive (of).

Gemälde [gɛ'mɛ:ldə], *n.* **(-s,** *pl.* **-)** picture, painting. **Gemälde|ausstellung,** *f.* exhibition of pictures. **–galerie,** *f.* picture gallery. **–händler,** *m.* art dealer.

Gemarkung [gə'markuŋ], *f.* landmark, boundary; precincts.

gemäß [gə'mɛ:s], **1.** *adj.* suitable, conformable, appropriate *(Dat.,* to). **2.** *prep.* *(with preceding (less frequently) or following Dat.)* according to, in accordance *or* agreement *or* conformity *or* compliance with; in consequence of, as a result of, *(Law)* in pursuance of, pursuant to; ***dem Zwecke nicht –,*** unsuitable to the purpose; ***der Natur –,*** according to nature; ***dem Befehl –,*** in conformity with the order; ***– Abschnitt 3,*** see para. 3, as provided under para. 3. **Gemäßheit,** *f.* conformity, accordance.

gemäßigt [gə'mɛ:sɪçt], *adj.* moderate, *(Geog.)* temperate; ***der –e Gürtel,*** the temperate zone.

Gemäuer [gə'mɔyər], *n.* *(Poet.)* masonry; ***altes –,*** ruins.

gemein [gə'maɪn], *adj.* 1. common, general, ordinary; ***auf –e Kosten die Reise machen,*** pool the expenses of the trip; ***der –e Mann,*** the man in the street; ***der –e Menschenverstand,*** common sense; ***mit ihm –e S. machen,*** make common cause with him, join him in an undertaking; ***–er Soldat,*** private (soldier); ***– haben mit,*** have in common with, share with; 2. low, vulgar, coarse, mean, base; *(coll.)* awful, beastly *(weather etc.)*; ***–e Ausdrücke,*** coarse remarks; ***–e Brüche,*** vulgar fractions; ***ein –er Streich,*** a shabby *or* dirty trick; ***sich – machen,*** demean o.s., lower o.s.; 3. *(dial.)* kind, friendly, condescending; ***– machen mit,*** become friendly with, chum up with, be hail fellow well met with; ***sich nicht – machen mit,*** keep *(a p.)* at a distance, hold aloof from *or* not be too familiar with *(a p.)*.

Gemein|besitz, *m.* public *or* common property. **–betrieb,** *m.* public utilities; communal farming.

Gemeinde [gə'maɪndə], *f.* community, *(Hist.)* commune; local authority, municipality; *(Eccl.)* parish; congregation, parishioners; corporate body; ***die christliche –,*** the Christian communion, the Church.

Gemeinde|abgaben, *f.pl.* local rates *or* *(Am.)* taxes. **–ammann,** *m.* *(Swiss)* mayor. **–anger,** *m.* common, village green. **–arbeiter,** *m.* municipal worker. **–behörde,** *f.* local authority, corporation, borough *or* municipal council, parish council. **–bezirk,** *m.* parish, borough, municipality, district. **–haus,** *n.* parish *or* village hall. **–land,** *n.* common. **–ordnung,** *f.* local bye-laws. **–rat,** *m.* 1. *See* **–behörde**; 2. alderman, town-councillor; (*Scots, Eccl.*) elder. **–schreiber,** *m.* town-clerk, parish clerk. **–schule,** *f.* council *or* elementary school, village school. **–steuer,** *f. See* **–abgaben. –unterstützung,** *f.* parish relief. **–verwaltung,** *f.* local government. **–vorstand,** *m.* local board, town *or* borough council. **–vorsteher,** *m.* mayor; chairman of urban *or* rural district council. **–wahl,** *f.* communal *or* local elections. **–weide,** *f.* common, village green. **–werk,** *n.* (*Swiss*) statute labour. **–wiese,** *f. See* **–weide.**

Gemeine(r) [gəˈmaɪnə(r)], *m., f.* (*obs.*) commoner; layman; (*Mil.*) private (soldier); (*Mil.*) ***die Gemeinen,*** the rank and file.

gemein|faßlich, *adj.* intelligible to all, popular, generally comprehensible, easy to understand, elementary. **–gefährlich,** *adj.* dangerous to the public; ***–er Mensch,*** public danger *or* enemy. **Gemein|geist,** *m.* public spirit, civic sense, esprit de corps. **–gläubiger,** *m.* bankrupt's creditor. **gemeingültig,** *adj.* generally admitted *or* accepted, current. **Gemeingut,** *n.* common *or* public property.

Gemeinheit [gəˈmaɪnhaɪt], *f.* vulgarity, coarseness, commonness; baseness, mean trick, vileness, meanness. **gemeinhin,** (*obs.*) **gemeiniglich,** *adv.* commonly, usually, generally (speaking).

Gemein|kosten, *pl.* overhead costs. **–nutz,** *m.* common good; ***– vor Eigennutz,*** service not self. **gemeinnützig,** *adj.* of public benefit, generally useful, of general utility; beneficial to the community; charitable, co-operative, non-profit making; (*of a p.*) public-spirited. **Gemein|nützigkeit,** *f.* general usefulness, public utility; (*esp. Swiss*) voluntary social work, private charity. **–platz,** *m.* commonplace, platitude, truism.

gemeinsam [gəˈmaɪnza:m], **1.** *adj.* (*Dat.*) common (to), held jointly *or* in common (with); joint, mutual; combined, collective; ***allen –,*** common to all; ***–e Aktion,*** joint *or* concerted action; ***–es Eigentum,*** joint *or* common property; ***–er Freund,*** mutual *or* common friend; ***–er Markt,*** common market; (*Math.*) ***–er Nenner,*** common denominator; ***–e Sache machen mit,*** make common cause with. **2.** *adv.* jointly, as one, together, in a body; ***– handeln mit,*** act jointly *or* together *or* in concert *or* concurrence with. **Gemeinsamkeit,** *f.* community, common interest *or* possession; mutuality.

Gemeinschaft [gəˈmaɪnʃaft], *f.* community; mutual participation, common possession *or* interest; communion; partnership, association; intercourse; ***– zwischen Seele und Leib,*** communion of soul and body; ***– haben mit,*** be connected, consort *or* have intercourse with; ***etwas in – haben,*** hold *or* have s.th. jointly *or* in common; ***in – mit,*** together *or* in co-operation with. **gemeinschaftlich,** *adj. See* **gemeinsam**; ***–es Konto, –e Rechnung,*** joint account; ***–es Unternehmen,*** concerted undertaking. **Gemeinschaftlichkeit,** *f.* community of interests *or* possession; solidarity, joint responsibility.

Gemeinschafts|anschluß, *m.* (*Tele.*) party line. **–arbeit,** *f.* team-work, co-operative work. **–betrieb,** *m.* joint enterprise. **–ehe,** *f.* companionate marriage. **–erziehung,** *f.* co-education. **–gefühl,** *n.* fellow-feeling, community of interests. **–geist,** *m.* team-spirit, esprit de corps, solidarity. **–konto,** *n.* joint account. **–küche,** *f.* canteen. **–kunde,** *f.* social studies. **–raum,** *m.* recreation room. **–schule,** *f.* co-educational school. **–speisung, –verpflegung,** *f.* communal feeding.

Gemein|schuldner, *m.* bankrupt. **–sinn,** *m.* public spirit, civic sense. **–sprache,** *f.* literary language (*as opposed to dialects*). **gemein|verständlich,** *adj. See* **–faßlich. Gemein|wesen,** *n.* public affairs; community; commonwealth, polity. **–wirtschaft,** *f.* social economy; collective farming. **–wohl,** *n.* common weal, public welfare.

Gemenge [gəˈmɛŋə], *n.* 1. mingling; mixture; aggregation; medley; 2. mêlée, hand-to-hand fight, brawl, (*sl.*) scrap. **Gemengestoff,** *m.* constituent parts, ingredients. **Gemengsel,** *n.* medley, hotchpotch.

gemessen [gəˈmɛsən], *adj.* measured, rated; precise, formal, solemn, grave, sedate; ***–er Befehl,*** express *or* strict order. **Gemessenheit,** *f.* precision, strictness; solemn *or* grave demeanour, gravity, sedateness, formality.

Gemetzel [gəˈmɛtsəl], *n.* slaughter, carnage, massacre, butchery, blood-bath.

gemieden [gəˈmi:dən], *see* **meiden.**

Gemisch [gəˈmɪʃ], *n.* **(-es,** *pl.* **-e)** mixture, composition, alloy; medley. **gemischt,** *adj.* mixed, diffused, combined. **Gemischtwaren,** *f.pl.* (*Austr.*) groceries.

Gemme [ˈgɛmə], *f.* gem, cameo. **Gemmen|abdruck, –abguß,** *m.* paste. **–kundige(r), –schneider,** *m.* lapidary.

gemocht [gəˈmɔxt], *see* **mögen.**

gemolken [gəˈmɔlkən], *see* **melken.**

Gemsbock [ˈgɛmsbɔk], *m.* chamois-buck. **Gemse** [ˈgɛmzə], *f.* chamois. **Gems|leder,** *n.* chamois leather, (*coll.*) shammy. **–tier,** *n.*, **–ziege,** *f.* doe of the chamois.

Gemunkel [gəˈmuŋkəl], *n.* talk, gossip, rumour, tittle-tattle.

Gemurmel [gəˈmurməl], *n.* murmuring, muttering, murmur.

Gemüse [gəˈmy:zə], *n.* **(-s,** *pl.* **-)** vegetable; vegetables, greens, (*Am.*) truck; (*coll.*) ***junges –,*** small fry. **Gemüse|bau,** *m.* vegetable gardening, (*Am.*) truck farming. **–garten,** *m.* kitchen *or* vegetable garden. **–gärtner,** *m.* market-gardener, (*Am.*) truck farmer. **–händler,** *m.* greengrocer.

gemüßigt [gəˈmy:sɪçt], *adj.* ***sich – sehen,*** find o.s., feel *or* be obliged *or* compelled.

gemußt [gəˈmust], *see* **müssen.**

gemustert [gəˈmustərt], *adj.* fancy, patterned, figured.

Gemüt [gəˈmy:t], *n.* **(-(e)s,** *pl.* **-er)** 1. (cast of) mind, soul, heart, disposition, nature, temperament, spirit, feeling, temper; ***sich*** (*Dat.*) ***etwas zu –e führen,*** take a th. to heart; (*hum.*) wrap o.s. around s.th. (*i.e.* eat it); ***ihm eine S. zu –e führen,*** remind him of a th., remonstrate with him about a th., bring s.th. home to him; 2. (*fig. usu. pl.*) person, individual, soul. **gemütlich,** *adj.* (*of a p.*) good-natured; genial, jovial, jolly, cheerful, sociable; easy-going, leisurely, placid; (*of a place*) pleasant, agreeable, restful, comfortable, cosy, snug; ***nur immer –!*** take it easy! (*sl.*) keep your hair *or* shirt on! ***es sich*** (*Dat.*) ***– machen,*** take things easy; make o.s. at home; ***–es Beisammensein,*** social gathering. **Gemütlichkeit,** *f.* good-natured *or* sanguine *or* easy-going disposition, good nature, kindliness, geniality, joviality, sociability; (*of a place*) snugness, comfort, cosiness; (*coll.*) ***da hört denn doch die – auf!*** this is too much! that's really the limit *or* (*coll.*) too steep; (*Prov.*) ***in Geldsachen hört die – auf,*** business is business. **gemütlos,** *adj.* heartless, unfeeling.

Gemüts|art, –beschaffenheit, *f.* character, disposition, turn *or* cast of mind, nature, temper, temperament. **–bewegung,** *f.* emotion, excitement, agitation. **gemütskrank,** *adj.* melancholic, emotionally disturbed. **Gemüts|krankheit,** *f.* melancholia. **–leben,** *n.* inner life. **–mensch,** *m.* man of feeling, sentimentalist. **–ruhe,** *f.* composure, calmness, tranquillity, placidity, peace of mind. **–verfassung,** *f.*, **–zustand,** *m.* frame of mind, humour. **gemütvoll,** *adj.* kindly, affectionate, tender-hearted.

Gen [ge:n], *n.* **(-s,** *pl.* **-e)** (*Biol.*) gene, factor.

gen, *prep.* (*Acc.*) (*Poet. abbr. of* **gegen**) towards, to; ***– Himmel,*** heavenwards; ***– Westen,*** to the west.

genabelt [gəˈna:bəlt], *adj.* (*Bot.*) umbilicate.

genannt [gəˈnant], *adj.* called, surnamed; referred to, above-mentioned, aforesaid, foregoing. *See* **nennen.**

genas [gəˈnaːs], *see* **genesen.**

genäschig [gəˈnɛʃɪç], *adj.* sweet-toothed.

genäse [gəˈnɛːzə], *see* **genesen.**

genau [gəˈnau], **1.** *adj.* exact, accurate, precise; detailed, in detail, minute; careful, meticulous, scrupulous, particular, punctilious; sparing, economical, parsimonious, close-fisted; (*Mech.*) true; ***–er Bericht,*** full *or* detailed account; ***–es Gewissen,*** scrupulous conscience; ***mit –er Not entkommen,*** have a narrow escape; (*Comm.*) ***–ester Preis,*** keenest price; ***die –e Zeit,*** the right *or* exact time; ***Genaueres,*** full particulars, further details, more precise information. **2.** *adv.* exactly, precisely, right, just; ***die Uhr geht –,*** the clock keeps good time; ***die Vorschriften – befolgen, sich an die Vorschriften – halten,*** follow the instructions closely; ***– kennen,*** know thoroughly *or* intimately *or* (*coll.*) inside out; ***es – nehmen mit,*** be particular *or* punctilious about; ***– genommen,*** strictly speaking; ***– so groß wie,*** just as big as; ***er tat es – so,*** he did it exactly *or* just like this; ***ich weiß es –,*** I know for certain *or* (*coll.*) sure, I am positive; ***etwas – überlegen,*** consider a th. carefully, give a th. careful consideration; ***aufs –este,*** as closely *or* strictly as possible, to a nicety *or* (*coll.*) a T. **Genauigkeit,** *f.* accuracy, precision, exactness; fidelity (*of a copy*); strictness, punctiliousness, carefulness; parsimony.

Gendarm [ʒanˈdarm], *m.* (**-en,** *pl.* **-en**) gendarme, constable, rural policeman. **Gendarmerie** [–əˈriː], *f.* constabulary, rural police; police station.

Genealogie [genealoˈgiː], *f.* genealogy. **genealogisch** [–ˈloːgɪʃ], *adj.* genealogical.

genehm [gəˈneːm], *adj.* acceptable, convenient, agreeable (*Dat.*, to), suitable (for); ***wenn es mir – ist,*** when it suits *or* will suit me.

genehmigen [gəˈneːmɪgən], *v.t.* approve (of), grant, concede; agree *or* consent *or* assent to, sanction, authorize, license; (*sl.*) okay; ratify (*an agreement*), (*Comm.*) accept (*a bill*); (*Comm.*) ***– Sie den Ausdruck meiner vorzüglichen Hochachtung,*** please accept the expression of my particular esteem; (*coll.*) ***sich*** (*Dat.*) ***einen –,*** wrap o.s. round a drink. **Genehmigung,** *f.* (*Gen.*) acceptance, approval, approbation, authorization; grant, ratification (of); assent, agreement, consent (to); permission, permit, licence (for). **genehmigungspflichtig,** *adj.* subject to authorization.

geneigt [gəˈnaɪkt], *adj.* 1. sloping, inclined; (*fig.*) inclined, prone, disposed (*zu*, to); with a propensity (for); ***zur Arbeit nicht –,*** disinclined to work; 2. (*with Dat.*) sympathetic *or* well-disposed *or* gracious *or* favourably inclined towards; ***das Glück ist ihm –,*** fortune favours him; ***–er Leser,*** kind *or* gentle reader; ***ihm ein –es Gehör geben,*** give him a favourable hearing. **Geneigtheit,** *f.* 1. inclination, propensity; 2. favour; goodwill, benevolence.

General [geneˈraːl], *m.* (**-s,** *pl.* **-e** (*less good* **¨-e**)) general, (supreme) commander. **General|admiral,** *m.* admiral commanding a fleet (*no equivalent British rank*). **–anwalt,** *m.* attorney-general. **–archivar,** *m.* chief archivist (*in England the Deputy Keeper of the Public Record Office*). **–arzt,** *m.* major-general (*of Med. Corps*). **–auditeur,** *m.* Judge Advocate General. **–baß,** *m.* (*Mus.*) thorough-bass. **–beichte,** *f.* universal confession. **–bevollmächtigte(r),** *m., f.* plenipotentiary; (*Law*) agent with full powers of attorney. **–bilanz,** *f.* annual balance. **–direktion,** *f.* board of management. **–direktor,** *m.* managing director, general manager. **–feldmarschall,** *m.* field-marshal, generalissimo. **–feldzeugmeister,** *m.* master-general of the ordnance; (*Austr.*) commander-in-chief. **–fiskal,** *m.* attorney- *or* solicitor-general. **–gouverneur,** *m.* governor-general. **–inspektion,** *f.* Inspector General's Department. **–intendant,** *m.* theatrical manager.

generalisieren [generaliˈziːrən], *v.i., v.t.* generalize.

Generalissimus [generaˈlɪsɪmus], *m.* (-, *pl.* **-mi** *or* **–se**) generalissimo.

Generalität [generaliˈtɛːt], *f.* general officers, the generals.

General|kommando, *n.* staff of an army corps; corps headquarters. **–konsul,** *m.* consul-general. **–kurs,** *m.* (*Navig.*) mean course. **–leutnant,** *m.* lieutenant-general; (*Av.*) air marshal; (*Am.*) major-general. **–major,** *m.* major-general; (*Av.*) air vice-marshal, (*Am.*) brigadier-general. **–nenner,** *m.* (*Math.*) common denominator; ***Brüche unter den – bringen,*** reduce fractions to a common denominator. **–oberst,** *m.* senior general (*no equivalent in British army*). **–pardon,** *m.* general amnesty. **–pause,** *f.* (*Mus.*) general rest. **–police,** *f.* comprehensive policy (*insurance*). **–postdirektor,** *m.* postmaster-general. **–probe,** *f.* (*Theat.*) dress rehearsal, (*Mus.*) full *or* final rehearsal. **–profos,** *m.* provost-marshal. **–quittung,** *f.* receipt in full. **–sekretär,** *m.* secretary-general. **–staaten,** *m.pl.* States-General (of Holland). **–stab,** *m.* (*Mil.*) general staff. **–stäbler,** *m.* staff officer. **–stabskarte,** *f.* ordnance map (scale 1:100,000), (*Am.*) strategic map. **–stabsoffizier,** *m.* staff officer. **–streik,** *m.* general strike. **–superintendent,** *m.* (*former designation of a Lutheran bishop*). **–unkosten,** *pl.* overhead expenses, (*coll.*) overheads. **–versammlung,** *f.* general meeting, company meeting, meeting of shareholders. **–vollmacht,** *f.* (*Law*) power of attorney, full authority.

Generation [generatsiˈoːn], *f.* generation; procreation.

Generator [geneˈraːtər], *m,* (**-s,** *pl.* **-en**) generator, alternator, dynamo. **Generatorgas,** *n.* producer gas.

generell [geneˈrɛl], **1.** *adj.* general; overall, (*coll.*) blanket. **2.** *adv.* generally, in general, in principle.

generisch [geˈneːrɪʃ], *adj.* generic.

generös [geneˈrøːs], *adj.* generous, liberal.

Genese [gəˈneːzə], *f.* genesis, formation.

genesen [gəˈneːzən], *irr.v.i.* (*aux.* s.) get well *or* better, recover, convalesce; ***eines Kindes –,*** be delivered of a child. **Genesung,** *f.* recovery; convalescence. **Genesungs|heim,** *n.* sanatorium. **–urlaub,** *m.* sick leave.

Genetik [geˈneːtɪk], *f.* genetics. **genetisch,** *adj.* genetic.

Genever [geˈneːvər], *m.* Hollands (*gin*).

Genf [gɛnf], *n.* (*Geog.*) Geneva. **Genfer, 1.** *m.* Genevese. **2.** *adj.* Geneva; ***– See,*** Lake Geneva.

genial [geniˈaːl], *adj.* (*of a p.*) highly gifted, brilliant; (*of a th.*) ingenious, brilliant. **Genialität** [–iˈtɛːt], *f.* (*of a p.*) genius, brilliance, originality, (*of a th.*) ingenuity.

Genick [gəˈnɪk], *n.* (**-(e)s,** *pl.* **-e**) nape *or* back *or* scruff of the neck; ***sich*** (*Dat.*) ***das – brechen,*** break one's neck; (*fig., coll.*) ruin one's chances; ***das brach ihm des –,*** that was his undoing. **Genickfänger,** *m.* hunting knife. **–schlag,** *m.* (*Boxing*) rabbit-punch. **–schmerz,** *m.* crick in the neck. **–starre,** *f.* (cerebrospinal) meningitis.

Genie [ʒeˈniː], *n.* (**-s,** *pl.* **-s**) genius; man of genius. **Genie|korps,** *n.* (*obs.*) engineer corps.

genieren [ʒeˈniːrən], **1.** *v.t.* embarrass, trouble, bother, inconvenience, incommode; ***geniert Sie mein Rauchen?*** do you mind my smoking? **2.** *v.r.* feel awkward *or* self-conscious *or* embarrassed, be shy; ***– Sie sich nicht,*** don't disturb yourself; make yourself at home.

genießbar [gəˈniːsbaːr], *adj.* enjoyable, agreeable; palatable, eatable, drinkable; ***er ist heute gar nicht –,*** today he is quite unbearable.

genießen [gəˈniːsən], *irr.v.t.* eat *or* drink; take (*nourishment*); enjoy, have the benefit *or* use of; ***recht –,*** savour, relish; ***nicht zu –,*** unpalatable, not fit to eat *or* drink; (*fig.*) intolerable, unbearable; ***– Sie doch ein wenig davon,*** do taste a little of it; ***er hat das Seinige*** or ***sein Gutes genossen,*** he has had his day, he has had his share of the good things of life. **Genießer,** *m.* epicure, gourmet, bon viveur.

Genie|streich, *m.* stroke of genius, (*coll.*) bright idea; ingenious trick. **–wesen,** *n.* (*obs.*) military engineering. **–zeit,** *f.* Storm and Stress Period (*in German literature 1770–85*).

Genist(e) [gəˈnɪst(ə)], *n.* 1. nest, hatch, brood;

2. waste, rubbish, sweepings; 3. brushwood, undergrowth; 4. broom, *see* **Ginster.**

Genitalien [geni'ta:liən], *pl.* genitals.

Genitiv ['ge:niti:f], *m.* (**-s,** *pl.* **-e**) (*Gram.*) genitive *or* possessive case. **genitivisch,** *adj.* genitival.

Genius ['ge:nius], *m.* (-, *pl.* **Genien**) spirit, guardian angel; *– einer Sprache,* genius of a language.

genommen [gə'nɔmən], *see* **nehmen.**

Genörgel [gə'nœrgəl], *n.* grumbling, nagging.

genormt [gə'nɔrmt], *adj.* standardized.

genoß [gə'nɔs], *see* **genießen.**

Genosse [gə'nɔsə], *m.* (**-n,** *pl.* **-n**) comrade, companion, colleague, partner, associate; (*coll.*) chum, mate, pal, (*Am.*) buddy; *– Pieck,* Comrade Pieck.

genösse [gə'nœsə], **genossen,** *see* **genießen.**

Genossenschaft [gə'nɔsənʃaft], *f.* company, fellowship, association; co-operative (society). **genossenschaftlich,** *adj.* co-operative. **Genossin,** *f. See* **Genosse. Genoßsame,** *f.* (*Swiss*) district, parish; village community, model estate.

Genoveva [geno'fe:fa], *f.* Genevieve.

Genre [ʒãr], *m. or n.* (**-s,** *pl.* **-s**) style, kind, genre. **Genrebild,** *n.* genre-painting.

Gent [gɛnt], *n.* (*Geog.*) Ghent.

Genua ['ge:nua], *n.* (*Geog.*) Genoa. **Genueser** [–'e:zər], *m.* Genoese. **genuesisch,** *adj.* Genoese.

genug [gə'nu:k], **1.** *indecl.adj., adv.* enough, sufficient(ly); *– der Tränen!* no more crying! *or* tears! *– des Streites,* a truce to quarrelling; *– davon!* let us have no more of this! *er ist Manns –,* he is man enough; *ich bin nicht Kenner* or *Künstler –, um zu,* I am not a sufficiently good judge *or* not enough of an artist to; *laß es – sein!* that will do! enough of that! put a stop to it! *mehr als –,* enough and to spare; *nicht – daß . . . sondern,* not only . . . but. **2.** *int.* enough! that will do! stop! in short, in a word.

Genüge [gə'ny:gə], *f. zur –,* enough, sufficiently, fully; *– tun* or *leisten* (*Dat.*), satisfy, content, give satisfaction to (*a p.*); comply with, fulfil, meet (*wishes*), come up to (*expectations*). **genügen,** *v.i.* (*Dat.*) be enough *or* sufficient (for), suffice, satisfy; *laß es dir –,* be content with that; *das genügt für meine Zwecke,* that will do for my purpose. **genügend,** *adj.* sufficient, enough; satisfying; satisfactory, fair. **genügsam,** *adj.* easily satisfied, contented; unassuming, unpretentious, modest; moderate, frugal. **Genügsamkeit,** *f.* contentedness, moderation.

genugtun [gə'nu:ktu:n], *irr. v.i.* (*Dat.*) give satisfaction, satisfy. **Genugtuung,** *f.* satisfaction; amends, redress, reparation; *zu meiner – erfahre ich,* I am gratified to learn; *ihm – geben,* give him satisfaction, make amends.

genung [gə'nuŋ], *adv.* (*obs., Poet.*) *see* **genug.**

Genus ['ge:nus], *n.* (-, *pl.* **Genera**) (*Biol.*) genus; (*Gram.*) gender.

Genuß [gə'nus], *m.* (**-(ss)es,** *pl.* **¨-(ss)e**) enjoyment, pleasure, delight, gratification, profit, use; taking, partaking (*of food etc.*); *lebenslänglicher –,* life interest. **Genuß|mensch,** *m.* epicure, epicurean, voluptuary, sensualist. **–mittel,** *n.* (*usu. pl.*) luxury articles, semi-luxuries; stimulants. **–recht,** *n.* (*Law*) right of usufruct. **genußreich,** *adj.* delightful, enjoyable, pleasurable. **Genußsucht,** *f.* craving for pleasure, pleasure-seeking, epicureanism, dissipation. **genußsüchtig,** *adj.* pleasure-seeking, epicurean, sensual.

Geodäsie [geodɛ'zi:], *f.* geodesy, surveying.

Geograph [geo'gra:f], *m.* (**-en,** *pl.* **-en**) geographer. **Geographie** [–'fi:], *f.* geography. **geographisch,** *adj.* geographical. **Geographisch-Nord,** *n.* true north.

Geologe [geo'lo:gə], *m.* (**-n,** *pl.* **-n**) geologist. **Geologie** [–'gi:], *f.* geology. **geologisch,** *adj.* geological.

Geometer [geo'me:tər], *m.* surveyor. **Geometrie** [–me'tri:], *f.* geometry. **geometrisch,** *adj.* geometrical.

geordnet [gə'ɔrdnət], *adj.* orderly, disciplined; systematic.

Georg ['ge:ɔrk, ge'ɔrk], *m.* George.

Georgia [ge'ɔrgia], *n.* (*Geog.*) Georgia (*U.S.A.*).

Georgien [ge'ɔrgiən], *n.* (*Geog.*) Georgia (*U.S.S.R.*).

Georgine [geɔr'gi:nə], *f.* dahlia.

Gepäck [gə'pɛk], *n.* (**-(e)s,** *pl.* **-e**) luggage, (*Am.*) baggage; (*Mil. etc.*) kit; (*coll.*) *ihm ins – fallen,* surprise him, come upon him unawares; *sein – aufgeben,* register one's luggage, (*Am.*) check one's baggage. **Gepäck|abfertigung,** *f.* luggage dispatch (office). **–annahme(stelle),** *f.* luggage registration (office). **–aufbewahrung,** *f.* left-luggage office. **–aufgabe,** *f.* luggage office. **–ausgabe,** *f.* (left-)luggage office (*auf-, an- indicate the receipt or 'in' side, aus- the delivery or 'out' side*). **–halter,** *m.* carrier (*on cycle*). **–netz,** *n.* luggage rack. **–schein,** *m.* luggage receipt, cloak-room *or* left-luggage ticket. **–stück,** *n.* parcel, package, bag, case, piece of luggage. **–träger,** *m.* (railway) porter; *see also* **–halter. –troß,** *m.* second-line transport, (*Mil.*) baggage train. **–wagen,** *m.* luggage-van, (*Am.*) baggage car. **–zettel,** *m.* luggage-label.

gepanzert [gə'pantsərt], *adj.* armoured, ironclad.

Gepard ['ge:part], *m.* (**-(e)s,** *pl.* **-e**) cheetah, hunting leopard (*Acinonyx*).

gepfiffen [gə'pfɪfən], *see* **pfeifen.**

gepflegt [gə'pfle:kt], *adj.* (*of a th.*) well cared for, tended, (*of a p.*) well-groomed, immaculate, (*fig.*) cultivated, refined, polished; *–er Wein,* seasoned wine.

Gepflogenheit [gə'pflo:gənhaɪt], *f.* custom, habit, usage, practice.

gepfropt [gə'pfrɔpft], *adj. – voll* (*von*), crammed *or* stuffed full (of), jammed chock-full (with).

Geplänkel [gə'plɛŋkəl], *n.* skirmishing, skirmish.

Geplapper [gə'plapər], *n.* babbling, chatter, prattle.

Geplätscher [gə'plɛtʃər], *n.* splashing, purling, gurgling.

Geplauder [gə'plaudər], *n.* small talk; chat, chatter, chatting.

Gepolter [gə'pɔltər], *n.* rumbling (noise), rumble, din.

Gepräge [gə'prɛ:gə], *n.* stamp, impression, imprint; coinage; characteristic (features), character; *einer S.* (*Dat.*) *ihr – aufdrücken,* put a stamp on a th., give a th. its (peculiar) character.

Gepränge [gə'prɛŋə], *n.* pageantry, pomp, splendour, ostentatious display.

Geprassel [gə'prasəl], *n.* crackling; clatter.

gepriesen [gə'pri:zən], *see* **preisen.**

gepunktet [gə'puŋktət], *adj.* dotted, spotted.

Gequassel [gə'kvasəl], **Gequatsch(e),** *n.* twaddle, gibberish, balderdash, (*coll.*) claptrap, hot air.

gequollen [gə'kvɔlən], *see* **quellen.**

Ger [ge:r], *m.* (**-(e)s,** *pl.* **-e**) spear; javelin.

gerade [gə'ra:də], **1.** *adj.* straight, direct; erect, upright; (*fig.*) straightforward, upright, sincere, honest; even (*numbers*); *fünf – sein lassen,* not be too particular, stretch a point; (*Navig.*) *–r Kurs,* rhumb line; *– Lichtstrahl,* direct ray of light; *– Linie,* straight line; (*Mus.*) *–r Takt,* binary measure; (*Prov.*) *der – Weg ist der beste,* honesty is the best policy. **2.** *adv.* precisely, exactly, just; *– in dem Augenblick,* (just at) that very moment; *ich bin – dabei, den Brief zu schreiben,* I am just about to write the letter; *– darum, weil,* just because, for the very reason that; *– entgegengesetzt,* directly *or* diametrically opposed; *– gegenüber,* directly opposite; *– das Gegenteil,* the very opposite, just the contrary; *er ist nicht – mein Freund,* he is not exactly a friend of mine; *nun – nicht,* not just now, certainly not now, now less than ever, not on any account; *nun –,* now especially, now more than ever; *– recht,* just right, the very thing; *– zur rechten Zeit,* just in time, in the nick of time; (*coll.*) *geschieht dir – recht,* serves you (jolly well) right; (*coll.*) *das hat mir – noch gefehlt,* that's really the last straw, (*iron.*) I could have done without that. **Gerade,** *f.* (*Geom.*) straight line; straight (*racecourse*); *linke* –, straight left (*boxing*).

geradeaus [gəˈraːdəaus], *adv.* straight ahead *or* on.

geradehalten [gəˈraːdəhaltən], *irr.v.r.* hold o.s. erect. **Geradehalter,** *m.* orthopaedic apparatus, back-board.

gerade|heraus, *adv.* bluntly, frankly, point-blank. **–so,** *adv.* just *or* exactly (the same); – *viel,* just as much.

geradestehen [gəˈraːdəʃteːən], *irr.v.i.* stand erect; (*fig.*) – *für,* accept *or* acknowledge responsibility for, answer for.

geradeswegs [gəˈraːdəsveːks], *adv.* (*Austr.*), **geradewegs,** *adv.* straightway, straight (away), at once, directly, on the spot; – *losgehen auf* (*Acc.*), make a beeline for.

geradezu [gəˈraːdətsuː], *adv.* straight on; immediately, directly; plainly, point-blank, flatly; candidly, frankly; plain, sheer, downright, nothing short of; *das ist – Wahnsinn,* that is sheer madness; – *frech,* downright cheeky.

Gerad|flügler, *m.* (*Ent.*) Orthoptera. **–führung,** *f.* slide-bar, slide; guides.

Geradheit [gəˈraːthaɪt], *f.* straightness, (*fig.*) straightforwardness, uprightness, rectitude.

gerad|läufig, *adj.* having a straight course, direct; (*Ent.*) orthopterous. **–linig,** *adj.* lineal (*descent*), (*Geom.*) straight-lined, rectilinear. **–sinnig,** *adj.* straightforward, upright, honest. **–zahlig,** *adj.* even-numbered.

Geräms [gəˈrɛms], *n.* (**-es,** *pl.* **-e**) (*dial.*) framework; porch.

Geranie [geˈraːniə], *f.*, **Geranium** [geˈraːnium], *n.* (**-s,** *pl.* **-ien**) geranium.

gerannt [gəˈrant], *see* **rennen.**

Gerassel [gəˈrasəl], *n.* clatter, rattle, clanking, clashing.

Gerät [gəˈrɛːt], *n.* (**-(e)s,** *pl.* **-e**) implement, tool, instrument; utensil(s), (household) effects, chattels; appliance, device, (*coll.*) gadget; equipment, apparatus, gear, (*Rad.*) set.

gerät, *see* **geraten.**

[1]**geraten** [gəˈraːtən], *irr.v.i.* (*aux.* s.) 1. get, fall, come (*in* (*Acc.*), into; *auf* (*Acc.*), to *or* upon); hit *or* happen (*auf* (*Acc.*), upon); *an eine falsche Adresse* –, be delivered at the wrong house *or* to the wrong p., (*fig.*) catch a Tartar; *aneinander* –, see *sich in die Haare* –; *außer sich* –, be beside o.s. (*vor* (*Dat.*), with), get worked up, fly into a rage (about *or* over); *an den Bettelstab* –, be reduced to beggary; *in Brand* –, catch fire; *in Entzücken* –, go into raptures; *in große Gefahr* –, run into danger; *in schlechte Gesellschaft* –, get into bad company; *gut* –, turn out well, be a success; *sich in die Haare* –, fall out; come to blows; *unter Räuber* –, fall among thieves; *an den rechten Mann* –, fall in with the right p., fall into good hands; *in Schulden* –, run into debt; *ins Stocken* –, come to a standstill; *an den Unrechten* –, catch a Tartar; *in Vergessenheit* –, become forgotten, sink into oblivion; *in Zorn* –, fly into a passion; 2. (*with Dat.*) turn out (well), be *or* prove a success, prosper, succeed, thrive; prove to be.

[2]**geraten,** *adj.* successful, advisable, commendable, profitable, advantageous; *das –ste wäre,* the best course would be. *See* **raten.**

Geräte|schalter, *m.* (*Elec.*) plug. **–schnur,** *f.* (*Elec.*) flexible cord *or* lead. **–stecker,** *m.* (*Elec.*) adapter plug. **–turnen,** *n.* gymnastics on the apparatus. **–wagen,** *m.* equipment van *or* truck.

Geratewohl [gəˈraːtəvoːl], *n. aufs* –, at random, haphazard, on the off-chance.

Gerätschaften [gəˈrɛːtʃaftən], *f.pl.* tools, implements, utensils.

gerätst [gəˈrɛːtst], *see* **geraten.**

gerauht [gəˈraut], *adj.* napped (*of fabrics*).

geraum [gəˈraum], *adj.* considerable, long; *–e Zeit,* long time; *vor –er Zeit,* some time ago.

Geräumde [gəˈrɔymdə], *n.* (**-s,** *pl.* **-en**) clearing (*in a wood*).

geräumig [gəˈrɔymɪç], *adj.* roomy, spacious. **Geräumigkeit,** *f.* roominess, spaciousness.

Geräusch [gəˈrɔyʃ], *n.* (**-es,** *pl.* **-e**) noise, sound. **Geräusch|kulisse,** *f.* background of sound. **–laut,** *m.* consonant (*not l, m, n, ng, r*). **geräuschlos,** *adj.* noiseless, silent. **geräuschvoll,** *adj.* noisy, loud, clamorous.

gerben [ˈgɛrbən], *v.t.* tan, dress, curry (*hides*); refine (*steel*); *weiß* –, taw; (*coll.*) *ihm das Fell* –, give him a good hiding *or* tanning. **Gerber,** *m.* tanner. **Gerberei** [–ˈraɪ], *f.* tannery, tan-yard; tanning. **Gerberlohe,** *f.* tan bark. **Gerb|säure,** *f.* tannic acid. **–stahl,** *m.* burnisher. **–stoff,** *m.* tannin.

gerecht [gəˈrɛçt], *adj.* 1. just, fair, equitable, impartial, righteous, legitimate, lawful, justified, well-deserved; *ihm – werden,* do justice to him; *einer S. – werden,* do justice to a th., take a th. into account; meet, satisfy (*a demand*); come *or* live up to, meet (*expectations*); cope with *or* master (*difficulty*); 2. fit, right, suitable; skilled; *in allen Sätteln* –, a match for anything. **Gerechte(r),** *m., f.* righteous man *or* woman. **gerechtfertigt,** *adj.* justified, justifiable. **Gerechtigkeit,** *f.* justice, right; righteousness, fairness, justness; justification; *ihm* or *einer S. – widerfahren lassen,* do justice to him *or* a th.; *der – ihren Lauf lassen,* let justice run its course; – *walten lassen,* dispense justice, (*fig.*) be just *or* fair.

Gerechtsame [gəˈrɛçtsaːmə], *f.* privilege, right, prerogative.

Gerede [gəˈreːdə], *n.* (idle) talk, gossip, tittle-tattle; report, rumour; *ins – kommen,* get talked about; *ins – bringen,* cause to be talked about; gossip about; *es geht das* –, the rumour is.

geregelt [gəˈreːgəlt], *adj.* well-ordered *or* -conducted, orderly; regular.

gereichen [gəˈraɪçən], *v.i.* (*zu*) contribute to, redound to; (will) be, (will) prove to be; *dies gereichte ihm zum Verderben,* this brought about *or* caused his ruin; *es gereicht ihm zur Ehre,* it does him credit *or* redounds to his honour.

gereizt [gəˈraɪtst], *adj.* irritated, (*coll.*) piqued, nettled; irritable. **Gereiztheit,** *f.* irritation.

gereuen [gəˈrɔyən], *v.t.imp. es gereut mich,* I regret it, I am sorry for *or* about it; *es wird Sie* –, you will repent it; *er läßt sich keine Mühe* –, he spares no trouble; *sich die Zeit nicht – lassen,* not grudge the time.

Gerfalke [ˈgeːrfalkə], *m.* (*Orn.*) Gyr falcon, (*Am.*) Gyrfalcon (*Falco rusticolus*).

Gerhard [ˈgeːrhart], *m.* Gerard, Gerald.

Gericht [gəˈrɪçt], *n.* (**-(e)s,** *pl.* **-e**) 1. court of justice, law-court; judgement, jurisdiction, tribunal; *ihn beim -e verklagen,* prosecute him; – *halten über* (*Acc.*), sit in *or* pass judgement on (*oft. fig.*); *mit ihm* (*streng* or *scharf*) *ins* or *zu – gehen,* haul him over the coals, take him to task; *das Jüngste* –, the Last Judgement, doomsday; *vor – bringen,* summon, bring an action against (*a p.*), go to law about (*a th.*); *vor – erscheinen,* appear in court; *vor – kommen,* (*of a matter*) come before the court(s), (*of a p.*) come to *or* go on trial; *vor – stellen,* arraign, bring to trial, put on trial, commit for trial; *zu – sitzen über* (*Acc.*), pass judgement on, bring to justice; *sich vor – verantworten,* stand trial; 2. dish, course.

gerichtlich [gəˈrɪçtlɪç], **1.** *adj.* judicial; legal, forensic; *–er Akkord,* bankrupt's certificate; *–e Medizin,* forensic medicine; *–e Tierarzneikunde,* veterinary jurisprudence; *–es Verfahren,* legal proceedings; *–e Verfügung,* order of the court; *–e Verfolgung,* prosecution; *–es Zeugnis ablegen,* give evidence in a court of law. **2.** *adv.* judicially; in legal form; by order of the court; – *vereidigt,* sworn; *ihn – belangen,* sue him at law, go to law with him; – *gegen ihn vorgehen,* start legal proceedings against him, take him to court.

Gerichts|akten, *f.pl.* records. **–assessor,** *m.* junior judge.

Gerichtsbarkeit [gə'rıçtsba:rkaıt], *f.* jurisdiction.

Gerichts|beamte(r), *m.* magistrate, justiciary. **–befehl,** *m.* writ, court order, legal warrant. **–beisitzer,** *m.* judge-lateral, assessor. **–bezirk,** *m.* circuit, jurisdiction. **–chemiker,** *m.* public analyst. **–diener,** *m.* court usher. **–ferien,** *pl.* vacation. **–gebäude,** *n.* law court, courthouse. **–gebühren,** *f.pl.*, **–gefälle,** *n.pl.* law charges, costs. **–herr,** *m.* supreme legal authority. **–hof,** *m.* law courts, court of justice, tribunal. **–kosten,** *pl.* legal expenses; ***ihn zu den – verurteilen,*** order him to pay costs. **–medizin,** *f.* forensic medicine. **–ordnung,** *f.* legal procedure. **–person,** *f.* magistrate, judge, court official *or* officer. **–posaune,** *f.* (*B.*) last trumpet. **–präsident,** *m.* presiding judge. **–rat,** *m.* justice (*a title*). **–saal,** *m.* court room. **–schreiber,** *m.* clerk of the court. **–sitzung,** *f.* session, hearing. **–sprengel,** *m.* jurisdiction, circuit. **–verfahren,** *n.* trial, proceedings at law. **–verhandlung,** *f.* trial, legal proceedings. **–vollzieher,** *m.* bailiff, sheriff. **–weg,** *m.* (*Hist.*) road to the gallows. **–wesen,** *n.* judiciary, judicial system. **–zwang,** *m.* legal sanction *or* authority.

gerieben [gə'ri:bən], *adj.* (*coll.*) ***–er Kunde,*** wily *or* shrewd customer, sly dog. *See* **reiben.**

Geriesel [gə'ri:zəl], *n.* drizzle; rippling, purling.

geriet [gə'ri:t], **geriete,** *see* **geraten.**

gering [gə'rıŋ], *adj.* small, little, trifling, scanty, negligible, petty, unimportant; mean, low, inferior, humble, modest; ***mit –en Ausnahmen,*** with but few exceptions; ***–e Aussicht,*** poor *or* slender *or* (*coll.*) slim chance; ***–e Entfernung,*** short distance; ***–es Interesse,*** little interest; ***–e Kenntnisse,*** slight *or* scanty *or* meagre knowledge; ***–e Kost,*** poor fare; ***–e Leute,*** people in humble circumstances; ***–er Preis,*** low price; ***– schätzen,*** estimate at a low value *or* price; ***das kostet – geschätzt 3 Mark,*** at a low estimate that will cost 3 marks (*see* **geringschätzen**); (*Naut.*) ***–er Tiefgang,*** shallow draught; ***mein –es Verdienst,*** my humble merit; ***wir kamen in nicht –e Verlegenheit,*** we were not a little embarrassed; ***kein –erer als er,*** no less a person than he; ***–er machen,*** lessen, diminish; ***nichts –eres als,*** nothing short of; ***ein –es,*** a trifle; ***sich*** (*Dat.*) ***nichts –es einbilden,*** think a great deal of o.s.; ***nicht das –ste,*** not the least bit, nothing at all; ***nicht im –sten,*** not in the least.

gering|achten, *v.t. See* **–schätzen. –fügig,** *adj.* insignificant, unimportant, trifling, negligible, paltry, trivial, petty. **Geringfügigkeit,** *f.* insignificance, paltriness; trifle. **geringhaltig,** *adj.* of little worth, low-grade, below standard, base, poor.

gering|schätzen, *v.t.* esteem lightly, attach little value to, think little of, have a low opinion of, look down on, scorn, despise. **–schätzig,** *adj.* deprecatory, derogatory, disparaging, disdainful, scornful, contemptuous; ***– abtun,*** treat with contempt, (*coll.*) pooh-pooh. **Geringschätzung,** *f.* deprecation, disparagement; scorn, disdain, contempt.

Gerinne [gə'rınə], *n.* (**-s,** *pl.* -) running, flowing; gutter, drain, conduit, mill-race, channel.

gerinnen, *irr.v.i.* (*aux.* s.) curdle (*as milk*), clot (*as blood*), set, coagulate, congeal. **Gerinnsel,** *n.* 1. curds; clot, coagulated mass; 2. rivulet; channel, watercourse.

Gerippe [gə'rıpə], *n.* (**-s,** *pl.* -) skeleton; framework; (*Av.*) air-frame.

gerippt [gə'rıpt], *adj.* ribbed; (*Archit.*) groined, fluted; (*Weav.*) corded; (*Bot., Zool.*) costate; ***–es Papier,*** laid paper.

gerissen [gə'rısən], *adj.* (*coll.*) *see* **gerieben.** *See* **reißen.**

geritten [gə'rıtən], *see* **reiten.**

Germ [gɛrm], *m.* (*Bav., Austr.*) yeast.

Germane [gɛr'ma:nə], *m.* Teuton. **germanisch,** *adj.* Germanic, Teutonic.

Germanist [gɛrma'nıst], *m.* (**-en,** *pl.* **-en**) student *or* teacher of German, Germanic philologist. **Germanistik** [–'nıstık], *f.* German philology.

gern(e) ['gɛrn(ə)], *adv.* (*comp.* **lieber**; *sup.* **am liebsten**) with pleasure, willingly, gladly, readily; (*obs.*) fain; (*dial.*) often; ***ich esse Obst –,*** I am fond of fruit; ***(es ist) – geschehen,*** you are very welcome (to it), don't mention it; ***das glaube ich –,*** I quite *or* can readily believe it; ***gut und –,*** easily, very well; ***– haben*** or ***mögen,*** like, be fond of, care for, (*coll.*) be keen on; (*iron.*) ***du kannst mich – haben,*** go to blazes! do as you damn well like! ***herzlich –, von Herzen –,*** with great pleasure, by all means, with all one's heart; ***etwas – tun,*** like *or* love to do s.th., be fond of doing s.th.; ***ich möchte – wissen,*** I wonder, I should like to know; ***– bereit sein,*** be glad *or* happy, be quite prepared (***zu tun,*** to do); ***er ist überall – gesehen,*** he is welcome everywhere; (*dial.*) ***er sagte –,*** he often said, he used to say; (*dial.*) ***der Baum wächst – am Wasser,*** this tree tends to grow at the water's edge; (*dial.*) ***dieses Holz verfault –,*** this wood is apt to rot.

Gernegroß ['gɛrnəgro:s], *m.* (-, *pl.* **-e**) upstart.

gerochen [gə'rɔxən], *see* **riechen.**

Geröll(e) [gə'rœl(ə)], *n.* rubble, pebbles, boulders, (*Geol.*) scree, rock-debris, detritus.

geronnen [gə'rınən], *see* **rinnen, gerinnen.**

Gerste ['gɛrstə], *f.* barley. **Gersten|ammer,** *f,* (*Orn.*) *see* **Grauammer. –graupen,** *f.pl.*. **–grütze,** *f.* pearl barley, Scotch barley. **–korn,** *n.* 1. barley-corn; 2. sty(e) (*in the eye*). **–mehl,** *n.* barley flour. **–saft,** *m.* (*Poet., hum.*) beer. **–schleim,** *m.* barley water. **–zucker,** *m.* barley-sugar.

Gerte ['gɛrtə], *f.* sapling, switch, rod, cane; whip, riding cane. **gertenschlank,** *adj.* slender as a wand *or* reed.

Geruch [gə'rux], *m.* (**-(e)s,** *pl.* **⸚e**) smell, odour, aroma, scent, perfume, fragrance, (*fig.*) reputation; ***im – der Heiligkeit,*** in the odour of sanctity; ***in dem – kommen,*** come under suspicion; ***er steht in schlechtem –,*** he is in bad odour. **geruchfrei, geruchlos,** *adj.* odourless; not scented; ***– machen,*** deodorize. **Geruchlosigkeit,** *f.* absence of smell, odourlessness. **Geruchs|nerv,** *m.* olfactory nerve. **–sinn,** *m.* sense of smell.

Gerücht [gə'ryçt], *n.* (**-(e)s,** *pl.* **-e**) rumour, report; ***es geht das –,*** it is rumoured *or* reported. **Gerüchtmacher,** *m.* rumour-monger. **gerüchtweise,** *adv.* according to report, as rumour has it, by hearsay; ***wie – verlautet,*** as the story goes, as is rumoured.

geruhen [gə'ru:ən], *v.i.* (*rare now except iron.*) condescend, deign, be pleased; ***Eure Majestät wollen allergnädigst –,*** may it please Your Majesty; ***Seine Majestät haben geruht,*** His Majesty has signified his pleasure.

geruhsam [gə'ru:za:m], *adj.* calm, peaceful, tranquil, restful, leisurely, relaxed, (*of a p.*) imperturbable, phlegmatic. **Geruhsamkeit,** *f.* leisureliness, imperturbability.

Gerümpel [gə'rympəl], *n.* lumber, rubbish, trash, junk.

Gerundium [ge'rundium], *n.* (**-s,** *pl.* **-dien**) gerund. **Gerundiv** [–'di:f], *n.* (**-s,** *pl.* **-e**), **Gerundivum,** *n.* (**-s,** *pl.* **-iva**) gerundive. **gerundivisch,** *adj.* gerundial, gerundival.

gerungen [gə'ruŋən], *see* **ringen.**

Gerüst [gə'ryst], *n.* (**-(e)s,** *pl.* **-e**) scaffold(ing), frame(work); stage, platform, stand; trestle, cradle, (*Biol.*) stoma, reticulum. **Gerüst|brücke,** *f.* trestle-bridge. **–künstler,** *m.* (*Theat.*) stage carpenter. **–stange,** *f.* scaffold pole.

Ges [gɛs], *n.* (*Mus.*) G-flat.

gesägt [gə'zɛ:kt], *adj.* (*Bot.*) serrate, serrated.

gesalzen [gə'zaltsən], *adj.* salted; (*coll.*) exorbitant (*price*); spicy, smutty, risqué (*joke etc.*).

gesamt [gə'zamt], *adj.* whole, entire, complete; united, joint, general, common; total, collective, aggregate, overall; ***das –e Volk,*** the whole nation, all the people; (*Comm.*) ***zur –en Hand,*** collective, joint (and several); ***Gesamte(s),*** the whole, the (sum) total.

Gesamt|ansicht, *f.* general view. **–auflage,** *f.* total circulation (*of newspaper*). **–ausgabe,** *f.* 1. complete edition; 2. *pl.* overall expenses. **–bedarf,** *m.*

total requirement(s). **-betrag,** *m.* sum *or* grand total. **-bewußtsein,** *n.* collective consciousness. **-bild,** *n.* overall *or* general view *or* picture. **-eindruck,** *m.* overall *or* general impression. **-einnahme,** *f.* total receipts. **-ertrag,** *m.* entire proceeds, total output. **-forderung,** *f.* total charges *or* claims.

gesamthaft [gə'zamthaft], *adj., adv.* (*Swiss*) *see* **gesamt, insgesamt.**

Gesamt|haftung, *f.* joint liability. **-haltung,** *f.* general attitude.

Gesamtheit [gə'zamthaɪt], *f.* totality, entirety, generality; the whole; all.

Gesamt|hubraum, *m.* (cubic) capacity (*of an engine*). **-lage,** *f.* general situation. **-länge,** *f.* overall length (*of ship etc.*). **-masse,** *f.* (*Comm.*) total estate. **-produkt,** *n.* gross national product. **-quittung,** *f.* receipt in full. **-schau,** *f.* overall view, synopsis. **-staat,** *m.* federal state. **-tonnengehalt,** *m.* total tonnage. **-übersicht,** *f.* general survey, comprehensive view. **-versicherung,** *f.* comprehensive insurance. **-wert,** *m.* aggregate value. **-wille(n),** *m.* collective will. **-wohl,** *n.* public welfare, common weal. **-zahl,** *f.* total number, sum total.

gesandt [gə'zant], *see* **senden. Gesandte(r),** *m., f.* envoy; ambassador, minister; ***päpstlicher Gesandter,*** the papal nuncio. **Gesandtschaft,** *f.* embassy, legation. **gesandtschaftlich,** *adj.* ambassadorial, diplomatic; ***-er Auftrag,*** diplomatic mission.

Gesang [gə'zaŋ], *m.* (**-es,** *pl.* **⸚e**) singing; vocal music, song; canto (*of a poem*); ***geistliche Gesänge,*** sacred songs, psalms, hymns; ***des -es Gabe,*** the gift of song *or* poesy; ***der - der Vögel,*** birdsong, singing of the birds; ***zweistimmiger -,*** (vocal) duet; ***mehrstimmiger -,*** part song; ***episches Gedicht in 9 Gesängen,*** epic poem in 9 cantos. **Gesang|buch,** *n.* hymn-book, song-book. **-lehrer,** *m,* singing-teacher. **gesanglich,** *adj.* vocal, choral. **Gesangprobe,** *f.* audition. **Gesangskunst,** *f.* vocal *or* choral art. **Gesang|stimme,** *f.* vocal part. **-stunde,** *f.*, **-unterricht,** *m.* singing lesson. **-verein,** *m.* choral society, glee club.

Gesäß [gə'zɛːs], *n.* (**-es,** *pl.* **-e**) seat; breech; buttocks, bottom, behind, (*vulg.*) backside. **Gesäß|bein,** *n.* (*Anat.*) ischium. **-wirbel,** *m.* sacral vertebra.

gesättigt [gə'zɛtɪçt], *adj.* (*Chem.*) saturated, (*fig.*) satiated.

Gesäuge [gə'zɔygə], *n.* udder, dugs (*animals with large litter*).

gesäumt [gə'zɔymt], *adj.* bordered, fimbriate; squared (*of timber*).

Gesäusel [gə'zɔyzəl], *n.* murmuring, rustling.

Geschabsel [gə'ʃaːpsəl], *n.* scrapings.

geschaffen [gə'ʃafən], *see* **schaffen**; (*coll.*) ***- für,*** cut out for.

Geschäft [gə'ʃɛft], *n.* (**-(e)s,** *pl.* **-e**) business, commerce, trade; transaction, deal, dealings, speculation; commercial *or* business house, firm, business, office, shop; business, employment, occupation, calling, job; ***welches - betreiben Sie?*** what line of business are you in? ***dunkles -,*** shady business; ***(gut)gehendes -,*** going concern; ***glänzendes -,*** roaring trade; ***sie geht ins -,*** she goes to business; (*fig.*) ***ein gewagtes -,*** a tricky business; ***große -e machen,*** do extensive business; ***ein gutes*** or ***vorteilhaftes - machen,*** make a bargain, make a good profit (*with a th.*); ***-e halber,*** on business; ***-e machen mit,*** do business with (*a p.*), deal in (*goods*); ***sich*** (*Dat.*) ***ein - daraus machen,*** do well out of it; (*fig.*) ***seinen -en nachgehen,*** go about one's business; ***offenes -,*** retail business; ***das - schließt um 7 Uhr,*** the shop *or* office closes at 7 o'clock; ***solides -,*** sound *or* reliable firm; (*fig.*) ***ein unsauberes -,*** a dirty business; (*coll.*) ***ein - verrichten,*** relieve o.s., relieve nature, (*nursery talk*) do one's business; (*nursery talk*) ***ein großes*** (***kleines***) ***-,*** 'big business' ('little business').

geschäftig [gə'ʃɛftɪç], *adj.* busy, active, industrious; energetic, pushing, officious bustling, fussy.

Geschäftigkeit, *f.* activity, industry, bustle, zeal; officiousness. **geschäftlich, 1.** *adj.* business, commercial, mercantile, business-like. **2.** *adv.* on business.

Geschäfts|abschluß, *m.* business transaction *or* deal. **-andrang,** *m.* pressure of business. **-anteil,** *m.* share in a business, business interest. **-aufsicht,** *f.* temporary receivership, judicial supervision, legal control. **-auftrag,** *m.* commission. **-bereich,** *m.* ***Minister ohne -,*** minister without portfolio. **-bericht,** *m.* market *or* company report. **-brief,** *m.* commercial letter. **-freund,** *m.* business connexion, correspondent; customer. **geschäftsführend,** *adj.* managing, executive; ***-e Regierung,*** caretaker government. **Geschäfts|führer,** *m.* manager, managing director. **-führung,** *f.* executive, management. **-gang,** *m.* 1. routine; 2. trend of affairs. **-gegend,** *f.* business quarter. **-geheimnis,** *n.* trade secret. **-gehilfe,** *m.* office clerk. **-geist,** *m.* head for business, business acumen. **-haus,** *n.* commercial firm; business premises. **-inhaber,** *m.* owner of a firm, principal. **-jahr,** *n.* financial *or* (*Am.*) fiscal year. **-kapital,** *n.* working capital. **-kreis,** *m.* sphere of activity, line of business, *pl.* business circles. **-lage,** *f.* (state of) business *or* trade *or* the market; commercial status. **-lokal,** *n.* business premises; office, shop. **geschäftslos,** *adj.* (*St. Exch.*) slack, lifeless, dull. **Geschäftsmann,** *m.* (-, *pl.* **-leute**) businessman, tradesman. **geschäftsmäßig,** *adj.* businesslike; routine, perfunctory.

Geschäfts|ordnung, *f.* standing orders, rules of procedure; agenda. **-personal,** *n.* staff, employees; (*Mil.*) clerical staff. **-reisende(r),** *m., f.* commercial traveller, travelling salesman. **-schluß,** *m.* closing-time. **-sitz,** *m.* place of business. **-sprache,** *f.* commercial language. **-stelle,** *f.* office, bureau, secretariat. **-stunden,** *f.pl.* business hours, office hours. **-teilhaber,** *m.* partner; ***stiller -,*** sleeping partner. **-träger,** *m.* (authorized) representative, agent (*of a firm*); chargé d'affaires (*diplomatic*). **geschäfts|tüchtig,** *adj.* efficient, enterprising, businesslike; ***-e Dame,*** good business-woman. **-unfähig,** *adj.* legally incapacitated. **Geschäfts|verbindung,** *f.* business connexion *or* relations. **-verkehr,** *m.* business dealings. **-viertel,** *n.* shopping centre, business quarter, (*Am.*) downtown. **-wagen,** *m.* commercial vehicle, delivery van. **-wert,** *m.* good will (*of a firm*). **-zeit,** *f.* office-hours. **-zentrum,** *n.* *See* **-viertel. -zimmer,** *n.* office; (*Mil.*) orderly room. **-zweig,** *m.* branch *or* line of business.

geschah [gə'ʃaː], **geschähe** [gə'ʃɛːə], *see* **geschehen.**

gescheckt [gə'ʃɛkt], *adj.* piebald; variegated.

geschehen [gə'ʃeːən], **1.** *irr.v.i.* (*aux.* s.) take place, happen, chance, come to pass, occur, be done; ***es geschehe!*** so be it! ***- ist -,*** what is done, is done; it's no good crying over spilt milk; ***es kann -, daß,*** it may chance that; ***- lassen,*** allow, permit, tolerate, suffer, shut one's eyes to; ***es geschieht ihm recht,*** it serves him right; ***es ist um ihn -,*** he is done for; ***es ist ein Unglück -,*** a misfortune *or* an accident has happened; ***es geschieht ihn ein Unrecht,*** he is wronged; ***es ist so gut wie -,*** it is as good as done; ***ich weiß nicht, wie mir geschieht,*** I don't know what's wrong with me; (*B.*) ***Dein Wille geschehe,*** Thy will be done; ***es geschehe, was da wolle,*** whatever may happen. **2.** *adj.* ***-e Dinge sind nicht zu ändern,*** what is done, cannot be undone; ***nach -er Arbeit,*** after one's work is over. **Geschehene(s),** *n.* what is done (and finished with), what has taken place, happening, event, accomplished fact; bygones.

Geschehnis [gə'ʃeːnɪs], *n.* (**-ses,** *pl.* **-se**) happening, event, incident, occurrence.

Gescheide [gə'ʃaɪdə], *n.* viscera, entrails, guts.

gescheit [gə'ʃaɪt], *adj.* clever, intelligent, (*coll.*) brainy, bright; wise, prudent, shrewd, sensible; ***nicht recht -,*** not all there, a bit cracked, out of one's mind, not in one's right senses; ***sei doch -!*** do be reasonable! ***ich kann nicht - daraus werden,***

I cannot make head or tail of it; ***daraus kann nichts Gescheites werden,*** no good can come of it, it won't lead to anything. **Gescheitheit,** *f.* cleverness, brains, commonsense.

Geschenk [gəˈʃɛŋk], *n.* **(-(e)s,** *pl.* **-e)** present, gift, donation; ***ihm ein – machen mit,*** make him a present of; ***ein – des Himmels,*** a heaven-sent blessing, a gift from the gods, a godsend, a windfall. **Geschenk|artikel,** *m.pl.* souvenirs, fancy goods. **-exemplar,** *n.* presentation copy (*of a book*).

Geschichte [gəˈʃɪçtə], *f.* history; story, tale, narrative, (*coll.*) event; affair, business, concern; ***alte –,*** ancient history; ***die alte –!*** the old story! (*coll.*) ***das sind alte –n,*** that is ancient history; ***biblische –,*** Scriptural history; ***eine dumme –,*** a nuisance, a stupid business; ***in die – eingehen,*** go down in history; (*coll.*) ***die ganze – kostet 5 DM,*** the whole caboodle costs 5 marks; (*coll.*) ***mache doch keine –n!*** don't make a fuss! don't be so silly! ***neuere –,*** modern history; (*iron.*) ***eine schöne –!*** a nice th. indeed! a pretty state of affairs. **Geschichten|-buch,** *n.* story-book. **-erzähler,** *m.* story-teller.

geschichtet [gəˈʃɪçtət], *adj.* stratified, laminated.

geschichtlich [gəˈʃɪçtlɪç], *adj.* historical, historically true. **Geschichtlichkeit,** *f.* authenticity; historical relevance.

Geschichts|buch, *n.* history book; historical work. **-forscher,** *m.* historian. **-forschung,** *f.* historical research. **-klitterung,** *f.* biased historical account. **-schreiber,** *m.* historian, historiographer, annalist. **-wissenschaft,** *f.* science of history.

Geschick [gəˈʃɪk], *n.* **(-es,** *pl.* **-e)** 1. fate, destiny; 2. *See* **Geschicklichkeit**; ***– zu*** or ***für etwas haben,*** have a knack *or* an aptitude for a th.

Geschicklichkeit [gəˈʃɪklɪçkaɪt], *f.* skill, facility, cleverness, aptitude, knack; dexterity, adroitness, deftness. **geschickt,** *adj.* skilful, clever (*zu,* at), adept, dexterous, adroit, deft.

Geschiebe [gəˈʃiːbə], *n.* **(-s,** *pl.* **-)** 1. boulder detritus; 2. pushing, shoving. **Geschiebe|mergel,** *m.* boulder clay. **-formation,** *f.* detrital *or* unstratified deposit. **-lehm,** *m.* glacial loam.

geschieden [gəˈʃiːdən], *adj.* separated; divorced (*a p.*), dissolved (*marriage*); (*coll.*) ***wir sind –e Leute,*** it's all over between us, we are through with each other. *See* **scheiden.**

geschieht [gəˈʃiːt], *see* **geschehen.**

geschienen [gəˈʃiːnən], *see* **scheinen.**

Geschirr [gəˈʃɪr], *n.* **(-(e)s,** *pl.* **-e)** 1. crockery, dishes, china, tableware; implements, utensils; ***das – abräumen (abwaschen) (abtrocknen),*** clear away (wash) (dry) the dishes *or* crocks; 2. harness (*of horses*); horse and cart, equipage; parachute harness; ***sich ins – legen, ins – gehen,*** pull hard (*of horses*); (*also fig.*) exert o.s., put one's shoulder to the wheel, put one's back into it. **Geschirr|-kammer,** *f.* harness-room. **-schrank,** *m.* sideboard, china cupboard. **-spülmaschine,** *f.* dishwasher.

geschissen [gəˈʃɪsən], *see* **scheißen.**

Geschlecht [gəˈʃlɛçt], *n.* **(-(e)s,** *pl.* **-er)** sex; genus, kind, species; lineage, race, family, stock, extraction; generation; (*Gram.*) gender; ***aus altem –,*** from an old line *or* family; ***kommende –r,*** future generations; ***männliches –,*** male sex; (*Gram.*) masculine gender; ***das menschliche –,*** the human race; ***das schöne (schwache) (zarte) –,*** the fair (weaker) (gentle) sex. **Geschlechterkunde,** *f.* genealogy.

geschlechtlich [gəˈʃlɛçtlɪç], *adj.* sexual, (*Biol.*) generic; ***–e Aufklärung,*** sex-education; ***–e Anziehungskraft,*** sex-appeal; ***–er Verkehr,*** sexual intercourse. **geschlechtlos,** *adj.* asexual; (*Gram.*) neuter; (*Bot.*) agamic.

Geschlechts|adel, *m.* hereditary nobility, nobility of blood. **-akt,** *m.* sexual intercourse, coition. **-art,** *f.* genus, kind, species, race; generic character. **-folge,** *f.* lineage. **geschlechtskrank,** *adj.* suffering from venereal disease. **Geschlechts|krankheit,** *f.* venereal disease. **-leben,** *n.* sex life. **geschlechtslos,** *adj. See* **geschlechtlos. Geschlechts|-lust,** *f.* carnal *or* sexual desire. **-merkmal,** *n.* sex characteristic. **-name,** *m.* family name, surname, (*Am.*) last name. **-organ,** *n.* sexual organ, genitals. **-register,** *n.* genealogical table, pedigree. **geschlechtsreif,** *adj.* pubescent, fully developed. **Geschlechtsreife,** *f.* puberty. **geschlechtsreizend,** *adj.* aphrodisiac. **Geschlechts|teile,** *m.pl.* sexual organs, genitals, private parts. **-trieb,** *m.* sex instinct *or* urge. **-verhältnis,** *n.* sex ratio. **-verkehr,** *m.* sexual intercourse. **-wort,** *n.* (*pl.* **-wörter**) (*Gram.*) article.

geschlichen [gəˈʃlɪçən], *see* **schleichen.**

geschliffen [gəˈʃlɪfən], *adj.* cut (*glass*), (*fig.*) polished, polite; (*Mil. sl.*) licked into shape, well drilled. *See* **schleifen.**

Geschlinge [gəˈʃlɪŋə], *n.* 1. (*Cul.*) pluck, giblets, offal; 2. festoon, garland, scroll; (*coll.*) twirls, twiddly-bits.

geschlissen [gəˈʃlɪsən], *see* **schleißen.**

geschlossen [gəˈʃlɔsən], **1.** *adj.* closed, (fully) enclosed; whole, complete, unbroken, continuous, uniform, consistent; united, unanimous, (*fig.*) compact, serried (*as ranks*); (*Hunt.*) close (*season*); ***in sich –,*** self-contained; ***–e Kette,*** endless chain; ***–e Gesellschaft,*** private circle; club; ***in –er Sitzung,*** in camera. **2.** *adv.* in a body, en bloc, to a man; unanimously; ***– hinter ihm stehen,*** be solidly behind him. *See* **schließen. Geschlossenheit,** *f.* compactness, inclusiveness, uniformity, consistency; continuity; unanimity.

Geschluchze [gəˈʃluxtsə], *n.* (prolonged) sobbing.

geschlungen [gəˈʃluŋən], *see* **schlingen.**

Geschmack [gəˈʃmak], *m.* **(-(e)s,** *pl.* **¨-e)** taste, flavour; savour, relish; (*fig.*) taste, fancy, liking (*an* (*Dat.*), for), good taste; ***dies hat einen guten –,*** this tastes good; ***– an einer S. finden,*** relish *or* like a th., take a fancy to a th.; ***einer S. keinen – abgewinnen können,*** not be able to acquire a taste for a th. *or* to develop a liking for a th.; ***der – des 18. Jahrhunderts,*** 18th-century taste; ***über den – läßt sich nicht streiten,*** there is no accounting for tastes; ***die Geschmäcke*** (*also coll.* ***Geschmäcker***) ***sind verschieden,*** tastes differ. **geschmacklich,** *adj.* as regards taste. **geschmacklos,** *adj.* tasteless, flavourless, insipid, flat, stale; in bad taste. **Geschmacklosigkeit,** *f.* lack of good taste, bad taste; *pl.* platitudes, inanities, tactlessness, bad form; ***das ist eine –,*** that is in bad taste.

Geschmacks|becher, *m.,* **-knopse,** *f.* taste bud. **-nerv,** *m.* gustatory nerve. **-sache,** *f.* matter *or* question of taste. **-sinn,** *m.* sense of taste; refinement, good taste. **-verirrung,** *f.* error in taste, misguided taste; outrage, travesty. **geschmackvoll,** *adj.* tasteful, elegant, stylish, in good taste.

Geschmatze [gəˈʃmatsə], *n.* champing, smacking of lips, noisy eating.

Geschmause [gəˈʃmauzə], *n.* banqueting, feasting, revelling.

Geschmeide [gəˈʃmaɪdə], *n.* jewellery, jewels, trinkets.

geschmeidig [gəˈʃmaɪdɪç], *adj.* soft, supple, lithe, lissome, pliant, pliable, flexible, (*of metals*) ductile, malleable; (*fig.*) smooth, yielding, elusive, (*coll.*) slick; supple, tractable, versatile. **Geschmeidigkeit,** *f.* suppleness, flexibility, pliancy, smoothness; ductility, malleability; tractability. **Geschmeidigkeitsübungen,** *f.pl.* (*Gymn.*) limbering-up exercises.

Geschmeiß [gəˈʃmaɪs], *n.* dirt, droppings; fly-blow, eggs (*of insects*); vermin; (*fig.*) scum, rabble, riffraff.

Geschmetter [gəˈʃmɛtər], *n.* flourish (*of trumpets*); warbling (*of a canary*).

Geschmier(e) [gəˈʃmiːr(ə)], *n.* scrawl, scribble; smear(ing); daub.

geschmissen [gəˈʃmɪsən], *see* **schmeißen.**

geschmolzen [gəˈʃmɔltsən], *see* **schmelzen.**

Geschmorte(s) [gəˈʃmoːrtə(s)], *n.* stew.

Geschmus(e) [gəˈʃmuːz(ə)], *n.* (*coll.*) fawning, wheedling, honeyed words, (*sl.*) soft soap.

Geschnatter [gəˈʃnatər], *n.* cackling, chatter.

geschniegelt [gə'ʃni:gəlt], *adj.* spruce, trim, smart, dapper; – *und gebügelt,* spick-and-span.

geschnitten [gə'ʃnɪtən], *see* **schneiden.**

geschnoben [gə'ʃno:bən], (*rare*) *see* **schnauben.**

Geschnörkel [gə'ʃnœrkəl], *n.* embellishment, trappings, arabesques; bombast, preciosity, flamboyance, mannerisms.

geschoben [gə'ʃo:bən], *see* **schieben.**

gescholten [gə'ʃɔltən], *see* **schelten.**

Geschöpf [gə'ʃœpf], *n.* (**-es,** *pl.* **-e**) creature; production, creation.

geschoren [gə'ʃo:rən], *see* **scheren.**

Geschoß [gə'ʃɔs], *n.* (**-(ss)es,** *pl.* **-(ss)e**) 1. projectile, missile, bullet, shell; *ferngesteuertes* –, guided missile; 2. storey, floor. **Geschoß|aufschlag,** *m.* impact (*of shell*). **–aufzug,** *m.* shell-hoist. **–bahn,** *f.* trajectory. **–bö,** *f.* shell blast.

geschossen [gə'ʃɔsən], *see* **schießen.**

Geschoß|garbe, *f.* cone of fire, dispersion. **–höhe,** *f.* height between floors. **–kammer,** *f.* magazine. **–mantel,** *m.* jacket (*of bullet*), shell-case. **–raum,** *m.* chamber (*of a gun*). **–trichter,** *m.* shell-crater, shell-hole. **–vorrat,** *m.* ammunition supply. **–wirkung,** *f.* burst effect (*of projectile*).

Geschräge [gə'ʃrɛ:gə], *n.* paling, hurdle.

geschränkt [gə'ʃrɛŋkt], *adj.* crossed, at an angle.

geschraubt [gə'ʃraupt], *adj.* screwed, bolted; (*fig.*) stilted, affected. **Geschraubtheit,** *f.* affectation.

Geschrei [gə'ʃraɪ], *n.* (**-s,** *pl.* **-e**) 1. screams, shrieks, cries, shouting, yelling, screaming; outcry, clamour, hue and cry, fuss, ado, stir; hubbub, hullabaloo; bray(ing) (*of ass*); *viel* or *ein großes – erheben,* make a great fuss, cry blue murder; *viel – um nichts,* (*Prov.*) *viel – und wenig Wolle,* much ado about nothing; 2. discredit, disrepute; *ins – bringen,* bring into disrepute; *ins – kommen,* get talked about, get a bad name.

Geschreibe [gə'ʃraɪbə], *n.* pen-pushing, quill-driving, scribbling. **Geschreibsel,** *n.* scribble, scrawl; pot-boiler, (*sl.*) tripe, bilge.

geschrieben [gə'ʃri:bən], *see* **schreiben.**

geschrie(e)n [gə'ʃri:ən], *see* **schreien.**

geschritten [gə'ʃrɪtən], *see* **schreiten.**

geschult [gə'ʃu:lt], *adj.* trained.

geschunden [gə'ʃundən], *see* **schinden.**

Geschür [gə'ʃy:r], *n.* dross, scoria.

Geschütz [gə'ʃyts], *n.* (**-es,** *pl.* **-e**) gun, cannon; piece (of ordnance); (*fig.*) *grobes* or *schweres – auffahren,* turn one's heavy guns (*gegen,* on), throw one's weight about; *das – auffahren* (*lassen*), bring the gun into action; *das – aufpflanzen,* mount the gun; *das – richten,* lay the gun; *das – in Stellung bringen,* emplace the gun.

Geschütz|aufstellung, *f.* (*Nav.*) disposition of guns, (*Artil.*) gun emplacement. **–bedienung,** *f.* gunners, gun-crew. **–bettung,** *f.* gun platform, mounting. **–bronze,** *f.* gun-metal. **–donner,** *m.* roar of the guns. **–exerzieren,** *n.* gun-drill. **–feuer,** *n.* barrage, gunfire, shelling, cannonade. **–führer,** *m.* (*Nav.*) gun captain, (*Artil.*) No. 1 gunner. **–kampf,** *m.* artillery duel. **–ladung,** *f.* propellent (charge). **–lafette,** *f.* gun-mounting. **–park,** *m.* ordnance park. **–pforte,** *f.* (*Nav.*) port-hole. **–probe,** *f.* firing test. **–protze,** *f.* gun carriage, limber. **–salve,** *f.* salvo, (*Nav.*) broadside. **–stand,** *m.*, **–stellung,** *f.* gun emplacement, firing position. **–turm,** *m.* gun turret. **–weite,** *f.* artillery range.

Geschwader [gə'ʃva:dər], *n.* (*Nav.*) squadron, (*Av.*) group, (*Am.*) wing. **Geschwader|flug,** *m.* formation flying. **–kommodore,** *m.* (*Av.*) Air Officer Commanding, (*Am.*) wing commander.

Geschwafel [gə'ʃva:fəl], *n.* (*coll.*) twaddle, tosh.

Geschwätz [gə'ʃvɛts], *n.* idle *or* empty talk; prattle, tittle-tattle, gossip; rigmarole; *was soll dies –?* what is the meaning of this babble? **geschwätzig,** *adj.* talkative, garrulous, loquacious, verbose, voluble; babbling (*brook*). **Geschwätzigkeit,** *f.* talkativeness, loquaciousness, loquacity, verbosity.

geschweift [gə'ʃvaɪft], *adj.* cranked, arched, curved; tailed.

geschweige [gə'ʃvaɪgə], *conj.* – *denn,* not to mention, let alone; much less; far from; to say nothing of.

geschweigen [gə'ʃvaɪgən], *irr.v.i.* (*obs.*) (*Gen.*) pass by in silence, say nothing of, not mention, omit; *anderer Vorzüge zu* –, not to speak of other advantages.

geschwiegen [gə'ʃvi:gən], *see* **schweigen.**

geschwind [gə'ʃvɪnt], *adj.* quick, swift, fast, speedy, rapid, hasty, prompt, immediate; *sie wußte nicht, was sie – sagen sollte,* she did not know at the moment what to say; *mach' –!* be quick!

Geschwindigkeit [gə'ʃvɪndɪçkaɪt], *f.* rapidity, haste, swiftness, quickness, promptness, expedition; pace, speed, rate, velocity, momentum; (*Naut.*) headway; *in der* –, hurriedly, on the spur of the moment; (*Prov.*) – *ist keine Hexerei,* sleight of hand is no magic. **Geschwindigkeits|abfall,** *m.* loss of speed, deceleration. **–grenze,** *f.* speed limit. **–messer,** *m.* speedometer, tachometer, (*Av.*) airspeed indicator. **–regler,** *m.* governor. **–rekord,** *m.* speed record. **–zunahme,** *f.* increase in speed, acceleration.

Geschwindschritt [gə'ʃvɪntʃrɪt], *m.* (*Mil.*) double-quick step, at the double.

Geschwirr(e) [gə'ʃvɪr(ə)], *n.* whirring, whizzing; buzz(ing).

Geschwister [gə'ʃvɪstər], *pl.* brother(s) and sister(s); *sie sind* –, they are brother and sister; *meine* –, my brother(s) and sister(s). **Geschwisterkind,** *n.* nephew *or* niece; first cousin. **geschwisterlich,** *adj.* brotherly, sisterly. **Geschwister|liebe,** *f.* love for brother(s) and sister(s). **–mord,** *m.* fratricide. **–paar,** *n.* brother and sister.

geschwollen [gə'ʃvɔlən], *adj.* thick, swollen, tumid; (*fig.*) inflated, bombastic, (*coll.*) highfalutin(g). *See* **schwellen.**

geschwommen [gə'ʃvɔmən], *see* **schwimmen.**

[1]**geschworen** [gə'ʃvo:rən], *adj.* sworn (*enemy etc.*); *Geschworene(r),* juror, jury-man *or* -woman; *die Geschworenen,* the jury. *See* **schwören.**

[2]**geschworen,** *adj.* (*obs.*) festered, ulcerated. *See* **schwären.**

Geschworenen|bank, *f.* jury-box. **–gericht,** *n.* jury. **–liste,** *f.* jury-list; panel; *auf die – setzen,* empanel. **–obmann,** *m.* foreman of the jury.

Geschwulst [gə'ʃvulst], *f.* (-, *pl.* **⸚e**) swelling, tumour, growth.

geschwunden [gə'ʃvundən], *see* **schwinden.**

geschwungen [gə'ʃvuŋən], *see* **schwingen.**

Geschwür [gə'ʃvy:r], *n.* (**-(e)s,** *pl.* **-e**) ulcer, abscess, boil, gathering, (running) sore; *bösartiges* –, malignant ulcer. **Geschwürbildung,** *f.* ulceration. **geschwürig,** *adj.* ulcerous.

gesegnen [gə'ze:gnən], *v.t.* (*Poet., dial.*) bless (*a p. or th.*); *Gott gesegne es!* God's blessing on his gifts (*grace after meal*); *gesegnete Mahlzeit!* (*a greeting at mealtimes; no English equivalent nearer than 'good appetite!'*); *gesegneten Leibes,* with child.

Geselchte(s) [gə'zɛlçtə(s)], *n.* (*Bav., Austr.*) smoked meat.

Geselle [gə'zɛlə], *m.* (**-n,** *pl.* **-n**) 1. companion, comrade, mate, fellow, brother member (*of a society*); 2. journeyman.

gesellen [gə'zɛlən], **1.** *v.t.* join, associate, ally. **2.** *v.r.* join *or* ally *or* associate (o.s.) (*zu,* with); keep company with; (*Prov.*) *gleich und gleich gesellt sich gern,* birds of a feather flock together. **Gesellen|herberge,** *f.* workingmen's lodging-house. **–jahre,** *n.pl.*, **–zeit,** *f.* time of service as journeyman.

gesellig [gə'zɛlɪç], *adj.* social, sociable; companionable, convivial; (*Zool.*) gregarious; *–es Beisammensein, –er Abend,* social gathering *or* evening; *man lebte* –, there was much social life. **Geselligkeit,** *f.* sociability, good fellowship, conviviality;

company, social life. **Geselligkeitstrieb,** *m.* social *or* gregarious instinct.

Gesellschaft [gəˈzɛlʃaft], *f.* society, community; society, association, union, fellowship, club; (*Comm.*) company, (*Am.*) corporation; partnership; party, social gathering, company, high society; ***eingetragene –,*** registered *or* incorporated society; (*coll.*) ***die ganze –,*** the whole bunch; ***eine – geben,*** give *or* (*coll.*) throw a party; ***geschlossene –,*** club; ***– mit beschränkter Haftung*** (*abbr.* ***GmbH***), limited liability company; ***die – Jesu,*** the Jesuit Order, the Society of Jesus; ***in seiner –,*** in his company, in company with him; ***ihm – leisten,*** keep him company, join him (***bei,*** in); ***schlechte – verdirbt gute Sitten,*** evil communications corrupt good manners; ***mit ihm in – treten,*** enter in(to) partnership with him; ***sich in – zeigen,*** appear in society. **Gesellschafter,** *m.* companion; associate, partner; member of a society *or* company; ***er ist ein guter –,*** he is good company; ***stiller –,*** sleeping *or* (*Am.*) silent partner. **Gesellschafterin,** *f.* lady companion.

gesellschaftlich [gəˈzɛlʃaftlɪç], *adj.* social, gregarious; co-operative; ***–e Produktion,*** co-operative *or* joint production; ***–er Schliff,*** social graces. **Gesellschaftlichkeit,** *f.* social life.

Gesellschafts|anzug, *m.* evening-dress, dress-suit. **–dame,** *f.* lady companion; chaperone. **gesellschaftsfähig,** *adj.* presentable; gentlemanly, ladylike. **Gesellschaftsfahrt,** *f.* conducted tour. **gesellschaftsfeindlich,** *adj.* antisocial. **Gesellschafts|haus,** *n.* club-house, casino. **–inseln,** *pl.* (*Geog.*) Society Islands. **–kapital,** *n.* (*Comm.*) joint *or* capital stock, share capital. **–klasse,** *f.* social class. **–klatsch,** *m.* society gossip. **–kleid,** *n.* (lady's) evening dress *or* gown, party dress. **–kreis,** *m.* circle of friends *or* acquaintances. **–lehre,** *f.* sociology. **–raum,** *m.* reception room, lounge. **–recht,** *n.* (*Comm.*) company law. **–register,** *n.* commercial register. **–reise,** *f.* conducted tour. **–satzungen,** *pl.* articles of association. **–spiel,** *n.* party game, round game. **–steuer,** *f.* corporation tax. **–tanz,** *m.* ballroom dancing. **–vertrag,** *m.* deed of partnership; (*Phil.*) social contract. **–wagen,** *m.* touring bus, (*obs.*) charabanc. **–wissenschaft,** *f.* sociology, *pl.* social sciences. **–zimmer,** *n.* reception-room, drawing-room; club-room.

Gesenk [gəˈzɛŋk], *n.* **(-(e)s,** *pl.* **-e)** stamp, die, swage; ***im – schmieden,*** drop-forge. **Gesenk|hammer,** *m.* drop hammer. **–schmiede,** *f.* drop forge.

gesessen [gəˈzɛsən], *see* **sitzen.**

Gesetz [gəˈzɛts], *n.* **(-es,** *pl.* **-e)** law; act, statute, decree; precept, rule, principle; ***das natürliche (göttliche) (bürgerliche) –,*** the natural (divine) (civil) law; ***ein – erlassen,*** enact a law; ***zum – werden,*** become law, pass into law; ***ein – tritt in Kraft,*** a law comes into force *or* becomes effective; ***– über das Verlagsrecht,*** law relating to publishing.

Gesetz|blatt, *n.* law gazette. **–buch,** *n.* statute-book; code; ***bürgerliches –,*** civil code. **–entwurf,** *m.* (*Parl.*) (draft of a) bill.

Gesetzes|kraft, *f.* force of law, legal force *or* sanction; ***– erhalten*** or ***erlangen,*** be enacted, be put on the statute-book, become law; ***– verleihen*** (*Dat.*), enact. **–schärfe,** *f.* rigour of the law. **–vorlage,** *f.* *See* **Gesetzentwurf.**

gesetzgebend [gəˈzɛtsgəːbənt], *adj.* legislative; ***–er Körper,*** legislative assembly *or* body, legislature. **Gesetz|geber,** *m.* legislator, law-giver. **–gebung,** *f.* legislation. **gesetz|kräftig,** *adj.* legally sanctioned, having the force of the law. **–kundig,** *adj.* versed in law.

gesetzlich [gəˈzɛtslɪç], *adj.* legal, statutory, lawful, legitimate; ***– geschützt,*** protected by law; copyright, patented. **Gesetzlichkeit,** *f.* 1. legality, lawfulness; 2. (system of) laws. **gesetzlos,** *adj.* lawless, anarchical. **Gesetzlosigkeit,** *f.* lawlessness, anarchy. **gesetzmäßig,** *adj.* 1. lawful, legitimate, legal, statutory; 2. (*fig.*) regular, conforming to *or* following a pattern, in accordance with theoretical principles. **Gesetzmäßigkeit,** *f.* 1. legality; 2. conformity, regularity. **Gesetzsammlung,** *f.* code *or* body of laws, statute-book.

gesetzt [gəˈzɛtst], *adj.* **1.** fixed, set, placed, established; (*Typ.*) in type, set up; steady, calm, composed, serious, staid, sober, grave, sedate; ***–es Alter, –e Jahre,*** years of discretion. **2.** *conj.* granted, supposing, in case; ***– den Fall,*** take the case, let us suppose, granting that it is so, provided such was the case; ***– es sei wahr,*** supposing it were *or* it to be true.

Gesetztafel [gəˈzɛtstaːfəl], *f.* table of laws; ***die (mosaischen) –n,*** decalogue.

Gesetztheit [gəˈzɛtsthaɪt], *f.* steadiness, sedateness, staidness gravity.

Gesetz|übertretung, *f.* infringement of the law. **–umgehung,** *f.* evasion of the law. **–vorlage,** *f.* *See* **–entwurf. gesetzwidrig,** *adj.* unlawful, illegal.

Gesicht [gəˈzɪçt], *n.* 1. **(-(e)s,** *no pl.*) sight; eyesight; ***aus dem – verlieren,*** lose sight of; ***kurzes – haben,*** be short-sighted; ***das – verlieren,*** lose one's sight; ***zu – bekommen,*** catch sight *or* a glimpse of, set eyes (up)on; ***zweites –,*** second sight; 2. **(-(e)s,** *pl.* **-er)** face, countenance, mien, physiognomy, look; (*fig.*) appearance, character, aspect; ***die S. kriegt ein anderes –,*** the matter takes on a different complexion; ***seinem Vater wie aus dem – geschnitten,*** the image of his father; ***ihm ins –,*** to his face; ***ins – fassen,*** face; ***seine Behauptung schlägt den Tatsachen ins –,*** his statement conflicts with *or* is at variance with *or* flatly contradicts the facts, the facts belie his *or* give the lie to his statement; ***ein böses – machen,*** scowl, look angry; ***ein freundliches – machen,*** look pleasant; ***ein langes – machen,*** pull a long face; ***ein saures – machen,*** look surly; ***–er schneiden,*** make *or* pull faces, grimace; ***ihm gut zu – stehen,*** suit him, be becoming to him; ***ihm schlecht zu – stehen,*** ill become him; ***das – wahren,*** save one's face; 3. **(-(e)s,** *pl.* **-e)** sight; vision, apparition; ***–e sehen,*** see visions.

Gesichts|ausdruck, *m.* facial expression. **–bildung,** *f.* physiognomy, features. **–eindruck,** *m.* visual impression. **–farbe,** *f.* complexion. **–feld,** *n.* visual field, field of vision *or* view. **–kreis,** *m.* (mental) range, horizon; ***seinen – erweitern,*** enlarge the range of one's ideas; ***er ist seit Jahren aus meinem – verschwunden,*** I have lost sight of him for years; ***das liegt außer seinem –,*** that is beyond him *or* his mental horizon. **–krem,** *m.* face cream. **–linie,** *f.* 1. facial line, lineament; 2. (*Opt.*) line of sight, visual line. **–nerv,** *m.* 1. optic nerve; 2. facial nerve. **–punkt,** *m.* point of view, viewpoint, aspect, (*coll.*) angle; criterion, factor, motive. **–rose,** *f.* (*Med.*) erysipelas. **–schmerz,** *m.* neuralgia, (*coll.*) face-ache. **–schnitt,** *m.* cast of features. **–spannung,** *f.* face-lifting. **–täuschung,** *f.* optical illusion. **–verletzung,** *f.* facial injury. **–wahrnehmung,** *f.* sight, visual perception. **–wasser,** *n.* face-lotion. **–weite,** *f.* visible range. **–winkel,** *m.* 1. (*Anat.*) facial angle; 2. (*Opt.*) visual angle; angle of vision; (*fig.*) *see* **–punkt. –zug,** *m.* (*usu. pl.*) feature, lineament.

Gesims [gəˈzɪms], *n.* **(-es,** *pl.* **-e)** cornice, moulding; shelf, ledge; lintel (*of door*), mantelpiece (*of fireplace*), window-sill.

Gesinde [gəˈzɪndə], *n.* (*obs.*) domestics, domestic servants; (*dial.*) farm-hands.

Gesindel [gəˈzɪndəl], *n.* rabble, mob, riffraff, (*coll.*) ragtag and bobtail.

gesinnt [gəˈzɪnt], *adj.* minded, disposed; ***gleich –,*** of the same mind *or* opinion; ***anders –,*** of different opinion, with different views (***als,*** from); ***freundlich –,*** well-disposed (*Dat.*, towards); ***Gustav Adolf war protestantisch –,*** Gustavus Adolphus had Protestant sympathies; ***feindlich –,*** ill-disposed, antipathetic, hostile, inimical; ***wie ist er –?*** what are his views?

Gesinnung [gəˈzɪnuŋ], *f.* disposition; sentiment(s), views, opinions, conviction(s), attitude, persuasion; character, mind, way of thinking; ***aufrichtige –,*** fair-mindedness; ***edle –,*** noble-mindedness;

niedere –, meanness, baseness; *treue* –, loyalty; *vaterländische* –, patriotism; *er zeigt nie seine wahre* –, he never shows his true face. **Gesinnungsgenosse,** *m.* partisan, adherent, follower; political friend. **gesinnungslos,** *adj.* unprincipled, characterless. **Gesinnungslosigkeit,** *f.* lack of principle *or* character. **Gesinnungslump,** *m.* turncoat, time-server; (*sl.*) rat. **gesinnungs|treu,** *adj.* loyal, true-hearted, constant, staunch. **–tüchtig,** *adj.* (*iron.*) sycophantic, fawning, cringing, time-serving. **Gesinnungs|tüchtigkeit,** *f.* sycophancy, obsequiousness. **–wechsel,** *m.* change of opinion *or* face *or* front, change in one's opinions.

gesittet [gə'zɪtət], *adj.* well-mannered, well-bred, polished, polite, courteous; civilized, cultured; moral. **Gesittung,** *f.* good manners, good breeding; civilization, culture; morality.

Gesöff [gə'zœf], *n.* (*sl.*) hooch.

gesoffen [gə'zɔfən], *see* **saufen.**

gesogen [gə'zo:gən], *see* **saugen.**

gesonnen [gə'zɔnən], *p.p.* – *sein,* intend, propose, have in mind, be inclined *or* resolved *or* disposed (*to do*). *See* **sinnen.**

gesotten [gə'zɔtən], *see* **sieden.**

gespalten [gə'ʃpaltən], *adj.* cleft.

Gespan [gə'ʃpa:n], *m.* 1. (**-(e)s** *or* **-en,** *pl.* **-e(n)**) (*obs., dial.*) colleague, assistant, comrade; 2. (**-(e)s,** *pl.* **-e**) Hungarian local official.

Gespann [gə'ʃpan], *n.* (**-(e)s,** *pl.* **-e**) team, yoke (*of horses etc.*); horse-drawn vehicle; carriage *or* coach and horses; (*fig.*) *ungleiches* –, bad match, incongruous pair *or* couple; incongruity, disparity. **Gespannführer,** *m.* teamster.

gespannt [gə'ʃpant], *adj.* stretched, tight, taut, strained, tense, under tension, cocked (*firearm*); intent, eager, anxious; – *sein,* be in suspense, be all agog, be on tenterhooks; – *sein auf* (*Acc.*), eagerly *or* anxiously await, be anxious for; – *sein ob,* wonder if, be curious to know if; *mit* –*er Aufmerksamkeit,* with close attention; –*e Verhältnisse,* strained relations; *auf* –*em Fuße mit ihm stehen,* be on bad terms with him. **Gespanntheit,** *f.* tension, tenseness, strained relations, estrangement, bad terms.

Gesparr(e) [gə'ʃpar(ə)], **Gespärre** [gə'ʃpɛrə], *n.* framework; rafters.

Gespenst [gə'ʃpɛnst], *n.* (**-es,** *pl.* **-er**) ghost, spectre, (*coll.*) spook; phantom, apparition; *es geht ein – in diesem Hause um,* this house is haunted; *das – der Arbeitslosigkeit,* the spectre of unemployment. **Gespenstergeschichte,** *f.* ghost-story. **gespensterhaft,** *adj.* ghostly, spectral, (*coll.*) spooky; ghostlike, ghastly. **Gespenster|reich,** *n.* spirit-world. **–schiff,** *n.* phantom ship. **–stunde,** *f.* witching-hour, midnight hour. **gespenstig, gespenstisch,** *adj. See* **gespensterhaft.**

Gesperr(e) [gə'ʃpɛr(ə)], *n.* (**-(e)s,** *pl.* **-e**) (*Hunt.*) brood of pheasants *etc.* **Gesperre,** *n.* (**-s,** *pl.* **-**) safety catch, stop, ratchet(-wheel) (*of a watch*), catch, clasp.

gespickt [gə'ʃpɪkt], *adj.* (*Cul.*) larded.

gespie(e)n [gə'ʃpi:ən], *see* **speien.**

Gespiele [gə'ʃpi:lə], *m.* (**-n,** *pl.* **-n**), **Gespielin,** *f.* (-, *pl.* **-nen**) playmate.

Gespinst [gə'ʃpɪnst], *n.* (**-es,** *pl.* **-e**) spun yarn, textile fabric; web, cocoon; (*fig.*) tissue (*of lies etc.*); *von feinem* –, fine-spun; (*Prov.*) *wie das –, so der Gewinnst,* no pains, no gains.

gesponnen [gə'ʃpɔnən], *see* **spinnen.**

Gespons [gə'ʃpɔns], *m. or n.* (**-es,** *pl.* **-e**) (*Poet., hum.*) spouse.

Gespött [gə'ʃpœt], *n.* mockery, derision; laughing-stock; *aller Leute – sein, allen Leuten zum – dienen,* be the laughing-stock of everyone; *ihn zum – machen, sein – mit ihm treiben,* mock *or* deride him, scoff at him, make a laughing-stock of him.

Gespräch [gə'ʃprɛ:ç], *n.* (**-(e)s,** *pl.* **-e**) conversation, talk, discussion, discourse, colloquy; dialogue, (*Tele.*) call; *sich mit ihm in ein – einlassen, ein – mit ihm anknüpfen,* enter into conversation with him; *ein – führen,* carry on a conversation; *es ist das – der ganzen Stadt,* it is the talk of the town, it is all over the town; *das – auf* (*einen Gegenstand*) *bringen,* lead the conversation round to (a subject), bring (a subject) into the conversation; (*Pol.*) –*e auf höchster Ebene,* summit talks. **gesprächig,** *adj.* talkative, communicative, garrulous; (*coll.*) chatty. **Gesprächigkeit,** *f.* talkativeness; garrulousness, garrulity. **Gesprächs|-form,** *f.* dialogue form. **–gegenstand, –stoff,** *m.* topic *or* subject of conversation. **gesprächsweise,** *adv.* in the course of (the) conversation; conversationally.

gespreizt [gə'ʃpraɪtst], *adj.* spread out, wide apart; (*fig.*) stilted, affected, pompous; *mit –en Beinen,* with legs astraddle. **Gespreiztheit,** *f.* affectation, pomposity.

gesprenkelt [gə'ʃprɛŋkəlt], *adj.* speckled, mottled, spotted.

gesprochen [gə'ʃprɔxən], *see* **sprechen.**

gesprossen [gə'ʃprɔsən], *see* **sprießen.**

gesprungen [gə'ʃpruŋən], *see* **springen.**

Gest [gɛst], *f.* (*dial.*) yeast, balm.

Gestade [gə'ʃta:də], *n.* (**-s,** *pl.* **-**) (*Poet.*) bank (*of lake or river*), shore (*of lake or sea*), beach (*of sea*), waterside.

gestaffelt [gə'ʃtafəlt], *adj.* staggered, distributed; (*Mil.*) echeloned.

Gestalt [gə'ʃtalt], *f.* (-, *pl.* **-en**) form, shape, contour; (*of physique*) figure, build, frame, stature; (*fig.*) kind, manner, way, fashion; (*in art or literature*) figure, character; (*in psychological contexts* 'Gestalt' *should not be translated*); (*feste*) – *annehmen,* take shape, materialize; *in – von,* in the form *or* shape *or* guise of; *das Abendmahl unter beiden –en* or *in beiderlei –,* communion in both kinds; *sich in seiner wahren – zeigen,* show one's true character *or* colours. **gestalt,** *adj.* (*rare*) shaped; *bei so –en Sachen,* such being the case.

gestalten [gə'ʃtaltən], **1.** *v.t.* form, fashion, mould, shape, (*fig.*) arrange, organize; *schöpferisch* –, create, produce; *dramatisch* –, dramatize, arrange for the stage. **2.** *v.r.* take shape, assume the form of, appear; develop (*zu,* into), become, turn out *or* prove (to be). **Gestalter,** *m.* fashioner, shaper; creator; organizer. **gestalterisch,** *adj.* creative, artistic. **gestaltet,** *adj.* shaped, fashioned, formed. **Gestaltlehre,** *f.* morphology. **gestaltlos,** *adj.* shapeless, formless, amorphous. **Gestaltpsychologie,** *f.* gestalt psychology.

Gestaltung [gə'ʃtaltuŋ], *f.* formation, forming, construction, shaping, fashioning, modelling; creation, production; form, figure, shape, style, fashion, features, configuration; situation, condition, state; organization, arrangement, development. **gestaltungsfähig,** *adj.* modifiable, variable; plastic. **Gestaltungs|kraft,** *f.* creative power; power of *or* gift for organization. **–trieb,** *m.* creative impulse.

Gestammel [gə'ʃtaməl], *n.* stammering, stuttering.

gestand [gə'ʃtant], **gestände** [gə'ʃtɛndə], *see* **gestehen.**

Geständе [gə'ʃtɛndə], *n.* (**-s,** *pl.* **-**) aerie, eyrie, nest (*of hawks, herons etc.*).

gestanden [gə'ʃtandən], *see* **stehen, gestehen.**

geständig [gə'ʃtɛndɪç], *adj.* confessing *or* admitting one's guilt; – *sein,* confess, plead guilty; (*Law*) –*er Verbrecher,* approver.

Geständnis [gə'ʃtɛntnɪs], *n.* (**-ses,** *pl.* **-se**) admission, acknowledgement, confession, avowal; *ein – ablegen über* (*Acc.*), make a confession *or* (*coll.*) a clean breast of. *See* **gestehen.**

Gestänge [gə'ʃtɛŋə], *n.* poles, rods, bars, rails, stakes, (*Mech.*) linkage gear, transmission shafts, (*Hunt.*) antlers.

Gestank [gə'ʃtaŋk], *m.* (**-(e)s,** *pl.* **⸚e**) bad *or* offensive smell, stench, stink.

gestatten [gə'ʃtatən], *v.t.* permit, allow, grant, consent to, approve (of), authorize; tolerate, suffer; *sich* (*Dat.*) – (*zu tun*), venture *or* presume (to do),

take the liberty (of doing); – ***Sie!*** excuse me! may I pass?
Geste ['gɛstə], *f.* gesture.
gestehen [gə'ʃte:ən], **1.** *irr.v.t.* own, confess, acknowledge, admit; ***offen gestanden,*** to speak frankly, to tell the truth. **2.** *irr.v.i.* confess, make a confession, own up, plead guilty, (*sl.*) come clean.
Gestehungs|kosten, *pl.* cost of production, prime cost, production costs. **–preis,** *m.* cost price.
Gestein [gə'ʃtaɪn], *n.* (**-(e)s,** *pl.* **-e**) rocks, mineral; (*Poet.*) rock, stone; (*Min.*) ***taubes –,*** deads. **Gesteins|gang,** *m.* vein, streak, lode. **–kunde, –lehre,** *f.* mineralogy, petrology. **–unterlage,** *f.* rocky subsoil.
Gestell [gə'ʃtɛl], *n.* (**-(e)s,** *pl.* **-e**) stand, rack, frame (*of umbrella, spectacles etc.*), framework, support, trestle, horse, mount, pedestal, holder, chassis, bedstead; hearth, crucible. **Gestellmacher,** *m.* wheelwright.
Gestellung [gə'ʃtɛluŋ], *f.* (*Mil.*) reporting (for duty); furnishing, making available. **Gestellungs|aufschub,** *m.* deferment (of call-up). **–befehl,** *m.* enlistment *or* mobilization order.
gestern ['gɛstərn], *adv.* yesterday; – ***vor vierzehn Tagen,*** yesterday fortnight; – ***abend,*** last night, yesterday evening; – ***früh,*** yesterday morning; early yesterday; (*coll.*) ***ich bin nicht von –,*** I wasn't born yesterday, I know what I'm about, I'm nobody's fool. **Gestern,** *n.* yesterday; the past.
gesternt [gə'ʃtɛrnt], *adj.* decorated *or* patterned with stars, starred.
gestiefelt [gə'ʃti:fəlt], *adj.* booted; ***Gestiefelter Kater,*** Puss in Boots; – ***und gespornt,*** booted and spurred.
gestiegen [gə'ʃti:gən], *see* **steigen.**
gestielt [gə'ʃti:lt], *adj.* helved; stalked, stemmed, petiolate, pedunculate.
gestikulieren [gɛstiku'li:rən], *v.t.* gesticulate, gesture.
Gestirn [gə'ʃtɪrn], *n.* (**-(e)s,** *pl.* **-e**) star; stars, heavenly body, constellation. **gestirnt,** *adj.* starry, starred.
gestoben [gə'ʃto:bən], *see* **stieben.**
Gestöber [gə'ʃtø:bər], *n.* drift, flurry (*of snow*); storm.
gestochen [gə'ʃtɔxən], *see* **stechen.**
gestohlen [gə'ʃto:lən], *p.p.* (*coll.*) ***das kann mir – bleiben,*** that leaves me cold, I don't care two hoots for that. *See* **stehlen.**
Gestöhn(e) [gə'ʃtø:n(ə)], *n.* moaning, groaning; groans.
Gestolper [gə'ʃtɔlpər], *n.* tottering, stumbling.
gestorben [gə'ʃtɔrbən], *see* **sterben.**
Gestotter [gə'ʃtɔtər], *n.* stammering, stuttering.
gestrahlt [gə'ʃtra:lt], *adj.* stellate, radiate.
Gestrampel [gə'ʃtrampəl], *n.* wriggling, fidgeting with one's legs.
gestrandet [gə'ʃtrandət], *adj.* (*Naut.*) ashore, aground.
Gesträuch [gə'ʃtrɔyç], *n.* (**-(e)s,** *pl.* **-e**) shrubs, bushes, shrubbery, thicket.
Gestrauchelte(r) [gə'ʃtrauxəltə(r)], *m., f.* petty offender.
gestreckt [gə'ʃtrɛkt], *adj.* procumbent, trailing, stretched, attenuate.
gestreift [gə'ʃtraɪft], *adj.* streaky, striped, striate(d).
gestreng [gə'ʃtrɛŋ], *adj.* (*obs.*) severe, strict, austere, puissant (*usu. in titles*); (*coll.*) ***die 3 –en Herren,*** the 3 severe days in May (*North Germany*: *May* 11, 12, 13, *Mamertus, Pancratius, Servatius*; *South Germany*: *Bonifatius, May* 14, *instead of Mamertus*).
gestrichen [gə'ʃtrɪçən], *adj.* ***frisch –,*** wet paint; ***–er Eßlöffel,*** level tablespoon; (*Mus.*) ***–e Note,*** ledger-line note; ***–es Papier,*** glazed *or* gloss paper; ***im Protokoll –,*** deleted *or* stricken from the records; – ***voll,*** full to the brim, brimful; ***–es Maß,*** level measure; strike-measure, strickle measure. *See* **streichen.**
gestrig ['gɛstrɪç], *adj.* of yesterday, yesterday's; ***am –en Abend,*** yesterday evening; ***am –en Tag,*** yesterday.
gestritten [gə'ʃtrɪtən], *see* **streiten.**
Gestrüpp [gə'ʃtryp], *n.* (**-(e)s,** *pl.* **-e**) bushes, underwood, undergrowth, brushwood, thicket, scrub, (*fig.*) maze, jungle.
Gestübe [gə'ʃty:bə], **Gestübbe** [gə'ʃtybə], *n.* combustible dust.
Gestühl [gə'ʃty:l], *n.* pew(s); (choir-)stalls.
Gestümper [gə'ʃtympər], *n.* bungling; bungled work.
gestunden [gə'ʃtundən], *v.t.* (*Comm.*) ***ihm etwas –,*** grant him delay *or* respite in (respect of) s.th. (*payment etc.*). **Gestundung,** *f.* respite, delay (*in payment*).
gestunken [gə'ʃtuŋkən], *see* **stinken.**
Gestürm [gə'ʃtyrm], *n.* (*Swiss*) commotion, hurly-burly; gabble.
Gestüt [gə'ʃty:t], *n.* (**-(e)s,** *pl.* **-e**) stud, stud-farm. **Gestüt|hengst,** *m.* stallion, stud-horse. **–stute,** *f.* brood-mare, stud-mare.
Gesuch [gə'zu:x], *n.* (**-(e)s,** *pl.* **-e**) application, petition, (formal) request, suit. **Gesuchsteller,** *m.* applicant, petitioner.
gesucht [gə'zu:xt], *adj.* 1. choice; studied, artificial, far-fetched, affected (*style*); 2. (*Comm.*) (much) sought after, in demand; (*in adverts, or by the police*) wanted.
Gesudel [gə'zu:dəl], *n.* dirty work; daub, scrawl.
Gesumm(e) [gə'zum(ə)], *n.* humming, buzzing.
gesund [gə'zunt], *adj.* healthy, in good health, sound (in wind and limb), well, (*coll.*) fit, able-bodied; financially sound, solvent; wholesome, beneficial, salutary, salubrious; ***–er Menschenverstand,*** commonsense; ***wieder – werden,*** get well again, recover, be restored to health; (*coll.*) ***das ist ihm –!*** that serves him right! – ***und munter,*** fit as a fiddle; – ***und wohlbehalten,*** safe and sound, (*coll.*) alive and kicking; ***frisch und –,*** hale and hearty; – ***wie ein Fisch im Wasser,*** in the pink of condition; ***ihn – schreiben,*** give him a clean bill of health. **Gesund|beten,** *n.*, **–beterei,** *f.* faith-healing. **–beter(in),** *m.* (*f.*) faith-healer. **–brunnen,** *m.* mineral spring *or* waters.
gesunden [gə'zundən], *v.i.* (*aux.* s.) regain *or* recover one's health, be restored to health, get well again, recover, recuperate, convalesce.
Gesundheit [gə'zunthaɪt], *f.* health; wholesomeness, soundness; ***bei guter – sein,*** be in good health; ***in bester –,*** in the best of health; ***auf Ihre –!*** your (very good) health! (***zur***) ***–!*** God bless you! (*to a p. sneezing*). **gesundheitlich,** *adj.* concerning health; hygienic, sanitary; ***aus –en Gründen,*** for reasons of health; ***–er Zustand,*** state of health, physical condition. **Gesundheits|amt,** *n.* Public Health Department. **–appell,** *m.* (*Mil.*) medical inspection. **–beamte(r),** *m.* public health officer. **–behörde,** *f.* Ministry of Health, (*Am.*) Health Department. **–dienst,** *m.* medical *or* public health service. **gesundheits|förderlich,** *adj.* conducive to health, healthy, wholesome, salubrious. **–halber,** *adv.* for reasons of health. **Gesundheits|lehre,** *f.* hygiene. **–paß,** *m. See* **–zeugnis. –pflege,** *f.* sanitation, hygiene; ***öffentliche –,*** public health service. **gesundheitsschädlich,** *adj.* injurious to health, noxious. **Gesundheitsvorschriften,** *f.pl.* sanitary regulations. **gesundheitswidrig,** *adj.* unwholesome. **Gesundheitszeugnis,** *n.* certificate of (good) health, clean bill of health; satisfactory report on sanitary conditions (*of a place*).
Gesundung [gə'zunduŋ], *f.* recovery, convalescence.
gesungen [gə'zuŋən], *see* **singen.**
gesunken [gə'zuŋkən], *see* **sinken.**
Getäfel [gə'tɛ:fəl], *n.* wainscot, wainscoting; inlaying, panelling; honeycomb (*bees*). **Getäfer,** *n.* (*Swiss*) *see* **Getäfel.**
getan [gə'ta:n], *p.p.* ***gesagt, –,*** no sooner said than done. *See* **tun.**

Getändel [gə'tɛndəl], *n.* trifling, dallying, toying, flirting, philandering.

Getier [gə'ti:r], *n.* animals, beasts; *(coll.)* animal.

getigert [gə'ti:gərt], *adj.* striped, streaked, marked; watered *(fabrics)*.

Getön [gə'tø:n], *n.* noise, din, clamour, clang.

getönt [gə'tø:nt], *adj.* tinted.

Getös(e) [gə'tø:z(ə)], **Getose** [gə'to:zə], *n.* (deafening) noise, din, uproar, turmoil, pandemonium, *(coll.)* racket; howling *(of wind)*, roaring *(of waves)*.

getragen [gə'tra:gən], *adj.* solemn, grave, measured, slow. *See* **tragen.**

Getrampel [gə'trampəl], *n.* stamping, trampling.

Getränk [gə'trɛŋk], *n.* **(-(e)s,** *pl.* **-e)** drink, beverage; potion; ***geistiges* –,** (spirituous) liquor; ***geistige* –*e*,** spirits.

getränkt [gə'trɛŋkt], *adj.* impregnated, saturated.

Getrappel [gə'trapəl], *n.* patter(ing) *(of feet)*, clatter *(of hoofs)*.

getrauen [gə'trauən], *v.r.* dare, venture, risk; feel confident; ***ich getraue mich*** (not ***mir***) ***nicht dahin,*** I dare not go there, I won't risk going there; ***ich getraue mir*** (not ***mich***) ***den Schritt nicht,*** I don't trust myself to take *or* I cannot venture this step; ***ich getraue mich*** (or ***mir***) ***nicht, dieses zu tun,*** I dare not do that, I hesitate to do that.

Getreide [gə'traɪdə], *n.* corn, grain, cereals. **Getreide|art,** *f.* cereal. **–bau,** *m.* corn-growing. **–boden,** *m.* cornland; granary. **–börse,** *f.* corn-exchange. **–brand,** *m.* smut *or* blight on corn. **–feld,** *n.* cornfield. **–händler,** *m.* corn-merchant. **–heber,** *m.* corn-elevator. **–kümmel,** *m.* cumin-brandy *(made of rye)*. **–land,** *n.* 1. corn-growing country; 2. cornland. **–(rohr)sänger,** *m.* *(Orn.)* *see* **Sumpfrohrsänger. –speicher,** *m.* granary, silo.

getreu [gə'trɔy], *adj.* faithful, true, trusty, loyal; staunch, accurate; ***–e Abschrift,*** true *or* faithful copy; ***–es Gedächtnis,*** retentive memory. **Getreue(r),** *m.* loyal *or* faithful follower. **getreulich,** *adj. See* **getreu.**

Getriebe [gə'tri:bə], *n.* 1. agitation, commotion, rush, whirl, bustle, fuss; ***– des Lebens,*** bustle of life; 2. motive power, mechanism, works, movement *(of clock)*; gear, pinion, gearing, gear-box, linkage, transmission; ***stufenloses –,*** variable-speed transmission. **Getriebe|bremse,** *f.* flywheel-brake. **–gehäuse,** *n.* gear-box, gear-casing, transmission housing.

getrieben [gə'tri:bən], *see* **treiben.**

Getriebe|rad, *n.* gear-wheel. **–welle,** *f.* transmission shaft.

getroffen [gə'trɔfən], *see* **treffen, triefen.**

getrogen [gə'tro:gən], *see* **trügen.**

getrost [gə'tro:st], **1.** *adj.* confident, hopeful; comforted; ***sei –!*** be of good courage *or* good cheer! **2.** *adv.* without hesitation, safely, easily.

getrösten [gə'trø:stən], *v.r.* *(obs.)* hope *(Gen.,* for), be confident (of); be solaced (***mit,*** by).

getrübt [gə'try:pt], *adj.* dull, cloudy, turbid, opaque.

getrunken [gə'truŋkən], *see* **trinken.**

Getue [gə'tu:ə], *n.* *(coll.)* doings, goings-on; pretence; affectation; fuss, bother, ado.

Getümmel [gə'tyməl], *n.* tumult; bustle, turmoil, hurly-burly.

getüpfelt [gə'typfəlt], *adj.* dotted, spotted, pitted.

geübt [gə'y:pt], *adj.* skilled, experienced, practised, versed, trained. **Geübtheit,** *f.* skill, practice, experience.

Gevatter [gə'fatər], *m.* **(-s,** *pl.* **-n)** 1. godfather, sponsor; ***– stehen,*** stand godfather *or* sponsor; 2. *(dial.)* good friend, neighbour, relative *(now implies a snobbish sneer)*; ***– Schneider und Handschuhmacher,*** shopkeepers and such-like people. **Gevatterschaft,** *f.* sponsorship. **Gevattersmann,** *m.* *(pl.* **-leute)** godfather.

geviert [gə'fi:rt], *adj.* quartered; squared; quaternary. **Geviert,** *n.* **(-(e)s,** *pl.* **-e)** square; quadrature; ***ins – bringen,*** square; ***es mißt 3 Zentimeter im –,*** it is 3 centimetres square. **Geviert|maß,** *n.* square measure. **–meter,** *n.* *(coll., dial. m.)* square metre. **–schein,** *m.* *(Astr.)* quartile aspect. **–wurzel,** *f.* square root.

Gewächs [gə'vɛks], *n.* **(-es,** *pl.* **-e)** plant, vegetable, herb; growth, produce; *(of wine)* vintage; *(Med.)* growth, tumour; ***ausländisches –,*** exotic plant; ***eigenes –,*** home produce; ***heuriges –,*** this year's vintage.

gewachsen [gə'vaksən], *adj.* ***ihm – sein,*** be a match for him; ***einer S.*** *(Dat.)* ***– sein,*** measure up to a th., be equal to a th. *See* **wachsen.**

Gewächshaus [gə'vɛkshaus], *n.* greenhouse, hothouse, conservatory.

gewagt [gə'va:kt], *adj.* risky, daring; risqué *(joke)*.

gewählt [gə'vɛ:lt], *adj.* selected, choice; select.

gewahr [gə'va:r], *adj.* ***– werden*** *(Gen.)*, become aware of; see, perceive, notice, observe, discern, catch sight of.

Gewähr [gə'vɛ:r], *f.* security, surety; warrant, guarantee, guaranty, bail; ***ohne –,*** no responsibility accepted, subject to change, without prejudice; ***– leisten (für)***, ensure, warrant, guarantee *(a th.)*.

gewahren [gə'va:rən], *v.t.* *(Poet.)* *see* ***gewahr werden.***

gewähren [gə'vɛ:rən], *v.t.* ***(ihm etwas)*** grant, allow, accord, concede, vouchsafe; give, furnish, offer, afford, yield, impart; ***ihn – lassen,*** let him alone; let him have his own way, indulge him; give him full scope; ***laß ihn –!*** let him do as he likes! ***(einen) Einblick – in*** *(Acc.)*, afford a view of; ***ihm Einlaß –,*** allow him to enter, admit him.

gewährleisten [gə'vɛ:rlaɪstən], *v.t.* ensure, guarantee, vouch for, warrant. **Gewährleistung,** *f.* acceptance of responsibility, warranty, guaranty.

Gewahrsam [gə'va:rza:m], *m. or n.* care, custody, safe keeping; detention, custody, control; ***es in – haben,*** have the control *or* care of it; ***ihn in – halten,*** hold him in custody; ***in – nehmen,*** take charge of *(a th.)*, take into custody *(a p.)*; ***in sicherem –,*** in safe keeping *or* custody.

Gewährs|mann, *m.* *(pl.* **-männer** *or* **-leute)** authority, informant; ***zuständiger –,*** competent authority. **–pflicht,** *f.* warranty. **–träger,** *m.* guarantor.

Gewährung [gə'vɛ:ruŋ], *f.* granting, concession; grant.

Gewalt [gə'valt], *f.* **(-,** *pl.* **-en)** power, authority, dominion, sway (***über*** *(Acc.)*, over), control (of *or* over); might; force, violence; ***– antun*** *(Dat.)*, do violence to; rape, violate, ravish *(a girl)*; ***einer Stelle – antun,*** do violence to a passage, distort the sense of a passage *(in a book etc.)*; ***sich*** *(Dat.)* ***– antun,*** restrain *or* constrain o.s.; lay (violent) hands upon o.s., commit suicide; ***ausübende*** or ***vollziehende –,*** executive (power *or* authority); ***höhere –,*** act of God *or* Providence, force majeure; ***in der – haben,*** master, be master of, have command of, have in one's power *or* under one's thumb; ***sich in der – haben,*** have o.s. under control, have self-control; ***mit –,*** by force, forcibly; ***mit aller –,*** with all one's might, with might and main; at all costs, by hook or by crook; ***nackte –,*** sheer *or* brute force; ***die – verlieren über*** *(Acc.)*, lose control over, lose one's hold on *or* over.

Gewalt|androhung, *f.* threat of violence. **–anmaßung,** *f.* usurpation of power. **–anwendung,** *f.* use of force; ***ohne –,*** without resort to force. **–friede,** *m.* enforced *or* dictated peace. **–haber,** *m.* holder of power, p. in authority, autocrat, dictator. **–herrschaft,** *f.* tyranny, despotism. **–herrscher,** *m.* tyrant, despot.

gewaltig [gə'valtɪç], *adj.* powerful, potent, mighty, strong; violent, vehement; *(coll.)* immense, enormous, gigantic, colossal, stupendous, prodigious, phenomenal, huge, vast, tremendous, terrific; ***–er Schlag,*** stunning *or* staggering blow; ***–er Unterschied,*** vast *or* *(coll.)* tremendous *or* terrific difference; ***sich – irren,*** be grossly mistaken. **gewaltlos,** *adj.* *(Pol.)* non-violent.

Gewalt|marsch, *m.* forced march. **–maßregel,** *f.*

coercive measure. **–mensch,** *m.* man who abuses authority; violent *or* brutal man, brute; terrorist.

gewaltsam [gə'valtza:m], *adj.* vigorous, forcible, violent, by force; – *verfahren,* use violence; *–e Schritte,* vigorous *or* strong measures; *–er Tod,* violent death. **Gewaltsamkeit,** *f.* violence, force.

Gewalt|streich, *m.* violent *or* illegal measure, arbitrary act, bold stroke, coup de main. **–tat,** *f.* act of violence, outrage, atrocity. **gewalttätig,** *adj.* violent, brutal, outrageous; *–er Angriff,* assault; *–er Mensch,* brutal *or* violent man. **Gewalt|tätigkeit,** *f.* violence, brutality; outrage, act of violence. **–verbrechen,** *n.* crime of violence. **–verbrecher,** *m.* violent criminal.

Gewand [gə'vant], *n.* **(-(e)s,** *pl.* **⸚er** (*Poet.* **-e**)) garment, dress, raiment, gown, robe, vestment. **Gewand|haus,** *n,* drapers' hall. **–meister,** *m.* (*Theat.*) wardrobe master.

gewandt [gə'vant], *adj.* active, agile, nimble; dexterous, deft, adroit, skilled, skilful, versatile; – *in* (*Dat.*), quick *or* clever *or* good at. *See* **wenden. Gewandtheit,** *f.* adroitness, dexterity, deftness, agility; versatility, fluency, knack, cleverness, skill, ingenuity.

gewann [gə'van], **gewänne** [gə'vɛnə], *see* **gewinnen.**

gewärtig [gə'vɛrtɪç], *adj.* (*with Gen.*) awaiting, expecting; expectant (of); – *sein, see* **gewärtigen. gewärtigen,** *v.t., v.i.* (*Gen.*) reckon with, be prepared for, be resigned to, expect, (*coll.*) be in for; *etwas zu – haben,* be liable for s.th.

Gewäsch [gə'vɛʃ], *n.* (*coll.*) twaddle, balderdash, poppycock, (*sl.*) bilge.

Gewässer [gə'vɛsər], *n.* water(s). **Gewässerkunde,** *f.* hydrology.

Gewebe [gə've:bə], *n.* weaving; web, (textile) fabric; texture; (*Anat., fig.*) tissue; (*dial.*) cells (*of bees*); *ein – von Lügen,* a tissue *or* pack of lies. **Gewebe|lehre,** *f.* histology. **–verletzung,** *f.* lesion.

geweckt [gə'vɛkt], *adj.* lively, alert, wide-awake; clever, (*coll.*) bright.

Gewehr [gə've:r], *n.* **(-(e)s,** *pl.* **-e**) rifle, musket; tusk (*of a boar*); (*Poet.*) weapon, arms; – *ab!* order arms! *an die –e!* stand to! to arms! *das – über!* shoulder arms! *präsentiert das –!* present arms! *das – strecken,* lay down one's arms; *die Mannschaft trat unters –,* the men stood to their arms. **Gewehr|appell,** *m.* rifle inspection. **–feuer,** *n.* rifle-fire. **–kolben,** *m.* butt. **–kugel,** *f.* rifle bullet. **–lauf,** *m.* gun-barrel. **–riemen,** *m.* rifle-sling. **–schaft,** *m.* gun-stock. **–schein,** *m.* gun licence. **–stärke,** *f.* combatant *or* rifle strength.

Geweih [gə'vaɪ], *n.* **(-(e)s,** *pl.* **-e**) horns, antlers; *ein – aufsetzen* (*Dat.*), cuckold, deceive (*one's husband*). **Geweih|sprosse,** *f.,* **–zacken,** *m.* prong *or* process of antlers.

Gewende [gə'vɛndə], *n.* **(-s,** *pl.* **-)** turn of the plough; length of the furrow; *ein – machen,* turn the plough.

Gewerbe [gə'vɛrbə], *n.* **(-s,** *pl.* **-)** trade, business, calling, profession, vocation, occupation; craft, industry; *er war seines –s ein Tischler,* he was a joiner by trade. **Gewerbe|aufsicht,** *f.* factory inspection. **–aufsichtsbeamte(r),** *m.* factory inspector. **–ausstellung,** *f.* industrial exhibition, industries fair. **–fleiß,** *m.* industry; industrial activity. **–freiheit,** *f.* licence to exercise a trade. **–gericht,** *n.* industrial council. **–kammer,** *f.* Chamber of Commerce. **–krankheit,** *f.* occupational disease. **–kunde,** *f.* technology. **–ordnung,** *f.* trade regulations. **–salz,** *n.* common salt. **–schein,** *m.* trade licence. **–schule,** *f.* trade *or* technical school. **–steuer,** *f.* trading licence. **gewerbetreibend,** *adj.* engaged in trade, trading, manufacturing, industrial. **Gewerbe|treibende(r),** *m., f.* tradesman, manufacturer, artisan, craftsman. **–zweig,** *m.* line (of business), (branch of) industry.

gewerblich [gə'vɛrplɪç], *adj.* industrial, commercial, trade. **gewerbsmäßig,** *adj.* professional; *–e Bettelei,* professional begging; *–e Unzucht,* prostitution. **gewerbtätig,** *adj. See* **gewerblich.**

Gewerk [gə'vɛrk], *n.* **(-(e)s,** *pl.* **-e**) (*obs.*) 1. works, machinery; 2. guild, corporation, craft. **Gewerke,** *m.* **(-n,** *pl.* **-n)** 1. member of miners' union; 2. (*Austr.*) manufacturer.

Gewerkschaft [gə'vɛrkʃaft], *f.* trade(s)-union, (*Am.*) labour union. **Gewerkschaftler,** *m.* trade(s)-unionist. **gewerkschaftlich,** *adj.* trade(s)-unionist. **Gewerkschafts|bund,** *m.* Trade(s)-Union Congress, (*Am.*) Federation of Labor. **–wesen,** *n.* trade(s)-unionism.

gewesen [gə've:zən], *p.p. mein –er Freund,* my friend that was, my former *or* erstwhile friend; *–e Schönheit,* faded beauty. *See* **sein.**

gewichen [gə'vɪçən], *see* **weichen.**

Gewicht [gə'vɪçt], *n.* **(-(e)s,** *pl.* **-e**) weight, heaviness; (*fig.*) weight, gravity, consequence, importance, moment; stress, load; *an – haben,* weigh; (*fig.*) *schwer ins – fallen,* be of *or* carry great weight, be of great consequence *or* importance, weigh heavily, count, matter (*bei,* with); *nicht ins – fallen,* be of no consequence, make no difference; (*fig.*) *– auf etwas legen,* consider a th. to be important, set (great) store by a th.; *spezifisches –,* specific gravity; *totes –,* tare; *an – verlieren,* lose (in) weight; *volles – geben,* give full weight.

Gewicht|heben, *n.* (*Spt.*) weight-lifting. **–heber,** *m.* weight-lifter. **gewichtig,** *adj.* heavy, weighty, ponderous; (*fig.*) weighty, important, momentous; influential.

Gewichts|abgang, *m.,* **–abnahme,** *f.* loss *or* decrease in weight. **–analyse,** *f.* (*Chem.*) gravimetric(al) analysis. **–einheit,** *f.* unit of weight. **–klasse,** *f.* (*Spt.*) weight. **–mangel,** *m.,* **–manko,** *n.* short weight, underweight, deficiency (in weight). **–satz,** *m.* set of weights. **–verlagerung,** *f.* (*fig.*) change *or* shift of emphasis. **–verlust,** *m. See* **–abnahme. –zunahme,** *f.* increase in weight.

gewickelt [gə'vɪkəlt], *p.p.* (*coll.*) *schief – sein,* be completely mistaken, be altogether on the wrong track, be barking up the wrong tree.

gewiegt [gə'vi:kt], *adj.* experienced, seasoned; clever, shrewd, smart.

Gewieher [gə'vi:ər], *n.* neighing; (*fig.*) horse-laugh.

gewiesen [gə'vi:zən], *see* **weisen.**

gewillt [gə'vɪlt], *adj.* willing, ready, prepared; disposed, inclined; determined.

Gewimmel [gə'vɪməl], *n.* swarming, crawling; crowd, swarm, multitude, throng.

Gewimmer [gə'vɪmər], *n.* whining, wailing, moaning, whimpering.

Gewinde [gə'vɪndə], *n.* **(-s,** *pl.* **-)** winding, coil, skein (*of thread*), festoon, garland, wreath; worm, (screw-)thread; (*Anat.*) labyrinth (*of the ear*); whorl (*of shells*). **Gewinde|bohrer,** *m.* screw tap. **–drehbank,** *f.* screw-cutting lathe. **–gang,** *m.* thread (*of a screw*). **–lehre,** *f.* screw gauge. **–schneider,** *m.* screw-die. **–steigung,** *f.* pitch (*of a screw*).

Gewinn [gə'vɪn], *m.* **(-(e)s,** *pl.* **-e**) gaining, winning; earnings, gain, profit, prize, winnings; yield, proceeds, returns; advantage, benefit; surplus, (profit) margin; *der reine –,* net profits; *Gewinn- und Verlustkonto,* profit and loss account; *mit – verkaufen,* sell to advantage, sell at a profit; *– abwerfen,* yield a profit, leave a margin; *das ist schon (ein) –,* that is s.th. gained. **Gewinn|abführungsgesetz,** *n.* excess profits tax. **–anteil,** *m.* share in the profits, dividend. **–beteiligung,** *f.* profit-sharing. **gewinnbringend,** *adj.* profitable, lucrative.

gewinnen [gə'vɪnən], **1.** *irr.v.t.* win, gain; obtain, get, secure, acquire, earn; (*Chem. etc.*) produce, extract, reclaim, recover, salvage; *den Anschein –,* appear, seem; *ihn für eine S. –,* interest him in, win him over to s.th.; *das Freie –,* gain *or* reach the open (field); *Interesse – für eine S.,* interest o.s. *or* become interested in s.th.; *das große Los –,* win *or* draw the first prize; *die Oberhand –,* gain *or* get the upper hand; *es über sich –,* bring o.s. (*zu tun,* to do); *ich habe Ehrfurcht vor ihm gewonnen,* he has inspired me with respect; ***den Vorsprung* –,** gain an advantage (*Dat.*, over), gain a lead (on); (*Prov.*) ***wie gewonnen, so zerronnen,*** easy come, easy go; ***ihn zum Freunde* –,** gain him as a friend; ***Zeit* –,** gain time; ***Zeit zu – suchen,*** temporize. **2.** *irr.v.i.* be victorious, gain the victory, win; ***an Bedeutung* –,** gain in importance; ***bei näherer Bekanntschaft* –,** improve on closer acquaintance; ***an Boden* –,** gain ground; ***an Klarheit* –,** gain in clarity; ***an Kraft* –,** gather force *or* strength; **– *durch*** or ***von etwas,*** benefit from *or* profit by a th. **gewinnend,** *adj.* (*fig.*) winning, engaging, fetching (*smile etc.*). **Gewinner,** *m.* winner, gainer. **Gewinnler,** *m.* profiteer.

Gewinn|liste, *f.* prize list. **–los,** *n.* **–nummer,** *f.* winning number. **–rechnung,** *f.* profit account. **gewinnreich,** *adj.* profitable, lucrative. **Gewinn|-spanne,** *f.* profit margin. **–sucht,** *f.* greed, avarice. **gewinnsüchtig,** *adj.* greedy, avaricious, covetous, mercenary.

Gewinnung [gə'vɪnuŋ], *f.* gaining, acquirement; (*Chem. etc.*) production; winning, extraction; reclamation (*of land*).

Gewinsel [gə'vɪnzəl], *n.* whining, moaning, whimpering.

Gewinst [gə'vɪnst], *m.* (**-es,** *pl.* **-e**) winnings, takings, gain, profit.

Gewirbel [gə'vɪrbəl], *n.* whirling; roll (*of drums*); (*Mus.*) roulade; warbling.

Gewirke [gə'vɪrkə], *n.* weaving; web, texture.

Gewirr(e) [gə'vɪr(ə)], *n.* confusion, entanglement; maze, jumble, tangle; whirl (*of ideas*).

gewiß [gə'vɪs], **1.** *adj.* (*with Gen.*) sure, certain, assured, positive, true, undoubted; stable, steady, fixed; ***sein Gewisses haben,*** have a fixed income; ***er behauptete es als* –,** he asserted it as a fact; ***ich bin dessen* –,** I am sure of it; ***in gewissen Fällen,*** in some *or* certain cases; ***in gewissem Sinne,*** in a sense; ***seine Stimme ist mir* –,** I am sure of his vote; ***sich*** (*Dat.*) ***seiner S. – sein,*** be sure of one's facts *or* one's ground. **2.** *adv.* certainly, surely, assuredly, indeed, to be sure, doubtless, no doubt; ***aber –!*** yes of course! by all means! to be sure! **– *nicht,*** certainly not, by no means; ***das ist – ein Streich von him,*** I dare say that is a trick of his; ***er hat – kein Geld,*** he is sure to have no money; ***Sie wollten uns – überraschen?*** you hoped to surprise us, didn't you?

Gewissen [gə'vɪsən], *n.* conscience; ***Sie haben es auf dem* –,** you are morally responsible for it *or* have it on your conscience; ***er macht sich*** (*Dat.*) ***kein – daraus zu betrügen,*** he has no scruples *or* does not think twice about cheating; ***ihm ins – reden,*** appeal to his conscience; ***sich mit seinem – abfinden,*** soothe one's conscience; (*Prov.*) ***ein gutes – ist ein sanftes Ruhekissen,*** a good conscience is a soft pillow; ***reines* –,** clear conscience; ***schlechtes* –,** bad *or* guilty conscience; ***ein weites – haben,*** be not overscrupulous, have an obliging conscience. **gewissenhaft,** *adj.* conscientious, scrupulous (*in* (*Dat.*), about). **Gewissenhaftigkeit,** *f.* conscientiousness. **gewissenlos,** *adj.* irresponsible, unscrupulous. **Gewissenlosigkeit,** *f.* irresponsibility, unscrupulousness.

Gewissens|angst, *f.* qualms of conscience, mental anguish. **–biß,** *m.* twinge of conscience; (*usu. pl.*) pangs of conscience, compunction, remorse; ***Gewissensbisse haben,*** be conscience-stricken. **–ehe,** *f.* morganatic marriage, cohabitation. **–frage,** *f.* moral issue, matter *or* question of conscience. **–freiheit,** *f.* freedom of conscience. **–konflikt,** *m.* inner *or* spiritual conflict. **–prüfung,** *f.* self-examination. **–sache,** *f.* matter of conscience. **–skrupel,** *m.* moral scruple. **–vorwurf,** *m.* self-reproach. **–zwang,** *m.* **1.** moral constraint; **2.** religious intolerance. **–zweifel,** *m.* doubt, scruple, qualm.

gewissermaßen [gə'vɪsərma:sən], *adv.* in a way, in a manner of speaking, to some extent, so to speak, as it were.

Gewißheit [gə'vɪshaɪt], *f.* certainty, assurance; ***innere* –,** certitude; ***ich werde mir – verschaffen,*** I shall make certain (***über*** (*Acc.*), about) *or* make sure (of); ***zur – werden,*** become certain *or* a certainty.

gewißlich [gə'vɪslɪç], *adv. See* **gewiß, 2.**

Gewitter [gə'vɪtər], *n.* thunderstorm, tempest, storm; ***ein – ist im Anzuge,*** a storm is gathering *or* brewing. **gewitterhaft, gewitterig,** *adj.* thundery, stormy, oppressive. **Gewitterluft,** *f.* sultriness before a thunderstorm, thunder in the air. **gewittern,** *v.i.imp.* ***es gewittert,*** there is a thunderstorm. **Gewitter|regen, –schauer,** *m.* thundershower. **gewitterschwül,** *adj.* sultry, oppressive. **Gewitter|schwüle,** *f.* sultriness. **–störungen,** *f.pl.* (*Rad.*) static, atmospherics. **–wolke,** *f.* thundercloud.

gewitz(ig)t [gə'vɪts(ɪg)t], *adj.* taught *or* made wise by experience, have learned one's lesson; shrewd.

gewoben [gə'vo:bən], *see* **weben.**

Gewoge [gə'vo:gə], *n.* billowing, surging; (*Poet.*) waves, (*fig.*) surging *or* milling throng.

gewogen [gə'vo:gən], *adj.* kindly *or* favourably *or* well-disposed, friendly, affectionate (*Dat.*, to(wards)); (*coll.*) ***bleib mir –!*** think of me from time to time! I'll be glad to hear from you (*farewell*). *See* **wiegen, wägen. Gewogenheit,** *f.* goodwill, friendliness, kindness, affection.

gewöhnen [gə'vø:nən], **1.** *v.t.* accustom, habituate, get used, inure (***an*** (*Acc.*), to), familiarize (with). **2.** *v.r.* get used *or* accustomed (***an*** (*Acc.*), to), become familiar (with), get into the habit (of); become acclimatized, acclimatize, (*Am.*) acclimate (to); ***gewöhnt sein,*** *see* **gewohnt.**

Gewohnheit [gə'vo:nhaɪt], *f.* habit, custom, usage, practice, fashion, wont; ***zur – werden,*** grow into *or* become a habit (*Dat.*, with); ***aus* –,** from habit; ***aus der – kommen,*** fall into disuse; get out of the habit *or* of practice; ***nach seiner* –,** according to his custom *or* practice; ***sich*** (*Dat.*) ***etwas zur – machen,*** make a practice *or* habit of s.th.; ***die – haben,*** be in the habit (***zu tun,*** of doing). **gewohnheitsmäßig, 1.** *adj.* customary, habitual, usual, normal, routine. **2.** *adv.* habitually, by *or* from habit, as is the custom.

Gewohnheits|mensch, *m.* creature *or* slave of habit. **–recht,** *n.* prescriptive law *or* right; common law. **–sünde,** *f.* besetting sin. **–tier,** *n.* (*Prov.*) ***der Mensch ist ein* –,** man is a creature of habit. **–trinker,** *m.* confirmed *or* habitual drunkard.

gewöhnlich [gə'vø:nlɪç], **1.** *adj.* usual, customary, habitual, normal, routine, conventional; common, general, ordinary, commonplace, average, mediocre; vulgar, low, common, ordinary; ***über das –e hinaus,*** out of the ordinary; ***der –e Sterbliche,*** the average mortal. **2.** *adv.* commonly, normally, generally, as a rule, in ordinary circumstances; ***wie* –,** as usual.

gewohnt [gə'vo:nt], *adj.* customary, habitual, usual, traditional; **– *sein,*** be accustomed *or* used (*Acc.*, to); be in the habit (***zu tun,*** of doing). **gewohntermaßen,** *adv.* as usual, as is customary.

Gewöhnung [gə'vø:nuŋ], *f.* habituation, addiction (*an* (*Acc.*), to); (*to hardship etc.*) inurement (to), (*to climate*) acclimatization, (*Am.*) acclimation (to); (*of animals*) training, breaking in, domestication. *See also* **Gewohnheit.**

Gewölbe [gə'vœlbə], *n.* (**-s,** *pl.* **-**) vault, arch; cellar; family vault; **– *des Himmels,*** vault of heaven. **Gewölbe|bogen,** *m.* arch of a vault. **–pfeiler,** *m.* buttress; shaft of an arch. **–stein,** *m.* vaulting-stone. **–stütze,** *f.* flying buttress. **–winkel,** *m.* haunch of an arch.

gewölbt [gə'vœlpt], *adj.* arched, vaulted; convex, domed; (*of road*) cambered.

Gewölk [gə'vœlk], *n.* clouds.

gewollt [gə'vɔlt], *adj.* deliberate, intentional, intended.

gewönne [gə'vœnə], **gewonnen** [gə'vɔnən], *see* **gewinnen.**

geworben [gə'vɔrbən], *adj.* raised, levied; ***–e Truppen,*** hired soldiers, levies. *See* **werben.**

geworden [gə'vɔrdən], *see* **werden.**

geworfen [gə'vɔrfən], *adj.* (*Naut.*) *–es Gut,* jetsam. *See* **werfen.**

Gewühl [gə'vy:l], *n.* tumult, bustle, throng, milling crowd.

gewunden [gə'vundən], *adj.* winding, wound, spiral, twisted; sinuous, (*fig.*) contorted, tortuous. *See* **winden.**

gewürfelt [gə'vyrfəlt], *adj.* chequered, tessellate, tessellated, tessellar.

Gewürge [gə'vyrgə], *n.* bloody battle, slaughter, bloodbath, (*coll.*) shambles.

Gewürm [gə'vyrm], *n.* worms; reptiles; vermin.

Gewürz [gə'vyrts], *n.* (**-es,** *pl.* **-e**) spice, condiment, seasoning. **gewürzartig,** *adj.* spicy, aromatic. **Gewürz|essig,** *m.* aromatic vinegar. **–fleisch,** *n.* curry, ragout. **gewürzhaft,** *adj.* spiced, seasoned, spicy, aromatic. **Gewürzhändler,** *m.* grocer. **gewürzig,** *adj. See* **gewürzhaft. Gewürz|krämer,** *m. See* **–händler. –kräuter,** *n.pl.* spices, aromatic plants. **–kuchen,** *m.* (spiced) gingerbread *or* cake. **–nelke,** *f.* clove. **gewürzt,** *adj.* spicy, seasoned, flavoured. **Gewürzwaren,** *f.pl.* groceries.

gewußt [gə'vust], *see* **wissen.**

gezackt [gə'tsakt], *adj.* notched, serrated, jagged, indented, scalloped.

Gezähe [gə'tsɛ:ə], *n.* (**-s,** *pl.* -) set of tools (*of miners*).

gezähn(el)t [gə'tsɛ:n(əl)t], **gezahnt** [gə'tsa:nt], *adj.* notched, cogged, toothed, serrated; indented, (*Bot.*) dentate, (*postage stamps*) perforated.

Gezänk [gə'tsɛŋk], **Gezanke** [gə'tsaŋkə], *n.* quarrel, squabble; quarrelling, wrangling.

Gezappel [gə'tsapəl], *n.* struggling, floundering; wriggling, squirming.

gezeichnet [gə'tsaɪçnət], *adj.* signed, subscribed; drawn; marked (*as face from blows*); ***vom Schicksal –,*** marked with the hand of fate.

Gezeiten [gə'tsaɪtən], *f.pl.* tide(s). **Gezeiten|hub,** *m.* range of the tides. **–strom,** *m.* tidal stream. **–tafel,** *f.* tide-tables.

Gezelt [gə'tsɛlt], *n.* (**-(e)s,** *pl.* **-e**) (*Poet.*) tent, canopy, pavilion.

Gezeter [gə'tse:tər], *n.* screaming, strident outcry, hue and cry; scolding, nagging.

Geziefer [gə'tsi:fər], *n.* vermin, insects.

geziehen [gə'tsi:ən], *see* **zeihen.**

geziemen [gə'tsi:mən], *v.i., v.r. imp.* be suitable *or* proper *or* seemly *or* fit *or* becoming (*Dat. or* ***für,*** for), befit, become. **geziemend, geziemlich,** *adj.* proper, fitting, becoming, due; decorous, seemly; ***mit –er Ehrfurcht,*** with due reverence; ***sich – aufführen,*** behave properly.

geziert [gə'tsi:rt], *adj.* affected, foppish; prim; studied. **Geziertheit,** *f.* affectation; mannerism, airs.

Gezirp(e) [gə'tsɪrp(ə)], *n.* chirping.

Gezisch [gə'tsɪʃ], *n.* hissing; whizzing. **Gezischel,** *n.* whispering, tittle-tattle, backbiting, scandalmongering.

gezogen [gə'tso:gən], *adj.* (*of gun barrel*) rifled. *See* **ziehen.**

Gezücht [gə'tsyçt], *n.* (**-(e)s,** *pl.* **-e**) brood, breed; race, set, lot, crew.

Gezweig [gə'tsvaɪk], *n.* branches, boughs (*of a tree*).

gezweit [gə'tsvaɪt], *adj.* binary, bipartite.

Gezwitscher [gə'tsvɪtʃər], *n.* chirping, twittering.

gezwungen [gə'tsvuŋən], *adj.* (en)forced, compulsory; forced, strained, unnatural, constrained, formal, stiff, affected; ***– lachen,*** force a laugh. *See* **zwingen. gezwungenermaßen,** *adv.* under compulsion *or* constraint, willy-nilly. **Gezwungenheit,** *f.* constraint; affectation; stiffness, formality.

gib [gi:p], *see* **geben.**

gibberig ['gɪbərɪç], *adj.* (*dial.*) ***nach einer S. – sein,*** hanker after a th.

gibst [gi:pst], **gibt,** *see* **geben.**

Gicht [gɪçt], *f.* 1. (-, *no pl.*) gout, arthritis; 2. (-, *pl* **-en**) furnace-mouth. **gicht|artig,** *adj.* gouty, arthritic (*swelling etc.*). **–brüchig,** *adj.* 1. *See* **–artig**; 2. (*B.*) paralytic, palsied; (*B.*) ***der Gichtbrüchige,*** the man of the palsy. **Gichter,** *pl.* (*dial.*) convulsive fits, convulsions. **gichterisch,** *adj.* convulsive. **Gichtgas,** *n.* blast-furnace gas. **gichtig, gichtisch, gichtkrank,** *adj.* gouty; arthritic (*person*). **Gichtrose,** *f.* (*Bot.*) rhododendron, peony (*Paeonia*).

Giebel ['gi:bəl], *m.* gable, gable-end; (*Archit.*) pediment; (*Poet.*) summit. **Giebel|balken,** *m.* roof-tree. **–dach,** *n.* gabled roof. **–feld,** *n.* (*Archit.*) pediment, tympanum. **–fenster,** *n.* attic- *or* dormer-window; gable-window.

Gier [gi:r], *f.* eagerness, avidity, greed(iness); inordinate desire, craving, lust, thirst, hunger (***nach,*** for). **Gierbrücke,** *f.* trail- *or* flying-bridge. **gieren,** *v.i.* 1. long, crave, thirst (***nach,*** for), lust, hunger (after *or* for), be greedy *or* avid (for); 2. (*Naut.*) deviate from course, sheer, yaw. **Gierfähre,** *f.* trail-ferry. **gierig,** *adj.* gluttonous, greedy; (*fig.*) greedy (***nach, auf*** (*Acc.*), for *or* after), eager (for), avid (for *or* of), covetous (of). **Gierigkeit,** *f.* greediness, gluttony; avidity.

Giersch [gi:rʃ], *m.* (*Bot.*) goatsfoot (*Aegopodium podagraria*).

Gießbach ['gi:sbax], *m.* (mountain) torrent.

gießen ['gi:sən], **1.** *irr.v.t.* 1. pour, water, shed, spill, sprinkle; ***Öl auf die Wogen –,*** pour oil on troubled waters; ***Öl ins Feuer –,*** add fuel to the flames, make things worse; ***es gießt sich schlecht aus diesem Topf,*** this pot pours badly; (*sl.*) ***eins hinter die Binde –,*** put one (*a drink*) down the hatch, wrap o.s. round (*a pint, a whisky etc.*); 2. cast, mould, found; ***er stand da wie aus Erz gegossen,*** he stood there rooted to the spot. **2.** *irr.v.i. imp.* ***es gießt,*** it is pouring with rain; (*coll.*) ***es gießt wie mit Scheffeln*** or ***mit Mollen,*** it is raining cats and dogs. **Gießer,** *m.* founder, caster, moulder. **Gießerei** [–'raɪ], *f.* foundry; casting.

Gieß|erz, *n.* bronze. **–form,** *f.* mould. **–hütte,** *f.* foundry. **–kanne,** *f.* watering-can. **–kannenaufsatz,** *m.* rose of a watering-can. **–kasten,** *m.* casting-mould. **–kopf,** *m.* (*Metall.*) dead head. **–mutter,** *f.* mould, matrix. **–ofen,** *m.* casting *or* foundry furnace. **–pfanne,** *f.* ladle. **–rinne,** *f.* spout. **–tiegel,** *m.* melting-pot, crucible.

Gift [gɪft], *n.* (**-(e)s,** *pl.* **-e**) 1. poison, toxin, virus, venom; (*coll.*) ***darauf kannst du – nehmen,*** you can bet your life on it; ***schleichendes –,*** slow poison; 2. (*fig. coll., dial. also m.*) venom, virulence, malice, spite; ***– und Galle speien,*** wreak fire and fury, foam with rage; (*coll.*) ***einen – auf ihn haben,*** be mad *or* furious with him. **giftabtreibend,** *adj.* antitoxic, antidotal. **Giftblase,** *f.* (*Zool.*) venom sac. **giftfrei,** *adj.* nonpoisonous. **Gift|gas,** *n.* poison gas. **–hahnenfuß,** *m.* (*Bot.*) marsh crowfoot (*Ranunculus sceleratus*). **gifthaltig,** *adj.* poisonous, venomous, toxic. **Gifthauch,** *m.* (*fig.*) blight.

giftig ['gɪftɪç], *adj.* 1. poisonous, venomous, (*Med.*) virulent, toxic; 2. (*fig.*) pernicious; malignant, baneful; malicious, spiteful; 3. (*coll.*) angry, furious. **Giftigkeit,** *f.* virulence, toxicity, poisonousness; malice, spitefulness, viciousness; (*coll.*) anger, fury.

Gift|kunde, –lehre, *f.* toxicology. **–mischer,** *m.* poisoner. **–mittel,** *n.* antidote. **–mord,** *m.* poisoning. **–nebel,** *m.* (*Mil.*) toxic smoke. **–pfeil,** *m.* poisoned arrow. **–pflanze,** *f.* poisonous plant. **–pilz,** *m.* poisonous toadstool. **–schlange,** *f.* poisonous *or* venomous snake. **–schwamm,** *m. See* **–pilz. –spinne,** *f.* poisonous spider. **–stachel,** *m.* poisonous sting. **–stoff,** *m.* toxin, toxic agent, venom, (*Med.*) virus. **–trank,** *m.* poisoned drink. **–zahn,** *m.* poison-fang. **–zunge,** *f.* (*fig.*) spiteful *or* venomous tongue.

Gigant [gi'gant], *m.* (**-en,** *pl.* **-en**) giant. **Gigantin,** *f.* giantess. **gigantisch,** *adj.* gigantic, colossal.

Gigerl ['gi:gərl], *m. or n.* (**-s,** *pl.* -) (*Austr.*) fop, dandy.

Gilbe ['gɪlbə], *f.* 1. yellowish colour; yellow ochre; 2. (*Bot.*) dyer's weed (*Reseda luteola*). **gilben,** *v.i.* turn yellow. **Gilbhard,** *m.* (*obs.*) October.

Gilde ['gɪldə], *f.* guild, corporation. **Gildenhalle,** *f.* guildhall.

Gilling ['gɪlɪŋ], *f.* (-, *pl.* **-e** *or* **-s**), **Gillung,** *f.* (-, *pl.* **-en** *or* **-s**) (*Naut.*) counter.

gilt [gɪlt], *see* **gelten.**

giltig ['gɪltɪç], *adj.* (*Austr.*) *see* **gültig.**

giltst [gɪltst], *see* **gelten.**

Gimpel ['gɪmpəl], *m.* (*Orn.*) bullfinch (*Pyrrhula pyrrhula*); (*coll.*) dunce, ninny, noodle, simpleton.

ging [gɪŋ], **ginge,** *see* **gehen.**

Ginster ['gɪnstər], *m.* (*Bot.*) the genus *Genista* (*N.B. not* broom *or* gorse); ***englischer –,*** petty whin, needle furze.

Gipfel ['gɪpfəl], *m.* summit, top (*of a mountain*), peak; (*fig.*) pinnacle, climax, culmination, zenith, peak, acme, apex; (*Swiss also*) tree-top; (*coll.*) ***das ist der –,*** that is the limit. **Gipfel|blüte,** *f.* terminal flower. **–gespräche,** *n.pl.* (*Pol.*) summit talks. **–höhe,** *f.* (*Av.*) ceiling. **–leistung,** *f.* record. **gipfeln,** *v.i.* culminate (***in*** (*Dat.*), in), reach the zenith *or* climax, rise to a peak. **Gipfelpunkt,** *m.* limit, culminating point, culmination. **gipfelständig,** *adj.* (*Bot.*) terminal, apical. **Gipfelung,** *f.* culmination.

Gips [gɪps], *m.* (**-es,** *pl.* **-e**) gypsum; plaster of Paris, stucco, calcium sulphate. **Gips|abdruck, –abguß,** *m.* plaster cast *or* impression. **–bewurf,** *m.* plastering. **–brennen,** *n.* calcination of plaster. **–decke,** *f.* plaster ceiling. **gipsen,** *v.t.* plaster.

Gipser ['gɪpsər], *m.* plasterer, stucco-worker.

Gips|guß, *m.* plaster casting. **–malerei,** *f.* painting in fresco. **–marmor,** *n.* stucco. **–mörtel,** *m.* plaster, stucco. **–platte,** *f.* plaster-board. **–verband,** *m.* (*Surg.*) plaster of Paris dressing, plaster (case).

Giraffe [gi'rafə, (*Austr.*) ʒi'rafə], *f.* giraffe.

Girant [ʒi'rant], *m.* (**-en,** *pl.* **-en**) (*Comm.*) endorser. **Girat,** *m.* (**-en,** *pl.* **-en**) endorsee. **girierbar,** *adj.* endorsable. **girieren,** *v.t.* put into circulation; ***einen Wechsel –,*** endorse a bill (***auf*** or ***an*** (*Acc.*), in favour of).

Girlande [gɪr'landə], *f.* garland.

Girlitz ['gɪrlɪts], *m.* (**-es,** *pl.* **-e**) (*Orn.*) serin (*Serinus canaria*).

Giro ['ʒi:ro], *n.* (**-s,** *pl.* **-s** *or* (*Austr.*) **Giri**) endorsement; ***sein – geben,*** endorse; ***unausgefülltes –,*** blank endorsement; ***sein – verweigern,*** refuse to back (a bill); ***ohne –,*** unendorsed. **Giro|abteilung,** *f.* cheque department. **–bank,** *f.* transfer *or* clearing bank. **–geschäft,** *n.* clearing-house business. **–konto,** *n.* current account. **–verkehr,** *m. See* **–geschäft. –zentrale,** *f.* clearing house, central bank. **–zettel,** *m.* bank statement.

girren ['gɪrən], *v.i.* coo.

Gis [gis], *n.* (*Mus.*) G-sharp.

gischen ['gɪʃən], *v.i.* foam, froth, effervesce, (*coll.*) fizz.

Gischt [gɪʃt], *m.* foam, spray; (*on beer etc.*) froth.

Giß [gɪs], *f.* (-, *pl.* **-(ss)en**) *or m.* (**-(ss)es,** *pl.* **-(ss)e**) (*Navig.*) estimated position. **gissen,** *v.i.* estimate one's position; ***gegißter Kurs,*** dead-reckoning course. **Gissung,** *f.* estimation of position, dead reckoning.

Gitarre [gi'tarə], *f.* guitar.

Gitter ['gɪtər], *n.* grating, lattice; railing, bars, fence, trellis, grille, (*Rad.*) grid, control electrode. **Gitter|bett,** *n.* cot. **–brücke,** *f.* girder bridge. **–draht,** *m.* wire netting. **–drossel,** *f.* (*Rad.*) grid resistor. **–fenster,** *n.* lattice window, barred window. **–gleichrichter,** *m.* (*Rad.*) grid-leak detector. **–kapazität,** *f.* (*Rad.*) (grid) input capacity. **–kreis,** *m.* (*Rad.*) grid *or* input circuit. **–kreisimpedenz,** *f.* (*Rad.*) input impedance. **–netz,** *n.* (*on maps*) grid (co-ordinates). **–steuerung,** *f.* (*Rad.*) grid control. **–tor,** *n.* iron gate. **–tür,** *f.* trellised door. **–werk,** *n.* trellis-work, lattice-work, grating. **–widerstand,** *m.* (*Rad.*) grid-leak resistance. **–zaun,** *m.* iron fence, railings.

Glacé [gla'se:], *m.* kid (*leather*). **Glacé|handschuhe,** *m.pl.* kid gloves; (*fig.*) ***mit –n anfassen,*** handle with kid gloves, treat gently. **–papier,** *n.* glazed paper.

Glanz [glants], *m.* brightness, brilliance, radiance; lustre, gleam, sheen, gloss, glossiness, polish; glitter, glare, glow, shine; (*fig.*) resplendence, spendour, glamour, distinction, glory, pomp, magnificence; ***– der Gesundheit,*** radiant *or* glowing health; ***seines –es beraubt,*** shorn of its glamour; ***mit – bestehen,*** pass (*examination*) with distinction. **Glanzbürste,** *f.* polishing brush, buffing wheel.

Glänze ['glɛntsə], *f.* 1. gloss, glaze; 2. glossing-machine, polishing material, polisher.

glänzen ['glɛntsən], **1.** *v.i.* 1. shine, glitter, glisten, gleam, glint, flash, sparkle (***vor*** (*Dat.*), with); (*Prov.*) ***es ist nicht alles Gold, was glänzt,*** all is not gold that glitters; 2. be distinguished *or* outstanding, excel, (*coll.*) shine (***durch,*** in); ***er will gern –,*** he likes to shine *or* to show off, he loves display; ***durch Abwesenheit –,*** be conspicuous by absence. **2.** *v.t.* gloss, glaze; polish, burnish. **glänzend,** *adj.* shiny, shining, glossy, glittering, gleaming, sparkling, radiant, lustrous, (*fig.*) brilliant, splendid, magnificent, glorious.

Glanz|farbe, *f.* glossy colour. **–firnis,** *m.* glazing varnish. **–gold,** *n.* gold-foil. **–kattun,** *m.* glazed calico. **–kohle,** *f.* anthracite. **–kopfmeise,** *f.* (*Orn.*) *see* **Sumpfmeise. –leder,** *n.* patent leather. **–leinen,** *n.* glazed linen. **–leistung,** *f.* brilliant feat *or* performance, outstanding *or* masterly achievement. **–lichter,** *n.pl.* (*Art*) highlights. **glanzlos,** *adj.* lustreless, dull, mat(t), dim, dead. **Glanz|nummer,** *f.* (*Theat. etc.*) main attraction, (*coll.*) hit. **–papier,** *n.* glazed paper. **–periode,** *f.* palmy days, heyday, golden age, most brilliant period. **–punkt,** *m.* highlight, climax. **–seite,** *f.* bright *or* shiny side. **–silber,** *n.* argenite. **–stoff,** *m.* artificial silk, rayon. **glanzvoll,** *adj.* splendid, resplendent, magnificent, glorious, brilliant. **Glanz|zeit,** *f. See* **–periode. –zwirn,** *m.* glacé thread.

[1]**Glas** [gla:s], *n.* (**-es,** *pl.* **-en**) (*Naut.*) half-hour bell; ***es schlägt 8 –en,*** it is 8 bells.

[2]**Glas,** *n.* (**-es,** *pl.* **⸚er**) glass; drinking-glass, tumbler; mirror, *pl.* (eye)glasses; ***ein – Wein,*** a glass of wine; ***er trank 3 – Bier,*** he drank 3 glasses of beer; ***er kaufte 3 Gläser,*** he bought 3 tumblers; ***die Gläser des Hirsches,*** the eyes of the stag; ***unter – und Rahmen bringen,*** frame; (*Prov.*) ***Glück und –, wie leicht bricht das,*** happiness is as fragile as glass; (*coll.*) ***gern ins – gucken,*** be fond of one's drink; (*coll.*) ***zu tief ins – gucken,*** have a drop too much. **glasartig,** *adj.* glassy, vitreous.

Glas|auge, *n.* glass eye. **–birne,** *f.* glass bulb, globe (*for electric lights*). **–bläser,** *m.* glass-blower.

Gläschen ['glɛ:sçən], *n.* little glass; (*coll.*) ***ein – zuviel,*** a drop too much (to drink).

glasen ['gla:zən], *v.i.* (*Naut.*) strike the (ship's) bell.

Glaser ['gla:zər], *m.* glazier. **Glaserkitt,** *m.* putty.

gläsern ['glɛ:zərn], *adj.* (of) glass, vitreous; glassy (*as eyes*).

Glas|fabrik, *f.* glassworks. **–faser,** *f.* spun glass, glass fibre, fibreglass. **–flasche,** *f.* glass bottle; decanter. **–flügler,** *m.* (*Ent.*) clearwing. **–gebläse,** *n.* glass-blower's blowpipe. **–geschirr,** *n.* glass, glassware. **–gespinst,** *n. See* **–faser. –glanz,** *m.* vitreous lustre. **–glocke,** *f.* bell-jar, glass cover. **glasgrün,** *adj.* bottle-green. **Glasharmonika,** *f.* musical glasses. **glashart,** *adj.* (as) brittle as glass. **Glas|haus,** *n.* hothouse, greenhouse, conservatory. **–haut,** *f.* cellophane. **–hütte,** *f.* glassworks.

glasieren [gla'zi:rən], *v.t.* glaze, gloss; enamel, varnish; (*Cul.*) ice.

glasig ['gla:zɪç], *adj.* glassy, vitreous; ***–er Blick,*** glassy stare.

Glas|kasten, *m.* glass case; show-case. **–kolben,** *m.* flask, carboy, demijohn. **–körper,** *m.* vitreous humour (*of the eye*). **–malerei,** *f.* glass-painting, painting on glass. **–ofen,** *m.* glass-furnace. **–papier,** *n.* glass-paper, sandpaper. **–perle,** *f.*

glass bead. **–röhre,** *f.* glass tube. **–scheibe,** *f.* pane of glass. **–scherbe,** *f.* piece of broken glass, glass splinter, *pl.* cullet. **–schleifen,** *n.* glass cutting *or* grinding. **–schrank,** *m.* cupboard with glass doors *or* for glassware. **–splitter,** *m.* splinter of glass. **–sturz,** *m. See* **–glocke.**

Glast [glast], *m.* (**-es,** *pl.* **-e**) (*dial., Poet.*) radiance.

Glastafel ['gla:sta:fəl], *f.* plate *or* square *or* pane of glass.

Glasur [gla'zu:r], *f.* glaze, gloss, glazing, varnish, enamel, (*Cul.*) icing.

Glas|versicherung, *f.* plate-glass insurance. **–wolle,** *f. See* **–faser. –zylinder,** *m.* lamp-chimney.

glatt [glat], **I.** *adj.* (*comp. –er, sup. –est, better than glätter, glättest, which also occur*) **I.** smooth, even, level, unruffled, flat, flush; sleek; ***–es Geschäft,*** even business; ***–es Gesicht,*** smooth *or* sleek face; ***–es Kinn,*** smooth *or* clean-shaven chin; ***–e Stirn,*** unruffled brow; 2. polished, slippery, glossy; ***es ist zu – zum Gehen,*** it is too slippery for walking; 3. plain, clear, obvious; downright, outright, absolute; ***–e Absage,*** flat refusal; ***–e Lüge,*** barefaced lie; ***–er Sieg,*** clear win *or* victory; ***–er Unsinn,*** sheer nonsense; 4. round (*number etc.*); ***–e 10 Pfund,*** all of £10; 5. (*fig.*) smooth, bland, oily, flattering; ***–e Worte,*** smooth *or* oily words; ***–e Zunge,*** smooth tongue; 6. (*Swiss*) splendid, capital. **2.** *adv.* **I.** smoothly; ***– anliegen,*** fit tightly *or* closely; be *or* lie flush (*an* (*Dat.*), with); ***die S. ging ganz –,*** the affair went (off) smoothly *or* without the slightest hitch, it was all plain sailing; 2. quite, entirely, thoroughly, (*coll.*) clean, plainly; unhesitatingly; ***– abschlagen,*** flatly refuse; ***– durchschneiden,*** cut clean through; ***– gewinnen,*** win hands down, win easily; ***– heraussagen,*** tell bluntly *or* plainly *or* frankly; ***ihm – ins Gesicht,*** to his face; (*coll.*) ***– vergessen,*** clean forget.

Glätte ['glɛtə], *f.* smoothness, sleekness; polish, gloss; slipperiness; (*fig.*) politeness, polish; smoothness, fluency.

Glatteis ['glatˀaɪs], *n.* (sheet) ice, frost, slippery surface; (*coll.*) ***ihn aufs – führen,*** mislead *or* trick him, lead him up the garden path.

Glätteisen ['glɛtˀaɪzən], *n.* smoothing iron.

glätten ['glɛtən], **I.** *v.t.* smooth, flatten, take out the creases; plane (*wood*), burnish (*metal*), glaze, gloss (*paper*), mangle, calender (*textiles*), polish, (*Swiss*) iron (*clothes*). **2.** *v.r.* become smooth *or* calm (*as waves*). **Glätter,** *m.* burnisher; polisher; polishing-tool. **Glättfeile,** *f.* smooth file.

glatthaarig ['glatha:rɪç], *adj.* smooth-haired. **Glatthobel,** *m.* smoothing plane. **glatt|köpfig,** *adj. See* **–haarig. –machen,** *v.t.* **I.** *See* **glätten**; 2. (*coll.*) pay off, settle (*a debt*).

Glättmaschine ['glɛtmaʃi:nə], *f.* (*Carp.*) planing machine; (*Pap.*) glazing machine; (*Text.*) sleeking machine.

glatt|rasiert, *adj.* smooth-shaven. **–stellen,** *v.t.* (*Comm.*) realize; settle, clear (*a debt*). **–streichen,** *irr.v.t.* flatten, smooth down, planish, flush. **–weg,** *adv.* plainly, flatly, bluntly, point-blank, (*coll.*) straight out. **–züngig,** *adj.* glib, plausible, smooth-tongued.

Glatze ['glatsə], *f.* bald spot *or* patch, bald head; tonsure. **Glatzkopf,** *m.* bald-headed person. **glatzköpfig,** *adj.* bald(-headed).

glau [glau], *adj.* (*dial.*) bright, lively, quick. **glauäugig,** *adj.* (*Poet.*) bright-eyed; keen-sighted.

Glaube ['glaubə], *m.* (**-ns,** *no pl.*) faith, confidence, trust, belief, credence (*an* (*Acc.*), in); religious faith *or* belief, religion; creed; ***von seinem –n abfallen*** or ***abgehen,*** see ***–n verleugnen***; ***einen –n bekennen,*** profess a faith; ***–n finden,*** be believed, find credence; ***in gutem –n,*** in good faith; ***–n schenken*** (*Dat.*), give credence to, believe; (*Prov.*) ***– macht selig,*** faith alone is bliss; ***auf Treu und –n,*** on trust, in good faith; ***seinen –n verleugnen,*** abjure *or* renounce one's faith, become an apostate.

glauben ['glaubən], **I.** *v.t.* believe, give credence to; think, suppose, imagine; ***ich glaube es nicht,*** I don't believe it; ***ich glaubte ihn gerettet,*** I thought he was saved. **2.** *v.i.* **I.** believe, trust, have faith (*an* (*Acc.*), in); ***an ihn –,*** have faith in *or* trust him; ***an Gott –,*** believe in God; (*coll.*) ***dran – müssen,*** (have to) die, lose one's life, come to grief; 2. ***ihm –,*** believe him; ***ich glaube dir aufs Wort,*** I'll take your word for it; ***es ist nicht zu –,*** it is incredible; ***ich glaube wohl,*** I dare say; (*coll.*) ***du kannst mir –,*** you can take it from me; ***er wollte uns – machen,*** he would have us believe.

Glaubens|abfall, *m.* apostasy. **–artikel,** *m.* article of faith, dogma. **–bekenntnis,** *n.* confession of faith, creed; ***apostolisches –,*** the Apostles' creed. **–bruder,** *m. See* **–genosse. –eifer,** *m.* religious zeal. **–freiheit,** *f.* religious liberty. **–genosse,** *m.* co-religionist; fellow-believer. **–lehre,** *f.* religious dogma *or* doctrine, dogmatic *or* doctrinal theology, dogmatics. **–sache,** *f.* matter of faith. **–satz,** *m.* dogma. **–spaltung,** *f.* schism. **glaubensstark,** *adj.* deeply religious. **Glaubensstreit,** *m.* religious controversy *or* strife. **glaubenswert,** *adj. See* **glaubwürdig. Glaubens|wut,** *f.* fanaticism. **–zeuge,** *m.* martyr. **–zwang,** *m.* religious intolerance *or* persecution. **–zwist,** *m. See* **–streit.**

Glaubersalz ['glaubərzalts], *n.* Glauber's salt sodium sulphate.

glaubhaft ['glauphaft], *adj.* credible, authentic, substantiated; ***– machen,*** substantiate, authenticate, make credible; ***dem Gericht – machen,*** satisfy the court. **Glaubhaftmachung,** *f.* substantiation, authentication.

gläubig ['glɔybɪç] (*dial.* **glaubig**), *adj.* **I.** believing, full of faith, devout, pious; 2. trustful, unsuspecting, credulous. **Gläubige(r),** *m., f.* true believer; ***die Gläubigen,*** the faithful.

Gläubiger(in) ['glɔybɪgər(ɪn)], *m.* (*f.*) (*Comm.*) creditor; mortgagee.

Gläubigkeit ['glɔybɪçkaɪt], *f.* full confidence; (*Eccl.*) faith, devoutness, piety.

glaublich ['glauplɪç], *adj.* credible, believable, likely. **glaubwürdig,** *adj.* authentic, reliable, credible; (*of a p.*) trustworthy; ***aus –er Quelle,*** on good authority, from a reliable source. **Glaubwürdigkeit,** *f.* authenticity, reliability, credibility; (*of a p.*) trustworthiness.

gleich [glaɪç], **I.** *adj.* same, like, identical, equal (*an* (*Dat.*), in); uniform, level, even; coincident; constant; alike, (very) similar; ***ich achte mich ihm –,*** I consider myself to be his equal; ***von –em Alter,*** of the same age; ***–er Boden,*** level ground; ***ins –e bringen,*** settle, arrange, put right *or* in order; (*Prov.*) ***–e Brüder, –e Kappen,*** like pot, like cover; (*Prov.*) ***– und – gesellt sich gern,*** birds of a feather flock together; ***–es*** or ***das –e gilt für dich,*** the same (rule) applies to you *or* applies in your case; ***es kommt aufs –e hinaus,*** it comes *or* amounts to the same thing (in the end), it is all one; ***in –em Maße,*** to the same degree *or* extent; ***das ist mir –,*** that makes no difference (to me), that is all the same *or* all one to me; ***das sieht ihm –,*** that is just like him; ***die Tochter sieht ihrer Mutter –,*** the daughter resembles her mother; ***Garbo ist der Cleopatra –,*** G. is C.'s equal *or* is on a par with C.; ***am –en Strange ziehen,*** have the same end in view; ***ein –es tun,*** do the same (thing), follow suit; ***ich werde ein –es für dich tun,*** I will do as much for you; ***–es mit –em vergelten*** give tit for tat; ***in –er Weise,*** likewise, in like manner, in the same way; ***von –em Werte,*** equivalent; ***in –em Werte stehen,*** be at par; ***zu –er Zeit,*** at the same time *or* moment, simultaneously. **2.** *adv.* **I.** alike, equally, exactly, just, in the same way; ***– alt,*** of the same age; ***– viel,*** just as much; ***– als ob,*** just as if; ***– gegenüber,*** right *or* directly opposite; ***– hier,*** just *or* right here; 2. immediately, at once, instantly, directly, presently; ***– als ich ihn sah,*** as soon as *or* the moment I saw him; ***– anfangs*** or ***– zu Beginn,*** at the very beginning; ***– bei der Hand,*** ready, at hand; ***das ist – geschehen,*** that is easily *or* soon done; ***– danach*** or ***– nachher,*** immediately, just *or* right afterwards; ***ich bin – wieder zurück,*** I shall return immediately, (*coll.*) I'll be back right away; ***willst du – still sein!***

be quiet this minute! *Frequently used idiomatically as a more or less meaningless particle, e.g.* ***ich dachte es –,*** I thought as much; ***wie ist doch – der Name?*** what is the name now? what did you say your name was *or* is? ***habe ich es nicht – gesagt!*** I told you so (already). **3.** *conj.* (*obs.*) although; ***ist er – nicht reich, so tut er doch . . .,*** although he is not rich, yet he acts . . .; ***wären Sie – mein Vater,*** even though you were my father.

gleich|altrig, *adj.* of the same age. **–artig,** *adj.* of the same kind, uniform, homogeneous; similar, analogous. **Gleichartigkeit,** *f.* uniformity, homogeneity; similarity. **gleich|bedeutend,** *adj.* synonymous (***mit,*** with), equivalent, tantamount (to); ***–e Wörter,*** synonyms. **–berechtigt,** *adj.* having equal right, equally entitled. **Gleichberechtigung,** *f.* equality of right(s).

gleich|bleiben, *irr.v.i., v.r.* remain unchanged *or* the same; ***das bleibt sich gleich,*** that makes no difference, that comes to the same thing. **–bleibend,** *adj.* constant, invariable.

Gleiche ['glaɪçə], *f.* (*rare*) evenness, equality; ***in die – bringen,*** see ***ins gleiche bringen*** *under* **gleich, 1.**

gleichen ['glaɪçən], *irr.v.i.* (*Dat.*) equal, be equal to, be alike; resemble, be like, be similar to; be comparable *or* analogous to, correspond to; ***die Zwillinge – einander völlig,*** the twins are absolutely alike; ***sie – sich wie ein Ei dem andern,*** they are as like as two peas.

Gleicher ['glaɪçər], *m.* (*obs.*) equator; equalizer, leveller.

gleicher|gestalt, –maßen, –weise, *adv.* in like manner, likewise.

gleich|falls, *adv.* likewise, too, as well, also, in the same way; ***danke –!*** the same to you, thanks! **–farbig,** *adj.* of the same colour, isochromatic. **–flächig,** *adj.* (*Math.*) isohedral. **–förmig,** *adj.* uniform, homogeneous, isomorphous; monotonous. **Gleichförmigkeit,** *f.* uniformity, conformity; monotony. **gleich|geschlechtlich,** *adj.* homosexual. **–gesinnt,** *adj.* like-minded, congenial, compatible. **–gestellt,** *adj.* co-ordinate; equal (in rank), on the same level, on a par (*Dat.*, with). **–gestimmt,** *adj.* (*Mus.*) tuned to the same pitch, (*fig.*) like-minded, congenial.

Gleichgewicht ['glaɪçgəvɪçt], *n.* balance, equilibrium, equipose; ***das europäische –,*** the balance of power in Europe; ***labiles –,*** unstable equilibrium; ***seelisches –,*** mental balance; ***ihm das – halten,*** counterbalance his influence, cope with him; ***das – behalten,*** keep *or* preserve one's balance; ***im – (er)halten,*** balance (equally), keep in equal balance; ***das – verlieren,*** lose one's balance; ***das – wiederherstellen,*** redress the balance; ***das – aufheben,*** turn the scales, upset the balance; ***im –,*** in (a state of) equilibrium, well-balanced; ***aus dem – bringen,*** throw out of balance, unbalance, (*fig.*) put *or* throw (*s.o.*) off his balance, disconcert, upset (*a p.*). **Gleichgewichts|lehre,** *f.* statics. **–organ,** *n.* (*Anat.*) labyrinth (of the inner ear). **–punkt,** *m.* centre of gravity. **–stange,** *f.* balancing pole. **–störung,** *f.* disturbance of equilibrium; (*fig.*) imbalance. **–übung,** *f.* balance exercise.

gleich|giltig (*Austr.*), **–gültig,** *adj.* indifferent (*Dat.* *or* ***gegen,*** to), unconcerned, nonchalant, casual (about), apathetic (towards); ***mir ist es –,*** it is all the same *or* is of no consequence *or* is a matter of indifference to me, it doesn't matter to me, I don't care. **Gleichgültigkeit,** *f.* indifference (***gegen,*** to), unconcern, apathy, nonchalance (about).

Gleichheit ['glaɪçhaɪt], *f.* equality, parity; equivalence, identity, similarity; uniformity, homogeneity; ***Freiheit, –, Brüderlichkeit,*** liberty, equality, fraternity; ***– vor dem Gesetz,*** equality before the law; ***die – der Winkel in einem Dreieck,*** the identity of the angles in a triangle. **Gleichheitszeichen,** *n.* sign of equality, (*coll.*) equals sign.

Gleichklang ['glaɪçklaŋ], *m.* unison, accord; harmony, consonance.

gleichkommen ['glaɪçkɔmən], *irr.v.i.* (*Dat.*) equal; come up to, be equivalent to, amount to; ***nicht –*** (*Dat.*), be no match for, fall short of.

Gleichlauf ['glaɪçlauf], *m.* synchronism; ***zum – bringen,*** synchronize. **gleichlaufend,** *adj.* (*time*) synchronous, synchronized; (*space*) parallel.

Gleichlaut ['glaɪçlaut], *m.* consonance. **gleichlautend, 1.** *adj.* identical, to the same effect, consonant; (*Gram.*) homonymous; ***–es Wort,*** homonym; ***–e Abschrift,*** duplicate, true copy. **2.** *adv.* in conformity, consonantly.

gleichmachen ['glaɪçmaxən], *v.t.* 1. make equal (*Dat.*, to), equalize (with), standardize; 2. ***dem Erdboden –,*** level *or* raze to the ground. **Gleich|macher,** *m.* (*Pol.*) egalitarian, leveller. **–macherei,** *f.* egalitarianism. **gleichmacherisch,** *adj.* egalitarian. **Gleichmachung,** *f.* 1. equalization; 2. levelling, razing.

Gleichmaß ['glaɪçma:s], *n.* symmetry, proportion; uniformity; commensurateness. **gleichmäßig,** *adj.* proportionate; symmetrical; uniform, constant, steady, level, regular, even, equable; homogeneous; ***–e Verteilung,*** uniform distribution; ***– marschieren,*** march at a steady pace. **Gleichmäßigkeit,** *f.* uniformity, regularity, continuity, evenness, steadiness, equability.

Gleichmut ['glaɪçmu:t], *m.* (*rarely f.*) equanimity, serenity, calmness, coolness, imperturbability, stoicism. **gleichmütig,** *adj.* even-tempered, calm, serene; imperturbable, stolid, cool, indifferent. **Gleichmütigkeit,** *f.* *See* **Gleichmut.**

gleichnamig ['glaɪçna:mɪç], *adj.* of *or* having the same name; (*Math.*) correspondent, (*Gram.*) homonymous.

Gleichnis ['glaɪçnɪs], *n.* (**-ses,** *pl.* **-se**) image, simile, metaphor, figure of speech; allegory, parable; ***Christi –se,*** the parables of Christ; ***in –sen reden,*** speak in riddles. **gleichnishaft,** *adj.* symbolical, allegorical. **gleichnisweise,** *adv.* allegorically, symbolically.

gleichrangig ['glaɪçraŋɪç], *adj.* equal, equivalent (***mit,*** to), on a par (with).

gleichrichten ['glaɪçrɪçtən], *v.t.* (*Rad.*) rectify. **Gleichrichter,** *m.* (*Rad.*) rectifier.

gleichsam ['glaɪçza:m], *adv.* as it were, so to speak, (just) as if *or* as though, almost.

gleichschalten ['glaɪçʃaltən], *v.t.* (*Pol.*) unify, coordinate, (*coll.*) bring into line, streamline; (*Tech.*) synchronize. **Gleichschaltung,** *f.* (*Pol.*) unification, coordination, (*Nat. Soc.*) elimination (of opposition); (*Tech.*) synchronization.

gleichschenkelig ['glaɪçʃɛnkəlɪç], *adj.* (*Math.*) isosceles.

Gleichschritt ['glaɪçʃrɪt], *m.* uniform step; (*Mil.*) ***im – marsch!*** by the left quick march! ***– halten,*** keep step.

gleichseitig ['glaɪçzaɪtɪç], *adj.* (*Math.*) equilateral.

gleichsetzen ['glaɪçzɛtsən], *v.t.* (*Dat.* *or* ***mit***) equate with; (*fig.*) put on a level with; compare *or* identify with. **Gleichsetzung,** *f.* equation *or* identification (***mit,*** with).

gleichsinnig ['glaɪçzɪnɪç], *adj.* in the same sense *or* direction.

Gleichstand ['glaɪçʃtant], *m.* (*Tenn.*) deuce. **gleich|stehen,** *irr.v.i.* (*Dat.*) equal; be equal to, be (on a) level *or* on a par *or* on the same footing with. **–stellen,** *v.t.* equate, put on a par, place on the same footing (*Dat.*, with). **Gleichstellung,** *f.* equalization; comparison.

gleichstimmig ['glaɪçʃtɪmɪç], *adj.* in unison; unanimous; congenial.

Gleichstrom ['glaɪçʃtro:m], *m.* (*Elec.*) direct current.

gleichtun ['glaɪçtu:n], *irr.v.t.* ***es ihm –,*** match *or* equal him, come up to him; ***es ihm – wollen,*** vie with him.

Gleichung ['glaɪçuŋ], *f.* equation; ***– des ersten Grades,*** linear equation; ***– des zweiten Grades,*** quadratic equation; ***– des dritten Grades,*** cubic equation.

gleich|viel, *adv.* no matter, all the same, all one.

-weit, *adj.* equidistant; ***er ist – entfernt, Unrecht zu tun, als . . .,*** he is as far from doing wrong as .... **-wertig,** *adj.* equivalent, equal (***mit,*** to), on a par (with). **Gleichwertigkeit,** *f.* equivalence, equality. **gleich|wie,** *adv.* like, just as, (even) as. **-wohl,** *adv.* nevertheless, notwithstanding, yet, however, all the same, for all that. **-zeitig, 1.** *adj.* contemporary, contemporaneous, simultaneous, synchronous. **2.** *adv.* together, at the same time, (*coll.*) at one blow. **Gleichzeitigkeit,** *f.* coexistence, contemporaneity; coincidence, simultaneousness; synchronism.

gleichziehen ['glaɪçtsi:ən], *irr.v.i.* (*Spt.*) overtake; draw level (*Dat.*, with).

gleichzu ['glaɪç'tsu:], *adv.* straightway, without ceremony.

Gleisanschluß ['glaɪsˀanʃlus], *m.* (*Railw.*) private siding. **Gleis(e),** *n. See* **Geleise.**

Gleisner ['glaɪsnər], *m.* hypocrite, dissembler, double-dealer, pharisee. **gleisnerisch,** *adj.* hypocritical, dissembling.

Gleiße ['glaɪsə], *f.* (*Bot.*) fool's-parsley (*Aethusa cynapium*).

gleißen ['glaɪsən], *reg. & irr.v.i.* glisten.

Gleit|aar, *m.* (*Orn.*) black-winged kite (*Elanus caerulens*). **-bahn,** *f.* slide, chute; (*Shipb.*) slip(s), slipway.

gleiten ['glaɪtən], *reg. & irr.v.i.* (*aux.* s. & h.) glide, slide; slip, (*Motor.*) skid, (*over surface*) skim; (*Metall.*) creep; – ***lassen,*** slip, slide (***in*** (*Acc.*), into); ***das Auge – lassen über,*** run one's eye(s) over; ***die Hand – lassen über,*** pass one's hand over; ***-de Preise*** (***Löhne***), sliding scale of prices (wages). **Gleiter,** *m. See* **Gleitflugzeug. Gleitertruppen,** *f.pl.* airborne *or* glider-borne troops.

Gleit|flieger, *m.* glider pilot. **-flug,** *m.* gliding flight; ***im – niedergehen,*** plane down. **-flugweite,** *f.* gliding range. **-flugzeug,** *n.* glider. **-kufe,** *f.* (*Av.*) landing skid. **-lager,** *n.* (*Tech.*) friction *or* sliding bearing. **-laut,** *m.* (*Phonet.*) glide. **-schiene,** *f.* (*Tech.*) skid, guide, slide-bar; (*typewriter*) carriage rail. **-schritt,** *m.* glissade. **-schutzreifen,** *m.* non-skid tyre. **-sitz,** *m.* sliding fit. **-verdeck,** *n.* (*Motor.*) sliding roof. **-zeit,** *f.* flexible working hours.

Gletscher ['glɛtʃər], *m.* glacier. **gletscherartig,** *adj.* glacial. **Gletscher|bildung,** *f.* glacial formation. **-brand,** *m.* sunburn (from reflected rays). **-brille,** *f.* snow-goggles. **-eis,** *n.* glacial ice. **-kunde,** *f.* glaciology. **-schutt,** *m.* moraine. **-spalte,** *f.* crevasse. **-zeit,** *f.* glacial period, ice age.

glich [glɪç], **gliche,** *see* **gleichen.**

Glied [gli:t], *n.* (**-(e)s,** *pl.* **-er**) **1.** limb, member; (*Anat.*) joint; ***ich habe meine geraden -er gerettet,*** I escaped without any bones broken; ***männliches –,*** penis; ***die -er recken,*** stretch o.s.; ***kein – rühren können,*** not be able to move hand or foot; ***mit steifen -ern erwachen,*** wake up stiff in every joint; ***an allen -ern zittern,*** tremble all over; **2.** (*Mil.*) rank, file; ***in -ern links,*** left wheel; ***in Reih und –,*** formed up (*on parade, for battle*), in formation; ***ins – treten,*** fall in; ***aus dem -e treten,*** step out of the ranks; **3.** (*Math., Log.*) term; link (*of chain*); ***äußere -er einer Verhältnisgleichung,*** extremes (*of a ratio*); ***Vettern im dritten -e,*** third cousins.

Glieder|abstand, *m.* (*Mil.*) space between the ranks. **-bau,** *m.* formation, structure, organization; articulation; frame, build. **-fahrzeug,** *n.* articulated vehicle. **-frucht,** *f.* (*Bot.*) loment(um). **-füß(l)er,** *m.pl. See* **-tiere. -gicht,** *f.* arthritis. **-hülse,** *f. See* **-frucht. gliederlahm,** *adj.* paralytic, palsied. **Gliederlähmung,** *f.* paralysis.

gliedern ['gli:dərn], **1.** *v.t.* joint, articulate; dispose, arrange, organize; classify, (sub)divide (***in*** (*Acc.*), into); (*Mil.*) form into ranks *or* files, form up. **2.** *v.r.* (***in*** (*Acc.*)) be composed of, be divided into.

Glieder|puppe, *f.* puppet, marionette, jointed doll. **-reißen,** *n.*, **-schmerz,** *m.* shooting pains, growing pains, rheumatism. **-schwund,** *m.* atrophy of the limbs. **-tiere,** *n.pl.* (*Zool.*) arthropods, articulated animals.

Gliederung ['gli:dəruŋ], *f.* organization, structure, system; pattern, disposition, arrangement, grouping, classification, distribution, division; (*Anat. etc.*) articulation; segmentation; (*Mil.*) formation; (*Gram.*) construction.

Glieder|zelle, *f.* articulate cell. **-zucken,** *n.* convulsion.

Glied|maßen, *f.pl.* limbs; ***gesunde – haben,*** be sound of limb; ***Mann von starken –,*** powerfully built man. **-staat,** *m.* constituent state (*in a federation*). **-wasser,** *n.* (*Anat.*) synovial fluid. **gliedweise,** *adv.* limb by limb; link by link; (*Mil.*) in files.

glimmen ['glɪmən], *reg. & irr.v.i.* glimmer, glow, smoulder; ***-de Asche,*** embers.

Glimmer ['glɪmər], *m.* **1.** faint glow, glimmer; **2.** (*Min.*) mica. **glimmer|artig, -haltig,** *adj.* micaceous. **Glimmerschiefer,** *m.* mica-slate, micaceous schist.

Glimm|lampe, -leuchtröhre, *f.*, **-licht,** *n.* fluorescent lamp *or* light. **-stengel,** *m.* (*sl.*) fag.

Glimpf ['glɪmpf], *m.* **1.** (**-s,** *no pl.*) (*obs.*) forbearance, gentleness; ***mit –,*** without harm *or* evil consequences; ***mit Fug und –,*** with right and justice; ***sich mit – aus der S. ziehen,*** extricate o.s. from a matter unscathed; **2.** (**-s,** *pl.* **-e**) (*Swiss*) bodkin. **glimpfig,** *adj.* (*Swiss*) pliant, pliable, elastic. **glimpflich, 1.** *adj.* forbearing, indulgent, lenient, mild, gentle, fair. **2.** *adv.* without difficulty *or* unpleasantness; – ***davonkommen,*** get off lightly.

Glitsche ['glɪtʃə], *f.* (*coll.*) slide. **glitschen,** *v.i.* (*aux.* h. & s.) (*coll.*) slide, glide, slip, slither, skid. **glitsch(er)ig,** *adj.* (*coll.*) slippery, slippy.

glitt [glɪt], **glitte,** *see* **gleiten.**

glitzern ['glɪtsərn], *v.i.* glitter, glisten, glint, sparkle; (*of stars*) twinkle.

Globus ['glo:bus], *m.* (- *or* **-ses,** *pl.* **Globen** *or* **-se**) globe.

Glocke ['glɔkə], *f.* bell, gong; glass shade, (*Chem.*) bell jar; any bell-shaped article; (*dial.*) clock; (*Bot.*) calyx, cup; ***etwas an die große – hängen,*** blazon *or* noise a th. abroad, broadcast a th., make a great fuss *or* a song (and dance) about a th.; ***die -n läuten,*** ring the bells; (*Prov.*) ***er hat die -n läuten hören, weiß aber nicht, wo sie hängen,*** he's been told, but doesn't take it in *or* doesn't see the point *or* doesn't grasp the idea; (*coll.*) ***ihm sagen, was die – geschlagen hat,*** tell him where he gets off; ***sie weiß, was die – geschlagen hat,*** she knows what she's in for *or* what's in store for her *or* where she stands; – ***zehn werde ich da sein,*** I shall be there on the stroke of ten.

Glocken|blume, *f.* (*Bot.*) Canterbury-bell, harebell, (*Scots*) bluebell (*Campanula rotundifolia*). **-boje,** *f.* (*Naut.*) bell buoy. **glockenförmig,** *adj.* bell-shaped. **Glocken|geläut(e),** *n.* chime, peal of bells; ***er hielt unter – seinen Einzug,*** all the bells were ringing as he made his entry. **-gießer,** *m.* bell-founder. **-gut,** *n.* bell-metal. **Glocken|hammer,** *m. See* **-klöppel. glocken|hell,** *adj. See* **-klar. -hut,** *m.* cloche (*lady's hat*). **glockenklar,** *adj.* clear as a bell. **Glocken|klöppel,** *m.* clapper (*of a bell*). **-rock,** *m.* pleated *or* gored skirt. **-schale,** *f.* gong. **-schlag,** *m.* chime, stroke of the clock *or* hour; ***mit dem –,*** punctually, (*coll.*) on the stroke *or* dot. **-schwengel,** *m. See* **-klöppel. -seil,** *n.* bell-rope. **-speise,** *f.* bell-metal. **-spiel,** *n.* chime(s), carillon. **-stube,** *f.*, **-stuhl,** *m.* bell-loft, belfry. **-tonne,** *f. See* **-boje. -turm,** *m.* bell-tower, belfry, campanile. **-zeichen,** *n.* call-bell. **-zug,** *m.* bell-pull, bell-rope; bell-stop (*in organs*).

Glöckner ['glœknər], *m.* sexton, bell-ringer.

glomm [glɔm], **glömme** ['glœmə], *see* **glimmen.**

Glorie ['glo:riə], *f.* glory; halo; (*coll.*) ***ihn seiner – entkleiden,*** debunk him. **Glorienschein,** *m.* (*fig.*) halo.

glorios [glori'o:s], *adj.* glorious; (*coll.*) excellent, capital.

glorreich ['glo:rraɪç], *adj.* glorious, illustrious, triumphant.

Glossar [glɔ'sa:r], *n.* (**-s**, *pl.* **-e** *or* **-ien**) glossary. **Glossator,** *m.* (**-s,** *pl.* **-en**) commentator; annotator. **Glosse,** *f.* gloss, annotation, marginal note; (*usu. pl.*) sneering remark, sarcastic comment; ***über alles -n machen,*** carp *or* scoff *or* jeer *or* sneer at *or* find fault with everything. **glossieren,** *v.t.* gloss, comment on; censure, criticize, find fault with.

Glottis ['glɔtɪs], *f.* (-, *pl.* **Glottes**) glottis. **Glottisschlag,** *m.* (*Phonet.*) glottal stop.

glotzäugig ['glɔts'ɔygɪç], *adj.* goggle-eyed, pop-eyed. **glotzen,** *v.i.* gape; stare, goggle.

Glück [glyk], *n.* (**-(e)s,** *as pl.* **Glücksfälle, Glücksumstände** *are oft. used*) (good) fortune, (good) luck, stroke of luck, (lucky) chance; success, prosperity; happiness, bliss, felicity; ***– ab!*** (*aviator's greeting*) happy landing! ***– auf!*** good luck! ***auf – oder Unglück,*** for better or for worse; ***– im Unglück,*** a blessing in disguise; ***alles auf das – ankommen lassen,*** leave everything to chance; (*Prov.*) ***– und Glas, wie leicht bricht das,*** fortune is brittle as glass; ***auf gut –,*** at random, at a venture, on the off-chance; ***– haben,*** be lucky, succeed (***mit,*** in); ***kein – haben,*** be unlucky, be out of luck, have no luck; ***das – haben zu tun,*** have the good luck *or* fortune to do; ***da hast du – gehabt,*** you were lucky; ***sein – machen,*** succeed, make one's fortune; ***Jagd nach dem –,*** fortune-hunting; ***da können Sie von – sagen,*** you may call *or* count *or* consider yourself lucky, you can thank your lucky star(s); (*Prov.*) ***jeder ist seines -es Schmied,*** every one is the architect of his own fortune; ***es war ein –,*** it was lucky *or* fortunate; ***es war ein wahres –,*** it was a mercy; ***dem – im Schoß sitzen,*** be Fortune's favourite; ***sein – verscherzen,*** forfeit one's chance of happiness; ***sein – versuchen,*** try one's luck; (*Prov.*) ***mancher hat mehr – als Verstand,*** Fortune favours fools; ***viel –!*** see ***– auf! – im Winkel,*** modest happiness, quiet serenity; ***ihm – wünschen,*** congratulate him (***zu,*** on); ***ich wünsche Ihnen viel – zum Geburtstage,*** I wish you many happy returns of the day; ***ich wünsche Ihnen – zum neuen Jahre,*** I wish you a happy New Year; ***– zu!*** see ***– auf! zum –,*** fortunately, luckily, as (good) luck would have it; ***zu meinem –,*** luckily for me; ***man kann niemanden zu seinem – zwingen,*** you can lead a horse to the water but you cannot make it drink. **glückbringend,** *adj.* lucky, fortunate, auspicious, propitious.

Glucke ['glukə], *f.* sitting *or* broody hen. **glucken,** *v.i.* cluck.

glücken ['glykən], *v.i. imp.* (*Dat.*) (*aux.* h. *&* s.) prosper, succeed, be successful, turn out well; ***es glückt ihm alles,*** everything succeeds with him; ***nicht –,*** fail, miscarry; ***es wollte nichts –,*** everything went wrong.

Gluckente ['gluk'ɛntə], *f.* (*Orn.*) Baikal teal (*Anas formosa*).

gluckern ['glukərn], *v.i.* gurgle.

Gluckhenne ['glukhɛnə], *f. See* **Glucke.**

glücklich ['glyklɪç], *adj.* fortunate, lucky, prosperous, successful; auspicious, favourable, propitious; felicitous; blissful, happy; ***-e Reise!*** bon voyage! ***sich – schätzen,*** count *or* consider o.s. lucky, congratulate o.s.; ***es – treffen,*** hit *or* strike it lucky; ***wenn ich – zurückkomme,*** if I return safe and sound *or* safely; ***– vonstatten gehen,*** come off *or* go well; (*Prov.*) ***dem Glücklichen schlägt keine Stunde,*** time passes quickly when one is happy. **glücklicherweise,** *adv.* by good fortune, fortunately, happily, luckily, mercifully, by a lucky chance, as luck would have it. **Glücksache,** *f.* matter of luck *or* chance.

Glücks|beutel, *m.* lucky dip. **-bote,** *m.*, **-botschaft,** *f.* glad tidings. **-bringer,** *m.* lucky mascot.

glückselig [glyk'ze:lɪç], *adj.* blissful, radiant, very happy, overjoyed, in ecstasies. **Glückseligkeit,** *f.* bliss, happiness, rapture, ecstasy.

Glücks|fall, *m.* lucky chance *or* (*coll.*) break, stroke of luck, windfall (*pl. oft. used as pl. of* **Glück**). **-göttin,** *f.* Fortune, Fortuna. **-güter,** *n.pl.* earthly goods *or* possessions, good things of this world, wealth. **-hafen,** *m.* safe port. **-kind,** *n.* Fortune's favourite, lucky person. **-klee,** *m.* four-leafed clover. **-pfennig,** *m.* lucky penny. **-pilz,** *m.* (*coll.*) lucky fellow, lucky chap, lucky dog. **-rad,** *n.* wheel of fortune. **-ritter,** *m.* adventurer, fortune-hunter. **-schweinchen,** *n.* lucky mascot. **-spiel,** *n.* game of chance *or* hazard, gamble. **-spinne,** *f.* money spider. **-stern,** *m.* lucky star. **-tag,** *m.* lucky *or* red-letter day.

glückstrahlend ['glykʃtra:lənt], *adj.* radiantly happy. **Glückssträhne,** *f.* streak of luck.

Glücks|treffer, *m.* stroke of luck. **-umstände,** *m.pl.* (*oft. used as pl. of* **Glück**) fortunate circumstances. **-wechsel,** *m.* vicissitude. **-wurf,** *m.* lucky shot *or* dip. **glückverheißend,** *adj.* propitious, auspicious, of good augury.

Glückwunsch ['glykvunʃ], *m.* congratulation, felicitation (***zu,*** on), good wishes (for), compliments (of the season); ***ihm seinen – abstatten*** or ***aussprechen,*** congratulate him; ***herzliche*** or ***beste Glückwünsche*** (***zu***), heartiest congratulations (on). **Glückwunschschreiben,** *n.* congratulatory letter.

Glüh|birne, *f.* (electric lamp) bulb. **-draht,** *m.* (electric) filament.

glühen ['gly:ən], **1.** *v.t.* make red-hot; anneal; mull (*wine*). **2.** *v.i.* glow, be red- *or* white-hot; (*fig.*) burn, glow, be aglow (***vor*** (*Dat.*), with). **glühend,** *adj.* glowing, incandescent, red- *or* white-hot; (*fig.*) glowing, burning, fiery, ardent, fervent, passionate, fervid; ***-e Hitze,*** scorching heat; ***-e Kohle,*** live coal; (*coll.*) ***wie auf -en Kohlen sitzen,*** be on thorns *or* tenter-hooks.

Glüh|faden, *m. See* **-draht. -frischen,** *n.* (*Metall.*) tempering. **-hitze,** *f.* red-heat, white-heat, (*fig.*) intense *or* scorching heat. **-kathodenröhre,** *f.* thermionic valve. **-kerze,** *f.*, **-kopf,** *m. See* **-zünder. -licht,** *n.* incandescent light. **-ofen,** *m.* annealing furnace. **-stahl,** *m.* malleable cast iron. **-strumpf,** *m.* incandescent mantle. **-wein,** *m.* mulled wine; negus. **-wind,** *m.* sirocco. **-wurm,** *m.*, **-würmchen,** *n.* glow-worm. **-zünder,** *m.* (*Motor.*) heater plug, hot bulb.

Glukose [glu'ko:zə], *f.* (*Chem.*) glucose.

glupen ['glu:pən], *v.i.* (*dial., coll.*) look sullen, scowl, lour, glower. **glupsch,** *adj.* (*dial., coll.*) sullen, louring, glowering, surly.

Glut [glu:t], *f.* (-, *pl.* **-en**) heat, glow, incandescence, glowing fire; (*fig.*) glow, fire, fervour, ardour, passion. **Glut|asche,** *f.* embers. **-auge,** *n.* fiery eye. **glutflüssig,** *adj.* molten, fused. **Glut|hauch,** *m.* scorching breath. **-hitze,** *f.* red *or* white heat. **-pfanne,** *f.* chafing-dish.

Glutt [glut], *m.* (*Orn.*) see **Grünschenkel.**

Glykose [gly'ko:zə], *f. See* **Glukose.**

Glypte ['glyptə], *f.* gem. **Glyptik,** *f.* gem-engraving, glyptography. **Glyptothek** [–'tɛ:k], *f.* (-, *pl.* **-en**) collection of gems; museum of antique sculpture.

Glyzerin [glytse'ri:n], *n.* (*Chem.*) glycerine.

Glyzine [gly'tsi:nə], *f.* (*Bot.*) wistaria (*Wistaria cinensis*).

Gnade ['gna:də], *f.* grace; clemency, mercy, (*Mil.*) quarter; favour; ***ihm auf – oder Ungnade ausgeliefert sein,*** be at his mercy; ***sich auf – oder Ungnade ergeben,*** surrender unconditionally; ***– für Recht ergehen lassen,*** temper justice with mercy; ***eine – erweisen*** or ***gewähren,*** grant a favour; ***Eure –n,*** your Honour, your Grace; ***– finden vor ihm,*** find favour in his eyes; ***von Gottes –n,*** by the grace of God; ***Königtum von Gottes –n,*** divine right of kings; (*obs.*) ***halten zu –n!*** if it pleases your Lordship! ***um – bitten,*** beg for mercy; ***in – stehen,*** be in favour. **gnaden,** *v.i.* (*Dat.*) (*obs.*) (*only in*) ***gnade uns Gott!*** God have mercy upon us!

Gnaden|akt, *m.* act of grace. **-beweis,** *m.*, **-bezeigung,** *f.* favour, grace. **-bild,** *n.* wonder-working *or* miraculous image, shrine. **-brief,** *m.* letter of pardon. **-brot,** *n.* bread of charity, pittance; ***– essen,*** live on sufferance. **-frist,** *f.* reprieve; respite, (days of) grace. **-gehalt, -geld,** *n.* allowance, gratuity. **-geschenk,** *n.* donation. **-gesuch,** *n.* appeal for mercy, petition for leniency *or* clemency.

-lohn, *m. See* **-gehalt. gnadenlos,** *adj.* relentless, merciless. **Gnaden|mittel,** *n.* (*Eccl.*) means of grace. **-ordnung,** *f.* (*Law*) rules of grace procedure. **-ort,** *m.* (*Eccl.*) place of pilgrimage. **gnadenreich,** *adj.* merciful, gracious. **Gnaden|-sold,** *m. See* **-gehalt. -stoß,** *m.* finishing stroke, death-blow, coup de grâce. **-tod,** *m.* mercy killing, euthanasia. **-wahl,** *f.* (*Eccl.*) predestination. **-weg,** *m. auf dem -,* as an act of grace. **-zeichen,** *n.* token of favour.

gnädig ['gnɛ:dɪç], *adj.* merciful, kind; favourable, gracious, condescending (*gegen,* to); lenient, mild (*as a verdict*); (*in title*) gracious; ***Gott sei uns -!*** God have mercy upon us! ***er ist noch - davongekommen,*** he got off easily *or* lightly; he has had a narrow escape; ***machen Sie es - mit ihm!*** do not be too hard on him! (*iron.*) ***du bist aber -!*** you are a nice one! ***-er Herr,*** Sir; ***-e Frau,*** Madam.

gnarren ['gnarən], *v.i.* (*dial.*) snarl; grizzle, whine.

gnatzig ['gnatsɪç], *adj.* (*coll.*) irritable, grumpy. **Gnatzkopf,** *m.* cross-patch.

gneisig ['gnaɪzɪç], *adj.* containing gneiss.

Gnom [gno:m], *m.* (**-en,** *pl.* **-en**) gnome.

Gnome ['gno:mə], *f.* maxim, apophthegm.

gnomenhaft ['gno:mənhaft], *adj.* dwarfish, misshapen.

Gnomiker ['gno:mɪkər], *m.* writer of sententious poetry. **gnomisch,** *adj.* sententious.

Gockel ['gɔkəl], *m.* (**-s, -**), **Gockelhahn,** *m.* (*dial.*) rooster, cock.

gokeln ['go:kəln], *v.i.* (*dial.*) play with fire.

Gold [gɔlt], *n.* gold; (*fig.*) ***nicht mit - zu bezahlen,*** invaluable, priceless; (*Prov.*) ***es ist nicht alles -, was glänzt,*** all is not gold that glitters; (*Prov.*) ***eigener Herd ist -es wert,*** there's no place like home; (*Prov.*) ***Morgenstunde hat - im Munde,*** the early bird catches the worm.

Gold|ader, *f.* 1. vein of gold; 2. (*Med.*) haemorrhoidal vein. **-adler,** *m.* (*Orn.*) *see* **Steinadler. -ammer,** *f.* (*Orn.*) yellow-hammer (*Emberiza citrinella*). **-anstrich,** *m.* gilding. **-apfel,** *m.* golden pippin. **-arbeiter,** *m.* goldsmith. **-barren,** *m.* gold ingot, bullion. **-barsch,** *m.* (*Ichth.*) ruff. **-bestand,** *m.* gold reserve. **-blatt, -blättchen,** *n.* gold foil *or* leaf. **-blockländer,** *n.pl.* hard-currency area. **-borte,** *f.* gold lace. **goldbraun,** *adj.* chestnut, auburn. **Gold|butt,** *m.* (*Ichth.*) plaice. **-drossel,** *f.* (*Orn.*) *see* **Erddrossel. -druck,** *m.* gold *or* gilt lettering.

golden ['gɔldən], *adj.* gold, golden; gilded, gilt; ***er ist noch - gegen seinen Bruder,*** he is an angel compared with his brother; ***-e Berge versprechen,*** promise the earth; ***sich*** (*Dat.*) ***-e Berge versprechen,*** cherish exaggerated hopes, expect to find Tom Tiddler's ground; ***-e Brille,*** gold-rimmed spectacles; ***dem Feinde -e Brücken bauen,*** leave a way open for reconciliation, leave a loophole open; (*sl.*) ***-e Füchse,*** gold pieces, yellow-boys; ***-es Haar,*** golden hair; ***-es Herz,*** heart of gold; ***-e Hochzeit,*** golden wedding; ***der -e Mittelweg,*** the golden mean; ***-e Regel,*** golden rule (*Matt.* 7. 12: *whatsoever ye would that men should do to you, do ye even so to them*); (*Math.*) ***der -e Schnitt,*** sectio aurea ($AB:AC = AC:BC$); ***-e Uhr,*** gold watch; ***-e Zeit,*** golden *or* idyllic age.

Gold|erde, *f.* auriferous earth. **-erz,** *n.* gold ore. **-feder,** *f.* gold nib. **-finger,** *m.* ring-finger. **-firnis,** *m.* gold size. **-fisch,** *m.* goldfish; (*coll.*) rich heiress. **-flimmer,** *m.* gold dust *or* grains (*as found in alluvial deposits*). **-flitter,** *m.* gold spangle, tinsel. **-fuchs,** *m.* yellow-dun horse; (*sl.*) gold coin. **goldführend,** *adj.* gold-bearing, auriferous. **Gold|gefäße,** *n.pl. See* **-geschirr. -gehalt,** *m.* gold content, percentage of gold. **goldgelb,** *adj.* golden (coloured), golden yellow. **Gold|geschirr,** *n.* gold plate. **-gespinst,** *n.* spun gold. **-gewicht,** *n.* troy weight. **-gewinn,** *m.* gold-output. **-gewinnung,** *f.* gold production. **-glanz,** *m.* golden lustre *or* sheen. **-grieß,** *m.* gold-dust. **-grube,** *f.* gold-mine; (*also fig. = highly profitable undertaking*), bonanza. **-grund,** *m.* gold size. **-haar,** *n.* golden hair; (*Bot.*) goldilocks. **-hähnchen,** *n.* 1. (*Orn.*) ***feuerköpfiges -,*** *see* **Sommergoldhähnchen**; ***gelbköpfiges -,*** *see* **Wintergoldhähnchen**; 2. (*Bot.*) yellow anemone. **-hähnchenlaubsänger,** *m.* (*Orn.*) Pallas's warbler (*Phylloscopus proregulus*). **goldhaltig,** *adj.* containing gold, gold-bearing, auriferous.

goldig ['gɔldɪç], *adj.* 1. golden (*colour*); 2. (*coll.*) sweet, precious, darling.

Gold|käfer, *m.* rose-chafer, gold-beetle. **-kies,** *m.* auriferous pyrites. **-kind,** *n.* sweet child, darling, cherub. **-klumpen,** *m.* nugget, gold ingot. **-lack,** *m.* 1. gold varnish; 2. (*Bot.*) wallflower (*Cheiranthus cheiri*). **-legierung,** *f.* gold alloy. **-leim,** *m.* gold size. **-leiste,** *f.* gilt cornice. **-macher,** *m.* alchemist. **-macherei, -macherkunst,** *f.* alchemy. **-milz,** *f.* (*Bot.*) golden saxifrage (*Chrysosplenium alternifolium*). **-münze,** *f.* gold coin; gold medal. **-niederschlag,** *m.* precipitate of gold. **-plattierung,** *f.* goldplating. **-pressung,** *f.* (*Bookb.*) gilt tooling. **-probe,** *f.* gold assay. **-rahmen,** *m.* gilt frame. **-regen,** *m.* (*Bot.*) laburnum (*Cytisus laburnum*). **-regenpfeifer,** *m.* (*Orn.*) (*Am.* Eurasian) golden plover (*Charadrius apricarius*); ***sibirischer -,*** Asiatic (*Am.* Pacific) golden plover (*Charadrius dominicus fulvus*). **-rute,** *f.* (*Bot.*) golden rod (*Solidago virga-aurea*). **-schaum,** *m.* gold leaf; tinsel. **-scheider,** *m.* gold-refiner. **-scheidewasser,** *n.* aqua regia. **-schlag,** *m.* gold leaf, gold foil. **-schläger,** *m.* gold-beater. **-schlägerhaut,** *f.* gold-beater's skin. **-schmied,** *m.* goldsmith. **-schnäpper,** *m.* (*Orn.*) Narcissus fly-catcher (*Ficedula narcissina*). **-schnitt,** *m.* gilt edge (*of a book*). **-stein,** *m.* chrysolite, olivine. **-stoff,** *m.* gold brocade; tinsel. **-stück,** *n.* gold coin *or* piece. **-stufe,** *f.* piece of gold ore. **-sucher,** *m.* prospector, gold-digger. **-tresse,** *f.* gold lace. **-waage,** *f.* gold-balance; (*coll.*) ***er legt jedes Wort auf die -,*** he weighs every word; ***du mußt nicht jedes Wort auf die - legen,*** you must take it with a pinch of salt. **-währung,** *f.* gold standard. **-waren,** *f.pl.* jewellery. **-wasser,** *n.* choice Danzig brandy, gold cordial. **-wolf,** *m.* jackal.

[1]**Golf** [gɔlf], *m.* (**-(e)s,** *pl.* **-e**) gulf.

[2]**Golf,** *n.* golf (*game*). **Golf|hose,** *f.* plus-fours. **-junge,** *m.* caddie. **-platz,** *m.* golf links. **-spiel,** *n. See* [2]**Golf. -spieler,** *m.* golfer.

Golfstrom ['gɔlfʃtro:m], *m.* the Gulf Stream.

Goller ['gɔlər], *m. See* **Koller.**

Göller ['gœlər], *m.* (*Swiss*) collar.

gölte ['gœltə], *see* **gelten.**

Gondel ['gɔndəl], *f.* (**-,** *pl.* **-n**) gondola; nacelle (*of an aircraft*). **Gondelführer,** *m.,* (*Austr.*) **Gondelier** [-'li:r], *m.* gondolier. **gondeln,** *v.i.* go in a gondola; (*coll.*) travel, cruise, go.

Gong [gɔŋ], *m. or n.* (**-s,** *pl.* **-s**) gong. **gongen,** *v.i.* sound *or* strike the gong. **Gongschlag,** *m.* sound *or* stroke of the gong.

gönnen ['gœnən], *v.t.* (*ihm etwas*) not to (be)-grudge, allow, grant, permit; ***nicht -,*** envy, grudge; ***ich gönne es dir von Herzen,*** I'm delighted for your sake; (*iron.*) it serves you right, much good may it do you; ***- Sie mir die Ehre Ihres Besuches,*** favour me with a visit; ***- Sie mir das Wort,*** permit me to speak. **Gönner,** *m.* patron, protector; well-wisher. **gönnerhaft,** *adj.* patronizing. **Gönnerschaft,** *f.* support, protection, patronage.

Göpel ['gø:pəl], *m.* winch; capstan; horse-gin, whim. **Göpel|hund,** *m.* whim-beam. **-knecht,** *m.* whim-stopper. **-rad,** *n.* pulley.

gor [go:r], *see* **gären.**

Gör [gø:r], *n.* (**-(e)s,** *pl.* **-en**) kid, urchin, brat.

gordisch ['gɔrdɪʃ], *adj.* ***der -e Knoten,*** the Gordian knot.

göre ['gø:rə], *see* **gären.**

Göre, *f. See* **Gör.**

Gösch [gœʃ], *f.* (**-,** *pl.* **-en**) (*Naut.*) jack (*small flag*); inset (*in a flag*). **Göschstock,** *m.* jackstaff.

Gose ['go:zə], *f.* Goslar-beer, pale and light ale.

goß [gɔs], **gösse** ['gœsə], *see* **gießen.**

Gosse [ˈɡɔsə], *f.* gutter, drain; ***ihn aus der – auflesen,*** rescue him from the gutter. **Gossenstein,** *m.* sink (*in a kitchen*).

Gote [ˈɡoːtə], *m.* (**-n,** *pl.* **-n**) Goth. **Gotik,** *f.* Gothic (style *or* architecture). **gotisch,** *adj.* Gothic; ***-e Schrift,*** Gothic *or* black-letter type.

Gott [ɡɔt], *m.* (**-es,** *pl.* **¨-er**) God; god, deity; ***ein Anblick für die Götter,*** a sight for the gods; ***– der Allmächtige,*** God *or* the Almighty; ***bei –!*** by God! I swear; ***– befohlen!*** good-bye! adieu! ***– bewahre*** or ***behüte!*** God *or* heaven forbid! not if I can help it; ***– sei Dank!*** thank God! thank goodness; (*as adv.*) fortunately, mercifully; (*coll.*) ***leben wie – in Frankreich,*** live like a king, be in clover; ***– gebe!*** God grant! ***von -es Gnaden,*** by the grace of God; ***großer –!*** great Scot! good heavens! (*dial.*) ***grüß' (dich) –!*** good day! ***so wahr mir – helfe!*** so help me God! ***– der Herr,*** our Lord God; ***Herr –!*** good gracious! ***leider -es!*** alas! sad to say, unfortunately; (*coll.*) ***den lieben – einen guten Mann sein lassen,*** not to worry about anything, trust in providence, let things take care of themselves *or* slide; ***mein –!*** good Heavens! ***O mein –!*** O God! ***– steh' uns bei!*** God help us; ***in -es Namen!*** for Heaven's sake! ***ganz von – verlassen,*** out of one's mind *or* senses; (*Prov.*) ***-es Wege sind wunderbar,*** the ways of Providence are strange; ***weiß –!*** God knows! ***– weiß wann,*** God (only) knows when; ***will's –! so – will!*** please God! ***um -es Willen,*** heaven forbid! for heaven's sake! ***wollte –!*** would to God! ***das Wort -es,*** the word of God, the Word.

gott|ähnlich, *adj.* godlike, divine. **-begnadet,** *adj.* divinely inspired.

Götter [ˈɡœtər], *pl. of* **Gott.**

Götter|bild, *n.* image of a god, idol, god-like figure. **-bote,** *m.* messenger of the gods, Mercury, Hermes. **-burg,** *f.* Valhalla. **-dämmerung,** *f.* twilight of the gods. **-dienst,** *m.* polytheism. **-funken,** *m.* divine spark.

gottergeben [ˈɡɔtˀɛrɡeːbən], *adj.* resigned to God's will, devout, pious.

Göttergestalt [ˈɡœtərɡəʃtalt], *f.* divine form. **göttergleich,** *adj.* divine, godlike, godly. **Götter|-lehre,** *f.* mythology. **-mahl,** *n.* feast for the gods. **-sage,** *f.* myth. **-sitz,** *m.* abode of the gods, Olympus. **-speise,** *f.* (*Myth.*) food of the gods, ambrosia, (*coll.*) trifle with whipped cream. **-spruch,** *m.* oracle. **-trank,** *m.* (*Myth.*) nectar. **-welt,** *f.* the gods; Olympus. **-wort,** *n.* oracle. **-zeichen,** *n.* omen, augury.

Gottes|acker, *m.* graveyard, churchyard. **-anbeterin,** *f.* (*Ent.*) praying mantis. **-dienst,** *m.* divine service, public worship. **-erde,** *f.* the earth; consecrated ground. **-furcht,** *f.* fear of God, piety. **gottesfürchtig,** *adj.* pious; God-fearing. **-gabe,** *f.* heaven-sent gift, godsend. **-gelehrsamkeit,** *f.* divinity, theology. **-gelehrte(r),** *m., f.* divine, theologian. **-gericht,** *n.* 1. divine judgement; 2. ordeal. **-glaube,** *m.* belief in God, theism. **-gnadentum,** *n.* divine right (of kings). **-haus,** *n.* place of worship, house of God, church, chapel. **-lästerer,** *m.* blasphemer. **gotteslästerlich,** *adj.* blasphemous. **Gottes|lästerung,** *f.* blasphemy. **-leugner,** *m.* atheist. **-leugnung,** *f.* atheism. **-lohn,** *m.* ***um einen –,*** for the love of God, for charity, for no reward. **-staat,** *m.* theocracy. **-urteil,** *n. See* **-gericht.**

Gottfried [ˈɡɔtfriːt], *m.* Godfrey, Geoffrey.

gottgefällig [ˈɡɔtɡəfɛlɪç], *adj.* pious. **Gott|gefälligkeit,** *f.* piety. **-gesandte(r),** *m.* the Messiah. **-gläubige,** *pl.* followers of modern German cult of pseudo-Humanism, a form of non-Christian theism.

Gotthard [ˈɡɔthart], *m.* Goddard; ***St. –,*** St. Gothard.

Gottheit [ˈɡɔthaɪt], *f.* deity; divinity; godhead.

Gotthold [ˈɡɔthɔlt], *m. See* **Gottlieb.**

Göttin [ˈɡœtɪn], *f.* goddess.

göttlich [ˈɡœtlɪç], *adj.* divine, godlike, heavenly; (*coll.*) divine, heavenly, capital, splendid. **Göttlichkeit,** *f.* divinity, godliness.

Gottlieb [ˈɡɔtliːp], *m.* Theophilus.

gottlob! [ˈɡɔtloːp], *int.* thank God! thank goodness! **gottlos,** *adj.* irreligious, ungodly, godless; wicked, impious, sinful; (*coll. of a th.*) ungodly, unholy, awful. **Gottlosigkeit,** *f.* ungodliness. **Gott|-mensch,** *m.* God incarnate, Christ. **-seibeiuns,** *m.* the devil, Old Nick. **gottselig,** *adj.* godly, pious; blessed. **Gottseligkeit,** *f.* godliness, piety. **gott|sträflich,** *adv.* (*coll.*) awfully. **-vergessen,** *adj.* ungodly, impious; (*coll.*) godforsaken, miserable, wretched. **-verhaßt,** *adj.* abominable, odious. **-verlassen,** *adj.* godforsaken. **-voll,** *adj.* (*coll.*) heavenly, priceless, splendid, capital, funny, too good to be true.

Götz [ɡœts], *m.* (*dim. of*) **Gottfried.**

Götze [ˈɡœtsə], *m.* (**-n,** *pl.* **-n**) idol, false god, heathen *or* pagan deity. **Götzen|bild,** *n.* graven image, idol. **-diener,** *m.* idolator. **-dienst,** *m.* idolatry. **-opfer,** *n.* an idolatrous sacrifice. **-zertrümmerer,** *m.* iconoclast.

Goudron [ɡuˈdrɔ̃], *m.* asphalt.

Gouvernante [ɡuvɛrˈnantə], *f.* governess; (*dial.*) manageress. **Gouvernement** [-əˈmɑ̃], *n.* (**-s,** *pl.* **-s**) government, province. **Gouverneur,** *m.* (**-s,** *pl.* **-e**) governor, commandant.

Grab [ɡraːp], *n.* (**-(e)s,** *pl.* **¨-er**) grave, tomb, sepulchre; (*fig.*) death, destruction, ruin; ***am -e,*** at the graveside; ***bis ins –,*** unto *or* till death; ***ihn ins – bringen,*** cause his death; (*coll.*) ***sie bringt mich noch ins –,*** she will be the death of me; ***ein feuchtes*** or ***nasses –,*** a watery grave; ***ihn zu -e geleiten,*** attend his funeral; ***die Kirche des heiligen -es,*** Church of the Holy Sepulchre; ***er nimmt sein Geheimnis mit ins –,*** he carries his secret with him to the grave; ***am Rande des -es*** or ***mit einem Bein*** or ***Fuß im -e stehen,*** have one foot in the grave, be at death's door; ***er gräbt*** or ***schaufelt sich*** (*Dat.*) ***selbst sein –,*** he is digging his own grave; ***ihn*** (or ***eine Hoffnung***) ***zu -e tragen,*** bury him (*or* one's hopes); ***über das – hinaus,*** beyond the grave; ***verschwiegen*** or ***schweigsam wie das –,*** secret *or* silent as the grave.

grabbeln [ˈɡrabəln], *v.i.* (*dial.*) grope, fumble (***nach,*** for), grab (at).

graben [ˈɡraːbən], **1.** *irr.v.t.* dig (*a grave, hole etc.*), sink (*a shaft or well*), dig (out), excavate (*foundations etc.*); engrave, cut (*in metal etc.*). **2.** *irr.v.i.* dig (***nach,*** for); dig *or* cut a trench *or* ditch, trench; ***ihm eine Grube –,*** lay a snare for him; (*Prov.*) ***wer andern eine Grube gräbt, fällt selbst hinein,*** the biter bit, (the engineer) hoist with his own petard; ***Kartoffeln –,*** dig potatoes; ***es ist mir ins Gedächtnis gegraben,*** it is engraved *or* imprinted *or* impressed on my mind *or* memory.

Graben, *m.* (**-s,** *pl.* **¨-**) ditch, (*also Mil.*) trench, (*of castle*) moat; dike, drain, culvert, canal; (*Geol.*) rift valley; (*Mil.*) ***vorderster –,*** front-line trench; ***zweiter –,*** support trench; ***dritter –,*** reserve trench. **Graben|bagger,** *m.* excavator, mechanical digger. **-bekleidung,** *f.* revetment. **-böschung,** *f.* counter-scarp. **-kampf,** *m.* trench-fighting. **-krieg,** *m.* trench warfare. **-mörser,** *m.* (*Mil.*) trench mortar. **-rost,** *n.* duck-board. **-schere,** *f.* tenaille. **-sohle,** *f.* trench bottom. **-stufe,** *f.* (*Mil.*) firestep, berm. **-wehr,** *f.* parapet.

[1]**Gräber** [ˈɡrɛːbər], *pl. of* **Grab.**

[2]**Gräber,** *m.* 1. digger, ditcher; 2. graving tool.

Gräber|dienst, *m.* War Graves Commission. **-fund,** *m.* relics (of *or* in a tomb).

Grabes|dunkel, *n.* sepulchral darkness. **-ruhe, -stille,** *f.* deathly *or* deathlike silence. **-stimme,** *f.* sepulchral voice.

Grab|geläut(e), *n.* (death-)knell. **-geleite,** *n.* funeral procession. **-gerüst,** *n.* catafalque. **-gesang,** *m.* dirge. **-gewölbe,** *n.* tomb, vault. **-hügel,** *m.* mound, tumulus. **-legung,** *f.* burial, interment, funeral. **-lied,** *n. See* **-gesang. -mal,** *n.* (**-s,** *pl.* **-male** *or* **-mäler**) sepulchre, tomb; monument. **-platte,** *f. See* **-stein. -rede,** *f.* funeral oration. **-schändung,** *f.* desecration of graves. **-scheit, n.** spade. **-schrift,** *f.* epitaph.

gräbst [ɡrɛːpst], *see* **graben.**

Grab|stätte, *f.* burial place, grave, tomb. **–stein,** *m.* gravestone, tombstone. **–stelle,** *f. See* **-stätte. –stichel,** *m* graver, graving tool.

gräbt [grɛ:pt], *see* **graben.**

Grabtuch ['gra:ptu:x], *n.* shroud, winding sheet, pall. **Grabung,** *f.* excavation. **Graburne,** *f.* funeral urn.

Gracchen ['graxən], *pl.* (*Hist.*) (the) Gracchi.

Gracht [graxt], *f.* (-, *pl.* **-en**) (*dial.*) ditch, drain, canal.

Grad [gra:t], *m.* (**-(e)s,** *pl.* **-e**) degree (*also Univ.*); rank, grade, stage; (*fig.*) degree, extent; (*Math.*) power; ***eine Verbrennung zweiten –es,*** second-degree burn; ***ein Vetter zweiten –es,*** second cousin; ***ein Winkel von 30 –,*** an angle of 30°; ***Wärme von 30 – Celsius,*** temperature of 30° centigrade; ***unter 30 – nördlicher Breite,*** latitude 30° N.; ***in hohem –e,*** highly, greatly, largely, extraordinarily; ***im höchsten –,*** exceedingly; ***im höchsten – zerstreut,*** absent-minded to a degree; ***bis zu einem gewissen –e,*** to a certain extent, up to a point; ***hoher – der Kultur,*** high level of civilization; ***der höchste – der Dummheit,*** the height of folly. *See also under* **Gleichung. Gradabzeichen,** *m.* (*Mil.*) badge of rank.

Gradation [gradatsi'o:n], *f.* gradation; (*Gram.*) comparison.

Grad|bogen, *m.* protractor, sextant. **–buch,** *n.* nautical almanac. **–einteilung,** *f.* graduation, scale. **–feld,** *n.* map square.

gradieren [gra'di:rən], *v.t.* refine (*gold*); graduate (*salt*). **Gradierung,** *f.* graduation. **Gradier|-waage,** *f.* areometer, hydrometer. **–werk,** *n.* graduation house (*salt*), (*Elec.*) cooling tower.

Grädigkeit ['grɛ:dıçkaıt], *f.* (*Chem.*) concentration, density.

Gradleiter ['gra:tlaıtər], *f.* (graduated) scale. **gradlinig,** *adj. See* **gerade. Grad|messer,** *m.* graduator, (*fig.*) indicator, indication. **–netz,** *n.* grid (*maps*).

Gradual [gradu'a:l], *n.* (**-s,** *pl.* **-e**) (*R.C.*) gradual, grail.

graduell [gradu'ɛl], *adj.* gradual.

graduieren [gradu'i:rən], *v.i.* graduate, take a *or* one's degree. **Graduierte(r),** *m., f.* graduate (*of a university*).

gradweise ['gra:tvaızə], *adv.* gradually, by degrees. **Gradzahl,** *f.* compass-bearing, direction.

Graf [gra:f], *m.* (**-en,** *pl.* **-en**) earl (*in England*), count (*foreign*); ***– und Gräfin W.,*** the Earl and Countess of W. **Grafenstand,** *m.* earldom.

Gräfin ['grɛ:fın], *f.* countess. **gräflich,** *adj.* of *or* belonging to an earl *or* count.

Grafschaft ['gra:fʃaft], *f.* 1. shire, county; 2. earldom.

Gral [gra:l], *m.* grail; (the) Sangreal, Holy Grail.

Gram [gra:m], *m.* grief, sorrow, affliction, sadness, melancholy; ***vor – vergehen,*** pine away; (*coll.*) ***er hat den –,*** he's (down) in the dumps, he has a fit of the blues *or* the miseries. **gram,** *pred.adj.* ***ihm – sein,*** be angry *or* cross with him, bear him ill-will *or* a grudge, have a grievance against him.

grämen ['grɛ:mən], **1.** *v.t.* grieve, worry, upset. (*usu.*) **2.** *v.r.* (***über*** (*Acc.*)) grieve (for *or* over *or* at), worry *or* fret (about *or* over), take to heart; ***sich zu Tode –,*** die of grief *or* of a broken heart, be broken-hearted.

gram|erfüllt, *adj.* grieved, sorrowful. **–gebeugt,** *adj.* bowed down with grief, grief-stricken, broken-hearted. **–gefurcht,** *adj.* careworn.

grämlich ['grɛ:mlıç], *adj.* peevish, morose, sullen, gloomy.

Gramm [gram], *n.* (**-s,** *pl.* **-e**) (*abbr.* **g.**) gram(me).

Grammatik [gra'matık], *f.* (-, *pl.* **-en**) grammar. **grammatikalisch** [–'ka:lıʃ], *adj.* grammatical. **Grammatiker,** *m.* grammarian. **grammatisch,** *adj. See* **grammatikalisch.**

Grammophon [gramo'fo:n], *n.* (**-s,** *pl.* **-e**) gramophone. **Grammophon|anschluß,** *m.* gramophone pick-up. **–platte,** *f.* (gramophone) record.

gramvoll ['gra:mvɔl], *adj.* sorrowful, grief-stricken, woebegone, careworn.

Gran [gra:n], *n.* (*Austr. m.*), **Grän,** *n.* (**-(e)s,** *pl.* **-e**) (*Pharm.*) grain.

Granalien [gra'na:liən], *f.pl.* (*Metall.*) granulated metal.

Granat [gra'na:t], *m.* 1. (**-(e)s,** *pl.* **-e** *or* **-en**) garnet (*jewel*); 2. (**-(e)s,** *pl.* **-e**) (*dial.*) shrimp. **Granat|-apfel,** *m.* pomegranate. **–baum,** *m.* pomegranate tree.

Granate [gra'na:tə], *f.* (*Mil.*) grenade, shell.

Granat|feuer, *n.* shellfire, shelling. **–hülse,** *f.* shell-case. **–loch,** *n. See* **–tricher. –splitter,** *m.* shell splinter. **–stein,** *m. See* **Granat,** 1. **–trichter,** *m.* shell crater *or* hole. **–werfer,** *m.* (*Mil.*) (trench) mortar.

Grand [grant], *m.* fine gravel, coarse sand.

Grande ['grandə], *m.* (**-n,** *pl.* **-n**) grandee.

Grandezza [gran'dɛtsa], *f.* sententiousness, solemn gravity, grandeur.

grandig ['grandıç], *adj.* gravelly.

grandios [grandi'o:s], *adj.* grand, grandiose, splendid, magnificent.

granieren [gra'ni:rən], *v.t. See* **granulieren.**

Granit [gra'nıt], *m.* (**-(e)s,** *pl.* **-e**) granite; (*coll.*) ***da beißt er auf –,*** he is running his head against a brick wall. **granitartig, graniten,** *adj.* granitic.

Granne ['granə], *f.* awn, beard, arista (*of corn*); whiskers (*of a cat*); bristle. **grannig,** *adj.* bearded.

Grans [grans], *m.* (**-es,** *pl.* **⸚e**), **Gransen** ['granzən], *m.* (*dial.*) bow (*of a ship*).

grantig ['grantıç], *adj.* (*coll.*) bad-tempered, surly, cross, irritable, peevish.

granulieren [granu'li:rən], *v.t.* granulate, pulverize. **granulös,** *adj.* granular.

Graphik ['gra:fık], *f.* (-, *pl.* **-en**) graphic arts. **Graphiker,** *m.* commercial artist, illustrator. **graphisch, 1.** *adj.* graphic; ***–e Darstellung,*** graphic representation, diagram, chart, graph; ***–e Farbe,*** printing ink, poster colour; ***–e Kunstanstalt,*** art printers. **2.** *adv.* graphically.

Graphit [gra'fi:t], *m.* graphite, black lead, plumbago. **Graphit|schmiere,** *f.* graphite lubricant. **–spitze,** *f.* carbon (*of arc lamp*).

Graphologe [grafo'lo:gə], *m.* (**-n,** *pl.* **-n**) graphologist, hand-writing expert.

grapschen ['grapʃən], **grapsen** ['grapsən], *v.t., v.i.* (*coll.*) snatch, grab, clutch (***nach,*** at).

Gras [gra:s], *n.* (**-es,** *pl.* **⸚er**) grass; (*coll.*) ***ins – beißen,*** bite the dust; (*coll.*) ***er hört das – wachsen,*** he thinks he is very clever, he fancies himself, he is a know-all; ***darüber ist (viel) – gewachsen,*** that is all forgotten, that is a th. of the past, that's dead and buried; ***ins – tun,*** put out to grass.

Gras|affe, *m.* young fool, stupid youngster. **–anger,** *m.* grass-plot, green. **–art,** *f.* kind *or* species of grass. **gras|artig,** *adj.* gramineous, graminaceous, herbaceous. **–bewachsen,** *adj.* grass-grown. **Grasebene,** *f.* grassy plain, prairie, steppe, savanna.

grasen ['gra:zən], *v.i.* graze (*of animals*); cut *or* mow grass; (*fig.*) ***nach einer S. –,*** aspire to a th.; (*fig.*) ***in einer S. –,*** steep o.s. in *or* satisfy o.s. with a th.

Grasfleck ['gra:sflɛk], *m.* 1. grass plot; 2. grass-stain. **grasfressend,** *adj.* herbivorous, graminivorous. **Gras|fresser,** *m.* (*Zool.*) graminivore. **–fütterung,** *f.* grass-feeding. **grasgrün,** *n.* grass-green. **Gras|halm,** *m.* blade of grass. **–hüpfer,** *m.* (*dial.*) grasshopper.

grasig ['gra:zıç], *adj.* grassy, grass-grown.

Gras|land, *n.* meadow-land, grassland. **–läufer,** *m.* (*Orn.*) buff-breasted sandpiper (*Tryngitis subruficollis*). **–mäher,** *m.,* **–mähmaschine,** *f.* grass-cutter, lawnmower. **–milbe,** *f.* harvest-tick *or* bug. **–mücke,** *f.* (*Orn.*) (bird of the) warbler (family) (*Silviidae*). *See* **Mönchsgrasmücke, Gartengrasmücke, Dorngrasmücke, Klappergrasmücke. –platz,** *m.* grass-plot, lawn, green.

graß [ɡraːs], *adj.* (*obs.*) *see* **gräßlich.**
Gras|schnecke, *f.* slug. **–scholle,** *f.* turf, sod, sward.
grassieren [ɡra'siːrən], *v.i.* prevail, spread, rage, be rampant; *–de Krankheit,* epidemic (disease).
gräßlich ['ɡrɛslɪç], *adj.* terrible, dreadful, frightful, awful, horrible, hideous, ghastly, atrocious, monstrous, heinous.
Gras|steppe, *f. See* **–ebene. –stück,** *n. See* **–platz. Grasung,** *f.* grazing. **Gras|weide,** *f.* pasture(-land). **–wirtschaft,** *f.* dairy farming.
Grat [ɡraːt], *m.* (**-es,** *pl.* **-e**) (sharp) edge; ridge, crest (*of a mountain*); roof-tree; wire edge, burr (*on metal*), (*Carp.*) tongue, (*Archit.*) arris, groin. **Grat|balken,** *m.* arris beam. **–bogen,** *m.* cross springer.
Gräte ['ɡrɛːtə], *f.* fish-bone. **gräten,** *v.i.* remove fish-bones. **Gräten|muster,** *n.* herringbone pattern. **–schritt,** *m.* herringbone step (*in ski-ing*).
Gratial(e) [ɡratsi'aːl(ə)], *n.* (**-s,** *pl.* **-e** *or* **-en**) thank offering, thanksgiving, donation; gratuity. **Gratias,** *n.* grace, thanksgiving; *das – sprechen,* return thanks.
Gratifikation [ɡratifikatsi'oːn], *f.* bonus, supplement, gratuity, ex gratia payment.
grätig ['ɡrɛːtɪç], *adj.* 1. full of fish-bones, bony; 2. (*Swiss*) *see* **grantig.**
gratis ['ɡraːtis], *adv.* free of charge, gratis. **Gratis|aktie,** *f.* bonus share. **–beilage,** *f.* free supplement. **–exemplar,** *n.* presentation copy, specimen copy. **–muster,** *n.* free sample.
Grätsche ['ɡrɛːtʃə], *f.* straddle, splits. **grätschen,** *v.i.* straddle, do the splits.
Gratulant [ɡratu'lant], *m.* (**-en,** *pl.* **-en**) well-wisher, congratulator. **Gratulation** [–tsi'oːn], *f.* congratulation. **Gratulationsschreiben,** *n.* congratulatory letter. **gratulieren,** *v.i.* *ihm zu etwas –*, congratulate him on a th.
grau [ɡrau], *adj.* grey, (*Am.*) gray; grizzled (*hair*); gloomy, dismal, sombre; venerable, ancient; *–er Alltag,* drab monotony, everyday routine; *–es Altertum,* remote *or* hoary antiquity; *–er Bär,* grizzly bear; (*coll.*) *das –e Elend,* hangover; *–e Gehirnsubstanz,* grey matter; (*coll.*) *darüber lasse ich mir keine –en Haare wachsen,* I do not trouble my head about that; I shan't lose any sleep over it; *– in – malen,* paint in the darkest colours, paint a gloomy *or* black picture; *–e Vorzeit,* prehistoric time, the dim distant past; *seit –er Vorzeit,* from time immemorial; *–e Zeiten,* olden time(s), times of yore; *–e Zukunft,* dim future. **Grau,** *n. See* **Grau(e).**
Grau|ammer, *f.* (*Orn.*) corn-bunting (*Emberiza calandra*). **–bart,** *m.* greybeard. **grau|blau,** *adj.* greyish-blue, slate-blue. **–braun,** *adj.* dun. **Grau|braunstein,** *m.* manganite. **–brot,** *n.* brown bread. **–bruststrandläufer,** *m.* (*Orn.*) pectoral sandpiper (*Calidris melanotus*). **–bürzelwasserläufer,** *m.* (*Orn.*) grey-rumped sandpiper (*Heteroscelus brevipes*).
Graubünden [ɡrau'byndən], *n.* (*Geog.*) the Grisons. **Graubündner,** *m.* inhabitant of the Grisons. **graubündnerisch,** *adj.* of the Grisons.
Grauchen ['ɡrauçən], *n.* Neddy (*pet name for a donkey*).
Grau(e) ['ɡrau(ə)], *n.* grey colour.
[1]**grauen** ['ɡrauən], *v.i.* 1. grow grey; 2. dawn, be dawning.
[2]**grauen,** *v.i. imp.* (*Dat.*); *es graut mir vor* (*Dat.*), I have a horror of *or* have an aversion to, I dread, I am afraid of, I shudder at; *es graut mir, wenn ich daran denke,* I shudder to think of it.
[1]**Grauen,** *n.* dawn(ing), daybreak.
[2]**Grauen,** *n.* horror, dread (*vor,* of).
grauenhaft ['ɡrauənhaft], **grauenvoll,** *adj.* horrible, awful, dreadful, ghastly, gruesome, (*coll.*) horrid.
Grau|fischer, *m.* (*Orn.*) pied kingfisher (*Ceryle rudis*). **–gans,** *f.* (*Orn.*) greylag goose (*Anser anser*). **–guß,** *m.* cast iron. **grauhaarig,** *adj.* grizzled, grey-haired.
graulen ['ɡraulən], **1.** *v.r.* (*coll.*) be afraid (*vor* (*Dat.*), of), have the creeps (at) (*esp. of ghosts, the dark etc.*). **2.** *v.imp.* (*coll.*) *see* [2]**grauen.**
[1]**graulich** ['ɡraulɪç], *adj.* horrifying, terrifying.
[2]**graulich, gräulich** ['ɡrɔylɪç], *adj.* greyish, grizzled.
Graupappel ['ɡraupapəl], *f.* (*Bot.*) white poplar.
Graupe ['ɡraupə], *f.* hulled grain, pearl barley, groats.
Graupel ['ɡraupəl], *f.* (-, *pl.* **-n**) (*usu. pl.*) sleet, hail. **graupelig,** *adj.* granular; sleety. **graupeln,** *v.i., imp.* sleet, hail; *es graupelt,* it is hailing, sleet is falling.
Graupen|grütze, *f.* barley groats. **–schleim,** *m.* barley water.
graurötlich ['ɡraurøːtlɪç], *adj.* sorrel, roan (*horse*).
[1]**Graus** [ɡraus], *m.* coarse sand, gravel, rubble; *in – zerfallen,* fall into decay.
[2]**Graus,** *m.* horror, dread.
grausam ['ɡrauzaːm], *adj.* cruel (*gegen,* to), inhuman, ferocious, fierce, (*coll.*) awful, horrible. **Grausamkeit,** *f.* cruelty, ferocity; atrocity.
Grau|schimmel, *m.* grey horse. **–schnäpper,** *m.* (*Orn.*) spotted flycatcher (*Muscicapa striata*).
grausen ['ɡrauzən], **Grausen,** *see* [2]**grauen,** [2]**Grauen.**
grausig ['ɡrauzɪç], *adj. See* **grauenhaft.**
Grau|specht, *m.* (*Orn.*) grey-headed woodpecker (*Picus canus*). **–tier,** *n.* donkey, ass. **–wacke,** *f.* (*Geol.*) greywacke. **–werk,** *n.* (Siberian) squirrel skin, miniver.
Gravelingen ['ɡravəlɪŋən], *n.*(*Geog.*) Gravelines.
Graveur [ɡra'vøːr], *m.* (**-s,** *pl.* **-e**) engraver. **gravieren,** *v.t.* 1. engrave; 2. aggravate. **gravierend,** *adj.* aggravating. **Gravierer,** *m.* engraver. **Gravier|kunst,** *f.* art of engraving. **–meißel,** *m.,* **–nadel,** *f.* engraving tool, graver.
Gravis ['ɡraːvɪs], *m.* (*Metr.*) grave accent.
Gravität [ɡravi'tɛːt], *f.* gravity, solemnity.
Gravitation(skraft) [ɡravitatsi'oːn(skraft)], *f.* (force of) gravity, gravitation.
gravitätisch [ɡravi'tɛːtɪʃ], *adj.* grave, solemn, ceremonious.
gravitieren [ɡravi'tiːrən], *v.i.* gravitate (*zu,* to(wards)).
Gravüre [ɡra'vyːrə], *f.* engraving.
Grazie ['ɡraːtsiə], *f.* grace, gracefulness, charm, elegance; *pl.* the Graces. **graziös** [–'øːs], *adj.* graceful, charming.
Gregor ['ɡreːɡɔr], *m.* Gregory. **gregorianisch** [–i'aːnɪʃ], *adj.* Gregorian (*chant*).
Greif [ɡraɪf], *m.* (**-(e)s,** *pl.* **-e**) griffin, condor.
greifbar ['ɡraɪfbaːr], *adj.* ready, available, on *or* to hand; seizable, (*fig.*) tangible, palpable, obvious; *nicht –*, intangible, impalpable; *–e Gestalt annehmen,* assume a definite form *or* shape, materialize; *– nahe, in –e Nähe gerückt,* near *or* close at hand.
greifen ['ɡraɪfən], **1.** *irr.v.t.* seize, grasp, catch (hold of); (*Mus.*) touch, strike (*a note*); *man kann es mit Händen –*, it is quite plain *or* evident, it meets the eye, it is clear as day; *es ist völlig aus der Luft gegriffen,* that is pure invention; *die Zahl ist zu hoch gegriffen,* the figure is put *or* has been fixed too high. **2.** *irr.v.i. – an* (*Acc.*), touch (*hat, heart etc.*); *– in* (*Acc.*), dip into, put one's hand in(to); (*fig.*) *in ein Wespennest –*, bring a hornets' nest about one's ears; (*fig.*) *in die Tasche –*, foot the bill, dip one's hand into one's pocket; *ins Leere –*, clutch at a straw; *– nach,* reach for, grasp *or* snatch *or* clutch at; *nach dem rettenden Strohhalm –*, clutch at a straw; (*fig.*) *mit beiden Händen – nach,* jump at (*a chance etc.*); *um sich –*, gain ground, spread; (*fig.*) *ihm unter die Arme –*, assist *or* help him, give him one's support; *– zu,* reach for; get hold of; select; (*fig.*) resort to, have recourse to; *zur Flasche –*, reach for the bottle, take to drink; *zu den Waffen –*, (*of a p.*) take up arms, (*of a group*) rise in arms; (*fig.*) *zum Äußersten –*, go to extremes. **Greifer,** *m.* catcher; (*Tech.*) lug, claw, grab; (*coll. of a p.*) bloodhound.

Greif|fuß, *m.* prehensile foot, gnathopod. **–haken,** *m.* grapple. **–holz,** *n.* wooden handle. **–klaue, –kralle,** *f.* hind claw, talon. **–schwanz,** *m.* prehensile tail. **–zange,** *f.* gripping pliers, pincers; (*Mil. bridging*) grip-strap. **–zirkel,** *m.* external callipers.

greinen ['graɪnən], *v.i.* (*coll.*) cry, weep, whine, blubber, whimper, grizzle.

greis [graɪs], *adj.* (*Poet.*) hoary, venerable, aged, senile. **Greis,** *m.* (**-es,** *pl.* **-e**) old man. **Greisenalter,** *n.* old age, senility. **greisenhaft,** *adj.* senile. **Greisenhaftigkeit,** *f.* senility.

Greißler ['graɪslər], *m.* (*Austr.*) *see* **Krämer**; (*fig.*) *see* **Kleinigkeitskrämer.**

grell [grɛl], *adj.* (*colours*) dazzling, glaring, crude, garish, loud, flashy; (*sounds*) harsh, piercing, strident, shrill; – ***gegen eine S. abstechen,*** contrast sharply *or* strongly with a th. **Grellheit,** *f.* vividness, dazzling brightness, glare, garishness; harshness, shrillness, stridency.

Gremium ['gre:mium], *n.* (**-s,** *pl.* **-mien**) panel, board, governing body.

Grenadier [grena'di:r], *m.* (**-s,** *pl.* **-e**) (*Mil.*) infantryman, rifleman.

Grenz|acker, *m.* boundary field. **–bahnhof,** *m.* frontier station. **–belastung,** *f.* (*Tech.*) critical load. **–bestimmung,** *f.* boundary settlement. **–bewohner,** *m.* borderer. **–bezirk,** *m.* frontier district.

Grenze ['grɛntsə], *f.* frontier; boundary, limit, border, edge, verge, limit, extremity, bounds, threshold; ***alles hat seine –n,*** there is a limit to everything, a line must be drawn somewhere; ***meine Geduld ist nicht ohne –n,*** there are limits to my patience; ***die –n des Möglichen überschreiten,*** exceed the bounds of possibility; ***einer S. feste –n ziehen*** or ***setzen,*** set a limit to *or* draw a line at s.th.; ***keine –n kennen,*** know no bounds.

grenzen ['grɛntsən], *v.i.* border (*an* (*Acc.*), on); be adjacent *or* contiguous (to), adjoin; be bounded (by), touch; (*fig.*) border *or* verge (on), be next door (to), come near (to being).

grenzenlos ['grɛntsənlo:s], *adj.* boundless, unlimited, infinite, immeasurable, immense, (*fig. only*) unbounded (*joy etc.*). **Grenzenlosigkeit,** *f.* boundlessness; immensity.

Grenz|fall, *m.* limiting case, extreme case; borderline case. **–festung,** *f.* frontier fortress. **–frequenz,** *f.* (*Rad.*) cut-off frequency. **–gänger,** *m.* (*Pol.*) illegal emigrant, refugee, escapee; worker whose home and employment are on different sides of a frontier. **–gegend,** *f.* frontier region, border area. **–gemeinschaft,** *f.* contiguity. **–jäger,** *m.* border patrolman. **–kämpfe,** *m.pl.* border warfare. **–kohlenwasserstoff,** *m.* (*Chem.*) saturated hydrocarbon. **–kontrolle,** *f.* passport control, customs inspection. **–konzentration,** *f.* (*Chem.*) threshold concentration. **–krieg,** *m. See* **–kämpfe. –land,** *n.* borderland, border-country. **–linie,** *f.* boundary-(line), borderline, line of demarcation. **–mark,** *f. See* **–land. –maß,** *n.* limiting size. **–mauer,** *f.* boundary- *or* party-wall. **–nachbar,** *m.* next-door neighbour. **–pfahl,** *m.* boundary post. **–polizei,** *f.* frontier police *or* guards. **–scheide,** *f.* boundary (line). **–schutz,** *m.* frontier defence(s). **–spannung,** *f.* limiting stress *or* (*Elec.*) voltage. **–sperre,** *f.* embargo on border traffic. **–stadt,** *f.* frontier town. **–station,** *f. See* **–bahnhof. –stein,** *m.* landmark, boundary marker. **–übergang,** *m.* (authorized) frontier crossing point. **–überschreitung,** *f.*, **–übertritt,** *m.* crossing of the frontier. **–verbindung,** *f.* (*Chem.*) saturated compound. **–verkehr,** *m.* frontier *or* border traffic. **–verletzung,** *f.* violation of the frontier. **–wache,** *f.* frontier-guard (*troops*). **–wächter,** *m.* frontier-guard (*soldier*). **–wert,** *m.* limit, limiting *or* threshold value. **–winkel,** *m.* critical angle. **–zoll,** *m.* (transit) duty, customs. **–zwischenfall,** *m.* frontier incident.

Gretchen ['gre:tçən], *n.*, **Grete,** *f.*, **Gretel,** *n.* (*dim. of* **Margarete**) Madge, Margery, Meg, Peggy.

Greuel ['grɔyəl], *m.* horror (***vor*** (*Dat.*), of); atrocity, abomination, outrage; (*coll. of a p.*) horror; ***es ist mir ein –,*** I abominate *or* loathe *or* abhor *or* detest it. **Greuel|märchen,** *n.*, **–propaganda,** *f.* (*Pol.*) atrocity story. **–tat,** *f.* atrocity.

greulich ['grɔylɪç], *adj.* horrible, abominable, detestable, frightful, atrocious, heinous, dreadful.

Grieben ['gri:bən], *f.pl.* crackling, greaves, tallow refuse.

Griebs [gri:ps], *m.* (**-es,** *pl.* **-e**) (*dial.*) core (*of fruit*); (*dial.*) Adam's apple.

Grieche ['gri:çə], *m.* (**-n,** *pl.* **-n**) Greek. **Griechenland,** *n.* Greece. **Griechentum,** *n.* Hellenism. **Griechin,** *f.* Greek woman. **griechisch,** *adj.* Greek, Grecian, Hellenic. **griechischkatholisch,** *adj.* Greek Orthodox.

Grien [gri:n], *n.* (**-s,** *no pl.*) (*Swiss*) gravel.

grienen ['gri:nən], *v.i.* (*dial.*) *see* **grinsen.**

gries [gri:s], *adj.* (*dial.*) grey. **grieseln,** *v.i. imp.* (*dial.*) shudder, shiver. **Griesgram,** *m.* grouser, grumbler, (*coll.*) sourpuss. **gries|grämig, –grämisch, –grämlich,** *adj.* peevish, morose, sullen, surly, glum, (*coll.*) grumpy.

Grieß [gri:s], *m.* (**-es,** *pl.* **-e**) 1. semolina, ground rice; 2. gravel, grit, coarse sand; 3. (*coal*) slack, dross; 4. (*corn*) groats, grits. **Grieß|brei,** *m.* thick (semolina) gruel. **–kohle,** *f.* singles, smalls, slack (*coal*). **–mehl,** *n.* semolina. **–pudding,** *m.* semolina-pudding. **–stein,** *m.* (*Med.*) urinary calculus, gravel. **–wärtel,** *m.* (*obs.*) marshal (*tournament*).

griff [grɪf], *see* **greifen.**

Griff, *m.* (**-(e)s,** *pl.* **-e**) grip, grasp, hold; catch, clutch, snatch (***nach,*** at); (hand- *or* foot-)hold (*mountaineering*); handful; handle, knob, lever, (*of sword*) hilt, (*of axe etc.*) haft, helve, (*of guitar*) fret, (*of fabric*) feel; (*wrestling*) hold; (*Mus.*) touch; (*Typ.*) rounce; (*Orn.*) talons, claws, clutch; *pl.* (*Mil.*) manual of arms; ***etwas im – haben,*** have the feel *or* knack of a th.; (*fig.*) ***ein kühner –,*** a bold stroke; ***einen falschen – tun,*** (*Mus.*) play a wrong note; make a mistake; (*fig. coll.*) pick the wrong man, do the wrong th.; ***einen – nach der*** or ***in die Tasche tun,*** go to one's pocket; (*Mil. sl.*) ***–e kloppen,*** do rifle-drill. **griffbereit,** *adj.* handy, ready to hand. **Griffbrett,** *n.* (*violin, guitar etc.*) finger-board; (*piano*) keyboard, (*organ*) manual.

griffe ['grɪfə], *see* **greifen.**

Griffel ['grɪfəl], *m.* stylus, graver; slate-pencil; (*Bot.*) style, pistil; (*fig.*) ***mit ehernem – eingetragen,*** recorded ineffaceably *or* indelibly. **griffel|artig, –förmig,** *adj.* styloid; (*Anat.*) ***griffelförmiger Fortsatz,*** styloid process. **griffellos,** *adj.* (*Bot.*) without styles *or* pistils, acephalous.

griffig ['grɪfɪç], *adj.* (*of fabric*) bulking well, (*of corn*) granular; (*of tools etc.*) gripping well, with a good purchase; easy to handle, handy. **Griffigkeit,** *f.* gripping capacity, grip; ***– der Reifen,*** tyre grip.

Griff|loch, *n.* keyhole (*of wind-instruments*). **–stück,** *n.* handle, grip, (*of pistol etc.*) stock.

Grille ['grɪlə], *f.* 1. (*Ent.*) cricket; 2. (*fig.*) whim, fad, caprice, fancy, crotchet; melancholy thought; ***sich mit –n plagen, –n fangen,*** be low-spirited *or* in low spirits, worry unnecessarily. **Grillenfänger,** *m.* capricious person, crank. **grillenhaft,** *adj.* crotchety, cranky, capricious.

Grimasse [gri'masə], *f.* grimace; ***–n schneiden,*** pull faces, grimace.

Grimm [grɪm], *m.* anger, fury, rage, wrath, ire. **grimm,** *adj.* (*Poet.*) *see* **grimmig.**

Grimmdarm ['grɪmdarm], *m.* (*Anat.*) colon. **Grimmdarm|anhang,** *m.* (*Anat.*) appendix. **–entzündung,** *f.* (*Med.*) colitis.

grimmen ['grɪmən], *v.i. imp.* (*rare*) enrage, infuriate; ***es grimmt mich im Bauche,*** I have the *or* a stomach-ache. **Grimmen,** *n.* (*Med.*) colic, (*coll.*) gripes. **grimmig,** *adj.* enraged, furious, wrathful, violent, ferocious, fierce, grim; ***es ist – kalt,*** it is bitterly cold; ***–e Schmerzen,*** excruciating pain; ***–er Hunger,*** fierce *or* gnawing hunger.

Grind [grɪnt], *m.* (**-(e)s,** *pl.* **-e**) 1. (*Vet.*) scab, mange; (*Med.*) impetigo; (*in hair*) scurf, dandruff; (*on* *wound*) scab, eschar; 2. (*Hunt.*) head (*of stag etc.*). **grindig,** *adj.* mangy, scabby, scurfy.

Grinsel [ˈgrɪnzəl], *n.* (**-s,** *pl.* **-(n)**) (*Austr.*) back-sight (*of rifle*).

grinsen [ˈgrɪnzən], *v.i.* 1. grin, smirk, sneer (*über* (*Acc.*), at); 2. (*coll.*) cry, whimper, grizzle; *see* **greinen. Grinsen,** *n.* grin, smirk, sneer.

Grippe [ˈgrɪpə], *f.* influenza, (*coll.*) flu.

Grips [grɪps], *m.* 1. (*coll.*) brains, sense; (*coll.*) ***er hat keinen – im Kopf,*** he is an empty-headed fool; 2. (*dial.*) neck; ***ihn beim – packen,*** seize him by the scruff of the neck.

Grit [grɪt], *m.* (**-s,** *pl.* **-e**) sandstone.

grob [gro:p], *adj.* (*comp.* ***gröber,*** *sup.* ***gröbst***) coarse(-grained), rough; raw, crude; (*fig.*) coarse, rough, uncouth, gross, churlish, rude, uncivil, blunt, bluff; clumsy, big, thick; ***ihn – anfahren,*** be abusive to him; ***aus dem –en arbeiten,*** rough-hew; ***–e Fahrlässigkeit,*** gross negligence; ***–er Fehler,*** gross *or* bad mistake; ***–es Geschütz,*** big *or* heavy guns; ***–er Scherz,*** coarse *or* broad joke; ***–e Lüge,*** flagrant lie; ***aus dem Gröbsten heraus sein,*** have got over the worst, have broken the back of it; ***–e Stimme,*** deep *or* gruff voice; ***etwas in –en Umrissen*** or ***Zügen schildern,*** give a rough picture of a th., depict a th. in broad outline; (*Law*) ***–er Unfug,*** disorderly conduct, public nuisance; ***–es Vergehen,*** serious *or* grievous offence.

Grob|abstimmung, *f. See* **–einstellung. –arbeiter,** *m.* manual *or* unskilled worker. **–blech,** *n.* thick *or* heavy metal plate. **–draht,** *m.* thick *or* heavy *or* coarse wire. **–einstellung,** *f.* coarse adjustment *or* (*Rad.*) tuning. **grob|fahrlässig,** *adj.* (*Law*) grossly negligent. **–faserig,** *adj.* coarse grained *or* fibred. **Grob|feile,** *f.* rasp. **–gewicht,** *n.* gross weight. **Grobheit,** *f.* coarseness, roughness, grossness, rudeness, insolence; ***–en sagen,*** be rude *or* abusive, insult. **Grobian,** *m.* (**-(e)s,** *pl.* **-e**) rude *or* coarse fellow, boor, ruffian. **grobjährig,** *adj.* broad-ringed (*of timber*). **Grobkeramik,** *f.* earthenware. **grobkörnig,** *adj.* coarse-grained.

gröblich [ˈgrø:plɪç], *adj.* gross, coarse, rude; ***– beleidigen,*** insult grossly; (***sich***) ***– irren,*** make a big *or* bad mistake; ***sich – vergehen,*** commit a faux pas, (*coll.*) put one's foot in it.

Groblunker [ˈgro:pluŋkər], *m.* (*Metall.*) cavity. **grobmaschig,** *adj.* coarse *or* wide-meshed.

Gröbs [grø:ps], *m. See* **Griebs.**

grobschlächtig [ˈgro:pʃlɛçtɪç], *adj.* boorish, uncouth, coarse. **Grob|schmied,** *m.* blacksmith. **–schnitt,** *m.* rough-cut tobacco. **–sicherung,** *f.* (*Elec.*) main fuse. **grob|sinnig,** *adj.* crude, coarse(grained), lacking refinement. **–sinnlich,** *adj.* gross, grossly sensual, voluptuous.

Groden [ˈgro:dən], *m.* (*dial.*) reclaimed land, alluvial land.

Grog [grɔk], *m.* (**-s,** *pl.* **-s**) grog.

grö(h)len [ˈgrø:lən], *v.t., v.i.* bawl, squall.

Groll [grɔl], *m.* hatred, resentment, animosity, rancour; ill-will, grudge; ***einen – auf ihn haben,*** harbour resentment *or* have a grievance against him; ***einen alten – hegen,*** nurse an old grievance, bear a grudge. **grollen,** *v.i.* (*usu. Dat. but also with* ***auf*** (*Acc.*), ***gegen*** or ***mit***) bear ill-will *or* a grudge; have a grievance (against); sulk, be resentful; be angry (with); (*of thunder*) rumble, roll. **grollend,** *adj.* sulky, resentful.

Grönland [ˈgrø:nlant], *n.* (*Geog.*) Greenland. **Grönländer,** *m.* Greenlander. **Grönlandfahrer,** *m.* whaler.

[1]**Gros** [gro:], *n.* gross; ***en gros,*** wholesale; ***– der Armee,*** main body.

[2]**Gros** [grɔs], *n.* (**-ses,** *pl.* **-se**) gross, twelve dozen.

Groschen [ˈgrɔʃən], *m.* smallest Austrian coin (100 = ***Schilling***); (*coll.*) penny, ten-pfennig piece; (*coll.*) ***der – ist gefallen,*** the penny has dropped, now I see; ***keinen – wert,*** not worth a jot; ***einen schönen*** or ***hübschen – verdienen,*** earn a pretty penny. **Groschen|automat,** *m.* (penny-in-the-)slot machine. **–roman,** *m.* penny dreadful, (*Am.*) dime novel. **–schreiber,** *m.* penny-a-liner, quill-driver.

groß [gro:s], (*comp.* ***größer,*** *sup.* ***größt***) 1. *adj.* tall, high; large, big, vast, huge, great, extensive, enormous, immense, spacious; large-scale, grand, major, important; (*fig.*) great, eminent; grown-up; ***–e Augen machen,*** stare (in surprise); ***–e Bohnen,*** broad beans; ***–er Buchstabe,*** capital letter; ***–es Einkommen,*** large income; (*Naut.*) ***–e Fahrt machen,*** sail full speed ahead; ***–er Fehler,*** great *or* big *or* gross *or* bad mistake; ***–e Ferien,*** long vacation; ***auf –em Fuße leben,*** live extravagantly *or* in a grand style; ***–es Geld,*** money in large denominations; ***die –e Welt,*** the fashionable world; (*Mil.*) ***–es Hauptquartier,*** General Headquarters; ***–e Havarie,*** general average; ***–e Kälte,*** severe cold; ***–e Kinder,*** grown-up children; ***–e Kleinigkeit,*** mere trifle; ***der Große Kurfürst,*** Friedrich Wilhelm, Elector of Brandenburg (1640–88); ***das –e Los,*** first (lottery) prize, winning draw; ***–e Mehrheit,*** vast majority; ***der Große Ozean,*** the Pacific (Ocean); ***das –e Publikum,*** the general public; (*Mus.*) ***–e Quarte,*** major fourth; ***–er Rat,*** full council; (*coll.*) ***–e Rosinen im Kopf haben,*** have one's head full of big *or* high-flown ideas; ***im –en Stil,*** on a large *or* grand scale; ***–e Stücke auf ihn halten,*** have a high opinion *or* (*coll.*) think a lot of him; ***zum –en Teil,*** largely, to a large extent; ***–e Toilette*** or (*Mil.*) ***Uniform,*** full dress; ***–er Unterschied,*** vast difference; ***–er Verlust,*** severe *or* heavy loss; ***eine –e Zahl (von),*** a large number (of), a great many; ***–e Zehe,*** big toe. **2.** *adv.* ***ihn – ansehen*** or ***anblicken,*** stare at him (in surprise), look at him in wide-eyed amazement; ***– auftreten,*** lord it, assume airs; ***– denken,*** think nobly; think highly *or* have a high opinion (***von,*** of); (*coll.*) ***sich nicht – darum kümmern,*** not bother much about it; (*coll.*) ***es nicht – nötig haben,*** have no great need of it; ***– schreiben,*** write in capitals *or* block letters, capitalize; ***– werden,*** grow up (*of children*); ***zu – werden für etwas,*** outgrow a th.

Groß|abnehmer, *m.* bulk purchaser. **–admiral,** *m.* Admiral of the Fleet. **großangelegt,** *adj.* large-scale, extensive. **Großangriff,** *m.* large-scale *or* all-out attack. **großartig,** *adj.* great, grand, splendid, marvellous, wonderful, magnificent; excellent, (*coll.*) first-rate; phenomenal, sublime, grandiose. **Großartigkeit,** *f.* grandeur, splendour, magnificence; excellence. **Groß|aufnahme,** *f.* (*Phot.*) close-up. **–bauer,** *m.* large-scale farmer. **–betrieb,** *m.* 1. large-scale enterprise *or* undertaking; 2. wholesale business. **–britannien,** *n.* Great Britain. **großbritannisch,** *adj.* British. **Großbuchstabe,** *m.* capital (letter), block capital.

Große [ˈgro:sə], *see* **Große(r), Große(s).**

Größe [ˈgrø:sə], *f.* 1. height, tallness, (*of a p.*) stature; size, largeness, vastness, spaciousness; dimension(s), bulk, (*of a vessel*) cubic contents; (*Astr.*) magnitude, (*Math.*) quantity; (*of a p.*) greatness; ***Stern erster –,*** star of the first magnitude; ***von mittlerer –,*** medium-sized, (*of a p.*) of medium height; ***in natürlicher –,*** life-size; ***in voller –,*** full-size; (*Math.*) ***unbekannte –,*** unknown quantity; 2. celebrity, notability; (*Theat., Spt.*) star.

Groß|einsatz, *m.* (*Mil.*) large-scale operation. **–eltern,** *pl.* grandparents. **–enkel,** *m.* great-grandson. **–enkelin,** *f.* great-granddaughter.

Größenordnung [ˈgrø:sənˀɔrdnuŋ], *f.* dimension, (*Astr.*) order of magnitude.

großenteils [ˈgro:səntaɪls], *adv.* mainly, mostly, largely, to a large *or* great extent, in a large measure, in large part.

Größen|verhältnis, *n.* ratio, proportion; *pl.* dimensions, proportions. **–verteilungskurve,** *f.* (*Stat.*) (frequency) distribution curve. **–wahn,** *f.* megalomania, (*coll.*) swelled head.

Große(r) [ˈgro:sə(r)], *m., f.* great (wo)man; *pl.* grown-ups, adults; those in high position, (*coll.*) big wigs *or* shots. **Große(s),** *n.* s.th. big *or* great, a great th. *or* achievement *or* feat; (*nursery talk*) ***Großes machen,*** do one's big business; ***im großen,*** on a large scale, wholesale; ***im Großen handeln,***

carry on wholesale trade; ***im großen und ganzen,*** on the whole, by and large, generally speaking.

größer ['grø:sər], *comp. adj. See* **groß.**

Groß|fabrikation, -fertigung, *f.* mass *or* large-scale production. **-feuer,** *n.* conflagration. **-finanz,** *f.* high finance. **-flughafen,** *m.* air terminal. **-funkstelle,** *f.* (*Rad.*) high-power transmitter. **-fürst,** *m.* Grand-Duke (*Russian*). **-fürstentum,** *m.* Grand-Duchy. **-grundbesitz,** *m.* landed property, estates. **-grundbesitzer,** *m.* landed proprietor, great landowner. **-handel,** *m.* wholesale trade. **-handelsindex,** *m.* wholesale price index. **-handelspreis,** *m.* wholesale price. **-handelsrabatt,** *m.* wholesale discount. **-händler,** *m.* wholesale merchant *or* dealer *or* distributor. **-handlung,** *f.* wholesale firm *or* distributors *or* suppliers. **groß|herrlich,** *adj.* seignorial, (*as title*) Most Excellent. **-herzig,** *adj.* generous, magnanimous. **Groß|herzigkeit,** *f.* generosity, magnanimity. **-herzog,** *m.* grand-duke (*German*). **-herzogtum,** *n.* grand-duchy. **-hirn,** *n.* (*Anat.*) cerebrum. **-hirnrinde,** *f.* (*Anat.*) cerebral cortex. **-industrie,** *f.* large-scale industry. **-industrielle(r),** *m.* big industrialist, captain of industry, industrial magnate.

Grossist [gro'sɪst], *m.* **(-en,** *pl.* **-en)** *see* **Großhändler.**

großjährig ['gro:sjɛ:rɪç], *adj.* of age; ***– werden,*** come of age. **Groß|jährigkeit,** *f.* coming of age; age of legal responsibility, majority. **-kämmerer, -kammerherr,** *m.* lord chamberlain. **-kampfschiff,** *n.* capital ship. **-kanzler,** *m.* Lord High Chancellor. **-kapital,** *n.* high finance, (*coll.*) big business. **-kapitalist,** *m.* business magnate, financier. **-kaufmann,** *m.* (wholesale) merchant. **-knecht,** *m.* head man, foreman (*on a farm*). **-küche,** *f.* feeding centre. **groß|leibig,** *adj.* big-bellied. **-lippig,** *adj.* thick-lipped. **Groß|luke,** *f.* (*Naut.*) main hatch. **-macht,** *f.* great power. **großmächtig, 1.** *adj.* high and mighty. **2.** *adv.* enormously. **Groß|magd,** *f.* head maid (*on a farm*). **-mama,** *f.* (*coll.*) grandma, grannie. **-mannssucht,** *f.* self-importance. **-mars,** *m.* (*Naut.*) main-top. **großmaschig,** *adj.* wide-meshed. **Groß|mast,** *m.* (*Naut.*) mainmast. **-maul,** *n.* braggart. **großmäulig,** *adj.* bragging, swaggering, boastful, loud-mouthed. **Groß|-meister,** *m.* Grand Master (*of an order*). **-mut,** *f.* magnanimity, generosity. **großmütig,** *adj.* magnanimous, generous. **Großmutter,** *f.* grandmother. **groß|mütterlich,** *adj.* grandmotherly. **-nasig,** *adj.* bottle-nosed; (*fig.*) arrogant.

Groß|oktav, *n.* large octavo; full organ. **-onkel,** *m.* great-uncle. **-papa,** *m.* (*coll.*) granddad, grandpa. **-quart,** *n.* large quarto. **-raum,** *m.* (*Nat. Soc.*) extra-territorial sphere of influence. **-raumkarte,** *f.* small-scale map. **-reihenfertigung,** *f.* mass production. **-reinemachen,** *n.* (spring) cleaning. **-schatzmeister,** *m.* Lord High Treasurer. **-schiffahrtsweg,** *m.* canal for sea-going vessels, ship canal. **-schreibung,** *f.* capitalization. **-siegelbewahrer,** *m.* Keeper of the Privy Seal (*in England the Lord Chancellor*). **-sprecher,** *m.* braggart, boaster, blusterer. **-sprecherei,** *f.* grandiloquence, magniloquence, boasting, bragging, bluster, (*coll.*) big talk. **groß|sprecherisch,** *adj.* boastful, bragging, blustering, swaggering; grandiloquent, magniloquent. **-spurig,** *adj.* arrogant, conceited, haughty, overbearing, (*coll.*) high-hat. **Groß|stadt,** *f.* large town (*over 100,000 inhabitants*). **-städter,** *m.* city-dweller. **großstädtisch,** *adj.* city, urban, metropolitan; fashionable. **Groß|stadtroman,** *m.* novel of metropolitan society. **-steingrab,** *n.* megalithic burial place.

größt [grø:st], *sup. adj. See* **groß.**

Groß|tante, *f.* great aunt. **-tat,** *f.* great deed *or* exploit, achievement, feat.

größtenteils ['grø:stəntaɪls], *adv.* mostly, chiefly, for the most part, in the main. **Größtmaß,** *n.* maximum size, size limit. **größtmöglich,** *adj.* greatest *or* largest possible, utmost.

Groß|tuer, *m.* braggart, (*coll.*) show-off, big-head. **-tuerei,** *f.* boastfulness, swagger(ing), pompousness, (*coll.*) big-headedness. **großtun,** *irr.v.i.* brag, boast, swagger, show off, give o.s. airs, (*coll.*) talk big; (***sich***) ***mit einer S. –,*** brag *or* boast about *or* of s.th., vaunt s.th. **Größtwert** ['grø:stve:rt], *m.* maximum *or* maximal value.

Großvater ['gro:sfa:tər], *m.* grandfather. **großväterlich,** *adj.* grandfatherly. **Groß|vaterstuhl,** *m.* high-backed arm-chair, easy-chair. **-verbraucher,** *m.* bulk consumer. **-versandgeschäft,** *n.* mail-order house *or* firm. **-verteiler,** *m.* wholesaler, wholesale distributor. **-vertrieb,** *m.* wholesale distribution. **-vieh,** *n.* horned cattle. **-wesir,** *m.* Grand Vizier. **-wild,** *n.* big game. **-wildjagd,** *f.* big-game shooting. **-würdenträger,** *m.* high dignitary. **groß|ziehen,** *irr.v.t.* bring up, rear, raise (*children etc.*). **-zügig,** *adj.* **1.** on a generous *or* grand *or* large *or* impressive scale; large-scale, (in) bold (outlines); grandiose; **2.** (*of a p.*) broad-minded, liberal; generous, liberal, open-handed. **Großzügigkeit,** *f.* (*of plans etc.*) grandiose scale, boldness of conception; (*of a p.*) broad-mindedness, liberality; generosity, open-handedness.

grotesk [gro'tɛsk], *adj.* grotesque. **Groteske,** *f.* grotesque(ness).

Grotte ['grɔtə], *f.* grotto.

grub [gru:p], *see* **graben.**

Grübchen ['gry:pçən], *n.* dimple; lacuna. **Grübchenbildung,** *f.* (*Metall.*) pitting.

Grube ['gru:bə], *f.* mine, colliery, pit; pit, hole, cavity, cave; excavation, quarry; (***ihm***) ***eine – graben,*** lay a snare (for him) (*see also under* **graben**); (*B.*) ***in die – fahren,*** go down to the grave.

grübe ['gry:bə], *see* **graben.**

Grübelei [gry:bə'laɪ], *f.* (-, *pl.* **-en**) musing, meditation, pensiveness, rumination, pondering, brooding; reflection, reverie, day-dream(ing). **grübeln** ['gry:bəln], *v.i.* ponder, brood, meditate, reflect, muse (***über*** (*Acc.*), on *or* over), ruminate (about), rack one's brains (about *or* over), (*coll.*) mull (over).

Gruben|arbeiter, *m.* collier, miner, pitman. **-axt,** *f.* miner's pick. **-besitzer,** *m.* mine-owner, colliery proprietor. **-brand,** *m.* underground *or* pit-fire. **-einbruch,** *m.* roof-fall. **-gas,** *n.* firedamp, marsh gas, methane. **-gezähe,** *n.* miner's tools. **-halde,** *f.* slag-heap, bing. **-klein,** *n.* smalls, slack (*coal*). **-lampe,** *f.* miner's (safety) lamp. **-schacht,** *f.* pit-shaft. **-schlacke,** *f.* slag. **-steiger** *m.* overseer of a mine. **-stempel,** *m.* pit-prop. **-unglück,** *n.* pit disaster. **-wasser,** *n.* seepage. **-wetter,** *n.* *See* **-gas.**

Grübler ['gry:blər], *m.* brooding *or* introspective p., (day)dreamer, melancholy brooder, one lost *or* sunk in pensive meditation. **grüblerisch,** *adj.* brooding, pensive, meditative, introspective.

Grude ['gru:də], *f.* lignite coke.

Gruft [gruft], *f.* (-, *pl.* **⸗e**) vault, tomb, (*Poet.*) grave.

Grum(me)t ['grum(mə)t], *n.* aftermath, second crop (*of hay*), (*Am.*) rowen.

grün [gry:n], *adj.* green, verdant; fresh, young, vigorous; raw, unripe, immature, inexperienced, (*coll.*) green; ***– bleiben,*** remain alive (*remembrance*); ***–e Bohne,*** French bean; ***es wird mir – und gelb vor den Augen,*** I have an attack of giddiness; ***– (und gelb) vor Neid,*** green with envy; ***– und gelb vor Wut sein,*** see red; ***– und gelb vor Ärger sein,*** be beside o.s. with annoyance, (*coll.*) blow one's top; ***ihn – und gelb schlagen,*** beat him black and blue; ***–e Häute,*** undressed skins; (*Austr.*) ***der –e Heinrich,*** see ***–e Minna***; ***–er Hering,*** fresh herring; ***–e Insel,*** Emerald Isle; ***–er Junge,*** greenhorn; (*coll.*) ***–e Minna,*** Black Maria; (*coll.*) ***ihm nicht – sein,*** have it in for him; ***–er Salat,*** lettuce; ***er setzt sich an meine –e Seite,*** he makes his appeal to my feelings *or* my better nature, he knows which is my soft spot, he knows how to win me over; ***vom –en Tisch aus,*** only in theory, bureaucratic (*decision*), armchair (*strategy*); (*Geog.*) ***–es Vorge-***

birge, Cape Verde. **Grün,** *n.* green colour, verdure; ***im –en,*** *(coll.)* ***bei Mutter –,*** in the country, in rural surroundings, in the open (air); *(coll.)* ***dasselbe in –,*** practically the same th., as near as no matter, *(sl.)* as near as dammit.

Grün|anlage, *f.* ornamental gardens, park; lawn, green. **–ästung,** *f.* pruning.

Grund [grunt], *m.* **(-es,** *pl.* **⸚e)** 1. ground, earth, soil; *(Naut.)* ***an – laufen, auf – geraten, auf den – fahren,*** run aground; *(Naut.)* ***wir sitzen am*** or ***auf dem –,*** we are aground; ***des Meeres tiefe Gründe,*** the depths of the ocean, the deep; ***ich habe keinen – mehr, ich habe den – unter den Füßen verloren,*** I am quite out of my depth; 2. land, (real) estate; (building) plot, terrain; 3. sediment, bottoms, grounds, dregs, lees; 4. bottom, base, foundation, basis, fundus, groundwork, rudiments, elements, first principles; ***einer S. auf den – gehen,*** get to the bottom *or* root of a matter; ***sich von – auf bessern,*** turn over a new leaf; ***die Nachricht entbehrt jedes –es,*** the news is without any foundation; ***im –e,*** at bottom, after all, fundamentally; ***im –e genommen,*** actually, in reality, strictly speaking, when all is said and done; ***den – legen zu,*** lay the foundation of; ***von – aus,*** thoroughly, radically, fundamentally, in its essentials, completely; 5. reason, cause, occasion, excuse, grounds, motive, argument; ***Gründe anführen,*** state one's case, advance arguments; ***auf – von,*** in virtue of, on account of, on the strength *or* basis *or* grounds of; *(Law)* pursuant to, under; ***aus dem –e,*** for this reason, that's why; ***mit gutem –,*** with reason, reasonably, justly; ***nicht ganz ohne –,*** not unreasonably; ***– zur Klage,*** cause for complaint; 6. background, ground, *(paint)* priming (coat).

Grund|abgabe, *f.* land tax. **–akkord,** *m.* *(Mus.)* fundamental chord. **–angeln,** *n.* bottom-fishing. **–anschauung,** *f.* basic conception, fundamental idea. **grundanständig,** *adj.* upright, high-principled. **Grund|anstrich,** *m.* first *or* ground *or* priming coat, undercoat. **–ausbildung,** *f.* *(Mil.)* basic training. **–baß,** *m.* *(Mus.)* thorough-bass. **–bau,** *m.* foundation; substructure; underpinning. **–bedeutung,** *f.* original meaning. **–bedingung,** *f.* fundamental *or* basic condition. **–begriff,** *m.* fundamental principle, basic idea *or* concept; *pl.* fundamentals, rudiments, principles. **–besitz,** *m.* real estate, landed property; ***freier –,*** freehold. **–besitzer,** *m.* landed proprietor, landowner. **–bestandteil,** *m.* primary *or* essential component *or* constituent. **–blei,** *n.* sounding-lead, plummet. **–bruch,** *m.* (soil) subsidence. **–buch,** *n.* land register. **–ebene,** *f.* datum level, ground-plane. **grundehrlich,** *adj.* thoroughly honest. **Grund|eigenschaft,** *f.* fundamental property *or* character. **–eigentum,** *n.* *See* **–besitz. –einheit,** *f.* absolute *or* fundamental unit. **–einkommen,** *n.* basic income. **–einstellung,** *f.* basic *or* fundamental attitude. **–eis,** *n.* ground-ice; *(vulg.)* ***ihm geht der Arsch mit –,*** he's frightened out of his wits.

gründen ['gryndən], **1.** *v.t.* establish, institute, found, create, *(coll.)* set up; *(Comm.)* promote, float, form *(a company)*, start, open, set up *(a business)*; launch, set on foot; *(fig.)* base *(argument* *(auf)* *(Acc.)*, on). **2.** *v.r.* rest, rely; be based *or* founded *or* grounded *(auf (Acc.)*, on). **3.** *v.i.* *(rare)* *(Naut.)* touch bottom; ***stille Wasser – tief,*** still waters run deep. **Gründer,** *m.* founder, originator, creator, *(Comm.)* promoter.

Grunderfordernis ['grunt?ɛrfɔrdənɪs], *n.* basic requirement.

Gründer|gesellschaft, *f.* *(Comm.)* parent company. **–jahre,** *n.pl.* *(Hist.)* years of rapid expansion *or* of lively financial speculation (1874–1914).

Grund|erwerb, *m.* acquisition of land. **–erzeugnis,** *n.* primary product. **grundfalsch,** *adj.* radically wrong, absolutely false. **Grund|farbe,** *f.* ground colour, priming; *(Opt.)* primary colour. **–fehler,** *m.* basic *or* fundamental error, radical fault. **–feste,** *f.* *(fig.)* basis, foundation; ***in den –n erschüttern,*** shake to its very foundation(s). **–feuchtigkeit,** *f.* *(Build.)* ground-damp. **–firnis,** *m.* priming-varnish. **–fläche,** *f.* base, basis; *(Geom.)* area; *(Build.)* ground space. **–form,** *f.* original *or* primary form. **–gedanke,** *m.* fundamental *or* leading *or* root idea. **–gehalt,** *n.* basic pay *or* salary. **–gerechtigkeit,** *f.* land-owner's rights, easement. **–geschwindigkeit,** *f.* *(Av.)* ground speed. **–gesetz,** *n.* statute; basic constitutional law. **grundgesetzlich,** *adj.* statutory. **Grund|gestein,** *n.* underlying rock(s). **–herr,** *m.* lord of the manor; landlord.

grundieren [grun'di:rən], *v.t.* size, prime, apply ground-coat. **Grundierfarbe,** *f.* priming colour.

Grund|irrtum, *m.* *See* **–fehler. –kapital,** *n.* (original) stock. **–kette,** *f.* *(Weav.)* ground-warp. **–körper,** *m.* fundamental substance. **–kraft,** *f.* primary force. **–kreis,** *m.* *(Geom.)* circumference of the base. **–lage,** *f.* foundation, base, basis, groundwork, data; rudiments, fundamentals, elements; *(Biol.)* matrix; ***auf der – von,*** on the basis of; ***die – bilden von,*** underlie; ***jeder – entbehren,*** be without any foundation. **–lagenforschung,** *f.* basic research. **grundlegend,** *adj.* fundamental, basic; ***–e wissenschaftliche Ausgabe,*** standard (critical) edition. **Grundlegung,** *f.* laying the foundation.

gründlich ['gryntlɪç], *adj.* thorough, painstaking, careful; thorough-going, radical, exhaustive, complete; solid, profound; ***–e Kenntnisse haben in*** *(Dat.)*, be thoroughly versed *or* well grounded in, *(coll.)* have *(s.th.)* at one's fingertips; ***ihm – die Meinung sagen,*** give him a piece of one's mind. **Gründlichkeit,** *f.* thoroughness, carefulness, diligence; exhaustiveness, solidity, profundity.

Gründling ['gryntlɪŋ], *m.* **(-s,** *pl.* **-e)** *(Ichth.)* gudgeon *(Gobis fluviatilis)*.

Grundlinie ['gruntli:niə], *f.* groundline, base, baseline; datum line, point of reference.

grundlos ['gruntlo:s], **1.** *adj.* bottomless, unfathomable, boundless; *(fig.)* unfounded, groundless, without foundation. **2.** *adv.* unreasonably, for no reason at all. **Grundlosigkeit,** *f.* *(fig.)* groundlessness.

Grund|maß, *n.* basic standard. **–masse,** *f.* *(Biol.)* stroma. **–mauer,** *f.* foundation-wall. **–nahrungsmittel,** *n.pl.* basic foodstuffs.

Gründonnerstag [gry:n'dɔnərsta:k], *m.* Maundy Thursday.

Grund|peilung, *f.* *(Naut.)* sounding. **–pfeiler,** *m.* foundation pillar; *(fig.)* mainstay, keystone. **–platte,** *f.* base-plate. **–preis,** *m.* basic price. **–prinzip,** *n.* basic *or* fundamental principle. **–problem,** *n.* fundamental problem. **–rechte,** *n.pl.* constitutional rights, rights of man. **–regel,** *f.* fundamental rule; axiom; basic principle. **–rente,** *f.* ground-rent. **–riß,** *m.* outline, sketch, layout, ground-plan *(of a building)*; summary, outline(s), epitome, compendium.

Grundsatz ['grundzats], *m.* principle, axiom; tenet, maxim; ***es sich*** *(Dat.)* ***zum – machen,*** make it a rule. **grundsätzlich, 1.** *adj.* fundamental, in *or* on principle. **2.** *adv.* as a general *or* on principle, basically; ***ich tue das – niemals,*** I have made a point never to do this.

Grund|schlamm, *m.* bottom mud. **–schoß,** *m.* land-tax. **–schuld,** *f.* encumbrance, mortgage. **–schule,** *f.* elementary *or* primary school. **–schwelle,** *f.* *(Archit.)* ground-sill; railway-sleeper. **–see,** *f.* ground-swell. **–stein,** *m.* foundation-stone; *(fig.)* corner-stone; *(fig.)* ***den – legen zu,*** lay the foundations of. **–steinlegung,** *f.* laying of the foundation-stone. **–stellung,** *f.* original *or* first position; *(Mil. command)* as you were! *(fencing)* on-guard. **–steuer,** *f.* land-tax, ground rent. **–stock,** *m.* matrix.

Grundstoff, *m.* *(Chem.)* element, base, radical; raw material; *(paper-making)* pulp. **Grundstoff|industrie,** *f.* basic industry. **–wechsel,** *m.* basal metabolism.

Grund|strich, *m.* down-stroke *(opp. to hair-stroke)*. **–stück,** *n.* real estate; lot, plot of land, (building) site; ***Haus mit –en,*** messuage. **–stückmakler,** *m.* (real-) estate agent. **–stufe,** *f.* **1.** lower classes of elementary school; 2. *(Gram.)* positive mood. **grundstürzend,** *adj.* destructive, revolutionary; ***–e Änderungen,*** fundamental *or* radical changes. **Grund|substanz,** *f.* (*Biol.*) matrix. **-taxe,** *f.* basic *or* flat rate. **-teilchen,** *n.* fundamental particle, atom. **-text,** *m.* original text. **-ton,** *m.* 1. (*Mus.*) keynote; 2. (*fig.*) prevailing mood *or* tone, undertone. **-tugend,** *f.* cardinal virtue. **-übel,** *n.* basic evil, the root of all evil.

Gründung ['gryndʊŋ], *f.* foundation, establishment, institution, creation, (*coll.*) setting-up; (*Comm.*) formation, promotion, flotation; incorporation. **Gründungs|kapital,** *n.* (*Comm.*) original stock. **-mitglied,** *n.* founder-member. **-stadium,** *n.* development stage. **-urkunde,** *f.*, **-vertrag,** *m.* articles of association *or* incorporation.

Grund|unterschied, *m.* basic difference. **-ursache,** *f.* primary cause. **grundverkehrt,** *adj.* totally *or* utterly mistaken *or* wrong. **Grundvermögen,** *n.* landed property; real estate; capital, principal. **grundverschieden,** *adj.* entirely *or* radically *or* utterly different. **Grund|verschiedenheit,** *f.* radical difference. **-wahrheit,** *f.* fundamental truth. **-wasser,** *n.* subsoil *or* underground water. **-wasserspiegel,** *m.* water table, ground water-level. **-wesen,** *n.* primary essence (*of a th.*). **-wort,** *n.* basic *or* determinative word (*of a compound*). **-zahl,** *f.* cardinal number; unit. **-zins,** *m.* ground-rent. **-zug,** *m.* main feature, characteristic (feature); *pl.* fundamentals, essentials.

Grüne ['gry:nə], *n.* greenness, verdure; *see* **Grün. grünen,** *v.i.* be green; become *or* turn green; (*fig.*) flourish, thrive, prosper. **Grüne(r),** *m.* (*sl.*) bobby, copper. **Grüne(s),** *n.* greens, vegetables.

Grün|fink, *m.* *See* **Grünling. -fläche,** *f.* lawn, green, greensward. **-futter,** *n.* green fodder. **-gürtel,** *m.* green belt (*round town*). **-kern,** *m.* green rye. **-kohl,** *m.* kale. **-kram,** *m.*, **-kraut,** *n.* greens, green vegetables. **-kreuz,** *n.*, **-kreuzkampfstoff,** *m.* (*Mil.*) choking gas. **grünlich,** *adj.* greenish.

Grünling ['gry:nlɪŋ], *m.* (**-s,** *pl.* **-e**) (*Orn.*) greenfinch (*Chloris chloris*); (*Bot.*) green agaric (*Tricholoma equestre*); (*fig.*) greenhorn.

Grün|schenkel, *m.* (*Orn.*) greenshank (*Tringa nebularia*). **-schnabel,** *m.* (*fig.*) whipper-snapper, greenhorn. **-span,** *m.* verdigris. **-specht,** *m.* (*Orn.*) green woodpecker (*Picus viridis*). **-streifen,** *m.* centre reservation (*of motorway*).

grunzen ['grʊntsən], *v.i.* grunt. **Grunzen,** *n.* grunt(ing). **Grunzer,** *m.* grunter, porker.

Grünzeug ['gry:ntsɔyk], *n.* greens, greenstuff; herbs.

Gruppe ['grʊpə], *f.* group, category; (*of workers etc.*) crew, gang, team; (*Mil.*) section, squad; (*Av.*) wing (= 3 *squadrons*), (*Am.*) group; (*of trees*) cluster, clump; (*of birds*) covey; (*Comm.*) syndicate. **Gruppen|aufnahme,** *f.* (*Phot.*) group. **-feuer,** *n.* (*Mil.*) volley firing. **-führer,** *m.* (*Mil.*) section *or* squad leader. **-schaltung,** *f.* (*Elec.*) series-parallel connexion. **gruppenweise,** *adv.* in groups *or* clusters; (*Mil.*) by *or* in sections *or* squads.

gruppieren [grʊ'pi:rən], **1.** *v.t.* group, arrange in groups, marshal, classify. **2.** *v.r.* form groups *or* a group, cluster, group o.s. **Gruppierung,** *f.* grouping, arrangement, disposition.

Grus [gru:s], *m.* (**-es,** *pl.* **-e**) grit, fine gravel; debris; smalls, (coal) slack.

gruselig ['gru:zəlɪç], *adj.* uncanny, weird, eerie, hair-raising, (*coll.*) creepy(-crawly). **gruseln,** *v.r.*, *v.i. imp.* ***mich*** or ***mir gruselt,*** my flesh creeps (*bei*, at), (*coll.*) it gives me the creeps. **Gruseln,** *n.* horrors, creeps.

Gruß [gru:s], *m.* (**-es,** *pl.* **¨-e**) greeting, salutation, salute; (*in letter*) ***mit bestem –,*** yours sincerely *or* faithfully *or* truly; ***herzliche Grüße,*** kind regards; ***von ihm einen – ausrichten*** or ***bestellen,*** convey his kind regards *or* best wishes (*an* (*Acc.*), to); (*B.*) ***der Englische –,*** Ave Maria.

grüßen ['gry:sən], *v.t.* greet; salute; present compliments to; ***– lassen,*** send one's respects *or* best wishes *or* kind regards (*Acc.*, to); ***bitte – Sie ihn von mir,*** please remember me to him, give him my kind regards; (*dial.*) ***grüß' Gott!*** greetings! farewell!

Grußform(el) ['gru:sfɔrm(əl)], *f.* form of salutation.

Grüßfuß ['gry:sfu:s], *m.* ***mit ihm auf dem – stehen,*** have a nodding acquaintance with him; know him just to speak to.

Grußpflicht ['gru:spflɪçt], *f.* (*Mil.*) obligation to salute.

Grütz|beutel ['gryts–], *m.* (*Med.*) wen, atheroma. **-brei,** *m.* gruel. **Grütze,** *f.* groats; (*coll.*) ***– im Kopfe haben,*** have gumption, be all there; ***rote –,*** fruit-flavoured blancmange. **Grütz|kopf,** *m.* blockhead. **-schleim,** *m.* *See* **-brei.**

Gschaftelhuber ['kʃaftlhu:bər], *m.* (*dial.*) busybody.

Guardian [guardi'a:n], *m.* (**-s,** *pl.* **-e**) (convent) prior, superior.

Guck [gʊk], *m.* (**-(e)s,** *pl.* **-e**) (*dial.*) look, peep. **gucken,** *v.i.* look, peep, peer; ***der Schelm guckt ihm aus den Augen,*** his looks bespeak the rogue he is. **Gucker,** *m.* peeper; eyeglass, spy-glass. **Guck|-kasten,** *m.* peep-show. **-loch,** *n.* peep-hole, spy-hole.

Gugelhupf ['gu:gəlhupf], *m.* (**-(e)s** *or* **-en,** *pl.* **-e(n)**) (*Austr.*) (*sort of*) cake.

Guido [gu'i:do], *m.* Guy.

guillotinieren [giljoti'ni:rən], *v.t.* guillotine.

Gulasch ['gu:laʃ], *n.* stewed steak (flavoured with paprika), goulash. **Gulaschkanone,** *f.* (*Mil. sl.*) field-kitchen.

Gulden ['gʊldən], *m.* florin, guilder.

gülden ['gyldən], *adj.* (*Poet.*) golden.

Gülle ['gylə], *f.* liquid manure.

Gully ['guli], *m.* (**-s,** *pl.* **-s**) street drain.

Gültbuch ['gyltbu:x], *n.* rent-roll. **Gülte,** *f.* (*dial.*) ground-rent; revenues of an estate; payment in kind. **Gültherr,** *m.* lord of the manor.

gültig ['gyltɪç], *adj.* valid, effective, in force, binding, lawful, legal; authentic, good, current; admissible, applicable; (*as a ticket*) ***– für,*** available *or* good for; ***– ab*** or ***vom,*** effective as from; (*Law*) ***eine Anklage für – erklären,*** bring in a true bill; ***– machen,*** legalize, render valid, ratify; ***– sein,*** *see* **gelten. Gültigkeit,** *f.* validity, legality, legal force; currency; availability; ***Fahrkarten mit dreißigtägiger –,*** tickets valid for thirty days; ***Behauptung von allgemeiner –,*** statement of universal validity. **Gültigkeitsdauer,** *f.* period of validity.

Gummi ['gumi], **1.** *n.* (india-)rubber, gum. **2.** *m.* (**-s,** *pl.* **-s**) india-rubber (eraser), (*coll.*) rubber. **Gummi|absatz,** *m.* rubber heel. **-arabikum,** *n.* gum (Arabic). **gummiartig,** *adj.* rubber-like, gummy. **Gummi|band,** *n.* elastic (band), rubber band. **-baum,** *m.* gum tree. **-boot,** *n.* rubber *or* inflatable dinghy. **-druck,** *m.* offset (printing).

gummieren [gu'mi:rən], *v.t.* gum; coat with rubber, rubberize; ***gummierte Briefumschläge,*** gummed *or* adhesive envelopes; ***gummierter Stoff,*** proofed fabric.

Gummi|ersatz, *m.* synthetic rubber, rubber substitute, factice. **-federung,** *f.* rubber shock-absorber. **-gutt,** *n.* gamboge. **-handschuh,** *m.* rubber glove. **-harz,** *n.* gum-resin. **-haut,** *f.* rubberized fabric. **-kabel,** *n.* insulated cable. **-knüppel,** *m.* rubber truncheon. **-lösung,** *f.* rubber solution *or* cement. **-mantel,** *m.* mackintosh, waterproof. **-reifen,** *m.* rubber tyre. **-schlauch,** *m.* rubber tube *or* tubing, hose; inner tube (*of tyre*). **-schleim,** *m.* mucilage, gum. **-schnur,** *f.* elastic thread. **-schuhe,** *m.pl.* galoshes, overshoes. **-seilstart,** *m.* catapult take-off (*gliders*). **-stempel,** *m.* rubber stamp. **-stiefel,** *m.pl.* gum boots. **-stöpsel,** *m.* rubber bung *or* stopper. **-überzug,** *m.* rubber coating, film of rubber. **-waren,** *f.pl.* rubber goods. **-zelle,** *f.* padded cell. **-zug,** *m.* elastic.

Gumpe ['gʊmpə], *f.* sump, grease-trap; (*dial.*) pool, deep (*in a watercourse*).

Gundel|beere ['gʊndəl–], *f.* *See* **-rebe. -kraut,** *n.* (*Bot.*) wild thyme (*Thymus serpyllum*). **-rebe,** *f.*, **Gundermann,** *m.* (*Bot.*) ground ivy (*Nepeta hederacea or glechoma*).

gunksen ['gʊŋksən], *v.t.* (*dial.*) nudge, push.

Günsel ['gynzəl], *m.* (*Bot.*) common bugle (*Ajuga reptans*).

Gunst [gunst], *f.* 1. favour, goodwill, kindness, affection; patronage, partiality; (*of weather etc.*) favourableness; 2. credit, advantage; *zu meinen -en*, to *or* in my favour, (*Comm.*) to my credit, to the credit of my account; *see also* **zugunsten**; *sich um seine - bewerben*, court his favour, curry favour with him; *ihm eine - erweisen*, do him a favour; *bei ihm in - stehen*, be in favour with him, be in his good graces *or* (*coll.*) books; 2. (*obs.*) leave, permission; *mit -*, with (your) permission, by (your) leave. **Gunstbezeigung,** *f.* (act of) favour *or* kindness.

günstig ['gynstɪç], *adj.* favourable, auspicious, opportune, propitious; promising, encouraging, reassuring; satisfactory, suitable, agreeable, convenient; advantageous, profitable, beneficial; *bei einer S. - abschneiden*, show up to advantage in a matter; *-e Gelegenheit*, (favourable *or* suitable) opportunity; *im -sten Falle*, at best; (*Comm.*) *zu -en Bedingungen*, on easy *or* favourable terms; *das Glück ist mir -*, luck is on my side; *bei -em Wetter*, weather permitting; *sich -er erweisen als ich dachte*, be not half as bad as I thought.

Günstling ['gynstlɪŋ], *m.* (**-s,** *pl.* **-e**) favourite, minion. **Günstlingswirtschaft,** *f.* favouritism.

Günther ['gyntər], *m.* Gunther.

Gurgel ['gurgəl], *f.* (-, *pl.* **-n**) throat, gullet, pharynx; *ihm die - abschneiden*, cut his throat; (*vulg.*) *durch die - jagen*, squander (*money*) in drink; (*fig.*) *ihm die - zuschnüren*, strangle him, ruin him economically. **Gurgel|ader,** *f.* jugular vein. **-bein,** *n.* collar bone, clavicle. **-klappe,** *f.* uvula. **gurgeln,** *v.i.* gargle; gurgle. **Gurgelwasser,** *n.* gargle.

Gurke ['gurkə], *f.* 1. cucumber, gherkin; 2. (*vulg.*) snitch, boko. **Gurken|hobel,** *m.* cucumber slicer. **-kraut,** *n.* borage. **-salat,** *m.* cucumber salad; (*Prov.*) *was versteht der Bauer von -?* this is quite above his head. **-zeit,** *f.* (*coll.*) *saure -*, silly season.

Gurre ['gurə], *f.* (*dial.*) nag, jade.

gurren ['gurən], *v.i.* coo.

Gurt [gurt], *m.* (**-(e)s,** *pl.* **-e**) girth, girdle, belt, sash, strap, webbing, harness (*parachute etc.*), machine-gun belt. **Gurt|anzug,** *m.* Norfolk suit. **-band,** *n.* straps, webbing. **-bogen,** *m.* (*Archit.*) transverse arch.

Gürtel ['gyrtəl], *m.* belt, girdle, sash; waistband; cordon; (*Geog.*) zone; (*Archit.*) fascia; (*fig.*) *den - enger schnallen*, tighten one's belt. **Gürtel|bahn,** *f.* ring railway (*in large towns*). **-kette,** *f.* chatelaine. **-reifen,** *m.* radial tyre. **-rose,** *f.* (*Med.*) shingles. **-schnalle,** *f.* clasp, buckle. **-tier,** *n.* (*Zool.*) armadillo (*Dasypodidae*).

gurten ['gurtən], *v.i.* fill ammunition *or* cartridge belt.

gürten ['gyrtən], **1.** *v.t.* gird, girdle. **2.** *v.r.* put on one's belt; (*fig.*) gird o.s., prepare, make ready.

Gurt|förderer, *m.* belt conveyor. **-gehenk,** *n.* sword-belt; belt ornaments, chatelaine. **-gewölbe,** *n.* (*Archit.*) ribbed vault. **-sims,** *m. or n.* (*Archit.*) plinth. **-strippe,** *f.* cinch strap (*harness*). **-zuführung,** *f.* belt-feed (*machine gun*).

Guß [gus], *m.* (**-(ss)es,** *pl.* **¨-(ss)e**) 1. gush, jet, downpour, torrent; 2. casting (process), founding, cast metal, cast iron, casting(s); *schmiedbarer -*, malleable cast iron; (*fig.*) *aus einem -*, homogeneous, harmonious, of a piece; 3. (*Typ.*) fount, (*Am.*) font; 4. (*Cul.*) icing.

Guß|abdruck, *m.* (*Typ.*) stereotype plate; cast. **-beton,** *m.* cast concrete. **-block,** *m.* ingot. **-bruch,** *m.* cast iron scrap. **-eisen,** *n.* cast iron, pig iron. **gußeisern,** *adj.* cast-iron. **Guß|form,** *f.* (casting-)mould. **-mutter,** *f.* (*Typ.*) matrix. **-stahl,** *m.* cast steel. **-stein,** *m.* (*dial.*) sink, gutter, drain. **-stück,** *n.* casting. **-waren,** *f.pl.* castings.

Gustav(us) ['gusta:f (gus'tavus)], *m.* Gustavus, Guy.

gut [gu:t] (*comp.* *besser*, *sup.* *best*), **1.** *adj.* good, excellent, fine, splendid; capable, efficient, serviceable; useful, profitable, advantageous, desirable, beneficial (*für*, to), conducive (to); pleasant, kind(-hearted), good-natured; considerable, substantial, adequate; respectable, virtuous; *-er Absatz*, ready sale; *-er Anzug*, best suit; *sein -es Auskommen haben*, make *or* earn a good deal of money; *auf - deutsch*, in plain English; *fröhlich und -er Dinge sein*, be of good cheer *or* in good spirits; (*Prov.*) *Ende -, alles -*, all's well that ends well; *aus -er Familie*, of *or* from a good family; *- zu Fuß*, a good walker; *für - finden*, think proper *or* fit; *ganz -*, quite good, not bad; *in -em Glauben*, in good faith, bona fide; *etwas auf - Glück tun*, do s.th. and hope for the best, do s.th. at a venture; *kein -es Haar an ihm lassen*, run him down, pull him to pieces; not have a good word to say for him; *für - halten*, approve of; *in -er Hand bei ihm sein*, be in good hands with him; *-er Hoffnung sein*, live in hope(s); be with child, be in the family way; *- bei Kasse*, be flush; *kurz und -*, in short; *zu -er Letzt*, finally, in the last resort; *-e Miene zum bösen Spiel machen*, put a good face on it; *-en Mutes*, of good cheer, in good spirits; *-e Nerven*, good *or* steady nerves; *der -e Ort*, (Jewish) cemetery; *-e Qualität*, good *or* high quality; *ein -er Rechner sein*, be good *or* quick at figures; *es mag für diesmal - sein*, I will overlook it this time; *ihm - sein*, be favourably disposed towards him, be attached to *or* like *or* care for *or* love him; *sie sind wieder -*, they have made it up *or* are friends again; *- sein mit ihm*, be on friendly terms with him; *- sein zu* or *gegen*, be good *or* kind to (*a p.*); *wozu ist das -?* what is the use of that? *so - wie nichts*, next to *or* practically nothing; *die -e Stube*, the best room, parlour, drawing-room; *eine -e Stunde*, fully *or* quite an hour, a good *or* full hour, an hour at least; *-e Tage haben*, have an easy life; (*Mus.*) *die -en Taktteile*, the strong accents; *ein -es Teil der Schuld liegt an mir*, I am largely responsible; *das hat -e Wege* or *Weile*, we need not trouble about that yet, there is plenty of time for that, that is (still) a long way off; *es wird schon alles - werden*, it will be all right, it will all turn out well; *er wird bald wieder -*, his anger won't last; *-es Wetter*, fine weather; *es ist sein -er Wille*, it is his wish *or* his own free will; *-e Worte*, fair words; (*Prov.*) *ein -es Wort findet eine -e Statt*, a good word goes a long way.

2. *adv.* well, excellently *etc.* (*see* **1** *above, adding ending* -ly); *- aussehen*, (*of a th.*) look good, (*of a p.*) be good-looking, (*health*) look well; *sich - halten*, (*of a th.*) keep well; (*of a p.*) hold o.s. erect *or* upright, (*fig.*) bear up, put up a good show; *den Klugen ist - predigen*, a word is enough to the wise; *du hast - reden*, it's easy for you to talk; *- riechen* (*schmecken*), smell (taste) good; *das tut mir -*, that does me the world of good; *du tätest - daran zu schweigen*, you would do well to keep silent, you had better keep silent; *- zustatten kommen*, stand in good stead, serve to good purpose; *- und gern*, easily, at least; *- 25 DM*, at least 25 marks, 25 marks or a little more; *- eine Viertelstunde*, fully a quarter of an hour; *ich kann ebenso - bleiben*, I may just as well stay; *sie schwimmt nicht so - wie ich*, she doesn't swim as well as I do; *schon -!* (that's) all right! never mind! that will do! that's enough! you need say no more! *laß es gut sein!* never mind! let it pass! don't mention it! let it be! leave it alone! have no more to do with it!

Gut, *n.* (**-es,** *pl.* **¨-er**) 1. good thing, blessing, treasure; *jenseits von - und Böse* (*Nietzsche*), beyond good and evil; (*Eccl.*) *das hochwürdige -*, the consecrated bread, the Host; *Gesundheit ist das höchste - auf Erden*, life's most precious gift is good health; 2. property, possession; estate, landed property, farm; *pl.* (*Law*) assets, effects; (*Comm.*) commodities, merchandise, goods, (*Am.*) freight; *- und Blut*, life and property; *ein erworbenes -*, an acquisition; *- und Geld, Geld und -*, wealth, possessions; *Hab und -*, goods and chattels; (*Law*) *heimgefallenes -*, escheat; (*Law*) *(un)bewegliche Güter*, (im)movables; (*Prov.*) *unrecht - gedeiht nicht*, ill-gotten gain never prospers; 3. (*Naut.*) rigging; *laufendes* (*stehendes*) *-*, running (standing) rigging.

Gut|achten, *n.* (expert) opinion, judgement, decision, award, verdict. **-achter,** *m.* consultant, arbitrator, expert; surveyor, valuer, assessor. **gut|-**

achtlich, *adv.* authoritative, expert. **–artig,** *adj.* good-natured, harmless, (*Med.*) benign, mild. **–aufgelegt,** *adj.* well disposed, in good humour. **–aussehend,** *adj.* good-looking. **Gutdünken,** *n.* opinion, judgement, estimation, discretion; ***nach* –,** at (one's own) discretion.

Gute, *see* **Gute(r), Gute(s).**

Güte ['gy:tə], *f.* kindness, kindliness, goodness (of heart), generosity; (*Eccl.*) loving kindness, (God's) grace; (intrinsic) worth, excellence, purity, (superior) quality; ***durch (die) – des Herrn Dr. W.,*** through the kindness *or* kind offices of Dr. W.; ***erster –,*** top-quality, first-rate, first-class; ***haben Sie die –,*** be so kind as (to); ***in –,*** amicably; by fair means; ***eine – ist der anderen wert,*** one good turn deserves another; ***meine –!*** good gracious! good Lord! **Güte|grad,** *m.*, **–klasse,** *f.* quality, grade, class, standard. **gütemäßig,** *adj.* in (respect of) quality.

Gute(r) ['gu:tə(r)], *m., f.* good (wo)man; ***die Guten,*** the good *or* righteous.

Güter ['gy:tər], *pl. of* **Gut. Güter|abfertigung,** *f.* despatch of goods; goods office. **–abtretung,** *f.* (*Law*) surrender of a bankrupt's estate. **–annahme,** *f.* goods office. **–bahnhof,** *m.* goods yard *or* station, (*Am.*) freight yard *or* depot. **–fernverkehr,** *n.* long-distance goods traffic. **–flugzeug,** *n.* freight-carrying aircraft. **–gemeinschaft,** *f.* property.

guterhalten ['gu:tˀɛrhaltən], *adj.* well preserved, in good condition *or* (state of) repair.

Güter|kraftverkehr, *n.* road haulage. **–makler,** *m.* estate *or* land agent, (*Am.*) realtor. **–markt,** *m.* commodity market. **–masse,** *f.* (*Law*) whole estate (of testator). **–recht,** *n.* law of property. **–schuppen,** *m.* warehouse, goods (*Am.* freight) shed *or* depot. **–sendung,** *f.* consignment. **–spedition,** *f.* goods department; forwarding agency, carriers. **–trennung,** *f.* (*Law*) antenuptial contract. **–verkehr,** *n.* goods (*Am.* freight) traffic. **–verlader,** *m.* shipping agent. **–wagen,** *m.* goods *or* luggage van *or* wag(g)on, (*Am.*) freight car. **–zug,** *m.* goods (*Am.* freight) train.

Gute(s) ['gu:tə(s)], *n.* good (th. *or* part); ***das Gute an der S.,*** the good thing about it; ***un das Gate der Geschichte*** the best of the joke; ***an das Gute glauben,*** have faith in (man's, God's) goodness; ***im Guten handeln,*** act in a friendly manner, be amicable; ***des Guten zuviel,*** too much of a good th.; ***des Guten zuviel tun,*** overshoot the mark, overdo it; ***Gutes mit Bösem vergelten,*** repay good with evil; ***nur Gutes sagen,*** only say nice things; ***sich zum Guten wenden,*** change for the better, take a turn for the better, turn out well; ***es hat auch sein Gutes,*** it has its good points too; ***alles Gute!*** good luck! I wish you well!

Güte|stelle, *f.* conciliation board. **–zeichen,** *n.* hallmark, guaranty seal.

gut|gelaunt, *adj.* in a good temper, good-humoured, in good spirits. **–gemeint,** *adj.* well-meant, well-intentioned. **–gesinnt,** *adj.* well-meaning; well-disposed (*Dat.*, to(wards)); right-minded, loyal. **Gutgewicht,** *n.* allowance, tret. **gutgläubig,** *adj.* credulous, (acting) in good faith, bona fide. **Gutgläubigkeit,** *f.* good faith; credulity. **Guthaben,** *n.* credit (balance), (bank) balance, assets, holdings; account; ***sein gegenwärtiges –,*** balance (standing) in his favour; ***kein –,*** no funds; ***ich habe noch ein kleines – bei Ihnen,*** a small sum still stands to my credit with you. **gutheißen,** *irr.v.t.* approve (of), sanction. **Gutheißung,** *f.* approbation, approval, consent, sanction. **gutherzig,** *adj.* good-natured *or* -hearted, kind-hearted. **Gutherzigkeit,** *f.* kind-heartedness, kindness, good nature.

gütig ['gy:tɪç], *adj.* good, kind, gracious; benevolent, charitable; indulgent; ***– gegen ihn,*** good to him; ***seien Sie – und geben es ihm,*** kindly give it to him; ***mit Ihrer –en Erlaubnis,*** with your kind permission; ***der Brief, den Sie mir –st geschrieben haben,*** the letter which you were kind enough to write me; ***–er Himmel!*** Good Heavens! Good Lord! **Gütigkeit,** *f.* goodness, kindness, graciousness; benevolence.

Gütler ['gy:tlər], *m.* (*dial.*) smallholder.

gütlich ['gy:tlɪç], *adj.* amicable, friendly; ***–er Vergleich,*** amicable settlement; ***sich*** (*Dat.*) ***– tun an einer S.,*** enjoy s.th., revel in a th.; ***– beilegen,*** settle amicably.

gut|machen, *v.t.* (***wieder***) –, make amends for, (*coll.*) make up for; make good, redress, repair. **–mütig,** *adj.* good-natured. **Gutmütigkeit,** *f.* good nature. **gutsagen,** *v.i.* vouch, answer, be answerable *or* responsible (***für,*** for).

Gutsbesitzer ['gu:tsbəzɪtsər], *m.* landowner, landed proprietor; squire, gentleman farmer.

Gutschein ['gu:tʃaɪn], *m.* voucher. **gutschreiben,** *irr.v.t.* credit; ***ihm etwas –,*** put s.th. to his account, place s.th. to his credit. **Gut|schrift,** *f.* credit(ing); ***zur –,*** to the credit of my (our) account. **–schriftsanzeige,** *f.*, **–schriftsbeleg,** *m.* credit note.

Guts|haus, *n.* farmhouse. **–herr,** *m.* squire, lord of the manor. *See* **–besitzer. gutsherrlich,** *adj.* ***–e Privilegien,*** manorial rights. **Gutshof,** *m.* estate, farm.

gut|situiert, *adj.* well-placed, in easy *or* comfortable circumstances. **–stehen,** *irr.v.i.* (***für***) *see* **–sagen.**

Guts|verwalter, *m.* manager of an estate, steward. **–verwaltung,** *f.* estate management; steward's office.

Guttapercha [guta'pɛrça], *f.* (*Austr. n.*) gutta-percha.

Guttat ['gu:tta:t], *f.* good deed, charitable act, kindness, benefit. **gut|tun,** *irr.v.i.* do good, (*as a child*) be good, behave, (*of medicine etc.*) do good, take effect, be soothing *or* a relief; ***das tut nicht gut,*** no good can come of it; ***das tut ihm gut,*** that does him (a world *or* power of) good. **–unterrichtet,** *adj.* well-informed. **–willig, 1.** *adj.* willing, obliging, complaisant. **2.** *adv.* willingly, readily, voluntarily, of one's own free will. **Gutwilligkeit,** *f.* willingness, complaisance.

Gymnasial|bildung [gymnazi'a:l–], *f.* classical education. **–direktor,** *m.* grammar-school headmaster. **–lehrer,** *m.* grammar-school master. **Gymnasiast,** *m.* (**-en,** *pl.* **-en**) grammar-school boy, secondary-school boy. **Gymnasiastin,** *f.* grammar-school girl. **Gymnasium** [–'na:zium], *n.* (**-s,** *pl.* **-sien**) grammar-school, classical secondary school.

Gymnastik [gym'nastɪk], *f.* gymnastics. **gymnastisch,** *adj.* gymnastic.

Gynäkologe [gynɛko'lo:gə], *m.* (**-n,** *pl.* **-n**) gynaecologist.

H

H, h [ha:], *n.* H, h; (*Mus.*) B, si.

Haag [ha:k], *m.* (*Geog.*) ***der or Den –,*** the Hague; ***in (Den) or im –,*** at the Hague.

Haar [ha:r], *n.* (**-(e)s,** *pl.* **-e**) hair; filament; (*of fabric*) nap, pile; wool, down, fluff; hairy *or* woolly side of skins; trifle; ***ihn an den –en ziehen,*** pull his hair; ***an den –en herbeiziehen,*** drag in willy-nilly; ***an den –en herbeigezogen, bei den –en herbeigeholt,*** far-fetched; ***es hing an einem –,*** it hung by a thread, it was touch and go; ***auf ein –, aufs –,*** to a T, exactly, precisely; ***das – aufwickeln,*** curl one's hair; ***deshalb lasse ich mir keine grauen –e wachsen,*** I shan't let that worry me, I shan't lose any sleep over that; ***sie läßt kein gutes – an ihm,*** she hasn't a good word to say for him, she pulls him to pieces *or* runs him down unmercifully; ***mit Haut***

und –(en), completely, entirely, altogether; lock, stock and barrel; ***sich in den –en liegen,*** be at loggerheads; (*coll.*) get in each other's hair; ***man hat ihm kein – gekrümmt,*** they have not touched a hair of his head; ***–e lassen müssen,*** suffer heavy loss(es), be fleeced; ***die –e standen*** or ***stiegen mir zu Berge,*** my hair stood on end; ***ein – in der Suppe,*** a fly in the ointment; ***um ein –,*** within an ace *or* a hair's breadth, very nearly, narrowly; ***nicht (um) ein –, (um) kein –,*** not a jot *or* bit *or* scrap, not in the least; ***–e auf den Zähnen haben,*** be aggressive *or* bare-faced *or* brazen.

Haar|ader, *f.* capillary vein. **–aufsatz,** *m.* false hair, toupee. **–(auf)wickler,** *m.* curling-pin; curl-paper; curling-tongs. **–ausfall,** *m.* loss of hair. **–balg,** *m.* hair follicle. **–beize,** *f.* depilatory. **–besatz,** *m.* hairy covering. **–beutel,** *m.* hair-bag; (*coll.*) ***einen – haben,*** be tipsy. **–bleiche,** *f.* hair bleach(ing). **–breit,** *n.* hair's breadth; ***nicht um ein – weichen,*** not budge an inch. **–bürste,** *f.* hair-brush. **–büschel,** *n.* tuft of hair. **–drüse,** *f.* sebaceous gland.

haaren ['ha:rən], *v.i., v.r.* lose hair; shed hair.

Haar|entferner, *m.,* **–entfernungsmittel,** *n. See* **–beize.**

Haaresbreite ['ha:rəsbraɪtə], *f.* hair's breadth; ***um –,*** by a hair's breadth; *see* **Haarbreit.**

Haar|farbe, *f.* colour of the hair. **–färbemittel,** *n.* hair-dye. **–färben,** *n.* hair dyeing *or* tinting. **–farn,** *m.* (*Bot.*) maidenhair fern (*Adiantum capillus veneris*). **–faser,** *f.* filament. **–feder,** *f.* (*of birds*) down, (*of clock*) hair-spring. **haarfein,** *adj.* fine as a hair; capillary, (*fig.*) delicate, extremely subtle. **Haar|flechte,** *f.* braid, tress, plait. **–fülle,** *f.* abundance *or* (*coll.*) mop of hair. **–gefäß,** *n.* capillary vessel. **haargenau,** *adj.* precise, exact, meticulous, to a nicety *or* a T. **haarig,** *adj.* 1. hairy, haired; hirsute; (*Bot.*) pilose, pilous; 2. (*Naut.*) hazy, obscured; 3. (*coll.*) colossal, monstrous, scandalous. **Haarklauberei,** *f.* hair-splitting. **haarklein,** *adv.* minutely, in detail, in all its details. **Haarlocke,** *f.* curl, ringlet, lock of hair. **haarlos,** *adj.* hairless, bald.

Haar|nadel, *f.* hairpin. **–nadelkurve,** *f.* hairpin bend. **–nest,** *n.* chignon. **–netz,** *n.* hair-net. **–öl,** *n.* hair-oil, brilliantine. **–pflege,** *f.* hairdressing. **–pflegemittel,** *n.* hair lotion *or* tonic. **–pinsel,** *m.* camel-hair brush. **–putz,** *m.* head-dress; coiffure; hair-ornament. **–riß,** *m.* hairline crack, craze. **–röhrchen,** *n.* capillary tube. **–röhrchenanziehung,** *f.* capillary attraction. **haarrissig,** *adj.* crazed. **Haarsalbe,** *f.* brilliantine, hair-cream. **haar|scharf, 1.** *adj.* very *or* razor sharp; (*fig.*) extremely precise *or* accurate. **2.** *adv.* (*fig.*) with mathematical precision; *see* **–genau. Haar|schneidemaschine,** *f.* hair clippers. **–schneiden,** *n.* haircutting; haircut. **–schneider,** *m.* barber, hairdresser. **–schnitt,** *m.* hair-style, (*coll.*) hair-do. **–schopf,** *m.* tuft of hair. **–schuppen,** *f.pl.* dandruff. **–schweif,** *m.* tail of a comet, coma. **–schwund,** *m.* loss of hair. **–sieb,** *n.* (*Cul.*) hair-sieve. **–spalterei,** *f.* hair-splitting, casuistry; ***– treiben,*** split hairs. **–spange,** *f.* hairslide. **–stern,** *m.* (*Zool.*) feather-star, sea-lily (*crinoid*). **haarsträubend,** *adj.* (*fig.*) hair-raising; incredible, outrageous, scandalous, atrocious, shocking. **Haar|strich,** *m.* up-stroke (*in writing*). **–tour, –tracht,** *f.* coiffure. **haartragend,** *adj.* (*Bot.*) capillary. **Haar|waschen,** *n.* shampoo. **–wasser,** *n.* hair-lotion. **–wechsel,** *m.* moulting. **–wickel,** *m.* curler, curl-paper. **–wickler,** *m. See* **–(auf)wickler. –wild,** *n.* ground game; ***– und Federwild,*** fur and feather. **–wuchs,** *m.* growth *or* head of hair; coat (*of animals*). **–wuchsmittel,** *n.* hair restorer. **–zange,** *f.* tweezers. **–zopf,** *m.* pigtail; plait.

Habakuk ['ha:bakuk], *m.* (*B.*) Habakkuk.

Habe ['ha:bə], *f.* property, goods, possessions, (personal) belongings, effects, (*Law*) personalty; ***Hab und Gut,*** goods and chattels, all one's belongings *or* property; ***bewegliche –,*** personal estate, movables; ***unbewegliche –,*** real estate, immovables.

haben ['ha:bən], **1.** *irr.v.t.* have; possess, be in possession of, own, hold; bear; ***er hat das so an sich,*** that is just his manner, he has that peculiarity about him; ***etwas auf sich –,*** be of significance *or* consequence, matter, signify; ***nichts auf sich –,*** be of no significance *or* consequence, not matter *or* signify; ***bei sich –,*** have about *or* with one; ***es bequem –,*** have an easy time; ***zum besten –,*** make a fool of, mock; (*coll.*) ***da hast du es!*** there you are! I told you so! what did I tell you? ***dafür ist er nicht zu –,*** he will have nothing to do with it; (*sl.*) count him out; ***ich habe nichts dagegen,*** I have no objection to it; ***nichts davon –,*** get nothing from it, gain *or* derive no benefit from it; ***was habe ich davon?*** what do I get out of it? what's in it for me? what good does it do me? ***das hat etwas für sich,*** that has its points, there's s.th. to be said for it; ***gern –,*** like, be fond of; (*coll.*) ***es im Halse –,*** have a sore throat; ***wo – Sie es her?*** how did you come by that? where have you picked that up? where did you get that from? ***hinter sich –,*** have done with; have experienced *or* undergone, (*coll.*) have gone through; ***das hat es in sich,*** there's a catch *or* difficulty in it, it's a tricky job; ***lieber –,*** prefer; ***am liebsten –,*** prefer above all; ***sie – es miteinander,*** they are having an affair; ***nötig –,*** need; ***nichts zu sagen –,*** not mean *or* signify much; ***es satt –,*** be sick of a th., (*coll.*) be fed to the teeth with a th., (*vulg.*) have had a belly-full; ***Gott habe ihn selig,*** God rest his soul! ***– zu*** (*inf.*), have to, be obliged *or* compelled to (*inf.*); ***es (nicht) für ungut –,*** (not) take amiss; ***unter sich –,*** have charge *or* control of; have care of; ***er hat viel von seinem Vater,*** he takes (a great deal) after his father; ***wen meinst du vor dir zu –?*** whom do you think you are speaking to? ***vor sich –,*** have still to do; face, await, (*coll.*) be in for; ***was hast du?*** what is the matter *or* (*coll.*) is up (with you)? (*sl.*) what's eating you? (*coll.*) ***hat sich was!*** nothing doing! not a hope! ***– wollen,*** wish, want, desire, require, demand. (*N.B. for expressions containing a noun object see the noun in question.*) **2.** *irr. v.r.* 1. (*coll.*) put on airs, (make a) fuss; 2. (*dial.*) there is, it is; ***es hat sich nichts zu danken,*** there's nothing to thank me for, you're welcome to it.

Haben, *n.* (*Comm.*) credit (side); ***Soll und –,*** debit and credit, liabilities and assets.

Habenichts ['ha:bənɪçts], *m.* (*- or* **-es,** *pl.* **-e**) beggar, s.o. without resources; *pl.* have-nots.

Haber ['ha:bər], *m.* (*dial.*) *see* **Hafer. Haber|-feldtreiben,** *n.* (*Hist.*) popular lynch justice (*among Bavarian peasants*). **–geiß,** *f.* (*dial.*) bog(e)y, spectre.

Habgier ['ha:pgi:r], *f.* greed(iness), avarice, covetousness. **habgierig,** *adj.* greedy, avaricious, covetous, (*coll.*) grasping. **habhaft,** *adj.* (*only in*) ***– werden*** (*Gen.*), get hold of, seize, take possession of, secure, catch.

Habicht ['ha:bɪçt], *m.* (**-(e)s,** *pl.* **-e**) (*Orn.*) goshawk (*Accipiter gentilis*). **Habichts|adler,** *m.* (*Orn.*) Bonelli's eagle (*Hieraætus fasciatus*). **–auge,** *n.* hawk-eye, keen eyesight. **–fang,** *m.* claw *or* pounce of a hawk. **–inseln,** *f.pl.* (*Geog.*) the Azores. **–kauz,** *m.* (*Orn.*) Ural owl (*Strix uralensis*). **–kraut,** *n.* (*Bot.*) hawkweed (*Hieracium*). **–nase,** *f.* hooked *or* aquiline nose.

Habilitation [habilitatsi'o:n], *f.* appointment as university lecturer. **Habilitationsschrift,** *f.* inaugural dissertation. **habilitieren** [–'ti:rən], *v.r.* qualify as university lecturer.

habituell [habitu'ɛl], *adj.* habitual, customary.

Habsburg ['ha:psburk], *f.* Hapsburg. **Habsburger,** *m.* member of the Hapsburg family; *pl.* the Hapsburg dynasty.

Hab|seligkeiten, *f.pl.* belongings, property, effects. **–sucht,** *f.,* **habsüchtig,** *adj. See* **Habgier, habgierig.**

Hachse ['haksə], *f.* back *or* hollow of the knee, lower leg, (*Cul.*) hock, leg (*of veal or pork*).

Hack [hak], *m.* (*dial.*) hack, stroke (*with axe etc.*); (*coll.*) ***– und Pack,*** ragtag and bobtail. **Hack|bau,** *m.* hoeing. **–beil,** *n.* chopper, cleaver, hand-axe. **–block,** *m.* chopping block. **–braten,** *m.* minced meat, mince. **–brett,** *n.* 1. chopping-board; 2. (*Mus.*) dulcimer.

[1]**Hacke** ['hakə], *f.* pickaxe, pick; mattock, hoe; hoeing time *or* season.

[2]**Hacke,** *f.*, **Hacken,** *m.* 1. afterpiece, shoulder; 2. heel *(of stocking, boot etc.)*; ***die –n zusammenschlagen,*** click one's heels; *(coll.)* ***sich*** *(Dat.)* ***die –n ablaufen,*** run one's feet off (***nach,*** for); ***er tritt mir unter die –n,*** he gets under my feet *or* heels; ***er ist mir dicht auf den –n,*** he is hard on my heels.

hacken ['hakən], *v.t.* chop, hack; *(Cul.)* hash, mince; hoe *(soil)*, cleave *(wood)*, pick, peck; ***Gehacktes,*** minced meat, mince. **Hackepeter,** *m.* *(dial.)* minced pork. **Hacker, Häcker,** *m.* *(dial.)* vine-grower.

Häckerling ['hɛkərlɪŋ], *m. See* **Häcksel.**

Hack|fleisch, *n.* minced meat, mince. **–frucht,** *f.* root-crops. **–klotz,** *m. See* **–block. –messer,** *n.* chopper, chopping-knife, cleaver.

Häcksel ['hɛksəl], *m.* *(Austr. n.)* chopped straw, chaff. **Häcksel(schneide)maschine,** *f.* chaff-cutter.

[1]**Hader** ['ha:dər], *m.* (**-s,** *pl.* **-n**) *(dial.)* rag, tatter; *pl.* rags *(paper-making)*.

[2]**Hader,** *m.* quarrel, brawl, feud, dispute, discord, strife. **hadern,** *v.i.* wrangle, quarrel, squabble, be at strife *or* feud (***mit,*** with).

Hafen ['ha:fən], *m.* (**-s,** *pl.* ¨) 1. (sea)port, harbour; *(fig.)* haven, refuge; ***einen – anlaufen,*** make for port; ***im – anlegen,*** harbour; 2. *(dial.)* earthen vessel, pot; *(Prov.)* ***jeder – findet seinen Deckel,*** every pot has its lid.

Hafen|amt, *n.* port authority. **–anlagen,** *f.pl.* port installations, docks. **–arbeiter,** *m.* docker, longshoreman. **–becken,** *n.* harbour-basin, wet dock. **–damm,** *m.* pier, jetty, mole, breakwater. **–gäste,** *m.pl.* foreign vessels (in a port). **–gatt,** *n.* harbour-mouth. **–gebühr,** *f.*, **–geld,** *n.* harbour-dues, anchorage (dues). **–sperre,** *f.* blockade, embargo; harbour-boom. **–stadt,** *f.* seaport (town). **–viertel,** *n.* dockquarter, waterfront. **–zoll,** *m. See* **–geld.**

Hafer ['ha:fər], *m.* oats; *(coll.)* ***der – sticht ihn,*** he is getting insolent *or* uppish *or* *(coll.)* cocky. **Hafer|-brei,** *m.* (oatmeal) porridge. **–flocken,** *f.pl.* rolled *or* porridge oats. **–grütze,** *f.* groats. **–mehl,** *n.* oatmeal. **–schleim,** *m.* oatmeal gruel. **–spreu,** *f.* oat-chaff. **–stroh,** *n.* oat-straw; ***grob wie –,*** abominably rude.

Haff [haf], *n.* (**-(e)s,** *pl.* **-e**) lagoon *(in the Baltic)*.

Hafner ['ha:fnər], *m.* 1. potter; 2. *(dial.)* plumber.

[1]**Haft** [haft], *m.* (**-(e)s,** *pl.* **-e**) fastening, clasp, clamp, tie; crotchet.

[2]**Haft,** *f.* custody, detention, imprisonment, confinement; arrest; ***aus der – entlassen,*** release, discharge from custody; ***in enger –,*** under close arrest, in close confinement *or* detention *or* custody; ***in – nehmen,*** (put under) arrest, take into custody, place under detention.

haftbar ['haftba:r], *adj.* responsible, liable, answerable (***für,*** for). **Haftbarkeit,** *f.* liability, responsibility.

Haft|befehl, –brief, *m.* warrant (for arrest). **–dauer,** *f.* period of detention, term of imprisonment.

haften ['haftən], *v.i.* 1. cling, adhere, stick (*an* *(Dat.)*, to); *(fig.)* be fixed *or* centred, persist *(as thoughts)*, rankle, haunt *(fears, doubts etc.)*; ***seine Blicke – lassen auf*** *(Dat.)*, have one's eyes fixed on, keep looking at; ***es haftet ein Verdacht auf ihm,*** suspicion rests on him; ***es haftet nichts an ihm*** or ***bei ihm,*** it goes in at one ear and out at the other, it goes over him like water off a duck's back; 2. *(Law)* ***– für,*** go bail for, bear the blame *or* be (held) responsible *or* liable *or* answerable for, answer for.

Haft|fähigkeit, –festigkeit, *f.* adhesive strength, adhesion, tenacity. **–geld,** *n.* *(dial.)* earnest money; retaining fee. **–gläser,** *n.pl.* contact lenses. **–hohlladung,** *f.* *(Mil., Naut.)* limpet bomb, sticky bomb.

Häftling ['hɛftlɪŋ], *m.* (**-s,** *pl.* **-e**) prisoner, detainee.

Haft|lokal, *n.* *(Mil.)* guard-room, detention room. **–pflicht,** *f.* liability, responsibility; ***solidare –,*** joint liability, solidarity; ***mit beschränkter –,*** limited (liability). **–pflichtgesetz,** *n.* Employers' Liability Act. **haftpflichtig,** *adj.* liable, responsible (***für,*** for). **Haftpflichtversicherung,** *f.* third-party insurance.

Haftung ['haftuŋ], *f.* 1. adhesion; 2. responsibility, liability, guarantee; ***mit beschränkter –,*** limited (liability).

Hag [ha:k], *m.* (**-(e)s,** *pl.* **-e**) hedge, fence; enclosure; *(Poet.)* bush, grove, coppice.

Hagebuche ['ha:gəbu:xə], *f.* *(Bot.)* hornbeam (*Carpinus betulus*). **hagebüchen, hagebuchen,** *adj.* coarse; clumsy; unheard-of, preposterous. **Hagel|-butte,** *f.* hip, haw. **–dorn,** *m.* *(dial.)* *(Bot.)* hawthorn (*Crataegus monogyna*).

Hagel ['ha:gəl], *m.* hail; *(obs.)* grape- *or* case-shot; ***ein – von Schimpfworten,*** a storm of abuse. **Hagelkorn,** *n.* hailstone; sty(e) *(in the eye)*. **hageln,** *v.i. imp.* hail; ***es hagelte Schläge,*** blows rained *or* hailed down. **Hagel|schaden, –schlag,** *m.* damage done by hail. **–schloßen,** *f.pl.* hailstones. **–wetter,** *n.* hailstorm.

hager ['ha:gər], *adj.* haggard, gaunt, spare, lean, lank, raw-boned, *(coll.)* lanky, scraggy. **Hagerkeit,** *f.* leanness, gauntness, lank(i)ness.

Häher ['hɛ:ər], *m.* *(Orn.)* *see* **Eichelhäher. Häherkuckuck,** *m.* great spotted cuckoo (*Clamator glandarius*).

Hahn [ha:n], *m.* (**-(e)s,** *pl.* **¨e** *or* (*rare except in mechanical sense*) **-en**) 1. cock, rooster; ***danach kräht kein –,*** nobody cares two hoots about it; ***– im Korbe sein,*** be cock of the roost *or* walk; ***den roten – aufs Dach setzen*** *(Dat.)*, set fire to *(a p.'s)* house, set *(s.o.'s)* house on fire; 2. stopcock, tap, spigot, *(Am.)* faucet; *(obs.)* cock *(on a gun etc.)*; ***den – (am Gewehr) spannen,*** cock a gun.

Hähnchen ['hɛ:nçən], *n.* cockerel.

Hahnen|balken, *m.* collar-beam. **–bart,** *m.* wattles. **–ei,** *n.* cock's egg, chimera, mare's nest; *(coll.)* very small egg. **–fuß,** *m.* *(Bot.)* ranunculus. **–kamm,** *m.* cockscomb; *(Bot.)* carob tree (*Erythrima abessinica*); *(Bot.)* common cockscomb (*Celosa eristata*); *(Bot.)* yellow rattle (*Rhinanthus cristagalli*). **–kampf,** *m.* cock-fight. **–plan,** *m.* cockpit. **–ruf,** *m.* cock-crowing, cock-crow. **–schlagen,** *n.* cock-shy. **–schrei,** *m. See* **–ruf. –sporn,** *m.* *(Bot.)* cockspur (*Crataegus crusgalli*). **–tritt,** *m.* copulation *(of fowl)*; tread *or* cicatricule *(of eggs)*; *(Vet.)* spring-halt.

Hahnrei ['ha:nraɪ], *m.* (**-s,** *pl.* **-e**) cuckold; ***zum – machen,*** cuckold.

Hai [haɪ], *m.* (**-(e)s,** *pl.* **-e**), **Haifisch,** *m.* shark (*also fig. = unscrupulous money-maker*).

Hain [haɪn], *m.* (**-(e)s,** *pl.* **-e**) *(Poet.)* grove, sylvan glade, bosket, boscage. **Hain|ampfer,** *m.* *(Bot.)* blood-wort (*Rumex sanguineus*). **–buche,** *f.* *(Bot.)* hornbeam (*Carpinus betulus*). **–bund,** *m.* poetic coterie of Göttingen undergraduates 1770–4.

Häkchen ['hɛ:kçən], *n.* little hook, crochet; *(Typ.)* apostrophe, tick; ***früh krümmt sich, was ein – werden will,*** as the twig is bent, so the tree will grow. **Häkelarbeit,** *f.* crochet-work. **Häkelei** [–'laɪ], *f.* 1. crochet-work; 2. *(fig.)* chaffing, teasing, taunting, fault-finding. **Häkel|garn,** *n.* crochet-thread. **–haken,** *m. See* **–nadel. häk(e)lig,** *adj.* 1. hooked, barbed, prickly; 2. *(fig.)* captious, critical. **häkeln,** *v.t., v.i.* crochet. **Häkelnadel,** *f.* crochet-hook *or* -needle.

Haken ['ha:kən], *m.* hook, hasp, clasp, clamp; grappling-iron; *(fig.)* catch, hitch, snag; ***die S. hat einen*** or ***ihren –,*** there is a catch *or* snag in it; *(Boxing)* ***ein rechter –,*** a right hook; ***– schlagen,*** *(Hunt.)* double *(as hares)*; *(Av.)* take evasive action. **haken, 1.** *v.i.* (*an* *(Acc.)*), *v.t.* hook, grapple (on to). **2.** *v.r.* catch, hook, get caught *or* hooked (up) (*an* *(Acc.)*, on). **3.** *v.i.imp.* ***da hakt es,*** there's the rub *or* the snag. **Hakenbüchse,** *f.* *(Hist.)* harquebus. **hakenförmig,** *adj.* hooked. **Haken|gimpel,** *m.* *(Orn.)* pine grosbeak (*Pinicola enucleator*). **–kreuz,** *n.* swastika, fylfot. **–kreuzler,** *m.* *(Austr.)* Nazi, Hitlerite. **–nase,** *f.* aquiline *or* hooked nose.

–schlüssel, *m.* picklock. **–spieß,** *m.* harpoon. **–zahn,** *m.* canine *or* eye tooth. **hakig,** *adj.* hooked.

häklig, *adj. See* **häk(e)lig.**

Halali [hala'li:], *int., n.* (**-s,** *pl.* **-(s)**) mort, kill, death (*hunting*).

halb [halp], **1.** *adj.* half; (*as pref.*) semi-, demi-; (*Naut.*) ***–e Fahrt,*** half-speed; ***auf –er Höhe,*** half-way up; ***mit –em Ohre zuhören,*** listen with half an ear, listen inattentively; ***zum –en Preise,*** at half the price, (at) half-price; ***es schlägt –,*** it strikes the half-hour; ***mit –er Stimme,*** in an undertone; (*Mus.*) mezza voce; ***eine –e Stunde,*** half an hour, a half-hour; ***alle –en Stunden,*** every half-hour; ***–er Ton,*** semitone; ***ihm auf –em Wege entgegenkommen,*** meet him halfway; ***– zehn,*** half-past nine. **2.** *adv.* by halves, half; ***– und –,*** nearly, tolerably, so-so, middling; ***– und – dazu entschlossen,*** half decided on; ***– geschenkt,*** practically *or* as good as given away, a gift at the price; ***– gewonnen,*** half the battle; ***– soviel,*** half as much; ***weder – noch ganz,*** neither one thing nor another.

halbamtlich ['halpˀamtlıç], *adj.* semi-official. **Halb|arier,** *m.* (*Nat. Soc.*) half-Jew (*distinguished from 'Halbjude' by the fact that Jewish parent was Christian at time of marriage*). **–ärmel,** *m.* short *or* elbow-length sleeve. **–band,** *m.* (*Bookb.*) boards. **halb|batzig,** *adj.* (*Swiss*) mediocre. **–befahren,** *adj.* ***–es Volk,*** common (*i.e. not* able) seamen. **Halb|bild,** *n.* half-length portrait, bust. **–bildung,** *f.* superficial culture; smattering of education. **–blut,** *n.* half-blood, half-caste. **–blüter,** *m.* half-breed (*horse*). **–bruder,** *m.* half-brother. **halbbürtig,** *adj.* half-caste; ***–e Schwester,*** (illegitimate) stepsister. **Halb|dach,** *n.* lean-to roof. **–deck,** *n.* quarter-deck. **halbdeckend,** *adj.* semi-opaque. **Halbdunkel,** *n.* dusk, semi-darkness, twilight. **halbdurchlässig,** *adj.* semi-permeable. **–durchsichtig,** *adj.* semi-transparent. **Halbedelstein,** *m.* semi-precious stone. **halberhaben,** *adj.* in basso relievo.

Halbe(s) ['halbə(s)], *n.* half, (*coll.*) small beer.

halb|fest, *adj.* semi-fluid. **–fett,** *adj.* (*Typ.*) medium-faced. **Halb|flügler,** *m.pl.* (*Ent.*) hemiptera. **–franzband,** *m.* half-calf binding. **halbgar,** *adj.* underdone. **Halbgeschoß,** *n.* entresol, mezzanine. **–gesicht,** *n.* profile. **–gott,** *m.* demigod. **–gut,** *n.* alloy of equal parts of tin and lead.

Halbheit ['halphaıt], *f.* incompleteness; imperfection; lukewarmness, half-heartedness; half-measure.

Halb|hemd, *n.* front, dicky. **–hose,** *f.* knickerbockers; bloomers (*of women*).

halbieren [hal'bi:rən], *v.t.* cut in half *or* halves, halve, (*Geom.*) bisect. **Halbierung,** *f.* halving, bisection. **Halbierungslinie,** *f.* bisecting line, bisector.

Halb|insel, *f.* peninsula. **–jahr,** *n.* half-year, six months. **halb|jährig,** *adj.* lasting six months; six months old. **–jährlich,** *adj.* occurring every six months, half-yearly. **Halb|kenner,** *m.* dabbler. **–kettenfahrzeug,** *n.* half-tracked vehicle. **–kreis,** *m.* semicircle. **halbkreisförmig,** *adj.* semicircular. **Halbkugel,** *f.* hemisphere. **halblaut,** *adj.* sotto voce, in an undertone. **Halb|leder,** *n.* half-calf. **–linke(r),** *m.* (*Footb.*) inside left (forward). **–mast,** *m.* (*of a flag*) ***auf –,*** (at) half-mast. **–mensch,** *m.* centaur; (*fig.*) brute. **–messer,** *m.* radius. **halbmilitärisch,** *adj.* paramilitary. **Halb|monatsschrift,** *f.* fortnightly (review *or* magazine). **–mond,** *m.* half-moon. **halb|mondförmig,** *adj.* crescent(-shaped). **–offen,** *adj.* half-open, (*of door*) ajar. **–part,** *adv.* ***– machen,*** go halves *or* (*coll.*) fifty-fifty. **–rund,** *adj.* semicircular. **Halb|schatten,** *m.* half-shade, half-shadow, penumbra. **–schlaf,** *m.* doze, dozing. **halbschreitig,** *adj.* (*Mus.*) chromatic. **Halbschuh,** *m.* shoe. **halbschürig,** *adj.* of second shearing; premature, imperfect; inferior; ***–es Lob,*** half-hearted praise. **Halb|schwergewicht,** *n.* (*Spt.*) light heavyweight. **–seide,** *f.* poplin. **–seitenlähmung,** *f.* (*Med.*) hemiplegia. **–sopran,** *m.* mezzo-soprano. **–starke(r),** *m.* (*coll.*) young rowdy, hooligan. **–stiefel,** *m.* ankle-boot. **halbstocks,** *adv.* half-mast. **Halbstrumpf,** *m.* ankle-sock. **halb|stündig,** *adj.* half-hour, (lasting) half an hour. **–stündlich,** *adj.* (occurring once) every half-hour, half-hourly.

halb|tägig, *adj.* (lasting) half a day, half a day's. **–täglich,** *adj.* occurring twice a day; lasting twelve hours. **Halb|tagsarbeit,** *f.* part-time work. **–ton,** *m.* (*Mus.*) semitone; (*Phot., Typ.*) half-tone. **halbtot,** *adj.* half-dead; (*coll.*) ***sich – lachen,*** kill o.s. laughing. **Halbtrauer,** *f.* half-mourning. **halbverdaut,** *adj.* partly digested. **Halb|verdeck,** *n.* quarter-deck. **–vers,** *m.* half-line, hemistich. **–vokal,** *m.* semi-vowel. **halbwach,** *adj.* dozing, half awake. **Halbwaise,** *f.* fatherless *or* motherless child. **halbwegs,** *adv.* half-way, midway; (*coll.*) tolerably, to a certain extent, middling. **Halb|welt,** *f.* demi-monde. **–weltdame,** *f.* demi-mondaine, demi-rep. **–wertzeit,** *f.* (*Phys.*) half-life (period). **–wissen,** *n.* smattering, superficial *or* imperfect knowledge. **halbwöchentlich,** *adj.* half-weekly, twice weekly. **Halbwolle,** *f.* linsey-woolsey. **halbwüchsig,** *adj.* adolescent, teen-age. **Halb|wüchsige(r),** *m., f.* adolescent, juvenile, teenager. **–zeit,** *f.* (*Spt.*) half-time. **–zug,** *m.* (*Mil.*) half-platoon, section.

Halde ['haldə], *f.* (*Poet.*) slope, declivity, hill-side; (*Min.*) slag-heap, dump.

half [half], *see* **helfen.**

Halfa ['halfa], *f.* esparto grass, alpha grass.

Hälfte ['hɛlftə], *f.* half, (*Law*) moiety; (*coll.*) ***bessere –,*** better half (*wife*); ***um die – teuerer,*** half as dear again; ***um die – weniger,*** less by half, only half; ***bis zur –,*** as far as the middle, half way; ***die Rechnung zur – tragen,*** go halves with the bill.

Halfter ['halftər], *f.* (**-,** *pl.* **-n**) (*Austr. sometimes m. or n.*) halter. **halftern,** *v.t.* (put on the) halter. **Halftertasche,** *f.* holster.

Hall [hal], *m.* (**-(e)s,** *pl.* **-e**) sound, resonance, peal, clang.

Halle ['halə], *f.* hall, great room; (*in hotel*) lounge, public room; lobby, vestibule; market-hall, emporium, bazaar; (*Tenn.*) covered court; (*Av.*) hangar.

hallen ['halən], *v.i.* (re)sound, echo.

Hallenbad ['halənba:t], *n.* indoor baths.

Hallenser [ha'lɛnzər], *m.* native of Halle.

Hallig ['halıç], **Halling** ['halıŋ], *f.* (**-,** *pl.* **-en**) (*Schleswig-Holstein dial.*) small island.

hallo! ['halo:, ha'lo:], *int.* hullo! **Hallo,** *n.* (*coll.*) hullabaloo, din.

Halm [halm], *m.* (**-(e)s,** *pl.* **-e**) blade; stalk, stem, straw; ***Getreide auf dem –,*** green corn; standing corn. **Halm|früchte,** *f.pl.* cereals. **–knoten,** *m.* joint *or* node of a stalk. **–lese,** *f.* gleaning. **–ziehen,** *n.* drawing lots.

Halogen [halo'ge:n], *n.* (**-s,** *pl.* **-e**) (*Chem.*) halogen, haloid. **Halogenid** [–'ni:t], *n.* (*Chem.*) halide. **halogenieren,** *v.t.* halinate, halogenate.

Hals [hals], *m.* (**-es,** *pl.* **⸗e**) neck; throat; tongue (*voice of hound*); ***ihm den – abdrehen*** or ***abschneiden,*** bring him to ruin; ***am – aufhängen,*** hang by the neck; ***das geht ihm an den –*** or ***kostet ihm den –,*** that may cost him his head; ***sich*** (*Dat.*) ***etwas an den – reden,*** bring s.th. upon o.s. by inconsiderate talk; (*fig.*) ***sich ihm an den – werfen,*** throw o.s. at his head; ***etwas auf dem – haben,*** be saddled with a th.; ***sich*** (*Dat.*) ***etwas auf den – laden*** or ***ziehen,*** bring a th. upon o.s., bring s.th. down on one's head; ***auf dem – sitzen*** (*Dat.*), importune, be a burden to; ***aus vollem –e lachen,*** roar with laughter, laugh heartily; ***aus vollem –e schreien,*** scream one's head off, shout at the top of one's voice; ***bis an den –,*** up to the eyes; ***böser –,*** sore throat; ***sich*** (*Dat.*) ***den – brechen,*** break one's neck; (*fig.*) ***das bricht ihm den –,*** that will be his undoing; ***einer Flasche den – brechen,*** crack a bottle; ***– geben,*** give tongue (*of hounds*); ***es wird ja nicht den – kosten,*** it is not a matter of life and death *or* a vital *or* serious *or* hanging matter; ***einen langen – machen,*** crane one's neck; ***die Lüge blieb ihm im –e stecken,*** the lie stuck in his throat; ***– über Kopf,*** head over heels;

(*fig.*) headlong, helter-skelter, precipitately; ***ihm um den – fallen,*** fall on his neck, embrace him; ***es geht um den –,*** it is a matter of life and death, it is a vital issue; ***ihm den – umdrehen,*** wring his neck; ***sich*** (*Dat.*) ***den – verrenken,*** crane one's neck (***nach,*** for); ***bleiben Sie mir damit vom –e,*** don't pester me with that; ***sich*** (*Dat.*) ***vom –e schaffen,*** rid o.s. of; ***das hängt*** or ***wächst mir zum – heraus,*** I'm fed up (to the teeth) with it, I am sick (and tired) of that.

Halsabschneider ['hals?apʃnaɪdər], *m.* 1. cut-throat; 2. usurer. **halsabschneiderisch,** *adj.* cut-throat (*competition*). **Hals|ader,** *f.* jugular vein. **–arterie,** *f.* carotid artery. **–ausschnitt,** *m.* neck-line (*of dress*). **–band,** *n.* collar (*for dogs*); necklace. **–bandfliegenfänger, –bandfliegenschnäpper,** *m. See* **–bandschnäpper. –bandfrankolin,** *m.* (*Orn.*) francolin (*Francolinus francolinus*). **–bandregenpfeifer,** *m. See* **Sandregenpfeifer. –bandsäger,** *m. See* **Mittelsäger. –bandschnäpper,** *m.* (*Orn.*) white-collared flycatcher (*Ficedula albicollis*). **–binde,** *f.* neck-tie, cravat, scarf. **–bräune,** *f.* quinsy. **halsbrecherisch,** *adj.* breakneck, dangerous, perilous. **Halsbund,** *m.* neckband (*on shirt*). **Halse,** *f. See* **Halsung. Halseisen,** *n.* iron collar (pillory).

halsen ['halzən], **1.** *v.t.* (*obs.*) embrace. **2.** *v.i.* (*Naut.*) gybe.

Hals|entzündung, *f.* tonsillitis, angina, sore throat. **–gericht,** *n.* (*obs.*) capital court. **–geschmeide,** *n.*, **–kette,** *f.* necklace. **–krause,** *f.* frill, ruff. **–mandel,** *f.* tonsil. **–muskel,** *m.* cervical muscle. **–priese,** *f. See* **–band. –schlagader,** *f. See* **–arterie. –schmuck,** *m.* necklace. **–starre,** *f.* stiffness of the neck. **halsstarrig,** *adj.* stiff-necked, stubborn, obstinate, headstrong. **Hals|-starrigkeit,** *f.* obstinacy, stubbornness. **–stück,** *n.* neck (*of meat*). **–tuch,** *n.* scarf, neckerchief, muffler. **Halsung,** *f.* (*Hunt.*) dog collar, leash. **Hals|vene,** *f.* jugular vein. **–weh,** *n.* sore throat. **–weite,** *f.* collar-size. **–wirbel,** *m.* cervical vertebra. **–zäpfchen,** *n.* uvula.

Halt [halt], *m.* (**-(e)s,** *pl.* **-e**) 1. hold, holding; footing, foothold, support; stability, steadiness, firmness; (*fig.*) (main)stay, support; ***Mensch ohne inneren –,*** unbalanced *or* vacillating *or* unstable p.; ***– geben*** (*Dat.*), support; 2. stop, halt, pause; ***ohne –,*** non-stop (*journey etc.*); ***– gebieten,*** call a halt (*Dat.*, to); ***– machen,*** stop, halt. **halt,** *adv., part.* (*dial.*) in my opinion, I think, I'm afraid, to be sure, you know; ***er wird – nicht kommen,*** I don't think he will come; ***er ist – ein Bummler,*** he is a loafer when all is said and done.

hält [hɛlt], *see* **halten.**

haltbar ['haltba:r], *adj.* tenable, defensible; strong, solid, firm, stable; durable, lasting, permanent, (*of colour*) fast; (*fig.*) tenable, valid. **Haltbarkeit,** *f.* defensibility; durability, serviceability, stability, firmness; strength, endurance, wear; (*of colour*) fastness; validity.

Halte|feder, *f.* retaining spring. **–gurt,** *m.* parachute harness. **–kabel,** *n.* mooring rope.

halten ['haltən], **1.** *irr.v.t.* 1. hold, keep, retain; detain, keep back, constrain; contain, include; observe, perform, celebrate; ***das Abendmahl –,*** celebrate *or* administer Holy Communion; ***ans Licht –,*** hold to the light; ***ein Auto –,*** keep *or* run a car; ***Freundschaft –,*** live on friendly terms; ***Frieden –,*** keep peace; ***Hochzeit –,*** celebrate one's marriage; ***in Ehren –,*** (hold in) honour; ***in Gang –,*** keep going; ***in Ordnung –,*** keep in order; ***Inventur –,*** take stock; ***Mahlzeit –,*** dine, sup, be at table; ***Maß –,*** observe moderation, be moderate; ***es mit ihm –,*** side *or* hold with him; ***Mund –,*** keep one's mouth shut; (*Mus.*) ***eine Note –,*** sustain a note; ***eine Rede –,*** make *or* deliver a speech, speak (*in public*); ***ihn schadlos –,*** indemnify him; ***sich schadlos –,*** recover one's losses; ***Schritt –,*** keep pace, walk in step; ***Stich –,*** stand the test; ***ein Kind über die Taufe –,*** stand sponsor to a child; ***Vorlesungen –,*** deliver *or* give lectures; ***Wasser –,*** be watertight, hold water; ***– Sie das wie Sie wollen,*** please yourself (about that); ***ihn bei seinem Worte –,*** hold *or* keep him to his word; ***im Zaume –,*** keep a tight hand on; ***eine Zeitschrift –,*** subscribe to a periodical; ***eine Zeitung –,*** take in a newspaper; ***ihn zum besten –,*** tease, make a fool of *or* deceive him; (*obs.*) ***– zu Gnaden,*** at your pleasure; 2. think, deem, consider; ***– für,*** look upon as, consider *or* regard as; think *or* believe *or* suppose *or* take to be; ***viel von ihm –,*** think highly *or* have a high opinion of him; ***nicht viel von ihm –,*** think little of *or* have a low *or* poor opinion of him.
2. *irr.v.i.* 1. stop, halt; pull *or* draw up; 2. last, be durable *or* lasting, endure, hold out, stand firm; (*coll.*) ***dicht –,*** keep quiet, keep one's mouth shut; ***das Eis hält noch nicht,*** the ice does not bear yet; ***das kann nicht lange –,*** that cannot last long; ***es hält schwer,*** it is difficult; ***der Stoff hält nicht,*** the material does not wear well; 3. ***an sich –,*** control *or* check *or* restrain o.s.; 4. ***auf seine Ehre –,*** be jealous of *or* set store by *or* attach value to *or* lay stress on one's honour; ***auf Träume –,*** pay heed *or* attention to *or* believe in dreams; ***auf sich –,*** be particular about one's appearance; 5. ***dafür – daß,*** hold *or* maintain that; 6. ***links*** (***rechts***) ***–,*** keep to the left (right).
3. *irr.v.r.* hold out, last, keep good; behave; take (good *or* bad) care of o.s.; ***sich – an*** (*Acc.*), (*to a th.*) hold on to, steady o.s. with; keep *or* (*coll.*) stick to, follow; (*fig.*) follow, observe, adhere to, comply with, abide by; (*to a p.*) have recourse to; ***sich aufrecht –,*** hold o.s. erect; ***sich bereit –,*** hold o.s. in readiness, be ready; ***die Festung hält sich,*** the fortress holds out; ***sich gut –,*** keep (well) (*as food*), wear well (*as clothes*), keep one's appearance (*of a p.*), hold one's ground, do well, (*coll.*) put up a good show (*of a p.*); ***sich links –,*** keep to the left; ***die Preise – sich,*** prices remain steady; ***das Wetter hält sich,*** the weather remains unchanged; ***sich zu Hause –,*** stay at home *or* indoors; (***sich***) ***zu einer Partei –,*** hold with *or* support a party.

Halte|platz, *m.* stopping-place, loading point, parking space. **–punkt,** *m.* 1. point of aim; 2. (*Railw.*) halt (= *small station*).

Halter ['haltər], *m.* 1. holder, keeper, (legal) owner; 2. hold, support, bracket, rack, clip, clamp; reservoir, receptacle; (*coll.*) penholder. **Halterung,** *f.* (*Tech.*) support, fixture, mounting.

Halte|seil, *n. See* **–tau. –signal,** *n.* (*Railw.*) block signal. **–stelle,** *f.* stopping-place *or* point, (bus) station, (tram *or* bus) stop; resting place; ***– für Taxis,*** taxi-stand. **–tau,** *n.* guy-line, guy-rope. **–zahn,** *m.* catch, locking pin.

-haltig ['haltɪç], *adj. suff.* (*in compounds* =) containing.

haltlos ['haltlo:s], *adj.* without support; unstable, unsteady, lax, unprincipled; baseless, unfounded; untenable. **Haltlosigkeit,** *f.* instability, unsteadiness; lack of principle(s), laxity. **haltmachen,** *v.i.* stop, pause, call *or* make a halt; (*Mil.*) ***– lassen,*** halt (*marchers*); ***vor nichts –,*** stop *or* stick at nothing.

hältst [hɛltst], *see* **halten.**

Haltung ['haltuŋ], *f.* bearing, attitude, posture, carriage, deportment; (*Art etc.*) pose, (*Spt.*) stance, style, (body-)position; (*fig.*) behaviour, demeanour, attitude (***gegenüber,*** towards); self-control, self-possession, poise, composure, (*Mil. etc.*) morale; standpoint, rôle, outlook, view(s), opinion(s); (*St. Exch.*) tendency, tone; ***matte –,*** flatness *or* dullness (of tone); ***feste –,*** firmness (of tone); ***– bewahren,*** maintain one's self-control, preserve one's dignity; keep a straight face (*instead of laughing*); keep a stiff upper-lip (*instead of showing weakness*); ***eine – einnehmen,*** assume an attitude, take up a point of view.

Halunke [ha'luŋkə], *m.* (**-n,** *pl.* **-n**) scoundrel, blackguard; (*coll.*) rascal, scamp.

Hämatit [hɛma'ti:t], *m.* (**-s,** *pl.* **-e**) bloodstone.

Hameln ['ha:məln], *n.* Hamelin; ***der Rattenfänger von –,*** the Pied Piper of Hamelin.

Hamen ['ha:mən], *m.* fish-hook; fishing *or* prawning net.

Hamfel ['hamfəl], *f.* (-, *pl.* **-n**) (*dial.*) handful.

hämisch ['hɛ:mɪʃ], *adj.* malicious, spiteful; gloating, sneering; *-es Lachen,* sneer, sardonic laugh; *-e Freude,* gloating.

Hämling ['hɛmlɪŋ], *m.* (**-s,** *pl.* **-e**) eunuch.

Hammel ['haməl], *m.* (**-s,** *pl.* - *or* ¨-) wether; mutton; (*coll.*) *süßer* –, duck, pet (*of a child*); (*coll.*) ***um auf besagten – zurückzukommen,*** to return to our subject. **Hammel|braten,** *m.* roast lamb *or* mutton. **–fleisch,** *n.* mutton, lamb. **–keule,** *f.* leg of mutton. **–kotelett, –rippchen,** *n.* mutton chop. **–schlegel,** *m. See* **–keule. –sprung,** *m.* (*Parl.*) division. **–talg,** *m.* mutton dripping, mutton suet.

Hammer ['hamər], *m.* (**-s,** *pl.* ¨-) hammer; (*auctioneer's, chairman's*) gavel; (*Anat.*) malleus (*of ear*); ***zwischen – und Amboß,*** twixt the devil and the deep blue sea; ***unter den – kommen,*** come under the hammer, come up for auction. **Hammerbahn,** *f.* face of a hammer.

hämmerbar ['hɛmərba:r], *adj.* malleable, ductile. **Hämmerer,** *m.* hammerer.

Hammer|hai, *m.* hammer-headed shark. **–herr,** *m.* owner of a foundry. **–hütte,** *f. See* **–werk.**

hämmern ['hɛmərn], *v.t., v.i.* hammer; forge; (*fig.*) thump, pound, (*also Motor.*) knock. **Hämmern,** *n.* hammering; (*fig.*) thumping, pounding, banging, knocking, thudding.

Hammer|schlag, *m.* 1. hammer-blow; 2. hammer-scale, iron oxide. **–schloß,** *n.* percussion-lock. **–schmied,** *m.* blacksmith, hammerman. **–schmiede,** *f. See* **–werk. –werfen,** *n.* (*Spt.*) throwing the hammer. **–werk,** *n.* foundry, ironworks.

Hämorrhoiden [hɛmoro'i:dən], *f.pl.* haemorrhoids, piles.

Hampelmann ['hampəlman], *m.* (*pl.* **–männer**) jumping Jack, puppet. **hampeln,** *v.i.* dither, prance about, flounder.

Hampfel ['hampfəl], *f. See* **Hamfel.**

Hamster ['hamstər], *m.* (*Zool.*) hamster, German marmot; (*fig.*) (*also* **Hamsterer,** *m.*) hoarder. **hamstern,** *v.t.* hoard.

Hand [hant], *f.* (-, *pl.* ¨-**e**) 1. hand; 2. handwriting; 3. side, direction; 4. source, origin; 5. *pl.* workmen. **(a)** (*with preps.*) **an** ***Händen und Füßen gebunden,*** bound hand and foot; ***ein Kind an der – führen,*** lead a child by the hand; ***ihm etwas an die – geben,*** supply *or* furnish him with s.th., place s.th. at his disposal; (*Comm.*) give him the refusal *or* option of a th.; ***ihm an die – gehen,*** lend *or* give him a hand, aid *or* assist him; ***– an etwas legen,*** take s.th. in hand; ***die letzte – an etwas legen,*** put the finishing touches to s.th.; ***– an ihn legen,*** lay hands on him; ***– ans Werk legen,*** get down to work; ***– an sich legen,*** commit suicide; ***an – von,*** with the aid of, in the light of, guided by, on the basis of, by means of; **auf** ***eigene –,*** on one's own responsibility; at one's expense; ***auf Händen und Füßen laufen,*** go on all fours; ***es liegt (klar) auf der –,*** it goes without saying, it is self-evident, quite obvious *or* as clear as daylight, (*coll.*) it sticks out a mile; ***ihm auf die – sehen,*** watch him closely; ***ihn auf (den) Händen tragen,*** treat him with every consideration, do all one can for him; ***Nachricht*** **aus** ***erster –,*** first-hand information; ***aus freier –,*** spontaneously, voluntarily; (*fig.*) ***ihm aus der – fressen,*** eat out of his hand; ***etwas aus der – geben,*** part with *or* relinquish s.th., waive one's rights to a th., leave a th. to others; ***aus bester –,*** on the best authority; ***etwas aus der – lassen,*** let s.th. slip from one's hand, lose one's control of *or* grip on s.th.; ***aus*** (or ***von***) ***der – in den Mund leben,*** live from hand to mouth; ***aus der – legen,*** put aside *or* away; ***aus zweiter – kaufen,*** buy second-hand; **bei** ***der –,*** at hand, handy, in readiness; ***er hat immer eine Antwort bei der –,*** he is always ready with an answer, he always has an answer pat, he is never at a loss for an answer; ***fest*** **in** ***der –,*** in hand, in *or* under one's control, (*coll.*) under one's thumb; in the hollow of one's hand, at one's mercy; (*Comm.*) ***in Händen,*** on hand; ***– in – gehen,*** go hand in hand; ***in die Hände bekommen,*** get hold of, gain control of; ***in die Hände klatschen,*** clap one's hands; (*of a horse*) ***schwer in der – liegen,*** pull hard at the bit; ***in die – nehmen,*** take control *or* charge of, take in hand; ***ihm in die Hände spielen,*** play into his hands; ***ihm etwas in die Hände spielen,*** help him to (gain *or* get) s.th.; ***in andere Hände übergehen,*** fall into other hands; **mit** ***der –,*** by hand; ***mit der – gemacht,*** hand-made; ***mit bewaffneter –,*** by force of arms; ***mit beiden Händen zugreifen,*** jump at the opportunity; ***mit vollen Händen,*** open-handedly, liberally, plentifully, lavishly, extravagantly; ***das ist mit Händen zu greifen,*** see ***auf der – liegen; mit leeren Händen,*** empty-handed; ***sich mit Händen und Füßen wehren,*** fight tooth and nail; **unter** ***der –,*** in secret, on the quiet, underhand; (*Comm.*) privately, by private contract; ***unter den Händen haben,*** have in hand; ***ihm unter die Hände kommen,*** fall into his power; **von** ***– gemalt,*** hand-painted; ***von langer –,*** long beforehand, for a long time (past); ***die Arbeit geht von der –,*** the work progresses rapidly; ***von der – weisen,*** reject *or* refuse out of hand; ***es ist nicht von der – zu weisen,*** it cannot be denied, (*coll.*) there's no getting away from it; **vor** ***der –,*** for the present, just now; meanwhile; ***vor die – nehmen,*** take in hand, set one's hand to; **zur** –, see ***bei der –***; (*on letters*) ***zu Händen*** (*Gen.*), care of; for the attention of; ***zur rechten (linken) –,*** on the right (left) hand *or* side; ***zu treuen Händen,*** in trust.

(b) (*with adjs.*) ***flache –,*** palm; ***ihm freie – lassen,*** leave him a free hand, leave him free play; ***Hände hoch!*** hands up! ***hohle –,*** hollow of the hand; ***Ehe zur linken –,*** morganatic *or* left-handed marriage; ***milde –,*** generosity; ***öffentliche –,*** public funds *or* authorities, government control; ***Politik der starken –,*** strong-arm policy; (*Law*) ***tote –,*** mortmain; ***die Hände voll zu tun haben,*** have one's hands full, be very busy.

(c) (*with verbs*) ***die – abziehen,*** withdraw one's support; ***– anlegen,*** lend a hand; ***die – ballen,*** clench one's fist; ***ihm die – drücken,*** press *or* squeeze his hand; ***darauf gebe ich (dir) die –,*** here's my hand on it; ***– und Fuß haben,*** be to the point *or* purpose, hold water; ***es hat weder – noch Fuß,*** it is without rhyme or reason, I can make neither head nor tail of it; ***er hat seine Hände im Spiel,*** he has a hand in it, he has a finger in the pie; ***durch Heben der Hände,*** by (a) show of hands; ***küß die –!*** (*Austr. form of greeting ladies*); ***die Hände im Schoß legen,*** fold one's hands, twiddle one's thumbs, remain idle, do nothing; ***ihm die – reichen,*** hold one's hand out to him, offer him one's hand; (*of a lady*) accept his hand *or* his offer of marriage; ***sich*** (*Dat.*) ***die Hände reichen,*** join hands, (*as greeting*) shake hands; ***ihm die – schütteln,*** shake his hand, shake hands with him; ***eine – wäscht die andere,*** one good turn deserves another.

Hand|anlasser, *m.* (*Motor.*) hand *or* self-starter. **–anlegung,** *f.* (*Law*) seizure. **–apparat,** *m.* (*Tele.*) handset. **–arbeit,** *f.* manual work *or* labour; handwork, handicraft; needlework; ***das ist –,*** that is hand-made. **–arbeiter,** *m.* workman, manual labourer; craftsman, mechanic. **–auf,** *n.* knock-on (*Rugby Footb.*). **–aufheben,** *n.* show of hands. **–auflegung,** *f.* (*Eccl.*) laying on of hands. **–ausgabe,** *f.* concise edition. **–ballen,** *m.* ball of the thumb. **–becken,** *n.* wash-handbasin. **–beil,** *n.* hatchet. **–besen,** *m.* hand-broom, brush. **–betrieb,** hand *or* manual operation. **–bewegung,** *f.* gesture, gesticulation. **–bibliothek,** *f.* reference library. **–bohrer,** *m.* gimlet. **–bohrmaschine,** *f.* hand-drill. **handbreit,** *adj.* of a hand's breadth. **Hand|-breite,** *f.* hand's breadth. **–bremse,** *f.* hand-brake. **–buch,** *n.* handbook, textbook, manual, compendium, vademecum; ***– für Reisende,*** travellers' guide. **–dienst,** *m.* service by manual labour. **–druck,** *m.* manual pressure; hand printing.

Hände ['hɛndə], *pl. of* **Hand. Hände|druck,** *m.* clasp of the hand, handshake. **–klatschen,** *m.* clapping, applause.

Handel ['handəl], *m.* (**-s,** *pl.* ¨-) 1. trade, traffic, commerce (***mit,*** in); transaction, business; affair, deal, bargain; litigation, lawsuit, action; ***einen – abschließen,*** conclude *or* strike a bargain; ***– mit dem Auslande,*** foreign trade; ***in den – bringen,*** put on the market; ***einen – mit ihm eingehen,*** make a bargain with him; ***– und Gewerbe,*** trade and industry; ***– im Großen,*** wholesale trade; ***– im Kleinen,*** retail trade; ***nicht im –,*** not for sale, not on the market; privately printed and published; ***in den – kommen,*** be put on the market; ***den – an sich reißen,*** capture the market; ***– treiben,*** (carry on) trade; ***– treiben mit,*** deal *or* trade in (*goods*), do business with (*a p.*); ***– und Wandel,*** business life; (*fig.*) general behaviour; 2. *pl.* quarrel, dispute, (*coll.*) squabble, brawl; ***Händel suchen,*** pick *or* seek a quarrel.

handeln ['handəln], **1.** *v.i.* take action, act, proceed; ***– um,*** bargain for *or* over, negotiate for *or* about, haggle over; ***– mit,*** trade *or* deal with (*a p.*), trade *or* deal *or* traffic in (*goods*); ***– von*** or ***über*** (*Acc.*), deal with, treat of (*subject matter*); ***mit sich – lassen,*** be open to an offer, be accommodating; ***als es zu – galt,*** when it came to the point, when the moment came to act; ***hier wird nicht gehandelt,*** prices are fixed, no reduction; ***die –den Personen des Dramas,*** the characters appearing in the play. **2.** *v.r. imp.* ***es handelt sich um,*** the question is, it is a question of; ***worum*** or ***um was handelt es sich?*** what is the (point in) question, what is it all about?

Handels|abkommen, *n.* trade agreement. **–adreßbuch,** *n.* commercial *or* trade directory. **–akademie,** *f.* commercial college, (*Am.*) school of business. **–amt,** *n.* Board of Trade. **–artikel,** *m.* commodity, merchandise; *pl.* goods. **–bericht,** *m.* commercial report, trade returns. **–besprechungen,** *f.pl.* trade talks. **–bezeichnung,** *f.* trade-name. **–beziehungen,** *f.pl.* trade relations. **–bilanz,** *f.* balance of trade; ***aktive*** (***passive***) **–,** favourable (unfavourable *or* adverse) balance of trade. **–blatt,** *n.* trade journal. **–brief,** *m.* business *or* commercial letter. **–buch,** *n.* ledger; account-book. **–dampfer,** *m.* cargo vessel, merchantman, tramp steamer. **handels|einig, –eins,** *pred.adj.* in agreement; ***– werden,*** come to terms. **Handels|-fach,** *n.* line of business, branch of trade. **–faktorei,** *f. See* **–niederlassung. –faktur,** *f.* trade invoice. **–firma,** *f.* commercial firm. **–flotte,** *f.* merchant shipping, mercantile marine. **–freiheit,** *f.* free trade; freedom of trade. **–gärtner,** *m.* market-gardener, (*Am.*) truck farmer. **–geist,** *m.* commercial spirit, commercialism. **–genossenschaft,** *f.* co-operative (enterprise). **–gericht,** *n.* (commercial) arbitration tribunal, commercial court. **–gesellschaft,** *f.* (trading) company; (business) corporation. **–gesetz,** *n.* commercial law. **–gesetzbuch,** *n.* commercial code. **–gesetzgebung,** *f.* commercial legislation. **–gewicht,** *n.* avoirdupois weight. **–gewinn,** *m.* trading profit.

Handels|hafen, *m.* commercial port. **–haus,** *n.* business house, trading firm. **–herr,** *m.* business magnate, head of a commercial house. **–hochschule,** *f.* commercial college. **–index,** *m.* business index. **–kammer,** *f.* Chamber of Commerce, (*Am.*) Board of Trade. **–kapital,** *n.* trading capital. **–korrespondent,** *m.* city correspondent (*newspaper*). **–korrespondenz,** *f.* commercial correspondence. **–krieg,** *m.* economic warfare. **–krise,** *f.* trade crisis. **–leute,** *pl.* tradespeople; merchants. **–mann,** *m.* (*pl.* **-leute**) merchant, trader, dealer. **–marine,** *f.* merchant navy *or* marine. **–minister,** *m.* Minister of Commerce (*Germany*), President of the Board of Trade (*England*), (*Am.*) Secretary of Commerce. **–ministerium,** *n.* Ministry of Commerce (*Germany*); Board of Trade (*England*); (*Am.*) Department of Commerce. **–nachrichten,** *f.pl.* commercial *or* City news. **–niederlassung,** *f.* trading station *or* post. **–platz,** *m.* trading post *or* centre; commercial centre. **–politik,** *f.* trade *or* commercial policy. **–recht,** *n.* commercial law. **–register,** *n.* commercial register; ***Eintragung in das –,*** incorporation. **–reisende(r),** *m.* commercial traveller, travelling salesman. **–schiff,** *n. See* **–dampfer. –schiffahrt,** *f.* merchant shipping. **–schranken,** *f.pl.* trade barriers. **–schule,** *f.* commercial school. **–sperre,** *f.* embargo (on trade). **–stand,** *m.* the business *or* trading classes. **–statistik,** *f.* Board of Trade returns. **–störer,** *m.* surface raider. **–straße,** *f.* trade route. **handelsüblich,** *adj.* usual in the trade; ***–e Bezeichnung,*** recognized trade-name; ***–e Qualität,*** commercial quality.

Händelsucht ['hɛndəlzuxt], *f.* quarrelsomeness, pugnacity. **händelsüchtig,** *adj.* quarrelsome, pugnacious.

Handels|umsatz, *m.* trade turnover. **–verbot,** *n. See* **–sperre. –verein,** *m.* commercial union. **–verkehr,** *m.* business dealings; commerce. **–vertrag,** *m.* commercial treaty, trade agreement. **–vertreter,** *m.* trade representative. **–waren,** *f.pl.* merchandise, commodities. **–wechsel,** *m.* trade-bill. **–weg,** *m.* trade-route; *pl.* trade channels. **–wert,** *m.* market value. **–zeichen,** *n.* trade-mark, brand. **–zweig,** *m. See* **–fach.**

handeltreibend ['handəltraɪbənt], *adj.* trading, commercial. **Handeltreibende(r),** *m. See* **Handelsmann.**

händeringend ['hɛndərɪŋənt], *adv.* wringing one's hands, beseechingly, imploringly; despairingly. **Händeschütteln,** *n.* handshake.

Hand|exemplar, *n.* 1. author's copy; 2. copy in regular use. **–fäustel,** *m.* miner's hammer. **–fertigkeit,** *f.* manual skill *or* dexterity. **–fertigkeitsunterricht,** *m.* manual training. **–fesseln,** *f.pl.* handcuffs. **handfest,** *adj.* sturdy, stalwart, robust, hefty; ***ihn – machen,*** take him into custody; ***–es Pferd,*** manageable *or* well-broken horse; ***–e Lüge,*** downright lie, (*coll.*) whopper. **Hand|feste,** *f.* (*obs.*) signed and sealed document. **–feuerwaffe,** *f.* pistol; *pl.* small-arms. **–fläche,** *f.* palm *or* flat of the hand. **–galopp,** *m.* canter. **–garn,** *n.* hand-spun yarn. **–gebrauch,** *m.* ordinary *or* everyday *or* daily use. **–geld,** *n.* earnest-money, handsel; (*Mil.*) bounty. **–gelenk,** *n.* wrist; ***aus dem –,*** with the greatest of ease, off the cuff. **handgemein,** *adj.* ***– werden,*** come to grips, blows *or* close quarters. **Hand|gemenge,** *n.* hand-to-hand fight(ing), mêlée; brawl, scrimmage, scuffle. **–gepäck,** *n.* hand-luggage, small luggage. **hand|gerecht,** *adj.* handy. **–geschöpft,** *adj.* hand-made (*paper*). **–geschrieben,** *adj.* handwritten, written by hand. **–gewebt, –gewirkt,** *adj.* hand-woven. **–greiflich,** *adj.* palpable, obvious, manifest, plain, evident. **Handgriff,** *m.* handle; grip, hold, grasp; manipulation; knack.

Handhabe ['hantha:bə], *f.* handle, hold, grip, (*fig.*) ways and means, pretext, evidence, proof; ***keine – haben,*** have not a leg to stand on; ***gesetzliche –,*** legal grounds. **handhaben,** *v.t.* (*insep.*) handle, wield, manipulate; operate; use, apply, administer (*justice*); (*fig.*) handle, manage, deal with; ***leicht*** or ***gut zu –,*** handy, easy to use, easily handled *or* managed. **Handhabung,** *f.* handling; use, application, operation, management; administration (*of justice*).

Handharmonika, *f.* (*Mus.*) accordion.

–händig ['hɛndɪç], *adj.suff.* (*in compounds*) -handed.

Hand|karren, *m.* hand-barrow, hand-cart, truck. **–kasse,** *f.* petty cash. **–kauf,** *m.* purchase in the lump; retail *or* cash transaction. **–koffer,** *m.* portmanteau, valise, suit-case, attaché case. **–korb,** *m.* work-basket; hand-basket. **–kurbel,** *f.* crank handle. **–kuß,** *m.* kiss on the hand; (*coll.*) ***mit –,*** gladly, with the greatest (of) pleasure. **–lampe,** *f.* inspection lamp. **–langer,** *m.* handyman, odd-job man, helper; workman's mate; (*Build.*) hodman; (*fig.*) underling, henchman, (*sl.*) stooge; drudge, hack. **–langerdienst,** *m.* fetching and carrying, (*coll.*) (doing) a p.'s dirty work (for him); drudgery. **–leiter,** *f.* step-ladder, (pair of) steps.

Händler [hɛndlər], *m.* trader, dealer, merchant, retailer, shopkeeper; (*St. Exch.*) stock jobber; ***fliegender –,*** hawker; (*oft. in compounds*) *e.g.* ***Buchhändler,*** bookseller; ***Fischhändler,*** fishmonger; ***Kohlenhändler,*** coal merchant; ***Zeitungshändler,*** news vendor. **Händlerpreis,** *m.* trade-price.

Hand|lesekunst, *f.* palmistry, chiromancy. **-leser(in),** *m.* (*f.*) palmist, palm-reader, chiromancer. **-leuchte,** *f. See* **-lampe. -leuchter,** *m.* portable candlestick. **-lexikon,** *n.* pocket dictionary.

handlich ['hantlɪç], *adj.* easy to use, handy, easily managed, manageable, compact.

Handlung ['handlʊŋ], *f.* 1. action, act, deed; (*of a play etc.*) action, story, plot; ***dramatische* –,** dramatic action, plot; ***heilige* –,** religious observance; ***strafbare* –,** criminal offence, punishable act; ***unerlaubte* –,** tort; 2. (*Comm.*) business, shop, store; (*oft. in compounds*) *e.g.* ***Blumenhandlung,*** flower *or* florist's shop; ***Musikalienhandlung,*** music shop.

Handlungs|bevollmächtigte(r), *m., f.* head-clerk, authorized representative. **-fähigkeit,** *f.* full authority. **-freiheit,** *f.* freedom of action, full discretion, (*coll.*) free play. **-gehilfe,** *m.* office-clerk; shop-assistant. **-reisende(r),** *m., f.* commercial traveller, travelling salesman. **-vollmacht,** *f.* power of attorney *or* procuration. **-weise,** *f.* (mode of) procedure, way of acting, methods, practices; attitude, conduct, behaviour.

Hand|maschinengewehr, *n.* sub-machine gun, tommy gun. **-nähmaschine,** *f.* hand *or* portable sewing-machine. **-pferd,** *n.* right-hand (*or* near-side) horse; led horse. **-pflege,** *f.* manicure. **-reichung,** *f.* assistance, help, aid. **-rücken,** *m.* back of the hand. **-schaltung,** *f.* (*Motor.*) hand-(gear)-change, manual gear-shift. **-schellen,** *f.pl.* handcuffs, manacles. **-schlag,** *m.* handshake, hand-clasp (*as a pledge*). **-schreiben,** *n.* autograph (letter). **-schrift,** *f.* handwriting, script; signature; manuscript. **-schriftendeutung,** *f.* graphology. **-schriftenkunde,** *f.* palaeography. **handschriftlich,** *adj.* in manuscript; in writing, (written) by hand, in long hand. **Hand|schuh,** *m.* glove, gauntlet; ***den* – *hinwerfen,*** throw down the gauntlet; ***den* – *aufnehmen,*** accept the challenge. **-schuhfach,** *n.* (*Motor.*) glove compartment. **-schuhmacher,** *m.* glover. **-seite,** *f.* near side (*in driving etc.*). **-siegel,** *n.* signet; ***Königliches* –,** privy seal. **-spake,** *f.* (*Naut.*) capstan bar. **-stand,** *m.* (*Gymn.*) handstand. **-standüberschlag,** *m.* (*Gymn.*) handspring. **-streich,** *m.* coup de main, sudden attack, surprise (onslaught), (*fig.*) bold stroke. **-stück,** *n.* specimen of a handy size. **-tasche,** *f.* (lady's) handbag, (*Am.*) purse. **-taschenräuber,** *m.* bag-snatcher. **-teller,** *m.* *See* **-fläche. -tuch,** *n.* towel; (*Boxing*) ***das* – *werfen,*** throw in the towel. **-tuchdrell,** *m.* towelling. **-umdrehen,** *n.* ***im* –,** in a flash, in the twinkling of an eye, in no time, (*coll.*) in a jiffy. **-voll,** *f.* handful. **-waffen,** *f.pl.* small-arms. **-wagen,** *m.* hand-cart, barrow. **-wahrsager,** *m. See* **-leser. -wahrsagerei,** *f. See* **-lesekunst. handwarm,** *adj.* luke-warm, tepid. **Hand|weberei,** *f.* hand-loom weaving. **-wechsel,** *m.* change of hands.

Handwerk ['hantvɛrk], *n.* handicraft; craft, trade; (craftsman's) guild; ***er ist seines -s ein Schneider,*** he is a tailor by trade; (*fig.*) ***ihm das* – *legen,*** put a stop to his activities, settle his business; (*fig.*) ***ihm ins* – *pfuschen,*** trespass on his preserves; (*fig.*) ***sein* – *verstehen,*** know one's business. **Handwerker,** *m.* craftsman; artisan, workman. **Handwerkerverein,** *m.* working men's club.

Handwerks|bursche, *m.* travelling artisan, journeyman. **-innung,** *f.* guild. **handwerksmäßig,** *adj.* workmanlike; (*fig.*) mechanical, by rule of thumb, without thinking. **Handwerks|meister,** *m.* master-craftsman. **-zeug,** *n.* tools, instruments. **-zunft,** *f. See* **-innung.**

Hand|wörterbuch, *n.* pocket dictionary. **-wurzel,** *f.* wrist. **-zeichen,** *n.* 1. monogram; initials, mark (*in lieu of signature*); 2. hand signal; 3. show of hands. **-zeichnung,** *f.* hand drawing, sketch, preliminary study (*for a painting etc.*). **-zettel,** *m.* leaflet, handbill.

hanebüchen ['ha:nəby:çən], *adj.* incredible, outrageous, (*coll.*) awful, the limit.

Hanf [hanf], *m.* (*Bot.*) hemp (*Cannabis sativa*); ***im* – *sitzen,*** be in clover, sit pretty. **hanfen, hänfen,** *adj.* hempen.

Hänfling ['hɛnflɪŋ], *m.* (*Orn.*) linnet (*Carduelis cannabina*).

Hanf|öl, *n.* hempseed oil. **-samen,** *m.* hempseed.

Hang [haŋ], *m.* (**-(e)s,** *pl.* **¨-e**) 1. slope, incline, declivity; 2. (*fig.*) tendency, bias, disposition (***zu,*** to), partiality, (natural) bent, propensity (for), inclination, proneness (to *or* for).

Hangar [haŋ'ga:r], *m.* (*Av.*) hangar, shed.

Hänge ['hɛŋə], *f.* drying-room, loft, (*Weav.*) tenter. **Hänge|antenne,** *f.* (*Rad.*) trailing aerial *or* (*Am.*) antenna. **-backe,** *f.* flabby cheek. **-bahn,** *f.* suspension *or* overhead railway. **-bauch,** *m.* paunch, (*sl.*) pot-belly. **-boden,** *m. See* **Hänge. -brücke,** *f.* suspension bridge. **-brust,** *f.* pendulous breasts. **-gerüst,** *n.* hanging scaffold. **-kette,** *f.* drag-chain. **-lampe,** *f.* hanging lamp. **-lippe,** *f.* pendulous lip.

hangeln ['haŋəln], *v.i.* (*Gymn.*) move hand over hand.

hangen ['haŋən], *irr.v.i.* (*aux.* s. & h.) (*In the pres. tense the correct forms have been superseded by the forms of* **hängen, 2.**).

hängen ['hɛŋən], **1.** *reg.v.t.* hang (up), suspend (***an*** (*Acc.*), on *or* by), attach, fasten, fix (to); ***gehängt werden,*** be hanged (*as a criminal*); ***sich* –,** hang o.s.; (*coll.*) ***den Mantel nach dem Winde* –,** sail with the wind, be a time-server; ***ihm den Brotkorb höher* –,** keep him on short rations; ***sein Herz an eine S.* –,** set one's heart on a th. **2.** *irr.v.i.* hang, be suspended (***an*** (*Dat.*), on *or* by; ***von,*** from); stick, adhere, cling (***an*** (*Dat.*), to), catch, be caught (on); (*fig.*) cling, be attached *or* devoted (***an*** (*Dat.*), to); ***woran hängt's?*** what's the trouble; ***sehr am Gelde* –,** be very fond of money; (*coll.*) ***an der Strippe* –,** have a long telephone call, hang on to the line. **hängenbleiben,** *irr.v.i.* (*aux.* s.) catch, be caught, get *or* be stuck (***an*** (*Dat.*), on; ***in*** (*Dat.*), in); (*Mech.*) seize, jam, lock; (*fig.*) be held up, be detained, (*coll.*) get stuck; ***die S. bleibt hängen,*** there's a hitch in the matter, it doesn't quite come off. **hängend,** *adj.* hanging, suspended, pendant; drooping, pendulous, sagging; ***-er Motor,*** inverted engine; ***-es Ventil,*** overhead valve. **hängenlassen,** *irr.v.t.* droop, (let) drop; ***den Kopf* –,** hang one's head.

Hänge|ohren, *n.pl.* drooping *or* lop ears. **-schloß,** *n.* padlock. **-weide,** *f.* (*Bot.*) weeping willow (*Salix babylonica*). **-werk,** *n.* truss (frame).

hängig ['hɛŋɪç], *adj.* (*Swiss*) see **anhängig.**

Hang|wind, *m.* up- *or* anabatic current. **-winkel,** *m.* gradient of a slope.

Hanke ['haŋkə], *f.* (*obs.*) haunch (*of horse*).

Hannchen ['hançən], *n.*, **Hanne** ['hanə], *f.*, **Hannele** ['hanələ], *n.* (*dim. of* **Johanna**) Hannah, Jane, Jenny, Jo.

Hannover [ha'no:fər], *n.* (*Geog.*) Hanover. **Hannoveraner** [–'ra:nər], *m.* Hanoverian. **hannover(i)sch,** *adj.* Hanoverian.

Hans [hans], *m.* Jack(ie), Johnnie; – ***bleibt* –,** you can't make a silk purse out of a sow's ear; (*coll.*) ***die großen -en,*** the big-wigs; – ***Dampf in allen Gassen,*** Jack of all trades; nosey-parker, busybody; – ***im Glück,*** lucky dog; – ***und Grete,*** Jack and Jill; – ***Guckindieluft,*** Johnnie Head-in-the-air; ***oder ich will* – *heißen,*** or I'm a Dutchman; – ***Liederlich,*** scapegrace, wastrel; – ***Sachte,*** slow-coach.

Hansa ['hanza], *f.* (*Hist.*) Hansa *or* Hanseatic League.

Hänschen ['hɛnsçən], *n.* (*dim. of* **Hans**) ***was* – *nicht lernt, lernt Hans nimmermehr,*** you can't teach an old dog new tricks.

Hanse, *f. See* **Hansa. hanseatisch** [hanze'a:tɪʃ], *adj.* (*Hist.*) Hanseatic.

hänseln ['hɛnzəln], *v.t.* chaff, tease, (*coll.*) pull (his *etc.*) leg, kid.

Hansestadt ['hanzəʃtat], *f.* Hanseatic town.

Hans|narr, *m.* tomfool. **-wurst,** *m.* (*Theat.*) clown, harlequin, merry andrew; (*coll.*) clown, buffoon.

Hantel ['hantəl], *f.* (-, *pl.* **-n**) *or* (*dial.*) *m.* dumb-bell.

hantieren [han'ti:rən], *v.i.* – *mit,* handle, wield, operate, busy o.s. with; fiddle *or* fidget with; – *an* (*Dat.*), manipulate, work on; potter about with. **Hantierung,** *f.* management, operation, handling, manipulation.

hantig ['hantıç], *adj.* (*Austr.*) bitter, sharp, harsh; quarrelsome.

haperig ['ha:pərıç], *adj.* embarrassing, frustrating. **hapern,** *v.i. imp.* go amiss, go *or* be wrong; ***es hapert am Gelde,*** lack of money is the stumbling block; ***da hapert es,*** there's the rub *or* snag; ***es hapert mit,*** there's a hitch in, there's s.th. wrong with.

Häppchen ['hɛpçən], *n.* morsel, bit.

Happen ['hapən], *m.* mouthful, morsel, titbit. **happig,** *adj.* greedy; (*coll.*) steep (*as of price*).

Härchen ['hɛ:rçən], *n.* tiny hair; cilium; ***man hat ihm kein – gekrümmt,*** not a hair of his head has been touched.

hären ['hɛ:rən], *adj.* (made of) hair; ***–es Gewand,*** hairshirt.

Häresie [hɛre'zi:], *f.* heresy. **Häretiker** [–'re:tıkər], *m.* heretic. **häretisch,** *adj.* heretical.

Harfe ['harfə], *f.* 1. harp; 2. corn-screen. **Harfenist** [–'nıst], *m.* (**-en,** *pl.* **-en**) *see* **Harfenspieler. Harfen|spiel,** *n.* harp-playing. **–spieler,** *m.* harp-player, harpist. **Harfner,** *m.* (*obs.*) harper, harpist.

Häring ['hɛ:rıŋ], *m.* (*dial.*) *see* **Hering,** 2.

Harke [harkə], *f.* rake; (*coll.*) ***ihm zeigen, was eine – ist,*** give him a piece of one's mind, tell him what's what. **harken,** *v.t., v.i.* rake.

Harlekin [harlə'ki:n], *m.* (**-s,** *pl.* **-e**) harlequin, clown. **Harlekinade** [–'na:də], *f.* harlequinade, buffoonery.

Harm [harm], *m.* grief, sorrow, affliction; injury, wrong. **härmen** ['hɛrmən], *v.r.* grieve, pine, fret, feel wretched (*um,* about *or* over). **harmlos,** *adj.* guileless, innocent; innocuous, harmless, inoffensive; insignificant.

Harmonie [harmo'ni:], *f.* harmony; agreement, concord. **Harmonie|gesetz,** *n.* tonal law; *pl.* laws of harmony. **–lehre,** *f.* harmony. **harmonieren,** *v.i.* harmonize, be in harmony (***mit,*** with); (*fig.*) agree, get on well, be in sympathy *or* in keeping (with).

Harmonika [har'mo:nika], *f.* (-, *pl.* **-s** *or* **-ken**) 1. *Orig.* musical glasses, *now* concertina; 2. harmonica.

harmonisch [har'mo:nıʃ], *adj.* harmonious; harmonic; (*Phys. etc.*) ***–e Komponenten*** or ***Teilschwingungen,*** harmonics. **harmonisieren** [–i'zi:rən], *v.t.* attune, harmonize, bring into harmony *or* accord.

Harmonium [har'mo:nium], *n.* (**-s,** *pl.* **-ien**) harmonium, parlour-organ.

Harn [harn], *m.* urine; – *lassen,* urinate, make *or* pass water. **Harn|abfluß,** *m. See* **–drang. –beschwerden,** *f.pl.* urinary disorder. **–blase,** *f.* (urinary) bladder. **–blasenentzündung,** *f.* cystitis. **–blasengang,** *m.* urethra. **–(blasen)gries,** *m.* gravel. **–drang,** *m.* incontinence, urgency, enuresis, micturition. **–fluß,** *m.* discharge of urine; ***unwillkürlicher –,*** *see* **–drang. –gang,** *m.* ureter. **–gries,** *m. See* **–(blasen)gries.**

Harnisch ['harnıʃ], *m.* (**-(e)s,** *pl.* **-e**) (suit of) armour; ***in – bringen,*** enrage, infuriate, exasperate, provoke, (*coll.*) get (his *etc.*) back up; ***in – geraten,*** fly into a rage.

Harn|kunde, *f.* urinology, urology. **–leiter,** *m.* ureter. **–probe,** *f.* urine sample; uric test. **–röhre,** *f.* urinary passage, urethra. **–ruhr,** *f.* polyuria (*diabetes insipidus*). **–säure,** *f.* uric acid. **–stein,** *m.* urinary calculus. **–stoff,** *m.* urea. **harntreibend,** *adj.* diuretic; ***–es Mittel,*** diuretic. **Harn|vergiftung,** *f.* uraemia. **–verhaltung,** *f.* retention of urine. **–zapfer,** *m.* catheter. **–zwang,** *m.* strangury, dysuria.

Harpune [har'pu:nə], *f.* harpoon. **Harpunengeschütz,** *n.* harpoon-gun, whaling-gun. **Harpunier** [–'ni:r], *m.* (**-s,** *pl.* **-e**) harpooner. **harpunieren,** *v.t.* harpoon.

Harpyie [har'py:jə], *f.* harpy, witch.

harren ['harən], *v.i.* 1. (*with Gen. or usu.* ***auf*** (*Acc.*)) look forward to impatiently, hope for, wait for, await; (*obs.*) ***ich harre des Herrn,*** I trust confidently in the Lord; ***diese Aufgabe harrt auf*** or ***nach Erledigung,*** it's high time this job was finished; 2. stay, tarry. **Harren,** *n.* waiting, hoping; perseverence, patience.

harsch [harʃ], *adj.* harsh, rough, brittle; frozen, crusted (*of snow*). **Harsch,** *m.* frozen snow.

hart [hart], (*comp.* ***härter,*** *sup.* ***härtest***) **1.** *adj.* 1. hard, difficult, troublesome, laborious; harsh, rough, severe, (*coll.*) tough; stern, austere; inflexible, adamant, pitiless, unfeeling; ***–er Kampf,*** hard *or* (*coll.*) stiff fight; ***–es Los,*** hard lot, cruel fate; ***–e Not,*** dire necessity; ***–er Schlag,*** heavy blow; ***durch eine –e Schule gegangen sein,*** have learnt it the hard way; ***einen –en Stand haben,*** have no easy time of it; ***–e Strafe,*** harsh *or* severe punishment; ***–es Wort,*** hard, harsh *or* unkind word; ***–e Zeiten,*** hard times; 2. hard, firm, solid, tough, hardy; (*Paint.*) crude; (*of water*) hard, chalky, calcareous; ***–er Dreiklang,*** major third; ***–es Geld,*** specie, coin; ***–e Kälte,*** severe *or* hard frost; ***einen –en Kopf haben,*** be headstrong; ***–e Laute,*** harsh *or* discordant sounds; ***einen –en Leibe haben,*** be constipated; ***eine –e Nuß,*** a tough nut to crack; ***–e Stirn,*** brazen face; ***–e Tatsachen,*** hard facts; ***–e Währung,*** hard currency. **2.** *adv.* – *an* (*Dat.*), hard *or* close by, close *or* near to; ***– am Feind,*** in the face of the enemy; ***– am Wind,*** close to the wind; ***– aneinander geraten,*** fly at each other; ***– anfassen,*** treat roughly, (*fig.*) deal severely with; ***ihn – ankommen,*** be hard on him, he finds it hard; ***– auf –,*** do or die, touch and go; ***– bedrängt,*** hard-pressed *or* -beset; ***– mitnehmen,*** have severe after-effects on.

Härte [hɛrtə], *f.* harshness, severity, rigour; hardness, toughness; (*Metall.*) temper; hardship. **Härte|bad,** *n.* tempering bath. **–grad,** *m.* (degree of) hardness, (*Metall.*) temper. **–mittel,** *n.* hardener, hardening agent. **härten, 1.** *v.t.* harden, (*Metall.*) temper, case-harden. **2.** *v.i., v.r.* harden, grow hard(er). **Härte|paragraph,** *m.* hardship clause. **–probe, –prüfung,** *f.,* **–versuch,** *m.* (*Metall.*) hardness test.

Hart|floß, *n.* (*Metall.*) specular iron. **–futter,** *n.* grain fodder. **hart|gefroren,** *adj.* frozen hard. **–gekocht,** *adj. See* **–gesotten. Hartgeld,** *n.* coins; specie. **hart|gelötet,** *adj.* silver-soldered. **–gesotten,** *adj.* hard-boiled (*egg*); ***–er Sünder,*** hardened sinner. **Hart|gummi,** *m.* vulcanized india-rubber, vulcanite, ebonite. **–guß,** *m.* chilled work, case-hardened castings. **hartherzig,** *adj.* hard-hearted, unfeeling. **Hart|herzigeit,** *f.* hard-heartedness. **–holz,** *n.* close-grained *or* hard-wood. **harthörig,** *adj.* (*dial.*) hard of hearing. **Harthörigkeit,** *f.* defective hearing, partial deafness. **hartköpfig,** *adj.* headstrong, obstinate, adamant. **Hartlage,** *f.* (*Naut.*) ***das Ruder in – legen,*** put the helm over. **hartleibig,** *adj.* constipated, costive. **Hart|leibigkeit,** *f.* constipation. **–lot,** *n.* hard solder. **hart|löten,** *v.t.* braze. **–mäulig,** *adj.* (*of horse*) hard-mouthed, unruly. **Hartmeißel,** *m.* cold chisel.

hartnäckig ['hartnɛkıç], *adj.* (*of a p.*) obstinate, stubborn, stiff-necked; dogged, persistent, pertinacious; (*of a th.*) obstinate, stubborn, refractory. **Hartnäckigkeit,** *f.* obstinacy, stubbornness; persistence, doggedness, pertinacity.

Hart|pappe, *f.* hardboard. **–platz,** *m.* (*Tenn.*) hard court. **–post,** *f.* typing *or* bank paper. **hartschalig,** *adj.* hard-shelled, testaceous. **Hartschier** ['hartʃi:r], *m.* (*Austr.*) *see* **Hatschier. Hart|schnaufen,** *n.* (*Vet.*) roaring. **–spiritus,** *m.* solid methylated spirits.

Hartung ['hartuŋ], *m.* (**-s,** *pl.* **-e**) (*obs.*) January.

Härtung ['hɛrtuŋ], *f.* hardening, (*Metall.*) tempering, case-hardening.

Hart|weizen, *m.* durum wheat. **–wurst,** *f.* hard-cured sausage. **–zinn,** *n.* pewter.

Harz [ha:rts], *n.* (**-es,** *pl.* **-e**) resin, (*Mus.*) rosin; gum. **harzen, 1.** *v.t.* collect *or* tap resin from (*pines*), (*Mus.*) rosin (*the bow*). **2.** *v.i.* 1. exude resin, be resinous; 2. (*Swiss*) stick; be difficult. **Harzgalle,** *f.* resinous exudation (*of wood*). **harzhaltig, harzig,** *adj.* resinous. **Harz|kohle,** *f.* resinous coal. **-reißen, -scharren,** *n.* extraction of resin (*from trees*). **-stoffe,** *m.pl.* resinoids.

Hasard [ha'zart], *n.* game of chance, betting game, (*fig.*) gamble. **hazardieren** [-'di:rən], *v.t.* risk, chance, hazard. **Hasardspiel,** *n. See* **Hasard.**

Haschee [ha'ʃe:], *n.* (**-s,** *pl.* **-s**) hash, minced meat.

haschen ['haʃən], **1.** *v.t.* catch, snatch, seize. **2.** *v.i.* *- nach,* snatch *or* grab at, grasp for; (*fig.*) strive for, strain after, aim at; ***nach Effekt -,*** play to the gallery *or* (*Am.*) grandstand; ***nach Komplimenten -,*** fish for compliments.

Häschen ['hɛ:sçən], *n.* young hare, leveret, (*Av., sl.*) novice pilot.

Häscher ['hɛʃər], *m.* (*obs.*) sheriff's officer, (bum) bailiff, catchpole; (*Poet.*) myrmidon, persecutor. **Häscherei** [-'raɪ], *f.* police-practices; (*sl.*) the cops.

Hascherl ['haʃərl], *n.* (**-s,** *pl.* -) (*Austr.*) beggar; poor wretch *or* creature *or* devil.

haschieren [ha'ʃi:rən], *v.t.* (*Cul.*) hash, mince.

Hase ['ha:zə], *m.* (**-n,** *pl.* **-n**) hare; (*sl.*) coward, funk; (*coll.*) ***alter -,*** old stager *or* hand; ***einen -n aufjagen,*** start a hare; ***falscher -,*** meat loaf, meat roll, mock duck; (*coll.*) ***heuriger -,*** greenhorn; ***sehen, wie der - läuft,*** see how the cat jumps *or* which way the wind blows; (*coll.*) ***da liegt der - im Pfeffer,*** there's the snag, that's the difficulty; (*coll.*) ***mein Name ist -,*** I haven't the faintest idea *or* notion.

Hasel ['ha:zəl], *f.* (-, *pl.* **-n**), **Hasel|busch,** *m. See* **-strauch. -huhn,** *n.* (*Orn.*) hazel-hen (*Tetrastes bonasia*). **-maus,** *f.* (*Zool.*) dormouse (*Muscardinus avellanarius*). **-nuß,** *f.* hazel-nut. **-strauch,** *m.* (*Bot.*) hazel(-tree), hazel-bush (*Corylus avellana*).

hasenartig ['ha:zənˀartɪç], *adj.* leporine. **Hasen|braten,** *m.* roast hare. **-fuß,** *m.* (*fig.*) poltroon, coward. **hasenfüßig, hasenhaft,** *adj.* faint-hearted, timid, cowardly. **Hasenhatz,** *f.* hare-hunting. **hasenherzig,** *adj. See* **hasenhaft. Hasen|hetze,** *f. See* **-hatz. -hund,** *m.* harrier. **-jagd,** *f. See* **-hatz**; ***dies ist ja keine -,*** there is no hurry about that, that can take its time. **-klein,** *n.* (*Cul.*) jugged hare. **-kurven,** *f.pl.* (*Av.*) evasive action. **-lager,** *n.* hare's form *or* lair. **-öhrchen,** *n.pl.* (*coll.*) inverted commas. **-panier,** *n.* ***das - ergreifen,*** take to one's heels. **-pfeffer,** *m. See* **-klein. hasenrein,** *adj.* (*coll.*) ***nicht ganz -,*** a bit fishy. **Hasen|scharte,** *f.* (*Med.*) harelip. **-weibchen,** *n.* female *or* doe hare.

Häsin ['hɛ:zɪn], *f. See* **Hasenweibchen.**

Haspe ['haspə], *f.* hasp, hinge; staple. **Haspel,** *f.* (-, *pl.* **-n**) (*also m.*) reel, winder; whim, windlass, winch; (*Naut.*) capstan; hinge-pin; turnstile. **haspeln, 1.** *v.t.* reel, wind (*on a reel etc.*). **2.** *v.i.* (*coll.*) (*movement*) bustle *or* fidget about; (*speech*) splutter, gabble.

Haß [has], *m.* hatred (***gegen,*** of *or* for), enmity, animosity (against), loathing (for), (*Poet.*) hate. **hassen,** *v.t.* hate, loathe, abhor, detest. **hassenswert,** *adj.* hateful, odious. **haßerfüllt,** *adj.* seething with hatred. **Haßgefühle,** *n.pl.* enmity, animosity, rancour.

hässig ['hɛsɪç], *adj.* (*Swiss*) irritable, disagreeable.

häßlich ['hɛslɪç], *adj.* ugly, misshapen, hideous, repulsive, (*of a p.*) plain, ill-favoured, (*Am.*) homely; unsightly, nasty, unpleasant, odious, loathsome, offensive; (*coll.*) mean, unkind; ***-er Anblick,*** eyesore; ***-e Antwort,*** unkind *or* rude answer; ***-es Benehmen,*** bad behaviour; ***-er Geruch,*** offensive smell; ***- von Gestalt,*** ill-formed; ***-e Geschichte,*** unpleasant affair; ***-e Gesinnung,*** nasty mind; ***-e Sitte,*** objectionable custom; ***-es Wetter,*** bad *or* dirty weather. **Häßlichkeit,** *f.* ugliness, unsightliness, loathsomeness; nastiness, offensiveness.

Hast [hast], *f.* haste, hurry; precipitation; ***in der -,*** in the rush; ***in wilder -,*** in a terrible hurry, helter-skelter. **hasten,** *v.i.* hurry, hasten, be in a hurry, scurry, rush. **hastig, 1.** *adj.* hasty, hurried; rash, precipitate, (*coll.*) slap-dash; nervous, excited, irritable. **2.** *adv.* hurriedly, in haste *or* a hurry. **Hastigkeit,** *f. See* **Hast**; hastiness, rashness, impetuosity; irritability.

hätscheln ['hɛtʃəln], *v.t.* coddle, pamper; pet, cuddle, caress, fondle.

Hatschier ['hatʃi:r], *m.* (**-s,** *pl.* **-e**) (*obs.*) halberdier; bodyguard.

hatte ['hatə], **hätte** ['hɛtə], *see* **haben.**

Hatz [hats], *f.* (-, *pl.* **-en**) 1. hunt, chase, coursing; 2. pack of hounds; 3. rout, tumultuous revelry.

Hau [hau], *m.* (**-(e)s.** *pl.* **-e**) 1. (*obs.*) cutting, felling; stroke, blow; 2. place where wood is felled; 3. *pl.* (*coll.*) beating, thrashing, whipping, spanking, hiding. **haubar,** *adj.* fit for felling.

Haube ['haubə], *f.* cap, bonnet, (*Hist.*) coif; hood, cowl; motoring *or* flying helmet; (*of birds*) crest, tuft, top; (*Build.*) dome, cupola (*of a roof*), crown, coping (*of a wall*); (*Mech.*) cover, cap; (*Motor.*) bonnet, (*Am.*) hood; (*Av.*) cowling; (*Naut.*) cabin top, sliding hatch; (*Railw.*) (steam-)dome; (*Bot.*) cupule; (*Zool.*) second stomach (*of ruminants*), reticulum; ***unter die - bringen,*** find a husband for, marry off; ***unter die - kommen,*** find a husband, get married, marry; (*Motor.*) ***die - aufklappen,*** raise the bonnet. **Hauben|lerche,** *f.* (*Orn.*) crested lark (*Galerida cristata*). **-meise,** *f.* (*Orn.*) crested tit (*Parus cristatus*). **-steißfuß, -taucher,** *m.* (*Orn.*) great crested grebe (*Podiceps cristatus*).

Haubitze [hau'bɪtsə], *f.* howitzer.

Hauch [haux], *m.* (**-(e)s,** *pl.* **-e**) breath, exhalation, breathing; breeze; puff; whiff; (*Phonet.*) aspiration; (*fig.*) tinge, trace, touch; haze, bloom, film. **hauchdünn,** *adj.* extremely thin (*coating*), filmy. **hauchen, 1.** *v.i.* breathe, exhale, respire. **2.** *v.t.* breathe out, exhale; (*fig.*) whisper, breathe, (*Phonet.*) aspirate. **Hauchlaut,** *m.* (*Phonet.*) spirant, aspirate. **hauchzart,** *adj.* flimsy, filmy, (extremely) delicate. **Hauchzeichen,** *n.* mark of aspiration.

Haudegen ['haude:gən], *m.* 1. (*Hist.*) broadsword; 2. (*coll.*) experienced fighter, veteran; fire-eater, bruiser.

Hauderer ['haudərər], *m.* (*dial.*) hackney-coachman, hired driver, cabby; (*fig.*) slow-coach. **haudern,** *v.i.* (*dial.*) ply for hire; go jogging along.

Haue ['hauə], *f.* hoe, mattock, pickaxe, pick. **hauen, 1.** *irr.v.t.* hew, cut, chop, cut down, fell; carve, chisel, dress (*stone*); whip, lash; hit, strike, beat, (*coll.*) thrash, spank; ***Fleisch -,*** cut up meat (for sale); ***ihn hinter die Ohren -,*** box his ears; (*coll.*) ***in die Pfanne -,*** put to the sword, cut to pieces; ***ihn übers Ohr -,*** cheat *or* outwit him. **2.** *irr.v.r.* (have a) fight. **3.** *irr.v.i.* ***um sich -,*** lay about one; ***über die Schnur*** or ***den Strang -,*** kick over the traces; ***nach einer S. -,*** strike at *or* lash out at a th.; ***- und stechen,*** cut and thrust; (*Prov.*) ***das ist weder gehauen noch gestochen,*** that is neither one thing nor the other, neither fish nor flesh; ***in die Eisen -,*** overreach (*of a horse*). **Hauer,** *m.* 1. wild boar; 2. cutting instrument; tusk, fang; 3. (*Austr.*) vine-grower. **Häuer,** *m.* (*Min.*) hewer, face-worker, miner.

Häufchen ['hɔyfçən], *n.* small heap *or* pile, small group *or* cluster; (*coll.*) ***wie ein - Unglück,*** woebegone, the picture of misery.

Haufe ['haufə], *m.* (**-ns,** *pl.* **-n**) *see* **Haufen.**

häufeln ['hɔyfəln], *v.t., v.i.* heap *or* pile (up), form into heaps, divide into piles; earth (*potatoes*).

Haufen ['haufən], *m.* heap, pile, accumulation, hoard; agglomeration, clutter, mass, stack (*of wood etc.*); (*of people*) crowd, band, great number, swarm, gang, troop; ***ein - Arbeit,*** a mass of work; ***Steine auf - legen,*** pile stones; ***Heu auf - setzen,*** stack hay; (*coll.*) ***auf einen -,*** in a jumble, higgledy-piggledy, all in *or* of a heap; ***ein - Geld,*** heaps *or* lots of *or* a lot of *or* pile of money; ***in -,*** in heaps; (*coll.*) ***in hellen -,*** in large numbers, in swarms; (*vulg.*) ***einen - setzen,*** evacuate the bowels; ***über den - schießen,*** shoot down, shoot out of hand;

über den – rennen, run down, knock *or* bowl over; *alle Bedenken über den – werfen,* cast aside all scruples, throw all scruples overboard *or* to the winds; *Pläne über den – werfen,* upset *or* overthrow plans, (*coll.*) knock plans on the head.

häufen ['hɔyfən], **1.** *v.t.* accumulate, amass, heap *or* pile (up). **2.** *v.r.* accumulate, increase, multiply, spread; *ein gehäufter Teelöffel,* a heaped teaspoonful.

Haufendorf ['haufəndɔrf], *n.* (*Geog.*) clustered village. **haufenweise,** *adv.* in heaps *or* crowds; (*coll.*) lots *or* piles of. **Haufenwolke,** *f.* cumulus (cloud); *geschichtete –,* stratocumulus.

häufig ['hɔyfɪç], **1.** *adj.* frequent, repeated; numerous, copious, abundant. **2.** *adv.* frequently, often; *– besuchen,* be a frequent visitor to, frequent; *– vorkommen,* occur frequently, be abundant *or* rife. **Häufigkeit,** *f.* frequency. **Häufigkeitskurve,** *f.* (*Stat.*) frequency (distribution) curve.

Häuflein ['hɔyflaɪn], *n.* (**-s,** *pl.* -) small group; little band, small body *or* a handful of men.

Häufung ['hɔyfuŋ], *f.* heaping, piling (up), accumulation; (*fig.*) accumulation, multiplication, increase, spread(ing), (*coll.*) piling up; frequent occurrence.

Haupt [haupt], *n.* (**-(e)s,** *pl.* **¨er**) head, leader, chief, principal; (*with numerals pl. oft.* –; *e.g. drei – Rinder,* three head of cattle); (*sl.*) *bemoostes –,* old student; *entblößten -es,* bared-headed, with head bared; *erhobenen -es,* with head erect; *gesenkten -es,* with bowed head; (*fig.*) *an – und Gliedern,* root and branch; *aufs – schlagen,* defeat utterly *or* decisively; *zu -en* (*Gen.*), at the head of.

Haupt|absicht, *f.* main object, ultimate aim. **-ader,** *f.* (*Anat.*) cephalic vein; (*Min.*) master lode. **-aktionär,** *m.* principal shareholder *or* (*Am.*) stockholder. **-altar,** *m.* high altar. **-amt,** *n.* (*Tele.*) central exchange. **hauptamtlich, 1.** *adj.* full-time (*occupation*). **2.** *adv.* on a full-time basis. **Haupt|anschluß,** *m.* (*Tele.*) (main) switchboard. **-artikel,** *m.* leading article, leader (*in newspaper*). **-attraktion,** *f.* main attraction, highlight, special feature. **-augenmerk,** *n. sein – richten auf* (*Acc.*), direct one's special attention to. **-bahnhof,** *m.* main *or* central station. **-balken,** *m.* (*Archit.*) main girder, architrave; *pl.* principals. **-bank,** *f.* head bank. **-belastungszeit,** *f.* peak hour (*of traffic*), peak load (*of electric supply etc.*). **-beruf,** *m.*, **-beschäftigung,** *f.* regular *or* full-time occupation. **-bestand,** *m.* main crop. **-bestandteil,** *m.* chief *or* main ingredient *or* component *or* constituent; *den – bilden von,* be part and parcel of. **-betrag,** *m.* sum total. **-buch,** *n.* ledger. **-buchhalter,** *m.* accountant. **-darsteller,** *m.* leading actor. **-deck,** *n.* main deck. **-eigenschaft,** *f.* leading *or* dominant feature, main attribute. **-einfahrt,** *f.*, **-eingang,** *m.* main entrance.

Häuptel ['hɔyptəl], *n.* (*dial.*) head (*of plant*). **Häuptelsalat,** *m.* (*dial.*) *see* **Kopfsalat.**

Haupt|erbe, *m.* residuary legatee, major beneficiary. **-erfordernis,** *n.* primary *or* chief requirement, prime *or* principal requisite. **-erzeugnis,** *n.* principal *or* staple product, main produce. **-fach,** *n.* principal *or* main subject, (*Am.*) major; *als – studieren,* take as one's main subject, (*Am.*) major in. **-farbe,** *f.* dominant colour, (*Opt.*) primary colour. **-feder,** *f.* mainspring. **-fehler,** *m.* main *or* chief *or* principal *or* cardinal fault *or* defect. **-feldwebel,** *m.* (*Mil.*) sergeant-major, (*Am.*) master sergeant. **-figur,** *f.* central *or* main figure, (*Theat.*) hero(ine), leading character. **-film,** *m.* feature (film). **-frage,** *f.* main issue *or* question *or* point. **-gebäude,** *n.* main building *or* block. **-gedanke,** *m.* leading idea, keynote. **-gericht,** *n.* main course (*of meal*). **-geschäftsstelle,** *f.* head-office. **-geschäftsstunden,** *f.pl.* rush hours. **-gesichtspunkt,** *m.* major consideration. **-gesims,** *n.* (*Archit.*) entablature. **-gewinn,** *m.* first prize (*in lottery*). **-gläubiger,** *m.* principal creditor. **-grund,** *m.* main reason, basic motive. **-haar,** *n.* hair of the head. **-hahn,** *m.* 1. main tap, stopcock; 2. (*Studs. sl.*) the life of the party. **-handelsartikel,** *m.* staple commodity. **-handlung,** *f.* (*Theat.*) main plot, principal action. **-inhalt,** *m.* principal contents, gist, substance; synopsis. **-interesse,** *n.* primary interest. **-jagd,** *f.* (*Hunt.*) battue. **-kabel,** *n.* main cable, mains. **-kartei,** *f.* master file. **-kassierer,** *m.* head cashier. **-kerl,** *m.* (*coll.*) splendid fellow. **-kontor,** *n.* head office. **-kräfte,** *f.pl.* (*Mil.*) main force. **-lager,** *n.* (*Mech.*) main bearing. **-lehrer,** *m.* senior master. **-leidenschaft,** *f.* ruling passion. **-leidtragende(r),** *m., f.* chief mourner. **-leitung,** *f.* (*Elec.*) main conductor, (*Elec., gas, water*) mains, (*Tele.*) trunk line.

Häuptling ['hɔyptlɪŋ], *m.* (**-s,** *pl.* **-e**) chief, chieftain, leader.

häuptlings ['hɔyptlɪŋs], *adv.* head-foremost, head over heels, headlong.

Haupt|linie, *f.* main *or* trunk line. **-macht,** *f.* (*Mil.*) main (striking) force, main body (*of troops*). **-mahlzeit,** *f.* principal meal (of the day). **-mann,** *m.* 1. (*pl.* **-leute**) (*Mil.*) captain, (*Hist.*) (Roman) centurion; chief, chieftain, leader (*of robbers, tribes etc.*); 2. (*pl.* **-männer**) (responsible) local government official. **-mannschaft,** *f.* (*Spt.*) first eleven, first fifteen *etc.* **-mannsrang,** *m.* (*Mil.*) captaincy. **-masse,** *f.* main body, bulk. **-mast,** *m.* (*Naut.*) mainmast. **-merkmal,** *n.* main, characteristic *or* distinctive feature, chief characteristic, criterion. **-messe,** *f.* (*Eccl.*) great mass. **-moment,** *n.* main point. **-nahrung,** *f.* staple food. **-nenner,** *m.* (*Math.*) common denominator. **-nervensystem,** *n.* central nervous system. **-niederlage,** *f.* main depot *or* warehouse. **-niederlassung,** *f.* (*Comm.*) head office, headquarters. **-pastor,** *m.* chief clergyman, pastor primarius. **-person,** *f.* principal *or* central figure, (*Theat.*) leading character. **-post,** *f.*, **-postamt,** *n.* general post-office. **-posten,** *m.* (*Comm.*) principal item. **-prämie,** *f.* first prize. **-probe,** *f.* (*Theat.*) dress rehearsal, (*Mus.*) general rehearsal. **-punkt,** *m.* main *or* cardinal point; chief feature. **-quartier,** *n.* (*Mil.*) headquarters; *großes –,* general headquarters (G.H.Q.). **-quelle,** *f.* main source; fountain-head. **-raum,** *m.* (*Naut.*) afterhold. **-redakteur,** *m.* chief editor, editor-in-chief. **-register,** *n.* index; (*of organ*) main stop. **-richtung,** *f.* main direction, trend. **-rippe,** *f.* midrib (*of leaf*). **-rohr,** *n.* main (supply-pipe). **-rolle,** *f.* leading rôle, (*Theat.*) chief part, lead, title-rôle; *die – spielen,* (*Theat.*) play the lead, star; (*fig.*) (*of a p.*) be the central figure, (*coll.*) run the show, play first fiddle; (*of a th.*) be all-important. **-rollendarsteller(in),** *m.* (*f.*) leading man, leading lady, lead, star (performer). **-ruder,** *n.* stroke-oar. **-ruderer,** *m.* stroke.

Hauptsache ['hauptzaxə], *f.* main point *or* issue, essential *or* most important point; *pl.* essentials; *in der –,* in the main, chiefly, on the whole; *der – nach,* in substance; *das ist die –,* that's all that matters; (*Law*) *zur – verhandeln,* deal with a case on its merits; (*Law*) *in der – entscheiden,* pass judg(e)ment on the merits of the case. **hauptsächlich, 1.** *adj.* chief, most important, essential, principal, main. **2.** *adv.* essentially, chiefly, mainly, especially, particularly, above all; *es kommt – darauf an,* the main point is.

Haupt|sängerin, *f.* prima donna. **-satz,** *m.* main proposition, axiom; (*Mus.*) leading theme; (*Gram.*) principal clause *or* sentence. **-schalter,** *m.* main *or* master switch. **-schiff,** *n.* (*Naut.*) flagship; (*Eccl.*) nave. **-schlacht,** *f.* decisive battle. **-schlagader,** *f.* (*Anat.*) aorta. **-schlager,** *m.* 1. theme song (*in film etc.*); 2. (*Comm.*) special bargain, main selling line. **-schlüssel,** *m.* master-key. **-schlußschaltung,** *f.* (*Elec.*) series winding. **-schriftleiter,** *m.* *See* **-redakteur. -schuld,** *f.* principal fault; *die – trifft ihn,* it is mainly his fault. **-schuldige(r),** *m., f.* major offender. **-schuldner,** *m.* principal debtor. **-schule,** *f.* intermediate school. **-schwingung,** *f.* fundamental oscillation. **-segel,** *n.* mainsail. **-sicherung,** *f.* (*Elec.*) main fuse. **-signal,** *n.* (*Railw.*) home signal. **-sitz,** *m.* (*Comm.*) head office, headquarters. **-sorge,** *f.* main concern. **-spaß,** *m.* capital joke, (*coll.*) lark. **-spule,**

f. (*Elec.*) primary winding. **–stadt,** *f.* metropolis, capital. **hauptstädtisch,** *adj.* metropolitan. **Haupt|straße,** *f.* main street, high street; highway, main *or* major *or* arterial road. **–strecke,** *f.* (*Railw.*) main *or* trunk line. **–streich,** *m.* masterstroke.

Hauptstrom ['hauptʃtro:m], *m.* main stream; (*Elec.*) primary current. **Hauptstrom|kreis,** *m.* (*Elec.*) primary circuit. **–motor,** *m.* (*Elec.*) series-wound *or* direct-current motor.

Haupt|stütze, *f.* main support, (*fig.*) mainstay. **–summe,** *f.* principal sum; (sum) total. **–sünde,** *f.* cardinal sin; besetting sin. **–ton,** *m.* (*Mus.*) keynote; (*Metr.*) principal accent, chief stress. **–träger,** *m.* *See* **–balken. –treffen,** *n.* *See* **–schlacht. –treffer,** *m.* first (lottery-)prize; (*coll.*) ***den – gewinnen,*** hit the jackpot. **–treppe,** *f.* main staircase. **–tribüne,** *f.* grandstand. **–triebfeder,** *f.* (*fig.*) mainspring. **–tugend,** *f.* cardinal virtue. **–-und-Staatsaktion,** *f.* (type of) blood-and-thunder Baroque drama; (*fig.*) great to-do *or* pother. **–uhr,** *f.* master clock. **–unterschied,** *m.* main *or* principal difference. **–untersuchung,** *f.* (*Law*) trial. **–ursache,** *f.* chief cause. **Haupt|verbrechen,** *n.* capital crime; major offence. **–verdienst,** *m.* chief merit. **–verkehrsstraße,** *f.* main *or* trunk *or* arterial road, main highway *or* thoroughfare. **–verkehrszeit,** *f.* peak traffic hour, rush hour. **–verlesen,** *n.* (*Swiss, Mil.*) roll-call. **–versammlung,** *f.* general business meeting. **–verzeichnis,** *n.* general catalogue. **–wache,** *f.* (*Mil.*) main-guard; main guard-house. **–welle,** *f.* (*Mech.*) transmission shaft. **–werk,** *n.* principal work, masterpiece. **–wirkung,** *f.* main effect. **–wort,** *n.* (*Gram.*) noun, substantive. **–wurzel,** *f.* tap-root. **–zahl,** *f.*, **–zahlwort,** *n.* cardinal number. **–zeuge,** *m.* principal witness. **–zug,** *m.* principal trait, chief characteristic, main feature. **–zweck,** *m.* chief purpose, main object.

Haus [haus], *n.* (**-es,** *pl.* **¨-er**) house, residence, dwelling(-house), home, household; family, house, dynasty; housing, casing, frame, shell; (*Comm.*) firm; (*coll.*) ***altes –,*** old chap *or* fellow; ***– an – wohnen,*** be next-door neighbours, live next door (***mit,*** to); ***aus gutem –e sein,*** come of a good family; ***außer dem –,*** outdoors, out of doors; ***außer –e essen,*** dine out; ***auf ihn kannst du Häuser bauen,*** you may pin your faith on him, you may trust him implicitly, he is absolutely reliable; ***beschlußfähiges –,*** quorum; ***sein – bestellen,*** put one's affairs in order; ***ein neues – beziehen,*** move to a new house; ***mit der Tür ins – fallen,*** go like a bull at a gate; (*coll.*) ***fideles –,*** cheery fellow; (*Comm.*) ***frei –,*** free delivery (to the door); (*coll.*) ***gelehrtes –,*** pundit, (*coll.*) know-all; ***ein großes – führen,*** live in great style, keep open house; ***der Herr vom –e,*** the master of the house; ***– und Hof,*** one's all, house and home; ***sie trieben ihn von – und Hof,*** they drove him from hearth and home; ***das – hüten,*** stay at home, stay indoors; ***im –e,*** indoors; on the premises; ***nach –e,*** homeward, home; ***ihn nach –e bringen,*** see him home; ***öffentliches –,*** house of ill-repute, disorderly house; ***von –e,*** from home; ***von – aus,*** from the very beginning, fundamentally, originally; by birth *or* nature; ***von – aus Vermögen haben,*** have property of one's own; ***von – aus begabt sein,*** be innately gifted, be born clever; ***von – zu –,*** from house to house, from door to door; ***mit herzlichen Grüßen von – zu –,*** with our kind regards to all of you; ***zu –e,*** at home, (*coll.*) in; ***nicht zu –e,*** away (from home), not at home, (*coll.*) out; ***bei uns zu –e,*** in our country, where I come from, at home; ***wo sind Sie zu –e?*** what nationality are you? where do you come from? ***nirgends zu –e sein,*** have no fixed abode; (*fig.*) ***zu –e sein in*** (*Dat.*), be well-versed *or* at home *or* (*coll.*) well up in; ***er fühlt sich wie zu –e,*** he feels quite at home; ***tut als ob ihr zu –e wäret,*** make yourselves at home.

Haus|andacht, *f.* family prayers. **–angestellte,** *f.* housemaid, domestic (servant); *pl.* domestics, servants. **–arbeit,** *f.* indoor work; house-work, domestic work; homework (*of schoolchildren*). **–arrest,** *m.* house arrest. **–arznei,** *f.* household remedy. **–arzt,** *m.* family doctor; (*at a spa*) resident doctor. **–aufgaben),** *f.*(*pl.*) homework. **hausbacken,** *adj.* home-baked, home-made; (*fig.*) homely, plain; prosaic, pedestrian. **Haus|bar,** *f.* cocktail cabinet. **–baumläufer,** *m.* (*Orn.*) *see* **Gartenbaumläufer. –bedarf,** *m.* household necessaries; ***für den –,*** for the home, for family use; ***nicht über den –,*** not above everyday domestic requirements. **–besitzer,** *m.* house-owner; landlord. **–bettelei,** *f.* door to door begging. **–biene,** *f.* domestic bee. **–boot,** *n.* houseboat. **–brot,** *n.* household bread. **–buch,** *n.* housekeeping-book.

Häuschen ['hɔysçən], *n.* small house, cottage, cabin, lodge; (*coll.*) outside lavatory, privy; (*fig.*) ***aus dem –,*** beside o.s., confused, overcome, (*coll.*) off one's head (***vor*** (*Dat.*), with); (*coll.*) ***aufs – gehen,*** go to the lavatory.

Haus|dame, *f.* housekeeper, lady's companion. **–diener,** *m.* manservant, valet; (*in hotel*) boots. **–drache,** *m.* (*coll.*) shrew, scold, vixen, termagant. **–durchbruch,** *m.* (*Mil.*) mouse-holing. **–durchsuchung,** *f.* domiciliary visit (*by the police*). **–eigentümer,** *m.* *See* **–besitzer. –einrichtung,** *f.* domestic fittings and furniture.

hausen ['hauzən], *v.i.* 1. house, lodge, reside, dwell; ***übel*** or ***schlimm –,*** ravage, devastate, play *or* wreak havoc; 2. (*Swiss*) save, economize.

Hausen, *m.* (*Ichth.*) sturgeon (*Acipenser huso*). **Hausenblase,** *f.* isinglass.

Hausente ['hausˀɛntə], *f.* domestic duck.

Hauser ['hauzər], *m.* (*Austr.*) *see* **Haushalter.**

Häuser ['hɔyzər], *pl. of* **Haus. Häuserblock,** *m.* block of houses. **Häuserin,** *f.* (*Austr.*) *see* **Haushälterin. Häuser|kampf,** *m.* house-to-house fighting. **–makler,** *m.* house agent, (real) estate agent, (*Am.*) realtor. **–viertel,** *n.* residential quarter.

Haus|fideikomiß, *n.* family trust. **–flur,** *m.* (*or Austr. f.*) (entrance) hall, vestibule. **–frau,** *f.* mistress *or* lady of the house; housewife; landlady. **–freund,** *m.* family friend. **–friede,** *m.* domestic peace, family concord. **–friedensbruch,** *m.* (*Law*) intrusion, trespass. **–garten,** *m.* back garden, backyard. **–gebrauch,** *m.* domestic use. **–gehilfin,** *f.* *See* **–angestellte. –genosse,** *m.* fellow-lodger. **–gerät,** *n.* household utensils. **–gesinde,** *n.* (*obs.*) domestic servants. **–glocke,** *f.* doorbell. **–gott,** *m.* household deity (*Roman* = penates). **–gottesdienst,** *m.* (family) prayers, family worship. **–grille,** *f.* (*Ent.*) cricket (*Gryllus domesticus*).

Haushalt ['haushalt], *m.* household; housekeeping; household budget; (*Pol.*) budget; ***den – führen,*** keep house, manage *or* run the house. **haushalten,** *irr.v.i.* keep house; ***– mit,*** economize *or* be economical with, husband; ***sie hält für ihn haus,*** she keeps house for him; ***gut –,*** be a good housekeeper. **Haushälterin,** *f.* housekeeper. **haushälterisch,** *adj.* economical, thrifty. **Haushaltkunde,** *f.* domestic science.

Haushalts|artikel, *m.pl.* household goods *or* supplies, (*Am.*) domestics. **–ausschuß,** *m.* (*Pol.*) Committee of Supply. **–beschränkungen,** *f.pl.* (*Pol.*) budgetary restraint. **–führung,** *f.* upkeep of home and family. **–geld,** *n.* housekeeping money *or* allowance. **–jahr,** *n.* (*Pol.*) financial *or* fiscal year. **–mittel,** *n.pl.* (*Pol.*) appropriations. **–plan,** *m.* (*Pol.*) budget; ***etwas im – vorsehen,*** budget for a th. **–tarif,** *m.* household tariff (*electricity*). **–voranschlag,** *m.* (*Pol.*) the estimates. **–zuweisung,** *f.* (*Pol.*) appropriation.

Haushaltung ['haushaltuŋ], *f.* *See* **Haushalt**; housekeeping, family budget. **Haushaltungs|kosten,** *pl.* household expenses. **–schule,** *f.* school of domestic science.

Hausherr ['haushɛr], *m.* master of the house, head of the family; householder; landlord. **haushoch,** *adj.* as high as a house, huge, enormous; ***– überlegen sein*** (*Dat.*), be head and shoulders above (*a p.*).

hausieren [hau'zi:rən], *v.i.* hawk, peddle (***mit etwas,*** s.th.). **Hausierer,** *m.* hawker, door-to-door salesman, pedlar.

Haus|industrie, *f.* cottage industry. **-kapelle,** *f.* private chapel; (*Mus.*) private orchestra. **-kleid,** *n.* house-dress. **-knecht,** *m.* porter; boots (*at an inn*). **-kost,** *f.* household fare. **-lehrer,** *m.* private tutor. **-lehrerin,** *f.* governess.

Häusler ['hɔyslər], *m.* cottager, landless labourer.

hauslich ['hauslıç], *adj.* (*Swiss*) economical.

häuslich ['hɔyslıç], **1.** *adj.* 1. domestic; *-e Aufgaben,* home work, home lessons (*of school-children*); *-er Kreis,* domestic circle; *im -en Kreise,* by the fire-side; 2. domesticated, home-loving, homely; 3. economical, thrifty, sparing. **2.** *adv. sich - einrichten,* set up house, (*fig.*) make o.s. at home; *sich - niederlassen an einem Orte,* make one's home *or* settle (down) in a place. **Häuslichkeit,** *f.* domesticity, family life.

Haus|macht, *f.* (*Pol.*) dynastic power. **-mädchen,** *n.* housemaid; maid. **-magd,** *f.* housemaid, maid of all work. **-mannskost,** *f.* plain *or* homely fare. **-marke,** *f.* proprietory sign, trade mark. **-meier,** *m.* (*Hist.*) major-domo. **-meister,** *m.* caretaker, porter, janitor. **-miete,** *f.* (house-)rent. **-mittel,** *n.* household remedy. **-mutter,** *f.* mother of a family; matron. **hausmütterlich,** *adj.* matronly, motherly. **Haus|mütze,** *f.* smoking cap. **-nummer,** *f.* street number. **-orden,** *m.* Royal Order. **-ordnung,** *f.* rule of the house, daily routine. **-pflanze,** *f.* indoor plant. **-pflege,** *f.* home-treatment; home-care, outdoor relief. **-postille,** *f.* book of family devotions. **-prediger,** *m.* family chaplain. **-rat,** *m.* household effects. **-recht,** *n.* domestic authority; *sein - brauchen,* show an intruder the door. **-rock,** *m.* house-coat; morning gown. **-rotschwanz,** *m.* (*Orn.*) black redstart (*Phoenicurus ochruros*). **-sammlung,** *f.* house-to-house *or* door-to-door collection. **-schabe,** *f.* cockroach. **-schatz,** *m.* privy purse (*of a prince*). **-schlüssel,** *m.* front-door key. **-schuh,** *m.* slipper, house-shoe. **-schwalbe,** *f. See* **Mehlschwalbe. -schwamm,** *m.* dry-rot.

Hausse ['(h)o:s(ə)], *f.* (*Comm.*) rise (in prices), boom, upward trend; *auf - spekulieren,* buy for a rise, bull.

Haussegen ['hausze:gən], *m.* 1. wall-text; 2. (*coll.*) children, family.

Hausse|kauf, *m.* (*Comm.*) bull purchase. **-markt,** *m.* boom market.

haußen ['hausən], *adv.* (*dial.*) outdoors, out of doors; (*fig.*) distasteful, irksome.

Hausse|spekulant, *m.* (*Comm.*) bull, (*Am.*) long. **-stimmung,** *f.* rising trend, lively tone (*of the market*).

Haussier [(h)o:'sje:], *m.* (**-s,** *pl.* **-s**) (*Comm.*) *see* **Haussespekulant.**

Haus|sperling, *m.* (*Orn.*) house-sparrow (*Passer domesticus*). **-stand,** *m.* household; *einen eigenen - gründen,* marry and settle down. **-suchung,** *f.* domiciliary visit (*by the police*), police raid. **-suchungsbefehl,** *m.* search-warrant. **-taufe,** *f.* private baptism. **-telefon,** *n.* internal telephone, (*coll.*) intercom. **-teufel,** *m.* termagant, shrew. **-tier,** *n.* domestic(ated) animal. **-tochter,** *f.* home-help, au-pair girl. **-trauung,** *f.* private wedding. **-truppen,** *f.pl.* household troops, life guards. **-tür,** *f.* street-door, front-door. **-tyrann,** *m.* domestic tyrant; *den - markieren,* play the heavy husband. **-unke,** *f.* rush-toad; (*fig.*) home-bird. **-vater,** *m.* father of a family, family-man. **-verstand,** *m.* (*coll.*) horse-sense. **-verwalter,** *m.* caretaker, janitor, house-superintendent. **-verwaltung,** *f.* property management. **-vogtei,** *f.* city-prison. **-wanze,** *f.* bed-bug. **-wappen,** *n.* family arms. **-wart,** *m. See* **-meister. -wäsche,** *f.* household washing. **-wesen,** *n.* domestic concerns; household (affairs). **-wirt,** *m.* householder; landlord. **-wirtin,** *f.* landlady. **-wirtschaft,** *f.* housekeeping; domestic economy; domestic science. **-zins,** *m.* house-rent.

Haut [haut], *f.* (-, *pl.* ⸚e) skin, (*Anat.*) cuticle, dermis, integument; (*of beasts*) hide; (*Bot. etc.*) membrane, pellicle; (*of liquids*) film; (*of a ship*) outer planking; *bis auf die - naß,* wet (through) *or* soaked to the skin, sopping wet; *er kann aus seiner - nicht heraus,* he cannot help being what he is, a leopard cannot change its spots; *aus der - fahren,* jump out of one's skin; *es ist um aus der - zu fahren, es ist zum Ausderhautfahren,* it's enough to drive one mad (*with impatience*); *auf bloßer - tragen,* wear next to the skin; *eine dicke - haben,* be thick-skinned; *ehrliche -,* honest fellow; *mit ganzer -,* safe and sound, unscathed, unharmed; *mit - und Haar,* altogether, utterly, completely, thoroughly, out and out, root and branch; *er kam mit heiler - davon,* he escaped unhurt *or* unscathed, he got off scot-free; (*Prov.*) *die - ist allweg näher als das Hemd,* charity begins at home; *er ist bloß noch - und Knochen,* he is a mere bag of bones *or* nothing but skin and bones; *auf der faulen - liegen,* loaf, take it easy; (*Anat.*) *obere -,* epidermis; *ihm die - über die Ohren ziehen,* flay him, fleece *or* cheat him; *seine (eigene) - retten,* save one's skin *or* bacon; *ich möchte nicht in seiner - stecken,* I should not like to be in his shoes *or* skin; *seine - zu Markte tragen,* do at one's own risk, risk one's hide; *seine - teuer verkaufen,* sell one's life dearly; *sich seiner - wehren,* defend o.s. to the last.

Haut|abschürfung, *f.* abrasion, excoriation. **-arzt,** *m.* dermatologist. **-ausschlag,** *m.* eruption, rash. **-bläschen,** *n.* papula, eczema.

Häutchen ['hɔytçən], *n.* thin coat(ing), film, (*Anat.*) membrane, tunicle, pellicle.

Haut|drüse, *f.* cutaneous *or* miliary gland. **-drüsenkrankheit,** *f.* scrofula.

häuten ['hɔytən], **1.** *v.t.* skin, flay. **2.** *v.r.* cast *or* shed the skin, (*of a snake*) (cast the) slough; (*Med.*) desquamate, peel.

hauteng ['hautˀɛŋ], *adj.* skin-tight. **Haut|entzündung,** *f.* dermatitis. **-falten,** *f.pl.* wrinkles. **-farbe,** *f.* complexion. **-flügler,** *pl.* (*Ent.*) hymenoptera. **-gewebe,** *n.* outer *or* dermal tissue, cuticle; (*Bot.*) periderm.

häutig ['hɔytıç], *adj.* membranous, cutaneous, cuticular; (*in compounds*) -skinned, *e.g. dunkelhäutig,* dark-skinned.

Haut|krankheit, *f.* skin disease. **-krem,** *f.* skin lotion. **-lehre,** *f.* dermatology. **-nährkrem,** *f.* skin food. **-nerv,** *m.* cutaneous nerve. **-pflege,** *f.* care of the skin, cosmetics. **-schere,** *f.* cuticle scissors. **-transplantation, -übertragung,** *f.* skin-grafting.

Häutung ['hɔytuŋ], *f.* skinning, casting *or* shedding of the skin, (*of snake*) sloughing; (*Anat.*) desquamation, peeling (of the skin).

Hauzahn ['hautsa:n], *m.* tusk, fang.

Havanna [ha'vana], **1.** *n.* (*Geog.*) Havana. **2.** *f.* (-, *pl.* **-s**) Havana cigar. **Havannazigarre,** *f. See* **Havanna, 2.**

Havarie [hava'ri:], *f.* damage by sea, loss at sea, average; *große -,* gross average; *besondere -,* particular average; *kleine -,* petty average; *- andienen,* notify average; *- aufmachen,* settle *or* adjust the average; *- erleiden,* suffer (sea-)damage. **Havarie|-attest,** *n.* certificate of average. **-kommissar,** *m.* average adjuster, claims agent.

Havelock ['ha:vəlɔk], *m.* (**-s,** *pl.* **-s**) ulster (*coat*).

Hebamme ['he:pˀamə], *f.* midwife.

Hebe|baum ['he:bə-], *m.* lever, handspike, crowbar. **-bock,** *m.* lifting gear, jack. **-daumen,** *m.* cam. **-eisen,** *n.* crowbar; (*Surg.*) elevatory. **-fahrzeug,** *n.* (*Naut.*) salvage vessel. **-kran,** *m.* hoisting winch, hoist.

Hebel ['he:bəl], *m.* lever; crank (handle); (*fig.*) *den - ansetzen,* set about, tackle; (*fig.*) *alle - in Bewegung setzen,* take all steps, use all means at one's disposal, move heaven and earth, leave no stone unturned. **Hebel|arm,** *m.* arm of a lever. **-kraft,** *f.*, **-moment,** *n.* leverage, purchase. **-stützpunkt,** *m.* fulcrum, point of leverage. **-verhältnis,** *n.* leverage.

Hebemuskel ['he:bəmuskəl], *m.* (*Anat.*) elevator.

heben ['he:bən], **1.** *irr.v.t.* lift, raise, elevate, hoist; heave; (*fig.*) enhance, add to, improve, put into relief, set off, accentuate, make prominent; (*Math.*) cancel, reduce (*fractions*); ***die Tür aus den Angeln –,*** take the door off its hinges; ***die Welt aus den Angeln –,*** put the world out of joint; ***den Ertrag –,*** increase output *or* yield; ***die Farbenwirkung –,*** enhance *or* accentuate the colouring; ***in den Himmel –,*** extol; praise *or* laud to the skies; ***aus dem Sattel –,*** unhorse; ***einen Schatz –,*** unearth a treasure; ***ein Schiff –,*** refloat a ship; ***aus der Taufe –,*** stand sponsor to; (*coll.*) ***einen –,*** put one down the hatch. **2.** *irr.v.r.* rise, raise o.s.; ***sich – und senken,*** rise and fall; ***sich wieder –,*** revive (*as trade*); ***das hebt sich,*** that cancels out, that levels things out, that makes this level *or* even, that makes us quits; (*B.*) ***heb' dich weg von mir Satan!*** get thee behind me Satan! *See* **gehoben. Heber,** *m.* lifter, raiser, heaver; (*Anat.*) elevator; (car-)jack; (*Chem. etc.*) siphon, pipette.

Hebe|rolle, *f.* (*Law*) register of dues and taxes. **–schiff,** *n. See* **–fahrzeug. –schraube,** *f.* lifting screw. **–stange,** *f. See* **–baum. –stelle,** *f.* inland revenue office. **–vorrichtung,** *f.*, **–werk,** *n.* jack, lifting tackle *or* gear. **–winde,** *f.* windlass. **–zeug,** *n. See* **–werk.**

–hebig ['he:bɪç], *adj.suff. e.g.* ***fünfhebiger Vers,*** verse with five stresses.

Hebräer [he'brɛ:ər], *m.* Hebrew. **hebräisch,** *adj.* Hebrew, Hebraic, Jewish; ***–e Sprache, das Hebräisch(e),*** Hebrew (language).

Hebung ['he:buŋ], *f.* 1. raising, lifting; (*fig.*) improvement, enhancement, increase, promotion; 2. cancellation; 3. encouragement; 4. revenue, tax; 5. elevation, rising ground; 6. (*Mus.*) arsis, (*Metr.*) accented syllable, accent, beat. **Hebungskammer,** *f.* inland-revenue department.

Hechel ['hɛçəl], *f.* (-, *pl.* **-n**) hackle, flax-comb; (*fig.*) ***durch die – ziehen,*** censure severely. **Hechelei** [–'laɪ], *f.* 1. hackling; 2. (*fig.*) heckling, carping. **hecheln,** *v.t.* 1. hackle, dress, comb (*flax*); 2. (*fig.*) censure severely, catechize, slate, criticize, heckle.

Hechse ['hɛksə], *f. See* **Hachse.**

Hecht [hɛçt], *m.* (**-(e)s,** *pl.* **-e**) 1. (*Ichth.*) pike (*Esocidae*); (*coll.*) ***ausgewachsener*** or ***feiner –,*** fop, dandy; (*coll.*) ***der – im Karpfenteich,*** one to goad *or* egg the others on; 2. (*coll.*) fug.

Heck [hɛk], *n.* (**-(e)s,** *pl.* **-e**) 1. (*Naut.*) after-deck, stern, poop; (*Motor.*) rear; (*Av.*) tail; 2. (*dial.*) trellis, fence; trellis-gate. **Heckantrieb,** *m.* (*Motor.*) rear drive. **–bauer,** *n.* breeding-cage.

[1]**Hecke** ['hɛkə], *f.* hedge, hedgerow; fence; ***lebendige –,*** quickset hedge; ***dichte –,*** thick-set (hedge); ***tote –,*** paling, fence.

[2]**Hecke,** *f.* 1. hatch, brood; 2. hatching, breeding-(time). **hecken,** *v.t., v.i.* hatch, breed; (*fig.*) produce.

Hecken|braunelle, *f.* (*Orn.*) hedge-sparrow (*Prunella modularis*). **–reiter,** *m.* (*Hist.*) highwayman. **–rose,** *f.* (*Bot.*) dog-rose (*Rosa canina*). **–sänger,** *m.* (*Orn.*) rufous warbler (*Agrobates galactotes*). **–schere,** *f.* hedge-clippers. **–schlehe,** *f.* sloe. **–schütze,** *m.* (*Mil.*) sniper. **–sichel,** *f.* bill-hook. **–springer,** *m.* (*Av.*) hedge-hopper, low-flying aircraft. **–sprung,** *m.* (*Av.*) hedge-hopping.

Heck|flagge, *f.* (Naut.) stern flag. **–geschütz,** *n.* (*Naut.*) stern-chaser, (*Av.*) rear *or* tail gun. **hecklastig,** *adj.* tail-heavy. **Heck|laterne,** *f.* (*Naut.*) poop lantern. **–motor,** *m.* rear engine. **–pfennig,** *m.* lucky penny, nest-egg. **–schütze,** *m.* (*Av.*) rear-gunner. **–stand,** *m.* (*Av.*) tail-turret. **–zeit,** *f.* breeding *or* pairing time.

Hede ['he:də], *f.* tow, oakum. **heden,** *adj.* of tow *or* oakum.

Hederich ['he:dərɪç], *m.* (**-(e)s,** *pl.* **-e**) (*Bot.*) hedge-mustard (*Raphanus raphanistrum*).

Heer [he:r], *n.* (**-(e)s,** *pl.* **-e**) army; (*fig.*) host, multitude; ***das wilde*** or ***wütende –,*** Wodan's (*or* Arthur's) chase; ***stehendes –,*** standing army; ***Dienst im aktiven –,*** service with the colours. **Heerbann,** *m.* (*obs.*) summons to arms; general levy; levies.

Heeres|bericht, *m.* army communiqué. **–betreuung,** *f.* army welfare. **–dienst,** *m.* military service. **–dienstvorschrift,** *f.* army manual, (*Engl.*) Queen's Regulations. **–führung, –leitung,** *f.*, army command; ***oberste –,*** Supreme Command. **–lieferant,** *m.* army contractor. **–macht,** *f.* military forces; troops. **–ministerium,** *n.* War Office, (*Am.*) Department of the Army. **–truppen,** *f.pl.* G.H.Q. troops. **–zeitung,** *f.* army gazette.

Heer|führer, *m.* commander-in-chief. **–lager,** *n.* camp, encampment; (*fig.*) party, faction, group. **–schar,** *f.* host, legion; ***die himmlischen –en,*** the heavenly host; ***der Herr der –en,*** the Lord of Hosts. **–schau,** *f.* military review, parade. **–schnepfe,** *f.* (*Orn.*) *see* **Zwergschnepfe. –straße,** *f.* main road, highway. **–verpflegungsamt,** *n.* commissariat. **–wagen,** *m.* baggage-wagon; (*Astr.*) Charles's Wain. **–wesen,** *n.* military affairs. **–wurm,** *m.* (*Zool.*) army-worm, grass-worm, snake-worm (*migrating host of larvae of Sciara militaris*).

Hefe ['he:fə], *f.* 1. yeast, barm; leaven; 2. dregs, sediment; (*fig.*) scum; lees, grounds, bottoms; ***bis auf die –,*** to the very dregs; ***die – des Volks,*** the scum of the people. **Hefe|gebäck,** *n.* leavened bread, raised pastry. **–pilz,** *m.* yeast fungus. **–teig,** *m.* leavened dough. **hefig,** *adj.* barmy, yeasty; yeast-like; full of lees.

Heft [hɛft], *n.* (**-(e)s,** *pl.* **-e**) 1. haft, handle, hilt; ***bis ans –,*** up to the hilt; ***ihm das – in die Hand geben,*** allow him to have all his own way; ***ihm das – entwinden*** or ***entreißen*** or ***aus der Hand nehmen,*** wrest the power from him; ***das – in der Hand haben,*** be master of the situation, hold the reins, hold the power in one's hands, have the whip-hand; 2. stitched *or* paper-covered book, booklet, pamphlet, brochure; exercise book, copy-book; instalment, number, part (*of serial publication*); ***die Zeitschrift erscheint in zwanglosen –en,*** the periodical appears in irregular instalments.

Heftel ['hɛftəl], *m. or n.* (*Austr. f.*) hook and eye. **hefteln,** *v.t.* fasten (*with hooks and eyes*), hook up.

heften ['hɛftən], *v.t.* fasten, fix (*an* (*Acc.*), to); (*Bookb.*) stitch; baste, tack (*sewing*); ***den Blick auf etwas –,*** fix *or* pin *or* rivet *or* glue one's eyes on s.th.; ***er heftet sich an meine Fersen,*** he dogs my footsteps, he sticks to my heels. **Hefter,** *m.* file, folder. **Heftfaden,** *m.* basting *or* tacking thread.

heftig ['hɛftɪç], *adj.* violent, severe, strong, keen, sharp, intense; vigorous, vehement, fierce, furious, hot-tempered, irascible, impetuous; passionate, fervent. **Heftigkeit,** *f.* vehemence, violence, fierceness, intensity, impetuosity, ardour.

Heft|klammer, *f.* paper-fastener *or* -clip; (wire) staple. **–lade,** *f.* bookbinder's sewing frame *or* press. **–maschine,** *f.* stapling machine, stapler. **–naht,** *f.* tacking. **–pflaster,** *n.* sticking *or* adhesive plaster, court-plaster. **–schnur,** *f.* pack-thread. **–stich,** *m.* (*Sewing*) tacking stitch. **heftweise,** *adv.* in (serial) parts. **Heftzwecke,** *f.* drawing-pin, (*Am.*) thumb-tack.

Hege ['he:gə], *f.* preservation, protection, care; preserve, reserve; close-season. **Hegemeister,** *m.* head gamekeeper.

hegen ['he:gən], *v.t.* enclose, preserve (*animals*), tend, nurse (*plants*), protect, guard, cherish, take care of; ***– und pflegen,*** cherish, foster, tend, bestow great care on; ***Verdacht –,*** harbour suspicion; ***Zweifel –,*** entertain doubts. **Heger,** *m.* keeper; forester; (*dial.*) hoarder; (*dial.*) small-holder, cottager.

Hege|reiter, *m.* mounted gamekeeper. **–säule,** *f.* landmark. **–schlag, –wald,** *m.* plantation, reservation. **–weide,** *f.* enclosed *or* controlled pasture. **–zeit,** *f.* close-season (*for game*).

Hehl [he:l], *n.* (*only in*) ***kein – machen aus,*** make no secret of; ***ohne –,*** openly, frankly, without subterfuge. **hehlen,** *v.i.* (*Law*) receive stolen goods. **Hehler,** *m.* receiver (of stolen goods), (*sl.*) fence. **Hehlerei** [–'raɪ], *f.* receiving stolen property.

hehr [he:r], *adj.* (*Poet.*) lofty, majestic, sublime; (*of* *a p.*) noble, exalted, august; ***hoch und –,*** high and commanding, lofty and dignified, imposing.

heida! ['haɪda], *int.* cheers!

[1]**Heide** ['haɪdə], *f.* 1. heath, moorland, moor; 2. (*Bot.*) Scotch heather *or* ling (*Calluna vulgaris*), (*Bot.*) bell heather (*Erica cinerea*), (*Bot.*) cross-leaved heather (*Erica tetralix*).

[2]**Heide,** *m.* (**-n,** *pl.* **-n**) heathen, pagan; (*B.*) ***Juden und –n,*** Jews and Gentiles.

Heide|ginster, *m.* (*Bot.*) gorse, furze (*Ulex europaeus*). **-korn,** *n.* buckwheat. **-kraut,** *n.* Scotch heather. **-land,** *n.* heath, moorland.

Heidelbeere ['haɪdəlbe:rə], *f.* (*Bot.*) bilberry; whortleberry, (*Am.*) blueberry, huckleberry (*Vaccinium myrtillis*).

Heidelerche ['haɪdəlɛrçə], *f.* (*Orn.*) woodlark (*Lullula arborea*).

Heiden|angst, *f.* mortal fright, (*coll.*) blue funk. **-apostel,** *m.* (*B.*) apostle to the Gentiles. **-bekehrung,** *f.* conversion of heathens, foreign missions, missionary work. **-bild,** *n.* idol. **-christ,** *m.* heathen proselyte (*of early Christianity*). **-geld,** *n.* (*coll.*) enormous sum of money, (*sl.*) a hell of a lot of money. **-haar,** *n.* first hair (*of newborn infant*). **-lärm,** *m.* (*coll.*) fearful *or* (*sl.*) hell of a noise, hullabaloo. **heidenmäßig,** *adj.* very large, very great, very much, tremendous, enormous, awful. **Heiden|mission,** *f.* foreign mission. **-spaß,** *m.* (*coll.*) a real scream. **-tempel,** *m.* pagan temple. **Heidentum,** *n.* heathendom, the pagan world, pagans; paganism.

Heideröslein ['haɪdərø:slaɪn], *n.* (*Bot.*) rock rose (*Helianthemum nummularium*).

Heidin ['haɪdɪn], *f. See* [2]**Heide.**

heidnisch ['haɪdnɪʃ], *adj.* heathen, heathenish, pagan, godless, (*fig.*) barbarous.

Heidschnucke ['haɪtʃnukə], *f.* (North German) moorland sheep.

heikel ['haɪkəl], **heiklig,** *adj.* (*of a th.*) ticklish, difficult, critical, delicate, (*of a p.*) fastidious, particular, exacting, finical, (*coll.*) choosy; squeamish.

heil [haɪl], *adj.* (*of a th.*) whole, intact; (*of a p.*) unhurt, safe and sound, uninjured, unscathed; healed (up), cured, restored.

Heil, 1. *n.* well-being, welfare; (*Eccl.*) salvation, redemption; ***das ewige –,*** eternal salvation; ***im Jahre des –s,*** in the year of grace, in the year of our Lord; ***sein – versuchen,*** try one's luck, (*coll.*) have a go; ***sein – in der Flucht suchen,*** seek safety in flight, take to one's heels; ***es gereichte*** or ***war mir zum –,*** it was lucky for me, it was to my good *or* benefit. 2. *int.* hail! good luck! ***– dem König!*** long live the king! God save the king! ***– dem Volke, welches . . .,*** happy the people that . . .; ***Sieg –!*** (*Nat. Soc. acclamation*) To Victory! ***Ski –!*** Good ski-ing!

Heiland ['haɪlant], *m.* (**-(e)s,** *pl.* **-e**) Saviour, Redeemer.

Heil|anstalt, *f.* sanatorium, hospital, clinic, asylum, convalescent home, nursing home (*usu.* mental home). **-bad,** *n.* medicinal baths, spa, watering place. **heilbar,** *adj.* curable; remediable. **Heilbehandlung,** *f.* (curative) treatment, cure. **heilbringend,** *adj.* salutary, beneficial. **Heil|brunnen,** *m.* mineral spring. **-butt,** *m.* (*Ichth.*) halibut (*Hippoglossus vulgaris*).

heilen [haɪlən], 1. *v.t.* heal (*a wound etc.*), cure (*a disease or a p.*) (***von,*** of). 2. *v.i.* (*aux.* s.) (*of a wound etc.*) heal (up), (*of a p. or a disease*) be cured.

Heilerfolg ['haɪlˀɛrfɔlk], *m.* successful treatment. **heilfroh,** *adj.* overjoyed, delighted. **Heilgymnastik,** *f.* physiotherapy, remedial gymnastics.

heilig ['haɪlɪç], *adj.* holy, godly, pious, sacred, hallowed; solemn, venerable, august; sacred, inviolable, sacrosanct; (*before proper names*) Saint; ***Heiliger Abend,*** Christmas Eve; ***das Heilige Abendmahl,*** the Lord's Supper, holy communion; ***Heiliges Bein,*** os sacrum; ***–e Bücher,*** sacred books; ***es ist mein –er Ernst,*** I am in dead earnest; ***der Heilige Geist,*** the Holy Ghost; ***den Sonntag – halten,*** keep the Sabbath day (holy); ***–e Handlung,*** sacred rite, sacrament; ***Heilige Jungfrau,*** the Blessed Virgin (Mary); ***das Heilige Land,*** the Holy Land; ***–er Ort,*** holy *or* sacred place; ***–e Pflicht,*** sacred duty; ***die Heilige Schrift,*** the (Holy) Scriptures; ***Heiliger Vater,*** the Holy Father, the Pope; ***hoch und – versprechen,*** promise solemnly; ***–er Zorn,*** righteous anger.

Heilige, *see* **Heilige(r), Heilige(s).**

heiligen ['haɪlɪɡən], *v.t.* hallow, sanctify, consecrate; canonize, beatify (*a p.*); keep holy, hold sacred; (*Prov.*) ***der Zweck heiligt die Mittel,*** the end justifies the means; (*B.*) ***geheiligt werde Dein Name,*** hallowed be Thy name.

Heiligen|bild, *n.* saint's image. **-buch,** *n.* book of legends of the saints, martyrology. **-dienst,** *m.* worship of saints, hagiolatry. **-geschichte,** *f.* hagiology. **-kalender,** *m.* calendar of saints. **-schein,** *m.* halo, glory, gloriole, (*Paint.*) auriole, auriola, (*fig.*) nimbus.

Heilige(r) ['haɪlɪɡə(r)], *m., f.* saint; (*coll.*) ***wunderlicher Heiliger,*** queer customer. **Heilige(s),** *n.* holy *or* sacred th.

heilighalten ['haɪlɪçhaltən], *irr.v.t.* hold sacred, keep holy. **Heilig|halten,** *n.,* **-haltung,** *f.* religious *or* (*fig.*) strict observance. **Heiligkeit,** *f.* holiness, saintliness, godliness; sanctity, sacredness; ***im Geruch der –,*** in the odour of sanctity; ***Seine –,*** His Holiness. **heiligsprechen,** *irr.v.t.* canonize. **Heilig|sprechung,** *f.* canonization. **-tuerei,** *f.* sanctimoniousness.

Heiligtum ['haɪlɪçtu:m], *n.* (**-s,** *pl.* **⸚er**) holy place, shrine, sanctuary; (sacred) relic; (*coll.*) sanctum. **Heiligtums|raub,** *m.,* **-schändung,** *f.* sacrilege.

Heiligung ['haɪlɪɡuŋ], *f.* consecration, sanctification, hallowing.

Heilkraft ['haɪlkraft], *f.* healing power. **heilkräftig,** *adj.* curative; medicinal, therapeutic. **Heil|kraut,** *n.* medicinal *or* officinal herb. **-kunde,** *f.* medical science, medicine, therapeutics. **heilkundig,** *adj.* skilled in medicine. **Heil|kunst,** *f. See* **-kunde. -künstler,** *m.* quack doctor.

heillos ['haɪllo:s], *adj.* unholy, godless; (*fig.*) terrible, dreadful; hopeless; (*coll.*) awful, enormous.

Heil|magnetismus, *m.* mesmerism, animal magnetism. **-mittel,** *n.* remedy, cure (***gegen,*** for); medicine, drug, medicament. **-mittellehre,** *f.* pharmacology, materia medica. **-pflanze,** *f. See* **-kraut. -pflaster,** *n.* medicated sticking-plaster. **-praktiker,** *m.* quack doctor. **-quelle,** *f. See* **-brunnen. -ruf,** *m.* cheer, acclamation.

heilsam ['haɪlza:m], *adj.* healing, curative; salubrious, wholesome, salutary, (*fig.*) good (***für,*** for), beneficial (to). **Heilsamkeit,** *f.* wholesomeness, salutariness, salutary effect; salubrity.

Heils|armee, *f.* Salvation Army. **-botschaft,** *f.* Christ's message to the world.

Heilserum ['haɪlze:rum], *n.* antitoxic serum, antitoxin.

Heils|geschichte, *f.* Passion and Salvation of Christ. **-lehre,** *f.* doctrine of salvation.

Heil|stätte, *f. See* **-anstalt** (*usu. for tubercular cases*). **-stoff,** *m. See* **-mittel.**

Heilung ['haɪluŋ], *f.* healing, curing, cure, recovery, successful treatment.

Heil|verfahren, *n.* medical treatment, therapy. **-wert,** *m.* therapeutic value.

heim [haɪm], *adv.* home, homeward. **Heim,** *n.* (**-(e)s,** *pl.* **-e**) home, residence, dwelling, abode, domicile; home, hostel; ***ein – gründen,*** set up house; ***– und Herd,*** hearth and home.

Heim|abend, *m.* club night. **-arbeit,** *f.* work done at home.

Heimat ['haɪma:t], *f.* (-, *pl.* **-en**) home; native land, country *or* place; homeland, (*Law*) domicile. **Heimat|dichter,** *m.* vernacular poet. **-flotte,** *f.* home fleet. **-hafen,** *m.* port of registry, home port. **-kunde,** *f.* local history and topography. **-land,** *n.* mother-country, native land *or* country. **heimat-**

lich, *adj.* native, (belonging to one's) home. **heimatlos,** *adj.* homeless; outcast. **Heimat|recht,** *n.* right of domicile. **-schein,** *m.* certificate of domicile. **-schlag,** *m.* homing loft (*of pigeons*). **-schuß,** *m.* (*Mil. sl.*) a Blighty one (1914–1918: *a wound that ensured repatriation*). **-schutz,** *m.* preservation of the countryside (*cf. National Trust*). **-sinn,** *m.* (*Zool.*) homing instinct. **-staat,** *m.* country of origin, native country. **-stadt,** *f.* home *or* native town. **-vertriebene(r),** *m., f.* refugee *or* expellee (from occupied territory).

heim|begeben, *irr.v.r.* go *or* return home. **-begleiten,** *v.t.* see (*s.o.*) home.

Heimchen ['haɪmçən], *n.* (*Zool.*) cricket.

heimelig ['haɪməlɪç], *adj.* comfy, cosy, snug, intimate.

Heim|fahrt, *f.* return *or* journey home, homeward journey, return trip. **-fall,** *m.* (*Law*) devolution, reversion, escheat. **heim|fallen,** *irr.v.i.* (*Law*) revert (*an* (*Acc.*), to). **-fällig,** *adj.* revertible, reversionary. **Heim|fallsberechtigte(r),** *m., f.* reversioner. **-fallsrecht,** *n.* right of escheat, reversionary right. **heim|finden,** *irr.v.r.* find one's way home *or* back. **-führen,** *v.t.* lead home; ***die Braut* –,** bring home one's bride. **Heim|gang,** *m.* going home; (*usu.*) death, decease. **-gegangene(r),** *m., f.* the deceased *or* departed. **heimgehen,** *irr.v.i.* (*aux.* s.) go home; die, pass away, depart this life. **Heimindustrie,** *f.* home *or* cottage industry.

heimisch ['haɪmɪʃ], *adj.* home, domestic; native, national, indigenous; ***-e Gewässer,*** home waters; ***– sein in*** (*Dat.*), be at home in; ***sich – machen,*** acclimatize o.s., make o.s. at home, settle down; ***sich – fühlen,*** feel at home.

Heimkehr ['haɪmkeːr], *f.* return home, homecoming. **heimkehren,** *v.i.* (*aux.* s.) return home. **Heimkehrer,** *m.* repatriated prisoner of war, returned soldier. **heim|kommen,** *irr.v.i.* (*aux.* s.) *see* **-kehren. Heim|kunft,** *f. See* **-kehr. -leiterin,** *f.* matron (*of a hostel*). **heimleuchten,** *v.t.* (*fig.*) ***ihm* –,** send him about his business, give him a piece of one's mind, tell him what's what, (*coll.*) tell him off.

heimlich ['haɪmlɪç], **1.** *adj.* 1. secret, hidden, concealed; stealthy, underhand, undercover, furtive, clandestine, surreptitious, secretive, (*coll.*) hush-hush; private, secluded; 2. comfy, cosy, snug. **2.** *adv.* secretly, by stealth, (*coll.*) on the quiet *or* sly; ***sich – entfernen,*** slip *or* steal away, take French leave; ***– lachen,*** laugh in one's sleeve; ***– tun,*** put on a knowing air. **Heimlichkeit,** *f.* secrecy, reticence; secretiveness, furtiveness, stealth(iness). **Heimlich|tuer,** *m.* mystery-monger. **-tuerei,** *f.* affectation of secrecy, mystification. **heimlichtun,** *irr.v.i.* be secretive (***mit,*** about), make a mystery (of).

Heim|reise, *f.* return *or* homeward journey, journey home. **-schule,** *f.* boarding school. **-stätte,** *f.* home; homestead. **heimsuchen,** *v.t.* (*fig.*) visit, afflict, plague (*as misfortune*), infest (*as vermin*), haunt (*as ghosts*), ravage, overrun (*as enemy troops*); ***heimgesucht,*** haunted, infested, racked, stricken. **Heim|suchung,** *f.* visitation, affliction, trial. **-tücke,** *f.* malice, insidiousness; treachery, perfidy, foul play. **heimtückisch,** *adj.* malicious, insidious; treacherous, perfidious, dastardly. **heimwärts,** *adv.* homeward. **Heim|weg,** *m.* way home, homeward journey. **-weh,** *n.* homesickness, (*fig.*) nostalgia (***nach,*** for); ***– haben,*** be homesick. **-wehr,** *f.* militia, (*Engl.*) Home Guard; (*Hist.*) Austrian fascist party. **heimzahlen,** *v.t.* ***ihm etwas* –,** pay him out *or* back, get even with him, be revenged on him (for s.th.).

Hein [haɪn], *m.* (*coll.*) ***Freund* –,** Death.

Heini ['haɪni], *m.* (*coll.*) dolt, numbskull.

Heinrich ['haɪnrɪç], *m.* Henry.

heint [haɪnt], *adv.* (*dial.*) tonight, last night; today.

Heinz [haɪnts], *m.* (**-en,** *pl.* **-en**), **Heinze,** *f.* rack *or* trestle for drying hay.

Heinzelmännchen ['haɪntsəlmɛnçən], *n.* brownie, sprite.

Heirat ['haɪraːt], *f.* (-, *pl.* **-en**) marriage, match; wedding; ***– aus Liebe,*** love-match. **heiraten,** **1.** *v.t.* marry, wed. **2.** *v.i.* marry, get married; (***wegen*** or ***nach***) ***Geld* –,** marry (for) money; ***in die Stadt* –,** marry a townsman; ***aufs Land* –,** marry a farmer; ***nach London* –,** marry a Londoner.

Heirats|antrag, *m.* offer of marriage, proposal; ***einer Dame einen – machen,*** propose to a lady. **-anzeige,** *f.* announcement of marriage. **-büro,** *n.* matrimonial agency. **heiratsfähig,** *adj.* marriageable. **Heirats|gut,** *n.* marriage portion, dowry. **-kandidat,** *m.* suitor, wooer. **heiratslustig,** *adj.* bent on marriage, eager to marry. **Heirats|markt,** *m.* marriage market. **-stifter,** *m.* matchmaker. **-urkunde,** *f.* marriage certificate *or* lines. **-vermittler,** *m.* go-between, matchmaker, matrimonial agent. **-versprechen,** *n.* promise to marry, engagement; ***Bruch des -s,*** breach of promise. **-vertrag,** *m.* marriage settlement.

heisa! ['haɪsa], *int.* cheers!

heischen ['haɪʃən], *v.t.* (*Poet.*) ask (for), beg, demand, request, require. **Heischesatz,** *m.* postulate; (*Gram.*) optative clause.

heiser ['haɪzər], *adj.* hoarse, husky, raucous, (*coll.*) croaking. **Heiserkeit,** *f.* hoarseness, raucousness.

heiß [haɪs], *adj.* hot, (*Geog.*) torrid; (*fig.*) hot, burning, fiery, ardent, fervent, fervid, vehement; ***-es Blut,*** hot blood *or* temper; ***der Boden wird mir zu* –,** things are getting too hot for me; ***wie die Katze um den -en Brei,*** like a cat on hot bricks; ***-er Dank,*** warm(est) thanks; ***das Eisen schmieden solange es – ist,*** strike while the iron is hot; ***-e Gebete,*** fervent prayers; ***glühend* –,** red-hot, (*fig.*) scorching (*as the sun*); (*coll.*) ***ihm die Hölle – machen,*** give it him hot, (*sl.*) give him hell; ***-er Kampf,*** fierce battle; ***-er Kopf,*** burning head; ***ihm den Kopf – machen,*** alarm *or* perturb him; ***-e Leitung,*** hot line; ***-e Liebe,*** ardent love; ***es lief mir – und kalt über den Rücken,*** I went all hot and cold; ***mir ist* –,** I feel hot; ***-e Tränen weinen,*** weep bitterly; ***was ich nicht weiß, macht mich nicht* –,** ignorance is bliss; ***-e Zone,*** torrid zone. **heißblütig,** *adj.* (*Zool.*) hot-blooded; (*fig.*) hot-blooded, hot-tempered, choleric. **Heißdampf,** *m.* superheated steam.

[1]**heißen** ['haɪsən], **1.** *irr.v.t.* 1. command, enjoin, bid, order, direct; ***ihn gehen* –,** bid him go; ***wer hat dich geheißen, das zu tun?*** at whose bidding are you doing this? ***ihn willkommen* –,** welcome him; 2. name, call, denominate. **2.** *irr.v.i.* 1. be called *or* named, go by the name of; ***er heißt,*** his name is; ***wie – Sie?*** what is your name? ***ich will ein Schuft –, wenn . . .,*** I'm a Dutchman if . . ., I'll eat my hat if . . .; 2. mean, signify, be tantamount to; ***das heißt,*** that is (to say); ***wie heißt das auf Deutsch?*** what is that in German? what is the German for this? ***was soll das –?*** what is the meaning of this? (*coll.*) what's the big idea? ***das will wenig*** or ***nicht viel* –,** that is of little consequence; ***das will schon etwas* –,** that is saying a great *or* good deal, that's indeed something. **3.** *irr.v.i.imp.* ***es heißt daß . . .,*** it is said *or* reported *or* rumoured that . . ., people *or* they say; ***wie es im Liede heißt,*** as the song says; ***hier heißt es mit Recht,*** one may well say here; ***nun heißt es aufhören!*** now it's time to stop! that's enough now!

[2]**heißen,** *v.t. See* **hissen.**

heiß|ersehnt, *adj.* ardently desired. **-geliebt,** *adj.* dearly loved *or* beloved. **Heißhunger,** *m.* ravenous hunger, voracious appetite, (*fig.*) craving, thirst (***nach,*** for). **heiß|hungrig,** *adj.* ravenous(ly hungry), voracious. **-laufen,** *irr.v.i.* (*aux. s.*), *v.r.* (*Mech.*) run hot, overheat, get overheated. **Heiß|luftdusche,** *f.* hair-dryer. **-sporn,** *m.* firebrand, hotspur. **-strahltriebwerk,** *n.* (*Av.*) thermojet engine. **-wasserheizung,** *f.* water-heater, geyser. **-wasserspeicher,** *m.* hot-water tank (with immersion heater).

Heister ['haɪstər], *m.* (*also f.* (-, *pl.* **-n**)) sapling, young tree, (*dial.*) young beech-tree.

heiter ['haɪtər], *adj.* clear, bright, fair, serene, (*of a p.*) happy, gay, merry, cheerful, (*of a story etc.*)

funny, amusing, humorous; – *werden,* brighten *or* clear up; (*coll.*) (*iron.*) *das kann ja – werden!* cheerful prospects *or* a bright outlook indeed! we may as well expect the worst! *–es Gemüt,* cheerful *or* happy disposition; *–e Stimmung,* merry *or* jovial mood; *–es Wetter,* fine, sunny weather; *wie ein Blitz aus –em Himmel,* like a bolt from the blue. **Heiterkeit,** *f.* brightness; clearness, serenity; gaiety, cheerfulness, merriment, mirth, amusement, glee.

Heiz|anlage ['haɪts–], *f.* heating-installation *or* plant. **–anzug,** *m.* (*Av.*) electrically heated flying suit. **–apparat,** *m.* heating-appliance *or* -apparatus, heater. **heizbar,** *adj.* heatable, easily heated; *–e Zimmer,* rooms with heating. **Heiz|batterie,** *f.* (*Rad.*) low-tension *or* filament battery. **–decke,** *f.* electric blanket.

heizen ['haɪtsən], *v.t., v.i.* heat; make a fire; *mit Holz –,* burn wood; *dieses Zimmer läßt sich gut –,* this room is easily heated; *diese Kohlen – gut,* this coal gives a good heat *or* burns well. **Heizer,** *m.* stoker, fireman; heating-apparatus.

Heiz|faden, *m.* (electric) filament. **–gas,** *n.* fuel gas. **–kessel,** *m.* boiler. **–kissen,** *n.* electric pillow *or* pad. **–körper,** *m.* (*Elec.*) heating element; heater, radiator. **–kraft,** *f.* calorific *or* heating power. **–loch,** *n.* stoke-hole. **–material,** *n.* fuel. **–platte,** *f.* hot-plate. **–raum,** *m.* boiler-house, (*Naut.*) stokehold. **–röhre,** *f.* fire-tube. **–sonne,** *f.* electric fire. **–strom,** *m.* (*Rad.*) filament *or* heater current. **Heizung,** *f.* heating, firing; central heating; *die – abstellen,* turn off the radiators. **Heizwert,** *m.* calorific value.

Hekatombe [heka'tɔmbə], *f.* hecatomb.

Hektar [hɛk'ta:r], *n.* (*Austr. also m.*) **(-s,** *pl.* **-e), Hektare,** *f.* (*Swiss*) hectare (= *just under* 2½ *acres*).

hektisch ['hɛktɪʃ], *adj.* hectic.

Hekto|gramm [hɛkto'gram], *n.* hectogramme (= *3 oz.*). **–graph,** *m.* hectograph; duplicator. **–liter,** *n.* (*Austr. m.*) hectolitre (= *22 gallons*).

Held [hɛlt], *m.* **(-en,** *pl.* **-en)** hero; champion; – *eines Romans,* hero *or* chief character of a novel.

Helden|buch, *n.* collection of medieval heroic poems. **–dichtung,** *f.* heroic *or* epic poetry. **–friedhof,** *m.* military cemetery. **–gedenktag,** *m.* Memorial (*Engl.* Armistice) Day. **–gedicht,** *n.* heroic epic. **heldenhaft,** *adj.* heroic, valiant. **Helden|keller,** *m.* (*sl.*) air-raid shelter, funk-hole. **–lied,** *n. See* **–gedicht. –mut,** *m.* heroism, valour, heroic spirit. **heldenmütig,** *adj. See* **heldenhaft. Helden|rolle,** *f.* (*Theat.*) part of the hero. **–sage,** *f.* heroic saga *or* legend. **–sinn,** *m.* heroism, heroic spirit. **–stück,** *n.*, **–tat,** *f.* heroic deed, bold exploit, feat. **–tod,** *m.* death in battle *or* action. **Heldentum,** *n.* heroism. **Heldenverehrung,** *f.* hero-worship.

Heldin ['hɛldɪn], *f.* heroine. **heldisch,** *adj.* heroic; *–e Dichtung,* (medieval) heroic *or* epic poetry.

helfen ['hɛlfən], *irr.v.i.* (*Dat.*) help, aid, assist, succour, promote, support; be of use, avail, profit, do good to; remedy; deliver; *so wahr mir Gott helfe!* so help me God! (*B.*) *was hülfe es dem Menschen wenn,* what is a man profited if; *da ist nicht zu –,* nothing can be done about it; *dem ist nicht* (*mehr*) *zu –,* he is past help; that is irremediable; *ich kann mir nicht –,* I cannot help it, I have no choice; *es hilft nichts,* it is no use, it is *or* does no good, that's no help; *es hilft Ihnen nichts zu . . .,* it is of no use for you to . . .; *ihm zu seinem Rechte –,* see that he gets his rights; *ihm auf die Spur –,* put him on the track; *er weiß sich zu –,* he can take care of himself, he is never beaten *or* nonplussed; *er weiß sich nicht* (*mehr*) *zu –,* he's at his wits' end *or* at the end of his tether, he doesn't know which way to turn, he's at a loss what to do.

Helfer ['hɛlfər], *m.* helper, assistant. **Helfershelfer,** *m.* accomplice, abettor.

Helge ['hɛlgə], *f.*, **Helgen,** *m.* (*dial.*) *see* **Helling.**

Helgoland ['hɛlgolant], *n.* (*Geog.*) Heligoland.

Heliograph [helio'gra:f], *m.* heliograph. **–gravüre,** *f.* photogravure. **–trop** [–'tro:p], *m.* **(-s,** *pl.* **-e)** heliotrope.

hell [hɛl], *adj.* (*of light*) clear, bright, shining, brilliant, luminous, pellucid; (*of sound*) ringing, clear, sonorous, high(-pitched); light, fair (*hair*); pale (*ale*); (*fig.*) bright, intelligent, clear-headed; *–e Augenblicke,* lucid intervals; *–e Farben,* light colours; *seine –e Freude an einer S. haben,* take a real pleasure in a th.; *–es Gelächter,* ringing laughter, hearty laugh; *in –en Haufen,* in large numbers, in swarms, in full force; *–er Kopf,* clear-headed person; *–er Mittag,* broad noon(day); *–er Neid,* pure jealousy; *am –en Tage,* in broad daylight; *–e Tränen,* brimming tears; *–er Unsinn,* sheer *or* downright nonsense; *–e Verzweiflung,* utter despair; *–er Wahnsinn,* sheer madness; *–e Wahrheit,* plain truth; *es wird schon –,* it is getting light, dawn is breaking.

hell|äugig, *adj.* bright-eyed; (*fig.*) clear-sighted. **–blau,** *adj.* light blue. **–blond,** *adj.* very fair, ash-blond. **–braun,** *adj.* light brown. **–dunkel,** *adj.* dim, half-lit, dusky; (*Paint.*) clair-obscure, chiaroscuro.

Helle ['hɛlə], *f.* brightness, lightness, clearness, luminosity, brilliance.

Hellebarde [hɛlə'bardə], *f.* halberd, halbert. **Hellebardier** [–'di:r], *m.* **(-s,** *pl.* **-e)** halberdier.

hellen ['hɛlən], *v.r.* (*Poet.*) *see* **erhellen.**

Hellene [hɛ'le:nə], *m.* (*Hist.*) Hellene, Greek. **hellenisch,** *adj.* Hellenic, Greek.

Heller ['hɛlər], *m.* small coin; farthing, (*B.*) mite; *kein roter –,* not a penny *or* farthing; *auf – und Pfennig,* to the last farthing *or* (*Am.*) cent; *keinen -wert,* not worth a rap.

Helle(s) ['hɛlə(s)], *n.* glass of pale ale.

helleuchtend ['hɛllɔyçtənt], *adj.* brilliant, luminous.

hell|farbig, *adj.* light-coloured. **–gelb,** *adj.* pale yellow. **–grün,** *adj.* pale *or* light green. **–hörig,** *adj.* (*of a p.*) keen of hearing; (*of walls*) not sound-proof; (*fig.*) *ihn – machen,* make him prick up his ears, arouse his suspicions.

hellicht ['hɛllɪçt], *adj. am –en Tage,* in broad daylight.

Helligkeit ['hɛlɪçkaɪt], *f. See* **Helle**; (*Opt.*) intensity (of light), brilliancy.

Helling ['hɛlɪŋ], *f.* (-, *pl.* **-en** *or* **Helligen**), *m.* **(-s,** *pl.* **-e)** (*Shipb.*) slip, slipway.

hellrot ['hɛlro:t], *adj.* light *or* bright red. **Hell|schreiber,** *m.* teleprinter. **–sehen,** *n.* clairvoyance. **hellsehend,** *adj.* clear-sighted, wide-awake. **Hell|seher(in),** *m.*(*f.*) clairvoyant(e). **hell|seherisch,** *adj.* clairvoyant. **–sichtig,** *adj. See* **–sehend.**

[1]**Helm** [hɛlm], *m.* **(-(e)s,** *pl.* **-e)** helmet, (*Poet.*) helm, casque; (*Archit.*) dome, cupola.

[2]**Helm,** *m. or n.* **(-(e)s,** *pl.* **-e)** handle, helve; (*Naut.*) helm, rudder.

Helm|busch, *m.* crest *or* plume of a helmet. **–dach,** *n.* vaulted roof, cupola. **–holz,** *n.* (*Naut.*) tiller. **–kamm,** *m.* crest. **–kolben,** *m.* distilling flask. **–schieber, –sturz,** *m.*, **–visier,** *n.* visor.

Helot(e) [he'lo:t(ə)], *m.* **(-en,** *pl.* **-en)** helot. **Helotentum,** *n.* helotry, helotism.

Hemd [hɛmt], *n.* **(-(e)s,** *pl.* **-en)** shirt; (under)vest (*man*), chemise, vest (*woman*); (*fig.*) *bis aufs – ausziehen,* fleece, plunder completely; *alles bis aufs – verlieren, kein* (*ganzes*) *– am* or *auf dem Leib* (*mehr*) *haben,* be left with not a shirt to one's back; (*Prov.*) *das – ist mir näher als der Rock,* blood is thicker than water; charity begins at home.

Hemd|ärmel, *m. See* **Hemdsärmel. –brust,** *f.*, **–einsatz,** *m.* shirt-front, dicky.

Hemden|knopf, *m.* shirt button; stud. **–matz,** *m.* (*hum.*) small child with a bare backside. **–stoff,** *m.* shirting.

Hemd|hose, *f.* combinations, camiknickers. **–knopf,** *m. See* **Hemdenknopf. –kragen,** *m.* shirt-collar.

Hemdsärmel ['hɛmtsʔɛrməl], *m.* shirt-sleeve. **hemdsärmelig,** *adj.* in shirt-sleeves.

Hemisphäre [hemi'sfɛ:rə], *f.* hemisphere. **hemisphärisch,** *adj.* hemispherical.

hemmen ['hɛmən], *v.t.* check, stop, arrest; handicap, hold up, hamper, impede, obstruct, delay, hinder; retard, slow up *or* down, put on the drag *or* brake; stop, stem, sta(u)nch *(blood)*, curb, check, restrain *(passions etc.)*, *(Psych.)* inhibit. **hemmend,** *adj.* obstructive, hampering, impeding, *(Psych.)* inhibitory. **Hemm|feder,** *f.* retaining spring. **-kette,** *f.* drag-chain.

Hemmnis ['hɛmnɪs], *n.* (**-ses,** *pl.* **-se**) check, obstruction, obstacle, hindrance, impediment, handicap.

Hemm|rad, *n.* *(Horol.)* escapement. **-schuh,** *m.* brake, drag, skid, scotch, *(fig.)* hindrance, impediment (*für*, to), drag (on).

Hemmung ['hɛmuŋ], *f.* restraint, check, stoppage, hindrance; *(Pysch.)* inhibition, *(fig.)* restraint, scruple(s); retardation *(of growth)*; *(Mech.)* detent, catch, stop; *(Horol.)* escapement; jam, stoppage *(of a gun)*. **hemmungslos,** *adj.* unchecked, unrestrained, without restraint, reckless, unscrupulous. **Hemmungs|spruch,** *m.*, **-urteil,** *n.* *(Law)* arrest of judgement.

Hendl [hɛndl], *n.* (**-s,** *pl.* **-(n)**) *(Austr.)* chicken.

Hengst [hɛŋst], *m.* (**-es,** *pl.* **-e**) stallion; jackass *(male of the horse, zebra, camel, or ass)*. **Hengst|füllen,** *n.* colt. **-geld,** *n.* covering-fee.

Henkel [hɛŋkəl], *m.* handle *(of a basket, pot etc.)*; ring, ear, lug; hanger, loop *(on clothes)*; shank *(of a button)*. **henkelig,** *adj.* with a handle, handled. **Henkel|korb,** *m.* basket with handles. **-krug,** *m.* jug, mug. **-ohren,** *n.pl.* *(coll.)* protruding ears. **-topf,** *m.* casserole.

henken [hɛŋkən], *v.t.* hang (by the neck). **Henker,** *m.* hangman, executioner; ***zum – damit!*** hang it! the deuce! *(sl.)* ***scher' dich*** or ***geh zum –!*** go to blazes *or* the devil! *(sl.)* ***ich frage den – danach, ich schere mich den – drum,*** I don't care a damn about it; *(coll.)* ***daraus werde der – klug!*** I cannot make head or tail of it. **Henkers|beil,** *n.* executioner's axe. **-hand,** *f.* ***von – sterben,*** die at the hands of the executioner. **-knecht,** *m.* tormentor, torturer. **-mahlzeit,** *f.* last meal (before execution); *(coll.)* farewell dinner.

Henne ['hɛnə], *f.* hen; ***junge –,*** pullet.

her [he:r], *adv.* 1. *(place)* hither, here, this way; ***– damit!*** out with it! hand it over! ***wo hat er das –?*** where did he get that (from)? ***die Hand –!*** give me your hand! ***hin und –,*** to and fro, hither and thither, up and down, there and back; ***ich dachte lange hin und –,*** I turned the matter over in my mind for a long time; ***hin und – sprechen,*** debate, argue; ***hinter ihm – sein,*** follow close upon his heels, dog his footsteps, *(fig.)* pester him, be after him; ***hinter einer S. – sein,*** be hot in pursuit of s.th.; ***rings um uns –,*** round about us; ***von oben (unten) –,*** from above (below); ***von weit –,*** from afar; *(coll.)* ***nicht weit – sein,*** be inferior, indifferent, mediocre, middling, insignificant, unimportant *or* of little value; *(coll.)* be no great shakes, not be up to much; *(sl.)* be nothing to write home about, be not so hot; *(coll.)* ***wo sind Sie –?*** where do you come from? ***– zu mir!*** come over here! 2. *(time)* since, ago; ***von alters –,*** from time immemorial, of old; ***vom Anfange –,*** from the very beginning; ***von früher –,*** from some time earlier, from earlier times; ***von je –,*** always; ***von meiner Jugend –,*** dating from my youth; ***wie lange ist es –?*** how long ago was it? ***noch keine Viertelstunde –,*** not a quarter of an hour ago (***daß,*** since *or* that); 3. *pref.* (a) *to prepositions (used adverbially), is unaccented; see* **herab, heran, herauf, heraus, herbei** *etc.*: *it refers the indicated motion in the direction of the speaker, cf. its opposite* **hin**; (b) *to verbs, it takes the accent and is separable; both as a simple prefix and as a component of the compound prefixes of* (a) *it usually implies the notion of 'hither'. Many compounds are of course quite idiomatic.*

herab [hɛ'rap], *adv., sep. pref.* *(indicates movement downwards as seen by the person below) (see also* **herunter**); down, down here; down from; downward; *(with preceding Acc.)* ***den Berg –,*** down (from) the mountain; ***die Treppe –,*** down the stairs, downstairs; ***von oben –,*** from (up) above, from on high, *(fig.)* condescendingly, in a superior manner *or* tone.

herab|blicken, *v.i. See* **-sehen. -drücken,** *v.t.* press down, depress; *(fig.)* beat *or* force down *(prices)*. **-gehen,** *irr.v.i.* descend, go *or* walk down; *(fig.)* extend downwards; *(Comm.)* fall, drop, go down, give way, sag *(of prices)*. **-hängen,** *irr.v.i.* hang down, be suspended, dangle. **-hängend,** *adj.* pendent, pendulous; flowing. **-kommen,** *irr.v.i.* descend, come down; be reduced in circumstance, be brought low. **-lassen, 1.** *irr.v.t.* lower, let down. **2.** *irr.v.r.* condescend, deign, stoop. **-lassend,** *adj.* condescending, affable (***gegen*** or ***zu,*** towards). **Herablassung,** *f.* condescension; affability. **-laufen,** *irr.v.i.* run down *(as clocks)*. **-mindern,** *v.t.* decrease, reduce, diminish; detract from, impair. **-schießen, 1.** *irr.v.t.* shoot down *(birds, aircraft etc.)*. **2.** *irr.v.i.* come shooting *or* running down. **-sehen,** *irr.v.i.* look down (***auf*** *(Acc.)*, at *or (fig.)* upon), despise. **-setzen,** *v.t.* lower, reduce, diminish, decrease, curtail, *(coll.)* cut down; *(in rank)* debase, degrade; *(fig.)* undervalue, minimize, disparage, depreciate, *(coll.)* run down; lower, reduce, curtail, cut, *(coll.)* slash *(prices)*. **-setzend,** *adj.* degrading, debasing; disparaging, derogatory, contemptuous. **Herabsetzung,** *f.* lowering, reduction, abatement, decrease, curtailment, cut; disparagement, depreciation, slight. **herab|sinken,** *irr.v.i.* sink (down); drop, *(of prices)* fall; debase *or* degrade o.s., be degraded. **-steigen,** *irr.v.i.* descend, climb *or* step down; dismount *(from horse)*. **-stoßen,** *irr.v.i.* *(of bird of prey)* swoop down. **-stürzen, 1.** *v.t.* throw *or* fling down. **2.** *v.r.* throw o.s. down, jump to one's death. **3.** *v.i.* rush *or* plunge down. **-transformieren,** *v.t.* *(Elec.)* step down. **-würdigen, 1.** *v.t.* degrade, abase, demean. **2.** *v.r.* lower o.s., demean o.s., stoop. **Herabwürdigung,** *f.* degradation, abasement.

Heraldik [he'raldɪk], *f.* heraldry. **heraldisch,** *adj.* heraldic.

heran [hɛ'ran], *adv., sep. pref.* *(indicates movement into the proximity of the speaker)*, near, along(side), (up) this way, towards, up *or* near to; ***er ging an sie –,*** he went up to them; ***nur –!*** come on! advance!

heran|arbeiten, *v.r.* work one's way *or* creep up (***an*** *(Acc.)*, to). **-bilden,** *v.t.* bring up, train, educate. **-brechen,** *irr.v.i.* approach, *(of day)* dawn. **-bringen,** *irr.v.t.* bring *or* move *or* carry up, transport. **-drängen,** *v.r.* press forward, jostle (***an*** *(Acc.)*, against). **-führen,** *v.t.* bring *or* lead up (to the spot), bring to bear (***an*** *(Acc.)*, on). **-gehen,** *irr.v.i.* go *or* walk up (***an*** *(Acc.)*, to), approach; ***an die Arbeit –,*** set about the task, tackle the job. **-kommen,** *irr.v.i.* come on *or* near, draw near, approach, get near to, near, *(Naut.)* come alongside; *(Spt.)* close in, gain (***an*** *(Acc.)*, on), overtake; ***an etwas –,*** get hold of *or* come by s.th.; *(fig.)* come *or* measure up to a th., come near *or* approximate to a th., approach s.th.; ***Dinge an sich – lassen,*** bide one's time, wait and see. **-machen,** *v.r.* (***an*** *(Acc.)*) undertake, set about, set to work on *(a task)*, approach, sidle up to *(a p.)*, *(fig.)* make up to, get to work on *(a p.)*. **-nahen,** *v.i.* *(aux.* s.) draw near, approach; be forthcoming *or* imminent *(of events)*. **-pirschen,** *v.r.* stalk *or* creep up (***an*** *(Acc.)*, to). **-reichen,** *v.i.* *(aux.* s.) (***an*** *(Acc.)*) come close *or* up to, reach (up to), touch; *(fig.)* equal, *(coll.)* touch, hold a candle to. **-reifen,** *v.i.* *(aux.* s.) grow to maturity, grow up, mature, ripen; ***– zu,*** develop *or* grow into. **-rücken, 1.** *v.t.* move *or* push *or* draw near *or* up. **2.** *v.i.* draw near, approach, come on; advance, push onwards. **-schaffen,** *v.t.* supply, furnish; *see also* **-bringen. -schleichen,** *irr.v.r.* sneak up, creep forward. **-treten,** *irr.v.i.* ***an ihn –,*** approach him *(also fig.)*. **-wachsen,** *irr.v.i.* *(aux.* s.) grow up; ***– zu,*** grow into, grow up to be; ***das -de Geschlecht,*** the rising generation. **-wagen,** *v.r.* (***an*** *(Acc.)*)

dare to approach, venture near; (*fig.*) try one's hand *or* luck with, (*coll.*) have a go at. **-ziehen, 1.** *irr.v.t.* (*a th.*) draw *or* pull *or* drag near; (*fig.*) requisition, draw upon, procure, use, apply (*materials*); refer to, rely (up)on, quote, cite (*sources*); (*a p.*) (*fig.*) mobilize, recruit (**zu**, for), enlist (*a p.'s*) services, interest (*a p.*) in, attract (*backers etc.*), summon, call in, consult (*doctor etc.*), call (up)on (*to do*); rear, raise, bring up (*young*). **2.** *irr.v.i.* draw near, approach, (*Mil.*) advance.

Herauch ['heːraux], *m.* haze.

herauf [hɛ'rauf], *adv., sep. pref.* (*indicates movement upwards as seen by the person above*), up, up to(wards), upwards; ***den Berg* –**, up the hill, uphill; ***die Treppe* –**, up the stairs, upstairs; ***von unten* –**, from below.

herauf|beschwören, *irr.v.t.* conjure up, evoke, (*fig.*) give rise to, bring on, cause, occasion. **-kommen,** *irr.v.i.* (*aux.* s.) come up; ***in der Welt* –**, get on *or* rise in the world. **-setzen,** *v.t.* put up (*prices*). **-steigen,** *irr.v.i.* come *or* climb up, mount, ascend; rise, gather, be brewing (*as a storm*). **-ziehen, 1.** *irr.v.t.* draw *or* pull *or* lift up. **2.** *irr.v.i.* (*aux.* s.) draw near, approach; rise, gather, be brewing (*of a storm*).

heraus [hɛ'raus], *adv., sep. pref.* (*indicates movement from inside a place as seen by the person outside*) out, from within, forth, from among; ***–!*** turn out! – ***mit der Sprache! – damit!*** out with it! speak out! (*sl.*) spill the beans! ***aus einem Gefühl*** (. . .) **–**, from a *or* out of a feeling (of . . .); **– *aus den Federn!*** get up! get out of bed! (*coll.*) ***er ist fein*** (or ***schön***) **–**, he is a lucky fellow, he is well out of it; ***von innen* –**, from within; ***es ist noch nicht* –**, it's not at all certain, (*coll.*) it's anybody's guess; (*coll.*) ***er hat es* –**, he has found it out; he understands it, (*coll.*) he's tumbled to it; ***gerade*** or ***offen*** or ***rund*** or ***frei*** –, frankly, openly, point-blank, flatly, bluntly, fearlessly; ***da* –**, this way out; ***zum Fenster* –**, out through the window.

heraus|arbeiten, 1. *v.t.* work out, (*fig.*) work out, elaborate (*ideas etc.*). **2.** *v.r.* work one's way out, extricate o.s. **-beißen, 1.** *irr.v.r.* extricate o.s. **2.** *irr.v.t.* lay stress on; ***er beißt immer den Offizier heraus,*** he won't let anyone forget that he is an officer. **-bekommen,** *irr.v.t.* get out (**aus,** of); (*fig.*) find out, discover, elicit; worm *or* ferret out; work *or* puzzle *or* figure out, (*coll.*) get the hang of; make out, arrive at (*the sense*); get back in exchange; ***einen Nagel aus dem Holz* –**, get *or* pull a nail out of the wood; ***ich bekomme eine Mark heraus,*** I get a mark change. **-bringen,** *irr.v.t.* turn out, bring out, get out, put on the market; bring out, publish, issue (*a book*), produce, (put on the) stage (*a play*); *see also* **-bekommen**; (*fig.*) ***seine Kosten* –**, cover one's expenses. **-drücken,** *v.t.* press *or* squeeze out; (*fig.*) stick *or* throw out (*one's chest*). **-fahren,** *irr.v.i.* (*aux.* s.) drive *or* sail out; rush *or* fly *or* burst out; slip out (*as an unpremeditated remark*). **-finden, 1.** *irr.v.t.* find out, discover. **2.** *irr.v.r.* find one's way out, extricate o.s. **-fordern,** *v.t.* challenge; provoke, defy; demand categorically; ***das Unglück* –**, court disaster. **-fordernd,** *adj.* challenging, defiant; provocative, provoking. **Herausforderung,** *f.* challenge; provocation, (open) defiance. **herausfühlen,** *v.t.* feel, sense. **Herausgabe,** *f.* surrender, retsitution; delivery; (*of a book*) issue, publication. **herausgeben,** *irr.v.t.* give *or* deliver up, hand over; give back, restore, return; edit, publish; ***Geld* – *auf,*** give change for. **Herausgeber,** *m.* editor, publisher. **heraus|gehen,** *irr.v.i.* go out, come out, leave; lead *or* open out (***auf*** (*Acc.*), on to); (*fig.*) ***aus sich* –**, thaw out, come out of one's shell; ***aus sich nicht* –**, be reserved *or* taciturn. **-greifen,** *irr.v.t.* choose, select, pick *or* single out.

heraus|haben, *irr.v.t.* have solved *or* discovered, know, understand, have the knack *or* (*coll.*) hang of. **-hängen, 1.** *v.t.* hang out (*washing, flags etc.*). **2.** *irr.v.i.* hang out (*as tongue with thirst*); (*coll.*) ***das hängt mir zum Halse heraus,*** I am fed up with it, I have had my fill of it; (*vulg.*) I've had a bellyful. **-heben,** *irr.v.t.* lift *or* take out; haul out, raise; (*fig.*) render prominent, make (*s.th.*) stand out *or* conspicuous, stress, accentuate, lay stress on, throw into relief, set off. **-holen,** *v.t.* get *or* take *or* draw *or* drag *or* force out (**aus,** of), extract, extricate (from), (*fig.*) elicit (*secret*) (from), worm out (of); ***das Äußerste*** or ***Letzte aus sich* –**, do one's utmost, give all one has, force o.s. to the limit, make an all-out effort. **-kehren,** *v.t. See* **-beißen**; ***er kehrt den Offizier nicht heraus,*** he does not flaunt his rank. **-kommen,** *irr.v.i.* (*aux.* s.) come out *or* forth; issue, emerge, appear; be issued *or* published, become known, (*coll.*) come out; result, amount to; ***was wird dabei –?*** what will be the use of it? what will be the upshot? ***aus sich* –**, loosen up, thaw out; ***aus etwas* –**, extricate o.s. from, (*coll.*) get out of; ***das kommt dabei heraus wenn man lügt,*** that is the result of telling lies; ***es kommt auf eins* –**, it is all the same *or* it amounts to the same in the end, it is all one. **-locken,** *v.t.* entice *or* lure out, (*fig.*) elicit.

heraus|machen, 1. *v.t.* remove; get *or* take out (*stains etc.*). **2.** *v.r.* come *or* get on (well), prosper, improve, show (good) progress, develop, (*coll.*) blossom out. **-nehmen,** *irr.v.t.* take out (**aus,** of), remove (from); (*teeth*) pull out, extract, remove; ***sich*** (*Dat.*) **–**, presume, make (so) bold, venture; ***sich*** (*Dat.*) ***Freiheiten* –**, take liberties (**gegen,** with), make free (with). **-platzen,** *v.i.* blurt out. **-pressen,** *v.t.* squeeze *or* wring *or* force out; express, extrude. **-putzen,** *v.t.* (*v.r.*) dress (o.s.) up, (*coll.*) spruce *or* (*sl.*) doll (o.s.) up. **-ragen,** *v.i.* protrude, project, jut *or* stand out (**aus,** from). **-reden, 1.** *v.i.* speak freely. **2.** *v.r.* make excuses. **-reißen,** *irr.v.t.* pull *or* tear *or* rip *or* wrench out; extract, free, deliver, extricate (**aus,** from). **-rücken, 1.** *v.t.* (*coll.*) fork out, (*sl.*) cough up (*money*). **2.** *v.i.* (*aux.* s.) *see* **1**; ***mit der Sprache* –**, speak out (freely), come out with, own up; ***nicht mit der Sprache* – *wollen,*** hedge, beat about the bush. **-rufen,** *irr.v.t.* (*Theat.*) call before the curtain; (*Mil.*) turn out (*the guard*).

heraus|sagen, *v.t.* speak one's mind; ***rund herausgesagt,*** to put it bluntly, in plain words. **-schälen,** *v.t.* (*fig.*) sift (**aus,** from), lay bare (*truth, facts etc.*). **-scheren,** *reg.v.i.* (*Av.*) peel off (*from a formation in flight*). **-schlagen, 1.** *irr.v.t.* knock out (**aus,** of); ***Funken aus dem Stein* –**, strike sparks from the stone; (*fig.*) ***Geld* –**, make money, make a profit (**aus,** from *or* by); ***die Kosten* –**, recover expenses; ***möglichst viel* – *aus,*** make the most of. **2.** *irr.v.i.* burst forth; ***die Flammen schlugen zum Dach heraus,*** the flames shot up through the roof. **-stecken,** *v.t.* put *or* hang out (*flags etc*); put *or* stick (*tongue*) out (*Dat.*, at). **-stellen, 1.** *v.t.* put out, expose, lay out, (*fig.*) lay down, expound, set forth (*ideas*), emphasize, give prominence to, throw into relief; publicize, feature, highlight, (*coll.*) play up (in a big way). **2.** *v.r.* turn out, prove (**als,** to be), appear, become apparent, come to light. **-strecken,** *v.t.* (*hand*) hold *or* reach out, (*tongue*) *see* **-stecken. -streichen,** *irr.v.t.* (*fig.*) eulogize, extol, praise. **-suchen,** *v.t.* choose, select, pick out. **-treten,** *irr.v.t.* step out (**aus,** of), emerge (from); protrude. **-wachsen,** *irr.v.i.* (*aux.* s.) grow out (**aus,** of), develop, sprout (from); (*coll.*) ***das wächst mir zum Halse heraus,*** *see* **-hängen**; ***aus den Kleidern* –**, outgrow one's clothes. **-winden,** *irr.v.r.* extricate o.s. (**aus,** from), (*coll.*) wriggle out (of). **-ziehen,** *irr.v.t.* extract, remove; (*Mil.*) disengage, withdraw, (*coll.*) pull out (*troops*).

herb [hɛrp], *adj.* acid, sour, sharp, tart, acrid; astringent; (*fig.*) dry (*of wine*); (*fig.*) harsh, austere, unpleasant, bitter, caustic; ***-e Not,*** dire necessity; ***-er Tod,*** grim death. **Herbe,** *f. See* **Herbheit.**

herbei [hɛr'baɪ], *adv., sep. pref.* (*indicates movement from a remoter to a nearer place with reference to the speaker or the point contemplated by him*) hither, here, near, on, this way, into the vicinity of; **–, *ihr Leute!*** gather round, folks!

herbei|bringen, *irr.v.t. See* **-schaffen. -eilen,** *v.i.* come running up, rush to the scene. **-führen,** *v.t.* bring about *or* on, induce, cause, produce, provide for; entail, lead to, give rise to. **-holen,** *v.t.* go for, fetch; call in (*a doctor*); **–** ***lassen,*** send for. **-lassen,** *irr.v.r.* condescend, deign (*zu*, to do). **-rufen,** *irr. v.t.* call in, send for, summon. **-schaffen,** *v.t.* bring *or* get here; transport, move *or* carry to the spot, collect, raise (*money*); procure, produce, supply, furnish, provide. **-strömen,** *v.i.* come in crowds, crowd *or* gather *or* flock round. **-ziehen,** *irr.v.t.* draw *or* pull near *or* towards; ***er zieht seine Beispiele an den Haaren herbei,*** his examples are far-fetched *or* fantastic *or* dragged in by the hair.

herbemühen ['he:rbəmy:ən], **1.** *v.t.* trouble (*a p.*) to come. **2.** *v.r.* take the trouble to come.

Herberge ['hɛrbɛrgə], *f.* shelter, lodging, quarters; inn, hostel. **herbergen,** *v.i.* (take) shelter, lodge (***bei***, with). **Herbergs|mutter,** *f.*, **-vater,** *m.* hostel warden.

herbestellen ['he:rbəʃtɛlən], *v.t.* order to come; send for, summon, make an appointment with (*a p.*).

Herbheit ['hɛrphaɪt], *f.* acidity, sourness, acerbity, astringency, (*of wine*) dryness; sharpness, bitterness; austerity.

herbringen ['he:rbrɪŋən], *irr.v.t.* bring hither *or* along *or* up. *See* **hergebracht.**

Herbst [hɛrpst], *m.* (**-es,** *pl.* **-e**) autumn; (*Am.*) fall; harvest time; (*dial.*) vine harvest. **Herbstblume,** *f.* autumn flower. **herbsten, 1.** *v.t.* (*dial.*) gather the vine harvest. **2.** *v.i. imp.* ***es herbstet,*** there are signs of autumn, the nights are drawing in. **Herbst|färbung,** *f.* autumnal tints. **-ferien,** *pl.* autumn holidays. **herbstlich,** *adj.* autumnal. **Herbstlichkeit,** *f.* autumn weather; autumnal look. **Herbstling,** *m.* (**-s,** *pl.* **-e**) autumn fruit; animal born in autumn. **Herbst|leute,** *pl.* (*dial.*) harvesters; vintagers. **-monat, -mond,** *m.* (*obs.*) September. **-rose,** *f.* (*Bot.*) hollyhock (*Althaea rosea*). **-tag,** *m.* autumn day. **--Tagundnachtgleiche,** *f.* autumn equinox. **-zeitlose,** *f.* (*Bot.*) meadow saffron, autumn crocus (*Colchicum autumnale*).

Herd [he:rt], *m.* (**-(e)s,** *pl.* **-e**) **1.** hearth, fireplace, fireside; kitchen-range, cooking stove; (*Prov.*) ***eigner – ist Goldes wert,*** there's no place like home; ***Heim und –,*** hearth and home; ***seinen eigenen – gründen,*** set up house, settle down; 2. (*fig.*) seat, focus (*of rebellion, disease etc.*); centre, source; 3. (*Naut.*) saddle (*of a block*).

Herde ['he:rdə], *f.* drove, flock, herd; (*fig.*) crowd, multitude; ***der – folgen,*** follow the crowd, be guided by herd instinct. **Herden|geist,** *m.* herd-mentality. **-mensch,** *m.* one of the common herd. **-tier,** *n.* gregarious animal. **-trieb,** *m.* herd instinct. **herdenweise,** *adv.* in flocks *or* herds.

Herd|frischen, *n.* (*Metall.*) refining (process). **-kohle,** *f.* household *or* domestic coal. **-platte,** *f.* hearth-plate, (*of stove*) hotplate. **-rost,** *m.* fire-grate.

herein [hɛ'raɪn], *adv., sep. pref.* (*indicates movement into a place as seen by the person inside*) in, in here; inward; ***–!*** come in! ***hier –,*** this way, in here; ***von (dr)außen –,*** from outside.

herein|bitten, *irr.v.t.* invite (*a p.*) to come in. **-brechen,** *irr.v.i.* (*aux.* s.) (*of night*) close in (***über*** (*Acc.*), upon), fall, (*of storm*) set in, come up, (*of misfortune etc.*) befall, overtake. **-bringen,** *irr.v.t.* bring in(doors); get *or* gather in (*crops*). **-fallen,** *irr.v.i.* (*aux* s.) 1. fall (***in*** (*Acc.*), into); 2. be cheated *or* swindled, (*coll.*) be taken in (***auf*** (*Acc.*), by), fall (for). **-führen,** *v.t.* show *or* usher in. **-lassen,** *irr.v.t.* admit, let in. **-legen,** *v.t.* (*coll.*) deceive, cheat, swindle, dupe, hoax, (*coll.*) take in, (*sl.*) take for a ride. **-nehmen,** *irr.v.t.* take in; (*Comm.*) book, accept. **-platzen,** *v.i.* (***in*** (*Acc.*)) burst in(to). **-schneien,** *v.i.* (*coll.*) arrive unexpectedly, blow *or* drop in. **-treten,** *irr.v.i.* step in, enter.

herfahren ['he:rfa:rən], **1.** *irr.v.i.* (*aux.* s.) come *or* travel *or* drive here; ***über ihn –,*** *see* **herfallen. 2.** *irr.v.t.* bring *or* drive here. **Herfahrt,** *f.* journey back (home), return journey. **her|fallen,** *irr.v.i.* (*aux.* s.) ***über ihn –,*** fall *or* set *or* pounce upon him, attack *or* assault *or* assail him. **-finden,** *irr.v.r.* find one's way here. **-führen,** *v.t.* bring *or* conduct here.

herfür [hɛr'fy:r], *adv.* (*Poet.*) *see* **hervor.**

Hergang ['he:rgaŋ], *m.* course of events, circumstances, proceedings; details of what happened, the whole story.

hergeben ['he:rge:bən], *irr.v.t.* give up, deliver, surrender, hand over; give away; give back, return; ***geben Sie mir gefälligst das Brot her,*** I'll thank you to pass me the bread; ***ich will mich nicht dazu –,*** I will not lend myself *or* be a party to that, I will have nothing to do with it; ***Waren – für,*** sell goods at.

hergebracht ['he:rgəbraxt], *adj.* usual, customary, conventional, traditional, established, ancient, handed down to us.

hergehen ['he:rge:ən], *irr.v.i.* (*aux.* s.) (*usu. as v. imp.*) come to pass, happen; go on, be going on, be carried on; ***vor etwas –,*** go before s.th. *or* at the head of s.th.; ***vor ihm –,*** go ahead of him; ***über etwas –,*** set to *or* set about s.th.; ***über ihn –,*** be down on him, treat him rough; ***da geht es heiß her,*** things are getting lively; ***da geht es hoch her,*** there are fine goings-on here; ***es geht lustig her,*** (we, they *etc.*) are having a high old time; ***so geht es (in der Welt) her,*** that's the way of the world, such is life; (*coll.*) ***geh' her!*** come off it!

her|gehören, *v.i.* be pertinent, be in place, be to the point *or* purpose; ***diese Bemerkungen gehören nicht her,*** these remarks are out of place (here). **-gehörig,** *adj.* apposite, pertinent, to the point.

hergelaufen ['he:rgəlaufən], *adj.* vagabond, vagrant, good-for-nothing.

her|halten, 1. *irr.v.t.* hold out, tender. **2.** *irr.v.i.* pay, suffer (for it *etc.*), bear the brunt (of it *etc.*), (*sl.*) stand the racket. **-holen,** *v.t.* fetch *or* bring here; ***– lassen,*** send for; ***weit hergeholt,*** far-fetched.

Hering ['he:rɪŋ], *m.* (**-s,** *pl.* **-e**) 1. herring; ***geräucherter –,*** smoked herring, bloater; ***gesalzener –,*** pickled herring; ***gedörrter –,*** kipper(ed herring); ***zusammengedrängt wie die –e,*** packed like sardines; 2. tent-peg; 3. (*coll.*) weedy fellow, little shrimp. **Herings|fang,** *m.* herring-fishery. **-fänger,** *m.* herring-smack. **-milch,** *f.* soft roe. **-möwe,** *f.* (*Orn.*) lesser black-backed gull (*Larus fuscus*). **-rogen,** *m.* hard roe.

herkommen ['he:rkɔmən], *irr.v.i.* (*aux.* s.) come hither *or* here, come *or* draw near, approach; ***– von,*** be due to, be caused by, be the consequence of, originate in, come *or* arise from, be derived from; ***wo kommt dieses Wort her?*** what is the origin *or* derivation of this word? ***wo kommen Sie her?*** where do you come *or* hail from? ***wo soll die Zeit –?*** how shall we find the time? **Herkommen,** *n.* origin, extraction, descent; tradition, custom, convention, usage. **herkömmlich** [–'kœmlɪç], *adj.* traditional, usual, customary, orthodox, conventional.

Herkunft ['he:rkunft], *f.* (*of a p.*) origin, descent, extraction, (*of a th.*) origin, provenance, (*of a word*) derivation.

herlaufen ['he:rlaufən], *irr.v.i.* (*aux.* s.) run here; ***hinter ihm –,*** run after him. *See* **hergelaufen.**

herleiern ['he:rlaɪərn], *v.t.* recite in a sing-song manner, reel *or* rattle off.

herleiten ['he:rlaɪtən], **1.** *v.t.* lead, conduct hither; (*fig.*) deduce, infer, derive (***von***, from). **2.** *v.r.* be derived (***von***, from), originate (in), be traceable *or* go back (to), descend *or* date (from). **Herleitung,** *f.* derivation; deduction, inference.

Herling ['hɛrlɪŋ], *m.* (**-s,** *pl.* **-e**) unripe grape; wild grape; (*B.*) sour grape.

her|locken, *v.t.* entice, lure, decoy. **-machen,** *v.r.* (***über etwas***) set about; work at, (*coll.*) tackle; (***über ihn***) fall upon, set about (him). *See also* **-fallen.**

Hermaphrodit [hɛrmafro'di:t], *m.* (**-en,** *pl.* **-en**) hermaphrodite.

Herme ['hɛrmə], *f.* (*Archit.*) herma.

Hermelin [hɛrmə'li:n], **1.** *n.* (**-s,** *pl.* **-e**) (*Zool.*) 1.

stoat, ermine (*Putorius ermineus*); 2. cream-coloured horse. **2.** *m.* (**-s,** *pl.* **-e**) ermine (*fur*).

hermetisch [hɛr'me:tɪʃ], *adj.* air-tight, hermetic; – *verschlossen,* hermetically sealed.

hernach [hɛr'na:x], *adv.* afterwards, hereafter; thereafter, later (on), subsequently, after this *or* that; *–?* what next? *den Tag –,* the day after.

hernehmen ['he:rne:mən], *irr.v.t.* take, get, draw (*von,* from); deduce, derive; (*coll.*) *ihn –,* take him to task, haul him over the coals.

hernieder [hɛr'ni:dər], *adv., sep. pref.* down.

Heroen [he'ro:ən], *pl. See* **Heros. Heroen|alter,** *n.* heroic age. **–kult(us),** *m.* hero-worship.

Heroin [hero'i:n], *n.* heroin (*drug*).

Heroine [hero'i:nə], *f.* (*Theat.*) heroine. **heroisch** [–'ro:ɪʃ], *adj.* heroic. **Heroismus,** *m.* heroism.

Herold ['he:rɔlt], *m.* (**-(e)s,** *pl.* **-e**) herald; harbinger. **Herolds|figuren,** *f.pl.* heraldic figures. **–kunst,** *f.* heraldry, heraldic art. **–mantel, –rock,** *m.* tabard. **–wissenschaft,** *f. See* **–kunst.**

Heros ['he:rɔs], *m.* (-, *pl.* **-roen** [–'ro:ən]) hero, demigod.

herplappern ['he:rplapərn], *v.t.* (*coll.*) reel *or* rattle off.

Herr [hɛr], *m.* (**-n,** *pl.* **-en**) master, (*coll.*) boss; lord, (*Eccl.*) Lord; ruler, sovereign; gentleman; sir (*in address*); Mr. (*before proper names*); (*coll.*) *sein alter –,* his father *or* governor; *die alten –en* (*einer Verbindung*), 'old boys', former students, alumni; *ich habe* (*es*) *–n Doktor B. versprochen,* I have promised (that to) Doctor B.; *sein eigner – sein,* stand on one's own feet; (*Prov.*) *gestrenge –en regieren nicht lange,* tyranny is shortlived; *die drei gestrengen –en, see* **gestreng**; *der – Gott,* God, our Lord, Lord God; *den großen –n spielen,* lord it, play the fine gentleman; *das Haus des –n,* the House of God; *Hochgeehrter –,* Sir, Dear Sir; *der junge –,* the young master, son of the house; (*Prov.*) *wie der –, so der Knecht,* like master, like man; *– der Lage sein,* be master of the situation; *in aller –en Ländern,* all the world over; *meine –en,* Gentlemen; (*iron.*) *die –en der Schöpfung,* the lords of creation; *– zur See sein,* rule the waves; *einer S.* or *von einer S.* or *über eine S. – sein,* be master of a th., have a th. at one's disposal *or* under one's control *or* in one's power; *– über Leben und Tod sein,* have power over life and death; *selig im –n sterben,* die blessed in the eyes of God; *der Tag des –n,* the Lord's day; *Ihr – Vater,* your father; *– Vorsitzender,* Mr. Chairman, (*Parl.*) Mr. Speaker; *einer S. – werden,* overcome *or* subdue *or* master s.th., get *or* bring s.th. under control.

Herrchen ['hɛrçən], *n.* young master, son of the house; fop, dandy.

her|rechnen, *v.t.* count *or* reckon up, enumerate. **–reichen,** *v.t.* pass, hand (over) (*Dat.,* to). **Herreise,** *f.* journey here; journey home, return journey.

Herren|abend, *m.* male gathering, smoking concert, (*coll.*) stag-party. **–anzug,** *m.* (gentle)man's suit. **–artikel,** *m.pl.* gentleman's outfitting *or* wear. **–ausstatter,** *m.* gentleman's outfitter. **–bank,** *f.* peers' bench. **–bekleidung,** *f.* men's wear. **–besuch,** *m.* gentleman caller. **–brot,** *n.* – *essen,* be in service, be dependent. **–diener,** *m.* gentleman's servant. **–dienst,** *m.* lord's service; forced service; service (*in a family*). **–doppel(spiel),** *n.* (*Tenn.*) men's doubles. **–einzel(spiel),** *n.* (*Tenn.*) men's singles. **–fahrer,** *m.* owner-driver (*of a motor-car*), amateur driver (*car-racing*). **–gülte,** *f.* (*Hist.*) tax paid to the lord of the manor. **–haus,** *n.,* **–hof,** *m.* manor(-house); mansion; country house; castle. **–konfektion,** *f.* men's ready-to-wear clothing. **–leben,** *n.* aristocratic *or* high life; *ein – führen,* live like a lord, live in grand style.

herrenlos ['hɛrənlo:s], *adj.* out of service *or* employment (*of servants*), without a master; ownerless, unowned; *–e Tiere,* stray animals; *–es Fahrzeug,* driverless vehicle; *–e Güter,* lost property, unclaimed goods.

Herren|mensch, *m.* masterful man. **–mode,** *f.* men's fashions. **–moral,** *f.* code of morality for men (but not women) *or* for masters (but not servants). **–pfarre,** *f.* benefice in private patronage. **–recht,** *n.* seigneurial right. **–reiten,** *n.* (*Equest.*) owners up, gentlemen's race. **–reiter,** *m.* (*Equest.*) gentleman rider. **–schneider,** *m.* men's tailor. **–schnitt,** *m.* Eton crop. **–sitz,** *m.* 1. *See* **–haus**; 2. *im – reiten,* ride astride (*opp. side-saddle*). **–stand,** *m.* rank of a lord; gentry. **–toilette,** *f.* men's lavatory. **–volk,** *n.* (*Nat. Soc.*) master race. **–zimmer,** *n.* study; smoking room.

Herrgott ['hɛrgɔt], *m.* Lord (our) God; (*coll.*) (*ach*) *–!* Lord! Good God! good heavens! good gracious! *den – einen guten Mann sein lassen,* let matters take their course; (*Prov.*) *er lebt wie der – in Frankreich,* he lives like a fighting cock. **Herrgotts|frühe,** *f.* (*coll.*) *in aller –,* at the crack of dawn, at an unearthly hour. **–käferchen,** *n.* lady-bird. **–schnitzer,** *m.* carver of crucifixes.

herrichten ['he:rrɪçtən], *v.t.* arrange, prepare, get ready; put in order, fit *or* (*coll.*) fix up.

Herrin ['hɛrɪn], *f.* lady, mistress.

herrisch ['hɛrɪʃ], *adj.* domineering, overbearing, masterful; arrogant, haughty, imperious; dictatorial, peremptory, commanding.

herrje! [hɛr'je:], *int.* (*coll.*) goodness gracious!

herrlich ['hɛrlɪç], *adj.* magnificent, splendid, glorious, marvellous, wonderful, excellent, capital, grand, exquisite, delicious, delightful, lovely, charming, (*coll.*) fine. **Herrlichkeit,** *f.* splendour, magnificence, grandeur, glory, excellence; *– Gottes,* majesty *or* glory of God.

Herrnhuter ['hɛrnhu:tər], *m.* Moravian; *pl.* the Moravian brethren.

Herrschaft ['hɛrʃaft], *f.* 1. dominion, power, sway, rule, sovereign authority (*über* (*Acc.*), over), (*fig.*) command, mastery, control (*über* (*Acc.*), of *or* over); supremacy, domination; *sich der – bemächtigen,* secure power *or* control; (*etwas*) *unter seine – bringen,* bring (a th.) under one's rule *or* dominion, subdue (a th.); *die – über sich verlieren,* lose one's self-control; 2. manor, estate, domain; 3. master and mistress, employers (*of servants*); p. *or* persons of rank; *ist die – zu Hause?* are your master and mistress (is your master *or* mistress) at home? *hohe –en,* people of high rank, illustrious persons; *die jungen –en,* the children of the master *or* lord; *meine –en!* ladies and gentlemen! **herrschaftlich,** *adj.* belonging to *or* referring to a lord *or* master, seigneurial, manorial; fit for a lord, lordly, high-class; *–e Gefälle,* seigneurial revenues; *–er Befehl,* lord's command; *–e Wohnung,* 'desirable' residence, fashionable *or* high-class dwelling-house. **Herrschaftsrecht,** *n.* sovereign authority *or* jurisdiction.

herrschen ['hɛrʃən], *v.i.* rule, reign, hold sway (*über* (*Acc.*), over), govern, control, dominate, be master (of); prevail, be prevalent, predominate; be rife *or* raging; be in vogue; exist; *es herrscht Schweigen,* silence reigns. **herrschend,** *adj.* ruling; predominant, dominant, prevailing.

Herrscher ['hɛrʃər], *m.* ruler, sovereign, lord, monarch, prince, governor; *willkürlicher –,* despot; *unumschränkter –,* autocrat. **Herrscher|blick,** *m.* commanding air, authoritative bearing. **–familie,** *f.* reigning family, dynasty. **–geschlecht,** *n. See* **–familie. –gewalt,** *f.* sovereign power. **–haus,** *n. See* **–familie. –miene,** *f. See* **–blick. –stab,** *m.* sceptre. **–wille,** *m.* sovereign will. **–willkür,** *f.* despotism, arbitrary rule.

Herrsch|gier, –sucht, *f.* love of power, lust for power, domineering nature. **herrschsüchtig,** *adj.* fond of power, tyrannical, domineering.

her|rücken, *v.i.* (*aux.* s.), *v.t.* move *or* draw near. **–rühren,** *v.i.* originate (*von,* in), derive, stem, spring, proceed, flow (from), be due (to). **–sagen,** *v.t.* recite, repeat; tell (*one's beads*); *das Tischgebet –,* say grace. **–schaffen,** *v.t.* bring hither; move near; produce, procure. **–stammen,** *v.i.* (*aux.* s.) descend, come, be derived (*von,* from); (*fig.*) *see* **–rühren.**

herstellen ['he:rʃtɛlən], *v.t.* 1. place here; 2. set up, establish, prepare, bring about; create, make, manufacture, build, produce; ***das läßt sich leicht –,*** that can be easily effected *or* produced; 3. (***wieder***) –, re-establish, repair, restore; ***er ist wieder ganz hergestellt,*** he is quite restored to health again. **Hersteller,** *m.* producer, manufacturer. **Herstellung,** *f.* 1. production, manufacture, preparation; establishment, creation; 2. recovery, repair, restoration. **Herstellungs|arbeit,** *f.* restoration work. **–fehler,** *m.* production fault, fault in manufacture. **–gang,** *m.* course *or* process of manufacture. **–kosten,** *f.pl.* cost of production, prime cost. **–mittel,** *n.* restorative. **–preis,** *m.* cost-price.

Herstrich ['he:rʃtrɪç], *m.* 1. (*Mus.*) down-bow; 2. (*Orn.*) return of migratory birds.

her|stürzen, *v.i.* (*aux.* s.) rush, fall (***über*** (*Acc.*), upon); *see* **–fallen. –treiben,** *irr.v.t.* (*coll.*) ***was treibt dich her?*** what brings you here? ***vor sich –,*** drive before one; (*Footb.*) dribble.

Hertz [hɛrts], *n.* (*Phys.*) cycles per second.

herüber [hɛ'ry:bər], *adv., sep. pref.* (*indicating movement across s.th. as seen by the p. approached*) over (here), to this side, across.

herum [hɛ'rum], *adv., sep. pref.* (*indicates* (a) *movement around as seen from the centre,* (b) *vague movement round about with no reference to a centre* (*see* **umher**), (c) *approximate time or amount*); round, round about, around, about; (*coll.*) finished, over; ***um das Haus –,*** round about *or* all round the house; ***hier –,*** hereabouts; ***hier –!*** this way round! ***in der ganzen Stadt –,*** all over the town; ***um zehn DM –,*** round (about) *or* about *or* roughly ten marks; ***rings*** or ***rund –,*** all around, round about; ***um die Zeit –,*** about that time.

herum|betteln, *v.i.* go around begging. **–bringen,** *irr.v.t.* bring *or* get round; win over (*a p.*), talk (*a p.*) round; ***die Zeit –,*** kill time. **–bummeln,** *v.i.* loaf *or* loiter about. **–dirigieren,** *v.t.* (*coll.*) boss around. **–doktern,** *v.i.* (*coll.*) – ***an*** (*Dat.*), try one's hand at. **–drehen, 1.** *v.t.* turn round; misconstrue. **2.** *v.r.* turn over (*in bed*). **–drücken,** *v.r.* (*coll.*) hang around, loiter; (***um***) shirk, dodge, run away from. **–fahren,** *irr.v.i.* (*aux.* s.) drive *or* sail around; dart *or* fly *or* rush about; ***mit den Händen –,*** gesticulate, wave one's arms about. **–fingern,** *v.i.* – ***an*** (*Dat.*), fumble with, finger. **–fragen,** *v.i.* make inquiries, ask everyone. **–führen,** *v.t.* lead *or* show around; – ***in*** (*Dat.*), show over; ***an*** or ***bei der Nase –,*** lead by the nose. **–geben,** *irr.v.t.* hand *or* pass round. **–gehen,** *irr.v.i.* (*aux.* s.) be current (*of reports*); be prevalent; ***– lassen,*** send *or* pass round; ***– um,*** go *or* walk round; (*Mil.*) make the round; (*fig.*) go *or* run round, surround; ***die Mauer ging einst um die ganze Stadt herum,*** the wall once enclosed the whole town; – ***in*** (*Dat.*), wander *or* walk about *or* around; ***es geht mir im Kopf herum,*** it is on *or* it haunts my mind, it goes round and round in my head; ***ich lasse mir die S. im Kopfe –,*** I am carefully considering the matter. **–horchen,** *v.i.* go about with one's ears open.

herum|kommen, *irr.v.i.* (*aux.* s.) come round (*a corner etc.*); do a lot of travelling, travel about; (*of rumour*) spread, get about, become known; (*fig.*) ***– um,*** avoid, evade; ***wir kommen um die Tatsache nicht herum,*** we cannot get away from the fact. **–kriegen,** *v.t.* (*coll.*) win round, talk over. **–laufen,** *irr.v.i.* (*aux.* s.) run about, rove, roam; ***– um,*** run around. **–liegen,** *irr.v.i.* lie around *or* about; ***– um,*** lie round, surround (*as a wall*). **–lungern,** *v.i.* loaf *or* lounge about, loiter. **–pfuschen,** *v.i.* (*coll.*) – ***an*** (*Acc.*), mess about with. **–reden,** *v.i.* ***– um,*** beat about the bush, hedge. **–reichen,** *v.t.* hand *or* pass round. **–reiten,** *v.i.* (*aux.* s.) (***auf*** (*Dat.*)) harp upon (*a th.*), ride a hobby-horse. **–schlagen,** *irr.v.r.* struggle, scuffle (***mit,*** with) (*a p.*), grapple, cope (with) (*a th.*). **–schnüffeln,** *v.i.* (*coll.*) snoop around. **–schweifen,** *v.i.* (*aux.* s.) roam *or* wander about. **–sprechen, 1.** *irr.v.t.* spread (*news*). **2.** *irr.v.r.* get around (*as news*). **–streichen,** *irr.v.i.* (*aux.* s.), **–streifen,** *v.i.*, roam (about), prowl. **–tanzen,** *v.i.* dance attendance (***um,*** on); (*coll.*) ***ihm auf der Nase –,*** plague *or* pester *or* tease *or* rag him. **–tasten,** *v.i.* grope (about) (***nach,*** for). **–tollen,** *v.i.* romp, frolic. **–tragen,** *irr.v.t.* carry around; ***seinen Kummer mit sich –,*** nurse one's grief. **–treiben,** *irr.v.r.* loiter, prowl around, knock *or* gad about, (*sl.*) stooge around. **–werfen, 1.** *irr.v.t.* throw *or* toss around; throw (*a switch*); *see* **–reißen. 2.** *irr. v.r.* turn sharply, slew round; toss and turn, toss about (*in bed*). **–wirtschaften,** *v.i.* (*coll.*) rummage *or* potter around. **–ziehen, 1.** *irr.v.t.* draw *or* pull round. **2.** *irr.v.i.* (*aux.* s.) roam *or* wander about; have no fixed abode. **–ziehend,** *adj.* itinerant, peripatetic, strolling; nomadic.

herunter [hɛ'runtər], *adv., sep. pref.* (*meaning similar to* **herab** *and* **hernieder,** *with fig. uses implying deterioration*) down, downward; off; ***– mit ihm!*** down with him! ***den Hut –!*** off with your hat! hats off!

herunter|bringen, *irr.v.t.* get down; bring down, lower, reduce. **–drücken,** *v.t.* lower, depress; force down (*prices*). **–fallen,** *irr.v.i.* (*aux.* s.) fall down; ***– von,*** fall *or* drop off. **–gehen,** *irr.v.i.* (*aux.* s.) go down, fall, drop; (*Av.*) come down, descend; (*Comm.*) (*prices*) fall, drop, ease off. **–handeln,** *v.t.* beat down (*in price*). **–hauen,** *irr.v.t.* (*coll.*) ***ihm eins –,*** slap his face; (*coll.*) ***eine Arbeit –,*** knock off a job in a hurry. **–holen,** *v.t.* fetch down; (*Hunt.*) bring down; (*Av.*) shoot down. **–klappen,** *v.t.* turn *or* fold down. **–kommen,** *irr.v.i.* (*aux.* s.) come down(stairs); (*fig.*) deteriorate, decline, decay, (*coll.*) fall off, run to seed, go to rack and ruin; (*health*) be run down, (*morally*) become depraved, sink low, (*economically*) come down in the world; (*fig.*) ***heruntergekommen,*** (*a p.*) shabby, down-at-heel, out-at-elbows, in reduced circumstances; demoralized, depraved; (*a th.*) run-down, on its last legs. **–langen,** *v.t. See* **–hauen. –lassen,** *irr.v.t.* lower, let down, drop. **–leiern,** *v.t.* reel *or* rattle off. **–machen, –putzen** (*coll.*), *v.t.* scold, upbraid, (*coll.*) give (*s.o.*) a dressing down, pull (*s.o.*) to pieces. **–reißen,** *irr.v.t.* pull *or* tear down; (*fig.*) pull to pieces, disparage. **–rutschen,** *v.i., v.t.* slide *or* slip down; (*coll.*) ***du kannst mir den Buckel –,*** I snap my finger at you; (*vulg.*) go and fry your face. **–schalten,** *v.i.* (*Motor.*) change down (***auf*** (*Acc.*), to). **–schlagen,** *irr.v.t.* knock *or* beat down; turn *or* fold down. **–schlucken,** *v.t.* swallow, gulp; stomach (*insults etc.*); smother, suppress (*what one would like to say*). **–sehen,** *irr.v.i.* look down (***auf*** (*Acc.*), at *or* (*fig.*) upon). **–sein,** *irr.v.i.* be run down (*in health*), be low (*in spirits*), be low-spirited, depressed *or* despondent; be in a bad way. **–setzen,** *v.t. See* **herabsetzen. –transformieren,** *v.t.* (*Elec.*) step down. **–werfen,** *irr.v.t.* throw down *or* off; throw (*a rider*). **–wirtschaften,** *v.t.* mismanage, ruin by bad management, bring to ruin, (*coll.*) run down. **–ziehen, 1.** *irr.v.t.* pull down. **2.** *irr.v.i.* (*aux.* s.) march down, descend.

hervor [hɛr'fo:r], *adv., sep. pref.* (*expressing movement forward as seen from out in front*) forth; out; ***aus . . . –,*** (from) out of; ***unter . . . –,*** from under.

hervor|blicken, *v.i.* peer *or* peep from behind; appear (out of), peep *or* show through. **–brechen,** *irr.v.i.* (*aux.* s.) burst forth, break out *or* through; rush out, (*Mil.*) sally forth, debouch. **–bringen,** *irr.v.t.* bring forth, produce, yield; draw forth, elicit; procreate, beget, bear, give birth to (*young*); create, generate, give rise to, cause, effect (*results*), utter (*words*). **Hervorbringung,** *f.* creation, generation, production, bringing *or* drawing forth. **hervor|dringen,** *irr.v.i.* proceed *or* issue (***von,*** from); *see also* **–brechen. –gehen,** *irr.v.i.* go *or* come forth; ***– aus,*** come, spring, arise *or* emerge from; proceed *or* result *or* follow from; ***als Sieger –,*** come off *or* out *or* emerge victorious; ***daraus geht hervor,*** hence it follows, this shows *or* proves, this goes to show *or* prove. **–heben, 1.** *irr.v.t.* give prominence to, bring into prominence, accentuate, lay stress on, stress, emphasize, throw into relief, display, set off, call special attention to. **2.** *irr.v.r.* stand out, be *or* become prominent *or* conspicuous. **–holen,** *v.t.* fetch *or* take out, produce.

hervor|kommen, *irr.v.i.* (*aux.* s.) come out *or* forth, emerge, appear (*aus,* from). **–leuchten,** *v.i.* shine forth; become clear *or* evident, be manifest. **–locken,** *v.t.* draw *or* lure *or* entice out; *Tränen –,* bring tears to one's eyes. **–quellen,** *irr.v.i.* well up, gush forth *or* out; bulge (out). **–ragen,** *v.i.* project, stand *or* stick out, jut forth *or* out (*aus,* from), be prominent; rise *or* tower above, overtop, tower up; exceed, surpass. **–ragend,** *adj.* prominent, protruding, salient, projecting; outstanding, distinguished, eminent, excellent, splendid, first-rate, superlative. **Hervorruf,** *m.* (*Theat.*) curtain call, recall. **hervor|rufen,** *irr.v.t.* evoke, call forth; cause, bring about, occasion, give rise to; (*Theat.*) recall, call before the curtain, encore. **–springen,** *irr.v.i.* leap out (*aus,* from); *see* **–stechen. –stechen,** *irr.v.i.* (*fig.*) stand *or* stick out (*aus,* from), be prominent *or* conspicuous, predominate. **–stechend,** *adj.* salient, prominent; conspicuous, striking, predominant, outstanding. **–stehen,** *irr. v.i.* (*aux.* s.) stand *or* stick *or* jut out, project, protrude, bulge; *–de Backenknochen,* high cheekbones. **–treten,** *irr.v.i.* (*aux.* s.) step forth *or* forward, come forward; protrude, bulge; stand out, be prominent; come to the fore, be much in evidence; (*of a p.*) make a name for o.s., distinguish o.s.; *– aus,* step out *or* emerge from; *– lassen,* throw into bold relief. **–tun,** *irr.v.r.* distinguish o.s., excel; come into prominence. **–zaubern,** *v.t.* conjure up.

herwagen ['he:rva:gən], *v.r.* venture near, venture to come here.

Herweg ['he:rve:k], *m.* way here, way back (*as seen from the starting place*).

Herz [hɛrts], *n.* (**-ens,** *pl.* **-en**) heart; breast, bosom; feeling, sympathy; mind, spirit, soul; courage; centre, vital part, marrow, (*Bot.*) pith; core, kernel; (*Cards*) hearts; darling; ***aus dem –en,*** sincerely, earnestly; ***sein – ausschütten,*** open one's heart, unbosom o.s.; ***es brennt mir auf dem –en,*** it wrings my heart; ***etwas übers – bringen,*** bring o.s. to do s.th., reconcile o.s. to a th., find it in one's heart to do a th.; ***ans – drücken,*** clasp to one's breast; ***sich*** (*Dat.*) ***das – erleichtern,*** unburden o.s.; ***schwer aufs – fallen,*** weigh heavily on (*a p.*); ***sich*** (*Dat.*) ***ein – fassen,*** take courage, take heart, pluck up courage; (*Bot.*) ***flammendes –,*** bleeding heart; ***das – am*** or ***auf dem rechten Fleck haben,*** have one's heart in the right place; ***frisch vom –en weg reden,*** speak one's mind freely; ***mit ganzem –en,*** whole-heartedly; ***von (ganzem) –en,*** with all my heart; ***ihm einen Stich ins – geben,*** cut him to the quick; ***sich*** (*Dat.*) ***zu –en gehen lassen,*** take to heart; ***ihm zu –en gehen,*** touch *or* stir his heart; ***goldenes –,*** heart of gold; ***im Grund seines –ens,*** at the bottom of his heart; ***ihm von –en gut sein,*** love him dearly; ***auf dem –en haben,*** have on one's mind; ***mit halbem –en bei einer S. sein,*** be half-hearted about a th.; ***Hand aufs –!*** cross (your, my *etc.*) heart! ***sein – an eine S. hängen,*** set one's heart on a th.; ***klopfenden –ens,*** with heart a-flutter; ***ihm etwas ans – legen,*** urge *or* enjoin a th. on him, recommend a th. warmly to him; ***kein – im Leibe haben,*** be without a heart *or* without feelings, be heartless; ***es wird mir leichter ums –,*** I feel easier in my mind; ***leichten –ens,*** light-heartedly, without misgivings; ***es liegt mir am –en,*** I have it at heart, I attach great importance to it; ***seinem –en Luft machen,*** give vent to one's feelings *or* opinions; ***ihm das – schwer machen,*** sadden *or* grieve him; ***mit dem –en bei einer S. sein,*** have one's heart in a thing; ***mit – und Hand,*** with heart and soul, sincerely, earnestly; ***ein Mann (recht) nach meinem –en,*** a man after my own heart; ***sich*** (*Dat.*) ***zu –en nehmen,*** take to heart; ***sein – in die Hände nehmen,*** take heart *or* courage; ***auf – und Nieren prüfen,*** put to the acid test; ***mein – schlug höher,*** my heart missed a beat; ***die –en höher schlagen lassen,*** thrill the hearts; ***ihn ins – schließen,*** take him to one's heart; ***es schneidet mir ins –,*** it cuts me to the quick *or* wrings my heart; ***ein – und eine Seele,*** bosom friends; ***ich weiß, wie es ihm ums – ist,*** I know how he feels; ***es fällt mir ein Stein vom –en,*** that's a weight *or* load off my mind; ***aus tiefstem –en,*** from the bottom of one's heart; ***ein Kind unter dem –en tragen,*** be with child; ***von –en gern,*** willingly, with the greatest (of) pleasure, heartily, cordially; ***dem –en wohl tun,*** warm the cockles of one's heart; ***es zerreißt mir das –,*** it wrings my heart; ***das – auf der Zunge tragen,*** wear one's heart on one's sleeve.

Herzader ['hɛrtsʔa:dər], *f.* (*Anat.*) aorta.

herzählen ['he:rtsɛ:lən], *v.t.* count *or* call off, enumerate.

herzallerliebst ['hɛrtsʔalərli:pst], *adj.* dearest beloved. **Herz|anfall,** *m.* heart-attack. **--As,** *n.* (*Cards*) ace of hearts. **–beklemmung,** *f.* oppression, anxiety. **herzbeklommen,** *adj.* anxious. **Herz|beutel,** *m.* pericardium. **–beutelentzündung,** *f.* pericarditis. **–blatt,** *n.* 1. (*Bot.*) unopened leaf bud; 2. (*coll.*) darling; (*Anat.*) ***inneres –,*** visceral pericardium; ***äußeres –,*** pareital pericardium. **–blättchen,** *n.* (*coll.*) *see* **–blatt,** 2. **–blut,** *n.* (*fig.*) life-blood. **–bräune,** *f.* (*Med.*) angina pectoris. **–bube,** *m.* (*Cards*) knave of hearts. **–dame,** *f.* (*Cards*) queen of hearts.

herzeigen ['he:rtsaɪgən], *v.t.* let be seen, show.

Herzeleid ['hɛrtsəlaɪt], *n.* grief, sorrow, woe, heart-ache.

herzen ['hɛrtsən], *v.t.* press to one's heart, embrace, hug, caress, cuddle, fondle.

Herzens|angelegenheit, *f.* love-affair, affair of the heart, romance. **–angst,** *f.* anguish of mind, deep anxiety. **–einfalt,** *f.* simple-mindedness. **–freude,** *f.* great joy, heart's delight. **–freund,** *m.* bosom friend. **herzens|froh,** *adj.* overjoyed, heartily glad. **–gut,** *adj.* kind-hearted; as good as gold. **Herzens|güte,** *f.* kindness of heart, kind-heartedness. **–lust,** *f.* ***nach –,*** to one's heart's content. **–wunsch,** *m.* heartfelt desire, heart's desire, fondest wish.

herz|erfreuend, *adj.* cheering, comforting, gladdening, heart-warming. **–ergreifend,** *adj.* heart-stirring, affecting, moving. **–erquickend,** *adj.* *See* **–erfreuend. –erschütternd,** *adj.* appalling, heart-rending. **Herz|erweiterung,** *f.* dilatation of the heart, hypertrophy. **–fehler,** *m.* organic disease of the heart, cardiac defect. **–fell,** *n.* pericardium. **herzförmig,** *adj.* heart-shaped. **Herz|-gegend,** *f.* cardiac region. **–geräusch,** *n.* cardiac murmur. **–grube,** *f.* pit of the stomach, (*Anat.*) epigastrium.

herzhaft ['hɛrtshaft], *adj.* courageous, valiant, bold, stout-hearted, brave; hearty, goodly. **Herzhaftigkeit,** *f.* courage, bravery, manliness.

herziehen ['he:rtsi:ən], **1.** *irr.v.t.* draw *or* drag here *or* near. **2.** *irr.v.i.* (*aux.* s.) move to this place, come to live here; (*fig.*) ***– über*** (*Acc.*), run down, pull to pieces, criticize unmercifully.

herzig ['hɛrtsɪç], *adj.* sweet, charming, lovely, dear, (*Am.*) cute; (*in compounds*) -hearted.

Herzinfarkt ['hɛrtsʔɪnfarkt], *m.* (*Med.*) cardiac infarction. **herzinniglich,** *adj.* hearty, heartfelt, cordial. **Herz|kammer,** *f.* ventricle of the heart. **–klappe,** *f.* cardiac valve. **–klappenfehler,** *m.* valvular disease of the heart. **–klopfen,** *n.* palpitation of the heart; (*fig.*) ***mit –,*** with beating heart. **–könig,** *m.* (*Cards*) king of hearts. **–krampf,** *m.* spasm of the heart. **herzkrank,** *adj.* suffering from heart trouble, with a weak heart; (*fig.*) sick at heart. **Herz|krankheit,** *f.*, **–leiden,** *n.* heart-disease, heart-trouble, cardiac disorder. **herz|leidend,** *adj.* *See* **–krank.**

herzlich ['hɛrtslɪç], *adj.* hearty, cordial, affectionate; heartfelt, sincere; ***– gern,*** gladly, willingly, with all one's heart; (*coll.*) ***– wenig,*** precious *or* mighty little; (*coll.*) ***– langweilig,*** awfully dull; ***wir haben es – satt,*** we are heartily sick of it; ***–e Grüße,*** kind regards, warmest greetings; ***–es Beileid,*** heartfelt *or* deepest sympathy. **Herzlichkeit,** *f.* cordiality, affection, sincerity.

Herzliebchen ['hɛrtsli:pçən], *n.* sweetheart.

herzlos ['hɛrtslo:s], *adj.* heartless, unfeeling, hard-hearted, unsympathetic. **Herzlosigkeit,** *f.* heartlessness, hard-heartedness, lack of feeling.

Herz|muschel, *f.* cockle (*Cardium edule*). **–muskel,** *m.* cardiac muscle. **–muskelentzündung,** *f.* myocarditis.

Herzog ['hɛrtso:k], *m.* (**-(e)s,** *pl.* **-e** *or* **¨-e**) duke. **Herzogin,** *f.* duchess. **herzoglich,** *adj.* ducal. **Herzogtum,** *n.* (**-s,** *pl.* **¨-er**) duchy, dukedom.

Herz|ohr, *n. See* **–vorhof. –pochen,** *n.* severe palpitations. **–reiz,** *m.* cardiac stimulant. **–schlag,** *m.* 1. heartbeat; 2. heart attack *or* failure, apoplexy, stroke, seizure. **–schwäche,** *f.* syncope. **–spezialist,** *m.* cardiologist. **–stück,** *n.* 1. (*Railw.*) crossing frog; 2. centre piece, core. **–tätigkeit,** *f.* heart-action, heart beat. **–ton,** *m. See* **–geräusch.**

herzu [hɛr'tsu:], *adv., sep. pref. See* **heran, herbei.**

Herz|verfettung, *f.* fatty (degeneration of the) heart. **–vergrößerung,** *f.* hypertrophy of the heart. **–verknöcherung,** *f.* ossification of the heart. **–vorhof,** *m.,* **–vorkammer,** *f.* auricle. **–weh,** *n.* heartache; grief. **–wurzel,** *f.* (*Bot.*) taproot. **herzzerreißend,** *adj.* heart-rending.

Hesse ['hɛsə], *m.* (**-n,** *pl.* **-n**) Hessian. **Hessen,** *n.* (*Geog.*) Hesse. **Hessin,** *f. See* **Hesse. hessisch,** *adj.* Hessian.

Hetäre [he'tɛ:rə], *f.* (Greek) courtesan.

heterodox [hetero'dɔks], *adj.* heterodox. **Heterodoxie** [–'ksi:], *f.* heterodoxy, heresy.

heterogen [hetero'ge:n], *adj.* heterogeneous; ***–e Befruchtung,*** cross-fertilization; ***–e Bestäubung,*** cross-pollination; ***–e Zeugung,*** heterogenesis.

Hetzblatt ['hɛtsblat], *n.* gutter press, yellow press; (*sl.*) rag. **Hetze,** *f.* baiting, agitation, instigation; mad rush, chase; *see also* **Hetzjagd.**

hetzen ['hɛtsən], **1.** *v.t.* hunt, course, chase, run after, pursue; agitate, provoke, incite, bait, hound, set on, (*coll.*) egg on; ***zu Tode gehetzt,*** harassed *or* worried to death; (*coll.*) ***mit allen Hunden gehetzt sein,*** be up to every dodge *or* trick. **2.** *v.i.* rush, hurry. **Hetzer,** *m.* instigator, inciter, agitator, (*coll.*) rabble rouser. **Hetzerei** [–'raɪ], *f.* baiting, harassing; stirring up strife; agitation, calumniation; (*coll.*) rush; – ***der Prüfungen,*** rush and worry of examinations. **hetzerisch,** *adj.* inflammatory, slanderous.

Hetz|garten, *m.* bullring, bear garden, baiting-place. **–hund,** *m.* staghound, sporting dog. **–jagd,** *f.* hunt, chase, coursing; (*coll.*) rush, great hurry. **–redner,** *m.* agitator. **–schrift,** *f.* inflammatory writing *or* pamphlet.

Heu [hɔy], *n.* hay; ***Geld wie –,*** money to burn. **Heu|boden,** *m.* hayloft. **–bühne,** *f.* (*Swiss*) *see* **–boden. –bund, –bündel,** *n.* truss of hay.

Heuchelei [hɔyçə'laɪ], *f.* (-, *pl.* **-en**) hypocrisy, dissimulation, duplicity, insincerity, cant.

heucheln ['hɔyçəln], **1.** *v.t.* feign, affect, simulate, sham. **2.** *v.i.* dissemble, play the hypocrite; pose (as a saint). **Heuchler,** *m.* hypocrite, dissembler. **heuchlerisch,** *adj.* hypocritical; false, deceitful, insincere, dissembling, (*coll.*) two-faced.

Heudiele, *f.* (*Swiss*) *see* **–boden.**

heuen ['hɔyən], *v.t.* make hay. **Heuen,** *n.* haymaking.

[1]**Heuer** ['hɔyər], *m.* haymaker.

[2]**Heuer,** *f.* (-, *pl.* **-n**) *see* **Heuerlohn.**

heuer, *adv.* (*Austr.*) (in) this year.

Heuerbaas ['hɔyərba:s], *m.* seaman's agent. **Heuerling,** *m.* (**-s,** *pl.* **-e**) (*dial.*) hired man, day-labourer. **Heuerlohn,** *m.* (*Naut.*) (seaman's) pay *or* wages. **heuern,** *v.t.* hire; charter (*a ship*), engage, take on (*seamen*).

Heuernte ['hɔyˀɛrntə], *f.* hay-harvest; hay-making (season). **Heue(r)t,** *m.* (*dial.*) July. **Heu|feim,** *m.* (**-s,** *pl.* **-e**), **–feime,** *f.,* **–feimen,** *m.* haystack, hayrick. **–fieber,** *n.* hay fever. **–gabel,** *f.* pitchfork.

Heulboje ['hɔylbo:jə], *f.* (*Naut.*) whistling buoy.

heulen ['hɔylən], *v.i.* howl; cry, blubber; scream (*as bombs*), roar, moan (*of wind*), hoot (*of owls*), wail (*of sirens*); ***mit den Wölfen –,*** follow the crowd. **Heulen,** *n.* howling, wailing, crying; (*B.*) – ***und Zähneklappern,*** weeping and gnashing of teeth.

Heul|kreisel, *m.* humming-top. **–meier, –michel,** *m.,* **–suse,** *f.* cry-baby. **–ton,** *m.* (*Rad.*) high-frequency hum. **–tonne,** *f. See* **–boje.**

Heu|monat, –mond, *m.* (*dial.*) July. **–pferd,** *n.* grasshopper.

heurig ['hɔyrɪç], *adj.* (*Austr.*) this year's *or* season's, of this year; ***–e Kartoffeln,*** new potatoes. **Heurigenschenke,** *f. See* **Heurige(r),** 2. **Heurige(r),** *m.* 1. young wine, this season's vintage; 2. Viennese suburban tavern (*kept by the grower*).

Heu|schnupfen, *m.* hayfever. **–schober,** *m.* hayrick, haystack. **–schrecke,** *f.* grasshopper, (*B.*) locust. **–schreckensänger,** *m.* (*Orn.*) *see* **Feldschwirl. –stadel, –stock,** *m.* (*Swiss*) *see* **–schober.**

heute ['hɔytə], *adv.* today, this day; – ***abend,*** tonight; – ***früh,*** this morning; ***das ist nicht von gestern und –,*** there is nothing new in that; (*Prov.*) – ***mir, morgen dir,*** every one in his turn; – ***morgen,*** this morning; ***nicht von – auf morgen zu erwarten,*** not to be expected overnight; – ***nacht,*** this night, tonight; (*Prov.*) – ***rot, morgen tot,*** here today, gone tomorrow; – ***über ein Jahr,*** a year hence, a year from today; – ***über vierzehn Tage*** or ***in vierzehn Tagen,*** today fortnight; – ***über vier Wochen,*** a month (from) today; ***Deutschland von –,*** present-day Germany; ***von – an,*** from today; – ***vor acht Tagen,*** a week ago today.

heutig ['hɔytɪç], *adj.* of today, today's; present (-day), actual, modern; ***mit der –en Post,*** by today's mail; ***am –en Tag,*** today, on this day; (*Comm.*) ***Ihr –es,*** your favour of today; (*Comm.*) ***unterm –en,*** under this day's date.

heutzutage ['hɔyttsuta:gə], *adv.* today, nowadays, in our times, in these days.

Hexaeder [hɛksa'e:dər], *n.* hexahedron, cube.

Hexameter [hɛ'ksa:me:tər], *m.* (dactylic) hexameter (verse). **hexametrisch** [–'me:trɪʃ], *adj.* hexameter.

Hexe ['hɛksə], *f.* witch, sorceress; hag. **hexen,** *v.i.* conjure, practise sorcery; ***ich kann nicht –,*** I cannot work miracles; ***wie gehext,*** like magic. **Hexen|glaube,** *m.* belief in witchcraft. **–jagd,** *f.* witch-hunt. **–kessel,** *m.* witch's cauldron; (*fig.*) inferno, hurly-burly, hubbub. **–kraut,** *n.* (*Bot.*) enchanter's nightshade (*Circaea lutetiana*). **–kreis,** *m.* magic circle; fairy-ring. **–küche,** *f.* witch's kitchen. **–kunst,** *f.* witchcraft, magic art. **–mehl,** *n.* lycopodium. **–meister,** *m.* wizard, sorcerer, magician. **–prozeß,** *m.* witchcraft trial. **–pulver,** *n. See* **–mehl. –sabbat,** *m.* witches' Sabbath. **–schuß,** *m.* lumbago. **–verbrennung,** *f.* witch-burning. **–verfolgung,** *f.* witch-hunt.

Hexerei [hɛksə'raɪ], *f.* witchcraft, sorcery, magic; (*Prov.*) ***Geschwindigkeit ist keine –,*** sleight-of-hand requires no magic; ***das ist keine –,*** there is nothing wonderful in that; – ***treiben,*** practise witchcraft.

hie [hi:], *adv.* (*obs.*) *see* **hier**; – ***und da,*** here and there, now and then; – ***Welf, – Weibling!*** a Guelph, a Ghibelline!

Hieb [hi:p], *m.* (**-(e)s,** *pl.* **-e**) blow, stroke, hit; slash, cut, gash; lash (*of whip*); (*fig.*) cutting remark; *pl.* thrashing, whipping; ***der – sitzt,*** the blow goes home; (*coll.*) ***auf den ersten –,*** at the first attempt *or* shot; (*Prov.*) ***auf den ersten – fällt kein Baum,*** Rome was not built in a day; (*Fenc.*) ***auf – und Stich gehen,*** cut and thrust; ***hieb- und stichfest,*** invulnerable, (*fig.*) watertight, cast-iron (*proof etc.*); ***freien – haben,*** be entitled to fell timber.

hieb [hi:p], **hiebe** ['hi:bə], *see* **hauen.**

Hieb|fechten, *n.* fighting with swords *or* sabres; ***Hieb- und Stoßfechten,*** cut and thrust. **–satz,** *m.* yield (*from felling*); amount felled. **–waffe,** *f.* cutting weapon, broadsword. **–wunde,** *f.* gash, slash, sword wound.

hielt [hi:lt], **hielte,** *see* **halten.**

hieng [hi:ŋ], *obs. for* **hing.**

hienieden [hi:'ni:dən], *adv.* (*Poet.*) here below, here on earth, in this life.

hier [hi:r], *adv.* here, present, in this place, at this point; (*fig.*) on this occasion, in this case; at these words; – ***und da,*** now and then, from time to time; – ***und dort,*** here and there; ***für – bestimmt,*** bound for this place; – ***herum,*** hereabouts; ***von – ab,*** starting here, from this point *or* place; ***ich bin nicht von –,*** I am a stranger here; (*coll.*) ***er ist nicht von –,*** he isn't all there; (*Tele.*) – ***Karl,*** Charles calling *or* speaking.

hier- (*N.B. In the following compounds* **hier-** *is nowadays normal in North Germany,* **hie-** *is obs. In South Germany and Austria* **hie-** *is still common, being in fact preferred where the second component commences with a consonant, e.g.* **hiegegen**).

hier|amts, *adv.* (*Austr.*) at *or* from this office (*official style*). **–an,** *adv.* hereupon; on, at, in, to *or* by this.

Hierarchie [hierar'çi:], *f.* hierarchy. **hierarchisch** [–'rarçɪʃ], *adj.* hierarchical.

hieratisch [hie'ratɪʃ], *adj.* hieratic, sacerdotal.

hier|auf, *adv.* hereupon, upon this, at this; after that, afterwards, then, now. **–aus,** *adv.* herefrom, out of this, from here, from this, hence, hereby, by this. **–bei,** *adv.* hereby, in doing so, herewith, in this connection, on this occasion; by, at, in, during *or* with this; enclosed, attached, appended, annexed. **–durch,** *adv.* this way, through here; by this means; by this, due to this, hereby, thereby. **–für,** *adv.* for this, for it, instead of this. **–gegen,** *adv.* against this *or* it; in return for this.

hierher [hi:r'he:r], *adv.* to this place, this way, hither, (over) here, to me; ***bis –,*** hitherto, till now, up to now, (up) to this day; up to here, so far, thus far. **hierhergehören,** *v.i.* belong here; ***nicht –,*** not be to the point, be off the point, be wide of the mark, not be relevant.

hier|herum, *adv.* this way round; hereabouts, in this neighbourhood. **–hin,** *adv.* in this direction, this way; hither; ***bald – bald dorthin,*** hither and thither, now here now there. **–in,** *adv.* herein; in this. **–mit,** *adv.* herewith, (along) with this; saying *or* doing this, with these words, on this. **–nach,** *adv.* after this; hereupon; hereafter; according to this.

Hieroglyphe [hiero'gly:fə], *f.* hieroglyph(ic).

hierorts ['hi:rˀɔrts], *adv.* here, in *or* of this place. **Hiersein,** *n.* being here, presence. **hier|selbst,** *adv.* here, in this very place; local (*in addresses*). **–über,** *adv.* over here; concerning *or* regarding this, about this, on this score *or* account. **–um,** *adv.* about *or* round this place, hereabout(s); about *or* concerning this. **–unter,** *adv.* hereunder; under(neath) *or* beneath this *or* it; in *or* by this; among these. **–von,** *adv.* hereof, herefrom; of *or* from this. **–zu,** *adv.* to this, hereto; add to this, in addition to this, moreover. **–zulande,** *adv.* in this country, in these parts. **–zwischen,** *adv.* between; between these.

hiesig ['hi:zɪç], *adj.* of *or* in this place *or* country, local, native, indigenous.

hieß [hi:s], **hieße,** *see* **heißen.**

hieven ['hi:vən], *v.t.* (*Naut.*) heave, haul.

Hift [hɪft], *m.* (**-(e)s,** *pl.* **-e**) (*rare*) sound given by the hunting-horn, bugle-call. **Hifthorn,** *n.* hunting-horn.

hilf [hɪlf], *see* **helfen.**

Hilfe ['hɪlfə], *f.* help, aid, assistance, succour, support; relief; ***ihn um – bitten,*** ask him for help, call in his assistance; ***erste –,*** first aid; ***ihm zu – kommen,*** come to his aid; – ***leisten*** (*Dat.*), help, aid, assist, succour, render aid *or* assistance; ***mit – der Nacht,*** under cover of night *or* darkness; ***ohne –,*** unaided, unassisted, single-handed, (*coll.*) by o.s. **hilfeflehend,** *adj.* suppliant. **Hilfe|leistung,** *f.* assistance, help; relief *or* rescue work. **–ruf,** *m.* cry *or* appeal for help.

hilflos ['hɪlflo:s], *adj.* helpless, defenceless, shiftless; destitute. **Hilflosigkeit,** *f.* helplessness. **hilfreich,** *adj.* helpful.

Hilfs|aktion, *f.* relief work. **–antrieb,** *m.* auxiliary drive. **–arbeiter,** *m.* temporary worker, auxiliary, assistant. **hilfsbedürftig,** *adj.* requiring help; needy, indigent. **Hilfsbedürftigkeit,** *f.* destitution, indigence. **hilfsbereit,** *adj.* helpful, co-operative, obliging. **Hilfs|bereitschaft,** *f.* helpfulness, goodwill; co-operative attitude. **–bischof,** *m.* suffragan bishop. **–dienst,** *m.* auxiliary (air-raid precaution) *or* emergency service. **–fallschirm,** *m.* pilot parachute. **–fonds,** *m.* relief fund. **–geistliche(r),** *m.* curate. **–geld,** *n.* subsidy. **–kasse,** *f. See* **–fonds. –kraft,** *f.* additional helper *or* worker, assistant, auxiliary. **–lehrer,** *m.* 1. assistant teacher *or* master (on probation); 2. replacement teacher, teacher on supply, part-time teacher. **–linie,** *f.* (*Math.*) auxiliary *or* subsidiary line; (*Mus.*) ledger-line. **–maschine,** *f.* auxiliary engine. **–maßnahmen,** *f.pl.* emergency *or* remedial measures. **–mittel,** *n.* remedy, resource, device, expedient, shift, means, aid, (*coll.*) stop-gap; ***letztes –,*** last resort. **–motor,** *m.* 1. *See* **–maschine**; 2. starting motor. **–polizei,** *f.* special constabulary, auxiliary police. **–prediger,** *m. See* **–geistliche(r). –quelle,** *f.* resources; expedient. **–satz,** *m.* (*Math.*) lemma. **–schiff,** *n.* auxiliary vessel, armed trawler. **–schule,** *f.* special school (for backward children). **–sprache,** *f.* auxiliary language (*Esperanto, Ido*).

hilfst [hɪlfst], *see* **helfen.**

Hilfs|truppen, *f.pl.* auxiliaries. **–vorrichtung,** *f.* auxiliary device, (*Mech.*) servo-mechanism. **–wache,** *f.* first-aid station. **hilfsweise,** *adv.* in an auxiliary *or* subsidiary *or* ancillary capacity. **Hilfs|-zeitwort,** *m.* auxiliary verb. **–zug,** *m.* relief *or* extra train.

hilft [hɪlft], *see* **helfen.**

Himalaja [hi'ma:laja], *m.* (*Geog.*) (the) Himalayas.

Himbeere ['hɪmbe:rə], *f.* raspberry. **Himbeer|-gelee,** *n.* raspberry jam. **–saft,** *m.* raspberry juice. **–strauch,** *m.* raspberry-bush *or* cane.

Himmel ['hɪməl], *m.* heaven; heavens, sky, firmament; canopy, tester; ***–!*** good heavens! ***am –,*** in the sky; ***bedeckter –,*** overcast sky; – ***und Hölle in Bewegung setzen,*** move heaven and earth; ***das Blaue vom – herunterlügen,*** lie impudently, swear black is white; ***dem – sei Dank, daß wir . . .!*** thank heaven, we . . .! ***aus allen –n fallen,*** be bitterly disappointed *or* cruelly disillusioned; ***wie vom – fallen,*** appear from nowhere *or* out of the blue, come like a bolt from the blue; ***unter freiem –,*** in the open (air); ***gerechter –!*** good heavens! (***bis***) ***in den – heben,*** praise to the skies; ***heiterer –,*** clear sky; ***ein Blitz aus heiterem –,*** a bolt from the blue; ***im –,*** in heaven; ***du lieber –!*** heavens above! (*int. of dismay*); ***das schreit zum –,*** it's a crying shame, it is scandalous *or* a disgrace; ***im siebenten – schweben,*** be in the seventh heaven (of delight), be beside o.s. for joy; ***es stinkt zum –,*** it stinks to high heaven; ***die Bäume wachsen nicht in den –,*** there is a limit to everything; ***so weit der – blaut*** or ***reicht,*** everywhere under the sun; ***weiß der –,*** heaven only knows; ***um –s Willen!*** for heaven's sake!

himmel|ab, *adv.* from heaven, from on high. **–an,** *adv.* heavenwards, to the skies. **–angst,** *adv.* (*coll.*) scared to death, in a blue funk. **Himmel|bett,** *n.* four-poster *or* tester bed. **–blau,** *n.* (*and adj.*) sky-blue, azure, cerulean. **–brot,** *n.* manna. **–fahrt,** *f.* Ascension; – ***Christi,*** Ascension Day; ***Mariä –,*** Assumption (of the Blessed Virgin). **–fahrtskommando,** *n.* (*sl.*) suicide squad, death-or-glory squad. **himmelhoch,** *adj.* sky-high, very high; – ***jauchzend,*** shouting to the skies with delight. **Himmelreich,** *n.* (kingdom of) heaven, paradise; bliss.

Himmels|achse, *f.* celestial axis. **–angel,** *f. See* **–pol. –bahn,** *f.* orbit. **–bogen,** *m.* (*Poet.*) vault of heaven; rainbow. **–braut,** *f.* (*Poet.*) nun. **–breite,** *f.* latitude.

himmelschreiend ['hɪməlʃraɪənt], *adj.* shameful, outrageous, atrocious; ***–e Schande,*** crying shame; ***–er Unsinn,*** utter nonsense.

Himmels|erscheinung, *f.* portent in the skies. **–feste,** *f.* (*Poet.*) firmament. **–gegend,** *f. See* **–richtung. –gewölbe,** *n.* firmament. **–globus,** *m.* celestial globe. **–haus,** *n.* firmament; (*Astrol.*)

house. **-heer,** *n.* heavenly host. **-höhe,** *f.* solar altitude (*vertical angle a star makes with the horizon*). **-karte,** *f.* star chart. **-königin,** *f.* (*Poet.*) Virgin Mary, mother of God. **-körper,** *m.* celestial body. **-kost,** *f.* ambrosia; the Sacrament. **-kugel,** *f.* celestial globe, firmament. **-kunde,** *f.* astronomy. **-länge,** *f.* astronomical longitude. **-lauf,** *m.* motion of the heavenly bodies. **-leiter,** *f.* Jacob's ladder. **-licht,** *n.* **1.** celestial orb; **2.** *pl.* luminaries. **-luft,** *f.* ether. **-ortung,** *f.* celestial navigation. **-pförtner,** *m.* St. Peter. **-pol,** *m.* celestial pole. **-punkt,** *m.* zenith. **-rand,** *m.* horizon. **-raum,** *m.* the heavens, space. **-reklame,** *f.* *See* **-schrift. -richtung,** *f.* cardinal point, point of the compass; direction. **-schlüssel,** *m.* **1.** keys of Heaven; **2.** (*Bot.*) cowslip (*Primula veris*). **-schrift,** *f.* (*Av.*) sky-writing. **-strich,** *m.* climate; latitude, zone, region, clime. **himmel(s)stürmend,** *adj.* titanic. **Himmels|trank,** *m.* nectar. **-wagen,** *m,* the Great Bear, Charles's Wain. **-zeichen,** *n.* sign of the zodiac. **-zelt,** *n.* (*Poet.*) canopy *or* vault of heaven.

himmelwärts ['hɪməlvɛrts], *adj.* heavenwards. **himmelweit** [-'vaɪt], *adj., adv.* (*fig.*) enormous(ly), vast(ly), immense(ly); – ***voneinander entfernt,*** miles apart; – ***verschieden sein,*** differ widely, be diametrically opposed; ***-er Unterschied,*** all the difference in the world.

himmlisch ['hɪmlɪʃ], *adj.* heavenly, celestial, divine; ethereal, beatific; (*coll.*) splendid, beautiful, lovely, glorious; ***-e Fügung,*** divine ordinance, decree of Providence; ***-e Geduld,*** the patience of Job; ***die -en Mächte,*** the powers above; ***-e Sehnsucht,*** longing for heaven, spiritual yearning; ***unser -er Vater,*** our Father in Heaven; ***-es Wetter,*** glorious weather.

hin [hɪn], *adv.* (a) *expressing motion away from the speaker or point contemplated; usu. with reference to a definite goal*; hence, thither, that way, over there; (b) *expressing duration of time into the future*; on, along; (c) *sometimes implying motion with no reference to direction*; along; (d) (*coll.*) gone, lost; spent; exhausted, broken; undone; ***auf*** (*Acc.*) . . . –, in consequence of, as a result of, following, on the strength of; ***auf die Gefahr*** –, at the risk of; ***auf Ihr Wort*** –, (relying) on your word; ***auf ein Ziel*** –, directed towards a goal; ***bis zum Baum*** –, up as far as the tree; – ***und her,*** to and fro, there and back, backwards and forwards, back and forth; – ***und her laufen,*** run to and fro, run all over the place (*N.B. **hin- und herlaufen,*** run there and back); – ***und her denken über*** (*Acc.*) or ***überlegen,*** rack one's brains about, turn over in one's mind; ***nach vielem Hin- und Herschreiben,*** after much correspondence; ***Mode –, Mode her, ich werde . . .,*** however the fashion may change, I shall . . .; – ***und her ist gleich weit,*** it's as broad as it's long; – ***ist*** –, what is gone is gone, it is no good crying over spilt milk; ***nach*** . . . –, to *or* towards . . .; (*coll.*) ***er ist*** –, he is lost *or* done for *or* ruined *or* dead, (*sl.*) he's a goner; ***ich bin ganz*** –, I'm all in, I'm dead beat; ***ich bin darüber ganz*** –, I'm in raptures about it; ***über das ganze Feld*** –, all over the field; ***still vor sich*** –, quietly to oneself (without interruption); ***es ist noch weit*** –, it is still far off *or* a long way off; – ***und wieder,*** now and then, from time to time; – ***und zurück,*** there and back, outward and return.

hin-, *pref. to verbs and to preps. (used adverbially), it has opposite meaning to* **her** (*q.v.*), *referring the motion away from the speaker; in compounds with verbs **hin** is sep. and has the accent; with preps. **or** advs. the accent is on the prep. or adv.*

hinab [hɪ'nap], *adv., sep. pref.* (*movement downwaras as seen from the starting place above*), down (there), downward(s); – ***mit dir!*** down! (*to dogs*); ***etwas weiter*** –, down a little; ***den Strom*** –, down the river, down-stream; ***die Treppe*** –, downstairs; *see* **hinunter. hinab|lassen,** *irr.v.t.* let down, lower. **-steigen,** *irr.v.i.* (*aux.* s.) descend. **-stürzen, 1.** *v.i.* (*aux.* s.) fall (*as on a mountain*). **2.** *v.t.* throw down, precipitate.

hinan [hɪ'nan], *adv., sep. pref.* (*rising movement to a summit or elevated position*) up (to), upward(s); *see* **hinauf.**

hinarbeiten ['hɪnˀarbaɪtən], *v.i.* (***auf*** (*Acc.*)) aim at, work for *or* towards, struggle towards.

hinauf [hɪ'nauf], *adv., sep. pref.* (*movement upwards as seen from the starting point below*) upward(s), up (to); ***bis*** –, up to; ***da*** –, ***dort*** –, up there; ***den Fluß*** –, up the river, up-stream; ***die Treppe*** –, upstairs.

hinauf|arbeiten, *v.r.* work one's way up. **-befördern,** *v.t.* hoist *or* carry up. **-begeben,** *irr.v.r.* go up(stairs). **-blicken,** *v.i.* look up (***zu,*** at *or* (*fig.*) to). **-gehen,** *irr.v.i.* (*aux.* s.) go *or* walk up, mount, ascend, go upstairs; (*fig. as prices*) rise, climb. **-schnellen,** *v.i.* (*aux.* s.) bounce *or* leap up, (*fig. as prices*) shoot up, soar *or* rocket (up). **-schrauben,** *v.t.* (*fig.*) screw *or* push up (*prices*), step *or* force up (*production*). **-setzen,** *v.t.* raise, put up (*prices*). **-steigen,** *irr.v.i.* (*aux.* s.) mount, ascend, climb up. **-stimmen,** *v.t.* (*Mus.*) raise the pitch of; raise, increase (*one's pretensions etc.*). **-transformieren,** *v.t.* (*Elec.*) step up (*voltage*). **-ziehen, 1.** *irr.v.t.* draw *or* pull up. **2.** *irr.v.i.* (*aux.* s.) move *or* go up (*of troops*).

hinaus [hɪ'naus], *adv., sep. pref.* (*movement outwards as seen from outside*) out (there), outside, forth; ***vorn*** –, out in (the) front, out at the front; ***hinten*** –, out at the back; – ***mit ihm!*** throw him out! ***dort*** –, out there; ***über*** . . . (*Acc.*) –, beyond, past, above, in excess of; (*fig.*) ***ich bin jetzt darüber*** –, I'm past that stage now; I have got over it now; ***auf Jahre*** –, for years (to come); ***über den Termin*** –, beyond the time limit; ***wo soll das noch –?*** where is that leading *or* will that lead to? ***worauf wollen Sie –?*** what are you driving at? (*fig.*) ***ich weißt nicht, wo*** –, I don't know what to do *or* which way to turn; ***zum Fenster*** –, out of the window.

hinaus|begleiten, *v.t.* see to the door, see out. **-beugen,** *v.r.* lean out (***zu,*** of). **-feuern,** *v.t.* (*coll.*) *see* **-werfen. -fliegen,** *irr.v.i.* (*aux.* s.) (*coll.*) get the sack, be sacked *or* fired, get flung out. **-gehen,** *irr.v.i.* (*aux.* s.) leave; go *or* walk out; – ***über*** (*Acc.*), surpass, exceed, go beyond, transcend; – ***auf*** (*Acc.*), aim at, have in view; ***das Zimmer geht auf den Garten hinaus,*** the room looks out over *or* looks out on *or* opens on *or* faces on the garden; ***die Rede ging darauf hinaus,*** the conversation turned on; the drift *or* purport of the speech was. **-geleiten,** *v.t.* show *or* usher out. **-greifen,** *irr.v.i.* (*fig.*) go *or* reach beyond. **-kommen, -laufen,** *irr.v.i.* (*aux.* s.) come out, run out; – ***auf*** (*Acc.*), come *or* amount to, (*coll.*) boil down to; ***auf eins*** or ***dasselbe*** –, come *or* amount to the same thing; ***darauf kommt*** or ***läuft es hinaus,*** that is what it's coming to; ***die Rede kam*** or ***lief darauf hinaus,*** *see* **-gehen. -ragen,** *v.i.* jut out, project (***über*** (*Acc.*), from), (*fig.*) tower, stand out (above). **-reichen,** *v.i.* reach, extend, stretch out (***über*** (*Acc.*), beyond). **-rücken,** *v.t.*, **-schieben,** *irr.v.t.* (*fig.*) delay, defer, postpone, (*coll.*) put off. **-schießen,** *irr.v.i.* (***über*** (*Acc.*)) go beyond, exceed; (***weit***) ***über das Ziel*** –, overshoot the mark; (*fig.*) be too much of a good thing, go too far. **-setzen,** *v.t.* *See* **-werfen. -stellen,** *v.t.* put out(side), (*Spt.*) order off the field. **-stoßen,** *irr.v.t.* eject, thrust out. **-trompeten,** *v.t.* trumpet forth. **-wachsen,** *irr.v.i.* (*aux.* s.) (***über*** (*Acc.*)) outgrow, (*fig.*) surpass. **-wagen,** *v.r.* venture out *or* forth. **-werfen,** *irr.v.t.* throw out (***aus,*** of), expel, eject (from); throw *or* turn *or* kick *or* (*coll.*) chuck (*a p.*) out, sack, fire (*s.o.*), give (*s.o.*) the sack *or* (*coll.*) boot; ***Geld zum Fenster*** –, squander money, throw one's money about. **-wollen,** *irr.v.i.* wish *or* want to go *or* get out (***aus,*** of), (*fig.*) aim at; ***wo wollte er hinaus?*** what was he driving at? ***wo will das hinaus?*** what will be the end *or* upshot of it? ***hoch*** –, aim high, aim at great things, have extravagant ambitions. **-ziehen, 1.** *irr.v.t.* stretch out, draw *or* drag out, prolong, protract. **2.** *irr.v.r.* be protracted, (*coll.*) go on and on. **3.** *irr.v.i.* (*aux.* s.) march *or* move *or* go out.

hin|begeben, *irr.v.r.* move, betake o.s., repair (***zu,*** to). **-bestellen,** *v.t.* order, tell, arrange for (*s.o.*) to go (***zu*** or ***nach,*** to) *or* to appear (at).

Hinblick ['hɪnblɪk], *m.* (*only in*) ***in*** or ***im – auf*** (*Acc.*), with *or* in regard to, with a view to, in consideration *or* in the light of, considering. **hinblicken,** *v.i.* (***auf*** (*Acc.*) or ***nach***) look towards, glance at; ***vor sich –,*** stare into space.

hin|bringen, *irr.v.t.* bring *or* carry away, convey (*a th.*); take *or* conduct *or* accompany there (*a p.*); ***die Zeit –,*** pass *or* spend the time, idle away *or* kill time. **–brüten,** *v.i.* ***vor sich –,*** be lost in thought. **–denken,** *irr.v.i.* let one's thoughts run away with one; ***wo denken Sie hin?*** whatever are you thinking of? it's quite out of the question!

hinderlich ['hɪndərlɪç], *adj.* hindering, impeding; obstructive, cumbersome, inconvenient, troublesome, embarrassing (*Dat.*, to), (*coll.*) in the way.

hindern ['hɪndərn], *v.t.* hinder, impede, hamper, handicap (***in*** (*Dat.*) *or* ***bei,*** in); prevent (***an*** (*Dat.*), from), interfere (with); block, obstruct, thwart, cross. **Hindernis,** *n.* (**-ses,** *pl.* **-se**) hindrance, impediment, handicap, encumbrance, stumbling block; obstacle, bar, barrier, check; (*Spt.*) hurdle, fence, jump; ***ohne –se,*** without a hitch. **Hindernis|lauf,** *m.* obstacle-race. **–rennen,** *n.* steeplechase, hurdle-race. **Hinderung,** *f.* interference, obstruction, hindrance; ***ohne –,*** without let or hindrance.

hindeuten ['hɪndɔytən], *v.i.* (***auf*** (*Acc.*)) point to, suggest, indicate, intimate, hint at, be indicative *or* suggestive of.

Hindin ['hɪndɪn], *f.* hind, doe.

hindurch [hɪn'durç], *adv., sep. pref.* through, throughout; during; ***den ganzen Tag –,*** all day long; ***die ganze Nacht –,*** all night (long), all through the night, the whole night long *or* through; ***das ganze Jahr –,*** all the year round.

hinein [hɪ'naɪn], *adv., sep. pref.* (*penetration into, sometimes as seen from outside, but oft. fig.*) in(side); ***– in*** (*Acc.*), into; ***bis*** or ***mitten – in*** (*Acc.*), right into the middle of; ***bis in den Sommer –,*** well into the summer; ***bis tief in die Nacht –,*** far into the night; (*fig.*) ***ins Blaue*** or ***Leere*** or ***in den Tag –,*** at random, without giving it a thought.

hinein|arbeiten, **1.** *v.t.* work, fit (***in*** (*Acc.*), in(to)). **2.** *v.r.* familiarize o.s. (***in*** (*Acc.*), with). **–denken,** *irr.v.r.* (***in*** (*Acc.*)) try to understand, go deeply into (*a matter*); try to follow, enter into (*a p.'s ideas*). **–drängen,** *v.r.* push *or* shoulder one's way (***in*** (*Acc.*), into). **–finden,** *irr.v.r.* (***in*** (*Acc.*)) get used to, familiarize o.s. with, grasp. **–gehen,** *irr.v.i.* (*aux.* s.) go in; ***etwa ein Liter geht in den Krug hinein,*** the jug holds about a litre; ***nur 20 Leute gehen in den Saal hinein,*** the hall only accommodates 20 people. **–knien,** *v.r.* (*fig.*)) get down to. **–leben,** *v.r.* ***sich in den Tag –,*** lead a carefree *or* happy-go-lucky existence. **–legen,** *v.t.* (*fig.*) *see* **hereinlegen. –reden,** **1.** *v.i.* ***ins Blaue –,*** talk without thinking, talk nonsense; ***in alles mit – wollen,*** wish to have a say *or* a voice *or* a finger in everything. **2.** *v.r.* ***sich in einen Zorn –,*** talk o.s. into a passion. **–reiten,** *irr.v.t. See* **–legen. –stecken,** *v.t.* put, sink (*money*) (***in*** (*Acc.*), into), invest (in); ***die Nase überall –,*** poke one's nose in everywhere. **–steigern,** *v.r.* (*coll.*) get (all) worked up (***wegen,*** over *or* about). **–tun,** *irr.v.t.* put (***in*** (*Acc.*), into), add (to), mix (with); ***einen Blick – in*** (*Acc.*), glance into. **–wollen,** *irr.v.i.* wish *or* be willing to go in; ***das will mir nicht in den Kopf hinein,*** I cannot get that into my head, that is beyond me. **–ziehen,** *irr.v.t.* pull, draw *or* drag in; (*fig.*) involve, implicate (*a p.*).

hinfahren ['hɪnfa:rən], **1.** *irr.v.i.* (*aux.* s.) go *or* travel *or* drive *or* sail *or* cycle there; (*Poet.*) die, pass away; ***fahre hin, Mitleid!*** farewell, pity! ***mit der Hand über eine S. –,*** pass one's hand over a th. **2.** *irr.v.t.* convey to. **Hinfahrt,** *f.* 1. journey there, passage out, outward journey; 2. decease.

hinfallen ['hɪnfalən], *irr.v.i.* (*aux.* s.) fall down; decay. **hinfällig,** *adj.* ready to fall, decaying; frail, feeble, weak, decrepit, infirm; (*Law*) null and void, invalid; untenable (*of opinions*); ***– machen,*** invalidate; ***– werden,*** come to nothing, fail. **Hinfälligkeit,** *f.* decrepitude, frailty; feebleness; weakness (*of arguments*).

hinfinden ['hɪnfɪndən], *irr.v.r.* find one's way to.

hinfort [hɪn'fɔrt], *adv.* henceforth, in future, from now on.

hing [hɪŋ], *see* **hangen; hängen, 2.**

Hin|gabe, *f.* submission; devotion (***an*** (*Acc.*), to). **–gang,** *m.* (*obs.*) departure; decease.

hinge ['hɪŋə], *see* **hangen; hängen, 2.**

hingeben ['hɪnge:bən], **1.** *irr.v.t.* give up, surrender, relinquish, abandon; sacrifice (*Dat.*, to); ***sein Leben für ihn –,*** sacrifice *or* lay down one's life for him. **2.** *irr.v.r.* (*Dat.*) abandon *or* resign o.s. to, give o.s. up *or* devote o.s. to; indulge in; submit, yield (*of a girl to a man's demands*); ***sie hat sich ihm hingegeben,*** she gave herself to him. **hingebend,** *adj.* devoted, self-sacrificing. **Hingebung,** *f.* self-denial; resignation; devotion. **hingebungsvoll,** *adj. See* **hingebend.**

hingegen [hɪn'ge:gən], *adv., conj.* on the contrary, on the other hand; whereas, however.

hin|gehen, *irr.v.i.* (*aux.* s.) go to that place; go *or* lead there; (*of time*) pass, elapse; (*fig.*) ***es geht hin,*** it is passable; (*fig.*) ***es mag –,*** it may pass; (*fig.*) ***etwas – lassen,*** let a th. pass, close one's eyes to a th., wink at a th. **–gehören.** *v.i.* ***wo gehört das hin?*** where does that go? **–geraten,** *irr.v.i.* (*aux.* s.) ***wo ist er –?*** where has he gone to? what has become of him? **–gerissen,** *adj.* carried away, enthralled, enraptured; *see* **–reißen. –halten,** *irr.v.t.* 1. proffer, tender, hold out (*a th.*); 2. (*fig.*) put off, delay; keep (*a p.*) waiting *or* in suspense. **–haltend,** *adj.* delaying; ***–er Widerstand,*** delaying action *or* tactics. **–hauen,** **1.** *irr.v.t.* (*coll.*) knock off, do in a slapdash manner. **2.** *irr.v.r.* (*coll.*) turn in, hit the hay. **3.** *irr.v.i.* (*coll.*) ***das haut hin,*** that's done the trick. **–hören,** *v.i.* prick up one's ears.

hinken ['hɪŋkən], *v.i.* (*aux.* h. *&* s.) (walk with a) limp, go lame, hobble; (*coll. of a th.*) be unsatisfactory *or* imperfect; ***auf*** or ***mit dem linken Fuß –,*** limp with the left leg. **hinkend,** *adj.* lame, halting, limping; ***der –e Bote,*** bad news; ***–e Verse,*** halting verse.

hin|knien, *v.i.* kneel down. **–kommen,** *irr.v.i.* (*aux.* s.) come *or* arrive *or* get there; (*coll.*) manage; ***nirgends –,*** not go anywhere, never go out; ***wo ist er hingekommen?*** where has he got to? what has become of him? (*coll.*) ***es kommt gerade*** or ***noch hin,*** it will be just enough; (*coll.*) ***ich komme damit nicht hin,*** I shan't manage with it, it won't be enough for me. **–langen,** **1.** *v.t.* ***ihm etwas –,*** hand over *or* give *or* pass s.th. to him. **2.** *v.i.* ***– nach,*** reach (out) for; ***–*** (***bis***) ***zu,*** reach (as far as), extend as far as; (*fig.*) be adequate, suffice. **–länglich,** *adj.* sufficient, adequate; ***–es Auskommen,*** sufficient means, a competence, living wage.

hinlegen ['hɪnle:gən], **1.** *v.t.* lay down; put away. **2.** *v.r.* lie down.

hin|machen ['hɪnmaxən], **1.** *v.t.* put (up) *or* make *or* fix there. **2.** *v.i.* (*coll.*) ***da hat der Hund hingemacht,*** the dog has made a *or* done its mess (*used only of animals and small children*). **–metzeln, –morden,** *v.t.* slaughter, massacre, butcher. **–nehmen,** *irr.v.t.* take, accept; ***als selbstverständlich –,*** take for granted, submit to, bear, suffer, put up with. **–neigen,** *v.i., v.r.* incline *or* bend *or* lean towards; (*fig. v.r. only*) incline *or* tend *or* gravitate towards.

hinnen ['hɪnən], *adv.* (*only in*) ***von –,*** away from here, from hence; ***von – scheiden,*** depart this life.

hin|opfern, *v.t.* sacrifice. **–passen,** *v.i.* fit in, suit, be apt *or* suitable *or* appropriate; ***nicht –,*** be out of place *or* inappropriate. **–pflanzen,** *v.t., v.r.* place *or* plant (o.s.) there. **–raffen,** *v.t.* (*of death*) carry off. **–reichen,** **1.** *v.t. See* **–langen. 2.** *v.i.* suffice, be sufficient, (*coll.*) do. **–reichend,** *adj.* sufficient, adequate, enough, ample.

Hinreise ['hɪnraɪzə], *f.* outward journey; ***Hin- und Rückreise,*** the double journey, outward and return journey, journey there and back. **hinreisen,** *v.i.* (*aux.* s.) go *or* travel there.

hin|reißen, *irr.v.t.* carry along *or* away *or* off; (*fig.*)

thrill, enrapture, captivate, fascinate, delight, charm, transport; (*fig.*) *sich – lassen,* be carried away (*von,* by), surrender, give way (to); *ihn – zu,* move *or* drive him to. **–reißend,** *adj.* ravishing, enchanting, thrilling, breath-taking. **–richten,** *v.t.* execute, put to death. **Hinrichtung,** *f.* execution.

hinscheiden ['hɪnʃaɪdən], *irr.v.i.* (*aux.* s.) depart this life, pass away; *der* (*die*) *Hingeschiedene,* the deceased. **Hinscheiden,** *n.* death, decease, passing. **Hinschied,** *m.* (*Swiss*) *see* **Hinscheiden.**

hin|schlachten, *v.t. See* **–metzeln. –schlagen,** *irr.v.i.* 1. (*aux.* s.) fall down heavily; (*coll.*) *lang –,* fall flat; (*coll.*) *da schlag einer lang hin!* blow me down! (you could) knock me down with a feather! 2. (*aux.* h.) hit *or* strike out. **–schleppen,** *v.t.* drag along *or* away, (*fig.*) drag out *or* on (and on). **–schmachten,** *v.i.* (*aux.* s.) languish on *or* away; linger on. **–schmeißen,** *irr.v.t.* (*coll.*) throw *or* fling down, (*coll.*) chuck it. **–schmieren,** *v.t.* scribble, scrawl; daub. **–schreiben,** *irr.v.t.* write *or* jot down, make a note of. **–schwinden,** *irr.v.i.* (*aux.* s.) pass away, vanish, dwindle. **–sehen,** *irr.v.i.* look towards *or* at, watch; *ohne hinzusehen,* without looking. **–setzen, 1.** *v.t.* set *or* put down. **2.** *v.r.* seat o.s., sit down, take a seat.

Hinsicht ['hɪnzɪçt], *f. in – auf* (*Acc.*), *see* **hinsichtlich**; *in mancher* or *vieler –* or *in vielen –en,* in many respects; *in gewisser –,* in a sense *or* way; *in dieser –,* in this respect *or* regard, on this score *or* point. **hinsichtlich,** *prep.* (*Gen.*) with regard *or* reference *or* in regard to, in respect of, in view of, with a view to, regarding, concerning, as *or* relating to, touching.

hin|siechen, *v.i.* go into a decline, waste away; pine away. **–sinken,** *irr.v.i.* (*aux.* s.) sink *or* fall down; collapse, swoon, faint; *tot –,* fall *or* drop down dead. **–sprechen,** *irr.v.t. nur so –,* say casually; *vor sich –,* say to o.s. **–stellen,** *v.t.* put *or* place (down); (*fig.*) set down *or* forth, make out to be, represent. **–streben,** *v.i.* strive (*nach,* for *or* after), (*fig.*) tend (towards). **–strecken, 1.** *v.t.* hold *or* stretch *or* reach out (*hand etc.*) (*Dat.,* to); knock down, lay low. **2.** *v.r.* lie down *or* stretch out at full length. **–strömen,** *v.i.* (*aux.* s.) pour *or* stream *or* flock *or* throng there. **–stürzen,** *v.i.* (*aux.* s.) fall headlong, tumble down; rush forward.

hintansetzen [hɪnt'anzɛtsən], *v.t.* treat slightingly, slight, set aside, ignore, disregard, neglect. **Hintansetzung,** *f.* neglect, disregard; slight; *mit* or *unter –* (*Gen.*), disregarding, regardless of, without regard to. **hintan|stellen,** *v.t. See* **–setzen. Hintan|stellung,** *f. See* **–setzung.**

hinten ['hɪntən], *adv.* behind; in the rear *or* background, at the back, at the end; (*Naut.*) aft; *von –,* from behind; *von – angreifen,* attack in the rear; *– anfügen,* add, append, annex; *– ausschlagen,* kick (*of horse*), (*fig.*) lash out, kick up one's heels; *sich – anstellen,* queue up, join the queue, wait one's turn; *– herum,* from behind *or* the rear; (*fig.*) surreptitiously, (*coll.*) on the quiet; (*nach*) *– hinaus wohnen,* live at the back of the house; *es hieß Herr B. – und vorn,* it was always Mr. B. here, Mr. B. there, Mr. B. everywhere; *ich habe doch – keine Augen,* I haven't eyes in the back of my head. **hinten|drein, –nach,** *adv.* after, afterwards, after the event; behind, in the rear; as an afterthought; last of all. **–über,** *adv.* (leaning) backwards; upside down.

hinter ['hɪntər], *prep., sep. pref.* (*with more or less literal meanings*) *and insep. pref.* (*with figurative meanings*) (*N.B. In the main the former are excluded from the list below*) (*place*) behind, (*time*) after; *ich habe es – mir,* I'm done *or* finished *or* (*coll.*) through with it; I have got over it; *– dem Berge halten,* keep (one's thoughts) to o.s., dissemble; *er brachte die Strecke in kurzer Zeit – sich,* he covered the distance in a short time; *– ihm her sein* or *hergehen,* be on his heels, (*fig.*) be constantly pestering him; *– eine S. kommen,* find a th. out, discover a th.; *ihn – sich lassen,* leave him behind, (*Spt.*) out-pace *or* out-distance him; *–s Licht führen,* dupe, deceive, take in; *sich – die Arbeit machen,* set to work with a will, get down to work, (*coll.*) tackle the job; *ich werde es mir – die Ohren schreiben,* I shall take good care to remember it, I shall certainly keep it in mind; (*coll.*) *er hat es faustdick – den Ohren,* there are no flies on him; *ihm – die Schliche kommen,* be up to his tricks *or* wiles; *– sich sehen,* look back; *er steckt – der S.,* he is at the bottom of it; *es steckt etwas – der S.,* there is more to it than meets the eye; *er steckt sich – mich,* he shelters behind me *or* uses me as his mouthpiece; *– einer S. stehen,* support *or* back a th.; *er steht – mir zurück,* he is inferior to me *or* does not come up to my level.

Hinter|achsantrieb, *m.* (*Motor.*) rear drive. **–achse,** *f.* rear axle. **–ansicht,** *f.* back-view, (*Archit.*) rear elevation. **hinteraus,** *adv.* (*Naut.*) astern. **Hinter|backe,** *f.* buttock; *pl.* (*vulg.*) bum, arse. **–backenzahn,** *m.* molar, grinder. **–bein,** *n.* hind leg; *sich auf die –e stellen,* stand on one's hind legs, (*of horse*) rear up; (*fig.*) show fight, dig one's heels in. **–bliebenenversorgung,** *f.* dependant's allowance. **–bliebene(r),** *m., f.* bereaved, dependant, survivor.

hinterbringen [hɪntər'brɪŋən], *irr.v.t.* (*insep.*) *ihm etwas –,* inform him of a th. secretly; *er hat es mir hinterbracht,* he has told me confidentially *or* in confidence. **Hinterbringer,** *m.* informer, telltale. **Hinterbringung,** *f.* 1. (secret) information, (confidential) communication; 2. denunciation.

Hinter|darm, *m.* rectum. **–deck,** *n.* (*Naut.*) poop.

hinterdrein [hɪntər'draɪn], *adv. See* **hinterher.**

hintere, *see* **hintere(r), hintere(s).**

hintereinander [hɪntəraɪn'andər], *adv.* one after the other *or* after another, one by one, in series *or* succession, successively; *– gehen,* go in single *or* Indian file; *– hereingehen,* file in; (*Elec.*) *– schalten,* connect in series; *zwei Wochen –,* two weeks running; *– weg,* without stopping to draw breath, uninterruptedly; *fünfmal –,* five times running *or* (*coll.*) in a row. **Hintereinanderschaltung,** *f.* (*Elec.*) series connexion.

hintere(r) ['hɪntərə(r)], *adj.* back, rear, posterior, hind, hinder; *am hinteren Ende,* at the far end. **Hintere(r),** *m.* (*coll.*) behind, bottom, backside, posterior, (*vulg.*) bum, arse. **hintere(s),** *see* **hintere(r).**

Hinter|fuß, *m.* hind foot. **–gaumen,** *m.* soft palate. **–gaumenlaut,** *m.* (*Phonet.*) guttural *or* velar sound. **–gebäude,** *n.* back premises. **–gedanke,** *m.* mental reservation, ulterior motive; *das war vielleicht sein –,* that was perhaps at the back of his mind.

hintergehen [hɪntər'geːən], *irr.v.t.* (*insep.*) deceive, cheat, impose on, dupe, (*coll.*) doublecross. **Hintergehung,** *f.* deception.

Hintergrund ['hɪntərgrunt], *m.* 1. background distance (*landscape, pictures*); (*Theat.*) backcloth, backdrops; 2. *pl.* hidden difficulties, moot *or* tricky points, (*sl.*) snags (*of problems*). **hintergründig,** *adj.* recondite, profound, enigmatic(al), cryptic, impenetrable.

Hinterhalt ['hɪntərhalt], *m.* ambush, trap; *aus dem – überfallen,* ambush; (*fig.*) *im – haben,* have in reserve *or* (*coll.*) up one's sleeve; *ohne –,* candidly, unreservedly, without reserve. **hinterhältig,** *adj. See* **hinterlistig.**

Hinter|hand, *f.* 1. hind quarter (*of a horse*); 2. (*Cards*) youngest hand. **–haupt,** *n. See* **–kopf. –haus,** *n.* rear part of a building, back premises.

hinterher [hɪntər'heːr], *adv.* (*place*) behind, in the rear; (*time*) after(wards), subsequently; when it is *or* was too late. **hinterher|gehen, –kommen,** *irr.v.i.* (*aux.* s.) walk *or* follow behind, bring up the rear.

Hinter|hof, *m.* backyard. **–Indien,** *n.* (*Geog.*) Further India, Indo-China. **–kante,** *f.* (*Av.*) trailing edge. **–kopf,** *m.* back of the head; (*Anat.*) occiput. **–lader,** *m.* breech-loader. **–lage,** *f.* (*Swiss*) deposit, pledge. **–lager,** *n.* (*Mech.*) rear bearing. **–land,** *n.* hinterland.

hinterlassen [hɪntər'lasən], **1.** *irr.v.t.* (*insep.*) leave (behind); leave (*word* or *a message*); leave (in one's will), bequeath; ***kein Testament –,*** leave no will, (*Law*) die intestate. **2.** *adj.* posthumous. **Hinterlassenschaft,** *f.* (testator's) estate.

hinterlastig ['hıntərlastıç], *adj.* (*Av.*) tail-heavy, (*Naut.*) stern-heavy.

hinterlegen [hıntər'le:gən], *v.t.* (*insep.*) deposit, consign, lodge, give in trust (***bei,*** with); ***hinterlegte Gelder,*** deposits. **Hinterleger,** *m.* depositor. **Hinterlegung,** *f.* deposit; deposition.

Hinter|leib, *m.* hind quarters, (*Ent.*) abdomen. **–leiste,** *f. See* **–kante. –list,** *f.* ruse, wile, stratagem, trick, (*coll.*) dodge; cunning, treachery, underhandedness. **hinterlistig,** *adj.* cunning, artful, wily, underhand, deceitful, false, perfidious. **Hinter|mann,** *m.* (*pl.* **-männer**) (*Mil.*) rear-rank man; (*Pol. etc.*) backer, supporter, (*coll.*) cover; endorser (*of cheques*), instigator; (*Cards, coll.*) ***wer ist mein –?*** who plays after me? **–mast,** *m.* mizzen-mast.

Hintern ['hıntərn], *m.* (*coll.*) *see* **Hintere(r).**

Hinter|pforte, *f.* back door, back gate. **–pommern,** *n.* (*Geog.*) Further Pomerania. **–rad,** *n.* back *or* rear wheel. **hinterrücks,** *adv.* from behind, from the back; (*fig.*) treacherously, stealthily, (*coll.*) in the back. **Hinter|saß, –säß,** *m.* **(-(ss)en,** *pl.* **-(ss)en), –sasse,** *m.* **(-n,** *pl.* **-n)** (*Swiss*) copyholder; smallholder, small farmer. **–satz,** *m.* (*Gram.*) apodosis. **–schiff,** *n.* (*Naut.*) stern. **hinter|schlingen,** *v.t.* gobble down, (*coll.*) bolt. **–schlucken,** *v.t.* (*coll.*) *see* **hinunterschlucken. –sinnen,** *irr.v.r.* (*Swiss*) be moody *or* melancholy. **–sinnig,** *adj.* (*Swiss*) brooding, gloomy, melancholy. **Hintersitz,** *m.* back *or* rear seat; pillion.

hinterst ['hıntərst], *sup. adj.* hindmost, last.

Hinter|steven, *m.* (*Naut.*) stern post. **–stück,** *n.* hind *or* back *or* tail piece. **–tau,** *n.* (*Naut.*) stern-fast. **–teil,** *n.* hind part, back part; buttock, crupper (*of horse*), stern (*of a ship*). **–treffen,** *n.* reserve; rearguard; ***ins – kommen,*** be pushed into the background, fall *or* lag behind, take a back seat, get the worst of it.

hintertreiben [hıntər'traıbən], *irr.v.t.* (*insep.*) prevent, frustrate, obstruct, hinder, baffle, thwart. **Hintertreibung,** *f.* frustration, obstruction, prevention, hindrance, thwarting.

Hintertreppe ['hıntərtrɛpə], *f.* backstairs. **Hintertreppen|politik,** *f.* backstairs politics. **–roman,** *m.* cheap thriller, penny dreadful, (*Am.*) dime novel.

Hinter|tür, *f.* back door; escape hatch; (*fig.*) loophole, escape, outlet. **–verdeck,** *n.* (*Naut.*) quarterdeck. **–wäldler,** *m.* backwoodsman, (*Am.*) hillbilly; (*fig. sl.*) fuddy-duddy, square.

hinterwärts ['hıntərvɛrts], *adv.* backwards; behind.

hinterziehen [hıntər'tsi:ən], *v.t.* (*insep.*) evade (*taxes*). **Hinterziehung,** *f.* (tax) evasion.

hin|träumen, *v.i.* ***vor sich –,*** be day-dreaming, be lost in thought. **–treten,** *irr.v.i.* (*aux.* s.) step up (***vor*** (*Acc.*), to), (take one's) stand (before). **–tun,** *irr.v.t.* (*coll.*) put, place; ***wo soll ich es –?*** where shall I put it? what shall I do with it?

hinüber [hı'ny:bər], *adv., sep. pref.* over there, across, beyond, to the other side; (*coll.*) dead; spoilt, no good, broken, worn-out; ***da –,*** over there, that way; ***er ist –,*** it's all over with him; ***die Vase ist –,*** the vase is broken; ***das Kleid ist –,*** the dress is worn out, (*sl.*) this dress has had it.

hinüber|bringen, *irr.v.t.* (*sep.*) take *or* bring across; (*Math.*) transpose. **–gehen,** *irr.v.i.* (*aux.* s.) go *or* walk over *or* across; (*fig.*) die, pass over *or* away; – ***über*** (*Acc.*), cross. **–kommen,** *irr.v.i.* (*aux.* s.) get over *or* across. **–wechseln,** *v.i.* move *or* go *or* change *or* shift *or* switch over.

hinunter [hı'nuntər], *adv., sep. pref.* down (there), downwards; ***die Treppe –,*** down the stairs, downstairs.

hinunter|blicken, *v.i. See* **–sehen. –führen, 1.** *v.t.* lead *or* take down. **2.** *v.i.* lead *or* run down. **–gehen,** *irr.v.i.* go *or* walk down. **–schauen,** *v.i.,* **–sehen,** *irr.v.i.* look down (***auf*** (*Acc.*), (up)on). **–stürzen, 1.** *v.i.* rush *or* fly down (*stairs etc.*); fall, tumble *or* crash down. **2.** *v.t.* gulp (down), toss off (*a drink*). **–würgen,** *v.t.* gulp *or* choke down.

Hinweg ['hınve:k], *m.* outward journey, way there.

hinweg [hın'vɛk], *adv., sep. pref.* away, off; – ***mit euch!*** be off! begone!

hinweg|bringen, *irr.v.t.* – ***über*** (*Acc.*), get *or* see *or* tide over (*troubles etc.*). **–gehen,** *irr.v.i.* (*aux.* s.) go away; (*fig.*) – ***über*** (*Acc.*), ignore, overlook, (*coll.*) skip; pass off with a shrug *or* laugh, shrug *or* laugh off. **–kommen,** *irr.v.i.* (*aux.* s.) – ***über*** (*Acc.*), get over (*also fig.*). **–raffen,** *v.t.* snatch away. **–sehen,** *irr.v.i.* look away; – ***über*** (*Acc.*), (manage to) see over (*an obstacle*); (*fig.*) take no notice of, overlook, shut one's eyes to. **–setzen,** *v.r.* (***über*** (*Acc.*)) disregard, ignore; override, dismiss, make light of, brush aside; *see also* **–gehen. –täuschen,** *v.t.* – ***über*** (*Acc.*), obscure (*the fact etc.*), delude, blind (*a p. to the fact*).

Hinweis ['hınvaıs], *m.* **(-es,** *pl.* **-e)** indication (***auf*** (*Acc.*), of), (*coll.*) pointer (to); comment, remark, notice, instruction, advice; reference, allusion (to), hint (at); ***unter – auf,*** referring to, in *or* with reference to.

hinweisen ['hınvaızən], **1.** *irr.v.i.* (***auf*** (*Acc.*)) point to *or* towards *or* at, indicate; (*fig.*) point out, indicate, refer *or* allude to. **2.** *irr.v.t.* draw *or* call (*a p.'s*) attention to, refer (*a p.*) to, point out to (*a p.*). **hinweisend,** *adj.* (*Gram.*) ***–es Fürwort,*** demonstrative pronoun. **Hinweisung,** *f. See* **Hinweis.**

hin|wenden, *irr.v.t., v.r.* turn (to(wards)). **–werfen,** *irr.v.t.* throw *or* fling to *or* down; scribble *or* jot down, dash off (hurriedly *or* with a few strokes), drop (*a word*) casually, make (*a remark*) in passing; ***hingeworfene Worte,*** casual *or* stray remarks.

hinwiederum [hın'vi:dərum], *adv.* again, once more; on the other hand, in return.

hinwirken ['hınvırkən], *v.i.* – ***auf*** (*Acc.*), use one's influence to, work towards.

Hinz [hınts], *m.* – ***und Kunz,*** Tom, Dick and Harry.

hin|zählen, *v.t.* count out. **–zeigen,** *v.i. See* **–weisen, 1. –ziehen, 1.** *irr.v.t.* draw along, extend, spread, stretch out; draw to(wards), attract, (*fig.*) delay, protract, (*coll.*) drag out; ***sich hingezogen fühlen,*** be *or* feel attracted *or* drawn (***zu,*** to). **2.** *irr.v.i.* (*aux.* s.) move off *or* away; move to; (*fig.*) drag on, go on and on.

hinzielen ['hıntsi:lən], *v.i.* (***auf*** (*Acc.*)) (*of a p.*) aim at, have in view, be out for; (*of a th.*) tend to, be intended for.

hinzu [hın'tsu:], *adv., sep. pref.* (*movement into the neighbourhood of or as an addition to s.th.*) to, towards, near; in addition, besides, moreover, (*coll.*) into the bargain.

hinzufügen [hın'tsu:fy:gən], *v.t.* add, append, attach, annex, enclose. **Hinzufügung,** *f.* addition; (*Gram.*) apposition. **hinzu|kommen,** *irr.v.i.* (*aux.* s.) be added, come up to; ***es kommt noch –, daß,*** add to this, that; what is more. **–kommend,** *adj.* additional, accessory, further, adventitious. **–nehmen,** *irr.v.t.* add, include. **Hinzunahme,** *f.* addition, inclusion. **hinzu|rechnen, –setzen,** *v.t. See* **–nehmen. –treten,** *irr.v.i.* (*aux.* s.) join (*others already there*); supervene; *see also* **–kommen. –wählen,** *v.t.* co-opt. **–zählen,** *v.t.* reckon in *or* count in (***zu,*** with). **–ziehen,** *irr.v.t.* take into consultation, call in (*a doctor*). **Hinzuziehung,** *f.* consultation; inclusion.

Hiob ['hi:ɔp], *m.* (*B.*) Job. **Hiobs|bote,** *m.* bearer of bad news. **–botschaft,** *f.* bad news, evil tidings. **–geduld,** *f.* patience of Job.

Hippe ['hıpə], *f.* 1. sickle, hedging *or* pruning knife, billhook, scythe; 2. (*dial.*) bread roll, croissant; 3. (*dial.*) goat.

Hippursäure [hı'pu:rzɔyrə], *f.* hippuric acid.

Hirn [hırn], *n.* **(-(e)s,** *pl.* **-e)** brain; brains, intellect; (*Cul.*) brains, *see* **Gehirn.**

Hirn|anhang, *m.* pituitary gland. **–bohrer,** *m.* (*Surg.*) trepan. **–deckel,** *m.* cranium. **–erschütterung,** *f.* concussion of the brain. **–falte,** *f.*

cephalic *or* cerebral lobe. **-geburt,** *f.*, **-gespinst,** *n.* (idle) fancy, whim, chimera, phantom; bog(e)y. **-haut,** *f.* meninges; ***die obere (untere)* -,** the dura (pia) mater. **-hautentzündung,** *f.* meningitis. **-holz,** *n.* cross-cut timber. **-kammer,** *f.* brain-cell, cerebral ventricle. **-kasten,** *m.* (*coll.*) brain-box, pate. **-lappen,** *m.* *See* **-falte.**

hirnlos ['hɪrnlo:s], *adj.* brainless, empty-headed. **Hirnlosigkeit,** *f.* empty-headedness.

Hirn|runde, *f.* cerebral cortex. **-säge,** *f.* cross-cut saw. **-schädel,** *m.* skull, cranium. **-schädelfuge,** *f.* suture. **-schädelhaut,** *f.* pericranium. **-schädelnaht,** *f.* *See* **-schädelfuge. -schale,** *f.* skull, cranium. **-schlag,** *m.* apoplectic fit. **-schnitt,** *m.* cross-section (*timber*). **-teil,** *n.* brain substance. **hirnverbrannt,** *adj.* (*coll.*) mad, crazy, crack-brained, (*coll.*) cracked, crack-pot. **Hirn|-verletzung,** *f.* contusion of the brain. **-windung,** *f.* cerebral convolution.

Hirsch [hɪrʃ], *m.* (**-es,** *pl.* **-e**) stag, hart; (red) deer; ***der – schreit*** or ***röhrt,*** the stag bellows.

Hirsch|antilope, *f.* *See* **-ziege. -bock,** *m.* stag, buck. **-braten,** *m.* venison. **-brunft, -brunst,** *f.* rutting (of deer). **-dorn,** *m.* (*Bot.*) buckthorn (*Rhamnus catharticus*). **-fänger,** *m.* hunting-knife, bowie knife. **-fleisch,** *n.* venison. **-geweih,** *n.* antlers. **-horn,** *n.* hartshorn. **-hornsalz,** *n.* carbonate of ammonia. **-käfer,** *m.* (*Ent.*) stag-beetle (*Lucanidae*). **-kalb,** *n.* fawn. **-keule,** *f.* haunch of venison. **-kuh,** *f.* hind, doe. **-leder,** *n.* buckskin, doeskin, deerskin. **hirschledern,** *adj.* deerskin, buckskin, doeskin. **Hirsch|sprung,** *m.* capriole (*haute école*). **-wurz,** *f.* (*Bot.*) mountain parsley (*Peucedanum cervaria*). **-ziege,** *f.* (*Zool.*) sasin, black buck, Indian gazelle (*Antilope cervicapra*). **-ziemer,** *m.* saddle of venison.

Hirse ['hɪrzə], *f.* millet. **Hirse|brei,** *m.* millet gruel. **-korn,** *n.* millet seed; stye (*on the eye*). **Hirse(n)-fieber,** *n.* miliary fever.

Hirt [hɪrt], *m.* (**-en,** *pl.* **-en**), (*Poet.*) **Hirte,** *m.* (**-n,** *pl.* **-n**) herdsman, shepherd; ***der Herr ist mein -e,*** the Lord is my shepherd; ***ich bin der gute -e,*** I am the Good Shepherd; ***wie der – so die Herde,*** like master like man. **hirten,** *v.i.* (*Swiss*) tend flocks.

Hirten|amt, *n.* pastorate. **-brief,** *m.* (bishop's) pastoral letter. **-dichtung,** *f.* pastoral *or* bucolic poetry. **-flöte,** *f.* Pan's pipe. **-gedicht,** *n.* pastoral poem, bucolic eclogue. **-gott,** *m.* Pan. **-hund,** *m.* sheep-dog. **-junge, -knabe,** *m.* shepherd boy. **-leben,** *n.* pastoral life, idyllic existence. **-lied,** *n.* pastoral song. **-mädchen,** *n.* shepherdess. **-pfeife,** *f.*, **-rohr,** *n.* *See* **-flöte. -spiel,** *n.* pastoral (play). **-stab,** *m.* shepherd's staff *or* crook; (*Eccl.*) (bishop's) crozier. **-tasche,** *f.*, **-täschel,** *n.* (*Bot.*) shepherd's purse (*Capsella bursa-pastoris*). **-volk,** *n.* pastoral *or* nomadic tribes.

Hirtin ['hɪrtɪn], *f.* shepherdess.

His [hɪs], *n.* (*Mus.*) B sharp.

Hisse ['hɪsə], *f.* pulley, tackle. **hissen,** *v.t.* hoist, set (*sail*). **Hissetau, Hißtau,** *n.* halyard.

hist! [hɪst], *int.* left! (*call to horse*); ***der eine will –, der andere hott,*** one pulls one way, the other another.

Histörchen [hɪs'tø:rçən], *n.* (**-s,** *pl.* **-**) funny story, anecdote.

Historie [hɪs'to:riə], *f.* history; (*obs.*) story, narrative. **Historienmalerei,** *f.* historical painting. **Historiker,** *m.* historian. **historisch,** *adj.* historic(al).

Hitsche ['hɪtʃə], *f.* (*dial.*) footstool; small sledge.

Hitz|ausschlag, *m.* heat-rash. **-bläschen,** *n.*, **-blatter,** *f.* heat-pimple.

Hitze ['hɪtsə], *f.* heat; ardour, fervour, passion; ***in der ersten –,*** in the first flush (of enthusiasm); ***in der – des Gefechts,*** in the heat of the moment; ***in – geraten,*** fly into a passion. **hitzebeständig,** *adj.* heat-proof, heat-resisting. **Hitzeeinheit,** *f.* unit of heat. **hitzeempfindlich,** *adj.* sensitive to heat. **Hitzeferien,** *f.pl.* holiday from school during heat wave. **hitzefrei,** *adj.* no school on account of heat. **Hitze|grad,** *m.* degree *or* intensity of heat. **-(grad)messer,** *m.* pyrometer. **-welle,** *f.* heat-wave, hot spell.

hitzig ['hɪtsɪç], *adj.* hot; (*fig.*) fiery, ardent, fervent, vehement, violent, hot-blooded, passionate; hot-headed, rash, hasty, hot-tempered, irascible, choleric; ***-es Fieber,*** high fever; ***-er Kopf,*** excitable fellow; ***-e Worte,*** heated words. **Hitzigkeit,** *f.* heat, rut; ardour, passion, temper, vehemence.

Hitzkopf ['hɪtskɔpf], *m.* hothead. **hitzköpfig,** *adj.* hot-headed. **Hitz|pickel,** *m.pl.*, **-pocken,** *f.pl.* heat rash, prickly heat. **-schlag,** *m.* heat-stroke.

hob [ho:p], **höbe** ['hø:bə], *see* **heben.**

Hobel ['ho:bəl], *m.* plane. **Hobel|bank,** *f.* joiner's *or* carpenter's bench. **-eisen,** *n.* plane-iron. **-maschine,** *f.* planing machine. **hobeln,** *v.t.* plane, smooth, surface. **Hobelspäne,** *m.pl.* shavings.

Hoboe [ho'bo:ə], *f.* (*obs.*) hautboy. **Hoboist** [-'ɪst], *m.* (**-en,** *pl.* **-en**) oboe-player.

hoch [ho:x], **1.** *adj.* (*when followed by* **e** *of the inflected cases* ch *becomes* h, *as*: ***hoher, hohe, hohes,*** *or* ***der, die, das Hohe***; *comp.* ***höher***; *sup.* ***höchst***) high; tall, lofty; noble, sublime; proud; expensive, dear; deep; important, great; ***das Hohe,*** the sublime; ***der hohe Adel,*** the peerage, the nobility; ***hohes Alter,*** advanced *or* old age; ***von hohem Ansehen,*** of high standing; ***ein hohes Ansehen genießen,*** be highly esteemed, enjoy a high reputation; ***hoher Baß,*** bass-baritone; ***hohe Blüte,*** full bloom; ***in hoher Blüte stehen,*** be flourishing, be at the height of (its) prosperity; ***die Dichtung stand in hoher Blüte,*** it was a golden age of poetry; (*coll.*) ***in hohem Bogen hinausfliegen,*** be thrown *or* flung out on one's ear; ***hohe Ehre,*** great honour; ***in hoher Fahrt,*** at top *or* full speed; ***hohe Farbe,*** bright colour; ***ein hoher Fünfziger,*** a man well on in the fifties; ***hoher Genuß,*** great enjoyment; ***hoher Gewinn,*** big prize (*in a lottery*); ***hohe Herrschaften,*** people of high rank; ***hohe Jagd,*** deer stalking, hunting large game; ***– an Jahren,*** advanced in years; (*coll.*) ***auf die hohe Kante legen,*** put aside, put on one side, put by (for a rainy day); ***ein hohes Lied singen auf*** (*Acc.*), sing the praises of; ***in hohem Maße,*** in a high degree, highly, largely; ***die Hohe Messe,*** high mass; ***eine hohe Meinung haben von,*** think highly of, have a high opinion of; ***hohes Neujahr,*** feast of Epiphany; ***– und niedrig,*** rich and poor; ***– oben im Norden, im hohen Norden,*** in the far north; ***die hohe Obrigkeit,*** the powers that be, the authorities; ***hoher Offizier,*** high-ranking officer; ***die Hohe Pforte,*** the Sublime Porte; ***die hohe Schule,*** haute école, equestrian gymnastics, advanced horsemanship; ***hohe See,*** open sea, the high seas; ***hoher Sinn,*** nobility of mind; ***bei hoher Strafe,*** under a heavy penalty; ***hohe Summe,*** large sum (of money); ***– am Tage, hoher Tag,*** broad daylight; (*sl.*) ***hohes Tier,*** big shot *or* bug; ***die hohe Woche,*** Holy Week; ***hohe Worte machen,*** make fine phrases.

2. *adv.* highly; (*Math.*) (raised) to the power of; ***2 hoch 3 gleicht 8,*** 2 to the power of 3 *or* 2 cubed equals 8; ***– anrechnen,*** value greatly, give full credit for; ***– aufhorchen,*** prick up one's ears; ***der Rhein geht –,*** the Rhine runs high; ***zu – gegriffen sein,*** be set *or* fixed too high; ***– gewinnen,*** win by a wide margin; ***Hände –!*** hands up! ***es geht – her,*** there is great excitement, things are pretty lively; ***– hinauswollen,*** be (over)ambitious; ***wenn es – kommt,*** at (the) most, at best; ***– lebe der König!*** long live the king! ***Kopf –!*** chin up! cheer up! never say die! ***drei Mann –,*** three men deep; ***– spielen,*** play for high stakes; ***– zu stehen kommen,*** cost dear, come expensive; ***das ist mir zu –,*** that is beyond me, that's above my head; ***den Kopf – tragen,*** hold one's head high; ***– verlieren,*** lose heavily; ***– und heilig versprechen,*** swear by all that's holy; ***zwei Treppen – wohnen,*** live two floors up, live on the second floor.

Hoch, *n.* **1.** cheer; toast; ***ein dreifaches – für,*** three cheers for; **2.** (*Meteor.*) anticyclone, high (pressure).

hoch|achtbar, *adj.* most honourable *or* estimable.

-achten, *v.t.* respect deeply, esteem highly. **Hochachtung,** *f.* (high) esteem, (deep) respect, regard, admiration, reverence; ***mit vorzüglicher –,*** yours respectfully *or* truly *or* faithfully (*at the end of a letter*); ***bei aller –,*** with all respect (***vor*** (*Dat.*), to); ***– zollen,*** pay respect (*Dat.*, to). **hochachtungsvoll,** *adv.* yours respectfully *or* truly *or* faithfully.

Hoch|altar, *m.* high altar. **-amt,** *n.* high mass. **-angriff,** *m.* (*Av.*) high-level attack. **hochansehnlich,** *adj.* *See* **-achtbar. Hochantenne,** *f.* (*Rad.*) outside aerial *or* (*Am.*) antenna. **hochaufgeschossen,** *adj.* lanky. **Hoch|aufschlag,** *m.* (*Tenn.*) overhand service. **-bahn,** *f.* overhead railway, high-level railway. **-bau,** *m.* superstructure; building construction (*as opp. to excavation*); ***Hoch- und Tiefbau,*** underground and surface engineering. **hoch|begabt,** *adj.* highly gifted, talented. **-bejahrt,** *adj.* *See* **-betagt. -berühmt,** *adj.* very famous, celebrated. **-betagt,** *adj.* aged, advanced in years. **Hochbetrieb,** *m.* intense *or* feverish activity, hustle, bustle; rush *or* peak hours (*of traffic, business etc.*), high season (*at resorts*). **hoch|bezahlt,** *adj.* highly paid. **-bringen,** *irr.v.t.* lift *or* raise (up), (*fig.*) raise, develop, bring to fruition. **-brisant,** *adj.* highly explosive. **Hoch|-burg,** *f.* (*fig.*) stronghold. **-decker,** *m.* (*Av.*) high-wing monoplane. **hochdeutsch,** *adj.* High German, standard German. **Hoch|druck,** *m.* 1. high pressure; ***mit – arbeiten,*** work energetically *or* at high pressure; 2. (*Typ.*) relief-printing. **-druckgebiet,** *n.* (*Meteor.*) high(-pressure area). **-ebene,** *f.* tableland, plateau. **hoch|edelgeboren,** *adj.* high-born; honourable (*obs. title*). **-elegant,** *adj.* very fashionable *or* stylish. **-empfindlich,** *adj.* (*Phot.*) highly sensitive, (*fig.*) hypersensitive. **-erfreut,** *adj.* highly delighted, overjoyed.

hoch|fahren, *irr.v.i.* (*aux.* s.) flare up, start up (suddenly). **-fahrend,** *adj.* haughty, arrogant, high-handed. **-farbig,** *adj.* highly coloured. **-fein,** *adj.* super-fine, exquisite, choice. **-fliegen,** *irr.v.i.* (*aux.* s.) soar (up), rise steeply, (*Av.*) zoom. **-fliegend,** *adj.* soaring, lofty, ambitious, (*coll.*) high-flying; exaggerated, high-flown. **Hoch|flut,** *f.* high tide, (*fig.*) floodtide. **-frequenz,** *f.* high *or* radio frequency. **-gebirge,** *n.* high mountain-chain. **-gebirgspflanze,** *f.* alpine plant. **hoch|geboren,** *adj.* high-born; (*as title*) Right Honourable. **-geehrt,** *adj.* highly honoured, highly respected; ***-er Herr,*** (Dear) Sir (*in letter*). **Hochgefühl,** *n.* exultation, elation.

hoch|gehen, *irr.v.i.* rise (*as curtain, prices etc.*), run high (*as sea*), soar, mount; fly into a *or* lose one's temper, (*sl.*) blow one's top. **-gehend,** *adj.* high (*of waves*), heavy (*sea*). **-gelehrt,** *adj.* very learned, erudite. **-gemut,** *adj.* high-spirited. **Hoch|genuß,** *m.* rapture, ecstasy, delight; luxury, treat. **-gericht,** *n.* supreme penal court; place of execution, gallows. **-gesang,** *m.* hymn, anthem. **hoch|geschätzt,** *adj.* (*of a p.*) highly esteemed, (*of a th.*) high appreciated. **-geschlossen,** *adj.* high-necked (*dress*). **-geschürzt,** *adj.* with skirts tucked up, (*fig.*) free-and-easy, sportive. **-gesinnt,** *adj.* high-minded, noble. **-gespannt,** *adj.* at high tension, (*of a p.*) highly strung; (*fig.*) exaggerated, high (*expectations etc.*). **-gestellt,** *adj.* high-ranking. **-gewachsen,** *adj.* tall, lanky. **-gezüchtet,** *adj.* (*Motor.*) high-compression. **Hochglanz,** *m.* lustre, high-gloss, brilliance, polish. **hoch|gradig,** *adj.* to *or* in a high degree, extreme, intense, high-grade, high quality.

hochhalten ['ho:xhaltən], *irr.v.t.* (*sep.*) hold up; (*fig.*) esteem *or* value highly, think highly of; (*Comm.*) peg (*prices*); ***sein Andenken –,*** cherish his memory. **Hochhaus,** *n.* sky-scraper. **hoch|-herzig,** *adj.* high-minded, noble, magnanimous. **-kant(ig),** *adj.* on end *or* edge, edgewise; ***– stellen,*** set (up) on end, (*coll.*) up-end. **-klappen,** *v.t.* fold *or* turn up. **-kommen,** *irr.v.i.* (*aux.* s.) get up, get on *or* struggle to one's feet; (*fig.*) make one's way in the world, get on; *see also* **heraufkommen. Hochkonjunktur,** *f.* business prosperity, boom. **hochkonzentriert,** *adj.* highly concentrated. **Hoch|lage,** *f.* high altitude. **-land,** *n.* highland, upland. **-länder,** *m.* highlander. **hochleben,** *v.i.* ***– lassen,*** give three cheers to, toast (*a p.*). **Hoch|leistung,** *f.* heavy duty, high capacity. **-leitung,** *f.* overhead line *or* wire.

höchlich ['hø:çlıç], *adv.* highly, greatly, exceedingly, grievously, mightily.

Hochmeister ['ho:xmaıstər], *m.* Grand Master. **hochmolekular,** *adj.* (*Chem.*) of high molecular weight. **Hochmut,** *m.* pride, superciliousness, arrogance, haughtiness; (*Prov.*) ***– kommt vor dem Fall,*** pride comes before a fall. **hochmütig,** *adj.* proud, arrogant, haughty, supercilious. **Hochmutsteufel,** *m.* demon of pride. **hoch|näsig,** *adj.* (*coll.*) stuck-up, snooty, (*sl.*) high-hat. **-nehmen,** *irr.v.t.* 1. lift (up), raise; 2. (*fig.*) tease, (*coll.*) rag, pull (*a p.'s*) leg, take (*a p.*) for a ride; take (*a p.*) in. **-notpeinlich,** *adj.* (*obs.*) penal, capital. **Hoch|-ofen,** *m.* blast furnace. **-parterre,** *n.* mezzanine. **hochprozentig,** *adj.* of a high percentage, (*of spirits*) high-proof; (*fig.*) in a large degree. **Hochrad,** *n.* penny-farthing bicycle. **hoch|ragend,** *adj.* towering, soaring, looming. **-rappeln,** *v.r.* struggle to one's feet. **-rot,** *adj.* bright *or* deep red, crimson. **Hoch|ruf,** *m.* cheer; ***sie wurden mit lauten -en begrüßt,*** they were loudly cheered. **hochrund,** *adj.* convex. **Hochsaison,** *f.* height of the season. **hochschätzen,** *v.t.* (*sep.*) esteem highly (*N.B.* ***– schätzen,*** set a high value on, make a high estimate of). **Hochschätzung,** *f.* high esteem. **hochschnellen,** *v.i.* spring, leap, jump *or* bounce up, (*of prices*) jump, rocket.

Hoch|schule, *f.* college, university; ***technische –,*** college of advanced technology, polytechnic; ***– für Landwirtschaft,*** agricultural college; ***– für Musik,*** academy of music; ***pädagogische –,*** teachers' training college. **-schüler,** *m.* university student, undergraduate. **-schulkursus,** *m.* extramural classes. **-schulreife,** *f.* matriculation standard. **-schulwesen,** *n.* university affairs.

hochschwanger ['ho:xʃvaŋər], *adj.* advanced in pregnancy.

Hochsee|fischerei, *f.* deep-sea fishery. **-flotte,** *f.* battle fleet. **-kabel,** *n.* deep-sea cable. **-schlepper,** *m.* ocean-going tug. **hochseetüchtig,** *adj.* sea- *or* ocean-going.

Hoch|silo, *m.* silo. **-sinn,** *n.* high-mindedness. **hochsinnig,** *adj.* high-minded. **Hoch|sommer,** *m.* midsummer. **-spannung,** *f.* high tension *or* voltage. **-spannungsleitung,** *f.* power *or* high-tension cables. **-sprache,** *f.* literary language, standard educated speech. **-sprung,** *m.* (*Spt.*) high-jump.

höchst [hø:çst], **1.** *sup.adj.* (*see* **hoch**) highest, uppermost, topmost; greatest, utmost, maximum, supreme, extreme; ***-e Instanz,*** last resort; ***-e Not,*** direst need, last extremity; ***in -en Tönen,*** in superlatives; ***-e Vollkommenheit,*** the peak of perfection; ***es ist -e Zeit,*** it is high time; ***es in einer S. aufs -e bringen,*** bring a th. to the height of perfection; ***wenn es aufs -e kommt,*** if the worst comes to the worst; ***das Leben ist der Güter -es nicht,*** life is not man's most precious possession (*Schiller*). **2.** *adv.* most, at the most, very, extremely, exceedingly, in the highest degree; ***– gemein,*** grossly vulgar; ***– schädlich,*** highly injurious. **Höchstalter,** *m.* maximum age.

hochstämmig ['ho:xʃtɛmıç], *adj.* (*of trees*) tall, lofty; (*of roses*) standard. **Hoch|stand,** *m.* high-water mark; (*Hunt.*) high stand; (*fig.*) fine condition; prosperity; high level *or* rate (*of prices*). **-stapelei,** *f.* fraud, swindling, embezzlement, confidence trick. **-stapler,** *m.* swindler, imposter, confidence trickster *or* man, (*sl.*) con man.

Höchst|beanspruchung, *f.* maximum stress *or* load. **-belastung,** *f.* maximum *or* (*Elec.*) peak load.

hochstehend ['ho:xʃte:ənt], *adj.* upright, (*Typ.*) superior, (*fig.*) (*of a th.*) superior, high-level, (*of a p.*) distinguished, notable, eminent.

höchst|eigen, *adj.* ***in -er Person,*** in person. **-eigenhändig,** *adj.* with (my, his *etc.*) own hand.

höchstens ['hø:çtəns], *adv.* at (the) most, at the

utmost *or* (*coll.*) outside, at best; (*with numerals*) not exceeding.

Höchst|fahrt, *f.* (*Naut.*) full *or* top speed. **–fall,** *m.* *im –, see* **höchstens. –form,** *f.* (*Spt.*) top form, peak of condition. **–frequenz(welle),** *f.* (*Rad.*) microwave. **–gebot,** *n.* highest bid. **–geschwindigkeit,** *f.* full *or* top *or* maximum speed; *zulässige –*, speed-limit. **–grenze,** *f.* upper limit, ceiling.

Hochstift ['ho:xʃtɪft], *n.* cathedral chapter, bishopric; academy.

Höchst|kommandierende(r), *m.* commander-in-chief. **–leistung,** *f.* (*Mech.*) peak power, maximum efficiency, (*Comm.*) maximum output, (*Spt.*) best performance, record (performance). **–maß,** *n.* maximum. **höchstpersönlich,** *adj.* by myself (himself *etc.*), in person. **Höchstpreis,** *m.* maximum price.

hochstrebend ['ho:xʃtre:bənt], *adj.* aspiring, ambitious; lofty, high-flying (*as plans*).

Höchststand ['hø:çstʃtant], *m.* peak, record level.

hoch|tönend, *adj.* high-sounding, high-flown, bombastic, grandiloquent. **–tönig,** *adj. See* **–näsig, –tönend. Hoch|tour,** *f.* high-altitude climb, alpine tour; (*fig.*) *auf –en,* at high *or* full speed, (*coll.*) in full swing. **–tourist,** *m.* mountaineer, climber, alpinist. **hoch|trabend,** *adj.* bombastic, pompous, high-sounding. **–trächtig, –tragend,** *adj.* great with young (*of animals*). **–treiben,** *irr.v.t.* force up, boost. **–verdient,** *adj.* highly meritorious *or* deserving, most worthy. **–verehrt,** *adj. See* **–geehrt. Hoch|verrat,** *m.* high treason. **–verräter,** *m.* traitor, rebel, treasonable felon. **hoch|verräterisch,** *adj.* treasonable. **–verzinslich,** *adj.* bearing a high rate of interest.

Hoch|wald, *m.* mountain *or* alpine *or* high-altitude forest, tree-covered mountain slope. **–wasser,** *n.* high tide *or* water; floods, flooding. **–wasserstand,** *m.* high-water mark; flood level. **hochwertig,** *adj.* high-grade *or* -quality, first-rate, (*Metall.*) high-tensile, (*Chem.*) of high valency. **Hochwild,** *n.* (red) deer, game. **hoch|winden,** *irr.v.t.* hoist, jack up. **–wohlgeboren,** *adj.* (*in titles, obs.*) *Ew. –,* Right Honourable Sir, Your Honour. **Hochwürden,** *m.* (*in titles*) *Ew. –,* Your Reverence, Reverend Sir. **hochwürdig,** *adj.* (*R.C.*) *das –ste Gut,* the Host. **Hochzahl,** *f.* (*Math.*) exponent.

Hochzeit ['hɔxtsaɪt], *f.* wedding, marriage; (*of birds*) pairing; *– machen* or *halten,* get married, celebrate one's wedding. **Hochzeiter,** *m.* (*dial.*) (bride)-groom. **Hochzeiterin,** *f.* (*dial.*) bride. **hochzeitlich,** *adj.* bridal, nuptial.

Hochzeits|feier(lichkeit), *f.*, **–fest(lichkeit),** *n.* (*f.*) wedding (celebration). **–flug,** *m.* (*Zool.*) nuptial flight. **–gedicht,** *n.* epithalamium. **–geschenk,** *n.* wedding present. **–kleid,** *n.* wedding dress. **–mahl,** *n.* wedding breakfast. **–nacht,** *f.* bridal *or* wedding night. **–reise,** *f.* honeymoon. **–reisende,** *pl.* honeymoon couple. **–tag,** *m.* wedding day; wedding anniversary; (*coll.*) *den – bestimmen,* name the day. **–zug,** *m.* bridal procession.

hochziehen ['ho:xtsi:ən], *irr.v.t.* pull *or* draw up, hoist; hitch up (*trousers etc.*); (*Av.*) zoom.

Hocke ['hɔkə], *f.* heap of sheaves, stook; (*Gymn.*) squatting position, crouch. **hocken, 1.** *v.t.* set up (*sheaves*) in piles *or* stooks. **2.** *v.i.* crouch, squat; *hinter dem Ofen* or *zu Hause –,* hug the fire, be a stay-at-home. **Hocker,** *m.* stool.

Höcker ['hœkər], *m.* protuberance, hump, bump, (*Anat.*) tuberosity, (*Bot.*) tubercle; *einen – haben,* be hunch-backed; (*B.*) *ich will die – eben machen,* I will make the crooked places straight.

Hockergrab ['hɔkərgra:p], *n.* prehistoric grave.

Höcker|hindernis, *n. See* **–sperre. höckerig,** *adj.* knobb(l)y, knotty, lumpy, bumpy, nodulated, gibbous, tuberculate, tuberous; (*of a p.*) hunch-backed. **Höcker|schwan,** *m.* (*Orn.*) mute swan (*Cygnus olor*). **–sperre,** *f.* (*Mil.*) tank obstacle, dragon's teeth. **–tier,** *m.* animal with a hump.

Hode ['ho:də], *f.* (-, *pl.* **-n**) *or m.* (**-n,** *pl.* **-n**), **Hoden,** *m.* testicle. **Hodensack,** *m.* scrotum.

Hof [ho:f], *m.* (**-es,** *pl.* **¨-e**) **1.** (court)yard; farm, country house, manor (house); palace, court; *am* or *bei –e,* at court; *ihr den – machen,* pay (one's) court to her; **2.** ring *or* circle (*under the eyes*), halo, corona, auriole.

Hof|arzt, *m.* court physician. **–bauer,** *m.* peasant proprietor. **–beamte(r),** *m.* court official. **–besitzer,** *m.* estate owner, freeholder. **–brauch,** *m. See* **–gebrauch. –burg,** *f.* Imperial Palace (*in Vienna*). **–dame,** *f.* maid of honour, lady in waiting. **–dichter,** *m.* court poet, poet laureate. **–dienst,** *m.* office at court, (*Hist.*) socage.

höfeln ['hø:fəln], *v.i.* (*Swiss*) (*Dat.*) *see* **hofieren.**

hoffähig ['ho:ffɛ:ɪç], *adj.* presentable at court, (*coll.*) presentable.

Hoffart ['hɔfart], *f.* pride, arrogance, haughtiness. **hoffärtig** [–ɛrtɪç], *adj.* arrogant, haughty.

hoffen ['hɔfən], *v.t., v.i.* (*auf* (*Acc.*)) hope (for), expect, look for, look forward to; *zuversichtlich –,* reckon on, trust in, be confident that; *verzweifelt –,* hope against hope; *ich hoffe es,* I hope so; *ich hoffe es von ihm,* I expect it of him; *ich hoffe nicht, ich will es nicht –,* I hope not; *das Beste –,* hope for the best; *was man hofft, glaubt man gern,* the wish is father to the thought; *der Mensch hofft solange er lebt,* while there is life there is hope; *es ist* or *steht zu –,* it is to be hoped. **Hoffen,** *n.* hope, hoping, expectation; (*Prov.*) *– und Harren macht manchen zum Narren,* he who lives on hope dies of hunger. **hoffentlich,** *adv.* it is to be hoped; (*as a reply*) I *or* let us hope so; *– nicht,* I hope not.

–höffig ['hœfɪç], *adj.suff.* rich in, *e.g. erdölhöffig,* oil-bearing. **höfflich,** *adj.* (*Min.*) rich.

Hoffnung ['hɔfnuŋ], *f.* hope (*auf* (*Acc.*), for *or* of), expectation, anticipation (of); prospect (of); hopefulness, trust; *die – aufgeben,* give up *or* abandon (all) hope; *berechtigte –en haben,* have good hopes; *zu den schönsten –en berechtigen,* justify the fondest hopes; *–en erwecken,* raise hopes (*in* (*Dat.*), in); *guter – sein,* be confident *or* full of hope, be of good cheer; (*of a woman*) be pregnant *or* expectant, (*coll.*) be expecting, be in the family way; *ihm –en machen auf* (*Acc.*), hold out hopes to him of, give him reason to hope for *or* to expect; *sich* (*Dat.*) *–en machen,* be hopeful *or* entertain hopes (that); *noch am Grabe pflanzt der Mensch die – auf,* hope springs eternal in the human breast (*Schiller*); *seine –en setzen auf* (*Acc.*), pin one's hopes on, (*coll.*) bank on; *Kap der Guten –,* Cape of Good Hope.

hoffnungsfreudig ['hɔfnuŋzfrɔydɪç], *adj.* hopeful, optimistic, sanguine. **hoffnungslos,** *adj.* hopeless, desperate; (*pred.*) past all hope. **Hoffnungslosigkeit,** *n.* hopelessness, despair. **Hoffnungs|schimmer, –strahl,** *m.* ray *or* gleam of hope. **hoffnungsvoll,** *adj.* hopeful, full of hope; promising.

Hof|fräulein, *n.* maid of honour. **–gänger,** *m.* (*obs.*) day-labourer. **–gebrauch,** *m.* court etiquette. **–geflügel,** *n.* farmyard poultry. **–gefolge,** *n.* courtiers, retinue. **–gesinde,** *n.* servants of the royal household; farm labourers. **–gut,** *n.* royal domain, demesne. **–haltung,** *f.* royal household, princely suite. **–herr,** *m.* lord of the manor. **–hund,** *m.* watchdog, yard-dog.

hofieren [ho'fi:rən], *v.i.* (*Dat.*) pay court to, flatter, fawn upon.

höfisch ['hø:fɪʃ], *adj.* courtly; *–e Lyrik,* courtly lyric; *–es Epos,* court epic.

Hof|junker, *m.* page, equerry. **–kanzlei,** *f.* court chancellery. **–kapelle,** *f.* **1.** royal chapel; **2.** court musicians. **–kaplan,** *m.* court chaplain. **–kasse,** *f.* prince's privy purse, civil list. **–kavalier,** *m.* courtier, gentleman-in-waiting. **–künste,** *pl. See* **–ränke. –leute,** *pl.* courtiers; (*Hist.*) bondsmen, socagers.

höflich ['hø:flɪç], *adj.* polite, courteous, civil (*gegen,* to); (*Comm.*) *ich teile Ihnen –st mit,* I beg to inform you. **Höflichkeit,** *f.* politeness, courtesy, civility; compliment.

Hoflieferant ['ho:fli:fərant], *m.* purveyor to the royal household.

Höfling ['hø:flɪŋ], *m.* (**-s,** *pl.* **-e**) courtier.

Hof|mann, *m.* courtier; *see* **–leute. –marschall,** *m.* master of ceremonies, (*Eng.*) Lord Chamberlain. **–meister,** *m.* 1. steward, (*Eng.*) Controller of the Royal Household; 2. private tutor. **–meisterei,** *f.* (*coll.*) pedantry. **hofmeistern,** *v.t.* (*coll.*) censure, find fault with. **Hof|narr,** *m.* court jester. **–prediger,** *m. See* **–kaplan. –ränke,** *pl.* court intrigues. **–rat,** *m.* Privy Councillor. **–raum,** *m.* courtyard. **–schranze,** *f.* courtier, flunkey, lickspittle. **–sitte,** *f.* court etiquette. **–staat,** *m.* royal *or* princely household; *see also* **–tracht.**

Höft [hø:ft], *n.* (**-es,** *pl.* **-e**) (*dial.*) foreland, headland; stage.

Hof|tor, *n.* yard-gate, back gate. **–tracht,** *f.* court-dress. **–trauer,** *f.* court-mourning. **–wohnung,** *f.* flat overlooking the courtyard.

hohe ['ho:ə], *see* **hoch.**

Höhe ['hø:ə], *f.* height, altitude, elevation, loftiness; summit, top, high place, hill, mountain; (*fig.*) amount (*of money*), level (*of price*), (*Rad.*) (level of) volume, (*Mus.*) pitch, (*Mus.*) upper register; (*fig.*) degree, extent, magnitude, importance, intensity; ***auf der – sein,*** be at the height of one's powers, be in top form; be up to date *or* to the mark; (*health*) be up to the mark; ***sich nicht auf der – fühlen,*** be off colour, not feel up to the mark; ***auf der – von,*** in the latitude of; (*Naut.*) ***auf der – von Dover,*** off Dover; ***auf gleicher – mit,*** on a level with; ***aus der –,*** from (up) above, from on high, from up aloft; ***in die – fahren,*** start *or* jump up, start *or* jump to one's feet; ***die – gewinnen,*** reach the summit; (*fig.*) ***in – von,*** at the rate of; to the amount *or* (*coll.*) tune of; ***in der –,*** up above *or* aloft, on high; ***in die –,*** up(ward), aloft; ***in die – gehen,*** rise, soar; (*coll.*) blow one's top; ***lichte –,*** headroom, clearance; (*Naut.*) ***die – von einem Kap nehmen,*** weather a cape; ***die – der Sonne nehmen,*** take an observation of the sun's altitude; ***die – des Meeres,*** offing; ***in die – richten,*** raise, set up(right); (*coll.*) ***das ist*** (***doch wirklich***) ***die –,*** that is the (absolute) limit, that beats everything; ***von der –,*** *see* ***aus der –.***

Hoheit ['ho:haɪt], *f.* 1. sublimity, nobility, grandeur, majesty; supreme power, sovereignty; high rank; 2. (*title*) Highness. **Hoheits|abzeichen,** *n.* (*Av.*) national markings. **–bereich,** *m.* jurisdiction. **–gebiet,** *n.* sovereign territory. **–gewässer,** *n.pl.* territorial waters. **–grenze,** *f.* limit of territorial waters. **–recht,** *n.* sovereign right *or* power, sovereignty; official authority; royal privilege *or* prerogative. **hoheitsvoll,** *adj.* majestic, dignified; imperious. **Hoheitszeichen,** *n.* national colours *or* emblem, insignia.

Hohelied [ho:ə'li:t], *n.* (*B.*) the Song of Solomon *or* Song of Songs.

Höhen|abstand, *m.* vertical interval. **–angabe,** *f.* altitude reading. **–anzug,** *m.* high-altitude flying-suit. **–atmer,** *m.* oxygen apparatus. **–darstellung,** *f.* relief (*on maps*). **–festigkeit,** *f.* altitude fitness (*of airmen*). **–flosse,** *f.* (*Av.*) tailplane, stabilizer. **–flug,** *m.* high-altitude flight. **–flugzeug,** *n.* high-altitude aircraft. **–kabine,** *f.* (*Av.*) pressurized cabin. **–karte,** *f.* relief map. **–klima,** *n.* alpine climate. **–krankheit,** *f.* mountain sickness, air sickness. **–kreis,** *m.* parallel of latitude. **–kurort,** *m.* mountain resort. **–lage,** *f.* altitude. **–leitwerk,** *n.* (*Av.*) elevator unit. **–linie,** *f.* contour (line). **–luft,** *f.* mountain air. **–messer,** *m.* (*Artil.*) height finder, (*Av.*) altimeter. **–messung,** *f.* altimetry, hysometry. **–rauch,** *m.* haze; *see* **Herrauch. –rekord,** *m.* altitude record. **–richtfeld,** *n.,* **–richtung,** *f.* (*Artil.*) (angle of) elevation; ***dem Geschütz das*** (or ***die***) ***– geben,*** elevate the gun. **–rücken,** *m.* ridge (of hills), mountain crest *or* chain. **–ruder,** *n.* (*Av.*) elevator, (*Naut.*) hydroplane. **–schichtlinie,** *f. See* **–linie. –schreiber,** *m.* barograph, altigraph. (*registered trade mark*) **–sonne,** *f.* ultraviolet *or* sunray lamp. **–steuer,** *n.* (*Av.*) elevator control. **–strahlen,** *m.pl.* cosmic rays. **–strahlung,** *f.* cosmic radiation. **–verhältnis,** *n.* (*Mus.*) interval. **–zug,** *m. See* **–rücken.**

Hohepriester ['ho:əpri:stər], *m.* (***ein Hoherpriester, des Hohenpriesters, die Hohenpriester, zwei Hohepriester***) high priest. **hohepriesterlich,** *adj.* pontifical. **Hohepriestertum,** *n.* pontificate.

Höhepunkt ['hø:əpuŋkt], *m.* (*fig.*) highest *or* critical *or* culminating point, culmination, pinnacle, peak, climax, zenith, acme, summit; (*Astr.*) culmination; highlight, heyday; ***auf dem –,*** at its height.

höher ['hø:ər], *comp.adj. See* **hoch**; higher (***als,*** than), superior (to); ***–er Beruf,*** (learned) profession; ***–e Berufstände,*** professional classes; ***–e Bildung,*** higher education; (*coll.*) ***–er Blödsinn,*** sheer *or* utter nonsense; ***–e Geometrie,*** analytic geometry; ***–e Gewalt,*** act of God; ***–e Instanz,*** higher authority, (*Law*) higher court; ***–e Macht,*** supernatural power; ***–e Mädchenschule,*** secondary *or* high school for girls; ***–er Offizier,*** superior officer; ***–en Orts,*** on higher authority, by authority; ***in –en Regionen schweben,*** live in the clouds; ***–e Schule,*** secondary school, (*Am.*) high school; ***von –er Warte,*** from a sovereign *or* pre-eminent position, from an exalted point of view. **höherwertig,** *adj.* (of) higher quality, of high value, (*Chem.*) of higher valency.

hohl [ho:l], *adj.* hollow, concave; (*fig.*) dull, vain, shallow, empty; (*Med.*) fistulous; ***die –e Hand,*** the hollow of the hand, palm; ***–er Klang,*** dull *or* hollow sound; ***–er Kopf,*** empty head, shallow mind; ***–e See,*** heavy swell; ***–e Seite,*** weak side. **hohl|äugig,** *adj.* hollow-eyed. **–backig,** *adj.* hollow-cheeked. **Hohldrüse,** *f.* (*Med.*) follicle.

Höhle ['hø:lə], *f.* cave, cavern, grotto; den, burrow, lair; cavity, hollow, hole, (*Anat.*) ventricle. **höhlen,** *v.t.* hollow out, excavate. **Höhlen|bewohner,** *m.* cave-dweller, cave-man, troglodyte. **–forscher,** *m.* speleologist, (*coll.*) pot-holer. **–tiere,** *n.pl.* troglodytic animals.

hohlerhaben ['ho:lˀɛrha:bən], *adj.* concavo-convex. **Hohl|fläche,** *f.* concave surface, concavity. **–gang,** *m.* (*Anat.*) fistula, canal. **hohlgeschliffen,** *adj.* hollow-ground, concave. **Hohl|geschoß,** *n.* shell, hollow projectile. **–geschwür,** *n.* fistula. **–gewinde,** *n.* female thread. **–guß,** *m.* hollow casting. **–kehle,** *f.* hollow, furrow, groove, channel. **hohlköpfig,** *adj.* empty-headed. **Hohl|körper,** *m.* hollow body. **–maß,** *n.* dry measure; cubic measure. **–naht,** *f. See* **–saum. –raum,** *m.* hollow space, cavity, well; lacuna. **–saum,** *m.* hemstitch, drawn-thread work. **–schiene,** *f.* U-shaped rail. **–schliff,** *m.* hollow grinding (*knives, lenses*). **–spiegel,** *m.* concave mirror. **–stab,** *m.* catheter. **–stempel,** *m.* matrix. **–taube,** *f.* (*Orn.*) stock-dove (*Columba oenas*). **–treppe,** *f.* spiral staircase.

Höhlung ['hø:luŋ], *f.* excavation, cavity, hollow; (*Med.*) fistula.

Hohlwalze ['ho:lvaltsə], *f.* hollow cylinder. **hohl|wangig,** *adj. See* **–backig. Hohl|weg,** *m.* gorge, defile, sunken road, narrow pass. **–zahn,** *m.* 1. (*Bot.*) hempnettle (*Galeopsis tetrahit*); 2. milk tooth. **–ziegel,** *m.* gutter-tile. **–zirkel,** *m.* inside callipers.

Hohn [ho:n], *m.* scorn, disdain, derision, mockery; gibe, jeer, sneer, insult; ***ihm zum –e,*** in defiance of him, to spite him; ***ein – auf*** (*Acc.*), a mockery of; ***zum Spott und – werden,*** become an object of derision, become a laughing-stock.

höhnen ['hø:nən], **1.** *v.i.* scoff, jeer, mock, sneer, laugh (***über*** (*Acc.*), at). **2.** *v.t.* deride, treat with scorn.

Hohngelächter ['ho:ngəlɛçtər], *n.* derision, mockery.

höhnisch ['hø:nɪʃ], *adj.* scornful, disdainful, sneering, mocking, sarcastic, derisive.

hohn|lächeln, –lachen, *v.i.* (*sep.*) *see* **höhnen. Hohnrede,** *f.* scornful language, insulting speech. **hohnsprechen,** *v.i.* (*sep.*) (*Dat.*) defy, flout, fly in the face of.

Höker ['hø:kər], *m.* huckster, costermonger, pedlar, hawker. **hökern,** *v.i.* retail (*small provisions*); hawk, huckster.

Hokuspokus [ho:kus'po:kus], *m.* hocus-pocus, mumbo-jumbo.

hold [hɔlt], *adj.* gracious, friendly; pleasing, charming, winsome, lovely; (*pred.*) well-disposed, favourable, propitious (*Dat.*, to); ***–er Friede,*** gentle peace; ***mein –es Mädchen,*** my sweet girl; ***ihm – sein,*** be attached to *or* (*coll.*) sweet on him. **Holde,** *f.* darling, sweetheart.

Holder ['hɔldə], *m.* (*dial.*) *see* **Holunder. Holder|blust,** *m., n. or f.,* **–blüte,** *f.* elder-blossom. **holdern,** *adj.* (of) elder-wood.

holdselig ['hɔltze:lıç], *adj.* gracious, charming, lovely, (*coll.*) sweet. **Holdseligkeit,** *f.* graciousness, charm, loveliness, (*coll.*) sweetness.

holen ['ho:lən], *v.t.* fetch, go *or* come for; get, catch, (*Naut.*) haul; ***Atem –,*** draw breath; ***– lassen,*** send for; ***sich*** (*Dat.*) ***Rat bei ihm –,*** consult him, ask him for advice; ***sich*** (*Dat.*) ***Trost bei ihm –,*** seek comfort from him; ***sich*** (*Dat.*) ***einen Korb –,*** get turned down (flat) (*by a girl*); (*coll.*) ***sich*** (*Dat.*) ***eine Nase –,*** come in for a rebuke; get snubbed; ***sich*** (*Dat.*) ***eine Erkältung –,*** catch a cold; ***hol's*** (***hol dich***) ***der Teufel!*** the devil take it (*or* you)! confound it (*or* you)!

Holk [hɔlk], *m.* (*dial.*) (**-es,** *pl.* **-e**) hulk, boat, barge.

holla! ['hɔla], *int.* halloo! holla! (*coll.*) ***und damit –!*** and there's an end of it!

Holland ['hɔlant], *n.* (*Geog.*) Holland, the Netherlands. **Holländer,** *m.* 1. Dutchman, *pl.* the Dutch (people); 2. (*dial.*) dairy-farmer; 3. (*Paperm.*) pulping machine. **Holländerei** [–'raı], *f.* dairy-farm. **holländern, 1.** *v.t.* pulp (*rags*). **2.** *v.i.* skate in the Dutch way. **holländisch,** *adj.* Dutch.

Holle ['hɔlə], *f.* (*dial.*) comb, wattle, crest.

Hölle ['hœlə], *f.* 1. hell, the infernal regions; ***Himmel und – aufbieten,*** move heaven and earth; ***ihm die – heiß machen,*** give him hell, make it hot for him; ***die – auf Erden,*** hell on earth; ***das Leben zur – machen,*** make life a perfect hell; ***die – war los,*** all hell broke loose; ***in die – kommen, zur – fahren,*** go to hell; 2. (*dial.*) space behind the stove, hot place in a furnace.

Höllen|angst, *f.* ***eine – haben,*** be scared to death, be in a mortal fright. **–brand,** *m.* hell-fire. **–brut,** *f.* infernal crew, scum, wretches, outcasts. **–fahrt,** *f.* (Christ's) descent into hell. **–fürst,** *m.* prince of darkness. **–hund,** *m.* hell-hound, Cerberus. **–lärm,** *m.* infernal noise. **–mächte,** *f.pl.* powers of darkness. **–maschine,** *f.* infernal machine. **–pein, –qual,** *f.* torments of hell; excruciating pain, agony. **–rachen, –schlund,** *m.* jaws of hell, bottomless pit. **–stein,** *m.* lunar caustic, silver nitrate. **–wut,** *f.* fury, satanic rage. **–zwang,** *m.* hell-charm, cabbalistic incantation, book of black magic.

Holler ['hɔlər], *m. See* **Holder.**

höllisch ['hœlıʃ], **1.** *adj.* hellish, infernal; devilish, fiendish; (*coll.*) terrible, awful, dreadful, abominable; ***das –e Feuer,*** the fires of hell; ***–e Qualen,*** torments of hell; (*coll.*) ***–e Angst,*** mortal fear. **2.** *adv.* (*coll.*) dreadfully, awfully; (*coll.*) ***– gescheit,*** devilish(ly) clever.

[1]**Holm** [hɔlm], *m.* (**-(e)s,** *pl.* **-e**) (*dial.*) islet, holm, eyot *or* ait; hill, hillock.

[2]**Holm,** *m.* (**-(e)s,** *pl.* **-e**) cross-beam, transom, spar, (*Av.*) longeron; helm, haft, handle; upright (*of ladder*); shaft (*of oar*); (*Gymn.*) (parallel) bar.

holp(e)rig ['hɔlp(ə)rıç], *adj.* rough, uneven, bumpy; clumsy, stumbling. **holpern,** *v.i.* jolt, stumble.

holter(die)polter ['hɔltər(di)'pɔltər], *adv.* helter-skelter, pell-mell.

Holunder [ho'lundər], *m.* (*Bot.*) elder (*Sambucus canadensis*); ***blauer*** or ***spanischer –,*** lilac. **Holunder|beere,** *f.* elderberry. **–blüte,** *f.* elder-blossom. **–strauch,** *m.* elder-bush. **–wein,** *m.* elderberry wine.

Holz [hɔlts], *n.* (**-es,** *pl.* **¨-er**) 1. wood; timber, (*Am.*) lumber; piece of wood; firewood; ***flüssiges –,*** plastic wood; ***– fällen,*** cut *or* fell timber; ***– hacken,*** chop wood; ***aus demselben – geschnitzt,*** a chip of the old block; (*Prov.*) ***wo man – haut, da fallen Späne,*** from chipping come chips; 2. thicket grove, copse, wood.

Holz|abfall, *m.* waste wood. **–alkohol,** *m.* methyl alcohol, wood spirit. **–anbau,** *m.* afforestation. **–apfel,** *m.* crab-apple. **–arbeiter,** *m.* woodworker. **holzarm,** *adj.* scantily wooded. **Holzart,** *f.* kind *or* species of wood. **holzartig,** *adj.* ligneous; woody. **Holz|bau,** *m.* 1. cultivation of timber; 2. timber-work; 3. wooden building. **–beize,** *f.* wood-stain. **–bildhauer, –bildner,** *m.* wood-carver. **–birne,** *f.* wild pear. **–blasinstrument,** *n.* (*Mus.*) wood-wind instrument. **–bock,** *m.* 1. sawing trestle; 2. (*Ent.*) capricorn-beetle, tick. **–boden,** *m.* 1. wooden floor; wood-loft; 2. soil for timber growing. **–bohrer,** *m.* 1. auger, drill, bit; 2. (*Ent.*) wood-beetle. **–brandmalerei,** *f.* poker-work. **–brei,** *m.* wood-pulp. **–bündel,** *n.* faggot. **–druck,** *m.* (*Typ.*) block-print.

holzen ['hɔltsən], **1.** *v.i.* fell *or* cut *or* gather wood; (*Spt.*) play rough, foul, charge (*in footb.*). **2.** *v.t.* thrash, (*coll.*) pile into. **Holzerei** [–'raı], *f.* (*coll.*) brawl, scrap, rough-house; (*Spt.*) rough *or* foul play.

hölzern ['hœltsərn], *adj.* wooden, (of) wood; (*fig.*) stiff, awkward, clumsy, wooden.

Holz|fäller, *m.* woodcutter, (*Am.*) lumberjack. **–faser,** *f.* wood fibre; grain. **–faserplatte,** *f.* fibre board, hardboard. **–faserstoff,** *m.* cellulose. **–fäule, –fäulnis,** *f.* dry-rot. **–feu(e)rung,** *f.* heating with wood-fires. **holzfrei,** *adj.* (*Paperm.*) wood-free. **Holz|frevel,** *m.* vandalism (*in cutting timber*); infringement of forest laws. **–fuhre,** *f.* carrying *or* conveying wood; cart-load of wood. **–gas,** *n.* producer gas. **–gefälle,** *n.pl.* yield from forests. **–geist,** *m. See* **–alkohol. –gerechtigkeit,** *f.* rights over a wood; free supply of wood (*from forest etc.*). **–gleite,** *f.* timber-shoot. **–hacker,** *m.* woodcutter. **holzhaltig,** *adj.* ligneous. **Holz|hammer,** *m.* mallet. **–handel,** *m.* timber-trade. **–händler,** *m.* timber-merchant, (*Am.*) lumberman. **–hau,** *m.* site of felling. **–hauer,** *m.* woodcutter; (*Am.*) lumberjack. **–hof,** *m.* wood-yard, timber-yard; (*Am.*) lumber-yard.

holzig ['hɔltsıç], *adj.* woody, ligneous, tough as wood.

Holz|klotz, *m.* block of wood, wood(en) block. **–kohle,** *f.* charcoal. **–kopf,** *m.* (*coll.*) blockhead. **–lager,** *n. See* **–hof. –masse,** *f.* wood-pulp. **–nagel,** *m. See* **–pflock. –pantine,** *f.* (*dial.*), **–pantoffel,** *m.* clog. **–papier,** *n.* wood-pulp paper. **–pflaster,** *n.* wood-block *or* parquet flooring. **–pflock,** *m.* peg, dowel. **–platz,** *m. See* **–hof. holzreich,** *adj.* (well-)wooded. **Holz|rost,** *m.* duckboard. **–säure,** *f.* (pyro)ligneous acid. **–scheit,** *n.* billet *or* log of (fire)wood. **–schlag,** *m.* felling area, trees marked for felling. **–schlägel,** *m.* mallet. **–schliff,** *m. See* **–brei. –schneider,** *m.* woodblock engraver. **–schnitt,** *m.* woodcut, wood engraving. **–schnitzer,** *m.* wood-carver. **–schnitzerei,** *f.* wood-carving. **–schraube,** *f.* wood-screw. **–schuh,** *m.* wooden shoe, clog, patten. **–schwamm,** *m.* dry-rot. **–späne,** *m.pl.* shavings. **–splitter,** *m.* splinter (of wood). **–stich,** *m. See* **–schnitt. –stock,** *m.* (*Typ.*) wood-block. **–stoff,** *m.* cellulose, wood pulp. **–stoß,** *m.* wood-pile, stack of wood. **–täf(e)lung,** *f.* wood panelling, wainscot(ing).

Holz|verkleidung, *f.* panelling, revetting; *see* **–täf(e)lung. –verkohlung,** *f.* charcoal burning. **–verschlag,** *m.* crate. **–wand,** *f.* wooden partition *or* wall. **–ware,** *f.* wooden article. **–weg,** *m.* 1. timber track (*for bringing down felled timber*), woodcutter's track; 2. (*fig.*) wrong track *or* tack; (***sehr*** or ***stark***) ***auf dem –e sein,*** be (quite) on the wrong track, be barking up the wrong tree. **–werk,** *n.* woodwork, timbers, framework; wainscoting. **–wolle,** *f.* wood wool, fine shavings. **–wurm,** *m.* wood-worm. **–zapfen,** *m.* plug, bung. **–zeit,** *f.* felling season. **–zellstoff,** *m.* lignocellulose. **–zucker,** *m.* xylose. **–zunder,** *m.* touchwood, tinder, punk.

homerisch [ho'me:rıʃ], *adj.* Homeric.

homogen [homo'ge:n], *adj.* homogeneous, uniform.

homogenisieren [–i'zi:rən], *v.t.* homogenize. **Homogenität** [–i'tɛ:t], *f.* homogeneity.

homolog [homo'lo:k], *adj.* homologous.

homonym [homo'ny:m], *adj.* homonymous. **Homonym,** *n.* **(-s,** *pl.* **-e)** homonym.

Homöopath [homøo'pa:t], *m.* **(-en,** *pl.* **-en)** homoeopath. **homöopathisch,** *adj.* homoeopathic.

Homosexualität [homozɛksuali'tɛ:t], *f.* homosexuality. **homosexuell** [–'ɛl], *adj.* homosexual. **Homosexuelle(r),** *m., f.* homosexual.

honett [hɔ'nɛt], *adj.* respectable, honourable, (*coll.*) decent.

Honig ['ho:nɪç], *m.* honey; ***ausgelassener –, geseimter –,*** liquid *or* strained honey; ***ihm – ums Maul schieren,*** wheedle *or* cajole *or* inveigle him (into doing s.th.), (*coll.*) soft-soap him, butter him up; (*Prov.*) ***– im Munde, Galle im Herzen*** or ***außen – innen Galle,*** honeyed words, hard heart.

Honig|behälter, *m.*, **–behältnis,** *n.* nectary (*of flowers*); honey pot. **–biene,** *f.* honey bee. **–brot,** *n.* gingerbread. **–gefäß,** *n.* honey-pot; nectary. **–kelch,** *m.* nectary. **–kuchen,** *m.* gingerbread. **–magen,** *m.* honey-sac, pollen basket (*of bees*). **–mond,** *m.* honeymoon. **–säure,** *f.* oxymel. **–scheibe,** *f.* honeycomb. **–schleuder,** *f.* honey extractor. **–seim,** *m.* virgin honey. **–stein,** *m.* mellite. **–steinsäure,** *f.* mellitic acid. **honigsüß,** *adj.* sweet as honey, honeyed, mellifluous. **Honig|tau,** *m.* honeydew. **–trank,** *m.* mead. **–wabe,** *f.* honeycomb. **–wasser,** *n.* hydromel. **–wochen,** *f.pl. See* **–mond. –zelle,** *f.* honey-cell; alveolus.

Honneurs [(h)ɔ'nø:rs], *n.pl.* (*Mil.*) ***die – machen,*** salute; do the honours.

Honorar [hono'ra:r], *n.* **(-s,** *pl.* **-e)** fee, remuneration, honorarium, (*to authors*) royalties. **Honorarprofessor,** *m.* titular professor, professor honoris causa.

Honoratioren [honoratsi'o:rən], *pl.* people of rank, dignitaries, notabilities.

honorieren [hono'ri:rən], *v.t.* 1. remunerate, pay (a fee to); 2. (*Comm.*) meet, honour (*a bill*). **Honorierung,** *f.* 1. remuneration, payment; 2. (*Comm.*) payment, acceptance (*of a bill*).

honorig [ho'no:rɪç], *adj.* (*Studs. sl.*) generous, honourable.

Hopfen ['hɔpfən], *m.* (*Bot.*) hop; hops; (*Prov.*) ***an ihm ist – und Malz verloren,*** nothing can be done with him, he's (a) hopeless (case). **Hopfen|bau,** *m.* hop-culture. **–bauer,** *m.* hop-grower. **–ernte,** *f.* hop-picking. **–stange,** *f.* hop-pole; (*fig.*) lanky p.

hopp! [hɔp], *int.* up! jump! jump to it! quick! away! hop it! beat it!

Hoppelpoppel ['hɔpəl'pɔpəl], *n.* egg-flip; scrambled egg dish.

hoppla! ['hɔpla], *int.* mind! steady! (*on stumbling*) clumsy!

hops [hɔps], *adv.* (*sl.*) ***– gehen,*** (*of a th.*) go to pot; (*of a p.*) peg out. **hopsasa!** *int.* (*coll.*) ups-a-daisy!

hopsen ['hɔpsən], *v.i.* (*coll.*) hop, jump, skip. **Hopser,** *m.* hop, jump, skip; (*dance*) hop, jig.

Hörapparat ['hø:rˀapara:t], *m.* hearing aid. **hörbar,** *adj.* audible; ***nicht –,*** inaudible; ***sich – machen,*** make o.s. heard. **Hörbarkeit,** *f.* audibility. **Hör|bericht,** *m.* radio report, running commentary. **–bild,** *n.* sound-picture.

horchen ['hɔrçən], *v.i.* listen (*Dat. or* ***auf*** (*Acc.*), to), (*Poet.*) give ear, hearken (to); eavesdrop. **Horcher,** *m.* listener; eavesdropper; (*Prov.*) ***– an der Wand hört seine eigne Schand',*** eavesdroppers hear no good of themselves. **Horch|gerät,** *n.* (*Mil.*) sound locator *or* detector, (*Nav.*) hydrophone, (*Rad.*) interception equipment. **–posten,** *m.* (*Mil.*) listening post.

Horde ['hɔrdə], *f.* 1. horde, nomadic tribe, (*coll.*) band, gang; 2. trestle, hurdle, lattice. **hordenweise,** *adv.* in hordes.

hören ['hø:rən], *v.t., v.i.* hear; listen; listen to; listen-in (to) (*radio*), attend (*lectures*), (*Law*) give a hearing to; ***– auf*** (*Acc.*), listen to, follow the advice of, heed, obey; ***alles hört auf mein Kommando!*** wait for the word of command! ***der Hund hört auf den Namen . . .,*** the dog answers to the name of . . .; (*Prov.*) ***wer nicht – will, muß fühlen,*** pay attention or take the consequences; ***er hört sich gern,*** he likes to hear himself talk, he likes to hear the sound of his own voice; ***ein Kolleg –,*** attend a course of lectures; ***ihn kommen –,*** hear him coming; ***das läßt sich –,*** that sounds all right, there is s.th. in that, that is worth considering; ***das läßt sich schon eher –,*** that's more like it, (*coll.*) now you're talking; ***sich – lassen,*** perform (play, sing *etc.*) (one's piece); ***von sich – lassen,*** send word *or* news, write; ***ich lasse von mir –,*** I'll let you know, I'll get in touch with you; ***laß dann und wann von dir –,*** let us hear from you now and then; (*coll.*) ***– Sie mal!*** (*expostulation*) I say! (*injunction*) look here! just listen to this! ***hört, hört!*** hear, hear! ***auf diesem Ohre höre ich nicht,*** I am deaf in this ear; ***ich habe sagen –,*** I have heard it said, I have been told; ***schwer –,*** be hard of hearing; ***soviel (wie) ich höre,*** from all I hear, from all accounts; ***er will nicht –,*** he will not listen; ***man kann sein eignes Wort nicht –,*** one cannot hear o.s. speak.

Hören, *n.* hearing; (*Rad.*) listening (in); ***es verging ihm – und Sehen,*** his senses left him. **Hörensagen,** *n.* hearsay, rumour. **Hörer,** *m.* 1. hearer; university student; *pl.* (radio) audience, listeners; 2. (*Tele.*) receiver, earphones, headset, headphones. **Hörerschaft,** *f.* hearers, students, audience.

Hör|fehler, *m.* 1. mistake in hearing, misapprehension; 2. defective hearing, hearing defect. **–folge,** *f.* (*Rad.*) radio series *or* serial. **–frequenz,** *f.* audiofrequency. **–gerät,** *n. See* **–apparat.**

hörig ['hø:rɪç], *pred.adj.* in bondage (*Dat.*, to), a slave (to), the slave (of). **Horige(r),** *m., f.* bondsman, serf, vassal, (*fig.*) slave (of *or* to). **Hörigkeit,** *f.* bondage, serfdom.

Horizont [hori'tsɔnt], *m.* **(-(e)s,** *pl.* **-e)** horizon; ***am –,*** on the horizon; (*fig.*) ***seinen – erweitern,*** broaden one's mind; ***das geht über meinen –,*** that is beyond me. **horizontal** [–'ta:l], *adj.* horizontal. **Horizontale,** *f.* (*Geom.*) horizontal line, (*Surv.*) level.

Hormon [hɔr'mo:n], *n.* **(-s,** *pl.* **-e)** hormone.

Hörmuschel ['hø:rmuʃəl], *f.* 1. (*Anat.*) (external) ear; 2. (*Tele.*) earpiece.

Horn [hɔrn], *n.* **(-(e)s,** *pl.* **⸚er)** 1. horn; ***sich*** (*Dat.*) ***die Hörner ablaufen*** or ***abstoßen,*** sow one's wild oats; (*fig.*) ***ihm die Hörner bieten*** or ***zeigen,*** show him one's teeth; ***den Stier an*** or ***bei den Hörnern packen*** or ***fassen,*** take the bull by the horns; ***Hörner tragen,*** be a cuckold; ***ihm (die) Hörner aufsetzen,*** cuckold him, make a cuckold of him; ***– des Überflusses,*** cornucopia; 2. bugle; ***mit ihm in ein*** or ***dasselbe*** or ***das gleiche – stoßen,*** chime in with him, agree with him; ***ins eigne – stoßen,*** blow one's own trumpet; 3. feeler (*of insects*); 4. hard *or* horny skin; (*dial.*) hoof (*of horses*); 5. (*dial.*) peak, cape, headland.

hornartig ['hɔrnˀartɪç], *adj.* horny. **Horn|auswuchs,** *m.* horny excrescence. **–baß,** *m.* horn-stop (*in organs*). **–baum,** *m.* (*Bot.*) hornbeam (*Carpinus betulus*). **–bläser,** *m.* horn-blower, bugler, trumpeter. **–blende,** *f.* hornblende, amphibole. **–brille,** *f.* horn-rimmed spectacles.

Hörnchen ['hœrnçən], *n.* 1. cornicle, little horn; 2. (*Cul.*) crescent, croissant.

hörnern ['hœrnərn], *adj.* horny, (of) horn.

Hörnerv ['hø:rnɛrf], *m.* auditory nerve.

Hornflügel ['hɔrnfly:gəl], *m.* elytra (*of insects*). **hornförmig,** *adj.* horn-shaped, corniform. **Hornhaut,** *f.* 1. horny skin, callosity; 2. (*Anat.*) cornea. **hornig,** *adj.* horny; horn-like; callous.

Hornisse [hɔr'nɪsə, 'hɔrnɪsə], *f.* hornet. **Hornissennest,** *n.* hornet's nest.

Hornist [hɔr'nɪst], *m.* horn player.

Horn|klee, *m.* (*Bot.*) bird's-foot trefoil (*Lotus corniculatus*). **–kraut,** *n.* (*Bot.*) mouse-ear, chickweed (*Cerastum vulgatum*). **–leiste,** *f.* ventral ridge (*of a feather*). **–ochs,** *m.* (*coll.*) blockhead. **–signal,** *n.* bugle-call, (*Motor.*) horn signal. **–spalte,** *f.* cleft of a hoof. **–taucher,** *m.* (*Orn.*) *see* **Ohrentaucher.**

Hornung [ˈhɔrnuŋ], *m.* (**-s,** *pl.* **-e**) February.

Hornvieh [ˈhɔrnfiː], *n.* horned cattle; (*coll.*) dolt, numskull, blockhead.

Hörorgan [ˈhøːrɔrgaːn], *n.* auditory organ.

Horoskop [horoˈskoːp], *n.* (**-s,** *pl.* **-e**) horoscope; ***ihm das – stellen,*** cast his horoscope.

Hörprobe [ˈhøːrproːbə], *f.* audition.

horrend [hɔˈrɛnt], *adj.* (*coll.*) enormous, terrific.

Hör|rohr, *n.* ear-trumpet, (*Med.*) stethoscope. **–saal,** *m.* auditorium, lecture-hall *or* -room. **–schwelle,** *f.* threshold of audibility. **–spiel,** *n.* radio play *or* drama.

Horst [hɔrst], *m.* (**-es,** *pl.* **-e**) 1. eyrie *or* aerie; mountain fortress; (*Av.*) (air) base; 2. shrubbery, thicket. **horsten,** *v.i.* build an eyrie, nest (*of birds of prey*).

Hort [hɔrt], *m.* (**-(e)s,** *pl.* **-e**) 1. day-nursery, play centre; (*Poet.*) safe retreat, refuge, shelter; 2. protection, bulwark, stronghold; shield, protector; 3. (*Poet.*) hoard, treasure. **horten,** *v.t.* hoard (up), accumulate.

Hortensie [hɔrˈtɛnziə], *f.* (*Bot.*) hydrangea (*Hortensis*).

Hortnerin [ˈhɔrtnərɪn], *f.* nursery-school teacher.

Hör|trichter, *m. See* **–rohr.**

Hortung [ˈhɔrtuŋ], *f.* hoarding, accumulation.

Hörweite [ˈhøːrvaɪtə], *f.* earshot; ***in –,*** within earshot; ***außer –,*** out of hearing *or* earshot.

Hose [ˈhoːzə], *f.* 1. (*usu. pl.*) trousers, (*Am.*) pants; breeches; knickers; thigh (*of horses and poultry*); ***kurze –n,*** shorts; ***lederne –n,*** leather breeches; (*coll.*) ***sie hat die –n an,*** she wears the breeches; ***die – durchsitzen,*** wear out the seat of one's trousers; (*coll*) ***das Herz fiel ihm in die –(n),*** his heart fell into his boots; (*coll.*) ***sich auf die –n setzen,*** get down to work; (*vulg.*) ***die –n voll haben,*** be in a blue funk; (*coll.*) ***ihm die –n stramm*** or ***straff ziehen,*** give him a spanking; 2. water spout; 3. (*dial.*) tub, pail; firkin.

Hosen|aufschlag, *m.* turn-up. **–bandorden,** *m.* Order of the Garter. **–bein,** *n.* trouser leg. **–boden,** *m.* seat of the trousers. **–boje,** *f.* (*Naut.*) breeches buoy. **–bund, –gurt,** *m.* waistband. **–klappe,** *f.*, **–latz,** *m.* fly.

hosenlos [ˈhoːzənloːs], *adj.* unbreeched. **Hosenlose(r),** *m., f.* sansculotte.

Hosen|matz, *m.* (*coll.*) little boy in first trousers. **–naht,** *f.* seam of the trouser-leg. **–rock,** *m.* divided skirt. **–rolle,** *m.* (*Theat.*) man's part (*for actress*). **–schlitz,** *m.* fly. **–stoff,** *m.* trousering. **–strecker,** *m.* trouser-press. **–tasche,** *f.* trouser pocket. **–träger,** *m.pl.* braces, (*Am.*) suspenders.

Hospital [hɔspɪˈtaːl], *n.* (**-s,** *pl.* **¨-er** *or Austr.* **-e**) hospital, home (for aged *or* infirm).

Hospitant [hɔspiˈtant], *m.* (**-en,** *pl.* **-en**) guest listener (*at lectures etc.*). **hospitieren,** *v.i.* (*bei*) sit in (at) (*lectures, lessons etc.*), supervise (*a p.'s work*).

Hospiz [hɔsˈpiːts], *n.* (**-es,** *pl.* **-e**) hostel; ***christliches –,*** temperance hostel *or* hotel.

Hostie [ˈhɔstiə], *f.* consecrated wafer, the Host. **Hostien|gefäß,** *n.* pyx. **–häuslein,** *n.* tabernacle. **–teller,** *m.* paten.

Hotel [hoˈtɛl], *n.* (**-s,** *pl.* **-s**) hotel. **Hotel|besitzer,** *m.* hotel-keeper. **–boy,** *m.* page, (*Am.*) bellboy, (*sl.*) bellhop. **Hotelier** [–ˈljeː], *m.* (**-s,** *pl.* **-s**) *see* **Hotelbesitzer.**

hott! [hɔt], *int.* gee up! to the right! (*to horses*). **Hott,** *n.* (**-s,** *pl.* **-s**) gee-gee (*children's word for horse*).

Hotte [ˈhɔtə], *f.* (*dial.*) vintager's butt; fruit-measure.

Hotzel [ˈhɔtsəl], *f. See* **Hutzel.**

hu! [huː], *int.* (*expressing horror*) ugh! whew!

hü! [hyː], *int.* whoa! (*to horses*).

Hub [huːp], *m.* (**-(e)s,** *pl.* **¨-e**) 1. lifting, raising, heaving; lift, heave; 2. impetus; 3. stroke, travel (*of a piston etc.*); ***aufgehender –,*** upstroke. **Hubbrücke,** *f.* drawbridge.

Hube [ˈhuːbə], *f.* (*dial.*) hide (*of land*). *See* **Hufe.**

Hübel [ˈhyːbəl], *m.* (*dial.*) hillock.

hüben [ˈhyːbən], *adv.* on this side; ***– und drüben,*** here, there and everywhere; on all sides; far and near.

Hub|höhe, *f.* 1. range of the tide; 2. (*Mech.*) (length of) stroke; 3. operating height, lift (*of cranes*). **–raum,** *m.* cylinder capacity, piston displacement.

hübsch [hypʃ], *adj.* (*of woman*) pretty, charming, lovely, beautiful; (*of man*) fine, handsome, good-looking; (*of a th.*) picturesque, pretty, pleasant, nice; (*coll.*) substantial, considerable; ***–e Summe,*** tidy sum; ***–es Vermögen,*** handsome *or* considerable fortune; ***sei – artig!*** there's a good boy (*or* girl)! ***das will ich – bleiben lassen,*** you won't catch me doing that; I'll take good care not to; ***eine –e Geschichte!*** a pretty kettle of fish! ***ein –es Stück Wegs,*** a tidy distance; ***das wirst du – sein lassen,*** you'll not do anything of the sort; ***es ist nicht –,*** it is not fair *or* not nice.

Hub|schrauber, *m.* helicopter. **–volumen,** *n.* (*Motor.*) piston displacement. **–weg,** *m.* (*Motor*), piston travel; (height of) valve lift. **–werk,** *n.* lifting *or* hoisting tackle. **–zahl,** *f.* (*Motor.*) number of strokes.

Hucke [ˈhukə], *f.* (*dial.*) load (*carried on back*); ***ihm die – vollügen,*** tell him a pack of lies. **hucken,** **1.** *v.t.* hump, carry on one's back. **2.** *v.i.* (*dial.*) *see* **hocken. huckepack,** *adv.* pick-a-back.

Hudel [ˈhuːdəl], *m.* (**-s,** *pl.* **-(n)**) rag, tatter; trash; (*dial.*) ragamuffin, scoundrel. **Hudelei** [–ˈlaɪ], *f.* careless *or* slipshod *or* botched work; bungling. **hudelig,** *adj.* ragged; paltry; botched, bungled. **hudeln,** *v.i.* be untidy *or* slipshod *or* slap-dash. **Hudler,** *m.* bungler.

Huf [huːf], *m.* (**-es,** *pl.* **-e**) hoof. **Hufbeschlag,** *m.* (horse-)shoeing.

Hufe [ˈhuːfə], *f.* hide (*of land*).

Hufeisen [ˈhuːfˀaɪzən], *n.* horseshoe; ***die – auflegen*** (*Dat.*), shoe (*a horse*). **hufeisenförmig,** *adj.* horseshoe(-shaped).

Hufen|geld, *n.* land-tax. **–meister,** *m.* collector of land-rents.

Huf|haar, *n.* fetlock. **–lattich,** *m.* (*Bot.*) coltsfoot (*Tussilago farfara*). **–nagel,** *m.* shoeing-nail, hobnail.

Hufner [ˈhuːfnər], **Hüfner** [ˈhyːfnər], *m.* smallholder.

Huf|schlag, *m.* 1. horse's kick; 2. beating of hoofs. **–schmied,** *m.* shoeing smith, farrier.

Hüft|ader [ˈhyft–], *f.* sciatic vein. **–bein, –blatt,** *n.* hip bone, ilium.

Hüfte [ˈhyftə], *f.* hip, (*of an animal*) haunch.

Hüft|gelenk, *n.* hip joint. **–gürtel, –halter,** *m.* suspender *or* (*Am.*) garter belt, girdle.

Huftier [ˈhuːftiːr], *n.* hoofed animal (*Ungulata*).

Hüft|nerv, *m.* sciatic nerve. **–pfanne,** *f.* socket of the hip-joint. **–schmerz,** *m. See* **–weh. –stück,** *n.* haunch (*of meat*). **–verrenkung,** *f.* dislocation of the hip. **–weh,** *n.* sciatic pains, sciatica.

Hügel [ˈhyːgəl], *m.* hill, hillock, knoll. **Hügelabhang,** *m.* hillside. **hügelig,** *adj.* hilly. **Hügel|kette,** *f.* chain *or* range of hills. **–land,** *n.* hilly *or* rolling country (*200–250 metres*).

Hugenotte [hugəˈnɔtə], *m.* (**-n,** *pl.* **-n**) (*Hist.*) Huguenot.

hüglig [ˈhyːglɪç], *adj. See* **hügelig.**

Huhn [huːn], *n.* (**-(e)s,** *pl.* **¨-er**) fowl, hen; (game) bird; (*coll.*) chap, fellow; *pl.* poultry; ***junges –,*** chicken, pullet; (*coll.*) ***er ist ein blindes –,*** he is as blind as a bat; (*coll.*) ***ein krankes –,*** a lame duck; (*coll.*) ***er ist ein verrücktes –,*** he is a crazy loon; (*coll.*) ***unsolides –,*** loose fish; ***zwei Völker Hühner,*** two covies of partridges; (*sl.*) ***vor die Hühner gehen,*** go to the dogs.

Hühnchen [ˈhyːnçən], *n.* chicken, pullet; (*coll.*) ***mit ihm ein – zu pflücken haben,*** have a bone to pick with him.

Hühner ['hy:nər], *pl. of* **Huhn. hühnerartig,** *adj.* gallinaceous. **Hühner|auge,** *n.* corn (*on the foot*); (*fig.*) ***ihm auf die –n treten,*** tread on his corns. **–blindheit,** *f.* night-blindness. **–braten,** *m.* roast chicken. **–brühe,** *f.* chicken broth. **–brust,** *f.* (*Med.*) pigeon chest. **–ei,** *n.* hen's egg. **–farm,** *f.* poultry *or* chicken farm. **–futter,** *n.* chicken-feed. **–habicht,** *m.* (*Orn.*) *see* **Habicht. –händler,** *m.* poulterer. **–haus,** *n.* hen-house, fowl-house. **–hof,** *m.* poultry-yard, chicken-run. **–hund,** *m.* pointer; setter. **–jagd,** *f.* partridge shooting. **–korb,** *m.* hen-coop. **–leiter,** *f.* hen-roost; (*coll.*) very steep and narrow staircase, breakneck stairs. **–markt,** *m.* poultry-market. **–pest, –seuche,** *f.* pip. **–stall,** *m.* hen-house, chicken-run. **–stange,** *f.* hen-roost, perch. **–stiege,** *f. See* **–leiter. –vieh,** *n.* poultry. **–vögel,** *m.pl.* gallinaceous birds. **–zucht,** *f.* poultry rearing, chicken farming.

hui! [huı], *int.* (*expressing pleasure, surprise, disgust*) ho! ha! oh! pooh! **Hui,** *m.* ***in einem*** or ***im –,*** in a twinkling, in a trice, in a flash.

Huld [hult], *f.* (-, *pl.* **-en**) grace, favour, clemency, benevolence, kindness; graciousness.

huldigen ['huldıgən], *v.i.* (*Dat.*) do homage, swear allegiance; pay homage *or* one's respects to; give (*a p.*) an ovation; hold, profess, embrace, subscribe to (*an opinion etc.*), indulge in, be addicted to (*alcohol etc.*); ***dem Fortschritte –,*** believe in progress; ***einer Dame –,*** pay one's attentions to *or* court a lady. **Huldigung,** *f.* homage; ovation; marked attention; favour. **Huldigungseid,** *m.* oath of allegiance *or* fealty.

huld|reich, –voll, *adj.* gracious, benevolent; favourable.

hülfe ['hylfə], *see* **helfen. Hülfe,** *f.* (*obs.*) *see* **Hilfe.**

Hulk [hulk], *m. See* **Holk.**

Hülle ['hylə], *f.* cover, covering, envelope, wrapper, jacket; wrapping, envelopment, mantle, integument; (*Bot.*) pod, husk, sheath; garment, raiment, jacket, tunic; cortex; veil, cloak, mask, bandage (*round the eyes*); ***irdische –,*** mortal frame, body; ***sterbliche –,*** (mortal) remains; ***– der Nacht,*** cover of night; ***die – und die Fülle,*** food and shelter, all that is needed; ***in – und Fülle,*** in plenty, in abundance; ***eine – fiel mir von den Augen,*** the scales fell from my eyes.

hüllen ['hylən], **1.** *v.t.* wrap (up), cover, envelop; hide, veil; ***in Dunkel gehüllt,*** shrouded in darkness, veiled in obscurity; ***in Flammen gehüllt,*** enveloped in flames; ***in Nebel gehüllt,*** shrouded *or* veiled in mist. **2.** *v.r.* wrap *or* muffle o.s. up; ***sich in Schweigen –,*** be wrapped in silence.

Hülse ['hylzə], *f.* pod, shell, husk; case, casing, housing, sleeve, bush; capsule, socket; shell *or* cartridge case. **hülsenartig,** *adj.* (*Bot.*) leguminous. **Hülsen|frucht,** *f.* legume, leguminous plant, pulse. **–schlüssel,** *m.* (*Mech.*) box spanner. **hülsig,** *adj. See* **hülsenartig.**

human [hu'ma:n], *adj.* humane; affable. **Humanismus,** *m.* humanism. **humanistisch,** *adj.* ***–e Bildung,*** classical education.

humanitär [humani'tɛ:r], *adj.* humanitarian. **Humanitarier** [–'ta:riər], *m.* humanitarian. **Humanität,** *f.* humanitarianism; humaneness, high-mindedness. **Humanitätsduselei,** *f.* sentimental humanitarianism.

Humbug ['humbuk], *m.* humbug, balderdash, swindle, hoax.

Hummel ['huməl], *f.* (-, *pl.* **-n**) bumble-bee; (*fig.*) tomboy, romp, hoyden; (*sl.*) ***–n im Hintern haben,*** have ants in one's pants, be restless *or* fidgety.

Hummer ['humər], *m.* (**-s,** *pl.* - *or Austr.* **-n**) lobster. **Hummerschere,** *f.* claw of a lobster.

Humor [hu'mo:r], *m.* sense of humour; humorous vein, comicality; ***feiner –, versteckter –,*** sly humour; ***derber –,*** broad humour; ***ausgelassener –,*** boisterous humour. **Humoreske** [–'rɛskə], *f.* humorous sketch, (*Mus.*) humoresque. **Humorist** [–'rıst], *m.* (**-en,** *pl.* **-en**) humorist, comedian; humorous *or* comic writer; funny *or* facetious p. **humoristisch,** *adj.* humorous, facetious, comical, droll, funny. **humorvoll,** *adj.* humorous.

humpeln ['humpəln], *v.i.* (*aux.* h. & s.) hobble, limp. **Humpelrock,** *m.* hobble-skirt.

Humpen ['humpən], *m.* bumper, tankard, goblet.

Humus ['hu:mus], *m.* vegetable mould, humus. **Humus|boden,** *m.* humus soil; arable land. **–decke,** *f.* leaf-mould. **–schicht,** *f.* top soil.

Hund [hunt], *m.* (**-(e)s,** *pl.* **-e**) **1.** dog, hound, (*fig.*) cur, beast, scoundrel; (*coll.*) ***mit den Nerven auf dem – sein,*** be a nervous wreck; (*coll.*) ***auf den – kommen,*** be down on one's luck; ***wie ein begossener –,*** with his tail between his legs, crest-fallen; (*Prov.*) ***–e die viel bellen, beißen nicht,*** his (*etc.*) bark is worse than his bite; (*Prov.*) ***blöder – wird selten fett,*** faint heart ne'er won fair lady; ***wie – und Katze leben,*** lead a cat-and-dog life; ***kein – nimmt ein Stück Brot von ihm,*** no one will have anything to do with him, he is beneath contempt; (*coll.*) ***da liegt der Knüppel beim –e,*** that goes without saying; (*coll.*) ***da liegt der – begraben,*** there's the rub! that's the snag *or* the root of the matter; (*coll.*) ***damit lockt man keinen – hinterm Ofen hervor,*** that won't get you anywhere; ***mit allen –en gehetzt sein,*** be wily, be up to all the tricks *or* dodges; ***wer mit –en zu Bette geht, steht mit Flöhen auf,*** as you make your bed, so you must lie in it; ***unter allem – sein,*** be as bad as it can be, be worse than awful; ***vor die –e gehen,*** go to the dogs; **2.** miner's truck.

Hundearbeit ['hundəarbaıt], *f.* (*coll.*) drudgery, fiendish job. **hundeelend,** *adj.* (*coll.*) rotten, miserable, wretched; ***– aussehen (sich fühlen),*** look (feel) like nothing on earth. **Hunde|futter,** *n.* dog's food, dog biscuits; (*fig.*) miserable fare. **–gattung,** *f.* breed of dog. **–hütte,** *f.* dog-kennel. **–kälte,** *f.* (*coll.*) bitter cold. **–koppel,** *f.* leash *or* pack (of hounds); *see also* **–leine. –kot,** *m.* dog dirt. **–kuchen,** *m.* dog biscuit. **–leben,** *n.* (*also fig.*) dog's life. **–leine,** *f.* leash, lead. **–liebhaber,** *m.* dog-fancier. **hundemüde,** *adj.* (*coll.*) dead *or* dog tired. **Hunderennen,** *n.* greyhound race, dog-racing.

hundert ['hundərt], *num.adj.* a *or* one hundred; ***– und aber –,*** hundreds and hundreds; ***zwei (einige) – Zigaretten,*** two (several) hundred cigarettes; ***– gegen eins wetten,*** bet *or* lay a hundred to one. **Hundert,** *n.* (**-s,** *pl.* **-e**) hundred; ***zu –en,*** in *or* by hundreds; ***–e von Pferden,*** hundreds of horses; ***zehn vom –,*** ten per cent; ***es geht in die –e,*** it runs into hundreds. **Hunderter,** *m.* hundred, three-figure number; hundred (mark, franc, dollar *etc.*) note. **hunderterlei,** *indecl.adj.* of a hundred kinds; (*coll.*) of all kinds.

hundert|fach, –fältig, *adj.* hundred-fold. **Hundert|fuß, –füßler,** *m.* centipede. **–jahrfeier,** *f.* centenary. **hundertjährig,** *adj.* centenary; ***der Hundertjährige Krieg,*** the hundreds years' war; ***die –e Feier von Schillers Geburt,*** the centenary celebration of Schiller's birth, the hundredth anniversary of Schiller's birthday. **Hundertjährige(r),** *m., f.* centenarian. **hundert|jährlich,** *adj.* centennial. **–mal,** *adv.* a hundred times, (*fig.*) very often. **–malig,** *adj.* done a hundred *or* (*fig.*) very many times. **–prozentig,** *adj., adv.* hundred per cent; (*fig.*) complete(ly), entire(ly), thorough(ly), out-and-out, utterly. **Hundertsatz,** *m.* percentage. **Hundertschaft,** *f.* an organized body of a hundred men.

hundertst ['hundərtst], *adj.* hundredth; ***vom Hundertsten ins Tausendste kommen,*** give a garbled account, talk *or* ramble on and on, not keep to the point; ***das weiß der Hundertste nicht,*** not one in a hundred knows that. **Hundertstel,** *n.* hundredth part. **hunderstens,** *adv.* in the hundredth place. **hunderttausend,** *num.adj.* a *or* one hundred thousand; ***Hunderttausende von Exemplaren,*** hundreds of thousands of copies.

Hunde|schlitten, *m.* dog sled(ge). **–schnauze,** *f.* dog's nose; (*coll.*) ***kalt wie eine –,*** cold as a fish. **–sperre,** *f.* muzzling order. **–staupe,** *f.* canine distemper. **–steuer,** *f.* dog licence. **–wache,** *f.* (*Naut.*) middle *or* graveyard watch (*24–04 hrs; N.B. not dog-watch*). **–wärter,** *m.* kennel-man.

-wetter, *n.* (*coll.*) wretched *or* beastly weather. **-zucht,** *f.* dog-breeding.

Hündin ['hyndɪn], *f.* bitch.

hündisch ['hyndɪʃ], *adj.* canine, (*coll.*) doggy; (*fig.*) cringing, fawning, toadying; vile, shameless; ***-e Angst,*** cringing fear; ***-e Treue,*** dog-like devotion.

Hunds|affe, *f.* baboon. **-blume,** *f.* dandelion. **-dolde,** *f.* (*Bot.*) fool's parsley (*Aethusa cynapium*). **-fott,** *m.* (*coll.*) cur, skunk. **hunds|föttisch, -gemein,** *adj.* (*coll.*) low-down, vile, caddish, (*sl.*) lousy. **Hunds|gleiße,** *f.* *See* **-dolde. -hai,** *m.* dogfish. **hunds|miserabel,** *adj.* (*coll.*) mean, paltry, pitiful, beggarly; *see also* **-gemein. -müde,** *adj.* *See* **hundemüde. Hunds|rose,** *f.* (*Bot.*) dog rose, wild brier (*Rosa canina*). **-stern,** *m.* Sirius, dog-star. **-tage,** *m.pl.* dog *or* canicular days. **-wut,** *f.* (*Med.*) rabies, hydrophobia.

Hüne ['hy:nə], *m.* **(-n,** *pl.* **-n)** giant. **Hünen|bett,** *n.* *See* **-grab. -gestalt,** *f.* (*fig.*) Herculean figure. **-grab,** *n.* prehistoric grave, barrow, cairn, mound. **hünenhaft,** *adj.* gigantic, colossal, huge.

Hunger ['huŋər], *m.* hunger, (*fig.*) craving, thirst (***nach,*** for); appetite (***auf*** (*Acc.*), for); starvation, famine; ***-s*** or ***vor - sterben,*** die of hunger, starve to death; ***- haben,*** be hungry; ***- leiden,*** go hungry; (*Prov.*) ***- ist der beste Koch,*** hunger is the best sauce.

Hunger|blockade, *f.* hunger-blockade. **-jahr,** *n.* year of famine. **-kandidat,** *m.* (*coll.*) unemployed graduate (*teacher etc.*). **-kur,** *f.* fasting cure, starvation diet. **-leben,** *n.* life below subsistence level, slow starvation. **-leider,** *m.* starveling; needy wretch; poor devil. **-lohn,** *m.* starvation wages, a mere pittance.

hungern ['huŋərn], **1.** *v.i.* hunger, be hungry, suffer hunger, go hungry, fast, diet (o.s.), starve; ***ich hungere,*** I go hungry, I am dieting; ***- nach,*** crave *or* long for; ***ihn - lassen,*** starve him. **2.** *v.imp.* ***mich hungert, es hungert mich,*** I am hungry.

Hunger|pfote, *f.* (*coll.*) ***an den -n saugen,*** be poverty-stricken *or* unable to make ends meet. **-ration,** *f.* starvation diet *or* rations.

Hungersnot ['huŋərsno:t], *f.* famine.

Hunger|streik, *m.* hunger-strike; ***in den - treten,*** go on hunger-strike. **-tod,** *m.* death from starvation. **-tuch,** *n.* black cloth covering the altar in Lent; (*coll.*) ***am - nagen,*** *see* **-pfote. -turm,** *m.* (*obs.*) dungeon.

hungrig ['huŋrɪç], *adj.* hungry, famished, starving; (*of soil*) poor, starved; ***- sein nach,*** have a craving for.

Hünin ['hy:nɪn], *f.* giantess.

Hunne ['hunə], *m.* **(-n,** *pl.* **-n)** (*Hist.*) Hun.

hunten ['huntən], *adv.* (*dial.*) below, down here.

Hupe ['hu:pə], *f.* motor-horn, siren, hooter. **hupen,** *v.i.* hoot, honk, sound the horn. **Hupensignal,** *n.* signal with the horn *or* hooter.

Hupf [hupf], *m.* **(-es,** *pl.* **-e)** hop, jump. **hupfen,** (*dial.*) *see* **hüpfen**; (*coll.*) ***das ist gehupft wie gesprungen,*** there's nothing to choose between them, it all comes to the same thing.

hüpfen ['hypfən], *v.i.* (*aux.* h. & s.) hop, jump, leap, skip, frisk about, gambol; (*of a th.*) bounce, bound; ***das Herz hüpfte ihr im Leibe*** or ***ihr vor Freude,*** her heart leapt with joy. **Hüpfer,** *m.* (*dial.*) grasshopper. **Hüpf|spiel,** *n.* hopscotch. **-steinspiel,** *n.* ducks and drakes.

Hürde ['hyrdə], *f.* hurdle; (*Racing*) fence; fold, pen, corral. **Hürden|lauf,** *m.* hurdle-race, hurdles. **-rennen,** *n.* steeplechase.

Hure ['hu:rə], *f.* prostitute, whore, harlot. **huren,** *v.i.* whore, fornicate. **Huren|haus,** *n.* brothel. **-kind,** *n.* bastard. **Hurer,** *m.* whoremonger, fornicator, lecher. **Hurerei** [-'raɪ], *f.* fornication, whoring; (*obs.*) prostitution.

hürnen ['hyrnən], *adj.* (*obs.*) horny, impenetrable, invulnerable.

hurra [hu'ra:], *int.* hurra(h)! **Hurra|geschrei,** *n.* *See* **-ruf. -patriot,** *m.* chauvinist. **hurrapatriotisch,** *adj.* chauvinistic, jingoistic. **Hurra|patriotismus,** *m.* jingoism, chauvinism. **-ruf,** *m.* cheer.

hurtig ['hurtɪç], *adj.* quick, swift, speedy, brisk, agile, nimble; lively, alert; (*Mus.*) presto. **Hurtigkeit,** *f.* quickness, briskness, swiftness, agility, nimbleness.

Husar [hu'za:r], *m.* **(-en,** *pl.* **-en)** hussar. **Husaren|jacke,** *f.* dolman. **-(pelz)mütze,** *f.* busby. **-stück,** *n.* (*fig.*) coup de main, (*coll.*) horse-play, shindy.

husch! [huʃ], *int.* quick! (*silence*) hush! (*intimidation*) shoo! ***- war er weg,*** he was gone in a flash. **Husche,** *f.* (*dial.*) sudden shower. **husch(el)ig,** *adj.* hasty, fleeting, superficial. **huscheln, huschen,** *v.i.* (*aux.* s.) flit, scurry, whisk.

Hüsing ['hy:zɪŋ], *n.* **(-(e)s,** *pl.* **-e)** *or f.* (-, *pl.* **-e)** (*Naut.*) housing.

hussa(h)! ['husa], *int.* huzza! ***- rufen,*** urge on.

hüst! [hyst], *int.* (*dial.*) left! (*drover's call to horses*).

hüsteln ['hystəln], *v.i.* cough slightly, clear one's throat.

husten ['hu:stən], **1.** *v.i.* (have a) cough, give a cough; (*coll.*) ***- auf*** (*Acc.*), not care a rap for, turn up one's nose at. **2.** *v.t.* cough *or* bring up; ***Blut -,*** spit blood; (*sl.*) ***ich werde dir was -,*** you can whistle for it, go and chase yourself. **Husten,** *m.* cough. **Husten|anfall,** *m.* fit of coughing, coughing fit. **-bonbon,** *m.* (*or Austr. n.*) cough sweet *or* drop, lozenge. **-fieber,** *n.* catarrhal fever. **-krampf,** *m.* convulsive cough. **-mittel,** *n.* cough cure *or* mixture. **hustenstillend,** *adj.* pectoral.

[1]**Hut** [hu:t], *m.* **(-(e)s,** *pl.* **⸚e)** hat; cap, cover, lid; top (*of a mushroom*); (*Orn.*) pileum, (*Archit.*) coping; ***den - vor ihm abnehmen,*** take off one's hat to him (*also fig.*); ***unter einen - bringen,*** reconcile, bring under one heading, reduce to a common formula; ***den*** or ***mit dem - in der Hand,*** hat in hand; (*coll.*) ***du kriegst was auf den -,*** you'll get your knuckles rapped; ***den - (vor Freude) schwingen,*** toss one's cap in the air (for joy); ***unter einem - stecken,*** be in the same boat.

[2]**Hut,** *f.* (-, *pl.* **-en)** 1. protection, shelter; custody, keeping, charge, care; tending (*of cattle*); ***unter meiner -,*** in my care; ***in Gottes - sein,*** be in God's keeping *or* under God's protection; ***auf der -*** or ***auf seiner - sein,*** be on one's guard (***vor*** (*Dat.*), against); 2. (*dial.*) pasture, pasturage; right of pasture; flock, herd.

Hut|ablage, *f.* hat-stand *or* -rack. **-boden,** *m.* crown (of a hat).

Hütchen ['hy:tçən], *n.* 1. capsule; 2. extinguisher.

hüten ['hy:tən], **1.** *v.t.* watch over, guard, take care of, look after, tend, keep; ***das Vieh -,*** tend the cattle; ***- vor*** (*Dat.*), protect *or* preserve from; ***das Bett (Zimmer, Hause) -,*** be confined to one's bed (one's room, the house); ***er hütete ihn wie seinen Augapfel,*** he cherished him as the apple of his eye; ***hüte deine Zunge!*** guard your tongue! **2.** *v.r.* be on one's guard, take care, beware (***vor*** (*Dat.*), of), watch out (for); ***- Sie sich vor ihm!*** (or ***vor Taschendieben!***) be on your guard against *or* beware of him! (*or* pick-pockets!); (*coll.*) ***ich werde mich -, das zu tun,*** I shall take (good) care not to do that! **Hüter,** *m.* keeper, guardian, custodian, warden; herdsman.

Hut|form, *f.* hat(ter's) block. **-geschäft,** *n.* hat shop, (*ladies*) milliners. **-kopf,** *m.* *See* **-boden. -krempe,** *f.* brim (of a hat). **-macher,** *m.* hatter. **-macherin,** *f.* milliner. **-nadel,** *f.* hat-pin. **-rand,** *m.* *See* **-krempe. -schachtel,** *f.* hat-box.

Hutsche ['hutʃə], *f.* (*dial.*) *see* **Hitsche**; (*also Austr.*) swing. **hutschen,** *v.i.* slip, slide; swing.

Hut|schleife, *f.* cockade. **-schnur,** *f.* (*coll.*) ***das geht über die -,*** that's going too far! that's past a joke! **-ständer,** *m.* *See* **-ablage.**

Hutte ['hutə], *f.* (*Swiss*) basket.

Hütte ['hytə], *f.* 1. cottage, hut, chalet, cabin, shelter, shanty, shack, shed; (*B.*) tent, tabernacle; 2. foundry, ironworks, steelworks; 3. (*Naut.*) poop. **Hütten|after,** *m.* slag, foundry waste. **-arbeiter,** *m.* foundryman, foundry-worker. **-bau,** *m.* smelting works, foundry. **-industrie,** *f.* iron and steel industry. **-ingenieur,** *m.* metallurgical engineer. **-koks,** *m.* metallurgical coke. **-kunde,** *f.* metallurgy. **-mehl,** *n.* white arsenic. **-meister,** *m.* foundry overseer. **-rauch,** *m.* furnace smoke, (arsenical) fumes, white arsenic. **-revier,** *n.* mining district. **-speise,** *f.* ore for smelting. **-technik,** *f.* metallurgical engineering. **-werk,** *n.* foundry, smelting works. **-wesen,** *n. See* **-technik. -wirt,** *m.* hut-warden (*on mountains*).

Hutzel ['hutsəl], *f.* (-, *pl.* **-n**) (*dial.*) dried fruit (*esp.* pears); wild pear; (*fig.*) wizened old hag. **hutz(e)lig,** *adj.* shrivelled, (*of a p.*) wizened, wrinkled. **Hutzelmännchen,** *n.* goblin. **hutzeln, 1.** *v.t.* dry (*fruit*). **2.** *v.i.* (*aux.* s.) shrivel, shrink, become shrivelled *or* wrinkled.

Hutzucker ['hu:ttsukər], *m.* loaf sugar.

Hyäne [hy'ɛ:nə], *f.* hyena; – ***des Schlachtfeldes,*** plunderer, despoiler (*of corpses and wounded*).

Hyazinth [hya'tsɪnt], *m.* (**-(e)s,** *pl.* **-e**) (*Min.*) hyacinth, jacinth. **Hyazinthe,** *f.* (*Bot.*) hyacinth.

hybrid [hy'bri:t], *adj.* hybrid, mongrel. **Hybride,** *f. or m.* (**-n,** *pl.* **-n**) hybrid, mongrel, cross. **hybridisch,** *adj. See* **hybrid.**

Hydrant [hy'drant], *m.* (**-en,** *pl.* **-en**) hydrant, fire-point, stand-pipe.

Hydrat [hy'dra:t], *n.* (**-(e)s,** *pl.* **-e**) hydrate, hydroxide. **Hydrat(at)ion** [–a(ta)tsi'o:n], *f.* hydration. **hydratisieren** [–'zi:rən], *v.t.* hydrate, form hydrates from. **Hydratwasser,** *n.* water of hydration.

Hydraulik [hy'draulik], *f.* hydraulics. **hydraulisch,** *adj.* hydraulic.

Hydrier|anlage [hy'dri:r–], *f. See* **-werk. hydrieren,** *v.t.* hydrogenate, hydrogenize. **Hydrierung,** *f.* hydrogenation. **Hydrierwerk,** *n.* hydrogenation plant.

Hydro|chinon [hydroçi'no:n], *n.* (*Phot.*) hydroquinone. **-chlorsäure,** *f.* hydrochloric acid.

hydrogenisieren [hydrogəni'zi:rən], *v.t. See* **hydrieren.**

Hydrolyse [hydro'ly:ze], *f.* hydrolysis. **hydrolytisch,** *adj.* hydrolytic.

Hydrometer [hydro'me:tər], *n.* hydrometer.

hydropisch [hy'dro:p'ɪʃ], *adj.* (*Med.*) dropsical. **Hydropsie** [–drɔ'psi:], *f.* dropsy.

Hydrostatik [hydro'sta:tik], *f.* hydrostatics. **hydrostatisch,** *adj.* hydrostatic.

Hyetometer [hyeto'me:tər], *n.* rain-gauge.

Hygiene [hygi'e:nə], *f.* hygiene, sanitation. **hygienisch,** *adj.* hygienic, sanitary.

Hymne ['hymnə], *f.* hymn, anthem. **hymnisch,** *adj.* hymnic, hymnal. **Hymnus,** *m.* (-, *pl.* **-nen**) *see* **Hymne.**

Hyperbel [hy'pɛrbəl], *f.* (-, *pl.* **-n**) 1. (*Math.*) hyperbola; 2. (*Log.*) hyperbole. **Hyperbelfunktion,** *f.* hyperbolic function. **hyperbolisch** [–'bo:lɪʃ], *adj.* hyperbolic(al).

hyper|kritisch [hypɛr–], *adj.* overcritical, hypercritical. **-modern,** *adj.* ultramodern. **-nervös,** *adj.* highly strung, oversensitive.

Hypnose [hyp'no:zə], *f.* hypnosis; ***für – empfänglich,*** hypnotizable. **hypnotisch,** *adj.* hypnotic; ***–e Mittel,*** hypnotics, hypnotic drugs; ***–er Zustand,*** hypnotic state; trance. **Hypnotiseur** [–ti'zø:r], *m.* (**-s,** *pl.* **-e**) hypnotist. **hypnotisieren,** *v.t.* hypnotize. **Hypnotisierung,** *f.* hypnotization. **Hypnotismus** [–'tɪsmus], *m.* hypnotism.

Hypochonder [hypo'xɔndər], *m.* hypochondriac. **Hypochondrei** [–'dri:], *f.* hypochondria. **hypochondrisch,** *adj.* hypochondriac(al).

Hypophyse [hypo'fy:zə], *f.* (*Anat.*) pituitary gland, hypophysis.

Hypotenuse [hypote'nu:zə], *f.* hypotenuse.

Hypothek [hypo'te:k], *f.* (-, *pl.* **-en**) mortgage; ***eine – aufnehmen,*** take out *or* raise a mortgage; ***mit –en belastet,*** encumbered with mortgages. **hypothekarisch** [–'ka:rɪʃ], *adj.* (by *or* on *or* as a) mortgage; ***–er Gläubiger,*** mortgagee; ***gegen –e Sicherheit,*** on mortgage security; – ***belastet,*** mortgaged.

Hypotheken|brief, *m.* mortgage (deed). **-forderung,** *f.* hypothecary claim. **hypothekenfrei,** *adj.* unencumbered. **Hypotheken|gläubiger,** *m.* mortgagee. **-schuldner,** *m.* mortgager *or* mortgagor.

Hypothese [hypo'te:zə], *f.* hypothesis, supposition. **hypothetisch,** *adj.* hypothetic(al).

Hysterie [hyste'ri:], *f.* hysteria, hysterics. **hysterisch** [–'ste:rɪʃ], *adj.* hysterical; ***einen –en Anfall bekommen,*** go (off) into hysterics.

I

I, i [i:], **1.** *n.* I, i. **2.** *int.* – ***bewahre! – wo!*** nothing of the kind *or* sort! certainly not! nonsense! rubbish! what next!

iah! [i'a:], *int.* hee-haw! (*bray of an ass*). **iahen,** *v.i.* bray, hee-haw.

iambisch [i'ambɪʃ], *adj.* **Iambus,** *m. See* **jambisch, Jambus.**

I-Barren ['i:barən], *m.* (*Metall.*) wire bar.

ich [ɪç], *pers.pron.* I; – ***selbst,*** I myself; – ***bin es,*** it is I, (*coll.*) it's me; – ***Elende(r)!*** miserable wretch that I am! **Ich,** *n.* self; ego; ***mein zweites*** or ***anderes –,*** my other self; my double. **ichbewußt,** *adj.* self-aware. **Ichbewußtsein,** *n.* self-awareness. **ichbezogen,** *adj.* self-centred, egocentric. **Ich|-bezogenheit,** *f.* self-centredness, egocentricity. **--Roman,** *m.* novel in the first person. **-sucht,** *f.* selfishness, egotism.

Ickerchen ['ikərcən], *n.pl.* toothy-pegs, (*children's word for teeth*).

Ideal [ide'a:l], *n.* (**-s,** *pl.* **-e**) 1. ideal; 2. model, pattern. **ideal,** *adj.* 1. ideal, perfect, Utopian; – ***angelegter Mensch,*** man of ideals, idealist; ***–er Ratschlag,*** council of perfection; ***–er Schauspieler,*** perfect actor; 2. conceptual, abstract; imaginary. **idealisieren** [–i'zi:rən], *v.t.* idealize. **Idealismus** [–'lɪsmus], *m.* idealism. **Idealist,** *m.* idealist. **idealistisch,** *adj.* idealistic. **Idealität** [–i'tɛ:t], *f.* ideality, conceptual realm.

Idee [i'de:], *f.* (-, *pl.* **-n**) idea, notion, conception; thought, fancy; intention, purpose; (*coll.*) trace, vestige; ***fixe –,*** obsession, idée fixe; ***gute –,*** good idea, brainwave; (*coll.*) ***keine –!*** by no means, certainly not! ***keine (blasse) – von einer S. haben,*** not have the faintest *or* least idea *or* notion of, be altogether in the dark about a th. **ideel** [–'ɛl], *adj.* notional, hypothetical, imaginary.

ideenarm [i'de:ən'ʔarm], *adj.* devoid of *or* lacking (in) ideas, unimaginative. **Ideen|folge,** *f.* sequence of ideas. **-gehalt,** *m.* thought content. **-geschichte,** *f.* history of ideas *or* thought. **-kreis,** *m.* range of ideas. **-reich,** *n.* realm of ideas. **ideenreich,** *adj.* inventive, resourceful. **Ideen|-reichtum,** *m.* invention, resourcefulness. **-verbindung,** *f.* association of ideas. **-welt,** *f.* ideal world, world of ideas.

Iden ['i:dən], *pl.* Ides (*in ancient Rome, the 15th day of March, May, July, October, and the 13th of the other months*).

identifizieren [idɛntifi'tsi:rən], *v.t., v.r.* identify (o.s.). **Identifizierung,** *f.* identification.

identisch [i'dɛntiʃ], *adj.* identical.

Identität [idɛnti'tɛ:t], *f.* identity. **Identitätsnachweis,** *m.* proof of identity; (*at customs*) certificate of identity.

Ideolog(e) [ideo'lo:g(ə)], *m.* (**-(e)n,** *pl.* **-(e)n)** ideologist. **Ideologie** [–'gi:], *f.* ideology. **ideologisch,** *adj.* ideological.

Idioblast [ideo'blast], *m.* (**-en,** *pl.* **-en**) germ plasm.

Idiom [idi'o:m], *n.* (**-s,** *pl.* **-e**) dialect, speech habits, manner of speech; idiom. **idiomatisch,** *adj.* dialectal, showing *or* referring to speech peculiarities (*of a class or group*); idiomatic.

Idiosynkrasie [idiozynkra'zi:], *f.* fixed aversion, allergy, antipathy.

Idiot [idi'o:t], *m.* (**-en,** *pl.* **-en**) idiot. **Idiotie** [–'ti:], *f.* idiocy. **idiotisch,** *adj.* idiotic. **Idiotismus** [–'tɪsmus], *m.* (-, *pl.* **-men**) 1. idiom; 2. (*rare*) stupid behaviour.

Idiotikon [idi'o:tikɔn], *n.* (**-s,** *pl.* **-ken** *or* **-ka**) dialect dictionary.

Idol [i'do:l], *n.* (**-s,** *pl.* **-e**) idol, graven image.

Idyll [i'dyl], *n.* (**-s,** *pl.* **-e**), **Idylle,** *f.* idyll. **idyllenhaft, idyllisch,** *adj.* idyllic, pastoral.

Igel ['i:gəl], *m.* 1. hedgehog; 2. harrow; 3. spiky brush; 4. surly *or* irritable p. **Igelstellung,** *f.* (*Mil.*) hedgehog position.

igitte! [i'gɪtə], *int.* (*coll.*) (*of abhorrence*) nasty! horrid! disgusting! (*nursery talk*) acky!

Ignorant [ɪgno'rant], *m.* (**-en,** *pl.* **-en**) ignoramus. **Ignoranz,** *f.* ignorance. **ignorieren,** *v.t.* ignore, disregard, take no notice of, (*coll. applied to a p. only*) cut (*s.o.*) dead.

ihm [i:m], *pers.pron.* (*Dat. sing. of* **er, es**) (to) him, (to) it; (*after prep.*) him.

ihn [i:n], *pers.pron.* (*Acc. sing. of* **er**) him; it.

ihnen ['i:nən], *pers. pron.* (*Dat. of* **sie,** *pl.*) (to) them; ***Ihnen,*** (*Dat. of* **Sie**) (to) you.

ihr [i:r], **1.** *pers.pron.* 1. (*Nom. pl. of* **du**) you, (*B.*) ye; 2. (*Dat. of* **sie,** *f. sing.*) (to) her, (to) it; (*after prep.*) her. **2.** *poss.adj.* (*and pron.*) her(s); its; their(s); ***Ihr,*** your(s).

ihre ['i:rə] (*der, die, das* –), *see* **ihrige.**

ihrer ['i:rər], **1.** *pers.pron.* 1. (*Gen. of* **sie,** *f. sing.*) of her, of it; 2. (*Gen. of* **sie,** *pl.*) of them; ***Ihrer,*** of you; ***es waren – viele,*** there were many of them; ***Gott wird sich – erbarmen,*** God will have compassion on them. **2.** *poss.adj.* (*Gen., Dat. sing. and Gen. pl. of* **ihr, 2.**) of her, to her; of its, to its; of their; ***Ihrer,*** of your. **ihrerseits,** *adv.* in her (its, their) turn; for *or* on her (its, their) part; as far as she (it, they) are concerned; ***Ihrerseits,*** for *or* on your part, in your turn, as far as you are concerned.

ihresgleichen ['i:rəsglaɪçən], *indecl.adj.* of her (its, their) kind; like (*or* the like(s) of) her (it, them); ***Ihresgleichen,*** of your kind; like you, the like(s) of you.

ihret|halben, –wegen, –willen, *adv.* on her (its, their) account *or* behalf; for her (its, their) sake; so far as she (*or* it) is *or* they are concerned, because of her (it, them); ***Ihrethalben*** *etc.*, on your account *etc.*

ihrige ['i:rɪgə] (***der, die, das*** **–**; ***die –n***) *poss. pron.* hers, its, theirs; ***Ihrige,*** yours; ***das –,*** your property; your duty *etc.*; ***die –n,*** your family; ***ich verbleibe stets der*** (***die***) **–**, I remain yours (very) truly *or* sincerely *etc.* (*at the end of a letter*).

Ikterus ['ɪktərus], *m.* (*Med.*) jaundice, (*Bot.* chlorosis.

Ilias ['i:lias], *f.* Iliad.

Ilk [ɪlk], *m.* (**-s,** *pl.* **-e**) (*dial.*) *see* **Iltis.**

illegal [ɪle'ga:l], *adj.* illegal; (*Pol.*) – ***werden,*** go underground.

illegitim [ɪlegi'ti:m], *adj.* unlawful, illegal; spurious, illegitimate.

illoyal [ɪlɔy'ja:l, ɪloa'ja:l], *adj.* disloyal. **Illoyalität** [–i'tɛ:t], *f.* disloyalty.

Illumination [ɪluminatsi'o:n], *f.* illumination. **illuminieren** [–'ni:rən], *v.t.* illuminate, light up.

Illusion [ɪluzi'o:n], *f.* illusion, delusion, self-deception. **illusorisch** [–'zo:rɪʃ], *adj.* illusory, illusive, deceptive.

illustrieren [ɪlus'tri:rən], *v.t.* illustrate, (*fig.*) exemplify, demonstrate. **Illustrierte,** *f.* illustrated (paper).

Iltis ['ɪltɪs], *m.* (**-ses,** *pl.* **-se**)polecat, fitchet.

im [ɪm], *contraction of* **in dem.**

imaginär [imagi'nɛ:r], *adj.* 1. imaginary; (*Math.*) ***–e Größe,*** imaginary quantity; 2. floating (*capital*).

Imber ['ɪmbər], *m.* ginger.

Imbiß ['ɪmbɪs], *m.* (**-(ss)es,** *pl.* **-(ss)e**) light meal, snack, (*coll.*) bite; light refreshments, (*Swiss*) lunch. **Imbiß|halle, –stube,** *f.* snack *or* refreshment-bar.

imitieren [imi'ti:rən], *v.t.* imitate; match.

Imker ['ɪmkər], *m.* bee-keeper, apiarist. **Imkerei** [–'raɪ], *f.* bee-keeping. **imkern,** *v.t.* keep *or* rear bees.

immanent [ɪma'nɛnt], *adj.* immanent, inherent.

immateriell [ɪmateri'ɛl], *adj.* immaterial.

Immatrikulation [ɪmatrikulatsi'o:n], *f.* matriculation, enrolment. **immatrikulieren** [–'li:rən], *v.t.* matriculate; enrol; ***sich – lassen,*** matriculate.

Imme ['ɪmə], *f.* (*dial., Poet.*) bee.

immediat [ɪmedi'a:t], *adj.* immediate. **Immediat|-bericht,** *m.*, **–eingabe,** *f.* direct report *or* petition (*to the highest authority without mediation*). **immediatisieren** [–ti'zi:rən], *v.t.* make free from intermediate control, make directly responsible (to the ultimate authority).

immens [ɪ'mɛns], *adj.* immense, enormous.

immer ['ɪmər], **1.** *adv.* always, (for) ever, every time; constantly, incessantly, perpetually, continually, (*coll.*) all the time; (*before comp.*) more and more; ***auf*** or ***für –,*** for ever, (*coll.*) for good; ***– besser,*** better and better; ***– und ewig,*** for ever and ever, eternally; ***– fort!*** *see* ***– zu;*** ***– gerade aus,*** keep straight ahead; ***– mehr,*** more and more; ***noch –,*** even now, still; ***noch – nicht,*** not yet, not even now; ***– schlimmer,*** worse and worse; ***– weiter reden,*** talk on and on, go on *or* keep (on) talking; ***– weniger,*** less and less; ***– wenn,*** every time, whenever; ***wenn*** (***auch***) **–**, although; ***wer*** (***auch***) **–**, who(so)ever; ***wie –,*** as usual; ***wie auch –,*** howsoever; ***– wieder,*** again *or* time and again, over and over again; ***wo*** (***auch*** or ***nur***) **–**, where(so)ever; ***– zu!*** keep *or* go on! (*coll.*) keep it up! keep going! **2.** *part.* in any case, under any circumstances, at all events, after all; as far as I am concerned, nevertheless, still, yet; ***er mag es – tun,*** he is welcome to do it; ***laß ihn nur – kommen,*** he can come for all I care, as far as I am concerned he can come; ***er ist doch – dein Vater,*** after all he is your father; ***wir wollen uns – setzen,*** at all events let us sit down; ***mag – sein Name vergessen werden, doch*** . . ., although his name may be forgotten, yet . . . .

immer|dar, *adv.* always, evermore, forever (and ever). **–fort,** *adv.* continuously, incessantly, unceasingly, uninterruptedly, perpetually, constantly, continually, (*coll.*) all the time; ***er redet –,*** he keeps on talking. **–grün,** *adj.* evergreen. **Immergrün,** *n.* (*Bot.*) large (*or* lesser) periwinkle (*Vinca major* (*minor*)). **immer|hin,** *adv., part.* for all that, still, after all; though, nonetheless, nevertheless, in spite of everything, at least; ***mag es – so sein,*** be that as it may; ***– mag die Welt wissen,*** the world is welcome to know. **–während,** *adj.* endless, eternal, everlasting, perpetual. **–zu,** *adv. See* **–fort.**

Immis ['ɪmɪs], *m.* (*dial.*) *see* **Imbiß.**

immobil ['ɪmobi:l, –'bi:l], *adj.* 1. immovable; 2. not ready for war. **Immobiliarvermögen** [–i'a:rfɛrmø:gən], *n.*, **Immobilien** [–'bi:ljən], *pl.* real estate, immovables; dead stock. **immobilisieren** [–'zi:rən], *v.t.* immobilize.

Immortelle [ɪmɔr'tɛlə], *f.* (*Bot.*) everlasting flower, immortelle (*Helychrysum*).

immun [ɪ'mu:n], *adj.* immune (***gegen,*** from) (*disease*), exempt (from) (*taxes*). **immunisieren** [–i'zi:rən], *v.t.* immunize, render immune. **Immunität** [–i'tɛ:t], *f.* immunity, exemption (***gegen,*** from); (*Parl.*) parliamentary privilege.

Impedanz [ɪmpe'dants], *f.* (*Rad.*) impedance. **Impedanzspule,** *f.* reactance (coil).

Imperativ ['ɪmperati:f, –'ti:f], *m.* (**-s,** *pl.* **-e**) imperative (mood). **imperativ(isch),** *adj.* imperative.

imperatorisch [impera'to:rɪʃ], *adj.* imperious.

Imperfekt(um) ['ɪmpɛrfɛkt(um)], *n.* (**-s,** *pl.* **-ta**) (*Gram.*) imperfect *or* past tense.

Imperialismus [ɪmperia'lɪsmus], *m.* imperialism. **imperialistisch,** *adj.* imperialistic. **Imperium** [–'pe:rium], *n.* (**-s,** *pl.* **-rien**) empire.

impertinent [ɪmpɛrti'nɛnt], *adj.* impertinent, insolent. **Impertinenz,** *f.* insolence, impertinence.

impfen ['ɪmpfən], *v.t.* inoculate, vaccinate; (*Hort.*) graft; (*fig.*) ***ihm den Haß ins Herz –,*** inspire him with hate. **Impfgesetz,** *n.* vaccination act. **Impfling,** *m.* (**-s,** *pl.* **-e**) child that has been *or* is due to be vaccinated. **Impf|reis,** *n.* (*Hort.*) graft-twig. **–schein,** *m.* certificate of vaccination. **–stoff,** *m.* vaccine, serum, lymph. **Impfung,** *f.* inoculation, vaccination. **Impfzwang,** *m.* compulsory vaccination.

implizieren [ɪmpli'tsi:rən], *v.i.* implicate (*a p.*), imply (*s.th.*).

imponderabel [ɪmpɔndə'ra:bəl], *adj.* imponderable. **Imponderabilien** [–'bi:ljən], *pl.* imponderables.

imponieren [ɪmpo'ni:rən], *v.i.* 1. be impressive *or* imposing, (*of a p.*) command respect; 2. (*Dat.*) impress (*a p.*), (*coll.*) strike, dazzle (*a p.*). **imponierend,** *adj.* imposing, impressive, (*coll.*) striking.

Import [ɪm'pɔrt], *m.* (**-(e)s,** *pl.* **-e**) import(ation), imports. **Importe,** *f.* imported Havana cigar. **Importeur** [–'tø:r], *m.* (**-s,** *pl.* **-e**) importer. **importieren** [–'ti:rən], *v.t.* import. **Importware,** *f.* imported article.

imposant [ɪmpo'zant], *adj.* impressive, imposing, majestic.

Impost [ɪm'pɔst], *m.* (**-es,** *pl.* **-en**) impost; *pl.* taxes, duties, customs.

Impotenz ['ɪmpotɛnts], *f.* impotency.

imprägnieren [ɪmprɛg'ni:rən], *v.t.* saturate, proof, impregnate. **Imprägnierung,** *f.* impregnation, proofing.

Imprimatur [ɪmpri'ma:tur], *n.* 1. Press! ***einem Druckbogen das – erteilen,*** mark a sheet for press; 2. (*R.C.*) authority to print.

Improvisator [ɪmprovi'za:tɔr], *m.* (**-s,** *pl.* **-en**) improviser, extemporizer. **improvisieren,** *v.t., v.i.* improvise, extemporize, (*coll.*) ad-lib.

Impuls [ɪm'puls], *m.* (**-es,** *pl.* **-e**) impulse. **impulsiv** [–'si:f], *adj.* impulsive.

imputieren [ɪmpu'ti:rən], *v.t.* ***ihn einer S.*** (*Gen.*) **–** impute s.th. to him, charge him with s.th.

Ims [ɪms], *m. See* **Imbiß.**

imstande [ɪm'ʃtandə], *pred.adj.* capable (of); able (to), in a position (to).

in [ɪn], *prep.* (*expressing rest or motion within a place* (*Dat.*)) in, at; (*implying change of state or motion to or towards* (*Acc.*)) into, to, within; – ***acht Tagen,*** in a week('s time), within a week; – ***etwas,*** a little, somewhat; – ***kurzem,*** shortly, in a short time, in the near future, before long; – ***die Schule gehen,*** go to school; – ***der Schule,*** at school; (*coll.*) ***das hat es – sich,*** there is a lot to it, it is difficult. (*For idioms using* **in,** *see under the characteristic word, usu. the governed noun.*)

inadäquat ['ɪnadɛkva:t, –'kva:t], *adj.* inadequate.

inaktiv ['ɪnakti:f, –'ti:f], *adj.* inactive, (*Chem.*) inert, neutral.

Inangriffnahme [ɪn'angrɪfna:mə], *f.* start, beginning made (*with a th.*), setting about (*a th.*), taking in hand, (*coll.*) tackling.

Inanspruchnahme [ɪn'anʃpruxna:mə], *f.* laying claim (*Gen. or* **von.** to); (*Mil.*) requisition; employment, use, utilization (of), reliance (on), resort (to); (*of means, power, resources*) demands, strain, drain (on); preoccupation, absorption (*of attention*); ***zur – des Kredits,*** for availment of credit; ***überaus starke geschäftliche –,*** heavy business claims on one's time.

inartikuliert ['ɪnartikuli:rt, –'li:rt], *adj.* unarticulated; inarticulate.

Inaugenscheinnahme [ɪn'augənʃaɪnna:mə], *f.* inspection, scrutiny.

inaugurieren [ɪnaugu'ri:rən], *v.t.* inaugurate.

Inbegriff ['ɪnbəgrɪf], *m.* contents; embodiment, substance, (quint)essence; sum, total, aggregate; ***mit – der Spesen,*** inclusive of charges. **inbegriffen,** *pred. adj.* including, included, inclusive of, implied.

Inbetrieb|nahme [inbə'tri:p–], **–setzung,** *f.* starting, opening, setting to work, (*coll.*) start-up.

Inbrunst ['ɪnbrunst], *f.* ardour, fervour. **inbrünstig** ['ɪnbrynstɪç], *adj.* ardent, fervent.

Inc. . . . *For words beginning with* **Inc** *see under* **Ink . . .** *or* **Inz. . . .**

indeklinabel [ɪndeklɪ'na:bəl], *adj.* indeclinable.

Indelikatesse [ɪndelika'tɛsə], *f.* indelicacy.

indem [ɪn'de:m], **1.** *adv. See* **indes. 2.** *conj.* (*simultaneity*) during the time that, whilst, while, **as;** (*instrumental*) in that, by (doing).

Indemnität [ɪndɛmni'tɛ:t], *f.* indemnity, exemption.

Inder ['ɪndər], *m.* Hindoo, Hindu, Indian.

indes [ɪn'dɛs], **indessen, 1.** *adv.* (in the) meantime, meanwhile. **2.** *conj.* however, yet, still, for all that, nevertheless, none the less; (*obs.*) whilst, while.

Indeterminismus [ɪndetɛrmi'nɪsmus], *m.* (*Phil.*) free will.

Index ['ɪndɛks], *m.* (**-(es),** *pl.* **-e** *or* **Indices**) index; ***auf den – setzen,*** (*R.C.*) proscribe (*a book*). **Index|-zahl, –ziffer,** *f.* index (number).

Indianer [ɪndi'a:nər], *m.* American (*or* Red) Indian. **indianisch,** *adj.* American (*or* Red) Indian. **Indien** ['ɪndiən], *n.* (*Geog.*) India.

Indienststellung [ɪn'di:nstʃtɛluŋ], *f.* mobilization; – ***eines Schiffes,*** commissioning of a (war-)ship.

Indier ['ɪndiər], *m. See* **Inder.**

indifferent ['ɪndɪferɛnt], *adj.* 1. passive, neutral, indifferent; 2. (*gas*) inert. **Indifferenz,** *f.* passivity, ineffectiveness.

indigen [ɪndi'ge:n], *adj.* indigenous, native. **Indigenat** [–'na:t], *n.* (**-s,** *pl.* **-e**) right of a native; denizenship.

indigniert [ɪndɪg'ni:rt], *adj.* indignant.

Indigo ['ɪndigo], *m.* indigo. **Indigo|blau,** *n.,* **–farbstoff,** *m.,* **–tin,** *n.* indigo blue.

Indikativ ['ɪndikati:f, –'ti:f], *m.* (**-s,** *pl.* **-e**) indicative (mood). **indikativisch** [–'ti:vɪʃ], *adj.* (*Gram.*) indicative.

indirekt ['ɪndirɛkt, –'rɛkt], *adj.* indirect.

indisch ['ɪndɪʃ], *adj.* Indian, Hindoo, Hindu.

indiskret ['ɪndɪskre:t, –'kre:t], *adj.* indiscreet, tactless, (*coll.*) nosy.

indiskutabel ['ɪndɪsku'ta:bəl], *adj.* not subject to discussion, out of the question.

indisponibel ['ɪndɪspo'ni:bəl], *adj.* not to be disposed of, not available.

indisponiert ['ɪndɪspo'ni:rt], *adj.* indisposed, out of sorts; disinclined (from).

Indisziplin ['ɪndɪstsipli:n], *f.* lack of discipline. **indiszipliniert** [–'ni:rt], *adj.* undisciplined.

individualisieren [ɪndividuali'zi:rən], *v.t.* individualize. **individualistisch** [–'lɪstɪʃ], *adj.* individualistic. **Individualität** [–i'tɛ:t], *f.* individuality, personality.

individuell [ɪndividu'ɛl], **1.** *adj.* individual, personal, private. **2.** *adv.* to one's personal requirements *or* taste.

Individuum [ɪndi'vi:duum], *n.* (**-s,** *pl.* **-duen**) individual, (*coll.*) doubtful *or* shady character *or* customer.

Indiz [ɪn'di:ts], *n.,* **Indizienbeweis,** *m.* circumstantial proof *or* evidence. **indizieren** [–'tsi:rən], *v.t.* indicate.

Indossament [ɪndɔsa'mɛnt], *n.* (**-es,** *pl.* **-e**) indorsement, endorsement. **Indossant** [–'sant], *m.* (**-en,** *pl.* **-en**) indorser, endorser. **Indossat,** *m.* (**-en,** *pl.* **-en**), **Indossatar** [–'ta:r], *m.* (**-s,** *pl.* **-e**) indorsee, endorsee. **indossieren** [–'sɪ:rən], *v.t.* indorse, endorse.

Induktion [ɪnduktsi'o:n], *f.* (*Log., Elec.*) induction. **Induktions|apparat,** *m.* inductor; magneto, induction coil. **–elektrizität,** *f.* induced electricity. **–funken,** *m.* induction spark. **–motor,** *m.* induction motor. **–spule,** *f.* (*Elec.*) induction coil, (*Rad.*) inductance (coil). **–strom,** *m.* induction *or* induced current. **Induktivität** [–tivi'tɛ:t], *f.* (*Elec. unit*) inductance. **Induktor** [–'duktɔr], *m.* *See* **Induktionsapparat.**

industrialisieren [ɪndustriali'zi:rən], *v.t.* industrialize. **Industrialisierung,** *f.* industrialization. **Industrialismus** [–'lɪsmus], *m.* industrialism.

Industrie [ɪndus'tri:], *f.* industry. **Industrie|-aktien,** *f.pl.* industrial shares *or* stocks, (*coll.*) industrials. **–arbeiter,** *m.* industrial worker. **–ausstellung,** *f.* industrial exhibition, industries fair. **–berater,** *m.* management consultant. **–betrieb,** *m.* manufacturing plant. **–bezirk,** *m.* *See* **–gebiet. –erzeugnisse,** *n.pl.* manufactured goods, manufactures. **–führer,** *m.* industrial magnate, captain of industry, (*sl.*) tycoon. **–gebiet,** *n.* manufacturing district, industrial area. **–gelände,** *n.* factory sites, industrial estate. **–kapitän,** *m.* *See* **–führer.**

industriell [ɪndustri'ɛl], *adj.* industrial. **Industrielle(r),** *m., f.* industrialist, manufacturer, factory owner.

Industrie|magnat, *m.* *See* **–führer. –messe,** *f.* *See* **–ausstellung. –papiere,** *n.pl.* *See* **–aktien. –ritter,** *m.* (*obs.*) racketeer, fraudulent speculator. **–staat,** *m.* industrial *or* manufacturing country. **–verband,** *m.* federation of industries. **–werk,** *n.* *See* **–betrieb. –werte,** *m.pl.* *See* **–aktien. –wirtschaft,** *f.* industrial sector of the economy. **–zweig,** *m.* (branch of) industry.

induzieren [ɪndu'tsi:rən], *v.t.* (*Log., Elec.*) induce. **induziert,** *adj.* (*Elec.*) induced, secondary.

inegal ['ɪnega:l, –'ga:l], *adj.* unequal; uneven.

ineinander [ɪnaɪn'andər], *adv., sep. pref.* into one another, into each other. **ineinander|fassen,** *v.i.* *See* **–greifen. –flechten,** *irr.v.t.* interlace, intertwine. **–fließen,** *irr.v.i.* flow *or* merge into one another, (*of colours*) run (into one another). **–fügen,** *v.t.* join, fit into each other. **–greifen,** *irr.v.i.* mesh, interlock, (*fig.*) work together; co-operate. **Ineinandergreifen,** *n.* (*fig.*) interplay, harmonious working; chain, concatenation (*of events*). **ineinander|passen,** *v.t.* fit together. **–schieben,** *irr.v.t.* telescope. **–stecken,** *See* **–passen.**

Inempfangnahme [ɪnɛm'pfaŋna:mə], *f.* reception, receiving.

Infam [ɪn'fa:m], *adj.* infamous. **Infamie** [–'mi:], *f.* infamy.

Infant [ɪn'fant], *m.* (**-en,** *pl.* **-en**) (*Hist.*) infante.

Infanterie [ɪnfantə'ri:], *f.* infantry. **Infanterie|-flieger,** *m.* army co-operation plane. **–geschütz,** *n.* close-support gun. **Infanterist,** *m.* (**-en,** *pl.* **-en**) infantryman.

infantil [ɪnfan'ti:l], *adj.* infantile, childish, retarded. **Infantin,** *f.* (*Hist.*) infanta.

Infektions|krankheit [infɛktsi'o:nz–], *f.* infectious disease. **–träger,** *m.* carrier.

Infel ['ɪnfəl], *f.* *See* **Inful.**

inferieren [ɪnfe'ri:rən], *v.t.* deduce, infer.

Inferioritätskomplex [ɪnferiori'tɛ:tskɔmplɛks], *m.* inferiority complex.

infiltrieren [ɪnfɪl'tri:rən], *v.i.* infiltrate.

Infinitesimalrechnung [ɪnfinitezi'ma:lrɛçnuŋ], *f.* infinitesimal calculus.

Infinitiv ['ɪnfiniti:f, –'ti:f], *m.* (**-s,** *pl.* **-e**) infinitive (mood). **infinitivisch** [–'ti:vɪʃ], *adj.* infinitive.

infizieren [ɪnfi'tsi:rən], **1.** *v.t.* infect. **2.** *v.r.* be *or* become infected.

inflationistisch [ɪnflatsio'nɪstɪʃ], *adj.* inflationary **Inflations|politik** [ɪnflatsi'o:nz–], *f.* inflationary policy. **–zeit,** *f.* period of inflation.

Influenz [ɪnflu'ɛnts], *f.* (*Elec.*) (electrostatic) induction.

Influenza [ɪnflu'ɛntsa], *f.* influenza, (*coll.*) flu.

infolge [ɪn'fɔlgə], *prep.* (*Gen.*) as a result of, in consequence of, due *or* owing to. **infolgedessen,** *adv.* hence, consequently, accordingly, as a result, owing to which, because of this.

Information [ɪnfɔrmatsi'o:n], *f.* information (*über* (*Acc.*), about *or* on); ***eine –***, a piece of information; *pl.* information. **informatorisch** [–'to:rɪʃ], *adj.* informative, instructive. **informieren** [–'mi:rən], **1.** *v.t.* inform, give information (*über* (*Acc.*), of, about *or* on), advise, notify (of), acquaint (with), instruct; (*Law, Mil.*) brief (on); ***falsch –***, misinform. **2.** *v.r.* inform o.s., make inquiries, gather information.

Infragestellung [ɪn'fra:gəʃtɛluŋ], *f.* casting doubts (up)on, questioning; endangering, imperilling.

Inful ['ɪnful], *f.* (-, *pl.* **-n**) (bishop's) mitre. **infulieren** [–'li:rən], *v.t.* invest (with episcopal robes).

Infus [ɪn'fu:s], *n.* (**-es,** *pl.* **-e** *or* **-a**), **Infusion** [–zi'o:n], *f.* infusion, decoction. **Infusionstierchen, Infusorien** [–'zo:riən], *pl.* infusoria.

Ingangsetzung [ɪn'gaŋzɛtsuŋ], *f.* starting, setting in motion (*of a machine*).

Ingenieur [ɪnʒeni'ø:r], *m.* (**-s,** *pl.* **-e**) engineer. **Ingenieur|schule,** *f.* school of engineering. **–wesen,** *n.* engineering.

Ingrediens [ɪn'gre:diɛns], *n.* (-, *pl.* **-dienzien** [–di'ɛntsiən]), **Ingredienz** [–'ɛnts], *f.* (-, *pl.* **-en**) (*usu. pl.*) ingredient, component.

Ingreß [ɪn'grɛs], *m.* (**-(ss)es,** *pl.* **-(ss)e**) entry, admission (*into religious order etc.*).

Ingrimm ['ɪngrɪm], *m.* rage, anger, wrath. **ingrimmig,** *adj.* furious, wrathful, very angry; fierce.

Ingwer ['ɪŋvər], *m.* ginger. **Ingwerbier,** *n.* ginger-ale *or* -beer.

Inhaber ['ɪnha:bər], *m.* possessor, (present) holder, proprietor; occupant, (*Comm.*) bearer (*of a bill*); ***– einer Pfründe,*** incumbent. **Inhaber|aktie,** *f.* bearer share. **–scheck,** *m.* cheque to bearer.

inhaftieren [ɪnhaf'ti:rən], *v.t.* take into custody, arrest. **Inhaftierung, Inhaftnahme** [ɪn'haftna:mə], *f.* arrest, imprisonment, detention.

inhalieren [ɪnha'li:rən], *v.t.* inhale.

Inhalt ['ɪnhalt], *m.* contents; content, capacity, extent, area, volume; (*fig.*) tenor, subject (matter), purport, substance, essence, gist, sense, meaning; ***des folgenden –s,*** to the following effect. **inhaltlich,** *adj.* with regard to the contents.

Inhalts|angabe, –anzeige, *f.* (table of) contents, summary, synopsis. **–anzeiger,** *m.* fuel gauge. **–bestimmung, –ermittlung,** *f.* determination of volume. **inhaltsleer, inhaltslos,** *adj.* empty, trivial, meaningless, of little consequence. **inhalts|reich, –schwer,** *adj.* weighty, significant, momentous, full of meaning, pregnant, (*coll.*) meaty. **Inhalts|verzeichnis,** *n.* index; *see also* **–angabe. inhalts|voll,** *adj.* *See* **–schwer.**

inhärent [ɪnhɛ'rɛnt], *adj.* inherent.

inhibieren [ɪnhi'bi:rən], *v.t.* check, stop, hinder, inhibit; (*Law*) ***einen Prozeß –***, stay proceedings. **Inhibitorium** [–'to:rium], *n.* (*Law*) inhibition.

Initial [ɪnitsi'a:l], *n.* (**-s,** *pl.* **-e**), (*usu.*) **Initiale,** *f.* 1. illuminated capital; 2. (*latter only*) initial *or* (*Bot.*) apical cell. **Initialzünder,** *m.* (*Artil.*) primer.

Initiativantrag [initsia'ti:fʔantra:k], *m.* (*Parl.*) private bill.

Initiative [initsia'ti:və], *f.* initiative, first step, (*Swiss*) (*Pol.*) right of initiative, obligatory referendum; ***auf eigene – hin*** or ***aus eigener –***, on one's own initiative, of one's own accord; ***die – ergreifen,*** take the initiative; ***private –***, private enterprise.

injizieren [ɪnji'tsi:rən], *v.t.* inject.

Injurie [ɪn'ju:riə], *f.* insult, slander, libel.

inkarnat [ɪnkar'na:t], *adj.* flesh-coloured, incarnative. **Inkarnat,** *n.* flesh-colour, pink. **inkarniert,** *adj.* incarnate, embodied.

Inkassant [ɪnka'sant], *m.* (**-en,** *pl.* **-en**) (*Austr.*) cashier. **Inkasso** [–'kaso], *n.* (**-s,** *pl.* **-s** (*Austr.*

-kassi)) (*Comm.*) encashment, cashing, collection; ***das – besorgen,*** collect, cash, get cashed, procure payment. **Inkasso|abteilung,** *f.* collection department. **–büro,** *n.* collection agency. **–geschäft,** *n.* collection business, collection of bills. **–spesen,** *pl.* collecting charges. **–wechsel,** *m.* bill for collection.

Inklination [ɪnklinatsi'o:n], *f.* dip (*of magnetic needle*); (*fig.*) inclination, predilection.

inklusive [ɪnklu'zi:və], **1.** *prep.* (*Gen.*) inclusive of, including. **2.** *adv.* inclusive.

inkohärent [ɪnkohɛ'rɛnt], *adj.* incoherent.

inkomplett ['ɪnkɔm'plɛt], *adj.* incomplete.

inkongruent ['ɪnkɔŋgru'ɛnt], *adj.* incongruous. **Inkongruenz,** *f.* (-, *pl.* **-en**) incongruity.

inkonsequent ['ɪnkɔnze'kvɛnt], *adj.* inconsistent, contradictory, inconsequential. **Inkonsequenz,** *f.* (-, *pl.* **-en**) inconsistency, contradiction.

inkorrekt ['ɪnkɔ'rɛkt], *adj.* incorrect.

Inkrafttreten [ɪn'krafttre:tən], *n.* coming into force, taking effect; ***Tag des –s,*** effective date.

Inkretion [ɪnkretsi'o:n], *f.* (*Med.*) internal secretion, endocrine secretion.

Inkubationszeit [ɪnkubatsi'o:nstsait], *f.* incubation period.

inkulant ['ɪnku'lant], *adj.* (*Comm.*) unaccommodating. **Inkulanz,** *f.* incivility, brusqueness.

Inkulpant [ɪnkul'pant], *m.* (**-en,** *pl.* **-en**) (*obs.*) prosecutor. **Inkulpat,** *m.* (**-en,** *pl.* **-en**) (*obs.*) accused, defendant.

Inkunabel [ɪnku'na:bəl], *f.* (-, *pl.* **-n**) early printed book, *pl.* incunabula.

Inland ['ɪnlant], *n.* inland, interior; native *or* home country, home; ***im In- und Auslande,*** at home and abroad; ***fürs – bestimmt,*** for home consumption. **Inland|absatz,** *m.* sales in the home market. **–anleihe,** *f.* internal loan. **–bedarf,** *m.* domestic requirements.

Inländer ['ɪnlɛndər], *m.* native. **inländisch,** *adj.* inland, internal, domestic, home, national; indigenous, native, home-bred, home-made; ***–es Fabrikat,*** home produce (*not foreign*).

Inlands– ['ɪnlants–], *pref. See* **inländisch.**

Inlaut ['ɪnlaut], *m.* (**-(e)s,** *pl.* **-e**) medial sound; ***im –,*** medially.

Inlett ['ɪnlɛt], *n.* (**-(e)s,** *pl.* **-e**; *Austr.* **-s,** *pl.* **-en**) bed-tick *or* ticking.

inliegend ['ɪnli:gənt], *adj.* enclosed, herewith.

inmitten [ɪn'mɪtən], *prep.* (*Gen.*) in the midst of, amidst, amid.

inne ['ɪnə], *adv., sep. pref.* within; ***mitten –,*** right in the middle *or* midst. **inne|haben,** *irr.v.t.* 1. occupy, possess, hold, be master of; 2. know, understand, be thoroughly acquainted with, have at one's finger-tips. **–halten, 1.** *irr.v.t.* maintain, keep to, observe. **2.** *irr.v.i.* stop, pause, leave off.

innen ['ɪnən], *adv.* within, (on the) inside; ***– und außen,*** inside and out(side), within and without, (*fig.*) through and through; ***nach –,*** inwards; ***von –,*** from within.

Innen|ansicht, *f.* interior view, view of the interior. **–antenne,** *f.* (*Rad.*) indoor aerial *or* (*Am.*) antenna. **–architektur, –ausstattung,** *f.* interior decoration. **–backenbremse,** *f.* (*Motor.*) internal expanding brake. **–bahn,** *f.* (*Spt.*) inside lane. **–dienst,** *m.* (*Mil.*) garrison duty. **–druck,** *m.* internal pressure. **–durchmesser,** *m.* inside diameter. **–einrichtung,** *f. See* **–ausstattung. –fläche,** *f. See* **–seite. –gewinde,** *n.* female *or* internal thread. **–leben,** *n.* inner life. **–leitung,** *f.* inside wiring, piping *etc.* **–lunker,** *m.* (*Metall.*) blow-hole. **–minister,** *m.* (*Eng.*) Home Secretary, (*Am.*) Secretary of the Interior. **–ministerium,** *n.* (*Eng.*) Home Office, (*Am.*) Department of the Interior. **–politik,** *f.* domestic *or* home policy. **innenpolitisch,** *adj.* internal, relating to home affairs. **Innen|raum,** *m.* interior (space). **–seite,** *f.* inner surface, inside; palm (of the hand). **–stadt,** *f.* city centre, (*Am.*) downtown. **–tasche,** *f.* inside pocket. **–welt,** *f. See* **–leben. –winkel,** *m.* interior angle.

inner ['ɪnər], *adj.* interior, internal, inner, inward, intestine, domestic; intrinsic, spiritual; (*Pol.*) ***–e Angelegenheiten,*** internal affairs; ***das –e Auge,*** the mind's eye; ***–er Durchmesser,*** internal diameter; ***–er Halt,*** moral backbone *or* fibre, (*coll.*) guts; ***–es Leiden,*** internal complaint; ***–er Mangel,*** inherent shortcoming; ***–e Mission,*** home mission; ***–e Schiffsladung,*** inboard cargo; ***die –e Stimme,*** inner voice, conscience; ***–er Verbrauch,*** home consumption; ***–er Wert,*** intrinsic value. **Innereien** [ɪnə'raiən], *f.pl.* offal, innards.

Innere(s) ['ɪnərə(s)], *n.* interior, inside; inner self, heart, soul, core; ***das Innere der Erde,*** the centre *or* bowels of the earth; ***Ministerium des Inneren,*** *see* **Innenministerium**; (*fig.*) ***im Inneren,*** at heart, secretly; ***im tiefsten Inneren,*** in the inmost recesses of the heart.

innerhalb ['ɪnərhalp], *adv., prep.* (*Gen.*) within, inside; ***– eines Jahres,*** within *or* (*coll.*) inside of a year (*but with Dat. when Gen. form is not recognizable, e.g.* ***– vier Jahren***).

innerlich ['ɪnərlɪç], *adj. See* **inner**; (*fig.*) mental, spiritual; introspective, contemplative; profound, heartfelt, sincere, cordial; intrinsic; ***– anzuwenden,*** to be taken internally. **Innerlichkeit,** *f.* inwardness, subjectivity, subjectiveness; profoundness; cordiality, warmth.

innerst ['ɪnərst], *adj.* (*sup. of* **inner**) inmost, innermost; ***meine –e Überzeugung,*** my firm *or* deepest conviction; ***meine –en Gedanken,*** my most secret thoughts; ***mein Innerstes,*** my inmost soul, the bottom of my heart; ***bis ins Innerste,*** to the very heart *or* core, to the foundations; ***im Innersten,*** in one's heart, at heart.

innert ['ɪnərt], *prep.* (*Swiss*) *see* **innerhalb.**

inne|werden, *irr.v.i.* (*Gen.*) become aware *or* conscious of, see, perceive, learn, awaken to. **–wohnen,** *v.t.* (*Dat.*) be characteristic of, be inherent in, be proper to.

innig ['ɪnɪç], *adj.* intimate, heartfelt, sincere; warm, tender, affectionate, cordial, fervent, ardent; ***–e Freundschaft,*** close friendship; ***– lieben,*** love dearly; (*Chem.*) ***–e Mischung,*** intimate mixture. **Innigkeit,** *f.* cordiality, warmth, tenderness, sincerity, fervour, ardour, intimacy. **inniglich,** *adv. See* **innig.**

Innung ['ɪnuŋ], *f.* guild, corporation. **Innungswesen,** *n.* guild system.

inoffiziell ['ɪnɔfi'tsjɛl, –i'ɛl], *adj.* unofficial, informal.

inokulieren [ɪnoku'li:rən], *v.t.* inoculate.

inopportun [ɪn'ɔpɔrtu:n, –'tu:n], *adj.* inopportune untimely, (*coll.*) out of place.

inquisitorisch [ɪnkvizi'to:rɪʃ], *adj.* inquisitorial.

ins [ɪns], *contr. for in das.*

Insasse ['ɪnzasə], *m.* (**-n,** *pl.* **-n**) inmate; inhabitant; passenger, occupant.

insbesondere [ɪnsbə'zɔndərə], *adv.* particularly, in particular, (e)specially, above all.

Inschrift ['ɪnʃrɪft], *f.* inscription; legend, caption, epigraph. **Inschriftenkunde,** *f.* epigraphy.

Insekt [ɪn'zɛkt], *n.* (**-(e)s,** *pl.* **-en**) insect. **Insekten|blütler,** *m.pl.* (*Bot.*) entomophilae. **–fraß,** *m.* damage *or* ravage by insects. **insektenfressend,** *adj.* insectivorous. **Insekten|kunde, –lehre,** *f.* entomology. **–pulver, –(vertilgungs)mittel,** *n.* insect powder, insecticide.

Insel ['ɪnzəl], *f.* (-, *pl.* **-n**) island, (*Poet. and in names*) isle. **Insel|bewohner,** *m.* islander. **Inselchen,** *n.* islet. **Insel|gruppe,** *f.* **–meer,** *n.* archipelago. **–reich,** *n.* island realm (*usu. refers to Denmark*). **inselreich,** *adj.* studded *or* dotted with islands. **Inselvolk,** *n.* islanders, insular race.

Inserat [ɪnze'ra:t], *n.* (**-(e)s,** *pl.* **-e**) advertisement. **Inseraten|büro,** *n.* advertising agency. **–teil,** *m. or n.* advertisement columns (*of newspaper*). **Inserent,** *m.* (**-en,** *pl.* **-en**) advertiser. **inserieren, 1.** *v.i.* insert an advertisement, advertise. **2.** *v.t.* advertise.

ins|geheim, *adv.* in secret, secretly, privily.

-gemein, *adv.* in general, generally, usually, commonly. **-gesamt,** *adv.* altogether, all together, in a body, collectively.

Insignien [ɪn'zigniən], *pl.* insignia, regalia, badge of office.

inskribieren [ɪnskri'bi:rən], **1.** *v.t.* inscribe. **2.** *v.r.* enter one's name, register.

insofern [ɪnzo'fɛrn], **1.** *adv.* to that extent, so far, as far as that goes, in this respect. **2.** *conj.* – *als,* in so far as, inasmuch as, in that.

Insolvenz [ɪnzɔl'vɛnts], *f.* insolvency.

insonderheit, *adv.* (*obs.*) *see* **insbesondere.**

insoweit, *adv. See* **insofern, 1.**

Inspekteur [ɪnspɛk'tø:r], *m.* (**-s,** *pl.* **-e**) *see* **Inspektor. Inspektion** [–si'o:n], *f.* inspection, supervision. **Inspektor,** *m.* (**-s,** *pl.* **-en**) inspector, supervisor, (*of an estate*) steward.

inspirieren [ɪnspi'ri:rən], *v.t.* inspire.

Inspizient [ɪnspitsi'ɛnt], *m.* (**-en,** *pl.* **-en**) (*Theat.*) stage-manager; inspector. **inspizieren** [–'tsi:rən], inspect, superintend.

Installateur [ɪnstala'tø:r], *m.* (**-s,** *pl.* **-e**) plumber, electrician, fitter. **installieren** [–'li:rən], *v.t.* install, fit, put in, mount.

instandhalten [ɪn'ʃtanthaltən], *irr.v.t.* keep in repair *or* good order, maintain, service, keep up. **Instandhaltung,** *f.* repair, maintenance, servicing, upkeep.

inständig ['ɪnʃtɛndɪç], *adj.* urgent, pressing, earnest (*only used of requests etc.*); – ***bitten,*** beseech, implore.

instandsetzen [ɪn'ʃtantzɛtsən], *v.t.* 1. repair, recondition, overhaul, restore, mend, (*coll.*) do up; 2. make ready; prepare; enable. **Instand|setzung,** *f.* maintenance, servicing, overhaul, repair, reconditioning, restoration. **-stellung,** *f.* (*Swiss*) *see* **-setzung.**

Instanz [ɪn'ʃtants], *f.* (-, *pl.* **-en**) authority, court (of justice); stage (*of proceedings*); ***höhere* –,** superior court; ***letzte* –,** last resort; ***von der – abgewiesen,*** out of court; ***von der – entbunden,*** discharged (*not acquitted*). **Instanzen|weg,** *m.* official channels; stage of appeal. **-zug,** *m.* successive appeal.

Inste, *m.* (**-n,** *pl.* **-n**) (*dial.*) *see* **Instmann.**

Inster ['ɪnstər], *m. or n.* (*dial.*) pluck, tripe, entrails, offal.

Instinkt [ɪn'stɪŋkt], *m.* (**-(e)s,** *pl.* **-e**) instinct; (*fig.*) – ***für,*** instinctive sense of, flair *or* feeling for. **instinktartig, instinktiv** [–'ti:f], **instinktmäßig,** *adv.* instinctive.

instituieren [ɪnstitu'i:rən], *v.t.* institute. **Institut** [–'tu:t], *n.* (**-s,** *pl.* **-e**) institution, establishment; institute (*of science or learning*), academy; boarding school. **institutionell** [–tsio'nɛl], *adj.* institutional.

Instmann ['ɪnstman], *m.* (**-es,** *pl.* **-leute**) (*dial.*) cottager.

instruieren [ɪnstru'i:rən], *v.t.* instruct, brief; (*Law*) ***einen Prozeß* –,** draw up *or* prepare a case. **Instruktion** [ɪnstruktsi'o:n], *f.* instruction(s), orders, regulations, directions, (*Law, Mil.*) briefing).

Instrument [ɪnstru'mɛnt], *n.* (**-(e)s,** *pl.* **-e**) instrument (*also Mus.*), implement, tool, (*Law*) (legal) instrument, deed. **instrumental** [–'ta:l], *adj.* instrumental. **Instrumentenbrett,** *n.* (*Motor.*) dashboard, control *or* instrument panel. **instrumentieren,** *v.t.* (*Mus.*) orchestrate, score.

Insulaner [ɪnzu'la:nər], *m.* islander, island dweller.

inszenieren [ɪntse'ni:rən], *v.t.* (*Theat.*) (put on the) stage, produce. **Inszenierung,** *f.* mise-en-scène, (*Theat.*) staging, production.

Intarsia [ɪn'tarzia], *f.* inlay, inlaid work, marquetry.

Integral|rechnung [ɪnte'gra:l–], *f.* integral calculus. **-zahl,** *f.* integer. **integrieren,** *v.t.* integrate.

Intellekt [ɪntɛ'lɛkt], *m.* (**-s,** *pl.* **-e**) intellect. **intellektuell** [–u'ɛl], *adj.* intellectual. **Intellektuelle(r),** *m., f.* intellectual, (*coll.*) high-brow, egg-head; *pl.* the intelligentsia.

intelligent [ɪntɛli'gɛnt], *adj.* intelligent, (*coll.*) brainy. **Intelligenz,** *f.* 1. intellect, brains, intelligence, understanding, cleverness; 2. intelligentsia, intellectuals. **Intelligenzblatt,** *n.* (*obs.*) advertiser (*newspaper*). **Intelligenzler,** *m. See* **Intellektuelle(r).**

Intendant [ɪntɛn'dant], *m.* (**-en,** *pl.* **-en**) director, superintendent; (theatrical) manager; (*Mil.*) administrative officer. **Intendantur** [–'tu:r], *f.* (-, *pl.* **-en**) superintendent's office *or* department; board of management, (*obs. Mil.*) Quartermaster-General's Department, commissariat.

Intensität [ɪntɛnzi'tɛ:t], *f.* intensity. **intensiv** [–'zi:f], *adj.* thorough, intensive. **intensivieren** [–'vi:rən], *v.t.* intensify.

interessant [ɪnterɛ'sant], *adj.* interesting, of interest (*für,* to). **Interesse** [–'rɛsə], *n.* (**-s,** *pl.* **-n**) 1. interest (***an*** (*Dat.*) *or* ***für,*** in); ***er hat – für,*** he is interested in; 2. advantages; 3. *pl.* (*obs.*) interest (*on money*). **Interessen|gemeinschaft,** *f.* community of interests; pooling agreement. **-gruppe,** *f.* (*Pol.*) pressure group. **-politik,** *f.* policy based on (commercial) interests. **-sphäre,** *f.* sphere of influence. **Interessent,** *m.* (**-en,** *pl.* **-en**) interested party, prospective customer; applicant (*for a post*); *pl.* vested interests.

interessieren [ɪnterɛ'si:rən], **1.** *v.t.* interest (***für,*** in), have *or* hold interest for (*a p.*), arouse the interest of (*a p.*) (in); ***interessiert sein an*** (*Dat.*), be interested in, be concerned in *or* with. **2.** *v.r.* interest o.s., show *or* take an interest (***für,*** in).

interimistisch [ɪnteri'mɪstɪʃ], *adj.* provisional, temporary, interim. **Interims|(anleihe)schein,** *m.* scrip. **-konto,** *n.* suspense account. **-regierung,** *f.* provisional government, interregnum. **-wechsel,** *m.* bill ad interim, provisional bill of exchange.

interkonfessionell [ɪntɛrkɔnfɛsio'nɛl], *adj.* interdenominational, undenominational.

intermediär [ɪntɛrmedi'ɛ:r], *adj.* intermediate, intermediary.

intermittierend [ɪntɛrmɪ'ti:rənt], *adj.* intermittent.

intern [ɪn'tɛrn], *adj.* internal. **Internat** [–'na:t], *n.* (**-s,** *pl.* **-e**) boarding school. **Interne(r),** *m., f.* boarder. **internieren,** *v.t.* intern, confine, detain; isolate (*cases of infectious disease*). **Internierte(r),** *m.* internee. **Internierung,** *f.* internment; isolation. **Internist** [–'nɪst], *m.* (**-en,** *pl.* **-en**) specialist for internal diseases.

interpellieren [ɪntɛrpɛ'li:rən], *v.t.* interrogate, interpellate.

interpolieren [ɪntɛrpo'li:rən], *v.t.* interpolate.

Interpret [ɪntɛr'pre:t], *m.* (**-en,** *pl.* **-en**) interpreter, expounder. **interpretieren** [–'ti:rən], *v.t.* interpret, explain, expound.

interpungieren [ɪntɛrpuŋ'gi:rən], **interpunktieren,** *v.t.* punctuate. **Interpunktion** [–tsi'o:n], *f.* punctuation. **Interpunktionszeichen,** *n.* punctuation mark.

Intervall [ɪntɛr'val], *n.* (**-s,** *pl.* **-e**) (*Mus.*) interval.

intervenieren [ɪntɛrve'ni:rən], *v.i.* intervene, interfere.

Interview [ɪntɛr'vju:], *n.* interview. **interviewen,** *v.t.* interview.

intim [ɪn'ti:m], *adj.* intimate, familiar; ***–e Bekanntschaft,*** close friendship. **Intimität** [–i'tɛ:t], *f.* intimacy, familiarity. **Intimus,** *m.* (-, *pl.* **-mi**) (*coll.*) intimate friend, chum.

Intoleranz ['ɪntole'rants], *f.* intolerance.

intonieren [ɪnto'ni:rən], *v.t.* intone, intonate.

Intrade [ɪn'tra:də], *f.* (*Mus.*) prelude; (trumpet-) flourish.

intransitiv ['ɪntranzi'ti:f], *adj.* intransitive. **Intransitiv,** *n.* (**-s,** *pl.* **-e**), **Intransitivum,** *n.* (**-ums,** *pl.* **-va**) intransitive verb.

intrigant [ɪntri'gant], *adj.* plotting, scheming, designing. **Intrigant,** *m.* (**-en,** *pl.* **-en**) intriguer, schemer, plotter. **Intrige** [–'tri:gə], *f.* intrigue, scheme, plot. **intrigieren,** *v.t.* intrigue, plot, scheme.

intuitiv [ɪntui'ti:f], *adj.* intuitive.

intus ['ɪntus], *adj.* (*coll.*) – ***haben,*** have understood, know full well.

invalid(e) [ɪnva'li:d(ə)], *adj.* disabled. **Invaliden|-heim,** *n.* home for disabled soldiers. **–liste,** *f.* retired *or* superannuated list. **–rente,** *f.* old age *or* disability pension. **–versicherung,** *f.* old age insurance. **Invalide(r),** *m.* disabled soldier, unemployable p. (*through old age or disability*).

invalidieren [ɪnvali'di:rən], *v.t.* invalidate. **Invalidierung,** *f.* invalidation, disallowance. **Invalidität** [–'tɛ:t], *f.* disability (*of a workman, soldier*).

Invariante [ɪnvari'antə], *f.* (*Math.*) invariable.

Inventar [ɪnvɛn'ta:r], *n.* (**-s,** *pl.* **-e** (*Austr.* **-ien**)) inventory, stock-list; ***ein – aufnehmen,*** draw up *or* take *or* make an inventory; ***lebendes –,*** livestock; ***totes –,*** fixtures. **inventarisieren** [–ri'zi:rən], **1.** *v.t.* list, catalogue. **2.** *v.i.* take stock; draw up *or* make *or* take an inventory. **Inventarverzeichnis,** *n.* stock-list *or* -book.

Inventur [ɪnvɛn'tu:r], *f.* (-, *pl.* **-en**) stock-taking; – ***machen,*** take stock. **Inventur|aufnahme,** *f. See* **Inventur. –ausverkauf,** *m.* stock-taking sale.

investieren [ɪnvɛs'ti:rən], *v.t.* invest (with). **Investierung,** *f.* investment, investiture.

Investition [ɪnvɛstitsi'o:n], *f.* (capital) investment. **Investitions|güter,** *n.pl.* capital goods. **–kredit,** *m.* capital development credit.

inwendig ['ɪnvɛndɪç], *adj.* interior, inside, inward; ***in- und auswendig kennen,*** know thoroughly, know completely by heart.

inwiefern [ɪnvi:'fɛrn], **inwieweit,** *adv.* to what extent, in what way *or* respect, (in) how far.

Inzahlungsnahme [ɪn'za:luŋsna:mə], *f.* trading-in.

Inzest [ɪn'tsɛst], *m.* (**-es,** *pl.* **-e**) incest, endogamy, inbreeding. **inzestuös** [–u'ø:z], *adj.* incestuous.

Inzicht [ɪn'tsɪçt], *f.* (-, *pl.* **-en**) (*obs.*) accusation; grounds for suspicion.

inzident [ɪntsi'dɛnt], *adj.* casual, incidental, incident (to). **Inzidentien,** *pl.* incidentals. **Inzidenz,** *f.* incidence. **Inzidenzwinkel,** *m.* angle of incidence. **inzidieren,** *v.i.* (*Math.*) (*mit*) be incident (*on a line*).

Inzucht ['ɪntsuxt], *f.* inbreeding; endogamy.

inzwischen [ɪn'tsvɪʃən], *adv.* in the meantime, meanwhile.

Ion [i'o:n], *n.* (**-s,** *pl.* **-en**) ion. **Ionen|bildung,** *f.* formation of ions. **–geschwindigkeit,** *f.* ionic velocity. **–reihe,** *f.* ionic series. **–spaltung,** *f.* ionization. **–wanderung,** *f.* ionic migration.

ionisch [i'o:nɪʃ], *adj.* (*Geog.*) Ionian, (*Archit.*) Ionic.

ionisieren [ioni'zi:rən], *v.t.* ionize. **Ionisierung,** *f.* ionization.

Iota, *n. See* **Jota.**

Iper ['ɪpər], *f.* (-, *pl.* **-n**) (*Bot.*) common elm (*Ulmus campestris*).

Irak [i'ra:k], *m.* Iraq. **Iraker,** *m.* Iraqi, Iraki. **irakisch,** *adj.* Iraqi, Iraki.

irden ['ɪrdən], *adj.* earthen(ware), made of earth *or* clay; ***–es Geschirr,*** earthenware, crockery; ***–e Pfeife,*** clay-pipe. **irdisch,** *adj.* earthly, worldly, terrestrial; temporal, mortal; ***–es Dasein,*** life on earth, temporal existence; ***–e Dinge,*** earthly things, temporal affairs; ***– gesinnt,*** worldly-minded; ***–e Hülle, –e Überreste,*** mortal remains.

Ire ['i:rə], *m.* (**-n,** *pl.* **-n**) Irishman.

irgend ['ɪrgənt], *adv.* **1.** (*frequently as pref.: see below*) (*intensifying indefiniteness of following pron. or pronominal comp.*) – ***jemand,*** anyone, anybody, somebody *or* s.o. or other; – ***etwas,*** anything whatever, s.th. or other; – (***woher***) ***wohin,*** (from) anywhere (whatever), (from) somewhere or other; **2.** (*after relatives: expresses* (*grudging*) *concession*) **–ever,** at all; ***was ich – tun kann,*** whatever I can do; ***wann*** (***wo***) ***es – vorkommt,*** whenever (wherever) it occurs; ***wenn – möglich,*** if at all possible; ***so gut wie – möglich,*** just as good as possible; ***ist – eine Hoffnung vorhanden?*** is there any hope (at all)?

irgend|ein, 1. *indef. pron.* someone (or other), anyone (you like). **2.** *indef. adj.* any (at all), any . . . you like, some sort of, (*coll.*) any old; ***auf –e Art,*** in some way or other, somehow. **–einmal, –wann,** *adv.* sometime, some time or other. **–was,** *pron.* (*coll.*) *see* ***irgend etwas.*** **–welch,** *indef. adj.* some, any (whatever *or* at all). **–wer,** *pron. See* ***irgend jemand.*** **–wie,** *adv.* somehow (or other), in some way (or other). **–wo,** *adv.* somewhere (or other), anywhere (whatever *or* at all), in some place or other. **–woher, –wohin,** *adv. See* ***irgend*** (***woher***) ***wohin.***

Irin ['i:rin], *f.* Irishwoman. **irisch,** *adj.* Irish.

irisierend [iri'zi:rənt], *adj.* iridescent.

Irland ['ɪrlant], *n.* Ireland, (*Poet.*) Erin. **Irländer,** *m. See* **Ire. irländisch,** *adj. See* **irisch.**

Ironie [iro'ni:], *f.* irony. **ironisch** [i'ro:nɪʃ], *adj.* ironical. **ironisieren** [–'zi:rən], *v.t.* treat with irony.

irr(e) ['ɪr(ə)], *adj.* in error, wrong, (*coll.*) off the mark, on the wrong track *or* tack; astray, wandering, lost; confused, puzzled, perplexed, disconcerted; wavering, uncertain; delirious, mentally deranged, out of one's mind, crazy, insane. **Irre,** *f.* (*only in*) ***in die – führen,*** lead astray; ***in die – gehen,*** go astray.

irreal ['ɪrea:l, –'a:l], *adj.* unreal, imaginary.

irre|führen, *v.t.* lead astray, mislead; hoodwink. deceive; ***sich – lassen,*** be misled *or* (*coll.*) taken in. **–führend,** *adj.* misleading, deceptive. **–gehen,** *irr.v.i.* (*aux.* s.) go astray, lose one's way, (*of letters etc.*) miscarry. **–leiten,** *v.t. See* **–führen. –machen,** *v.t.* bewilder, confuse, puzzle, perplex.

irren ['ɪrən], **1.** *v.i.* (*aux.* h. *&* s.) go astray, lose one's way; err, be mistaken *or* wrong, make a mistake. **2.** *v.r.* be mistaken, be wrong; make a mistake; ***sich in ihm –,*** be mistaken in *or* about him, be disappointed in him. **Irren,** *n. See* **Irrtum**; ***– ist menschlich,*** to err is human.

Irren|anstalt, *f.* mental hospital. **–arzt,** *m.* psychiatrist, alienist. **–haus,** *n.* (*fig.*) madhouse.

Irre(r) ['ɪrə(r)], *m., f.* madman, lunatic.

irrereden ['ɪrəre:dən], *v.i.* rave, talk incoherently. **Irresein,** *n.* insanity, mental instability. **irrewerden,** *irr.v.i.* (*aux.* s.) – ***an*** (*Dat.*), not know what to make of, have one's doubts about, begin to doubt, lose confidence *or* faith in.

Irr|fahrt, *f.* helpless wandering about. **–gang,** *m.* aberration, fruitless *or* bootless errand; (*usu. pl.*) maze, labyrinth. **–garten,** *m.* maze, labyrinth. **–gast,** *m.* (*Orn.*) accidental migrant. **–glaube,** *m.* heresy; heterodoxy. **irrgläubig,** *adj.* heterodox, heretical. **Irrgläubige(r),** *m., f.* heretic.

irrig ['ɪrɪç], *adj.* erroneous, false, incorrect, wrong. **irrigerweise,** *adv.* by mistake, erroneously.

irritieren [ɪri'ti:rən], *v.t.* irritate, annoy, exasperate; upset, disturb, puzzle, intrigue.

Irr|läufer, *m.* letter delivered to the wrong address. **–lehre,** *f. See* **–glaube. –licht,** *n.* will-o'-the-wisp, jack-o'-lantern. **irrlichter(e)n,** *v.i.* dart about like a will-o'-the-wisp. **Irrpfad,** *m.* wrong path. **Irrsal,** *n.* (**-s,** *pl.* **-e**) erring, sin, error. **Irrsinn,** *m.* insanity, madness, mental derangement. **irrsinnig,** *adj.* insane, mad, (*coll.*) crazy. **Irrsinnige(r),** *m., f. See* **Irre(r).**

Irrtum ['ɪrtu:m], *m.* (**-s,** *pl.* **⸚er**) error, mistake, oversight, (*coll.*) slip; misunderstanding, erroneous idea; ***ihm seinen – benehmen,*** undeceive him, disabuse his mind; (*coll.*) – ***vorbehalten,*** errors excepted; ***ein – von mir,*** my mistake. **irrtümlich,** *adj.* erroneous, mistaken, false.

Irrung ['ɪruŋ], *f.* error, mistake; misunderstanding, difference; dispute. **Irr|wahn,** *m.* delusion, erroneous opinion. **–weg,** *m.* wrong way; ***auf –e geraten,*** lose one's way. **–wisch,** *m. See* **–licht**; (*also coll.*) flibbertigibbet, flighty p.

Isabellfarbe [ɪza'bɛlfarbə], *f.* buff, dun, cream-colour.

Ischias ['ɪʃias], *f.* sciatica. **Ischiasnerv,** *m.* sciatic nerve.

Island ['i:slant], *n.* (*Geog.*) Iceland. **Isländer,** *m.* Icelander. **isländisch,** *adj.* Icelandic.

Isobare [izo'ba:rə], *f.* (*Meteor.*) isobar.

isochron [izo'kro:n], *adj.* isochronous, isochronic.

Isogon [izo'go:n], *n.* (**-s,** *pl.* **-e**) equiangular and equilateral polygon.

Isolation [izolatsi'o:n], *f.* isolation, (*Elec.*) insulation. **Isolator** [-'la:tɔr], *m.* (**-s,** *pl.* **-en**) (*Elec.*) insulator, insulating material.

Isolier|band [izo'li:r-], *n.* insulating tape. **-baracke,** *f.* isolation ward *or* hospital. **isolieren,** *v.t.* isolate, quarantine; (*Elec.*) insulate; (*Rad.*) screen; lag (*plumbing*). **Isolier|flasche,** *f.* vacuum *or* thermos flask. **-haft,** *f.* solitary confinement. **-schicht,** *f.* insulating layer. **-schutz,** *m.* insulation. **-station,** *f.* isolation ward. **Isolierung,** *f.* isolation, quarantine; insulation; lagging. **Isolierzelle,** *f.* padded cell, solitary confinement *or* punishment cell.

isomer [izo'me:r], *adj.* isomeric. **isomorph,** *adj.* isomorphic, isomorphous. **Isotop,** *n.* (**-s,** *pl.* **-e**) isotope. **isotrop,** *adj.* isotropic.

Israel ['ɪsraɛl], *n.* (*Geog.*) Israel. **Israeli** [isra'e:li], *m.* (**-s,** *pl.* **-s**) Israeli. **israelisch,** *adj.* Israeli. **Israelit** [-'li:t], *m.* (**-en,** *pl.* **-en**) Israelite. **israelitisch,** *adj.* Israelite.

issest ['ɪsəst], **ißt,** *see* **essen.**

ist [ɪst], *see* **sein. Ist|ausgabe,** *f.* actual issue. **-bestand,** *m.* stock in hand. **-eingänge,** *m.pl.*, **-einnahmen,** *f.pl.* clear income, net receipts. **-stand,** *m.*, **-stärke,** *f.* (*Mil.*) effective strength, actual strength.

Italien [i'ta:liən], *n.* (*Geog.*) Italy. **Italiener** [-'e:nər], *m.* Italian. **italienisch** [-'e:nɪʃ], *adj.* Italian.

itze ['ɪtsə], **itzo** ['ɪtso], **itzt** [ɪtst], *adv.* (*obs., dial.*) now, at present. **itzig,** *adj.* (*dial.*) the same; *– **und allein,*** solely, by itself.

Itzig ['ɪtzɪç], *m.* (*sl.*) sheeny.

J

J, j [jɔt], *n.* J, j.

ja [ja:], *adv., part.* yes, (*Naut.*) aye, (*B., Poet.*) yea; truly, really, indeed, certainly; by all means, of course, (*obs.*) forsooth; even; well; you know.

(a) (*with emphasis*) ***nimm dich – in acht,*** be sure to take care; ***geh – nicht dahin,*** do not go there on any account; ***das mußt du – tun,*** you must do that without fail *or* in any case *or* at all events *or* come what may; ***sei doch – so gut!*** please be so good *or* kind; ***daß du es – nicht wieder tust,*** see to it *or* make sure *or* mind that you don't do that again; ***– doch!*** to be sure, really; ***– freilich,*** *see* **jawohl**; ***wenn –,*** if so, if this is the case, in that case.

(b) (*without emphasis*) ***er ist – mein Freund,*** after all he is my friend; ***ich gebe mir – Mühe,*** I do take pains; ***da ist er –!*** well, there he is; ***Sie sehen – ganz blaß aus,*** you certainly look quite pale; ***– wenn es sein muß,*** if it must needs be; ***wenn er – kommt,*** if indeed he comes at all, even if he should come; ***ich sage es –,*** in any case I am telling you; ***ich wünsche, daß du es tust, – ich bitte darum,*** I wish, I even beg you to do it, (*obs.*) I wish, nay I beg, that you would do it; ***warum schreibst du nicht? Ich schreibe –,*** Why are you not writing? But I am! ***er ist hier – zu Hause,*** this is his home, you know; ***ich habe es dir – schon gesagt,*** well, I have told you before; ***– was ich sagen wollte,*** by the way I was going to tell you; ***– was wollen sie denn eigentlich?*** well *or* why, what do you want anyway?

Ja, *n.* (**-s,** *pl.* **-s**) assent, consent, approval; affirmation; ***– sagen,*** give one's consent; ***mit einem – beantworten,*** answer in the affirmative. **Jabruder,** *m.* (*coll.*) yes-man.

jach [jax], (*Poet., obs.*) *see* **jäh.**

jachern ['jaxərn], *v.i.* (*dial.*) romp, roister.

Jacht [jaxt], *f.* (-, *pl.* **-en**) yacht.

jachtern ['jaxtərn], *v.i.* (*dial.*) *see* **jachern.**

Jachtklub ['jaxtklup], *m.* yacht *or* sailing club.

Jäckchen ['jɛkçən], *n.* vest, jacket, short coat, coatee.

Jacke ['jakə], *f.* jacket; coat; jerkin; (*coll.*) ***ihm die – voll klopfen,*** thrash him soundly; (*coll.*) ***ihm die – voll lügen,*** stuff him with lies; (*coll.*) ***das ist – wie Hose,*** that is much of a muchness, it's all one *or* all the same. **Jackenkleid,** *n.* (ladies') costume, two-piece.

Jackett [ʒa'kɛt], *n.* (**-(e)s,** *pl.* **-e** *or* **-s**) (short) coat, jacket (*for men*). **Jackettanzug,** *m.* lounge suit.

Jagd [ja:kt], *f.* (-, *pl.* **-en**) chase, hunt, pursuit; shooting, hunting-party, hunting expedition; the huntsmen, hounds, the hunt; (*coll.*) rush; ***auf die – gehen,*** go hunting *or* shooting; ***– machen auf*** (*Acc.*), give chase to, hunt; chase *or* run after; ***hohe –,*** deer-stalking; ***– nach dem Glück,*** pursuit of happiness.

Jagd|abwehr, *f.* (*Av.*) fighter defence. **-aufseher,** *m.* gamekeeper. **jagdbar,** *adj.* fit for the chase, fair game. **jagdberechtigt,** *adj.* licensed to shoot. **Jagd|berechtigung,** *f.* shooting-licence. **-beute,** *f.* bag, booty, quarry. **-bezirk,** *m.* hunting-ground, preserve. **-bomber,** *m.* (*Av.*) fighter-bomber. **-büchse,** *f.* sporting gun. **-einsitzer,** *m.* (*Av.*) single-seater fighter. **-flieger,** *m.* (*Av.*) fighter pilot. **-flinte,** *f.* *See* **-büchse,** (*obs.*) fowling piece. **-flugzeug,** *n.* (*Av.*) fighter (plane), (*Am.*) pursuit plane. **-freund,** *m.* keen huntsman. **-frevel,** *m.* poaching. **jagdgerecht,** *adj.* skilled in the chase; broken in (*of dogs*). **Jagd|gerechtigkeit,** *f.* shooting rights. **-geschichte,** *f.* (hunter's) tall story. **-geschwader,** *n.* (*Av.*) fighter group, (*Am.*) pursuit wing. **-gesellschaft,** *f.* shooting-party. **-gesetz,** *n.* game law. **-gewehr,** *n.* sporting-gun. **-gründe,** *m.pl.* hunting grounds; (*coll.*) ***in die ewigen –,*** to the happy hunting-grounds. **-gruppe,** *f.* (*Av.*) fighter wing, (*Am.*) pursuit group. **-haus,** *n.* shooting-lodge. **-horn,** *n.* hunting-horn. **-hund,** *m.* hound, setter. **-hütte,** *f.* shooting-box. **-messer,** *n.* hunting-knife. **-partie,** *f.* hunting-party. **-pferd,** *n.* hunter. **-recht,** *n.* game-laws. **-rennen,** *n.* steeplechase. **-revier,** *n.* *See* **-bezirk.** **-schein,** *m.* shooting licence. **-schloß,** *n.* hunting lodge. **-schutz,** *m.*, **-sicherung,** *f.* (*Av.*) fighter escort. **-sitz,** *m.* *See* **-schloß.** **-staffel,** *f.* (*Av.*) fighter (*or Am.* pursuit) squadron *or* unit. **-stück,** *n.* picture of a hunt *etc.* **-tasche,** *f.* game-bag. **-verband,** *m.* (*Av.*) fighter (*or Am.* pursuit) formation. **-zeit,** *f.* hunting season. **-zusammenkunft,** *f.* (*Hunt.*) meet.

jagen ['ja:gən], **1.** *v.t.* hunt, (give) chase (to), pursue, drive; stalk; shoot; ***ein Witz jagte den anderen,*** one witty remark followed on the other; ***aus dem Hause –,*** turn out of doors; ***ihm eine Kugel durch den Kopf –,*** blow his brains out; ***in die Flucht –,*** put to flight; ***zum Teufel –,*** send to the devil; ***ihm den Dolch in den Leib –,*** run *or* drive the dagger into him. **2.** *v.i.* (*aux.* s. & h.) go hunting, hunt; (*Motor. coll.*) scorch, speed; rush, race, gallop; ***– nach,*** pursue, rush after, (*coll.*) go all out to get; ***davon –,*** scamper away; ***vorbei –,*** gallop past, sweep by; ***(auf) Hasen –,*** go coursing hares, go hare-shooting; ***(auf) Füchse –,*** go fox-hunting; ***(auf) Rotwild –,*** go deer-stalking; ***gut gejagt haben,*** have had good sport. **3.** *v.r.* follow one another in rapid succession. **Jagen,** *n.* hurry, rush, hot pursuit, galloping; hunting, chasing, shooting; shooting preserve, game reserve.

Jager ['ja:gər], *m.* (*Naut.*) flying jib; herring-smack.

Jäger ['jɛ:gər], *m.* hunter, huntsman, sportsman; gamekeeper, ranger; (*Mil.*) rifleman, fusilier; (*Av.*) fighter (pilot *or* plane). **Jägerbataillon,** *n.* rifle brigade. **Jägerei** [-'raɪ], *f.* hunting, shooting, huntsmanship, (*obs.*) venery, woodcraft. **Jäger|-haus,** *n.* gamekeeper's house. **–joppe,** *f.* shooting-jacket. **–latein,** *n.* huntsmen's slang; tall stories. **–meister,** *m.* chief ranger; master of hounds. **Jägersmann,** *m.* (*pl.* **-leute**) hunter, huntsman. **Jägersprache,** *f.* hunting jargon.

jäh(e) [jɛ:(ə)], *adj.* sudden, abrupt, rapid, quick; (*of a p.*) hasty, rash, impetuous, hot-tempered, irascible, precipitate; (*of a slope*) steep, precipitous; *–es Ende,* sudden *or* violent end; *–e Flucht,* headlong flight; *–er Schrecken,* panic; *–er Tod,* sudden death; *–e Höhe,* precipitous peak. **jählings,** *adv.* abruptly; suddenly, precipitously, (*coll.*) all of a sudden; headlong, in violent haste.

Jahn [ja:n], *m.* (*dial.*) strip of land, swath(e).

Jahr [ja:r], *n.* (**-(e)s,** *pl.* **-e**) year; ***alle –e,*** see ***– für –***; ***anderthalb –e,*** eighteen months; ***er ist schon bei –en,*** he is already advanced in years; ***dreiviertel –,*** nine months; (*B.*) ***fette –e,*** prosperous years; ***– für –,*** year by year, every year; ***– des Heils,*** year of grace; ***– des Herrn,*** year of our Lord; ***in die –e kommen,*** begin to grow old, be getting on in years; ***in den besten –en,*** in the prime of life; ***es geht ins vierte – daß,*** it is more than three years since; ***zwei –e lang,*** for two (whole) years; ***im Laufe der –e,*** through *or* over the years; ***nach – und Tag,*** a full *or* whole year later; ***nach –en,*** after many years; ***seit –en,*** for years; ***seit einigen –en,*** of late years, for some years; ***seit undenklichen –en,*** since time immemorial, time out of mind; ***seit – und Tag,*** for many a year, (*coll.*) for ages; ***übers –,*** a year hence, next year; ***über – und Tag,*** (sometime) in the future; ***ein – ums*** or ***übers andere,*** every year, year after *or* by year; ***vor einem –,*** a year ago; ***vor –en,*** years ago; ***vor – und Tag,*** quite a year ago; a long time ago; ***zu –en kommen,*** begin to grow old. **jahraus,** *adv.* ***–, jahrein,*** year after year. **Jahrbuch,** *n.* year-book, annual, almanac. **jahrein,** *adv.* *See* **jahraus. jahrelang,** *adv.* (lasting) for years.

jähren [ˈjɛ:rən], *v.r.* ***der Tag*** or ***es jährt sich heute daß . . .,*** it is a year (ago) today that *or* since . . . .

Jahres|abonnement, *n.* annual subscription (*to a journal etc.*). **–abschluß,** *m.* annual balance sheet, annual statement of account. **–anfang,** *m.* beginning of the year. **–beitrag,** *m.* annual subscription (*to a society*). **–bericht,** *m.* annual report. **–durchschnitt,** *m.* yearly average. **–einkommen,** *n.* annual income. **–ende,** *n.* end *or* close of the year. **–feier,** *f.* anniversary. **–folge,** *f.* ***nach –,*** in chronological order. **–frist,** *f.* space of a year; ***nach –,*** in a year's time; ***binnen*** or ***innerhalb –,*** within a year. **–gehalt,** *n.* *See* **–einkommen. –hälfte,** *f.* half-year. **–klasse,** *f.* mobilization *or* (*coll.*) call-up group. **–lohn,** *m.* annual wages. **–pensum,** *n.* (year's) curriculum. **–rente,** *f.* annuity. **–ring,** *m.* annual ring (*of trees*). **–schluß,** *m.* *See* **–ende. –schrift,** *f.* annual (periodical). **–tag,** *m.* anniversary. **–versammlung,** *f.* annual meeting. **–viertel,** *n.* quarter (of a year). **–vierteltag,** *m.* quarter-day. **–wechsel,** *m.,* **–wende,** *f.* turn of the year, new year; ***Wünsche zum Jahreswechsel,*** New Year's greetings. **–zahl,** *f.* (year's) date, year. **–zeit,** *f.* season. **jahreszeitlich,** *adj.* seasonal.

Jahr|fünft, *n.* lustrum, quinquennium, quinquenniad, quinquennial period. **–gang,** *m.* age-group; (year's) class; year of publication *or* issue; (year's) vintage. **–gänger,** *m.* (*Swiss*) p. born in the same year, coeval. **–gebung,** *f.* (*Law*) judicial declaration of (*a p.'s*) majority. **–geld,** *n.* annual allowance, annuity; annual dues. **–hundert,** *n.* (**-s,** *pl.* **-e**) century; ***jahrhundertelang,*** for centuries. **–hundertfeier,** *f.* centenary, (*Am.*) centennial. **–hundertwende,** *f.* turn of the century.

jährig [ˈjɛ:rɪç], *adj.* a year old; lasting a year; (*usu. in compounds*) *e.g.* ***zwei–,*** two years old. **jährlich,** **1.** *adj.* yearly, annual. **2.** *adv.* each *or* every year, per annum. **Jährling,** *m.* (**-s,** *pl.* **-e**) (*animal*) yearling, (*plant*) annual.

Jahr|markt, *m.* annual fair. **–schuß,** *m.* *See* **–wuchs. –tausend,** *n.* (**-s,** *pl.* **-e**) millenium. **jahrweise,** *adv.* annually, year by year. **Jahr|wuchs,** *m.* year's growth. **–zehnt,** *n.* (**-s,** *p* . **-e**) decennium, decade, space of ten years; ***jahrzehntelang,*** (lasting) for decades.

jähstotzig [ˈjɛ:ʃtɔtsɪç], *adj.* (*dial.*) precipitous. **Jähzorn,** *m.* sudden *or* violent anger, fit of passion; irascibility, hot-temper. **jähzornig,** *adj.* violently angry, furious, irascible, hot-tempered.

Jakob [ˈja:kɔp], *m.* James, (*B.*) Jacob; (*coll.*) ***der wahre –,*** (*sl.*) the real McCoy.

Jakobiner [jakoˈbi:nər], *m.* (*Hist.*) Jacobin. **Jakobinermönch,** *m.* Dominican (friar).

Jakobsleiter [ˈja:kɔpslaɪtər], *f.* Jacob's ladder.

Jalousie [ʒaluˈzi], *f.* Venetian blind.

Jambe [ˈjambə], *m.* (**-n,** *pl.* **-n**) (*Metr.*) iambus. **jambisch,** *adj.* iambic. **Jambus,** *m.* (-, *pl.* **-ben**) *see* **Jambe.**

Jammer [ˈjamər], *m.* lamentation; misery, distress, wretchedness, affliction, woe; (*coll.*) ***es ist ein –,*** it's a pity *or* a crying shame. **Jammer|blick,** *m.* piteous look. **–geheul, –geschrei,** *n.* wail of lamentation. **–gesicht,** *n.* piteous look, rueful countenance. **–gestalt,** *f.* pitiable sight *or* figure, picture of misery. **–lappen,** *m.* (*coll.*) sissy. **–leben,** *n.* miserable *or* wretched life, life of misery.

jämmerlich [ˈjɛmərlɪç], *adj.* miserable, wretched, pitiable; deplorable, lamentable, piteous. **Jämmerling,** *m.* miserable wretch.

jammern [ˈjamərn], **1.** *v.i.* lament, mourn (***über*** (*Acc.*), over; ***um,*** for); cry, wail, moan, whine; ***– über*** (*Acc.*), bewail, bemoan. **2.** *v.t.* pity; be *or* feel sorry for; move to pity; (*B.*) ***meine Seele jammerte der Armen,*** my soul was grieved for the poor; ***mich jammert seine Not,*** I pity his distress; ***meine Freunde – mich,*** I am sorry for my friends; ***es jammert mich,*** I am moved to pity. **jammerns|-wert, –würdig,** *adj.* *See* **jammervoll.**

jammerschade [ˈjamərʃa:də], *adv.* a very great pity, a thousand pities, (*coll.*) just too bad. **Jammertal,** *m.* (*Poet.*) vale of tears *or* woe. **jammervoll,** *adj.* lamentable, pitiable, piteous, heart-rending; woebegone, wretched, miserable. **Jammerzustand,** *m.* piteous condition.

Janhagel [ˈjanˈha:gəl], *m.* rabble, mob, riff-raff.

Janitschar [janiˈtʃa:r], *m.* (**-en,** *pl.* **-en**) janizary, janissary.

janken [ˈjaŋkən], *v.i.* (*dial.*) whine (***nach,*** for), hanker (after).

Jänner, *m.* (*Austr.*) *see* **Januar.**

Januar [ˈjanua:r], *m.* (**-s,** *pl.* **-e**) January.

Japan [ˈja:pan], *n.* Japan. **Japaner** [–ˈpa:nər], *m.* Japanese, (*pej.*) Jap. **japanisch,** *adj.* Japanese. **Japan|lack,** *m.* japan(ning). **–papier,** *n.* India paper.

jappen [ˈjapən], **japsen** [ˈjapsən], *v.i.* (*dial.*) pant, gasp (***nach,*** for).

Jargon [ʒarˈgɔ̃], *m.* (**-s,** *pl.* **-s**) jargon, parlance, (*coll.*) lingo; gibberish.

Jasmin [jasˈmi:n], *m.* (**-s,** *pl.* **-e**) jasmine, jessamine; ***gemeiner –,*** white syringa.

Jaspis [ˈjaspɪs], *m.* (**-(ses),** *pl.* **-se**) jasper.

Jaß [jas], *m.* a (kind of) Swiss card game. **jassen,** *v.i.* play (this game).

Ja-Stimme, *f.* (*Parl.*) aye, vote for (a motion).

jäten [ˈjɛ:tən], *v.t.* weed, clear of weeds. **Jät|-hacke, –haue,** *f.* hoe.

Jauche [ˈjauxə], *f.* dung water, liquid manure, (*Med.*) ichor. **Jauchgrube,** *f.* cesspool.

jauchzen [ˈjauxtsən], *v.i.* rejoice, shout with *or* for joy, cheer; exult, triumph. **Jauchzen,** *n.* rejoicing, joyful shouts *or* shouting, cheers, cheering; jubilation, exultation. **jauchzend,** *adj.* cheering, jubilant, exultant. **Jauchzer,** *m.* shout of joy *or* jubilation.

jaulen [ˈjaulən], *v.i.* (*coll.*) whine, howl (*as dogs*).

Jause [ˈjauzə], *f.* (*Austr.*) afternoon tea (*or* coffee). **jausen,** *v.i.* have *or* take tea (*or* coffee).

Java [ˈja:va], *n.* Java. **Javaner** [–ˈva:nər], *m.* Javanese. **javanisch,** *adj.* Javanese.

jawohl [jaˈvo:l], *adv.* yes, indeed, to be sure; quite so, certainly, exactly, (*coll.*) for sure.

Jawort ['ja:vɔrt], *n.* consent, affirmation; *ihm das – geben,* accept his offer of marriage *or* his proposal, accept him, (*coll.*) say yes.

Jazz [dʒɛs], *m.* jazz. **Jazz|kapelle,** *f.* dance *or* jazz band. **–sänger,** *m.* jazz singer, crooner.

[1]**je** [je:], *adv., conj.* 1. *seit –, seit eh und –,* always, at all times, from time immemorial; *– und –,* on and on, for ever (and a day); 2. ever, at any time; *hast du – so was gesehen,* have you ever seen the like; *ohne das Wort – gesagt zu haben,* without ever having *or* without having once said that word; 3. (*distributive*) *– zwei,* two at a time, two by two, in twos *or* pairs; *er gab ihnen – zwei Äpfel,* he gave them two apples each *or* (*coll.*) apiece; *– Stück bis 10 kg,* each piece up to 10 kg.; *7 Pf. – km,* 7 pfennigs a kilometre; *1 DM – 6 Wörter,* 1 mark for every 6 words; *– nach,* according to, depending on; *– nachdem,* (*conj.*) in proportion as, according as; (*adv.*) as the case may be, according to circumstances, that (all) depends; 4. (*with comp.*) *– . . . desto, – . . . – . . .,* the . . . the . . .; *– mehr er hat, desto* or *– mehr will er,* the more he has, the more he wants; *– eher, – lieber* or *desto lieber* or *um so lieber,* the sooner the better; *ich habe sie – länger – lieber,* the longer I know her the more I love her.

[2]**je!** (*abbr. of* **Jesus**), *int.* heavens! gracious! *– nun,* well now, well then; now then! really!

jede ['je:də], 1. *adj.* each, every, either, any; *auf –n* or *in –m Fall, see* **jedenfalls**; *zu –r Zeit,* at all times; *an –m Orte,* in every place, everywhere; *– leiseste Berührung,* the least *or* slightest touch; *– beliebige Sorte,* any kind that you may choose. 2. *pron.* each, each *or* every one; either (one); everyone, everybody; *alles und –s, alle und –,* one and all; *– zehn Minuten,* every ten minutes; *–m das Seine,* to every man his due; (*Prov.*) *–r ist seines Glückes Schmied,* every man is the architect of his own fortune; (*Prov.*) *–r ist sich selbst der Nächste,* charity begins at home.

jedenfalls ['je:dənfals], *adv.* at all events, in any case, at any rate, however it is *or* it may be.

jeder ['je:dər], *see* **jede.**

jederlei ['je:dərlaɪ], *indecl.adj.* of every *or* any kind. **jeder|mann,** *pron.* everyone, everybody; anyone, anybody. **–zeit,** *adv.* at any time, always.

jedes ['je:dəs], *see* **jede.**

jedesmal ['je:dəsma:l], *adv.* each time, every time, always; *– wenn,* whenever, as often as. **jedesmalig,** *adj.* existing, actual, prevailing; in each *or* every case, respective; *wie es die –en Zustände erheischen,* according to the (then) prevailing circumstances, as circumstances demand; *see* **jeweilig.**

jedoch [je'dɔx], *adv.* however, nevertheless, notwithstanding, for all that, yet, still.

jedwed(e, -er, -es) ['je:t've:d(ə, -ər, -əs)], **jeglich(e, -er, -es)** ['je:klɪç(ə, -ər, -əs)], *adj., pron.* (*elevated style*) *see* **jede.**

jeher ['je:he:r], *adv. von –,* at all times, from time immemorial, (*coll.*) all along.

Jelängerjelieber [je'lɛŋərje'li:bər], *m.* (*Austr. n.*) (*Bot.*) honeysuckle, woodbine (*Lonicera caprifolium*).

jemals ['je:ma:ls], *adv.* ever, at any time.

jemand ['je:mant], *indef.pron.* (*Acc. – or –en; Gen. –es; Dat. – or –em*), somebody, someone; anybody, anyone; *– anders or sonst –,* somebody *or* anybody else; *irgend –,* anyone, anybody; *– Fremdes,* some stranger.

jene ['je:nə], 1. *dem.adj.* that, *pl.* those; *auf –r Seite des Flusses,* on the other side of the river; *in –m Leben, in –r Welt,* in the life to come, in the other world. 2. *dem.pron.* that one; *pl.* those ones; the former; *–, welche,* those who; *bald dieses, bald –s,* now one thing, now the other *or* another; *von diesem und –m sprechen,* talk of this and that. **jener, jenes,** *see* **jene.**

jenseitig ['je:nzaɪtɪç], *adj.* (lying) on the other side, opposite; ulterior; (*fig.*) otherworldly. **jenseits,** 1. *adv.* on the other side, beyond, yonder. 2. *prep.* on the other side of, beyond, across. **Jenseits,** *n.* the next world, the life to come, the hereafter, (*coll.*) kingdom come.

Jeremiade [jeremi'a:də], *f.* jeremiad, doleful lament, (*coll.*) wailing and gnashing of teeth, (*sl.*) belly-aching.

jerum! ['je:rum], *int.* (*for* **Jesus**); *o –!* dear me!

Jesuit [jezu'i:t], *m.* (**-en,** *pl.* **-en**) Jesuit. **Jesuiten|-orden,** *m.* Jesuit Order, Society of Jesus. **–schule,** *f.* Jesuit college. **jesuitisch,** *adj.* Jesuit.

Jesus ['je:zus], *m.* Jesus. **Jesuskind,** *n.* (the) infant *or* baby Jesus.

jetzig ['jɛtsɪç], *adj.* present, now existing, actual, current, prevailing; *in der –en Zeit,* nowadays; *der –e König,* the reigning *or* present king; *zum –en Kurs,* at the current rate of exchange.

jetzt [jɛtst], *adv.* now, at present, at the present time; *gleich –, gerade –,* instantly, this very moment, at once, (*coll.*) right away; *erst –,* only now; *für –,* for the present; *von – an,* from now on, from this time, henceforth; *bis –,* till now, up to now, as yet, hitherto, (*coll.*) so far; *noch –,* even now, to this day; *nur – erst, eben –,* only just, just now. **Jetztzeit,** *f.* the present (time), the present day, modern times, these days.

jeweilig ['je:'vaɪlɪç], 1. *adj.* of *or* at the moment, respective; *der –e Direktor,* the headmaster at the time concerned, (whoever may be) the headmaster at the moment, the headmaster of the day; *unter den –en Umständen,* as the circumstances may require. 2. *or* **jeweils,** *adv.* at times, from time to time, at any given time; respectively, in each case; *die – gültigen Bestimmungen,* such regulations as may from time to time be in force.

Jiddisch ['jɪdɪʃ], *n.* Yiddish.

Joch [jɔx], *n.* (**-(e)s,** *pl.* **-e**) yoke (*also fig.*), (*fig.*) burden, load; cross-beam, transom, pile (*bridges*); saddle (*mountains*), mountain ridge; land measure; *ins – spannen,* yoke; *sich ins – spannen,* work hard, slave; *zwei – Ochsen,* two pair *or* two yoke of oxen. **Joch|balken,** *m.* tie-beam, cross-beam, girder, transom, bay (*of a bridge*). **–bein,** *n.* cheek-bone. **–brücke,** *f.* pile-bridge. **jochen,** *v.t.* yoke. **Joch|hölzer,** *n.pl.* crossbars. **–spannung,** *f.* span (*of bridge*). **–straße,** *f.* mountain pass. **–träger,** *m.* cross-beam.

Jockei ['dʒɔki], *m.* (**-s,** *pl.* **-s**) jockey.

Jod [jo:t], *n.* iodine; *mit – behandeln, see* **jodieren.**

jodeln ['jo:dəln], *v.i., v.t.* yodel.

jodhaltig ['jo:thaltɪç], *adj.* iodiferous. **jodieren,** *v.t.* (*Chem.*) iodate, (*Phot.*) iodize. **Jodkali(um),** *n.* potassium iodide.

Jodler ['jo:dlər], *m.* 1. yodel(l)er; 2. yodel, yodelling cry.

Jodoform [jodo'fɔrm], *f.* iodoform. **Jodtinktur,** *f.* tincture of iodine.

Joghurt ['jogurt], *m. or n.* yoghurt.

Johanni(s) [jo'hani(s)], *n.* midsummer day. **Johannis|beere,** *f.* currant. **–brot,** *n.* carob-bean. **–fest,** *n. See* **Johanni(s). –käfer,** *m.* glow-worm. **–kraut,** *n.* (*Bot.*) St. John's wort (*Hypericum perforatum*). **–nacht,** *f.* midsummer night. **–tag,** *m.* midsummer day. **–trieb,** *m.* second bloom; late love. **–würmchen,** *n. See* **–käfer.**

Johanniter [joha'ni:tər], *m.* Knight Hospitaller, Knight of St. John of Jerusalem.

johlen ['jo:lən], *v.i.* howl, yell, bawl, hoot, (*of an audience*) boo.

Jolle ['jɔlə], *f.* dinghy, jolly-boat. **Jollenführer,** *m.* boatman, waterman.

Jongleur [ʒɔ̃'glø:r], *m.* (**-s,** *pl.* **-e**) juggler. **jonglieren,** *v.t.* · *v.i.* juggle (with).

Joppe ['jɔpə], *f.* jerkin, jacket.

Jordanien [jɔr'da:niən], *n.* (*Geog.*) Jordan.

Jot [jɔt], *n.* (**-s,** *pl.* **-n**) letter J. **Jota** ['jo:ta], *n.* (**-s,** *pl.* **-s**) iota; jot, whit.

Journal [ʒur'na:l], *n.* (**-s,** *pl.* **-e**) newspaper; (*Comm.*) daybook, (*Naut. etc.*) logbook. **Journalismus** [–'lɪsmus], *m.* journalism. **Journalist** [–'lɪst], *m.* (**-en,** *pl.* **-en**) journalist, reporter. **Journalisten-**

stil, *m.* journalese. **Journalistik,** *f.* journalism, the press. **journalistisch,** *adj.* journalistic.

jovial [jovi'a:l], *adj.* jovial, affable. **Jovialität** [–i'tɛ:t], *f.* joviality.

Jubel ['ju:bəl], *m.* rejoicing, exultation, jubilation. **Jubel|feier,** *f.*, **–fest,** *n.* jubilee. **–greis,** *m. See* **Jubilar**; (*coll.*) gay old cock *or* spark. **–jahr,** *n.* jubilee; (*coll.*) ***alle –e einmal,*** once in a blue moon. **jubeln,** *v.i.* rejoice, shout with *or* for joy, exult (*über* (*Acc.*), at). **Jubel|paar,** *n.* couple celebrating their silver *or* golden wedding. **–ruf,** *m.* acclamation, shout of joy.

Jubilar [jubi'la:r], *m.* (**-s,** *pl.* **-e**) p. celebrating his jubilee. **Jubiläum,** *n.* (**-s,** *pl.* **-äen**) jubilee, anniversary. **jubilieren,** *v.i. See* **jubeln,** (*coll.*) crow (*über* (*Acc.*), over).

juchhe! [jux'he:], **juchhei(sa)!** [jux'haɪ(sa)], **juchheirassa(ssa)!** [jux'haɪrasa(sa)], *int.* hurrah!

Juchten ['juxtən], *n.* (*Austr. m.*) Russia leather. **juchten,** *adj.* in *or* made of Russia leather. **Juchten(ein)band,** *m.* Russia(n)-leather binding.

Juchzer ['juxtsər], *m.* shout of joy, cheer.

jucken ['jukən], **1.** *v.i., imp.* itch, irritate; ***es juckt mich*** or ***mir am Arm,*** my arm itches; ***die Ohren – ihm,*** he is inquisitive; ***es juckt mir die Fingern,*** my fingers itch to be (***nach,*** at); ***das Fell juckt ihn*** or ***ihm,*** he is itching for a fight; ***die Hand juckt ihm,*** he expects a tip *or* present; (*Prov.*) ***wen's*** or ***wem's juckt, der kratze sich,*** let those whom the cap fits wear it. **2.** *v.t., v.r.* (*dial.*) scratch (o.s.). **Jucken,** *n.* itching, itch.

Jucker ['jukər], *m.* carriage horse. **Juckerzug,** *m.* four-in-hand.

Judaskuß ['ju:daskus], *m.* traitor's kiss.

Jude ['ju:də], *m.* (**-n,** *pl.* **-n**) Jew; ***der Ewige –,*** the Wandering Jew; (*coll.*) ***haust du meinen –n, hau ich deinen –n,*** tit for tat. **Juden|deutsch,** *n.* Yiddish. **–feind,** *m.* anti-Semite. **–hetze,** *f.* Jew-baiting. **–kirsche,** *f.* winter cherry. **–schule,** *f.* Jewish school; (*coll.*) ***ein Lärm wie in einer –,*** hubbub, hullaballoo, babel, cat's concert. **–tum,** *n.* Jewry, Judaism. **–verfolgung,** *f.* persecution of the Jews, pogrom. **–viertel,** *n.* Jewish quarter, ghetto.

Jüdin ['jy:dɪn], *f.* Jewess. **jüdisch,** *adj.* Jewish; (*coll.*) ***nur keine –e Hast!*** keep your shirt on! what's the rush?

Jugend ['ju:gənt], *f.* youth, adolescence; early period; the rising generation, young people; (*Prov.*) ***– hat keine Tugend,*** you cannot put an old head on young shoulders; boys will be boys; ***von – auf,*** from the earliest years.

Jugend|alter, *n.* (days of) youth. **–amt,** *n.* youth welfare *or* employment office. **–bewegung,** *f.* youth movement. **–blüte,** *f.* flush of youth. **–buch,** *n.* children's book, book for the young. **–erinnerung,** *f.* childhood memory. **–erziehung,** *f.* education of youth, early education. **–freund,** *m.* friend of one's youth, old school-friend, playmate. **–frische,** *f.* bloom of youth. **–führer,** *m.* youth leader. **–fülle,** *f.* exuberance of youth. **–fürsorge,** *f.* young people's welfare, juvenile care. **–gefährte, –genosse,** *m.* companion of one's youth. **–gericht,** *n.* juvenile court. **–herberge,** *f.* youth hostel. **–jahre,** *n.pl.* early years. **–kraft,** *f.* youthful strength. **–kriminalität,** *f.* juvenile delinquency. **–lager,** *n.* youth camp.

jugendlich ['ju:gəntlɪç], *adj.* youthful, juvenile; ***–er Verbrecher,*** juvenile delinquent. **Jugendliche(r),** *m., f.* young person, juvenile, adolescent, (*coll.*) teen-ager. **Jugendlichkeit,** *f.* youthfulness.

Jugend|liebe, *f.* early love, first love, calf-love; old sweetheart, old flame. **–pflege,** *f.* youth welfare work. **–schriften,** *f.pl.* books for the young. **–schriftsteller,** *m.* writer of books for the young. **–streich,** *m.* youthful prank. **–sünde,** *f.* sin (excusable because) of one's youth. **–torheit,** *f.* youthful folly. **–werk,** *n.* early work (*of a writer*), (*pl.*) juvenilia. **–wohlfahrt,** *f. See* **–pflege. –zeit,** *f.* youth, early *or* young days.

Jugoslawe [jugo'sla:və], *m.* Yugoslav. **Jugoslawien,** *n.* (*Geog.*) Yugoslavia. **Jugoslawin,** *f. See* **Jugoslawe. jugoslawisch,** *adj.* Yugoslav.

juhe! [ju'he:], (*int.*) (*Swiss*) *see* **juchhe.**

Jul– [ju:l], *pref.* Yule. **–block,** *m.* Yule log. **–fest,** *n.* Christmas festivities. **–feuer,** *n.* ceremonial fire for the winter solstice.

Juli ['ju:li], *m.* (**-s,** *no pl.*) July.

Jul|klapp, *n.* (*dial.*) Christmas present traditionally thrown in at the window. **–monat, –mond,** *m.* December.

jung [juŋ], *adj.* (*comp. jünger, sup. jüngst*) young, youthful; new, fresh; recent; early; ***–e Erbsen,*** green peas; ***–es Gemüse,*** fresh vegetables, (*fig., coll.*) young fry; (*fig.*) ***–es Blut,*** young person, youngster; ***–er Boden,*** reclaimed land; ***–er Morgen,*** early morning; ***–er Wein,*** new wine; ***die –e Frau,*** newly married woman, young wife, bride; ***in meinen –en Jahren,*** in my early days, in my youth; (*Prov.*) ***– gewohnt, alt getan,*** what is bred in the bone will come out in the flesh. **Jungbrunnen,** *m.* fountain of youth. **Junge,** *m.* (**-n,** *pl.* **-n** *or* (*dial., coll.*) **-ns** *or* **Jungs**) boy, lad, youth, youngster, young fellow; apprentice, errand *or* message boy; (*Cards*) knave, jack; ***alter –!*** old fellow! old boy! old chap! ***die blauen Jungs,*** the boys in blue; ***grüner –,*** whippersnapper; ***schwerer –,*** jail-bird, crook; blackguard, ruffian. **jungen,** *v.i.* bring forth young (*of animals*). **jungenhaft,** *adj.* boyish.

jünger ['jyŋər], *comp.adj.* (*see* **jung**) younger, junior, (*Her.*) puisne; (*fig.*) newer, later; ***– aussehen als man ist,*** not look one's age; ***–en Datums,*** of a later date; ***–er Teilhaber,*** junior partner; ***einige Jahre – als ich,*** my junior by several years.

Jünger, *m.* disciple, follower, adherent; (*B.*) ***die zwölf –,*** the twelve apostles. **Jüngerschaft,** *f.* (body of) disciples, followers *or* adherents.

Junge(s) ['juŋə(s)], *n.* young, offspring (*of animals*), cub, puppy, calf, whelp *etc.*; ***ein Junges,*** a young one; ***Junge werfen,*** *see* **jungen.**

Jungfer ['juŋfər], *f.* (-, *pl.* **-n**) virgin, maid(en); spinster, (*coll.*) old maid; (*obs.*) lady's maid; ***alte –,*** old maid. **jüngferlich,** *adj.* virginal, maidenly, chaste; spinster-like, (*coll.*) old maidish; (*fig.*) demure, coy, prim (and proper), prudish.

Jungfern|erde, *f.* virgin soil. **–fahrt,** *f.* maiden voyage. **–flug,** *m.* maiden flight. **–geburt,** *f.* parthenogenesis, (*Eccl.*) virgin birth. **–glas,** *n.* selenit. **–häutchen,** *n.* (*Anat.*) hymen, (*coll.*) maidenhead. **–honig,** *m.* virgin honey. **–käfer,** *m.* ladybird. **–kind,** *n.* illegitimate *or* natural child; first-born. **–kranich,** *m.* (*Orn.*) demoiselle crane (*Anthropoides virgo*). **–kranz,** *m.* bridal wreath. **–metall,** *n.* native metal. **–raub,** *m.* rape. **–rede,** *f.* maiden speech. **–schaft,** *f.* maidenhood, virginity. **–stand,** *m.* spinsterhood. **–zeugung,** *f. See* **–geburt.**

Jungfrau ['juŋfrau], *f.* virgin; maid, maiden; (*Astr.*) Virgo; ***Heilige –,*** Blessed Virgin; ***– von Orleans,*** Maid of Orleans; (*B.*) ***von der – Maria geboren,*** born of the Virgin Mary. **jungfräulich,** *adj.* virginal, maidenly, chaste, pure, (*Eccl.*) immaculate; (*fig.*) virgin. **Jungfräulichkeit,** *f.* virginity, maidenhood, virginal purity, maidenly modesty, demureness, coyness.

Junggesell(e) ['juŋgəzɛl(ə)], *m.* (**-(e)n,** *pl.* **-(e)n**) bachelor; junior journeyman. **Junggesellen|leben,** *n.*, **–stand,** *m.*, **Junggesellentum,** *n.* bachelorhood. **Junggesellin,** *f.* bachelor-girl.

Jung|herr, *m.* (*Hist.*) young nobleman. **–lehrer,** *m.* assistant teacher.

Jüngling ['jyŋlɪŋ], *m.* (**-s,** *pl.* **-e**) youth, youngster, young man; stripling. **Jünglingsalter,** *n.* youth, early manhood; adolescence, (*coll.*) teens.

Jung|mädchen, *n.* (*Swiss*) girl. **–mädel,** *n.* (*Nat. Soc.*) young member of girls' organization, Nazi 'Girl Guide'. **–mann,** *m.* (*pl.* **¨-er** *or* **-en**) (*Nat. Soc.*) pupils of political training establishment, party probationers *or* cadets.

jüngst [jyŋst], **1.** *sup.adj.* (*see* **jung**) youngest; last, latest, (most) recent; ***Jüngstes Gericht,*** Judgement

Day, Doomsday, Last Judgement; ***die –en Ereignisse,*** the latest happenings; ***Ihr –es Schreiben,*** your last *or* most recent letter; ***die –e Vergangenheit,*** the recent past; ***–er Tag,*** see ***–es Gericht***; ***sein –es Werk,*** his latest work; (*coll.*) ***sie ist nicht mehr die –e,*** she is no chicken. **2.** *adv.* lately, (quite) recently, of late, (*coll.*) the other day.

Jungsteinzeit ['juŋʃtaɪntsaɪt], *f.* neolithic age. **jungsteinzeitlich,** *adj.* neolithic.

Jüngstenrecht ['jyŋstənrɛçt], *n.* (*Law*) right of juniority (*opp. of primogeniture*). **jüngstens, jüngsthin,** *adv. See* **jüngst, 2.**

Jungtertiär ['juŋtɛrtsiɛ:r], *n.* miocene period. **jungvermählt,** *adj.* newly wed(ded), newly married. **Jung|vieh,** *n.* young cattle. **–wuchs,** *m.* young growth. **–wuchsgrenze,** *f.* timber line.

Juni ['ju:ni], *m.* (**-s,** *no pl.*) June.

Junker ['juŋkər], *m.* country squire; titled landowner; (*pl.*) Junkers, aristocratic landowners (*in Prussian territories*). **Junker|herrschaft,** *f.*, **–tum,** *n.* squirearchy.

[1]**Jura** ['ju:ra], *n.pl.* law; – ***studieren,*** study law.

[2]**Jura,** *m.* **1.** (*Geol.*) Jurassic (period *or* system); **2.** (*Geog.*), **Jura|gebirge,** *n.* Jura Mtns. **–kalk,** *m.* Jurassic *or* oolitic limestone.

Jurat [ju'ra:t], *m.* (**-en,** *pl.* **-en**) (*Law*) deponent (*on oath*). **jurato,** *adv.* (*Law*) upon oath.

Juridisch [ju'ri:dɪʃ], *adj.* juridical. **Jurist,** *m.* (**-en,** *pl.* **-en**) lawyer, jurist; law student. **Juristensprache,** *f.* legal jargon. **juristisch,** *adj.* legal, of *or* in law, juridical; ***–e Fakultät,*** faculty *or* school of law, board of legal studies; ***–e Person,*** corporate body, corporation.

Jus [ju:s], *n. See* [1]**Jura.**

just [just], **1.** *adv.* just, exactly; just now, only just, even now. **2.** *adj.* proper, right; ***nicht –,*** uncanny; ***das ist – nicht nötig,*** that is not altogether necessary.

justieren [jus'ti:rən], *v.t.* adjust; (*Typ.*) justify. **Justier|gewicht,** *n.* standard (weight). **–schraube,** *f.* adjusting *or* set screw. **–waage,** *f.* adjusting balance.

justifizieren [justifi'tsi:rən], *v.t.* justify. **Justitiar** [justitsi'a:r], (*Austr.* **Justitiär**), *m.* (**-s,** *pl.* **-e**) justiciary.

Justiz [jus'ti:ts], *f.* administration of justice *or* of the law. **Justiz|beamte(r),** *m.* officer of the court, judicial officer. **–gebäude,** *n.* law courts. **–gewalt,** *f.* power of the judiciary. **–inspektor,** *m.* senior judicial officer. **–irrtum,** *m.* miscarriage of justice. **–kommissär,** *m.* (*obs.*) attorney-at-law. **–minister,** *m.* Minister of Justice (*combines the functions of British Lord Chancellor, Attorney-General and Solicitor-General*). **–mord,** *m.* judicial murder, execution of an innocent person. **–palast,** *m.* Central Law Courts. **–pflege,** *f.* administration of justice. **–rat,** *m.* King's *or* Queen's Counsel. **–versehen,** *n. See* **–irrtum. –verwaltung,** *f. See* **–pflege. –wesen,** *n.* judicial *or* legal system, judicature; the law.

Jütland ['jy:tlant], *n.* (*Geog.*) Jutland.

Juwel [ju've:l], *m. or n.* (**-s,** *pl.* **-e(n)**) jewel, gem, precious stone; *pl.* jewellery; (*fig.*) (*only n.* (*pl.***-e**)) treasure, priceless gift (*of a friend, servant etc.*). **Juwelen|diebstahl,** *m.* jewel robbery. **–händler, Juwelier** [–'li:r], *m.* (**-s,** *pl.* **-e**) jeweller.

Jux [juks], *m.* (**-es,** *pl.* **-e**) (*coll.*) lark, spree, practical joke; (*dial.*) filth, muck. **juxen, 1.** *v.i.* (*coll.*) lark, frolic, play practical jokes. **2.** *v.t.* (*coll.*) ***ihn –,*** pull his leg.

K

See also under C.

K, k [ka:], *n.* K, k.

Kabale [ka'ba:lə], *f.* intrigue, conspiracy, cabal; ***–n schmieden,*** hatch a plot, intrigue.

Kabarett [kaba'rɛt], *n.* (**-s,** *pl.* **-e**) cabaret; entré dish. **Kabarettist** [–'tɪst], *m.* (**-en,** *pl.* **-en**) cabaret artiste.

Kabbala ['kabala], *f.* cab(b)ala, Jewish oral tradition; occult lore. **kabbalistisch,** *adj.* cab(b)alistic, occult, esoteric.

Kabbelei [kabə'laɪ], *f.* (-, *pl.* **-en**) (*dial.*) squabble, quarrel. **kabbelig** ['kabəlɪç], *adj.* choppy (*of sea*). **kabbeln,** *v.i.* (*dial.*) bandy words, squabble, quarrel; ***die See kabbelt*** or ***geht –,*** the sea is choppy.

[1]**Kabel** ['ka:bəl], *f.* (-, *pl.* **-n**) (*dial.*) lot, share.

[2]**Kabel,** *n.* cable; ***oberirdisches –,*** overland cable; ***unterirdisches –,*** underground cable; ***unterseeisches –,*** submarine cable; ***– abrollen,*** pay out cable; ***– auslegen,*** lay cable(s); ***bewehrtes –,*** armoured cable.

Kabel|aufführung, *f.* point where cable emerges. **-brunnen,** *m.* cable manhole. **–dampfer,** *m.* cable layer, cable-laying vessel. **–depesche,** *f.* cable(gram); ***eine – senden,*** cable. **–gatt,** *n.* (**-s,** *pl.* **–e**) (*Naut.*) cable locker.

Kabeljau ['ka:bəljau], *m.* (**-s,** *pl.* **-s** *or* **-e**) cod. **Kabeljau(leber)tran,** *m.* cod-liver oil.

Kabel|klüse, *f.* (*Naut.*) hawse-pipe. **–länge,** *f.* cable's length (*100 fathoms*). **–legung,** *f.* laying of a (telegraphic) cable. **–muffe,** *f.* cable coupling.

kabeln ['ka:bəln], *v.t., v.i.* cable, send a cablegram.

Kabel|nachricht, *f.* news *or* information sent by cable. **–rohr,** *n.* cable conduit. **–schacht,** *f.* manhole. **–schnur,** *f.* flex. **–seil,** *n. See* **–tau. –tanz,** *m.* sailor's hornpipe. **–tau,** *n.* cable. **–trommel,** *f.* cable-drum *or* reel. **–verbindung,** *f.* (*Naut.*) cable splice.

Kabine [ka'bi:nə], *f.* (*Naut.*) cabin, (*Av.*) cockpit; cage (*of a lift etc.*); (*Film.*) projection room; cubicle (*at hairdressers*), bathing hut, cubicle.

Kabinett [kabi'nɛt], *n.* (**-s,** *pl.* **-er**) cabinet, closet, (*Pol.*) cabinet (ministers); collection (*of coins, gems etc.*); section *or* department (of a museum); (*obs.*) water-closet; (*obs.*) ***aufs – gehen,*** go to the lavatory. **Kabinett|auslese,** *f.* choice wine. **–photographie,** *f.* cabinet photograph. **Kabinetts|befehl,** *m.* order in council. **–frage,** *f.* vital question; question involving the cabinet; (*Parl.*) ***die – stellen,*** propose a motion of confidence; (*fig.*) ***aus einer S. eine – machen,*** make a vital issue of a matter. **–rat,** *m.* cabinet council. **–sitzung,** *f.* cabinet meeting. **Kabinettstück,** *n.* museum piece.

Kabriolett [kabrio'lɛt], *n.* (**-(e)s,** *pl.* **-e**) cabriolet, (*Motor.*) roadster, convertible.

Kabuse [ka'bu:zə], *f.* (*coll., dial.*) shack, shanty, small hut; (*Naut.*) galley, caboose. *See* **Kombüse.**

Kachel ['kaxəl], *f.* (-, *pl.* **-n**) (glazed) tile. **Kachelofen,** *m.* tiled stove.

Kacke ['kakə], *f.* (*vulg.*) excrement, stool. **kacken,** *v.t.* (*vulg.*) go to stool.

Kadaver [ka'da:vər], *m.* carcass, carrion. **Kadaver|fliege,** *f.* carrion-fly. **–gehorsam,** *m.* utter subordination, slavish submission *or* obedience, abject submissiveness.

Kadenz [ka'dɛnts], *f.* (-, *pl.* **-en**) (*Mus.*) cadence.

Kader ['ka:dər], *m.* (*Mil.*) cadre.

Kadett [ka'dɛt], *m.* (**-en,** *pl.* **-en**) (*Mil.*) cadet, (*Naut.*) midshipman. **Kadetten|anstalt,** *f.* officer's training-school, cadet college. **–korps,** *n.* cadet corps. **–(schul)schiff,** *n.* training-ship.

kaduk [ka'du:k], *adj.* frail, broken (down). **kaduzieren** [–'tsi:rən], *v.t.* declare forfeited, condemn (as worthless).

Käfer ['kɛ:fər], *m.* 1. beetle; 2. (*sl.*) bird, skirt; (*sl.*) ***sie ist ein netter* –,** she is a nice bit of stuff. **käferartig,** *adj.* coleopterous. **Käferschnecke,** *f.* (*Mollusc.*) Chitonidae.

Kaff [kaf], *n. or m.* **(-(e)s,** *pl.* **-e)** (*dial.*) rubbish, nonsense, bosh; (*n. only*) (*sl.*) god-forsaken place.

Kaffee ['kafe:, ka'fe:], **1.** *m.* coffee; ***wollen Sie morgen nachmittag zum – kommen?*** will you come to tea tomorrow? – ***verkehrt,*** coffee dash. **2.** *n.* coffee-house, café. **Kaffee|base,** *f. See* **–schwester. –bohne,** *f.* coffee-bean. **–brenner,** *m.* coffee-roaster. **–brötchen,** *n.* breakfast roll. **–dick,** *n.* (*dial.*) *see* **–satz. –gebäck,** *n.* fancy cakes. **–geschirr,** *n.* coffee-service. **–grund,** *m. See* **–satz. –haus,** *n.* café. **–kanne,** *f.* coffee-pot. **–klatsch,** *m.* (*coll.*) gossip over a cup of coffee, (ladies) afternoon-tea party. **–kränzchen,** *n.* coffee party. **–löffel,** *m.* coffee-spoon, teaspoon. **–maschine,** *f.* coffee-percolator. **–mühle,** *f.* coffee-mill *or* grinder; (*Av. sl.*) dog fight. **–muhme,** *f. See* **–schwester. -pflanzung,** *f,* coffee plantation, **–röster,** *m. See* **–brenner. –satz,** *m.* coffee-grounds. **–schwester,** *f.* (*coll.*) coffee-lover; gossip. **–seiher,** *m.,* **–sieb,** *n.* coffee-strainer. **–sorten,** *f.pl.* brands of coffee. **-tasse,** *f.* coffee-cup. **–topf,** *m.* coffee-pot. **–trichter,** *m.* coffee-filter. **–trommel,** *f. See* **–brenner.**

Kaffein [kafə'i:n], *n,* **(-s)** caffeine.

Käfig ['kɛ:fıç], *m.* **(-s,** *pl.* **-e)** cage; bird-cage; (*sl.*) prison; ***im goldenen* –,** in a gilded cage. **Käfigmotor,** *m.* (*Elec.*) squirrel-cage (induction) motor.

Kaftan ['kaftan], *m.* **(-s,** *pl.* **-e** (*Austr.* **-s**)) caftan.

kahl [ka:l], *adj.* bald, shorn, (*fig.*) bare, naked, blank, empty; unfledged (*of birds*); dismantled (*of ships*), barren, bleak, treeless, leafless (*as landscape*); paltry, poor, sorry, threadbare; (*sl.*) skint; ***–e Ausflucht,*** poor excuse; – ***bestehen,*** come off poorly; ***–es Geschwätz,*** empty *or* idle talk. **Kahl|bäuche,** *m.pl.* (*Ichth.*) apodes. **–fläche,** *f. See* **–schlag. kahl|fleckig,** *adj.* having threadbare spots. **–geschoren,** *adj.* close cropped. **Kahlheit,** *f.* baldness, alopecia; (*fig.*) bareness, bleakness, barrenness. **Kahlkopf,** *m.* bald head, baldheaded p. **kahlköpfig,** *adj.* bald-headed. **Kahl|schlag, –trieb,** *m.* complete deforestation, clearing.

Kahm [ka:m], *m.* mould (*on liquids*). **kahmen,** *v.i.* (*aux.* h. & s.) grow mouldy. **kahmig,** *adj.* mouldy, musty, stale, ropy (*of wine*).

[1]**Kahn** [ka:n], *m.* (*dial.*) *see* **Kahm.**

[2]**Kahn,** *m.* **(-(e)s,** *pl.* **⸚e)** 1. boat, barge, canoe, skiff; 2. (*Surg.*) scapha. **Kahnbein,** *n.* scaphoid bone, navicular bone. **kahnfahren,** *irr.v.i.* go boating. **Kahnfahrt,** *f.* boat trip.

Kai [kaı], *m.* **(-s,** *pl.* **-e** (*Austr.* **-s**)) quay, wharf; pier, jetty. **Kai|arbeiter,** *m.* docker, longshoreman. **–gebühr,** *f.,* **–geld,** *n.* wharfage, harbour dues.

Kaiman ['kaiman], *m.* **(-s,** *pl.* **-e** (*Austr.* **-s**)) alligator, cayman.

Kai|mauer, *f.* quayside, jetty-wall. **–meister,** *m.* harbour master.

Kain [kaın], *m.* (*B.*) Cain. **Kains|mal, –zeichen,** *n.* mark of Cain.

Kairo ['kaıro], *n.* (*Geog.*) Cairo.

Kaiser ['kaızər], *m.* emperor; ***der frühere* –,** the ex-Kaiser; ***den – einem guten Mann sein lassen,*** let matters take their course; ***sich um des –s Bart streiten,*** quarrel about nothing, split hairs; ***auf den alten – borgen,*** borrow with no intention of repaying, abuse one's credit; (*B.*) ***gebt dem – was des –s ist,*** render unto Caesar the things which are Caesar's; (*Prov.*) ***wo nichts ist, hat (selbst) der – sein Recht verloren,*** where nought's to be got, kings lose their scot; you cannot get blood out of a stone.

Kaiser|adler, *m.* (*Orn.*) imperial eagle (*Aquila heliaca*). **–bart,** *m.* dundreary, mutton-chop whiskers. **–blau,** *n.* smalt. **–format,** *n.* imperial (paper) (22″×32″). **–haus,** *n.* imperial family *or* house. **Kaiserin,** *f.* empress; ***die –mutter*** or ***–witwe,*** the Dowager Empress. **Kaiserkrone,** *f.* imperial crown; (*Bot.*) crown imperial (*Fritillaria imperialis*).

kaiserlich ['kaızərlıç], *adj.* imperial; ***die Kaiserlichen,*** the imperial troops; ***—königlich,*** royal and imperial (*title of the Hapsburgs*); (***gut***) – ***gesinnt,*** siding with the emperor; supporting the imperial party. **Kaiserling,** *m.* **(-s,** *pl.* **-e)** 1. would-be emperor; 2. (*Bot.*) golden agaric (*Amanita caesarea*). **kaiserlos,** *adj.* ***die –e Zeit,*** Interregnum (1150–73).

Kaiser|mantel, *m.* 1. cloak, ulster; 2. (*Ent.*) mother-of-pearl butterfly (*Argynnis paphia*). **–reich,** *n.* empire. **–schlange,** *f.* boa-constrictor. **–schnitt,** *m.* Caesarean section *or* operation. **–schrift,** *f.* (*Typ.*) great primer. **–schwamm,** *m. See* **Kaiserling,** 2. **Kaisertum,** *n.* **(-s,** *pl.* **⸚er)** 1. empire; 2. *See* **–würde. Kaiser|wahl,** *f.* election of the emperor. **–wetter,** *n.* (*coll.*) glorious weather. **–würde,** *f.* imperial dignity.

Kajak ['ka:jak], *m. or n.* **(-s,** *pl.* **-e, -s)** folding *or* collapsible canoe, kayak (*of Esquimaux*).

Kaje ['ka:jə], *f.* (*dial.*) dyke, embankment.

Kajüte [ka'jy:tə], *f.* cabin, berth; ***erste* –,** saloon. **Kajütentreppe,** *f.* companion way.

Kakadu ['kaka'du], *m.* **(-s,** *pl.* **-s,** (*rare*) **-e)** cockatoo.

Kakao [ka'ka:o], *m.* cocoa (*the product*); cacao (*the tree, seed*); (*coll.*) ***ihn durch den – ziehen,*** make him look ridiculous.

Kakerlak ['ka:kərlak], *m.* **(-s** *or* **-en,** *pl.* **-en)** 1. cockroach; 2. (*dial.*) albino.

Kako– ['kako], *pref.* bad. **Kakokratie** [–'ti:], *f.* bad government. **Kakophonie** [–'ni:], *f.* cacophony.

Kaktee [kak'te:ə], *f.,* **Kaktus,** *m.* (-, *pl.* **-teen** [–'te:ən], (*Austr.*) **-ses,** *pl.* **-se)** cactus.

Kalamität [kalami'tɛ:t], *f.* calamity.

Kalander [ka'landər], *m.* calendering machine, glazing rollers. **kalandern,** *v.t.* calender.

Kalauer [ka'lauər], *m.* (*coll.*) pun, stale joke, chestnut. **kalauern,** *v.i.* make puns.

Kalb [kalp], *n.* **(-(e)s,** *pl.* **⸚er)** calf; fawn; (*fig.*) ninny; (*fig.*) ***das – ins Auge schlagen,*** tread on someone's toes; ***das goldene – anbeten,*** worship the golden calf; (*B.*) ***mit fremdem –e pflügen,*** plough with another p.'s heifer, profit by another's work, plagiarize.

Kalbe ['kalbə], *f.* heifer. **kalben,** *v.i.* calve. **kalberig,** *adj.* giggling. **kalbern,** *v.i.* romp, be frolicsome, behave foolishly; snigger, titter, giggle. **kälbern, 1.** *v.i.* 1. *See* **kalben**; 2. *See* **kalbern. 2.** *adj.* (of) calf *or* veal. **Kälberne(s),** *n.* veal.

Kalb|fell, *n.* calfskin; drum; ***dem – folgen,*** follow the call of the army, follow the colours. **–fleisch,** *n.* veal. **–leder,** *n.* calf (leather); ***in – gebunden,*** bound in calf.

Kalbs|braten, *m.* roast veal. **–bröschen,** *n. See* **–milch. –brust,** *f.* breast of veal. **–hachse, –haxe, –keule,** *f.* leg of veal. **–kotelett,** *n.* veal chop *or* cutlet. **–leber,** *f.* calf's liver. **–lende,** *f.* fillet of veal. **–milch,** *f.* sweetbread. **–nierenbraten,** *m.* loin of veal. **–schlegel,** *m. See* **–keule. –schnitte,** *f.,* **–schnitzel,** *n.* veal cutlet.

Kaldaunen [kal'daunən], *f.pl.* (*dial.*) intestines, (*Cul.*) tripe.

Kalebasse [kale'basə], *f.* calabash.

Kalender [ka'lɛndər], *m.* calendar, almanac; ***das steht nicht in meinem –,*** that is nothing to me, I know nothing of that. **Kalender|block,** *m.* tear-off calendar. **–rechnung,** *f.* ***Russische –,*** old style.

Kalesche [ka'lɛʃə], *f.* light carriage, chaise.

Kalfakter [kal'faktər], *m.* **(-s,** *pl.* **-), Kalfaktor,** *m.* **(-s,** *pl.* **-en)** boilerman, caretaker; toady, spy.

kalfatern [kal'fa:tərn], *v.i.* (*Naut.*) caulk.

Kali ['ka:li], *n.* potash; ***ätzendes* –,** caustic potash, potassium hydrate; ***blausaures* –,** cyanide of potassium; ***chlorsaures* –,** chlorate of potassium.

Kaliber [ka'li:bər], *n.* calibre, bore, (*fig.*) gauge; (*coll.*) sort, kind. **kalibermäßig,** *adj.* true to gauge.

kalibrieren [kali'bri:rən], *v.t.* gauge; calibrate, standardize.

Kalidünger ['ka:lidyŋər], *m.* potash manure, fertilizer.

Kalif [ka'li:f], *m.* (**-en,** *pl.* **-en**) caliph. **Kalifat** [–'fa:t], *n.* (**-(e)s,** *pl.* **-e**) caliphate.

Kalifornien [kali'fɔrniən], *n.* (*Geog.*) California. **kalifornisch,** *adj.* Californian.

Kalihydrat ['ka:lihydra:t], *n.* potassium hydrate.

Kaliko ['kaliko], *m.* (**-s,** *pl.* **-s**) calico.

Kali|lauge, *f.* potash *or* caustic lye. **–nitrat,** *n.* saltpetre, nitre, potassium nitrate. **–salz,** *n.* potassium salt. **Kalium,** *n. See* **Kali.**

Kalk [kalk], *m.* (**-(e)s,** *pl.* **-e**) lime, limestone, chalk, calcium; ***ätzender*** or ***gebrannter*** **–,** quicklime, unslaked *or* anhydrous lime; ***gelöschter*** **–,** slaked lime; ***kohlensaurer*** **–,** carbonate of lime; ***verwitterter*** **–,** see ***gelöschter*** **–;** **–** ***brennen,*** calcine lime; ***mit*** **–** ***bewerfen,*** roughcast; ***mit*** **–** ***tünchen,*** limewash.

Kalk|ablagerung, *f.* calcareous *or* lime deposit. **–anlagerung,** *f.* calcification. **kalk|arm,** *adj.* deficient in lime *or* calcium. **–artig,** *adj.* calcareous, chalky, limy. **Kalk|bewurf,** *m.* plaster(ing), roughcast. **–boden,** *m.* calcareous soil. **–brennerei,** *f.* lime-kiln. **–bruch,** *m.* limestone quarry. **–düngung,** *f.* liming (*the soil*).

kalken ['kalkən], *v.t.* dress *or* cover with lime, whitewash.

Kalk|erde, *f.* calcareous earth, calcium oxide. **–farbe,** *f.* distemper. **–fels,** *m.* limestone. **–grube,** *f.* lime-pit. **kalkhaltig,** *adj.* calcareous, hard (*of water*). **Kalk|hütte,** *f.* lime-kiln. **–hydrat,** *n.* slaked lime. **kalkig,** *adj. See* **kalkhaltig. Kalk|mangel,** *m.* lime *or* calcium deficiency. **–milch,** *f.* slaked lime, whitewash. **–mulde,** *f.* mortar-trough. **–ofen,** *m.* lime-kiln. **–schicht,** *f.* chalk layer. **–stein,** *m.* limestone. **–tünche,** *f.* whitewash.

Kalkül [kal'ky:l], *m.* (**-s,** *pl.* **-e**) calculation, assessment, estimate. **Kalkulation** [–latsi'o:n], *f.* calculation, computation, (*Comm.*) cost accounting; ***falsche*** **–,** miscalculation. **kalkulieren** [–'li:rən], *v.t.* calculate, compute, reckon, estimate.

Kalkwand ['kalkvand], *f.* plaster-wall.

Kall [kal], *m.* (*dial.*) chatter, prattle.

Kalle ['kalə], *f.* (*vulg.*) mistress, kept woman.

kallen ['kalən], *v.i.* (*dial.*) chatter, prattle.

Kalligraphie [kaligra'fi:], *f.* calligraphy.

kallös [ka'lø:s], *adj.* (*Med., Bot.*) callous, hard, hardened. **Kallus** ['kalus], *m.* (-, *pl.* **-se**) callosity, hardening (*of skin*).

Kalmäuser ['kalmɔyzər], *m.* grumbler, grouser, misanthrope. **Kalmäuserei** [–'raɪ], *f.* moping, misanthropy. **kalmäusern,** *v.i.* mope.

Kalme ['kalmə], *f.* (*Naut.*) calm, windless period. **Kalmengürtel,** *m.* (*Naut.*) doldrums.

Kalmus ['kalmus], *m.* (-, *pl.* **-se**) (*Bot.*) calamus (*Acorus calamus*).

Kalomel [kalo'mɛl], *n.* mercurious chloride, calomel.

Kalorie [kalo'ri:], *f.* thermal unit, calorie. **Kalorifer** [–'fe:r], *m.* (**-s,** *pl.* **-s**) heating element, radiator. **Kalorimetrie** [–me'tri:], *f.* measurement of heat.

Kalotte [ka'lɔtə], *f.* (priest's) skull-cap.

kalt [kalt], *adj.* (*comp. kälter, sup. kältest*) cold, cool, chill, chilly; (*fig.*) cold, frosty, frigid, indifferent, callous, restrained, calm; ***–e Angst,*** chill of terror; **–** ***bleiben,*** keep cool, keep one's temper; ***–en Blutes,*** callously, in cold blood; ***–er Brand,*** gangrene, mortification; ***–e Ente,*** cold punch; (*Hunt.*) ***–e Fährte,*** cold scent; ***–es Fieber,*** ague; **–** ***keilen,*** quarry without blasting; ***–er Krieg,*** cold war; ***–e Küche,*** cold dishes, cold foods; ***–e Schale,*** *see* **Kaltschale;** ***–er Schlag,*** lightning that strikes without igniting; ***mir ist*** **–,** I am *or* feel cold; **–** ***stellen,*** put into cold storage; shelve (*a th.*), *see* **kaltstellen;** ***es überläuft mich*** **–,** ***es läuft mir*** **–** ***über den Rücken,*** a cold shudder runs down my back; ***mir wird*** **–,** I am getting cold; (*of a th.*) **–** ***werden,*** grow cold, cool down; ***–e Zone,*** frigid zone.

Kalt|blüter, *m.pl. See* **–blütler. kaltblütig, 1.** *adj.* cold-blooded; calm, composed, cool-headed. **2.** *adv.* in cold blood, callously. **Kalt|blütigkeit,** *f.* cold-bloodedness; sangfroid, composure. **–blütler,** *m.* cold-blooded animal. **kaltbrüchig,** *adj.* (*Metall.*) cold-short.

Kälte ['kɛltə], *f.* cold, chilliness, frost, frostiness, (*fig.*) coldness, coolness, indifference, frigidity; ***zwei Grad*** **–,** two degrees of frost; ***vor*** **–** ***zittern,*** shiver with cold.

Kälteanlage ['kɛltəʔanla:gə], *f.* refrigeration plant. **kältebeständig,** *adj.* cold-resistant, non-freezing. **Kälteeinbruch,** *m.* cold snap. **kälte|empfindlich,** *adj.* sensitive to cold. **–erzeugend,** *adj.* frigorific. **Kälte|erzeugung,** *f.* refrigeration. **–gefühl,** *n.* sensation of cold. **–grad,** *m.* degree of frost, degree below zero (centigrade). **–industrie,** *f.* cold-storage industry. **–maschine,** *f.* refrigerator. **–mischung,** *f.* freezing-mixture. **–mittel,** *n.* freezing *or* cooling agent. **kälten,** *v.t.* chill, make cold. **Kälte|schutzmittel,** *n.* (*Motor.*) antifreeze mixture. **–technik,** *f.* refrigeration engineering. **–welle,** *f.* cold spell.

kalt|gezogen, *adj.* (*Metall.*) cold-drawn. **–hämmerbar,** *adj.* malleable. **–härtend,** *adj.* cold-setting *or* drying. **–herzig,** *adj.* hard-hearted. **–lächelnd, 1.** *adj.* cynical. **2.** *adv.* without turning a hair. **Kalt|lagerung,** *f.* cold storage. **–leim,** *m.* cold (-setting) glue. **–luft,** *f.* (*Meteor.*) polar air(-stream). **–luftfront,** *f.* (*Meteor.*) cold front. **kaltmachen,** *v.t.* (*coll.*) bump (*a p.*) off, make cold meat of (*a p.*). **Kalt|nadelarbeit,** *f.* dry-point etching. **–schale,** *f.* cold fruit soup. **–schmied,** *m.* coppersmith, wrought-iron worker. **kaltschnäuzig, 1.** *adj.* cool, (*coll.*) snooty. **2.** *adv.* coolly, as cool as you please. **Kaltsinn,** *m.* coldness, indifference, insensibility. **kalt|sinnig,** *adj.* cold, indifferent. **–stellen,** *v.t.* 1. put into cold storage, put on ice, put in a cold place, keep cool; 2. (*fig.*) remove (*a p.*) from office, debar (*a p.*) from having influence, (*coll.*) shelve (*a p.*), leave (*a p.*) out in the cold; prevent (*a p.*) from interfering. **Kalt|verarbeitung,** *f.* (*Metall.*) cold working. **–walzen,** *n.* (*Metall.*) cold rolling. **–wasserheilanstalt,** *f.* hydropathic (establishment). **–wasserkur,** *f.* hydropathic treatment. **kaltziehen,** *irr.v.t.* (*Metall.*) cold-draw.

Kalvarienberg [kal'fa:riənbɛrk], *m.* (*B.*) (Mount) Calvary.

Kalvinist [kalfi'nɪst], *m.* (**-en,** *pl.* **-en**) Calvinist.

kalzinieren [kaltsi'ni:rən], *v.t.* calcine.

Kalzium ['kaltsium], *n.* calcium.

kam [ka:m], *see* **kommen.**

Kamarilla [kama'rilja], *f.* (-, *pl.* **-llen**) camarilla, court-party.

kambieren [kam'bi:rən], *v.i.* deal in bills, do exchange business. **Kambist,** *m.* (**-en,** *pl.* **-en**) money-changer, financier.

kambrisch ['kambrɪʃ], *adj.* (*Geol.*) Cambrian.

Kambüse [kam'by:zə], *f. See* **Kombüse.**

käme ['kɛ:mə], *see* **kommen.**

Kamee [ka'me:ə], *f.* cameo.

Kamel [ka'me:l], *n.* (**-s,** *pl.* **-e**) camel; (*coll.*) blockhead, duffer, numskull, dolt; ***Mücken zu –en machen,*** make mountains out of molehills. **Kamel|abteilung,** *f.* camel corps. **–füllen,** *n.* young camel. **–garn,** *n.* mohair. **–haar,** *n.* camel-hair. **–hengst,** *m.* male camel.

Kamelie [ka'me:liə], *f.* (*Bot.*) camellia.

Kamel|kuh, *f. See* **–stute.**

Kamelopard [kamelo'part], *m.* (**-en** *or* **-(e)s,** *pl.* **-e(n)**) giraffe, (*obs.*) camelopard.

Kamelott [kamə'lɔt], *m.* (**-(e)s,** *pl.* **-e**) Angora cloth, camlet.

Kamel|stute, *f.* female camel. **–ziege,** *f.* Angora goat.

Kamera ['kamәra], *f.* (-, *pl.* **-s**) (*Phot.*) camera.

Kamerad [kamə'ra:t], *m.* (**-en,** *pl.* **-en**) comrade, mate, companion, colleague, fellow (worker *etc.*); (*coll.*) chum, pal, (*Am.*) buddy. **Kameradschaft,** *f.* comradeship, fellowship, companionship, camaraderie; (*Nat. Soc.*) squad of Hitler Youth. **kameradschaftlich, 1.** *adj.* companionable, friendly, (*coll.*) pally, matey, chummy. **2.** *adv.* as comrades. **Kameradschaftlichkeit,** *f. See* **Kameradschaftsgeist. Kameradschafts|ehe,** *f.* companionate marriage. **-geist,** *m.* team spirit, camaraderie, fellow-feeling. **-haus,** *n.* students' union.

Kameralien [kame'ra:liən], *pl. See* **Kameralistik. Kameralist** [–'lɪst], *m.* (**-en,** *pl.* **-en**) (*obs.*) student of public affairs. **Kameralistik,** *f.* public finance and administration. **Kameral|wesen,** *n.* fiscal affairs. **-wissenschaft,** *f. See* **Kameralistik.**

Kamerun [kamə'ru:n], *n.* (*Geog.*) Cameroon.

kamest ['ka:məst], *see* **kommen.**

kamig, *adj. See* **kahmig.**

Kamille [ka'mɪlə], *f.* (*Bot.*) camomile (*Matricaria chamomilla*).

Kamin [ka'mi:n], *m.* (**-s,** *pl.* **-e**) chimney, flue; fireplace, fireside; (*Mount.*) chimney; (*coll.*) ***das kannst in den – schreiben,*** that's as good as lost, that's up the chimney. **Kamin|aufsatz,** *m.* mantelpiece, overmantel. **-ecke,** *f.* chimney-corner. **-feger,** *m.* chimney-sweep. **-feuer,** *n.* open fire. **-gerät,** *n.* fire-irons. **-gesims,** *n.* mantelpiece. **-gestell,** *n.* fire-dogs. **-gitter,** *n.* fender; fire-guard. **-kehrer,** *m. See* **-feger. -platte,** *f.* back of the chimney. **-rost,** *m.* grate. **-schirm,** *m.* fire-screen. **-sims,** *n. See* **-gesims. -teppich,** *m.* hearth-rug. **-vorsatz, -vorsetzer,** *m.* fender, fireguard, fire screen.

Kamm [kam], *m.* (**-es,** *pl.* **⸚e**) comb; ridge (*of hills*); crest (*of waves*); cog, cam, tappet; mane (*of a horse*); back of neck (*of oxen*); tuft, crest (*of birds etc.*); comb (*of a cock*); (*Zool.*) pecten; weaver's reed, carding machine (*for wool*); (*dial.*) stalk (*of grapes*); ***enger –,*** fine comb; ***der – schwillt ihm,*** he bristles with rage, he sees red; he gives himself airs, (*sl.*) he gets cocky; ***alle*** (***alles***) ***über einen – scheren,*** treat *or* judge all (everything) alike; ***weiter –,*** coarse(-toothed) comb. **kammartig,** *adj.* pectinate. **Kammbläßhuhn,** *n.* (*Orn.*) crested coot (*Fulica cristata*).

kämmen ['kɛmən], **1.** *v.t.* comb; card (*wool*). **2.** *v.r.* comb o.s. *or* one's hair.

Kammer ['kamər], *f.* (-, *pl.* **-n**) (small unheated) room, closet, chamber, cabinet, cubicle, (*coll.*) cubby-hole; compartment; chamber (*of a gun etc.*); cavity, hollow, ventricle (*of the heart*); chamber (*of deputies etc.*); board, panel; (*Mil.*) quartermaster's store; ***Stube und –,*** sitting-room and bedroom; ***dunkle –,*** camera obscura; (*Parl.*) ***erste –,*** Upper House, House of Lords; ***zweite –,*** Lower House, House of Commons.

Kammer|archiv, *n.* the rolls. **-beamte(r),** *m.* finance *or* treasury clerk. **-bediente(r),** *m.* valet de chambre. **-dame,** *f.* lady of the bedchamber. **-degen,** *m.* dress-sword. **-diener,** *m.* valet, groom, personal servant.

Kämmerei [kɛmə'raɪ], *f.* finance *or* treasury department, (city) chamberlain's office. **Kämmerer** ['kɛmərər], *m.* (city) treasurer, (*Hist.*) chamberlain.

Kammer|frau, *f.,* **-fräulein,** *n.* lady's maid, chambermaid. **-gefälle,** *n.pl.* revenues of a prince's domains. **-gericht,** *n.* supreme court (*in Prussia*). **-gut,** *n.* crown land. **-herr,** *m.* chamberlain; gentleman of the bedchamber. **-höhe,** *f. See* **-ton. -jäger,** *m.* vermin-killer, fumigator. **-jungfer,** *f. See* **-frau. -junker,** *m. See* **-herr. -kätzchen,** *n.* (*coll.*) *see* **-frau. -klappe,** *f.* ventricular valve (*of heart*). **-kollegium,** *n.* treasury board. **-lehen,** *n.* fief of the crown. **-mädchen,** *n. See* **-frau. -musik,** *f.* chamber music. **-orchester,** *n.* chamber orchestra. **-pächter,** *m.* crown-land tenant. **-sänger,** *m.,* **-sängerin,** *f.* concert singer (*also as title given to singers*). **-schreiber,** *m.* treasury clerk. **-spiele,** *n.pl.* intimate theatre. **-ton,** *m.* (*Mus.*) concert-pitch. **-tuch,** *n.* cambric. **-unteroffizier,** *m.* (*Mil.*) NCO in charge of stores, (*Am.*) supply serjeant. **-wasser,** *n.* aqueous humour (*of eye*). **-zofe,** *f. See* **-frau.**

Kamm|flosser, *m.* (*Ichth.*) pecten. **-garn,** *n.* worsted (yarn). **-garngewebe,** *n.,* **-garnstoff,** *m.* worsted; ***gerippter –,*** whipcord. **-haar,** *n.* (horse's) mane. **-rad,** *n.* cog-wheel. **-stück,** *n.* neck (*of meat*). **Kammuschel,** *f.* scallop (*Pectinidae*). **Kammwolle,** *f.* carded wool.

Kamp [kamp], *m.* (**-(e)s,** *pl.* **⸚e**) (*dial.*) enclosure, preserve.

Kampanje [kam'panjə], *f.* (*Naut.*) (*obs.*) poop. **Kampanjetreppe,** *f.* (*Naut.*) companion(way).

Kämpe ['kɛmpə], *m.* (**-n,** *pl.* **-n**) 1. (*Poet.*) champion, warrior; (*coll.*) ***alter –,*** old hand, (*Mil.*) old sweat; 2. (*dial.*) hog.

kampeln ['kampəln], *v.i.* (*dial.*) quarrel, squabble, tussle.

Kampescheholz [kam'pɛʃəhɔlts], *n.* campeachy-wood, logwood.

Kampf [kampf], *m.* (**-(e)s,** *pl.* **⸚e**) combat, fight; contest, engagement, action, encounter, battle, conflict, feud, strife, struggle (***um,*** for); ***den – ansagen*** (*Dat.*), challenge, throw down the gauntlet to; ***den – eröffnen,*** open hostilities; ***– ums Dasein,*** struggle for existence; ***– bis aufs Messer,*** war to the knife; ***wo der – am heißesten tobt,*** the thick of the battle *or* fight; ***– der Anschauungen,*** conflict of opinions; ***– auf Leben und Tod,*** fight to the death, life-and-death struggle.

Kampf|abschnitt, *m.* combat sector. **-ansage,** *f.* challenge (***an*** (*Acc.*), to). **-aufstellung,** *f.* battle array. **-auftrag,** *m.* combat mission. **-bahn,** *f.* stadium, arena. **-begier(de),** *f.* bellicosity, pugnacity. **kampf|begierig,** *adj.* pugnacious, bellicose. **-bereit,** *adj.* ready *or* (*Naut.*) clear for action. **Kampf|einheit,** *f.* combat unit. **-einsatz,** *m.* commitment (*of troops*); combat, action.

kämpfen ['kɛmpfən], *v.i.* fight, strive, struggle, do battle (***für*** *or* ***um,*** for); engage in battle *or* combat; (*fig.*) ***– mit,*** struggle *or* wrestle *or* grapple *or* contend with; ***gut –,*** put up a good fight.

Kampfer ['kampfər], *m.* camphor.

Kämpfer ['kɛmpfər], *m.* 1. fighter, combatant, warrior; boxer, prize-fighter, pugilist; wrestler; (*Spt.*) contestant; (*Nat. Soc.*) ***alter –,*** original party member; 2. (*Archit.*) abutment. **kämpferisch,** *adj.* fighting, warlike, militant, combative, bellicose, pugnacious, aggressive.

kampferprobt ['kampfˀɛrpro:pt], *adj.* seasoned, veteran, tried in battle.

kampfersauer [kampfər'zauər], *adj.* (*Chem.*) camphorated.

kampffähig ['kampffɛ:ɪç], *adj.* (*Mil.*) effective; (*coll.*) fighting fit, in fighting trim; ***ein Schiff – machen,*** clear a ship for action. **Kampf|flieger,** *m.* member of aircrew. **-flugzeug,** *n.* military *or* operational *or* (*Am.*) combat aircraft. **-front,** *f.* (*Mil.*) front line. **-gas,** *n.* (*Mil.*) poison gas. **-geist,** *m.* fighting spirit; (*coll.*) ***– zeigen,*** show fight. **-geschrei,** *n.* war-cry, battle-cry. **-geschwader,** *n.* fighter squadron. **-gewühl,** *n.* mêlée; ***im –,*** in the thick of the fight. **-gruppe,** *f.* (*Mil.*) task force. **-hahn,** *m.* fighting *or* game cock (*also fig.*). **-handlung,** *f.* engagement, (military) operation, *pl.* (military) action. **-kraft,** *f.* fighting strength. **-lage,** *f.* tactical situation. **-läufer,** *m.* (*Orn.*) (*male*) ruff, (*female*) reeve (*Philomachus pugnax*). **kampflos,** *adv.* without a fight. **Kampflust,** *f.* pugnacity, aggressiveness, bellicosity. **kampf|lustig,** *adj.* pugnacious, aggressive, bellicose. **-müde,** *adj.* battle-weary. **Kampf|ordnung,** *f.* order of battle. **-platz,** *m.* battlefield; (*fig.*) scene of action, arena, cockpit; ***den – betreten,*** enter the lists. **-preis,** *m.* 1. prize (*contested for*); 2. (*Comm.*) cut price. **-richter,** *m.* umpire, referee, judge. **-ruf,** *m.* war-cry. **-schwimmer,** *m.* (*Mil.*) frogman. **-spiel,** *n.* jousting, tilting, tournament; prize-fighting, prize-fight; *pl.* athletic contest, sports meeting. **-stoff,** *m.* (*Mil.*) poison gas. **-übung,** *f.* (*Mil.*) manœuvres. **kampfunfähig,** *adj.* (*of a p.*) disabled, (*of a th.*) out of action; ***– machen,*** disable; knock out, put out of action. **-wagen,** *m.* armoured car. **-ziel,** *n.,* **-zweck,** *m.* tactical objective.

kampieren [kam'pi:rən], *v.i.* camp (out), be encamped; (*coll.*) ***auf dem Sofa –,*** shake down on the sofa.
kamst [ka:mst], *see* **kommen.**
Kanada ['kanada], *n.* Canada. **Kanadier** [–'na:diər], *m.* 1. Canadian; 2. Canadian canoe. **kanadisch,** *adj.* Canadian.
Kanal [ka'na:l], *m.* (**-s,** *pl.* **⸚e**) canal; ditch, conduit, drain, sewer; cutting; channel. **Kanal|arbeiter,** *m.* navvy. **–dampfer,** *m.* cross-channel steamer. **–gas,** *n.* sewer gas. **–inseln,** *f.pl.* Channel Islands.
Kanalisation [kanalizatsi'o:n], *f.* canalization, drainage, sewerage; drains. **Kanalisationsanlage,** *f.* sewage system. **kanalisieren** [–'zi:rən], *v.t.* drain, canalize. **Kanalisierung,** *f.* drainage.
Kanal|netz, *n.* canal system. **–schiffahrt,** *f.* canal-navigation. **–schleuse,** *f.* canal-lock. **–schwimmer,** *m.* Channel swimmer. **–system,** *n.* drainage system. **–wähler,** *m.* (*Rad.*) channel selector (switch). **–wasser,** *n.* sewage.
Kanapee ['kanape, –'pe:], *n.* (**-s,** *pl.* **-s**) sofa, settee.
Kanarien|hahn [ka'na:riən–], *m.*, **–männchen,** *n.* cock canary. **–vogel,** *m.* canary. **–weibchen,** *n.* hen canary.
Kanarische Inseln [ka'na:riʃə], *f.pl.* Canary Islands.
Kanaster [ka'nastər], *m.* (*obs.*) *see* **Knaster.**
Kandare [kan'da:rə], *f.* curb(-bit), double bridle; (*fig.*) ***an die – nehmen*** or ***legen, an der – halten,*** take in hand, take a strong line with, put a curb on; (***ein Pferd***) ***an die – legen*** or ***nehmen,*** (***einem Pferd***) ***die – anlegen,*** put on the curb *or* bridlebit, curb (*a horse*).
Kandelaber [kandə'la:bər], *m.* candelabrum, chandelier.
kandeln ['kandəln], *v.t.* groove, channel, flute.
Kandelzucker ['kandəltsukər], *m.* *See* **Kandiszucker.**
Kandidat [kandi'da:t], *m.* (**-en,** *pl.* **-en**) candidate, applicant, aspirant; probationer; ***cand. phil.*** = ***– der Philosophie,*** final year arts student; ***aufgestellter –,*** nominee; ***als –en aufstellen,*** nominate; ***als – (für eine Stelle) auftreten,*** submit one's application (for a post), submit o.s. as a candidate. **Kandidatur** [–'tu:r], *f.* (-, *pl.* **-en**) candidature, (*Am.*) candidacy, application. **kandidieren,** *v.i.* be a candidate (***für,*** for), submit one's application (for) (*a post*); stand, run, (*coll.*) put up (for) (*election*), contest (*a seat*).
kandieren [kan'di:rən], *v.t.* candy. **Kandis(zucker),** *m.* sugar candy.
Kaneel [ka'ne:l], *m.* cinnamon.
Kanevas ['kanəvas], *m.* (**-ses,** *pl.* **-se**) canvas.
Känguruh ['kɛŋguru], *n.* (**-s,** *pl.* **-s**) kangaroo.
Kaninchen [ka'ni:nçən], *n.* rabbit. **Kaninchen|bau,** *m.* rabbit-burrow. **–gehege,** *n.* rabbit-warren. **–höhle,** *f.* *See* **–bau. –kasten, –stall,** *m.* rabbit-hutch.
Kanister [ka'nɪstər], *m.* can, tin, canister, (metal) container.
Kanker ['kaŋkər], *m.* canker (*on trees*).
kann [kan], *see* **können.**
Kännchen ['kɛnçən], *n.* jug; small can *or* tin.
Kanne ['kanə], *f.* can, tankard, mug, jug, pot, canister; quart, litre (*liquid measure*); (*studs. sl.*) ***in die – steigen,*** be called upon to drink (*students' drinking ritual*); ***es gießt mit –n,*** it is raining cats and dogs. **Kanne|gießer,** *m.* (*coll.*) tub-thumper. **–gießerei,** *f.* political hot air. **kannegießern,** *v.i.* rant.
Kännel ['kɛnəl], *m.* (*Swiss*) roof gutter.
kannelieren [kane'li:rən], *v.t.* channel, flute, groove. **Kannelüre** [–'ly:rə], *f.* flute, groove (*of a pillar*); (*pl.*) fluting.
Kannengießer ['kanəngi:sər], *m.* pewterer.
Kannibale [kani'ba:lə], *m.* (**-n,** *pl.* **-n**) cannibal. **kannibalisch,** *adj.* man-eating, cannibal, (*fig.*) savage, ferocious; (*sl.*) enormous, terrific, awful, beastly; (*sl.*) ***ich habe –en Hunger,*** I am ravenously hungry; (*sl.*) ***–e Hitze,*** terrific heat.

kannst [kanst], *see* **können.**
kannte ['kantə], **kanntest,** *see* **kennen.**
Kannvorschrift ['kanfo:rʃrɪft], *f.* (*Law*) permissive *or* discretionary provision.
Kanon ['ka:nɔn], *m.* (**-s,** *pl.* **-s**) 1. canon (*of Holy Scriptures*); 2. (*Mus.*) canon, round.
Kanonade [kano'na:də], *f.* cannonade, bombardment.
Kanone [ka'no:nə], *f.* 1. cannon, gun; (*sl.*) ***ein Paar –n,*** a pair of riding-boots; 2. (*coll.*) master-mind, big shot, (*Spt.*) ace, star, crack; (*coll.*) ***große –,*** big shot, big gun, big bug, big noise; 3. (*coll.*) ***unter aller –,*** beneath contempt, (*sl.*) lousy.
Kanonen|boot, *n.* gunboat, naval sloop *or* pinnace. **–donner,** *m.* boom *or* roar of cannon; cannonade. **–feuer,** *n.* artillery fire, gunfire, cannonade. **–fieber,** *n.* nervousness under fire; (*coll.*) ***– haben,*** get cold feet. **–futter,** *n.* cannon-fodder. **–gießerei,** *f.* gun-foundry. **–gut,** *n.* gun-metal. **–kugel,** *f.* cannonball. **–ofen,** *m.* high-pressure furnace. **–schlag,** *m.* bursting-charge; maroon (*fireworks*). **–schuß,** *m.* cannon-shot; ***mit – begrüßen,*** honour with a salute of guns. **–stiefel,** *m.pl.* jackboots.
Kanonier [kano'ni:r], *m.* (**-s,** *pl.* **-e**) gunner.
Kanonikat [kanoni'ka:t], *n.* (**-(e)s,** *pl.* **-e**) canonry, prebend. **Kanoniker** [–'no:nikər], *m.* (**-s,** *pl.* -), **Kanonikus,** *m.* (-, *pl.* **-ker**) canon, prebender. **kanonisch** [–'no:nɪʃ], *adj.* canonical; ***–es Recht,*** canon law. **kanonisieren** [–'zi:rən], *v.t.* canonize. **Kanonisse** [–'nɪsə], **Kanonissin,** *f.* canoness.
Kantate [kan'ta:tə], *f.* cantata.
Kante ['kantə], *f.* edge, corner; edging, lace; brim, border, margin, ledge; selvage (*of cloth*); crust (*of bread*); ***spitze –,*** corner; ***flache –,*** face, side; ***auf die hohe – legen,*** put by (for a rainy day); ***mit –n besetzen,*** trim with lace. **Kantel,** *m. or n.* square ruler. **Kanten,** *m.* (*dial.*) crust (*of a loaf*). **kanten,** *v.t.* edge, border; turn *or* set on edge, tilt, cant; square (*a stone*); ***nicht –!*** this side up (*on boxes*).
Kanten|besatz, *m.* trimming, edging. **–kleid,** *n.* dress trimmed with lace. **–länge,** *f.* length of side. **–schienen,** *f.pl.* (*Railw.*) edge-rails. **–winkel,** *m.* angle formed by two planes.
Kanter ['kantər], *m.* canter. **kantern,** *v.i.* canter.
Kanthaken ['kantha:kən], *m.* (*Naut.*) cant-hook; (*sl.*) ***ihn beim – fassen,*** seize him by the scruff of the neck.
Kantharide [kanta'ri:də], *f.* Spanish fly.
Kantholz ['kanthɔlts], *n.* squared timber. **kantig,** *adj.* edged, angular, squared.
Kantine [kan'ti:nə], *f.* canteen, mess.
Kanton [kan'to:n], *m.* (**-s,** *pl.* **-e**) (*Swiss*) canton; district, province. **kantonieren** [–'ni:rən], *v.i.* (*obs.*) (*Mil.*) be quartered *or* billeted, be in cantonment. **Kantonierung,** *f.* cantonment, billet. **Kantonist** [–'nɪst], *m.* (**-en,** *pl.* **-en**) (*sl.*) ***unsicherer –,*** shifty fellow, unreliable customer.
Kantönligeist [kan'tø:nligaɪst], *m.* (*Swiss*) narrow particularism.
Kantor ['kantɔr], *m.* (**-s,** *pl.* **-en**) precentor; choir-master; village schoolmaster and organist; (*Jew.*) cantor.
Kantschu ['kantʃu], *m.* (**-s,** *pl.* **-s**) short whip, knout.
Kanu [ka'nu:], *n.* (**-s,** *pl.* **-s**) canoe.
Kanüle [ka'ny:lə], *f.* hypodermic syringe; tube, cannula.
Kanzel ['kantsəl], *f.* (-, *pl.* **-n**) 1. pulpit; ***sich von der – ablesen lassen,*** have the banns published; 2. (*Av.*) turret, cockpit; 3. (*Univ.*) chair. **Kanzel|rede,** *f.* sermon. **–redner,** *m.* preacher, pulpit orator.
Kanzlei [kants'laɪ], *f.* (-, *pl.* **-en**) chancellery, lawyer's office, government office. **Kanzlei|archiv,** *n.* rolls, archives, government records. **–beamte(r),** *m.* chancery clerk, government official. **–dekret,** *n.* departmental order. **–diener,** *m.* government servant, tipstaff. **–format,** *n.* foolscap. **–gericht(shof),** *n.* (*m.*) court of chancery.

-papier, *n.* foolscap paper. **-schreiben,** *n.* writ of chancery. **-schreiber,** *m. See* **-beamte(r). -sprache,** *f.*, **-stil,** *m.* official *or* legal language, officialese.

Kanzler ['kantslər], *m.* chancellor. **Kanzlist** [-'lɪst], *m.* (**-en,** *pl.* **-en**) *see* **Kanzleibeamte(r).**

Kaolin [kao'li:n], *m. or n.* china clay, porcelain clay.

Kap [kap], *n.* (**-s,** *pl.* **-e** *or* **-s**) cape, headland.

Kapaun [ka'paun], *m.* (**-s,** *pl.* **-e**) capon; (*coll.*) quarrelsome youngster. **kapaunen,** *v.t.* castrate.

Kapazität [kapatsi'tɛ:t], *f.* capacity (*also Elec.*), (*Elec.*) capacitance; authority; ***eine – ersten Ranges,*** a leading authority.

Kapee [ka'pe:], *n.* (*sl.*) ***schwer von – sein,*** be dull of comprehension, be slow on the uptake.

Kapellan [kapɛ'la:n], *m.* (**-s,** *pl.* **-e**) (*Austr.*) *see* **Kaplan.**

Kapelle [ka'pɛlə], *f.* 1. (*Rel.*) chapel; 2. (*Mus.*) band, orchestra; church choir; 3. (*Metall.*) cupel. **Kapellen|abfall,** *m.* loss in cupellation. **-gold,** *n.* fine gold. **kapellieren** [-'li:rən], *v.t.* refine, cupel (*gold etc.*). **Kapellmeister,** *m.* bandmaster, conductor.

[1]**Kaper** ['ka:pər], *m.* pirate, freebooter, corsair, privateer, sea raider.

[2]**Kaper,** *f.* (-, *pl.* **-n**) (*Bot., Cul.*) caper.

Kaperbrief ['ka:pərbri:f], *m.* letters of marque (and reprisal). **Kaperei** [-'raɪ], *f.* privateering, freebootery, piracy. **kapern,** *v.t.* seize, capture (*a ship*); (*fig.*) commandeer, (*coll.*) collar, bag; ***sie hat endlich einen Mann gekapert,*** she has collared a husband at last.

Kapern|soße, *f.* caper sauce. **-strauch,** *m.* (*Bot.*) *Capparis spinosa.* **-tunke,** *f. See* **-soße.**

Kaperschiff, *n. See* [1]**Kaper.**

kapieren [ka'pi:rən], *v.t.* (*coll.*) grasp, catch on to, tumble to, get it, (*sl.*) savvy.

kapillar [kapi'la:r], *adj.* capillary. **kapillaraktiv,** *adj.* tending to reduce surface tension. **Kapillargefäß,** *n.* capillary (vessel). **kapillarinaktiv,** *adj.* tending to increase surface tension. **Kapillarität** [-i'tɛ:t], **Kapillarkraft,** *f.* capillary attraction.

Kapital [kapi'ta:l], *n.* (**-s,** *pl.* **-e, -ien**) capital, principal, stock, funds; ***eingeschossenes –,*** deposit; ***eisernes –,*** capital invested *or* sunk; ***flüssiges –,*** available funds; ***imaginäres –,*** floating capital; (*fig.*) ***– aus einer S. schlagen,*** profit by *or* make capital out of a th., turn s.th. to account, (*coll.*) cash in on a th.; ***totes –,*** unemployed capital; ***– und Zinsen,*** principal and interest. **kapital,** *adj.* (*coll.*) capital, excellent, first-rate.

Kapital|abfindung, *f.* lump sum settlement. **-abgabe,** *f.* capital levy. **-abschöpfung,** *f.* depletion of capital. **-abwanderung,** *f. See* **-flucht. -anlage,** *f.* investment. **-bilanz,** *f.* net capital movement. **-bildung,** *f.* formation of (new) capital. **-einkommen,** *n.* unearned income. **-einlage,** *f.* invested capital. **-ertragssteuer,** *f.* capital gains tax. **-flucht,** *f.* flight of capital (to foreign markets). **-geber,** *m.* investor, financier. **-gesellschaft,** *f.* joint-stock company. **-güter,** *n.pl.* capital goods. **-hirsch,** *m.* royal stag. **Kapitalien,** *pl. of* **Kapital**; ***Umsatz von –,*** stock operations.

kapitalisieren [kapitali'zi:rən], *v.t.* capitalize, finance; convert into capital, realize (*investments*). **Kapitalisierung,** *f.* capitalization; realization. **Kapitalisierungsanleihe,** *f.* funding loan.

Kapitalismus [kapita'lɪsmus], *m.* capitalism. **Kapitalist,** *m.* (**-en,** *pl.* **-en**) capitalist. **kapitalistisch,** *adj.* capitalist(ic).

Kapital|knappheit, *f.* money shortage. **-kraft,** *f.* financial soundness. **kapitalkräftig,** *adj.* well-funded, financially sound. **Kapital|markt,** *m.* money *or* stock market. **-verbrechen,** *n.* capital crime. **-verkehr,** *m.* turnover of capital. **-vermögen,** *n.* capital assets. **-zins,** *m.* interest on capital. **-zufluß,** *m.* influx of capital.

Kapitäl [kapi'tɛ:l], *n.* (**-s,** *pl.* **-e(r)**) (*Austr.*) *see* **Kapitell. Kapitälchen,** *n.* (*Typ.*) small capitals.

Kapitän [kapi'tɛ:n], *m.* (**-s,** *pl.* **-e**) (*Navy*) captain, skipper (*also Spt.*). **Kapitänleutnant,** *m.* (*Navy*) lieutenant.

Kapitel [ka'pɪtəl], *n.* chapter (*book*); (*Eccl.*) chapter; (*fig.*) topic; ***das ist ein – für sich,*** that is another story; ***ein – halten,*** hold a chapter, convene the canons. **kapitelfest,** *adj.* well-versed. **Kapitelhaus,** *n.* chapter-house.

Kapitell [kapi'tɛl], *n.* (**-s,** *pl.* **-e**) (*Archit.*) capital.

Kapitulant [kapɪtu'lant], *m.* (**-en,** *pl.* **-en**) (*obs.*) re-enlisted soldier. **Kapitulation** [-tsi'o:n], *f.* 1. capitulation, surrender; 2. (*obs.*) (re-)enlistment. **kapitulieren** [-'li:rən], *v.i.* 1. capitulate, surrender; 2. (*obs.*) (re-)engage, (re-)enlist.

Kaplan [ka'pla:n], *m.* (**-s,** *pl.* **⸚e**) (*R.C.*) chaplain, assistant priest.

kapores [ka'po:rəs], *adj.* (*sl.*) spoilt, broken; ***– gehen,*** get broken *etc.*

Kapotte [ka'pɔtə], *f.* hood.

Kappe ['kapə], *f.* cap, hood, bonnet; (*Archit.*) cowl, dome; (*obs.*) hooded mantle, cape; crown (*of a tooth*); horn (*of a sea-mine*); (*Fort.*) coping, bonnet; toe-piece (*of shoe*); heel-piece (*of a sock*), heel-plate; (*Bot.*) sheath, calyptra; (*coll.*) ***etwas auf seine – nehmen,*** answer for a th., make o.s. responsible *or* shoulder the responsibility for a th.; (*Prov.*) ***gleiche Brüder gleiche –n,*** birds of a feather flock together. **kappen,** *v.t.* (*partic. Naut.*) chop, sever, cut away; lop, top, trim (*a hedge*); castrate, caponize (*poultry*); tip, cap (*a shoe*), heel (*a sock*).

Kappenammer ['kapənˀamər], *f.* (*Orn.*) black-headed bunting (*Emberiza melanocephala*). **kappenförmig,** *adj.* hood-shaped, cowled, (*Bot., Zool.*) cucullate. **Kappenmantel,** *m.* hooded cloak, cape. **-mine,** *f.* (*Navy*) horned mine. **-robbe,** *f.* hooded seal. **-säger,** *m.* (*Orn.*) hooded merganser (*Lophodytes cucullatus*). **-stiefel,** *m.pl.* top-boots.

Kapp|fenster, *n.* dormer window. **-hahn,** *m.* capon.

Käppi ['kɛpi], *n.* (**-s,** *pl.* **-s**) military cap, kepi, shako.

Kapp|naht, *f.* flat *or* lap seam, hem. **-zaum,** *m.* cavesson (*harness*).

Kapriole [kapri'o:lə], *f.* capriole (*haute école*), (*coll.*) caper; ***–n machen,*** cut capers.

kaprizieren [kapri'tsi:rən], *v.r.* ***sich – auf*** (*Acc.*), take it into one's head (to do), set one's heart on, be obstinate about. **kapriziös** [-i'ø:s], *adj.* capricious.

Kapschaf ['kapʃa:f], *n.* (*Orn.*) wandering albatross (*Diomedea exulans*).

Kapsel ['kapsəl], *f.* (-, *pl.* **-n**) cover, case, box; (*Med., Bot., rocketry*) capsule; (*Artil.*) detonator; (*Metall.*) chill; (*pottery*) sagger; cap (*of a bottle*); (*hum. sl.*) bed. **kapsel|artig, -förmig,** *adj.* capsular. **Kapselguß,** *m.* chill-casting. **kapseltragend,** *adj.* capsulated, capsuliferous.

Kap|stadt ['ka:p-], *n.* Cape Town. **-sturmvogel,** *m.* (*Orn.*) Cape pigeon, (*Am.*) Cape petrel (*Daption capensis*).

Kaput [ka'put], *m.* (**-s,** *pl.* **-e**) (*Austr., Swiss*) soldier's greatcoat *or* cape.

kaputt [ka'put], *adj.* (*coll.*) (*of a p.*) done up, played *or* fagged out, all in, dead-beat; done for, dead; (*of a th.*) spoilt, ruined, broken, in pieces; ***– gehen,*** come to pieces; (*of a p.*) go to pieces *or* (*sl.*) to pot; ***– machen,*** spoil, ruin, smash (up), knock to pieces; ***das macht einen –,*** that's more than one can bear, that knocks the stuffing out of you.

Kapuze [ka'pu:tsə], *f.* cowl; cape, hood. **Kapuzinade** [-'na:də], *f.* popular sermon; tirade, severe lecture. **Kapuziner** [-'tsi:nər], *m.* 1. capuchin monk; 2. (*Austr. coll.*) coffee with little milk. **Kapuziner|affe,** *m.* capuchin monkey. **-kresse,** *f.* (*Bot.*) nasturtium (*Tropaeolum majus*). **-predigt,** *f. See* **Kapuzinade.**

Karabiner [kara'bi:nər], *m.* carbine, rifle. **Karabinerhaken,** *m.* snaphook, swivel. **Karabinier** [-'nje:], *m.* (**-s,** *pl.* **-s**) carbineer, carabineer, dragoon. **Karabiniere** [-ni'ɛ:rə], *m.* (**-(s),** *pl.* **-ri**) Italian gendarme.

Karaffe [ka'rafə], **Karaffine** [kara'fi:nə], *f.* (cut-glass) carafe, decanter.

Karambolage [karambo'la:ʒə], *f.* (*billiards*) cannon, (*Am.*) carom; collision. **karambolieren,** *v.i.* cannon, (*Am.*) carom; collide.

Karat [ka'ra:t], *n.* (**-(e)s,** *pl.* **-e**) carat. **Karat|gewicht,** *n.* troy weight. **-gold,** *n.* alloyed gold. **karätig,** *suff., e.g. zehn-,* ten carat.

Karausche [ka'rauʃə], *f.* (*Ichth.*) crucian (carp) (*Carassius vulgaris*).

Karawane [kara'va:nə], *f.* caravan. **Karawanserei** [-se'raɪ], (*Austr.* **Karawanserai**), *f.* caravanserai.

Karbatsche [kar'ba:tʃə], *f.* whip, scourge. **karbatschen,** *v.t.* whip, flog.

Karbid [kar'bi:t], *n.* (**-(e)s,** *pl.* **-e**) carbide. **Karbidlampe,** *f.* carbide *or* acetylene lamp.

Karbol, *n.* (*coll.*) *see* **Karbolsäure. Karbolineum** [-'ne:um], *n.* creosote. **Karbol|säure,** *f.* phenol, carbolic acid. **-seife,** *f.* carbolic soap.

Karbonade [karbo'na:də], *f.* chop, cutlet.

Karbonat [karbo'na:t], *n.* (**-(e)s,** *pl.* **-e**) carbonate.

Karbonsäure [kar'bo:nzɔyrə], *f.* carbonic acid.

Karborund [karbo'runt], *m.* (**-s,** *pl.* **-e**) carborundum.

Karbunkel [kar'buŋkəl], *m.* carbuncle, furuncle. **Karbunkelkrankheit,** *f.* anthrax.

Kärcher ['kɛrçər], *m.* (*dial.*) *see* **Kärrner.**

Kardangelenk [kar'da:ngəlɛŋk], *n.* universal joint. **kardanische Aufhängung,** *f.* gimbals. **Kardanwelle,** *f.* jointed *or* flexible shaft.

Kardätsche [kar'dɛ:tʃə], *f.* carding-comb; curry-comb, curry-brush, horse-brush. **kardätschen,** *v.t.* card (*wool*); curry (*a horse*).

Karde ['kardə], *f.* (*Bot.*) teasel (*Dipsacus sativus*); teasel brush; carding instrument.

Kardeel [kar'de:l], *f.* (-, *pl.* **-e**) (*Naut.*) strand of a hawser.

karden ['kardən], **kardieren** [-'di:rən], *v.t.* comb, card (*wool*).

Kardinal [kardi'na:l], *m.* (**-s,** *pl.* **⸗e**) (*R.C.*) cardinal. **Kardinalskollegium,** *n.* college of cardinals. **Kardinal|tugend,** *f.* cardinal virtue. **-zahlen,** *f.pl.* cardinal numbers.

Kardiogramm [kardio'gram], *n.* (*Med.*) cardiogram.

Karenz [ka'rɛnts], *f.* (-, *pl.* **-en**), **Karenzzeit,** *f.* (*Comm. Law*) period of restriction *or* non-availability, waiting-period (*before benefits mature*).

karessieren [karɛ'si:rən], *v.t.* caress, fondle, hug.

Karfiol [karfi'o:l], *m.* (**-s,** *pl.* **-e**) (*Austr.*) cauliflower.

Karfreitag [ka:r'fraɪta:k], *m.* Good Friday.

Karfunkel [kar'fuŋkəl], *m.* 1. carbuncle, almandite (*gem*); 2. (*coll.*) *see* **Karbunkel.**

karg [kark], *adj.* (*comp.* ***kärger*** or ***karger***; *sup.* ***kärgst*** or ***kargst*** (*Austr. only the latter*)) scanty, poor, paltry, meagre; poor, sterile (*soil*); miserly, niggardly, mean, sparing, parsimonious, (*coll.*) stingy; ***-e Antwort,*** short answer. **kargen,** *v.t.* be stingy *or* niggardly (***mit,*** with), be sparing (of); ***nicht – mit,*** be generous *or* lavish with. **Kargheit,** *f.* parsimony, meanness, stinginess; poverty (*of soil*); meagreness, scantiness.

kärglich ['kɛrklɪç], *adj.* scanty, meagre, poor, paltry, wretched; ***-e Kost,*** scanty rations, short commons.

Karibisches Meer [ka'ri:biʃəs], *n.* Caribbean Sea.

kariert [ka'ri:rt], *adj.* chequered, (*Am.*) checkered; check(ed); ***-e Artikel,*** checks; tartans.

Karies ['ka:riəs], *f.* (*Med.*) caries.

Karikatur [karika'tu:r], *f.* (-, *pl.* **-en**) caricature, cartoon. **karikieren** [-'ki:rən], *v.t.* caricature, lampoon.

kariös [kari'ø:s], *adj.* (*Med.*) decayed, carious.

karitativ [karita'ti:f], *adj.* charitable, benevolent.

Karkasse [kar'kasə], *f.* carcass; form (*for hats*); casing (*of tyres*).

Karl [karl], *m.* Charles; – ***der Große,*** Charlemagne.

karmesin(rot) [karme'zi:n(rot)], *adj.* crimson.

Karmin [kar'mi:n], *n.* (*Austr. m.*) carmine. **Karmingimpel,** *m.* (*Orn.*) scarlet grosbeak (*Erythrina erythrina*).

Karneol [karne'o:l], *m.* (**-s,** *pl.* **-e**) carnelian (*gem*).

Karneval ['karneval], *m.* (**-s,** *pl.* **-e** (*Austr.* **-s**)) carnival, Shrovetide festivities.

Karnickel [kar'nɪkəl], *n.* (*coll. Austr.*) rabbit, bunny; scapegoat; (*coll.*) ***wer war das –?*** who began it (*the trouble*)? who is to blame? (*coll.*) ***das – hat angefangen,*** the cat did it.

Karnies [kar'ni:s], *n.* (**-es,** *pl.* **-e**) (*Archit.*) cornice, moulding; pelmet, valance, curtain runner.

Kärnten ['kɛrntən], *n.* (*Geog.*) Carinthia. **Kärntner,** *m.*, **kärntnerisch,** *adj.* Carinthian.

Karo ['ka:ro], *n.* (**-s,** *pl.* **-s**) diamond (*shape*), square, (*fabrics*) check; (*cards*) diamonds. **Karokönigin,** *f.* queen of diamonds.

Karolinger ['ka:rolɪŋər], *m.*, **karolingisch,** *adj.* (*Hist.*) Carolingian.

Karosse [ka'rɔsə], *f.* state-coach. **Karosserie** [-'ri:], *f.* body, coachwork, bodywork (*motor-car*). **Karossier** [-'sje:], *m.* (**-s,** *pl.* **-s**) coach-horse.

Karotte [ka'rɔtə], *f.* carrot.

Karpaten [kar'pa:tən], *pl.* (*Geog.*) Carpathian Mtns.

Karpfen ['karpfən], *m.* carp.

Karre ['karə], *f.* *See* **Karren;** (*coll.*) ***alte –,*** bone-shaker; (*Am.*) jalopy.

Karree [ka're:], *n.* (*Mil.*) square; (*dancing*) set.

Karren ['karən], *m.* cart, (wheel-)barrow; (*Typ.*) carriage; (*fig.*) ***den – festfahren*** or ***in den Dreck fahren,*** come to a deadlock, get stuck; ***an demselben – ziehen,*** be in the same boat; ***den –, einfach laufen lassen,*** let matters take their course, let matters slide. **karren,** *v.t.* cart. **Karren|-führer,** *m.* drayman, carter. **-gaul,** *m.* cart-horse. **-schieber,** *m.* barrowman.

Karrer ['karər], *m.* (*Swiss*) *see* **Kärrner.**

Karrete [ka're:tə], *f.* (*Austr.*) bone-shaker, jalopy.

Karrette [ka'rɛtə], *f.* (*Swiss*) wheelbarrow.

Karriere [kari'ɛ:rə], *f.* career; course; full gallop; – ***machen,*** get on (in the world), be quickly promoted.

karriert, *adj.* (*Austr.*) *see* **kariert.**

Karriol [kari'o:l], *n.* (**-s,** *pl.* **-s**), **Karriole,** *f.* two-wheel(ed) chaise, gig; dog-cart; curricle. **karriolen,** *v.i.* rush about, tear up and down, drive madly *or* recklessly.

Kärrner ['kɛrnər], *m.* carter, carrier. drayman.

[1]**Karst** [karst], *m.* (*Geol.*) chalk formation.

[2]**Karst,** *m.* (**-es,** *pl.* **-e**) mattock; two-pronged fork. **karsten,** *v.t.* hoe, work with a mattock. **Karsthans,** *m.* (*obs.*) peasant.

Kartätsche [kar'tɛ:tʃə], *f.* canister-shot, case-shot, grape-shot, shrapnel.

Kartäuser [kar'tɔyzər], *m.* (*Eccl.*) Carthusian. **Kartäuserlikör,** *m.* Chartreuse.

Karte ['kartə], *f.* card, postcard, visiting card, playing-card; map, (*Naut.*) chart; ticket (of admission); menu, bill of fare; ***ein Spiel -n,*** a pack *or* (*Am.*) deck of cards; ***seine – abgeben,*** leave one's (visiting) card; ***die -n abheben,*** cut the cards; ***seine -n aufdecken,*** show one's hand; ***eine – ausspielen,*** play one's card; ***-n geben,*** deal the cards; ***schlechte -n haben,*** have a poor hand; ***-n legen,*** tell one's fortune; ***-n mischen,*** shuffle the cards; ***alles auf eine – setzen,*** stake everything on one throw, put all one's eggs in one basket; ***auf die falsche – setzen,*** back the wrong horse; ***-(n) spielen,*** play cards; (*fig.*) ***mit offenen -n spielen,*** put one's cards on the table; ***-n schlagen,*** tell fortunes by cards; (*coll.*) ***ihm in die -n sehen,*** see through his game; ***die -n durchschauen,*** be in the secret *or* the know; ***nach der – speisen,*** dine à la carte.

Kartei [kar'taɪ], *f.* (-, *pl.* **-en**) card-index, filing cabinet, file; – ***führen über*** (*Acc.*), keep files on. **Kartei|karte,** *f.* record card. **-reiter,** *m.* index tab.

Kartell [kar'tɛl], *n.* (**-s,** *pl.* **-e**) 1. (*Comm.*) cartel, trust, combine, syndicate, ring; 2. (*Hist.*) agreement (between enemies); 3. (*obs.*) challenge (*to single combat*). **Kartell|schiff,** *n.* ship with a flag of truce. **–träger,** *m.* second, bearer of a challenge (*for a duel*).

Karten|ausgabe, *f.* ticket-office, booking-office. **–blatt,** *n.* (single) card; map sheet. **–brief,** *m.* letter-card. **–folge,** *f.* sequence; – *von 5 Karten,* quint. **–gitter,** *n.* (map) grid. **–haus,** *n.* 1. house of cards; castle in the air; 2. (*Naut.*) chart room. **–kunde,** *f.* map-reading. **–kunststück,** *n.* card-trick. **–legerin,** *f.* fortune-teller (with cards). **–lesen,** *n. See* **–kunde. –spiel,** *n.* card-playing; card-game; pack *or* (*Am.*) deck of cards. **–stelle,** *f.* issuing office for ration cards. **–tasche,** *f.* map-case. **–tisch,** *m.* card-table. **–verkauf,** *m.* sale of tickets. **–werk,** *n.* atlas. **–zeichen,** *n.* conventional sign. **–zeichner,** *m.* cartographer.

Kartoffel [kar'tɔfəl], *f.* (-, *pl.* **-n**) potato; ***junge –,*** new potato; ***–n schälen,*** peel potatoes; ***–n stecken,*** plant potatoes; (*sl.*) ***sich*** (*Dat.*) ***die –n von unten ansehen,*** be pushing up the daisies. **Kartoffel|-ausschuß,** *m.* small potatoes. **–bau,** *m.* potato growing. **–brei,** *m.* mashed potatoes. **–fäule,** *f. See* **–pest. –flocken,** *f.pl.* potato crisps. **–käfer,** *m.* Colorado beetle. **–kloß,** *f.*, **–knödel,** *m.* potato-dumpling. **–kraut,** *n.* potato-tops *or* stalks. **–mehl,** *n.* potato flour, farina. **–mus,** *n. See* **–brei. –puffer,** *m.* potato pancake. **–püree,** *n. See* **–brei. –salat,** *m.* potato salad. **–schale,** *f.* potato peel(ing).

kartographisch [karto'gra:fɪʃ], *adj.* cartographic(al), map-making; ***–e Verlagsanstalt,*** publishing house for maps; – ***erfaßt,*** mapped.

Karton [kar'to:n], *m.* (**-s,** *pl.* **-s**) 1. cardboard, paste-board, (*coll.*) carton, cardboard box; 2. (*Bookb.*) boards; 3. cartoon. **Kartonage** [–'na:ʒə], *f.* boarding, packing, wrapping. **kartonieren** [–'ni:rən], *v.t.* bind in boards. **kartoniert,** *adj.* (bound) in boards, hard-cover.

Kartothek [karto'te:k], *f. See* **Kartei.**

Kartusche [kar'tuʃə], *f.* cartridge, charge. **Kartuschenhülse,** *f.* cartridge case. **Kartusch|munition,** *f.* (*Artil.*) semi-fixed ammunition. **–raum,** *m.* powder chamber.

Karussell [karu'sɛl], *n.* (**-s,** *pl.* **-e**) roundabout, merry-go-round. **Karusselldrehbank,** *f.* vertical turret drilling machine.

Karwoche [ka:r'vɔxə], *f.* Holy *or* Passion Week.

Karzer [kartzər], *n.* (*Austr. m.*) (*Univ.*) lock-up, (*sl.*) jug, clink.

Kaschemme [ka'ʃɛmə], *f.* tavern, pot-house, (*sl.*) low dive.

Käscher, *m. See* **Kescher.**

kaschieren [ka'ʃi:rən], *v.t.* line, cover, conceal.

Kaschmir ['kaʃmir], *m.* (**-s,** *pl.* **-e**) 1. (*Geog.*) Kashmir; 2. (*fabric*) cashmere.

Käse ['kɛ:zə], *m.* (**-s,** *pl.* -) 1. cheese; 2. curds; 3. flower (*of cauliflower*); 4. seed (*of poplars or mallows*); 5. crown (*of artichokes*); 6. (*coll.*) balderdash, rot. **Käse|bereitung,** *f.* cheesemaking. **–blatt,** *n.* local newspaper, (*coll.*) local rag. **–butter,** *f.* curds; cream-cheese. **–form,** *f.* cheese-mould. **–glocke,** *f.* cheese-dish, cheese-cover.

Kasel ['ka:zəl], *f.* (-, *pl.* **-n**) chasuble.

Käse|lab, *n.* rennet. **–laib,** *m.* whole cheese. **–made,** *f. See* **–milbe.**

Kasematte [ka:zə'matə], *f.* casemate, barbettes, (*Nav.*) gun turret.

Käse|messer, *n.* (*coll.*) large knife, cheese cutter, (*sl.*) cut-throat. **–milbe,** *f.* cheese-mite, maggot. **käsen,** *v.i.* (*aux.* h. *&* s.) curdle, curd, coagulate. **Käse|pappel,** *f.* mallow. **–platte,** *f.* dish of assorted cheeses. **Käserei** [–'raɪ], *f.* dairy; trade of cheese-making.

Kaserne [ka'zɛrnə], *f.* barracks. **Kasernen|arrest,** *m.* confinement to barracks. **–hof,** *m.* barrack-square. **–hofblüten,** *f.pl.* barrack-room expressions; N.C.O.'s howlers. **kasernieren** [–'ni:rən], *v.t.* quarter in barracks.

Käse|säure, *f.* lactic acid, caseic acid. **–stange,** *f.* cheese-straw. **–stoff,** *m.* casein. **–wasser,** *n.* (*dial.*) whey. **käsig,** *adj.* caseous, cheesy; curdled; sallow (*of the complexion*).

Kasino [ka'zi:no], *n.* (**-s,** *pl.* **-s**) clubhouse, club-room, (*Mil.*) officers' mess; casino.

Kasko ['kasko], *m.* (**-s,** *pl.* **-s**) hull (*of ship*). **Kasko-versicherung,** *f.* insurance on hull (*i.e. not on cargo*), (*Motor.*) comprehensive insurance.

Kasperle ['kaspɛrlə], *m. or n.* Punch. **Kasperle-theater,** *n.* Punch and Judy show.

Kaspisches Meer ['kaspɪʃəs], *n.* Caspian Sea.

Kassa ['kasa], *f.* (*obs., Austr.*) *see* **Kasse. Kassa|-geschäft,** *n.* cash sale *or* transaction. **–kurs,** *m.* spot price. **–skonto,** *n.* cash discount.

Kassation [kasatsɪ'o:n], *f.* (*Law*) cassation, quashing; discharge, dismissal, (*Mil.*) cashiering. **Kassationsurteil,** *n.* reversal of judgement, annulment.

Kasse ['kasə], *f.* 1. cash-box, till; cash-desk, cash register, counting-house, pay-office; ticket-office, booking-office, box-office; ***an der –,*** at the booking office *or* cash desk; ***die – führen,*** keep the cash, act as cashier *or* treasurer; 2. ready money, cash (in hand); fund; ***schlecht bei – sein,*** be hard up; (***gut***) ***bei – sein,*** be in funds, (*sl.*) be flush; – ***machen,*** make up the cash account; ***gemeinschaftliche –,*** joint account; ***gemeinschaftliche – machen,*** pool *or* share the expenses; – ***bei Lieferung,*** cash on delivery; ***netto –,*** net cash; ***gegen – verkaufen,*** sell for cash.

Kassen|abschluß, *m.* closing cash account, cash balance. **–anweisung,** *f.* treasury bond. **–arzt,** *m.* panel doctor. **–beamte(r),** *m., f.* cashier, (*banks*) teller. **–beleg,** *m.* cash voucher. **–bestand,** *m.* cash balance, cash in hand. **–bote,** *m.* bank-messenger. **–buch,** *n.* cash-book. **–defizit,** *n.* adverse cash balance, cash deficit. **–diebstahl,** *m.* embezzlement. **–eingänge,** *m.pl.* cash receipts. **–erfolg,** *m.* (*Theat.*) box-office success. **–führer,** *m.* cashier. **–patient,** *m.* panel patient. **–prüfer,** *m.* auditor. **–prüfung,** *f.* audit(ing). **–rabatt,** *m.* cash rebate. **–raub,** *m.* pay-roll robbery. **–revision,** *f. See* **–prüfung. –revisor,** *m. See* **–prüfer. –schalter,** *m.* cash-desk, cash-office. **–scheck,** *m.* open *or* uncrossed cheque. **–schein,** *m.* treasury note; cash voucher. **–schlager,** *m.* box-office draw *or* hit. **–schrank,** *m.* (fire-proof) safe. **–sturz,** *m.* audit; adding up the cash; – ***machen,*** make up *or* count the cash. **–wart,** *m.* treasurer (*of a society*). **–zettel,** *m.* (*in shops*) sales slip, check.

Kasserolle [kasə'rɔlə], *f.* stew-pot, stewpan, casserole.

Kassette [ka'sɛtə], *f.* cash-box, deed-box; casket, coffer; (protective) case (*for books*); (*Phot.*) (film-pack) adapter, plate-holder; (*sound*) cassette.

Kassia ['kasia], **Kassie** [–sjə], *f.* cassia. **Kassien|-blüte,** *f.* cassia bud. **–öl,** *n.* oil of cassia.

Kassiber [ka'si:bər], *m.* clandestine communication between prisoners; letter smuggled into a prisoner's cell.

Kassier [ka'si:r], *m.* (**-s,** *pl.* **-e**) (*S. German*) *see* **Kassierer. kassieren,** *v.t.* 1. receive (*money*), cash (*a bill*); 2. annul, set aside, quash (*a will, a judgement*); 3. (*Mil.*) cashier, dismiss. **Kassierer,** *m.* cashier, treasurer, (*Naut.*) purser. **Kassierung,** *f. See* **Kassation.**

Kastagnette [kastan'jɛtə], *f.* castanet; (*pl. coll.*) bones.

Kastanie [kas'ta:niə], *f.* chestnut; ***eßbare –,*** sweet chestnut; (*Prov.*) ***für ihn die –n aus dem Feuer holen,*** be made a cat's-paw of by him, do his dirty work. **Kastanienbaum,** *m.* chestnut-tree; ***bitterer*** (***wilder***) –, *see* **Roßkastanie. kastanienbraun,** *adj.* chestnut (brown), auburn, maroon.

Kästchen ['kɛstçən], *n. See* **Kasten**; 1. little box, casket; 2. (*Anat.*) alveolus; 3. (*in documents*) (inset) square.

Kaste ['kastə], *f.* caste; corporation.

Käste ['kɛstə], *f.* (*dial.*) *see* **Kastanie.**

kasteien [kas'taɪən], *v.t.* (*v.r.*) castigate *or* mortify (o.s.). **Kasteiung,** *f.* (self-)castigation, mortification (of the flesh), penance.

Kastell [kas'tɛl], *n.* (**-(e)s,** *pl.* **-e**) fort, fortification, citadel, castle. **Kastellan** [–'la:n], *m.* (**-s,** *pl.* **-e**) castellan, steward.

Kasten ['kastən], *m.* (**-s,** *pl.* - (*Austr.* ⁻̈)) 1. box, chest, case, housing, crate, coffer; locker, press, cupboard, drawer; hutch; boot (*of a coach*); setting (*of jewels etc.*); pillar-box; body, frame (*of coaches etc.*), windchest, sounding-board (*organ*); – ***der Zähne,*** socket of teeth; (*sl.*) ***er hat was auf dem –,*** he's on the ball, he's with it; 2. (*dial., coll.*) fund; 3. (*Mil., sl.*) guard-room, detention barracks, clink, jug; 4. (*coll.*) tumbledown house, hovel; unseaworthy ship, hulk; (*vehicle*) old crock, boneshaker; (*Av.*) crate; 5. (*of a p.*) hulk of a fellow, blowsy female.

Kästenbaum ['kɛstənbaum], *m.* (*coll.*) *see* **Kastanienbaum.**

Kasten|drachen, *m.* box-kite. **–geist,** *m.* caste feeling, (*coll.*) clannishness. **–kamera,** *f.* box-camera. **–lautsprecher,** *m.* (*Rad.*) cabinet speaker. **Kastentum,** *n.* caste system. **Kastenwagen,** *m.* box cart, (*Railw.*) box car, (*Motor.*) (delivery) van.

Kastrat [kas'tra:t], *m.* (**-en,** *pl.* **-en**) eunuch. **kastrieren,** *v.t.* 1. castrate (*a p.*), geld (*animals*); 2. expurgate (*books*).

Kasualien [kazu'a:liən], *pl.* occasional emoluments, incidental fees.

Kasuar [kazu'a:r], *m.* (**-s,** *pl.* **-e**) (*Orn.*) cassowary.

Kasuistik [kazu'ɪstɪk], *f.* casuistry.

Kasus ['ka:zus], *m.* (-, *pl.* -) (*Gram.*) case; (*coll.*) case, incident.

Katafalk [kata'falk], *m.* (**-s,** *pl.* **-e**) tomb of state; catafalque.

Katakombe [kata'kɔmbə], *f.* catacomb.

Katalog [kata'lo:k], *m.* (**-s,** *pl.* **-e**) catalogue, list. **katalogisieren** [–'logi'zi:rən], *v.t.* catalogue.

Katalysator [kataly'za:tɔr], *m.* (**-s,** *pl.* **-en**) catalyst, catalytic agent. **Katalyse** [–'ly:zə], *f.* catalysis. **katalysieren,** *v.t.* catalyse. **katalytisch,** *adj.* catalytic.

katapultieren [katapul'ti:rən], *v.t.* catapult, launch (*aircraft*) by catapult. **Katapultstart** [–'pultʃtart], *m.* (*Av.*) catapult take-off.

Katarakt [kata'rakt], *m.* (**-(e)s,** *pl.* **-e**) waterfall, cataract, rapids. **Katarakt(e),** *f.* (*Med.*) cataract (*of the eye*).

Katarrh [ka'tar], *m.* (**-s,** *pl.* **-e**) catarrh, cold in the head, common cold. **Katarrhalfieber** [–'ra:l-fi:bər], *n.* feverish cold; (*Vet.*) catarrh of cattle.

Kataster [ka'tastər], *n.* (*Austr. m.*) land-register, register of assessment. **Katasteramt,** *n.* land-registry office, rates *or* rating office.

katastrophal [katastro'fa:l], *adj.* catastrophic, disastrous, (*coll.*) terrible, appalling, awful. **Katastrophe** [–'stro:fə], *f.* catastrophe, disaster.

Kate ['ka:tə], *f.* (tied) cottage.

Katechese [katɛ'çe:zə], *f.* catechesis. **Katechet,** *m.* (**-en,** *pl.* **-en**) (*R.C.*) catechist, religious instructor. **katechisieren** [–çi'zi:rən], *v.t.* catechize. **Katechismus** [–'çɪsmus], *m.* (-, *pl.* **-men**) catechism.

Kategorie [katego'ri:], *f.* category. **kategorisch** [–'go:rɪʃ], *adj.* categorical, positive, unconditional. **kategorisieren** [–ri'zi:rən], *v.t.* classify (according to categories).

Kater ['ka:tər], *m.* 1. tom-cat; ***der gestiefelte –,*** Puss in Boots; 2. (*sl.*) hang-over; ***moralischer –,*** qualms of conscience, self-reproach. **Kateridee,** *f.* (*sl.*) crazy idea.

Katheder [ka'te:dər], *m. or n.* rostrum, reading-desk; (*fig.*) (*Univ.*) chair; ***vom –,*** ex cathedra. **Katheder|blüte,** *f.* lecturer's howler. **–held,** *m.* unworldly theorizer. **–sozialismus,** *m.* armchair socialism. **–weisheit,** *f.* theoretical knowledge, unpractical views.

Kathedrale [kate'dra:lə], *f.* cathedral.

Kathete [ka'te:tə], *f.* (*Geom.*) short side of a rectangular triangle.

Katheter [ka'te:tər], *m.* (*Surg.*) catheter, bougie.

Kathode [ka'to:də], *f.* cathode. **Kathoden|röhre,** *f.* thermionic valve. **–strahl,** *m.* cathode ray. **–verstärker,** *m.* cathode follower.

Katholik [kato'li:k], *m.* (**-en,** *pl.* **-en**) (Roman) Catholic. **katholisch** [–'to:lɪʃ], *adj.* 1. (Roman) Catholic; – ***werden,*** turn (Roman) Catholic; 2. catholic, all-embracing. **Katholizismus** [–'tsɪsmus], *m.* (Roman) Catholicism.

Kätner ['kɛ:tnər], *m.* cottager, farm labourer.

katschen ['katʃən], *v.i.* (*Austr.*) smack one's lips, eat noisily.

Katt|anker ['kat–], *m.* (*Naut.*) kedge. **–block,** *m.* (*Naut.*) cathead. **katten,** *v.t.* (*Naut.*) cat (*the anchor*).

Kattun [ka'tu:n], *m.* (**-s,** *pl.* **-e**) cotton, calico; chintz; ***bedruckter –,*** print. **Kattun|kleid,** *n.* print *or* cotton frock. **–papier,** *n.* chintz paper.

katzbalgen ['katsbalgən], *v.r.* brawl, scuffle, scrap; romp. **Katzbalgerei** [–'raɪ], *f.* brawl(ing), scrap, tussle. **katzbuckeln,** *v.i.* cringe, toady (***vor*** (*Dat.*), to), bow and scrape (to).

Kätzchen ['kɛtsçən], *n.* 1. kitten; 2. (*Bot.*) catkin. **Kätzchenblütler,** *m.* (*Bot.*) amentaceous *or* amentiferous plant.

Katze ['katsə], *f.* 1. cat; (*coll.*) puss; ***wie die – um den heißen Brei gehen,*** beat about the bush; ***falsch wie eine –,*** false as a serpent, sly as a fox; (*coll.*) ***das ist für die –,*** that is a complete waste, that is as good as useless; ***sie vertragen sich wie – und Hund,*** they lead a cat and dog life; ***sieht doch die Katz(e) den Kaiser an,*** a cat may look at a king; ***wenn die – fort ist, tanzen die Mäuse,*** when the cat's away the mice will play; (*Prov.*) ***bei Nacht sind alle –n grau,*** all cats are grey in the dark; ***neunschwänzige –,*** cat-o'-nine-tails; (*coll.*) ***die – läuft ihm den Rücken hinauf,*** it gives him the creeps, it makes his flesh creep; (*Prov.*) ***die – im Sack kaufen,*** buy a pig in a poke; ***die – aus dem Sack lassen,*** let the cat out of the bag; 2. (*dial.*) battering-ram; 3. pouch, money-bag.

katzenartig ['katsənartɪç], *adj.* cat-like, feline. **Katzen|auge,** *n.* cat's-eye (*semi-precious stone, traffic indicator*), red light, rear reflector (*cycle*). **–balken,** *m.* ridge pole, roof-tree. **–buckel,** *m.* crouching position, arched back; broken back (*of a ship*); ***einen – machen,*** arch one's back; bow and scrape (*see* **katzbuckeln**). **–darm,** *m.* catgut. **katzenfreundlich,** *adj.* friendly to one's face only. **Katzen|freundschaft,** *f.* cupboard love. **–gedächtnis,** *n.* bad memory. **–geschlecht,** *n.* cat tribe, feline family. **–geschrei,** *n.* caterwauling. **–glimmer,** *m.,* **–gold,** *n.* yellow mica. **–jammer,** *m.* hang-over; (*coll.*) ***einen moralischen – haben,*** have qualms of conscience *or* a touch of compunction; resolve to mend one's ways. **–kopf,** *m.* (*coll.*) box on the ear; *see also* **Kattblock. –musik,** *f.* caterwauling, catcalls. **–pfötchen,** *n.* (*Bot.*) mountain everlasting, catsfoot (*Antennaria dioica*). **–silber,** *n.* Argentine mica. **–sprung,** *m.* a stone's throw. **–steg, –steig,** *m.* narrow path; cat-walk. **–tisch,** *m.* (*coll.*) children's table; ***am – essen,*** eat at the little folk's table; eat alone in a corner (*punishment for children*). **–tritt,** *m.* cat-like tread, stealthy footsteps. **–vogel,** *m.* (*Orn.*) catbird (*Dumetella carolinensis*). **–wäsche,** *f.* cat-lick, lick and a promise.

kaudern ['kaudərn], *v.i.* gobble (*as a turkey*); talk gibberish; act as middleman *or* go-between, profiteer. **Kauderwelsch,** *n.* gibberish, nonsense, double Dutch. **kauderwelschen,** *v.i.* talk gibberish *or* double Dutch, jabber.

Kaue ['kauə], *f.* (*Min.*) pithead.

kauen ['kauən], *v.t.* chew, masticate; mouth (*one's words*); ***die Nägel*** *or* ***an den Nägeln –,*** bite one's nails; (*fig.*) – ***an*** (*Dat.*), rack one's brains over, plod away at; (*fig.*) ***ihm etwas zu – geben,*** give him a hard nut to crack, give him s.th. to keep him busy. **Kauen,** *n.* mastication, chewing; ***das – auf dem Gebiß,*** champing the bit.

kauern ['kauərn], *v.i.* (*aux.* s.), *v.r.* squat, crouch, cower. **kauernd,** *adj.* (*Her.*) couchant.

Kauf [kauf], *m.* (**-(e)s,** *pl.* **⸚e**) buying, purchase; bargain; ***einen – abschließen,*** complete a purchase; ***zum – anbieten,*** offer for sale; ***durch – an sich*** (*Acc.*) ***bringen,*** acquire by purchase; ***leichten –es davonkommen,*** get off lightly *or* cheaply; ***durch –,*** by purchase; ***in den – geben,*** throw into the bargain, (*coll.*) throw in; ***in den –,*** over and above, into the bargain; ***einen wohlfeilen*** or ***guten – machen,*** get a bargain; ***in*** (***den***) ***– nehmen,*** make allowance for; (***mit***) ***in – nehmen,*** (have to) put up with; ***– auf*** or ***nach*** or ***zur Probe,*** sale on appro.; ***– ist –,*** a bargain is a bargain; ***ihm in den – treten,*** outbid him; ***– mit Vorbehalt,*** qualified purchase; ***zum –,*** for sale. **Kaufauftrag,** *m.* buying order. **kaufbar,** *adj.* for sale, purchasable. **Kauf|bedingungen,** *f.pl.* conditions of sale. **–brief,** *m.* bill of sale.

kaufen ['kaufən], *v.t., v.i.* buy, purchase (***von, bei,*** from); (*sl.*) ***sich*** (*Dat.*) ***einen Affen –,*** get tipsy; ***auf Borg*** or ***Kredit –,*** buy on credit *or* (*coll.*) on tick; ***einen Beamten –,*** buy over *or* bribe an official; ***bei wem – Sie gewöhnlich?*** with whom do you deal as a rule? (*sl.*) ***was ich mir dafür kaufe!*** a fat lot of good that does! that cuts no ice with me; ***für teures Geld –,*** pay a lot *or* (*coll.*) pay through the nose for; (*sl.*) ***den werde ich mir –!*** I'll let him have it (in no uncertain terms); (*coll.*) ***auf Stottern –,*** buy on the never-never.

Käufer ['kɔyfər], *m.* buyer, purchaser, customer; ***ohne –,*** no bidders *or* takers. **Käufermarkt,** *m.* buyers' market.

Kauf|fahrer, *m. See* **–fahrteischiff. –fahrtei,** *f.* (*obs.*) sea trade. **–fahrteiflotte,** *f.* merchant fleet. **–fahrteischiff,** *n.* merchantman, merchant ship. **–geld,** *n.* purchase-money. **–gut,** *n.* merchandise. **–halle,** *f.* market hall, bazaar, saleroom. **–handel,** *m.* commerce, trade, traffic. **–haus,** *n.* department store, stores. **–herr,** *m.* merchant. **–kontrakt,** *m.* bill of sale. **–kraft,** *f.* purchasing power (*of money*), spending power (*of customer*). **kaufkräftig,** *adj.* able to buy, wealthy, moneyed. **Kauf|kraftüberhang,** *m.* surplus spending *or* purchasing power. **–laden,** *m.* shop, store. **–leute,** *pl. See* **–mann.**

käuflich ['kɔyflɪç], **1.** *adj.* marketable, saleable; to be sold, for *or* on sale; (*fig. of a p.*) venal, corruptible. **2.** *adv.* by purchase; ***– erwerben*** or ***an sich bringen,*** buy, (acquire by) purchase; ***– überlassen,*** sell. **Käuflichkeit,** *f.* corruptibility, venality.

Kauf|lust, *f.* wish to buy; (*St. Exch.*) buoyancy; ***rege –,*** brisk demand. **–lustige(r),** *m., f.* intending purchaser, keen customer.

Kaufmann ['kaufman], *m.* (**-s,** *pl.* **-leute**) merchant, business-man; trader, tradesman, shopkeeper, dealer; ***– werden,*** go into business. **kaufmännisch,** *adj.* mercantile, commercial; businesslike; ***–er Angestellter,*** clerk (*in business concern*); ***–er Direktor,*** business manager; ***–e Regel,*** rule of business; ***in –er Hinsicht,*** commercially, from a business point of view. **Kaufmannschaft,** *f.* trades council, Chamber of Commerce. **Kaufmanns|deutsch,** *n.* commercial German. **–geist,** *m.* commercial spirit. **–innung,** *f.* trading company, guild. **–stand,** *m.* merchant class.

Kauf|motiv, *n.* reason for buying, customer's motivation. **–muster,** *n.* salesman's sample. **–preis,** *m.* purchase-price, cost price, first cost. **–schilling,** *m.* (*obs.*) earnest-money. **–steuer,** *f.* (*Law*) stamp duty (on conveyance). **–summe,** *f.* purchase-money. **–unlust,** *f.* sales resistance. **–vertrag,** *m. See* **–kontrakt. –wut,** *f.* buying *or* spending craze. **–zwang,** *m.* obligation to purchase; ***ohne –,*** on approval, without obligation to purchase; inspection invited.

Kaugummi ['kaugumi], *m.* chewing-gum.

Kaukasier [kau'ka:ziər], *m.,* **kaukasisch,** *adj.* Caucasian. **Kaukasus** ['kaukazus], *m.* Caucasus.

Kaulbarsch ['kaulbarʃ], *m.* (*Ichth.*) ruffe, pope (*Acerina cernua*). **Kaule,** *f.* (*dial.*) see **Kuhle. Kaulquappe,** *f.* tadpole.

kaum [kaum], *adv.* hardly, scarcely, barely, with difficulty; no sooner . . . than; only just, just now; ***– je,*** hardly *or* scarcely ever; ***– noch,*** just a moment ago; ***–*** (***der Gefahr***) ***entgehen*** or ***entwischen,*** have a very narrow escape; ***– glaublich,*** hard to believe; ***– war er fort, da*** or ***so . . .,*** he was no sooner gone than. . . .

kaupeln ['kaupəln], *v.i.* (*Austr.*) barter, swap, trade.

kausal [kau'za:l], *adj.* causal, causative. **Kausal|gesetz,** *n.* law of causation. **–konjunktion,** *f.* (*Gram.*) causal conjunction. **–nexus,** *m.* connection between cause and effect, causality. **–satz,** *m.* (*Gram.*) causal clause. **–verbum,** *n.* (*Gram.*) causative *or* factitive verb. **–zusammenhang,** *m.* causal relationship; (*Law*) proximate connection.

Kausch(e) ['kauʃ(ə)], *f.* (*Naut.*) eyelet, thimble (*on rope*).

kaustifizieren [kaustifi'tsi:rən], *v.t.* cauterize, corrode. **Kaustik** ['kaustɪk], *f.* (*obs.*) (art of) etching. **Kaustika,** *pl.* corrosive substances, caustics. **kaustisch,** *adj.* caustic, corrosive; (*fig.*) caustic, biting, satirical, mocking.

Kautabak ['kautabak], *f.* chewing-tobacco.

Kautel [kau'te:l], *f.* (-, *pl.* **-en**) caution; precaution, safeguard, reservation.

kauterisieren [kauteri'zi:rən], *v.t.* cauterize, sear. **Kauterium** [–'te:rium], *n.* (**-s,** *pl.* **-ien**) cautery; caustic.

Kaution [kautsi'o:n], *f.* security, surety, bond, guarantee; (*Law*) bail; caution money; ***unter –,*** under bond; ***gegen gute –,*** on good security; ***gegen – entlassen,*** release on bail; ***– stellen,*** go bail, stand security. **kautions|fähig,** *adj.* able to give bail *or* provide security. **–pflichtig,** *adj.* liable for bail; conditional on security being offered.

Kautschuk ['kautʃuk], *m. or n.* (**-s,** *pl.* **-e**) caoutchouc, (india)rubber. **Kautschukmilch,** *f.* rubber latex.

Kauwerkzeuge ['kauvɛrktsɔygə], *n.pl.* (*Anat.*) masticators.

Kauz [kauts], *m.* (**-es,** *pl.* **⸚e**) (*Orn.*) (*coll.*) owl; queer fellow, odd fish, eccentric, crank, (*Am.*) screwball.

Kavalier [kava'li:r], *m.* (**-s,** *pl.* **-e**) cavalier, gallant, knight; gentleman, ladies' man; admirer, beau. **kavaliermäßig,** *adj.* gentlemanly, gallant. **Kavaliertuch,** *n.* (*coll.*) breast-pocket handkerchief.

Kavalkade [kaval'ka:də], *f.* cavalcade, (mounted) procession.

Kavallerie [kavalə'ri:], *f.* cavalry, horsemen, (*collect.*) horse. **Kavallerist,** *m.* (**-en,** *pl.* **-en**) cavalryman, trooper.

Kavent [ka'vɛnt], *m.* (**-en,** *pl.* **-en**) guarantor. **kaventieren** [–'ti:rən], *v.i.* ***– für,*** offer surety *or* give security for, guarantee.

Kaviar ['kaviar], *m.* caviare; (*Prov.*) ***– fürs Volk,*** caviare to the general.

Kebse ['ke:psə], *f.* concubine, mistress. **Kebs|ehe,** *f.* concubinage. **–kind,** *n.* (*obs.*) illegitimate child, bastard. **–weib,** *n. See* **Kebse.**

keck [kɛk], *adj.* 1. bold, daring, audacious, (*coll.*) plucky; pert, forward, brazen, impudent, (*coll.*) saucy, cheeky; ***mit –er Stirn,*** with brazen assurance; 2. (*dial.*) firm, sound (*of fruit*). **Keckheit,** *f.* boldness, audacity, daring, (*coll.*) pluck; pertness, impudence, brazenness, (*coll.*) sauce, cheek.

Kegel ['ke:gəl], *m.* 1. (*Geom.*) cone; ***abgestumpfter –,*** truncated cone; 2. taper; 3. skittle, nine-pin; 4. shoulder-bone (*of a horse*); 5. (*obs.*) illegitimate child; ***mit Kind und –,*** with bag and baggage; 6. (*Typ.*) depth (*of type*). **Kegelbahn,** *f.* skittle- *or* bowling-alley. **kegelförmig,** *adj. See* **kegelig. Kegelgetriebe,** *n.* bevel gear *or* pinions. **kegelig,** *adj.* conical, cone-shaped, tapering. **Kegel|kugel,** *f.* skittle-ball. **–kupplung,** *f.* (*Motor.*) cone clutch. **kegeln, 1.** *v.i.* play at ninepins *or* skittles; roll head over heels, turn a somersault. **2.** *v.t.* bowl, roll. **Kegelrad,** *n.* bevel wheel. **kegel|scheiben,** *v.i.* (*dial.*), **–schieben,** *irr.v.i. See* **kegeln, 1. Kegel|schnitt,** *m.* conic section; ***Lehre von den –en,*** conics. **–schub,** *m. See* **–bahn. –spiel,** *n.,* **–sport,** *m.* (game of) skittles, skittle-playing. **–stumpf,** *m.* frustrum, truncated cone. **–ventil,** *n.* conical valve.

Kegler ['ke:glər], *m.* skittle-player.

Kehl|ader [–'ke:l–], *f.* (*Anat.*) jugular vein. **–deckel,** *m.* (*Anat.*) epiglottis.

Kehle ['ke:lə], *f.* throat, gullet, throttle; flute, fluting, channel, gutter; (*Fort.*) gorge, breast of a bastion; chamfer; ***aus voller –,*** heartily, loudly, at the top of one's voice; ***ihm geht's an die –,*** he is up against it; ***sein ganzes Geld durch die – jagen,*** spend all his money on drink; ***in die unrechte – kommen,*** go down the wrong way; ***an der – packen,*** seize by the throat; ***ihm die – zuschnüren*** or ***abschneiden,*** strangle *or* bleed him (*through usury*); ***ihm das Messer an die – setzen,*** hold a knife at his throat; ***ihm an der – sitzen,*** have a stranglehold on him.

kehlen ['ke:lən], *v.t.* flute, groove, channel.

Kehl|hauch, *m.* aspirate 'h', spirant. **–hobel,** *m.* grooving plane. **Kehlkopf** ['ke:lkɔpf], *m.* larynx. **Kehlkopf|bänder,** *n.pl.* vocal chords. **–eingang,** *m.* glottis. **–entzündung,** *f.* laryngitis. **–krebs,** *m.* cancer of the throat. **–spiegel,** *m.* laryngoscope. **–verschluß(laut),** *m.* (*Phonet.*) glottal stop.

Kehl|lappen, *pl.* wattles. **–laut,** *m.* (*Phonet.*) guttural (sound). **–leiste,** *f.* (*Archit.*) moulding. **–riemen,** *m.* throat latch (*of harness*). **–rinne,** *f.* gutter. **–schweißnaht,** *f.* (*Metall.*) fillet weld. **–stimme,** *f.* guttural voice. **Kehlung,** *f.* channel, groove, fluting, moulding. **Kehlziegel,** *m.* gutter-tile.

Kehr|aus ['ke:r–], *m.* (-, *pl.* -) last dance, (*fig.*) clearing out, clean(ing) out. **–besen,** *m.* (sweeping) broom. **–bild,** *n.* (*Phot.*) negative.

Kehre ['ke:rə], *f.* sharp turn, (hairpin) bend, corner; (*Av., skiing*) turn; (*Gymn.*) side *or* flank vault; (*dial.*) ***ganz aus der –,*** quite wrong, in the contrary direction.

[1]**kehren** ['ke:rən], **1.** *v.t.* turn (over); ***das Schwert in die Scheide –,*** return the sword to the scabbard; ***ihm den Rücken –,*** turn one's back on him; ***eine S. zum besten –,*** turn s.th. to account *or* advantage, make the best of a th.; ***die rauhe Seite nach außen –,*** show one's worst side, behave brusquely, be abrupt *or* blunt; ***das Oberste zuunterst –,*** turn (everything) upside down; ***die Maschinen –,*** reverse the engines. **2.** *v.r.* turn (round); (*fig.*) ***sich – an*** (*Acc.*), heed, mind, pay attention to, (have) regard (to), follow; ***an ihn kehre ich mich nicht,*** I pay no attention to him, (*sl.*) I don't give a damn for him. **3.** *v.i.* ***in sich –,*** retire into o.s., be lost *or* wrapt in thought, brood, meditate, commune with o.s.; (*Eccl.*) ***kehre in dich!*** repent! (*Mil.*) ***kehrt!*** about turn! (*Am.*) about face!

[2]**kehren,** *v.t.* sweep, brush; turn out, dust, tidy (*a room*); (*Prov.*) ***neue Besen – gut,*** new brooms sweep clean; ***kehre vor deiner eignen Tür!*** mind your own business!

Kehricht ['ke:rɪçt], *m., n.* sweepings, rubbish, refuse; dirt, dust. **Kehricht|eimer,** *m.* refuse bucket *or* pail. **–haufe(n),** *m.* rubbish heap, dump; heap of rubbish. **–kasten,** *m.* dust-bin, (*Am.*) ash-can; refuse *or* rubbish bin. **–schaufel,** *f.* dust-pan.

Kehr|maschine, *f.* sweeping machine, road sweeper. **–punkt,** *m.* (*Astr.*) apsis. **–reim,** *m.* refrain. **–seite,** *f.* reverse (side), back (*of the sheet*); other *or* wrong side; seamy side (*of life*); (*fig.*) drawback, disadvantage; ***die – der Medaille,*** the reverse of the medal.

kehrtmachen ['ke:rtmaxən], *v.i.* turn round, face about, turn on one's heels; turn back, turn in one's tracks.

Kehrtunnel ['ke:rtunəl], *m.* loop-tunnel.

Kehrtwendung ['ke:rtvɛnduŋ], *f.* (*Mil.*) about turn *or* (*Am.*) about face; (*Av.*) turn; (*fig.*) about-face.

Kehr|wert, *m.* (*Math.*) reciprocal value. **–wieder,** *n. or m.* blind alley.

keifen ['kaɪfən], *v.i.* scold, upbraid, chide; nag, wrangle, squabble.

Keil [kaɪl], *m.* **(-(e)s,** *pl.* **-e)** wedge; (*Dressm.*) gusset, gore, (*of stocking*) clock; (*Archit.*) keystone; (thunder)bolt; (*Tech.*) key, dowel, cotter(pin); (*Av.*) V-formation; (*Typ.*) quoin; *pl.* (*coll.*) thrashing; ***das spitze Ende eines –es,*** the thin end of the wedge; (*coll.*) ***es gibt –e!*** they are coming to blows! (*coll.*) ***–e kriegen,*** get thrashed; (*Prov.*) ***auf einen groben Klotz gehört ein grober –,*** give tit for tat; (*Prov.*) ***ein – treibt den andern,*** it is just one thing after another. **Keilabsatz,** *m.* wedge heel. **keil|artig,** *adj. See* **–förmig.**

keilen ['kaɪlən], **1.** *v.t.* wedge, fasten with a wedge, (*Tech.*) key; (*Typ.*) quoin; cleave, split with a wedge; (*coll.*) thrash; (*coll.*) canvass, win over. **2.** *v.r.* come to blows, fight, scuffle, brawl, scrap.

Keiler ['kaɪlər], *m.* wild boar.

Keilerei [kaɪlə'raɪ], *f.* brawl, fight, fisticuffs, rough-and-tumble, (*sl.*) scrap.

Keil|flosse, *f.* (*Av.*) triangular tail fin. **–form,** *f.* V-formation. **keilförmig,** *adj.* wedge-shaped, cuneiform, sphenoidal, cuneate; (*Dressm.*) ***– zuschneiden,*** gore. **Keil|hacke,** *f. See* **–haue. –haken,** *m.* (*Orn.*) *see* ***großer*** **Brachvogel. –haue,** *f.* pickaxe, mattock. **–inschrift,** *f.* cuneiform inscription. **–kissen,** *n. See* **–polster. –nute,** *f.* (*Tech.*) keyway. **–polster,** *n.* (*Austr. m.*) wedge-shaped bolster. **–riemen,** *m.* (*Tech.*) V-belt. **–schrift,** *f.* cuneiform characters. **–schwanz-regenpfeifer,** *m.* (*Orn.*) killdeer plover, (*Am.*) killdeer (*Charadrius vociferus*). **–stück,** *n.* (*Dressm.*) gore, gusset. **–welle,** *f.* (*Tech.*) keyed shaft.

Keim [kaɪm], *m.* **(-(e)s,** *pl.* **-e)** germ; (*Bot.*) bud, spore, sprout, shoot; (*Biol.*) embryo; (*of crystals*) nucleus; (*fig.*) germ, seed, origin; ***im –e ersticken,*** nip in the bud; ***–e treiben,*** germinate; ***im –e vorhanden,*** in embryo. **Keim|anlage,** *f.* blastoderm. **–blatt,** *n.* cotyledon. **–drüse,** *f.* gonad. **keimen,** *v.i.* (*aux.* h. & s.) germinate, sprout, bud; arise, spring up, develop, begin to show itself, stir. **keimend,** *adj.* germinating, nascent, (*fig.*) budding, rising, growing, developing. **keimfrei,** *adj.* sterile, sterilized, aseptic; ***– machen,*** sterilize. **Keim|hülle,** *f.* perisperm. **–kapsel,** *f.* spore. **–knospe,** *f.* germinal bud, ovule. **–korn,** *n. See* **–kapsel. –kraft,** *f.* vitality, viability. **–lager,** *n.* stroma.

Keimling ['kaɪmlɪŋ], *m.* **(-s,** *pl.* **-e)** germ-bud, seedling, embryo. **Keim|sack,** *m.* amnion. **–stock,** *m.* ovary. **keimtötend,** *adj.* disinfectant, antiseptic, germicidal; ***–es Mittel,*** germicide, disinfectant, antiseptic. **Keimträger,** *m.* (*Med.*) carrier. **Keimung,** *f.* germination. **Keim|wurzel,** *f.* radicle. **–zelle,** *f.* germ cell, spore.

kein [kaɪn], **1.** *adj.* no, not a, not one, not any; ***– anderer als,*** none other but; (*coll.*) ***– Gedanke!*** no such thing! that's not to be thought of! nonsense! ***– einziger,*** not a single one; ***– Mensch,*** no one; ***auf –en Fall,*** see **keinesfalls**; ***es ist –e so wichtige S.,*** it is not so important a matter; ***er ist – Student mehr,*** he is no longer a student; ***–e halbe Stunde vor dem Anfang der Prüfung,*** within half an hour of the beginning of the examination; ***es sind noch –e acht Tage,*** it is not a week yet; ***– Geschäftstag,*** dies non. **2.** *pron.* *–er, –e, –(e)s,* nobody, no one, not anyone, none; nothing, not anything; ***er ist –er der Stärksten,*** he is not of the strongest; ***–er von beiden,*** neither of them; ***er gibt –em etwas nach,*** he is inferior to none; ***–es dieser Bücher gefällt ihm,*** he likes none of these books.

keinerlei ['kaɪnərlaɪ], *indecl. adj.* of no sort, not any; ***auf – Weise,*** by no means whatever, in no way at all.

keinesfalls ['kaɪnəsfals], (*less good* **keinenfalls**), *adv.* in no case, on no account *or* condition; (*in reply*) by no means. **keineswegs,** *adv.* by no means, not at all, not in the least, in no way; ***er ist – gescheit,*** he is anything but clever.

keinmal ['kaɪnma:l], *adv.* not (even) once, never; (*Prov.*) ***einmal ist –,*** once does not count, the exception proves the rule.

Keks [ke:ks], *m. or n.* **(-(es),** *pl.* **-(e))** biscuit.

Kelch [kɛlç], *m.* **(-es,** *pl.* **-e)** cup, goblet, (*Eccl.*) chalice, communion cup; (*Bot.*) calyx; (*Prov.*) ***zwischen Lipp' und –es Rand schwebt der finstern Mächte Hand,*** there's many a slip 'twixt cup and lip. **Kelch|blatt,** *n.* sepal. **–blüter,** *m.pl.* (*Bot.*) Calcyciflorae. **kelchförmig,** *adj.* cup-shaped, calciform. **Kelch|glas,** *n.* (crystal) goblet. **–weihe,** *f.* consecration of the communion-cup.

Kelle ['kɛlə], *f.* trowel; scoop, ladle; fish-slice. **kellen,** *v.t.* scoop, ladle.

Keller ['kɛlər], *m.* cellar; tavern, wine-cellar; ***Küche und –,*** food and drink. **Kellerassel,** *f.* wood-louse. **Kellerei** [–'raɪ], *f.* cellarage; wine-cellar. **Kellerer,** *m.* keeper of a wine-cellar; cellarer (*in monasteries*), butler. **Keller|geschoß,** *n.* basement. **–gewölbe,** *n.* vault. **–hals,** *m.* covered entrance to a cellar. **–knecht,** *m.* cellar-man. **–meister,** *m. See* **Kellerer. –miete,** *f.* cellarage. **–schnecke,** *f.* slug. **–wechsel,** *m.* (*Comm.*) accommodation bill, (*coll.*) kite. **–wirtschaft,** *f.* basement restaurant. **–wohnung,** *f.* basement (dwelling).

Kellner ['kɛlnər], *m.* waiter, barman, bartender. **Kellnerin,** *f.* waitress, barmaid.

Kelte ['kɛltə], *m.* Celt.

Kelter ['kɛltər], *f.* (-, *pl.* **-n**) wine-press; ***die – treten,*** work the wine-press, tread the grapes. **Kelterei** [–'raɪ], *f. See* **Kelterhaus. Kelter|faß,** *n. See* **–zuber. –haus,** *n.* press-house. **keltern,** *v.t.* tread *or* press (*grapes*). **Kelterzuber.** *m.* wine-dosser.

keltisch ['kɛltɪʃ], *adj.* Celtic.

Kem(e)nate [kem(e)'na:tə], *f.* (*Hist.*) living-room (*of a castle*); (*Poet.*) ladies' bower.

kennbar ['kɛnba:r], *adj.* recognizable, distinguishable, discernible. **Kenn|buchstabe,** *m.* identification letter. **–daten,** *n.pl.* data.

kennen ['kɛnən], *irr.v.t.* know, be acquainted with; be aware of, be conversant with, understand, (*coll.*) be at home in; (*Law*) have cognizance of; ***wir – uns,*** we know one another *or* each other; ***von Ansehen –,*** know by sight; (*coll.*) ***das kenne ich!*** you're telling me! **kennenlernen,** *v.t.* get *or* come to know, become acquainted with, make the acquaintance of; (*coll.*) ***du sollst mich –!*** I'll give you what for! **kennenswert,** *adj.* worth knowing.

Kenner ['kɛnər], *m.* connoisseur, (good) judge (*Gen.*, of), expert, specialist (in). **Kenner|blick,** *m.* eye of a connoisseur *or* expert. **–miene,** *f.* air of a connoisseur.

Kenn|karte, *f.* identity card. **–licht,** *n.* (*Av., Naut.*) navigation light. **–linie,** *f.* graph, characteristic (curve). **–marke,** *f.* identification label *or* tag. **–melodie, –musik,** *f.* signature tune.

kenntlich ['kɛntlɪç], *adj.* (easily) recognizable, discernible, distinguishable; conspicuous, marked, distinct; ***– machen,*** mark; ***sich – machen,*** make o.s. known. **Kenntlichmachung,** *f.* characterization, labelling, marking.

Kenntnis ['kɛntnɪs], *f.* (-, *pl.* **-se**) knowledge, notice, awareness, cognizance (*Gen.*, of), acquaintance (with); ***zur – nehmen*** or ***– nehmen von,*** take cognizance *or* notice *or* note of; ***ihn in – setzen von,*** inform *or* notify *or* advise *or* apprise him of; ***ihm etwas zur – bringen*** or ***geben,*** bring s.th. to his notice *or* attention; ***sich von etwas in – setzen,*** inform o.s. about s.th.; ***Mann von vielen –sen,*** man of wide *or* much knowledge; ***er hat gute philologische –se,*** he knows a great deal about philology, he has a thorough knowledge of philology. **Kenntnisnahme,** *f.* cognizance, notice; information; (*coll.*) ***zu Ihrer –,*** for your information *or* guidance. **kenntnisreich,** *adj.* well-informed, learned.

Kennummer ['kɛnnumər], *f.* reference number, (*newspapers*) box number.

Kennung ['kɛnuŋ], *f.* (*Av. etc.*) recognition signal, (*Naut.*) landmark, beacon; characteristic. **Kenn|wert,** *m.* characteristic value. **–wort,** *n.* password, code word, motto. **–zahl,** *f. See* **–ziffer. –zeichen,** *n.* distinguishing mark, characteristic; sign, token, badge, emblem; (*Med.*) symptom; criterion; (*Motor.*) ***polizeiliches –,*** number plate. **kenn|zeichnen,** *v.t.* mark, characterize, identify, label. **–zeichnend,** *adj.* characteristic. **Kennziffer,** *f.* index of a logarithm, coefficient; reference number, code number.

kentern ['kɛntərn], *v.i.* (*Naut.*) capsize, overturn, keel over.

Keramik [ke'ra:mɪk], *f.* (-, *pl.* **-en**) ceramics, pottery.

Kerbe ['kɛrbə], *f.* notch, nick, (in)dent, indentation, groove; ***er haut in dieselbe – wie ich,*** he is working along *or* on the same lines as I am.

Kerbel ['kɛrbəl], *m.* (*Bot.*) chervil (*Anthriscus and Chaerophyllum*).

kerben ['kɛrbən], *v.t.* notch, channel, indent, dent; mill (*edge of coins*); (*Bot.*) ***gekerbt,*** crenate(d).

Kerbholz ['kɛrphɔlts], *n.* notched stick; tally; ***viel*** or ***einiges auf dem – haben,*** have a lot to answer for; have a (police) record. **kerbschlagfest,** *adj.* (*Metall.*) impact-resistant. **Kerb|schlag(versuch),** *m.* (*Metall.*) notched bar impact test. **–schnitzerei,** *f.* chip-carving. **–tier,** *n.* insect. **–tierkunde, –tierlehre,** *f.* entomology. **kerbzähnig,** *adj.* notched, crenate, indented.

Kerf, *m.* (**-s,** *pl.* **-e**), **Kerfe,** *f. See* **Kerbtier.**

Kerker ['kɛrkər], *m.* (*Poet.*) prison, dungeon; (*Austr.*) imprisonment with hard labour. **Kerker|fieber,** *n.* jail-fever. **–haft,** *f.* imprisonment. **–meister,** *m.* gaoler, jailer. **–turm,** *m.* donjon, keep.

Kerl [kɛrl], *m.* (**-(e)s,** *pl.* **-e** (*coll. and dial.* **-s**)) fellow; (*coll.*) chap; (*Am.*) guy; ***ein ganzer –,*** a man indeed, quite a fellow; (*sl.*) ***sie ist ein lieber –,*** she is a dear.

Kern [kɛrn], *m.* (**-(e)s,** *pl.* **-e**) kernel, core, pip, stone (*of fruit*); heart (*of lettuce*), grain (*of corn*), pith (*of wood*), heartwood; (*fig.*) heart, essence, pith, core, bottom, root (*of a matter*); main issue, gist, best part; élite, flower, picked men (*of an army*); core (*of cable*), bore (*of cannon*), nucleus (*of atom*).

Kern|abstand, *m.* inter-nuclear distance. **–aufbau,** *m.* nuclear synthesis. **–beißer,** *m.* (*Orn.*) hawfinch (*Coccothraustes coccothraustes*). **kern|deutsch,** *adj.* thoroughly German, German to the core. **–echt,** *adj.* true to type. **–faul,** *adj.* (*Bot.*) rotten at the core; (*coll.*) bone idle. **–fern,** *adj.* (*Phys.*) planetary (*of electrons*). **–fest,** *adj.* very firm *or* solid. **Kern|fleisch,** *n.* 1. choice meat, prime cut; 2. pulp, pith. **–forschung,** *f.* nuclear research. **–frage,** *f.* crucial question. **–frucht,** *f.* stone-fruit. **–gedanke,** *m.* central *or* basic idea. **–gehäuse,** *n.* (apple *etc.*) core. **–geschoß,** *n.* armour-piercing bullet. **kern|gesund,** *adj.* thoroughly sound *or* healthy, (*coll.*) sound as a bell, fit as a fiddle. **–haft,** *adj.* substantial, sound, healthy, robust, solid; pithy, vigorous, energetic, forcible. **Kern|haus,** *n.* (*Bot.*) core. **–holz,** *n.* heartwood.

kernig ['kɛrnɪç], *adj.* full of kernels *or* pips; *see* **kernhaft.**

Kern|ladung, *f.* (*Artil.*) main charge, (*Phys.*) nuclear charge. **–ladungszahl,** *f.* atomic number. **–leder,** *n.* best *or* bend leather. **kernlos,** *adj.* (*Bot.*) seedless. **Kern|mehl,** *n.* best grade flour, firsts. **–munition,** *f. See* **–geschoß. –obst,** *n. See* **–frucht. –physik,** *f.* nuclear physics. **–punkt,** *m.* essential *or* central *or* decisive point; (*Mil.*) strong point. **–reaktion,** *f.* nuclear reaction. **–reaktor,** *m.* (nuclear) reactor. **–rohr,** *n.* (*Artil.*) liner. **–schatten,** *m.* (*Astr.*) umbra. **–schuß,** *m.* point-blank shot. **–schußweite,** *f.* point-blank range. **–seife,** *f.* best quality soap, curd soap. **–spaltung,** *f.* nuclear fission. **–spruch,** *m.* pithy saying. **–stäbchen,** *n.* chromosome. **–stück,** *n.* principal item, essential part. **–teilchen,** *n.* nuclear particle. **–truppen,** *f.pl.* picked *or* crack troops. **–waffe,** *f.* nuclear weapon. **kernweich,** *adj.* soft-boiled (*egg*). **Kern|wolle,** *f.* prime wool. **–wuchs,** *m.* seedling. **kernwüchsig,** *adj.* sprung from seed.

Kerze ['kɛrtsə], *f.* candle, taper; (*Motor.*) sparkin- (*or Am.* spark) plug; (*Footb. etc.*) lob. **kerzeng gerade,** *adj.* straight as a ramrod, bolt upright; ***– zugehen auf*** (*Acc.*), make a bee-line for. **Kerzen|gießer,** *m.* chandler. **–halter, –leuchter,** *m.* candlestick. **–licht,** *n.* candle-light. **–stärke,** *f.* candle-power.

Kescher ['kɛʃər], *m.* fishing net.

keß [kɛs], *adj.* (*coll.*) saucy, pert; smart, jaunty.

Kessel ['kɛsəl], *m.* 1. kettle; cauldron, copper,

boiler; (*Chem.*) retort; 2. (*Geol.*) valley, depression, hollow; 3. cover, burrow, den, kennel (*of wild animals*); excavation; crater; basin (*of a fountain etc.*); 4. (*Mil.*) pocket (*of troops*).

Kessel|asche, *f.* potash. **–dampf,** *m.* live steam. **–druck,** *m.* boiler pressure. **–flicker,** *m.* tinker. **–gewölbe,** *n.* (*Archit.*) cupola. **–haken,** *m.* pot-hook. **–haus,** *n.* boiler-house. **–jagen,** *n.* battue-shooting. **–kohle,** *f.* steam coal. **kesseln,** *v.i.* hollow out; root up the ground (*of boars*). **Kessel|pauke,** *f.* kettle-drum. **–schlacht,** *f.* (battle of) encirclement. **–schmied,** *m.* coppersmith, brazier; boilermaker. **–stein,** *m.* deposit, scale (*on boilers*), fur (*on kettles*). **–tal,** *n.* valley enclosed by mountains. **–treiben,** *n.* battue-beating (*hunted game*), (*Mil.*) encirclement and extermination; hunting down (*of a criminal*). **–wagen,** *m.* tanker, fuel truck.

Keßler ['kɛslər], *m.* (*dial.*) *see* **Kesselschmied.**

Ketsch [kɛtʃ], *f.* (-, *pl.* **-en**) (*Naut.*) ketch.

Kette ['kɛtə], *f.* chain; necklace; (*Mil.*) track (*of tracked vehicles*); (*Weav.*) warp; (*fig.*) chain, series, train, concatenation; covey (*of birds*); flight (*of 3 aircraft*); chain, range (*of mountains*), (*Mil.*) cordon; (*obs.*) chain (*measure = 10 metres*); *pl.* fetters, bondage, slavery; ***an die – legen***, chain up; ***in –n legen*** or ***schlagen***, put in irons, shackle, fetter; ***eine – bilden***, form a chain *or* line; ***– und Schuß***, warp and woof.

Kettel|haken ['kɛtəl–], *m. See* **–nadel. ketteln,** *v.t.* embroider with chain-stitch; link together *or* pick up (stitches). **Kettelnadel,** *f.* embroidery needle.

ketten ['kɛtən], *v.t.* chain (**an** (*Acc.*), to), tie on (to), link (to *or* with), connect (with).

Ketten|antrieb, *m.* chain drive. **–brief,** *m.* chain-letter. **–bruch,** *m.* (*Math.*) continued fraction. **–brücke,** *f.* suspension-bridge. **–faden,** *m.* (*Weav.*) warp. **–fahrzeug,** *n.* tracked vehicle. **–feier,** *f.* (*R.C.*) ***Petri –***, St. Peter's chains, Lammas. **kettenförmig,** *adj.* (*Chem.*) aliphatic. **Ketten|gebirge,** *n.* mountain-chain. **–gelenk,** *n. See* **–glied. –geschäft,** *n.* chain- *or* multiple-store. **–glied,** *n.* link (*of a chain*). **–handel,** *m.* transaction passing through hands of numerous middlemen. **–hemd,** *n. See* **–panzer. –hund,** *m.* yard dog; watch-dog. **–kasten,** *m.* (*Cycl.*) chain cover. **–kugel,** *f.* (*Hist.*) chain-shot. **–linie,** *f.* catenary. **–panzer,** *m.* (*Hist.*) coat of mail. **–rad,** *n.* sprocket wheel. **–raucher,** *m.* chain-smoker. **–reaktion,** *f.* chain-reaction. **–rechnung, –regel,** *f.* (*Math.*) chain-rule, compound rule of three. **–schluß,** *m.* (*Log.*) sorites, chain-syllogism. **–stich,** *m.* chain-stitch. **–sträfling,** *m.* shackled *or* fettered convict; *pl.* chain-gang. **–triller,** *m.* (*Mus.*) sustained shake. **–wirkung,** *f. See* **–reaktion.**

Kett|faden, *m.*, **–garn,** *n.* warp.

Ketzer ['kɛtsər], *m.* heretic. **Ketzerei** [–'raɪ], *f.* heresy. **Ketzergericht,** *n.* (court of) inquisition. **ketzerisch,** *adj.* heretical, heterodox. **Ketzer|macherei,** *f.* intolerance of dissentients. **–meister,** *m.* grand inquisitor. **–richter,** *m.* inquisitor. **–riecher,** *m.* heresy-hunter. **–verbrennung,** *f.* burning of heretics, auto-da-fé.

keuchen ['kɔyçən], *v.i.* pant, gasp, puff, wheeze. **Keuchhusten,** *m.* whooping-cough.

Keule ['kɔylə], *f.* club, cudgel; pestle; hind leg, thigh (*of a beast*); leg, joint (*of meat*). **keulen,** *v.t.* (*Swiss*) slaughter (*beasts*). **keulenförmig,** *adj.* club-shaped. **Keulen|hieb, –schlag,** *m.* blow of a club, (*fig.*) crushing blow. **–schwingen,** *n.* (*Gymn.*) (Indian) club swinging. **–stück,** *n.* cut off the leg (*of meat*).

Keuper ['kɔypər], *m.* (*Geol.*) red marl, keuper.

keusch [kɔyʃ], *adj.* chaste, pure, virgin(al), maidenly. **Keuschheit,** *f.* chastity, purity, virginity; ***Priesterin der –***, vestal virgin. **Keuschheitsgelübde,** *n.* vow of chastity.

Kichererbse ['kɪçərɛrpsə], *f.* (*Bot.*) chick-pea (*Cicer arietinum*).

kichern ['kɪçərn], *v.i.* giggle, titter, snigger.

Kicks [kɪks], *m.* (**-es,** *pl.* **-e**) (*Bill.*) miscue; (*coll.*) botched job. **kicksen,** *v.i.* miscue; (*coll.*) fluff *or* botch it. **Kickser,** *m. See* **Kicks.**

Kiebitz ['ki:bɪts], *m.* (**-es,** *pl.* **-e**) (*Orn.*) lapwing, peewit, green plover (*Vanellus vanellus*). **kiebitzen,** *v.i.* look over players' shoulders as a spectator (*cards*). **Kiebitzregenpfeifer,** *m.* (*Orn.*) grey (*or Am.* black-bellied) plover (*Charadrius squatarola*).

[1]**Kiefer** ['ki:fər], *m.* jaw; jawbone; (*Anat.*) maxilla, (*Ent.*) mandible.

[2]**Kiefer,** *f.* (-, *pl.* **-n**) (*Bot.*) Scots pine (*Pinus silvestris*), stone pine (*Pinus pinea*).

Kiefer|bruch, *m.* fracture of the (lower) jaw. **–drüse,** *f.* submaxillary gland. **–knochen,** *m.* jawbone. **–muskel,** *m.* maxillary muscle.

kiefern ['ki:fərn], *adj.* (made of) pine(wood). **Kiefern|eule,** *f.* (*Ent.*) pine moth. **–holz,** *n.* pinewood, yellow pine, pitch-pine. **–kreuzschnabel,** *m.* (*Orn.*) parrot-crossbill (*Loxia pytyopsittacus*). **–nadel,** *f.* pine-needle. **–spanner,** *m.* pine shoot moth. **–wald,** *m.* pine wood, pine forest. **–zapfen,** *m.* pine-cone.

Kiefer|sperre, *f.* lockjaw. **–winkel,** *m.* angle of the jaw.

Kieke ['ki:kə], *f.* (*dial.*) foot-warmer.

kieken ['ki:kən], *v.i.* (*dial., coll.*) peep, have a look. **Kieker,** *m.* (*sl.*) telescope, spy-glass; ***ihn auf dem – haben***, keep one's eye on him; have a down on him. **Kiekindiewelt,** *m.* (**-s,** *pl.* **-s**) (*coll.*) jackanapes, greenhorn.

Kiel [ki:l], *m.* (**-s,** *pl.* **-e**) 1. quill (pen); 2. keel; (*Bot.*) carina; ***den – legen***, lay down the keel; ***mit breitem –***, broad-bottomed; ***auf ebenem –***, on an even keel. **kielbrüchig,** *adj.* broken-backed (*of a ship*). **kielen, 1.** *v.t.* feather (*an arrow*). **2.** *v.i.* become fledged. **Kiel|feder,** *f.* quill feather; quill pen. **–flosse,** *f.* tail fin. **kielförmig,** *adj.* (*Bot.*) carinate. **Kielgeld,** *n.* keelage. **kielholen,** *v.t.* 1. careen (*a vessel*); 2. (*obs.*) keelhaul (*a sailor*). **Kiel|kropf,** *m.* (*dial.*) changeling; abortion, monster. **–linie,** *f.* ***in – fahren***, sail line-ahead. **kieloben,** *adv.* bottom up. **Kiel|raum,** *m.* (ship's) hold. **–richtung,** *f.* fore and aft (line). **–schwein,** *n.* keelson. **–wasser,** *n.* wake (*of a ship*). **–wasserströmung,** *f.* back wash.

Kieme ['ki:mə], *f.* gill (*of fish*); branchia. **kiemenatmend,** *adj.*, **Kiemenatmung,** *f.* gill-breathing. **–spalte,** *f.* gill-slit.

Kien [ki:n], *m.* (**-(e)s,** *pl.* **-e**) 1. resinous pine-wood; pine-resin; 2. (*coll.*) balderdash, bosh, tosh. **Kien|apfel,** *m.* pine-cone. **–baum,** *n.* Scots pine. **–harz,** *n.* pine-resin. **–holz,** *n.* resinous wood. **kienig,** *adj.* resinous. **Kien|öl,** *n.* oil of turpentine. **–ruß,** *m.* lamp-black. **–span,** *m.* pine torch.

Kiepe ['ki:pə], *f.* (*dial.*) wicker basket (*carried like rucksack*), dosser.

Kies [ki:s], *m.* (**-es,** *pl.* **-e**) gravel; shingle, scree; (*Min.*) pyrites, quartz; (*sl.*) dough, lolly. **kiesartig,** *adj.* gravelly, shingly; (*Min.*) pyritous. **Kies|boden,** *m.* gravelly soil. **–brenner,** *m.* pyrites burner.

Kiesel ['ki:zəl], *m.* pebble, flint; (*Min.*) silex, silica; (*dial., coll.*) top (*plaything*). **kieselartig,** *adj.* siliceous. **Kiesel|erde,** *f.* siliceous earth, silica. **–glas,** *n.* flint-glass. **–grund,** *m.* pebbly ground *or* bottom. **–gur,** *f.* (*Geol.*) infusorial earth. **kieselhart,** *adj.* hard as flint. **kieselig,** *adj.* flinty, pebbly, siliceous.

kieseln ['ki:zəln], *v.i.* (*dial., coll.*) play (whip and) top.

Kiesel|sand, *m.* coarse gravel. **–sandstein,** *m.* siliceous sandstone. **kieselsauer,** *adj.* silicic, silicate of. **Kiesel|säure,** *f.* silicic acid. **–stein,** *m.* pebble(-stone), flint. **–stoff,** *m.* silicon. **–verbindung,** *f.* silicate.

kiesen ['ki:zən], *irr.v.t.* (*obs., Poet.*) select, choose, elect.

Kiesgrube ['ki:sgru:bə], *f.* gravel-pit. **kieshaltig, kiesig,** *adj.* gravelly, (*Min.*) pyritiferous. **Kies|sand,** *m.* coarse sand. **–schicht,** *f.* layer of gravel. **–weg,** *m.* gravel path.

kikeriki! [kɪkəri'ki:], *int.* cock-a-doodle-doo!

Kilo ['ki:lo], *n.* (**-s,** *pl.* **-**) (*coll.*), **Kilo|gramm,** *n.* (**-s,** *pl.* **-e**) kilogram(me). **–hertz,** *n.* kilocycles per second. **-meter,** *n. or m.* kilometre. **-meterfresser,** *m.* (*coll.*) road hog. **-meterstand,** *m.* mileage reading. **-meterstein,** *m.* milestone. **-meterzahl,** *f.* mileage. **-meterzähler,** *m.* cyclometer, mileage meter *or* indicator. **-wattstunde,** *f.* kilowatt hour.

Kilt [kɪlt], *m.* (**-s,** *pl.* **-e**) (*dial.*) bundling. **kilten,** *v.i.* go bundling. **Kiltgang,** *m. See* **Kilt.**

Kimm [kɪm], *f.* (*m. is common though incorrect*) (*Naut.*) 1. (visual) horizon; 2. bilge (*of a ship*).

Kimme ['kɪmə], *f.* saw-cut, kerf, notch, nick; backsight (*of rifle*); *über – und Korn feuern,* fire over open sights. **kimmen,** *v.t.* nick, notch.

Kimmung ['kɪmuŋ], *f.* 1. mirage; 2. *See* **Kimm. Kimmwasser,** *n.* bilge-water.

Kind [kɪnt], *n.* (**-(e)s,** *pl.* **-er**) child; *pl.* children, offspring; family, (*Law*) issue; (*under 7 yrs.*) infant; (*Law*) (*under 21 yrs.*) minor; ***ein – abtreiben,*** procure abortion; (*Prov.*) ***das – mit dem Bade ausschütten,*** throw out the baby with the bathwater; ***ein – bekommen,*** have a child; ***Berliner –,*** native of Berlin; (*Prov.*) ***wenn das – ertrunken ist, wird der Brunnen zugedeckt,*** lock the stable door when the horse is gone; ***ein – erwarten,*** be expecting a baby, (*coll.*) be in the family way; ***wes Geistes – ist er?*** what sort of a person is he? ***eines –es genesen,*** be delivered of a child; ***– des Glückes,*** lucky dog; ***ein – unter dem Herzen haben,*** see ***ein – erwarten;*** ***mit – und Kegel,*** bag and baggage; ***er hat weder – noch Kegel,*** he has neither kith nor kin; ***sie wird kein – mehr haben,*** she is past child-bearing; ***kleines –,*** baby; ***– der Liebe,*** natural *or* illegitimate child; ***sich lieb – machen bei,*** ingratiate o.s. with, curry favour with; ***mein –!*** my dear, my dear child! ***– im Mutterleibe,*** embryo, foetus, unborn child; ***das – beim rechten*** or ***bei seinem Namen nennen,*** call a spade a spade; ***kein – mehr sein,*** be no longer a child; ***– des Todes,*** one doomed to death, (*sl.*) goner; ***unmündiges –,*** minor; ***von – auf,*** from childhood, from infancy; (***wieder***) ***zum – werden,*** grow childish.

Kindbett ['kɪntbɛt], *n.* childbed; ***ins – kommen,*** be brought to bed (with child). **Kindbetterin,** *f.* lying-in patient, woman that has just been delivered. **Kindbettfieber,** *n.* puerperal fever.

Kindel|bier ['kɪndəl–], *n.* (*dial.*) christening-feast. **-mutter,** *f.* (*dial.*) midwife. **kindeln,** *v.i.* (*dial.*) trifle, act childishly.

Kinder|amme ['kɪndər–], *f.* wet-nurse. **-arbeit,** *f.* child-labour. **-arzt,** *m.* children's specialist, pediatrician. **-beihilfe,** *f.* children's allowance. **-bekleidung,** *f. See* **-kleidung. -bett,** *n.* crib, cot. **-bewahranstalt,** *f. See* **-hort. -brei,** *m.* pap. **-buch,** *n.* book for children, children's book. **-dieb,** *m.* kidnapper (of children).

Kinderei [kɪndə'raɪ], *f.* nonsense, stupidity, childishness, childish behaviour, silly trick, (*fig.*) trifle.

Kinder|entführer, *m. See* **-dieb. -ernährung,** *f.* baby *or* infant feeding. **-feind,** *m.* child-hater. **-fest,** *n.* children's party. **-frau,** *f.*, **-fräulein,** *n.* nurse, nursery governess, nanny. **-freund,** *m.* child-lover. **-fürsorge,** *f.* child welfare. **-garten,** *m.* kindergarten, nursery school. **-gärtnerin,** *f.* kindergarten *or* infant teacher. **-glaube,** *m.* childish faith. **-gottesdienst,** *m.* children's service. **-heilkunde,** *f.* pediatrics. **-hort,** *m.* day-nursery, crèche. **-husten,** *m.* whooping cough. **-jahre,** *n.pl.* (years of) childhood. **-kleidung,** *f.* children's wear. **-krankheit,** *f.* children's ailment, *pl.* (*fig.*) teething troubles. **-krippe,** *f. See* **-hort. -lähmung,** *f.* infantile paralysis; ***spinale –,*** polio(myelitis). **-landverschickung,** *f.* evacuation of children from towns (*in wartime*). **-lätzchen,** *n.* bib. **-lehre,** *f.* instruction in the catechism; Sunday-school (teaching). **kinder|leicht,** *adj.* very easy, child's play. **-lieb,** *adj.* fond of children. **Kinder|liebe,** *f.* 1. love of children; 2. filial *or* parental affection. **-lied,** *n.* nursery rhyme. **kinderlos,** *adj.* childless, (*Law*) without issue.

Kinder|mädchen, *n. See* **-frau. -mord,** *m.* child murder, (*at birth*) infanticide; ***der Bethlehemitische –,*** the Massacre of the Innocents. **-nahrung,** *f.* infant *or* baby food. **-narr,** *m.* ***er ist ein –,*** he dotes on children. **-pech,** *n.* meconium. **-pferd,** *n.* hobby-horse. **-pflege,** *f.* child care. **-raub,** *m.* kidnapping. **-räuber,** *m. See* **-dieb. kinderreich,** *adj.* prolific, blessed with a large family; ***-e Familie,*** large family. **-reim,** *m.* nursery rhyme. **-schreck,** *m.* bog(e)y(man).

Kinder|schuhe, *m.pl.* children's shoes; ***die – ausgetreten*** or ***abgelegt haben, den -n entwachsen sein,*** be no longer a child, have put away childish things; ***noch in den – stecken,*** be still a child, be tied to one's mother's apron-strings; (*usu. fig.*) not have progressed *or* advanced beyond the early stages, be still in its beginnings *or* infancy. **-seife,** *f.* nursery soap, baby-soap. **-spiel,** *n.* children's game; (*fig.*) child's play, easy matter; trifle; ***es ist kein –,*** it is not easy, that is no joke. **-sprache,** *f.* nursery talk, child language. **-sterblichkeit,** *f.* infant mortality. **-stube,** *f.* nursery; (*fig.*) manners, upbringing. **-tag,** *m.* (*Eccl.*) Innocents' Day. **-wagen,** *m.* perambulator, baby carriage, (*coll.*) pram. **-wäsche,** *f.* baby-linen. **-wiege,** *f.* cradle. **-zahl,** *f.* ***Beschränkung der –,*** family planning, birth-control. **-zahn,** *m.* milk-tooth. **-zeit,** *f.* (early) childhood. **-zeug,** *n.* playthings; trifles; baby-linen. **-zimmer,** *n.* nursery, playroom. **-zulage,** *f. See* **-beilage.**

Kindes|alter, *n.* infancy, childhood. **-annahme,** *f.* adoption. **-beine,** *n.pl.* (*only in*) ***von -n an,*** from infancy *or* earliest childhood. **-kind,** *n.* grandchild; *pl.* grandchildren; posterity. **-liebe,** *f.* filial love. **-mord,** *m.* infanticide; *see* **Kindermord. -mörderin,** *f.* woman guilty of infanticide, woman who kills her new-born child. **-nöte,** *f.pl.* labour, travail; ***in -n sterben,*** die in childbed. **-pflicht,** *f.* filial duty. **-räuber,** *m.* baby-snatcher; *see* **Kinderraub. -recht,** *n.* portion (of inheritance) due to a child. **-statt,** *f.* ***Annahme an –,*** adoption. **-teil,** *n. See* **-recht. -tötung,** *f.* infanticide (*among primitive peoples*). **-wasser,** *n.* amniotic fluid.

kindhaft ['kɪnthaft], *adj.* childlike, childish.

Kindheit ['kɪnthaɪt], *f.* childhood, infancy; ***von – an,*** from infancy *or* childhood, from a child.

kindisch ['kɪndɪʃ], *adj.* childish, babyish, puerile; ***sei nicht –!*** be your age! **kindlich,** *adj.* childlike, innocent, naïve, simple(-minded); (*in relation to parents*) filial; ***sich – freuen,*** be as pleased as Punch. **Kindschaft,** *f.* relation of a child to its parents; filiation; (*B.*) adoption.

Kinds|kopf, *m.* (*coll.*) silly ass, fool, numskull. **-lage,** *f.* foetal position. **-mutter,** *f.* (*Law*) unmarried *or* natural mother. **-pech,** *n.* meconium.

Kindtaufe ['kɪnttaufə], *f.* christening, baptism.

Kinematograph [kinemato'gra:f], *m.* (**-en,** *pl.* **-en**) cinematograph.

Kinetik [ki'ne:tik], *f.* kinetics. **kinetisch,** *adj.* kinetic.

Kinkerlitzchen ['kɪŋkərlɪtsçən], *n.pl.* (*coll.*) trifles, trivialities; knicknacks; ***mach mir keine –!*** none of your tricks! don't make a silly fuss!

Kinn [kɪn], *n.* (**-(e)s,** *pl.* **-e**) 1. chin; lower jaw; 2. spout (*of a gutter*). **Kinn|backe(n),** *m.* jaw, jawbone, mandible. **-backendrüse,** *f.* submaxillary gland. **-backenkrampf,** *m.* lockjaw, trismus. **-bart,** *m.* beard on the chin; imperial, goatee. **-grube,** *f.* dimple; mental fossa. **-haken,** *m.* (*Boxing*) upper cut. **-kette,** *f.* curb. **-kettenstange,** *f.* curb-bit. **-lade,** *f.* jaw-bone, maxilla. **-riemen,** *m.* chin-strap.

[1]**Kino** ['ki:no], *n.* (**-s,** *no pl.*) (gum)kino.

[2]**Kino,** *n.* (**-s,** *pl.* **-s**) (*coll.*) cinema, the pictures, (*Am.*) motion pictures, the movies. **Kino|besucher,** *m.* picture-goer. **-vorstellung,** *f.* cinema performance *or* show.

Kintopp ['ki:ntɔp], *m.* (*sl.*) the flicks.

Kiosk [ki'ɔsk], *m.* (**-(e)s,** *pl.* **-e**) kiosk, bookstall, (*Am.*) newsstand.

Kipf [kɪpf], *m.* (**-es,** *pl.* **-e**), **Kipfel,** *n.* (*dial.*) (horn-shaped) roll, croissant.

Kippe ['kɪpə], *f.* 1. (*dial.*) see-saw; (*fig.*) ***auf der –***

stehen, hang in the balance, be touch and go; be on the verge (*of falling, of disaster*); 2. (*sl.*) fag-end, stub, butt. **kippelig,** *adj.* unstable, labile; (*coll.*) tottering, wobbly, shaky, (*sl.*) dicey. **kippen, 1.** *v.t.* 1. tilt, tip over, upset, tip up; tip, dump (*rubbish etc.*); 2. break (*a gun*); 3. (*dial.*) cut the edges off, clip, lop. **2.** *v.i.* (*aux.* h. *&* s.) tip *or* topple over, lose one's balance; upset, overturn. **Kipper,** *m.* 1. *See* **Kippwagen**; 2. (*obs.*) money-clipper.

Kipp|fenster, *n.* hinge- *or* swivel-window. **-hebel,** *m.* (*Motor. etc.*) rocker arm. **-karren,** *m.* tip-cart. **-lager,** *n.* rocker bearing. **-laufgewehr,** *n.* break-joint gun. **kipplig,** *adj.* (*coll.*) *see* **kippelig. Kipp|-schalter,** *m.* tumbler switch. **-schwimmer,** *m.* (*Motor.*) carburettor float. **-spannung,** *f.* (*Rad.*) saw-tooth *or* sweep *or* time-base voltage. **-vorrichtung,** *f.* tipping *or* rocker *or* swivelling device *or* mechanism; hinge-fitting. **-wagen,** *m.* tip-cart, tip(ping) wag(g)on, (*Am.*) dump truck.

Kirche ['kırçə], *f.* church, (*nonconformist*) chapel; (divine) service; ***in der –,*** at church; ***nach der –,*** after the service, after church; ***streitende –,*** church militant; ***herrschende –,*** established church.

Kirchen|älteste(r), *m.* churchwarden, elder. **-amt,** *n.* church office, ecclesiastical function. **-bann,** *m.* excommunication; interdict; ***in den – tun,*** excommunicate, interdict. **-besuch,** *m.* attendance at church. **-besucher,** *m.* churchgoer. **-buch,** *n.* church *or* parish register. **-buße,** *f.* church penance. **-chor,** *m.* (church) choir. **-diener,** *m.* church officer; sexton; sacristan, verger. **kirchendienstlich,** *adj.* ***-e Handlung,*** religious observance *or* ceremony. **Kirchenfahne,** *f.* church banner. **kirchenfeindlich,** *adj.* anti-clerical. **Kirchen|-fürst,** *m.* high dignitary of the church; prelate. **-gebet,** *n.* common prayer. **-gemeinde,** *f.* parish; congregation. **-gericht,** *n.* ecclesiastical court, consistory. **-gesang,** *m.* hymn; chorale; ***liturgischer –,*** psalmody; ***Gregorianischer –,*** Gregorian chant. **-geschichte,** *f.* ecclesiastical history. **-gesetz,** *n.* canon; *pl.* decretals. **-gestühl,** *n.* pews. **-grund,** *m.* glebe. **-jahr,** *n.* ecclesiastical year. **-konvent,** *m.* convocation. **-konzert,** *n.* recital of sacred music.

Kirchen|lehen, *n.* ecclesiastical fief. **-lehre,** *f.* church doctrine. **-licht,** *n.* ***kein – sein,*** be no shining light, be not (a) very bright (spark). **-lied,** *n.* hymn. **-maus,** *f.* ***arm wie eine – sein,*** be as poor as a church mouse. **-musik,** *f.* sacred music. **-ornat,** *n.* canonicals. **-rat,** *m.* consistory, church committee, ecclesiastical court; member of a consistory *or* church committee. **-raub,** *m.* sacrilege. **-recht,** *n.* canon law. **kirchenrechtlich,** *adj.* canonical. **Kirchen|schändung,** *f.* *See* **-raub. -schiff,** *n.* nave. **-seitenschiff,** *n.* aisle. **-sitz,** *m.* pew. **-spaltung,** *f.* schism. **-staat,** *m.* Papal territory, Pontifical State. **-steuer,** *f.* church-rate. **-streit,** *m.* religious controversy; dissension in the church. **-stuhl,** *m.* pew. **-vater,** *m.* father of the church; *pl.* the early fathers. **-versammlung,** *f.* synod; convocation; vestry. **-vorstand,** *m.* vestry board. **-vorsteher,** *m.* churchwarden, elder.

Kirch|gang, *m.* churchgoing; ***– halten,*** be churched. **-gänger,** *m.* churchgoer. **-hof,** *m.* churchyard; cemetery, graveyard.

kirchlich ['kırçlıç], *adj.* ecclesiastical, church; (*of the service*) ritual; (*of the clergy*) clerical; (*of a p.*) religious, devout; ***-es Begräbnis,*** Christian burial; ***ohne -e Bindung,*** (*of a p.*) unaffiliated.

Kirch|spiel, *n.* parish; ***zum – gehörig,*** parochial. **-sprengel,** *m.* diocese. **-turm,** *m.* church tower *or* spire *or* steeple. **-turmpolitik,** *f.* parochialism, parish-pump politics. **-turmspitze,** *f.* spire, steeple. **-weih(e),** *f.*, **-weihfest,** *n.* church-festival, (annual) parish fair.

Kirmes ['kırmɛs], *f.* (-, *pl.* **-sen**), (*Austr.*) **Kirmeß,** *f.* (-, *pl.* **-(ss)en**) *see* **Kirchweihe.**

kirnen ['kırnən], *v.t.* churn (*butter*).

kirre ['kırə], *adj.* tame; docile, tractable, submissive; ***ihn – machen,*** bring him to heel, make him eat humble pie. **kirren, 1.** *v.t.* tame, bring to heel; bait, decoy. **2.** *v.i.* (*dial.*) coo.

Kirsch [kırʃ], *m.* *See* **Kirschgeist. Kirsch|baum,** *m.* cherry tree. **-branntwein,** *m.* *See* **-geist. Kirsche,** *f.* cherry; (*Prov.*) ***mit ihm ist nicht gut -n essen,*** he is not an easy man to deal with *or* to get on with; ***sich wie reife -n verkaufen,*** sell like hot cakes; ***saure –,*** morello. **Kirsch|geist,** *m.* cherry-brandy. **-kern,** *m.* cherry-stone. **-kernbeißer,** *m.* *See* **Kernbeißer. -kuchen,** *m.* cherry-tart. **kirschrot,** *adj.* cherry-coloured, cerise. **Kirsch|-saft,** *m.* cherry-juice. **-wasser,** *n.* kirsch.

Kissen ['kısən], *n.* cushion, pillow, bolster, pad, padding. **Kissen|bezug, -überzug,** *m.*, **-ziehe,** *f.* pillow-slip *or* case, cushion cover.

Kiste ['kıstə], *f.* 1. box, chest, coffer, trunk, crate, packing-case; ***eine – Zigarren,*** a box of cigars; 2. (*sl.*) job, matter, affair; (*sl.*) ***die – wird gemacht,*** the job is on; 3. (*sl.*) crate (= *car or aircraft*). **Kisten|pfand,** *n.* (*Law*) daughter's portion. **-verschlag,** *m.* crate.

Kitsch [kıtʃ], *m.* rubbish, trash; (*picture*) daub, (*story*) slush, sob-stuff. **kitschig,** *adj.* rubbishy, trashy, shoddy, tawdry, mawkish, sloppy.

Kitt [kıt], *m.* (**-(e)s,** *pl.* **-e**) cement; putty; lute, luting; (*sl.*) ***der ganze –,*** the whole shoot, the whole boiling.

Kittchen ['kıtçən], *n.* (*sl.*) clink, jug.

Kittel ['kıtəl], *m.* smock, overall; frock, blouse; (*dial.*) jacket (*of a suit*); (*sl.*) ***hinter jedem – herlaufen,*** trail after every skirt.

kitten ['kıtən], *v.t.* cement, lute, fasten with putty, stick *or* glue together. **Kittmesser,** *n.* putty-knife.

Kitz [kıts], *n.* (**-es,** *pl.* **-e**), (*Austr.*) **Kitze,** *f.* kid, fawn.

Kitzel ['kıtsəl], *m.* tickle, itching, itch, tickling, titillation; longing, (inordinate) desire, appetite; pruriency; ***der – sticht ihn danach,*** he has a longing for it. **kitzelig,** *adj.* *See* **kitzlig. kitzeln,** *v.t.* tickle, titillate; gratify, flatter (*vanity etc.*). **Kitzler,** *m.* (*Anat.*) clitoris. **kitzlig,** *adj.* ticklish, delicate, difficult, tricky.

klabastern [kla'bastərn], *v.i.* (*dial.*) blunder along.

Klabautermann [kla'bautərman], *m.* bogy man, hobgoblin.

Klack [klak], *m.* (**-(e)s,** *pl.* **⸚e**) (*dial.*) crack, chap (*in skin*).

klack(s)! [klak(s)], *int.* slap-bang!

Klacks [klaks], *m.* (**-es,** *pl.* **-e**) (*coll.*) blob.

Kladde ['kladə], *f.* rough draft, rough copy; rough notebook, scribbling jotter; (*Comm.*) daybook, log.

Kladderadatsch [kladəra'da:tʃ], *m.* (*coll.*) mess, muddle, mix-up.

klaffen ['klafən], *v.i.* (*aux.* h. *&* s.) gape, yawn; split open; (*of skin*) chap; (*of door*) be ajar; ***hier klafft ein Widerspruch,*** there is a contradiction here.

kläffen ['klɛfən], *v.i.* bark, yap, yelp; (*fig.*) squabble, bicker.

klaffend ['klafənt], *adj.* gaping, yawning, loosely fitting; (*of door*) ajar; (*Bot.*) dehiscent.

Klafter ['klaftər], *f.* (-, *pl.* **-n**) (*Naut.*) fathom; cord (*of wood*); span (*with outstretched arms*). **Klafterholz,** *n.* cord-wood. **klaftern,** *v.i., v.t.* span (*with outspread arms or wings*); cord (up) (*wood*). **klaftertief,** *adj.* many fathoms deep.

Klag|abweisung ['kla:k-], *f.* (*Law*) dismissal of an action; non-suit. **-anspruch,** *m.* claim. **-antrag,** *m.* application, endorsement of claim. **klagbar,** *adj.* (*Law*) actionable; (*of a debt*) recoverable; ***– machen,*** sue; ***– werden,*** go to law, bring an action.

Klage ['kla:gə], *f.* complaint; lament, lamentation; grievance, ground of *or* for complaint; (*Law*) suit, action, charge, accusation, impeachment, indictment; ***– erheben gegen,*** enter *or* bring an action, institute proceedings *or* file a suit against, sue (***wegen,*** for); ***– auf Schadenersatz,*** action for damages; ***mit einer – abgewiesen werden,*** be nonsuited; – *führen über* (*Acc.*), lodge a complaint about, complain of.

Klage|gesang, *m. See* **–lied. –grund,** *m.* grievance, ground of complaint, (*Law*) cause of action. **–laut,** *m.* plaintive sound, whimper, moan. **–lied,** *n.* dirge, lamentation, elegy, threnody. **–mauer,** *f.* Wailing Wall (*at Jerusalem*).

klagen ['kla:gən], **1.** *v.t.* bewail, complain of, bemoan; ***sein Leid –,*** pour out one's troubles (*Dat.*, to). **2.** *v.i.* complain (***über*** (*Acc.*), of; ***bei,*** to); utter complaints, (*coll.*) moan; (*Law*) bring an action, sue (***auf*** (*Acc.*), ***wegen,*** for), go to law (about). **klagend,** *adj.* plaintive, complaining; ***der –e Teil,*** plaintiff. **Klagende(r),** *m., f.* (*Law*) plaintiff.

Klagepunkt ['kla:gəpuŋkt], *m.* count (of an indictment), grievance.

Kläger ['klɛ:gər], *m.* (*Law*) plaintiff, petitioner; ***Öffentlicher –,*** Public Prosecutor. **klägerisch,** *adj.* (*Law*) of *or* for the plaintiff. **klägerischerseits,** *adv.* on the part of the plaintiff.

Klage|sache, *f.* civil case, lawsuit, action at law. **–schrift,** *f.* writ, written complaint, statement of claim. **–ton,** *m. See* **–laut. –weib,** *n.* (hired) mourner.

Klaggesang ['kla:kgə'zaŋ], *m. See* **Klagelied.**

kläglich ['klɛ:klɪç], *adj.* lamentable, deplorable, pitiable; doleful, plaintive, piteous; miserable, wretched, pitiful.

Klamauk [kla'mauk], *m.* (*coll.*) din, row, rumpus, racket, hullabaloo; (*fig.*) ballyhoo (*of advertising etc.*).

klamm [klam], *adj.* stiff (with cold), numb; (*dial.*) clammy; scarce, short; (*coll.*) – ***sein,*** be hard-up.

Klamm, *f.* (-, *pl.* **-en**) ravine, gorge, canyon.

Klammer ['klamər], *f.* (-, *pl.* **-n**) clamp, clasp, cramp; (paper-)clip; (clothes-)peg; (*Typ.*) parenthesis, bracket; ***eckige –,*** square bracket; ***zusammenfassende –,*** brace; ***in –n setzen,*** put in brackets *or* parentheses; (*Math.*) ***löse zuerst die –n auf,*** get rid of the brackets.

Klammer|affe, *m.* (*Zool.*) spider-monkey (*Ateles*); (*sl.*) pillion-rider. **–ausdruck,** *m.* parenthetical expression. **–fuß,** *m.* prehensile claw.

klammern ['klamərn], **1.** *v.t.* fasten, clip, clasp, clamp (***an*** (*Acc.*), to). **2.** *v.i.* (*Boxing*) clinch. **3.** *v.r.* cling (***an*** (*Acc.*), to).

Klamotten [kla'mɔtən], *f.pl.* (*coll.*) belongings, things, goods and chattels.

Klampe ['klampə], *f.* clamp, cramp, hasp, clasp, holdfast, *pl.* (*Naut.*) cleats.

Klampfe ['klampfə], *f.* guitar, lute.

klang ['klaŋ], *see* **klingen.**

Klang, *m.* **(-(e)s,** *pl.* **⸚e)** sound, tone; (*of bells*) peal, ringing, clang; (*Mus., Phonet.*) timbre, ring; (*fig.*) ***von gutem –,*** of good repute; (*fig.*) ***keinen guten – haben,*** be held in poor *or* low repute; (*fig.*) ***mit Sang und –,*** with a flourish of trumpets. **Klangbild,** *n.* sound pattern.

klänge ['klɛŋə], **klang(e)st** ['klaŋ(ə)st], *see* **klingen.**

Klang|farbe, *f.* timbre. **–fülle,** *f.* sonority, resonance. **–lehre,** *f.* acoustics. **klanglich,** *adj.* tonal. **klanglos,** *adj.* toneless, hollow; soundless, mute; unaccented; (*fig.*) without a word of praise. **klangreich,** *adj.* sonorous, full-sounding, rich, rolling. **Klangtreue,** *f.* (tonal) fidelity; ***von höchster –,*** high-fidelity. **klang|voll,** *adj. See* **–reich. Klangwelle,** *f.* sound-wave.

klappbar ['klapba:r], *adj.* folding, hinged, collapsible. **Klapp|bett,** *n.* camp-bed, folding bed. **–blende,** *f.* drop-shutter. **–brücke,** *f.* drawbridge. **–deckel,** *m.* snap-lid.

Klappe ['klapə], *f.* flap; shutter, hatch, trap, trapdoor; tailboard (*of wagon*), ramp (*of landing-craft*); lid, valve, damper (*of boiler*), (*Mus.*) key, stop; (*sl.*) trap (= *mouth*); (*Prov.*) ***zwei Fliegen mit einer – treffen,*** kill two birds with one stone; (*sl.*) ***halt die –!*** shut up! hold your trap! (*sl.*) ***in die – gehen*** or ***steigen,*** turn in, hit the hay.

klappen ['klapən], **1.** *v.t.* fold, tip, tilt; ***in die Höhe –,*** tip up (*seat etc.*); ***nach vorne –,*** tilt *or* fold forwards. **2.** *v.i.* (*coll.*) tally, work well *or* smoothly, go smoothly, go without a hitch; be all right, work out, come off, (*sl.*) click; ***es klappt,*** it works; ***es klappt nicht,*** something is wrong, it doesn't work, there's a hitch; ***alles klappte,*** it was all plain sailing.

Klappen|horn, *n. See* **Klapphorn. –schrank,** *m.* (telephone) switchboard. **–text,** *m.* blurb. **–ventil,** *n. See* **Klappventil.**

Klapper ['klapər], *f.* (-, *pl.* **-n**) rattle, clapper; (*Weav.*) flier. **Klapperbein,** *n.* skeleton, Death. **klapperdürr,** *adj.* spindly, thin as a rake. **Klappergrasmücke,** *f.* (*Orn.*) lesser whitethroat (*Sylvia curruca*). **klapperig,** *adj.* clattering, rattling; (*fig.*) weak, shaky, rickety. **Klapperkasten,** *m.* (*coll.*) old *or* out-of-tune piano; boneshaker (*car*).

klappern ['klapərn], *v.i.* clatter, rattle, click, clack; chatter (*of teeth*); ***ihm – die Zähne, er klappert mit den Zähnen,*** his teeth are chattering; ***Klappern gehört zum Handwerk,*** you must blow your own trumpet.

Klapper|schlange, *f.* rattlesnake, (*Am.*) rattler. **–storch,** *m.* (*coll.*) stork (*partic. the one that brings babies*).

Klapp|fenster, *n.* trap *or* skylight window. **–horn,** *n.* (*Mus.*) cornet-à-piston. **–hornvers,** *m.* limerick. **–hut,** *m.* opera- *or* crush-hat. **–kamera,** *f.* folding camera. **–kragen,** *m.* turn-down collar. **–messer,** *n.* clasp *or* jack-knife.

klapprig, *adj. See* **klapperig.**

Klapp|sitz, *m.* tip-up seat. **–stuhl,** *m.* folding chair, camp-stool. **–tisch,** *m.* gate-leg table, folding table. **–tür,** *f.* trap-door. **Klappult,** *n.* folding desk. **Klappventil,** *n.* flap *or* clack-valve.

Klaps [klaps], *m.* **(-es,** *pl.* **⸚e** (*Austr.*) **-e)** smack, slap, clap; (*coll.*) ***du hast wohl einen –!*** you're cracked *or* nuts *or* crackers, you've a screw loose. **klapsen,** *v.t.* slap, smack, clap. **Klapsmühle,** *f.* (*sl.*) loony bin.

klar [kla:r], *adj.* clear, limpid, transparent; bright (*as weather*); pure, unsullied; (*fig.*) clear, distinct; obvious, evident, manifest, plain, intelligible, lucid; fine (ground) (*of sugar, sand etc.*); (*Naut.*) ready; (*N.B. with verbs: used as an adverb with literal meanings, as a sep. pref. when figurative; see below*); – ***zum Gefecht,*** ready *or* clear for action; – ***Schiff!*** clear the decks! ***an sich –,*** self-evident; ***es ist ja –,*** it stands to reason, you (must) surely realize; (*coll.*) ***na –!*** of course! sure! you bet! (*coll.*) – ***wie Kloßbrühe,*** as clear as mud; ***er muß sich darüber – werden,*** he must make up his mind about it; ***ihm –en Wein einschenken,*** tell him the plain truth; (*fig.*) ***ins klare bringen,*** clear up, settle (*problems*); ***ins klare kommen über*** (*Acc.*), become clear about, see clearly; ***mit ihm ins klare kommen,*** come to *or* reach an understanding with him; ***sich*** (*Dat.*) ***im klaren sein über*** (*Acc.*), realize, be (fully) aware of, (*coll.*) be alive to; see one's way (*to do*). **2.** *adv.* – ***zum Ausdruck bringen,*** make clear *or* plain; – ***zutage treten,*** be obvious *or* apparent *or* evident, meet the eye.

Klär|anlage ['klɛ:r–], *f.* sewage(-disposal) works; purification plant. **–becken,** *m.* filter-bed.

klarblickend ['kla:rblɪkənt], *adj.* clear-sighted.

Klärbottich ['klɛ:rbɔtɪç], *m.* settling vat *or* tank.

Kläre ['klɛ:rə], *f.* (*Poet.*) clearness, purity, brightness; clarifier; clear liquid. **klären, 1.** *v.t.* clear, clarify, purify, (*fig.*) clarify, settle, clear up (*problems*). **2.** *v.r.* settle, become clear.

Klare(s) ['kla:r(ə)s], *n.* (*dial.*) white (of an egg).

Klär|flasche, *f.*, **–gefäß,** *n. See* **–bottich.**

Klarheit ['kla:rhaɪt], *f.* clearness, brightness, transparency; purity, fineness; (*fig.*) clarity, lucidity, distinctness; (*fig.*) – ***bringen in*** (*Acc.*), shed light on (*problems*).

klarieren [kla'ri:rən], *v.t.* (*Naut.*) clear (*ship at customs*). **Klarierung,** *f.* clearance.

Klarinette [klari'nɛtə], *f.* clarinet. **Klarinettist** [–'tɪst], *m.* **(-en,** *pl.* **-en)** clarinettist.

klar|legen, *v.t.* (*fig.*) make clear, elucidate, clear up, point out (*difficulties*). **–machen, 1.** *v.t.* make clear *or* plain, point out, explain, bring home (*Dat.*, to); *sich* (*Dat.*) –, (come to) realize. **2.** *v.t.*, *v.i.* (*Naut.*) make *or* get ready (*zu*, for), clear (*ropes*), get clear (*lifeboat*), ship (*oars*).

Klär|mittel, *n.* clarifying agent. **–schlamm,** *m.* sludge, deposit.

klar|sehen, *irr.v.i.* (*fig.*) see one's way clear, (*coll.*) see daylight. **–stellen,** *v.t. See* **–legen. Klartext,** *m.* text in clear.

Klärung ['klɛ:ruŋ], *f.* clarification; elucidation.

klarwerden ['kla:rve:rdən], **1.** *irr.v.i.* (*fig.*) become clear; ***es wurde ihm klar,*** he realized, it dawned on him, it came home to him. **2.** *irr.v.r.* make up one's mind (***über*** (*Acc.*), about); understand, realize, grasp.

Klasse ['klasə], *f.* class, rank, order, division, grade, rating, category, quality, type; (*in school*) class, form, (*Am.*) grade; ***in –n einteilen,*** classify; ***erster –,*** first class *or* rate, first *or* top grade; (*coll.*) ***ganz großer –,*** high class, tip-top; ***Wechsel erster –,*** A1 bill.

Klassen|älteste(r), *m., f.* top-boy *or* -girl (of the form). **–arbeit,** *f.* school *or* class work. **klassenbewußt,** *adj.* class-conscious. **Klassen|einteilung,** *f.* classification. **–kamerad,** *m.* class-mate. **–kampf,** *m.* class war(fare), class-conflict. **–lehrer,** *m.* form-master. **–ordnung,** *f.* classification. **–unterschied,** *m.* class distinction. **–zimmer,** *n.* schoolroom, classroom.

klassieren [kla'si:rən], *v.t.* size (*ore*).

klassifizieren [klasifi'tsi:rən], *v.t.* classify.

Klassik ['klasɪk], *f.* classical period (*of art, literature etc.*). **Klassiker,** *m.* classical author; classical scholar; classic (*work of literature*); standard author. **klassisch,** *adj.* classical, (*coll.*) classic; ***ein –es Beispiel,*** a classic example.

Klatsch [klatʃ], *m.* (**-es,** *pl.* **-e**) 1. slap, clap, smack; crack (*of a whip*); 2. (*coll.*) tittle-tattle, gossip. **klatsch!** *int.* crack! smack! **Klatschbase,** *f.* gossip, tale-bearer, scandal-monger. **Klatsche,** *f.* 1. fly-swatter; 2. *See* **Klatschbase**; (*at school*) tell-tale, sneak. **klatschen,** *v.t., v.i.* 1. smack, slap, clap; crack (*whip*); applaud; swat (*flies*); ***Beifall –,*** applaud, clap (*Dat.*, a p.); ***in die Hände –,*** clap one's hands; 2. (*coll.*) gossip, spread stories, tell tales, blab. **Klatscherei** [–'raɪ], *f.* gossip, scandal, prattle, tittle-tattle. **klatschhaft,** *adj.* gossiping, gossipy.

Klatsch|maul, *n. See* **–base. –mohn,** *m.* (*Bot.*) corn-poppy (*Papaver rhoeas*). **klatschnaß,** *adj.* sopping *or* dripping *or* soaking wet, drenched, soaked (to the skin). **Klatsch|rose,** *f. See* **–mohn. –sucht,** *f.* love of gossiping. **–weib,** *n. See* **–base.**

klauben ['klaubən], *v.t.* pick, pick out, sort, cull; ***Worte –,*** quibble, cavil, split hairs.

Klaue ['klauə], *f.* claw, talon, fang; fluke (*of an anchor*); hoof, paw, clutch; jaw; (*sl.*) paw, mitt (= *hand*); (*sl.*) scrawl, fist (= *handwriting*); (*fig.*) ***ihn in meine –n bekommen,*** get my hands on him, get him into my clutches. **klauen,** *v.t.* (*sl.*) pilfer, pinch, swipe. **Klauen|fett,** *n.* neatsfoot oil. **–kupplung,** *f.* dog clutch. **–seuche,** *f.* foot-and-mouth disease.

Klause ['klauzə], *f.* cell, hermitage, (*coll.*) den; mountain-pass. defile.

Klausel ['klauzəl], *f.* (-, *pl.* **-n**) clause; stipulation, proviso, condition.

Klausner ['klausnər], *m.* hermit, recluse.

Klausur [klau'zu:r], *f.* confinement, seclusion; ***unter –,*** under supervision (*as examinations*). **Klausurarbeit,** *f.* class exercise (*under examination conditions*); examination-paper, test-paper.

Klaviatur [klavia'tu:r], *f.* (-, *pl.* **-en**) key-board, keys (*of a piano*); manual (*of an organ*).

Klavier [kla'vi:r], *n.* (**-s,** *pl.* **-e**) piano(forte). **Klavier|auszug,** *m.* piano score. **–konzert,** *n.* piano(forte) recital. **–lehrer,** *m.* piano teacher. **–schule,** *f.* manual of exercises for the piano. **–sessel,** *m.* piano-stool. **–spiel,** *n.* piano-playing. **–spieler,** *m.* pianist. **–stimmer,** *m.* piano tuner. **–stück,** *n.* piece of music for the piano. **–stuhl,** *m. See* **–sessel. –stunde,** *f.*, **–unterricht,** *m.* piano-lesson. **–vortrag,** *m. See* **–konzert.**

Klebäther ['kle:pʔɛ:tər], *m.* (*Chem.*) collodion.

Klebe|band ['kle:bə–], *n. See* **–streifen. –blatt,** *n.* sticker, poster. **–ecke,** *f.* (*Phot.*) corner-mount. **–flugzeug,** *n.* (*coll.*) intruder (aircraft). **klebefrei,** *adj.* non-tacky. **Klebe|garn,** *n.* springe. **–lack,** *m.* (*Av.*) fabric dope. **–mittel,** *n. See* **Klebstoff.**

kleben ['kle:bən], **1.** *v.t.* paste, glue, gum, stick; splice (*film or sound-tape*); (*sl.*) ***ihm eine –,*** give him a fourpenny one. **2.** *v.i.* stick, adhere (***an*** (*Dat.*), to); ***es bleibt nichts bei ihm –,*** he has a memory like a sieve; ***am Irdischen –,*** be worldly-minded; ***an der Scholle –,*** be bound to the soil; ***am Buchstaben –,*** stick to the letter; (*coll.*) ***schon seit 3 Jahren –,*** have been insured *or* covered (*i.e. sticking on insurance stamps*) for 3 years. **klebenbleiben,** *irr. v.i.* stick fast, stay stuck; (*coll.*) stay down (*at school*). **klebend,** *adj.* adhesive, sticky, tacky.

Klebepflaster ['kle:bəpflastər], *n.* adhesive *or* sticking-plaster; court-plaster.

Kleber ['kle:bər], *m.* 1. bill-poster; 2. adhesive; 3. (*coll.*) sticker (= *persistent p.*); 4. (*Bot.*) gluten. **kleberig,** *adj.* adhesive; sticky, viscid, viscous, glutinous; clammy, tacky. **Kleberigkeit,** *f.* stickiness, viscidity, viscosity, tackiness.

Klebe|rute, *f.* lime-twig (*for catching birds*). **–stoff,** *m. See* **Klebstoff. –streifen,** *m.* adhesive tape, (*coll.*) sticky tape. **–tisch,** *m.* (*Film etc.*) splicing table. **–zettel,** *m.* poster, sticker, sticky *or* gummed label.

klebfähig ['kle:pfɛ:ɪç], *adj.* adhesive. **Kleb|garn,** *n. See* **Klebegarn. –kraft,** *f.* adhesive strength *or* property. **–lack,** *m. See* **Klebelack. –mittel,** *n. See* **–stoff. klebrig,** *adj. See* **kleberig. Kleb|sand,** *m.* luting sand. **–stoff,** *m.* adhesive, gum, glue, paste, cement.

kleckern ['klɛkərn], *v.i.* (*coll.*) dribble, drop (*one's food*), spill (*one's drink*), slobber; (*sl.*) (*Nav.*) lay mines.

Klecks [klɛks], *m.* (**-es,** *pl.* **-e**) blot, (ink) stain, spot, blotch, blur; ***voller –e,*** full of blots. **klecksen, 1.** *v.t.* smudge, blot, stain. **2.** *v.i.* make blots *or* smudges; daub, scrawl. **Kleckser,** *m.* scrawler, scribbler, dauber. **Kleckserei** [–'raɪ], *f.* scrawl, untidy writing; daubing, daub (*bad painting*).

Klee [kle:], *m.* clover, trefoil, shamrock; (*Cards*) clubs; ***über den grünen – loben,*** boost, praise to the skies. **Klee|blatt,** *n.* clover-leaf; (*fig.*) trio, triplet. **–blattbogen,** *m.* (*Archit.*) trefoil arch. **kleeblattförmig,** *adj.* trifoliate. **Klee|salz,** *n.* sorrel-salt, potassium acid oxalite, salts of lemon. **–salzkraut,** *n.* (*Bot.*) wood-sorrel (*Oxalis acetosella*). **–säure,** *f.* oxalic acid.

Klei [klaɪ], *m.* clay, loam, marl. **Kleiacker,** *m.* clay-land. (*See also under* **Kleie.**)

kleiben ['klaɪbən], *irr.v.t.* daub (*wattles*), smear; (*dial.*) *also v.i. See* **kleben. Kleiber,** *m.* 1. daub; daub and wattle worker; 2. (*Orn.*) nuthatch (*Sitta europaea*). **Kleiberlehm,** *m.* daub (*for wattles*). **Kleib(er)werk,** *n.* daub and wattle (*fence, wall etc.*).

Kleid [klaɪt], *n.* (**-(e)s,** *pl.* **-er**) garment, (*Poet.*) raiment, attire, garb, habit, frock, dress, gown, robe; costume; clothes, garments; (*Prov.*) ***–er machen Leute,*** fine feathers make fine birds; ***abgetragene –er,*** cast-off clothing.

kleiden ['klaɪdən], **1.** *v.t.* clothe, dress, attire; ***in Worte –,*** clothe *or* couch in words. **2.** *v.t., v.i.* suit, become, look well on (*a p.*). **3.** *v.r.* get dressed, dress o.s.; ***sich gut –,*** dress well.

Kleider|ablage, *f.* cloak-room. **–bestand,** *m.* ward-robe (*i.e. all one's clothes*). **–bezugschein,** *m.* clothing coupon. **–bügel,** *m.* clothes- *or* coat-hanger. **–bürste,** *f.* clothes-brush. **–geld,** *n.* clothing allowance. **–geschäft,** *n.* outfitters. **–haken,** *m.* coat-hook. **–handel,** *m.* old-clothes trade. **-motte,** *f.* (clothes) moth. **-narr,** *m.* fop, dandy. **-ordnung,** *f.* sumptuary law affecting (clerical) dress. **-puppe,** *f.* lay-figure (*as used by artists*), tailor's dummy. **-schrank,** *m.* wardrobe. **-schützer,** *m.* (*Cycl.*) dress-guard. **-schwimmen,** *n.* swimming fully dressed. **-ständer,** *m.* hall-stand, hat and coat stand. **-stoff,** *m.* clothing material, dress material, cloth. **-trödler,** *m.* old-clothes man. **-verleiher,** *m.* theatrical costumer.

kleidsam ['klaɪtza:m], *adj.* fitting well, smart, becoming; ***nicht* –,** unbecoming.

Kleidung ['klaɪdʊŋ], *f.* clothing, clothes, dress, wearing apparel; (*Poet.*) attire, raiment, costume, garb; drapery. **Kleidungsstück,** *n.* article of clothing *or* dress, garment; *pl.* clothes, wearing apparel.

Kleie ['klaɪə], *f.* bran. **Kleienmehl,** *n.* pollard. **kleiig,** *adj.* branny, clayey, loamy. (*See* **Klei.**)

klein [klaɪn], **1.** *adj.* little, small, tiny, minute, diminutive; short (*stature*); trifling, paltry, insignificant, petty; mean, narrow-minded; exact; scanty; neat, nice; (*Mus.*) minor; ***-e Anzeigen,*** small *or* classified advertisements (*in newspaper*); ***-e Augen machen,*** look tired; ***-e Auslagen,*** petty expenses; (*coll.*) ***ein – bißchen,*** (a) very little, a little *or* tiny *or* wee bit; to a slight extent *or* degree; (*Naut.*) ***-e Fahrt,*** dead slow; ***-er Fehler,*** trifling error; ***-er Finger,*** little finger; ***-es Geld,*** (small) change; ***groß und –,*** young and old; (*fig.*) high and low, great and small; ***-e Leiden,*** petty annoyances; ***die -en Leute*** or ***der -e Mann,*** the lower middle-class, the poorer classes, the common man; ***-e Propheten,*** minor prophets; (*coll.*) ***eine -e Stunde,*** barely an hour; ***-e Terz,*** minor third; ***-es Verbrechen,*** petty crime, minor offence; ***von – ab*** or ***an*** or ***auf,*** from infancy *or* childhood, from a child, from an early age; ***ein – wenig,*** see ***ein – bißchen***; ***– werden,*** grow small, shrink, grow less, lessen, diminish, decrease, subside; (*fig.*) (*of a p.*) come down a peg. **2.** *adv.* ***– anfangen,*** begin in a small way, make a modest start; ***– beigeben,*** give way, yield, eat humble pie; ***– denken,*** have narrow views, be narrow-minded; ***von ihm – denken,*** think little of him, have a poor opinion of him; ***bei ihm geht's – her,*** he's in a poor way, he's badly off; ***sich – kriegen lassen,*** be worsted, admit defeat; ***kurz und – schlagen,*** (*a th.*) knock to pieces, smash to bits; (*a p.*) beat, beat-up, (*sl.*) beat the daylights out of. **3.** *n.* ***im -en,*** in a small way, on a small scale; in miniature; in detail; ***im -en verkaufen,*** sell (by) retail; ***bis ins -ste,*** down to the (very) last detail; ***über ein -es,*** after a little while, in a short time; ***um ein -es,*** very nearly, by a hair's breadth; ***um ein -es zu kurz,*** a shade too short.

Klein, *n.* **(-s,** *no pl.*) (*Cul.*) giblets.

Klein|anzeigen, *f.pl. See* ***-e Anzeigen.*** **-arbeit,** *f.* detail(ed work); (*coll.*) spade-work. **-asien,** *n.* Asia Minor. **-auto,** *n. See* **-wagen. -bahn,** *f.* narrow-gauge *or* light railway. **-bauer,** *m.* peasant farmer, smallholder. **-betrieb,** *m.* small business; smallholding; work on a small scale. **-bild,** *n.* miniature. **-bogenform,** *f.* small folio. **-bürger,** *m.* petty bourgeois, little man; philistine. **kleinbürgerlich,** *adj.* ***-e Ansichten,*** narrow-minded views. **Kleinbürgertum,** *n.* petty bourgeoisie. **klein|denkend,** *adj.* narrow-minded, petty. **-deutsch,** *adj.* (*Hist.*) supporting the policy of (German) unification with the exclusion of Austria. **Kleinempfänger,** *m.* (*Rad.*) midget receiver.

Kleine(r) ['klaɪnə(r)], *m., f.* little boy; little girl; ***die Kleinen,*** the little ones.

kleinern ['klaɪnərn], *v.t.* (*Math.*) reduce (*fractions*).

Kleine(s) ['klaɪnə(s)], *n.* little thing, trifle.

Klein|flugzeug, *n.* light aeroplane. **-garten,** *m.* allotment. **-geld,** *n.* (small) change. **-gewerbe,** *n.* small-scale industry. **kleingläubig,** *adj.* of little faith, faint-hearted. **Klein|gläubigkeit,** *f.* lack of faith, faint-heartedness. **-handel,** *m.* retail trade. **-handelspreis,** *m.* retail price. **-händler,** *m.* retailer. **-heit,** *f.* littleness, smallness; pettiness, meanness, insignificance. **-hirn,** *n.* (*Anat.*) cerebellum. **-holz,** *n.* firewood, sticks, kindling, matchwood; (*sl., Av.*) ***– machen,*** prang; (*sl.*) ***– aus ihm machen,*** beat him to pulp *or* to a jelly, tear him limb from limb.

Kleinigkeit ['klaɪnɪçkaɪt], *f.* trifle, trifling *or* petty matter, bagatelle, (*sl.*) chickenfeed; (*coll.*) bite, snack; ***sich mit -en abgeben,*** fritter one's time away; ***für eine – kaufen,*** buy for a mere song. **Kleinigkeits|krämer,** *m.* stickler for details, pedant, pettifogger. **-krämerei,** *f.* pedantry, hair-splitting.

Klein|kaliberschießen, *n.* small-bore *or* sub-calibre rifle shooting. **-kind,** *n.* toddler, pre-school child (*under six years*). **-kinderbewahranstalt,** *f.* day-nursery, crèche. **-kinderschule,** *f.* infant school. **-kinderwäsche,** *f.* baby-linen. **-kohle,** *f.* slack, small coal. **kleinkörnig,** *adj.* fine-grained. **Klein|kraftrad,** *n.* auto-cycle. **-kraftwagen,** *m. See* **-wagen. -kram,** *m.* trifles, pettifogging details. **-krieg,** *m.* guerrilla warfare. **-küche,** *f.* kitchenette. **-kunstbühne,** *f.* intimate theatre, cabaret. **kleinlaut,** *adj.* meek, subdued, low-spirited, dejected, downcast; ***– werden,*** come off one's high horse. **Kleinlebewesen,** *n.* micro-organism.

kleinlich ['klaɪnlɪç], *adj.* paltry, petty; fussy, pedantic. **Kleinlichkeit,** *f.* pettiness, paltriness; pedantry. **kleinmaschig,** *adj.* fine meshed. **Kleinmut,** *m.* (*rare f.*) despondency, dejection; faint-heartedness, pusillanimity. **kleinmütig,** *adj.* faint-hearted, pusillanimous; dejected, despondent.

Kleinod ['klaɪno:t], *n.* **(-s,** *pl.* **-e** *or* **-ien)** jewel, gem; (*fig.*) treasure.

Klein|pferd, *n.* pony. **-rentner,** *m.* 1. pensioner; 2. small investor. **-schmied,** *m.* (*dial.*) tool-maker, mechanic. **-siedler,** *m.* smallholder. **-siedlung,** *f.* smallholding. **-specht,** *m.* (*Orn.*) lesser spotted woodpecker (*Dendrocopus minor*). **-staat,** *m.* minor state, petty state. **-staaterei,** *f.* particularism. **-stadt,** *f.* small provincial town (*under 20,000 inhabitants*). **kleinstädtisch,** *adj.* provincial. **Kleinsteller,** *m.* by-pass (*of gas burner*).

Kleinst|haus, *n.* small (one-family) house. **-kind,** *n.* infant, baby, babe(-in-arms). **-maß,** *n.* minimum. **-wagen,** *m.* minicar, (*coll.*) mini.

Klein|verdiener, *m.* (*usu. pl.*) low-income group. **-verkauf,** *m.* retail trade. **-vieh,** *n.* small live-stock (*i.e. sheep, goats, pigs*). **-wagen,** *m.* small *or* family car. **-ware,** *f.* hardware. **-wild,** *n.* small game.

Kleister ['klaɪstər], *m.* paste, size, gum, adhesive. **kleist(e)rig,** *adj.* pasty, sticky. **kleistern,** *v.t.* paste. **Kleister|pinsel,** *m.* paste-brush. **-tiegel, -topf,** *m.* paste-pot.

Klemme ['klɛmə], *f.* 1. clip, clamp, vice, hold-fast; 2. (*Elec.*) terminal; 3. (*fig.*) shortage, difficulty, quandary, dilemma, straits, (*coll.*) jam, fix, tight corner; ***in der -e sein,*** be in a fix *or* a jam *or* a corner. **klemmen, 1.** *reg. & irr.v.t.* 1. squeeze, pinch, clamp, cramp; ***sich*** (*Dat.*) ***den Finger –,*** pinch one's finger; 2. (*sl.*) pilfer, pinch, swipe. **2.** *reg. & irr. v.r.* get caught *or* jammed *or* locked, jam, bind, catch.

Klemmen|brett, *n.* terminal board. **-dose,** *f.*, **-kasten,** *m.* terminal box. **-spannung,** *f.* terminal voltage. **Klemmer,** *m.* 1. pince-nez; 2. cycle-clip. **Klemm|haken,** *m.* cramp-iron, holdfast. **-schraube,** *f.* set-screw, binding-screw. **Klemmung,** *f.* stoppage (*of a gun*).

Klempner ['klɛmpnər], *m.* plumber; sheet-metal worker, tinsmith. **Klempnerei** [–'raɪ], *f.* plumber's trade *or* workshop. **Klempner(ei)-arbeit,** *f.* plumbing. **klempnern,** *v.i.* do sheet-metal work, work in sheet-metal, do plumbing.

Klepper ['klɛpər], *m.* nag, hack.

Kleptomane [klɛpto'ma:nə], *m.* **(-n,** *pl.* **-n)** kleptomaniac. **Kleptomanie** [–'ni:], *f.* kleptomania.

Kleriker ['kle:rikər], *m.* (*R.C.*) cleric, priest, clergyman. **Klerisei** [–'zaɪ], *f.* clerical set, clergy, (*coll.*) clique, hangers-on. **Klerus,** *m.* (*R.C.*) clergy.

Klette ['klɛtə], *f.* (*Bot.*) bur, burdock (*Arctium lappa*); ***sich wie eine – an ihn hängen,*** stick to him like a leech. **Kletten|bombe,** *f.* sticky *or* limpet bomb. **–wurzelöl,** *n.* burdock oil.

Kletterer ['klɛtərər], *m.* (rock) climber, mountaineer.

klettern ['klɛtərn], *v.i.* (*aux.* h. & s.) climb; clamber, scramble; ***auf einen Baum –,*** climb (up) a tree; ***auf eine Mauer –,*** climb *or* scale a wall. **kletternd,** *adj.* (*Bot.*) climbing, creeping, (*Orn.*) scansorial. **Kletter|pflanze,** *f.* climber, creeper. **–rose,** *f.* rambler. **–schuhe,** *m.pl.* climbing-boots. **–seil,** *n.* climbing-rope. **–stange,** *f.* climbing-pole; greasy pole. **–vögel,** *m.pl.* (*Orn.*) climbers, scansores. **–waldsänger,** *m.* (*Orn.*) black and white warbler (*Mniotilta varia*).

Kliebeisen ['kli:pˀaɪzən], *n.* cleaver. **klieben,** *reg. & irr.v.t.* (*dial.*) cleave, split. **Kliebholz,** *n.* sawn logs (*fit for splitting*). **kliebig,** *adj.* easily split.

klieren ['kli:rən], *v.i.* (*coll.*) scrawl, scribble.

Klima ['kli:ma], *n.* (**-s,** *pl.* **-s** (*Austr.* **-te** [–'ma:tə]) climate; (***sich***) ***an das – gewöhnen,*** acclimatize, (*Am.*) acclimate, get acclimatized. **Klimaanlage,** *f.* air-conditioning plant.

Klimakterium [klimak'te:rium], *n.* (*Med.*) climacteric, change of life.

Klimate [kli'ma:tə], *pl.* (*Austr.*) *see* **Klima. klimatisch,** *adj.* climatic.

Klimbim [klɪm'bɪm], *m., n.* (*coll.*) pother, fuss (and bother); to-do, goings-on.

Klimme ['klɪmə], *f.* wild grape.

klimmen ['klɪmən], *reg. or* (*usu.*) *irr.v.i.* (*aux.* h. & s.) (*usu. fig.*) climb, aspire (***auf*** (*Acc.*), to); ***er ist bis zum Gipfel des Ruhms geklommen,*** he has reached *or* raised himself to the pinnacle of fame. **Klimm|ziehen,** *n.,* **–zug,** *m.* (*Gymn.*) climbing hand over hand; short-arm stretch (*on the horizontal bar*).

Klimperkasten ['klɪmpərkastən], *m.* (*coll.*) jangly piano. **klimperklein,** *adj.* tiny, wee. **klimpern,** *v.i.* jingle, jangle, clink, chink, tinkle; (*Mus.*) strum.

Klinge ['klɪŋə], *f.* blade; sword; ***vor die – fordern,*** challenge; ***mit der – entscheiden,*** decide by the sword; ***die –n kreuzen mit,*** cross swords with; ***über die – springen,*** be put to the sword; ***den Feind über die – springen lassen,*** put the enemy to the sword; ***eine gute – führen*** (or ***schlagen***), be a good swordsman, (*fig.*) be able to defend o.s. *or* to hold one's own.

Klingel ['klɪŋəl], *f.* (-, *pl.* **-n**) small bell, handbell. **Klingel|beutel,** *m.* collection-bag, offertory bag. **–knopf,** *m.* bell-push. **klingeln,** *v.i.* tinkle, ring, (*Motor.*) pink; ***es klingelt,*** there is a ring at the door; ***es wurde nach dem Diener geklingelt,*** the bell was rung for the servant. **Klingel|schnur,** *f.* bell-rope. **–strom,** *m.* (*Tele.*) ringing current. **–ton,** *m.* (*Tele.*) ringing (tone). **–zug,** *m.* bell-pull.

klingen ['klɪŋən], *irr.v.i.* (*aux.* h.) (*usu. 3rd pers. only*) ring, chime, sound, tinkle, jingle, clink; ***diese Frage klingt sonderbar,*** that sounds a strange question; ***das klingt wahr,*** that rings true; ***die Gläser – lassen,*** clink *or* touch glasses (*in drinking*); ***die Ohren – mir,*** there is a ringing in my ears, my ears are burning; (*coll.*) ***klingt es nicht, so klappert's doch,*** it's s.th. at any rate, it is better than nothing. **klingend,** *adj.* resonant, ringing; (*B.*) ***tönendes Erz oder –e Schelle,*** sounding brass or a tinkling cymbal; ***–e Worte,*** high-sounding *or* fine words; ***–e Münze,*** (hard) cash, ready money; ***mit –em Spiele,*** drums beating, with full band, triumphantly; (*Metr.*) ***–er Reim,*** feminine rhyme. **Klingklang,** *m.* ding-dong, jangle, jingle.

Klinik ['kli:nɪk], *f.* (-, *pl.* **-en**) clinic(al hospital), nursing-home. **Kliniker,** *m.* clinician. **Klinikum,** *n.* (**-s,** *pl.* **-ken**) clinical lecture *or* demonstration. **klinisch,** *adj.* clinical.

Klinke ['klɪŋkə], *f.* latch, door handle, (*Mech.*) catch, pawl, (*Elec.*) jack. **klinken,** *v.i.* press the latch.

Klinker ['klɪŋkər], *m.* (Dutch) clinker, hard brick. **Klinker|bau,** *m.* brick building; clinker construction (*of boats*). **–boot,** *n.* clinker-built boat.

Klinse ['klɪnzə], (*Austr.* **Klinze**) *f.* cleft, crack, chink, gap, fissure.

Klipp [klɪp], *m.* (**-(e)s,** *pl.* **-e**) clip, clasp. **klipp!** *int.* snip, snap; (*coll.*) ***– und klar,*** (*pred.adj.*) quite plain, obvious, clear as daylight; (*adv.*) point-blank, plainly, (*coll.*) straight from the shoulder.

Klippe ['klɪpə], *f.* cliff, crag, rock, reef; (*fig.*) stumbling-block, hurdle, obstacle, (*coll.*) snag; ***blinde –,*** sunken rock. **Klippen|küste,** *f.* rocky coast. **–reihe,** *f.* ledge of rocks, reef. **–strandläufer,** *m.* (*Orn.*) *see* **Meerstrandläufer. –wand,** *f.* rocky wall, escarpment.

Klipper ['klɪpər], *m.* sculptor's mallet; fast-sailing merchantman; flying-boat.

Klippfisch ['klɪpfɪʃ], *m.* dried cod.

klippig ['klɪpɪç], *adj.* rocky, craggy.

klirren ['klɪrən], *v.i.* clink, clank, clash, jingle, clatter, rattle; ***mit –den Sporen,*** with clanking spurs.

Klischee [kli'ʃe:], *n.* (**-s,** *pl.* **-s**) 1. (*Typ.*) stereo(type)plate, block; electro, cliché; 2. (*fig.*) cliché, hackneyed phrase. **Klischeeabzug,** *m.* engraver's proof. **klischieren,** *v.t.* (*Typ.*) stereotype, cut *or* make a block of.

Klistier [klɪs'ti:r], *n.* (**-s,** *pl.* **-e**) enema, (*rare*) clyster. **klistieren,** *v.t.* give an enema (to). **Klistierspritze,** *f.* enema.

klitsch! [klɪtʃ], *int.* slap! slop! splash! **Klitsch,** *m.* (**-es,** *pl.* **-e**) soggy mass, (*coll.*) doughy bread, sad cake. **klitsch(e)naß,** *adj.* sopping wet, soaked (to the skin), drenched. **klitschig,** *adj.* (*coll.*) doughy, soggy, sad; sodden, clayey.

Klitter ['klɪtər], *m.* blur, smudge, mess. **klittern,** *v.t., v.i.* 1. enter into details; 2. smear, daub, smudge.

Klo [klo:], *n.* (**-s,** *pl.* **-s**) (*coll.*) lav, loo.

Kloake [klo'a:kə], *f.* 1. sewer, sink, drain, cesspool; 2. (*Zool., Orn.*) cloaca. **Kloakentiere,** *n.pl.* (*Zool.*) monotremes.

klob [klo:p], **klöbe** ['klø:bə], *see* **klieben.**

Kloben ['klo:bən], *m.* (**-s,** *pl.* -) log, billet (*of wood*); (*Mech.*) block, pulley; hand-vice, clamp; cheek (*of a balance*); pivot (*of hinge*); (*coll., fig.*) boor, lout.

klobest ['klo:bəst], *see* **klieben.**

klobig ['klo:bɪç], *adj.* bulky, clumsy; (*of a p.*) clumsy, crude, loutish, boorish.

klomm [klɔm], **klömme** ['klœmə], **klomm(e)st,** *see* **klimmen.**

klönen ['klø:nən], *v.i.* (*coll.*) talk and talk, chat, (*sl.*) natter, chinwag.

Klöpfel ['klœpfəl], *m. See* **Klöppel,** 2.

klopfen ['klɔpfən], **1.** *v.t.* beat (*clothes, carpets etc.*), break (*stones*), knock, drive (*a nail etc.*); (*Typ.*) ***die Form –,*** plane down. **2.** *v.i.* knock (*also Motor.*) (***an*** or ***auf*** (*Acc.*), at *or* on); throb, pulsate, palpitate (***vor*** (*Dat.*), with); ***es klopft,*** there's a knock at the door; ***ihm auf die Finger –,*** rap him over the knuckles (*also fig.*); ***ihm auf die Schultern –,*** pat *or* slap his back; (*fig.*) ***auf den Busch –,*** draw a bow at a venture; ***bei ihm auf den Busch –,*** pump *or* sound him. **Klopfen,** *n.* knocking, beating, throbbing, palpitation, pulsation. **Klopfer,** *m.* 1. (carpet) beater; (door) knocker; 2. *See* **Klopfholz. klopffest,** *adj.* (*Motor.*) anti-pinking, anti-knock. **Klopf|holz,** *n.* mallet, beetle; (*Typ.*) planer. **–käfer,** *m.* death-watch beetle (*Anobidae*). **–see,** *f.* heavy *or* choppy sea. **–wert,** *m.* octane rating (*of petrol*).

Kloppe ['klɔpə], *f.* (*dial.*) beating, thrashing.

Klöppel ['klœpəl], *m.* 1. bobbin; 2. tongue, clapper (*of a bell*); (door) knocker; mallet, cudgel, drumstick. **Klöppel|arbeit,** *f.* pillow lace. **–garn,** *n.* thread used in lace-making. **–holz,** *n.* bobbin. **klöppeln,** *v.i.* make pillow lace. **Klöppelspitze,** *f.* pillow lace.

Klops [klɔps], *m.* (**-es,** *pl.* **-e**) (*dial.*) meat ball.

Klosett [klo'zɛt], *n.* (**-s,** *pl.* **-e**) lavatory, (water-) closet (*abbr.* W.C.), toilet. **Klosett|becken,** *n.*

lavatory pan. **–deckel,** *m.* lid *or* cover of a lavatory. **–muschel,** *f. See* **–becken. –papier,** *n.* lavatory *or* toilet paper.

Kloß [klo:s], *m.* (**-es,** *pl.* **¨-e**) clod, lump; meat ball; dumpling; (*coll.*) ***einen – im Hals haben,*** have a lump in one's throat. **Kloßbrühe,** *f.* (*coll.*) ***klar wie –,*** as clear as mud.

Kloster [ˈklo:stər], *n.* (**-s,** *pl.* **¨**) monastery, cloister (*for monks*), nunnery, convent (*for nuns*); ***ins – gehen,*** enter a monastery *or* convent, take the veil (*of nuns*), turn monk. **Kloster|bogen,** *m.* Gothic arch. **–bruder,** *m.* monk, friar. **–frau,** *f.*, **–fräulein,** *n.* nun. **–gang,** *m.* cloister(s). **–gelübde,** *n.* monastic vow. **–gemeinde,** *f.* fraternity (*monks*), sisterhood (*nuns*). **–gut,** *n.* estate belonging to a convent. **–leben,** *n.* monastic life. **–leute,** *pl.* conventuals, monks, nuns.

klösterlich [ˈklø:stərlıç], *adj.* monastic, conventual; (*fig.*) cloistered, secluded.

Kloster|schule, *f.* monastery *or* convent school. **–schwester,** *f.* lay sister; nun.

Klotz [klɔts], *m.* (**-es,** *pl.* **¨-e**) 1. block; log, lump, chunk (*of wood*); ***ein – am Bein,*** a millstone round one's neck; (*Prov.*) ***auf einen groben – gehört ein grober Keil,*** pay him back in his own coin, tit for tat; 2. (*fig.*) boor, lout, clod, blockhead. **klotzig,** *adj.* massive, bulky, heavy, clumsy, (*of a p.*) lumpish, coarse-grained; boorish, (*sl.*) mighty, enormous; (*sl.*) ***– viel,*** an awful lot of; ***– viel Geld haben,*** be stiff with money, be stinking rich; ***– viel Geld kosten,*** cost no end of money, cost the earth.

Klub [klup], *m.* (**-s,** *pl.* **-s**) club. **Klub|haus, –lokal,** *n.* clubhouse, clubroom. **–sessel,** *m.* easy- *or* lounge-chair.

Klucke [ˈklukə], *f.* (*dial.*) sitting *or* broody hen.

kluckern [ˈklukərn], *v.i.* gurgle, babble (*as water*).

[1]**Kluft** [kluft], *f.* (-, *pl.* **-en**) (*sl.*) togs, duds, rig-out.

[2]**Kluft,** *f.* (-, *pl.* **¨-e**) cleft, crevice, crack, fissure, gap, cleavage; chasm, gulf, ravine, abyss, gorge. **klüften,** *v.t.* (*dial.*) cleave, split, (*fig.*) rift. **kluftig, klüftig,** *adj.* cleft, split; cracked. **Klüftung,** *f.* cleavage, segmentation.

klug [klu:k], *adj.* (*comp. klüger, sup. klügst*) intelligent, gifted, talented, able; clever, astute, alert, (*coll.*) bright, smart; sagacious, cunning, shrewd, clear-sighted, discerning, (*coll.*) sharp; judicious, wise, sensible, prudent; (*coll.*) ***er ist nicht recht –,*** he is not all there; ***aus ihm werde ich nicht –,*** I cannot make him out; ***daraus kann ich nicht – werden,*** I can make neither head nor tail of it; ***genau so – wie zuvor*** or ***vorher,*** none the wiser; (*Prov.*) ***durch Schaden wird man –,*** a burnt child dreads the fire; ***das klügste wäre nun wohl,*** it would probably be best.

Klügelei [kly:gəˈlaı], *f.* (-, *pl.* **-en**) sophistry, casuistry, quibbling, cavilling, special pleading, chicanery, hypercriticism. **klügeln,** *v.i.* quibble, cavil, split hairs, subtilize.

Klugheit [ˈklu:khaıt], *f.* prudence, discretion, wisdom, good sense; intelligence, cleverness, sagacity, astuteness, shrewdness.

Klügler [ˈkly:klər], *m.* sophist, caviller, carper, quibbler, wiseacre. **klüglich,** *adv.* prudently, sensibly, wisely, shrewdly, astutely.

klug|reden, –schnacken, *v.i.* (*coll.*) be too clever by half, wisecrack. **Klugschnack(er),** *m.* wiseacre, know-all, (*coll.*) smart aleck, wise guy.

Klump [klump], *m.* (**-(e)s,** *pl.* **-e**) (*rare*) *see* **Klumpen.**

Klümpchen [ˈklympçən], *n.* (**-s,** *pl.* **-** *or* **Klümperchen**) little lump *or* clot; globule, nodule; ***– bilden,*** clot; (*coll.*) (***wie***) ***ein – Unglück,*** (like) a picture of misery.

Klumpen [ˈklumpən], *m.* 1. clod (*of earth*), clot (*of blood*), lump; ingot, nugget (*of gold*); cluster, heap, ball; ***in – hauen,*** smash to smithereens; ***auf einem –,*** all of a heap; 2. *pl.* clogs, pattens. **klumpenweise,** *adv.* in lumps *or* clusters.

klümp(e)rig [ˈklympərıç], *adj.* lumpy, clotted; ***– werden,*** clot.

Klumpfuß [ˈklumpfus], *m.* club-foot. **klumpig,** *adj.* clotted, in lumps, lumpy, caked (*flour*).

klümprig, *adj. See* **klümp(e)rig.**

Klüngel [ˈklyŋəl], *m.* clique, coterie, faction; ***der ganze –,*** the whole caboodle.

Klunker [ˈkluŋkər], *f.* (-, *pl.* **-n**) *or m.* tassel; cake, clod (*of dirt*). **klunkerig,** *adj.* caked with mud, bespattered, bedraggled. **Klunkermilch,** *f.* (*dial.*) clotted milk, sour milk.

Kluppe [ˈklupə], *f.* 1. die-stock; 2. pincers, nippers, tongs; callipers; (*Austr.*) clothes-peg. **kluppen,** *v.t.* squeeze into a slit *or* fissure, pinch. **kluppieren,** *v.t., v.i.* measure the girth (of). **Kluppzange,** *f.* forceps.

Klus [klu:s], *f.* (-, *pl.* **-en**) (*Swiss*) gorge, ravine, chasm.

Klüse [ˈkly:zə], *f.* (*Naut.*) hawse, hawse-pipe.

Klutter [ˈklutər], *f.* (-, *pl.* **-n**) decoy-whistle, bird-call.

Klüver [ˈkly:vər], *m.* (*Naut.*) jib; fan-tail (*of windmill*). **Klüver|baum,** *m.* jib-boom. **–fall,** *m.* jib-halyard. **–schote,** *f.* jib-sheet, head-sheet; ***–n los!*** ease off the jib!

Klystier, *n. See* **Klistier.**

knabbern [ˈknabərn], *v.t., v.i.* nibble, gnaw, munch (*an* (*Dat.*), at).

Knabe [ˈkna:bə], *m.* (**-n,** *pl.* **-n**) boy, lad; ***alter –,*** old boy, old fellow; old fogy; ***braver –,*** fine lad. **Knabenalter,** *n.* boyhood. **knabenhaft,** *adj.* boyish. **Knabenhaftigkeit,** *f.* boyishness. **Knaben|kraut,** *n.* (*Bot.*) orchis. **–liebe,** *f.* pederasty. **–schule,** *f.* boys' school. **–streich,** *m.* boyish trick.

knack! [knak], *int.* crack! snap! **Knackbeere,** *f.* wild strawberry (*Fragaria viridis*).

Knäckebrot [ˈknɛkəbro:t], *n.* crispbread.

knacken [ˈknakən], **1.** *v.t.* crack (open); solve (*riddles*). **2.** *v.i.* click, crackle, crepitate. **Knacker,** *m.* (*coll.*) ***alter –,*** old fogy, old codger. **Knack|laut,** *m.* (*Phonet.*) glottal stop. **–mandel,** *f.* almond in the shell.

knacks! [knaks], *int. See* **knack. Knacks,** *m.* crack; (*coll.*) ***einen – kriegen,*** crack up; (*coll.*) ***er hat seinen – weg,*** his health (*or* nerves) have cracked up, he's had a breakdown.

Knackwurst [ˈknakvurst], *f.* saveloy.

Knagge [ˈknagə], *f.* stay, bracket; (*Mach.*) cam, tappet.

Knäkente [ˈknɛ:kʔɛntə], *f.* (*Orn.*) garganey (*Anas querquedula*).

Knall [knal], *m.* (**-(e)s,** *pl.* **-e**) report, bang, pop, clap, thud, crack (*of whip*); detonation, explosion; (*coll.*) ***– und Fall,*** all at once, (all) of a sudden, without notice *or* warning; (*coll.*) ***er hat wohl einen –,*** he's cracked *or* crazy, he's off his rocker, (*Am.*) he's nuts. **Knall|bonbon,** *m. or n.* (Christmas) cracker. **–büchse,** *f.* popgun. **–dämpfer,** *m.* (*Motor.*) silencer. **–effekt,** *m.* coup de théâtre; unexpected turn in events, sensation.

knallen [knalən], **1.** *v.i.* burst, explode, detonate, fulminate; crack (*as whip*), bang (*as door*), pop; ***mit der Peitsche –,*** crack the whip; (*aux.* s.) ***der Pulverturm knallte in die Luft,*** the powder-magazine blew up with a loud report. **2.** *v.t.* (*coll.*) ***den Ball ins Tor –,*** land the ball in the net; (*coll.*) ***ich knalle dir eine!*** I'll land you one!

Knall|erbse, *f.* cracker (*firework*). **–gas,** *n.* oxy-hydrogen gas. **–gasgebläse,** *n.* oxyhydrogen blow-pipe. **–gold,** *n.* fulminating gold. **knallig,** *adj.* (*coll.*) gaudy, flashy, glaring, striking. **Knall|kapsel,** *f.* (*Railw.*) fog-signal. **–körper,** *m.* detonator. **–pulver,** *n.* fulminating powder. **–quecksilber,** *n.* fulminate of mercury. **knallrot,** *adj.* glaring red. **Knall|salpeter,** *m.* ammonium nitrate. **–satz,** *m.* explosive mixture. **knallscheu,** *adj.* gun-shy. **Knall|signal,** *n. See* **–kapsel. –silber,** *n.* fulminating silver. **–zündmittel,** *n.* primer, detonator.

knapp [knap], **1.** *adj.* 1. close(-fitting), narrow, tight (*as clothes*); 2. scant(y), scarce, (*coll.*) tight (*as supplies*); spare, meagre, paltry, stringent, limited, barely sufficient; ***sein –es Auskommen haben,*** make a bare living, have barely enough to live on; *das Geld ist – bei ihm, er ist – bei Kasse,* he's short of money, he's hard up; *-e Kost,* barely sufficient food; short rations; *eine -e Mehrheit,* a bare majority; *mit -er (Mühe und) Not,* barely, only just, with great difficulty; *mit -er Not davonkommen,* have a narrow escape, (*coll.*) escape by the skin of one's teeth; *– sein,* be in short supply; *– werden,* be running short; *-er Wind,* scant wind; *-e Zeiten,* hard times; 3. accurate, exact, concise, terse, brief (*style*). **2.** *adv.* barely, only just; a little less than, just under, not quite; *– bemessen,* give short measure; *meine Zeit ist – bemessen,* I am pressed for time, my time is limited; *– berechnen,* cut it fine; *– berechnet,* at most; *– gewinnen (verlieren),* win (lose) by a narrow margin; *ihn – halten,* keep him short (of); *– sitzen,* be a tight fit, fit tight; (*sl.*) *aber nicht zu –!* and how!

Knappe ['knapə], *m.* (**-n,** *pl.* **-n**) (*Hist.*) squire, page; miner; miller's boy *or* apprentice.

Knappheit ['knaphaɪt], *f.* shortage, scarcity, scantiness, deficiency, stringency; tightness; terseness, conciseness.

Knappschaft ['knapʃaft], *f.* (body of) miners. **Knappschafts|kasse,** *f.* miners' provident fund. **-verband,** *m.* miners' union.

knapsen ['knapsən], *v.i.* pinch, stint, go short.

Knarre ['knarə], *f.* rattle; ratchet; (*sl.*) gun, pea-shooter. **knarren,** *v.i.* creak, grate, squeak; groan.

Knast [knast], *m.* (**-(e)s,** *pl.* **-e**) 1. (*dial.*) knot (*in wood*); stub, stump, crust (*of bread*); (*sl.*) *einen – sägen,* snore; 2. *See* **Knaster,** 2. **Knaster,** *m.* 1. shag, (stinking) weed (= *tobacco*); 2. *or* **Knasterbart,** *m.* (old) curmudgeon.

knattern ['knatərn], *v.i.* rattle, clatter, (*Motor.*) chug.

Knäuel ['knɔyəl], *n. or m.* ball, hank, clew, skein (*of thread*), coil (*of wire*), (*Bot.*) fascicle, spireme; (*fig.*) snarl, tangle; (*of people*) cluster, throng, crowd; (*Bot.*) Scleranthus. **Knäuelbinse,** *f.* (*Bot.*) common rush (*Juncus conglomeratus*). **knäuelförmig,** *adj.* globular, glomerate; in a coil, coiled, convoluted. **knäueln,** *v.t., v.r.* form into a ball, ball up, coil up.

Knauf [knauf], *m.* (**-(e)s,** *pl.* **¨-e**) (*Archit.*) capital; knob; pommel (*of a sword's hilt*).

Knaul [knaul], *m. or n.* (**-s,** *pl.* **-e** *or* **¨-e**) (*dial.*) *see* **Knäuel.**

knaupeln ['knaupəln], *v.t., v.i.* nibble; crunch; scrabble.

Knauser ['knauzər], *m.* miser, skinflint, niggard. **Knauserei** [–'raɪ], *f.* stinginess, cheese-paring, niggardliness. **knauserig,** *adj.* niggardly, mean, stingy, close(-fisted), cheese-paring; churlish. **knausern,** *v.i.* be stingy *or* miserly *or* mean *or* niggardly, stint, grudge.

knautschen ['knautʃən], *v.t.* crumple, crease.

Knebel ['kne:bəl], *m.* club, cudgel, stick; toggle, tommy-bar, frog; gag (*for the mouth*); clapper (*of a bell*); twisted moustache; (*dial.*) knuckles of clenched fist. **Knebel|anschraubung,** *f.* tommy-bar adjustment. **-bart,** *m.* (twisted) moustache. **-gebiß,** *n.* snaffle-bit. **knebeln,** *v.t.* fasten with a toggle; gag, (*fig.*) suppress; *die Presse –,* muzzle the press. **Knebel|presse,** *f.,* **-verband,** *m.* tourniquet.

Knecht [knɛçt], *m.* (**-(e)s,** *pl.* **-e**) 1. farm-hand, farm-labourer, ploughman; stable-hand, servant, menial; (*Hist.*) serf, bondsman, slave; *fauler –,* ready reckoner; *– Ruprecht,* Santa Claus, St. Nicholas; *lieber ein kleiner Herr als ein großer –,* better a big fish in a little pond than a little fish in a big pond; *wie der Herr so der –,* like master like man; 2. (*Mech.*) trestle, jack. **knechten,** *v.t.* reduce to servitude, subjugate, enslave, oppress, (*fig.*) trample under foot. **knechtisch,** *adj.* menial; submissive, slavish; servile, crawling. **Knechtschaft,** *f.* servitude, bondage, slavery; serfdom. **Knechtung,** *f.* enthralment, enslavement, subjugation, oppression.

Kneif [knaɪf], *m.* (**-s,** *pl.* **-e**) cobbler's knife.

kneifen ['knaɪfən], **1.** *irr.v.t.* pinch, squeeze, nip, gripe; cog (*dice*); *den Schwanz zwischen die Beine gekniffen,* with its tail between its legs; *Preise –,* force down prices; *den Wind –,* hug the wind. **2.** *irr.v.i.* (*aux.* h. & s.) (*coll.*) flinch, wriggle *or* back out, funk it; shirk, skrimshank. **Kneifer,** *m.* pince-nez; work-dodger, shirker. **Kneifzange,** *f.* cutting pliers, nippers, pincers; tweezers.

Kneip [knaɪp], *m.* (**-s,** *pl.* **-e**) (*Austr.*) *see* **Kneif.**

Kneip|abend, *m.* (students') drinking party. **-bruder,** *m.* toper, tippler.

Kneipe ['knaɪpə], *f.* tavern, public-house, (*coll.*) pub; saloon, bar; (students') beer party; *auf der –,* in the bar. **kneipen,** *v.i.* 1. (*dial.*) pinch, nip, gripe; *es kneipt ihm im Bauche,* he has the gripes *or* colly-wobbles; 2. go drinking, carouse; (*sl.*) go on the beer; booze, tipple. **Kneipen,** *n.* 1. colic, gripes; 2. *or* **Kneiperei** [–'raɪ], *f.* (beer) drinking; (*sl.*) boozing.

Kneip|lied, *n.* drinking-song. **-wart,** *m.* student officiating with the drinks. **-wirt,** *m.* publican.

Kneller ['knɛlər], *m.* (*dial.*) cheap tobacco, (*coll.*) weed.

knetbar ['kne:tba:r], *adj.* kneadable, plastic. **Knete,** *f.* plasticine. **kneten,** *v.t.* knead, mill, pug. **Kneter,** *m.* churn, dough mixer. **Knetmasse,** *f.* *See* **Knete.**

Knick [knɪk], *m.* (**-(e)s,** *pl.* **-e**) 1. crack, break, flaw; fold, crease (*in paper*), kink (*in wire*), dent, buckle (*in metal*), sharp bend (*of a road*); 2. (*dial. with pl. also* **-s**) quick-set hedge. **knickbeinig,** *adj.* knock-kneed. **knicken, 1.** *v.t.* crease, bend, fold (*paper*); crack, break, snap (*twig etc.*), split, burst; (*fig.*) *ihn –,* break him, break his spirit *or* resistance; *Eier –,* crack eggs; *einen Hasen –,* break the neck of a hare. **2.** *v.i.* (*aux.* h. & s.) crack, break, split, burst; give way, buckle, sag; (*fig.*) be broken *or* cast down (*of courage, hope etc.*); be niggardly; *geknicktes Dasein,* blighted life; *geknickter Mann,* broken man.

Knicker ['knɪkər], *m.* 1. *See* **Knauser**; 2. grumbler, grouser; 3. clasp-knife; 4. (*dial.*) marble, taw. **Knickerei** [–'raɪ], *f.,* **knickerig,** *adj. See* **Knauserei, knauserig. knickern,** *v.i.* 1. *See* **knausern**; 2. haggle, chaffer; 3. (*dial.*) play marbles.

Knick|festigkeit, *f.* (*Metall.*) buckling strength. **-flügel,** *m.* (*Av.*) gull-wing. **-last,** *f.* buckling load. **-punkt,** *m.* break (*in a curve*).

Knicks [knɪks], *m.* (**-es,** *pl.* **-e**) curtsy. **knicksen,** *v.i.* curtsy, make a curtsy.

Knickstütz ['knɪkʃtyts], *m.* (*Gymn.*) bent-arm rest. **knickung,** *f.* bending, buckling, flexion. **Knickversuch,** *m.* (*Metall.*) buckling test.

Knie [kni:], *n.* (**-s,** *pl.* **-** *or dial.* **-e**) 1. knee; (*Poet.*) *euch lege ich's auf die –,* I leave the decision in your hands; (*fig.*) *etwas übers – brechen,* hurry a matter through, rush a th., rush one's fences, make short work of a th.; *auf den -n bitten,* beg on one's bended knee; *auf* or *in die – fallen* or *sinken,* go down on *or* fall on *or* drop to one's knees; *ihn auf* or *in die – zwingen,* force him to his knees; *ein Kind übers – legen,* put a child across one's knee; *mir schlottern die –,* my knees are knocking; 2. bend (*of a road*), (*Mil.*) salient; 3. (*of a pipe etc.*) elbow, bend, angle, joint; (*Mech.*) crank.

Knie|band, *n.* 1. garter; 2. ligament of the knee. **-beuge,** *f.* bend of the knee, popliteal space; (*Gymn.*) knees-bend. **-beugung,** *f.,* **-fall,** *m.* genuflexion; *einen Kniefall tun,* prostrate o.s., make *or* do *or* pay obeisance. **kniefällig,** *adv.* upon one's knees, on bended knee. **Knieflechse,** *f.* hamstring. **kniefrei,** *adj.* leaving the knees free; *-er Rock,* knee-length skirt. **Knie|galgen,** *m.* gibbet. **-geige,** *f.* viola da gamba. **-gelenk,** *n.* knee-joint. **kniehoch,** *adj.* up to the knees, knee-deep (in); knee-high (*grass etc.*). **Knie|holz,** *n.* scrub. **-hose,** *f.* knee-breeches, knickerbockers. **-kehle,** *f. See* **-beuge. -kissen,** *n.* hassock.

knien ['kni:ən], *v.i.* be on one's knees, be kneeling, kneel; (*aux.* s.) go down on one's knees, kneel down; (*Eccl.*) genuflect; (*coll.*) *sich – in* (*Acc.*), get *or* buckle down to (*work etc.*). **kniend,** *adj.* kneeling, on one's knees, on bended knee; with bended knees; (*Mil.*) *-er Anschlag,* kneeling position (*for firing*).

Kniepaugen, *pl.* (*coll.*) – **machen,** be hardly able to keep one's eyes open.

Knie|riem(en), *m.* shoemaker's stirrup. **-rohr,** *n.* elbow bend (*of a pipe*). **-scheibe,** *f.* knee-cap, patella. **-schützer,** *m.* knee-pad. **-strumpf,** *m.* knee-length stocking. **-stück,** *n.* 1. knee-piece, angle-joint (*of a pipe*); *see* **-rohr**; 2. three-quarter length portrait. **knieweich,** *adj.* weak-kneed.

kniff [knɪf], *see* **kneifen.**

Kniff, *m.* (**-(e)s,** *pl.* **-e**) 1. crease, fold, dent (*in hat*); 2. (*fig.*) trick, dodge, device, artifice, stratagem, ruse; short-cut, knack; (*coll.*) *den – heraushaben,* have the knack of it, know the ropes.

kniffe ['knɪfə], *see* **kneifen.**

kniffen ['knɪfən], *v.t.* (*dial.*) fold, crease.

kniff(e)lig ['knɪf(ə)lɪç], *adj.* difficult, intricate, (*coll.*) tricky.

kniff(e)st ['knɪf(ə)st], *see* **kneifen.**

knipsen ['knɪpsən], **1.** *v.t.* punch (*a ticket*); (*coll.*) *ihn –,* take a snapshot of him. **2.** *v.i.* (*mit*) snip (*with scissors*), snap (*one's fingers*). **Knipszange,** *f.* ticket-punch.

Knirps [knɪrps], *m.* (**-es,** *pl.* **-e**) 1. dwarf, pigmy; manikin, midget, hop-o'-my-thumb; little fellow, whippersnapper; 2. (*coll.*) collapsible umbrella.

knirschen ['knɪrʃən], *v.i.* crunch, grind, grate, creak; crackle, rustle; *mit den Zähnen –,* gnash *or* grind one's teeth.

Knistergold ['knɪstərgɔlt], *n.* tinsel. **knistern,** *v.i.* crackle, rustle; (*Chem.*) crepitate.

Knittel ['knɪtəl], *m.* *See* **Knüttel.**

Knitter ['knɪtər], *m.* crease, crumple, ruck. **knitterfrei,** *adj.* non-creasing, crease-resisting. **Knittergold,** *n.* tinsel. **knitterig,** *adj.* creased, rucked, wrinkled, crumpled, (*fig.*) irritable. **knittern,** *v.t.* crumple, crease, ruck. **2.** *v.r.* get crumpled, creased *or* rucked. **Knitterpapier,** *n.* crinkled *or* crêpe paper.

Knobel ['kno:bəl], *m.pl.* dice, (*dial.*) knuckles. **Knobelbecher,** *m.* dice-box; *pl.* (*sl., Mil.*) jack-boots. **knobeln,** *v.i.* throw dice, toss (*um,* for), (*fig.*) rack one's brains (*an* (*Dat.*), over).

Knoblauch ['kno:plaux], *m.* garlic. **Knoblauchzehe,** *f.* clove of garlic.

Knöchel ['knœçəl], *m.* knuckle; ankle (bone); (*dial.*) *pl.* dice, bones; *bis an die –,* ankle deep. **Knöchelchen,** *n.* ossicle; small joint. **Knöchelgelenk,** *n.* ankle-joint. **knöchellang,** *adj.* ankle-length (*skirt*). **knöcheln,** *v.i.* play with dice. **Knöchel|spiel,** *n.* game with dice. **-zerrung,** *f.* strained ankle.

Knochen ['knɔxən], *m.* bone; *in – verwandeln* (*v.t.*), *zu – werden* (*v.i.*), ossify; *stark von –,* bony, strong-limbed; *seine – schonen,* take good care of o.s.; *naß bis auf die –,* wet to the skin; *bis in die –,* to the core, through and through; *er ist nichts als Haut und –,* he is a mere bag of bones, he is all skin and bones. **knochenartig,** *adj.* bony, osseous.

Knochen|band, *n.* ligament. **-bau,** *m.* skeleton, frame. **-beschreibung,** *f.* osteology, osteography. **-brand,** *m.* necrosis. **-bruch,** *m.* fracture. **-dünger,** *m.,* **-dungmehl,** *n.* bone manure. **knochen|dürr,** *adj.* *See* **-trocken. Knochen|-erweichung,** *f.* osteomalacia. **-fortsatz,** *m.* bony process, apophysis. **-fraß,** *m.* caries. **-fuge,** *f.* symphysis. **-gerüst,** *n.* skeleton, (*coll.*) (*of a p.*) living skeleton. **-gewebe,** *n.* bony tissue. **knochenhart,** *adj.* hard as rock *or* brick. **Knochen|-haus,** *n.* charnel-house. **-haut,** *f.* periosteum. **-hautentzündung,** *f.* periostitis. **-kohle,** *f.* animal charcoal, bone black. **-kunde, -lehre,** *f.* osteology. **-leim,** *m.* bone glue. **-mark,** *n.* marrow. **-markentzündung,** *f.* osteomyelitis. **-mehl,** *n.* bone-meal. **-mühle,** *f.* (*sl.*) 1. sweat-shop; 2. boneshaker. **-naht,** *f.* suture. **-öl,** *n.* neatsfoot oil. **-pfanne,** *f.* glenoid cavity. **-säure,** *f.* phosphoric acid. **-schwund,** *m.* atrophy of the bones. **knochentrocken,** *adj.* bone-dry, dry as a bone. **Knochenwuchs,** *m.* ossification.

knöcherig ['knœçərɪç], *adj.* (*of a p.*) bony, scraggy. **knöchern,** *adj.* (made of) bone, osseous.

knochig ['knɔxɪç], *adj.* bony, osseous; (*of a p.*) big-boned.

Knödel ['knø:dəl], *m.* (*dial.*) dumpling.

Knolle ['knɔlə], *f.,* **Knollen,** *m.* clod, lump; (*Cul.*) dumpling; protuberance, knot, knob, nodule; (*Bot.*) bulb, tuber. **knollenartig,** *adj.* bulbous, globular. **Knollen|fäule,** *f.* potato rot, tuber rot. **-gewächs,** *n.* bulbous plant. **-zwiebel,** *f.* corm. **knollig,** *adj.* knotty, knobby, lumpy, (*Bot.*) tuberous, bulbous.

Knopf [knɔpf], *m.* (**-es,** *pl.* **⸚e**) 1. button, knob, stud, boss, head (*of a pin*); pommel (*of sword*); *auf den – drücken,* press the button; (*coll.*) *Knöpfe haben,* be in the money; *übersponnene* or *überzogene Knöpfe,* covered buttons; (*coll.*) *den – auf dem Beutel halten,* keep one's hand on the purse-strings; (*Mil.*) *die Knöpfe bekommen,* be made a lance-corporal, get one's stripe; (*coll.*) *mit den Knöpfen herausrücken,* pay up; (*coll.*) *der – geht ihm auf,* the penny has dropped; 2. (*Austr.*) knot; 3. (*dial.*) bud; 4. (*Swiss*) dumpling; 5. (*coll.*) fellow, (*Am.*) guy.

knöpfen ['knœpfən], *v.t.* button; (*dial.*) tie (in a knot), knot. **Knöpfer,** *m.* button-hook.

Knopf|loch, *n.* buttonhole. **-nadel,** *f.* (*dial.*) pin. **-naht,** *f.* (*Surg.*) suture.

Knöpfschuh ['knœpfʃu:], *m.* buttoned shoe *or* boot.

Knopfsteuerung ['knɔpfʃtɔyəruŋ], *f.* push-button control.

Knöpf|stiefel, *m.* *See* **-schuh.**

knorke ['knɔrkə], *pred.adj.* (*no longer in current use*) (*coll.*) top-hole, first-rate, priceless, pukka, wizard, smashing.

Knorpel ['knɔrpəl], *m.* cartilage, gristle. **knorpelartig,** *adj.* gristly, cartilaginous. **Knorpel|band,** *n.* (*Anat.*) fibrocartilage, synchondrosis. **-gelenk,** *n.* (*Anat.*) cartilaginous joint, symphysis. **-haut,** *f.* (*Anat.*) perichondrium. **knorpelig,** *adj.* *See* **knorpelartig. Knorpelwerk,** *n.* (*Archit.*) scroll, volute.

Knorrbremse ['knɔrbrɛmzə], *f.* pneumatic brake.

Knorren ['knɔrən], *m.* knotty excrescence *or* protuberance; knot, gnarled branch, tree stump. **knorrig,** *adj.* knotty, knobby, gnarled, (*fig. of a p.*) coarse, uncouth.

Knorz [knɔrts], *m.* (**-es,** *pl.* **-e**) knot (*in wood*). **knorzig,** *adj.* knotty.

Knospe ['knɔspə], *f.* bud; burgeon, gemma, gemmule; *pl.* (*Archit.*) leafage (*of a capital*). **knospen,** *v.i.* bud, sprout, gemmate. **Knospen|behälter,** *m.* (*Bot.*) conceptacle. **-bildung,** *f.* gemmation. **knospentragend,** *adj.* gemmiferous.

Knötchen ['knø:tçən], *n.* nodule, little lump, pimple; tubercle. **Knötchenausschlag,** *m.* heat rash.

Knote ['kno:tə], *m.* (**-n,** *pl.* **-n**), *see* [1]**Knoten.**

[1]**Knoten** ['kno:tən], *m.* boor, clod-hopper, lout, (*Am.*) roughneck.

[2]**Knoten,** *m.* knot, (*Naut.*) hitch; (*Naut.*) knot (= *measure of speed*); bun (*of hair*); (*Bot.*) node, nodule, joint; (*Anat.*) condyle; (*Med.*) ganglion, growth, tubercle; (*fig.*) hitch, catch, rub, snag, tangle, difficulty; (*Theat.*) plot, intrigue; *zehn – laufen,* make ten knots; *einen – binden* or *knüpfen,* tie a knot; *einen – lösen,* undo *or* untie a knot; (*fig.*) solve a difficulty; (*fig.*) *den – durchhauen,* cut the knot; (*Theat.*) *Lösung des -s,* dénouement; (*Theat.*) *Schürzung des -s,* thickening of the plot, epitasis; (*coll.*) *da steckt der –,* there's the snag. **knoten,** *v.t., v.i.* knot, tie in a knot.

Knoten|ader, *f.* sciatic vein. **-leben,** *n.* (*sl.*) dissolute life. **-punkt,** *m.* nodal point; (*Railw.*) junction, intersection (*of roads*). **-stock,** *m.* knobbed stick, knotty stick. **-strick,** *m.* Franciscan's girdle. **-stück,** *n.* knot (*in wood*).

Knöterich ['knø:tərɪç], *m.* (*Bot.*) knotgrass, knotweed (*Polygonum aviculare*).

knotig [ˈkno:tɪç], *adj. See* **knorrig**; (*Bot.*) nodulated, nodular; 2. (*Med.*) tubercular; 3. (*fig.*) boorish, uncouth, coarse, vulgar.

Knubbe [ˈknubə], *f.* (*Austr.*) **Knubben,** *m.* knot (*in wood*). **knubbig,** *adj.* huge.

Knuff [knuf], *m.* (**-(e)s,** *pl.* **⸚e**) buffet, cuff, thump, push, nudge, shove. **knuffen,** *v.t.* cuff, buffet, pummel, pommel, thump; push, nudge, shove. **knuffig,** *adj.* (*coll.*) churlish, crusty, cross.

Knülch [knylç], *m.* (*sl.*) lout, boor.

knüll(e) [ˈknyl(ə)], *adj.* (*sl.*) drunk, soused. **knüllen,** *v.t.* crumple, crease, ruck. **Knüller,** *m.* (*coll.*) scoop, hit.

knüpfen [ˈknypfən], *v.t.* tie, knot; join, attach, fasten (*an* (*Acc.*), to); join, fasten, tie *or* knit together; (*fig.*) ***ein Bündnis* –,** form an alliance; (*fig.*) ***sich* – *an*** (*Acc.*), be connected *or* associated with; ***daran* – *sich keine Bedingungen,*** no conditions (are) attach(ed) to it.

Knüppel [ˈknypəl], *m.* 1. club, cudgel, truncheon; sculptor's *or* carpenter's mallet; billet (*of wood*), round timber, log; (*Metall.*) wire bar; ***der* – *liegt beim Hunde,*** there is no choice, that goes without saying; ***ihm einen* – *zwischen die Beine werfen,*** put difficulties in his way, put a spoke in his wheel; 2. (*Cul.*) French roll; 3. (*Av.*) joystick; 4. boor. **Knüppel|brücke,** *f.* corduroy bridge. **–damm,** *m.* corduroy road. **knüppeldick,** *adv.* (*coll.*) thick and fast; ***er bekam es* –,** it (= *misfortune*) has hit him good and proper; ***er hat es* – *hinter den Ohren,*** he is a thorough scoundrel; – ***voll,*** crammed full; ***ich hab's* –,** I'm sick (and tired) of it, I'm fed up (to the back teeth). **Knüppel|holz,** *n.* logs, faggots. **–regiment,** *n.* club law. **–steig, –weg,** *m. See* **–damm.**

knuppern [ˈknupərn], *v.t., v.i. See* **knabbern, knuspern.**

knurren [ˈknurən], *v.i.* growl, snarl; grumble, grunt; rumble (*of one's stomach*). **knurrig,** *adj.* growling, grumbling, disagreeable, snarling, irritable.

knusp(e)rig [ˈknusp(ə)rɪç], *adj.* crisp, crunchy, crackling; (*sl.*) ***ein* –*es Mädchen,*** a snappy piece, a nice bit of crackling *or* stuff. **knuspern,** *v.t.* nibble, crunch.

Knut [knu:t], *m.* (*Hist.*) Canute.

Knute [ˈknu:tə], *f.* knout; (*fig.*) terrorism; ***die* – *bekommen,*** be knouted. **knuten,** *v.t.* (lash with the) knout.

knutschen [ˈknu:tʃən], *v.t.* 1. crumple; 2. (*coll.*) cuddle, hug, pet, (*sl.*) neck, smooch.

Knutt [knut], *m.* (*Orn.*) knot (*Calidris canutus*).

Knüttel [ˈknytəl], *m.* cudgel, club, big stick. **Knüttel|reim, –vers,** *m.* doggerel.

knütten [ˈknytən], *v.t., v.i.* (*dial.*) knit.

Kobalt [ˈko:balt], *m.* cobalt. **Kobalt|blau,** *n.* cobalt blue, smalt. **–spiegel,** *m.* transparent cobalt ore. **–stahl,** *m.* (*Metall.*) high-speed steel. **–stufe,** *f.* piece of cobalt ore.

Kobel [ˈko:bəl], *m.* (*dial.*) shed, hut; dove-cote.

Koben [ˈko:bən], *m.* shed, hut; pigsty; pen, hen-coop.

Kober [ˈko:bər], *m.* (*dial.*) two-handled basket, hamper.

Kobold [ˈko:bɔlt], *m.* (**-(e)s,** *pl.* **-e**) goblin, hobgoblin, sprite, imp; (*Av. sl.*) gremlin.

Kobolz [ˈko:bɔlts], *m.* (*only in*) (*einen*) – ***schießen,*** go head over heels, turn a somersault.

Koch [kɔx], *m.* (**-es,** *pl.* **⸚e**) cook; (*Prov.*) ***viele Köche verderben den Brei,*** too many cooks spoil the broth; (*Prov.*) ***Hunger ist der beste* –,** hunger is the best sauce. **Koch|apfel,** *m.* cooking apple. **–birne,** *f.* stewing pear. **koch|beständig,** *adj. See* **–echt. Kochbuch,** *n.* cookery book. **kochecht,** *adj.* fast to boiling (*of dyes*).

kochen [ˈkɔxən], **1.** *v.i.* cook, boil, stew, be cooking, boiling *or* stewing; bubble up, seethe; ripen (*of grapes*); (*of a woman*) do the cooking; ***vor Wut* –,** boil *or* seethe with rage; ***sie kocht schlecht,*** she is a bad cook; ***gekochtes Obst,*** stewed fruit; (*Prov.*) ***es wird überall mit Wasser gekocht,*** people are the same everywhere; ***hier wird auch nur mit Wasser gekocht,*** you cannot expect the impossible; ***dieses Fleisch kocht sich gut,*** this meat stews well. **2.** *v.t.* cook, boil; stew (*fruit*), poach (*egg*), make (*tea etc.*). **Kochen,** *n.* cooking, boiling; ***zum* – *bringen,*** bring to the boil *or* (*Chem.*) to boiling-point; (*fig.*) bring to a head, rouse, inflame (*tempers, spirits etc.*). **kochend,** *adj.* boiling; seething, boiling (*rage*), raging, boiling (*surf*); – ***heiß,*** boiling *or* scalding hot. **Kocher,** *m.* cooker, boiler.

Köcher [ˈkœçər], *m.* quiver; golf-bag.

koch|fertig, *adj.* ready for the pot, (ready) prepared, instant. **–fest,** *adj. See* **–echt. Koch|fett,** *n.* cooking-fat, shortening. **–gefäß,** *n.* cooking vessel *or* pot. **–gelegenheit,** *f.* cooking facilities. **–gerät, –geschirr,** *n.* kitchen *or* cooking utensils, pots and pans, (*Mil.*) mess tin. **–herd,** *m.* kitchen-range, cooking-stove, cooker.

Köchin [ˈkœçɪn], *f.* (female)cook.

Koch|kessel, *m.* cauldron, copper, digester. **–kiste,** *f.* haybox. **–kunst,** *f.* culinary art. **–löffel,** *m.* ladle. **–nische,** *f.* kitchenette. **–obst,** *n.* fruit for stewing. **–platte,** *f.* hotplate. **–punkt,** *m.* boiling-point. **–salz,** *n.* table salt. **–schule,** *f.* school of cookery. **–topf,** *m.* cooking-pot, saucepan. **–vergütung,** *f.* (*Metall.*) ageing at 100° C. **–zeug,** *n.* kitchen utensils. **–zucker,** *m.* brown sugar.

koddrig [ˈkɔdrɪç], *adj.* (*dial.*) 1. shabby, scruffy, unkempt; 2. impudent, cheeky; (*vulg.*) ***–e Schnauze,*** insolence, big mouth; 3. ill, sick, queasy.

Köder [ˈkø:dər], *m.* bait, lure, decoy; ***auf den* – *anbeißen,*** rise to *or* take the bait. **ködern,** *v.t.* bait, lure, decoy, entice.

Kodex [ˈko:dɛks], *m.* (**-es,** *pl.* **-e** *or* **Kodices**) codex, old manuscript; code (*of laws*).

kodifizieren [kodifiˈtsi:rən], *v.t.* codify, systematize. **Kodifizierung,** *f.* codification.

Kodizill [kodiˈtsɪl], *n.* (**-s,** *pl.* **-e**) codicil.

Kofel [ˈko:fəl], *m.* (*dial.*) summit, knoll.

Kofen [ˈko:fən], *m.* (*dial.*) *see* **Koben.**

Kofent [ˈko:fɛnt], *m.* (**-s,** *pl.* **-e**) small *or* weak beer.

Koffein [kɔfeˈi:n], *n.* caffeine.

Koffer [ˈkɔfər], *m.* trunk, coffer, portmanteau, (suit-)case, bag, (*Am.*) grip. **Koffer|grammophon,** *n.* portable record player. **–raum,** *m.* luggage *or* (*Am.*) baggage compartment; (*Motor.*) boot (*Am.* trunk). **–zettel,** *m.* luggage label.

Kog [ˈko:k], *m.* (**-s,** *pl.* **⸚e**) *see* **Koog. Köge,** *pl. of* **Koog.**

Kohärenz [koheˈrɛnts], *f.* coherence. **kohärieren,** *v.i.* cohere. **kohärierend,** *adj.* cohesive. **Kohäsion** [–ziˈo:n], *f.* cohesion, cohesiveness. **Kohäsionskraft,** *f.* cohesive strength, cohesiveness.

Kohl [ko:l], *m.* (**-(es),** *pl.* **-e**) cabbage, kale; (*coll.*) rigmarole, stuff and nonsense, twaddle, bosh, rot, hooey; ***aufgewärmter* –,** same old story; (*coll.*) – ***machen,*** blunder; (*coll.*) ***das macht den* – *nicht fett,*** that doesn't help much; (*coll.*) ***schöne Worte machen den* – *nicht fett,*** fair words butter no parsnips. **Kohldampf,** *m.* (*sl.*) hunger; – ***schieben,*** be hungry.

Kohle [ˈko:lə], *f.* charcoal; coal; (*Chem.*) carbon; ***abgeschwefelte* –,** coke; ***ausgebrannte*** or ***ausgeglühte* –,** cinder; ***glimmende* –,** ember; ***glühende* –,** live coal; ***–n einnehmen,*** coal (*of ships*); ***zu* – *werden,*** become charred *or* carbonized; ***in* – *verwandeln,*** char, carbonize; (*fig.*) ***auf*** (***glühenden***) ***–n sein*** or ***sitzen,*** be on thorns *or* tenterhooks; (*B.*) ***feurige*** or (*coll.*) ***glühende –n auf sein Haupt sammeln,*** heap coals of fire on his head.

kohleartig [ˈko:ləartɪç], *adj.* (*Chem.*) carbonaceous. **Kohle|bürste,** *f.* (*Elec.*) carbon brush. **–hydrat,** *n.* (*Chem.*) carbohydrate. **–mikrophon,** *n.* (*Elec.*) carbon microphone.

[1]**kohlen** [ˈko:lən], **1.** *v.t., v.i.* char, carbonize. **2.** *v.i.* 1. make charcoal; blacken, turn black, burn badly (*of a cigar or wick*); 2. (*Naut.*) (take on) coal.

[2]**kohlen,** *v.i.* (*coll.*) talk rubbish *or* rot *or* bosh. (*See* **Kohl.**)

Kohlen|abbau, *m.* coal-mining. **-arbeiter,** *m.* coal-miner, pitman, collier. **-becken,** *n.* coalfield; brazier. **-behälter,** *m.* coal-bin. **-bergbau,** *m.* coal-mining (industry). **-bergwerk,** *n.* coal-mine, colliery. **-blende,** *f.* anthracite. **-brenner,** *m.* charcoal-burner. **-dampf, -dunst,** *m.* charcoal fumes. **-eimer,** *m.* coal-scuttle *or* bucket *or* box. **-fadenbirne,** *f.* carbon filament lamp. **-flöz,** *n.* coal-seam. **-gas,** *n.* coal gas; (*Motor.*) producer gas. **-gestübe,** *n.*, **-gries,** *m. See* **-grus. -grube,** *f.* coal-mine *or* -pit. **-grus,** *m.* slack, small coal. **kohlenhaltig,** *adj.* carboniferous, containing coal. **Kohlen|händler,** *m.* coal merchant, coalman. **-hauer,** *m.* face worker, pitman. **-hütte,** *f.* charcoal-kiln. **-kalk,** *m.* carboniferous limestone. **-kasten,** *m. See* **-eimer. -klein,** *n. See* **-grus.**

Kohlen|lager, *n.* (*Geol.*) coal seam; coal depot *or* dump. **-lösche,** *f.* coal-dust. **-luke,** *f.* (*Naut.*) coaling hatch. **-meiler,** *m.* charcoal pile. **-mulm,** *m. See* **-grus. -oxyd,** *n.* carbon monoxide. **-papier,** *n. See* **Kohlepapier. -revier,** *n.* coal-mining district. **kohlensauer,** *adj.* **-es** *Salz,* carbonate; **-es** *Soda,* carbonate of soda; **-er** *Kalk,* calcium carbonate; **-es** *Wasser,* aerated water. **Kohlen|säure,** *f.* carbonic acid. **-säuregas,** *n.* carbon dioxide. **kohlensäurehaltig,** *adj.* carbonated. **Kohlen|-schiefer,** *m.* bituminous shale. **-schiff,** *n.* collier, coal barge. **-schuppen,** *m.* coal-shed. **-station,** *f.* coaling-station. **-stift,** *m.* carbon (*for arc-lamp*). **-stoff,** *m.* carbon. **-stoffstahl,** *m.* (*Metall.*) carbon steel. **-wasserstoff,** *m.* hydrocarbon. **-zeche,** *f.* coal-pit, colliery.

Kohlepapier [ˈkoːləpapiːr], *n.* carbon paper.

Köhler [ˈkøːlər], *m. See* **Kohlenbrenner. Köhlerei** [–ˈraɪ], *f.* charcoal works. **Köhlerglaube,** *m.* (*coll.*) blind faith.

Kohle|stift, *m.* 1. charcoal pencil; 2. (*Elec.*) carbon. **-zeichnung,** *f.* charcoal drawing. **-zinksammler,** *m.* (*Elec.*) dry cell.

Kohl|garten, *m.* kitchen-garden. **-kopf,** *m.* head of cabbage, (*coll.*) duffer, blockhead. **-meise,** *f.* (*Orn.*) great tit(mouse) (*Parus major*). **kohl(pech)-(raben)schwarz,** *adj.* (*coll.*) coal- *or* jet-black, black as a crow.

Kohlrabi [koːlˈraːbi], *m.* (**-s,** *pl.* **-s**) kohlrabi.

Kohl|rübe, *f.* swede. **-weißling,** *m.* (*Ent.*) cabbage butterfly.

Kohorte [koˈhɔrtə], *f.* cohort.

Koitus [ˈkoːitus], *m.* coition, coitus, copulation.

Koje [ˈkoːjə], *f.* (*Naut.*) berth, bunk; stand, stall (*in a market etc.*).

Kokain [kokaˈiːn], *n.* cocaine.

Kokarde [koˈkardə], *f.* cockade.

Kokerei [koːkəˈraɪ], *f.* carbonization *or* coking plant.

kokett [koˈkɛt], *adj.* coquettish, flirtatious. **Kokette,** *f.* flirt, coquette, demi-monde. **Koketterie** [–təˈriː], *f.* coquetry, flirtation. **kokettieren** [–ˈtiːrən], *v.i.* (*of a woman*) be coquettish; (*fig.*) – *mit,* flirt *or* toy with (*s.th. extraneous, ideas etc.*), make a demonstration of, show off (*s.th. one owns*).

Kokille [koˈkɪlə], *f.* (ingot) mould, die. **Kokillenguß,** *m.* chill casting.

Kokon [koˈkɔ̃], *n.* (**-s,** *pl.* **-s**) cocoon.

Kokos|baum [ˈkoːkos–], *m.* coconut palm. **-faser,** *f.* coir, coconut fibre. **-fett,** *n.* coconut oil. **-nuß,** *f.* coconut. **-palme,** *f. See* **-baum.**

Koks [koːks], *m.* (**-es,** *pl.* **-e**) (*Austr. also f.*) 1. coke; 2. (*sl.*) (= ***Kokain***) snow; 3. (*sl.*) (= ***Geld***) dough.

Kolben [ˈkɔlbən], *m.* 1. club, mace, mallet; butt-end, butt (*of rifle*); burnisher; soldering-iron; (*Mech.*) piston; 2. (*Chem.*) flask, still, demijohn, retort, alembic; 3. (*Bot.*) spadix; 4. (*Ent.*) feeler; 5. immature stag's horn. **kolben,** *v.i.* grow horns (*as young stag*), develop a head (*as maize or rushes*).

Kolben|antrieb, *m.* piston drive. **-aufgang,** *m.* upstroke of a piston. **-bolzen,** *m.* (*Motor.*) gudgeon pin. **-ente,** *f.* (*Orn.*) red-crested pochard, (*Am.*) rufous-crested duck (*Netta rufina*). **-hub,** *m.* piston-stroke. **-kappe,** *f.* butt-plate (*of rifle*). **-niedergang,** *m.* down-stroke of the piston. **-schieber,** *m. See* **-ventil. -schlag,** *m. See* **-stoß. -spiel,** *n.* motion of the piston. **-stange,** *f.* piston-rod. **-stoß, -streich,** *m.* blow with a club *or* butt-end. **kolbentragend,** *adj.* (*Bot.*) spadiceous. **Kolben|träger,** *m.* 1. mace-bearer; 2. (*Chem.*) retort stand. **-ventil,** *n.* piston-valve. **-verdichter,** *m.* reciprocating compressor.

kolbig [ˈkɔlbɪç], *adj.* club-like; knotty, knobbly, nodular.

Kolchose [kɔlˈçoːzə], *f.* collective farm. **Kolchosenwirtschaft,** *f.* collective farming.

Kolibri [ˈkoːlibri], *m.* (**-s,** *pl.* **-s**) humming-bird.

kolieren [koˈliːrən], *v.t.* filter, strain. **Koliertuch,** *n.* filter, strainer.

Kolk [kɔlk], *m.* (**-(e)s,** *pl.* **-e**) (*dial.*) deep hole, depression, pool. **Kolkrabe,** *m.* (*Orn.*) raven (*Corvus corax*).

Kollaps [kɔˈlaps], *m.* (**-es,** *pl.* **-e**) (*Med.*) collapse, fainting fit.

kollationieren [kɔlatsioˈniːrən], *v.t.* collate, compare, check (off) against.

Kolleg [kɔˈleːk], *n.* (**-s,** *pl.* **-ien**) (course of) lectures; *see also* **Kollegium**; – ***halten*** or ***lesen,*** give (*or* deliver) a course of lectures, lecture (***über*** (*Acc.*), on); – ***hören,*** hear (*or* attend) a course of lectures *or* a lecture; – ***belegen,*** register for a course of lectures; – ***schinden,*** attend lectures without paying fees; – ***schwänzen,*** cut lectures; – ***testieren,*** testify to attendance at lectures; – ***nachschreiben,*** take (down) lecture notes.

Kollege [kɔˈleːgə], *m.* (**-n,** *pl.* **-n**) colleague; ***Herr*** – or ***Lieber*** –, *form of address in academic circles.*

Kolleg|geld, *n.* lecture-fee. **-heft,** *n.* lecture notebook.

kollegial [kɔleˈgjaːl], (*obs.*) **kollegialisch,** *adj.* friendly, loyal, as a good colleague. **Kollegialität** [–liˈtɛːt], *f.* esprit de corps among colleagues. **Kollegin** [–ˈleːgɪn], *f.* (lady) colleague.

Kollegium [kɔˈleːgium], *n.* (**-s,** *pl.* **-gien**) corporation, assembly, committee, council, board; teaching staff, (*Am.*) faculty.

Kollektaneen [kɔlɛkˈtaːneən], *pl.* literary gleanings, miscellany, collectanea. **Kollektaneenbuch,** *n.* commonplace-book.

Kollekte [kɔˈlɛktə], *f.* collection; flag day; (*Eccl.*) collect, short prayer.

kollektiv [kɔlɛkˈtiːf], *adv.* collective, joint. **Kollektiv|begriff,** *m.* (*Gram.*) collective. **-gesellschaft,** *f.* (*Comm.*) partnership. **kollektivieren** [–ˈviːrən], *v.t.* collectivize. **Kollektivismus** [–ˈvɪsmus], *m.* collectivism. **Kollektor** [–ˈlɛktɔr], *m.* (**-s,** *pl.* **-en**) (*Elec.*) commutator. **Kollektur** [–ˈtuːr], *f.* (-, *pl.* **-en**) (*Austr.*) assembly *or* collecting point, depot, dump.

[1]**Koller** [ˈkɔlər], *n.* jerkin, doublet; waistcoat; bodice.

[2]**Koller,** *m.* frenzy, rage, choler; giddiness, vertigo, (*Vet.*) staggers. **Kollergang,** *m.* crushing rollers. **kollern, 1.** *v.i.* (*Vet.*) have the staggers; rage, rave, storm; rumble (*abdominally*); coo (*of pigeons*); gobble (*of turkeys*); (*aux.* s.) roll (about). **2.** *v.t.* grind, crush. **Kollerstein,** *m.* millstone, roller.

Kollett [kɔˈlɛt], *n.* (**-(e)s,** *pl.* **-e** *or* (*dial.*) **-s**) *see* [1]**Koller.**

kollidieren [kɔliˈdiːrən], *v.i.* (*aux.* s.) come into collision (with), collide, clash, conflict (*as lectures etc. held at the same time, or opposing views*), be incompatible.

Kollier [kɔliˈeː], *n.* (**-s,** *pl.* **-s**) necklace.

kollieren [kɔˈliːrən], *v.t.* (*Bill.*) lay (*the ball*) under the cushion.

Kollo [ˈkɔlo], *n.* (**-s,** *pl.* **-s** *or* **Kolli**) (*obs.*) bale, package, parcel, bundle.

Kollodium [kɔˈloːdium], *n.* (*Chem.*) collodion.

Kolloquium [kɔˈloːkvium], *n.* (**-s,** *pl.* **-quien**) colloquy, discussion (group).

kolludieren [kɔluˈdiːrən], *v.i.* act in collusion with.

Köln [kœln], *n.* Cologne. **kölnisch,** *adj.* (of) Cologne.
Kolon ['ko:lɔn], *n.* (**-s,** *pl.* **-(s)**) (*Anat., Typ.*) colon.
Kolonel [kolo'nɛl], *f.* (*Typ.*) minion.
kolonial [koloni'a:l], *adj.* colonial. **Kolonial|minister,** *m.* Secretary of State for the Colonies, Colonial Secretary. **-ministerium,** *n.* Colonial Office. **-waren,** *f.pl.* grocery, groceries. **-warenhändler,** *m.* grocer, provision merchant. **-zucker,** *m.* cane sugar.
Kolonie [kolo'ni:], *f.* colony. **kolonisieren** [-'zi:rən], *v.t.* colonize. **Kolonist,** *m.* (**-en,** *pl.* **-en**) colonist, (colonial) settler.
Kolonne [ko'lɔnə], *f.* column, gang, crew (*of workers*); (*Pol.*) ***Mitglied der Fünften –,*** Fifth Columnist. **Kolonnen|gebiet,** *n.* (*Mil.*) rear area. **-staffel,** *f.* (*Mil.*) rear echelon. **-steller,** *m.* tabulator (*typewriter*).
Kolophonium [kolo'fo:nium], *n.* colophony, rosin.
Koloratur [kolora'tu:r], *f.* (**-,** *pl.* **-en**) (*Mus.*) coloratura; *pl.* grace-notes. **Koloratursängerin,** *f.* coloratura soprano, prima-donna.
kolorieren [kolo'ri:rən], *v.t.* colour, illuminate. **Kolorit,** *n.* (**-s,** *pl.* **-e**) colouring, hue, shade, colour-effect.
Koloß [ko'lɔs], *m.* (**-(ss)es,** *pl.* **-(ss)e**) colossus. **kolossal** [-'sa:l], **1.** *adj.* colossal, gigantic, huge, enormous; (*coll.*) ***er hat –es Schwein,*** he has fantastic luck. **2.** *adv.* (*coll.*) extremely, immensely; ***es freut mich –,*** I'm ever so pleased.
Kolportage [kɔlpɔr'ta:ʒə], *f.* door-to-door sale of books, colportage (*esp. of religious tracts*); sensational rubbish, popular trash (*of literature*). **Kolportageroman,** *m.* penny-dreadful, trashy novel, (*Am.*) dime-novel. **Kolporteur,** *m.* (**-s,** *pl.* **-e**) itinerant bookseller. **kolportieren,** *v.t.* hawk, sell in the street; (*fig.*) retail, spread (*news*).
[1]**Kolter** ['kɔltər], *m.* quilt, coverlet.
[2]**Kolter,** *n.* ploughshare.
Kolumne [ko'lumnə], *f.* (*Typ., Archit.*) column. **Kolumnen|maß,** *n.* (*Typ.*) type-scale *or* -rule. **-titel,** *m.* running head *or* title, heading, headline. **-ziffer,** *f.* (*Typ.*) folio.
Kombination [kɔmbinatsi'o:n], *f.* **1.** surmise, conclusion, inference, deduction, conjecture; **2.** combination, teamwork; **3.** scheme, project; **4.** combinations (*underwear*), overall, (*Av.*) flying-suit. **Kombinations|gabe,** *f.* acumen, perspicacity, discernment, (*coll.*) gumption, mother-wit. **-lehre,** *f.* (*Math.*) (permutations and) combinations. **-schloß,** *n.* combination lock. **-spiel,** *n.* good combination, teamwork.
kombinieren [kɔmbi'ni:rən], *v.t., v.i.* **1.** combine; **2.** surmise, conclude, infer, deduce, conjecture.
Kombiwagen ['kɔmbiva:gən], *m.* (*coll.*) estate car, station wagon.
Kombüse [kɔm'by:zə], *f.* (*Naut.*) galley, caboose.
Komet [ko'me:t], *m.* (**-en,** *pl.* **-en**) comet. **Kometen|bahn,** *f.* orbit of a comet. **-schweif,** *m.* tail of a comet.
Komfort [kɔm'fo:r, -'fɔrt], *m.* (**-(e)s,** *no pl.*) ease, luxury. **komfortabel** [-'ta:bəl], *adj.* luxurious, comfortable. **Komfortwohnung,** *f.* luxury-flat.
Komik ['ko:mɪk], *f.* comicality; fun, humour, funny ways. **Komiker,** *m.* comedian, comedy turn; comic writer. **Komikerin,** *f.* comedienne. **komisch,** *adj.* comic(al), funny, humorous, droll; funny, peculiar, queer, strange; ***ein –er Kauz,*** a queer fish; ***–es Epos,*** mock-heroic *or* burlesque epic; ***–e Oper,*** comic opera.
Komitat [komi'ta:t], *m. or n.* (**-(e)s,** *pl.* **-e**) **1.** suite, attendance; **2.** (*in Hungary*) county.
Komitee [komi'te:], *n.* (**-s,** *pl.* **-s**) committee, board.
Komma ['kɔma], *n.* (**-s,** *pl.* **-s** *or* **-ta** [-'ma:tə]) (*Typ.*) comma, (*Math.*) decimal point; ***sechs – zwei,*** six point two; ***null – sechs,*** point six.
Kommandant [kɔman'dant], *m.* (**-en,** *pl.* **-en**) commander (*of a ship*), commandant (*of a garrison*). **Kommandantur** [-'tu:r], *f.* commandant's office, garrison headquarters. **Kommandeur** [-'dø:r], *m.* (**-s,** *pl.* **-e**) commanding officer, officer commanding (*of military unit*). **kommandieren,** *v.t., v.i.* give orders, be in command (of).
Kommanditär [kɔmandi'tɛ:r], *m.* (**-s,** *pl.* **-e**) (*Comm.*) **1.** branch manager; **2.** (*Swiss*) *see* **Kommanditist. Kommandite** [-'di:tə], *f.* branch establishment. **Kommanditgesellschaft,** *f.* limited partnership; company in which liability of one partner is limited (*in commendum*). **Kommanditist** [-'tɪst], *m.* (**-en,** *pl.* **-en**) partner with limited liability. **Kommanditsumme,** *f.* amount for which limited partner is liable.
Kommando [kɔ'mando], *n.* (**-s,** *pl.* **-s**) **1.** (word of) command, order; (*coll.*) ***wie auf –,*** with one accord; **2.** command, headquarters; **3.** squad, detail, detachment. **Kommando|brücke,** *f.* (*Naut.*) bridge. **-gerät,** *n.* (anti-aircraft) predictor. **-pfeife,** *f.* (*Naut.*) boatswain's whistle. **-stand,** *m.* (anti-aircraft) command post. **-trupp,** *m.* (*Mil.*) task force, raiding party. **-truppe,** *f.* (*Mil.*) Commandos. **-turm,** *m.* (*Av.*) control tower, (*Naut.*) fighting top, (*submarine*) conning tower. **-wagen,** *m.* (*Mil.*) command car.
kommen ['kɔmən], *irr.v.i.* (*aux.* s.) come, arrive; approach, draw near; come to pass, come about, arise, occur, happen, take place.
(a) (*with adv.*) ***abhanden –,*** get lost *or* mislaid; ***sie sind mir abhanden gekommen,*** I have lost *or* mislaid them; ***es kann nicht anders – als daß er . . .,*** he cannot (help) but . . .; ***es wird noch ganz anders –,*** there is still worse to come; ***es kommt bloß daher da . . .,*** it is entirely due to the (fact that) . . .; ***wie es gerade kommt,*** as the case may be, just as it turns out; ***hierzu kommt noch daß . . .,*** added to it that, in addition; ***wenn es hoch kommt,*** at the most; ***zu kurz –,*** come off the loser; ***. . . daß es soweit – konnte, . . .*** that things could get so bad; ***spät –,*** be late; ***weit – mit,*** get far with; ***es ist weit mit ihm gekommen,*** he has fallen *or* sunk very low, he has come to a pretty pass; ***weit –,*** have made good *or* great progress; ***weiter –,*** get on, advance, (make) progress.
(b) (*with imp. sub.*) ***es kommt ein Gewitter,*** a storm is brewing; ***es mag – was (da) will,*** come what may, whatever happens; ***es kann – daß . . .,*** it is possible that . . .; ***wie(so)*** or ***woher kommt es daß . . .,*** how is it *or* how do you explain it that . . .
(c) (*with Dat. of p.*) ***mir kam der Gedanke,*** it occurred to me, the thought crossed my mind; ***das kommt ihm gerade recht,*** that suits him perfectly *or* admirably; (*coll.*) ***komm mir nicht so!*** don't speak to me like that! don't treat me in this way! (*coll.*) ***der soll mir wieder –!*** just let him show his face here again!
(d) (*with lassen*) ***ihn – lassen,*** send for him; ***es – lassen,*** have it sent *or* brought, order it.
(e) (*with p.p.*) ***gegangen, gelaufen, gefahren*** or ***geritten etc. –,*** come on foot, come running *or* driving *or* riding *etc.*; ***wie gerufen –,*** come opportunely.
(f) (*with prep.*) ***– an*** (*Acc.*), get *or* come to, arrive at, reach; *see under* **Bettelstab, Land, Licht, Reihe, Stelle, Ufer, Unrechten**; ***– auf*** (*Acc.*), (come to) think of, hit upon; (come to) mention, touch upon; remember; (*of amounts*) amount *or* come to, add up to, total; ***wie kommst du darauf?*** what put that idea into your head? ***darauf wäre er nie gekommen,*** it would never have occurred to him; (*coll.*) ***ich lasse auf dich nichts –,*** I'll stand by you, I'll take your part, I'll back you to the hilt; *see also* **Gedanke, Kosten, Spur, Welt**; ***aus der Mode –,*** go out of fashion; *see also* **Auge**; ***außer Atem –,*** get out of breath; *see also* **Fassung**; ***hinter das Geheimnis –,*** penetrate the secret; ***hinter seine Schliche –,*** see through his tricks; ***hinter die Wahrheit –,*** discover *or* (*coll.*) get at the truth; ***– in*** (*Acc.*), go *or* come *or* get into, enter; ***in Bewegung –,*** get moving *or* going *or* under way; (*Naut.*) ***in Fahrt –,*** get under way; ***in andere Hände –,*** pass into other hands; ***in den Himmel –,*** go to heaven; *see also* **Betracht, Frage, Gang, Gerede, Kehle, klar, Lage, Quere, rein, Schule, Schwung, Sinn, Verfall,**

Verlegenheit, Weg, Woche; (*coll.*) – *Sie mir nicht damit!* don't you come that one on me! I'll have none of that! – *nach,* get to; *nach Hause* –, get home; – *über* (*Acc.*), fall upon, (*fig.*) befall, be seized with; *see also* **Lippe, Schwelle**; – *um,* lose, be deprived of, (*coll.*) be done *or* cheated out of; *see also* **Leben**; *unter die Leute* –, mix with *or* meet people; (*of news*) be spread abroad, be made known, (*coll.*) get around; – *von,* come from, be due to, be caused by; *see also* **Fleck, Kraft, Seite, Sinn, Stelle**; *du sollst mir nicht wieder vor die Augen* –, I never want to see you again; – *zu,* come by, get hold of (*a th.*); find time for, (*coll.*) get round to; *zur Ansicht* –, come to the view *or* conclusion; *zur Beratung* –, come up for discussion; (*coll.*) *wie kommst du dazu!* you've got a cheek! *zu nichts* –, come to nothing; *zu sich* –, recover one's senses, (*coll.*) come round; *see also* **Atem, Besinnung, Fall, Ohr, Rede, Ruhe, Sprache, Treffen, Vermögen, Verwendung, Vorschein, Wort.**

Kommen, *n.* coming, arrival, (*Poet.*) advent; *das – und Gehen,* coming(s) and going(s). **kommend,** *adj.* coming, approaching, future; *–e Generation,* future *or* rising generation; *–e Woche,* next week; *in den –en Wochen,* in the weeks to come.

Kommende [kɔˈmɛndə], *f.* prebend.

Komment [kɔˈmã], *m.* (**-s,** *pl.* **-s**) students' customs; code of corporate behaviour, Bacchanalian ritual (*among German students*); (*sl.*) – *reiten,* be a stickler for formality.

Kommentar [kɔmɛnˈtaːr], *m.* (**-s,** *pl.* **-e**) commentary. **kommentieren,** *v.t.* comment (up)on; annotate.

Kommers [kɔˈmɛrs], *m.* (**-es,** *pl.* **-e**) students' festive gathering; drinking session. **Kommers|-buch,** *n.* students' song book. **–lied,** *n.* students' song.

Kommerz [kɔˈmɛrts], *m.* commerce. **kommerzialisieren** [–ialiˈziːrən], *v.t.* convert into a negotiable loan. **kommerziell** [–iˈɛl], *adj.* commercial.

Kommilitone [kɔmiliˈtoːnə], *m.* (**-n,** *pl.* **-n**) fellow-student.

Kommis [kɔˈmiː], *m.* (-, *pl.* -) clerk, salesman, (*Am.*) salesclerk.

Kommiß, *m.* (**-(ss)es,** *no pl.*) (*coll.*) army life, soldiering, (*sl.*) spit and polish; (*coll.*) *er ist beim* –, he is a soldier.

Kommissar [kɔmɪˈsaːr], (*Austr.*) **Kommissär,** *m.* (**-s,** *pl.* **-e**) commissary, commissioner, (*Russia*) commissar; police inspector. **Kommissariat** [–riˈaːt], *n.* (**-s,** *pl.* **-e**) territory *or* office of commissioner, (*dial.*) police station. **kommissarisch,** *adj.* provisional.

Kommiß|brot, *n.* (*sl.*) army bread. **–hengst,** *m.* disciplinarian, martinet.

Kommission [kɔmɪsiˈoːn], *f.* 1. commission, committee *or* board of inquiry; *eine – berufen* or *ernennen,* appoint *or* set up a commission; 2. commission, order; *eine – erteilen,* give an order; 3. commission, percentage. **Kommissionär** [–ˈnɛːr], *m.* (**-s,** *pl.* **-e**) factor, (commission) agent. **Kommissions|bericht,** *m.* report of a commission. **–buch,** *n.* order-book. **–gebühr,** *f.* commission (charges), percentage. **–geschäft,** *n.* commission business, business on commission.

Kommittent [kɔmɪˈtɛnt], *m.* (**-en,** *pl.* **-en**) (*Comm.*) person *or* party giving an order; employer of an agent (*commission business*), consignor.

kömmlich [ˈkœmlɪç], *adj.* (*dial.*) convenient, comfortable.

kommod [kɔˈmoːt], *adj.* (*coll.*) comfortable, cosy, snug. **Kommode,** *f.* chest of drawers, tallboy.

kömmst [kœmst], **kömmt,** (*dial.*) *see* **kommen.**

kommunal [kɔmuˈnaːl], *adj.* communal, municipal. **Kommunal|beamte(r),** *m., f.* local (government) official, municipal employee. **–steuer,** *f.* (local) rate(s).

Kommune [kɔˈmuːnə], *f.* 1. commune, municipality; 2. (*pej.*) the Reds *or* Commies.

Kommunikant [kɔmuniˈkant], *m.* (**-en,** *pl.* **-en**) (*Eccl.*) communicant. **Kommunion,** *f.* (*Eccl.*) (holy) communion.

Kommunismus [kɔmuˈnɪsmus], *m.* communism. **Kommunist,** *m.* (**-en,** *pl.* **-en**) communist. **kommunistisch,** *adj.* communist(ic).

kommunizieren [kɔmuniˈtsiːrən], *v.i.* communicate, partake of *or* receive the sacrament.

Komödiant [komødiˈant], *m.* (**-en,** *pl.* **-en**) comedian; actor; (*fig.*) play-actor, buffoon, clown, humbug. **Komödiantin,** *f.* comedienne, actress. **Komödie** [–ˈmøːdiə], *f.* comedy; play, (*fig.*) farce; (*fig.*) – *spielen,* put on an act, play-act.

Kompagnie [kɔmpaˈniː], *f.* (*Mil.*) company squadron; (*Comm.*) company. **Kompagnie|-chef, –führer,** *m.* company commander. **–geschäft,** *n.* joint-business, partnership. **–mutter,** *f.* (*sl.*) sergeant.

Kompagnon [kɔmpaˈnjɔ̃], *m.* (**-s,** *pl.* **-s**) partner, associate; *stiller* –, sleeping ((*Am.*) silent) partner.

kompakt [kɔmˈpakt], *adj.* compact, solid. **Kompaktheit,** *f.* compactness, solidity.

Kompanie, *See* **Kompagnie.**

Komparation [kɔmparatsiˈoːn], *f.* (*Gram.*) comparison.

Komparse [kɔmˈparzə], *m.* (**-n,** *pl.* **-n**) (*Theat.*) super(numerary). **Komparserie** [–ˈriː], *f.* mute actors, supers.

Kompaß [ˈkɔmpas], *m.* (**-(ss)es,** *pl.* **-(ss)e**) compass. **Kompaß|häuschen,** *n.* binnacle. **–peilung,** *f.* compass bearing. **–strich,** *m.* point of the compass.

Kompensation [kɔmpɛnzatsiˈoːn], *f.* compensation. **Kompensations|abkommen,** *n.* barter arrangement. **–geschäft,** *n.* barter.

kompetent [kɔmpeˈtɛnt], *adj.* competent, responsible, authoritative. **Kompetenz,** *f.* competence; competency, jurisdiction; – *eines Falliten,* bankrupt's allowance. **Kompetenzstreit,** *m.* question of jurisdiction.

Kompilator [kɔmpiˈlaːtor], *m.* (**-s,** *pl.* **-en**) compiler. **kompilieren,** *v.t.* compile.

Komplementär [kɔmplemɛnˈtɛːr], *m.* (*Comm*) unlimited partner (of company '*in commendam*'). **Komplementär|farbe,** *f.* complementary colour. **–winkel,** *m.* complement of an angle.

Komplet [kɔmˈpleːt], *n.* (**-s,** *pl.* **-s**) (*Dressm.*) ensemble.

komplett [kɔmˈplɛt], *adj.* complete, all included; *–es Frühstück,* full breakfast.

Komplex [kɔmˈplɛks], *m.* (**-es,** *pl.* **-e**) complex; aggregate, entirety; block (*of houses*).

Komplice [kɔmˈpliːtsə], *m.* (**-n,** *pl.* **-n**) accomplice, accessory.

Kompliment [kɔmpliˈmɛnt], *n.* (**-s,** *pl.* **-e**) compliment; greeting; bow, obeisance; **keine –e!** no ceremony! **komplimentieren** [–ˈtiːrən], *v.t.* pay one's compliments *or* respects to.

Komplize, *m. See* **Komplice. komplizieren** [kɔmpliˈtsiːrən], *v.t.* complicate. **kompliziert,** *adj.* complicated, intricate, complex; (*Med.*) *–er Bruch,* compound fracture. **Kompliziertheit,** *f.* complexity.

Komplott [kɔmˈplɔt], *n.* (**-(e)s,** *pl.* **-e**) plot, conspiracy; *ein – schmieden,* hatch a plot, conspire (together).

Komponente [kɔmpoˈnɛntə], *f.* component, ingredient, constituent.

komponieren [kɔmpoˈniːrən], *v.t., v.i.* compose, set to music. **Komponist,** *m.* (**-en,** *pl.* **-en**), (*Austr.*) **Kompositeur** [–poziˈtøːr], *m.* (**-s,** *pl.* **-e**) composer. **Komposition** [–zitsiˈoːn], *f.* 1. (*Mus.*) composition, composing; 2. (*Typ.*) make-up, layout.

Kompositum [kɔmˈpɔzitum], *n.* (**-s,** *pl.* **-ta**) (*Gram.*) compound.

Kompott [kɔmˈpɔt], *n.* (**-s,** *pl.* **-e**) stewed *or* preserved fruit.

Kompresse [kɔmˈprɛsə], *f.* compress, poultice.

Komprette [kɔmˈprɛtə], *f.* pill, tablet.

komprimierbar [kɔmpri'mi:rba:r], *adj.* compressible. **komprimieren,** *v.t.* compress, condense.

Kompromiß [kɔmpro'mɪs], *m. or n.* **(-(ss)es,** *pl.* **-(ss)e)** compromise. **kompromittieren** [–'ti:rən], **1.** *v.t.* compromise. **2.** *v.r.* commit *or* compromise o.s.

Komteß [kɔm'tɛs], *f.* (-, *pl.* **-(ss)en), Komtesse,** *f.* countess, daughter of a count.

Komtur [kɔm'tu:r], *m.* **(-s,** *pl.* **-e)** (Grand) Commander (of an order). **Komturei** [–'raɪ], *f.* estate (under jurisdiction) of a knightly order.

Kondensator [kɔndɛn'za:tɔr], *m.* **(-s,** *pl.* **-en)** (*Elec., Rad.*) capacitor, condenser. **kondensieren,** *v.t.* condense. **Kondensierung,** *f.* condensation.

Kondens|milch [kɔn'dɛns–], *f.* condensed *or* evaporated *or* tinned milk. **–streifen,** *m.* (*Av.*) vapour trail. **–wasser,** *n.* condensed water, water of condensation.

Kondition [kɔndɪtsi'o:n], *f.* condition, stipulation; (*coll.*) situation; (*obs.*) ***in – gehen,*** enter service. **konditionieren, 1.** *v.t.* condition. **2.** *v.i.* (*obs.*) ***bei ihm –,*** be in his employment.

Konditor [kɔn'di:tɔr], *m.* **(-s,** *pl.* **-en)** pastry-cook, confectioner. **Konditorei** [–'raɪ], *f.* confectioner's shop. **Konditoreiwaren,** *pl.* confectionery.

Kondolenz [kɔndo'lɛnts], *f.* (-, *pl.* **-en)** condolence. **Kondolenz|besuch,** *m.* visit of condolence. **–brief,** *m.* letter of condolence. **kondolieren,** *v.i.* condole (with), express one's sympathy (with).

Kondom [kɔn'do:m], *m.* **(-s,** *pl.* **-s)** condom, rubber sheath, contraceptive.

Kondukt [kɔn'dukt], *m.* **(-(e)s,** *pl.* **-e)** funeral train, cortège. **Kondukteur** [–'tø:r], *m.* **(-s,** *pl.* **-e)** (*Swiss, Austr.*) (tram *or* bus) conductor. **Konduktor,** *m.* **(-s,** *pl.* **-en)** (electrical) conductor.

Konfekt [kɔn'fɛkt], *n.* **(-(e)s,** *pl.* **-e)** confectionery, chocolates, sweets, sweetmeats, (*Am.*) candy.

Konfektion [kɔnfɛktsi'o:n], *f.* ready-made clothes. **Konfektionär** [–'nɛ:r], *m.* **(-s,** *pl.* **-e)** outfitter, clothier. **Konfektions|artikel,** *m.pl. See* **Konfektion. –geschäft,** *n.* ready-made clothier's. **–waren,** *f.pl. See* **Konfektion.**

Konferenz [kɔnfe'rɛnts], *f.* (-, *pl.* **-en)** conference. **konferieren,** *v.i.* confer (together) (***über*** (*Acc.*), on), hold talks, meet for talks, go into conference (about), deliberate, discuss.

Konfession [kɔnfɛsi'o:n], *f.* confession (of faith), creed; denomination. **konfessionell** [–'nɛl], *adj.* confessional, denominational. **konfessionslos,** *adj.* undenominational.

Konfirmand [kɔnfɪr'mant], *m.* **(-en,** *pl.* **-en)** candidate for confirmation. **Konfirmandenunterricht,** *m.* confirmation classes. **Konfirmandin,** *f. See* **Konfirmand. konfirmieren,** *v.t.* confirm.

konfiszieren [kɔnfɪs'tsi:rən], *v.t.* confiscate, appropriate, sequester, seize. **Konfiszierung,** *f.* confiscation, appropriation, sequestration, seizure.

Konfitüre [kɔnfi'ty:rə], *f.* (*usu. pl.*) jam, marmalade, preserves; sweetmeats, confectionery.

Konflikt [kɔn'flɪkt], *m.* **(-(e)s,** *pl.* **-e)** conflict, controversy; ***in – geraten,*** come into conflict.

Konföderation [kɔnføderatsi'o:n], *f.* confederacy.

konform [kɔn'fɔrm], *adj.* in conformity, coinciding, uniform, in agreement (*mit or Dat.*, with), conforming, conformable, corresponding (to).

konfrontieren [kɔnfrɔn'ti:rən], *v.t.* confront, face, bring face to face (*mit,* with).

konfus [kɔn'fu:s], *adj.* (*of a p.*) puzzled, muddle-headed, (*of a p. or th.*) in confusion, confused, muddled.

kongenial [kɔngeni'a:l], *adj.* congenial, like-minded.

Konglomerat [kɔnglomə'ra:t], *n.* **(-(e)s,** *pl.* **-e)** (*Geol.*) conglomerate; (*fig.*) conglomeration, aggregation, accumulation, lump, mass.

Kongreß [kɔn'grɛs], *m.* **(-(ss)es,** *pl.* **-(ss)e)** congress, convention. **Kongreß|mitglied,** *n.* member of congress, (*Am.*) Congressman. **–polen,** *n.* (*Hist.*) Russian Poland (1815–1918).

Kongruenz [kɔngru'ɛnts], *f.* congruity, perfect equality; (*Math.*) congruence, isometry. **kongruieren,** *v.i.* agree; (*Math.*) coincide, be congruent.

König ['kø:nɪç], *m.* **(-s,** *pl.* **-e)** 1. king; (*Eccl.*) ***die heilige drei –e,*** the three Magi; (*B.*) ***das erste Buch der –e,*** the first book of Kings; ***zum – machen*** or ***einsetzen,*** make *or* create king, raise to the throne; ***des –s Rock,*** the king's uniform; 2. (*Chem.*) regulus.

Königin ['kø:nɪgɪn], *f.* queen. **Königin|mutter,** *f.* queen mother. **–suppe,** *f.* (*Cul.*) cream of chicken soup. **–witwe,** *f.* queen dowager.

königlich ['kø:nɪklɪç], **1.** *adj.* royal, kingly, queenly, regal, sovereign; ***–e Hoheit,*** Royal Highness; ***– Gesinnte(r),*** royalist. **2.** *adv.* (*coll.*) ***sich – freuen,*** be as happy as a sandboy *or* as pleased as Punch; (*coll.*) ***sich – amüsieren,*** enjoy o.s. immensely. **Königliche,** *pl.* Royalists. **Königreich,** *n.* kingdom, realm.

königsblau ['kø:nɪçsblau], *adj.* royal blue. **Königs|hof,** *m.* royal palace *or* court. **–kerze,** *f.* (*Bot.*) mullein (*Verbascum thrapsus*). **–krankheit,** *f.* king's evil, scrofula. **–krone,** *f.* 1. royal crown; 2. (*Bot.*) crown imperial. **–mord,** *m.* regicide. **–mörder,** *m.* regicide. **–schießen,** *n.* (rifle) shooting competition. **–schuß,** *m.* best shot. **–sitz,** *m.* throne; royal seat *or* residence. **–sohn,** *m.* prince of royal blood. **–tiger,** *m.* (*Zool.*) Bengal tiger. **königstreu.** *adj.* loyal to the throne. **Königs|treue(r),** *m., f.* royalist, loyalist. **–wasser,** *n.* (*Chem.*) aqua regia. **–weihe,** *f.* (*Orn.*) *see* ***roter Milan.*** **–würde,** *f.* royal dignity; kingship.

Königtum ['kø:nɪçtu:m], *n.* kingship, royalty; monarchical principle; ***– von Gottes Gnaden,*** kingship by divine right *or* by divine grace.

konisch ['ko:nɪʃ], *adj.* conical, tapered. **Konizität** [–nɪtsi'tɛ:t], *f.* taper.

Konjugation [kɔnjugatsi'o:n], *f.* conjugation. **kongjugieren** [–'gi:rən], *v.t.* conjugate.

Konjunktiv ['kɔnjuŋkti:f], *m.* **(-s,** *pl.* **-e)** subjunctive (mood).

Konjunktur [kɔnjuŋk'tu:r], *f.* business outlook *or* trend, trade cycle, industrial fluctuation, state of business; (*coll.*) prosperity, boom; (*fig.*) ***die günstige – ausnützen,*** make the most of a favourable opportunity; ***sinkende –,*** trade recession, depression, slump. **Konjunktur|bericht,** *m.* economic survey. **–bewegung,** *f.* economic trend, trade cycle. **–forschung,** *f.* market research. **–gewinn,** *m.* market *or* competitive profit. **–ritter,** *m.* (*coll.*) big time operator, profiteer. **–schwankung,** *f.* (*usu. pl.*) market fluctuation. **–verkauf,** *m.* seasonal sale. **–verlauf,** *m. See* **–bewegung.**

konkav [kɔn'ka:f], *adj.* concave. **konkavkonvex,** *adj.* concavo-convex.

Konkordat [kɔnkɔr'da:t], *n.* **(-(e)s,** *pl.* **-e)** concordat, treaty between (R.C.) Church and State.

konkret [kɔn'kre:t], *adj.* concrete; tangible, actual, real; ***– gesprochen,*** in factual terms.

Konkubinat [kɔnkubi'na:t], *m. or n.* **(-(e)s,** *pl.* **-e)** concubinage.

Konkurrent [kɔnku'rɛnt], *m.* **(-en,** *pl.* **-en)** competitor, rival; (*Spt.*) contestant. **Konkurrenz,** *f.* (-, *pl.* **-en)** competition; rivalry, opposition; competitors, rivals; ***– machen,*** compete, enter into competition (*Dat.*, with). **konkurrenzfähig,** *adj.* able to compete, competitive. **konkurrenzieren** [–'tsi:rən], *v.i.* (*Swiss, Austr.*) *see* **konkurrieren. Konkurrenz|geschäft,** *n.* rival firm, business competitor. **–kampf,** *m.* (business) competition, (trade) rivalry. **konkurrenzlos,** *adj.* unrivalled, unchallenged, matchless. **Konkurrenz|neid,** *m.* professional jealousy. **–preis,** *m.* competitive price. **–prüfung,** *f.* competitive examination.

konkurrieren [kɔnku'ri:rən], *v.i.* compete (*mit,* with), rival. **konkurrierend,** *adj.* competitive.

Konkurs [kɔn'kurs], *m.* **(-es,** *pl.* **-e)** bankruptcy, insolvency, failure; ***es ist ein – eröffnet worden,*** a fiat of bankruptcy has been issued; ***Erkennung des –es,*** judicial assignment of an insolvent's property; ***in – gehen*** or ***geraten,*** go bankrupt, become insolvent, fail; – ***anmelden,*** declare o.s. bankrupt; – ***erklären,*** file a petition in bankruptcy. **Konkurs|behörde,** *f.* commission of bankruptcy. **–erklärung,** *f.* declaration of insolvency. **–eröffnung,** *f.* opening of bankruptcy proceedings. **–forderung,** *f.* claim against a bankrupt's estate. **–gericht,** *n.* court of bankruptcy. **–masse,** *f.* bankrupt's assets *or* estate. **–verfahren,** *n.* proceedings in bankruptcy. **–verwalter,** *m.* (creditor's) trustee in bankruptcy; official receiver, liquidator, (*Am.*) judicial factor.

können ['kœnən], **1.** *irr.v.t.* know, understand (*how to do*), be proficient in, have skill in, know how to, be able to; ***er kann nichts,*** he knows nothing; he can do nothing; ***er kann nichts dafür,*** he can't help it, it isn't his fault; (*coll.*) ***laufe was du kannst,*** run as fast as you can; ***Englisch –,*** have command of *or* know English. **2.** *irr.v.i.* **(a)** (*ability*) be able (to), be capable (of); **(b)** (*permission*) be allowed *or* permitted (to), be in a position (to); **(c)** (*possibility*) may; ***nicht –,*** be unable (to), be incapable (of); ***es kann sein,*** it is possible, it may be; ***ich kann mich irren,*** I may be mistaken; ***ich konnte nicht anders als,*** I could not (help) but; I couldn't do otherwise than; ***ich kann nicht umhin zu bemerken,*** I cannot help *or* avoid remarking; ***ich kann nicht mehr,*** I can do no more, I can't go on, I'm at the end of my tether; I am quite knocked up, I am all in; ***ich tue was ich kann,*** I'm doing my best, I'm doing all I can; ***nicht weiter –,*** be at a standstill; ***man kann hoffen,*** it is to be hoped.

Können, *n.* ability, faculty, knowledge, power, skill, efficiency. **Könner,** *m.* adept, expert, master (hand); very able man, master-mind.

Konnex [kɔ'nɛks], *m.* **(-es,** *pl.* **-e)** connection, relation; nexus. **Konnexion** [–si'o:n], *f.* (*usu. pl.*) ***–en haben,*** have influential contacts *or* connections *or* friends.

Konnossement [kɔnɔsə'mɛnt, –'mã], *n.* **(-(e)s,** *pl.* **-e)** (*Comm.*) bill of lading.

konnte ['kɔntə], **konntest,** *see* **können.**

Konrektor ['kɔnrɛktɔr], *m.* **(-s,** *pl.* **-en)** deputy *or* assistant headmaster.

Konsens [kɔn'zɛns], *m.* **(-es,** *pl.* **-e)** consent, assent, approval.

konsequent [kɔnze'kvɛnt], *adj.* consistent, (*Log.*) consequent; thoroughgoing, persistent; ***–er Naturalismus,*** thoroughgoing naturalism. **Konsequenz,** *f.* **(-,** *pl.* **-en)** consistency; result, consequence; ***die –en tragen,*** accept responsibility, acknowledge *or* take the consequences; ***die –en ziehen,*** draw one's conclusions, act accordingly.

Konservator [kɔnzɛr'va:tɔr], *m.* **(-s,** *pl.* **-en)** keeper, curator (*of museum*).

Konservatorist [kɔnzɛrvato'rɪst], *m.* **(-en,** *pl.* **-en)** music student. **Konservatorium** [–'to:rium], *n.* **(-s,** *pl.* **-rien)** conservatoire, academy of music.

Konserve [kɔn'zɛrvə], *f.* tinned *or* (*Am.*) canned food. **Konserven|büchse, –dose,** *f.* can, tin. **–fabrik,** *f.* tinning factory, cannery. **–glas,** *n.* preserving jar. **–musik,** *f.* (*coll.*) canned music. **–verpflegung,** *f.* (*Mil.*) tinned rations.

konservieren [kɔnzɛr'vi:rən], *v.t.* conserve, preserve, keep; tin, can (*food*). **Konservierung,** *f.* preservation; tinning, canning. **Konservierungsmittel,** *n.* preservative.

Konsignant [kɔnzɪɡ'nant], *m.* **(-en,** *pl.* **-en)** (*Comm.*) consignor. **Konsignatar** [–'ta:r], **Konsignatär,** *m.* **(-s,** *pl.* **-e)** (*Comm.*) consignee. **Konsignation** [–natsi'o:n], *f.* consignment, delivery (*from wholesaler to retailer*). **konsignieren,** *v.t.* consign, deliver, forward.

Konsilium [kɔn'zi:lium], *n.* **(-s,** *pl.* **-lien)** consultation (of experts); expert opinion.

konsistent [kɔnzɪs'tɛnt], *adj.* firm, solid, durable, viscous; ***–es Fett,*** grease, solid lubricant. **Konsistenz,** *f.* consistency, consistence, body, viscosity.

Konsistorium [kɔnzɪs'to:rium], *n.* **(-s,** *pl.* **-rien)** consistory; (Lutheran) Church Council.

konskribieren [kɔnskri'bi:rən], *v.t.* levy (*troops*). **Konskribierte(r),** *m.* conscript.

Konsole [kɔn'zo:lə], *f.* console; (*Archit.*) corbel; bracket, support.

konsolidieren [kɔnzoli'di:rən], *v.t., v.r.* consolidate; ***konsolidierte Staatspapiere,*** consolidated funds *or* annuities, consols; ***konsolidierte Schuld,*** funded debt. **Konsolidierung,** *f.* consolidation.

konsonant [kɔnzo'nant], *adj.* consonant; agreeing. **Konsonant,** *m.* **(-en,** *pl.* **-en)** (*Phonet.*) consonant. **konsonantisch,** *adj.* consonantal. **Konsonanz,** *f.* agreement, concord.

Konsorten [kɔn'zɔrtən], *m.pl.* associates, participants, members of a syndicate, (*Law*) parties; (*coll.*) ***Z. und –,*** Z. and those he consorts with, Z. and his like. **Konsortium,** *n.* **(-s,** *pl.* **-tien)** syndicate, association.

Konstabler [kɔn'sta:blər], *m.* (*dial.*) constable; (*obs.*) armourer.

konstant [kɔn'stant], *adj.* constant, steady, stable, invariable. **Konstante,** *f.* (*Math.*) constant. **Konstanz,** *f.* constancy, invariability, stability.

konstatieren [kɔnsta'ti:rən], *v.t.* state, establish, (*coll.*) find; (*Med.*) diagnose.

konsterniert [kɔnstɛr'ni:rt], *adj.* disconcerted, dismayed, stupified, taken aback.

konstituieren [kɔnstitu'i:rən], *v.t.* (*v.r.*) constitute (o.s.), establish (o.s.), organize (o.s.). **konstitutionell** [–tsio'nɛl], *adj.* (*Pol.*) constitutional. **Konstitutionswasser** [–tsi'o:nzvasər], *n.* (*Chem.*) water of crystallization. **konstitutiv** [–'ti:f], *adj.* structural, intrinsic, fundamental, (*Law*) conclusive, probative, evidential.

konstruieren [kɔnstru'i:rən], *v.t.* construct, design; (*Gram.*) construe, parse; ***konstruierte Fall,*** hypothetical *or* fictitious case. **Konstrukteur** [–'tø:r], *m.* **(-s,** *pl.* **-e)** design engineer, technical designer.

Konstruktions|büro [kɔnstruktsi'o:nz–], *n.* drawing office. **–einzelheit,** *f.* structural detail. **–fehler,** *m.* faulty design, structural defect. **–leiter,** *m.* chief designer. **–merkmal,** *n.* structural feature. **konstruktionstechnisch,** *adj.* structural. **Konstruktions|zeichner,** *m.* designer, (technical) draughtsman *or* (*Am.*) draftsman. **–zeichnung,** *f.* technical *or* workshop drawing.

konstruktiv [kɔnstruk'ti:f], *adj.* constructional, structural. **Konstruktivismus** [–ti'vɪsmus], *m.* (*Art.*) modernism, cubism.

Konsul ['kɔnzul], *m.* **(-s,** *pl.* **-n)** consul. **konsularisch** [–la:rɪʃ], *adj.* consular. **Konsulat** [–'la:t], *n.* **(-(e)s,** *pl.* **-e)** consulate.

Konsulent [kɔnzu'lɛnt], *m.* **(-en,** *pl.* **-en)** legal adviser, counsel, consultant. **konsultativ** [–ta'ti:f], *adj.* advisory. **konsultieren,** *v.t.* consult.

Konsum [kɔn'zu:m], *m.* 1. **(-s,** *no pl.*) consumption; 2. (*pl.* **-s**) (*coll.*) *see* **Konsumverein. Konsument** [–'mɛnt], *m.* **(-en,** *pl.* **-en)** consumer, user. **Konsumgüter,** *n.pl.* consumer goods. **konsumieren** [–'mi:rən], *v.t.* consume, use. **Konsumverein,** *m.* (consumers') co-operative society, (*coll.*) co-op.

Kontakt [kɔn'takt], *m.* **(-s,** *pl.* **-e)** contact; (*Elec.*) contact, terminal; (*Elec.*) ***den – herstellen (unterbrechen),*** make (break) the contact; (*fig.*) – ***aufnehmen mit,*** make contact with, get into touch with, contact. **Kontakt|abzug,** *m.* (*Phot.*) contact print. **–draht,** *m.* contact *or* trolley wire (*of tramcars*). **–fläche,** *f.* surface of contact. **–mittel,** *n.* (*Chem.*) catalyst. **–schlüssel,** *m.* (*Motor.*) ignition key. **–schnur,** *f.* flex.

kontant [kɔn'tant], *adv.* (*Comm.*) for cash *or* ready-money, (in) cash. **Kontanten,** *pl.* cash, ready money.

Konten ['kɔntən], *pl. See* **Konto.**

Konteradmiral ['kɔntərˀadmira:l], *m.* rear-admiral. **konterband,** *adj.* contraband. **Konter|bande,** *f.* contraband, smuggled goods. **–eskarpe,** *f.* counterscarp. **–fei,** *n.* **(-(e)s,** *pl.* **-e)** (*obs.*) image, portrait, likeness. **–revolution,** *f.* counter revolution, forces of reaction. **–tanz,** *m.* quadrille, square-dance.

Kontinent ['kɔntinɛnt, –'nɛnt], *m.* **(-(e)s,** *pl.* **-e)** continent.

Kontingent [kɔntɪŋˈgɛnt], *n.* (**-(e)s,** *pl.* **-e**) contingent, quota, allotment, share. **kontingent,** *adj.* contingent, incidental, accidental, fortuitous, chance. **kontingentieren** [–ˈti:rən], *v.t.* fix the quota for, allocate, ration, limit; *kontingentierte Einfuhren,* quota imports. **Kontingenz,** *f.* (-, *pl.* **-ien**) contingency, uncertainty.

kontinuierlich [kɔntinuˈi:rlɪç], *adj.* continuous, uninterrupted. **Kontinuität** [–iˈtɛ:t], *f.* continuity.

Konto [ˈkɔnto], *n.* (**-s,** *pl.* **-s** *or* **Konten**) account; *ein – belasten,* debit *or* charge an account; *ein – führen,* keep an account; (*fig.*) *das geht auf dein –,* that's your doing, you are to blame (for it); *ein – saldieren,* balance an account. **Konto|auszug,** *m.* statement of account. **–buch,** *n.* account book. **–gegenbuch,** *n.* deposit *or* pass-book. **–inhaber,** *m.* account-holder. **–korrent,** *n.* (**-(e)s,** *pl.* **-e**) current account, (*Am.*) account current.

Kontor [kɔnˈto:r], *n.* (**-s,** *pl.* **-e**) counting-house; trading post (*in foreign country*); office; (*coll.*) *ein Schlag ins –,* a slap in the eye.

Kontorist [–ˈrɪst], *m.* (**-en,** *pl.* **-en**), **Kontoristin,** *f.* clerk.

Konto|saldo [ˈkɔntozaldo], *n.* balance account. **–stand,** *m.* state of one's account, amount to (one's) credit.

kontra [ˈkɔntra], **1.** *prep.* contra, against, versus. **2.** *adv.* (*Cards*) *– geben,* double, (*sl.*) talk back, tell (*s.o.*) where he gets off. **Kontra,** *n.* (**-s,** *pl.* **-s**) rebuttal, refutation, confutation, disproof, retort; (*Comm.*) credit side (of an account); (*coll.*) *per –,* against which.

Kontra|baß, *m.* (*Mus.*) double-bass, bass viol. **–buch,** *n.* *See* **Kontogegenbuch. –fagott,** *n.* double bassoon (*organ stop*). **–hage** [–ˈha:ʒə] *f.* (*obs.*) challenge (to a duel).

Kontrahent [kɔntraˈhɛnt], *m.* (**-en,** *pl.* **-en**) 1. contracting party, party to a contract; 2. (*obs.*) opponent (in a duel). **kontrahieren,** *v.t., v.i.* 1. contract, reach a bargain; stipulate; 2. (*obs.*) challenge (to a duel).

kontrakt [kɔnˈtrakt], *adj.* (*Med.*) contracted, shortened, stiffened.

Kontrakt, *m.* (**-(e)s,** *pl.* **-e**) contract, agreement, bargain. **Kontraktbruch,** *m.* breach of contract. **kontraktbrüchig,** *adj.* *– werden,* break *or* violate an agreement *or* contract. **kontraktlich, 1.** *adj.* contractual, stipulated, agreed. **2.** *adv.* by contract.

Kontraktur [kɔntrakˈtu:r], *f.* (-, *pl.* **-en**) (*Med.*) muscular contraction, shortening.

kontraktwidrig [kɔnˈtraktvi:drɪç], *adj.* contrary to *or* in breach of contract.

Kontrapunkt [ˈkɔntrapuŋkt], *m.* (*Mus.*) counterpoint. **kontrapunktisch,** *adj.* contrapuntal.

konträr [kɔnˈtrɛ:r], *adj.* contrary, adverse, antithetical; (*coll.*) (*of a p.*) captious, perverse, contrary.

Kontrast [kɔnˈtrast], *m.* (**-(e)s,** *pl.* **-e**) contrast. **kontrastieren** [–ˈti:rən], *v.t., v.i.* contrast.

Kontroll|abschnitt, *m. See* **–blatt. Kontrollampe,** *f.* (*Tech.*) pilot light. **Kontroll|beamte(r),** *m. See* **Kontrolleur. –blatt,** *n.* counterfoil, (*coll.*) stub.

Kontrolle [kɔnˈtrɔlə], *f.* control, supervision; revision, check; *die – verlieren über* (*Acc.*), lose control of; *unter –,* under control, in hand.

Kontrolleur [kɔntrɔˈlø:r], *m.* (**-s,** *pl.* **-e**) controller, comptroller; supervisor, inspector; (*Railw.*) ticket collector; (*Comm.*) auditor.

Kontroll|gang, *m.* (*police*) beat. **–gerät,** *n.* monitoring device, monitor. **–gesellschaft,** *f.* (*Comm.*) holding company.

kontrollierbar [kɔntrɔˈli:rba:r], *adj.* controllable. **kontrollieren,** *v.t.* control, have control over, be in control of; supervise, check, verify, (*coll.*) keep track of, keep tabs on; (*Comm.*) audit.

Kontroll|karte, *f.* time-sheet. **–kasse,** *f.* cash-register. **–muster,** *n.* checking sample. **–posten, –punkt,** *m.* control *or* check point. **–schein,** *m. See* **–blatt. –stelle,** *f. See* **–punkt. –turm,** *m.* (*Av.*) control tower. **–versuch,** *m.* control test, spot check.

Kontroverse [kɔntroˈvɛrzə], *f.* controversy.

Kontumaz [kɔntuˈma:ts], *f.* (*Law*) contempt of court, contumacy.

Kontur [kɔnˈtu:r], *f.* (-, *pl.* **-en**) contour, outline.

konvenieren [kɔnveˈni:rən], *v.i.* 1. (*of a p.*) come to an agreement *or* arrangement (*mit,* with); 2. (*of a th.*) be convenient *or* suitable (*Dat.,* for *or* to), suit.

Konvent [kɔnˈvɛnt], *m.* (**-(e)s,** *pl.* **-e**) gathering, meeting, assembly, convention. **Konvention** [–tsiˈo:n], *f.* arrangement, agreement, settlement, treaty, convention. **Konventionalstrafe** [–ˈna:l-ʃtra:fə], *f.* (*Law*) liquidated damages. **konventionell** [–ˈnɛl], *adj.* conventional, traditional.

konvergieren [kɔnvɛrˈgi:rən], *v.i.* converge, come *or* run together *or* to a point.

Konversations|lexikon [kɔnvɛrzatsiˈo:nz–], *n.* encyclopaedia. **–stück,** *n.* (*Theat.*) drawing-room comedy, comedy of errors.

konvertierbar [kɔnvɛrˈti:rba:r], *adj.* (*Comm.*) convertible. **konvertieren,** *v.t.* (*Comm., Eccl.*) convert. **Konvertierung,** *f.* conversion. **Konvertit,** *m.* (**-en,** *pl.* **-en**) (*Eccl.*) convert.

konvex [kɔnˈvɛks], *adj.* convex. **Konvexität,** *f.* convexity.

Konvikt [kɔnˈvɪkt], *n.* (**-(e)s,** *pl.* **-e**) (*R.C.*) theological seminary.

Konvoi [ˈkɔnvɔy], *m.* (**-s,** *pl.* **-s**) convoy.

Konvolut [kɔnvoˈlu:t], *n.* (**-(e)s,** *pl.* **-e**) bundle *or* sheaf *or* file *or* roll of papers.

konzedieren [kɔntseˈdi:rən], *v.t.* concede, allow, acknowledge, make a concession *or* concessions.

Konzentrat [kɔntsɛnˈtra:t], *n.* (**-(e)s,** *pl.* **-e**) (*Chem.*) concentration, concentrate.

Konzentrations|fähigkeit [kɔntsɛntratsiˈo:nz–], *f.* power(s) of concentration. **–lager,** *n.* concentration camp.

konzentrieren [kɔntsɛnˈtri:rən], **1.** *v.t.* concentrate, condense; (*fig.*) focus (*attention*), mass (*troops*) (*auf* (*Acc.*), on). **2.** *v.r.* concentrate, centre (*auf* (*Acc.*), on); (*Mil.*) *sich rückwärts –,* fall back, withdraw; (*hum.*) run away, take to one's heels.

konzentrisch [kɔnˈtsɛntrɪʃ], *adj.* concentric.

Konzept [kɔnˈtsɛpt], *n.* (**-(e)s,** *pl.* **-e**) rough copy, first *or* rough draft; notes (*of a speech*); *ihn aus dem – bringen,* confuse *or* disconcert him, (*coll.*) put him off, rattle him; *aus dem – kommen,* become confused, lose the drift *or* thread; *in sein* or *ihm ins – passen,* fit *or* suit his plans. **Konzept|-heft,** *n.* rough notebook, jotter. **–papier,** *n.* scribbling-paper, rough-paper.

Konzern [kɔnˈtsɛrn], *m.* (**-s,** *pl.* **-e**) (*Comm.*) combine.

Konzert [kɔnˈtsɛrt], *n.* (**-(e)s,** *pl.* **-e**) concert (*also Pol.*), recital; concerto; *im –,* at the concert; *ins – gehen,* go to the concert. **Konzert|besucher,** *m.* concert-goer. **–flügel,** *m.* grand-piano, concert grand. **–haus,** *n.* concert hall. **konzertieren** [–ˈti:rən], *v.i.* play in *or* give a concert. **Konzert|-meister,** *m.* first-violin(ist), leader (of the orchestra). **–saal,** *m. See* **–haus.**

Konzession [kɔntsɛsiˈo:n], *f.* concession, privilege, charter, grant, patent, licence, (*Am.*) franchise; *–en machen,* make concessions *or* allowances; *eine – haben,* be licensed *or* (*Am.*) franchised. **konzessioniert** [–ˈni:rt], *adj.* licensed, (*Am.*) franchised; authorized. **Konzessionsinhaber,** *m.* licence-holder, licensee, concessionaire, (*Am.*) franchised dealer.

Konzil [kɔnˈtsi:l], *n.* (**-s,** *pl.* **-e** *or* **-ien**) (church) council.

konziliant [kɔntsiliˈant], *adj.* conciliatory.

Konzilium [kɔnˈtsi:lium], *m.* (**-s,** *pl.* **-lien**) (*Austr.*) *see* **Konzil.**

konzipieren [kɔntsiˈpi:rən], **1.** *v.r.* formulate, draft, draw up, outline, plan. **2.** *v.i.* (*obs.*) conceive, become pregnant.

Koog [ko:k], *m.* (**-(e)s,** *pl.* **Köge**) (*dial.*) reclaimed land, polder.

kooptieren [ko'ɔp'ti:rən], *v.t.* co-opt.

Koordinate [ko'ɔrdi'na:tə], *f.* co-ordinate. **Koordinaten|papier,** *n.* graph paper. **–system,** *n.* system of co-ordinates. **koordinieren,** *v.t.* co-ordinate.

Kopeke [ko'pe:kə], *f.* copeck.

Kopenhagen [kopən'ha:gən], *n.* Copenhagen.

Köper ['kø:pər], *m.* (*Weav.*) twill, tweel. **köpern,** *v.t.* twill.

Kopf [kɔpf], *m.* (**-es,** *pl.* **⸚e**) 1. head; top, crown (*of hat*), bowl (*of pipe*), nose (*of aircraft*), warhead (*of missile*); (*Typ.*) heading, title, letterhead; 2. (*fig.*) brains, ability; understanding, judgement, sense; memory; will; 3. (*of a p.*) great mind, (able) thinker; head, leader.

(a) (*with verbs*) ***ihm den – abschlagen,*** chop off his head; ***den – oben behalten,*** not lose heart, (*coll.*) keep one's chin *or* (*sl.*) pecker up; ***seinen – durchsetzen,*** have (it) one's own way, carry the day; ***die Köpfe erhitzen sich,*** tempers run high; ***seinem eigenen – folgen,*** follow one's bent, suit o.s.; ***es geht um*** or ***gilt seinen –,*** his life is at stake; ***es geht um – und Kragen,*** it's a hanging matter, (*coll.*) it's a matter of life and death; ***den – hängen lassen,*** hang one's head; (*fig.*) be disgruntled *or* downcast *or* despondent *or* (*coll.*) down in the mouth; ***sich*** (*Dat.*) ***blutige Köpfe holen,*** be the worse for wear; ***den – in den Sand stecken,*** hide one's head in the sand; ***der – steht darauf,*** it's a capital offence; ***ich weiß nicht wo mir der – steht,*** I don't know which way to turn, I don't know whether I'm coming or going; ***mir steht der – nicht danach,*** I don't feel like it, I have no inclination for it; ***ihm den – verdrehen,*** turn his head; ***den – verlieren,*** lose one's head; ***den – nicht verlieren,*** keep one's head; ***ihm den – waschen,*** wash his hair; (*fig., coll.*) take him to task, give him a good dressing down *or* a piece of one's mind; ***den – zerbrechen,*** rack one's brains; ***ihm den – zurechtweisen,*** bring him to his senses.

(b) (*with preps.*) ***– an –,*** shoulder to shoulder, packed *or* crowded together; ***auf dem – stehen,*** be inverted *or* upside-down, (*fig.*) be topsy-turvy *or* at sixes and sevens *or* in a muddle; ***auf den – stellen,*** turn upside-down, upturn, invert; (*fig.*) disarrange, muddle, jumble, upset, throw into disorder *or* confusion; stand (*facts*) on their head; paint (*the town*) red; ***er ist nicht auf den – gefallen,*** he's no fool, he's all there; ***ihm etwas auf den – zusagen,*** tell him s.th. to his face; ***aus dem –,*** by heart *or* rote, from memory; ***sich*** (*Dat.*) ***etwas aus dem – schlagen,*** put s.th. out of one's *or* banish *or* dismiss s.th. from one's mind *or* thoughts; ***es will mir nicht aus dem –,*** I cannot get it out of my head *or* mind; ***sich*** (*Dat.*) ***etwas durch den – gehen lassen,*** think s.th. over in one's mind; ***Grillen*** or ***große Rosinen im – haben,*** have one's head full of crazy ideas; ***Grütze im – haben,*** have one's wits about one; ***sich*** (*Dat.*) ***etwas in den – setzen,*** take s.th. into one's head; ***in den – steigen,*** go to one's head; ***es will mir nicht in den –,*** I cannot believe *or* credit it, it is past my understanding; ***mit dem – gegen die Wand rennen,*** run one's head against a brick wall; ***mir bis über den –,*** right over my head (*as water*); ***über den – in Schulden stecken,*** be up to one's eyes *or* ears in debt; ***ihm über den – wachsen,*** be too much for him; ***über seinen – hinweg,*** (*promotion*) over his head; ***Hals über –,*** headlong, head over heels; ***es geht um seinen –,*** his life is at stake; ***von – bis Fuß,*** from head to foot, from top to toe; ***wie vor den – geschlagen,*** speechless, thunderstruck; ***ein Brett vor dem – haben,*** be obtuse *or* dim-witted *or* blockheaded *or* fatuous; ***ihn vor den – stoßen,*** give offence to him, offend *or* shock *or* antagonize him; ***zu –e steigen,*** go to one's head.

(c) (*enumerating*) ***pro –,*** per capita *or* head, a head, each; ***es kommen 10 Mark auf den –,*** that's 10 marks each; ***viel(e) Köpfe viel(e) Sinne,*** many heads many minds.

(d) ***– hoch!*** chin up! bear up! keep smiling! ***– oder Schrift*** or ***Wappen?*** heads or tails? ***er ist ein kluger –,*** he has a good head on his shoulders.

Kopf|arbeit, *f.* brain-work. **–arbeiter,** *m.* brain-worker, white-collar worker. **–bahnhof,** *m.* terminus, railhead. **–ball,** *m.* (*Footb.*) header. **–bedeckung,** *f.* headgear. **–besteuerung,** *f.* capitation tax. **–blüte,** *f.* aggregate blossom, (*Bot.*) capitulum. **–bogen,** *m.* letterhead sheet (*of notepaper*).

Köpfchen ['kœpfçən], *n.* 1. (*Bot.*) *see* **Kopfblüte**; 2. (*coll.*) brains, resourcefulness; (*coll.*) ***er hat –,*** he has brains, he's a smart lad; (*iron.*) ***–! –!*** that's very clever! brilliant!

Kopf|drüse, *f.* (*Anat.*) cephalic gland. **–düngung,** *f.* top dressing.

köpfen ['kœpfən], **1.** *v.t.* 1. behead, decapitate; truncate, pollard, poll, lop, top (*plants*); 2. (*Footb.*) head. **2.** *v.i.* form *or* develop a head (*of plants*).

Kopf|ende, *n.* head (*of a bed etc.*). **–füßer,** *m.* (*Zool.*) cuttle fish (*Cephalopoda*). **–geld,** *n.* poll-tax; blood money, money on (*s.o.'s*) head. **–gewand,** *n.* (*Eccl.*) amice. **–grind,** *m.* (*Med.*) scald-head, porrigo. **–grippe,** *f.* (*Med.*) influenza. **–haar,** *n.* hair of the head. **–hänger,** *m.* moper, (*coll.*) misery. **kopfhängerisch,** *adj.* low-spirited, dejected. **Kopf|haube,** *f.* tuft, crest, hood. **–haut,** *f.* scalp. **–hörer,** *m.* (*Rad.*) headphones, earphones, (*Tele.*) headset.

-köpfig ['kœpfɪç], *adj.suff.* -headed, -cephalous; of . . . (persons).

Kopf|kissen, *n.* pillow. **–kissenbezug,** *m.* pillow-case *or* -slip. **–kohl,** *m.* common *or* red cabbage. **–länge,** *f.* ***um eine –,*** by a head. **kopflastig,** *adj.* (*Av.*) nose-heavy, (*Naut.*) down by the bow, (*coll.*) top-heavy. **kopflos,** *adj.* headless; acephalous; (*fig.*) panic-stricken, (*coll.*) panicky; ***–e Flucht,*** headlong flight, stampede. **Kopf|naht,** *f.* (*Anat.*) cranial suture. **–nicken,** *n.* nod. **–nuß,** *f.* (*coll.*) clout, cuff, box on the ear. **–pfühl,** *m.* bolster; pillow. **–putz,** *m.* coiffure; head-dress. **–rechnen,** *n.* mental arithmetic. **–rose,** *f.* (*Med.*) erysipelas. **–salat,** *m.* cabbage- *or* garden-lettuce. **kopfscheu,** *adj.* apprehensive, timid; restive (*as horses*); ***– machen,*** disconcert, unnerve, intimidate. **Kopf|-schmerzen,** *m.pl.* headache. **–schuppen,** *f.pl.* dandruff. **–schütteln,** *n.* shake *or* shaking of the head, (*fig.*) misgiving, disapproval. **–schützer,** *m.* Balaclava helmet. **–sprung,** *m.* header. **–stand,** *m.* (*Gymn.*) standing on one's head.

kopfstehen ['kɔpfʃte:hən], *irr.v.i.* (*sep.*) (*of a p.*) stand on one's head; (*of a th.*) be upside down *or* inverted; (*fig.*) be beside o.s. *or* amazed.

Kopf|steinpflaster, *n.* cobbled pavement. **–steuer,** *f.* poll-tax. **–stimme,** *f.* falsetto. **–stoß,** *m.* (*Footb.*) header, (*Boxing*) butt, (*Bill.*) massé. **–sturz,** *m.* (*Av.*) nose-dive. **–tuch,** *n.* kerchief, shawl, scarf. **kopfüber,** *adv.* head foremost *or* first; (*also* ***– kopfunter***) (*fig.*) head over heels, headlong. **Kopf|-wäsche,** *f.*, **–waschen,** *n.* shampoo(ing); (*coll. fig.*) dressing-down, telling-off. **–wasser,** *n.* hair wash *or* lotion, shampoo. **–wassersucht,** *f.* (*Med.*) hydrocephalus, (*coll.*) water on the brain. **–weh,** *n.* headache. **–weide,** *f.* pollard willow. **–zahl,** *f.* number of persons. **–zerbrechen,** *n.* ***ihm – machen,*** puzzle *or* nonplus him, (*coll.*) give him s.th. to worry about, give him quite a headache; ***ohne viel –,*** without giving it a second thought.

Kopie [ko'pi:], *f.* copy, reproduction, facsimile; transcript, duplicate, carbon copy; (*Phot.*) (contact) print. **Kopier|anstalt,** *f.* (photographic) processing laboratory; copying-office. **–farbe,** *f.* *See* **–tinte. –maschine,** *f.* copying-press. **–papier,** *n.* (*Phot.*) printing-paper. **–rahmen,** *m.* (*Phot.*) printing-frame. **–stift,** *m.* copying-(ink) pencil. **–tinte,** *f.* copying-ink. **Kopist,** *m.* (**-en,** *pl.* **-en**) copyist.

Koppe ['kɔpə], *f.* (*dial.*) *see* **Kuppe.**

[1]**Koppel** ['kɔpəl], *f.* (-, *pl.* **-n**) 1. pack, string, leash (*of dogs*); 2. pen, paddock, enclosure; 3. (*Austr.*) *see* [2]**Koppel.**

[2]**Koppel,** *n.* sword-belt, (*Mil., coll.*) webbing.

Koppel|balken, *m.* tie-beam. **–band,** *n.* leash. **–kette,** *f.* drag-chain. **–kurs,** *m.* (*Naut.*) dead-reckoning. **koppeln,** *v.t.* leash, couple, tie *or* string together; fence in, enclose; (*Rad.*) couple, connect; (*fig.*) couple, tie in. **Koppel|recht,** *n.* joint right. **–schloß,** *n.* buckle. **Koppelung,** *f.* coupling, linkage; double-main (*organ stop*).

Koppler ['kɔplər], *m.* (*Rad.*) coupler. **Kopplung,** *f. See* **Koppelung. Kopplungsspule,** *f.* (*Rad.*) coupling coil.

Kopulation [kopulatsi'o:n], *f.* union, mating, marriage, pairing, (*Hort.*) grafting. **kopulativ** [–'ti:f], *adj.* (*Gram.*) copulative. **kopulieren** [–'li:rən], **1.** *v.t.* unite, pair, mate, (*Hort.*) graft, (*obs.*) marry. **2.** *v.i.* pair, mate, (*obs.*) marry.

kor [ko:r], *see* **kiesen.**

Koralle [ko'ralə], *f.* coral. **korallen,** *adj.* coral(line). **Korallen|bank,** *f. See* **–riff. –fischer,** *m.* coral-diver *or* -fisher. **–riff,** *n.* coral reef. **–schnur,** *f.* string of coral beads, coral necklace. **–tiere,** *n.pl.* coral polyps, Actinozoa, Anthozoa.

koranzen [ko'rantsən], *v.t. See* **kuranzen.**

Korb [kɔrp], *m.* **(–(e)s,** *pl.* **¨e)** 1. basket, (*for food*) hamper, (*on pack-animals*) pannier, (*for packing goods*) crate, (*for fish*) creel; (*of sabre*) guard, (*of hoisting gear*) cage; ***Hahn im –e sein,*** be cock of the walk; 2. (*coll.*) rebuff, refusal; ***einen – bekommen,*** receive a refusal, be turned down; ***ihm einen – geben,*** reject his offer of marriage, turn him down.

Korb|arbeit, *f.* basket-work, wickerwork; basket-making. **–ball,** *m.* basketball. **–blütler,** *m. pl.* (*Bot.*) compositae.

Korber ['kɔrbər], *m.* (*Swiss*) basket maker.

Korb|flasche, *f.* carboy, demijohn. **–flechter,** *m.* basket maker. **–geflecht,** *n.* wickerwork. **–möbel,** *n.pl.* wicker furniture. **–sessel, –stuhl,** *m.* wicker chair. **–wagen,** *m.* basket-carriage. **–weide,** *f.* (*Bot.*) osier (*Salix viminalis*).

Kord [kɔrt], *m.* **(–(e)s,** *pl.* **–e)** corduroy.

Korde ['kɔrdə], *f.* (ornamental) cord, piping. **Kordel,** *f.* **(–,** *pl.* **–n)** (*dial.*) cord, twine, string.

Kordhose ['kɔrtho:zə], *f.* corduroy trousers, cords.

Kordon [kɔr'dõ], *m.* **(–s,** *pl.* **–s** (*Austr.* **–e**)) cordon, barrier, barricade.

Kordsamt ['kɔrtzamt], *m. See* **Kord.**

Korduan ['kɔrdua:n], *m.* **(–s,** *pl.* **–e)** (*obs.*) cordwain, cordova leather.

köre ['kø:rə], *see* **kiesen.**

Korea [ko're:a], *n.* (*Geog.*) Korea. **Koreaner** [–'a:nər], *m.*, **koreanisch,** *adj.* Korean.

kören ['kø:rən], *v.t.* assay, inspect, select (*animals for breeding*).

korest ['ko:rəst], *see* **kiesen.**

Körhengst ['kø:rhɛŋst], *m.* selected stallion.

Korinthe [ko'rɪntə], *f.* (dried) currant.

Kork [kɔrk], *m.* **(–(e)s,** *pl.* **–e)** cork, stopper; ***nach dem – schmecken,*** (*of wine*) be corky *or* corked. **korkartig,** *adj. See* **korkig. Korkeiche,** *f.* cork-tree, cork-oak. **korken, 1.** *adj.* (of) cork. **2.** *v.t.* cork (up). **Korkenzieher,** *m. See* **Korkzieher. Kork|geld,** *n.* corkage. **–gürtel,** *m.* lifebelt. **korkig,** *adj.* corky, corklike, (*Bot.*) suberous, suberose. **Kork|stöpsel,** *m.* cork(-stopper). **–weste,** *f.* lifejacket. **–zieher,** *m.* corkscrew; (*fig.*) (*Av.*) spin, spiral dive.

Kormoran [kɔrmo'ra:n], *m.* **(–s,** *pl.* **–e)** (*Orn.*) (*Am.* great) cormorant (*Phalacrocorax carbo*).

[1]**Korn** [kɔrn], *n.* **(–(e)s,** *pl.* **¨er** (= *grains*) *and* **–e** (= *cereals*)) 1. grain, corn, cereal; (grain of) seed, kernel; rye, (*Am.*) maize; ***die Flinte ins – werfen,*** throw in one's hand, throw in the towel; 2. standard (*of metal*); ***das Schrot und –,*** weight and fineness (*of coin*); ***Mann von altem*** or ***echtem Schrot und –,*** man of sterling character *or* (*coll.*) of the right sort; 3. foresight (*of a rifle*) (*pl. rare* **–e**); ***aufs – nehmen,*** (take) aim at, (*sl.*) draw a bead on; (*fig.*) fix one's eye on, fix with one's eye, make the target of one's remarks; mark for one's attack.

[2]**Korn,** *m.* (*coll.*) *see* **Kornbranntwein.**

Kornähre ['kɔrnʔɛ:rə], *f.* ear of corn; (*Astr.*) Spica. **kornartig,** *adj.* frumentaceous. **Korn|bau,** *m.* cultivation of grain. **–bildung,** *f.* crystallization, granulation. **–blume,** *f.* (*Bot.*) cornflower (*Centaurea cyanus*). **–boden,** *m.* granary. **–börse,** *f.* corn-exchange. **–brand,** *m.* blight, smut. **–branntwein,** *m.* rye whisky.

Körnchen ['kœrnçən], *n.* granule, spore; (*fig.*) ***kein –,*** not a grain *or* atom (*of truth etc.*). **körneln,** *v.t.* granulate. **Körnelung,** *f. See* **Körnung. körnen, 1.** *v.t.* granulate; grain (*leather*), tool (*metal*); (*Tech.*) mark with a centre-punch. **2.** *v.i., v.r.* form into grains, granulate; run to seed.

[1]**Körner** ['kœrnər], *m.* (*Tech.*) centre-punch; centre-mark, punch-mark.

[2]**Körner,** *pl. of* [1]**Korn. körner|fressend,** *adj.* granivorous. **–tragend,** *adj.* graniferous.

[1]**Kornett** [kɔr'nɛt], *m.* **(–(e)s,** *pl.* **–e** (*Austr.* **–s**)) standard bearer, (*obs.*) cornet.

[2]**Kornett,** *n.* **(–s,** *pl.* **–e)** (*Mus.*) cornet.

Korn|feld, *n.* cornfield. **–fraß,** *m. See* **–brand. –früchte,** *f.pl.* cereals, grain. **–garbe,** *f.* sheaf of corn. **–händler,** *m.* corn-merchant.

körnig ['kœrnɪç], *adj.* granular, granulated; gritty; (*as suff.*) -grained.

Korn|käfer, *m.* grain-weavil. **–kammer,** *f.* granary. **–kasten,** *m.*, **–lade,** *f.* corn-bin. **–mutter,** *f.* ergot. **–rade,** *f.* (*Bot.*) corn-cockle, corn campion (*Agrostemma* or *Lychnis githago*). **–schnaps,** *m.* rye whisky. **–schwinge,** *f.* winnowing machine. **–speicher,** *m.* granary. **–spitze,** *f.* (*Mech.*) dead-centre.

Körnung ['kœrnuŋ], *f.* granulation; graining; grain-size, granularity.

Kornweihe ['kɔrnvaiə], *f.* (*Orn.*) hen-harrier, (*Am.*) marsh hawk (*Circus cyaneus*).

Korona [ko'ro:na], *f.* **(–,** *pl.* **–nen)** 1. (*Univ. sl.*) circle of listeners, audience; 2. (*Astr.*) corona. **Korona-entladung,** *f.* (*Elec.*) corona discharge.

Körper ['kœrpər], *m.* body; bulk; matter, substance; (*Geom.*) solid; ***der gesetzgebende –,*** legislative body; ***flüssiger –,*** liquid substance; ***fester –,*** solid matter, solid (body); ***am ganzen – zittern,*** tremble all over.

Körper|anlage, *f.* constitution; temperament. **–bau,** *m.* bodily structure. frame, build; ***von kräftigem –,*** of sturdy physique, powerfully built. **körperbehindert,** *adj.* physically handicapped. **Körper|beschaffenheit,** *f.* physique, constitution. **–bildung,** *f.* physical development; body-building. **Körperchen,** *n.* particle, corpuscule, corpuscle. **Körper|fülle,** *f.* corpulence, plumpness. **–gehalt,** *n. or m.* solid content, body. **–geruch,** *m.* body odour. **–gewicht,** *n.* body-weight. **–größe,** *f.* stature. **–haltung,** *f.* deportment, bearing, posture, carriage. **–inhalt,** *m.* solid content, volume. **–kraft,** *f.* physical strength. **–kultur,** *f.* physical culture. **–lehre,** *f.* 1. (*Med.*) somatology; 2. (*Math.*) solid geometry, stereometry.

körperlich ['kœrpərlɪç], *adj.* bodily, physical; corporeal, substantial, material; (*Geom.*) solid, (*Med.*) somatic; ***–e Betätigung,*** physical activity; ***–er Winkel,*** solid angle; ***–er Eid,*** verbal oath, oath taken in person; ***–e Strafe,*** corporal punishment; ***– leidend,*** physically ailing. **Körperlichkeit,** *f.* corporeality, concreteness. **körperlos,** *adj.* incorporeal.

Körper|maß, *n.* 1. cubic measure; 2. *pl.* (physical) measurements (*of a p.*). **–messung,** *f.* stereometry, mensuration of solids. **–pflege,** *f.* beauty culture, personal hygiene. **–puder,** *m.* talcum powder. **–schaft,** *f.* corporate body, corporation. **–schulung,** *f.* physical training *or* culture, body-building exercises. **–schwäche,** *f.* debility, frailness. **–stellung,** *f.* posture. **–strafe,** *f.* corporal punishment. **–teil,** *m.* part of the body. **–teilchen,** *n.* particle, molecule. **–treffer,** *m.* body-blow. **–übung,** *f.* physical exercise, gymnastics. **–verletzung,** *f.* bodily injury; (*Law*) ***schwere –,*** grievous bodily harm. **–wärme,** *f.* body heat. **–wuchs,** *m.* stature, build, physique.

Korporal [kɔrpo'ra:l], *m.* **(–s,** *pl.* **–e)** corporal. **Korporalschaft,** *f.* (*Mil.*) section, squad.

Korporation [korporatsi'o:n], *f.* corporation, (*Univ.*) students' society, (*Am.*) fraternity.

Korps [ko:r], *n.* (-, *pl.* - [*Gen. and pl.* ko:rs]) (army) corps; ***fliegendes –***, flying column. **Korps|geist,** *m.* esprit de corps; (*Pol.*) party spirit. **–student,** *m.* (*coll.*) member of a student body. (*See* **Korporation.**)

[1]**Korpus** ['korpus], *m. or n.* (-, *pl.* **-pora**) body, totality, entirety, mass.

[2]**Korpus, Korpusschrift,** *f.* (*Typ.*) long primer.

korrekt [ko'rɛkt], *adj.* correct, proper, irreproachable. **Korrektheit,** *f.* correctness. **Korrektionshaus** [–tsi'o:nzhaus], *n.* remand home. **korrektiv** [–'ti:f], *adj.* correctional, corrective.

Korrektor [ko'rɛktor], *m.* (**-s,** *pl.* **-en**) press-corrector, proof reader. **Korrektur** [–'tu:r], *f.* (–, *pl.* **-en**) correction, revision, (*Typ.*) proof (sheet); *–(en) lesen,* correct proofs; ***zweite –***, revise; ***letzte –***, press proof. **Korrektur|abzug, –bogen,** *m.* printer's proof, proof(-sheet). **–fahne,** *f.* galley proof. **–zeichen,** *n.* (mark of) correction.

Korrespondent [korɛspon'dɛnt], *m.* (**-en,** *pl.* **-en**) correspondent. **Korrespondenz,** *f.* (-, *pl.* **-en**) correspondence. **Korrespondenzbüro,** *n.* news- *or* press-agency. **korrespondieren,** *v.i.* correspond, be in correspondence, exchange letters (*mit*, with); correspond (*mit*, to), agree (with) (*a th.*).

korrigieren [kori'gi:rən], *v.t.* correct, rectify, alter, adjust; (*Typ.*) correct, read (*proofs*).

korrumpieren [korum'pi:rən], *v.t.* corrupt.

Korsar [kor'za:r], *m.* (**-en,** *pl.* **-en**) pirate, corsair, buccaneer.

Korse ['korzə], *m.* (**-n,** *pl.* **-n**) Corsican.

Korsett [kor'zɛt], *n.* (**-(e)s,** *pl.* **-e**) corset, stays. **Korsettstange,** *f.* corset-busk *or* bone.

korsisch ['korzɪʃ], *adj.* Corsican.

Korund [ko'runt], *m.* (*Mil.*) corundum.

Korvette [kor'vɛtə], *f.* corvette. **Korvettenkapitän,** *m.* lieutenant-commander.

Koryphäe [kori'fɛ:ə], *f.* (-, *pl.* **-en**), *m.* (**-n,** *pl.* **-n**) star, celebrity; authority (*für*, on); (*m. only*) (*Antiquity*) corypheus.

Kosak [ko'zak], *m.* (**-en,** *pl.* **-en**) Cossack.

Koschenille [koʃə'niljə], *f.* cochineal.

koscher ['ko:ʃər], *adj.* kosher; (*coll.*) ***nicht ganz –***, rather fishy, not quite on the level.

kosen ['ko:zən], **1.** *v.t.* (*Poet.*) caress, fondle. **2.** *v.i.* – ***mit***, *see* **1. Kose|name,** *m.* pet name. **–wort,** *n.* term of endearment.

Kosinus ['ko:zinus], *m.* (-, *pl.* -) cosine.

Kosmetik [kos'me:tɪk], *f.* cosmetics. **kosmetisch,** *adj.* cosmetic.

kosmisch ['kosmɪʃ], *adj.* cosmic.

Kosmopolit [kosmopo'li:t], *m.* (**-en,** *pl.* **-en**) cosmopolitan. **kosmopolitisch,** *adj.* cosmopolitan.

Kosmos ['kosmos], *m.* cosmos, universe.

Kossat [ko'sa:t], (**-en,** *pl.* **-en**), **Kossäte** [ko'sɛ:tə], *m.* (**-n,** *pl.* **-n**) (*Hist.*) cottager, cotter, cottar.

Kost [kost], *f.* food, diet, fare, victuals, board; ***in*** (***der***) ***– sein*** (***bei***), board (with); ***in*** (***die***) ***– geben*** or ***tun,*** board out, put out to board; ***ihn in*** (***die***) ***– nehmen*** or ***ihm die – geben,*** board him, take him as a boarder; ***kräftige –***, rich diet; ***magere*** or ***schmale –***, slender *or* scanty fare, low *or* poor diet; ***– und Wohnung*** (or ***Logis***), board and lodging *or* residence; ***französische –***, French food *or* cooking; ***reichliche –***, plentiful *or* full diet; (*fig.*) ***leichte –***, light fare.

kostbar ['kostba:r], *adj.* precious, valuable, costly, expensive; luxurious, sumptuous, splendid; (*fig., coll.*) priceless (*joke etc.*). **Kostbarkeit,** *f.* costliness, expensiveness; object of value, precious object, treasure; *pl.* valuables.

[1]**kosten** ['kostən], *v.t.* taste, sip, sample, try; (*fig.*) have a taste of, enjoy.

[2]**kosten,** *v.i.* cost; (*fig.*) require, take; ***was*** or ***wieviel kostet das?*** how much is this? what is the price of this? how much *or* what do you charge for this? (*subsequently*) how much was it? what did you pay for it? what did it cost? ***es kostet Zeit,*** it takes time; ***es kostete mich*** or ***mir einen harten Kampf,*** it cost me a hard struggle; ***es koste was es wolle,*** at any price, cost what it may; ***das kostete mich*** or ***mir viel Geld,*** that cost me a lot of money.

Kosten, *pl.* cost(s), (*Law*) costs; expense(s), expenditure, outlay; fee(s), charges; ***auf meine –***, at my expense; ***die – bestreiten*** or ***tragen, für die – aufkommen,*** pay *or* bear *or* defray *or* meet the expense; ***keine – scheuen,*** spare no expense; (*Law*) ***in die*** or ***zu den – verurteilen,*** condemn to pay all costs; ***auf seine – kommen,*** cover one's outlay, (re)cover one's expenses; (*fig.*) get value for one's money, get one's money's worth; ***sich in – stürzen,*** go to *or* incur (great) expense; ***auf – des Staats,*** at public expense; ***auf – seiner Ehre,*** at the expense of his honour.

Kosten|anschlag, *m.* estimate, quotation, tender. **–aufstellung,** *f.* cost account. **–aufwand,** *m.* expenditure; ***mit einem – von,*** at a cost *or* an outlay of. **–berechnung,** *f.* calculation of cost, cost accounting, costing. **–ersatz,** *m.*, **–erstattung,** *f.* compensation for outlay, reimbursement of expenses, indemnification. **kostenfrei, kostenlos, 1.** *adj.* (cost) free. **2.** *adv.* free of *or* without charge, (*coll.*) free, for nothing. **kostenpflichtig,** *adj.* (*Law*) liable for costs; ***– abweisen,*** dismiss with costs. **Kosten|preis,** *m.* cost price, prime cost; ***unter – verkaufen,*** sell at a loss. **–punkt,** *m.* (matter of) expense(s); ***was den – anbetrifft,*** as to expenses. **–voranschlag,** *m.* estimate.

kostfrei ['kostfraɪ], *adj.* with free board. **Kost|gänger,** *m.* boarder. **–geld,** *n.* 1. (cost of) board, (*coll.*) keep; (*servants*) board-wages, allowance for board; 2. (*St. Exch.*) contango.

köstlich ['kœstlɪç], *adj.* exquisite, choice; delightful, wonderful, charming; (*of food*) delicious, tasty; ***sich – amüsieren,*** have a wonderful time.

Kostprobe ['kostpro:bə], *f.* sample (to taste), (*coll.*) a taste.

kostspielig ['kostʃpi:lɪç], *adj.* costly, expensive, dear; lavish, sumptuous. **Kostspieligkeit,** *f.* costliness, expensiveness; lavishness, sumptuousness.

Kostüm [kos'ty:m], *n.* (**-s,** *pl.* **-e**) costume, dress; fancy-dress; (ladies') tailor-made dress, coat and skirt, two-piece. **Kostüm|ball,** *m.*, **–fest,** *n.* fancy-dress ball; ***historisches Kostümfest,*** historical pageant. **kostümieren** [–'mi:rən], *v.t., v.r.* dress (o.s.) up. **Kostüm|probe,** *f.* dress-rehearsal. **–stück,** *n.* (*Theat.*) period-piece. **–zeichner,** *m.* dress-designer.

Kostverächter ['kostfɛrˀɛçtər], *m.* (*coll.*) ***er ist kein –***, he likes his food; (*hum.*) he's fond of the girls.

[1]**Kot** [ko:t], *n.* (**-(e)s,** *pl.* **-e**) (*dial.*) hut, cot, hovel, shed.

[2]**Kot,** *m.* (*no pl.*) dirt, filth; mire, mud; muck, manure, droppings, dung; excrement, faeces. **Kot|abgang,** *m.* defaecation. **–blech,** *n.* *See* **–flügel.**

[1]**Kote** ['ko:tə], *f.* (*dial.*) *see* [1]**Kot.**

[2]**Kote,** *f.* (*Geom.*) z-coordinate; (*Surv.*) triangulation point.

Köte ['kø:tə], *f.* (*dial.*) fetlock.

Kotelett [kotə'lɛt], *n.* (**-(e)s,** *pl.* **-e**) cutlet, chop. **Kotelette,** *f.* (*usu. pl.*) side *or* mutton-chop whiskers.

Köten|gelenk, *n.*, **–schopf, –zopf,** *m.* *See* **Köte.**

Köter ['kø:tər], *m.* cur; mongrel.

Kot|fliege, *f.* dung-fly. **–flügel,** *m.* (*Motor.*) mudguard, wing, (*Am.*) fender. **–grube,** *f.* cesspool, sewer.

Kothurn [ko'turn], *m.* (**-s,** *pl.* **-e**) cothurnus, buskin; (*fig.*) ***auf hohem –***, in a grandiloquent *or* pompous style.

kotieren [ko'ti:rən], **1.** *v.t.* (*Comm.*) quote (*prices etc.*). **2.** *v.i.* (*Geog.*) measure altitude.

kotig ['ko:tɪç], *adj.* dirty, filthy, (*coll.*) mucky; muddy, begrimed; faecal.

Kötner ['kø:tnər], **Kot|saß** (**-(ss)en**, *pl.* **-(ss)en**), **–sasse** (**-n**, *pl.* **-n**), *m. See* **Kätner.**

[1]**Kotze** ['kɔtsə], *f.* (*dial.*) coarse blanket, woollen cape.

[2]**Kotze,** *f.* (*no pl.*) (*vulg.*) vomit, spew.

Kötze ['kœtzə], *f.* (*dial.*) dosser, pannier.

kotzen ['kɔtsən], *v.r.*, *v.i.* (*vulg.*) vomit, spew, puke; (*coll.*) ***es ist zum –,*** it's enough to make you sick.

Kotzen, *m.* (*dial.*) *see* [1]**Kotze.**

Krabbe ['krabə], *f.* crab; shrimp; (*coll.*) little child, lively girl. **krabbelig,** *adj.* lively, frisky; itchy, prickly. **krabbeln,** **1.** *v.i.* scramble, clamber, scurry, scuttle; crawl, wriggle; (*aux.* s.) grope, fumble, scrabble (**nach,** for). **2.** *v.t.*, *v.i. imp.* itch, tickle; scratch; ***es krabbelt mir*** or ***mich am Halse,*** my neck itches.

Krabbentaucher ['krabəntauxər], *m.* (*Orn.*) little auk, (*Am.*) dovekie (*Plautus alle*).

Krach [krax], *m.* (**-(e)s,** *pl.* **-e** (*coll.* **¨e**)) crash; noise, din, (*coll.*) row, racket, rumpus; quarrel, (*coll.*) row, tiff, scene; bankruptcy, failure, commercial crisis, (*coll.*) crash, smash; – ***machen,*** make a din *or* row; (*coll.*) – ***schlagen,*** kick up a row, (*sl.*) raise hell; ***mit Ach und –,*** with great difficulty. **krachen,** **1.** *v.i.* crack, bang, roar, thunder; (*aux.* s.) smash, crash (*also Comm.*). **2.** *v.r.* (*coll.*) quarrel.

[1]**Krachen** ['kraxən], *n.* crack, crash, roar, thunder.

[2]**Krachen,** *m.* (*Swiss*) gorge, ravine.

Kracher ['kraxər], *m.* (*coll.*) old dodderer.

Kracherl ['kraxərl], *n.* (*Austr.*) aerated *or* soda water, (*coll.*) pop, fizzy drink. **Krachmandel,** *f.* (*dial.*) soft-shelled almond.

krächzen ['krɛçtsən], *v.i.* croak, caw; ***die Krähe krächzt,*** the crow caws; ***der Rabe krächzt,*** the raven croaks.

Kracke ['krakə], *f.* (*dial.*) jade, nag; screw.

Kraft [kraft], *f.* (-, *pl.* **¨e**) strength; power, force (*also Mil.*), vigour, energy; efficacy, validity; worker, employee; (*Naut.*, *fig.*) ***aus eigener –,*** under one's own steam; ***außer – setzen,*** annul, abrogate, rescind; ***außer – treten,*** expire, lapse, cease to be effective; ***was in meinen Kräften steht,*** my utmost, as far as I can; ***in – setzen,*** enact, put into force *or* operation; ***in – treten,*** become effective; come into operation *or* effect *or* force; ***in voller –,*** in full force *or* operation; ***mit aller –,*** with all one's might; ***mit der – der Verzweiflung,*** with strength born of despair; ***nach besten Kräften,*** to the best of one's ability; ***rohe –,*** brute force; ***treibende –,*** motive power, prime mover; ***das geht über meine Kräfte,*** that lies outside my power *or* is too much for me; ***von Kräften kommen,*** lose strength; ***zu Kräften kommen,*** regain one's strength.

kraft, *prep.* (*Gen.*) in *or* by virtue of, on the strength of; by authority of.

Kraft|anlage, *f.* power-plant, power-station. **–anstrengung,** *f.* effort. **–antrieb,** *m.* power drive. **–aufbietung,** *f.*, **–aufwand,** *m.* exertion, effort, expenditure of energy. **–ausdruck,** *m.* swear-word, *pl.* strong language. **–äußerung,** *f.* manifestation of force *or* strength. **–bedarf,** *m.* (*of a machine*) input; power requirement. **–brühe,** *f.* beef-tea. **–droschke,** *f.* taxi-cab.

Kräfte ['krɛftə], *pl. of* **Kraft. Kräftebedarf,** *m.* manpower requirements.

Krafteck, *n.* polygon of forces.

Kräfte|dreieck, *n.* triangle of forces. **–einsatz,** *m.* (*Mil.*) commitment of forces.

Krafteinheit ['kraftʔaınhaıt], *f.* unit of force *or* work.

Kräfte|mangel, *m.* shortage of manpower *or* labour **–parallelogramm,** *n.* parallelogram of forces. **–verfall,** *m.* loss of strength. **–vergeudung,** *f.* waste of energy. **–verteilung,** *f.* division *or* distribution of forces. **–vieleck,** *n.* polygon of forces. **–zersplitterung,** *f. See* **–verteilung.**

Kraft|fahrer, *m.* motorist. **–fahrtruppe,** *f.* (*Mil.*) motorized troops. **–fahrzeug,** *n.* motor vehicle. **–feld,** *n.* (*Phys.*) field of force. **–fülle,** *f.* exuberance. **–futter,** *n.* concentrated feed. **–gefühl,** *n.* feeling of strength. **kraftgeladen,** *adj.* dynamic, (*coll.*) power-packed.

kräftig ['krɛftıç], *adj.* strong, robust, sturdy, powerful; (*of a p. only*) vigorous, energetic, stalwart, brawny, (*coll.*) hefty, husky; (*fig.*) forceful, forcible; efficacious; (*of food*) nourishing, strengthening, rich; (*of colour*) rich, full. **kräftigen,** **1.** *v.t.* strengthen, invigorate; restore, revive, refresh; fortify, steel, harden. **2.** *v.r.* gain strength. **kräftigend,** *adj.* invigorating, bracing, refreshing, (*Med.*) tonic. **Kräftigkeit,** *f.* strength, energy, vigour; efficaciousness, full force. **Kräftigung,** *f.* strengthening, invigoration, restoration. **Kräftigungsmittel,** *n.* (*Med.*) restorative.

Kraft|lastwagen, *m.* (motor) lorry, (*Am.*) truck. **–lehre,** *f.* dynamics. **–linie,** *f.* (*Elec.*) line of force. **kraftlos,** *adj.* weak, feeble, powerless, exhausted, languid, enervated, faint, limp, (*coll. of style*) wishy-washy; ineffectual, impotent; (*Law*) (null and) void, invalid. **Kraft|meier, –mensch,** *m.* he-man. **–messer,** *m.* dynamometer. **–mittel,** *n.* forceful means; powerful remedy. **–post,** *f.* (motor) bus. **–probe,** *f.* trial of strength. **–quelle,** *f.* source of power *or* energy; generator unit. **–rad,** *n.* motor-cycle. **–reserve(n),** *f.*(*pl.*) (*of a p.*) reserve of strength. **–sprache,** *f.* powerful *or* forceful *or* pithy language. **–stoff,** *m.* fuel, petrol, (*Am.*) gas. **–stoffverbrauch,** *m.* fuel consumption. **–strom,** *m.* (*Elec.*) power supply *or* current. **kraftstrotzend,** *adj.* lusty, vigorous, (*coll.*) full of beans. **Kraft|stück,** *n.* stunt. **–übertragung,** *f.* power transmission. **–verkehr,** *m.* motor traffic. **kraftvoll,** *adj.* vigorous, powerful; (*fig.*) (*of style*) terse, pithy. **Kraft|wagen,** *m.* (motor-)car, motor vehicle, (*Am.*) automobile. **–werk,** *n.* (*Elec.*) power-station. **–wort,** *n. See* **–ausdruck.**

Kragen ['kra:gən], *m.* (**-s,** *pl.* - (*dial.* ¨)) collar; cape; ***am – packen,*** collar, seize by the scruff of the neck; (*fig.*) ***beim – nehmen*** or ***fassen,*** call to account; ***es geht ihm an den –,*** it will cost him his life, he will be called to account; (*coll.*) ***da platzte mir der –,*** that was the last straw, (*sl.*) I blew my top. **Kragen|knopf,** *m.* collar-stud. **–patten,** *f.pl.*, **–spiegel,** *m.* (*Mil.*) tab, facing, collar insignia. **–weite,** *f.* collar-size.

Krag|stein ['kra:k–], *m.* (*Archit.*) corbel, console, bracket. **–träger,** *m.* cantilever beam.

Krähe ['krɛ:ə], *f.* crow; rook; (*Prov.*) ***eine – hackt der andern nicht die Augen aus,*** there's honour among thieves, dog won't eat dog. **krähen,** *v.t.* crow, (*fig.*) (*of a child*) squall, squawk; ***danach kräht kein Hahn,*** nobody troubles about it. **Krähen|auge,** *n.* nux vomica, (*dial.*) corn (*on the foot*). **–füße,** *m.pl.* scrawl; crow's feet, wrinkles. **–kolonie,** *f.* rookery. **–nest,** *n.* (*Naut.*) crow's nest. **–scharbe,** *f.* (*Orn.*) shag (*Phalacrocorax aristotelis*).

Krähwinkel [krɛ'vıŋkəl], *n.* Gotham.

Krakau ['krakau], *n.* Cracow. **Krakauer** [–'kauər], *m.*, **krakauisch,** *adj.* Cracovian.

Krake ['kra:kə], *m.* (**-n,** *pl.* **-n**) octopus.

Krakeel [kra'ke:l], *m.* (**-s,** *pl.* **-e**) (*coll.*) squabble, brawl; row, racket. **krakeelen,** *v.i.* brawl, (*coll.*) kick up a row. **Krakeeler,** *m.* rowdy, brawler.

Krakelfüße ['kra:kəlfy:sə], *m.pl.* (*coll.*) illegible handwriting, scrawl.

Kral [kra:l], *m.* (**-s,** *pl.* **-e**) kraal.

Kralle ['kralə], *f.* claw, talon, clutch; (*fig.*) ***die –n zeigen,*** show one's claws *or* teeth; (*fig.*) ***in die –n bekommen,*** get one's clutches *or* claws on. **krallen,** **1.** *v.i.* claw, clutch (**an** (*Acc.*), at), scratch; (*coll.*) steal; (*dial.*) clamber. **2.** *v.r.* ***sich – an*** (*Acc.*), cling to, clutch. (at).

Kram [kra:m], *m.* (**-(e)s,** *pl.* **¨e**) 1. retail goods; haberdashery, small wares; (*fig.*) stuff, rubbish, trumpery, trash, odds and ends, lumber; (*coll.*) affair, business; retail trade; shop; (*coll.*) ***das paßt gerade in meinen –,*** that suits me down to the ground *or* me to a T., it's just what I want(ed); ***es paßte (ihm) nicht in seinen –,*** it did not suit his plans *or* purpose; ***der ganze –,*** the whole bag of tricks, (*sl.*) the whole shoot *or* caboodle; ***den – zumachen,*** shut up shop; 2. (*dial.*) childbed.

Kram|bude, *f. See* **-laden. kramen,** *v.i.* 1. rummage (*in* (*Dat.*), in; *unter* (*Dat.*), among), fumble (*nach*, for); (*dial.*) hawk, sell; 2. (*dial.*) be brought to childbed. **Kramer,** *m.* (*dial.*), **Krämer** ['krɛ:mər], *m.* (shifty) tradesman, pettifogger; (*obs.*) (small) shopkeeper; (*coll.*) grocer.

Krämer|geist, *m.* petty *or* mercenary spirit. **-latein,** *n.* dog-Latin. **-seele,** *f.* mercenary creature. **-volk,** *n.* small-minded people, (*obs.*) nation of shopkeepers.

Kramladen ['kra:mla:dən], *m.* small shop, general stores, grocer's shop.

Krammetsvogel, *m. See* **Wacholderdrossel.**

Krampe ['krampə], *f.* staple, U-bolt.

Krampf [krampf], *m.* (**-(e)s,** *pl.* **-̈e**) 1. cramp, spasm, convulsion, paroxysm, fit; 2. (*coll.*) thieving, pilfering. **Krampfader,** *f.* varicose vein. **krampfartig,** *adj. See* **Krampfhaft. krampfen,** *v.t.*, *v.r.* clench, clasp convulsively, contract spasmodically; (*coll.*) thieve, pilfer. **krampfhaft,** *adj.* convulsive, spasmodic; (*fig.*) frantic, desperate, feverish, frenzied; *– schluchzen,* sob convulsively, be seized with a fit of sobbing; *–es Lachen,* forced laughter; *–e Zuckung,* convulsion. **Krampfhusten,** *m.* convulsive cough, whooping cough. **krampfstillend,** *adj.* sedative, soothing, anti-spasmodic.

Kramwaren ['kra:mva:rən], *f.pl.* small wares, (*coll.*) groceries.

Kran [kra:n], *m.* (**-(e)s,** *pl.* **-e** (*Austr.* **-̈e**)) 1. crane, hoist; 2. (*dial.*) (stop-)cock, faucet. **Kran|arm, -ausleger,** *m.* crane-jib. **-bahn, -brücke,** *f.* gantry. **-geld,** *n.* cranage.

krängen ['krɛŋən], *v.i.* (*Naut.*) heel over.

Kranich ['kra:nɪç], *m.* (**-s,** *pl.* **-e**) (*Orn.*) crane (*Grus grus*).

krank [kraŋk], *adj.* (*comp. kränker, sup. kränk(e)st*) ill, sick, afflicted (*an* (*Dat.*), with), suffering, ailing (from); in poor *or* bad *or* ill health; (*of organ etc.*) diseased; *– zu Bett liegen,* be ill in bed; (*Mil.*) *sich – melden,* report sick; *– werden,* fall *or* be taken ill; *sich – stellen,* feign illness, (*Mil.*) malinger; *sich – lachen,* split one's sides with laughing; *– schreiben,* certify as ill, issue a doctor's certificate.

Kränke ['krɛŋkə], *f.* (*dial.*) epilepsy, (*obs.*) falling sickness.

kränkeln ['krɛŋkəln], *v.i.* be ailing *or* sickly *or* in poor health *or* poor in health *or* (*coll.*) poorly. **Kränkeln,** *n.* poor health, sickliness, (*coll.*) poorliness.

kranken ['kraŋkən], *v.i.* suffer (*an* (*Dat.*), from), be ill *or* (*fig.*) afflicted (with).

kränken ['krɛŋkən], **1.** *v.t.* offend, hurt (*s.o.'s*) feelings, insult; (ag)grieve, mortify; vex, annoy; *das kränkt,* that hurts; *es kränkte mich tief,* it cut me to the quick; *gekränkte Unschuld,* injured innocence. **2.** *v.r.* feel hurt *or* aggrieved, be mortified.

Kranken|anstalt, *f.* hospital. **-auto,** *n.* motor ambulance. **-bahre,** *f.* stretcher, litter. **-bericht,** *m.* bulletin; hospital report. **-besuch,** *m.* sick visiting; doctor's visit *or* attendance. **-bett,** *n.* sick-bed; *am –,* at the patient's bedside; *ans – gefesselt,* bedridden, confined to bed.

kränkend ['krɛŋkənt], *adj.* insulting, hurtful, offensive; vexing, annoying, mortifying.

Kranken|geld, *n.* medical *or* sick benefit, (*Mil.*) sick pay. **-haus,** *n.* infirmary, hospital. **-kasse,** *f.* health insurance, sick fund, (*coll.*) panel. **-kost,** *f.* invalid diet. **-lager,** *n. See* **-bett. -pflege,** *f.* (sick-)nursing. **-pflegerin,** *f. See* **-schwester. -revier,** *n.* (*Mil.*) sick-bay; medical centre. **-schein,** *m.* (*Mil.*) sick report; medical certificate, doctor's certificate *or* (*coll.*) note. **-schwester,** *f.* (hospital) nurse. **-stube,** *f.* sick-room; (*Mil.*) sick-bay. **-stuhl,** *m.* invalid chair. **-träger,** *m.* ambulance-man, stretcher-bearer. **-urlaub,** *m.* (*Mil.*) sick-leave. **-versicherung,** *f.* health insurance. **-wagen,** *m.* ambulance. **-wärter,** *m.* male nurse, hospital orderly, (*Mil.*) medical orderly. **-zimmer,** *n.* sick-room. **-zug,** *m.* hospital train.

Kranke(r) ['kraŋkə(r)], *m., f.* invalid, patient, sick person; casualty, case.

krankhaft ['kraŋkhaft], *adj.* pathological, diseased, abnormal, morbid; (*of mind*) unhealthy, psychopathic. **Krankhaftigkeit,** *f.* abnormality, pathological *or* diseased state, morbidity.

Krankheit ['kraŋkhaɪt], *f.* illness, sickness, disease, malady, ailment, complaint; *sich* (*Dat.*) *eine – zuziehen,* contract a disease, be taken *or* fall ill; *an einer – sterben,* die of an illness. **Krankheits|-bericht,** *m.* doctor's report. **-erreger,** *m.* pathogenic agent. **-erscheinung,** *f.* (pathological) symptom. **-fall,** *m.* case of sickness. **krankheitshalber,** *adv.* on account of *or* through *or* because of *or* owing to illness. **Krankheits|herd,** *m.* seat of disease. **-lehre,** *f.* pathology. **-stoff,** *m.* morbid *or* contagious matter. **-träger,** *m.* (*Med.*) carrier. **-übertragung,** *f.* infection, contagion. **-verlauf,** *m.* course of disease. **-vortäuschung,** *f.* (*Mil.*) malingering. **-zeichen,** *n.* symptom. **-zustand,** *m.* diseased *or* morbid state.

kränklich ['krɛŋklɪç], *adj.* sickly, ailing, infirm, valetudinarian, (*coll.*) poorly.

Kränkung ['krɛŋkuŋ], *f.* insult, offence, wrong, outrage, mortification, vexation.

Kranwagen ['kra:nva:gən], *m.* mobile crane, breakdown lorry; (*Mil.*) salvage truck, recovery vehicle.

Kranz [krants], *m.* (**-es,** *pl.* **-̈e**) garland, wreath; (*Archit.*) cornice; festoon, cincture; rim (*of wheel*), (mounting) ring, revolving mount (*of gun*); border, areola; edge, crest, ridge; valance; (*fig.*) group, circle (*of onlookers etc.*); *– von schönen Frauen,* galaxy of beauty; *einen – spenden,* send a wreath (*funeral*).

Kranz|arterie, *f.* (*Anat.*) coronary artery. **-brenner,** *m.* ring-burner, (gas)ring.

Kränzchen ['krɛntsçən], *n.* little garland; small gathering, bee, coffee-party; girls' *or* ladies' club. **kränzen,** *v.t.* (*Poet.*) crown, wreathe, garland, bedeck.

kranzförmig ['krantsfœrmɪç], *adj.* wreath-like; coronoid. **Kranz|gesims,** *n.* cornice. **-jungfer,** *f.* bridesmaid. **-spende,** *f.* funeral wreath.

Krapfen ['krapfən], *m.* fritter; doughnut.

Krapp [krap], *m.* madder (*dye*).

kraß [kras], *adj.* crass, flagrant, blatant, gross, drastic, striking, pronounced; *–(ss)e Unwissenheit,* gross ignorance; *–(ss)er Fuchs,* freshman, fresher; *–(ss)er Widerspruch,* flagrant contradiction; *–(ss)e Lüge,* blatant untruth; *–(ss)er Philister,* crass materialist.

Kratz [krats], *m.* (**-es,** *pl.* **-e** (*coll.* **-̈e**)) scratch, score, striation. **Kratz|beere,** *f.* (*dial.*) bramble, blackberry. **-bürste,** *f.* 1. scrubbing-brush; scratch-brush, wire-brush; 2. (*fig.*) (*coll.*) crosspatch. **kratzbürstig,** *adj.* (*coll.*) irritable, quick-tempered, cross; (*sl.*) snooty. **Kratze,** *f.* scraper; carding-comb.

Krätze ['krɛtzə], *f.* itch, scabies, scab, mange; (*Metall.*) scrapings, clippings, skimmings, dross.

kratzen ['kratsən], *v.t.*, *v.i.* scratch, scrape, striate; card, tease; (*as sound*) rasp, grate; scrawl, scribble; itch, tickle; *sich hinter dem Ohr –,* scratch one's head; *der Rauch kratzt mir im Halse,* the smoke irritates *or* (*coll.*) catches my throat; *auf einen Haufen –,* scrape together into a heap; *der Wein kratzt,* the wine is tart *or* harsh to the taste. **Kratzer,** *m.* 1. scraper, scratcher; 2. intestinal worm; 3. *See* **Kratzwunde.**

Krätzer ['krɛtsər], *m.* harsh *or* sour *or* tart wine.

Kratzfuß ['kratsfu:s], *m.* bow, obeisance.

kratzig ['kratsɪç], *adj.* scratchy; (*coll.*) *see* **kratzbürstig.**

krätzig ['krɛtsɪç], *adj.* (*Med.*) scabious, psoric; itchy.

Kratz|maschine, *f.* carding-machine. **-wunde,** *f.* surface wound, scratch.

krauchen ['krauxən], *v.i.* (*coll.*) *see* **kriechen.**

kraue(l)n ['krauə(l)n], *v.t.* rub *or* scratch gently, stroke.

kraul(schwimm)en ['kraul(ʃvɪm)ən], *irr.v.i.* swim the crawl.

kraus [kraus], *adj.* curly, crinkled, curled, frizz(l)y; corrugated; irregular, ruffled, tangled, confused, intricate; ***–es Durcheinander,*** inextricable tangle; ***ein –es Gesicht machen, die Stirne – ziehen,*** knit one's brow; ***er macht (treibt) es zu –,*** he carries things too far.

Krause ['krauzə], *f.* frill, ruff, ruffle.

Kräuseleisen ['krɔyzəlʔaɪzən], *n.* crimping-iron, curling-tongs. **kräuseln, 1.** *v.t.* curl, crinkle, crimp, goffer, pucker; mill (*coin*); fold, plait. **2.** *v.r.* curl (up), pucker, be ruffled.

krausen ['krauzən], *v.i., v.r. See* **kräuseln, 2.**

Kraus|gummi, *m.* crêpe rubber. **–haar,** *n.* curly hair. **kraushaarig,** *adj.* curly-haired. **Kraus|-kopf,** *m.* curly-head; curly-headed person. **–putz,** *m.* rough-cast. **–salat,** *m.* endive. **–tabak,** *m.* shag.

Kraut [kraut], *n.* (**-(e)s,** *pl.* **⸚er**) herb, plant, vegetable, weed, leaves *or* tops (*of root crops*); sumac; (*dial.*) cabbage; (*dial.*) purée; (*Prov.*) ***gegen den Tod ist kein – gewachsen,*** there is no cure for death; (*Prov.*) ***Muß ist ein bitter –,*** necessity is painful, compulsion is unpleasant; ***durcheinander wie – und Rüben,*** higgledy-piggledy; ***ins – schießen,*** run to leaf; ***das macht das – nicht fett,*** that does not help matters. **krautartig,** *adj.* herbaceous. **krauten,** *v.t., v.i.* hoe, weed. **Krauten,** *n.* weeding. **Krauter,** *m.* eccentric, crank, oddity.

Kräuter ['krɔytər], *pl. of* **Kraut. Kräuter|buch,** *n.* herbal. **–essig,** *m.* aromatic vinegar. **kräuterfressend,** *adj.* herbivorous. **Kräuter|käse,** *m.* green cheese. **–kenner,** *m.* herbalist, botanist. **–kenntnis,** *f.* botanical knowledge. **–kunde,** *f.* botany. **–sammler,** *m.* herbalist. **–sammlung,** *f.* herbarium. **–suppe,** *f.* vegetable soup. **–tee,** *m.* herb tea. **–wein,** *m.* medicated wine.

Kraut|garten, *m.* kitchen-garden. **–hacke,** *f.* hoe. **–junker,** *m.* (*coll.*) country squire.

Kräutler ['krɔytlər], *m.* (*Austr.*) greengrocer.

Krawall [kra'val], *m.* (**-s,** *pl.* **-e**) (*coll.*) riot, disturbance, brawl; row, uproar, (*sl.*) rumpus, shindy. **krawallen,** *v.i.* brawl, kick up a row. **Krawallmacher,** *m.* rowdy, hooligan.

Krawatte [kra'vatə], *f.* (neck)tie, cravat. **Krawattenmacher,** *m.* (*coll.*) moneylender, usurer.

kraweelgebaut [kra've:lgəbaut], *adj.* carvel-built (*of boats*).

kraxeln ['kraksəln], *v.i.* (*aux.* s.) (*coll.*) climb, clamber, scramble.

Kräze ['krɛ:tsə], *f.* (*Swiss*) dosser, pannier.

Kreatur [krea'tu:r], *f.* (**-,** *pl.* **-en**) creature, created man, (*Poet.*) all living creatures; vassal, dependant; ***feile –,*** hireling, minion.

Krebs [kre:ps], *m.* (**-es,** *pl.* **-e**) 1. crab, crayfish, (*Am.*) crawfish; *pl.* crustaceans; 2. (*Astr.*) Cancer; ***Wendekreis des –es,*** Tropic of Cancer; 3. (*Med.*) cancer; (*Bot.*) canker; 4. (*of a book*) unsold copy, remainder; 5. (*B.*) breastplate (of faith).

krebsartig ['kre:psʔartɪç], *adj.* 1. (*Zool.*) crustaceous; 2. (*Med.*) cancerous, (*Bot.*) cankerous. **Krebsbildung,** *f.* cancerous growth. **krebseln,** *v.i.* crawl, clamber. **krebsen,** *v.i.* 1. catch crayfish; 2. (*fig.*) have an uphill struggle, go to a lot of trouble in vain; 3. (*sl.*) ***– mit,*** turn to one's own advantage.

Krebs|gang, *m.* crab's walk; movement backwards, retrogression, decline. **–geschwür,** *n.* cancerous growth, carcinoma. **krebskrank,** *adj.* suffering from cancer. **Krebskranke(r),** *m., f.* cancer-patient. **krebsrot,** *adj.* red as a lobster *or* turkey-cock. **Krebs|schaden,** *m.* (*obs.*) cancerous sore; (*fig.*) inveterate evil, canker. **–schere,** *f.* crayfish's *or* crab's claw. **–tiere,** *n.pl.* crustacea.

Kredenz [kre'dɛnts], *f.* (**-,** *pl.* **-en**) sideboard. **kredenzen,** *v.t.* (*obs.*) taste (*wine before serving*); (*Poet.*) offer, serve, present. **Kredenzer,** *m.* foretaster; cupbearer. **Kredenz|teller,** *m.* salver. **–tisch,** *m.* sideboard, serving table.

[1]**Kredit** [kre'di:t], *m.* (**-(e)s,** *pl.* **-e**) credit, loan; (*fig.*) standing, reputation; ***laufender –,*** open credit; ***den – überziehen*** or ***überschreiten*** or ***übertreiben,*** overdraw one's account, exceed one's credit.

[2]**Kredit** ['kre:dɪt], *s.* (**-s,** *pl.* **-s**) (*Comm.*) credit (side) (*of account*).

Kredit|anstalt, *f.* bank. **–aufnahme,** *f.* raising credit, borrowing. **–ausweitung,** *f.* (*euphemism for*) inflation. **–brief,** *m.* letter of credit. **kreditfähig,** *adj.* solvent, sound, trustworthy. **Kredit|fähigkeit,** *f.* credit standing, solvency, soundness, trustworthiness. **–genossenschaft,** *f.* mutual loan society, co-operative credit association.

kreditieren [kredi'ti:rən], **1.** *v.t.* credit, place to the credit of. **2.** *v.i.* give *or* allow *or* extend credit. **Kreditierung,** *f.* crediting; credit note *or* advice.

Kreditiv [kredi'ti:f], *n.* (**-s,** *pl.* **-e**) credentials, warrant, authority.

Kredit|mittel, *n.pl.* borrowed money, loan funds. **–posten,** *m.* credit entry. **–saldo,** *m.* credit balance. **–sperre,** *f.* credit squeeze. **kredit|-würdig,** *adj. See* **–fähig.**

kregel ['kre:gəl], *adj.* (*dial.*) sound, hale; lively, brisk, frisky.

Kreide ['kraɪdə], *f.* chalk; crayon; calcium carbonate, whiting; (*coll.*) ***mit 12 Mark bei ihm in der – stehen,*** be 12 marks in the red with him; (*coll.*) ***tief in der – stehen*** or ***sitzen,*** be up to the ears in debt. **kreide|bleich,** *adj. See* **–weiß. Kreide|-boden,** *m.* chalky soil. **–fels,** *m.* chalk cliff. **–formation,** *f.,* **–gebilde,** *n.* (*Geol.*) chalk-formation; cretaceous group. **–stift,** *m.* chalk, crayon. **kreideweiß,** *adj.* deathly pale, white as a sheet. **Kreidezeichnung,** *f.* crayon drawing. **kreidig,** *adj.* chalky, cretaceous.

kreieren [kre'i:rən], *v.t.* create, make, produce.

Kreis [kraɪs], *m.* (**-es,** *pl.* **-e**) circle, ring, (*Astr.*) orbit; circuit (*also Elec.*); cycle; district; sphere, range, zone (*of action etc.*); ***städtischer (ländlicher) –,*** urban (rural) district; (*Geom.*) ***einen – ziehen,*** describe a circle; ***das liegt außer meinem –e,*** that is not within my province *or* ken; ***im –e seiner Familie,*** in the bosom of his family; ***aus unseren –en,*** from among our circle (of friends); ***in allen –en des Lebens,*** in every walk of life; ***die höchsten –e,*** the upper ten (thousand), high society; ***sich in einen – stellen*** or ***treten,*** form a circle; ***seine –e weiter ziehen,*** enlarge one's horizon; ***sich im –e bewegen*** or ***drehen,*** revolve, rotate, circle round, turn round and round; (*fig.*) go round in circles, make no headway.

Kreis|abschnitt, *m.* (*Geom.*) segment (of a circle). **–amtmann,** *m.* chairman of a district council. **–arzt,** *m.* local doctor. **–ausschnitt,** *m.* (*Geom.*) sector (of a circle). **–ausschuß,** *m.* district council. **–bahn,** *f.* orbit. **–behörde,** *f.* local *or* district council. **–bewegung,** *f.* rotation, circular *or* rotary motion. **–bogen,** *m.* (*Archit.*) circular arch; (*Geom.*) arc (of a circle).

kreischen ['kraɪʃən], *irr.v.i.* shriek, screech, scream; (*as a hinge etc.*) squeak, creak, grate (on the ear), (*of colours*) be glaring *or* garish; ***–de Stimme,*** shrill voice.

Kreis|drehung, *f. See* **–bewegung. –einteilung,** *f.* (*Geom.*) division of the circle, (*Pol.*) division into districts.

Kreisel ['kraɪzəl], *m.* (spinning) top, gyroscope; ***den – schlagen,*** spin a top. **Kreisel|bewegung,** *f.* gyration. **–horizont,** *m.* (*Naut.*) artificial horizon. **–kompaß,** *m.* gyro-compass. **kreiseln,** *v.i.* gyrate, rotate, revolve, spin *or* whirl round; spin a top. **Kreisel|pumpe,** *f.* centrifugal pump. **–rad,** *n.* turbine, rotor. **–verdichter,** *m.* turbo-compressor.

kreisen ['kraɪzən], *v.i.* move in circles *or* in a circle, circle, rotate, revolve, whirl round; (*as money, blood etc.*) circulate; ***die Flasche – lassen,*** pass the bottle round.

Kreisfläche ['kraɪsflɛçə], *f.* (*Geom.*) area of the circle. **kreisförmig,** *adj.* circular, round, annular. **Kreis|frequenz,** *f.* angular velocity. **–fuge,** *f.* (*Mus.*) round canon. **–gericht,** *n.* district-court; (*Eng.*) county court, petty sessions. **–hauptmann,** *m.* (*dial.*) prefect of a district. **–lauf,** *m.* rotation, revolution; (*of blood etc.*) circulation; course, cycle, circuit, orbit; series, succession (*of the seasons etc.*). **–leitung,** *f.* (*Elec., Rad.*) closed circuit. **–linie,** *f.* circumference. **kreisrund,** *adj.* circular. **Kreissäge,** *f.* circular saw.

kreißen [ˈkraɪsən], *v.i.* be in labour. **Kreißen,** *n.* labour (pains). **Kreißende,** *f.* woman in labour. **Kreißsaal,** *m.* labour ward.

Kreis|stadt, *f.* chief town of a district, (*Eng.*) county town. **–strom,** *m.* (*Elec.*) circuit current. **–tag,** *m.* local council meeting. **–umfang,** *m.* circumference, periphery. **–verkehr,** *m.* one-way traffic; traffic on a roundabout. **–viertel,** *n.* quadrant.

Krem [kreːm], *m.* (**-s,** *pl.* **-s** *or* **-e**) *or f.* (-, *pl.* **-s**) cream (filling), custard. **Kreme,** *f.* 1. ointment, (face) cream, (tooth) paste, (shoe) polish; 2. (*dial.*) cream (*of milk*).

kremieren [kreˈmiːrən], *v.t.* cremate.

Kreml [kreːml], *m.* the Kremlin.

Krempe [ˈkrɛmpə], *f.* edge, border, brim (*of hat*), turn-up (*of trousers*), (*Mech.*) flange.

[1]**Krempel** [ˈkrɛmpəl], *m.* (*coll.*) rubbish; stuff.

[2]**Krempel,** *f.* (-, *pl.* **-n**) card, carding-comb. **krempeln,** *v.t.* card (*wool*), tease(l), teazle (*cloth*).

Kremser [ˈkrɛmzər], *m.* (*dial.*) charabanc.

Kren [kreːn], *m.* (*Austr.*) horse-radish.

krepieren [kreˈpiːrən], **1.** *v.i.* (*aux.* s.) 1. die (*of animals*), (*vulg.*) peg out, kick the bucket; 2. explode; burst (*of shells*). **2.** *v.t.* (*dial.*) annoy, irritate.

Krepp [krɛp], *m.* (**-s,** *pl.* **-e**) crêpe, crape.

Kreppapier, *n.* crêpe paper. **kreppen,** *v.t.* crêpe, crisp, crinkle; nap (*cloth*); curl, wave. **Kreppseide,** *f.* crêpe-de-chine.

kreß [krɛs], *adj.* orange(-coloured).

Kresse [ˈkrɛsə], *f.* (*Bot.*) cress (*Lepidium sativum*).

Krethi und Plethi [ˈkreːti], all the world and his wife; rag-tag and bobtail; Tom, Dick and Harry.

Kretscham [ˈkrɛtʃam], *m.* (**-s,** *pl.* **-e**) (*dial.*) village tavern.

kreuch [krɔyç], **kreuchst, kreucht,** *see* **kriechen.**

Kreuz [krɔyts], *n.* (**-es,** *pl.* **-e**) cross, crucifix, crosier; cross-bar; (*Anat.*) sacral region, small of the back, loins, rump; (*of horse*) croup, crupper; (*of cow*) chine; (*Cards*) club; (*Mus.*) sharp; (*Typ.*) dagger, obelus; (*fig.*) burden, affliction; ***ans – schlagen,*** fix *or* nail to the cross; (***sich*** (*Dat.*)) ***das – brechen,*** break one's back; (*coll.*) ***drei –e hinter ihm machen,*** be glad to see the back of him; ***ins – legen,*** lay crosswise; ***ins – segeln,*** tack; ***das – machen,*** cross o.s., make the sign of the cross; (*fig.*) ***sein – auf sich nehmen,*** take up one's cross; ***ein – schlagen,*** see ***das – machen; zu –e kriechen,*** humble o.s., submit, (*coll.*) knuckle under, truckle (***vor*** (*Dat.*), to), eat humble pie.

kreuz, *adv.* ***– und quer,*** in all directions, this way and that, criss-cross; ***– und quer durchwandern,*** travel the length and breadth of.

Kreuz|abnahme, *f.* descent *or* deposition from the cross. **–arm,** *m.* cross-bar. **–band,** *n.* 1. (*Carp.*) notched joint; 2. postal *or* newspaper wrapper; ***unter –,*** as printed matter, by book-post. **–bein,** *n.* (*Anat.*) sacrum. **–berg,** *m.* Calvary. **–bild,** *n.* effigy of the Cross. **–blütler,** *m.pl.* cruciferous plants. **–bogen,** *m.* (*Archit.*) ogive, groined arch. **kreuzbrav,** *adj.* thoroughly honest, worthy, (*of child*) very well-behaved. **Kreuz|bube,** *m.* knave of clubs. **–dame,** *f.* queen of clubs. **–dorn,** *m.* (*Bot.*) buckthorn (*Rhamnus cathartica*).

kreuzen [ˈkrɔytsən], **1.** *v.t.* mark with a cross, cross (*one's legs*), fold (*one's arms*); (*fig.*) thwart, cross; (*Biol.*) cross, hybridize, interbreed; (*Elec.*) cross-connect. **2.** *v.r.* make the sign of the cross; intersect, cross *or* cut one another, traverse, meet; clash; (*Biol.*) interbreed. **3.** *v.i.* (*Naut.*) cruise; (*Naut.*) tack.

Kreuzer [ˈkrɔytsər], *m.* 1. (*Naut.*) cruiser; 2. (*obs.*) groat, farthing.

Kreuz|erhöhung, *f.* elevation of the cross. **–fahrer,** *m.* crusader. **–feuer,** *n.* (*Mil.*) crossfire; (*fig.*) ***ins – nehmen,*** take *or* catch between two fires.

kreuz|fidel, *adj.* merry as a cricket, pleased as Punch. **–förmig,** *adj.* cruciform, cross-shaped. **Kreuz|gang,** *m.* 1. cloisters; 2. (*Min.*) cross-lode. **–gegend,** *f.* lumbar region. **–gelenk,** *n.* (*Mech.*) universal joint. **–gewölbe,** *n.* cruciform vault, cross vaulting.

kreuzigen [ˈkrɔytsɪgən], *v.t.* crucify. **Kreuzigung,** *f.* crucifixion.

Kreuz|kirche, *f.* 1. church on cruciform plan; 2. church of the Holy Cross. **–kopf,** *m.* (*Motor.*) big-end. **kreuzlahm,** *adj.* (*Vet.*) suffering from azoturia, (*coll.*) broken-backed; (*fig.*) ***ich bin ganz –,*** my back is killing me. **Kreuz|mast,** *m.* (*Naut.*) mizzen (*when square-rigged*). **–maß,** *n.* T-square; (*Typ.*) gauge. **–naht,** *f.* cross-stiched seam. **–otter,** *f.* viper, adder. **–peilung,** *f.* cross-bearing. **–punkt,** *m.* (*Geom.*) point of intersection, (*Railw. etc.*) crossing, intersection. **–ritter,** *m.* Knight of the Cross, crusader. **kreuzsaitig,** *adj.* overstrung (*piano*). **Kreuz|schiff,** *n.* transept. **–schmerz,** *m.* lumbago. **–schnabel,** *m.* (*Orn.*) *see* **Fichtenkreuzschnabel**; ***großer –,*** *see* **Kiefernkreuzschnabel. –schraffierung, –schraffur,** *f.* cross-hatching. **–spinne,** *f.* garden spider. **–stab,** *m.* crosier. **–stellung,** *f.* (*dancing*) pas croisé. **–stenge,** *f.* (*Naut.*) mizzen topmast. **–stich,** *m.* cross-stitch.

Kreuzung [ˈkrɔytsuŋ], *f.* crossing, intersection, crossroads; (*Biol.*) cross-breeding, inter-breeding, hybridization; cross-breed, hybrid, mongrel.

kreuzunglücklich [krɔytsˈunglyklɪç], *adj.* thoroughly wretched *or* miserable *or* despondent *or* downcast. **Kreuz|verhör,** *n.* cross-examination; ***ins – nehmen,*** cross-examine. **–verweis,** *m.* cross-reference. **–weg,** *m.* crossing, crossroad; (*Eccl.*) way *or* stations of the Cross. **kreuzweise,** *adv.* crosswise, transverse, across. **Kreuz|woche,** *f.* Rogation week. **–worträtsel,** *n.* crossword puzzle. **–zeichen,** *n.* sign of the cross. **–zug,** *m.* crusade.

Kribbel [ˈkrɪbəl], *m.* itching, irritation, impatience. **kribb(e)lig,** *adj.* (*coll.*) irritable, touchy; fidgety, jumpy, jittery. **Kribbelkrankheit,** *f.* (*coll.*) ergot poisoning. **kribbeln,** *v.i.* (*coll.*) 1. creep, crawl, swarm; 2. (*imp.*) itch, tickle, prickle, tingle; ***es kribbelt mir,*** I have pins and needles; (*fig.*) I am itching (*to do*).

Kribskrabs [ˈkrɪpskraps], *m. or n.* hotch-potch, medley, gibberish.

Krickelei [krɪkəˈlaɪ], *f.* (*dial.*) 1. scrawl, scribble; 2. provocations, annoyances; fretfulness, peevishness, cavilling. **krickeln** [ˈkrɪkəln], *v.i.* 1. be fretful *or* querulous *or* peevish *or* captious; 2. scrawl, scribble.

Krickente [ˈkrɪkˀɛntə], *f.* (*Orn.*) (*Am.* European) teal (*Anas crecca*).

Krida [ˈkriːda], *f.* (*Austr.*) bankruptcy. **Kridar** [kriˈdaːr], *m.* (**-s,** *pl.* **-e**) bankrupt.

Kriech [kriːç], *m.* (*Metall.*) creep. **kriechen,** *irr.v.i.* (*aux.* h. & s.) creep, crawl; cringe, grovel, fawn; ***aus dem Ei –,*** hatch (out). **Kriecher,** *m.* sneak, toady, sycophant, lickspittle. **Kriecherei** [–ˈraɪ], *f.* servility, fawning, cringing, grovelling. **kriecherisch,** *adj.* servile, grovelling, fawning, cringing.

Kriech|funken, *m.* (*Elec.*) flash-over, surface discharge. **–geschwindigkeit,** *f.* (*Metall.*) creep rate. **–pflanze,** *f.* creeper. **–strecke,** *f.* (*Elec.*) leakage path. **–strom,** *m.* (*Elec.*) surface leakage. **–tier,** *n.* reptile. **–weg,** *m.* *See* **–strecke.**

Krieg [kriːk], *m.* (**-(e)s,** *pl.* **-e**) war, warfare, hostilities, feud, strife; ***den – wieder anfangen,*** resume hostilities; ***den – erklären,*** declare war (*Dat.*, on); ***– führen*** (***gegen*** (*Acc.*) or ***mit***), wage war (with *or* against), be at war (with), make war (on); ***geistiger –,*** psychological warfare; ***im –,*** at war; ***– in der Luft,*** aerial warfare; ***in den – ziehen,*** go to war (***gegen*** (*Acc.*), against); ***– bis aufs Messer, – auf Tod und Leben,*** war to the knife; ***– zu Lande,*** land warfare; ***– zur See,*** war at sea, maritime *or* naval warfare

[1]**kriegen** [ˈkriːgən], *v.i.* (*rare*) wage war.

[2]**kriegen,** *v.t.* (*coll.*) get (hold of); catch (*a disease*

etc.); *wir werden's schon* –, we'll manage it all right; *gleich kriegst du was!* you'll catch it!

Krieger ['kri:gər], *m.* warrior, fighter, combatant; *ehemaliger* or (*coll.*) *alter* –, ex-serviceman. **Krieger|denkmal,** *n.* war-memorial. **–grab,** *n.* war-grave.

kriegerisch ['kri:gərɪʃ], *adj.* militant, bellicose; warlike, martial.

Krieger|verein, *m.* ex-servicemen's *or* old comrades' association. **–waise,** *f.* war-orphan. **–witwe,** *f.* war-widow.

kriegführend ['kri:kfy:rənt], *adj.* belligerent. **Kriegführung,** *f.* strategy (of war); warfare.

Kriegs|akademie, *f.* military academy; staff college. **–anleihe,** *f.* war loan. **–artikel,** *m.pl.* articles of war. **–ausbruch,** *m.* outbreak of war. **–ausrüstung,** *f.* war equipment. **–auszeichnung,** *f.* war decoration. **–bedarf,** *m.* military stores. **–beil,** *n.* (*Hist.*) battle-axe; (*fig.*) *das – begraben,* bury the hatchet. **–bemalung,** *f.* warpaint. **kriegsbereit,** *adj.* prepared for war. **Kriegs|bereitschaft,** *f.* readiness for war, state of mobilization. **–bericht,** *m.* war communiqué. **–berichterstatter,** *m.* war correspondent. **kriegs|beschädigt,** *adj.* *See* **–versehrt. Kriegs|beute,** *f.* spoils of war, booty. **–blinde(r),** *m.* blind ex-serviceman. **–dienst,** *m.* military service. **–dienstpflichtige(r),** *m.* conscript. **–dienstverweigerer,** *m.* conscientious objector. **–einwirkung,** *f.* enemy action. **–entschädigung,** *f.* reparations, war indemnity. **–erklärung,** *f.* declaration of war. **–eröffnung,** *f.* commencement of hostilities. **–etat,** *m.* military estimates. **–fahne,** *f.* regimental colours. **–fall,** *m.* case of war. **–flotte,** *f.* navy, fleet, naval force. **–freiwillige(r),** *m.* war time volunteer. **–führung,** *f.* conduct of war. **–fuß,** *m.* war footing; *auf (dem)* –, on a war footing, (*fig.*) at daggers drawn; *auf – setzen,* mobilize; put (*a ship*) in commission.

Kriegs|gebiet, *n.* war area *or* zone. **–gefahr,** *f.* danger *or* risk of war. **–gefährte,** *m.* *See* **–kamerad. –gefangene(r),** *m.* prisoner of war. **–gefangenschaft,** *f.* captivity. **–geist,** *m.* martial spirit. **–genosse,** *m.* *See* **–kamerad. –gerät,** *n.*, **–gerätschaften,** *f.pl.* warlike stores, war material. **–gericht,** *n.* court-martial; *vor ein – stellen,* court martial. **kriegsgerichtlich,** *adv.* by court martial. **Kriegs|gerichtsrat,** *m.* judge advocate. **–geschrei,** *n.* war-cry, battle-cry. **–gesetz,** *n.* martial law. **–gewinnler,** *m.* war profiteer. **–glück,** *n.* fortune of war; military success. **–gott,** *m.* god of war, Mars. **–gräberfürsorge,** *f.* war graves commission. **–greuel,** *m.pl.* atrocities (*of war*). **–hafen,** *m.* naval base *or* station. **–handwerk,** *n.* profession of arms, military profession. **–heer,** *n.* field-army, (*B.*) host. **–held,** *m.* great warrior, war-hero. **–herr,** *m.* supreme commander, commander-in-chief; generalissimo, war lord. **–hetze,** *f.* warmongering. **–hetzer,** *m.* warmonger. **–hinterbliebene,** *m.pl.* next-of-kin of war casualties, war-widows and orphans. **–industrie,** *f.* war industry.

Kriegs|kamerad, *m.* fellow-soldier, comrade in arms. **–kind,** *n.* war baby. **–knecht,** *m.* (*Hist.*) mercenary. **–kost,** *f.* war-time rations. **–kunst,** *f.* military science; art of war, generalship, tactics and strategy. **–lage,** *f.* strategic situation. **–lärm,** *m.* rumours of war. **–lazarett,** *n.* military hospital. **–list,** *f.* stratagem. **–lüge,** *f.* lying war propaganda. **kriegslustig,** *adj.* bellicose. **Kriegs|macht,** *f.* fighting strength, war potential; forces, troops; (*Pol.*) belligerent power. **–marine,** *f.* navy. **–minister,** *m.* (*Eng.*) Secretary of State for War, (*Am.*) Secretary of War. **–ministerium,** *n.* (*Eng.*) War Office, (*Am.*) War Department. **–müdigkeit,** *f.* war-weariness. **–neurose,** *f.* shell-shock, battle fatigue. **–opfer,** *n.* war casualty *or* victim. **–orden,** *m.* war-time decoration. **–pfad,** *m.* (*fig.*) *auf* –, on the warpath. **kriegspflichtig,** *adj.* liable for military service. **Kriegs|rat,** *m.* war council; (*fig.*) *– halten,* hold a council of war. **–recht,** *n.* martial law. **–rente,** *f.* war pension. **–ruf,** *m.* war-cry; summons to arms. **–ruhm,** *m.* military glory.

Kriegs|schaden, *m.* war-damage. **–schauplatz,** *m.* seat of war, theatre of operations. **–schiff,** *n.* man-of-war, warship. **–schuld,** *f.* war guilt. **–schulden,** *f.pl.* war-debts. **–schuldverschreibung,** *f.* war-bond. **–schule,** *f.* military academy. **–spiel,** *n.* 1. manœuvre; 2. prisoner's base (*game*). **–stand,** *m.*, **–stärke,** *f.* war(time) establishment. **–tanz,** *m.* war-dance. **–teilnehmer,** *m.* *See* **Krieger. –trauung,** *f.* wartime wedding. **–treiber,** *m.* *See* **–hetzer. –übung,** *f.* manœuvres. **kriegs|unbrauchbar,** *adj.* unfit for service (*equipment*). **–untauglich,** *adj.* unfit for active service (*personnel*). **Kriegs|verbrechen,** *n.* war-crime. **–verbrecher,** *m.* war-criminal. **–verluste,** *m.pl.* casualties. **kriegsversehrt,** *adj.* disabled, wounded. **Kriegsversehrte(r),** *m.* disabled ex-serviceman, *pl.* war-wounded. **kriegsverwendungsfähig,** *adj.* fit for active service. **Kriegsvorrat,** *m.* war reserves. **kriegswichtig,** *adj.* strategic, of military importance; *–es Ziel,* military target. **Kriegs|wirtschaft,** *f.* war(time) economy. **–wissenschaft,** *f.* military science. **–wucher,** *m.* war profiteering. **–zeit,** *f.* wartime; *in –en,* in times of war. **–ziel,** *n.* war aim *or* objective. **–zug,** *n.* campaign, military expedition. **–zulage,** *f.* field-allowance. **–zustand,** *m.* state of war; military preparedness. **–zwecke,** *m.pl.* military purposes.

Krim [krɪm], *f.* (*Geog.*) Crimea.

kriminal [krimi'na:l], *adj.* criminal, penal. **Kriminal,** *n.* (**-s,** *pl.* **-e**) (*Austr.*) prison. **Kriminal|abteilung,** *f.* criminal investigation department. **–beamte(r),** *m.* detective, plainclothes man. **Kriminalist** [–'lɪst], *m.* (**-en,** *pl.* **-en**) criminologist. **Kriminalistik,** *f.* criminology. **Kriminalität** [–i'tɛ:t], *f.* criminality. **Kriminal|polizei,** *f.* *See* **–abteilung. –recht,** *n.* penal *or* criminal law. **–roman,** *m.* detective novel. **–vergehen,** *n.* indictable offence. **kriminell,** *adj.* criminal, culpable.

Krimkrieg ['krɪmkri:k], *m.* Crimean War.

krimmeln ['krɪməln], *v.i.* (*dial.*) (*only in*) *es krimmelt und wimmelt* (*von*), it is crawling (with), it swarms (of).

Krimmer ['krɪmər], *m.* astrakhan, Persian lamb (skin).

Krimpe ['krɪmpə], *f.* shrinking; *in die – gehen,* shrink. **krimpen, 1.** *v.t.* shrink (*cloth*). **2.** *v.r., v.i.* (*aux.* s.) shrink; back (*of wind*); shrivel. **krimpfrei,** *adj.* non-shrink(ing).

Krimskrams ['krɪmskrams], *m.* (*coll.*) *see* **Kribskrabs.**

Krimstecher ['krɪmʃtɛçər], *m.* (*obs.*) field-glass.

Kringel ['krɪŋəl], *m.* 1. (*bakery*) cracknel; 2. curl, squiggle; kink, loop (*in rope*).

Krippe ['krɪpə], *f.* crib, manger, feeding trough; (*dial.*) hurdle-work, fence; (*coll.*) crèche, day-nursery. **krippen,** *v.t.* fence with hurdles; strengthen (*a dike*) with hurdle-work. **Krippen|beißer,** *m.* crib-biter, wind-sucker, unsound horse. **–reiter,** *m.* parasite. **–setzer,** *m.* *See* **–beißer. –spiel,** *n.* nativity play.

Krise ['kr:zə], *f.* crisis, turning point; (*Comm.*) depression. **kriseln,** *v.i. imp.* take a critical turn, approach a crisis. **krisenfest,** *adj.* stable. **Krisenfürsorge,** *f.* unemployment relief. **Krisis,** *f.* (-, *pl.* **Krisen**) *see* **Krise** (*esp. Med.*).

krispeln ['krɪspəln], *v.t.* crinkle, grain (*leather etc.*).

Kristall [krɪs'tal], **1.** *m.* (**-s,** *pl.* **-e**) crystal; *–e bilden,* crystallize. **2.** *n.* *See* **Kristallglas. kristall|ähnlich, –artig,** *adj.* crystal-like, crystalline. **Kristall|bau,** *m.* crystal structure. **–bildung,** *f.* crystallization. **Kristallehre,** *f.* crystallography. **Kristallempfänger,** *m.* (*Rad.*) crystal set. **kristallen,** *adj.* crystal clear; crystalline, crystal-like. **Kristall|flasche,** *f.* cut-glass decanter. **–glas,** *n.* cut-glass, crystal. **kristallhell,** *adj.* clear as crystal; transparent. **kristallinisch** [–'li:nɪʃ], *adj.* crystalline.

kristallisierbar [krɪstali'zi:rba:r], *adj.* crystallizable. **kristallisieren,** *v.t., v.i.* crystallize. **Kristallisierung,** *f.* crystallization.

kristall|klar, *adj.* *See* **–hell. Kristall|kunde,**

f. crystallography. **–wasser,** *n.* water of crystallization.

Kriterium [kri'te:rium], *n.* (**-s,** *pl.* **-rien**) criterion.

Kritik [kri'ti:k], *f.* (-, *pl.* **-en**) criticism (*über* (*Acc.*) *or* ***an*** (*Dat.*), of), censure; review, critique; ***einer – unterziehen,*** criticize; review (*a book*); ***unter aller –,*** beneath contempt; ***gute –en haben,*** have good notices (*of a book etc.*). **Kritikaster** [–'kastər], *m.* carping critic, fault-finder. **Kritiker** ['kri:tikər], *m.* critic, reviewer. **kritiklos,** *adj.* uncritical, undiscriminating. **Kritiklosigkeit,** *f.* lack of discrimination.

kritisch ['kri:tɪʃ], *adj.* critical (***gegenüber,*** of); discerning, discriminating; critical, grave, serious; ***–e Temperatur,*** critical temperature; ***–er Augenblick,*** crucial moment; ***das –e Alter,*** change of life, menopause, climacteric. **kritisieren** [–'zi:rən], *v.t.* criticize, comment on; review (*a book*); censure; ***abfällig –,*** disparage, impugn, decry, vilify, speak ill of.

Krittelei [krɪtə'laɪ], *f.* carping criticism, fault-finding, cavilling. **Kritt(e)ler** ['krɪt(ə)lər], *m.* fault-finder, captious *or* (*coll.*) niggling critic, grouser, (*sl.*) nark. **kritteln,** *v.i.* (***an*** (*Dat.*)), criticize, cavil *or* carp (at), find fault (with).

Kritz [krɪts], *m.* (**-es,** *pl.* **-e**) scratch, scrawl. **Kritzelei** [–'laɪ], *f.* scrawl, scribble. **kritzeln,** *v.i.* scribble, scrawl; scratch, splutter (*as pens*).

Kroate [kro'a:tə], *m.* (**-n,** *pl.* **-n**) Croat. **Kroatien,** *n.* Croatia. **kroatisch,** *adj.* Croatian.

kroch [krɔx], **kroch(e)st, kröche** ['krœçə], *see* **kriechen.**

Kroki [kro'ki:], *n.* (**-s,** *pl.* **-s**) (*Mil.*) sketch map. **krokieren,** *v.t., v.i.* sketch, make a sketch map.

krollen ['krɔlən], *v.t., v.r.* (*dial.*) crisp, curl (up).

Kron|anwalt ['kro:n–], *m.* (*Hist.*) counsel for the crown, public prosecutor; attorney-general. **–beamte(r),** *m.* officer of the crown. **–bewerber,** *m.* aspirant to the crown.

Krone ['kro:nə], *f.* crown; coronet; tiara; (*fig.*) diadem; tonsure. (*fig.*) head; chandelier; (*coin*) crown, (*dentistry*) crown(-cap); florin; (*Anat., Archit., Bot.*) corona; (*Bot.*) perianth; crest (*of waves*), coping (*of wall*), crown (*of road*); top, tree-top, (*fig.*) acme, apotheosis, consummation, crowning achievement *or* glory, paragon; glory, halo; ***das setzt der S. die – auf,*** that puts the lid on it, that's the last straw; ***dem Verdienste seine –,*** honour to whom honour is due; (*coll.*) ***was ist ihm in die – gefahren?*** what has upset him? what's the matter with him? (*sl.*) what's got into *or* eating him?

krönen ['krø:nən], *v.t.* crown; (*fig.*) crown, finish, cap, top, put the finishing touch(es) to; ***ihn zum König –,*** crown him king; ***gekrönter Dichter,*** poet laureate.

Kronen|bein, *n.* coronoid bone. **–gold,** *n.* 18-carat gold. **kronenlos,** *adj.* uncrowned; (*Bot.*) apetalous. **Kronenträger,** *m.* crowned head, sovereign.

Kron|erbe, *m.* heir to the crown. **–glas,** *n.* crown-glass. **–gut,** *n.* crown-lands, royal domain. **–juwelen,** *n.pl.* crown jewels. **–kolonie,** *f.* crown colony. **–lehen,** *n.* fief of the crown. **–leuchter,** *m.* lustre, chandelier. **–prinz,** *m.* crown prince; (*Eng.*) Prince of Wales. **–prinzessin,** *f.* (*Eng.*) Princess Royal. **–rat,** *m.* (*Eng.*) Privy Council. **–rede,** *f.* speech from the throne.

Kronsbeere ['kro:nsbe:rə], *f.* (*dial.*) cranberry.

Kron|schatz, *m.* *See* **–juwelen. –schnepfe,** *f.* *See* ***großer Brachvogel.***

Krönung ['krø:nuŋ], *f.* 1. crowning, coronation (ceremony); 2. (*fig.*) crowning achievement *or* event, culmination, climax, acme; 3. finishing touch(es).

Kron|werk, *n.* (*Mil.*) outworks. **–zeuge,** *m.* king's *or* queen's (*Am.* state's) evidence; chief witness.

Kropf [krɔpf], *m.* (**-(e)s,** *pl.* **⸚e**) crop, craw, maw (*of birds*); (*Med.*) wen, goitre; (*Bot.*) excrescence; (*Vet.*) bunches, glanders; bow (*of ship*); projecting part, top (*of a wall*). **Kropfader,** *f.* varicose vein. **kropfartig,** *adj.* goitrous. **Kropfdrüse,** *f.* thyroid gland.

kröpfen ['krœpfən], **1.** *v.t.* 1. (*Tech.*) bend at right angles, crank, offset; 2. cram (*poultry*). **2.** *v.i.* gorge, feed (*of birds of prey*). **Kröpfer,** *m.* male pouter pigeon.

kropfig ['krɔpfɪç], **kröpfig** ['krœpfɪç], *adj.* (*Med.*) strumous, goitrous.

Kropf|mittel, *n.* antistrumatic. **–rohr,** *n.* bent tube. **–stein,** *m.* voussoir. **–sucht,** *f.* cretinism. **–taube,** *f.* pouter pigeon.

Kröpfung ['krœpfuŋ], *f.* 1. (*Archit.*) corner-moulding; (*Tech.*) bend, offset, shoulder, crank; 2. cramming (*of poultry*).

Kroppzeug ['krɔptsɔyk], *n.* (*coll.*) rag-tag and bob-tail; small fry; ***das kleine –,*** pack of young brats.

Kroquis, *n.* (-, *pl.* -) (*Austr.*) *see* **Kroki.**

Kröseleisen ['krø:zəlʔaɪzən], *n.* glazier's iron; croze(-iron). **kröseln,** *v.t.* trim (*glass*).

Krösus ['krø:zus], *m.* Croesus.

Kröte ['krø:tə], *f.* toad; (*coll.*) ***ich habe nur noch ein paar –n in der Tasche,*** I have only a few coppers in my pocket; (*sl.*) ***niedliche kleine –,*** attractive little piece.

Krücke ['krykə], *f.* crutch; (*fig.*) prop; (croupier's) rake; (*of violin*) peg; (*Bill.*) bridge; ***an –n gehen,*** walk with *or* on crutches; ***ihm die – reichen,*** hold out a helping hand to him. **Krück(en)stock,** *m.* crutch; crooked-stick.

Krug [kru:k], *m.* (**-(e)s,** *pl.* **⸚e**) pitcher, jug; mug, tankard, pot, jar, urn; public-house, tavern; (*Prov.*) ***der – geht so lange zum Wasser bis er bricht,*** you'll do that once too often.

Kruke ['kru:kə], *f.* 1. stone jar *or* (hot-water) bottle; 2. (*coll.*) oddity, crank, queer card *or* fish.

Krulle ['krulə], *f.* (*obs.*) ruffle, ruff.

krüllen ['krylən], *v.t.* (*dial.*) shell (*peas*). **Krüllschnitt(tabak),** *m.* curly cut (tobacco).

Krume ['kru:mə], *f.* 1. crumb (*of bread*); 2. topsoil, tilth, vegetable mould.

Krümel ['kry:məl], *m.* *See* **Krume. krüm(e)lig,** *adj.* crumbling, friable, crumbly, crumby. **krümeln,** *v.r.,v.i.* crumble. **Krümel|schokolade,** *f.* broken chocolate. **–zucker,** *m.* granulated sugar.

krumig ['kru:mɪç], *adj.* *See* **krümelig.**

krumm [krum], *adj.* (*comp.* ***–er*** *or* ***⸚er,*** *sup.* ***–st*** *or* ***⸚st***) crooked, bent, curved, wry, twisted, hooked, bowed, arched; circuitous, devious, tortuous, winding; ***ihn – ansehen,*** look askance at him; ***–er Buckel,*** flunkyism, fawning, sycophancy; ***er dreht –e Dinger,*** he's up to his tricks; ***–e Finger machen,*** be light-fingered; ***keinen –en Finger machen,*** not raise a finger; ***eine –e Haltung haben,*** stoop; ***–e Knie,*** knock-knees; (*coll.*) ***sich – legen,*** cut one's coat according to one's cloth; (*coll.*) ***– liegen,*** be in a bad way; ***–e Linie,*** curve; ***–es Maul,*** wry mouth; ***–er Rücken,*** see ***–er Buckel;*** (*fig.*) ***er macht den Rücken –,*** he bends over backwards; ***ihn – und lahm schlagen,*** beat the living daylights out of him; ***– sitzen,*** cower, loll, sit doubled up; (*coll.*) ***eine –e Tour,*** a shady business; ***–e Wege,*** crooked *or* underhand ways.

krumm|ästig, *adj.* gnarled. **–beinig,** *adj.* bow- *or* bandy-legged. **Krummdarm,** *m.* (*Anat.*) ileum.

Krumme ['krumə], *m.* (**-n,** *pl.* **-n**) (*dial.*) hare.

Krümme ['krymə], *f.* crookedness; turning, bend (*in a road*). **krümmen, 1.** *v.t.* bend, twist, curve, crumple; ***niemand soll dir ein Haar –,*** no one shall hurt a hair of your head. **2.** *v.r.* grow crooked, (*as wood*) warp; (*of a p.*) wriggle, writhe, squirm; (*of a river*) wind, meander; (*fig.*) cringe, grovel, fawn; ***sich vor Schmerzen –,*** writhe with pain; ***sich vor Lachen –,*** double up *or* be convulsed with laughter; (*Prov.*) ***auch ein Wurm krümmt sich,*** even a worm will turn. **Krümmer,** *m.* pipe-joint, manifold; bend, elbow; harrow.

krumm|faserig, *adj.* cross-grained. **–halsig,** *adj.* wry-necked. **Krumm|holz,** *n.* dwarf mountain pine; knee-timber, scrub. **–horn,** *n.* 1. animal with crumpled horns; 2. (*Mus.*) crumhorn; (*organ-stop*) cromorne, cremona. **krumm|linig,** *adj.* curvilinear, non-linear. **–nasig,** *adj.* hook-nosed. **–nehmen,** *irr.v.t.* take amiss, take offence *or* umbrage at. **Krumm|säbel,** *m.* scimitar. **–stab,** *m.* crook; crosier; (*fig.*) episcopal authority.

Krümmung ['krymuŋ], *f.* bend, curve, curvature, flexure; turn, winding, twist; crookedness, sinuosity; contortion. **Krümmungshalbmesser,** *m.* radius of curvature.

Krummzirkel ['krumtsɪrkəl], *m.* bow-compasses, callipers.

krumpeln ['krumpəln], **krümpeln** ['krympəln], *v.t.* crumple, crinkle, ruffle, pucker.

Krümper|pferd ['krympər–], *n.* (*Mil.*) reserve horse. **–system,** *n.* (*Hist.*) short-service training of conscripts.

krumpfen ['krumpfən], *v.t.* pre-shrink.

Krupp [krup], *m.* (**-s,** *no pl.*) (*Med.*) (*coll.*) croup.

Kruppe ['krupə], *f.* crupper, croup (*of a horse*).

Krüppel ['krypəl], *m.* cripple; ***zum – machen,*** cripple, maim; ***zum – werden,*** be crippled *or* maimed. **krüppelhaft, krüppelig,** *adj.* crippled, maimed, deformed, stunted. **Krüppelwuchs,** *m.* scrub, dwarf timber.

Kruste ['krustə], *f.* crust, scab, scale, incrustation, (*on the head*) scurf; (*on a boiler etc.*) fur; ***sich mit einer – überziehen,*** become (en)crusted. **Krusten|-bildung,** *f.* incrustation. **–tier,** *n.* crustacean. **krustig,** *adj.* crusty, crusted.

Kruzifix [krutsi'fɪks, 'kru:tsifɪks], *n.* (**-es,** *pl.* **-e**) crucifix.

Krypta ['krypta], *f.* (-, *pl.* **-ten**), **Krypte,** *f.* crypt.

Kryptogame [krypto'ga:mə], *f.* (*Bot.*) cryptogam. **kryptogamisch,** *adj.* cryptogamous.

Kuba ['ku:ba], *n.* (*Geog.*) Cuba. **Kubaner** [–'ba:nər], *m.*, **kubanisch,** *adj.* Cuban.

Kübel ['ky:bəl], *m.* bucket, pail, tub, vat; ***es gießt wie mit –n,*** it's pouring *or* teeming with rain. **Kübelwagen,** *m.* (*Mil.*) jeep.

kubieren [ku'bi:rən], *v.t.* 1. determine the cubic measure *or* content(s) of; 2. (*Math.*) cube, raise to the third power. **Kubierung,** *f.* cubation.

Kubik|berechnung [ku'bi:k–], *f.* cubature. **–gehalt, –inhalt,** *m.* cubic *or* solid content, volume. **–maß,** *n.* cubic measure. **–meter,** *m. or n.* cubic metre. **–wurzel,** *f.* cube-root. **–zahl,** *f.* cube; ***auf die – erheben,*** cube, raise to the third power.

kubisch ['ku:bɪʃ], *adj.* cubic(al). **Kubismus** [–'bɪsmus], *m.* (*Art*) cubism. **Kubist** [–'bɪst], *m.* (**-en,** *pl.* **-en**) cubist. **kubistisch,** *adj.* cubist(ic). **Kubus,** *m.* (-, *pl.* **-ben**) (*Geom.*) cube.

Küche ['kyçə], *f.* kitchen; cooking, cookery, cuisine, culinary art; ***eine gute – führen,*** keep a good table; ***schwarze –,*** alchemist's laboratory; ***bürgerliche –,*** plain fare, plain cooking; ***kalte –,*** cold meat(s); (*coll.*) ***in des Teufels – kommen,*** get into a hell of a mess.

Kuchen ['ku:xən], *m.* 1. cake, pastry, tart; (*coll.*) ***ja –!*** what a hope! nothing doing! 2. clot (*of blood*); placenta.

küchen ['ky:çən], *v.i.* (*Swiss*) bake cakes.

Küchen|abfall, *m.* kitchen refuse. **–artikel,** *m.pl.* kitchenware.

Kuchenblech ['ku:xənblɛç], *n.* baking-tin.

Küchen|benutzung, *f.* ***mit –,*** with use of the kitchen, with kitchen facilities. **–bulle,** *m.* (*sl.*) (*Mil.*) mess sergeant. **–chef,** *m.* chef. **–einrichtung,** *f.* kitchen furniture.

kuchenfertig ['ku:xənfɛrtɪç], *adj.* ***–es Mehl,*** self-raising flour. **Kuchenform,** *f.* cake-tin.

Küchen|garten, *m.* vegetable *or* kitchen-garden. **–gerät, –geschirr,** *n.* kitchen utensils.

Kuchenheber ['ku:xənhe:bər], *m.* pastry-server.

Küchen|herd, *m.* (kitchen-)range, cooking stove, (gas *or* electric) cooker. **–kräuter,** *pl.* pot-herbs. **–latein,** *n.* dog-Latin. **–mädchen,** *n.*, **–magd,** *f.* kitchen-maid, scullion. **–meister,** *m.* head-cook, chef; ***bei uns ist Schmalhans –,*** we're on short rations. **–personal,** *n.* kitchen staff. **–schabe,** *f.* cockroach. **–schrank,** *m.* kitchen-cupboard *or* dresser; pantry, larder.

Kuchenteig ['ku:xəntaɪk], *m.* cake mixture.

Küchenzettel ['kyçəntsɛtəl], *m.* bill of fare, menu.

Küchlein ['kyçlaɪn], *n.* (**-s,** *pl.* -) chicken, chick.

Küchler ['kyçlər], *m.* pastry cook.

Kücken ['kykən], *n.* 1. *See* **Küchlein**; 2. (*coll.*) young girl; 3. (*Tech.*) plug. **Kückenhahn,** *m.* stop-cock.

Kuckuck ['kukuk], *m.* (**-(e)s,** *pl.* **-e**) (*Orn.*) cuckoo (*Cuculus canorus*); (*coll.*) ***der – und sein Küster,*** Old Nick; ***hol' ihn der –!*** devil take him! to blazes with him! ***zum –!*** confound it! hang it! ***wie, zum – . . .?*** how in the world . . .? ***das mag der – wissen,*** how the devil should I know? that's anybody's guess! heaven only knows! **Kuckucks|blume,** *f.* (*Bot.*) ragged robin (*Lychnis flos-cuculi*). **–ei,** *n.* cuckoo's egg; (*fig.*) ***ihm ein – ins Nest legen,*** render him a doubtful service, sow the seeds of future trouble for him. **–uhr,** *f.* cuckoo clock.

Kuddelmuddel ['kudəlmudəl], *m.* (*coll.*) medley, hotchpotch, muddle, mess.

Kufe ['ku:fə], *f.* 1. vat, tub, barrel; 2. runner, skid (*of a sledge*); rocker (*of cradle, rocking chair*).

Küfer ['ky:fər], *m.* 1. cellarman; 2. (*dial.*) cooper.

Kugel ['ku:gəl], *f.* (-, *pl.* **-n**) 1. globe, sphere, globule; 2. ball; (*coll.*) ***eine ruhige – schieben,*** have it cushy; 3. bullet, (cannon)ball, shot; ***mit goldenen –n schießen,*** let one's money talk; ***–n und Granaten,*** shot and shell; ***matte –,*** spent bullet; ***sich*** (*Dat.*) ***eine – durch den Kopf jagen,*** blow one's brains out; (*Prov.*) ***nicht alle –n treffen,*** not every bullet finds its billet; ***–n wechseln,*** exchange shots; 4. (*Spt.*) shot, weight; 5. (*Anat.*) head (*of bone*); 6. ballot; ***man hat ihm eine schwarze – geworfen,*** he was black-balled; ***die schwarze – ziehen,*** have bad luck.

Kugel|abschnitt, *m.* spherical segment. **–ausschnitt,** *m.* cone with spherical base. **–bahn,** *f.* trajectory; bowling-alley. **–blitz,** *m.* ball lightning. **–büchse,** *f.* shot-gun.

Kügelchen ['ky:gəlçən], *n.* globule, globulet; pellet.

Kugel|dreieck, *n.* spherical triangle. **–durchmesser,** *m.* diameter of a sphere. **–fallhahn,** *m.* ball-cock. **–fang,** *m.* butts, (*Am.*) backstop. **kugelfest,** *adj.* bullet-proof. **Kugel|fläche,** *f.* surface of a sphere. **–form,** *f.* spherical form; bullet-mould. **kugelförmig,** *adj.* globular, spherical. **Kugel|gelenk,** *n.* (*Anat.*) sphenoid *or* ball and socket (joint); (*Tech.*) ball joint. **–gewölbe,** *n.* cupola. **–haube,** *f.* (*Eccl.*) spherical calotte. **–helm,** *m.* (*Archit.*) tholus, cupola. **kugelig,** *adj. See* **kugelförmig. Kugel|kalotte, –kappe,** *f. See* **–haube. –lage,** *f.* position of bullet (*in wound*). **–lager,** *n.* ball-bearing. **–loch,** *n.* (*Bill.*) pocket. **–los,** *n.* decision by ballot.

kugeln ['ku:gəln], **1.** *v.i.* (*aux.* s.) roll; (*aux.* h.) play bowls *or* skittles; ballot. **2.** *v.t.* roll; make globular, form into a ball. **3.** *v.r.* roll, assume a globular form; (*coll.*) ***sich – vor Lachen,*** double up with laughter; (*coll.*) ***das ist zum Kugeln,*** that's a scream.

Kugel|patrone, *f.* ball-cartridge. **–regen,** *m.* shower *or* hail of bullets. **kugelrund,** *adj.* globular, quite round, round as a ball. **Kugel|schicht,** *f.* frustrum of a sphere. **–schnitt,** *m.* spherical section. **–schreiber,** *m.* ball-point pen. **kugel|sicher,** *adj. See* **–fest. Kugel|spiel,** *n.* bowling, bowls. **–stoßen,** *n.* putting the shot *or* weight. **–ventil,** *n.* ball-valve. **–wahl,** *f.* (election by) ballot. **–wechsel,** *m.* exchange of shots. **–zange,** *f.* ball-extractor, bullet-forceps. **–zapfen,** *m.* ball-pivot.

Kuh [ku:], *f.* (-, *pl.* **¨-e**) cow (*also female of deer, elephant etc.*); ***junge –,*** heifer; (*coll.*) ***dumme –,*** silly goose; ***blinde –,*** blindman's-buff; ***er sieht es an wie die – das neue Tor,*** he stares at it like a stuffed dummy; (*B.*) ***fette*** or ***magere Kühe,*** fat *or* lean kine. **Kuhblume,** *f.* marsh-marigold (*Caltha palustris*).

Küher ['ky:ər], *m.* (*Swiss*) cowherd.

Kuh|fladen, *m.* cow-dung. **–fuß,** *m.* crowbar; (*obs.*) old gun, rifle. **–glocke,** *f. See* **–schelle. –handel,** *m.* (*fig.*) shady business, wire-pulling, log-rolling, horse-trading. **–haut,** *f.* cowhide; (*coll.*) ***das geht auf keine –,*** that beggars description; that cannot be described.

kuhhessig ['ku:hɛsɪç], *adj.* (*Vet.*) knock-kneed. **Kuh|hirt,** *m.* cowherd, (*Am.*) cowboy, cow-puncher. **–hürde,** *f.* cow-stall.

kühl [ky:l], *adj.* cool; fresh; (*fig.*) lukewarm, chilly, half-hearted; (*coll.*) ***eine –e Blonde,*** a glass of pale ale. **Kühl|anlage,** *f.* cold-storage plant. **–apparat,** *m.* refrigerator. **–bottich,** *m.* cooling vat.

Kuhle ['ku:lə], *f.* deep hole, pit.

Kühle ['ky:lə], *f.* coolness; freshness, cool; (*fig.*) coldness, half-heartedness.

Kühleimer ['ky:lʔaɪmər], *m.* cooler, ice-pail.

kühlen ['ky:lən], **1.** *v.t.* cool, refresh; (*food*) chill, keep in cold store; ***den Durst –,*** quench one's thirst; ***sein Mütchen an ihm –,*** vent one's rage on him. **2.** *v.r.* grow cool, cool down. **Kühler,** *m.* (*Motor.*) radiator; cooler, condenser. **Kühler-haube,** *f.* (*Motor.*) bonnet, (*Am.*) hood.

Kühl|fleisch, *n.* chilled meat. **–halle,** *f.*, **–haus,** *n.* cold store, cold-storage depot. **–mantel,** *m.* (*Motor.*) water-jacket. **–mittel,** *n.* (*Med.*) cooling draught; (*Tech.*) coolant, refrigerant. **–ofen,** *m.* annealing oven. **–raum,** *m.* refrigerating *or* cold-storage chamber. **–schiff,** *n.* refrigerator ship. **–schlange,** *f.* condensing coil. **–schrank,** *m.* refrigerator.

Kühlte ['ky:ltə], *f.* (*Naut.*) fresh breeze. **Kühlung,** *f.* cooling, refrigeration; cooling *or* refreshing breeze.

Kühl|wagen, *m.* (*Railw.*) refrigerator car. **–wasser,** *n.* cooling water.

Kuh|magd, *f.* milkmaid, dairy maid. **–milch,** *f.* cow's milk. **–mist,** *m.* cow-dung. **–molken,** *f.pl.* whey.

kühn [ky:n], *adj.* bold, brave, fearless, intrepid, courageous, dashing, daring, audacious; ***– machen,*** embolden; ***–es Unternehmen,*** risky *or* hazardous undertaking; ***–ste Träume,*** fondest dreams. **Kühnheit,** *f.* boldness, fearlessness, bravery, daring, dash, intrepidity; audacity. **kühnlich,** *adv.* boldly.

Kuh|pocken, *f.pl.* cow-pox. **–pockenimpfung,** *f.* vaccination. **–pockenstoff,** *m.* vaccine lymph. **–reigen, –reihen,** *m.* dance (music) of Alpine cowherds. **–reiher,** *m.* (*Orn.*) cattle egret (*Ardeola ibis*). **–schelle,** *f.* cow-bell. **–schluck,** *m.* (*vulg.*) large draught (*of beer etc.*). **–stall,** *m.* cow-shed, byre. **–stelze,** *f.* (*Orn.*) *see* **Schafstelze. –weide,** *f.* cattle pasture.

Kujon [ku'jo:n], *m.* (**-s,** *pl.* **-e**) scoundrel, rogue. **kujonieren** [–'ni:rən], *v.t.* treat shabbily, exploit, bully.

Küken, (*dial.*) *see* **Kücken.**

Kukuruz ['ku:kuruts], *m.* (*Austr.*) maize.

kulant [ku:'lant], *adj.* (*Comm.*) accommodating, obliging, fair. **Kulanz,** *f.* fair dealing, readiness to oblige.

Kule, *f. See* **Kuhle.**

Kuli ['ku:li], *m.* (**-s,** *pl.* **-s**) coolie.

Kulisse [ku'lɪsə], *f.* **1.** (*Theat.*) wing; side-scene, backdrop; (*fig.*) background (*also of music*); ***in die – sprechen,*** make an aside; ***hinter den –n,*** (*Theat.*) back-stage; (*fig.*) behind the scenes, in secret; ***hinter die –n schauen,*** know the ins and outs of, have a glimpse behind the scenes; 2. (*fig.*) outward show, front, (*sl.*) eyewash; ***das ist nur –,*** that is only outward show; 3. (*St. Exch.*) unofficial market; 4. (*Tech.*) connecting-link.

Kulissen|fieber, *n.* stage-fright. **–geschwätz,** *n.* green-room talk. **–maler,** *m.* scene-painter. **–reißer,** *m.* ham (actor), ranter. **–reißerei,** *f.* playing to the gallery. **–schaltung,** *f.* (*Motor.*) gate-change (gear-shift). **–schieber,** *m.* scene-shifter. **–tisch,** *m.* extending table. **–tür,** *f.* stage-door.

Kulm [kulm], *m.* (**-s,** *pl.* **-e**) (*dial.*) summit, knoll.

Kulminationspunkt [kulminatsi'o:nspuŋkt], *m.* culminating point, culmination, zenith, (*fig.*) peak, pinnacle, acme. **kulminieren** [–'ni:rən], *v.i.* culminate (*in* (*Dat.*), in), reach the climax (with).

Kult [kult], *n.* (**-(e)s,** *pl.* **-e**) worship; cult.

kultivieren [kulti'vi:rən], *v.t.* cultivate, till. **kulti-viert,** *adj.* civilized, refined, cultured.

Kultstätte ['kultʃtɛtə], *f.* place of worship.

Kultur [kul'tu:r], *f.* **1.** cultivation, tilling, growing, breeding, (*of bacteria etc.*) culture; afforestation, (forest) plantation; ***in – nehmen,*** bring under cultivation; 2. culture, civilization. (*N.B. Orig. with connotations of 'learning' and 'literary', Nat. Soc. perverted it in two directions*: (1) 'folklore', 'race culture'; (2) 'decadent intellectualism', western democratic materialism'.)

Kultur|abkommen, *n.* cultural agreement. **–ar-beit,** *f.* cultural activity, creative work. **–aufgabe,** *f.* civilizing mission, cultural task. **–austausch,** *m.* cultural exchange. **–bolschewismus,** *m.* (*Nat. Soc.*) intellectual (and artistic) nihilism, modernism (in art), decadence.

kulturell [kultu'rɛl], *adj.* cultural.

kultur|fähig, *adj.* 1. cultivable, arable; 2. amenable to civilization, open *or* accessible to cultural influences. **–feindlich,** *adj.* hostile to culture *or* civilization. **Kultur|film,** *m.* documentary. **–gebiet,** *n.* civilized region. **–geschichte,** *f.* history of civilization. **kulturgeschichtlich,** *adj.* relating to the history of civilization. **Kultur|gut,** *n.* cultural asset. **–kammer,** *f.* (*Nat. Soc.*) 'Chamber of Culture' (*acting as censor over all cultural life*). **–kampf,** *m.* (Bismarck's) conflict between State and R.C. Church. **–mensch,** *m.* civilized man. **–pflanze,** *f.* cultivated plant. **–schaffende(r),** *m.*, *f.* intellectual; creative artist; performing artist; (*N.B. the approved Communist word for workers outside production or organization*). **–staat,** *m.* civilized country. **–stufe,** *f.* stage of civilization, level of culture. **–träger,** *m.* upholder of civilization. **–volk,** *n.* civilized nation. **–zentrum,** *n.* cultural centre.

Kultus ['kultus], *m.* (**-,** *pl.* **Kulte**) *see* **Kult. Kultus|-freiheit,** *f.* freedom of worship. **–minister,** *m.* Minister of Public Worship and Education.

Kumme ['kumə], *f.* (*dial.*) basin, bowl.

Kümmel ['kyməl], *m.* **1.** caraway *or* cumin(-seed); **2.** *See* **Kümmelschnaps. Kümmel|brot,** *n.* bread flavoured with caraway-seeds. **–käse,** *m.* cheese flavoured with caraway-seeds. **–kuchen,** *m.* seed-cake. **kümmeln,** *v.i.* (*coll.*) tipple. **Küm-mel|schnaps,** *m.* kummel (*liqueur*). **–türke,** *m.* (*coll.*) philistine, 'petit bourgeois'; braggart.

Kummer ['kumər], *m.* **1.** (*no pl.*) grief, sorrow, sadness, affliction, trouble, worry, care; ***– und Sorge,*** trouble and worry; ***– und Not,*** grief and misery; ***sich*** (*Dat.*) ***– machen über*** (*Acc.*), grieve about; ***das ist mein geringster –,*** that is the least of my worries *or* troubles; ***ihm viel – machen*** or ***bereiten*** or ***verursachen,*** cause him much grief, grieve him sorely; ***das macht mir wenig –,*** I do not worry (my head) about that, that doesn't trouble me; (*dial.*) ***sie hatte –, es könnte ihm etwas passieren,*** she feared s.th. might happen to him; 2. (*dial.*) (heap of) rubble *or* rubbish.

kümmerlich ['kymərlɪç], **1.** *adj.* miserable, wretched, pitiful; poor, paltry, meagre, (*coll.*) measly; stunted. **2.** *adv.* scarcely, barely, with great trouble; ***sich – durchschlagen,*** make a bare *or* scanty living, eke out a living. **Kümmerling,** *m.* (**-s,** *pl.* **-e**) stunted plant *or* animal; (*coll.*) (*of a p.*) weedy specimen, shrimp.

kümmern ['kymərn], **1.** *v.t.* grieve, afflict, trouble; worry, concern; ***was kümmert mich das?*** what is that to me? what do I care? **2.** *v.r.* ***sich – um,*** mind, look after, care for, take care of, attend to, see to; care *or* trouble *or* bother about; pay heed to; ***ich kümmere mich nicht darum,*** I do not trouble my head about it; ***– Sie sich nicht um ihn,*** do not take any notice of him, pay no attention to him, ignore *or* disregard him, don't bother about him;

– Sie sich nicht um Dinge, die Sie nichts angehen! do not poke your nose into *or* meddle in other people's affairs! mind your own business! ***kümmere dich nicht um ungelegte Eier!*** don't count your chickens before they are hatched! **Kümmernis,** *f.* (-, *pl.* **-se**) *see* **Kummer.**

kummervoll ['kumərfəl], *adj.* sorrowful, doleful, woebegone; woeful, grievous.

Kummet ['kumət], *n. See* **Kumt.**

Kump [kump], *n.* (**-s,** *pl.* **-e**) (*dial.*) *see* **Kumpf.**

Kumpan [kum'pa:n], *m.* (**-s,** *pl.* **-e**) companion, crony, mate, pal, (*Am.*) buddy.

Kumpel ['kumpəl], *m.* (*dial.*) coal-miner, collier; (*coll.*) *see* **Kumpan.**

Kumpen ['kumpən], *m.* (**-s,** *pl.* -), **Kumpf** [kumpf], *m.* (**-(e)s,** *pl.* **-e** *or* **⸗e**) (*dial.*) deep basin, bowl; feeding trough.

Kumt [kumt], *n.* (**-(e)s,** *pl.* **-e**) horse-collar. **Kumtpferd,** *n.* draught-horse.

kund [kunt], *indecl. pred. adj.* known, public; ***die S. ist –,*** it is generally known; (*Law*) ***– und zu wissen sei hiemit,*** know all men by these presents. **kundbar,** *adj.* (*dial.*) notorious, (well-)known; manifest.

kündbar ['kyntba:r], *adj.* (*Comm.*) (*money*) at call, subject to call; (*mortgage*) subject to foreclosure, terminable; (*loan*) redeemable.

[1]**Kunde** ['kundə], *f.* information, notice; news, tidings, intelligence; ***ihm – geben von,*** inform him of, send him word of *or* about; ***– von etwas nehmen,*** take cognizance of a th.

[2]**Kunde,** *m.* (**-n,** *pl.* **-n**) customer, client; (*fig.*) ***übler –,*** ugly customer, nasty piece of work; (*fig.*) ***schlauer*** or ***geriebener –,*** sharp one, shrewd customer; ***fester –,*** patron, regular customer; ***zufälliger –,*** chance buyer; ***du bist mir ja ein netter –,*** well you're a nice one.

-kunde, *suff.* -ology, -graphy, science of . . . .

künden ['kyndən], **1.** *v.t.* (*Poet.*) announce, herald, tell of. **2.** *v.i.* (*Poet.*) ***– von,*** tell of, bear witness to. *See also* **kündigen.**

Kunden|dienst, *m.* (after-sales) service. **–fang,** *m.* touting (for custom). **–kreis,** *m.* clients, clientele, customers; (*Comm.*) goodwill. **–werber,** *m.* tout, canvasser. **–werbung,** *f.* advertising *or* publicity (campaign), sales-talk.

Kund|gabe, *f. See* **–gebung. kundgeben, 1.** *irr.v.t.* notify, give notice of, make known, declare, announce, proclaim, publish, set forth. **2.** *irr.v.r.* proclaim itself (as), prove itself (to be), become manifest. **Kundgebung,** *f.* (*Pol.*) demonstration, rally; (*of views*) declaration, proclamation, announcement; manifestation.

kundig ['kundıç], *adj.* (*Gen.*) versed, skilled, experienced (in), expert (in *or* at), (well-)informed (about), acquainted, familiar (with).

kündigen ['kyndıgən], **1.** *v.i.* (*Dat.*) give notice (to quit), (*coll.*) sack; (*coll.*) (*of employee*) give *or* hand in one's notice. **2.** *v.t.* (*Comm.*) recall, call in (*money*), terminate, cancel, revoke (*agreement*), denounce (*treaty*), foreclose (*mortgage*), (*coll.*) dismiss, sack; (*coll.*) ***die Wohnung –,*** (*of landlord*) give notice to quit, (*of tenant*) give notice that one is leaving. **Kundige(r)** ['kundıgə(r)], *m., f.* initiate, expert; *pl.* (*coll.*) those in the know.

Kündigung ['kyndıguŋ], *f.* notice (to quit); dismissal (*of employee*); termination, cancellation; foreclosure, notice of redemption; ***mit halbjähriger –,*** at *or* subject to six months' notice; ***mit vierwöchiger – angestellt,*** engaged on a monthly basis; ***Geld auf tägliche –,*** day-to-day money, call-money. **Kündigungs|frist,** *f.* period of notice. **–termin,** *m.* last day for giving notice.

Kundin ['kundın], *f. See* [2]**Kunde.**

kund|machen, *v.t.* (*Austr., Swiss*) *see* **–geben. Kund|machung,** *f. see* **–gebung.**

Kundschaft ['kuntʃaft], *f.* 1. custom, patronage; customers, clients, clientele; (*Comm.*) goodwill; 2. (*obs.*) information; (*Mil.*) ***auf – ausgehen,*** go out to reconnoitre *or* on reconnaissance; ***– einziehen,*** collect information. **kundschaften,** *v.i.* (*Mil.*) scout, reconnoitre, make a reconnaissance. **Kundschafter,** *m.* (*Mil.*) spy, scout; emissary.

kund|tun, *irr.v.t. See* **–geben. –werden,** *irr.v.i.* become (generally) known *or* public, come to light *or* notice, come to be known, transpire.

künftig ['kynftıç], **1.** *adj.* future; coming, to come, next; prospective; ***–e Zeiten,*** time(s) to come; ***–e Woche,*** next week; ***das –e Leben,*** the next life, the life to come; ***seine –e Frau,*** his wife to be; his intended. **2.** *or* **künftighin,** *adv.* for the future, in future, henceforth, from now on, hereafter.

Kunkel ['kuŋkəl], *f.* (-, *pl.* **-n**) distaff; (*obs.*) womankind. **Kunkel|lehen,** *n.* (*Law*) petticoat tenure. **–magen,** *m.pl.* (*Law*) maternal relations.

Kunst [kunst], *f.* (-, *pl.* **⸗e**) 1. art; ***angewandte –,*** applied art; ***bildende Künste,*** pictorial *or* graphic arts; (*Prov.*) ***– geht nach Brot,*** art follows the public; (*fig.*) ***brotlose –,*** profitless business, thankless task; ***darstellende –,*** representational art; ***die freien Künste,*** the liberal arts; ***redende Künste,*** rhetorical arts; ***schöne Künste,*** fine arts; ***schwarze –,*** black magic, necromancy; 2. skill, dexterity, ingenuity; trick, knack, artifice, sleight-of-hand; (*coll.*) ***das ist keine –,*** that is easy (enough), that's nothing, there's nothing to it *or* nothing difficult in that; ***er ist mit seinen Künsten zu Ende,*** he is at his wits' end; ***nach –, nicht nach Gunst gehen,*** depend on merit rather than influence; ***seine – an einer S. versuchen,*** try one's skill *or* one's hand at a th.; 3. (*obs.*) machine, engine, waterwork.

Kunst|akademie, *f.* art school. **–anlage,** *f.* artistic bent. **–anstalt,** *f.* art publisher. **–ausdruck,** *m.* technical term. **–ausstellung,** *f.* art exhibition. **–bäcker,** *m.* fancy baker, confectioner. **–ballade,** *f.* literary ballad. **–beflissene(r),** *m., f.* student of art. **–beilage,** *f.* pictorial *or* art supplement. **–brut,** *f.* artificial incubation. **–butter,** *f.* synthetic butter, margarine. **–darm,** *m.* synthetic sausage-skin. **–dichtung,** *f.* literary poetry (*opp. folk-poetry*). **–druckerei,** *f.* fine art printers. **–druckpapier,** *n.* art-paper. **–dünger,** *m.* artificial manure, fertilizer.

Künstelei [kynstə'laı], *f.* (-, *pl.* **-en**) affectation, mannerism, artificiality, affected ways; over-refinement, over-elaboration. **künsteln** ['kynstəln], **1.** *v.t.* elaborate; over-refine, subtilize; ***gekünstelt,*** artificial, elaborate, affected. **2.** *v.i.* ***– an*** (*Dat.*), bestow great pains on.

Kunst|epos, *n.* literary epic. **–erziehung,** *f.* aesthetic education. **–fahrer,** *m.* trick cyclist. **–faser,** *f.* man-made fibre. **–fehler,** *m.* technical error. **kunstfertig,** *adj.* skilful, skilled, workmanlike. **Kunst|fertigkeit,** *f.* artistic *or* technical skill; craftsmanship. **–flieger,** *m.* stunt flier. **–flug,** *m.* stunt-flying, aerobatics. **–freund,** *m.* art-lover, patron of the arts. **–gärtner,** *m.* florist, horticulturist, nursery-gardener. **–gärtnerei,** *f.* horticulture. **–gefühl,** *n.* artistic feeling, taste for art. **–gegenstand,** *m.* objet d'art. **kunstgemäß,** *adj.* skilful, workmanlike, technically correct. **Kunstgenuß,** *m.* aesthetic enjoyment; (artistic) treat; ***es war ein musikalischer –,*** it was a musical treat. **kunst|gerecht,** *adj. See* **–gemäß.**

Kunst|geschichte, *f.* history of art. **–geschmack,** *m.* artistic taste. **–gewerbe,** *n.* arts and crafts, handicrafts, applied art, useful art. **–gewerbeschule,** *f.* school of arts and crafts. **–gewerbler,** *m.* craftsman. **–glied,** *n.* artificial limb. **–graben,** *m.* canal, conduit, aqueduct. **–griff,** *m.* knack, trick, (*coll.*) dodge; artifice, device. **–gummi,** *n.* synthetic rubber. **–halle,** *f.* art gallery. **–handel,** *m.* fine art trade. **–händler,** *m.* art dealer. **–handlung,** *f.* print-shop, picture shop, fine-art dealers. **–handwerk,** *n.* skilled craft. **–handwerker,** *m.* skilled craftsman. **–harz,** *n.* synthetic resin, plastic. **–historiker,** *m.* art historian. **–horn,** *n.* celluloid. **–kenner,** *m.* connoisseur. **–kniff,** *m. See* **–griff. –kritik,** *f.* art criticism. **–kritiker,** *m.* art critic. **–lauf,** *m.,* **–laufen,** *n.* figure-skating. **–leder,** *n.* imitation leather, leatherette.

Künstler ['kynstlər], *m.,* **Künstlerin,** *f.* artist;

virtuoso; (*Theat.*) artiste, performer. **künstlerisch,** *adj.* artistic. **Künstlername,** *m.* stage-name. **Künstlertum,** *n.* artistry; artistic gift *or* power *or* greatness *or* genius. **Künstlerwerkstatt,** *f.* studio.

künstlich ['kynstlɪç], **1.** *adj.* artificial; imitated, false, spurious, fake; synthetic, man-made; *–e Atmung,* artificial respiration; *–es Auge,* artificial eye; *–e Befruchtung,* artificial insemination; *–e Beleuchtung,* artificial lighting; *–e Blumen,* artificial flowers; *–er Diamant,* paste (diamond); *–e Glieder,* artificial limbs; *–e Haare,* false hair; *–es Lachen,* forced laughter; *–e Zähne,* false *or* artificial teeth, dentures. **2.** *adv.* *– gehaltene Preise,* pegged prices; *– (in die Höhe) treiben,* force (*vegetables, flowers*).

Kunst|liebhaber, *m.* art lover, amateur artist. **–liebhaberei,** *f.* artistic hobby. **kunstlos,** *adj.* tasteless, amateurish, crude; artless, naïve; unsophisticated. **Kunstlosigkeit,** *f.* crudity, tastelessness, poor taste; artlessness. **kunst|mäßig,** *adj. See* **–gemäß. Kunst|meister,** *m.* (*obs.*) hydraulic engineer. **–mittel,** *n.* artificial means. **–pause,** *f.* pause for effect; (*iron.*) awkward pause. **–pflege,** *f.* patronage *or* promotion of art. **–poesie,** *f. See* **–dichtung. –produkt,** *n.* artificial product. **–prosa,** *f.* rhythmic prose. **kunstreich,** *adj.* ornate, elaborate. **Kunst|reiter,** *m.* circus-rider. **–richter,** *m.* critic. **–richtung,** *f.* art trend, artistic school. **–sammlung,** *f.* art collection. **–schlosser,** *m.* art metal worker. **–schreiner,** *m.* cabinet-maker. **–schule,** *f.* school of arts; artists' coterie. **–seide,** *f.* artificial silk, rayon. **–sinn,** *m.* artistic sense, taste for *or* appreciation of art. **kunstsinnig,** *adj.* art-loving, with artistic taste, appreciative of art. **Kunst|sprache,** *f.* artificial language; literary language; technical language. **–springen,** *n.* springboard diving. **–stein,** *m.* artificial stone. **–stickerei,** *f.* art needlework, embroidery. **–stoff,** *m.* plastics, synthetic material. **–stopfen,** *n.* invisible mending. **–stück,** *n.* (clever) trick, feat, cunning device; *das ist kein –!* that's nothing wonderful! there is nothing clever in that! **–tischler,** *m.* cabinet-maker. **–verein,** *m.* art club, art union. **–verlag,** *m.* fine art publishers. **–verleger,** *m.* fine art publisher. **–verständige(r),** *m., f.* art expert; connoisseur. **kunstvoll,** *adj.* elaborate, intricate, ornate; skilful. **Kunst|wabe,** *f.* comb foundation. **–werk,** *n.* 1. work of art, artistic production; 2. (*obs.*) machine, engine; waterwork. **–wissenschaft,** *f.* aesthetics. **–wolle,** *f.* artificial wool, shoddy. **–wort,** *n.* technical term. **–zweig,** *m.* branch of art.

kunterbunt ['kuntərbunt], *adj.* topsy-turvy, higgledy-piggledy; motley, multi- *or* parti-coloured; (*coll.*) *er redet –es Zeug,* he talks incoherent rubbish; (*coll.*) *bei X. geht es – her* or *zu,* at X.'s things are pretty hectic.

Küpe ['ky:pə], *f.* 1. large tub, vat, copper, boiler; 2. dyeing liquor.

Kupee [ku'pe:], *n.* (**-s,** *pl.* **-s**) (*Railw.*) compartment. **Kupeekoffer,** *m.* dressing-case.

Küper ['ky:pər], *m.* (*dial.*) *see* **Küfer.**

Kupfer ['kupfər], *n.* copper; copper coin; (*obs.*) copperplate print; *in – stechen,* engrave on copper; *mit – beschlagen,* copper-bottomed.

Kupfer|ader, *f.* (*Min.*) vein of copper. **–bergwerk,** *n.* copper mine. **–beschlag,** *m.* copper sheathing. **–blatt,** *n.* copper foil. **–blech,** *n.* sheet copper. **–draht,** *m.* copper wire. **–druck,** *m.* copperplate (printing *or* print). **–erz,** *n.* copper ore. **kupfer|farben, –farbig,** *adj.* copper-coloured. **Kupfer|gang,** *m.* copper lode. **–(geld),** *n.* copper money; *nur etwas –,* only a few coppers. **–grün,** *n.* verdigris. **kupferhaltig,** *adj.* cupreous, cupriferous. **Kupfer|kalk,** *m.* oxide of copper. **–kies,** *m.* copper pyrites. **–legierung,** *f.* copper alloy. **–münze,** *f.* copper (coin). **kupfern,** *adj.* (of) copper. **Kupfer|oxyd,** *n.* black oxide of copper, cupric oxide. **–oxydul,** *n.* red oxide of copper, cuprous oxide; *salzsaures –,* cuprous chloride. **–platte,** *f.* copperplate. **–rost,** *m.* verdigris. **–rot,** *n.* red oxide of copper. **kupferrot,** *adj.* copper-coloured. **Kupfer|röte,** *f.* 1. virgin copper; 2. copper-colour. **–sammlung,** *f.* collection of engravings. **–schmied,** *m.* brazier, coppersmith. **–stecher,** *m.* (copperplate) engraver. **–stich,** *m.* (copperplate) engraving. **–verhüttung,** *f.* copper smelting. **–vitriol,** *n.* copper sulphate, blue vitriol.

Kupido [ku'pi:do], *m.* Cupid.

kupieren [ku'pi:rən], *v.t.* (*Austr.*) cut off; dock (*tail*), (*obs.*) punch (*tickets*), clip; adulterate (*wine*).

Kupon [ku'pɔ̃], *m.* (**-s,** *pl.* **-s**) coupon, counterfoil.

Kuppe ['kupə], *f.* summit, knoll, hilltop; round head (*of a nail*); finger-end.

Kuppel ['kupəl], *f.* (-, *pl.* **-n**) cupola, dome. **kuppelartig,** *adj.* with a round(ed) end, dome-shaped.

Kuppelei [kupə'laɪ], *f.* match-making; pandering, procuring. **kuppeln** ['kupəln], **1.** *v.i.* 1. pander, procure; 2. (*Motor.*) declutch, depress the clutch. **2.** *v.t. See* **koppeln. Kuppel|pelz,** *m.* *sich* (*Dat.*) *einen – verdienen,* bring about a match, succeed in bringing (*lovers*) together. **–stange,** *f.* connecting-rod, tie-rod. **Kuppler,** *m.,* **Kupplerin,** *f.* match-maker, pander, procurer (*f.* procuress).

Kupplung ['kupluŋ], *f.* coupling, joint, (*Motor.*) clutch. **Kupplungs|(fuß)hebel,** *m.* clutch-pedal. **–stecker,** *m.* (*Elec.*) adapter (plug).

[1]**Kur** [ku:r], *f.* (-, *pl.* **-en**) (course of) treatment, cure; (*obs.*) course of baths, taking the waters; *in der – haben,* treat; *er war in Karlsbad zur* (or *Swiss in der*) *–,* he was drinking the waters *or* undergoing treatment at Karlsbad; *eine – machen,* undergo (medical) treatment; (*fig.*) *in die – nehmen,* work on, (*sl.*) give (*a p.*) the works.

[2]**Kur,** *f.* *einer Dame die – machen* or *schneiden,* court *or* woo a lady.

Kür [ky:r], *f.* (-, *pl.* **-en**) 1. (*Hist.*) election; 2. (*Gymn.*) optional exercise; free skating.

Kuranstalt ['ku:rˀanʃtalt], *f.* sanatorium.

kurant [ku'rant], *adj.* (*Comm.*) current, in demand.

[1]**Kurant,** *n.* (**-s,** *pl.* **-e**) currency, coin of the realm.

[2]**Kurant,** *m.* (**-en,** *pl.* **-en**) (*Swiss*) *see* **Kurgast.**

Kurantgeld [ku'rantgɛlt], *n. See* [1]**Kurant.**

kuranzen [ku'rantsən], *v.t.* (*coll.*) scold, punish.

Kurarzt ['ku:rˀartst], *m.* resident medical adviser (at a spa).

Küraß ['ky:ras], *m.* (**-(ss)es,** *pl.* **-(ss)e**) cuirass. **Kurassier** [–'si:r], *m.* (**-s,** *pl.* **-e**) cuirassier, dragoon.

Kuratel [kura'te:l], *f.* (-, *pl.* **-en**) guardianship, trusteeship, tutelage; *ihn unter – stellen,* put him in charge of a guardian, appoint a trustee for him.

Kurator [ku'ra:tɔr], *m.* (**-s,** *pl.* **-en**) 1. curator (*of museum*); 2. (*Law*) guardian, trustee. **Kuratorium** [–'to:rium], *n.* (**-s,** *pl.* **-rien**) board of trustees; board of control, governing body.

Kurbel ['kurbəl], *f.* (-, *pl.* **-n**) crank (handle), (*Motor.*) starting-handle. **Kurbel|anlasser,** *m.* crank starter. **–gehäuse,** *n.* crankcase. **–gelenk,** *n.* toggle joint. **–kasten,** *m.* (*sl.*) film camera.

kurbeln ['kurbəln], *v.i., v.t.* crank, wind; (*film*) reel off; (*coll.*) *einen Film –,* run off *or* take *or* shoot a film.

Kurbel|pumpe, *f.* reciprocating pump. **–rad,** *n.* handwheel. **–stange,** *f.* (*Mech.*) connecting-rod. **–welle,** *f.* crankshaft.

Kurbette [kur'bɛtə], *f.* curvet (*of horse*). **kurbettieren** [–'ti:rən], *v.i.* curvet.

Kürbis ['kyrbɪs], *m.* (**-ses,** *pl.* **-se**) 1. pumpkin, gourd, (*Am.*) squash; 2. (*sl.*) loaf, nut (= *head*). **Kürbis|baum,** *m.* calabash-tree. **–flasche,** *f.* gourd. **–gewächs,** *n.* cucurbitaceous plant.

Kurbrandenburg ['ku:rbrandənburk], *n.* (*Hist.*) Electorate of Brandenburg.

küren ['ky:rən], *v.t.* (*Hist., Poet.*) choose, elect.

Kur|fürst, *m.* (*Hist.*) Elector (*in the German Empire*). **–fürstentag,** *m.* (*Hist.*) Diet. **–fürstentum,** *n.* (*Hist.*) Electorate. **kurfürstlich,** *adj.* (*Hist.*) Electoral.

Kur|gast, *m.* patient, visitor (*at a spa*); holiday visitor, holidaymaker. **–halle,** *f.* pump-room. **–haus,** *n.* spa hotel; casino.

Kur|hessen, *n.* (*Hist.*) Electorate of Hesse. **–hut,** *m.* electoral crown.

Kurie [ˈkuːriə], *f.* Curia.

Kurier [kuˈriːr], *m.* (**-s,** *pl.* **-e**) courier, (express) messenger.

kurieren [kuˈriːrən], *v.t.* cure, restore to health.

kurios [kuriˈoːs], *adj.* curious, strange, queer, odd, quaint, singular, (*coll.*) funny. **Kuriosität** [–iˈtɛːt], *f.* 1. (*no pl.*) strangeness, queerness, oddness, quaintness; 2. curiosity, rarity, curio. **Kuriosum,** *n.* (**-s,** *pl.* **-sa**) curious *or* queer *or* odd thing *or* fact; oddity, curiosity, freak.

Kur|lande, –länder, *n.pl.* (*Hist.*) electoral domains.

Kürlauf [ˈkyːrlauf], *m.* free-style skating.

Kurort [ˈkuːrˀɔrt], *m.* health-resort, watering-place, spa; holiday resort.

Kurpfalz [ˈkuːrpfalts], *f.* (*Hist.*) the Palatinate; ***der Kurfürst von –,*** the Elector Palatine.

Kur|pfuscher, *m.* quack (doctor). **–pfuscherei,** *f.* quackery, quack practices.

Kurprinz [ˈkuːrprɪnts], *m.* (*Hist.*) Elector's heir.

Kurre [ˈkurə], *f.* 1. trawl, dredge, trammel (*fishing*); 2. (*dial.*) turkey-hen. **kurren,** *v.i.* (*dial.*) coo; gobble.

Kurrendaner [kurɛnˈdaːnər], *m.* (*obs.*) itinerant choir-boy. **Kurrende** [–ˈrɛndə], *f.* 1. (*obs.*) itinerant boys' choir; 2. round robin, circular letter.

kurrent [kuˈrɛnt], *adj.* cursive. **Kurrent|schrift,** *f.* script, running hand. **–schuld,** *f.* running score.

Kurrhahn [ˈkurhaːn], *m.* (*dial.*) turkey-cock.

kurrig [ˈkurɪç], *adj.* untamed, fiery, excitable; sulky, surly, moody.

Kurs [kurs], *m.* (**-es,** *pl.* **-e**) 1. (*Comm.*) (rate of) exchange, price, quotation; currency, circulation; ***welchen – geben Sie für diesen Wechsel?*** what rate do you give for this bill? ***die –e sind gefallen,*** the exchange has fallen; ***der – ist pari,*** exchange is at par; ***hoch im – stehen,*** be at a premium; (*fig.*) rate high; ***niedrig im – stehen,*** be at a discount; (*fig.*) rate low; ***in – setzen,*** put in circulation; ***außer – setzen,*** withdraw from circulation, call in; ***zum –e von,*** at the rate of; 2. course, route, track; ***rechtweisender –,*** true course; ***mißweisender –,*** magnetic course; ***den – besetzen*** or ***bestimmen,*** plot a course; ***den – absetzen*** or ***nehmen,*** shape a course (***auf*** (*Acc.*), for); ***vom – abkommen*** or ***abweichen,*** deviate from course; 3. *See* **Kursus.**

Kursaal [ˈkuːrzaːl], *m.* casino.

Kurs|abschlag, *m.* fall *or* drop in prices, (*St. Exch.*) backwardation. **–änderung,** *f.* change of course. **–bericht,** *m.* market quotations *or* report. **–buch,** *n.* time-table, railway guide.

Kürsch [kyrʃ], *n.* (*Her.*) fur. **Kürschner,** *m.* furrier. **Kürschnerware,** *f.* furs and skins.

Kursentwicklung [ˈkursˀɛntvɪkluŋ], *f.* price trend. **kursfähig,** *adj.* current, in circulation. **Kursfestsetzung,** *f.* rate-fixing. **kursieren** [–ˈziːrən], *v.i.* circulate, be current, (*as rumour*) be in the air, go round.

kursiv [kurˈziːf], **1.** *adj.* italic. **2.** *adv.* in italics; ***– setzen,*** italicize. **Kursive, Kursivschrift,** *f.* italics; ***in – setzen,*** italicize.

Kurs|makler, *m.* stockbroker, inside broker. **–niveau,** *n.* price level. **–notierung,** *f.* market quotation.

kursorisch [kurˈzoːrɪʃ], *adj.* cursory.

Kurs|rückgang, *m.* decline in prices. **–schwankung,** *f.* fluctuation in price. **–steuerung,** *f.* (*Av.*) autopilot, (*Naut.*) automatic steering gear. **–sturz,** *m.* sudden fall in prices, slump. **–treiberei,** *f.* market rigging, share pushing.

Kursus [ˈkurzus], *m.* (-, *pl.* **Kurse**) course (of instruction *or* lectures), class.

Kurs|wagen, *m.* (*Railw.*) through carriage. **–wechsel,** *m.* change of course (*also fig.*). **–wert,** *m.* market *or* exchange value.

Kurtaxe [ˈkuːrtaksə], *f.* visitors' tax.

Kurtine [kurˈtiːnə], *f.* (*Mil.*) curtain.

Kurtisan [kurtiˈzaːn], *m.* (**-s,** *pl.* **-e**) (*obs.*) courtier; parasite. **Kurtisane,** *f.* courtesan.

Kürturnen [ˈkyːrturnən], *n.* (*Gymn.*) optional exercises.

Kurve [ˈkurvə], *f.* curve, bend, turn; (*Av.*) ***eine – fliegen,*** do a banking turn; (*Av.*) ***in die – gehen,*** bank; (*Av.*) ***gezogene –,*** climbing turn; ***ballistische –,*** trajectory; ***scharfe –,*** hairpin bend. **kurven,** *v.i.* turn, swerve, (*Av.*) bank, go into a turn.

Kurven|bild, *n.*, **–darstellung,** *f.* graph. **–gleitflug,** *m.* (*Av.*) spiral glide. **–kampf,** *m.* (*Av.*) dogfight. **–lineal,** *n.* curve template *or* templet. **–radius,** *m.* (*Motor.*) half turning-circle. **kurvenreich,** *adj.* winding, twisting; (*hum.*) curvaceous (*of a girl's figure*); ***–e Strecke,*** (*traffic warning*) bends ahead! **Kurven|schar,** *f.* set *or* system of curves *or* graphs. **–scheibe,** *f.* cam. **–vorgabe,** *f.* (*Spt.*) stagger(ed start).

kurz [kurts], *adj., adv.* (*comp.* ***kürzer,*** *sup.* ***kürzest***) short; brief, succinct, abrupt, laconic, curt, summary, concise, compendious; ***– abbrechen,*** break off *or* end abruptly; ***– abfertigen,*** be short with, dismiss abruptly; ***– abweisen,*** cut (*a p.*) short; ***– angebunden sein,*** be curt *or* brusque; ***–en Atem haben,*** be asthmatic *or* short of breath; ***–er Besuch,*** flying visit; ***binnen –em,*** within a short time, in the near future, before long; ***– und bündig,*** brief(ly), concise(ly), succinct(ly); blunt(ly), flat(ly), pointblank; ***– danach*** or ***darauf,*** a little while *or* shortly *or* not long after(wards); ***sich – fassen,*** be brief, express o.s. briefly; ***–es Futter,*** corn, oats *etc.* (*opp. to* ***langes Futter*** = hay, straw *etc.*); ***–er Galopp,*** canter; ***–es Gedächtnis,*** short memory; ***– und gut,*** in a word, in short, to come to the point, to put it briefly *or* in a nutshell; ***ihn – halten,*** keep him short (*of money etc.*); ***–e Hose,*** shorts; ***in –em,*** soon, shortly, (*Poet.*) ere long; ***– und klein hauen*** or ***schlagen,*** cut to pieces, smash to bits; (*coll.*) ***etwas – kriegen,*** get the knack of a th.; ***über – oder lang,*** sooner or later; ***kürzer machen,*** shorten; (*Comm.*) ***–es Papier,*** short(-dated) bills; ***–en Prozeß machen mit,*** make short work of; ***um es – zu sagen,*** to come to the point, to cut a long story short, to sum up; (*Naut.*) ***–e See,*** choppy sea; ***seit –em,*** lately, of late, for some (little) time now; ***der langen Rede –er Sinn,*** the gist of the matter; (*Mil.*) ***– treten,*** mark time; ***vor –em,*** recently, the other day, not long ago, a short time ago; ***– vor,*** just before (reaching); ***– vorher,*** shortly *or* a little time *or* little while before, a short time previously; ***–e Wechsel*** (*pl.*), *see* ***–es Papier***; ***den kürzeren ziehen,*** get the worst of it, be worsted, come off second-best; ***zu – kommen,*** come off the loser *or* badly; ***–e Zusammenfassung,*** brief summary; short resumé.

Kurzarbeit [ˈkurtsˀarbaɪt], *f.* short-time (work). **kurz|arbeiten,** *v.i.* be on *or* work short-time. **–ärmelig,** *adj.* short-sleeved. **–atmig,** *adj.* short-winded, (*Med.*) asthmatic, (*Vet.*) broken-winded. **–brüchig,** *adj.* brittle, (*of pastry*) short. **Kurzausgabe,** *f.* abridged edition.

Kürze [ˈkyrtsə], *f.* shortness, brevity, conciseness; short duration, short space of time; (*Metr.*) short syllable; ***in –,*** shortly, soon, in the near future, before long; ***der – halber,*** to save time *or* space; ***in aller –,*** promptly, with all possible dispatch; ***sich der – befleißigen,*** express o.s. briefly; (*Prov.*) ***in der – liegt die Würze,*** brevity is the soul of wit.

Kürzel [ˈkyrtsəl], *n.* (*shorthand*) logogram, grammalogue, short form.

kürzen [ˈkyrtsən], *v.t.* shorten (***um,*** by); condense, abbreviate, abridge; curtail, reduce, diminish, cut (down); (*Math.*) simplify; (*dial.*) ***ihn um etwas –,*** withhold s.th. from him, refuse to grant him s.th.

kurzerhand [ˈkurtsərhant], *adv.* abruptly; without hesitation, on the spot; ***– abtun,*** make short work of.

Kurz|fangsperber, *m.* (*Orn.*) Levant sparrow hawk

(*Accipiter brevipes*). **–fassung,** *f.* abridged *or* shortened version. **–form,** *f.* abbreviated *or* shortened form, abbreviation. **kurz|fristig,** *adj.* (*Comm.*) short-dated, at short sight; short-term, of short duration; at short notice, immediate. **–gefaßt,** *adj.* brief, concise, briefly worded, succinct. **Kurzgeschichte,** *f.* short story. **kurz|geschoren,** *adj.* close(ly)-cropped. **–haarig,** *adj.* short-haired. **–lebig,** *adj.* short-lived, ephemeral, perishable.

kürzlich ['kyrtslıç], *adv.* lately, recently, not long ago, the other day; ***erst –,*** quite recently.

Kurz|meldung, *f.* news flash. **–nachrichten,** *f.pl.* news summary, news in brief. **kurzschädelig,** *adj.* brachycephalic. **Kurz|schließer,** *m.* (*Elec.*) cut-out, earth switch. **–schluß,** *m.* (*Elec.*) short-circuit. **–schlußhandlung,** *f.* (*fig.*) panic (re)action. **–schlußklemme,** *f.* (*Elec.*) shunt. **–schlußkontakt,** *m.* (*Elec.*) arcing contact. **–schlußläufermotor,** *m.* (*Elec.*) squirrel-cage (induction) motor. **–schnabelgans,** *f.* (*Orn.*) pink-footed goose (*Anser brachyrhynchus*). **–schrift,** *f.* shorthand, stenography. **kurzsichtig,** *adj.* short- *or* near-sighted, (*Med.*) myopic, (*fig.*) short-sighted. **Kurzsichtigkeit,** *f.* short- *or* near-sightedness, myopia. **kurz|silbig,** *adj.* (*fig.*) taciturn, reserved, (*pred.*) of few words. **–sinnig,** *adj.* narrow-minded. **Kurz|streckenlauf,** *m.* sprint. **–streckenläufer,** *m.* sprinter.

kurzum ['kurts'um], *adv.* in short, in a word, to sum up.

Kürzung ['kyrtsuŋ], *f.* shortening, curtailment; reduction, retrenchment, cut; abridgement, condensation, cutting; abbreviation.

Kurzwaren ['kurtsva:rən], *f.pl.* haberdashery, (*Am.*) dry goods. **kurzweg** [–'vɛk], *adv.* plainly, abruptly, without ceremony, unceremoniously, curtly, offhand; simply, for short. **Kurzweil,** *f.* pastime, amusement, fun, entertainment, diversion. **kurzweilig,** *adj.* amusing, entertaining, diverting, funny. **Kurz|welle,** *f.* (*Rad.*) short-wave (band). **–wellensender,** *m.* short-wave transmitter. **–woche,** *f.* short working week, short-time. **–wort,** *n.* acronym. **–zehenlerche,** *f.* (*Orn.*) short-toed lark (*Calandrella brachydactyla*).

kuscheln ['kuʃəln], *v.r.* cuddle *or* snuggle up (***an*** (*Acc.*), to *or* against).

kuschen ['kuʃən], *v.i., v.r.* (*of dog*) lie down, crouch; (*fig.*) knuckle under.

Kusine [ku'zi:nə], *f.* (female) cousin.

Kuß [kus], *m.* **(-(ss)es,** *pl.* **¨-(ss)e)** kiss. **kuß|echt,** *adj. See* **–fest.**

küssen ['kysən], *v.t.* kiss; ***zum Abschied –,*** kiss goodbye; ***sie – sich,*** they kiss (each other).

kußfest ['kusfɛst], *adj.* kiss-proof. **Kußhand,** *f.* ***ihm eine – zuwerfen,*** blow him a kiss; (*fig.*) ***mit –,*** with alacrity, with the greatest of pleasure.

Küste ['kystə], *f.* coast, (sea)shore; ***das Land längs der –,*** the littoral; ***an der – entlangfahren,*** coast, sail along the coast; ***die – entlang,*** coastwise; ***angesichts der Waliser –,*** off the Welsh coast.

Küsten|artillerie, *f.* coast(al) artillery. **–batterie,** *f.* shore battery. **–befestigungen,** *f.pl.* coastal defences. **–befeu(e)rung,** *f.* shore lights. **–bewohner,** *m.pl.* coast-dwellers, (*Biol.*) shore forms. **–dampfer, –fahrer,** *m.* coaster, coastal *or* coasting vessel. **–fahrt,** *f.* coasting. **–feuer,** *n.* shore light. **–fischerei,** *f.* inshore fishing. **–gebiet,** *n.* coastal area, seaboard, littoral. **–gewässer,** *n.pl.* coastal waters. **–handel,** *m.* coastal trade. **–land,** *n. See* **–gebiet. –lotse,** *m.* inshore pilot. **–provinz,** *f.* maritime province. **–schiffahrt,** *f.* coastal shipping. **–schutzflottille,** *f.* light coastal forces. **–seeschwalbe,** *f.* (*Orn.*) Arctic tern (*Sterna macrura*). **–strich,** *m.* coastline, strip of coast. **–versetzung,** *f.* change in the coastline. **–verteidigung,** *f.* coast defence. **–wache,** *f.* coastguard; coastguard station. **–wachschiff,** *n.* coastal patrol vessel.

Küster ['kystər], *m.* verger, sexton, sacristan.

Kustos ['kustɔs], *m.* (-, *pl.* **Kustoden** [-'to:dən]) 1. keeper, custodian, curator; 2. (*Typ.*) catchword; 3. (*Mus.*) direction.

Kute ['ku:tə], *f.* (*dial.*) pit, hole.

Kutschbock ['kutʃbɔk], *m.* coachman's seat, box. **Kutsche,** *f.* carriage, coach. **kutschen,** *v.i. See* **kutschieren. Kutscher,** *m.* coachman, driver, (*Av.*) (*sl.*) pilot. **Kutscher(spiel),** *n.* (*coll.*) (*Cards*) game with a very good hand. **kutschieren** [–'tʃi:rən], *v.i.* (*aux.* h. & s.) go driving, drive (in) a carriage *or* coach.

Kutte ['kutə], *f.* cowl; ***die – anlegen,*** don the cowl, turn monk; (*Prov.*) ***die – macht nicht den Mönch,*** all is not gold that glitters.

Kuttel ['kutəl], *f.* (-, *pl.* **-n**) (*dial.*) entrails. **Kuttel|fleck,** *m.* **(-(e)s,** *pl.* **-e)** tripe, offal. **–kraut,** *n.* (*Austr.*) thyme. **Kutteln,** *f.pl. See* **–fleck.**

Kuttengeier ['kutəŋgaıər], *m.* (*Orn.*) *see* **Mönchsgeier.**

Kutter ['kutər], *m.* (*Naut.*) cutter.

Kuvert [ku'vɛrt, –'vɛ:r], *n.* **(-(e)s,** *pl.* **-s** [–'vɛ:rs] *or* **-e** [–'vɛrtə]) envelope, wrapper; cover (*plate, knife, fork etc.*); ***trockne –,*** dinner exclusive of wine. **kuvertieren** [–'ti:rən], *v.t.* put in an envelope, pack for posting.

Küvette [ky'vɛtə], *f.* tray, trough, vessel, wash-bowl; (*Fort.*) draining trench; (inner) dust cover (*of watch-case*).

Kux [kuks], *m.* **(-es,** *pl.* **-e)** mining share.

Kybernetik [kybɛr'ne:tık], *f.* cybernetics.

L

L, l [ɛl], *n.* L, l.

Lab [la:p], *n.* **(-(e)s,** *pl.* **-e)** rennet.

Labbe ['labə], *f.* hanging lip; (*vulg.*) mouth, gob. **labb(e)rig,** *adj.* pappy, sloppy, wishy-washy. **labbern,** *v.t., v.i.* lap, lick up, slobber; talk twaddle, blab.

Labdrüse ['la:pdry:zə], *f.* peptic gland.

Labe ['la:bə], *f.* (*Poet.*) *see* **Labsal. laben, 1.** *v.t.* refresh, revive, restore; comfort, delight. **2.** *v.r.* ***sich mit Speisen –,*** take some refreshment; ***sich an einer Speise –,*** enjoy a dish thoroughly; ***seine Augen – sich an dem Anblick,*** he feasts his eyes on the sight. **3.** *v.i.* (*dial.*) *see* **labbern.**

Laberdan [labər'da:n], *m.* **(-s,** *pl.* **-e)** salted cod.

Labetrunk ['la:bətruŋk], *m.* refreshing draught, cordial.

labil [la'bi:l], *adj.* labile, variable, unstable, changeable, unsteady, vacillating, unsettled. **Labilität** [–bili'tɛ:t], *f.* instability, lability.

Lab|kraut, *n.* (*Bot.*) galium, bedstraw. **–magen,** *m.* abomasum.

Labor [la'bo:r], *n.* **(-s,** *pl.* **-s** *or* **-e)** (*coll.*) *see* **Laboratorium. Laborant** [–'rant], *m.* **(-en,** *pl.* **-en)** laboratory assistant *or* technician. **Laboratorium** [–'to:rium], *n.* **(-s,** *pl.* **-rien)** laboratory. **laborieren** [–'ri:rən], *v.i.* do laboratory work *or* experiments; (*coll.*) be afflicted (***an*** or ***unter*** (*Dat.*), with), suffer (from), labour (under).

Labsal ['la:pza:l], *n.* **(-s,** *pl.* **-e), Labung** ['la:buŋ], *f.* refreshment, restorative; (*fig.*) comfort.

Lachanfall ['laxanfal], *m.* fit of laughter, laughing fit.

Lachbaum ['laxbaum], *m.* blazed *or* marked tree, boundary-tree.

[1]**Lache** ['laxə], *f.* laughter, laugh; ***eine – anschlagen,*** burst out laughing, give a laugh.

[2]**Lache,** *f.* blaze, notch, mark (*on a tree*).

[3]**Lache,** *f.* puddle, pool.

lächeln [ˈlɛçəln], *v.i.* smile (*über* (*Acc.*), at); ***albern* –,** simper, snigger; ***geziert* –,** smirk; ***höhnisch*** or ***spöttisch* –,** sneer; ***spitzbübisch* –,** grin; (*fig.*) – (*Dat.*), smile upon (*as fortune*). **Lächeln,** *n.* smile, simper, snigger, smirk, grin.

lachen [ˈlaxən], *v.i.* laugh (*über* (*Acc.*), at); ***brüllend* –,** roar with laughter; ***laut* –,** laugh out loud; ***leise*** (***vor sich hin***) **–,** chuckle (to o.s.); ***häßlich* –,** give an ugly laugh; ***aus vollem Halse* –,** laugh heartily *or* uproariously; ***sie – daß ihnen die Augen übergehen,*** they laugh till the tears come to their eyes; ***in die Faust –, sich*** (*Dat.*) ***ins Fäustchen –,*** laugh in one's sleeve; (*coll.*) ***daß ich nicht lache!*** don't make me laugh! ***du hast gut –,*** it's all very well for you to laugh; ***du kannst wohl –,*** you may consider yourself lucky; ***da ist nichts zu –,*** there is nothing to laugh at; ***ihm lacht das Herz im Leibe,*** his heart leaps for joy, his heart rejoices; ***das Glück lacht ihm,*** Fortune smiles upon him; (*Prov.*) ***wer zuletzt lacht, lacht am besten,*** he who laughs last laughs longest; ***sich tot*** or ***schief*** or ***krumm*** or ***krank*** or ***bucklig –, sich*** (*Dat.*) ***den Buckel voll –,*** split one's sides with *or* die with laughing, laugh o.s. silly; ***es wäre doch gelacht wenn . . .,*** it would be too silly for words if. . . .

Lachen, *n.* laughter, laugh; ***ein – hervorrufen,*** draw *or* raise a laugh; ***das ist zum –,*** that is ridiculous; ***das ist nicht zum –,*** it is no joke *or* no laughing matter; ***ihn zum – bringen,*** make him laugh; ***sich des –s nicht erwehren können,*** not be able to restrain one's laughter *or* to contain o.s. for laughter; ***nicht aus dem – kommen,*** not be able to stop laughing; ***sich*** (*Dat.*) ***das – verbeißen,*** stifle *or* suppress one's laughter; ***ich werde dir das – abgewöhnen,*** I'll make you laugh on the other side of your face, I'll teach you to laugh; ***sich vor – biegen*** or ***kugeln,*** be doubled up with laughter; ***unter –,*** laughingly.

lachend [ˈlaxənt], *adj.* laughing, smiling; glad, joyful; ***– über etwas hinweggehen,*** laugh s.th. off. **Lacher,** *m. See* [1]**Lache**; ***ich habe die – auf meiner Seite,*** the laugh is on my side.

lächerlich [ˈlɛçərlɪç], *adj.* laughable, ridiculous, ludicrous, absurd, derisory; funny, droll, comical; ***sich – machen,*** make a fool *or* an ass of o.s.; ***etwas ins – ziehen,*** make s.th. appear ridiculous; ***ihn – machen,*** make fun of him, hold him up to ridicule; ***mir ist gar nicht – zumute,*** I am in no laughing mood; ***– billig,*** ridiculously cheap. **Lächerlichkeit,** *f.* absurdity, ridiculousness; ridicule; ***er kümmert sich nicht um solche –en,*** he does not bother about such trivialities.

lächern [ˈlɛçərn], *v.t.* (*coll.*) ***es lächert mich,*** it makes me laugh.

Lachgas [ˈlaxgaːs], *n.* laughing-gas. **lachhaft,** *adj.* laughable, ridiculous. **Lach|krampf,** *m.* fit *or* paroxysm of laughter, laughing-fit; ***einen – bekommen,*** be convulsed with laughter. **–lust,** *f.* hilarity, merriness, light-heartedness. **lachlustig,** *adj.* hilarious, merry, light-hearted. **Lach|möwe,** *f.* (*Orn.*) black-headed gull (*Larus ridibundus*). **–muskel,** *m.* risible muscle.

Lachs [laks], *m.* **(-es,** ***pl.*** **-e)** 1. salmon; 2. (a kind of) Danzig brandy.

Lachsalve [ˈlaxzalvə], *f.* peal of laughter.

Lachsbrut [ˈlaksbruːt], *f.* salmon fry.

Lachseeschwalbe [ˈlaxzeːʃvalbə], *f.* (*Orn.*) gull-billed tern (*Gelochelidon nilotica*).

Lachsfang [ˈlaksfaŋ], *m.* salmon-fishing. **lachs|-farben, –farbig,** *adj.* salmon-pink. **Lachs|forelle,** *f.* salmon-trout. **–schinken,** *m.* lightly salted and smoked cut of lean pork.

Lachter [ˈlaxtər], *f.* (-, ***pl.*** **-n**) *or n.* (*obs.*) fathom.

Lack [lak], *m.* **(-(e)s,** ***pl.*** **-e)** varnish, lacquer, enamel; lac; ***der – der Zivilisation,*** the veneer of civilization; (*coll.*) ***fertig ist der –!*** there you have it! there you are! **Lack|anstrich,** *m.* coat of varnish. **–arbeit,** *f.* japanned *or* lacquered work. **–draht,** *m.* enamelled wire.

Lackel [ˈlakəl], *m.* (*coll.*) boor, oaf, yokel.

Lack|farbe, *f.* enamel paint. **–firnis,** *m.* lacquer, varnish. **lackieren** [–ˈkiːrən], *v.t.* lacquer, varnish, enamel, japan; (*coll.*) cheat, impose upon, hoodwink, dupe, hoax, take in; (*coll.*) ***der Lackierte sein,*** be the mug *or* sucker. **Lackleder,** *n.* patent leather.

Lackmus [ˈlakmus], *n.* litmus.

Lackschuhe [ˈlakʃuːə], *m.pl.* patent-leather shoes, dress shoes.

Lade [ˈlaːdə], *f.* box, chest, case; drawer; sounding board (*of organs*).

Lade|anlage, *f.* loading ramp. **–batterie,** *f.* storage battery, (*Am.*) accumulator. **–baum,** *m.* derrick, jib. **–brief,** *m.* bill of lading. **–bühne,** *f. See* **–anlage. –damm,** *m.* jetty, landing stage. **ladefähig,** *adj.* serviceable (*of ammunition*). **Lade|-fähigkeit,** *f.* loading capacity, (*Naut.*) tonnage. **–gebühr,** *f.*, **–geld,** *n.* lading charges. **–gewicht,** *n.* (*Naut.*) weight loaded, deadweight tonnage. **–hemmung,** *f.* jam, stoppage (*of gun*). **–höhe,** *f.* maximum loading height. **–klappe,** *f.* (*Motor.*) tailboard. **–linie,** *f.* loadline, Plimsoll('s) mark. **–liste,** *f.* (*Naut.*) manifest. **–loch,** *n.* (*Artil.*) chamber. **–luke,** *f.* (*Naut.*) hatch(way). **–maschine,** *f.* (*Elec.*) battery charger.

[1]**laden** [ˈlaːdən], *irr.v.t.* load, lade, (*Naut.*) ship, freight; load (*a gun*); (*Elec.*) charge; ***blind* –,** load with blank cartridge; ***scharf* –,** load with ball; (*sl.*) ***er hat schwer*** or ***schief geladen,*** he is half-seas-over; ***auf sich*** (*Acc.*) **–,** bring down upon o.s., incur, burden *or* saddle o.s. with; (*coll.*) ***geladen sein,*** be mad (***auf*** (*Acc.*), at), have it in (for).

[2]**laden,** *irr.v.t.* invite, (*Law*) summon, cite, subpoena.

Laden, *m.* **(-s,** ***pl.*** **-** ***or*** **¨)** 1. (*pl. usu.* -) (window-) shutter; 2. (*pl. usu.* ¨) shop, store, stall; ***einen – aufmachen,*** set up shop; (*fig.*) ***den – zumachen,*** shut up shop, (*coll.*) pack it in; (*sl.*) ***den – schmeißen,*** run the (whole) show.

Laden|angestellte(r), *m., f.* shop assistant. **–besitzer,** *m.* shopkeeper, (*Am.*) storekeeper. **–dieb,** *m.* shoplifter. **–diebstahl,** *m.* shoplifting. **–diener,** *m.* (*obs.*) *see* **–angestellte(r). –einbruch,** *m.* smash-and-grab raid. **–fenster,** *n.* shop window. **–gaumer,** *m.* (*Swiss*) *see* **–hüter. –geschäft,** *n. See* **Laden,** 2. **–hüter,** *m.* dead stock, drug in *or* on the market. **–inhaber,** *m. See* **–besitzer. –kasse,** *f.* cash-desk, till. **–mädchen,** *n.* shop assistant, shopgirl. **–preis,** *m.* retail *or* selling-price, (*of books*) published price. **–schluß,** *m.* closing-time; ***nach* –,** after hours. **–schwengel,** *m.* (*coll.*) counter-jumper. **–tisch,** *m.* counter. **–tochter,** *f.* (*Swiss*) *see* **–mädchen. –verkauf,** *m.* retail sale.

Lade|platz, *m.* loading point *or* space, (*Railw.*) goods platform, (*Naut.*) wharf, landing stage. **–rampe,** *f.* loading ramp *or* platform. **–raum,** *m.* (ship's) hold; cargo space; tonnage; (*Av.*) stowage compartment; (*Artil.*) chamber. **–schein,** *m. See* **–brief. –schütze,** *m.* (*Artil.*) loader. **–spannung,** *f.* (*Elec.*) charging voltage. **–station, –stelle,** *f.* (battery-)charging station. **–stock,** *m.* (*Artil.*) ramrod. **–streifen,** *m.* cartridge clip (*rifle*), cartridge belt (*machine gun*). **–strom,** *m.* (*Elec.*) charging current. **–tisch,** *m.* (*Artil.*) loading tray. **–trommel,** *f.* cartridge drum (*machine gun*).

lädieren [lɛˈdiːrən], *v.t.* injure, damage, hurt.

Ladnerin [ˈlaːtnərɪn], *f.* (*Austr.*) *see* **Ladenmädchen.**

lädst [lɛːtst], **lädt,** *see* **laden.**

[1]**Ladung** [ˈlaːduŋ], *f.* loading, lading; load, freight, (*Naut.*) cargo, shipment; (*ammunition, Elec.*) charge; ***in – liegen nach,*** be loading for; ***die – anbrechen,*** break bulk; ***– einnehmen,*** load, (*Naut.*) take on cargo *or* freight; ***ohne –,*** empty, in ballast; ***volle –,*** full freight; ***geballte –,*** concentrated charge; ***gestreckte –,*** distributed charge.

[2]**Ladung,** *f.* (*Law*) summons, citation, subpoena.

Ladungs|aufseher, *m.* (*Naut.*) supercargo. **–empfänger,** *m.* consignee. **–flasche,** *f.* Leyden jar.

-**interessent,** *m.* part-owner of a cargo. **–verzeichnis,** *n.* ship's manifest, freight-list.

Lafette [la'fɛtə], *f.* gun-carriage; ***auf die – bringen*** or ***heben,*** mount (*a gun*); ***von der – abheben,*** dismount (*a gun*). **Lafetten|kreuz,** *n.* outriggers, gunlegs. **–schwanz,** *m.* trail. **–sporn,** *m.* trail spade.

[1]**Laffe** ['lafə], *f.* (*dial.*) bowl (*of a spoon*).

[2]**Laffe,** *m.* **(-n,** *pl.* **-n)** fop, dandy, popinjay.

lag [la:k], **läge** ['lɛ:gə], *see* **liegen.**

Lage ['la:gə], *f.* 1. situation, position, site, locality, location, attitude, posture; (*Med.*) presentation (*at birth*); (*Fenc.*) guard; (*fig.*) state (of affairs), outlook, condition, circumstances; (*Geol.*) bed, deposit, layer, stratum; tier, course; ***ihn in die – versetzen,*** enable him, make it possible for him (to); ***versetzen Sie sich in meine –,*** put yourself in my position; ***in der – sein,*** be in a position *or* be able (to); ***in die – kommen,*** be enabled, be put in a position (to); ***das ändert die*** (***ganze***) ***–,*** that puts (quite) a new face on things; ***nach – der Dinge,*** as things stand, in *or* under the circumstances; ***schiefe*** or ***mißliche –,*** predicament, plight, awkward position; (*Fenc.*) ***außer –,*** off one's guard; ***ungeschütze –,*** exposure; ***rechtliche –,*** legal status *or* position; 2. covering, film, coat (*of paint*); ***ein Schiff mit drei –n,*** a three-decker; 3. (*Mus.*) harmonic arrangement (*of a chord*); (*Mus.*) register, compass; position (*of fingering with stringed instruments*); 4. quire (*of paper*); round (*of drinks*); salvo, volley (*of shots*); (*Naut.*) ***volle –,*** broadside.

Lagebesprechung ['la:gəbəʃprɛçuŋ], *f.* (*Mil.*) briefing.

Lagen|feuer, *n.* salvo, continuous fire. **–staffel,** *f.* (*Swimming*) medley relay race. **lagenweise,** *adv.* in layers; in tiers; in strata. **Lageplan,** *m.* plan of a site, ground plan, layout.

Lägel ['lɛ:gəl], *n.* (*dial.*) barrel, keg, cask; hank (*of cord*); (*Naut.*) cringle.

Lager ['la:gər], *n.* **(-s,** *pl.* **-** (*Comm.* ⸚)) 1. storehouse, warehouse, depot, dump, store, stock(s), supply; ***auf(s) – bringen,*** warehouse, put into store; ***das – aufnehmen,*** take an inventory of stock in hand; ***auf – haben,*** stock, have on hand, keep in stock; (*fig., coll.*) have up one's sleeve; ***dies fehlt auf –,*** this is out of stock; 2. camp, encampment; (*fig.*) party, side; ***ein – aufschlagen*** (***abstecken***), pitch (mark out) a camp, pitch one's tent *or* tents; ***– abbrechen,*** strike camp; ***ein – beziehen,*** move into camp; ***ins feindliche – übergehen,*** go over to the enemy; 3. stratum, stroma, layer; 4. couch, bed; lair; den, hole, cover (*of beasts*); ***ein unruhiges – haben,*** be a restless sleeper, have a restless night; ***vom – aufstehen,*** rise from a bed of sickness; 5. dregs, sediments; 6. (*Tech.*) bearing.

Lager|arrest, *m.* confinement to camp *or* barracks, (*sl.*) jankers. **–aufnahme,** *f.* stock-taking, inventory. **–aufseher,** *m.* store-keeper. **–bestand,** *m.* inventory, stock (on hand). **–bier,** *n.* lager (beer). **–buch,** *n.* stock-book. **–buchse,** *f.* (*Tech.*) bushing. **–diener,** *m. See* **–halter. lager|fähig, –fest,** *adj.* storable, unaffected by storage. **Lagerfeuer,** *n.* camp-fire. **lagerförmig,** *adj.* in layers *or* strata. **Lager|gebühren,** *f.pl.*, **–geld,** *n.* charge for storage, warehouse charges, demurrage. **–halter,** *m.* warehouse- *or* store-clerk; stockist, distributor. **–haus,** *n.* warehouse.

Lagerist [la:gə'rɪst], *m.* **(-en,** *pl.* **-en)** warehouse-clerk, store-keeper.

Lager|kosten, *f.pl.* warehouse charges. **–leben,** *n.* camp-life. **–meister,** *m.* storeman.

lagern ['la:gərn], **1.** *v.i.* (*aux.* h. *&* s.), *v.r.* lie down, rest; camp, be encamped; be stored *or* warehoused, be in store, be deposited, lie spread out, (*fig.*) (*as clouds*) lie, hang. **2.** *v.t.* lay down; deposit, pile, place, post; encamp (*troops*), pitch (*tents*); store, lay-up (*goods*); (*Tech.*) seat, mount (in bearings), pivot, support, bed.

Lager|ort, –platz, *m.* storage place, depot, dump; (*Geol.*) bed; camping place, camp site; resting-place. **–raum,** *m.* store-room, warehouse. **–reibung,** *f.* (*Tech.*) bearing friction. **–schale,** *f.* bearing-housing, axle-box. **–schuppen,** *m.* storage shed. **–statt, –stätte, –stelle,** *f.* resting-place; couch, bed; lodging; encampment.

Lagerung ['la:gəruŋ], *f.* arrangement; orientation; recumbent position; storing, storage, warehousing; (*Geol.*) stratification; (*Tech.*) seating, mounting, support.

Lager|verwalter, *m. See* **–meister. –vorrat,** *m.* stock in hand, supply. **–zapfen,** *m.* (*Tech.*) pivot-pin, trunnion, journal.

–lägerig ['lɛ:gərɪç], *adj.suff.* -lying; *e.g.* ***bettlägerig,*** *adj.* lying in bed, confined to one's bed.

Lagune [la'gu:nə], *f.* lagoon.

lahm [la:m], *adj.* lame, limping, crippled; paralysed, (*obs.*) halt; (*fig.*) weak, impotent, feeble, dull, sluggish; ***eine –e Entschuldigung,*** a lame *or* poor excuse. **lahmen,** *v.i.* (walk with a) limp, be lame *or* crippled.

lähmen ['lɛ:mən], *v.t.* (make) lame, cripple, paralyse; (*fig.*) obstruct, immobilize, hinder, (*coll.*) hamstring; (*fig.*) ***gelähmt,*** paralysed (***vor*** (*Dat.*), with); (*as business*) lifeless, stagnant.

Lahme(r) ['la:mə(r)], *m., f.* cripple, paralytic. **lahm|legen,** *v.t.* paralyse, cripple, bring to a standstill, make useless. **–schießen,** *irr.v.t.* damage *or* cripple (*a vehicle etc.*) by gunfire.

Lähmung ['lɛ:muŋ], *f.* lameness, paralysis, (*obs.*) palsy.

Lahn [la:n], *m.* **(-(e)s,** *pl.* **-e)** metal foil, tinsel.

Lai [laɪ], *n.* **(-s,** *pl.* **-s)** (*usu. pl.*) lay, song (*of Celtic and Old French minstrels*).

Laib [laɪp], *m.* **(-(e)s,** *pl.* **-e)** loaf (*of bread*); ***ein – Käse,*** a whole cheese.

Laich [laɪç], *m.* **(-(e)s,** *pl.* **-e)** spawn, (*oysters*) spat. **Laiche,** *f.* spawning-time. **laichen,** *v.i.* spawn, (*oysters*) spat. **Laich|kraut,** *n.* (*Bot.*) pond-weed (*Pontamogeton*). **–teich,** *m.* breeding-pond. **–zeit,** *f. See* **Laiche.**

Laie ['laɪə], *m.* **(-n,** *pl.* **-n)** layman; novice, amateur; *pl.* the laity. **Laien|bruder,** *m.* lay-brother. **–güter,** *n.pl.* temporalities. **laienhaft,** *adj.* lay; non-professional; amateurish. **Laien|priester,** *m.* lay-reader. **–richter,** *m.* lay-judge, magistrate, (*Eng.*) Justice of the Peace. **–spiel,** *n.* amateur theatricals. **–stand,** *m.*, **–welt,** *f.* laity, laymen.

Lakai [la'kaɪ], *m.* **(-en,** *pl.* **-en)** footman, lackey, flunkey. **lakaienhaft,** *adj.* flunkey-like, cringing. **Lakaien|seele,** *f.* (*fig.*) flunkey. **–sitz,** *m.* dicky, rumble.

Lake ['la:kə], *f.* brine, pickle.

Laken ['la:kən], *m. or n.* (*dial.*) dust-cloth, sheet; tablecloth; shroud.

lakonisch [la'ko:nɪʃ], *adj.* laconic.

Lakritze [la'krɪtsə], *f.* (*Austr.*), **Lakritzen,** *m.* (Spanish) liquorice.

lala ['la'la], *adv.* (*coll.*) *so–*, so-so, middling, pretty well, not so bad, nothing to boast of, (*sl.*) not so dusty.

lallen ['lalən], *v.t., v.i.* stammer, stutter, mumble, babble.

[1]**Lama** ['la:ma], *m.* **(-(s),** *pl.* **-s)** lama (*Buddhist priest*).

[2]**Lama,** *n.* **(-s,** *pl.* **-s)** (*Zool.*) llama.

Lambertsnuß ['lambɛrtsnus], *f.* filbert, hazel-nut.

Lamelle [la'mɛlə], *f.* lamella, (*Elec.*) lamina, lamination; (*of fungus*) gill, (*Tech.*) blade, leaf, plate, layer, segment. **lamellenförmig,** *adj.* laminated, lamellar, laminar. **Lamellenkupplung,** *f.* (*Motor.*) disc-clutch. **lamellieren** [–'li:rən], *v.t.* laminate.

lamentieren [lamɛn'ti:rən], *v.i.* lament (***um,*** for; ***über*** (*Acc.*), over), complain (***um,*** about), (*coll.*) moan, (*sl.*) belly-ache (over *or* about). **Lamento** [–'mɛnto], *n.* **(-(s),** *pl.* **-s)** lamentation, wailing, complaining.

Lametta [la'mɛta], *f.* lametta, tinsel, angels' hair (*decoration on Christmas-trees*).

laminieren [lami'ni:rən], *v.t.* flatten (*metal*), laminate.

Lamm [lam], *n.* (**-(e)s,** *pl.* **¨-er**) lamb. **–braten,** *m.* roast lamb.

Lämmer ['lɛmər], *pl. of* **Lamm. Lämmerchen,** *n.* 1. lambkin; 2. *pl.* lambs' tails, fleecy clouds; catkins. **Lämmer|geier,** *m.* (*Orn.*) *see* **Bartgeier. –hüpfen,** *n.* (*coll.*) dancing, frisking, frolicking (*of young girls without male partners*). **–schwänzchen,** *n.* lamb's tail, (*Bot.*) yarrow; (*coll.*) ***lustig wie ein –,*** merry as a cricket. **–wolke,** *f.* cirrus.

Lamm(e)sgeduld ['lam(ə)sgədult], *f.* patience of Job. **Lamm|fell,** *n.* lambskin. **–fleisch,** *n.* lamb. **lamm|fromm, –herzig,** *adj.* gentle *or* meek as a lamb. **Lamm|wolle,** *f.* lamb's wool. **–zeit,** *f.* lambing-time.

Lampe ['lampə], *f.* lamp; *pl.* (*Theat.*) footlights. **Lampen|docht,** *m.* (lamp-)wick. **–faden,** *m.* lighting filament. **–fassung,** *f.* light- *or* lamp-fitting, lamp-socket. **–fieber,** *n.* stage-fright. **–glocke,** *f.* lampshade, globe. **–licht,** *n.* lamplight, artificial light. **–ruß,** *m.* lamp-black. **–schirm,** *m.* lampshade. **–zylinder,** *m.* (lamp-)chimney.

Lampion [lãpi'õ], *m. or n.* (**-s,** *pl.* **-s**) Chinese lantern.

Lamprete [lam'pre:tə], *f.* lamprey; (*coll.*) tit-bit, luxury.

lancieren [lã'si:rən], *v.t.* fling, thrust, fire, launch; float (*a loan*). **Lancierrohr,** *n.* torpedo-tube.

Land [lant], *n.* 1. (**-(e)s,** *no pl.*) land (*as opp. to water*); country(side) (*as opp. to town*); soil, earth, ground, arable land; piece of land, landed property; ***an – gehen*** or ***ans – steigen,*** land, go ashore; ***auf das – gehen,*** go into the country; ***auf dem*** (*Austr.* ***am***) ***–e,*** in the country; ***festes –,*** terra firma, mainland; (*coll.*) ***seitdem sind viele Tage ins – gegangen,*** since then much water has flowed under the bridge; ***plattes*** or ***flaches –,*** low country, plain; ***– sehen,*** be near one's goal; ***über –,*** overland; ***vom –e stoßen,*** put to sea, push off from the bank; ***Einfalt*** (or ***Unschuld*** or ***Gänschen***) ***vom –e,*** simple country maid, country cousin; ***zu –e,*** by land; 2. (**-(e)s,** *pl.* **¨-er,** (*Poet.* **-e**)) land, country, region, realm, territory, province, state, nation; ***aus aller Herren Ländern,*** from all parts of the globe, from all over the world; ***außer –es,*** abroad; ***– der Elfen,*** fairyland; ***das Gelobte –,*** the Promised Land; ***das Heilige –,*** the Holy Land; ***– und Leute regieren,*** govern a country; ***– der Träume,*** dreamland; ***des –es verwiesen,*** exiled.

Land|adel, *m.* landed aristocracy *or* gentry. **–ammann,** *m.* (*pl.* **-männer**) (*Swiss*) cantonal president. **–anker,** *m.* shore-anchor. **–anwachs,** *m.* alluvium. **–arbeit,** *f.* agricultural work, farming. **–arbeiter,** *m.* farm *or* agricultural labourer, farm-hand. **–armee,** *f.* land forces. **–arzt,** *m.* country doctor.

Landauer ['landauər], *m.* landau.

Landaufenthalt ['lantˀaufɛnthalt], *m.* stay in the country. **landaus,** *adv.* ***–, landein,*** far afield, far and wide. **Land|bau,** *m.* agriculture. **–besitz,** *m.* landed property, (*Law*) real estate. **–besitzer,** *m.* landowner, landed proprietor. **–bevölkerung,** *f.* rural population. **–bewohner,** *m.* country dweller. **–bezirk,** *m.* rural district. **–buch,** *n.* land register. **–bund,** *m.* Farmers' Union. **–butter,** *f.* farm butter.

Lande|bahn ['landə–], *f.* (*Av.*) runway. **–brücke,** *f.* landing stage, pier, jetty, quay. **–deck,** *n.* (*Naut.*) flight deck.

Landedelmann ['lantˀe:dəlman], *m.* country squire.

Lande|erlaubnis, *f.* landing permit. **–geschwindigkeit,** *f.* (*Av.*) land speed.

Land|eigentum, *n.* landed property. **–eigentümer, –eig(e)ner,** *m.* landed proprietor. **landeinwärts,** *adv.* up country, (further) inland.

Lande|klappe, *f.* (*Av.*) landing flap. **–kopf,** *m.* (*Mil.*) beachhead. **–licht,** *n.* (*Av.*) landing light.

landen ['landən], **1.** *v.i.* (*aux.* h. *&* s.) land, disembark, get ashore; (*Av.*) make a landing, land; alight, land (*on one's feet*); (*fig.*) land (up), end (*in prison etc.*); touch down. **2.** *v.t.* land (*troops, a blow*).

länden ['lɛndən], *v.t.* 1. bring ashore, wash ashore; 2. (*Swiss*) *see* **landen.**

Landenge ['lantˀɛŋə], *f.* isthmus.

Lande|piste, *f. See* **–bahn. –platz,** *m.* (*Naut.*) *see* **–brücke,** (*Av.*) landing ground *or* field.

Länder ['lɛndər], *pl. of* **Land.**

Landerad ['landəra:t], *n.* (*Av.*) landing wheel.

Länderei [lɛndə'raɪ], *f.* (*usu. pl.*) landed property, estates. **Länder|kampf,** *m.* (*Spt.*) international contest *or* meeting *or* match. **–kunde,** *f.* geography. **–mannschaft,** *f.* national team. **–spiel,** *n.* international match.

Landerziehungsheim ['lantˀɛrtsi:uŋshaɪm], *n.* country boarding-school.

Landes|arbeitsgericht, *n.* Regional Labour Court. **–archiv,** *n.* provincial archives. **–aufnahme,** *f.* topographical *or* ordnance survey. **–bank,** *f.* national bank. **–behörde,** *f.* provincial authority. **–beschreibung,** *f.* topography. **–brauch,** *m.* national custom. **landeseigen,** *adj.* state-owned. **Landes|erzeugnis,** *n.* home produce. **–farben,** *f.pl.* national colours. **–flagge,** *f.* national flag. **–fürst,** *m.* reigning prince, sovereign. **–gebiet,** *n.* national territory. **–gericht,** *n.* assize court. **–gesetz,** *n.* law of the land. **–grenze,** *f.* national frontier. **–herr,** *m. See* **–fürst. –hoheit,** *f.* sovereignty, the Crown. **–kind,** *n.* native (of the country). **–kirche,** *f.* established church. **–mutter,** *f.* wife of a sovereign, sovereign (lady). **–obrigkeit,** *f.* supreme authority, authorities, government. **–polizei,** *f.* state police. **–regierung,** *f.* central government, (*Germany*) state *or* provincial government. **–sitte,** *f.* national custom. **–sozialgericht,** *n.* Regional Social Court. **–sprache,** *f.* vernacular.

Lande|steg, *m. See* **–brücke. –stelle,** *f.* landing place *or* point.

Landes|tracht, *f.* national costume *or* dress. **–trauer,** *f.* public *or* national mourning.

Landestreifen ['landəʃtraɪfən], *m.* (*Av.*) landing strip.

landesüblich ['landəsˀy:plɪç], *adj.* customary, (according to the practice) usual (in a country). **Landes|vater,** *m.* sovereign. **–vermessung,** *f.* ordnance *or* topographical survey. **–verrat,** *m.* high treason. **–verräter,** *m.* traitor (to his country). **landesverräterisch,** *adj.* treasonable. **Landes|verteidigung,** *f.* national *or* home defence. **–verwalter,** *m. See* **–verweser. –verwaltung,** *f.* provincial administration. **–verweisung,** *f.* banishment, exile. **–verweser,** *m.* governor, viceroy. **landesverwiesen,** *adj.* banished, exiled. **Landeswährung,** *f.* national *or* legal currency.

Landflucht ['lantfluxt], *f.* migration from the country (*to the town*), rural exodus. **landflüchtig,** *adj.* fugitive; ***– werden,*** flee one's country, go into voluntary exile. **Land|flugzeug,** *n.* land-plane. **–frachtwesen,** *n.* (over)land carrying trade. **landfremd,** *adj.* foreign *or* strange to *or* a stranger in a country; (*fig.*) quite strange *or* new. **Land|frieden,** *m.* public peace (*proclaimed by the Emperor in medieval times*); (*coll.*) ***dem – nicht trauen,*** be on one's guard. **–friedensbruch,** *m.* breach of the peace. **–geistliche(r),** *m.* country clergyman. **–gemeinde,** *f.* rural community; country parish. **–gemeindeordnung,** *f.* local government regulations. **–gericht,** *n.* county court, petty sessions; (*in Germany*) Regional Court. **–graf,** *m.* (**-en,** *pl.* **-en**) count, landgrave. **–gräfin,** *f.* countess, landgravine. **–grenze,** *f.* landmark; boundary. **landgültig,** *adj.* valid, legal; ***–es Gesetz,*** common law, law of the land. **Land|gut,** *n.* estate, manor, country-seat. **–haus,** *n.* villa, country-house; week-end house *or* cottage. **–heer,** *n.* land-forces. **–helfer,** *m.* (*Nat. Soc.*) youngster during year's land service. **–hilfe,** *f.* (*Nat. Soc.*) land service for girls; land-girl. **–hunger,** *m.* (*Pol.*) expansionist urge. **–innere(s),** *n.* up-country, interior. **–jäger,** *m.* gendarme; country constable. **–jahr,** *n.* (*Nat. Soc.*) year of compulsory service on the land. **–junker,** *m.* (country) squire. **–karte,** *f.* map. **–kartenkunde,** *f.* map-reading. **–kennung,**

f. navigational aids (*in coastal waters*). **–krankheit,** *f.* endemic disease. **–kreis,** *m.* rural district. **–krieg,** *m.* land warfare. **–kriegordnung,** *f. Haager –,* Hague Convention. **land|kundig,** *adj.* knowing the country well; well-known, notorious. **–läufig,** *adj.* customary, ordinary, common, generally accepted, current. **Landleben,** *n.* rural *or* country life.

Ländler [ˈlɛndlər], *m.* (*Mus.*) (slow) country waltz.

Landleute [ˈlantlɔytə], *pl.* country people, peasant farmers.

ländlich [ˈlɛntlɪç], *adj.* rural, rustic, (*Poet.*) bucolic, (*coll.*) countrified; (*Prov.*) **–,** ***sittlich,*** other countries, other customs; do in Rome as the Romans do; (*coll.*) **–,** ***schändlich,*** cheap and nasty. **Ländlichkeit,** *f.* rusticity, rural *or* rustic simplicity, rural character, country ways.

Land|macht, *f.* (*Mil.*) land forces; land power. **–makler,** *m.* (real-) estate agent. **–mann,** *m.* (*pl.* **–leute**) farmer, countryman, peasant. **–maschinen,** *f.pl.* farming equipment, agricultural machinery. **–messer,** *m.* surveyor. **–miliz,** *f.* yeomanry, provincial militia. **–mine,** *f.* (*Mil.*) landmine. **–nähe,** *f.* (*Naut.*) landfall. **–nahme,** *f.* annexation of territory; land rush. **–partie,** *f.* picnic, outing, excursion. **–peilung,** *f.* (*Naut.*) shore bearing. **–pfarre,** *f.* country living *or* parsonage. **–pfarrer,** *m.* country parson. **–pfleger,** *m.* (*B.*) governor, prefect. **–plage,** *f.* scourge, calamity, (*coll.*) public nuisance. **–polizei,** *f.* rural police, gendarmerie. **–pomeranze,** *f.* (*coll.*) country wench. **–rasse,** *f.* indigenous breed. **–rat,** *m.* 1. district magistrate, chairman of rural district council; 2. cantonal government (*in Switzerland*). **–ratte,** *f.* (*coll.*) landlubber. **–recht,** *n.* common law. **–regen,** *m.* widespread and persistent rain. **–reise,** *f.* overland journey. **–reiter,** *m.* mounted gendarme. **–rücken,** *m.* ridge of hills. **–sasse,** *m.* (*Hist.*) freeholder; feudal lord.

Landschaft [ˈlantʃaft], *f.* landscape, scenery; countryside; district, region. **landschaftlich,** *adj.* provincial; scenic, of the landscape. **Landschafts|bild,** *n.* scene, landscape(-painting). **–gärtner,** *m.* landscape-gardener. **–gärtnerei,** *f.* landscape-gardening. **–maler,** *m.* landscape-painter. **–malerei,** *f.* landscape-painting.

Land|schnecke, *f.* common snail. **–schreiber,** *m.* (*Swiss*) magistrate's clerk. **–schule,** *f.* country *or* village-school. **–schulheim,** *n.* country boarding school. **–see,** *m.* inland lake.

Landser [ˈlantsər], *m.* (*coll.*) infantryman, footslogger; common soldier, (*Am.*) doughboy.

Landsgemeinde [ˈlantsgəmaɪndə], *f.* (*Swiss*) annual assembly of all voters in a canton.

Landsitz [ˈlantzɪts], *m.* country seat.

Lands|knecht, *m.* (*Hist.*) mercenary, (16th century) lansquenet; ***fluchen wie ein –,*** swear like a trooper. **–mann,** *m.* (*pl.* **–leute**) compatriot, fellow countryman; ***was für ein – sind Sie?*** where do you come from? where is your home? what is your native country? ***er ist Ihr –,*** he is a countryman of yours. **–mannschaft,** *f.* student organization with local affiliations; organization of expellees from occupied territories with revisionist aims.

Land|spitze, *f.* cape, headland, promontory. **–stände,** *m.pl.* (*Hist.*) representative body, provincial diet. **–straße,** *f.* main road, highway. **–strecke,** *f.* tract of land, region. **–streicher,** *m.* tramp, vagrant. **–streicherei,** *f.* vagrancy. **–streitkräfte,** *f.pl.* (*Mil.*) land *or* ground forces. **–strich,** *m. See* **–strecke. –sturm,** *m.* army reserve (*men over 45*), local militia. **–tag,** *m.* provincial diet. **–tier,** *n.* land animal. **–transport,** *m.* overland transport. **–truppen,** *f.pl.* land forces, ground troops.

Landung [ˈlanduŋ], *f.* landing, disembarkation. **Landungs|boot,** *n.* landing barge *or* craft, (*Mil.*) assault boat. **–brücke,** *f.* landing-stage, pier, jetty. **–platz,** *m.* landing place. **–steg,** *m.* gangway, gang-plank. **–truppen,** *f.pl.* landing force, beach assault troops.

Land|urlaub, *m.* (*Naut.*) shore leave. **–vermessung,** *f.* land survey. **–verschickung,** *f.* evacuation to the country. **–vogt,** *m.* (*Hist.*) provincial governor. **–volk,** *n.* country people; peasantry. **landwärts,** *adv.* landward; inshore. **Land|weg,** *m.* (over)land route; country road, secondary road; ***auf dem –,*** by land. **–wehr,** *f.* militia, yeomanry; Territorial Reserve (*men between 35 and 45*). **–wind,** *m.* off-shore wind. **–wirt,** *m.* farmer. **–wirtschaft,** *f.* farming, agriculture, husbandry. **landwirtschaftlich** *adj.* agricultural. **Land|-zunge** *f.* spit (of land). **–zwang** *m.* (*obs.*) breach of the peace, public nuisance.

lang [laŋ], **1.** *adj.* (*comp. länger, sup. längst*) (*space*) long; tall; high, lofty; (*time*) long, (for) a long time, prolonged, protracted, lengthy; (*of wine*) ropy; ***auf die –e Bank schieben,*** shelve, pigeonhole, postpone, delay, (*coll.*) put off; ***das Lange und Kurze der S.,*** the long and the short of the matter; ***ein –es und breites*** (*Austr. with caps.*) ***reden*** or ***schwatzen,*** talk at great length; ***sich des –en und breiten über etwas auslassen,*** discuss a th. from all angles, enlarge on a th.; ***–e Finger machen,*** steal, pilfer; ***er machte ein –es Gesicht,*** he pulled a long face, his face fell; ***einen –en Hals machen,*** crane one's neck; (*coll.*) ***eine –e Leitung haben,*** be slow on the uptake; ***–e Ohren machen,*** be inquisitive; ***ihm eine –e Nase machen,*** cock a snook at him; ***der –en Rede kurzer Sinn,*** to cut a long story short; ***auf –e Sicht,*** long-sighted *or* -dated (*bills*); far-sighted; ***den lieben –en Tag,*** the live-long day; ***in nicht zu –er Zeit,*** in the not too distant future; ***vor –en Jahren*** or ***vor –er Zeit,*** long ago; ***ihm wird die Zeit –,*** time hangs heavy on his hands. **2.** *adv., prep.* (*preceded by Acc.*) long; for, during; ***eine Zeit –,*** for a time; ***drei Jahre –,*** for three years; ***sein Leben –,*** all his life, till the end of his days; (*coll.*) ***den Fluß – gehen,*** walk along the river. **3.** (*also lange*), *adv.* (*comp. länger, sup. am längsten, längst*) *see also* **längst–**; a long while, long; by far; ***auf –e,*** for a long time; ***nicht –(e) darauf,*** shortly after; ***den muß man nicht erst –(e) fragen,*** he does not wait to be asked; ***wer wird erst –(e) fragen?*** who would hesitate? (*coll.*) ***es ist für mich –e gut,*** it is quite good enough for me; ***–e machen,*** take one's time; (*coll.*) ***er wird es nicht mehr –e machen,*** he has not long to live; ***–e nicht so gut,*** not nearly so good; ***noch –e nicht,*** not for a long time yet, not by a long way, far from (it); ***noch –e nicht fertig,*** not nearly ready; ***er ist noch –e kein Goethe,*** he is far from being a Goethe; ***ohne sich –e zu besinnen,*** without any hesitation; ***seit –em,*** for a long time (past); ***schon –e bereit,*** ready long ago; ***schon –e her,*** a long time ago; ***es ist schon –e her daß . . .,*** it has been a long time since *or* that . . .; ***schon –e vorbei,*** all over *or* past, long since; ***so –e wie*** or ***als,*** as long as; ***so –e bis,*** until (such time as), till; ***über kurz oder –,*** sooner or later; ***von –e her,*** of long standing, of old; (*coll.*) ***da kannst du –e warten,*** you can whistle for it, you can wait till you're blue in the face; ***wie –e wohnen Sie hier?*** how long have you been living here?

lang|anhaltend, *adj.* lasting, continuous, enduring. **–atmig,** *adj.* long-winded. **–blätterig,** *adj.* long-leaved, macrophyllous. **Langbrennweite** *f.* long focus. **lang|dauernd** *adj. See* **–anhaltend.**

lange, *adv. See* **lang, 3**.

Länge [ˈlɛŋə], *f.* (*space*) length; tallness, size, (*Geog.*) longitude; (*time*) length, duration, (*Metr.*) quantity, long syllable; (*fig.*) tedious passage (*in a book*); ***der – nach,*** lengthwise, longitudinally; ***der – nach hinfallen,*** fall full length, (*coll.*) go sprawling; (*fig.*) ***auf die –,*** in the long run; ***in die – ziehen,*** draw out, elongate; drag *or* spin out, protract; ***sich in die – ziehen,*** drag on (and on); ***20 Meter in der –,*** 20 m. long *or* in length; (*Spt.*) ***um eine – siegen,*** win by a length. **längeland,** *adv.* (at) full length; ***– hinfallen, see der Länge nach hinfallen.***

langen [ˈlaŋən], **1.** *v.i.* 1. be enough *or* sufficient, suffice, (*coll.*) will do, will last; ***langt das?*** will that do? 2. ***– nach,*** reach for, stretch out the hand for; ***das Kleid langt kaum bis an die Knie,*** the dress scarcely reaches the knees; ***lange zu!*** help yourself! ***in die Tasche –,*** put one's hand in one's pocket. **2.** *v.t.* ***ihm eine (Ohrfeige) –,*** box his ears, give him a clout; ***lange mir den Hut!*** reach *or* hand *or* pass me my hat.

längen ['lɛŋən], *v.t.* (*Tech.*) extend, lengthen, elongate; (*Cul.*) roll out (*dough*), thin (*soup*).

Längen|abweichung, *f.* (*Artil.*) ranging error. **–ausdehnung,** *f.* linear expansion. **–bruch,** *m.* longitudinal fracture. **–durchschnitt,** *m.* longitudinal section. **–einheit,** *f.* unit of length. **–grad,** *m.* degree of longitude. **–kreis,** *m.* meridian. **–maß,** *n.* linear measure.

länger ['lɛŋər], *comp.adj., adv.* longer (*see* **lang**); rather long; ***auf –e Zeit,*** for some (considerable) time; ***– machen,*** lengthen, extend, prolong; ***wenn er es noch – so macht,*** if he goes on in this way; ***– werden,*** grow longer, lengthen, draw out (*as the days*); ***je – je lieber,*** the longer the better.

lang|ersehnt, –erwünscht, *adj.* long-desired, long-wished for.

Länge|strich, *m. See* **–zeichen.**

Langette [laŋ'gɛtə], *f.* scallop, scalloping. **langettieren** [–'ti:rən], *v.t.* scallop.

Langeweile ['laŋəvaɪlə], *f.* tediousness, tedium, boredom, ennui; ***vor*** or ***aus (lauter) Lange(r)weile,*** from (sheer) boredom; ***– haben,*** be *or* feel bored; ***sich*** (*Dat.*) ***die – vertreiben,*** while away *or* (*coll.*) kill the time.

Längezeichen ['lɛŋətsaɪçən], *n.* (*Metr.*) macron.

Langezeit ['laŋətsaɪt], *f.* (*Swiss*) home-sickness.

Langfinger ['laŋfɪŋər], *m.* (*coll.*) thief, pickpocket, pilferer. **lang|fingerig,** *adj.* (*coll.*) long-fingered; light-fingered. **–fristig,** *adj.* long-sighted *or* -dated (*bills*), long-term, long-range (*weather forecast etc.*). **–gestreckt, –gezogen,** *adj.* elongated, extended, long-drawn-out. **–haarig,** *adj.* long-haired; shaggy. **Lang|haus,** *n.* main aisle (*of a church*). **–holz,** *n.* (*Naut.*) timbers, beams and planks. **lang|jährig,** *adj.* of long standing; ***–er Freund,*** old friend; ***–e Erfahrung,*** (many) years of experience, long experience. **–köpfig,** *adj.* dolichocephalic. **–lebig,** *adj.* long-lived, durable, (*Biol.*) macrobiotic. **Langlebigkeit,** *f.* longevity, durability; macrobiosis.

länglich ['lɛŋlɪç], *adj.* elongated; longish; oblong. **länglichrund,** *adj.* elliptical, oval, ovate.

Lang|loch, *n.* slot. **–mut,** *f.* forbearance, patience, long-suffering. **langmütig,** *adj.* long-suffering, forbearing, indulgent, patient. **Lang|mütigkeit,** *f. See* **–mut. –ohr,** *m.* **(-(e)s,** *pl.* **-e)** *or n.* **(-(e)s,** *pl.* **-en)** long-eared p. *or* beast; ass; (*Prov.*) ***ein Esel nennt den anderen –,*** the pot calls the kettle black.

längs [lɛŋs], *adv., prep.* (*Dat. or Gen.*) along, alongside (of); (*Naut.*) ***– der Küste fahren,*** hug the coast. **Längsachse,** *f.* longitudinal *or* longer axis.

langsam ['laŋza:m], *adj.* slow; tardy; ***– backen,*** bake in a slow oven; ***– kochen,*** simmer; ***nur – begreifen,*** be slow *or* dull of comprehension; (*coll.*) be slow on the uptake; ***– laufen,*** tick over (*of an engine*). **Langsamkeit,** *f.* slowness, tardiness; dullness. **Langsamtreten,** *n.* (*coll.*) go-slow (strike), working to rule.

lang|schädelig, *adj. See* **–köpfig. Langschäfter,** *m.pl.* topboots, Wellington boots. **langschaftig,** *adj.* longboled (*trees*). **Lang|schiff,** *n.* nave. **–schläfer,** *m.* late-riser; (*coll.*) slug-abed. **–schliff,** *m.* fibrous (wood) pulp. **–schwelle,** *f.* (*Railw.*) groundplate.

Längsfeuer ['lɛŋsfɔyər], *n.* (*Artil.*) enfilade fire.

lang|sichtig, *adj.* (*Comm.*) *see* **–fristig.**

Längslager ['lɛŋsla:gər], *n.* (*Tech.*) axial *or* thrust bearing.

Langspielplatte ['laŋʃpi:lplatə], *f.* long-playing record.

Längsrichtung ['lɛŋsrɪçtuŋ], *f.* longitudinal direction, (*coll.*) along the length. **längsschiffs,** *adv.* (*Naut.*) fore and aft. **Längsschnitt,** *m.* longitudinal section, (*Archit.*) sectional elevation. **längsseit(s),** *adv., prep.* (*Gen.*) (*Naut.*) alongside (of).

längst [lɛŋst], *adv.* long ago, long since; (*fig.*) ***– nicht,*** not nearly, not by a long way, far from (being); ***ich hätte es – sagen sollen,*** I ought to have mentioned it before; ***ich weiß es schon –,*** I have known it for a long time. **längstens,** *adv.* at the furthest, at the most; at the latest; ***er kommt – in einer Woche zurück,*** he will return in a week at the latest.

langstielig ['laŋʃti:lɪç], *adj.* 1. long-stemmed, long-stalked; long-handled; 2. (*coll.*) tiresome, tedious, circumstantial. **Lang|streckenflug,** *m.* long-distance flight. **–streckenjäger,** *m.* (*Av.*) long-range fighter. **–streckenläufer, –streckler,** *m.* long-distance runner.

Languste [laŋ'gustə], *f.* lobster.

Langweile ['laŋvaɪlə], *f. See* **Langeweile. lang|weilen, 1.** *v.t.* tire, bore, weary. **2.** *v.r.* be *or* feel bored. **–weilig,** *adj.* boring, tedious, tiresome, wearisome, irksome; ***–e Person,*** bore. **Langwellen,** *f.pl.* (*Rad.*) long waves. **langwierig,** *adj.* lengthy, protracted, long-drawn-out, unending, tedious, wearisome; (*Med.*) lingering, chronic. **Lang|zeile,** *f.* (*Metr.*) ***stabreimende –,*** alliterative (long) line. **–zeitzünder,** *m.* delayed-action fuse. **–ziehen,** *n.* lengthening; (*Mus.*) allargando.

Lanthan [lan'ta:n], *n.* lanthanum.

Lanze ['lantsə], *f.* lance, spear; (*fig.*) ***eine – brechen für,*** stand up for, champion; ***Schwadron von 100 –n,*** squadron of 100 lancers. **Lanzen|brechen,** *n. See* **–stechen. lanzenförmig,** *adj.* (*Bot.*) lanceolate. **Lanzen|reiter,** *m.* lancer; uhlan. **–schuh,** *m.* bucket of a lance. **–stechen,** *n.* joust, tournament, tilting.

Lanzettbogen [lan'tsɛtbo:gən], *m.* Gothic arch. **Lanzette,** *f.* lance. **lanzettförmig** *adj.* (*Bot.*) lanceolate.

lapidar [lapi'da:r], *adj.* lapidary; concise, pithy.

Lappalie [la'pa:liə], *f.* trifle, bagatelle; bauble.

Lappen ['lapən], *m.* rag, cloth, duster; patch; (*Anat., Bot.*) lobe; (*Mech.*) flange; (*pl.*) ears (*of hounds*); (*pl.*) wattles (*of poultry*); (*coll.*) ***durch die – gehen,*** clear out, beat it, do a bunk, give (*Dat.*, a p.) the slip.

läppen ['lɛpən], *v.t.* (*Tech.*) lap.

Lappenhaut ['lapənhaut], *f.* web (*between toes*). **lappenlos,** *adj.* (*Bot.*) acotyledonous.

läppern ['lɛpərn], *v.t., v.i.* sip, lap; (*coll.*) ***sich (zusammen) –,*** mount *or* run up, accumulate.

lappig ['lapɪç], *adj.* flabby, flaccid; ragged, tattered; (*Bot. etc.*) lobed, lobate, lobular.

läppisch ['lɛpɪʃ], *adj.* silly, childish, foolish, trifling.

Lappland ['laplant], *n.* Lapland. **Lappländer,** *m.* Laplander, Lapp. **lappländisch,** *adj.* Lapp. **Lapplands|eule,** *f.* (*Orn.*) *see* **Bartkauz. –meise,** *f.* (*Orn.*) Siberian tit, (*Am.*) gray-headed chickadee (*Parus cinctus*).

Lärche ['lɛrçə], *f.* (*Bot.*) larch (*Larix europoea*).

Laren ['la:rən], *m.pl.* household gods, Lares.

Larifari [lari'fa:ri], *n.* prattle, nonsensical talk. **larifari!** *int.* stuff and nonsense! fiddlesticks!

Lärm [lɛrm], *m.* 1. noise, din, uproar, (*coll.*) racket, row; clamour, hubbub, hullaballoo, fuss; tumult, bustle; ***viel – um nichts,*** much ado about nothing; 2. (*obs.*) alarm; ***blinder –,*** false alarm; ***– blasen*** or ***schlagen,*** sound *or* raise the alarm; ***blinden – schlagen,*** cry wolf. **Lärmbekämpfung,** *f.* noise abatement campaign. **lärmen,** *v.i.* make a noise *or* racket, be noisy, (*coll.*) kick up a row; shout, yell; (*as children*) romp, (*as rowdies*) brawl. **lärmend,** *adj.* uproarious, tumultuous, noisy, unruly. **Lärmer, Lärmmacher,** *m.* noisy person; roisterer, rowdy. **Lärmzeichen,** *n.* alarm (signal).

Larve ['larfə], *f.* 1. mask, (*obs.*) face; ***ihm die – abziehen*** or ***abnehmen,*** unmask him; 2. (*Zool.*) larva, grub; 3. (*Poet.*) spectre, ghoul. **Larven|mantel,** *m.* domino. **–zustand,** *m.* chrysalis state.

las [la:s], *see* **lesen.**

lasch [laʃ], *adj.* (*coll.*) lax, limp, loose, flabby, languid; (*of food*) insipid.

Lasche ['laʃə], *f.* flap, lappet; (*Dressm.*) gusset;

tongue (*of a shoe*); (*Naut.*) lashing, (*Carp.*) groove; (*Tech.*) shackle, clip, strap-joint; (*Railw.*) fishplate. **laschen,** *v.t.* sew in a lappet; join (*wood*) in a groove, butt-joint. **Laschenkette,** *f.* sprocket chain.

Lase [ˈlaːzə], *f.* (*dial.*) pitcher, jug, can (*with spout*).

läse [ˈlɛːzə], *see* **lesen.**

lasieren [laˈziːrən], *v.t.* glaze (*paint, pottery etc.*).

[1]**laß** [las], *adj.* lax, slack; weary; spiritless; (*B.*) slothful.

[2]**laß,** *see* **lassen.**

lassen [ˈlasən], **1.** *irr.v.t.* leave (*in a certain state*); let go, part with, abandon, relinquish.
(a) (*with nouns*) ***Blut –,*** bleed, let blood; ***keinen guten Faden*** or ***kein gutes Haar an ihm –,*** not have a good word to say for him; ***Haar(e) –,*** pay dearly, be fleeced, (*gambling*) lose heavily; ***– Sie die Hand*** or ***Hände davon!*** hands off! don't meddle! ***ihm freie Hand –,*** give him a free hand; ***laß den Lärm!*** stop that noise! ***den Tränen freien Lauf –,*** give vent to *or* abandon o.s. to one's tears; ***sein Leben –,*** lay down *or* give *or* sacrifice one's life; ***Wasser –,*** make *or* pass water; ***ihm Zeit –,*** give *or* allow him (sufficient) time; ***sich*** (*Dat.*) ***Zeit –,*** take (one's) time.
(b) (*with preps.*) ***nicht aus den Augen –,*** not let out of one's sight; ***aus der Hand*** or ***den Händen –,*** drop, let go *or* slip; ***aus dem Hause –,*** let out, see to the door; ***aus dem Spiele –,*** leave out of the question; ***außer acht –,*** disregard, take no notice of; ***alles beim alten –,*** leave matters as they were; ***ihn bei seiner Meinung –,*** leave him to his opinion; ***wir wollen es dabei –,*** we will leave it at that; ***ich ließ ihn in die Stube,*** I let him into the room; ***ich ließ ihn in der Stube,*** I left him in the room; ***vom Stapel –,*** launch; ***Wein vom Fasse –,*** draw wine from a cask; ***zur Ader –,*** see ***Blut –***; ***zu sich –,*** admit to one's presence.
(c) (*other idioms*) ***laß das!*** stop it! don't! (*coll.*) lay off! cut it out! ***laß nur!*** never mind! ***laß (es) gut sein!*** leave it at that! ***laß mich (zufrieden)!*** leave *or* let me alone! don't bother me! ***es ihm –,*** let him have it; ***das muß man ihm –,*** you have to grant him that *or* give him credit for that; ***ich kann es nicht –,*** I can't help (doing) it, (*coll.*) I can't keep off it; ***tun was man nicht – kann,*** do what one cannot help (doing); ***mit sich reden –,*** listen to reason, be reasonable, not be obstinate; ***unerwähnt –,*** pass over in silence, not mention; ***das läßt alles weit hinter sich,*** that knocks everything into a cocked hat.
2. *irr. v. aux.* (*with inf. without zu*)
1. let (*do*), allow, permit, suffer (*to do*), not prevent from, tolerate (*doing*); ***bleiben –,*** leave alone; ***fahren –,*** let slip, let go; ***fallen –,*** drop; ***das laß ich mir gefallen,*** that will suit me, I agree with it *or* approve of it *or* consent to it, (*coll.*) it's all right by me; ***das laß ich mir nicht gefallen,*** I will not put up with that, I won't stand for it; ***gehen –,*** let go; ***gelten –,*** allow, admit as valid; ***geschehen –,*** allow to happen; ***gut sein –,*** let pass, approve of; ***– Sie von sich hören,*** let us hear from you; (*coll.*) ***laß ihm nur kommen!*** just let him show himself *or* his face! ***liegen –,*** leave behind, forget (*umbrella etc.*); ***sich*** (*Dat.*) ***nichts merken –,*** seem to know nothing, not show *or* betray one's feelings, look unconcerned, act as if nothing had happened; ***etwas sein –,*** refrain from doing s.th., not do s.th.; ***fünf gerade sein –,*** not be too particular; ***die Zügel schießen –,*** give (the horse) its head, (*fig.*) give full rein (*Dat.*, to); ***laß dir's gut schmecken,*** I hope you enjoy it (= *the food*), bon appetit! ***seine Worte – mich vermuten,*** his words give *or* lead me to suppose; ***Milde walten –,*** show clemency, be indulgent; ***ihn warten –,*** keep him waiting; ***ihn wissen –,*** inform him, let him know.
2. make (*do*), cause (*to do*), get, have (*done*); ***sich*** (*Dat.*) ***einfallen –,*** get it into one's head; ***fragen –,*** have inquiries made, set inquiries afoot; ***grüßen –,*** send greetings to; ***kommen –,*** send for; (***sich*** (*Dat.*)) ***machen –,*** have *or* get made; order to be done; ***sich einen Anzug machen –,*** have a suit made (to order); ***sich*** (*Dat.*) ***sagen –,*** be told; ***sich*** (*Dat.*) ***nichts sagen –,*** ignore all advice, be deaf to entreaty; ***laß dir das gesagt sein!*** mark my words! ***ihm sagen –,*** send word to him, send him word; (***sich*** (*Dat.*)) ***schicken –,*** have sent, order to be delivered; ***ins Reine schreiben –,*** have a fair copy made; (*fig.*) ***alle Minen springen –,*** do one's utmost *or* (*sl.*) damnedest; ***das hätte ich mir nicht träumen –,*** I should never have thought such a th. were possible; ***die Zeugen verhören –,*** cause *or* order the witnesses to be examined; ***die Truppen vorrücken –,*** order the troops to advance; ***sich*** (*Dat.*) ***einen Zahn ziehen –,*** have a tooth extracted;
3. (*refl.*) ***sich abschrecken –,*** be intimidated; ***sich nicht beschreiben –,*** defy description; ***das läßt sich nichts biegen,*** that cannot *or* must not be bent; ***sich bitten –,*** wait to be asked *or* pressed; ***das läßt sich denken,*** I can well imagine it, that is quite conceivable, I should think so; ***sich hören –,*** speak, sing, play *etc.* in company; ***das läßt sich (schon) hören,*** that sounds good *or* all right; ***es läßt sich nicht leugnen,*** there's no denying (the fact), it cannot be denied; ***das läßt sich (schon) machen,*** it can be arranged *or* managed (all right); ***darüber läßt sich weiter reden,*** that admits of further discussion; ***sich sehen –,*** show o.s., put in an appearance; ***der Wein läßt sich trinken,*** the wine is drinkable *or* (*coll.*) isn't at all bad; ***sich trösten –,*** be comforted; ***es läßt sich nicht übersetzen,*** it is untranslatable, it defies translation; ***es läßt sich nicht umgehen,*** it cannot be avoided, it is unavoidable; ***– Sie es sich nicht verdrießen,*** do not let yourself be dissuaded *or* (*coll.*) put off; ***sich keine Mühe verdrießen –,*** spare no effort, make every effort, go to great trouble, take great pains; ***es läßt sich vielfach verwenden,*** it can be used for various purposes.
3. *irr.v.i.* ***– von,*** renounce, abandon, relinquish; part with, give up, let go; desist *or* refrain *or* abstain from; ***von seiner Meinung –,*** change one's opinion.
4. *irr.v.i.* (*obs., dial.*) look, appear, become, suit; ***es läßt ihr nicht übel,*** it is rather becoming to her; ***du läßt jünger denn je,*** you look younger than ever.

Lassen, *n.* ***unser Tun und –,*** our commissions and omissions, what we have done and what we have left undone, our entire behaviour.

lässest [ˈlɛsəst], *see* **lassen.**

lässig [ˈlɛsɪç], *adj.* indolent, lazy, idle; remiss, slack, careless, negligent. **Lässigkeit,** *f.* laziness, indolence; remissness, slackness, carelessness, negligence.

läßlich [ˈlɛslɪç], *adj.* pardonable, venial; ***–e Sünden,*** venial sins, peccadilloes.

laßt [last], **läßt** [lɛst], *see* **lassen.**

Last [last], *f.* (-, *pl.* **-en**) load, burden, weight; load, cargo, freight, tonnage; charge, encumbrance, tax, impost; (*fig.*) onus, burden, weight, nuisance, trouble; (*obs.*) (approx.) 2 tons (*measure of shipping tonnage*); ***das Schiff ist bei seiner –,*** the ship is freighted; ***die – brechen,*** break bulk; ***zur – fallen,*** be a burden to *or* a charge on; ***der Gemeinde zur – fallen,*** be a charge on the parish; ***ihm etwas zur – legen,*** lay s.th. to his charge, charge *or* tax him with a th., blame a th. on him, (*coll.*) lay a th. at his door; ***zu seinen –en buchen*** or ***ihm zur – schreiben,*** charge to his account; ***zu –en von,*** to the debit of; ***nach Abzug der –en,*** deducting all charges; ***ein Schiff von 200 –,*** a ship of ***400*** tons burden.

Last|anhänger, *m.* (*Motor.*) (load-carrying) trailer. **–auto,** *n.* (motor-)lorry, (*Am.*) truck. **lastbar,** *adj.* (*Poet.*) load-bearing; ***–e Tiere,*** beasts of burden.

lasten [ˈlastən], *v.i.* ***auf*** (*Dat.*), weigh on, press heavily upon, oppress; encumber, burden; (*of responsibility*) rest on (*his*) shoulders.

Lasten|aufzug, *m.* goods lift, (*Am.*) freight elevator. **–ausgleich,** *m.* (*Pol.*) equalization of burdens. **lastenfrei,** *adj.* unencumbered.

[1]**Laster** [ˈlastər], *n.* vice; depravity; (*fig. of a p.*) bad lot; slut, trollop.

[2]**Laster,** *m.* (*coll.*) *see* **Lastkraftwagen.**

Lästerer [ˈlɛstərər], *m.* slanderer, calumniator; (*Eccl.*) blasphemer.

lasterhaft [ˈlastərhaft], *adj.* wicked, vicious, depraved, corrupt. **Lasterhaftigkeit,** *f.* wickedness, viciousness, depravity, corruptness. **Laster|höhle,** *f.* den of vice *or* iniquity. **–leben,** *n.* life of wickedness *or* depravity.

lästerlich ['lɛstərlıç], *adj.* slanderous, abusive, calumnious; (*Eccl.*) blasphemous; (*fig.*) abominable, disgraceful, shameful, scandalous. **Lästermaul,** *n.* (*coll.*) slanderer, scandalmonger, backbiter.

lästern ['lɛstərn], *v.t., v.i.* slander, calumniate, defame, revile, abuse, (*coll.*) run down; (*Eccl.*) blaspheme. **Lästerung,** *f.* slander, calumny; (*Eccl.*) blasphemy. **Läster|zunge,** *f.* slanderous tongue; *see also* **–maul.**

Last|esel, *m.* sumpter-mule, (*fig.*) drudge. **–fahrzeug,** *n.* heavy goods vehicle. **–flugzeug,** *n.* (*Av.*) freight carrier. **–fuhre,** *f.* See **–fahrzeug. –geld,** *n.* tonnage.

–lastig ['lastıç], *adj.suff.* freighted, weighted; (*Naut.*) of 2 tons burden; *e.g.* ***gleich–,*** on an even keel; ***zwei–,*** of 4 tons burden; (*Av.*) ***schwanz–,*** tail-heavy.

lästig ['lɛstıç], *adj.* burdensome, onerous, cumbersome; troublesome, irksome, tiresome, (*coll.*) bothersome; tedious, inconvenient, uncomfortable; ***–er Ausländer,*** undesirable alien; ***–e Person,*** nuisance, bore, (*sl.*) pain in the neck; ***ihm – fallen*** or ***werden,*** be a nuisance *or* trouble *or* burden to him, (*sl.*) be a pain in the neck to him; bore *or* bother *or* molest him.

Lastigkeit ['lastıçkaıt], *f.* (*Naut.*) tonnage, burden; trim (*of a ship in the water*); (*Av.*) trimming.

Lästigkeit ['lɛstıçkaıt], *f.* troublesomeness, irksomeness, inconvenience, bother, annoyance.

Last|kahn, *m.* barge, lighter. **–kraftwagen,** *m.* (motor-)lorry, (*Am.*) truck. **–pferd,** *n.* pack-horse. **–sand,** *m.* ballast (sand). **–schiff,** *n.* freighter, cargo-boat. **–schrift,** *f.* (*Comm.*) debit-note; debit-entry. **–tier,** *n.* pack-animal, beast of burden; (*fig.*) ***wie ein – arbeiten,*** slave, drudge, work like a slave. **–wagen,** *m.* wagon, van; *see also* **–kraftwagen. –wagenfahrer,** *m.* lorry *or* (*Am.*) truck driver. **–zug,** *m.* tractor-trailer unit, (*Am.*) trailer truck; lorry with trailer, (*Am.*) motor freight car train.

[1]**Lasur** [la'zu:r], *f.* (–, *pl.* **-en**) glaze, glazing.

[2]**Lasur,** *m.* (**-s,** *pl.* **-e**) *see* **Lasurstein. lasur|blau, –farben,** *adj.* ultramarine; azure, sky-blue. **Lasur|lack,** *m.* transparent *or* glazing varnish. **–meise,** *f.* (*Orn.*) azure tit (*Parus cyarius*). **–stein,** *m.* lapis lazuli, azurite.

lasziv [las'tsi:f], *adj.* lascivious.

Latein [la'taın], *n.* Latin; (*coll.*) ***mit seinem – am Ende sein,*** be at his wit's end. **Lateinamerika,** *n.* Latin America. **Lateiner,** *m.* Latinist, Latin scholar. **lateinisch,** *adj.* Latin; ***–e Buchstaben,*** Roman letters *or* characters; ***–es Segel,*** lateen sail; ***–e Volkssprache,*** Vulgar Latin. **Lateinschule,** *f.* (classical) grammar school.

latent [la'tɛnt], *adj.* latent; dormant, potential; ***–e Kraft,*** latent force, (*fig.*) potentiality. **Latenz,** *f.* latency. **Latenz|stadium,** *n.,* **–zeit,** *f.* (*Med.*) incubation period.

Laterne [la'tɛrnə], *f.* lantern, lamp; street-lamp. **Laternen|halter,** *m.* (*cycle*) lamp-bracket. **–pfahl,** *m.* lamp-post; (*coll.*) ***Wink mit dem –,*** broad hint.

Latinum [la'ti:num], *n.* qualification in Latin; ***großes –,*** Higher Latin; ***kleines –,*** Lower *or* Intermediate Latin.

Latsch [la:tʃ], *m.* (**-es,** *pl.* **-e**) 1. (*coll.*) slovenly fellow; slut; 2. (*dial.*) weak coffee.

[1]**Latsche** ['la:tʃə], *f.* dwarf-pine.

[2]**Latsche,** *f.,* **Latschen,** *m.* (*usu. pl.*) (old) slipper, down-at-heel shoe; feathered foot (*of fowl*). **latschen,** *v.i.* (*coll.*) shuffle *or* slouch along, drag one's feet. **latschig,** *adj.* shuffling, slouching; slovenly, slipshod.

Latte ['latə], *f.* lath, slat, batten, strip-board; (*Footb.*) (cross)bar, (*high jump*) bar; (*Av. sl.*) prop; ***die – reißen*** (***überqueren***), dislodge (clear) the bar; (*coll.*) ***lange –,*** lanky p. **Latten|holz,** *n.* lath-wood. **–kiste,** *f.* crate. **–punkt,** *m.* (*Surv.*) bench-mark. **–rost, –steg,** *m.* duck-boards. **–verschlag,** *m.* latticed partition. **–werk,** *n.* trellis. **–zaun,** *m.* paling(s), railings, fence.

Lattich ['latıç], *m.* (**-s,** *pl.* **-e**) (*Bot.*) genus *Lactuca*; lettuce (*Lactuca sativa*).

Latwerge [lat'vɛrgə], *f.* electuary.

Latz [lats], *m.* (**-es,** *pl.* **-e** (*Austr.* **¨-e**)) bib; pinafore; flap, (*of trousers*) fly.

lau [lau], *adj.* lukewarm, tepid; (*of weather*) mild; (*fig.*) lukewarm, half-hearted, indifferent.

Laub [laup], *n.* (**-(e)s,** *pl.* **-e**) foliage, leaves; (*Art*) leafage. **Laub|baum,** *m.* deciduous tree. **–dach,** *n.* canopy of leaves, leafy canopy. **–decke,** *f.* carpet of leaves.

Laube ['laubə], *f.* summer-house, arbour, bower; arcade, covered way, pergola; portico, porch; loggia, (*Theat.*) arcade box; (*coll.*) ***fertig ist die –!*** there you have it! what did I tell you!

Lauben|gang, *m.* arcade, covered way, pergola. **–garten,** *m.* allotment (garden). **–kolonie,** *f.* allotments, allotment gardens.

Laub|entfaltung, *f.* foliation. **–erde,** *f.* leaf- *or* vegetable-mould. **–fall,** *m.* fall of the leaf, defoliation. **–frosch,** *m.* tree-frog. **–gehänge, –gewinde,** *n.* festoon, garland. **laubgrün,** *adj.* leaf-green. **Laub|grün,** *n.* chlorophyll. **–holz,** *n.* deciduous trees. **–hütte,** *f.* bower, (*B.*) tabernacle. **–hüttenfest,** *n.* (*Eccl.*) Feast of the Tabernacles. **laubig,** *adj.* leaved, leafy, foliate, foliaceous. **Laubkäfer,** *m.* (*Swiss*) cockchafer. **laublos,** *adj.* leafless. **laubreich,** *adj.* leafy. **Laub|säge,** *f.* fretsaw. **–sägearbeit,** *f.* fretwork. **–sänger,** *m.* (*Orn.*) ***dunkler –,*** dusky warbler (*Phylloscopus fuscatus*); ***grüner –,*** greenish warbler (*Ph. trochiloides*); ***nordischer –,*** Arctic warbler (*Ph. borealis*). **–vogel,** *m.* (*Orn.*) ***gelbbrauiger –,*** *see* **Gelbbrauenlaubsänger. –wald,** *m.* deciduous forest. **–werk,** *n.* (*Art*) foliage, leaves, trees; (*Archit.*) crocket.

Lauch [laux], *m.* (**-(e)s,** *pl.* **-e**) (*Bot.*) leek (*Allium porrum*).

Laue ['lauə], *f.* (–, *pl.* **-nen**), **Lauene,** *f.* (*Swiss*) avalanche, landslide.

[1]**Lauer** ['lauər], *m.* wine from the second pressing, sour wine.

[2]**Lauer,** *f.* ***auf der – sein*** or ***liegen,*** lie in wait *or* ambush, be on the watch *or* lookout, lurk. **lauern,** *v.i.* watch (out), be on the lookout; lie in ambush, lie in wait (***auf*** (*Acc.*), for). **lauernd,** *adj.* lurking, watchful, wary

Lauf [lauf], *m.* (**-(e)s,** *pl.* **¨-e**) 1. running, run, (*Spt.*) race; current, circulation, flow (*of liquid*); track, path, orbit (*of solid body*); progress, movement, motion, travel, action; ***freien – lassen*** (*Dat.*), give full scope to, give vent *or* free play to, let (*s.th.*) take its course, (*coll.*) let (*s.th.*) slide; ***– der Begebenheiten,*** course of events; ***das ist der – der Welt,*** that is the way of the world, such is life; ***im – der Zeit,*** in the course of time; ***ruhiger – des Motors,*** smooth *or* silent running of the engine; (*Spt.*) ***einen einzelnen – machen,*** run a heat; ***am Ende seines –es,*** at the close of his career; ***in vollem –e,*** at top *or* full speed, in full career; 2. barrel (*of a rifle*); ***ein Gewehr mit zwei Läufen,*** a double-barrelled gun; 3. course, bed (*of a river*); 4. (*Mus.*) run, arpeggio; 5. (*dial.*) rutting season; 6. (*Hunt.*) leg, foot (*of furred game*).

Lauf|achse, *f.* free (running) axle, (*Railw.*) carrying axle. **–bahn,** *f.* racecourse; course, (*Astr.*) orbit, (*Spt.*) lane, (*Av.*) runway; track, wake (*of torpedo*); (*fig.*) career. **–band,** *n.* tread (*of a tyre*). **–bohne,** *f.* scarlet runner. **–brett,** *n.* running-board; (*Typ.*) carriage (*of a press*). **–bretter,** *n.pl.* duck-boards. **–brief,** *m.* circular. **–brücke,** *f.* foot-bridge, (*Naut.*) gangway. **–bursche,** *m.* errand-boy, messenger-boy; printer's devil.

laufen ['laufən], **1.** *irr.v.i.* (*aux.* h. & s.) 1. run; (*dial*) walk, go on foot; (*of machines*) go, work, function; (*of moving parts*) travel, move; (*of liquids*) run, flow, ooze, leak, run out, run down, gutter; (*in space*) extend, cover, stretch; (*in time*) go by, pass, elapse; circulate, be in circulation; (*fig.*) ***ihm in die Arme –,*** bump into him, run into *or* across him; ***zu Ende –,*** run out, come to an end, expire; ***das läuft ins Geld,*** that runs away with money; ***es läuft ein Gerücht, daß,*** it is rumoured that; ***auf Grund –,*** run aground; ***sehen wie der Hase läuft,*** see how the cat jumps; ***gelaufen kommen,*** come running; ***– lassen,*** let go, set free; let (*s.th.*) slide; ***ein Pferd – lassen,*** give a horse its head; ***es läuft mir eiskalt über den Rücken,*** a cold shiver runs down my back, it makes my flesh creep; ***hinter die Schule –,*** play truant; ***vom*** or ***von Stapel –,*** be launched; ***das läuft wider die gesunde Vernunft,*** that flies in the face of reason; ***der Wechsel läuft noch,*** the bill has still some time to run; ***um die Wette –,*** race; 2. rut; 3. rise (*of dough*); ***der Teig läuft,*** the dough is rising. **2.** *irr.v.t.* ***die Sonne läuft ihre Bahn,*** the sun moves in its orbit; ***Gänge*** or ***Wege –,*** run errands; ***Gefahr –,*** run a risk; ***sich müde –,*** tire o.s. out by running about; ***es läuft sich hier schlecht,*** this is not a good place for running; ***Schlittschuh –,*** skate; ***Spießruten –,*** run the gauntlet; ***Sturm – auf*** (*Acc.*), assail, assault, storm; ***sich*** (*Dat.*) ***die Füße wund –,*** get sore-footed *or* footsore, get a blister.

laufend [ˈlaufənt], *adj.* current, running, continuous, steady, regular, day-to-day, routine, (*of numbers*) serial, consecutive; ***auf dem –en bleiben*** or ***sein,*** be conversant *or* well acquainted (with), keep abreast (of affairs), be up to date; ***–e Ausgaben,*** day-to-day expenses; ***das –e Band,*** conveyor belt, assembly line; (*Naut.*) ***das –e Gut,*** running tackle, halyards and sheets; ***das –e Jahr,*** the current year; ***vom 3. –en Monats,*** of the 3rd inst.; ***zum –en Preise,*** at the current rate of exchange, at the market price; ***–e Rechnung,*** current account; ***–e Wartung,*** routine maintenance; ***–e Wechsel,*** bills in circulation.

Läufer [ˈlɔyfər], *m.* 1. runner; 2. (*obs.*) footman, messenger; 3. (*Footb.*) half-back, (*Rugby Footb.*) three-quarter (back); 4. (*Chess*) bishop; 5. (*Bot.*) runner, tendril, shoot; 6. stair-carpet, runner, strip of carpet; table-runner, drugget; 7. (*Mus.*) run, glissando; 8. (*slide-rule*) cursor, slider; 9. (*crane*) over-head tackle; 10. (*scales*) sliding weight; 11. (*Elec.*) rotor, armature; 12. (*Build.*) stretcher, binder; 13. (*Zool.*) young pig, porker.

Lauferei [laufəˈraɪ], *f.* running about, running to and fro.

Läufer|reihe, *f.* (*Footb.*) half-back *or* (*Rugby Footb.*) three-quarter line. **–stange,** *f.* stair-rod. **–stoff,** *m.* (stair-)carpeting. **–wicklung,** *f.* (*Elec.*) armature winding. **–zug,** *m.* (*Chess*) bishop's move.

Lauf|feuer, *n.* heath *or* grass fire; (*Mil.*) running fire; train of gunpowder; ***sich wie ein – verbreiten,*** spread like wildfire. **–fläche,** *f.* (*Mech.*) bearing surface, journal, (*of tyre*) tread. **–gang,** *m.* gangway, catwalk, gallery; (*Railw.*) corridor. **–gewicht,** *n.* sliding weight; counterpoise. **–graben,** *m.* (*Mil.*) communication trench. **–grabenspiegel,** *m.* trench-periscope.

läufig [ˈlɔyfɪç], **läufisch,** *adj.* (*Zool.*) ruttish, in *or* on heat.

Lauf|junge, *m. See* **–bursche. –käfer,** *m.* ground-beetle (*Carabidae*). **–karren,** *m.* (*dial.*) wheelbarrow. **–katze,** *f.* crane-crab, overhead tackle. **–kette,** *f.* (caterpillar (*regd. trade name*)) track. **–kran,** *m.* travelling crane. **–kundschaft,** *f.* passing trade, casual customers. **–masche,** *f.* ladder, run (*in stockings*), dropped stitch. **–nummer,** *f.* serial number. **–paß,** *m.* ***ihm den – geben,*** give him his marching orders. **–planke,** *f.* gangway, gangplank. **–rad,** *n.* (*Railw.*) bogey, carrying wheel; rotor (*of turbine*), caster (*of furniture*), (*Av.*) landing wheel. **–riemen,** *m.* driving-belt. **–ring,** *m.* ball-race. **–rolle,** *f.* bogie; caster. **–schiene,** *f.* guide-rail. **–schritt,** *m.* (*Mil.*) double(-quick step), (*coll.*) jogtrot; ***im –,*** at the double. **–seele,** *f.* bore (*of gun*). **–sitz,** *m.* (*Tech.*) clearance, easy fit.

läufst [lɔyfst], *see* **laufen.**

Lauf|ställchen, *n.* playpen. **–steg,** *m.* footbridge, footpath, (*Naut.*) gangway.

läuft [lɔyft], *see* **laufen.**

Lauf|werk, *n.* mechanism, drive (assembly), movement (*of a clock*). **–zeit,** *f.* rutting season; (*Spt.*) time; (*Comm.*) currency, term; (*of film etc.*) run; time of operation, running time; serviceable life; transit *or* transmission time. **–zettel,** *m.* circular (letter), post-office circular (*to recover misdelivered letters*).

Lauge [ˈlaugə], *f.* caustic solution, lye, buck, leach; (*Chem.*) lixivium; (*coll.*) brine; (soap-)suds; (*fig.*) ***die – seines Spottes,*** his biting sarcasm, his caustic wit. **laugen,** *v.t.* soak *or* steep in lye, leach, lixiviate, buck. **laugenartig,** *adj.* lixivial, alkaline. **Laugen|asche,** *f.* alkaline ashes, potash. **–salz,** *n.* alkaline salt, alkali, soda. **–wasser,** *n.* lye, suds, liquor, caustic *or* alkaline solution.

Laune [ˈlaunə], *f.* 1. mood, humour, temper, frame of mind; ***gleiche –,*** even temper; ***bei*** (***guter***) ***–,*** in a good humour *or* mood, in good spirits; ***nicht bei –,*** out of temper, in a bad mood; ***nicht in der – für,*** not in the mood *or* humour for; ***er hat heute seine –,*** he is in one of his (bad) moods today; 2. whim, caprice; ***– des Glückes,*** freak of fortune. **launenhaft,** *adj.* moody, capricious, fickle, wayward, unaccountable, erratic, changeable. **Launenhaftigkeit,** *f.* moodiness, capriciousness, fickleness, waywardness, unaccountability.

launig [ˈlaunɪç], *adj.* whimsical, playful, skittish; humorous, witty, comical, funny, droll.

launisch [ˈlaunɪʃ], *adj.* ill-humoured, bad-tempered, peevish, (*coll.*) grumpy; *see also* **launenhaft.**

Laus [laus], *f.* (-, *pl.* ¨-**e**) louse; (*coll.*) ***ihm eine – in den Pelz setzen,*** give him trouble, cause him annoyance; (*coll.*) ***eine – läuft ihm über die Leber,*** s.th. is eating him. **Laus|bub(e),** *m.* little rogue *or* rascal, (*coll.*) young devil. **–büberei,** *f.* mischievousness.

Lausche [ˈlauʃə], *f.* (*obs.*) 1. lurking, eavesdropping, lying in wait; 2. hiding-place; cosy nook. **lauschen,** *v.i.* 1. listen (*Dat. or* ***auf*** (*Acc.*), to), take careful note (of); prick up *or* strain one's ears; hang on (*s.o.'s*) words; spy (on), eavesdrop; (*dial.*) lie in wait (for); 2. (*dial.*) doze, slumber. **Lauscher,** *m.* 1. listener, eavesdropper; 2. *pl.* (*Hunt.*) ears (*of the wolf, fox, deer etc.*). **Lauschgerät,** *n.* (*Mil.*) interceptor set.

lauschig [ˈlauʃɪç], *adj.* snug, cosy, secluded, peaceful, tranquil.

Lauschposten [ˈlauʃpɔstən], *m.* (*Mil.*) listening post.

Lausejunge [ˈlauzəjuŋə], *m.* blackguard, lout, hobbledehoy.

Läusekraut [ˈlɔyzəkraut], *n.* (*Bot.*) louse-wort, larkspur.

lausen [ˈlauzən], *v.t.* delouse; (*sl.*) fleece.

Läuse|pulver, *n.* insect-powder, insecticide. **–sucht,** *f.* Herodian *or* pedicular disease; lice disease (*of plants*).

lausig [ˈlauzɪç], *adj.* (*vulg.*) lousy, miserable; perishing, awful.

Lausitz [ˈlauzɪts], *f.* Lusatia. **Lausitzer,** *m.*, **lausitzisch,** *adj.* Lusatian.

[1]**laut** [laut], **1.** *adj.* (*comp.* ***-er,*** *sup.* ***-est***) loud, noisy; audible; sonorous; (*of a p.*) loud-voiced, (*sl.*) loud-mouthed. **2.** *adv.* (*Mus.*) forte; aloud, in a loud voice; ***– werden,*** (*fig.*) become public *or* known, get about *or* abroad, (*coll.*) leak out; (*Hunt.*) give tongue (*of hounds*); ***– werden lassen,*** divulge, betray, breathe a word of *or* about, (*sl.*) let on about; ***seine Gefühle – werden lassen,*** show *or* express one's feelings; ***ich sage es –,*** I say it openly.

[2]**laut,** *prep.* (*Gen., occ. Dat.*) according to, in accordance *or* conformity with; by virtue of, on the strength of, in consequence of, (*Law*) in persuance of, (*Comm.*) as per; ***– Befehl,*** as ordered, by order; ***– Rechnung,*** as per invoice; ***– Verfügung,*** as directed.

Laut, *m.* (**-(e)s,** *pl.* **-e**) sound, tone; ***keinen – von sich geben,*** not utter a sound; ***– geben,*** give tongue (*hounds*). **Lautangleichung,** *f.* (*Phonet.*) assimilation of sounds. **lautbar,** *adj.* – *werden,* be noised abroad, become known *or* public. **Laut|bezeichnung,** *f.* sound-notation. **–bildung,** *f.* articulation.

Laute ['lautə], *f.* lute.

lauten ['lautən], *v.i.* sound, run, read; *die Worte – so,* the words run thus *or* as follows; *das lautet seltsam,* that sounds strange; *wie lautet sein Name?* what is his name? *wie lautet das dritte Gebot?* what does the third commandment say? *die Antwort lautete günstig,* the answer was favourable; *das Urteil lautete auf ein Jahr Gefängnis,* the verdict was for one year's imprisonment; *auf den Inhaber –de Aktien,* shares made out *or* issued *or* payable to bearer.

läuten ['lɔytən], *v.t., v.i.* ring, peal, toll, sound; *zur Kirche –,* ring the bells for church; *der Fernsprecher läutet,* the telephone is ringing; *etwas – hören,* hear a rumour of s.th.; have an inkling of s.th., hear s.th. to that effect. **Läuten,** *n.* ringing, tolling.

Lautenspieler ['lautənʃpi:lər], *m.* lute-player, lutanist.

Lauter ['lautər], *m.* (*obs.*) (*Phonet.*) sound.

[1]**lauter,** *comp. adj. See* [1]**laut.**

[2]**lauter,** 1. *adj.* clear; pure, unmixed, unalloyed, undefiled; (*of gems*) flawless; (*fig.*) genuine, sincere, candid, honest; *–e Absichten,* disinterested motives; *–e Wahrheit,* plain *or* unvarnished truth. 2. *adv.* (*used as indecl. adj.*) only, nothing but, pure and simple, downright, mere, sheer, rank; *er trinkt – Wein,* he drinks nothing but wine; *es sind – Lügen,* it is nothing but *or* is all lies; *aus – Neid,* out of sheer envy; *er sieht den Wald vor – Bäumen nicht,* he cannot see the wood for the trees. **Lauterkeit,** *f.* purity, pureness, clearness; uprightness, integrity, sincerity, candour.

läutern ['lɔytərn], *v.t.* purify, refine, clear, clarify, strain, rectify (*spirits*); cleanse, purge; thin (*a wood*); (*fig.*) purify, chasten, ennoble. **Läuterung,** *f.* purification; refining, clarification, rectification; (*fig.*) cleansing, purging, chastening. **Läuterungs|mittel,** *n.* purifying agent. **–prozeß, –vorgang,** *m.* refining process.

Läute|werk, *n.* alarm-bell, electric bell. **–zeichen,** *n.* ring(ing).

Lautgesetz ['lautgəzɛts], *n.* phonetic law. **lautgetreu,** *adj.* phonetically correct, orthophonic, (*Rad. etc.*) high-fidelity. **Lautheit,** *f.* loudness, sonorousness.

lautieren [lau'ti:rən], *v.i.* read *or* spell phonetically. **Lautiermethode,** *f.* phonetic method, phonetic spelling.

Lautlehre ['lautle:rə], *f.* phonology; phonetics.

lautlich ['lautlıç], *adj.* phonetic. **lautlos,** *adj.* soundless, noiseless, silent, mute; *es herrschte –e Stille,* all was hushed. **Lautlosigkeit,** *f.* silence.

Laut|malerei, –nachahmung, –nachbildung, *f.* onomatopœia. **–schrift,** *f.* phonetic transcription *or* spelling. **–sprechanlage,** *f.* public address system. **–sprecher,** *m.* loudspeaker. **–stand,** *m.* phonetic structure (*of a language*). **–stärke,** *f.* intensity *or* volume of sound, signal-strength, (*Rad.*) volume. **–stärkeregler,** *m.* (*Rad.*) volume-control. **–verschiebung,** *f.* sound-shift, Grimm's law; *erste –,* Germanic sound-shift; *zweite –,* High-German sound-shift. **–verstärker,** *m.* (*Rad.*) audio-amplifier. **–wandel, –wechsel,** *m.* sound change, mutation. **–zeichen,** *n.* phonetic symbol.

lauwarm ['lauvarm], *adj. See* **lau.**

Lavendel [la'vɛndəl], *m.* lavender. **Lavendelöl,** *n.* spike-oil.

lavieren [la'vi:rən], *v.i.* (*Naut.*) tack; (*coll.*) wriggle *or* wangle (through).

Lawine [la'vi:nə], *f.* avalanche.

lax [laks], *adj.* lax, loose; *–e Moral,* easy morals; *–e Sitten,* loose living. **Laxheit,** *f.* laxity, looseness.

laxierend [la'ksi:rənt], *adj.* aperient, laxative. **Laxiermittel,** *n.* aperient, laxative, purge.

Lazarett [latsa'rɛt], *n.* (**-s,** *pl.* **-e**) military hospital, sick bay. **Lazarett|aufnahme, –behandlung,** *f.* hospital treatment, (*Am.*) hospitalization. **–fieber,** *n.* hospital fever. **–gehilfe,** *m.* hospital orderly. **–schiff,** *n.* hospital-ship. **–wagen,** *m.* ambulance. **–zug,** *m.* hospital-train.

Laz(z)arone [latsa'ro:nə], *m.* (**-(n)** *or* **-s,** *pl.* **-n**) beggar, pauper.

Lebe|dame ['le:bə–], *f.* society lady; demi-mondaine. **–hoch,** *n.* cheers; *dreimaliges –,* three cheers. **–mann,** *m.* man of the world, man about town, bon vivant, worldling, (*coll.*) playboy.

leben ['le:bən], 1. *v.i.* live, be alive, exist, pass one's life; dwell, live, reside, (*esp. Scots*) stay; *er lebt auf großem Fuße,* he lives in (a) grand style; *für sich –,* live alone; (*B.*) *der Gerechte wird seines Glaubens –,* the just shall live by faith; *so wahr Gott lebt,* as sure as there is a God; *er ist sein Vater, wie er leibt und lebt,* he is the living *or* very image of his father; *er hat zu –,* he is provided for, he has enough to live on; *– und – lassen,* live and let live; *er lebt in dem Glauben,* he firmly believes, he is convinced; *sein Andenken lebt im Herzen des Volkes,* his memory lives on in the people's hearts; *in den Tag hinein –,* live for the moment; *es lebe der König! der König soll –! der König lebe hoch!* long live the King! *so etwas lebt nicht!* things like that don't happen, (*sl.*) you're telling me! *– von,* feed *or* live *or* subsist on; make *or* earn one's living by, support o.s. *or* live by; *von der Hand in den Mund –,* live from hand to mouth; *so wahr ich lebe,* as sure as I am alive; *er weiß zu –,* he is a man of the world, (*coll.*) he knows his way around; *wie Hund und Katze –,* lead a cat-and-dog life; *leb(e) wohl! – Sie wohl!* farewell! 2. *v.r. sich satt –* or *sich satt gelebt haben,* be weary of life; *hier lebt sich's gut,* it is pleasant living here.

Leben, *n.* 1. life, existence, being; living being *or* creature; *am – bleiben,* survive, stay alive; *am – erhalten,* keep alive; *am – sein,* be alive; *auf – und Tod,* a matter of life and death; *Kampf auf – und Tod,* mortal combat; *aus dem – gegriffen,* taken from real life; (*coll.*) *ein neues – beginnen,* turn over a new leaf; *bei meinem –,* as I live; *bei Leib und –,* upon pain of death; *für sein – gern tun,* be passionately fond of *or* (*coll.*) crazy about; *ich darf es für mein – nicht tun,* I dare not do it for the life of me; *im öffentlichen – stehen,* be a public figure; *in diesem und in jenem –,* in his life and the life hereafter *or* to come; *ins – rufen,* call into being *or* existence, originate, start, establish, launch, (*Comm.*) set on foot, float; *ins – treten,* be started *or* established, be set up; *sein – lassen,* lay down one's life, die; *nach dem –,* from life; *ihm nach dem – trachten,* be after his blood; *sich* (*Dat.*) *das – nehmen,* commit suicide, kill o.s.; *ihm das – schenken,* give birth to him (*a child*); spare his life; *ums – bringen,* kill, do away with; *ums – kommen,* lose one's life, be killed, die, perish; *zeit meines –s,* all my life long; 2. vitality, vigour; animation, activity, vivacity, liveliness, stir; (*coll.*) *– in die Bude bringen,* make things lively *or* interesting, (*coll.*) make things hum, stir things up a bit; 3. living flesh, the quick; *bis aufs –,* to the quick; 4. biography.

lebend ['le:bənt], *adj.* living, live; (*pred.*) alive; *–er Bestand,* (inventory of) livestock; *–e Bilder,* tableaux vivants; *–e Hecke,* quickset hedge; *–e Sprache,* living *or* modern language; *kein –es Wesen,* not a living soul. **Lebende(r),** *m., f.* living person; (*B.*) *die Lebenden und die Toten,* the quick and the dead; *unter den noch Lebenden,* among the survivors. **lebendgebärend,** *adj.* viviparous. **Lebendgewicht,** *n.* live weight (*of cattle*).

lebendig [le'bɛndıç], *adj.* living, live, (*pred.*) alive; full of life, active, lively, vivacious; *–e Anteilnahme,* warm *or* lively interest; *fünf –e Kinder,* five children living; *–e Kraft,* kinetic energy; *–en Leibes* or *bei –em Leibe,* (while still) alive; (*B.*) *der –e Odem,* the breath of life; *es wird schon – auf der Straße,* the street is already astir; *mehr tot als –,* more dead than alive; *–e Unterhaltung,* animated *or* lively conversation; (*Naut.*) *das –e Werk,* below the waterline. **Lebendigkeit,** *f. See* **Lebhaftig-**

keit. lebendigmachend, *adj.* vivifying, enlivening; *-e Gnade,* quickening grace.

Lebens|abend, *m.* decline of life, old age. **-abriß,** *m.* biographical sketch. **-ader,** *f.* (*fig.*) life-line. **-alter,** *n.* age, period of life. **-anschauung,** *f.* outlook on life. **-art,** *f.* manner *or* mode of living; manners, good breeding; ***ohne* -,** ill-bred. **-auffassung,** *f.* view *or* philosophy of life. **-aufgabe,** *f.* life-work. **-bahn,** *f.* course, career. **-baum,** *m.* tree of life, (*Bot.*) arbor vitae. **-bedingung,** *f.* condition essential for life; (*fig.*) condition of vital importance, *pl.* living conditions. **-bedürfnisse,** *n.pl.* necessaries of life. **lebensbejahend,** *adj.* optimistic, virile. **Lebens|beschreibung,** *f.* biography, life(-story). **-bild,** *n.* short biography, biographical sketch. **-dauer,** *f.* duration of life, durability, lifetime, life-span; ***auf* -,** for life. **-ende,** *n.* end of life; ***bis an mein* -,** to the end of my days. **-erfahrung,** *f.* experience of life. **-erhaltungstrieb,** *m.* instinct of self-preservation. **-erwartung,** *f.* expectation of life. **lebensfähig,** *adj.* viable. **Lebens|fähigkeit,** *f.* viability, vitality. **-frage,** *f.* vital question. **lebensfremd,** *adj.* ill-equipped for life; unsociable, retiring, solitary. **Lebensfreude,** *f.* zest for life, joy of living. **lebens|freudig,** *adj. See* **-froh. Lebensfrist,** *f.* lease of life. **lebensfroh,** *adj.* light-hearted, vivacious. **Lebens|führung,** *f.* style of living, (conduct of) life. **-funktion,** *f.* vital function. **-gefahr,** *f.* danger to life, danger of death, mortal danger; ***mit*** or ***unter* -,** at the risk *or* peril of one's life. **lebensgefährlich,** *adj.* perilous, highly dangerous, (*Law*) involving danger to life and limb; (*Med.*) dangerous, very serious *or* grave. **Lebens|gefährte,** *m.*, **-gefährtin,** *f.* life's companion, partner for life. **-geister,** *m.pl.* animal spirits; ***die* - *wecken*** (*Gen.*), put life into. **-gewohnheiten,** *f.pl.* lifelong habits. **lebensgroß,** *adj.* life-sized, (*fig.*) (as) large as life. **Lebensgröße,** *f.* life-size, real *or* actual size.

Lebens|haltung, *f.* standard of living *or* life. **-haltungskosten,** *pl.* cost of living, living expenses. **-holz,** *n.* lignum vitae. **-hunger,** *m.* zest for life. **-interesse,** *n.* vital interest (*usu. pl.*). **-jahr,** *n.* year (of one's life); ***im 20.* -,** at the age of 20. **lebensklug,** *adj.* worldly-wise. **Lebens|klugheit,** *f.* worldly wisdom. **-kraft,** *f.* vigour, vital energy; vitality. **-kunde,** *f.* biology. **-lage,** *f.* situation, position; ***in jeder* -,** in every emergency, in all situations. **lebens|lang,** *adv.* ***auf* -,** for life. **-länglich,** *adj.* lifelong, for life, perpetual; ***-e Freiheitsstrafe,*** life imprisonment; ***-es Gnadengehalt,*** life pension, pension for life; ***-es Mitglied,*** life-member; ***-e Rente,*** life annuity. **Lebens|lauf,** *m.* curriculum vitae, personal record; career. **-linie,** *f.* (*Palmistry*) line of life. **-lust,** *f.* vivacity, exhilaration, high spirits, love of life, zest. **lebens|lustig,** *adj. See* **-freudig. Lebensmark,** *n.* (*fig.*) vitals.

Lebensmittel ['le:bənsmɪtəl], *n.pl.* food; provisions, foodstuffs, victuals. **Lebensmittel|geschäft,** *n.* provision merchants', food shop. **-karte,** *f.* ration-card. **-knappheit,** *f.* food shortage. **-lieferant,** *m.* caterer. **-versorgung,** *f.* food supply.

lebensmüde ['le:bənsmy:də], *adj.* tired of life, dispirited, dejected, disconsolate, despondent, depressed. **Lebens|mut,** *m.* courage to face life, optimism. **-nerv,** *m.* (*fig.*) mainspring. **-notdurft** *f.* (bare) necessaries of life. **lebensnotwendig,** *adj.* essential, vital. **Lebens|notwendigkeit,** *f.* vital necessity. **-ordnung,** *f.* diet, regimen. **-prozeß,** *m.* vital functions. **-raum,** *m.* environment, milieu; living space. **-regel,** *f.* rule of conduct, maxim, precept. **-rente,** *f.* life-annuity. **-retter,** *m.* life-saver; oxygen apparatus. **-rettungsgerät,** *n.* life-saving equipment. **-rettungsmedaille,** *f.* life-saving medal. **lebenssprühend,** *adj.* exuberant. **Lebens|standard,** *m.* standard of living, living standard. **-stellung,** *f.* life appointment, permanent position, (*coll.*) life-time job; social status, position in life. **-stil,** *m. See* **-art. -trieb,** *m.* vitality, vital urge. **lebensüberdrüssig,** *adj.* sick *or* tired of life. **Lebens|unterhalt,** *m.* livelihood, living, subsistence. **-versicherung,** *f.* life-insurance *or* assurance. **-versicherungspolice,** *f.* life-policy. **lebens|voll,** *adj.* full of life, vigorous, active, spirited, lively, vivacious. **-wahr,** *adj.* true to life, life-like. **Lebens|wandel,** *m.* mode of life, moral attitudes, conduct. **-weg,** *m.* path through life. **-weise,** *f.* mode of life, way of living, habits. **-weisheit,** *f. See* **-klugheit. -werk,** *n.* life-work. **lebens|wichtig,** *adj. See* **-notwendig. Lebens|wille,** *m.* will to live. **-zeichen,** *n.* sign of life. **-zeit,** *f.* age; lifetime; ***auf* -,** for life; ***bei* -,** during life, in life. **-ziel,** *n.*, **-zweck,** *m.* aim in life.

Leber ['le:bər], *f.* (-, *pl.* **-n**) liver; ***frei von der - weg sprechen,*** speak one's mind (frankly), speak out bluntly. **Leber|anschwellung,** *f.* enlargement of the liver. **-blümchen,** *n.* (*Bot.*) three-leaved *or* noble agrimony (*Anemone hepatica*). **-entzündung,** *f.* (*Med.*) hepatitis. **-fleck(en),** *m.* mole, birth mark. **-gang,** *m.* hepatic duct. **-krank,** *adj.* suffering from a liver complaint. **-moose,** *n.pl.* (*Bot.*) liverworts (*Hepaticae*). **-tran,** *m.* cod-liver oil. **-wurst,** *f.* liver-sausage.

Lebe|wesen, *n.* living creature, living *or* animate being, organism; ***kleinstes* -,** micro-organism. **-wohl,** *n.* farewell.

lebhaft ['le:phaft], **1.** *adj.* lively, full of life, vivacious; active, brisk, animated, spirited, sprightly; (*as colour*) gay, bright, vivid; ***-es Interesse,*** keen *or* lively interest; ***-e Erinnerung,*** vivid memory; ***-e Nachfrage,*** brisk demand; ***-e Straße,*** much frequented *or* busy street; ***-er Streit,*** heated discussion, violent quarrel. **2.** *adv.* **- *vor Augen haben,*** have a clear picture of; **- *bedauern,*** sincerely regret; **- *begrüßen,*** warmly welcome; **- *empfinden,*** be alive to; ***sich*** (*Dat.*) **- *vorstellen,*** easily imagine. **Lebhaftigkeit,** *f.* liveliness, animation, vivacity, sprightliness, briskness, activity.

Lebkuchen ['le:pku:xən], *m.* gingerbread.

leblos ['le:plo:s], *adj.* lifeless, inanimate; (*fig.*) lifeless, spiritless, heavy, dull, flat; (*Comm.*) inactive, dull. **Leblosigkeit,** *f.* lifelessness, stagnation, dullness.

Leb|tag, *m.* ***mein(e)* -(*e*),** all my life, in all my born days. **-zeiten,** *f.pl.* ***bei*** or ***zu meinen* -,** in my lifetime.

lechzen ['lɛçtsən], *v.i.* 1. be parched with thirst; 2. languish, long, yearn (***nach,*** for); ***nach Blut* -,** thirst for blood.

leck [lɛk], *adj.* leaky, leaking; **- *werden,*** spring a leak. **Leck,** *n. or m.* (**-(e)s,** *pl.* **-e**) leak; leakage; ***ein(en)* - *bekommen,*** spring a leak.

Leckarsch ['lɛkˀarʃ], *m.* (*vulg.*) lickspittle, toady, (*vulg.*) arse-crawler.

[1]**lecken** ['lɛkən], *v.i.* (*obs.*) (*B.*) ***wider den Stachel* -,** kick against the pricks.

[2]**lecken,** *v.i.* let in water, leak; (*aux.* s.) leak, run *or* drip *or* trickle out; gutter (*as a candle*).

[3]**lecken,** *v.t., v.i.* lick; ***an den Fingern* -, *sich*** (*Dat.*) ***die Finger* -,** lick one's fingers; ***sich*** (*Dat.*) ***die Finger nach etwas* -,** hanker after a th.; ***wie geleckt,*** very neat *or* spruce.

lecker ['lɛkər], *adj.* nice, tasty, delicious, appetizing, savoury; dainty, fastidious.

Lecker, *m.* 1. gourmet, sweet-tooth; 2. toady, fawner, lickspittle; 3. (*Hunt.*) tongue (*of furred game*). **Leckerbissen,** *m.*, **Leckerei** [-'raɪ], *f.* titbit, dainty, delicacy, choice morsel. **leckerhaft,** *adj.* lickerisch, fastidious, dainty. **Leckerli,** *n.pl.* (*Swiss*) gingerbread. **Lecker|maul, -mäulchen,** *n.* sweet-tooth.

leckern ['lɛkərn], *v.i.* be fastidious; **- *nach,*** hanker after, long *or* crave for.

Leder ['le:dər], *n.* leather; skin; (*coll.*) leather apron, leather seat of trousers; football; ***weiche* -,** kid; ***in* - *gebunden,*** in leather binding; ***vom* - *ziehen,*** (*Hist.*) draw one's sword, (*coll.*) let (*him*) have it straight from the shoulder, not pull one's punches; (*coll.*) ***ihm das* - *gerben,*** give him a good tanning. **Leder|band, 1.** *m.* leather binding. **2.** *n.* leather strap *or* thong. **-bereitung,** *f.*

leather dressing. **–dichtung,** *f. See* **–ring. Lederer,** *m.* (*dial.*) tanner. **lederfarbig,** *adj.* buff(-coloured). **Leder|fett,** *n.* dubbin(g). **–gamaschen,** *f.pl.* leggings. **–haut,** *f.* (*Anat.*) cutis vera, corium, derma. **–hose,** *f.* leather breeches *or* shorts.

ledern ['le:dərn], *adj.* 1. leather, leathern; leathery, tough; coriaceous; 2. (*coll.*) dull, tedious, pedestrian.

Leder|riemen, *m.* leather strap *or* belt; strop (*for shaving*). **–ring,** *m.* leather washer. **–rücken,** *m.* leather back (*of book or chair*). **–scheibe,** *f. See* **–ring. –schmiere,** *f. See* **–fett. –waren,** *f.pl.* leather goods. **–zeug,** *m.* (*Mil.*) leather equipment. **–zucker,** *m.* ***weißer –,*** marshmallow; ***schwarzer (brauner) –,*** liquorice. **–zurichtung,** *f. See* **–bereitung.**

ledig ['le:dıç], *adj.* 1. unmarried, single, (*obs.*) illegitimate (*child*); ***– bleiben,*** remain single, (*coll.*) be left on the shelf (*of girls*); ***ich bleibe –,*** I shall not marry; ***–es Frauenzimmer,*** spinster; ***–er Mann,*** bachelor; ***–e Mutter,*** unmarried mother; ***–er Stand,*** celibacy; (*coll.*) single blessedness; 2. devoid, rid (*Gen.*, of), free, exempt (from); ***aller Pflichten los und –,*** exempt from all duties; ***los und – sprechen,*** absolve, acquit; 3. (*dial.*) empty, unoccupied, vacant. **Ledigensteuer,** *f.* bachelor's tax. **lediglich,** *adv.* exclusively, solely, merely, purely, simply. **Ledigsprechung,** *f.* 1. acquittal; 2. granting the freedom of a company.

Lee [le:], *f.* (*Naut.*) lee, lee-side; ***das Ruder in –!*** ease the helm! ***in – fallen,*** drive to leeward. **leegierig,** *adj.* (*Naut.*) carrying lee helm.

leer [le:r], *adj.* empty, vacant, void, evacuated, unoccupied; inane; ***–es Blatt,*** blank *or* clean sheet of paper; ***–e Drohung,*** empty *or* vain *or* hollow threat; ***mit –en Händen,*** empty-handed; ***– ausgehen,*** leave empty-handed; ***–er Raum,*** void *or* empty space; blank space; vacuum; ***–es Stroh,*** threshed straw; (*fig.*) ***–es Stroh dreschen, –e Worte machen,*** beat the air, pour water into a sieve; ***–es Gerücht,*** idle talk, unfounded rumour. **Leerdarm,** *m.* (*Anat.*) jejunum.

Leere ['le:rə], *f.* void, emptiness, vacancy, vacuity, blank(ness), nothingness; vacuum. **leeren** *v.t.* empty, evacuate, clear, clear out, drain; ***der Saal leerte sich in fünf Minuten,*** the room was cleared in five minutes.

Leer|gang, *m.* (*Mech.*) lost motion, backlash, (*Motor.*) neutral gear; *see also* **–lauf. –gewicht,** *n.* dead weight, weight empty, tare. **–gut,** *n.* empties. **Leerheit,** *f.* emptiness, futility; (*Med.*) inanition. **Leer|lauf,** *m.* (*Tech.*) idle motion, idling, ticking-over, (*Motor.*) neutral gear, (*Elec.*) no-load working. **–laufen,** *irr.v.i.* empty, drain dry (*tank etc.*), (*Tech.*) idle, be idling, (*Naut.*) sail in ballast. **Leerpackung,** *f.* dummy package. **leerstehend,** *adj.* unoccupied, empty, vacant (*dwelling*). **Leer|takt,** *m.* (*Tech.*) idle stroke. **–taste** *f.* dead key. **Leerung,** *f.* emptying, clearing, clearance, evacuation. **Leerverkauf,** *m.* (*Comm.*) short sale.

Leesegel ['le:ze:gəl], *n.* (*Naut.*) studding sail.

Lefzen ['lɛftsən], *f.pl.* flews.

legal [le'ga:l], *adj.* legal, lawful. **legalisieren** [–li'zi:rən], *v.t.* legalize, validate. **Legalität** *f.* legality.

[1]**Legat** [le'ga:t], *m.* **(-en,** *pl.* **-en)** legate.

[2]**Legat,** *n.* **(-(e)s,** *pl.* **-e)** legacy, devise; ***bedingtes –,*** contingent bequest. **Legatar** [–'ta:r], *m.* **(-s** *pl.* **-e)** legatee, divisee.

Legation [legatsi'o:n], *f.* legation, embassy.

Lege|geld, *n.* (*dial.*) entrance-fee. **–henne,** *f. See* **Leger.**

Legel, *m.* (*Austr.*) *see* **Lägel.**

legen ['le:gən], **1.** *v.t.* lay, put, place; deposit; set, sow, plant (*potatoes etc.*); ***Hand – an*** (*Acc.*), turn one's hand to, take in hand; lay hands on (*a p.*); ***Hand an sich –,*** commit suicide; ***letzte Hand – an*** (*Acc.*), put the finishing touches to; ***ihm (etwas) ans Herz –,*** bring (s.th.) home to him, urge *or* enjoin *or* impress (s.th.) upon him, recommend (s.th.) warmly to him; ***an die Kette –,*** chain up; ***Geld auf die hohe Kante –,*** put money aside; ***etwas aus der Hand –,*** put a th. down, lay a th. aside; ***Eier –,*** lay eggs; ***einen Fußboden –,*** lay a floor; ***ihm das Handwerk –,*** put a stop to his activities, (*coll.*) settle his hash, put a spoke in his wheel; ***in Asche –,*** reduce to ashes; ***in den Mund –*** (*Dat.*), suggest to, prompt, give the cue to; ***die Hände in den Schoß –,*** sit with one's hands in one's lap, twiddle one's fingers *or* thumbs; ***den Kopf – an*** (*Acc.*), rest one's head against; ***ihm die Karte(n) –,*** tell his fortune from cards; ***Nachdruck – auf*** (*Acc.*), lay stress *or* emphasis on, stress, emphasize; ***einen Teppich –,*** lay a carpet; ***von sich –,*** lay aside; ***ihm den Kopf vor die Füße –,*** strike off his head; ***ein Schloß vor die Tür –,*** put the bolt on the door; ***Wert – auf*** (*Acc.*), set store by, attach importance to. **2.** *v.r.* lie down; cease; die *or* go down, subside, ebb, abate, settle, slacken; be quiet; ***sich – auf*** (*Acc.*), devote *or* apply o.s. to, give o.s. up to, have recourse to; specialize in, (*coll.*) go in for, take up; ***sich mir aufs Gemüt –,*** begin to prey on my mind; ***sich aufs Bitten –,*** implore *or* entreat earnestly; (*coll.*) ***sich auf die faule Haut –,*** take it easy, be lazy; ***sich auf die Seite*** or ***aufs Ohr –,*** have *or* take a nap, (*sl.*) get some shut-eye; ***sich ins Mittel –,*** intervene, mediate, (*coll.*) step in; interfere, interpose; (*coll.*) ***sich mächtig ins Zeug –,*** go all out for; ***sich vor Anker –,*** cast anchor; ***sich schlafen –,*** go to bed.

legendar [legɛn'da:r], **legendär,** *adj.* legendary, mythical. **Legende** [–'gɛndə], *f.* 1. legend, myth; 2. inscription, caption, legend.

Leger ['le:gər], *m.* good layer, laying hen. **Lege|röhre,** *f.* ovipositor. **–zeit,** *f.* laying-season.

legieren [le'gi:rən], *v.t.* alloy (*metals*), blend, compound (*oil*); (*Cul.*) thicken (*soup*). **Legierung,** *f.* alloy(ing).

Legion [legi'o:n], *f.* legion. **Legionär** [–'nɛ:r], *m.* **(-s,** *pl.* **-e)** legionary.

Legislative [legısla'ti:və], *f.* legislature. **legislatorisch,** *adj.* legislative. **Legislatur,** *f.* legislature.

legitim [legi'ti:m], *adj.* legitimate, lawful. **Legitimation** [–matsi'o:n], *f.* authority (to act); credentials; acknowledgement of legitimacy, proof of identity. **Legitimations|karte,** *f.*, **–papiere,** *n.pl.* identity card, identification papers. **legitimieren** [–'mi:rən], **1.** *v.t.* prove the identity of; authorize; legitimize; make lawful. **2.** *v.r.* prove one's identity. **Legitimität** [–i'tɛ:t], *f.* legitimacy, legality.

Lehde ['le:də], *f.* (*dial.*) waste *or* fallow land.

Leh(e)n ['le:(ə)n], *n.* fief, feudal tenure; ***als – besitzen, zu – tragen,*** hold in fee; ***zu – geben,*** enfeoff, invest with; ***unbedingtes*** or ***freies –,*** fee simple. **Leh(e)ngut,** *n.*, **Leh(e)ns|besitz,** *m. See* **–gut. –dienst,** *m.* feudal service, vassalage, socage. **–eid,** *m.* oath of allegiance *or* fealty. **–erbe, 1.** *m.* successor to a fief. **2.** *n.* hereditary fief. **–gut,** *n.* copyhold. **–herr,** *m.* feudal lord. **leh(e)nsherrlich,** *adj.* seignorial. **Leh(e)ns|hof,** *m.* court leet. **–leute,** *pl.* vassals, feudal tenants. **–mann,** *m.* vassal. **leh(e)nspflichtig,** *adj.* feudatory. **Leh(e)ns|recht,** *n.* feudal law. **–treue,** *f.* allegiance. **–verhältnis,** *n.* vassalage, socage. **–wesen,** *n.* feudalism.

Lehm [le:m], *m.* **(-(e)s,** *pl.* **-e)** loam, clay; mud. **lehmartig,** *adj.* loamy. **Lehm|boden,** *m.* loamy *or* clay soil; clay floor. **–grube,** *f.* clay *or* loam-pit. **–hütte,** *f.* mud-hut. **lehmig,** *adj.* loamy, clayey, argillaceous. **Lehm|kalk,** *m.* argillaceous limestone. **–mergel,** *m.* loamy marl. **–stein,** *m.* (unbaked) clay brick. **–wand,** *f.* mud wall. **–ziegel,** *m.* sun-dried brick.

Lehn, *n. See* **Leh(e)n.**

Lehne ['le:nə], *f.* 1. arm *or* back (*of a chair*), support, rest, prop; hand-rail, balustrade, railing; 2. (*Typ.*) gallows; 3. (*dial.*) slope, inclined plane, declivity. **lehnen, 1.** *v.t.* lean, rest, prop. **2.** *v.i.* (*aux.* h. *&* s.) *v.r.* lean, recline (**an** (*Acc.*), against), rest, support o.s. (***auf*** (*Acc.*), on). **Lehn|satz,** *m.* (*Math.*) lemma. **–sessel, –stuhl,** *m.* easy chair, armchair. **–wort,** *n.* loan-word.

Lehr [le:r], *n.* (**-(e)s,** *pl.* **-e**) pattern, model, gauge. *See* **Lehre. Lehr|amt,** *n.* teacher's post, professorship; teaching profession. **–anstalt,** *f.* educational establishment. **–aufgabe,** *f.* programme of work; *– der Obersekunda,* work to be done in the Upper Fifth. **–auftrag,** *m.* professorship; *einen – erhalten,* be appointed professor. **–befähigung,** *f.* qualification to teach (*a subject*). **–behelf,** *m. See* **–mittel. –beruf,** *m.* teaching *or* scholastic profession. **–bogen,** *m.* (*Archit.*) centre, centering. **–brett,** *n.* templet, template; mould, pattern. **–brief,** *m.* indentures. **–buch,** *n.* textbook. **–bursche,** *m.* apprentice.

Lehre ['le:rə], *f.* 1. instruction, tuition; moral, warning, lesson, precept; *laßt euch dies zur – dienen!* let this be a warning *or* lesson to you! 2. teaching, doctrine, dogma, system, tenets, theory, science; *die – Christi,* Christ's teaching; *die – vom Schall,* the theory of sound; 3. apprenticeship; *in die – geben* or *tun,* apprentice (*bei,* to *or* with); *er ist bei Herrn N. in der –,* he is serving his time with Mr. N.; 4. (*Tech.*) gauge, calibre, size, pattern.

lehren ['le:rən], *v.t. ihn etwas –,* teach him a th., instruct him in a th., show him how to do a th.; *ihn lesen –,* teach him to read; *so wurde es mir gelehrt,* that was the way I was taught; *die Zeit wird es –,* time will show.

Lehrer ['le:rər], *m.* teacher, schoolmaster, instructor, tutor. **Lehrer|bildungsanstalt,** *f. See* **–seminar. Lehrerin,** *f.* schoolmistress, woman teacher. **Lehrer|kollegium,** *n.* staff (*of a school*). **–konferenz,** *f.* staff(-room) meeting. **–prüfung,** *f.* examination for teachers. **Lehrerschaft,** *f.* body of teachers; staff. **Lehrer|seminar,** *n.* (teachers') training college. **–stand,** *m.* scholastic profession; members of the teaching profession. **–stelle,** *f.* teaching post *or* appointment.

Lehr|fach, *n.* subject, branch of study; teaching profession. **–film,** *m.* instructional *or* educational film. **–freiheit,** *f.* freedom of teaching. **–gang,** *m.* course (*of instruction*). **–gebäude,** *n.* system (*of a science etc.*). **–gedicht,** *n.* didactic poem. **–gegenstand,** *m.* subject taught, branch of study. **–geld,** *n.* fees, apprentice's premium; (*fig.*) *– bezahlen,* learn it the hard way, pay for one's experience. **–gerüst,** *n.* (*Archit.*) matrix, frame, scantling.

lehrhaft ['le:rhaft], *adj.* didactic; instructive.

Lehr|herr, *m.* master, (*coll.*) boss (*of an apprentice*). **–jahre,** *n.pl.* (term of *or* years of) apprenticeship; *seine – durchmachen,* serve one's apprenticeship, serve out one's time. **–junge,** *m.* apprentice. **–kanzel,** *f.* (*Austr.*) *see* **–stuhl. –körper,** *m.* teaching staff, professoriate. **–kraft,** *f.* teacher. **–kurs(us),** *m.* course of instruction.

Lehrling ['le:rlıŋ], *m.* (**-s,** *pl.* **-e**) apprentice, pupil; beginner, novice, tyro.

Lehr|mädchen, *n.* girl-apprentice. **–meister,** *m.* master (*of a trade*). **–mittel,** *n.* educational *or* teaching aid, appliances, material, apparatus (*for instruction*). **–personal,** *n. See* **Lehrerschaft. –plan,** *m.* course of instruction, syllabus, school curriculum. **–probe,** *f.* (time of) probation, novitiate; trial lesson. **lehrreich,** *adj.* instructive, informative. **Lehr|saal,** *m.* lecture-room; classroom, school-room. **–satz,** *m.* thesis, dogma, doctrine, proposition, theorem, precept. **–spruch,** *m.* maxim, adage. **–stand,** *m. See* **Lehrerstand. –stelle,** *f.* apprenticeship. **–stoff,** *m.* subject matter (of instruction). **–stuhl,** *m.* professorship, professorial chair. **–stunde,** *f.* period of instruction, lesson, lecture. **–tätigkeit,** *f.* educational work, instruction, teaching. **–tochter,** *f.* (*Swiss*) *see* **–mädchen. –vertrag,** *m.* indentures. **–weise,** *f.* method of instruction, teaching method. **–zeit,** *f. See* **–jahre. –zwang,** *m.* compulsory indoctrination, compulsory education.

Lei [laı], *f.* (-, *pl.* **-en**) (*dial.*) slate (*e.g. Erpeler Lei, Lorelei*).

Leib [laıp], *m.* (**-(e)s,** *pl.* **-er**) body; abdomen, belly, bowels; womb; waist, trunk; *– und Leben,* life and limb; *auf dem bloßen –e,* next to one's skin; *am ganzen –e zittern,* tremble all over; *kein Hemd auf dem –e haben,* not have a shirt to one's back; (*Austr.*) *bei –e nicht!* not on your life; not on any account! *lebendigen –es, bei lebendigem –e,* while (still) alive; *gesegneten –es,* pregnant, with child, in the family way; *harten – haben,* be constipated; *der – des Herrn,* the Host, the consecrated wafer *or* bread; *mit – und Seele,* with heart and soul; *sich* (*Dat.*) *ihn vom –e halten,* keep him at arm's length; *bleib mir vom –e!* keep your distance! keep off! *bleib mir damit vom –e!* don't bother me about that; *ihm* (*scharf*) *zu –e gehen, ihm* (*hart*) *auf den – rücken,* attack him (sharply), grapple with *or* tackle him; press him hard; close in on him.

Leib|arzt, *m.* physician in ordinary (*Gen.,* to). **–binde,** *f.* 1. waistband, sash; 2. abdominal belt *or* bandage, body-belt. **–bursch,** *m.* elder student who has a younger one to fag for him. **Leibchen,** *n.* bodice, vest, corset. **Leibdiener,** *m.* page, valet de chambre. **leibeigen,** *adj.* in bondage *or* thrall *or* villeinage. **Leib|eigene(r),** *m.* serf, bondman. **–eigenschaft,** *f.* bondage, serfdom.

leiben ['laıbən], (*only in*) *wie er leibt und lebt,* the very image of him, his very self.

Leiberl ['laıbərl], *n.* (*dial.*) rissole.

Leibes|beschaffenheit, *f.* (physical) constitution, physique. **–erbe,** *m.* legitimate heir; offspring; (*pl.*) issue. **–erziehung,** *f.* physical training. **–frucht,** *f.* foetus, embryo, (*Poet.*) offspring; *Abtreibung* or *Tötung der –,* procuring abortion. **–höhle,** *f.* abdominal cavity. **–kraft,** *f.* bodily *or* physical strength; *aus ¨–en,* with might and main; *aus ¨–en schreien,* shout at the top of one's voice. **–öffnung,** *f.* opening of the bowels, motion. **–pflege,** *f.* care of the body. **–schüssel,** *f.* bed-pan.

Leibessen ['laıpˀɛsən], *n.* (*coll.*) favourite dish.

Leibes|strafe, *f.* corporal punishment. **–übung,** *f.* (*usu. pl.*) physical exercise *or* training, gymnastics. **–umfang,** *m.* corpulence. **–visitation,** *f.* bodily search.

Leib|fuchs, *m.* freshmen who acts as fag to an older student. **–garde,** *f.* bodyguard, life-guards. **–gedinge,** *n.* jointure, dower, appanage, settlement, (*dial.*) pension, life-annuity. **–geleit,** *n.* safe-conduct. **–gericht,** *n.* (*coll.*) *see* **–essen. –gurt, –gürtel,** *m. See* **–binde.**

leibhaft(ig) ['laıphaft(ıç)], **1.** *adj.* embodied, corporeal, personified; living, real, true, incarnate; *der –e Teufel,* the devil incarnate. **2.** *adv.* personally, in person, in the flesh; *– erscheinen,* appear in person.

leibig ['laıbıç], *adj.* 1. (*dial.*) fat, corpulent; 2. (*as suff.*) having a . . . body, *e.g.* **dickleibig,** corpulent.

Leib|jäger, *m.* prince's own huntsman *or* gamekeeper; (*Mil.*) chasseur. **–knecht,** *m.* groom of the royal stables. **–kompa(g)nie,** *f.* colonel's own company, first company of a regiment.

leiblich ['laıplıç], *adj.* 1. bodily, material, corporeal; somatic; *–es Wohl,* physical well-being; 2. consanguineous; *sein –er Sohn,* his own son; *mit –en Augen sehen,* see with one's own eyes; *–er Bruder,* own brother; *–er Vetter,* first cousin, cousin german; 3. temporal, earthly, worldly; (*B.*) *–e Güter,* carnal things; earthly goods. **Leiblichkeit,** *f.* corporeality.

Leib|regiment, *n.* prince's own regiment. **–rente,** *f.* (life) annuity. **–rock,** *m.* (*obs.*) frock-coat. **–schmerz,** *m.* (*usu. pl.*), **–schneiden,** *n.* stomach-ache, gripes, colic. **–schüssel,** *f.* bed-pan. **–speise,** *f.* (*coll.*) *see* **–gericht. –spruch,** *m.* (*coll.*) favourite saying *or* maxim. **–standarte,** *f.* (*Nat. Soc.*) Hitler's bodyguard.

Leibung ['laıbuŋ], *f.* (*Archit.*) inner face of arches and wall openings (*windows, doors etc.*).

Leib|wache, *f.* bodyguard. **–wächter,** *m.* soldier of the bodyguard; satellite. **–wäsche,** *f.* linen, underwear, (*women*) lingerie. **–weh,** *n. See* **–schmerz. –zucht,** *f.* (*obs.*) *see* **–gedinge.**

Leich [laıç], *m.* (**-(e)s,** *pl.* **-e**) (*obs.*) lay.

Leichdorn ['laıçdɔrn], *m.* (**-s,** *pl.* **¨–er** (*Austr.* **-e**)) (*dial.*) corn (*on the foot*).

Leiche ['laɪçə], *f.* 1. (dead) body, corpse, cadaver, (mortal) remains, (*of animal*) carcass; ***über –n gehen,*** ride roughshod, stick at nothing; (*coll.*) ***nur über meine –!*** over my dead body! (*coll.*) ***wandelnde –,*** walking skeleton; 2. (*dial.*) funeral; (*dial.*) ***zur – gehen,*** attend a funeral; 3. (*Typ.*) omitted word(s).

Leichenacker ['laɪçənʔakər], *m.* (*dial.*) churchyard, burying-ground, cemetery, necropolis. **leichenartig,** *adj.* cadaverous. **Leichen|ausgrabung,** *f.* exhumation. **–begängnis,** *n.* funeral, burial. **–begleiter,** *m.* mourner. **–begleitung,** *f.* funeral procession. **–beschauer,** *m.* coroner. **–besorger, –bestatter,** *m.* undertaker, (*Am.*) mortician. **–bestattung,** *f.* *See* **–begängnis. –bittergesicht,** *n.*, **–bittermiene,** *f.* woebegone look. **leichenblaß,** *adj.* pale as death, deathly pale. **Leichen|blässe,** *f.* deathly *or* deathlike pallor. **–dieb,** *m.* body-snatcher. **–farbe,** *f.* *See* **–blässe. –feier,** *f.* obsequies, exequies, funeral service. **–feld,** *n.* field strewed with corpses, battlefield. **–fledderer,** *m.* looter of corpses. **–frau,** *f.* layer-out.

Leichen|geleit, *n.* *See* **–begleitung. –geruch,** *m.* cadaverous smell. **–gerüst,** *n.* catafalque. **–gewand,** *n.* *See* **–hemd. –gewölbe,** *n.* burial-vault, catacomb. **–gift,** *n.* ptomaine. **–gruft,** *f.* *See* **–gewölbe. –halle,** *f.*, **–haus,** *n.* mortuary, morgue. **–hemd,** *n.* shroud, winding sheet. **–öffnung,** *f.* autopsy, post-mortem (examination). **–predigt,** *f.* funeral sermon. **–raub,** *m.* body-snatching. **–räuber.** *m.* *See* **–dieb. –rede,** *f.* funeral oration. **–schändung,** *f.* desecration of corpses. **–schau,** *f.* coroner's inquest; post-mortem (examination). **–schauhaus,** *n.* *See* **–haus. –schmaus,** *m.* funeral banquet *or* repast. **–starre,** *f.* rigor mortis. **–stein,** *m.* tombstone. **–träger,** *m.* (pall) bearer. **–tuch,** *n.* *See* **–hemd. –untersuchung,** *f.* *See* **–schau. –verbrennung,** *f.* cremation. **–wagen,** *m.* hearse. **–zug,** *m.* funeral procession.

Leichnam ['laɪçna:m], *m.* **(-s,** *pl.* **-e)** *see* **Leiche**; (*hum.*) ***seines –s pflegen,*** do o.s. well.

leicht [laɪçt], *adj.* light (*in weight*), light-weight, (*Tech. etc.*) light-duty; (*fig.*) light, easy, effortless, facile; mild (*of tobacco or beer*), small (*of beer*); slight, moderate, gentle, trifling, petty, minor, insignificant, superficial; light-minded, easy-going, fickle, frivolous, flighty; ***–en Absatz finden,*** meet with a ready sale, sell readily; ***etwas auf die –e Achsel*** or ***Schulter nehmen,*** take *or* treat a th. lightly, make light of a th., (*coll.*) pooh-pooh a th.; ***–e Bewegung,*** easy *or* graceful movement; ***mit –er Bewegung des Kopfes,*** with a slight movement of the head; ***–er Bruder,*** loose character; ***–er Diebstahl,*** petty larceny; ***–e Erkältung,*** slight cold; ***–en Fußes,*** light-footed, nimbly, trippingly; ***–en Kaufs davon kommen,*** get *or* come off lightly; ***–e Kost,*** light diet, (*fig.*) meagre fare; ***–er Panzer,*** light tank; ***–er Sieg*** or ***–es Spiel,*** walkover; ***–er Sinn,*** cheerful temperament. **2.** *adv.* lightly, easily, effortlessly, without effort; slightly; ***–(er) machen,*** make lighter, lighten, clear (*the head*); facilitate, render easy *or* easier; ***es sich*** (*Dat.*) ***– machen,*** take it easy; choose the easy way out; ***es – nehmen,*** take it easy; ***– möglich sein,*** be quite probable, be easily possible, may well be possible; ***–er gesagt als getan,*** easier said than done; (*fig.*) ***gewogen und zu – befunden,*** weighed and found wanting; ***das passiert nicht so – wieder,*** that is unlikely *or* not likely to happen again; ***– ums Herz sein*** or ***werden,*** feel relieved, feel easier in one's mind; ***mir – von der Hand gehen,*** come easy *or* easily to me; ***sich – erkälten,*** be apt *or* prone *or* liable to catch cold, catch cold easily; ***– zugänglich,*** easily accessible, easy of access.

Leicht|athletik, *f.* athletics, track and field events. **–bauweise,** *f.* lightweight construction. **leicht|-beschädigt,** *adj.* slightly damaged. **–beschwingt,** *adj.* (*fig.*) jaunty, (*pred.*) on air. **–bewaffnet,** *adj.* lightly armed. **–beweglich,** *adj.* easily movable, very mobile. **–blütig,** *adj.* sanguine, light-hearted.

leichten ['laɪçtən], *v.t.* weigh (*the anchor*). *See* [2]**lichten.**

leichtentzündlich ['laɪçtʔɛnttsyntlɪç], *adj.* highly inflammable.

Leichter ['laɪçtər], *m.* (*Naut.*) lighter, barge. **Leichtergeld,** *n.* lighterage. **leichtern,** *v.t.* unload (*a ship*).

leicht|faßlich, *adj.* easily understood, popular. **–fertig, 1.** *adj.* careless, thoughtless, inconsiderate, light-minded, irresponsible; frivolous, wanton, feckless, fickle; loose (*talk*), flippant (*word, behaviour*), loose, fast (*woman*). **2.** *adv.* ***– behandeln,*** treat lightly, make light of. **Leichtfertigkeit,** *f.* carelessness, thoughtlessness, irresponsibility; frivolity, flippancy, fickleness, wantonness. **leichtflüchtig,** *adj.* highly volatile. **Leichtflugzeug,** *n.* light (aero)plane. **leichtflüssig,** *adj.* easily fusible, easily dissolved; thin (*liquid*). **Leichtfuß,** *m.* bright spark, happy-go-lucky fellow. **leicht|füßig,** *adj.* nimble, light-footed. **–geschürzt,** *adj.* lightly draped (*i.e. the Muse*). **Leicht|gewicht,** *n.*, **–gewichtler,** *m.* (*Spt.*) lightweight. **leichtgläubig,** *adj.* credulous, gullible. **Leichtgläubigkeit,** *f.* credulity, gullibility. **leicht|herzig,** *adj.* cheerful, light-hearted. **–hin,** *adv.* lightly, casually, carelessly, superficially.

Leichtigkeit ['laɪçtɪçkaɪt], *f.* lightness, ease, easiness, facility, readiness; ***mit größter –,*** with effortless ease *or* the greatest of ease; ***mit – gewinnen,*** win easily *or* (*coll.*) hands down.

leicht|lebig, *adj.* happy-go-lucky, easy-going. **–löslich,** *adj.* easily soluble. **Leicht|matrose,** *m.* ordinary seaman. **–metall,** *n.* light metal. **–sinn,** *m.* rashness, recklessness, imprudence; *see also* **–fertigkeit. leicht|sinnig,** *adj.* reckless, rash, (*coll.*) devil-may-care; imprudent, irresponsible; *see also* **–fertig. –sinnigerweise,** *adv.* rashly, recklessly *etc.* **Leichtsinnigkeit,** *f.* *See* **–sinn. leicht|verdaulich,** *adj.* easily digestible. **–verderblich,** *adj.* perishable (*of goods*). **–verständlich,** *adj.* easy to understand, easily understood. **Leichtverwundete,** *pl.* walking wounded.

leid [laɪt], *adj.* painful, disagreeable (*only pred. with* ***sein, tun, werden,*** *and Dat.*); (*Swiss*) *used attrib.*, unpleasant, bad; ***es ist*** or ***tut mir –,*** I am sorry (***um,*** for), I regret; ***er tut mir –,*** I am sorry for him; (*Poet.*) ***ich bin es –,*** I shrink from it, I cannot bear it; ***laß dir das nicht – sein,*** do not regret having done it.

Leid, *n.* **(-(e)s,** *no pl.*) 1. harm, hurt, injury, wrong; ***ihm ein –(s) antun*** or ***zufügen,*** harm *or* injure him; ***sich*** (*Dat.*) ***ein –(s) antun,*** lay hands on o.s.; 2. pain, sorrow, grief, mourning; ***in Lieb und –,*** through thick and thin; ***ihm sein – klagen,*** pour out one's troubles to him; ***vor – vergehen,*** die of a broken heart; ***– tragen,*** mourn *or* be in mourning (***um,*** for); ***keinem zu –e und keinem zu Liebe,*** without fear or favour.

Leideform ['laɪdəfɔrm], *f.* (*Gram.*) passive voice.

Leiden ['laɪdən], *n.* suffering, affliction, tribulation, trouble; disease, ailment, malady, (chronic) complaint; ***das –Christi,*** the Passion of our Lord.

leiden, 1. *irr.v.t.* 1. suffer, bear, tolerate, (*coll.*) stand, put up with; ***Hunger –,*** suffer from hunger; ***Schaden –,*** sustain loss *or* injury; ***ich leide es nicht,*** I can't *or* won't put up with it; ***es litt mich nicht länger dort,*** I could not bear to stay there any longer; 2. allow, permit, admit, tolerate; ***keinen Aufschub –,*** admit of *or* brook no delay; 3. – (***mögen*** or ***können***), like, care for, be fond of; ***ich kann ihn nicht –,*** I cannot bear *or* stand him; ***ich mag ihn wohl –,*** I rather like him. **2.** *irr.v.i.* be in pain; suffer (***an*** or ***unter*** (*Dat.*), from), be afflicted (with), complain (of); be subject *or* liable (to); ***seine Gesundheit wird darunter –,*** his health will suffer *or* will be affected, (*coll.*) it will tell on his health.

leidend ['laɪdənt], *adj.* 1. ailing, sickly, suffering, ill; 2. (*Gram.*) passive.

Leidenschaft ['laɪdənʃaft], *f.* passion. **leidenschaftlich,** *adj.* passionate; vehement, ardent, fervent, impassioned, burning, glowing; impulsive, hot-headed, hot-tempered; enthusiastic.

Leidenschaftlichkeit, *f.* impulsiveness, vehemence, ardour, fervour, hot-headedness, hot-temper. **leidenschaftslos,** *adj.* impassive, apathetic; dispassionate, detached, matter-of-fact, cool, calm.

Leidens|gefährte, -genosse, *m.* fellow-sufferer, companion in misfortune. **-geschichte,** *f.* tale of woe; (*Eccl.*) Christ's Passion. **-stationen,** *f.pl.* (*Eccl.*) Stations of the Cross. **-weg,** *m.* (*Eccl.*) Way of the Cross; (*fig.*) life of suffering. **-woche,** *f.* Passion Week. **-zeit,** *f.* ordeal.

leider ['laɪdər], *adv., int.* unfortunately, I am sorry to say; alas! – ***Gottes!*** most unfortunately! – ***sehen wir, daß . . .,*** we are sorry to see that . . .; – ***müssen wir zugeben,*** much to our regret we must admit; – ***muß ich gehen,*** I am afraid I have to go.

leiderfüllt ['laɪtˀɛrfylt], *adj.* griefstricken, sorrowful; woebegone (*appearance*).

leidig ['laɪdɪç], *adj.* tiresome, unpleasant, disagreeable; grievous, distressing; nasty, confounded, accursed; ***-er Trost,*** cold comfort, poor consolation.

leidlich ['laɪtlɪç], **1.** *adj.* tolerable, bearable, passable, (*coll.*) middling. **2.** *adv.* fairly well, not too badly. **leidsam,** *adj.* (*dial.*) tolerant, patient; tolerable.

Leidtragende(r) ['laɪttra:gəndə(r)], *m., f.* mourner; (*fig.*) ***der Leidtragende dabei sein,*** be the one to suffer. **leid|voll,** *adj. See* **-erfüllt. -werken,** *v.i.* (*Dat.*) (*Swiss*) make difficulties (for), annoy. **Leidwesen,** *n.* ***zu unserm –,*** to our sorrow *or* distress *or* regret.

Leier ['laɪər], *f.* (-, *pl.* **-n**) lyre; (*Astr.*) Lyra; (*fig.*) ***die alte –,*** the same old story; ***immer bei der alten – bleiben,*** be always on about the same thing. **Leier|bohrer,** *m.* (carpenter's) brace. **-kasten,** *m.* barrel-organ, (*coll.*) hurdy-gurdy. **-kastenmann,** *m.* organ-grinder. **leiern,** *v.t., v.i.* grind a barrel-organ; turn (with) a crank(-handle); (*coll.*) drawl on; ***ihm die Ohren voll –,*** din perpetually into his ears; ***besser geleiert als gefeiert,*** anything is better than nothing.

Leih|amt ['laɪ-], *n.*, **-anstalt,** *f. See* **-haus. -bibliothek, -bücherei,** *f.* lending *or* circulating library.

Leihe ['laɪə], *f.* loan; (*coll.*) pawnshop. **leihen,** *irr.v.t.* lend (out), loan; advance (*money*); borrow, hire; ***er leiht es mir,*** he lends it to me; ***ich leihe es (mir) von ihm,*** I borrow it from him.

Leih|gebinde, *n.* (*Comm.*) returnable container. **-gebühr,** *f.* hiring fee, charge for lending. **-geld,** *n.* (*Comm.*) loans. **-geschäft,** *n.* money-lending business. **-haus,** *n.* loan-office, pawnshop. **--Pacht-Gesetz,** *n.* Lend-Lease Act. **-schein,** *m.* pawn-ticket; library ticket. **leihweise,** *adv.* as a loan, by way of a loan, on hire.

Leikauf ['laɪkauf], *m.* (*dial.*) drink to seal a bargain.

Leim [laɪm], *m.* **(-(e)s,** *pl.* **-e)** glue; size; bird-lime; gelatine; – ***sieden,*** boil glue; (*fig.*) be engaged in *or* on unprofitable work; (*coll.*) ***auf den – führen,*** hoodwink; (*coll.*) ***auf den – gehen,*** fall into the trap, (*coll.*) fall for it; (*coll.*) ***auf den – krieche*** (or ***gehe***) ***ich nicht,*** I shall not let myself in for that, you will not catch me there; (*coll.*) ***aus dem -e gehen,*** fall apart, fall to pieces, come to grief. **leimartig,** *adj.* glutinous, gelatinous. **leimen,** *v.t.* glue, cement; size; (*coll.*) ***geleimt werden,*** be tricked *or* cheated *or* hoodwinked *or* taken in. **Leimfarbe,** *f.* water-paint, distemper. **leimig,** *adj.* gluey, viscous, glutinous. **Leim|kitt,** *m.* plastic wood. **-ring,** *m.* grease band (*on fruit trees*). **-rute,** *f.* lime-twig. **-sieder,** *m.* glue-maker; (*hum.*) bore. **-stoff,** *m.* gluten. **-tiegel, -topf,** *m.* glue-pot. **-zucker,** *m.* glycocoll, glycocin.

Lein [laɪn], *m.* **(-(e)s,** *pl.* **-e)** (*Bot.*) flax; linseed.

Leine ['laɪnə], *f.* cord, line, rope; clothes-line; (dog's) lead, leash; ***an der – haben,*** hold by a string; (*fig.*) lead by the nose; ***an der – führen,*** keep on a lead, (*fig.*) keep in tow; ***eine – ziehen,*** hang out a clothes line; (*sl.*) – ***ziehen,*** beat it, do a bunk.

leinen ['laɪnən], *adj.* (of) linen. **Leinen,** *n.* linen; linen goods. **Leinen|band, 1.** *n.* linen tape. **2.** *m.* cloth binding. **-garn,** *n.* linen thread *or* yarn. **-papier,** *n.* linen-paper. **-schuh,** *m.* canvas shoe. **-zeug,** *n.* linen (material).

Lein|fink, *m.* (*Orn.*) ***grönländischer –,*** greater redpoll (*Carduelis flammea rostrata*). **-firnis,** *m.* linseed varnish. **-kraut,** *n.* (*Bot.*) wild flax (*Linaria vulgaris*). **-kuchen,** *m.* oil-cake. **-öl,** *n.* linseed-oil. **-pfad,** *m.* towing-path, towpath. **-same(n),** *m.* flax-seed, linseed. **-tuch,** *n.* linen (cloth); (bed-)sheet. **-wand,** *f.* linen (cloth); (*Paint.*) canvas; (*Films*) screen; ***grobe –,*** sackcloth, bale-cloth; ***gesteifte –,*** buckram; ***auf – ziehen,*** mount on canvas; ***auf die – bringen,*** put on the screen; ***über die – gehen,*** appear *or* be shown on the screen. **-zeisig,** *m.* (*Orn.*) *see* **Birkenzeisig.**

leise ['laɪzə], **1.** *adj.* low, soft, faint; slight, light, imperceptible; gentle, fine, delicate; ***-r Schlaf,*** light sleep; ***mit -r Stimme,*** in a low voice, in an undertone; ***nicht der -ste Laut,*** not the least *or* faintest sound; ***nicht die -ste Ahnung,*** not the least *or* slightest *or* faintest idea *or* suspicion; ***nicht im -sten zweifeln,*** not have a shadow of doubt; – ***sein,*** be quiet. **2.** *adv.* – ***auftreten,*** tread noiselessly *or* softly, (*fig.*) proceed cautiously; (*fig.*) – ***berühren,*** touch lightly upon; ***-r sprechen,*** lower one's voice; (*Rad.*) ***-r stellen,*** turn the volume down. **Leisetreter,** *m.* sneak, (*Am.*) pussyfoot.

Leist [laɪst], *m.* (**-es,** *pl.* **-e**) (*Swiss*) club, association.

Leiste ['laɪstə], *f.* 1. beading, moulding, fillet; ridge, ledge; 2. (*Bot., Zool.*) carina; 3. (*dial.*) slope, incline; 4. (*Anat.*) groin; 5. (*Weav.*) list, selvage.

leisten ['laɪstən], *v.t.* do, fulfil, carry out, perform, execute, achieve, accomplish; effect, realize; afford, give; produce; ***Beistand –,*** render assistance; ***Bürgschaft –,*** give bail; ***Buße –,*** do penance; ***Dienste –,*** render service; ***den Eid der Treue –,*** take the oath of allegiance; ***Ersatz –,*** supply a substitute, act as substitute; ***Folge –,*** obey; ***einer gerichtlichen Aufforderung Folge –,*** answer a summons; ***Genugtuung –,*** give satisfaction; ***Gesellschaft –,*** keep (*s.o.*) company; ***Gewähr –,*** vouch for, guarantee; ***Hilfe –,*** help, assist, give help *or* assistance, (*coll.*) give a hand; ***Tüchtiges –,*** do a good job, render good service; ***Vorschuß –,*** make an advance (*auf* (*Acc.*), on); ***Verzicht auf eine S. –,*** renounce *or* give up *or* do without a th.; ***Widerstand –,*** offer resistance; ***Zahlung –,*** make payment; (*coll.*) ***ich kann mir das –,*** I can afford (to do) it; (*coll.*) ***er hat sich einen neuen Hut geleistet,*** he has treated himself to a new hat.

Leisten, *m.* shoemaker's last, boot-tree; ***auf*** or ***über den – schlagen,*** put on the last; ***alles über einen – schlagen,*** treat all alike; ***sie sind alle über einen – geschlagen,*** they are all of the same stamp.

Leisten|bruch, *m.* rupture (in the groin), inguinal hernia. **-gegend,** *f.* groin, inguinal region. **-werk,** *n.* (*Archit.*) coping, moulding, beading, bordering.

Leistung ['laɪstuŋ], *f.* performance, execution; achievement, attainment, accomplishment, feat, work (done); production, output, capacity, efficiency, (*Elec.*) power, wattage, (*Mech.*) brake horse-power; (*Comm.*) payment; delivery; contribution; result, effect; ***höchste –,*** record, peak performance; ***tüchtige –,*** creditable performance, excellent piece of work; ***gegen – einer Bürgschaft,*** on bail.

Leistungs|abgabe, *f.* (*Elec.*) power output. **-aufnahme,** *f.* (*Elec.*) power input. **-einheit,** *f.* unit of power. **leistungsfähig,** *adj.* efficient, productive, (*Comm.*) sound, solvent, (*Mech.*) powerful. **Leistungs|fähigkeit,** *f.* efficiency, productivity, capacity; performance, output; (*Comm.*) soundness, solvency, (*Mech.*) power; (*of microscope*) resolving power. **-faktor,** *m.* (*Elec.*) power factor. **-grundsatz,** *m.* Bedaux principle. **-messer,** *m.* (*Elec.*) output meter. **-norm,** *f.* standard of performance. **-prämie,** *f.* efficiency bonus. **-prüfung,** *f.* performance *or* efficiency test. **-soll,** *n.* output target. **-steigerung,** *f.* increased efficiency *or* productivity, increased production *or* output. **-system,** *n.* piecework system. **-vermögen,** *n.*

See **–fähigkeit. –wettbewerb,** *m.* efficiency drive. **–wille,** *m.* will to work. **–zulage,** *f. See* **–prämie.**

Leit|artikel ['laɪt–], *m.* leading article, leader. **–blech,** *n.* deflecting plate, baffle.

Leite ['laɪtə], *f.* (*dial.*) declivity, slope (*of a hill*).

leiten ['laɪtən], *v.t.* lead, guide, conduct; direct, manage, control, be in charge of, (*coll.*) run; head, preside over, govern; ***sich – lassen,*** be led *or* guided *or* actuated (***von,*** by). **leitend,** *adj.* 1. leading, chief, (*coll.*) key; (*Comm.*) managerial, executive; ***die –en Kreise,*** influential circles, the governing classes, those in authority; 2. (*Elec.*) conducting; ***nicht –,*** non-conducting.

[1]**Leiter** ['laɪtər], *m.* 1. leader. guide, conductor; superintendent, director, manager, governor, principal, head, chief; 2. (*Elec.*) conductor.

[2]**Leiter,** *f.* (-, *pl.* **-n**) 1. ladder; 2. (*Mus.*) scale, gamut.

leiter|artig, *adj.* (*Bot., Zool.*) scalariform. **Leiter|-baum,** *m. See* **–stange. –förmig,** *See* **–artig. –netz,** *n.* (*Elec.*) conducting network. **–sprosse,** *f.* rung of a ladder. **–stange,** *f.* ladder upright.

Leitfaden ['laɪtfa:dən], *m.* guide, manual; textbook, primer; clue. **leitfähig,** *adj.* (*Elec.*) conductive. **Leit|fähigkeit,** *f.* conductivity, conductance. **–feuer,** *n.* (*Naut.*) leading light; slow-match, safety-fuse. **–flosse,** *f.* (*Av.*) tail fin. **–fossil,** *n.* characteristic fossil. **–gedanke,** *m.* leading *or* basic *or* fundamental *or* main idea, keynote. **–hammel,** *m.* bell-wether. **–kante,** *f.* (*Av.*) leading edge. **–karte,** *f.* index card. **–kauf,** *m. See* **Leikauf. –motiv,** *n.* (*Mus.*) leitmotiv. **–satz,** *m.* guiding principle. **–schiene,** *f.* (*Railw.*) live rail, guide rail. **–seil,** *n.* guide-rope. **–spruch,** *m.* motto. **–stand,** *m.* control post, (*Mil.*) fire-control centre, command post. **–stange,** *f.* guide-rod, (*Railw.*) conducting rod, trolley-pole. **–stelle,** *f.* army post-office. **–stern,** *m.* guiding-star; pole-star. **–strahl,** *m.* (*Geom.*) radius vector. **–tier,** *n.* (*Hunt.*) leader.

Leitung ['laɪtuŋ], *f.* 1. lead(ing), conducting; guidance, direction; administration, directorate; command, control, management, charge, care; ***– der öffentlichen Angelegenheiten,*** conduct of public affairs; ***die – haben,*** lead, be in *or* have charge of; (*Tele.*) ***die – ist besetzt,*** the line is engaged; (*coll.*) ***heiße –,*** hot line; (*Mus.*) ***unter der – von K.,*** conducted by K.; ***die – in die Hand nehmen,*** take the lead, take charge, take the reins; (*coll.*) ***eine lange – haben,*** be slow on the uptake, be dull of comprehension; 2. pipeline, conduit, pipe, piping, tubing, duct; (*dial.*) tap, standpipe; (*Elec.*) line, wire, lead, cable, wiring, circuit; mains (*of gas, water, elec.*), (*Phys.*) supply, conduction, transmission.

Leitungs|aufseher, *m.* (*Tele.*) lineman. **–draht,** *m.* lead, conductor, conducting-wire. **–fähigkeit,** *f.* (*Elec.*) conductivity, conductance. **–fehler,** *m. See* **–störung. –hahn,** *m.* water-tap. **–mast,** *m.* (*Elec.*) pylon. **–netz,** *n.* (*Elec.*) supply network, (*Rad.*) circuit. **–plan,** *m.* wiring diagram. **–rohr,** *n.*, **–röhre,** *f.* supply-pipe; conduit, main. **–schnur,** *f.* (*Elec.*) flex, lead. **–spannung,** *f.* line voltage. **–störung,** *f.* (*Tele.*) line-fault, (*Rad.*) circuit fault. **–vermögen,** *n. See* **–fähigkeit. –wasser,** *n.* tap-water.

Leitwerk ['laɪtvɛrk], *n.* (*Av.*) tail unit, empennage.

Lektion [lɛktsi'o:n], *f.* lesson; (*coll.*) rebuke; ***ihm eine – lesen,*** give him a lecture *or* a good scolding.

Lektor ['lɛktɔr], *m.* (**-s,** *pl.* **-en**) 1. lecturer, lector, teacher (of mother tongue abroad); 2. publisher's reader.

Lektüre [lɛk'ty:rə], *f.* 1. reading; 2. reading matter, books, literature.

Lemma ['lɛma], *n.* (**-s,** *pl.* **-s**) 1. assumption, proposition, (*Log.*) lemma; 2. caption, legend, heading.

Lemur(e) [le'mu:r(ə)], *m.* (**-s,** *pl.* **-(e)n**) 1. (*Zool.*) maki, lemur; 2. evil spirit, ghost, spook.

Lende ['lɛndə], *f.* loin, loins, lumbar region; haunch, hip, (*coll.*) thigh. **Lenden|braten,** *m.* roast sirloin; rump of beef. **–gegend,** *f.* lumbar region. **–knochen,** *m.* hip-bone. **lendenlahm,** *adj.* hobbling, crippled, worn out (*from walking*); (*fig.*) halting, lame (*as an excuse*). **Lenden|schnitte,** *f.* rumpsteak. **–schurz,** *m.* loin-cloth. **–stück,** *n.* loin, fillet, undercut, (*Am.*) tenderloin. **–wirbel,** *m.* lumbar vertebra.

Lenk|achse, *f.* steering axle. **–ballon,** *m.* dirigible (balloon). **lenkbar,** *adj.* steerable, manoeuvrable, manageable, controllable, (*of airship*) dirigible; (*fig.*) manageable, tractable, docile.

lenken ['lɛŋkən], *v.t.* turn, guide, direct; (*Motor.*) drive, steer, (*Naut.*) navigate, pilot; govern, rule, lead, control, manage; turn (***in*** (*Acc.*), into); ***einen Wagen –,*** drive a car; ***die Schritte –,*** wend one's way, turn one's steps, turn, go (***nach,*** towards); ***das Gespräch auf einen Gegenstand –,*** turn the conversation round to a subject; ***die Aufmerksamkeit auf sich –,*** attract attention, call *or* draw attention to o.s.; (*Prov.*) ***der Mensch denkt, Gott lenkt,*** man proposes, God disposes; ***gelenkte Wirtschaft,*** planned economy. **Lenker,** *m.* ruler, disposer, (*Motor.*) driver.

Lenk|gehäuse, *n.* steering gear housing. **–knüppel,** *m.* (*Av.*) (*coll.*) joy-stick. **–rad,** *n.* 1. (*Motor.*) steering-wheel; 2. (*Cycl.*) front wheel. **–rolle,** *f.* caster. **lenksam,** *adj. See* **lenkbar. Lenk|säule,** *f.* steering column. **–seil,** *n.* guide-rope. **–stange,** *f.* (*Motor.*) tie-rod; *pl.* steering suspension, (*Cycl.*) handle-bars. **–stelle,** *f.* planning office.

Lenkung ['lɛŋkuŋ], *f.* controlling, steering; guidance, control, direction, governing; management, planning; (*Motor.*) steering assembly.

[1]**Lenz** [lɛnts], *m.* (**-es,** *pl.* **-e**) (*Poet.*) spring; (*fig.*) prime, bloom (*of life*); *pl.* years (*of age*).

[2]**Lenz,** *f.* (*Austr.*) indolence; leisure.

lenz, *adj.* (*dial.*) dry, empty.

[1]**lenzen** ['lɛntsən], *v.imp.* (*Poet.*) become spring; ***es lenzt,*** spring comes.

[2]**lenzen,** 1. *v.t.* pump (*bilges*), blow (*tanks of submarine*). 2. *v.i.* (*Naut.*) run before the wind, scud.

[3]**lenzen,** *v.i.* (*Austr.*) laze, be idle; lounge, loaf.

Lenzing ['lɛntsɪŋ], **Lenzmond,** *m.* (*Poet.*) March.

Lenzpumpe ['lɛntspumpə], *f.* bilge-pump.

Leopard [leo'part], *m.* (**-en,** *pl.* **-en**) leopard, panther.

Lepra ['le:pra], *f.* leprosy. **Leprakranke(r),** *m., f.* leper.

Lerche ['lɛrçə], *f.* (*Orn.*) *see* **Feldlerche**; (*fig.*) ***eine – schießen,*** take a toss, fall head over heels; ***–n streichen,*** catch larks with a net. **Lerchen|falke,** *m.* (*Orn.*) *see* **Baumfalke. –garn,** *n.* net for catching larks. **–spornammer,** *f.* (*Orn.*) *see* **Spornammer. –strandläufer,** *m.* (*Orn.*) Temminck's stint (*Calidris temminckii*). **–streichen,** *n.* netting of larks. **–strich,** *m.* flight *or* migration of larks.

Lernbegier(de) ['lɛrnbəgi:r(də)], *f.* studiousness. **lernbegierig,** *adj.* studious, eager to learn. **Lern|eifer,** *m.* zest for learning; *see* **–begier(de).**

lernen ['lɛrnən], *v.t., v.i.* learn; study; (*dial., coll.*) teach; (*coll.*) serve one's apprenticeship *or* one's time (***bei,*** with); ***ich habe vieles entbehren*** – or ***gelernt,*** I have learnt to do without many things; ***lesen –,*** learn reading *or* to read; ***schätzen –,*** come to esteem; ***gelernt,*** trained, expert, skilled. **Lernen,** *n.* learning, study; ***das – wird ihm schwer,*** he learns with difficulty. **lernfähig,** *adj.* amenable to instruction, teachable. **Lern|freiheit,** *f.* uncontrolled study (*as in German universities*). **–schwester,** *f.* student nurse. **–zeit,** *f.* time for study; apprenticeship.

Lesart ['le:sˀart], *f.* version, reading; ***kritischer Text mit allen abweichenden –en,*** critical text with all variants. **lesbar,** *adj.* 1. legible, decipherable; 2. readable, worth reading. **Lesbarkeit,** *f.* legibility.

lesbisch ['lɛsbɪʃ], *adj.* Lesbian.

Lese ['le:zə], *f.* gleaning, gathering, collecting; (*of wine*) vintage; (*fig.*) gatherings, harvest.

Lese|abstand, *m.* reading-distance. **–brille,** *f.* reading-glasses. **–buch,** *n.* reading-book, reader.

–fibel, *f.* primer, first reader. **–freund,** *m.* great reader. **–früchte,** *f.pl.* anthology of selections. **–gesellschaft,** *f.* book-club. **–glas,** *n.* reading-glass. **–halle,** *f.* reading-room. **lesehungrig,** *adj.* avid for reading-matter. **Lese|kränzchen,** *n.*, **–kreis,** *m.* reading-circle. **–lampe,** *f.* reading-lamp. **–lupe,** *f. See* **–glas.**

[1]**lesen** ['le:zən], *irr.v.t., v.i.* read; (*Univ.*) lecture, give lectures (*über* (*Acc.*), on); ***ihm den Text*** or ***die Epistel*** or ***ein Kapitel*** or ***die Leviten –,*** haul him over the coals, give him a dressing down, read him the riot act; ***die Messe –,*** say mass; ***für sich –,*** read to o.s.; ***sich leicht – lassen,*** be easily read, be very readable; ***das Buch liest sich gut,*** the book is *or* makes interesting reading *or* is very readable; ***seine Schrift ist nicht zu –,*** his handwriting is unreadable *or* illegible; ***was liest du aus diesem Briefe?*** what do you make of this letter? (*Univ.*) ***heute wird nicht gelesen,*** there are no lectures today.

[2]**lesen,** *irr.v.t.* glean, gather; pick (over), sort; ***Ähren –,*** glean; ***den Acker –,*** clear the ground of stones; ***Wein –,*** gather grapes.

[1]**Lesen,** *n.* reading; lecturing.

[2]**Lesen,** *n.* gleaning, gathering, picking.

lesens|wert, –würdig, *adj.* worth reading.

Lese|probe, *f.* 1. (*Theat.*) rehearsal; 2. sample text, extract (*in a bookseller's catalogue*). **–pult,** *n.* reading-desk, lectern.

[1]**Leser** ['le:zər], *m.* reader.

[2]**Leser,** *m.* gleaner; vintager.

Leseratte ['le:zəʔratə], *f.* (*coll.*) bookworm.

[1]**Leserin** ['le:zərɪn], *f. See* [1]**Leser.**

[2]**Leserin,** *f. See* [2]**Leser.**

Leser|karte, *f.* reader's ticket, library ticket. **–kreis,** *m.* readers (*collect.*), public (*for newspapers and periodicals*). **leserlich,** *adj.* legible. **Leserlichkeit,** *f.* legibility. **Leserschaft,** *f. See* **Leserkreis.**

Lese|saal, *m.* reading-room. **–stoff,** *m.* reading-matter. **–stücke,** *n.pl.* selections for reading. **–stunde,** *f.* reading-lesson. **–welt,** *f.* reading public. **–zeichen,** *n.* book-mark(er). **–zimmer,** *n.* reading-room. **–zirkel,** *m. See* **–gesellschaft, –kreis.**

Lesung ['le:zuŋ], *f.* reading; ***der Gesetzentwurf kam zur zweiten –,*** the bill came up for a second reading.

Lette ['lɛtə], *m.* (**-n,** *pl.* **-n**) Latvian, Lett.

Letten ['lɛtən], *m.* potter's clay, loam.

Letter ['lɛtər], *f.* (-, *pl.* **-n**) letter, character; type; ***lateinische (deutsche) –n,*** Roman (Gothic) type. **Lettern|druck,** *m.* printing, letterpress. **–gut,** *n. See* **–metall. –kasten,** *m.* lower case. **–metall,** *n.* type-metal. **–setzmaschine,** *f.* monotype machine.

Lettin ['lɛtɪn], *f. See* **Lette. lettisch,** *adj.* Latvian. **Lettland,** *n.* Latvia.

Lettner ['lɛtnər], *m.* rood-loft, rood screen (*between nave and choir in church*).

letzen ['lɛtsən], *v.t.* (*Poet.*) gratify, refresh, comfort; ***sich – (an einer S.),*** enjoy *or* relish (a th.).

letzt [lɛtst], *adj.* 1. last, latest, ultimate, final; extreme; ***im –en Augenblick,*** at the last moment, at the eleventh hour; ***–er Ausweg,*** last resort; ***–en Endes,*** after all, ultimately, in the last analysis, when all's said and done; ***–e Erklärung,*** ultimatum; ***–e Hand,*** see ***–er Schliff;*** ***auf dem –en Loch pfeifen,*** be on one's last legs; ***in den –en Jahren,*** in recent years; ***bis auf den –en Mann,*** to a man, to the last man; ***–en Mittwoch,*** last Wednesday; (*Comm.*) ***–en Monats,*** ultimo; ***–e Nachrichten,*** latest *or* stop-press news; (*R.C.*) ***–e Ölung,*** extreme unction; ***bis auf den –en Platz gefüllt,*** filled to capacity, packed; ***–er Schliff,*** final *or* finishing touch; (*coll.*) ***der –e Schrei sein,*** be the latest *or* all the rage; ***das –e Wort behalten,*** have the last word; ***in –er*** or ***der –en Zeit,*** of late, recently, lately; ***in den –en Zügen liegen,*** be breathing one's last, be at death's door; 2. ***der, die, das Letzte,*** (the) last one *or* th.; ***der Letzte (in) der Klasse,*** bottom in *or* of the class; ***den Letzten beißen die Hunde,*** devil take the hindmost; ***das Letzte,*** the last thing, the end, the last extremity; ***der Letzte des Monats,*** the last (day) of the month; ***sein Letztes hergeben,*** do one's utmost, give of one's best, make an all-out effort; ***er gäbe das Letzte hin,*** he would sacrifice everything *or* his all; ***zu guter Letzt,*** finally, last but not least, to sum up, to cap it all.

letztens ['lɛtstəns], *adv.* finally, lastly, in the last place; lately, of late, latterly, the other day, recently. **letztere(r, -s),** *adj.* (the) latter. **letzt|-erwähnt, –genannt,** *adj.* last-named *or* -mentioned, latter. **–hin, letztlich,** *adv. See* **letztens. letztwillig, 1.** *adj.* testamentary; ***–e Verfügung,*** last will and testament; ***ohne –e Verfügung gestorben,*** died intestate. **2.** *adv.* by will.

Leu [lɔy], *m.* (**-en,** *pl.* **-en**) (*Poet.*) lion.

Leucht|bake ['lɔyçt–], **–boje,** *f.* (*Naut.*) light-buoy. **–bombe,** *f.* (*Av.*) flare. **–draht,** *m.* (lamp *or* light) filament.

Leuchte ['lɔyçtə], *f.* luminary, light, lamp; (*Naut. etc.*) flare, beacon; (*fig.*) shining light, star.

leuchten ['lɔyçtən], *v.i.* shine (forth), light, illuminate; radiate, emit *or* give light; beam, gleam, glow, burn, glare, glimmer, sparkle; phosphoresce (*of the sea*); ***ihm die Treppe hinunter –,*** light him downstairs; ***in alle Winkel –,*** shine a light into all the corners; ***– auf*** (*Acc.*), shine on, illuminate; ***sein Auge leuchtete vor Zorn,*** his eyes flashed *or* blazed with anger. **Leuchten,** *n.* shining, light, gleam, glare, glow, illumination, coruscation; phosphorescence, luminosity. **leuchtend,** *adj.* shining, brilliant, bright, luminous, lustrous; ***ein –es Beispiel,*** an illuminating example. **Leuchter,** *m.* candlestick, chandelier, lustre. **Leuchter|arm,** *m.* branch of a chandelier. **–krone,** *f.* chandelier, lustre.

Leucht|fackel, *f.* flare. **–faden,** *m. See* **–draht. –fallschirm,** *m.* parachute-flare. **–farbe,** *f.* luminous paint. **–feuer,** *n.* (*Av.*) beacon, flare, (*Naut.*) light. **–gas,** *n.* coal gas (*for lighting*). **–geschoß,** *n.*, **–granate,** *f.* (*Mil.*) star-shell. **–käfer,** *m.* glow-worm, fire-fly. **–körper,** *n.* light, lamp. **–kraft,** *f.* luminosity, illuminating power. **–kugel,** *f.* fire-ball; (*Mil.*) star-shell, Very light. **–öl, –petroleum,** *n.* lamp oil, naphtha, kerosene. **–pfad,** *m.* (*Av.*) flare path. **–pistole,** *f.* Very pistol. **–rakete,** *f.* signal rocket. **–reklame,** *f.* neon lights *or* signs. **–röhre,** *f.* neon tube, fluorescent tube. **–schiff,** *n.* lightship. **–schirm,** *m.* fluorescent screen. **–skala,** *f.* luminous dial. **–spur,** *f.* (*Mil.*) tracer (fire). **–spurgeschoß,** *n.*, **–spurgranate,** *f.* tracer shell. **–stab,** *m.* flashlamp, torch. **–stein,** *m.* Bologna-stone; lithophosphor. **–stoff,** *m.* luminous matter. **–stofflampe,** *f.* fluorescent lamp. **–stoffröhre,** *f.* fluorescent tube. **–tonne,** *f. See* **–bake. –turm,** *m.* lighthouse. **–uhr,** *f.* luminous clock *or* watch. **–zifferblatt,** *n. See* **–skala.**

leugnen ['lɔygnən], *v.t.* deny; disavow, disclaim, contest, gainsay; ***nicht zu –,*** undeniable; ***das Gesagte –,*** eat one's words. **Leugnen,** *n.*, **Leugnung,** *f.* disavowal, denial, disclaimer.

Leukämie [lɔykɛ'mi:], *f.* (*Med.*) leukaemia.

Leukoplast [lɔyko'plast], *n.* adhesive tape.

Leukozyten [lɔyko'tsy:tən], *pl.* (*Anat.*) leukocytes.

Leumund ['lɔymunt], *m.* reputation, repute, character; ***guter –,*** good name. **Leumundszeugnis,** *n.* testimonial, certificate of good conduct, character reference.

Leute ['lɔytə], *pl.* people, persons, folk, men, the (general) public, the world; servants, domestics; hands, rank and file, men; ***meine –,*** my folks; ***– von Stand,*** gentlefolk, persons of standing *or* quality; ***vor allen –n,*** openly, publicly, before all the world; ***unter die – gehen*** or ***kommen,*** mix with people, get about; ***unter die – bringen,*** spread abroad, make widely known; ***es fehlt ihm an –n, er hat nicht genug –,*** he is short-handed; ***er kennt seine –,*** he knows whom he has to deal with, he is a good judge of character; ***wir sind geschiedene –,*** it is all over between us; ***Kleider machen –,*** clothes make the man. **Leute|schinder,** *m.* extortioner, bloodsucker, slave-driver. **–stube,** *f.* servants' quarters.

Leutnant ['lɔytnant], *m.* (**-s,** *pl.* **-s** (*Austr.* **-e**)) (*Mil.*) second lieutenant, (*Av.*) pilot officer; – ***zur See,*** sub-lieutenant.

Leutpriester ['lɔytpri:stər], *m.* (*Swiss*) lay priest.

leutselig ['lɔytze:lɪç], *adj.* affable, genial, familiar, condescending. **Leutseligkeit,** *f.* affability, geniality, good nature, familiarity, condescension.

Levit [le'vi:t], *m.* (**-en,** *pl.* **-en**) Levite; ***ihm die*** (*Austr.* ***den***) ***-en lesen,*** lecture him, give him a good dressing down, haul him over the coals.

Levkoje [lɛf'ko:jə], *f.* (*Bot.*) gillyflower, stock (*Matthiola incana*).

Lexikalien [lɛksi'ka:liən], *pl.* lexicographical *or* lexical material. **lexikalisch,** *adj.* lexical, lexicographical. **Lexikograph** [–ko'gra:f], *m.* (**-en,** *pl.* **-en**) lexicographer. **Lexikon** ['lɛksikɔn], *n.* (**-s,** *pl.* **-ka** *or* **-ken**) dictionary, (en)cyclopaedia; ***ein wandelndes –,*** a walking encyclopaedia.

Libanese [liba'ne:zə], *m.* (**-n,** *pl.* **-n**), **libanesisch,** *adj.* Lebanese. **Libanon** ['li:banɔn], *m.* (*Geog.*) Lebanon.

Libell [li'bɛl], *n.* (**-s,** *pl.* **-e**) libel.

Libelle [li'bɛlə], *f.* 1. (*Ent.*) dragonfly; 2. (*Mech.*) spirit-level.

Libellist [libɛ'lɪst], *m.* (**-en,** *pl.* **-en**) libeller, lampooner.

licht [lɪçt], *adj.* light, shining, bright, luminous, clear; thin, sparse, open; ***-er Augenblick,*** lucid interval; ***-er Durchmesser,*** inside diameter; ***-e Fassung,*** open setting (*jewels*); ***-e Höhe,*** clearance, headroom (*bridges etc.*); ***-e Maschen,*** wide mesh; ***am -en Tag,*** in broad daylight; ***-e Weite,*** width in the clear; – ***werden,*** grow clear; get light; ***-e Zukunft,*** bright future.

[1]**Licht,** *n.* (**-(e)s,** *pl.* **-er**) 1. light, illumination, lighting; (*Art*) highlight; ***ans – bringen,*** bring to light, divulge; ***– bringen in*** (*Acc.*), throw *or* shed light on; ***ans – kommen,*** come to light, become known; ***jetzt geht mir ein – auf,*** now I (begin to) see, now it dawns *or* begins to dawn on me; ***ihm ein – aufstecken über*** (*Acc.*), open his eyes to, (*coll.*) put him wise to; ***ihm aus dem – gehen,*** stand *or* get out of his light; ***bei -e,*** by day, in daylight; ***bei -e besehen*** or ***betrachtet,*** looked at closely, on closer inspection; strictly speaking, on careful consideration; ***hinters – führen,*** humbug, hoodwink, deceive, dupe, impose on, (*coll.*) take in; ***in milderndem – sehen,*** see through rose-tinted spectacles; ***in ein falsches – setzen*** or ***stellen*** or ***rücken,*** misrepresent; ***ihm*** (or ***sich*** (*Dat.*) ***selbst***) ***im – stehen,*** stand in his (*or* one's own) light; – ***machen,*** strike a light, switch on the light(s); (*Prov.*) ***wo viel – ist, ist starker Schatten,*** the brighter the light, the deeper the shadow; ***sein – unter den Scheffel stellen,*** hide one's light under a bushel; ***ein schlechtes – werfen auf*** (*Acc.*), reflect on, cast a reflection on; ***das – der Welt erblicken,*** see the light of day; (*B.*) ***es werde –!*** let there be light! ***sich im wahren – zeigen,*** show one's true colours; ***im besten – zeigen,*** show up to the best advantage; 2. luminary; ***er ist ein großes –,*** he is an outstanding figure; ***er ist kein großes –,*** he is no great shining light; 3. (*dial.*) opening, window; 4. *pl.* (*Hunt.*) eyes (*of game*).

[2]**Licht,** *n.* (**-(e)s,** *pl.* **-e** (*Austr.* **-er**)) candle, taper, dip.

Licht|anlage, *f.* lighting plant *or* system. **-bad,** *n.* (*Med.*) solar bath, insolation. **-behandlung,** *f.* sun-ray treatment. **lichtbeständig,** *adj.* fast to light, non-fading. **Licht|beugung,** *f.* refraction (of light). **-bild,** *n.* photograph; (lantern-)slide. **-bilderkundung,** *f.* (*Mil.*) photographic reconnaissance. **-bildervortrag,** *m.* lantern-lecture. **-bildner,** *m.* photographer. **-bildung,** *f.* production of light, photogenesis. **lichtblau** (*etc.*), *adj.* pale *or* light blue (*etc.*). **Licht|blende,** *f.* (*Phot.*) stop. **-blick,** *m.* ray of hope. **lichtblond,** *adj.* ash-blond. **Licht|bogen,** *m.* (*Elec.*) arc. **-bogenbildung,** *f.* (*Elec.*) arcing. **lichtbrechend,** *adj.* refracting, refractive, dioptric. **Licht|brechung,** *f.* refraction (of light). **-bündel, -büschel,** *n.* light-beam, pencil of light. **lichtdicht,** *adj.* light-proof, light-tight. **Lichtdruck,** *m.* (*Typ.*) phototype, collotype. **licht|durchlässig,** *adj.* transparent, translucent. **-echt,** *adj. See* **-beständig. -elektrisch,** *adj.* photo-electric. **-empfindlich,** *adj.* sensitive to light; (*Phot.*) sensitized; – ***machen,*** sensitize. **Lichtempfindlichkeit,** *f.* (*Phot.*) sensitivity, speed.

[1]**lichten** ['lɪçtən], 1. *v.t.* thin out, clear (*a wood*), thin (*the ranks*). 2. *v.r.* grow *or* get thinner; get brighter *or* clearer, clear up.

[2]**lichten,** *v.t.* lighten, unload, (*Naut.*) weigh (*anchor*).

[1]**Lichter** ['lɪçtər], *m.* (*Naut.*) lighter, barge.

[2]**Lichter,** *pl. of* [1]**Licht. Lichterbaum,** *m.* Christmas tree. **lichterloh,** *adv.* blazing, ablaze, in full blaze; – ***brennen,*** be ablaze. **Lichtermeer,** *n.* sea of light(s).

Licht|erscheinung, *f.* optical phenomenon. **-farbendruck,** *m.* (*Typ.*) photomechanical colour-print(ing). **lichtfarbig,** *adj.* pale *or* light coloured. **Licht|filter,** *m.* (*Phot.*) light filter. **-form,** *f.* mould for candles. **-geschwindigkeit,** *f.* velocity of light. **-gießer,** *m.* chandler. **-glanz,** *m.* lustre, brightness. **-heilverfahren,** *n. See* **-behandlung. lichthell,** *adj.* lit *or* lighted up; very bright. **Licht|hieb,** *m.* clearing, thinning (*a wood*). **-hof,** *m.* well of a courtyard; (*Phot.*) halation. **lichthoffrei,** *adj.* (*Phot.*) non-halating. **-hütchen,** *n.* extinguisher. **-jahr,** *n.* (*Astr.*) light-year. **-kegel,** *m.* cone of light, searchlight beam. **-kranz,** *m.* corona (*of sun*). **-kreis,** *m.* halo. **-lehre,** *f.* optics. **-leitung,** *f.* lighting circuit. **-maschine,** *f.* (*Motor.*) dynamo, lighting generator. **-meß,** *f.* Candlemas. **-messen,** *n.* (*Artil.*) flash-spotting. **-messer,** *m.* photometer. **-nelke,** *f.* lychnis. **-pausapparat,** *m.* photographic copying apparatus. **-pause,** *f.* blue-print, photostatic reproduction. **-pausverfahren,** *n.* heliographic printing. **-punkt,** *m.* luminous point, focus; (*fig.*) ray (*of hope*). **-putze,** *f.* snuffers. **-quant,** *n.* (*Phys.*) photon. **-quelle,** *f.* source of light. **-reklame,** *f.* illuminated advertisement *or* advertising.

Licht|schacht, *m.* light-shaft. **-schalter,** *m.* light-switch. **-schein,** *m.* lustre, glow; gleam of light. **-schere,** *f. See* **-putze. lichtscheu,** *adj.* shunning the light, aphotic; (*fig.*) shady, furtive, skulking. **Licht|schirm,** *m.* lamp-shade, eye-protector, screen. **-schwingung,** *f.* light-wave. **-seite,** *f.* (*fig.*) bright side. **-signal,** *n.* traffic light; (*Naut.*) flare. **-spiel,** *n.* (cinematograph) film. **-spieltheater,** *n.* cinema, picture house, (*Am.*) motion picture theatre. **-spur,** *f.* luminous trail. **-spurgeschoß,** *n.* tracer bullet. **-stärke,** *f.* intensity of light, (*of electric lamp*) candlepower; (*Phot.*) speed. **-strahl,** *m.* ray, beam (*of light*), streamer (*of the aurora borealis*). **-strahlung,** *f.* radiation. **-stumpf,** *m.* candle-end. **-träger,** *m.* candle-holder, candlestick. **licht|umflossen,** *adj.* bathed in light, radiant. **-undurchlässig,** *adj.* opaque.

Lichtung ['lɪçtuŋ], *f.* clearing, glade.

Licht|weite, *f.* clearance, width in the clear. **-welle,** *f.* light-wave. **-zeichen,** *n.* illuminated sign. **-zelle,** *f.* photo-electric cell. **-zerstreuung,** *f.* dispersion of light. **-zieher,** *m.* chandler.

Lid [li:t], *n.* (**-(e)s,** *pl.* **-er**) lid, eyelid; ***die -er schließen,*** close one's eyes.

lidern ['li:dərn], *v.t.* (*obs.*) garnish *or* line *or* pack with leather. **Liderung,** *f.* 1. packing, washer, gasket; 2. (*Artil.*) gas check, obdurator.

lieb [li:p], *adj.* 1. dear, (dearly) beloved; charming, nice, (*coll.*) sweet; kind, good, well-behaved; ***das Kind ist gar zu –,*** the child really is too sweet for anything; ***er will sich – Kind bei mir machen,*** he is trying to ingratiate himself with me *or* to curry favour with me; ***wenn Ihnen Ihr Leben – ist,*** as you value your life; ***das ist aber – von Ihnen,*** that is indeed most kind of you; (*coll.*) ***mein Lieber,*** my dear fellow; ***meine Liebe,*** my dear woman *or* girl; ***meine Lieben,*** my beloved ones; dear friends! ***etwas Liebes,*** anything *or* something pleasing; ***ihm Liebes und Gutes tun*** or ***erweisen,*** be very kind to him; ***ich weiß nur Liebes von ihm,*** I can only speak well of him; 2. (*when used as pred.*) pleasant, attractive, agreeable; ***es ist mir –, daß,*** I am glad that; ***es***

ist mir nicht –, I am sorry, I regret; *es wäre mir –,* I should appreciate it, I should be glad; *das wäre Ihnen gewiß nicht –,* you would not like that, I'm sure; *es mag ihm – oder leid sein,* whether he likes it or not; 3. (*also used pleonastically in familiar phrases*), *e.g.* ***um das –e Brot arbeiten,*** work for one's bare subsistence; ***unsere –e Frau,*** Our Lady, the Virgin Mary; ***um des –en Friedens willen,*** for the sake of peace and quiet; ***der –e Gott,*** God (Almighty); ***das weiß der –e Himmel,*** heaven only knows; ***wir haben unsere –e Not mit ihm,*** he causes us no end of trouble; ***den –en lang Tag,*** the live-long day; ***du –e Zeit!*** dear me! good gracious! ***ums –e Leben rennen,*** run for dear life.

liebäugeln ['li:pˀɔygəln], *v.i.* (*insep.*) – ***mit,*** ogle, (*sl.*) give (*a p.*) the glad eye; toy, flirt (*with an idea*). **Liebchen,** *n.* sweetheart, pet, darling, love. **Liebden,** *f.* (*obs. form of address among sovereigns*) ***Euer –,*** my dear prince.

Liebe ['li:bə], *f.* 1. love (***zu, für,*** of *or* for), affection, fondness, liking (for); ***in – und Leid,*** in joy and sorrow, for better or for worse; ***abgöttische –,*** idolatry; ***aus –,*** for love; ***aus – zu.*** for love of; ***kindliche –,*** filial love *or* piety; ***christliche –,*** christian charity, love for others; ***– zum Vaterlande,*** love for one's country; ***ein Kind der –,*** a love-child, an illegitimate child; ***mit Lust und – tun,*** do with all one's heart; (*Prov.*) ***alte – rostet nicht,*** old love is never forgotten; (*Prov.*) ***– macht erfinderisch,*** love will find out a way, love laughs at locksmiths; 2. kindness, favour; ***tun Sie mir die –,*** do me the favour, have the kindness (*to do*), oblige me (*by doing*); (*Prov.*) ***eine – ist der andern wert,*** one good turn deserves another; 3. beloved, love; ***eine alte –,*** an old sweetheart *or* (*coll.*) flame.

liebebedürftig ['li:bəbədyrftɪç], *adj.* craving for love. **Liebe|diener,** *m.* time-server. **–dienerei,** *f.* cringing servility, obsequiousness, fawning, toadyism. **liebe|dienerisch,** *adj.* servile, obsequious, cringing, fawning, grovelling. **–dienern,** *v.i.* cringe, fawn, grovel, toady. **–leer,** *adj.* loveless, lacking in love.

Liebelei [li:bə'laɪ], *f.* (-, *pl.* **-en**) flirtation, dalliance. **liebeln** ['li:bəln], *v.i.* flirt, dally (***mit,*** with).

lieben ['li:bən], **1.** *v.t.* love, be in love with; be attached to, be fond of, like; fancy, cherish (*an idea etc.*); ***sich –,*** be in love with *or* love each other; ***meine geliebte Frau,*** my dearly beloved wife. **2.** *v.i.* be in love. **liebend,** *adj.* loving, fond, affectionate; ***Deine Dich –e Schwester,*** your loving *or* affectionate sister; ***Dein Dich –er Wilhelm,*** yours affectionately, William; ***die beiden Liebenden,*** the two lovers, the loving couple. **liebens|wert,** *adj.* lovable. **–würdig,** *adj.* kind, amiable, obliging, charming. **–würdigerweise,** *adv.* kindly. **Liebenswürdigkeit,** *f.* 1. amiability, kindness, charm; 2. compliment, kind words.

lieber ['li:bər], **1.** *comp. adj. See* **lieb. 2.** *adv.* (*comp. of* **gern**) rather, sooner; ***je länger je –,*** the longer the better; ***ich täte es – selbst,*** I would rather do it myself; ***es ist mir –, ich habe*** or ***mag es –,*** I prefer (it); ***– sterben als leiden,*** better die than suffer; ***um so –, weil,*** the more so since; ***es ist mir um so –,*** I like it all the better.

Liebes|abenteuer, *n.* love-affair, romance, liaison, intrigue. **–angelegenheiten,** *f.pl.* love-affairs, affairs of the heart. **–antrag,** *m.* proposal. **–apfel,** *m.* (*obs.*) tomato. **–band,** *n.* bond of love. **–bedürfnis,** *n.* desire for love. **–blick,** *m.* loving glance. **–bote,** *m.* harbinger of love. **–brief,** *m.* love-letter. **–dienst,** *m.* good turn, kind act, act of kindness; ***ihm einen – erweisen,*** do him a good turn *or* a kindness. **–erklärung,** *f.* declaration of love; ***eine – machen,*** declare one's love. **–erlebnis,** *n.* romance; sexual experience, (*coll.*) affair. **–gabe,** *f.* gift parcel; *pl.* comforts (*for troops*). **–gedicht,** *n.* love-poem. **–genuß,** *m.* sexual indulgence. **–geschichte,** *f.* love-story; love-affair, romance. **–geständnis,** *n.* protestation of love. **–glück,** *n.* success in love, lover's bliss. **–glut,** *f.* ardour, amorous rapture. **–gott,** *m.* Cupid, Amor, Eros; *pl.* (*Archit.*) amoretti, cupids, putti. **–göttin,** *f.* Venus, Aphrodite. **–handel,** *m. See* **–abenteuer.** **–heirat,** *f.* love-match. **–knoten,** *m.* lovers' knot. **liebeskrank,** *adj.* love-sick, love-lorn. **Liebes|kummer,** *m.* heartache, a broken heart. **–künste,** *f.pl.* techniques of love-making. **–leben,** *n.* love-life, sex-life, sexual experience. **–lied,** *n.* love-song.

Liebes|mahl, *n.* love-feast, agape; banquet; regimental dinner. **–mühe,** *f.* ***Verlorene –,*** Love's Labour's Lost (*Shakespeare*), (*fig.*) vain *or* fruitless *or* futile efforts. **–paar,** *n.* lovers, (courting) couple. **–pfand,** *n.* love-token; pledge of love; (*Poet.*) child. **–pfeil,** *m.* love-dart, Cupid's dart. **–pflicht,** *f.* Christian duty. **–qual,** *f.* pangs of love. **–rausch,** *m.* overwhelming passion, transport of love. **–ritter,** *m.* knight-errant; gay Lothario, Don Juan. **–roman,** *m.* love-story, romance; erotic novel. **–schwur,** *m.* lover's pledge. **–sehnsucht,** *f.* love-sickness. **–spiel,** *n.* amorous play, dalliance, flirtation. **–stöckel,** *m.* (*Bot.*) lovage (*Levisticum officinale*). **–szene,** *f.* (*Theat.*) love-scene. **–trank,** *m.* love-potion, philtre. **liebestrunken,** *adj.* rapturous, crazed with love. **Liebes|verhältnis,** *n. See* **–abenteuer. –werben,** *n.*, **–werbung,** *f.* wooing, courtship. **–werk,** *n.* work of charity, Christian act. **–worte,** *n.pl.* loving words. **–zeichen,** *n.* love-token.

liebevoll ['li:bəfɔl], *adj.* loving, kind(-hearted), tender, affectionate.

Liebfrauen|kirche, *f.* church of Our Lady. **–milch,** *f.* a (kind of) choice Rhenish wine, Liebfraumilch.

lieb|gewinnen, *irr.v.t.* (*sep.*) take a fancy to, get to like, grow fond of. **–haben,** *irr.v.t.* (*sep.*) be fond of, like; love.

Liebhaber ['li:pha:bər], *m.* 1. lover, admirer, gallant, beau, sweetheart; (*Theat.*) ***erster –,*** hero; (*Theat.*) ***jugendlicher –,*** juvenile lead; 2. dilettante, amateur; fancier; ***– finden,*** find buyers. **Liebhaberausgabe,** *f.* edition de luxe. **Liebhaberei** [–'raɪ], *f.* fondness, fancy, passion, liking (***für,*** for), inclination, partiality (for *or* to), hobby, favourite amusement; dilettantism. **Liebhaber|konzert,** *n.* amateur concert. **–preis,** *m.* fancy price. **–rolle,** *f.* (*Theat.*) lover's part. **–theater,** *n.* private *or* studio theatre; amateur theatricals, dramatic club. **–wert,** *m.* collector's value, sentimental value.

liebkosen ['li:pko:zən], *v.t.* (*insep.*) pet, caress, fondle, cuddle, hug. **Liebkosung,** *f.* caress, cuddle, hug; caressing, fondling, cuddling, hugging, petting.

lieblich ['li:plɪç], *adj.* lovely; charming, delightful, delicious; winsome, pleasing, sweet. **Lieblichkeit,** *f.* charm, loveliness, sweetness, winsomeness, pleasantness.

Liebling ['li:plɪŋ], *m.* (**-s,** *pl.* **-e**) darling, dear; favourite, pet. **Lieblings|beschäftigung,** *f.* favourite occupation, hobby. **–gedanke,** *m.*, **–idee,** *f.* pet idea. **–nahrung,** *f.* favourite food.

lieblos ['li:plo:s], *adj.* unloving, unkind, hard-hearted, cold; careless, (*coll.*) slap-happy. **Lieblosigkeit,** *f.* uncharitableness, unkindness, coldness. **liebreich,** *adj.* loving, affectionate, tender; amiable, kind. **Liebreiz,** *m.* charm, attractiveness. **liebreizend,** *adj.* charming, winning. **Liebschaft,** *f.* 1. love-affair, liaison, amour; ***flüchtige –,*** flirtation; 2. sweetheart, (*coll.*) flame.

liebst [li:pst], **1.** *sup. adj. See* **lieb**; ***meine –e Beschäftigung,*** my favourite occupation; ***der*** or ***die Liebste,*** dearest, beloved, lover, love, sweetheart; ***das Liebste,*** the most precious th. **2.** *adv. sup. of* **gern**; ***das esse ich am –en,*** this is my favourite dish; ***am –en haben,*** love or like best.

Liebstöckel [li:pʃtœkəl], *m. See* **Liebesstöckel.**

lieb|tätig, *adj.* charitable, beneficent. **–wert,** *adj.* (*obs.*) highly esteemed, beloved.

Lied [li:t], *n.* (**-(e)s,** *pl.* **-er**) song; air, tune; poem, ditty; ***geistliches –,*** hymn, psalm; ***das Hohe – (Salomonis),*** Song of Solomon, Song of Songs; ***immer das alte –,*** always the same old story; ***davon kann ich auch ein – singen,*** there's s.th. I can tell you about that; (*Prov.*) ***wes Brot einer ißt, des – er singt,*** never quarrel with your bread and butter; ***ein anderes – anstimmen,*** change one's tune; ***das –***

ist aus, it is all over; *das Ende vom –e,* the end of the matter, the upshot.

Lieder|abend, *m.* ballad concert, song recital. **–buch,** *n.* song-book; hymn-book. **–dichter,** *m.* lyric poet; song writer. **–kranz,** *m. See* **–tafel.**

liederlich ['li:dərlɪç], *adj.* slovenly, disorderly; lewd, debauched, dissipated, dissolute, immoral, loose; (*dial.*) wretched, miserable; *–er Mensch* or *Kerl* or *Patron* or *Bruder,* rake, loose-liver, debauchee; *–e Person,* sloven, slut; loose woman. **Liederlichkeit,** *f.* slovenliness, disorderliness; debauchery, dissipation, dissoluteness, loose living, immoral conduct.

Lieder|sammlung, *f. See* **–buch. –sänger,** *m.* ballad singer. **–tafel,** *f.* glee club, choral society.

lief [li:f], **liefe,** *see* **laufen.**

Lieferant [li:fə'rant], *m.* **(-en,** *pl.* **-en)** supplier, distributor, purveyor; contractor; caterer. **lieferbar** ['li:fərba:r], *adj.* available (for delivery), in supply. **Liefer|bedingungen,** *f.pl.* terms of delivery. **–frist,** *f. See* **–zeit. –gebühr,** *f.* delivery charge. **–gewicht,** *n.* net weight. **–hafen,** *m.* port of delivery. **–menge,** *f.* amount *or* quantity supplied.

liefern ['li:fərn], *v.t.* deliver, hand over (*Dat.,* **an** (*Acc.*), to), furnish, supply (*ihm etwas,* him with a th.), afford, yield, produce; *einen harten Kampf –,* put up a stiff fight; *ein Werk in Heften –,* publish a work in numbers; *einen Beweis –,* furnish proof; *eine Schlacht –,* give battle; *zu – an mich,* to be delivered to me; (*coll.*) *er ist geliefert,* he is lost *or* ruined *or* done for *or* (*sl.*) sunk.

Lieferschein ['li:fərʃaɪn], *m.* delivery note, receipt.

Lieferung ['li:fərʊŋ], *f.* delivery, supply, consignment; lot, parcel, carload, shipment, cargo; issue, part, number (*of a publication*); (*St. Exch.*) *auf –,* forward; *zahlbar bei –,* payment on delivery; *sofortige –,* for immediate delivery. **Lieferungs|-geschäft,** *n.* time bargain, futures; option deal. **–tag,** *m.* 1. *See* **Lieferzeit**; 2. (*St. Exch.*) settling-day. **–termin,** *m. See* **Lieferzeit. lieferungsweise,** *adv.* in parts *or* instalments, serially. **Lieferungs|werk,** *n.* serial publication. **–zustand,** *m.* condition on delivery, condition as received. (*For other compounds see under* **Liefer–**.)

Liefer|wagen, *m.* delivery van. **–zeit,** *f.* delivery-date; term for delivery.

Liege ['li:gə], *f.* couch, chaise-longue. **Liege|deck,** *n.* (*Naut.*) lounge deck. **–geld,** *n.* (*Naut.*) demurrage. **–hafen,** *m.* (*Naut.*) base. **–kur,** *f.* (*Med.*) rest-cure.

liegen ['li:gən], *irr.v.i.* (*aux.* h. *&* *dial.* s.) lie, be lying, rest, repose, be recumbent; be located, placed *or* situated, be; (*Mil.*) be stationed *or* quartered *or* billeted; *wie liegt die Sache?* what is the position? how does the matter stand? *wie die Sache liegt* or *die Dinge –,* as things *or* matters stand; *das liegt mir nicht,* that is not in my line, that doesn't suit me at all; *nichts liegt mir ferner,* nothing is further from my mind; (*coll.*) *da liegt der Hase im Pfeffer* or *der Hund begraben,* that's the snag *or* the stumbling-block, there you have it, that's the fly in the ointment; *krank –,* lie ill in bed; *gefangen –,* lie in prison.
(*with preps.*) *– an* (*Dat.*), lie near *or* at, lie on (*a river*); (*fig.*) be due to, depend on; *woran liegt es daß . . .?* how does it come that . . .? what is the reason for *or* cause of . . .? *an wem liegt es?* whose fault is it? *es liegt nun einmal daran daß . . .,* that is due to the fact that . . .; *es liegt nichts daran,* it doesn't matter, it is of no consequence; *es liegt mir daran, es ist mir daran gelegen,* I am anxious (*to do*), I am concerned (*that . . .*); *es liegt mir sehr viel daran,* it means *or* matters a great deal *or* a lot to me; *soviel an mir liegt,* as far as (it) lies in my power, as far as I am concerned; *es liegt mir nichts daran,* that doesn't concern *or* interest me; *das liegt mir am Herzen,* it is of interest to me, I am deeply interested in that; *der Hund liegt an der Kette,* the dog is on the chain; *es liegt am Tage,* it is obvious *or* as clear as day; *auf Flaschen –,* be in bottles; *auf der Hand –,* be plain *or* obvious; *der Ton liegt auf der letzten Silbe,* the accent is on the last syllable; *ihm auf der Tasche –,* be a heavy expense *or* burden to him; *ihm auf der Zunge –,* be on the tip of his tongue; *es liegt schon hinter uns,* it is over *or* done with, that's past history; *es liegt schon darin,* it is implied; *es liegt in meiner Absicht,* it is my intention; *es liegt im Blute* or *in der Familie,* it runs in the blood *or* in the family; *das Pferd liegt schwer in der Faust,* the horse is hard-mouthed; *einander in den Haaren –,* be at loggerheads; *das liegt mir noch immer im Sinne,* I cannot get that out of my head *or* mind; *damit richtig –,* be on the right lines *or* track; *nach Osten –,* face east; *das Schiff liegt vor Anker,* the ship lies *or* rides at anchor; *klar vor Augen –,* be apparent; *vor einer Festung –,* besiege *or* invest a fortress; *zu Bett –,* be in bed, be confined to (one's) bed, be bedridden, keep one's bed, (*coll.*) be laid up; *ihm zur Last –,* be a burden *or* nuisance to him, importune him. *See also* **gelegen.**

liegenbleiben ['li:gənblaɪbən], *irr.v.i.* (*aux.* s.) stay *or* keep lying down; stay in bed, not get up; (*of a th.*) be neglected *or* forgotten *or* left behind, (*Comm.*) not sell, be left on one's hands, (*of work*) not get done, fall behind; (*of a boxer*) stay down, (*of a car*) break down; *unter der Last –,* sink under the burden.

liegend ['li:gənt], *adj.* recumbent, prostrate, prone, reclining, horizontal; situated; *–es Geld,* idle money; *–e Güter, see* **Liegenschaften**; *–e Schrift,* italics.

liegenlassen ['li:gənlasən], *irr.v.i.* let lie, neglect; forget, leave behind *or* lying about; abandon, give up; leave off, discontinue; let *or* leave alone; *links –,* neglect, disregard, by-pass (*a th.*), ignore, cut, cold-shoulder (*a p.*). **Liegenschaften,** *f.pl.* (*Law*) real estate, landed property, immovables. **Liegeplatz,** *m.* berth, staple (*of a ship*). **Lieger,** *m.* 1. ship lying up; 2. ship's caretaker; 3. large water butt. **Liege|stuhl,** *m.* deck-chair. **–stütz,** *m.* (*Gymn.*) push-up. **–wiese,** *f.* space for sun-bathing (*in open-air baths*). **–zeit,** *f.* time of lying (*of wine*); quarantine; (*Naut.*) lay days, days of demurrage.

lieh [li:], **liehe,** *see* **leihen.**

lies [li:s], **liesest,** *see* **lesen.**

ließ [li:s], **ließe,** *see* **lassen.**

liest [li:st], *see* **lesen.**

Lietze, *f.* (*Orn.*) *see* **Bläßhuhn.**

Lift [lɪft], *m.* **(-(e)s,** *pl.* **-e** *or* **-s)** lift, (*Am.*) elevator.

Liga ['li:ga], *f.* (-, *pl.* **-gen)** league. **Ligaspiel,** *n.* league-match.

Liguster [li'gʊstər], *m.* (*Bot.*) privet.

liieren [li'i:rən], *v.r.* ally, unite, combine (*mit,* with), become a partner (of), (*of the sexes*) take up (with).

Likör [li'kø:r], *m.* **(-s,** *pl.* **-e)** liqueur, (*coll.*) highball. **Likörbonbon,** *n.* brandy-ball.

Lila ['li:la], *n.* lilac (colour). **lila,** *adj.* lilac(-coloured), pale violet; (*coll.*) *es geht mir –,* I'm pretty well *or* not bad *or* so so. **Lilak,** *m.* **(-s,** *pl.* **-s)** (*Bot.*) lilac.

Lilie ['li:liə], *f.* lily; (*Her.*) fleur-de-lis. **lilienartig,** *adj.* liliaceous. **Lilienbaum,** *m.* magnolia. **lilienblaß,** *adj.* lily-white. **Lilienhaut,** *f.* lily-white skin. **lilien|weiß,** *adj. See* **–blaß.**

Limetta [li'mɛta], *f.* (-, *pl.* **-ten)** (*Bot.*) lime.

Limit ['lɪmɪt], *n.* **(-(e)s,** *pl.* **-e), Limite** [li'mi:tə], *f. See* **Limitum. limitieren** [–'ti:rən], *v.t.* limit, restrict, control (*prices*). **Limitum,** *n.* **(-s,** *pl.* **-ta)** (*Comm.*) fixed price, reserve price, price limit *or* ceiling.

Limonade [limo'na:də], *f.* lemonade, lemon squash, soft drink. **Limone** [–'mo:nə], *f.* citron; *süße –,* lime; *saure* or *eigentliche –,* lemon.

lind [lɪnt], (*Austr.* **linde**), *adj.* soft, gentle, mild.

Linde ['lɪndə], *f.* lime-tree, (*Poet.*) linden (tree). **linden,** *adj.* (made) of linden-wood. **Linden|-allee,** *f.* avenue of lime-trees. **–baum,** *m. See* **Linde. –blütentee,** *m.* lime-blossom tea.

lindern ['lɪndərn], *v.t.* mitigate, alleviate, soften, ease; soothe, allay, assuage, appease, palliate, relieve, temper, moderate. **Linderung,** *f.* alleviation, easing, softening, mitigation, palliation; relief, comfort. **Linderungsmittel,** *n.* palliative, anodyne.

Lindwurm [ˈlɪntvurm], *m.* (*Poet.*) dragon.

Lineal [lineˈaːl], *n.* (**-s,** *pl.* **-e**) rule(r), straight edge.

linear [lineˈaːr], *adj.* linear. **Linear|maßstab,** *m.* linear scale. **–zeichnung,** *f.* line-drawing, outline.

Linie [ˈliːniə], *f.* 1. line; (*Mil.*) rank; (*Naut.*) equator; (*Typ.*) (composing) rule; route, (*fig.*) trend, course, policy, party-line; ***punktierte –,*** dotted line; ***gestrichelte –,*** line of dashes; ***–n ziehen,*** draw lines, rule (*paper etc.*); ***in gerader –,*** in a straight line; as the crow flies, in the direct line; ***auf der ganzen –,*** all down *or* along the line; ***in der ersten –,*** in the first rank; ***in erster –,*** in the first place, first of all, above all, primarily; ***in letzter –,*** finally, in the last analysis; ***in vorderster –,*** in the front rank, in the firing line; ***auf gleicher – mit,*** on a level with, on the same footing as; ***eine mittlere – einschlagen*** or ***einhalten,*** follow a middle course; 2. lineage, descent, ancestry.

Linienblatt [ˈliːniənblat], *n.* lined sheet (*guide lines in writing*). **linienförmig,** *adj.* linear. **Linien|führung,** *f.* (*Tech.*) shape, form, outline; streamlining. **–papier,** *n.* ruled paper. **–richter,** *m.* (*Footb.*) linesman. **–schiff,** *n.* ship of the line, battleship. **–spannung,** *f.* (*Elec.*) line voltage. **linientreu,** *adj.* following the party-line. **Linien|truppen,** *f.pl.* troops of the line, regular troops, (*coll.*) regulars. **–umschalter,** *m.* (*Elec.*) commutator, switch.

linieren [liˈniːrən], **liniieren** [–niˈiːrən], *v.t.* rule (lines). **Lin(i)ierung,** *f.* ruling.

link [lɪŋk], *adj.* left; left-hand; (*Her.*) sinister; (*dial.*) left-handed; ***–e Seite,*** left-hand side, left; reverse *or* wrong side (*of cloth etc.*), reverse (*of coins*); near side (*of horse*), port (side) (*of ship*); ***mit dem –en Fuß zuerst aufstehen,*** get out of bed on the wrong side; ***sich zur –en Hand trauen lassen,*** contract a morganatic marriage. **Linke,** *f.* left hand, left; left wing, (*Pol.*) the Left; ***zur –n,*** on *or* to the left. **Linke(r),** *m.* left-handed blow *or* punch, left; ***gerader Linker,*** straight left.

linkisch [ˈlɪnkɪʃ], *adj.* awkward, clumsy, gauche.

links [lɪŋks], *adv.* 1. to the left, on the left; ***nach –,*** to the left; ***– schwenkt!*** left wheel! ***– um!*** left turn! (*Am.*) left face! ***– um kehrt!*** left about turn! ***– oben,*** top left (*of a picture*); ***– unten,*** bottom left; ***weder – noch rechts sehen,*** look neither to right nor to left; ***– fahren*** or ***gehen,*** keep to the left; (*Pol.*) ***– eingestellt sein, – stehen,*** be leftist *or* have left-wing sympathies; 2. wrong side out, inside out; on the wrong *or* reverse side; ***ihn – liegen lassen,*** give him the cold shoulder; ignore *or* cold-shoulder *or* bypass *or* cut him; (*coll.*) ***da sind Sie weit –,*** there you are wide of the mark *or* very much mistaken.

Links|außen(stürmer), *m.* (*Footb.*) outside left. **–drall,** *m.* counter-clockwise rifling (*of gun*), left-hand twist. **linksdrehend,** *adj.* laevorotatory, anti- *or* counter-clockwise. **Linksdrehung,** *f.* laevorotation, anti- *or* counter-clockwise rotation, (*Phys.*) left-handed polarization.

Linkser [ˈlɪŋksər], *m.* (*coll.*) *see* **Linkshänder.**

links|gängig, *adj.* *See* **–läufig. –gerichtet,** *adj.* (*Pol.*) leftist. **Links|gewinde,** *n.* left-handed (screw) thread. **–händer,** *m.* left-handed person. **links|händig,** *adj.* left-handed. **–herum,** *adv.* (round) to the left, anti- *or* counter-clockwise. **–läufig,** *adj.* anti- *or* counter-clockwise. **Linkspartei,** *f.* left-wing party. **linksradikal,** *adj.* (extreme) left-wing. **Links|radikale(r),** *m., f.* (extreme) left-winger. **–steuerung,** *f.* (*Motor.*) left-hand drive. **–stricken,** *n.* (*knitting*) purl (stitches). **–verkehr,** *m.* left-hand traffic.

Linnen [ˈlɪnən], *n.*, **linnen,** *adj.* linen. *See* **Leinen.**

Linoleum [liˈnoːleum], *n.* linoleum. **Linoleumschnitt,** *m.* lino-cut.

Linon [liˈnɔ̃ː], *m.* (**-s,** *pl.* **-s**) (French) lawn.

Linse [ˈlɪnzə], *f.* 1. lentil; 2. (*Opt.*) lens; 3. pendulum-bob; 4. (*sl.*) dough, tin. **linsenförmig,** *adj.* lenticular, lens-shaped. **Linsen|gericht,** *n.* pea soup; (*B.*) mess of pottage. **–paar,** *n.* paired lenses. **–weite,** *f.* aperture.

Lippe [ˈlɪpə], *f.* lip; (*Anat.*) labium; edge, border; ***es soll nicht über meine –n kommen,*** it shall not pass my lips, I won't breathe a word (of it); ***sich (auf) die –n beißen,*** bite one's lips (*in frustration*); ***die –n hängen lassen,*** mope, sulk; ***die –n aufwerfen*** or ***schürzen,*** curl one's lip (*in scorn*); sneer; (*coll.*) ***eine – riskieren,*** speak out of turn, (*sl.*) stick one's neck out; ***über die –n bringen,*** utter; ***an seinen –n hängen,*** hang on his words; ***die –n spitzen,*** purse one's lips; ***das Herz auf den –n haben,*** wear one's heart on one's sleeve; ***ihm auf den –n schweben,*** be on the tip of his tongue; (*Prov.*) ***zwischen Lipp' und Kelches Rand schwebt der finstern Mächte Hand,*** there's many a slip 'twixt cup and lip; ***von den –n lesen,*** lip-read (*by the deaf and dumb*).

Lippen|bekenntnis, *n.* *See* **–dienst. –blütler,** *m.* (*Bot.*) labiate flower. **–dienst,** *m.* lip-service. **lippenförmig,** *adj.* labiate. **Lippen|laut,** *m.* (*Phonet.*) labial. **–pomade,** *f.* lip-salve. **–stift,** *m.* lipstick.

lippig [ˈlɪpɪç], *adj.suff.* -lipped; *e.g.* ***dünnlippig,*** thin-lipped.

liquid [liˈkviːt], *adj.* (*Comm.*) unpaid, payable, due; ***–e Forderungen,*** debts due.

Liquida [ˈliːkvida], *f.* (-, *pl.* **-dä** *or* **-den**) (*Phonet.*) liquid (sound).

Liquidation [likvidatsiˈoːn], *f.* 1. charge, fee, costing; 2. liquidation, winding up (*of a business*). **Liquidations|guthaben,** *n.* clearing balance. **–wert,** *m.* realization value. **Liquidator** [–ˈdaːtɔr], *m.* (**-s,** *pl.* **-en**) liquidator, receiver (*in bankruptcy cases*). **liquidieren** [–ˈdiːrən], *v.t.* 1. liquidate, wind up, settle; 2. charge (*a fee*). **Liquidierung,** *f.* *See* **Liquidation.**

lismen [ˈlɪsmɛn], *v.t., v.i.* (*Swiss*) knit.

lispeln [ˈlɪspəln], *v.t., v.i.* 1. (have a) lisp; 2. whisper, murmur softly.

Lissabon [ˈlɪsabɔn], *n.* (*Geog.*) Lisbon.

List [lɪst], *f.* (-, *pl.* **-en**) cunning, craftiness, craft, artfulness; artifice, (underhand) trick, ruse, stratagem; (*Prov.*) ***– gegen*** or ***über –,*** diamond cut diamond.

Liste [ˈlɪstə], *f.* list, register, schedule, catalogue, inventory, (*Mil.*) roll, roster, (*Law*) panel (*of jurors*); ***schwarze –,*** black list; ***auf die schwarze – setzen,*** blacklist; ***eine – führen*** or ***aufstellen,*** draw up a list, keep a register; ***in eine – eintragen,*** enrol, register. **Listen|preis,** *m.* catalogue *or* list price. **–wahl,** *f.* 'ticket' election.

listig [ˈlɪstɪç], *adj.* cunning, crafty, artful, wily, sly, deceitful, (*coll.*) tricky.

Litanei [litaˈnaɪ], *f.* (-, *pl.* **-en**) 1. litany; – (***von Klagen***), jeremiad; 2. (*coll.*) rigmarole.

Litauen [ˈliːtauən], *n.* (*Geog.*) Lithuania. **Litauer,** *m.*, **litauisch,** *adj.* Lithuanian.

Liter [ˈliːtər], *n.* (*Austr., Swiss m.*) litre (= 1¾ pints).

literarisch [litəˈraːrɪʃ], *adj.* literary; ***–er Diebstahl,*** plagiarism; ***–es Eigentum,*** copyright. **Literat,** *m.* (**-en,** *pl.* **-en**) man of letters, literary man, writer; *pl.* literati.

Literatur [litəraˈtuːr], *f.* (-, *pl.* **-en**) 1. literature, letters; 2. bibliography. **Literatur|angaben,** *f.pl.* bibliographical data. **–beilage,** *f.* literary supplement. **–geschichte,** *f.* history of literature. **–historiker,** *m.* historian of literature. **–nachweis,** *m.*, **–verzeichnis,** *n.* bibliography, reading list, books consulted.

literweise [ˈliːtərvaɪzə], *adv.* by the litre.

Litewka [liˈtɛfka], *f.* (-, *pl.* **-ken**) battledress blouse *or* tunic.

Litfaßsäule [ˈlitfaszɔylə], *f.* advertisement pillar.

Lithographie [litograˈfiː], *f.* 1. lithograph; 2. lithography. **lithographieren,** *v.t.* lithograph. **lithographisch** [–ˈgraːfɪʃ], *adj.* lithographic.

litt [lɪt], **litte,** *see* **leiden.**

Liturgie [liturˈgiː], *f.* liturgy; responses. **liturgisch** [–ˈtuːrgɪʃ], *adj.* liturgical.

Litze [ˈlɪtsə], *f.* braid, cord, lace, piping; strand (*of* *wire*). **litzen,** *v.t.* (*Swiss*) fold *or* turn up. **Litzen|-besatz,** *m.* braiding; lace-trimming. **-draht,** *m.* stranded wire, flex.

Live-Sendung ['laɪf-], *f.* (*Rad., T.V.*) live broadcast.

Livius ['li:vius], *m.* Livy.

Livland ['li:flant], *n.* (*Geog.*) Livonia. **Livländer,** *m.*, **livländisch,** *adj.* Livonian.

Livorno [li'vorno], *n.* (*Geog.*) Leghorn.

Livree [li'vre:], *f.* livery. **Livreediener,** *m.* liveried servant, (*coll.*) buttons, (*Am.*) bellboy.

Lizentiat [litsɛntsi'a:t], *m.* (**-en,** *pl.* **-en**) licentiate.

Lizenz [li'tsɛnts], *f.* (-, *pl.* **-en**) licence, (*Am.*) license; concession; *in* **–**, under licence. **Lizenz|-bau,** *m.* licensed construction, manufacture under licence. **-gebühr,** *f.* licence-fee, royalty. **-inhaber,** *m.* licensee.

Lob [lo:p], *n.* praise, commendation, eulogy; approval, applause; fame, reputation; ***des -es voll,*** full of praise (*über* (*Acc.*), for); ***über alles – erhaben,*** above *or* beyond praise; ***zum -e*** (*Gen.*), in praise of; ***zu seinem -e,*** to his credit, in his praise; ***das gereicht ihm zum -e,*** that does him credit; ***Gott sei –!*** Heaven be praised!

Lobby ['lɔbi], *f.* *or* *m.* (*Parl.*) lobby. **Lobbyismus** [-i'ɪsmus], *m.* lobbying (*of M.P.s*).

loben ['lo:bən], *v.t.* praise, speak highly of, commend, eulogize, laud; (*B.*) glorify, extol; (*dial.*) value, estimate; ***das ist an ihm zu –,*** that is praiseworthy in him; ***über den grünen Klee –,*** laud to the skies; (*coll.*) ***ich lobe mir den Frieden!*** thank goodness for peace! (*coll.*) ***da lobe ich mir ein warmes Bett!*** there is nothing like a warm bed! ***das Werk lobt den Meister,*** the work reflects honour upon its maker; ***gelobt sei Gott!*** God be praised! **lobenswert,** *adj.* praiseworthy, laudable, commendable.

lobesam ['lo:bəza:m], *adj.* (*Poet.*) honourable, worthy; laudable; (*Poet.*) ***Kaiser Rotbart Lobesam,*** the noble emperor Frederic Barbarossa.

Lobeserhebung ['lo:bəsˀɛrhe:buŋ], *f.* high praise, eulogy, encomium.

Lob|gesang, *m.* song of praise, hymn of praise; panegyric. **-hudelei,** *f.* adulation, fulsome praise, base flattery. **lobhudeln,** *v.t.* (*insep.*) flatter, toady to, praise fulsomely *or* extravagantly. **Lobhudler,** *m.* toady, sycophant, flatterer.

löblich ['lø:plɪç], *adj.* praiseworthy, laudable, commendable; (*obs. as form of address*) worthy, honourable, estimable.

Lob|lied, *n.* *See* **-gesang. lobpreisen,** *irr.v.t.* (*insep.*) praise, sing the praises of, extol, eulogize. **Lob|preisung,** *f.* praise, glorification. **-rede,** *f.* panegyric, eulogy. **lobsingen,** *irr.v.i.* (*sep.*) (*B.*) sing praises (*Dat.*, to). **Lob|spruch,** *m.* *See* **-rede.**

Loch [lɔx], *n.* (**-es,** *pl.* **⸚er**) hole, cavity, opening, orifice, aperture; gap, breach; slot, pit; pore, eye; perforation, puncture; (*Bill.*) pocket; (*sl.*) quod, clink, jug; (*coll.*) den, hovel; (*Anat.*) foramen; (*vulg.*) arse; ***ihm ein – in den Bauch reden*** (or ***fragen***), pester him with one's chatter (*or* one's questions); ***sich*** (*Dat.*) ***ein – in den Bauch reden,*** talk one's head off, talk the hind legs off a donkey; (*Hunt.*) ***aus dem – jagen,*** draw, unearth (*fox etc.*); (*Bill.*) ***ins – spielen,*** pocket; (*coll.*) ***ihm zeigen wo der Zimmermann das – gelassen hat,*** show him the door; ***ein – stopfen*** or ***zumachen,*** stop a hole *or* gap; ***ein – mit einem anderen stopfen, ein – aufmachen um ein anderes zu schleißen, ein – zu- und ein anderes aufmachen,*** rob Peter to pay Paul; ***aus einem anderen – pfeifen,*** change one's tune; ***auf dem letzten – pfeifen,*** be on one's last legs; ***ein – in die Luft schlagen,*** be wide of the mark, miss by a mile.

Loch|bohrer, *m.* borer, auger. **-eisen,** *n.* (hollow) punch.

Löchelchen ['lœçəlçən], *n.* small hole; eyelet; (*Anat.*) foramen; dimple.

lochen [lɔxən], *v.t.* perforate, pierce (holes in), punch. **Locher,** *m.* punch, perforator.

löch(e)rig ['lœç(ə)rɪç], *adj.* full of holes; perforated; porous, pitted; (*fig.*) untenable, shaky (*as arguments*).

Loch|fraß, *m.* (*Metall.*) pitting. **-karte,** *f.* punched card. **-lehre,** *f.* *See* **-winkel. -säge,** *f.* pad-saw, keyhole saw. **Lochung,** *f.* punching, perforation (*of tickets etc.*). **Loch|weite,** *f.* width of opening, inside diameter. **-winkel,** *m.* hole-gauge. **-zange,** *f.* (ticket) punch.

Locke ['lɔkə], *f.* lock (*of hair*), curl, ringlet; flock (*of wool etc.*); ***in -n legen,*** curl (*hair*).

[1]**locken** ['lɔkən], *v.t.*, *v.r.* curl.

[2]**locken,** *v.t.*, *v.i.* bait, decoy; (*fig.*) attract, entice, allure, coax, tempt; ***ihm Tränen aus den Augen –,*** bring tears to his eyes; ***einen Hund –,*** call *or* whistle to a dog; (*coll.*) ***damit kann man keinen Hund vom Ofen –,*** that's no use whatever.

Locken|haar, *n.* curly hair. **-kopf,** *m.* curly head; curly-headed p. **lockenköpfig,** *adj.* curly-headed, curly-haired. **Locken|wickel, -wickler,** *m.* curler, curl-paper.

locker ['lɔkər], *adj.* loose, slack; light, porous, spongy; (*fig.*) loose, lax, frivolous, dissolute; ***– machen,*** loosen, slacken; ***– werden,*** get *or* work loose; (*coll.*) ***-er Zeisig,*** loose fish, rake. **Lockerheit,** *f.* looseness, slackness; lightness, porosity, sponginess; (*fig.*) laxity, dissipation. **lockerlassen,** *irr.v.t.*, *v.i.* (*fig.*) give in, give way, relent, yield; ***nicht –,*** not yield *or* relent, remain firm, insist, stick to one's point *or* (*coll.*) one's guns. **lockern, 1.** *v.t.* loosen, slacken, relax (*one's hold*); break up, loosen, hoe (*soil*). **2.** *v.r.* (be)come *or* work loose, loosen, (*fig.*) relax. **Lockerung,** *f.* loosening, slackening; relaxation.

lockig ['lɔkɪç], *adj.* curled, curly; (*pred.*) in curls.

Lock|mittel, *n.* bait, lure, inducement. **-pfeife,** *f.* bird-call. **-ruf,** *m.* call-note, mating call. **-speise,** *f.* bait, lure. **-spitzel,** *m.* agent provocateur, (*coll.*) stool-pigeon. **Lockung,** *f.* attraction, enticement, allurement. **Lockvogel,** *m.* decoy-bird, (*fig.*) decoy.

Lode ['lo:də], *f.* sprout, sprig, sapling, young shoot.

Loden ['lo:dən], *m.* coarse woollen cloth.

lodern ['lo:dərn], *v.i.* blaze, flame *or* flare up, (*fig.*) glow, burn.

Löffel ['lœfəl], *m.* spoon; ladle, scoop; bucket (*of dredger etc.*); (*Hunt.*) ear (*of hare etc.*); (*coll.*) ***zu einem – Suppe kommen,*** come and take pot-luck; (*coll.*) ***ihn über den – barbieren,*** cheat him, do him one in the eye, do him down, take him for a ride; ***tun als hätte man die Weisheit mit -n gegessen,*** play the wiseacre, make a great show of wisdom *or* learning.

Löffel|bohrer, *m.* spoon bit. **-ente,** *f.* (*Orn.*) shoveller (*Spatula clypeata*). **löffelförmig,** *adj.* spoon-shaped, cochlear(iform). **Löffelkraut,** *n.* (*Bot.*) scurvy-grass (*Cochlearia*). **löffeln,** *v.t.* spoon up; ladle out; (*Studs. sl.*) ***sich –,*** drink in response to a toast; return a favour. **Löffel|reiher,** *m.* *See* **Löffler. -stiel,** *m.* spoon-handle. **-voll,** *m.* spoonful. **löffelweise,** *adv.* in spoonfuls, spoonful by spoonful.

Löffler ['lœflər], *m.* (*Orn.*) spoonbill, (*Am.*) white spoonbill (*Platalae leucorodia*).

log [lo:k], *see* **lügen.**

Log [lɔk], *n.* (**-s,** *pl.* **-e**) (*Naut.*) log.

Logarithmentafel [loga'rɪtmənta:fəl], *f.* table of logarithms. **logarithmisch,** *adj.* logarithmic. **Logarithmus,** *m.* (-, *pl.* **-men**) logarithm.

Logbuch ['lɔkbu:x], *n.* (*Naut.*) log(-book), ship's log.

Loge ['lo:ʒə], *f.* **1.** (private) box (*in theatre*); **2.** (Masonic) lodge.

löge ['lø:gə], *see* **lügen.**

Logen|bruder ['lo:ʒən-], *m.* (brother) mason. **-meister,** *m.* master of a lodge. **-schließer, -wärter,** *m.* attendant (*in the theatre*).

Logge ['lɔgə], *f.* *See* **Log.**

loggen ['lɔgən], *v.i.* (*Naut.*) heave the log. **Logger,** *m.* (*Naut.*) lugger.

logieren [lo'ʒi:rən], *v.i.* lodge, stay, put up, (*Am.*)

room (*bei*, with *or* at). **Logierzimmer,** *n.* spare room, guest-room.

Logik ['lo:gɪk], *f.* logic. **Logiker,** *m.* logician.

Logis [lo'ʒi:], *n.* (- [**-s**], *pl.* - [**-s**]) lodging(s), (*sl.*) digs; (*Naut.*) mess-deck, crew space.

logisch ['lo:gɪʃ], *adj.* logical. **logischerweise,** *adv.* logically.

Logistik [lo'gɪstɪk], *f.* logistics.

loh [lo:], *adj.* (*obs.*) blazing, flaming, flaring, burning.

Loh|beize, *f.* tanning; tan liquor. **-brühe,** *f.* ooze, tannin.

[1]**Lohe** ['lo:ə], *f.* tanning-bark, tan (liquor).

[2]**Lohe,** *f.* blaze, flame, (*fig.*) ardour.

[1]**lohen** ['lo:ən], *v.i.* blaze *or* flare up.

[2]**lohen,** *v.t.* tan; steep.

Lohfarbe ['lo:farbə], *f.* tan (*colour*). **loh|farben,** *adj.* tan(-coloured). **-gar,** *adj.* tanned. **Loh|gerber,** *m.* tanner. **-gerberei,** *f.* tannery; tanning. **-grube,** *f.* tan-pit.

Lohn ['lo:n], *m.* (**-(e)s,** *pl.* **¨-e**) reward, recompense, compensation, requital; payment, remuneration; pay, salary, wages; (*Prov.*) ***Undank ist der Welt(en)*** **-**, one meets with nothing but ingratitude in this world; ***der Arbeiter ist seines -es wert,*** the labourer is worthy of his hire.

Lohn|abbau, *m.* reduction in wages, wage-cut. **-abrechnung,** *f.* statement of earnings, pay-slip. **-abzug,** *m.* deduction (from wages). **-arbeit,** *f.* hired labour. **-arbeiter,** *m.* labourer, workman, jobber. **-auftrag,** *m.* jobbing order. **-büro,** *n.* wages *or* pay office. **-diener,** *m.* hired servant. **-drückerei,** *f.* exploitation, (*coll.*) sweating. **-empfänger,** *m.* wage-earner.

lohnen ['lo:nən], *v.t.*, *v.i.* remunerate, reward, recompense, compensate, requite; pay, repay, be worth; (*obs.*) ***ihn -,*** pay him (*for work*); ***ihm etwas -,*** reward *or* recompense *or* requite him for s.th.; ***ihm mit Undank -,*** repay him with ingratitude; ***Gott lohn' es dir!*** may God reward you for it! ***es lohnt die Mühe*** or ***sich der Mühe,*** it is worth the trouble; ***das lohnt sich nicht,*** that does not pay, that is not worth while; ***es lohnt (sich) nicht darüber zu reden,*** it is not worth talking about.

löhnen ['lø:nən], *v.t.* pay (wages to).

lohnend ['lo:nənt], *adj.* paying, remunerative, lucrative, profitable; advantageous, rewarding, worthwhile, (*pred.*) worth while.

Lohn|erhöhung, *f.* wage increase, rise (in wages). **-forderung,** *f.* wage claim. **-herr,** *m.* employer. **-kampf,** *m.* wages dispute. **-kellner,** *m.* day-waiter. **-klasse,** *f.* wage group. **-kosten,** *pl.* rate for the job; labour costs. **-kürzung,** *f.* reduction *or* (*coll.*) cut in wages. **-kutsche,** *f.* hackney-cab. **-kutscher,** *m.* cabman. **-liste,** *f.* wages-sheet; pay-roll. **-politik,** *f.* wages policy. **-satz,** *m.* rate of pay. **-schreiber,** *m.* literary hack. **-steuer,** *f.* tax on wages. **-stopp,** *m.* wages freeze; wage ceiling. **-tag,** *m.* pay-day. **-tarif,** *m.* rate of pay. **-tüte,** *f.* pay packet.

Löhnung ['lø:nuŋ], *f.* payment (*of wages*), (*Mil.*) pay. **Löhnungs|appell,** *m.* (*Mil.*) pay-parade. **-tag,** *m.* *See* **Lohntag.**

Lohrinde ['lo:rɪndə], *f.* tanning-bark.

Lok, *f.* (-, *pl.* **-s**) (*coll.*) *see* **Lokomotive.**

lokal [lo'ka:l], **1.** *adj.* local; ***Lokale(s),*** local concerns, local news. **Lokal,** *n.* (**-(e)s,** *pl.* **-e**) 1. public house, (*coll.*) pub; 2. locality, place; premises. **Lokal|bahn,** *f.* local *or* suburban railway. **-behörden,** *f.pl.* local authorities. **-blatt,** *n.* local (news)paper. **lokalisieren** [-i'zi:rən], *v.t.* localize, locate, determine the position of. **Lokalität** [-i'tɛ:t], *f.* locality. **Lokal|patriotismus,** *m.* local patriotism; parochialism. **-termin,** *m.* (*Law*) on-the-spot investigation. **-verhältnisse,** *n.pl.* local conditions. **-wirkung,** *f.* local action. **-zug,** *m.* local *or* suburban train.

Lokogeschäft ['lo:kogəʃɛft], *n.* (*Comm.*) spot-business.

Lokomobile [lokomo'bi:lə], *f.* traction engine. **Lokomotive,** *f.* locomotive, railway *or* train engine. **Lokomotivführer,** *m.* engine-driver, (*Am.*) engineer.

Lokowaren ['lo:kova:rən], *f.pl.* (*Comm.*) spots, spot goods.

Lokus ['lo:kus], *m.* (-, *pl.* - *or* **-se**) (*sl.*) rear, bog, loo.

Lolch [lɔlç], *m.* (**-(e)s,** *pl.* **-e**) (*Bot.*) darnel, ray-grass (*Lolium*).

Lombard ['lɔmbart], *m. or n.* (**-s,** *pl.* **-e**) (*Comm.*) collateral loan, loan against security; (*dial.*) pawn-shop; loan office. **Lombardbestände,** *m.pl.* advances of money against security.

Lombardei [lɔmbar'daɪ], *f.* (*Geog.*) Lombardy.

Lombardgeschäft ['lɔmbartgəʃɛft], *n.* collateral loan business. **lombardieren** [-'di:rən], *v.t.* pawn, pledge, lodge as security, deposit against a loan; lend *or* advance against security. **Lombard|satz,** *m.* bank rate, (*Am.*) lending rate. **-zettel,** *m.* pawn ticket. **-zinsfuß,** *m.* pawnbroker's rate of interest.

Lomber ['lɔmbər], *n.* (*Cards*) ombre.

Lompenzucker ['lɔmpəntsukər], *m.* *See* **Lumpenzucker.**

Lorbeer ['lɔrbe:r], *m.* (**-s,** *pl.* **-en**) (*Bot.*) laurel, bay; (*fig.*) fame, repute; ***auf seinen -en ausruhen,*** rest on one's laurels. **Lorbeer|baum,** *m.* laurel, bay-tree. **-kranz,** *m.* laurel-wreath. **-rose,** *f.* (*Bot.*) oleander (*Kalmia augustifolia*). **-spiritus,** *m.* bay rum.

Lorch [lɔrç], *m.* (**-(e)s,** *pl.* **-e**) (*dial.*) *see* **Lurch.**

Lore ['lo:rə], *f.* truck, trolley, lorry.

Lorenz ['lo:rɛnts], *m.* Lawrence, Laurence. **Lorenzstrom,** *m.* (*Geog.*) St. Lawrence River.

Los [lo:s], *n.* (**-es,** *pl.* **-e**) **1.** lot, share, allotment, portion; lottery ticket *or* prize; ***das - werfen,*** cast lots; ***das große - ziehen,*** win the first prize, draw the winner, (*coll.*) hit the jackpot; ***das - ist geworfen,*** the die is cast; ***das - ziehen,*** draw lots; ***durchs - entscheiden,*** decide by lot; 2. fate, destiny, lot; ***ihm wurde ein glückliches - zuteil,*** his lot was a happy one.

los, 1. *pred. adj., adv.* loose, slack; free, disengaged, released; ***- sein*** (*Acc.*), be rid of (*a th. or a p.*); ***- werden*** (*Acc.*) or ***von,*** get loose *or* free from; get rid *or* (*coll.*) shut of; ***aller Bande -,*** free of *or* freed from all restraint; ***- und ledig,*** rid of once and for all; (*coll.*) ***was ist -?*** what is the matter? what is wrong? what is going on? (*coll.*) what's cooking? what's up? ***der Teufel ist -,*** all hell is let loose; ***es muß etwas - sein,*** something must be afoot, there is s.th. in the wind; (*coll.*) ***hier ist viel -,*** there is plenty going on *or* doing here; (*coll.*) ***mit ihm ist nicht viel -,*** he is not up to much; (*coll.*) ***etwas - haben,*** know what one's talking about, (*coll.*) know one's stuff, (*sl.*) be on the ball. **2.** *int.* go on! fire away! (*sl.*) shoot! ***also*** or ***nun -!*** here goes! (*Spt.*) ***Achtung, fertig, -!*** on your marks, ready, go!

los-, *sep. pref. meaning* **(a)** *separation*; **(b)** *commencement*; **(c)** *violence, lack of restraint*; *with last meaning it can be added adverbially to most verbs of action (not listed here) e.g.* ***drauf-leben,*** live from hand to mouth, live carelessly; ***wacker -lügen,*** lie shamelessly; ***-trinken!*** drink up! drink to your heart's content! drink your fill!

losarbeiten ['lo:sˀarbaɪtən], **1.** *v.t.* loosen, work loose, disengage. **2.** *v.r.* extricate o.s., get free. **3.** *v.i.* work on *or* away (***auf*** (*Acc.*), at).

lösbar ['lø:sba:r], *adj.* (*Chem. etc.*) soluble, (*fig.*) (*of a problem*) solvable, resolvable.

los|binden, *irr.v.t.* untie, unfasten, undo; loosen, unfurl. **-brechen, 1.** *irr.v.t.* break off *or* loose. **2.** *v.i.* (*aux.* s.) break loose *or* away, break *or* burst forth *or* out. **-bröckeln,** *v.t., v.i.* (*aux.* s.) crumble off.

Lösch|blatt ['lœʃ-], *n.* (sheet of) blotting paper. **-boot,** *n.* fire-boat, fire-tender.

Lösche ['lœʃə], *f.* coal *or* charcoal dust, slack, dross; cinder, clinker.

Löscheimer ['lœʃˀaɪmər], *m.* fire-bucket.

[1]**löschen** ['lœʃən], *v.t.* extinguish, quench, put out; liquidate, discharge, cancel (*a debt*); delete, erase, blot out, efface, obliterate; slake (*lime, one's thirst*).

²löschen, *v.t.* (*Naut.*) unload, discharge (*cargo*).

Löscher ['lœʃər], *m.* 1. extinguisher; blotter; 2. docker, stevedore, longshoreman.

Lösch|gebühren, *f.pl.*, **-geld,** *n.* landing charges, wharfage. **-gerät,** *n.* fire extinguisher, fire-fighting equipment. **-hafen,** *m.* port of discharge. **-kalk,** *m.* slaked lime. **-kopf,** *m.* erasure head (*of tape-recorder*). **-mannschaft,** *f.* fire-fighting squad, fire-brigade. **-papier,** *n.* blotting paper. **-platz,** *m.* wharf; *see also* **-hafen. -schaum,** *m.* foam extinguisher.

Löschung ['lœʃuŋ], *f.* 1. extinguishing; extinction, dissolution; cancellation, deletion; discharge (*of debt*); 2. landing, unloading, discharging (*of cargo*).

Lösch|zug, *m. See* **-mannschaft.**

los|drehen, *v.t.* twist off. **-drücken,** *v.i.* pull the trigger.

lose ['lo:zə], *adj.* 1. loose, slack, movable, shifting; ***-s Haar,*** flowing *or* dishevelled hair; ***-r Kalk,*** untempered mortar; 2. (*Comm.*) unpacked, bulk, unpackaged; ***- Blätter,*** loose *or* unbound sheets; ***- Waren,*** bulk goods; 3. (*fig.*) wanton, dissolute, frivolous, irresponsible, mischievous, roguish, naughty; ***-s Gesindel,*** vagabonds, blackguards; ***-s Geschwätz,*** irresponsible chatter; ***-s Mädchen,*** fast *or* loose girl; (*coll.*) ***-s Maul*** or ***- Zunge,*** loose *or* abusive tongue; ***-r Streich,*** reckless prank; ***-r Vogel,*** bawdy fellow, rake. **Lose,** *n.* (*Naut.*) free end (*of rope*).

Lösegeld ['lø:zəgɛlt], *n.* ransom.

loseisen ['lo:sʔaɪzən], *v.t.* (*coll.*) wangle (***von,*** out of).

¹losen ['lo:zən], *v.i.* draw *or* cast lots, toss (***um,*** for).

²losen, *v.i.* (*dial.*) listen, overhear, eavesdrop.

lösen ['lø:zən], **1.** *v.t.* 1. loosen, slacken, untie, unfasten, undo; ***den Knoten eines Schauspieles -,*** unravel the plot of a play; ***ein Siegel -,*** break a seal; ***seine Zunge -,*** make him speak; 2. release, relax; ***Gefangene -,*** set prisoners free; 3. break off, sever (*relationship*), (*fig.*) absolve (*a p.*) (***von,*** from), set aside, rescind, annul, cancel (*agreement*); ***eine Ehe -,*** dissolve *or* annul a marriage; ***eine Verlobung -,*** break off an engagement; ***den Zauber -,*** break the spell; 4. solve, answer (*a riddle etc.*), (*Math.*) resolve; ***eine Frage -,*** settle *or* answer a question; ***Rätsel -,*** solve *or* guess riddles; ***eine Schwierigkeit -,*** settle *or* overcome a difficulty; ***die Verwirrung -,*** dispel the confusion; ***einen Widerspruch -,*** resolve a contradiction; ***Zweifel -,*** clear away doubt; 5. redeem, ransom; ***ein Pfand -,*** redeem a pledge; ***sein Versprechen -,*** fulfil *or* keep one's promise; 6. discharge, fire (*a shot*); 7. take, buy (*a ticket*); ***im voraus -,*** book in advance; 8. (*Chem.*) dissolve. **2.** *v.r.* free *or* disengage o.s. (***von,*** from), (*of a th.*) get *or* come loose; (*Chem.*) dissolve; ***die Freundschaft löst sich,*** the friendship goes to pieces; ***der Verband löst sich,*** the bandage gets loose; ***Zucker löst sich in Wasser,*** sugar dissolves in water; ***sie löste sich in Tränen,*** she dissolved into tears; ***das Rätsel löst sich sehr einfach,*** the riddle is easy to solve.

los|fahren, *irr.v.i.* (*aux.* s.) depart, set off; (*fig.*) ***auf ihn -,*** make for him, fly (out) at him; (***gerade***) ***auf das Land -,*** make (straight) for land. **-gehen,** *irr.v.i.* (*aux.* s.) 1. set out, begin; ***auf ihn -,*** go straight up to him; (*coll.*) pitch into him, go for him; 2. come off *or* undone, become loose; (*of firearms*) explode, go off; (*coll.*) ***jetzt geht's los,*** now the fun starts. **Losgehen,** *n.* explosion, deflagration; ***verspätetes -,*** hang-fire; ***vorzeitiges -,*** premature discharge. **los|haken,** *v.t.* unclasp, unhook. **-kaufen,** *v.t.* redeem, ransom, buy off; ***sich -,*** buy one's freedom, buy o.s. off. **-ketten,** *v.t.* unchain. **-knüpfen,** *v.t.* untie, unknot. **-kommen,** *irr.v.i.* (*aux,* s.) get *or* come off *or* loose; get rid of; get free, be set free, escape, get away; ***- von,*** get rid of. **-lassen,** *irr.v.t.* let loose, let go, release, set free; let off (*a gun*); (*fig., coll.*) utter, break out into; (*coll.*) ***einen Brief -,*** write a letter; (*coll.*) ***eine Rede -,*** deliver a speech; (*coll.*) ***einen Witz -,*** make a joke; ***laß mich los!*** let go! let me go! **-legen,** *v.i.* (*coll.*) set to, get going, fire away, (*sl.*) step on the gas; ***- gegen,*** *see* **-ziehen.**

löslich ['lø:slɪç], *adj.* (*Chem.*) soluble. **Löslichkeit,** *f.* solubility.

loslösen ['lo:slø:zən], **1.** *v.t.* loosen, detach, separate. **2.** *v.r.* disengage o.s., break away, become detached; come *or* peel off. **Loslösung,** *f.* separation, dissociation. **los|löten,** *v.t.* unsolder. **-machen, 1.** *v.t.* loosen, undo, unfasten, untie, (*Naut.*) cast off, unmoor; disengage; detach, separate; set at liberty, free. **2.** *v.r.* get away; disengage *or* extricate o.s. (***von,*** from); get rid (of); get free (from). **-platzen.** *v.i.* (*aux.* s.) burst *or* blurt out; explode. **-reißen, 1.** *irr.v.t.* pull *or* tear *or* rip off *or* away. **2.** *irr.v.r.* break loose, break away; (*Naut.*) part anchor, go adrift; tear o.s. away (***von,*** from).

Löß [lœs], *m.* **(-(ss)es,** *pl.* **-(ss)e)** (*Geol.*) loess.

lossagen ['lo:sza:gən], *v.r.* ***sich - von,*** renounce, give up, withdraw *or* secede from, dissociate o.s. from, break with, have nothing more to do with. **Lossagung,** *f.* renunciation, withdrawal. **los|schießen, 1.** *irr.v.t.* fire off, discharge; (*coll.*) fire away. **2.** *irr.v.i.* (*aux.* s.) (*fig.*) ***- auf*** (*Acc.*), *see* **-ziehen** (*fig.*). **-schlagen, 1.** *irr.v.t.* 1. knock off; 2. (*Comm.*) dispose of, sell (cheap), sell off. **2.** *irr. v.i.* ***- auf*** (*Acc.*), let fly at, attack, belabour. **-schnallen,** *v.t.* unbuckle. **-schrauben,** *v.t.* unscrew, screw off. **-sprechen,** *irr.v.t.* acquit (***von,*** of), absolve (from), release, free, set free (from). **Lossprechung,** *f.* acquittal; absolution; release. **los|sprengen,** *v.t.* blast off *or* loose. **-springen,** *irr.v.i.* (*aux.* s.) fly off, burst loose, crack; ***- auf*** (*Acc.*), fly at, pounce *or* rush upon. **-steuern,** *v.i.* ***- auf*** (*Acc.*), set course for, head for, make (straight) for; (*fig.*) (*of remarks*) be driving at. **-stürmen,** *v.i.* (*aux.* s.) rush (***auf*** (*Acc.*), upon *or* at); rush forth; ***auf seine Gesundheit -,*** play ducks and drakes with one's health. **-stürzen,** *v.i.* dash (***auf*** (*Acc.*), at), pounce (upon). **-trennen,** *v.t.* undo, unsew, unstitch; separate, sever. **Lostrennung,** *f.* separation, severance.

Losung ['lo:zuŋ], *f.* 1. watchword, password; battle-cry, (*fig.*) slogan, catchword; 2. (*Comm., obs.*) cash takings; 3. (*Hunt.*) droppings, fumets.

Lösung ['lø:zuŋ], *f.* 1. loosening, detachment; 2. (*Chem.*) solution; 3. (*fig.*) solution, explanation, answer, (*Theat.*) dénouement, unravelling (*of a plot*); 4. (*Poet.*) ransom; redemption (*of a pledge*); 5. absolution. **Lösungsmittel,** *n.* solvent.

los|werden, *irr.v.i.* (*aux.* s.) get rid of, (*Comm.*) dispose of (*goods*). **-wickeln, 1.** *v.t.* unwind, untwist, unravel, unwrap. **2.** *v.r.* disentangle *or* extricate o.s. **-winden, 1.** *irr.v.t.* unwind, untwist, extricate. **2.** *irr.v.r.* wriggle free. **-ziehen,** *irr.v.t.* (*aux.* s.) set out (***auf*** (*Acc.*), for), move *or* march off (towards); (*fig., coll.*) rail, inveigh (***gegen, über*** (*Acc.*), against); (*coll.*) ***über ihn -,*** run him down, pull him to pieces, tear him to shreds.

Lot [lo:t], *n.* **(-(e)s,** *pl.* **-e)** 1. perpendicular (line); plumb-line, plummet, (*Naut.*) sounding-lead; ***aus dem -,*** out of plumb, (*fig., coll.*) out of order; ***im -,*** perpendicular, (*fig., coll.*) in apple-pie order; ***ins - bringen,*** set to rights; (*coll.*) ***er ist nicht ganz im -,*** he is not all there; 2. solder; 3 (*obs.*) small weight (= 10 grams); ***es gehen 100 auf ein -,*** they are as light as a feather.

Löt|blei ['lø:t-], *n.* soft solder. **-eisen,** *n.* soldering-iron.

loten ['lo:tən], *v.t., v.i.* (*Naut.*) sound, take soundings; plumb; test for perpendicular.

löten ['lø:tən], *v.t.* solder, braze.

Löt|fett, *n.*, **-flüssigkeit,** *f.* flux.

Lothringen ['lo:trɪŋən], *n.* (*Geog.*) Lorraine.

Lötkolben ['lø:tkɔlbən], *m.* soldering-iron.

-lotig ['lo:tɪç], *adj.suff.* weighing half an ounce, of due alloy, of full weight; ***das feinste Silber ist 16 lotig,*** the finest silver is of 12 dwt. **Lotigkeit,** *f.* fineness (*of silver*).

Lötlampe ['lø:tlampə], *f.* blowlamp, (*Am.*) blowtorch.

Lotleine ['lo:tlaɪnə], *f.* plumb-line, sounding line.

Löt|naht, *f. See* **-stelle.**

lotrecht ['lo:trɛçt], *adj.* perpendicular, vertical.
Lötrohr ['lø:tro:r], *n.* blowpipe.
Lotse ['lo:tsə], *m.* (**-n,** *pl.* **-n**) pilot. **lotsen,** *v.t.* pilot. **Lotsen|gebühr,** *f.*, **-geld,** *n.* pilotage.
Lötstelle ['lø:tʃtɛlə], *f.* soldered joint.
Lotter|bett ['lɔtər-], *n.* (*obs.*) couch; (*fig.*) ***auf dem – liegen,*** be sunk in indolence. **-bube,** *m.* rascal, good-for-nothing, rapscallion; (*dial.*) vagabond.
Lotterie [lɔtə'ri:], *f.* lottery; ***in der – spielen,*** take a lottery-ticket; (*coll.*) have a flutter. **Lotterie|-gewinn,** *m.* winning number; prize in a lottery. **-los,** *n.* lottery-ticket.
lotterig ['lɔtərɪç], *adj.* slovenly, sluttish, slatternly; dissolute. **Lotterleben,** *n.* dissolute life. **lottern,** *v.i.* loaf about, sow one's wild oats. **Lotterwirtschaft,** *f.* hugger-mugger, slovenliness; maladministration, mismanagement; disreputable goings-on.
Lotung ['lo:tuŋ], *f.* sounding, plumbing.
Lötung ['lø:tuŋ], *f.* soldering, brazing. **Lötwasser,** *n.* chlorate of zinc.
Löwe ['lø:və], *m.* (**-n,** *pl.* **-n**) lion; (*Astrol.*) Leo.
Löwen ['lø:vən], *n.* (*Geog.*) Louvain.
Löwen|anteil, *m.* lion's share. **-bändiger,** *m.* lion-tamer. **-grube,** *f.* lions' den. **löwenhaft,** *adj.* leonine. **Löwen|herz,** *n.* (*fig.*) valour, fortitude; man of mettle, Cœur de Lion. **-maul,** *n.* (*Bot.*) snapdragon (*Antirrhinum*). **-mut,** *m.* lion-hearted *or* stout-hearted courage. **-stärke,** *f.* stubborn *or* invincible *or* unsurpassed *or* sovereign strength. **-zahn,** *m.* (*Bot.*) dandelion (*Taraxacum officinale*).
Löwin ['lø:vɪn], *f.* lioness.
loyal [loa'ja:l], *adj.* loyal. **Loyalität** [-i'tɛ:t], *f.* loyalty.
Luch [lux], *n.* (**-(e)s,** *pl.* **-e**) *or f.* (-, *pl.* **⸗e**) (*dial.*) marsh, bog; ***– und Bruch,*** moorland.
Luchs [luks], *m.* (**-es,** *pl.* **-e**) lynx. **luchsäugig,** *adj.* hawk-eyed, sharp-eyed. **luchsen,** *v.t., v.i.* **1.** (*coll.*) watch intently, watch like a hawk, peer, be all eyes; **2.** (*coll.*) steal, pilfer.
Lücke ['lykə], *f.* gap, break, breach, opening, space, void, cavity, hole, interstice, lacuna; blank, omission, deficiency, deficit; interval, hiatus; ***eine – reißen,*** leave a gap; (*fig.*) ***eine – schließen*** or ***füllen,*** (*of a th.*) fill *or* stop a gap, supply a want, (*of a p.*) step into the breach. **Lückenbüßer,** *m.* stopgap, standby, makeshift (*things*); stand-in (*persons*). **lückenhaft,** *adj.* defective, incomplete; full of gaps, broken, interrupted; fragmentary, meagre. **lückenlos,** *adj.* uninterrupted, unbroken, complete, consistent.
lud [lu:t], **lüde** ['ly:də], *see* **laden.**
Luder ['lu:dər], *n.* (*obs., dial.*) carrion; bait, lure, decoy; (*coll.*) wretch, beast; slut, hussy; (*coll.*) ***das ist unter allem –,*** that beggars description. **luderhaft,** *adj.* disgusting, abominable. **Luderleben,** *n.* dissolute life. **ludern, 1.** *v.t.* (*dial.*) lure, bait. **2.** *v.i.* (*dial.*) feed on carrion, (*coll.*) lead a dissolute life.
Ludwig ['lu:tvɪç], *m.* Lewis, Louis.
Lues ['lu:ɛs], *f.* syphilis.
Luft [luft], *f.* (-, *pl.* **⸗e**) air, atmosphere; breeze, zephyr, breath; (*Mech.*) (amount of) slackness (*of fitting parts*); ***keine – bekommen,*** not be able to breathe; ***an die – bringen,*** air; (*coll.*) ***dicke –,*** trouble, threatening atmosphere; ***in die – fliegen,*** be blown up; ***in freier –,*** in the open air; ***an die – gehen,*** take an airing; (*fig.*) ***in die – gehen,*** go up in the air, blow up, explode (*with anger*), (*sl.*) blow one's top; ***aus der – greifen,*** fabricate, invent; ***gute – haben,*** draw well (*of a chimney etc.*); ***keine – haben,*** be out of breath, be winded; ***das hängt*** or ***schwebt in der –,*** it is all in the air, that is still undecided; ***es liegt etwas in der –,*** there's s.th. in the wind; ***– machen,*** give vent (*Dat.*, to) (*anger etc.*); ***aus der – nehmen,*** volley (*a ball*); ***die – ist rein,*** the coast is clear; ***– schaffen*** (*Dat.*), give breathing space; ***wieder – schöpfen,*** recover one's breath; ***(frische) – schöpfen*** or (*coll.*) ***schnappen,*** get a breath of (fresh) air; ***nach – schnappen,*** pant, gasp for breath; ***er ist für mich –,*** he just does not exist for me, as far as I am concerned he might not be there; ***ihn an die – setzen,*** throw *or* turn him out; ***in die – sprengen,*** blow up.
Luft|abschirmung, *f.* (*Av.*) air-umbrella. **-abschluß,** *m.* hermetic seal. **-abwehr,** *f.* anti-aircraft, air defence. **-akrobatik,** *f.* (*Av.*) stunt flying, aerobatics. **-angriff,** *m.* air-raid, aerial attack. **-ansicht,** *f.* aerial view. **-antenne,** *f.* overhead aerial. **luftartig,** *adj.* aeriform; gaseous. **Luft|-aufklärung,** *f.* air-reconnaissance. **-aufnahme,** *f.* aerial photograph. **-aufsicht,** *f.* air-traffic control. **-ballon,** *m.* balloon. **-behälter,** *m.* compressed-air tank; (*Orn.*) airsack. **-bereifung,** *f.* pneumatic tyres. **-beschaffenheit,** *f.* climatic conditions. **-bewegung,** *f.* flow of air. **-bild,** *n.* vision, fancy, fantasy; *see also* **-aufnahme. -bildaufklärung,** *f.* photographic reconnaissance. **-bläschen,** *n.* (*Anat.*) pulmonary vesicle. **-blase,** *f.* (air) bubble; (*Bot.*) vesicle; (*Ichth.*) air-bladder. **-bremse,** *f.* air *or* pneumatic brake. **-brücke,** *f.* (*Av.*) air-lift.
Lüftchen ['lyftçən], *n.* light *or* gentle breeze, breath of air.
luftdicht ['luftdɪçt], *adj.* air-tight, hermetically sealed; ***– verpackt,*** vacuum-packed. **Luft|dichte,** *f.* density of the air, atmospheric pressure. **-dichtigkeitsmesser,** *m.* manometer. **luftdienstuntauglich,** *adj.* (*Av.*) grounded. **Luft|druck,** *m.* **1.** atmospheric pressure; **2.** blast (*of explosion*). **-druckbremse,** *f.* compressed air *or* pneumatic brake. **-druckgefälle,** *n.* pressure gradient. **-druckpumpe,** *f.* air-compressor, pneumatic pump. **luftdurchlässig,** *adj.* porous, permeable. **Luft|düse,** *f.* air-vent, air-nozzle. **-einlaß,** *m.* air-intake.
lüften ['lyftən], **1.** *v.t.* ventilate, (expose to the) air; aerate; raise, lift (*hat, veil etc.*); (*fig.*) unveil, disclose, reveal, lay bare (*secret*). **2.** *v.r.* lift. **Lüfter,** *m.* ventilator, fan.
Luftfahrt ['luftfa:rt], *f.* aviation; aeronautics; air-navigation. **luftfahrtbegeistert,** *adj.* air-minded. **Luftfahrtminister,** *m.* air minister.
Luft|fahrzeug, *n.* aircraft. **-feuchtigkeit,** *f.* humidity of the atmosphere. **-feuchtigkeitsmesser,** *m.* hygrometer. **-flotte,** *f.* air force, air armada. **luft|förmig,** *adj. See* **-artig. -gekühlt,** *adj.* air-cooled. **Luft|gespinst,** *n.* airy nothing, chimera. **-gewehr,** *n.* air-gun, air-rifle. **-gitter,** *n. See* **-sperre. -hafen,** *m.* airport. **-hahn,** *m.* air-cock, air-valve. **lufthaltig,** *adj.* charged with air, aeriferous. **Luft|hauch,** *m.* breath of air. **-heizung,** *f.* air-conditioning, controlled ventilation. **-herrschaft,** *f.* air-supremacy. **-hülle,** *f.* atmosphere.
luftig ['luftɪç], *adj.* airy, breezy, windy; vaporous, gaseous; (*fig.*) light, thin, flimsy; (*of a p.*) flighty.
Luftikus ['luftikus], *m.* (-, *pl.* **-se**) (*coll.*) **1.** harum-scarum; **2.** windbag.
Luft|kabel, *n.* overhead cable. **-kampf,** *m.* aerial combat. **-kanal,** *m.* air-vent *or* -duct. **-kissen,** *n.* air- *or* pneumatic cushion. **-klappe,** *f.* ventilation-flap; air-valve. **-krankheit,** *f.* air-sickness. **-krieg,** *m.* war in the air, aerial war(fare). **-kurort,** *m.* high-altitude *or* mountain resort. **-landetruppen,** *f.pl.* airborne troops. **luftleer,** *adj.* exhausted, evacuated, void of air; ***-er Raum,*** vacuum. **Luft|-leiter,** *m.* (*Rad.*) overhead aerial, (*Am.*) antenna. **-leitung,** *f.* overhead wire(s). **-linie,** *f.* bee-line; ***in der –,*** as the crow flies. **-loch,** *n.* air-hole, vent, breathing-hole; (*Av.*) air-pocket; register (*of a chimney*); (*Ent.*) stigma. **-messer,** *m.* aerometer. **-parade,** *f.* (*Av.*) fly-past. **-post,** *f.* airmail. **-pumpe,** *f.* pneumatic pump. **-raum,** *m.* atmosphere, (*Av.*) air-space. **-raumüberwachung,** *f. See* **-aufsicht. -reifen,** *m.* pneumatic tyre. **-reiniger,** *m.* air filter. **-reinigung,** *f.* air-conditioning. **-reise,** *f.* journey by air, flight. **-reisende(r),** *m., f.* air-passenger. **-reklame,** *f.* sky-writing. **-rohr,** *n.* vent-pipe.
Luftröhre ['luftrø:rə], *f.* air-tube; (*Anat.*) trachea, windpipe; (*Bot.*) air-vessel. **Luftröhren|äste,** *m.pl.* bronchiae, bronchial tubes. **-deckel,** *m.* epiglottis. **-entzündung,** *f.* bronchitis. **-katarrh,**

m. tracheal catarrh. **-kopf,** *m.* larynx. **-schnitt,** *m.* tracheotomy.

Luft|sack, *m.* wind sleeve *or* sock. **-sauger,** *m.* aspirator. **-saugpumpe,** *f.* suction pump. **-säure,** *f.* carbonic acid. **-schacht,** *m.* air-shaft (*in tunnels*). **-schaukel,** *f.* swing-boat. **-schicht,** *f.* layer of air. **-schiff,** *n.* airship. **-schiffahrt,** *f.* aerial navigation, aeronautics. **-schlange,** *f.* paper streamer. **-schlauch,** *m.* (inner) tube (*of tyre*). **-schleuse,** *f.* air-chamber. **-schlitz,** *m.* louvre. **-schlösser,** *m.pl.* castles in the air. **-schraube,** *f.* propeller, airscrew.

Luftschutz ['luftʃuts], *m.* (passive) air defence, air-raid precautions. **Luftschutz|bottich,** *m.* static water tank. **-bunker, -keller, -raum,** *m.* air-raid shelter. **-wart,** *m.* air-raid warden.

Luft|spalt, *m.* air-gap. **-sperre,** *f.* balloon barrage. **-spiegelung,** *f.* mirage. **-sport,** *m.* amateur flying. **-sprünge,** *m.pl.* **– *machen,*** leap about, gambol, cut capers. **-stauung, -stockung,** *f.* air-lock. **-störung,** *f.* (*Rad.*) atmospherics, static. **-stoß,** *m.* gust of air, (*explosion*) blast. **-strahl,** *m.* jet of air. **-strahlantrieb,** *m.* jet propulsion. **-streitkräfte,** *f.pl.* air force. **-strom,** *m.*, **-strömung,** *f.* slipstream, air current. **-stützpunkt,** *m.* (*Av.*) air-base. **-tanken,** *n.* refuelling in the air. **luft|trocken,** *adj.* air-dried, seasoned. **-trocknen,** *v.t.* season. **-tüchtig,** *adj.* (*Av.*) airworthy.

Lüftung ['lyftuŋ], *f.* ventilation; airing, exposure to the air; aeration; (*fig.*) disclosure. **Lüftungsanlage,** *f.* ventilation system.

Luft|veränderung, *f,* change of air. **-verdichter,** *m.* air compressor. **-verkehr,** *m.* air-traffic. **-verkehrsgesellschaft,** *f.* airline company. **-verkehrslinie,** *f.* airline, air-route. **-vermessung,** *f.* aerial survey. **-verteidigung,** *f.* air-defence. **-verunreinigung,** *f.* air pollution. **-waffe,** *f.* (German) air force. **-warnung,** *f.* air-raid warning. **-wechsel,** *m.* change of air. **-weg,** *m.* 1. (*Anat.*) respiratory tract; 2. (*Av.*) air-route; ***auf dem* –,** by air. **-widerstand,** *m.* air resistance, (*Av.*) drag. **-wirbel,** *m.* vortex, eddy, turbulence. **-wurzel,** *f.* (*Bot.*) aerial *or* exposed root. **-ziegel,** *m.* air-dried brick. **-zufuhr,** *f.* air supply. **-zug,** *m.* draught, current of air. **-zurichtung,** *f.* *See* **-reinigung.** **-zutritt,** *m.* access of air; air inlet.

1**Lug** [lu:k], *m.* (*obs., only in*) **– *und Trug,*** falsehood and deceit.

2**Lug,** *m.* **(-(e)s,** *pl.* **-e)** opening; peep-hole, spy-hole. **Lugaus,** *m.* (-, *pl.* -) (*dial.*) *see* **Luginsland.**

Lüge ['ly:gə], *f.* lie, falsehood, untruth; (*coll.*) story, fib; ***ihn –n strafen,*** give the lie to him, (*Am.*) belie his words; ***fromme* –,** white lie; ***–n haben kurze Beine,*** you will not get anywhere with lies *or* with lying.

lugen ['lu:gən], *v.i.* (*of a p.*) look out (***nach,*** for); (*of a th.*) peep, show, be visible (***von, aus,*** from).

lügen ['ly:gən], *irr.v.i.* lie, tell lies, tell a lie, (*coll.*) tell stories, fib, tell fibs *or* a fib; ***in seinen Beutel* –,** lie to one's own advantage; ***ich will gern gelogen haben,*** I wish I could deny it, it is unfortunately all too true; ***daß ich nicht lüge,*** to tell the truth, really; ***er lügt daß sich die Balken biegen, er lügt wie gedruckt,*** he lies like a gas-meter. **Lügen,** *n.* lying, deceitfulness. **Lügen|bold,** *m.* habitual liar. **-detektor,** *m.* lie detector. **-fürst, -geist,** *m.* Satan. **-geschichte,** *f.* cock-and-bull story. **-gewebe,** *n.* tissue of lies. **lügenhaft,** *adj.* (*of a th.*) lying, false, untrue; (*of a p.*) lying, deceitful, mendacious. **Lügenhaftigkeit,** *f.* (*of a th.*) falsehood, untruth; (*of a p.*) deceitfulness, mendacity, falseness. **Lügen|maul,** *n.* impudent *or* brazen *or* barefaced liar. **-prophet,** *m.* false prophet. **-vater,** *m.* *See* **-fürst.**

Lugger ['lugər], *m.* (*Naut.*) lugger.

Luginsland ['lu:kˀɪnslant], *m.* (-, *pl.* -) (*dial.*) watchtower, lookout.

Lügner ['ly:gnər], *m.* liar; ***er wurde zum – an mir,*** he did not keep his word to me, he deceived me; ***ihn zum – machen,*** make him out to be a liar. **lügnerisch,** *adj.* (*of a p.*) lying, deceitful, mendacious.

Lukas ['lu:kas], *m.* Lucas, Luke; ***der heilige* –,** St. Luke. **Lukasevangelium,** *n.* Gospel according to St. Luke.

Luke ['lu:kə], *f.* dormer-window; (*dial.*) trap-door; (*Naut.*) hatch. **Luken|deckel,** *m.* (*Naut.*) hatch-cover. **-öffnung,** *f.* (*Naut.*) hatchway.

Lukrez [lu:'krets], *m.* Lucretius.

Lulatsch ['lu:latʃ], *m.* **(-es,** *pl.* **-e)** (*coll.*) bag of bones, bean-pole.

lullen ['lulən], *v.t.* lull, sing to sleep.

Lumme ['lumə], *f.* (*Orn.*) *see* **Trottellumme.**

Lümmel ['lyməl], *m.* lout, ruffian, boor, hooligan, hoodlum. **Lümmelei** [–'laɪ], *f.* boorishness, loutish behaviour. **lümmelhaft,** *adj.* loutish, ruffianly, boorish. **lümmeln,** *v.r.* (*v.i.*) behave badly; loll (about), lounge.

Lump [lump], *m.* **(-(e)s** *or* **-en,** *pl.* **-e(n))** rascal, scoundrel, blackguard; cad, (*sl.*) rat, heel.

Lumpazius [lum'pa:tsius], *m.* (-, *pl.* **-se**), **Lumpazivagabundus** [–'bundus], *m.* (-, *pl.* **-se** *or* **-di**) (*hum.*) vagabond, tramp, scoundrel.

Lumpen ['lumpən], *m.* 1. rag, tatter, clout; *pl.* ragged clothes, rags and tatters; lumber, trash; 2. (*coll.*) thingamy, thingumajig, thingumbob, thingummy; 3. (*dial.*) handkerchief. **lumpen, 1.** *v.i.* (*sl.*) go on the binge. **2.** *v.r.* (*only in*) ***sich nicht – lassen,*** not act shabbily, do the thing decently, do the decent thing, come down handsomely.

Lumpen|baron, *m.* shabby-genteel person. **-brei,** *m.* (*Paperm.*) paper pulp, first stuff. **-geld,** *n.* paltry sum; ***für ein* –,** dirt-cheap. **-gesindel,** *n.* riff-raff, rabble, rag-tag and bobtail. **-händler,** *m.* rag-and-bone man. **-hund, -kerl,** *m.* *See* **Lump.** **-kram,** *m.* *See* **-zeug.** **-pack,** *n.* *See* **-gesindel.** **-papier,** *n.* rag-paper. **-sammler,** *m.* ragpicker; rag-and-bone man, (*coll.*) last tram *or* last bus (*at night*). **-volk,** *n.* *See* **-gesindel.** **-wolf,** *m.* (*Paperm.*) rag-tearing machine, devil. **-wolle,** *f.* shoddy. **-zeug,** *n.* trash, stuff. **-zucker,** *m.* lump *or* loaf sugar.

Lumperei [lumpə'raɪ], *f.* 1. rascality; shabby trick, meanness; 2. trifle, bagatelle.

lumpig ['lumpɪç], *adj.* ragged, tattered, shabby; (*fig.*) (*of a p.*) mean, stingy, shabby, (*of a th.*) paltry, trifling; (*coll.*) ***die –en paar Mark,*** those few miserable marks.

Lund [lunt], *m.* **(-(e)s,** *pl.* **-e)** (*Orn.*) *see* **Papageitaucher.**

Lünette [ly'nɛtə], *f.* skylight, fanlight (*above doors and windows*); (*Fort.*) lunette.

Lunge ['luŋə], *f.* lung(s); (*of beasts*) lights; ***eiserne* –,** iron lung; ***aus voller – schreien,*** shout at the top of one's voice; ***auf – rauchen,*** inhale (smoke).

Lungen|arterie, *f.* pulmonary artery. **-bläschen,** *n.* vesicle of the lungs. **-braten,** *m.* (*dial.*) loin (of beef). **-entzündung,** *f.* pneumonia. **-fell,** *n.* pleura. **-fellentzündung,** *f.* pleurisy. **-flügel,** *m.* lobe of the lungs. **-heilanstalt, -heilstätte,** *f.* sanatorium for consumptives. **-kammer,** *f.* right ventricle (*of heart*). **lungenkrank,** *adj.* consumptive. **Lungen|krankheit,** *f.* *See* **-leiden.** **-krebs,** *m.* lung cancer. **-leiden,** *n.* pulmonary disease. **-pfeifer,** *m.* (*Vet.*) whistler, roarer (*horse*). **-(schwind)sucht,** *f.* tuberculosis, phthisis. **lungensüchtig,** *adj.* consumptive.

Lungerer ['luŋərər], *m.* loafer, loiterer, idler. **lungern,** *v.i.* (*aux.* h. *&* s.) 1. loll *or* lounge about, loiter; 2. (*dial.*) crave (***nach,*** for).

Lunker ['luŋkər], *m.* cavity, (*Metall.*) pipe, shrink-hole. **lunkern,** *v.i.* develop cavities.

Lünse ['lynzə], *f.* linchpin, axle-pin.

Lunte ['luntə], *f.* slow-match, fuse; (*Hunt.*) (fox's) brush; (*coll.*) **– *riechen,*** smell a rat.

Lupe ['lu:pə], *f.* magnifying glass; ***unter die – nehmen,*** examine closely, scrutinize, take a good look at.

lupfen ['lupfən] (*dial.*), **lüpfen** (*Austr.*), *v.t.* lift, raise.

Luppe ['lupə], *f.* (*Found.*) loop, ball, lump (*ore*), bloom. **Luppenfeuer,** *n.* smelting-furnace.

Lurch [lurç], *m.* **(-(e)s,** *pl.* **-e)** batrachian; amphibious animal.

Lust [lust], *f.* (-, *pl.* ⸚**e**) pleasure, enjoyment, delight; joy, gaiety, mirth; disposition, fancy, inclination; carnal pleasure *or* desire *or* appetite, lust; ***seinen Lüsten frönen,*** indulge *or* gratify one's desires; – ***an einer S. finden, seine – an einer S. haben,*** take a delight *or* take pleasure in a th.; – ***haben (zu tun),*** be disposed, feel inclined *or* have a mind (to do), feel like, be in the mood for (doing); ***beinahe – haben (zu tun),*** have half a mind (to do); ***keine – haben (zu tun),*** not be disposed, feel disinclined (to do), not feel like, not be in the mood for, (*coll.*) not be keen on (doing); ***in – und Leid,*** in joy and sorrow; ***mit – und Liebe,*** with heart and soul; ***ihm – zu etwas machen,*** excite his desire for a th., give him a taste for a th.; ***ihm die – nehmen,*** spoil his pleasure (***an*** (*Dat.*), in); ***ich hatte nicht übel –,*** I had a good mind to . . .; ***alle – verlieren an*** (*Dat.*), lose all interest in; ***er zeigte wenig –,*** he showed little liking *or* inclination.

Lustbarkeit ['lustba:rkaɪt], *f.* amusement, entertainment, diversion; festivity, *pl.* revels. **Lustbarkeitssteuer,** *f.* entertainment tax.

Lustempfindung ['lustˀɛmpfɪnduŋ], *f.* pleasurable sensation.

lüsten ['lystən], *v.t. imp.* (*obs.*) ***es lüstet mich sehr danach,*** I covet it, I would fain have *or* do it; *see* **gelüsten.**

Lüster ['lystər], *m.* 1. chandelier; 2. *See* **Glanz, Schmelz. Lüsterglanz,** *m.* lustre, sheen, glaze, gloss.

lüstern ['lystərn], *adj.* greedy (***nach,*** for); desirous, covetous (of); lustful, lecherous, lascivious, lewd; ***–e Erzählung,*** indecent *or* ribald *or* bawdy *or* smutty *or* Rabelaisian story; ***mit –en Augen,*** with prurient *or* lascivious *or* lustful *or* lecherous *or* salacious glances. **Lüsternheit,** *f.* concupiscence, lasciviousness, lewdness, prurience, lubricity; lust, greed.

lusterregend ['lustˀɛrre:gənt], *adj.* erogenous. **Lust|fahrt,** *f.* pleasure-trip, outing; joy-ride. **–garten,** *m.* pleasure-gardens *or* -grounds. **–gefühl,** *n. See* **–empfindung. –haus, –häuschen,** *n.* summer-house.

lustig ['lustɪç], *adj.* merry, gay, joyous, jolly, jovial, cheerful; amusing, funny, droll, comical; ***–er Bruder,*** jolly fellow, joker, merry-andrew; ***–e Geschichte,*** funny story; ***sich über ihn – machen,*** make fun of *or* poke fun at him; (*Theat.*) ***–e Person,*** clown, fool; ***– sein,*** make merry; (*iron.*) ***das kann ja – werden,*** this is a pretty kettle of fish. **Lustigkeit,** *f.* gaiety, mirth, merriment, hilarity; fun, jollity, cheerfulness. **Lustigmacher,** *m.* buffoon, wag, clown, jester, merry-andrew.

Lüstling ['lystlɪŋ], *m.* (**-s,** *pl.* **-e**) voluptuary, sensualist; debauchee, lecher, rake, libertine.

lustlos ['lustlo:s], *adj.* spiritless, listless; (*Comm.*) dull, flat, inactive, lifeless. **Lustlosigkeit,** *f.* lack of spirit, listlessness; (*Comm.*) dullness, flatness, inactivity.

Lust|mord, *m.* murder and rape, sex murder. **–partie,** *f.* pleasure trip. **–schiff,** *n.* yacht, pleasure-boat. **–schloß,** *n.* country seat. **–seuche,** *f.* (*obs.*) venereal disease. **–sitz,** *m. See* **–schloß. –spiel,** *n.* (*Theat.*) comedy. **lustwandeln,** *v.i.* (*aux.* h. & s.) (*insep.*) stroll, go for a stroll *or* walk.

Lutheraner [lutə'ra:nər], *m.*, **lutheranisch,** *adj.* Lutheran.

lutschen ['lutʃən], *v.t., v.i.* suck. **Lutscher,** *m.* dummy, comforter.

lütt [lyt], *adj.* (*dial.*) *see* **lüttje.**

Lutter ['lutər], *m.* singlings (*brandy*).

Lüttich ['lytɪç], *n.* (*Geog.*) Liège.

lüttje ['lytjə], *adj.* (*dial.*) small, little, wee; (*dial.*) ***– Lage,*** beer with brandy.

Luv [lu:f], *f.* (*Naut.*) luff, weather side. **luven,** *v.i.* luff, ply to windward. **Luv|küste,** *f.* weather shore. **–seite,** *f.* (*Naut.*) weather side; windward slope (*of a hill*). **–winkel,** *m.* (*Naut.*) drift angle, allowance for wind.

luxurieren [luksu'ri:rən], *v.i.* luxuriate, revel, wallow. **luxuriös** [–ri'ø:s], *adj.* luxurious.

Luxus ['luksus], *m.* luxury, sumptuousness, extravagance. **Luxus|artikel,** *m.* luxury article; *pl.* luxuries, fancy goods. **–ausführung,** *f.* de-luxe model. **–ausgabe,** *f.* edition de luxe. **–ausgaben,** *f.pl.* luxury spending. **–kabine,** *f.* (*Naut.*) state-room. **–steuer,** *f.* luxury tax. **–verbot,** *n.* sumptuary law. **–wagen,** *m.* (*Motor.*) de-luxe model. **–ware,** *f. See* **–artikel. –zug** (*abbr.* **L-Zug**), *m.* saloon-train.

Luzern [lu'tsɛrn], *n.* (*Geog.*) Lucerne.

Lymphdrüse ['lymfdry:zə], *f.* lymphatic gland. **Lymphe,** *f.* lymph, vaccine. **Lymph|gefäß,** *n.* lymphatic vessel, lymph duct. **–körperchen,** *n.* lymph-corpuscle, leucocyte.

lynchen ['lynçən, 'lɪnçən], *v.t.* lynch. **Lynchjustiz,** *f.* mob law.

Lyra ['ly:ra], *f.* (-, *pl.* **-ren**) lyre; (*Astr.*) Lyra.

Lyrik ['ly:rɪk], *f.* lyric poetry. **Lyriker,** *m.* lyric poet. **lyrisch,** *adj.* lyric(al).

Lyssa ['lysa], *f.* rabies.

Lyzeum [ly'tse:um], *n.* (**-s,** *pl.* **-zeen**) girls' secondary school *or* high school.

L-Zug, *m. See* **Luxuszug.**

M

M, m [ɛm], *n.* M, m. *See Index of Abbreviations.*

Maar [ma:r], *n.* (**-es,** *pl.* **-e**) crater, volcanic lake, (*Scots*) corrie.

Maas [ma:s], *f.* (*Geog.*) River Meuse. **Maastricht,** *n.* (*Geog.*) Maestricht.

Maat [ma:t], *m.* (**-s,** *pl.* **-s** *or* **-en**) (*Naut.*) mate, petty-officer; (*coll.*) comrade, pal. **Maatschaft,** *f.* (*dial.*) mates, crew, (*coll.*) clique.

Machandelbaum [ma'xandəlbaum], *m.* (*dial.*) juniper.

Machart ['maxˀart], *f.* pattern, type, make, design, style.

Mache ['maxə], *f.* making, production, manufacture; (*fig.*) show, pretence, make-believe, (*coll.*) window-dressing, (*sl.*) eyewash; ***in die – nehmen,*** take in hand, set about, (*coll.*) give (*a p.*) a going-over, (*sl.*) give (*a p.*) the works; ***in der – haben,*** have in hand; ***in der – sein,*** be in hand; (*coll.*) ***er versteht sich auf die –,*** he knows how to beat the big drum *or* to blow his own trumpet.

machen ['maxən], **1.** *v.t.* make, do; manufacture, fabricate, prepare, produce, construct, form, create; cause, effect; constitute, amount *or* come to. **(a)** (*with nouns*) ***Anspruch – auf*** (*Acc.*), lay claim to; ***große Augen –,*** stare wide-eyed; ***einen Ausflug –,*** go on *or* for an excursion; ***einen Begriff – von,*** form an idea of; (*coll.*) ***ihm Beine –,*** make him find his legs, put one's toe behind him; ***einen Besuch –,*** pay a visit (***bei,*** to); ***ein Ende –,*** put an end (*Dat.*, to); ***Epoche –,*** make a stir, create a sensation; ***Ernst – mit,*** set about seriously, go ahead with; (*fig.*) ***Feuer hinter ihm –,*** put pressure on him; ***Freude –,*** give pleasure (*Dat.*, to); ***sich*** (*Dat.*) ***Gedanken – über*** (*Acc.*), wonder *or* worry about; ***Geschäfte – mit,*** do business with; ***sein Glück –,*** make one's fortune; ***sich*** (*Dat.*) ***das Haar –,*** do one's hair; ***Platz –,*** make way *or* room (*Dat.*, for); ***gemeinsame Sache – mit,*** make common cause with; ***Spaß –,*** joke; ***es macht mir Spaß,*** it amuses me; ***es macht keinen Spaß,*** it is a dull *or* dreary business; ***viel Wesens –,*** make a fuss (***von,*** about); ***nicht viel Wesens – mit,*** deal with *or* treat perfunctorily.

(b) (*with prons.*) ***so macht es jeder,*** everyone does it; ***so macht man es,*** that is how it's done; ***mache es mir nicht noch einmal so,*** don't let me catch you doing it again; ***so etwas macht man nicht,*** it (just) isn't done; (*coll.*) ***was macht das?*** what does it matter? (*sl.*) so what? ***was – Sie?*** what are you doing *or* are you up to? ***das macht nichts,*** never mind, that's all right; (*coll.*) ***das macht mir nichts,*** that's nothing to me, I don't care *or* mind; ***dagegen kann man nichts –,*** you can't do a thing about it, it cannot be helped; (*coll.*) ***nichts zu –!*** nothing doing! ***sich*** (*Dat.*) ***viel zu schaffen –,*** give o.s. *or* go to a lot of *or* no end of trouble.
(c) (*with adjs. etc.*) ***er macht es zu arg,*** he goes too far; ***sich beliebt –,*** ingratiate o.s. (***bei,*** with); ***gesund –,*** cure, restore to health; ***es ihm recht –,*** satisfy *or* please him; (*coll.*) ***mach schnell!*** hurry up! make haste! be quick! look sharp! (*sl.*) step on it! make it snappy! get a move on!
(d) (*with preps.*) ***sich*** (*Dat.*) ***viel*** (or ***wenig***) ***daraus –,*** make much (*or* little) of it, attach great (*or* little) importance to it, care much (*or* little) about it, mind (*or* not mind) much about it; ***– zu,*** change *or* turn *or* convert into; ***ihn zum Feind –,*** make an enemy of him; ***zu Geld –,*** sell, turn into money; ***es sich*** (*Dat.*) ***zum Gesetz –,*** make it one's rule; ***ihn zum König –,*** make him king.
(e) (*amount*) ***drei mal drei macht neun,*** three times three is *or* are nine; ***was macht die Rechnung?*** how much does the bill come to? ***wieviel macht es?*** how much is it *or* does it come to? ***das macht vier Mark,*** that amounts *or* comes to four marks.
(f) (*as p.p. and adj.*) ***gemacht,*** made (***aus,*** of); artificial, simulated, false; ***wird gemacht,*** it shall be done, I (*or* we) shall do it; ***das ist ihm wie gemacht,*** that suits him perfectly *or* to a T, that fits him like a glove; ***gemachte Begeisterung,*** simulated enthusiasm; ***gemachte Blumen,*** artificial flowers; ***ein gemachter Mann,*** a made man; ***gemacht!*** agreed! (*coll.*) right-oh! okay! ***gut gemacht!*** well done! good work!
2. *v.r.* 1. do well, get on; progress; ***der Junge macht sich jetzt,*** the boy is doing *or* shaping nicely *or* is getting on well; 2. come about, happen; ***es macht sich nicht, es läßt sich nicht –,*** it cannot be done *or* managed, it is not practicable *or* feasible; ***es wird sich schon –,*** it will come right in time; ***es macht sich,*** things are looking up, it's all plain sailing now; (*as reply to inquiry*) (*coll.*) so-so! not too badly! not bad! pretty well! 3. (*with preps.*) ***sich – an*** (*Acc.*), apply o.s. to, take in hand, set *or* go about, (*coll.*) tackle (*a task*); come *or* get near to, approach (*a p.*); ***sich auf die Beine –,*** be on the point of leaving, be about to set off; ***sich auf den Weg –,*** set out, depart; ***sich aus dem Staube –,*** take to one's heels.
3. *v.i.* do; ***mach daß du fortkommst!*** be off with you! (*sl.*) beat it! scram! ***lassen Sie mich nur –!*** just let me have my own way! just leave it to me! (*coll.*) ***ins Bett*** (or ***in die Hosen***) ***–,*** soiled the bed (*or* one's trousers); ***– in*** (*Dat.*), deal in; ***in Politik –,*** dabble in politics; ***in Wolle –,*** deal in wool, be in the woollen business.

Machenschaften ['maxənʃaftən], *f.pl.* machinations, intrigues.

Macher ['maxər], *m.* maker, manager, (*Pol. etc.*) wire-puller. **Macherlohn,** *m.* cost of *or* charge for making.

machiavellistisch [makiavɛ'lɪstɪʃ], *adj.* Machiavellian.

Macht [maxt], *f.* (-, *pl.* ⸚e) might; authority, influence, sway (***über*** (*Acc.*), over), control (of), grip (on); force, strength, power; (military) forces; (*Pol.*) ***an der –,*** in power; ***an die – kommen,*** rise to *or* come into power; ***aus eigner –,*** on one's own responsibility, by one's own authority; ***es steht nicht in meiner –,*** it is not in my power; ***mit aller –,*** with all one's might, with might and main; (*Prov.*) ***– geht vor Recht,*** might is right; ***die – der Gewohnheit,*** the force of habit.

Macht|befugnis, *f.* competency, authority, power. **-bereich,** *m.* sphere of influence. **-ergreifung,** *f. See* **-übernahme. -frage,** *f.* trial of strength. **-fülle,** *f.* fullness of strength. **-gebot,** *n.* authoritative *or* despotic order. **-gier,** *f.* greed for power. **-haber,** *m.* lord, ruler, dictator. **machthaberisch,** *adj.* dictatorial, despotic. **Machtherrscher,** *m.* despot. **machthungrig,** *adj.* power-hungry.

mächtig ['mɛçtɪç], **1.** *adj.* mighty, strong, powerful; vast, enormous, huge, immense; considerable; (*Min.*) rich, thick; ***einer S. – sein,*** be master of *or* have the mastery of a th., have authority over a th., control a th.; ***sie ist des Deutschen vollkommen –,*** she has a thorough command of German. **2.** *adv.* (*coll.*) extremely, intensely, awfully; ***– arbeiten,*** work like a horse *or* slave.

Machtkampf ['maxtkampf], *m.* struggle for power. **machtlos,** *adj.* powerless, weak, impotent. **Machtlosigkeit,** *f.* impotence, powerlessness, weakness. **Macht|politik,** *f.* power politics. **-probe,** *f. See* **-frage. -spruch,** *m.* authoritative decision, decree. **-stellung,** *f.* strong position; political power; predominance. **-trieb,** *m.* lust for power. **-übernahme,** *f.* seizure of power. **-verhältnis,** *n.* balance of power. **machtvoll,** *adj.* effective. **Macht|vollkommenheit,** *f.* authority, absolute power; ***aus eigner –,*** on one's own authority. **-weib,** *n.* virago, amazon. **-wort,** *n.* peremptory order, word of command; ***ein – sprechen,*** exert one's authority, (*coll.*) put one's foot down.

Machwerk ['maxvɛrk], *n.* concoction, (*coll.*) put-up job; clumsy *or* botched work.

Madagaskar [mada'gaskar], *n.* Madagasca. **Madagasse,** *m.* **(-n,** *pl.* **-n), madagassisch,** *adj.* Madagascan.

Mädchen ['mɛ:tçən], *n.* girl; (*dial.*) servant (girl), maid(-servant); maiden, maid; sweetheart; ***– für alles,*** maid-of-all-work, general servant. **mädchenhaft,** *adj.* girlish; maidenly, bashful. **Mädchen|handel,** *m.* white-slave traffic. **-kammer,** *f.* servants' bedroom. **-name,** *m.* maiden name. **-pensionat,** *n.* boarding school for young ladies. **-schändung,** *f.* violation, seduction (*of a girl under the age of 16 years*).

Made ['ma:də], *f.* maggot, mite; worm; ***wie die – im Speck sitzen,*** be (sitting) in clover.

Mädel ['mɛ:dəl], *n.* (*dial.*) girl, (*Scots*) lass.

madig ['ma:dɪç], *adj.* worm-eaten; maggoty; (*sl.*) ***ihn – machen,*** make mincemeat of him; (*sl.*) ***-er Kerl,*** heel, cad.

Madonnenbild [ma'dɔnənbɪlt], *n.* image of the Virgin Mary. **madonnenhaft,** *adj.* Madonna-like. **Madonnen|kultus,** *m.*, **-verehrung,** *f.* worship of the Virgin.

mag [ma:k], *see* **mögen.**

Magazin [maga'tsi:n], *n.* **(-s,** *pl.* **-e)** 1. warehouse; storehouse, depot, (*Mil.*) stores; repository; 2. magazine (*of gun*); 3. magazine, periodical. **Magazin|aufseher, -verwalter,** *m.* storeman, storekeeper, warehouse superintendent.

Magd [ma:kt], *f.* (-, *pl.* ⸚**e**) maid, maidservant, general servant; (*B.*) handmaid; (*Poet.*) maiden, virgin.

Mägdlein ['mɛ:ktlaɪn], *n.* (*Poet.*) little girl, lassie.

Mage ['ma:gə], *m.* **(-n,** *pl.* **-n)** (*obs.*) kinsman.

Magen ['ma:gən], *m.* **(-s,** *pl.* - (*dial.* ⸚)) stomach; (*of beasts*) maw, (*of birds*) gizzard; ***sich*** (*Dat.*) ***den – verderben,*** get indigestion, upset one's stomach; (*coll.*) ***im – haben,*** be sick and tired of, hate the mention of, be fed to the teeth with, (*sl.*) have had a bellyful of.

Magen|arznei, *f.* stomachic. **-ausgang,** *m.* pylorus. **-beschwerden,** *f.pl.* indigestion, gastric *or* stomach trouble. **-bewegung,** *f.* gastric movement. **-bitter,** *m.* bitters. **-brei,** *m.* chyme. **-brennen,** *n.* heartburn, pyrosis. **-eingang,** *m.* cardia. **-entzündung,** *f.* gastritis. **-erkältung,** *f.* chill on the stomach. **-fieber,** *n.* gastric fever. **-flüssigkeit,** *f.* gastric fluid *or* juice. **-gegend,** *f.* epigastrium. **-geschwür,** *n.* gastric ulcer. **-grube,** *f.* pit of the stomach. **-knurren,** *n.* rumbling in the bowels, (*coll.*) tummy rumbles. **magenkrank,** *adj.* dyspeptic. **Magen|krankheit,** *f.* gastric trouble, stomach disorder. **–krebs,** *m.* cancer of the stomach. **–lab,** *n.* rennet. **–leiden,** *n.* *See* **–krankheit. magen|leidend,** *adj. See* **–krank. Magen|-mittel,** *n. See* **–arznei. –mund,** *m. See* **–eingang. –pförtner,** *m. See* **–ausgang. –rohr,** *n.* œsophagus. **–saft,** *m. See* **–flüssigkeit. –säure,** *f.* acidity. **–schlund,** *m. See* **–rohr. –schmerzen,** *m.pl.* stomach-ache. **–schnitt,** *m.* gastrotomy. **–schwäche,** *f.* dyspepsia. **–stärkung,** *f. See* **–arznei. –übersäuerung,** *f. See* **–säure. –verstimmung,** *f.* stomach upset, indigestion.

mager ['ma:gər], *adj.* thin, lean, spare, gaunt, (*coll.*) skinny, scrawny; (*of meat*) lean; (*fig.*) poor, meagre, scanty; *–e Kost,* poor *or* slender fare; *–er Kalk,* poor lime; *–e Lauge,* weak lye; *–er Stoff,* short pulp. **Mager|fleisch,** *n.* lean (meat). **–käse,** *m.* non-fatty cheese. **Magerkeit,** *f.* leanness. **Mager|kohle,** *f.* semi-bituminous *or* non-coking coal. **–milch,** *f.* skim milk.

Magie [ma'gi:], *f.* magic. **Magier** ['ma:giə], *m.* magician; *pl.* Magi. **magisch** ['ma:gɪʃ], *adj.* magic(al).

Magister [ma'gɪstər], *m.* schoolmaster; tutor, (*Scots*) dominie; *– der freien Künste,* Master of Arts (*M.A.*). **magisterhaft,** *adj.* pedantic, didactic, pragmatic(al).

Magistrat [magɪs'tra:t], *m.* (**-(e)s,** *pl.* **-e**) town *or* city *or* borough *or* municipal council. **Magistrats|-beamte(r),** *m.* municipal officer, local government official. **–mitglied,** *n.*, **–person,** *f.* town councillor. **Magistratur** [–stra'tu:r], *f.* (-, *pl.* **-en**) municipal *or* local (government) authority.

Magnat [mag'na:t], *m.* (**-en,** *pl.* **-en**) magnate, grandee, (*coll.*) tycoon.

Magnesia [mag'ne:zia], *f.* magnesia, magnesium oxide; *doppeltkohlensaure –,* bicarbonate of magnesia. **Magnesium,** *n.* magnesium. **Magnesium|-licht,** *n.* flash-light. **–sulphat,** *m.* Epsom salt.

Magnet [mag'ne:t], *m.* (**-s** *or* **-en,** *pl.* **-e(n)**) magnet (*also fig.*); (*Motor.*) magneto; *natürlicher –,* lodestone. **Magnet|eisenerz,** *n.* magnetite. **–feld,** *n.* magnetic field. **magnetisch,** *adj.* magnetic; *–e Abweichung,* declination; *–er Schlaf,* mesmeric trance.

Magnetiseur [magneti'zø:r], *m.* (**-s,** *pl.* **-e**) mesmerist. **magnetisieren,** *v.t.* magnetize (*a th.*), mesmerize (*a p.*). **Magnetisierungsstärke,** *f.* intensity of magnetization. **Magnetismus** [–'tɪsmus], *m.* magnetism; mesmerism. **Magnetismus-menge,** *f.* intensity of magnetization.

Magnet|kies, *m.* magnetic pyrites. **–nadel,** *f.* magnetic needle, compass needle.

Magnetophon [magneto'fo:n], *n.* (**-s,** *pl.* **-e**) tape recorder. **Magnetophonband,** *n.* recording tape.

Magnet|regler, *m.* rheostat. **–schalter,** *m.* (*Motor.*) ignition switch. **–spule,** *f.* electromagnet, solenoid. **–stab,** *m.* bar magnet. **–stein,** *m.* lodestone. **–wicklung,** *f.* field coil. **–zündung,** *f.* magneto-ignition.

Magnolie [mag'no:liə], *f.* (*Bot.*) magnolia.

magst [ma:kst], *see* **mögen.**

mäh! [mɛ:], *int.* bah (*of sheep*).

Mahagoni [maha'go:ni], *n.* mahogany.

Maharadscha [maha'ra:dʒa], *m.* (**-s,** *pl.* **-s**) maharajah.

Mähbinder ['mɛ:bɪndər], *m.* reaper-binder.

1**Mahd** [ma:t], *f.* (-, *pl.* **-en**) mowing; swath(e); hay crop; hay-making time.

2**Mahd,** *n.* (**-es,** *pl.* **¨-er**) (*Swiss*) alpine pasture.

Mähder ['mɛ:dər], *m.* (*dial.*) *see* **Mäher.**

Mähdrescher ['mɛ:drɛʃər], *m.* combine harvester, (*Am.*) harvester combine.

1**mähen** ['mɛ:ən], *v.i.* bleat.

2**mähen,** *v.t., v.i.* mow, cut, reap. **Mäher,** *m.* mower, reaper, haymaker. **Mähfeuer,** *n.* (*Mil.*) shifting fire.

Mahl [ma:l], *n.* (**-(e)s,** *pl.* **-e** *or* **¨-er**) meal, repast, banquet, feast.

mahlen ['ma:lən], *reg. & irr.v.t. & v.i.* grind, mill, pound, crush, bruise, bray, beat; powder, pulverize; (*of wheels in mud*) spin; *gemahlener Kaffee,* ground coffee; (*Prov.*) *wer zuerst kommt, mahlt zuerst,* first come, first served.

Mahl|feinheit, *f.* fineness of grinding. **–gang,** *m.* millstones. **–geld,** *n.* miller's fee. **–gut,** *n. See* **–korn.**

mählich ['mɛ:lɪç], *adj.* (*obs.*) *see* **allmählich.**

Mahl|knecht, *m.* miller's man. **–korn,** *n.* grist.

Mahlschatz ['ma:lʃats], *m.* (*obs.*) dowry.

Mahlstrom ['ma:lʃtro:m], *m.* maelstrom, vortex, whirlpool.

Mahl|werk, *n.* grinding mill. **–zahn,** *m.* molar.

Mahlzeit ['ma:ltsaɪt], *f.* meal; *gesegnete –!* good appetite! (*coll.*) *prost –!* there we are! and that's that!

Mähmaschine ['mɛ:maʃi:nə], *f.* mowing *or* reaping machine; lawn-mower.

Mahnbrief ['ma:nbri:f], *m.* request for payment, dunning letter, reminder, demand-note.

Mähne ['mɛ:nə], *f.* mane.

mahnen ['ma:nən], *v.t.* remind; warn, admonish; exhort, urge; *ihn an seine Pflicht –,* remind him of his duty; *wegen einer Schuld –,* press for payment, demand payment from, dun.

Mähnenbusch ['mɛ:nənbuʃ], *m.* (helmet) plume.

mahnend ['ma:nənt], *adj.* warning, admonitory. **Mahner,** *m.* admonisher, warning voice; (*for payment*) dun(ner). **Mahn|gebühr,** *f.* library fine. **–mal,** *n.* memorial (stone *etc.*). **–ruf,** *m.* warning cry. **–schreiben,** *n. See* **Mahnbrief. Mahnung,** *f.* reminder; warning, admonition; dunning. **Mahn|verfahren,** *n.* (*Law*) hortatory proceedings. **–wort,** *n.* warning, exhortation. **–zeichen,** *n.* the writing on the wall. **–zettel,** *m.* reminder, demand note.

Mahr [ma:r], *m.* (**-(e)s,** *pl.* **-e**) (*dial.*) nightmare.

Mähre ['mɛ:rə], *f.* mare, (*coll.*) jade, hack.

Mähren ['mɛ:rən], *n.* (*Geog.*) Moravia. **mährisch,** *adj.* Moravian.

Mai [maɪ], *m.* (**-s,** *pl.* **-e**) (*Poet.* **-en,** *pl.* **-en**) May; *im –,* in (the month of) May; *der erste –,* the first of May, Mayday. **Mai|baum,** *m.* maypole. **–blume,** *f.* (*Bot.*) lily of the valley (*Convallaria majalis*).

Maid [maɪt], *f.* (-, *pl.* **-en**) *Poet. for* **Magd, Mädchen.**

Maie ['maɪə], *f.*, *Austr. m.* (**-n,** *pl.* **-n**) 1. maypole; 2. Mayday festivities; 3. greenery, leaves (*for decoration*); (*dial.*) birch twigs, birch sapling. **Maien,** *m.* (*Swiss*) posy, bouquet. **Maien|blüte,** *f.* (*fig.*) blossom-time, spring-time. **–königin,** *f.* Queen of the May. **–säß,** *n.* (**-es,** *pl.* **-e**) (*Swiss*) spring pasture.

Mai|feier, *f.*, **–fest,** *n.* Mayday celebration. **–glöckchen,** *n. See* **–blume. –käfer,** *m.* (*Ent.*) cockchafer (*Melolontha vulgaris*); *grinsen wie ein –,* grin like a Cheshire cat. **maikäfern,** *v.i.* (*sl.*) ponder, ruminate, rack one's brains. **Mai|kätzchen,** *n.* catkin (*of birches etc.*). **–königin,** *f. See* **Maienkönigin.**

Mailand ['maɪlant], *n.* (*Geog.*) Milan. **mailändisch,** *adj.* Milanese.

Mainz [maɪnts], *n.* (*Geog.*) Mayence.

Mais [maɪs], *m.* Indian corn, maize.

Maischbottich ['maɪʃbɔtɪç], *m.* mash(ing)-tub *or* -vat. **Maische,** *f.* mash. **maischen,** *v.t.* mash.

Mais|flocken, *f.pl.* cornflakes. **–kolben,** *m.* corn (-on-the-)cob. **–mehl,** *n.* cornflour.

Majestät [majɛs'tɛ:t], *f.* (-, *pl.* **-en**) majesty. **majestätisch,** *adj.* majestic. **Majestätsbeleidigung,** *f.* lèse-majesté.

Major [ma'jo:r], *m.* (**-s,** *pl.* **-e**) (*Mil.*) major, (*Av.*) squadron-leader.

Majoran [majo'ra:n], *m.* (**-s,** *pl.* **-e**) (*Bot.*) marjoram.

Majorat [majo'ra:t], *n.* (**-s,** *pl.* **-e**) primogeniture; entail. **Majorats|gut,** *n.* property entailed on the eldest child. **–herr,** *m.* owner of an entailed estate. **majorenn,** *adj.* of age.

Majorin [ma'jo:rɪn], *f.* major's wife.

majorisieren [majori'zi:rən], *v.t.* carry by a majority. **Majorität,** *f.* majority (*of votes etc.*). **Majoritätsbeschluß,** *m.* resolution carried by a majority.

Majuskel [ma'juskəl], *f.* (-, *pl.* **-n**) capital (letter), upper case, majuscule; (*Typ.*) small cap.

makadamisieren [makadami'zi:rən], *v.t.* macadamize, metal (*roads*).

Makel ['ma:kəl], *m.* stain, spot, blot, taint, blemish, flaw, defect, fault.

Mäkelei [mɛ:kə'laɪ], *f.* fault-finding, censoriousness; – ***im Essen,*** fastidiousness. **mäkelig,** *adj.* censorious, carping; fastidious, fussy, finicky.

makellos ['ma:kəllo:s], *adj.* spotless, unblemished, impeccable, immaculate.

mäkeln ['mɛ:kəln], *v.i.* – *an* (*Dat.*), find fault with, carp *or* cavil at, (*coll.*) run down.

makeln ['ma:kəln], *v.i.* act as a broker *or* go-between, negotiate; ***mit seinem Gewissen*** –, compound with one's conscience.

Makkaroni [maka'ro:ni], *pl.* macaroni.

makkaronisch [maka'ro:nɪʃ], *adj.* macaronic, burlesque (*of verse etc.*).

Makler ['ma:klər], (*Swiss* **Mäkler**), *m.* broker, middleman, jobber, factor, (commission-)agent. **Makler|gebühr,** *f.* brokerage, commission. **–geschäft,** *n.* broker's business.

Makrele [ma'kre:lə], *f.* mackerel.

Makrone [ma'kro:nə], *f.* macaroon.

Makulatur [makula'tu:r], *f.* (-, *pl.* **-en**) waste paper, scrap. **Makulaturbogen,** *m.* (*Typ.*) waste sheet. **makulieren** [–'li:rən], *v.t.* pulp (*paper*).

[1]**Mal** [ma:l], *n.* (**-(e)s,** *pl.* **-e** *or* **¨-er**) sign, mark; landmark, monument; stigma, stain, spot, birthmark, mole; (*Spt.*) goal, base, start(ing point *or* post).

[2]**Mal,** *n.* (**-(e)s,** *pl.* **-e**) time, occasion; ***das erste*** –, the first time; ***zum dritten –e,*** for the third time; ***dieses eine*** –, this once, on this occasion; ***mit einem*** –, all at once, suddenly, (*coll.*) all of a sudden; ***zu wiederholten –en, ein – über das andre,*** time after time, time and again, again and again, repeatedly, time out of number; ***ein ums andre*** –, by turns, alternately.

mal, *adv.* 1. (*in multiplication*) times, multiplied by; ***2 – 5 ist 10,*** twice 5 are 10; ***3 – 5 ist 15,*** three times 5 is 15; 2. (*coll. for* **einmal**); ***es ist nun – nicht anders in der Welt,*** that is (just) the way of the world; ***sie ist nicht – hübsch,*** she is not even pretty; ***hör' –!*** just listen! ***kommen Sie – her!*** just come here!

-mal, *adj.suff.* (*with meanings as* [2]**Mal**); ***drei– bis viermal*** (***3– bis 4mal***), on three or four occasions; *see* **allemal, diesmal, einmal, zweimal** *etc.*, **erstemal, etlichemal, letztenmal** *etc.*, **manchmal, wievielmal, x-mal** *etc.*

Malaie [ma'laɪə], *m.* (**-n,** *pl.* **-n**), **malaiisch,** *adj.* Malay, Malayan.

malen ['ma:lən], **1.** *v.t.* paint; portray, depict, represent, delineate; ***sich – lassen,*** sit for one's portrait, have one's portrait painted; (*Prov.*) ***den Teufel an die Wand –,*** talk of the devil; ***sie ist zum Malen,*** she is a picture; ***es ist wie gemalt,*** it is like a picture *or* as pretty as a picture. **2.** *v.r.* (*fig.*) show itself, be reflected.

Maler ['ma:lər], *m.* painter, artist. **Malerei** [–'raɪ], *f.* painting; picture. **Maler|farbe,** *f.* artists' colour, paint. **–gold,** *n.* ormolu. **malerisch,** *adj.* picturesque, artistic; pictorial, graphic. **Maler|leinwand,** *f.* artist's canvas. **–meister,** *m.* (house-)painter, painter and decorator. **–pinsel,** *m.* paint-brush. **–scheibe,** *f.* palette. **–schule,** *f.* school of painting *or* painters; school of art. **–staffelei,** *f.* easel. **–stock,** *m.* maulstick.

Malheur [ma'lø:r], *n.* (**-s,** *pl.* **-e**) (*coll.*) misfortune, mishap.

-malig ['ma:lɪç], *adj.suff.* (*with meanings as* [2]**Mal**) -fold; *e.g.* ***dreimalig*** (***3malig***), threefold.

maliziös [malitsi'ø:s], *adj.* malicious.

Malkasten ['ma:lkastən], *m.* paintbox.

Mall [mal], *n.* (**-es,** *pl.* **-e**) (*Naut.*) model, mould. **Mallbrief,** *m.* (*Naut.*) building contract.

Malmann ['ma:lman], *m.* (*Spt.*) scratch runner.

malnehmen ['ma:lne:mən], *irr.v.t.* multiply.

Malter ['maltər], *m. or n.* (*obs.*) corn-measure (*about 150 litres*); cord (*of wood*). **maltern,** *v.t.* cord (*wood*).

Malteser [mal'te:zər], *m.* Maltese. **Malteserkreuz,** *n.* Maltese cross. **maltesisch,** *adj.* Maltese.

Malvasier [malva'zi:r], *m.* malmsey (*grape or wine*).

Malve ['malvə], *f.* (*Bot.*) mallow. **malvern|artig,** *adj.* (*Bot.*) malvaceous. **–farbig,** *adj.* mauve, heliotrope.

Malz [malts], *n.* (**-es,** *pl.* **-e**) malt; (*Prov.*) ***an ihm ist Hopfen und – verloren,*** he is (quite) hopeless. **Malz|auszug,** *m.* malt-extract. **–bier,** *n.* malt-beer. **–bonbon,** *m. or n.* cough-lozenge. **–darre,** *f.* malt-kiln.

Malzeichen ['ma:ltsaɪçən], *n.* multiplication sign.

Mälzer ['mɛltsər], *m.* maltster. **Mälzerei** [–'raɪ], *f.* 1. malting; 2. malt-house.

Malz|kaffee, *m.* malt coffee. **–milch,** *f.* malted milk. **–schrot,** *m. or n.* crushed malt, grist. **–tenne,** *f.* malt-floor. **–zucker,** *m.* (*Chem.*) maltose.

Mama [ma'ma:], *f.* (-, *pl.* **-s**) (*coll.*) mamma, mummy, mom, ma.

Mammon ['mamɔn], *m.* mammon, lucre; ***schnöder*** –, filthy lucre. **Mammons|diener, –knecht,** *m.* mammon-worshipper, worldling, self-seeker, time-server, fortune hunter.

Mammut ['mamut], *n.* (**-(e)s,** *pl.* **-s** *or* **-e**) mammoth.

mampfen ['mampfən], *v.i.* (*coll.*) eat with one's mouth full.

Mamsell [mam'zɛl], *f.* (-, *pl.* **-en** *or* **-s**) (*coll.*) miss, damsel; shopgirl; housekeeper, stewardess (*on a farm*).

[1]**man** [man], *indef. pron.* (*used only in the Nom. sing.*; *in other cases an oblique case of* **einer** *is used*) 1. (*with 1st pers. reference*) one, we, you; 2. (*with 3rd pers. reference*) someone, somebody, they, people; 3. (*rendered by passive construction*); 4. (*formal imper.*) – ***sagt,*** it is said, they say; – ***hat mir gesagt,*** I was *or* have been told; – ***muß es tun,*** it must be done; – ***kann nicht wissen,*** there is no knowing; – ***schneide AD im Punkte B,*** bisect *AD* at the point *B*; – ***nehme eine Tablette,*** take one tablet.

[2]**man,** *adv.* (*dial.*) only, but; ***das ist – wenig,*** that is but little; ***geh – ja nicht hin!*** mind you do not go! (*coll.*) ***denn – los!*** here goes!

managen ['mɛnɪdʒən], *v.t.* (*coll.*) have under one's thumb; bring off, wangle, work. **Managerkrankheit,** *f.* (*coll.*) thrombosis, stress disease.

manch [manç], *indef.adj., pron.* many a (one), many a thing; – ***einer,*** many a one; ***das habe ich – liebes mal gehört,*** I have heard that many a time; ***das wird –em leid sein,*** that will grieve many a one; ***ich habe Ihnen –es zu erzählen,*** I have a good deal to tell you; ***–es ist dabei zu bedenken,*** many things must be considered; ***in –em hast du recht,*** in many things *or* to a great *or* large extent you are right. **manche,** *pl.* many; some, several.

mancherlei [mançər'laɪ], *indecl.adj.* all sorts of, many different, various, sundry, divers; ***auf – Art,*** in sundry *or* various ways; ***er sagte mir –,*** he told me many things.

Manchester ['mɛntʃɛstər], *m.* corduroy, (*coll.*) cord; velveteen.

manchmal ['mançma:l], *adv.* sometimes, now and again, from time to time, at times.

Mandant [man'dant], *m.* (**-en,** *pl.* **-en**) customer, client.

Mandarine [manda'ri:nə], *f.* mandarin orange, tangerine.

Mandat [man'da:t], *n.* (**-(e)s,** *pl.* **-e**) mandate, (*Pol.*) seat; authorization, (*Law*) brief; (*Austr.*) order to pay. **Mandatar** [–'ta:r], *m.* (**-s,** *pl.* **-e**) proxy, mandatary, attorney. **Mandatarmacht,** *f.* mandatory power *or* authority. **Mandatsgebiet,** *n.* mandated territory.

[1]**Mandel** ['mandəl], *f.* (-, *pl.* **-n**) 1. (*Bot.*) almond; 2. (*Anat.*) tonsil.

[2]**Mandel,** *f.* (-, *pl.* **-(n)**), *Austr. m.* (**-s,** *pl.* **-n**) set of 15, 15 sheaves.

Mandel|entfernung, *f.* (*Med.*) tonsilectomy. **–entzündung,** *f.* tonsilitis. **–kern,** *m.* almond. **–kleie,** *f.* ground almonds. **–krähe,** *f.* (*Orn.*) *see* **Blauracke.**

mandeln ['mandəln], *v.t.* put up in heaps *or* shocks of 15 sheaves; count by fifteens. **mandelweise,** *adv.* by fifteens.

Mandoline [mando'li:nə], *f.* mandolin.

Mandragora [man'dra:gora], *f.* (-, *pl.* **-ren**) (*Bot.*) mandrake.

Mandschurei [mandʒu'raɪ], *f.* (*Geog.*) Manchuria.

Manege [ma'nɛ:ʒə], *f.* riding-school; circus ring.

Manen ['ma:nən], *pl.* manes, shades.

Mangan [maŋ'ga:n], *n.* manganese. **mangansauer,** *adj.* manganate of. **Mangan|säure,** *f.* manganic acid. **–stahl,** *m.* manganese steel.

Mange ['maŋə], *f.* (*dial.*) *see* [1]**Mangel.**

[1]**Mangel** ['maŋəl], *f.* (-, *pl.* **-n**) mangle, wringer; calender, rolling-press.

[2]**Mangel,** *m.* (**-s,** *pl.* **¨-e**) want, lack, need, shortage, scarcity, dearth, deficiency, absence, defect, blemish, imperfection, flaw, fault, short-coming; *– haben an* (*Dat.*), be short of *or* in need *or* want of; *aus – an, see* **mangels**; *– leiden,* be destitute, suffer privation; *in – geraten,* be reduced to want *or* penury.

Mangel|erkrankung, *f. See* **–krankheit. –güter,** *n.pl.* goods in short supply. **mangelhaft,** *adj.* defective (*also Gram.*), imperfect, faulty, deficient, incomplete, inadequate, unsatisfactory. **Mangelhaftigkeit,** *f.* inadequacy, incompleteness, defectiveness, faultiness, imperfection. **Mangelkrankheit,** *f.* deficiency disease, malnutrition, vitamin deficiency, avitaminosis.

[1]**mangeln** ['maŋəln], *v.t.* mangle, wring (*laundry*), calender (*cloth*).

[2]**mangeln,** *imp.v.i.* want, lack, be wanting *or* lacking, be deficient; *an mir soll es nicht –,* I shall not fail, I shall do my part; *er läßt es sich* (*Dat.*) *an nichts –,* he denies himself nothing, he goes short of nothing; *es mangelt mir an barem Geld,* I am short of *or* in need of ready money; *wegen –der Nachfrage,* in absence of demand.

Mängelrüge ['mɛŋəlry:gə], *f.* (dissatisfied customer's) complaint.

mangels ['maŋəls], *prep.* (*Gen.*) for want *or* lack of, in the absence *or* in default of; *– Annahme,* for non-acceptance.

Mangel|ware, *f.* scarce commodity; *see* **–güter.**

Mangold ['maŋgɔlt], *m.* (**-s,** *pl.* **-e**) silver *or* stock beet, mangel-wurzel.

Manie [ma'ni:], *f.* mania; craze; *es ist ihm zur – geworden,* it is a mania with him.

Manier [ma'ni:r], *f.* (-, *pl.* **-en**) manner; fashion, mode, style; mannerism; (*Mus.*) grace notes; *pl.* manners, good behaviour; *mit guter –,* with a good grace; *das ist keine –,* that is not the way to behave. **manieriert** [–'ri:rt], *adj.* affected, stilted, pretentious, meretricious, ornate, flamboyant, pompous, bombastic, grandiloquent, highfalutin(g). **manierlich,** *adj.* well-mannered, well-bred, well-behaved, mannerly, genteel, civil.

Manifest [mani'fɛst], *n.* (**-es,** *pl.* **-e**) manifesto; (*Naut.*) ship's manifest.

Manifestant [manifɛs'tant], *m.* (**-en,** *pl.* **-en**) demonstrator. **Manifestationseid** [–tatsi'o:ns-ʔaɪt], *m.* (*obs.*) sworn declaration of insolvency. **manifestieren,** *v.t.* 1. manifest; 2. (*obs.*) (*Law*) swear an affidavit to one's insolvency; 3. make a demonstration, demonstrate (*für,* in favour of; *gegen,* against).

Maniküre [mani'ky:rə], *f.* 1. manicure; 2. manicurist. **maniküren,** *v.t.* manicure.

Manipel [ma'nɪpəl], *f.* (-, *pl.* **-n**) (*Eccl.*) maniple. **Manipulation** [–pulatsi'o:n], *f.* manipulation, treatment. **manipulieren** [–'li:rən], *v.t.* manipulate, treat, work.

manisch ['ma:nɪʃ], *adj.* manic, maniac.

Manko ['maŋko], *n.* (**-s,** *pl.* **-s**) deficit, deficiency, short measure *or* weight, shortage.

Mann [man], *m.* 1. (**-(e)s,** *pl.* **¨-er**) man; husband; 2. (**-es,** *pl.* **-en**) (*Poet.*) retainer, vassal; *die Soldaten standen drei – hoch,* the soldiers were drawn up three deep; *mit dreitausend –,* with three thousand troops; *tausend – zu Fuß,* a thousand foot-(soldiers) *or* infantrymen; (*Naut.*) *alle – an Deck!* all hands on deck! *so viel auf den –,* so much per *or* a head; *an den – bringen,* find a purchaser for, dispose of, place (*goods*); find a husband for, dispose of in marriage (*one's daughter*); *seinen – finden,* find *or* meet one's match; *– für –,* man for man; *– gegen –,* hand to hand (*fight*); *er ist –s genug,* he is man enough; *den lieben Gott einen guten – sein lassen,* let things take their course; *der kleine –,* the common man, the man in the street; *wenn Not am – ist,* in case of need *or* necessity, if the worst comes to the worst; (*Cards*) *wollen Sie den vierten – machen?* will you make the fourth? *mit – und Maus untergehen,* go down with all hands; *du wärst nie mein –,* you would never do for me, you are not the man for me; *seinen – stehen,* hold one's own, stand one's ground; *seinen – stellen,* pull one's weight, do one's share; *du bist ein – des Todes, wenn . . .,* you are a dead man if . . .; *das Volk erhob sich wie ein –,* the nation rose as one man; *der wilde –,* the wild man of the woods; (*Prov.*) *ein – ein Wort,* an honest man is as good as his word.

mannbar ['manba:r], *adj.* marriageable. **Mannbarkeit,** *f.* sexual maturity, puberty, marriageable age.

Männchen ['mɛnçən], *n.* (**-s,** *pl.* - *or* **männerchen**) little man, manikin; male (*of beasts, birds etc.*); *mein –,* my dear hubby; *– machen,* sit up, beg (*as a dog*); *Männerchen sehen,* see pink elephants.

Männer ['mɛnər], *pl. of* **Mann. Männer|chor,** *m.* male(-voice) choir. **–gesangverein,** *m.* men's choral society. **–riege,** *f.* (*Gymn.*) men's section. **–stimme,** *f.* man's voice, male part. **–treu,** *f.* (*Bot.*) black orchis (*Nigritella nigra*). **–volk,** *n.,* **–welt,** *f.* men(folk).

Mannes|alter, *n.* (years of) manhood; *im besten –,* in the prime of life. **–kraft,** *f.* manly vigour, virility. **–stamm,** *m.* male line. **–stolz,** *m.* manly pride. **–wort,** *n.* honest man's word. **–würde,** *f.* manly dignity.

mannhaft ['manhaft], *adj.* manly, brave, valiant; resolute, stout. **Mannhaftigkeit,** *f.* manliness; bravery, courage. **Mannheit,** *f.* manhood, masculinity, virility.

mannig|fach ['manɪç–], **–faltig,** *adj.* various, manifold, diverse, multifarious. **Mannigfaltigkeit,** *f.* multiplicity, variety, diversity.

männiglich ['mɛnɪçlɪç], *indecl.adj.* (*Law*) every man, everybody; one and all; individually and collectively.

Männin ['mɛnɪn], *f.* virago; (*B.*) woman. **männisch,** *adj.* unwomanly, mannish (*of a woman*).

Männlein ['mɛnlaɪn], *n.* little fellow; *– und Weiblein,* man, woman, and child.

männlich ['mɛnlɪç], *adj.* male, manly; (*Gram.*) masculine; *–e Kleidung,* man's clothes. **Männlichkeit,** *f.* masculinity, maleness; manliness, virility.

Mannsbild ['mansbɪlt], *n.* (*coll.*) man, male.

Mannschaft ['manʃaft], *f.* (body of) men, personnel, troops, crew; (*Spt.*) team; *pl.* (*Mil.*) rank and file, other ranks; (*Naut.*) the lower deck, ratings. **Mannschafts|führer,** *m.* (*Spt.*) (team) captain. **–geist,** *m.* team-spirit. **–kost,** *f.* troops' rations. **–rennen,** *n.* team-race. **–schlitten,** *m.* bobsleigh. **–wagen,** *m.* (*Mil.*) troop carrier.

mannshoch ['mansho:x], *adj.* tall as a man. **Manns|leute,** *pl.* menfolk, men. **–person,** *f.* man, male. **mannstoll,** *adj.* mad about men, nymphomaniac. **Manns|tollheit,** *f.* nymphomania. **–treu,** *f.* (*Bot.*) eryngo, sea-holly (*Eryngium maritimum*). **–volk,** *n. See* **–leute. –zucht,** *f.* (military) discipline.

Mannweib ['manvaɪp], *n.* virago, amazon.

Manometer [mano'meːtər], *n.* manometer; steam-gauge, pressure-gauge.

Manöver [ma'nøːvər], *n.* manœuvre; military exercise; (*fig.*) trick, feint. **manövrieren** [–'vriːrən], *v.i.* manœuvre. **manövrierfähig,** *adj.* manœuvrable. **Manövrierfreiheit,** *f.* freedom of manœuvre. **manövrierunfähig,** *adj.* out of control.

Mansarde [man'zardə], *f.* attic, garret. **Mansarden|dach,** *n.* mansard-roof. **–fenster,** *n.* attic-window, dormer-window. **–wohnung,** *f.* garret.

Mansch [manʃ], *m.* (**-(e)s,** *pl.* **-e**) mixture, hotchpotch, squash, (*coll.*) mess, slop. **manschen,** *v.t., v.i.* paddle about, splash (about), dabble, mix up, knead. **Manscherei** [–'raɪ], *f.* dabbling, splashing, mixing, kneading.

Manschester, *m. See* **Manchester.**

Manschette [man'ʃɛtə], *f.* cuff; (*Mech.*) collar, sleeve; (*coll.*) ***–n haben*** (***vor*** (*Dat.*)), funk; (*coll.*) ***–n bekommen,*** get cold feet. **Manschetten|fieber,** *n.* (*coll.*) funk. **–knopf,** *m.* cuff-link.

Mantel ['mantəl], *m.* (**-s,** *pl.* **¨-**) overcoat, greatcoat, top coat; cloak, robe; (*Zool.*) pallium; mantle, pall; envelope, sheathing, case, shell, jacket, sleeve, casing; outer cover (*of a tyre*); (*fig.*) mantle, cloak, pretence; ***den – nach dem Winde hängen,*** temporize, trim one's sails according to the wind.

Mäntelchen ['mɛntəlçən], *n.* short cloak, cape; ***ein – umhängen*** (*Dat.*), gloss over, palliate.

Mantel|geschoß, *n.* (*Artil.*) shell. **–gesetz,** *n.* skeleton law. **–möwe,** *f.* (*Orn.*) Greater (*Am.* Great) black-backed gull (*Larus marinus*). **–sack,** *m.* portmanteau, valise. **–schicht,** *f.* protective layer. **–stoff,** *m.* mantling, coat-material. **–tarif,** *m.* skeleton agreement. **–träger,** *m.* time-server, turncoat. **–tuch,** *n. See* **–stoff.**

Mantille [man'tɪljə], *f.* mantilla.

Mantsch, mantschen, *see* **Mansch, manschen.**

Manual [manu'aːl], *n.* (**-s,** *pl.* **-e**) 1. handbook; (*Comm.*) journal, day-book; 2. (*Mus.*) keyboard; (organ-)manual. **manuell,** *adj.* manual (*skill*).

Manufaktur [manufak'tuːr], *f.* (-, *pl.* **-en**) 1. manufacture, manufacturing; 2. hand-made article; 3. (*obs.*) factory. **Manufakturist,** *m.* (**-en,** *pl.* **-en**) manufacturer; dealer in textiles. **Manufakturwaren,** *f.pl.* textiles, drapery, (*Am.*) dry-goods.

Manuskript [manu'skrɪpt], *n.* (**-(e)s,** *pl.* **-e**) (*Typ.*) manuscript; copy; (*Films*) script, scenario; ***als – gedruckt,*** printed for private circulation only; (*Theat.*) acting rights reserved.

Mappe ['mapə], *f.* portfolio, briefcase, satchel; letter- *or* writing-case; folder, file.

Mär [mɛːr], *f.* (-, *pl.* **-en**) news, tidings, rumour, report, story.

Marasmus [ma'rasmus], *m.* (-, *pl.* **-men**) marasmus, wasting, bodily decay. **marastisch,** *adj.* marasmic, wasted, decrepit.

Marbel ['marbəl], **Märbel,** *m. See* **Marmel.**

Märchen ['mɛːrçən], *n.* fairy-tale; fable, legend; tale, story; fib. **märchenhaft,** *adj.* fabulous, legendary; (*fig.*) fictitious. **Märchenwelt,** *f.* fabulous world, world of romance, Wonderland.

Marder ['mardər], *m.* (*Zool.*) pine marten; marten-fur.

Märe ['mɛːrə], *f. See* **Mär.**

Margarine [marga'riːnə], *f.* margarine. **margarinsauer,** *adj.* (*Chem.*) margaric, margarate of.

Marien|bild [ma'riːən–], *n.* Madonna, image of the Virgin Mary. **–dienst,** *m. See* **–kult. –distel,** *f.* (*Bot.*) milk thistle (*Silybum marignum*). **–fäden,** *m.pl.* gossamer. **–fest,** *n.* Lady Day. **–flachs,** *m.* (*Bot.*) toadflax (*Linaria*). **–garn,** *n. See* **–fäden. –glas,** *n.* mica. **–käfer,** *m.* ladybird, (*Am.*) ladybug (*Coccinellidae*). **–kapelle,** *f.* Lady chapel. **–kult,** *m.* mariolatry.

Marille [ma'rɪlə], *f.* (*Austr.*) apricot.

Marine [ma'riːnə], *f.* navy, naval forces; (*in Germany combined navy and merchant fleet*); ***bei der – dienen,*** serve in the navy. **Marine|akademie,** *f.* (Royal) Naval College. **–artillerie,** *f.* naval artillery (*in Germany,* coastal artillery). **–blau,** *n.* navy blue. **–etat,** *m.* naval estimates. **–flugwesen,** *n.* Fleet Air Arm. **–flugzeug,** *n.* naval aircraft, plane of the Fleet Air Arm. **–infanterie,** *f.* marines. **–minister,** *m.* (*Eng.*) First Lord of the Admiralty; (*Am.*) Secretary of the Navy. **–ministerium,** *n.* (*Eng.*) Admiralty, (*Am.*) Navy Department. **–offizier,** *m.* naval officer. **–soldat,** *m.* marine. **–station,** *f.*, **–stützpunkt,** *m.* naval base. **–truppen,** *f.pl.* marines. **–werft,** *f.* navy-yard, naval dockyard. **–wesen,** *f.* naval affairs.

marinieren [mari'niːrən], *v.t.* pickle, marinate.

Marionette [mario'nɛtə], *f.* puppet, marionette. **Marionetten|regierung,** *f.* puppet government. **–spiel,** *n.* puppet-show. **–theater,** *n.* marionette- *or* puppet-theatre.

1**Mark** [mark], *f.* (-, *pl.* **-en**) boundary, frontier, limit; border, border-country, marches; wood *or* pasture held in common; (*Rugby footb.*) touch-(line); (*Geog.*) ***die –*** (***Brandenburg***), Brandenburg.

2**Mark,** *f.* (-, *pl.* **–stücke,** (*as measure of value*) – (*e.g.* 5 –, 5 marks)) mark (*coin*).

3**Mark,** *n.* marrow, medulla; (*of wood*) pith; (*of fruit*) pulp; (*fig.*) core, heart, essence; (*coll.*) ***– in den Knochen haben,*** have guts; ***ihm durch – und Bein gehen,*** set his teeth on edge; ***ins – treffen,*** cut to the quick; ***bis ins –,*** to the marrow *or* (*fig.*) core.

markant [mar'kant], *adj.* striking, prominent, (well-)marked, salient, characteristic; ***–e Persönlichkeit,*** outstanding personality, man of mark.

Marke ['markə], *f.* 1. mark, token, sign; countermark, label, chit, chip, check, counter, ticket, coupon; trade-mark; 2. grade, quality, sort; growth, vintage; type, brand, make; (*coll.*) ***sie ist eine –,*** she's a (queer) character; 3. (postage) stamp.

Markenartikel ['markənˀartɪkəl], *m.* proprietary article. **markenfrei, 1.** *adj.* non-rationed, coupon-free. **2.** *adv.* off the ration. **Markenname,** *m.* proprietary name, brand. **markenpflichtig,** *adj.* rationed. **Marken|sammler,** *m.* stamp collector, philatelist. **–schutz,** *m.* trade-mark, registration. **–ware,** *f. See* **–artikel.**

Märker ['mɛrkər], *m.* frontier dweller; Brandenburger.

markerschütternd ['markˀɛrʃytərnt], *adj.* blood-curdling.

Marketender [markə'tɛndər], *m.* (*Hist.*) canteen proprietor, (*obs.*) sutler. **Marketenderin,** *f.* (*Hist.*) camp-follower.

Mark|graf, *m.* margrave. **–gräfin,** *f.* margravine.

Markholz ['markhɔlts], *n.* heartwood.

markieren [mar'kiːrən], *v.t.* 1. mark, label, stamp, brand; indicate, designate, earmark; 2. accentuate; 3. (*coll.*) simulate, sham, put on. **Markierung,** *f.* marking (*of footpaths etc.*), marker, route-indicator.

markig ['markɪç], *adj.* marrowy, (*fig.*) pithy, vigorous, emphatic.

märkisch ['mɛrkɪʃ], *adj.* (*Geog.*) (of) Brandenburg.

Markise [mar'kiːzə], *f.* blind, awning.

Markknochen ['markknɔxən], *m.* marrow-bone. **marklos,** *adj.* marrowless, (*fig.*) spineless, spiritless.

Markör [mar'køːr], *m.* (**-s,** *pl.* **-e**) 1. billiard-marker, billiard-hall attendant; 2. (*Austr.*) waiter.

Mark|scheider, *m.* mining surveyor. **–stein,** *m.* boundary-stone *or* -marker, landmark, milestone; (*fig.*) crucial *or* deciding factor, turning-point.

Markstrahlen ['markʃtraːlən], *m.pl.* medullary rays.

Markt [markt], *m.* (**-(e)s,** *pl.* **¨-e**) market, market-place, market-town; mart, emporium, trading centre; business, trade, outlet; fair; ***auf den – bringen,*** put on the market, offer for sale; issue (*a loan*); ***auf den – kommen,*** come on (to) the market; ***auf dem*** or ***am – sein,*** be on the market, be for sale; ***im – sein,*** be in the market, be a prospective customer; ***seine Haut zu –e tragen,*** risk one's neck.

Markt|analyse, *f.* market research. **–bericht,** *m.* market report. **–bude,** *f.* stall, stand, booth. **markten,** *v.i.* (*dial.*) bargain (*um,* for), haggle (over); market, sell in the market. **marktfähig,** *adj.* marketable, saleable. **Markt|flecken,** *m.* small market-town. **–forschung,** *f. See* **–analyse. markt|gängig,** *adj.* (*of goods*) *see* **–fähig**; *–er Preis,* current *or* market-price. **Markt|geld,** *n.* stall-rent. **–gut,** *n.* market wares. **–halle,** *f.* covered market, market-hall. **–korb,** *m.* shopping basket. **–kurs,** *m.* market quotation. **–lage,** *f.* state of the market. **–ordnung,** *f.* market regulation(s). **–platz,** *m.* market-place *or* -square. **–preis,** *m.* current *or* market-price. **–schreier,** *m.* quack, charlatan, cheap-jack. **marktschreierisch,** *adj.* quack, charlatan, cheap-jack, showy. **Markt|-schwankung,** *f.* fluctuation of the market. **–tag,** *m.* market-day. **–tasche,** *f. See* **–korb. –verband,** *m.* marketing board. **–wert,** *m.* market value, value on the open market. **–wirtschaft,** *f. freie –,* free enterprise; *gebundene –,* controlled economy. **–zettel,** *m.* market report, price-list.

Markung ['markuŋ], *f. See* [1]**Mark.**

Markus ['markus], *m.* Mark. **Markusevangelium,** *n.* Gospel according to St. Mark.

Markzelle ['marktsɛlə], *f.* medullary cell.

Marmel ['marməl], *m.* (*obs.*) marble; marble (*boy's toy*). **marmeln, 1.** *v.t.* (*Art*) vein, marble. **2.** *v.i.* play (at) marbles. **Marmelstein,** *m. See* **Marmel.**

Marmor ['marmɔr], *m.* (**-s,** *pl.* **-e**) marble. **Marmor|bild,** *m.* marble statue *or* bust. **–bruch,** *m.* marble quarry. **marmorglatt,** *adj.* (as) smooth as marble. **marmorieren** [–'ri:rən], *v.t.* marble, grain, vein, mottle. **marmorn,** *adj.* (made of) marble. **Marmor|platte,** *f.* marble slab. **–säule,** *f.* marble pillar *or* column. **–schnitt,** *m.* marbled edge (*of book*). **–tafel,** *f. See* **–platte.**

marode [ma'ro:də], *adj.* weary, exhausted, tired out; (*coll.*) knocked up, dead-beat. **Marodeur** [–'dø:r], *m.* (**-s,** *pl.* **-e**) pillager, looter, marauder. **marodieren,** *v.i.* pillage, loot, maraud.

Marokkaner [marɔ'ka:nər], *m.,* **marokkanisch,** *adj.* Moroccan. **Marokko** [–'rɔko], *n.* Morocco.

Marone [ma'ro:nə], *f.* sweet chestnut.

Maroquin [maro'kɛ̃], *m.* Morocco leather.

Marotte [ma'rɔtə], *f.* whim, fad, caprice, crotchet, hobby-horse.

Marquis [mar'ki:], *m.* (- [–'ki:(s)], *pl.* - [–'ki:s]) marquess. **Marquise,** *f.* marchioness.

Mars [mars], *m.* (-, *pl.* **-e**) (*Naut.*) top; *großer –,* main-top.

Marsbewohner ['marsbəvo:nər], *m.* Martian.

[1]**Marsch** [marʃ], *f.* (-, *pl.* **-en**) fen(land), alluvial land.

[2]**Marsch,** *m.* (**-es,** *pl.* **¨e**) march (*also Mus.*); *auf dem –,* on the march, (*fig.*) under way, in progress; *den – blasen,* strike up a march; (*coll.*) *ihm den – blasen,* send him about his business, send him packing; *den – schließen,* bring up the rear; *sich in – setzen,* march off, set out.

marsch! *int.* (*Mil.*) march! –, –! (*Mil.*) at the double! (*coll.*) (*with 1st pers. reference*) hurry up! what are we waiting for? come on! let's go! (*with 3rd pers. reference*) clear off *or* out! beat it! scram! shake a leg!

Marschall ['marʃal], *m.* (**-s,** *pl.* **¨e**) marshal.

Marschbefehl ['marʃbəfe:l], *m.* marching orders, movement order, (*Am.*) travel orders; *– haben,* be under marching orders. **marsch|bereit,** *adj. See* **–fertig.**

Marsch|bewohner, *m.* fen-dweller. **–boden,** *m.* alluvial soil, marshland.

marschfertig ['marʃfɛrtɪç], *adj.* ready to march *or* move off. **Marsch|folge,** *f.* order of march. **–gepäck,** *n.* full pack, full marching order. **–geschwindigkeit,** *f.* rate of marching, (marching) pace, (*Naut., Av.*) cruising speed. **marschieren** [–'ʃi:rən], *v.i.* (*aux.* h. & s.) march, (*coll.*) stride, pace.

marschig ['marʃɪç], *adj.* marshy.

Marsch|kolonne, *f.* column on the march, column of route. **–kompaß,** *m.* prismatic compass.

Marsch|land, *n.* (**-s,** *pl.* **¨er**) *see* [1]**Marsch. –länder,** *m. See* **–bewohner.**

Marsch|leistung, *f.* distance marched. **–lied,** *n.* marching song. **–linie,** *f.* line of march. **marschmäßig,** *adj.* in marching order. **Marsch|ordnung,** *f.* order of march. **–pause,** *f.* halt on the march. **–richtung,** *f.* direction (of march), route (*oft. fig.*). **–route,** *f.* (*usu. fig.*) orders, instructions. **–stiefel,** *pl.* marching-boots. **–tempo,** *n.* (*Mus.*) march time. **–verpflegung,** *f.* haversack *or* (*Am.*) travel ration.

Mars|rahe, *f.* (*Naut.*) topsail yard. **–schoten,** *f.pl.* topsail sheets. **–segel,** *n.* topsail.

Marstall ['marʃtal], *m.* (**-s,** *pl.* **¨e**) (royal *or* duke's) stables.

Marter ['martər], *f.* (-, *pl.* **-n**) torture; torment, ordeal, agony, pang. **Marterl,** *n.* (**-s,** *pl.* **-(n)**) (*dial.*) memorial tablet. **martern,** *v.t.* torment; torture, inflict torture on. **Marter|pfahl,** *m.* the stake. **–tod,** *m.* death by torture, martyr's death; painful death. **–werkzeuge,** *n.pl.* instruments of torture.

martialisch [martsi'a:lɪʃ], *adj.* martial, warlike.

Martini [mar'ti:ni], **Martins|fest,** *n.,* **–tag,** *m.* Martinmas.

Märtyrer ['mɛrtyrər], *m.,* **Martyr(er)in,** *f.* martyr. **Märtyrertum,** *n. See* **Martyrium.**

Martyrium [mar'ty:rium], *n.* (**-s,** *pl.* **-rien**) martyrdom.

Marunke [ma'ruŋkə], *f.* (*Austr.*) egg-plum.

Marxismus [mar'ksɪsmus], *m.* Marxism. **marxistisch,** *adj.* Marxist.

März [mɛrts], *m.* March. **März(en)bier,** *n.* strong beer. **März|ente,** *f. See* **Stockente. –feld,** *n.* national assembly of the Franks. **–tage,** *m.pl.* revolution of 1848. **–veilchen,** *n.* sweet violet.

Masche ['maʃə], *f.* 1. mesh, stitch; *eine – fallen lassen* (*aufnehmen*), drop (pick up) a stitch (*in knitting*); 2. interstice; 3. (*dial.*) bow, bow-tie; 4. (*Hist.*) link (*of mail*); 5. (*coll.*) line, racket; (*coll.*) *seine neueste –,* his latest (trick); (*coll.*) *das ist nicht die –,* that won't work, it's no go. **Maschendraht,** *m.* wire-netting. **maschenfest,** *adj.* ladder-proof (*hosiery*). **Maschen|panzer,** *m.* chain-mail. **–weite,** *f.* width of mesh. **maschig,** *adj.* meshy, meshed, netted, reticulated.

Maschine [ma'ʃi:nə], *f.* machine, engine, *pl.* machinery; appliance, apparatus; typewriter; *mit der – geschrieben,* typewritten. **maschinell** [–'nɛl], *adj.* mechanical; *–e Bearbeitung,* machining.

Maschinen|anlage, *f.* power-plant. **–antrieb,** *m.* mechanical drive; *mit –,* power-driven, machine-driven. **–bau,** *m.* mechanical engineering. **–bauer,** *m.* mechanical engineer. **–bauschule,** *f.* engineering school. **–fabrik,** *f.* engineering works. **–garn,** *n.* machine-spun yarn, (mule-)twist. **–gewehr,** *n.* machine-gun. **–gewehrschütze,** *m.* machine-gunner. **–gewehrstand,** *m.* machine-gun emplacement. **–haus,** *n.* engine-shed, power-house. **–kunde, –lehre,** *f.* (science of) mechanical engineering. **maschinenmäßig,** *adj.* mechanical, automatic. **Maschinen|meister,** *m.* machinist; (*Railw.*) superintendent of rolling-stock; (*Theat.*) stage-mechanic; (*Typ.*) pressman. **–mensch,** *m.* robot.

Maschinen|öl, *n.* lubricating oil. **–park,** *m.* machinery, mechanical equipment. **–personal,** *n.* engine-room staff. **–pistole,** *f.* submachine gun, tommy-gun. **–raum, –saal,** *m.* engine-room; (*Typ.*) press-room. **–satz,** *m.* generating plant, generator, power-unit; (*Typ.*) machine-set type. **–schaden,** *m.* mechanical breakdown *or* failure, engine trouble. **–schlosser,** *m.* engine-fitter, mechanic. **–schreiben,** *n.* typing, typewriting. **–schreiber,** *m.* typist. **–schrift,** *f.* typescript. **–setzer,** *m.* (*Typ.*) machine compositor. **–teil,** *m.* engine component. **–wärter,** *m.* machine-minder, machine operator. **–webstuhl,** *m.* power-loom. **–werkstatt,** *f.* machine-shop. **–wesen,** *n.* (mechanical) engineering. **–zeichnen,** *n.* engineering drawing. **–zeitalter,** *n.* Machine Age. **–zentrale,** *f.* central power-plant.

Maschinerie [maʃi:nəˈri:], *f.* machinery, works, drive, wheels. **Machinist** [–ˈnɪst], *m.* **(-en,** *pl.* **-en)** machinist, operator; (*Railw.*) engine driver, (*Am.*) engineer; (*Theat.*) stage mechanic.

Maser [ˈma:zər], *f.* (-, *pl.* **-n**) *or m.* vein, streak, grain (*in wood*); speck, speckle, spot. **Maserholz,** *n.* veined wood, bird's-eye wood. **maserig,** *adj.* mottled, veined, grained, streaky, speckled. **masern,** *v.t.* grain, vein.

Masern [ˈma:zərn], *pl.* (*Med.*) measles.

Maserung [ˈma:zəruŋ], *f.* veining, graining.

Maske [ˈmaskə], *f.* mask; (*fig.*) guise, pretence, pretext; (*Mil.*) camouflage, screen; fancy dress *or* costume; (*Theat.*) make-up; ***ihm die – vom Gesicht reißen,*** unmask him; ***die – fallen lassen,*** drop pretence, show one's true face, come into the open; ***in der –*** (*Gen.*), in *or* under the guise of.

Masken|ammer, *f.* (*Orn.*) masked bunting (*Emberiza spodocephala*). **–ball,** *m.* fancy-dress ball. **–bildner,** *m.* (*Theat.*) make-up man. **–brille,** *f.* (*Mil.*) anti-gas goggles. **–kleid, –kostüm,** *n.* fancy-dress. **–stelze,** *f.* (*Orn.*) black-headed wagtail (*Motacilla flava feldegg*). **–verleih,** *m.* hire of fancy costumes *or* theatrical properties. **–würger,** *m.* (*Orn.*) masked shrike (*Lanius nubicus*). **–zug,** *m.* fancy-dress parade.

Maskerade [maskəˈra:də], *f.* mummery, fancy dress, masquerade.

maskieren [masˈki:rən], **1.** *v.t.* mask, screen, camouflage; disguise, conceal. **2.** *v.r.* put on a mask; disguise o.s., dress (o.s.) up. **Maskierung,** *f.* camouflage, screening.

maß [ma:s], *see* **messen.**

[1]**Maß,** *f.* (-, *pl.* **-(e)**) quart, tankard.

[2]**Maß,** *n.* (**-es,** *pl.* **-e**) measure, measurement, size, dimension, gauge; extent, quantity, volume, degree, criterion, standard, rate, (*fig.*) proportion, moderation; (*Math.*) ***das kleinste gemeinsame –,*** least common measure; ***in dem –e wie,*** in the same proportion *or* manner as, to the same extent as; ***in dem –e daß,*** to such an extent *or* such a degree that *or* as to, so far as to, so that; ***in nicht geringem –,*** in no small measure; ***in gleichem –e,*** to the same extent; ***in großem –e,*** to a large extent, on a large scale; ***in hohem –e,*** in a high degree, highly; ***in höherem –e,*** to a greater extent; ***in rechtem –,*** in due proportion; ***in reichem –e,*** in full measure; ***in solchem –e,*** to such an extent, to such a degree; ***in verjüngtem –e,*** on a reduced scale, in miniature; ***in vollem –e,*** in full measure, fully, amply, completely; ***mit – und Ziel,*** in reason *or* moderation; ***Anzug nach –,*** suit made to measure; ***(das) – nehmen,*** measure him *or* take his measurement(s) (***zu,*** for); ***das rechte – haben,*** be the right size; ***über alle –en,*** excessively, beyond all measure *or* bounds; ***das – überschreiten,*** overshoot the mark, go too far; ***das – ist voll,*** my patience is exhausted, that's the limit *or* the last straw; ***das – vollmachen,*** fill the cup to the brim; ***weder – noch Ziel kennen,*** know no bounds.

Maßabteilung [ˈma:sˀaptaɪluŋ], *f.* bespoke department.

Massaker [maˈsa:kər], *n.* massacre. **massakrieren** [–ˈkri:rən], *v.t.* massacre, slaughter.

Maß|analyse, *f.* (*Chem.*) volumetric analysis. **–anzug,** *m.* tailor-made suit, suit made to measure. **–arbeit,** *f.* bespoke tailoring.

mäße [ˈmɛ:sə], *see* **messen.**

Masse [ˈmasə], *f.* 1. mass, heap, quantity, number; multitude, horde, the masses, the people; lump, block, bulk; (*Mil.*) ***in –n aufstellen,*** mass; ***in –n herstellen,*** mass-produce; ***– der Nation,*** bulk of the nation; (*Prov.*) ***die – muß es bringen,*** small profits and large returns; 2. substance, compound, paste, dough; pulp, stuff; 3. (*Law*) property, estate, assets; ***sich zur – melden,*** lodge a claim (*on a bankrupt's estate*); ***Kreditoren der –*** creditors of the estate. **Massegläubiger,** *pl.* bankrupt's creditors.

Maßseinheit [ˈma:sˀaɪnhaɪt], *f.* unit of measurement, measuring unit.

Masseleisen [ˈmasəlˀaɪzən], *n.* pig-iron.

Massen|absatz, *m.* wholesale selling. **–abwurf,** *m.* (*Av.*) mass bombing. **–angriff,** *m.* mass attack. **–anziehung,** *f.* gravitation. **–artikel,** *m.* wholesale *or* bulk article. **–aufgebot,** *f.* (*Mil.*) levy en masse, general levy. **–auflage,** *f.* mass circulation. **–aufmarsch,** *m.* mass rally. **–beeinflussung,** *f.* propaganda. **–erzeugung, –fabrikation,** *f.* mass-production. **–flucht,** *f.* stampede. **–grab,** *n.* common grave. **–güter,** *n.pl.* bulk goods. **massenhaft,** *adj.* in a mass, in bulk, in large quantities, wholesale.

Massen|herstellung, *f. See* **–erzeugung. –kundgebung,** *f.* mass meeting *or* demonstration. **–mord,** *m.* general massacre, mass *or* wholesale murder. **–psychologie,** *f.* mass psychology. **–quartier,** *n.* billets for a large number. **–streik,** *m.* general strike. **–trägheit,** *f.* (*Phys.*) moment of inertia. **–verbrauch,** *m.* bulk consumption. **–verhaftungen,** *f.pl.* wholesale arrests. **–verkauf,** *m.* bulk sale. **–versammlung,** *f.* mass-meeting. **–verwalter,** *m.* (*Law*) (official) receiver. **massenweise,** *adv.* en masse, in large numbers, in heaps *or* (*coll.*) shoals, in a lump, wholesale. **Massenzusammenstoß,** *m.* (*Motor.*) (*coll.*) pile-up.

Maßgabe [ˈma:sga:bə], *f.* measure, proportion; ***nach –*** (*Gen.*), according to; (*Law*) as provided in, under (the terms of); ***mit den folgenden –n,*** subject to the undermentioned conditions. **maß|gebend, –geblich,** *adj.* authoritative, decisive, controlling, influential, leading, competent; relevant, important, substantial, authentic, determining; standard; applicable (***für,*** to); ***–e Beteiligung,*** controlling interest; ***–en Orts,*** in an authoritative quarter; ***die –en Kreise,*** influential circles, those in authority. **–gerecht,** *adj.* true to size. **–halten,** *irr.v.i.* be moderate, observe moderation, keep within bounds *or* limits. **Maßhaltung,** *f.* moderation, restraint, sobriety.

Maßholder [ˈma:shɔldər], *m.* (*dial.*) common maple.

[1]**massieren** [maˈsi:rən], *v.t.* massage.

[2]**massieren,** *v.t., v.r.* mass, concentrate (*troops etc.*).

massig [ˈmasɪç], *adj.* bulky, massive, solid, voluminous.

mäßig [ˈmɛ:sɪç], **1.** *adj.* 1. moderate; frugal, modest; temperate; ***zu –em Preise,*** at a reasonable figure; 2. mediocre, middling; 3. (*Mus.*) andante. **2.** *adv.* fairly, moderately.

–mäßig, *adj.suff.* -like (*e.g.* ***heldenmäßig,*** like a hero).

mäßigen [ˈmɛ:sɪgən], **1.** *v.t.* moderate, temper; ease, mitigate, allay, assuage; restrain, check, control, tone down, soften down; slacken (*speed*); ***gemäßigte Zone,*** temperate zone. **2.** *v.r.* restrain *or* check *or* control *or* calm o.s., keep one's temper, be moderate. **Mäßigkeit,** *f.* moderation, temperance, sobriety, frugality; mediocrity; *see also* **Mäßigung. Mäßigung,** *f.* moderation, restraint, self-control.

massiv [maˈsi:f], *adj.* massive, solid; (*coll.*) ***– werden,*** cut up rough. **Massiv,** *n.* (**-s,** *pl.* **-e**) (*Geol.*) massif. **Massiv|bau,** *m.* solid construction *or* structure. **–gold,** *n.* solid gold.

Maß|krug, *m.* beer-mug, tankard. **–liebchen,** *n.* (*Bot.*) ox-eye daisy (*Chrysanthemum leucanthemum*). **maßlos,** *adj.* boundless, immoderate, excessive, extravagant, exorbitant. **Maßlosigkeit,** *f.* lack of moderation, excess, extravagance, vehemence. **Maß|nahme, –regel,** *f.* measure, step, move, action, provision, precaution, preventive measure, expedient; ***–n ergreifen*** or ***treffen,*** take steps *or* action *or* precautions. **maßregeln,** *v.t.* (*insep.*) reprimand, take to task, discipline, inflict disciplinary punishment on. **Maß|regelung,** *f.* reprimand, disciplinary punishment. **–röhre,** *f.* (*Chem.*) burette. **–schneiderei,** *f.* bespoke tailoring. **–stab,** *m.* ruler, rule, measure; (*fig.*) standard, yardstick, criterion; scale, representative fraction (*on maps*); ***in großem –,*** on a large scale; ***verjüngter –,*** reduced scale; ***in vergrößertem –,*** on an enlarged scale. **maß|stabgerecht,** *adj.* true to scale. **–voll,**

adj. moderate, discreet, sober, temperate. **Maß|-werk,** *n.* (*Archit.*) tracery. **-zeichnung,** *f.* dimensional *or* scale drawing.

¹**Mast** [mast], *m.* (**-es,** *pl.* **-e(n)**) mast (*also Naut.*), pole, pylon, tower.

²**Mast,** *f.* mast, acorns, beech-nuts *etc.*; feeding-stuff, fattening (*pigs etc.*); ***zur – halten, auf der – haben,*** fatten.

Mastbaum ['mastbaum], *m.* (*Naut.*) mast.

Mastdarm ['mastdarm], *m.* (*Anat.*) rectum.

mästen ['mɛstən], **1.** *v.t.* fatten, feed (up), cram; (*B.*) ***das gemästete Kalb schlachten,*** kill the fatted calf. **2.** *v.r.* overfeed, feed on the fat of the land.

Mast|futter, *n.* fattening (food), mast. **-geld,** *n.* pannage. **-huhn,** *n.* fattened chicken. **mastig,** *adj.* sleek, fat, well-fed; thick (*of corn etc.*), lush (*of pasture*).

Mastix ['mastɪks], *m.* mastic.

Mastkorb ['mastkɔrp], *m.* (*Naut.*) masthead, top, crow's nest.

Mast|kur, *f.* fattening diet. **-nutzung,** *f.* pannage. **-recht,** *n.* right of pannage.

Mästung ['mɛstuŋ], *f.* fattening; fattening food.

Mastvieh ['mastfi:], *n.* fattened cattle.

Mast|wächter, *m.* (*Naut.*) masthead lookout (man). **-wurf,** *m.* (*Naut.*) clove hitch.

Masurka [ma'zurka], *f.* (-, *pl.* **-s**) mazurka.

Matador [mata'do:r], *m.* (**-s** *or* **-en,** *pl.* **-e(n)**) matador; (*coll.*) ace *or* crack (player); (*sl.*) big shot.

Material [materi'a:l], *n.* (**-s,** *pl.* **-ien**) material, matter, substance, stuff; stock (in trade), plant; (*Mil.*) matériel, equipment; *pl.* stores, (raw) materials, ingredients, products, (*fig.*) information, evidence, experimental data; (*Railw.*) ***rollendes –,*** rolling-stock; ***liegendes –,*** railway-plant. **material,** *adj.* material. **Materialanforderung,** *f.* (*Mil.*) indent *or* requisition for stores. **Materialien-depot,** *n.* (*Mil.*) supply depot, ordnance stores.

materialisieren [materiali'zi:rən], *v.t., v.r.* materialize. **Materialismus** [–'lɪsmus], *m.* materialism. **Materialist,** *m.* (**-en,** *pl.* **-en**) **1.** materialist, worldling; **2.** (*dial.*) druggist, grocer. **materi-alistisch,** *adj.* materialistic.

Material|prüfungsamt, *n.* testing laboratory. **-sammelstelle,** *f.* salvage dump. **-schaden,** *m.* material damage. **-schlacht,** *f.* battle in which superior equipment is decisive. **-waren,** *f.pl.* **1.** household goods; **2.** (*dial.*) groceries, colonial produce; drugs.

Materie [ma'te:riə], *f.* matter, stuff, substance; subject, cause; (*Med.*) matter, pus. **materiell** [–ri'ɛl], **1.** *adj.* material, real, intrinsic; pecuniary, financial, materialistic; ***-es Recht,*** substantive law; ***-er Mensch,*** materialist. **2.** *adv.* in fact *or* reality.

Mathematik [matema'ti:k], *f.* mathematics. **Mathe-matiker** [–'ma:tikər], *m.* mathematician. **mathe-matisch,** *adj.* mathematical.

Matjeshering ['matjəshe:rɪŋ], *m.* (**-s,** *pl.* **-e**) white herring.

Matratze [ma'tratsə], *f.* mattress.

Mätresse [mɛ'trɛsə], *f.* (kept) mistress, kept woman. **Mätressenwirtschaft,** *f.* petticoat government.

Matrikel [ma'tri:kəl], *f.* (-, *pl.* **-n**) roll, register; matriculation; ***in die – eintragen,*** matriculate.

Matrize [ma'tri:tsə], *f.* matrix, mould; die, stencil.

Matrone [ma'tro:nə], *f.* matron, elderly lady. **matronenhaft,** *adj.* matronly.

Matrose [ma'tro:zə], *m.* (**-n,** *pl.* **-n**) sailor, seaman; naval rating, (*coll.*) bluejacket, jack-tar.

Matrosen|anzug, *m.* sailor suit. **-heuer,** *f.* sailor's wages. **-jacke,** *f.* pea-jacket. **-lied,** *n.* sea-shanty. **-tanz,** *m.* sailor's hornpipe.

Matsch [matʃ], *m.* (**-es,** *pl.* **-e**) **1.** (*coll.*) mash, squash, pulp; mud, mire, slush; **2.** (*Cards*) capot; ***– machen,*** make all the tricks; (*fig.*) sweep the board; ***– werden,*** lose all the tricks (*at cards*). **matschen,** *v.t.* **1.** squash, mash, bruise; **2.** (*Cards*) capot, win all the tricks. **matschig,** *adj.* sloppy, mashed; muddy, slushy.

matt [mat], *adj.* **1.** faint, weak, feeble, languid, exhausted, jaded, subdued; flat, stale, insipid, jejune, tasteless; dull, dim, mat(t), lustreless, dead; frosted (*as glass*), tarnished (*as metal*), dull, lifeless, slack (*as the market*), spent (*as bullets*); **2.** (*pred. only*) (*Chess*) checkmate; (*Chess*) ***– setzen,*** checkmate; (*fig.*) thwart, frustrate. **mattblau,** *adj.* pale blue.

¹**Matte** ['matə], *f.* mat, matting.

²**Matte,** *f.* (*dial.*) alpine meadow, pasture, (*Poet.*) mead. **Mattenklee,** *m.* red clover.

mattgeschliffen ['matgəʃlɪfən], *adj.* ground, frosted (*of glass*). **Matt|glanz,** *m.* dull finish. **-glas,** *n.* ground *or* frosted glass. **-gold,** *n.* old gold.

Matthäus [ma'te:us], *m.* Matthew. **Matthäus-evangelium,** *m.* Gospel according to St. Matthew.

Mattheit ['mathaɪt], *f.* dullness, dimness, faintness; tiredness, lassitude, lifelessness. **mattherzig,** *adj.* faint-hearted, spiritless. **mattieren** [–'ti:rən], *v.t.* dull, deaden, frost (*glass*), tarnish (*metal*), give a mat(t) finish to. **Mattigkeit,** *f.* faintness, feebleness, weakness, exhaustion, debility, lassitude, languor.

Matt|kopfmeise, *f.* (*Orn.*) *see* **Weidenmeise. -scheibe,** *f.* **1.** (*Phot.*) ground-glass *or* focussing screen; **2.** (*coll.*) fuzziness in the head. **-setzen,** *n.* (*Chess*) checkmating. **mattweiß,** *adj.* off-white.

Matura [ma'tu:ra], *f.* (*Austr.*) school-leaving examination. **Maturant** [–'rant], *m.* (**-en,** *pl.* **-en**) (*Austr., Swiss*) school-leaver. **maturieren, 1.** *v.t.* mature. **2.** *v.i.* (*Austr.*) sit *or* take the school-leaving examination. **Maturität** [–ri'tɛ:t], *f.* maturity. **Maturitäts|prüfung,** *f.* *See* **Matura. -zeugnis,** *n.* school-leaving certificate.

Matz [mats], *m.* (**-es,** *pl.* **-e** *or* **⸚e**) (*coll.*) brat, kid, nipper; ***oder ich will – heißen,*** or I'm a Dutchman.

Mätzchen ['mɛtsçən], *n.* prank, antic; ***– machen,*** be up to one's tricks, make trouble; ***keine –!*** none of your monkey-tricks! no monkey-business!

Matze ['matsə], *f.,* **Matzen,** *m.* unleavened bread.

mau [mau], *pred.adj.* (*coll.*) middling, indifferent.

Mauer ['mauər], *f.* (-, *pl.* **-n**) wall, (*Fort.*) battlement. **Mauer|absatz,** *m.* offset. **-anker,** *m.* cramp-iron. **-anschlag,** *m.* placard, poster. **-blende,** *f.* niche. **-blümchen,** *n.* (*coll.*) wall-flower. **-brüstung,** *f.,* **-dach,** *n.,* **-hut,** *m.,* **-kappe,** *f.* coping(-stone). **-kalk,** *m.* mortar. **-kelle,** *f.* trowel. **-kitt,** *m.* *See* **-kalk. -klammer,** *f.* cramp-iron. **-krone,** *f.* mural crown. **-läufer,** *m.* (*Orn.*) wall-creeper (*Trichodroma muraria*).

mauern ['mauərn], **1.** *v.i.* **1.** build a wall, lay bricks; **2.** (*fig.*) play a waiting game, give nothing away, stone-wall. **2.** *v.t.* build (*with stone or brick*).

Mauer|pfeffer, *m.* (*Bot.*) stonecrop (*Sedum*). **-polier,** *m.* foreman bricklayer, head-mason. **-schwalbe,** *f.,* **-segler,** *m.* (*Orn.*) swift (*Apus apus*). **-speise,** *f.* mortar. **-stein,** *m.* building stone; brick. **-werk,** *n.* masonry, stonework; brickwork; (*coll.*) walls. **-ziegel,** *m.* brick.

Mauke ['maukə], *f.* (*Vet.*) scurf, malanders.

Maul [maul], *n.* (**-s,** *pl.* **⸚er**) mouth, jaws, muzzle, snout (*of animals*); (*vulg. of persons*) trap; (*Bot.*) peristoma; ***das – aufreißen,*** talk big, brag, blow one's own trumpet; ***– und Nase aufsperren,*** be flabbergasted; ***alle bösen Mäuler des Dorfes,*** all the malicious tongues of the village; ***er ist nicht aufs – gefallen,*** he has the gift of the gab, he has a glib tongue, he is always ready with an answer, he can talk himself out of anything; (*Prov.*) ***einem geschenkten Gaul sieht man nicht ins –,*** don't look a gift horse in the mouth; ***ein grobes (loses) –,*** a coarse (loose) tongue; ***halt's –!*** hold your tongue! shut up! ***sich selbst aufs – schlagen,*** contradict o.s.; (*fig.*) ***ihm das – stopfen,*** muzzle *or* gag him, stop his mouth; ***ihm übers – fahren,*** cut him short, shout him down; ***sich*** (*Dat.*) ***das – verbrennen,*** say the wrong thing, put one's foot in it; ***das – vollnehmen,*** see ***das – aufreißen;*** ***ihm das – wäßrig machen,*** make his mouth water.

Maul|affe, *m.* (gawping) booby; ***–n feilhalten,*** stand around gaping; lounge about (with one's hands in one's pockets). **-beerbaum,** *m.* mulberry tree.

Mäulchen ['mɔylçən], *n.* pursed lips, (*coll.*) kiss; ***ein – machen,*** pout, sulk.

maulen ['maulən], *v.i.* (*coll.*) sulk, pout; grouse, moan, whine. **Maulesel,** *m.* hinny. **maulfaul,** *adj.* laconic, taciturn, reserved, (*coll.*) close, buttoned up. **Maul|fäule,** *f.* (*Vet.*) flaps. **–held,** *m.* braggart, boaster. **–korb,** *m.* muzzle. **–schelle,** *f.* slap on the face, box on the ear. **–schlüssel,** *m.* open-ended spanner. **–sperre,** *f.* lockjaw, tetanus. **–tasche,** *f. See* **–schelle. –tier,** *n.* mule. **–trommel,** *f.* Jew's harp. **–werk,** *n.* (*vulg.*) ***gutes –,*** gift of the gab.

Maulwurf ['maulvurf], *m.* mole; (*coll.*) ***wie ein – schlafen,*** sleep like a top. **Maulwurfs|haufen, –hügel,** *m.* molehill.

Maurer ['maurər], *m.* mason, bricklayer. **Maurer|-arbeit,** *f.* masonry, bricklaying. **–gesell(e),** *m.* journeyman mason. **–handwerk,** *n.* building-trade. **–kelle,** *f. See* **Mauerkelle. –meister,** *m.* building contractor. **–polier,** *m. See* **Mauerpolier.**

maurisch ['maurɪʃ], *adj.* Moorish.

Maus [maus], *f.* (–, *pl.* **¨e**) 1. mouse; (*Prov.*) ***wenn die Katze nicht zu Hause ist, tanzen die Mäuse,*** when the cat's away the mice will play; (*Prov.*) ***mit Speck fängt man Mäuse,*** good bait catches fine fish; ***Mäuse im Kopfe,*** a bee in one's bonnet; (*coll.*) ***da beißt keine – den Faden*** or ***die – keinen Faden ab,*** nothing can be changed, that's settled and done with; 2. (*Anat.*) ball of the thumb, thenar; 3. hairy mole.

mauscheln ['mauʃəln], *v.i.* talk with a Jewish accent; (*coll.*) jabber.

Mäuschen ['mɔysçən], *n.* 1. little mouse, mousie; (*coll.*) ***mein –,*** my darling *or* pet, honey; 2. (*Anat.*) funny-bone. **mäuschenstill,** *adj.* quiet as a mouse, stock-still, so that one could hear a pin drop.

Mäuse ['mɔyzə], *pl. of* **Maus. Mäuse|bussard,** *m.* (*Orn.*) (*Am.* European) buzzard (*Buteo buteo*). **–falle** (*also* **Mausefalle**), *f.* mousetrap. **–fänger,** *m.* mouse-catcher, mouser. **–fraß,** *m.* damage done by mice; (*coll.*) bald patch. **–gift,** *n.* ratsbane. **–loch** (*also* **Mauseloch**), *n.* mouse-hole.

mausen ['mauzən], **1.** *v.i.* catch mice (*of cats*). **2.** *v.t.* (*sl.*) filch, swipe, pinch.

Mauser ['mauzər], *f.* moulting; moulting-season; ***in der – sein,*** be moulting.

Mauserei [mauzə'raɪ], *f.* (*sl.*) filching, swiping, pinching.

Mäuserich ['mɔyzərɪç], *m.* (**-s,** *pl.* **-e**) male mouse.

mauserig ['mauzərɪç], *adj.* (*Swiss*) peevish, irritable, bad-tempered.

[1]**mausern** ['mauzərn], *v.r.* (*Swiss*) be peevish *or* irritable.

[2]**mausern,** *v.i.*, *v.r.* moult. **Mauserung,** *f.* moulting.

mausetot ['mauzəto:t], *adj.* stone-dead, dead as a doornail.

maus|farbig, –grau, *adj.* mousy grey, dun, drab.

mausig ['mauzɪç], *adj.* uppish, cocky, (*sl.*) snooty; ***sich – machen,*** put on airs, be uppish *or* cocky *or* (*sl.*) snooty.

Mausloch ['mauslɔx], *n. See* **Mäuseloch.**

Maut [maut], *f.* (–, *pl.* **-en**) (*dial.*) duty, excise, toll; custom-house. **Mautamt,** *n.* custom-house. **mautfrei,** *adj.* duty-free. **Mautner,** *m.* customs-officer.

Maximal– [maksi'ma:l], *pref.* maximum. **–betrag,** *m.* highest amount; (*Comm.*) limit.

Maxime [ma'ksi:mə], *f.* maxim, precept, principle.

Maximum ['maksimum], *n.* (**-s,** *pl.* **-ma**) maximum (amount).

Mazedonien [matsə'do:niən], *n.* (*Geog.*) Macedonia. **Mazedonier,** *m.*, **mazedonisch,** *adj.* Macedonian.

Mäzen [mɛ'tse:n], *m.* (**-s,** *pl.* **-e**) Maecenas, patron. **Mäzenatentum** [–'na:təntu:m], *n.* patronage.

Mechanik [me'ça:nɪk], *f.* (–, *pl.* **-en**) mechanics; (*coll.*) mechanism. **Mechaniker,** *m.* mechanic, fitter, artificer. **mechanisch,** *adj.* mechanical; ***–er Webstuhl,*** power-loom. **Mechanisierung** [–'zi:ruŋ], *f.* mechanization. **Mechanismus** [–'nɪsmus], *m.* mechanism, works.

Mecheln ['mɛçəln], *n.* (*Geog.*) Malines, Mechlin.

meckern ['mɛkərn], *v.i.* (*of sheep*) bleat, (*of snipe*) drum; (*fig.*) grumble, grouse, carp, nag.

Medaille [me'daljə], *f.* medal; seal; ***die Kehrseite der –,*** the dark side of the picture; ***Träger der goldenen –,*** gold medallist. **Medaillon** [–'jɔ̃], *n.* (**-s,** *pl.* **-s**) locket, medallion.

Median|ader [medi'a:n–], *f.* (*Anat.*) median vein. **–folio,** *n.* demi-folio. **–oktav,** *n.* demi-octavo.

Mediante [medi'antə], *f.* (*Mus.*) mediant.

Medianwert [medi'a:nve:rt], *m.* (*Stat.*) median.

Medikament [medika'mɛnt], *n.* (**-(e)s,** *pl.* **-e**) medicine, drug, physic, medicant. **Medikus** ['me:dikus], *m.* (–, *pl.* **Medizi**) medical man, doctor.

Medium ['me:dium], *n.* (**-s,** *pl.* **-dien**) 1. (psychic) medium; 2. (*Phys*) agent.

Medizin [medi'tsi:n], *f.* (–, *pl.* **-en**) (science of) medicine; (*coll.*) physic, medicine, medicament.

Medizinal|behörde [meditsi'na:l–], *f.* Board of Health. **–gewicht,** *n.* troy weight. **–rat,** *m.* public health officer. **–waren,** *f.pl.* medicinal drugs. **–wein,** *m.* medicated wine.

Medizinball [medi'tsi:nbal], *m.* medicine-ball. **Mediziner,** *m.* medical man; medical student. **medizinisch,** *adj.* medical; medicinal; ***–e Fakultät,*** faculty of medicine; ***–e Seife,*** medicated soap. **Medizinmann,** *m.* medicine-man, magician.

Meer [me:r], *n.* (**-es,** *pl.* **-e**) sea; ocean; ***am –e,*** on the seashore; at *or* by the seaside; maritime; ***auf dem –e,*** (out) at sea, on the sea, on the main; ***das hohe*** or ***offene –,*** the main, the high sea(s); ***ein Tropfen im –e,*** a drop in the ocean; ***ein – von Tränen,*** a flood of tears; ***übers – gehen,*** go overseas; ***unter dem –e,*** submarine.

Meer|busen, *m.* gulf, bay. **–enge,** *f.* straits, channel, narrows.

Meeres|alge, *f.* seaweed, alga. **–arm,** *m.* arm *or* inlet of the sea. **–boden,** *m. See* **–grund. –brandung,** *f.* surf, breakers. **–gebiet,** *n.* maritime basin. **–grund,** *m.* bottom of the sea, sea-bed, sea-bottom, (*coll.*) Davy Jones's locker. **–höhe,** *f. See* **–spiegel. –kunde,** *f.* oceanography, hydrography. **–küste,** *f.* sea-coast, seashore. **–leuchten,** *n.* marine phosphorescence. **–schlund,** *m.* the deep. **–spiegel,** *m.* sea-level; ***über dem –,*** above sea-level. **–stille,** *f.* (*Naut.*) dead calm. **–strand,** *m.* beach, seashore. **–strömung,** *f.* ocean-current. **–ufer,** *n. See* **–strand.**

Meer|gewächs, *n.* marine plant. **–gott,** *m.* sea-god, Neptune. **meergrün,** *adj.* sea-green, glaucous. **Meer|jungfer,** *f.* mermaid, siren. **–katze,** *f.* (*Zool.*) long-tailed monkey (*Cercopithecus*). **–kohl,** *m.* (*Bot.*) sea-kale (*Crambe*). **–muschel,** *f.* sea-shell. **–rettich,** *m.* (*Bot.*) horse-radish (*Armoracia lapathifolia*). **–schaum,** *m.* meerschaum. **–schwein,** *n.* porpoise. **–schweinchen,** *n.* (*Zool.*) guinea-pig (*Cavia porcellus*). **–stern,** *m.* starfish. **–strandläufer,** *m.* (*Orn.*) purple sandpiper (*Calidris maritima*). **–straße,** *f.* strait. **meerumschlungen,** *adj.* sea-girt. **Meerungeheuer,** *n.* sea-monster. **meerwärts,** *adv.* seawards. **Meer|-wasser,** *n.* sea-water. **–weibchen,** *n. See* **–jungfer.**

Megahertz ['me:gahɛrts], *n.* (*Rad.*) megacycles per second.

Megäre [me'gɛ:rə], *f.* (*Myth.*) Fury; (*coll.*) vixen, shrew, termagant.

Mehl [me:l], *n.* (**-s,** *pl.* **-e**) 1. flour, meal, farina; 2. dust, powder. **Mehl|beutel,** *m.* bolter, sifter. **–brei,** *m.* pap. **–faß,** *n.* flour-barrel.

mehlig ['me:lɪç], *adj.* floury, farinaceous.

Mehl|käfer, *m.* (*Ent.*) meal beetle (*Tenebrio molitor*). **–kleister,** *m.* flour paste. **–kloß,** *m.* plain dumpling. **–körper,** *m.* endosperm. **–kreide,** *f.* infusorial earth. **–sack,** *m.* flour-bag. **–schwalbe,** *f.* (*Orn.*) house martin (*Delichon urbica*). **–sieb,** *n. See* **–beutel. –speise,** *f.* (*Austr.*) pudding. **–suppe,** *f.* gruel. **–tau,** *m.* powdery mildew (*see* **Meltau**).

–wurm, *m.* meal-worm. **–zucker,** *m.* caster *or* castor sugar.

mehr [me:r], *indecl.num.adj., adv.* more; – *als,* more than; – *groß als klein,* tall rather than short; *und andere –,* and a few others; *und dergleichen –,* and the like, et cetera; – *denn je,* more than ever; *immer –,* more and more, increasingly; *kein Kind –,* no longer a child; *kein Wort –!* not another word! *nicht lange –, nicht – lange,* not much longer; – *und –,* see *immer –*; *nicht –,* (*of numbers*) no more, (*of time*) no longer; *ich kann nicht –,* I'm at the end of my tether; (*coll.*) I'm all in; *es ist nicht – als billig,* it is only fair; *nichts –,* nothing more, nothing further; *noch –,* even more, still more; – *noch,* what is more, (still) further; (*dial.*) *nur –,* nothing but, only; – *rechts,* farther to the right; *um so –,* so much the more; *um so – als,* all the more as. **Mehr,** *n.* **(-(s),** *no pl.*) majority; increase; surplus, excess.

Mehr|achsantrieb, *m.* multiple-axle drive. **–arbeit,** *f.* overtime; (*Marxism*) surplus work, work producing profit for the employer; *see* **–wert. –aufwand,** *m.,* **–ausgaben,** *f.pl.* additional expenditure. **mehrbändig,** *adj.* in several volumes. **Mehr|-bedarf,** *m.* additional requirement, excess demand. **–betrag,** *m.* surplus, excess; extra charge. **mehr-deutig,** *adj.* ambiguous. **Mehr|deutigkeit,** *f.* ambiguity. **–einnahme,** *f.* surplus of receipts.

mehren [me:rən], **1.** *v.t.* increase, augment, multiply. **2.** *v.r.* increase, multiply; grow, propagate. **mehrenteils,** *adv.* for the most part, mostly.

mehrere ['me:rərə], *adj., indef.pron.* several, some, a few, sundry, divers; *–s,* various *or* sundry things. **mehrerlei,** *indecl.adj.* of more than one kind, various, diverse, sundry, divers.

mehrfach ['me:rfax], **1.** *adj.* manifold, repeated, multiple. **2.** *adv.* repeatedly, over and over again, more than once. **Mehrfach–,** *pref.* (*Tech., Elec. etc.*) multiple.

Mehrfarbendruck ['me:rfarbəndruk], *m.* colour-printing. **mehrfarbig,** *adj.* polychromatic. **Mehr|forderung,** *f.* increased demand, higher claim. **–frontenkrieg,** *m.* war on several fronts. **–gebot,** *n.* overbid; higher bid. **–gepäck,** *n.* excess baggage. **–gewicht,** *n.* overweight, excess weight. **–gitterröhre,** *f.* (*Rad.*) multigrid valve. **mehr|-gleisig,** *adj.* multi-tracked. **–gliederig,** *adj.* (*Math.*) complex.

Mehrheit ['me:rhaıt], *f.* majority, plurality. **Mehr-heits|beschluß,** *m.,* **–entscheidung,** *f.* majority decision; (*Parl.*) *durch –,* by a majority (of votes).

mehrjährig ['me:rjɛ:rıç], *adj.* several years old, (*Bot.*) perennial. **Mehr|kosten,** *pl.* additional expenses. **–ladegewehr,** *n.,* **–lader,** *m.* magazine rifle, repeater. **–leistung,** *f.* increased efficiency, *or* performance *or* output; (*Insur.*) extended benefits. **mehr|malig,** *adj.* repeated, reiterated. **–mals,** *adv.* again and again, repeatedly, more than once, several times. **–motorig,** *adj.* multi-engined. **Mehr|phasenstrom,** *m.* (*Elec.*) polyphase current. **–porto,** *n.* postage due. **–preis,** *m.* extra charge. **mehr|samig,** *adj.* polyspermous. **–schichtig,** *adj.* multi-layered. **–seitig,** *adj.* polygonal, many-sided, (*Pol.*) multilateral. **–silbig,** *adj.* polysyllabic. **–sprachig,** *adj.* polyglot. **–stellig,** *adj.* with more than one digit. **–stimmig,** *adj.* (arranged) for several voices; part (*song*). **–stöckig,** *adj.* multi-storey. **Mehrstufe,** *f.* (*Gram.*) comparative degree. **mehr|stufig,** *adj.* multi-stage. **–stündig, (–tägig),** *adj.* of several hours' (days') duration. **Mehrumsatz,** *m.* increase in turnover.

Mehrung ['me:ruŋ], *f.* increase, multiplication, augmentation; propagation. **Mehr|verbrauch,** *m.* increased consumption. **–wert,** *m.* 1. surplus value; 2. (*Marxism*) ratio between work necessary for workers' needs and work producing profit for employer (*see* **–arbeit**). **mehrwertig,** *adj.* (*Chem.*) polyvalent. **Mehr|wertsteuer,** *f.* value-added tax. **–zahl,** *f.* majority, greater part; (*Gram.*) plural; *die überwiegende – von,* the great majority of, the bulk of, most of. **–zweck–,** *pref.* multi-purpose, general-purpose, general-utility.

meiden ['maıdən], *irr.v.t.* avoid, shun, flee from, keep clear of.

Meier ['maıər], *m.* steward (*of an estate*); tenant of a (dairy-)farm, (dairy-)farmer. **Meierei** [–'raı], *f.* (dairy-)farm. **Meiereierzeugnisse,** *n.pl.* dairy-produce.

meiern ['maıərn], *v.t.* (*coll.*) *ihn –,* take him in, pull the wool over his eyes.

Meile ['maılə], *f.* (*obs.*) league (*5.556 metres, 3 nautical or 3.456 statute miles*); *englische –,* English *or* statute mile (*1,610 metres*); *geographische –,* geographical *or* nautical mile (*1,853 metres*). **Meilen|stein,** *m.* milestone. **–stiefel,** *m.pl.* seven-league boots. **meilenweit,** *adj., adv.* miles and miles of, (extending) for miles; miles away; – *auseinander,* miles apart; (*fig.*) – *überlegen* (*Dat.*), head and shoulders above.

Meiler ['maılər], *m.* charcoal-kiln *or* -pile. **Meiler|-kohle,** *f.* charcoal. **–köhler,** *m.* charcoal-burner.

mein [maın], **1.** *poss.adj.* my, mine; *–es Wissens,* so far as I know; *dieser – Sohn,* my son here; *–e vielen Freunde,* my numerous friends. **2.** *poss.pron.* mine; *dieses Haus ist –,* this house is mine; – *ist die Schande,* mine is the shame. **3.** *obs. Gen. sing. of ich* (*see* **meiner**); *gedenke –,* think of me; *vergiß – nicht!* do not forget me! **Mein,** *n.* my own, my property; *das – und Dein,* what is mine and what is thine. **4.** *poss.pron. der, die* or *das –e,* mine; *nicht dein Bruder, sondern –er* or *der –e,* not your brother but mine; *das –e,* my own, my share, my belongings *or* property; *die –en,* my family *or* folks; *ich habe das –e getan,* I have done my part.

Meineid ['maınaıt], *m.* perjury; *einen – leisten* or *schwören,* perjure *or* foreswear o.s., commit perjury. **meineidig,** *adj.* perjured; – *werden,* commit perjury, perjure *or* foreswear o.s. **Meineidige(r),** *m., f.* perjurer.

meinen ['maınən], *v.t., v.i.* 1. be of the opinion, believe, think, suppose, (*Am.*) reckon, guess; assert, say, suggest; mean, intend, have in view, purpose; – *Sie?* do you think so? *es nicht böse –,* mean no harm (*mit,* to); *den Sack schlagen und den Esel –,* put the blame on an innocent p.; *er meint es gut,* he means well; *damit sind Sie gemeint,* that is meant for you; *man sollte –,* one would think; *so war es nicht gemeint,* it was not meant in that way; *was – Sie dazu?* what do you think of *or* (*coll.*) say to it? *was – Sie damit?* see *wie – Sie das? wie Sie –,* just as you like, if you say so; *wie – Sie?* what did you say? I beg your pardon? *wie – Sie das?* what do you mean by that? *das will ich –,* I should think so (indeed); *er meinte wunder, was er täte,* he thought he was doing s.th. marvellous *or* great; *sie meint wunder, wer sie ist,* she thinks she is the last word; 2. (*Poet.*) love; *Freiheit, die ich meine,* Freedom that I love.

meiner ['maınər], *Gen. of ich* (*see* **mein, 3**); *erbarme dich –,* have pity upon me; *ich war – nicht mehr mächtig,* I had lost control over myself. **meinerseits,** *adv.* for my part, so far as I am concerned. **meines|gleichen,** *indecl.adj. or pron.* my equals, such as I, people like me, the likes of me. **–teils,** *adv.* for *or* on my part, as for me. **meinet|-halben, –wegen, –willen,** *adv.* (*also um meinetwillen*) for my sake, on my behalf *or* account; so far as I am concerned, for all *or* aught I care; by all means.

meinige ['maınıgə], *poss.pron. See der, die, das meine.*

Meinung ['maınuŋ], *f.* opinion, view (*über* (*Acc.*), *von,* of *or* about); idea, notion (of); judgement (on); belief; meaning, intention; *nach meiner –* or *meiner – nach,* in my opinion, as I see it, to my mind; *anderer – sein mit,* disagree with; *wir sind derselben* or *einer –,* we are of one opinion, we see eye to eye, we agree with one another, we share the same opinion; *geteilter – sein,* be in two minds (*über* (*Acc.*), about); *die – ändern,* change one's mind (*über* (*Acc.*), about), revise one's opinion (of); *die öffentliche –,* public opinion; *ihm die – sagen,* give him a piece of one's mind; *der – sein, daß . . .,* be of the opinion *or* hold (the view) that . . .; *vorgefaßte –,* preconceived idea, prejudice.

Meinungs|äußerung, *f.* expression of opinion. **-austausch,** *m.* exchange of views *or* ideas (*über* (*Acc.*), on). **-befragung, -forschung,** *f.* opinion poll. **-streit,** *m.* conflict of opinion. **-verschiedenheit,** *f.* difference (of opinion), disparity *or* divergence of views; dissension, disagreement (*über* (*Acc.*), about). **-wechsel,** *m.* change of opinion *or* mind.

Meise ['maɪzə], *f.* (*Orn.*) (member of the) tit (family) (*Paridae*). **Meisensänger,** *m.* (*Orn.*) Parula warbler (*Parula americana*).

[1]**Meißel** ['maɪsəl], *f.* (-, *pl.* **-n**) (*dial.*) plug *or* wad of lint, (*Surg.*) pledget.

[2]**Meißel,** *m.* chisel. **meißeln,** *v.t.* chisel, carve.

meist [maɪst], **1.** *adj.* (*sup. of* **mehr**) most; ***die -en,*** the majority of them, most people; ***die -en Schüler,*** most of the pupils; ***seine -e Zeit,*** most of his time; ***das -e,*** the greater *or* best part of it, most *or* the bulk of it. **2.** *adv.* generally, usually, as a rule, in most cases, mostly, for the most part; ***am -en,*** most (of all); ***am -en bekannt,*** best known.

Meist|begünstigung, *f.* preference, preferential treatment. **-begünstigungsklausel,** *f.* most-favoured-nation clause. **meistbietend,** *adj.* bidding highest, offering most; ***- verkaufen,*** sell to the highest bidder, sell by auction. **Meistbietende(r),** *m., f.* highest bidder. **meistens, meistenteils,** *adv. See* **meist, 2.**

Meister ['maɪstər], *m.* master; foreman, (*sl.*) boss; (*Spt.*) champion; (*Naut.*) shipwright; ***am Werke erkennt man den -,*** the master's hand is seen in the finished work; (*Prov.*) ***Übung macht den -,*** practice makes perfect; ***er hat in ihm seinen - gefunden,*** he has met his match in him; (*Prov.*) ***es ist noch kein - vom Himmel gefallen,*** no man is born a master of his craft; ***- vom Stuhl,*** master of the lodge; (*fig.*) ***- werden*** (*Gen.*), control, master, get under control; ***ein wahrer -,*** a past-master.

Meister|fahrer, *m.* crack driver. **-gesang,** *m.* poetry of the mastersingers. **-grad,** *m.* 1. (*Univ.*) degree of M.A.; 2. (*Freem.*) grade of master; freedom (*of a guild*). **meisterhaft, 1.** *adj.* masterly, excellent, accomplished, skilful. **2.** *adv.* in a masterly manner, in perfect style, brilliantly. **Meisterhand,** *f.* master-hand, masterly hand. **Meisterin,** *f.* 1. mistress, master's wife; 2. (*Spt.*) woman champion. **meisterlich,** *adj., adv. See* **meisterhaft. meisterlos,** *adj.* (*Swiss*) headstrong.

meistern ['maɪstərn], *v.t.* master, get the better of, control; outdo, surpass; ***er kann seine Zunge nicht -,*** he cannot keep a rein on his tongue.

Meister|prüfung, *f.* examination for the (*Univ.*) degree *or* (*guilds*) grade of Master. **-recht,** *n.* freedom of a company. **-sänger,** *m.* mastersinger.

Meisterschaft ['maɪstərʃaft], *f.* mastery, masterly skill; freedom (*of a guild etc.*); masters of a lodge *or* trade-guild; (*Spt.*) championship. **Meisterschafts|anwärter,** *m.* aspirant to the title of Master. **-kampf,** *m.* championship bout. **-spiel,** *n.* championship match.

Meister|schütze, *m.* champion marksman, crack-shot. **-singer,** *m. See* **-sänger. -stück, -werk,** *n.* masterpiece. **-zug,** *m.* (*Chess, Pol.*) master-stroke.

Meistgebot ['maɪstgəbo:t], *n.* best offer, highest bid. **meist|gekauft,** *adj.* best *or* largest selling, most in demand. **-gelesen,** *adj.* most widely read. **-verkauft,** *adj. See* **-gekauft.**

Melancholie [melaŋko'li:], *f.* melancholy, melancholia. **Melancholiker** [-'ko:likər], *m.* p. of melancholy disposition. **melancholisch,** *adj.* melancholy.

Melange [me'lã:ʒə], *f.* mixture, blend, (*Austr.*) coffee with milk.

Melasse [me'lasə], *f.* molasses, treacle.

Melde|amt ['mɛldə-], *n.* registration office. **-block,** *m.* message pad. **-dienst,** *m.* (*Av.*) early-warning system. **-fahrer,** *m.* dispatch-rider. **-frist,** *f.* last date for registration. **-gänger,** *m.* (dispatch-) runner, messenger. **-kette,** *f.* relay of runners. **-kopf,** *m.* (*Mil.*) message-centre. **-liste,** *f.* (*Spt.*) list of entries.

melden ['mɛldən], **1.** *v.t., v.i.* 1. ***ihm etwas -,*** inform *or* advise *or* apprise him of a th., notify *or* report *or* announce s.th. to him, send him word of s.th.; 2. recount, tell, state (*news etc.*); 3. announce (*a p.*) (*Dat.*, to); report (*a p. to the police etc.*); 4. (*Cards*) ***Sie haben zu -,*** it is your call. **2.** *v.r.* announce o.s. (***bei,*** to), come forward, make a claim (*of creditors*); (*Mil.*) report; (*Spt.*) enter (***zu,*** for); register (***bei,*** with); answer (*on the phone*); (*fig.*) make itself felt; (*Mil.*) ***sich krank -,*** report sick; ***sich freiwillig -,*** volunteer (***zu*** or ***für,*** for); ***sich - lassen,*** send in one's name *or* card, have o.s. announced; ***sich zur Arbeit -,*** report for work; ***sich auf ein Inserat -,*** answer an advertisement; ***sich zu einer Prüfung -,*** enter for an examination; ***man muß sich zeitig -,*** early application is necessary; ***der Winter meldet sich dieses Jahr zeitig,*** winter is setting in early this year; ***der Hunger meldet sich,*** hunger makes itself felt; ***sich zum Wort -,*** announce one's wish to speak, catch the chairman's eye, (*in school*) raise one's hand.

Meldepflicht ['mɛldəpflɪçt], *f.* obligation to report *or* register. **meldepflichtig,** *adj.* subject to registration, notifiable. **Meldequadrat,** *n.* reference square (*map*). **Melder,** *m.* dispatch-rider, runner, messenger; alarm (equipment). **Melde|reiter,** *m.* mounted orderly; dispatch-rider. **-schluß,** *m.* closing date for entries. **-stelle,** *f.* reporting centre, registration office. **-vorschriften,** *f.pl.* regulations for applicants. **-zettel,** *m.* registration form.

Meldung ['mɛlduŋ], *f.* message, advice, notice, notification; announcement, news, report; registration, application, (*Spt.*) entry.

melieren [me'li:rən], *v.t.* mix, mingle, blend, mottle; shuffle; ***grau meliert,*** mixed with gray, (*coll.*) pepper and salt. **Melierpapier,** *n.* mottled *or* marbled paper.

Melinit [meli'ni:t], *n.* (*Chem.*) picric acid, melinite.

Melioration [melioratsi'o:n], *f.* soil enrichment. **meliorieren** [-'ri:rən], *v.t.* ameliorate.

Melisse [me'lɪsə], *f.* balm, balm-mint.

Meliszucker ['me:lɪstsukər], *m.* (coarse) loaf-sugar.

melk [mɛlk], *adj.* milch, giving milk. **Melk|eimer,** *m. See* **-kübel. melken,** *reg. & irr.v.t.* milk; (*coll.*) bleed, fleece; ***frisch gemolkene Milch,*** milk fresh from the cow. **Melk|kübel,** *m.* milking-pail. **-kuh,** *f.* milch-cow (*also fig.*). **-maschine,** *f.* milking-machine. **-schemel,** *m.* milking-stool. **-vieh,** *n.* milch-cattle. **-zeit,** *f.* milking time.

Melodie [melo'di:], *f.* melody, tune, air. **melodisch** [-'lo:dɪʃ], *adj.* melodious, tuneful.

Melone [me'lo:nə], *f.* 1. melon; 2. (*coll.*) bowler hat, (*Am.*) derby.

Meltau ['me:ltau], *m.* mildew, blight.

Membran(e) [mɛm'bra:n(ə)], *f.* (*Anat.*) membrane; (*Tech.*) diaphragm.

Memme ['mɛmə], *f.* coward, poltroon. **memmenhaft,** *adj.* cowardly.

Memoire [memo'a:rə], *n.* (**-s,** *pl.* **-s**) memorial address *or* publication. **Memoiren,** *pl.* memoirs, reminiscences.

Memorabilien [memora'bi:liən], *pl. See* **Denkwürdigkeiten.**

Memorandum [memo'randum], *n.* (**-s,** *pl.* **-da** *or* **-den**) note, memorandum. **memorieren,** *v.t.* memorize, commit to memory, learn by heart.

Menage [me'na:ʒə], *f.* set of dishes; cruet; (*dial.*) household, (*Mil.*) mess.

Menge ['mɛŋə], *f.* quantity, number, amount; (*Math.*) aggregate; multitude, crowd, (*coll.*) heap, pile; ***eine ganze -,*** quite a lot; ***in großer -,*** in abundance, abundantly; ***eine - Geld, Geld in -(n),*** plenty of *or* a lot of money, (*coll.*) lots *or* heaps *or* piles of money; ***eine - Bücher,*** a lot of *or* a great many books; ***die - muß es bringen,*** small profits, quick returns.

mengen ['mɛŋən], **1.** *v.t.* mix, mingle, blend, admix (***unter*** (*Acc.*), ***mit,*** with); shuffle (*cards*); ***eins ins andere -,*** give a garbled account. **2.** *v.r.* mix, mingle; ***sich - in*** (*Acc.*), meddle with, interfere in;

er mengt sich in alles, he pokes his nose in everywhere, he is a busybody.

Mengen|bestimmung, *f.* quantitative analysis. **-einheit,** *f.* unit of quantity. **mengenmäßig,** *adj.* quantitative. **Mengen|rabatt,** *m.* discount *or* rebate on bulk order. **–verhältnis,** *n.* ratio, proportion.

Meng|futter, *n.* mixed feed *or* fodder. **–gestein,** *n.* (*Geol.*) conglomerate.

Mengsel ['mɛŋsəl], *m.* medley; mess, hodge-podge, hotch-potch.

Mennig ['mɛnɪç], *m.*, **Mennige,** *f.* minium, red lead.

Mensa ['mɛnza], *f.* (-, *pl.* **-sen**) (*Univ.*) students' refectory.

1**Mensch** [mɛnʃ], *m.* (**-en,** *pl.* **-en**) human being, man; individual person; *pl.* people, mankind; ***kein –,*** nobody, not a (living) soul; ***eine Menge –en,*** a crowd of people; ***er ist auch nur ein –,*** he is only human; ***unter die –en kommen,*** mix with people, mix in society; ***einen neuen –en anziehen,*** turn over a new leaf; ***der innere –,*** the inner man; (*Prov.*) ***der – denkt, Gott lenkt,*** man proposes, God disposes.

2**Mensch,** *n.* (**-es,** *pl.* **-er**) (*vulg.*) wench, hussy, slut, baggage.

Menschenaffe ['mɛnʃənˀafə], *m.* anthropoid ape. **menschenähnlich,** *adj.* anthropoid, anthropomorphous. **Menschen|alter,** *n.* generation, age, lifetime. **–art,** *f.* race of men, kind *or* species of man; ***das ist –,*** such are men, such is human nature. **–blut,** *n.* human blood. **–familie,** *f.* human race. **–feind,** *m.* misanthropist. **menschen|feindlich,** *adj.* misanthropic. **–fressend,** *adj.* anthropophagous. **Menschen|fresser,** *m.* man-eater, cannibal. **–freund,** *m.* philanthropist, humanitarian. **menschenfreundlich,** *adj.* affable, sociable; philanthropic, humanitarian. **Menschen|freundlichkeit,** *f.* affability, sociability; kindness, benevolence, philanthropy. **–führung,** *f.* personnel management. **–gedenken,** *n.* ***seit –,*** from time immemorial; in living memory. **–geschlecht,** *n.* human race, mankind. **–gestalt,** *f.* human shape *or* form. **–gewühl,** *n.* throng, milling crowd.

Menschen|handel, *m.* slave-trade. **–händler,** *m.* slave-dealer. **–haß,** *m.* misanthropy. **–hasser,** *m.* misanthrope. **–jagd,** *f.* manhunt. **–kenner,** *m.* (good) judge of men, keen observer of human nature. **–kenntnis,** *f.* knowledge of human nature. **–kind,** *n.* human being, creature. **–kunde,** *f.* anthropology. **–leben,** *n.* lifetime; human life; life of man; ***Verlust an –,*** loss of life. **menschenleer,** *adj.* deserted. **Menschen|liebe,** *f.* philanthropy, charity, human kindness, love of one's fellow man. **–masse,** *f.* crowd of people, (*coll.*) mob. **–material,** *n.* (*Mil.*) man-power. **–menge,** *f.* *See* **–masse. menschenmöglich,** *adj.* humanly possible; ***das menschenmögliche,*** all that is humanly possible, (*coll.*) every mortal thing.

Menschen|opfer, *n.* human sacrifice. **–pack,** *n.* rabble. **–potential,** *n.* human resources, manpower (reserves). **–raub,** *m.* kidnapping, abduction, (*Poet.*) rape. **–rechte,** *n.pl.* rights of man, human rights. **menschen|reich,** *adj.* populous. **–scheu,** *adj.* unsociable, shy. **Menschen|scheu,** *f.* unsociableness, shyness. **–schinder,** *m.* oppressor, extortioner, (*coll.*) slave-driver. **–schlag,** *m.* race of men, type *or* breed of men. **–seele,** *f.* ***keine –,*** not a living soul.

Menschenskind! ['mɛnʃənskɪnt], *int.* (*coll.*) man alive! wow!

Menschensohn ['mɛnʃənzo:n], *m.* (*Eccl.*) Son of Man. **menschenunwürdig,** *adj.* degrading. **Menschen|verächter,** *m.* cynic. **–verstand,** *m.* human understanding; ***gesunder –,*** common sense. **–werk,** *n.* (fugitive *or* transitory) works of man. **–wohl,** *n.* human weal. **–würde,** *f.* human dignity. **menschenwürdig,** *adj.* honourable, dignified.

Menschheit ['mɛnʃhaɪt], *f.* human race, humanity, mankind; ***der Abschaum*** or ***Auswurf der –,*** the scum of the earth.

menschlich ['mɛnʃlɪç], *adj.* human; humane; ***nach –em Ermessen,*** as far as can be foreseen; (*Prov.*) ***irren ist –,*** to err is human; ***etwas –es begehen,*** be guilty of a human weakness. **Menschlichkeit,** *f.* human nature; humanity, humaneness; (*also pl.*) human weakness, human frailties; ***Verbrechen gegen die –,*** crime against humanity.

Menschwerdung ['mɛnʃve:rduŋ], *f.* incarnation, anthropogenesis.

menstruieren [mɛnstru'i:rən], *v.i.* menstruate.

Mensur [mɛn'zu:r], *f.* (-, *pl.* **-en**) measure, mensuration; (*Chem.*) measuring vessel; proper distance (between duellists); (*dancing*) measure; (*Mus.*) duration of a note; standard size and thickness (*of organ-pipes, wind instruments*); (*Univ.*) students' duel. **Mensurglas,** *n.* measuring glass.

Mentalität [mɛntali'tɛ:t], *f.* mentality, way of thinking.

Menü [me'ny:], (*Austr., Swiss*) **Menu,** *n.* (**-s,** *pl.* **-s**) menu, table d'hôte.

Menuett [menu'ɛt], *n.* (**-s,** *pl.* **-e**) minuet.

Mergel ['mɛrgəl], *m.* marl. **Mergel|boden,** *m.* marly soil. **–grube,** *f.* marl-pit. **mergeln,** *v.t.* manure with marl.

merkantil [mɛrkan'ti:l], *adj.* mercantile. **merkantilisch,** *adj.* commercial. **Merkantilismus** [–'lɪsmus], *m.* controlled economy, system of state control of all economic life.

merkbar ['mɛrkba:r], *adj.* noticeable, perceptible, evident. **Merk|blatt,** *n.* leaflet, instruction sheet, book of instructions. **–buch,** *n.* notebook, memo(randum) book.

merken ['mɛrkən], **1.** *v.t.* observe, notice, perceive; be aware of, realize, sense, feel; ***sich*** (*Dat.*) ***etwas –,*** make a mental note of s.th., keep *or* bear s.th. in mind; ***– lassen,*** show, reveal, betray (*one's feelings etc.*); ***sich*** (*Dat.*) ***nichts – lassen,*** act as if one knew nothing, act as if nothing had happened, look unconcerned; ***merke dir das!*** mark my words! remember what I've said! ***es war zu – daß . . .,*** it was noticeable that. . . . **2.** *v.i.* ***– auf*** (*Acc.*), pay attention *or* listen to.

merklich ['mɛrklɪç], *adj.* marked, distinct, noticeable, evident, visible, perceptible, appreciable, considerable.

Merkmal ['mɛrkma:l], *n.* (**-s,** *pl.* **-e**) sign, mark, indication, symptom; feature, attribute, property, characteristic, criterion, (*Biol.*) character. **Merkmalsträger,** *m.* (*Biol.*) gene.

Merkur [mɛr'ku:r], *m.* (*Myth., Astr.*) Mercury.

Merkwort ['mɛrkvɔrt], *n.* catchword; (*Theat.*) cue.

merkwürdig ['mɛrkvy:rdɪç], *adj.* remarkable, noteworthy, striking; odd, strange, curious, peculiar. **merkwürdigerweise,** *adv.* strange to say, oddly *or* strangely enough. **Merkwürdigkeit,** *f.* strangeness, peculiarity; curiosity, remarkable thing; salient point.

Merkzeichen ['mɛrktsaɪçən], *n.* mark, sign, stamp, characteristic.

Merle ['mɛrlə], *f.* (*dial.*) blackbird.

Merlin [mɛr'li:n], *m.* (**-s,** *pl.* **-e**) (*Orn.*) merlin, (*Am.*) pigeon hawk (*Falco columbarius*).

Merzschaf ['mɛrtsʃa:f], *n.* cast-off sheep.

meschugge [me'ʃugə], *inv. adj.* (*sl.*) crazy, cracked, nuts, crackers.

Mesmer, *m.* (*Swiss*) *see* **Mesner.**

Mesner ['mɛsnər], *m.* (*R.C.*) sacristan, sexton.

Meß|amt ['mɛs–], *n.* 1. calibration office; 2. (*R.C.*) celebration of mass. **–analyse,** *f.* (*Chem.*) volumetric analysis. **–apparat,** *m.* measuring apparatus. **–band,** *n.* tape-measure. **meßbar,** *adj.* measurable, commensurable. **Meß|becher,** *m.* (*Chem.*) graduated beaker. **–blatt,** *n.* calibration sheet. **–brücke,** *f.* (*Elec.*) Wheatstone bridge. **–buch,** *n.* (*Eccl.*) missal. **–diener,** *m.* (*Eccl.*) acolyte.

Messe ['mɛsə], *f.* 1. (*R.C.*) mass; (*Mus.*) mass; ***hohe –,*** high *or* grand mass; ***stille –,*** low mass; ***in die – gehen, die – hören,*** go to mass; ***die – lesen,*** say mass; 2. fair, market; ***die – besuchen,*** attend the fair; ***die – beschicken,*** send goods to the fair; 3. (*Mil.*) mess, (*Naut.*) wardroom. **Messe|besucher,** *m.* visitor to a fair. **-gelände,** *n.* fairground.

messen ['mɛsən], **1.** *irr.v.t.* measure, take the measurement(s) of, gauge, (*Elec. etc.*) (*with apparatus*) meter; (*fig.*) measure, eye, (*coll.*) size up; ***er maß mich vom Scheitel bis zur Sohle,*** he eyed me from top to toe, he took stock of me; ***an ihm gemessen bist du . . .,*** compared with him you are. . . . **2.** *irr.v.i.* measure, be . . . long (*or* high *or* broad *etc.*). **3.** *irr.v.r.* ***sich – mit,*** compete with, try one's strength with, try conclusions with, pit o.s. against; ***sich nicht – können mit,*** be no match for (*a p.*), not stand comparison with (*a th.*).

[1]**Messer** ['mɛsər], *m.* 1. measurer, surveyor; 2. gauge, meter.

[2]**Messer,** *n.* knife; ***das große – führen,*** draw the long bow; ***das – sitzt ihm an der Kehle,*** he is face to face with ruin; ***Krieg bis aufs –,*** war to the knife; ***auf des -s Schneide,*** on the razor's edge.

Messer|bänkchen, *n.* knife-rest. **-griff,** *m.*, **-heft,** *n.* knife-handle. **-held,** *m.* cut-throat. **-klinge,** *f.* blade. **-kopf,** *m.* (*Tech.*) cutter-head. **-rücken,** *m.* back of a knife. **messerscharf,** *adj.* razor-sharp, razor-edged. **Messer|schmied,** *m.* cutler. **-(schmiede)waren,** *f.pl.* cutlery. **-spitze,** *f.* point of a knife. **-stecher,** *m.* *See* **-held.** **-stecherei,** *f.* knife-fight, knifing. **-stich,** *m.* stab. **-stiel,** *m.* *See* **-griff.**

Meß|fahne, *f.* (surveyor's) marker-flag. **-fehler,** *m.* error in measurement. **-freiheit,** *f.* right to hold a fair. **-gefäß,** *n.* graduated vessel. **-gerät,** *n.* measuring instrument, gauge, meter. **-gewand,** *n.* (*Eccl.*) vestment, chasuble. **-glas,** *n.* burette. **-gut,** *n.* goods exhibited at a fair. **-hemd,** *n.* (*Eccl.*) alb, alba.

Messias [me'si:as], *m.* Messiah.

Messing ['mɛsɪŋ], *n.* (**-s,** *pl.* **-e**) brass; ***mit – löten,*** braze. **Messing|blech,** *n.* sheet brass, brass plate. **-draht,** *m.* brass wire. **messingen,** *adj.* brazen, (of) brass. **Messing|gießer,** *m.* brass-founder. **-gießerei, -hütte,** *f.* brass-foundry. **-schmied,** *m.* brazier. **-waren,** *f.pl.* brass ware. **-werk,** *n.* *See* **-hütte.**

Meß|kelch, *m.* (*Eccl.*) chalice. **-kette,** *f.* surveyor's chain. **-kunst,** *f.* surveying. **-latte,** *f.* surveyor's rod *or* pole. **-leine,** *f.* measuring line. **-opfer,** *n.* (*Eccl.*) (sacrifice of the) mass. **-stab,** *m.* (*Motor.*) dipstick. **-stelle,** *f.* computing centre. **-tisch,** *m.* plane table. **-tischblatt,** *n.* ordnance-survey map (1:25,000). **-trupp,** *m.* (*Mil.*) survey section. **-tuch,** *n.* (*Eccl.*) communion-cloth. **-uhr,** *f.* meter.

Messung ['mɛsuŋ], *f.* measurement; measuring; survey(ing); mensuration; (*Naut.*) sounding. **Meßverfahren,** *n.* (*Artil.*) range finding, ranging.

Mestize [mɛs'ti:tsə], *m.* (**-n,** *pl.* **-n**) mestizo.

Met [me:t], *m.* (**-(e)s,** *pl.* **-e**) mead.

Metall [me'tal], *n.* (**-(e)s,** *pl.* **-e**) 1. metal; ***edle -e,*** precious metals; ***unedle -e,*** base metals; 2. timbre (*of the voice*).

Metall|arbeiter, *m.* metal-worker. **-beschlag,** *m.* metal sheathing *or* plating, *pl.* metal fittings. **-bestand,** *m.* specie, bullion. **-blech,** *m.* sheet metal, metal plate. **Metallegierung,** *f.* alloy. **metallen,** *adj.* metal, metallic; ***ein -er Klang,*** a metallic sound; (*fig.*) ***das hat einen -en Beigeschmack,*** that smacks of bribery. **Metall|farbe,** *f.* metallic pigment. **-folie,** *f.* metal foil. **-gehalt,** *m.* metal content. **-geld,** *n.* specie. **-glanz,** *m.* metallic lustre. **metallhaltig,** *adj.* metalliferous, **metallisch,** *adj.* metallic; ***eine -e Stimme,*** a harsh *or* jarring *or* strident voice. **Metall|kunde,** *f.* metallurgy. **-oxyd,** *n.* metallic oxide. **-probe,** *f.* assay. **-säge,** *f.* hacksaw. **-spritzverfahren,** *n.* metallization.

Metallurg [meta'lurk], *m.* (**-en,** *pl.* **-en**) metallurgist. **Metallurgie** [–'gi:], *f.* metallurgy. **metallurgisch,** *adj.* metallurgical.

Metall|verarbeitung, *f.* metal-working. **-verbindung,** *f.* (*Chem.*) metallic compound. **-vergiftung,** *f.* metallic poisoning. **-vorrat,** *m.* bullion reserve. **-waren,** *f.pl.* hardware, metal goods.

Metamorphose [metamɔr'fo:zə], *f.* metamorphosis.

Metapher [me'tafər], *f.* (-, *pl.* **-n**) metaphor.

metaphrastisch [meta'frastɪʃ], *adj.* periphrastic, circumlocutory.

Metaphysik [metafy'zi:k], *f.* metaphysics. **metaphysisch** [–'fy:zɪʃ], *adj.* metaphysical.

Metastase [meta'sta:zə], *f.* metastasis.

Meteor [mete'o:r], *n.* (**-s,** *pl.* **-e**) meteor. **Meteorologe** [–ro'lo:gə], *m.* (**-n,** *pl.* **-n**) meteorologist. **Meteorologie** [–lo'gi:], *f.* meteorology. **meteorologisch,** *adj.* meteorological. **Meteorstein,** *m.* aerolite, meteorite.

Meter ['me:tər], *n.* (*Swiss, Austr. m.*) metre. **Meter|kilogramm,** *n.* kilogram-meter. **-maß,** *n.* 1. metric measure; 2. tape-measure. **-sekunde,** *f.* metres per second. **-system,** *n.* metric system. **meterweise,** *adv.* by the metre. **Meterzentner,** *m.* 100 kilos (*approx.* 0·1 ton).

Methode [me'to:də], *f.* method; way (of doing things), procedure, system, policy; (*Tech.*) technique, process. **Methodenlehre, Methodik,** *f.* theory of method, methodology. **methodisch,** *adj.* methodical.

Methodismus [meto'dɪsmus], *m.* (*Eccl.*) Methodism. **Methodist,** *m.* (**-en,** *pl.* **-en**), **methodistisch,** *adj.* Methodist.

Metrik ['me:trɪk], *f.* versification, metrics, prosody. **metrisch,** *adj.* metrical; metric (*cf.* **Meter**).

Metropole [metro'po:lə], *f.* metropolis. **Metropolit** [–'li:t], *m.* (**-en,** *pl.* **-en**) archbishop. **Metropolitankirche** [–i'ta:nkɪrçə], *f.* Cathedral.

Metrum ['me:trum], (**-s,** *pl.* **-tra** *or* **-tren**) (*Pros.*) metre.

Mette ['mɛtə], *f.* matins; early morning service.

Mettwurst ['mɛtvurst], *f.* Bologna sausage, polony.

[1]**Metze** ['mɛtsə], *f.* (*obs.*) harlot, strumpet.

[2]**Metze,** *f.*, *m.* (*obs.*) peck (= *3·44 litre*).

Metzelei [mɛtsə'laɪ], *f.* (-, *pl.* **-en**) massacre, slaughter, butchery. **metzeln** ['mɛtsəln], *v.t.* butcher, slaughter, massacre, cut to pieces. **Metzelsuppe,** *f.* (*dial.*) broth.

Metzen ['mɛtsən], *m.* *See* [2]**Metze.**

Metzge ['mɛtsgə], *f.* (*dial.*) slaughter-house, shambles. **metzgen,** *v.t.* (*dial.*) slaughter. **Metzger,** *m.* butcher. **Metzgerei** [–'raɪ], *f.* butcher's shop. **Metzger(s)gang,** *m.* (*dial.*) fool's errand.

Meuchelmord ['mɔyçəlmɔrt], *m.* assassination. **Meuchelmörder,** *m.* assassin. **meucheln,** *v.t.* assassinate. **Meuchler,** *m.* assassin. **meuchlerisch,** *adj.*, **meuchlings,** *adv.* treacherous(ly), dastardly.

Meute ['mɔytə], *f.* pack of hounds, (*fig.*) gang, pack, rabble.

Meuterei [mɔytə'raɪ], *f.* mutiny. **Meuterer** ['mɔytərər], *m.* mutineer. **meuterisch,** *adj.* mutinous. **meutern,** *v.i.* mutiny. **meuternd,** *adj.* *See* **meuterisch.**

miauen [mi'auən], *v.i.* mew; caterwaul.

mich [mɪç], (*Acc. of* **ich**) me.

Michaeli(s) [mɪça'e:lɪ(s)], *n.* Michaelmas.

Michel ['mɪçəl], *m.* ***der deutsche –,*** the ordinary *or* average German, Fritz.

mied [mi:t], **miede** ['mi:də], *see* **meiden.**

Mieder ['mi:dər], *n.* bodice, corset.

Mief [mi:f], *m.* (*sl.*) fug.

Miene ['mi:nə], *f.* countenance; air, look, expression; bearing, mien; ***ernste –,*** stern *or* solemn appearance; ***finstere –,*** black looks, scowling expression; ***fromme –,*** pious looks; ***gute – zum bösen Spiele machen,*** make the best of a bad job, put a good face on it, make a virtue of necessity; ***kecke –,*** bold front; ***– machen (zu tun),*** be about, offer, threaten (to do), show signs (of doing), make a move (to do); ***saure –,*** scowl; ***ohne die – zu verziehen,*** without turning a hair, without flinching, (*coll.*) without batting an eyelid; ***überlegene –,*** superior air. **Mienenspiel,** *n.* play of the features, pantomime, dumb show; ***Mienen- und Gebärdenspiel,*** by-play (*of an actor*).

Miere [ˈmiːrə], *f.* chickweed.

mies [miːs], *adj.* (*coll.*) out of sorts, seedy, poorly; poor, bad, wretched, (*coll.*) awful.

Mies [ˈmiːs], *f.* (-, *pl.* **-en**), **Mieschen,** *n.*, **Miesekatze,** *f. See* **Miez.**

Miesepeter [ˈmiːzəpeːtər], *m.* (*coll.*) cross-patch, sour-puss. **miesepetrig,** *adj.* morose, churlish, sullen, moody, grumpy, irritable, disgruntled. **Miesmacher,** *m.* (*coll.*) grouser, defeatist, alarmist, (*Am.*) croaker, calamity, howler.

Miesmuschel [ˈmiːsmuʃəl], *f.* mussel.

Miet|ausfall [ˈmiːt–], *m.* loss of rent. **–auto,** *n.* hired car. **–besitz,** *m.* tenancy. **–dauer,** *f.* (period of) tenancy, period of lease.

[1]**Miete** [ˈmiːtə], *f.* hire; rent; lease; ***die – aufsagen,*** give notice; ***fällige –,*** rent due; ***in der – haben,*** have on hire, hold on lease; ***in – nehmen,*** hire, rent; ***rückständige –,*** arrears of rent; ***zur – geben,*** let out; ***zur – wohnen,*** be a tenant, live in lodgings.

[2]**Miete,** *f.* (*dial.*) mite.

[3]**Miete,** *f.* stack, shock, rick (*of corn etc.*), clamp (*of potatoes*).

mietefrei [ˈmiːtəfraɪ], *adj.* rent-free. **Mieteinnahme,** *f.* (income from) rent. **mieten,** *v.t.* hire, rent, (take on) lease; engage (*a taxi etc.*); charter (*a ship*). **Mieter,** *m.* hirer; tenant, lodger, (*Am.*) roomer, (*Law*) lessee.

Mieterschaft [ˈmiːtərʃaft], *f.* tenantry. **Mieter|schutz,** *m.* rent control *or* restriction. **–vereinigung,** *f.* tenant's association.

Mietflugzeug [ˈmiːtfluːktsɔyk], *n.* charter-plane. **mietfrei,** *adj. See* **mietefrei. Miet|haus,** *n.* block of flats, tenement, (*Am.*) apartment-house. **–herr,** *m.* landlord. **–kaserne,** *f.* (*coll.*) *see* **–haus. –kutsche,** *f.* hackney carriage.

Mietling [ˈmiːtlɪŋ], *m.* (**-s,** *pl.* **-e**) (*Hist.*) mercenary, (*coll.*) hireling.

Miet|preis, *m.* rent, hire-charge. **–preispolitik,** *f.* rent policy. **–recht,** *n.* tenants' rights.

Miets|bedingungen, *f.pl.* terms of lease *or* of hire. **–haus,** *n.*, **–kaserne,** *f.*, *See* **Miet|haus, –kaserne. Miets|mann,** *m.* (*pl.* **-leute**) lodger, tenant. **–wohnung,** *f. See* **Mietwohnung.**

Miet|truppen, *f.pl.* mercenaries. **–verhältnis,** *n.* tenancy. **–verlust,** *m.* loss of rent. **–vertrag,** *m.* tenancy agreement, lease, (*Naut.*) charter party. **–wagen,** *m.* hired car. **–wagenverleih,** *m.* car-hire service. **mietweise,** *adv.* (*of dwelling*) on lease, (*of th.*) on hire. **Miet|wohnung,** *f.* rented house, lodgings, flat, (*Am.*) apartment. **–zins,** *m.* (**-es,** *pl.* **-e**) (house-)rent.

Miez [miːts], *f.* (-, *pl.* **-en**), **Mieze, Miezekatze,** *f.* pussy(cat), puss. **miezeln,** *v.i.* (*coll.*) spoon, canoodle, bill and coo.

Migräne [miˈgrɛːnə], *f.* sick headache, migraine.

Mikrobe [mɪˈkroːbə], *f.* microbe.

Mikro|biologie [mikro–], *f.* bacteriology, microbiology. **–kosmos, –kosmus,** *m.* microcosm. **–organismus,** *m.* micro-organism.

Mikrophon [mikroˈfoːn], *n.* (**-s,** *pl.* **-e**) microphone.

Mikroskop [mikroˈskoːp], *n.* (**-s,** *pl.* **-e**) microscope. **mikroskopisch,** *adj.* microscopic; ***– untersuchen,*** examine under the microscope.

Mikrowelle [mikroˈvɛlə], *f.* (*Rad.*) microwave.

Milan [ˈmiːlan], *m.* (**-s,** *pl.* **-e**) (*Orn.*) ***brauner*** or ***schwarzer –,*** black kite (*Milvus migrans*); ***roter –,*** kite (*Milvus milvus*).

Milbe [ˈmɪlbə], *f.* (*Ent.*) mite (*Acarus*).

Milch [mɪlç], *f.* milk; (*Chem.*) emulsion; (*Ichth.*) milt, soft roe; (*Bot.*) juice; ***saure –, geronnene –, dicke –,*** curdled milk, sour milk; ***abgerahmte –,*** skimmed milk; ***wie – und Blut,*** like cream and roses; ***in die – geben,*** put out to nurse.

Milchader [ˈmɪlçˀaːdə], *f.* lacteal vein. **milch|ähnlich, –artig,** *adj.* milk-like, milky, lacteal. **Milch|bar,** *f.* milk-bar. **–bart,** *m.* greenhorn, milksop. **–brei,** *m.* gruel, pap. **–brot, –brötchen,** *n.* French roll. **–bruder,** *m.* foster-brother. **–drüse,** *f.* lacteal *or* mammary gland. **–eimer,** *m.* milk-pail.

milchen [ˈmɪlçən], *v.i.* give milk. **Milcher,** *m.* 1. (*Ichth.*) milter, male fish; 2. (*dial.*) milker, dairy-hand.

Milch|erzeugnisse, *n.pl.* dairy produce *or* products. **–ferkel,** *n.* sucking pig. **–fieber,** *n.* lacteal fever. **–frau,** *f.* dairywoman. **–gefäß,** *n.* 1. milk-pan; 2. (*Anat.*) lacteal vessel. **–geschäft,** *n.* dairy, creamery. **–gesicht,** *n.* baby face. **–gewinnung,** *f.* milk production. **–glas,** *n.* opalescent *or* frosted glass; glass for milk. **–halle,** *f. See* **–bar. milchhaltig,** *adj.* lactiferous. **Milch|händler,** *m.* milkman, dairyman. **–handlung,** *f. See* **–geschäft. milchig,** *adj* milky. **Milch|kaffee,** *m.* coffee with milk. **–kuh,** *f.* milch cow, milker. **–kur,** milk diet. **–laden,** *m. See* **–geschäft. –leistung,** *f.* milk yield. **Milchling** [ˈmɪlçlɪŋ], *m.* (**-s.** *pl.* **-e**) milky top (*fungus*) (*Lactaria*); *see* **Brätling, Reizker.**

Milch|mädchen, *n.*, **–magd,** *f.* dairymaid, milkmaid. **–mann,** *m.* milkman, dairyman. **–messer,** *m.* lactometer. **–napf,** *m.* milk-saucepan. **–pulver,** *n.* evaporated *or* dried milk. **–reis,** *m.* rice pudding. **–ruhr,** *f.* infantile diarrhoea. **–saft,** *m.* milky juice, chyle; latex. **milchsauer,** *adj.* lactate of. **Milch|säure,** *f.* lactic acid. **–schleuder,** *m.* (cream) separator. **–schwester,** *f.* foster-sister. **–straße,** *f.* Milky Way. **–suppe,** *f.* (*sl.*) pea-souper (*fog*). **–topf,** *m.* milk-jug. **–vieh,** *n.* dairy cattle. **milchweiß,** *adj.* milk-white. **Milch|wirtschaft,** *f.* dairy-farm(ing). **–zahn,** *m.* milk-tooth. **–zucker,** *m.* sugar of milk, lactose.

mild(e) [ˈmɪld(ə)], **1.** *adj.* mild, soft, mellow, gentle; lenient, indulgent, charitable; ***–e Beiträge,*** donations, benefactions; ***–e Gabe,*** charitable gift, alms; ***–e Hand,*** generosity, clemency; ***–e Stiftung,*** charitable institution; benefaction; ***–e Strafe,*** light *or* lenient punishment. **2.** *adv.* ***– gesagt,*** to put it mildly; ***– beurteilen,*** take a lenient view of. **Milde,** *f.* mildness, gentleness, softness; indulgence, leniency, kindness, clemency.

mildern [ˈmɪldərn], *v.t.* soften, moderate, ease, relax, mollify, mitigate; soothe, relieve, alleviate, assuage, temper; qualify, (*Law*) commute (*a sentence*), (*coll.*) tone down; ***–de Umstände,*** extenuating *or* mitigating circumstances.

Milderung [ˈmɪldərʊŋ], *f.* mitigation, alleviation; mollification; softening, relaxation, moderation; qualification (*of a statement*). **Milderungs|ausdruck,** *m.* euphemism. **–gründe,** *m.pl.* extenuating *or* mitigating circumstances. **–mittel,** *n.* lenitive, mitigant, palliative, demulcant.

mildherzig [ˈmɪlthɛrtsɪç], *adj.* tender *or* kind-hearted, indulgent, charitable. **Mildherzigkeit,** *f.* kind-heartedness, indulgence. **mildtätig,** *adj.* generous, benevolent, beneficent, charitable; ***–e Zwecke,*** charities. **Mildtätigkeit,** *f.* beneficence, liberality, generosity, charity.

Milieu [miliˈøː], *n.* (**-s,** *pl.* **-s**) (social) surroundings, background, environment, local colour. **milieubedingt,** *adj.* environmental. **Milieu|einfluß,** *m.* influence of environment.

Militär [miliˈtɛːr], **1.** *m.* (**-s,** *pl.* **-s**) (*coll.*) military man, soldier. **2.** *n.* the military, armed forces; military personnel, soldiery, army, soldiers.

militärähnlich [miliˈtɛrˀɛːnlɪç], *adj.* para-military. **Militär|anwärter,** *m.* long-service N.C.O. (entitled on discharge to low-grade civil-service employment). **–arzt,** *m.* army doctor, medical officer. **–behörden,** *pl.* military authorities. **–dienst,** *m.* active *or* military service. **–etat,** *m.* army estimates. **–fahrschein,** *m.* railway warrant. **–geistliche(r),** *m.* army chaplain. **–gericht,** *n.* military court, court martial. **–gerichtsbarkeit,** *f.* military jurisdiction. **–größe,** *f.* minimum height for military service.

militärisch [miliˈtɛːrɪʃ], *adj.* military; soldierly, martial; ***–es Aussehen,*** soldierly *or* martial bearing; ***– besetzt,*** occupied by troops.

militarisieren [militariˈziːrən], *v.t.* militarize. **Militarisierung,** *f.* militarization. **Militarismus** [–ˈrɪsmus], *m.* militarism.

Militär|kapelle, *f.* military band. **–macht,** *f.* military power. **–maß,** *n. See* **–größe. –musik,** *f.* martial music; military band. **–musiker,** *m.* bandsman. **–pflicht,** *f. See* **Wehrpflicht. militärpflichtig,** *adj.* liable for military service. **Militär|putsch,** *m.* military coup. **–recht,** *n.* military law. **–staat,** *m.* militarized state. **–stand,** *m.* profession of arms. **–strafanstalt,** *f.* detention barracks. **–vorlage,** *f.* army bill.

Miliz [mi'li:ts], *f.* (-, *pl.* **-en**) militia; yeomanry. **Milizsoldat,** *m.* militiaman.

Milliardär [mɪliar'dɛ:r], *m.* (**-s,** *pl.* **-e**) multi-millionaire. **Milliarde** [–'ardə], *f.* milliard, (*Am.*) billion. **Million** [–'o:n], *f.* million. **Millionär** [–'ne:r], *m.* (**-s,** *pl.* **-e**) millionaire.

Milz [mɪlts], *f.* (-, *pl.* **-en**) spleen; ***mich sticht die –,*** I have the stitch, I have a stitch in my side. **Milzbrand,** *m.* (*Vet.*) anthrax. **milzkrank,** *adj.* splenetic. **Milz|krankheit,** *f. See* **–sucht. –stechen,** *n.* stitch (in the side). **–sucht,** *f.* (*obs.*) hypochondria, spleen, melancholia. **milz|süchtig,** *adj. See* **–krank.**

Mime ['mi:mə], *m.* (**-n,** *pl.* **-n**) mimic, actor. **mimen,** *v.t.* act (*in plays*), personate, mimic, pose as, feign, pretend. **Mimik,** *f.* mimicry, miming. **Mimiker,** *m.* mimic. **mimisch,** *adj.* mimic.

Mimose [mi'mo:zə], *f.* (*Bot.*) mimosa. **mimosenhaft,** *adj.* highly sensitive, (*coll.*) touchy.

minder ['mɪndər], **1.** *adj.* less; lesser, smaller, inferior, minor. **2.** *adv.* less; ***nicht mehr, nicht –,*** neither more nor less; ***– gut,*** inferior, of lower quality.

Minderbedarf ['mɪndərbədarf], *m.* smaller *or* reduced demand. **minder|begabt,** *adj.* handicapped, sub-normal. **–bemittelt,** *adj.* of moderate means. **Minder|betrag,** *m.* deficiency, shortage, deficit. **–bewertung,** *f.* under-valuation, depreciation. **–einnahme,** *f.* drop in earnings *or* receipts. **–ertrag,** *m.* falling-off in output. **–gewicht,** *n.* short weight.

Minderheit ['mɪndərhaɪt], *f.* minority. **Minderheiten|frage,** *f.* problem of minorities. **–kabinett,** *n.* cabinet of the minority party.

minderjährig ['mɪndərjɛ:rɪç], *adj.* under age; ***er ist –,*** he is a minor. **Minder|jährige(r),** *m., f.* minor. **–jährigkeit,** *f.* minority.

mindern ['mɪndərn], **1.** *v.t.* diminish, lower, reduce, depreciate, decrease, lessen. **2.** *v.r.* decrease, abate, diminish, grow less.

Minderung ['mɪndəruŋ], *f.* decrease, reduction, diminution, abatement, depreciation.

Minderwert ['mɪndərve:rt], *m.* inferiority, undervalue. **minderwertig,** *adj.* inferior, of poor quality, low-grade, sub-standard; (*Chem.*) of lower valence. **Minderwertigkeit,** *f.* inferiority, poor quality. **Minderwertigkeits|gefühl,** *n.* sense of inferiority, self-disparagement. **–komplex,** *m.* inferiority complex. **Minderzahl,** *f.* minority; ***in der – sein,*** be in the minority.

mindest ['mɪndəst], **1.** *adj.* least, smallest, lowest, slightest, minimum. **2.** *adv.* least, lowest, smallest; ***nicht das –e,*** not the slightest, nothing at all; ***zum –en,*** at least, at the (very) least; ***nicht im –en,*** not in the least, not at all, by no means.

Mindest–, *pref.* minimum. **–bietende(r),** *m., f.* lowest bidder. **mindestens,** *adv.* at least, at the (very) least; (*before numbers*) not less than. **Mindest|gebot,** *n.* lowest bid. **–maß,** *n.* (indispensable) minimum; ***auf ein – herabsetzen,*** minimize. **–zahl,** *f.* minimum; (*in meetings*) quorum.

Mine ['mi:nə], *f.* 1. (*Min., Mil., Naut.*) mine; ***auf eine – laufen,*** hit a mine; (*Mil.*) ***–n ausbauen,*** clear a minefield; (*Naut.*) ***–n räumen,*** sweep for mines; (*fig.*) ***alle –n springen lassen,*** leave no stone unturned; 2. refill, lead (*for propelling pencil*).

Minen|abweiser, *m.* (*Naut.*) paravane. **–aktie,** *f.* mining share. **–falle,** *f.* (*Mil.*) booby trap. **–feld,** *n.* minefield. **–gasse,** *f.* lane in a minefield. **–leger,** *m.* (*Naut.*) minelayer. **–räumboot,** *n.* minesweeper. **–sperre,** *f.* minefield. **–suchboot,** *n. See* **–räumboot. –suchgerät,** *n.* mine detector. **–werfer,** *m.* (*Mil.*) trench mortar.

Mineral [mine'ra:l], *n.* (**-s,** *pl.* **-e** *or* **-ien**) mineral. **Mineral|bad,** *n.*, **–brunnen,** *m.* mineral springs.

Mineralien [mine'ra:liən], *pl. of* **Mineral. Mineralien|kunde,** *f.* mineralogy. **–sammlung,** *f.* collection of geological specimens.

mineralisch [mine'ra:lɪʃ], *adj.* mineral.

Mineraloge [minera'lo:gə], *m.* (**-n,** *pl.* **-n**) mineralogist. **Mineralogie** [–'gi:], *f.* mineralogy. **mineralogisch,** *adj.* mineralogical.

Mineral|öl, *n.* mineral oil, petroleum. **–quelle,** *f. See* **–bad. –reich,** *n.* mineral kingdom. **–stoffwechsel,** *m.* inorganic metabolism. **–wasser,** *n.* (*pl.* **–wässer**) mineral water.

Mineur [mi'nø:r], *m.* (**-s,** *pl.* **-e**) sapper, miner. **Mineurpflug,** *m.* deep plough.

Miniatur [minia'tu:r], *f.* (-, *pl.* **-en**) miniature. **Miniatur|ausgabe,** *f.* pocket-edition. **–bild,** *n.* miniature.

Minierarbeit [mi'ni:rˀarbaɪt], *f.* (*Mil.*) sapping; (*fig.*) intrigue, plotting, (*coll.*) skulduggery. **minieren,** *v.t.* sap, (under)mine.

minimal [mini'ma:l], *adj.* minimum; minute, tiny, insignificant, trifling. **Minimal|betrag,** *m.* mimimum (amount), lowest amount. **–satz,** *m.* lowest rate. **Minimum** ['mi:nimum], *n.* (**-s,** *pl.* **-ma**) 1. minimum; 2. (*Meteor.*) low, depression.

Minister [mi'nɪstər], *m.* minister; (*Eng.*) Secretary of State, (*Am.*) Secretary; ***bevollmächtiger –,*** plenipotentiary; ***erster –,*** Prime Minister, Premier; ***– ohne Geschäftsbereich,*** minister without portfolio.

Ministerial|ausschuß [minɪsteri'a:l-], *m.* ministerial committee. **–beamte(r),** *m.* departmental official. **–direktor,** *m.* head of a government department. **–erlaß,** *m.* ministerial order; order in Council. **–gebäude,** *n.* Government offices. **–rat,** *m.* senior civil servant.

ministeriell [minɪsteri'ɛl], *adj.* ministerial.

Ministerium [minɪs'te:rium], *n.* (**-s,** *pl.* **-rien**) ministry; government department; ***– des Inneren,*** Home Office; ***im – sein,*** be in the ministry *or* cabinet, be in office, hold office.

Minister|präsident, *m.* president of the cabinet council; Prime Minister, Premier. **–rat,** *m.* cabinet council.

Ministrant [minɪs'trant], *m.* (**-en,** *pl.* **-en**) (*Eccl.*) acolyte, altar-boy. **ministrieren,** *v.i.* minister, officiate.

Minne ['mɪnə], *f.* (*Poet.*) love. **Minne|lied,** *n.*, **–sang,** *m.* medi(a)eval German love poem. **–sänger, –singer,** *m.* minnesinger (*German lyric poet of the 12th to 14th centuries*), minstrel. **minnig(lich),** *adj.* (*Poet.*) lovely, charming; lovable.

minorenn [mino'rɛn], *adj.* under age, minor. **Minorennität** [–i'tɛ:t], *f.* minority (*of a person*).

Minorität [minori'tɛ:t], *f.* minority. **Minoritätenproblem,** *n.* problem of minorities. **Minoritätsgutachten,** *n.* minority report.

minus ['mi:nus], *adv.* minus, less; ***7 – 3,*** 7 minus *or* less 3. **Minus,** *n.* deficit, deficiency; shortage. **Minus|betrag,** *m.* (*Math.*) minus quantity, (*Comm.*) deficiency, shortage, deficit. **–glas,** *n.* (*Opt.*) concave lens.

Minuskel [mi'nuskəl], *f.* (-, *pl.* **-n**) small letter; minuscule.

Minus|pol, *m.* (*Elec.*) negative terminal. **–seite,** *f.* (*Comm.*) debit side (*also fig.*). **–zeichen,** *n.* (*Math.*) minus sign (—).

Minute [mi'nu:tə], *f.* minute; ***auf die – (genau),*** to the minute, (*coll.*) on the dot; ***ein Grad dreißig –n,*** 1° 30′ (*angle*). **minuten|lang,** *adj.* for (several) minutes. **–weise,** *adv.* minute by minute, from minute to minute. **Minutenzeiger,** *m.* minute-hand.

minuziös [minutsi'ø:s], *adj.* minute, tiny; detailed, painstaking.

Minze ['mɪntsə], *f.* (*Bot.*) mint (*Mentha*).

mir [mi:r], *Dat. of* **ich,** me, to me; (*refl.*) (to) myself; ***ein Buch von –,*** a book belonging to me *or* written by me; a book of mine; ***– ist kalt,*** I feel cold; ***ich will – die Hände waschen,*** I want to wash my hands; ***jetzt ist es an –,*** now it is my turn; ***von – aus,*** as far as I am concerned, for all I care; ***– nichts, dir nichts,*** without (more) ado, without ceremony, (*coll.*) as cool as you please; ***laß – das bleiben,*** just leave that alone; ***wie du –, so ich dir,*** what's sauce for the goose is sauce for the gander; tit for tat; (*Prov.*) ***heute –, morgen dir,*** everyone in his turn.

Mirabelle [mira'bɛlə], *f.* yellow plum.

Mirakel [mi'ra:kəl], *n.* miracle. **Mirakelspiel,** *n.* (medi(a)eval) miracle play.

Misanthrop [mizan'tro:p], *m.* (**-en,** *pl.* **-en**) misanthropist. **misanthropisch,** *adj.* misanthropic.

Mischart ['mɪʃʔart], *f.* crossbreed, mongrel. **mischbar,** *adj.* mixable, miscible, combinable. **Mischbarkeit,** *f.* miscibility. **Misch|becher,** *m.* shaker. **–behälter,** *m.* mixing tank. **–bestand,** *m.* mixed crop. **–ehe,** *f.* mixed marriage.

mischen ['mɪʃən], **1.** *v.t.* mix, mingle; blend, combine, compound; adulterate; alloy (*metals*), cross (*breeds*), (*Cards*) shuffle. **2.** *v.r.* mix, mingle, join in (***unter*** (*Acc.*), with); (*of things*) blend, combine, be miscible; interfere (***in*** (*Acc.*), in *or* with), meddle (with); ***sich ins Gespräch –,*** join *or* (*coll.*) butt in the conversation; *see* **gemischt.**

Misch|farbe, *f.* mixed *or* combination colour. **–futter,** *n.* mixed fodder. **–gericht,** *n.* ragout.

Mischling ['mɪʃlɪŋ], *m.* (**-s,** *pl.* **-e**) (*Zool.*) mongrel, cross(breed), (*Bot.*) hybrid, (*of men*) half-breed, half-caste.

Mischmasch ['mɪʃmaʃ], *m.* (**-es,** *no pl.*) jumble, medley, hotchpotch.

Misch|maschine, *f.* mixer, mixing machine. **–pult,** *n.* (*Rad. etc.*) control desk. **–rasse,** *f.* mongrel race, crossbreed.

Mischung ['mɪʃuŋ], *f.* mixture, blend; compound; composition, combination; (*of metals*) alloy. **Mischungs|bestandteil,** *m.* component, ingredient, constituent. **–verhältnis,** *n.* ratio of components.

Misch|volk, *m.* mixed race *or* breed. **–wald,** *m.* mixed woodland.

miserabel [mize'ra:bəl], *adj.* wretched, miserable; (*coll.*) rotten, awful.

Misere [mi'ze:rə], *f.* calamity; miseries.

Misogyn [mizo'gy:n], *m.* (**-en,** *pl.* **-en,** *Austr.* **-(e)s,** *pl.* **-e**) misogynist.

Mispel ['mɪspəl], *f.* (**-,** *pl.* **-n**) (*Bot.*) medlar (*Mespilus germanica*).

Miß [mɪs], *f.* (**-,** *pl.* **-(ss)es**) (*coll.*) Miss (*as title*).

miß—, *pref.* = mis-, dis-, bad, ill, amiss, false, wrong; *cannot be described as either sep. or insep.; p.p. is best without ge–, e.g.* ***mißachtet,*** *though both other forms occur, e.g.* ***gemißhandelt, mißgetönt;*** *inf. is sometimes as sep., sometimes as insep., e.g.* ***mißzustimmen, zu mißbilden,*** *depending on the stress; sep. when the contrast with its opposite is emphasized.*

mißachten [mɪs'axtən], *v.t.* (*p.p.* ***mißachtet***) disregard, ignore, neglect; esteem lightly, undervalue, slight, despise, disdain. **Mißachtung,** *f.* disregard, disrespect, disdain; neglect; (*Law*) ***– des Gerichts,*** contempt of court.

Missal [mi'sa:l], *n.* (**-s,** *pl.* **-e**), **Missale,** *n.* (**-s,** *pl.* **-n**) (*R.C.*) missal.

mißarten [mɪs'a:rtən], *v.i.* (*p.p.* ***miß(ge)artet***) (*aux.* s.) degenerate. **Mißartung,** *f.* degeneracy.

Mißbegriff ['mɪsbəgrɪf], *m.* misconception, wrong idea.

mißbehagen ['mɪsbəha:gən], *v.imp.* (*p.p.* ***mißbehagt***) (*Dat.*) displease. **Mißbehagen,** *n.* discomfort, uncomfortable feeling, uneasiness; dislike, displeasure, discontent.

mißbilden [mɪs'bɪldən], *v.t.* (*p.p.* ***mißgebildet***) deform, malform. **Mißbildung,** *f.* deformity, malformation, disfigurement.

mißbilligen [mɪs'bɪlɪgən], *v.t.* (*p.p.* ***mißbilligt,*** *also* ***gemißbilligt***) disapprove (of), object (to), disallow, condemn. **Mißbilligung,** *f.* disapproval, disapprobation.

Mißbrauch ['mɪsbraux], *m.* misuse; abuse, malpractice, improper *or* unauthorized use. **mißbrauchen,** *v.t.* 1. (*p.p.* ***mißbraucht,*** *also* ***gemißbraucht***) misapply, misuse, abuse; 2. (*p.p.* ***mißbraucht***) take (unfair) advantage of; ***den Namen des Herrn –,*** take the Lord's name in vain. **mißbräuchlich,** *adj.*, **mißbräuchlicherweise,** *adv.* wrong(ly), improper(ly).

mißdeuten [mɪs'dɔytən], *v.t.* (*p.p.* ***mißdeutet***) misinterpret, misconstrue. **Mißdeutung,** *f.* misinterpretation, false construction.

missen ['mɪsən], *v.t.* 1. be *or* do without, dispense with; 2. miss, feel the lack of.

Miß|erfolg, *m.* failure, fiasco, (*coll.*) flop. **–ernte,** *f.* bad *or* poor harvest.

missest ['mɪsəst], *see* **messen.**

Missetat ['mɪsəta:t], *f.* (*B.*) sin, misdeed, crime. **Missetäter,** *m.* (*B.*) evildoer, sinner, malefactor; (*Law*) offender, delinquent.

mißfallen [mɪs'falən], *irr.v.i.* (*p.p.* ***mißfallen***) (*Dat.*) displease, be displeasing to, offend; ***es mißfällt mir,*** I dislike it. **Mißfallen** ['mɪsfalən], *n.* dislike, displeasure, dissatisfaction; ***– erregen,*** displease, meet with displeasure. **mißfällig** ['mɪsfɛlɪç], *adj.* displeasing, disagreeable, offensive; disparaging, deprecatory, unfavourable; ***sich – äußern über*** (*Acc.*), speak ill of, find fault with.

mißfarbig ['mɪsfarbɪç], *adj.* discoloured. **Mißfarbung,** *f.* discolo(u)ration.

Mißgeburt ['mɪsgəburt], *f.* (*fig.*) freak, monstrosity, monster, abortion.

mißgelaunt ['mɪsgəlaunt], *adj.* ill-humoured, bad-tempered.

Mißgeschick ['mɪsgəʃɪk], *n.* misfortune, bad luck; misadventure, mishap.

Mißgestalt ['mɪsgəʃtalt], *f.* monster. **mißgestalt,** *adj.* deformed, misshapen. **mißgestalten,** *v.t.* (*p.p.* ***mißgestaltet***) disfigure, mutilate, deform.

miß|gestimmt, *adj. See* **–gelaunt.**

mißglücken [mɪs'glykən], *v.i.* (*p.p.* ***mißglückt***) (*aux.* s.) (*Dat.*) fail, not succeed, miscarry. **mißglückt,** *adj.* unsuccessful, abortive.

mißgönnen [mɪs'gœnən], *v.t.* (*p.p.* ***mißgönnt***) (*Dat. of a p.*) (be)grudge, envy.

Mißgriff ['mɪsgrɪf], *m.* failure; mistake, blunder.

Mißgunst ['mɪsgunst], *f.* grudge, envy, jealousy; (*rare*) ill-will, disfavour. **mißgünstig,** *adj.* envious, jealous.

mißhandeln [mɪs'handəln], **1.** *v.i.* (*p.p.* ***mißgehandelt***) do wrong. **2.** *v.t.* (*p.p.* ***mißhandelt***) abuse, mishandle; ill-treat, maltreat, (*coll.*) manhandle. **Mißhandlung,** *f.* ill-treatment, maltreatment, ill-usage, abuse; misdeed; (*Law*) battery.

Mißheirat ['mɪshaɪra:t], *f.* misalliance.

mißhellig ['mɪshɛlɪç], *adj.* disagreeing, dissentient, dissonant, discordant. **Mißhelligkeit,** *f.* (*usu. pl.*) disagreement, difference, dissension, discord, (*coll.*) unpleasantness.

Mission [mɪsi'o:n], *f.* mission, ***Innere*** (***Äußere***) –, Home (Foreign) mission. **Missionar** [–'na:r], (*Austr.*) **Missionär,** *m.* (**-s,** *pl.* **-e**) missionary. **Missions|anstalt,** *f.* mission (house). **–gesellschaft,** *f.* missionary society. **–predige(r),** *m.* evangelist. **–werk,** *n.* missionary work.

Miß|jahr, *n.* bad year *or* harvest. **–klang,** *m.* dissonance, discord, discordant note. **–kredit,** *m.* discredit; ***in – bringen,*** discredit, bring discredit upon, bring into ill-repute.

mißlang [mɪs'laŋ], *see* **mißlingen.**

Mißlaut ['mɪslaut], *m.* discordant sound, cacophony.

mißleiten [mɪs'laɪtən], *v.t.* (*p.p.* ***mißleitet,*** *also* ***mißgeleitet***) mislead, lead astray.

mißlich ['mɪslɪç], *adj.* unpleasant, inconvenient, awkward; difficult, precarious, critical, dangerous;

(*coll.*) touchy, tricky, ticklish; *–e Lage*, predicament, quandary, (*coll.*) fix, jam. **Mißlichkeit,** *f.* unpleasantness, inconvenience, awkwardness; difficulty, critical situation.

mißliebig ['mɪsli:bɪç], *adj.* unpopular, out of *or* not in favour; *– aufnehmen,* take amiss *or* ill; *sich bei ihm – machen,* get into his bad books.

mißlingen [mɪs'lɪŋən], *irr.v.i.* (*aux.* s.) (*p.p. mißlungen*) fail, not succeed, be *or* prove unsuccessful, miscarry, (*coll.*) not come off; *es ist mir mißlungen,* I failed. **Mißlingen,** *n.* failure.

mißlungen [mɪs'luŋən] *see* **mißlingen.**

Mißmut ['mɪsmu:t], *m.* ill-humour, discontent, despondence. **mißmutig,** *adj.* ill-humoured, discontented; bad-tempered, peevish, (*coll.*) cross; despondent, sullen, morose.

mißraten [mɪs'ra:tən], **1.** *irr.v.i.* (*aux.* s.) (*p.p. mißraten*) (*Dat.*) turn out badly (for), fail, miscarry. **2.** *adj.* (*as children*) ill-bred, badly brought up, naughty, wayward; *–er Mensch,* misfit, a square peg in a round hole.

Mißstand ['mɪsʃtant], *m.* deplorable state of affairs; nuisance, inconvenience, grievance; *Mißstände beseitigen,* remedy grievances *or* abuses.

mißstimmen ['mɪsʃtɪmən], *v.t.* (*p.p. mißgestimmt*) upset, irritate, put out of humour. **Mißstimmung,** *f.* friction, strife; *see also* **Mißmut.**

mißt [mɪst], *see* **messen.**

Miß|ton, *m.* *See* **–klang, –laut. miß|tönend, –tönig,** *adj.* discordant, dissonant, jarring, cacophonous.

mißtrauen [mɪs'trauən], *v.i.* (*p.p. mißtraut*) (*Dat.*) distrust, mistrust, have no confidence in, suspect, have one's doubts about. **Mißtrauen** ['mɪstrauən], *n.* distrust, mistrust, suspicion (*gegen,* of), doubts, misgiving(s) (about). **Mißtrauensvotum,** *n.* (*Parl.*) vote of censure *or* no confidence. **mißtrauisch,** *adj.* distrustful, suspicious; doubtful, diffident, wary.

Mißvergnügen ['mɪsfɛrgny:gən], *n.* displeasure, discontent, dissatisfaction. **mißvergnügt,** *adj.* displeased, discontented, dissatisfied (*über* (*Acc.*), *mit,* with), malcontent.

Mißverhältnis ['mɪsfɛrhɛltnɪs], *n.* (*of things*) disproportion, disparity, incongruity; (*of persons*) tension, unfriendly relations; *in einem – stehen,* be out of proportion (*zu,* to).

mißverständlich ['mɪsfɛrʃtɛntlɪç], *adj.* erroneous; misleading, ambiguous. **Mißverständnis,** *n.* misunderstanding, misapprehension, misconception; (*coll.*) difference (of opinion), tiff. **mißverstehen,** *irr.v.t.* (*p.p. mißverstanden*) misunderstand (*a p. or th.*); misapprehend, misconceive, misconstrue, mistake (*th. only*).

Miß|wachs, *m.* *See* **–ernte. mißwachsen,** *adj.* misshapen, ill-formed.

Mißweisung ['mɪsvaɪzuŋ], *f.* magnetic declination. **mißweisend,** *adj. –er Kurs,* magnetic *or* compass course.

Mißwirtschaft ['mɪsvɪrtʃaft], *f.* maladministration, mismanagement.

Mißwuchs ['mɪsvu:ks], *m.* malformation.

Mist [mɪst], *m.* (**-es,** *pl.* **-e**) 1. dung, manure, (*coll.*) muck; (*sl.*) trash, bosh, twaddle, rot, bilge; 2. (*Naut.*) mist, haze. **Mist|beet,** *n.* hotbed. **–beetkasten,** *m.* forcing frame.

Mistel ['mɪstəl], *f.* (-, *pl.* **-n**) mistletoe. **Mistel|-drossel,** *f.* (*Orn.*) mistle-thrush (*Turdus viscivorus*). **–zweig,** *m.* mistletoe bough.

[1]**misten** ['mɪstən], *v.t.* 1. manure, spread dung on (*fields*); 2. clean (*cattle*), clean out (*stables*).

[2]**misten,** *v.imp.* (*Naut.*) *es mistet,* there is a haze, it is hazy.

Mist|fink, *m.* (*coll.*) dirty brat, filthy beast, pig. **–fuhre,** *f.* load of manure. **–gabel,** *f.* pitch-fork, dung-fork. **–grube,** *f.*, **–haufen,** *m.* dunghill, dung-heap.

mistig ['mɪstɪç], *adj.* 1. (*coll.*) caddish, low-down, shabby, scurvy, vile; 2. (*Naut.*) hazy, misty; 3. (*dial.*) filthy.

Mist|jauche, *f.* liquid manure. **–käfer,** *m.* dung-beetle. **–stock,** *m.* (*Swiss*) *see* **–haufen. –vieh,** *n.* (*vulg.*) filthy beast. **–wagen,** *m.* muck-cart.

Miszellaneen [mɪstsɛ'laneən], **Miszellen** [–'tsɛlən], *f.pl.* miscellanies.

mit [mɪt], **1.** *prep.* (*Dat.*) 1. with, along with, in company with, in the company of; 2. with, by (means of); *– Absicht,* intentionally; *– Gewalt,* by force; *– dem Glockenschlage,* on the stroke *or* dot; *– 15 Jahren,* at the age of 15; *– Lebensgefahr,* at the risk of one's life; *– einem Male* or *– einemmal,* suddenly, all at once; *– Muße,* at leisure; *– Namen,* by name; *– der Post,* by post; *– Protest,* under protest; *– einem Schlage,* at a blow; *– Tinte schreiben,* write in ink; *was ist – ihm?* what is the matter with him? *– lauter Stimme,* in a loud voice; *– Verlust,* at a loss; *was hat er – ihr vor?* what plans has he regarding her? *– einem Wort,* in a word. **2.** *adv.* along with, together *or* in company with; jointly; likewise, also, too; simultaneously; *die Kosten sind – berechnet,* the charge is included; *das ist – die beste Lösung,* that is one of the best solutions; *– dabei sein,* be (one) of the party, be there too, participate; *das gehört – dazu,* that belongs to it also; that is part of it; *da kann ich nicht –,* that is beyond me, that is too much for me (*i.e.* my understanding); I cannot manage that (*i.e.* exceeds my powers *or* pocket); *ich will –,* I want to go (*or* come) too.

Mit–, mit–, *pref. with nouns and some adjs.* = fellow-, joint-, co-; *sep. pref. with practically any verb* = in company with, in common with, simultaneously.

Mitangeklagte(r) ['mɪtˀangəkla:ktə(r)], *m., f.* (*Law*) co-defendant.

Mitarbeit ['mɪtˀarbaɪt], *f.* co-operation, collaboration (*bei,* in). **mitarbeiten,** *v.i.* collaborate, co-operate, assist, give assistance, take part (*an* (*Dat.*), in); contribute (to). **Mitarbeiter,** *m.* colleague, collaborator, co-worker; contributor (*to a journal*).

mitbedacht ['mɪtbədaxt], *adj.* also remembered (in the will); *Mitbedachter,* co-legatee.

Mitbeklagte(r) ['mɪtbəkla:ktə(r)], *m.* co-defendant.

mitbekommen ['mɪtbəkɔmən], *irr.v.t.* receive when leaving; get as dowry; (*coll.*) get, catch.

mitbenutzen ['mɪtbənutsən], *v.t.* use jointly *or* in common. **Mitbenutzer,** *m.* joint user. **Mitbenutzungsrecht,** *n.* right to joint use.

Mit|besitz, *m.* joint property. **–besitzer,** *m.* joint-owner *or* proprietor.

mitbestimmen ['mɪtbəʃtɪmən], *v.i.* (*of a th.*) be a contributory factor; (*of a p.*) participate in the management, have a say *or* voice in the matter. **Mitbestimmungsrecht,** *n.* co-partnership (*of workers in industry*).

mitbeteiligt ['mɪtbətaɪlɪçt], *adj.* participating, taking part, interested (*an* (*Dat.*), in). **Mitbeteiligte(r),** *m., f.* interested party; associate, partner.

mitbewerben ['mɪtbəvɛrbən], *irr.v.r.* compete, enter into competition (*um,* for). **Mitbewerber,** *m.* competitor.

Mitbewohner ['mɪtbəvo:nər], *m.* fellow-lodger.

mitbringen ['mɪtbrɪŋən], *irr.v.t.* 1. bring along with (one); bring as dowry; produce (*evidence etc.*); *das Mitgebrachte,* bride's dowry; 2. (*fig.*) be endowed with (*qualities*); *für diese Stellung bringt er gar nichts mit,* he has not any qualifications for this post. **Mitbringsel,** *n.* (*coll.*) present, souvenir.

Mitbürge ['mɪtbyrgə], *m.* co-surety, joint security.

Mitbürger ['mɪtbyrgər], *m.* fellow-citizen.

Mit|eigentum, *n.* joint property. **–eigentümer,** *m.* co-owner, joint proprietor.

miteinander ['mɪtˀaɪnandər], *adv.* with one another, with each other, together, jointly; simultaneously, at the same time; *alle –,* one and all.

miteinbegriffen ['mɪtˀaɪnbəgrɪfən], *adj.* included, inclusive.

mitempfinden ['mɪtˀɛmpfɪndən], *irr.v.t.* share, sympathize with (*s.o.'s feelings*). **Mitempfinden,** *n.* sympathy, compassion, fellow-feeling.

Mit|erbe, *m.* co-heir, joint heir. **–erbin,** *f.* co-heiress, joint heiress.

miterleben ['mɪtˀɛrle:bən], *v.t.* witness, experience at first hand.

mitessen ['mɪtˀɛsən], *irr.v.t., v.i.* eat *or* dine with s.o., share a meal with s.o. **Mitesser,** *m.* 1. (*Med.*) blackhead; 2. fellow-diner.

mitfahren ['mɪtfa:rən], *irr.v.i.* (*aux.* s.) go *or* ride *or* drive with s.o.; ***ihn – lassen,*** give him a lift. **Mitfahrer,** *m.* fellow-passenger.

mitfühlen, *v.i.* share, be sympathetic to (*s.o.'s feelings*); ***ein –des Herz,*** a feeling heart.

mitführen ['mɪtfy:rən], *v.t.* bring *or* carry along with one.

mitgeben ['mɪtge:bən], *irr.v.t.* give (*Dat.*, to) (*s.o. departing*); send (with); give as dowry; (*fig.*) impart (to), bestow (on).

Mitgefangene(r) ['mɪtgəfaŋənə(r)], *m., f.* fellow-prisoner; *see also under* **mitgehen.**

Mitgefühl ['mɪtgəfy:l], *n.* sympathy, compassion; condolences.

mitgehen ['mɪtge:ən], *irr.v.i.* (*aux.* s.) go with; accompany; be with; agree with; ***mit dem Redner –,*** be carried away by the speaker, be in complete agreement with the speaker; (*coll.*) ***eine S. – heißen,*** pocket a th., help o.s. to s.th.; ***mitgegangen, mitgefangen, mitgehangen,*** together through thick and thin.

mitgenommen ['mɪtgənɔmən], *see* **mitnehmen.**

Mitgift ['mɪtgɪft], *f.* dowry, marriage portion. **Mitgiftjäger,** *m.* fortune-hunter.

Mitglied ['mɪtgli:t], *n.* member; fellow (*of a learned society*); ***– auf Lebenszeit,*** life-member; ***förderndes –,*** corresponding member; ***ordentliches –,*** full member; ***zahlendes –,*** subscribing member. **Mitglieder|versammlung,** *f.* general meeting. **–zahl,** *f.* (total) membership. **Mitgliedsbeitrag,** *m.* (membership) subscription, (*Am.*) dues. **Mitgliedschaft,** *f.* membership; fellowship (*of a learned society*). **Mitgliedskarte,** *f.* membership card. **Mitgliedstaat,** *m.* (*Pol.*) member state.

Mithafte ['mɪthaftə], *m.* (**-n,** *pl.* **-n**) (*Swiss*) underwriter. **Mithaftung,** *f.* joint liability.

mithalten ['mɪthaltən], *irr.v.i.* (*coll.*) be one of a party, be there; side with s.o.; ***ich halte mit,*** I'm with you; ***ich kann nicht –,*** I cannot keep up (the pace); ***wacker –,*** hold one's own.

mithelfen ['mɪthɛlfən], *irr.v.i.* help, aid, assist; co-operate with s.o. **Mithelfer,** *m.* assistant, helper.

Mitherausgeber ['mɪthɛrausge:bər], *m.* co-editor, joint editor.

Mithilfe ['mɪthɪlfə], *f.* help, aid, assistance; co-operation.

mithin [mɪt'hɪn], *adv.* thus, so, consequently, then, therefore, hence.

mithören ['mɪthø:rən], *v.t.* overhear; (*Tele., Rad.*) monitor, (*Mil. etc.*) intercept.

mitkämpfen ['mɪtkɛmpfən], *v.i.* join in the battle *or* struggle. **Mitkämpfer,** *m.* fellow-soldier, comrade-in-arms.

Mitkläger ['mɪtklɛ:gər], *m.* co-plaintiff.

mitklingen ['mɪtklɪŋən], *irr.v.i.* resonate.

mitkommen ['mɪtkɔmən], *irr.v.i.* (*aux.* s.) come along (with), accompany; be able to follow (*the lesson etc.*); keep up (with), keep pace (with); ***– mit,*** catch (*a train etc.*).

mit|kriegen, *v.t.* (*coll.*) *see* **–bekommen.**

mitlachen ['mɪtlaxən], *v.i.* join in the laugh(ter).

mitlaufen ['mɪtlaufən], *irr.v.i.* (*aux.* s.) run along with, join in the race; (*sl.*) ***– lassen,*** swipe, lift. **Mitläufer,** *m.* time-server, hanger-on, (*Pol.*) fellow-traveller.

Mitlaut(er) ['mɪtlaut(ər)], *m.* (*Gram.*) consonant.

Mitleid(en) ['mɪtlaɪt (–dən)], *n.* pity, compassion, sympathy; ***– haben mit,*** have pity on, be sorry for, pity. **Mitleidenschaft,** *f.* ***in – ziehen,*** affect, involve, implicate; impair, damage. **mitleidig,** *adj.* sympathetic, compassionate. **Mitleidsbezeigung,** *f.* condolence, expression of sympathy. **mitleidslos,** *adj.* pitiless, merciless, ruthless, unfeeling. **mitleidsvoll,** *adj.* sympathetic, compassionate.

mitmachen ['mɪtmaxən], **1.** *v.i.* go along *or* join in (with); keep pace (with); respond, follow suit, do as others do, do the same; ***ich mache nicht mit,*** I shall keep out of it; ***ich mache mit,*** I'll join you, (*coll.*) count me in. **2.** *v.t.* take part in, join *or* participate in, be a party to; ***alle Moden –,*** go with *or* follow every fashion; ***er hat viel mitgemacht,*** he has been *or* gone through a lot.

Mitmensch ['mɪtmɛnʃ], *m.* fellow-man, fellow-creature; (*B.*) neighbour.

mitnehmen ['mɪtne:mən], *irr.v.t.* 1. take along with (one); ***ihn im Wagen –,*** give him a lift in the car; ***mitgenommen werden,*** get a lift; ***einen Ort –,*** call at a place (*en route*); ***einen Verdienst –,*** avail o.s. of the opportunity of doing a stroke of business, (*coll.*) turn an honest penny; 2. (*fig.*) affect, impair, (*coll.*) be rough on; ***ihn arg –,*** deal with him harshly, (*coll.*) treat him rough, let him have it; 3. wear (out), exhaust; ***mitgenommen sein,*** be worn out *or* exhausted (***von,*** by), (*coll.*) be *or* look the worse for wear (as a result of), be *or* have been hard hit (by); ***die letzte Krankheit hat mich sehr mitgenommen,*** the last illness has taken a lot out of me *or* has pulled me down a great deal. **Mitnehmer,** *m.* 1. (*Mech.*) cam, dog; 2. follower, driver.

mitnichten [mɪt'nɪçtən], *adv.* by no means, in no way, not at all.

Mitra ['mi:tra], *f.* (-, *pl.* **-ren**) (*Eccl.*) mitre.

mitrechnen ['mɪtrɛçnən], **1.** *v.t.* include (in the account); ***nicht –,*** leave out of account. **2.** *v.i.* ***das rechnet nicht mit,*** that does not count.

mitreden ['mɪtre:dən], **1.** *v.i.* join in the conversation *or* discussion, put in a word (or two). **2.** *v.t.* ***ein Wort mitzureden haben,*** have a word to say (***bei,*** in); ***nichts mitzureden haben,*** have no say in the matter.

mitreisen ['mɪtraɪzən], *v.i.* travel with s.o. **Mitreisende(r),** *m., f.* fellow-traveller *or* -passenger.

mitreißen ['mɪtraɪsən], *irr.v.t.* drag *or* sweep *or* carry along; (*fig.*) thrill, grip, electrify (*as enthusiasm*). **mitreißend,** *adj.* thrilling, gripping, breath-taking.

mitsamt [mɪt'zamt], *prep.* (*Dat.*) together with.

mit|schicken, *v.t.* enclose (*in letter etc.*). **–schleppen,** *v.t.* drag *or* take along (with). **–schreiben,** *irr.v.t., v.i.* write *or* take down, take *or* make notes (of).

Mitschuld ['mɪtʃult], *f.* complicity, share of guilt (***an*** (*Dat.*), in). **mitschuldig,** *adj.* accessory (***an*** (*Dat.*), to), implicated (in). **Mitschuldige(r),** *m., f.* accessory (***an*** (*Dat.*), to), accomplice (in). **Mitschuldner,** *m.* joint debtor.

Mitschüler ['mɪtʃy:lər], *m.* schoolfellow, classmate, fellow-pupil.

mitschwingen ['mɪtʃvɪŋən], *irr.v.i.* resonate. **Mitschwingen,** *n.* resonance.

mitsingen ['mɪtzɪŋən], *irr.v.i.* join in the singing.

mitspielen ['mɪtʃpi:lən], *v.t., v.i.* take part in *or* join in a game; (*Spt.*) play in a game, be in the team; (*Theat.*) appear in, take part *or* have a part in (*a play*); (*Mus.*) play with (*an orchestra*); (*Cards*) take a hand; (*fig.*) play a part in, be involved in; ***ihm arg*** or ***übel –,*** play a dirty trick on him, (*sl.*) do the dirty on him. **Mitspieler,** *m.* partner, (*Theat.*) supporting player.

mit|sprechen, *irr.v.t., v.i. See* **–reden.**

[1]**Mittag** ['mɪta:k], *m.* (**-s,** *pl.* **-e**) midday, noon; (*Astr.*) meridian, (*Poet.*) south; ***gegen –,*** around midday, (*Poet.*) southwards; ***heller –,*** broad noon; ***heute –,*** at noon *or* midday today; ***zu – essen,*** lunch, dine, have lunch *or* dinner, take one's midday meal.

[2]**Mittag,** *n.* (*coll.*) lunch, midday meal; ***– machen,*** break for lunch.

Mittagessen ['mɪta:kˀɛsən], *n.* midday meal, lunch, (early) dinner.

mittäglich ['mɪtɛ:klɪç], *adj.* midday, noonday; (*Astr.*) meridional, (*Poet.*) southern.

mittags ['mɪta:ks], *adv.* at midday *or* noon, at lunch-time.

Mittags|ausgabe, *f.* midday edition. **-blatt,** *n.* midday paper. **-gesellschaft,** *f.* luncheon party. **-glut, -hitze,** *f.* midday *or* noonday heat. **-höhe,** *f.* (*Astr.*) meridian altitude. **-kreis,** *m.*, **-linie,** *f.* meridian. **-mahl(zeit),** *n.* (*f.*) midday meal. **-pause,** *f.* lunch-break, dinner-break, lunch-hour. **-ruhe,** *f.*, **-schlaf,** *m.*, **-schläfchen,** *n.* after-dinner nap, siesta. **-sonne,** *f.* midday *or* noonday sun. **-stunde,** *f. See* **-pause. -tisch,** *m.* lunch, dinner; luncheon club. **-zeit,** *f.* noon(tide); lunch-time, dinner-hour; ***um die* -,** about *or* around noon.

mittanzen ['mɪttantsən], *v.i.* join in the dance. **Mittänzer(in),** *m.* (*f.*) (dancing) partner.

Mittäter ['mɪttɛ:tər], *m.* accomplice, accessory (to the crime). **Mittäterschaft,** *f.* complicity.

Mitte ['mɪtə], *f.* middle, centre, (*of a crowd*) midst; (*Stat.*) mean, medium; (*Footb.*) centre; ***- Fünfzig, - der Fünfziger,*** in one's middle fifties; ***die goldene -,*** the golden *or* happy mean; ***- Juli,*** in the middle of July, in mid July; ***die - des 20. Jahrhunderts,*** the mid 20th century; ***in unserer -,*** in our midst, among us; (*Mil.*) ***in die - nehmen,*** attack from both sides; ***das Reich der -,*** the Middle Kingdom.

mitteilbar ['mɪttaɪlba:r], *adj.* communicable; (*Med.*) contagious. **mitteilen, 1.** *v.t.* ***ihm etwas -,*** communicate *or* impart *or* pass on s.th. to him; inform *or* apprise *or* notify him of a th.; tell him s.th. **2.** *v.r.* communicate one's thoughts, unbosom o.s.; spread, communicate itself, be contagious. **mitteilsam,** *adj.* communicative. **Mitteilung,** *f.* announcement, pronouncement, communication, information, news, intimation, notification, notice, note, intelligence.

Mittel ['mɪtəl], *n.* 1. means, measures, medium, instrument, device, expedient, method, (*coll.*) way; ***sich ins - legen*** or ***schlagen,*** interpose, intervene, mediate, (*coll.*) step in; ***als letztes -,*** as a last resort; ***mir ist jedes - recht,*** I shall stick at nothing, I shall go to any length; ***als - zum Zweck,*** as a means to the end; (*Prov.*) ***der Zweck heiligt die -,*** the end justifies the means; ***- und Wege finden,*** find ways and means, manage, contrive; ***alle - und Wege versuchen,*** leave no stone unturned, explore every avenue; 2. (*Math.*) mean, average; ***arithmetisches -,*** arithmetic mean; 3. (*Phys.*) medium, agent; 4. (*Med.*) remedy, medicine (***gegen,*** for); ***ein unfehlbares -,*** an infallible remedy, a specific; 5. *pl.* means, resources, funds, capital; money, wealth; ***bescheidene -,*** moderate means; ***aus öffentlichen -n,*** from the public purse; ***meine - erlauben es (mir) nicht,*** I cannot afford it; 6. (*Typ.*) English.

mittel, *adj.* (*comp.* ***mittler,*** *sup.* ***mittelst;*** *rarely used in the positive, see* **mittler**) middle, mid, central; mean, average, medium, (*coll.*) middling; intermediate.

Mittelalter ['mɪtəlʔaltər], *n.* Middle Ages. **mittelalterlich,** *adj.* medi(a)eval. **Mittel|amerika,** *n.* Central America. **-arrest,** *n.* (*Mil.*) light field-punishment. **-asien,** *n.* Central Asia.

mittelbar ['mɪtəlba:r], *adj.* mediate, indirect; consequential, collateral. **Mittelbarkeit,** *f.* indirectness.

Mittel|darm, *m.* intestine. **-decker,** *m.* (*Av.*) mid-wing monoplane. **-deutschland,** *n.* Central Germany (*post-war West German designation for the German Democratic Republic*). **-ding,** *n.* s.th. between, intermediate th., cross. **-ente,** *f.* (*Orn.*) *see* **Schnatterente. -europa,** *n.* Central Europe. **-farbe,** *f.* secondary colour. **-fehler,** *m.* mean error. **-feld,** *n.* (*Footb.*) mid-field. **-finger,** *m.* middle finger. **mittelflüssig,** *adj.* semi-fluid, viscous. **Mittelfrequenz,** *f.* (*Rad.*) medium frequency. **mittelfristig,** *adj.* (*Comm.*) medium-term (*loan etc.*). **Mittel|fuß,** *m.* (*Anat.*) metatarsus. **-gebirge,** *n.* medium-altitude *or* sub-alpine mountain range. **-geschwindigkeit,** *f.* mean velocity. **-gewicht,** *n.* (*Boxing*) middle-weight. **-glied,** *n.* 1. (*Anat.*) middle phalanx; 2. (*Log.*) middle term; intermediate member. **mittelgroß,** *adj.* medium-sized. **Mittelgröße,** *f.* medium size. **mittelgut,** *adj.* of medium quality, middling, second-rate. **Mittel|hand,** *f.* (*Anat.*) metacarpus. **-hochdeutsch,** *n.* Middle High German. **-höhe,** *f.* mean height. **-klassen,** *f.pl.* the middle school. **-kraft,** *f.* resultant (force). **-kurs,** *m.* average rate *or* price. **-lage,** *f.* mid-position, (*Mus.*) middle voice. **mittelländisch,** *adj.* Mediterranean. **Mittel|latein,** *n.* Medi(a)eval Latin. **-läufer,** *m.* (*Footb.*) centre-half. **-leib,** *m.* (*Ent.*) thorax. **-linie,** *f.* axis, median line, (*Geom.*) bisector, (*Footb.*) centre (line), (*Tenn.*) centre service line.

mittellos ['mɪtəllo:s], *adj.* destitute, impecunious, without means. **Mittellosigkeit,** *f.* lack of means, destitution.

Mittel|mächte, *f.pl.* Central Powers. **-maß,** *n.* average, medium size. **mittelmäßig,** *adj.* middling, indifferent, mediocre; moderate, average. **Mittelmäßigkeit,** *f.* mediocrity. **Mittel|meer,** *n.* Mediterranean (Sea). **-meersteinschmätzer,** *m.* (*Orn.*) black-eared wheatear (*Oenanthe hispanica*). **-ohr,** *n.* middle ear, tympanum. **-partei,** *f.* (*Pol.*) centre *or* moderate party. **-punkt,** *m.* centre, central point, (*fig.*) focus, centre of interest *or* attraction; hub (*of affairs*).

mittels ['mɪtəls], *prep.* (*Gen.*) by (means *or* virtue of), with (the help of), through.

Mittel|säger, *m.* (*Orn.*) red-breasted merganser (*Mergus serrator*). **-schicht,** *f.* intermediate layer. **-schiff,** *n.* central aisle. **-schlag,** *m. See* **-sorte. -schule,** *f.* intermediate school, (*Austr.*) secondary school. **-schwein,** *n.* (*Shipb.*) main keelson. **mittelschwer,** *adj.* medium-weight.

Mittels|mann, *m.* (*pl.* **-männer**) mediator, intermediary, (*coll.*) go-between; (*Comm.*) middleman.

Mittel|sorte, *f.* medium quality, middle grade. **-specht,** *m.* (*Orn.*) middle spotted woodpecker (*Dendrocopus medius*).

Mittels|person, *f. See* **-mann.**

mittelst ['mɪtəlst], *prep. See* **mittels.**

Mittel|stadt, *f.* medium-size town. **-stand,** *m.* middle class(es). **-stands-,** *pref.* middle-class. **mittel|ständig,** *adj.* (*Bot.*) intermediate, perigynous. **-stark,** *adj.* moderately strong. **Mittel|steinzeit,** *f.* (*Geol.*) mesolithic age. **-stellung,** *f.* mid position. **-straße,** *f.* (*fig.*) middle road *or* course, mean, compromise; ***die goldene -,*** the golden mean; ***ich halte mich auf der -,*** I steer the middle course. **-streckenlauf,** *m.* medium distance race. **-streckenrakete,** *f.* (*Mil.*) intermediate-range missile. **-streckler,** *m.* medium-distance runner. **-stück,** *n.* middle cut (*of meat*); central portion. **-stufe,** *f.* intermediate step *or* stage; (*in school*) intermediate grade. **-stürmer,** *m.* (*Footb.*) centre forward. **-ton,** *m.* 1. (*Mus.*) mediant; 2. (*Art*) half-tint. **-wand,** *f.* partition wall. **-weg,** *m. See* **-straße**; ***einen - einschlagen,*** adopt a middle course, make a compromise. **-welle,** *f.* (*Rad.*) medium wave. **-wert,** *m.* average *or* mean (value), median. **-wort,** *n.* (*Gram.*) participle.

mitten ['mɪtən], *adv.* (*used with prep. following*) midway; ***- am Tag,*** in broad daylight; ***- auf der Straße,*** in *or* on the open street; ***- aus,*** from amidst *or* among, from the midst of; ***- entzwei,*** right in two, (*coll.*) clean through the middle; ***- im Ozean,*** in mid-ocean; ***- in der Luft,*** in mid-air; ***- in der Nacht,*** in the middle *or* dead of the night; ***- im Winter,*** in the middle *or* depth of (the) winter; ***- ins Herz,*** right to the heart; (*Austr.*) ***- inne,*** right in the middle, amidst; ***- unter,*** among(st), amid(st), in the midst of. **mitten|d(a)rin, -d(a)runter,** *adv.* right in the middle *or* midst, in the centre. **-hindurch,** *adv. See* ***mitten entzwei.***

Mitternacht ['mɪtərnaxt], *f.* midnight; (*Poet.*) north. **mitter|nächtig,** *adj.* nocturnal, midnight, (*fig.*) gloomy. **-nächtlich,** *adj.* (happening every) midnight; (*Poet.*) northern. **-nachts,** *adv.* at midnight. **Mitternachtssonne,** *f.* midnight sun.

mittig ['mɪtɪç], *adj.* (*Tech.*) concentric.
mittler ['mɪtlər] (*comp. of* **mittel** *which it has supplanted*) middle, central; intermediate, medium, average, mean; middling, mediocre; (*Stat.*) ***–e Abweichung,*** mean deviation; ***–er Beamter,*** middle-grade civil servant; ***–e Ortszeit,*** local time; ***–er Osten,*** Middle East; ***–e Qualität,*** medium quality; ***Person von –en Jahren,*** middle-aged person; ***–e Schnelligkeit,*** average speed; (*Stat.*) ***–e Streuung,*** mean scatter.
Mittler, *m.* mediator, intercessor; third party; ***unser –,*** Christ our Mediator. **Mittlertod,** *m.* (*Eccl.*) expiatory death.
mittlerweile ['mɪtlərvaɪlə], *adv.* (in the) meantime, meanwhile.
mittragen ['mɪttra:gən], *irr.v.t.* carry with others, help to carry, (*fig.*) share (*burden etc.*).
mittschiffs ['mɪtʃɪfs], *adv.* (*Naut.*) (a)midships.
mit|tun, *irr.v.i. See* **–machen.**
Mittwoch ['mɪtvɔx], *m.* **(-(e)s,** *pl.* **-e)** Wednesday. **mittwochs,** *adv.* on Wednesday(s).
mitunter [mɪt'untər], *adv.* now and then, sometimes, at times, occasionally.
mitunterschreiben ['mɪtʔuntərʃraɪbən], *irr.v.t., v.i.* add one's signature, countersign. **Mitunterschrift,** *f.* joint-signature. **mit|unterzeichen,** *v.t., v.i. See* **–unterschreiben. Mitunterzeichner,** *m.* co-signatory.
mitverantwortlich ['mɪtfɛrantvɔrtlɪç], *adj.* sharing responsibility, guilty with others. **Mitverantwortung,** *f.* joint responsibility.
Mitverfasser ['mɪtfɛrfasər], *m.* co-author.
Mitverschulden ['mɪtfɛrʃuldən], *n.* (*Law*) ***fahrlässiges –,*** contributory negligence.
Mitverschworene(r) ['mɪtfɛrʃvo:rənə(r)], *m., f.* fellow-conspirator, accomplice.
Mitwelt ['mɪtvɛlt], *f.* the age we live in, our age, our own times, the present generation, our contemporaries.
mitwirken ['mɪtvɪrkən], *v.i.* co-operate, concur, assist, contribute towards, collaborate, take part, take a part (*in a concert etc.*). **mitwirkend,** *adj.* contributory, concurrent; co-operative, co-operating. **Mitwirkende(r),** *m., f.* member (of the cast), actor, player, performer; *pl.* the cast. **Mitwirkung,** *f.* co-operation, assistance, participation.
Mitwissen ['mɪtvɪsən], *n.* cognizance; ***ohne mein –,*** without my knowledge, unknown to me. **Mitwisser,** *m.* one in the secret; confidant, accessory. **Mitwisserschaft,** *f.* collusion, complicity.
mit|zählen, *v.t., v.i. See* **–rechnen.**
Mixbecher [mɪksbɛçər], *m.* cocktail shaker. **mixen,** *v.t.* mix (*drinks*). **Mixer,** *m.* 1. barman; 2. (*Cul.*) liquidizer. **Mixtur** [–'tu:r], *f.* (-, *pl.* **-en**) (*Pharm.*) mixture, draught, potion.
Möbel ['mø:bəl], *n.* piece of furniture; *pl.* furniture; (*coll.*) ***altes –,*** old fogy, fixture, stick-in-the-mud. **Möbel|geschäft,** *n.* furniture shop, furnishing house. **–händler,** *m.* furniture dealer. **–lack,** *m.* cabinet varnish. **–laden,** *m. See* **–geschäft. –politur,** *f.* furniture polish. **–spediteur,** *m.* furniture remover. **–speicher,** *m.* repository. **–stoff,** *m.* furnishing fabric. **–stück,** *n. See* **Möbel. –tischler,** *m.* cabinet maker. **–transportgeschäft,** *n.* removal contractors, (firm of) furniture removers. **–wagen,** *m.* furniture van, removal van, pantechnicon.
mobil [mo'bi:l], *adj.* movable, (*Mil.*) mobile, (*coll.*) active, nimble; ***– machen,*** put in motion, (*Mil.*) mobilize; ***es wurde – gemacht,*** the reserves were called out; ***für eine S. – machen,*** make an appeal for a th., rouse support *or* sympathy for a th.
Mobiliar [mobili'a:r], *n.* furniture. **Mobiliar|erbe,** *m.* heir to personal property. **–masse,** *f.* personalty of a bankrupt. **–vermögen,** *n.* personal property, personalty.
Mobilien [mo'bi:liən], *pl.* movables, effects, goods and chattels.
mobilisieren [mobili'zi:rən], *v.t., v.i.* 1. (*Mil.*) mobilize; 2. (*Law*) realize (*real estate*). **Mobilisierung,** *f.* 1. (*Mil.*) mobilization; 2. (*Law*) realization. **Mobilmachung** [mo'bi:lmaxuŋ], *f.* (*Mil. only*) mobilization.
möblieren [mø'bli:rən], *v.t.* furnish; (*coll.*) ***möblierter Herr,*** gentleman lodger; ***möbliertes Zimmer,*** furnished room; ***möbliert wohnen,*** live in lodgings.
mochte ['mɔxtə], **möchte** ['mœçtə], *see* **mögen.**
modal [mo'da:l], *adj.* modal. **Modalität** [–dali'tɛ:t], *f.* modality; proviso, arrangement.
Modder ['mɔdər], *m.* (*dial.*) bog, marsh, swamp. **moddrig,** *adj.* (*dial.*) boggy, marshy, swampy.
Mode ['mo:də], *f.* fashion, vogue, mode, custom; ***– werden*** (or ***sein***), come into (*or* be in) fashion *or* vogue; ***die – angeben,*** set the fashion; ***die – mitmachen,*** follow the fashion; ***nach der –,*** in the latest style *or* fashion; ***aus der – kommen,*** go out of fashion; ***in –,*** in fashion *or* vogue, fashionable; ***in – kommen,*** *see* ***– werden; die große – sein,*** be (all) the rage, be the (latest) craze *or* fad.
Mode|artikel, *m.pl.* novelties, fancy goods. **–ausdruck,** *m. See* **–wort. –dame,** *f.* lady of fashion. **–geschäft, –haus,** *n.* fashion house. **–krankheit,** *f.* fashionable complaint. **–künstler,** *m.* couturier.
Model ['mo:dəl], *m.* pattern, mould, matrix, block.
Modell [mo'dɛl], *n.* **(-s,** *pl.* **-e)** model; pattern, prototype; type, style, design; form, mould; (artist's) model; fashion model, mannequin; ***als – dienen,*** serve as a model *or* pattern; ***– stehen,*** pose (*Dat.*, for), (*fig.*) serve as a model (for). **Modell|bau,** *m.* pattern making. **–druck,** *m.* block printing. **–eisenbahn,** *f.* model railway.
Modellierbogen [modɛ'li:rbo:gən], *m.* cutting-out pattern. **modellieren,** *v.t.* form, fashion, model, mould. **Modellier|masse,** *f.,* **–ton,** *m.* modelling clay, plasticine.
Modell|kleid, *n.* model(led) dress. **–macher,** *m.* pattern maker. **–puppe,** *f.* lay-figure, dressmaker's dummy. **–schuhe,** *m.pl.* bespoke shoes. **–tischler,** *m. See* **–macher.**
modeln ['mo:dəln], *v.t.* shape, form, mould; figure *or* work *or* embroider a pattern on (*fabric etc.*). **Modeltuch,** *n.* stencilled pattern (*for embroidery*).
Moden|bild, –blatt, *n.* fashion plate. **–schau,** *f.* fashion *or* mannequin parade. **–zeichner,** *m.* dress designer. **–zeitung,** *f.* fashion magazine.
Moder ['mo:dər], *m.* 1. dry-rot, mould; mouldering, decay, putrefaction, rottenness; (*on wine*) mother; damp(ness), musty atmosphere; 2. (*dial.*) bog, marsh. **Modererde,** *f.* mould, compost. **moderfleckig,** *adj.* mildewed, (*of paper*) foxed. **Modergeruch,** *m.* musty smell. **moderig,** *adj.* 1. mouldy, putrid, decaying, rotten; musty; 2. (*dial.*) boggy, marshy.
[1]**modern** ['mo:dərn], *v.i.* (*aux.* s. & h.) decay, rot, moulder, putrefy.
[2]**modern** [mo'dɛrn], *adj.* modern, up-to-date, progressive; fashionable, stylish. elegant; ***die Moderne,*** modernity, the modern trend. **modernisieren** [–ni'zi:rən], modernize, bring up to date.
Mode|salon, *m.* fashion house. **–schau,** *f. See* **Modenschau. –schöpfer,** *m.* dress designer, couturier. **–schöpfung,** *f.* latest creation. **–schriftsteller,** *m.* popular writer. **–stil,** *m.* new look. **–torheit,** *f.* fashionable craze. **–waren,** *f.pl. See* **–artikel. –welt,** *f.* world of fashion, fashionable world. **–wort,** *n.* vogue-word. **–zeichner,** *m.,* **–zeitung,** *f. See* **Moden|zeichner, –zeitung.**
modifizieren [modifi'tsi:rən], *v.t.* modify, qualify. **Modifizierung,** *f.* modification, qualification.
modisch ['mo:dɪʃ], *adj.* fashionable, stylish, elegant.
Modistin [mo'dɪstɪn], *f.* milliner.
modrig ['mo:drɪç], *adj.* (*Austr.*) *see* **moderig.**
Modul ['mo:dul], *m.* **(-s,** *pl.* **-n)** 1. (*Archit.*) module; 2. (*Math.*) modulus.
Modulation [modulatsi'o:n], *f.* modulation, intonation, inflexion. **Modulations|fähigkeit,** *f.* adapta-

bility (*of voice etc.*). **-frequenz,** *f.* (*Rad.*) modulating frequency. **modulieren** [–'li:rən], *v.t.* modulate.

Modus ['mo:dus], *m.* (-, *pl.* **-di**) (*Gram.*) mood; mode, manner, method.

Mogelei [mo:gə'laɪ], *f.* (*coll.*) cheating. **mogeln** ['mo:gəln], *v.i.* (*coll.*) cheat, diddle.

mögen ['mø:gən], **1.** *irr.v.t.* 1. want, wish, desire; 2. be fond of, be partial to; ***nicht* –,** dislike, not care for, (*coll.*) not be keen on; ***lieber* –,** like better, prefer.
2. *irr.v.i.* be willing, have a mind to, be inclined; ***nicht* –,** not want to, not like to; ***ich mag nicht,*** I would rather not.
3. *irr.v. aux.* may, might; ***leiden* –,** like well enough, find acceptable, tolerate; (*coll.*) ***ich mag es nicht leiden,*** I can't stand it *or* put up with it.
(a) (*pres. indic.*) ***es mag (wohl) sein,*** it may (well) be true, it is (indeed) possible; ***mag er*** or ***er mag tun was er will,*** let him do what(ever) he wants; ***was ich auch tun mag,*** whatever I do, no matter what I do; ***wie dem auch sein mag,*** be that as it may; ***wer mag das sein?*** who might that be?
(b) (*pres. subj.*) ***möge es ihm wohl bekommen!*** much good may it do him! ***möge er sich in Acht nehmen!*** let him beware *or* (*coll.*) look out! ***möge es dir gelingen!*** let us hope you'll be successful! ***möge kommen was da will!*** come what may!
(c) (*imperf. indic.*) ***es mochte wohl schon 4 Uhr sein,*** it was perhaps *or* it would be as late as 4 o'clock; ***X, Y, Z, und wie sie alle heißen mochten,*** X, Y, Z, or whatever their names might have been; ***ich mochte es ihm nicht sagen,*** I did not like to tell him.
(d) (*imperf. subj.*) ***ich möchte gern bleiben,*** I should like to stay; ***ich möchte lieber bleiben,*** I would rather stay; ***ich möchte wissen,*** I should like to know, I wonder; ***sagen Sie ihm, er möchte kommen,*** tell him (he is) to come; (*coll.*) ***man möchte aus der Haut fahren,*** it's enough to drive one crazy; ***das Herz möchte mir zerspringen,*** my heart is ready to break.
(e) (*inf. used for p.p. when immediately preceded by another inf.*) ***ich habe es nicht tun* –,** I did not like *or* care to do it; ***ich hatte es ihm nicht sagen* –,** I should not have liked to tell him.

Mogler ['mo:glər], *m.* (*coll.*) cheat.

möglich ['mø:klɪç], **1.** *adj.* possible; feasible, practicable; likely, potential, eventual; ***alle –en,*** all kinds *or* sorts of; ***alles –e,*** everything possible, all sorts *or* kinds of things, every conceivable thing; ***alles –e tun,*** do everything in one's power, use all possible means, try everything; ***sein –stes tun,*** do one's best *or* utmost; ***das ist eher* –,** that is more likely; ***das ist leicht*** or ***wohl* –,** that may well be so, that is quite possible; ***es – machen,*** make it possible *or* feasible; ***nicht –!*** impossible! surely not! it can't be! (*coll.*) you don't say (so)! (*sl.*) no kidding! ***es war mir nicht – zu kommen,*** I wasn't able to come. **2.** *adv.* ***so bald wie (nur)* –, *–st bald,*** as soon as (ever) possible, (*Comm.*) at your earliest convenience; ***–st klein,*** (*attrib.*) the smallest possible, a minimum of, (*pred.*) as small as possible; ***–st wenig,*** the least possible. **möglichenfalls, möglicherweise,** *adv.* possibly, if possible, as far as possible, perhaps.

Möglichkeit ['mø:klɪçkaɪt], *f.* possibility, feasibility, practicability; contingency, eventuality, potentiality; ***außerhalb des Bereichs der* –,** outside the bounds of possibility; ***ihm die –en bieten,*** offer him facilities (***zu,*** for), give him the chance (to); ***es ist keine – (vorhanden),*** there is no chance; ***nach* –,** as far as possible, as far as lies in one's power; ***es besteht die* –,** it is possible (***daß,*** that), there is a chance (of). **Möglichkeitsform,** *f.* (*Gram.*) subjunctive *or* conditional mood. **möglichst,** *adv.* *See* **möglich.**

Mohammedaner [mohamə'da:nər], *m.*, **mohammedanisch,** *adj.* Mohammedan, Moslem, Muslim.

Mohär [mo'hɛ:r], *m.* (**-s,** *pl.* **-e**) mohair.

Mohn [mo:n], *m.* (**-s,** *pl.* **-e**) (*Bot.*) poppy (*Papaver*). **Mohn|blume,** *f.* poppy. **-kapsel,** *f.*, **-kopf,** *m.* poppy-head. **-säure,** *f.* meconic acid. **-stoff,** *m.* narcotic.

Mohr [mo:r], *m.* (**-en,** *pl.* **-en**) Moor; Negro; (*pej.*) darky; ***das heißt einen –en bleichen*** or ***weißwaschen,*** that is attempting the impossible.

Möhre ['mø:rə], *f.* carrot.

Mohrenlerche ['mo:rənlɛrçə], *f.* (*Orn.*) black lark (*Melanocorypha yeltonensis*). **mohrenschwarz,** *adj.* jet *or* pitch black. **Mohrenwäsche,** *f.* (*fig.*) (*coll.*) white-washing.

Mohrrübe ['mo:rry:bə], *f.* carrot.

Moiré [moa're:], *m. or n.* (**-s,** *pl.* **-s**) moiré, watered *or* shot silk; moreen. **moirieren,** *v.t.* water, cloud (*silk*).

mokant [mo'kant], *adj.* sarcastic, sneering, mocking. **mokieren,** *v.r.* sneer (***über*** (*Acc.*), at), mock.

Mokka ['mɔka], *m.* (**-s,** *pl.* **-s**) Mocha (coffee). **Mokkatasse,** *f.* small coffee-cup.

Molch [mɔlç], *m.* (**-es,** *pl.* **-e**) salamander; (*fig., coll.*) monster.

Moldau ['mɔldau], *f.* (*Geog.*) Moldavia.

Mole ['mo:lə], *f.* mole, breakwater; jetty, pier.

Molekel [mo'le:kəl], *f.* (-, *pl.* **-n**) *or* (*Austr.*) *n.*, **Molekül** [–'ky:l], *n.* (**-s,** *pl.* **-e**) molecule. **molekular** [–'la:r], *adj.*, **Molekular–,** *pref.* molecular. **Molekülbau,** *m.* molecular structure.

molk [mɔlk], **mölke** ['mœlkə], *see* **melken.**

Molke ['mɔlkə], *f.*, **Molken,** *m.* whey. **Molkensäure,** *f.* lactic acid.

Molkerei [mɔlkə'raɪ], *f.* dairy. **Molkerei|erzeugnisse,** *n.pl.* dairy-produce. **-genossenschaft,** *f.* dairy-farmers' association.

molkig ['mɔlkɪç], *adj.* containing *or* like whey, wheyish.

Moll [mɔl], *n.* (*Mus.*) minor (key); ***a-Moll,*** A minor. **Mollakkord,** *m.* minor chord.

Molle ['mɔlə], *f.* 1. (*dial.*) *see* **Mulde**; 2. beer-glass, glass of beer; (*coll.*) ***mit –n gießen,*** rain cats and dogs; 3. (*dial.*) bed.

mollig ['mɔlɪç], *adj.* (*coll.*) comfortable, cosy, snug; soft; (*of a p.*) (well-)rounded, chubby, buxom.

Moll|tonart, *f.* (*Mus.*) minor key. **-tonleiter,** *f.* minor scale.

Molluske [mɔ'luskə], *f.* mollusc.

Mollymauk ['mɔlɪmauk], *m.* (*Orn.*) black-browed albatross (*Diomedea melanophris*).

Molybdän [molyp'dɛ:n], *n.* (*Chem.*) molybdenum.

[1]**Moment** [mo'mɛnt], *m.* (**-(e)s,** *pl.* **-e**) moment, instant; (*coll.*) ***– mal!*** just a moment, (*sl.*) half a tick *or* mo.

[2]**Moment,** *n.* (**-(e)s,** *pl.* **-e**) (*Phys.*) moment; force, impetus, impulse; motive, factor, element; ***das ausschlaggebende* –,** the decisive factor; (*Theat.*) ***das erregende* –,** the initial impulse (bringing about the development of the dramatic action), the starting-point of the plot; ***das psychologische* –,** the psychological motive.

momentan [momɛn'ta:n], **1.** *adj.* 1. momentary, instantaneous; 2. actual, present. **2.** *adv.* at the moment, for the time being, for the present, just now. **Momentanwert,** *m.* instantaneous value.

Moment|aufnahme, *f.* snapshot. **-verschluß,** *m.* (*Phot.*) instantaneous shutter.

Monade [mo'na:də], *f.* monad. **Monadenlehre,** *f.* (*Phil., esp. Leibniz*) theory of monads, monadium.

Monarch [mo'narç], *m.* (**-en,** *pl.* **-en**) monarch. **Monarchie** [–'çi:], *f.* monarchy. **monarchisch,** *adj.* monarchic(al). **Monarchist** [–'çɪst], *m.* (**-en,** *pl.* **-en**) monarchist, royalist. **monarchistisch,** *adj.* pro-monarchic, royalist.

Monat ['mo:nat], *m.* (**-s,** *pl.* **-e**) month; ***vor anderthalb –en,*** a month and a half ago, six weeks ago; (*Comm.*) ***laufenden –s,*** of the current month (*abbr.* inst.); ***alle zwei –e,*** every second month, alternate months; ***– für* –,** month after month. **monatelang, 1.** *adj.* months of, lasting for months. **2.** *adv.* for months. **monatlich,** *adj., adv.* monthly; menstrual, every month; ***–e Lieferung,*** monthly instalment (*of a publication*); ***–e Zahlung,*** monthly instalment (*of payments*); *er bekommt sein –es (Gehalt) am 15.*, his salary is paid monthly on the 15th.

Monats|abschluß, *m.* monthly balance. **–aufstellung,** *f.*, **–ausweis,** *m.* monthly statement *or* return. **–bericht,** *m.* monthly report. **–binde,** *f.* sanitary towel. **–fluß,** *m.* menses, menstruation, (monthly) period. **–frist,** *f.* space *or* respite of a month; *binnen –*, within a month. **–gehalt,** *n.* monthly salary *or* wages. **–heft,** *n.* monthly number (*of a periodical*). **–karte,** *f.* monthly season-ticket. **–name,** *m.* name of the month. **–schrift,** *f.* monthly (magazine). **–wechsel,** *m.* (student's) monthly allowance.

monatweise ['mo:natvaɪzə], *adv.* by the month, month by month, monthly.

Mönch [mœnç], *m.* (**-es,** *pl.* **-e**) 1. monk, friar; 2. spindle (*of spiral staircase*). **mönchisch,** *adj.* monastic, monkish.

Mönchs|geier, *m.* (*Orn.*) black vulture (*Aegypius monachus*). **–grasmücke,** *f.* (*Orn.*) blackcap (*Sylvia atricapilla*). **–kloster,** *n.* monastery. **–kranich,** *m.* (*Orn.*) *see* **Schneekranich. –kutte,** *f.* cowl, capuche; *ohne –*, unfrocked, uncowled; *die – anlegen,* turn monk. **–latein,** *n.* dog Latin. **–leben,** *n.* monastic life. **–meise,** *f.* (*Orn.*) *see* **Weidenmeise. –orden,** *m.* religious *or* monastic order. **–schrift,** *f.* (*Typ.*) black letter. **Mönch(s)tum, Mönchswesen,** *n.* monachism, monasticism, monastic life.

Mond [mo:nd], *m.* (**-es,** *pl.* **-e**) 1. moon; satellite; *den – anbellen,* give way to impotent rage; (*fig.*) *auf dem – sein,* be up in the clouds; (*coll.*) *hinter dem – sein* or *leben,* be a square, be behind the times; *ein Loch in den – bohren,* swindle one's creditors; (*coll.*) *du kannst in den – gucken,* you can whistle for it; *nach dem – verlangen,* cry for the moon; 2. (*Geom.*) lune; 3. (*Poet.*) month; 4. (*coll.*) bald patch *or* spot.

mondän [mɔn'dɛ:n], *adj.* modish, stylish, (*coll.*) swell. **Mondäne,** *f.* society-woman, mondaine.

Mondbahn ['mo:ndba:n], *f.* moon's *or* lunar orbit. **mondbeglänzt,** *adj.* moonlit. **Mondfinsternis,** *f.* eclipse of the moon. **mondförmig,** *adj.* moon-shaped; (*Bot.*) lunate. **Mondgebirge,** *n.* mountains of the moon. **mond|hell,** *adj. See* **–beglänzt. Mond|jahr,** *n.* lunar year. **–kalb,** *n.* premature issue; (*fig.*) moon-calf, born fool. **–licht,** *n. See* **–schein. –nacht,** *f.* moonlit night. **–phasen,** *f.pl.* phases of the moon. **–scheibe,** *f.* face of the moon. **–schein,** *m.* moonlight; (*coll.*) bald spot. **–sichel,** *f.* crescent moon. **–stein,** *m.* moonstone, selenite. **–strahl,** *m.* moonbeam. **–sucht,** *f.* sleep-walking, somnambulism. **mondsüchtig,** *adj.* given to sleep-walking, somnambulistic; (*fig.*) moon-struck. **Mond|tafeln,** *f.pl.* lunar tables. **–umlauf,** *m.* lunar revolution. **–viertel,** *n.* quarter of the moon; (*Astr.*) quadrature. **–wechsel,** *m.* change of the moon. **–zirkel,** *m.* lunar cycle.

Moneten [mo'ne:tən], *pl.* (*sl.*) dough, cash.

Mongole [mɔŋ'go:lə], *m.* (**-n,** *pl.* **-n**) Mongol(ian). **Mongolei** [–'laɪ], *f. die –*, Mongolia. **Mongolin,** *f. See* **Mongole. mongolisch,** *adj.* Mongol(ian).

monieren [mo'ni:rən], *v.t.* warn, censure, criticize; (*Comm.*) dun, send a reminder to.

Monogamie [monoga'mi:], *f.* monogamy. **monogam(isch)** [–'ga:m(ɪʃ)], *adj.* monogamous.

Monogonie [monogo'ni:], *f.* asexual reproduction.

Monogramm [mono'gram], *n.* (**-s,** *pl.* **-e**) monogram.

Monographie [monogra'fi:], *f.* monograph, treatise.

Monokel [mo'nɔkəl], *n.* monocle.

Monolog [mono'lo:k], *m.* (**-s,** *pl.* **-e**) monologue, soliloquy.

Monomanie [monoma'ni:], *f.* monomania.

monophasisch [mono'fa:zɪʃ], *adj.* (*Elec.*) single-phase.

Monopol [mono'po:l], *n.* (**-s,** *pl.* **-e**) monopoly; exclusive control (*auf* (*Dat.*), of). **Monopolerzeugnis,** *n.* proprietory product. **monopolisieren** [–'zi:rən], *v.t.* monopolize. **Monopolstellung,** *f. See* **Monopol.**

Monotheismus [monote'ɪsmus], *m.* monotheism.

monoton [mono'to:n], *adj.* monotonous, (*fig.*) humdrum. **Monotonie** [–'ni:], *f.* monotony.

Monstranz [mɔn'strants], *f.* (-, *pl.* **-en**) (*Eccl.*) monstrance, pyx.

monströs [mɔn'strø:s], *adj.* monstrous, hideous, odious, frightful, misshapen. **Monstrosität** [–i'tɛ:t], *f.* deformity, uncouthness, monstrosity, unsightliness, repulsiveness. **Monstrum** ['mɔnstrum], *n.* (**-s,** *pl.* **-ren** (*Austr.* **-ra**)) monster, horror.

Monsun [mɔn'zu:n], *m.* (**-s,** *pl.* **-e**) monsoon.

Montag ['mo:nta:k], *m.* Monday; *der blaue –*, holiday Monday; (*Prov.*) *– wird nicht wochenalt,* Monday does not outlast the week.

Montage [mɔn'ta:ʒə], *f.* setting *or* fitting up, mounting, installing, erection, assembly, installation; (*Phot. etc.*) montage. **Montage|bahn,** *f.*, **–band,** *n.* assembly line. **–gestell,** *n.* jig. **–halle,** *f.* assembly-shop. **–hebel,** *m.* (*Motor.*) tyre lever. **–werk,** *n.* assembly plant.

montags ['mo:nta:ks], *adv.* on Monday(s), every Monday.

Montan|industrie [mɔn'ta:n–], *f.* coal, iron and steel industries. **–union,** *f.* (*Pol.*) European Coal and Steel Community.

Monteur [mɔn'tø:r], *m.* (**-s,** *pl.* **-e**) (engine) fitter, mechanic, assembly hand, (*Elec.*) electrician, (*Av.*) rigger. **Monteuranzug,** *m.* overall(s).

montieren [mɔn'ti:rən], *v.t.* set *or* fit up, erect, mount, install, assemble; (*Mil.*) equip, fit out (*troops*). **Montierung,** *f. See* **Montage**; (*of jewels*) mount, setting; (*Mil.*) equipment.

Montur [mɔn'tu:r], *f.* (-, *pl.* **-en**) uniform, livery, (*Mil.*) regimentals.

Moor [mo:r], *n.* (**-s,** *pl.* **-e**) bog, fen, swamp; peat-bog, moorland. **Moor|bad,** *n.* mud-bath. **–boden,** *m.* marshy soil. **–eiche,** *f.* bog-oak. **–ente,** *f.* (*Orn.*) white-eyed pochard (*Aythya nyroca*). **–eule,** *f.* (*Orn.*) *see* **Sumpfohreule. –gegend,** *f.* fen-country, marshy land. **moorig,** *adj.* marshy, boggy, swampy. **Moor|kultur,** *f.* moorland cultivation. **–land,** *n. See* **–gegend. –packung,** *f.* mud-pack. **–schneehuhn,** *n.* (*Orn.*) willow grouse *or* (*Am.*) ptarmigan (*Lagopus lagopus*); *schottisches –*, red grouse (*Lagopus scoticus*). **–wasser,** *n.* brackish water.

Moos [mo:s], *n.* (**-es,** *pl.* **-e**) 1. moss, lichen; *irländisches –*, Carragheen moss; 2. (*dial.*) peat-bog; 3. (*sl.*) cash, dough. **moosbedeckt,** *adj.* moss-grown. **Moosbeere,** *f.* (*Bot.*) cranberry (*Vaccinium oxycoccus*). **moos|bewachsen,** *adj. See* **–bedeckt. –grün,** *adj.* moss-green. **moosig,** *adj.* mossy, moss-grown.

Mop [mɔp], *m.* (**-(e)s,** *pl.* **-s**) mop.

Moped ['mo:pɛt], *n.* (**-s,** *pl.* **-s**) motor-scooter.

moppen ['mɔpən], *v.t., v.i.* mop.

Mops [mɔps], *m.* (**-es,** *pl.* **⸚e**) pug.

mopsen ['mɔpsən], **1.** *v.t.* (*sl.*) pinch, swipe. **2.** *v.r.* (*sl.*) be bored; *sich schauderhaft –*, be bored stiff.

mopsig ['mɔpsɪç], *adj.* pug-nosed; (*sl.*) snooty, cocky; (*sl.*) *sich – machen,* become a pain in the neck.

Moral [mo'ra:l], *f.* morals, morality; ethics, moral philosophy; moral, lesson; morale; *die – lesen* or *– predigen,* moralize, sermonize, point the moral. **moralisch,** *adj.* moral; *einen –en Druck auf ihn ausüben,* bring moral pressure to bear on him; (*coll.*) *einen –en (Kater) haben,* have qualms of conscience; *eine –e Ohrfeige,* a dressing-down; *– unmöglich,* morally impossible. **moralisieren** [–li'zi:rən], *v.i.* moralize. **Moralist** [–'lɪst], *m.* (**-en,** *pl.* **-en**) moral philosopher, moralist. **Moralität** [–i'tɛ:t], *f.* morality; morality play.

Moral|pauke, *f.* reprimand, lecture; *ihm eine – halten,* read him the riot act. **–philosophie,** *f.* moral philosophy, ethics. **–predigt,** *f. See* **–pauke.**

Moräne [mo'rɛːnə], *f.* moraine.

Morast [mo'rast], *m.* (**-es**, *pl.* **⸚e** *or* **-e**) morass, quagmire, bog, (*Poet.*) slough; ***im – waten,*** wallow in the mire. **morastig,** *adj.* muddy, boggy, marshy.

Morchel ['mɔrçəl], *f.* (-, *pl.* **-n**) morel (*edible fungus*).

Mord [mɔrt], *m.* (**-s,** *pl.* **-e**) murder (***an*** (*Dat.*), of), (*Law*) (culpable) homicide; assassination; (*Law*) ***schwerer –,*** first-degree murder; ***der – des Ehemannes an der Frau,*** the murder of his wife by the husband; ***einen – begehen,*** commit a murder; (*coll.*) ***es gibt – und Totschlag,*** it will end in bloodshed; (*coll.*) ***das ist der rein(st)e –,*** that is a hopeless *or* impossible task; (*coll.*) ***Zeter und – schreien,*** cry blue murder.

Mord|anschlag, *m.* murderous assault, attempted murder. **–brenner,** *m.* incendiary, (*Scots*) fire-raiser. **–brennerei,** *f.* incendiarism, arson, (*Scots*) wilful fire-raising. **–bube,** *m.* assassin, cut-throat. **morden,** *v.t., v.i.* murder, kill, slay, assassinate.

Mörder ['mœrdər], *m.* murderer, killer, assassin. **Mördergrube,** *f.* den of thieves *or* cut-throats; (*coll.*) ***aus seinem Herzen keine – machen,*** wear one's heart on one's sleeve, be very outspoken, make no bones about it. **mörderisch,** *adj.* murderous, (*fig.*) deadly, (*coll.*) killing, wicked, (*of speed*) breakneck, (*of competition etc.*) cut-throat. **mörderlich,** *adj.* (*coll.*) fearful, awful, terrible; enormous, terrific; ***ihn – verhauen,*** beat him to within an inch of his life.

Mord|geschichte, *f.* murder story. **–gier,** *f.* *See* **–lust. mordgierig,** *adj.* bloodthirsty; homicidal. **Mordio!** *int.* murder! help! **Mord|kommission,** *f.* homicide squad. **–lust,** *f.* homicidal mania; bloodthirstiness. **mord|lustig,** *adj.* *See* **–gierig. Mordraupe,** *f.* carnivorous caterpillar.

Mords– [mɔrts], *pref.* (*coll.*) terrible, fearful. **–angst,** *f.* mortal fear, (*coll.*) blue funk. **–ding,** *n.* (*sl.*) killer, humdinger. **–geschichte,** *f.* cock-and-bull story. **–geschrei,** *n.* fearful outcry. **mordskalt,** *adj.* fearfully *or* terribly cold. **Mords|kerl,** *m.* devil of a fellow. **–lärm,** *m.* *See* **–spektakel. mordsmäßig,** *adj.* awful, terrific, enormous. **Mords|spaß,** *m.* great fun. **–spektakel,** *m.* hullaballoo, awful din *or* racket.

Mord|sucht, *f.* *See* **–lust. mord|süchtig,** *adj.* *See* **–gierig.**

mordswenig ['mɔrtsveːnɪç], *adv.* (*coll.*) precious *or* mighty little.

Mord|tat, *f.* murder, murderous assault. **–verdacht,** *m.* suspicion of murder. **–versuch,** *m.* attempted murder. **–waffe,** *f.*, **–werkzeug,** *n.* murder weapon, (*fig.*) murderous weapon.

Morelle [mo'rɛlə], *f.* morello (cherry).

Mores ['moːrɛs], *pl.* (good) manners; (*coll.*) ***ihn – lehren,*** teach him what's what.

morganatisch [mɔrga'naːtɪʃ], *adj.* morganatic, (*coll.*) left-handed (*marriage*).

[1]**Morgen** ['mɔrgən], *m.* 1. morning, forenoon; ***heute morgen,*** this morning; ***vorgestern morgen,*** the morning before yesterday; 2. dawn, daybreak; ***es wird –,*** it is getting light, the day *or* dawn is breaking; 3. (*Poet.*) east.

[2]**Morgen,** *m.* a land measure (*local variations from 0.6 to 0.9 acre*).

[3]**Morgen,** *n.* (the) future, (*Poet.*) (the) morrow.

morgen, *adv.* tomorrow; ***– früh,*** tomorrow morning; ***– über acht Tage,*** tomorrow week; ***– ist auch ein Tag,*** there's always tomorrow.

Morgen|andacht, *f.* morning prayers, matins. **–ausgabe,** *f.*, **–blatt,** *n.* morning paper. **–brot,** *n.* (*dial.*) breakfast. **–dämmerung,** *f.* dawn, daybreak. **morgendlich,** *adj.* morning, matitudinal. **Morgen|essen,** *n.* (*Swiss*) breakfast. **–grauen,** *n.* *See* **–dämmerung**; break of day, crack of dawn. **–kleid,** *n.* house-gown. **–land,** *n.* Orient, East, Levant. **morgenländisch,** *adj.* Oriental, Eastern. **Morgen|luft,** *f.* morning air; (*coll.*) ***– wittern,*** become hopeful. **–post,** *f.* early morning post, first delivery. **–rock,** *m.* dressing-gown, house-coat. **–rot,** *n.*, **–röte,** *f.* dawn, sunrise, (*Poet.*) aurora.

morgens ['mɔrgəns], *adv.* in the morning; every morning.

Morgen|seite, *f.* eastern aspect. **–sonne,** *f.* morning *or* rising sun. **–stern,** *m.* morning star, Venus. **–stunde,** *f.* (*Prov.*) ***– hat Gold im Munde,*** the early bird catches the worm; ***frühe –n,*** the small hours (of the morning).

morgig ['mɔrgɪç], *adj.* of tomorrow, tomorrow's; ***der –e Tag,*** tomorrow.

Mormone [mɔr'moːnə], *m.* (**-n,** *pl.* **-n**) Mormon.

Mornellregenpfeifer [mɔr'nɛlreːgənpfaɪfər], *m.* (*Orn.*) dotterel (*Charadrius morinellus*).

moros [mo'roːs], *adj.* morose, glum, ill-tempered.

Morphin [mɔr'fiːn], *n.* (*Austr.*) *see* **Morphium.**

Morphium ['mɔrfium], *n.* morphine, morphia. **Morphium|einspritzung,** *f.* morphia injection. **–sucht,** *f.* morphinism. **–süchtige(r),** *m., f.* morphia addict.

morsch [mɔrʃ], *adj.* decaying, decayed, decomposed, rotten; frail, fragile, brittle; ***– werden,*** decay, rot; crumble.

morsen ['mɔrzən], *v.t., v.i.* signal by Morse code.

Mörser ['mœrzər], *m.* mortar; (*Artil.*) howitzer. **Mörser|keule,** *f.*, **–stößel,** *m.* pestle.

Morse|schrift, *f.* Morse code. **–zeichen,** *n.* Morse signal.

Mörtel ['mœrtəl], *m.* mortar; plaster; ***mit – bewerfen,*** plaster, rough-cast. **Mörtel|kelle,** *f.* trowel. **–maschine,** *f.* cement mixer. **–trog,** *m.* hod.

Mosaik [moza'iːk], *n.* (**-s,** *pl.* **-e**), **Mosaik|arbeit,** *f.* mosaic(-work), inlaid work. **–fußboden,** *m.* tessellated pavement. **–spiel,** *n.* jig-saw puzzle.

mosaisch [mo'zaːɪʃ], *adj.* (*B.*) Mosaic.

Mosch [mɔʃ], *m.* (*dial.*) waste, rubbish, scraps.

Moschee [mɔ'ʃeː], *f.* mosque.

Moschus ['mɔʃus], *m.* musk. **Moschus|ochse,** *m.* musk-ox. **–tier,** *n.* musk-deer.

Moskito [mɔs'kiːto], *m.* (**-s,** *pl.* **-s**) mosquito.

Most [mɔst], *m.* (**-es,** *pl.* **-e**) fruit juice, new wine, must; cider; ***wissen, wo Barthel den – holt,*** be in the know, be behind the scenes, know on which side one's bread is buttered. **Most|kelter, –presse,** *f.* wine-press; cider-press.

Mostrich ['mɔstrɪç], *m.* (*dial.*) French mustard.

Motette [mo'tɛtə], *f.* motet.

Motion [motsi'oːn], *f.* 1. movement, exercise; ***sich*** (*Dat.*) ***(eine kleine) – machen,*** take some exercise; 2. motion (*in parliament etc.*).

Motiv [mo'tiːf], *n.* (**-s,** *pl.* **-e**) motive, reason, cause; subject, theme, (*Mus.*) motif. **Motivforschung,** *f.* (*Comm.*) motivation research. **motivieren** [–'viːrən], *v.t.* motivate. **Motivierung,** *f.* motivation.

Motor ['moːtɔr], *m.* (**-s,** *pl.* **-en**) motor, engine; ***elektromagnetischer –,*** dynamo; ***hochverdichteter –,*** high-compression engine; ***sternförmiger –,*** radial engine; ***untersetzter –,*** geared motor; ***der – setzt aus*** or (*sl.*) ***muckt*** or ***stottert,*** the engine cuts out; ***der – springt an,*** the engine picks up; ***den – voll beanspruchen,*** run the engine full *or* flat out.

Motor|aufhängung, *f.* engine suspension. **–ausfall,** *m.* engine failure. **–boot,** *n.* motor-boat, motor-launch, speed-boat. **–defekt,** *m.* *See* **–ausfall. –drehmoment,** *n.* engine torque. **–drehzahl,** *f.* engine *or* motor speed.

Motoren|anlage, *f.* power-plant. **–betriebsstoff,** *m.* motor fuel. **–gondel,** *f.* (*Av.*) engine nacelle. **–halle,** *f.* engine-house, power-house. **–haube,** *f.* bonnet, (*Am.*) hood, (*Av.*) engine cowling. **–haus,** *n.* *See* **–halle.**

motorig [mo'toːrɪç], *adj.suff.* -engined, *e.g.* ***zweimotorig,*** twin-engined. **motorisch,** *adj.* motor, motive, kinetic; motor-driven, power-operated. **motorisieren** [–i'ziːrən], *v.t.* motorize, mechanize.

Motor|leistung, *f.* engine performance *or* power. **–pflug,** *m.* motor-plough. **–rad,** *n.* motor-cycle.

-roller, *m.* motor-scooter. **-säge,** *f.* power saw. **-schaden,** *m. See* **-ausfall. -sport,** *m.* motoring. **-störung,** *f.* engine trouble.

Motte ['mɔtə], *f.* moth; (*coll.*) ***du hast die -n,*** you've a bee in your bonnet. **Motten|fraß,** *m.* damage done by moths. **-pulver,** *n.* insect-powder, insecticide. **motten|sicher,** *adj.* mothproof. **-zerfressen,** *adj.* moth-eaten.

Motthühnchen ['mɔthy:nçən], *n.* (*Orn.*) *see* ***kleines* Sumpfhuhn.**

moussieren [mu'si:rən], *v.i.* effervesce, sparkle, froth, fizz; ***-der Champagner,*** sparkling champagne, (*sl.*) bubbly.

Möwe ['mø:və], *f.* (sea)gull; (*Orn.*) ***dünnschnäbelige -,*** slender-billed gull (*Larus geneï*).

Muck [muk], *m.* (**-(e)s,** *pl.* **-e**) faint *or* suppressed sound; ***keinen - tun,*** not utter a sound; (*coll.*) ***nicht - sagen,*** not say bo to a goose.

[1]**Mucke** ['mukə], *f.* whim, crotchet, caprice; ***ein Pferd, das -n hat,*** a vicious horse; ***er hat seine -n,*** he has his little moods; ***das Ding hat seine -n,*** the matter has its snags.

[2]**Mucke,** *f.* (*dial.*) *see* **Mücke**; (*Prov.*) ***mit Geduld und Spucke fängt man eine -,*** softly, softly, catchee monkey.

Mücke ['mykə], *f.* 1. gnat, midge; (*Prov.*) ***aus einer - einen Elefanten machen,*** make a mountain of a molehill; ***-n seihen und Kamele verschlucken,*** strain at a gnat and swallow a camel; 2. (*obs.*) foresight (*of a gun*).

mucken ['mukən], *v.i.* grumble, murmur, mutter; be up in arms, rebel; ***nicht gemuckt! mucke nicht!*** not another word *or* sound!

Mücken|fett, *n.* mare's nest, pigeon's milk; ***ihn nach - schicken,*** send him on a fool's errand. **-netz,** *n.*, **-schleier,** *m.* mosquito net. **-stich,** *m.* midge *or* gnat bite.

Mucker ['mukər], *m.* bigot, hypocrite. **Muckerei** [-'raɪ], *f.* cant, hypocrisy. **muckerhaft, muckerisch,** *adj.* canting, sanctimonious, hypocritical, self-righteous, pharisaical, bigoted. **muckern,** *v.i.* (*coll.*) be a bigot *or* hypocrite; whine hypocritically. **Muckertum,** *n. See* **Muckerei.**

Mucks [muks], *m.* (*coll.*) ***keinen - tun,*** not budge (an inch); *see also under* **Muck. mucksen,** *v.i., v.r.* budge, stir, move. **mucksmäuschenstill,** *adj.* (*coll.*) quiet as a mouse.

müde ['my:də], *adj.* weary, tired, exhausted, fatigued, (*coll.*) worn out; ***ich bin des Wartens -,*** I am tired of waiting; ***ich bin es -,*** I am tired of it; ***zum Umfallen -,*** tired to death, fit to drop; ***sich - arbeiten,*** work till one is tired; ***- machen,*** tire out, fatigue, weary; ***- werden,*** grow weary, get tired. **Müdigkeit,** *f.* weariness, fatigue, exhaustion, lassitude; ***von der - übermannt werden,*** be overcome with exhaustion.

Muff [muf], *m.* (**-es,** *pl.* **-e**) muff (*for the hands*). **Muffe,** *f.* (*Tech.*) socket, coupling, sleeve.

[1]**Muffel** ['mufəl], *m.* snout, muzzle.

[2]**Muffel,** *f.* (-, *pl.* **-n**) (*Tech., Chem.*) muffle, crucible.

muffeln ['mufəln], *v.t., v.i.* mumble, mutter, gabble; champ, munch (*one's food*); mope, sulk.

müffeln ['myfəln], *v.i.* smell musty *or* fusty.

muffig ['mufɪç], *adj.* musty, fusty; (*of air*) close, stifling; (*of a p.*) sullen, sulky, disgruntled. **mufflig,** *adj.* (*dial.*) sullen, sulky, disgruntled.

Mühe ['my:ə], *f.* trouble, pains, toil, labour, effort, exertion, difficulty; ***sich*** (*Dat.*) ***- geben,*** take pains (***mit, um,*** with *or* over); ***es lohnt die -,*** it is quite worth while; ***ihm - machen,*** give *or* cause him trouble, make trouble for him; ***machen Sie sich keine -!*** do not go to any trouble; ***mit - und Not,*** barely, only just, with difficulty; ***keine -(n) scheuen, sich*** (*Acc.*) ***keine - verdrießen lassen,*** spare no pains; ***die*** or ***seine - umsonst haben,*** have all the trouble in vain *or* to no purpose; ***verlorene -,*** waste of effort; ***nicht der - wert,*** not worth while, not worth the trouble. **mühelos, 1.** *adj.* easy, effortless, without trouble. **2.** *adv.* easily, with ease. **Mühelosigkeit,** *f.* ease, easiness, facility.

muhen ['mu:ən], *v.i.* low (*of cattle*).

mühen ['my:ən], *v.r.* work hard, exert o.s., take pains *or* trouble. **mühevoll,** *adj.* laborious, hard, difficult, troublesome, irksome. **Mühewaltung,** *f.* care *or* trouble *or* pains (taken), assiduity; ***für seine -,*** for the trouble he has taken.

Mühlbach ['my:lbax], *m.* mill-stream. **Mühle,** *f.* 1. mill; crusher, grinder; ***das ist Wasser auf seine -,*** that is grist to his mill; 2. (a kind of) game played with draughtsmen.

Mühlen|arbeiter, *m.* millhand. **-bauer,** *m.* millwright. **-rad, -stein, -teich, -wehr,** *see under* **Mühl-.**

Mühlespiel ['my:ləʃpi:l], *n. See* **Mühle,** 2.

Mühl|gang, *m.* run of millstones. **-graben,** *m.* mill-race. **-rad,** *n.* mill-wheel. **-stein,** *m.* millstone. **-steinkragen,** *m.* ruffle. **-teich,** *m.* millpond. **-wehr,** *n.* mill-dam. **-werk,** *n.* grinding mechanism.

Muhme ['mu:mə], *f.* (*obs.*) aunt; elderly female relation.

Mühsal ['my:za:l], *f.* (-, *pl.* **-e**) toil, drudgery; trouble, difficulty, hardship, strain.

mühsam ['my:za:m], **mühselig, 1.** *adj.* troublesome, laborious, hard, difficult; tiresome, irksome. **2.** *adv.* with difficulty; ***sich - erheben,*** struggle to one's feet; ***sich - ernähren,*** eke out a living, make a bare living. **Mühseligkeit,** *f.* toil, hardship, difficulty.

Mulatte [mu'latə], *m.* (**-n,** *pl.* **-n**) mulatto.

Mulde ['muldə], *f.* tray, trough, mould, tub, bowl; (*Geog., Geol.*) hollow, basin, gully, depression, re-entrant; ***eine - Blei,*** a pig of lead; (*coll.*) ***es gießt wie mit -n,*** it is raining cats and dogs. **Muldenblei,** *n.* pig-lead.

Mull [mul], *m.* (**-s,** *pl.* **-e**) gauze, mull.

Müll [myl], *m.* 1. dust, sweepings, rubbish, refuse, (*Am.*) garbage; 2. humus, mould. **Müll|abfuhr,** *f.* refuse *or* (*Am.*) garbage disposal. **-abfuhrwagen,** *m. See* **-wagen. -eimer,** *m.* dustbin, (*Am.*) garbage can.

Müller ['mylər], *m.* 1. miller; 2. (*Ent.*) meal-worm. **Müllerchen,** *n.* (*Orn.*) *see* **Klappergrasmücke. Müllerei** [-'raɪ], *f.* miller's trade. **Mülleresel,** *m.* (*coll.*) drudge; dunce. **Müllerin,** *f.* miller's wife.

Müll|fahrer, *m.* dustman, (*Am.*) garbageman. **-grube,** *f.* ashpit. **-haufen,** *m.* rubbish heap *or* dump. **-kasten,** *m. See* **-eimer. -kutscher,** *m. See* **-fahrer. -schaufel,** *f.* dustpan. **-schlucker,** *m.* waste-disposer. **-verbrennungsofen,** *m.* incinerator, destructor. **-wagen,** *m.* dustcart, (*Am.*) garbage truck.

Mulm [mulm], *m.* (**-(e)s,** *pl.* **-e**) decay, rot; rotten wood; mould, humus; ore-dust. **mulmen, 1.** *v.t.* pulverize. **2.** *v.i.* (*aux.* s.) turn to dust, crumble. **mulmig,** *adj.* worm-eaten, decayed, rotten, mouldy; (*fig.*) precarious, ticklish, (*coll.*) rotten.

Multiplikation [multiplikatsi'o:n], *f.* multiplication. **Multiplikator** [-'ka:tɔr], *m.* (**-s,** *pl.* **-en**) multiplier. **multiplizieren** [-'zi:rən], *v.t.* multiply (***mit,*** by). **Multiplum** ['multiplum], *n.* (**-s,** *pl.* **-pla**) multiple.

Mulus ['mu:lus], *m.* (-, *pl.* **-li**) (*Studs. sl.*) fresher, university entrant.

Mumie ['mu:miə], *f.* mummy. **mumienhaft,** *adj.* mummified. **mumifizieren** [-fi'tsi:rən], *v.t.* mummify, embalm.

Mumm [mum], *m.* (*sl.*) ***-*** (***in den Knochen***) ***haben,*** have guts *or* spunk.

[1]**Mumme** ['mumə], *f.* (a kind of) strong beer.

[2]**Mumme,** *f.* (*dial.*) disguise, mask; masquerader.

Mummel ['muməl], *f.* (-, *pl.* **-n**) (*dial.*) (*Bot.*) water-lily. **Mummelgreis,** *m.* (*coll.*) old fogy *or* geezer.

mummen ['mumən], *v.t.* muffle up; mask, disguise. **Mummen|schanz,** *m.*, **-spiel,** *n. See* **Mummerei. Mummer,** *m.* masquerader, mummer. **Mummerei** [-'raɪ], *f.* mummery; masquerade.

Mumpitz ['mumpɪts], *m.* (*sl.*) bosh, balderdash, stuff and nonsense.

München ['mynçən], *n.* Munich. **Münchner, 1.** *m.* inhabitant of Munich. **2.** *adj.* – *Bier,* Munich beer.

Mund [munt], *m.* (**-es,** *pl.* **-e** *or* **⸚er**) mouth; muzzle, os, orifice, stoma, opening, aperture, vent; – ***und Nase*** or ***den – aufsperren,*** stand gaping, be dumbfounded *or* flabbergasted; ***ihm über den – fahren,*** cut him short; ***nicht auf den – gefallen sein,*** have a ready *or* glib tongue; ***wie aus einem -e,*** as one man; ***aus dem -e riechen,*** have bad breath; ***im -e führen,*** always be talking about; ***den – halten,*** hold one's tongue, (*sl.*) shut *or* dry up; ***reinen – halten über etwas,*** keep a th. a secret; ***von*** or ***aus der Hand in den – leben,*** live from hand to mouth; ***ihm in den – legen,*** suggest to him, give him the cue; ***in aller*** (***Leute***) ***– sein,*** be much talked of, be on everybody's lips; ***Sie nehmen mir das Wort aus dem -e,*** that is just what I was going to say, you took the words out of my mouth; ***ich mag das Wort nicht in den – nehmen,*** I cannot bring myself to use that word; ***kein Blatt vor den – nehmen,*** call a spade a spade, not choose one's words; ***offenen -es,*** open-mouthed, agape; ***sich*** (*Dat.*) ***den – fusselig reden,*** talk o.s. hoarse; ***ihm nach dem -e reden,*** chime in with his views; flatter him, fawn upon him, (*coll.*) butter him up; ***auf den – schlagen,*** contradict flatly; ***er ist wie auf den – geschlagen,*** he is quite dumbstruck; ***ihm etwas in den – schmieren,*** leave him no choice but to believe s.th.; ***ihm das Wort im -e umdrehen,*** twist his words *or* meaning; ***sich den – verbrennen,*** put one's foot in it; ***den – vollnehmen,*** brag, boast, talk big; ***ihm den – wässerig machen,*** make his mouth water.

Mundart ['muntˀart], *f.* dialect. **mundartlich,** *adj.* dialectal, provincial.

Mund|bäcker, *m.* (*Hist.*) royal baker. **-bedarf,** *m.* provisions, victuals.

Mündel ['myndəl], *m.* (*Austr. n.*), (*when female also f.* (-, *pl.* **-n**)) ward, minor. **Mündelgeld,** *n.* trust-money. **mündelsicher,** *adj.* absolutely safe (*of investments etc.*); ***-e Anlage,*** trustee investment; ***-e Papiere,*** gilt-edged securities. **Mündelstand,** *m.* pupilage.

munden ['mundən], *v.i.* taste good, be appetizing *or* delicious; ***es mundet mir,*** I relish that, I like it.

münden ['myndən], *v.i.* – ***in*** (*Acc.*), (*as river*) fall *or* flow *or* empty into, (*of street*) run into; (*fig.*) lead to, end in.

mundfaul ['muntfaul], *adj.* taciturn, tongue-tied. **Mundfäule,** *f.* (*Med.*) thrush, stomatitis. **mund|-fertig,** *adj.* glib. **-gerecht,** *adj.* easy (to pronounce); palatable, fit *or* suitable for eating; (*fig.*) suitable, attractive. **Mund|geruch,** *m.* bad breath, (*Med.*) halitosis. **-harmonika,** *f.* mouth-organ. **-höhle,** *f.* oral cavity.

mundieren [mun'di:rən], *v.t.* (*Law*) engross, (*coll.*) make a fair copy of. **Mundierung,** *f.* engrossment, engrossing.

mündig ['myndɪç], *adj.* – ***sein,*** be of age; – ***werden,*** come of age, attain one's majority; ***ihn für – erklären, ihn – sprechen,*** declare him to be of age. **Mündigkeit,** *f.* full age, majority. **Mündigsprechung,** *f.* declaration of (*a p.'s*) majority, (*fig.*) emancipation.

mündlich ['myntlɪç], *adj.* oral, verbal, by word of mouth, viva-voce, (*Law*) by parol; ***-e Prüfung,*** oral *or* viva-voce examination; ***-er Vertrag,*** verbal *or* (*Law*) parol contract; (*Law*) ***-e Verhandlung,*** oral hearing *or* proceedings.

Mund|loch, *n.* blow-hole (*of a flute*). **-pflege,** *f.* dental care. **-raub,** *m.* pilfering of food, picking. **-schenk,** *m.* (*Hist.*) cupbearer. **-sperre,** *f.* lockjaw. **-stellung,** *f.* (*Phonet.*) position of the mouth. **-stück,** *n.* mouth-piece; nozzle; tip (*of cigarettes*); bridle-bit; (*vulg.*) trap. **mundtot,** *adj.* dead in law; silenced, reduced to silence, prevented from speaking; ***ihn – machen,*** silence him, reduce him to silence, (*coll.*) gag *or* muzzle him. **Mundtuch,** *n.* (table)napkin, serviette.

Mundum ['mundum], *n.* (**-s,** *pl.* **-da**) (*Law*) fair copy, engrossment.

Mündung ['myndʊŋ], *f.* mouth (*of a river*), estuary; muzzle (*of a gun*); opening, orifice, aperture, outlet. **Mündungs|bremse,** *f.* muzzle brake. **-feuer,** *n.* gun flash. **-gebiet,** *n.* delta. **-geschwindigkeit,** *f.* muzzle velocity. **-rohr,** *n.* torpedo tube. **-waag(e)rechte,** *f.* (*Artil.*) chord of trajectory.

Mund|voll, *m.* mouthful. **-vorrat,** *m.* victuals, provisions. **-wasser,** *n.* mouth-wash, gargle. **-werk,** *n.* (*coll.*) glib tongue; (*coll.*) ***ein gutes – haben,*** have the gift of the gab. **-winkel,** *m.* corner of the mouth.

Munition [munitsi'o:n], *f.* ammunition, military *or* naval stores; – ***vorbringen,*** bring up ammunition. **Munitions|arbeiter,** *m.* munition-worker. **-aufzug,** *m.* ammunition hoist. **-einsatz,** *m.* expenditure of ammunition. **-ergänzung,** *f.*, **-ersatz,** *m.* replenishment of ammunition. **-kammer,** *f.* magazine. **-kolonne,** *f.* ammunition column *or* train. **-lager,** *n.* ammunition depot *or* dump. **-nachschub,** *m. See* **-versorgung. -verbrauch,** *m. See* **-einsatz. -versorgung,** *f.* ammunition supply.

munkeln ['muŋkəln], *v.t., v.i.* whisper, mutter; ***man munkelt,*** it is rumoured; (*Prov.*) ***im Dunkeln ist gut –,*** night is the friend of lovers; (*coll.*) ***das Wetter munkelt,*** the weather is threatening.

Münster ['mynstər], *n.* (*rare m.*) cathedral, minster.

munter ['muntər], *adj.* (wide-)awake, up and about, up and doing; sprightly, lively, brisk, (*coll.*) frisky; gay, cheerful, jolly, merry; (*of colours*) gay, bright; (*Mus.*) lively, allegro; ***du bist wohl nicht ganz –?*** are you mad? ***gesund und –,*** hale and hearty, (as) fit as a fiddle; ***er war früh –,*** he was up early. **Munterkeit,** *f.* liveliness, briskness, sprightliness; cheerfulness, gaiety, high spirits.

Münze ['myntsə], *f.* coin, coinage; small change; medal; mint; ***bare –,*** ready cash; ***falsche –,*** base coin; ***gangbare –,*** current coin; ***klingende –,*** hard cash; ***ihm mit gleicher – heimzahlen,*** pay him back in his own coin; ***für bare – nehmen,*** take for gospel truth, believe implicitly, take at its face value.

Münz|einheit, *f.* monetary unit, standard of currency. **-einwurf,** *m.* coin slot (*on slot-machines*). **münzen,** *v.t.* coin, mint (*money*); ***gemünztes Geld,*** specie; (*fig.*) ***es war auf ihn gemünzt,*** that was meant for *or* aimed at him. **Münz(en)sammlung,** *f.* collection of coins. **Münzer, Münz|fälscher,** *m.* coiner, forger. **-fälschung,** *f.* uttering false coin, forging, counterfeiting. **-fernsprecher,** *m.* coin-box telephone; telephone-kiosk, public call-box. **-freiheit,** *f.* right to strike coinage. **-fuß,** *m.* unit *or* standard of currency. **-gehalt,** *m.* standard of alloy, fineness (*of coins*). **-kabinett,** *n.* collection of coins. **-kunde,** *f.* numismatics. **-kundige(r),** *m., f.* numismatist. **-meister,** *m.* mint-master. **-probe,** *f.* assay (*of coin*). **-recht, -regal,** *n. See* **-freiheit. -stempel,** *m.* die. **-stück,** *n.* coin; planchet. **-verbrechen,** *n.*, **-verfälschung,** *f.* uttering base coin. **-vertrag,** *m.* monetary convention. **-wardein,** *m.* assay-master. **-wert,** *m.* nominal value. **-wesen,** *n.* monetary system. **-zeichen,** *n.* mint mark.

mürb(e) ['myrp (-bə)], *adj.* 1. mellow; tender, ripe, soft; 2. well-cooked; crisp, brittle, friable; short (*of pastry*); 3. unsound (*of ice*); suffering from dry-rot; 4. (*fig.*) weary, worn out; demoralized, unnerved; (*fig.*) – ***machen,*** (*a p.*) wear down, make pliable, break (*a p.'s*) resistance *or* spirit; unnerve; (*Mil.*) soften up; – ***werden,*** give in. **Mürb(e)braten,** *m.* roast sirloin. **Mürbekuchen,** *m.* shortbread, shortcake. **Mürb(e)teig,** *m.* short pastry. **Mürbheit,** *f.* mellowness; tenderness; dry-rot; friability; crispness, (*of pastry*) shortness.

Murbruch ['mu:rbrux], *m.* (*dial.*) landslide. **Mur(e),** *f.* scree. **Mur|gang,** *m. See* **-bruch.**

murksen ['murksən], *v.i.* (*coll.*) botch *or* bungle the job.

Murmel ['murməl], *m.* (*dial.*) marble (*boy's toy*).

murmeln ['murməln], *v.t., v.i.* murmur, mutter. **Murmeltier,** *n.* marmot, (*Am.*) wood-chuck; ***schlafen wie ein –,*** sleep like a dormouse *or* a top.

murren ['murən], *v.t.*, *v.i.* murmur, grouse, grumble (*über* (*Acc.*), at).
mürrisch ['myrɪʃ], *adj.* sullen, surly, disgruntled, morose, (*coll.*) grumpy.
Murr|kater, -kopf, *m.* grouser, grumbler. **murrköpfig,** *adj.* *See* **mürrisch.**
Mus [mu:s], *n.* (**-es,** *pl.* **-e**) purée, pulp; jam; stewed fruit; ***zu – schlagen,*** beat to a pulp *or* jelly.
Muschel ['muʃəl], *f.* (-, *pl.* **-n**) 1. mussel, shell-fish; shell; (*Tele.*) ear-piece; (*Anat.*) conch; 2. thumb (*of a latch*); 3. lavatory pan *or* pedestal, wash-handbasin. **muschel|artig,** *adj.* *See* **-förmig. Muschelbein,** *n.* (*Anat.*) turbinate bone. **muschelförmig,** *adj.* shell-like, conchoidal. **Muschel|gehäuse,** *n.* shell (*of mussels etc.*). **-kalk,** *m.* (*Geol.*) shell lime(stone). **-kenner,** *m.* conchologist. **-kunde,** *f.* conchology. **-linie,** *f.* (*Math.*) conchoid. **-schale,** *f.* *See* **-gehäuse. -schieber,** *m.* (*Motor.*) side-valve. **-tier,** *n.* mollusc, shell-fish.
Muse ['mu:zə], *f.* Muse; ***leichte –,*** lightly draped Muse, light entertainment, variety. **Musen|almanach,** *m.* poetical annual. **-berg,** *m.* Parnassus, Helicon. **-born,** *m.* *See* **-quell. -freund,** *m.* poetry lover, patron of poetry. **-gott,** *m.* Apollo. **-quell,** *m.* Hippocrene. **-roß,** *n.* Pegasus. **-sitz,** *m.* seat of the Muses; academy, university. **-sohn,** *m.* poet; university student. **-stadt,** *f.* university town.
Museum [mu'ze:um], *n.* (**-s,** *pl.* **-seen**) museum.
Musik [mu'zi:k], *f.* music; band; ***in – setzen,*** set to music; (*coll.*) ***ohne – abziehen,*** steal *or* sneak away; ***da kommt die –,*** there comes the band. **Musikalien** [-'ka:liən], *pl.* music (books), printed music. **Musikalienhandlung,** *f.* music-shop. **musikalisch,** *adj.* musical; ***-es Gehör,*** good ear for music. **Musikalität** [-kali'tɛ:t], *f.* musicality.
Musikant [muzi'kant], *m.* (**-en,** *pl.* **-en**) (*Poet.*) musician; performer; ***herumziehende -en,*** itinerant musicians; (*coll.*) ***hier liegt ein – begraben!*** I tripped over s.th.; ***da sitzen die -en!*** there's the rub! **Musikantenknochen,** *m.* funny-bone.
Musik|aufführung, *f.* musical performance. **-automat,** *m.* musical box, juke box. **-begleitung,** *f.* (musical) accompaniment. **-direktor,** *m.* conductor; (*Mil.*) bandmaster. **-dose,** *f.* musical box.
Musiker ['mu:zikər], *m.* musician; (*Mil.*) bandsman.
Musik|fest, *n.* music(al) festival. **-freund,** *m.* music lover. **-hochschule,** *f.* academy of music, conservatoire. **-instrument,** *n.* musical instrument. **-kenner,** *m.* connoisseur of music. **-korps,** *n.* band (of musicians). **-lehrer,** *m.* music teacher. **-liebhaber,** *m.* music lover, amateur musician. **-mappe,** *f.* music-case. **-meister,** *m.* director of music, bandmaster. **-pavillon,** *m.* bandstand. **-saal,** *m.* concert hall. **-schrank,** *m.* radiogram. **-stunde,** *f.* music lesson. **-truhe,** *f.* *See* **-schrank. -unterricht,** *m.* music lesson.
Musikus ['mu:zikus], *m.* (-, *pl.* **Musiker** *or* **Musizi**) (*obs.*) *see* **Musiker.**
Musik|veranstaltung, *f.* *See* **-aufführung. -verein,** *m.* musical society. **-werk,** *n.* (musical) composition; musical box. **-wissenschaft,** *f.* musicology.
musisch ['mu:zɪʃ], *adj.* sacred *or* devoted to the Muses; favoured by the Muses, poetic, artistic, musical.
musivisch [mu'zi:vɪʃ], *adj.* inlaid, mosaic.
musizieren [muzi'tsi:rən], *v.i.* play *or* make music; ***des Abends wurde stets musiziert,*** we always had music in the evenings.
Muskat [mus'ka:t], *m.* (**-s,** *pl.* **-e**), **Muskate,** *f.* mace, nutmeg. **Muskateller(wein)** [-'tɛlər], *m.* muscatel, muscadel. **Muskat(en)blüte,** *f.* mace. **Muskatnuß,** *f.* nutmeg.
Muskel ['muskəl], *m.* (**-s,** *pl.* **-n**) *or f.* (-, *pl.* **-n**) muscle. **Muskel|ansatz,** *m.* strenuous work. **-anstrengung,** *f.* muscular exertion. **-band,** *n.* ligament, tendon. **-bau,** *m.* muscles. **-eiweiß,** *n.* myosia. **-faser,** *f.* muscular *or* muscle fibre. **-gewebe,** *n.* muscular tissue. **-haut,** *f.* muscular membrane. **-kater,** *m.* stiffness, soreness, (*Med.*) myalgia. **-kraft,** *f.* muscular strength. **-lehre,** *f.* myology. **-magen,** *m.* gizzard. **-mann,** *m.* skinned figure (*for study of muscles*). **-mensch, -protz,** *m.* (*coll.*) muscle-man, he-man, Tarzan. **-riß,** *m.* torn *or* ruptured muscle. **-schwund,** *m.* muscular atrophy. **muskelstark,** *adj.* muscular. **Muskel|stärke,** *f.* muscular strength. **-stoff,** *m.* sarcosine. **-zergliederung, -zerlegung,** *f.* myotomy. **-zerrung,** *f.* strained *or* pulled muscle. **-zucker,** *m.* inositol.
Muskete [mus'ke:tə], *f.* musket. **Musketier** [-e'ti:r], *m.* (**-s,** *pl.* **-e**) musketeer.
Muskulatur [muskula'tu:r], *f.* (-, *pl.* **-en**) muscular system, muscles. **muskulös** [-'lø:s], *adj.* muscular, (*coll.*) brawny.
muß [mus], *see* **müssen. Muß,** *n.* (*Austr. m.*) (*indecl.*) necessity, compulsion; ***es ist kein – dabei,*** there is no real need for it; (*Prov.*) ***– ist eine harte Nuß,*** necessity is a hard master; ***– ist ein bitter Kraut,*** compulsion is always hard to swallow.
Mußbaier ['musbaɪər], *m.* native of Franconia.
Muße ['mu:sə], *f.* leisure, spare time; ***in*** (***aller***) ***–, mit –,*** at (one's) leisure, in a leisurely manner; ***– haben,*** have leisure, be at leisure.
Musselin [musə'li:n], *m.* (**-s,** *pl.* **-e**) muslin. **musselinen,** *adj.* (of) muslin.
müssen ['mysən], *v.i.*, *v.aux.* must, have to; be obliged *or* compelled *or* forced *or* bound to.
(a) (*indic.*) ***ich muß,*** I must, I have to, I cannot help it; ***ich muß gehen,*** I must go, I have to go, I am obliged to go; ***ich muß nicht*** (***gehen***), I don't have to (go), I need not (go); ***ich mußte,*** I had to, I couldn't help it; ***ich mußte gehen,*** I had to go, I couldn't help but go *or* (*coll.*) help going; ***ich mußte nicht*** (***gehen***), I didn't have to *or* need to (go); ***ich werde –,*** I shall have to, I shall not be able to help it; ***ich werde gehen –,*** I shall have to go; ***ich werde nicht gehen –,*** I shall not have to *or* need to go; ***wenn es*** (***eigentlich***) ***sein muß,*** if it cannot be helped; ***das muß man sagen,*** it must be admitted, to be sure; ***eine Frau wie sie sein muß,*** a woman *or* wife such as one would wish, a paragon of a woman, a model wife; ***kein Mensch muß –,*** no one has to submit to compulsion; ***es mußte sich gerade so fügen daß . . .,*** chance would have it that. . . .
(b) (*subj.*) ***ich müßte*** (***eigentlich***) ***bleiben,*** I ought to stay; ***ich müßte*** (***eigentlich***) ***nicht bleiben,*** I shouldn't have to *or* need to stay; ***ich müßte mich sehr irren wenn . . .,*** I should be very much mistaken if . . .; ***er tut es nicht, er müßte sonst*** or ***denn verrückt sein,*** he won't do it unless he is quite crazy.
(c) (*ellipt.*) ***ich muß fort,*** I must go *or* leave; ***der Brief muß zur Post,*** the letter must go to the post *or* must be posted.
(d) (*preceded by another inf. – is used for p.p.* ***gemußt***) ***ich habe es tun –,*** I have had to do it; ***ich habe es nicht tun –,*** I haven't had to do it, I didn't have to do it; ***ich hätte es*** (***nicht***) ***tun –,*** I ought (not) to have done it.
Mußestunde ['mu:səʃtundə], *f.* leisure-hour, spare time.
müßig ['my:sɪç], *adj.* idle; vain, useless, futile, superfluous; ***-e Frage,*** idle question; ***sich*** (*Dat.*) ***-e Gedanken machen,*** speculate idly; ***-es Kapital,*** unproductive capital; ***es wäre –,*** it would not be worth while, it would be futile *or* superfluous. **müßigen,** *v.t.* (*only in*) ***sich gemüßigt sehen,*** find o.s. compelled, be left with no alternative but. **Müßiggang,** *m.* idleness, sloth, indolence; (*Prov.*) ***– ist aller Laster Anfang,*** idleness is the root of all evil; ***– ist des Teufels Ruhebank,*** the devil finds work for idle hands. **Müßiggänger,** *m.* idler, loafer
Mußpreuße ['musprɔysə], *m.* rative of region annexed by Prussia (*i.e. Hanover, Schleswig-Holstein*).
mußt [must], **mußte, müßte** ['mystə], *see* **müssen.**
Mußteil ['mustaɪl], (*Austr.*) **Musteil.** *m.* (**-s,** *pl.* **-e**) widow's portion.

Muster ['mustər], *n.* model, example, ideal, paragon; pattern, model, sample, specimen; type, design, pattern; standard, norm; – *ohne Wert,* sample with no commercial value; *sich (Dat.) zum – nehmen,* take as a model; *nach einem – arbeiten,* work to *or* from a pattern; *nach –,* according to pattern, as per sample.

Muster|beispiel, *n.* typical example (*für,* of). **–betrieb,** *m.* model plant. **–bild,** *n.* paragon, ideal. **–buch,** *n.* book of patterns. **–exemplar,** *n.* specimen copy. **mustergültig, musterhaft,** *adj.* model, exemplary, ideal, perfect; standard. **Muster|karte,** *f.* pattern-card, sample-card. **–klammer,** *f.* paper-fastener. **–knabe,** *m.* model boy, prig. **–koffer,** *m.* sample-bag. **–kollektion,** *f.* range of samples. **–lager,** *n.* showroom(s); stock of samples. **–leistung,** *f.* splendid achievement, record.

mustern ['mustərn], *v.t.* 1. survey, examine (critically), inspect, scrutinize, muster; (*Mil.*) (pass in) review, inspect; 2. figure, pattern; *gemusterter Stoff,* patterned *or* figured material.

Muster|prozeß, *m.* (*Law*) test case. **–schule,** *f.* model school. **–schüler,** *m.* model pupil. **–schutz,** *m.* registered design, trademark, patent, copyright. **–sendung,** *f.* parcel of samples. **–stück,** *n.* model, pattern, specimen; perfect example.

Musterung ['mustəruŋ], *f.* 1. inspection, scrutiny, (critical) examination; (*Mil.*) inspection, review; 2. (*Weav.*) pattern, design. **Musterungs|bescheid,** *m.* recruitment order. **–kommission,** *f.* recruiting board.

Muster|wort, *n.* (*Gram.*) paradigm. **–zeichner,** *m.* pattern-maker, designer. **–zeichnung,** *f.* design, pattern.

Mut [mu:t], *m.* courage, valour, gallantry, daring, (*coll.*) pluck; prowess, fortitude, heart, spirit, (*coll.*) grit; *angetrunkener –,* Dutch courage; – *fassen,* summon up *or* (*coll.*) pluck up courage, take heart; *ihm – machen,* fill *or* inspire him with courage; *ihm neuen – einflößen,* reassure him; *ihm den – nehmen,* discourage *or* dishearten him; *den – sinken lassen,* lose heart *or* courage, be discouraged, despair; *guten –es sein,* be of good cheer, be full of hope; *mich verließ der –,* my heart sank into my boots; *nur nicht den – verlieren!* keep up your courage! don't lose heart! never say die! (*coll.*) keep your chin up! (*see* **zumute**).

Mütchen ['my:tçən], *n. sein – kühlen an (Dat.),* vent one's anger *or* spite on, (*coll.*) take it out on.

muten ['mu:tən], *v.t.* demand, sue for, claim; (*Min.*) (*um*) *eine Grube –,* stake a claim; (*Hist.*) *das Meisterstück –,* submit a masterpiece to one's guild. **Muter,** *m.* petitioner, claimant.

mutieren [mu'ti:rən], *v.i.* (*of voice*) break.

mutig ['mu:tıç], *adj.* courageous, brave, gallant, daring, valiant, stout-hearted, (*coll.*) plucky, game; *–!* courage! (*Prov.*) *dem Mutigen gehört die Welt,* Fortune favours the brave.

Mutjahr ['mu:tja:r], *n.* (*obs.*) journeyman's travel year.

mutlos ['mu:tlo:s], *adj.* despondent, discouraged, dejected, disheartened. **Mutlosigkeit,** *f.* despondency, discouragement, dejection.

mutmaßen ['mu:tma:sən], *v.t.* (*insep.*) have an idea of, guess, suppose, presume, surmise, conjecture. **mutmaßlich,** *adj.* probable, conjectural, presumable, supposed, apparent, (*partic. Law*) putative, presumptive. **Mutmaßung,** *f.* guess, surmise, conjecture, supposition, suspicion; speculation, guesswork. **mutmaßungsweise,** *adv.* at *or* as a guess.

[1]**Mutter** ['mutər], *f.* (-, *pl.* ¨) mother, (*of animals*) dam; (*Found.*) matrix; *sie fühlt sich –,* she is pregnant, she is with child; *ledige –,* unmarried mother; *werdende –,* expectant mother; *zur – machen,* put in the family way; *bei – Grün übernachten,* sleep *or* pass the night in the open; *sie wird –,* she is going to become a mother, she is having a child; *–s Geburtstag,* mother's birthday; (*coll.*) *er hat's dort wie bei seiner –,* he is treated as one of the family.

[2]**Mutter,** *f.* (-, *pl.* **-n**) (*Tech.*) (screw-)nut, female screw.

Mütterberatungsstelle ['mytərbəra:tuŋsʃtɛlə], *f.* maternity centre, ante-natal clinic.

Mutter|boden, *m.* native soil, (*Med.*) parent tissue, matrix. **–bruder,** *m.* maternal uncle. **–brust,** *f.* mother's breast.

Mütterchen ['mytərçən], *n.* (*coll.*) old woman, granny.

Mutter|erde, *f.* garden mould, top-soil, (*fig.*) native soil. **–freuden,** *f.pl.* joys of motherhood; – *entgegensehen,* be expecting, be in a certain condition. **–füllen,** *n.* filly. **–fürsorge,** *f.* maternity welfare. **–gesellschaft,** *f.* (*Comm.*) parent company. **–gewinde,** *n.* (*Tech.*) female thread. **–gottes,** *f.* Blessed Virgin. **–hals,** *m.* neck of the uterus. **–kalb,** *n.* heifer calf. **–kind,** *n.* mother's pet *or* darling, spoilt child, (*coll.*) sissy. **–kirche,** *f.* mother church. **–kompaß,** *m.* master compass. **–korn,** *n.* (**-s,** *pl.* **-e**) ergot. **–kuchen,** *m.* placenta. **–lamm,** *n.* ewe lamb. **–land,** *n.* mother country. **–lauge,** *f.* mother-lye, mother-liquor. **–leib,** *m.* womb, uterus; *vom –e an,* from birth.

mütterlich ['mytərlıç], *adj.* motherly, maternal. **mütterlicherseits,** *adv.* on *or* from the mother's side, (*as uncle*) maternal. **Mütterlichkeit,** *f.* motherliness.

Mutterliebe ['mutərli:bə], *f.* motherly love, mother-love. **mutterlos,** *adj.* motherless. **Mutter|mal,** *n.* (-, *pl.* **-e**) birthmark, mole. **–milch,** *f.* mother's milk; *mit der – einsaugen,* have bred in the bone, imbibe from earliest infancy. **–mord,** *m.* matricide (*act*). **–mörder,** *m.* matricide (*person*). **–mund,** *m.* orifice of the uterus.

Mutternschlüssel ['mutərnʃlysəl], *m.* spanner, wrench.

Mutter|pferd, *n.* mare. **–pflicht,** *f.* maternal duty. **–schaf,** *n.* ewe. **Mutterschaft,** *f.* motherhood, maternity. **Mutter|scheide,** *f.* vagina. **–schiff,** *n.* parent ship, depot ship. **–schmerz,** *m.* (*Med.*) hysteralgia. **–schoß,** *m.* mother's lap, (*fig.*) womb. **–schraube,** *f.* nut, female screw. **–schutz,** *m.* ante-natal care. **–schwein,** *n.* sow. **–schwester,** *f.* maternal aunt. **mutterseelenallein,** *pred.adj., adv.* quite *or* utterly *or* all alone. **Mutter|söhnchen,** *n.* mother's darling (boy); spoilt child, mollycoddle. **–spiegel,** *m.* (*Med.*) uterine speculum. **–sprache,** *f.* mother tongue, native language. **–stand,** *m.* maternity. **–stelle,** *f.* – *vertreten bei* or *an* (*Dat.*), be a (second) mother to. **–substanz,** *f.* matrix, stroma. **–tag,** *m.* Mother's Day, Mothering Sunday. **–teil,** *m.* maternal inheritance *or* portion. **–trompete,** *f.* Fallopian tube. **–uhr,** *f.* master clock.

Mütterverschickung ['mytərfɛrʃıkuŋ], *f.* evacuation of expectant mothers (*from air-raids*).

Mutter|witz, *m.* mother-wit, common sense, (*coll.*) gumption. **–zelle,** *f.* parent cell.

Mutti ['muti], *f.* (*coll.*) mummy, mama.

Mutung ['mu:tuŋ], *f.* (*Min.*) claim; appeal, application (*for a concession*).

Mutwille ['mu:tvılə], *m.* mischievousness, playfulness, devilry, wantonness. **mutwillig,** 1. *adj.* mischievous, playful; wanton, malicious; *–e Beschädigung,* wanton damage. 2. *adv. sich – in Gefahr stürzen,* rush headlong *or* blindly into danger.

Mütze ['mytsə], *f.* cap; (*Bot.*) calyptra; (*dial.*) reticulum (*of ruminants*); (*fig.*) *die – vor ihm abziehen,* take one's hat off to him; (*coll.*) *das war ihm nicht nach der –,* that did not suit him, he did not like that; (*Naut.*) *eine – Wind,* a capful of wind. **Mützen|band,** *n.* chin strap. **–schild,** *n.,* **–schirm,** *m.* peak (*of a cap*).

Myriade [myri'a:də], *f.* myriad.

Myrrhe ['myrə], *f.* myrrh.

Myrte ['myrtə], *f.* myrtle; *eine jungfräuliche –,* a bridal wreath.

mysteriös [mysteri'ø:s], *adj.* mysterious. **Mysterium** [–'ste:rium], *n.* (**-s,** *pl.* **-rien**) mystery. **mystifizieren** [–ifi'tsi:rən], *v.t.* mystify.

Mystik ['mystık], *f.* mystics, mysticism. **Mystiker,**

m. mystic. **mystisch,** *adj.* mystic(al). **Mystizismus** [–'tsɪsmus], *m.* mysticism.

Mythe ['my:tə], *f.* myth, fable. **mythenhaft, mythisch,** *adj.* mythical. **Mythologie** [–tolo'gi:], *f.* mythology. **mythologisch** [–'lo:gɪʃ], *adj.* mythological. **Mythos, Mythus,** *m.* (-, *pl.* **-then**) *see* **Mythe.**

N

N, n [ɛn], N, n. (*See Index of Abbreviations.*)

na! [na], *int.* well! (come) now! – ***also!*** what did I tell you! there you are! – ***gut!*** all right! if that's what you think! –***!*** –***!*** come (now)! take it easy! – (***und***) ***ob!*** I should think so! rather! most certainly! (*sl.*) and how! – ***und?*** what of it? so what? – ***so was!*** did you ever hear such a thing! oh, nonsense!

Nabe ['na:bə], *f.* nave, hub (*of a wheel*), boss (*of a propeller*).

Nabel ['na:bəl], *m.* (**-s,** *pl.* - *or* ⸚) navel, (*Bot.*) hilum; umbo, boss (*of a shield*); (*Her.*) nombril. **Nabel|binde,** *f.* navel-bandage. **–bruch,** *m.* omphalocele. **nabelförmig,** *adj.* umbilicate. **Nabel|schnur,** *f.*, **–strang,** *m.* umbilical cord, funiculus.

Naben|bremse, *f.* hub brake. **–haube, –kappe,** *f.* hub cap.

nach [na:x], **1.** *prep.* (*Dat.*)
(a) (*precedes the word it governs*) (*time and place*) after, following, (*place*) behind; ***ein Viertel – fünf,*** a quarter past five; – ***einer Woche,*** a week later, after a week; – ***20 Minuten,*** in 20 minutes; – ***10 Jahren,*** 10 years from now, in 10 years; – ***Tisch,*** after the meal; ***im Jahre 600 – Christi Geburt,*** in the year 600 of our Lord; (*Comm.*) – ***Empfang des Gegenwärtigen,*** on receipt of this.
(b) (*oft. followed by adv. or adv. pref.* ***hin*** *or* ***zu***) towards, to, (bound) for; ***die Flucht – Ägypten,*** the flight into Egypt; – ***Deutschland bestimmte Postsendungen,*** the mails for Germany; ***die Jagd – dem Glück,*** the pursuit of happiness; – ***Hause,*** home(wards); – ***oben,*** upwards, (*Poet.*) on high; – ***rechts,*** to(wards) the right; – ***Süden,*** towards the south, southwards; – ***Deutschland reisen,*** go to Germany; – ***Deutschland abreisen,*** leave for Germany; ***dieser Zug fährt – Hamburg,*** this train is (bound) for Hamburg; – ***der Straße hin,*** facing the street; – ***jeder Richtung,*** in every direction, in all directions; – ***dem Arzt schicken,*** send for the doctor.
(c) (*sometimes follows the word it governs*) in accordance *or* conformity with, according to; as regards, considering; after the manner of; on the authority of; – ***allem was ich höre,*** as far as my information goes, according to all that I hear; ***seinem Aussehen –,*** to judge by his appearance; – ***Bedarf,*** as required; – ***Belieben,*** at one's discretion; – ***dem Englischen übersetzt,*** translated from the English; – ***dem Gedächtnis,*** from memory; – ***meinem Geschmack,*** to my taste; – ***dem französischen Geschmack,*** in the French style *or* fashion *or* manner; ***sich – dem Gesetz richten,*** conform to the law; – ***den bestehenden Gesetzen,*** under existing laws; – ***dem Gewicht,*** by weight; ***meiner Meinung –,*** in my opinion; ***nur dem Namen –,*** by name only; – ***der Natur zeichnen,*** draw from nature; – ***Noten spielen,*** play from music; ***der Reihe –,*** in turn, by turns; – ***meiner Uhr,*** by my watch; – ***seiner Weise,*** in his (usual) way; – ***bestem Wissen,*** to the best of one's knowledge; – ***Wunsch,*** as one desires.
(d) (*in idiomatic association with verbs*) *e.g.* ***fragen –,*** ask for, inquire about; ***riechen*** (***schmecken***) ***–,*** smell (taste) of; ***schreien –,*** cry for; ***werfen –,*** throw at; *etc. See the relevant verbs.*
2. *adv.* after, behind; – ***und*** –, gradually, little by little, by degrees; – ***wie vor,*** as usual, the same as ever *or* before, now as ever, still; ***mir –!*** follow me! after me!

nach–, Nach–, *pref.* (*may be added to most verbs and many abstract nouns formed from verbs. Compounds not found below should be derived by adding the notion of 'after' in time or space to the simplex*).

Nachachtung ['na:xˀaxtuŋ], *f.* ***Ihnen zur –,*** for your guidance.

nachäffen ['na:xˀɛfən], *v.t.* ape, mimic; *see* **nachahmen. Nach|äfferei, –äffung,** *f.* aping, mimicry.

nachahmen ['na:xˀa:mən], *v.t.* imitate, copy; simulate; ***ihn –,*** imitate *or* copy him; ***ihn – in*** (*Dat.*), imitate him in, follow his example in; ***nachgeahmt,*** imitated, copied, counterfeit, artificial, spurious. **nachahmenswert,** *adj.* worthy of imitation, worth imitating, exemplary. **Nachahmer,** *m.* imitator, copyist, (*coll.*) copy-cat. **Nachahmung,** *f.* imitation, copy; counterfeit, fake; imitation, copying, emulation. **Nachahmungstrieb,** *m.* imitative instinct.

Nacharbeit ['na:xˀarbaɪt], *f.* extra work; subsequent *or* additional work, retouching, finishing; repair, maintenance; copy, replica. **nacharbeiten, 1.** *v.t.* copy, follow (*a pattern*); work over, touch up, put the finishing touches to (*unsatisfactory work*); ***das Versäumte –,*** make up for lost time. **2.** *v.i.* (*Dat.*) work from *or* according to (*a pattern*), follow the example *or* guidance of (*an instructor*); do extra work, work after school.

nacharten ['na:xˀartən], *v.i.* (*aux.* s.) (*Dat.*) resemble, take after.

Nachbar ['naxba:r], *m.* (**-s** *or* **-n,** *pl.* **-n**) neighbour; ***nächster –,*** next-door neighbour. **Nachbar|-division,** *f.* (*Mil.*) flanking division. **–dorf,** *n.* neighbouring village. **–haus,** *n.* adjoining house, house next door. **–kanal,** *m.* (*Rad.*) adjacent channel. **–land,** *n.* neighbouring country. **nachbarlich, 1.** *adj.* neighbourly; neighbouring. **2.** *adv.* – ***verkehren mit,*** live on neighbourly terms with. **Nachbarschaft,** *f.* neighbourhood, vicinity, proximity; (*coll.*) neighbours; ***in der nächsten –,*** in the immediate neighbourhood; ***die ganze –,*** all the neighbours. **Nachbars|kind,** *n.* child next door. **–leute,** *pl.* neighbours. **Nachbar|staat,** *m.* neighbouring state. **–zimmer,** *n.* adjoining room.

Nach|bearbeitung, *f.* finishing, dressing. **–behandlung,** *f.* after-treatment.

nachbessern ['na:xbɛsərn], *v.t.* mend, repair, improve (on), touch up. **Nachbesserung,** *f.* repair, improvement, touching up.

nach|bestellen, *v.t.* order some more of *or* a fresh supply of, repeat the order for. **Nachbestellung,** *f.* repeat order.

nachbeten ['na:xbe:tən], *v.t.* repeat mechanically *or* (*coll.*) parrot-fashion.

nachbezahlen ['na:xbətsa:lən], *v.t.* pay afterwards; pay the rest. **Nachbezahlung,** *f.* subsequent *or* additional payment.

Nachbild ['na:xbɪlt], *n.* copy, imitation; (*Psych.*) after-image. **nachbilden,** *v.t.* copy, imitate, reproduce; counterfeit. **Nachbildung,** *f.* copy, imitation, reproduction; dummy, (*coll.*) mock-up; ***genaue –,*** replica, facsimile.

nachbleiben ['na:xblaɪbən], *irr.v.i.* (*aux.* s.) remain *or* lag behind; be left over; (*at school*) be kept in; – ***lassen,*** (*at school*) keep in; – ***müssen,*** (*at school*) have to stay in, be kept in. **nachbleibend,** *adj.* residual, residuary; redundant, superfluous. **Nachbleibsel,** *n.* remainder, remains, surplus.

nachblicken ['na:xblɪkən], *v.i.* (*Dat.*) look *or* gaze after, follow with one's eyes.

Nach|blüte, *f.* second blossom(ing), (*fig.*) aftermath. **–blutung,** *f.* secondary bleeding.

nachbrennen ['na:xbrɛnən], *irr.v.i.* smoulder. **Nachbrenner,** *m.* (*Artil.*) hangfire.

nachbringen ['na:xbrɪŋən], *irr.v.t.* supply (subsequently *or* as an afterthought), supplement with.

Nach|bürge, -bürgschaft, *f.* collateral surety.

nachdatieren ['na:xdati:rən], *v.t.* postdate (*letter etc.*).

nachdem [na:x'de:m], **1.** *adv.* after that, afterwards, subsequently; (*coll.*) ***je –***, that depends, according to circumstances. **2.** *conj.* (*time*) after, when; (*degree*) (*je*) –, depending on, according as; ***je – es sich trifft,*** according to (the) circumstances, as the case may be, depending on how it turns out.

nachdenken ['na:xdɛŋkən], *irr.v.i.* muse, meditate, reflect (*über* (*Acc.*), on), ponder, cogitate, (*coll.*) mull (over), think (about *or* over), consider; ***denk mal nach!*** think it over! try to think back! **Nachdenken,** *n.* reflection, meditation, contemplation, deep thought, musing. **nachdenklich,** *adj.* reflective, contemplative, meditative, thoughtful, pensive, lost in thought; (*of a th.*) thought-provoking; ***ihn – machen,*** set him thinking.

Nachdichtung ['na:xdɪçtuŋ], *f.* paraphrase, free rendering.

nachdrängen ['na:xdrɛŋən], *v.i.* (*Dat.*) push *or* press *or* crowd after; pursue closely, follow eagerly.

Nachdruck ['na:xdruk], *m.* 1. stress, emphasis; force, vigour, energy; ***mit –,*** forcefully, energetically, emphatically; ***– legen auf*** (*Acc.*), lay stress on, stress, emphasize; 2. (*Typ.*) reprint(ing), reproduction (*of a book*), pirated edition; ***– verboten,*** all rights reserved. **nachdrucken,** *v.t.* reprint; pirate (*a book*). **Nachdrucker,** *m.* piratical printer *or* publisher, literary pirate. **nachdrücklich, 1.** *adj.* emphatic, forcible, energetic, vigorous. **2.** *adv.* ***– sagen,*** state emphatically; ***– handeln,*** act forcibly *or* vigorously; ***– empfehlen,*** urge (*Dat.*, upon); ***– verlangen,*** insist on, make a point of; ***– abraten von,*** strongly advise against. **Nachdrucksrecht,** *n.* copyright. **nachdrucksvoll,** *adj. See* **nachdrücklich.**

nachdunkeln ['na:xduŋkəln], *v.i.* darken, deepen, grow darker, (*Dye.*) sadden.

Nacheiferer ['na:xˀaɪfərər], *m.* rival, emulator. **nacheifern,** *v.i.* (*Dat.*) emulate; vie *or* compete with. **Nacheiferung,** *f.* emulation.

nacheilen ['na:xˀaɪlən], *v.i.* (*aux.* s.) 1. hurry *or* hasten after; 2. (*Elec.*) lag.

nacheinander ['na:xˀaɪnandər], *adv.* one after another, successively, in turn(s); ***fünf Tage –,*** for five days running *or* on end.

nachempfinden ['na:xˀɛmpfɪndən], **1.** *irr.v.t.* enter into, have a feeling for. **2.** *irr.v.i. See* **nachfühlen.**

Nachen ['na:xən], *m.* (small) boat, skiff.

Nach|erbe, *m.* (*Law*) reversionary heir; ***ihm als –n zufallen,*** revert to him. **-erbenrecht,** *n.* (right of) reversion. **-ernte,** *f.* second crop, aftermath.

nacherzählen ['na:xˀɛrtsɛ:lən], *v.t.* retell, repeat; ***dem Englischen nacherzählt,*** adapted from the English; ***Schlimmes wird ihm nacherzählt,*** awful things are being said about him. **Nacherzählung,** *f.* (free) adaptation.

nachexerzieren ['na:xˀɛksɛrtsi:rən], *v.i.* (*Mil.*) do extra drill; (*coll.*) go on after (all) the others have finished.

Nachfahr ['na:xfa:r], *m.* (**-s** *or* **-en,** *pl.* **-en**) (*Poet.*) successor, descendant. **nachfahren,** *irr.v.i.* (*aux.* s.) (*Dat.*) follow, come on after.

nach|färben, *v.t.* add colour to; re-dye, re-dip. **-fassen,** *v.t., v.i.* have a second helping (of). **-feiern,** *v.t., v.i.* celebrate after the event. **-feilen,** *v.t.* (*fig.*) retouch, put the finishing touch(es) to.

Nachfolge ['na:xfɔlgə], *f.* sequence; succession (*in office etc.*), (*Law*) reversion; ***– Christi,*** Imitation of Christ. **nachfolgen,** *v.i.* (*aux.* s.) (*Dat.*) follow, pursue, succeed (*in office*), (*fig.*) follow the example *or* in the steps of, emulate, imitate. **nachfolgend,** *adj.* following; undermentioned; ***im –en,*** in the following, (*Law*) hereinafter. **Nachfolger,** *m.* follower, successor; ***als – von,*** in succession to. **Nachfolgerschaft,** *f.* successors. **Nachfolgestaaten,** *m.pl.* succession states.

nachfordern ['na:xfɔrdərn], *v.t.* charge extra, claim subsequently. **Nachforderung,** *f.* extra charge, subsequent claim.

nachforschen ['na:xfɔrʃən], *v.i.* inquire *or* look into, make inquiries, investigate, conduct an investigation; search for, make inquiries about (*a p.*). **Nachforschung,** *f.* inquiry, investigation, search, quest; ***-en anstellen,*** *see* **nachforschen.**

Nachfrage ['na:xfra:gə], *f.* inquiry; (*Comm.*) demand (***nach,*** for); ***Angebot und –,*** supply and demand. **Nachfragebelebung,** *f.* rise in demand. **nachfragen,** *v.i.* inquire (***nach,*** after *or* about), ask (after).

Nachfrist ['na:xfrɪst], *f.* respite, extension (of time).

nachfühlen ['na:xfy:lən], *v.t.* feel for *or* with, sympathize with, enter into *or* understand (*a p.'s*) feelings; ***ich kann es ihm recht –,*** I know well what he must have felt, I can share his feelings.

nachfüllen ['na:xfylən], *v.t.* refill, replenish, fill *or* (*coll.*) top up.

Nachgärung ['na:xgɛ:ruŋ], *f.* secondary fermentation.

nachgeben ['na:xge:bən], *irr.v.i.* (*Dat.*) give way *or* in, yield, submit (to), comply (with); humour, indulge (*a p.*); (*of a th.*) slacken, relax, (*coll.*) give; (*Comm.*) (*of the market*) slacken, decline; ***ihm nichts –,*** be in no way inferior to him.

nachgeboren ['na:xgəbo:rən], *adj.* posthumous (*of a p.*).

Nach|gebühr, *f.* excess postage, surcharge, postage due. **-geburt,** *f.* placenta, afterbirth.

nachgehen ['na:xge:ən], *irr.v.i.* (*aux.* s.) (*Dat.*) go after, follow, be behind; (*of clocks*) be slow, lose; pursue, follow (*line of inquiry, career etc.*), attend to, apply o.s. to, mind (*one's business*), indulge in, be addicted to (*pleasures etc.*), investigate, look *or* inquire into, check, trace, (*coll.*) follow up (*problems etc.*); (*coll.*) ***es geht ihm nach,*** it preys on his mind, he can't get over it. **nachgehends,** *adv.* afterwards, subsequently, hereafter.

nach|gelassen, *adj.* posthumous (*work*). **-gemacht,** *adj.* imitation, artificial, false, fake, counterfeit, bogus, sham, (*coll.*) phoney. **-geordnet,** *adj.* subordinate. **-genannt,** *adj.* undermentioned. **-gerade,** *adv.* gradually, at length, by degrees; by this time, by now, after all; really, in fact. **Nach|gesang,** *m.* (*Pros.*) epode. **-geschmack,** *m.* aftertaste. **nachgewiesenermaßen,** *adv.* as has been shown *or* proved.

nachgiebig ['na:xgi:bɪç], *adj.* 1. pliable, flexible, elastic; yielding, compliant, tractable; complaisant, indulgent, forebearing, obliging, easy-going (*gegen,* to(wards)); 2. (*Comm.*) declining. **Nachgiebigkeit,** *f.* pliability, flexibility, elasticity; compliance, complaisance, tractability, indulgence.

nach|gießen, *irr.v.t., v.i. See* **-füllen. -glühen, 1.** *v.t.* temper, anneal. **2.** *v.i.* smoulder. **-grübeln,** *v.i.* ponder *or* brood (*Dat. or* ***über*** (*Acc.*), over), muse (on).

Nachhall ['nax:hal], *m.* echo, reverberation; resonance; (*fig.*) response. **nachhallen,** *v.i.* echo, resound, reverberate.

nachhaltig ['na:xhaltɪç], *adj.* lasting, enduring, sustained, protracted, persistent; strong, vigorous, effective.

Nachhang ['na:xhaŋ], *m.* postscript, addendum. **nach|hangen, -hängen,** *irr.v.i.* 1. (*Dat.*) give o.s. up to, give way to, indulge in, be addicted to; ***seinen Gedanken –,*** be immersed in one's thoughts, be lost in thought, give free play to one's thoughts; 2. (*space*) lag behind, hang back.

Nachhausegehen [na:x'hauzəge:ən], *n.* ***beim –,*** on the way *or* walk home.

nachhelfen ['na:xhɛlfən], *irr.v.i.* (*Dat.*) lend a helping hand, help (on), assist, (*coll.*) egg on, give a leg-up.

nachher ['na:xhe:r, na:x'he:r], *adv.* afterwards, after that, later (on), then, subsequently, hereafter, thereafter; (*coll.*) ***bis –!*** see you later! so long! **nachherig,** *adj.* subsequent, following, ensuing, later, future; posterior.

Nachhilfe ['na:xhɪlfə], *f.* aid, help, assistance. **Nachhilfe|kurs(us),** *m.* supplementary course. **–lehrer,** *m.* private tutor, coach. **–stunden,** *f.pl.*, **–unterricht,** *m.* private tuition *or* lessons, (private) coaching.

nachhinken ['na:xhɪŋkən], *v.i.* (*aux.* s.) (*Dat.*) hobble *or* limp along behind, (*usu. fig.*) lag behind. **Nachhinken,** *n.* time-lag.

Nachholbedarf ['na:xho:lbədarf], *m.* backlog. **nachholen,** *v.t.* bring *or* fetch later, (*fig.*) retrieve, make good, make up for (*s.th. omitted*), do *or* finish later (*a task*).

Nachhut ['na:xhu:t], *f.* rearguard; ***den – bilden,*** bring up the rear. **Nachhutgefecht,** *n.* rearguard action.

Nachimpfung ['na:xʔɪmpfuŋ], *f.* re-vaccination, re-inoculation.

nachjagen ['na:xja:gən], **1.** *v.i.* (*aux.* s.) (*Dat.*) chase, pursue. **2.** *v.t.* (*coll.*) send after (*bullet, telegram etc.*).

Nachklang ['na:xklaŋ], *m.* echo, reverberation, resonance, (*fig.*) reminiscence; after-effect.

nachklingen ['na:xklɪŋən], *irr.v.i.* (re-)echo, reverberate, resound; linger in one's ear.

Nachkomme ['na:xkɔmə], *m.* (**-n,** *pl.* **-n**) descendant, offspring, successor, (*Law*) issue; ***ohne –n,*** without issue. **nachkommen,** *irr.v.i.* (*aux.* s.) (*Dat.*) come after, come later, follow (on); overtake, come up with; keep up with, keep pace with; (*fig.*) comply with, accede to, grant (*a wish*), comply with, adhere to, observe, fulfil, obey, (*coll.*) act up to (*instructions*), meet (*obligations*), keep (*promises*); ***ich komme in fünf Minuten nach,*** I'll join you in five minutes. **Nachkommenschaft,** *f.* descendants, posterity, offspring, progeny, (*Law*) issue. **Nachkömmling,** *m.* (**-s,** *pl.* **-e**) descendant; later child.

Nachkriegs– ['na:xkri:ks–], *pref.* post-war, *e.g.* **–jahre,** *n.pl.*, **–zeit,** *f.* post-war period.

Nachkur ['na:xku:r], *f.* after-treatment; rest after treatment, convalescence.

nachladen ['na:xla:dən], *irr.v.t.* recharge (*battery etc.*).

Nachlaß ['na:xlas], *m.* (**-(ss)es,** *pl.* **-(ss)e** *or* **¨-(ss)e**) 1. remission (*of sentence*), reduction, abatement; rebate, allowance, discount (*of charges*); ***unter – von,*** allowing, deducting; 2. legacy, heritage; deceased's remains *or* estate *or* assets; residue of inheritance; literary remains, posthumous works (*of author*).

nachlassen ['na:xlasən], **1.** *irr.v.t.* 1. loosen, slacken, relax, (*coll.*) let go; 2. (*Comm.*) make a reduction of, allow (a discount of); 3. (*Law*) bequeath, devise, (*coll.*) leave (behind). **2.** *irr.v.i.* decrease, diminish, decline, subside, abate, slacken, grow less, fall *or* ease off, slow down; weaken, deteriorate, wane, flag, ebb, fail, give way; cease, (*coll.*) give over; (*of prices*) drop, fall, sag; (*coll.*) ***laß doch nach!*** do stop! give over! ***nicht –!*** keep it up! keep at it! don't give up! **Nachlassen,** *n.* relaxation; decrease, diminution, reduction, abatement, subsidence, weakening, flagging; cessation, (*coll.*) let-up.

Nachlaßgericht ['na:xlasgərɪct], *n.* (*Law*) probate court.

nachlässig ['na:xlɛsɪç], *adj.* neglectful (*in* (*Dat.*), of), negligent, careless, remiss, lax, (*coll.*) slack (about); slovenly, slipshod, (*coll.*) sloppy. **Nachlässigkeit,** *f.* negligence, carelessness, laxity, slovenliness; neglect, remissness, indolence.

Nachlaß|pfleger, *m. See* **–verwalter. –steuer,** *f.* death duty, (*Am.*) inheritance tax. **–verwalter,** *m.* executor.

Nachlauf ['na:xlauf], *m.* last drips, (*distilling*) tails. **nachlaufen,** *irr.v.i.* (*aux.* s.) (*Dat.*) follow, run after; (*fig.*) ***den Mädchen –,*** run after the girls.

nach|leben, *v.i.* (*Dat.*) observe, conform to, live up to. **–legen,** *v.i.* make up *or* stoke the fire, put on more coal.

Nachlese ['na:xle:zə], *f.* gleaning; gleanings; (*fig.*) second sorting; (*Lit.*) supplement, addendum.

nachlesen, *irr.v.t., v.i.* glean; re-read, read over (again); look up (*in a book*).

nachliefern ['na:xli:fərn], *v.t.* supply *or* deliver subsequently, make a further delivery; (add as a) supplement. **Nachlieferung,** *f.* subsequent delivery; supplement.

nachlösen ['na:xlø:zən], **1.** *v.i.* take a supplementary ticket. **2.** *v.t.* ***eine Fahrkarte –,*** *see* **1.**

nachmachen ['na:xmaxən], *v.t.* copy, imitate, mimic; counterfeit, fake, forge; ***mach es mir nach!*** do (the same) as I do! ***das soll mir einer –,*** I defy anyone to do *or* I'd like to see anyone do as well *or* do any better; ***nachgemachte Blumen,*** artificial *or* imitation flowers.

Nachmahd ['na:xma:t], *f.* (*dial.*) aftermath.

nachmalig ['na:xma:lɪç], *adj.* subsequent. **nachmals,** *adv.* subsequently, afterwards, later on.

nachmessen ['na:xmɛsən], *irr.v.t.* re-measure, measure again, check (the measurements of).

Nachmittag ['na:xmɪta:k], *m.* (**-(e)s,** *pl.* **-e**) afternoon. **nachmittags,** *adv.* in the afternoon. **Nachmittags|schläfchen,** *n.* afternoon nap, siesta. **–vorstellung,** *f.* afternoon performance, matinée.

Nachnahme ['na:xna:mə], *f.* cash *or* (*Am.*) collect on delivery (*abbr.* C.O.D.); ***gegen*** *or* (*coll.*) ***per –,*** C.O.D.; ***unter – Ihrer Spesen,*** carrying your charges forward. **Nachnahme|gebühr,** *f.* C.O.D. charge, collection fee. **–sendung,** *f.* C.O.D. parcel.

Nachname ['na:xna:mə], *m.* surname, last name.

nachnehmen ['na:xne:mən], *irr.v.t.* charge forward, collect (charges) on delivery.

nachordnen ['na:xʔɔrdnən], *v.t.* subordinate, place subordinate to.

nachplappern ['na:xplapərn], *v.t.* repeat mechanically *or* parrot-fashion.

Nachporto ['na:xpɔrto:], *n.* (**-s,** *pl.* **-s** *or* **-ti**) postage due, surcharge, excess postage.

nachprüfbar ['na:xpry:fba:r], *adj.* verifiable. **nachprüfen,** *v.t.* check, verify, make sure about; inspect, investigate, examine; (*Law*) review. **Nachprüfung,** *f.* check, verification; inspection, investigation, examination, test(ing); (*Law*) review(al); (*Univ. etc.*) re-examination, (*coll.*) re-sit.

nachrechnen ['na:xrɛçnən], *v.t.* check (the working), add up again.

Nachrede ['na:xre:də], *f.* 1. (*Law*) defamation (of character), slander, libel; ***üble –,*** vile gossip; ***in üble – bringen,*** bring into disrepute, cast aspersions on; 2. (*Theat.*) epilogue. **nachreden,** *v.t., v.i.* repeat (*what has been said*); ***Übles –*** (*Dat.*), *see* ***in üble Nachrede bringen.***

nach|reichen, *v.i.* serve second helpings. **–reifen,** *v.i.* ripen in storage.

Nachricht ['na:xrɪçt], *f.* (-, *pl.* **-en**) news, message, communication, report, account, notice, advice, (*Mil.*) intelligence, (*Poet.*) tidings; ***eine –,*** a piece of news; ***letzte –en,*** stop-press (news); ***– bekommen von,*** receive news *or* (*coll.*) get word from, hear from; ***– geben,*** inform, advise, send word *or* news, let (*a p.*) know (***über*** (*Acc.*), ***von,*** of *or* about).

Nachrichten|abteilung, *f.* (*Mil.*) signals unit. **–agentur,** *f.* news *or* press agency. **–amt,** *n.* intelligence department. **–blatt,** *n.* information sheet, gazette, bulletin. **–büro,** *n. See* **–agentur. –dienst,** *m.* (*Press, Rad.*) news service; (*Mil.*) signals, intelligence. **–helferin,** *f.* (German Air Force) woman auxiliary. **–netz,** *n.* communications network. **–offizier,** *m.* (*Mil.*) intelligence officer. **–sendung,** *f.* (*Rad.*) news broadcast. **–sperre,** *f.* ban on news, news black-out. **–sprecher,** *m.* (*Rad.*) news-reader, newscaster. **–stelle,** *f.* information centre. **–technik,** *f.* telecommunications engineering. **–truppe,** *f.* (*Mil.*) corps of signals. **–übersicht,** *f.* summary of the news. **–wesen,** *n.* communications (system). **–zentrale,** *f. See* **–stelle.**

nachrücken ['na:xrykən], *v.i.* (*aux.* s.) (*Dat.*) move on, follow; (*Mil.*) follow up; (*in rank*) move up.

Nachruf ['na:xru:f], *m.* obituary (notice), memorial address; in memoriam; posthumous fame. **nachrufen,** *irr.v.i.* (*Dat.*) shout *or* call after.

Nachruhm ['na:xru:m], *m.* posthumous fame. **nachrühmen,** *v.i.* (*Dat.*) say to (*a p.'s*) credit, say in praise of.

nachsagen ['na:xza:gən], **1.** *v.i.* (*Dat.*) credit with; ***man sagt ihm nach, daß er übermäßig trinkt,*** he has a reputation for excessive drinking, he is said to drink excessively; ***ich lasse es mir nicht –,*** I won't have it said about me (*see also* **nachreden**). **2.** *v.t. See* **nachplappern.**

Nach|saison, *f.* late season. **–satz,** *m.* 1. (*Log.*) minor proposition; 2. (*Gram.*) final clause; *see* **–schrift.**

nachschauen ['na:xʃauən], *v.i.* (go and) see, have a look; (*Dat.*) follow with one's eyes, gaze after; ***schau mal nach, ob er kommt,*** (look and) see if he is coming.

nach|schicken, *v.t. See* **–senden.**

nachschieben ['na:xʃi:bən], *irr.v.t.* (*Mil.*) send in (*reinforcements*). **Nachschieber,** *m.* (*Ent.*) caudal disk.

nachschießen ['na:xʃi:sən], *irr.v.t.* ***Gelder –,*** make further payments, pay an additional sum.

Nachschlag ['na:xʃla:k], *m.* 1. (*Mus.*) grace-note; 2. (*Boxing*) counter(-punch). **Nachschlage|buch,** *n.* work of reference, reference book. **nachschlagen, 1.** *irr.v.t.* consult, refer to (*a book*), look up (*a word in a book*). **2.** *irr.v.i.* 1. (*Boxing*) counter; 2. ***ihm –,*** take after him, resemble him. **Nachschlage|werk,** *n. See* **–buch.**

nach|schleichen, *irr.v.i.* (*Dat.*) steal *or* slink after, (*coll.*) shadow, tail. **–schleifen,** *irr.v.t.* regrind, reface, reseat (*valves etc.*). **–schleppen,** *v.t.* drag *or* trail after; (take in) tow.

Nachschlüssel ['na:xʃlysəl], *m.* master-key, skeleton key, picklock.

nachschreiben ['na:xʃraɪbən], *irr.v.t., v.i.* copy, transcribe, write out; write from dictation; take *or* write down.

Nachschrift ['na:xʃrɪft], *f.* 1. copy, transcript; 2. postscript.

Nachschub ['na:xʃu:p], *m.* (*Mil.*) replacements, reserves, reinforcements; (fresh) supply. **Nachschub|kolonne,** *f.* supply column *or* train. **–lager,** *n.* supply depot *or* dump. **–linie,** *f.*, **–weg,** *m.* line of communications.

Nach|schuß, *m. See* **–zahlung**; (*with loans*) additional cover. **nachschußpflichtig,** *adj.* contributory.

nachsehen ['na:xze:ən], **1.** *irr.v.i.* (*Dat.*) look *or* gaze after, follow with one's eyes; look and see, go and see, make sure, see to it; look up (*in a book*); *see* **nachschlagen. 2.** *irr.v.t.* 1. examine, inspect, check, revise, correct, overhaul, look over; 2. take no notice of, close one's eyes to, overlook, condone, pardon, excuse (***ihm etwas,*** s.th. in him). **Nachsehen,** *n.* ***das*** (***leere***) ***– haben,*** have (all) one's trouble for nothing; ***nun bleibt dir das –,*** now you may whistle for it; ***ihm das – geben,*** beat him to it, outdo *or* outpoint him.

Nachsendeanschrift ['na:xzɛndəˀanʃrɪft], *f.* forwarding address. **nachsenden,** *irr.v.t.* re-address, forward, send on (*letters*); ***bitte –!*** please forward!

nachsetzen ['na:xzɛtsən], **1.** *v.t.* 1. put *or* place behind; (*fig.*) think less of, consider inferior; 2. (*gambling*) increase one's stake. **2.** *v.i.* (*aux.* s.) (*Dat.*) pursue, chase; run *or* make after.

Nachsicht ['na:xzɪçt], *f.* indulgence, forbearance, leniency, patience; ***– üben,*** stretch a point, bear and forbear, make allowance(s) (***mit,*** for), have patience, be lenient (with), be indulgent (towards); ***ich bitte um –,*** I crave your indulgence. **nachsichtig, nachsichtsvoll,** *adj.* considerate, indulgent, lenient, forbearing, patient. **Nachsichtwechsel,** *m.* (*Comm.*) aftersight bill.

Nachsilbe ['na:xzɪlbə], *f.* (*Gram.*) suffix.

nach|sinnen, *irr.v.i.* reflect, meditate, muse (***über*** (*Acc.*), on), ponder (over). **–sitzen,** *irr.v.i.* (*in school*) – (***müssen***), be kept in; ***– lassen,*** keep in.

Nach|sommer, *m.* Indian *or* St. Martin's summer. **–speise,** *f.* dessert, sweet. **–spiel,** *n.* (*Theat.*) epilogue, (*Mus.*) voluntary, (*fig.*) sequel; ***das geht nicht ohne – ab,*** we haven't heard the last of it.

nachspüren ['na:xʃpy:rən], *v.i.* (*Dat.*) trace, track down, inquire into, investigate (*a th.*); spy on (*a p.*).

nächst [nɛ:çst], **1.** *adj.* (*sup. of* **nah**) next, following, nearest, closest, shortest; ***im –en Augenblick,*** the next moment; ***der –e beste,*** the first to hand; ***aus –er Entfernung,*** at (very) close range; ***bei –er Gelegenheit,*** at the first opportunity; ***im –en Haus,*** next door; ***das –e Mal,*** (the) next time; (*Comm.*) ***–en Monat(s),*** proximo; ***–en Sonntag,*** next Sunday, Sunday next; ***die –e Stadt,*** the nearest town; (*Comm.*) ***in unserem –en Schreiben,*** in our next; ***in den –en Tagen,*** in the next few days; ***die –en Verwandten,*** the nearest relatives, the next of kin; ***der –e Weg,*** the nearest *or* shortest way; ***in –er Zeit,*** in the near future, very soon; ***der –e Zweck,*** the immediate purpose. **2.** *adv.* ***am –en,*** next, nearest (*Dat.*, to); ***fürs –e,*** for the present, for the time being. **3.** *prep.* (*Dat.*) next to *or* after, close to. **nächstbest,** *adj.* second best, next best.

nachstehen ['na:xʃte:ən], *irr.v.i.* (*Dat.*) follow, come after; (*fig.*) be inferior to, fall short of; ***keinem –,*** be second to none; ***ihm in nichts –,*** be in no way inferior to him. **nachstehend,** *adj.* following, undermentioned; ***im –en,*** in the following, in what follows, (*Law*) hereinafter; ***wie – bemerkt,*** as mentioned below.

nachsteigen ['na:xʃtaɪgən], *irr.v.i.* (*aux.* s.) (*Dat.*) (*coll.*) go *or* be after, chase (*girls*).

nachstellbar ['na:xʃtɛlba:r], *adj.* adjustable. **nachstellen, 1.** *v.t.* adjust; put back (*a clock*); place after *or* behind. **2.** *v.i.* (*Dat.*) lie in wait for, waylay, (*coll.*) be after; set a trap for, lay a snare for; persecute, hound. **Nachstellschraube,** *f.* adjusting screw, screw adjustment. **Nachstellung,** *f.* 1. persecution; ambush, snare, trap ; 2. (*Tech.*) adjustment.

Nächstenliebe ['nɛ:çstənli:bə], *f.* (Christian) charity, love of one's fellow-man.

nächstens ['nɛ:çstəns], *adv.* (very) soon, shortly, before long, in the (very) near future. **Nächste(r),** *m., f.* fellow man *or* creature, (*B.*) neighbour; (*Prov.*) ***jeder ist sich selbst der Nächste,*** charity begins at home; ***das Nächste,*** the first *or* next *or* immediate th. **nächst|folgend,** *adj.* (immediately *or* next) following, succeeding, next (in order); ***am –en Tage,*** the next *or* following day, the day following. **–liegend,** *adj.* nearest (at hand).

Nachstoß ['na:xʃto:s], *m.* (*Fenc.*) riposte. **nachstoßen,** *irr.v.i.* (*Fenc.*) riposte, (*Mil.*) pursue, follow up, push forward.

nachstreben ['na:xʃtre:bən], *v.i.* (*Dat.*) strive after, aspire to (*a th.*), emulate (*a p.*).

Nächsttreffer ['nɛ:çsttrɛfər], *m.* near-hit, near-miss.

nachsuchen ['na:xzu:xən], *v.t., v.i.* search *or* look for; ***– um,*** apply *or* petition *or* sue for, request, seek, solicit. **Nachsuchung,** *f.* search, inquiry; petition, application, request.

Nacht [naxt], *f.* (-, *pl.* ¨**-e**) night; (*fig.*) darkness; ***bei –,*** in *or* during the night, at night; ***bei – und Nebel,*** under cover of darkness; (*Prov.*) ***bei – sind alle Katzen grau,*** all cats are grey in the dark; ***des –s,*** *see* ***bei –***; ***gute – sagen,*** bid goodnight; ***heute nacht,*** tonight; ***bis in die – arbeiten,*** burn the midnight oil; ***in der –,*** *see* ***bei –***; ***in tiefer –,*** at dead of night; ***mit einbrechender –,*** at nightfall; ***Märchen von 'Tausendundeiner –',*** the Arabian Nights; ***über –,*** overnight, (*fig.*) from one day to the next; quite suddenly, without warning; ***über – bleiben,*** stay the night; ***es wird –,*** it is growing *or* getting dark; ***es wurde mir – vor den Augen,*** everything went black; ***häßlich wie die –,*** as ugly as sin; ***zu – essen,*** have supper.

Nacht|angriff, *m.* night-attack. **–arbeit,** *f.* night-work. **–ausgabe,** *f.* late edition. **–blindheit,** *f.* night-blindness. **–blütler,** *m.* night-flowering plant. **–dienst,** *m.* night-service; night duty.

Nachteil ['na:xtaɪl], *m.* (**-s,** *pl.* **-e**) disadvantage, drawback, shortcoming; loss, detriment, prejudice; (*Spt., fig.*) handicap; ***im – sein,*** be at a disadvantage, be handicapped; ***zum – von allen Anwesenden,*** to the prejudice *or* disadvantage of everyone present; ***zum – gereichen*** (*Dat.*), prove a handicap *or* disadvantage to, be detrimental to; ***mit – verkaufen,*** sell at a loss; (*Law*) ***ohne – für,*** without prejudice to. **nachteilig, 1.** *adj.* disadvantageous, prejudicial, detrimental (***für,*** to); adverse, unfavourable, hurtful, derogatory. **2.** *adv.* ***– beeinflussen,*** affect adversely, prejudice; ***– sprechen,*** speak disparagingly *or* unfavourably.

nächtelang [ˈnɛçtəlaŋ], *adv.* night after night, for nights on end.

Nacht|essen, *n.* supper. **–falke,** *m.* (*Orn.*) nighthawk, (*Am.*) common nighthawk (*Chordeiles minor*). **–falter,** *m.* moth. **–flug,** *m.* night flight. **–gebet,** *n.* evening-prayer. **–geschirr,** *n.* chamber (-pot). **–gleiche,** *f.* equinox. **–haus,** *n.* (*Naut.*) binnacle. **–hemd,** *n.* nightshirt (*men*); night-dress, night-gown (*women*).

Nachtigall [ˈnaxtɪgal], *f.* (*Orn.*) nightingale (*Luscinia megarhynchos*). **Nachtigallschwirl,** *m. See* **Rohrschwirl.**

nächtigen [ˈnɛçtɪgən], *v.i.* pass *or* spend the night.

Nachtisch [ˈna:xtɪʃ], *m.* sweet, dessert.

Nacht|jäger, *m.* (*Av.*) night-fighter. **–kleid,** *n. See* **–hemd. –lager,** *n.* night's lodging, quarters, bed for the night; (*Mil.*) ***ein – aufschlagen,*** bivouac. **–leben,** *n.* night-life.

nächtlich [ˈnɛçtlɪç], *adj.* nightly, nocturnal. **nächtlicherweile,** *adv.* at night(-time).

Nacht|licht, *n.* night-light. **–lokal,** *n.* night-club. **–mahl,** *n.* (*Austr.*) supper. **nachtmahlen,** *v.i.* (*Austr.*) have supper. **Nacht|mahr,** *m.* nightmare. **–mette,** *f.* (*Eccl.*) nocturn. **–musik,** *f.* serenade. **–mütze,** *f.* night-cap, (*coll.*) dimwit, dolt. **–pfauenauge,** *n.* emperor-moth. **–quartier,** *n.* overnight accommodation, night quarters; ***ihm – geben,*** put him up for the night.

nachtönen [ˈna:xtø:nən], *v.i.* resound, (re-)echo, reverberate; linger in one's ear.

Nachtrab [ˈna:xtra:p], *m.* (*Mil.*) rear(guard). **nachtraben,** *v.i.* (*aux.* s.) (*Dat.*) follow at a trot, trot at (*a p.'s*) heels.

Nachtrag [ˈna:xtra:k], *m.* **(-(e)s,** *pl.* **⸚e)** supplement, postscript, addendum, (*Law*) codicil; *pl.* addenda. **nachtragen,** *irr.v.t.* carry after; add, append, make a supplementary entry; (*fig.*) ***es ihm –,*** bear him a grudge, resent him for it; ***es ihm nicht –,*** bear him no grudge, not hold it against him. **nachträgerisch,** *adj.* resentful, vindictive, rancorous. **nachträglich, 1.** *adj.* supplementary, additional; subsequent, extra, later; belated. **2.** *adv.* subsequently, later, further, by way of addition. **Nachtrags–,** *pref.* supplementary, additional, subsequent.

Nacht|reiher, *m.* (*Orn.*) night heron (*Nycticorax nycticorax*). **–ruhe,** *f.* sleep, night's rest. **–runde,** *f.* night-patrol.

nachts [naxts], *adv.* by *or* at night, in *or* during the night.

Nacht|schatten, *m.* (*Bot.*) nightshade (*Solanum*). **–schattengewächse,** *n.pl.* (*Bot.*) Solanaceae. **–schicht,** *f.* night shift. **nachtschlafend,** *adj.* (*coll.*) ***zu –er Zeit,*** when everyone is asleep, in the middle of the night. **Nacht|schwalbe,** *f. See* **Ziegenmelker. –schwärmer,** *m. See* **–falter**; (*fig.*) night-reveller, (*coll.*) fly-by-night. **–schwester,** *f.* night nurse. **–seite,** *f.* (*fig.*) dark *or* seamy side. **–sicht,** *f.* night vision. **–sitzung,** *f.* all-night sitting. **–stuhl,** *m.* night-stool, commode. **–tisch(chen),** *m.* (*n.*) bedside table. **–topf,** *m. See* **–geschirr. –übung,** *f.* (*Mil.*) night manœuvres.

nachtun [ˈna:xtu:n], *irr.v.t.* ***es ihm –,*** copy *or* imitate *or* emulate him; *see* **nachmachen.**

Nacht|viole, *f.* (*Bot.*) dame's violet. **–vorstellung,** *f.* (*Theat.*) midnight matinée. **–wache,** *f.* night-watch, vigil; ***– halten bei,*** keep vigil over. **–wächter,** *m.* night-watchman; (*coll.*) dolt, slowcoach; (*sl.*) ***unter dem –,*** beneath criticism. **nachtwandeln,** *v.i.* (*insep.*) walk in one's sleep. **Nacht|wandeln,** *n.* sleep-walking, somnambulism. **–wandler,** *m.* sleep-walker, somnambulist. **nachtwandlerisch,** *adj.* somnambulistic; (*fig.*) ***mit –er Sicherheit,*** with uncanny sureness, unerringly. **Nacht|zeug,** *n.* (*coll.*) night-clothes, night-things. **–zuschlag,** *m.* extra pay for night work.

Nach|untersuchung, *f.* follow-up, check-up. **–urlaub,** *m.* extension of leave. **–wahl,** *f.* by-election, (*Am.*) special election. **–wehen,** *f.pl.* (*Med.*) after-pains, (*fig.*) painful consequences, evil after-effects, aftermath.

nachweinen [ˈna:xvaɪnən], *v.t., v.i.* (*Dat.*) mourn over, lament *or* bewail the loss *or* death of; (*coll.*) ***ich werde ihm keine Träne –,*** I shan't be sorry to see him go, I shan't shed any tears over his departure.

Nachweis [ˈna:xvaɪs], *m.* **(-es,** *pl.* **-e)** proof, evidence; certificate, voucher, record; ***den – erbringen*** or ***führen,*** prove, furnish proof, demonstrate, show evidence. **nachweisbar, 1.** *adj.* provable, demonstrable, ascertainable, assignable, authenticated; evident, manifest; (*Chem. etc.*) traceable, detectable. **2.** *adv.* as can be proved *or* shown. **nachweisen,** *irr.v.t.* prove, establish, authenticate; (*Chem. etc.*) detect, trace, identify; ***ihm etwas –,*** point out *or* demonstrate s.th. to him, bring s.th. home to him. **nachweislich,** *adj. See* **nachweisbar. Nachweisung,** *f.* proof, demonstration; establishment, detection; information, reference.

Nachwelt [ˈna:xvɛlt], *f.* posterity, future generations.

nachwirken [ˈna:xvɪrkən], *v.i.* act *or* operate *or* be felt afterwards; take effect later; have *or* leave *or* produce an after-effect. **Nachwirkung,** *f.* after-effect, secondary effect; consequences, aftermath (of), (*coll.*) hangover (from).

Nach|wort, *n.* epilogue, concluding remarks. **–wuchs,** *m.* second growth, young wood; (*fig.*) recruits, trainees, junior staff, rising generation, (*coll.*) new blood, young talent. **–wuchs–,** *pref.* junior, trainee.

nach|zahlen, *v.t., v.i.* pay later *or* extra *or* in addition. **–zählen,** *v.t.* count over (again), check (over). **Nachzahlung,** *f.* later *or* extra *or* additional payment, (*Comm.*) fresh call.

nach|zeichnen, *v.t.* (draw from a) copy, trace. **–ziehen, 1.** *irr.v.t.* 1. pull along after; drag (*one's feet*); 2. tighten (up) (*screw*); 3. trace (*a line*), pencil (in) (*eyebrows etc.*). **2.** *irr.v.i.* (*aux.* s.) (*Dat.*) follow, move after, (*Chess*) have the next move; ***der Tochter nach London –,*** move to London in the steps of one's daughter, go and settle in London to be with one's daughter. **–zotteln,** *v.i.* (*aux.* s.) (*Dat.*) lag behind.

Nach|zug, *m.* (*obs. Mil.*) rearguard. **–zügler,** *m.* straggler, late-comer. **–zugsaktie,** *f.* (*Comm.*) deferred share. **–zündung,** *f.* (*Motor.*) retarded ignition.

Nackedei [ˈnakədaɪ], *m.* **(-(e)s,** *pl.* **-e** *or* **-s)** (*coll.*) naked child.

Nacken [ˈnakən], *m.* nape of the neck, (*Anat.*) cervix; neck, scrag (*of mutton etc.*); ***ihm auf dem*** or ***ihm im – sitzen*** or ***liegen,*** be on his heels, press *or* harass him; (*fig.*) be a burden to him, plague *or* pester him; ***den Kopf in den – werfen,*** throw back one's head; ***ihn im – haben,*** have him hard on one's heels; (*fig.*) be plagued *or* pestered by him; ***den Schelm im – haben,*** be full of mischief; ***einen harten – haben,*** be unyielding *or* recalcitrant *or* refractory; ***den – unter das Joch beugen,*** submit to the yoke.

nackend [ˈnakənt], *adj.* (*Poet.*) *see* **nackt.**

Nacken|haar, *n.* back hair. **–hebel,** *m.* (*wrestling*) nelson. **–muskel,** *m.* (*Anat.*) splenius. **–schlag,** *m.* blow from behind, (*coll.*) rabbit-punch; (*fig.*) shock, blow, setback. **–stachel,** *m.* (*Ichth.*) dorsal spine. **–starre,** *f.* stiff neck. **–wirbel,** *m.* (*Anat.*) cervical vertebra.

nackt [nakt], *adj.* naked, bare, nude; callow, unfledged (*of birds*); ***mit –em Auge,*** with the naked *or* unaided eye; (*fig.*) – ***und bloß,*** stripped, fleeced, penniless, destitute; ***das –e Leben retten,*** barely escape with one's life; ***–e Lüge,*** bare-faced lie; ***–e Tatsachen,*** hard *or* blunt facts; ***die –e Wahrheit,*** the plain *or* naked *or* blunt *or* unadorned truth; ***die –en Wände,*** the bare walls; ***mit –en Worten,*** in plain words, bluntly, openly. **Nacktheit,** *f.* nakedness, nudity; *pl.* nudes. **Nacktkultur,** *f.* nudism. **nacktstengelig,** *adj.* (*Bot.*) non-leafy.

Nadel ['na:dəl], *f.* (-, *pl.* **-n**) needle; pin, brooch; (*of conifers*) needle; (*of mountain*) pinnacle; (*of a gun*) striker; (*of instruments*) pointer, needle; (*Engr.*) style; ***mit –n befestigen,*** pin; ***mit –n abstecken,*** pinpoint (*on a map*); ***das ist mit der heißen – genäht,*** that was done in a hurry, that was a rush job; ***wie auf –n sitzen,*** be on thorns *or* on pins and needles *or* on tenterhooks.

Nadel|abweichung, *f.* magnetic declination. **–arbeit,** *f.* needlework. **–ausschlag,** *m.* deflexion of needle *or* pointer. **–baum,** *m.* conifer. **–brief,** *m.* paper of pins. **nadelförmig,** *adj.* needle-shaped, acicular. **Nadel|futteral,** *n.* needle-case. **–geld,** *n.* pin-money, dress-allowance. **–holz,** *n.* conifers, conifer forest. **–holzteer,** *m.* pine tar. **–kissen,** *n.* pin-cushion. **–knopf, –kopf,** *m.* pin's head. **–öhr,** *n.* eye of a needle. **–spitze,** *f.* point of a needle. **–stein,** *m.* lodestone. **–stich,** *m.* prick; (*sewing*) stitch; (*Med.*) acupuncture; (*fig.*) pin-prick, petty annoyance. **–stockung,** *f.* repeating groove (*on a gramophone record*). **–wald,** *m.* coniferous forest. **–zahl,** *f.* azimuth reading.

Nagel ['na:gəl], *m.* (**-s,** *pl.* ¨-) nail, stud, (carpet) tack; spike, peg; (*Anat.*) nail; ***keinen – breit,*** not an inch; ***es brennt mir auf den Nägeln,*** the matter is urgent *or* pressing, I am very rushed *or* hard pressed; (*sl.*) ***einen – haben,*** have a high opinion of o.s.; (*coll.*) ***etwas an den – hängen,*** give *or* (*sl.*) chuck a th. up; ***an den Nägeln kauen,*** bite one's (finger-)nails; (*fig.*) ***den – auf den Kopf treffen,*** hit the nail on the head; ***sich*** (*Dat.*) ***die Nägel schneiden,*** cut one's nails.

Nagel|bohrer, *m.* gimlet. **–bürste,** *f.* nail-brush.

Nägelchen ['nɛ:gəlçən], *n.* tack, brad; (*dial.*) clove.

Nagelfeile ['na:gəlfaɪlə], *f.* nail-file. **nagel|fest,** *adj.* nailed; immovable; ***niet- und –e Gegenstände,*** fixtures. **–förmig,** *adj.* unguiform. **Nagel|geschwür,** *n.* whitlow. **–gras,** *n.* chickweed. **–haut,** *f.* cuticle. **–kuppe,** *f.* nail-head, head of a nail. **–lack,** *m.* nail-varnish.

nageln ['na:gəln], *v.t.* nail (*an* or *auf* (*Acc.*), to); (*coll.*) ***ich nagele ihn fest,*** I'll pin him down.

nagelneu ['na:gəlnɔy], *adj.* brand-new. **Nagel|-pflege,** *f.* manicure. **–probe,** *f.* ***die – machen,*** show that one's glass is empty by ringing it with the finger-nail; (*fig.*) crucial test; ***nicht die – ist im Glase geblieben,*** not a heeltap is left in the glass. **–schere,** *f.* nail-scissors. **–schmied,** *m.* nail-maker. **–schuhe,** *m.pl.* (*Spt.*) spiked shoes, (*coll.*) spikes. **–weiß,** *n.* lunula, moon (*of the nail*). **–wurzel,** *f.* root of a nail. **–zange,** *f.* nippers. **–zieher,** *m.* nail-extractor. **–zwang,** *m.* (*coll.*) ingrowing nails.

nagen ['na:gən], *v.t., v.i.* gnaw, nibble (*an* (*Dat.*), at); (*Chem., Geol.*) corrode, erode, eat into; (*fig.*) rankle; ***–de Sorgen,*** carking cares; ***Kummer nagt ihm am Herzen*** or ***nagt an ihm,*** he is eaten up with worry; ***am Hungertuche –,*** be starving *or* destitute. **Nager,** *m.*, **Nage|tier,** *n.* (*Zool.*) rodent. **–zahn,** *m.* incisor tooth.

Näglein ['nɛ:klaɪn], *n.* (**-s,** *pl.* **-**) *see* **Nägelchen.**

nah [na:], **1.** *adj.* (*comp. näher, sup. nächst*) near, close (*Dat. or* ***bei,*** to); (*time*) forthcoming, approaching, impending, imminent; ***–e an*** (*Dat., Acc.*), close on; ***–e aneinander,*** close to one another; ***–e dabei,*** nearby; ***–(e) daran sein,*** be on the point of, be near (***zu tun,*** doing); ***es war – daran daß*** . . ., it was touch and go whether . . .; ***von – und fern,*** from far and near; ***– und fern,*** far and wide; ***–er Freund,*** close friend; ***–e Gefahr,*** impending danger; ***das Weinen war ihr sehr –e,*** she was very nearly crying. **2.** *adv.* (*written separately when it has literal meaning of proximity or when qualified by* ***zu, sehr*** *etc.*) *e.g.* ***ihm zu –e treten,*** offend him, hurt his feelings, (*coll.*) tread on his corns; ***von –em ansehen,*** look at closely; ***wie – sind Sie verwandt?*** how closely are you related? (*When it has a figurative meaning, it is used as a separable prefix; see entries below.*)

Nahangriff ['na:ˀangrɪf], *m.* (*Mil.*) close-range attack.

Näharbeit ['nɛ:ˀarbaɪt], *f.* needlework, sewing.

Nah|aufklärung, *f.* (*Mil.*) close reconnaissance. **–aufnahme,** *f.* close-up.

nahe, *adj. See* **nah.**

Nähe ['nɛ:ə], *f.* nearness, proximity; neighbourhood, surroundings, vicinity; (*of relationship*) propinquity; ***aus der –,*** at close range, from close up; ***in der –,*** nearby, close by, near *or* close at hand; ***in nächster –,*** at one's elbow; within call; ***in erreichbarer –,*** within reasonable *or* striking distance; ***in der – betrachten,*** look at closely; ***in meiner –,*** near me; ***in der – der Kirche,*** close to *or* near the church.

nahebei ['na:əbaɪ], *adv.* nearby, close by.

nahe|gehen, *irr.v.i.* (*aux.* s.) (*Dat.*) affect, grieve; ***sich*** (*Dat.*) ***– lassen,*** take to heart. **–gelegen,** *adj.* nearby, neighbouring.

Naheinstellung ['na:ˀaɪnʃtɛluŋ], *f.* (*Phot.*) short focus, close-up.

nahe|kommen, *irr.v.i.* (*aux.* s.) (*Dat.*) approach, come near (to); ***der Wahrheit –,*** get at the truth. **–legen,** *v.t.* suggest, make plain, bring home (*Dat.*, to), urge (upon), give (*s.o.*) to understand that. **–liegen,** *irr.v.i.* (*fig.*) suggest itself, be obvious *or* patent *or* manifest. **–liegend,** *adj.* nearby, near *or* close at hand; (*fig.*) obvious, manifest, patent, inescapable; ***–e Annahme,*** reasonable assumption.

nahen ['na:ən], *v.i., v.r.* (*Dat.*) (*Poet.*) draw near, draw near (to), approach.

nähen ['nɛ:ən], **1.** *v.t.* sew, stitch. **2.** *v.i.* sew, do sewing *or* needlework; ***überwendlich –,*** overcast, whip-stitch.

näher ['nɛ:ər], *comp.adj. See* **nah**; nearer, closer; shorter, more direct (*route*); more precise *or* specific *or* detailed, further (*information, details etc.*); ***–e Angaben,*** further particulars, fuller *or* more precise details; ***– ausführen,*** go into detail(s), elaborate (upon); ***–e Auskunft,*** further information, more particulars; ***–e Bekanntschaft,*** close acquaintance, familiarity, intimacy; ***mit ihm – bekannt werden,*** become closely acquainted with him; ***bei –er Betrachtung,*** on further consideration; ***darauf kann ich nicht – eingehen,*** I cannot go into the matter any further; ***um der Sache – zu kommen,*** to come to the point, to get to the root *or* bottom of a matter; ***–e Rechte,*** prior rights *or* claims; ***treten Sie –!*** step this way! ***die –e Umgebung,*** the immediate vicinity; ***–e Umstände,*** particulars, details.

Näherei [nɛ:ə'raɪ], *f.* sewing, needlework. **Näherin** ['nɛ:ərɪn], *f.* needlewoman, seamstress.

Nähere(s) ['nɛ:ərə(s)], *n.* details, the precise circumstances, (further) particulars; ***das Nähere wollen Sie ersehen aus*** . . ., for particulars please refer to . . ..

nähern ['ne:ərn], **1.** *v.t.* bring *or* place near (*Dat.*, to). **2.** *v.r.* come *or* draw nearer, approach, near, close in. **nähertreten,** *irr.v.i.* (*Dat.*) (*fig.*) approach. **Näherung,** *f.* approach, (*Math. etc.*) approximation. **Näherungswert,** *m.* approximate value, approximation.

nahestehend ['na:əʃte:ənt], *adj.* closely associated, connected (*Dat.*, with).

nahezu ['na:ətsu:], *adv.* almost, nearly; – ***unmöglich,*** next to impossible.

Nähgarn ['nɛ:ˀgarn], *n.* sewing-cotton.

Nah|gespräch, *n.* (*Tele.*) toll call. **–kampf,** *m.* hand-to-hand fighting, close combat, (*Av. coll.*) dog-fight, (*Boxing*) infighting. **–kampfartillerei,** *f.* close-support artillery.

Näh|kästchen, *n.* work-box. **–korb,** *m.* work-basket. **–kränzchen,** *n.* sewing-bee.

nahm [na:m], *see* **nehmen.**

Nähmaschine [ˈnɛ:maʃi:nə], *f.* sewing-machine.
nähme [ˈnɛ:mə], **nahmest** [ˈna:məst], *see* **nehmen.**
Nähnadel [ˈnɛ:na:dəl], *f.* sewing-needle.
Nährboden [ˈnɛ:rbo:dən], *m.* fertile soil; (*Biol.*) culture medium; (*fig.*) hotbed (*of vice, crime etc.*).
nähren [ˈnɛ:rən], **1.** *v.t.* feed, provide *or* supply with nourishment, nourish; (*a child*) breast-feed, nurse, suckle; (*a family*) keep, support; (*fig.*) foster, harbour, cherish, entertain (*hope etc.*); ***ein Handwerk, das seinen Mann nährt,*** a trade by which a man may support himself. **2.** *v.r.* earn one's living *or* livelihood; maintain *or* keep *or* support o.s. (***von,*** by), live, feed (on); ***sich kümmerlich –,*** earn a scanty living, have great difficulty in making both ends meet. **3.** *v.i.* be nourishing. **nährend,** *adj.* nutritious, nutritive, nourishing, nutrient.
nahrhaft [ˈna:rhaft], *adj. See* **nährend**; (*of soil etc.*) productive; (*fig.*) lucrative.
Nährkraft [ˈnɛ:rkraft], *f.* nutritive power. **nährkräftig,** *adj. See* **nährend. Nähr|krem,** *f.* skin-food. **–mittel,** *n.* nutriment, nutrient; (*usu. pl.*) articles of food; processed foodstuffs. **–mittelchemie,** *f.* chemistry of food. **–mittelfabrik,** *f.* food-processing plant. **–präparat,** *n.* patent food. **–saft,** *m.* nutrient juice, chyme, sap. **–salz,** *n.* nutrient salt. **–sorgen,** *f.pl.* difficulty in making a living. **–stand,** *m.* the producers, the peasants. **–stoff,** *m.* nutrient.
Nahrung [ˈna:ruŋ], *f.* nourishment, nutriment, food; diet; subsistence, livelihood; ***in – setzen,*** give employment to, find work for; ***seiner – nachgehen,*** strive to gain a livelihood.
Nahrungs|aufnahme, *f.* food intake. **–bedarf,** *m.* food requirement. **–bedürfnis,** *n.* need of nourishment. **–freiheit,** *f.* agrarian self-sufficiency, independence of foodstuffs from abroad. **–mangel,** *m.* food shortage, scarcity of food. **–mittel,** *n.* article of food; *pl.* means of subsistence, food supplies; food, eatables, provisions, victuals, foodstuffs. **–mittelchemie,** *f. See* **Nährmittelchemie. –mittelfälschung,** *f.* adulteration of food. **–mittelkarte,** *f.* ration card. **–mittelzufuhr,** *f.* food supply. **–sorgen,** *f.pl. See* **Nährsorgen. –verweigerung,** *f.* hunger-strike; (*Med.*) sitiophobia. **–vorschrift,** *f.* diet, regimen.
Nährwert [ˈnɛ:rve:rt], *m.* nutritive *or* food value.
Nähseide [ˈnɛ:zaɪdə], *f.* sewing-silk.
Nahsender [ˈna:zɛndər], *m.* (*Rad.*) local transmitter.
Naht [na:t], *f.* (-, *pl.* **¨e**) seam; (*Anat., Bot., Surg.*) suture; (*Tech.*) join, joint, weld; (*Mil.*) sector boundary; ***aufgetrennte –,*** split down the seam; ***die – ist aufgegangen,*** the seam has come undone; (*coll.*) ***ihm auf die – fühlen*** or ***gehen,*** sound him; ***ihm auf die Nähte rücken,*** press home one's attack on him.
Nähtäschchen [ˈnɛ:tɛʃçən], *n.* needle-case, housewife, (*coll.*) hussif.
Nähterin [ˈnɛ:tərɪn], *f.* (*dial.*) *see* **Näherin.**
Nahtkompagnie [ˈna:tkɔmpanji], *f.* (*Mil.*) contact company. **nahtlos,** *adj.* seamless. **Naht|schweißung,** *f.* seam welding. **–stelle,** *f.* (*Mil.*) boundary between sectors.
Nahverkehr [ˈna:fɛrke:r], *m.* (*Railw.*) local *or* suburban traffic, (*Motor.*) short-haul traffic, (*Tele.*) toll service.
Nähzeug [ˈnɛ:tsɔyk], *n.* sewing-kit *or* things.
Nahziel [ˈna:tsi:l], *n.* (*Mil,*) immediate objective.
naiv [naˈi:f], *adj.* naive, naïve, ingenuous, artless, simple. **Naive** [–ˈi:və], *f.* (*Theat.*) ingénue. **Naivität** [–iˈtɛ:t], *f.* naivety, naïvety, naiveté, simplicity, ingenuousness.
Najade [naˈja:də], *f.* naiad, water-nymph.
Name [ˈna:mə], *m.* (**-ns,** *pl.* **-n**) name, designation, title, appellation; character, reputation, good name; ***auf –n meiner Frau,*** under my wife's name; (*Comm.*) ***auf den –n lautend,*** not negotiable, payable to order; ***dem –n nach,*** nominal(ly), by name; ***Dinge*** or ***gas Kind beim rechten*** or ***richtigen –n nennen,*** call a spade a spade, not mince matters; ***seinen –n daruntersetzen,*** set one's name to s.th.; ***den –n für etwas hergeben,*** lend one's name to s.th.; ***in Gottes –n,*** in the name of God, for God's sake; ***im –n des Königs,*** in the king's name, by order of the king; ***sich*** (*Dat.*) ***einen –n machen,*** gain a name for o.s.; ***er geht unter dem –n, er trägt den –n,*** he is known as, he goes by the name of; (*Comm.*) ***unter unsern vereinten –n,*** under our joint signature; ***wie ist Ihr*** (*werter*) ***–?*** what is your name?
Namen [ˈna:mən], *m.* (*Austr.*) *see* **Name. Namen|aktie,** *f.* (*Comm.*) registered share. **–forschung,** *f.* study of (place *or* personal) names. **–gebung,** *f.* naming, nomenclature; christening. **–gedächtnis,** *n.* memory for names. **–kunde,** *f. See* **–forschung. –liste,** *f.* list of names, roll, (*with doctors, jurors*) panel, (*Pol.*) poll. **namenlos,** *adj.* anonymous, nameless; (*fig.*) ineffable, unutterable, unspeakable, inexpressible, indescribable, dreadful. **Namen|nennung,** *f.* specifying by name, giving (of) the name. **–register,** *n. See* **–liste**; index of names.
namens [ˈna:məns], **1.** *adv.* called, named, by (the) name of. **2.** *prep.* (*Gen.*) in the name of, on behalf of.
Namens|aktie, *f. See* **Namenaktie. –aufruf,** *m.* roll-call. **–fest,** *n.*, **–tag,** *m.* (*R.C.*) Saint's day, name-day, (*coll.*) birthday. **–vetter,** *m.* namesake. **–zug,** *m.* signature, monogram.
namentlich [na:məntlɪç], *adj.* (*rare*), *adv.* by name, nominal(ly); in particular, particularly, especially.
Namen|verzeichnis, *n. See* **–register. –wechsel,** *m.* change of name.
namhaft [ˈna:mhaft], *adj.* well-known, noted, notable, renowned; worth mentioning, noteworthy, considerable; ***– machen,*** name, specify, mention by name.
nämlich [ˈnɛ:mlɪç], **1.** *adj.* ***der, die, das –e,*** the (self-)same. **2.** *adv.* namely, that is (to say); of course, (*obs.*) to wit.
Nänie [ˈnɛ:niə], *f.* elegy, dirge.
Nanking [ˈnaŋkɪŋ], *m.* (**-s,** *pl.* **-e** *or* **-s**) nankeen.
nannte [ˈnantə], **nanntest,** *see* **nennen.**
nanu! [ˈnanu], *int.* well I never! what next! I say!
Napf [napf], *m.* (**-es,** *pl.* **¨e**) basin, bowl. **Napfkuchen,** *m.* large cake.
Narbe [ˈnarbə], *f.* 1. scar; (*Med.*) cicatrice; 2. topsoil; 3. grain (*in leather*); 4. (*Bot.*) stigma, hilum. **narben, 1.** *v.t.* scar, mark, grain (*leather*). **2.** *v.r.* ***sich –,*** cicatrice, form a scar, scar over. **Narben|bildung,** *f.* cicatrization; pitting (*of metals*). **narbenlos,** *adj.* unmarked; unscarred. **Narbenseite,** *f.* grain-side (*of leather*).
Narde [ˈnardə], *f.* nard, spikenard. **Nardenöl,** *n.* nard-oil.
Narkose [narˈko:zə], *f.* narcosis, anaesthesia. **Narkotikum,** *n.* (**-s,** *pl.* **-ka**) narcotic. **narkotisch,** *adj.* narcotic; ***–e Mittel,*** narcotics. **narkotisieren** [–tiˈzi:rən], *v.t.* narcotize, anaesthetize.
Narr [nar], *m.* (**-en,** *pl.* **-en**) fool, foolish person; clown, jester, buffoon; ***ein – von Hause aus,*** a born fool; ***den – abgeben,*** play the fool; (*coll.*) ***einen –en an ihm fressen,*** dote on him, be infatuated with him, have taken a great fancy to him; ***ihn zum –en haben*** or ***halten,*** make a fool of him; ***sich zum –en hergeben*** or ***machen,*** make a fool of o.s., make o.s. a laughing-stock. **narren,** *v.t.* fool, hoax, dupe, make a fool of.
Narren|fest, *n.* All Fools' Day. **–geschwätz,** *n.* stuff and nonsense, balderdash. **–haus,** *n.* madhouse. **–kappe,** *f.* fool's cap, cap and bells. **-posse,** *f.* (*usu. pl.*) (tom)foolery, buffoonery, silly trick; ***–n treiben,*** play the fool, fool about, get up to mad pranks. **–seil,** *n.* ***am– führen,*** make a fool of, lead by the nose. **narrensicher,** *adj.* foolproof. **Narrenstreich,** *m.* foolish trick, stupid th. to do.
Narretei [narəˈtaɪ], *f.* madness, foolery, fooling, folly.
Narrheit [ˈnarhaɪt], *f.* foolishness, folly, madness, craziness.

Närrin ['nɛrɪn], *f.* foolish woman, fool. **närrisch,** *adj.* (*of a th.*) foolish, silly, mad, crazy; (*of a p.*) eccentric, peculiar, strange, (*coll.*) odd, funny; ***man möchte – werden,*** it's enough to drive one mad; ***ganz – sein auf*** (*Acc.*), be quite dotty about, dote on.

Narzisse [nar'tsɪsə], *f.* (*Bot.*) narcissus; ***gelbe –,*** daffodil.

Narzißmus [nar'tsɪsmus], *m.* narcissism, self-adoration.

nasal [na'za:l], *adj.* (*Phonet.*) nasal. **Nasal(laut),** *m.* nasal (sound).

naschen ['naʃən], *v.t., v.i.* eat (*sweets or dainties*) on the sly, nibble (***an*** (*Dat.*), at); ***gern –,*** have a sweet tooth. **Nascher** ['naʃər], *m.* sweet tooth. **Nascherei,** *f.* eating (sweets) on the sly; sweets, dainties. **naschhaft,** *adj.* sweet-toothed, fond of dainties *or* of sweet things. **Nasch|katze,** *f. See* **Nascher. –lust,** *f.* fondness for dainties. **–maul,** *n. See* **Nascher. –werk,** *n.* sweets, (*Am.*) candy.

Nase ['na:zə], *f.* nose, (*of animals*) snout, proboscis; (*fig. of dog etc.*) scent; nozzle, spout; (*Tech.*) lug, cam, tappet; (*obs.*) beak (*of a ship*); (*fig.*) sharp rebuke; ***man kann es ihm an der – ansehen,*** it is written all over his face; ***an die eigene – fassen,*** blame o.s.; ***an der – herumführen,*** lead by the nose; ***es ihm auf die – binden,*** tell it him to his face; ***ihm auf der – herumtanzen,*** ride roughshod over him, play fast and loose *or* play Old Harry with him; ***auf der – liegen,*** be laid up, lie ill in bed; ***Mund und – aufsperren,*** stand agape *or* aghast; ***ihm die Würmer aus der – ziehen,*** worm the secret out of him; ***sich*** (*Dat.*) ***die – begießen,*** booze, guzzle; ***eine – bekommen,*** get on the scent of (*of dogs*); ***ihm eine – drehen,*** cock a snook at him, thumb one's nose at him, put one's fingers to one's nose at him; ***eine feine – haben,*** have a good nose *or* a keen sense of smell, (*fig.*) have a flair *or* (*coll.*) a nose (***für,*** for); not miss much; ***die – hochtragen,*** be stuck-up; ***in die – steigen,*** be noticeable (*of smells*); ***ihm eine lange – machen,*** *see* ***ihm eine – drehen***; ***mit langer – abziehen,*** retire crestfallen; ***der – nachgehen,*** follow one's nose; ***die – rümpfen,*** turn up one's nose (***über*** (*Acc.*), at); ***es sticht mir in die*** or ***steckt mir in der –,*** I have set my heart on it; ***er steckt die – gern in Bücher,*** he keeps his nose buried in books; ***seine – in alles*** or (*coll.*) ***in jeden Quark*** or ***Dreck stecken,*** poke *or* stick one's nose into everything; ***ihn mit der – darauf stoßen,*** rub his nose in it, push it under his nose, (*coll.*) rub it in; ***es steigt mir in die –,*** it sticks in my throat *or* gullet; ***er hat sich*** (*Dat.*) ***viel Wind um die – wehen lassen,*** he has knocked around a good deal; ***es ihm unter die – reiben,*** cast it in his teeth, fling it in his face, rub his nose in it, bring it home to him, (*coll.*) rub it in; ***es ihm unter die – binden,*** bamboozle him about it; ***die – voll haben von,*** be fed up with *or* sick to death of; ***ihm vor die – halten,*** *see* ***unter die – reiben***; ***mir vor der –,*** under my very nose; ***ihm die Tür vor der – zuwerfen,*** slam the door in his face; ***zieh*** or ***zupf dich an deiner*** (***eigenen***) ***–!*** mind your own business! ***sich*** (*Dat.*) ***die – zuhalten,*** hold one's nose.

näseln ['nɛ:zəln], *v.i.* speak through one's nose, (*Phonet.*) nasalize. **Näseln,** *n.* nasal twang. **näselnd,** *adj.* nasal(ized).

Nasen|bein, *n.* nasal bone. **–bluten,** *n.* nose-bleeding. **–flügel,** *m.* side *or* wing of the nose. **–gewächs,** *n.* nasal polypus. **–höhle,** *f.* nasal cavity. **nasenlang,** *adj.* (*sl.*) ***alle –,*** very frequently, every minute. **Nasen|länge,** *f.* (***mit einer***) or (***um***) ***eine – voraus sein,*** win by a short head. **–laut,** *m.* (*Phonet.*) nasal (sound). **–leiste,** *f.* (*Av.*) leading edge (*of wing*). **–loch,** *n.* nostril. **–rücken,** *m.* bridge of the nose. **–scheidewand,** *f.* nasal septum. **–schleim,** *m.* nasal mucous. **–spitze,** *f.* tip of the nose; ***es ihm an der – ansehen,*** see it (written) in his face. **–stüber,** *m.* snub, rap on the knuckles. **–ton,** *m.* nasal sound; twang.

naseweis ['na:zəvaɪs], *adj.* pert, saucy, impertinent, (*coll.*) cheeky. **Naseweisheit,** *f.* pertness, forwardness, sauciness; impudence, (*coll.*) cheek.

nasführen ['na:sfy:rən], *v.t.* (*sep.*) dupe, fool, bamboozle, lead by the nose.

Nashorn ['na:shɔrn], *n.* (*Zool.*) rhinoceros.

naß [nas], *adj.* (*comp.* ***nässer,*** *also Austr.* ***nasser,*** *sup.* ***nässest,*** *also Austr.* ***nassest***) wet, damp, humid, moist; ***es wird nasse Augen setzen*** or ***geben,*** many a tear will be shed; ***er hat das Bett – gemacht,*** he has wet the bed; ***nasser Boden,*** marshy *or* low-lying ground; ***nasser Bruder,*** tippler, toper, drunkard, sot, (*sl.*) boozer; (*coll.*) ***für –,*** buckshee; ***ein nasses Grab,*** a watery grave; ***Vergoldung auf nassem Wege,*** water-gilding; ***– werden,*** get soaked *or* drenched. **Naß,** *n.* (**-(ss)es,** *no pl.*) (*Poet.*) humidity, wetness; liquid, water.

Nassauer ['nasauər], *m.* (*coll.*) scrounger, sponger. **nassauern,** *v.i.* (*coll.*) sponge (***bei,*** on), scrounge.

Naßdampf ['nasdampf], *m.* saturated *or* wet steam.

Nässe ['nɛsə], *f.* wet(ness), damp(ness), moisture, humidity. **nässen, 1.** *v.t.* wet, moisten, soak. **2.** *v.i.* 1. ooze, discharge (*of wounds*); 2. make *or* pass water; 3. drizzle.

Naßfäule ['nasfɔylə], *f.* wet rot. **naßkalt,** *adj.* raw, damp and cold (*as weather*), clammy (*as hands*). **Naßverfahren,** *n.* wet process.

naszierend [nas'tsi:rənt], *adj.* (*Chem.*) nascent.

Nation [natsi'o:n], *f.* nation. **national** [–'na:l], *adj.* national. **National|bewußtsein,** *n.* national consciousness. **–charakter,** *m.* national character. **nationalchinesisch,** *adj.* Chinese Nationalist. **Nationale,** *n.* (*obs.*) identification papers. **National|farben,** *f.pl.,* **–flagge,** *f.* national colours *or* flag. **–gefühl,** *n.* patriotic feelings. **–held,** *m.* national hero. **–hymne,** *f.* national anthem.

nationalisieren [natsionali'zi:rən], *v.t.* nationalize. **Nationalisierung,** *f.* nationalization. **Nationalismus** [–'lɪsmus], *m.* nationalism. **nationalistisch,** *adj.* nationalistic. **Nationalität** [–i'tɛ:t], *f.* nationality.

National|mannschaft, *f.* national team. **–ökonom,** *m.* (political) economist. **–ökonomie,** *f.* political economy. **–rat,** *m.* (*Swiss*) representative assembly. **–schuld,** *f.* national debt. **–sozialismus,** *m.* National Socialism. **–sozialist,** *m.* National Socialist, (*coll.*) Hitlerite, Nazi. **nationalsozialistisch,** *adj.* National Socialist. **National|staat,** *m.* nation state. **–stolz,** *m.* national pride. **–tracht,** *f.* national costume. **–versammlung,** *f.* National Assembly.

Nativität [nativi'tɛ:t], *f.* nativity; horoscope; ***ihm die – stellen,*** cast his horoscope. **Nativitätensteller,** *m.* astrologer.

Natrium ['na:trium], *n.* sodium. **Natrium|-chlorid,** *n.* sodium chloride, common salt. **–hydroxyd,** *n.* sodium hydrate, (*coll.*) caustic soda. **–karbonat,** *n.* sodium carbonate, (*coll.*) washing soda. **–nitrat,** *n.* sodium nitrate, (*coll.*) Chili saltpetre. **–sulfat,** *n.* sodium sulphate, (*coll.*) Glauber's salt.

Natron ['na:trɔn], *n.* (*obs.*) *see* **Natrium**; (*coll.*) sodium bicarbonate; ***kohlensaures –,*** sodium carbonate; ***doppeltkohlensaures –,*** sodium bicarbonate; ***salpetersaures –,*** Chili saltpetre, sodium nitrate; ***salzsaures –,*** sodium chloride. **Natronlauge,** *f.* caustic soda solution, soda-lye.

Natter ['natər], *f.* (-, *pl.* **-n**) adder, viper; ***eine – am Busen nähren,*** cherish a snake in one's bosom.

Natur [na'tu:r], *f.* (-, *pl.* **-en**) nature; (*of a p.*) nature, character, temperament, disposition, temper, frame of mind, constitution; (natural) scenery; ***in der freien –,*** in the open country; ***hitzige –,*** fiery temperament; ***es liegt in der – der S.,*** it is in the nature of things; ***nach der – zeichnen,*** draw from life *or* from nature; ***es ist seiner – nach kalt,*** it is naturally *or* by nature cold; ***von –*** (***aus***), by nature, constitutionally, congenitally; ***ein von – fester Ort,*** a natural stronghold; ***das ist mir von – zuwider,*** I have a natural aversion to that; ***es geht mir wider die –,*** it goes against my nature *or* against the grain; ***der – seinen Tribut zahlen,*** pay one's debt to nature; ***ihm zur zweiten – werden,*** become second nature with him.

Natura [na'tu:ra], *f. in – bezahlen,* pay in kind.

Naturalbezüge [natu'ra:lbətsy:gə], *m.pl.* remuneration in kind.

Naturalien [natu'ra:liən], *pl.* 1. natural produce, fruits of the soil; 2. natural history specimens. **Naturaliensammlung,** *f.* natural history collection, museum of natural curiosities.

naturalisieren [naturali'zi:rən], *v.t.* naturalize; *sich – lassen,* become naturalized. **Naturalisierung,** *f.* naturalization.

Naturalismus [natura'lɪsmus], *m.* naturalism; natural religion. **naturalistisch,** *adj.* naturalistic.

Natural|leistung, *f.* payment *or* delivery in kind. **–lohn,** *m.* remuneration in kind. **–verpflegung,** *f.* (*Mil.*) supply of provisions. **–wert,** *m.* value in kind.

Natur|anlage, *f.* (natural) disposition, temperament; talent, gifts. **–begebenheit,** *f.* natural phenomenon. **–beschreibung,** *f.* natural description, description of nature. **–bleiche,** *f.* grass bleach, sun bleach. **–bursche,** *m.* child of nature. **–butter,** *f.* genuine butter. **–dichtung,** *f.* nature-poetry. **–ei,** *n.* shell-egg.

Naturell [natu'rɛl], *n.* (**-s,** *pl.* **-e**) nature, (natural) disposition, temper(ament).

Natur|ereignis, *n.,* **–erscheinung,** *f. See* **–begebenheit. –farbe,** *f.* natural colour; self-colour. **naturfarben,** *adj.* natural-coloured; *–e Wolle,* natural wool. **Natur|forscher,** *m.* naturalist, scientist; natural philosopher. **–freund,** *m.* nature-lover. **–gabe,** *f. See* **–anlage. –gas,** *n.* natural gas. **–gefühl,** *n.* feeling for nature. **naturgemäß,** *adj., adv.* according to nature, natural(ly). **Natur|geschichte,** *f. See* **–kunde. –gesetz,** *n.* law of nature, natural law. **naturgetreu,** *adj.* true to nature, true to life, life-like, natural. **Natur|heilkunde,** *f.* nature cure. **–heilkundige(r),** *m., f.* nature healer. **–historiker,** *m.* writer of natural history. **–kind,** *n.* child of nature. **–kraft,** *f.* natural force; natural strength. **–kunde,** *f.* natural history. **–lehre,** *f.* natural philosophy, physics.

natürlich [na'ty:rlɪç], **1.** *adj.* natural, native, innate; normal, genuine, unaffected, uninhibited, unsophisticated, artless; *ein –es Bedürfnis befriedigen,* satisfy nature's call, ease nature; *–e Größe,* natural *or* actual *or* real *or* full size; *–e Tochter,* natural *or* illegitimate daughter; *eines –en Todes sterben,* die a natural death; *–e Tonleiter,* natural key (*without sharp or flat*); (*Biol.*) *–e Zuchtwahl,* natural selection; *das geht ganz – zu,* that is quite natural *or* normal, it stands to reason; *das geht nicht –* or *nicht mit –en Dingen zu,* there is something strange *or* uncanny *or* (*coll.*) fishy in this; *in –em Zustand,* in a state of nature, in the natural state. **2.** *or* **natürlicherweise,** *adv.* of course, certainly, naturally, to be sure. **Natürlichkeit,** *f.* naturalness, genuineness, artlessness, simplicity.

Natur|mensch, *m.* primitive man; nature worshipper. **–notwendigkeit,** *f.* physical necessity. **–produkte,** *n.pl.* natural products *or* produce. **–recht,** *n.* natural right, natural law, law of nature. **–reich,** *n.* kingdom of nature. **–religion,** *f.* natural religion. **–schätze,** *m.pl.* natural resources. **–schutz,** *m.* preservation *or* conservation of natural beauty and wild life. **–schutzgebiet,** *n.* preserve, sanctuary, national trust property. **–schutzpark,** *m.* national (preserved) park. **–stoff,** *m.* native *or* natural substance. **–theater,** *n.* open-air theatre. **–treue,** *f.* fidelity to nature. **–trieb,** *m.* instinct. **–volk,** *n.* primitive race. **naturwidrig,** *adj.* unnatural; abnormal. **Natur|wissenschaft,** *f.* (natural *or* physical) science. **–wissenschaft(l)er,** *m.* scientist. **natur|wissenschaftlich,** *adj.* scientific. **–wüchsig,** *adj.* indigenous, original, natural, unforced. **Natur|wunder,** *n.* prodigy. **–zustand,** *m.* natural *or* primitive state.

Nautik ['nautɪk], *f.* art of navigation; nautical affairs. **nautisch,** *adj.* nautical.

Navigations|anlage [navigatsi'o:ns–], *f.* navigation system. **–karte,** *f.* chart. **–offizier,** *m.* (*Naut.*) navigation officer, (*Av.*) navigator. **–raum,** *m.* chart-room. **-schule,** *f.* naval college.

ne! *int. See* **nee!**

Neapel [ne'a:pəl], *n.* (*Geog.*) Naples. **Neapolitaner** [–poli'ta:nər], *m.,* **neapolitanisch,** *adj.* Neapolitan.

Nebel ['ne:bəl], *m.* mist, fog, haze; (*Astr.*) nebula; (*fig.*) veil, cloud; *der – fällt,* the mist comes down; *künstlicher –,* smoke-screen; *– legen* or *abblasen,* lay a smoke-screen; *bei Nacht und –,* stealthily, like a thief in the night.

Nebel|bank, *f.* fog-bank. **–boje,** *f.* smoke-buoy. **-bombe,** *f.* smoke-bomb. **–fleck,** *m.* (*Astr.*) nebula. **–granate,** *f.* (*Mil.*) smoke-shell. **nebelgrau,** *adj.* misty grey. **nebelhaft,** *adj.* misty, hazy, nebulous, dim. **Nebelhorn,** *n.* fog-horn. **nebelig,** *adj.* foggy, misty, hazy. **Nebel|kammer,** *f.* (*Phys.*) cloud-chamber. **–kappe,** *f.* magic cloak of invisibility; (*on mountain*) shroud of mist. **–krähe,** *f.* (*Orn.*) hooded crow (*Corvus corone cornix*). **–lampe, –leuchte,** *f.* (*Motor.*) fog lamp. **–monat, –mond,** *m.* (*Poet.*) month of fogs, November.

nebeln ['ne:bəln], *v.i.* 1. be *or* grow foggy; 2. (*Mil.*) put down *or* lay a smoke-screen.

Nebel|regen, *m.* drizzle. **–schleier,** *m.* veil of mist; smoke-screen. **–signal,** *n.* fog-signal.

Nebelung ['ne:bəluŋ], *m.* (**-s,** *pl.* **-e**) (*Poet.*) November.

Nebel|vorhang, *m.,* **–wand,** *f.* (*Mil.*) smoke-screen. **–wetter,** *n.* foggy weather.

neben ['ne:bən], *prep.* (*with Acc. when expressing motion absolutely; with Dat. when expressing rest or limited motion*) beside, by (the side of), side by side with, alongside; next to, close by, near *or* close to; compared with, as against; apart *or* (*Am.*) aside from, in addition to, besides; *– mir,* at my side, beside me; in addition to me; compared with me; *stellen Sie es – mich,* put it beside me; *er stand* (*ging*) *– mir,* he stood (walked) by my side; *er trat – mich,* he came up alongside me; *– andern Dingen,* amongst other things.

Neben|abrede, *f.* collateral agreement. **–abschnitt,** *m.* adjacent sector. **–absicht,** *f.* secondary objective *or* aim. **–achse,** *f.* secondary *or* lateral axis. **–amt,** *n.* sub-office; (*Tele.*) branch exchange; subsidiary appointment. **nebenamtlich,** *adj.* part-time.

nebenan [ne:bən'an], *adv.* close by, alongside; in the next room; next-door.

Neben|angriff, *m.* (*Mil.*) diversionary attack. **–anschluß,** *m.* (*Tele.*) extension, (*Elec.*) shunt. **–arbeit,** *f.* work of secondary importance; extra work. **–ausgaben,** *f.pl.* incidental expenses. **–ausgang,** *m.* side-exit. **–bedeutung,** *f.* secondary meaning. **–bedingung,** *f.* secondary *or* accessory factor. **–begriff,** *m.* subordinate *or* collateral idea.

nebenbei [ne:bən'baɪ], *adv. See* **nebenan**; by the way, incidentally, besides, moreover, by the by.

Nebenberuf ['ne:bənbəru:f], *m.* part-time occupation, sideline, avocation. **nebenberuflich,** **1.** *attrib.adj.* part-time, spare-time. **2.** *adv.* in one's spare time, as a side-line. **Neben|beschäftigung,** *f. See* **–beruf. –bestandteil,** *m.* secondary *or* accessory ingredient *or* constituent. **–blatt,** *n.* (*Bot.*) stipule, bract. **–buhler,** *m.* rival, competitor. **–buhlerschaft,** *f.* rivalry. **–bürgschaft,** *f.* collateral surety.

nebeneinander [ne:bənˀaɪn'andər], *adv.* side by side, abreast, neck and neck; close together, in proximity *or* juxtaposition; (*time*) concurrently, simultaneously; *– bestehen,* coexist. **Nebeneinander,** *n.* co-existence. **nebeneinanderschalten,** *v.t.* (*Elec.*) connect in parallel. **Nebeneinanderschaltung,** *f.* parallel connection. **nebeneinanderstellen,** *v.t.* put *or* place side by side; compare. **Nebeneinanderstellung,** *f.* juxtaposition; comparison.

Neben|eingang, *m.* side-entrance. **–einkünfte,** *f.pl.,* **–einnahme,** *f.,* **–erwerb,** *m.* perquisites, casual emoluments *or* earnings, additional income. **–erzeugnis,** *n.* by-product, residual product.

-fach, *n.* subsidiary subject. **-farbe,** *f.* secondary *or* complementary colour. **-figur,** *f.* subordinate figure, accessory. **-fluß,** *m.* tributory, affluent. **-folge,** *f.* indirect result, secondary effect. **-forderung,** *f.* accessory claim. **-frage,** *f.* secondary question, side-issue. **-frau,** *f.* concubine. **-gang,** *m.* byway, passage; (*Min.*) side lode, lateral vein. **-gasse,** *f.* side-street, by-lane. **-gebäude,** *n.* outbuilding, annex; adjacent building. **-gebühren,** *f.pl.* extras, supplementary fees, incidental charges. **-gedanke,** *m.* subordinate idea; mental reservation. **-geleise,** *n.* (*Railw.*) siding; (*fig.*) side-track. **-geräusche,** *n.pl.* (*Rad.*) noise, crackling, interference, atmospherics, static. **-gericht,** *n.* entremets, side-dish. **-geschmack,** *m.* after-taste. **-gewinn,** *m.* extra *or* incidental profit. **-gleis,** *n.* (*Railw.*) siding. **-handlung,** *f.* (*Theat.*) subordinate *or* subsidiary action; (*fig.*) episode, sideshow. **-haus,** *n.* adjoining house, house next-door.

neben|her, *adv. See* **-bei. -hergehend,** *adj.* additional, extra, secondary, accessory, subordinate, minor. **-hin,** *adv. See* **-her.**

Neben|kläger, *m.* co-plaintiff. **-kosten,** *pl.* extras, incidentals, petty expenses. **-linie,** *f.* (*Genealogy*) collateral line; (*Railw.*) branch line. **-mann,** *m.* next man (*in line*); (*Mil.*) man right *or* left of one. **-mensch,** *m.* fellow-creature. **-niere,** *f.* (*Anat.*) suprarenal *or* adrenal gland. **-person,** *f.* (*Theat.*) subordinate character; person of no consequence. **-postamt,** *n.* branch post-office. **-produkt,** *n. See* **-erzeugnis. -programm,** *n.* (*Films*) supporting programme. **-räume,** *m.pl.* offices (*i.e. rooms of a house other than living-rooms*). **-reaktion,** *f.* secondary *or* side reaction. **-rolle,** *f.* (*Theat.*) *see* **-person. -sache,** *f.* matter of minor importance. **nebensächlich,** *adj.* unimportant, immaterial, irrelevant; incidental, accessory, subordinate, subsidiary; (*pred.*) of no importance *or* consequence, not essential; ***eine -e Rolle spielen,*** be of secondary importance. **Neben|sächlichkeit,** *f.* unimportance, insignificance; triviality. **-satz,** *m.* (*Gram.*) subordinate *or* dependent clause. **-schluß,** *m. See* **-schaltung. -schlußmotor,** *m.* (*Elec.*) shunt motor. **-schößling,** *m.* sucker, offshoot. **-sonne,** *f.* mock-sun, parhelion. **-sprechen,** *n.* (*Rad.*) cross-talk. **-sproß,** *m. See* **-schößling.**

neben|ständig, *adj.* accessory, collateral. **-stehend,** *adj.* following, annexed, appended, marginal; (*pred.*) in the margin; ***wie - abgebildet,*** as in the accompanying illustration *or* in the illustration opposite.

Neben|stelle, *f.* sub- *or* branch-office. **-straße,** *f.* side-street, by-road. **-strom,** *m.* tributary, feeder; (*Elec.*) shunt-current. **-titel,** *m.* subtitle. **-ton,** *m.* secondary stress. **-tür,** *f.* side-door. **-umstand,** *m.* accidental circumstance, minor *or* accessory detail, incident. **-ursache,** *f.* incidental cause; secondary reason. **-verdienst,** *m. See* **-einkünfte. -versicherung,** *f.* collateral assurance, underwriting. **-weg,** *m.* by-way, side- *or* branch-road; *pl.* (*fig.*) indirect means. **-weib,** *n. See* **-frau. nebenweibig,** *adj.* (*Bot.*) perigynous. **-widerstand,** *m.* (*Elec.*) shunt, shunt resistance. **Neben|-winkel,** *m.* adjacent angle. **-wirkung,** *f.* secondary effect *or* action. **-wurzel,** *f.* adventitious root. **-zimmer,** *n.* next *or* adjoining room. **-zweck,** *m.* secondary aim.

neblig, *adj. See* **nebelig. Neblung,** *m. See* **Nebelung.**

nebst [ne:pst], *prep.* (*Dat.*) with, together *or* along with, in addition to, besides, including.

necken ['nɛkən], *v.t.* tease, chaff, (*coll.*) kid. **Neckerei** [-'raɪ], *f.* banter, raillery, chaffing, teasing. **neckisch,** *adj.* fond of teasing, roguish, playful; droll, funny.

nee! [ne:], *int.* (*dial., coll.*) no.

Neffe ['nɛfə], *m.* (**-n,** *pl.* **-n**) nephew.

Negation [negatsi'o:n], *f.* negation. **negativ** [-'ti:f], *adj.* (*Math., Elec., Phot.*) negative; (*coll.*) fruitless, unsuccessful. **Negativ,** *n.* (**-s,** *pl.* **-e**) (*Phot.*) negative.

Neger ['ne:gər], *m.* negro. **Neger|chor,** *m.* Negro-minstrels. **-handel,** *m.* slave-trade. **Negerin,** *f.* Negress, Negro black woman *or* girl.

negieren [ne'gi:rən], *v.t.* deny, answer in the negative, negate, negative (*a proposal*). **Negierung,** *f.* denial, negation.

Neglige [negli'ʒe:], *n.* (**-s,** *pl.* **-s**) 1. néglige, dishabille; 2. (*obs.*) informal dress, undress.

Negoziant [negotsi'ant], *m.* (**-en,** *pl.* **-en**) negotiator, agent, trader, merchant. **negoziieren, 1.** *v.t.* arrange, bring about; negotiate (*bills*). **2.** *v.i.* negotiate, traffic.

nehmen ['ne:mən], *irr.v.t.* take (*Dat.*, from), seize, appropriate, capture, lay hold of; receive, accept; take, clear (*an obstacle*), take, negotiate (*a corner*); (*at table*) help o.s. to; ***an sich -,*** take into (one's) safe keeping; purloin, misappropriate; ***auf sich*** (*Acc.*) **-,** take upon o.s., undertake, assume (*a charge or burden*); ***eine Verantwortung auf sich -,*** shoulder a responsibility; ***die Folgen auf sich -,*** answer for the consequences, (*coll.*) face the music; (*coll.*) ***auf seine Kappe -,*** accept responsibility for; ***ihn beim Worte -,*** take him at his word; ***es ernst - mit,*** be serious about; *for idioms with in see under* **Acht, Angriff, Anspruch, Empfang, Gebet, Grund, Kauf, Kost, Obhut, Pacht**; ***ich lasse es mir nicht -,*** I (must) insist upon it, I will not be talked out of it, I will not give way; ***er weiß seine Leute zu -,*** he understands how to handle people, he has a way with people; ***sie - sich*** (*Dat.*) ***beide nichts,*** there is nothing to choose between them, the one is as good as the other; ***über sich -,*** *see* ***auf sich -***; ***zu sich -,*** take into one's house; partake (of) *or* take (*food*), eat *or* drink (*s.th.*), have (*s.th.*) to eat *or* drink; ***sie zur Frau -,*** make her one's wife; ***etwas zur Hand -,*** take s.th. in hand, set about a th., make a start with a th.; ***sich*** (*Dat.*) ***etwas zu Herzen -,*** take a th. to heart; ***es genau -,*** be very particular *or* pedantic; ***genau*** or ***streng genommen,*** strictly speaking; ***- wir den Fall,*** let us assume *or* suppose; ***Urlaub -,*** be granted leave.
For other idioms see under **Anstand, Augenschein, Beispiel, Ende, Interesse, Mühe, Mund, Partei, Platz, Reißaus, Rücksicht, Schaden, Sicht, Stellung, Wort.**

Nehmen, *n.* (*Boxing*) ***er ist gut*** or ***hart im -,*** he can take a lot of punishment.

Nehrung ['ne:ruŋ], *f.* narrow tongue of land, spit.

Neid [naɪt], *m.* envy, jealousy (***gegen,*** of), grudge (against); ***das muß ihm der - lassen,*** (even) his worst enemy must admit that, (*coll.*) you've got to hand it to him; ***vor - vergehen,*** be eaten up with envy; ***- gegen ihn hegen,*** be envious of him; ***blaß*** or ***gelb*** or ***grau vor -,*** green with envy.

neiden ['naɪdən], *v.t.* ***ihm etwas -,*** envy *or* (be)-grudge him s.th. **Neider,** (*coll.*) **Neid|hammel, -hart,** *m.* envious p., (*coll.*) dog in a manger. **neidisch,** *adj.* envious, jealous (***auf*** (*Acc.*), of). **neidlos,** *adj.* free from envy, not envious, ungrudging.

Neidnagel ['naɪtna:gəl], *m.* (*dial.*) *see* **Niednagel.**

Neige ['naɪgə], *f.* 1. slope, decline, declivity; ***auf der -,*** aslant, atilt, on the slope; ***ein Faß auf die - setzen,*** tilt a barrel; 2. sediment, dregs; ***den Becher bis zur - leeren,*** drain the cup to the dregs; 3. depression, wane; ***zur*** or ***auf die - geben,*** come *or* draw *or* be coming to an end, run low *or* short, be on the decline.

neigen ['naɪgən], **1.** *v.t.* tilt, bend (over); incline, tilt, bow (down), lower. **2.** *v.r.* bow, dip, lean, slant, slope, incline; ***sich zum Ende -,*** draw to a close. **3.** *v.i.* ***- zu,*** lean *or* tend *or* incline to; be liable *or* subject *or* prone to; be given to, have a propensity for; ***er neigt zu Erkältungen,*** he is very apt to catch cold, he is subject *or* prone to chills; ***der geneigte Leser,*** the sympathetic *or* kind reader; ***ein geneigtes Ohr,*** a ready *or* sympathetic ear.

Neigung ['naɪguŋ], *f.* 1. incline, declivity, slope, gradient, tilt, slant; dip, pitch, list (*of ship*); (*Math., Astr.*) inclination; 2. (*fig.*) inclination, propensity (***zu,*** to *or* for), taste, liking, preference, bent (for), leaning, tendency, bias, trend (towards), disposition, proneness, proclivity, liability (to); – ***haben*** or ***fassen zu,*** take a fancy to.

Neigungs|ebene, *f.* inclined plane. **–ehe,** *f.* love-match. **–linie,** *f.* gradient. **–lot,** *n.* axis of incidence. **–messer,** *m.* clinometer. **–winkel,** *m.* angle of inclination.

nein [naɪn], *adv.* no; – ***und abermals –!*** no! a thousand times no! – ***doch!*** no, indeed! no, certainly not! **Nein,** *n.* refusal, denial; ***mit (einem) – beantworten,*** say no, answer in the negative, refuse; deny (it).

Nekrolog [nekro'lo:k], *m.* (**-s,** *pl.* **-e**) obituary (notice), necrology.

Nekromant [nekro'mant], *m.* (**-en,** *pl.* **-en**) necromancer. **Nekromantie** [–'ti:], *f.* necromancy.

Nekrose [ne'kro:zə], *f.* (*Med.*) necrosis, gangrene, mortification.

Nelke ['nɛlkə], *f.* (*Bot.*) pink, carnation (*Dianthus caryophyllus*), (*Bot.*) clove (*Eugenia caryophyllata*); ***gefüllte –,*** double carnation. **Nelken|öl,** *n.* oil of cloves. **–pfeffer,** *n.* allspice, pimento.

nennbar ['nɛnba:r], *adj.* mentionable; ***nicht –,*** unmentionable. **Nenn|belastung,** *f.* nominal load. **–drehzahl,** *f.* rated speed (*of an engine*).

nennen ['nɛnən], *irr.v.t.* name, call, designate, dub, term, style, denominate; mention (by name), quote, speak of; nominate (*a candidate*); (*Spt.*) enter (*für,* for); ***sich –,*** be named *or* called, go by the name of; ***er nennt sich Professor,*** he calls *or* styles himself a professor; ***das nenne ich Glück,*** that's what I call lucky; ***einer der nicht genannt sein will,*** one who does not wish to be named *or* wish his name to be known, one who wishes to remain anonymous; ***das Kind beim Namen –*** or ***das Ding beim rechten Namen –,*** call a spade a spade; ***Karl genannt der Kühne,*** Charles surnamed the Bold; *see* **genannt. nennenswert,** *adj.* worth mentioning, noteworthy, appreciable, considerable; ***nicht –,*** negligible, inconsiderable.

Nenner ['nɛnər], *m.* denominator; ***auf einen gemeinsamen – bringen,*** reduce to a common denominator (*also fig.*).

Nenn|fall, *m.* (*Gram.*) nominative (case). **–form,** *f.* (*Gram.*) infinitive (mood). **–geld,** *n.* (*Spt.*) entry fee. **–kurs,** *m.* (*Comm.*) par value. **–leistung,** *f.* rated power *or* output. **–tante,** *f.* titular aunt.

Nennung ['nɛnuŋ], *f.* mention, naming, designation; nomination, registration, (*Spt.*) entry. **Nennungs|liste,** *f.* list of entries *or* competitors. **–schluß,** *m.* (*Spt.*) close of entries.

Nennwert ['nɛnve:rt], *m.* nominal *or* face value; denomination (*of coin*); (*Comm.*) ***zum –,*** at par. **nennwertlos,** *adj.* (*Comm.*) no-par. **Nennwort,** *n.* (*Gram.*) noun, substantive.

Neologismus [neolo'gɪsmus], *m.* (**-,** *pl.* **-men**) neology, neologism, verbal innovation, newly coined word.

neppen ['nɛpən], *v.t.* (*sl.*) swindle, diddle, fleece, take in, do brown. **Nepplokal,** *n.* (*sl.*) gyp-joint.

Nereide [nere'i:də], *f.* nereid, sea-nymph.

nergeln ['nɛrgəln], *v.i. See* **nörgeln.**

Nerv [nɛrf], *m.* (**-(e)s** *or* **-en,** *pl.* **-en**) 1. nerve; ***ihm auf die –en fallen*** or ***gehen,*** get on his nerves; ***die –en verlieren,*** lose one's nerve; ***ich bin mit den –en herunter,*** I'm run down, I'm all nerves; ***eiserne –en,*** nerves of steel; (*coll.*) ***die hat vielleicht –en!*** she's got a nerve! 2. (*obs.*) sinew; 3. (*Bot.*) vein, rib (*of leaf*); 4. fibre, filament; 5. string (*of a bow*).

Nervatur [nɛrva'tu:r], *f.* (*Bot.*) venation.

Nerven|anfall, *m.* attack of nerves, nervous fit. **–arzt,** *m.* nerve specialist, neurologist. **–aufregung,** *f.* nervous excitement. **nervenaufreibend,** *adj.* nerve-racking. **Nerven|bündel,** *n.* (*Anat.*) nerve-fascicle; (*coll., fig.*) bag of nerves. **–entzündung,** *f.* neuritis. **–faser,** *f.* nerve fibre. **–fieber,** *n.* (unspecified) nervous disease; (*obs.*) typhus. **–heilanstalt,** *f.* clinic for nervous diseases. **–kitzel,** *m.* sensation, thrill. **–knoten,** *m.* ganglion. **nervenkrank,** *adj.* neurotic. **Nerven|kranke(r),** *m., f.* neurotic. **–krankheit,** *f.* neurosis. **–krieg,** *m.* war of nerves. **–leiden,** *n.* nervous disorder *or* complaint. **–probe,** *f.* test of nerves, trying affair, trial, ordeal. **–reiz,** *m.* nervous irritation. **–schmerz,** *m.* (*usu. pl.*) neuralgia. **–schnitt,** *m.* neurotomy. **–schock,** *m.* (nervous) shock. **nervenschwach,** *adj.* nervous, neurasthenic. **Nerven|schwäche,** *f.* nervous debility, neurasthenia. **–strang,** *m.* nerve-centre. **–system,** *n.* nervous system. **–zelle,** *f.* nerve cell. **–zentrum,** *n.* nerve centre (*also fig.*). **nervenzerrüttend,** *adj.* nerve-racking. **Nerven|zerrüttung,** *f.* shattered nerves. **–zucken,** *n.* nervous twitch(ing). **–zusammenbruch,** *m.* nervous breakdown.

nervig ['nɛrfɪç], *adj.* (*Bot.*) veined, ribbed; (*fig.*) sinewy, pithy, vigorous.

nervös [nɛr'vø:s], *adj.* nervous, excitable, fidgety, (*coll.*) nervy, edgy, jumpy, jittery; (*pred.*) on edge, keyed-up. **Nervosität** [–vosi'tɛ:t], *f.* nervousness, excitability.

Nerz [nɛrts], *m.* (**-es,** *pl.* **-e**) (*Zool.*) mink.

Nessel ['nɛsəl], *f.* (**-,** *pl.* **-n**) nettle; (*coll.*) ***sich in die –n setzen,*** get into trouble *or* into hot water, put one's foot in it. **Nessel|ausschlag,** *m.* nettle-rash, (*Med.*) urticaria. **–brand,** *m.* nettle-sting. **–fieber,** *n.*, **–sucht,** *f. See* **–ausschlag. –tuch,** *n.* muslin, cheese-cloth.

Nest [nɛst], *n.* (**-es,** *pl.* **-er**) 1. nest; (*of birds of prey*) eyrie, aerie; (*Prov.*) ***eigen – ist stets das best,*** there's no place like home; ***–er ausnehmen,*** go bird-nesting; ***sein eigenes – beschmutzen,*** foul one's own nest; (*fig.*) ***das – leer finden,*** find the bird(s) flown; (*sl.*) ***ins – gehen,*** turn in, hit the hay; 2. (*fig.*) god-forsaken place, backwater, (*sl.*) awful hole *or* dump; 3. (*Mil.*) emplacement; 4. (*Min.*) rosette, cluster; 5. (*of hair*) chignon.

Nestel ['nɛstəl], *f.* (**-,** *pl.* **-n**) thong, thread, string, lace. **Nestel|beschlag,** *m.* tag (*of a lace*). **–loch,** *n.* eyelet(-hole). **nesteln, 1.** *v.t.* lace (up), thong, tie, fasten. **2.** *v.i.* – ***an*** (*Dat.*), fuss *or* fiddle with. **Nestelnadel,** *f.* bodkin.

Nest|feder, *f.* down. **–flüchter,** *m.* autophagous bird, *pl.* autophagi. **–häkchen,** *n.* nestling, (*fig.*) spoilt child, pet, baby of the family. **–hocker,** *m.* insessorial *or* heterophagous bird, *pl.* insessores. **Nestling,** *m.* (**-s,** *pl.* **-e**) nestling. **Nestwurz,** *f.* (*Bot.*) bird's-nest orchis (*Neottia nidus avis*).

nett [nɛt], *adj.* nice, pretty; neat, tidy, trim, spruce; pleasant, amiable, kind; (*iron.*) ***–e Zustände,*** a fine state of affairs, a pretty kettle of fish.

netto ['nɛto], *adv.* (*Comm.*) net(t), clear (of all charges); – ***Kassa im voraus,*** net cash in advance. **Netto|betrag,** *m.* net amount. **–einnahme,** *f.*, **–ertrag,** *m.* net proceeds *or* receipts. **–gewicht,** *n.* net weight. **–gewinn,** *m.* clear profit. **–preis,** *m.* net price; – ***3 Pfund,*** 3 pounds net. **–registertonnen,** *pl.* net register tonnage.

Netz [nɛts], *n.* (**-es,** *pl.* **-e**) net, netting, mesh, gauze; lattice, grid, network; (*Opt.*) reticle, reticule; (*Anat.*) plexus, caul, reticulum, omentum; (*Elec.*) mains; luggage-rack; (*Hist.*) caul, reticule; (*fig.*) ***ins – gehen,*** walk into the trap; (*fig.*) ***ins – locken,*** win over; ***ins – schlagen*** or ***spielen,*** send *or* play (*the ball*) into the net; ***ein – von Lügen,*** a tangle *or* tissue of lies.

Netzanschluß ['nɛtsˀanʃlus], *m.* (*Elec.*) mains-connection, power-supply. **netzartig,** *adj.* reticular, reticulate. **Netz|auge,** *n.* (*Ent.*) compound eye. **–ball,** *m.* (*Tenn.*) net ball. **–ballspiel,** *n.* (*obs.*) lawn-tennis. **–brumm,** *m.* (*Rad.*) mains hum. **–empfänger,** *m.* (*Rad.*) mains receiver.

netzen ['nɛtsən], *v.t.* wet, moisten, sprinkle.

Netz|flügler, *m.pl.* (*Ent.*) neuroptera. **–funk,** *m.* (*Rad.*) line-relay service. **–gerät,** *n.* (*Rad.*) all-mains set. **–gleichrichter,** *m.* (*Elec.*) A.C. eliminator. **–haut,** *f.* (*Anat.*) retina; (*coll.*) ***das Bett im –,*** come-hither look. **–hautspiegel,** *m.* ophthalmoscope. **–hemd,** *n.* cellular shirt. **–karte,** *f.* unrestricted season ticket. **–magen,** *m.* (*Zool.*) reticulum (*of ruminants*). **–spannung,** *f.* (*Elec.*) mains *or* line voltage. **–steckdose,** *f.* (*Elec.*) mains socket *or* output. **–stecker,** *m.* (*Elec.*) mains plug. **–stoff,** *m.* cellular fabric, netting. **–strom,**

m. (*Elec.*) mains *or* line current. **–werk,** *n.* network, netting; (*Archit.*) reticulation.

neu [nɔy], **1.** *adj.* new, fresh; recent, latest, modern, novel; ***ein –er Anfang,*** a fresh start; ***die –(er)e Geschichte,*** modern history; ***–este Mode,*** latest fashion; ***–en Mut fassen,*** gain fresh courage; ***–este Nachrichten,*** the latest news; ***–ere Sprachen,*** modern languages; ***in –erer Zeit,*** in recent times, of late; ***in –ester Zeit,*** very recently, (*coll.*) no time ago; ***was gibt's Neues?*** what's the news? (*coll.*) what's new? (*sl.*) what's cooking? ***aufs –e*** or ***von –em,*** anew, afresh, (over) again, once more. **2.** *adv.* newly, afresh, anew. (*With finite verbs adv. is usu. written separately, e.g.* ***– aufgelegt,*** reprinted; ***ein Schauspiel – besetzen,*** re-cast a play; *with participles used attributively usu. as a pref., e.g.* ***–hinzukommende Mitglieder,*** members newly enrolling; ***ein –eröffnetes Geschäft,*** a recently opened business.)

Neu|ankömmling, *m.* new arrival, newcomer. **–anschaffung,** *f.* new purchase, acquisition. **–ansiedling,** *f.* resettlement. **neuartig,** *adj.* new-fashioned, new-style, modern, novel. **Neu|-auflage, –ausgabe,** *f.* new edition, reprint. **–bau,** *m.* reconstruction, rebuilding; building under construction; new(ly erected) building. **–bauten,** *pl.* new buildings. **–bauwohnung,** *f.* flat in a new block. **–bearbeitung,** *f.* revised edition, revision. **–bekehrte(r),** *m., f.* neophyte. **–belebung,** *f.* revival. **–besetzung,** *f.* new appointment (*to a post*), (*Theat.*) new cast(ing). **–bildung,** *f.* new growth *or* formation, (*Gram.*) neologism, (*Med.*) neoplasm. **–bruch,** *m.* newly cleared *or* broken ground. **–druck,** *m.* reprint. **–einstellung,** *f.* readjustment; replacement.

Neuenburg [ˈnɔyənburk], *n.* Neuchatel.

neuerdings [ˈnɔyərdɪŋs], *adv.* lately, of late, latterly, recently.

Neu(e)rer [ˈnɔy(ə)rər], *m.* innovator.

neuerlich [ˈnɔyərlɪç], **1.** *adj.* recent, fresh, renewed. **2.** *adv. See* **neuerdings.**

Neuerscheinung [ˈnɔyˀɛrʃaɪnuŋ], *f.* new publication.

Neuerung [ˈnɔyəruŋ], *f.* innovation, change, reform. **Neuerungssucht,** *f.* mania for change, craze for novelty, modernism. **neuerungssüchtig,** *adj.* bent on change.

Neu|erwerbung, *f. See* **–anschaffung.**

neuestens [ˈnɔyəstəns], *adv.* very recently.

Neu|fassung, *f.* revised text, revision, (*Law, Pol.*) amendment. **–fundland,** *n.* (*Geog.*) Newfoundland. **neu|gebacken,** *adj.* newly baked, freshly made, new (*bread etc.*), (*fig.*) newly-fledged, new-fangled. **–geboren,** *adj.* new-born; ***sich wie – fühlen,*** feel like a new man. **–gestalten,** *v.t.* reorganize; re-design, modify. **Neugestaltung,** *f.* reorganisation; modification.

Neugier(de) [ˈnɔygiːr(də)], *f.* curiosity, inquisitiveness. **neugierig,** *adj.* curious, inquisitive (***auf*** (*Acc.*), about); ***ihn – machen,*** arouse his curiosity; ***ich bin – ob,*** I wonder whether.

Neu|griechisch, *n.* modern Greek (*language*). **–gründung,** *f.* re-establishment; new foundation. **–gruppierung,** *f.* reorganisation, regrouping, reshuffling.

Neuheit [ˈnɔyhaɪt], *f.* novelty, originality, newness, freshness.

Neuhochdeutsch [ˈnɔyhoːxdɔytʃ], *n.* Modern High German (*language*).

Neuigkeit [ˈnɔyɪçkaɪt], *f.* (piece of) news; new production, novelty; ***–en des Tages,*** current events.

Neu|inszenierung, *f.* (*Theat.*) revival, new staging. **–jahr,** *n.* New Year('s Day); ***Prosit –!*** a happy New Year! **–jahrsabend,** *m.* New Year's Eve. **–jahrswunsch,** *m.* New Year's greeting (card). **–land,** *n.* fresh ground, virgin soil, (*fig.*) new territory *or* ground; ***– erschließen,*** reclaim land *or* the soil, (*fig.*) break new ground, make a new departure. **–landgewinnung,** *f.* reclamation of land *or* the soil.

neulich [ˈnɔylɪç], *adv.* recently, (*in E. Germany*) the other day, a day or two ago, (*in W. Germany*) the other week, a week or so ago; ***– abends,*** the other evening.

Neuling [ˈnɔylɪŋ], *m.* (**-s,** *pl.* **-e**) novice, beginner, tyro, (*coll.*) new hand.

neumodisch [ˈnɔymoːdɪʃ], *adj.* fashionable, new-fangled. **Neumond,** *m.* new moon.

neun [nɔyn], *num.adj.* nine; ***alle –(e) schieben*** or ***werfen,*** throw down the whole nine (*at skittles*). **Neun,** *f.* (-, *pl.* **-en**) (number) nine. **Neun|auge,** *n.* lamprey. **–eck,** *n.* nonagon. **neuneckig,** *adj.* nonagonal.

Neuner [ˈnɔynər], *m.* the figure nine; one of nine. **neunerlei,** *indecl.adj.* of 9 (different) sorts, 9 (different) kinds of.

neun|fach, –fältig, *adj.* ninefold. **–hundert,** *num. adj.* nine hundred. **–jährig,** *adj.* (*attrib.*) nine-year-old; (*pred.*) 9 years old. **–jährlich,** *adj.* recurring every ninth year, novennial. **–mal,** *adv.* 9 times. **–malklug,** *adj.* would-be clever, sapient. **Neunmalkluge(r),** *m., f.* know-all, wiseacre, (*coll.*) smart aleck. **neun|schwänzig,** *adj.* ***–e Katze,*** cat-o'-nine-tails. **–tägig,** *adj.* nine-day, nine days old. **–tausend,** *num.adj.* nine thousand.

neunt [nɔynt], *adj.* ninth. **neuntehalb,** *indecl.adj.* eight and a half. **Neuntel,** *n.* (*Swiss m.*) ninth (part). **neuntens,** *adv.* in the ninth place, ninthly. **Neuntöter,** *m.* (*Orn.*) red-backed shrike (*Lanius cristatus*). **neun|wertig,** *adj.* (*Chem.*) nonavalent. **–zehn,** *num.adj.* nineteen.

neunzig [ˈnɔyntsɪç], *num.adj.* ninety; ***in den –er Jahren,*** in the nineties. **Neunziger,** *m.* nonagenarian. **neunzigjährig,** *adj.* 90 years old. **Neunzigjährige(r),** *m., f.* nonagenarian. **neunzigst,** *num.adj.* ninetieth. **Neunzigstel,** *n.* ninetieth (part).

Neu|ordnung, *f.* reorganization, rearrangement, readjustment, reform. **–orientierung,** *f.* reorientation, readjustment; new approach *or* course *or* policy. **–philologe,** *m.* modern language specialist. **–platoniker,** *m.* Neo-platonist.

Neuralgie [nɔyralˈgiː], *f.* neuralgia. **neuralgisch** [–ˈralgɪʃ], *adj.* neuralgic. **Neurasthenie** [–teˈniː], *f.* neurasthenia. **Neurastheniker** [–ˈteːnikər], *m.* neurasthenic.

Neu|regelung, *f. See* **–ordnung. –reiche(r),** *m., f.* parvenu, (wealthy) upstart, *pl.* new rich, nouveaux riches.

Neurer, *m. See* **Neu(e)rer.**

Neurose [nɔyˈroːzə], *f.* neurosis. **Neurotiker,** *m.* neurotic.

Neu|schätzung, *f.* revaluation, reassessment. **–schnee,** *m.* new(ly fallen) snow, névé. **–schöpfung,** *f.* new creation. **–schottland,** *n.* (*Geog.*) Nova Scotia. **–seeland,** *n.* (*Geog.*) New Zealand. **–silber,** *m.* German *or* nickel silver, argentin. **–sprachler,** *m. See* **–philologe. neu|sprachlich,** *adj.* modern-language. **–steinzeitlich,** *adj.* neolithic. **Neusüdwales,** *n.* (*Geog.*) New South Wales. **neutestamentlich,** *adj.* New Testament.

neutral [nɔyˈtraːl], *adj.* neutral, impartial. **neutralisieren** [–iˈziːrən], *v.t.* neutralize, saturate. **Neutralität** [–iˈtɛːt], *f.* neutrality. **Neutralitäts|-erklärung,** *f.* declaration of neutrality. **–verletzung,** *f.* violation of neutrality. **Neutrum** [ˈnɔytrum], *n.* (**-s,** *pl.* **-ra** *or* **-ren**) (*Gram.*) neuter (gender).

neuvermählt [ˈnɔyfɛrmɛːlt], *adj.* newly married *or* wed. **Neu|wahl,** *f.* new election; re-election. **–wert,** *m.* value (when *or* as) new. **neuwertig,** *adj.* as good as new, practically new. **Neuzeit,** *f.* modern times. **neuzeitlich,** *adj.* modern, up-to-date; of modern times.

nicht [nɪçt], *adv.* 1. not (*only used to negative v. aux. e.g.* ***ich habe – geschrieben,*** I have not *or* (*coll.*) haven't written; ***ich bin – dort gewesen,*** I was not *or* (*coll.*) wasn't there; ***wird*** – or ***will –,*** will not, (*coll.*) won't; ***darf –,*** must not, (*coll.*) mustn't; may not; ***kann –,*** cannot, (*coll.*) can't; *see under the other modal aux. esp.* **müssen**). *With other verbs the extended form of negation with 'do' is necessary* (*except B. or Poet.*), *e.g.* ***ich schwimme –,*** I do not *or* (*coll.*) don't swim; ***fuhren Sie danach – nach Berlin?*** did you not *or* (*coll.*) didn't you then go to Berlin? ***nein, ich fuhr – dorthin,*** no I did not *or* (*coll.*) didn't (go there); 2. (*before comp.*) no; not any; ***– besser als,*** no better *or* not any better; ***– mehr,*** no more, not any more; 3. (*before adjs.*) in-, un-, non-; ***– zusammendrückbar,*** incompressible; ***– berufsmäßig,*** unprofessional; ***am Kampf – beteiligt,*** non-combatant; (*for the more commonly negated adjs. see compounds with* ***nicht–*** *below*); 4. (*coll. idiomatic usage*) ***und ich auch –,*** nor *or* neither do (*or* did) I, no more do (*or* did) I; ***bitte –!*** please don't! ***– doch!*** (*beseeching*) (please) don't! (*categoric*) certainly not! ***durchaus –,*** not at all, by no means, on no condition; in no way, not in the least; ***– einmal,*** not even, (***ganz und***) ***gar –,*** *see* ***durchaus –; noch –,*** not (as) yet; ***nur das –!*** anything but that; (*sl.*) ***das ist – ohne,*** that's not bad, that's not so dusty, that's not to be sneezed at; ***– wahr?*** is it not so? (*coll.*) isn't it? ***Sie kommen doch, – wahr?*** you will come, won't you? ***wir kennen ihn, – wahr?*** we know him, don't we? ***er kennt uns –, – wahr?*** he doesn't know us, does he? ***– wenige von ihnen ertranken,*** not a few of *or* quite a number of them were drowned; 5. (*Poet.*) to be sure, (*or oft. redundant*) ***wie schön ist – die Eintracht!*** how beautiful is concord! (is it not?); ***verhüt' es Gott, daß ich – Hilfe brauche!*** God forbid that I should need help!

nicht–, *adj.pref.*, **Nicht–,** *noun pref. See* **nicht,** 3.

Nichtachtung ['nɪçtˀaxtuŋ], *f.* disregard, disrespect; (*Law*) contempt. **nichtamtlich,** *adj.* unofficial. **Nichtanerkennung,** *f.* disavowal; repudiation (*of debts*). **nichtangreifend,** *adj.* non-corroding, inert. **Nicht|angriffspakt,** *m.* non-aggression pact. **–annahme,** *f.* non-acceptance. **–arier,** *m.*, **nichtarisch,** *adj.* (*Nat. Soc.*) non-Aryan, Jewish. **Nichtbeachtung,** *f.* non-observance (*Gen.*, of), failure to comply (with). **nichtbeamtet,** *adj.* unestablished, not on the permanent staff. **Nicht|befolgung,** *f. See* **–beachtung. –berechtigte(r),** *m.*, *f.* unauthorized p. **nichtbewirtschaftet,** *adj.* non-rationed. **Nichtbezahlung,** *f.* non-payment, failure to pay.

Nichte ['nɪçtə], *f.* niece.

Nicht|eignung, *f.* unfitness, unsuitability. **–eingeweihte(r),** *m.*, *f.* uninitiated *or* uninformed p. **–einhaltung,** *f.* non-compliance, failure to comply (with). **–einmischung,** *f.* non-intervention. **–eisenmetall,** *n.* non-ferrous metal. **–erfüllung,** *f.* default, non-performance. **–erscheinen,** *n.* non-appearance, failure to attend, absence, (*Law*) default. **–fachmann,** *m.* layman, amateur. **nichtflüchtig,** *adj.* non-volatile. **Nichtgebrauch,** *m.* ***bei –,*** when not in use. **Nicht-Ich,** *n.* (*Phil.*) non-ego, world of objective reality.

nichtig ['nɪçtɪç], *adj.* null, void, invalid; vain, futile, empty, idle; ***–e Vorwände,*** empty *or* idle *or* flimsy excuses; ***für*** (***null und***) ***– erklären,*** annul, quash, invalidate, declare (null and) void. **Nichtigkeit,** *f.* nothingness, futility, emptiness, vanity; (*Law*) nullity, invalidity. **Nichtigkeits|beschwerde,** *f.* (*Law*) plea of nullity. **–erklärung,** *f.* annulment, nullification.

Nicht|kämpfer, *m.* non-combatant. **–leiter,** *m.* (*Elec.*) non-conductor. **–metall,** *m.* metalloid. **nichtmetallisch,** *adj.* non-metallic. **Nichtmitglied,** *n.* non-member. **nicht|öffentlich,** *adj.* private; ***in –er Sitzung,*** in closed session, in camera. **–periodisch,** *adj.* aperiodic. **Nicht|raucher,** *m.* non-smoker. **–raucherabteil,** *n.* non-smoking compartment. **nicht|reduzierbar,** *adj.* irreducible. **–rostend,** *adj.* non-corroding, rust-proof, (*of steel*) stainless.

nichts [nɪçts], *indef. indecl. pron.* nothing, not . . . anything, (*Poet.*) naught; ***– als,*** nothing but; ***es ist – daran,*** it is of no consequence; there is no truth in it; ***– anderes als,*** nothing else but; ***– daraus machen,*** not take too seriously; ***– dergleichen,*** nothing of the kind *or* sort, no such thing; ***fast*** (***gar***) ***–,*** hardly anything; ***das ist – für mich,*** that's not for me, that is of no use to me, it's not in my line; ***für – und wieder –,*** for no (earthly) reason at all; (***ganz und***) ***gar –,*** nothing at all, nothing whatever; ***– mehr,*** no(thing) more, not any more; ***mir – dir –,*** without more ado, as cool as you please, as cool as a cucumber, bold as brass; ***es ist – damit,*** it's no go; ***– Neues,*** nothing new; ***soviel wie –,*** practically nothing, next to nothing; ***um – gebessert,*** in no way *or* wise improved; ***um – spielen,*** play for love; ***– für ungut!*** don't take it amiss; ***– davon!*** not a word *or* don't talk about it; ***wenn es weiter – ist,*** if that is all, if it's nothing more than that; ***– weniger als,*** anything but; (*coll.*) ***wie –,*** like nobody's business; ***– zu machen!*** there's nothing (more) can be done *or* (more) to be done about it, (*coll.*) nothing doing! ***es macht –,*** it doesn't matter, never mind! ***es nützt –,*** it's no use *or* no good, it doesn't help (at all); ***das hat – zu sagen,*** that's beside the point; ***es schadet –,*** there's no harm in that; *see also* ***es macht –; es bleibt mir – übrig,*** I have no choice in the matter, I am left with no alternative; ***zu – werden,*** come to nothing.

[1]**Nichts,** *n.* nothing(ness), emptiness, void; (*of a th.*) trifle, bagatelle, mere nothing; (*of a p.*) nonentity, cipher; ***aus dem –,*** from nowhere; ***vor dem – stehen,*** be face to face with ruin, not have a leg to stand on, be past hope.

[2]**Nichts,** *n.* (*Chem.*) zinc oxide, flowers of zinc.

nichtsahnend ['nɪçtsˀa:nənt], *adj.* unsuspecting.

Nichtschwimmer ['nɪçtʃvɪmər], *m.* non-swimmer.

nichts|destominder, –destoweniger, *adv.* none the less, nevertheless, notwithstanding, just the same.

Nichtsein ['nɪçtzaɪn], *n.* non-existence, non-entity, nullity.

Nichtser ['nɪçtsər], *m.* (*coll.*) *see* **Nichtsnutz.**

Nichtskönner ['nɪçtskœnər], *m.* ignoramus, dunce, (*coll.*) duffer; blockhead, nincompoop; muddler.

Nichtsnutz ['nɪçtsnuts], *m.* (**-es,** *pl.* **-e**) good-for-nothing, ne'er-do-well. **nichtsnutz(ig),** *adj.* useless, worthless, good-for-nothing. **Nichtsnutzigkeit,** *f.* uselessness, worthlessness.

nichtssagend ['nɪçtsza:gənt], *adj.* meaningless, insignificant, (*of statements*) trite, trivial, non-committal, (*of appearance*) empty, indeterminate, vague, colourless, expressionless, vacuous.

Nichts|tuer, *m.* idler, loafer, slacker. **–tun,** *n.* idleness, indolence, inaction, idling; ***mit – verbringen,*** idle away (*one's time*).

nichtswürdig ['nɪçtsvyrdɪç], *adj.* worthless, base, vile, infamous; contemptible. **Nichtswürdigkeit,** *f.* worthlessness, baseness, infamy, villainy.

nicht|tropfend, *adj.* non-drip. **–versichert,** *adj.* uninsured. **Nicht|vollziehung,** *f. See* **–erfüllung. –vorbestrafte(r),** *m.*, *f.* first offender. **–vorhandensein,** *n.* absence, (complete) lack, (*Phil.*) non-existence. **–wissen,** *n.* ignorance. **–wollen,** *n.* unwillingness. **–zahlung,** *f.* non-payment; ***bei –,*** in default of payment. **nichtzielend,** *adj.* (*Gram.*) intransitive. **Nichtzutreffende(s),** *n.* that which is inapplicable.

[1]**Nickel** ['nɪkəl], *n.* (*Austr. m.*) (*Chem.*) nickel.

[2]**Nickel,** *m.* (*coll.*) small coin, copper, (*Am.*) dime.

[3]**Nickel,** *m.* (*dial.*) dwarf; pigheaded fellow; scamp.

Nickel|chromstahl, *m.* chrome-nickel steel. **–stahl,** *m.* nickel-steel. **–überzug,** *f.* nickel-plating.

nicken ['nɪkən], *v.i.* nod (one's head); (*coll.*) doze (off), snooze, nod. **Nickerchen,** *n.* (*coll.*) nap, snooze, forty winks.

nid, *prep.* (*dial.*) *see* **nied.**

nie [ni:], *adv.* never, at no time; ***– und nimmer,*** never at any time, never yet; ***fast –,*** hardly ever; ***jetzt oder –,*** now or never.

nied ['ni:t], *prep.*, *adv.* (*dial.*) below, beneath. **nieden** [–dən], *adv.* (*Poet.*) here below, here on earth.

nieder ['ni:dər], **1.** *adj.* low, inferior; mean, base, vulgar, common; ***hoch und –,*** high and low, great and small, rich and poor; ***der –e Adel,*** the gentry; ***von –er Geburt,*** low-born, of low birth, of humble origin. **2.** *adv.* down, low; ***auf und –,*** up and down; ***– mit den Verrätern!*** down with the traitors!

nieder|beugen, **1.** *v.t.* bend down, depress, (*fig.*) weigh *or* cast down; humiliate. **2.** *v.r.* bow *or* bend (down *or* low). **–brechen,** *irr.v.i.* (*aux.* s.), *v.t.* break down. **–brennen,** *irr.v.i.* (*aux.* s.), *v.t.* burn down, burn to the ground. **–brüllen,** *v.t.* howl down, boo.

niederdeutsch [ˈniːdərdɔytʃ], *adj.* Low German, North German.

Niederdruck [ˈniːdərdruk], *m* low pressure. **nieder|drücken,** *v.t.* press *or* weigh down, depress; oppress, keep down; (*fig.*) depress, prey on the mind; *see* **–gedrückt.**

nieder|fahren, *irr.v.i.* (*aux.* s.) descend. **–fallen,** *irr.v.i.* (*aux.* s.) fall *or* drop (down); (*of birds*) settle, alight; (*Chem.*) precipitate (out); ***vor ihm –,*** throw o.s. *or* fall at his feet.

Nieder|frequenz, *f.* (*Elec.*) low frequency, (*Rad.*) audio- *or* speech-frequency. **–gang,** *m.* 1. downfall, decline, decay; (*Mech.*) down-stroke; (*of sun etc.*) setting; 2. (*Naut.*) companion-way.

nieder|gedrückt, *adj.* depressed. **–gehen,** *irr.v.i.* (*aux.* s.) go down, descend; (*of sun etc.*) set, sink; (*of storm*) burst, break; (*Av.*) touch down, land, alight.

niedergeschlagen [ˈniːdərgəʃlaːgən], *adj.* downcast (*as eyes, also fig.*), (*fig.*) down-hearted, crestfallen, dejected, despondent, depressed, low-spirited, cast-down. **Niedergeschlagenheit,** *f.* depression, dejection, despondency, low spirits.

nieder|halten, *irr.v.t.* hold *or* keep down, suppress; fasten down; (*Mil.*) pin down, neutralize. **–holen,** *v.t.* haul down, lower (*a flag*).

Niederholz [ˈniːdərhɔlts], *n.* undergrowth, brushwood, scrub.

nieder|kämpfen, *v.t.* overcome, overpower, subdue, get the better of; (*Mil.*) silence (*enemy fire*), reduce (*a fortress*), put out of action. **–knallen,** *v.t.* shoot down, (*sl.*) bump off.

niederkommen [ˈniːdərkɔmən], *irr.v.i.* (*aux.* s.) be confined (***mit,*** with), be delivered (of) (*a child*). **Niederkunft,** *f.* (-, *pl.* **¨-e**) delivery, confinement.

Niederlage [ˈniːdərlaːgə], *f.* 1. warehouse, depot, (*Comm.*) agency, branch (establishment); 2. (*Mil.*) defeat, overthrow, rout, (*coll.*) beating.

Nieder|lande, *pl.* the Netherlands, the Low Countries. **–länder,** *m.* Dutchman.

niederlassen [ˈniːdərlasən], **1.** *irr.v.t.* let down, lower, drop. **2.** *irr.v.r.* take a seat, sit down; (*of birds*) alight, perch; settle (down), take up one's abode; establish o.s., set up in business. **Niederlassung,** *f.* establishment; settlement, colony; (*Comm.*) branch, agency.

niederlegen [ˈniːdərleːgən], **1.** *v.t.* 1. lay *or* put down, deposit; store, warehouse (*goods*); ***schriftlich –,*** set forth *or* put (down) in writing; 2. resign, retire from, (*coll.*) give up (*a post*), abdicate (*throne*), lay down (*arms, laws*); (*coll.*) ***die Arbeit –,*** (go on) strike, down tools, walk out. **2.** *v.r.* lie down, go to bed. **Niederlegung,** *f.* 1. deposition; resignation; 2. abdication.

nieder|machen, –metzeln, *v.t.* slay, massacre, butcher, cut down, wipe out. **–reißen,** *irr.v.t.* pull *or* tear down, demolish. **–ringen,** *irr.v.t.* overpower, overcome, wear down (*opposition*). **–schießen, 1.** *irr.v.t.* shoot down. **2.** *irr.v.i.* (*aux.s.*) shoot *or* swoop down (*from the sky*).

Niederschlag [ˈniːdərʃlaːk], *m.* precipitation, rainfall; (radioactive) fall-out; (*Boxing*) knock-out; (*Chem.*) deposit, sediment, precipitate; (*Mus.*) beat, fall; (*fig.*) result, outcome, upshot; ***seinen – finden in*** (*Dat.*), be reflected *or* embodied in, find expression in. **nieder|schlagen, 1.** *irr.v.t.* strike *or* knock down, fell, (*Boxing*) floor, knock out; suppress, quell, put down (*a rising*); refute, quash (*a claim*); (*fig.*) prostrate, cast down. dishearten, depress; *see* **–geschlagen. 2.** *irr.v.r.* (*Chem.*) precipitate (out), be deposited; (*fig.*) *see* ***seinen Niederschlag finden.*** **–schlagend,** *adj.* disheartening, depressing. **Niederschlag|mittel,** *n.* (*Chem.*) precipitant, precipitating agent. **Niederschlag(s)-messer,** *m.* rain-gauge. **Niederschlagung,** *f.* cancellation, quashing; suppression (*of rebellion*). **Niederschlagwasser,** *n.* condensate, water of condensation, condensed water.

nieder|schmettern, *v.t.* strike down, dash to the ground; (*fig.*) overwhelm, crush. **–schmetternd,** *adj.* crushing, shattering (*news etc.*). **–schreiben,** *irr.v.t.* record, write down. **–schreien,** *irr.v.t.* shout down.

Niederschrift [ˈniːdərʃrɪft], *f.* writing (down); record, written copy, notes.

nieder|setzen, 1. *v.t.* set *or* put down, deposit; (*Mil.*) ground (*arms*). **2.** *v.r.* sit down, (*of birds*) perch, alight. **–sinken,** *irr.v.i.* (*aux.* s.) sink *or* drop down, drop, sink, droop, collapse.

Niederspannung [ˈniːdərʃpanuŋ], *f.* (*Elec.*) low voltage, low tension.

nieder|steigen, *irr.v.i.* (*aux.* s.) descend, step down. **–stimmen,** *v.t.* outvote, vote down. **–stoßen, 1.** *irr.v.t.* push *or* knock down. **2.** *irr.v.i.* (*aux.* s.) swoop *or* pounce down (***auf*** (*Acc.*), upon). **–strecken,** *v.t.* strike *or* stretch to the ground, prostrate; fell, floor. **–stürzen, 1.** *v.t.* throw *or* hurl down. **2.** *v.i.* (*aux.* s.) tumble down.

Niedertracht [ˈniːdərtraxt], *f.* meanness, baseness. **niederträchtig,** *adj.* low, base, mean, abject, vile. **Niederträchtigkeit,** *f.* base act, vile action, (*coll.*) dirty trick; *see also* **Niedertracht.**

niedertreten [ˈniːdərtreːtən], *irr.v.t.* tread *or* trample down; wear down (*heels of shoes*).

Niederung [ˈniːdəruŋ], *f.* lowland, plain, low ground, marsh.

niederwärts [ˈniːdərvɛrts], *adv.* downwards; (*Her.*) *– gekehrt,* reversed.

niederwerfen [ˈniːdərvɛrfən], **1.** *irr.v.t.* throw *or* cast *or* fling down; (*fig.*) put down, suppress, overcome, crush (*a rising*); ***von einer Krankheit niedergeworfen werden,*** be prostrated by *or* (*coll.*) laid up with an illness. **2.** *irr.v.r.* prostrate *or* hurl o.s. (***vor ihm,*** at his feet). **Niederwerfung,** *f.* suppression.

Niederwild [ˈniːdərvɪlt], *n.* small game.

niedlich [ˈniːtlɪç], *adj.* pretty, nice, dainty, neat, (*coll.*) sweet, cute. **Niedlichkeit,** *f.* prettiness, daintiness, neatness.

Niednagel [ˈniːtnaːgəl], *m.* agnail, hangnail, torn quick (*of nail*).

niedrig [ˈniːdrɪç], *adj.* low; lowly, humble, obscure; inferior; mean, base, abject, vile, vulgar; ***hoch und –,*** great and small; one and all; (*Comm.*) ***–e Prämie,*** short premium; ***– halten,*** keep down (*prices*); ***von –em Stande,*** of low birth; of poor standing; ***von ihm – denken,*** have a poor *or* low opinion of him. **niedriger,** *comp.adj.* lower; inferior; ***– hängen,*** (*fig.*) remove from its pedestal, show in its true light, (*sl.*) debunk; ***ausländische Fonds gingen –,*** foreign stocks fell; ***– machen,*** lower, reduce. **Niedrigkeit,** *f.* lowness, low level; lowliness; baseness. **niedrigst,** *sup.adj.* lowest, minimum, bottom. **Niedrigwasser,** *n.* low tide *or* water.

niemals [ˈniːmaːls], *adv. See* **nie.**

niemand [ˈniːmant], *pron.* (*Gen.* **-(e)s,** *Dat.* **-em** *or* (*obs.*) **-en,** *Acc.* **-** *or* **-en**) nobody, no one; no man, none, not anybody, (*coll.*) not a soul; ***– als,*** no one *or* none but; ***– anders,*** nobody else, no one else. **Niemandsland,** *n.* no-man's-land.

Niere [ˈniːrə], *f.* 1. kidney; *pl.* loins; ***wandernde –,*** floating kidney; ***auf Herz und –n prüfen,*** put to the acid test; 2. (*Min.*) nodule, concretion. **Nieren|-braten,** *m.* roast loin. **–entzündung,** *f.* nephritis. **–fett,** *n.* suet. **nierenförmig,** *adj.* reniform, kidney-shaped. **Nieren|grieß,** *m.* renal gravel. **–stein,** *m.* renal calculus. **–stück,** *n.* loin of veal. **–talg,** *m.* suet.

nieseln [ˈniːzəln], *v.i.* 1. drizzle; 2. (*dial.*) dawdle.

niesen [ˈniːzən], *v.i.* sneeze. **Niesen,** *n.* sneeze; sneezing.

Nies|kraut [ˈniːs–], *n.* (*Bot.*) sneezewort (*Achillea ptarmica*). **–pulver,** *n.* sneezing-powder; sternutative, snuff.

Nieß|brauch [ˈniːs–], *m.* usufruct; ***lebenslänglicher***

–, life-interest. **–braucher, –nutzer,** *m.* usufructuary. **–nutzung,** *f. See* **–brauch.**

Nieswurz ['ni:svurts], *f.* (*Bot., Chem.*) hellebore (root).

Niet [ni:t], *m.* **(-(e)s,** *pl.* **-e)** (*Tech.*) rivet.

[1]**Niete** ['ni:tə], *f.* (*coll.*) *see* **Niet.**

[2]**Niete,** *f.* blank (*in a lottery*); failure, (*sl.*) washout, flop.

nieten ['ni:tən], *v.t.* rivet. **Nieter,** *m.* riveter. **Nietstelle,** *f.* riveted joint. **niet- und nagelfest,** *adj.* (*coll.*) firmly fixed *or* fastened, (*fig.*) clinched. **Niet|verbindung,** *f. See* **–stelle.**

Nil [ni:l], *m.* (*Geog.*) the (River) Nile. **Nilpferd,** *n.* hippopotamus.

Nimbus ['nɪmbus], *m.* (*Meteor.*) nimbus (cloud); halo, aureole, nimbus, (*fig.*) halo, aura; prestige.

nimm [nɪm], *see* **nehmen**; (*coll.*) ***er ist vom Stamme Nimm,*** he is very greedy, he has a grasping nature.

nimmer ['nɪmər], *adv.* never; *see* **nie. Nimmer|leinstag,** *m. See* **–mehrstag. nimmermehr,** *adv.* nevermore; never (again); on no account, by no means, not at all. **Nimmermehrstag,** *m.* (*coll.*) when the cows come home, doomsday, the Greek Calends. **nimmer|müde,** *adj.* indefatigable. **–satt,** *adj.* insatiable. **Nimmersatt,** *m.* (- *or* **-(e)s,** *pl.* **-e**) glutton. **Nimmerwiedersehen,** *n.* ***auf –,*** never to meet again; ***er verschwand auf –,*** he left for good.

nimmst [nɪmst], **nimmt,** *see* **nehmen.**

Nipp ['nɪp], *m.* **(-(e)s,** *pl.* **-e)** nip, sip. **nippen,** *v.t., v.i.* 1. (*an* (*Dat.*)) (take a) sip, taste; (*dial.*) tipple; 2. (*dial.*) nod, snooze.

Nippflut ['nɪpflu:t], *f.* (*Naut.*) neap-tide.

Nipp|sachen, *f.pl.* knick-knacks, trinkets. **–tisch,** *m.* what-not.

nirgend(s) ['nɪrgənt(s)], **nirgendwo(hin),** *adv.* nowhere (at all), not anywhere.

Nische ['ni:ʃə], *f.* niche, recess.

Niß [nɪs], *f.* (-, *pl.* **-(ss)e**), **Nisse,** *f.* nit. **nissig,** *adj.* lousy, nitty; (*fig.*) mean.

nisten ['nɪstən], *v.i.* nest, build a nest. **Nistkasten,** *m.* nesting-box.

Nitrat [ni'tra:t], *n.* **(-(e)s,** *pl.* **-e)** nitrate. **nitrieren,** *v.t.* (*Chem.*) nitrate, (*Metall.*) nitrify. **Nitrierung,** *f.* (*Chem.*) nitration, (*Metall.*) nitridation.

Nitro|glyzerin [nitro–], *n.* nitroglycerine. **–toluol,** *n.* nitrotoluene. **–zellulose,** *f.* nitrocellulose, guncotton.

Niveau [ni'vo:], *n.* **(-s,** *pl.* **-s)** level; (*fig.*) standard; ***unter dem –,*** not up to standard; (*coll.*) ***– haben,*** be above average, be of a high order, have class.

nivellieren [nivɛ'li:rən], *v.t.* level, grade. **Nivellier|latte,** *f.* (*Surv.*) stadia(-rod). **–waage,** *f.* spirit-level.

Nix [nɪks], *m.* **(-es,** *pl.* **-e)** water-sprite. **Nixe,** *f.* water-nymph, mermaid.

nix, (*dial., coll.*) *see* **nichts.**

Nizza ['nɪtsa], *n.* (*Geog.*) Nice.

nobel ['no:bəl], *adj.* (*comp.* ***nobler***) noble, distinguished, grand, stylish, elegant; (*coll.*) generous, open-handed; (*coll.*) ***sich – zeigen,*** come down handsomely.

Nobis|haus ['no:bɪs–], *n.*, **–krug,** *m.* (*sl.*) purgatory.

noch [nɔx], **1.** *adv.* 1. still, yet; ***– besser wäre es wenn ...,*** it would be still *or* even better if ...; ***– gestern,*** only yesterday; ***– heute,*** even today, this very day; ***– immer,*** still; ***– im 19. Jahrhundert,*** as late as the 19th century; ***– jetzt,*** even now; ***– keine Nachricht,*** no news (as) yet; ***– nicht,*** not yet; ***– lange nicht,*** not by a long way; ***– nie,*** never (before); ***nur – ein paar Gröschen übrig,*** only a few pence left; ***– vor kurzem,*** until recently; (*coll.*) ***das hat mir gerade – gefehlt,*** that's just what I needed, (*iron.*) that's the last straw, that's the giddy limit; (*coll.*) ***ich habe Zeit – und –,*** I've plenty of time, I have time and to spare; 2. in addition (to that); besides, further; ***– dazu,*** in addition, over and above that, (and) what is more, into the bargain; ***– einer,*** one more, (still) another; ***– einmal,*** once more, once again; ***– einmal so viel,*** as much again, twice as much; ***– eins*** or ***etwas,*** just one more *or* one final point; ***– etwas?*** is there anything else *or* something more? ***wer kommt –?*** who else is coming? ***was wollen Sie –?*** what more do you want? 3. ***– so,*** ever so; ***sei es – so wichtig,*** however important it may be, no matter how important it is, be it ever so important. **2.** *conj.* ***weder ... –,*** neither ... nor.

Nochgeschäft ['nɔxgəʃɛft], *n.* (*St. Exch.*) put, call. **nochmalig,** *adj.* repeated, renewed, reiterated, re-; ***–e Durchsicht,*** revision, re-examination; ***bei –er Überlegung,*** on second thoughts. **nochmals,** *adv.* once more, (once) again, over again, a second time, re-.

Nock [nɔk], *n.* **(-(e)s,** *pl.* **-e)** *or f.* (-, *pl.* **-en**) (*Naut.*) yard-arm.

Nöck [nœk], *m.* **(-(e)s,** *pl.* **-e)** *see* **Nix.**

Nocke ['nɔkə], *f.* (*dial.*) dumpling.

Nocken ['nɔkən], *m.* cam, lifter. **Nockenwelle,** *f.* camshaft.

Nockerl ['nɔkərl], *n.* **(-s,** *pl.* **-(n))** (*dial.*) *see* **Nocke.**

Noddiseeschwalbe [nɔdi'ze:ʃvalbə], *f.* (*Orn.*) noddy, (*Am.*) noddy tern (*Anous stolidus*).

nölen ['nø:lən], *v.t.* (*dial.*) dawdle, drawl. **Nöl|peter,** *m.*, **–suse,** *f.* (*coll.*), slowcoach.

Nomade [no'ma:də], *m.* **(-n,** *pl.* **-n)** nomad. **Nomadenleben, Nomadentum,** *n.* nomadic life. **nomadisch,** *adj.* nomadic.

Nomen ['no:mɛn], *n.* **(-s,** *pl.* **Nomina)** noun, substantive. **Nomenklatur** [–kla'tu:r], *f.* (-, *pl.* **-en**) nomenclature, technical terms.

nominal [nomi'na:l], *adj.* nominal. **Nominalwert,** *m.* nominal *or* face value. **Nominativ** [–'ti:f], *m.* **(-s,** *pl.* **-e)** nominative (case).

nominell [nomi'nɛl], *adj. See* **nominal.**

nominieren [nomi'ni:rən], *v.t.* nominate.

None ['no:nə], *f.* 1. (*Mus.*) ninth; 2. (*R.C.*) nones.

Nonius ['no:nius], *m.* (-, *pl.* **-se** *or* **-nien**) vernier.

Nonne ['nɔnə], *f.* 1. nun; 2. (*Ent.*) night-moth; 3. (*Metall.*) pot-mould. **Nonnen|gans,** *f.* (*Orn.*) *see* **Weißwangengans. –kloster,** *n.* nunnery, convent. **–meise,** *f.* (*Orn.*) *see* **Sumpfmeise. –steinschmätzer,** *m.* (*Orn.*) pied wheatear (*Oenanthe leucomela*).

Noppe ['nɔpə], *f.* nap, burl (*in cloth*). **noppen,** *v.t.* burl, nap.

Nord [nɔrt], *m.* 1. north; (*Naut.*) ***– zum Westen,*** north by west; 2. **(-(e)s,** *pl.* **-e)** (*Poet.*) north wind. **Nord|amerika,** *n.* America. **–atlantikpakt,** *m.* North Atlantic Treaty Organization. **Norden,** *m.* the North; ***gegen*** or ***gen*** or ***nach –,*** to the North, in a northerly direction; ***im –,*** to the north (***von*** *or Gen.*, of). **Nordersonne,** *f.* (*Naut.*) midnight sun.

nordisch ['nɔrdɪʃ], *adj.* Norse (= *Scandinavian*); Nordic (*race*), Teutonic (*language*).

Nord|kap, *n.* North Cape. **–länder, 1.** *m.* Northerner. **2.** *m. pl.* Northern nations.

nördlich ['nœrtlɪç], **1.** *adj.* northern, northerly; arctic; ***–e Breite,*** north latitude; ***–e Halbkugel,*** northern hemisphere; ***–es Eismeer,*** Arctic Ocean. **2.** *adv.* (to the) north (***von*** *or Gen.*, of).

Nord|licht, *n.* aurora borealis, northern lights. **–mark,** *f.* (*Nat. Soc.*) Schleswig-Holstein. **–ost(en),** *m.* north-east. **nordöstlich,** *adj.* north-east(ern). **Nord|ostseekanal,** *m.* Kiel Canal. **–pol,** *m.* North Pole. **–polarkreis,** *m.* Arctic Circle. **–polfahrer,** *m.* arctic explorer. **–polfahrt,** *f.* arctic expedition. **–schein,** *m.* zodiacal light. **–see,** *f.* North Sea. **–seetaucher,** *m.* (*Orn.*) *see* **Sterntaucher. –staaten,** *m.pl.* Northern states (*of America*). **–stern,** *m.* pole star. **nordwärts,** *adv.* northward. **Nordwest(en),** *m.* north-west. **nordwestlich,** *adj.* northwest(erly). **Nordwind,** *m.* north wind.

Nörgelei [nœrgə'laɪ], *f.* nagging, fault-finding, carping; grumbling, (*coll.*) grousing. **nörgelig** ['nœrgəlɪç], *adj.* nagging, fault-finding, carping; grumbling, grousing. **nörgeln,** *v.i.* grumble, grouse; nag; find fault (***an*** (*Dat.*), with), carp (at).

Nörgler, *m.* grumbler, fault-finder, carper, malcontent.

Norm [nɔrm], *f.* (-, *pl.* **-en**) 1. rule, standard; measure, rate, quota, norm; criterion; yardstick; 2. (*Typ.*) signature.

normal [nɔr'maːl], *adj.* 1. normal, standard, regular; 2. perpendicular, at right angles. **Normalbelastung,** *f.* normal load. **Normale,** *f.* perpendicular (line). **Normalelement,** *n.* (*Elec.*) standard cell. **normalerweise,** *adv.* normally. **Normal|fall,** *m.* normal case; *im* –, normally. **–fluglage,** *f.* (*Av.*) level flight. **–geschwindigkeit,** *f.* normal *or* permitted speed. **–gewicht,** *n.* standard weight. **–größe,** *f.* normal *or* standard size.

normalisieren [nɔrmali'ziːrən], *v.t.* normalize.

Normal|kerze, *f.* standard candle. **–klasse,** *f.* (*Spt.*) scratch. **–maß,** *n.* standard (measure). **–null,** *n.* (mean) sea-level. **–spur,** *f.* standard gauge. **–stärke,** *f.* proof strength (*of spirits*). **–uhr,** *f.* standard clock. **–zeile,** *f.* (*Typ.*) direction line. **–zeit,** *f.* mean *or* standard *or* correct time. **–zustand,** *m.* normal state *or* conditions, normality, normalcy.

normen ['nɔrmən], *v.t.* standardize. **Normenvorschrift,** *f.* standard specifications.

normgerecht ['nɔrmgərɛçt], *adj.* complying with the standards *or* specifications.

normieren [nɔr'miːrən], *v.t. See* **normen. Normierung, Normung,** *f.* standardization.

Norwegen ['nɔrveːgən], *n.* Norway. **Norweger,** *m.*, **norwegisch,** *adj.* Norwegian.

Nörz [nœrts], *m.* (*Austr.*) *see* **Nerz.**

Nößel ['nøːsəl], *m. or n.* (*obs.*) pint.

Not [noːt], *f.* (-, *pl.* ¨**e**) need, want, privation, indigence; care, sorrow, misery, affliction; trouble, difficulty, plight, predicament, emergency, extremity; danger, peril, distress; necessity, exigency, urgency; ***aus –,*** from necessity; ***aus der – eine Tugend machen,*** make a virtue of necessity; (*Prov.*) ***– bricht Eisen,*** necessity is the mother of invention; ***wenn es die – erfordert,*** if need be; ***die – fernhalten,*** keep the wolf from the door; (*Prov.*) ***wenn die – am größten, ist Gottes Hilfe am nächsten,*** man's extremity is God's opportunity; ***seine liebe – haben mit,*** have no end of trouble with; ***ein Freund in der –,*** a friend in need; ***in – sein,*** be in distress *or* danger: (*coll.*) be dishonoured (*of a cheque*); ***in –*** or ***Nöten sein,*** be in trouble, be hard pressed; (*Prov.*) ***– kennt kein Gebot,*** necessity knows no law; (*Prov.*) ***in der – frißt der Teufel Fliegen,*** beggars can't be choosers; ***– leiden,*** suffer want *or* privation; ***einen Wechsel – leiden lassen,*** dishonour a bill; ***wenn – am Mann ist,*** if need be, in case of need, when necessity *or* the need arises, in the last resort, if the worst comes to the worst; ***– macht erfinderisch,*** *see* ***– bricht Eisen;*** ***mit (knapper) –,*** with difficulty, barely, narrowly; ***ohne –,*** unnecessarily, needlessly, without cause; ***zur –,*** at a pinch, at the worst, if need be.

not, *pred.adj.* needful, necessary; ***mir ist*** or ***tut –,*** I want *or* need; ***wenn es – tut,*** in case of necessity *or* need; ***es tut – daß,*** it is necessary *or* urgent *or* imperative that.

Nota ['noːta], *f.* (-, *pl.* **-s**) (*Comm.*) 1. invoice, bill; 2. memo(randum).

Not|adresse, *f.* emergency address. **–anker,** *m.* sheet-anchor.

Notar [no'taːr], *m.* (**-s,** *pl.* **-e**) notary; ***öffentlicher –,*** notary public, conveyancer, commissioner for oaths. **Notariat** [–ri'aːt], *n.* (**-(e)s,** *pl.* **-e**) notary's office. **notariell,** *adj.* notarial; ***– beglaubigt,*** legally certified *or* attested; ***–e Vollmacht,*** power of attorney.

Not|ausgang, *m.* emergency exit. **–ausstieg,** *m.* escape hatch. **–behelf,** *m.* makeshift, expedient, (*coll.*) stopgap. **–bremse,** *f.* emergency brake; (*Railw.*) communication cord. **–brücke,** *f.* temporary bridge. **–durft,** *f.* necessity, pressing need; ***seine – verrichten,*** ease o.s., relieve nature. **notdürftig,** *adj.* scanty; needy, necessitous, indigent; makeshift, improvised, (*coll.*) rough-and-ready. **Notdürftigkeit,** *f.* scantiness; indigence, want.

Note ['noːtə], *f.* 1. note, memorandum; diplomatic note; 2. mark; report (*at school*); ***gute –,*** high *or* good marks, a good report; 3. bank-note; 4. (musical) note; *pl.* music; ***ganze –,*** semibreve; ***geschwänzte –,*** quaver; ***halbe –,*** minim; ***schwarze –,*** crotchet; ***in –n setzen,*** set to music; ***nach –n spielen,*** play at sight; (*coll.*) ***nach –n,*** properly, thoroughly, with a vengeance; 5. (*fig.*) character, feature, style, stamp; ***persönliche –,*** personal trait *or* stamp.

Noten|ausgabe, *f.* issue of (bank-)notes. **–austausch,** *m.* (*Pol.*) exchange of notes. **–bank,** *f.* bank of issue, issuing bank. **–beilage,** *f.* musical supplement. **–bezeichnung,** *f.* musical notation. **–blatt,** *n.* sheet of music. **–druck,** *m.* music-printing; printed music. **–halter,** *m.* music-stand. **–handlung,** *f.* music shop. **–lesen,** *n.* reading of music. **–linie,** *f.* (*Mus.*) line (of the staff). **–papier,** *n.* music *or* manuscript paper. **–schlüssel,** *m.* (*Mus.*) clef. **–ständer,** *m. See* **–halter. –system,** *n.* (*Mus.*) staff. **–umlauf,** *m.* circulation of (bank-)notes. **–wechsel,** *m. See* **–austausch.**

Notfall ['noːtfal], *m.* emergency, case of need *or* necessity; ***im –,*** in case of need, if necessary. **notfalls,** *adv. See* **nötigenfalls. Notflagge,** *f.* flag of distress. **notgedrungen, 1.** *adj.* compulsory, forced. **2.** *adv.* necessarily, perforce, under compulsion. **Not|geld,** *n.* emergency *or* token money. **–gemeinschaft,** *f.* emergency association. **–gesetz,** *n.* provisional *or* emergency decree. **–groschen,** *n. See* **–pfennig. –hafen,** *m.* harbour of refuge. **–helfer,** *m.* helper in (time of) need. **–hilfe,** *f.* help in need, emergency service.

notieren [no'tiːrən], **1.** *v.t.* note (down), make *or* take a note of, (*coll.*) put *or* take down; (*Comm.*) quote. **2.** *v.i.* (*Comm.*) be quoted at. **Notierung,** *f.* noting, booking, entry, (*Comm.*) quotation.

nötig ['nøːtɪç], *adj.* needed, needful, necessary, required, requisite; ***– haben,*** need, be *or* stand in need of, require; (*coll.*) ***das habe ich nicht –,*** I don't have to stand for that; (*coll.*) ***er hat es sehr –,*** he needs the lavatory badly; ***es ist nicht – daß,*** there is no need for; ***das Nötige,*** the wherewithal, all that is required, what is necessary.

nötigen ['nøːtɪgən], *v.t.* oblige, force, coerce, compel; urge, entreat, press; ***sich – lassen,*** stand upon ceremony, need pressing; ***lassen Sie sich nicht –!*** do not wait to be asked, help yourself. **nötigenfalls,** *adj.* if need be, if necessary, in case of need, in an emergency, in the last resort. **Nötigung,** *f.* compulsion, coercion, constraint; entreaty, pressing *or* urgent request; (*Law*) duress.

Notiz [no'tiːts], *f.* (-, *pl.* **-en**) 1. notice, cognizance; ***– nehmen von,*** pay attention to, take notice *or* cognizance of, note; ***keine – nehmen von,*** ignore; 2. note, memo(randum); ***sich*** (*Dat.*) ***–en machen,*** take *or* make notes. **Notiz|block,** *m.* scribbling pad, jotter. **–buch,** *n.* notebook.

Not|klausel, *f.* escape-clause. **–lage,** *f.* predicament, plight, distress, calamity. **–lager,** *n.* makeshift *or* shakedown bed. **notlanden,** *v.i.* (*insep.*) (*p.p.* ***notgelandet***) (*Av.*) make a forced landing. **Not|landeplatz,** *m.* emergency landing ground. **–landung,** *f.* forced landing. **notleidend,** *adj.* 1. needy, destitute; suffering, distressed; 2. (*Comm.*) dishonoured (*of bills*). **Not|leine,** *f.* (*Railw.*) communication cord. **–lüge,** *f.* unavoidable lie, white lie. **–luke,** *f.* escape hatch. **–maßnahme,** *f. See* **–mittel. –mast,** *m.* jury-mast. **–mittel,** *n.* shift, expedient, emergency measure, last resort.

notorisch [no'toːrɪʃ], *adj.* notorious, acknowledged.

Not|pfennig, *m.* savings; nest-egg; ***einen – zurücklegen,*** lay *or* put by (money) for a rainy day. **–ruf,** *m.* distress call, (*Tele.*) emergency call. **–schlachtung,** *f.* forced slaughter (*of diseased or starving animals*). **–schrei,** *m.* cry of distress, shout for help. **–signal,** *n.* distress signal, SOS. **–sitz,** *m.* emergency seat, (*Motor.*) dickey (*Am.* rumble) seat.

Notstand ['noːtʃtant], *m.* state of distress, critical state, emergency. **Notstands|arbeiten,** *f.pl.* relief works. **–gebiet,** *n.* distressed area. **–gesetz,** *n.* Emergency Powers Act, emergency bill.

Not|taufe, *f.* private baptism (*in emergency*). **–treppe,** *f.* fire escape. **–verband,** *m.* first-aid *or* temporary dressing, (*Mil.*) first field dressing. **–verordnung,** *f.* emergency decree. **notwassern,** *v.i.* (*insep.*) (*p.p.* ***notgewassert***) make a forced landing on the sea, (*sl.*) ditch a plane. **Notwehr,** *f.* self-defence; (*Law*) ***Totschlag aus –,*** justifiable homicide.

notwendig ['no:tvɛndɪç], *adj.* necessary, requisite, essential, indispensable, inevitable. **notwendigenfalls,** *adv.* in case of necessity. **notwendigerweise,** *adv.* necessarily, of necessity. **Notwendigkeit,** *f.* necessity, requirement.

Not|wurf, *m.* (*Av.*) jettisoning (*of bombs*). **–zeichen,** *n.* distress signal. **–zucht,** *f.* indecent assault, rape. **notzüchtigen,** *v.t.* (*insep.*) (*p.p.* ***genotzüchtigt***) rape, ravish, violate; (*Law*) assault. **Notzwang,** *m.* force of circumstances.

Novelle [no'vɛlə], *f.* 1. short story, short novel; 2. (*Law*) supplementary law *or* clause, amendment; ***die –n des Justinian,*** the constitutions *or* laws of Justinian. **Novellette** [–'lɛtə], *f.* anecdote, sketch. **novellieren,** *v.t.* (*Austr.*) amend, modify, reorganize. **Novellist** [–'lɪst], *m.* writer of short stories *or* sketches. **novellistisch,** *adj.* fictional; diverting; mawkish.

November [no'vɛmbər], *m.* November.

Novität [novi'tɛ:t], *f.* novelty; new publication; new play.

Novize [no'vi:tsə], *m.* (**-n,** *pl.* **-n**) *or f.* novice, probationer, acolyte. **Noviziat** [–i'a:t], *n.* (**-es,** *pl.* **-e**) novitiate.

Novum ['no:vum], *n.* (-, *pl.* **-va**) s.th. quite new, unheard-of fact; (*Law*) fresh evidence; *see also* **Novität.**

nu! [nu:], *int.* (*dial., coll.*) well! well now! **Nu,** *m.* moment, instant; ***im*** or ***in einem –,*** in an instant, in a trice, in no time, (*coll.*) in the twinkling of an eye, in a flash *or* jiffy.

Nuance [ny'ãsə], *f.* shade, tint, hue, tinge, cast. **nuancieren** [–'si:rən], *v.t.* shade, tint, tinge.

nüchtern ['nyçtərn], *adj.* 1. (on an) empty (stomach); 2. sober, dispassionate, temperate, moderate, calm, reasonable, sensible, level-headed, clear-headed; ***wieder – werden,*** sober up; ***–es Urteil,*** sober *or* dispassionate judgement; 3. vapid, flat, insipid, dry, dull, jejune, matter-of-fact, prosaic, Philistine. **Nüchternheit,** *f.* 1. sobriety; (*fig.*) soberness, common sense, calmness; 2. prosiness; 3. emptiness, dullness, dryness.

Nucke ['nukə], **Nücke** ['nykə], *f.* (*dial.*) whim, fad, crotchet, fancy; wilfulness, obstinacy.

Nuckel ['nukəl], *m.* (*coll.*) comforter, dummy (*for babies*). **nuckeln,** *v.i.* (*coll.*) suck.

Nudel ['nu:dəl], *f.* (-, *pl.* **-n**) 1. vermicelli, macaroni, (*Am.*) noodles; stuffing (*for poultry*); 2. (*coll.*) gay spark. **Nudel|brett,** *n.* pastry-board. **–holz,** *n. See* **–walze. nudeln,** *v.t.* cram, feed up; stuff (*poultry*); (*vulg.*) ***ich bin genudelt,*** I am full. **Nudel|suppe,** *f.* vermicelli soup. **–walze,** *f.* rolling pin.

null [nul], *indecl.adj.* nil, null; ***– und nichtig,*** null and void; ***– und nichtig machen,*** annul. **Null,** *f.* (-, *pl.* **-en**) nought, zero, cipher; blank; ***er ist eine wahre –,*** he is a nonentity *or* nobody *or* a mere cipher. **Nulleiter,** *m.* (*Elec.*) neutral conductor. **Null|partie,** *f.* (*Tenn.*) love-set. **–punkt,** *m.* zero, nadir, neutral point; freezing point. **–spiel,** *n.* (*Tenn.*) love-game. **–stellung,** *f.* zero-position. **–strich,** *m.* zero-mark. **–zeit,** *f.* zero-hour.

Numerale [nume'ra:lə], *n.* (**-s,** *pl.* **-lien** (*Austr.* **-lia**)) numeral adjective. **numerieren,** *v.t.* number; ***numerierter Sitz,*** reserved seat. **Numerierung,** *f.* numbering, numeration; notation. **numerisch** [–'me:rɪʃ], *adj.* numerical. **Numerus** ['nu:merus], *m.* (-, *pl.* **-ri**) (*Gram.*) number.

Numismatik [numɪs'ma:tɪk], *f.* numismatics.

Nummer ['numər], *f.* (-, *pl.* **-n**) number; part, issue, copy (*of a journal*); lottery-ticket; size (*in clothing*); (*Spt.*) event; (*coll.*) ***eine große – sein,*** be influential, have influence; (*coll.*) ***eine gute – haben,*** be well thought of (***bei,*** by); (*coll.*) ***keine – haben,*** have no say, be without influence; (*coll.*) ***eine nette*** or ***feine – sein,*** be quite a character; (*coll.*) ***er ist auf – Sicher,*** he is in jug *or* the clink. **Nummern|folge,** *f.* numerical order. **–scheibe,** *f.* (*Tele.*) dial. **–schild,** *n.* (*Motor.*) number-plate.

nun [nu:n], **1.** *adv.* now, at present; then, henceforth; ***von – an,*** from now *or* then on, (t)henceforth; ***– erst gestand er,*** it was only then that he confessed; ***– und nimmer,*** never, nevermore. **2.** *part.* now, well; ***er mag – kommen oder nicht,*** whether or not he comes; ***–, und?*** and then what? ***– also?*** well then! ***– ja!*** that's true enough, granted; ***wenn –,*** supposing, now if. **3.** (*coll., dial.*) *conj.* (= ***da***) ***– es einmal so ist,*** since it is so; ***– du mich kennst,*** now that you know me. **nun|mehr,** *adv., conj.* now, at present, at this stage, by this time; henceforth, then, since then. **–mehrig,** *adj.* present, actual. **–mehro,** *adv., conj.* (*obs.*) *see* **–mehr.**

Nuntius ['nuntsius], **Nunzius,** *m.* (-, *pl.* **-tien** (*Austr.* **-tii**)) (papal) nuncio.

nur [nu:r], *adv., part.* only, alone, simply, merely, solely, exclusively; (nothing) but, except; ***– einmal,*** only *or* just once; ***geh –!*** do go! by all means go! ***er mag – gehen!*** let him go by all means! he is quite at liberty to go! ***soviel ich – kann,*** as much as ever I can *or* as I possibly can; ***laßt mich – machen!*** (just) let me do it! let me alone! ***sehen Sie –, was Sie gemacht haben,*** just look at what you have done; (*coll., Austr.*) ***– mehr,*** still, only; ***– nicht ängstlich!*** do not fear! ***alle, – er nicht,*** all but *or* all except him; ***alles, – nicht das,*** anything but *or* rather than that; ***nicht – . . ., sondern auch*** . . ., not only . . ., but also; ***– noch eine Zeile,*** only *or* just one line more; ***– so,*** easily, rapidly, perfectly; ***es klappte – so,*** everything fitted in admirably; ***es ging – so,*** it went off first-rate *or* without a hitch; ***es – so tun,*** pretend to do it, do it in a slipshod manner; not take any trouble about it; ***warte –!*** you just wait! ***was er – damit meint?*** whatever *or* what on earth can he mean? ***– weiter!*** carry on! that's all right so far! ***wenn –,*** if only, provided (that), would that; ***wer – (immer),*** whoever, who on earth; ***wie kommt er – hierher?*** however *or* how on earth did he get there? ***wo du – hinkommst,*** wherever you may go; ***– zu!*** go on! get on! make a start! (*coll.*) jump to it! **Nurflügelflugzeug,** *n.* (*Av.*) flying wing.

Nürnberg ['nyrnbɛrk], *n.* (*Geog.*) Nuremberg; ***–er Trichter,*** the royal road to learning.

nuscheln ['nuʃəln], *v.i.* mumble, slur one's words.

Nuß [nus], *f.* (-, *pl.* **¨(ss)e**) nut (*also Mech.*); walnut; ***taube –,*** empty nut; ***keine taube – wert,*** not worth a straw *or* fig; (*fig.*) ***harte –,*** hard nut to crack, tough job; ***Nüsse auskernen,*** shell nuts. **Nußbaum,** *m.* walnut-tree. **nußbraun,** *adj.* nut-brown, hazel. **Nuß|häher,** *m.* (*Orn.*) *see* **Tannenhäher. –kern,** *m.* kernel (*of a nut*). **–knacker,** *m.* nutcracker(s); (*coll.*) ***alter –,*** old fogy. **–kohle,** *f.* small coal, (kitchen) nuts. **–schale,** *f.* 1. nutshell; 2. cockleshell (*small boat*). **–staude,** *f.* hazel-tree.

Nüstern ['ny(:)stərn], *f.pl.* nostrils (*of horses*).

Nut [nu:t], *f.* (-, *pl.* **-en**), (*coll.*) **Nute,** *f.* groove, notch, furrow, rabbet, slot, flute; keyway; ***– und Feder,*** tongue and groove. **nuten,** *v.t.* slot, flute, groove. **Nuthobel,** *m.* rabbet- *or* grooving-plane.

Nutschbeutel ['nu:tʃbɔytəl], *m.* feeding-bottle. **Nutsche,** *f.* (*Chem.*) suction filter. **nutschen,** *v.t.* (*rare*) filter by suction; (*dial.*) suck. **Nutscher,** *m.* (*coll.*) suckling.

nutz [nuts], *pred.adj.* useful, of use, profitable; ***das ist zu nichts –,*** that is good for nothing *or* is quite useless. **Nutz,** *m.* (*obs.*) *see* **Nutzen**; (*Poet.*) ***zu – und Frommen*** (*Gen.*), for the benefit *or* good of, to the advantage of.

Nutz|anwendung, *f.* utilization; practical application. **–arbeit,** *f.* (*Mech.*) effective work. **nutzbar,** *adj.* utilizable, usable, fit for use; useful, profitable, productive, effective; ***sich*** (*Dat.*) ***– machen,*** make use of, utilize, turn to account, take advantage of. **Nutzbarkeit,** *f.* fitness for use, usefulness, effectiveness. **Nutzbarmachung,** *f.* utilization.

nutzbringend, *adj.* profitable, advantageous. **nutze, nütze,** *see* **nutz. Nutzeffekt,** *m.* (*Mech.*) efficiency.

nutzen ['nutsən], **nützen** ['nytsən], **1.** *v.t.* make use of, use, utilize, put *or* turn to account, exploit. **2.** *v.i.* be of use, be useful (*ihm,* to him; *zu etwas,* for s.th.), serve, benefit (him), be of advantage *or* benefit (to him); ***was nützt es?*** what is the use *or* good of it? what use *or* good is it? ***es nützt nichts,*** it is no use *or* good; it is useless *or* of no avail; ***wenig –,*** not be much use, not do much good, not help very much, avail little.

Nutzen, *m.* use, utility; profit, gain, yield, returns, benefit, advantage; ***– bringen*** or ***tragen,*** show *or* yield a profit; ***großer Umsatz, kleiner –,*** a large turnover with small profit; ***von – sein,*** be of benefit *or* advantage (***für,*** to), be of use *or* service (to); ***– ziehen aus,*** derive profit *or* benefit from; (*fig.*) turn to advantage, make capital out of, (*coll.*) cash in on; ***zum – von,*** for the benefit of.

Nutz|fahrzeug, *n.* utility (vehicle). **–fläche,** *f.* effective area; acreage under cultivation. **–garten,** *m.* kitchen-garden. **–holz,** *n.* commercial timber. **–inhalt,** *m.* useful capacity. **–kraft,** *f.* effective power. **–last,** *f.* loading capacity, working load, payload. **–leistung,** *f.* (*Mech.*) effective work, useful power, output, (*Motor.*) brake horsepower.

nützlich ['nytslıç], *adj.* useful, of use, serviceable, profitable, advantageous, beneficial, conducive (*Dat.*, to); ***das Angenehme mit dem Nützlichen verbinden,*** combine pleasure with profit; ***sich – machen,*** make o.s. useful. **Nützlichkeit,** *f.* utility, use, usefulness, advantage, profitableness. **Nützlichkeits|prinzip,** *n.* utilitarianism. **–rücksichten,** *f.pl.* considerations of utility, utilitarian *or* practical considerations. **–system,** *n.* *See* **–prinzip.**

nutzlos ['nutslo:s], *adj.* useless, (of) no use, futile, unavailing, unprofitable. **Nutzlosigkeit,** *f.* uselessness, futility.

Nutz|nießer, *m.* beneficiary, usufructuary. **–nießung,** *f.* usufruct. **–pflanze,** *f.* useful plant, plant useful as *or* for fodder.

Nutzung ['nutsuŋ], *f.* using, utilization; *see also* **Nutzbarmachung, Nutznießung**; yield, produce, revenue. **Nutzungs|dauer,** *f.* useful *or* service life. **–ertrag,** *m.* revenue. **–güter,** *n.pl.* consumer goods. **–recht,** *n.* right of usufruct.

Nutz|vieh, *n.* domestic cattle. **–wert,** *m.* economic value.

Nymphe ['nymfə], *f.* 1. nymph, fairy, elf; 2. (*Ent.*) chrysalis, pupa. **Nymphomanie** [–oma'ni:], *f.* nymphomania.

O

O, o [o:], **1.** *n.* O, o; ***das A und O,*** the beginning and end; the whole *or* entire. **2.** *int.* o! oh! *See Index of Abbreviations.*

Oase [o'a:zə], *f.* oasis.

[1]**ob** [ɔp], *conj.* if, whether; ***es fragt sich –,*** I wonder whether, it is a question whether; ***wer weiß, – er nicht krank ist,*** who knows but he may be ill; ***– er wohl wieder kommt?*** will he come back, do you think? (*coll.*) (***na***) ***und –!*** rather! I should say so! (*sl.*) you bet! and how! ***als –,*** as if, as though; ***nicht als –,*** not that; ***tun als –,*** pretend, make believe; ***– . . ., oder nicht,*** whether . . . or not.

[2]**ob,** *prep.* 1. (*Dat.*) (*dial.*) over, above, on, upon; ***Rothenburg – der Tauber,*** Rothenburg on Tauber; 2. (*Gen. or Dat.*) (*obs.*) on account of; ***er zürnte mir – meines Freimuts,*** he was angry with me on account of my frankness; ***er zürnte – solchem Frevel,*** he was angry at such sacrilege.

Obacht ['o:baxt], *f.* attention, care, heed; ***in – nehmen,*** take heed of; ***– geben auf*** (*Acc.*), keep a watchful eye on, take care of; ***–!*** take care! look out!

Obdach ['ɔpdax], *n.* shelter; lodging; ***unter – bringen,*** place under shelter. **obdachlos,** *adj.* homeless. **Obdachlose(r),** *m., f.* casual (pauper); homeless p.; ***Asyl für Obdachlose,*** casual ward.

Obduktion [ɔpduktsi'o:n], *f.* post-mortem examination, autopsy. **obduzieren** [–'tsi:rən], *v.t.* hold a post-mortem examination *or* autopsy on.

Obedienz [obedi'ɛnts], *f.* (*R.C.*) obedience.

O-Beine ['o:baınə], *n.pl.* bandy *or* bow legs. **O-beinig,** *adj.* bandy- *or* bow-legged.

oben ['o:bən], *adv.* above, aloft, overhead, on high; upstairs; at the top; on the surface; ***– abschöpfen,*** skim (off); (*fig.*) treat superficially; ***den Kopf – behalten,*** remain calm and collected; ***von – bis unten,*** from top to bottom; (*of a p.*) from top to toe, from head to foot; (*coll.*) ***mir steht die ganze Wirtschaft bis hier –,*** I am heartily sick of the whole affair; ***dort –,*** up there; ***– erwähnt,*** mentioned above, aforesaid; ***von – herab behandeln,*** treat condescendingly *or* with condescension; ***nach –,*** upward, up, upstairs, on high; ***von – nach unten,*** downward, from above; ***von –,*** from the top.

oben|an [–'an], *adv.* at the top *or* head; in the first place. **–auf,** *adv.* at the top *or* head, above; on the surface; uppermost; ***– sein,*** be in great form, be going strong. **–drein,** *adv.* besides, over and above, in addition, into the bargain, what is more. **–erwähnt, –genannt, –gesagt,** *adj.* aforesaid, above-mentioned. **–gesteuert,** *adj.* (*Motor.*) overhead (*valve*). **–hin,** *adv.* on the surface, casually, superficially, cursorily, perfunctorily. **–hinaus,** *adv.* ***– wollen,*** have extravagant *or* ambitious notions. **–stehend,** *adj.* *See* **–erwähnt.**

ober ['o:bər], **1.** *prep.* (*Dat.*) (*Austr.*) over, above, beyond. **2.** *adj.* situated above, upper, higher, superior; supreme, chief, principal, senior, leading; *see* **oberst. Ober,** *m.* 1. (*Cards*) trump knave, highest knave; 2. (head) waiter; (***Herr***) ***–!*** waiter!

Ober|appellationsgericht, *n.* High Court of Appeal. **–arm,** *m.* upper arm. **–armbein,** *n.* (*Anat.*) humerus. **–armgelenk,** *n.* shoulder joint. **–armknochen,** *m.* *See* **–armbein. –arzt,** *m.* head-physician. **–aufseher,** *m.* superintendent, inspector-general. **–aufsicht,** *f.* superintendence. **–bau,** *m.* superstructure; (*Railw.*) roadbed. **–bauch,** *m.* (*Anat.*) epigastrum. **–befehl,** *m.* supreme command. **–befehlshaber,** *m.* commander-in-chief, supreme commander. **–begriff,** *m.* generic term. **–bett,** *n.* coverlet. **–bootsmaat,** *m.* (*Naut.*) boatswain's mate. **–bootsmann,** *m.* (*Naut.*) chief boatswain's mate. **–bramsegel,** *n.* (*Naut.*) main-royal. **–bürgermeister,** *m.* (*England*) lord mayor; (*Scotland*) lord provost; (*foreign*) chief burgomaster. **–deck,** *n.* upper deck. **oberdeutsch,** *adj.* Upper German, South German.

Obere(r) ['o:bərə(r)], *m., f.* 1. chief, superior; ***die Oberen,*** those in authority; (*Eccl.*) Father Superior. **Obere(s),** *n.* top; ***das Obere zuunterst kehren,*** turn everything upside-down *or* topsy-turvy.

Ober|feldwebel, *m.* (*Mil.*) sergeant-major, warrant officer; (*Nav.*) chief petty officer; (*Av.*) flight-sergeant. **–feuerwerker,** *m.* (*Artil.*) chief gunner's mate.

Oberfläche ['o:bərflɛçə], *f.* surface (area), face. **Oberflächen|bearbeitung, –behandlung,** *f.* finish(ing). **–härtung,** *f.* case-hardening. **–reibung,** *f.* skin-friction. **–spannung,** *f.* surface-tension. **oberflächlich,** *adj.* superficial, perfunctory, cursory, casual; ***–e Bekanntschaft,*** casual acquaintance; ***–e Kenntnisse,*** superficial knowledge, smattering; ***nach –er Schätzung,*** at a rough estimate.

Ober|gärtner, *m.* head-gardener. **–gefreite(r),** *m.* (*Mil.*) corporal; (*Nav.*) leading seaman; (*Av.*) leading aircraftman. **–gericht,** *n.* (*Swiss*) Supreme *or* High Court. **–geschoß,** *n.* upper storey. **–gewalt,** *f.* supreme power *or* authority; supremacy, sovereignty. **–glied,** *n.* (*Log.*) major term. **–gurt,** *m.* (*Naut.*) top boom.

oberhalb ['o:bərhalp], *prep.* (*Gen.*) above, at the upper part of.

Ober|hals, *m.* cervical region. **–hand,** *f.* 1. back of the hand; metacarpus; 2. (*fig.*) upper hand, ascendancy; ***die – haben,*** have the upper hand *or* whip-hand, predominate, (*coll.*) be top dog; ***die – gewinnen,*** get the better (***über*** (*Acc.*), of), prevail (over). **–haupt,** *n.* 1. head, chief, leader, master; 2. vertex. **–haus,** *n.* House of Lords, upper house *or* chamber. **–haut,** *f.*, **–häutchen,** *n.* cuticle, epidermis. **–heizer,** *m.* (*Nav.*) leading stoker. **–hemd,** *n.* (dress) shirt. **–herr,** *m.* supreme lord, sovereign. **–herrschaft,** *f.* sovereignty, supremacy. **–hofgericht,** *n.* supreme court of judicature. **–hofmeister,** *m.* Lord High Steward; tutor to a prince. **–hoheit,** *f. See* **–herrschaft.**

Oberin ['o:bərɪn], *f.* (*R.C.*) Mother Superior; hospital matron.

oberirdisch ['o:bərˀɪrdɪʃ], *adj.* above ground, surface; aerial; overhead (*cable*). **Ober|italien,** *n.* Northern Italy. **–jägermeister,** *m.* master of the hunt *or* of hounds. **–kämmerer, –kammerherr,** *m.* lord high chamberlain. **–kante,** *f.* upper edge. **–kellner,** *m.* head-waiter. **–kiefer,** *m.*, **–kinnlade,** *f.* upper jaw. **–kirchenrat,** *m.* High Consistory; member of a High Consistory. **–klasse,** *f.* upper class (*of society*); (*pl.*) upper *or* fifth and sixth forms (*school*). **–kleid,** *n.* outer garment. **–kommando,** *n.* supreme *or* high command. **–körper,** *m.* upper part of the body, trunk. **–land,** *n.* upland, highland. **–landesgericht,** *n.* Higher Regional Court. **oberlastig,** *adj.* top-heavy. **Ober|lauf,** *m.* upper course (*of a river*). **–leder,** *n.* uppers (*of boots*). **–lehrer,** *m.* senior assistant master, secondary school teacher; (*Austr.*) headmaster. **–leib,** *m.* upper part of the body, trunk; bodice (*of a dress*). **–leitung,** *f.* 1. direction, management; 2. (*Elec.*) overhead system. **–leitungsbus,** *m.* trolley bus. **–leutnant,** *m.* (*Mil.*) (1st) lieutenant; (*Av.*) flying-officer; (*Nav.*) – ***zur See,*** lieutenant. **–licht,** *n.* skylight (*in roof*), fanlight (*above door*). **–lippe,** *f.* upper lip. **–pfarrer,** *m.* rector. **–postmeister,** *m.* postmaster-general. **–priester,** *m.* high priest. **–prima,** *f.* upper VI form (*in school*). **–primaner,** *m.* upper-sixth-form boy. **–realschule,** *f.* modern *or* non-classical secondary school. **–regierungsrat,** *m.* senior civil servant, senior government official. **–rinde,** *f.* outer bark; upper crust.

Obers ['o:bərs], *n.* (*Austr.*) whipped cream.

Ober|satz, *m.* major term (*of a syllogism*). **–schenkel,** *m.* thigh. **–schenkelbein,** *n.*, **–schenkelknochen,** *m.* (*Anat.*) femur. **–schicht,** *f.* (*Geol.*) upper stratum; (*fig.*) upper classes. **oberschlächtig,** *adj.* overshot (*of a mill*). **Ober|schule,** *f.* modern *or* non-classical secondary school. **–schwester,** *f.* (ward) sister. **–schwingung,** *f.* harmonic, overtone. **–seite,** *f.* top side, right side. **–sekundaner,** *m.* upper-fifth-form boy.

oberst ['o:bərst], *adj.* (*sup. of* ***ober***) top, topmost, uppermost, highest; chief, head, first, principal, supreme; ***–es Gericht,*** supreme court; ***–er Grundsatz,*** leading principle; ***–e Heeresleitung,*** supreme command; ***das Oberste zuunterst kehren,*** turn everything upside-down *or* topsy-turvy.

Oberst, *m.* (**-en** *or* **-s,** *pl.* **-en**) (*Mil.*) colonel; (*Av.*) group-captain.

Ober|staatsanwalt, *m.* attorney-general. **–stabsarzt,** *m.* (*Mil.*) regimental medical officer. **–stabsfeldwebel,** *m.* (*Mil.*) regimental sergeant major, warrant officer class 1; (*Av.*) warrant officer, (*Am.*) chief master sergeant. **–stallmeister,** *m.* master of the horse. **–steuermann,** *m.* (*Naut.*) first mate. **–stimme,** *f.* treble, soprano.

Oberstleutnant ['o:bərstlɔytnant], *m.* (*Mil.*) lieutenant-colonel; (*Av.*) wing-commander.

Ober|stübchen, *n.* (*coll.*) ***bei ihm stimmt was nicht im –,*** he is not quite right in the head. **–studiendirektor,** *m.* headmaster (of a secondary school). **–studienrat,** *m.* senior assistant master. **–stufe,** *f.* higher *or* highest grade; upper school. **–tasse,** *f.* cup. **–tertianer,** *m.* upper-fourth-form boy. **–ton,** *m.* harmonic, overtone. **–trumpf,** *m.* (*Cards*) matador. **–verwaltungsgericht,** *n.* Higher Regional Court. **–vormundschaftsgericht,** *n.* Court of Chancery. **–wasser,** *n.* upper water (*weir*); (*fig.*) ***– haben*** or ***bekommen,*** have *or* get the upper hand. **–wasserverdrängung,** *f.* surface displacement. **–welle,** *f. See* **–schwingung.** **–zähne,** *m.pl.* upper teeth. **–zeug,** *n.* outer garments. **–zimmermeister,** *m.* (*Nav.*) chief shipwright.

obgleich [ɔp'glaɪç], *conj.* though, although.

Obhut ['ɔphu:t], *f.* care, protection, custody, guard, keeping; ***in seine – nehmen,*** take charge *or* care of, take under one's charge *or* care *or* (*coll.*) wing.

obig ['o:bɪç], *adj.* above, foregoing, above-mentioned.

Objekt [ɔp'jɛkt], *n.* (**-s,** *pl.* **-e**) 1. object (*also Gram.*); 2. project, objective; 3. (*Law*) property; 4. (*Comm.*) transaction. **Objekt|abstand,** *m.* working distance. **–glas,** *n.* (microscopic) slide *or* mount.

objektiv [ɔpjɛk'ti:f], *adj.* objective, impartial, unbiassed, detached, dispassionate; actual, factual. **Objektiv,** *n.* (**-s,** *pl.* **-e**) 1. (*Gram.*) objective case; 2. (*Opt.*) object lens, objective. **Objektivität** [–tivi'tɛ:t], *f.* objectivity, objectiveness, impartiality. **Objektivverschluß,** *m.* (*Phot.*) instantaneous shutter.

Objektträger [ɔp'jɛkttrɛ:gər], *m.* slide, mount, stand.

Oblate [o'bla:tə], *f.* wafer; (*Eccl.*) consecrated wafer, Host. **Oblaten|schachtel,** *f.* pyx. **–teller,** *m.* paten.

obliegen ['ɔpli:gən], *irr.v.i.* (*sep.*) (*Dat.*) 1. apply o.s., be devoted (to); be (one's) duty; be incumbent, devolve (on); 2. (*B.*) (*aux.* s.) prevail (over). **Obliegenheit,** *f.* obligation, incumbency, duty.

obligat [obli'ga:t], *adj.* obligatory, indispensable, necessary; inevitable; (*Mus.*) ***mit –er Flöte,*** with flute obligato.

Obligation [obligatsi'o:n], *f.* obligation; bond, debenture, promissory note. **Obligations|inhaber,** *m.* bond-holder. **–konto,** *n.* debenture book. **–schein,** *m.* bond. **–schuld,** *f.* bond(ed) debt. **–schuldner,** *m.* obligor. **obligatorisch** [–'to:rɪʃ], *adj.* obligatory (***für,*** on), compulsory, mandatory (for).

Obligo ['o:bligo], *n.* (**-s,** *pl.* **-s**) (*Law*) obligation to pay, liability; (*Comm.*) commitment, engagement; (*Comm.*) ***ohne –,*** without recourse.

Obmacht ['ɔpmaxt], *f.* (*obs.*) supremacy, supreme power *or* authority.

Obmann ['ɔpman], *m.* (*pl.* **–̈er** *or* **-leute**) chairman (*of committee*), foreman (*of jury*), umpire, spokesman, shop steward (*in factory*), steward, overseer, head man.

Oboe [o'bo:ə], *f.* oboe, (*obs.*) hautboy. **Oboist** [–'ɪst], *m.* (**-en,** *pl.* **-en**) oboe player.

Obrigkeit ['o:brɪçkaɪt], *f.* ruling body, government, the authorities, (*coll.*) the powers that be; magistrate; ***von –s wegen,*** by order of the authorities. **obrigkeitlich, 1.** *adj.* magisterial, authoritative, official, governmental; ***–er Befehl,*** government order; ***–e Genehmigung,*** official permission. **2.** *adv.* officially, by authority; ***– gestempelt,*** with the official stamp. **Obrigkeitsstaat,** *m.* authoritarian state.

Obrist [o'brɪst], *m.* (*obs.*) *see* **Oberst.**

obschon [ɔp'ʃo:n], *conj. See* **obgleich.**

Observanz [ɔpsɛr'vants], *f.* (-, *pl.* **-en**) observance, conformance; usage, convention, custom.

Observatorium [ɔpzɛrva'to:rium], *n.* (**-s,** *pl.* **-rien**) observatory.

obsiegen ['ɔpzi:gən], *v.i.* (*sep.*) (*Dat.*) triumph (over), get the better (of); be victorious, carry the day.

obskur [ɔps'kuːr], *adj.* obscure; (*coll.*) ***eine –e Größe,*** a dark horse. **Obskurant** [–'rant], *m.* (**-en,** *pl.* **-en**) obscurantist.

Obst [oːpst], *n.* (**-es,** *pl.* **-arten**) fruit; (*coll.*) ***ich danke für –,*** nothing doing! **Obst|bau,** *m.* fruit-growing. **–baum,** *m.* fruit-tree. **–ernte,** *f.* fruit picking; fruit crop. **–garten,** *m.* orchard. **–händler,** *m.* fruiterer. **–kern,** *m.* kernel, stone, pip. **–kuchen,** *m.* fruit-tart, flan. **Obstler, Öbstler** ['øːpstlər], *m.* (*Austr.*) fruiterer. **Obst|lese,** *f. See* **–ernte. obstreich,** *adj.* abounding in fruit.

Obstruktion [ɔpstruktsi'oːn], *f.* blockage, stoppage, obstruction; (*coll.*) – ***treiben,*** go slow (*at work*). **Obstruktions|stelle,** *f.* (*coll.*) bottle-neck. **–taktik,** *f.* obstructionism.

Obst|schale, *f.* fruit skin, peel, paring. **–wein,** *m.* friut drink, fermented fruit juice. **–züchter,** *m.* fruit-grower. **–zucker,** *m.* laevulose.

obszön [ɔps'tsøːn], *adj.* obscene. **Obszönität** [–i'tɛːt], *f.* obscenity; smutty joke.

O-Bus ['oːbus], *m.* (*coll.*) trolley bus.

obwalten ['ɔpvaltən], *v.i.* (*sep.*) prevail, exist; ***unter den –den Umständen,*** under the (prevailing) circumstances.

ob|wohl, –zwar, *conj. See* **–gleich.**

Ochs [ɔks], *m.* (**-en,** *pl.* **-en**) (*Austr.*) *see* **Ochse.**

Ochse ['ɔksə], *m.* (**-n,** *pl.* **-n**) ox, bull, bullock; (*fig.*) duffer, blockhead; ***die –n hinter den Pflug spannen,*** put the cart before the horse; (*coll.*) ***er steht da wie der – am Berge*** or ***vorm neuen Tor,*** he stands there like a duck in a thunderstorm.

ochsen ['ɔksən], *v.i.* (*sl.*) grind, cram, swot. **Ochsen|-auge,** *n.* (*Naut.*) bull's eye; (*Bot.*) ox-eye; (*Archit.*) oval *or* round window; (*Cul.*) fried egg. **–fiesel,** *m. See* **–ziemer. –fleisch,** *n.* beef. **–frosch,** *m.* bull-frog. **–gespann,** *n.* team of oxen. **–klauenöl,** *n.* neatsfoot oil. **–kopf,** *m.* (*fig.*) blockhead. **–post,** *f.* (*coll.*) slow journey. **–schwanz,** *m.* ox-tail. **–treiber,** *m.* drover. **–ziemer,** *m.* (*obs.*) bull's pizzle; horsewhip. **–zunge,** *f.* ox-tongue.

Ocker ['ɔkər], *m.* (*Min.*) ochre. **Ockergelb,** *n.* yellow ochre.

Ode ['oːdə], *f.* ode.

öd(e) [øːt ('øːdə)], *adj.* waste, empty, bare, bleak, desolate, deserted; (*fig.*) tedious, dull, dreary. **Öde,** *f.* waste(land), desert, solitude, (*fig.*) bleakness, dreariness, tedium.

Odem ['oːdəm], *m.* (*Poet.*) breath.

Ödem [ø'deːm], *n.* (**-s,** *pl.* **-e**) oedema. **ödematös** [–ma'tøːs], *adj.* oedematic, oedematose, oedematous.

oder ['oːdər], *conj.* or; or else, otherwise; – ***aber,*** or instead, or on the other hand.

Odermennig ['oːdərmɛnɪç], *m.* (*Bot.*) agrimony.

Odinshühnchen ['oːdɪnshyːnçən], *n.* (*Orn.*) red-necked (*Am.* northern) phalarope (*Phalaropus lobatus*).

Ödland ['øːtlant], *n.* wasteland, barren *or* fallow land.

Odyssee [ody'seː], *f.* Odyssey.

Ofen ['oːfən], *m.* (**-s,** *pl.* ⸗) 1. stove, oven, furnace, kiln; ***hinter dem – hocken,*** be a stay-at-home; ***damit lockt man keinen Hund hinterm – vor,*** that has no attraction at all, that leaves (me, him *etc.*) quite cold; (*B.*) ***der feurige –,*** the fiery furnace; 2. (*Min.*) mine-chamber.

Ofen|bank, *f.* fireside seat, chimney-corner. **–emaille,** *f. See* **–lack. –farbe,** *f. See* **–schwärze. –geld,** *n.* charge for using baker's oven. **–hocker,** *m.* stay-at-home, mollycoddle. **–kachel,** *f.* Dutch tile. **–klappe,** *f.* damper. **–lack,** *m.* stove enamel. **–loch,** *n.* stove-vent. **–rohr,** *n.* stovepipe; recess for keeping things warm; (*Mil. coll.*) bazooka. **–röhre,** *f.* cooking-oven. **–rost,** *m.* grate. **–schaufel, –schippe,** *f.* fire-shovel. **–schirm,** *m.* fire-screen. **–schwärze,** *f.* blacklead, stove-polish. **–setzer,** *m.* stove-fitter. **–trocknung,** *f.* stoving, kiln-drying. **–vorsetzer,** *m.* fender. **–ziegel,** *m.* firebrick.

offen ['ɔfən], *adj.* open; frank, outspoken, sincere, candid; clear, overt, public; vacant, free, spaced, exposed, denuded, bare; ***–er Brief,*** unsealed *or* open letter; ***–er Dampf,*** live steam; ***–es Eis,*** loose ice; ***bei –en Fenstern schlafen,*** sleep with the windows open; ***–es Feuer,*** open fire; ***–e Flamme,*** open *or* naked flame; ***–e Fragen,*** unsolved problems; ***–es Geheimnis,*** open secret; – ***gesagt*** or ***gestanden,*** frankly speaking; (*Comm.*) ***–es Giro,*** blank endorsement; ***–e Handelsgesellschaft,*** private firm; ***–er Leib,*** open bowels; ***–e Police,*** floating policy; ***–e Rechnung,*** current account; outstanding account; ***auf –er See,*** on the open sea; ***einen –en Sinn für eine S. haben,*** be receptive to a th.; ***–e Stadt,*** unfortified town; ***–e Stelle,*** vacancy, gap; ***auf –er Straße,*** in the open street, in public; ***auf –er Strecke,*** on the open road; (*Railw.*) between stations; (*Theat.*) ***bei –er Szene,*** in the middle of the performance; ***–e Tafel halten,*** keep open house; ***– zu Tage liegen,*** be evident; ***–e Türen einrennen,*** fight shadows; (*fig.*) ***mit –em Visier,*** openly, without ulterior motive; ***–er Wechsel,*** blank cheque; ***–er Wein,*** wine from the barrel; (*Hunt.*) ***–e Zeit,*** open season.

offenbar ['ɔfənbaːr, –'baːr], *adj.* apparent, manifest, evident, plain, clear, obvious, palpable; declared (*enemy*). **offenbaren** [–'baːrən], *v.t.* disclose, reveal, unveil, show, manifest, discover; proclaim, publish; ***sein Herz*** or ***sich –,*** open one's heart, unbosom o.s.; ***geoffenbarte Religion,*** revealed religion. **Offenbarung** [–'baːruŋ], *f.* manifestation; disclosure; revelation. **Offenbarungs|eid,** *m.* oath of manifestation, pauper's oath. **–glaube,** *m.* belief in revealed religion.

offenhalten ['ɔfənhaltən], *irr.v.i.* (*sep.*) (*Dat.*) (*fig.*) keep *or* leave open *or* undecided; reserve the right (to).

Offenheit ['ɔfənhaɪt], *f.* frankness, candour.

offenherzig ['ɔfənhɛrtsɪç], *adj.* candid, frank, outspoken, sincere. **Offenherzigkeit,** *f.* frankness, candour, outspokenness, sincerity; (*hum.*) ***sein Rock hat einige –en,*** his coat is more holy than righteous.

offenkundig ['ɔfənkundɪç], *adj.* public, well-known; evident, overt, patent, flagrant, blatant; notorious. **Offenkundigkeit,** *f.* publicity, overtness, notoriety.

offenlassen ['ɔfənlasən], *irr.v.t.* (*sep.*) leave open, unfinished, unsettled, undecided *or* in abeyance.

offensichtlich ['ɔfənzɪçtlɪç], *adj.* obvious, apparent, evident, manifest.

offensiv [ɔfɛn'ziːf], *adj.* offensive, aggressive. **Offensive,** *f.* offensive, attack; ***die – ergreifen,*** take the offensive.

offenstehen ['ɔfənʃteːən], *irr.v.i.* (*sep.*) be *or* stand open; (*fig.*) remain unpaid; remain unsettled *or* undecided; ***es steht mir offen,*** I am free *or* at liberty (*to do*). **offenstehend,** *adj.* open; undecided; outstanding (*account*).

öffentlich ['œfəntlɪç], **1.** *adj.* public; ***–e Bekanntmachung,*** public announcement; ***–e Betriebe,*** public utilities; ***–es Geheimnis,*** open secret; ***–e Hand,*** public enterprise; ***–es Haus,*** brothel, disorderly house; ***–e Person,*** public figure; ***–es Recht,*** law applying to public bodies; ***–e Schule,*** free *or* state school; ***–e Vorlesung,*** open *or* public lecture. **2.** *adv.* publicly, in public; – ***bekanntmachen,*** publicize, make public. **Öffentlichkeit,** *f.* publicity; public opinion; the general public; ***sich in die – flüchten,*** rush into print; ***an*** or ***vor die – treten,*** appear publicly *or* in public; publish, be published, come before the public; ***in aller –,*** in public; ***im Lichte der –,*** in the public eye, in the limelight.

offerieren [ɔfe'riːrən], *v.t.* bid, tender, (make an) offer. **Offert** [ɔ'fɛrt], *n.* (**-(e)s,** *pl.* **-e**) (*Austr.*), **Offerte,** *f.* offer, tender, bid, proposal.

Offizial [ɔfitsi'aːl], *m.* (**-s,** *pl.* **-e**) ecclesiastical official. **Offizialverteidiger,** *m.* poor defendant's council. **Offiziant,** *m.* (**-en,** *pl.* **-en**) minor official. **offiziell,** *adj.* official; authoritative.

Offizier [ɔfi'tsiːr], *m.* (**-s,** *pl.* **-e**) 1. (commissioned) officer; ***aktiver –,*** regular officer; ***hoher –,*** high-ranking officer; ***er ist – geworden,*** he has obtained his commission; ***– vom Dienst,*** orderly officer; ***zur Disposition gestellter –,*** officer on the retired list; ***vom Gemeinen zum – emporsteigen,*** rise from the ranks; 2. any of the chessmen except king and pawns. **Offiziers|anwärter,** *m.* officer cadet. **–bursche,** *m.* orderly, batman. **–deck,** *n.* quarter-deck. **–kasino,** *n.* officers' mess. **–messe,** *f.* (*Mil.*) officers' mess, (*Nav.*) ward-room. **–patent,** *n.* commission.

Offizin [ɔfi'tsi:n], *f.* (-, *pl.* **-en**) 1. laboratory; 2. dispensary, chemist's shop; 3. printing-office. **offizinell** [–'nɛl], *adj.* medicinal, officinal.

offiziös [ɔfitsi'ø:s], *adj.* semi-official.

öffnen ['œfnən], *v.t., v.r.* open; unlock, unseal; (*Surg.*) dissect (*a body*); ***ihm die Wege –,*** pave the way for him; ***dem Laster Tür und Tor –,*** give full licence to vice. **öffnend,** *adj.* opening; (*Med.*) aperient, laxative. **Öffnung,** *f.* opening, hole, aperture, gap; mouth, orifice; outlet; (*Bot.*) dehiscence; (*Med.*) evacuation; (*Surg.*) dissection. **Öffnungs|mittel,** *n.* (*Med.*) aperient. **–zeiten,** *f.pl.* hours of business, opening hours *or* time.

oft [ɔft], *adv.* (*comp.* *öfter, sup. öftest*) often, frequently, repeatedly; time and again; ***so – du kommst,*** every time you come; ***wie – ist 3 in 6 enthalten?*** how many times does 3 go into 6? ***ziemlich –,*** not infrequently.

öfter ['œftər], 1. *adj.* (*comp. of* **oft**) repeated; ***sein –es Kommen,*** his repeated *or* frequent visits. 2. *adv.* more frequently; oftener; ***je – ich ihn sehe, desto mehr . . .,*** the more I see of him, the more . . . *etc.*; ***–s, des –en,*** *see* **oft.**

oftmalig ['ɔftmalıç], *adj.* frequent, repeated. **oftmals,** *adv.* *See* **oft.**

Oheim ['o:haım], *m.* (**-s,** *pl.* **-e**) *see* [1]**Ohm.**

[1]**Ohm** [o:m], *m.* (**-s,** *pl.* **-e**) (*Poet., dial.*) uncle.

[2]**Ohm,** *n.* (**-(e)s,** *pl.* **-e**) (*obs.*) liquid measure (*approx.* = 35 *gallons* = 168 *l.*).

[3]**Ohm,** *n.* (**-(s),** *pl.* -) (*Elec.*) ohm.

Öhm [ø:m], *m.* (**-s,** *pl.* **-e**) (*dial.*) *see* [1]**Ohm.**

Öhmd [ø:mt], *n.* (*dial.*) second mowing (*of grass*). **öhmen,** *v.t., v.i.* mow for the second time.

ohne ['o:nə], 1. *prep.* (*Acc.*) without, devoid *or* innocent of, lacking; apart from, excluding, not counting, not to speak of, but for; ***– Arbeit,*** out of work; (*Comm.*) ***– Bericht,*** for want of advice; ***– Frage,*** doubtless; ***– Jahr,*** no date (*of publication*); (*coll.*) ***– mich!*** count me out! (*coll.*) ***die S. ist nicht –,*** there is a good deal to be said for that, it is not at all bad; (*Mil.*) ***– Tritt marsch!*** break step! ***– weiteres,*** without more ado, forthwith, at once; easily, readily. 2. *conj.* ***– daß,*** without, save, unless; ***– daß ich es wußte,*** without my knowledge, unknown to me; ***– ein Wort zu sagen,*** without saying a word.

ohne|dem, (*obs.*), **–dies, –hin,** *adv.* besides; all the same, anyway, anyhow, moreover. **–gleichen,** *adj.* unequalled, matchless, peerless. **Ohnehalt–,** *pref.* non-stop.

Ohnmacht ['o:nmaxt], *f.* (-, *pl.* **-en**) faint, fainting fit, swoon, syncope, unconsciousness; impotency, impotence, powerlessness, weakness; ***in – fallen,*** swoon. **ohnmächtig,** *adj.* swooning, unconscious; faint, weak, helpless, powerless, feeble; ***– werden,*** faint, swoon, (*coll.*) pass out. **Ohnmachtsanfall,** *m.* fainting fit.

Ohr [o:r], *n.* (**-(e)s,** *pl.* **-en**) ear; auricle; hearing; handle; (*coll.*) ***sich aufs – legen,*** lie down, have a nap; (*coll.*) ***ihn bei den –en nehmen,*** pin his ears down; ***ganz – sein,*** be all ears; ***ein geneigtes – finden,*** find a sympathetic ear; ***die –en hängen lassen,*** look crestfallen, be downcast *or* (*coll.*) down in the mouth; ***er hat es (faustdick) hinter den –en,*** he is a very wily, he is a sly *or* cunning dog; ***ihn hinter die –en hauen,*** box his ears; ***sich hinter dem – kratzen,*** scratch one's head (*embarrassed or puzzled*); ***sich*** (*Dat.*) ***etwas hinter die –en schreiben,*** make a special note of s.th., take a th. to heart; ***noch nicht trocken hinter den –en,*** still wet behind the ears; ***ein – in ein Buch einschlagen,*** turn down the corner of a page; ***mir klingen die –en, es klingt mir in den –en,*** my ears are tingling *or* burning, someone is walking over my grave; ***ihm in den –en liegen,*** pester him, keep dinning (*s.th.*) into his ears; ***ihm einen Floh ins – setzen,*** unsettle his mind; ***lange –en machen,*** listen inquisitively; ***die –en spitzen,*** prick up one's ears; (*coll.*) ***die –en steif halten,*** keep a stiff upper lip, keep one's pecker up; ***bis über die –en,*** up to the eyes; ***sie wurde bis über die –en rot,*** she blushed to the roots of her hair; ***bis über die –en verliebt,*** head over heels in love; ***ihn übers – hauen,*** cheat him, (*sl.*) do him in the eye; ***ihm das Fell über die –en ziehen,*** fleece him; ***sich die Nacht um die –en schlagen,*** not get a wink of sleep, toss and turn all night; ***ihm die –en vollschreien,*** din in his ears; ***vor meinen –en,*** in my hearing; ***ihm zu –en kommen,*** come to his knowledge *or* hearing; ***von einem – zum anderen,*** from ear to ear; ***zu einem – hinein, zum andern hinaus,*** in at one ear and out at the other.

Öhr [ø:r], *n.* (**-(e)s,** *pl.* **-e**) eye (*of needle*), eyelet; handle, catch, lug.

Ohren|arzt, *m.* ear specialist. **–beichte,** *f.* auricular confession. **ohrenbetäubend,** *adj.* deafening, ear-splitting. **Ohren|bläser,** *m.* tale-bearer, scandal-monger, slanderer. **–drüse,** *f.* parotid gland. **ohrenfällig,** *adj.* impressive-sounding. **Ohren|geier,** *m.* (*Orn.*) lappet-faced vulture (*Torgos tracheliotus*). **–höhle,** *f.* cavity of the ear. **–klingen,** *n.* *See* **–sausen. –leiden,** *n.* disease of the ear. **–lerche,** *f.* (*Orn.*) shore (*Am.* horned) lark (*Eremophila alpestris*). **–nerv,** *m.* auditory nerve. **–qualle,** *f.* (*Mollusc.*) auricula. **–reißen,** *n.* *See* **–schmerz. –sausen,** *n.* buzzing in the ears, (*Med.*) tinnitus. **–schmalz,** *n.* earwax, cerumen. **–schmaus,** *m.* musical treat, (*fig.*) delightful news. **–schmerz,** *m.* earache. **–schützer,** *m.pl.* ear-muffs. **–sessel,** *m.* wing chair. **–spiegel,** *m.* otoscope. **–steißfuß, –taucher,** *m.* (*Orn.*) Slavonian (*Am.* horned) grebe (*Podiceps auritus*). **ohrenzerreißend,** *adj.* ear-splitting. **Ohrenzeuge,** *m.* auricular witness.

Ohrfeige ['o:rfaıgə], *f.* slap in the face, box on the ear. **ohr|feigen,** *v.t.* (*insep.*) box (*a p.'s*) ears, slap (*a p.'s*) face. **–förmig,** *adj.* auriculate, auriform. **Ohr|gehänge,** *n.* ear-ring. **–hammer,** *m.* (*Anat.*) malleus.

-ohrig ['o:rıç], *adj.suff.* -eared.

Ohr|kanal, *m.* auditory canal. **–läppchen,** *n.* lobe of the ear. **–leiste,** *f.* (*Anat.*) helix. **–muschel,** *f.* external ear, pinna, ear conch, auricle. **–ring,** *m.* ear-ring. **–schnecke,** *f.* (*Anat.*) cochlea. **–speicheldrüse,** *f.* parotid gland. **–trompete,** *f.* (*Anat.*) Eustachian tube. **–wurm,** *m.* (*Ent.*) earwig.

Okkasion [ɔkazi'o:n], *f.* opportunity, occasion; (*Comm.*) (good) bargain.

Okkupation [ɔkupatsi'o:n], *f.* occupation, seizure.

Ökonom [øko'no:m], *m.* (**-en,** *pl.* **-en**) farmer, agriculturist; manager, steward, housekeeper. **Ökonomie** [–'mi:], *f.* economics; economy; domestic economy, housekeeping; farming. **Ökonomiegebäude,** *n.* farm-building(s). **ökonomisch,** *adj.* economic, economical, thrifty.

Oktaeder [ɔkta'e:dər], *n.* octahedron. **oktaedrisch,** *adj.* octahedral.

Oktav [ɔk'ta:f], *n.* (**-s,** *pl.* **-e**) octavo; ***breites –,*** crown octavo. **Oktav|band,** *m.* octavo volume.

Oktave [ɔk'ta:və], *f.* (*Mus.*) octave.

Oktavformat [ɔk'ta:fforma:t], *n.* *See* **Oktav.**

oktavieren [ɔkta'vi:rən], *v.i.* be overblown (*of a note on a wind instrument*).

Oktett [ɔk'tɛt], *n.* (**-(e)s,** *pl.* **-e**) (*Mus.*) octet.

Oktober [ɔk'to:bər], *m.* October.

Oktogon [ɔkto'go:n], *n.* (**-s,** *pl* **-e**) octagon. **oktogonal** [–'na:l], *adj.* octagonal.

oktroyieren [ɔktroa'ji:rən], *v.t.* dictate, impose (*Dat.,* on) from above, force (upon).

okular [oku'la:r], *adj.* ocular. **Okular,** *n.* (**-s,** *pl.* **-e**),

Okular|glas, *n.* eyepiece. **–schätzung,** *f.* visual estimate.
okulieren [oku'li:rən], *v.t.* (*Bot.*) graft, inoculate. **Okuliermesser,** *n.* grafting-knife.
ökumenisch [øku'me:nɪʃ], *adj.* oecumenical.
Okzident ['ɔktsidɛnt], *m.* occident.
Öl [ø:l], *n.* (**-s,** *pl.* **-e**) oil; ***ätherische –e,*** essential oils; ***fette –e,*** fatty oils; ***heiliges –,*** chrism; ***flüchtige –e,*** *see* ***ätherische –e***; (*fig.*) – ***ins Feuer gießen,*** add fuel to the flames, pour oil on the flames; – ***auf die Wellen gießen,*** pour oil on the waters; ***in – malen,*** paint in oil(s); ***auf – stoßen,*** strike oil.
Öl|ablaß, *m.* oil drain *or* outlet. **–abscheider,** *m.* oil trap. **–anstrich,** *m.* coat of oil-paint. **–anzug,** *m. See* **–zeug. –bauer,** *m.* owner of an olive-grove. **–baum,** *m.* olive-tree; ***wilder*** or ***falscher –,*** oleaster. **–beere,** *f.* olive. **–behälter,** *m.* oil-receptacle (*in a lamp*), oil-tank. **–berg,** *m.* Mount of Olives. **–blatt,** *n.* olive-leaf. **–bohrung,** *f.* oil-well. **–druck,** *m.* 1. oil pressure; 2. *See* **–druckbild. –druckanzeiger,** *m.* oil-pressure gauge. **–druckbild,** *n.* oleograph, chromolithograph. **–druckstoßdämpfer,** *m.* oil *or* oleo shock-absorber.
ölen ['ø:lən], *v.t.* oil, lubricate; (*Eccl.*) anoint; (*fig.*) ***wie geölt,*** smoothly, without a hitch; (*fig.*) ***wie ein geölter Blitz,*** like greased lightning. **Öler,** *m.* lubricating point, nipple; oil-can.
Öl|farbe, *f.* oil-colour. **–farbendruck,** *m.* oleography; oleograph. **–feuerung,** *f.* oil-fuel. **–fläschchen,** *n.* oil-cruet. **–garten,** *m.* olive grove. **–geläge,** *n. See* **–schlamm. –gemälde,** *n.* oil-painting. **–gewinnung,** *f.* oil production. **–götze,** *m.* (*coll.*) ***wie ein –,*** like a stuffed dummy. **ölhaltig,** *adj.* oily, oleiferous. **ölig,** *adj.* oily; (*fig.*) unctuous.
olim ['o:lɪm], *adv.* (*obs.*) *see* **ehemals. Olim,** *m.* (*coll.*) ***seit –s Zeit,*** from time immemorial, from the year dot; (*coll.*) ***zu –s Zeiten,*** in days of yore.
Olive [o'li:və], *f.* (*Bot.*) olive. **oliven|farbig, –grün,** *adj.* olive-green. **Oliven|öl,** *n.* olive oil. **–spötter,** *m.* (*Orn.*) olive-tree warbler (*Hippolais olivetorum*).
Öl|kohle, *f.* carbon (*inside cylinders*). **–kuchen,** *m.* oilcake. **–leitung,** *f.* oil pipe-line, (*Motor.*) oil-feed. **–lese,** *f.* olive-harvest. **–malerei,** *f.* painting in oil. **–meßstab,** *m.* dipstick. **–motor,** *m.* oil-engine, diesel engine. **–papier,** *n.* transparent (oiled) paper, grease-proof paper. **–quelle,** *f. See* **–bohrung. –ruß,** *m.* lamp-black. **–sardinen,** *f.pl.* sardines in olive oil. **ölsauer,** *adj.* ***–es Salz,*** oleate. **Öl|säure,** *f.* oleic acid. **–schiefer,** *m.* (*Min.*) shale. **–schlamm,** *m.* sludge, oil-foots *or* -dregs. **–stand,** *m.* oil-level. **–standmesser,** *m.* oil gauge. **–stein,** *m.* oilstone. **–süß,** *n.* glycerin(e), glycerol. **–tuch,** *n.* oilcloth.
Ölung ['ø:luŋ], *f.* oiling, lubrication; (*Eccl.*) anointment; ***letzte –,*** extreme unction.
Öl|verbrauch, *m.* oil consumption. **–vorkommen,** *n.* oil resources. **–wanne,** *f.* (*Motor.*) sump, oil-bath.
Olymp [o'lymp], *m.* 1. Olympus; 2. (*coll. Theat.*) the gods. **Olympiade** [–i'a:də], *f.* Olympiad, Olympic Games. **olympisch,** *adj.* Olympian, (*Spt.*) Olympic.
Öl|zeug, *n.* oilskin (clothing), oilskins. **–zucker,** *m. See* **–süß. –zuführung,** *f.* (*Motor.*) oil-feed, oil supply. **–zweig,** *m.* (*fig.*) olive branch (*symbol of peace and goodwill*).
Oma ['o:ma], *f.* (-, *pl.* **-s**) (*coll.*) grandma, granny.
Omelett [ɔm(ə)'lɛt], *n.* (**-(e)s,** *pl.* **-e**), **Omelette,** *f.* (-, *pl.* **-n**) omelet.
ominös [omi'nø:s], *adj.* ominous.
Omnibus ['ɔmnibus], *m.* (**-ses,** *pl.* **-se**) omnibus, (*coll.*) bus.
Onanie [ona'ni:], *f.* onanism, masturbation, self-abuse. **onanieren,** *v.i.* masturbate.
ondulieren [ɔndu'li:rən], *v.t.* wave (*hair*).
Onkel ['ɔŋkəl], *m.* uncle; (*sl.*) old chap; (*sl.*) ***er ist ein gemütlicher –,*** he is a jolly old boy. **onkelhaft,** *adj.* avuncular.
Onomatopöie [onomatopø'i:], *f.* onomatopoeia.
Oolith [oo'li:t], *m.* (**-(e)s** *or* **-en,** *pl.* **-e(n)**) oolite.
Opa ['o:pa], *m.* (**-s,** *pl.* **-s**) (*coll.*) gran(d-)dad, grandpa.
opak [o'pa:k], *adj.* opaque.
Opal [o'pa:l], *m.* (**-s,** *pl.* **-e**) opal. **opaleszieren** [–lɛs'zi:rən], **opalisieren,** *v.i.* opalesce. **opalisierend,** *adj.* opalescent.
Oper ['o:pər], *f.* (-, *pl.* **-n**) opera; opera-house.
Operateur [opera'tø:r], *m.* (**-s,** *pl.* **-e**) operator (*cinematograph etc.*); operating surgeon.
Operation [operatsi'o:n], *f.* (military) operation, (surgical) operation, (*Comm. etc.*) transaction. **Operationsbasis,** *f.* base of operations. **operationsfähig,** *adj.* (*Surg.*) operable; ***nicht –,*** inoperable. **Operations|gebiet,** *n.* (*Mil.*) theatre of operations. **–narbe,** *f.* (*Surg.*) post-operative scar. **–plan,** *m.* plan of campaign. **–saal,** *m.* (*Surg.*) operating theatre. **–schwester,** *f.* (*Surg.*) theatre nurse. **–tisch,** *m.* (*Surg.*) operating table. **–ziel,** *n.* (*Mil.*) tactical objective.
operativ [opera'ti:f], *adj.* (*Mil.*) operational, strategic, (*Surg.*) surgical, operative.
Operette [ope'rɛtə], *f.* operetta, musical (comedy).
operieren [ope'ri:rən], **1.** *v.i.* (*Surg.*) operate, perform an operation; (*Mil., fig.*) operate, proceed. **2.** *v.t.* (*Surg.*) operate on; ***sich – lassen,*** undergo an operation. **Operierung,** *f.* operation (*Gen.*, on).
Opern|dichter, *m.* librettist. **–glas,** *n.*, **–gucker,** *m.* opera-glasses. **opernhaft,** *adj.* operatic, (*fig.*) stagy. **Opern|haus,** *n.* opera-house. **–musik,** *f.* operatic music. **–sänger,** *m.*, **–sängerin,** *f.* opera-singer, operatic singer. **–text,** *m.* libretto.
Opfer ['ɔpfər], *n.* offering, sacrifice; victim; ***zum – fallen*** (*Dat.*), fall a victim to; ***ein – bringen,*** make a sacrifice (*Dat.*, for). **Opferaltar,** *m.* sacrificial altar. **opferbereit,** *adj.* unselfish, self-sacrificing, devoted, self-forgetful. **Opfer|brot,** *n.* consecrated bread *or* wafer; showbread (*of Mosaic ritual*). **–büchse,** *f.* offering box. **–flamme,** *f.* sacrificial flame. **–dienst,** *m.* worship by sacrifices. **opfer|freudig,** *adj. See* **–bereit. Opfer|gabe,** *f.* offering. **–gebet,** *n.* offertory. **–geld,** *n.* money-offering. **–gesang,** *m.* offertory. **–kasten,** *m.* poor-box. **–lamm,** *n.* sacrificial lamb; the Lamb (Jesus); (*fig.*) innocent victim. **–mut,** *m.* spirit of sacrifice.
opfern ['ɔpfərn], *v.t., v.i.* sacrifice, offer as a sacrifice, offer up, immolate; ***sein Leben – für,*** give one's life for; ***sich für etwas –,*** sacrifice o.s. for a th.
Opfer|priester, *m.* sacrificer. **–schale,** *f.* offering cup. **–stätte,** *f.* place of sacrifices. **–stock,** *m. See* **–kasten. –tag,** *m.* flag-day. **–tier,** *n.* sacrificial victim. **–tod,** *m.* sacrifice of one's life, supreme sacrifice; expiatory death (*of Christ*).
Opferung ['ɔpfəruŋ], *f.* immolation, sacrifice.
opfer|willig, *adj. See* **–bereit.**
Ophthalmie [ɔftal'mi:], *f.* (*Med.*) ophthalmia.
Opiat [opi'a:t], *n.* (**-(e)s,** *pl.* **-e**) opiate. **Opium** ['o:pium], *n.* opium. **Opium|höhle,** *f.* opium-den. **–tinktur,** *f.* laudanum.
Opponent [ɔpo'nɛnt], *m.* (**-en,** *pl.* **-en**) objector (*in disputations*). **opponieren,** *v.t.* resist, oppose, offer resistance to. **Opposition** [–zitsi'o:n], *f.* (*Pol., Astr.*) opposition. **oppositionell** [–'nɛl], *adj.* opposed, opposing.
opportun [ɔpɔr'tu:n], *adj.* opportune. **Opportunismus** [–'nɪsmus], *m.* opportunism. **Opportunität** [–i'tɛ:t], *f.* expediency. **Opportunitätspolitik,** *f.* political time-serving.
optieren [ɔp'ti:rən], *v.i.* choose, decide, opt (***für,*** in favour of).
Optik ['ɔptɪk], *f.* 1. optics; 2. lens; 3. gun-sight. **Optiker,** *m.* optician.
optimal [ɔpti'ma:l], *adj.* optimum, maximum, highest, best, most favourable. **Optimat,** *m.* (**-en,** *pl.* **-en**) dignitary.
Optimismus [ɔpti'mɪsmus], *m.* optimism. **optimistisch,** *adj.* optimistic.

Optimum ['ɔptimum], *n.* (**-s,** *pl.* **-tima**) optimum, best.

optisch ['ɔptɪʃ], *adj.* optical; *-es Signal,* visual signal; *-e Brechung,* refraction; *-e Täuschung,* optical illusion.

Orakel [o'ra:kəl], *n.* oracle. **orakelhaft,** *adj.* oracular, cryptic. **orakeln,** *v.i.* speak in riddles. **Orakelspruch,** *m. See* **Orakel.**

Orange [o'rãʒə], *f.* orange. **Orangeat** [–'ʒa:t], *n.* candied peel. **orange(farben),** *adj.* orange-(coloured). **Orangen|blüte,** *f.* orange-blossom. **–schale,** *f.* orange-peel.

Orang-Utan ['o:raŋ'u:tan], *m.* (**-s,** *pl.* **-e** *or* **-s**) orang-outang.

oratorisch [ora'to:rɪʃ], *adj.* oratorical.

Oratorium [ora'to:rium], *n.* (**-s,** *pl.* **-rien**) (*Mus.*) oratorio; (*R.C.*) oratory.

Orchester [ɔr'kɛstər], *n.* orchestra; band; (*Theat.*) orchestra pit. **Orchester|begleitung,** *f.* orchestration, orchestral accompaniment. **–sessel,** *m.* (*Theat.*) (orchestra) stall. **orchestrieren** [–'tri:rən], *v.t.* orchestrate, score.

Orchidee [ɔrçi'de:ə], *f.* orchid.

Ordal [ɔr'da:l], *n.* (**-s,** *pl.* **-ien**) (*usu. pl.*) (judgement by) ordeal.

Orden ['ɔrdən], *m.* order; decoration, distinction, medal. **Ordens|band,** *n.* ribbon of an order. **–bruder,** *m.* member of an order; friar, monk. **–burg,** *f.* castle of (*Teutonic etc.*) order; (*Nat. Soc.*) training school for political leaders. **–geistliche(r),** *m.* regular. **–gelübde,** *n.* monastic vow, profession. **–kleid,** *n.* monastic garb *or* habit. **–regel,** *f.* statute(s) of an order. **–ritter,** *m.* knight of an order. **–schwester,** *f.* sister, nun. **–zeichen,** *n.* badge, order.

ordentlich ['ɔrdəntlɪç], **1.** *adj.* orderly, neat, tidy, well kept, (*pred.*) in good order, regular, ordinary, proper, usual; (*coll.*) respectable, decent; real, sound, downright, out-and-out; *-er Kerl,* a decent *or* honest fellow; *-e Mahlzeit,* proper *or* (*coll.*) decent meal; *-es Mitglied,* ordinary *or* full member; *-er Professor,* university professor (in ordinary); *-e Schlacht,* pitched battle; *-e Tracht Prügel,* sound thrashing. **2.** *adv.* really, properly, duly, soundly, thoroughly; *– froh,* downright *or* (*coll.*) awfully glad; *es ihm – geben,* really let him have it; (*coll.*) *ihm – den Kopf waschen,* give him a good blowing up *or* dressing down. **Ordentlichkeit,** *f.* orderliness; respectability.

Order ['ɔrdər], *f.* (-, *pl.* **-n**) (*Mil., Comm.*) order, command; *bis auf weitere –,* until further orders; (*coll.*) *– parieren,* obey, carry out orders; (*Comm.*) *eine – erteilen,* place an order; (*Comm.*) *an – stellen,* issue to order; *für mich an die – des* or *von ...,* pay to the order of. . . .

Ordinale [ɔrdi'na:lə], *n.* (**-s,** *pl.* **-lia**), **Ordinalzahl,** *f.* ordinal (number).

ordinär [ɔrdi'nɛ:r], *adj.* common, ordinary, base, low, vulgar; (*Comm.*) *-e Havarie,* petty average; *-er Mensch,* vulgar fellow; *-er Preis,* published price (*of books*).

Ordinariat [ɔrdinari'a:t], *n.* professorship.

Ordinarium [ɔrdi'na:rium], *n.* budget, standing charge.

Ordinarius [ɔrdi'na:rius], *m.* (-, *pl.* **-rien**) professor; (*Eccl.*) ordinary.

Ordinate [ɔrdi'na:tə], *f.* (*Geom.*) ordinate, offset, *y*-axis.

Ordination [ɔrdinatsi'o:n], *f.* 1. ordination, investment; 2. surgery hours. **Ordinationszimmer,** *n.* doctor's surgery. **ordinieren** [–'ni:rən], *v.t.* ordain; *sich – lassen,* take (holy) orders. **ordiniert,** *adj.* in (holy) orders.

ordnen ['ɔrdnən], *v.t.* arrange, (set in *or* put in) order; classify, sift, sort; (*Comm.*) file (*papers*), (*Mil.*) marshall (*troops*); regulate, settle, organize, (*coll.*) put straight. **Ordner,** *m.* 1. organizer, supervisor, regulator, arranger; prefect, monitor (*schools*); 2. (letter) file.

Ordnung ['ɔrdnuŋ], *f.* arrangement; classification, order, system, array; tidiness, orderliness; class, rank; order, succession, series; rules, regulations; *auf – halten,* enforce good order; *aus der –,* disarranged, out of order; (*Mil.*) *geöffnete –,* extended order; (*Mil.*) *geschlossene –,* close order; *in –,* in order, correct, right, settled, arranged; (*coll.*) all right; (*coll. of a p.*) a decent sort; *nicht in –,* not in order, out of order, faulty, wrong, amiss, (*of a p.*) out of sorts, off colour, not up to the mark; *in – bringen,* arrange, settle, put *or* set right, put straight *or* in order, (*coll.*) straighten out, fix up; (*Parl.*) *zur – rufen,* call to order.

Ordnungsdienst ['ɔrdnuŋsdi:nst], *m.* security police. **ordnungs|gemäß,** *adj. See* **–mäßig. Ordnungsliebe,** *f.* orderliness, tidiness (*of a p.*). **ordnungsmäßig, 1.** *adj.* regular, orderly, methodical; lawful, in order. **2.** *adv.* properly, duly. **Ordnungs|ruf,** *m.* (*Parl.*) call to order. **–sinn,** *m.* orderliness, sense of order. **–strafe,** *f.* fine, penalty for breach of the peace. **ordnungswidrig,** *adj.* contrary to orders, illegal, irregular. **Ordnungszahl,** *f.* 1. ordinal (number); 2. (*Phys.*) atomic number, number in a series.

Ordonnanz [ɔrdɔ'nants], *f.* (-, *pl.* **-en**) 1. (*Mil.*) orderly, runner; *auf – sein,* be on orderly duty; 2. (*obs.*) order, instruction; announcement. **Ordonnanz|dienst,** *m.* orderly duty. **–offizier,** *m.* orderly officer.

Ordre ['ɔrdər], *f.* (*obs.*) *see* **Order.**

Organ [ɔr'ga:n], *n.* (**-s,** *pl.* **-e**) organ; organon; agent, agency; mouthpiece of opinion, publication, periodical, journal (*expressing specific views*); voice; *kein – für Musik,* no ear for music.

Organiker [ɔr'ga:nikər], *m.* organic chemist.

Organisation [ɔrganizatsi'o:n], *f.* organization. **Organisator** [–'za:tɔr], *m.* organizer. **organisatorisch** [–'to:rɪʃ], *adj.* organizing, organizational.

organisch [ɔr'ga:nɪʃ], *adj.* organic, structural.

organisieren [ɔrgani'zi:rən], *v.t.* organize; (*sl.*) organize, get hold of, pinch, swipe. **organisiert,** *adj.* organized, affiliated to an organization.

Organismus [ɔrga'nɪsmus], *m.* (-, *pl.* **-men**) organism, structure, system.

Organist [ɔrga'nɪst], *m.* (**-en,** *pl.* **-en**) organist.

Orgasmus [ɔr'gasmus], *m.* (-, *pl.* **-men**) orgasm, (*coll.*) climax.

Orgel ['ɔrgəl], *f.* (-, *pl.* **-n**) (*Mus.*) organ. **Orgel|bauer,** *m.* organ-builder. **–chor,** *n.* organ-loft. **–geschütz,** *n.* multiple-barrel gun. **–konzert,** *n.* organ-recital. **orgeln,** *v.i.* play the organ; grind a barrel-organ; (*contemptuously*) play *or* sing badly. **Orgel|pfeife,** *f.* organ-pipe. **–punkt,** *m.* pedal-note. **–spiel,** *n.* organ-playing. **–spieler,** *m.* organist. **–stimme,** *f.* register, organ-stop.

orgiastisch [ɔrgi'astɪʃ], *adj.* wild, dissolute, crapulous, sybaritical. **Orgie** ['ɔrgiə], *f.* orgy, dissipation, debauch(ery).

Orient ['o:riɛnt], *m.* orient. **Orientale** [–'ta:lə], *m.* (**-n,** *pl.* **-n**) oriental. **orientalisch,** *adj.* oriental, eastern.

orientieren [oriɛn'ti:rən], **1.** *v.t.* locate, fix, orient; (put) right, orientate, inform, instruct, brief; guide, give direction to, determine the trend of. **2.** *v.r.* get *or* find one's bearings, find one's way about, learn how the land lies; inform o.s. (*über* (*Acc.*), of *or* about), make inquiries (about), make o.s. acquainted (with); *eine Politik nach gewissen Grundsätzen –,* guide policy along certain channels, give a policy a certain bias; *gut orientiert über* (*Acc.*), familiar with, well-informed about; *religiös orientiert,* with a religious bias; *falsch orientiert,* incorrectly informed, misinformed. **Orientierung,** *f.* orientation, direction; information, guidance. **Orientierungs|linie,** *f.* datum line. **–punkt,** *m.* reference point; landmark. **–sinn,** *m.*, **–vermögen,** *n.* sense of direction; homing instinct (*of birds etc.*).

original [origi'na:l], *adj.* 1. original, initial; 2. genuine, innate, inherent. **Original,** *n.* (**-s,** *pl.* **-e**) 1. autograph (copy), holograph; 2. (*of a p.*) original, oddity, eccentric. **Originalausgabe,** *f.* first edition. **Originalität** [-i'tɛ:t], *f.* originality. **Original|kopie,** *f.* (*Films*) master copy. **–sendung,** *f.* (*Rad.*) live transmission. **–treue,** *f.* high fidelity.

originell [origi'nɛl], *adj.* creative, inventive, original; amusing, peculiar, eccentric; ingenious.

Orkan [ɔr'ka:n], *m.* (**-s,** *pl.* **-e**) hurricane, typhoon.

Ornat [ɔr'na:t], *m.* (**-(e)s,** *pl.* **-e**) official robes, gown, vestments, canonicals; (*coll.*) ***in vollem –,*** in full array.

Orpheus|grasmücke ['ɔrfɔys–], *f.* (*Orn.*) Orphean warbler (*Sylvia hortensis*). **–spötter,** *m.* (*Orn.*) melodious warbler (*Hippolais polyglotta*).

[1]**Ort** [ɔrt], *m.* **1.** (**-(e)s,** *pl.* **-e**) place, spot, point, site; (*Geom.*) locus; ***an allen -en,*** everywhere; ***am angegebenen –,*** as mentioned above, loc. cit.; ***geeigneten -es empfehlen,*** recommend in the proper quarter; (*Theat.*) ***– der Handlung,*** scene of action; ***der Plan ist höheren -es genehmigt,*** the authorities have approved of the project; ***recht am -e,*** in the right place; ***das ist hier sehr am –,*** that is very fitting *or* appropriate *or* quite suitable here; ***an – und Stelle,*** on the spot, here and now; ***am unrechten -e,*** in the wrong place, out of place, misplaced; **2.** (**-(e)s,** *pl.* **¨-er**) village, small town, region, locality.

[2]**Ort,** *n.* (**-(e)s,** *pl.* **¨-er**) (*Min.*) coal face, head of a working; ***vor –,*** at the (coal-)face.

[3]**Ort,** *m. or n.* (**-(e)s,** *pl.* **-e**) (*dial.*) shoemaker's awl.

Örtchen ['œrtçən], *n.* (*coll.*) lavatory, W.C.

orten ['ɔrtən], **1.** *v.i.* take bearings, fix one's position. **2.** *v.t.* take a bearing on, get a fix on, locate, (*coll.*) pin-point.

orthodox [ɔrtɔ'dɔks], *adj.* orthodox. **Orthodoxie** [–'ksi:], *f.* orthodoxy.

Orthographie [ɔrtogra'fi], *f.* orthography, (correct) spelling. **orthographisch** [–'gra:fɪʃ], *adj.* orthographic(al); ***-e Reform,*** spelling reform; ***– richtig,*** correctly spelt, spelt correctly.

örtlich ['œrtlɪç], *adj.* local, endemic; ***-e Betäubung,*** local anaesthetic; ***-e Zuständigkeit,*** venue, territorial jurisdiction; ***– begrenzen,*** localize. **Örtlichkeit,** *f.* place, locality; locale.

Ortolan [ɔrto'la:n], *m.* (**-s,** *pl.* **-e**) (*Orn.*) Ortolan bunting (*Emberiza hortulana*); ***grauer –,*** Cretzschmar's bunting (*Emberiza caesia*).

Orts|amt, *n.* (*Tele.*) local exchange. **–angabe,** *f.* indication of place, map reference; (*on letters*) address. **–anruf,** *m.* (*Tele.*) local call. **ortsansässig,** *adj.* resident (in the locality). **Orts|beschaffenheit,** *f.* nature of a place. **–beschreibung,** *f.* topography. **–bestimmung,** *f.* position-finding, orientation, bearing.

Ortschaft ['ɔrtʃaft], *f.* (inhabited) place; village; market-town.

Ortscheit ['ɔrtʃaɪt], *n.* splinter-bar, swingle-tree.

orts|fest, *adj.* fixed, static, stationary, permanent. **–fremd,** *adj.* strange to a place, unknown in a place, non-resident. **Orts|gedächtnis,** *n.* sense of direction. **–gespräch,** *n.* (*Tele.*) local call. **–gruppe,** *f.* local branch. **–kenntnis,** *f.* local knowledge, knowledge of a place. **ortskundig,** *adj.* familiar *or* acquainted with a locality. **Orts|name,** *m.* place-name. **–quartier,** *n.* (*Mil.*) billet. **–sender,** *m.* (*Rad.*) local transmitter. **–sinn,** *m.* sense of direction. **ortsüblich,** *adj.* (according to) the local custom, customary in a place. **Orts|unterkunft,** *f.* (*Mil.*) billets. **–veränderung,** *f.* change of place *or* habitat, migration, locomotion. **–verkehr,** *m.* local traffic. **–verweisung,** *f.* expulsion *or* banishment from a place. **–vorsteher,** *m.* village magistrate, mayor. **–zeit,** *f.* local time.

Ortung ['ɔrtuŋ], *f.* orientation, location, position-finding; radio-location. **Ortungsgerät,** *n.* radar equipment.

Öse ['ø:zə], *f.* ring, loop, eye, eyelet; lug, ear, hook, catch; ***Haken und -n,*** hooks and eyes. **Ösenschraube,** *f.* eyebolt.

Oskar ['ɔskar], *m.* (*coll.*) ***frech wie –,*** as bold as brass.

Osmane [ɔs'ma:nə], *m.* (**-n;** *pl.* **-n**), **osmanisch,** *adj.* Ottoman.

Osmose [ɔs'mo:zə], *f.* osmosis.

Ost [ɔst], *m.* (**-es,** *pl.* **-e**) east; (*Poet.*) East wind; ***– zu Nord,*** east by north.

Ost|asien, *n.* Eastern Asia, the Far East. **–elbien,** *n.* territories east of the Elbe. **–elbier,** *m.* Prussian landowner, Junker.

Osten ['ɔstən], *m.* east, Orient; ***der Nahe*** (***Ferne, Mittlere***) ***–,*** the Near (Far, Middle) East.

Ostende [ɔst'ɛndə], *n.* (*Geog.*) Ostend.

ostentativ [ɔstɛnta'ti:f], *adj.* explicit, (*of a p.*) ostentatious.

Oster|abend ['o:stər–], *m.* Easter eve, the eve of Easter. **–ei,** *n.* Easter egg. **–ferien,** *pl.* Easter holiday *or* vacation. **–fest,** *n.* Easter, (*Jewish*) Passover. **–fladen,** *m.* Passover bread. **–glocke,** *f.* (*Bot.*) Easter lily. **–hase,** *m.* (fabulous) hare that lays the Easter egg. **–lamm,** *n.* (*Jewish*) paschal lamb.

österlich ['ø:stərlɪç], *adj.* (of) Easter; paschal.

Oster|monat, –mond, *m.* (*obs.*) April. **–montag,** *m.* Easter Monday.

Ostern ['o:stərn], *n.* (*also, esp. Austr., Swiss, as pl.*) Easter, (*Jewish*) Passover.

Österreich ['ø:stəraɪç], *n.* Austria. **Österreicher,** *m.*, **österreichisch,** *adj.* Austrian; ***-ungarisch,*** Austro-Hungarian.

Oster|(sonn)tag, *m.* Easter Day *or* Sunday. **–woche,** *f.* Easter Week. **–zeit,** *f.* Eastertide.

Ost|europa, *n.* Eastern Europe. **–flüchtling,** *m.* refugee from the East. **–frage,** *f.* problem of German minorities beyond the eastern frontier. **–friese,** *m.* (**-n,** *pl.* **-n**), **ostfriesisch,** *adj.* East Frisian. **Ost|friesland,** *n.* East Frisia. **–gote,** *m.* Ostrogoth. **–hilfe,** *f.* subsidies to maintain the Eastern provinces. **–indien,** *n.* the East Indies. **–indienfahrer,** *n.* (*Naut.*) East-Indiaman. **ostindisch,** *adj.* ***-e Archipel,*** Malay Archipelago; ***-e Kompagnie,*** East India Company.

ostisch ['ɔstɪʃ], *adj.* (*Ethn.*) Alpine.

Ostjude ['ɔstju:də], *m.* Polish *or* Galician Jew.

östlich ['œstlɪç], *adj.* eastern, easterly; Oriental; ***– von,*** (to the) east of.

Ost|mark, *f.* **1.** (*obs., Nat. Soc.*) Austria; **2.** German Democratic Republic mark (*currency*). **–preußen,** *n.* East Prussia. **–raum,** *m.* (*Nat. Soc.*) Eastern Europe. **oströmisch,** *adj.* ***-es Reich,*** (Roman) Empire of the East, Byzantine Empire. **Ost|see,** *f.* Baltic Sea. **–vertriebene(r),** *m., f.* displaced p. from eastern territory. **–währung,** *f.* *See* **–mark,** 2. **ostwärts,** *adv.* eastward. **Ost|wind,** *m.* east wind. **–zone,** *f.* Eastern *or* Soviet Zone.

Oszillation [ɔstsɪlatsi'o:n], *f.* oscillation, vibration. **Oszillator** [–'la:tɔr], *m.* (**-s,** *pl.* **-en**) oscillator. **oszillieren,** *v.i.* oscillate, vibrate. **Oszillograph** [–o'gra:f], *m.* (**-en.** *pl.* **-en**) oscillograph.

Otter ['ɔtər], **1.** *m.* (*rare, f.* (-, *pl.* **-n**)) otter. **2.** *f.* (-, *pl.* **-n**) viper, adder.

Ouvertüre [uvɛr'ty:rə], (*Austr.* **Ouverture**) *f.* (*Mus., fig.*) overture.

Ovarium [o'va:rium], *n.* (**-s,** *pl.* **-rien**) (*Anat.*) ovary.

Oxalsäure [ɔk'sa:lzɔyrə], *f.* (*Chem.*) oxalic acid.

Oxhoft ['ɔkshɔft], *n.* (**-(e)s,** *pl.* **-e**) hogshead.

Oxyd [ɔ'ksy:t], *n.* (**-(e)s,** *pl.* **-e**) oxide. **Oxydation** [–datsi'o:n], *f.* oxidation. **oxydationsfest,** *adj.* non-oxidizing. **Oxydationsmittel,** *n.* oxidizing agent. **oxydieren** [–'di:rən], *v.t., v.i.* (*aux.* h. *&* s.) oxidize. **Oxydiermittel,** *n.* *See* **Oxydationsmittel. Oxydierung,** *f.* oxidation. **Oxydul** [–'du:l], *n.* (**-s,** *pl.* **-e**) protoxide.

Ozean ['o:tsea:n], *m.* (**-s,** *pl.* **-e**) ocean; (*hum.*) ***dem – Tribut zahlen,*** be seasick. **Ozean|dampfer,** *m.* ocean(-going) liner. **–fahrt,** *f.* ocean cruise. **–flug,** *m.* trans-oceanic flight. **ozeanisch** [–'a:nɪʃ], *adj.* oceanic; ***-es Klima,*** marine climate. **Ozeanographie** [–ogra'fi:], *f.* oceanography.

Ozon [o'tso:n], *n.* ozone; ***in – verwandeln,*** ozonify. **ozonhaltig,** *adj.* ozoniferous. **ozonisieren** [–i'zi:rən], *v.t.* ozonize.

P

P, p [pi:], *n.* P, p. *See list of abbreviations.*

Paar [pa:r], *n.* (**-s,** *pl.* **-e**) pair, couple, brace; ***20 – Rebhühnchen,*** 20 brace of partridges; ***ein – Pistolen,*** a brace of pistols; ***ein – Strümpfe,*** a pair of stockings; ***sie sind ein schönes –,*** they are a handsome couple; ***ein – bilden mit,*** pair off with; ***sie werden wohl ein – werden,*** it looks like a match; ***zu –en treiben,*** scatter, rout, put to flight.

paar, 1. *adj.* (*rare or dial.*) like, matching; ***– oder unpaar,*** odd or even; (*dial.*) ***–e Zahlen,*** even numbers. **2.** *num.adj.* (*indecl.*) some, a few; ***die – Mark,*** those few shillings; ***mit ein – Worten,*** in a few words; ***in ein – Tagen,*** in a few days.

paaren ['pa:rən], **1.** *v.t.* match; pair, couple, join, mate, unite. **2.** *v.r.* pair, couple, copulate, mate; (*fig.*) join, unite; (*Bot.*) ***gepaart,*** conjugate; paired. **paarig,** *adj.* in pairs, paired. **Paarlaufen,** *n.* pair-skating. **Paarling,** *m.* (**-s,** *pl.* **-e**) one of a pair, allelomorph.

paarmal ['pa:rma:l], *adv.* several times.

Paarung ['pa:ruŋ], *f.* 1. pairing, matching; 2. coupling, mating, copulation; 3. conjugation. **Paarungs|ausfall,** *m.* product of mating, offspring. **–zeit,** *f.* mating season.

paarweise ['pa:rvaɪzə], *adv.* in pairs, in couples, two by two; ***– ordnen,*** pair off (*v.t.*); ***– wegtreten,*** pair off (*v.i.*). **Paarzeher,** *m.* artiodactyl.

Pacht ['paxt], *f.* (-, *pl.* **-en**) *or m.* (**-(e)s,** *pl.* **-e**) tenure, lease; tenancy; rent; ***in – geben,*** let on lease; ***in – nehmen,*** take a lease of, take on lease; ***in – haben,*** hold under lease. **Pacht|bauer,** *m.* tenant-farmer. **–besitz,** *m.* leasehold property. **–brief,** *m.* *See* **–vertrag. –dauer,** *f.* (term of) lease, tenancy.

pachten ['paxtən], *v.t.* lease, rent; farm; (*fig.*) monopolize; (*sl.*) ***sich*** (*Dat.*) ***etwas –,*** commandeer; (*coll.*) ***als ob er die Weisheit gepachtet hätte,*** as if he knew all the answers. **Pachter, Pächter,** *m.* leaseholder, lessee; tenant (farmer). **pachtfrei,** *adj.* rent-free. **Pacht|geld,** *n.* (farm) rent. **–gut,** *n.* farm, leasehold estate. **–herr,** *m.* landlord. **–hof,** *m.* *See* **–gut. –leute,** *pl.* tenants, tenantry.

Pachtung ['paxtuŋ], *f.* leasing, renting, farming; leasehold estate. **Pachtvertrag,** *m.* lease, deed of conveyance. **pachtweise,** *adv.* on lease. **Pacht|wert,** *m.* rental value. **–zins,** *m.* rent.

Pack [pak], **1.** *m. or n.* (**-(e)s,** *pl.* **-e** *or* **¨-e**) packet, parcel, package, pack, bundle, bale; (*Mil.*) baggage; ***mit Sack und –,*** with bag and baggage. **2.** *n.* mob, rabble, pack; (*Prov.*) ***– schlägt sich, – verträgt sich,*** the mob is fickle.

Päckchen ['pɛkçən], *n.* (postal) package, parcel; (*fig.*) load, burden (*of worries*); ***– Zigaretten,*** packet of cigarettes.

Pack|darm, *m.* rectum. **–eis,** *n.* pack-ice.

Packen ['pakən], *m.* bale.

packen, 1. *v.t.* 1. pack (up), wrap up; stow away; 2. lay hold of, seize, come to grips with, pounce on, clutch, grasp, (*fig.*) thrill, grip, hold (spell-bound). **2.** *v.r.* (*coll.*) pack off, clear out, be gone; ***pack' dich!*** be gone! get away! clear out! **packend,** *adj.* thrilling, stirring, gripping, absorbing, breath-taking. **Packer,** *m.* packer.

Pack|esel, *m.* sumpter *or* baggage mule; (*fig.*) drudge. **–garn,** *n.* packthread. **–haus,** *n.* warehouse; packing-room. **–hof,** *m.* custom-house; bonded warehouse. **–kasten,** *m.* packing-case. **–korb,** *m.* crate, hamper. **–kosten,** *pl.* charges for packing. **–lack,** *m. or n.* sealing wax. **–leinen,** *n.*, **–leinwand,** *f.* packing-cloth, sacking. **–nadel,** *f.* packing-needle. **–papier,** *n.* packing *or* wrapping paper; brown paper. **–pferd,** *n.* pack-horse, baggage-horse. **–raum,** *m.* packing room, (*Naut.*) stowage compartment. **–sattel,** *m.* pack-saddle. **–schnur,** *f.* cord, twine. **–stoff,** *m.* packing (material). **–tasche,** *f.* saddle-bag. **–träger,** *m.* (*dial.*) porter.

Packung ['pakuŋ], *f.* packing, wrapper; package, packet; fomentation, poultice; (*Mech.*) gasket, lagging (*of pipes*).

Pack|wagen, *m.* baggage waggon, luggage-van, goods-van. **–zeug,** *n.* *See* **–stoff.**

Pädagoge [pɛda'go:gə], *m.* (**-n,** *pl.* **-n**) pedagogue. **Pädagogik,** *f.* pedagogy, educational theory. **pädagogisch,** *adj.* educational, pedagogic(al); ***–e Akademie,*** teachers' training college.

Padde ['padə], *f.* (*dial.*) frog; toad.

Paddel ['padəl], *n.* paddle. **Paddelboot,** *n.* canoe. **paddeln,** *v.i.* paddle, canoe.

paff! [paf], *int.* pop! bang! plop! **paffen,** *v.t., v.i.* puff (away at); (*coll.*) ***daß es*** (***nur so***) ***pafft,*** with a vengeance.

Page ['pa:ʒə], *m.* (**-n,** *pl.* **-n**) page. **Pagen|frisur,** *f.*, **–kopf,** *m.* bobbed hair.

paginieren [pagi'ni:rən], *v.t.* number (*the pages*). **Paginierung,** *f.* pagination.

Pagode [pa'go:də], *f.* pagoda.

Pair [pɛ:r], *m.* (**-s,** *pl.* **-s**) peer. **Pairsschub,** *m.* nomination of new peers (*for political purposes*), (wholesale) creation of peers.

Paket [pa'ke:t], *n.* (**-s,** *pl.* **-e**) packet, package, parcel, bundle. **Paket|annahme,** *f.* parcels receiving-office. **–ausgabe,** *f.* parcels issuing office. **–beförderung,** *f.* parcels-delivery. **–boot,** *n.* mail-boat, steam-packet. **–karte,** *f.* parcel form. **–post,** *f.* parcel-post.

Pakt [pakt], *m.* (**-s,** *pl.* **-e(n)**) pact, agreement, compact. **paktieren** [–'ti:rən], *v.i.* agree (***über*** (*Acc.*), on), come to an agreement (on) *or* to terms (about).

Palais [pa'lɛ:], *n.* (-, *pl.* -) (*obs.*), **Palast** [pa'last], *m.* (**-es,** *pl.* **¨-e**) palace. **palastartig,** *adj.* palatial. **Palastdame,** *f.* lady in waiting.

Palästina [palɛ'sti:na], *n.* Palestine.

Palastrevolution [pa'lastrevolutsi'o:n], *f.* court-revolution.

Palatschinke [pala'tʃɪŋkə], *f.* (*usu. pl.*) (*Austr.*) pancake with filling.

Paletot ['palə̆to], *m.* (**-s,** *pl.* **-s**) overcoat; greatcoat.

Palette [pa'lɛtə], *f.* palette.

Palisade [pali'za:də], *f.* palisade, stockade. **palisadieren** [–'di:rən], *v.t.* fence in, palisade.

Palisanderholz [pali'zandərhɔlts], *n.* rosewood.

Pallasch ['palaʃ], *m.* (**-es,** *pl.* **-e**) broadsword.

Palm [palm], *m.* (**-s,** *pl.* **-e**) (*obs.*) palm, hand-breadth (*measure*).

Palmarum [pal'ma:rum], *m.* *See* **Palmsonntag.**

Palme ['palmə], *f.* palm(-tree); ***die – des Sieges erringen,*** carry off the palm. **Palm(en)gewächse,** *n.pl.* palms.

Palmin [pal'mi:n], (*regd. trade name*) *n.* coconut butter.

Palm|kätzchen, *n.* (*dial.*) willow catkin. **–(nuß)öl,** *n.* coconut oil. **–sonntag,** *m.* Palm Sunday. **–wedel,** *m.* palm branch (*symbol of victory*). **–weide,** *f.* (*Bot.*) sallow (*Salix capraea*). **–woche,** *f.* Holy Week.

Pampelmuse ['pampəlmu:zə], *f.* grapefruit.

Pamphlet [pam'fle:t], *n.* (**-(e)s,** *pl.* **-e**) lampoon. **Pamphletist** [–'tɪst], *m.* (**-en,** *pl.* **-en**) pamphleteer; lampoonist.

Panaschiersystem [pana'ʃi:rzyste:m], *n.* alternative voting, proportional representation. **panaschiert,** *adj.* mottled, variegated. **Panaschierung,** *f.* mottling, variegation (*in plants*).

Pandekten [pan'dɛktən], *pl.* pandects. **Pandekten|reiter** (*coll.*), **–wurm,** *m.* student of law.

Paneel [pa'ne:l], *n.* (**-s,** *pl.* **-e**) panel(ling), wainscot. **paneelieren** [–'li:rən], *v.t.* wainscot, panel.

Panier [pa'ni:r], *n.* (**-s,** *pl.* **-e**) banner, standard.

panieren [pa'ni:rən], *v.t.* dress (*meat, fish*), sprinkle with egg, bread-crumbs *etc.*

Panik ['pa:nɪk], *f.* panic. **panikartig,** *adj.* panicky. **panisch,** *adj.* panic, (*coll.*) panicky; ***–er Schrecken,*** panic.

Panne ['panə], *f.* (*Motor.*) break-down, engine

failure *or* trouble; puncture, flat tyre; (*fig.*) blunder, mishap.

Panoptikum [pa'nɔptikum], *n.* (**-s**, *pl.* **-ken**) waxworks.

panschen, *v.t., v.i.* (*Austr.*) *see* **pantschen.**

Pansen ['panzən], *m.* (*Zool.*) rumen, (*coll.*) paunch, belly.

Pantine [pan'ti:nə], *f.* (*dial.*) clog, patten.

Pantoffel [pan'tɔfəl], *m.* (**-s**, *pl.* **-(n)**) slipper; ***dem Papste den – küssen,*** kiss the pope's toe; (*coll.*) ***unter dem – stehen,*** be henpecked. **Pantoffel|blume,** *f.* (*Bot.*) slipper-wort (*Calceolaria*). **–held,** *m.* henpecked husband. **–regiment,** *n.* petticoat government. **–tierchen,** *n.* (*Zool.*) slipper animalcule (*Paramaecium*).

Pantomime [panto'mi:mə], *f.* mime, pantomime; dumb show.

pantschen ['pantʃən], **1.** *v.t.* adulterate, water down. **2.** *v.i.* (*dial.*) dabble, splash.

Panzen ['pantsən], (*dial.*) *see* **Pansen.**

Panzer ['pantsər], *m.* 1. armour, cuirass, coat of mail; (*Mil.*) armour plating *or* plate; 2. tank. **Panzer|abwehr,** *f.* anti-tank defence. **–abwehrkanone,** *f.* anti-tank gun. **–batterie,** *f.* armoured battery. **–blech,** *n.* armour-plate. **panzerbrechend,** *adj.* armour-piercing. **Panzer|büchse,** *f.* anti-tank rifle. **–drehturm,** *m.* revolving gun turret (*of tank*). **–falle,** *f.* tank trap. **–faust,** *f.* anti-tank weapon, bazooka. **–flotte,** *f.* (*obs.*) ironclads. **–führer,** *m.* tank commander. **–geschoß,** *n.* armour-piercing shell. **–gewölbe,** *n.* strong-room, vault (*of a bank*). **–glas,** *n.* bullet-proof glass. **–graben,** *m.* anti-tank ditch. **–granate,** *f.* *See* **–geschoß.** **–hemd,** *n.* coat of mail. **–jäger,** *m.* anti-tank gunner. **–kabel,** *n.* (*Elec.*) armoured cable. **–kampfwagen,** *m.* armoured fighting vehicle. **–kette,** *f.* tank track. **–knacker,** *m.* (*coll.*) tank buster. **–korps,** *n.* armoured corps. **–kraftwagen,** *m.* armoured car. **–kreuzer,** *m.* pocket battleship. **–kuppel,** *f.* *See* **–turm.** **–mine,** *f.* antitank mine.

panzern ['pantsərn], **1.** *v.t.* arm, armour, plate (*a ship*). **2.** *v.r.* put on armour, (*fig.*) arm o.s. (***gegen,*** against); ***gepanzert,*** armoured; ***gepanzerte Faust,*** mailed fist.

Panzer|platte, *f.* armour-plate. **–schiff,** *n.* armoured vessel, dreadnought. **–schrank,** *m.* safe, strong-box. **–schütze,** *m.* tank gunner. **–träger,** *m.* tank-landing ship. **–truppe,** *f.* tank corps. **–turm,** *m.* gun turret (*of a tank*). **Panzerung,** *f.* armour-plating, (*Hist.*) (coat of) mail. **Panzer|waffe,** *f.* tank force. **–wagen,** *m.* tank, armoured car. **–wanne,** *f.* hull (*of tank*). **–weste,** *f.* bullet-proof vest. **–zug,** *m.* armoured train.

Päonie [pɛ'o:niə], *f.* peony.

Papa [pa'pa:], *m.* (**-s**, *pl.* **-s**) (*coll.*) dad(dy), pa(pa), pop.

Papagei [papa'gaɪ], *m.* (**-s** *or* **-en**, *pl.* **-en**) parrot. **Papageialk,** *m.* (*Orn.*) paraquet (*Am.* parakeet) auklet (*Cyclorrhynchus psittacula*). **papageienhaft,** *adj.* parrot-like. **Papageienkrankheit,** *f.* psittacosis. **Papageitaucher,** *m.* (*Orn.*) puffin (*Am.* common puffin) (*Fratercula arctica*).

Papier [pa'pi:r], *n.* (**-s**, *pl.* **-e**) paper; document; *pl.* identity papers; (*Comm.*) stocks, securities; ***das steht nur auf dem –,*** that is only on paper; ***gemachtes –,*** bills ready for endorsement; ***zu – bringen,*** write down; commit to paper, put on record; ***fettdichtes –,*** grease-proof paper; ***glattes*** or ***geglättetes*** or ***satiniertes –,*** calendered paper, glazed paper; ***geleimtes –,*** sized paper; ***gemasertes –,*** grained paper; ***geprägtes –,*** embossed paper; ***geripptes –,*** laid paper; ***geschöpftes –,*** handmade paper; ***gewelltes –,*** corrugated paper; ***lichtempfindliches –,*** sensitized paper.

Papier|abfälle, *m.pl.*, **–abgänge,** *m.pl.* paper waste. **–adel,** *m.* peerage by letters patent. **–beutel,** *m.* paper bag. **–blatt,** *n.*, **–bogen,** *m.* sheet of paper. **–brei,** *m.* paper pulp.

papieren [pa'pi:rən], *adj.* (made of) paper; papery, paper-like; ***–er Stil,*** prosy *or* bookish *or* wooden style.

Papier|fabrik, *f.* paper-mill. **–fetzen,** *m.* scrap of paper. **–geld,** *n.* paper money, bank-note(s). **–händler,** *m.* stationer. **–handlung,** *f.* stationer's shop. **–holz,** *n.* *See* **–brei.** **–korb,** *m.* waste-paper basket. **–krieg,** *m.* red-tape. **–masse,** *f.* *See* **–brei.** **–mühle,** *f.* pulp mill. **–schlange,** *f.* paper streamer. **–schnitzel,** *n.pl.* paper shavings. **–tüte,** *f.* paper bag. **–umlauf,** *m.* paper circulation. **–währung,** *f.* paper currency. **–waren,** *f.pl.* stationery. **–wert,** *m.* nominal *or* paper value. **–wisch,** *m.* *See* **–fetzen.** **–zeichen,** *n.* watermark. **–zeug,** *n.* *See* **–brei.**

Papillote [papi'jo:tə], *f.* curl-paper.

Papismus [pa'pɪsmus], *m.* popery. **papistisch,** *adj.* popish.

Papp [pap], *m.* (**-es**, *pl.* **-e**) (*dial., coll.*) *see* **Pappe.** **Papp|band,** *m.* (book bound in) boards. **–bogen,** *m.* sheet of cardboard *or* pasteboard. **–deckel,** *m.* (cover in) boards. **Pappe,** *f.* pasteboard, cardboard, millboard; paste, pap; ***in – gebunden,*** bound in boards; (*coll.*) ***nicht von –,*** not to be sneezed at. **Pappeinband,** *m.* (binding in) boards.

Pappel ['papəl], *f.* (**-**, *pl.* **-n**) (*Bot.*) poplar.

pappeln ['papəln], *v.i.* (*coll.*) babble, blether.

päppeln ['pɛpəln], *v.t.* feed (with pap); (*fig.*) pamper, coddle.

Pappelweide ['papəlvaɪdə], *f.* (*Bot.*) black poplar.

pappen ['papən], **1.** *v.t.* paste, stick (with paste). **2.** *v.i.* stick, clog, be tacky.

Pappenheimer ['papənhaɪmər], *m.pl.* (*coll.*) ***ich kenne meine –,*** I know (and can trust) them, I know my troops.

Pappenstiel ['papənʃti:l], *m.* trifle; (*coll.*) ***um einen –,*** for a mere song, dirt-cheap.

papperlapapp! [papərla'pap], *int.* (*coll.*) bosh! rubbish! fiddlesticks!

pappig ['papɪç], *adj.* sticky, pasty, pappy. **Papp|masse,** *f.* papier-mâché. **–schachtel,** *f.* cardboard box. **–schädel,** *m.* (*coll.*) blockhead, dunderhead. **–schnee,** *m.* soggy *or* caking snow. **–teller,** *m.* paper plate.

Paprika ['paprika], *m.* red pepper.

Papst [pa:pst], *m.* (**-es**, *pl.* **⸗e**) pope, pontiff; Holy Father. **Papstkrone,** *f.* tiara, triple crown.

päpstlich ['pɛ:pstlɪç], *adj.* papal, pontifical; *see also* **papistisch**; ***–er Stuhl,*** Holy See; ***–er als der Papst sein,*** overdo it.

Papsttum ['pa:psttu:m], *n.* papacy, pontificate. **Papstwürde,** *f.* papal dignity.

Parabel [pa'ra:bəl], *f.* (**-**, *pl.* **-n**) 1. parable, simile; 2. (*Geom.*) parabola. **parabolisch** [–'bo:lɪʃ], *adj.* 1. parabolic; 2. figurative, allegorical.

Parade [pa'ra:də], *f.* parade; display; (military) review, (*Av.*) fly-past; (*Fenc.*) parry; ***eine – abnehmen,*** take the salute, hold a review; ***ihm in die – fahren,*** upset his plans *or* calculations, put a spoke in his wheel. **Parade|anzug,** *m.* (full-)dress uniform, gala uniform, (*coll.*) full dress. **–aufstellung,** *f.* review order. **–bett,** *n.* catafalque; ***auf dem – liegen,*** lie in state. **–flug,** *m.* fly-past.

Paradeis [para'daɪs], **1.** *n.* (*obs.*) *see* **Paradies.** **2.** *m.* (**-**, *pl.* **-er**), **Paradeisapfel, Paradeiser,** *m.* (*dial.*) tomato.

Parade|marsch, *m.* march-past. **–pferd,** *n.* (*fig.*) showpiece (*of a p.*). **–platz,** *m.* parade ground. **–schritt,** *m.* slow march, (*coll.*) goose-step. **–stückchen,** *n.* (*fig.*) showpiece (*of a th.*).

paradieren [para'di:rən], *v.i.* parade, (*fig.*) make a show; ***– mit,*** parade, show off, make a show of.

Paradies [para'di:s], *n.* (**-es**, *pl.* **-e**) paradise; (*Theat. sl.*) the gods; ***das Verlorene –,*** Paradise Lost. **Paradiesapfel,** *m.* (*dial.*) *see* **Paradeis, 2.** **paradiesisch,** *adj.* heavenly, delightful. **Paradies|seeschwalbe,** *f.* (*Orn.*) *see* **Rosenseeschwalbe.** **–vogel,** *m.* bird of paradise.

Paradigma [para'dɪgma], *n.* (**-s**, *pl.* **-men**) (*Gram.*) paradigm.

paradox [para'dɔks], *adj.* paradoxical. **Paradox,** *n.* (**-es**, *pl.* **-e**), **Paradoxon,** *n.* (**-s**, *pl.* **-xa**) paradox.

Paraffin [para'fi:n], *n.* (**-s**, *pl.* **-e**) paraffin.

Paragraph [para'gra:f], *m.* (**-en,** *pl.* **-en**) paragraph, section, article. **Paragraphenreiter,** *m.* stickler for the letter of the law, pettifogger, pedant.

parallel [para'le:l], *adj.* parallel (*zu, mit,* to). **Parallele,** *f.* (*Math.*) parallel; (*fig.*) parallel, comparison. **Parallel|erscheinung,** *f.* analogous form. **-fall,** *m.* parallel case. **Parallelismus** [-'lɪsmus], *m.*, **Parallelität** [-i'tɛ:t], *f.* parallelism, coextension. **Parallel|kreis,** *m.* parallel (*of latitude*). **-linie,** *f.* parallel (line). **-schaltung,** *f.* (*Elec.*) parallel connection. **-stelle,** *f.* parallel passage, literary parallel. **-trapez,** *n.* trapezium. **-versammlung,** *f.* overflow meeting. **-währung,** *f.* dual currency.

Paralyse [para'ly:zə], *f.* general paralysis (of the insane). **paralysieren** [-'zi:rən], *v.t.* paralyse. **Paralytiker,** *m.* paralytic. **paralytisch,** *adj.* paralytic, paralysed.

Paranuß ['paranus], *f.* Brazil-nut.

Paraphe [pa'ra:fə], *f.* flourish, paraph. **paraphieren** [-'fi:rən], *v.t.* sign (*with a flourish*); sign provisionally.

Parasit [para'zi:t], *m.* (**-en,** *pl.* **-en**) parasite. **parasitär** [-'tɛ:r], **parasitisch,** *adj.* parasitic.

parat [pa'ra:t], *adj.* (*coll.*) prepared, ready.

Paratyphus ['pa:raty:fus], *m.* paratyphoid fever.

Pärchen ['pɛ:rçən], *n.* (loving) couple, lovers.

pardautz! [par'dauts], *int.* bang! crash!

Pardel ['pardəl], **Parder,** *m.* leopard, panther.

Pardon [par'dɔ̃], *m.* (**-s,** *pl.* **-s**) pardon, grace, clemency, mercy; ***keinen – geben,*** give no quarter; (*dial.*) *–!* excuse me!

Parenthese [parɛn'te:zə], *f.* parenthesis, brackets.

Parforce|jagd [par'fɔrs–], *f.* hunting with hounds, coursing. **-kur,** *f.* (*coll.*) drastic cure. **-ritt,** *m.* steeplechase, (*coll.*) mad ride.

Parfum [par'fœ], *n.* (**-s,** *pl.* **-s**), *usu.* **Parfüm** [par'fy:m], *n.* (**-(e)s,** *pl.* **-e**) perfume, scent. **Parfümfläschchen,** *n.* scent-bottle. **parfümieren** [-'mi:rən], *v.t.* scent, perfume.

pari ['pa:ri], *adv.* at par; ***unter –,*** below par, at a discount; ***über –,*** above par, at a premium. **Pari,** *n.* par value.

Paria ['pa:ria], *m.* (**-s,** *pl.* **-s**) pariah.

parieren [pa'ri:rən], **1.** *v.i.* (*Fenc.*) parry; rein in; (*fig.*) (*Dat.*) obey, follow (*orders*); toe the line, fall in line, knuckle under. **2.** *v.t.* parry, ward off (*a blow*); rein in (*a horse*).

Parikurs ['pa:rikurs], *m.* (*Comm.*) par.

Pariser [pa'ri:zər], *m.* Parisian; *– **Mode,*** Paris fashions; (*Typ.*) *– **Schrift,*** ruby, (*Am.*) agate.

Parität [pari'tɛ:t], *f.* (*Comm.*) parity; religious equality. **paritätisch,** *adj.* on a par, on a footing of equality; proportional, pro rata; ***-e Schule,*** undenominational school; ***-er Staat,*** state with religious equality.

Pariwert ['pa:rive:rt], *m.* (*Comm.*) par *or* nominal value.

Park [park], *m.* (**-(e)s,** *pl.* **-e**) park; (*Mil.*) depot, dump, distributing point. **Park|anlagen,** *f.pl.* public gardens, pleasure-grounds. **-aufseher,** *m.* park-keeper. **-bremse,** *f.* (*Motor.*) parking brake. **parken,** *v.t., v.i.* park (*motor-cars*).

Parkett [par'kɛt], *n.* (**-(e)s,** *pl.* **-e**) parquet (floor); (*Theat.*) (orchestra) stalls. **parkettieren,** *v.t.* inlay, lay with parquet. **Parkettwachs,** *n.* floor polish.

Parkgebühren ['parkgəby:rən], *f.pl.* parking fee. **parkieren** [-'ki:rən], *v.t., v.i.* (*Swiss*) *see* **parken.** **Park|platz,** *m.* car-park, parking place *or* (*Am.*) lot. **-uhr,** *f.* parking meter. **-verbot,** *n.* ban on parking, 'no parking!' **-wache,** *f.* car-park attendant.

Parlament [parla'mɛnt], *n.* (**-(e)s,** *pl.* **-e**) parliament.

Parlamentär [parlamɛn'tɛ:r], *m.* (**-s,** *pl.* **-e**) (*Mil.*) bearer of a flag of truce, (*fig.*) intermediary. **Parlamentärflagge,** *f.* flag of truce, white flag.

Parlamentarier [parlamɛn'ta:riər], *m.* parliamentarian. **parlamentarisch,** *adj.* parliamentary. **Parlamentarismus** [-'rɪzmus], *m.* parliamentary system.

parlamentieren [parlamɛn'ti:rən], *v.i.* (*Mil.*) parley; (*coll.*) talk round the subject.

Parlaments|beschluß, *m.* vote of parliament, parliamentary decision *or* enactment. **-ferien,** *pl.* recess. **-mitglied,** *n.* member of parliament, (*Am.*) congressman. **-sitzung,** *f.* parliamentary session. **-verhandlung,** *f.* parliamentary debate.

Parnaß [par'nas], *m.* Parnassus.

Parodie [paro'di:], *f.* parody, travesty (***auf*** (*Acc.*), on). **parodieren,** *v.t.* parody, travesty.

Parole [pa'ro:lə], *f.* parole, catchword; (*Mil.*) password; watchword, slogan.

Paroli ['pa:roli], *n.* (**-s,** *pl.* **-s**) doubling first stake (*in faro*); (*coll.*) ***ihm – bieten,*** defy him, (*coll.*) stick up to him.

Part [part], *n.* (*Austr. m.*) (**-(e)s,** *pl.* **-e**) part; share.

Parte ['partə], *f.* (*Austr.*) obituary notice.

Partei [par'taɪ], *f.* (-, *pl.* **-en**) faction, party, side; (*Law*) plaintiff *or* defendant; tenant; *– **ergreifen*** or ***nehmen für,*** side with, take (*s.o.'s*) part; ***es mit keiner – halten, sich zu keiner – schlagen,*** stand aside from the conflict, not take sides, remain neutral, (*coll.*) sit on the fence; ***in einer S. – sein,*** be an interested party; ***gegnerische –,*** opponent(s), opposite side; ***vertragschließende -en,*** contracting parties.

Partei|abzeichen, *n.* party insignia *or* badge. **-anhänglichkeit,** *f.* partisanship. **-apparat,** *m.* party machine. **-bonze,** *m.* (*coll.*) party boss. **-buch,** *n.* membership-book. **-buchbeamte(r),** *m., f.* official appointed on party grounds. **-führer,** *m.* party leader. **-gänger,** *m.* partisan, follower. **-geist,** *m.* party spirit. **-genosse,** *m.* fellow member (of a party) (*associated now irredeemably with Nat. Soc. Party*). **-grundsätze,** *m.pl.* party-line. **-gruppe,** *f.* faction, splinter-party. **-herrschaft,** *f.* party rule.

parteiisch [par'taɪɪʃ], *adj. See* **parteilich. Parteileitung,** *f.* party headquarters; party leaders. **parteilich,** *adj.* partial (***für,*** to), biased, prejudiced (***für,*** in favour of; ***gegen,*** against); one-sided; factious. **Parteilichkeit,** *f.* partiality, bias. **parteilos,** *adj.* impartial, neutral; (*Pol.*) non-party, non-aligned, independent. **Parteilosigkeit,** *f.* impartiality, neutrality; (*Pol.*) non-alignment, independence.

Partei|mitglied, *n.* party-member. **-nahme,** *f.* partisanship (***für,*** for), support (for *or* of). **-politik,** *f.* party politics. **parteipolitisch,** *adj.* party-political. **Partei|sucht,** *f.* factiousness. **-tag,** *m.* party conference. **-vorbringen,** *n.* (*Law*) pleadings. **-wesen,** *n.* party system. **-wirtschaft,** *f.* (*coll.*) party racket. **-zugehörigkeit,** *f.* party affiliation(s).

Parterre [par'tɛr], *n.* (**-s,** *pl.* **-s**) ground-floor, (*Am.*) first floor; (*Theat.*) pit; (*Hort.*) flower-bed; (*Theat.*) ***erstes –,*** stalls. **Parterre|loge,** *f.* (*Theat.*) lower box. **-wohnung,** *f.* ground-floor flat.

partial [partsi'a:l], *adj.* (*Austr.*) *see* **partiell.**

Partie [par'ti:], *f.* **1.** parcel, batch, lot; ***in -n von 6 bis 12 Stück,*** in lots of from 6 to 12 pieces; ***in -n billiger,*** cheaper in bulk; 2. passage (*in a book or piece of music*); 3. (*Theat.*) part, rôle; party, outing, picnic, excursion; game (*of whist etc.*); (*Tenn.*) set; (*Spt.*) match; ***eine gute – machen,*** marry well, make a good match; ***sie hat mehrere -n ausgeschlagen,*** she has refused several offers of marriage; (*coll.*) ***bei*** or ***mit*** or ***von der – sein,*** be in on a th.; (*Tenn.*) *– **mit Spiel vor,*** advantage set; 4. (*Anat.*) region, area. **Partiegeld,** *n.* expenses (*for the table, cards etc.*) at play; (*Bill.*) ***wir spielen nur ums –,*** we are only playing for the table (*i.e. there are no stakes*).

partiell [partsi'ɛl], **1.** *adj.* partial, one-sided. **2.** *adv.* partly, in part, partially, not entirely.

Partie|preis, *m.* (special) price for the lot *or* set. **-waren,** *f.pl.* (*Comm.*) sub-standard goods; remainders (*books*).

Partikel [par'ti:kəl], *f.* (-, *pl.* **-n**) (*Gram.*) particle.
Partikular [partiku'la:r], *m.* (**-s**, *pl.* **-e**) (*Swiss*) *see* **Partikülier. partikularisieren** [–ri'zi:rən], *v.t.* particularize. **Partikularismus** [–'rɪsmus], *m.* (*Pol.*) particularism, separatist movement.
Partikülier [partikyli'e:] (*Austr.* **Partikulier**), *m.* (**-s**, *pl.* **-s**) private individual, man of private means.
Partisan [parti'za:n], *m.* (**-s**, *pl.* **-e**) partisan, guerilla (fighter).
Partisane [parti'za:nə], *f.* halberd.
Partitur [parti'tu:r], *f.* (-, *pl.* **-en**) (*Mus.*) full score.
Partizip [parti'tsi:p], *n.* (**-s**, *pl.* **-e** *or* **-ien**) (*Gram.*) participle.
Partizipationsgeschäft [partitsipatsi'o:nsgəʃɛft], *n.* (*Comm.*) business on joint account. **partizipieren** [–'pi:rən], *v.i.* participate, share (*an* (*Dat.*), in).
Partizipium, *n.* (**-s**, *pl.* **-pien**) *see* **Partizip.**
Partner ['partnər], *m.*, **Partnerin,** *f.* partner. **Partnerschaft,** *f.* partnership.
partout [par'tu:], *adv.* (*coll.*) by all means, at any cost.
Parvenü [parve'ny:], *m.* (**-s**, *pl.* **-s**) upstart, parvenu.
Parze ['partsə], *f.* destiny, fate; *die –n,* the Fates, the weird sisters.
Parzelle [par'tsɛlə], *f.* parcel, lot (*of ground*), plot, allotment. **parzellieren** [–'li:rən], *v.t.* parcel out, divide into lots.
Pasch [paʃ], *m.* (**-es**, *pl.* **-e** *or* **¨-e**) dice; doublets (*at dice*); (*dominoes*) *einen – setzen,* make the numbers at each end the same; – *werfen* or *würfeln,* throw doublets (*at dice*).
Pascha ['paʃa], *m.* (**-s**, *pl.* **-s**) pasha, pacha.
[1]**paschen** ['paʃən], *v.i.* throw doublets (*at dice*); (*Austr.*) clap one's hands, slap.
[2]**paschen,** *v.t., v.i.* smuggle. **Pascher,** *m.* smuggler.
pascholl! [pa'ʃɔl], *int.* (*coll.*) vamose! vamoos(e)! hop it!
Paspel ['paspəl], *f.* (-, *pl.* **-n**) *or m.* piping, braid, edging (*on a dress etc.*). **paspelieren** [–'li:rən], *v.t.* pipe (*a dress*).
Pasquill [pas'kvil], *n.* (**-s**, *pl.* **-e**) lampoon. **Pasquillant** [–'lant], *m.* (**-en**, *pl.* **-en**) lampooner, satirist. **pasquillieren,** *v.t., v.i.* lampoon.
Paß [pas], *m.* (**-(ss)es**, *pl.* **¨-(ss)e**) 1. pace, amble; *den – gehen,* amble, pace; 2. pass, defile, passage; (*Naut.*) narrows; 3. passport, papers, pass, permit; 4. measuring glass.
paß, *adv.* (*coll.*) *mir zu – kommen,* suit me perfectly, come in handy for me, suit my book, serve my turn.
passabel [pa'sa:bəl], *adj.* passable, tolerable, admissible, practicable.
Passage [pa'sa:ʒə], *f.* passage, thoroughfare; arcade, covered way; (*Mus.*) run, passage.
Passagier [pasa'ʒi:r], *m.* (**-s**, *pl.* **-e**) passenger; *blinder –,* stowaway, (*coll.*) deadhead. **Passagier|-dampfer,** *m.* passenger-steamer, liner. **-fahrt,** *f.* tour, trip, (*Naut.*) cruise. **-flugzeug,** *n.* passenger plane, air-liner. **-gut,** *n.* passenger's luggage.
Passah ['pasa], *n.* (-, *pl.* **-s**), **Passahfest,** *n.* (Feast of the) Passover.
Paßamt ['pasˀamt], *n.* passport office.
Passant [pa'sant], *m.* (**-en**, *pl.* **-en**) passer-by, through-traveller.
Passat [pa'sa:t], *m.* (**-(e)s**, *pl.* **-e**), **Passat|wind,** *m.* trade-wind. **-strömung,** *f.* equatorial current.
Paßbild ['pasbɪlt], *n.* passport photograph.
Passe ['pasə], *f.* yoke (*of dress*).
passen ['pasən], **1.** *v.i.* 1. (*Dat.*) fit, suit, be suited to, become; be suitable *or* convenient for (*a p.*); – *auf* (*Acc.*) or *für* or *zu,* fit, fit in with, be suited to *or* suitable for (*a th.*), (*coll.*) go with (*a th.*); agree, harmonize, tally, (*esp. of colours*) match; *nicht –,* (*esp. of colours*) clash; *gut zueinander –,* be well-matched, (*coll.*) go well together; *nur wenn es mir* (*in den Kram*) *paßt,* only if I feel like it *or* if it suits me *or* suits my purpose; *das paßt wie die Faust aufs Auge,* that's entirely out of place; 2. – *auf* (*Acc.*), wait *or* watch for, be attentive *or* pay attention to; 3. (*Cards*) pass. **2.** *v.r.* be proper *or* seemly *or* becoming; *es paßt sich einfach nicht,* it just isn't done, it's just bad form; *es paßt sich nicht für mich,* it ill befits *or* becomes me.
passend ['pasənt], *adj.* appropriate, suited (*für,* to), fit, fitting, suitable (for), convenient (to *or* for); (*of clothes*) becoming, well-fitting; (*of occasion*) timely, seasonable, apt, opportune, to the purpose; (*of demeanour*) proper, seemly, becoming; *das –e Wort,* the right word; *für – halten,* think fit *or* proper; *dazu –,* matching, to match.
Passepartout [paspar'tu:], *m. or n.* (**-(s)**, *pl.* **-s**) 1. master-key, free (admission) ticket; 2. mount (*for photos etc.*).
Paß|form, *f.* fit (*of clothes*). **-gang,** *m.* amble. **-gänger,** *m.* ambler, ambling nag. **-höhe,** *f.* height of a pass.
passierbar [pa'si:rba:r], *adj.* passable, traversable, practicable.
passieren [pa'si:rən], **1.** *v.t.* pass, go *or* travel over, through *or* across; cross; (*Naut.*) clear; (*durch ein Sieb*) –, sieve, filter, strain, pass through a sieve. **2.** *v.i.* (*aux.* s.) (*coll.*) come to pass, take place, happen, occur; *es mag –,* it will (just) *or* may do; (*coll.*) *was ist ihm passiert?* what has happened to him? (*coll.*) *ist nichts Neues passiert?* is there no news? *jetzt ist's passiert,* now the fat is in the fire. **Passier|gefecht,** *n.* running fight. **-gewicht,** *n.* mint-allowance, tolerated deficiency. **-schein,** *m.* pass, permit.
Passion [pasi'o:n], *f.* passion (*also Eccl.*), (*coll.*) craze. **passioniert** [–'ni:rt], *adj.* impassioned, ardent, keen. **Passions|betrachtung,** *f.* Lenten meditation. **-blume,** *f.* passion-flower (*Passiflora coerulea*). **-predigt,** *f.* Good Friday sermon. **-spiel,** *n.* Passion play. **-woche,** *f.* Holy Week.
passiv ['pasi:f, –'si:f], *adj.* passive, inert, inactive; *–er Widerstand,* passive resistance; ca'canny; *–e Bestechung,* taking bribes, (*coll.*) graft; *–e Bilanz,* debit balance; *–es Wahlrecht,* eligibility for election; *–er Wortschatz,* reading *or* recognition vocabulary. **Passiv,** *n.* (**-s**, *pl.* **-e** (*Austr.* **-a**)) (*Gram.*) passive (voice), passive verb.
Passiva [pa'si:va], **Passiven,** *pl.* (*Comm.*) liabilities. **passivieren** [–'vi:rən], **1.** *v.t.* (*Comm.*) enter on the debit side. **2.** *v.r.* (*Comm.*) (*of balance*) become adverse. **passivisch,** *adv.* passively. **Passivität** [–i'tɛ:t], *f.* passivity, inertness, inactivity. **Passiv|-posten,** *m.* (*Comm.*) debit entry. **-saldo,** *m.* debit balance. **-seite,** *f.* left side (*of ledger*).
Passivum [pa'si:vum], *n.* (**-s**, *pl.* **-va** *or* **-ven**) *see* **Passiv.**
Paßkontrolle ['paskɔntrɔlə], *f.* examination of passports. **paßlich,** *adj.* fit, suitable, seemly, proper. **Paß|sitz,** *m.* (*of clothes*) good *or* snug fit. **-stelle,** *f.* passport office. **-stück,** *n.* (*Mech.*) adapter, fitting.
Passung ['pasuŋ], *f.* (*Mech.*) fit.
Passus ['pasus], *m.* (-, *pl.* -) passage (*in a book*), paragraph; case, instance.
Paßzwang ['pastsvaŋ], *m.* obligation to carry a passport.
Paste ['pastə], *f.* paste; impress, replica, facsimile.
Pastell [pas'tɛl], **1.** *m.* (**-s**, *pl.* **-e**) pastel, crayon. **2.** *n.* (**-s**, *pl.* **-e**) pastel *or* crayon drawing. **Pastell-farben,** *f.pl.* pastel colours, coloured crayons. **pastellfarbig,** *adj.* pastel-coloured, of delicate shade.
Pastete [pa'ste:tə], *f.* pie, pastry; (*coll.*) *da haben wir die –!* here's a pretty kettle of fish! **Pasteten|-bäcker,** *m.* pastrycook. **-kruste,** *f.* piecrust.
pasteurisieren [pastøri'zi:rən], *v.t.* pasteurize.
Pastille [pa'stɪlə], *f.* pastille, lozenge.
Pastinak ['pastinak], *m.* (**-(e)s**, *pl.* **-e**), **Pastinake** [–'na:kə], *f.* parsnip.
Pastor ['pastɔr], *m.* (**-s**, *pl.* **-en**) pastor, clergyman, vicar, minister. **Pastorale** [–'ra:lə], *n.* (**-s**, *pl.* **-s**) *or f.* idyll, eclogue, pastoral; (*Eccl.*) pastoral (letter).

Pastorat, *n.* (**-s,** *pl.* **-e**) parsonage, vicarage, (*Scots*) manse; incumbency. **Pastorin,** *f.* minister's wife.

Patchen ['pa:tçən], *n.* godchild. **Pate,** **1.** *m.* (**-n,** *pl.* **-n**) godfather, sponsor; godchild. **2.** *f. See* **Patin**; – ***stehen bei,*** stand sponsor *or* act as godparent to (*a child*). **Paten|geld, -geschenk,** *n.*, **-groschen,** *m.* christening present. **-kind,** *n.* godchild. **-pfennig,** *m. See* **-geld. Patenschaft, Patenstelle,** *f.* sponsorship; ***Patenschaft vertreten bei,*** *see* ***Pate stehen bei.***

Patent [pa'tɛnt], *n.* (**-s,** *pl.* **-e**) (letters) patent (***auf*** (*Acc.*), for), charter; (*Mil.*) commission; ***ein – anmelden,*** apply for a patent; ***ein – nehmen,*** take out a patent.

patent, *adj.* (*coll.*) fine, splendid, (*sl.*) nifty.

Patent|amt, *n.* patent-office. **-anmeldung,** *f.* application for a patent. **-anwalt,** *m.* patent-attorney *or* agent. **-beschreibung,** *f.* patent-specification. **-erteilung,** *f.* issue of letters patent. **-fatzke,** *m.* (*coll.*) dandy, fop. **-gebühr,** *f.* patent-fee.

patentieren [patɛn'ti:rən], *v.t.* (protect by) patent; grant a patent to; ***etwas – lassen,*** take out a patent for s.th.

Patent|inhaber, *m.* patent holder, patentee. **-lösung,** *f.* (*coll.*) pat solution. **patentrechtlich,** *adv.* – ***geschützt,*** patented, protected (by patent). **Patent|schutz,** *m.* protection by patent. **-schutzgesetz,** *n.* Patent Act. **-urkunde,** *f.* letters patent. **-verletzung,** *f.* infringement of a patent. **-verschluß,** *m.* patent stopper, patent cork.

Paternoster [patər'nɔstər], *n.* (**-s** (*Austr.* -), *pl.* -) paternoster. **Paternoster|aufzug,** *m.* hoist, lift. **-werk,** *n.* bucket chain.

pathetisch [pa'te:tɪʃ], *adj.* lofty, elevated, solemn, expressive.

pathogen [pato'ge:n], *adj.* pathogenic. **Pathogenese** [–'ne:zə], *f.* pathogenesis.

Pathologe [pato'lo:gə], *m.* (**-n,** *pl.* **-n**) pathologist. **Pathologie** [–'gi:], *f.* pathology. **pathologisch,** *adj.* pathological.

Pathos ['pa:tɔs], *n.* solemnity, fervour, ardour, vehemence, emotion, pathos, transport, animation, exuberance.

Patience [pasi'ãs], *f.* (*Cards*) patience, solitaire.

Patient [patsi'ɛnt], *m.* (**-en,** *pl.* **-en**), **Patientin,** *f.* patient; – ***sein,*** be under (medical) treatment; ***ambulante(r)*** –, out-patient; ***stationäre(r)*** –, in-patient.

Patin ['pa:tɪn], *f.* godmother.

Patina ['pa:tina], *f.* patina, verd-antique. **patiniert** [–'ni:rt], *adj.* patinated, patinous.

Patriarch [patri'arç], *m.* (**-en,** *pl.* **-en**) patriarch. **patriarchalisch** [–'ça:lɪʃ], *adj.* patriarchal. **Patrimonium,** *n.* (**-s,** *pl.* **-nien**) patrimony.

Patriot [patri'o:t], *m.* (**-en,** *pl.* **-en**), **Patriotin,** *f.* patriot. **patriotisch,** *adj.* patriotic. **Patriotismus** [–'tɪsmus], *m.* patriotism.

Patrize [pa'tri:tsə], *f.* punch, counter-die.

Patrizier [pa'tri:tsiər], *m.*, **Patrizierin,** *f.* patrician. **patrizisch,** *adj.* patrician.

Patron [pa'tro:n], *m.* (**-s,** *pl.* **-e**) patron; patron saint; (*coll.*) fellow; ***unzuverlässiger*** –, shifty customer; ***lustiger*** –, jolly character. **Patronat** [–'na:t], *n.* (**-en,** *pl.* **-en**) advowson. **patronatsberechtigt,** *adj.* (*Eccl.*) having the gift of a living *or* the right of presentation. **Patronats|herr,** *m.* (*Eccl.*) patron (of a living). **-recht,** *n.* patronage.

Patrone [pa'tro:nə], *f.* (*Mil.*) cartridge, round (of ammunition); pattern, stencil, mandrel; ***scharfe*** –, ball-cartridge. **Patronen|auswerfer,** *m.* ejector. **-auszieher,** *m.* extractor. **-gurt,** *m.* cartridge-belt, bandolier. **-hülse,** *f.* cartridge-case. **-tasche,** *f.* ammunition pouch. **-trommel,** *f.* cartridge drum. **-zuführung,** *f.* cartridge feed.

Patronin [pa'tro:nɪn], *f.* patroness.

Patrouille [pa'truljə], *f.* patrol. **patrouillieren** [–'lji:rən], *v.i.* (*aux.* h. & s.) patrol.

patsch! [patʃ], *int.* slap! smack! **Patsch,** *m.* (**-es,** *pl.* **-e**) (*coll.*) smack, clap; (*dial.*) hand.

Patsche ['patʃə], *f.* (*coll.*) **1.** hand, (*sl.*) paw, mitt; slap on the face, box on the ears; **2.** mire, slush, puddle, (*fig.*) scrape, jam, pickle, fix, mess; (*coll.*) ***in die – geraten,*** get into hot water, get into a scrape; (*coll.*) ***in der – sitzen,*** be in a fix *or* jam; (*coll.*) ***ihn in der – sitzen lassen,*** leave him in the lurch. **patschen,** **1.** *v.i.* (*aux.* h. & s.) make a slapping noise, clap; splash *or* paddle about; patter down (*of rain*). **2.** *v.t.* smack, slap; splash. **patsch(e)naß,** *adj.* soaked to the skin, drenched, dripping wet. **Patsch|hand,** *f.*, **-händchen,** *n.* tiny hand (*of a baby*).

Patschuli ['patʃuli], *n.* patchouli.

patt [pat], *indecl.adj.*, **Patt,** *n.* (**-s,** *pl.* **-s**) (*Chess*) stalemate; – ***machen*** or ***setzen,*** stalemate; – ***sein,*** be stalemated.

Patte ['patə], *f.* 1. lapel, revers (*of coat*), flap (*of pocket*); 2. (*dial.*) paw.

patzen ['patsən], *v.i.* (*coll.*) bungle *or* botch *or* muff it, (*sl.*) codge; (*Theat. etc.*) fluff. **patzig,** *adj.* rude, impudent, insolent; (*sl.*) snotty; ***sich – tun,*** behave insolently.

Paukant [pau'kant], *m.* (**-en,** *pl.* **-en**) (*Univ. sl.*) duellist. **Pauk|arzt,** *m.* doctor in attendance at students' duel. **-boden,** *m.* duelling arena.

Pauke ['paukə], *f.* (*Mus.*) kettle-drum; (*Anat.*) tympanum; (*coll.*) lecture, harangue, dressing-down; ***mit -n und Trompeten,*** with drums beating and trumpets sounding, with full honours; (*iron.*) ignominiously; (*coll.*) ***auf die – hauen,*** paint the town red, make whoopee. **pauken,** *v.i.* beat the kettle-drum; (*sl. also v.t.*) cram, swot; (*Univ. sl.*) fight a duel; thump, drum (***auf*** (*Dat.*), on).

Pauken|fell, *n.* tympanic membrane; drum skin, drumhead. **-höhle,** *f.* tympanic cavity. **-klöppel, -schläger, -schlegel,** *m.* drumstick. **-wirbel,** *m.* roll of the kettle-drum.

Pauker ['paukər], *m.* kettle-drummer; duellist; (*sl.*) school-teacher; coach, crammer. **Paukerei** [–'raɪ], *f.* students' duel; brawl, scrap, row; (*sl.*) cramming, swotting.

Pauk|handschuh, *m.* fencing-glove. **-komment,** *m.* duelling rules.

Paus|back ['paus–], *m.* (**-(e)s,** *pl.* **-e**) chubby-faced person. **-backen,** *f.pl.* chubby face *or* cheeks. **paus|backig,** *Austr.* **-bäckig,** *adj.* chubby-faced.

Pausch- ['pauʃ–], *pref. See under* **Pauschal-.**

pauschal [pau'ʃa:l], **1.** *adj.* lump-sum, all-inclusive, overall. **2.** *adv.* all inclusive, (*coll.*) all in. **Pauschale,** *n.* (**-s,** *pl.* **-lien**) lump sum; all-inclusive price. **Pauschal|gebühr,** *f.* flat rate. **-kauf,** *m.* bulk purchase. **-reise,** *f.* all-in tour. **-summe,** *f. See* **Pauschale. -versicherung,** *f.* comprehensive *or* blanket insurance.

Pausche ['pauʃə], *f.* pommel (*of saddle etc.*).

[1]**Pause** ['pauzə], *f.* pause, stop, interruption, lull, rest (*also Mus.*); (*Theat., Mus.*) interval, (*Am.*) intermission; break, playtime, recess (*schools*); ***ganze*** –, semibreve rest; ***halbe*** –, minim rest; ***viertel*** –, crotchet rest.

[2]**Pause,** *f.* tracing; traced design; blueprint. **pausen,** *v.t.* trace.

pausenlos ['pauzənlo:s], *adj.* without pause, uninterrupted, ceaseless, incessant, non-stop. **Pausenzeichen,** *n.* (*Rad.*) interval signal.

pausieren [pau'zi:rən], *v.i.* (take a) rest, (make a) pause.

Pauspapier ['pauspapi:r], *n.* tracing-paper.

Pavian ['pa:vian], *m.* (**-s,** *pl.* **-e**) baboon.

Pavillon ['paviljɔ̃], *m.* (**-s,** *pl.* **-s**) pavilion, arbour.

Pazifismus [patsi'fɪsmus], *m.* pacificism. **Pazifist,** *m.* (**-en,** *pl.* **-en**) pacifist. **pazifistisch,** *adj.* pacifist. **pazifizieren** [–'tsi:rən], *v.i.* come to terms *or* to an agreement (***mit,*** with).

Paziszenten [patsis'tsɛntən], *m.pl.* contracting parties. **paziszieren,** *v.i.* make a contract.

Pech [pɛç], *n.* 1. pitch; cobbler's wax; (*Prov.*) ***wer – angreift, besudelt sich,*** who touches pitch will be defiled; *wie – und Schwefel zusammenhalten,* stick together through thick and thin; 2. (*coll.*) hard, ill *or* bad luck; hard lines; – *haben,* be unlucky, have no luck, (*coll.*) be down on one's luck, (*sl.*) have a tough break. **pechartig,** *adj.* bituminous. **Pech|blende,** *f.* pitchblende. **–draht,** *m.* cobbler's thread. **pechdunkel,** *adj.* pitch-dark. **Pech|erde,** *f.* bituminous earth. **–fackel,** *f.* torch. **pechig,** *adj.* bituminous; pitchy. **Pech|kiefer,** *f.* pitch-pine. **–kohle,** *f.* bituminous coal. **–nelke,** *f.* (*Bot.*) catch-fly. **pech(raben)schwarz,** *adj.* pitch-black. **Pech|strähne,** *f.* (*coll.*) run of bad luck. **–tanne,** *f.* common spruce; American pitch-pine. **–uran,** *n.* pitchblende. **–vogel,** *m.* (*coll.*) unlucky person.

Pedal [pe'da:l], *n.* (**-s,** *pl.* **-e**) pedal; (*coll.*) *in die –e treten,* step on the pedals. **Pedalharfe,** *f.* double-actioned harp.

Pedant [pe'dant], *m.* (**-en,** *pl.* **-en**) pedant. **pedant,** *adj.* (*Austr.*) *see* **pedantisch. Pedanterie** [–ə'ri:], *f.* pedantry. **pedantisch,** *adj.* pedantic; precise, meticulous, punctilious.

Pedell [pe'dɛl], *m.* (**-s** *or* **-en,** *pl.* **-e(n)** (*Austr.* **-(e)s,** *pl.* **-e**)) beadle, porter, janitor, proctor's man, (*Univ. sl.*) bulldog.

Pediküre [pedi'ky:rə], *f.* pedicure.

Pegel ['pe:gəl], *m.* water-gauge, tide-gauge, water-mark. **Pegelstand,** *m.* water-mark *or* level.

Peilantenne ['paɪlˀantɛnə], *f.* (*Rad.*) directional aerial *or* (*Am.*) antenna.

peilen ['paɪlən], *v.t.* take bearings, get a fix; take soundings; sound; *das Land –,* take the bearings of the coast; *die Sonne –,* take the sun's altitude. **Peiler,** *m.* bearing-compass, direction finder. **Peil|funk,** *m.* radio-beam; radar, radio direction finding. **–gerät,** *n.* direction finding *or* radar equipment. **–lot,** *n.* plummet, sounding lead. **–station, –stelle,** *f.* radar station. **–tisch,** *m.* plotting board *or* table.

Peilung ['paɪluŋ], *f.* (radio) bearing, (*coll.*) fix; direction-finding; (*Naut.*) sounding; *optische –,* visual bearing.

Pein [paɪn], *f.* pain, agony, torture, torment, anguish, suffering(s). **peinigen,** *v.t.* torture; torment, (*fig.*) tantalize, pester, harass. **Peiniger,** *m.* torturer, tormentor; (*coll.*) plague. **Peinigung,** *f.* torture; torment.

peinlich ['paɪnlɪç], **1.** *adj.* 1. painful, distressing, embarrassing, awkward (*Dat.,* for); *–e Frage,* awkward *or* embarrassing question; 2. precise, painstaking, exact, meticulous, punctilious, scrupulous; 3. (*Law*) capital, penal, on pain of death; (*obs.*) by torture; (*obs.*) *–e Gerichtsbarkeit,* criminal jurisdiction. **2.** *adv.* – *anklagen,* accuse on a capital charge; (*obs.*) – *befragen,* put to torture; – *berührt,* pained, distressed, embarrassed; – *genau,* scrupulously exact. **Peinlichkeit,** *f.* 1. painfulness; awkwardness, embarrassment; 2. scrupulousness, punctiliousness.

Peitsche ['paɪtʃə], *f.* whip, lash, (*fig.*) scourge; cat-o'-nine-tails; *mit der – klatschen* or *knallen,* crack a whip. **peitschen, 1.** *v.t.* (horse-)whip, flog, lash; (*fig.*) scourge. **2.** *v.i.* flap (*of sails*); pelt (*of rain*). **Peitschen|hieb,** *m.* lash *or* cut of the whip. **–knall,** *m.* crack of a whip. **–riemen,** *m.,* **–schnur,** *f.* thong of a whip.

pekuniär [pɛkuni'ɛ:r], *adj.* pecuniary.

Pelerine [pelə'ri:nə], *f.* (fur) cape.

Pelikan ['pe:lika:n, –'ka:n], *m.* (**-s,** *pl.* **-e**) pelican.

Pelle ['pɛlə], *f.* (*dial.*) peel, skin, husk. **pellen,** *v.t.* (*dial.*) peel, skin; *wie aus dem Ei gepellt,* spick and span. **Pellkartoffeln,** *f.pl.* potatoes in their jackets.

Peloton [pelo'tɔ̃], *n.* (**-s,** *pl.* **-s**) (*obs.*) (*Mil.*) file, platoon, firing party.

Pelz [pɛlts], *m.* (**-es,** *pl.* **-e**) fur, pelt, hide, skin; fur coat; (*coll.*) skin; *ihm den – ausklopfen,* give him a good thrashing; *ihm Läuse in den – setzen,* give him cause for anxiety; *ihm (dicht) auf den – rücken,* importune him. **Pelzbesatz,** *m.* fur trimming. **pelzbesetzt,** *adj.* trimmed with fur, fur-trimmed. **Pelzfutter,** *n.* fur lining. **pelzgefüttert,** *adj.* fur-lined. **Pelzhändler,** *m.* furrier. **pelzig,** *adj.* furry, (*of tongue*) furred, coated, (*of limbs*) numb, (*of vegetables*) stringy. **Pelz|jäger,** *m.* trapper. **–mantel,** *m.* fur coat. **–märtel** (*dial.*), **–nickel,** *m.* Santa Claus. **–tiere,** *n.pl.* fur-bearing animals. **–ware,** *f.,* **–werk,** *n.* furriery, furs.

Pendel ['pɛndəl], *n. or m.* pendulum. **Pendel|ausschlag,** *m.* (*Phys.*) amplitude of swing. **–länge,** *f.* length of pendulum. **–linse,** *f.* pendulum-bob. **pendeln,** *v.i.* oscillate, swing; sway, undulate, (*Boxing etc.*) weave; (*Railw.*) travel backwards and forwards, operate a shuttle-service, (*of passengers*) commute. **Pendel|schlag,** *m.,* **–schwingung,** *f.* swing of the pendulum, (*Phys.*) oscillation. **–tür,** *f.* swing(ing) door. **–uhr,** *f.* pendulum-clock. **–verkehr,** *m.* shuttle-service, commuter service. **–zug,** *m.* commuter train.

Pendler ['pɛndlər], *m.* commuter.

penetrant [pene'trant], *adj.* penetrating.

penibel [pe'ni:bəl], *adj.* (*of a p.*) difficult, fussy, (*coll.*) pernickerty.

Pennal [pɛ'na:l], **1.** *n.* (**-s,** *pl.* **-e**) 1. pencil case; 2. (grammar-)school. **2.** *m.* (*Studs. sl.*) (*also* **Pennäler**) grammar-school boy.

Pennbruder ['pɛnbru:dər], *m.* (*coll.*) tramp, (*sl.*) hobo, bum.

Penne ['pɛnə], *f.* tramps' lodging-house; (*coll.*) doss-house; (*sl.*) school. **pennen,** *v.i.* (*sl.*) kip, hit the hay.

Pension [pɛnzi'o:n, pã'sjɔ̃], *f.* (retiring) pension, (*Mil.*) retired pay; private hotel, boarding-house; boarding-school; board and lodging; *mit – verabschiedet,* pensioned off; *in – sein,* be retired, live in retirement; *in – gehen,* retire.

Pensionär [pãsjɔ̃'nɛ:r], *m.* (**-s,** *pl.* **-e**) pensioner; boarder (*at school or boarding house*). **Pensionat,** *n.* (**-s,** *pl.* **-e**) boarding-school. **pensionieren,** *v.t.* pension (off), superannuate, (*Mil.*) put on the retired list *or* on half-pay; *sich – lassen,* retire. **Pensionierte(r),** *m., f.* pensioner. **Pensionierung,** *f.* pensioning off, superannuation. **Pensionist,** *m.* (**-en,** *pl.* **-en**) (*Austr.*) pensioner.

Pensionsalter [pɛnzi'o:nsˀaltər], *n.* retiring age. **pensionsberechtigt,** *adj.* pensionable. **Pensions|berechtigung,** *f.* entitlement to a pension. **–fonds,** *m.* pension *or* superannuation fund. **–gast,** *m.* boarder. **–kasse,** *f. See* **–fonds. –liste,** *f.* (*Mil.*) retired list. **–preis,** *m.* (full) board, terms for residents. **pensionsreif,** *adj.* due for retirement.

Pensum ['pɛnzum], *n.* (**-s,** *pl.* **-sa** *or* **-sen**) task, lesson; curriculum.

Pentaeder [pɛnta'e:dər], *n.* pentahedron. **Pentagramm,** *n.* pentacle.

per [pɛr], *prep.* – *Achse,* by road (transport); – *Adresse,* care of; – *Bahn,* by rail; (*coll.*) – *Fuß,* on foot; *zweimal – Jahr,* twice a year; (*Comm.*) – *Kasse,* on payment in cash; – *Post,* by post.

pereat! ['pe:reat], *int.* (*Studs. sl.*) down with . . .! **Pereat,** *n.* (**-s,** *pl.* **-s**) *ihm ein – bringen,* throw mud at *or* hiss him; *ein – dem . . .!* three groans for . . .!

peremptorisch [perɛmp'to:rɪʃ], *adj.* peremptory.

perennierend [perɛ'ni:rənt], *adj.* perennial.

perfekt [pɛr'fɛkt], *adj.* perfect, complete, concluded, settled; – *machen,* clinch (*a deal*). **Perfekt,** *n.* (**-(e)s,** *pl.* **-e**), **Perfektum,** *n.* (**-s,** *pl.* **-s**) (*Gram.*) perfect tense.

perfid [pɛr'fi:t], *adj.* perfidious, insidious. **Perfidie** [–'di:], **Perfidität,** *f.* perfidy, perfidiousness; insidiousness.

perforieren [pɛrfo'ri:rən], *v.t.* perforate.

Pergament [pɛrga'mɛnt], *n.* (**-(e)s,** *pl.* **-e**) parchment, vellum. **pergamenten,** *adj.* (of) parchment. **Pergament|papier,** *n.* thick vellum; grease-proof paper. **–rolle,** *f.* parchment scroll.

Pergamin [pɛrga'mi:n], *n.* imitation parchment.

Periode [peri'o:də], *f.* period, (*coll.*) spell; (*Gram.*) sentence, phrase; (*Mus.*) repetend; (*Elec.*) (complete) cycle; (*Med.*) menstrual *or* monthly period, menses.

Perioden|umformer, *m.* (*Elec.*) frequency changer. **-zahl,** *f.* (*Elec.*) frequency. **periodisch,** *adj.* periodic(al); *-er Dezimalbruch,* recurring decimal; (*Chem.*) *-es System,* periodic law; *– erscheinende Zeitschrift,* periodical (magazine). **Periodizität** [–ditsi'tɛ:t], *f.* periodicity.

Peripetie [peripe'ti:], *f.* (*Theat.*) climax, turning-point (*of dramatic action*).

peripher [peri'fe:r], *adj.* peripheral; (*Mil.*) *-e Verteidigung,* perimeter defence. **Peripherie** [–'ri:], *f.* periphery, circumference; *– einer Stadt,* outer suburbs *or* outskirts of a town.

Periskop [peri'sko:p], *n.* (**-s,** *pl.* **-e**) periscope.

Perl [pɛrl], *f.* (*Typ.*) nonpareil, pearl.

Perle ['pɛrlə], *f.* pearl; bead; sparkling bubble; (*fig.*) gem, jewel; *-n vor die Säue werfen,* cast pearls before swine.

perlen ['pɛrlən], *v.i.* sparkle, glisten; ripple (*laughter*); form bubbles, effervesce; (*aux.* s.) appear in drops *or* beads; *die Träne perlte aus ihrem Auge,* the tear-drop rolled from her eye.

Perlen|fischer, *m.* pearl-fisher *or* diver. **-glanz,** *m.* pearly *or* nacrous lustre. **-kette, -schnur,** *f.* string of pearls, pearl necklace *or* necklet. **-stickerei,** *f.* beading.

perlgrau ['pɛrlgrau], *adj.* pearl-grey. **Perl|graupe,** *f.* pearl-barley. **-huhn,** *n.* guinea-fowl. **-korn,** *n.* bead-sight (*of rifle*). **-muschel,** *f.* pearl-oyster. **-mutt,** *n.*, **-mutter,** *f.* mother of pearl. **-samen,** *m.* seed pearl. **-schrift,** *f. See* **Perl.**

perlustrieren [pɛrlus'tri:rən], *v.t.* examine closely, investigate.

permanent [pɛrma'nɛnt], *adj.* permanent, lasting, enduring, durable. **Permanenz,** *f.* permanency, permanence, persistence, durability, stability; *sich in – erklären,* prolong one's power, authority *etc.*, (*Pol.*) sit *sine die.* **Permanenzkarte,** *f.* (*Austr.*) season-ticket.

permutieren [pɛrmu'ti:rən], *v.r.* permute, exchange, interchange. **Permutierung,** *f.* permutation.

perniziös [pɛrnitsi'ø:s], *adj.* (*Med.*) pernicious.

Perpendikel [pɛrpɛn'di:kəl], *m. or n.* perpendicular (line); pendulum; plummet-line.

perplex [pɛr'plɛks], *adj.* (*coll.*) confused, perplexed, bewildered, dumbfounded.

Perron [pɛ'rõ], *m.* (**-s,** *pl.* **-s**) (*dial.*) railway platform.

Persenning [pɛr'zɛnɪŋ], *f.* (-, *pl.* **-en**) tarpaulin.

Perser ['pɛrzər], *m.*, **Perserin,** *f.* Persian. **Perserteppich,** *m.* Persian carpet. **Persianer** [–i'a:nər], *m.* Persian lamb(skin). **Persien,** *n.* Persia.

Persiflage [pɛrzi'fla:ʒə], *f.* persiflage, satire. **persiflieren,** *v.t.* satirize, burlesque.

persisch ['pɛrzɪʃ], *adj.* Persian.

Person [pɛr'zo:n], *f.* (-, *pl.* **-en**) person, individual, personage; (*Law., coll.*) party; (*Theat.*) rôle, character, part; (*Theat.*) *stumme –,* silent part; (*Theat.*) *lustige –,* clown, fool; *juristische –,* corporation, body politic; *klein von –,* of short stature; *die handelnden -en,* dramatis personae; *in* (*eigener*) *–,* in person, personally, himself *or* herself; *von – kennen,* know by sight; *ich für meine –,* I for my part *or* for one, as for me; *5 Mark pro –,* 5 marks a head; (*Law*) *dritte –,* third party; (*Law*) *die beteiligten -en,* the parties; *ohne Ansehen der –,* without respect of persons.

Personal [pɛrzo'na:l], *n.* (**-s,** *no pl.*) staff, employees, personnel; servants, attendants; *ständiges –,* permanent staff; (*Av.*) *fliegendes –,* air-crew(s), flying personnel. **Personal|abbau,** *m.* reduction of *or* in staff. **-abteilung,** *f.* personnel division. **-amt,** *n.* (*Engl.*) Records Office, (*Am.*) Personnel Division. **-angaben,** *f.pl.* personal data. **-aufwendungen,** *f.pl.* (*Comm.*) wages and salaries. **-ausweis,** *m.* identity card. **-bestand,** *m.* number of staff. **-chef,** *m.* personnel manager.

Personalien [pɛrzo'na:liən], *pl.* personal particulars *or* data. **Personalität** [–nali'tɛ:t], *f. See* **Persönlichkeit. personaliter** [–'nalitər], *adv.* personally, in person.

Personal|pronomen, *n.* (*Gram.*) personal pronoun. **-wechsel,** *m.* (*Mil. etc.*) relief (*of guards etc.*).

Personen|aufzug, *m.* passenger lift. **-beförderung,** *f.* passenger service, conveyance of passengers. **-kraftwagen,** *m.* private (motor-)car, passenger vehicle. **-kreis,** *m.* category of persons, circle. **-name,** *m.* (*Gram.*) proper name *or* noun. **-schaden,** *m.* personal injury. **-stand,** *m.* family status. **-standsregister,** *n.* register of births, marriages and deaths. **-verkehr,** *m.* passenger traffic. **-verwechs(e)lung,** *f.* mistaken identity. **-verzeichnis,** *n.* register of persons; (*Theat.*) dramatis personae. **-waage,** *f.* weighing-machine. **-zug,** *m.* passenger-train, local train.

Personifikation [pɛrzonifikatsi'o:n], *f.* personification, embodiment. **personifizieren** [–'tsi:rən], *v.t.* personify, embody; impersonate.

persönlich [pɛr'zø:nlɪç], **1.** *adj.* personal; *-e Auslagen,* out-of-pocket expenses; *-e Meinung,* private opinion; *– werden,* make personal remarks, become personal (*in a quarrel*). **2.** *adv.* in person, personally; *– haften,* be personally liable *or* individually answerable. **Persönlichkeit,** *f.* personality; personage. **persönlichkeitsbewußt,** *adj.* self-assured. **Persönlichkeitsspaltung,** *f.* split *or* dual personality.

Perspektiv [pɛrspɛk'ti:f], *n.* (**-s,** *pl.* **-e**) telescope, field-glass. **Perspektive** [–'ti:və], *f.* perspective; (*fig.*) view, prospect (*of the future*). **perspektivisch,** *adj.* perspective, (*fig.*) prospective.

Pertinenzien [pɛrti'nɛntsiən], *pl.* belongings, appurtenances.

Peru [pə'ru:], *n.* Peru. **Peruaner,** *m.*, **Peruanerin,** *f.*, **peruanisch,** *adj.* Peruvian.

Perücke [pe'rykə], *f.* wig; *ihm in die – fahren,* show him up as he really is, strip him of all his pretensions. **Perückenstock,** *m.* wig-block.

pervers [pɛr'vɛrs], *adj.* perverse, unnatural. **Perversität** [–i'tɛ:t], *f.* perverseness, perversity, aberration.

Perzeption [pɛrtsɛptsi'o:n], *f.* perception. **perzeptorisch** [–'to:rɪʃ], *adj.* perceptual, perceptive. **perzipieren** [–'pi:rən], *v.t.* 1. perceive, apprehend, conceive of; 2. (*Law*) collect (*money, rent etc.*).

Pesel ['pe:zəl], *m.* (*dial.*) (unheated) parlour.

pesen ['pe:zən], *v.i.* (*dial.*) hurry, rush.

Pessar [pe'sa:r], *n.* (**-s,** *pl.* **-e**) pessary.

Pessimismus [pɛsi'mɪsmus], *m.* pessimism. **Pessimist,** *m.* (**-en,** *pl.* **-en**), **Pessimistin,** *f.* pessimist. **pessimistisch,** *adj.* pessimistic.

Pest [pɛst], *f.* (-, *pl.* **-en**) plague, pestilence; contagion, epidemic; (*fig.*) pest, nuisance; *daß dich die –!* a plague on you! *ihn wie die – fliehen,* avoid him like the plague; *wie die – hassen,* hate like poison. **pestartig,** *adj.* pestilential. **Pest|beule,** *f.* (*Med.*) bubo; (*fig.*) plague-spot. **-geruch, -hauch,** *m.* miasma, pestilential smell *or* stench. **-haus,** *n.* (*obs.*) plague hospital.

Pestilenz [pɛsti'lɛnts], *f.* pestilence.

pestkrank ['pɛstkraŋk], *adj.* plague-infected, plague-stricken. **Pestluft,** *f.* foul *or* pestilential air.

Petent [pe'tɛnt], *m.* (**-en,** *pl.* **-en**) petitioner.

Petersilie [petər'zi:liə], *f.* parsley; (*coll.*) *ihm ist die – verhagelt,* he has come unstuck *or* come a cropper; (*coll.*) *sie pflückt –,* she is on the shelf, she is a wallflower.

Peters|kirche ['pe:tərs-], *f.* St. Peter's (church). **-vogel,** *m.* (*Orn.*) *see* **Sturmschwalbe.**

Petit [pə'ti:], *f.* (*Typ.*) brevier.

petitionieren [petitsio'ni:rən], *v.i.* petition (*um,* for).

Petrefakt [petre'fakt], *n.* (**-(e)s,** *pl.* **-e(n)**) fossil. **Petrefaktenkunde,** *f.* palaeontology.

Petroleum [pe'tro:leum], *n.* petroleum, crude oil, mineral oil, rock oil; paraffin(-oil), lamp oil, (*Am.*)

kerosene. **Petroleumquelle,** *f.* petroleum-spring, oil well.

Petschaft ['pɛtʃaft], *n.* (**-s,** *pl.* **-e**) seal, signet. **Petschaft|ring,** *m.* signet-ring. **–stecher,** *m.* seal-engraver.

Petsche ['pɛtʃə], *f.* drying rack *or* frame.

petto ['pɛto], (*coll.*) ***in – haben,*** have in mind, intend.

Petz [pɛts], *m.* Bruin. **Petze,** *f.* 1. she-bear; (*dial.*) bitch; 2. (*coll.*) sneak, tell-tale. **petzen,** *v.t., v.i.* (*sl.*) tell tales (***gegen,*** about), inform (against); (*sl.*) sneak (about *or* against), peach (on), shop. **Petzer,** *m.* sneak, tell-tale.

Pfad [pfa:t], *m.* (**-es,** *pl.* **-e**) path, track, lane. **Pfader,** *m.* (*Swiss*), **Pfad|finder,** *m.* Boy Scout. **–finderin,** *f.* Girl Guide, (*Am.*) Girl Scout.

Pfaff(e) ['pfaf(ə)], *m.* (**-en,** *pl.* **-en**) priest; cleric, parson. **Pfaffen|geschmeiß, –gezücht,** *n.* (*pej.*) priests, clerics, parsons **–herrschaft,** *f.* clerical rule. **–knecht,** *m.* slavish adherent of the clergy. **–platte,** *f.* priest's tonsure. **Pfaffentum,** *n.* clericalism; (*collect.*) priests.

pfäffisch ['pfɛfɪʃ], *adj.* priest-like; clerical; priest-ridden.

Pfahl [pfa:l], *m.* (**-s,** *pl.* **⸚e**) stake, stick, post, pale, pole, pile, prop, picket; (*Hist.*) pillory; ***in meinen vier Pfählen,*** within my own four walls, in my own house; ***ein – im Fleische,*** a thorn in the flesh. **Pfahl|bau,** *m.* lake-dwelling, building on piles. **–bauer,** *m.* lake-dweller. **–bauten,** *m.pl.* lake-dwellings. **–bürger,** *m.* Philistine; stick-in-the-mud. **–dorf,** *n.* lake-village.

pfählen ['pfɛ:lən], *v.t.* 1. enclose (with a paling), fence in; 2. prop, support (*on stakes*); 3. impale.

Pfahl|graben, *m.* palisaded ditch. **–gründung,** *f.* pile foundation. **–hecke,** *f.* palisade, paling. **–jochbrücke,** *f.* trestle-bridge, pile bridge. **–ramme,** *f.*, **–rammler,** *m.* pile-driver. **–rost,** *m.* pile support *or* framework.

Pfählung ['pfɛ:luŋ], *f.* impalement.

Pfahl|werk, *n.* paling, stockade, palisade. **–wurzel,** *f.* (*Bot.*) tap-root. **–zaun,** *m.* paling, railing, rail *or* picket fence, stockade.

Pfalz [pfalts], *f.* (*Geog.*) the Palatinate; ***Kurfürst von der –,*** Elector Palatinate. **Pfalzgraf,** *m.* Count Palatine. **pfälzisch,** *adj.* Palatine, of the Palatinate.

Pfand [pfant], *n.* (**-es,** *pl.* **⸚er**) pledge, security, forfeit, pawn; (*on real estate*) mortgage; deposit, guarantee; ***Pfänder spielen,*** play at forfeits; ***auf – geben,*** supply against security; ***zum –e setzen,*** pawn, mortgage; (*fig.*) pledge (*one's honour, word*), stake (*one's life*).

pfändbar ['pfɛntba:r], *adj.* distrainable.

Pfandbrief ['pfantbri:f], *m.* (deed of) mortgage, mortgage bond.

pfänden ['pfɛndən], *v.t.* seize, distrain upon, attach, impound, take as security, take in pledge. **Pfänder,** *m.* (*dial.*) bailiff, executor. **Pfänderspiel,** *n.* game of forfeits.

Pfand|geber, *m.*, **–geberin,** *f.* *See* **–schuldner. –gebühr,** *f.* interest on mortgage; pledge-money. **–gläubiger,** *m.* mortgagee. **–haus,** *n.* pawnshop, (*Am.*) loan office. **–leiher,** *m.* pawnbroker. **–leihgeschäft,** *n.* pawnbroker's business; pawnshop. **–nehmer,** *m.*, **–nehmerin,** *f.* *See* **–gläubiger. –recht,** *n.* lien; hypothecary law. **pfandrechtlich,** *adj.* hypothecary. **Pfand|schein,** *m.* pawn-ticket. **–schuld,** *f.* debt on a mortgage. **–schuldner,** *m.*, **–schuldnerin,** *f.* mortgagor. **–sicherheit,** *f.* collateral security. **–stück,** *n.* pledge.

Pfändung ['pfɛnduŋ], *f.* seizure, attachment, distraint, distress. **Pfändungsbefehl,** *m.* distress warrant.

Pfand|verschreibung, *f.*, **–vertrag,** *m.* mortgage deed.

Pfanne ['pfanə], *f.* pan, bowl, cauldron, copper, boiler; (*Anat.*) socket; (*coll.*) ***den Feind in die – hauen,*** cut the enemy to pieces; ***etwas auf der – haben,*** have s.th. pat. **Pfannen|flicker,** *m.* tinker. **–schmied,** *m.* tinsmith. **–stein,** *m.* boiler scale. **–werk,** *n.* saltworks. **–ziegel,** *m.* pantile.

Pfannkuchen ['pfanku:xən], *m.* pancake; fritter; (*dial.*) doughnut.

Pfarr|acker ['pfar–], *m.* glebe land. **–amt,** *n.* incumbency. **–besetzungsrecht,** *n.* patronage. **–bezirk,** *m.* parish. **–buch,** *n.* parish register.

Pfarre ['pfarə], **Pfarrei** [–'raɪ], *f.* (church) living, benefice, incumbency; parsonage, vicarage; parish. **Pfarrer,** *m.* clergyman, parson; rector, vicar; minister; priest.

Pfarr|gemeinde, *f.* *See* **–bezirk. –gut,** *n.* *See* **–acker. –haus,** *n.* parsonage; rectory, vicarage; (*Scots*) manse. **–kind,** *n.* parishioner. **–kirche,** *f.* parish church. **–land,** *n.* *See* **–acker. –schule,** *f.* church school, village school. **–sprengel,** *m.* *See* **–bezirk. –stelle,** *f.* *See* **–amt. –zehnte,** *m.* parochial tithe.

Pfau [pfau], *m.* (**-(e)s** *or* **-en,** *pl.* **-e** *or* **-en**) peacock; ***der – schlägt (ein) Rad,*** the peacock spreads its tail. **Pfauen|auge,** *n.* 1. (*Ent.*) peacock-butterfly; 2. spot in a peacock's tail. **–henne,** *f.* peahen. **–rad,** *n.*, **–schweif,** *m.* peacock's tail *or* fan.

Pfeffer ['pfɛfər], *m.* pepper; (*Prov.*) ***da liegt der Hase im –,*** there's the rub *or* snag; (*coll.*) ***das ist starker –,*** that's going too far, that's a bit too thick; that is really the limit; (*coll.*) ***im – sein,*** be in a pickle *or* a jam; (*coll.*) ***wo der – wächst,*** the back of beyond, Jericho.

Pfeffer|büchse, *f.* pepper-caster *or* box. **–fresser,** *m.* (*Orn.*) toucan. **–gurke,** *f.* (pickled) gherkin. **–korn,** *n.* peppercorn. **pfefferig,** *adj.* peppery. **Pfeffer|kraut,** *n.* (*Bot.*) savory. **–kuchen,** *m.* gingerbread. **–land,** *n.* (*coll.*) Jericho.

Pfefferling ['pfɛfərlɪŋ], *m.* (**-s,** *pl.* **-e**) *see* **Pfifferling.**

Pfefferminz, 1. *m.* essence of peppermint. 2. *n.* (**-es,** *pl.* **-e**) peppermint (*sweet*). **–minze,** *f.* (pepper)-mint (*plant*).

pfeffern ['pfɛfərn], *v.t.* pepper; season with pepper; (*coll.*) chuck, pelt, fling, let fly (***auf*** (*Acc.*), at); ***die Preise sind gepfeffert,*** the prices are exorbitant *or* (*coll.*) steep; ***gepfefferte Witze,*** spicy *or* (*coll.*) blue jokes; ***gepfefferte Worte,*** bitter *or* biting words.

Pfeffer|nuß, *f.* ginger biscuit. **–staude,** *f.*, **–strauch,** *m.* pepper-plant. **–streuer,** *m.* *See* **–büchse.**

Pfeife ['pfaɪfə], *f.* pipe; blowpipe; organ-pipe; whistle; ***eine – stopfen,*** fill a pipe; ***nach seiner – tanzen,*** dance to his tune; (*Prov.*) ***man muß sich –n schneiden, während man im Rohr sitzt,*** make hay while the sun shines.

pfeifen ['pfaɪfən], *irr.v.t. & v.i.* whistle, (*Theat.*) hiss, (*Rad.*) squeal, howl; ***tanzen müssen wie er pfeift,*** have to dance to his tune; (*fig.*) ***also daher pfeift der Wind?*** so that's the way the wind is blowing! (*coll.*) ***ich will dir eins*** or ***was –!*** you can whistle for it! (*coll.*) ***– auf*** (*Acc.*), not care two hoots *or* a rap *or* a straw for; ***auf dem letzten Loch –,*** be at the end of one's tether.

Pfeifen|halter, *m.* pipe-rack. **–kopf,** *m.* pipe-bowl. **–reiniger,** *m.* pipe-cleaner. **–stiel,** *m.* pipe-stem.

Pfeifente ['pfaɪfˀɛntə], *f.* (*Orn.*) wigeon, (*Am.*) European widgeon (*Anas penelope*).

Pfeifen|ton, *m.* pipe-clay, Fuller's earth. **–werk,** *n.* organ-pipes.

Pfeifer ['pfaɪfər], *m.* fife-player, piper; whistler.

Pfeif|kessel, *m.* whistling kettle. **–konzert,** *n.* hissing, catcalls. **–signal,** *n.* whistle signal.

Pfeil ['pfaɪl], *m.* (**-s,** *pl.* **-e**) 1. arrow, dart; bolt, shaft; 2. camber (*of an arch*).

Pfeiler ['pfaɪlər], *m.* pillar (*also fig.*), column; pier (*of bridge*), prop, standard, upright; door-post, jamb. **Pfeiler|bogen,** *m.* pier-arch. **–brücke,** *f.* pier-bridge. **–weite,** *f.* (*Archit.*) distance between columns.

Pfeil|flügel, *m.* (*Av.*) swept-back wing. **–form,** *f.* arrow *or* wedge formation, (*Av.*) sweep-back (*of wings*). **pfeil|förmig,** *adj.* arrow- *or* wedge-shaped. **–gerade,** 1. *adj.* (as) straight as an arrow. 2. *adv.* ***– zukommen auf*** (*Acc.*), make a beeline for. **Pfeil|höhe,** *f.* (*Archit.*) height of crown, rise. **–motor,** *m.* V-type engine. **pfeilschnell,** *adj.* (as) swift as an arrow. **Pfeil|schuß,** *m.* bowshot. **–schütze,** *m.* archer. **–spitze,** *f.* arrowhead, (*fig.*) spearhead. **–verhältnis,** *n.* (*Archit.*) ratio of rise to span (*of an arch*). **–verzahnung,** *f.* herring-bone gear. **–wurz,** *f.* (*Bot.*) arrowroot.

Pfennig ['pfɛnɪç], *m.* (**-s,** *pl.* **-e**) one-hundredth part of a mark; farthing, (*Am.*) cent; (*Prov.*) ***wer den – nicht ehrt, ist des Talers nicht wert,*** take care of the pence and the pounds will take care of themselves. **Pfennig|fuchser,** *m.* (*coll.*) pinch-penny, skinflint, money-grubber. **–fuchserei,** *f.* stinginess. **pfennigweise,** *adv.* in pennyworths.

Pferch [pfɛrç], *m.* (**-es,** *pl.* **-e**) fold, pen. **pferchen,** *v.t.* pen, fold, (*fig.*) coop up, pack closely, cram.

Pferd [pfe:rt], *n.* (**-es,** *pl.* **-e**) horse; vaulting-horse; (*Chess*) knight; ***zu –e,*** mounted, on horseback; ***zu –e!*** to horse! ***vom –e auf den Esel kommen,*** come down in the world; ***nicht*** or ***keine vier*** or ***sechs*** or ***zehn –e bringen mich dahin,*** wild horses won't drag me there; ***das – beim Schwanze aufzäumen, das – hinter den Wagen spannen,*** put the cart before the horse; ***wie ein – arbeiten,*** work like a horse; ***sich aufs hohe – setzen,*** get on one's high horse.

Pferde|arbeit, *f.* drudgery. **–ausstellung,** *f.* horse show. **–bändiger,** *m.* horse-breaker. **–behang,** *m.* harness, trappings. **–beschlag,** *m.* horseshoeing; horseshoes. **pferdebespannt,** *adj.* horse-drawn. **Pferde|bremse,** *f.* horse-fly, cleg. **–decke,** *f.* horse-blanket. **–fleisch,** *n.* horseflesh. **–fuhrwerk,** *n.* horse-drawn vehicle. **–fuß,** *m.* club-foot; (*fig.*) cloven foot. **–futter,** *n.* fodder, provender. **–geschirr,** *n.* harness. **–händler,** *m.* horse-dealer. **–huf,** *m.* horse's hoof. **–junge,** *m.* stable-boy. **–knecht,** *m.* ostler, groom. **–koppel,** *f.* paddock. **–kraft,** *f. See* **–stärke. –länge,** *f.* ***um 2 –n,*** by 2 lengths. **pferdemäßig,** *adj.* (*sl.*) excessive. **Pferde|milch,** *f.* mare's milk. **–mist,** *m.* horse manure, horse droppings. **–rennbahn,** *f.* race-course, race-track. **–rennen,** *n.* horse-race; horse-racing. **–schwanz, –schweif,** *m.* horse's tail. **–schwemme,** *f.* horse-pond. **–seuche,** *f.* murrain. **–stall,** *m.* stable. **–stärke,** *f.* (*Mech.*) horse-power. **–(transport)wagen,** *m.* horse-box. **–verleih,** *m.* livery stables. **–verstand,** *m.* (*coll.*) horse sense. **–wechsel,** *m.* relay of horses. **–zucht,** *f.* horse breeding.

-pferdig ['pfe:rdɪç], *adj.suff.* (*coll.*) horse-powered; ***ein 50pferdiger Motor,*** a 50 horse-power engine.

Pfette ['pfɛtə], *f.* (*Archit.*) purlin, templet.

Pfiff ['pfɪf], *m.* (**-es,** *pl.* **-e**) 1. whistle, whistling; ***einen – tun,*** give a whistle; ***ihm auf den – gehorchen,*** come at his call; 2. nip (*of wine, spirits etc.*); 3. trick; ***den – verstehen,*** know *or* be up to all the tricks (of the trade); ***keine –e!*** no nonsense!

pfiff, pfiffe, *see* **pfeifen.**

Pfifferling ['pfɪfərlɪŋ], *m.* (**-s,** *pl.* **-e**) (*Bot.*) chanterelle; ***keinen – wert,*** not worth a rap *or* a straw.

pfiffest ['pfɪfəst], *see* **pfeifen.**

pfiffig ['pfɪfɪç], *adj.* sly, artful, cunning, crafty; knowing (*smile etc.*). **Pfiffigkeit,** *f.* slyness, artfulness, cunning, craftiness.

Pfiffikus ['pfɪfɪkus], *m.* (**-,** *pl.* **-se**) (*coll.*) sly dog, artful dodger, slyboots.

Pfingsten ['pfɪŋstən], *n.* (*Austr.f.*) *or pl.* Whitsuntide, (*Eccl.*) Pentecost. **Pfingst|ferien,** *pl.* Whitsun holidays, (*Parl.*) Whitsuntide recess. **–fest,** *n. See* **Pfingsten. –montag,** *m.* Whit-Monday. **–ochs,** *m.* (*coll.*) ***geputzt wie ein –,*** dressed up to the nines. **–rose,** *f.* (*Bot.*) peony. **–sonntag,** *m.* Whit-Sunday. **–woche,** *f.* Whit-week. **–zeit,** *f.* Whitsun.

Pfirsche ['pfɪrʃə], *f.* (*dial.*) *see* **Pfirsich.**

Pfirsich ['pfɪrzɪç], *m.* (**-s,** *pl.* **-e**) *or* (*dial.*) *f.* (**-,** *pl.* **-e**), **Pfirsiche,** *f.* peach. **Pfirsichkern,** *m.* peach-stone.

Pflanze ['pflantsə], *f.* 1. plant; 2. (*coll.*) person, fellow; ***du bist eine saubere –!*** you're a nice so-and-so! **pflanzen,** *v.t.* plant; (*fig.*) set, implant.

Pflanzen|anatomie, *f.* phytotomy. **–art,** *f.* species of plants. **–buch,** *n.* herbal, flora. **–butter,** *f.* vegetable butter. **–chemie,** *f.* chemistry of plants, phytochemistry. **–daunen,** *f.pl.* kapok. **–eiweiß,** *n.* vegetable protein. **–erde,** *f.* vegetable mould, humus. **–farbe,** *f.* vegetable dye. **–faser,** *f.* vegetable fibre. **pflanzenfressend,** *adj.* graminivorous, herbivorous. **Pflanzen|gattung,** *f.* genus of plants. **–gift,** *n.* vegetable poison. **–grün,** *n.* chlorophyll. **–kenner,** *m.* botanist. **–kost,** *f.* vegetarian diet. **–kunde,** *f.* botany. **–leben,** *n.* plant life, vegetation; ***ein – führen,*** vegetate. **–lehre,** *f. See* **–kunde. –öl,** *n.* vegetable oil. **–reich,** *n.* vegetable kingdom, flora. **pflanzenreich,** *adj.* rich in flora. **Pflanzen|reste,** *m.pl.* fossil plants. **–saft,** *m.* sap. **–sammlung,** *f.* herbarium. **–schädling,** *m.* plant pest. **–schleim,** *m.* mucilage. **–stecher,** *m.* dibble. **–stoff,** *m.* vegetable matter; *pl.* vegetable remains. **–stoffwechsel,** *m.* plant metabolism. **–system,** *n.* classification of plants. **–tier,** *n.* zoophyte. **–welt,** *f. See* **–reich. –wuchs,** *m.* vegetation. **–zucht,** *f.* plant cultivation. **–züchter,** *m.* nurseryman.

Pflanzer ['pflantsər], *m.* planter; settler, colonist.

Pflanzkartoffel ['pflantskartɔfəl], *f.* seed potato. **pflanzlich,** *adj.* vegetable.

Pflänzling ['pflɛntslɪŋ], *m.* (**-s,** *pl.* **-e**) seedling, young plant.

Pflanz|schule, *f.* nursery; plantation. **–stadt,** *f.* daughter-town, development area. **–stätte,** *f.* (*fig.*) hotbed, source, nucleus. **–stock,** *m.* dibble.

Pflanzung ['pflantsuŋ], *f.* planting; plantation; settlement, colony.

Pflaster ['pflastər], *n.* 1. plaster; patch; (*fig.*) sop, salve; ***englisches –,*** court-plaster; 2. pavement, paving, flagstones; ***eingelegtes –,*** tessellated pavement; ***das – treten,*** loaf about; (*coll.*) ***London ist ein teures –,*** London is an expensive place. **Pflasterbohrer,** *m.* road drill. **Pflasterer,** *m.* paviour, paver. **Pflaster|geld,** *n.* road charges. **–kasten,** *m.* (*hum.*) sawbones, (*Mil.*) medical orderly.

pflastern ['pflastərn], *v.t.* 1. put a plaster *or* patch on; 2. pave; (*Prov.*) ***der Weg zur Hölle ist mit guten Vorsätzen gepflastert,*** the way to hell is paved with good intentions.

Pflaster|ramme, *f.* paving-beetle. **–stein,** *m.* paving-stone, cobble stone. **–treter,** *m.* (*coll.*) loiterer, loafer, street-corner lounger.

Pflaume ['pflaumə], *f.* plum; ***gedörrte –,*** prune; ***geschmorte –n,*** stewed prunes. **Pflaumen|kern,** *m.* plum-stone. **–mus,** *n.* plum jam. **–spanner,** *m.* (*Ent.*) orange-moth. **pflaumenweich,** *adj.* soft as butter, (*fig.*) weak-kneed, spineless.

Pflege ['pfle:gə], *f.* care, attention; tending, nursing; rearing, bringing up; fostering, cultivation, encouragement (*of arts etc.*); (*Mech.*) maintenance; ***in – geben,*** put out to nurse (*of babies*); put out to board (***bei,*** with); ***in – nehmen,*** take charge of; ***– des Haares,*** care of the hair. **pflegebedürftig,** *adj.* needing care. **Pflege|befohlene(r),** *m., f.* charge, ward. **–dienst,** *m.* (*Motor.*) service, servicing. **–eltern,** *pl.* foster-parents. **–kind,** *n.* foster-child. **–mittel,** *n.* dressing (*for hair, leather etc.*). **–mutter,** *f.* foster-mother; nurse.

pflegen ['pfle:gən], **1.** *v.t.* (*reg.*) (*with Gen. obs. except in stock phrases*) tend, nurse, cherish, care for, attend to, take care of; cultivate, foster, (*fig.*) apply o.s. to, carry on, keep up, (*coll.*) go in for (*also Poet. and obs. irr.*); ***seines Amts –,*** perform the duties of one's office; ***Rat –,*** take counsel; ***der Ruhe –,*** rest, take one's ease; ***Umgang – mit,*** associate with, (*coll.*) see a good deal of; *see* **gepflegt. 2.** *v.r.* take care of o.s., pamper o.s. **3.** *v.i.* (*with inf.*) (*reg. only*) be used to, be accustomed to, be in the habit of, be given to; (*Poet.*) be wont to; ***er pflegt zu sagen,*** he is used to saying; ***er pflegte zu sagen,*** he used to say; ***er pflegte der erste zu sein,*** he was usually *or* used to be the first. **Pfleger,** *m.* (male) nurse; guardian, curator, trustee, promotor. **Pflegerin,** *f.* nurse; *see* **Pfleger.**

Pflege|schwester, *f.* visiting nurse. **–sohn,** *m.* foster-son. **–tier,** *n.* (animal) foster-parent.

–tochter, *f.* foster-daughter. **–vater,** *m.* foster-father.

pfleglich ['pfle:klıç], **1.** *adj.* 1. careful, attentive; 2. (*dial.*) usual, customary. **2.** *adv.* – ***behandeln,*** take good care of, husband, nurse, conserve (*one's resources etc.*).

Pflegling ['pfle:klıŋ], *m.* (**-s,** *pl.* **-e**) ward, charge, foster-child. **pflegsam,** *adj.* careful, attentive.

Pflegschaft, *f.* guardianship; trust(eeship).

Pflicht [pflıçt], *f.* (-, *pl.* **-en**) duty, obligation (***gegen,*** to), responsibility, liability; ***es ihm zur – machen,*** make him responsible for it; ***– und Schuldigkeit,*** bounden duty. **pflichtbewußt,** *adj.* responsible. **Pflicht|bewußtsein,** *n.* sense of duty. **–eifer,** *m.* zeal. **pflichteifrig,** *adj.* zealous. **Pflicht|erfüllung,** *f.* performance of a duty. **–exemplar,** *n.* presentation copy. **–fach,** *n.* compulsory subject. **–gefühl,** *n.* sense of duty. **pflicht|gemäß, 1.** *adj.* in conformity with one's duty, incumbent, due. **2.** *adv.* duly, dutifully, as in duty bound. **–getreu,** *adj.* dutiful, loyal, conscientious.

pflichtig ['pflıçtıç], *adj.* *See* **pflichtschuldig.**

pflicht|mäßig, *adj.* *See* **–gemäß. –schuldig,** *adj.* obligatory, in duty bound. **Pflichtteil,** *m.* lawful share; (*Law*) inalienable (portion of) inheritance, entail. **pflichttreu,** *adj.* conscientious, dutiful. **Pflicht|treue,** *f.* loyalty, dutifulness, (*Hist.*) fealty. **–übung,** *f.* (*skating*) set figure. **pflichtvergessen,** *adj.* disloyal, undutiful, unfaithful. **Pflicht|vergessenheit,** *f.* dereliction of duty; disloyalty. **–verletzung,** *f.* violation of duty. **–versäumnis,** *f.* neglect of one's duty. **–vorlesung,** *f.* compulsory *or* prescribed lecture. **pflichtwidrig,** *adj.* contrary to duty; undutiful, disloyal.

Pflock [pflɔk], *m.* (**-(e)s,** *pl.* **⸚e**) (tent-)peg; (wooden) pin, stake, picket; plug; (*coll.*) ***einige Pflöcke zurückstecken,*** come down a peg, climb down.

pflöcken ['pflœkən], *v.t.* fasten with pegs, peg.

pflog [pflo:k], **pflöge** ['pflø:gə], (*obs.*) *see* **pflegen.**

pflücken ['pflykən], *v.t.* pluck, pick, gather, cull; (*obs.*) pluck (*fowls etc.*); (*coll.*) ***ich habe ein Sträußchen (Hühnchen) mit ihm zu –,*** I have a bone to pick with him.

Pflug ['pflu:k], *m.* (**-(e)s,** *pl.* **⸚e**) plough, (*Am.*) plow; ***Land unter dem –,*** arable land, land under the plough.

pflügbar ['pfly:kba:r], *adj.* arable.

Pflug|dienst, *m.* (*Hist.*) socage. **–eisen,** *n.* coulter.

pflügen ['pfly:gən], *v.t., v.i.* plough, (*Am.*) plow; till; ***mit fremdem Kalb(e) –,*** plough with another man's heifer; ***den Sand*** or ***das Wasser –,*** beat the air; (*fig.*) ***sich – durch,*** plough through (*as a ship through the waves*). **Pflüger,** *m.* ploughman.

Pflug|messer, *n.* *See* **–eisen. –schar,** *f.* ploughshare. **–sterz,** *m.* (*Austr.* **–sterze,** *f.*) plough-handle, stilt. **–tiefe,** *f.* depth of furrow. **–treiber,** *m.* ploughboy.

Pfortader ['pfɔrtˀa:dər], *f.* (*Anat.*) portal vein.

Pförtchen ['pfœrtçən], *n.* little door; wicket-gate.

Pforte ['pfɔrtə], *f.* gate, door; orifice, entrance; (*Naut.*) porthole; ***die Hohe –,*** the Sublime Porte.

Pförtner ['pfœrtnər], *n.* 1. doorkeeper, doorman, porter, janitor; gatekeeper, gateman; 2. (*Anat.*) pylorus.

Pfoste ['pfɔstə], *f.*, **Pfosten,** *m.* post, pale, stake; upright, standard; jamb (*of doors*); main-piece (*of rudders*).

Pfote ['pfo:tə], *f.* paw; (*coll.*) (= *handwriting*) scrawl, fist, (*sl.*) (= *hand*) fist, mitt, paw; ***sich die –n verbrennen,*** burn one's fingers; ***ihm etwas auf die –n geben, ihn auf die –n klopfen,*** rap him over the knuckles.

Pfriem [pfri:m], *m.* (**-(e)s,** *pl.* **-e**), (*Austr.*) **Pfrieme,** *f.*, **Pfriemen,** *m.* 1. awl, bradawl; 2. (*Bot.*) German broom. **pfriemen,** *v.t.* bore. **Pfriemengras,** *n.* esparto grass.

Pfropf [pfrɔpf], *m.* (**-(e)s,** *pl.* **-e** *or* **⸚e**) stopper, cork, bung, plug; (*Med.*) clot, thrombus, embolus; (*Surg.*) wad, wadding, tampon; (*Artil.*) tampion; (*coll.*) tubby p. **Pfropfbastard,** *m.* (*Bot.*) graft hybrid. **Pfropfen,** *m.* *See* **Pfropf. pfropfen,** *v.t.* cram into, stuff full of; cork, plug; (*Hort.*) graft; (*fig.*) ***gepfropft voll,*** crammed (full). **Pfropfen|geld,** *n.* corkage. **–zieher,** *m.* corkscrew. **Pfropf|messer,** *n.* grafting knife. **–reis,** *n.* graft, scion, shoot, slip. **–spalt,** *m.* graft-slit.

Pfröpfling ['pfrœpflıŋ], *m.* (**-s,** *pl.* **-e**) *see* **Pfropfreis.**

Pfründe ['pfryndə], *f.* benefice, living; prebend; maintenance, keep (*in an institution*); (*fig.*) sinecure. **Pfründen|besetzungsrecht,** *n.* advowson. **–handel,** *m.* simony. **Pfründer,** *m.* (*Swiss*), **Pfründner,** *m.* beneficiary; prebendary; incumbent, beneficed clergyman.

Pfuhl [pfu:l], *m.* (**-(e)s,** *pl.* **-e**) pool; puddle, (*fig.*) sink, slough. **Pfuhlschnepfe,** *f.* (*Orn.*) bar-tailed godwit (*Limosa lapponica*).

Pfühl [pfy:l], *m. or n.* (**-(e)s,** *pl.* **-e**) (*Poet.*) bolster, pillow, cushion; couch; (*Archit.*) torus, column-moulding.

pfui! [pfuı], *int.* fie! shame! boo! – ***über ihn!*** shame on him!

Pfulmen ['pfulmən], *m.* (*Swiss*) pillow.

Pfund [pfunt], *n.* (**-(e)s,** *pl.* **-e**) 1. pound (*weight*); half a kilogram, metric pound (*unofficial except in Austr.*); ***drei – Fleisch,*** three pounds of meat; 2. pound (*sterling*); 3. (*B.*) talent; (*fig.*) ***sein – vergraben,*** hide one's talent. **Pfund|geld,** *n.* poundage. **–gewicht,** *n.* pound-weight.

pfundig ['pfundıç], *adj.* (*coll.*) splendid, fine, first-rate.

Pfundkurs ['pfuntkurs], *m.* sterling exchange.

Pfunds–, *pref.* (*sl. expressing approval*). **–essen,** *n.* excellent food. **–kerl,** *m.* fine fellow, great guy. **–sache,** *f.* stunner, knockout.

pfuschen ['pfuʃən], *v.t., v.i.* bungle, botch; – ***in*** (*Acc.*), meddle with, dabble in; ***ihm ins Handwerk –,*** poke one's nose in his affairs. **Pfuscher,** *m.* bungler, dabbler; poor workman; quack. **Pfuscherei** [–'raı], *f.* bungling, inferior *or* scamped work.

Pfütze ['pfytsə], *f.* puddle, pool, pot-hole.

Phänomen [fɛno'me:n], *n.* (**-s,** *pl.* **-e**) phenomenon, (*coll.*) miracle. **phänomenal** [–'na:l], *adj.* phenomenal; (*coll.*) remarkable, prodigious.

Phantasie [fanta'zi:], *f.* imagination, fancy, inventiveness; (fantastic) vision, fantasy, chimera; (*Mus.*) fantasia, impromptu, improvisation. **Phantasie|bild, –gebilde,** *n.* vision. **phantasielos,** *adj.* unimaginative. **Phantasielosigkeit,** *f.* unimaginativeness, lack of imagination. **Phantasiepapier,** *n.* fancy (coloured) paper. **–preis,** *m.* fancy price. **phantasiereich,** *adj.* imaginative, fanciful. **phantasieren,** *v.t., v.i.* indulge in reveries *or* fancies; imagine, dream; rave, ramble (***von,*** about), be delirious; (*Mus.*) improvise. **phantasie|voll,** *adj.* *See* **–reich.**

Phantast [fan'tast], *m.* (**-en,** *pl.* **-en**) visionary; dreamer; oddity. **phantastisch,** *adj.* fanciful, fantastic, visionary, (*coll.*) splendid, fine, terrific.

Phantom [fan'to:m], *n.* (**-s,** *pl.* **-e**) 1. phantom, chimera; 2. (*Med.*) manikin, anatomical model.

Pharisäer [fari'zɛ:ər], *m.* Pharisee. **pharisäisch,** *adj.* pharisaic(al), self-righteous.

Pharmakologe [farmako'lo:gə], *m.* (**-n,** *pl.* **-n**) pharmacologist. **Pharmakologie** [–'gi:], *f.* pharmacology. **Pharmakopöe** [–ko'pø:(ə)], *f.* pharmacopoeia.

Pharmazeut [farma'tsɔyt], *m.* (**-en,** *pl.* **-en**) apothecary, druggist, pharmacist. **pharmazeutisch,** *adj.* pharmaceutical. **Pharmazie,** *f.* pharmacy.

Pharo(spiel) ['fa:ro(ʃpi:l)], *n.* faro.

Phase ['fa:zə], *f.* (*Elec., of moon etc.*) phase, (*fig.*) stage. **Phasenänderung,** *f.* phase-change. **phasen|frei,** *adj.* (*Elec.*) non-reactive. **–gleich,** *adj.* of the same *or* of like phase, (*pred.*) in phase. **Phasen|messer,** *m.* phase-meter. **–schieber,** *m.* phase-converter. **–unterschied,** *m.* phase difference. **–verzögerung,** *f.* phase lag.

Philanthrop [filan'tro:p], *m.* (**-en,** *pl.* **-en**) philanthropist. **philanthropisch,** *adj.* philanthropic.

Philister [fi'lıstər], *m.* Philistine, vulgarian; (*sl.*) square, (*Studs. sl.*) townsman; *– und Studenten,* town and gown. **philisterhaft,** *adj.* philistine, pedantic, unimaginative, uncultured, narrow-minded. **Philisterium** [–'ste:rium], *n.* (*Studs. sl.*) life after leaving the university; (*collect.*) old students, graduates; *ins – treten,* go down.

Philologe [filo'lo:gə], *m.* **(-n,** *pl.* **-n)** philologist, linguist. **Philologie** [–'gi:], *f.* philology, language studies. **philologisch,** *adj.* philological, linguistic.

Philosoph [filo'zo:f], *m.* **(-en,** *pl.* **-en)** philosopher; *– von Sanssouci,* King Frederick II (the Great) of Prussia. **Philosophie** [–'fi:], *f.* philosophy. **philosophieren,** *v.i.* philosophize. **philosophisch,** *adj.* philosophical.

Phiole [fi'o:lə], *f.* phial, vial.

Phlegma ['flɛgma], *n.* 1. phlegm; 2. apathy, sluggishness, dullness. **Phlegmatiker** [–'ma:tikər], *m.* phlegmatic person. **phlegmatisch,** *adj.* phlegmatic.

Phonetik [fo'ne:tik], *f.* phonetics. **Phonetiker,** *m.* phonetician. **phonetisch,** *adj.* phonetic.

Phönix ['fø:nıks], *m.* **(-(es),** *pl.* **-e)** phoenix.

Phönizier [fø'ni:tsiər], *m.,* **phönizisch,** *adj.* Phoenician.

Phosgen [fɔs'ge:n], *n.* phosgene gas.

Phosphat [fɔs'fa:t], *n.* phosphate.

Phosphor ['fɔsfɔr], *m.* phosphorus. **Phosphoreszenz** [–rɛs'tsɛnts], *f.* phosphorescence. **phosphoreszieren,** *v.i.* phosphoresce. **phosphorhaltig,** *adj.* phosphorated. **phosphorig,** *adj.* phosphorous. **phosphorisch,** *adj.* phosphoric. **phosphorsauer,** *adj.* phosphate of. **Phosphor|säure,** *f.* phosphoric acid. **–wasserstoff,** *m.* phosphoretted hydrogen.

Photo ['fo:to], *n.* **(-s,** *pl.* **-s)** photo. **Photo|album,** *n.* photo(graph) album. **–apparat,** *m.* camera. **–chemie,** *f.* photochemistry. **photogen** [–'ge:n], *adj.* (*Biol., coll.*) photogenic.

Photograph [foto'gra:f], *m.* **(-en,** *pl.* **-en)** photographer. **Photographie** [–'fi:], *f.* photograph; photography. **photographieren,** *v.t.* photograph, take a picture *or* (*coll.*) snap of; *sich – lassen,* have one's photograph taken; *sie läßt sich gut –,* she photographs well, she takes a good picture. **photographisch, 1.** *adj.* photographic. **2.** *adv.* by photography.

Photo|gravüre, *f.* photo-engraving. **–händler,** *m.* dealer in photographic materials. **–kopie,** *f.* photoprint, photostat. **–montage,** *f.* photographic layout. **–sphäre,** *f.* (*Astr.*) photosphere. **–therapie,** *f.* sun-ray treatment. **–zelle,** *f.* photo-electric cell.

Phrase ['fra:zə], *f.* phrase; catchphrase, cliché; *leere –n,* empty talk, clap-trap; *–n dreschen,* talk hot air, (*sl.*) shoot off one's mouth. **Phrasendrescher,** *m.* windbag, gasbag, phrase-monger. **phrasenhaft,** *adj.* rambling, long-winded, prosy, prolix, verbose.

phrasieren [fra'zi:rən], *v.t.* (*Mus.*) phrase. **Phrasierung,** *f.* (*Mus.*) phrasing.

phrenetisch, *adj. See* **frenetisch.**

Physik [fy'zi:k], *f.* physics, physical science, natural philosophy. **physikalisch** [–'ka:lıʃ], *adj.* physical. **Physiker** ['fy:zikər], *m.* physicist, physical scientist. **Physikum,** *n.* **(-s,** *pl.* **-ka)** pre-medical (examination). **Physikus,** *m.* (-, *pl.* **-se)** (district) medical officer.

Physiognomie [fyziogno'mi:], *f.* physiognomy.

Physiologe [fyzio'lo:gə], *m.* **(-n,** *pl.* **-n)** physiologist. **Physiologie** [–'gi:], *f.* physiology. **physiologisch,** *adj.* physiological.

physisch ['fy:zıʃ], *adj.* physical, bodily, material.

Pianino [pia'ni:no], *n.* **(-s,** *pl.* **-s)** upright piano. **Pianist,** *m.* **(-en,** *pl.* **-en), Pianistin,** *f.* pianist. **Piano** [–'a:no], *n.* **(-s,** *pl.* **-s), Pianoforte** [–'fɔrte], *n.* **(-s,** *pl.* **-s)** piano(forte). **Pianola,** *n.* **(-s,** *pl.* **-s)** pianola, player-piano.

picheln ['pıçəln], *v.i.* (*coll.*) tipple, tope, booze.

pichen ['pıçən], *v.t.* (smear with) pitch. **Pichwachs,** *n.* heel-ball.

Pick [pık], *m.* **(-s,** *pl.* **-e)** picking; peck; (*dial.*) secret grudge (*see* **Pik, Pike**).

Picke ['pıkə], *f.* pickaxe, pick.

Pickel ['pıkəl], *m.* 1. pimple; 2. pickaxe, ice-axe. **Pickel|flöte,** *f.* piccolo. **–haube,** *f.* spiked helmet. **–hering,** *m.* 1. pickled herring; 2. clown, buffoon. **pick(e)lig,** *adj.* pimply, blotched.

picken ['pıkən], *v.i.* peck, pick; (*coll.*) stick, bind, be sticky *or* tacky.

Picknick ['pıknık], *n.* **(-s,** *pl.* **-e** (*Austr.-, pl.* **-s))** picnic.

Piek [pi:k], *f.* (-, *pl.* **-en)** (*Naut.*) peak (*of sail*).

pieken ['pi:kən], *v.t., v.i.* (*coll.*) prick, (*of insects*) sting. **piekfein,** *adj. See* **pikfein.**

piepe ['pi:pə], *adj.* (*coll.*) *das ist mir –,* that's all one *or* all the same to me, I don't give a damn.

piepen ['pi:pən], *v.i.* chirp, chirrup, cheep, squeak; (*Rad.*) bleep; (*coll.*) *es ist zum Piepen,* it's a perfect scream; (*coll.*) *bei dir piept's wohl,* you are off your head, you're dotty *or* nuts. **Piep|matz,** *m. See* **–vogel. piepsen,** *v.i.* 1. *See* **piepen;** 2. (*coll.*) be poorly, be off colour. **piepsig,** *adj.* 1. chirping, squeaking, piping; 2. (*coll.*) weakly, ailing, poorly. **Piepvogel,** *m.* (*coll.*) dicky-bird.

piesacken ['pi:zakən], *v.t.* (*sl.*) harass, badger, plague.

Pietät [pie'tɛ:t], *f.* reverence, deference; piety. **pietätlos,** *adj.* irreverent, disrepectful. **Pietätlosigkeit,** *f.* irreverence, disrespect; outrage. **pietätvoll,** *adj.* reverent, deferent(ial).

Pietismus [pie'tısmus], *m.* pietism. **pietistisch,** *adj.* pietistic(al).

Pik [pi:k], **1.** *m.* **(-s,** *pl.* **-s)** 1. pique; rancour, grudge (*see* **Pick, Pike**); (*coll.*) *einen – auf ihn haben,* bear him a grudge, have it in for him; 2. peak (*of mountain*). **2.** *n.* **(-s,** *pl.* **-s)** (*Cards*) spade(s).

pikant [pi'ka:nt], *adj.* piquant, pungent, biting, highly seasoned *or* spiced; (*coll.*) racy, spicy, suggestive, risqué. **Pikanterie** [–ə'ri:], *f.* risqué remark, racy joke *or* story.

Pik|-As, *n.* (*Cards*) ace of spades. **–dame,** *f.* queen of spades.

Pike ['pi:kə], *f.* pike, lance; (*fig.*) *von der – auf dienen,* rise from the ranks.

Pikee [pi'ke:], *m.* piqué.

Pikett [pi'kɛt], *n.* **(-(e)s,** *pl.* **-e)** 1. (*Cards*) piquet; 2. (*Swiss*) (*Mil.*) picket, squad.

pikfein ['pi:kfaın], *adj.* (*coll.*) tiptop, posh, (*sl.*) slap-up, snazzy.

pikieren [pi'ki:rən], *v.t.* 1. pique, nettle; 2. (*Hort.*) plant out, transplant. **pikiert,** *adj.* piqued, touchy (*über* (*Acc.*), about).

Pikkolo ['pıkolo], **1.** *m.* **(-s,** *pl.* **-s)** boy waiter, piccolo. **2.** *m. or n.* **(-s,** *pl.* **-s), Pikkoloflöte,** *f.* (*Mus.*) piccolo.

Pikrinsäure [pi'kri:nzɔyrə], *f.* picric acid.

Pilatus [pi'la:tus], *m.* (*B.*) Pilate; (*coll.*) *von Pontius zu –,* from pillar to post.

Pilger ['pılgər], *m.* pilgrim. **Pilgerfahrt,** *f.* pilgrimage. **Pilgerin,** *f. See* **Pilger. pilgern,** *v.i.* (*aux.* h. *&* s.) go on a pilgrimage; (*fig.*) flock, troop. **Pilgerschaft,** *f.* pilgrimage. **Pilgerstab,** *m.* pilgrim's staff.

Pille ['pılə], *f.* pill; *eine bittere – versüßen,* sugar a pill. **Pillen|dreher,** *m.* 1. (*Ent.*) scarabaeus; 2. (*hum.*) apothecary. **–schachtel,** *f.* pill-box.

Pilot [pi'lo:t], *m.* **(-en,** *pl.* **-en)** (*Naut., Av.*) pilot. **Pilotschirm,** *m.* pilot-parachute.

Pilz [pılts], *m.* **(-es,** *pl.* **-e)** fungus; (*edible*) mushroom, (*poisonous*) toadstool; (*coll.*) *in die –e gehen,* vamoose, disappear. **pilzartig, pilzig,** *adj.* fungoid, mushroom-like. **Pilz|keim,** *m.* fungus spore. **–krankheit,** *f.* mycosis. **–kunde,** *f.* mycology.

Piment [pi'mɛnt], *m. or n.* **(-(e)s,** *pl.* **-e)** allspice, pimento, Jamaica pepper. **Pimentrum,** *m.* bay rum.

Pimpelei [pɪmpə'laɪ], *f.* (*coll.*) effeminacy.
Pimpelfritz ['pɪmpəlfrɪts], *m.* (*coll.*) delicate *or* sickly p., (*sl.*) cissy, sissy. **pimpelig,** *adj.* soft, flabby, effeminate; weakly, sickly; whining, complaining. **Pimpel|liese,** *f. See* **–fritz. pimpeln,** *v.i.* (*coll.*) whine, complain, (*sl.*) belly-ache; be a cissy.
Pimpernuß ['pɪmpərnus], *f.* pistachio *or* bladder-nut (*Staphylaea*).
Pimpf [pɪmpf], *m.* **(-(e)s, -en,** *pl.* **-e)** (*Nat. Soc.*) (*analogous to*) wolf-cub.
Pinakothek [pinako'te:k], *f.* (-, *pl.* **-en**) art *or* picture gallery.
Pinasse [pi'nasə], *f.* pinnace.
Pinguin [pɪŋgu'i:n], *m.* **(-s,** *pl.* **-e)** (*Orn.*) penguin (*Aptenodytes*).
Pinie ['pi:niə], *f.* (*Bot.*) stone-pine (*Pinus pinea*).
Pinke ['pɪŋkə], *f.* (*sl.*) brass, dough, lolly; (*dial.*) blacksmith.
pinkeln ['pɪŋkəln], *v.i.* (*coll.*) piddle.
Pinne ['pɪnə], *f.* 1. brad, tack; pivot, centre-pin (*of compass needle*); 2. (*Naut.*) tiller; 3. quill feather.
Pinscher ['pɪnʃər], *m.* fox-terrier, rough-haired terrier.
Pinsel ['pɪnzəl], *m.* 1. (paint-)brush; 2. simpleton, noddle, numskull, fathead. **Pinselei** [–'laɪ], *f.* daub(ing); stupidity. **Pinsel|führung,** *f.* brush-work, touch. **pinseln,** *v.t., v.i.* brush; paint; daub; play the fool. **Pinsel|stiel,** *m.* brush handle. **–strich,** *m.* stroke of the brush, brushmark.
Pinzette [pɪn'tsɛtə], *f.* forceps, (pair of) tweezers, pincers, nippers.
Pionier [pio'ni:r], *m.* **(-s,** *pl.* **-e)** (*Mil.*) engineer, sapper; (*fig.*) pioneer. **Pionier|arbeit,** *f.* (*fig.*) spadework. **–park,** *m.* (*Mil.*) engineer stores.
Pipe ['pi:pə], *f.* butt, wine cask.
Pips [pɪps], *m.* pip (*in fowls*).
Pirat [pi'ra:t], *m.* **(-en,** *pl.* **-en)** pirate. **Piraten|-flagge,** *f.* Jolly Roger. **–küste,** *f.* (*Geog.*) Trucial Coast. **Piraterie** [–ə'ri:], *f.* piracy.
Pirol [pi'ro:l], *m.* **(-s,** *pl.* **-e)** (*Orn.*) golden oriole (*Oriolus oriolus*).
Pirsch [pɪrʃ], *f.* hunting, deer-stalking. **pirschen,** *v.i.* go deer-stalking, stalk, hunt.
Pisang ['pi:zaŋ], *m.* **(-s,** *pl.* **-e)** banana, plantain (-tree).
pispern ['pɪspərn], *v.i.* (*dial.*) whisper.
Pisse ['pɪsə], *f.* (*vulg.*) piss; (*Med.*) ***die kalte –,*** strangury. **pissen,** *v.i.* (*vulg.*) piss. **Pissoir** [–o'a:r], **Pißort,** *m.* urinal.
Pistazie [pɪs'ta:tsiə], *f.* pistachio-nut *or* tree.
Piste ['pɪstə], *f.* beaten track, (*Spt.*) cinder track, ski-run, (*Av.*) runway.
Pistill [pɪs'tɪl], *n.* **(-s,** *pl.* **-e)** 1. (*Bot.*) pistill; 2. pestle.
Pistol [pɪs'to:l], *n.* **(-s,** *pl.* **-e)** (*obs.*), **Pistole,** *f.* pistol; ***wie aus der – geschossen,*** like a shot; (*fig.*) ***ihm die – auf die Brust setzen,*** hold a pistol to his head. **Pistolen|griff,** *m.* pistol grip. **–schußweite,** *f.* pistol-shot. **–tasche,** *f.* holster.
Piston [pɪs'tõ], *n.* **(-s,** *pl.* **-s)** (*Mech.*) piston; (*Mus.*) cornet-à-piston.
pitsch(e)naß ['pɪtʃ(ə)'nas], *adj.* (*coll.*) wet through, sopping wet, wet to the skin.
pittoresk [pɪto'rɛsk], *adj.* picturesque.
Pivot|lafette [pi'vo:–], *f.* pivot mounting, rotating mount. **–lager,** *n.* trunnion bearing. **–zapfen,** *m.* trunnion.
placieren [pla'si:rən], **1.** *v.t.* (*Comm.*) place, negotiate. **2.** *v.r.* be placed. **placiert,** *adj.* (*Spt.*) well-placed.
Plack [plak], *m.* **(-es,** *pl.* **-e), Placke,** *f.* **Placken,** *m.* (*dial.*) patch, piece; blot, stain; ***see also*** **Plage. placken, 1.** *v.t.* (*dial.*) patch, stick; post up, placard; flatten, ram down. **2.** *v.t., v.r. See* **plagen. Plackerei** [–'raɪ], *f.* harassment, vexation; toil, drudgery; extortion, oppression.
pladdern ['pladərn], *v.i.* (*dial.*) rain in torrents.

Plädeur [plɛ'dø:r], *m.* **(-s,** *pl.* **-e)** counsel for the defence. **plädieren,** *v.i.* plead (***für, auf*** (*Acc.*), for). **Plädoyer** [–doa'je:], *n.* **(-s,** *pl.* **-s)** speech for the defence.
Plage ['pla:gə], *f.* vexation; torment, trouble, nuisance, annoyance, bother; (*B.*) plague, pest, calamity; (*Prov.*) ***jeder Tag hat seine –,*** sufficient unto the day is the evil thereof. **Plagegeist,** *m.* tormentor, nuisance, pest, plague, tiresome p., bore. **plagen, 1.** *v.t.* torment; vex, annoy; harass, pester, trouble, bother; (*of cares*) worry, haunt, prey on (*one's*) mind. **2.** *v.r.* toil (and moil), drudge, slave; take trouble *or* pains (***mit,*** with *or* about); ***geplagt werden von,*** be afflicted with (*a disease*).
Plagge ['plagə], *f.* (*dial.*) sod, turf.
Plagiar [plagi'a:r], *m.* **(-s,** *pl.* **-e)** *see* **Plagiator. Plagiat,** *n.* **(-es,** *pl.* **-e)** plagiarism; ***ein – begehen,*** plagiarize. **Plagiator,** *m.* **(-s,** *pl.* **-en)** plagiarist.
Plaid [ple:t], *m. or n.* **(-s,** *pl.* **-s)** plaid, travelling-rug.
plaidieren, *v.i.* (*Austr.*) *see* **plädieren.**
Plakat [pla'ka:t], *n.* **(-(e)s,** *pl.* **-e)** bill, placard, poster. **Plakat|ankleber,** *m.* bill-sticker. **–anschlag,** *m.* bill-posting, poster display. **–farbe,** *f.* poster colour.
plakatieren [plaka'ti:rən], **1.** *v.t.* placard. **2.** *v.i.* stick bills.
Plakat|malerei, *f.* poster-painting. **–säule,** *f.* advertisement *or* advertising pillar. **–schild,** *n.* showcard. **–schrift,** *f.* poster-lettering. **–träger,** *m.* sandwich-man.
plan [pla:n], *adj.* plain, clear, open; level, flat, plane, horizontal.
Plan, *m.* **(-(e)s,** *pl.* **⸚e)** 1. plane, level ground, plain; arena, battlefield; glade, clearing (*in a wood*); ***auf den – treten,*** appear, turn up, put in an *or* make one's appearance; ***der grüne –,*** the greensward, meadow; 2. ground-plan, map, chart, plan, design, layout, diagram, blueprint; (*fig.*) project, scheme, design, plan, intention; ***tief durchdachter –,*** carefully thought-out scheme; ***gedruckter –,*** prospectus; ***entgegengesetzte Pläne,*** cross-purposes; ***Pläne schmieden,*** make plans.
Plandrehbank ['pla:ndre:baŋk], *f.* (*Mech.*) facing lathe. **plandrehen,** *v.t.* face (down).
Plane ['pla:nə], *f.* awning, tarpaulin, canvas cover, tilt.
Pläne|macher, *m. See* **–schmied.**
planen ['pla:nən], *v.t.* plan, project; plot, scheme, design, work *or* map out; propose, envisage.
Pläneschmied ['plɛ:nəʃmi:t], *m.* schemer.
Planet [pla'ne:t], *m.* **(-en,** *pl.* **-en)** planet; asteroid. **planetarisch** [–'ta:rɪʃ], *adj.* planetary. **Planetarium,** *n.* **(-s,** *pl.* **-rien)** planetarium, orrery. **Planeten|bahn,** *f.* orbit of a planet. **–getriebe,** *n.* (*Mech.*) planetary *or* epicyclic gear(ing). **–jahr,** *n.* planetary year. **–stand,** position of a planet, (*Astr.*) aspect.
Plan|feuer, *n.* (*Artil.*) curtain of fire. **–film,** *m.* (*Phot.*) flat film, film-pack. **–fräsmaschine,** *f.* horizontal milling machine. **–hammer,** *m.* planishing-hammer.
Planieramboß, *m.* planishing-anvil. **planieren** [pla'ni:rən], *v.t.* level, plane, grade; smooth, planish (*metal*), size (*paper*). **Planier|maschine,** *f.* leveller, grader, bulldozer. **–presse,** *f.* size-press. **–raupe,** *f. See* **–maschine. –wasser,** *n.* size; glue-water.
Planke ['plaŋkə], *f.* plank, board.
Plänkelei [plɛŋkə'laɪ], *f.* (-, *pl.* **-en)** skirmish(ing). **plänkeln** ['plɛŋkəln], *v.i.* skirmish. **Plänkler,** *m.* skirmisher.
planliegend ['pla:nli:gənt], *adj.* (*Phot.*) non-curling. **planlos, 1.** *adj.* planless, purposeless, aimless, unsystematic, haphazard. **2.** *adv.* at random, without any plan. **Planlosigkeit,** *f.* aimlessness, desultoriness. **planmäßig, 1.** *adj.* methodical, systematic; (well-)planned; scheduled (*as trains*); established (*of an appointment*). **2.** *adv.* as planned, according to

plan, (*in time*) according to schedule. **Plan|mäßigkeit,** *f.* methodicalness; method, system, systematic arrangement. **–pause,** *f.* blueprint. **–quadrat,** *n.* map square *or* grid.

Planschbecken ['planʃbɛkən], *n.* paddling pool. **planschen,** *v.t., v.i.* splash, paddle.

Plan|schießen, *n.* (*Mil.*) map firing. **–sektor,** *m.* map protractor. **–soll,** *n.* quota, target. **–spiegel,** *m.* plane mirror. **–spiel,** *n.* (*Mil.*) map-reading exercise. **–stärke,** *f.* (*Mil.*) establishment. **–stelle,** *f.* post *or* position on the establishment.

Plantage [plan'ta:ʒə], *f.* plantation.

Planum ['pla:num], *n.* levelled ground, road-bed.

Planung ['pla:nuŋ], *f.* plan(ning); budget(ing); layout, blueprint. **Planungs|amt,** *n.* planning authority. **–forschung,** *f.* operational research. **–ingenieur,** *m.* production engineer.

planvoll ['pla:nfɔl], *adj.* planned, concerted; methodical, systematic.

Plan|vorschub, *m.* (*Mech.*) transverse feed. **–wagen,** *m.* covered *or* tilt wagon. **–wirtschaft,** *f.* planned economy, economic planning. **–zeichnen,** *n.* map drawing, field-sketching, plotting. **–ziel,** *n.* planned output, output target.

Plapperei [plapə'raɪ], *f.* babbling, prattle, chatter, blether. **plapperhaft** ['plapərhaft], *adj.* talkative, chatty, garrulous. **Plapper|liese,** *f.*, **–maul,** *n. See* **–tasche. plappern,** *v.t., v.i.* babble, chatter, prattle, jabber. **Plappertasche,** *f.* chatterbox, prattler, gossip.

plärren ['plɛrən], *v.i.* blubber, cry, whine.

Plastik ['plastɪk], *f.* (-, *pl.* **-en**) plastic art; (piece of) sculpture; plastic (material); (*fig.*) plasticity, graphic power.

Plastilin [plasti'li:n], *n.*, **Plastilina,** *f.* plasticine.

plastisch ['plastɪʃ], *adj.* plastic; (*fig.*) graphic; ***–e Chirurgie,*** plastic surgery; ***–e Landkarte,*** relief map.

Platane [pla'ta:nə], *f.* plane-tree.

Platin [pla'ti:n], *n.* platinum. **platinhaltig,** *adj.* platiniferous. **platinieren** [–'ni:rən], *v.t.* coat with platinum.

Platoniker [pla'to:nikər], *m.* Platonist. **platonisch,** *adj.* Platonic, unworldly, spiritual.

platsch! [platʃ], *int.* splash! **platschen,** *v.i.* splash. **plätschern,** *v.i.* splash *or* paddle about; (*of water*) ripple, babble. **platschnaß,** *adj.* sopping wet, drenched.

platt [plat], *adj.* flat, flattened (out), plain, level, even; (*fig.*) dull, flat, stale, insipid; commonplace, trite, trivial, silly; low (*of a dialect*); (*coll.*) dumbfounded, flabbergasted, taken aback; *– **abschlagen,*** give a flat refusal; *– **auf der Erde liegen,*** lie flat on the ground; *– **drücken,*** flatten (out); ***ich sagte es ihm – heraus,*** I told it him straight out; ***–es Land,*** flat *or* open country; (*coll.*) ***ich war ganz –,*** you could have knocked me down with a feather; ***–e Wahrheit,*** plain *or* naked truth; ***–er Widerspruch,*** downright *or* flat contradiction. **Platt,** *n. See* **Plattdeutsch.**

Plättbrett ['plɛtbrɛt], *n.* ironing-board.

Plättchen ['plɛtçən], *n.* (*Anat.*) lamina, (*Bot.*) lamella.

Plattdeutsch ['platdɔytʃ], *n.*, **platt|deutsch,** *adj.* Low German (*dialect*). **–drücken,** *v.t.* flatten (out).

Platte ['platə], *f.* plate; dish; tray, salver; bald head, tonsure; clearing (*in a wood*); cleared *or* bare patch; sheet (*of metal*); panel (*of wood*), slab, flag(stone), tile; (*Archit.*) plinth; plaque; planchet, disk; gramophone record; photographic plate; platform, ledge (*of rock*), plateau, tableland; leaf (*of a table*); ***kalte –e,*** (plate of) cold meat.

Plätte ['plɛtə], *f.* (*dial.*), **Plätteisen,** *n.* flat-iron, (smoothing-)iron. **plätten,** *v.t.* flatten; iron (*laundry*), (*Mech.*) laminate.

Platten|abzug, *m.* stereotyped proof. **–belag,** *m.* layer *or* covering of flag(stone)s *or* tiles. **–druck,** *m.* stereotype (printing). **–geräusch,** *n.* surface scratch (*gramophone*). **–gummi,** *n.* sheet rubber. **–halter,** *m.*, **–kassette,** *f.* (*Phot.*) plate-holder. **–leger,** *m.* paver, paviour, tiler. **–rüstung,** *f.* plate-armour. **–spieler,** *m.* record player. **–teller,** *m.* turntable (*gramophone*). **–wechsler,** *m.* automatic record changer.

platterdings ['platərdɪŋs], *adv.* utterly, absolutely, decidedly, positively, by all means, downright; – ***nicht,*** not by any means, in no case.

Plätterin ['plɛtərɪn], *f.* ironer.

Platt|fisch, *m.* flat-fish, plaice, flounder. **–form,** *f.* platform.

Plättfrau ['plɛtfrau], *f. See* **Plätterin.**

Platt|fuß, *m.* flat-foot; (*coll. Motor.*) puncture, flat. **–fußeinlage,** *f.* arch-support. **plattfüßig,** *adj.* flat-footed.

Plattheit ['platharɪt], *f.* flatness, levelness; (*usu. fig.*) triviality, dullness, staleness, insipidity; trite expression, platitude, banality, commonplace.

plattieren [pla'ti:rən], *v.t.* plate.

Plattler ['platlər], *m. See* **Schuhplattler.**

Platt|mönch, *m. See* **Mönchsgrasmücke. –stich,** *m.* satin-stitch. **–stickerei,** *f.* plain embroidery.

Plätt|wäsche, *f.*, **–zeug,** *n.* (laundry for) ironing.

Platz [plats], *m.* (**-es,** *pl.* **⸚e**) place, locality, spot, site, location; room, space; stand (*for carriages*); (market) square; (*Theat. etc.*) seat; post; position; ***am –e,*** in this place, here; (*fig.*) in place *or* order, suitable, pertinent, opportune; ***nicht am –e,*** unwanted, uncalled for, irrelevant; ***500 blieben auf dem –e,*** 500 were slain; (*Spt.*) ***auf eigenem –,*** at home; (*Spt.*) ***auf gegnerischem –,*** away; (*Spt.*) ***auf die Plätze!*** on your marks! – ***behalten,*** keep one's seat, stay *or* remain seated; ***den – behaupten,*** hold one's own, stand one's ground; (*Spt.*) ***den zweiten – belegen,*** come in second; – ***da!*** make way there! ***fester –,*** fortress, stronghold, fortified place; ***freier –,*** open space, esplanade; – ***greifen,*** gain ground, spread, take effect; (*Theat.*) ***einen guten – haben,*** have a good seat; ***hier ist kein – mehr,*** there is no more room here; – ***machen,*** make way *or* room, clear the way (*Dat.*, for); – ***nehmen,*** sit down; be seated, take a seat; ***öffentlicher –,*** public place *or* square.

Platz|angst, *f.* agoraphobia. **–anweiser,** *m.* usher. **–anweiserin,** *f.* usherette. **–bedarf,** *m.* local requirements; requisite floor-space.

Plätzchen ['plɛtsçən], *n.* 1. pastille, lozenge, tablet; biscuit; 2. snug little spot, cozy corner.

platzen ['platsən], *v.i.* (*aux.* s.) burst, explode; split, crack, rupture, (*of tyre*) puncture; (*coll.*) come to nothing, be exploded, collapse (*as a theory*); (*coll.*) ***geplatzt sein,*** bounce (*as a cheque*); ***ins Zimmer –,*** burst into the room; (*coll.*) ***mir platzte der Kragen,*** I blew my top; ***ihm ist eine Ader geplatzt,*** he burst a blood-vessel; ***mir ist ein Reifen geplatzt,*** I had a puncture.

Platz|feuer, *n.* airfield lights. **–geschäft,** *n.* local business. **–herren,** *m.pl.* (*Spt.*) home team. **–karte,** *f.* (reserved) seat ticket. **–kommandant,** **–major,** *m.* local commandant, town-major. **–mangel,** *m.* shortage *or* lack of space *or* room. **–meister,** *m.* (*Spt.*) groundsman. **–notierung,** *f.* (*Comm.*) spot quotation. **–nummer,** *f.* (*Chem.*) atomic number. **–patrone,** *f.* blank cartridge. **platzraubend,** *adj.* taking up too much room. **Platz|regen,** *m.* cloudburst, downpour. **–runde,** *f.* (*Av.*) circling flight (*before landing*). **–wart,** *m. See* **–meister. –wechsel,** *m.* 1. change of place, migration; (*Spt.*) change of ends; 2. (*Comm.*) local bill.

Plauderei [plaudə'raɪ], *f.* chat, small talk, tittle-tattle, gossip; (*Rad.*) discussion, talk.

Plauderer ['plaudərər], *m.* conversationalist, talker; chatterer, chatterbox. **plauderhaft,** *adj.* chatty, talkative. **Plauder|hans,** *m.*, **–liese,** *f.*, **–maul,** *n. See* **–tasche. plaudern,** *v.i.* (have a) chat (***mit,*** with), talk (to *or* with), prattle, chatter, gossip (with); ***aus der Schule –,*** tell tales (out of school). **Plauder|stündchen,** *n.* cosy chat. **–tasche,** *f.* (*coll.*) chatter-box. **–ton,** *m.* conversational tone.

Plaue ['plauə], *f.* (*Austr.*) *see* **Plane.**

Plausch [plauʃ], *m.* (**-es,** *pl.* **-e**) (*dial.*) chat. **plauschen,** *v.i.* (*dial.*) *see* **plaudern.**

plausibel [plau'zi:bəl], *adj.* plausible, feasible, specious; – *machen,* make plausible, give colour to.

plauz! [plauts], *int.* bang! smash!

Plazenta [pla'tsɛnta], *f.* (-, *pl.* **-s**) (*Anat.*) placenta.

plazieren [pla'tsi:rən], *v.t. See* **placieren.**

Plebejer [ple'be:jər], *m.,* **Plebejerin,** *f.* plebeian; (*coll.*) cad, bounder. **plebejisch,** *adj.* plebeian, low, vulgar.

Plebiszit [plebɪs'tsi:t], *n.* (**-s,** *pl.* **-e**) plebiscite.

Plebs [plɛps], *f.* (*coll. m.*) plebs; mob, rabble.

Pleite ['plaɪtə], *f.* (*coll.*) bankruptcy, smash, (*fig.*) failure; (*sl.*) washout, flop; – *machen,* go bankrupt *or* (*sl.*) broke *or* bust. **pleite,** *adj.* (*coll.*) (dead) broke; (*coll.*) – *gehen, see Pleite machen.* **Pleitegeier,** *m.* misfortune, impending disaster.

Plejade [ple'ja:də], *f.* pleiad.

Plempe ['plɛmpə], *f.* (*Mil. sl.*) short sword; (*coll.*) thin coffee, wishy-washy drink.

plemplem [plɛm'plɛm], *adj.* (*sl.*) nuts, barmy, gaga.

plempern ['plɛmpərn], **1.** *v.i.* (*dial.*) lounge about. **2.** *v.t.* (*coll.*) splash, spray, water.

Plenarsitzung [ple'na:rzitsuŋ], *f.,* **Plenum** ['ple:-num], *n.* full assembly, plenary session

Pleuelstange ['plɔyəlʃtaŋə], *f.* (*Mech.*) connecting rod, piston rod.

Plicht [plɪçt], *f.* (-, *pl.* **-en**) (*Naut.*) cockpit.

plinkern ['plɪŋkərn], *v.i.* (*coll.*) blink, wink.

Plinse ['plɪnzə], *f.* (*Austr.*) fritter, pancake, omelet.

plinsen ['plɪnzən], *v.i.* (*dial.*) weep, cry.

Plinze, *f. See* **Plinse.**

Pliozän [plio'tsɛ:n], *n.,* **pliozän,** *adj.* (*Geol.*) pliocene.

Plissee [plɪ'se:], *n.* (**-s,** *pl.* **-s**) pleating. **Plisseerock,** *m.* pleated skirt. **plissieren,** *v.t.* pleat.

Plombe ['plɔmbə], *f.* lead, (lead) seal; plug; stopping, filling (*for a tooth*). **plombieren** [–'bi:rən], *v.t.* (affix lead) seal (to); plug; fill, stop (*a tooth*).

Plötze ['plœtsə], *f.* (*Ichth.*) roach (*Leuciscus rutilus*).

plötzlich ['plœtslɪç], **1.** *adj.* sudden, abrupt, unexpected. **2.** *adv.* all of a sudden, all at once. **Plötzlichkeit,** *f.* suddenness, abruptness.

Pluderhosen ['plu:dərho:zən], *f.pl.* baggy trousers, plus-fours. **pludern,** *v.i.* be baggy, bag (*of clothes*).

Plumeau [ply'mo:], *n.* (**-s,** *pl.* **-s**) feather bed, eiderdown (quilt).

plump [plump], *adj.* podgy; clumsy, awkward, shapeless, heavy; crude, coarse, ill-bred; tactless, blunt; ponderous (*style*); *–e Schmeichelei,* gross flattery; – *heraussagen,* blurt out. **Plumpheit,** *f.* shapelessness, heaviness, crudeness, clumsiness; bluntness. **Plumps,** *m.* (**-s,** *pl.* **-e**) thump, thud. **plumps!** *int.* plump! bump! thump! thud! **plumpsen,** *v.i.* (*aux.* h. & s.) fall plump *or* with a thud, plump down; bounce, burst (*in* (*Acc.*), into).

Plunder ['plundər], *m.* lumber, litter, old clothes *or* rags, trash, rubbish, junk; (*coll.*) *der ganze* –, the whole bag of tricks, the whole boiling *or* shoot. **Plunderkammer,** *f.* lumber-room.

Plünderer ['plyndərər], *m.* plunderer, pillager. **plündern,** *v.t., v.i.* plunder, pillage, sack, loot; strip, rifle, despoil, rob. **Plünderung,** *f.* plundering, looting, pillage, sack.

Plural [plu'ra:l], *m.* (**-s,** *pl.* **-e**), **Pluralis,** *m.* (-, *pl.* **-lia**) plural (number). **pluralisch,** *adj.* (in the) plural.

Plus [plus], *n.* plus, surplus; (*fig.*) advantage, asset. **plus,** *adv.* plus, in addition. **Plus|betrag,** *m.* surplus. **–leitung,** *f.* (*Elec.*) positive lead. **–macher,** *m.* (*coll.*) financial schemer, profiteer. **–pol,** *m.* (*Elec.*) positive pole *or* terminal. **–punkt,** *m.* (*coll.*) asset, plus. **–quamperfekt(um),** *n.* pluperfect (tense).

Plüsch [ply(:)ʃ], *m.* (**-es,** *pl.* **-e**) plush. **Plüsch|-kopfente,** *f.* (*Orn.*) spectacled eider (*Somateria fischeri*). **–teppich,** *m.* Wilton carpet.

plusterig ['plu:stərɪç], *adj.* tousled, ruffled. **plustern,** *v.i., v.r.* ruffle one's feathers, bristle.

Pluszeichen ['plustsaɪçən], *n.* plus *or* addition sign.

Pneu [pnɔy], *m.* (**-s,** *pl.* **-s**), **Pneumatik** [–'ma:tɪk], **1.** *m.* (**-s,** *pl.* **-s**) (*Austr. f.* (-, *pl.* **-en**)) (pneumatic) tyre. **2.** *f.* (science of) pneumatics. **pneumatisch,** *adj.* pneumatic.

Pöbel ['pø:bəl], *m.* mob, populace, rabble. **pöbelhaft,** *adj.* vulgar, low, plebeian. **Pöbelhaftigkeit,** *f.* vulgarity, coarseness. **Pöbel|haufe,** *m.* rabble. **–herrschaft,** *f.* mob-rule. **–justiz,** *f.* lynch-law. **pöbeln,** *v.i.* (*coll.*) indulge in a slanging match.

Poch, *n. or m. See* **Pochspiel.**

Poche ['pɔxə], *pl.* (*dial.*) thrashing.

pochen ['pɔxən], **1.** *v.t.* crush, pound, batter. **2.** *v.t., v.i.* 1. knock, rap; beat, throb (*of the heart*); *man pocht,* there is a knock at the door; *mir pocht das Herz,* my heart beats *or* throbs; (*fig.*) – *auf* (*Acc.*), boast *or* brag about; boast of, presume upon; *auf sein gutes Recht* –, stand on one's rights; 2. play poker.

Poch|erz, *n.* crude ore. **–hammer,** *m.* crusher. **–mehl,** *n.* pulverized ore. **–mühle,** *f.* stamping-mill. **–satz,** *m.* ore sludge. **–schlägel,** *m. See* **–hammer. –schlamm, –schlick,** *m. See* **–satz. –spiel,** *n.* poker (*cards*). **–stempel,** *m.* stamp (die). **–werk,** *n. See* **–mühle.**

Pocke ['pɔkə], *f.* pock; pockmark; *die –n,* smallpox. **Pocken|gift,** *n.* smallpox virus. **–holz,** *n.* lignum vitae. **–impfung,** *f.* vaccination. **pockenkrank,** *adj.* suffering from smallpox. **Pocken|-lymphe,** *f.* vaccine. **–narbe,** *f.* pockmark. **pockennarbig, pockig,** *adj.* pockmarked.

Podagra ['po:dagra], *n.* gout, podagra.

Podest [po'dɛst], *m., n.* (**-es,** *pl.* **-e**) landing (*of staircase*); stage, platform, pedestal (*also fig.*); (*fig.*) *von seinem – stoßen,* debunk.

Podex ['po:dɛks], *m.* (**-(es),** *pl.* **-e**) posterior, buttocks, backside.

Podium ['po:dium], *n.* (**-s,** *pl.* **-dien**) rostrum, platform.

Poesie [poe'zi:], *f.* poetry; piece of poetry, poem. **poesielos,** *adj.* unpoetical; prosaic, (*coll.*) prosy; pedestrian, dull, commonplace.

Poet [po'e:t], *m.* (**-en,** *pl.* **-en**) (*high style*) poet. **Poetik,** *f.* theory of poetry, poetics. **Poetin,** *f.* poetess. **poetisch,** *adj.* poetic(al).

Pogge ['pɔgə], *f.* (*dial.*) frog. **Poggenstuhl,** *m.* toadstool.

Pointe [po'ɛ̃tə], *f.* point (*of a joke*), (*sl.*) punch line. **pointieren** [–'ti:rən], *v.t.* give point to, express in a pointed manner, emphasize.

Pokal [po'ka:l], *m.* (**-s,** *pl.* **-e**) goblet, cup; trophy. **Pokal|endspiel,** *m.* (*Spt.*) cup final. **–spiel,** *n.* (*Spt.*) cup-tie.

Pökel ['pø:kəl], *m.* brine, pickle. **Pökel|faß,** *n.* pickling vat. **–fleisch,** *n.* salt(ed) *or* cured meat. **–hering,** *m.* pickled herring. **pökeln,** *v.t.* salt, cure, pickle.

pokulieren [poku'li:rən], *v.i.* drink, carouse, (*sl.*) booze.

Pol [po:l], *m.* (**-s,** *pl.* **-e**) (*Astr., Magnet.*) pole; (*Elec.*) terminal; (*fig.*) *der ruhende* –, the one constant factor.

polar [po'la:r], *adj.* polar. **Polar|eis,** *n.* polar ice. **–forscher,** *m.* polar explorer. **–forschung,** *f.* polar exploration. **–fuchs,** *m.* arctic fox. **–gegend,** *f.* polar regions. **–gürtel,** *m.* frigid zone. **–hund,** *m.* husky, Eskimo dog.

Polarisation [polarizatsi'o:n], *f.* polarization. **Polarisations|ebene,** *f.* plane of polarization. **–farbe,** *f.* colour of polarized light. **polarisieren** [–'zi:rən], *v.t.* polarize. **Polarität** [–'tɛ:t], *f.* polarity.

Polar|kreis, *m.* polar circle. **–licht,** *n.* northern lights, aurora borealis. **–meer,** *n.* Arctic ocean; *südliches* –, Antarctic ocean. **–möwe,** *f.* (*Orn.*) Iceland gull (*Larus glaucoides*). **–(see)taucher,** *m.* (*Orn.*) *see* **Prachttaucher. –stern,** *m.* Pole star, (*Poet.*) lodestar.

Polder ['pɔldər], *m.* reclaimed land.

Pole ['po:lə], *m.* (**-n,** *pl.* **-n**) Pole.

Polemik [po'le:mɪk], *f.* (-, *pl.* **-en**) polemics, controversy. **Polemiker,** *m.* controversialist. **polemisch,** *adj.* polemic(al). **polemisieren** [–'zi:rən], *v.i.* carry on a controversy (*gegen*, with) (*a p.*), controvert (*a th.*).

Polen ['po:lən], *n.* Poland.

polen, *v.t.* (*Elec.*) polarize. **Pol|ende,** *n.* (*Elec.*) electrode. **–höhe,** *f.* (*Astr.*) latitude.

Police [po'li:s(ə)], *f.* (insurance) policy.

Polier [po'li:r], *m.* (**-s,** *pl.* **-e**) building trade foreman.

polieren [po'li:rən], *v.t.* polish, burnish; furbish. **Polierer,** *m.* burnisher; French-polisher. **Polier|mittel,** *n.* polish. **–rot,** *n.* (jeweller's) rouge, colcothar. **–scheibe,** *f.* polishing wheel, buff-wheel. **–stahl,** *m.* burnisher. **–stock,** *m.* polishing stick, buff-stick. **–wachs,** *n.* polishing wax.

Poliklinik ['po:likli:nɪk], *f.* outpatients' department (*of hospital*).

Polin ['po:lɪn], *f.* *See* **Pole.**

Politik [poli'ti:k], *f.* politics; policy. **Politikaster** [–'kastər], *m.* armchair politician. **Politiker** [–'li:tikər], *m.* politician. **Politikus,** *m.* (-, *pl.* **-se**) (*fig.*) diplomatist, sly old fox. **politisch,** *adj.* political; (*fig.*) judicious, politic. **politisieren** [–'zi:rən], **1.** *v.i.* dabble in *or* talk politics. **2.** *v.t.* give political character to, make politically-minded.

Politur [poli'tu:r], *f.* (-, *pl.* **-en**) polish, gloss, lustre, varnish; (*fig.*) polish, refinement.

Polizei [poli'tsaɪ], *f.* police; *berittene –*, mounted police. **Polizei|amt,** *n.* police-station. **–aufsicht,** *f.* police supervision, surveillance, (*coll.*) ticket of leave. **–beamte(r),** *m., f.* police-officer. **–behörde,** *f.* police (authorities). **–gefängnis,** *n.* cells, lock-up. **–gericht,** *n.* police-court, magistrate's court. **–gewahrsam,** *n.* *See* **–gefängnis. –kommissar, –kommissär, –leutnant,** *m.* police-inspector.

polizeilich [poli'tsaɪlɪç], *adj., adv.* police; *– verboten,* forbidden, prohibited; *–e Bedeckung, –er Schutz,* police protection; *–e Aufsicht, see* **Polizeiaufsicht**; *–e Anmeldung* (*Abmeldung*), report of (change of) address to the police.

Polizei|präsident, *m.* chief constable. **–präsidium,** *n.* police headquarters. **–revier,** *n.* *See* **–amt. –richter,** *m.* magistrate. **–spitzel,** *m.* police spy, (*sl.*) stool pigeon. **–strafe,** *f.* fine. **–streife,** *f.* police raid. **–stunde,** *f.* closing time, curfew. **–(ver)ordnung,** *f.* police regulation(s). **–wache,** *f.* *See* **–amt. –wachtmeister,** *m.* police-sergeant. **polizeiwidrig,** *adj.* contrary to police regulations, unlicensed, unauthorized; (*coll.*) *– dumm,* incredibly stupid.

Polizist [poli'tsɪst], *m.* (**-en,** *pl.* **-en**) policeman, constable. **Polizistin,** *f.* policewoman.

Polizze [po'lɪtsə], *f.* (*Austr.*) *see* **Police.**

Polklemme ['po:lklɛmə], *f.* (*Elec.*) terminal, binding-screw.

Poller ['pɔlər], *m.* (*Naut.*) bollard, mooring post.

polnisch ['pɔlnɪʃ], *adj.* Polish; (*coll.*) *–e Wirtschaft,* awful mess.

Pol|schuh, *m.* (*Elec.*) pole-piece. **–stein,** *m.* loadstone, lodestone.

Polster ['pɔlstər], *n.* (*Austr. m.*) cushion, pillow, bolster; stuffing, pad, padding. **Polsterbank,** *f.* cushioned bench. **Polsterer,** *m.* upholsterer. **polsterförmig,** *adj.* (*Archit., Bot.*) pulvinate. **Polster|kammer,** *f.* padded cell. **–klasse,** *f.* upholstered class (*in German trains the first and second*). **–möbel,** *n.pl.* upholstered furniture. **polstern,** *v.t.* stuff, pad, cushion, upholster. **Polster|sessel,** *m.* *See* **–stuhl. –sitz,** *m.* cushioned *or* padded seat. **–stuhl,** *m.* upholstered *or* easy chair.

Polsterung ['pɔlstəruŋ], *f.* upholstery, stuffing, padding.

Polterabend ['pɔltərˀa:bənt], *m.* eve-of-the-wedding party. **Polterer,** *m.* rowdy *or* unruly fellow, blusterer. **Polter|geist,** *m.* poltergeist. **–kammer,** *f.* lumber-room. **poltern,** *v.i.* make a row *or* racket; knock, thump, pound; (*of a p.*) bluster, (*coll.*) kick up a shindy; (*aux.* s.) rattle, rumble, thunder, thud; (*of a p.*) come pounding *or* thumping *or* clumping.

Polwechsler, *m.* (*Elec.*) polarity inverter.

polyandrisch [poly'andrɪʃ], *adj.* (*Bot.*) polyandrous. **polychrom(atisch),** *adj.* polychromatic, polychrome.

Polyeder [poly'e:dər], *n.* polyhedron. **polyedrisch,** *adj.* polyhedral.

Polygamie [polyga'mi:], *f.* polygamy. **polygam(isch)** [–'ga:m(ɪʃ)], *adj.* polygamous.

Polyglotte [poly'glɔtə], *f.* polyglot (*Bible, dictionary etc.*). **polyglott(isch),** *adj.* polyglot.

polygonal [polygo'na:l], *adj.* polygonal, multangular.

Polygraphic, *f.* the printing trade.

polymer, *adj.* (*Chem.*) polymeric.

polymorph [poly'mɔrf], *adj.* polymorphous. **Polymorphie** [–'fi:], *f.* polymorphism.

Polynesien [poly'ne:ziən], *n.* Polynesia. **Polynesier,** *m.*, **polynesisch,** *adj.* Polynesian.

Polyp [po'ly:p], *m.* (**-en,** *pl.* **-en**) **1.** (*Zool.*) polyp; (*Med.*) polypus; **2.** (*Studs. sl.*) cop, bobby.

Polysklerose, *f.* (*Med.*) multiple sclerosis.

Polytechnik [poly'tɛçnɪk], *f.* polytechnics. **Polytechniker,** *m.* engineering student. **Polytechnikum,** *n.* technical *or* engineering college.

Pomade [po'ma:də], *f.* hair-oil, brilliantine, pomade; (*sl.*) coolness, smoothness, aplomb. **Pomadenhengst,** *m.* dandy, fop. **pomadig,** *adj.* (*coll.*) phlegmatic, indifferent, leisurely, easy-going, lazy.

Pomeranze [pomə'rantsə], *f.* (Seville) orange. **Pomeranzenlikör,** *m.* curaçao.

Pommer ['pɔmər], *m.*, **pommer(i)sch,** *adj.* Pomeranian. **Pommern,** *n.* (*Geog.*) Pomerania.

Pomp [pɔmp], *m.* pomp, splendour. **pomphaft,** *adj.* pompous, stately, (*coll.*) showy. **pompös** [–'pø:s], *adj.* splendid, magnificent.

ponieren [po'ni:rən], *v.t.* postulate, assume; (*Studs. sl.*) pay for.

Ponton [pɔ̃'tɔ̃], *m.* (**-s,** *pl.* **-s**) pontoon. **Pontonbrücke,** *f.* pontoon bridge.

Pony ['pɔni], *m., n.* (**-s,** *pl.* **-s** *or* (*Austr.*) **Ponies**) pony; (*coll.*) fringe (*hair style*).

Popanz ['po:pants], *m.* (**-es,** *pl.* **-e**) bugbear, bogy, scarecrow.

Pope ['po:pə], *m.* (**-n,** *pl.* **-n**) priest of the Greek church.

Popel ['po:pəl], *m.* (*dial., coll.*) **1.** snot; **2.** guttersnipe. **popeln,** *v.i.* (*coll.*) pick one's nose.

Popo [po'po:], *m.* (**-s,** *pl.* **-s**) (*coll.*) backside, bottom, behind, bum.

populär [popu'lɛ:r], *adj.* popular; *– machen,* popularize; *sich – machen,* make o.s. a general favourite, ingratiate o.s. with everyone; *–wissenschaftliche Vorlesung,* scientific lecture for the general public. **popularisieren** [–lari'zi:rən], *v.t.* popularize, bring (down) to the level of the masses. **Popularität,** *f.* popularity.

Pore ['po:rə], *f.* pore, foramen. **Porenzelle,** *f.* guard cell. **porös** [–'rø:s], *adj.* porous, permeable. **Porosität** [–rosi'tɛ:t], *f.* porosity.

Porphyr ['pɔrfyr], *m.* (**-s,** *pl.* **-e**) porphyry.

Porree ['pɔre], *m.* (**-s,** *pl.* **-s**) leek.

Port [pɔrt], *m.* (**-(e)s,** *pl.* **-e**) harbour, port.

Portal [pɔr'ta:l], *n.* (**-s,** *pl.* **-e**) portal, main entrance.

Porte|chaise [pɔrt'ʃɛ:zə], *f.* sedan chair. **–feuille** [–'fø:j], *n.* portfolio (*also Comm., Parl.*). **–monnaie** [–mɔ'nɛ:], *n.* purse.

porten ['pɔrtən], **1.** *v.t.* (*Swiss*) nominate (for election). **2.** *v.r.* interest o.s., show an interest (*für*, in).

Portepée [pɔrte'pe:], *n.* sword-knot. **Portepeéfähnrich,** *m.* ensign.

Portier [pɔrti'e:], *m.* (**-s,** *pl.* **-s** *or* (*Austr.*) **-e**) porter, doorkeeper, doorman. **Portière** [–'ɛ:rə], *f.* door curtain.

Portion [pɔrtsi'o:n], *f.* portion, share, allowance; serving, helping, ration; ***eine – Tee und zwei Tassen,*** a pot of tea and two cups; ***zwei –en Kaffee,*** coffee for two; ***eine – Frechheit,*** a good dose of cheek; (*sl.*) ***halbe –,*** little runt.

Porto ['pɔrto], *n.* (**-s,** *pl.* **-s** *or* **Porti**) postage; mail charges, carriage. **portofrei,** *adj.* prepaid, post-free. **Porto|gebühr,** *f.* postal rates. **–kasse,** *f.* petty cash. **portopflichtig,** *adj.* subject to postage. **Porto|satz,** *m.* postal charge. **–vergütung,** *f.* refunding of postage. **–zuschlag,** *m.* excess postage, surcharge.

Porträt [pɔr'trɛ:(t)], *n.* (**-(e)s,** *pl.* **-s** *or* **-e**) portrait, likeness. **porträtieren** [–'ti:rən], *v.t.* portray, paint a portrait of. **Porträtmaler,** *m.* portrait-painter.

Portugal ['pɔrtugal], *n.* Portugal. **Portugiese** [–'gi:zə], *m.* (**-n,** *pl.* **-n**), **Portugiesin,** *f.*, **portugiesisch,** *adj.* Portuguese.

Portulak ['pɔrtulak], *m.* (**-s,** *pl.* **-e** *or* **-s**) (*Bot.*) purslane.

Portwein ['pɔrtvaɪn], *m.* port(-wine).

Porzellan [pɔrtsɛ'la:n], *n.* (**-s,** *pl.* **-e**) china(-ware), porcelain; (*fig.*) ***unnötig – zerschlagen,*** wash one's dirty linen in public. **porzellanblau,** *adj.* china-blue. **porzellanen,** *adj.* (of) porcelain, china. **Porzellan|erde,** *f.* china-clay, kaolin. **–geschirr,** *n.* china(-ware), crockery. **–laden,** *m.* china-shop; (*coll.*) ***wie der Elefant im –,*** like a bull in a china-shop. **–ofen,** *m.* porcelain-kiln. **–schnecke,** *f.* (*Zool.*) cowrie.

Posament [poza'mɛnt], *n.* (**-(e)s,** *pl.* **-en**) (*usu. pl.*) gold *or* silver lace, braid, gimp, galloon. **Posamenter, Posamentier** [–'ti:r], *m.* (**-s,** *pl.* **-e**), **Posamentierer** (*Austr.*), *m.* haberdasher. **Posamentwaren,** *f.pl.* haberdashery.

Posaune [po'zaunə], *f.* trombone; (*fig.*) trumpet; ***letzte –,*** last trump(et), trump of doom. **posaunen, 1.** *v.i.* play the trombone, **2.** *v.t.* (*fig.*) trumpet, sound, proclaim aloud. **Posaunen|bläser,** *m.* trombone player. **–engel,** *m.* (*coll.*) angelic chubby-faced baby.

[1]**Pose** ['po:zə], *f.* pose, attitude.

[2]**Pose,** *f.* quill (feather); (*coll.*) feather; (*coll.*) ***'raus aus den –n!*** get out of (your) bed!

posieren [po'zi:rən], *v.i.* pose, sit (*Dat.,* for); strike an attitude *or* pose, attitudinize, put on airs.

Position [pozitsi'o:n], *f.* 1. position, (social) standing; (*Mil.*) station; 2. (*Comm.*) entry, item. **Positionslicht,** *n.* navigation light, recognition light, (*Motor.*) side light.

positiv ['po:ziti:f], *adj.* positive; ***–e Einstellung,*** goodwill; ***–e Größe,*** positive *or* affirmative quantity; ***–es Recht,*** statute law; ***–es Wissen,*** exact science, (*coll.*) solid knowledge; ***nichts Positives,*** nothing definite. **Positiv, 1.** *m.* (**-s,** *pl.* **-e**) (*Gram.*) positive (*degree*). **2.** *n.* (**-s,** *pl.* **-e**), 1. harmonium; 2. (*Phot.*) positive (picture); print.

Positur [pozi'tu:r], *f.* (-, *pl.* **-en**) posture; defensive attitude; ***sich in – setzen*** or ***stellen,*** strike an attitude, attitudinize; (*Fenc. etc.*) stand on one's guard.

Posse ['pɔsə], *f.* (*Theat.*) burlesque, farce; jest, joke, antic, buffoonery, (tom)foolery. **Possen,** *m.* trick, prank, practical joke; ***– reißen,*** play the fool, clown (about); ***– treiben mit,*** play tricks on; ***ihm etwas zum – tun,*** do a th. to spite him. **possenhaft,** *adj.* comical, farcical. **Possen|-reißer,** *m.* buffoon, clown, jester, tomfool. **–spiel,** *n. See* **Posse. possierlich** [–'si:rlɪç], *adj.* droll, quaint, comic, funny, waggish.

Post [pɔst], *f.* (-, *pl.* **-en**) post-office; postal service; post, mail; (*Poet.*) news; ***mit der ersten –,*** by the first delivery; (*obs.*) ***mit der – fahren,*** travel by post-chaise; ***mit gewöhnlicher –,*** by surface mail; ***mit gleicher –,*** under separate cover; ***mit der heutigen –,*** by today's post; ***mit umgehender*** or ***wendender –,*** by return (of post); ***auf die – geben,*** (take to the) post; ***mit der – schicken,*** send by post, mail. **Postadreßbuch,** *n.* post-office directory. **postalisch** [–'sta:lɪʃ], *adj.* postal.

Postament [pɔsta'mɛnt], *n.* (**-s,** *pl.* **-e**) base, pedestal.

Post|amt, *n.* post-office. **–annahme(stelle),** *f.* receiving-office (*for parcels etc.*). **–annahmestempel,** *m.* cancellation, date stamp. **–antwortschein,** *m.* reply coupon. **–anweisung,** *f.* postal order, money-order. **–auftrag,** *m.* cash on delivery order. **–auto,** *n.* motor-bus (*carrying mail as well*). **–beamte(r),** *m., f.* post-office official *or* clerk. **–beförderung,** *f.* postal delivery. **–beförderungsdienst,** *m.* postal service. **–behörde,** *f.* post-office authorities. **–(bestell)bezirk,** *m.* postal district. **–bezug,** *m.* mail order(ing) (*of goods*), postal subscription (*of newspapers*). **–bote,** *m.* postman. **–dampfer,** *m.* mailboat, packet (steamer).

postdatieren [pɔstda'ti:rən], *v.t.* post-date.

Post|debit, *n.* postal delivery of newspapers. **–diebstahl,** *m.* mail robbery. **–dienst,** *m.* postal service, mail-service. **–dienststunden,** *f.pl.* post-office hours of business. **–direktion,** *f.* General Post-Office. **–direktor,** *m.* Minister of Posts and Telecommunication. **–einlieferungsschein,** *m.* post-office receipt, certificate of posting.

Posten ['pɔstən], *m.* 1. post, position, situation, (*coll.*) job; (*Mil.*) sentry, guard, sentinel, picket (*also industrial*), outpost; (*Mil.*) ***auf – ziehen,*** go on *or* mount guard; (*coll.*) ***auf dem – sein,*** be on the alert *or* on one's toes; feel well, be in good form, be fighting fit; (*coll.*) ***nicht recht auf dem – sein,*** not feel quite up to the mark, feel groggy *or* under the weather; (*Mil.*) ***– aufstellen,*** post a sentry; (*Mil.*) ***– ablösen,*** change guard; (*Mil.*) ***– stehen,*** stand sentry, be on guard; (*Mil. sl.*) ***schlauer –,*** cushy job, soft billet; (*fig.*) ***verlorener –,*** forlorn hope; ***auf verlorenem – kämpfen,*** fight a losing battle, fight for a lost cause; (*Mil.*) ***– vor Gewehr,*** armed sentry; 2. (*Comm.*) parcel, lot, batch, (*in ledger*) item, entry, sum, amount.

posten, *v.i.* (*Swiss*) go *or* run errands.

Posten|dienst, *m.* (*Mil.*) sentry *or* guard duty. **–jäger,** *m.* place-seeker. **–kette, –linie,** *f.* line of sentries, cordon, outposts. **postenweise,** *adv.* (*Comm.*) in lots *or* parcels; item by item; ***– aufführen,*** itemize.

Post|fach, *n.* post-office box. **–fachnummer,** *f.* box number. **–festkonto,** *n.* post-office deposit account. **–flugzeug,** *n.* mailplane. **postfrei,** *adj.* postage paid; post-free. **Post|gebühr,** *f.* postal charge, postage. **–gebühren,** *f.pl.* postal rates. **–gefälle,** *n.pl.* post-office revenues. **–gehilfe,** *m.* post-office assistant.

postglazial [pɔstglatsi'a:l], *adj.* post glacial.

Post|gut, *n. See* **–sachen. –halter,** *m.* (*obs.*) keeper of post-horses *or* posting house. **–haltestelle,** *f.* stage. **–handbuch,** *n.* post-office guide. **–haus,** *n.* (*obs.*) posting house, post stage. **–hilfsstelle,** *f.* sub-office (*in a shop etc.*). **–horn,** *n.* posthorn, postilion's horn.

postieren [pɔs'ti:rən], *v.t.* (*v.r.*) post (o.s.), place (o.s.), position (o.s.), station (o.s.); ***sich –,*** (take one's) stand.

Postille [pɔs'tɪlə], *f.* book of prayers *or* sermons.

Postillion [pɔstɪl'jo:n], *m.* (**-s,** *pl.* **-e**) postilion.

Post|karte, *f.* postcard. **–konto,** *n.* post-office account. **–kraftwagen,** *m. See* **–auto. –kutsche,** *f.* mail- *or* stage-coach; postchaise. **postlagernd,** *adv.* to be called for; poste restante, (*Am.*) general delivery. **Post|leitzahl,** *f.* postal code. **–meister,** *m.* postmaster. **–nachnahme,** *f.* ***gegen –,*** cash *or* (*Am.* collection) on delivery.

postnumerando [pɔstnume'rando], *adv.* payable on receipt.

Postpaket, *n.* postal package. **–regal,** *n.* post-office monopoly. **–reisende(r),** *m., f.* (*obs.*) passenger by mail-coach. **–reiter,** *m.* (*obs.*) courier. **–sachen,** *f.pl.* post, mail. **–sack,** *m.* mail-bag. **–schalter,** *m.* post-office counter. **–scheck,** *m.* postal cheque. **–scheckkonto,** *n.* post-office transfer *or* cash account. **–schiff,** *n. See* **–dampfer. –schließfach,** *n.* post-office box. **–schluß,** *m.* last collection, post-office closing time. **–sendung,** *f.* letter *or* parcel sent by post.

Postskript [pɔst'skrɪpt], *n.* **(-(e)s,** *pl.* **-e), Postskriptum,** *n.* **(-s,** *pl.* **-ta)** postscript, P.S.

Postsparbuch, *n.* post-office savings book. **–sparkasse,** *f.* post-office savings-bank. **–sparschein,** *m.* savings-certificate. **–sperre,** *f.* interruption of postal services. **–stempel,** *m.* post-mark. **–stunden,** *f.pl.* hours of business at a post-office. **–tag,** *m.* mail-day. **–tarif,** *m.* postal rates *or* charges.

Postulat [pɔstu'la:t], *n.* **(-(e)s,** *pl.* **-e)** postulate. **postulieren,** *v.t.* postulate.

postum [pɔs'tu:m], *adj.* posthumous.

Post|verkehr, *m.* postal service. **–versandhaus,** *n.* mail-order firm. **–verwaltung,** *f.* postal administration. **–wagen,** *m.* mail van, *(Am.)* postal car; *(obs.)* mail-coach, stage-coach. **–wechsel,** *m.* *(obs.)* change of post horses. **postwendend,** *adv.* by return (of post). **Post|wertzeichen,** *n.* postage-stamp. **–wesen,** *n.* postal system. **–wurfsendung,** *f.* mail circular. **–zahlschein,** *m.* postal order. **–zug,** *m.* mail-train.

Potentat [potɛn'ta:t], *m.* **(-en,** *pl.* **-en)** potentate.

Potential [potɛntsi'a:l], *n.* **(-s,** *pl.* **-e)** *(Elec.)* potential, voltage. **Potential|abfall,** *m.* *(Elec.)* potential drop. **–exponent,** *m.* *(Math.)* index. **–sprung,** *m.* *(Elec.)* potential difference.

potentiell [potɛntsi'ɛl], *adj.* potential, latent.

Potenz [po'tɛnts], *f.* (-, *pl.* **-en)** *(Math.)* power; *(fig.)* potency; ***zweite –,*** square; ***dritte –,*** cube; ***vierte –,*** fourth power, *(fig., coll.)* *n*th power, uttermost limit. **potenzieren** [–'tsi:rən], *v.t.* *(Math.)* raise to a higher power, *(fig.)* magnify. **Potenzierung,** *f.* involution. **Potenzreihe,** *f.* *(Math.)* exponential series.

Potpourri ['pɔtpuri], *n.* **(-s,** *pl.* **-s)** *(Mus.)* medley, potpourri.

Pott [pɔt], *m.* **(-(e)s,** *pl.* **⸗e)** *(dial.)* pot. **Pott|asche,** *f.* potash, potassium carbonate. **–fisch,** *m.* sperm-whale. **–fischtran,** *m.* sperm oil. **–lot,** *n.* graphite, blacklead. **–wal,** *m. See* **–fisch.**

potz|tausend! [pɔts–] **– Wetter!** *int.* good God! good gracious!

Poule ['pu:l(ə)], *f.* pool *(game).*

poussieren [pu'si:rən], **1.** *v.i.* flirt. **2.** *v.t.* *(coll.)* butter up, soft-soap.

Prä [prɛ:], *n.* preference; *(coll.)* ***ein – vor ihm haben,*** come *or* rank first, have an advantage over him.

Präambel [prɛ'ambəl], *f.* preamble.

Präbende [prɛ'bɛndə], *f. See* **Pfründe.**

Pracht [praxt], *f.* pomp, display, state, rich array, luxury, *(coll.)* glitter; spendour, magnificence; *(coll.)* ***das ist eine (wahre) –!*** that is splendid! that's (just) great!

Pracht|ammer, *f.* *(Orn.)* yellow-browed bunting *(Emberiza chrysophrys).* **–aufwand,** *f.* magnificent display, sumptuousness. **–ausgabe,** *f.* édition-de-luxe. **–bau,** *m.* palatial building. **–bett,** *n.* state-bed. **–eiderente,** *f.* *(Orn.)* king-eider *(Somateria spectabilis).* **–exemplar,** *n.* fine specimen. **–fregattvogel,** *m.* *(Orn.)* magnificent man-o'-war bird, *(Am.)* magnificent frigate-bird *(Fregata magnificens).*

prächtig ['prɛ:çtɪç], *adj.* magnificent, splendid; gorgeous, sumptuous, pompous; *(coll.)* brilliant, superb, dazzling, glorious, lovely, fine, great, grand, capital.

Pracht|kerl, *m.* splendid fellow, *(coll.)* great guy, sport, brick. **–liebe,** *f.* love of splendour, fondness for show, ostentation, showiness. **prachtliebend,** *adj.* fond of show, ostentatious, showy. **Pracht|stück,** *n.* fine specimen, choice piece, *(coll.)* beauty. **–taucher,** *m.* *(Orn.)* black-throated diver, *(Am.)* Arctic loon *(Gavia arctica).* **prachtvoll,** *adj. See* **prächtig. Prachtzimmer,** *n.* state-room.

Prädikant [prɛdi'ka:nt], *m.* **(-en,** *pl.* **-en)** preacher.

Prädikat [prɛdi'ka:t], *n.* **(-(e)s,** *pl.* **-e) 1.** *(Gram.)* predicate; **2.** *(school)* mark(s), report; **3.** attribute, title. **Prädikatsnomen,** *n.* *(Gram.)* complement.

prädisponieren [prɛdispo'ni:rən], *v.t.* predispose *(für,* to).

Präfekt [prɛ'fɛkt], *m.* **(-(e)s** *(Austr.* **-en),** *pl.* **-en)** prefect, governor.

Präfix ['prɛ:fɪks], *n.* **(-es,** *pl.* **-e)** prefix.

Prag ['pra:k], *n.* *(Geog.)* Prague.

Präge|anstalt ['prɛ:gə–], *f.* mint. **–druck,** *m.* *(Typ.)* embossed *or* relief print(ing). **–form,** *f.* matrix, die. **prägen,** *v.t.* coin; stamp, emboss; *(fig.)* impress, imprint, engrave ***(in*** *(Acc.),* on). **Präg(e)|recht,** *n.* right of coinage. **–stanze,** *f.,* **–stempel, –stock,** *m.* matrix, die.

Pragmatik, *f.* *(Austr.)* (Civil Service) grades *or* grading.

pragmatisch [prag'ma:tɪʃ], *adj.* pragmatic(al).

pragmatisieren, *v.t.* *(Austr.)* appoint *(a p.)* to the permanent staff.

prägnant [prɛg'nant], *adj.* **1.** pregnant *(with meaning),* fraught with meaning, suggestive; **2.** precise, exact, to the point, terse, pithy. **Prägnanz,** *f.* precision, terseness.

prähistorisch [prɛ:hɪs'tɔ:rɪʃ], *adj.* prehistoric.

prahlen ['pra:lən], *v.i.* boast, brag ***(mit,*** of), parade, vaunt; show off, swagger; ***mit einer S. –,*** parade *or* make a parade *or* show of a th. **Prahler,** *m.* boaster, braggart, swaggerer, *(coll.)* show-off. **Prahlerei** [–'raɪ], *f.* boast(ing), bragging; ostentation. **prahlerisch,** *adj.* boastful, bragging; swaggering, ostentatious. **Prahl|hans,** *m. See* **Prahler. –sucht,** *f.* boastfulness, ostentation.

Prahm [pra:m], *m.* **(-(e)s,** *pl.* **-e), Prahme,** *f.* barge, lighter. **Prahmgeld,** *n.* lighterage.

praien, *v.t. See* **preien.**

Präjudiz [prɛju'di:ts], *n.* **(-es,** *pl.* **-e)** prejudice, *(Law)* precedent. **präjudizieren** [–'tsi:rən], *v.t.* prejudge. **Präjudizrecht,** *n.* *(Law)* case-law.

Praktik ['praktɪk], *f.* (-, *pl.* **-en)** practice, (manner of) execution, exercise; *pl.* machinations, tricks, sharp practice. **Praktikant** [–'kant], *m.* **(-en,** *pl.* **-en), Pratikantin,** *f.* **1.** probationer; **2.** laboratory assistant. **Praktiker,** *m.* practitioner; practical men; expert, experienced p. **Praktikum,** *n.* **(-s,** *pl.* **-ka** *or* **-ken)** practical work, (course of) laboratory work; practical handbook, laboratory manual. **Praktikus,** *m.* (-, *pl.* **-se)** *(coll.)* ***alter –,*** old hand, old stager.

praktisch ['praktɪʃ], **1.** *adj.* practical, experimental; *(of a th.)* useful, serviceable, handy, ready-to-use, easy-to-use; *(of a p.)* practical-minded, handy; *(fig., coll.)* virtual; ***–er Arzt,*** general practitioner; ***–e Ausbildung,*** practical training; ***–es Beispiel,*** practical *or* working example; ***–er Sinn,*** practical-mindedness; ***–er Versuch,*** field trial. **2.** *adv.* practically, virtually, as good as, for *or* to all practical purposes.

praktizieren [prakti'tsi:rən], *v.t., v.i.* practise *(one's profession),* *(Med.)* practise medicine, *(Law)* practise at the bar; *(coll.)* ***ihm etwas aus der Tasche –,*** extract s.th. from his pocket.

Prälat [prɛ'la:t], *m.* **(-en,** *pl.* **-en)** *(Eccl.)* prelate.

präliminar [prɛlimi'na:r], *adj.* preliminary. **Präliminarien,** *pl.* preliminaries.

Praline [pra'li:nə], *f.,* **Praliné,** *(Austr., Swiss)* **Pralinee** [–li'ne:], *n.* **(-s,** *pl.* **-s)** chocolate (cream).

prall [pral], *adj.* tight, taut, stretched, tense; chubby, plump, well-rounded; ***–e Sonne,*** blazing sunshine, full glare of the sun.

Prall, *m.* **(-s,** *pl.* **-e)** shock, impact, collision; bounce, rebound, recoil. **prallen,** *v.i.* *(aux.* h. *&* s.) rebound, recoil, bounce ***(auf*** *(Acc.),* against), *(Artil.)* ricochet; *(of the sun)* beat down ***(auf*** *(Acc.),* on). **Prallblech,** *n.* baffle (plate). **Prallheit,** *f.* tightness, tautness; roundness, plumpness. **Prall|kraft,** *f.* elasticity, resilience. **–schuß,** *m.* *(Artil.)* ricochet. **–triller,** *m.* *(Mus.)* mordent. **–winkel,** *m.* angle of reflection *or* recoil.

Präludium [prɛ'lu:dium], *n.* **(-s,** *pl.* **-dien)** *(Mus.)* prelude.

Prämie ['prɛ:miə], *f.* award, reward, prize, (*Comm.*) premium, bonus, option-money, (*Mil.*) bounty. **Prämien|geschäft,** *n.* option-business. **-satz,** *m.* (rate of) premium. **-schein,** *m.* premium bond. **-system,** *n.* incentive bonus system (*of wage payment*). **prämiieren** [-i'i:rən], *v.t.* award a prize to; place a premium on.

Prämisse [prɛ'mɪsə], *f.* premise.

prangen ['praŋən], *v.i.* be resplendent, make a show, look fine, (*coll.*) shine; (*of a p.*) show off, boast; (*Naut.*) crowd all sails.

Pranger ['praŋər], *m.* pillory, whipping-post; ***an den – stellen,*** (put in the) pillory, (*fig.*) pillory, expose publicly.

Pranke ['praŋkə], *f.* claw, clutch, fore-paw.

pränumerando [prɛnume'rando], *adv.* (payable)in advance. **Pränumerant,** *m.* subscriber. **pränumerieren,** *v.t.* subscribe to.

Präparat [prɛpa'ra:t], *n.* (**-es,** *pl.* **-e**) 1. (*Chem. etc.*) preparation, compound; (*Med.*) patent medicine, mixture; 2. (microscope) slide. **präparieren, 1.** *v.t.* prepare (***auf*** (*Acc.*), for), (*Anat.*) dissect. **2.** *v.r.* prepare o.s., make (one's) preparations (***auf*** (*Acc.*), for).

Präposition [prɛpozitsi'o:n], *f.* (*Gram.*) preposition.

Prärie [prɛ'ri:], *f.* prairie.

Prärogativ [prɛroga'ti:f], *n.* (**-s,** *pl.* **-e**), **Prärogative,** *f.* prerogative.

Präsens ['prɛ:zɛns], *n.* (-, *pl.* **Präsentia**) (*Gram.*) present (tense).

Präsentant [prɛzɛn'tant], *m.* (**-en,** *pl.* **-en**) (*Comm.*) presenter, holder (*of a bill*). **präsentieren,** *v.t.* present, tender, offer; (*Mil.*) ***präsentiert das Gewehr!*** present arms! **Präsentierteller,** *m.* tray, salver; (*fig.*) ***wie auf dem –,*** in full view.

Präsenz [prɛ'zɛnts], *f.* presence. **Präsenz|bibliothek,** *f.* reference library. **-liste,** *f.* list of participants, (*Mil.*) muster-roll. **-stärke,** *f.* (*Mil.*) effective strength, effectives.

Präses ['prɛ:zɛs], *m.* (-, *pl.* **Präsiden**), **Präside** [-'zi:də], *m.* (**-n,** *pl.* **-n**), **Präsident** [-'dɛnt], *m.* (**-en,** *pl.* **-en**) president, chairman, (*Parl.*) Speaker, (*Scots Eccl.*) moderator. **Präsidenten|stuhl,** *m.* presidential chair. **-wahl,** *f.* presidential election. **Präsidentschaft,** *f.* presidency, chairmanship. **Präsidentschaftskandidat,** *m.* presidential candidate. **präsidieren,** *v.i.* (*Swiss v.t.*) preside (***über*** (*Acc.*), over), be in *or* take the chair; (*coll.*) chair (*a meeting*). **Präsidium** [-'zi:dium], *n.* (**-s,** *pl.* **-dien**) presidency, chairmanship, (*coll.*) the chair.

prasseln ['prasəln], *v.i.* patter (*as rain*), rattle (*as hail*), crackle (*as fire*), hail, rain (*as shots*).

prassen ['prasən], *v.i.* feast, carouse, revel; live in luxury *or* debauchery. **Prasser,** *m.* glutton; reveller; spendthrift; rake. **Prasserei** [-'raɪ], *f.* feasting, gluttony; revelry; dissipation, debauchery.

Prätendent [pretɛn'dɛnt], *m.* (**-en,** *pl.* **-en**) pretender, claimant (***auf*** (*Acc.*), to).

Präteritum [prɛ'te:ritum], *n.* (**-s,** *pl.* **-ta**) (*Gram.*) preterite (tense), past tense.

Prätur [prɛ'tu:r], *f.* (*Hist.*) praetorship.

Pratze ['pratsə], *f.* paw.

Präventiv|behandlung [prɛvɛn'ti:f-], *f.* prophylactic treatment. **-impfung,** *f.* immunization. **-krieg,** *m.* preventive war. **-maßnahme,** *f.*, **-mittel,** *n.* preventive measure.

Praxis ['praksɪs], *f.* practice, exercise; usage, experience, practice, custom; (*Med.*) patients, practice, (*Law*) clients.

Präzedenz [prɛtse'dɛnts], *f.* (-, *pl.* **-ien**) precedence, precedent. **Präzedenzfall,** *m.* precedent.

präzis [prɛ'tsi:s], *adj.* exact, precise. **präzisieren** [-'zi:rən], *v.t.* specify, define (exactly), make precise. **Präzision** [-zi'o:n], *f.* precision, exactitude, accuracy. **Präzisions|arbeit,** *f.* precision work. **-waage,** *f.* precision balance. **Präziswechsel,** *m.* (*Comm.*) bill drawn and payable on the same day.

predigen ['pre:dɪgən], *v.t.*, *v.i.* preach; (*coll.*) rant, sermonize; (*Prov.*) ***Gelehrten ist gut –,*** a word to the wise is enough. **Prediger,** *m.* preacher; clergyman, minister; ***der – in der Wüste,*** a voice crying in the wilderness. **Predigt,** *f.* (-, *pl.* **-en**) sermon, (*fig.*) lecture; ***eine – halten,*** preach a sermon; (*fig.*) ***ihm eine – halten,*** give him a lecture *or* a good talking to *or* a dressing-down.

preien ['praɪən], *v.t.* (*Naut.*) hail.

[1]**Preis** [praɪs], *m.* (**-es,** *pl.* **-e**) 1. price, cost, charge, terms, fee, rate, fare; ***um jeden –,*** at any price, at all costs; ***um keinen –,*** not at any price, not for all the world; ***zum -e von,*** at the price of, selling for, priced at; ***zivile -e,*** moderate charges, reasonable prices; ***äußerster –,*** lowest possible *or* (*coll.*) rock-bottom price, keenest price; 2. prize, award, trophy; (*motor-racing*) ***großer –,*** Grand Prix; ***den – davontragen,*** take the prize, (*coll.*) carry off the prize; 3. praise, glory

[2]**Preis,** *m.* (**-es,** *pl.* **-e**) *see* **Preise.**

Preis|abbau, *m.* reduction in price. **-änderung,** *f.* alteration in price; ***-en vorbehalten,*** terms subject to alteration. **-angabe,** *f.* quotation (of prices); ***ohne –,*** not priced *or* marked. **-anstieg,** *m.* rise in prices. **-aufgabe,** *f.* *See* **-ausschreiben. -aufschlag,** *m.* rise in price, supplement(ary charge). **-auftrieb,** *m.* upward trend (of prices). **-ausschreiben,** *n.* open competition. **-bewerber,** *m.* competitor, contestant. **-bewerbung,** *f.* competition, contest. **-bildung,** *f.* price control *or* fixing, pricing. **-bindung,** *f.* price restriction. **-druck,** *m.* downward trend of prices. **-drücker,** *m.* price-cutter. **-drückerei,** *f.* price-cutting.

Preise ['praɪzə], *f.* border(ing), edging.

Preiseinbruch, *m.* *See* **-sturz.**

Preiselbeere ['praɪzəlbe:rə], *f.* bilberry, whortleberry, cranberry.

preisen ['praɪzən], *irr.v.t.* praise, commend; extol, exalt, laud, glorify, eulogize; ***Gott sei gepriesen!*** glory be to God! ***sich glücklich –,*** call *or* consider o.s. lucky.

Preis|entwicklung, *f.* trend of prices. **-erhöhung,** *f.* *See* **-aufschlag. -ermäßigung,** *f.* reduction in price, (*coll.*) price cut; discount, rebate. **-frage,** *f.* 1. subject *or* question set for competition; 2. matter of price.

Preis|gabe, *f.* *See* **-gebung. preisgeben,** *irr.v.t.* give up, surrender, relinquish, hand over; reveal, expose; abandon, sacrifice; ***alles –,*** let everything go to rack and ruin, (*coll.*) let everything slide; ***sich –,*** deliver o.s. up; prostitute o.s.; ***(dem) Wind und (den) Wellen preisgegeben,*** at the mercy of the wind and waves. **Preisgebung,** *f.* surrender, abandonment; exposure; prostitution.

Preisgefüge ['praɪsgəfy:gə], *n.* price-structure. **preisgekrönt,** *adj.* prize-winning. **Preis|gericht,** *n.* jury, tribunal, committee of adjudicators, the judges. **-grenze,** *f.* price limit; ***obere –,*** ceiling. **preis|günstig,** *adj.* *See* **-wert. Preis|höhe,** *f.* level of prices. **-lage,** *f.* price range; ***in jeder –,*** at all prices. **-liste,** *f.* price-list. **-nachlaß,** *m.* rebate, discount. **-notierung,** *f.* quotation. **-richter,** *m.* judge, arbiter, umpire. **-rückgang,** *m.* fall in prices. **-schere,** *f.* (*Comm.*) relation between prime costs and selling price of product. **-schießen,** *n.* shooting-match. **-schild,** *n.* price tag. **-schrift,** *f.* prize essay. **-schwankung,** *f.* fluctuation of prices.

Preißelbeere, *f.* (*Austr.*) see **Preiselbeere.**

Preis|senkung, *f.* fall *or* drop in price. **-steigerung,** *f.* rise in prices. **-stopp,** *m.* price freeze *or* pegging. **-sturz,** *m.* sudden fall in price(s), slump. **-tafel,** *f.* list of rates *or* charges, price list. **-träger,** *m.* prize-winner. **-treiberei,** *f.* forcing up of prices, profiteering. **-überhöhung,** *f.* excessive *or* extortionate prices. **-überwachung,** *f.* price control. **-unterbietung,** *f.* underselling, dumping. **-verteilung,** *f.* distribution of prizes. **-verzeichnis,** *n.* *See* **-liste. preis|wert, -würdig,** *adj.* worth the money *or* price, good value. **Preis|zettel,** *m.* *See* **-schild. -zuschlag,** *m.* supplement, additional charge.

Prellbock ['prɛlbɔk], *m.* (*Railw.*) buffer.
prellen, *v.t.* make rebound; toss (in a blanket); (*Med.*) contuse, bruise; (*fig.*) humbug, dupe, cheat, swindle, (*coll.*) take in.
Prell|schuß, *m.* (*Artil.*) ricochet. **-stein,** *m.* kerb-(stone), guardstone.
Premiere [prəmi'ɛ:rə], *f.* (*Theat.*) first night, first performance. **Premierminister** [-mi'e:-], *m.* prime minister, premier.
preschen ['prɛʃən], *v.i.* (*coll.*) hurry, scurry.
Presenning [pre'zɛnɪŋ], *f.* *See* **Persenning.**
Presse ['prɛsə], *f.* 1. press; 2. gloss, lustre; 3. journalism, the press; ***unter der –***, in the press, being printed; ***in die – gehen,*** go to press; 4. (*coll.*) coach, crammer, tutorial *or* cramming college.
Presse|agentur, *f.* press agency. **-amt,** *n.* public relations office. **-dienst,** *m.* news service. **-freiheit,** *f.* freedom of the press. **-meldung,** *f.* news item.
pressen ['prɛsən], *v.t.* press, squeeze, compress; strain, extrude; stamp, emboss; block (*a hat*); (*fig.*) press, urge, force, oppress; ***das preßt ihm Tränen aus den Augen,*** that draws tears from him; ***Matrosen –***, (im)press sailors; ***gepreßt voll,*** crammed full; ***gepreßtes Lachen,*** forced laugh; ***mit gepreßter Stimme,*** in a choked voice.
Presse|stelle, *f.* *See* **-amt. -stimme,** *f.* press comment(ary). **-tribüne,** *f.* (*Parl.*) press gallery. **-verlautbarung,** *f.* news *or* press release. **-vertreter,** *m.* pressman, reporter; public relations officer.
Preß|form, *f.* mould, matrix. **-futter,** *n.* compressed fodder. **-gas,** *n.* high-pressure gas. **-glanz,** *m.* gloss. **-glas,** *n.* moulded glass. **-holz,** *n.* chip-board.
pressieren [prɛ'si:rən], *v.i.* be pressing *or* urgent; (*of a p.*) be in a hurry; ***es pressiert sehr,*** there is no time to be lost; ***es pressiert nicht,*** there is no hurry.
Preß|kohle, *f.* briquette. **-kopf,** *m.* brawn, chawl. **-lauge,** *f.* expressed liquor. **-luft,** *f.* compressed air. **-luftanlage,** *f.* air compressor. **-lufthammer,** *m.* pneumatic hammer. **-masse,** *f.* *See* **-stoff. -ölschmierung,** *f.* forced-feed lubrication. **-stempel,** *m.* press die, dolly. **-stoff,** *m.* plastic (moulding compound). **-stroh,** *n.* baled straw. **-teil,** *m.* pressed section. **-torf,** *m.* pressed peat.
Pressung ['prɛsuŋ], *f.* pressing, pressure, compression.
Preßwalze ['presvaltsə], *f.* pressure-roller.
Preuße ['prɔysə], *m.* (**-n,** *pl.* **-n**) Prussian. **Preußen,** *n.* Prussia. **Preußin,** *f.* *See* **Preuße. preußisch,** *adj.* Prussian.
Pricke ['prɪkə], *f.* (*Ichth.*) lamprey. **prick(e)lig,** *adj.* prickly; pungent. **prickeln,** *v.t., v.i.* prick, prickle, sting, itch, tingle; tickle (the palate), be pungent. **Prickeln,** *n.* tingling (sensation), (*coll.*) pins and needles; pungency. **prickelnd,** *adj.* prickly; tickling; sharp, pungent; (*fig.*) thrilling, gripping; piquant, spicy.
Priel [pri:l], *m.* (**-(e)s,** *pl.* **-e**), **Priele,** *f.* (-, *pl.* **-n**) rill; channel.
Priem [pri:m], *m.* (**-(e)s,** *pl.* **-e**), **Prieme,** *f.* quid, plug (of tobacco), chew, (*vulg.*) chaw. **priemen,** *v.i.* chew (tobacco).
pries [pri:s], *see* **preisen.**
Priese ['pri:zə], *f.* neckband (*of shirt*).
priese(st) ['pri:zə(st)], *see* **preisen.**
Priester ['pri:stər], *m.* priest. **Priester|amt,** *n.* priesthood, priestly office. **-gewand,** *n.* vestment. **-hemd,** *n.* alb, surplice. **-herrschaft,** *f.* hierarchy. **Priesterin,** *f.* priestess. **priesterlich,** *adj.* priestly, sacerdotal. **Priester|rock,** *m.* cassock, vestment. **Priesterschaft,** *f.*, **Priestertum,** *n.* priesthood, clergy. **-weihe,** *f.* ordination; ***die – empfangen,*** take orders.
Prima ['pri:ma], *f.* (-, *pl.* **-men**) sixth *or* top form. **prima,** *adj.* (*Comm.*) prime, first grade, (*coll.*) first rate, A1, (*sl.*) great, swell.
Primaner [pri'ma:nər], *m.*, **Primanerin,** *f.* sixth-form boy (*or* girl).
primär [pri'mɛ:r], *adj.* (*Med.*) primary, idiopathic; (*Geol.*) protogenic. **Primär|element,** *n.* (*Elec.*) primary cell.
Primarius [pri'ma:rius], *m.* (-, *pl.* **-rien**) (*Austr.*) chief surgeon.
Primärkreis, *m.* (*Elec.*) primary circuit.
Primarschule [pri'ma:rʃu:lə], *f.* (*Swiss*) primary school, public elementary school.
Primär|spannung, *f.* (*Elec.*) primary voltage. **-strom,** *m.* (*Elec.*) primary current. **-wicklung,** *f.* (*Elec.*) primary winding.
Primas ['pri:mas], *m.* (-, *pl.* **-maten**) (*Eccl.*) primate.
Primat [pri'ma:t], **1.** *m. or n.* primacy. **2.** *m.* (**-en,** *pl.* **-en**) (*Biol.*) primate.
prima vista ['pri:ma'vɪsta], *adv.* (*Mus., Comm.*) at sight.
Prima|ware, *f.* superior *or* high grade *or* top quality goods. **-wechsel,** *m.* (*Comm.*) first of exchange, prime bill.
Primel ['pri:məl], *f.* (-, *pl.* **-n**) primrose, primula.
Primgeld ['pri:mgɛlt], *n.* (*Naut.*) primage.
primitiv [primi'ti:f], *adj.* primitive. **Primitiven,** *pl.* primitive peoples *or* races. **Primitivität** [-tivi'tɛ:t], *f.* primitiveness.
Primus ['pri:mus], *m.* head (boy) *or* top (boy) of the form.
Primzahl ['pri:mtsa:l], *f.* prime number.
Prinz [prɪnts], *m.* (**-en,** *pl.* **-en**) prince; ***– von Geblüt,*** prince of the blood. **Prinzessin** [-'tsɛsɪn], *f.* princess. **Prinzgemahl,** *m.* prince consort.
Prinzip [prɪn'tsi:p], *n.* (**-s,** *pl.* **-e** *or* **-pien**) principle; ***aus –***, on principle; ***im –***, in principle, essentially, basically. **Prinzipal** [-'pa:l], *m.* (**-s,** *pl.* **-e**) principal, chief; employer, head (*of a firm*), manager. **prinzipiell** [-pi'ɛl], *adj., adv.* *See* ***aus Prinzip.*** **Prinzipien|frage,** *f.* question of principle. **-reiter,** *m.* (*coll.*) stickler for principles, pedant, dogmatist.
prinzlich ['prɪntslɪç], *adj.* princely.
Prior ['pri:ɔr], *m.* (**-s,** *pl.* **-en**) prior. **Priorin** [-'o:rɪn], *f.* prioress.
Priorität [priori'tɛ:t], *f.* priority. **Prioritäts|-aktie,** *f.* preference share. **-anleihe,** *f.* loan on a mortgage. **-anspruch,** *m.* prior(ity) claim. **-beleg,** *m.* certified copy of documents. **-gläubiger,** *m.* privileged creditor. **-obligation,** *f.* preference bond, debenture. **-papiere,** *n.pl.* preferential stock.
Prise ['pri:zə], *f.* 1. (*Naut.*) prize; 2. pinch (*of snuff, salt etc.*). **Prisen|gelder,** *n.pl.* (*Naut.*) prize-money. **-gericht,** *n.*, **-hof,** *m.* prize-court. **-kommando,** *n.* prize-crew. **-mannschaft,** *f.* boarding party. **-recht,** *n.* right of capture.
Prisma ['prɪsma], *n.* (**-s,** *pl.* **-men**) prism. **prismatisch,** *adj.* prismatic. **Prismen|glas,** *n.* prism glass; prismatic telescope *or* binoculars. **-spektrum,** *n.* prismatic spectrum.
Pritsche ['prɪtʃə], *f.* (harlequin's) wooden sword; bat; back-seat (*of a sledge*); plank-bed; (*Mil.*) guard-bed. **pritschen,** *v.t.* slap, beat, drub; ***ich bin gepritscht,*** my hopes are dashed, I have been let down. **Pritschenwagen,** *m.* light carriage.
privat [pri'va:t], *adj.* private; personal, confidential. **Privat|adresse,** *f.* home *or* private address. **-angelegenheit,** *f.* personal matter, private affair. **-angestellte(r),** *m., f.* employee of a private firm. **-arzt,** *m.* doctor in private practice. **-bank,** *f.* private *or* commercial bank. **-besitz,** *m.* *See* **-eigentum. -dozent,** *m.* (unestablished) university lecturer. **-eigentum,** *n.* personal *or* private property. **-einkommen,** *n.* private income. **-gelehrte(r),** *m., f.* independent scholar.
Privatier [privati'e:], *m.* (**-s,** *pl.* **-s**) man of independent means.
privatim [pri'va:tim], *adv.* privately; tête-à-tête; private and confidential.

Privat|initiative, *f.* private venture; personal initiative. **–interesse,** *n.* private interest; *–n verfolgen,* have an axe to grind.

privatisieren [privatiˈziːrən], **1.** *v.i.* live on one's private income. **2.** *v.t.* return to private ownership, denationalize.

Privatissimum [privaˈtɪsimum], *n.* (**-s,** *pl.* **-ma**) (*Univ.*) individual tutorial.

Privat|klage, *f.* (*Law*) civil action. **–klinik,** *f.* nursing home. **–leben,** *n.* private life, personal life. **–lehrer,** *m.* private tutor. **–mann,** *m.* private person *or* individual. **–patient,** *m.* (*Med.*) private patient. **–person,** *f. See* **–mann. –recht,** *n.* civil law. **privatrechtlich,** *adj.* under civil law. **Privat|rücksichten,** *f.pl.* personal grounds. **–sache,** *f.* private *or* personal matter. **–schatulle,** *f.* privy purse. **–stunde,** *f.* private lesson. **–unternehmen,** *n.* private enterprise. **–unterricht,** *m.* private tuition *or* coaching, private lessons. **–wirtschaft,** *f.* free enterprise. **–wohnung,** *f.* private residence.

Privileg [priviˈleːk], *n.* (**-s,** *pl.* **-ien**) privilege, licence, charter. **privilegieren** [–ˈgiːrən], *v.t.* privilege; license, charter. **Privilegium,** *n.* (**-s,** *pl.* **-gien**) *see* **Privileg.**

pro [proː], *prep.* per; *– Jahr,* per annum; *– Kopf,* per capita, (*coll.*) per head; *– Quadratmeile,* to the square mile; *50 Pf. – Stück,* 50 pfennigs a piece *or* each. **Pro,** *n. das – und Kontra,* the pros and cons.

probat [proˈbaːt], *adj.* proved, tried, tested.

Probe [ˈproːbə], *f.* 1. trial, test, experiment, (*coll.*) try-out; probation, proof, ordeal; exhibition, demonstration (*of skill*); *eine – ablegen,* give proof of; *auf –,* on probation, on trial, (*Comm.*) on appro(val); *die – bestehen,* stand the test; *es gilt die –!* let us try it! *auf die – stellen,* (put to the) test; *zur –,* as a sample; on approval; 2. pattern, sample, specimen, test-piece, (*Metal.*) assay; (*coll. of food*) taste; *–n nehmen,* take samples; 3. (*Mus.*) audition, (*Theat.*) rehearsal; *–n (ab)halten,* rehearse, have a rehearsal; 4. (trade) mark, stamp.

Probe|abdruck, –abzug, *m.* proof (sheet). **–aufnahme,** *f.* (*Films*) screen test. **–auftrag,** *m.* trial order. **–belastung,** *f.* test load. **–bogen,** *m. See* **–abdruck. –exemplar,** *n.* specimen copy. **–fahrt,** *f.* trial run, (*Motor.*) road test. **–fall,** *m.* test-case. **–flug,** *m.* test flight. **–jahr,** *n.* year of probation. **–kandidat,** *m.* probationer, assistant master (*during year of probation*). **–muster,** *n.* experimental model, sample.

proben [ˈproːbən], *v.t., v.i.* (*Theat.*) rehearse.

Probe|nummer, *f.* specimen number *or* copy. **–schuß,** *m.* (*Artil.*) sighting shot. **–sendung,** *f.* sample sent on approval. **–stück,** *n.* sample, pattern, specimen. **probeweise,** *adv.* on approval, on trial, as a specimen, (*of a p.*) on probation. **Probezeit,** *f.* time of probation, noviciate, qualifying period.

probieren [proˈbiːrən], *v.t.* test, prove, put to the test *or* proof, (*Metal.*) assay, (*of food*) taste; (*coll.*) attempt, try. **Probieren,** *n.* (method of) trial and error; (*Prov.*) *– geht über Studieren,* practice is better than theory, the proof of the pudding is in the eating. **Probier|glas,** *n.* test-tube. **–nadel,** *f.* touch-needle. **–ofen,** *m.* assay-furnace. **–stein,** *m.* touchstone. **–tiegel,** *m.* crucible. **–waage,** *f.* assay-balance.

Problem [proˈbleːm], *n.* (**-s,** *pl.* **-e**) problem. **Problematik** [–ˈmaːtɪk], *f.* uncertainty, dubiousness, ambiguity, difficulty (in arriving at a solution). **problematisch,** *adj.* problematic(al).

Probst, *m. See* **Propst.**

Produkt [proˈdukt], *n.* (**-(e)s,** *pl.* **-e**) produce; product, result, outcome, upshot. **Produkten|börse,** *f.* produce-exchange. **–handel,** *m.* trade in home (agricultural) produce.

Produktion [produktsiˈoːn], *f.* production, yield, output. **Produktions|ausfall,** *m.* fall in *or* loss of production. **–fähigkeit,** *f.* productivity, productive capacity. **–kosten,** *pl.* cost of production. **–kraft,** *f.* productive power. **–leiter,** *m.* production manager, (*Films*) producer. **–menge,** *f.* output. **–mittel,** *n.pl.* means of production.

produktiv [produkˈtiːf], *adj.* productive, (*as a writer*) prolific. **Produktivität** [–tiviˈtɛːt], *f.* productivity.

Produzent [produˈtsɛnt], *m.* (**-en,** *pl.* **-en**) grower, producer; manufacturer. **produzieren, 1.** *v.t.* produce, grow; (*fig.*) yield, bring forward, furnish (*proofs*). **2.** *v.r.* perform *or* exhibit *or* appear in public; (*coll.*) show off, make an exhibition of o.s.

profan [proˈfaːn], *adj.* profane, secular. **Profanbau,** *m.* secular building. **profanieren** [–ˈniːrən], *v.t.* profane. **Profanierung,** *f.* profanation.

Profeß [proˈfɛs], *f.* (-, *pl.* **-(ss)e**) (*Eccl.*) profession, vow; *– tun,* take vows, take the veil.

Profession [profɛsiˈoːn], *f.* trade; profession, vocation; *Spieler von –,* professional gambler. **professionell** [–nɛl], **professioniert,** *adj.* professional; by trade, in business as. **Professionist,** *m.* (**-en,** *pl.* **-en**) (*Austr.*) tradesman, artisan.

Professor [proˈfɛsɔr], *m.* (**-s,** *pl.* **-en**) university professor; *ordentlicher –,* professor in ordinary; *außerordentlicher –,* assistant professor. **professorisch** [–ˈsoːrɪʃ], *adj.* professorial. **Professur** [–ˈsuːr], *f.* (-, *pl.* **-en**) professorship, (academic) chair.

Profi [ˈproːfi], *m.* (**-s,** *pl.* **-s**) (*Spt., coll.*) pro.

Profil [proˈfiːl], *n.* (**-s,** *pl.* **-e**) profile; side-view, section; (*of tyre*) tread; (*Av.*) airfoil section. **Profileisen,** *n.* sectional *or* structural iron, iron girders.

profilieren [profiˈliːrən], *v.t.* sketch in profile; (*Mech.*) shape; streamline; (*fig.*) outline clearly. **profiliert,** *adj.* shaped; streamlined, (*of tyres*) non-skid; (*fig.*) clearly defined, salient. **Profilierung,** *f.* (*of tyres*) tread; (*Av.*) fairing.

Profit [proˈfiːt], *m.* (**-(e)s,** *pl.* **-e**) profit, (net) proceeds. **profitabel** [–ˈtaːbəl], *adj.* profitable, lucrative. **profitgierig,** *adj.* profit-seeking. **profitieren,** *v.i.* profit, gain (*von,* by), make *or* clear a profit (from). **Profitjäger,** *m. See* **–macher. profitlich,** *adj.* (*coll.*) *see* **profitgierig;** (*dial.*) mean, stingy. **Profit|macher,** *m.* profiteer. **–macherei,** *f.* profiteering.

Profos [proˈfoːs], *m.* (**-en,** *pl.* **-en** (*Austr.* **-es,** *pl.* **-e**)) (*obs.*) provost.

Prognose [proˈgnoːzə], *f.* (*Med.*) prognosis; (*Meteor.*) forecast. **Prognostikon,** *n.* (**-s,** *pl.* **-ka** *or* **-ken**) prognostic. **prognostizieren** [–iˈtsiːrən], *v.t., v.i.* prognosticate, predict, foretell.

Programm [proˈgram], *n.* (**-s,** *pl.* **-e**) programme, prospectus; lecture, paper (*read annually in German schools*). **programmäßig, programmatisch** [–ˈmaːtɪʃ], **programmgemäß,** *adj.* according to plan *or* programme, (*coll.*) without a hitch. **Programmgestaltung,** *f.* arrangement of the programme, programming. **Programmierer,** *m.* programmer (*computers*). **Programmusik,** *f.* incidental *or* programme music. **Programmvorschau,** *f.* (*film*) trailer.

Progymnasium [proːgymˈnaːzium], *n.* (**-s,** *pl.* **-sien**) secondary school with curtailed (classical) curriculum.

Prohibitorium [prohibiˈtoːrium], *n.* (-s, *pl.* **-rien**) (*Law*) writ of prohibition.

Projekt [proˈjɛkt], *n.* (**-(e)s,** *pl.* **-e**) project, plan, proposal. **projektieren** [–ˈtiːrən], *v.t.* project, plan, propose, design.

Projektil [projɛkˈtiːl], *n.* (**-s,** *pl.* **-e**) projectile.

Projektions|apparat [projɛktsiˈoːns–], *m.* magic lantern, projector. **–bild,** *n.* lantern slide. **–mattscheibe,** *f.* ground-glass screen. **–schirm,** *m.* screen.

projizieren [projiˈtsiːrən], *v.t.* project (*a picture*), throw on the screen.

proklamieren [proklaˈmiːrən], *v.t.* proclaim.

Prokura [proˈkuːra], *f.* (*Comm.*) proxy, procuration, power of attorney. **Prokurator** [–ˈraːtɔr], *m.* (**-s,** *pl.* **-en**) proxy, attorney, procurator. **Prokurist** [–ˈrɪst], *m.* (**-en,** *pl.* **-en**) confidential *or* head clerk, deputy.

Prolet [pro'le:t], *m.* (**-en,** *pl.* **-en**) commoner; (*coll.*) clod, lout, cad. **Proletariat** [-tari'a:t], *n.* (**-(e)s,** *pl.* **-e**) proletariat, the lower classes, the workers. **Proletarier** [–'ta:riər], *m.* worker, member of the working classes, proletarian. **proletarisch,** *adj.* proletarian, lower- *or* working-class. **proletarisieren** [–'zi:rən], *v.t.* proletarianize.

Prolog [pro'lo:k], *m.* (**-s,** *pl.* **-e**) prologue.

Prolongation [prolɔŋgatsi'o:n], *f.* (*Comm.*) extension, renewal. **Prolongations|gebühr,** *f.* contango. **–geschäft,** *n.* contango business. **prolongieren** [–'gi:rɛn], *v.t.* extend, renew.

Promemoria [prome'mo:ria], *n.* (**-s,** *pl.* **-s** *or* **-rien**) memorandum; memorial.

Promenade [promə'na:də], *f.* promenade, avenue; walk, stroll. **promenieren,** *v.i.* go *or* take a walk *or* a stroll.

Promesse [pro'mɛsə], *f.* (*Comm.*) promissory note.

prominent [promi'nɛnt], *adj.* prominent, outstanding. **Prominente(r),** *m., f.* prominent p., celebrity, notable, leading figure. **Prominenz,** *f.* prominence; celebrities, leading figures, civic heads, high society.

Promotion [promotsi'o:n], *f.* (*Univ.*) graduation. **promovieren** [–'vi:rən], **1.** *v.t.* confer a degree on. **2.** *v.i.* graduate, take a degree (*an* (*Dat.*), at, (*Am.*) from).

prompt [prɔmpt], *adj.* prompt, punctual, ready, quick; – ***bezahlen,*** pay without delay, pay cash. **Promptheit,** *f.* promptness, promptitude.

Pronomen [pro'no:mən], *n.* (**-s,** *pl.* **-mina**) (*Gram.*) pronoun.

Propaganda [propa'ganda], *f.* propaganda, publicity, advertising, sales promotion. **Propagandarummel,** *m.* (*coll.*) ballyhoo. **propagieren,** *v.t.* propagate, spread, publicize.

Propeller [pro'pɛlər], *m.* propeller, air-screw. **Propeller|antrieb,** *m.* ***mit*** –, propeller-driven. **–blatt,** *n. See* **–flügel. –bö,** *f.* (*Av.*) slipstream. **–flügel,** *m.* propeller blade. **–nabe,** *f.* propeller hub. **–steigung,** *f.* propeller pitch. **–turbine,** *f.* turbo-prop. **–wind,** *m. See* **–bö.**

Prophet [pro'fe:t], *m.* (**-en,** *pl.* **-en**) prophet; (*sl.*) ***Moses und die –en,*** ready cash; ***die kleinen –en,*** the minor prophets; (*Prov.*) ***ein – gilt nichts in seinem Vaterlande,*** a prophet has no honour in his own country. **Prophetie** [–'ti:], *f. See* **Prophezeiung. Prophetin,** *f.* prophetess. **prophetisch,** *adj.* prophetic. **prophezeien** [–'tsaɪən], *v.t.* prophesy, foretell, predict. **Prophezeiung** [–'tsaɪuŋ], *f.* prophecy, prediction.

proportional [propɔrtsio'na:l], *adj.* proportionate, proportional. **Proportionalwahlrecht,** *n.* proportional representation. **proportioniert,** *adj.* proportional, proportionate; well-proportioned. **Proportionsrechnung,** *f.* (*Math.*) proportion. **Proporzwahlrecht,** *n.* (*Austr., Swiss*) *see* **Proportionalwahlrecht.**

Propst [pro:pst], *m.* (**-es,** *pl.* **⸚e**) prior; provost. **Propstei** [–'staɪ], *f.* diocese, jurisdiction *or* dwelling of a provost.

Prosa ['pro:za], *f.* prose. **Prosadichtung,** *f.* prose fiction, novel-writing. **Prosaiker** [–'za:ikər], *m.* prose-writer. **prosaisch,** *adj.* prosaic, (*coll.*) prosy. **Prosaist** [–'ɪst], *m.* (**-en,** *pl.* **-en**) *see* **Prosaiker.**

Proselyt [proze'ly:t], *m.* (**-en,** *pl.* **-en**) proselyte. **Proselytenmacherei,** *f.* proselytism.

prosit! ['pro:zit], *int.* your health! (*coll.*) cheers! (*sl.*) bottoms up! here's mud in your eye! – ***Mahlzeit,*** good appetite! (*iron.*) you may whistle for it! fiddlesticks! (*Am.*) applesauce! – ***Neujahr!*** a Happy New Year.

Prospekt [pro'spɛkt], *m.* (**-(e)s,** *pl.* **-e**) 1. prospectus, leaflet; 2. prospect, (distant) view; 3. (*Theat.*) backcloth; organ screen.

prost! [pro:st], *int. See* **prosit.**

prostituieren [prostitu'i:rən], *v.t.* prostitute. **Prostituierte,** *f.* prostitute. **Prostitution** [–tsi'o:n], *f.* prostitution.

Proszenium [pro'stse:nium], *n.* (**-s,** *pl.* **-nien**) (*Theat.*) proscenium. **Proszeniumsloge,** *f.* stage-box.

protegieren [prote'ʒi:rən], *v.t.* patronize, (*coll.*) take under one's wing.

Protektion [protɛktsi'o:n], *f.* protection, patronage. **Protektionswirtschaft,** *f.* protectionism.

Protektorat [protɛkto'ra:t], *n.* protectorate; ***unter dem – von,*** under the patronage *or* auspices of.

Protest [pro'tɛst], *m.* (**-es,** *pl.* **-e**) protest; ***zu – gehen lassen,*** dishonour (*a cheque*); ***mit – zurückkommen,*** be dishonoured; – ***mangels Annahme,*** protest for non-acceptance; – ***erheben,*** protest, raise *or* enter a protest; – ***einlegen,*** lodge a protest.

Protestant [protɛs'tant], *m.* (**-en,** *pl.* **-en**) Protestant. **protestantisch,** *adj.* Protestant. **Protestantismus** [–'tɪsmus], *m.* Protestantism.

protestieren [protɛs'ti:rən], **1.** *v.i.* protest (***gegen,*** against), object (to), take objection (to) *or* exception (at). **2.** *v.t.* protest (*a bill etc.*); ***einen Wechsel – lassen,*** have a bill protested.

Protest|sturm, *m.* storm of protest, outcry. **–versammlung,** *f.* indignation meeting.

Prothese [pro'te:zə], *f.* artificial limb; artificial teeth, denture.

Protokoll [proto'kɔl], *n.* (**-s,** *pl.* **-e**) record, transcript; protocol, proceedings, minutes; ***im –,*** on record; ***in das – eintragen,*** *see* **protokollieren;** (***das***) ***– führen,*** take down *or* draw up the minutes; ***zu – geben,*** depose, place on record, state in evidence; ***zu – nehmen,*** record, take down (*a deposition*). **protokollarisch** [–'la:rɪʃ], *adj.* (entered) in the minutes, on record. **Protokoll|aufnahme,** *f.* record(ing), report (*of a meeting*). **–buch,** *n.* minute-book. **–eintragung,** *f.* minute; entry in the minute-book. **–führer,** *m.* (minutes-)secretary; (*Law*) clerk of the court, recorder. **protokollieren,** *v.t.* enter in *or* keep the minutes; take down (on record), (enter in the) record.

Proto|plasma [proto-], *n.* protoplasma. **–typ,** *m.* prototype. **Protozoen** [–'tso:ən], *n.pl.* protozoa.

Protuberanz [protube'rants], *f.* (-, *pl.* **-en**) protuberance; (*Astr.*) (solar) prominence.

Protz ['prɔts], *m.* (**-en,** *pl.* **-en**) ostentatious person, snob, (*coll.*) toff.

Protze ['prɔtsə], *f.* (*Artil.*) limber.

protzen ['prɔtsən], *v.i.* be a snob, be purse-proud, put on airs, flaunt one's wealth; – ***mit,*** flaunt, parade, make a show of, show off with. **protzenhaft,** *adj.* snobbish, purse-proud. **Protzentum,** *n.* snobbism, snobbishness.

protzig ['prɔtsɪç], *adj. See* **protzenhaft;** ostentatious, (*coll.*) showy; (*of a p.*) stuck-up.

Provenienz [provəni'ɛnts], *f.* origin, source, derivation, provenance.

Proviant [provi'ant], *m.* provisions, victuals; (*Mil.*) rations, supplies, stores. **Proviant|amt,** *n.* (*Mil.*) supply depot. **–kolonne,** *f.* (*Mil.*) supply column. **–lager,** *n.* (*Mil.*) ration store. **–sack,** *m.* haversack. **–wagen,** *m.* (*Mil.*) ration truck. **–wesen,** *n.* (*Mil.*) commissariat.

Provinz [pro'vɪnts], *f.* (-, *pl.* **-en**) province, provinces; ***in der – leben,*** live in the country. **provinzial** [–i'a:l], *adj.* provincial, regional. **Provinzial,** *m.* (**-s,** *pl.* **-e**) (*Eccl.*) provincial, father superior. **Provinzialismus** [–'lɪsmus], *m.* (-, *pl.* **-men**) provincialism, dialect word. **provinziell** [–'ɛl], *adj.* provincial, narrow-minded, unenlightened. **Provinzler,** *m.* provincial, country cousin, country bumpkin.

Provision [provizi'o:n], *f.* commission, brokerage. **provisions|frei,** *adj.* free of commission. **–pflichtig,** *adj.* subject to commission.

Provisor [pro'vi:zɔr], *m.* (**-s,** *pl.* **-en**) dispenser; chemist's *or* pharmacist's assistant.

provisorisch [provi'zo:rɪʃ], *adj.* provisional, temporary, makeshift; ***–e Regierung,*** caretaker government. **Provisorium,** *n.* (**-s,** *pl.* **-rien**) provisional *or* temporary arrangement, makeshift.

Provokation [provokatsi'o:n], *f.* provocation. **provozieren** [–'tsi:rən], *v.t.* provoke; challenge. **provozierend,** *adj.* provocative.

Prozedur [protse'du:r], *f.* procedure; (*Law*) proceedings.

Prozent [pro'tsɛnt], *n.* (*Swiss m.*) (**-s,** *pl.* **-e**) per cent., percentage; ***zu sechs –,*** at six per cent.; ***wie viel –?*** what percentage? ***zu hohen –en,*** at a high rate of interest. **-prozentig,** *adj.suff.* per cent. **Prozentsatz,** *m.* percentage, rate of interest, (*coll.*) proportion, part. **prozentual** [–u'a:l], *adj.* (expressed as) percentage; proportional.

Prozeß [pro'tsɛs], *m.* (**-(ss)es,** *pl.* **-(ss)e**) (*Law*) action, lawsuit, trial, (legal) proceedings; operation, procedure, process; ***einen – mit ihm anfangen, ihm einen – anhängen, einen – gegen ihn anhängig machen*** or ***gegen ihn anstrengen,*** bring an action against him, institute (legal) proceedings against him; ***im – liegen,*** be at law, be involved in a lawsuit; ***ihm den – machen wegen,*** put him on trial for; ***einen – führen,*** conduct a case; (*fig.*) ***kurzen – machen mit,*** make short work of; ***der – schwebt noch,*** the case is still pending *or* sub judice; ***einen – gewinnen,*** gain one's case. **Prozeßbevollmächtige(r),** *m., f.* attorney (for the plaintiff). **prozeßfähig,** *adj.* actionable. **Prozeß|führer,** *m.* plaintiff; plaintiff's counsel. **-führung,** *f.* conduct of the case. **-gegner,** *m.* opposing party.

prozessieren [protsɛ'si:rən], *v.i.* carry on a lawsuit, be at *or* go to law (with), litigate.

Prozession [protsɛsi'o:n], *f.* procession.

Prozeß|kosten, *pl.* legal charges, (law-)costs. **-krämer,** *m.* (*coll.*) litigious person. **-vollmacht,** *f.* power of attorney.

prüde ['pry:də], *adj.* prudish. **Prüderie** [–'ri:], *f.* prudishness, prudery.

prüfen ['pry:fən], *v.t.* test, examine (*also at school etc.*), inspect, scrutinize, investigate, (*coll.*) look into; audit, check (*an account*); assay (*ore*); review (*a decision*); (*Tech.*) inspect, check, control; (*fig.*) (put to the) test, try; weigh, consider; ***geprüfte Lehrerin,*** certificated teacher; ***auf Herz und Nieren –,*** (*B.*) try the heart and the reins; (*coll.*) put to a searching test; ***auf Richtigkeit –,*** verify. **Prüfer,** *m.* examiner, inspector, tester, checker, (*Comm.*) auditor, (*Min.*) assayer.

Prüf|feld, *n.* (*Tech.*) test-bay. **-gerät,** *n.* test(ing) equipment. **Prüfling,** *m.* (**-s,** *pl.* **-e**) examinee, (examination) candidate; *see also* **Prüfstück. Prüf|stand,** *m.* test-bench. **-standversuch,** *m.* (*Motor.*) bench *or* (*Am.*) block test. **-stein,** *m.* touchstone, criterion, test.

Prüfung ['pry:fuŋ], *f.* examination (*also at school etc.*), scrutiny, investigation; check, test, trial; inspection, checking, verification, (*coll.*) check-up; (*Comm.*) audit, (*Law*) review; (*fig.*) visitation, affliction, ordeal; ***eine – machen,*** (*coll.*) ***in die – steigen,*** sit *or* take an *or* (*coll.*) go in for an examination; ***die – bestehen,*** pass the examination; ***in der – durchfallen,*** fail the examination; (***in***) ***einer – unterliegen,*** fail to get through a test, succumb to temptation. **Prüfungs|arbeit,** *f.* examination paper. **-ausschuß,** *m.,* **-behörde,** *f.* board of examiners, examination board. **-bericht,** *m.* test-report; auditor's report. **-bestimmungen,** *f.pl.* regulations for the conduct of an examination. **-ergebnis,** *n.* examination results. **-fach,** *n.* examination subject. **-kommission,** *f. See* **-ausschuß. -ordnung,** *f. See* **-bestimmungen. -zeugnis,** *n.* certificate, diploma.

Prügel ['pry:gəl], *m.* cudgel, stick; *pl.* thrashing, caning; ***einen Tracht –,*** a sound thrashing. **Prügelei** [–'laɪ], *f.* brawl, (*coll.*) row, scrap. **Prügel|junge, -knabe,** *m.* scapegoat; whipping-boy. **prügeln, 1.** *v.t.* beat, thrash, cane. **2.** *v.r.* fight, (*coll.*) scrap. **Prügel|strafe,** *f.* corporal punishment, caning, birching, flogging. **-weg,** *m.* (*Mil.*) corduroy road.

Prünelle [pry'nɛlə], *f.* prune.

Prunk [pruŋk], *m.* pomp, splendour, magnificence, state, show, display. **Prunkbett,** *n.* bed of state. **prunken,** *v.i.* be resplendent; ***– mit,*** flaunt, parade, make a show of, show off; boast of, vaunt. **Prunk|gemach,** *n. See* **-saal. -gewand,** *n.* state-attire. **prunkhaft,** *adj.* ostentatious, showy. **prunklos,** *adj.* unostentatious, unpretentious. **Prunk|saal,** *m.* stateroom. **-stück,** *n.* (*coll.*) show-piece. **-sucht,** *f.* ostentation. **prunk|süchtig,** *adj.* pompous, ostentatious. **-voll,** *adj.* splendid, gorgeous.

prusten ['pru:stən], *v.i.* snort; sneeze violently; burst out laughing.

Pseudonym [psɔydo'ny:m], *n.* (**-s,** *pl.* **-e**) pseudonym, nom-de-plume, assumed name. **pseudonym,** *adj.* pseudonymous, fictitious.

pst! [pst], *int.* hush!

Psychiater [psyçi'a:tər], *m.* psychiatrist.

psychisch ['psyçɪʃ], *adj.* psychic(al).

Psycho|analyse [psyço–], *f.* psycho-analysis. **-analytiker,** *m.* psycho-analyst. **Psychologe,** *m.* (**-n,** *pl.* **-n**) psychologist. **psychologisch,** *adj.* psychological.

Psychose [psy'ço:zə], *f.* psychosis.

Pubertät [pubɛr'tɛ:t], *f.* puberty.

publik [pu'bli:k], *adj.* public; ***– machen,*** publicize. **Publikation** [–katsi'o:n], *f.* publication, publishing; published paper *or* book.

Publikum ['pu:blikum], *n.* 1. (**-s,** *no pl.*) public; audience, spectators, bystanders; readers; ***das große*** or ***breite –,*** the general public; 2. (**-s,** *pl.* **-ka**) open *or* public lecture.

publizieren [publi'tsi:rən], *v.t.* publish; make public, promulgate; prove (*a will*). **Publizist,** *m.* (**-en,** *pl.* **-en**) political commentator, publicist, journalist. **Publizistik,** *f.* (political) journalism.

Puddeleisen ['pudəlaɪzən], *n.* puddled iron. **puddeln,** *v.t.* puddle (*metal*); (*dial.*) paddle, splash; potter about. **Puddelofen,** *m.* puddling furnace.

Pudding ['pudɪŋ], *m.* (**-s,** *pl.* **-e** *or* **-s**) pudding, (*usu.*) custard, blancmange.

Pudel ['pu:dəl], *m.* 1. poodle; ***wie ein begossener – abziehen,*** slink off with one's tail between one's legs; ***wie ein begossener – dastehen,*** look crestfallen, stand aghast; ***des -s Kern,*** the gist of the matter; 2. drudge, (*sl.*) skivvy; 3. blunder; miss (*at skittles*); 4. (*Studs. sl.*) university beadle, bulldog. **pudeln,** *v.i.* miss (*at skittles*). **pudel|nackt,** *adj.* stark naked. **-naß,** *adj.* drenched, dripping *or* sopping wet. **-wohl,** *adj.* (*coll.*) ***sich – fühlen,*** feel great, feel on top of the world.

Puder ['pu:dər], *m.* (toilet) powder. **Puder|dose,** *f.* vanity-case, compact. **-mantel,** *m.* peignoir. **pudern,** *v.t.* (*v.r.*) powder (o.s. *or* one's face). **Puderquaste,** *f.* powder-puff.

puff! [puf], *int.* puff! bang! **Puff, 1.** *m.* (**-(e)s,** *pl.* **¨-e**) 1. bump, crash, bang; 2. cuff, thump, blow; push, nudge; ***er kann einen (guten) – vertragen,*** he can take a lot, he is thick-skinned. **2.** *m.* (**-(e)s,** *pl.* **-e**) pouffe, (*sl.*) brothel. **3.** *n.* backgammon. **Puff|ärmel,** *m.* puffed sleeve. **-bohne,** *f.* horsebean. **-brett,** *n.* backgammon-board.

puffen ['pufən], **1.** *v.t.* shove, jostle, push, nudge; thump, whack, cuff. **2.** *v.i.* 1. chuff, chug, puff; pop, go bang; (*coll.*) ***daß es pufft,*** with a vengeance; 2. play backgammon.

Puffer ['pufər], *m.* 1. buffer, cushion; 2. (*dial.*) potato-fritter; 3. popgun. **Puffer|batterie,** *f.* (*Elec.*) balancing battery. **-staat,** *m.* buffer state.

Puff|mais, *m.* popcorn. **-spiel,** *n.* backgammon.

pulen ['pu:lən], *v.i.* (*dial.*) pick, finger.

Pulk [pulk], *m.* (**-s,** *pl.* **-e**) (*Av.*) group, formation.

Pulle ['pulə], *f.* (*dial.*) bottle.

pullen ['pulən], *v.i.* 1. (*dial.*) row; 2. pull *or* rein in (*a horse*); 3. (*coll.*) piddle.

Puls [puls], *m.* (**-es,** *pl.* **-e**) pulse; ***erhöhter –,*** high pulse; ***ihm den – fühlen,*** feel his pulse, (*fig.*) sound him. **Puls|ader,** *f.* artery; ***die große –,*** aorta. **pulsen, pulsieren** [–'si:rən], *v.i.* pulsate, vibrate, throb, (*fig.*) pulse (***von,*** with). **Puls|schlag,** *m.* pulsation, pulse (beat). **-stillstand,** *m.,* **-stockung,** *f.* cessation of the pulse. **-wärmer,** *m.* mitten, wristlet. **-zahl,** *f.* pulse rate.

Pult [pult], *n.* (**-(e)s,** *pl.* **-e**) desk, lectern, reading-desk. **Pultdach,** *n.* lean-to roof.

Pulver ['pulfər], *n.* powder; gunpowder; (*sl.*) brass, dough; ***zu – und Blei verurteilt,*** condemned to be shot; (*coll.*) ***er hat das – nicht erfunden,*** he will never set the Thames on fire; ***ein Schuß –,*** a whiff of powder; ***sein – unnütz verschießen,*** labour in vain; ***sein – (vorzeitig) verschießen,*** shoot one's bolt; ***keinen Schuß – wert,*** not worth powder and shot, not worth a rap, no good at all; ***er hat – gerochen,*** he has been in the front line.

pulverartig ['pulfərˀartıç], *adj.* powdery. **Pulver|-dampf,** *m.* powder-smoke. **–faß,** *n.* powder-barrel *or* keg; ***auf dem – sitzen,*** sit on top of a volcano. **–form,** *f. in –*, pulverized. **pulverisieren** [–ri'zi:rən], *v.t.* pulverize, (reduce to) powder. **Pulver|kammer,** *f.* powder-magazine. **–korn,** *n.* percussion primer; grain of powder. **–ladung,** *f.* powder charge. **pulvern, 1.** *v.t. See* **pulverisieren. 2.** *v.i.* fire, shoot (*with a gun*). **Pulver|satz,** *m.* powder train. **–schnee,** *m.* dry powdery snow. **–turm,** *m. See* **–kammer.**

Pummel ['puməl], *m.* (*coll.*) plump little person. **pummelig,** *adj.* plump, chubby, (*coll.*) roly-poly.

Pump [pump], *m.* (**-(e)s,** *pl.* **-e**) 1. hollow sound; 2. (*coll.*) credit, trust, (*sl.*) tick; (*sl.*) ***auf –,*** on tick.

Pumpe ['pumpə], *f.* pump. **pumpen,** *v.t., v.i.* pump; (*coll.*) lend, loan, give *or* let have on tick; (*coll.*) ***sich*** (*Dat.*) ***– von,*** borrow from, have on loan from, touch for (*money*). **Pumpenschwengel,** *m.* pump-handle.

Pumpernickel ['pumpərnıkəl], *m.* (black) Westphalian ryebread.

Pump|hose(n), *f.(pl.)* baggy trousers, plus-fours. **–station,** *f.*, **–werk,** *n.* pumping station.

Punkt [puŋkt], *m.* (**-(e)s,** *pl.* **-e**) point, dot, spot; place, spot; (*Typ.*) full stop; period, (*fig.*) point, topic, item, matter, subject; (*Comm., Law*) article, clause, head(ing), (*Law*) charge, count, (*Spt. etc.*) point, mark; ***auf dem –e, wo die Sachen stehen,*** as matters stand; (***bis***) ***auf den –,*** to a T, exactly; ***bis zu einem*** (***gewissen***) ***–,*** up to a point; ***– für –,*** point by point, item by item, in detail; ***höchster –,*** climax; ***in vielen –en,*** in many respects, on many points; (*Geom.*) ***sich in einem – schneiden,*** intersect at a point; ***den – aufs i setzen,*** dot one's *i*'s, be meticulous; (*Boxing*) ***nach –en siegen,*** win on points; ***der springende –,*** the salient point; ***der strittige –,*** (point at) issue; ***auf dem toten –,*** at a deadlock, (*Mech.*) at dead centre; ***– zehn Uhr,*** on the stroke of ten; (*Boxing*) ***nach –en verlieren,*** be outpointed; ***der wunde –,*** the weak *or* sore point.

Punktation [puŋktatsi'o:n], *f.* draft agreement.

Punktfeuer ['puŋktfɔyər], *n.* (*Artil.*) converging *or* concentrated fire, (*machine gun*) single rounds. **punkt|förmig,** *adj.* punctate. **–frei,** *adj.* (*of commodities*) off-the-ration, unrationed.

punktieren [puŋk'ti:rən], *v.t.* point, dot; (*Gram., Typ.*) punctuate; (*Med.*) puncture, tap; (*Art*) spot, speckle, stipple; (*Typ.*) ***punktierte Linie,*** dotted rule *or* (*coll.*) line. **Punktier|kunst,** *f.* geomancy; stippling. **–nadel,** *f.* (*Med.*) puncture needle, (*Art*) stipple. **–rädchen,** *n.* dotting-wheel.

Punktion [puŋktsi'o:n], *f. See* **Punktur.**

pünktlich ['pyŋktlıç], *adj.* punctual, prompt; exact, accurate, precise, painstaking, conscientious; ***– (da) sein,*** be on time; ***–er Gehorsam,*** strict obedience. **Pünktlichkeit,** *f.* punctuality; conscientiousness; ***mit militärischer –,*** with military precision.

Punkt|linie, *f.* dotted line. **–muster,** *n.* polka-dot pattern. **–niederlage,** *f.* (*Boxing*) defeat on points. **punktpflichtig,** *adj.* (*of rationed goods*) available on points. **Punkt|richter,** *m.* (*Boxing*) (ringside) judge. **–schweißung,** *f.* spot-welding. **–sieg,** *m.* (*Boxing*) win on points. **–sieger,** *m.* winner on points. **–system,** *n.* points rationing scheme.

Punktum ['puŋktum], *n.* (*Typ.*) full stop, period; (*coll.*) ***und damit –!*** that's that! let's have no more of that! there's the end of it! that's flat!

Punktur [puŋk'tu:r], *f.* (-, *pl.* **-en**) (*Med.*) puncture, tap(ping).

Punkt|zahl, *f.* (*Spt.*) score. **–ziel,** *n.* (*Mil.*) individual *or* pin-pointed target.

Punsch [punʃ], *m.* (**-es,** *pl.* **-e** *or* **¨-e**) punch (*drink*). **Punsch|bowle, –schüssel,** *f.* punch-bowl.

Punzarbeit ['puntsˀarbaıt], *f.* tooling. **Punze,** *f.* (*Austr.*), **Punzen,** *m.* punch (*tool*). **punzen, punzieren** [–'tsi:rən], *v.t.* punch, tool, chase, emboss; hallmark.

Pup [pu:p], *m.* (**-(e)s,** *pl.* **-e**) (*vulg.*) fart. **pupen,** *v.i.* break wind, (*vulg.*) fart.

pupillarisch [pupi'la:rıʃ], *adj.* pupil(l)ar(y).

[1]**Pupille** [pu'pılə], *f.* (*obs.*) orphan, ward.

[2]**Pupille,** *f.* pupil (*of the eye*).

Pupillen|abstand, *m.* distance between *or* separation of the pupils. **–erweiterung,** *f.* dilation of the pupil. **–gelder,** *n.pl.* property of a ward *or* of a minor. **–gericht,** *n.* court of chancery. **–verengung,** *f.* contraction of the pupil.

Püppchen ['pypçən], *n.* little doll; (*coll.*) pet, (*sl.*) popsy.

Puppe ['pupə], *f.* doll, puppet (*also fig.*), marionette; lay figure, dummy; (*Ent.*) chrysalis, pupa; stack, stook (*hay, corn*); (*sl.*) ***bis in die –n,*** till the cows come home. **Puppen|gesicht,** *n.* pretty face, face like a doll. **–haus,** *n.* doll's house. **–hülle,** *f.* (*Ent.*) cocoon. **–spiel,** *n. See* **–theater. –stand,** *m.* (*Ent.*) chrysalis state. **–stube,** *f. See* **–haus. –theater,** *n.* puppet-show; puppet-play. **–wagen,** *m.* doll's pram.

puppern ['pupərn], *v.i.* (*dial.*) throb; tremble, palpitate.

Pups [pu:ps], *m.* (**-es,** *pl.* **-e**), **pupsen,** *v.i.* (*vulg.*) *see* **Pup, pupen.**

pur [pu:r], *adj.* pure, sheer; neat (*drink*).

Püree [py're:], *n.* (**-s,** *pl.* **-s**) *or f.* (-, *pl.* **-s**) purée, mash.

Purgans ['purgans], *n.* (-, *pl.* **-ganzien** *or* **-gantia**), (*Austr.*) **Purganz** [pur'gants], *f.* (-, *pl.* **-en**), **Purgativ** [purga'ti:f], *n.* (**-s,** *pl.* **-e**) purgative, laxative, aperient. **purgieren** [–'gi:rən], *v.t., v.i.* purge; boil off. **Purgiermittel,** *n. See* **Purgativ.**

Puritaner [puri'ta:nər], *m.* Puritan. **puritanisch,** *adj.* puritan(ical). **Puritanismus** [–'nısmus], *m.* Puritanism.

Purpur ['purpur], *m.* 1. purple; crimson, scarlet; 2. purple *or* scarlet robe. **Purpurhuhn,** *n.* (*Orn.*) purple gallinule (*Porphyrio porphyrio*). **purpur|-farben, –farbig, purpurn,** *adj.* purple, scarlet, crimson. **Purpurreiher,** *m.* (*Orn.*) purple heron (*Ardea purpurea*). **purpur|rot,** *adj. See* **–farben.**

purren ['purən], **1.** *v.i.* purr, hum, buzz. **2.** *v.t.* 1. (*Naut.*) call out (*the watch*); 2. poke, stir up (*fire*), (*fig.*) tease, incite.

Pürsch [pyrʃ], *f. See* **Pirsch.**

Purzelbaum ['purtsəlbaum], *m.* somersault; ***einen – schlagen,*** turn a somersault. **purzeln,** *v.i.* tumble (head over heels), stumble, trip. **Purzeltaube,** *f.* tumbler (pigeon).

pusselig ['pusəlıç], *adj.* (*dial.*) sweet, darling, pretty; fiddling, footling. **pusseln,** *v.i.* (*coll.*) potter about, fiddle (about *or* with), footle. **pußlig,** *adj. See* **pusselig.**

Puste ['pu:st], *f.* (*coll.*) breath; (*coll.*) ***er hat keine – mehr, die – geht ihm aus,*** he is out of breath.

Pustel ['pustəl], *f.* (-, *pl.* **-n**) pustule, pimple.

pusten ['pu:stən], *v.i.* (*coll.*) puff, blow, pant; (*Draughts*) huff; (*coll.*) ***darauf puste ich,*** I snap my fingers at it. **Pusterohr,** *n.* blowpipe; pea-shooter.

Putchen ['pu:tçən], *n.* (*nursery talk*) chuckie, chuck-chuck. **Pute** ['pu:tə], *f.* turkey-hen; (*coll.*) ***dumme –,*** silly goose. **Puter,** *m.* turkey-cock. **Puterbraten,** *m.* roast turkey. **puterrot,** *adj.* (as) red as turkey-cock *or* a lobster. **Puthahn,** *m. See* **Puter. Putput,** *n.* (**-s,** *pl.* -) *see* **Putchen.**

Putsch [putʃ], *m.* (**-es,** *pl.* **-e**) armed (up)rising, insurrection, coup, riot; (*Swiss*) push, shove. **putschen,** *v.i.* riot, (rise in) revolt. **Putschist** [–'tʃıst], *m.* (**-en,** *pl.* **-en**) rioter.

Putte ['putə], *f.* (*Art*) putto (*usu. pl.* putti).

Putz [puts], *m.* 1. (elegant) attire, finery; trimming, ornaments, adornment; ***im –,*** in full dress; ***dem –***

ergeben, fond of dress; dressy; 2. (*Build.*) plaster, rough-cast; *unter* –, plastered over. **Putz|arbeit,** *f.* plasterwork. **–artikel,** *m.pl.* millinery.

putzen ['putsən], **1.** *v.t.* 1. clean, cleanse, scour, scrub, polish, brighten, furbish up; clean, polish (*shoes*); snuff (*a candle*), trim (*a lamp*), blow *or* wipe (*one's nose*), brush (*one's teeth*); curry, groom (*a horse*); prune, lop (*tree*); pluck (*fowl*); 2. decorate, adorn; 3. plaster, rough-cast (*a wall*). **2.** *v.r.* dress up, smarten o.s. up.

Putzer ['putsər], *m.*, **Putzerin,** *f.* cleaner; (*Mil.*) batman. **Putz|frau,** *f.* charwoman, (*Am.*) scrub-woman. **–geschäft,** *n.* milliner's (shop). **–händlerin,** *f.* milliner.

putzig ['putsıç], *adj.* (*coll.*) funny, queer, quaint, droll; (*dial.*) small, tiny.

Putz|kram, *m.* millinery, finery. **–lappen,** *m.* cleaning rag, duster. **–leiste,** *f.* (decorative) window-frame. **–macherin,** *f.* milliner. **–mittel,** *n.* cleaner, cleansing agent, detergent; polish, polishing material. **–pulver,** *n.* scouring powder. **–schere,** *f.* (candle) snuffers. **–stein,** *m.* bath-brick. **–stock,** *m.* cleaning-rod (*of a gun*). **–sucht,** *f.* dressiness, love of finery. **putzsüchtig,** *adj.* dressy, fond of finery. **Putz|tuch,** *n.* polishing cloth. **–waren,** *f.pl. See* **–kram. –werg,** *n.*, **–wolle,** *f.* cotton waste. **–zeug,** *n.* cleaning utensils *or* materials.

Pygmäe [py'gmε:ə], *m.* (**-n,** *pl.* **-n**) pigmy. **pygmäenhaft,** *adj.* pigmy.

Pyjama [pi'dʒa:ma], *m.* (**-s,** *pl.* **-s**) pyjamas.

Pyramide [pyra'mi:də], *f.* pyramid; stack (*of rifles*); (*Mil.*) – *ansetzen, die Gewehre in –n* (*zusammen*)*setzen,* pile arms. **Pyramidenwürfel,** *m.* octahedron.

Pyrenäen [pyre'nε:ən], *pl.* Pyrenees. **pyrenäisch,** *adj.* Pyrenean; *–e Halbinsel,* Iberian Peninsular.

Pyrit [py'ri:t], *m.* (**-es,** *pl.* **-e**) pyrites.

pyrogen [pyro'ge:n], *adj.* pyrogenic. **pyrophor,** *adj.* pyrophoric, pyrophorus. **Pyrosilin,** *n.* guncotton, nitrocellulose, pyroxylin. **Pyrotechnik,** *f.* pyrotechnics, fireworks.

Pyrrhussieg ['pyruszi:k], *m.* Pyrrhic victory.

pythagoreisch [pytago're:ıʃ], *adj.* Pythagorean; *–er Lehrsatz,* Pythagoras' theorem.

Q

Q, q [ku:], *n.* Q, q. (*See Index of Abbreviations.*)

Quabbe ['kvabə], *f.* fatty growth, wen; tadpole; quagmire. **Quabbel,** *m.* flabby mass. **quabbelig,** *adj.* flabby, wobbly, jelly-like. **quabbeln,** *v.i.* wobble, quiver, shake like a jelly; be flabby (*of flesh*); (*dial.*) *ich quabbele,* I feel queasy. **quabblig,** *adj. See* **quabbelig.**

Quackelei [kvakə'laı], *f.* (-, *pl.* **-en**) silly talk, nonsense. **Quackel|fritz,** *m.*, **–liese,** *f.* (*coll.*) chatterbox; pernickerty p., niggler. **quackeln,** *v.i.* (*coll.*) chatter, babble, prattle (*see* **quakeln**); shilly-shally, dilly-dally, hum and ha.

Quacksalber ['kvakzalbər], *m.* quack (doctor), charlatan. **Quacksalberei** [–'raı], *f.* quackery. **Quacksalbermittel,** *n.* quack remedy *or* medicine. **quacksalbern,** *v.i.* practise quackery; dabble (*mit*, in); – *an* (*Dat.*), doctor (*a p.*).

Quaddel ['kvadəl], *f.* (-, *pl.* **-n**) itchy swelling *or* lump. **Quaddelsucht,** *f.* nettle-rash.

Quader ['kva:dər,] *f.* (-, *pl.* **-n**) *or m.* squared stone; freestone, ashlar. **Quader|stein,** *m.* ashlar. **–werk,** *n.* bound masonry.

Quadrant [kva'drant], *m.* (**-en,** *pl.* **-en**) quadrant; (*Surv.*) clinometer.

Quadrat [kva'dra:t], *n.* (**-s,** *pl.* **-e**) square; (*Mus.*) natural; (*Typ.*) quadrat; block (*of houses*); *zum* or *auf das* or *ins – erheben,* square (*a number*); *im – der Entfernung,* as the square of the distance. **quadrat,** *adj. See* **quadratisch. Quadrätchen,** *n.* (*Typ.*) M-quadrat; *halbes* –, N-quadrat. **quadratisch,** *adj.* square, quadratic; tetragonal. **Quadrat|meter,** *n.* square metre. **–pyramide,** *f.* pentahedron. **–schein,** *m.* (*Astr.*) quartile.

Quadratur [kvadra'tu:r], *f.* quadrature, squaring (*of the circle*).

Quadrat|würzel, *f.* square root. **–zahl,** *f.* square (number).

quadrieren [kva'dri:rən], *v.t.* (*Math.*) square.

Quadriga [kva'dri:ga], *f.* (–, *pl.* **-gen**) quadriga, four-in-hand. **Quadrille** [–'drıljə, (*Austr.*) –'drıl], *f.* quadrille. **Quadrillion** [–i'o:n], *f.* a million million million million, 10 to the power of 24. **quadrupel** [–'ru:pəl], *adj.* quadruple.

quakeln ['kva:kəln], *v.i.* (*dial.*) chatter, babble, blether.

quaken ['kva:kən], *v.i.* quack (*ducks*); croak (*frogs*); (*coll.*) *see* **quakeln, quackeln.**

quäken ['kvε:kən], *v.i.* squeak; *–de Stimme,* squeaky voice.

Quäker ['kvε:kər], *m.* Quaker. **Quäker|bund,** *m.* Society of Friends. **–speisung,** *f.* Friends Relief Organization. **Quäkertum,** *n.* Quakerism.

Qual ['kva:l], *f.* (-, *pl.* **-en**) torment, torture, agony, pangs, (excruciating) pain; (*mental*) anguish, suffering, ordeal, tribulation, affliction; (*coll.*) drudgery, burden.

quälen ['kvε:lən], **1.** *v.t.* torture, torment; agonize, rack; (*mental*) afflict, harrow, distress, cause pain; prey on the mind, haunt; (*coll.*) tantalize, pester, molest, harass, annoy, bother, plague, worry; *zu Tode* –, kill by (slow) torture; (*fig.*) worry to death, worry the life out of. **2.** *v.r.* toil, slave, drudge; *sich umsonst* –, labour in vain. **Quäler,** *m.* tormentor, torturer; bore. **Quälerei** [–'raı], *f.* tormenting; torments, torture; vexation, annoyance, pestering, persecution; drudgery. **quälerisch,** *adj.* tormenting; vexatious. **Quälgeist,** *m.* tormentor, bore, nuisance, plague, pest.

Qualifikation [kvalifikatsi'o:n], *f.* qualification; eligibility, fitness, competence, capacity. **Qualifikations|freilos,** *n.* (*Spt.*) bye. **–kampf,** *m.* qualifying contest. **qualifizieren** [–'tsi:rən], **1.** *v.t.* qualify, fit, make eligible (*zu*, for); mark, denote, define, describe (*als*, as). **2.** *v.r.* qualify, (show *or* prove o.s. to) be fit *or* eligible *or* suitable (*zu*, for).

Qualität [kvali'tε:t], *f.* 1. quality; grade, brand, sort; *erster* –, high-grade, top-quality, (*coll.*) first-rate; *mittlerer* –, middling, mediocre; *schlechter* –, low-grade-, poor-quality; 2. (*Chess*) capture of castle by bishop or knight; *kleine* –, capture of bishop by knight.

qualitativ [kvalita'ti:f], *adj.* in quality, qualitative.

Qualitäts|arbeit, *f.* high-quality work(manship). **–fehler,** *m.* defect, flaw. **–stahl,** *m.* high-grade steel. **–ware,** *f.* high-class article, top-quality product, (*coll.*) good value.

Qualle ['kvalə], *f.* 1. jellyfish, medusa; 2. (*vulg.*) phlegm, gob.

Qualm [kvalm], *m.* thick *or* dense smoke; fumes. **qualmen, 1.** *v.i.* steam; smoke; (*fig.*) be in a towering rage. **2.** *v.t.* smoke (*cigars etc.*) heavily. **Qualmer,** *m.* (*coll.*) inveterate smoker. **qualmig,** *adj.* steaming; smoky.

Qualster ['kvalstər], *m.* (*vulg.*) *see* **Qualle,** 2.

qualvoll ['kva:lfəl], *adj.* very painful, agonizing, excruciating; (*mental*) harrowing, distressing.

Quandel ['kvandəl], *m.* chimney vent (*in a kiln*).

quängeln, *v.i. See* **quengeln.**

Quantentheorie ['kvantənteori:], *f.* quantum theory.

Quantität [kvanti'tε:t], *f.* quantity, amount.

quantitativ [–ta'ti:f], *adj.* numerical, quantitative. **Quantitätsbestimmung,** *f.* quantitative determination.

quantitieren [kvanti'ti:rən], *v.i.* (*Pros.*) measure syllables.

Quantum ['kvantum], *n.* (**-s,** *pl.* **-ten** *or* (*Austr.*) **-ta**) (*Phys.*) quantum; quantity, amount; share, portion, quota.

Quappe ['kvapə], *f.* eel-pout; tadpole.

Quarantäne [kvarã'tɛ:nə], *f.* quarantine; – ***halten,*** undergo *or* be subjected to quarantine; ***in – liegen,*** be in quarantine; ***die – auferlegen*** (*Dat.*), ***in – legen*** or ***versetzen, unter – stellen, der – unterwerfen,*** put *or* place in quarantine.

Quark [kvark], *m.* curd, curds; (*fig., sl.*) bilge, tripe, trash; (*sl.*) ***du verstehst einen – davon,*** you understand damn-all about it; (*fig.*) ***den alten – aufrühren,*** stir up mud. **Quarkkäse,** *m.* soft *or* cream cheese.

Quarre ['kvarə], *f.* (*dial.*) squalling child, nagging wife, shrew; (*Prov.*) ***erst die Pfarre, dann die –,*** first a living, then a wife. **quarren,** *v.i.* whine, squall, squawk; croak (*frogs*); nag. **quarrig,** *adj.* squalling, whining, squawking; nagging.

Quart [kvart], **1.** *n.* (**-(e)s,** *pl.* **-e**) 1. (*obs.*) quart (= *approx. 1 litre*); 2. (*Typ.*) quarto. **2.** *f. See* **Quarte.**

Quarta ['kvarta], *f.* (-, *pl.* **-ten**) third form (*in secondary schools*).

Quartal [kvar'ta:l], *n.* (**-s,** *pl.* **-e**) 1. quarter (*of a year*), (*in schools*) term; 2. quarter-day. **Quartal|gericht,** *n.* quarter-sessions. **–kündigung,** *f.* three-months' notice. **Quartal(s)|abschluß,** *m.* quarter's balance, quarterly stock-taking. **–geld,** *n.* quarterly allowance. **–tag,** *m.* quarter-day. **quartal(s)weise,** *adv.* quarterly.

Quartaner [kvar'ta:nər], *m.*, **Quartanerin,** *f.* third-form boy (girl).

quartär [kvar'tɛ:r], *adj.* (*Geol.*) quarternary.

Quart|band, *n.* quarto volume. **–blatt,** *n.*, **–bogen,** *m.* quarto sheet.

Quarte ['kvartə], *f.* (*Cards, Fenc.*) carte, quart; (*Mus.*) fourth.

Quartett [kvar'tɛt], *n.* (**-(e)s,** *pl.* **-e**) (*Mus.*) quartet, (*Cards*) four.

Quartformat ['kvartfɔrma:t], *n.* (*Typ.*) quarto.

Quartier [kvar'ti:r], *n.* (**-s,** *pl.* **-e**) 1. lodging, accommodation, (*Mil.*) quarters, billet; (*of a town*) quarter, district, ward; (*Naut.*) watch below decks; ***in – liegen bei . . .,*** be quartered *or* billeted on . . .; ***– nehmen*** or ***beziehen,*** take up quarters, take lodgings; 2. (*obs.*) quarter, mercy, clemency. **Quartier|arrest,** *m.* (*Mil.*) confinement to quarters. **–macher,** *m.* (*Mil.*) billeting officer. **–meister,** *m.* (*Mil.*) quartermaster. **–zettel,** *m.* requisition for billets.

Quartstoß ['kvartʃto:s], *m.* (*Fenc.*) thrust in carte.

Quarz [kva:rts], *m.* (**-es,** *pl.* **-e**) quartz, (*Rad.*) crystal. **Quarzdrüse,** *f.* crystallized quartz. **quarz|gesteuert,** *adj.* (*Rad.*) crystal-controlled. **–haltig,** *adj.* quartziferous. **quarzig,** *adj.* quartzy, of quartz. **Quarzkristall,** *n.* rock-crystal

quasi ['kva:zi], *adv.* as it were, so to speak, in a way. **Quasigelehrte(r),** *m* would-be scholar.

Quasimodogeniti [kvazimodo'ge:niti], *m.* Low Sunday.

quasseln ['kvasəln], *v.t., v.i.* (*sl.*) prattle, chatter, blether. **Quasselstrippe,** *f.* (*sl.*) prattler, blatherer; telephone.

Quast [kvast], *m.* (**-es,** *pl.* **-e**), **Quaste,** *f.* tuft, tassel; soft brush, puff. **Quastenbehang,** *m.* tasselled hangings.

Quästor ['kvɛ:stɔr], *m.* (**-s,** *pl.* **-en**) quaestor, university finance officer. **Quästur** [–'stu:r], *f.* (-, *pl.* **-en**) university finance office.

Quatember [kva'tɛmbər], *m.* quarter-day, emberday; (*as pref.*) quarterly.

quaternär [kvatər'nɛ:r], *adj.* (*Chem.*) quaternary, compounded of four parts. **Quaterne** [–'tɛrnə], *f.* quaternity, run *or* set of four.

Quatsch [kvatʃ], *m.* (*coll.*) twaddle, nonsense, balderdash, rubbish, gibberish, rot, (*Am.*) boloney, (*sl.*) bosh, tripe, bilge. **quatschen, 1.** *v.i., v.t.* (*coll.*) talk nonsense *or* bosh, twaddle, blether; (have a) gossip. **2.** *v.i.* squelch, splash. **Quatschkopf,** *m.* (*coll.*) gossip, bletherer, twaddler.

Quecke ['kvɛkə], *f.* (*Bot.*) couch-grass (*Agropyrum repens*).

Quecksilber ['kvɛkzɪlbər], *n.* quicksilver, mercury. **Quecksilber|chlorür,** *n.* mercurous chloride, calomel. **–dampf,** *m.* mercury vapour. **quecksilberhaltig,** *adj.* (*Chem.*) mercurial. **quecksilberig,** *adj.* (*fig.*) lively, restless, fidgety, mercurial. **Quecksilberlegierung,** *f.* amalgam. **quecksilbern,** *adj.* of quicksilver, mercurial. **Quecksilber|oxyd,** *n.* mercuric oxide. **–oxydul,** *n.* mercurous oxide. **–salbe,** *f.* mercurial ointment, blue ointment. **–säule,** *f.* column of mercury. **–vergiftung,** *f.* mercurial poisoning. **quecksilbrig,** *adj. See* **quecksilberig.**

Quell [kvɛl], *m.* (**-(e)s,** *pl.* **-e**) (*Poet.*) *see* **Quelle. Quell|bach,** *m.* source of a river. **–bottich,** *m.* steeping-vat.

Quelle ['kvɛlə], *f.* spring, source, fountain, well; (*fig.*) source, fountain-head, origin; informant, authority; (*Navig. sl.*) fix; ***aus guter –,*** from a reliable source, on good authority.

quellen ['kvɛlən], **1.** *irr.v.i.* (*aux.* s. *&* h.) gush (forth), well (up); issue, flow, arise, spring (***aus,*** from); (*fig.*) arise, emanate, originate, spring (***in*** (*Dat.*), from); bulge, swell; ***die Augen – ihm fast aus dem Kopfe,*** his eyes are popping out of his head; ***Tränen – ihr aus den Augen,*** tears well from her eyes. **2.** *reg. & irr.v.t.* (cause to) swell; soak, steep.

Quellen|angabe, *f.* (list of) references (to one's authorities). **–forschung,** *f.* study of sources, original research. **quellenmäßig,** *adj.* on good authority, according to the most reliable sources, authentic. **Quellen|material,** *n.* authentic *or* source-material. **–nachweis,** *m. See* **–angabe. –studium,** *n. See* **–forschung.**

Quell|fähigkeit, *f.* absorption capacity. **–fluß,** *m. See* **–bach. –gebiet,** *n.* headwaters. **–sand,** *m.* quicksand, driftsand. **Quellung,** *f.* swelling, soaking, tumefaction. **Quellwasser,** *n.* spring water.

Quendel ['kvɛndəl], *m.* wild thyme.

Quengelei [kvɛŋgə'laɪ], *f.* complaining, (*coll.*) grousing, whining; fault-finding, carping, nagging. **quengeln** ['kvɛŋəln], *v.i.* complain, grumble, (*coll.*) grouse, whine; (*sl.*) belly-ache, moan; nag, pester.

Quent [kvɛnt], *n.* (**-(e)s,** *pl.* **-e**) (*obs.*) drachm, dram.

quer [kve:r], **1.** *adj.* cross, transverse, lateral, oblique, slanting, diagonal. **2.** *adv.* athwart, crosswise, obliquely, diagonally; ***– über*** (*Acc.*), across; (*fig.*) ***– gehen,*** go amiss *or* wrong; ***kreuz und –,*** hither and thither, to and fro, in all directions; ***es kommt mir –,*** I am put out by this, it thwarts my plans *or* puts a spoke in my wheel.

querab [kve:r'ap], *adv.* (*Naut.*) abeam, on the beam. **Quer|achse,** *f.* lateral *or* transverse axis. **–axt,** *f.* twibill, mattock. **–balken,** *m.* cross-beam, transom; architrave; (*Her.*) bar. **–baum,** *m.* cross-bar. **quer|beet,** *adv.* (*coll.*) across country (*of tanks etc.*). **–durch,** *adv.* right *or* straight across. **Querdurchschnitt,** *m.* transverse section *or* diameter (*of a conic section*).

Quere ['kve:rə], *f.* diagonal; oblique *or* transverse direction, breadth (*rarely used except in stock phrases*); ***in die –, der – nach,*** athwart, across, crosswise; ***die Länge und die –,*** the length and breadth; ***ihm in die – kommen,*** cross his path, get in his way, thwart his plans, queer his pitch. **queren,** *v.i., v.t.* cross (over), cut across; (*Mount.*) traverse.

Querfaser ['kve:rfa:zər], *f.* transverse fibre. **quer|feldein,** *adv. See* **–beet. Quer|feldeinlauf,** *m.* cross-country running *or* run. **–feldeinritt,** *m.* point-to-point racing *or* meeting. **–feuer,** *n.* (*Mil.*) enfilading fire. **–flöte,** *f.* (German) flute. **–format,** *n.* (*Typ.*) broadside. **–frage,** *f.* interposed *or* interjected question, cross-question. **–gang,** *m.* alley way, (*sl.*) cut; (*Mount.*) traverse. **–giebel,** *m.* side gable. **–holz,** *n.* transom; (*Crick.*) bail. **–kopf,** *m.* contrary fellow; crank. **querköpfig,** *adj.* contrary, (*coll.*) pig-headed; cranky. **Quer|kraft,** *f.* shearing force. **–lage,** *f.* (*Med.*) (*of birth*) transverse presentation. **–lager,** *n.* (*Tech.*) radial bearing. **–latte,** *f.* (*Footb.*) cross-bar. **–leiste,** *f.* cross-piece, strut, transverse ridge. **–linie,** *f.* diagonal.

Quer|pfeife, *f.* fife. **–ruder,** *n.* (*Av.*) aileron. **–säge,** *f.* cross-cut saw. **–sattel,** *m.* side-saddle. **–schiff,** *n.* transept. **querschiffs,** *adv.* (*Naut.*) athwartships. **Quer|schläger,** *m.* ricochet. **–schnitt,** *m.* cross-section, transverse section, profile, cross-cut, (*of wire*) gauge. **–schnittansicht,** *f.* (cross-)sectional view. **–schott,** *n.* (transverse) bulkhead. **–schub,** *m.* lateral thrust. **–steuer,** *n.* (*Av.*) aileron control. **–stollen,** *m.* (*Min.*) transverse gallery. **–straße,** *f.* crossroad; ***erste – links,*** first turning to the left. **–strich,** *m.* dash, stroke, (*Typ.*) break; (cross-) line (*in fractions*); (*fig.*) ***einen – machen durch,*** frustrate, thwart, nip in the bud. **–summe,** *f.* total of the digits of a number. **–träger,** *m.* transverse (bearer *or* girder). **–treiber,** *m.* obstructionist, intriguer. **–treiberei,** *f.* obstruction(ism), intrigue(s). **querüber,** *adv.* diagonally opposite, right across.

Querulant [kveru'lant], *m.* (**-en,** *pl.* **-en**) querulous person, grumbler. **querulieren,** *v.i.* be querulous *or* contentious, grumble, complain, (*sl.*) moan, gripe, belly-ache.

Quer|verbindung, *f.* cross link *or* connection, intercommunication. **–wall,** *m.* (*Fort.*) traverse. **–wand,** *f.* transverse wall, partition. **–weg,** *m.* cross-country path *or* lane, crossroad. **–welle,** *f.* transverse shaft.

Quese ['kve:zə], *f.* (*dial.*) blister, blood-blister.

Quetsche ['kvɛtʃə], *f.* 1. crusher, presser, wringer; 2. (*dial.*) plum (*see* **Zwetschge**); 3. (*coll.*) cramped space, poky hole; small shop. **quetschen,** *v.t.* (*Med.*) bruise, contuse; mash, crush, press; squeeze, squash, pinch, nip; (*Bill.*) ***einen Ball an die Bande –,*** strike a ball against the cushion.

Quetsch|hahn, *m.* pinch-cock, spring clip. **–kartoffeln,** *f.pl.* mashed potatoes. **–kommode,** *f.* (*sl.*) squeeze-box. **–laut,** *m.* (*Phonet.*) affricate, affricative.

Quetschung ['kvɛtʃuŋ], *f.* crushing; bruise, contusion; (*Bill.*) cushion.

Quetsch|werk, *n.* crushing-mill. **–wunde,** *f.* contused wound.

Queue [kø:], **1.** *n.* (**-s,** *pl.* **-s**) (*Bill.*) cue. **2.** *f.* (**-,** *pl.* **-s**) queue.

quick [kvɪk], *adj.* (*dial.*) lively, brisk. **Quick,** *m.* (*dial.*) quicksilver. **Quick|arbeit,** *f.* amalgamation. **–born,** *m.* (*Poet.*) fountain of youth. **–brei,** *m.* amalgam. **quicken,** *v.t.* amalgamate. **Quickerz,** *n.* mercury ore. **quicklebendig,** *adj.* spirited, vivacious, lively. **Quick|sand,** *m.* quicksand. **–wasser,** *n.* mercurial solution.

Quidam ['kvi:dam], *m.* (**-s,** *pl.* **-**) a certain person, somebody, so-and-so.

Quiek [kvi:k], *m.* (**-es,** *pl.* **-e**) squeak. **quieken, quieksen,** *v.i.* (*coll.*) squeak.

quietschen ['kvi:tʃən], *v.i.* squeal, squeak, (*as doors, floor etc.*) creak, (*of brakes*) screech. **quietschvergnügt,** *adj.* as pleased as Punch.

quill [kvɪl], **quillst, quillt,** *see* **quellen.**

Quinta ['kvɪnta], *f.* (**-,** *pl.* **-ten**) second form, (*Austr.*) fifth form. **Quintaner** [kvɪn'ta:nər], *m.* second-form boy.

Quinte ['kvɪntə], *f.* (*Mus.*) fifth; first string, E string (*of violins*); (*Fenc.*) quinte; (*Cards*) quint; trick, feint.

Quintessenz ['kvɪnt'ɛsɛnts], *f.* quintessence, pith, gist.

Quintett [kvɪn'tɛt], *n.* (**-s,** *pl.* **-e**) (*Mus.*) quintet.

Quirl [kvɪrl], *m.* (**-(e)s,** *pl.* **-e**) (*Cul.*) whisk, beater; (*Bot.*) verticil, whirl, whorl; one year's growth of firs; (*coll.*) restless person; (*fig.*) whirlwind. **quirlen, 1.** *v.i.* (*aux.* h. & s.) twirl round, whirl. **2.** *v.t.* whisk, beat (*eggs etc.*), stir, agitate, twirl.

quitt [kvɪt], *pred.adj.* quits, even (***mit,*** with), rid, free (of).

Quitte ['kvɪtə], *f.* quince. **quittengelb,** *adj.* brilliant *or* bright yellow.

quittieren [kvɪ'ti:rən], *v.t.* receipt (*a bill*), give a receipt for; quit, leave, abandon; ***quittierte Rechnung,*** receipted bill; (*coll.*) ***den Vorwurf mit einem Lächeln –,*** acknowledge the rebuke with a smile.

Quittung ['kvɪtuŋ], *f.* receipt, acknowledgement; discharge.

quoll [kvɔl], **quollest, quölle** ['kvœlə], *see* **quellen.**

Quote ['kvo:tə], *f.* quota, share, portion, contingent; dividend.

Quotient [kvotsi'ɛnt], *m.* (**-en,** *pl.* **-en**) quotient.

quotieren [kvo'ti:rən], *v.t.* quote (*prices*).

R

R, r [ɛr], *n.* R, r (*see Index of Abbreviations*).

Raa [ra:], *f.* *See* **Rahe.**

rabantern [ra'bantərn], **rabangen, rabaschen, rabastern,** *v.i.* (*coll.*) move about noisily, be busy, be restless.

Rabatt [ra'bat], *m.* (**-(e)s,** *pl.* **-e**) (trade-)discount, rebate, allowance; deduction; ***davon geht noch – ab,*** discount to be deducted; ***einem – unterworfen,*** subject to a discount.

Rabatte [ra'batə], *f.* facing (*of a coat*); cuff; (*Hort.*) border, bed.

rabattieren [raba'ti:rən], *v.t.* reduce in price, make a deduction, allow discount on. **Rabattmarke,** *f.* discount voucher.

Rabatz [ra'bats], *m.* (*coll.*) row, din, racket. **rabatzen,** *v.i.* (*coll.*) see **rabantern** *etc.*

Rabbi ['rabi], *m.* (**-s,** *pl.* **-nen** *or* **-s**), **Rabbiner** [–'bi:nər], *m.* rabbi. **rabbinisch,** *adj.* rabbinical.

Rabe, *m.* (**-n,** *pl.* **-n**) (*Orn.*) see **Kolkrabe**; (*Astr.*) Corvus; (*coll.*) ***weißer –,*** rare bird, blue moon; ***alt wie ein –,*** as old as the hills; ***er stiehlt wie ein –,*** he steals like a magpie. **Raben|aas,** *n.* carrion; (*fig.*) gallows-bird. **–eltern,** *pl.* unnatural parents. **–haar,** *n.* raven(-black) hair. **–krähe,** *f.* carrion crow (*Corvus corone corone*). **–mutter,** *f.* cruel mother. **rabenschwarz,** *adj.* jet-black, pitch-black *or* dark; ***–e Locken,*** raven locks. **Rabenstein,** *m.* (*obs.*) place of execution, gallows.

rabiat [rabi'a:t], *adj.* furious, raving, rabid, mad with rage.

Rabulist [rabu'lɪst], *m.* (**-en,** *pl.* **-en**) pettifogger, hair-splitter.

Rache ['raxə], *f.* vengeance, revenge, retaliation; ***– üben*** or ***nehmen,*** take (one's) revenge, have revenge, revenge o.s. (***an*** (*Dat.*), on). **Rache|durst,** *m.* vengefulness, vindictiveness. **–engel,** *m.* avenging angel. **–göttin,** *f.* Fury.

Rachen ['raxən], *m.* jaws, mouth (*of beasts*); throat, cavity of the mouth; (*fig.*) yawning abyss; ***ihm den – stopfen,*** stop his mouth.

rächen ['rɛçən], **1.** *v.t.* (*irr. obs.*) avenge, revenge, take revenge for. **2.** *v.r.* take revenge *or* vengeance, be revenged, revenge o.s. (***an*** (*Dat.*), on; ***wegen,*** for), (*coll.*) get one's own back; ***es wird sich an ihm –,*** it will come home *or* be brought home to him, he will pay (the penalty) for *or* suffer for it.

Rachen|abstrich, *m.* (*Med.*) throat-swab. **–blütler,**

m.pl. (*Bot.*) labiatae. **-bräune,** *f.* (*Med.*) quinsy. **rachenförmig,** *adj.* (*Bot.*) labiate. **Rachen|-höhle,** *f.* pharynx. **-katarrh,** *m.* sore throat, pharyngitis. **-putzer,** *m.* (*coll.*) sour wine, raw spirits.

Rächer ['rɛçər], *m.* avenger.

Rachgier ['raxgi:r], *f.* *See* **Rachedurst. rachgierig,** *adj.* (re)vengeful, vindictive. **Rachsucht,** *f.* *See* **Rachedurst. rach|süchtig,** *adj.* *See* **-gierig.**

Rachitis [ra'xi:tɪs], *f.* rickets. **rachitisch,** *adj.* rickety, rachitic.

Racker ['rakər], *m.* (young) rogue, (little) rascal *or* scamp, (*of a girl*) minx.

Rad [ra:t], *n.* (**-s,** *pl.* **¨-er**) **1.** wheel; ***das – an der Welle,*** wheel and axle; ***ein – schlagen,*** turn a cartwheel; (*of peacocks*) spread the tail; (*fig.*) ***unter die Räder kommen,*** go to the dogs; ***das – der Geschichte,*** the wheels of history; (*coll.*) ***bei ihm fehlt ein –,*** he's got a screw loose; (*Hist.*) ***zum -e verurteilen,*** condemn to be broken on the wheel; (*Hist.*) ***aufs – flechten,*** break on the wheel; ***das fünfte – am Wagen sein,*** be redundant *or* superfluous, be out of place, not be wanted; **2.** (*coll.*) cycle, bike. **Rad|abstand,** *m.* wheel-base. **-achse,** *f.* axle-tree.

Radar [ra'da:r], *m. or n.* radiolocation, radar. **Radar|navigationsgerät,** *n.* plan-position indicator. **-warnnetz,** *n.* radar warning network.

Radau ['ra'dau], *m.* (*coll.*) row, din, hullabaloo, racket. **Radau|bruder,** *m.* ruffian, rowdy, (*sl.*) tough. **-komödie,** *f.* slapstick comedy. **-macher,** *m.* *See* **-bruder. -presse,** *f.* gutter *or* yellow press.

Radber ['ra:tbe:r], *f.* (-, *pl.* **-en**) (*Austr.*) wheelbarrow.

Rädchen ['rɛ:tçən], *n.* small wheel; (*on furniture*) castor, caster; (*on spurs*) rowel; (*Dressm.*) perforating wheel; (*coll.*) ***bei dir ist ein – locker,*** you've got a screw loose.

Rad|dampfer, *m.* paddle-steamer. **-drehung,** *f.* rotation, torsion.

Rade ['ra:də], *f.* (*Bot.*) (corn-)cockle (*Agrostemma githago*).

Rade|ber, -berge, *f.* *See* **Radber.**

radebrechen ['ra:dəbrɛçən], *irr.v.t.* (*insep.*) mangle *or* murder (*a language*); ***deutsch –,*** speak broken German.

radeln ['ra:dəln], *v.i.* (*aux.* s.) (*coll.*) cycle, ride a bicycle.

Rädelsführer ['rɛ:dəlsfy:rər], *m.* ringleader.

Räder|fahrzeug, *n.* wheeled vehicle. **-getriebe,** *n.* gears, gearing. **-kasten,** *m.* (*on engines*) gear-box, (*on machinery*) safety cage *or* cover. **-kettenfahrzeug,** *n.* half-track vehicle.

-räd(e)rig ['rɛ:d(ə)rɪç], *adj.suff.* -wheeled.

rädern ['rɛ:dərn], *v.t.* (*Hist.*) break on the wheel; (*coll.*) ***wie gerädert sein,*** be fagged out, be knocked up *or* done in.

Räder|tierchen, *n.* (*Zool.*) rotifer, wheel-animalcule. **-untersetzung,** *f.* gear reduction. **-werk,** *n.* gearing, gears, wheels, clockwork.

radfahren ['ra:tfa:rən], *irr.v.i.* (*aux.* s. & h.) cycle, ride a bicycle. **Radfahrer,** *m.*, **Radfahrerin,** *f.* cyclist, (*Am.*) cycler. **Radfahrweg,** *m.* cycle-track.

Radfelge ['ra:tfɛlgə], *f.* (wheel-)rim, felly, felloe. **radförmig,** *adj.* wheel-shaped, radial, (*Bot.*) rotate.

radial [radi'a:l], *adj.* radial.

radieren [ra'di:rən], *v.t.* etch; erase, rub out. **Radier|gummi,** *n.* (india-)rubber, eraser. **-kunst,** *f.* (art of) etching. **-messer,** *n.* eraser, penknife. **-nadel,** *f.* etching-needle, dry needle. **Radierung,** *f.* etching.

Radieschen [ra'di:sçən], *n.* radish; (*coll.*) ***sich*** (*Dat.*) ***die – von unten ansehen,*** be pushing up the daisies.

radikal [radi'ka:l], *adj.* radical, root, basic, fundamental, inherent; utterly, ruthlessly. **Radikale(r),** *m., f.* radical (*in politics*), extremist. **Radikalessig,** *m.* glacial acetic acid. **Radikalismus** [–'lɪsmus], *m.* radicalism.

Radikand [radi'kant], *m.* (**-en,** *pl.* **-en**) (*Math.*) number of which the root is to be found.

Radio ['ra:dio], *n.* (*Swiss m.*) (**-s,** *pl.* **-s**) radio, wireless; ***– hören,*** listen in, listen to the radio; ***im –,*** on the radio; ***im – sprechen,*** speak on the radio.

radioaktiv [radioak'ti:f], *adj.* radioactive; ***-er Niederschlag,*** fallout; ***-e Zerfallsreihe,*** radioactive series. **Radio|aktivität,** *f.* radioactivity. **-apparat,** *m.* *See* **-gerät. -frequenz,** *f.* radio-frequency. **-gerät,** *n.* wireless set, radio.

Radiogramm [radio'gram], *n.* radio telegram. **Radiogrammophon,** *n.* radiogram.

Radiologe [radio'lo:gə], *m.* (**-n,** *pl.* **-n**) radiologist.

Radio|mechaniker, *m.* radio-mechanic *or* technician. **-peilgerät,** *n.* (radio) direction-finder. **-peilung,** *f.* (radio) direction-finding, radiolocation. **-publikum,** *n.* listeners, radio audience. **-sender,** *m.* radio transmitter, broadcasting station. **—sendung,** *f.* transmission, broadcast. **-technik,** *f.* radio engineering. **-telegraphie.** *f.* wireless telegraphy.

Radium ['ra:dium], *n.* radium. **Radium|behandlung,** *f.*, **-heilverfahren,** *n.* radiotherapy.

Radius ['ra:dius], *m.* (-, *pl.* **-ien**) (*Math., Anat.*) radius. **radizieren** [–'tsi:rən], *v.t.* extract the root of.

Rad|kappe, *f.* hub-cap. **-kasten,** *m.* wheel-case; (*on boats*) paddle-box. **-kranz,** *m.* *See* **-felge.**

Radler ['ra:tlər], *m.* (*coll.*) see **Radfahrer.**

Rad|linie, *f.* (*Geom.*) cycloid. **-mutter,** *f.* wheel-nut. **-nabe,** *f.* hub. **-reifen,** *m.* tyre. **-rennbahn,** *f.* cycling track. **-rennen,** *n.* cycle race. **-schalter,** *m.* rotary switch. **-schaufel,** *f.* paddle-board, (*of a watermill*) sweep. **radschlagen,** *irr.v.i.* *See* ***Rad schlagen.*** **Rad|schlüssel,** *m.* ratchet wrench. **-schuh,** *m.* skid, wheel-drag. **-speiche,** *f.* spoke. **-sperre,** *f.* drag-chain. **-sporn,** *m.* (*Av.*) tail-wheel. **-sport,** *m.* cycling. **-spur,** *f.* wheel mark *or* track, rut. **-stand,** *m.* *See* **-abstand. -sturz,** *m.* camber. **-welle,** *f.* pulley shaft, (*on boats*) paddle shaft. **-zahn,** *m.* cog.

Räf, *n.* (**-s,** *pl.* **-e**) (*Swiss*) see **Reff.**

Raff [raf], *m.* (**-(e)s,** *pl.* **-e**) (*coll.*) grab, handful.

Raffel ['rafəl], *f.* (-, *pl.* **-n**) raffle-net (*for turbot*); rattle; chatterbox; grater, scraper; flax-comb. **raffeln, 1.** *v.t.* rake, ripple (*flax*); grate, scrape. **2.** *v.i.* chatter, gossip.

raffen ['rafən], **1.** *v.t.* snatch up, carry off, gather up; (*Dressm.*) take in *or* up. **2.** *v.i.* snatch (***nach,*** at). **Raffgier,** *f.* greed, rapacity. **raffig,** *adj.* grasping, greedy, rapacious.

Raffinade [rafi'na:də], *f.* refined sugar. **Raffination** [–tsi'o:n], *f.* refining. **Raffinerie** [–ə'ri:], *f.* refinery.

Raffinesse [rafi'nɛsə], *f.* finesse, subtlety, cleverness; polish, elegance, refinement, discrimination.

raffinieren [rafi'ni:rən], *v.t.* refine, purify. **raffiniert,** *adj.* refined; (*fig.*) subtle, artful, cunning, crafty; ***-e Bosheit,*** studied malice. **Raffiniertheit,** *f.* *See* **Raffinesse.**

Raffzahn ['raftsa:n], *m.* (*Zool.*) laniary *or* canine tooth (*of carnivores*), (*coll.*) projecting front tooth.

ragen ['ra:gən], *v.i.* tower (up), project.

Ragout [ra'gu], *n.* (**–s,** *pl.* **–s**) stew, hotch-potch.

Rahe ['ra:ə], *f.* (*Naut.*) yard, spar; spreader; ***große –,*** main yard.

Rahm [ra:m], *m.* **1.** cream; ***– ansetzen,*** form cream; ***– abnehmen,*** skim the cream; 2. soot. **Rahmbonbon,** *m.* (milk) toffee.

[1]**rahmen** ['ra:mən], **1.** *v.i.* form cream. **2.** *v.t.* skim.

[2]**rahmen,** *v.t.* frame, mount (*pictures*).

Rahmen, *m.* frame; housing; casement (*of windows*), welt (*of shoes*); edge, border; framework, structure; (*fig.*) frame(work), background, setting, surroundings, milieu; compass, scope; (*fig.*) ***in engem –,*** within a close compass; (*fig.*) ***im – von,*** within the limits *or* scope *or* framework of, for the purposes of; in the course of; (*fig.*) ***aus dem – fallen,*** be out of place; (*fig.*) ***den – sprengen,*** be beyond the scope (*Gen.*, of).

Rahmen|abkommen, *n.* skeleton agreement. **-antenne,** *f.* (*Rad.*) frame-aerial, loop aerial. **-arbeit,** *f.* welted footwear. **-darbietung,** *f.* supporting item(s). **-erzählung,** *f.* stories within a story. **-gesetz,** *n.* skeleton law. **-heer,** *n.* cadre. **-rohr,** *n.* (*Cycl.*) *oberes –*, cross-bar. **-schuh,** *m.* welted shoe. **-spiegel,** *m.* framed mirror. **-stickerei,** *f.* frame-embroidery. **-sucher,** *m.* (*Phot.*) view-finder. **-vertrag,** *m.* skeleton agreement.

rahmig ['ra:mɪç], *adj.* 1. creamy; 2. sooty. **Rahmkäse,** *m.* cream cheese.

Rahsegel ['ra:ze:gəl], *n.* (*Naut.*) square sail.

Rain [raɪn], *m.* **(-(e)s,** *pl.* **-e)** balk, ridge, bank (*between fields*); (*Poet.*) limit, border, edge. **rainen,** *v.t.* fix boundaries of (*fields*), demarcate. **Rain|farn,** *m.* (*Bot.*) tansy (*Tanacetum vulgare*). **-stein,** *m.* boundary-stone. **-weide,** *f.* (*Bot.*) privet (*Ligustrum vulgare*).

rajolen [ra'jo:lən], *v.t. See* **rigolen.**

räkeln, *v.r. See* **rekeln.**

Rakete [ra'ke:tə], *f.* rocket; *– für Erdzielbeschuß,* air-to-ground rocket; *– für Luftkampf,* air-to-air rocket. **Raketen|abwehrrakete,** *f.* anti-missile missile. **-antrieb,** *m.* rocket propulsion; *mit –*, rocket-propelled. **-bombe,** *f.* guided missile. **-brennkammer,** *f.* rocket-motor. **-flugzeug,** *n.* rocket-plane. **-forschung,** *f.* rocketry. **-geschoß,** *n. See* **-bombe. -start,** *m.* rocket-assisted take-off. **-werfer,** *m.* rocket-apparatus (*on lifeboats etc.*).

Rakett [ra'kɛt], *n.* **(-(e)s,** *pl.* **-e** *or* (*Austr.*) **-s)** (*Tenn.*) racket.

Ralle ['ralə], *f.* (*Orn.*) *see* **Wasseralle.**

Ramm [ram], *m.* **(-(e)s,** *pl.* **-e)** (*dial.*) ram. **Ramm|-bär, -bock,** *m. See* **Ramme. rammdösig,** *adj.* (*coll.*) excitable, hysterical. **Ramme,** *f.* pile-driver, drop hammer, rammer. **Rammel,** *m.* 1. *See* **Ramme**; 2. (*dial.*) lout, hooligan. **Rammelei** [–'laɪ], *f.* (*vulg.*) randiness. **rammelig,** *adj.* (*dial.*) in *or* on heat (*partic. of rabbits*), (*vulg.*) randy. **rammeln, 1.** *v.t. See* **rammen. 2.** *v.i.* rut, be in *or* on heat (*partic. of rabbits*). **rammen,** *v.t.* drive *or* ram in; ram (*a ship*); beat *or* stamp down (*soil*). **Rammler,** *m.* buck hare *or* rabbit; tomcat. **Rammsporn,** *m.* (*Naut.*) ram.

Rampe ['rampə], *f.* platform, ramp, slope, ascent; (*Theat.*) apron. **Rampenlicht,** *n.* footlight, (*fig.*) limelight.

ramponieren [rampo'ni:rən], *v.t.* spoil, mar, damage, crumple, batter, bash.

Ramsch [ramʃ], *m.* job-lot; odds and ends, (*coll.*) junk, trash; (*Studs. sl.*) quarrel; **im –**, in bulk, in the lump. **ramschen,** *v.t.* 1. buy in bulk, buy cheap; 2. (*Studs. sl.*) challenge. **Ramsch|geschäft,** *n. See* **-laden. -händler,** *m.* junk dealer. **-laden,** *m.* junk shop. **-verkauf,** *m.* jumble sale. **-ware,** *f.* sale-price goods, odds and ends, cheap junk.

ran [ran], *adv. See* **heran.**

Rand [rant], *m.* **(-es,** *pl.* **¨er)** edge, border, verge, brink, margin (*of page*), brim (*of hat*), rim (*of spectacles*), fringe, flange, lip, ledge, (*Mil.*) perimeter; (*fig.*) *am –e* (*bemerkt*), by the way; (*fig.*) *am –e bemerken,* remark in passing; *am –e des Grabes,* at death's door; *am –e des Verderbens,* on the verge of ruin; *am –e der Stadt,* on the outskirts of the town; (*coll.*) *das versteht sich am –e,* that is a matter of course, that goes without saying; *außer – und Band,* quite *or* completely out of hand, unmanageable; *außer – und Band geraten,* go crazy, be beside o.s. (*vor* (*Dat.*), with); *bis zum –e voll,* full to the brim, brimful; (*dunkle*) *Ränder um die* or *unter den Augen,* dark rings *or* circles under the eyes; (*sl.*) *den – halten,* hold one's tongue; (*Prov.*) *zwischen Lipp' und Kelches – schwebt der dunklen Mächte Hand,* there's many a slip 'twixt cup and lip; (*coll.*) *zu –e kommen mit,* cope with, manage, make a go of.

Randal [ran'da:l], *m.* (*coll.*) row, din, racket, hullabaloo. **randalieren** [–da'li:rən], *v.i.* (*coll.*) kick up a row *or* shindy; riot, royster.

Rand|auslösung, *f.* (*typewriter*) margin-release. **-bemerkung,** *f.* marginal note, gloss, (*fig.*) aside.

Rande ['randə], *f.* (*Swiss*) beetroot.

Rand|einsteller, *m. See* **-steller.**

rändeln ['rɛndəln], *v.t.* border, edge; mill (*coins*), knurl. **Rändelrad,** *n.* knurling *or* milling tool.

rändern ['rɛndərn], *v.t. See* **rändeln.**

Randgebiet ['rantgəbi:t], *n.* borderland, (*of a town*) surroundings, outskirts. **randgenäht,** *adj.* (*of shoes*) welted. **Rand|glosse,** *f. See* **-bemerkung**; (*fig.*) *–n machen,* comment on. **randlos,** *adj.* (*of spectacles*) rimless. **Rand|schärfe,** *f.* (*Phot.*) sharpness of outline. **-schrift,** *f.* edge-legend (*on coins etc.*). **-siedlung,** *f.* suburban housing estate. **randständig,** *adj.* marginal, peripheral. **Rand|-stein,** *m.* kerb(stone), curbstone. **-steller,** *m.* (*typewriter*) margin-stop. **-stellung,** *f.* (*Mil.*) perimeter position. **-verzierung,** *f.* ornamental border. **-widerstand,** *m.* (*Av.*) induced drag. **-zeichnung,** *f.* marginal sketch.

Ranft [ranft], *m.* **(-es,** *pl.* **¨e)** crust (*of bread*); (*Poet.*) edge, border.

Rang [raŋ], *m.* **(-(e)s,** *pl.* **¨e)** 1. rank (*also Mil.*), rating, grade, status, station, position, order, class, rate, quality, degree; (*fig.*) *ihm den – ablaufen,* outrun *or* outstrip *or* outdo him, get the better of him, (*coll.*) steal a march on him; (*fig.*) *ersten –es,* first-class, first-rate, of the first order; *ihm den – streitig machen,* compete with him, dispute his position; 2. (*Theat.*) tier, gallery, circle; *erster –*, dress circle, (*Am.*) first balcony; *zweiter –*, upper circle, (*Am.*) second gallery.

rang, *see* **ringen.**

Rang|abzeichen, *n.* (*Mil.*) badge of rank. **-älteste(r),** *m.* (*Mil.*) senior officer.

Range ['raŋə], *m.* **(-n,** *pl.* **-n)** *or f.* (*of boys*) scamp, (*of girls*) tom-boy, romp.

Rang|erhöhung, *f.* promotion. **-folge,** *f.* order, sequence.

Rangierbahnhof [rã'ʒi:rba:nho:f], *m.* shunting *or* marshalling *or* (*Am.*) switching yard. **rangieren, 1.** *v.t.* arrange, classify; (*Railw.*) shunt, (*Am.*) switch. **2.** *v.i.* rank; *– mit,* rank *or* be classed with. **Rangierer,** *m.* shunter, (*Am.*) switchman. **Rangier|geleise, -gleis,** *n.* (*Railw.*) siding, (*Am.*) switching track. **-lokomotive, -maschine,** *f.* shunting *or* (*Am.*) switcher engine.

Rang|liste, *f.* (*Mil.*) Army *or* Navy *or* Air Force List, (*Spt.*) position table. **-ordnung,** *f.* order of precedence, hierarchy. **-stufe,** *f.* grade, rank, degree. **-verlust,** *m.* (*Mil.*) loss of rank.

rank [raŋk], *adj.* (*dial.*) slim, slender.

Rank, *m.* **(-(e)s,** *pl.* **¨e)** 1. (*dial.*) turning, bend (*in road*); (*Swiss*) *den – ausfinden,* find a way out; 2. (*usu. pl.*) (*fig.*) *see* **Ränke.**

Ranke ['raŋkə], *f.* (*Bot.*) tendril, shoot; runner, climber.

Ränke ['rɛŋkə], *pl.* tricks, wiles, machinations, intrigue(s); *– schmeiden* or *spinnen,* hatch plots, plot, scheme, intrigue.

ranken ['raŋkən], *v.r.*, *v.i.* (*aux.* h. & s.) creep, climb; send forth tendrils. **Ranken|gewächs,** *n.* creeper, climber. **-verzierung,** *f.*, **-werk,** *n.* scroll, interlaced ornament.

Ränke|schmied, *m.* intriguer, plotter, schemer. **-spiel,** *n.* intrigue. **-sucht,** *f.* deceitfulness, insincerity, shiftiness, duplicity, guile. **ränke|süchtig, -voll,** *adj.* deceitful, sly, designing, scheming.

rankig ['raŋkɪç], *adj.* having tendrils.

rann [ran], **ränne** ['rɛnə], **rannest,** *see* **rinnen.**

rannte ['rantə], **ranntest,** *see* **rennen.**

Ranunkel [ra'nuŋkəl], *f.* (-, *pl.* **-n)** ranunculus, buttercup, crowfoot.

Ränzel ['rɛntsəl], *n.*, **Ranzen** ['rantsən], *m.* knapsack, satchel, schoolbag; (*vulg.*) belly, paunch; *seinen – schnüren,* pack (up) one's traps.

ranzen, *v.i.* (*Hunt.*) rut, be in rut.

Ranzer ['rantsər], *m.* (*coll.*) dressing down, wigging.

ranzig ['rantsɪç], *adj.* rancid, rank.

Ranzion [rantsi'o:n], *f.* ransom. **ranzionieren** [–'ni:rən], *v.t.* redeem, ransom, buy off.

Ranzzeit ['rantstsaɪt], *f.* rut, rutting season.

Rappe ['rapə], *m.* **(-n,** *pl.* **-n)** black horse; *(coll.)* ***auf Schusters -n reiten,*** go on Shanks's pony.

Rappel ['rapəl], *m.* *(coll.)* fit of madness, rage; *(coll.)* tantrums; *(coll.)* ***er hat einen -,*** he is off his head, he is cracked *or* dotty *or* *(Am.)* nuts; *(coll.)* ***er hat seinen -,*** he is in one of his fits *or* tantrums. **rappelig,** *adj.* *(coll.)* hare-brained, crazy, hot-headed, headstrong. **Rappelkopf,** *m.* madcap, hothead. **rappelköpfig,** *adj.* *See* **rappelig. rappeln,** *v.i.* rattle; *(coll.)* ***bei ihm rappelt's,*** he is cracked *or* dotty, he's off his nut *or* head.

Rappen ['rapən], *m.* *(Swiss)* centime.

Rapport [ra'pɔrt], *m.* **(-s,** *pl.* **-e)** report, notice, announcement; ***sich zum - melden,*** come in to report, make one's report. **rapportieren** [-'ti:rən], *v.t.* report, announce, make an announcement *or* a report.

Raps [raps], *m.* **(-es,** *pl.* **-e)** *(Bot.)* rape, colza *(Brassica napus).* **Rapsöl,** *n.* rape-oil.

Raptus ['raptus], *m.* (-, *pl.* **-se)** *see* **Rappel.**

Rapunze [ra'puntsə], *f.*, **Rapunzel,** *f.* (-, *pl.* **-n)** *or* *m.* *(Bot.)* lamb's lettuce, rampion *(Varianella olitoria).*

rar [ra:r], *adj.* rare, scarce; exquisite; *(coll.)* ***Sie machen sich -,*** you are quite a stranger. **Rarität** [rari'tɛ:t], *f.* rarity, curiosity; curio. **Raritätenhändler,** *m.* dealer in curios.

rasant [ra'zant], *adj.* flat(-trajectory), *(Artil.)* grazing. **Rasanz,** *f.* flat trajectory, flatness of trajectory.

rasaunen [ra'zaunən], *v.i.* *(dial.)* make a din, raise a hullabaloo.

Rasch [raʃ], *m.* **(-es,** *pl.* **-e)** serge.

rasch, *adj.* quick, swift, speedy, rapid, prompt, *(coll.)* snappy; hasty, rash; lively, brisk, nimble.

rascheln ['raʃəln], *v.i.* rustle, crackle.

Raschheit ['raʃhaɪt], *f.* quickness, swiftness, speed, rapidity, promptness; haste, rashness.

rasen ['ra:zən], *v.i.* rave, rage, storm, fume, be frantic; *(coll.)* speed, tear, dash, scorch. **rasend,** *adj.* raving; furious; mad, frantic; ***-er Hunger,*** furious *or* raging hunger; ***-e Schmerzen,*** violent pains; ***- werden,*** go mad, see red, *(sl.)* blow one's top; ***- machen,*** enrage, drive mad.

Rasen, *m.* lawn, grass(-plot), *(Poet.)* (green)sward; turf, sod; ***auf dem -,*** on the lawn; ***unter dem -,*** under the sod. **Rasen|bekleidung,** *f.* *(Fort.)* turf-lining, sod-revetment. **-bleiche,** *f.* bleaching-ground; sun bleaching. **-eisenerz,** *n.*, **-eisenstein,** *m.* limonite, bog iron ore. **-hacke,** *f.* sod-cutter. **-hügel,** *m.* grassy knoll. **-mähmaschine,** *f.* lawn-mower. **-plagge,** *f.* sod, turf. **-platz,** *m.* lawn, grass-plot, green. **-sport,** *m.* outdoor sport *or* game. **-sprenger,** *m.* lawn-sprinkler. **-stecher,** *m.* *See* **-hacke. -stück,** *n.* sod; grass-plot. **-walze,** *f.* lawn-roller.

Raserei [ra:zə'raɪ], *f.* fury, (towering) rage, frenzy; (raving) madness; *(coll.)* reckless driving, speeding, scorching.

Rasierapparat [ra'zi:rapara:t], *m.* safety-razor; ***elektrischer -,*** electric razor *or* shaver, dry-shaver.

rasieren [ra'zi:rən], *v.t.* shave; *(Mil.)* raze; ***sich - lassen,*** get shaved. **Rasier|flechte,** *f.* ringworm, barber's rash. **-klinge,** *f.* razor-blade. **-krem,** *f.* shaving cream. **-messer,** *n.* razor. **-pinsel,** *m.* shaving-brush. **-seife,** *f.* shaving-soap *or* -stick. **-zeug,** *n.* shaving-things.

Räson [rɛ'zɔ̃], *f.* reason, common sense; ***er will keine - annehmen,*** he will not listen to reason. **Räsoneur** [rɛzo'nø:r], *m.* **(-s,** *pl.* **-e)** grumbler; argumentative person. **räsonieren,** *v.i.* reason, argue, wrangle, grumble *(über (Acc.),* about).

Raspel ['raspəl], *f.* (-, *pl.* **-n)** rasp, *(Cul.)* grater. **raspeln,** *v.t.* rasp, scrape, grate; *(coll.)* ***Süßholz -,*** say sweet nothings, flirt, spoon. **Raspelspäne,** *m.pl.* filings, scrapings.

Rasse ['rasə], *f.* race, *(of animals)* stock, breed; ***von reiner -,*** thoroughbred; ***das Mädchen hat -,*** the girl has quality. **Rassebewußtsein,** *n.* racialism. **rasseecht,** *adj.* thoroughbred. **Rassehund,** *m.* pedigree dog.

Rassel ['rasəl], *f.* (-, *pl.* **-n)** rattle. **Rasselgeräusche,** *n.pl.* *(Med.)* rattle, rattling (sounds). **rasseln,** *v.i.* 1. rattle, clatter; clank, clash; ***mit den Ketten -,*** clank one's chains; 2. *(aux.* s.) *(coll.)* be ploughed, *(Am.)* flunk *(in an examination)*; ***- lassen,*** plough, flunk *(examination candidate).*

Rassen|frage, *f.* race *or* racial question. **-haß,** *m.* race *or* racial hatred. **-hygiene,** *f.* eugenics. **-kampf,** *m.* race *or* racial conflict. **-kreuzung,** *f.* cross-breeding *(of animals).* **-kunde,** *f.* ethnology. **-mischung,** *f.* racial mixture, miscegenation. **-schranke,** *f.* colour bar. **-theorie,** *f.* racialism. **-trennung,** *f.* racial segregation.

Rassepferd ['rasəpfe:rt], *n.* thoroughbred horse. **rasse|rein,** *adj.* *See* **-echt. Rasse|reinheit,** *f.* purity of breed *(of animals),* racial purity. **-vieh,** *n.* pedigree cattle.

rassig ['rasɪç], *adj.* thoroughbred, *(fig., coll.)* racy, *(sl.)* super, snazzy.

rassisch ['rasɪʃ], *adj.* racial.

Rast [rast], *f.* (-, *pl.* **-en)** 1. rest, repose, relaxation; rest, break, pause, halt *(on march)*; resting place; *(dial.)* stage *(of a journey)*; ***- machen,*** take a rest, *(Mil.)* (make a) halt; ***ohne - und Ruh,*** restlessly, never at rest; 2. *(Mech.)* notch, groove, stop; bosh *(of blast-furnace).*

Raste ['rastə], *f.* *(Mech.)* stop, catch, detent.

Rastelbinder ['rastəlbɪndər], *m.* *(dial.)* itinerant tinker.

rasten ['rastən], *v.i., v.r.* take rest, (take a) rest, *(Mil.)* (make a) halt.

Raster ['rastər], *m.* screen *(photo-engraving), (T.V.)* frame. **Raster|bild,** *n.* *(T.V.)* frame. **-druck,** *m.* screen-process, autotypy. **rastern,** *v.t.* print by screen-process, *(T.V.)* scan. **Rasterung,** *f.* *(T.V.)* definition; scanning.

Rast|gärung, *f.* incomplete fermentation. **-haus,** *n.* road-house. **rastlos,** *adj.* restless, *(coll.)* fidgety; indefatigable. **Rast|losigkeit,** *f.* restlessness, *(coll.)* fidgetiness; indefatigable industry. **Rastort,** *m.* resting place; stage *(of a journey)*; *(Mil.)* halting place.

Rastral [ras'tra:l], *n.* **(-s,** *pl.* **-e)** pen for ruling music.

Rast|stätte, *f.* *See* **-haus. -tag,** *m.* day of rest.

Rasur [ra'zu:r], *f.* (-, *pl.* **-en)** erasure; shave.

Rat [ra:t], *m.* 1. **(-(e)s,** *pl.* **Ratschläge)** counsel, advice, suggestion, recommendation; *(pl.* **Beratungen)** deliberation, consultation; remedy, means, expedient, ways and means, *(coll.)* way out; ***seinen - befolgen,*** take his advice; ***ihm - erteilen,*** give him advice; ***um - fragen,*** ask advice; ***mit sich zu -e gehen,*** debate with o.s., think things over; *(coll.)* ***da ist guter - teuer,*** what a mess (we're in)! what are we to do now? ***- halten,*** deliberate, take counsel; ***etwas zu -e halten,*** be sparing with a th., not waste a th., economize with *or* husband a th.; ***sich (Dat.) - holen*** or *(obs.)* ***-s erholen bei,*** consult *(a p.)*; turn to *(s.o.)* for advice; *(Prov.)* ***kommt Zeit kommt -,*** all in good time; ***-s pflegen,*** *see* ***zu -e gehen***; ***- schaffen,*** find ways and means, devise means; ***mit - und Tat,*** by word and deed; ***- wissen,*** know what to do; ***keinen - mehr wissen,*** be at a loss (what to do), be at one's wit's end; ***zu -e ziehen,*** consult, *(coll.)* call in *(a doctor etc.)*; 2. *(pl.* **Ratsversammlungen)** senate, assembly, board, council; 3. *(pl.* **-̈e)** councillor; ***Frau -,*** councillor's wife; ***vortragender -,*** privy councillor, counsellor; 4. *(pl.* **Ratsherrn)** alderman, senator.

rät [rɛ:t], *see* **raten.**

Rate ['ra:tə], *f.* instalment; ratio, quota, proportion; ***in -n,*** by instalments.

raten ['ra:tən], *irr.v.t., irr.v.i.* *(Dat.)* 1. advise, counsel, recommend, give advice; ***ihm etwas*** or ***zu einer S. -,*** advise him on a th.; ***damit ist mir nicht geraten,*** that does not help me much; ***sich (Dat.) - lassen,*** listen to reason, take advice, be advised; ***ich wußte mir nicht zu -,*** I was at my wits' end; 2. guess, conjecture, solve *(a riddle)*; ***ihm etwas zu - geben,*** give him s.th. to think about; ***hin und her -,*** make random guesses; *(coll.)* ***-e mal!***

have a guess! ***geraten!*** you have guessed it! right! 3. (*obs.*) help; ***geschehenen Dingen ist nicht zu –,*** what's done can't be helped *or* undone, it's no use crying over spilt milk.

Ratenkauf ['ra:tənkauf], *m.* hire-purchase. **ratenweise,** *adv.* by instalments. **Ratenzahlung,** *f.* instalment (payment); ***auf –,*** on the instalment plan, on hire-purchase.

Räte|regierung, *f.* Soviet government. **–republik,** *f.* Soviet republic.

Ratespiel ['ra:təʃpi:l], *n.* guessing-game.

Rat|geber, *m.*, **–geberin,** *f.* adviser, counsellor; (*Law*) counsel. **–haus,** *n.* town-hall, guildhall, (*Am.*) city hall.

ratifizieren [ratifi'tsi:rən], *v.t.* ratify. **Ratifizierung,** *f.* ratification.

Rätin ['rɛ:tɪn], *f.* councillor's *or* senator's wife.

Ration [ratsi'o:n], *f.* ration, portion, share, allowance; rations; (*Mil.*) ***eiserne –,*** iron *or* emergency rations.

rationalisieren [ratsionali'zi:rən], *v.t.* rationalize. **Rationalisierung,** *f.* rationalization. **Rationalisierungsfachmann,** *m.* efficiency expert, methods-study adviser, time-and-motion study expert. **Rationalismus** [–'lɪsmus], *m.* rationalism. **rationalistisch,** *adj.* rationalist(ic).

rationell [ratsio'nɛl], *adj.* rational, reasonable, economical, efficient, expedient,

rationieren [ratsio'ni:rən], *v.t.* ration, allot. **Rationierung,** *f.* rationing; ***Aufheben der –,*** derationing.

rätlich ['rɛ:tlɪç], *adj.* advisable, expedient; *see* **ratsam.**

ratlos ['ra:tlo:s], *adj.* perplexed, helpless, embarrassed, (*pred.*) at a loss, at sea. **Ratlosigkeit,** *f.* perplexity, helplessness.

ratsam ['ra:tza:m], *adj.* advisable, commendable; expedient, fit, useful, (*dial.*) prudent, wise. **Ratsamkeit,** *f.* advisability, expediency; suitability.

Ratschlag ['ra:tʃla:k], *m.* (piece of) advice, counsel, suggestion, recommendation. **ratschlagen,** *reg. v.i.* (*insep.*) deliberate, take counsel, consult (together).

Ratschluß ['ra:tʃlus], *m.* resolution, decision; decree; ***Gottes –,*** the ways of the Lord.

Ratsdiener ['ra:tsdi:nər], *m.* beadle.

Rätsel ['rɛ:tsəl], *n.* riddle, puzzle, conundrum, mystery, enigma; ***er ist ein –,*** he is an enigma; ***das ist mir ein –,*** that puzzles me, (*coll.*) that beats me, I can't make it out. **Rätselaufgabe,** *f.* problem, riddle, conundrum. **rätselhaft,** *adj.* puzzling, enigmatic(al), mysterious, incomprehensible, obscure, cryptic. **Rätsel|raten,** *n.* guessing(-game); guesswork. **–spruch,** *m.*, **–wort,** *n.* enigma, cryptic remark.

Rats|erlaß, *m.* decree of the council. **–herr,** *m.* (town) councillor, alderman, senator. **–keller,** *m.* town-hall (cellar) restaurant. **–schreiber,** *m.* town-clerk. **–sitzung,** *f.* council meeting.

rätst [rɛ:tst], *see* **raten.**

Rats|versammlung, *f. See* **–sitzung.**

Ratte ['ratə], *f.* 1. rat; ***wie eine – schlafen,*** sleep like a top *or* log; 2. miss, mis-throw (*skittles*).

rätten ['rɛtən], *v.t.* riddle, screen, sift, sieve.

Ratten|falle, *f.* rat-trap. **–fänger,** *m.* rat-catcher; ***der – von Hameln,*** the Pied Piper of Hamelin. **–gift,** *n.* ratsbane, rat poison. **rattenkahl,** *adj.* bald as a coot, quite bare. **Ratten|könig,** *m.* (*fig.*) a perfect maze, tangle, farrago, jumble, concatenation. **–schwanz,** *m.* rat's tail; (*Tech.*) rat-tail (file); (*fig.*) ***ein ganzer – von,*** no end of, a whole string of.

rattern ['ratərn], *v.t.* clatter, rattle.

Ratz [rats], *m.* **(-es,** *pl.* **-e)** (*dial.*) rat; marmot; polecat; ***schlafen wie ein –,*** sleep like a top *or* log.

Ratze ['ratsə], *f.* (*coll.*) *see* **Ratte. ratzekahl,** *adj. See* **rattenkahl.**

Raub [raup], *m.* **(-(e)s,** *pl.* (*rare*) **-e)** 1. robbery; plundering, pillaging, rapine; kidnapping, abduction; rape; (*literary etc.*) piracy; ***auf – ausgehen,*** go on the prowl; ***gewaltsamer –,*** robbery with violence; 2. spoils, loot, booty, plunder, pillage, (*fig.*) prey; ***zum –e werden,*** fall victim *or* a prey (to); ***ein – der Flammen werden,*** be consumed *or* destroyed by fire. **Raub|anfall,** *m.* (armed) hold-up, (*Hist.*) highway robbery. **–bau,** *m.* exhaustion (*of the soil*), uncontrolled cutting (*of woods*); despoiling (*a mine*), (*fig.*) ruthless exploitation; ***– treiben mit,*** ruthlessly exploit; undermine (*one's health*).

rauben ['raubən], 1. *v.i.* steal, take by force, carry off; kidnap, abduct; ravish; (*Dat.*) rob *or* deprive of. 2. *v.i.* rob, commit robbery; plunder, pillage.

Räuber ['rɔybər], *m.* robber, thief; (*literary etc.*) pirate; (*Hist.*) highwayman, brigand; (*Hort.*) sucker; ***– und Gendarm spielen,*** play cops and robbers. **Räuberbande,** *f.* gang of thieves, band of robbers. **Räuberei** [–'raɪ], *f.* robbery; brigandage; pillage. **Räuber|geschichte,** *f.* penny-dreadful; cock-and-bull story. **–hauptmann,** *m.* robber chief. **–höhle,** *f.* den of thieves. **räuberisch,** *adj.* thievish, rapacious, predatory.

Raub|fisch, *m.* predatory fish. **–gesindel,** *n.* pack of thieves. **–gier,** *f.* rapacity. **raubgierig,** *adj.* rapacious. **Raub|gut,** *n.* booty; stolen goods. **–krieg,** *m.* predatory war. **–mord,** *m.* murder and robbery. **–möwe,** *f.* (*Orn.*) ***breitschwanzige –,*** see ***mittlere –; große –,*** great skua, (*Am.*) skua (*Stercorarius skua*); ***kleine –,*** long-tailed skua *or* (*Am.*) jaeger (*S. longicaudus*); ***landschwanzige*** or ***lanzettschwanzige –,*** see ***kleine –; mittlere –,*** pomatorhine skua, (*Am.*) pomarine jaeger (*S. pomarinus*); *see also* **Schmarotzerraubmöwe. –ritter,** *m.* robber knight. **–schiff,** *n.* pirate-ship, corsair. **–seeschwalbe,** *f.* (*Orn.*) Caspian tern (*Hydroprogne caspia*).

Raubstaaten ['raupʃta:tən], *m.pl.* Barbary States.

Raub|sucht, *f. See* **–gier. raub|süchtig,** *adj. See* **–gierig. Raub|tier,** *n.* beast of prey. **–überfall,** *m. See* **–anfall. –vogel,** *m.* bird of prey. **–wirtschaft,** *f.* ruinous exploitation. **–würger,** *m.* (*Orn.*) great grey shrike, (*Am.*) northern shrike (*Lanius excubitor*). **–zug,** *m.* raid.

rauch [raux], *adj.* (*used mainly in compounds*) shaggy.

Rauch, *m.* smoke; fume, vapour, steam; (*dial.*) soot; (*Poet.*) haze; ***in den – hängen,*** smoke(-dry); (*fig.*) disregard; ***in – aufgehen,*** go up in smoke, (*fig.*) end in smoke, come to nothing. **Rauch|abzug,** *m.* flue. **–bekämpfung,** *f.* smoke abatement. **–bombe,** *f.* smoke-shell. **rauchen,** 1. *v.i.* smoke, fume, give off smoke *or* fumes, reek; (*coll.*) ***daß es nur so rauchte,*** with a vengeance, like nobody's business. 2. *v.t.* smoke (*cigar etc.*). **Rauchen,** *n.* smoking; ***– verboten!*** no smoking! **Raucher,** *m.* smoker; (*coll.*) smoking-compartment.

Räucheraal ['rɔyçərʔa:l], *m.* smoked eel.

Raucherabteil ['rauxərʔaptaɪl], *n.* (*Railw.*) smoking-compartment.

Räucher|essig, *m.* aromatic vinegar. **–faß,** *n. See* **Rauchfaß. –hering,** *m.* smoked herring, kipper, bloater.

Raucherhusten ['rauxərhu:stən], *m.* smoker's cough.

Räucher|kammer, *f.* smoking- *or* curing-room. **–kerze,** *f.* fumigating candle. **–mittel,** *n.* fumigating agent. **räuchern,** 1. *v.t.* smoke(-dry), cure; fumigate. 2. *v.i.* burn incense. **Räucherung,** *f.* smoking, curing; fumigation. **Räucherwerk,** *n.* (*B.*) frankincense.

Rauch|fahne, *f.* trail of smoke. **–fang,** *m.* chimney, flue. **–faß,** *n.* censer. **–fleisch,** *n.* smoked meat. **rauch|frei,** *adj.* smokeless. **–füßig,** *adj.* hairy-footed, (*Orn.*) plumiped. **Rauchgas,** *n.* flue-gas, fumes. **rauchgeschwärzt,** *adj.* smoke-stained. **Rauch|glas,** *n.* smoked glass. **–helm,** *m.* smoke-helmet.

rauchig ['rauxɪç], *adj.* smoky.

Rauch|kammer, *f.* smoke-box (*in engines*). **–kanal,** *m.* smoke-flue, funnel. **rauchlos,** *adj. See* **rauchfrei. Rauch|nächte,** *f.pl.* (*dial.*) nights when spirits walk. **–opfer,** *n.* incense offering. **–pfanne,** *f. See* **–faß. –säule,** *f.* pillar *or* column of smoke.

-schieber, *m.* damper, register (*of furnace*). **-schrift,** *f.* (*Av.*) sky-writing. **rauch|schwach,** *adj. See* **-frei. Rauch|schwaden,** *m.pl.* wisps of smoke. **-schwalbe,** *f,* (*Orn.*) swallow, (*Am.*) barn swallow (*Hirundo rustica*). **rauchschwarz,** *adj.* black as soot. **Rauch|tabak,** *m.* tobacco. **-verbot,** *n.* ban on smoking. **-verbrennung,** *f.* consumption *or* elimination of smoke. **-verzehrer,** *m.* smoke-consumer *or* eliminator *or* remover. **-vorhang,** *m.,* **-wand,** *f.* (*Mil.*) smoke-screen. **-waren,** *f.pl.* 1. tobacco products; 2. (*also* **-werk,** *n.*) furs, peltry. **-zimmer,** *n.* smoke-room.

Räude ['rɔydə], *f.* scab, mange (*of dogs*), rubbers (*of sheep*). **räudig,** *adj.* scabby; mangy; (*fig.*) rotten, lousy, foul; (*fig.*) ***-es Schaf,*** black sheep.

rauf [rauf], *adv., sep. pref.* (*coll.*) *see* **darauf, herauf.**

Rauf|bold, *m.* **(-(e)s,** *pl.* **-e),** **-degen,** *m.* rowdy, brawler, ruffian, (*coll.*) tough.

Raufe ['raufə], *f.* hay-rack; hackle.

raufen ['raufən], **1.** *v.t.* pluck, pull out; *sich* (*Dat.*) ***die Haare -,*** tear one's hair. **2.** *v.i., v.r.* fight, brawl; scuffle, tussle. **Rauferei** [-'raı], *f.,* **Rauf|handel,** *m.* scuffle, fight, brawl. **-lust,** *f.* rowdiness, pugnacity. **rauflustig,** *adj.* pugnacious.

rauh [rau], *adj.* rough, uneven, rugged; (*of weather*) inclement, raw, (*of cold*) bitter, biting, (*of winter*) severe, (*of voice*) hoarse, (*of throat*) sore; (*fig.*) coarse; rude; harsh; (*dial.*) raw, uncooked; ***aus dem -en arbeiten,*** rough-hew; ***-e Behandlung,*** harsh treatment; ***-es Benehmen,*** coarse behaviour; ***-e Gegenden,*** wild, mountainous countryside; ***-es Klima,*** bleak climate; (*coll.*) ***in -en Mengen,*** galore; ***-er Pfad,*** rugged *or* bumpy path; ***-e Sitten,*** uncultivated manners; ***-e Tugend,*** austere virtue; ***-e Tatsachen, die -e Wirklichkeit,*** harsh reality, the hard facts.

Rauh|bank, *f.* (*Carp.*) jack-plane. **-bein,** *n.* (*fig.*) rough diamond, tough egg, roughneck. **rauhbeinig,** *adj.* caddish, loutish.

Rauhe ['rauə], *f. See* **Rauhzeit. Rauheit,** *f.* roughness, ruggedness, unevenness; inclemency, severity; rudeness, coarseness; hoarseness, harshness, acerbity; *see* **rauh. rauhen, 1.** *v.t.* roughen; card, tease, nap, dress (*cloth*). **2.** *v.i., v.r.* (*dial.*) moult.

Rauh|frost, *m.* (*dial.*) *see* **-reif. -fußbussard,** *m.* (*Orn.*) rough-legged buzzard *or* (*Am.*) hawk (*Buteo lagopus*). **-futter,** *n.* course fodder, roughage. **rauhhaarig,** *adj.* shaggy, hirsute; wire-haired (*dog*). **Rauh|nächte,** *f.pl. See* **Rauchnächte. -reif,** *m.* rime, hoar-frost. **-zeit,** *f.* (*dial.*) moulting season.

Rauke ['raukə], *f.* (*Bot.*) hedge mustard (*Eruca sativa*).

Raum [raum], *m.* **(-(e)s,** *pl.* **-̈e)** room, space; place, locality, district, zone, area; width, expanse; capacity, volume; hold (*of a ship*); accommodation, premises, room, hall, chamber; (*Tech.*) clearance, play; (*fig.*) scope, opportunity, sphere; ***- bieten*** (*Dat.*) *or* ***für,*** hold, accommodate, admit; (*Mil.*) ***bestrichener -,*** danger zone; (*Mil.*) ***feuerleerer*** or ***gedeckter -,*** dead space; ***luftleerer -,*** vacuum; (*fig.*) ***- geben*** (*Dat.*), give way to, indulge in; ***einer Bitte - geben,*** yield to *or* grant a request; ***seinen Neigungen - geben,*** follow one's bent *or* inclinations; ***einer Hoffnung - geben,*** indulge in a hope; ***- und Zeit,*** space and time. **raum,** *adj.* (*Naut.*) ***-e See,*** open sea; ***-er Wind,*** following *or* favourable wind; ***-es Feld,*** open *or* clear field.

Raum|analyse, *f.* volumetric analysis. **-anordnung,** *f.* floor plan, layout of rooms. **-bedarf,** *m.* space requirement. **-bild,** *n.* stereoscopic *or* panoramic picture, three-dimensional diagram.

Räumboot ['rɔymbo:t], *n.* mine-sweeper.

Raumeinheit ['raumˀaınhaıt], *f.* unit of volume.

raumen ['raumən], *v.i.* (*Naut.*) veer *or* draw aft (*of wind*).

räumen ['rɔymən], *v.t.* clear away, remove; sweep (*mines*); sell off (cheap) (*goods*); clear, clean up (*a room*), dredge (*a river*); make room; quit, leave, vacate (*a house*), evacuate (*a district*); (*Tech.*) broach; ***aus dem Wege -,*** remove (*obstacle*), make away with, dispose of (*a p.*); ***das Feld -,*** quit the field; ***beiseite -,*** put aside.

Raum|ersparnis, *f.* saving of space. **-flug,** *m.* space-flight. **-gehalt,** *m. See* **-inhalt. -geometrie,** *f.* solid geometry. **-gestalter,** *m.* interior decorator. **-gestaltung,** *f.* interior decoration. **-gewinn,** *m.* (*Mil.*) ground gained, advance.

räumig ['rɔymıç], *adj.* (*dial.*) roomy, spacious.

Raum|inhalt, *m.* cubic content, volume, capacity. **-kunst,** *f. See* **-gestaltung. -lehre,** *f.* geometry.

räumlich ['rɔymlıç], *adj.* spatial; three-dimensional, in space; (*Chem.*) volumetric, (*Opt.*) stereoscopic; ***-e Wirkung,*** stereoscopic effect. **Räumlichkeit,** *f.* 1. extent, space; spaciousness; 2. locality; *pl.* rooms, premises.

Raum|mangel, *m.* lack of space *or* room. **-maß,** *n.* measure of capacity; dimensions. **-messung,** *f.* stereometry. **-meter,** *n. or m.* cubic metre.

Räumpflug ['rɔympflu:k], *m.* bulldozer.

Raum|politik, *f.* geopolitics. **-raffer,** *m.* telephoto lens. **-schiff,** *n.* space-ship. **-schiffahrt,** *f.* space-travel.

Räumte ['rɔymtə], *f.* (*Naut.*) offing, open sea; ship's hold, loading space; ***die - suchen,*** stand out to sea.

Raum|temperatur, *f.* room temperature. **-tonne,** *f.* (*Naut.*) freight ton. **-tonwirkung,** *f.* (*Rad.*) stereoscopic effect.

Räumtrupp ['rɔymtrup], *m.* demolition party. **Räumung,** *f.* removal, clearing; leaving, vacating, quitting (*voluntarily*), eviction (*under compulsion*); evacuation (*of population*), (*Comm.*) clearance (*of goods*); (*Law*) ***Vollstreckung durch -,*** execution by a writ of possession. **Räumungs|(aus)verkauf,** *m.* clearance sale. **-befehl,** *m.* eviction order. **-gebiet,** *n.* (*Mil.*) territory (to be) evacuated.

Raum|verschwendung, *f.* waste of space. **-verteilung,** *f.* layout (*of rooms*), disposition of space; (*Typ.*) spacing. **-welle,** *f.* (*Rad.*) space- *or* propagating *or* non-directional wave.

raunen ['raunən], *v.t., v.i.* whisper, murmur; ***man raunt*** (***sich*** (*Dat.*) ***ins Ohr***), it is rumoured, rumour has it.

raunzen ['rauntsən], *v.i.* (*coll.*) grumble, find fault, niggle, nag.

Raupe ['raupə], *f.* 1. caterpillar; grub, maggot; (*coll.*) ***-n im Kopf haben,*** have a bee in one's bonnet; 2. caterpillar-track (*vehicle*); 3. helmet-crest. **Raupen|antrieb,** *m.* caterpillar-drive. **-fahrzeug,** *n.* full-tracked vehicle. **-fraß,** *m.* damage done by caterpillars. **raupengängig,** *adj.* tracked (*of vehicles*). **Raupen|helm,** *m.* dragoon's crested helmet. **-kette,** *f.* caterpillar-track. **-schlepper,** *m.* (*regd. trade name*) caterpillar-tractor.

raus [raus], *adv., sep. pref.* (*coll.*) *see* **heraus.**

Rausch [rauʃ], *m.* **(-es,** *pl.* **-̈e)** drunken fit, drunkenness, intoxication; (*fig.*) frenzy, transport, ecstasy; ***einen - haben,*** be drunk; ***im -e,*** in one's cups; ***sich*** (*Dat.*) ***einen - antrinken,*** get tipsy; ***seinen - ausschlafen,*** sleep it off; ***im ersten -,*** in the first rapture *or* transport *or* flush (of enthusiasm). **Rauschbeere,** *f.* (*Bot.*) crowberry (*Empetrum nigrum*).

rauschen ['rauʃən], *v.i.* rush (*wind, water*), rustle, murmur (*breeze*), roar (*storm*), rustle (*leaves, silk etc.*), thunder (*applause*), (*Poet.*) sough; (*fig.*) (*aux.* s.) sweep, sail. **Rauschen,** *n.* rushing (noise), rustle, roar; (*Rad.*) (background) noise. **rauschend,** *adj.* rustling; noisy; ***-er Beifall,*** thunderous applause; ***-e Vergnügungen,*** boisterous pleasures.

Rausch|faktor, *m.* (*Rad.*) signal-to-noise ratio. **-gelb,** *n.* orpiment.

Rauschgift ['rauʃgıft], *n.* (narcotic) drug, (*sl.*) dope. **Rauschgift|handel,** *m.* drug-traffic. **-sucht,** *f.* drug-addiction. **rauschgiftsüchtig,** *adj.* addicted to drugs. **Rauschgiftsüchtige(r),** *m., f.* drug-addict, (*sl.*) junkie.

Rausch|gold, *n.* tinsel. **-mittel,** *n.* intoxicant. **-pfeife,** *f.,* **-werk,** *n.* loud alto (*in organs*).

räuspern ['rɔyspərn], *v.r.* clear one's throat.

Raus|reißer, *m.* (*coll.*) good selling line. **-schmeißer,** *m.* (*coll.*) 1. chucker-out, (*Am.*) bouncer; 2. last dance.

[1]**Raute** ['rautə], *f.* (*Bot.*) rue (*Ruta*).

[2]**Raute,** *f.* (*Her.*) lozenge(-shaped figure), (*Cards*) diamond, (*Geom.*) rhombus, rhomb(oid). **Rauten|bauer,** *m.* (*Cards*) knave of diamonds. **-fläche,** *f.* rhomb; facet. **rautenförmig,** *adj.* rhomboid, rhombic, lozenge-shaped; – *schneiden,* cut in facets.

Rayon [rɛ'jɔ̃], *m.* (**-s,** *pl.* **-s**) (*Artil.*) radius, range; district, area. **Rayonchef,** *m.* departmental head *or* manager. **rayonieren** [-jo'ni:rən], *v.t.* allocate, distribute.

Razzia ['ratsia], *f.* (-, *pl.* **-ien** *or* (*Austr.*) **-ias**) police-raid, (*coll.*) round-up; (*fig.*) swoop, crack-down (*auf* (*Acc.*), on).

Reagenz [rea'gɛnts], *n.* (-, *pl.* **-ien**) reagent. **Reagenz|glas,** *n.* test-tube. **-papier,** *n.* test-paper, litmus paper. **reagibel,** *adj.* sensitive. **reagieren,** *v.i.* react (*auf* (*Acc.*), on), (*fig.*) respond (to); show a reaction.

Reaktanz [reak'tants], *f.* (*Elec.*) reactance.

Reaktion [reaktsi'o:n], *f.* reaction (*auf* (*Acc.*), on) (*also Pol.*), (*fig.*) response (to). **reaktionär** [-'nɛ:r], *adj.* (*Pol.*) reactionary. **Reaktionär,** *m.* (**-s,** *pl.* **-e**), **Reaktionärin,** *f.* (*Pol.*) reactionary, reactionist. **Reaktions|fähigkeit,** *f.* sensitivity, responsiveness, (*Chem.*) reactivity. **-kette,** *f.* chain-reaction. **-mittel,** *n.* (*Chem.*) reagent. **-moment,** *n.* (engine) torque. **reaktions|schnell,** *adj.* susceptible, impressionable, responsive; lively, mettlesome, highly-strung. **-träge,** *adj.* slow to react, unresponsive, unimpressionable, torpid.

real [re'a:l], *adj.* real, actual, concrete, substantial; material, tangible. **Realgymnasium,** *n.* secondary school with scientific bias. **Realien,** *pl.* realities, real facts; exact sciences; institutions and customs. **Realinjurie,** *f.* assault and battery.

realisierbar [reali'zi:rba:r], *adj.* realizable, (*assets*) liquid; *nicht -e Aktiven,* frozen assets. **realisieren,** *v.t.* realize; dispose of (*assets*), convert *or* (*coll.*) turn into money. **Realisierung,** *f.* realization, disposal (*of assets*), conversion into money.

Realismus [rea'lɪsmus], *m.* realism. **realistisch,** *adj.* realistic.

Realität [reali'tɛ:t], *f.* 1. reality; 2. *pl.* (*dial.*) real estate, landed property. **realiter** [-'a:litɛr], *adv.* in reality.

Real|katalog, *m.* subject catalogue. **-kenntnisse,** *f.pl.* factual knowledge. **-konkurrenz,** *f.* (*Law*) cumulation. **-kredit,** *m.* mortgage. **-lexikon,** *n.* encyclopaedia. **-lohn,** *m.* real wages, commodities in lieu of wages. **-obligation,** *f.* mortgage (bond). **-politik,** *f.* realist politics. **-schule,** *f.* science *or* modern secondary school. **-steuer,** *f.* tax on real estate and commercial transactions. **-wert,** *m.* actual value.

Rebe ['re:bə], *f.* vine, grape tendril.

Rebell [re'bɛl], *m.* (**-en,** *pl.* **-en**) rebel; mutineer. **rebellieren** [-'li:rən], *v.i.* rebel, revolt, mutiny. **Rebellion** [-i'o:n], *f.* rebellion. **rebellisch,** *adj.* rebellious.

rebeln ['re:bəln], *v.i.* (*dial.*) gather grapes.

Reben|blatt, *n.* vine leaf. **-geländer,** *n.* vine-trellis. **-gott,** *m.* Bacchus. **-hügel,** *m.* vine-clad hill. **-saft,** *m.* grape-juice; (*Poet.*) wine.

Reb|huhn ['re:p-], *n.* (*Orn.*) partridge, (*Am.*) gray partridge (*Perdix perdix*). **-hühnervolk,** *n.* covey of partridges. **-laus,** *f.* phylloxera vastatrix. **-stock,** *m.* vine.

Rechen ['rɛçən], *m.* rake; rack (*for clothes*); grating (*of a weir*). **rechen,** *v.t.* rake.

Rechen|aufgabe, *f.* sum, arithmetical problem. **-brett,** *n.* abacus. **-buch,** *n.* arithmetic book. **-exempel,** *n. See* **-aufgabe. -fehler,** *m.* miscalculation, arithmetical error, (*coll.*) mistake. **-heft,** *n.* sum book, arithmetic book. **-kammer,** *f.* audit-office. **-knecht,** *m. See* **-tabelle. -kunst,** *f.* arithmetic. **-künstler,** *m.* arithmetician, person good at figures. **-lehrer,** *m.* arithmetic teacher. **-maschine,** *f.* adding *or* calculating-machine, computer. **-pfennig,** *m.* counter (*at cards*).

Rechenschaft ['rɛçənʃaft], *f.* account; *ihm – schuldig sein,* be accountable to him; *ihn zur – ziehen* or *fordern,* call him to account (*wegen,* for); – *ablegen* or *geben über* (*Acc.*), answer *or* account for, give an account of; *sich der – entziehen,* evade *or* (*coll.*) dodge the consequences. **Rechenschaftsbericht,** *m.* statement of accounts, report (of activities). **rechenschaftspflichtig,** *adj.* accountable.

Rechen|schieber, *m.* slide-rule. **-stelle,** *f.* computing centre. **-stunde,** *f.* arithmetic lesson. **-tabelle,** *f.* ready reckoner. **-tafel,** *f.* slate.

Recherchen [re'ʃɛrʃən], *f.pl.* inquiries, investigation.

rechnen ['rɛçnən], *v.t., v.i.* count, calculate, reckon, (*coll.*) work out; compute, figure, estimate; (*v.i.*) do sums; (*fig.*) esteem, consider, hold (to be); rank, class (*unter* (*Acc.*) *or zu,* with *or* among); – *auf* (*Acc.*), reckon *or* count *or* depend *or* rely on; *an einer Aufgabe –,* work out a sum; *falsch –,* miscalculate; *hoch gerechnet,* at the most; *eins fürs* or *ins andre gerechnet,* taking *or* counting each (item) separately, omitting nothing; with one th. and another, considering everything; *alles in allem gerechnet,* considering everything, (taking) all in all, on the whole; *– lernen,* learn arithmetic; *– mit,* reckon with; *mit ihm ist nicht zu –,* he cannot be relied on, there is no relying on him, you do not know where you are with him; *wir müssen damit –, daß . . .,* we must take into account that . . ., we must be prepared for . . ., we must face the possibility that . . ., it may happen *or* may be that . . .; *mit dazu gerechnet,* inclusive of, thrown in; *wir – es uns zur Ehre,* we consider *or* (*Poet.*) deem it an honour. **Rechnen,** *n.* calculation(s), arithmetic.

Rechner ['rɛçnər], *m.* 1. p. good at figures, arithmetician; 2. computer. **rechnerisch,** *adj.* mathematical, arithmetical; analytical.

Rechnung ['rɛçnuŋ], *f.* calculation, computation; sum; account, bill, invoice, (*coll.*) reckoning; calculus; opinion; – *ablegen,* render an account; *eine – ausgleichen,* balance *or* settle *or* (*coll.*) square an account; (*coll.*) *die – geht nicht auf,* it won't *or* can't work out; *eine – aufgehen lassen,* strike a balance; *auf eigne –,* at one's own risk; *– führen,* keep accounts *or* an account; *auf – und Gefahr,* for account and risk; (*coll.*) *das geht auf meine –,* that is on me; *auf – kaufen,* buy on credit, have an account; *auf seine – kommen,* benefit (*bei,* from *or* by), profit (from); *auf – setzen,* charge *or* place to account; *eine – begleichen, see eine – ausgleichen*; *ihm einen Strich durch die – machen,* frustrate his plans, put an end to his (little) game, put a spoke in his wheel; *gemeinschaftliche –,* joint account; *in – bringen* or *stellen, see auf – setzen*; *auf* or *in feste – liefern,* supply and charge to account; *in – stehen mit,* have a running *or* ledger account with; (*fig.*) *in – ziehen,* take into consideration *or* account; *laufende –,* current account; *laut –,* as per account; (*coll.*) *die – ohne den Wirt machen,* reckon without one's host; *eine – saldieren, see eine – ausgleichen*; *– tragen* (*Dat.*), allow for, take into account, make allowance(s) for.

Rechnungs|ablegung, *f.* rendering of accounts. **-abnahme,** *f.* audit(ing of accounts). **-abschluß,** *m.* balancing *or* closing of accounts, balance-sheet. **-art,** *f.* method of calculation; (*Arith.*) *die vier -en,* the four rules. **-ausschuß,** *m.* audit-board. **-auszug,** *m.* abstract *or* statement of accounts. **-beleg,** *m.* voucher. **-betrag,** *m.* invoice figure. **-buch,** *n.* account-book. **-führer,** *m.* accountant, book-keeper; (*Mil.*) pay sergeant. **-führung,** *f.* accountancy, accounting. **-jahr,** *n.* financial *or* fiscal year. **-kammer,** *f.* government audit-office. **-prüfer,** *m.* auditor, comptroller. **-prüfung,** *f.* audit, auditing. **-revisor,** *m. See* **-prüfer**; *vereidigter –,* chartered accountant. **-stelle,** *f.* accounting-office. **-wesen,** *n.* book-keeping, accountancy, accounting, auditing, actuarial matters.

recht [rɛçt], **1.** *adj.*
1. right(-hand); **–er Hand,** on the right; **die Rechte,** right hand; right(-hand) side; (*Pol.*) the Right; **mit erhobener Rechten,** with the right hand uplifted; **zur Rechten,** on *or* to the right; (*Boxing*) **mit einem blitzschnellen Rechten,** with a lightning right;
2. right, proper, correct, due, fitting, befitting, agreeable, suitable; true, real, sound, thorough, genuine; just, lawful, legitimate; ***nur – und billig,*** only just and reasonable, only fair; ***–er Bruder,*** my own brother (*opp. to half-brother*); ***das geht nicht mit –en Dingen zu,*** there is something queer *or* not quite right there; ***–e Ehefrau,*** lawful wife; ***der –e Glaube,*** the true faith; ***ihm ist jedes Mittel –,*** he sticks at nothing; ***er ist ein –er Narr,*** he is a proper fool; ***mir ist es –,*** I agree to *or* with it, I am agreeable, that suits me fine, it's all right with me; ***wenn es Ihnen – ist,*** if it is agreeable to *or* all right with you; ***ist es so –?*** will that do? ***so ist's –!*** that's all right! (*sl.*) O.K.! that's the stuff! ***was dem einen –st, ist dem andern billig,*** what's sauce for the goose is sauce for the gander; ***–er Winkel,*** right angle; ***zu –er Zeit,*** in (good) time, punctually; ***zur –en Zeit,*** at the proper time, at the right moment, just in time, in the nick of time;
der or ***die Rechte,*** the right *or* very p.; (*iron.*) ***du bist mir der Rechte!*** you're a fine fellow *or* (*coll.*) a nice one! ***an den Rechten kommen,*** meet one's match; ***das Rechte,*** the proper *or* right *or* appropriate th.; ***er dünkt sich was Rechtes,*** he thinks himself somebody; (*iron.*) ***das ist was Rechtes!*** that's not so wonderful, that's nothing to be proud about *or* (*coll.*) to write home about; (*iron.*) ***das half ihm auch was Rechtes!*** that was a great help, I'm sure! (*coll.*) ***nichts Rechtes wissen,*** have no idea; ***das Rechte meinen,*** have the right idea; ***das Rechte treffen,*** hit the mark; ***nach dem Rechten sehen,*** see that everything is all right *or* in order, look after things.
2. *adv.* well, right(ly), greatly, remarkably, very; quite, rather, really, downright; properly, correctly, thoroughly, soundly; ***wenn ich es – bedenke,*** when I come to think of it; ***– behalten,*** be right in the end; ***erst –,*** all the more, more than ever; (*coll.*) with a vengeance; ***ganz –!*** quite (so)! exactly! ***ihm – geben,*** acknowledge *or* admit that he is right, agree with him; ***– gern,*** gladly, with pleasure; (*coll.*) ***nicht – gescheit,*** not all there; ***das geschieht dir –,*** that serves you right; ***– gut,*** very good, quite well, (*coll.*) not (at all) bad; ***– haben,*** be (in the) right; (*iron.*) ***da kommst du mir –!*** just what I expected; ***es tut mir – leid,*** I am truly sorry; ***es nicht – machen können*** (*Dat.*), not able to do anything right for, not able to please; (***so***) ***– als ob,*** just as if; ***schlecht und –,*** fairly good, not bad; ***tue – und scheue niemand,*** do (what is) right and shame the devil; ***ich weiß nicht –,*** I'm not so sure; ***sie kommen – zeitig,*** you (have) come very early (*see* **rechtzeitig**).

Recht, *n.* **(-es,** *pl.* **-e)** right, privilege; title (***auf*** (*Acc.*), to), claim (on), interest (in); authority, power; law; justice; administration of justice; ***angestammtes –,*** birthright; ***bürgerliches –,*** civil law; ***für – befinden,*** hold *or* find (to be); ***für – erkennen*** or ***erklären,*** adjudge, decree, determine, order; ***gemeines –,*** common law; ***geschriebenes –,*** statute law; ***im – sein,*** be in the right, be within one's rights, have right *or* justice on one's side; ***mit –,*** justly, rightly, with (good) reason(s); ***mit – sagen,*** be correct in saying; ***ohne –,*** unjustly; ***– sprechen,*** administer *or* dispense justice; ***– über Leben und Tod,*** power over life and death; ***sich*** (*Dat.*) ***selbst – verschaffen,*** take the law into one's own hands; ***von –s wegen,*** by rights, in justice, (*Law*) de jure; ***ihm – widerfahren lassen,*** do him justice; ***zu – bestehen,*** be legitimate *or* justified *or* valid; ***zu seinem –e kommen,*** come into one's own (again); ***zu – erkennen,*** *see* ***für – befinden.***

Rechte, *see* **recht.**

Rechteck [ˈrɛçtˀɛk], *n.* rectangle. **rechteckig,** *adj.* rectangular.

rechten [ˈrɛçtən], *v.i.* contest, dispute, remonstrate, demand one's right. **rechtens,** *adv.* lawfully, by law, right and proper; ***im Wege –,*** by the due processes of law.

Rechter [ˈrɛçtər], *m.* (*Boxing*) right. **Rechte(r), Rechte(s),** *see* **recht.**

rechtfertigen [ˈrɛçtfɛrtɪgən], **1.** *v.t.* (*insep.*) justify, vindicate. **2.** *v.r.* justify *or* vindicate o.s.; exculpate *or* (*coll.*) clear o.s. **Rechtfertigung,** *f.* justification, vindication; ***zu seiner –,*** in his defence, in justice to him. **Rechtfertigungsgrund,** *m.* excuse, (legal) justification.

rechtgläubig [ˈrɛçtglɔybɪç], *adj.* orthodox. **Rechtgläubigkeit,** *f.* orthodoxy.

Recht|haber, *m.* disputatious *or* dogmatic person, dogmatist, (*coll.*) know-all. **–haberei,** *f.* disputatiousness, dogmatism, obstinacy. **rechthaberisch,** *adj.* obstinate, disputatious, dogmatic(al).

rechtläufig [ˈrɛçtlɔyfɪç], *adv.* clockwise, running the normal course.

rechtlich [ˈrɛçtlɪç], *adj.* lawful, legal, judicial, juridical; valid, legitimate; honest, upright, righteous; just, fair, proper. **Rechtlichkeit,** *f.* lawfulness, legality; validity, rightness; probity, integrity, honesty; fair play.

rechtlinig [ˈrɛçtli:nɪç], *adj.* rectilinear.

rechtlos [ˈrɛçtlo:s], *adj.* illegal, unlawful; without rights, outside the pale of the law, outlawed. **Rechtlosigkeit,** *f.* absence *or* lack of rights; unlawfulness, illegality; outlawry.

rechtmäßig [ˈrɛçtmɛ:sɪç], *adj.* legal, lawful, rightful, legitimate; just, fair. **Rechtmäßigkeit,** *f.* lawfulness, legality; legitimacy, rightfulness.

rechts [rɛçts], *adv.* on the right (hand); to the right; ***nach –,*** to the right; ***– halten!*** keep to the right! ***gleich – um die Ecke,*** (take) the first turning on *or* to the right; ***die erste Straße –,*** the first street on the right; ***– von ihm,*** to *or* on his right.

rechtsanhängig [ˈrɛçtsˀanhɛŋɪç], *adj.* pending (judicial decision), sub judice. **Rechts|anspruch,** *m.* legal claim (***auf*** (*Acc.*), on *or* to), title (to). **–anwalt,** *m.* lawyer, solicitor; barrister(-at-law), (*Am.*) attorney-at-law; ***– für den Beklagten*** (***Kläger***), counsel for the defence (plaintiff). **–anwaltschaft,** *f.* the bar. **–anwaltskammer,** *f.* Bar Association. **–ausdruck,** *m.* legal term. **–außen(stürmer),** *m.* (*Footb.*) outside right. **–beflissene(r),** *m.* (*obs.*) law-student. **–befugnis,** *f.* competency. **–begehren,** *n.* petition. **–behelf,** *m.* protest, remonstrance, demurrer, legal remedy. **–beistand,** *m.* counsel; legal adviser. **–belehrung,** *f.* legal instructions; direction of the jury, (judge's) summing up. **–beratung, –betreuung,** *f.* legal aid. **–beugung,** *f.* defeating the ends of the law, perversion of justice. **–bruch,** *m.* infringement *or* breach of the law.

rechtschaffen [ˈrɛçtʃafən], **1.** *adj.* righteous, upright, honest; (*fig.*) solid, thorough. **2.** *adv.* (*also coll.*) thoroughly, downright, awfully, mighty, mightily. **Rechtschaffenheit,** *f.* integrity, honesty, probity, uprightness.

rechtschreiben [ˈrɛçtʃraɪbən], *irr. v.i.* (*sep.*) (*rare*) spell correctly; (*but cf. **er kann nicht recht schreiben,*** he cannot write properly, his writing is bad). **Rechtschreibung,** *f.* spelling, orthography.

Rechtsdrall [ˈrɛçtsdral], *m.* clockwise rifling. **rechtsdrehend,** *adj.* clockwise, dextrorotatory. **Rechts|drehung,** *f.* clockwise rotation. **–einwand,** *m.* demurrer, traverse, plea.

Rechtser [ˈrɛçtsər], *m.* (*coll.*) right-handed p.

rechtsfähig [ˈrɛçtsfɛ:ɪç], *adj.* competent; with legal competency; ***–er Verband,*** incorporated society. **Rechts|fähigkeit,** *f.* competency, competence, legal rights. **–fall,** *m.* suit, cause, (court-)case. **–frage,** *f.* legal question, point of law. **–gang,** *m.* 1. legal procedure; proceedings; 2. (*Mech.*) clockwise action *or* operation. **rechts|gängig,** *adj.* right-handed (*thread*); *see* **–drehend. Rechts|gefühl,** *n.* sense of justice. **–gelehrsamkeit,** *f.* jurisprudence. **–gelehrte(r),** *m., f.* lawyer, jurist. **–geschäft,** *n.* legal transaction. **–gewinde,** *n.* right-hand thread. **–gleichheit,** *f.* equality in the eyes of the *or* before the law. **–grund,** *m.* legal argument; title (*auf* (*Acc.*), to). **–grundlage,** *f.* legal basis *or* foundation. **–grundsatz,** *m.* legal maxim. **rechts|gültig, 1.** *adj.* legal, valid, good in law; *see* **–kräftig. 2.** *adv.* – *ausfertigen,* execute; – *machen,* validate. **Rechts|gültigkeit,** *f.* legality, validity. **–gutachten,** *n.* legal *or* counsel's opinion. **Rechts|handel,** *m.* (legal) action, lawsuit, litigation. **–händer,** *m.* right-handed p. **rechtshändig,** *adj.* right-handed. **Rechts|innen(stürmer),** *m.* (*Footb.*) inside right. **–kraft,** *f.* force of law, validity; – *erlangen,* become valid *or* final *or* effective, come into effect; – *erteilen,* confirm, validate; – *haben,* be conclusive. **rechtskräftig,** *adj.* legally binding, legal, valid. **Rechts|kurve,** *f.* right-hand bend. **–lage,** *f.* legal status *or* position. **–lauf,** *m.* *See* **–drehung. –mangel,** *m.* defect of title. **–mittel,** *n.* legal remedy, right of appeal; – *einlegen,* lodge an appeal. **–nachfolger,** *m.* assign. **–person,** *f.* body corporate. **–pflege,** *f.* administration of justice. **–pfleger,** *m.* judicial administrator, registrar.

Rechtsprechung ['rɛçtʃprɛçuŋ], *f.* administration of justice; jurisdiction.

rechtsradikal ['rɛçtsradi'ka:l], *adj.* (*Pol.*) (extreme) right-wing. **Rechts|radikale(r),** *m., f.* (extreme) right-winger. **–säure,** *f.* (*Chem.*) dextro-acid. **–schutz,** *m.* legal protection. **–schwenkung,** *f.* (*Mil.*) movement to the right. **–sprache,** *f.* legal terminology. **–spruch,** *m.* legal decision; (*criminal*) sentence, (*civil*) judgement, (*of a jury*) verdict. **–staat,** *m.* constitutional state. **–steuerung,** *f.* (*Motor.*) right-hand drive. **–streit,** *m.* litigation, action, lawsuit. **–titel,** *m.* legal title.

rechtsum [rɛçts'um], *adv.* (*Mil.*) – *schwenkt!* right wheel! – (*kehrt*)*!* right about turn *or* (*Am.*) face!

rechtsunfähig ['rɛçtsˀunfɛ:ıç], *adj.* legally disabled. **Rechtsunfähigkeit,** *f.* legal disability. **rechts|-ungültig,** *adj.* illegal, invalid. **–unwirksam,** *adj.* without legal force, ineffective. **–verbindlich,** *adj.* legally binding (*für,* on). **Rechts|verdreher,** *m.* pettifogging lawyer. **–verfassung,** *f.* judicial system, judiciary, judicature. **–verhältnis,** *n.* legal relationship; *pl.* legal position. **–verkehr,** *m.* (*Motor.*) right-hand traffic. **–verletzung,** *f.* infringement of rights. **–vertreter,** *m.* proxy, authorized agent, attorney. **–weg,** *m.* course of law, legal procedure; *den – beschreiten,* go to law, take legal action *or* proceedings *or* steps; *unter Ausschluß des –es,* admitting of no appeal. **rechts|weisend,** *adj.* (*Naut. etc.*) true (*of a course*). **–widrig,** *adj.* illegal, illicit, unlawful. **Rechtswidrigkeit,** *f.* illegality, unlawfulness. **rechts|wirksam,** *adj.* *See* **–kräftig. Rechtswissenschaft,** *f.* jurisprudence.

recht|wink(e)lig, *adj.* right-angled (*triangle*), rectangular. **–zeitig, 1.** *adj.* timely, well-timed, opportune, seasonable. **2.** *adv.* on time, in (good) time, punctually, (*coll.*) in the nick of time.

Reck [rɛk], *n.* **(-(e)s,** *pl.* **-e)** (*Gymn.*) horizontal bar; rack, stretcher.

Recke ['rɛkə], *m.* **(-n,** *pl.* **-n)** valiant warrior, hero.

recken ['rɛkən], **1.** *v.t.* stretch, extend; rack; *die Glieder –,* stretch one's limbs; *den Kopf in die Höhe –,* crane one's neck. **2.** *v.r.* stretch o.s.

reckenhaft ['rɛkənhaft], *adj.* valiant, doughty.

Redakteur [redak'tø:r], *m.* **(-s,** *pl.* **-e** *or* **-s)** editor. **Redaktion** [–tsi'o:n], *f.* editing; editorship; editor's office; editorial staff; wording, drafting, drawing up (*of deeds etc.*). **redaktionell** [–'nɛl], *adj.* editorial. **Redaktionsschluß,** *m.* time of going to press; – *machen,* put a paper to bed; *nach – eingegangen,* stop-press (news).

Rede ['re:də], *f.* speech, utterance, words, talk, discourse, conversation; speech, address, oration; report, rumour; *alltägliche –,* common parlance; (*Gram.*) *direkte –,* direct speech; *gebundene –,* verse, poetry; *die – geht,* it is said, rumour has it; *gehobene –,* elevated style; *eine – halten,* make a speech, deliver an address *or* oration; (*coll.*) *große –n halten,* talk big; *ihm in die – fallen,* interrupt him, cut him short; *davon ist nicht die –,* that is not the point; *wenn die – darauf kommen soll(te),* if the subject should be mentioned; *die – kam auf* (*Acc.*), the conversation came round *or* got on to; *ihn zur – kommen lassen,* let him speak; *wovon ist die – ?* what are you talking about? what is the point at issue? *davon kann keine – sein,* that is out of the question; (*coll.*) *keine – !* nothing of the kind! by no means! *der langen – kurzer Sinn,* the long and the short of it; – (*und Antwort*) *stehen,* be answerable, (have to) answer (*über* (*Acc.*), for), give an account (of); *in – stehen,* be under discussion; *der in – stehende Gegenstand,* the subject under discussion *or* in question; *ungebundene –,* prose; *nicht der – wert,* not worth mentioning; *es wird die – davon sein,* we shall speak of it, we shall turn to this point; *zur – stellen,* call to account, take to task.

rede|begabt, *adj.* eloquent. **–fertig,** *adj.* fluent, glib. **Rede|figur,** *f.* figure of speech, metaphorical expression. **–fluß,** *m.* flow of words, fluency, volubility. **–freiheit,** *f.* liberty of speech. **–gabe,** *f.* fluency, eloquence, (*coll.*) gift of the gab. **rede|-gewandt,** *adj.* *See* **–fertig. Redekunst,** *f.* rhetoric.

reden ['re:dən], *v.t., v.i.* speak, talk (*mit,* to), converse, discourse (with) (*über* (*Acc.*), about *or* on (*a subject*)); *sich* (*Dat.*) *einen Prozeß an den Hals –,* talk o.s. into trouble; *Sie haben gut* or *leicht –,* it is all very well *or* is easy for you to talk; *ihm ins Gewissen –,* appeal to his conscience; *in den Tag hinein –,* talk at random; *in den Wind –,* beat the air; *in die Wolle hinein –,* talk into the blue; *darüber läßt sich –,* we can talk about that (later), that sounds reasonable enough; *mit sich – lassen,* listen to reason; *mit Zungen –,* talk with the voice of angels; *viel von sich – machen,* cause a great stir, give rise to comment; *ihm nach dem Munde –,* echo his opinion, talk in a way that suits *or* pleases him; (*sl.*) – *wie einem der Schnabel gewachsen ist,* shoot off one's mouth; *keine Silbe –,* not say a word, not utter a sound; *aus ihm redet die Verzweiflung,* his is the language of despair; *das Wort –* (*Gen.*), put in a (good) word for, hold a brief for, support, defend, advocate, recommend.

Reden, *n.* talking, speaking; speech; *viel –s von etwas machen,* make a great pother *or* fuss about a th.; *all' Ihr – ist umsonst,* you are wasting your breath; *das – wird ihm schwer,* he speaks with difficulty. **redend,** *adj.* speaking; (*fig.*) expressive; *die –e Person,* the interlocutor *or* speaker; *–e Künste,* poetry and music, the communicative arts. **Redensart,** *f.* expression, phrase; idiom, figure of speech; phraseology; *allgemeine –,* common saying; *bloße –en,* mere words, empty talk *or* phrases; *feste –,* stock phrase; *sprichwörtliche –,* proverb, saying. **Rederei** [–'raı], *f.* empty prattle, idle talk.

Rede|schmuck, *m.* rhetorical embellishment. **–schwall,** *m.* *See* **–strom. –schwulst,** *m.* bombast. **–schwung,** *m.* rhetorical flight. **–strom,** *m.* flood of words, verbosity. **–teil,** *m.* (*Gram.*) part of speech. **–übung,** *f.* exercise in declamation. **–weise,** *f.* manner of speaking, mode of expression, style, language. **–wendung,** *f.* turn of speech, phrase, expression, idiom.

redigieren [redi'gi:rən], *v.t.* edit, prepare for the press, revise.

redlich ['re:tlıç], *adj.* honest; sincere, upright, candid, just. **Redlichkeit,** *f.* honesty, probity, integrity, uprightness, sincerity.

Redner ['re:dnər], *m.* speaker, orator. **Redner|-bühne,** *f.* platform, rostrum. **–gabe,** *f.* *See* **Redegabe. rednerisch,** *adj.* oratorical, rhetorical.

Redoute [redu'te], *f.* **1.** (*Fort.*) redoubt; **2.** fancy-dress ball.

redselig ['re:tze:lıç], *adj.* talkative, loquacious, garrulous, (*coll.*) chatty. **Redseligkeit,** *f.* talkativeness, loquacity, (*coll.*) chattiness.

Reduktion [reduktsi'o:n], *f.* reduction, diminution. **Reduktions|mittel,** *n.* reducing agent. **–teilung,** *f.* (*Biol.*) meiosis. **–ventil,** *n.* reduction valve.

reduzierbar [redu'tsi:rba:r], *adj.* reducible. **redu-**

zieren, I. *v.t.* reduce, diminish, lower (*auf* (*Acc.*), to). 2. *v.r.* be(come) reduced, diminish, decrease, atrophy. **reduziert,** *adj.* reduced, diminished, vestigial; (*coll.*) *er sieht sehr – aus,* he looks very down-at-heel.

ree! [re:], *int.* (*Naut.*) about ship!

Reede ['re:də], *f.* (*Naut.*) roadstead, roads; *auf der – liegen,* ride at anchor (*in the roads*). **reeden,** *v.t.* fit out (*ship*). **Reeder,** *m.* shipowner. **Reederei** [–'raɪ], *f.* I. shipping-office; shipping company *or* line; – *betreiben,* be in (the) shipping (business); 2. fitting out (*of a ship*). **Reedereiflagge,** *f.* house flag.

Reef [re:f], *n.* *See* **Reff,** 2.

Reeling, *f.* *See* **Reling.**

reell [re'ɛl], *adj.* safe, sound, solid, reliable, respectable; practicable, workable; fair, honest, just; *–e Bedienung,* fair dealing, good value for one's money; *–es Geschäft,* respectable *or* reliable firm; *–e Waren,* sound wares. **Reelität** [–i'tɛ:t], *f.* (*Comm.*) soundness, reliability, trustworthiness,

Reep [re:p], *n.* (**-(e)s,** *pl.* **-e**) (*dial.*) rope.

Refektorium [refɛk'to:rium], *n.* (**-s,** *pl.* **-rien**) refectory.

Referat [refe'ra:t], *n.* (**-(e)s,** *pl.* **-e**) lecture, talk, report (*usu. verbal*); abstract, review (*of a book*); (*Univ. etc.*) *ein – halten,* read a paper.

Referendar [referɛn'da:r], *m.* (**-s,** *pl.* **-e**), **Referendarin,** *f.* junior barrister; teacher on probation.

Referendum [refe'rɛndum], *n.* (-s, *pl.* **-den** *or* **-da**) (*Swiss*) plebiscite.

Referent [refe'rɛnt], *m.* (**-en,** *pl.* **-en**) expert (adviser), consultant; reviewer (*of a book*); speaker, lecturer, reader of a (scholarly) paper (*at a meeting*). **Referenz,** *f.* (-, *pl.* **-en**) reference, testimonial; referee (*p. supplying a reference*). **referieren,** *v.i.* report, read a paper, (give a) lecture (*über* (*Acc.*), on).

Reff [rɛf], *n.* (**-s,** *pl.* **-e**) I. frame for carrying loads on the back; 2. (*Naut.*) reef; 3. (*coll.*) crone, baggage. **reffen,** *v.t.* (*Naut.*) reef.

Reflektant [reflɛk'tant], *m.* (**-en,** *pl.* **-en**) prospective purchaser *or* customer. **reflektieren,** I. *v.t.* (*Phys., Opt.*) reflect. 2. *v.i.* reflect (*über* (*Acc.*), upon), consider, ponder; – *auf* (*Acc.*), be interested in, think of buying, (*coll.*) have in view, have one's eye on.

Reflex [re'flɛks], *m.* (**-es,** *pl.* **-e**) reflex, reflection. **Reflexbewegung,** *f.* reflex action *or* movement.

Reflexion [reflɛksi'o:n], *f.* reflection, reflex, (*radar*) echo. **Reflexionswinkel,** *m.* angle of reflection.

Reflexivpronomen [reflɛ'ksi:fprono:mən], *n.*, **Reflexivum,** *n.* (**-s,** *pl.* **-va**) (*Gram.*) reflexive pronoun.

Reflex|kamera, *f.* (*Phot.*) reflex camera. **–kette,** *f.* chain of reflexes. **–licht,** *n.* reflected light.

Reform [re'fɔrm], *f.* (-, *pl.* **-en**) reform. **Reformation** [–matsi'o:n], *f.* reformation. **Reformator** [–'ma:tɔr], *m.* (**-s,** *pl.* **-en**) (religious) reformer. **reformatorisch** [–'to:rɪʃ], *adj.* reformatory. **Reformbestrebungen,** *f.pl.* programme of social reform. **Reformer,** *m.* (social) reformer. **Reformhaus,** *n.* health-food shop. **reformieren** [–'mi:rən], *v.t.* reform. **Reformierte(r),** *m., f.* Calvinist, member of the Reformed Church. **Reformkleidung,** *f.* rational dress.

refraktär [refrak'tɛ:r], *adj.* refractory. **Refraktion** [–tsi'o:n], *f.* refraction. **Refraktor** [re'fraktɔr], *m.* (**-s,** *pl.* **-en**) refracting telescope.

refrigieren [refri'gi:rən], *v.t., v.i.* freeze, refrigerate.

[1]**Regal** [re'ga:l], *n.* (**-(e)s,** *pl.* **-ien**) royal prerogative.

[2]**Regal,** *n.* (**-s,** *pl.* **-e**) I. bookshelf; 2. portable organ.

rege ['re:gə], *adj.* astir, in motion, animated; lively, alert, quick, nimble, brisk, active, busy, bustling, industrious; – *machen,* stir up, rouse, excite; – *sein,* be up and doing; – *werden,* arise, make itself felt; *– Kauflust,* brisk demand; *–r Verstand,* alert *or* active mind.

Regel ['re:gəl], *f.* (-, *pl.* **-n**) I. rule, standard; regulation, precept, principle, law; *in der –,* as a rule, ordinarily, usually; *–n des Fußballspiels,* rules of football; 2. (*Med.*) menses, menstruation. **Regelausführung,** *f.* standard design *or* model. **regelbar,** *adj.* adjustable, controllable, variable. **Regel|belastung,** *f.* (*Tech.*) normal *or* permissible load. **–buch,** *n.* book of rules.

Regeldetri [re:gəlde'tri:], *f.* (*Arith.*) rule of three.

Regel|fall, *m.* normal case. **–getriebe,** *n.* (*Tech.*) *stufenloses –,* variable-speed transmission. **regellos,** *adj.* disorderly, irregular, anomalous. **Regellosigkeit,** *f.* disorderliness, irregularity, anomaly. **regelmäßig,** I. *adj.* regular, regulated, orderly, well-proportioned; ordinary, normal. 2. *adv.* regularly, every time, always. **Regelmäßigkeit,** *f.* regularity, orderliness.

regeln ['re:gəln], I. *v.t.* regulate, adjust, control; arrange, settle, (put in) order, fix, determine, direct, govern. 2. *v.r.* *sich – nach,* be ruled *or* regulated *or* governed *or* guided by; *es wird sich schon –,* it will come right in the end.

regelrecht ['re:gəlrɛçt], *adj.* normal, regular, proper, correct; thoroughgoing, downright, nothing short of; *–e Schlacht,* pitched battle.

Regel|spur, *f.* (*Railw.*) standard gauge. **–tank,** *m.* (*Naut.*) trimming *or* stabilizing tank. **Regelung,** *f.* adjustment, regulation, control; arrangement, settlement; provision, ruling. **Regelwiderstand,** *m.* (*Elec.*) variable resistor, rheostat. **regelwidrig,** *adj.* contrary to rule, irregular, abnormal; *see* **regellos;** (*Spt.*) foul. **Regel|widrigkeit,** *f.* abnormality, irregularity, (*Spt.*) foul. **–zelle,** *f.* *See* **–tank.**

regen ['re:gən], I. *v.t.* move, stir, rouse, animate. 2. *v.r.* move, stir; bestir o.s., be active; (*fig.*) be roused, spring up, arise, make itself felt.

Regen, *m.* rain, (*Meteor.*) precipitation; (*fig.*) rain, hail; *feiner –,* light rain, drizzle; *starker –,* heavy rain, downpour; *vom – in die Traufe,* out of the frying-pan into the fire; *auf – folgt Sonnenschein,* every cloud has a silver lining.

regenarm ['re:gənʔarm], *adj.* rainless (*region*). **Regen|bogen,** *m.* rainbow. **–bogenfarben,** *f.pl.* colours of the rainbow, prismatic colours, iridescence. **regenbogenfarbig,** *adj.* rainbow-coloured, iridescent. **Regen|bogenhaut,** *f.* (*Anat.*) iris. **–brachvogel,** *m.* (*Orn.*) whimbrel (*Numenius phaeopus*). **–dach,** *n.* lean-to roof, shelter. **–decke,** *f.* rainproof cover, tarpaulin. **regendicht,** *adj.* rainproof, waterproof.

Regenerat [regene'ra:t], *n.* (**-s,** *pl.* **-e**) reclaimed material. **regenerieren,** *v.t.* reclaim, regenerate.

Regen|fall, *m.* rainfall, precipitation. **–fang,** *m.* rainwater cistern. **–faß,** *n.* water-butt. **–guß,** *m.* downpour, heavy shower (of rain). **–haut,** *f.* oilskin, plastic mac. **–mantel,** *m.* raincoat, mackintosh, waterproof. **–menge,** *f.* rainfall. **–messer,** *m.* rain-gauge. **–pfeifer,** *m.* (*Orn.*) plover (*Charadriidae*).

Regensburg ['re:gənsburk], *n.* Ratisbon.

Regen|schauer, *m.* shower (of rain). **–schirm,** *m.* umbrella; (*coll.*) *gespannt wie ein –,* all agog. **–schirmgestell,** *n.* umbrella-frame. **–schirmständer,** *m.* umbrella-stand. **–sturm,** *m.* rainstorm.

Regent [re'gɛnt], *m.* (**-en,** *pl.* **-en**), **Regentin,** *f.* regent; sovereign, reigning prince(ss).

Regen|tag, *m.* rainy day. **–tonne,** *f.* *See* **–faß.** **–tropfen,** *m.* raindrop.

Regentschaft [re'gɛntʃaft], *f.* regency; sovereignty.

Regen|verdeck, *n.* carriage-hood. **–wasser,** *n.* rainwater. **–wetter,** *n.* rainy *or* wet weather. **–wolke,** *f.* raincloud. **–wurm,** *m.* earthworm. **–zeit,** *f.* rainy *or* wet season, (*in the tropics*) the rains.

Regie [re'ʒi:], *f.* I. management, administration, (*Theat.*) stage-direction, (*film etc.*) direction; (*Theat. etc.*) *unter der – von,* directed by; 2. state monopoly. **Regie|assistent,** *m.* (*Theat. etc.*) assistant director. **–betrieb,** *m.* state *or* public undertaking. **–fehler,** *m.* (*coll.*) bad management.

–kosten, *f.pl.* overhead expenses, *(coll.)* overheads. **–pult,** *n. (Rad. etc.)* mixing desk.

regieren [re'gi:rən], **1.** *v.t.* rule *or* reign over, govern; manage, control, direct, conduct. **2.** *v.i.* rule, reign; *(fig.)* prevail. **Regierung,** *f.* government; rule, reign; administration; ***an der –,*** in power; ***unter der – von,*** in the reign of, under (the rule of); ***zur – gelangen,*** come into power, come to the throne.

Regierungs|antritt, *m.* accession (to the throne). **–beamte(r),** *m., f.* government official, civil-servant. **–bezirk,** *m.* administrative district. **–blatt,** *n.* official gazette. **–form,** *f.* regime, form of government. **–gebäude,** *n.* government offices. **–kreise,** *m.pl.* governmental circles. **–partei,** *f.* party in power. **–präsident,** *m.* president of an administrative district. **–rat,** *m.* privy councillor. **–sitz,** *m.* seat of government. **–stelle,** *f.* government agency. **–umbildung,** *f.* cabinet changes. **–wechsel,** *m.* change of government. **–zeit,** *f.* reign.

Regie|spesen, *pl. See* **–kosten.**

Regiment [regi'mɛnt], *n.* 1. **(-s,** *pl.* **-e)** power, authority, rule, government control; ***das – haben*** or ***führen,*** be in *or* have control, rule, command; *(coll.)* ***sie führt das –,*** she wears the trousers; 2. **(-s,** *pl.* **-er)** *(Mil.)* regiment, *(German equiv.)* brigade. **Regiments|arzt,** *m.* regimental medical officer. **–chef,** *m.* colonel-in-chief, honorary colonel. **–kapelle,** *f.* regimental band. **–kommandeur,** *m.* regimental commander, colonel. **–musik,** *f. See* **–kapelle. –schreiber,** *m.* orderly-room sergeant. **–stab,** *m.* regimental headquarters. **–unkosten,** *pl. (coll.)* ***auf –,*** at other people's expense.

Region [regi'o:n], *f.* region; *(fig.)* ***in höheren –en schweben,*** live in the clouds.

Regisseur [reʒɪ'sø:r], *m.* **(-s,** *pl.* **-e)** *(Theat.)* stage-manager, *(film)* director, *(Rad. etc.)* producer.

Register [re'gɪstər], *n.* 1. *(in books)* index, table of contents; register, record; list, catalogue; *(coll.)* ***ins alte – gehören,*** be old-hat, be a square; ***ich stehe bei ihr im schwarzen –,*** I am in her bad books; 2. damper; (organ) stop; *(fig.)* ***alle – spielen lassen*** or ***ziehen,*** pull out all the stops, *(sl.)* go it strong, do one's damnedest. **Register|stimme,** *f. See* **–zug, –tonnen,** *f.pl. (Naut.)* tons burden, register tons. **–zug,** *m.* (organ-)register.

Registrande [regɪs'trandə], *f.* order-book. **Registrator,** *m,* **(-s,** *pl.* **-en)** registrar, recorder; (letter-) file. **Registratur** [–'tu:r], *f.* (-, *pl.* **-en)** registry *or* record-office, registrar's office; filing cabinet; *(collect.)* files and records. **Registrier|apparat,** *m.* recording instrument. **–ballon,** *m. (Meteor.)* sounding balloon. **registrieren,** *v.t.* record, register, place on record; index, enter (in the record). **Registrier|kasse,** *f.* cash-register. **–thermometer,** *n.* self-registering thermometer. **Registrierung,** *f.* registration, recording; reading *(on instrument)*, entry *(in the record)*.

Reglement [reglə'mã], *n.* **(-s,** *pl.* **-s)** regulation(s). **reglementarisch** [–mɛn'ta:rɪʃ], *adj. See* **reglementmäßig. reglementieren,** *v.t.* bring under official control *or* supervision, regiment. **reglementmäßig,** *adj.* according to regulations.

Regler ['re:glər], *m. (Mech.)* regulator, control, governor, trimmer, compensator; *(Artil.)* corrector. **Regler|tank,** *m. (Naut.)* trimming tank. **–teilung,** *f. (Artil.)* correction scale.

reglos ['re:klo:s], *adj.* motionless. **Reglung,** *f. See* **Regelung.**

regnen ['re:gnən], **1.** *v.i. (imp.)* rain. **2.** *v.t. (fig.)* rain, hail. **Regnerdüse,** *f.* spray nozzle. **regnerisch,** *adj.* rainy, showery.

Regreß [re'grɛs], *m.* **(-(ss)es,** *pl.* **-(ss)e)** recourse, (legal) remedy; (recovery of) damages; ***– nehmen an*** *(Dat.)* or ***gegen,*** have recourse to, make claim on. **Regreß|anspruch,** *m.* right of recourse, right to compensation. **–nehmer,** *m.* claimant, p. seeking redress. **regreßpflichtig,** *adj.* liable for compensation *or* to recourse; ***ihn – machen,*** have recourse to him. **Regreß|recht,** *n. See* **–anspruch.**

regsam ['re:kza:m], *adj.* active, agile, nimble; *(fig.)* quick, alert *(mind)*. **Regsamkeit,** *f.* activity, agility; quickness, alertness.

regulär [regu'lɛ:r], *adj.* regular. **Regulativ** [–la'ti:f], *n.* **(-s,** *pl.* **-e)** regulation, rule. **Regulator** [–'la:tɔr], *m.* **(-s,** *pl.* **-en)** *see* **Regler. regulierbar,** *adj.* adjustable, controllable. **regulieren,** *v.t.* regulate, adjust, control, set. **Regulier|hebel,** *m.* adjusting handle *or* lever *or* knob. **–schraube,** *f.* adjusting screw, set-screw. **Regulierung,** *f. See* **Regelung.**

Regung ['re:guŋ], *f.* movement, motion, stirring; *(fig.)* impulse; agitation, emotion, feeling. **regungslos,** *adj. See* **reglos.**

Reh [re:], *n.* **(-(e)s,** *pl.* **-e)** roe (deer); ***ein Rudel –e,*** a herd of deer. **Reh|blatt,** *n.* shoulder of venison. **–bock,** *m.* roebuck. **–braten,** *m.* roast venison. **reh|braun.** *See* **–farben. Rehe** ['re:ə], *f.* 1. *(Vet.)* founder; 2. *(dial.)* plough-tail; 3. *(dial.)* doe. **rehfarben,** *adj.* fawn(-coloured). **Reh|fell,** *n.* doeskin. **–fleisch,** *n.* venison. **–geiß,** *f.* doe. **–kalb,** *n,* fawn. **–keule,** *f.* haunch of venison. **–kitz,** *n.,* **–kitze,** *f. See* **–kalb. –leder,** *n.* doeskin, buckskin.

Reh|ling ['re:lɪŋ], *m.* **(-s,** *pl.* **-e)** young deer; *(Bot.)* chanterelle. **–posten,** *pl.* buckshot. **–rücken,** *m.* saddle of venison. **–schlegel,** *m. See* **–keule. –wild,** *n.* deer. **–ziege,** *f.* doe. **–ziemer,** *m.* loin of venison.

Reibahle ['raɪpˀa:lə], *f.* broach, reamer. **Reibe** ['raɪbə], *f.,* **Reibeisen,** *n.* grater, scraper, rasp. **Reibe|laut,** *m. (Phonet.)* fricative (consonant), spirant. **–mühle,** *f.* grinding mill.

reiben ['raɪbən], **1.** *irr.v.t.* rub, massage; grate, grind; bray, pulverize; gall, chafe; ***sich*** *(Dat.)* ***die Hände wund –,*** rub the skin off one's hands, chafe one's hands; ***ihm etwas unter die Nase –,*** bring a th. home to him, *(coll.)* rub it in; ***ein ganz geriebener Kerl,*** a smooth customer. **2.** *irr. v.r.* ***sich an ihm –,*** provoke *or* annoy *or* irritate him, *(sl.)* get in his hair; ***sich wund –,*** chafe o.s. **Reiberei** [–'raɪ], *f.* *(fig.)* provocation, (constant) friction, squabbling, *(coll.)* tiff.

Reib|festigkeit, *f.* resistance to abrasion. **–fläche,** *f.* rubbing *or* striking surface; cartridge-base. **–keule,** *f.* pestle. **–schale,** *f.* mortar.

Reibsel ['raɪpsəl], *n.* scourings, scrapings.

Reib|stein, *m. See* **–keule. –stellen,** *pl.* abrasion marks.

Reibung ['raɪbuŋ], *f.* rubbing, friction; abrasion, attrition; trituration; *(fig.)* clash, friction, tension. **Reibungs|beiwert,** *m.* coefficient of friction. **–bremse,** *f.* friction-brake. **–elektrizität,** *f.* frictional electricity. **–fläche,** *f.* friction surface; *(fig.) see* **–punkt. –koeffizient,** *m. See* **–beiwert. –kupplung,** *f.* friction-clutch. **reibungslos, 1.** *adj.* frictionless, *(fig.)* smooth, smooth-running. **2.** *adv. (fig.)* smoothly, without a hitch. **Reibungs|punkt,** *m. (fig.)* point of friction, source of irritation, cause of annoyance. **–verlust,** *m.* loss by friction. **–widerstand,** *m.* frictional resistance.

Reibzünder ['raɪptsyndər], *m.* friction primer.

reich [raɪç], *adj.* rich, wealthy, *(coll.)* well-to-do; abundant, copious, ample; sumptuous, opulent, plentiful, fertile; *(Chem.)* concentrated; ***– an*** *(Dat.)*, rich *or* abounding in, with a wealth of; ***–e Anzahl,*** large number; ***–e Auswahl,*** wide selection; *(Motor.)* ***–es Gemisch,*** rich mixture; ***in –em Maße,*** amply, copiously.

Reich, *n.* **(-(e)s,** *pl.* **-e)** empire, kingdom, realm *(also fig.)*; ***Deutsches –,*** Germany, *(Hist.)* German Empire; ***das Dritte –,*** the Third Reich; ***– der Geister,*** realm of spirits, spirit world; ***das – Gottes,*** the Kingdom of Heaven; ***das Heilige Römische – (Deutscher Nation),*** the Holy Roman Empire *(843–1806)*; ***das – der Mitte,*** China; ***das – der Schatten,*** the shades, Hades, the underworld.

reich|bebildert, *adj.* richly *or* profusely illustrated. **–begütert,** *adj.* (very) wealthy, affluent, propertied. **–besetzt,** *adj.* well-spread *(table)*.

reichen ['raɪçən], **1.** *v.t.* reach; ***(ihm etwas) –,*** hand *or* pass; give, offer, hold out, present *(s.th. to* *him*); ***das Abendmahl –***, administer the sacrament; ***Almosen –***, bestow alms; (*fig.*) ***er kann ihm das Wasser nicht –***, he is not fit to hold a candle to him, he is no match for him. **2.** *v.i.* reach, extend (*bis*, to); suffice; be enough, (*coll.*) do; last (out), hold out; ***– nach***, stretch out one's hand for *or* towards; ***das reicht***, that will do; ***reicht das nicht?*** is that not enough? ***er reicht mir bis an die Schulter***, he comes up to my shoulder; ***so weit das Auge reicht***, as far as the eye can see.

Reiche(r) ['raɪçə(r)], *m., f.* wealthy *or* rich man *or* woman; ***die Reichen***, the wealthy, the well-to-do.

reichhaltig ['raɪçhaltɪç], *adj.* copious, abundant, plentiful, profuse, rich; ***ein –es Buch***, a book with a wealth of information. **Reichhaltigkeit,** *f.* copiousness, abundance, richness, great variety.

reichlich ['raɪçlɪç], **1.** *adj.* ample, profuse, copious, plentiful, abundant; (*pred.*) enough and to spare; ***sein –es Auskommen haben***, be sufficiently well-off. **2.** *adv.* 1. amply *etc.*; ***– Zeit haben***, have plenty of time; 2. (*coll.*) rather, fairly; ***– dick***, on the fat side; ***– die Hälfte***, a good half. **Reichlichkeit,** *f.* plentifulness, abundance.

Reichs– [raɪçs–], *pref.* (*before 1918*) Imperial, (*subsequently*) National, Federal, State. **Reichs|acht,** *f.* (*Hist.*) imperial ban; ***in die – tun***, outlaw. **–adel,** *m.* (*Hist.*) nobility of the Empire. **–adler,** *m.* German eagle, Imperial eagle. **–angehörige(r),** *m., f.* German subject *or* national. **–angehörigkeit,** *f.* German nationality. **–apfel,** *m.* (*Hist.*) Imperial orb. **–archiv,** *n.* National Records Office. **–autobahn,** *f.* arterial motorway, express highway. **–bahn,** *f.* German *or* Federal Railway. **–bank,** *f.* German National Bank. **–banner,** *n.* (*Hist.*) German ex-servicemen's association (*1924–33*). **–bürger,** *m. See* **–angehörige(r). –deutsche(r),** *m., f.* German (*i.e. not Austrian*). **–erbhofgesetz,** *n.* (*Nat. Soc.*) law of entail. **–farben,** *f.pl.*, **–flagge,** *f.* German national flag. **–freiherr, –fürst,** *m.* (*Hist.*) prince of the Holy Roman Empire. **–gericht,** *n.* Supreme Court of Justice. **–gesetz,** *n.* Federal law. **–hauptstadt,** *f.* Federal capital. **–hilfe,** *f.* (federal) government subsidy. **–kammergericht,** *n.* (*Hist.*) Supreme Court (*of Holy Roman Empire*). **–kanzlei,** *f.* State Chancery. **–kanzler,** *m.* Chancellor. **–kleinodien,** *n.pl.* (*Hist.*) Imperial insignia, crown jewels. **–kulturkammer,** *f.* (*Nat. Soc.*) Chamber for Arts and Culture, (*coll.*) propaganda ministry. **–kurzschrift,** *f.* official shorthand system. **–land,** *n.* (*Hist.*) ***die –e***, the Imperial provinces (*i.e. Alsace and Lorraine, 1871–1918*). **–lehen,** *n.* (*Hist.*) fief of the Empire. **–marine,** *f.* German (Imperial) navy. **–mark,** *f.* (*Hist.*) German mark, stabilized currency (*after 1924*). **–minister,** *m.* Federal minister. **–partei,** *f.* (*Hist.*) National(ist) Party (*1871–1933*). **–post,** *f.* German postal service. **–post-direktion,** *f.* Postmaster General's department. **–präsident,** *m.* President of the Republic. **–rat,** *m.* (*Hist.*) Federal Council (*1918–33*). **–ritter,** *m.* (*Hist.*) knight of the (Holy Roman) Empire. **–sender,** *m.* German radio station. **–stadt,** *f.* imperial *or* free city. **–stadthalter,** *m.* Federal representative in the states. **–stände,** *m.pl.* (*Hist.*) princes and dignitaries of the Imperial Diet. **–tag,** *m.* German parliament, (*Hist*). Imperial Diet (of the Holy Roman Empire). **–tagsabgeordnete(r),** *m., f.* member of parliament. **–truppen,** *f.pl.* (*Hist.*) Imperial troops. **reichsunmittelbar,** *adj.* (*Hist.*) subject to the Emperor alone. **Reichs|verband,** *m.* National federation. **–verfassung,** *f.* constitution of the Reich. **–verweser,** *m.* (*Hist.*) Imperial Administrator (*1848–49*). **–währung,** *f.* standard (German) currency. **–wappen,** *n.* (*Hist.*) Imperial arms. **–wehr,** *f.* (*Hist.*) German armed forces (*1919–33*).

Reichtum ['raɪçtu:m], *m.* **(-s,** *pl.* **¨-er)** riches, wealth, fortune, opulence; (*fig.*) wealth, abundance (***an*** (*Dat.*), of), richness, great variety.

reichverziert ['raɪçfɛrtsi:rt], *adj.* richly *or* profusely *or* ornately decorated, florid.

Reichweite ['raɪçvaɪtə], *f.* reach, (*Mil.*) range (*of guns*), operational range *or* radius (*of ships or aircraft*), (*Rad.*) range, coverage; ***in –***, within reach *or* (*Mil.*) range, close at hand, to hand; ***außer –***, out of reach *or* (*Mil.*) range.

reif [raɪf], *adj.* ripe, mature, mellow; fully developed, ready; ***– werden***, become ripe, ripen, mature, season, mellow; ***ein Mann von*** or ***in –eren Jahren***, a middle-aged man.

[1]**Reif,** *m.* **(-(e)s,** *pl.* **-e)** hoar-frost; bloom (*on fruit*).

[2]**Reif,** *m.* (*Poet.*) *see* **Reifen.**

Reife ['raɪfə], *f.* maturity; puberty; ripeness, mellowness; ***zur – bringen*** (*v.t.*), ***zur – kommen*** (*v.i.*), ripen, mature.

reifeln ['raɪfəln], *v.t.* (*Archit.*) flute, groove, channel. **Reif(e)lung,** *f.* flute, fluting.

[1]**reifen** ['raɪfən], **1.** *v.t.* ripen, bring to maturity. **2.** *v.i.* (*aux.* s.) mature, ripen, mellow; reach puberty; (*of an abscess*) come to a head.

[2]**reifen,** *v.i.* (*imp.*) ***es reift***, there is a hoar-frost.

[3]**reifen,** *v.t.* (*dial.*) fix a hoop *or* rim on, tyre (*a wheel*).

Reifen, *m.* ring, circle, collar, hoop; (*Motor, etc.*) tyre; ***– legen um***, hoop (*a cask etc.*); ***den – schlagen, mit dem – spielen***, bowl *or* trundle a hoop. **Reifen|-decke,** *f.* (*Motor.*) outer cover. **–defekt,** *m.* tyre trouble, puncture. **–druckmesser,** *m.* tyre gauge. **–heber,** *m.* tyre lever. **–mantel,** *m. See* **–decke. –profil,** *n.* tread (*of a tyre*). **–schaden,** *m. See* **–defekt, –spiel,** *n.* trundling *or* bowling a hoop. **–springen,** *n.* jumping through hoops.

Reife|prüfung, *f.* school-leaving *or* school-certificate *or* matriculation examination. **–zeugnis,** *n.* (school-)leaving *or* matriculation certificate.

reiflich ['raɪflɪç], *adj.* careful, mature, thorough.

Reifrock ['raɪfrɔk], *m.* crinoline.

Reifung ['raɪfuŋ], *f.* curing, maturing (*of cheese*).

Reigen ['raɪgən], *m.* round-dance, roundelay; ***den – eröffnen***, lead the dance, (*fig.*) lead off.

Reihe ['raɪə], *f.* row, line, (*Mil.*) file (*one behind the other*), rank (*side by side*); tier (*of layers*), row (*of seats*), suite (*of rooms*), range (*of hills*), queue (*Am.* line) (*of people*), succession, series, set (*of things in order*), (*Math.*) progression; sequence, train (*of thought etc.*), string (*of beads*); (*Crick.*) innings; ***die – ist an mir, ich bin an der –***, it is my turn; ***Sie werden an die – kommen, die – kommt an dich***, your turn will come; (*fig.*) ***aus der – tanzen***, go one's own way; ***aus den –n von***, from among; ***aus*** or ***außer der –***, out of (one's) turn, out of order; ***bunte –***, paired off, ladies and gentlemen alternately; (*coll.*) ***eine ganze – von***, a long *or* whole string of, a lot of; ***in Reih und Glied***, in rank and file; (*Elec.*) ***in –***, in series; ***nach der –, der – nach***, in succession, successively, one after the other, in rotation, in turn, by turns; ***in der vordersten –***, in the front row, (*fig.*) in the forefront.

Reihen ['raɪən], *m.* 1. (*dial.*) *see* **Reigen**; ***der nächtliche –***, the nocturnal dance; 2. arch of the foot.

reihen, 1. *v.t.* arrange in a row *or* series; range; string (*beads etc.*); (*Dressm.*) tack, baste. **2.** *v.r.* form a row; ***eins reiht sich ans andere***, one thing follows another.

Reihen|abwurf, *m. See* **–wurf. –arbeit,** *f.* repetition work. **–band,** *m.* volume in a set *or* series. **–dorf,** *n.* Franconian form of settlement. **–fabrikation, –fertigung,** *f. See* **–herstellung. –folge,** *f.* (order of) succession, order, sequence, series. **–häuserbau,** *m.* ribbon building *or* development. **–herstellung,** *f.* serial *or* series production. **–motor,** *m.* (*Mech.*) in-line engine, (*Elec.*) series motor. **–schaltung,** *f.* (*Elec.*) series connection. **–schlußmotor,** *m. See* **–motor** (*Elec.*). **–standmotor,** *m. See* **–motor** (*Mech.*). **–tanz,** *m.* round-dance. **reihenweise,** *adv.* in rows; by turns. **Reihenwurf,** *m.* (*Av.*) stick *or* salvo of bombs, salvo bombing.

Reiher ['raɪər], *m.* (*Orn.*) heron (*Ardeidae*); ***grauer –***, *see* **Fischreiher. Reiher|busch,** *m.* tuft of heron's feathers. **–ente,** *f.* (*Orn.*) tufted duck

(*Aythya fuligula*). **–feder,** *f.* aigrette. **–horst,** *m.* heronry. **–schnabel,** *m.* (*Bot.*) cranesbill.

Reihfaden [ˈraɪfa:dən], *m.* tacking *or* basting thread.

–reihig [ˈraɪɪç], *adj. suff.* -breasted (*of a jacket*).

reihum [–ˈum], *adv.* in succession, in *or* by turns.

Reim [raɪm], *m.* **(-(e)s,** *pl.* **-e)** rhyme; ***männlicher*** or ***stumpfer –,*** masculine rhyme; ***weibliche*** or ***klingender –,*** feminine rhyme; ***rührender –,*** identical rhyme; (*coll.*) ***ich kann keinen – darauf finden,*** there's no rhyme or reason in it, I can't make head or tail of it, it doesn't make sense (to me). **reimen,** *v.t., v.i., v.r.* rhyme (***auf*** (*Acc.*), with); (*v.r. only*) (*fig.*) make sense, agree *or* tally (with); ***wie reimt sich das zusammen?*** how do you reconcile that? **Reimer,** *m.* versifier, rhym(st)er, poetaster. **Reimerei** [–ˈraɪ], *f.* doggerel. **Reim|geklingel,** *n.* jingle. **–kunst,** *f.* rhyming. **reimlos,** *adj.* unrhymed, blank (*verse*).

Reims [raɪmz], *n.* Rheims.

Reim|schmied, *m. See* **Reimer. –silbe,** *f.* rhyming syllable. **–wort,** *n.* rhyming word. **–wörterbuch,** *n.* rhyming dictionary, dictionary of rhymes.

[1]**rein** [raɪn], **1.** *adj.* clean, neat, tidy; pure (*also fig. of a p.*); clear, unadulterated, undiluted, unalloyed; (*Comm.*) net; (*coll.*) pure, sheer, mere; ***–er Alkohol,*** absolute alcohol; ***–e Bahn machen,*** clear the way, make a clean sweep; ***–e Bilanz,*** clear balance; ***–er Bogen,*** clean *or* blank sheet; ***–e Freude,*** unadulterated pleasure; ***–e Gesichtsfarbe,*** clear complexion; ***–er Gewinn,*** net profit; ***der –e Hohn,*** sheer mockery; (*coll.*) ***die Luft ist –,*** the coast is clear; ***–e Lüge,*** downright lie; ***–e Mathematik,*** pure mathematics; ***aus –em Mitleid,*** out of sheer compassion; ***–en Mund halten,*** hold one's tongue, keep a secret; ***–en Tisch machen,*** make a clean sweep (of it); ***–e Wahrheit,*** plain *or* unvarnished truth; (*fig.*) ***vom –sten Wasser,*** of the first water; (*fig.*) ***ihm –en Wein einschenken,*** tell him the plain *or* unvarnished truth; ***–er Zufall,*** sheer luck, pure chance. **2.** *adv.* purely *etc.*; (*coll.*) quite, utterly; ***– heraus,*** clearly and to the point; ***– (gar) nichts,*** absolutely nothing at all; ***– unmöglich,*** utterly impossible; (*coll.*) ***er war – weg,*** he was flabbergasted.

[2]**rein,** *adv., sep.pref.* (*coll.*) *see* **herein.**

Reindruck [ˈraɪndruk], *m.* (*Typ.*) clean proof. **Reine,** *f.* (*Poet.*) *see* **Reinheit.**

Reineclaude [rɛ:nəˈklo:də], *f.* (*Austr.*) *see* **Reneklode.**

Reinemachen, *n. See* **Reinmachen.**

reinerbig [ˈraɪnˀɛrbɪç], *adj.* (*Biol.*) homozygotic. **Reinertrag,** *m.* (*Comm.*) net yield *or* proceeds, net *or* clear profit.

Reine(s) [ˈraɪnə(s)], *n.* ***ins Reine bringen,*** clear up, settle, (*coll.*) get to the bottom of; ***ins Reine kommen,*** come to an understanding *or* to terms; ***mit sich ins Reine kommen,*** make up one's mind (***über*** (*Acc.*), about); ***ins Reine schreiben,*** make a fair *or* neat copy of.

Reinfall [ˈraɪnfal], *m.* (*coll.*) let-down, flop, wash-out.

reinfallen [ˈraɪnfalən], *irr. v.i.* (*coll.*) *see* **hereinfallen**; be diddled.

Rein|gewicht, *n.* (*Comm.*) net weight. **–gewinn,** *m. See* **–ertrag.**

Reinheit [ˈraɪnhaɪt], *f.* purity, pureness; cleanness, cleanliness, clearness; (*fig.*) innocence; (*Rad. etc.*) fidelity.

reinigen [ˈraɪnɪgən], *v.t.* clean, cleanse; purge; disinfect; refine, clear, purify, clarify, rectify; ***chemisch –,*** dry-clean; ***er reinigte sich von jedem Verdacht,*** he cleared himself of all suspicion. **reinigend** *adj.* cleansing, detergent; (*Med.*) purging; (*Chem.*) abluent.

Reinigung [ˈraɪnɪguŋ], *f.* purification; cleaning, cleansing; refinement, rectification; purging, disinfection; ***chemische –,*** dry-cleaning; (*coll.*) ***in der –,*** at the cleaners; (*Med.*) ***monatliche –,*** menses, menstruation. **Reinigungs|anstalt,** *f.* dry-cleaners. **–eid,** *m.* oath of purgation. **–krem,** *f.* cleansing cream. **–mittel,** *n.* cleanser, detergent; purgative, aperient. **–opfer,** *n.* lustration.

Reinkultur [ˈraɪnkultu:r], *f.* bacilli-culture, (*fig.*) the purest form.

reinlegen [ˈraɪnle:gən], *v.t.* (*coll.*) *see* **hereinlegen**; diddle, doublecross.

reinlich [ˈraɪnlɪç], *adj.* clean, neat, tidy, clean-cut, distinct. **Reinlichkeit,** *f.* cleanliness, neatness, tidiness. **Reinmachefrau,** *f.* charwoman. **Reinmachen,** *n.* cleaning (*the house*), tidying up, scrubbing (*floors*); (*fig.*) cleaning up. **reinrassig,** *adj.* pure-bred, pedigree, thoroughbred. **Reinschrift,** *f.* fair *or* neat copy. **rein|seiden,** *adj.* pure- *or* all-silk. **–waschen,** *irr. v.t.* (*fig.*) vindicate, clear, (*coll.*) whitewash. **–weg,** *adv.* flatly, completely, absolutely, altogether. **–wollen,** *adj.* pure- *or* all-wool.

[1]**Reis** [raɪs], *n.* **(-es,** *pl.* **-er)** twig, sprig; shoot, scion.

[2]**Reis,** *m.* rice.

Reis|auflauf, *m.* rice pudding. **–bau,** *m.* cultivation of rice. **–bündel,** *n.* faggot.

Reise [ˈraɪzə], *f.* journey, tour, trip, (sea) voyage; ***auf –n sein,*** be travelling; ***eine – machen,*** go on a journey, make *or* take a trip; ***sich auf die – begeben*** or ***machen,*** set out; ***wo geht die – hin?*** where are you bound for? ***glückliche –!*** pleasant journey! (*coll.*) ***etwas auf die – schicken,*** set s.th. going, get a.th. started.

Reise|andenken, *n.* souvenir (of one's travels). **–anzug,** *m.* travelling-clothes. **–apotheke,** *f.* medicine-chest, first-aid kit. **–bedarf,** *m.* travelling requirements *or* requisites. **–begleiter,** *m.* travelling-companion. **–beschreibung,** *f.* travel book; (*film etc.*) travelogue. **–büro,** *n.* travel agency, tourist office. **–decke,** *f.* travelling-rug. **reisefertig,** *adj.* ready to set out. **Reise|führer,** *m.* guide; guide-book. **–gefährte,** *m.*, **gefährtin,** *f.* fellow-traveller. **–gefolge,** *n.* suite (*of a prince*). **–genehmigung,** *f.* travel permit. **–gepäck,** *n.* luggage. **–geschwindigkeit,** *f.* (*Av., Naut.*) cruising speed. **–gesellschaft,** *f.* party of tourists, travelling companions. **–karte,** *f.* touring-map. **–koffer,** *m.* trunk; ***kleiner –,*** portmanteau, travelling-case. **–korb,** *m.* hamper. **–kosten,** *f.pl.* travelling-expenses. **reiselustig,** *adj.* fond of travelling. **Reise|marsch,** *m.* (*Mil.*) route-march. **–marschall,** *m.* (royal) courier.

reisen [ˈraɪzən], *v.i.* (*aux.* h. *&* s.) travel, (go on *or* make a) journey (*or* trip), take a trip, (go on a) voyage, go on a cruise (***nach,*** to); ***– nach,*** (*also*) be bound for, go to; leave *or* depart *or* start for; ***– über*** (*Acc.*), go by way of, go via; ***aufs Land –,*** leave for the country; ***ins Ausland –,*** go abroad, leave for abroad; ***in die Ferien –,*** go on one's holidays; ***zu den Kindern –,*** go to see the children; ***zum Vergnügen –,*** travel for pleasure; ***unsre Firma läßt nicht –,*** our firm does not employ travellers. **reisend,** *adj.* travelling, itinerant. **Reisende(r),** *m., f.* traveller, tourist, passenger; (*Comm.*) commercial traveller, agent, representative.

Reise|necessaire, *n.* dressing-case. **–paß,** *m.* passport. **–prospekt,** *m.* travel brochure. **–route,** *f.* route, itinerary. **–scheck,** *m.* traveller's cheque. **–spesen,** *pl.* travelling-expenses. **–stipendium,** *n.* travelling-scholarship. **–tasche,** *f.* travelling-bag. **–verkehr,** *m.* tourist traffic. **–zeit,** *f.* tourist season. **–ziel,** *n.* destination.

Reisig [ˈraɪzɪç], *n.* brushwood, twigs. **Reisig|besen,** *m.* birch-broom, besom. **–bündel,** *n. See* **Reisbündel.**

Reisige(r) [ˈraɪzɪgə(r)], *m.* (*Hist.*) knight on horseback, mounted mercenary.

Reis|lauf, *m.* (*Hist.*) enlistment (*of foreign troops*) as mercenaries. **–läufer,** *m.* foreign mercenary.

Reiß|aus [ˈraɪs–], *m.* (*coll.*) ***– nehmen,*** take to one's heels, (*sl.*) beat it, do a bunk. **–blei,** *n.* blacklead, graphite. **–brett,** *n.* drawing-board.

reißen [ˈraɪsən], **1.** *irr.v.t.* 1. tear, rip, rend, rupture; ***sich*** (*Dat.*) ***den Finger blutig –,*** gash one's finger; ***eine große Lücke –,*** leave a great gap; ***in Stücke –,*** tear to pieces; 2. pull, drag, tug, snatch, jerk, (*coll.*) yank; ***an sich*** (*Acc.*) ***–,*** seize upon, seize *or* lay hold of, snatch up; (*fig.*) monopolize, seize, usurp; ***aus der Gefahr –,*** snatch from danger; ***zu Boden –,*** knock down, floor; ***Grimassen –,*** pull a face *or* faces; (*Spt.*) ***die Latte –,*** knock down *or* dislodge the bar; 3. ***Witze –,*** crack jokes; ***Zoten –,*** talk smut, tell dirty stories; 4. (*obs.*) sketch, draw, trace, scribe. **2.** *irr.v.i.* (*aux.* h. *&* s.) burst, rupture, break, snap, crack, split, tear, get torn; ***– an*** (*Dat.*), tear *or* tug at; ***wenn alle Stränge*** or ***Stricke –,*** in the last resort, if the worst come to the worst; ***mir reißt's in allen Gliedern,*** I have rheumatic pains in all my limbs; ***da riß mir die Geduld,*** at this I lost all patience; (*coll.*) ***das reißt*** (***sehr***) ***ins Geld,*** that runs away with a lot of money. **3.** *irr.v.r.* get scratched, scratch o.s.; ***sich – um,*** scramble *or* struggle for.

Reißen, *n.* 1. tearing, rending; 2. acute *or* sharp pain, racking *or* rheumatic pains, rheumatism. **reißend,** *adj.* rapid; impetuous, tumultuous; (*of pain*) acute, racking; (*of animals*) ravening, rapacious; ***–er Strom,*** torrent; (*coll.*) ***–en Absatz finden, – abgehen,*** sell like hot cakes. **Reißer,** *m.* (*coll.*) (*Theat.*) draw, box-office success *or* (*coll.*) hit.

Reiß|feder, *f.* drawing-pen. **–festigkeit,** *f.* breaking *or* tensile strength. **–kohle,** *f.* charcoal crayon. **–leine,** *f.* rip-cord (*parachute*). **–linie,** *f.* perforation. **–nagel,** *m.* drawing-pin, (*Am.*) thumbtack. **–schiene,** *f.* T-square. **–verschluß,** *m.* zip-fastener. **–zahn,** *m.* canine *or* laniary tooth, fang. **–zeug,** *n.* mathematical *or* drawing instruments, geometry set. **–zirkel,** *m.* drawing-compasses. **–zwecke,** *f. See* **–nadel.**

Reit|anzug ['raɪt–], *m.* riding-habit. **–bahn,** *f.* riding-school, manège.

reiten ['raɪtən], **1.** *irr.v.i.* (*aux.* h. *&* s.) ride, go on horseback; ***geritten kommen,*** come on horseback; ***schlecht –,*** be a poor rider *or* horseman; ***auf dem Apostelpferde –,*** go on Shanks's pony; ***im Galopp –,*** gallop; ***im Schritt –,*** pace, amble, trot; ***vor Anker –,*** ride at achor. **2.** *irr.v.t.* ride (*a horse*); ***ihn zu Boden*** or ***über den Haufen –,*** ride him down; ***ein Pferd zu Schanden –,*** override *or* founder a horse; ***sich*** (*Acc.*) ***wund –, sich*** (*Dat.*) ***einen Wolf –,*** gall o.s. in riding; ***ihn in die Tinte –,*** drive him into a corner; ***Prinzipien*** or ***ein Prinzip –,*** have a bee in one's bonnet, work an idea to death; (*Comm. coll.*) ***Wechsel –,*** fly a kite; ***der Teufel muß ihn –,*** he must have the devil in him.

Reiten, *n.* riding, equitation. **reitend,** *adj.* on horseback; mounted; equestrian; ***–e Artillerie,*** horse-artillery.

[1]**Reiter** ['raɪtər], *m.* 1. rider, horseman, (*Mil.*) cavalryman, trooper; (*Mil.*) ***spanische –,*** chevaux-de-frise; (*Mil.*) ***leichte –,*** (*pl.*) light horse; 2. (*Mech.*) slider; tab (*of card-index*).

[2]**Reiter,** *f.* (-, *pl.* **-n**) (*dial.*) coarse sieve, riddle.

Reiterei [raɪtə'raɪ], *f.* cavalry, mounted troops, horse. **Reiterin** ['raɪtərɪn], *f.* horsewoman.

reitern ['raɪtərn], *v.t.* (*dial.*) riddle, sift, screen (*corn*).

Reiter|regiment, *n.* cavalry regiment. **–säbel,** *m.* cavalry sabre. **–schar,** *f.* troop of horse, cavalcade. **Reitersmann,** *m.* (*pl.* **⸚er**) horseman. **Reiterstandbild,** *n.* equestrian statue.

Reit|gerte, *f.* riding-crop, whip, switch. **–gurt,** *m.* saddle-girth. **–handschuh,** *m.* riding-glove. **–hose,** *f.* riding-breeches. **–kleid,** *n.* (ladies') riding-habit. **–knecht,** *m.* groom. **–kunst,** *f.* horsemanship, equitation. **–peitsche,** *f.* horsewhip. **–pferd,** *n.* riding-horse, saddle-horse, mount. **–post,** *f.* (*Hist.*) courier. **–schule,** *f.* 1. riding-school; 2. (*Swiss*) merry-go-round. **–sport,** *m.* riding. **–stunden,** *f.pl.*, **–unterricht,** *m.* riding-lessons. **–wechsel,** *m.* (*Comm.*) accommodation bill, (*sl.*) kite. **–weg,** *m.* bridle-path.

Reiz [raɪts], *m.* (**-es,** *pl.* **-e**) charm, attraction, attractiveness, fascination, appeal; lure, temptation, allurement; enticement, incentive, stimulus; stimulation, irritation; (*Phys.*) impulse; ***den – verlieren,*** pall (***für,*** on). **reizbar,** *adj.* sensitive, susceptible; excitable, irritable, irascible, testy, short-tempered, (*coll.*) touchy; (*Med.*) inflammable. **Reizbarkeit,** *f.* susceptibility, sensitiveness; irritability, irascibility, testiness, (*coll.*) touchiness.

reizen ['raɪtsən], *v.t.* 1. excite, stimulate, rouse, provoke, stir up, irritate, (*coll.*) nettle; ***reize sie nicht zur Wut,*** do not exasperate them; 2. charm, attract, fascinate, allure, lure, entice, tempt, whet, ***die Aufgabe reizt mich,*** the task appeals to me *or* is a challenge to me. **reizend,** *adj.* 1. charming, (*appetite*), tickle (*palate*); ***es reizt mich, sie zu sehen,*** I am eager to see her *or* (*coll.*) keen on seeing her; attractive, delightful, (*coll.*) fetching, lovely, cute, smart; 2. inflammatory, irritating, irritant.

Reiz|gas, *n.* irritant gas. **–husten,** *m.* irritating cough.

Reizker ['raɪtskər], *m.* orange-agaric.

reizlos, *adj.* 1. non-irritant; 2. unattractive, insipid, (*pred.*) not worth while. **Reiz|mittel,** *n.* stimulant, irritant; incentive, stimulus. **–schwelle,** *f.* (*Physiol.*) threshold of sensation. **–stoff,** *m.* 1. *See* **–gas**; 2. stimulant, adjuvant.

Reizung ['raɪtsuŋ], *f.* irritation, stimulation, excitation; incitement, provocation, enticement, inducement. **reizvoll,** *adj.* graceful, charming, attractive, fascinating, seductive, tempting, alluring, exciting. **Reizwirkung,** *f.* irritant effect.

rekeln ['re:kəln], **1.** *v.t.* sprawl, stretch (*limbs*). **2.** *v.r.* sprawl, lounge, loll about.

Reklamation [reklamatsi'o:n], *f.* complaint, protest, objection; reclamation, claim.

Reklame [re'kla:mə], *f.* advertisement; advertising, publicity, (sales) promotion; propaganda; (*fig., coll.*) ballyhoo, window-dressing; ***– machen für*** advertise, make propaganda for, (*coll.*) boost. **Reklame|chef,** *m.* advertising manager. **–fachmann,** *m.* publicity expert. **–feldzug,** *m.* advertising drive *or* campaign. **–sendung,** *f.* (*Rad.*) commercial programme. **–stück,** *n.* (*coll.*) show-piece. **–zeichner,** *m.* poster artist. **–zettel,** *m.* handbill.

reklamieren [rekla'mi:rən], **1.** *v.t.* reclaim. **2.** *v.i.* 1. complain (***wegen,*** about); protest (***gegen,*** against), object (to); 2. apply for exemption (*from military service*). **reklamiert,** *adj.* exempt from military service, reserved (for essential work).

rekognoszieren [rekɔgnɔs'tsi:rən], *v.t.* (*Mil.*) reconnoitre.

rekommandieren [rekɔman'di:rən], *v.t.* 1. (*obs. or dial.*) recommend; 2. (*Austr.*) register (*a letter etc.*).

rekonstruieren [rekɔnstru'i:rən], *v.t.* reconstruct, (*Law*) re-enact (*a crime*).

Rekonvaleszent [rekɔnvalɛs'tsɛnt], *m.* convalescent. **Rekonvaleszenz,** *f.* convalescence.

Rekord [re'kɔrt], *m.* (**-s,** *pl.* **-e** *or* (*Austr.*) **-s**) (*Spt.*) record; ***einen – aufstellen,*** establish a *or* set up a record; ***den – schlagen*** or ***brechen,*** break *or* smash *or* beat the record; ***den – einstellen,*** equal the record; ***den – verbessern,*** better the record; ***auf – laufen,*** attack *or* (*coll.*) go for the record. **Rekord|besuch,** *m.* record attendance. **–versuch,** *m.* attempt on the record.

Rekrut [re'kru:t], *m.* (**-en,** *pl.* **-en**) recruit; conscript. **Rekrutenausbildung,** *f.* basic training. **rekrutieren** [–'ti:rən], **1.** *v.t.* recruit. **2.** *v.r.* be recruited (***von,*** from). **Rekrutierung,** *f.* recruiting; recruitment.

Rekta– ['rɛkta], *pref.* (*Comm.*) restrictive. **–papier,** *n.*, **–wechsel,** *m.* non-negotiable bill.

Rektion [rɛktsi'o:n], *f.* (*Gram.*) complement, agreement, dependence.

Rektor ['rɛktɔr], *m.* (**-s,** *pl.* **-en**) (*Univ.*) vice-chancellor, (*Am.*) president; (*school*) rector, headmaster, (*Am.*) principal. **Rektorat** [–'ra:t], *n.* (**-s,** *pl.* **-e**) vice-chancellor's office; headmastership.

Rekurs [re'kurs], *m.* (**-es,** *pl.* **-e**) (*Law*) appeal; redress.

Relais [rə'lɛ:], *n.* (- [–s], *pl.* - [–s]) (*Elec.*) relay (*also obs. of horses*). **Relaissender,** *m.* (*Rad.*) relay *or* repeater station.

relativ [rela'ti:f], **1.** *adj.* relative, relating (to);

respective. **2.** *adv.* relatively, comparatively; respectively. **Relativ,** *n.* **(-s,** *pl.* **-e)** *see* **Relativpronomen. Relativität** [–tivi'tɛ:t], *f.* relativism, relativity. **Relativitätstheorie,** *f.* theory of relativity. **Relativ|pronomen,** *n.* relative pronoun. **–satz,** *m.* relative clause. **Relativum,** *n.* **(-s,** *pl.* **-va)** *see* **Relativpronomen.**

Relegation [relegatsi'o:n], *f.* (*Univ.*) expulsion; rustication. **relegieren** [–'gi:rən], *v.t.* expel; send down, rusticate (*a student*).

Relief [reli'ɛf], *n.* **(-s,** *pl.* **-s** *or* **-e)** relief, relievo. **Relief|druck,** *m.* (*Typ.*) relief *or* embossed printing. **–tapete,** *f.* embossed wallpaper.

Religion [religi'o:n], *f.* religion. **Religions|-bekenntnis,** *n.* religious profession *or* faith. **–freiheit,** *f.* religious liberty. **–gemeinschaft,** *f.* religious community, sect. **–lehre,** *f.* doctrine. **–lehrer,** *m.* divine; scripture teacher, teacher of religious knowledge. **religionslos,** *adj.* irreligious. **Religionslosigkeit,** *f.* irreligion. **Religions|streit,** *m.* religious controversy. **–stunde,** *f.* religious instruction, scripture (lesson). **–trennung,** *f.* schism. **–unterricht,** *m.* *See* **–stunde. –verfolgung,** *f.* religious persecution. **–wissenschaft,** *f.* theology, divinity.

religiös [religi'ø:s], *adj.* religious, devout, pious; *–er Eiferer,* religious fanatic; *–er Wahnsinn,* religious mania. **Religiosität** [–ozi'tɛ:t], *f.* piety, religiosity.

Reling ['re:lɪŋ], *f.* (-, *pl.* **-e**) (*Naut.*) bulwark(s).

Reliquie [re'li:kviə], *f.* relic. **Reliquien|dienst,** *m.* worship of relics. **–schrein,** *m.* reliquary.

Remanenz [rema'nɛnts], *f.* residual magnetism. **Remanenzspannung,** *f.* residual voltage.

Rembours [rã'bu:r], *m.* (-, *pl.* -) (*Comm.*) remittance.

Reminiszenz [reminɪs'tsɛnts], *f.* (-, *pl.* **-en**) reminiscence, recollection, memory.

remis [rə'mi:], *adj.* (*Chess*) drawn. **Remis,** *n.* (-, *pl.* - *or* **-en** [–zən]) drawn game; – *machen,* leave the game drawn, agree a draw.

Remise [rə'mi:zə], *f.* coach-house, shed; (*Hunt.*) cover.

Remittende [remɪ'tɛndə], *f.* remainder; (*books*) surplus *or* return copy. **Remittent,** *m.* **(-en,** *pl.* **-en)** (*Comm.*) remitter, payee. **remittieren,** *v.t.* return, send back (*goods*), remit (*money*).

remontant [remɔn'tant], *adj.* *See* **remontierend. Remonte** [–'mɔntə], *f.*, **Remontepferd,** *n.* (*Mil.*) remount. **remontieren, 1.** *v t.* remount (*cavalry*). **2.** *v.i.* (*Hort.*) bloom a second time. **remontierend,** *adj.* (*Hort.*) perpetual, perennial.

Remontoiruhr [remɔ̃to'a:rʔu:r], *f.* keyless watch.

Remoulade [remu'la:də], *f.* salad cream, mayonnaise.

Rempelei [rɛmpə'laɪ], *f.* jostling, scuffle, (*coll.*) rough-house. **rempeln** ['rɛmpəln], *v.t.* jostle; bump *or* (*coll.*) barge into.

Rem(p)ter ['rɛm(p)tər], *m.* (*Hist.*) refectory, assembly hall (*in castles, monasteries*).

Remulade, *see* **Remoulade.**

Ren [rɛn], *n.* **(-s,** *pl.* **-e)** reindeer.

Rendant [rɛn'dant], *m.* **(-en,** *pl.* **-en)** treasurer, paymaster, cashier, accountant.

Rendement [rãdə'mã], *m.* (*Comm.*) output, yield.

Rendezvous [rãde'vu:], *n.* (- [–(s)], *pl.* - [–s]) rendezvous, meeting, (*obs.*) tryst; (*sl.*) date; *ein – verabreden mit,* make an appointment with, arrange *or* (*coll.*) fix a meeting with, (*sl.*) date (*a girl*).

Rendite [rɛn'di:tə], *f.* (*Comm.*) yield.

Renegat [rene'ga:t], *m.* **(-en,** *pl.* **-en)** renegade.

Reneklode [rɛ:nə'klo:də], *f.* greengage.

Renette [re'nɛtə], *f.* rennett(-apple).

renitent [reni'tɛnt], *adj.* refractory. **Renitenz,** *f.* refractoriness, obstinacy.

renken ['rɛŋkən], *v.t.* turn, bend, twist, wrench.

Renkontre [rã'kɔ̃:tər], *n.* **(-s,** *pl.* **-s)** encounter *or* (*coll.*) clash with the enemy.

Renk(verschluß) ['rɛŋk–], *m.* bayonet catch.

Renn|arbeit, *f.* (*Metall.*) direct process (*of ore extraction*). **–bahn,** *f.* racecourse, race-track. **–boot,** *n.* racing boat, speedboat.

rennen ['rɛnən], **1.** *irr.v.i.* (*aux.* h. *&* s.) run, race, rush, dash; (run a) race; *– an* (*Acc.*) or *gegen* or *wider,* dash against, crash into; *sich ein Loch in den Kopf –,* injure one's head in a collision; *mit dem Kopf – gegen,* run one's head against; *ins Verderben –,* rush (headlong) into disaster. **2.** *irr.v.t., v.r. eine Meile in fünf Minuten –,* run a mile in five minutes; *sich außer Atem –,* run o.s. out of breath; *ihn zu Boden –,* run him over *or* down; *ihm den Degen durch den Leib –,* run one's sword through his body. **3.** *irr.v.t.* (*Metall.*) smelt. **Rennen,** *n.* run, running; race; (*fig.*) *aus dem – fallen,* be out of the running; *das – machen,* win the race, come in first, be the winner, (*fig.*) make the running; (*esp. fig.*) *das – aufgehen,* give up, throw up the sponge; *totes –,* dead-heat. **Rennerei** [–'raɪ], *f.* (*coll.*) dashing hither and thither, rushing about.

Renn|fahrer, *m.* racing cyclist; racing driver. **–pferd,** *n.* racehorse. **–platz,** *m.* *See* **–bahn. –rad,** *n.* (*Cycl.*) racer. **–schlitten,** *m.* bobsleigh. **–schuhe,** *m.pl.* spiked *or* track shoes, (*coll.*) spikes. **–sport,** *m.* racing, the turf. **–stahl,** *m.* (*Metall.*) direct-process steel. **–stall,** *m.* racing-stables. **–strecke,** *f.* course, distance (to be run). **–termin,** *m.* racing-fixture. **–tier,** *n.* *See* **Ren. –wagen,** *m.* racing car.

Renommage [renɔ'ma:ʒə], *f.* (*obs.*) boasting, bragging, big talk; (*Studs. sl.*) good form, proper behaviour. **Renommee,** *n.* repute, renown, reputation, name. **renommieren,** *v.i.* boast, brag (*mit,* of). **renommiert,** *adj.* renowned, well-known, noted (*wegen,* for), (*pred.*) of good repute. **Renommist,** *m.* **(-en,** *pl.* **-en)** (*obs.*) boaster, braggart.

Renonce [rə'nɔ̃s(ə)], *f.* (*Cards*) revoking.

renovieren [reno'vi:rən], *v.t.* renew, renovate, redecorate, (*coll.*) do up. **Renovierung,** *f.* renovation, redecoration.

rentabel [rɛn'ta:bəl], *adj.* profitable, remunerative, lucrative, paying, productive; *eine S. – machen,* make a th. pay, make a th. a paying proposition. **Rentabilität** [–bili'tɛ:t], *f.* productiveness, profitableness. **Rentabilitätsrechnung,** *f.* calculation of profits.

Rentamt ['rɛntʔamt], *n.* finance *or* revenue office.

Rente ['rɛntə], *f.* income, revenue; interest; annuity, pension; (*pl.*) stocks, bonds; *lebenslängliche –,* life annuity; *jährliche –,* annuity; *auf –n legen,* invest, put out at interest. **Rentei** [–'taɪ], *f.* (*obs.*) *see* **Rentamt. Renten|bank,** *f.* annuity-office. **–empfänger,** *m.* *See* **Rentner. –mark,** *f.* (*Hist.*) (stabilized) mark (based on land values) (1923). **–papiere,** *n.pl.* fixed-interest bonds. **–versicherung,** *f.* pension insurance fund.

[1]**Rentier** ['rɛnti:r], *n.* *See* **Ren.**

[2]**Rentier** [rɛnti'e:], *m.* **(-s,** *pl.* **-s), Rentiere** [–'ɛ:rə], *f.* man *or* woman of private means. **rentieren** [–'ti:rən], *v.i., v.r.* yield a profit *or* revenue, be profitable, pay (its way); (*fig.*) *das rentiert sich nicht,* it doesn't pay, it isn't worth while.

Rentner ['rɛntnər], *m.*, **Rentnerin,** *f.* pensioner, annuitant, recipient of a pension *or* annuity; p. of *or* with private *or* independent means.

Rentrant [rã'trã], *m.* (*Geom.*) re-entrant angle.

reorganisieren [reɔrgani'zi:rən], *v.t.* reorganize. **Reorganisierung,** *f.* reorganization.

Reparation [reparatsi'o:n], *f.* reparation, (war) indemnity.

Reparatur [repara'tu:r], *f.* repair(s); *in –,* under repair; *in – geben,* have repaired. **reparatur|-bedürftig,** *adj.* in need of repair, out of repair. **–fähig,** *adj.* repairable. **Reparaturwerkstatt,** *f.* repair shop, (*Motor.*) service station. **reparieren** [–'ri:rən], *v.t.* mend, repair.

repassieren [repa'si:rən], *v.t., v.i.* repair ladders (in stockings); pick up stitches, do invisible mending (*on stockings*).

repatriieren [repatri'i:rən], *v.t.* repatriate. **Repatriierte(r),** *m., f.* repatriate. **Repatriierung,** *f.* repatriation.

Repertoire [repɛrto'a:r], *n.* (**-s,** *pl.* **-s**) (*Theat.*) repertoire, repertory. **Repertoire|stück,** *n.* stock-play. **–theater,** *n.* repertory theatre.

Repetent [repe'tɛnt], *m.* (**-en,** *pl.* **-en**) pupil repeating a year; *see also* **Repetitor. repetieren,** *v.t., v.i.* repeat. **Repetieruhr,** *f.* repeater. **Repetition** [-titsi'o:n], *f.* recapitulation, revision. **Repetitor** [–'ti:tɔr], *m.* (**-s,** *pl.* **-en**) coach, tutor. **Repetitorium** [–'to:rium], *n.* (**-s,** *pl.* **-rien**) refresher *or* revision (course) (*on a subject*).

Replik [re'pli:k], *f.* (-, *pl.* **-en**) (*Law*) counter-plea, reply.

reponieren [repo'ni:rən], *v.t.* replace, put in its place; (*Surg.*) set (*a limb*); reduce.

Report [re'pɔrt], *m.* (**-s,** *pl.* **-e**) (*Comm.*) contango.

Reportage [repɔr'ta:ʒə], *f.* eyewitness account, on-the-spot reporting, (running) commentary, coverage of day-to-day events.

Repositorium [repozi'to:rium], *n.* (**-s,** *pl.* **-rien**) (set of) bookshelves; music-stand, canterbury.

Repräsentant [reprɛzɛn'tant], *m.* (**-en,** *pl.* **-en**) representative.

repräsentationsfähig [reprɛzɛntatsi'o:nsfɛ:ɪç], *adj.* presentable. **Repräsentations|figur,** *f.* figure-head. **–gelder,** *n.pl.* allowance for representation, upkeep allowance. **repräsentativ** [–ta'ti:f], *adj.* 1. representative (*für*, of); 2. stately, imposing. **repräsentieren** [–'ti:rən], **1.** *v.t.* represent. **2.** *v.i.* keep up appearances; (*coll.*) cut a fine figure, make a show.

Repressalie [reprɛ'sa:liə], *f.* reprisal, retaliation; ***–n ergreifen gegen,*** make reprisals on.

Reprise [re'pri:zə], *f.* (*Mus.*) repeat; (*Theat.*) repeat performance; (*Films*) re-issue.

Reproduktion [reproduktsi'o:n], *f.* reproduction. **reproduzieren** [–'tsi:rən], *v.t.* reproduce.

Reps, *m.* (*dial.*) *see* **Raps** *and* **Rips.**

Reptil [rɛp'ti:l], *n.* (**-s,** *pl.* **-ien** *or* (*Austr.*) **-e**) reptile.

Republik [repu'bli:k], *f.* (-, *pl.* **-en**) republic. **Republikaner** [–'ka:nər], *m.* republican. **republikanisch,** *adj.* republican.

Repunze [re'puntsə], *f.* hall-mark.

reputierlich [repu'ti:rlɪç], *adj.* reputable, respectable, (*coll.*) decent; ***nicht –,*** disreputable.

requirieren [rekvi'ri:rən], *v.t.* demand, request; (*Mil.*) requisition, commandeer, confiscate.

Requisit [rekvi'zi:t], *n.* (**-(e)s,** *pl.* **-en** *or* (*Austr.*) **-e**) requisite, requirement, indispensable item; *pl.* (*Theat.*) properties.

resch [rɛʃ], *adj.* (*dial.*) crisp, crusty (*bread*); tough (*meat*); acid, tart (*wine*); pithy, lively, gay.

Reseda [re'ze:da], *f.* (-, *pl.* **-s**), **Resede,** *f.* (*Bot.*) mignonette (*Reseda odorata*).

Resektion [rezɛktsi'o:n], *f.* surgical removal.

Reservage [rezɛr'va:ʒə], *f.* resist, reserve, resist-paste.

Reservat [rezɛr'va:t], *n.* reservation, proviso.

Reserve [re'zɛrvə], *f.* 1. reserve, (*Mil.*) reserves; ***in – liegen,*** be in reserve, be in stock; ***stille –n,*** hidden reserves; 2. (*fig.*) reserve, restraint, guarded manner. **Reserve|batterie,** *f.* spare battery. **–fonds,** *m.* reserve-fund. **–mannschaft,** *f.* (*Mil.*) reserves, replacements. **–offizier,** *m.* officer in the reserve. **–rad,** *n.* spare wheel. **–teil,** *m.* replacement, spare (part). **–truppen,** *f.pl. See* **–mannschaft.**

reservieren [rezɛr'vi:rən], *v.t.* reserve, secure, make sure of; book (in advance). **reserviert,** *adj.* (*also fig.*) reserved, retiring, restrained, aloof (*of manner*).

Reservist [rezɛr'vɪst], *m.* (**-en,** *pl.* **-en**) (*Mil.*) reservist.

Reservoir [rezɛrvo'a:r], *n.* (**-s,** *pl.* **-e**) reservoir, cistern, tank, (*fig.*) resources.

Resident [rezi'dɛnt], *m.* (**-en,** *pl.* **-en**) agent on the spot; resident ambassador *or* minister. **Residenz,** *f.* (-, *pl.* **-en**) (prince's) residence; seat of the court, capital. **Residenzstadt,** *f.* seat of the court, capital (town). **residieren,** *v.i.* reside, be in residence.

Residuum [re'zi:duum], *n.* (**-s,** *pl.* **-duen**) residue.

resignieren [rezɪ'gni:rən], *v.i.* renounce *or* forgo one's right; be resigned, acquiesce, (*coll.*) give up.

Resonanz [rezo'nants], *f.* (-, *pl.* **-en**) resonance; (*fig.*) echo, understanding. **Resonanz|boden,** *m.* sounding-board. **–frequenz,** *f.* resonant frequency. **–kreis,** *m.* (*Rad.*) resonant circuit.

resorbieren [rezɔr'bi:rən], *v.t., v.i.* reabsorb. **Resorbierung, Resorption** [–zɔrptsi'o:n], *f.* reabsorption.

Respekt [re'spɛkt], *m.* 1. respect; ***mit – zu melden*** or ***zu sagen,*** with all due respect, if I may (be allowed to) say so, if you will excuse the language; 2. (*obs.*) wide border *or* margin. **respektabel** [–'ta:bəl], *adj.* estimable, respectable, (*coll.*) fairly big, decent-sized, sizeable. **Respektblatt,** *n.* fly-leaf. **respektieren,** *v.t.* respect, esteem; have respect for; (*Comm.*) honour (*bills*). **respektierlich,** *adj.* respectable, honourable.

respektiv [respɛk'ti:f], *adj.* respective. **respektive,** *adv.* respectively; or (rather).

respektlos [re'spɛktlo:s], *adj.* without respect, irreverent. **Respektlosigkeit,** *f.* irreverence, lack *or* want of respect. **Respektsperson,** *f.* person held in *or* commanding respect, notability. **Respekttage,** *m.pl.* days of grace. **respekt|voll,** *adj.* respectful, deferential. **–widrig,** *adj.* disrespectful.

Responsorium [rɛspɔn'zo:rium], *n.* (**-s,** *pl.* **-ien**) (*Eccl.*) response, antiphon.

Ressentiment [rɛsãti'mã], *n.* (**-s,** *pl.* **-s**) resentment, grudge, rancour, ill-will.

Ressort [rɛ'so:r], *n.* (**-s,** *pl.* **-s**) department; (*fig.*) purview, sphere, province. **ressortmäßig,** *adj.* departmental.

Rest [rɛst], *m.* 1. (**-es,** *pl.* **-e**) rest, residue, remains; (*Math.*) remainder; difference; (*Comm.*) balance; (*dial.*) arrears; 2. (*usu. pl.* **-er,** (*Austr., Swiss*) **-en**) remnant (*of cloth, food etc.*); dregs (*of liquid*), (*coll.*) leftovers (*of meal*), vestige; ***das wird ihm den – geben,*** that will do for him *or* finish him off; ***sterbliche*** or ***irdische –e,*** earthly *or* mortal remains; ***der letzte –,*** the last vestiges.

Restant [rɛs'tant], *m.* (**-en,** *pl.* **-en**) defaulter; *pl.* arrears, suspense items.

Restauflage ['rɛstˀauf'la:gə], *f.* remainders.

Restaurant [rɛsto'rã], *n.* (**-s,** *pl.* **-s**) restaurant. **Restaurateur** [rɛstora'tø:r], *m.* (**-s,** *pl.* **-e**) restaurant proprietor. **Restauration** [–ratsi'o:n], *f.* 1. refreshment room; 2. (*Pol., Art*) restoration. **Restaurator** [–'ra:tɔr], *m.* (**-s,** *pl.* **-en**) restorer (*of pictures*). **restaurieren, 1.** *v.t.* restore, repair. **2.** *v.r.* take refreshment.

Rest|bestand, –betrag, *m.* balance, remainder. **–forderung,** *f.* residual claim.

restieren [rɛs'ti:rən], *v.i.* (*obs.*) remain, be left; be in arrears; owe.

restituieren [rɛstitu'i:rən], *v.t.* restore.

restlich ['rɛstlɪç], *adj.* residual, remaining, (*pred.*) left over; (*Comm.*) ***–er Betrag,*** balance; (*Law*) ***–er Nachlaß,*** residue (of the estate). **restlos, 1.** *adj.* total, complete. **2.** *adv.* totally, thoroughly, completely, entirely, absolutely, altogether; (*coll.*) ***– erledigt,*** dead-beat, all in. **Rest|posten,** *m.* surplus stock. **–summe,** *f. See* **–betrag.**

Resultante [rezul'tantə], *f.* (*Phys.*) resultant. **Resultat** [rezul'ta:t], *n.* (**-(e)s,** *pl.* **-e**) result, outcome; (*Spt.*) score. **resultieren,** *v.i.* result (***aus,*** from).

Resümee [rezy'me:], *n.* (**-s,** *pl.* **-s**) summary. **resümieren,** *v.t., v.i.* recapitulate, sum up.

retablieren [reta'bli:rən], *v.t.* re-establish. **Retablissement** [–bli:smã], *n.* re-establishment.

retardieren [retar'di:rən], **1.** *v.t.* retard, check, impede; ***–des Moment,*** retardation in the progress of the (dramatic) action. **2.** *v.i.* go slow (*of watches etc.*).

Retentionsrecht [retɛntsi'o:nsrɛçt], *n.* (*Law*) lien.
Retirade [reti'ra:də], *f.* (*obs.*) retreat, withdrawal; latrine.
Retorte [re'tɔrtə], *f.* (*Chem.*) retort, alembic.
retour [re'tu:r], *adv.* back. **Retourbillet,** *n.* (*Swiss*) return-ticket. **Retouren,** *f.pl.* empties; returns. **Retourkutsche,** *f.* (*sl.*) knock-down argument; (*sl.*) – ***selber eins!*** same to you! **retournieren** [–'ni:rən], *v.t.* (*Comm.*) return, send back.
Retraite [rə'trɛ:t(ə)], *f.* (*obs.*) retreat; tattoo.
retten ['rɛtən], **1.** *v.t.* save, rescue (***vor*** (*Dat.*), from), deliver, (set) free (***aus,*** from); recover, retrieve, salvage. **2.** *v.r.* escape, save o.s.; ***seine Ehre*** –, vindicate one's honour; ***rette sich wer kann!*** everyone for himself! **Retter,** *m.* rescuer, deliverer; (*Eccl.*) Saviour, Redeemer.
Rettich ['rɛtɪç], *m.* (**-s,** *pl.* **-e**) radish.
Rettung ['rɛtuŋ], *f.* preservation; salvage, recovery; deliverance, rescue; escape; (*Eccl.*) salvation; ***ohne*** –, past help. **Rettungs|anker,** *m.* sheet-anchor, (*fig.*) lifeline. **–apparat,** *m.* life-saving apparatus. **–arbeiten,** *f.pl.* rescue operations. **–boje,** *f.* lifebuoy. **–boot,** *n.* life boat. **–gürtel,** *m.* life-belt. **–leine,** *f.* life-line. **–leiter,** *f.* fire-escape. **rettungslos,** *adj.* irrecoverable, irremediable, irretrievable, past help, beyond hope, beyond recovery. **Rettungs|mannschaft,** *f.* rescue party. **–medaille,** *f.* life-saving medal. **–ring,** *m.* life-belt. **–schwimmen,** *n.* life-saving. **–schwimmer,** *m.* lifeguard. **–station,** *f.* first-aid post. **–versuch,** *m.* attempted rescue.
Retusche [re'tuʃə], *f.* (*Phot.*) retouching. **retuschieren** [–'ʃi:rən], *v.t.* retouch.
Reue ['rɔyə], *f.* repentance (***über*** (*Acc.*), for), regret (at), remorse (for *or* over). **Reuegefühl,** *n.* compunction, remorse, penitence, contrition. **reuelos,** *adj.* impenitent. **reuen,** *v.i. imp.* regret, be sorry (for), repent (of), feel remorse (at *or* over); ***es reut mich,*** I am sorry about it, I regret it. **reuevoll,** *adj. See* **reuig. Reugeld,** *n.* forfeit, penalty, (*St. Exch.*) option money. **reuig,** *adj.* remorseful, penitent, contrite. **Reu|kauf,** *m. See* **–geld**; (*fig.*) discomfiture, fiasco. **reumütig,** *adj. See* **reuig.**
Reuse ['rɔyzə], *f.* weir-basket; oyster-basket, eel-pot.
Reute ['rɔytə], *f.* (*dial.*) clearing. **reuten,** *v.t.* root out (*weeds*), plough *or* turn up (*land*), clear (*a wood*). **Reut|feld,** *n.* newly reclaimed land, virgin soil. **–hacke, –haue,** *f.* hoe, mattock.
Revanche [re'vãʃ(ə)], *f.* revenge, satisfaction. **Revanchespiel,** *n.* return-match. **revanchieren** [–'ʃi:rən], *v.r.* have *or* take one's revenge, be revenged (***an*** (*Dat.*), on), (*coll.*) get one's own back; (*fig.*) ***sich – für,*** reciprocate (*a present*), return (*a kindness*).
Reverenz [reve'rɛnts], *f.* (-, *pl.* **-en**) reverence, respect; obeisance.
Revers [re'vɛ:r], *m.* (**-es,** *pl.* **-e**) 1. reverse (*of coin*), lapel, revers (*of coat*); 2. (*Law*) reciprocal bond, declaration, written undertaking.
revidieren [revi'di:rən], *v.t.* revise, check, control, examine, review (*a decision*), audit (*accounts*).
Revier [re'vi:r], *n.* (**-s,** *pl.* **-e**) 1. quarter, district, precinct, territory; (*police*) beat, (*postman*) round; (*Hunt.*) preserve, hunting ground; 2. (*Mil.*) sick-bay, medical centre; (*Mil.*) – ***bekommen,*** be put on the sick-list. **Revierdienst,** *m.* (*Mil.*) light duties. **revieren,** *v.t.* (*Hunt.*) quarter (*hounds*). **Revier|-forster,** *m.* gamekeeper. **-kranke(r),** *m.* (*Mil.*) soldier sick in quarters.
Revision [revizi'o:n], *f.* revision; (*Law*) revisal, review, re-hearing; (*Comm.*) audit(ing); (custom's) examination (*of luggage*); (*Law*) – ***einlegen,*** appeal on a point of law. **Revisor** [re'vi:zɔr], *m.* (**-s,** *pl.* **-en**) inspector, examiner, auditor; ***qualifizierter*** –, chartered accountant.
Revolte [re'vɔltə], *f.* revolt, insurrection. **revoltieren** [–'ti:rən], *v.i.* (rise in) revolt.
Revolution [revolutsi'o:n], *f.* revolution. **Revolutionär** [–'nɛ:r], *m.* (**-s,** *pl.* **-e**) revolutionary. **revolutionär,** *adj.* revolutionary. **revolutionieren,** *v.t.* revolutionize.
Revolver [re'vɔlvər], *m.* revolver. **Revolver|blatt,** *n.* (*coll.*) scandal-sheet, rag. **–drehbank,** *f.* turret *or* capstan-lathe. **–held,** *m.* (*coll.*) gunman, thug, hoodlum. **–presse,** *f.* yellow press, gutter-press.
revozieren [revo'tsi:rən], **1.** *v.t.* revoke, retract, recall. **2.** *v.i.* retract one's words.
Revue [rə'vy:], *f.* 1. (*Theat.*) revue, musical; 2. (*obs.*) review, muster; – ***passieren lassen,*** pass in review.
Rezensent [retsɛn'zɛnt], *m.* (**-en,** *pl.* **-en**) critic, reviewer. **rezensieren,** *v.t.* criticize, review. **Rezension,** *f.* critique, criticism, review. **Rezensionsexemplar,** *n.* review(er's) copy.
Rezepisse [retse'pɪsə], *f.* receipt, acquittance.
Rezept [re'tsɛpt], *n.* (**-s,** *pl.* **-e**) (*Cul.*) recipe, (*Med.*) prescription, (*Chem.*) formula.
rezeptieren [retsɛp'ti:rən], *v.t., v.i.* prescribe. **Rezeptor** [–'tsɛptɔr], *m.* (**-s,** *pl.* **-en**) receiver, collector; (*Anat.*) receptor organ. **Rezeptur** [–'tu:r], *f.* receivership; dispensing (*of medicines*).
Rezeß [re'tsɛs], *m.* (**-(ss)es,** *pl.* **-(ss)e**) compact, treaty.
reziprok [retsi'pro:k], *adj.* reciprocal, converse.
Rezitativ [retsita'ti:f], *n.* (**-s,** *pl.* **-e**) (*Mus.*) recitative. **Rezitator** [–'ta:tɔr], *m.* (**-s,** *pl.* **-en**) reciter. **rezitieren,** *v.t.* recite.
Rhabarber [ra'barbər], *m.* rhubarb.
Rhapsode [ra'pso:də], *m.* (**-n,** *pl.* **-n**) rhapsodist. **Rhapsodie** [–'di:], *f.* rhapsody.
Rhein [raɪn], *m.* (*Geog.*) Rhine. **Rhein|bund,** *m.* (*Hist.*) Confederation of the Rhine (*1806–13*). **–franken,** *n.* Rhenish Franconia. **rheinfränkisch,** *adj.* Rheno-Franconian. **Rheinhessen,** *n.* Rhenish Hesse. **rheinisch,** *adj.* Rhenish. **Rhein|-land,** *n.* Rheinland. **–länder,** *m.* Rhinelander. **rheinländisch,** *adj. See* **rheinisch. Rhein|pfalz,** *f.* Rhenish Palatinate. **–wein,** *m.* Rhine wine, hock.
rhetorisch [re'to:rɪʃ], *adj.* rhetorical.
Rheuma ['rɔyma], *n.* (*coll.*) *see* **Rheumatismus. rheumatisch** [–'ma:tɪʃ], *adj.* rheumatic. **Rheumatismus** [–'tɪsmus], *m.* rheumatism, (*coll.*) rheumatics.
Rhinozeros [ri'no:tserɔs], *n.* (- *or* **-ses,** *pl.* **-se**) rhinoceros.
rhombisch ['rɔmbɪʃ], *adj.* rhombic. **Rhombus,** *m.* (-, *pl.* **-ben**) rhomb(us).
rhythmisch ['rytmɪʃ], *adj.* rhythmic(al). **Rhythmus,** *m.* (-, *pl.* **-men**) rhythm; ***steigender*** –, iambic rhythm; ***fallender*** –, trochaic rhythm.
Ribisel ['ri:bizəl], *f.* (-, *pl.* **-n**) (*Austr.*) redcurrant.
Richt|antenne ['rɪçt–], *f.* (*Rad.*) directional aerial. **–bake,** *f.* direction-finding beacon. **–beil,** *n.* executioner's axe. **–blei,** *n.* plumb-line, plummet. **–block,** *m.* executioner's block.
Richte ['rɪçtə], *f.* straight *or* direct line, shortest distance; normal *or* proper position; ***wieder in die – bringen,*** adjust, put straight; ***in die – gehen,*** take a short cut, go as the crow flies; ***aus der – kommen,*** go astray, (*fig.*) get in a muddle.
richten ['rɪçtən], **1.** *v.t.* 1. set right, adjust, arrange, put in order, straighten; repair, (*coll.*) fix; make (*a bed*), prepare (*a meal*), settle (*a dispute*), trim (*sails*), set, regulate (*a watch*); (*Mil.*) dress (*ranks*); 2. direct, point (***gegen,*** at *or* towards), turn (on *or* towards), level, point, aim (*a gun*) (***auf*** (*Acc.*), at), lay, sight, train (*cannon*) (on), turn, direct (*attention*) (to), focus, concentrate (on), address (*letter, remarks*) (***an*** (*Acc.*), to), address, put (*question*) (to); ***in die Höhe*** –, lift up, raise; ***das war auf mich gerichtet,*** that was aimed at *or* meant for me; ***den Blick gen Himmel*** –, turn one's eyes towards Heaven; ***die Segel nach dem Winde*** –, trim the sails to the wind (*also fig.*), be a timeserver. **2.** *v.r.* ***sich in die Höhe*** –, raise o.s. up; (*Mil.*) ***Augen rechts, richt euch!*** eyes right, dress! ***sich – an*** (*Acc.*), address o.s. to; ***sich – auf*** (*Acc.*), be prepared for; ***sich – gegen,*** be levelled at; ***sich – nach,*** act according to *or* in harmony *or* conformity with,

be governed *or* determined by, conform to *or* with, depend *or* be conditional on, be guided by, take one's bearings from; ***ich richte mich nach dir,*** I'll leave it to you, just as you like, anything you say; ***das Eigenschaftswort richtet sich nach dem Hauptwort,*** the adjective agrees with the noun. **3.** *v.t., v.i.* sit in judgement, judge, try; pass *or* pronounce sentence on, condemn; (*obs.*) execute (*a criminal*).

Richter ['rɪçtər], *m.* judge (*über* (*Acc.*), of), magistrate; (*Spt.*) umpire; ***sich zum – aufwerfen,*** constitute o.s. a judge. **Richter|amt,** *n.* judicial office, judgeship. **-kollegium,** *n.* the Bench. **richterlich,** *adj.* judicial; judiciary. **Richter|spruch,** *m.* (*civil*) judgement, (*criminal*) sentence; (judicial) decision. **-stand,** *m.* judicature, the Bench. **-stuhl,** *m.* tribunal; ***das gehört nicht vor seinen –,*** that is not within his jurisdiction.

Richt|fall, *m.* (*Gram.*) required form. **-fehler,** *m.* error in aiming, bad aim. **-feier,** *f. See* **-fest. -fernrohr,** *n.* tracking telescope, telescopic sight. **-fest,** *n.* (*Build.*) topping-out ceremony. **-funkbake,** *f.* radio beacon. **-gerät,** *n.* laying *or* aiming gear. **-hebel,** *m.* elevating lever. **-hörer,** *m.* (*Mil.*) sound locator.

richtig ['rɪçtɪç], **1,** *adj.* right, correct, true, accurate, exact, faithful; fair, just, due, appropriate, suitable, proper, adequate; genuine, real, regular, (*coll.*) out and out; in order, settled; ***–e Abschrift,*** accurate *or* faithful copy; ***es ist alles –,*** all is well; ***–er Londoner,*** regular Cockney; (*coll.*) ***mit dem Ort ist es nicht –,*** there's s.th. queer *or* (*sl.*) fishy about this place; (*coll.*) ***es ist nicht – mit ihm, er ist nicht ganz –,*** he is not quite right in the head; ***–e Zeit,*** right *or* correct time. **2.** *adv.* duly, properly, thoroughly, soundly, (*coll.*) quite right, certainly, just so, sure enough; ***er hat es – vergessen,*** he has quite forgotten it; ***die Uhr geht –,*** the clock keeps good time; ***für – halten,*** see *or* think fit; ***und –! da kam er,*** and sure enough he came.

Richtigbefund ['rɪçtɪçbəfunt], *m.* (*Comm.*) ***nach –,*** if verified, if found correct. **richtiggehend,** *adj.* accurate (*clocks*), (*coll.*) real, regular, out and out, honest-to-goodness. **Richtigkeit,** *f.* correctness, accuracy, exactness; justness, rightness, fairness; ***die – nachweisen*** (*Gen.*), verify, confirm; ***in – bringen,*** adjust, settle, put right *or* in order; ***es ist alles in –,*** everything is in order *or* is arranged *or* settled; ***die S. hat ihre –, es hat damit seine –,*** it is quite true, it is a fact. **richtigstellen,** *v.t.* put *or* set right, rectify.

Richt|kanonier, *m.* gun-layer. **-kranz,** *m.* garland erected to crown the rafters (*at topping-out ceremony, see* **-fest**). **-kreis,** *m.* azimuth circle. **-linie,** *f.* (*usu. pl.*) (general) direction, rule, guiding principle, instruction. **-lot,** *n.* plumb-line. **-maß,** *n.* standard gauge. **-platz,** *m.* (*Hist.*) place of execution. **-preis,** *m.* standard price. **-punkt,** *m.* aiming point, aim. **-scheit,** *n.* ruler, straight edge, level, (*Typ.*) justifier. **-schmaus,** *m. See* **-fest. -schnur,** *f.* plumb line, (*fig.*) rule of conduct, guiding principle. **-schraube,** *f.* elevating screw. **-schwert,** *n.* (*Hist.*) executioner's sword. **-sendung,** *f.* (*Rad.*) beam transmission. **-stätte,** *f.* (*Hist.*) *see* **-platz. -strahl,** *m.* directional beam. **-strahlantenne,** *f.*, **-strahler,** *m.* beam *or* directional aerial.

Richtung ['rɪçtuŋ], *f.* direction, route, way; aim, alignment, bearing, course, (*fig.*) trend, orientation, course, tendency, line, bent, turn; ***neuere –,*** modern lines *or* methods; ***in jeder –, nach allen –en,*** in all directions; ***nach beiden –en,*** both ways; ***in gerader –,*** in a straight line, straight on; ***gerade –,*** alignment, (*Mil.*) dressing. **richtunggebend,** *adj.* trend-setting, prevailing, leading.

Richtungs|änderung, *f.* change of direction. **-anzeiger,** *m.* (*Motor.*) trafficator. **-linie,** *f.* line of direction, base-line. **-pfeil, -weiser,** *m.* signpost, marker, direction indicator, arrow. **-winkel,** *m.* angle of sight. **richtungweisend,** *adj.* directional, guiding, leading.

Richt|waage, *f.* (*Tech.*) level. **-weg,** *m.* short cut. **-wert,** *m.* standard value. **-zahl,** *f.* coefficient.

Ricke ['rɪkə], *f.* doe.

rieb [ri:p], *see* **reiben.**

riechen ['ri:çən], **1.** *irr.v.t.* smell, scent; sniff, nose out; (*coll.*) ***ich kann ihn nicht –,*** I can't stand (the sight of) him; (*coll.*) ***das kann ich doch nicht –!*** how am I to know? I can't be expected to know that! (*coll.*) ***Lunte –,*** smell a rat; (*coll.*) ***den Braten –,*** get wind of it, see through it; ***er kann kein Pulver –,*** he's a funk, he is chicken-hearted. **2.** *irr. v.i.* smell (***nach,*** of); ***– an*** (*Dat.*), smell, sniff (at) (*a th.*); ***er riecht aus dem Munde,*** his breath smells; ***es riecht angebrannt,*** it smells burnt; ***gut –,*** have a pleasant smell, (*coll.*) smell good; ***stark –,*** give off a powerful smell; ***übel –,*** have an unpleasant smell, (*coll.*) smell awful; (*sl.*) ***daran kannst du –!*** put that in your pipe and smoke it!

riechend ['ri:çənt], *adj.* smelling, odorous, perfumed, fragrant, redolent; strong, high (*of meat*). **Riecher,** *m.* (*sl.*) nose. **Riech|essig,** *m.* aromatic vinegar. **-fläschchen,** *n.* smelling-bottle. **-nerv,** *m.* olfactory nerve. **-salz,** *n.* smelling-salt(s). **-spur,** *f.* scent (*for dogs*). **-stoffe,** *m.pl.* scents, perfumes. **-werkzeuge,** *n.pl.* olfactory organs.

Ried [ri:t], *n.* (**-(e)s,** *pl.* **-e**) marsh, bog; reed. **Riedgras,** *n.* sedge.

rief [ri:f], **riefe,** *see* **rufen.**

Riefe ['ri:fə], *f.* groove, chamfer, channel; flute (*of a pillar*). **riefeln, riefen,** *v.t.* chamfer, channel, flute; groove; rifle (*a gun*); knurl, mill, striate.

riefest ['ri:fəst], *see* **rufen.**

Riege ['ri:gə], *f.* (*Gymn.*) section, squad.

Riegel ['ri:gəl], *m.* bolt; rail, bar, cross-bar, tie-(beam); bar, cake (*of soap*); ***unter Schloß und –,*** bolted and barred; (*fig.*) ***einen – vorschieben*** (*Dat.*), put an end *or* stop to (*s.th.*), check (*a p.*), put an obstacle in (*a p.'s*) way. **riegelfest,** *adj.* (securely) bolted, barred. **riegeln,** *v.t.* bar, bolt. **Riegelschloß,** *n.* stock-lock.

Riegen|führer, *m.* section leader. **-turnen,** *n.* squad drill.

Riemen ['ri:mən], *m.* 1. strap, (rifle) sling; belt; thong, shoelace; (*fig.*) ***sich den – enger schnallen,*** tighten one's belt; 2. oar; ***die – klar machen,*** ship the oars. **Riemen|antrieb,** *m.* belt-drive *or* transmission. **-bügel,** *m.* (sling) swivel. **-scheibe,** *f.* belt-pulley. **-schlag,** *m.* stroke of the oar. **-schneider,** *m. See* **Riemer. -schuh,** *m.* sandal. **-werk, -zeug,** *n.* straps, harness.

Riemer ['ri:mər], *m.* saddler, leather-worker, harness-maker.

Ries [ri:s], *n.* (**-es,** *pl.* **-e**) (*orig.*) ream (*of paper*), (*now*) 1,000 sheets.

[1]**Riese** ['ri:zə], *m.* (**-n,** *pl.* **-n**) giant, ogre.

[2]**Riese,** *f.* timber-slide.

Riesel|feld ['ri:zəl–], *n.* irrigated field. **-gut,** *n.* sewage-farm. **-jauche,** *f.* sewage (fertilizer). **rieseln,** *v.i.* (*aux.* h. & s.) ripple; trickle; (*of tears*) roll, run; ***es rieselt,*** it is drizzling; ***ein Schauer rieselt mir durchs Gebein,*** a shiver goes down my back. **Riesel|regen,** *m.* drizzle, drizzling rain. **-schutt,** *m.* shifting scree.

Riesen– ['ri:zən], *pref.* giant, gigantic, enormous, colossal, oversize, outsize. **-alk,** *m.* (*Orn.*) great auk (*Pinguinus impennis*). **-arbeit,** *f.* Herculean task. **-erfolg,** *m.* tremendous success, (*sl.*) smash-hit. **-faultier,** *n.* megatherium. **-fehler,** *m.* (*coll.*) howling blunder. **-geschlecht,** *n.* race of giants. **-gestalt,** *f.* colossus. **riesen|groß, -haft,** *adj. See* **riesig. Riesen|haftigkeit,** *f.* gigantic proportions *or* size. **-kraft,** *f.* Herculean strength. **-maß,** *n. See* **-haftigkeit. -rad,** *n.* giant wheel. **-schlange,** *f.* boa-constrictor, python, anaconda. **-schritt,** *m.* giant stride; (*fig.*) ***mit –en,*** at a tremendous pace. **-schwirl,** *m.* (*Orn.*) Gray's grasshopper warbler (*Locustella fasciolata*). **-wuchs,** *m.* (*Med.*) hypophysia.

riesig ['ri:zɪç], **1.** *adj.* gigantic, enormous, huge, immense, vast, colossal. **2.** *adv.* (*coll.*) immensely, tremendously, awfully.

Riesin ['ri:zin], *f.* giantess.

Riester ['ri:stər], *m.* 1. patch (*on a shoe etc.*); 2. (*dial.*) stilt (*of a plough*). **riestern,** *v.t.* (put on a) patch, mend.

riet [ri:t], **riete, rietest,** *see* **raten.**

Riff [rɪf], *n.* **(-(e)s,** *pl.* **-e)** reef, ridge, shelf, ledge, sandbank.

Riffel ['rɪfəl], *f.* (-, *pl.* **-n**) flax-comb, ripple. **Riffelblech,** *n.* corrugated iron. **riffeln,** *v.t.* ripple (*flax*); rib, channel, groove, corrugate, chamfer, flute. **Riffelwalze,** *f.* fluted roller.

Rigole [ri'go:lə], *f.* deep furrow. **rigolen,** *v.t.* trench(-plough). **Rigolpflug,** *m.* trench-plough.

rigoristisch [rigo'rɪstɪʃ], **rigoros,** *adj.* rigorous, severe, drastic, rigid, strict. **Rigorosum,** *n.* **(-s,** *pl.* **-sa)** oral examination (*for the doctor's degree*).

Rikoschet(t) [rɪkɔ'ʃɛt], *n.* **(-s,** *pl.* **-s)** ricochet. **rikoschet(t)ieren** [–'ti:rən], *v.i.* ricochet, rebound.

Rille ['rɪlə], *f.* rill; furrow; (*Hort.*) drill; (*Tech.*) flute, chamfer; groove (*of gramophone record*); (*Naut.*) narrow channel. **rillen,** *v.t.* groove, furrow, flute, (*Hort.*) drill.

Rimesse [ri'mɛsə], *f.* (*Comm.*) remittance.

Rind [rɪnt], *n.* **(-es,** *pl.* **-er)** ox, cow; *pl.* (horned) cattle, (*after numerals*) head of cattle.

Rinde ['rɪndə], *f.* bark (*of tree*), crust (*of bread*), rind (*of fruit, cheese*), (*Anat.*) cortex.

Rinder|braten, *m.* roast beef. **–brust,** *f.* brisket of beef. **–fett,** *n.* beef dripping. **–galle,** *f.* ox-gall. **–hirt,** *m.* cowherd, (*Am.*) cowboy. **rindern,** *v.i.* desire the bull (*of cows*). **Rinder|pest, –seuche,** *f.* cattle-plague. **–talg,** *m.* beef-suet *or* -tallow. **–zucht,** *f.* cattle breeding.

Rind|fleisch, *n.* beef. **–fleischbrühe,** *f.* beef-tea.

Rindsbraten ['rɪntsbra:tən], *m.* (*dial.*) roast beef. **Rind(s)leder,** *n.* cowhide. **Rindstalg,** *m.* *See* **Rindertalg.**

Rindvieh ['rɪntfi:], *n.* (horned) cattle; (*vulg.*) (*pl.* **-viecher**) idiot, blockhead.

Ring [rɪŋ], *m.* **(-(e)s,** *pl.* **-e)** 1. ring; circle; arena, (*Boxing*) (prize-)ring; (*Archit.*) astragal; loop, coil (*of wire etc.*); washer; link (*of chain*); ferrule, band, hoop, annulus; ruff (*in pigeons*); *pl.* dark rings (*round the eyes*); (*Boxing*) ***– frei!*** seconds out of the ring! ***einen – bilden,*** form a circle; ***–e in die Luft blasen,*** blow smoke-rings; (*fig.*) ***den – betreten,*** enter the arena; 2. (*Comm.*) ring, combine, trust, syndicate, pool. **Ring|amsel,** *f.* *See* **–drossel. –bahn,** *f.* circular railway. **–buch,** *n.* loose-leaf *or* ring-book. **–drossel,** *f.* (*Orn.*) ring-ouzel (*Turdus torquatus*).

Ringel ['rɪŋəl], *m.* small ring; ringlet, curl. **Ringel|blume,** *f.* (*Bot.*) marigold. **Ringelchen,** *n.* *See* **Ringel. Ringel|gans,** *f.* (*Orn.*) brent goose, (*Am.*) brant (*Branta bernicla*). **–locke,** *f.* ringlet, curl. **ringeln, 1.** *v.t.* curl (*hair*); ring. **2.** *v.r.* curl (*as hair*); wreathe, wind (*smoke*). **Ringel|natter,** *f.* grass-snake, ring-snake. **–reigen, –reihen,** *m.* *See* **–tanz. –reiten,** *n.* *See* **–stechen. –spiel,** *n.* (*Austr.*) roundabout, merry-go-round. **–stechen,** *n.* tilting at the ring. **–tanz,** *m.* round-dance. **–taube,** *f.* (*Orn.*) woodpigeon (*Columba palumbus*).

ringen ['rɪŋən], **1.** *irr.v.i.* wrestle; struggle, grapple; ***– um,*** strive after *or* for, struggle *or* fight for; ***nach Atem –,*** gasp for breath; ***mit dem Tode –,*** be in the grip *or* throes of death, be in one's last throes. **2.** *v.t.* twist, wring; ***die Hände –,*** wring one's hands. **Ringen,** *n.* wrestling; (*fig.*) (hard) struggle. **Ringer,** *m.* wrestler. **Ringergriff,** *m.* wrestling hold.

Ring|feder, *f.* annular spring. **–finger,** *m.* ring-finger. **ringförmig,** *adj.* annular, circular, ring-like, cyclic. **Ringhaube,** *f.* (*Av.*) cowling ring. **ringhörig,** *adj.* (*Swiss*) sound-conducting. **Ring|kampf,** *m.* wrestling match. **–kämpfer,** *m.* *See* **Ringer. –knorpel,** *m.* (*Anat.*) annular *or* cricoid cartilage. **–lotte,** *f.* (*Austr.*) greengage. **–mauer,** *f.* town *or* city wall. **–richter,** *m.* (*Boxing*) referee.

rings [rɪŋs], *adv.* (a)round.

Ring|scheibe, *f.* (rifle-)target. **–schießen,** *n.* target-shooting. **–sendung,** *f.* (*Rad.*) nation-wide relay, (*coll.*) national hook-up.

rings(her)um ['rɪŋs(hɛr)um], *adv.* all (a)round, round about, on all sides, everywhere.

Ring|straße, *f.* circular road, ring-road. **–tennis,** *n.* deck-tennis.

rings|um(her), *adv.* *See* **–(her)um.**

Ring|verbindung, *f.* (*Chem.*) cyclic compound. **–wall,** *m.* rampart(s).

Rinne ['rɪnə], *f.* gutter, drain, sewer, gully, conduit, duct, channel, chute; channel, groove; furrow; (*Archit.*) flute. **rinnen,** *irr.v.i.* (*aux.* s.) run, flow; trickle, drip; (*aux.* h.) leak; gutter (*of candles*), run (*of nose*). **Rinnsal,** *n.* **(-s,** *pl.* **-e)** watercourse, channel; rill, rivulet. **Rinnstein,** *m.* gutter (*in the street*); sink (*in the kitchen*).

Rippchen ['rɪpçən], *n.* (*Cul.*) cutlet, chop.

Rippe ['rɪpə], *f.* (*Anat.*) rib; vein (*of a leaf*); (*Archit.*) groin; bar (*of chocolate*); (*coll.*) ***ich kann es mir nicht aus den –n schneiden,*** I cannot do the impossible, you can't squeeze blood from a stone. **rippen,** *v.t.* rib, groin; ***gerippt,*** ribbed, fluted, corded. **Rippen|bogen,** *m.* (*Anat.*) costal arch. **–braten,** *m.* roast loin. **–bruch,** *m.* fracture of a rib. **–fell,** *n.* (*Anat.*) pleura. **–fellentzündung,** *f.* pleurisy. **–gewölbe,** *n.* (*Archit.*) rib-vaulting. **–knorpel,** *m.* (*Anat.*) costal cartilage. **–stoß,** *m.* dig in the ribs. **–stück,** *n.* rib (*of meat*), chop. **–zwischenraum,** *m.* (*Anat.*) intercostal space.

Rippespeer ['rɪpəʃpe:r], *m.* *or* *n.* smoked ribs of pork.

Rips [rɪps], *m.* **(-es,** *pl.* **-e)** rep.

ripsraps ['rɪpsraps], *adv., int.* (*coll.*) in a twinkling.

Risiko ['ri:ziko], *n.* **(-s,** *pl.* **-ken** (*Austr.* **-s**)) risk; ***auf eigenes –,*** at one's own risk; ***ein – eingehen,*** run *or* take a risk.

riskant [rɪs'kant], *adj.* risky, dangerous, precarious. **riskieren,** *v.t.* risk, chance.

Rispe ['rɪspə], *f.* (*Bot.*) panicle.

Riß [rɪs], *m.* **(-(ss)es,** *pl.* **-(ss)e)** 1. tear, rent, laceration; cleft, crevice, fissure, chink, gap; break, crack, flaw; (*fig.*) breach, rift, rupture, split, schism (*in relationships*); (*coll.*) ***das gab mir einen –,*** that shook me to the core, that pained me deeply; 2. plan, design, technical drawing, draft, sketch, outline.

riß, risse, rissest, *see* **reißen.**

rissig ['rɪsɪç], *adj.* torn, cracked, fissured; (*of skin*) chapped; ***– werden,*** crack, get brittle; (*of skin*) become chapped. **Rißwunde,** *f.* laceration.

Rist [rɪst], *m.* **(-es,** *pl.* **-e)** instep, arch (*of foot*); back of the hand. **Ristgriff,** *m.* (*Gymn.*) hold with fingers upwards.

ristornieren [rɪstɔr'ni:rən], *v.t.* (*Comm.*) transfer (*an item*) from one account to another; cancel (*an insurance policy*). **Ristorno** [–'stɔrno], *m.* *or* *n.* **(-s,** *pl.* **-s)** transfer to another account; return of premium; cancellation (*of insurance*).

Ritornell [ritɔr'nɛl], *n.* **(-s,** *pl.* **-e)** (*Mus.*) ritornello, (*Pros.*) triad, triplet.

Ritratte [ri'tratə], *f.* (*Comm.*) re-exchange, redraft.

ritschratsch! ['rɪtʃratʃ], *int.* snip! snap!

Ritt [rɪt], *m.* **(-(e)s,** *pl.* **-e)** ride (on horseback); ***einen – machen,*** go for *or* take a ride; (*coll.*) ***in einem –e,*** at one go, without a break.

ritt, ritte, *see* **reiten.**

Ritter ['rɪtər], *m.* knight; (*fig.*) cavalier; ***fahrender –,*** knight-errant; ***– ohne Furcht und Tadel,*** knight without fear and without reproach (*Bayard*); ***– von der traurigen Gestalt,*** knight of the woeful countenance (*Don Quixote*); ***ihn zum – schlagen,*** knight him, dub him a knight; (*Cul.*) ***arme –,*** fritters.

Ritter|burg, *f.* knight's castle. **–gut,** *n.* nobleman's estate, manor. **–gutsbesitzer,** *m.* lord of the manor. **–kreuz,** *n.* Knight's Cross (*decoration*).

ritterlich ['rɪtərlɪç], *adj.* knightly; (*fig.*) chivalrous, gallant. **Ritterlichkeit,** *f.* (*fig.*) gallantry, chivalry.

Ritter|orden, *m.* knightly order, order of knighthood. **–roman,** *m.* romance of chivalry. **Ritter-**

schaft, *f.* knighthood, body of knights. **Ritterschlag,** *m.* dubbing, knighting, accolade.
Rittersmann ['rɪtərsman], *m.* (*pl.* **-leute**) knight.
Ritter|spiel, *n.* tournament; jousting. **–sporn,** *m.* (*Bot.*) larkspur. **–stand,** *m.* knighthood. **Rittertum,** *n.* chivalry. **Ritterzeit,** *f.* age of chivalry.
rittest ['rɪtəst], *see* **reiten.**
Ritual [rɪtu'a:l], *n.* (**-s,** *pl.* **-e**) ritual. **rituell,** *adj.* ritual. **Ritus** ['ri:tus], *m.* (-, *pl.* **-ten**) rite.
Ritz [rɪts], *m.* (**-es,** *pl.* **-e**), **Ritze,** *f.* cleft, fissure, crack, crevice, rift, chink, slit; scratch.
Ritzel ['rɪtsəl], *n.* (*Mech.*) pinion.
ritzen ['rɪtsən], *v.t.* cratch, graze, cut, etch. **ritzig,** *adj.* cracked; crannied; scratched.
Rival [ri'va:l], *m.* (**-s** *or* **-en,** *pl.* **-e** *or* **-en**), **Rivale,** *m.* (**-n,** *pl.* **-n**), **Rivalin,** *f.* rival. **rivalisieren** [-li'zi:rən], *v.i.* – *mit,* compete *or* vie with, rival. **Rivalität,** *f.* rivalry.
Rizinusöl ['ri:tsinusø:l], *n.* castor-oil.
Robbe ['rɔbə], *f.* (*Zool.*) seal.
Robber ['rɔbər], *m.* rubber (*of whist*).
Robinsonade [robɪnzo'na:də], *f.* far-fetched adventure story; (*Footb., coll.*) full-length save.
Robot ['rɔbɔt], *m.* (**-(e)s,** *pl.* **-e**), *Austr. f.* (-, *pl.* **-e**) (*Hist.*) ville(i)nage, forced labour. **Roboter,** *m.* (**-s,** *pl.* -) robot; (*Hist.*) forced labourer, villein.
roch [rɔx], *see* **riechen.**
Rochade [rɔ'xa:de, –'ʃa:də], *f.* (*Chess*) castling.
Roche, *m.* (**-n(s),** *pl.* **-n**) *see* **Rochen.**
röche [rœçə], *see* **riechen.**
röcheln ['rœçəln], **1.** *v.i.* rattle in the throat. **2.** *v.t.* (*coll.*) gasp out. **Röcheln,** *n.* death-rattle.
Rochen ['rɔxən], *m.* (*Ichth.*) ray (*Raiidae*).
rochest ['rɔxəst], *see* **riechen.**
rochieren [rɔ'xi:rən, –'ʃi:rən], *v.i.,v.t.* (*Chess*) castle.
Rock [rɔk], *m.* (**-(e)s,** *pl.* **⸚e**) coat (*for men*), skirt (*for women*); ***geteilter –,*** divided skirt; ***kniefreier –,*** knee-length skirt; ***des Königs –,*** the King's uniform; (*obs.*) ***der bunte –,*** military uniform; ***den bunten – anziehen,*** join the colours.
Röckchen ['rœkçən], *n.* frock; (*coll.*) ***ganz ohne –,*** naked and unashamed.
Rocken ['rɔkən], *m.* distaff; ***Werg am – haben,*** be mixed up in a th., have one's finger in the pie.
Rocken|politik, *f.* women's wiles, petticoat government. **–stube,** *f.* spinning-room. **–weisheit,** *f.* old wives' tale.
Rock|falte, *f.* pleat. **–schoß,** *m.* coat-tail; (*usu. fig.*) ***sich ihm an die Rockschösse hängen,*** hang on his coat-tails, follow him round. **–zipfel,** *m.* lappet of a coat; ***der Mutter am –*** or ***an Mutters – hängen,*** be tied to one's mother's apron strings.
Rodeland ['ro:dəlant], *n. See* **Rodung.**
Rodel ['ro:dəl], *f.* (-, *pl.* **-n**) *or m.* toboggan.
Rodelbahn, *f.* toboggan-run.
Rödelbalken ['rø:dəlbalkən], *m.* (*Mech.*) rack, racking-balk, side rail, wheel guide.
rodeln ['ro:dəln], *v.i.* toboggan, go tobogganing. **Rodeln,** *n.* tobogganing.
rödeln ['rø:dəln], *v.t.* (*Mech.*) rack down.
Rodelschlitten ['ro:dəlʃlɪtən], *m. See* **Rodel.**
roden ['ro:dən], *v.t., v.i.* root out, clear (*a wood*), make arable.
Rodler ['ro:dlər], *m.* tobogganer.
Rodung ['ro:duŋ], *f.* clearing, woodland cleared for cultivation, virgin soil.
Rodomontade [rodomɔn'ta:də], *f.* swagger, bragging, bluster, braggadocio, rodomontade. **rodomontieren,** *v.i.* swagger, brag, (*coll.*) talk big; swank, blow one's own trumpet; (*sl.*) shoot off one's mouth.
Rogen ['ro:gən], *m.* (hard) roe, spawn. **Rog(e)ner,** *m.* spawner. **Rogenstein,** *m.* oolite.
Roggen ['rɔgən], *m.* rye. **Roggen|bau,** *m.* rye-growing. **–brot,** *n.* rye-bread.
roh [ro:], *adj.* raw, unrefined, in native state, unbroken (*horse*), unbleached (*textiles*), undressed (*hides*), (*Bookb.*) in sheets, (*Comm.*) gross, (*Metall.*) unwrought, crude; (*fig.*) rough, rude, coarse, gross, uncouth, vulgar; barbarous, brutal, cruel; (*fig.*) ***wie ein –es Ei behandeln,*** handle with kid gloves; ***mit –er Gewalt,*** with brute force.
Roh|bau, *m.* bare *or* rough brickwork. **–bilanz,** *f.* trial balance. **–block,** *m.* (*Metall.*) ingot. **–einnahme,** *f.* gross receipts. **–eisen,** *n.* pig-iron.
Roheit ['ro:haɪt], *f.* rawness, crudeness, raw *or* crude state; (*fig.*) rudeness, roughness, coarseness, crudity; brutality; piece of rudeness; brutal act.
Roh|ertrag, *m.* gross yield. **–erzeugnis,** *n.* raw product. **–faser,** *f.* crude fibre. **–formel,** *f.* empirical formula. **–frucht,** *f.* unprocessed *or* untreated produce. **–gewicht,** *n.* gross weight. **–gewinn,** *m.* gross profit. **–gummi,** *m.* crude rubber. **–guß,** *m.* (*Metall.*) pig. **–haut,** *f.* rawhide. **–kost,** *f.* uncooked (vegetarian) food. **–köstler,** *m.* vegetarian. **–leder,** *n.* untanned leather.
Rohling ['ro:lɪŋ], *m.* (**-s,** *pl.* **-e**) brute, coarse lout, ruffian; (*Metall.*) slug.
Roh|material, *n.* raw material. **–metall,** *n.* crude metal. **–öl,** *n.* crude oil.
Rohr [ro:r], *n.* (**-(e)s,** *pl.* **-e**) **1.** reed, cane; ***spanisches –,*** Spanish reed, cane; ***indisches –,*** bamboo; (*fig.*) ***schwank(end)es –,*** vacillating *or* unstable *or* erratic p., chameleon, weathercock; **2.** tube, pipe; tubing, piping; duct, flue, (gun-)barrel; ***geschweißtes –,*** welded tube; ***gezogenes –,*** rifled bore *or* barrel; (*Prov.*) ***wer im – sitzt, hat gut Pfeifen schneiden,*** it's all right for you to talk.
Rohr|ammer, *f.* (*Orn.*) reed-bunting (*Emberiza schoeniclus*). **–anschluß,** *m.* pipe-joint. **–bruch,** *m.* burst pipe. **–brunnen,** *m.* artesian well. **–dommel,** *f.* (*Orn.*) ***große –,*** bittern (*Botaurus stellaris*). **–drossel,** *f. See* **Drosselrohrsänger.**
Röhre ['rø:rə], *f.* pipe, tube; (wireless) valve, (*Am.*) tube; canal, duct, conduit; shaft, tunnel; small recess in a stove (*for baking or keeping things warm*). **röhren,** *v.i.* bell (*of stags*) **Röhren|apparat,** *m.* valve-set. **–bewässerung,** *f.* piped water supply. **–fassung,** *f.* valve holder. **röhrenförmig,** *adj.* fistular, tubular. **Röhren|gang,** *m.* conduit, piping. **–kennlinie,** *f.* (*Rad.*) valve characteristics. **–kessel,** *m.* cylindrical boiler. **–knochen,** *m.* hollow bone. **–leitung,** *f.* *See* **Rohrleitung.** **–pilz,** *m.* (*Bot.*) boletus. **–rauschen,** *n.* (*Rad.*) valve noise. **–sender,** *m.* valve-transmitter. **–sockel,** *m.* valve base. **–walzwerk,** *n.* tube-rolling mill. **–wasser,** *n.* piped *or* tap water. **–werk,** *n.* tubing, piping.
Rohrflöte ['ro:rflø:tə], *f.* reed-pipe. **rohrförmig,** *adj.* tubular. **Rohr|geflecht,** *n.* wickerwork, basket work. **–huhn,** *n. See* **Teichhuhn.**
Röhricht ['rø:rɪçt], *n.* (bank *or* bed of) reeds.
Rohr|kolben, *m.* (*Bot.*) reed-mace. **–krepierer,** *m.* (*Artil.*) barrel burst. **–leger,** *m.* pipe-fitter, plumber. **–leitung,** *f.* pipe-line, conduit; *see* **–netz;** (*pl.*) (*in the house*) pipes, piping, plumbing. **–matte,** *f.* rush-mat. **–mündung,** *f.* muzzle (*of a gun*). **–netz,** *n.* pipes, piping, (gas *or* water) mains. **–post,** *f.* pneumatic post (*in large stores etc.*). **–rahmen,** *m.* (*Motor.*) tubular chassis. **–rücklauf,** *m.* barrel recoil. **–schelle,** *f.* pipe-clip. **–schieber,** *m.* sleeve-valve. **–schilf,** *n.* reed. **–schlange,** *f.* coiled tube. **–schlitten,** *m.* (*Artil.*) barrel slide. **–schlosser,** *m.* pipe-fitter. **–schmied,** *m.* gun-barrel-maker. **–schwirl,** *m.* (*Orn.*) Savi's warbler (*Locustella luscinioides*). **–seele,** *f.* bore (*of a gun*). **–spatz,** *m.* (*coll.*) ***wie ein – schimpfen,*** scold like a fishwife. **–stiefel,** *m.* high *or* knee-boot. **–stock,** *m.* cane, bamboo. **–stuhl,** *m.* cane *or* wicker *or* basket-chair. **–walzwerk,** *n. See* **Röhrenwalzwerk.** **–weihe,** *m.* (*Orn.*) marsh-harrier (*Circus aeruginosus*). **–weite,** *f.* bore, calibre. **–werk,** *n.* **1.** *See* **Röhrenwerk**; **2.** (*Org.*) reed-stop. **–zange,** *f.* pipe wrench. **–zerspringer,** *m. See* **–krepierer.** **–zucker,** *m.* cane-sugar.
Roh|schwefel, *m.* native *or* rock sulphur. **–seide,** *f.* tussore silk. **–stoff,** *m.* raw-material, natural produce. **–zucker,** *m.* unrefined sugar. **–zustand,** *m.* raw *or* natural state.

Rokoko ['rɔkoko], *n.* (**-s,** *no pl.*) rococo.

Rolladen ['rɔlla:dən], *m.* roller-shutter.

Roll|bahn, *f.* (*Av.*) runway, landing-strip. **-bahre,** *f.* wheeled stretcher. **-binde,** *f.* roller bandage. **-dach,** *n.* (*Motor.*) sliding *or* sunshine roof.

Rolle ['rɔlə], *f.* 1. roll; cylinder, roller; caster, castor (*on furniture*), pulley, reel, spool; mangle, calender; coil (*of rope, wire*), bolt (*of cloth*), scroll (*of parchment*); 2. (*Theat.*) rôle, part; register, roll, list (of personnel), (*Mil.*) duty roster; ***aus der – fallen,*** act out of character, show one's true face, misbehave, (*coll.*) drop a brick; ***eine – spielen,*** act a part; (*fig.*) play a part, be of importance, be a factor, figure (***bei,*** in); (*fig.*) ***keine – spielen,*** be of no importance *or* consequence, (*of a th.*) make no difference, not matter at all; ***eine große – spielen,*** be of great importance, have considerable influence, (*of a th.*) figure large; ***eine jämmerliche – spielen,*** (*of a p.*) cut a poor figure.

rollen ['rɔlən], **1.** *v.i.* (*aux.* s. *&* h.) 1. roll, lurch; revolve, rotate, (*Av.*) taxi; 2. (*as thunder*) roll, rumble, roar. **2.** *v.t.* roll, wheel, trundle; mangle, calender (*cloth*); ***die Augen –,*** roll one's eyes; ***das R –,*** roll *or* trill one r's. **3.** *v.r.* roll up, curl (up). **Rollen,** *n.* rolling; (*fig.*) ***etwas ins – bringen,*** get s.th. started *or* under way, set the ball rolling; ***ins – kommen,*** get going, get under way.

Rollenbesetzung ['rɔlənbəzɛtsuŋ], *f.* (*Theat.*) cast.

rollend ['rɔlənt], *adj.* rolling; (*Mil.*) ***-er Angriff,*** attack in waves; (*fig.*) ***in -em Einsatz,*** in waves; (*Railw.*) ***-es Material,*** rolling stock.

rollen|förmig, *adj.* cylindrical; coiled, convoluted. **-gelagert,** *adj.* (*Mech.*) mounted on roller bearings. **Rollen|lager,** *n.* (*Mech.*) roller bearing. **-verteilung,** *f.* (*Theat.*) allocation of parts. **-zug,** *m.* block and tackle.

Roller ['rɔlər], *m.* 1. (*Naut.*) rolling sea; 2. (*Spt., coll.*) daisy-cutter, grub-hunter; 3. scooter; 4. canary. **rollern,** *v.t.* play with *or* ride on a scooter; ride *or* drive a motor-scooter.

Roll|feld, *n. See* **-bahn. -film,** *m.* roll-film. **-fuhrmann,** *m.* carter, carrier, vanman. **-fuhrunternehmen,** *n.* carrier's business, transport firm. **-fuhrwerk,** *n. See* **-wagen. -geld,** *n.* cartage, delivery charge; charge for mangling. **-geschäft,** *n. See* **-fuhrunternehmen. -handtuch,** *n.* roller-towel. **-holz,** *n.* rolling-pin. **-jalousie,** *f.* roller blind. **-kommando,** *n.* raiding party; organized hecklers (*to break up meetings*). **-kragen,** *m.* roll-neck collar. **-kutscher,** *m. See* **-fuhrmann. -mops,** *m.* pickled *or* soused herring. **-muskel,** *m. or f.* trochlear *or* rotator muscle. **-schinken,** *m.* rolled ham. **-schuh,** *m.* roller-skate. **-schuhlaufen,** *n.* roller-skating. **-sitz,** *m.* sliding seat. **-stein,** *m.* boulder. **-straße,** *f. See* **-bahn. -stuhl,** *m.* bath chair, invalid chair, wheel-chair. **-treppe,** *f.* escalator, moving staircase. **-tür,** *f.* sliding door. **-verband,** *m. See* **-binde. -verschluß,** *m.* sliding lid; ***Schreibtisch mit –,*** roll-top desk. **-wagen,** lorry, truck, trolley, dray. **-wäsche,** *f.* clothes for mangling.

Rom [ro:m], *n.* Rome.

Roman [ro'ma:n], *m.* (**-s,** *pl.* **-e**) novel, work of fiction, romance.

Romanen [ro'ma:nən], *pl.* Romance nations, Latin races.

romanhaft [ro'ma:nhaft], *adj.* fictitious, fanciful, fantastic.

romanisch [ro'ma:nɪʃ], *adv.* Romance, neo-Latin. **Romanist** [–'nɪst], *m.* (**-en,** *pl.* **-en**) teacher *or* student of Romance languages.

Romanschriftsteller [ro'ma:nʃrɪftʃtɛlər], *m.* novelist, fiction writer.

Romantik [ro'mantɪk], *f.* Romantic poetry; Romantic period, Romanticism. **Romantiker,** *m.* Romantic author *or* poet, Romanticist; *pl.* the Romantics, Romanticists. **romantisch,** *adj.* romantic. **Romanze,** *f.* poetic romance; ballad.

[1]**Römer** ['rø:mər], *m.* large drinking-glass, rummer.

[2]**Römer,** *m.*, **Römerin,** *f.* Roman. **römisch** *adj.* Roman. **römisch-katholisch,** *adj.* Roman Catholic.

Rommé [rɔ'me:], *n.* (*Cards*) rummy.

Ronde ['rɔndə, 'rɔ̃də], *f.* round, patrol; (*Mech.*) circular shape. **Rondell** [rɔn'dɛl], *n.* (**-s,** *pl.* **-e**) circular flower-bed *or* plot; round tower, bastion.

röntgen ['rœntgən], *v.t.* X-ray. **Röntgen|anlage,** *f.* X-ray apparatus. **-assistent,** *m.* radiographer. **-aufnahme,** *f.* X-ray photograph. **-behandlung, -bestrahlung,** *f.* X-ray treatment, radiotherapy. **-bild,** *n. See* **-aufnahme. -durchleuchtung,** *f.* X-ray examination. **röntgenisieren** [–ni'zi:rən], *v.t.* (*Austr.*) X-ray. **Röntgenstrahlen,** *m.pl.* X-rays.

rören, *v.i. See* **röhren.**

rosa ['ro:za], *indecl.adj.* rose-coloured, pink; (*fig.*) ***durch eine – Brille,*** through rose-tinted spectacles. **Rosapelikan,** *m.* (*Orn.*) white pelican (*Pelecanus onocrotalus*).

Rose ['ro:zə], *f.* rose; (*Med.*) erysipelas; rose-window; compass-rose; rosette; ***wilde –,*** sweet-brier, dog-rose; (*Prov.*) ***keine – ohne Dornen,*** no rose without a thorn; ***auf -n gebettet,*** on a bed of roses.

rosenartig ['ro:zənˀartɪç], *adj.* rosaceous; like a rose. **Rosen|busch,** *m.* rose-bush, rose-tree. **-essenz,** *f. See* **-öl. rosen|farben, -farbig,** *adj.* rose-coloured. **Rosen|gimpel,** *m.* (*Orn.*) rose-finch (*Erynthrina rosea*). **-holz,** *n.* rosewood. **-kohl,** *m.* Brussels sprouts. **-kranz,** *m.* 1. garland of roses; 2. (*Eccl.*) rosary; ***seinen – beten,*** tell one's beads. **-kreuzer,** *m.* Rosicrucian. **-montag,** *m.* Monday before Lent. **-möwe,** *f.* (*Orn.*) Ross's gull (*Rhodostethia rosea*). **-öl,** *n.* attar of roses. **-seeschwalbe,** *f.* (*Orn.*) roseate tern (*Sterna dougallii*). **-stock,** *m.* standard rose-tree; ***wilder –,*** eglantine. **-zeit,** *f.* (*fig.*) blossom time, youth. **-zucht,** *f.* cultivation of roses.

Rosette [ro'zɛtə], *f.* rosette; centre-piece (*of a ceiling*); rose-diamond.

rosig ['ro:zɪç], *adj.* rosy, rose-coloured, roseate; ***in der -sten Laune,*** in the sweetest of tempers; ***die Dinge im -sten Lichte sehen,*** look on the bright side of things, see things through rose-tinted spectacles.

Rosine [ro'zi:nə], *f.* raisin, sultana; (*coll.*) (***große***) ***-n im Kopfe haben,*** plan great things, have big ideas, be full of o.s.

Röslein ['rø:slaɪn], *n.* rosebud, little rose.

Rosmarin [rɔsma'ri:n], *m.* rosemary.

Roß [rɔs], *n.* (**-(ss)es,** *pl.* **-(ss)e**) (*Poet.*) steed, charger; (*pl.* **¨-(ss)er**) (*dial.*) horse; (*coll.*) blockhead; ***sich aufs hohe – setzen,*** get on one's high horse. **Roß|apfel,** *m.* horse-manure. **-arzt,** *m.* veterinary surgeon.

Rossebändiger ['rɔsəbɛndɪgər], *m.* horse-breaker.

Rösselsprung ['rœsəlʃpruŋ], *m.* (*Chess*) knight's move.

rossen ['rɔsən], *v.i.* desire the stallion (*of mares*).

Roß|haar, *n.* horsehair. **-händler,** *m.* horse-dealer.

rossig [rɔsɪç], *adj.* desiring the stallion (*of mares*).

Roß|kamm, *m.* curry-comb. **-kastanie,** *f.* horse-chestnut. **-kur,** *f.* (*fig.*) drastic treatment. **-markt,** *m.* horse-fair. **-schweif,** *m.* horse's tail.

[1]**Rost** [rɔst], *m.* (**-es,** *pl.* **-e**) (fire) grate; gridiron, grill; grating, duckboard; ***auf dem – braten,*** grill.

[2]**Rost,** *m.* rust (*on metal*), (*Bot.*) blight, smut, mildew; ***– ansetzen,*** rust, get rusty, (*fig.*) get rusty.

rostbeständig ['rɔstbəʃtɛndɪç], *adj.* rust-proof, non-corroding. **Rost|bildung,** *f.* corrosion. **-braten,** *m.* (roast) joint. **rostbraun,** *adj.* rusty brown, russet.

Röstbrot ['rø:stbro:t], *n.* toast. **Röste,** *f.* steeping, retting (*flax*); flax-hole, rettery.

rosten ['rɔstən], *v.i.* (*aux.* s. *&* h.) rust, get rusty, (*Chem.*) oxidize. **Rosten,** *n.* rusting.

rösten ['rø:stən], *v.t.* grill (*meat*), roast (*coffee*), toast (*bread*), fry (*potatoes*); steep, ret (*flax*); (*Metall.*) roast, torrefy, calcine.

rost|farben, -farbig, *adj. See* **-braun. Rostfleck,** *m.* rust stain, (*on linen*) iron-mould. **rostfleckig,**

adj. rust-stained, (*linen*) stained with iron-mould. **Rost|flügeldrossel,** *f.* (*Orn.*) dusky thrush (*Turdus naumanni eunomus*). **–fraß,** *m. See* **–bildung. rostfrei,** *adj.* rust-proof, stainless (*steel*). **Rostgans,** *f.* (*Orn.*) ruddy sheld-duck (*Casarca ferruginea*). **rostig,** *adj.* rusty, rusted, corroded.

Röst|kartoffeln, *f.pl.* fried potatoes. **–ofen,** *m.* (*Metall.*) roasting *or* calcining furnace, kiln. **–pfanne,** *f.* frying-pan.

Rost|schutz, *m.* rust-proofing. **–schutzfarbe,** *f.* anti-rust paint, rust-preventive.

rot [ro:t], *adj.* red; (*complexion*) ruddy; rubicund; (*fig.*) – ***anstreichen,*** make a special note of; ***die –e Armee,*** the Red Army; ***die –e Erde,*** Westphalia; (*fig.*) ***–er Faden,*** unbroken thread; ***den –en Hahn aufs Dach setzen,*** set fire to s.o.'s house; ***–es Haar*** or ***–e Haare,*** red hair; ***er hat keinen –en Heller,*** he hasn't a bean *or* a brass farthing; ***–es Kreuz,*** Red Cross; ***–e Ruhr,*** dysentry; (*Prov.*) ***heute –, morgen tot,*** here today, gone tomorrow; (*fig.*) ***–es Warnlicht,*** the red light; – ***werden,*** go *or* turn red, blush, colour up. **Rot,** *n.* red (colour), redness; rouge; (*Cards*) red suit.

Rotation [rotatsi'o:n], *f.* rotation. **Rotations|achse,** *f.* axis of rotation. **–bewegung,** *f.* rotary motion. **–maschine,** *f.* rotary press. **–pumpe,** *f.* rotary pump.

Rotauge ['ro:tʔaugə], *n.* (*Ichth.*) roach (*Leuciscus*). **rot|äugig,** *adj.* red-eyed. **–backig, –bäckig,** *adj.* rosy-cheeked, ruddy. **–blond,** *adj.* auburn, sandy. **–braun,** *adj.* reddish-brown, russet, (*of horse*) sorrel, bay. **Rotbruch,** *m.* (*Metall.*) red-shortness. **rotbrüchig,** *adj.* (*Metall.*) red-short. **Rot|buche,** *f.* (common) beech. **–dorn,** *m.* pink hawthorn. **–drossel,** *f.* (*Orn.*) redwing (*Turdus musicus*).

Röte ['rø:tə], *f.* red (colour), redness; (*of face*) flush (*through heat*), blush (*embarrassment*); ***die – stieg ihr ins Gesicht,*** the colour rushed to her face, she coloured up.

Rote-Kreuz– ['ro:tə'krɔyts], *pref.* (*pl.* **Rote(n)-**. . .) Red-Cross.

Rötel ['rø:təl], *m.* 1. red ochre, ruddle; 2. *See* **Rötelstift. Rötel|ammer,** *f.* (*Orn.*) rufous bunting (*Emberiza rutila*). **–falke,** *m.* (*Orn.*) lesser kestrel (*Falco naumanni*).

Röteli ['rø:təli:], *n.* (-, *pl.* -) (*dial.*) robin.

Röteln ['rø:təln], *pl.* German measles, rubella.

röteln, *v.t.* mark with red pencil.

Rötel|schwalbe, *f.* (*Orn.*) red-rumped swallow (*Hirundo daurica*). **–stift,** *m.* red pencil *or* chalk *or* crayon.

röten ['rø:tən], **1.** *v.t.* redden, colour *or* dye red. **2.** *v.r.* turn *or* go red, redden; get flushed, flush.

Rote(r) ['ro:tə(r)], *m., f.* (*Pol.*) Red, communist, bolshevik.

Rot|fuchs, *m.* bay *or* sorrel horse, chestnut. **–fußfalke,** *m.* (*Orn.*) red-footed falcon (*Falco vespertinus*). **rotgelb,** *adj.* orange (coloured). **Rot|gerber,** *m.* tanner. **–gießer,** *m.* copper-founder, brazier. **rot|glühen,** *v.t.* heat to redness. **–glühend,** *adj.* red-hot. **Rot|glühhitze, –glut,** *f.* red-heat. **–guß,** *m.* red brass, bronze. **rothaarig,** *adj.* red-haired, red-headed, (*coll.*) sandy. **Rot|halsgans,** *f.* (*Orn.*) red-breasted goose (*Branta ruficollis*). **–halstaucher,** *m.* (*Orn.*) red-necked grebe (*Podiceps griseigena*). **–halsziegenmelker,** *m.* (*Orn.*) red-necked nightjar (*Caprimulgus ruficollis*). **–haut,** *f.* redskin. **–hirsch,** *m.* red deer. **–holz,** *n.* (*Bot.*) Sappan wood (*Caesalpinia sappa*); Brazil wood (*Caesalpinia echinata*); Wellingtonia, Mammoth tree (*Sequoia*); camwood, redwood. **–huhn,** *n.* (*Orn.*) red-legged partridge (*Alectoris rufa*).

rotieren [ro'ti:rən], *v.i.* revolve, rotate.

Rot|kabis, *m.* (*Swiss*) red cabbage. **–käppchen,** *n.* Red Riding Hood. **–kehlchen,** *n.* (*Orn.*) robin (*Erithacus rubecula*). **–kehlpieper,** *m.* (*Orn.*) red-throated pipit (*Anthus cervinus*). **–kehltaucher,** *m.* (*Orn.*) *see* **Sterntaucher. –kohl,** *m.* red cabbage. **–kopfwürger,** *m.* (*Orn.*) woodchat-shrike (*Lanius senator*). **–lauf,** *m.* erysipelas; (*Vet.*) red murrain.

rötlich ['rø:tlɪç], *adj,* reddish, ruddy; (*Pol. coll.*) pink.

Rot|liegende(s), *n.* (*Geol.*) lower new red sandstone. **–rauschgelb,** *n.* realgar. **–salz,** *n.* sodium acetate. **–schenkel,** *m.* (*Orn.*) redshank (*Tringa totanus*); ***großer –,*** spotted redshank (*Tringa erythropus*). **–schimmel,** *m.* roan. **–specht,** *m.* (*Orn.*) *see* **Buntspecht. –spon,** *m.* (*dial.*) claret. **–spießglanz,** *m.* kermesite. **–stift,** *m.* red pencil. **–tanne,** *f.* (*Bot.*) spruce-fir (*Picea excelsa*).

Rotte ['rɔtə], *f.* (*Mil.*) file, squad, two aircraft, two ships (*operating together*); gang (*of workers*), pack (*of hounds*), (*coll.*) band, gang, mob, horde, rabble; (*Mil.*) ***blinde –,*** blank file. **rotten,** *v.r.* flock *or* band together; troop, (*coll.*) gang up. **Rotten|aufmarsch,** *m.* deployment in file. **–feuer,** *n.* volley. **–führer,** *m.* file-leader, (*Nat. Soc.*) corporal; (*of workmen*) ganger, foreman. **rottenweise,** *adv.* in gangs *or* (*Mil.*) files.

Rottgans ['rɔtgans], *f.* (*Orn.*) *see* **Ringelgans.**

Rötung ['rø:tuŋ], *f.* reddening.

Rotverschiebung ['ro:tfɛrʃi:buŋ], *f.* red shift.

rot|wangig, *adj. See* **–backig. Rot|wein,** *m.* red wine, claret. **–welsch,** *n.* thieves' slang. **–wild,** *n.* red deer.

Rotz [rɔts], *m.* nasal mucus, (*vulg.*) snot; (*Vet.*) glanders. **rotzen,** *v.i.* have a running nose, (*vulg.*) blow one's nose. **rotzig,** *adj.* (*vulg.*) snotty-nosed, (*fig.*) snotty; (*Vet.*) glandered. **Rotz|junge, –löffel,** *m.* cheeky young brat. **–nase,** *f.* (*vulg.*) snotty nose; (*fig.*) brat.

Roulade [ru'la:də], *f.* rolled meat; (*Mus.*) trill.

Rouleau [ru'lo:], *n.* (**-s,** *pl.* **-s**) roller-blind.

routinemäßig [ru'ti:nəmɛ:sɪç], *adj.* routine. **routiniert** [–'ni:rt], *adj.* experienced, versed; well trained.

Rübe ['ry:bə], *f.* rape; ***weiße –,*** turnip; ***gelbe –,*** carrot; ***rote –,*** beetroot; (*coll.*) pate, nob; ***durcheinander wie Kraut und –n,*** higgledy-piggledy.

Rubel ['ru:bəl], *m.* rouble.

Rüben|kraut, *n.* turnip tops. **–zucker,** *m.* beet-sugar.

rüber, *adv.* (*coll.*) *see* **herüber.**

Rubin [ru'bi:n], *m.* (**-s,** *pl.* **-e**) ruby. **Rubin|fluß,** *m.,* **–glas,** *n.* ruby-glass. **rubinrot,** *adj.* ruby(-red).

Rüb|kohl, *m.* (*Swiss*) kohlrabi. **–öl,** *n.* rape-oil.

Rubrik [ru'bri:k], *f.* (-, *pl.* **-en**) heading; column, rubric; (*fig.*) class, category. **rubrizieren** [–'tsi:rən], *v.t.* supply headings to; arrange in columns.

Rüb|saat, *f.,* **–samen,** *m.* rape-seed (*Brassica rapus*).

ruchbar ['ru:xba:r], *adj.* notorious; known, public; – ***machen,*** noise abroad; – ***werden,*** become known, get about. **Ruchbarkeit,** *f.* notoriety. **ruchlos,** *adj.* wicked, nefarious, infamous, impious, profligate. **Ruchlosigkeit,** *f.* wickedness, profligacy, infamy.

Ruck [ruk], *m.* (**-(e)s,** *pl.* **-e**) jolt, jerk, tug, sudden push *or* movement, start, shock; ***sich einen – geben,*** pull o.s. together; ***mit*** or ***in einem –, auf einen –,*** all at once, at one go. **ruckartig, 1.** *adj.* jerky. **2.** *adv.* abruptly, without warning *or* notice.

Rück– [ryk], *pref.* (*with nouns*) (*for corresponding verbs see* **zurück–**). **rück–,** *pref.* (*with verbs*) *Poet. only, see* **zurück–.**

Rück|ansicht, *f.* rear view. **–antwort,** *f.* reply; ***Postkarte mit –,*** reply postcard; ***Telegramm mit –,*** reply-paid telegram. **–beförderung,** *f.* (*Mil.*) evacuation to the rear. **–berufung,** *f.* recall. **–bewegung,** *f.* (*Mech.*) return stoke. **rückbezüglich,** *adj.* (*Gram.*) reflexive. **Rück|bildung,** *f.* (*Gram.*) back-formation; (*Math.*) involution; (*Biol.*) retrogressive metamorphosis, (*coll.*) reversion to type. **–blendung,** *f.* (*Films*) flash-back. **–blick,** *m.* backward glance, glance back (***auf*** (*Acc.*), at), (*fig.*) retrospective view, (view in) retrospect; survey, review. **–blickspiegel,** *m.* (*Motor.*) driving mirror. **–bürge,** *m.,* **–bürgschaft,** *f.* collateral security. **rückdatieren,** *v.t.* antedate.

rücken, 1. *v.t.* move, shift, pull, push, change the

place of. **2.** *v.i.* (*aux.* s. & h.) move, proceed; (*Mil.*) ***ins Feld –***, take the field, go into action; ***näher –***, draw near, approach; ***nicht von der Stelle –***, not budge an inch; ***ihm zu Leibe –***, press him hard.

Rücken ['rykən], *m.* back, (*Mil.*) rear; ridge (*of hills*), bridge (*of nose*), back, spine (*of book*), chine (*of beef*), saddle (*of mutton*); ***– an –***, back to back, (*Her.*) addorsed; ***ihm den – decken***, cover *or* protect his rear; ***ihm den – kehren***, turn one's back on him; ***ihm in den – fallen***, attack him from *or* in the rear, (*fig.*) stab him in the back; ***sich*** (*Dat.*) ***den – freihalten***, cover one's rear, secure one's line of retreat; (*fig.*) not commit o.s. absolutely, (*coll.*) play it safe; ***den – beugen***, bend down, stoop; (*fig.*) cringe; (*fig.*) ***einen krummen – machen***, cringe; ***es läuft mir kalt über den –***, a shiver runs down my spine.

Rücken|angriff, *m.* attack from *or* in the rear. **–band,** *n.* (*Anat.*) dorsal ligament. **–blatt,** *n.* (*Archit.*) reredos. **–deckung,** *f.* (*Mil.*) parados, rear cover; (*fig.*) covering, backing, support. **–feuer,** *n.* (*Mil.*) (enemy) fire from the rear. **–flosse,** *f.* dorsal fin. **–flug,** *m.* (*Av.*) inverted flight *or* flying. **rückenfrei,** *adj.* backless (*dress*). **Rücken|kraul,** *m.* (*swimming*) back crawl. **–lage,** *f.* supine position. **–lehne,** *f.* back(-rest) (*of chair etc.*). **–mark,** *n.* (*Anat.*) spinal cord. **–muskel,** *m.* dorsal muscle. **–schild,** *m.* (*Zool.*) carapace. **–schmerzen,** *m.pl.* backache. **–schwimmen,** *n.* backstroke, swimming on the back. **rückenständig,** *adj.* dorsal. **Rücken|stück,** *n.* saddle (*of mutton*), chine (*of beef*). **–titel,** *m.* (*Bookb.*) spine lettering. **–wende,** *f.* (*swimming*) backstroke turn. **–wind,** *m.* following *or* tail wind. **–wirbel,** *m.* (*Anat.*) dorsal vertebra.

Rück|erinnerung, *f.* reminiscence.**–erstattung,** *f.* restitution, (*of money*) reimbursement, refund. **–fahrkarte,** *f.*, **–fahrschein,** *m.* return-ticket. **–fahrt,** *f.* return journey. **–fall,** *m.* (*Law*) reversion; (*Med.*) relapse; (*of a culprit*) recidivism, (*coll.*) backsliding; ***Einbruch im zweiten –***, second conviction for housebreaking. **rückfällig,** *adj.* (*Law*) revertible; (*Med.*) ***– werden,*** have a relapse. **Rück|fällige(r),** *m., f.* recidivist, (*coll.*) backslider. **–fenster,** *n.* (*Motor.*) rear window. **–flug,** *m.* return flight. **–forderung,** *f.* reclamation; counter-demand. **–frage,** *f.* query, further inquiry, check-back. **–führung,** *f.* (*Mech.*) restoring mechanism, follow-up device; ***– in die Heimat***, repatriation. **–gabe,** *f.* return, restoration, restitution. **–gang,** *m.* decrease, falling-off, (*Comm.*) decline, recession, downward movement; relapse, retrogression. **rückgängig,** *adj.* retrograde, retrogressive; declining, downward; ***– machen***, render null and void, rescind, cancel, annul, revoke, (*coll.*) break off, put an end to, undo. **Rück|gewinnung,** *f.* recovery, salvage.

Rückgrat ['rykɡra:t], *n.* **(-(e)s,** *pl.* **-e)** backbone, spine, spinal *or* vertebral column. **rückgratlos,** *adj.* (*fig.*) spineless. **Rückgrats(ver)krümmung,** *f.* curvature of the spine.

Rück|griff, *m.* recourse (***gegen,*** against), resort (***auf*** (*Acc.*), to). **–griffsanspruch,** *m.* claim for indemnification. **–griffsrecht,** *n.* right of recourse. **–halt,** *m.* prop, stay, backing, support; (*Mil.*) reserve (force); (*obs.*) restraint, reserve. **rückhaltlos,** *adj.* unreserved, without reserve *or* restraint; point-blank, plain, open, frank. **Rück|hand(schlag),** *f.* (*m.*) (*Tenn.*) backhand stroke. **–kauf,** *m.* repurchase; redemption. **rückkäuflich,** *adj.* redeemable. **Rück|kaufswert,** *m.* redemption *or* surrender value; resale price. **–kehr,** *f.* return. **–kopp(e)lung,** *f.* (*Rad.*) reaction (coupling), regeneration, feed-back. **–kunft,** *f.* *See* **–kehr.** **–lage,** *f.* reserve (fund). **–lauf,** *m.* (*Mech.*) return stroke, (*oscillograph*) flyback, (*gun*) recoil. **–laufbremse,** *f.* (*Artil.*) recoil buffer. **rückläufig,** *adj.* retrograde, retrogressive; (*Surg.*) ***–er Verband***, figure of eight bandage; ***–e Sendung***, (postal package) to be returned to sender. **Rück|leitung,** *f.* (*Elec.*) return (line). **–licht,** *n.* (*Motor.*) rear *or* tail light. **rücklings,** *adv.* from behind; backwards. **Rück|marsch,** *m.* march back, retreat. **–nahme,** *f.* re-acceptance; withdrawal. **–porto,** *n.* return-postage. **–prall,** *m.* repercussion, rebound; recoil; reaction. **–prämie,** *f.* seller's option. **–reise,** *f.* return journey, journey home. **–ruf,** *m.* recall.

Rucksack ['rukzak], *m.* rucksack, knapsack.

Rück|schau, *f.* *See* **–blick.** **–schlag,** *m.* recoil, kick (*of a gun*); rebound; (*Motor.*) back-fire; (*fig.*) check, set-back, reverse; reaction, (*Biol.*) atavism, reversion to type. **–schlagventil,** *n.* non-return valve. **–schluß,** *m.* conclusion, inference. **–schreiben,** *n.* (letter in) reply, answer. **–schritt,** *m.* retrogression, recession; (*Pol.*) reaction; (*Mil.*) pace back; (*fig.*) set-back, relapse, falling off. **rückschrittlich,** *adj.* reactionary. **Rückseite,** *f.* back; reverse, wrong side.

rucksen ['ruksən], *v.i.* coo (*of pigeons*).

Rücksendung ['rykzɛnduŋ], *f.* return (*of goods*).

Rücksicht, *f.* respect, regard, consideration; notice; discretion; ***aus – gegen***, in deference to, out of regard for; ***aus*** or ***mit – auf*** (*Acc.*), with regard to, in consideration of, considering; ***ohne – auf***, irrespective *or* regardless of, notwithstanding, without regard for; ***– nehmen auf*** (*Acc.*), take into consideration, make allowance(s) for, allow for; have regard for *or* to, have *or* show consideration for. **rücksichtlich,** *prep.* (*Gen.*) with regard to, considering. **Rücksichtnahme,** *f.* respect, consideration (***auf*** (*Acc.*), for); ***– im Verkehr***, road courtesy. **rücksichtslos, 1.** *adj.* without consideration (***gegen***, for), regardless (of); inconsiderate (of), thoughtless, reckless, high-handed; unfeeling, callous, ruthless, relentless; ***–es Fahren***, reckless driving. **2.** *adv.* thoughtlessly, recklessly *etc.*; relentlessly, at all costs, (*coll.*) (*after verb*) regardless; ***– einschreiten***, resort to drastic measures, act without counting the cost. **Rücksichtslosigkeit,** *f.* lack of consideration, inconsiderateness, thoughtlessness, recklessness; relentlessness, ruthlessness. **rücksichtsvoll,** *adj.* considerate, regardful (***gegen***, of); thoughtful.

Rück|sitz, *m.* back seat, (*coll.*) dickey, (*Motor-cycle*) pillion. **–spiegel,** *m.* driving mirror. **–spiel,** *n.* return-match. **–sprache,** *f.* discussion, consultation; ***– nehmen***, consult, confer (***wegen, über*** (*Acc.*), about), discuss, talk over.

Rückstand ['rykʃtant], *m.* arrears, outstanding debt; residue, sediment, remains; remainder; ***im – sein***, be behindhand *or* in arrears (*with s.th.*). **rückständig,** *adj.* outstanding, overdue, in arrears; residual; (*fig.*) under-developed, backward; behindhand, behind the times, antiquated, old-fashioned. **Rückständigkeit,** *f.* backwardness.

Rück|stelltaste, *f.* back-spacer (*typewriter*). **–stoß,** *m.* recoil, backstroke; repulsion. **–stoßantrieb,** *m.* (*Av.*) jet-propulsion. **–stoßdämpfer,** *m.* (*Artil.*) muzzle brake. **–stoßmotor,** *m.* (*Av.*) jet engine. **–strahler,** *m.* (*Cycl.*) reflector; (*on roads*) cat's eye. **–taste,** *f.* *See* **–stelltaste.** **–tritt,** *m.* retirement, withdrawal, retreat, retrogression; resignation (*from a post*); (*Mil.*) ***– in den Stand der Mannschaften***, reduction to the ranks. **–trittbremse,** *f.* (*Cycl.*) back-pedalling brake. **–trittsgesuch,** *n.* submission of one's resignation. **–übersetzung,** *f.* re-translation. **–vergütung,** *f.* refund, repayment, reimbursement. **–versicherung,** *f.* reinsurance. **–wand,** *f.* back (wall). **–wanderer,** *m.* returning emigrant.

rückwärtig ['rykvɛrtɪç], *adj.* rear(ward), (*Mil.*) behind the lines. **rückwärts,** *adv.* backward(s), back; (*Motor.*) ***– fahren***, reverse, (*coll.*) back (up). **Rückwärts|bewegung,** *f.* backward movement, retrogression, retrograde motion. **–gang,** *m.* reverse gear. **rückwärtsgehen,** *irr.v.i.* (*aux.* s.) (*fig.*) decline, deteriorate, (*coll.*) fall off, go down.

Rückweg ['rykve:k], *m.* return route, way back.

ruckweise ['rukvaɪzə], *adv.* by *or* in fits and starts, in jerks.

Rückwiderstand ['rykvi:dərʃtant], *m.* (*Rad.*) reactance. **rückwirkend,** *adj.* retroactive, retrospective; ***–es Gesetz***, ex post facto law. **Rück|-**

wirkung, *f.* 1. (*Rad.*) reaction, feedback; 2. (*Law*) retrospectiveness, retroaction; 3. repercussion. **–zahlung,** *f.* repayment, redemption, amortization. **–zieher,** *m.* (*Anat.*) retractor muscle; (*coll.*) ***einen – machen,*** climb down. **rückzielend,** *adj.* (*Gram.*) reflexive. **Rück|zollgüter,** *n.pl.* debenture goods. **–zollschein,** *m.* certificate of drawback. **–zug,** *m.* (*Mil.*) retreat, withdrawal; (*fig.*) climb-down. **–zündung,** *f.* backfire.

Rüde ['ry:də], *m.* (**-n,** *pl.* **-n**) large hound; male dog *or* fox *or* wolf.

rüde, *adj.* rude, coarse, vulgar, brutal.

Rudel ['ru:dəl], *n.* flock, herd, (*also of submarines*) pack.

Ruder ['ru:dər], *n.* rudder, helm; (*coll.*) oar; (*fig.*) ***am – sein,*** be at the helm; (*fig.*) ***ans – kommen,*** come into power; ***sich ins – legen,*** row hard; (*fig.*) put one's back into it. **Ruder|bank,** *f.* thwart. **–blatt,** *n.* oar-blade. **–boot,** *n.* rowing boat. **–dolle,** *f.* rowlock, thole-pin. **–ente,** *f.* (*Orn.*) white-headed duck (*Oxyura leucocephala*). **Ruderer,** *m.* rower, oarsman. **Ruder|fuß,** *m.* (*Orn.*) webbed foot. **–gänger,** *m.* helmsman, steersman. **–klub,** *m. See* **–verein. –kommando,** *n.* steering order. **ruderlos,** *adj.* ***–es Schiff,*** disabled ship. **rudern, 1.** *v.t., v.i.* row, paddle; ***lang –,*** pull a long stroke; ***rückwärts –,*** back water. **2.** *v.i.* (*aux.* s.) go for a row. **Ruder|pinne,** *f.* tiller. **–schlag,** *m.* stroke of the oar. **–schwanz,** *m.* (*Ichth.*) caudal fin. **–sport,** *m.* rowing. **–verein,** *m.* rowing club.

rudimentär [rudimɛn'tɛ:r], *adj.* rudimentary. **Rudimentärorgan,** *n.* vestigial organ.

Ruf [ru:f], *m.* (**-(e)s,** *pl.* **-e**) 1. call, shout, cry, summons; ***der Professor hat einen – nach Berlin erhalten,*** the professor has been offered a chair at Berlin; 2. repute, reputation, name, fame, renown, (*Comm.*) credit, standing; ***ihn in üblen – bringen,*** give him a bad name; ***dem –e nach,*** by repute; ***im –e stehen,*** be reputed (*to be*), have a reputation (*for being*); ***in gutem –e stehen,*** have a good name, stand in high repute (***bei,*** with).

rufen ['ru:fən], **1.** *irr.v.t.* call, summon, (*coll.*) call in (*doctor etc.*); call to, hail; ***ins Gedächtnis –,*** call to mind; ***ins Gewehr –,*** call to arms; ***ins Leben –,*** call into being; ***ihn wieder ins Leben –,*** recall him to life; (*coll.*) ***wie gerufen kommen,*** come in the nick of time; come in handy. **2.** *irr.v.i.* call (out), cry out, shout, exclaim; ***ihn – lassen,*** send for him, have him fetched; ***er rief (nach) mir,*** he called for *or* to me; ***um Hilfe –,*** call *or* cry for help.

Rüffel ['ryfəl], *m.* (*coll.*) reprimand, wigging, telling-off, dressing-down. **rüffeln,** *v.t.* (*coll.*) reprimand, upbraid, take to task.

Ruf|name, *m.* Christian name. **–nummer,** *f.* telephone number. **–strom,** *m.* (*Tele.*) ringing current. **–weite,** *f.* ***in –,*** within call *or* earshot. **–zeichen,** *n.* call-signal, call-sign.

Rüge ['ry:gə], *f.* censure, reproach, blame, admonition, reproof, (*Spt.*) caution. **rügen,** *v.t.* censure, reprove, reprimand, blame (***wegen,*** for), find fault with, (*Spt.*) warn, caution.

Ruhe ['ru:ə], *f.* rest, repose, sleep; stillness, peace, quiet, silence, calm, tranquillity; (*fig.*) calm, composure, equanimity, imperturbability, coolness; ***er ist nicht aus seiner – zu bringen,*** nothing disturbs his equanimity; ***keine – haben vor*** (*Dat.*), have no peace with; ***– halten,*** keep quiet *or* silent; ***laß mich in –!*** don't bother me! let *or* leave me alone! ***in aller –,*** very calmly; ***ihm keine – gönnen,*** give him no rest; ***ihm keine – lassen,*** haunt him, prey on his mind; ***Störung der öffentlichen – und Ordnung,*** disturbance of the peace; ***– vor dem Sturm,*** lull before the storm; ***ihm eine angenehme – wünschen,*** wish him a good night; ***zur – bringen,*** silence, quiet, hush, calm; ***sich zur – begeben,*** retire to rest, go to bed; ***zur – (ein)gehen,*** go to one's *or* be laid to rest; ***nicht zur – kommen,*** not get any peace *or* rest; ***sich zur – setzen,*** retire (*from office*).

ruhebedürftig ['ru:əbədyrftɪç], *adj.* in need of rest. **Ruhe|bett,** *n.* sofa, couch. **–gehalt,** *n.* (retirement) pension. **–haltung,** *f.* position at rest, normal position. **–lage,** *f. See* **–stellung. –lager,** *n.* rest-camp. **ruhelos,** *adj.* restless, (*coll.*) fidgety. **Ruhelosigkeit,** *f.* restlessness.

ruhen ['ru:ən], *v.i.* rest, repose, (*fig.*) sleep, be dormant, (*Law*) be suspended, be in abeyance; come to *or* be at a standstill; be idle, lie fallow; ***– auf*** (*Dat.*), be supported by, rest on; (*fig.*) rest on (*as a glance*), be founded *or* based on; ***hier ruht,*** here lies; ***hier ruht sich's gut,*** here is a good place to rest *or* good resting-place; ***– lassen,*** leave, (let) drop (*discussion etc.*), suspend, leave unfinished (*project*); ***ich wünsche wohl zu –,*** I wish you a good night's rest. **ruhend,** *adj.* static, stationary, latent; ***–es Kapital,*** unused *or* uninvested capital.

Ruhe|pause, *f.* pause, lull; interval *or* break for rest, (*coll.*) breather. **–platz,** *m.* resting-place. **–posten,** *m.* sinecure. **–punkt,** *m.* resting-point, point of rest; (*Mus.*) rest, (*Metr.*) caesura; (*Phys.*) fulcrum, centre of gravity. **–quartier,** *n.* (*Mil.*) rest billets. **–sessel,** *m.* easy-chair. **–spannung,** *f.* (*Elec.*) open-circuit voltage. **–stand,** *m.* retirement; ***in den – versetzen,*** superannuate, pension off; ***in den – treten,*** retire (*from business*). **–statt, –stätte,** *f.* place of rest, resting-place. **–stellung,** *f.* (*Mil.*) at-ease position; (*Mech.*) idle *or* neutral *or* normal position. **–störer,** *m.* disturber of the peace. **–störung,** *f.* breach of the peace, disturbance, disorderly conduct. **–stunde,** *f.* leisure hour. **–tag,** *m.* day of rest, sabbath; holiday, (*coll.*) day off. **ruhevoll,** *adj.* quiet, peaceful. **Ruhe|zeichen,** *n.* (*Mus.*) pause, rest. **–zeit,** *f.* leisure time, (*coll.*) time off; off-season. **–zustand,** *m.* state of rest, dormancy.

ruhig ['ru:ɪç], **1.** *adj.* (*sound*) quiet, silent, still, (*movement*) still, at rest, motionless; tranquil, peaceful, (*of sea*) calm, smooth; (*fig.*) serene, calm, composed, placid, even-tempered, unruffled, imperturbable, cool-headed; ***–!*** quiet! silence! hush! ***–(es) Blut bewahren,*** keep a cool head; (*Mil.*) ***–es Feuer,*** deliberate fire; ***–es Gewissen,*** easy conscience; (*Comm.*) ***das Geschäft liegt –,*** business is dull; ***bei –er Überlegung,*** on calm reflection. **2.** *adv.* 1. ***– bleiben,*** keep calm, keep one's temper; ***– schlafen,*** sleep soundly *or* peacefully; ***sich – verhalten,*** keep one's mouth shut, hold one's peace; ***– verlaufen,*** be uneventful, pass off without more ado; 2. (*coll.*) safely, unhesitatingly; ***du kannst – mitkommen,*** it will be all right for you to come.

Ruhm [ru:m], *m.* glory, fame, renown; ***den – muß man ihm lassen, daß . . .,*** it must be said in his favour *or* to his credit, that . . .; ***ihm zum –e gereichen,*** redound to his honour. **ruhmbedeckt,** *adj.* crowned with glory. **Ruhmbegier(de),** *f.* thirst for glory, ambition.

rühmen ['ry:mən], **1.** *v.t.* praise, commend; extol, glorify, sing the praises of, (*Poet.*) laud; ***man rühmt ihn als tapfer,*** he is said to be brave; ***–d erwähnt werden,*** receive honourable mention. **2.** *v.r.* (*Gen.*) boast (of), pride o.s. (on), brag (about); ***ohne mich zu –,*** without boasting; ***ich rühme mich, sein Freund zu sein,*** I am proud to call myself his friend. **Rühmen,** *n.* praise(s); ***viel –s machen von,*** sing the praises of, (*coll.*) make a fuss about. **rühmenswert,** *adj.* praiseworthy, laudable.

Ruhmes|blatt, *n.* honourable page (*in annals*); ***es ist für ihn kein –,*** it does him no credit. **–halle,** *f.* pantheon, hall *or* temple of fame. **–titel,** *m.* claim to glory.

rühmlich ['ry:mlɪç], *adj.* laudable, creditable, praiseworthy; honourable, glorious.

ruhmlos ['ru:mlo:s], *adj.* inglorious, ignominious; obscure, unnoticed. **Ruhmlosigkeit,** *f.* ignominy, obloquy, opprobrium, discredit; obscurity. **ruhm|redig,** *adj.* vainglorious, boastful. **–reich,** *adj.* glorious. **Ruhm|sucht,** *f. See* **–begier(de). ruhmvoll,** *adj. See* **rühmlich.**

Ruhr [ru:r], *f.* dysentery.

Rühr|apparat ['ry:r–], *m.* mixer, agitator. **–ei,** *n.* scrambled egg.

rühren ['ry:rən], **1.** *v.i.* ***an etwas*** (*Acc.*) ***–,*** finger *or* touch a th., come into contact with a th.; (*fig.*) make reference to a th.; ***daher rührt es,*** it follows as a consequence. **2.** *v.t.* stir, move; touch, strike, beat;

set in motion, agitate; affect, make an impression on; turn up (*the ground*), rake (*hay etc.*); ***keinen Finger –,*** not raise *or* lift a finger; ***kein Glied – können,*** not be able to move *or* stir; ***die Trommel –,*** beat the drum; ***zu Tränen –,*** move to tears; ***vom Schlage gerührt,*** seized with an apoplectic fit; ***wie vom Donner gerührt,*** thunderstruck; ***das rührt mich gar nicht,*** that leaves me cold; ***rühr' nicht daran!*** let sleeping dogs lie! ***Eier –,*** beat eggs; ***Sahne –,*** whip cream. **3.** *v.r.* stir, move; bestir o.s., be active, be up and doing, make a move, take steps; (*Mil.*) ***rührt Euch!*** stand easy! stand at ease! ***sich nicht*** (***vom Fleck***) **–,** not budge (an inch), (*coll.*) sit tight; (*fig.*) make no move; ***es rührt sein Gewissen,*** his conscience pricks him. **Rühren,** *n.* ***ein menschliches –,*** a physical need *or* urge; a touch of human feeling.

rührend ['ry:rənt], *adj.* moving, touching, heart-rending, pathetic; ***–er Reim,*** identical rhyme.

Ruhrgebiet ['ru:rgəbi:t], *n.* (*Geog.*) the Ruhr (territory).

rührig ['ry:rɪç], *adj.* stirring, busy, active, bustling, nimble, brisk, energetic, eager, alert, enterprising, (*coll.*) go-ahead. **Rührigkeit,** *f.* activity; agility; nimbleness.

ruhrkrank ['ru:rkraŋk], *adj.* suffering from dysentery, dysenteric.

Rühr|löffel, *m.* stirring-ladle. **--mich-nicht-an,** *n.* (*Bot.*) noli-me-tangere; (*fig.*) aloof *or* touchy person. **–scheit,** *n.* stirrer, rod, paddle, spatula. **rührselig,** *adj.* very emotional, sentimental, lachrymose. **Rühr|seligkeit,** *f.* sentimentality. **–stück,** *n.* melodrama, (*sl.*) sob-stuff. **Rührung,** *f.* compassion, sympathy, feeling, emotion; ***unter – der Trommeln,*** with drums beating.

Ruin [ru'i:n], *m.* ruin, downfall, decay. **Ruine,** *f.* ruins, ruin, (*fig.*) (*of a p.*) wreck. **ruinenhaft,** *adj.* ruinous, in ruins, dilapidated, (*coll.*) tumbledown. **ruinieren** [–'ni:rən], *v.t.* ruin, destroy, wreck, spoil.

Rülps [rylps], *m.* (**-es,** *pl.* **-e**) 1. eructation, belch; 2. (*fig.*) lout. **rülpsen,** *v.i.* belch.

'rum [rum], *adv., sep.pref., coll. for* **herum.**

Rum, *m.* (**-s,** *pl.* **-s** *or* **-e**) rum.

Rumäne [ru'mɛ:nə], *m.* (**-n,** *pl.* **-n**) Rumanian. **Rumänien,** *n.* Rumania. **Rumänin,** *f. See* **Rumäne. rumänisch,** *adj.* Rumanian.

Rummel ['ruməl], *m.* hubbub, hullabaloo, racket, row, din; bustle, hurly-burly, stir, to-do; *see also* **Rummelplatz**; (*coll.*) ***der ganze –,*** the whole bag of tricks, the whole bunch *or* shoot *or* boiling; (*coll.*) ***er versteht*** or ***kennt den –,*** he knows what's what, he knows all about it. **Rummelplatz,** *m.* fair-ground, fun-fair, amusement park.

Rumor [ru'mo:r], *m.* (**-s,** *pl.* **-e**) noise, uproar. **rumoren,** *v.i.* make a noise, (*coll.*) kick up a row; ***es rumorte,*** there was growing unrest.

Rumpel ['rumpəl], **1.** *m.* (*dial.*) rubbish, lumber, junk. **2.** *f.* (**-,** *pl.* **-n**) (*dial.*) scrubbing board. **rumpelig.** *adj.* bumpy, lumpy, uneven, rugged. **Rumpel|kammer,** *f.* lumber-room, junk-room. **–kasten,** *m.* (*coll.*) rattletrap, bone-shaker; worn-out piano. **rumpeln, 1.** *v.i.* rumble, jolt; rummage. **2.** *v.t.* (*dial.*) scrub (*washing*). **Rumpelstilzchen,** *n.* hobgoblin.

Rumpf [rumpf], *m.* (**-(e)s,** *pl.* **¨-e**) trunk, torso; carcass (*of meat*); hull (*of a vessel*); (*Av.*) fuselage; (*fig.*) ***mit – und Stumpf,*** root and branch. **Rumpfbeuge,** *f.* (*Gymn.*) trunk-bending.

rümpfen ['rympfən], *v.t.* ***die Nase –,*** sneer, turn up one's nose (***über*** (*Acc.*), at).

Rumpf|ende, *n.* (*Av.*) tail of fuselage. **–holm,** *m.* (*Av.*) longeron. **–kanzel,** *f.* (*Av.*) cockpit. **rumpflastig,** *adj.* (*Av.*) tail-heavy. **Rumpf|spant,** *n.* (*Av.*) fuselage frame. **–spitze,** *f.* (*Av.*) nose of fuselage. **–stück,** *n.* rump steak.

rumplig, *adj. See* **rumpelig.**

rund [runt], **1.** *adj.* 1. round; circular, spherical; ***Besprechung am –en Tisch,*** round-table conference; ***–e Summe,*** round sum; 2. frank, plain; ***gib mir auf meine –e Frage eine –e Antwort,*** give me a plain answer to a plain question; 3. rotund, plump, (*coll.*) podgy. **2.** *adv.* ***– um den Park,*** (all a)round the park; ***– heraussagen,*** say straight out, state plainly *or* bluntly; ***– abschlagen,*** refuse flatly; ***– 10 Meilen,*** about 10 miles, 10 miles or so.

Rund, *n.* (**-(e)s,** *pl.* **-e**) globe, orb, sphere, circle.

Runda ['runda], *n.* (**-s,** *pl.* **-s**) (*dial.*) roundelay, chorus, drinking-song.

Rund|bau, *m.* (*pl.* **-ten**) rotunda, circular building. **–bild,** *n.* panoramic view. **–blick,** *m.* view all round, panorama. **–blickfernrohr,** *n.* panoramic sight. **–blickscheinwerfer,** *m.* revolving beacon. **–bogen,** *m.* Romanesque *or* Norman arch; Roman arch. **–bogenstil,** *m.* Romanesque style. **–brenner,** *m.* ring-burner. **–dorf,** *n. See* **Rundling.**

Runde ['rundə], *f.* circle; company, party; (*racing*) lap, (*Boxing*) round, (*Spt.*) heat; patrol, beat; ***eine – spenden,*** stand a round (*of drinks*); ***die – machen,*** be passed round, be circulated (*round the table*), go the rounds; ***10 Meilen in die –,*** 10 miles round; ***rings in der –,*** all around, round about.

Ründe ['ryndə], *f.* roundness, rotundity, curve (*of an arch*).

Rundeisen ['runtʔaɪzən], *n.* iron rod. **runden, ründen, 1.** *v.t.* round, (*fig.*) round off. **2.** *v.r.* round itself off, fill out, become complete. **runderhaben,** *adj.* convex. **Rund|erlaß,** *m.* circular (*notice*). **–fahrt,** *f.* circular tour. **–feile,** *f.* round file. **–flug,** *m.* round flight. **–frage,** *f.* inquiry, questionnaire.

Rundfunk ['runtfuŋk], *m.* wireless, radio, broadcasting; ***im*** or ***durch –,*** on *or* over the radio *or* air; ***– hören,*** listen-in, listen to the radio. **Rundfunk|-anlage,** *f.* wireless installation. **–ansager,** *m.* wireless announcer. **–gebühr,** *f.* wireless licence. **–gerät,** *n.* wireless set, radio. **–gesellschaft,** *f.* broadcasting company, (*Am.*) radio corporation. **–hörer,** *m.* listener(-in), *pl.* radio audience. **–sender,** *m.* wireless transmitter. **–sendung,** *f.* transmission, broadcast; wireless *or* radio programme. **–teilnehmer,** *m.* (radio) licence-holder. **–übertragung,** *f. See* **–sendung. –werbung,** *f.* radio advertising. **–wesen,** *n.* broadcasting.

Rund|gang, *m.* (*Mil. etc.*) round; stroll. **–gesang,** *m.* round, roundelay, glee. **Rundheit,** *f.* roundness. **rund|heraus,** *adv.* in plain terms, plainly, point-blank, flatly, bluntly, straight out. **–herum,** *adv.* all around, round about. **–hohl,** *adj.* concave. **Rund|holz,** *n.* round timber, logs. **–kopfschraube,** *f.* round-headed screw. **–lauf,** *m.* circular motion, (*Mech.*) concentric running; (*Gymn.*) giant-stride. **rundlich,** *adj.* roundish, rotund, plump, chubby.

Rundling ['runtlɪŋ], *m.* (**-(e)s,** *pl.* **-e**) radial form of settlement.

Rund|reise, *f.* circular tour, round trip. **–reisebillett,** *n.,* **–reisekarte,** *f.* round-trip *or* circular ticket. **rundschädelig,** *adj.* round-headed, mesocephalic. **Rund|schau,** *f.* panorama; review; ***literarische –,*** literary review. **–schreiben,** *n.* circular (letter); ***durch – benachrichtigen,*** circularize. **–schrift,** *f.* round-hand (*writing*). **–spruch,** *m.* (*Swiss*) *see* **Rundfunk. –stab,** *m.* (*Archit.*) astragal, (*Mech.*) rod, post. **–stange,** *f.* (*Metall.*) rod, round section bar. **–strahlantenne,** *f.* (*Rad.*) non-directional aerial. **–strickmaschine,** *f.* circular knitting machine, hosiery frame. **–stück,** *n.* (*dial.*) (breakfast) roll. **rundum(her),** *adv.* round about, all (a)round, on all sides. **Rund|-umverteidigung,** *f.* all-round defence.

Rundung ['runduŋ], *f.* roundness, curve; (*Phonet.*) labialization.

rund|weg, *adv. See* **–heraus. Rundzange,** *f.* round-nosed pliers.

Rune ['ru:nə], *f.* rune, runic letter. **Runen|schrift,** *f.* runes, runic characters *or* inscription. **–stein,** *m.* runic stone.

Runge ['ruŋə], *f.* stanchion, upright (*on sides of open goods van*). **Rungenwagen,** *m.* (*Railw.*) platform *or* flat wagon.

Runke ['ruŋkə], **Runkel,** *f.* (-, *pl.* **-n**) (*coll.*) lump, chunk. **Runkelrübe,** *f.* beet(-root). **Runken,** *m.* (*coll.*) thick slice, wad. **Runks,** *m.* (**-es,** *pl.* **-e**) (*coll.*) lout. **runksen,** *v.i.* (*dial.*) behave like a boor, (*Spt. sl.*) play dirty.

'runter ['runtər], *adv., sep.pref., coll. for* **herunter.**

Runzel ['runtsəl], *f.* (-, *pl.* **-n**) wrinkle, pucker, fold; ***–n um die Augen,*** crows' feet. **runzelig,** *adj.* wrinkled, shrivelled (up), puckered; (*Bot.*) rugose. **runzeln,** *v.t., v.i.* wrinkle, pucker, shrivel; ***die Stirn –,*** knit one's brows, frown. **runzlig,** *adj. See* **runzelig.**

Rüpel ['ry:pəl], *m.* boor, lout. **Rüpelei** [–'laɪ], *f.* loutishness, boorishness; rudeness, coarseness. **rüpelhaft,** *adj.* boorish, loutish, coarse, rude.

rupfen ['rupfən], *v.t.* pluck, pull up *or* out, pick; (*coll.*) ***ihn –,*** fleece him; (*coll.*) ***ein Hühnchen mit ihm zu – haben,*** have a bone to pick with him. **Rupfen,** *m. or n.* hessian (*cloth*).

Rupie ['ru:piə], *f.* rupee.

ruppig ['rupɪç], *adj.* coarse, rude, unmannerly; (*dial.*) ragged, shabby, unkempt.

Ruprecht ['ru:prɛçt], *m.* ***Knecht –,*** Santa Claus, Father Christmas.

Rusch [ruʃ], *m.* (**-es,** *pl.* **-e**) (*dial.*) rush, reed; ***– und Busch,*** brake and briar.

Rüsche ['ry:ʃə], *f.* ruche, frill, ruffle.

Ruschel ['ruʃəl], *f.* (-, *pl.* **-n**) *or m.* (*dial.*) scatter-brain, harum-scarum. **ruschelig,** *adj.* slap-dash, scatterbrained, happy-go-lucky, (*sl.*) slap-happy. **Ruschelkopf,** *m.* (*coll.*) *see* **Ruschel. ruscheln,** *v.i.* 1. rustle; 2. do a clumsy job, work hastily *or* carelessly.

rüschen ['ry:ʃən], *v.t* crimp, goffer.

Ruß [ru:s], *m.* (**-es,** *pl.* **-e**) soot, lamp-black; (*Bot.*) smut.

Russe ['rusə], *m.* (**-n,** *pl.* **-n**) Russian.

Rüssel ['rysəl], *m.* snout (*of pig*), trunk (*of elephant*), proboscis (*of insects*); nozzle. **rüsselartig, rüsselig,** *adj.* snout-like. **Rüssel|käfer,** *m.* weevil. **–tier,** *n.* proboscidian.

rußen ['ru:sən], **1.** *v.t.* blacken (with soot). **2.** *v.i.* (*of lamp*) smoke, get sooty, get caked with soot. **Ruß|farbe,** *f.* lamp-black, bistre. **–fleck,** *m.* smut. **rußig,** *adj.* sooty, (*Bot.*) smutty.

Russin ['rusɪn], *f. See* **Russe. russisch,** *adj.* Russian. **Rußland,** *n.* Russia.

Rußseeschwalbe ['ru:sze:ʃvalbə], *f.* (*Orn.*) sooty tern (*Sterna fuscata*).

Rüstbaum ['rystbaum], *m.* scaffold pole.

Rüste ['rystə], *f.* (*Poet.*) ***zu*** or ***zur – gehen,*** sink, set (*of the sun*); go to rest, expire.

rüsten ['rystən], **1.** *v.t* prepare, equip (***auf*** (*Acc*), ***zu,*** for). **2.** *v.i., v.r.* make preparations, prepare, make *or* get ready (***auf*** (*Acc.*), ***zu,*** for), (*Mil.*) arm, mobilize, prepare for war; ***gerüstet,*** armed, ready, prepared.

¹**Ruster** ['rystər], *m. See* **Rüstmann.**

²**Rüster,** *f.* (-, *pl.* **-n**) elm (tree). **rüstern,** *adj.* (of) elm.

Rüst|gewicht, *n.* (*Av.*) structural weight. **–halle,** *f.*, **–haus,** *n.* (*Hist.*) arsenal, armoury. **–holz,** *n.* (*Min.*) prop, shore.

rüstig ['rystɪç], *adj.* vigorous, robust, hale and hearty, active, alert, brisk, nimble, (*coll.*) spry; ***er ist noch –,*** he is well-preserved, he is active for his years.

Rüst|kammer, *f.* (*obs.*) armoury, arsenal. **–mann,** *m.* assembly man (*in a factory*). **–material,** *n.* scaffolding. **–meister,** *m.* (*Hist.*) armourer. **–saal,** *m. See* **–kammer. –stange,** *f. See* **–baum.**

Rüstung ['rystuŋ], *f.* armaments, arms, munitions; mobilization, preparation for war; (*Hist. also fig.*) armour, panoply; (*Build.*) scaffolding; (*fig.*) preparations; equipment, implements.

Rüstungs|auftrag, *m.* defence contract. **–beschränkung,** *f.* restriction of military expenditure. **–fabrik,** *f.* armaments *or* munitions factory. **–industrie,** *f.* armaments *or* war industry. **–material,** *n.* war material. **–stand,** *m.* state of preparedness (for war). **–werk,** *n. See* **–fabrik. –wettbewerb,** *m.* armament race.

Rüstzeug ['rysttsɔyk], *n.* (set of) tools, implements; (*fig.*) (mental) equipment.

Rute ['ru:tə], *f.* 1. rod, twig, switch, wand, birch (rod); ***sich die – selbst flechten,*** make a rod for one's own back; ***einem Kind die – geben,*** give a child the stick; ***mit eiserner – regieren,*** rule with a rod of iron; 2. brush (*of foxes*); 3. (*Anat.*) penis; 4. (*obs. land measure*) rod, pole *or* perch. **Ruten|bündel,** *n.* bundle of rods, faggot; (*Hist.*) fasces. **–gänger,** *m.* dowser, water-diviner.

Rutsch [rutʃ], *m.* (**-es,** *pl.* **-e**) slip, slide; landslip, landslide. **Rutschbahn, Rutsche,** *f.* slide; chute. **rutschen,** *v.i.* (*aux.* h. *&* s.) slide, glide, slip, (*Motor.*) skid, (*Av.*) sideslip; (*coll.*) make (some) headway; (*coll.*) ***aufs Land –,*** pop *or* slip into the country. **rutschig,** *adj.* slippery, (*coll.*) slippy. **Rutschpartie,** *f.* (*coll.*) jaunt, trip.

Rüttelfalke ['rytəlfalkə], *m.* (*Orn.*) *see* **Turmfalke.**

rütteln ['rytəln], *v.t., v.i.* shake; jog, jolt, vibrate; winnow (*corn*); (*fig.*) ***– an*** (*Dat.*), assail, undermine; ***daran ist nicht zu –,*** that is absolutely fixed, that is an unalterable *or* unassailable fact, you will not change that; ***gerüttelt voll,*** heaped; ***gerüttelt und geschüttelt Maß,*** full *or* good measure.

Rüttelstroh, *n.* loose straw, litter.

Rüttler ['rytlər], *m.* (*Tech.*) vibrator.

S

S, s [ɛs], *n.* S, s. (*See List of Abbreviations.*)

–s (*in elision*) = **das**; *e.g.* ***ins = in das; ans = an das; aufs, durchs, fürs*** *etc.*

's (*in elision*) = **es**; *e.g.* ***geht's = geht es; ist's = ist es; hat's, wenn's, ob's*** *etc.*

Saal [za:l], *m.* (**-(e)s,** *pl.* **Säle**) hall, assembly room, (large) room; (hospital) ward; (operating-)theatre; (*Univ.*) (lecture-)theatre. **Saal|öffnung,** *f.* (*Theat. etc.*) opening time. **–tochter,** *f.* (*Swiss*) waitress.

Saat [za:t], *f.* (-, *pl.* **-en**) sowing; seed (*also fig.*); standing crops; ***Zeit zur –,*** time for sowing; ***in – schießen,*** run *or* go to seed. **Saatbestellung,** *f.* sowing. **Saatenstand,** *m.* state of the crops.

Saat|erbse, *f.* (*Bot.*) field pea (*Pisum arvense*). **–feld,** *n.* field of corn. **–gans,** *f.* (*Orn.*) bean goose (*Anser fabalis*). **–getreide,** *n.* seed-corn. **–gut,** *n.* seeds, seedlings. **–kartoffel,** *f.* seed-potato. **–korn,** *n.* (**-s,** *pl.* **⸚er**) single seed. **–krähe,** *f.* (*Orn.*) rook (*Corvus frugilegus*). **–krankheit,** *f.* seed-borne disease. **–schule,** *f.* (*Hort.*) nursery. **–zeit,** *f.* sowing season.

Sabbat ['zabat], *m.* (**-(e)s,** *pl.* **-e**) (*Jew.*) Sabbath; (*Poet.*) Sunday; ***den – heiligen,*** keep the Sabbath; ***den – entheiligen,*** break the Sabbath. **Sabbat|jahr,** *n.* Sabbatical year. **–schänder,** *m.* Sabbath-breaker.

Sabbel ['zabəl], *m. See* **Sabber. sabbeln,** *v.i. See* **sabbern.**

Sabber ['zabər], *m.* (*dial.*) dribble, spittle. **Sabberlätzchen,** *n.* feeder, bib. **sabbern,** *v.i.* (*dial.*) dribble, slobber, slaver, drivel, drool.

Säbel ['zɛ:bəl], *m.* sabre, broadsword. **Säbel|bajonett,** *n.* sword-bayonet. **–beine,** *n.pl.* bandy *or* bow-legs. **säbelbeinig,** *adj.* bandy- *or* bow-legged. **Säbel|fechten,** *n.* sabre-fencing. **–gerassel,** *n.* sabre-rattling, jingoism, chauvinism. **–hieb,** *m.* sword-cut. **säbeln,** *v.t.* sabre, (*coll.*) cut, slash, hack. **Säbel|raßler,** *m.* swashbuckler; sabre-rattler, jingoist, chauvinist. **–schnäbler,** *m.* (*Orn.*) avocet (*Recurvirostra avosetta*). **–troddel,** *f.* sword-knot.

Sabotage [zabo'ta:ʒə], *f.* sabotage; *– treiben,* (commit) sabotage. **Sabotage|abwehr,** *m.* counter-sabotage. **–akt,** *m.* act of sabotage. **sabotieren,** *v.t.* sabotage (*also fig.*), (*fig.*) torpedo.

Sach|anlagevermögen ['zax–], *n.* (*Law*) tangible fixed assets. **–bearbeiter,** *m.* official in charge; (*social work*) case-worker. **–beschädigung,** *f.* wilful destruction, damage to property, vandalism. **–bezüge,** *m.pl.* payment in kind. **–darstellung,** *f.* (*Law*) statement of facts. **sachdienlich,** *adj.* relevant, pertinent; appropriate, suitable; useful, helpful.

Sache ['zaxə], *f.* thing, object, article; (*Law*) cause, action, case; subject, matter, affair, business, concern; event, fact, point, circumstance; *pl.* chattels, belongings, (*coll.*) things; ***bei der – bleiben,*** stick to the point; ***bei der – sein,*** be attentive (to) *or* intent (on), pay attention (to); be heart and soul (in); (*sl.*) be on the job; ***nicht bei der – sein,*** be inattentive *or* absent-minded; (*Law*) ***fremde –n,*** other people's property; (*Law*) ***eine – führen,*** plead a cause; ***gemeinsame – machen mit,*** make common cause with; ***seiner – sicher*** or ***gewiß sein,*** know what one is about, (*coll.*) be sure of one's ground; ***seine – gut machen,*** acquit o.s. well, do one's job well, play a part well, (*sl.*) put up a good show; ***das ist seine –,*** that is his affair, that is his look-out; ***Lügen ist nicht seine –,*** he is not given to lying; ***jede – hat zwei Seiten,*** there are two sides to every question; ***meine sieben –n,*** my belongings, all my things; (*Motor. sl.*) ***mit 100 –n,*** at 60 m.p.h.; (*coll.*) ***mach keine –n!*** you don't say so! not on your life! (*sl.*) don't pull that one on me! (*sl.*) ***das ist –!*** that's (just) the stuff, that's hot stuff; ***es geht um die –, nicht die Person,*** the issue is above personalities; ***kümmere dich um deine (eigenen) –n,*** mind your own business; ***unverrichteter – zurückkommen,*** come back empty-handed; ***so steht die –, die – verhält sich so,*** matters stand *or* the matter stands thus; ***das gehört nicht zur –,*** that has nothing to do with it; ***zur – kommen,*** come to the point, (*coll.*) get down to business *or* (*sl.*) to brass tacks; ***das tut nichts zur –,*** that is beside the point *or* is insignificant *or* irrelevant, that makes no difference.

Sach|entscheidung, *f.* (*Law*) decision on the merits of the case. **–erklärung,** *f.* factual explanation. **–gebiet,** *n.* department *or* field of knowledge, subject. **sachgemäß, 1.** *adj.* relevant, pertinent, appropriate, proper. **2.** *adv.* appropriately, properly, in a suitable manner. **Sach|katalog,** *m.* subject catalogue. **–kenner,** *m.* *See* **–kundige(r). –kenntnis, –kunde,** *f.* special *or* expert knowledge, (professional) experience. **sachkundig,** *adj.* experienced, skilled, expert, versed, competent. **Sach|kundige(r),** *m., f.* expert, competent judge, (*of art*) connoisseur. **–lage,** *f.* state of things *or* affairs, position; facts, circumstances; ***bei dieser –,*** as matters stand, under *or* in these circumstances. **–leistung,** *f.* *See* **–bezüge.**

sachlich ['zaxlɪç], **1.** *adj.* real, material, factual, objective; essential, relevant, pertinent, (*pred.*) to the point; realistic, matter-of-fact, businesslike; unbiased, impartial, objective, detached (*attitude*); practical, functional, technical (*style*); ***aus –en Gründen,*** for practical reasons, on material grounds; ***–e Zuständigkeit für,*** jurisdiction over. **2.** *adv.* to the point; ***– richtig,*** factually correct.

sächlich ['zɛçlɪç], *adj.* (*Gram.*) neuter.

Sachlichkeit ['zaxlɪçkaɪt], *f.* reality, objectivity; relevance, pertinence; realism, practicality, functionalism; impartiality, objectivity; (*Liter.*) ***die Neue –,*** the New Realism.

Sach|register, *n.* table of contents, subject index. **–schaden,** *m.* damage to property, material damage. **–schadenersatz,** *m.* indemnity.

Sachse ['zaksə], *m.* **(-n,** *pl.* **-n)** Saxon. **Sachsen,** *n.* Saxony. **Sächsin,** *f.* *See* **Sachse.**

sacht(e) ['zaxt(ə)], **1.** *adv.* softly, gently, cautiously, (*coll.*) gingerly; by degrees, gradually, slowly. **2.** *adj.* (*obs.*) *see* **sanft.**

Sach|verhalt, *m.* state of affairs, circumstances, facts (of the case). **–vermögen,** *n.* (*Law*) real assets. **sach|verständig,** *adj.* *See* **–kundig. Sach|verständige(r),** *m., f.* expert, authority, specialist, (*Law*) expert witness (***in*** (*Dat.*), ***für,*** on). **–walter,** *m.* legal adviser, counsel, attorney, solicitor; agent, trustee, administrator. **–wert,** *m.* real value; *pl.* real assets. **–wörterbuch,** *n.* encyclopaedia.

Sack [zak], *m.* **(-(e)s,** *pl.* **⸚e)** sack, bag; (*Anat. etc.*) sac, cyst, pouch; (*dial.*) purse, pocket; ***zwanzig – Korn,*** twenty sacks of corn; ***in – und Asche,*** in sackcloth and ashes; (*coll. fig.*) ***etwas im – haben,*** have a th. in one's pocket; (*coll.*) ***in den – hauen,*** throw in one's hand, (*sl.*) chuck it; ***eine Katze im – kaufen,*** buy a pig in a poke; (*coll.*) ***in den – stecken,*** have him under one's thumb, get the better of him, be one up on him; ***mit – und Pack,*** with bag and baggage; ***wie ein – schlafen,*** sleep like a log *or* top; ***den – schlagen und den Esel meinen,*** say one thing and mean another.

Säckel ['zɛkəl], *m.* purse, money-bag.

sacken ['zakən], **1.** *v.t.* put into sacks, bag. **2.** *v.i., v.r.* sink, sag, subside, settle, give way; (*of clothes*) become baggy *or* puckered.

sackerlot! [zakər'lo:t], **sackerment!** *int.* *See* **sapperlot! sapperment!**

Sack|gasse, *f.* blind alley; cul-de-sac, dead-end; (*fig.*) deadlock, impasse. **–geschwulst,** *f.* encysted tumour. **sackgrob,** *adj.* exceedingly rude. **Sack|-hüpfen,** *n.* sack-race. **–landung,** *f.* (*Av.*) pancake landing. **–leinen,** *n.,* **–leinwand,** *f.* sack-cloth, sacking. **–pfeife,** *f.* bagpipe. **–tuch,** *n.* sacking; (*dial.*) (pocket-)handkerchief.

Sackung ['zakuŋ], *f.* sagging, subsidence. **sackweise,** *adv.* by the bagful *or* sackful. **Sackzwirn,** *m.* twine, packing-thread.

säen ['zɛ:ən], *v.t., v.i.* sow.

Safe [se:f], *m. or n.* **(-s,** *pl.* **-s)** safe, strong-room; safe-deposit (box).

Saffian ['zafian], *m.* morocco (leather).

Saflor [za'flo:r], *m.* **(-s,** *pl.* **-e)** (*Bot.*) safflower, bastard saffron (*Carthamus tinctorius*).

Safran ['zafran], *m.* **(-s,** *pl.* **-e)** (*Bot.*) saffron (*Crocus sativus*). **safran|farben, –farbig, –gelb,** *adj.* saffron(-yellow).

Saft [zaft], *m.* **(-(e)s,** *pl.* **⸚e)** juice (*of fruit*), sap (*of tree etc.*), gravy (*of meat*), (*Med.*) humour, lymph; ***im – stehen,*** be in sap; (*fig.*) ***ohne – und Kraft,*** fit *or* good for nothing, spineless, (*coll.*) wishy-washy. **saftgrün,** *adj.* sap-green. **Safthalter,** *m.* (*Bot.*) nectary. **saftig,** *adj.* juicy, luscious, succulent; (*coll.*) spicy (*of joke*); ***eine –e Ohrfeige,*** a sound box on the ear. **saftlos,** *adj.* sapless; (*fig.*) dry, insipid. **Saft|pflanze,** *f.* succulent plant. **–röhre,** *f.* lymphatic vessel. **saftvoll,** *adj.* *See* **saftig. Saftzelle,** *f.* lymph cell.

Saga ['za:ga], *f.* (-, *pl.* **-s)** saga.

Sage ['za:gə], *f.* legend, fable, myth; tradition; (*coll.*) tale, rumour; ***es geht die –,*** the story goes, it is rumoured.

Säge ['zɛ:gə], *f.* saw. **sägeartig,** *adj.* saw-like, serrate(d). **Säge|blatt,** *n.* saw-blade. **–bock,** *m.* sawing-trestle. **–fisch,** *m.* saw-fish. **säge|förmig,** *adj.* *See* **–artig. Säge|grube,** *f.* saw-pit. **–maschine,** *f.* mechanical saw. **–mehl,** *n.* sawdust. **–mühle,** *f.* saw-mill.

sagen ['za:gən], **1.** *v.t.* say, tell; ***ihm –,*** say to him, tell him; (*iron.*) ***wem – Sie das?*** you're telling me! ***Dank –,*** express *or* return one's thanks, render thanks; ***ihm gehörig die Meinung –,*** give him a piece of one's mind; ***etwas dabei zu – haben,*** have a say in the matter; ***auf alles etwas zu – wissen,*** have an answer to everything; ***sagt dir das etwas?*** does it mean anything to you? ***ihm – lassen,*** send him word, let him know; ***laß dir das gesagt sein,*** let it be a warning to you; ***er läßt sich*** (*Dat.*) ***nichts –,*** he will listen to no advice *or* to no one, he won't listen to reason; ***ich ließ mir das nicht zweimal –,*** I did not wait to be told twice, I jumped at it; ***das kann man wohl –,*** you may well say so; ***das sagt***

man nicht, that's not a nice *or* the proper thing to say; ***was Sie nicht –!*** you don't say! ***das will nichts –, es hat nichts zu –,*** it does not signify, it is of no great importance *or* consequence, it makes no difference, it does not matter; ***Sie haben mir nichts zu –,*** I won't be ordered about by you; ***wie sagt man es auf deutsch?*** how do you say *or* put it in German? what is the German for it? ***was wollen Sie damit –?*** what do you mean by that? ***das will viel –, das ist viel gesagt,*** that is saying a lot; ***das will ich nicht gesagt haben,*** I did not mean that; ***was ich – wollte,*** as I was about to say, what I was going to say. **2.** *v.i.* say; ***man sagt, er sei . . .,*** it is said that he is . . ., he is said to be . . .; ***ich habe mir – lassen,*** I am told, I have been told; ***laß dir von mir –,*** take it from me; ***es läßt sich nicht –,*** it is beyond words; there is no saying; ***es ist nicht gesagt, daß . . .,*** that is not to say that . . ., that does not necessarily mean that . . .; ***es ist nicht zu –,*** it's incredible *or* fantastic, words fail me; ***sage und schreibe eine ganze Stunde,*** a solid hour, believe it or believe it not; ***wenn ich so – darf,*** if I may say so, if I may be permitted the expression; ***du sagst nur so,*** you don't really mean it; ***mit Verlaub zu –,*** excuse the language; ***er kann von Glück –,*** he can count himself lucky; ***wie man so sagt,*** as the saying is *or* goes; ***wie sagt man?*** how does it go? what's it called? what's its name? ***das will*** (***nicht***) ***–,*** that is (not) to say; ***das Gesagte,*** what I have said, what has been said, the aforesaid; ***beiläufig gesagt,*** by the way, as was mentioned in passing; ***offen gesagt,*** to put it plainly, in plain language; ***richtiger gesagt,*** properly speaking; ***gesagt, getan,*** no sooner said than done; ***unter uns gesagt,*** between you and me, in confidence; ***wie gesagt,*** as I said.

sägen ['zɛ:gən], **1.** *v.t., v.i.* saw. **2.** *v.i.* (*coll.*) snore.

sagenhaft ['za:gənhaft], *adj.* legendary, mythical, fabulous, (*coll.*) marvellous, incredible. **Sagen|-kreis,** *m.* legendary cycle, epic cycle. **–kunde,** *f.* legendary lore; folklore. **–schatz,** *m.* legends; folklore. **–zeit,** *f.* legendary *or* heroic age; fabulous age.

Säger ['zɛ:gər], *m.* (*Orn.*) ***großer –,*** *see* **Gänsesäger**; ***kleiner –,*** *see* **Zwergsäger.**

Säge|schnitt, *m.* saw cut. **–späne,** *m.pl.* sawdust. **–werk,** *n.* saw-mill. **–zahn,** *m.* saw-tooth, indentation. **sägezähnig,** *adj.* serrate. **Sägezahnspannung,** *f.* sawtooth *or* time-base *or* trip voltage.

Sago ['za:go], *m.* sago.

sah [za:], **sähe** ['zɛ:ə], *see* **sehen.**

Sahne ['za:nə], *f.* cream. **Sahne|bonbon,** *m.* (*Austr. n.*) cream toffee. **–butter,** *f.* dairy butter. **Sahnen|eis,** *n.* ice-cream. **–käse,** *m.* cream cheese. **–kuchen,** *m.* cream-tart *or* cake. **sahnig,** *adj.* creamy.

Saibling ['zaɪplɪŋ], *m.* **(-s,** *pl.* **-e)** (*Ichth.*) char.

Saison [zɛ'zɔ̃], *f.* (-, *pl.* **-s**) season; ***die stille*** or ***tote –,*** the quiet *or* off-season. **Saison|arbeiter,** *m.* seasonal worker. **–ausverkauf,** *m.* clearance *or* stock-taking sale. **saison|bedingt, –mäßig,** *adj.* seasonal.

Saite ['zaɪtə], *f.* (*Mus.*) string; (*fig.*) chord; (*fig.*) ***andere –n aufziehen,*** change one's tone *or* tune; ***–n auf eine Geige aufziehen,*** string a violin; ***besponnene –,*** silver string, covered string; (*fig.*) ***gelindere*** or ***mildere –n aufziehen,*** climb down a peg; (*fig.*) ***die –n zu hoch spannen,*** take too much for granted. **Saiten|bezug,** *m.* set of strings. **–halter,** *m.* tail-piece (*of a violin etc.*). **–instrument,** *n.* stringed instrument. **–spiel,** *n.* **1.** string music; 2. (*Hist.*) lyre.

Sakko ['zako], *m.* (*Austr. n.*) **(-s,** *pl.* **-s)** lounge-jacket. **Sakkoanzug,** *m.* lounge-suit.

sakral [za'kra:l], *adj.* (*Anat.*) sacral.

Sakrament [zakra'mɛnt], *n.* **(-(e)s,** *pl.* **-e)** sacrament; consecrated Host.

Sakristan [zakrɪs'ta:n], *m.* **(-s,** *pl.* **-e)** sacristan, sexton. **Sakristei,** *f.* (-, *pl.* **-en**) vestry.

säkular [zɛku'la:r], *adj.* **1.** secular; 2. centennial. **Säkularfeier,** *f.* centenary (celebration). **säkularisieren** [–ri'zi:rən], *v.t.* secularize. **Säkulum** ['zɛ:kulum], *n.* **(-s,** *pl.* **-la)** century.

Salamander [zala'mandər], *m.* salamander; (*Studs. sl.*) ***einen – reiben auf*** (*Acc.*), toast with due ceremony.

Salär [za'lɛ:r], *n.* **(-s,** *pl.* **-e)** (*Austr., Swiss*) salary. **salarieren** [–la'ri:rən], *v.t.* pay a salary to.

Salat [za'la:t], *m.* **(-(e)s,** *pl.* **-e)** salad; lettuce; ***den – anmachen,*** dress the salad; (*coll.*) ***da haben wir den –,*** that's a nice mess *or* a fine *or* pretty how-do-you-do! **Salat|besteck,** *n.* salad-servers. **–blatt,** *n.* lettuce leaf. **–kopf,** *m.* head of lettuce. **–öl,** *n.* salad-oil. **–pflanze,** *f.* salad vegetable.

Salbader [zal'ba:dər], *m.* quack; bore. **Salbaderei** [–'raɪ], *f.* quackery; interminable talk, twaddle. **salbadern,** *v.i.* prate, talk nonsense *or* bosh *or* twaddle.

Salband ['za:lbant], *n.* **(-es,** *pl.* **⸚er)** selvage.

Salbe ['zalbə], *f.* ointment, salve; scented oil, pomade.

Salbei [zal'baɪ], *m. or f.* (*Bot.*) sage.

salben ['zalbən], *v.t.* apply ointment to; (*fig.*) ***– zu,*** anoint (as); (*fig., coll.*) ***ihm die Hände –,*** grease his palm. **Salben|büchse,** *f.* ointment pot. **–öl,** *n.* anointing oil, consecrated oil. **Salbung,** *f.* **1.** anointing; 2. (*fig.*) unction, pomposity, fulsomeness. **salbungsvoll,** *adj.* unctuous, ingratiating, fulsome, (*sl.*) smarmy, smalmy.

saldieren [zal'di:rən], *v.t.* pay, balance, settle, clear; ***– mit,*** set off against. **Saldierung,** *f.* balancing, settlement.

Saldo ['zaldo], *m.* **(-s,** *pl.* **-s** *or* **Salden** (*or Austr.* **Saldi**)) balance (of an account); ***einen – aufweisen,*** show a balance; ***– vorgetragen,*** balance carried forward; ***– zu unseren Gunsten,*** balance in our favour; ***– zu unseren Lasten,*** debit balance; ***in – sein*** or ***bleiben,*** have debts outstanding, be in debt; ***den – ziehen,*** strike the balance. **Saldo|guthaben,** *n.* credit balance. **–übertrag,** *m.* balance brought forward. **–vortrag,** *m.* balance carried forward. **–wechsel,** *m.* draft for the balance. **–zahlung,** *f.* settlement.

Saline [za'li:nə], *f.* salt-works, salt-pit. **salinisch,** *adj.* saline.

salisch ['za:lɪʃ], *adj.* (*Hist.*) Salic.

Salizylsäure [zali'tsy:lzɔyrə], *f.* salicylic acid.

Salleiste ['za:llaɪstə], *f. See* **Salband.**

[1]**Salm** ['zalm], *m.* **(-s,** *pl.* **-e)** salmon.

[2]**Salm,** *m.* (*coll.*) ***langer –,*** rigmarole; ***einen langen – machen,*** spin a long yarn, be long-winded; (*coll.*) ***mache keinen –! nur keinen –!*** come to the point!

Salmiak ['zalmiak, –'ak], *m.* sal-ammoniac, ammonium chloride. **Salmiak|geist,** *m.* liquid ammonia. **–salz,** *n.* sal volatile.

Salomo ['za:lomo], *m.* (*B.*) Solomon; ***das Hohe Lied Salomonis,*** the Song of Solomon.

Salon [za'lɔ̃], *m.* **(-s,** *pl.* **-s)** drawing-room, parlour; saloon (*in ships, hairdressing etc.*); salon. **Salon|-bolschewik,** *m.* white-collar socialist. **–bruch,** *m.* (*Av. sl.*) slight damage. **salonfähig,** *adj.* presentable, fit for (good) society, (*coll.*) drawing-room. **Salon|held, –löwe,** *m.* lady's *or* ladies' man. **–wagen,** *m.* saloon carriage, Pullman car.

salopp [za'lɔp], *adj.* casual, slovenly, shabby, (*coll.*) sloppy.

Salpeter [zal'pe:tər], *m.* nitre, saltpetre, potassium nitrate. **salpeterartig,** *adj.* nitrous. **Salpeter|-bildung,** *f.*, **–blumen,** *f.pl.* nitrous exhalation (*on walls etc.*). **–erde,** *f.* nitrous earth. **salpeterhaltig,** *adj.* nitrous. **Salpetersalzsäure,** *f.* aqua regia, nitro-hydrochloric acid. **salpetersauer,** *adj.* nitric, nitrate of; ***–es Salz,*** nitrate. **Salpeter-säure,** *f.* nitric acid. **salpetrig,** *adj.* nitrous; ***–e Säure,*** nitrous acid; ***–saures Natron,*** sodium nitrate.

Salto (mortale) ['zalto mɔr'ta:lə], *m.* (-(-), *pl.* **-ti (-li)** *or* -(-)) vault, somersault, breakneck leap.

Salut [za'lu:t], *m.* **(-(e)s,** *pl.* **-e)** salute, salutation. **salutieren** [–'ti:rən], *v.t., v.i.* salute.

Salve ['zalvə], *f.* salute *or* discharge of guns; burst of fire (*or* of applause); salvo (*of guns*), volley (*rifle*); round (*of applause*); ***eine – abgeben,*** fire a volley *or* salvo. **Salven|feuer,** *n.* volley firing. **–geschütz,** *n.* multiple-barrel gun.

Salweide [ˈzaːlvaɪdə], *f.* (*Bot.*) sallow (*Salix caprea*).

Salz [zalts], *n.* (**-es,** *pl.* **-e**) salt; ***englisches –,*** Epsom salts; ***basisches –,*** subsalt; ***weder – noch Schmalz haben,*** be without body, be tasteless *or* insipid; (*coll.*) ***er liegt tüchtig im –,*** he is in a proper mess; (*coll.*) ***du hast es noch im –*** (***liegen***), you have it in store for you, you have it coming to you.

Salz|abgabe, *f.* salt-tax. **–ablagerung,** *f.* salt deposit. **salzartig,** *adv.* saline. **Salz|äther,** *m.* muriatic ether, ethyl chloride. **–bäder,** *n.pl.* brine *or* sea-water baths. **–bergwerk,** *n.* salt-mine. **salzbildend,** *adj.* halogenous. **Salz|bild(n)er,** *m.* halogen. **–bildung,** *f.* salification, halogenation. **–brühe,** *f.* brine, pickle. **–brunnen,** *m.* saline spring.

salzen [ˈzaltsən], *irr.v.t., reg.v.t.* (*p.p. always irr. when fig.*) salt; pickle; spice, season (*with wit etc.*); (*coll.*) ***ihm den Buckel –,*** give it him good and hard; ***gesalzen,*** piquant, spicy, strong; ***gesalzener Hering,*** salt herring; ***gesalzene Preise,*** exorbitant *or* (*coll.*) steep prices.

Salz|faß, –fäßchen, *n.* salt-cellar. **–fleisch,** *n.* salt(ed) meat. **–gehalt,** *m.* saline matter; proportion *or* percentage of salt. **–gehaltsmessung,** *f.* halometry. **–geschmack,** *m.* salty taste; brackishness. **–grube,** *f.* salt-pit. **–gurke,** *f.* pickled cucumber.

salzhaltig [ˈzaltshaltɪç], *adj.* saline, saliferous. **salzig,** *adj.* saline, salt(y), (*of water*) brackish. **Salzigkeit,** *f.* saltiness, salinity, salty taste.

Salz|korn, *n.* grain of salt. **–lager,** *n.* salt deposits. **–lake, –lauge,** *f.* brine, pickle. **–lecke,** *f.* salt-lick (*for cattle etc.*). **–pflanze,** *f.* halophyte. **–quelle,** *f.* saline spring. **salzsauer,** *adj.* (hydro)chloride of, hydrochlorate, muriatic; ***–es Salz,*** chloride. **Salz|säure,** *f.* hydrochloric *or* muriatic acid. **–siederei,** *f.* salt-works. **–sole,** *f.* brine, salt-spring. **–stange,** *f.* hard-baked white bread (strongly flavoured with salt and caraway seed). **–waage,** *f.* salinometer, brine-gauge. **–wasser,** *n.* salt-water, sea-water, brine. **–werk,** *n.* salt-works; salt-mine.

Sämann [ˈzɛːman], *m.* (*pl.* **-männer**) sower.

Samariter [zamaˈriːtər], *m.* (*B.*) Samaritan.

Sämaschine [ˈzɛːmaʃiːnə], *f.* sowing-machine, corn-drill.

Same [ˈzaːmə], *m.* (**-ns,** *pl.* **-n**), **Samen,** *m.* seed, grain; (*Zool.*) sperm, (*of man*) semen; (*of fish*) fry, spawn; (*fig.*) germ, source; (*B.*) seed, offspring, descendants.

Samen|anlage, *f.* gemmule, ovule; placenta. **–behälter,** *m.* (*Bot.*) seed-vessel, pericarp; (*Anat.*) seminal vesicle. **samenbeständig,** *adj.* true to type, homozygotous. **Samen|drüse,** *f.* (*Anat.*) testicle, spermatic gland. **–eiweiß,** *n.* endosperm, albumen. **–erguß,** *m.* seminal discharge. **–faden,** *m.* spermatozoon. **–flüssigkeit,** *f.* seminal fluid. **–gang,** *m.* spermatic duct, vas deferens. **–gärtner,** *m.* nurseryman. **–gehäuse,** *n.* *See* **–behälter** (*Bot.*). **–händler,** *m.* seedsman. **–hülle,** *f.* perisperm, seed-case. **–hülse,** *f.* seed-vessel, husk, shell, pod. **–kapsel,** *f.* capsule, seed-pod. **–keim,** *m.* germ-embryo. **–kelch,** *m.* seed-cup. **–kern,** *m.* sperm-nucleus, endosperm. **–knospe,** *f.* ovule, gemmule. **–korn,** *n.* grain of seed, single seed. **–lappen,** *m.* seed-lobe, cotyledon. **–lehre,** *f.* spermatology. **–leiter,** *m.* (*Anat.*) spermatic duct, vas deferens. **–öl,** *n.* rapeseed oil. **–pflanze,** *f.* seedling. **–schießen,** *n.* running to seed. **–schote,** *f.* *See* **–hülse. –schule,** *f.* (*Hort.*) nursery. **–staub,** *m.* pollen. **–stiel,** *m.* funicle. **–strang,** *m.* (*Anat.*) spermatic cord. **–tierchen,** *n.* spermatozoon. **samentragend,** *adj.* seed-bearing, spermatophorous. **Samen|träger,** *m.* (*Bot., Biol.*) spermatophore. **–zelle,** *f.* sperm-cell. **–zwiebel,** *f.* seed-bulb.

Sämereien [zɛːməˈraɪən], *pl.* (*Hort.*) seeds. **Sämereihändler,** *m.* seedsman.

sämig [ˈzɛːmɪç], *adj.* (*dial.*) thick, viscid, creamy.

sämisch [ˈzɛːmɪʃ], *adj.* chamois-dressed, (*coll.*) shammy (*leather*); fawn, beige (*colour*). **Sämisch|gerber,** *m.* chamois-dresser. **–leder,** *n.* chamois leather; wash-leather.

Sammel|aktion, *f.* salvage drive (*for goods*), fund-raising campaign (*for money*). **–album,** *n.* scrap-book. **–anschluß,** *m.* (*Tele.*) party-line. **–band,** *m.* omnibus volume. **–becken,** *n.* reservoir, storage tank, collecting vessel, (*Geog.*) catchment area. **–bezeichnung,** *f.* collective name. **–büchse,** *f.* collecting-box. **–fahrschein,** *m.* group ticket. **–gebiet,** *n.* catchment *or* drainage area. **–güter,** *n.pl.* mixed consignment, miscellaneous goods. **–konto,** *n.* general account. **–lager,** *n.* assembly camp, collecting centre. **–lazarett,** *n.* (*Mil.*) casualty collecting centre. **–linse,** *f.* converging *or* convex lens. **–mappe,** *f.* file, folder, portfolio. **–meldung,** *f.* (*Mil.*) situation report.

sammeln [ˈzaməln], **1.** *v.t.* gather, collect, pick (*flowers etc.*); hoard (up), amass, accumulate; collect (*postage stamps etc.*); assemble, rally, concentrate, mass (*troops etc.*); canvass for (*votes*); (*Opt.*) focus. **2.** *v.i.* collect money, make a collection. **3.** *v.r.* collect, gather, meet, assemble, rally, flock together (*of persons*), collect, gather, accumulate (*of things*); (*fig.*) concentrate, collect one's thoughts, regain one's self-possession *or* composure, compose o.s.

Sammel|name, *m.* collective name. **–platz,** *m.* (*Mil.*) assembly point, rendezvous, (*for goods*) collecting point, depot, dump. **–punkt,** *m.* (*oft. fig.*) rallying-point. **–schiene,** *f.* (*Elec.*) bus-bar. **–stelle,** *f.* (*for goods*) *see* **–platz.**

Sammelsurium [zaməlˈzuːrium], *n.* (**-s,** *pl.* **-rien**) medley, jumble, hotch-potch, omnium-gatherum.

Sammel|tag, *m.* flag-day. **–teller,** *m.* collection plate. **–transport,** *m.* group transport. **–werk,** *n.* compilation. **–wort,** *n.* collective noun.

Sammet [ˈzamət], *m.* *See* **Samt.**

Sammler [ˈzamlər], *m.* collector; (*Elec.*) accumulator, secondary cell. **Sammler|batterie,** *f.* storage-battery. **–stück,** *n.* collector's piece.

Sammlung [ˈzamluŋ], *f.* **1.** gathering, collecting; collection; compilation, anthology, selection, (*Law*) digest; **2.** (*fig.*) concentration; composure, collectedness. **Sammlungsdatum,** *n.* date of compilation (*on maps*).

Samstag [ˈzamstaːk], *m.* Saturday.

samt [zamt], **1.** *adv.* ***– und sonders,*** all of them (*or* you), each *or* one and all, the whole lot, (all) to a man, (all) without exception, jointly and severally. **2.** *prep.* (*Dat.*) (together *or* along) with, including.

Samt, *m.* (**-(e)s,** *pl.* **-e**) velvet; ***baumwollener –,*** velveteen. **samtartig,** *adj.* velvety. **Samtband,** *n.* velvet ribbon; ribbon velvet. **samten,** *adj.* *See* **samtartig. Samt|ente,** *f.* (*Orn.*) velvet scoter (*Melanitta fusca*). **–handschuh,** *m.* (*fig.*) ***mit –en anfassen,*** handle with kid-gloves. **–kopfgrasmücke,** *f.* (*Orn.*) Sardinian warbler (*Sylvia melanocephala*).

sämtlich [ˈzɛmtlɪç], **1.** *adj.* complete, entire, whole, all (together); ***–e Werke,*** complete works. **2.** *adv.* all (of them), all together, to a man, in a body.

Samt|manchester, *m.* velveteen. **–pfötchen,** *n.pl.* ***– machen,*** draw in claws (*of cat*); (*fig.*) be all smiles, play the hypocrite. **samt|schwarz,** *adj.* black as night. **–weich,** *adj.* velvety, soft as velvet.

Samum [zaˈmuːm], *m.* (**-s,** *pl.* **-s** *or* **-e**) simoom.

Sand [zant], *m.* (**-(e)s,** *pl.* **-e**) sand, grit; ***auf den – geraten, auf dem –e sitzen,*** (*Naut.*) be aground *or* stranded; (*fig.*) be left in the lurch; ***auf den – setzen,*** run *or* put (*a ship*) aground; bring (*one's opponent*) to the ground; (*fig.*) place (*s.o.*) in an awkward predicament; ***ihm – in die Augen streuen,*** throw dust in his eyes, hoodwink him; (*fig.*) ***in – schreiben,*** dismiss from one's mind; ***im –e verlaufen,*** peter *or* fizzle out, dry up, come to nothing.

Sandale [zanˈdaːlə], *f.* sandal.

Sand|bahn, *f.* (*Motor.*) dirt-track. **–bank,** *f.* sand-bank. **–blatt,** *n.* shrub-leaf (*used for covering cigars*). **–boden,** *m.* sandy soil. **–dorn,** *m.* (*Bot.*) sea-buckthorn (*Hippophaë rhamnoides*). **–dünen,** *f.pl.* sand-dunes.

Sandelholz ['zandəlhɔlts], *n.* sandalwood.
sandfarben ['zantfarbən], *adj.* sand(y)-coloured, sandy. **Sand|fliege,** *f.* sand-fly. **–floh,** *m.* sand-flea. **–flughuhn,** *n.* (*Orn.*) black-bellied sand-grouse (*Pterocles orientalis*). **–form,** *f.* sand-mould. **–grieß,** *m.* grit, fine gravel, coarse sand. **–grube,** *f.* sand-pit. **–guß,** *m.* sand-casting. **–hase,** *m.* (*sl.*) miss (*at nine-pins*); (*Mil. sl.*) *see* **–latscher. –hose,** *f.* sand-spout.
sandig ['zandıç], *adj.* sandy, gravelly.
Sand|kasten, *m.* sand-box (*for childten's play*), (*Mil.*) sand-table. **–korn,** *n.* grain of sand. **–kraut,** *n.* (*Bot.*) sandwort (*Arenaria*). **–kuchen,** *m. See* **–torte. –latscher,** *m.* (*sl.*) foot-slogger. **–(lauf)-käfer,** *m.* (*Ent.*) tigerbeetle (*Cicindelidae*). **–lerche,** *f.* (*Orn.*) desert lark (*Ammomanes deserti*). **–mann,** *m.* (*nursery talk*) sandman. **–meer,** *n.* (sandy) desert. **–papier,** *n.* sand- *or* glass-paper. **–regenpfeifer,** *m.* (*Orn.*) ringed plover (*Charadrius hiaticula*). **–sack,** *m.* sand-bag; (*Boxing*) punch-bag. **–stein,** *m.* sandstone. **–strahlgebläse,** *n.* sand-blasting equipment. **–strahlputzen,** *n.* sand-blasting. **–strandläufer,** *m.* (*Orn.*) semi-palmated sandpiper (*Calidris pusilla*). **–sturm,** *m.* sand-storm.
sandte ['zantə], *see* **senden.**
Sand|torte, *f.* Madeira cake. **–uhr,** *f.* hour-glass. **–webe, –wehe,** *f.* sand-drift. **–wüste,** *f. See* **–meer. –zucker,** *m.* brown sugar.
sanft [zanft], *adj.* gentle, easy; smooth, soft; (*of character*) placid, calm, meek, good-natured, (*coll.*) sweet, bland, mild; slight.
Sänfte ['zɛnftə], *f.* sedan-chair, litter.
Sanftheit ['zanfthaıt], *f.* softness; mildness, gentleness.
sänftigen ['zɛnftıgən], *v.t.* (*obs.*) soften, appease, mitigate.
Sanftmut ['zanftmu:t], *f.* (*of character*) gentleness, meekness, sweet temper. **sanftmütig,** *adj.* gentle, mild, meek, sweet-tempered.
Sang [zaŋ], *m.* **(-(e)s,** *pl.* **⸚e)** (*Poet.*) song, chant, singing; ***mit – und Klang,*** with a flourish, with pomp and circumstance; ***ohne – und Klang,*** unsung, unheralded, unceremoniously; ***ohne – und Klang abziehen,*** sneak off.
sang, *see* **singen.**
Sänger ['zɛŋər], *m.* singer, vocalist; (*Poet.*) minstrel, bard, poet; (*Orn.*) songbird, songster. **Sänger|-bund,** *m.* choral society, glee club. **–fest,** *n.* choral festival. **–grasmücke,** *f.* (*Orn.*) *see* **Orpheus-grasmücke. Sängerin,** *f. See* **Sänger. Sänger|-laubvogel,** *m.* (*Orn.*) *see* **Orpheusspötter. Sängerschaft,** *f. See* **Sängerbund.**
Sanguiniker [zaŋgu'i:nıkər], *m.* sanguine person. **sanguinisch,** *adj.* sanguine.
sanieren [za'ni:rən], *v.t.* cure; reclaim, restore, reorganize, reconstruct; stabilize (*currency*); clear (*slums*). **Sanierung,** *f.* reorganization, reconstruction, restoration, stabilization. **Sanierungsviertel,** *n.* slum-clearance area.
sanitär [zani'tɛ:r], *adj.* sanitary, hygienic; ***–e Anlagen,*** sanitation, plumbing (*in a house*). **sanitarisch,** *adj.* (*Swiss*) *see* **sanitär. Sanität,** *f.* (*Swiss*) army medical service. **Sanitäter,** *m.* (*Mil.*) medical orderly, ambulance man.
Sanitäts|artikel, *m.pl. See* **–bedarf. –auto,** *n. See* **–wagen. –beamte(r),** *m., f.* public health officer, medical officer, sanitary inspector. **–bedarf,** *m.* medical supplies. **–behörde,** *f.* public health department. **–dienst,** *m.* army medical service. **–flugzeug,** *n.* air ambulance. **–hund,** *m.* first-aid dog. **–kasten,** *m.* medicine chest, first-aid kit. **–kolonne,** *f.* first-aid squad, ambulance detachment. **–korps,** *n.* army medical corps. **–offizier,** *m.* (*Mil.*) medical officer. **–pack,** *n. See* **–tasche. –personal,** *n.* (*Mil.*) medical personnel. **–pflege,** *f.* (*Mil.*) army nursing; sanitation. **–polizei,** *f.* sanitary inspectors. **–rat,** *m.* member of the public health department; title conferred on German medical practitioners. **–soldat,** *m. See* **Sanitäter. –staffel,** *f.* (*Mil.*) medical personnel (*at division level*). **–tasche,** *f.* first-aid outfit. **–truppe,** *f. See* **–korps. –unterstand,** *m.* (*Mil.*) field dressing-station. **–wache,** *f.* ambulance station; first-aid post. **–wagen,** *m.* motor ambulance. **–wesen,** *n.* public health services. **–zug,** *m.* (*Mil.*) hospital train.
sank [zaŋk], **sänke** ['zɛŋkə], *see* **sinken.**
Sankt [zaŋkt], *indecl.adj.* Saint.
Sanktion [zaŋktsi'o:n], *f.* sanction, ratification; *pl.* sanctions, reprisals. **sanktionieren** [–'ni:rən], *v.t.* sanction, ratify.
Sanktissimum [zank'tısimum], *n.* (*Eccl.*) consecrated Host. **Sanktuarium** [–u'a:rium], *n.* **(-s,** *pl.* **-rien)** sanctuary, reliquary.
sann [zan], **sänne** ['zɛnə], *see* **sinnen.**
Saphir ['za:fır], *m.* **(-s,** *pl.* **-e)** sapphire.
Sappe ['zapə], *f.* (*Mil.*) sap-trench. **Sappenkopf,** *m.* saphead.
sapperlot! [zapər'lo:t], **sapperment!** *int.* (*coll.*) the devil! the dickens!
Sappeur [za'pø:r], *m.* **(-s,** *pl.* **-e)** (*obs. Mil.*) sapper.
Sarazene [zara'tse:nə], *m.* **(-n,** *pl.* **-n)** Saracen.
Sardelle [zar'dɛlə], *f.* anchovy. **Sardellen|butter, –paste,** *f.* anchovy paste.
Sardengrasmücke ['zardəngra:smykə], *f.* (*Orn.*) Marmora's warbler (*Sylvia sarda*).
Sardine [zar'di:nə], *f.* sardine.
Sardinien [zar'di:niən], *n.* (*Geog.*) Sardinia.
sardonisch [zar'do:nıʃ], *adj.* sardonic.
Sarg [zark], *m.* **(-(e)s,** *pl.* **⸚e)** coffin. **Sarg|deckel,** *m.* coffin-lid. **–träger,** *m.* coffin-bearer. **–tuch,** *n.* pall.
Sarkasmus [zar'kasmus], *m.* **(-,** *pl.* **-men)** sarcasm. **sarkastisch,** *adj.* sarcastic.
Sarkom [zar'ko:m], *n.* **(-s,** *pl.* **-e)** (*Med.*) sarcoma.
Sarkophag [zarko'fa:k], *m.* **(-s,** *pl.* **-e)** sarcophagus.
Sarraß ['zaras], *m.* **(-(ss)es,** *pl.* **-(ss)e)** sabre, broadsword.
Sarsche ['zarʃə], *f. See* **Serge.**
saß [za:s], *see* **sitzen.**
Saß [zas], *m.* **(-(ss)en,** *pl.* **-(ss)en),** (*Austr.*) **Sasse,** *m.* **(-n,** *pl.* **-n)** (*obs.*) (*usu. as suff.*) settler, tenant, freeholder.
säßig ['zɛ:sıç], *adj.* (*obs.*) settled, established, resident.
Satan ['za:tan], *m.* **(-s,** *pl.* **-e)** Satan, devil. **satanisch** [–'ta:nıʃ], *adj.* satanic, diabolical. **Satans|-brut,** *f.* limb of Satan. **–tücke,** *f.* devilish wiles.
Satellit [zatɛ'li:t], *m.* **(-en,** *pl.* **-en)** satellite (*also fig.*). **Satellitenstaat,** *m.* satellite state.
Satin [sa'tɛ̃], *m.* **(-s,** *pl.* **-s)** satin, sateen. **Satinage** [–ti'na:ʒə], *f.* glaze, glazing, finish, gloss. **satinieren,** *v.t.* glaze, gloss; (*paper*) glaze, calender.
Satire [za'ti:rə], *f.* satire. **Satiriker,** *m.* satirist. **satirisch,** *adj.* satirical.
satisfaktionsfähig [zatısfaktsi'o:nsfɛ:ıç], *adj.* (*of a p.*) of the sort who may be expected to make amends *or* from whom one may expect satisfaction (*partic. duelling, also fig.*).
satt [zat], *adj.* 1. satisfied, full, satiated; ***des Lärmes –,*** sick of the noise; ***sich – essen,*** eat one's fill *or* to one's heart's content; ***es (gründlich) – haben*** or ***bekommen*** or ***kriegen,*** have had enough of it, have had one's fill, get tired *or* sick of it, (*coll.*) be fed up with it, (*sl.*) have had a bellyful, be cheesed *or* brassed off; ***er hat nicht – zu essen,*** he does not get enough to eat; ***ich kann mich daran nicht – sehen,*** I cannot take my eyes off it; ***ich bin –,*** I have had sufficient (to eat); 2. (*Chem.*) saturated; 3. dark, deep, heavy, intens(iv)e, rich (*of colour*). **Satt-dampf,** *m.* saturated steam.
Satte ['zatə], *f.* (*dial.*) milk-pan *or* -bowl.
Sattel ['zatəl], *m.* **(-s,** *pl.* **⸚)** saddle (*also Geol., Geog.*), (*Mech.*) cross-beam; (*Dressm.*) yoke; bridge (*of nose*), nut (*of violin*); ***in allen Sätteln gerecht sein,*** be able to turn one's hand to anything, be good at everything; ***aus dem – heben,*** unhorse; (*fig.*) unseat, oust, supplant, supersede; ***fest im – sitzen,***

have a firm seat; (*fig.*) be firmly established, have the situation well in hand, be master of the situation.

Sattel|baum, *m.* saddle-tree. **–bekleidung,** *f.* saddle trappings. **–bock,** *m. See* **–baum. –bogen,** *m.* saddle-bow. **–dach,** *n.* span-roof, gable-roof. **–decke,** *f.* saddle-cloth. **–federn,** *f.pl.* (*Cycl.*) springs. **sattel|fertig,** *adj.* ready to mount. **–fest,** *adj.* – ***sein,*** sit one's horse well, have a good seat; (*fig.*) – ***sein in*** (*Dat.*), have (*a th.*) at one's finger-tips, be well up in (*s.th.*). **Sattel|gurt,** *m.* girth. **–holz,** *n.* transverse beam. **–kammer,** *f.* harness-room. **–kissen,** *n.* pillion. **–knecht,** *m.* groom. **–knopf,** *m.* pommel.

satteln ['zatəln], **1.** *v.t.* saddle. **2.** *v.r.* (*fig.*) make *or* get ready, prepare (*für,* for).

Sattel|pausche, *f.* cantle. **–pferd,** *n.* riding-horse; near-(side) horse (*of a team*). **–pistolen,** *f.pl.* horse-pistols. **–platz,** *m.* paddock. **–riemen,** *m.* girth leather. **–schlepper,** *m.* articulated lorry. **–seite,** *f.* near side (*of a horse*). **–stück,** *n.* saddle (*of mutton etc.*). **–stütze,** *f.* (*Cycl.*) seat-pillar. **–tasche,** *f.* saddle-bag. **–zeug,** *n.* saddle and harness, saddlery.

Sattheit ['zathaɪt], *f.* fullness, satiety; (*of colour*) fullness, richness, intensity.

sättigen ['zɛtɪgən], **1.** *v.t.* fill, satisfy, appease, satiate, sate; (*Chem.*) saturate, impregnate. **2.** *v.r.* satisfy *or* appease one's hunger. **sättigend,** *adj.* (*of food*) satisfying, nourishing, (*coll.*) filling. **Sättigung,** *f.* satisfaction, appeasement (*of hunger*); satiety, satiation; (*Chem.*) saturation, neutralization. **Sättigungspunkt,** *m.* saturation point.

Sattler ['zatlər], *m.* saddler, harness-maker. **Sattlerware,** *f.* saddlery.

sattsam ['zatza:m], *adv.* sufficiently, enough.

saturieren [zatu'ri:rən], *v.t.* saturate; satiate.

Satyr ['za:tyr], *m.* (**-s** *or* **-n,** *pl.* **-e** *or* **-n**) satyr. **satyrartig,** *adj.* satyric(al).

Satz [zats], *m.* (**-es,** *pl.* **¨-e**) 1. jump, leap, bound, vault; ***einen – machen*** or ***tun,*** (take a) jump *or* leap; 2. (*Typ.*) setting, composition; copy, matter; ***in – geben,*** send to the printer; 3. batch, lot, assortment, set, nest (*of boxes etc.*), (*Tenn.*) set; litter (*of animals*), fry (*of fish*); 4. charge, price, rate; (*coll.*) ***einen – geben,*** stand a treat; 5. stake, allocation; 6. dregs, grounds, sediment, deposit; 7. (*Gram.*) sentence, clause, period, (*Mus.*) passage, phrase, movement; 8. (*Log.*) proposition, tenet, theme, thesis, theorem, maxim, principle; ***seinen – behaupten,*** maintain one's point.

Satz|aussage, *f.* (*Gram.*) predicate. **–ball,** *m.* (*Tenn.*) set point. **–bau,** *m.*, **–bildung,** *f.* sentence structure *or* construction. **–fehler,** *m.* compositor's *or* printer's error, misprint. **–gefüge,** *n.* complex sentence. **–gegenstand,** *m.* (*Gram.*) subject. **–glied,** *n.* part of a sentence. **–kosten,** *pl.* (*Typ.*) cost of setting up. **–lehre,** *f.* syntax. **satzreif,** *adj.* ready for the press. **Satz|spiegel,** *m.* (*Typ.*) face, type area. **–teich,** *m.* breeding-pond (*for fishes*). **–teil,** *m. See* **–glied.**

Satzung ['zatsuŋ], *f.* (*Law*) statute, charter; by-law, standing rule, ordinance, precept; ***–en eines Vereins,*** articles of an association, rules of a society. **satzungs|gemäß, –mäßig,** *adj.* statutory. **–widrig,** *adj.* unconstitutional, ultra vires.

satzweise ['zatsvaɪzə], *adv.* sentence by sentence; by leaps and bounds, intermittently. **Satz|zeichen,** *n.* punctuation mark. **–zeit,** *f.* breeding *or* spawning time.

Sau [zau], *f.* 1. (-, *pl.* **¨-e**) sow (*also Metall.*), (*fig.*) filthy pig, swine, slut; 2. (-, *pl.* **-en**) wild sow; blot (*of ink*), bad blunder, howler; (*sl.*) ***es ist unter aller –,*** it stinks, it's lousy; (*sl. Mil. etc.*) ***zur – machen,*** smash up, crack open, (*fig. of a p.*) let (him) have it, do (him), give (him) the works. **Sau|arbeit,** *f.* (*coll.*) dirty *or* disgusting work, drudgery, tough job. **–beller,** *m.* boar-hound.

sauber ['zaubər], *adj.* clean; cleanly, neat, tidy; (*dial.*) pretty; (*iron.*) fine, nice, rare; ***eine –e Bescherung!*** a fine mess! a pretty kettle of fish! ***–e Abschrift,*** fair copy. **Sauberkeit,** *f.* cleanness, cleanliness, neatness, tidiness; (*fig.*) integrity.

säuberlich ['zɔybərlɪç], *adj. See* **sauber**; (*fig.*) decent, proper; careful, cautious, wary. **säubern,** *v.t.* clean, cleanse; clear (***von,*** of); clean up, tidy (*a room*); (*Pol.*) purge, (*Mil.*) mop up. **Säuberung,** *f.* cleansing, cleaning, clearing. **Säuberungsaktion,** *f.* (*Pol.*) purge, (*Mil.*) mopping-up operation.

Sau|bohne, *f.* horse-bean, vetch. **–borste,** *f.* hog's bristle.

Sauce ['zo:sə], *f. See* **Soße. Sauciere** [zosi'ɛ:rə], *f.* sauce-boat. **Saucischen** [zo'si:sçən], *n.* cocktail sausage.

saudumm ['zaudum], *adj.* (*coll.*) painfully stupid, thick-headed.

sauen ['zauən], *v.i.* 1. (*of pigs*) farrow; 2. (*fig.*) be filthy, talk smut.

sauer ['zauər], **1.** *adj.* (*comp.* ***saurer,*** *sup.* ***sauerst***) sour, acid (*also Chem.*), acrid, tart; acidulous, acetous; (*as Chem. suff.* = bi, *e.g.* ***chrom–,*** bichromate; ***schweflig–,*** bisulphide); (*fig.*) cross, morose, surly, peevish, crabbed; hard, bitter, troublesome, painful, (*coll.*) tough; ***saure Arbeit,*** hard work, grind; (*coll.*) ***in den sauren Apfel beißen,*** swallow a bitter pill; ***–er Boden,*** marshy land; ***ein saures Gesicht machen,*** pull a long face; ***saure Gurken,*** pickled cucumbers; ***ihm das Leben – machen,*** embitter his life; ***saure Miene,*** disgusted expression; ***saure Pflicht,*** painful duty; ***saure Probe,*** hard *or* difficult task, trial; ***saurer Schweiß,*** sweat of the brow. **2.** *adv.* – ***machen,*** acidify; (make) sour; ***es kommt ihn – an,*** it goes hard *or* against the grain with him, he finds it difficult *or* trying; – ***erworbenes Geld,*** money earned with the sweat of one's brow; – ***reagieren auf*** (*Acc.*), take amiss, take in bad part; – ***werden,*** turn sour, (*of milk*) curdle; ***ich lasse es mir – werden,*** I take great pains *or* a great deal of trouble (over); (*sl.*) ***ihm Saures geben,*** let him have it. **Sauer,** *n.* giblets prepared with vinegar; (*dial.*) vinegar; yeast.

Sauer|ampfer, *m.* (*Bot.*) sorrel (*Rumex acetosa*). **–braten,** *m.* stewed pickled beef. **–brunnen,** *m.* (acidulous) mineral water; chalybeate spring.

Sauerei [zauə'raɪ], *f.* beastliness, filth, smut.

Sauer|futter, *n.* ensilage. **–honig,** *m.* oxymel. **–kirsche,** *f.* (*Bot.*) morello cherry (*Prunus cerasus*). **–klee,** *m.* (*Bot.*) wood-sorrel (*Oxalis acetosella*). **–kleesalz,** *n.* salt of lemon, potassium binoxalate. **–kleesäure,** *f.* oxalic acid. **–kohl,** *m.*, **–kraut,** *n.* pickled (white) cabbage.

säuerlich ['zɔyərlɪç], *adj.* sourish, tart, (*Chem.*) acidulous, sub-acid, acetous. **Säuerling,** *m.* (**-s,** *pl.* **-e**) acidulous (medicinal) spring; sour wine.

Sauermilch ['zauərmɪlç], *f.* curdled milk.

säuern ['zɔyərn], **1.** *v.t.* make sour, (*Chem.*) acidify, acidulate, oxidize; (*Bak.*) leaven. **2.** *v.i.* turn sour, curdle.

Sauerstoff ['zauərʃtɔf], *m.* oxygen. **Sauerstoff|abgabe,** *f.* evolution of oxygen. **–apparat,** *m.* oxygen-apparatus. **–äther,** *m.* aldehyde. **–atmung,** *f.* oxygen-breathing, aerobic respiration. **–aufnahme,** *f.* oxygen absorption, oxygenation. **–entzug,** *m.* reduced oxygen supply; de-oxygenation. **–gerät,** *n. See* **–apparat. sauerstoffhaltig,** *adj.* oxygenated, oxidized. **Sauerstoff|ion,** *n.* anion. **–mangel,** *m.* oxygen starvation. **–messer,** *m.* eudiometer. **–verbindung,** *f.* oxide, oxygen compound. **–zufuhr,** *f.* oxygenation; oxygen supply.

sauersüß ['zauərzy:s], *adj.* bitter-sweet. **Sauer|teig,** *m.* leaven, yeast. **–topf,** *m.* (*coll.*) morose *or* grumpy fellow, (*sl.*) sourpuss. **sauertöpfisch,** *adj.* peevish, crabbed, cross, sullen, surly, morose.

Säuerung ['zɔyəruŋ], *f.* acidification, acidulation; oxygenation; (*Bak.*) leavening. **Säuerungsgrad,** *m.* degree of acidity.

Sauer|wasser, *n. See* **–brunnen. –wein,** *m.* verjuice.

Sauf|aus, *m.* (-, *pl.* -), **-bold,** *m.* (**-(e)s,** *pl.* **-e**) drunkard, toper, sot. **-bruder,** *m.* drinking- *or* boon-companion, crony; *see also* **-bold. saufen,** *irr.v.t., v.i.* drink (*of beasts, vulg. of men*), (*coll.*) guzzle, booze, soak, hit the bottle; ***zu – geben,*** water (*horses*); (*vulg.*) ***sich voll –,*** get boozed (up); ***– wie ein Loch,*** drink like a fish.

Säufer ['zɔyfər], *m.*, **Säuferin,** *f.* drunkard, alcoholic, dipsomaniac, (*coll.*) boozer.

Sauferei [zaufə'raı], *f.* (*vulg.*) boozing (session).

Säufer|nase, *f.* bottle-nose. **-wahnsinn,** *m.* delirium tremens, (*coll.*) the jim-jams.

Saufgelage ['zaufgəla:gə], *n.* drinking-bout, orgy, (*coll.*) binge, (*sl.*) booze-up.

Sau|fleisch, *n.* (wild) boar's meat. **-fraß,** *m.* (*vulg.*) terrible food, wretched meal.

Säugamme ['zɔykˀamə], *f.* wet-nurse.

Saugbagger ['zaukbagər], *m.* suction dredger. **saugen,** *irr.v.t., v.i.* (*an* (*Dat.*) suck; ***an sich –,*** absorb, suck up; ***in sich –,*** suck in, imbibe; (*coll.*) ***sich etwas aus den Fingern –,*** make up *or* invent s.th.; (*coll.*) ***an den Klauen –,*** be hard put to it to make ends meet. **Saugen,** *n.* suction, absorption.

säugen ['zɔygən], *v.t.* suckle, nurse, feed at the breast, give the breast to. **Säugen,** *n.* suckling, nursing, breast-feeding, (*Med.*) lactation.

Sauger ['zaugər], *m.* sucker, suction apparatus, aspirator; nipple, teat (*of feeding-bottle*).

Säuge|tier, *n.* mammal. **-zeit,** *f.* lactation period.

saugfähig ['zaukfɛ:ıç], *adj.* absorbent, absorptive. **Saug|fähigkeit,** *f.* absorptive strength. **-flasche,** *f.* feeding-bottle. **-füßchen,** *n.* (*Zool.*) sucker-foot. **-glas,** *n.* suction bottle, breast-pump. **-heber,** *m.* siphon. **-höhe,** *f.* suction-head, capillary rise. **-hub,** *m.* (*Mech.*) intake *or* induction stroke. **-klappe,** *f.* suction-valve. **-leistung,** *f.* suction (capacity). **-leitung,** *f.* suction-pipe, (*Mech.*) intake duct, induction pipe.

Säugling ['zɔyklıŋ], *m.* (**-s,** *pl.* **-e**) infant, suckling. **Säuglings|ausstattung,** *f.* layette. **-fürsorge,** *f.* infant-welfare (work). **-heim,** *n.* crèche. **-pflege,** *f.* baby-care. **-sterblichkeit,** *f.* infant mortality.

Saug|luft, *f.* (*Av.*) inflow. **-papier,** *n.* absorbent paper. **-pfropfen,** *m.* (rubber) teat, comforter, dummy. **-pumpe,** *f.* suction pump.

saugrob ['zaugro:p], *adj.* (*vulg.*) abominably rude.

Saug|rohr, *n.* suction pipe, siphon. **-rüssel,** *m.* (*Ent.*) proboscis, (*coll.*) sucker. **-ventil,** *n. See* **-klappe. -wirkung,** *f.* suction. **-wurzel,** *f.* (*Bot.*) haustorium. **-zug,** *m.* induced draught.

Sau|hatz, -hetze, *f.* boar hunt(ing). **-hirt,** *m.* swineherd.

sauigeln ['zauˀi:gəln], *v.i.* (*coll.*) talk smut.

säuisch ['zɔyıʃ], *adj.* filthy, swinish.

Sau|kerl, *m.* (*vulg.*) swine, skunk, cur. **-koben,** *m.* *See* **-stall.**

Säule ['zɔylə], *f.* column (*also Mil.*), pillar, support, pile, prop, post, upright, jamb; (*fig.*) pillar, prop, support; prism; (*Elec. etc.*) pile. **Säulenachse,** *f.* prismatic axis. **säulen|artig, -förmig,** *adj.* columnar; prismatic. **Säulen|fuß,** *m.* pedestal. **-gang,** *m.* colonnade, arcade. **-halle,** *f.* portico. **-heilige(r),** *m., f.* stylite. **-knauf, -knopf, -kopf,** *m.* (*Archit.*) capital. **-ordnung,** *f.* type of column (*Doric, Ionic etc.*). **-platte,** *f.* (*Archit.*) abacus, plinth. **-reihe,** *f.* peristyle, row of columns. **-schaft,** *m.* shaft of a column. **-ständer,** *m.* post, upright. **-weite,** *f.* separation between columns. **-wulst,** *m.* (*Archit.*) astragal.

¹**Saum** [zaum], *m.* (**-(e)s,** *pl.* **⸚e**) hem, seam; margin, border, edge, (*Weav.*) selvage, (*Archit.*) fillet, (*fig.*) brink, fringe, (*Bot., Zool.*) fimbris; ***– eines Kleides,*** hem of a dress; ***– des Waldes,*** edge *or* fringe of the forest; ***– einer Stadt,*** outskirts of a town.

²**Saum,** *m.* (**-(e)s,** *pl.* **⸚e**) (*obs.*) load, burden.

¹**säumen** ['zɔymən], *v.t.* hem, edge, border, skirt; (*fig.*) fringe, skirt.

²**säumen,** *v.t.* (*dial.*) drive (*pack animals*), convey (*goods*) by pack animals.

³**säumen,** *v.i.* linger, tarry, delay, hesitate, (*coll.*) dally, dawdle. **Säumen,** *n.* delay, hesitation, tarrying.

Saum|esel, *m.* sumpter mule. **-farn,** *m.* (*Bot.*) bracken (*Pteris aquilina*).

säumig ['zɔymıç], *adj. See* **saumselig. Säumnis,** *f.* (-, *pl.* **-se**) delay, dilatoriness; default, negligence.

Saum|pfad, *m.* mule-track. **-pferd,** *n.* pack-horse. **-sattel,** *m.* pack-saddle.

saumselig ['zaumzəlıç], *adj.* slow, tardy, dilatory, (*coll.*) dawdling; sluggish, lazy, negligent, (*coll.*) slack. **Saumseligkeit,** *f.* tardiness, dilatoriness; negligence, (*coll.*) slackness.

Saum|stich, *m.* hemming stitch. **-tier,** *n.* pack-animal, beast of burden.

Säure ['zɔyrə], *f.* acid; sourness, acidity, tartness; (*fig.*) acrimony. **Säure|äther,** *m.* ester. **-ballon,** *m.* carboy. **-batterie,** *f.* (*Elec.*) lead-acid battery. **säure|beständig,** *adj.* acid-proof. **-bildend,** *adj.* acidifying. **Säure|bildung,** *f.* acidification. **-dampf,** *m.* acid fumes. **-dichte,** *f.* specific gravity of acid. **säure|fest,** *adj. See* **-beständig. -frei,** *adj.* non-acid. **Säuregehalt,** *m.* acidity.

Sauregurkenzeit [zaurə'gurkəntsaıt], *f.* silly season.

säure|haltig, *adj.* acidiferous. **-löslich,** *adj.* acid-soluble. **Säure|messer,** *m.* acidimeter. **-rest,** *m.* acid radical. **säurewidrig,** *adj.* ant(i-)acid.

Saurier ['zauriər], *m.* saurian.

Saus [zaus], *m.* ***in – und Braus leben,*** live riotously, live on the fat of the land.

säuseln ['zɔyzəln], *v.i.* rustle, whisper, murmur, sigh.

sausen ['zauzən], *v.i.* (*aux.* h. *&* s.) rush, boil (*as water*), whistle, howl, sough (*as wind*); whistle, whiz (*as arrows*); (*coll.*) rush, dash, flit; ***mir – die Ohren, es saust mir in den Ohren,*** I have a ringing in my ears; ***es saust mir im Kopf,*** my head sings *or* buzzes. **Sausen,** *n.* rush(ing), buzz(ing), singing (*in the ears*). **Sauser,** *m.* 1. (*sl.*) pub-crawl; 2. (*Swiss*) fermented apple juice.

Sau|stall, *m.* pigsty, (*fig. coll.*) disgusting mess, piggery. **-wetter,** *n.* (*coll.*) filthy *or* beastly weather. **-wirtschaft,** *f.* (*coll.*) utter chaos, disgusting state of affairs, (*sl.*) hell of a mess. **sauwohl,** *adv.* (*sl.*) in the pink, the tops, on the top of the world.

Savanne [za'vanə], *f.* (*Geog.*) savanna(h).

Saxophon [zakso'fo:n], *n.* (**-s,** *pl.* **-e**) saxophone.

Schabbes ['ʃabəs], *m.* (-, *pl.* -) (*coll.*) (*Jew.*) Sabbath.

¹**Schabe** ['ʃa:bə], *f.* cockroach; (*dial.*) moth.

²**Schabe,** *f. See* **Schabeisen. Schabefleisch,** *n.* (*dial.*) minced meat. **Schabeisen,** *n.* grater, scraper, parer, peeler. **Schabemesser,** *n.* scraping-knife, (vegetable) peeler. **schaben,** *v.t.* scrape, grate; scratch, abrade, rasp; shave (*skins*). **Schaber,** *m. See* **Schabeisen.**

Schabernack ['ʃa:bərnak], *m.* (**-(e)s,** *pl.* **-e**) trick, hoax, prank, practical joke; ***ihm einen – spielen,*** play a practical joke on him.

schäbig ['ʃɛ:bıç], *adj.* shabby, worn(-out), threadbare, (*fig.*) shabby, mean, stingy. **Schäbigkeit,** *f.* shabbiness; meanness.

Schablone [ʃa'blo:nə], *f.* model, pattern; jig, template, templet, stencil; (*fig.*) routine; ***nach der – arbeiten,*** work mechanically *or* according to pattern *or* like a machine. **schablonenhaft, schablonenmäßig,** *adj.* stereotyped, mechanical; according to pattern. **Schablonenzeichnung,** *f.* stencil drawing. **schablon(is)ieren** [-'ni:rən (-ni'zi:rən)], *v.t.* stencil, make to pattern.

Schabmesser ['ʃa:pmɛsər], *n. See* **Schabemesser.**

Schabracke [ʃa'brakə], *f.* caparison, shabrack, saddlecloth.

Schabsel ['ʃa:psəl], *n.* shavings, scrapings, parings.

Schach [ʃax], *n.* chess; check; ***dem Könige – bieten,*** give check to the king; (*fig.*) ***ihm – bieten,*** defy him; – ***dem König!*** check! – ***(und) matt!*** checkmate! ***in*** or ***im – halten,*** keep *or* hold in check. **Schach|-aufgabe,** *f.* chess problem. **–brett,** *n.* chess-board. **schachbrettartig,** *adj.* chequered; tessellated.

Schacher [ˈʃaxər], *m.* haggling, chaffering; hawking; petty dealing(s); (political) jobbery.

Schächer [ˈʃɛçər], *m.* (*B.*) thief, robber; malefactor, felon; (*coll.*) ***armer –,*** poor wretch *or* devil.

Schacherei [ʃaxəˈraɪ], *f.* *See* **Schacher. Schacherer** [ˈʃaxərər], *m.* haggler, vendor, broker. **schachern,** *v.i.* haggle, chaffer; barter, peddle.

Schach|feld, *n.* square (*of chess-board*). **–figur,** *f.* chessman; (*fig.*) pawn. **schachmatt,** *adj.* checkmate; (*fig.*) played out, knocked out, worn-out, (*coll.*) dead-beat; – ***setzen,*** checkmate. **Schach|-meisterschaft,** *f.* chess championship. **–partie,** *f.* game of chess. **–spiel,** *n.* game of chess; chess-board and men. **–spieler,** *m.* chess-player.

Schacht [ʃaxt], *m.* **(-(e)s,** *pl.* **¨e)** shaft, well, pit; manhole; dip, depression, hollow; (*Top.*) gorge, ravine. **Schacht|abdeckung,** *f.* manhole-cover. **–arbeiter,** *m.* pitman; navvy. **–einfahrt,** *f.* pit-head.

Schachtel [ˈʃaxtəl], *f.* (**-,** *pl.* **-n**) box, case; (*coll.*) ***alte –,*** old maid, old frump. **Schachtel|deckel,** *m.* box-lid. **–halm,** *m.*, **–kraut,** *n.* (*Bot.*) horse-tail, shave-grass (*Equisetum*). **–männchen,** *n.* Jack-in-the-box. **schachteln,** *v.t.* (*coll.*) pack. **Schachtel|-satz,** *m.* (*Gram.*) involved period. **–wort,** *n.* portmanteau word.

schächten [ˈʃɛçtən], *v.t.* slaughter (*cattle according to Jewish ritual*). **Schächter,** *m.* kosher butcher.

Schacht|förderung, *f.* shaft *or* pit hauling. **–ofen,** *m.* cupola (furnace). **–turm,** *m.* pit-head derrick.

Schächtung [ˈʃɛçtuŋ], *f.* kosher butchering.

Schach|turnier, *n.* chess tournament. **–zug,** *m.* move (at chess); (*fig.*) ***geschickter –,*** clever move.

Schadchen [ˈʃaːtçən], *m. or n.* (*Jew.*) matchmaker.

schade [ˈʃaːdə], *pred.adj.* ***(es ist sehr) –,*** it is a (great) pity, it's (most) unfortunate, (*coll.*) it's too bad; ***es ist ewig –!*** it is a thousand pities! – ***um die verlorene Zeit,*** it is a pity that so much time has been lost; ***um das ist's nicht –,*** that's no (great) loss; ***wie –,*** what a pity, how unfortunate; ***zu – für,*** too good for.

Schade, *m.* *See* **Schaden.**

Schädel [ˈʃɛːdəl], *m.* skull, (*Anat.*) cranium; ***ihm den – einschlagen,*** bash his head in; ***sich*** (*Dat.*) ***den – einrennen,*** run one's head against a brick wall. **Schädel|basis,** *f.* base of the skull. **–bohrer,** *m.* trepan. **–bruch,** *m.* fracture of the skull, fractured skull. **–dach,** *n.* (*Anat.*) vault of the cranium. **–decke,** *f.* scalp. **–haut,** *f.* (*Anat.*) pericranium. **–knochen,** *m.* cranial bone. **–lehre,** *f.* phrenology, craniology. **–messung,** *f.* craniometry. **–naht,** *f.* cranial *or* coronal suture.

schaden [ˈʃaːdən], *v.i.* (*Dat.*) harm, damage, injure, hurt; prejudice, be prejudicial *or* detrimental *or* injurious to; ***das schadet nichts,*** it does not matter, no matter, never mind; ***das schadet dir nichts,*** that serves *or* will serve you right, that will teach you a lesson; ***das schadet dir nicht,*** that won't affect you, you won't suffer; ***was schadet es?*** what harm is there? what does it matter? ***was schadet es wenn . . .?*** what (does it matter) if . . .?

Schaden, *m.* **(-s,** *pl.* **¨)** damage, harm, injury (***an*** (*Dat.*), to); defect, hurt, mischief, wrong, havoc, *pl.* ravages; disadvantage, detriment, loss, prejudice (***für,*** to); – ***anrichten,*** do *or* cause damage; – ***erleiden*** or ***nehmen, zu – kommen,*** come to harm, sustain injury, suffer loss, be damaged; ***mit – verkaufen,*** sell at a loss; – ***zufügen*** (*Dat.*), cause damage to (*a th.*), do harm *or* injury to, inflict losses on (*a p.*); (*Prov.*) ***durch – wird man klug,*** a burnt child dreads the fire, once bitten twice shy; (*Prov.*) ***wer den – hat, braucht für den Spott nicht zu sorgen,*** the laugh is always on the losers.

Schaden|abschätzung, *f.* appraisal *or* estimate of damages. **–ersatz,** *m.* reparation, compensation, damages, indemnity, indemnification; – ***leisten,*** pay damages, make amends; ***auf – (ver)klagen,*** sue for damages. **–ersatzanspruch,** *m.*, **–ersatzforderung,** *f.* claim for damages, (*Law*) claim in tort. **–ersatzklage,** *f.* action for damages. **schadenersatzpflichtig,** *adj.* liable for damages. **Schaden|feststellung,** *f.* assessment of damage. **–feuer,** *n.* destructive fire. **–freude,** *f.* malicious joy *or* glee *or* pleasure, gloating. **schadenfroh,** *adj.* gloating, malicious. **Schadenrechnung,** *f.* statement of damage.

schadhaft [ˈʃaːthaft], *adj.* damaged, injured; spoilt, defective, faulty; dilapidated, in (a) bad (state of) repair, decayed. **Schadhaftigkeit,** *f.* damaged condition, defectiveness, dilapidation.

schädigen [ˈʃɛːdɪgən], *v.t.* harm, hurt, injure, damage, wrong, impair, prejudice. **Schädigung,** *f.* damage, injury (*Gen.*, to), impairment (of), detriment, prejudice (to).

schädlich [ˈʃɛːtlɪç], *adj.* (*Dat.*) detrimental, deleterious, prejudicial, disadvantageous, injurious, poisonous, noxious, harmful, pernicious, destructive, dangerous. **Schädlichkeit,** *f.* harmfulness, destructiveness, perniciousness, noxiousness.

Schädling [ˈʃɛːtlɪŋ], *m.* **(-s,** *pl.* **-e)** pest, vermin, parasite, weed, noxious plant *or* animal; vile person. **Schädlings|bekämpfung,** *f.* pest control. **–bekämpfungsmittel,** *n.* insecticide, fungicide, pesticide.

schadlos [ˈʃaːtloːs], *adj.* indemnified; – ***halten,*** indemnify, compensate; ***sich – halten,*** recoup o.s. (***an*** (*Dat.*), from). **Schadloshaltung,** *f.* indemnification, compensation.

Schaf [ʃaːf], *n.* **(-(e)s,** *pl.* **-e)** sheep, ewe; (*fig.*) dolt, simpleton, nincompoop, ninny; ***die –e von den Böcken scheiden,*** separate the sheep from the goats. **Schaf|blattern,** *pl.* chicken-pox; sheep pox, ovinia. **–bock,** *m.* ram. **–bremse,** *f.* sheep-bot(t).

Schäfchen [ˈʃɛːfçən], *n.* 1. lamb(kin); (*fig.*) ***sein – scheren*** or ***ins Trockene bringen,*** feather one's nest; 2. (*Bot.*) catkin, (*coll.*) pussy-willow; 3. (*Meteor.*) cirrus (clouds), (*coll.*) fleecy clouds, mackerel sky. **Schäfchenwolken,** *f.pl.* *See* **Schäfchen,** 3.

Schäfer [ˈʃɛːfər], *m.* shepherd; (*fig.*) amorous swain. **Schäferdichtung,** *f.* pastoral *or* bucolic poetry. **Schäferei** [–ˈraɪ], *f.* sheep-farm. **Schäfer|-gedicht,** *n.* pastoral (poem), eclogue, idyll. **–hund,** *m.* sheepdog, shepherd's dog; ***deutscher –,*** Alsatian (dog); ***schottischer –,*** collie (dog). **Schäferin,** *f.* shepherdess. **Schäfer|spiel,** *n.* pastoral play. **–stab,** *m.* shepherd's crook. **–stunde,** *f.* hour for lovers. **–welt,** *f.* Arcadia, Golden Age.

Schaff [ʃaf], *n.* **(-(e)s,** *pl.* **-e)** (*dial.*) tub, vat; (*dial.*) cupboard.

Schaf|fäule, *f.* sheep-rot. **–fell,** *n.* sheepskin, fleece.

schaffen [ˈʃafən], **1.** *irr.v.t., v.i.* create; produce, call into being, set up; ***wie geschaffen für,*** made *or* destined for; ***er ist für diesen Posten wie geschaffen,*** he is the very man for this post, he is cut out for this post. **2.** *reg.v.t.* do, accomplish; procure, provide, get, find, furnish with, let have; bring, carry, move, put, convey, transport; reach, manage, succeed, (*sl.*) make it; (*coll.*) ***er hat's geschafft,*** he has done it *or* managed it *or* has succeeded; ***einen Koffer zur Bahn –,*** convey *or* bring *or* get a trunk to the station; ***auf die Seite –,*** put aside, hide; (*fig.*) embezzle; ***ich habe nichts damit zu –,*** that is no business *or* no concern of mine, I wash my hands of it; ***sich*** (*Dat.*) ***vom Halse –,*** shake off, get rid of; ***Linderung –,*** bring relief, be soothing; ***Ordnung –,*** establish (some) order; ***Rat –,*** find a way (out), not be at a loss, know what to do; ***Vergnügen –,*** afford pleasure; ***etwas aus dem Wege –,*** move *or* get a th. out of the way, remove s.th., (*fig.*) manage (to do) s.th., cope with s.th.; ***ihn aus dem Wege*** or ***der Welt –,*** make away with *or* dispose of him. **3.** *reg.v.i.* (*dial.*) do, work, be busy, (*sl., Naut.*) eat; ***ihm zu – geben*** or ***machen,*** give *or* cause him trouble; ***mit ihm zu – haben,*** have business *or* have to do with him; ***sich*** (*Dat.*) ***zu – machen,*** occupy o.s., be busy, (*coll.*) potter about; ***das Rheuma macht mir zu –,*** I am bothered *or* troubled with rheumatism.

Schaffen, *n.* activity, work(ing); creative work, creation, production. **schaffend,** *adj.* productive, creative, working. **Schaffens|drang,** *m.* creative urge *or* impulse. **–kraft,** *f.* creative power.

Schaffer ['ʃafər], *m.* 1. hard-working man; 2. (*Naut.*) steward; 3. (*Austr.*) *see* **Schaffner. Schafferei** [–'raɪ], *f.* (*Naut.*) bread-room. **schaffig,** *adj.* (*Swiss*) busy, industrious.

Schaffleisch ['ʃa:fflaɪʃ], *n.* mutton, lamb.

Schäffler ['ʃɛflər], *m.* (*dial.*) cooper..

Schaffner ['ʃafnər], *m.* conductor (*tram etc.*), (*Railw.*) guard; (*obs.*) housekeeper, manager, steward. **Schaffnerin,** *f.* conductress; (*obs.*) housekeeper, manageress, stewardess.

Schaffung ['ʃafuŋ], *f.* production, creation; establishment, provision.

Schaf|garbe, *f.* (*Bot.*) yarrow (*Achillea millefolium*). **–haut,** *f.* sheepskin, (*Anat.*) amnion. **–herde,** *f.* flock of sheep. **–hirt,** *m.* shepherd. **–hürde,** *f.* sheep-pen, fold. **–käse,** *m.* ewe's-milk cheese. **–leder,** *n.* sheepskin; (*coll.*) ***ausreißen wie –***, make o.s. scarce. **schafledern,** *adj.* (of) sheepskin. **Schaf|milch,** *f.* ewe's milk. **–mutter,** *f.* ewe.

Schafott [ʃa'fɔt], *n.* **(-(e)s,** *pl.* **-e)** scaffold.

Schaf|pelz, *m.* sheepskin (fur); (*fig.*) ***Wolf im –***, wolf in sheep's clothing. **–pocken,** *f.pl.* sheep-pox, ovinia. **–räude,** *f.* scab. **–schere,** *f.* (pair of) sheep-shears. **–schur,** *f.* sheep-shearing. **–schweiß,** *m.* suint, yolk of wool. **–seuche,** *f.* sheep-rot.

Schafskopf ['ʃa:fskɔpf], *n.* (*coll.*) duffer, blockhead, numskull. **schafsköpfig,** *adj.* block-headed, stupid, silly.

Schaf|stall, *m.* sheep-pen, fold. **–stand,** *m.* head of sheep. **–stelze,** *f.* (*Orn.*) blue-headed (*Am.* yellow) wagtail (*Motacilla flava flava*); ***englische –***, yellow wagtail (*Motacilla flava flavissima*); ***grünköpfige –***, see –; ***nordische –***, grey wagtail (*Motacilla cinerea*).

Schaft [ʃaft], *m.* **(-(e)s,** *pl.* **⸚e)** shaft (*of spear, feather, pillar*), stock (*of a rifle*), handle, shank; leg (*of a boot*); stick; stalk, stem, trunk (*of a tree*); (*Bot., Zool.*) peduncle.

schäften ['ʃɛftən], *v.t.* fit with a stock, a handle *etc.*; (*dial.*) give the stick to, cane; (*Naut.*) splice; (*Hort.*) graft; fit new legs on (*boots*).

schaftrein ['ʃaftraɪn], *adj.* branchless, clear-boled. **Schaftreinigung,** *f.* self-pruning.

Schaf|trift, *f.* *See* **–weide.**

Schaft|rinne, *f.* fluting (*of a column*). **–stiefel,** *m.* top-boot, knee-boot.

Schaf|waschmittel, *n.* sheep-dip. **–wasser,** *n.* amniotic *or* amnionic fluid. **–weide,** *f.* sheep-run. **–wolle,** *f.* sheep's wool. **–zucht,** *f.* sheep-farming *or* rearing. **–züchter,** *m.* sheep-farmer.

Schah [ʃa:], *m.* **(-s, -s)** shah.

Schakal [ʃa'ka:l], *m.* **(-s, -e)** jackal.

Schake ['ʃa:kə], *f.* (*Naut.*) link (of chain).

Schäkel ['ʃɛ:kəl], *m.* (*Naut.*) shackle, link.

Schäker ['ʃɛ:kər], *m.* jester, wag, joker; flirt. **Schäkerei** [–'raɪ], *f.* badinage, teasing, philandering, dalliance, flirtation. **schäkerhaft,** *adj.* playful, waggish. **Schäkerin,** *f.* *see* **Schaker. schäkern,** *v.i.* jest, joke; tease; dally, flirt, philander.

Schal [ʃa:l], *m.* **(-s, -e)** shawl; scarf, muffler.

schal, *adj.* stale, flat, dull; insipid, vapid, spiritless; commonplace, trite, hackneyed.

Schalbrett ['ʃa:lbrɛt], *n.* outside plank (with bark).

Schale ['ʃa:lə], *f.* 1. skin, peel (*of fruit*), husk, hull, pod (*of vegetables*), shell (*of eggs, nuts*), cup (*of acorn*), rind, bark (*of tree*), crust, shell, carapace (*of crustacea*); peelings, parings (*from peeled vegetables*), (*fig.*) covering, shell, outside (surface), superficies; (*coll.*) ***sich in – werfen,*** don the glad rags, spruce o.s. up; 2. dish, bowl, basin, pan, tray, vessel; scale (*of a balance*); (*Mech.*) bush(ing); (*Austr.*) tea *or* coffee cup; cloven hoof; *pl.* (*Naut.*) fishes; (*B.*) ***die – seines Zornes ausgießen,*** pour out the vials of one's wrath; ***die – senkt sich zu seinen Gunsten,*** the scale tipped in his favour. **schalen,** *v.t.* plank, line with timber, revet.

schälen ['ʃɛ:lən], **1.** *v.t.* skin, pare, peel (*fruit etc.*), shell (*peas*); blanch (*almonds*); remove bark from; ***sie ist wie aus dem Ei geschält,*** she is as fresh as a daisy *or* looks spick and span. **2.** *v.r.* peel *or* scale off, exfoliate; cast one's skin *or* shell, shed the bark.

Schalen|bau(weise), (*f.*) *m.* (*Av.*) monocoque *or* stressed-skin construction. **–bretter,** *n.pl.* form-board (*for concrete*). **–frucht,** *f.* shell-fruit, caryopsis. **–gehäuse,** *n.* shell (*of snails*). **–guß,** *m.* chill-casting. **schalenhart,** *adj.* (*Metall.*) chilled. **Schalen|haut,** *f.* (*Anat.*) chorion. **–kreuz,** *n.* cup-anemometer, wind gauge. **–lack,** *m.* shellac. **–lederhaut,** *f.* *See* **–haut. –obst,** *n.* *See* **–frucht. –wild,** *n.* cloven-hoofed game.

Schälerzeugnisse ['ʃɛ:lˀɛr'tsɔyknɪsə], *pl.* prepared cereals.

Schalfrucht ['ʃa:lfruxt], *f.* *See* **Schalenfrucht.**

Schalheit ['ʃa:lhaɪt], *f.* flatness, staleness, insipidity, vapidity.

Schälhengst ['ʃɛ:lhɛŋst], *m.* stallion.

Schal|holz, *n.* timber with bark, outer planks; *see* **–brett.**

Schalk [ʃalk], *m.* **(-(e)s,** *pl.* **-e** (*dial.* **⸚e**)) (little) rascal, scoundrel, scamp, rogue, wag; ***er hat den –*** or ***ihm sitzt der – im Nacken,*** he is full of mischief; ***der – sieht*** or ***lacht ihm aus den Augen,*** there's a mischievous twinkle in his eye. **schalkhaft,** *adj.* roguish, waggish. **Schalkhaftigkeit, Schalkheit,** *f.* roguishness, mischief; (*obs.*) roguery, guile, villainy. **Schalks|knecht,** *m.* (*B.*) unfaithful servant. **–narr,** *m.* buffoon.

Schall [ʃal], *m.* **(-(e)s,** *pl.* **-e** (*Austr.*) **⸚e)** sound, ring, peal, resonance, noise; ***– dämpfen,*** muffle *or* deaden *or* damp the sound, silence; ***schneller als –***, supersonic. **Schall|aufnahme,** *f.* sound-recording. **–becken,** *n.* cymbal. **–boden,** *m.* sound(ing)-board. **–brett,** *n.* baffle. **–dämpfer,** *m.* silencer, muffler. **–deckel,** *m.* sound-board. **schalldicht,** *adj.* sound-proof. **Schalldose,** *f.* sound-box, (gramophone) pick-up.

Schallehre ['ʃalle:rə], *f.* acoustics.

schallen ['ʃalən], *reg.v.i.* (*Austr. irr.v.i.*) (*aux.* h. & s.) sound, resound, ring, peal. **schallend,** *adj.* resonant, resounding; ***–es Gelächter,*** peal(s) of laughter.

Schall|fenster, *n.* louvre-board. **–fülle,** *f.* sonority. **–geschwindigkeit,** *f.* velocity of sound. **–glas,** *n.* musical glass. **–grenze,** *f.* *See* **–mauer. –ingenieur,** *m.* sound engineer. **–mauer,** *f.* (*Av.*) sound-barrier. **–messer,** *m.* sonometer. **–meßtrupp,** *m.* (*Mil.*) sound-ranging section. **–mine,** *f.* acoustic mine. **schallnachahmend,** *adj.* onomatopoeic. **Schallnachahmung,** *f.* onomatopoeia.

Schalloch ['ʃallɔx], *n.* sound-hole (*in violins etc.*); louvre-window (*in a belfry*).

Schallplatte ['ʃalplatə], *f.* gramophone (*Am.* phonograph) record. **Schallplatten|aufnahme,** *f.* recording. **–musik,** *f.* recorded *or* (*sl.*) canned music. **–sendung, –übertragung,** *f.* (*Rad.*) record programme.

Schall|quelle, *f.* sound-source. **–raum,** *m.* sound-chamber. **–schwingung,** *f.* sound-vibration. **–stärke,** *f.* intensity of sound. **–trichter,** *m.* bell-mouth, horn, trumpet, megaphone. **–welle,** *f.* sound-wave. **–wort,** *n.* onomatopoeic word.

Schalm [ʃalm], *m.* **(-(e)s,** *pl.* **-e)** blaze, mark (*on a tree*).

Schälmaschine ['ʃɛ:lmaʃi:nə], *f.* stripping machine (*for timber*), decorticator.

Schalmei [ʃal'maɪ], *f.* (-, *pl.* **-en**) (*obs.*) (*Mus.*) shawm.

schalmen ['ʃalmən], *v.t.* blaze, mark (*a tree*).

Schalotte [ʃa'lɔtə], *f.* shallot.

Schälpflug ['ʃɛ:lpflu:k], *m.* shallow plough.

schalt [ʃalt], *see* **schelten.**

Schalt|ader, *f.* spurious vein, (*Elec.*) cross-connection. **–anlage,** *f.* switchgear. **–bild,** *n.* wiring *or* circuit *or* switching diagram. **-brett,** *n.* switchboard, control panel, (*Motor.*) dashboard, (*Av.*) instrument panel. **-dose,** *f.* switchbox, electric(-) light switch.

schalten ['ʃaltən], **1.** *v.i.* 1. direct, govern, rule; *– und walten,* manage; *ihn – und walten lassen,* let him do as he likes, give him plenty of rope; *– mit,* do as one likes with, deal with, dispose of; 2. (*Motor.*) change gear, (*Elec.*) switch; (*fig. coll.*) do some quick thinking; (*Motor.*) *hart –,* clash the gears. **2.** *v.t.* operate, actuate, control; (*Elec.*) wire, connect; switch.

Schalter ['ʃaltər], *m.* 1. sliding shutter *or* hatch; ticket *or* booking office; counter, desk, window (*at post office etc.*); 2. (*Elec.*) switch, circuit-breaker, cut-out. **Schalter|beamte(r),** *m., f.* desk- *or* counter-clerk, cashier. **-dienst,** *m.* counter-service. **-raum,** *m.* booking-hall.

schaltest ['ʃaltəst], *see* **schelten.**

Schalt|getriebe, *n.* control-gear, (*Motor.*) gearbox. **-hebel,** *m.* (*Motor.*) gear-lever, (*Elec.*) contact- *or* switch-lever.

Schaltier ['ʃa:lti:r], *n.* (*Zool.*) crustacean, testacean, shellfish.

Schalt|jahr, *n.* leap-year. **-kasten,** *m.* switch-box. **-klinke,** *f.* (*Mech.*) ratchet, pawl. **-knopf,** *m.* control button, press-button. **-kulisse,** *f.* gate of gear-shift. **-kupplung,** *f.* clutch-coupling. **-nocke,** *f.* (*Mech.*) trip-dog. **-plan,** *m.* circuit *or* wiring *or* switching diagram. **-pult,** *n.* control-panel *or* desk. **-schema,** *n.* *See* **-plan, -tafel,** *f.* *See* **-brett. -tag,** *m.* intercalary day.

Schaltung ['ʃaltuŋ], *f.* (*Elec.*) switching; circuit, connection(s), wiring; (*Motor.*) gear-changing; gear-change, gear-shift. **Schaltwort,** *n.* interpolated word.

Schalung ['ʃa:luŋ], *f.* sheathing, mould, form (*for concrete*).

Schaluppe [ʃa'lupə], *f.* sloop; longboat.

Scham [ʃa:m], *f.* 1. shame, modesty, bashfulness; *vor – erröten,* blush with shame; *vor – vergehen,* die of shame; *aller – bar,* shameless, dead to all sense of shame, past shame; 2. (*Anat.*) genitals, pudenda, private *or* privy parts; 3. (*B.*) nakedness.

Schamade [ʃa'ma:də], *f.* (*Mil.*) parley; *– schlagen* or *blasen,* sound a parley, (*fig.*) capitulate, give in.

Scham|bein, *n.* pubic bone. **-berg,** *m.* mons pubis, mons Veneris, pubes. **-bogen,** *m.* pubic arch.

schämen ['ʃɛ:mən], *v.r.* be *or* feel ashamed (*Gen., wegen, über* (*Acc.*), of); *schäme dich!* for shame! shame on you! you ought to be ashamed of yourself! *ich brauche mich deshalb* or *dessen nicht zu –,* I have no reason to be ashamed of that; *sich vor sich selbst –,* be ashamed of o.s.; *sich zu Tode –,* die of shame.

schamfilen [ʃam'fi:lən], *v.t., v.r.* (*Naut.*) chafe (*of ropes*).

Scham|gefühl, *n.* sense of shame, modesty. **-gegend,** *f.* pubic region. **-haare,** *n.pl.* pubic hair. **schamhaft,** *adj.* modest, bashful, coy, prim, prudish, shamefaced; chaste. **Schamhaftigkeit,** *f.* modesty, bashfulness, coyness, primness, prudishness, shamefacedness; chastity.

schämig ['ʃɛmıç], *adj.* (*dial.*) *see* **schamhaft.**

Scham|kapsel, *f.* (*Hist.*) codpiece. **-lippen,** *f.pl.* vulva. **schamlos,** *adj.* shameless, impudent, brazen. **Schamlosigkeit,** *f.* shamelessness, impudence.

Schamotte [ʃa'mɔtə], *f.* fire-clay. **Schamotten|-stein, -ziegel,** *m.* fire-brick.

schampunieren [ʃampu'ni:rən], *v.t.* shampoo.

Schampus ['ʃampus], *m.* (*coll.*) champagne.

schamrot ['ʃa:mro:t], *adj.* blushing, red with shame; *– machen,* put to the blush; *– werden,* blush (with shame). **Scham|röte,** *f.* blush. **-teile,** *n.pl.* genitals, pudenda, private *or* privy parts.

schandbar ['ʃantba:r], *adj.* *See* **schändlich. Schand|brief,** *m.* slanderous letter. **-bube,** *m.* villain, scoundrel.

Schande ['ʃandə], *f.* shame, disgrace, dishonour, discredit, infamy, ignominy; *– auf sich laden,* bring disgrace *or* dishonour upon o.s.; *ihm – machen,* be a disgrace to him, bring disgrace *or* discredit upon him; *mit Schimpf und –,* in disgrace, with ignominy; *Schmach und –,* shame and dishonour; *– über dich!* shame on you! *zu meiner – muß ich bekennen,* I am ashamed to acknowledge.

schänden ['ʃɛndən], *v.t.* violate, rape, ravish (*a girl*); profane, desecrate (*a holy place*), defame, disgrace, dishonour, revile; disfigure, deface, sully, soil.

schande(n)halber ['ʃandə(n)halbər], *adv.* (*dial.*) for decency's sake, for the sake of appearances. **Schänder,** *m.* ravisher, violator, profaner, desecrator; slanderer, traducer; blasphemer; *der – meiner Ehre,* the defiler of my honour.

Schand|fleck, *m.* blemish, blot, stain, disgrace; eyesore. **-geld,** *n.* scandalous price, ridiculous(ly low) sum; *für ein –,* dirt-cheap, for a (mere) song.

schändlich ['ʃɛntlıç], **1.** *adj.* shameful, disgraceful, infamous, abominable, foul, despicable, vile, base. **2.** *adv.* (*coll.*) extremely, intensely, dreadfully, infernally, awfully. **Schändlichkeit,** *f.* infamy, ignominy, disgrace; baseness, disgraceful act *or* conduct.

Schand|lied, *n.* infamous *or* obscene song. **-mal,** *n.* (**-s,** *pl.* **-e** *or* **⸚er**) brand (of infamy), stigma. **-maul,** *n.* evil *or* slanderous tongue; scandal-monger, backbiter, slanderer. **-pfahl,** *m.* pillory. **-preis,** *m.* *See* **-geld. -schrift,** *f.* libel, lampoon. **-tat,** *f.* foul deed *or* crime; (*hum.*) *er ist zu jeder – bereit,* he's a good sport, he's game for anything.

Schändung ['ʃɛnduŋ], *f.* violation, rape; desecration, profanation; despoilment, disfigurement.

Schank [ʃaŋk], *m.* sale of liquor. **Schankbier,** *n.* draught beer.

Schanker ['ʃaŋkər], *m.* (*Med.*) chancre.

Schank|gerechtigkeit, *f.* licence to sell intoxicants. **-gesetz,** *n.* licensing act. **-mädchen,** *n.* barmaid. **-stätte,** *f.* licensed premises, public house. **-stube,** *f.* tap room, bar parlour. **-tisch,** *m.* bar. **-wirt,** *m.* publican. **-wirtschaft,** *f.* *See* **-stätte.**

Schanz|arbeiten, *f.pl.* *See* **-bau. -arbeiter,** *m.* sapper. **-bau,** *m.* fortifications, field-works, entrenchment.

Schanze ['ʃantsə], *f.* 1. (*Mil.*) entrenchment, redoubt, field-works; (*fig.*) *in die – schlagen,* stake, risk, hazard; 2. (*Naut.*) quarter-deck; 3. ski-jump. **schanzen,** *v.i.* throw up entrenchments, entrench, (*coll.*) dig in; (*fig. coll.*) slave, slog, work like a navvy. **Schanzentisch,** *m.* (*ski-ing*) jump-off platform.

Schanz|gerät, *n.* entrenching tools. **-korb,** *m.* (*Hist.*) gabion. **-pfahl,** *m.* palisade. **-wehr,** *f.* bulwark. **-werk,** *n.* entrenchment. **-zeug,** *n.* *See* **-gerät.**

Schar [ʃa:r], *f.* (-, *pl.* **-en**) 1. troop, band, group, (*coll.*) bunch, party, gang; (*Nat. Soc.*) squad, platoon; crowd, horde, multitude, (*of birds*) flight, flock, (*partridges etc.*) covey; 2. ploughshare.

Scharade [ʃa'ra:də], *f.* charade.

Scharbe ['ʃarbə], *f.* *See* **Kormoran.**

scharben ['ʃarbən], **schärben,** *v.t.* (*dial.*) (*Cul.*) cut into strips.

Scharbock ['ʃa:rbɔk], *m.* (*obs.*) scurvy. **Scharbockskraut,** *n.* (*Bot.*) figwort.

scharen ['ʃa:rən], *v.t.* assemble, gather, collect, congregate; *sich – um,* flock (a)round; *– um sich,* rally (round).

Schären ['ʃɛ:rən], *f. pl.* cliffs, rocky promontories.

scharenweise ['ʃa:rənvaızə], *adv.* in bands *or* groups *or* hordes *or* crowds.

scharf [ʃarf], **1.** *adj.* (*comp.* *schärfer, sup.* *schärfst*) sharp, keen, sharp-edged (*knife*); sharp, pointed, acute (*corner*); caustic, corrosive, mordant (*acid*); sharp, harsh, pungent, acrid (*taste, smell*), piquant, hot (*as food*); piercing, shrill, strident (*sound*); (*fig.*) biting, cutting, slashing, caustic, trenchant (*as criticism*), precise, exact, abrupt, sharp (*of behaviour*), (*Phot., Opt.*) sharply-defined, (well-) focussed; well-defined, pronounced, salient (*as outlines*), strict, severe, rigorous, drastic (*of treat-*

ment); (*Mil.*) live (*ammunition*), primed, armed (*bomb*).
(a) (*with nouns*) *-e Antwort,* cutting reply; *-er Beobachter,* keen observer; *-er Blick,* keen eye; *eine -e Brille,* strong spectacles; *-e Flüssigkeit,* corrosive liquid; *-er Gegensatz,* sharp contrast; *-es Gehör,* sharp *or* quick ears, acute hearing; *-e Kälte,* biting *or* bitter cold; *-er Kampf,* hotly-contested battle; *-e Konkurrenz,* keen *or* (*coll.*) cut-throat competition; *-e Kurve,* sharp bend; *-e Linien,* well-defined lines; *-e Luft,* keen air; *-e Stimme,* strident voice; *-es Tempo,* sharp pace; *-e Umrisse,* clear outlines; *-e Untersuchung,* strict *or* searching examination; *-es Urteil,* keen judgement; *-er Verstand,* keen intelligence, penetrating mind; *-er Widerstand,* bitter resistance; *-er Wind,* keen *or* biting *or* cutting wind; *-e Zucht,* stern *or* rigid *or* iron discipline; *-e Zucht halten,* rule with a rod of iron; *-e Züge,* sharp-cut features; *-e Zunge,* sharp tongue.
(b) (*with sein*) (*coll.*) *– sein auf* (*Acc.*), be (very) keen on; (*coll.*) *hinter dem Gelde – her sein,* have an eye to the main chance.
2. *adv.* (*fig.*) *ihn – anfassen,* deal strictly with him; *– ansehen,* look at hard *or* closely; *– aufpassen,* pay close attention, (*coll.*) prick up one's ears; be on the alert, (*coll.*) watch *or* look out; *– auswirken,* have a telling effect; *– im Auge behalten,* keep a sharp *or* close watch on; *– beschlagen,* rough-shoe (*a horse*); *– betonen,* emphasize strongly; *– bewachen,* keep close guard on, guard closely; *– einstellen,* (bring into) focus; *– entgegentreten,* oppose vigorously; *– ins Auge fassen,* look straight in the face; (*coll.*) *– ins Zeug gehen,* not pull one's punches, (*sl.*) come it strong; *ihm – zu Leibe gehen,* press him hard; *– geladen haben,* be loaded with live ammunition; *– machen,* prime, arm; fuse (*explosives*), activate (*a fuse*); (*Prov.*) *allzu – macht schartig,* a bow long bent at last grows weak; *– nachdenken,* consider closely; *– reiten,* ride hard; *– schießen,* fire *or* shoot with live ammunition; *– verurteilen,* condemn strongly *or* roundly; *– vorgehen,* take vigorous steps *or* energetic measures; *sich – wenden gegen,* take strong issue with.

Scharf, *n.* (**-(e)s,** *pl.* **-e**) tapered *or* pointed end.

Scharf|abstimmung, *f.* (*Rad.*) fine tuning. **–blick,** *m.* piercing look, penetrating glance; (*fig.*) quick eye, acuteness, perspicacity. **scharf|blickend,** *adj.* *See* **–sichtig.**

Schärfe ['ʃɛrfə], *f.* sharpness, keenness, edge (*of knife*); (*fig.*) keenness, acuteness; trenchancy, point; pungency, piquancy; severity, harshness, rigour, stringency, acrimony; (*Opt.*) definition (*of image*), resolving power (*of lens*); (*fig.*) *– verleihen* (*Dat.*), give an edge (to); (*fig.*) *die – nehmen* (*Dat.*), take the edge off.

scharfeckig ['ʃarfˀɛkɪç], *adj.* sharp-cornered, acute-angled. **Scharfeinstellung,** *f.* (*Opt.*) focus-control; sharp focussing.

schärfen ['ʃɛrfən], *v.t.* sharpen, whet, grind, put an edge on (*knife*), strop, set (*razor*); prime, arm (*bomb*); (*fig.*) intensify, increase, heighten; aggravate; strengthen (*memory*); *ihm das Gewissen –,* appeal to his conscience; *ihm den Blick –,* widen his horizon, open his eyes. **Schärfentiefe,** *f.* depth of focus.

scharf|kantig, *adj.* sharp-edged, sharp-cornered; (*Phot.*) sharply defined. **–machen,** *v.t.* **1.** *See scharf machen*; **2.** (*fig.*) instigate; *mich gegen ihn –,* set me against him. **Scharf|macher,** *m.* agitator, firebrand. **–macherei,** *f.* (political) agitation. **scharf|randig,** *adj.* *See* **–kantig. Scharf|richter,** *m.* executioner, hangman. **–schießen,** *n.* firing with live ammunition. **–schütze,** *m.* marksman, (*coll.*) crack shot; (*Mil.*) sharpshooter, sniper. **–schützenfeuer,** *n.* (*Mil.*) accurate *or* independent rifle fire. **–sicht,** *f.* keen *or* sharp-sightedness; (*fig.*) clear-sightedness, penetration, perspicacity. **scharfsichtig,** *adj.* keen *or* sharp-sighted, (*fig.*) clear-sighted, penetrating, perspicacious. **Scharfsinn,** *n.* sagacity, discernment, acuteness, acumen, shrewdness, penetration. **scharfsinnig,** *adj.* sharp-witted, shrewd, penetrating, discerning, subtle, sagacious. **Scharf|sinnigkeit,** *f.* *See* **–sinn. scharf|umrissen,** *adj.* clear-cut. **–winkelig,** *adj.* acute-angled.

Scharlach ['ʃarlax], **1.** *m.* scarlet. **2.** *m. or n.* *See* **Scharlachfieber. Scharlachexanthem,** *n.* scarlet-fever rash. **scharlach|farben, –farbig,** *adj.* *See* **–rot. Scharlachfieber,** *n.* scarlet-fever; scarlatina. **scharlachrot,** *adj.* scarlet, vermilion.

Scharlatan ['ʃarlatan], *m.* (**-s,** *pl.* **-e**) charlatan; mountebank; quack (doctor). **Scharlatanerie,** [-ə'ri:] *f.* charlatanism, quackery.

Scharm [ʃarm], *m.* charm. **scharmant** [–'mant], *adj.* charming, engaging, endearing. **scharmieren,** *v.t., v.i.* (*obs.*) charm, (be) endear(ing).

Scharmützel [ʃar'mytsəl], *n.* skirmish. **scharmützeln,** *v.i.* skirmish.

Scharnier [ʃar'ni:r], *n.* (**-s,** *pl.* **-e**) hinge, joint. **Scharnier|deckel,** *m.* hinged lid. **–gelenk,** *n.* rule-joint; (*Anat.*) hinge-like joint. **–stift,** *m.* hinge-pin. **–ventil,** *n.* flap valve.

Schärpe ['ʃɛrpə], *f.* scarf, sash; sling.

Scharpie [ʃar'pi:], *f.* (*Med.*) lint.

Scharre ['ʃarə], *f.* rake, raker, scraper. **Scharreisen,** *n.* scraper. **scharren,** *v.t., v.i.* scrape, scratch; rake; paw (*of horses*); shuffle the feet. **Scharrfuß,** *m.* claw of gallinaceous birds; digging claw, (*fig.*) obsequious bow.

Scharte ['ʃartə], *f.* notch, nick, slot; gap, crack, fissure, dent, indentation; (*Mil.*) loophole, embrasure; *eine – auswetzen,* wipe out a disgrace, make amends (for), (*coll.*) make up (for), make good (*a mistake etc.*).

Scharteke [ʃar'te:kə], *f.* (trashy) old book; trash, junk; old frump.

schartig ['ʃartɪç], *adj.* jagged, notched, dented.

Scharwenzel [ʃar'vɛntsəl], *m.* knave (*at cards*); busybody, toady. **scharwenzeln,** *v.i.* bow and scrape; toady, fawn; dance attendance (*um,* (up)on).

schassen ['ʃasən], *v.t.* (*obs.*) expel (*from school etc.*).

Schatten ['ʃatən], *m.* shadow, shade; (*Poet.*) phantom, spirit; *in den – stellen,* place in the shade, (*fig.*) put into the shade, eclipse, push into the background; *er macht mir –,* he stands in my light. **schatten,** *v.i.* (*obs.*) throw a shadow, afford shade.

Schatten|bild, *n.* silhouette, outline; (*fig.*) phantom. **–blume,** *f.* (*Bot.*) bifoliate lily of the valley (*Maianthemum bifolium*). **–dasein,** *n.* unreal *or* shadowy existence. **schattenhaft,** *adj.* shadowy, indistinct; ghostly, unreal. **Schatten|industrie,** *f.* shadow factories. **–land,** *n.* the hereafter, realm of shades, Hades, the Underworld. **schattenlos,** *adj.* without shadow; shadeless. **Schatten|pflanze,** *f.* heliophobous plant. **–reich,** *n.* *See* **–land. schattenreich,** *adj.* shady, umbrageous. **Schatten|riß,** *m.* silhouette; outline. **–seite,** *f.* shady side, side in shadow; (*fig.*) dark *or* seamy side; drawback. **schattenspendend,** *adj.* throwing a shadow, shady. **Schatten|spiel,** *n.* shadow-play, (*fig.*) phantasmagoria.

schattieren [ʃa'ti:rən], *v.t.* shade (*of colours etc.*); tint; hatch (*maps*). **Schattierung,** *f.* gradation of colour, shading; hatching (*maps*); shade, tint, hue; *in allen –en,* in all shades.

schattig ['ʃatɪç], *adj.* shady, shaded.

Schatulle [ʃa'tulə], *f.* cash box, strong-box; casket, jewel case; privy purse (*of a prince*).

Schatz [ʃats], *m.* (**-es,** *pl.* **⸚e**) **1.** treasure, (*fig.*) wealth, (rich) store (*an* (*Dat.*), of); **2.** (*coll.*) sweetheart, love, darling. **Schatz|amt,** *n.* treasury, exchequer. **–anweisung,** *f.* exchequer bond.

schätzbar ['ʃɛtsba:r], *adj.* assessable; estimable, valuable, precious. **Schätzbarkeit,** *f.* assessability; value.

Schätzchen ['ʃɛtsçən], *n.* *See* **Schatz, 2.**

schatzen ['ʃatsən], *v.t.* (*dial.*) tax, impose tax *or* fine on.

schätzen ['ʃɛtsən], *v.t.* **1.** value, appraise, estimate, assess (*auf* (*Acc.*), at), compute, rate, price (at), (*coll.*) reckon, consider (to be); ***es sich*** (*Dat.*) ***zur Ehre –***, esteem it an honour; ***sich glücklich –***, consider o.s. fortunate, be delighted; ***wie alt – Sie ihn?*** how old do you suppose he is? 2. appreciate, esteem, think highly of, respect, set great store by, prize; ***zu hoch –***, overrate, overestimate; ***ich schätze das gar nicht,*** I don't like that at all. **schätzenswert,** *adj.* estimable, valuable, precious. **Schätzer,** *m.* (expert) valuer, (*Insur.*) adjuster.

Schatz|gräber, *m.* treasure-seeker. **–kammer,** *f.* treasury (vault); – ***der Natur,*** nature's rich storehouse; *see* **–amt. –kanzler,** *m.* Chancellor of the Exchequer, (*Am.*) Secretary of the Treasury. **–kästlein,** *n.* (*fig.*) collection of gems, treasury (*as title of anthology*). **–meister,** *m.* treasurer (*of a society*). **schatzpflichtig,** *adj.* taxable, rateable. **Schatzschein,** *m.* treasury *or* exchequer bond.

Schatzung ['ʃatsuŋ], *f.* taxation.

Schätzung ['ʃɛtsuŋ], *f.* 1. (e)valuation, assessment, estimation, computation, appraisal; 2. (*for taxation*) assessment, assessed valuation; estimate; 3. (*fig.*) appreciation, estimation, esteem, high opinion. **Schätzungsfehler,** *m.* computing error. **schätzungsweise,** *adv.* at a rough estimate, approximately, (*coll.*) roughly. **Schätzungswert,** *m.* estimated *or* assessed value.

Schatz|wechsel, *m. See* **–schein.**

Schau [ʃau], *f.* (-, *pl.* **-en**) sight, view; inspection, (*Mil.*) review; display, show, spectacle, exhibition; ***nur zur –***, only for show; ***zur – stehen,*** be on display *or* show; ***zur – stellen,*** exhibit, (put on) display *or* show; ***zur – tragen,*** (make) display (of), parade, flaunt.

Schaub [ʃaup], *m.* **(-(e)s,** *pl.* **-e** (*Austr.* **¨-e**)) (*dial.*) bundle of straw, sheaf.

Schaube ['ʃaubə], *f.* (*Hist.*) long cloak *or* mantle open in front.

Schaubendach ['ʃaubəndax], *n.* (*dial.*) thatched roof.

Schau|bild, *n.* diagram, chart, graph. **–brot,** *n.* (*Jew.*) shewbread. **–bude,** *f.* booth, stall (*at fair*). **–bühne,** *f.* stage, theatre.

Schauder ['ʃaudər], *m.* shuddering, shivering; shudder, tremor; (*fig.*) horror, terror, fright; (*Poet.*) awe; ***– erregen (in*** (*Dat.*), ***bei***), make (*a p.'s*) flesh creep. **schauderbar** (*coll.*), **schaudererregend, schauderhaft,** *adj.* horrible, frightful, terrible, dreadful, (*coll.*) awful; horrifying, atrocious. **schaudern,** *v.i.* (*aux.* h. & s.) *v.imp.* shudder, shiver (***vor*** (*Dat.*), at), feel dread, be awed; ***mir*** or ***mich schaudert bei dem Gedanken,*** I shudder *or* my flesh creeps at the thought; ***vor Kälte –***, shiver with cold.

schauen ['ʃauən], (*coll. in Southern dial., otherwise elev. style*) **1.** *v.t.* see, perceive, behold, view. **2.** *v.i.* look, gaze; – ***auf*** (*Acc.*), look *or* gaze at; (*fig.*) look up to, look upon; (*coll.*) ***schau mal!*** I say! well I never! what do you know! (*coll.*) ***schau mal her!*** just look at this! (*coll.*) ***schau, daß du wegkommst!*** be off with you! (*coll.*) ***schau, daß du dich nicht verirrst!*** see (to it) that *or* mind you don't get lost!

[1]**Schauer** ['ʃauər], *m.* 1. shower, (*dial.*) hail; 2. shudder, thrill, shiver, spasm, fit, attack, paroxysm; *see* **Schauder.**

[2]**Schauer,** *m. or n.* (*dial.*) shed, shelter, barn; ***unter – gehen,*** take shelter.

Schauerdrama ['ʃauərdrama], *n.* blood-and-thunder melodrama. **schauerlich,** *adj.* horrible, ghastly, gruesome, terrible, (*coll.*) horrid, awful.

Schauermann ['ʃauərman], *m.* (*pl.* **-leute**) docker, dock labourer, stevedore, (*Am.*) longshoreman.

schauern ['ʃauərn], *v.i.* 1. *See* **schaudern**; 2. (*dial.*) hail. **Schauerroman,** *m.* thriller, shocker, penny-dreadful.

Schaufel ['ʃaufəl], *f.* (-, *pl.* **-n**) shovel, scoop; paddle, (*of turbine*) blade, vane, (*of anchor*) fluke, (*of antlers*) palm; ***zwei –n Kohlen,*** two shovel(ful)s of coal. **Schaufel|bagger,** *m.* shovel-dredger. **–geweih,** *n.* palmed antlers. **–hirsch,** *m.* fallow deer over two years. **schaufeln,** *v.t., v.i.* shovel, dig. **Schaufelrad,** *n.* paddle-wheel. **schaufelweise,** *adv.* by the shovelful. **Schaufelzahn,** *m.* broad incisor.

Schaufenster ['ʃaufenstər], *n.* shop-window, show-case. **Schaufenster|auslage,** *f.* window display. **–bummel,** *m.* window-shopping. **–dekorateur,** *m. See* **–gestalter. –dekoration,** *f. See* **–gestaltung. –einbruch,** *m.* smash-and-grab raid. **–gestalter,** *m.* window-dresser. **–gestaltung,** *f.* window-dressing.

Schaufler ['ʃauflər], *m. See* **Schaufelhirsch.**

Schau|fliegen, *n.*, **–flug,** *m.* air-display, aerial pageant. **–gerüst,** *n.* stage; grandstand. **–haus,** *n.* morgue, mortuary. **–kampf,** *m.* (*Boxing etc.*) exhibition bout. **–kasten,** *m.* show-case.

Schaukel ['ʃaukəl], *f.* (-, *pl.* **-n**) swing. **Schaukelbrett,** *n.* seesaw. **Schaukelei** [–'laɪ], *f.* rolling and pitching, pitching and tossing. **schaukeln, 1.** *v.i.* swing, rock, sway, seesaw, (*Naut.*) roll. **2.** *v.t.* 1. swing, rock; 2. (*sl.*) swing, wangle. **Schaukel|pferd,** *n.* rocking-horse. **–stuhl,** *m.* rocking-chair, rocker.

Schau|klappe, *f.* inspection flap *or* door. **–linie,** *f.* graph, curve, characteristic. **–loch,** *n.* peep-hole. **–lust,** *f.* curiosity. **schaulustig,** *adj.* curious. **Schaulustige(r),** *m., f.* sightseer, onlooker, bystander.

Schaum [ʃaum], *m.* **(-(e)s,** *pl.* **¨-e)** foam, spray, spume (*also Med.*), (*as on beer*) froth, head, (*of soap*) lather, bubbles; (*Tech.*) scum, skimmings; ***zu – schlagen,*** beat up, whip, whisk; (*Prov.*) ***Träume sind Schäume,*** dreams are like bubbles. **Schaum|bad,** *n.* bubble-bath. **–beton,** *m.* aero-concrete. **–blase,** *f.* bubble; (*fig.*) delusion, airy nothings.

schäumen ['ʃɔymən], **1.** *v.i.* foam, froth, (*of soap*) lather; (*of drinks*) effervesce, sparkle, (*coll.*) fizz; ***vor Wut –***, foam *or* boil with rage. **2.** *v.t.* skim. **schäumend,** *adj.* foaming, frothy; (*of drinks*) effervescent, (*coll.*) fizzy, (*wine*) sparkling.

Schaum|gebäck, *n.* meringue(s). **–gold,** *n.* tinsel. **–gummi,** *n.* foam- *or* sponge-rubber. **–haube,** *f.* (*Brew.*) head. **schaumig,** *adj.* foaming, frothy. **Schaum|kelle,** *f.* skimming-ladle. **–kraut,** *n.* (*Bot.*) cardamine (*Cardamine pratensis*). **–krone,** *f.* white crest (*of waves*), white horses. **–löffel,** *m.* *See* **–kelle. schaumlos,** *adj.* without foam *or* froth; without a head, flat (*of beer*). **Schaum|schläger,** *m.* egg-whisk; (*fig.*) wind-bag, gas-bag. **–schlägerei,** *f.* (*fig.*) empty talk, hot air, humbug. **–stand,** *m. See* **–haube.**

Schaumünze ['ʃaumyntsə], *f.* (commemorative) medal, medallion.

Schaum|wein, *m.* sparkling wine; champagne, (*coll.*) bubbly. **–zirpe,** *f.* (*Ent.*) froghopper (*Aphrophora*).

Schau|packung, *f.* dummy (package). **–platz,** *m.* scene (of action), theatre (*of war*), arena. **–prozeß,** *m.* (*Law*) propaganda *or* show trial.

schaurig ['ʃaurɪç], *adj.* horrible, (*coll.*) horrid, frightening, hair-raising, weird.

Schauspiel ['ʃauʃpi:l], *n.* sight, spectacle, (*Theat.*) drama, (stage-)play; ***ein trauriges –***, a sorry sight. **Schauspiel|dichter,** *m.* dramatist, playwright. **–dichtung,** *f.* drama, dramatic poetry. **Schauspieler,** *m.* actor, performer, player; (*fig.*) play-actor; *pl.* the cast. **Schauspielerei,** *f.* play-acting, affectation. **Schauspielerin,** *f.* actress. **schauspielerisch,** *adj.* theatrical, histrionic. **schauspielern,** *v.t., v.i.* act a part, put on an act, play-act, feign, sham, (*coll.*) put (it) on. **Schauspiel|haus,** *n.* theatre, playhouse. **–kunst,** *f.* dramatic art, the drama.

Schau|steller, *m.* showman, exhibitor. **–stellung,** *f.* show, exhibition. **–stück,** *n.* show-piece, exhibit, (fine) specimen, (*Theat.*) lavish stage spectacle. **–tafel,** *f. See* **–bild.**

Schaute ['ʃautə], *m.* **(-n,** *pl.* **-n)** (*sl.*) fool.

Schauturnen ['ʃauturnən], *n.* acrobatic display.

Schawatte [ʃa'vatə], *f.* bed-plate, anvil block.

[1]**Scheck** [ʃɛk], *m.* **(-en,** *pl.* **-en)** *see* **Schecke.**

[2]**Scheck,** *m.* **(-s,** *pl.* **-e** *or* **-s)** cheque, (*Am.*) check (*auf* or *über* (*Acc.*), for). **Scheckbuch,** *n.* cheque-book.

Schecke [ˈʃɛkə], *f.* piebald *or* dappled animal. **Scheckenbildung,** *f.* piebald spotting, partial albinism.

Scheck|fähigkeit, *f.* acceptability as holder of a current account. **-formular,** *n.* blank cheque.

scheckig [ˈʃɛkɪç], *adj.* spotted, speckled, mottled, brindled, (*of animals*) dappled, piebald; (*coll.*) ***sich – lachen,*** split one's sides with laughing.

Scheck|inhaber, *m.* bearer. **-konto,** *n.* current *or* (*Am.*) checking account. **-verkehr,** *m.* cheque transactions. **-zahlung,** *f.* payment by cheque.

scheel [ʃe:l], *adj.* envious; (*dial.*) cross-eyed, squinting; ***– zu etwas sehen, etwas mit -en Augen ansehen,*** look askance at. **scheel|äugig,** *adj.* cross-eyed, squinting; (*fig.*) *see* **-süchtig. -süchtig,** *adj.* envious, jealous.

Scheffel [ˈʃɛfəl], *m.* bushel. **scheffeln, 1.** *v.t.* (*coll.*) heap up, rake in; measure by the bushel. **2.** *v.i.* yield in abundance. **scheffelweise,** *adv.* by the bushel; abundantly.

Scheg [ʃe:k], *m.* **(-(e)s,** *pl.* **-e)** (*Naut.*) foremost part of the cutwater; ***– des Steuers,*** after-piece of the rudder.

Scheibe [ˈʃaɪbə], *f.* disk, (*Tech.*) disc, washer, gasket, round plate, (*Astr.*) orb; slice (*of bread etc.*); pane (*of glass*); (honey)comb; target; face (*of a clock etc.*); card (*of compass*), dial (*of telephone*); quoit, (*hockey*) puck; pulley, wheel, potter's wheel, sheave (*of a block*); coil (*of rope*); (*coll.*) ***du kannst dir (bei ihm) eine – abschneiden,*** you can take a leaf out of (his *etc.*) book, you can learn a lot from (him *etc.*); (*fig.*) ***an der – vorbeischießen,*** miss the mark; (*vulg.*) ***ja –!*** for crying out loud! bulsh!

scheiben [ˈʃaɪbən], *v.i.* (*dial.*) *see* **schieben.**

Scheiben|blei, *n.* glazier's lead. **-(elektrisier)-maschine,** *f.* (*Elec.*) Wimshurst machine. **scheibenförmig,** *adj.* disk-shaped. **Scheiben|gardinen,** *f.pl.* casement-curtains. **-glas,** *n.* plate-glass, window glass. **-honig,** *m.* honey in the comb. **-könig,** *m.* champion shot. **-kupplung,** *f.* (*Motor.*) disc- *or* plate-clutch. **-schießen,** *n.* target practice. **-spule,** *f.* flanged spool. **-stand,** *m.* (rifle) butts, firing-range. **scheibenweise,** *adv.* in slices. **Scheiben|werfen,** *n.* quoit-throwing. **-wischer,** *m.* (*Motor.*) windscreen- *or* (*Am.*) windshield-wiper.

Scheich [ʃaɪç], *m.* **(-s,** *pl.* **-e)** sheik.

Scheide [ˈʃaɪdə], *f.* **1.** boundary, border(line), limit, divide, parting; **2.** case, sheath (*also Bot.*), scabbard; **3.** (*Anat.*) vagina. **Scheide|anstalt,** *f.* refinery. **-bad,** *n.* (*Chem.*) separating bath. **-bank,** *f.* (*ore*) sorting table. **-brief,** *m.* farewell letter; (*Law*) bill of divorce. **-erz,** *n.* picked *or* screened ore. **-feuer,** *n.* refining furnace. **-gruß,** *m.* farewell. **-kunst,** *f.* (*obs.*) analytical chemistry. **-linie,** *f.* line of demarcation, separating line. **-mauer,** *f.* partition (wall). **-münze,** *f.* small coin, (small) change.

scheiden [ˈʃaɪdən], **1.** *irr.v.i.* (*aux.* s.), *v.r.* separate, part; depart, go away, leave, take leave of each other; (*fig.*) ***hier – sich die Wege,*** here the roads part; ***aus dem Dienst –,*** resign, retire from service; ***aus dem Leben –,*** depart this life; ***aus der Firma –,*** leave the firm. **2.** *irr.v.t.* **1.** separate, divide, (*ore etc.*) pick, sort, sift; part, sever, (*Law*) divorce (*persons*), dissolve (*a marriage*); ***sich – lassen,*** sue for *or* seek a divorce; ***geschieden werden,*** be granted *or* obtain a judicial separation, get divorced; (*fig.*) ***wir sind geschiedene Leute,*** we have nothing more to do with one another; **2.** (*Chem.*) analyse, refine, clarify; **3.** decompose, defecate. **Scheiden,** *n.* parting, separation; ***vor seinem –,*** before leaving; previous to his departure *or* death.

scheidend [ˈʃaɪdənt], *adj.* parting, farewell; ***das -e Jahr,*** the closing year.

Scheiden|entzündung, *f.* (*Med.*) vaginitis. **-spekulum,** *n.*, **-spiegel,** *m.* (*Med.*) vaginal speculum. **-vorfall,** *m.* (*Med.*) vaginal prolapsus.

Scheide|punkt, *m.* point of separation *or* divergence. **-stunde,** *f.* hour of parting *or* death. **-wand,** *f.* partition (wall), dividing wall; (*Anat.*) septum; (*Naut.*) bulkhead; (*fig.*) barrier. **-wasser,** *n.* (*Chem.*) aqua fortis, nitric acid. **-weg,** *m.* crossroads, forked road; ***am – stehen,*** stand at the parting of the ways *or* at the crossroads; be in a quandary *or* dilemma.

Scheiding [ˈʃaɪdɪŋ], *m.* (*obs.*) September.

Scheidung [ˈʃaɪdʊŋ], *f.* **1.** separation, parting; (*Law*) divorce (*of people*), dissolution (*of a marriage*); ***– von Tisch und Bett,*** judicial separation; ***auf – klagen,*** sue for divorce; **2.** (*Tech.*) refining, clarifying, (*ore etc.*) sorting, picking; decomposition, defecation; chemical analysis. **Scheidungs|-begehren,** *n.* petition for divorce. **-erkenntnis,** *n.* decree nisi. **-grund,** *m.* grounds for divorce. **-klage,** *f.* divorce suit. **-prozeß,** *m.* divorce-case *or* proceedings.

Schein [ʃaɪn], *m.* **(-(e)s,** *pl.* **-e) 1.** shine, light, brilliance, gleam, lustre, bloom, sheen; **2.** (*fig.*) appearance, air, look; (mere) show, pretence, semblance, pretext, (*coll.*) sham, make-believe, blind; ***zum -e, des -es wegen,*** pro forma; ***den – wahren,*** keep up appearances, save one's face; ***unter dem -e der Freundschaft,*** under the guise *or* cloak of friendship; ***kein – von Hoffnung,*** no glimmer of hope; ***es hat den –, als ob . . .,*** it looks as if . . .; ***dem -e nach,*** apparently, on the face of it, to all intents and purposes; ***sich*** (*Dat.*) ***den – geben,*** pretend, feign, give the impression; ***das ist alles nur –,*** that is all pretence; ***der – spricht gegen ihn,*** appearances are against him; (*Prov.*) ***der – trügt,*** appearances are deceptive; **3.** (*Comm. etc.*) banknote, (*Am.*) bill; receipt, document, paper, ticket, form, certificate; ***-e und Hartgeld,*** notes and coin.

Schein|angriff, *m.* mock attack. **-anlage,** *f.* (*Mil.*) decoy, dummy works. **-argument,** *n.* specious argument.

scheinbar [ˈʃaɪnba:r], **1.** *adj.* seeming, apparent, ostensible, likely, plausible; pretended, fictitious, false; ***-er Horizont,*** apparent horizon. **2.** *adv.* seemingly, apparently *etc.*, on the face of it.

Schein|bewegung, *f.* deceptive movement, feint. **-bild,** *n.* delusion, illusion; phantom. **-blüte,** *f.* (*Comm.*) apparent prosperity, false boom. **-ehe,** *f.* fictitious *or* mock marriage.

scheinen [ˈʃaɪnən], *irr.v.i.* **1.** shine, give light, gleam; ***die Sonne scheint warm,*** the sun is hot; **2.** (*fig.*) (*Dat.*) seem, appear, look; ***sie – reich zu sein,*** they seem to be rich; ***wie scheint dir die Geschichte?*** what do you think of the story? ***wie es scheint,*** as it seems.

Scheinergrad [ˈʃaɪnərgra:t], *m.* **(-es,** *pl.* **-e)** photometric unit (*after Julius Scheiner*).

Schein|farben, *f.pl.* (*Opt.*) accidental colours. **-flugplatz,** *m.* decoy airfield. **-friede,** *m.* hollow peace. **-frucht,** *f.* spurious fruit. **-funk,** *m.* (*Rad.*) spoof transmission. **-fuß,** *m.* (*Zool.*) pseudopodium. **-gefecht,** *n.* mock fight. **-gelehrsamkeit,** *f.* would-be learning, pretended erudition. **-gelenk,** *n.* false articulation. **-gericht,** *n.* mock trial. **-geschäft,** *n.* fictitious transaction. **-gewinn,** *m.* apparent profit. **-glück,** *n.* seeming happiness. **-gold,** *n.* artificial gold. **-grund,** *m.* apparent reason; pretext, sophism. **scheinheilig,** *adj.* hypocritical, sanctimonious, canting. **Schein|-heilige(r),** *m., f.* hypocrite. **-heiligkeit,** *f.* hypocrisy, sanctimoniousness, cant. **-hoffnung,** *f.* delusive hope. **-kampf,** *m.* mock fight. **-krankheit,** *f.* feigned illness. **-leben,** *n.* semblance of life; empty life. **-tod,** *m.* apparent death. suspended animation, trance. **scheintot,** *adj.* seemingly dead, in a trance. **Schein|verkauf,** *m.* pro forma sale, fictitious sale. **-wechsel,** *m.* accommodation bill. **-werfer,** *m.* reflector, projector, (*Mil. etc.*) searchlight, floodlight; (*Motor.*) headlight, headlamp; (*Theat.*) spotlight. **-werferkegel,** *m.* searchlight beam. **-widerstand,** *m.* (*Elec.*) impedance. **-zwiebel,** *f.* (*Bot.*) aerial tuber. **-zwitter,** *m.* pseudo-hermaphrodite.

Scheiße [ˈʃaɪsə], *f.* (*vulg.*) shit. **scheißen,** *irr.v.i.*

(*vulg.*) shit, crap. **Scheißkerl,** *m.* (*vulg.*) bugger, bastard, (lily-livered) skunk.

Scheit [ʃaɪt], *n.* (**-(e)s,** *pl.* **-e, -er**) log, billet, stick (of firewood).

Scheitel [ˈʃaɪtəl], *m.* 1. top, summit; 2. peak, apex, (*Geom.*) vertex; (*Math.*) origin of coordinates; 3. crown *or* top of the head, parting (*of the hair*); ***vom – bis zur Sohle,*** from head to foot, from top to toe. **Scheitel|bein,** *n.* parietal bone. **-fläche,** *f.* vertical plane. **-kreis,** *m.* vertical circle, azimuth. **-lappen,** *m.* parietal lobe. **scheiteln,** *v.t.* part (*the hair*). **Scheitel|naht,** *f.* parietal suture. **-punkt,** *m.* (*Geom.*) vertex, (*Astr.*) zenith, summit, apex (*of trajectory*). **-wert,** *m.* peak amplitude. **-winkel,** *m.* vertical *or* opposite angle. **-zelle,** *f.* apical cell.

scheiten [ˈʃaɪtən], *v.i.* (*Swiss*) split logs.

Scheiterhaufen [ˈʃaɪtərhaufən], *m.* funeral pile, pyre; stake.

scheitern [ˈʃaɪtərn], *v.i.* (*aux.* h. & s.) (*Naut.*) run aground, be lost *or* wrecked, founder, become a wreck; (*fig.*) be frustrated (***an*** (*Dat.*), by), miscarry, fail, prove unavailing; ***daran scheitert meine (ganze) Kunst,*** that is beyond me, that beats me. **Scheitern,** *n.* shipwreck; (*fig.*) miscarriage, failure, breakdown.

Schelfe [ˈʃɛlfə], *f.* husk, shell, pod (*of fruits*). **schelfen, schelfern,** *v.t., v.i., v.r.* peel (off), scale (off).

Schellack [ˈʃɛlak], *m.* shellac. **Schellackpolitur,** *f.* French polish.

Schelladler [ˈʃɛlˀa:dlər], *m.* (*Orn.*) spotted eagle (*Aquila clanga*).

Schelle [ˈʃɛlə], *f.* 1. (little) bell, handbell; (*Cards*) *pl.* diamonds; (*B.*) ***wie eine klingende –,*** as a tinkling cymbal; (*Prov.*) ***der Katze die – umhängen,*** bell the cat; 2. clamp, clip, collar, manacle, handcuff; 3. (*coll.*) box on the ears. **schellen,** *v.t., v.i.* ring, ring the bell; tinkle; ***es hat geschellt,*** the bell rang; ***ich habe geschellt,*** I have rung. **Schellen|bube,** *m.* (*Cards*) knave *or* jack of diamonds. **-geläut(e),** *n.* jingling, tinkling; sleigh-bells; bell-harness (*of a horse*). **-kappe,** *f.* (fool's) cap and bells. **-könig,** *m.* (*Cards*) king of diamonds; ***über den – loben,*** praise to the skies.

Schellente [ˈʃɛlˀɛntə], *f.* (*Orn.*) (*Am.* European) golden-eye (*Bucephala clangula*).

Schellentrommel [ˈʃɛləntrɔməl], *m.* tambourine, timbrel.

Schell|fisch, *m.* (*Ichth.*) haddock (*Gadus aeglefinus*). **-hengst,** *m. See* **Schälhengst. -kraut,** *n.* (*dial.*) *see* **Schöllkraut.**

Schelm [ʃɛlm], *m.* (**-(e)s,** *pl.* **-e**) rogue; (*obs.*) rascal, knave, scoundrel; ***zum – machen,*** sully (*a p.'s*) good name; (*Prov.*) ***ein –, der besser macht*** (or ***mehr gibt*** or ***tut***) ***als er kann,*** you must not expect impossibilities; (*Prov.*) ***auf einen – anderthalben setzen,*** set a thief to catch a thief; ***ein – der Schlechtes dabei denkt,*** honi soit qui mal y pense; ***ihm sitzt der – im Nacken,*** *see* **Schalk.**

Schelmen|roman, *m.* picaresque novel. **-sprache,** *f.* thieves' slang. **-streich,** *m.*, **-stück,** *n.* prank. **-zunft,** *f.* all rogues. **Schelmerei** [–ˈraɪ], *f.* roguishness, roguish ways; *see also* **Schelmenstreich**; (*obs.*) roguery, knavery. **schelmisch,** *adj.* roguish, waggish, impish, arch.

Schelte [ˈʃɛltə], *f.* scolding; ***– bekommen,*** be scolded, get a scolding. **schelten,** *irr.v.t.* scold, chide, reprimand, upbraid, reproach, (*dial.*) call, nickname; ***ihn einen Dummkopf –,*** call him stupid *or* a blockhead. **Schelt|rede,** *f.* philippic, invective, abuse. **-wort,** *n.* invective.

Schema [ˈʃe:ma], *n.* (**-s,** *pl.* **-s** *or* **-men** *or* **-ta**) schedule, diagram, model, scheme, pattern, arrangement, system, (*coll.*) set-up; ***nach – F,*** according to rule, without discrimination. **schematisch** [–ˈma:tɪʃ], *adj.* diagrammatic, schematic, systematic, reduced to a norm, undifferentiated. **schematisieren** [–tiˈzi:rən], *v.t.* sketch out, (describe in) outline, (*coll.*) lump together. **Schematismus** [–ˈtɪsmus], *m.* lack of discrimination, formalism.

Schembart [ˈʃɛmba:rt], *m.* false beard, bearded mask.

Schemel [ˈʃe:məl], *m.* (foot-)stool.

Schemen [ˈʃe:mən], *m.* phantom, shadow, delusion. **schemenhaft,** *adj.* shadowy, ghostly, unreal.

Schenk [ʃɛŋk], *m.* (**-en,** *pl.* **-en**) cup-bearer; publican. **Schenke,** *f.* inn, tavern, public house.

Schenkel [ˈʃɛŋkəl], *m.* 1. thigh; shank; 2. side (*of angles*); 3. hinged leg, arm, limb, side-piece. **Schenkel|beuge,** *f.* groin, inguinal furrow. **-blutader,** *f.* femoral artery. **-bruch,** *m.* fracture of the femur. **-gelenk,** *n.* hip joint. **-knochen,** *m.* thigh-bone, femur. **-muskel,** *m.* crural muscle. **schenkelrecht,** *adj.* tractable (*of horses*). **Schenkelrohr,** *n.* (*Tech.*) elbow-joint.

schenken [ˈʃɛŋkən], *v.t.* 1. give, present, make a present of, donate, bestow, grant, endow; ***etwas zu Weihnachten geschenkt bekommen,*** get s.th. as a Christmas present; ***etwas beinahe geschenkt bekommen,*** buy a th. for next to nothing, get s.th. dirt-cheap *or* practically given away; ***ihm die Freiheit –,*** set him free *or* at liberty; ***ihm das Herz –,*** give him one's heart; ***ich möchte es nicht (einmal) geschenkt haben,*** I would not have it as a gift; 2. remit, forgive, acquit of, excuse from, (*coll.*) let off; (*coll.*) ***es soll dir geschenkt sein,*** I will let you off this time; (*coll.*) ***das kannst du dir –,*** you can cut that out *or* skip that; ***den Rest der Geschichte schenke ich dir,*** I will spare you the rest of the story; 3. pour out; retail (*liquor*). **Schenk-,** *suff. see under* **Schank-. Schenker,** *m.* donor. **Schenkung,** *f.* donation, gift, endowment. **Schenkungsurkunde,** *f.* deed of gift. **schenkungsweise,** *adv.* by way of donation, as a gift.

scheppern [ˈʃɛpərn], *v.i.* (*coll.*) clatter, rattle; (*sl. Motor.*) (have a) crash.

Scherbe [ˈʃɛrbə], *f.* fragment (*of glass, earthenware etc.*), potsherd, shard; (*dial.*) earthenware vessel; flower-pot; (*sl.*) monocle; *pl.* broken pieces, debris; ***in -n gehen,*** go to pieces.

Scherbeanspruchung [ˈʃe:rbəanʃpru:xuŋ], *f.* (*Tech.*) shear(ing) stress.

Scherbel [ˈʃɛrbəl], **Scherben,** *m. See* **Scherbe.**

Scherben|gericht, *n.* ostracism. **-gewächs,** *n.* pot-plant. **-haufen,** *m.* heap of fragments, (*fig., coll.*) shambles.

Schere [ˈʃe:rə], *f.* 1. (a pair of) scissors *or* shears, clippers; shafts (*of a carriage*); claw (*of crabs etc.*); (*Wrestling*) scissors; 2. (*fig.*) reciprocal relationship. **scheren, 1.** *irr.* (*rare reg.*) *v.t.* 1. shear, cut, clip, prune, trim, mow, shave; (*Weav.*) warp; (*Naut.*) reeve; ***sein Schäfchen –,*** feather one's nest; ***laß mich ungeschoren!*** let me alone! ***alles über einen Kamm –,*** treat all alike, make no distinction, (*coll.*) tar with the same brush; 2. (*fig.*) *v.imp.* (*usu. reg.*) concern; ***was schert*** or ***schiert mich das?*** what's that to me? (*sl.*) so what? ***sich – um,*** trouble o.s. *or* bother about, be bothered about, be concerned for. **2.** *irr.v.i.* (*Naut.*) sheer, yaw. **3.** *reg.v.r.* (*coll.*) clear off, (*sl.*) beat it, do a bunk; ***er mag sich zum Teufel –,*** he can go to the devil.

Scheren|bewegung, *f.* (*Comm.*) reciprocal movement (*of prices etc.*). **-fernrohr,** *n.* stereotelescope. **-gitter,** *n.* folding trellis. **-schlag,** *m.* (*Footb.*) scissors kick. **-schleifer,** *m.* knife-grinder. **-schnitt,** *m.* silhouette. **-werk,** *n.* (*Fort.*) tenaille. **-zange,** *f.* wire cutters.

Schererei [ʃe:rəˈraɪ], *f.* (*coll.*) trouble, bother, vexation, annoyance.

Scherfestigkeit [ˈʃe:rfɛstɪçkaɪt], *f.* shearing strength.

Scherflein [ˈʃɛrflaɪn], *n.* (**-s,** *pl.* **-**) mite; ***sein – beitragen,*** do one's bit.

Scher|gang, *m.* (*Naut.*) sheerstrake. **-garn,** *n.* (*Weav.*) warp-thread.

Scherge [ˈʃɛrgə], *m.* (**-n,** *pl.* **-n**) (*obs.*) beadle, constable; hangman's assistant, myrmidon; ***des Gesetzes -n,*** myrmidons of the law. **Schergendienste,** *m.pl.* ***– tun,*** do all the dirty work.

Scherling [ˈʃe:rlɪŋ], *m.* (**-s,** *pl.* **-e**) shorn fleece.

Scher|maschine, *f.* (*Weav.*) shearing maschine.

–maus, *f.* (*Zool.*) mole (*Arvicola scherman*). **–messer,** *n.* shearing-knife, (*obs.*) razor. **–stift,** *m.* (*Mech.*) shearing-pin. **–tau,** *n.* (*Naut.*) sheer-line. **–versuch,** *m.* (*Tech.*) shear(ing) test.

Scherwenzel [ʃɛrˈvɛntsəl], *m.* *See* **Scharwenzel.**

Scher|winkel, *m.* (*Naut.*) angle of yaw. **–wolle,** *f.* shearings.

Scherz [ʃɛrts], *m.* (**-es,** *pl.* **-e**) jest, joke, pleasantry, witticism, (*coll.*) wisecrack; fun, raillery, badinage, banter, chaff; ***im*** or ***zum* –,** in *or* for fun, as a joke, in jest; – ***beiseite,*** joking apart; ***er versteht keinen* –,** he cannot take *or* see a joke; ***seinen – treiben mit,*** make fun of. **Scherzartikel,** *m.* (*Comm.*) trick.

Scherzel [ˈʃɛrtsəl], *n.* (*Austr.*) crust (*of bread etc.*).

scherzen [ˈʃɛrtsən], *v.i.* jest, joke (***über*** (*Acc.*), about), make merry *or* have fun (with), make fun (of); crack jokes; ***Sie*** – or ***Sie belieben wohl zu* –,** you are joking, you surely don't mean it; ***er läßt nicht mit sich*** – or ***mit ihm ist nicht zu* –,** he is not to be trifled with; ***es ist nicht zum* –,** it is no joking matter.

Scherz|frage, *f.* jocular question. **–gedicht,** *n.* comic *or* burlesque poem. **scherzhaft,** *adj.* joking, facetious, playful, humorous, jocular; comical, waggish, droll, jocose. **Scherzhaftigkeit,** *f.* facetiousness, playfulness, waggishness, jocularity. **Scherz|lied,** *n.* comic song. **–name,** *m.* nickname. **scherzweise,** *adv.* in *or* for fun, in jest. **Scherzwort,** *n.* witticism, word spoken in jest.

scheu [ʃɔy], *adj.* shy, timid, timorous, nervous; bashful, reserved, unsociable; (*of horse*) skittish, shying; – ***machen,*** startle, frighten; – ***werden,*** shy, take fright (***durch,*** at). **Scheu,** *f.* 1. shyness, timidity, nervousness; 2. awe, dread (***vor*** (*Dat.*), of), respect (for), aversion (to).

Scheuche [ˈʃɔyçə], *f.* scarecrow, (*fig.*) bugbear. **scheuchen,** *v.t.* scare; frighten *or* chase *or* (*coll.*) shoo away.

scheuen [ˈʃɔyən], **1.** *v.t.* be afraid of, fear, dread, shun, avoid, shrink from, fight shy of; ***keine Mühe* –,** spare no pains. **2.** *v.r.* be afraid (***vor*** (*Dat.*), of); hesitate (***zu tun,*** to do), be shy *or* timid (about doing). **3.** *v.i.* take fright, shy, balk (***vor*** (*Dat.*), at).

Scheuer [ˈʃɔyər], *f.* (-, *pl.* **-n**) *see* **Scheune.**

Scheuer|besen, *m.*, **–bürste,** *f.* scrubbing-brush. **–festigkeit,** *f.* (*Tech.*) abrasion resistance. **–frau,** *f.* charwoman, (*coll.*) char, (*Am.*) scrubwoman. **–lappen,** *m.* floor-cloth; dish-cloth. **–leiste,** *f.* skirting-board. **–mittel,** *n.* scouring agent.

scheuern [ˈʃɔyərn], **1.** *v.t.* scrub, scour; ***das Hemd scheuert mir den Rücken wund,*** the shirt rubs the skin off my back. **2.** *v.i., v.r.* rub, chafe. **Scheuer|-pulver,** *n.* scouring powder. **–tuch,** *n.* *See* **–lappen.**

Scheu|klappe, *f.*, **–leder,** *n.* blinker, (*Am.*) blinder.

Scheune [ˈʃɔynə], *f.* barn, granary, hayloft, shed. **Scheunen|drescher,** *m.* (*coll.*) ***essen wie ein* –,** eat like a horse. **–tenne,** *f.* threshing-floor. **–tor,** *n.* barn door; ***ihm mit dem – winken,*** give him a broad hint *or* the broadest of hints. **–viertel,** *n.* (*coll.*) slums.

Scheusal [ˈʃɔyza:l], *n.* (**-(e)s,** *pl.* **-e**) monster, horrible creature, (*coll. of a p.*) beast, horror, holy terror, (*ugly p.*) fright.

scheußlich [ˈʃɔyslɪç], **1.** *adj.* horrible, frightful, abominable, atrocious, loathsome, revolting, vile, (*appearance*) hideous, (*crime*) heinous, bestial, foul; (*coll.*) horrid, foul, awful, beastly. **2.** *adv.* (*coll.*) awfully, frightfully, abominably. **Scheußlichkeit,** *f.* frightfulness, loathsomeness, vileness, beastliness, hideousness, abomination; atrocity, horrible *or* heinous deed, (*coll.*) horror.

Schi [ʃi:], *m.* *See* **Ski.**

Schicht [ʃɪçt], *f.* (-, *pl.* **-en**) 1. (*Geol.*) layer, bed, stratum; (*in liquids*) sediment; (*Build.*) course, tier, (*of paint etc.*) film, coat, (*Phot.*) coating, emulsion; (*of wood etc.*) pile, stack, (*in an oven*) batch, charge; 2. (*of work*) turn, spell, shift, (*of workers*) shift, gang; – ***machen,*** knock off (work); ***in –en arbeiten,*** work in shifts; (*fig.*) ***in einer* –,** uninterruptedly, without pause *or* break; 3. (*fig.*) level, class, social stratum; ***aus allen –en,*** from all walks of life; ***breite –en der Bevölkerung,*** wide sections of the population. **Schichtarbeit,** *f.* shift-work. **Schichte,** *f.* (*Austr.*) *see* **Schicht. Schichtebene,** *f.* plane of stratification.

schichten [ˈʃɪçtən], **1.** *v.t.* put into *or* arrange in layers, (*Geol.*) stratify; pile (up), stack (*wood etc.*), stow (*cargo*), charge (*furnace*); (*fig.*) classify, arrange. **2.** *v.i.* (*coll.*) work shifts, be on shift.

Schichten|aufbau, *m.*, **–bildung,** *f.* stratification. **–folge,** *f.* geological structure, archaeological sequence. **–kopf,** *m.* (*Geol.*) outcrop. **–plan,** *m.* relief *or* contour map. **schichtenweise,** *adv.* *See* **schichtweise.**

Schicht|gestein, *n.* stratified rock. **–glas,** *n.* laminated glass. **–holz,** *n.* stacked wood; plywood. **schichtig,** *adj.* laminated, lamellar; (*as suff.*) -layered, (*of plywood*) -ply. **Schicht|leistung,** *f.* output per shift. **–linie,** *f.* contour line. **–lohn,** *m.* wages per shift. **–meister,** *m.* overseer, foreman, ganger. **–seite,** *f.* (*Phot.*) sensitized side (*of film*). **–stoff,** *m.* laminated plastic.

Schichtung [ˈʃɪçtuŋ], *f.* 1. (*Geol. also fig.*) stratification; arrangement (in layers), piling, stacking; 2. (*fig.*) classification; ***soziale* –,** social strata; 3. second dentition. **Schichtungsebene,** *f.* *See* **Schichtebene. schichtweise,** *adv.* in layers, layer by layer; (*of work*) in shifts. **Schicht|wolke,** *f.* stratus (cloud). **–zahn,** *m.* milk-tooth.

Schick [ʃɪk], *m.* chic, style, elegance, taste; (due) order, fitness; skill, dexterity; tact; (*coll.*) ***wieder in – bringen,*** put in order again; (*coll.*) ***er hat seinen rechten – nicht,*** he is not quite himself; (*coll.*) ***er ist nicht auf dem* –,** he is off colour, he is out of sorts. **schick,** *adj.* chic, stylish, elegant, smart, (*sl.*) swanky, swell.

schicken [ˈʃɪkən], **1.** *v.t.* send, dispatch; remit (*money*); ***ins Parlament* –,** return to parliament; ***ein Buch in die Welt* –,** publish a book; ***Waren ins Haus* –,** deliver goods to the door; ***in den April* –,** make an April fool of; ***der Zufall schickte es,*** it so happened, it chanced. **2.** *v.r.* come to pass, happen, chance; ***sich – für,*** be fitting for, be adapted to, suit, befit, be becoming in, behove, (*Am.*) behoove; ***sich – in*** (*Acc.*), agree with, submit *or* conform to, adapt *or* accommodate o.s. to, resign o.s. to, be reconciled with, (*coll.*) put up with; ***es schickt sich nicht,*** it's not good form, it isn't done, it's not the proper thing to do; ***es schickte sich daß*** . . ., luck *or* chance would have it that . . .; ***sich in die Zeit* –,** move with the times; ***je nachdem es sich schickt,*** just as the case may be; ***wenn es sich gerade so schickt,*** if things will turn out that way; ***es wird sich schon* –,** it will all come right some day; (*Prov.*) ***eines schickt sich nicht für alle,*** one man's meat is another man's poison.

schicklich [ˈʃɪklɪç], *adj.* proper, correct, seemly, decent, becoming; appropriate, convenient, suitable, (*obs.*) meet. **Schicklichkeit,** *f.* fitness, propriety, decorum, seemliness, decency, good-breeding. **Schicklichkeitsgefühl,** *n.* tact, sense of propriety.

Schicksal [ˈʃɪkza:l], *n.* destiny, entelechy; fate, fortune, lot; ***sein – ist besiegelt,*** his fate is sealed; ***das gleiche – erfahren,*** share the same fate, fare alike; ***das – herausfordern,*** tempt providence, court disaster; ***mich meinem – überlassen,*** leave me to my fate; ***es ist mein* –,** I am fated (***zu tun,*** to do). **schicksalhaft,** *adj.* fateful. **schicksalreich,** *adj.* chequered.

Schicksals|frage, *f.* fateful *or* vital issue. **–fügung,** *f.* act of providence. **–gefährte, –genosse,** *m.* companion in misfortune, fellow-sufferer. **–glaube,** *m.* fatalism. **–göttinnen,** *f.pl.* Fatal Sisters, the Fates, the Parcae. **–prüfung,** *f.* sore trial, ordeal, visitation. **–schlag,** *m.* heavy blow, blow *or* buffet of fate, reverse. **–tag,** *m.* fateful day. **–wechsel,** *m.* change of fortune, vicissitude(s). **–weg,** *m.* march of destiny. **–wort,** *n.* decree of Providence; oracle.

Schickse [ˈʃɪksə], *f.* (*coll.*) non-Jewish girl (*among Jews*); *also* **Schicksel,** *n.* (*coll.*) young Jewess (*among non-Jews*); girl of doubtful repute, (*sl.*) baggage, pick-up.

Schickung [ˈʃɪkuŋ], *f.* Providence, fate, dispensation; divine ordinance *or* decree, the finger of God.

Schiebe|bühne, *f.* travelling platform. **–dach,** *n.* sliding roof. **–fenster,** *n.* sash-window.

schieben [ˈʃi:bən], *irr.v.t., v.r., v.i.* (*aux.* h. & s.) push, thrust, shove; slide, move, put, slip; (*coll.*) profiteer, sell on the black-market; (*coll.*) wangle; (*coll.*) ***wir werden es schon –,*** we'll wangle it somehow; ***er muß immer geschoben werden,*** he always needs s.o. behind him; ***etwas auf die lange Bank –,*** postpone *or* defer *or* (*coll.*) put off a th.; (*sl., Mil.*) ***Dienst*** (or ***Wache***) **–,** be on (guard) duty; ***ihn über die Grenze –,*** get him out of the country; ***Kegel –,*** play at skittles; (*Mil. sl.*) ***Kohldampf –,*** be hungry; (*coll.*) ***ihm etwas in die Schuhe –,*** pin s.th. on him; ***die Schuld auf ihn –,*** put *or* lay the blame on him; ***einen Stein –,*** make a move (*at draughts*). **Schieber,** *m.* 1. slide, slider, carriage; oven-peel; damper; bar, bolt; running-loop; slide *or* sleeve valve; slide-rule; 2. (*coll.*) racketeer, profiteer, black-marketeer. **Schieber|geschäft,** *n.* profiteering, graft, racket.

Schieberohr [ˈʃi:bəro:r], *n.* (*Mech.*) sleeve.

Schiebertum [ˈʃi:bərtu:m], *n.* profiteering, racketeering, graft.

Schieber|ventil, *n.* slide valve. **–weg,** *m.* slide-valve travel.

Schiebe|sitz, *m.* sliding seat. **–tür,** *f.* sliding door. **–wind,** *m.* (*Av.*) tail-wind.

Schieb|karren, *m.* wheelbarrow. **–lehre,** *f.* (carpenter's) adjustable square.

Schiebung [ˈʃi:buŋ], *f.* 1. profiteering, racketeering, sharp practice, underhand dealings, (*coll.*) wangling; political jobbery, racket, graft, wangle, put-up job; 2. (*Tech.*) ***spezifische –,*** shearing strain.

schiech [ʃi:ç], *adj.* (*dial.*) ugly, terrifying.

schied [ʃi:t], **schiede** [ˈʃi:də], *see* **scheiden.**

schiedlich [ˈʃi:tlɪç], *adv.* (*only in*) **–** ***und friedlich,*** amenable to discussion, amicable, reasonable, pacific.

Schiedsgericht [ˈʃi:tsgərɪçt], *n.* court of arbitration, arbitration committee, (*Spt.*) the judges. **Schiedsgerichtsbarkeit,** *f.* arbitration. **Schiedsgerichts|hof,** *m.* ***Ständiger Internationaler –,*** Permanent Court of International Justice. **–klausel,** *f.* arbitration clause.

Schiedsrichter [ˈʃi:tsrɪçtər], *m.* arbiter, (*Spt.*) judge, (*Crick., Tenn.*) umpire, (*Footb., Boxing*) referee. **schieds|richterlich,** *adj., adv.* by arbitration. **–richtern,** *v.i.* arbitrate, act as arbiter, (*Spt.*) judge, umpire, referee.

Schieds|spruch, *m.* ruling, decision, arbitration award. **–vertrag,** *m.* arbitration treaty.

schief [ʃi:f], **1.** *adj.* oblique, diagonal, slanting, sloping, inclined; bent, crooked, distorted, wry, (*coll.*) lop-sided, (*sl.*) cock-eyed; (*fig.*) bad, wrong, false; ***–e Ebene,*** inclined plane; (*Railw.*) gradient; ***auf die –e Ebene kommen*** or ***geraten,*** go off the straight and narrow path, start on the downward path; (*fig.*) ***–e Lage,*** awkward *or* false position; ***ein –es Gesicht machen,*** make a wry face; ***in –es Licht kommen,*** be misjudged, be shown up *or* put in a bad light; ***in ein –es Licht setzen,*** put in a bad light; ***der –e Turm,*** the leaning tower. **2.** *adv.* obliquely, aslant, awry, askew, across, cross-wise; (*fig.*) amiss; ***etwas – anfangen,*** set about a th. the wrong way; **–** ***ansehen,*** look askance at, frown upon; **–** ***gehen,*** go wrong, turn out badly; (*coll.*) **–** ***gewickelt sein,*** be very much mistaken, be on the wrong tack *or* track; ***den Hut – aufsetzen,*** wear one's hat at an angle; ***seine Stiefel – laufen*** or ***treten,*** tread one's boots down at the heels; (*coll.*) **–** ***nehmen,*** take amiss; ***es steht – darum,*** there is something wrong with it. **Schiefblatt,** *n.* (*Bot.*) begonia, elephant's ear. **Schiefe,** *f.* inclination, obliquity, obliqueness, crookedness; inclined plane, slope, incline, slant; (*fig.*) wrongness, perversity.

Schiefer [ˈʃi:fər], *m.* slate, shale, schist; (*dial.*) splinter, (*Scots*) skelf. **schiefer|artig,** *adj.* slaty, schistous. **–blau,** *adj.* slate-blue, slate-coloured. **Schiefer|bruch,** *m.* slate quarry. **–dach,** *n.* slate roof. **–decker,** *m.* slater. **–griffel,** *m.* *See* **–stift. schief(e)rig,** *adj.* slate-like; slaty, schistous; splintery, scaly, flaky, foliated. **schiefern,** *v.i.* peel *or* scale off, exfoliate. **Schiefer|spat,** *m.* schistous spar. **–stein,** *m.* slate, lithographic stone. **–stift,** *m.* slate-pencil. **–tafel,** *f.* slate (*school*). **–ton,** *m.* slate clay, shale.

Schieferung [ˈʃi:fəruŋ], *f.* scaling, exfoliation.

schief|gehen, *irr.v.i.* go wrong, turn out badly, (*coll.*) not come off; (*hum.*) ***nur Mut! es wird schon –,*** cheer up, there's worse to come! **–geladen,** *adj.* (*sl.*) tipsy, plastered, half-seas over.

Schiefheit [ˈʃi:fhaɪt], *f.* *See* **Schiefe.**

schief|laufen, *irr.v.t.* *See* **–treten. –liegend,** *adj.* aslant, askew, oblique, inclined, sloping, tilted. **schiefrig,** *adj.* *See* **schief(e)rig. schieftreten,** *irr.v.t.* wear *or* tread (*shoes*) down at the heels.

schieg [ʃi:k], *adj.* (*dial.*) *see* **schiech. schiegbeinig,** *adj.* (*dial.*) knock-kneed. **schiegen** (*dial.*), (*Swiss*) **schieggen,** *v.i.* turn in one's foot, walk on the side of one's foot.

schielen [ˈʃi:lən], *v.i.* 1. squint, be cross-eyed; 2. leer, cast a furtive *or* sidelong glance (***nach*** (*Dat.*), ***auf*** (*Acc.*), at), (*fig.*) have an eye (to), hanker (after). **Schielen,** *n.* squint(ing), cast in the eye, (*Med.*) strabismus. **schielend,** *adj.* cross-eyed, squint-eyed; leering; (*obs.*) ***–er Vergleich,*** inappropriate comparison. **Schieloperation,** *f.* strabotomy.

Schiemann [ˈʃi:man], *m.* (*pl.* **¨er**) sailor, seaman. **Schiemannsgarn,** *n.* cordage, (*usu. fig.*) fisherman's story, tall story.

schien [ʃi:n], *see* **scheinen.**

Schienbein [ˈʃi:nbaɪn], *n.* shin(-bone), (*Anat.*) tibia. **Schienbeinschützer,** *m.* (*Spt.*) shin-guard, (shin-)pad.

schiene [ˈʃi:nə], *see* **scheinen.**

Schiene, *f.* (*Med.*) splint; iron band *or* hoop, (*of wheel*) iron rim *or* tyre; bar, rail; (*Railw.*) rail, *pl.* track, metals, rails; (wooden) slat, (*of umbrella*) rib; ***aus den –n springen,*** run off the rails, leave the rails; ***sein Arm liegt in –n,*** his arm is in splints. **schienen,** *v.t.* put in splints; tyre (*wheels*).

Schienen|bus, *m.* rail-bus. **–eisen,** *n.* iron (in) bars. **schienengleich,** *adj.* ***–er Übergang,*** level (*Am.* grade) crossing. **Schienen|kopf,** *m.* railhead. **–lasche,** *f.* fish-plate. **–leger,** *m.* (*Railw.*) platelayer. **–netz,** *n.* railway (*Am.* railroad) system. **–räumer,** *m.* cow-catcher (*on engines*). **–reibung,** *f.* rolling-friction. **–strang,** *m.* track, railway line, metals. **–weg,** *m.* permanent way. **–weite,** *f.* gauge.

[1]**schier** [ʃi:r], *adj.* 1. (*rare*) clear; ***–es Fleisch,*** meat without fat or bones; 2. (*usu. fig.*) sheer, pure; ***–e Unmöglichkeit,*** sheer *or* pure impossibility.

[2]**schier,** *see* **scheren.**

[3]**schier,** *adv.* (*coll.*) almost, nearly, barely, (*also with negative*) next to.

Schierling [ˈʃi:rlɪŋ], *m.* (**-s,** *pl.* **-e**) (*Bot.*) hemlock (*Conium maculatum*). **Schierlingstanne,** *f.* (*Bot.*) Canadian hemlock, hemlock spruce (*Tsuga canadensis*).

schierst [ʃi:rst], **schiert,** *see* **scheren.**

Schiertuch [ˈʃi:rtu:x], *n.* canvas.

Schieß|ausbildung [ˈʃi:s–], *f.* gunnery *or* musketry training. **–bahn,** *f.* firing lane (*of marksman*), (*collect.*) rifle-range. **–baumwolle,** *f.* guncotton, nitrocellulose, pyroxylin. **–bedarf,** *m.* ammunition. **–befehl,** *m.* firing-order. **–bude,** *f.* shooting-gallery.

schießen [ˈʃi:sən], **1.** *irr.v.i.* (*aux.* s.) shoot (*as stars or pain*), dash, swoop, dart, rush, (*of plants*) sprout, spring up, burst forth; ***das Blut schoß ihm ins Gesicht,*** the blood rushed to his face; ***in die Höhe –,*** spring *or* shoot up; ***ein Gedanke schoß mir durch den Kopf,*** a thought flashed through my mind *or* crossed my mind in a flash; ***ins Kraut –,*** run to leaf, (*fig.*) run wild; **–** ***lassen,*** let go, let fly; let loose, pay out (*rope*); (*fig.*) relinquish, forgo, give up, throw to the wind; ***die Zügel – lassen*** (*Dat.*), give (*a horse*) its head; (*fig.*) give full rein to; ***in Samen –***, run to seed. **2.** *irr.v.i.* shoot, fire, open fire; – ***auf*** (*Acc.*), shoot *or* fire at, take a shot at; ***blind –***, shoot with blank cartridges; ***das Gewehr schießt schlecht,*** the rifle fires badly; ***gut –***, be a good shot; ***scharf –***, shoot with live ammunition; ***weit –***, carry far; (*coll.*) – ***Sie los!*** fire away! (*Am.*) shoot! **3.** *irr.v.t.* shoot; ***einen Blick – auf*** (*Acc.*), shoot a glance at; (*fig.*) ***einen Bock –***, commit a blunder *or* (*coll.*) bloomer; ***Brot in den Ofen –***, shove (a batch of) bread in the oven; ***in Grund und Boden –***, batter down with cannonfire; ***Kugeln –***, fire bullets; ***sich*** (*Dat.*) ***eine Kugel durch den Kopf –***, blow one's brains out; ***Pfeile –***, shoot arrows; ***einen Purzelbaum –***, turn a somersault; ***sich mit ihm –***, fight a pistol duel with him; (*Naut.*) ***die Sonne –***, take the sun's altitude; ***einen Vogel im Fluge –***, shoot a bird on the wing; ***ihn tot –***, shoot him, kill him with a shot; (*Footb.*) ***ein Tor –***, shoot a goal, score (a goal).

Schießen, *n.* shooting, firing, shots, gunfire; shooting match *or* contest; (*coll.*) ***es ist zum –***, it's a perfect scream, it's too funny for words. **Schießerei** [–'raɪ], *f.* continuous *or* repeated firing *or* shooting, gunfight.

Schieß|gerechtigkeit, *f.* shooting rights. **–gewehr,** *n.* firearm; ***spiele nicht mit dem –!*** don't play with fire. **–hund,** *m.* pointer; (*coll.*) ***aufpassen wie ein –***, watch like a lynx. **–hütte,** *f.* shooting-box. **–kunst,** *f.* marksmanship. **–lehre,** *f.* ballistics. **–patrone,** *f.* cartridge, charge. **–platz,** *m.* rifle-range, artillery-range. **–prügel,** *m.* (*coll.*) shooting-iron. **–pulver,** *n.* gunpowder. **–scharte,** *f.* loophole, embrasure, firing slit *or* port. **–scheibe,** *f.* target. **–schlitz,** *m. See* **–scharte. –schule,** *f.* school of musketry *or* gunnery. **–sport,** *m.* shooting. **–stand,** *m.* rifle-range, butts. **–tabelle,** *f.* range-table. **–übungen,** *f.pl.* musketry *or* shooting *or* target practice, artillery *or* firing practice. **–vorschrift,** *f.* gunnery *or* musketry manual. **–wettbewerb,** *m.* shooting contest. **–zeit,** *f.* shooting season.

Schiff [ʃɪf], *n.* (**-(e)s,** *pl.* **-e**) **1.** ship, boat, vessel; ***auf dem –***, on board ship; ***zu – gehen,*** embark, go on board, board ship (***nach,*** for); ***klar –***, decks cleared for action; ***kleine –e,*** small craft; ***ein – vom Stapel lassen,*** launch a ship; – ***voraus,*** ship ahoy; ***das – verlassen,*** abandon ship; ***zu – versenden,*** send by ship *or* by water; 2. (*Archit.*) nave (*of a church*); 3. (*Weav.*) shuttle; 4. (*Typ.*) galley.

Schiffahrt ['ʃɪffart], *f.* shipping; navigation. **Schiffahrts|ausschuß,** *m.* maritime commission. **–gesellschaft,** *f.* shipping company *or* line. **–kanal,** *m.* ship-canal. **–linie,** *f. See* **–gesellschaft. –straße,** *f.* navigable waterway. **–weg,** *m.* shipping route *or* lane. **schiffahrttreibend,** *adj.* seafaring.

schiffbar ['ʃɪfba:r], *adj.* navigable. **Schiffbarkeit,** *f.* navigability. **Schiffbarmachung,** *f.* dredging, opening up (*a waterway*).

Schiff|bau, *m.* shipbuilding. **–bauer,** *m.* shipbuilder, naval architect. **–baukunst,** *f.* naval architecture. **–baumeister,** *m.* master shipwright. **–bein,** *n.* (*Anat.*) scaphoid bone. **–bruch,** *m.* shipwreck (*also fig.*); – ***erleiden,*** be (ship)wrecked, (*fig.*) fail, founder. **schiffbrüchig,** *adj.* shipwrecked. **Schiff|brüchige(r),** *m.* shipwrecked mariner, castaway. **–brücke,** *f.* pontoon bridge.

Schiffchen ['ʃɪfçən], *n.* **1.** little ship *or* vessel; 2. (*Bot.*) carina; 3. (*Anat.*) scapha; 4. (*Weav.*) shuttle; 5. (*Mil.*) forage cap.

schiffen ['ʃɪfən], **1.** *v.t.* (*rare*) ship (*goods etc.*). **2.** *v.i.* (*aux.* s.) 1. navigate, sail (on); 2. (*vulg.*) piss, pump ship.

Schiffer ['ʃɪfər], *m.* mariner, sailor, seaman; (*in merchant marine*) skipper, master. **Schiffer|ausdruck,** *m.* nautical term. **–klavier,** *n.* concertina, accordion. **–knoten,** *m.* sailor's knot. **–patent,** *n.* master's certificate. **–sprache,** *f.* seamen's jargon. **–stange,** *f.* boathook.

Schiffs|arrest, *m.* seizure (of a ship), embargo. **–artillerie,** *f.* naval artillery. **–arzt,** *m.* ship's doctor *or* surgeon. **–bau,** *m.* (*Austr.*) *see* **Schiffbau. –bedarf,** *m.* naval *or* ship's stores. **–befrachter,** *m.* shipper, freighter, charterer. **–befrachtung,** *f.* freightage, chartering. **–besatzung,** *f.* crew. **–beute,** *f.* maritime prize. **–bewuchs,** *m.* underwater growth. **–breite,** *f.* beam. **–brücke,** *f.* (captain's) bridge. **–eigentümer, –eigner,** *m.* shipowner. **–fracht,** *f.* freight, cargo. **–frachtbrief,** *m.* bill of lading. **–geleit(e),** *n.* convoy. **–geschütz,** *n.* naval gun, *pl.* armament. **–haken,** *m.* grappling-iron. **–händler,** *m.* ship's chandler. **–hebewerk,** *n.* ship hoist (*on canals*). **–hinterteil,** *n.* poop, stern. **–journal,** *n.* log-book. **–junge,** *m.* cabin-boy. **–kapitän,** *m.* (sea) captain, master, skipper. **–klasse,** *f.* (ship's) rating. **–körper,** *m. See* **–rumpf. –küche,** *f.* galley, caboose. **–kurs,** *m.* steered course. **–ladung,** *f. See* **–fracht. –lazarett,** *n.* sick-bay. **–leim,** *m.* marine glue. **–leute,** *pl.* crew, sailors, seamen. **–liegeplatz,** *m.* (loading) berth. **–liste,** *f.* ship's register. **–makler,** *m.* shipbroker. **–mannschaft,** *f.* crew. **–maschine,** *f.*, **–motor,** *m.* marine engine. **–panzer,** *m.* armour-plating. **–papiere,** *n.pl.* ship's papers. **–pfandbrief,** *m.* bottomry bond. **–prediger,** *m.* naval chaplain. **–raum,** *m.* hold; tonnage, displacement. **–reeder,** *m.* shipowner. **–rolle,** *f.* muster-roll. **–route,** *f.* sea-route *or* -lane. **–rumpf,** *m.* hull. **–rüstung,** *f.* naval armament. **–schaukel,** *f.* swing-boat. **–schnabel,** *m.* cutwater, prow. **–schraube,** *f.* propellor, screw. **–spediteur,** *m.* shipping agent. **–spur,** *f.* wake (of a ship). **–tagebuch,** *n.* ship's log. **–tau,** *n.* hawser, cable. **–verkehr,** *m.* shipping. **–vermietung,** *f.* chartering, freighting. **–verzeichnis,** *n.* shipping-list. **–verzollung,** *f.* (custom's) clearance. **–volk,** *n.* crew. **–vorderteil,** *n.* forecastle, prow, bows. **–wache,** *f.* look-out; watch. **–werft,** *f.* shipbuilding yard, shipyard; naval dockyard, (*Am.*) navy yard. **–winde,** *f.* capstan, windlass. **–zeughaus,** *n.* naval arsenal. **–zoll,** *m.* tonnage-duty, freightage. **–zwieback,** *m.* ship's biscuit.

schiften ['ʃɪftən], *v.t.* join, pin (*rafters*).

Schikane [ʃi'ka:nə], *f.* annoyance, persecution, chicanery, underhand dealing, (*coll.*) dirty trick; (*sl.*) ***mit allen –n,*** with all the frills *or* trimmings. **schikanieren** [–'ni:rən], *v.t.* vex, annoy, irritate, torment; play tricks upon. **schikanös** [–'nø:s], *adj.* annoying, vexatious, tiresome, trying; spiteful.

¹**Schild** [ʃɪlt], **1.** *m.* (**-(e)s,** *pl.* **-e**) shield, buckler; escutcheon, coat of arms; shell, (*Zool.*) carapace, scutum; ***auf den – (er)heben,*** choose as leader; ***den – der Ehre blank*** or ***rein erhalten,*** maintain one's reputation untarnished, have no blot on one's escutcheon; ***einen Eber im –e führen,*** bear the wild boar on one's coat of arms; (*fig.*) ***etwas im –e führen,*** be up to s.th., have s.th. up one's sleeve; ***Schirm und – sein,*** be shield and protector; ***zum –e geboren sein,*** be of noble birth.

²**Schild,** *n.* (**-(e)s,** *pl.* **-er**) sign-board, fascia; (brass) plate, door-plate, name-plate; badge, label, ticket; peak (*of a cap*); ***das – aushängen*** (***einziehen***), open (shut up) business *or* a shop.

Schild|abteilung, *f. See* **–teilung. –amsel,** *f. See* **Ringdrossel. –blume,** *f.* (*Bot.*) aspidistra (*Chelone obliqua*). **–bogen,** *m.* arcaded arch. **–bürger,** *m.* Gothamite. **–decke,** *f.* (*Her.*) mantle of the shield. **–drüse,** *f.* (*Anat.*) thyroid gland.

Schilder|haus, *n.* sentry-box. **–maler,** *m.* sign-painter.

schildern ['ʃɪldərn], *v.t.* describe, depict, delineate, portray, give an account of; draw, outline, sketch, (*dial.*) paint. **Schilderung,** *f.* description, delineation, representation, portrayal, account; sketch, outline.

schildförmig ['ʃɪltfœrmɪç], *adj.* shield-shaped, (*Bot.*) scutiform, (*Zool.*) clypeate, clypeiform. **Schild|halter,** *m. See* **–knappe;** *pl.* (*Her.*) supporters. **–haupt,** *n.* (*Her.*) chief. **–jungfrau,** *f.* battle-maiden, Valkyrie. **–käfer,** *m.* (*Ent.*) tortoise-beetle (*Cassididae*). **–knappe, –knecht,** *m.* shield-bearer, squire. **–knorpel,** *m.* thyroid cartilage, shield cartilage, Adam's apple. **–krot,** *n. See* **–patt. –kröte,** *f.* tortoise (*land*); turtle (*sea*). **–kröten-suppe,** *f.* turtle soup. **–lager,** *n.* (*Artil.*) trunnion bearing. **–laus,** *f.* (*Ent.*) shield-louse, scale-insect (*Coccidae*). **–lehen,** *n.* knight's fief. **–patt,** *n.* tortoise-shell. **–rand,** *m.* (*Her.*) bordure. **–teilung,** *f.* (*Her.*) quartering. **–träger,** *m. See* **–knappe. –wache,** *f.* sentinel, sentry; – ***zu Pferde,*** vedette; – ***stehen,*** stand guard *or* sentry. **–wacht,** *f.* sentry-go; sentry. **–zapfen,** *m.* (*Artil.*) trunnion.

Schilf [ʃɪlf], *n.* **(-(e)s,** *pl.* **-e)** reed, rush, bulrush. **schilfartig,** *adj.* arundinaceous, reedy. **Schilf-decke,** *f.* rush-mat.

Schilfe [ˈʃɪlfə], *f. See* **Schelfe.**

schilfen [ˈʃɪlfən], *v.t.* clear of reeds. **Schilfgras,** *n.* sedge. **schilfig,** *adj.* reedy, sedgy. **Schilf|meer,** *n.* (*B.*) Red Sea. **–rohr,** *n.* reed; (*Bot.*) reeds, sedge (*Phragmites communis*). **–rohrsänger,** *m.* (*Orn.*) sedge-warbler (*Acrocephalus schoenobaenus*).

Schiller [ˈʃɪlər], *m.* play of colours; iridescence. **Schillerfalter,** *m.* (*Ent.*) purple emperor (*Apatura iris*).

Schillerkragen [ˈʃɪlərkraːgən], *m.* open collar.

schillern [ˈʃɪlərn], *v.i.* opalesce, scintillate, be iridescent *or* opalescent. **schillernd,** *adj.* iridescent, opalescent, scintillating, glittering. **Schiller|-seide,** *f.* shot silk. **–wein,** *m.* mixed red and white wine.

Schilling [ˈʃɪlɪŋ], *m.* **(-s,** *pl.* **-e)** shilling.

schilt [ʃɪlt], **schilt(e)st,** *see* **schelten.**

Schimäre [ʃiˈmɛːrə], *f.* chimera. **schimärisch,** *adj.* chimerical.

Schimmel [ˈʃɪməl], *m.* 1. mould, mildew; 2. grey *or* white horse. **Schimmelflecken,** *m.pl.* mildew stains. **schimmelig,** *adj.* mouldy, mildewed, musty. **schimmeln,** *v.i.* (*aux.* h. & s.) grow mouldy, moulder; (*coll.*) ***das Mädchen schimmelt,*** the girl is a wallflower. **Schimmelpilz,** *m.* mould (fungus), mildew, mycoderin.

Schimmer [ˈʃɪmər], *m.* glitter, shine, shimmer, glimmer, gleam, glint, lustre; (*dial.*) twilight, dusk; (*coll.*) ***ich habe keinen (blassen) – (davon),*** I have not the faintest idea; (*coll.*) ***kein – von Aussicht,*** not the ghost of a chance; ***ein – von Hoffnung,*** a flicker *or* gleam of hope. **schimmern,** *v.i.* glitter, glisten, gleam, glint, glimmer, shine.

Schimpanse [ʃɪmˈpanzə], *m.* **(-n,** *pl.* **-n)** chimpanzee.

Schimpf [ʃɪmpf], *m.* **(-(e)s,** *pl.* **-e)** insult, affront; disgrace, outrage; (*dial.*) joke, jest, fun; ***ihm einen – antun,*** insult him; ***einen – auf sich*** (*Dat.*) ***sitzen lassen,*** swallow an insult; ***mit – und Schande,*** ignominiously; ***ihm – und Schande nachsagen,*** disparage *or* vilify *or* speak ill of him.

schimpfen [ˈʃɪmpfən], **1.** *v.t.* insult, abuse, revile; ***ihn einen Schurken –,*** call him a blackguard. **2.** *v.i.* (***auf*** or ***über*** (*Acc.*)) grumble (about), scold; rail *or* swear (at). **Schimpfen,** *n.*, **Schimpferei,** *f.* grumbling, scolding, reviling, abusive language. **Schimpfgedicht,** *n.* lampoon. **schimpfieren** [–ˈfiːrən], *v.t.* (*coll.*) insult, malign, revile. **schimpflich,** *adj.* disgraceful, ignominious, outrageous, infamous; (*dial.*) joking. **Schimpf|-name,** *m.*, **–wort,** *n.* rude name, term of abuse, swear-word, invective.

Schinakel [ʃiˈnakəl], *n.* (*Austr.*) (little) boat, skiff.

Schind|aas, *n.* carrion. **–anger,** *m.* knacker's yard.

Schindel [ˈʃɪndəl], *f.* (-, *pl.* **-n)** shingle, wooden tile *or* slat; (*Her.*) billet. **Schindeldach,** *n.* shingle roof. **schindeln,** *v.t.* cover *or* roof with shingles; (*Med.*) put in splints.

schinden [ˈʃɪndən], **1.** *irr.v.t.* skin, flay; (*fig.*) oppress, ill-treat; (*coll.*) wangle, try to get (*s.th.*) for nothing; (*sl.*) ***Eindruck –,*** show off, be out to impress; (*sl.*) ***das Fahrgeld –,*** travel without a ticket; (*Univ. sl.*) ***Kolleg –,*** gatecrash a lecture; (*sl.*) ***Lokal –,*** sit in a restaurant without ordering anything; (*sl.*) ***Zeilen –,*** do hack writing; ***Zeit –,*** temporize, play for time. **2.** *irr.v.r.* work o.s. to death, drudge, slave.

Schinder [ˈʃɪndər], *m.* knacker; (*fig.*) oppressor, sweater, (*coll.*) slave-driver. **Schinderei** [–ˈraɪ], *f.* (*fig.*) oppression, ill-treatment, sweating; grind, drudgery.

schindern [ˈʃɪndərn], *v.i.* (*aux.* s.) (*dial.*) slide (on ice).

Schind|grube, *f. See* **–anger. –luder,** *n.* broken-down *or* worn-out animal; (*fig.*) ***– treiben mit,*** play fast and loose with, play old Harry with. **–mähre,** *f.* miserable jade.

Schinken [ˈʃɪŋkən], *m.* 1. ham; ***mit der Wurst nach dem – werfen,*** use a sprat to catch a mackerel; – ***mit Ei,*** ham and eggs; 2. (*sl.*) wretched daub; 3. (*sl.*) fat tome; (*sl.*) fat backside. **Schinken|brot, –brötchen,** *n.* ham-sandwich, ham-roll. **–schnitte,** *f.* slice of ham.

Schinn [ˈʃɪn], *m.* **(-(e)s,** *pl.* **-e), Schinne,** *f.* (*usu. pl.*) scurf, dandruff. **schinnen,** *v.r.* scratch one's head.

Schippe [ˈʃɪpə], *f.* shovel, scoop, (child's) spade; (*Cards*) spade; (*coll.*) ***eine – machen,*** pout. **schippen,** *v.t.* 1. shovel, scoop; 2. (*coll.*) tease, rag, rib. **Schipper,** *m.* (*Mil., coll.*) fatigue man, soldier on fatigues.

Schirm [ʃɪrm], *m.* **(-(e)s,** *pl.* **-e)** umbrella; parasol, sunshade; (lamp-)shade; screen, shield, protective cover; (*Rad., T.V., Films*) screen; peak (*of a cap*); (*Bot.*) umbel; (*fig.*) shield, shelter, protection; ***Schutz und –,*** protection, protector, safeguard; ***unter seinem Schutz und –,*** under his patronage *or* protection.

Schirm|bezug, *m.* (umbrella-)cover. **–bildverfahren,** *n.* mass radiography. **–dach,** *n.* shelter, shed; tilt.

schirmen [ˈʃɪrmən], *v.t.* screen, shield, shelter, protect (***vor*** (*Dat.*), from *or* against), defend, guard (against).

Schirmfläche [ˈʃɪrmflɛçə], *f.* shaded area, covered space. **schirmförmig,** *adj.* (*Bot.*) umbellate, umbelliform. **Schirm|gestell,** *n.* umbrella-frame. **–gitter,** *n.* (*Rad.*) screen grid. **–gitterröhre,** *f.* (*Rad.*) tetrode. **–herr,** *m.* protector, patron. **–herrin,** *f.* protectress, patroness. **–herrschaft,** *f.* patronage, auspices. **–mütze,** *f.* peaked cap. **–palme,** *f.* (*Bot.*) fan-palm, talipot (*Corypha umbraculifera*). **–pflanze,** *f.* umbelliferous plant. **–ständer,** *m.* umbrella-stand.

Schirokko [ʃiˈrɔko], *m.* sirocco.

schirren [ˈʃɪrən], *v.t.* harness. **Schirr|kammer,** *f.* harness-room. **–kette,** *f.* pole-chain. **–macher,** *m.* cartwright. **–meister,** *m.* head ostler; (*Mil.*) M.T. sergeant.

Schirting [ˈʃɪrtɪŋ], *m.* **(-s,** *pl.* **-e** (*Austr.* **-s))** shirting.

Schisma [ˈʃɪsma], *n.* **(-s,** *pl.* **-men** (*Austr.* **-mata))** schism. **schismatisch** [–ˈmaːtɪʃ], *adj.* schismatic.

Schiß [ʃɪs], *m.* **(-(ss)es,** *no pl.*) (*vulg.*) shit; (*fig. coll.*) funk, (*vulg.*) the shits; (*vulg.*) – ***(in den Hosen) haben,*** shit o.s. with fright, have the shits.

schizophren [ʃɪtsoˈfreːn], *adj.* schizophrenic. **Schizophrenie** [–ˈniː], *f.* schizophrenia.

schlabb(e)rig, *adj.* sloppy, watery. **schlabbern** [ˈʃlabərn], *v.i.* slobber, slaver; (*Tech.*) overflow; (*coll.*) jabber, babble. **Schlabber|rohr,** *n.* overflow-pipe. **–ventil,** *n.* check-valve.

Schlacht [ʃlaxt], *f.* (-, *pl.* **-en)** battle (***bei,*** of); ***regelrechte –,*** pitched battle; ***eine – liefern*** or ***schlagen,*** give battle, fight a battle.

Schlacht|bank, *f.* shambles, slaughter-house; (*fig.*) ***zur – führen,*** lead like a lamb to the slaughter. **–beil,** *n.* poleaxe.

schlachten [ˈʃlaxtən], *v.t., v.i.* kill, slaughter (*animals*), slay, sacrifice, immolate (*a victim*), (*fig.*) butcher, slaughter, massacre (*the enemy*).

Schlachten|bummler, *m.* camp-follower. **–glück,** *n.* fortune of war. **–gott,** *m.* God of battles, Mars. **–lenker,** *m.* God of Hosts. **–maler,** *m.* painter of battle-scenes.

Schlachter [ˈʃlaxtər], **Schlächter** [ˈʃlɛçtər], *m.* (*dial.*) butcher. **Schlächterei** [–ˈraɪ], *f.* butcher's shop, (*fig.*) butchery, massacre, slaughter.

Schlacht|feld, *n.* battlefield; *auf dem – bleiben,* fall in battle; *das – behaupten,* be victorious. **-flieger-bombe,** *f.* anti-personnel bomb. **-fliegergruppe,** *f.* (*Av.*) army-cooperation unit. **-gemälde,** *n.* *See* **-stück. -gesang,** *m.* battle-song. **-geschrei,** *n.* war-cry. **-getöse,** *n.* din of battle. **-getümmel,** *n.* mêlée; *mitten im –,* in the thick of the fight. **-gewicht,** *n.* dead weight, carcass weight. **-gewühl,** *n.* *See* **getümmel. -haus,** *n.*, **-hof,** *m.* slaughter-house, abattoir. **-linie,** *f.* line of battle. **-messer,** *n.* butcher's knife. **-opfer,** *n.* victim, sacrifice. **-ordnung,** *f.* order of battle, battle array. **-plan,** *m.* plan of action *or* operations. **-reihe,** *f.* *See* **-linie. -roß,** *n.* war-horse, charger. **-ruf,** *m.* battle *or* war-cry. **-schiff,** *n.* battleship. **-schwert,** *n.* broadsword. **-stück,** *n.* (*Paint.*) battle-scene. **Schlachtung,** *f.* slaughtering. **Schlachtvieh,** *n.* fat stock.

Schlack [ʃlak], *m.* (*dial.*) sleet, slush, slushy weather. **schlack,** *adj.* (*dial.*) *see* **schlaff. Schlack-darm,** *m.* rectum.

Schlacke [ˈʃlakə], *f.* 1. dross (*also fig.*), slag, scoria, cinders, clinker; waste matter; 2. (*dial.*) rectum. **schlacken,** *v.i.* leave dross, form slag, precipitate sediment; (*dial.*) *es schlackt,* it is sleeting.

Schlacken|bahn, *f.* (*Spt.*) cinder-track. **-bildung,** *f.* scorification. **schlackenfrei,** *adj.* free from dross. **Schlacken|halde,** *f.* slag-heap. **-sand,** *m.* ground clinker. **-sieb,** *n.* clinker screen. **-staub,** *m.* coal dust, slack, dross. **-stein,** *m.* slag-stone. **-wolle,** *f.* mineral wool.

schlackerig [ˈʃlakərɪç], *adj.* 1. (*dial.*) dangling, tottering; 2. sleety, slushy. **schlackern,** *v.i.* 1. (*dial.*) slouch, dangle, totter; 2. *es schlackert,* it is sleeting. **Schlackerwetter,** *n.* (*dial.*) slushy *or* sleety weather.

schlackig [ˈʃlakɪç], *adj.* slaggy, drossy, scoriaceous; (*dial.*) slushy.

Schlack|wetter, *n.* *See* **Schlackerwetter. -wurst,** *f.* (fat) North German sausage.

Schlaf [ʃla:f], *m.* sleep, slumber; *sie hat einen bleiernen –,* she sleeps like a log; *das wäre mir nicht im -e eingefallen,* I should never have dreamt of such a thing; *fester –,* sound *or* heavy sleep; *einen festen – haben,* be a sound *or* heavy sleeper; *im -e,* while asleep, in one's sleep; (*fig.*) *im -e tun können,* do blindfold, do (standing) on one's head; *die ganze Nacht ist kein – in meine Augen gekommen,* I have not slept a wink all night; *er hat einen leichten –,* he is a light sleeper; *hypnotischer –,* hypnotic trance; *in – sinken,* fall asleep, drop off to sleep; *in – wiegen* (*singen*), rock (sing, lull) to sleep.

Schlaf|abteil, *n.* sleeping-compartment, (*coll.*) sleeper. **-anzug,** *m.* sleeping-suit, pyjamas, (*Am.*) pajamas.

Schläfchen [ˈʃlɛ:fçən], *n.* doze, nap, snooze, (*coll.*) forty winks, catnap, (*sl.*) shut-eye; *ein – machen,* take *or* have a nap *or* snooze, have forty winks, (*sl.*) get some shut-eye.

Schlafdecke [ˈʃla:fdɛkə], *f.* blanket.

Schläfe [ˈʃlɛ:fə], *f.* (*Anat.*) temple.

schlafen [ˈʃla:fən], *irr.v.i.* sleep, be asleep; slumber, rest, repose; be *or* lie dormant; *auswärts –,* sleep out; *bei ihm –,* sleep with him, spend the night with him; *fest –,* be fast asleep; *– gehen,* go to bed; (*coll.*) turn in; *länger –,* sleep late *or* (*coll.*) in; *zu lange –,* oversleep; (*fig.*) *eine Sache – lassen,* let a matter rest *or* drop; *– legen,* put to bed; *sich – legen,* go to bed. **schlafend,** *adj.* sleeping, (*pred.*) asleep, (*fig.*) dormant.

Schläfen- [ˈʃlɛ:fən], *pref.* temporal; *see* **Schläfe.**

Schlafengehen [ˈʃla:fənge:ən], *n.* *vor dem –,* before going to bed, before retiring. **Schlafenszeit,** *f.* bedtime.

Schläfer [ˈʃlɛ:fər], *m.* sleeper.

schläfern [ˈʃlɛ:fərn], *v.imp.* *es schläfert mich,* I am *or* feel sleepy *or* drowsy.

schlaferzeugend [ˈʃla:fˀɛrtsɔygənt], *adj.* soporific, sleep-inducing.

schlaff [ʃlaf], *adj.* slack, loose, limp; flabby, flaccid; (*fig.*) lax, loose (*as morals*), slack (*of behaviour*), flabby (*as style*), (*St. Exch.*) sluggish, slack; *– machen* (*v.t.*), *– werden* (*v.i.*), slacken, relax. **Schlaff-heit,** *f.* slackness, limpness, flabbiness, flaccidity, (*fig.*) laxity, looseness; indolence, (*Med.*) atony.

Schlaf|gänger, -gast, *m.* night lodger, overnight visitor (*in hotel*). **-gefährte,** *m.* bedfellow. **-gelegenheit,** *f.* sleeping accommodation. **-ge-mach,** *n.* *See* **-zimmer. -genosse, -gesell,** *m.* *See* **-gefährte.**

Schlafittchen [ʃlaˈfɪtçən], *n.* (*coll.*) coat-tails; *ihn beim – nehmen* or *packen,* (seize by the) collar, seize by the scruff of the neck.

Schlaf|kamerad, *m.* bedfellow. **-kammer,** *f.* (small) bedroom, bed-recess. **-koje,** *f.* (sleeping) berth, bunk. **-krankheit,** *f.* sleeping sickness, epidemic encephalitis. **-lied,** *n.* lullaby.

schlaflos [ˈʃla:flo:s], *adj.* sleepless. **Schlaflosig-keit,** *f.* insomnia.

Schlaf|mittel, *n.* sleeping-tablet, soporific, narcotic. **-mütze,** *f.* 1. night-cap; 2. (*fig.*) slowcoach, sleepyhead. **schlafmützig,** *adj.* sleepy, (*fig.*) dull, slow. **Schlaf|pille,** *f.* *See* **-mittel. -ratte,** *f.*, **-ratz,** *m.*, **-ratze,** *f.* sound sleeper; dormouse; slowcoach.

schläfrig [ˈʃlɛ:frɪç], *adj.* sleepy, drowsy, somnolent, (*fig.*) dull, slow, indolent. **Schläfrigkeit,** *f.* sleepiness, drowsiness, somnolence, (*fig.*) dullness, indolence.

Schlaf|rock, *m.* dressing-gown; *Apfel im –,* apple-dumpling. **-saal,** *m.* dormitory. **-sack,** *m.* sleeping-bag. **-sofa,** *n.* bed-settee. **-stätte, -stelle,** *f.* night's lodging, overnight accommodation; lodging house. **-stellung,** *f.* sleeping *or* nocturnal position. **-störung,** *f.* troubled sleep. **-stube,** *f.* *See* **-zimmer. -sucht,** *f.* somnolence, lethargy. **schlafsüchtig,** *adj.* somnolent, drowsy, lethargic. **Schlaf|tablette,** *f.* *See* **-mittel. -trank,** *m.* sleeping draught. **-trunk,** *m.* drink before retiring, (*coll.*) night-cap. **schlaftrunken,** *adj.* overcome with sleep, very drowsy. **Schlaf|wachen,** *n.* somnambulism. **-wagen,** *m.* (*Railw.*) sleeping-car, (*coll.*) sleeper. **schlafwandeln,** *etc.* *See* **nacht-wandeln. Schlaf|zeug,** *n.* (*coll.*) night-things. **-zimmer,** *n.* bedroom.

Schlag [ʃla:k], *m.* **(-(e)s,** *pl.* **¨-e)** 1. blow, knock, bang, (*coll.*) whack, biff; tap, rap, slap, smack, (*coll.*) cuff; punch, (*sl.*) sock; kick; beat (*also Mus.*), oscillation, pulsation; stroke (*of chiming clock, piston, oar*); shock, impact, hit; (*Med.*) apoplectic fit, (*coll.*) stroke; clap (*of thunder*), chime (*of clocks*), song (*of birds*); *von einem andern -e,* cast in a different mould; *auf einen –,* see *mit einem –* (*fig.*); *– auf –,* one after the other, in rapid succession; *Schläge bekommen,* get a (good) beating; *elektrischer –,* electric shock; *– ins Gesicht,* slap in the face; *einen großen – machen,* have great success, make *or* be a (great) hit; undertake great things; *zwei Herzen und ein –,* two hearts that beat as one; *kalter –,* flash of lightning that blasts without igniting; *mit einem –,* with a crash *or* bang, (*fig.*) at one blow *or* (*coll.*) go, all at once; *– 10 Uhr,* on the stroke of 10, at 10 sharp, punctually at 10; *– ins Wasser,* vain attempt, wild-goose chase, (*coll.*) flop; 2. carriage-door; 3. pigeon loft, dovecot; 4. plot, strip, parcel (*of land*); helping, (*sl.*) whack (*of food*); clearing (*in forest*); 5. (*Naut.*) tack; coil, turn, bend, bight (*in rope*); 6. (*fig.*) stamp, kind, sort, type, breed, stock; coinage, stamping; *der gewöhnliche –,* the common run (*of men etc.*); *vom alten -e,* of the old school; *von gleichem -e,* of the same sort *or* stamp *or* character; *schoner – Pferde,* fine breed of horses; 7. (*Min.*) horizontal workings.

Schlag|ader, *f.* artery. **-anfall,** *m.* apoplectic fit, stroke. **schlagartig, 1.** *adj.* sudden, abrupt, violent. **2.** *adv.* all of a sudden, at a moment's notice, (*sl.*) with a bang. **Schlag|ball,** *m.* rounders. **-band,** *n.* (*Swiss*) sword knot. **-baum,** *m.* turnpike. **-biegefestigkeit,** *f.* (*Tech.*) impact bending strength. **-bolzen,** *m.* firing-pin, striker.

schlagen [ˈʃla:gən], **1.** *irr.v.t.* beat, strike, hit, punch, (*Poet.*) smite, (*coll.*) biff, (*sl.*) sock; knock, rap, clap, tap, pat; smack, *(coll.)* cuff, spank, whack, *(at school)* cane; kick; beat, whip, whisk *(eggs etc.)*; fell, cut *(trees)*; coin, stamp *(money)*; toll *(a bell)*, *(Mus.)* touch, strike *(a note)*; beat, defeat, rout, trounce, *(sl.)* lick *(an enemy)*; ***Alarm –,*** sound the alarm; ***– an*** *(Acc.)*, fasten to, nail on; ***ans Kreuz –,*** crucify, nail to the cross; ***den Feind aufs Haupt –,*** defeat *or* overthrow the enemy; ***seine Unkosten auf die Ware –,*** add *or* *(coll.)* clap one's expenses to the price of a th.; ***ihm etwas aus der Hand –,*** knock s.th. out of his hand; ***sich*** *(Dat.)* ***etwas aus den Gedanken*** or ***dem Kopfe*** or ***Sinne –,*** dismiss something from one's thoughts *or* mind, put s.th. out of one's mind; ***eine Brücke – über*** *(Acc.)*, throw a bridge across; ***durch ein Sieb –,*** pass through a sieve; ***Falten –,*** wrinkle, get creased; ***zwei Fliegen mit einer Klappe –,*** kill two birds with one stone; ***die Arme (Hände) ineinander –,*** fold one's arms (clasp one's hands); ***in Fesseln –,*** put in irons; ***die Augen in die Höhe –,*** raise one's eyes; ***in Papier –,*** wrap up in paper; ***sein Leben in die Schanze –,*** risk his life; ***in den Wind –,*** cast to the four winds; ***aus einer S. Kapital –,*** make capital out of a th., turn s.th. to account; ***die Karten –,*** read the cards, tell fortunes with cards; ***den Kopf – an*** *(Acc.)*, knock *or* bang *or* bump one's head against *or* on; ***kurz und klein –,*** smash to pieces; ***mit Blindheit –,*** strike blind, smite with blindness; ***einen Nagel – in*** *(Acc.)*, drive a nail into; ***einen Purzelbaum –,*** turn a somersault; *(Spt.)* ***einen Rekord –,*** break a record; ***Schaum –,*** whip into froth; *(fig.)* talk rubbish, *(coll.)* blether; ***eine Schlacht –,*** fight a battle, give battle; ***ihm ein Schnippchen –,*** play a trick on him; ***den Takt –,*** beat time; ***diese Uhr schlägt die Stunden,*** this clock strikes the hours; ***sich*** *(Dat.)* ***die Nacht um die Ohren –,*** sit *or* stay up all night, drink *or* carouse the whole night through; ***sich*** *(Dat.)* ***die Welt um die Ohren –,*** go out into the wide world, let the wind blow round one's ears; ***um die Schultern –,*** throw round one's shoulders; ***Wurzel –,*** take root; ***zu Boden –,*** knock down, floor *(a p.)*; ***die Augen zu Boden –,*** cast down one's eyes; ***einen Zweifel zu Boden –,*** silence a misgiving, overcome a scruple, remove a doubt; ***die Zinsen zum Kapital –,*** add the interest to the capital; ***ihn zum Ritter –,*** dub him a knight, invest him with knighthood; ***ein geschlagener Mann,*** a ruined *or* broken man; ***eine geschlagene Stunde,*** a full *or* whole *or* *(coll.)* solid hour; ***den ganzen geschlagenen Tag,*** the livelong day.

2. *irr.v.r.* hit, knock, bang, bump *or* *(coll.)* biff o.s.; *(of two p.)* come to blows, (have *or* start a) fight; fence, fight a duel; ***sich an die Brust –,*** beat one's breast; ***sich an die Stirn –,*** clutch *or* smite one's brow; ***die Erkältung schlägt sich auf den Magen,*** the cold settles on the stomach; ***sich auf die Seite der Verschworenen –,*** take the part of *or* join the conspirators; ***sich recht und schlecht durchs Leben –,*** make one's way in the world after a fashion; ***sich ins Mittel –,*** interpose, mediate; ***sich links –,*** turn to the left; ***sich tapfer*** or ***gut –,*** hold one's own, stand one's ground, fight well, *(coll.)* put up a good show; ***sich – zu,*** take sides with, side with, go over to, join.

3. *irr.v.i.* beat *(also of heart* , strike *(also of clocks)*; throb; sing *(of some birds)*; kick, lash out *(of a horse)*; ***liebliche Töne schlugen an mein Ohr,*** sweet sounds fell upon my ear; ***bei ihm auf den Busch –,*** tap him, put out feelers; ***der Qualm schlägt ihm auf die Brust*** or ***Lunge,*** the fumes catch his chest *or* make him choke; ***ihm auf die Finger –,*** rap his knuckles; ***mit der Faust auf den Tisch –,*** thump the table, bang one's fist on the table; ***aus der Art –,*** go one's own way(s), be different from the others; *(coll.)* ***nun schlägt es aber 13!*** that's the limit! I can't stand any more! ***die Tinte schlägt durchs Papier,*** the ink soaks through the paper; ***sein Herz schlägt warm für . . .,*** he has a soft spot for . . .; ***die Flammen – gen*** or ***zum Himmel,*** the flames shoot up to the sky; ***das Gewehr schlägt stark,*** the rifle has a strong kick; ***das Gewissen schlägt ihm,*** his conscience pricks him, he is stung with remorse; ***er weiß, was die Glocke geschlagen hat,*** he is (well) aware of the situation, he has no illusions about the matter; ***das Herz schlägt mir,*** my heart is pounding *or* thumping; ***der Blitz schlägt in das Haus,*** the lightning strikes the house; ***das schlägt nicht in mein Fach,*** that is not in my line; ***einer S. ins Gesicht –,*** set s.th. at naught, make a mock of a th., scoff at *or* deride a th.; ***mit den Flügeln –,*** flap *or* beat one's wings; ***die Nachtigall schlägt,*** the nightingale is singing; *(Chess)* ***die Bauern ziehen geradeaus, – aber schräg,*** pawns move forwards but take diagonally; *(fig.)* ***– nach,*** take after; ***seine Stunde hat geschlagen,*** his hour has come; ***dem Glücklichen schlägt keine Stunde,*** a happy man is oblivious to time; ***über den Strang*** or ***die Stränge –,*** kick over the traces; ***die Uhr schlug,*** the clock struck; ***heftig um sich –,*** lay about one with *or* set to with one's fists; ***wie vor den Kopf geschlagen sein,*** be dumbfounded, be at a loss; ***der Wagen schlägt,*** the carriage jolts.

Schlagen, *n.* striking, beating; pulsation, throbbing; singing, warbling *(of birds)*; kicking *(of horses)*; fighting; construction *(of a bridge)*; felling *(of timber)*. **schlagend,** *adj.* striking, impressive; ***–e Antwort,*** irrefutable answer; ***–er Beweis,*** conclusive *or* compelling evidence, convincing proof; ***–er Grund,*** cogent reason; *(Univ.)* ***–e Verbindung,*** duelling club; *(Min.)* ***–e Wetter*** *(pl.)*, firedamp.

Schlager ['ʃla:gər], *m.* pop(ular) song, *(coll.)* hit, *(Theat.)* box-office draw, *(sl.)* smash hit; good selling line *(in shops)*.

Schläger ['ʃlɛ:gər], *m.* 1. hitter, striker, batsman; kicker *(said of horses)*; rowdy, brawler, *(coll.)* tough, bruiser, *(sl.)* hoodlum; 2. sword, rapier; (cricket) bat, (hockey) stick, (tennis-)racket; (golf-)club; 3. singing-bird, warbler. **Schlägerei** [–'raɪ], *f* free fight, brawl, scuffle, *(sl.)* roughhouse, free-for-all.

Schlager|komponist, *m.* pop(ular)-song writer. **–melodie,** *f.* pop-song, *pl.* pop-music.

schlägern ['ʃlɛ:gərn], *v.t.* *(Austr.)* fell *(trees)*.

Schlager|parade, *f.* hit-parade, top of the pops. **–preis,** *m.* rock-bottom *or* give-away price. **–sänger,** *m.* pop-singer.

Schlagfeder ['ʃla:kfe:dər], *f.* striking-spring *(in clocks)*; striker-spring *(in a gun)*. **schlagfertig,** *adj.* ready with one's tongue, quick-witted, quick at repartee; ***–e Antwort,*** repartee; *(sl.)* snappy come-back. **Schlag|fertigkeit,** *f.* 1. ready wit, quickness of repartee; 2. *(Mil.)* tactical readiness. **–festigkeit,** *f.* *(Metall.)* impact strength. **–fluß,** *m.* apoplectic fit, apoplexy. **–holz,** *n.* 1. (cricket-)bat; 2. copse, wood for felling. **–instrument,** *n.* percussion instrument. **–kraft,** *f.* force of impact, hitting *or* striking power, *(Mil.)* fighting power, *(fig.)* effectiveness, *(coll.)* punch, drive. **schlagkräftig,** *adj.* powerful, striking, effective, efficient; ***–er Beweis,*** *see under* **schlagend.**

Schlag|licht, *n.* strong *or* glaring light, glare. **–loch,** *n.* pot-hole, *pl.* bad surface *(of road)*. **–lot,** *n.* hard solder. **–mann,** *m.* stroke *(in rowing)*. **–matrize,** *f.* stamping die. **–mühle,** *f.* crusher *(for ore)*. **–obers,** *n.* *(Austr.)* whipped cream. **–pulver,** *n.* fulminating powder. **–rahm,** *m.* whipped cream. **–regen,** *m.* downpour, pelting rain. **–reim,** *m.* rhyme of successive words. **–ring,** *m.* 1. *(Mus.)* plectrum; 2. knuckle-duster. **–röhre,** *f.* *(Artil.)* friction igniter, primer. **–sahne,** *f.* whipped cream. **–schatten,** *m.* cast shadow. **–schatz,** *m.* brassage. **–schwirl,** *m.* *(Orn.)* river warbler *(Lucustella fluviatilis)*. **–seite,** *f.* *(Naut.)* list; *(sl.)* ***– haben,*** be half-seas over. **–uhr,** *f.* repeater; striking-clock. **–wärter,** *m.* toll-keeper. **–wasser,** *n.* bilge-water. **–weite,** *f.* *(Artil.)* striking distance, effective range; *(Elec.)* spark distance. **–welle,** *f.* 1. surge, roller; 2. camber. **–werk,** *n.* striking mechanism *(of clock)*. **–wetter,** *n.* firedamp. **–wort,** *n.* catchword, slogan; catch-phrase, caption, heading; shibboleth. **–wortkatalog,** *m.* subject catalogue. **–wunde,** *f.* contused wound. **–zeile,** *f.* headline. **–zeit,** *f.* felling time. **–zeug,** *n.* percussion (instruments). **–zeuger,** *m.* timpanist. **–zünder,** *m.* percussion-fuse.

Schlaks [ʃla:ks], *m.* (**-es**, *pl.* **-e**) (*coll.*) gangling *or* ungainly fellow. **schlaksig,** *adj.* (*coll.*) lanky, gangling.

Schlamassel [ʃla'masəl], *m.* (*sl.*) scrape, fix, mess, jam.

Schlamm [ʃlam], *m.* mud, slime, mire, ooze, sediment, (*Pott.*) slip, (*Motor.*) sludge. **Schlamm|bad,** *n.* mud-bath. **-beißer,** *m.* (*Ichth.*) mud-fish (*Cobites fossilis*).

schlämmen ['ʃlɛmən], *v.t.* dredge (*harbour*), clear mud from (*dock, etc.*), wash, buddle (*ore*), (*Chem.*) elutriate.

Schlammherd ['ʃlamhe:rt], **Schlämmherd,** *m.* (*Metall.*) buddle. **schlammig,** *adj.* muddy, slushy, miry, slimy, oozy.

Schlämm|kohle, *f.* washed coal. **-kreide,** *f.* whiting, whitening.

Schlamm|läufer, *m.* (*Orn.*) red-breasted snipe, (*Am.*) short-billed dowitcher (*Limnodromus griseus*). **-loch,** *n.* mud-hole. **-netz,** *n.* drag-net.

Schlämmpflanze ['ʃlɛmpflantsə], *f.* mud-plant.

Schlamm|pfütze, *f. See* **-loch.**

Schlämmschnecke ['ʃlɛmʃnɛkə], *f.* pond-snail.

Schlamp ['ʃlamp], *m.* (**-(e)s,** *pl.* **-e**) (*coll.*) slovenly fellow, sloven, oaf, lout.

schlampampen [ʃlam'pampən], *v.i.* (*coll.*) gorge o.s., guzzle.

Schlampe ['ʃlampə], *f.* 1. slut, slattern, sloven; 2. slipper, house-shoe (*see also* **Schlempe**). **schlampen,** *v.i.* do a slovenly job, bungle; be slovenly; (*aux.* s.) slouch, slummock. **Schlampen,** *m.* (*dial.*) rags, tatters. **Schlamper,** *m.* (*dial.*) *see* **Schlamp. Schlamperei** [–'raɪ], *f.* sluttishness, slatternly behaviour, slovenliness, shiftlessness, untidiness; (*coll.*) slackness, carelessness, unpunctuality; (*coll.*) mess, muddle. **schlampig,** *adj.* (*of a woman*) sluttish, slatternly, (*coll.*) frowzy; slovenly, untidy, unkempt; (*coll.*) slack, shiftless, careless, slipshod, sloppy.

schlang [ʃlaŋ], **schlänge** ['ʃlɛŋə], *see* **schlingen.**

Schlange ['ʃlaŋə], *f.* snake, serpent; coil, worm (*of a still*); queue, (*Am.*) line; (*fig.*) snake in the grass, viper; *– stehen,* queue (up), line up (*nach,* for).

schlängeln ['ʃlɛŋəln], *v.r.* twist, wind (in and out), meander; wriggle; (*fig.*) worm one's way (into), wriggle (out of). **schlängelnd,** *adj.* winding, twisting, meandering, sinuous, serpentine.

Schlangenadler ['ʃlaŋənˀa:tlər], *m.* (*Orn.*) short-toed eagle (*Circaetus gallicus*). **schlangen|ähnlich, -artig,** *adj.* serpentine, snake-like, snaky. **Schlangen|beschwörer,** *m.* snake-charmer. **-biß,** *m.* snakebite. **-bohrer,** *m.* spiral drill. **-geschlecht,** *n.* ophidians. **-gift,** *n.* snake venom. **-haar,** *n.* serpent locks (*of Medusa*). **-haut,** *f.* snake skin. **-kraut,** *n.* (*Bot.*) marsh-calla, bog-arum (*Calla palustris*). **-kühler,** *m.* spiral condenser.**-leder,** *n.* snake skin (leather). **-linie,** *f.* wavy line, (*Typ.*) waved rule. **-mensch,** *m.* contortionist, **-rohr,** *n.* worm (*of a still*). **-stab,** *m.* caduceus (*of Mercury*), Hermes' wand. **-stein,** *m.* ophite, serpentine. **-träger,** *m.* (*Astr.*) Ophiucus. **-weg,** *m.* winding *or* meandering path, serpentine. **-zunge,** *f.* (*Bot.*) adder's tongue (*Ophioglossum vulgatum*); (*fig.*) malicious *or* wicked tongue.

schlank [ʃlaŋk], *adj.* slim, slender; *-e Linie,* slimming line (*fashion*); *– machen,* slim; give a slim appearance, make one look slim (*of clothes*).

Schlankel ['ʃlaŋkəl], *m.* (*Austr.*) *see* **Schelm, Schlingel.**

Schlankheit ['ʃlaŋkhaɪt], *f.* slimness, slenderness, slim figure. **Schlankheitskur,** *f.* slimming *or* reducing treatment. **schlank|machend,** *adj.* slimming. **-weg,** *adv. See* **rundweg.**

schlapp [ʃlap], *adj.* (*coll.*) slack, limp, flabby, soft; (*fig.*) jaded, (*coll.*) done in; weak-kneed, spineless; (*coll.*) *– machen,* give way *or* up, droop, wilt, flag, (*sl.*) crock.

Schlappe ['ʃlapə], *f.* 1. blow, rebuff, check, setback; reverse, defeat, beating; (financial) loss; (*dial.*) slap; *eine – erhalten* or *erleiden,* be worsted *or* rebuffed, suffer a set-back *or* blow *or* defeat *or* loss *or* reverse; 2. (*dial.*) slipper; 3. (*dial.*) fainting fit.

schlappen ['ʃlapən], **1.** *v.i.* dangle, flap, slop about (*as ill-fitting shoes*). **2.** *v.t.* (*dial.*) swig, swill, guzzle (*liquids noisily*).

Schlappen, *m.* (*coll.*) slipper.

Schlapp|hut, *m.* slouch-hat. **-macher,** *m.* (*coll.*) slacker, quitter. **-ohr,** *n.* floppy ear. **-schuh,** *m. See* **Schlappen. -schwanz,** *m.* (*sl.*) weakling, coward, sissy.

Schlaraffen|land [ʃla'rafən–], *n.* Cockaigne, fool's paradise, land of milk and honey. **-leben,** *n.* life of idle luxury.

schlau [ʃlau], *adj.* sly, cunning, crafty, wily, artful, (*coll.*) smart, slick; (*coll.*) *er wird nie –,* he'll never learn; (*coll.*) *ich werde daraus nicht –,* I can't make head or tail of it.

Schlaube ['ʃlaubə], *f.* (*dial.*) husk.

Schlauberger, *m.* (sly) old fox, sly dog, sly-boots, artful dodger, (*sl.*) smart-aleck, smartie,s mart *or* slick operator.

Schlauch [ʃlaux], *m.* (**-es,** *pl.* **⸚e**) 1. tube, tubing, pipe, hose; (*of tyre*) inner tube; leathern bottle *or* skin; 2. (*Bot.*) ampulla, utricle; 3. (*sl.*) toper, guzzler; *er trinkt wie ein –,* he drinks like a fish; 4. (*coll.*) fag, strain, tough job; 5. (*sl.*) crib, (*Am.*) pony. **Schlauch|anschluß,** *m.* hose-coupling. **-balg,** *m.* (*Bot., Zool., Anat.*) utricle. **-boot,** *n.* inflatable dinghy. **schlauchen,** *v.t.* fill (*barrels etc.*) by a pipe; (*coll.*) give it (*a p.*) hot and strong, give (*a p.*) hell *or* (*Am.*) chicken. **Schlauchventil,** *n.* tyre-valve.

Schlauder ['ʃlaudər], *f.* (**-,** *pl.* **-n**) brace, iron tie.

Schläue ['ʃlɔyə], *f.* (*rare*) *see* **Schlauheit.**

schlauerweise ['ʃlauərvaɪzə], *adv.* cunningly, craftily; wisely, prudently.

Schlauf [ʃlauf], *m.* (**-s,** *pl.* **-e**), **Schlaufe,** *f. See* **Schleife.**

Schlauheit ['ʃlauhaɪt], *f.* slyness, cunning, craftiness, wiliness, artfulness, (*coll.*) smartness. **Schlau|kopf, -meier,** *m. See* **-berger.**

schlecht [ʃlɛçt], **1.** *adj.* bad, wicked, evil, base; poor, inferior, wretched; (*dial.*) straight, plain, simple; (*coll.*) angry; *-er Absatz,* poor demand *or* sale; *-e Aussichten,* poor prospects; *-e Behandlung,* ill-treatment; *billig und –,* cheap and nasty; *ihm -en Dank wissen,* give him no thanks; *ihm einen -en Dienst erweisen,* do him an ill service; *-e Führung,* bad behaviour, misconduct; *-es Haus,* house of ill repute, disorderly house; *-e Papiere,* worthless stocks *or* bills; *-er Trost,* cold comfort; *– werden,* turn sour, go bad; *-er werden,* get worse, worsen, deteriorate; *es kann einem dabei – werden,* it's sickening, it is enough to make one feel sick; *-e Zeiten,* hard times. **2.** *adv.* badly, poorly, ill; *– aussehen,* look bad, (*of a p.*) look ill; *bei ihm – angeschrieben sein,* be in his bad books; *ihm – bekommen,* do him no good; *das soll ihm – bekommen!* he'll pay for this! he won't get away with this! *– beraten,* ill-advised; *– gehen,* (*of a clock*) keep poor time; *es geht mir –,* I'm not well; *immer -er,* from bad to worse; *ich kann es mir – leisten,* I can ill afford (*to do*); *– und recht,* after a fashion, as well as may be, somehow, (*coll.*) so-so; *es ist mir –,* I feel ill; *– zu sprechen sein auf* (*Acc.*), be ill-disposed towards, (*coll.*) have it in for; *es steht – um ihn,* he is in a bad way; *es steht dir – an,* it ill becomes you (*to do*); (*coll.*) *ich staunte nicht –,* I wasn't half surprised; *– dabei wegkommen,* come off badly.

schlechterdings ['ʃlɛçtərdɪŋs], *adv.* by all means, downright, utterly, positively, absolutely; *– nicht,* not by any means, by no means.

schlechtgelaunt ['ʃlɛçtgəlaunt], *adj.* in a bad temper *or* mood, ill-humoured, (*coll.*) cross. **Schlechtheit,** *f.* badness, poorness, worthlessness, inferior quality; *see* **Schlechtigkeit. schlechthin,** *adv.* simply, merely, plainly, quite, absolutely, downright, (*coll.*) purely and simply. **Schlechtigkeit,** *f.* badness, baseness, wickedness, depravity; base act, (*coll.*) mean trick. **schlecht|machen,** *v.t.* speak ill of, malign, (*coll.*) run down. **-weg,** *adv.*

See **–hin. Schlechtwetterperiode,** *f.* spell of bad weather.

Schlecker ['ʃlɛkər], *m.* sweet-tooth. **Schleckerei** [–'raɪ], *f.* daintiness; *pl.* sweets, dainties. **schleckern, 1.** *v.i.* be dainty *or* pampered, be fond of sweet things. **2.** *v.t.* lick; (*coll.*) kiss.

Schlegel ['ʃle:gəl], *m.* mallet, club; beetle; drumstick; clapper (*of bell*); (*dial.*) leg (*of veal etc.*). **schlegeln, 1.** *v.i.* 1. (*dial.*) limp, hobble; 2. make a bad mistake. **2.** *v.t.* beat, stamp.

Schlehdorn ['ʃle:dɔrn], *m.* (*Bot.*) sloe-tree, blackthorn (*Prunus spinosa*). **Schlehe,** *f.* sloe, wild plum. **schlehweiß,** *adj.* snow-white.

Schlei [ʃlaɪ], *m.* **(-(e)s,** *pl.* **-e)** (*Ichth.*) tench (*Finca vulgaris*).

Schleiche ['ʃlaɪçə], *f.* (*Zool.*) anguid.

schleichen ['ʃlaɪçən], *irr.v.r.*, *v.i.* (*aux.* s.) crawl, creep; slink, sneak, skulk, steal, prowl; ***sich in sein Vertrauen –,*** worm o.s. into his confidence. **schleichend,** *adj.* sneaking, creeping, insidious, furtive; slow (*poison, fever*), lingering, chronic (*disease*). **Schleicher,** *m.* prowler, crawler; (*fig.*) sneak; intriguer, (*Am.*) pussyfooter. **Schleicherei** [–'raɪ], *f.* sneaking, intrigue(s), underhand dealing.

Schleich|gut, *n.* contraband. **–handel,** *m.* black market, (*obs.*) smuggling. **–händler,** *m.* blackmarketeer, (*obs.*) smuggler. **–ware,** *f.* *See* **–gut. –weg,** *m.* (*fig.*) secret ways, underhand *or* devious means; ***auf –en,*** surreptitiously.

Schleie ['ʃlaɪə], *f.* *See* **Schlei.**

Schleier ['ʃlaɪər], *m.* veil; (*fig.*) cloak, screen; haze, mist (*before the eyes*); (*Phot.*) film; (*Mil.*) smokescreen; ***den – nehmen,*** take the veil, become a nun; ***den – über eine S. ziehen,*** draw a veil over s.th., hush s.th. up. **Schleier|eule,** *f.* (*Orn.*) barn-owl (*Tyto alba*). **–flor,** *m.* crape; lawn, voile, veiling. **schleierhaft,** *adj.* veiled, mysterious, inexplicable; ***das ist mir einfach –,*** that is beyond me, that beats me, that is a complete mystery to me. **schleiern,** *v.t.* veil; (*Phot.*) fog. **Schleier|tuch,** *n.* *See* **–flor.**

Schleif|arbeit ['ʃlaɪf–], *f.* grinding (operation). **–antenne,** *f.* (*Rad.*) loop aerial. **–bahn,** *f.* slide. **–bank,** *f.* grinding lathe.

Schleife ['ʃlaɪfə], *f.* 1. loop, slip-knot, noose, (*in ribbon etc.*) bow, (*fancy paper*) (paper) streamer, (*accidentally in rope*) kink; (*fig.*) loop, S- *or* horseshoe bend, (*Railw.*) loop line, (*Av.*) looping; 2. sled(ge); 3. slide.

[1]**schleifen** ['ʃlaɪfən], **1.** *v.t.* drag along, trail; demolish, raze (to the ground) (*buildings*); (*Mus.*) slur (*notes*); (*Motor.*) ***die Kupplung – lassen,*** ride the clutch. **2.** *v.i.* (*aux.* s. *&* h.) drag (along), slide, skid.

[2]**schleifen,** *irr.v.t.* grind, abrade, polish, smooth, rub down, (*wood*) sand(paper); (*knife*) grind, sharpen, whet, (*razor*) set, (*gems*) cut; (*sl.*) ***ihn –,*** put him through his paces, give him hell *or* (*Am.*) chicken; ***geschliffen,*** (*fig. of manners, language etc.*) polished.

Schleifen|flug, *m.* (*Av.*) looping. **–kurve,** *f.* S- *or* horse-shoe bend.

Schleifer ['ʃlaɪfər], *m.* 1. grinder, polisher; gemcutter; 2. (*Mech.*) slip-ring; (*Mus.*) slurred note; 3. (*fig.*) martinet, (*sl.*) slave driver. **Schleiferei** [–'raɪ], *f.* grinding; grinding shop; (*Paperm.*) pulping; pulp-mill.

Schleif|knoten, *m.* slip-knot, running knot, noose. **–kontakt,** *m.* (*Elec.*) sliding contact. **–lack,** *m.* body *or* flatting varnish. **–mittel,** *n.* abrasive. **–mühle,** *f.* pulp-mill. **–papier,** *n.* abrasive *or* emery- *or* sand-paper. **–rad,** *n.* grinding *or* polishing wheel. **–ring,** *m.* (*Elec.*) slip-ring. **–scheibe,** *f.* polishing *or* buffing disk. **–schritt,** *m.* (*dancing*) glissade. **–sporn,** *m.* (*Av.*) tail-skid. **–stein,** *m.* grindstone, emery-wheel; whetstone, hone. **–stoff,** *m.* paper-pulp.

Schleifung ['ʃlaɪfuŋ], *f.* demolition, dismantling, razing (to the ground). **Schleifungszeichen,** *n.* (*Mus.*) slur.

Schleim [ʃlaɪm], *m.* **(-(e)s,** *pl.* **-e)** slime; (*Med.*) phlegm, mucus; (*Bot.*) mucilage. **Schleim|-absonderung,** *f.* mucous secretion, blennorrhoea. **–auswurf,** *m.* expectoration (*of mucus*). **–beutel,** *m.* *See* **–sack. –drüse,** *f.* mucous gland.

schleimen ['ʃlaɪmən], **1.** *v.i.* produce phlegm; form a scum (*in boiling*). **2.** *v.t.* clear of slime; clean (*fish*), remove the scum from.

Schleim|fluß, *m.* *See* **–absonderung. –haut,** *f.* mucous membrane. **schleimig,** *adj.* slimy, viscous, mucilaginous. **schleimlösend,** *adj.* expectorant. **Schleim|sack,** *m.* (*Anat.*) mucous follicle, fluid vesicle, bursa. **–suppe,** *f.* gruel. **–tier,** *n.* mollusc. **–zucker,** *m.* l(a)evulose.

Schleiße ['ʃlaɪsə], *f.* 1. (*dial.*) splinter, splint; quill (*of a feather*); 2. lint. **schleißen, 1.** *irr.v.t.* split; slit; ***Federn –,*** strip quills. **2.** *irr.v.i.* (*aux.* s.) 1. wear out; 2. (*dial.*) slide. **schleißig,** *adj.* (*dial.*) cut to pieces, worn out.

Schlemm [ʃlɛm], *m.* **(-s,** *pl.* **-e)** (*Cards*) grand slam.

Schlemmboden ['ʃlɛmbo:dən], *m.* (*Geol.*) diluvial soil.

schlemmen ['ʃlɛmən], **1.** *v.i.* revel, carouse; gormandize, guzzle. **2.** *v.t.* *See* **schlämmen. Schlemmer,** *m.* gormandizer, glutton, gourmand, gourmet. **Schlemmerei** [–'raɪ], *f.* gluttony, feasting.

Schlempe ['ʃlɛmpə], *f.* distiller's wash; swill, slops.

schlendern ['ʃlɛndərn], *v.i.* (*aux.* h. *&* s.) dawdle, lounge, loiter, saunter, stroll about. **Schlendrian,** *m.* **(-s,** *pl.* **-e)** old humdrum way, routine, groove, beaten track; muddling on.

schlenkern ['ʃlɛŋkərn], **1.** *v.i.* dangle; shamble (*in walking*); ***mit den Armen –,*** swing one's arms. **2.** *v.t.* dangle, swing; (*dial.*) shake off, jerk, toss, sling, fling.

Schlepp|antenne ['ʃlɛp–], *f.* (*Rad.*) trailing aerial. **–boot,** *n.* tug(boat). **–busch,** *m.* brush harrow. **–dampfer,** *m.* *See* **–boot.**

Schleppe ['ʃlɛpə], *f.* 1. train (*of a dress*); 2. (*Hunt.*) trail; 3. sledge.

schleppen ['ʃlɛpən], **1.** *v.t.* drag, trail; tow, haul, tug, (*coll.*) lug; (*Naut.*) ***den Anker –,*** drag the anchor. **2.** *v.r.* drag o.s. along, trudge *or* plod on; (*fig.*) struggle, be burdened, have trouble (***mit,*** with). **schleppend,** *adj.* slow, sluggish; (*fig.*) tedious, wearisome, (*of speech*) drawling; (*of gait*) shuffling, dawdling. **Schleppen|kleid,** *n.* dress with train. **–träger,** *m.* train-bearer.

Schlepper ['ʃlɛpər], *m.* 1. hauler; tractor; tug(boat); 2. tout (*of customers*); 3. prime mover.

Schlepp|flugzeug, *n.* towing plane. **–geschwindigkeit,** *f.* towing speed. **–kabel,** *n.* tow-rope, hawser. **–kahn,** *m.* barge, lighter. **–kante,** *f.* (*Av.*) trailing edge. **–kraft,** *f.* tractive force. **–leine,** *f.* *See* **–kabel. –netz,** *n.* trawl, drag-net. **–schacht,** *m.* inclined gallery (*in mines*). **–scheibe,** *f.* towed target; (*Av.*) sleeve, drogue. **–seil,** *n.* drag; (*Artil.*) drag-rope; trail-rope (*of a balloon*). **–start,** *m.* towed take-off (*gliders*). **–tau,** *n.* hawser; (*fig.*) ***ins – nehmen,*** take in tow. **–wagen,** *m.* towing vehicle, recovery vehicle. **–winde,** *f.* towing winch. **–ziel,** *n.* *See* **–scheibe. –zug,** *m.* train of barges.

Schlesien ['ʃle:ziən], *n.* Silesia. **Schlesier,** *m.*, **schlesisch,** *adj.* Silesian.

Schleuder ['ʃlɔydər], *f.* (-, *pl.* **-n**) 1. sling, catapult; 2. (*Mech.*) centrifuge, hydro-extractor, (cream) separator. **Schleuder|arbeit,** *f.* bungled work. **–artikel,** *m.* *See* **–ware. –ausfuhr,** *f.* dumping. **–guß,** *m.* centrifugal casting. **–honig,** *m.* extracted honey. **–konkurrenz,** *f.* unfair competition. **–kraft,** *f.* centrifugal force. **–maschine,** *f.* *See* **Schleuder,** 2.

schleudern ['ʃlɔydərn], **1.** *v.t.* 1. sling, catapult; fling, throw, hurl, toss, project, send, shoot, dart; 2. centrifuge, hydro-extract; strain (*honey*), spin-dry (*laundry*). **2.** *v.i.* 1. shake, swing; 2. (*Motor.*) skid, side-slip, (*Naut.*) roll; 3. (*Comm.*) undersell, cut prices, dump.

Schleuder|preis, *m.* cut price, give-away price; ***zu –en verkaufen,*** sell at a sacrifice, sell dirt-cheap. **–pumpe,** *f.* centrifugal pump. **–sitz,** *m.* (*Av.*)

ejector seat. **–spur,** *f.* skid marks. **–start,** *m.* catapult take-off (*of gliders*). **–verkauf,** *m.* underselling, dumping. **–waffe,** *f.* missile. **–ware,** *f.* bargain (article).

schleunig [ˈʃlɔynɪç], **1.** *adj.* quick, speedy, prompt, ready, swift; immediate. **2.** *adv.* immediately, forthwith, (*coll.*) right away; posthaste, in all haste, as soon as possible; ***aufs –ste,*** with the utmost dispatch.

Schleuse [ˈʃlɔyzə], *f.* 1. sluice, floodgate, (*on canals*) lock; 2. drain, sewer. **schleusen,** *v.t.* tow *or* pass (*ships*) through locks, (*fig.*) channel. **Schleusen|gas,** *n.* sewer gas. **–geld,** *n.* lock-dues. **–hafen,** *m.* wet-dock. **–kammer,** *f.* lock-basin. **–meister,** *m.* lock-keeper. **–tor,** *n.* sluice-gate, lock-gate. **–treppe,** *f.* chain of locks, **–wärter,** *m. See* **–meister. –zoll,** *m. See* **–geld.**

Schlich [ʃlɪç], *m.* **(-(e)s,** *pl.* **-e)** 1. secret way, by(e)-way; *pl.* tricks, dodges, ruses; (*coll.*) ***alle –e kennen,*** be up to all the tricks; know all the ins and outs; ***ihm auf die –e kommen,*** find him out; 2. (*dial.*) *see* **Schlick.**

schlich, schliche, *see* **schleichen.**

schlicht [ʃlɪçt], *adj.* plain, homely, simple, modest, unpretentious, straightforward; (*of a meal*) frugal; (*as hair*) sleek, smooth; ***–er Menschenverstand,*** plain common-sense; (*Mil.*) ***–er Abschied,*** unceremonious dismissal; ***–e Erzählung,*** plain unvarnished tale.

Schlichte [ˈʃlɪçtə], *f.* dressing, size.

schlichten [ˈʃlɪçtən], *v.t.* 1. plane, level, smooth, (*Weav.*) planish, dress (*yarn*); 2. arrange, adjust, settle, put right, make up (*quarrels etc.*), settle by arbitration. **Schlichter,** *m.* 1. planisher, dresser; 2. mediator, arbitrator, peacemaker, (*coll.*) trouble-shooter.

Schlicht|feile, *f.* smoothing file. **–hammer,** *m.* planishing-hammer. **Schlichtheit,** *f.* plainness, smoothness, sleekness; (*fig.*) unpretentiousness, simplicity. **Schlicht|hobel,** *m.* smoothing-plane. **–leim,** *m.* size. **–maschine,** *f.* dressing *or* sizing machine. **–rahmen,** *m.* tanner's stretching-frame.

Schlichtung [ˈʃlɪçtuŋ], *f.* mediation, arbitration, conciliation, settlement, amicable arrangement. **Schlichtungs|ausschuß,** *m.*, **–stelle,** *f.* arbitration board.

Schlick [ʃlɪk], *m.* **(-(e)s,** *pl.* **-e)** slime, ooze, silt, mud. **schlicken,** *v.r.* silt up. **schlick(e)rig,** *adj.* muddy, slimy. **Schlickermilch,** *f.* (*dial.*) curdled milk. **schlickern,** *v.i.* 1. *imp.* sleet; 2. (*dial.*) curdle. **Schlickgrund,** *m.* mud bottom. **schlick(r)ig,** *adj. See* **schlick(e)rig. Schlickwatt,** *n.* mud-flat.

Schlief [ʃli:f], *m.* **(-(e)s,** *pl.* **-e)** sad *or* soggy lump (*in bread etc.*); (*coll.*) ***– backen,*** make a hash of.

schlief, schliefe, *see* **schlafen.**

Schliefer [ˈʃli:fər], *m.* badger-hound.

schliefig [ˈʃli:fɪç], *adj.* sad, soggy (*of bread etc.*).

Schliere [ˈʃli:rə], *f.* (*Glassw., Phot.*) streak *or* flaw in glass *or* negative.

schlieren [ˈʃli:rən], *v.i.* (*Naut.*) slip (*of knots, rope etc.*).

schließbar [ˈʃli:sba:r], *adj.* lockable. **Schließbaum,** *m.* bar, boom (*of a harbour*).

Schließe [ˈʃli:sə], *f.* catch, latch, clasp, fastening, fastener; shutter (*of a sluice etc.*).

schließen [ˈʃli:sən], **1.** *irr.v.t.* 1. shut, close; lock, bolt; ***an die Brust –,*** press to one's heart; ***hieran – wir die Bemerkung,*** to this we add the remark; ***in die Arme –,*** embrace, clasp in one's arms; ***in sein Herz –,*** take a fancy *or* liking to; ***in sich –,*** include, comprise; imply; ***den Laden –,*** shut up shop; ***die Rede mit einem Witz –,*** wind up the speech with a joke; *see* **geschlossen**; ***die Reihen –,*** close the ranks; 2. finish, end, conclude, terminate; 3. (*fig.*) contract (*marriage etc.*); (*Comm.*) make (*a deal*), strike (*a bargain*); come to, reach (*an agreement*), enter into, conclude (*a treaty*), conclude, make (*peace*); enter into, form (*alliance*); (*Comm.*) close (*an account*), (*Elec.*) close (*a circuit*); form (*a circle*); ***er schließt jetzt die dritte Ehe,*** he is marrying for the third time; ***Freundschaft – mit,*** become friends *or* friendly with. **2.** *irr.v.r.* close, shut; lock; knit, heal up (*as wounds*); come to an end; ***sich – an*** (*Acc.*), follow on, come next to; (*fig.*) ***der Kreis schließt sich,*** it comes full circle. **3.** *irr.v.i.* 1. shut, close; fit well *or* close, join well; stop, end, conclude; break up (*from school*); ***da*** or ***hiermit schließt die Geschichte,*** here the story ends, that is the end of the story; ***der Markt schloß fest,*** the market closed firm; ***der Schlüssel schließt nicht,*** the key does not fit (the lock); 2. ***– auf*** (*Acc.*), infer, conclude, (*coll.*) gather (***aus,*** from); ***– lassen auf*** (*Acc.*), point to, indicate, suggest; ***von sich auf andre –,*** judge others by o.s.

Schließer [ˈʃli:sər], *m.* 1. door-keeper, (house) porter; turnkey, jailer (*in a prison*); 2. latch; 3. constrictor, sphincter.

Schließ|fach, *n.* safe-deposit, post-office box. **–feder,** *f.* locking-spring, spring-catch; spring-bolt. **–hahn,** *m.* stop-cock. **–haken,** *m. See* **Schließe. –kappe,** *f.* staple (*of a lock*). **–kopf,** *m.* rivet-head. **–korb,** *m.* hamper.

schließlich [ˈʃli:slɪç], **1.** *adj.* last, final, definitive, conclusive, ultimate, eventual. **2.** *adv.* finally, at last, in conclusion, in the end, eventually, ultimately, (*coll.*) in the long run; ***– doch*** or ***– und endlich,*** after all, when all is said and done.

Schließ|muskel, *m. or f.* sphincter, constrictor. **–rahmen,** *m.* (*Typ.*) chase. **–riegel,** *m.* dead-bolt. **–rohr,** *n.*, **–röhre,** *f.* sealed tube.

Schließung [ˈʃli:suŋ], *f.* closing, close, conclusion; closure, shut-down; breaking-up.

Schliff [ʃlɪf], *m.* **(-(e)s,** *pl.* **-e)** grinding, sharpening, smoothing, polishing; ground *or* polished surface; polish, smoothness, (*fig.*) polish, refinement, style, cut; micro-section; grindings; wood-pulp; (*see also* **Schlief**); ***Mensch ohne –,*** man without manners *or* refinement; (*fig.*) ***den letzten – geben*** (*Dat.*), put the finishing touch(es) to.

schliff, schliffe, *see* ²**schleifen.**

schlimm [ʃlɪm], *adj., adv.* bad, naughty, evil, wicked; grave, severe, serious; sore, painful; unpleasant, nasty, annoying; ***immer –er,*** from bad to worse, worse and worse; ***um so –er,*** so much the worse; ***im –sten Falle,*** *see* **schlimmstenfalls**; ***ich bin – daran,*** I am in a bad way; ***–e Augen,*** sore eyes; ***auf das –ste gefaßt sein,*** be prepared for the worst; ***ein –es Ende nehmen,*** come to a bad *or* (*coll.*) sticky end; (*coll.*) ***– hinter etwas her sein,*** be set *or* bent upon s.th. **schlimmstenfalls,** *adv.* if the worst comes to the worst, at the worst.

Schlinge [ˈʃlɪŋə], *f.* (running) knot, slip-knot, noose; loop, coil; (*Hunt.*) snare; (*Surg.*) sling; (*fig.*) trap, snare; ***in die – gehen,*** fall into the trap; ***–n legen,*** set snares; ***den Kopf*** or ***Hals in die – stecken,*** run one's head into the noose; ***sich aus der – ziehen,*** get out of a difficulty *or* scrape, get one's head out of the noose, (*coll.*) wriggle out of it; ***sich in der eignen – fangen,*** be hoist with one's own petard.

Schlingel [ˈʃlɪŋəl], *m.* rascal; naughty boy, (*coll.*) scallywag.

¹**schlingen** [ˈʃlɪŋən], **1.** *irr.v.t.* wind, twist, twine, entwine, weave, plait, tie; ***die Arme – um,*** fling one's arms round; ***ein Band in eine Schleife –,*** tie a ribbon into a bow. **2.** *irr.v.r.* coil, wind, twine.

²**schlingen,** *irr.v.t.* swallow (greedily), gulp (down), devour, (*coll.*) gobble, bolt; (*fig.*) engulf.

Schlingenfalle [ˈʃlɪŋənfalə], *f.* gin-trap.

Schlinger|bewegung, *f.* rolling (motion) (*of ships*). **–dämpfungsanlage,** *f.* (*Naut.*) stabilizer. **–kiel,** *m.* bilge-keel. **–kreisel,** *m.* gyroscopic stabilizer. **schlingern,** *v.i.* roll (*of ships*), sway, rock, lurch (*of vehicles*).

Schling|gewächs, *n.*, **–pflanze,** *f.* creeper, climber, climbing plant, liana.

Schlipf [ʃlɪpf], *m.* **(-(e)s,** *pl.* **-e)** (*Swiss*) landslide.

Schlippe [ˈʃlɪpə], *f.* 1. (*Austr.*) alley, passage; **2.** (*dial.*) coat-tail.

Schlipper [ˈʃlɪpər], *m.* (*Austr.*) *see* **Schlipper-**

milch. schlipperig, *adj.* (*dial.*) curdled. **Schlippermilch,** *f.* (*dial.*) curdled milk.

Schlips [ʃlɪps], *m.* (**-es,** *pl.* **-e**) (neck-)tie, cravat; (*coll.*) ***ihm auf den – treten,*** tread on his corns *or* toes; (*coll.*) ***das haut einen auf den –,*** that's more than one can stand *or* swallow, that's going too far.

schliß [ʃlɪs], **schlisse,** *see* **schleißen.**

schlitteln [ˈʃlɪtəln], *v.i.* (*Swiss*) go sledging.

Schlitten [ˈʃlɪtən], *m.* sledge, sled, sleigh, toboggan; (*Av.*) skids; (*Mech.*) sliding carriage, cradle, (*of typewriter*) carriage; (*coll.*) ***unter den – kommen,*** come to grief, go to the bad; (*coll.*) ***mit ihm – fahren,*** lead him up the garden path, take him for a ride; ***– fahren,*** go sledging. **Schlitten|bahn,** *f.* sledge-run; ***es wird bald – geben,*** we shall soon be able to sledge. **-fahren,** *n.*, **-fahrt,** *f.* sledging, sledge-run, sleigh-ride. **-geläute,** *n.* sleigh-bells. **-kufe,** *f.* sledge-runner, (*Av.*) skid.

schlittern [ˈʃlɪtərn], *v.i.* (*aux.* s. & h.) slide; (*of a vehicle*) skid; (*fig.*) ***in einen Streit –,*** stumble into a quarrel.

Schlittschuh [ˈʃlɪtʃu:], *m.* skate; ***– laufen*** or ***fahren,*** skate. **Schlittschuh|bahn,** *f.* ice- *or* skating-rink. **-laufen,** *n.* skating. **-läufer(in),** *m.* (*f.*) skater.

Schlitz [ʃlɪts], *m.* (**-es,** *pl.* **-e**) slit, slash, (*of trousers*) fly; rift, cleft, notch, aperture, crack, fissure, (*Archit.*) glyph, (*Mech.*) port, louvre, (*for coins*) slot. **Schlitzauge,** *n.* slit (of an) eye. **schlitzäugig,** *adj.* narrow-eyed. **Schlitz|brenner,** *m.* fantail-burner. **-bruch,** *m.* longitudinal fracture. **schlitzen,** *v.t.* slit, slash, (*Mech.*) slot; split, cleave, rip open; ***geschlitztes Kleid,*** divided skirt. **Schlitz|flügel,** *m.* (*Av.*) slotted wing. **-verschluß,** *m.* (*Phot.*) focal-plane shutter.

schlohweiß [ˈʃlo:vaɪs], *adj.* snow-white.

Schloß [ʃlɔs], *n.* (**-(ss)es,** *pl.* **¨-(ss)er**) 1. castle, palace; chateau, manor-house; ***Schlösser im Mond,*** castles in the air *or* in Spain, (*coll.*) pie in the sky; 2. lock (*of doors, firearms*); buckle (*of belt*); hinge (*of shells*); ***ins – fallen,*** slam shut *or* to; ***ein – vor dem Mund haben,*** have one's lips sealed; be tongue-tied, not have a word to say; ***hinter – und Riegel,*** under lock and key; behind bars.

schloß, *see* **schließen.**

Schloß|aufseher, *m.* castellan. **-band,** *n.* hinge-ligament. **-beamte(r),** *m.* court official. **-blatt, -blech,** *n.* lock-plate, key-plate.

Schloße [ˈʃlo:sə], *f.* hailstone. **schloßen,** *v.i.* hail.

Schlosser [ˈʃlɔsər], *m.* locksmith; mechanic, fitter. **Schlosserei** [–ˈraɪ], *f.* locksmith's shop; workshop; repair shop, garage. **schlossern,** *v.i.* work, tinker (*an* (*Dat.*), at).

Schloß|feder, *f.* spring of a lock. **-fortsatz,** *m.* cardinal process. **-freiheit,** *f.* precincts of a castle. **-graben,** *m.* castle-moat. **-herr,** *m.* (**-herrin,** *f.*) lord (lady) of the manor. **-hof,** *m.* castle-yard, courtyard. **-hund,** *m.* (*coll.*) ***heulen wie ein –,*** weep buckets. **-platz,** *m.* palace-yard. **-verwalter, -vogt,** *m.* castellan. **-wache,** *f.* palace-guard. **-zirkel,** *m.* reduction compasses.

Schlot [ʃlo:t], *m.* (**-(e)s,** *pl.* **-e** *or* **¨-e**) 1. chimney, flue; (*Railw., Naut.*) funnel, smokestack; ***rauchen wie ein –,*** smoke like a chimney; 2. (*coll.*) lout, bounder. **Schlot|baron,** *m.* industrial magnate, (*coll.*) tycoon. **-feger,** *m. See* **-kehrer. -gang,** *m.* (*Geol.*) neck. **-junker,** *m. See* **-baron. -kehrer,** *m.* chimney-sweep.

Schlotte [ˈʃlɔtə], *f.* hollow stalk; soil-pipe (*of lavatories*); *see also* **Schlotgang.**

[1]**Schlotter** [ˈʃlɔtər], *m.* 1. (*dial.*) trembling, tremors; 2. sediment (from boiling).

[2]**Schlotter,** *f.* (-, *pl.* **-n**) (*dial.*) (child's) rattle.

schlotterbeinig [ˈʃlɔtərbaɪnɪç], *adj.* unsteady on the legs, shambling. **Schlottergang,** *m.* unsteady *or* shambling *or* shuffling gait. **schlott(e)rig,** *adj.* shaky, shaking, wobbly, wobbling, tottering; loose, dangling, flabby, floppy; (*fig.*) slovenly, (*coll.*) sloppy; (*with age*) doddering. **Schlottermilch,** *f.* (*dial.*) curdled milk.

schlottern [ˈʃlɔtərn], *v.i.* flap, dangle, hang loose(ly), fit loosely; shake, tremble, shiver (*with cold*); wobble, totter; ***vor Angst –,*** tremble with fear; ***mit –den Knien,*** shaking at the knees.

Schlucht [ʃluxt], *f.* (-, *pl.* **-en** (*Poet.* **¨-e**)) ravine, gorge, gully, defile, canyon; (*fig.*) abyss, chasm.

schluchzen [ˈʃluxtsən], *v.i.* sob; (*dial.*) hiccup. **Schluchzen,** *n.* sobbing. **Schluchzer,** *m.* sob.

Schluck [ʃluk], *m.* (**-(e)s,** *pl.* **-e** *or* **¨-e**) sip, gulp, mouthful, draught; ***einen – über den Durst trinken,*** take a drop too much, have one over the eight. **Schluck|akt,** *m.* act of swallowing. **-apparat,** *m.* organs of deglutition. **-auf,** *m.* hiccup. **-beschwerden,** *f.pl.* difficulty in swallowing, (*Med.*) dysphagia. **schlucken,** 1. *v.t.* swallow, gulp (down), drink down; (*Tech.*) absorb; (*fig.*) swallow, pocket (*an insult etc.*). 2. *v.i.* have the hiccups, hiccup. **Schlucken,** *m.* hiccups. **Schlucker,** *m.* hiccup; (*coll.*) ***armer –,*** poor wretch. **schlucksen,** *v.i. See* **schlucken, 2. Schluckung,** *f.* (*Tech.*) absorption. **schluckweise,** *adv.* by mouthfuls *or* draughts, in gulps, sip by sip.

schludern [ˈʃlu:dərn], *v.i.* work carelessly, bungle; botch *or* scamp *or* bungle the job. **schlud(e)rig,** *adj.* botched, bungled, slapdash.

Schluft, *f.* (-, *pl.* **¨-e**) (*dial.*) *see* **Schlucht, Schlupfwinkel.**

schlug [ʃlu:k], **schlüge** [ˈʃly:gə], *see* **schlagen.**

Schlummer [ˈʃlumər], *m.* slumber, nap. **Schlummer|kissen,** *n.* (soft) pillow. **-körner,** *n.pl.* poppy-seeds. **-lied,** *n.* lullaby. **schlummern,** *v.i.* slumber, sleep, doze, snooze, (take a) nap; (*fig.*) lie dormant. **schlummernd,** *adj.* (*fig.*) slumbering; latent, dormant; ***-e Kräfte,*** potentialities. **Schlummerrolle,** *f.* small bolster.

Schlumpe [ˈʃlumpə], *f.* slut, slattern, sloven. **schlumpen,** *v.i.* (*aux.* h. & s.) be untidy; draggle, hang untidily, dangle; *see also* **schludern. Schlumper,** *m.* (*dial.*) wrap, shawl. **schlumpig,** *adj.* slovenly, (*coll.*) draggle-tailed.

Schlund [ʃlunt], *m.* (**-(e)s,** *pl.* **¨-e**) pharynx, throat, œsophagus, gullet; (*fig.*) chasm, gorge, gulf, abyss, crater; ***er jagt sein Geld durch den –,*** he pours his money down the drain; ***– der Hölle,*** jaws of hell; ***– der Kanone,*** mouth of the cannon. **Schlund|kopf,** *m.* pharynx. **-kopfschnitt,** *m.* pharyngotomy. **-röhre,** *f.* œsophagus. **-sonde,** *f.*, **-stößer,** *m.* probang.

Schlunze, *f.*, **schlunzig,** *adj.* (*dial.*) *see* **Schlumpe, schlumpig.**

Schlup [ʃlu:p], *f.* (-, *pl.* **-s** *or* **-en**) (*Naut.*) sloop.

Schlupf [ʃlupf], *m.* (**-(e)s,** *pl.* **¨-e**) 1. slip, slipping; (*Tech.*) backlash, play, slop; 2. (*Naut.*) running knot, noose; *see* **Unterschlupf.**

schlüpfen [ˈʃlypfən] (*dial.* **schlupfen**), *v.i.* (*aux.* s.) slip, slide, glide; ***in die Kleider –,*** slip into one's clothes.

Schlüpfer [ˈʃlypfər], *m.* 1. raglan (coat); 2. (pair of) knickers, (*coll.*) panties, briefs.

schlüpf(e)rig [ˈʃlypf(ə)rɪç], *adj.* 1. slippery, (*coll.*) slippy; 2. (*fig.*) indecent, risqué, (*coll.*) blue. **Schlüpf(e)rigkeit,** *f.* slipperiness, (*coll.*) slippiness; (*fig.*) indelicacy, lubricity, obscenity. **Schlüpfgrasmücke,** *f.* (*Orn.*) Dartford warbler (*Sylvia undata*).

Schlupf|hafen, *m.* creek. **-jacke,** *f.* sweater. **-loch,** *n.* loophole (*for escape*); hiding-place, (*coll.*) hide-out. **-wespe,** *f.* (*Ent.*) ichneumon-fly. **-winkel,** *m.* hiding-place, haunt, refuge; recess, nook.

Schluppe [ˈʃlupə], *f.* (*dial.*) bow (*of ribbon*).

schlurfen [ˈʃlurfən], *v.i.* (*aux.* h. & s.) shuffle.

schlürfen [ˈʃlyrfən], 1. *v.t.* sip, lap, quaff, swig; eat *or* drink noisily. 2. *v.i.* (*dial.*) *see* **schlurfen.**

Schlurpen [ˈʃlurpən], *m.* (*dial.*) slipper.

Schlurre [ˈʃlurə], *f.* (*dial.*) slipper.

Schluß [ʃlus], *m.* (**-(ss)es,** *pl.* **¨-(ss)e**) shutting, closing; end, close, finish, termination, conclusion; breaking-up (*of schools etc.*), winding-up (*of business*); (*Elec., Mech.*) contact, connection; keystone (*of a vault*); (*Mus.*) cadence, (*fig.*) conclusion, inference, deduction, (*Log.*) syllogism; upshot, result, issue; consequence; ***einen guten – haben,*** have a good *or* firm seat (*on horseback*); ***– machen mit,*** stop, finish with, put an end to, have done with; (*coll.*) ***– machen,*** do away with o.s.; knock off (*work*); ***den – bilden,*** bring up the rear; ***– folgt,*** to be concluded; ***– damit!*** enough of that! that will do! stop it! ***zu dem – kommen*** or ***gelangen,*** come to *or* arrive at the conclusion; ***nach – der Redaktion,*** before going to press; ***einen – ziehen,*** draw a conclusion, make an inference; ***zum –,*** finally, in the end, in conclusion.

Schluß|abrechnung, *f.* final settlement. **–akt,** *m.* 1. closing ceremony, (*at school*) speech-day; 2. (*Theat.*) final act. **–antrag,** *m.* (*Parl.*) motion for closure. **–bemerkung,** *f.* final observation. **–bilanz,** *f.* annual balance(-sheet). **–effekt,** *m.* upshot, outcome.

Schlüssel ['ʃlysəl], *m.* 1. key (*zu,* of, (*fig.*) to); ***falscher –,*** skeleton key, picklock; 2. (*Mus.*) clef; 3. (*Mech.*) spanner, wrench; 4. ratio; code, cipher. **Schlüssel|bart,** *m.* key-bit. **–bein,** *n.* collar-bone, clavicle. **–blume,** *f.* (*Bot.*) cowslip, primrose (*Primula officinalis*). **–bolzen,** *m.* retaining pin. **–bund,** *n. or m.* **(-es,** *pl.* **-e)** bunch of keys. **schlüsselfertig,** *adj.* ready for immediate occupation (*of new houses*). **Schlüssel|gewalt,** *f.* (*Eccl.*) power of the keys. **–industrie,** *f.* key industry. **–loch,** *n.* keyhole. **schlüsseln,** *v.t., v.i.* encode, encipher. **Schlüssel|ring,** *m.* key-ring. **–roman,** *m.* novel in which living persons figure under fictitious names. **–soldaten,** *m.pl.* papal soldiers. **–stellung,** *f.* key position. **–text,** *m.* coded text. **Schlüsselung,** *f.* encoding. **Schlüssel|weite,** *f.* (*Mech.*) calibre of a spanner, width over flats (*of nuts etc.*). **–wort,** *n.* keyword, code word. **–zahl,** *f.* code number, index number.

Schluß|ergebnis, *f. See* **–effekt. –fang,** *m.* safety-catch (*of rifle*). **–feier,** *f. See* **–akt. –folge(rung),** *f.* argument(ation), (line of) reasoning; deduction, inference, conclusion. **–formel,** *f.* closing phrase; ending (*of a letter*).

schlüssig ['ʃlysıç], *adj.* resolved, determined, decided; ***–er Beweis,*** conclusive proof *or* evidence; ***sich*** (*Dat.*) ***– werden,*** make up one's mind (***über*** (*Acc.*), about).

Schluß|kurs, *m.* (*St. Exch.*) closing price. **–licht,** *n.* (*Motor.*) tail-light; (*coll.*) ***das – bilden,*** bring up the rear. **–note,** *f.* broker's *or* contract-note. **–notierung,** *f. See* **–kurs**; contract price. **–pfiff,** *m.* (*Footb.*) final whistle. **–prüfung,** *f.* (*Univ.*) final examination. **–punkt,** *m.* full stop, period. **–rechnung,** *f.* final account; (*Arith.*) proportion. **–rede,** *f.* closing speech; epilogue. **–reim,** *m.* (*Metr.*) end-rhyme. **–runde,** *f.* (*Spt.*) final, (*Boxing*) last *or* final round. **–rundenteilnehmer,** *m.* (*Spt.*) finalist. **–satz,** *m.* 1. (*Log.*) consequent (*of a syllogism*); 2. closing *or* concluding sentence; 3. (*Tenn.*) final set; 4. (*Mus.*) last movement, finale. **–schein,** *m. See* **–note. –stand,** *m.* (*Spt.*) final score. **–stein,** *m.* coping-stone, keystone (*also fig.*). **–strich,** *m.* (*fig.*) ***einen – ziehen unter*** (*Acc.*), bring to an end, draw a line underneath; (*fig.*) ***einen – ziehen,*** put an end to it, draw the line. **–verkauf,** *m.* (*Comm.*) end-of-season sale. **–vignette,** *f.* (*Typ.*) tailpiece. **–wort,** *n.* last *or* final word; summary. **–zeichen,** *n.* signal for the end; (*Mus.*) double-bar, fine; *see also* **–punkt. –zettel,** *m. See* **–note.**

Schmach [ʃma:x], *f.* shame, disgrace, humiliation, insult, affront, outrage. **Schmachfrieden,** *m.* ignominious *or* humiliating peace (treaty).

schmachten ['ʃmaxtən], *v.i.* languish, pine away (***vor*** (*Dat.*), with); ***– nach,*** long *or* pine for, yearn after; ***vor Durst –,*** be parched with thirst. **schmachtend,** *adj.* languishing. **Schmacht|-fetzen,** *m.* (*coll.*) tear-jerker.

schmächtig ['ʃmɛçtıç], *adj.* delicate, slight, slender, slim, (*coll.*) weedy.

Schmacht|lappen, *m.* lovesick swain, (*coll.*) mawkish fellow. **–locke,** *f.* lovelock, kiss(ing)-curl. **–riemen,** *m.* (*coll.*) ***den – enger schnallen,*** tighten one's belt.

schmachvoll ['ʃma:xfɔl], *adj.* shameful, disgraceful, humiliating, ignominious.

Schmack [ʃmak], *m.* **(-(e)s,** *pl.* **-e)** sumac(-tree).

Schmack(e) ['ʃmak(ə)], *f.* (-, *pl.* **-(e)n)** (*Naut.*) smack.

schmacken ['ʃmakən], *v.t., v.i.* treat with sumac. **schmackgar,** *adj.* boiled in sumac.

schmackhaft ['ʃmakhaft], *adj.* tasty, savoury; palatable, appetizing. **Schmackhaftigkeit,** *f.* savouriness; savour, taste.

Schmadder ['ʃmadər], *m.* (*dial.*) wet dirt. **schmaddern,** *v.t.* daub, soil; scrawl.

Schmähbrief ['ʃmɛ:bri:f], *m.* insulting letter.

schmähen ['ʃmɛ:ən], *v.t., v.i.* abuse, revile, decry, disparage, belittle, (*coll.*) run down; calumniate, defame, slander, inveigh against. **schmählich,** 1. *adj. See* **schmachvoll.** 2. *adv.* (*coll.*) frightfully, awfully, beastly, terribly. **Schmäh|rede,** *f.* invective, abuse, diatribe. **–schrift,** *f.* libel; lampoon. **schmähsüchtig,** *adj.* slanderous, abusive, calumnious. **Schmähung,** *f.* (*pl. also used as pl. of* **Schmach**) abuse, invective, slander, calumny, vituperation, defamation; ***Klage wegen –,*** action for libel. **Schmähwort,** *n.* invective.

schmal [ʃma:l], *adj.* (*comp.* ***-er, ⁻er,*** *sup* ***-st, ⁻st***) narrow, thin, slim, slender; (*fig.*) small, poor, scanty, meagre; ***auf die –e Seite legen,*** lay edgewise; ***–e Bissen*** or ***Kost haben,*** fare badly, be on short commons. **schmalbrüstig,** *adj.* narrow-chested.

schmälen ['ʃmɛ:lən], 1. *v.t.* scold, chide. 2. *v.i.* bleat (*of deer*); ***– auf*** (*Acc.*), declaim against, nag.

schmälern ['ʃmɛ:lərn], *v.t.* lessen, diminish, curtail, narrow; (*fig.*) impair, detract from, belittle. **Schmälerung,** *f.* lessening, diminution, curtailment, narrowing; detraction, impairment.

Schmal|film, *m.* (*Phot.*) 8-mm. film. **–hans,** *m.* ***heute ist – bei uns Küchenmeister,*** we are on short commons today. **–leder,** *n.* upper leather (*for shoes*). **–spur,** *f.* narrow gauge. **–spurbahn,** *f.* narrow-gauge railway, light railway. **schmalspurig,** *adj.* narrow-gauged. **Schmalspursoldat,** *m.* (*sl.*) short-service soldier.

Schmalt ['ʃmalt], *m. See* **Schmelz,** 1. **Schmaltblau,** *n.,* **Schmalte,** *f.* smalt blue, azure. **schmalten,** *v.t., v.i.* enamel.

Schmaltier ['ʃma:lti:r], *n.* hind in her second year, hind before calving. **schmalwangig,** *adj.* hollow-cheeked.

Schmalz [ʃmalts], *n.* melted fat *or* grease, dripping, lard; (*fig.*) sentimental mush, sloppy sentiment; unctuousness; (*coll.*) ***ohne Salz und –,*** wishy-washy. **Schmalz|birn(e),** *f.* butter-pear. **–brot,** *n.* slice of bread and dripping. **–butter,** *f.* melted butter. **schmalzen** (*Austr.*), **schmälzen** ['ʃmɛltsən], *v.t.* (*p.p. often* ***geschmalzen***) grease, butter, lard, oil; cook with lard *etc.* **Schmalz|-gebackene(s),** *n.* food fried in lard; *see* **–kuchen. schmalzig,** *adj.* greasy; (*fig.*) maudlin, mawkish, sloppy, unctuous, sentimental. **Schmalzkuchen,** *m.* dripping- *or* short-cake.

Schmand [ʃmant], **Schmant,** *m.* **(-(e)s,** *pl.* **-e)** (*dial.*) cream; slime, ooze, sludge.

schmarotzen [ʃma'rɔtsən], *v.i.* live as a parasite, sponge (***bei,*** on). **Schmarotzer,** *m.* (*Bot.*) parasite; sponger. **schmarotzerhaft, schmarotzerisch,** *adj.* parasitic(al). **Schmarotzer|pflanze,** *f.* parasitic plant, parasite. **–raubmöwe,** *f.* (*Orn.*) Arctic skua, (*Am.*) parasitic jaeger (*Stercorarius parasiticus*). **–tier,** *n.* animal parasite. **Schmarotzertum,** *n.* parasitism.

Schmarre ['ʃmarə], *f.* slash, gash, cut, scar.

Schmarren ['ʃmarən], *m.* 1. (*dial.*) omelet, pancake; 2. (*coll.*) trash; shocker (*book*).

Schmasche ['ʃmaʃə], *f.* dressed lambskin. **Schmaschenleder,** *n.* chamois-leather, shammy(-leather).

Schmatz [ʃmats], *m.* **(-es,** *pl.* **-e** *or* **⁻e)** smack(er), hearty kiss.

Schmatz(e) ['ʃmats(ə)], *f.* (-, *pl.* **-(en)n)** (*dial.*) tree-stump.

schmatzen ['ʃmatsən], *v.i.* eat noisily, smack the lips; give a hearty kiss.

Schmauch ['ʃmaux], *m.* (**-(e)s**, *pl.* **-e**) thick *or* dense smoke. **schmauchen,** *v.t., v.i.* smoke, puff away at (*pipe etc.*).

Schmaus [ʃmaus], *m.* (**-es**, *pl.* **⸚e**) feast, banquet; (*fig.*) treat; ***ihm einen – geben,*** feast *or* treat him, give a dinner in his honour. **schmausen,** *v.i.* feast, banquet.

schmecken ['ʃmɛkən], **1.** *v.t.* taste; try by tasting; (*fig.*) sample, experience. **2.** *v.i.* taste (***nach,*** of), smack, savour (of); taste good, be pleasant to the taste; (*dial.*) smell; ***gut –,*** taste good; ***süß –,*** taste sweet, have a sweet taste; ***wie schmeckt es dir?*** how do you like it? are you enjoying it? ***dieser Wein schmeckt mir,*** I like this wine; ***ihm will nichts –,*** he has no appetite, nothing is to his taste; ***er läßt es sich –,*** he eats it with relish; ***es hat mir vortrefflich geschmeckt,*** I have thoroughly enjoyed it; ***das schmeckt nach mehr,*** it is so good that I should like some more of it, (*sl.*) it is morish; ***es schmeckt nach nichts,*** it has no taste; (*coll.*) ***diese Nachricht schmeckte ihm gar nicht,*** he did not relish that piece of news at all.

Schmeiche ['ʃmaɪçə], *f.* (*Weav.*) size, dressing.

Schmeichelei [ʃmaɪçə'laɪ], *f.* flattery, adulation; coaxing, wheedling, cajolery, (*coll.*) soft soap.

schmeichelhaft ['ʃmaɪçəlhaft], *adj.* flattering, complimentary; adulatory, wheedling, coaxing. **Schmeichel|kätzchen,** *n.*, **-katze,** *f.* wheedler, flatterer, coaxer, cajoler. **schmeicheln,** *v.i.* (*Dat.*) flatter (***mit,*** with), compliment ((up)on); coax, cajole, wheedle; fawn upon, (*coll.*) soft-soap, play up to; caress, fondle, pet; ***sich*** (*Dat.*) ***in eitlen Hoffnungen –,*** flatter o.s. with foolish hopes; ***das Bild ist geschmeichelt,*** the picture is flattering. **Schmeichel|name,** *m.* flattering name. **-rede,** *f.*, **-worte,** *n.pl.* honeyed words, (*coll.*) soft soap. **Schmeichler,** *m.* flatterer, wheedler, sycophant, toady. **schmeichlerisch,** *adj. See* **schmeichelhaft.**

schmeidig ['ʃmaɪdɪç], *adj.* (*Poet., dial.*) *see* **geschmeidig.**

schmeißen ['ʃmaɪsən], *irr.v.t., v.i.* fling, hurl, dash, slam; (*of insects*) deposit eggs; (*sl.*) ***eine Runde –,*** stand a round of drinks; (*sl.*) ***den Laden –,*** run the show; (*sl.*) ***die Sache*** (***schon***) ***–,*** pull it off, put it across; ***mit dem Geld um sich –,*** throw one's money about. **Schmeiße, Schmeißfliege,** *f.* blow-fly, bluebottle, meat-fly.

Schmelz [ʃmɛlts], *m.* 1. enamel, glaze, glazing; 2. fusion, melting; 3. (*fig.*) mellowness; ***melodischer – einer Stimme,*** melting sweetness of a voice. **Schmelzarbeit,** *f.* 1. smelting (process); 2. enamelling. **schmelzbar,** *adj.* fusible; ***schwer –,*** refractory. **Schmelzdraht,** *m.* (*Elec.*) fuse wire. **Schmelze,** *f.* 1. thaw, melting, (*Metall.*) smelting, fusion; molten *or* fused mass; batch, charge (*of metal*); composition (*of glass*); 2. foundry.

schmelzen ['ʃmɛltsən], **1.** *irr.v.i.* (*aux.* s.) 1. melt, fuse; 2. diminish, melt away; 3. soften (*of heart*). **2.** *reg. & irr.v.t.* 1. melt, liquefy, smelt; 2. fuse, blend. **schmelzend,** *adj.* 1. melting, liquefying, liquescent; 2. (*fig.*) languishing, soul-stirring, touching, sentimental, (*of sound*) melodious, mellow, dulcet, sweet. **Schmelzer,** *m.* smelter, founder. **Schmelzerei** [–'raɪ], *f.* foundry, smelting works.

Schmelz|farbe, *f.* vitrifiable pigment, enamel-colour. **-feuer,** *n.* refinery. **-fluß,** *m.* enamel; fused mass. **schmelzflüssig,** *adj.* molten. **Schmelz|glas,** *n.*, **-glasur,** *f.* enamel. **-grad,** *m.*, **-hitze,** *f.* smelting heat. **-hütte,** *f. See* **Schmelzerei. -koks,** *m.* foundry-coke. **-mittel,** *n.* flux. **-ofen,** *m.* smelting furnace. **-perle,** *f.* bugle. **-punkt,** *m.* melting-point, fusing temperature *or* (*Elec.*) load. **-schupper,** *m.* (*Ichth.*) ganoid. **-sicherung,** *f.* (*Elec.*) fuse. **-tiegel,** *m.* crucible. **-wärme,** *f.* heat of fusion. **-wasser,** *n.* melting *or* melted snow. **-zement,** *m. or n.* aluminous cement.

Schmer [ʃme:r], *n.* fat, grease, suet. **Schmerbauch,** *m.* paunch, (*coll.*) pot-belly, corporation.

Schmergel ['ʃmɛrgəl], *m. See* **Schmirgel.**

Schmerle ['ʃmɛrlə], *f.* (*Ichth.*) stone-loach.

Schmerz [ʃmɛrts], *m.* (**-es**, *pl.* **-en**) pain, ache, smart; (*fig.*) grief, suffering, sorrow; ***-en haben,*** be in pain; (*coll.*) ***hast du sonst noch -en?*** what do you think I am? do you take me for a sucker? **Schmerzbekämpfung,** *f.* alleviation of pain. **schmerz|beladen,** *adj.* (*fig.*) deeply afflicted *or* grieved. **-betäubend,** *adj.* analgesic. **-empfindlich,** *adj.* sensitive to pain.

schmerzen ['ʃmɛrtsən], **1.** *v.t.* pain, hurt, distress, grieve; ***es schmerzt mich, das zu sagen,*** it pains me to say so. **2.** *v.i.* (*3rd. pers. only*) be painful, hurt, smart, ache; ***mir schmerzt der Kopf,*** my head aches.

Schmerzens|geld, *n.* smart-money, compensation. **-kind,** *n.* child of sorrow. **-lager,** *n.* bed of suffering. **-schrei,** *m.* cry of pain.

schmerz|erfüllt, *adj. See* **-beladen. -frei,** *adj. See* **schmerzlos. schmerzhaft,** *adj.* painful; (*fig.*) distressing, grievous; ***-e Stelle,*** sore spot *or* place, tender *or* sensitive spot. **schmerzlich,** *adj.* (*usu. fig.*) sad, grievous, painful. **schmerzlindernd,** *adj.* soothing, analgesic, anodyne. **schmerzlos,** *adj.* painless; (*Med.*) indolent, sluggish. **schmerz|stillend,** *adj. See* **-lindernd. -voll,** *adj.* painful, agonizing.

Schmetterling ['ʃmɛtərlɪŋ], *m.* (**-s**, *pl.* **-e**) butterfly. **Schmetterlings|blütler,** *m.* papilionaceous flower. **-sammlung,** *f.* butterfly collection. **-schwimmen,** *n.*, **-stil,** *m.* (*Swimming*) butterfly stroke.

schmettern ['ʃmɛtərn], **1.** *v.i.* (*aux.* h. & s.) crash; resound, (*of bells*) ring out, (*of trumpet*) blare out, (*of birds*) warble. **2.** *v.t.* dash, smash, throw down violently; ***ein Lied –,*** give lusty voice to a song; (*sl.*) ***einen –,*** knock one back (*a drink*); ***zu Boden –,*** dash to the ground. **Schmetterschlag,** *m.* (*Tenn.*) smash.

Schmicke ['ʃmɪkə], *f.* whip-lash.

Schmied [ʃmi:t], *m.* (**-(e)s**, *pl.* **-e**) (black)smith; (*fig.*) founder, author; (*Prov.*) ***jeder ist seines Glückes –,*** every man is the architect of his own fortune. **schmiedbar,** *adj.* malleable. **Schmiedbarkeit,** *f.* malleability.

Schmiede ['ʃmi:də], *f.* smithy, forge; ***er kam vor die rechte –,*** he hit upon *or* got hold of the right person. **Schmiede|amboß,** *m.* anvil. **-arbeit,** *f.* smith's work, wrought-iron work. **-eisen,** *n.* wrought-iron. **schmiedeeisern,** *adj.* wrought-iron. **Schmiede|esse,** *f.* forge. **-hammer,** *m.* sledge-hammer.

schmieden ['ʃmi:dən], *v.t.* forge, hammer; (*fig.*) frame, devise, hatch, concoct; ***in Ketten*** or ***Eisen –,*** put in irons; ***Lügen –,*** concoct lies; ***Pläne –,*** devise plans; ***Ränke –,*** (hatch a) plot, scheme; ***Verse –,*** put together *or* pen verses; (*Prov.*) ***man muß das Eisen –, solange es heiß ist,*** strike while the iron is hot; ***sein eigenes Unglück –,*** be the author of one's own misfortune.

Schmiede|presse, *f.* forging press. **-stahl,** *m.* forged steel. **-stück,** *n.* forging. **-ware,** *f.* hardware. **-werkstatt,** *f. See* **Schmiede.**

Schmiege ['ʃmi:gə], *f.* 1. bevel; 2. folding rule. **schmiegen, 1.** *v.t.* bevel. **2.** *v.r.* (*fig.*) yield, bend; cringe; ***sich – an*** (*Acc.*), press close to, nestle against, cling to, (*coll.*) snuggle up to; ***sich – in*** (*Acc.*), (*of a th.*) fit snugly in(to); ***sich – und biegen,*** give in on every point, climb down. **schmiegsam,** *adj.* pliant, flexible, lithe, supple; (*fig.*) submissive, yielding. **Schmiegsamkeit,** *f.* pliancy, suppleness, flexibility.

Schmiele ['ʃmi:lə], *f.* 1. (*Bot.*) hair-grass (*Deschampsia*); 2. weal.

Schmier|anlage, *f.* lubricating system. **-buch,** *n.* rough notebook, scrapbook, jotter. **-büchse,** *f.* grease-cup, lubricator.

Schmiere ['ʃmi:rə], *f.* grease, lubricant, (*sl.*) spread (*for bread*), (*sl.*) troupe of strolling players, (*sl.*) thrashing, hiding; bribery; (*sl.*) ***– stehen,*** keep cave; (*sl.*) ***die ganze –,*** the whole shoot *or* boiling.

schmieren ['ʃmi:rən], **1.** *v.t.* grease, oil, lubricate; (*coll.*) spread (*butter etc.*), smear, (*of a painter*) daub, (*of a writer*) scribble, scrawl; (*sl.*) tip heavily, bribe, grease (*a p.'s*) palm; (*sl.*) ***ihm eine –***, swipe him (a fourpenny) one; (*sl.*) ***sich*** (*Dat.*) ***die Kehle –***, wet one's whistle; (*coll.*) ***ihm etwas ins Maul –***, rub his nose in s.th.; ***ihm Honig*** or ***Brei ums Maul –***, butter him up, soft-soap him; (*coll.*) ***wie geschmiert,*** like clockwork, without a hitch. **2.** *v.i.* rub off, smear. **Schmierenschauspieler,** *m.* strolling player. **Schmierer,** *m.* greaser; (*coll.*) (*writer*) scribbler, hack, (*painter*) dauber. **Schmiererei** [–'raɪ], *f.* daub; scribble, scrawl.

Schmier|fett, *n.* axle-grease. **–fink,** *m.* (*coll.*) dirty pig. **–geld,** *n.* tip, bribe. **schmierig,** *adj.* greasy, oily, viscous; (*coll.*) dirty, messy, grimy, sticky; (*fig.*) smutty, filthy; (*fig.*) sordid, mean, (*sl.*) smarmy. **Schmier|kanne,** *f.* oilcan. **–käse,** *m.* soft *or* spreading cheese. **–mittel,** *n.* lubricant; ointment, liniment; (*fig.*) bribe, tip. **–öl,** *n.* lubricating oil. **–pistole,** *f. See* **–presse. –plan,** *m.* lubrication chart. **–presse,** *f.* grease-gun. **–salbe,** *f.* ointment. **–seife,** *f.* soft soap. **–stelle,** *f.* lubrication point. **–stoff,** *m.* lubricant, (*Med.*) liniment. **Schmierung,** *f.* lubrication. **Schmiervorrichtung,** *f.* lubricator, oil-feed.

schmilz [ʃmɪlts], **schmilzt,** *see* **schmelzen.**

Schminke ['ʃmɪŋkə], *f.* (grease-)paint; rouge, cosmetic, make-up. **schminken,** *v.t., v.r.* paint one's face, powder one's face, make (o.s.) up, use make-up, (*fig.*) colour, adorn, embellish (*an account etc.*). **Schminkpflästerchen,** *n.* beauty-patch.

Schmirgel ['ʃmɪrgəl], *m.* emery. **Schmirgelleinen,** *n.* emery cloth. **schmirgeln,** *v.t.* rub *or* polish *or* grind with emery. **Schmirgelscheibe,** *f.* emery-wheel.

Schmiß [ʃmɪs], *m.* (**-(ss)es,** *pl.* **-(ss)e**) **1.** cut, gash; duelling scar; **2.** (*fig.*) verve, go, dash, pep.

schmiß [ʃmɪs], **schmisse,** *see* **schmeißen.**

schmissig ['ʃmɪsɪç], *adj.* racy, dashing, full of go.

Schmitz [ʃmɪts], *m.* (**-es,** *pl.* **-e**) blow, cut, lash; spot, blot, splash, blur. **Schmitze,** *f.* (*dial.*) *see* **Schmicke. schmitzen, 1.** *v.t.* lash, whip. **2.** *v.t., v.i.* soil, stain, splash; smudge, blur.

Schmöker ['ʃmø:kər], *m.* (*coll.*) old book, trashy novel. **schmökern,** *v.i.* browse, pore over old books.

schmollen ['ʃmɔlən], *v.i.* pout, sulk, be sulky.

Schmollis ['ʃmɔlɪs], *n.* ***mit ihm – trinken,*** have a drink with him, hobnob with him; (*Studs. sl.*) ***ein – den Sängern!*** a toast to the singers!

schmolz [ʃmɔlts], **schmölze** ['ʃmœltsə], *see* **schmelzen, 1.**

Schmorbraten ['ʃmo:rbra:tən], *m.* stewed *or* braised steak.

schmoren ['ʃmo:rən], **1.** *v.t.* stew, braise. **2.** *v.i.* (*coll. fig.*) swelter, be stewed *or* suffocated *or* baked *or* roasted (*with the heat*); (*coll.*) ***ihn – lassen,*** leave him to *or* let him stew in his own juice. **Schmor|pfanne,** *f.*, **–topf,** *m.* stewpan, stew-pot.

Schmu [ʃmu:], *m.* (*coll.*) unfair gain, illicit profit; ***– machen,*** swindle, diddle, doublecross.

Schmuck [ʃmuk], *m.* (**-(e)s,** *pl.* **-e**) ornament, decoration, adornment, finery; jewels, jewellery, ornaments, trinkets. **schmuck,** *adj.* spruce, tidy, trim, neat, smart, dapper, spick and span; pretty, nice, (*coll.*) dinky.

schmücken ['ʃmykən], **1.** *v.t.* decorate, adorn, set off, embellish, ornament. **2.** *v.r.* deck o.s. out, dress up, spruce *or* smarten o.s. up.

Schmuck|feder, *f.* plume. **–händler,** *m.* jeweller. **–kästchen,** *n.* jewel-case. **–laden,** *m.* jeweller's shop. **schmucklos,** *adj.* unadorned, plain, simple, austere. **Schmucklosigkeit,** *f.* plainness, simplicity. **Schmuck|nadel,** *f.* tiepin, breastpin, brooch. **–platz,** *m.* ornamental gardens. **–sachen,** *f.pl.* jewels, trinkets, ornaments, finery. **–stein,** *m.* gem. **–stück,** *n.* piece of jewellery. **schmuckvoll,** *adj.* ornate, ornamental. **Schmuck|waren,** *f.pl.* *See* **–sachen.**

Schmuddel ['ʃmudəl], *m.* (*coll.*) dirtiness, muckiness, grime. **schmuddelig,** *adj.* (*coll.*) dirty, dingy, grimy.

Schmuggel ['ʃmugəl], *m.*, **Schmuggelei** [–'laɪ], *f.* smuggling. **schmuggeln,** *v.t., v.i.* smuggle. **Schmuggelware,** *f.* smuggled goods, contraband. **Schmuggler,** *m.* smuggler.

schmunzeln ['ʃmuntsəln], *v.i.* smirk, grin, look pleased.

Schmus [ʃmu:s], *m.* empty chatter, prattle; (*sl.*) blarney, soft-soap. **schmusen,** *v.i.* 1. (*coll.*) chatter, prattle, babble; lay it on thick; 2. (*sl.*) spoon, neck; 3. ***– mit,*** fawn upon, butter (*a p.*) up, curry favour with, soft-soap (*a p.*). **Schmuser,** *m.* chatterbox; lickspittle, toady.

Schmutz [ʃmuts], *m.* dirt, filth; mud, muck; (*fig.*) smut; (*fig.*) ***mit – bewerfen,*** sling mud at; (*fig.*) ***in den – ziehen,*** drag through the mire *or* mud. **Schmutz|ärmel,** *m.pl.* sleeve protectors. **–blech,** *m.* (*Cycl.*) mudguard. **–bogen,** *m.* (*Typ.*) slur, waste sheet.

schmutzen ['ʃmutsən], *v.i.* get dirty (easily), soil (easily). **Schmutzerei** [–'raɪ], *f.* dirty job, filthiness; (*fig.*) filth, obscenity, smut.

Schmutz|farbe, *f.* dingy *or* drab colour. **–fink(e),** *m.* (*coll.*) dirty fellow, pig. **–fleck,** *m.* spot, stain, smudge, smear; (*fig.*) stain, blemish. **–geier,** *m.* (*Orn.*) Egyptian vulture (*Neophron percuopterus*).

schmutzig [ʃmutsɪç], *adj.* dirty, filthy, mucky, muddy, soiled, grimy; (*fig.*) base, sordid, low, mean, shabby; filthy, obscene, smutty; (*Typ.*) ***–er Abdruck,*** smudged *or* uneven proof; ***–er Eigennutz,*** sordid self-interest; ***–e Geschichte,*** dirty story; ***–er Wucher,*** filthy lucre; ***–e Wäsche,*** soiled *or* dirty linen.

Schmutz|kittel, *m.* overall. **–konkurrenz,** *f.* unfair competition. **–literatur,** *f.* pornography, (*coll.*) smut. **–presse,** *f.* gutter press. **–schrift,** *f.* obscene publication. **–seite,** *f.* (*Typ.*) sham page. **–titel,** *m.* (*Typ.*) bastard title, half-title. **–wasser,** *n.* waste water, sewage. **–zulage,** *f.* bonus (payment) for dirty work, (*coll.*) dirty-money.

Schnabel ['ʃna:bəl], *m.* (**-s,** *pl.* **⸚**) bill, beak; nozzle, snout; prow, cutwater (*of a ship*); (*vulg.*) mouth, trap, gob; (*vulg.*) ***halt' den –,*** hold your trap; ***seinen – an allem wetzen,*** poke one's nose into everything; (*coll.*) ***er spricht wie ihm der – gewachsen ist,*** he speaks according to his lights, he does not mince matters. **schnabelförmig,** *adj.* beak-shaped, rostrate. **schnabelieren** [–'li:rən], *v.i.* *See* **schnabulieren. Schnabelkerfe,** *f.* (*Ent.*) hemiptera.

schnäbeln ['ʃnɛ:bəln], *v.i.* (*coll.*) bill and coo.

Schnabel|schuhe, *m.pl.* (*Hist.*) pointed shoes *12th–15th centuries*). **–tasse,** *f.* (invalid's) feeding cup. **–tier,** *n.* (*Zool.*) duckbill platypus. **–zange,** *f.* (*Surg.*) rostrum.

schnabulieren [ʃnabu'li:rən], *v.i.* (*coll.*) eat heartily *or* with relish.

Schnack [ʃnak], *m.* (**-(e)s,** *pl.* **-e** *or* **⸚e**) (*coll., dial.*) chit-chat, stuff and nonsense, fiddlesticks, twaddle.

schnackeln, *v.i.* (*dial.*) *see* **schnalzen. schnacken,** *v.t., v.i.* (*dial., coll.*) (have a) chat, chatter, gossip, prattle, natter.

Schnadahüpf(e)l ['ʃna:dahypf(ə)l], **Schnaderhüpfe(r)l,** *n.* Alpine folk-song.

Schnake ['ʃna:kə], *f.* 1. jest, joke, piece of nonsense; fun; 2. (*Ent.*) cranefly; (*dial.*) gnat, midge. **Schnakenstich,** *m.* gnat bite. **schnakig, schnakisch,** *adj.* funny, amusing, comical.

Schnalle ['ʃnalə], *f.* buckle, clasp; latch, catch (*of a door*). **schnallen,** *v.t.* buckle, strap, fasten. **Schnallen|dorn,** *m.* tongue *or* tooth *or* pin of a buckle. **–haken,** *m.* chape. **–schuh,** *m.* buckled shoe.

schnalzen ['ʃnaltsən], *v.i.* ***– mit,*** crack (*a whip*), click (*the tongue*), snap (*the fingers*). **Schnalzlaut,** *m.* (*Phonet.*) click.

schnapp! [ʃnap], *int.* snap! snip! before you can say 'Jack Robinson'! **Schnapp,** *m.* (**-s,** *pl.* **-e**) (*coll.*) snap, fillip; mouthful. **schnappen, 1.** *v.i.*

(*aux.* h. & s.) snap (to), engage, click (in position), close with a snap; snatch, grab, (*as dogs*) snap (**nach,** at); ***nach Luft* –,** gasp for breath; (*coll.*) ***jetzt hat's aber geschnappt,*** but now there is an end of it, I'll not put up with it *or* stand it any longer. **2.** *v.t.* (*coll.*) catch, grab, get hold of, nab.

Schnäpper ['ʃnɛpər], *m.* **1.** snap, catch, latch; 2. (*Med.*) cupping instrument; 3. (*Orn.*) flycatcher (*Muscicapidae*).

Schnapp|feder, *f.* spring-catch. **–messer,** *n.* flick-knife. **–sack,** *m.* knapsack. **–schloß,** *n.* spring-lock, (*of necklace*) spring-catch *or* -fastening. **–schuß,** *m.* (*Phot.*) snapshot, (*coll.*) snap.

Schnaps [ʃnaps], *m.* (**-es,** *pl.* **⸗e**) spirits, brandy, gin, liquor. **Schnaps|bruder,** *m.* (*coll.*) tippler, toper. **–bude,** *f.* gin-shop. **schnapsen,** *v.i.* tipple. **Schnaps|idee,** *f.* (*coll.*) crazy notion, hare-brained scheme. **–nase,** *f.* bottle-nose.

schnarchen ['ʃnarçən], *v.i.* snore. **Schnarchen,** *n.* snoring. **Schnarchventil,** *n.* snifting-valve, sniffle-valve.

Schnarre ['ʃnarə], *f.* rattle. **schnarren,** *v.i.* rattle, (speak with a) burr; jar, rasp; ***das r* –,** roll *or* burr the r. **Schnarr|saite,** *f.* snare (*on drums*). **–werk,** *n.* bourdon, reed-stops (*of an organ*).

Schnattergans ['ʃnatərgans], *f.* (*coll.*) chatterbox. **schnattern,** *v.i.* chatter (*also of teeth with cold*); gabble; quack, cackle (*of geese*).

schnauben ['ʃnaubən], **1.** (*obs., Austr. irr.*) *v.t., v.i.* pant, puff, blow, breathe heavily, snort; (***vor***) ***Wut* –,** foam *or* fume with rage; (***nach***) ***Rache* –,** breathe vengeance. **2.** *v.r.* (*dial.*) blow one's nose.

schnäubig ['ʃnɔybɪç], *adj.* (*dial.*) choosy, fussy (*about food*).

schnaufen ['ʃnaufən], *v.i.* breathe heavily *or* hard, pant, gasp, wheeze, snort. **Schnaufer,** *m.* (*coll.*) breath; ***bis zum letzen* –,** to the last gasp.

Schnauzbart ['ʃnautsbart], *m.* moustache.

Schnauze ['ʃnautsə], *f.* snout, muzzle; spout, nozzle; (*vulg.*) nose, beak, (*vulg.*) gob, trap, snitch; (*sl.*) lip, cheek; (*vulg.*) ***die – halten,*** hold one's trap, put a sock in it; (*sl.*) ***die – voll haben,*** be fed up to the teeth, have had a bellyful; (*sl.*) ***ihm eins auf die – geben,*** give him a sock on the jaw. **schnauzen,** *v.i.* (*coll.*) snap, bawl, throw one's weight about. **Schnauzer,** *n.* rough-haired terrier.

Schnecke ['ʃnɛkə], *f.* **1.** snail, slug; 2. (*Anat.*) cochlea (*of the ear*); (*Archit.*) spiral, scroll, volute; fusee (*of clock*); Archimedes' screw; worm-gear.

Schnecken|antrieb, *m.* worm-drive. **–feder,** *f.* coiled spring. **schneckenförmig,** *adj.* helical, spiral. **Schnecken|fraß,** *n.* damage done by slugs. **–gang,** *m.* snail's pace; circuitous path. **–getriebe,** *n.* worm-gear. **–gewinde,** *n.* helix, whorl; (*Mech.*) worm, endless screw. **–haus,** *n.* snail-shell. **–linie,** *f.* spiral, helix. **–muschel,** *f.* conch shell. **–post,** *f.* (*fig.*) ***mit der* –,** at a snail's pace. **–rad,** *n.* worm-wheel. **–tempo,** *n.* (*fig.*) ***im* –,** at a snail's pace.

Schnee [ʃne:], *m.* snow; ***vom – eingeschlossen,*** snowed up, snow-bound; ***Eiweiß zu – schlagen,*** beat the white of egg to a froth. **Schnee|ammer,** *f.* (*Orn.*) snow-bunting (*Plectrophenax nivalis*). **–ball,** *m.* **1.** snowball; 2. (*pl.* **-ballen**) (*Bot.*) guelder-rose (*Viburnum*). **schnee|ballen,** *v.t.* (*v.r.*) (*insep.*) snowball (one another). **–bedeckt,** *adj.* snow-covered *or* -capped (*of mountains*). **Schnee|beere,** *f.* (*Bot.*) snow-berry (*Symphoricarpus racemosus*). **–berg,** *m.* snow-capped mountain. **–besen,** *m.* egg-beater, whisk. **–blindheit,** *f.* snow-blindness. **–brille,** *f.* dark glasses, snow-goggles. **–decke,** *f.* blanket of snow. **–Eule,** *f.* (*Orn.*) snowy owl (*Nyctea scandiaca*). **–fink,** *m.* (*Orn.*) snow-finch (*Montifringilla nivalis*). **–flocke,** *f.* snowflake. **–gans,** *f.* (*Orn.*) snow-goose (*Anser caerulescens*); (*coll.*) silly goose. **–gestöber,** *n.* snow flurry. **–glöckchen,** *n.* (*Bot.*) snowdrop (*Galanthus nivalis*). **–grenze,** *f.* snowline. **–hase,** *m.* (*Zool.*) Alpine hare (*Lepus timidus*). **–höhe,** *f.* depth of snow. **–huhn,** *n.* (*Orn.*) *see* **Alpenschneehuhn.** **–hütte,** *f.* igloo.

schneeig ['ʃne:ɪç], *adj.* snowy, snow-covered.

Schnee|kette, *f.* (*Motor.*) non-skid chain. **–könig,** *m.* (*dial.*) wren; (*coll.*) ***sich freuen wie ein* –,** be as merry as a lark *or* cricket, be as pleased as Punch. **–koppe,** *f.* *See* **–kuppe.** **–kranich,** *m.* (*Orn.*) Asiatic white crane (*Grus leucogeranus*). **–kufe,** *f.* (*Av.*) landing-skid. **–kuppe,** *f.* snow-capped peak. **–lawine,** *f.* avalanche. **–mann,** *m.* snowman. **–pflug,** *m.* snow-plough. **–schipper,** *m.* snow-sweeper. **–schläger,** *m.* *See* **–besen.** **–schmelze,** *f.* thaw. **–schuh,** *m.* snow-shoe, ski. **–schüpper,** *m.* *See* **–schipper.** **–sturm,** *m.,* **–treiben,** *n.* snowstorm, blizzard. **–wasser,** *n.* melted snow, slush. **–wehe,** *f.* snowdrift. **schneeweiß,** *adj.* snow-white, (as) white as snow. **Schnee|wetter,** *n.* snowy weather; snowstorm. **–wittchen,** *n.* Snow White (*fairy tale*). **–zeisig,** *m.* (*Orn.*) Hornemann's redpoll (*Carduelis hornemanni*).

Schnegel ['ʃne:gəl], *m.* (*dial.*) slug.

Schneid [ʃnaɪt], *m.* (*dial. f.*) pluck, dash, (*coll.*) go, (*sl.*) guts.

Schneidbrenner ['ʃnaɪtbrɛnər], *m.* blow-torch.

Schneide ['ʃnaɪdə], *f.* edge (*of a knife etc.*), cutting edge, knife-edge; ***auf des Messers* –,** at a critical juncture, hanging by a thread, on the razor's edge, (*coll.*) touch and go. **Schneide|backen,** *pl.* screw-dies. **–bank,** *f.* chopping-block. **–bohnen,** *pl.* French beans. **–brett,** *n.* bread-board. **–maschine,** *f.* cutting machine, bacon slicer *or* cutter. **–mühle,** *f.* sawmill.

schneiden ['ʃnaɪdən], **1.** *irr.v.t., v.i.* cut, mow, trim, carve, engrave; ***ihn* –,** cut him (dead); (*Cards*) ***mit der Dame* –,** finesse the queen; ***eine Ecke* –,** cut (off) a corner; ***Fleisch* –,** carve meat; ***ins lebendige Fleisch* –,** cut to the quick; ***Fratzen*** or ***Gesichter*** or ***Grimassen*** or ***ein Gesicht* –,** pull *or* make faces *or* a face; ***sich*** (*Dat.*) ***die Haare – lassen,*** have one's hair cut; (*fig.*) ***das schneidet mir ins Herz,*** that cuts me to the quick; ***in Holz* –,** carve (in) wood; ***die Kur* –,** pay court (*Dat.,* to); ***sich*** (*Dat.*) ***die Nägel* –,** cut one's nails; ***ein Tier* –,** castrate an animal; ***er ist seinem Vater wie aus den Augen*** or ***dem Gesicht geschnitten,*** he is the very image of his father. **2.** *irr.v.r.* (*of lines*) cut each other, intersect, meet; (*fig.*) ***da schneidest du dich aber gewaltig,*** that's where you make your big mistake; ***sich in den Finger* –,** cut one's finger. **schneidend,** *adj.* cutting, sharp, (*as wind*) keen, piercing, biting, penetrating; (*as remarks*) cutting, bitter, sarcastic, (*of sarcasm*) biting; (*of voice*) strident.

Schneider ['ʃnaɪdər], *m.* **1.** tailor; cutter; (*coll.*) ***wir froren wie ein* –,** we were perished with cold; 2. (*fig.*) poltroon; 3. (*Ent.*) daddy-long-legs; 4. (*Cards, Bill.*) ***aus dem – heraus kommen,*** gain more than half the points; (*coll.*) ***sie ist aus dem* –,** she will not see thirty again. **Schneiderei** [-'raɪ], *f.* tailoring (*for men*); dressmaking (*for ladies*). **Schneiderin,** *f.* dressmaker. **Schneider|kleid,** *n.* tailor-made dress. **–kostüm,** *n.* tailor-made outfit. **–meister,** *m.* master-tailor. **schneidern,** *v.i.* do tailoring *or* dressmaking. **Schneider|puppe,** *f.* tailor's dummy. **–seele,** *f.* (*fig.*) timorous spirit.

Schneide|stahl, *m.,* **–werkzeug,** *n.* cutting tool. **–zahn,** *m.* incisor.

schneidig ['ʃnaɪdɪç], *adj.* spirited, dashing, plucky; keen, alert, smart. **Schneidigkeit,** *f.* *See* **Schneid**; smartness, keenness.

schneien ['ʃnaɪən], *v.i.* (*aux.* h. & s.) snow; ***es hat viel geschneit,*** it has snowed heavily; (*coll.*) ***er ist uns ins Haus geschneit,*** he dropped in on us unexpectedly, (*sl.*) he blew in.

Schneise ['ʃnaɪzə], *f.* cutting, ride, aisle (*in a forest*); (*Mil.*) lane; (*Av.*) flying-lane.

schneiteln ['ʃnaɪtəln], *v.t.* lop, prune, trim.

schnell [ʃnɛl], **1.** *adj.* rapid, swift, fast, quick, speedy, (*Poet.*) fleet; prompt, sudden, abrupt, hasty, (*Comm.*) brisk; ***–e Bahn,*** fast course; ***–e Bedienung,*** quick *or* prompt service; ***in –er Folge,*** in rapid succession; ***–er Strom,*** swift stream; ***–er Verkauf,*** brisk sale; ***–e Zahlung,*** prompt payment. **2.** *adv.* fast, quickly, rapidly, swiftly, speedily, (*Mus.*) presto; promptly, hastily, suddenly, abruptly; – ***denken,*** do some quick thinking; – ***handeln,*** act without delay, act promptly; (*coll.*) ***das ist – gegangen,*** that was quick; ***mach –!*** hurry up! make haste! look sharp! (*sl.*) step on it! make it snappy!

Schnellader ['ʃnɛlla:dər], *m.* quick-firing gun, pom-pom. **Schnellauf,** *m.* sprint. **schnellaufend,** *adj.* high-speed, fast-running. **Schnelläufer,** *m.* sprinter.

Schnell|bahn, *f.* high-speed railway. **–betrieb,** *m.* express service. **–binder,** *m.* quick-setting cement. **–bleiche,** *f.* chemical bleaching. **–boot,** *n.* speed-boat, (*Mil.*) motor torpedo-boat. **–büfett,** *n.* snack-bar. **–dampfer,** *m.* express steamer. **–dienst,** *m.* *See* **–betrieb. –drehlegierung,** *f.* high-speed alloy.

Schnelle ['ʃnɛlə], *f.* *See* **Schnelligkeit. Schnellen,** *pl.* rapids.

schnellen ['ʃnɛlən], **1.** *v.i.* (*aux.* s.) bounce, spring, jerk, fly, snap; ***in die Höhe –,*** shoot into the air, fly *or* tip up. **2.** *v.t.* 1. fling, let fly; toss, flick, jerk; 2. snap one's fingers; 3. (*coll.*) bamboozle, diddle, cheat. **Schneller,** *m.* 1. snap of the finger; 2. (*Mus.*) mordant; 3. trigger (*of crossbow*); 4. (*dial.*) marble (*toy*).

Schnell|feuer, *n.* (*Mil.*) rapid fire, running fire. **–feuergeschütz,** *n.* quick-firing gun, pom-pom. **–flugzeug,** *n.* high-speed aircraft. **schnell|flussig,** *adj.* easily *or* readily fusible. **–füßig,** *adj.* swift (-footed), nimble. **Schnell|gang,** *m.* (*Mech.*) overdrive. **–ganggetriebe,** *n.* (*Motor.*) high-speed gear-box. **–gaststätte,** *f.* self-service restaurant, cafeteria. **–gericht,** *n.* summary court. **–hefter,** *m.* letter-file.

Schnelligkeit ['ʃnɛlıçkaıt], *f.* velocity, speed, rate, pace; quickness, swiftness, rapidity; promptness, dispatch, haste, suddenness.

Schnell|imbiß, *m.* snack. **–imbißstube,** *f.* snack-bar. **–käfer,** *m.* (*Ent.*) click-beetle (*Elateridae*). **–kocher,** *m.* pressure-cooker. **–kraft,** *f.* elasticity, springiness, resilience. **Schnellot,** *n.* soft solder.

Schnell|presse, *f.* high-speed press. **–reinigung,** *f.* express dry-cleaning. **–richter,** *m.* magistrate with power of summary jurisdiction. **–schrift,** *f.* (*obs.*) shorthand, steno- graphy. **–schritt,** *m.* (*Mil.*) quick march. **–stahl,** *m.* high-speed steel. **–triebwagen,** *m.* express diesel train. **schnelltrocknend,** *adj.* quick-drying. **Schnell|truppen,** *f.* mobile task-force. **–verband,** *m.* (*Med.*) adhesive dressing. **–verfahren,** *n.* 1. (*Law*) summary procedure; 2. rapid *or* quick method. **–verkehr,** *m.* express traffic **–waage,** *f.* steelyard. **–zug,** *m.* express (train).

Schnepfe ['ʃnɛpfə], *f.* 1. (*Orn.*) *see* **Doppelschnepfe, Waldschnepfe, Zwergschnepfe**; 2. (*vulg.*) tart. **Schnepfen|dreck,** *m.* roast giblets (of snipe *or* woodcock). **–läufer,** *m.* (*Orn.*) *see* **Schlammläufer.**

Schneppe ['ʃnɛpə], *f.* 1. nozzle, spout, lip; peak (*of a cap*); 2. (*dial.*) *see* **Schnepfe.**

Schnepper, *m.* (*Austr.*) *see* **Schnäpper.**

Schnerfer ['ʃnɛrfər], *m.* (*Austr.*) rucksack.

schneuzen ['ʃnɔytsən], **1.** *v.t.* snuff (*a candle*). **2.** *v.r.* blow one's nose.

Schnickschnack ['ʃnıkʃnak], *m.* chit-chat, tittle-tattle.

schniegeln ['ʃni:gəln], *v.r.* (*coll.*) dress up, deck o.s. out, smarten o.s. up; ***geschniegelt und gebügelt,*** spick and span.

Schniepel ['ʃni:pəl], *m.* (*coll.*) tailcoat, dandy.

Schnipfel ['ʃnıpfəl], *m.* (*dial.*) shred, scrap. **schnipfeln,** *v.t.* shred, cut up, slice.

schnipp! [ʃnıp], *int.* snip! flip! flick! **Schnippchen,** *n.* snap of the fingers; ***ihm ein – schlagen,*** play a trick on him, outwit *or* outdo *or* fox him. **Schnippel,** *m. or n.* (*coll.*) shred, scrap, bit, chip, slice. **schnippeln,** *v.t.* shred, cut up, snip, slice. **schnippen,** *v.t., v.i.* snap one's fingers; flip, flick, jerk.

schnippisch ['ʃnıpıʃ], *adj.* impertinent, pert, saucy, (*coll.*) cheeky.

Schnipsel ['ʃnıpsəl], *n.,* **schnipseln,** *v.t.* (*coll.*) *see* **Schnippel, schnippeln. schnipsen,** *v.t., v.i.* (*dial.*) *see* **schnippen.**

Schnitt [ʃnıt], *m.* **(-(e)s,** *pl.* **-e)** 1. cut, gash, slash; notch, slice; (*Surg.*) incision, operation; 2. (*Geom. etc.*) intersection, section, (*Tech.*) sectional view; (*Dressm.*) (paper) pattern, (*fig.*) cut, style, fashion, make; ***der goldene –,*** medial section; 3. (*Bookb.*) edge(s); 4. cutting; reaping, harvest, crop; 5. (*Films*) cutting and editing; 6. (*dial.*) small glass of beer; 7. (*Comm., coll.*) profit, (*sl.*) cut; (*coll.*) ***seinen – an*** or ***bei einer S. machen,*** make a packet *or* get one's cut out of a th.

schnitt, *see* **schneiden.**

Schnitt|ansicht, *f.* sectional view. **–ball,** *m.* (*Tenn. etc.*) cut. **–blumen,** *f.pl.* cut flowers. **–bohne,** *f.* French bean. **–breite,** *f.* breadth of cut, (*of a saw*) width of kerf. **–dicke,** *f.* thickness of sections.

Schnitte ['ʃnıtə], *f.* cut, (*of bread*) slice, (*coll.*) piece, (*of meat*) steak, cutlet, chop, (*of bacon*) rasher.

Schnitter ['ʃnıtər], *m.,* **Schnitterin,** *f.* harvester, mower, reaper.

schnittfest ['ʃnıtfɛst], *adj.* firm enough to cut (*as tomatoes*). **Schnittfläche,** *f.* sectional plane *or* area. **schnitthaltig,** *adj.* (*Tech.*) true to size. **Schnittholz,** *n.* cut *or* sawn timber.

schnittig ['ʃnıtıç], *adj.* stylish, elegant, smart, (*coll.*) racy, streamlined.

Schnitt|kante, *f.* cutting edge. **–kurve,** *f.* intersecting curve. **–lauch,** *m.* (*Bot.*) chive. **–linie,** *f.* intersecting line, secant.

Schnittling ['ʃnıtlıŋ], *m.* **(-s,** *pl.* **-e)** 1. (*Bot.*) cutting; 2. (*animal*) gelding.

Schnitt|meister, *m.* (*Films*) cutter, editor. **–messer,** *n.* (*Surg.*) scalpel. **–muster,** *n.* dress *or* paper pattern. **–punkt,** *m.* (point of) intersection, vertex. **schnittreif,** *adj.* ready for cutting *or* reaping. **Schnitt|waren,** *f.pl.* drapery, (*Am.*) dry goods; haberdashery. **–warenhändler,** *m.* draper. **schnittweise,** *adv.* cut by cut, in slices. **Schnitt|-winkel,** *m.* angle of intersection. **–wunde,** *f.* cut, gash, laceration. **–zeichnung,** *f.* sectional drawing.

Schnitz [ʃnıts], *m.* **(-es,** *pl.* **-e)** (*dial.*) slice, cut; chop, cutlet, steak. **Schnitzarbeit,** *f.* wood-carving.

Schnitzel ['ʃnıtzəl], *n.* chip, scrap, shred, slice; *pl.* clippings, parings, shavings; ***Wiener –,*** fillet of veal, veal cutlet. **Schnitzel|jagd,** *f.* paper-chase. **–maschine,** *f.* slicer, shredder. **schnitzeln,** *v.t., v.i.* carve, whittle, chip, cut finely, shred.

schnitzen ['ʃnıtsən], *v.t., v.i.* carve, whittle. **Schnitzer,** *m.* 1. wood-carver; 2. carving-knife; 3. (*coll.*) blunder, howler, slip. **Schnitzerei** [–'raı], *f.* wood-carving; piece of carving, carved work. **Schnitz|holz,** *n.* wood for carving. **–kunst,** *f.* art of carving in wood. **–messer,** *n.* carving-tool. **–werk,** *n.* *See* **Schnitzerei.**

schnob [ʃno:p], **schnöbe** ['ʃnø:bə], *see* **schnauben.**

schnobern ['ʃno:bərn], *v.i.* *See* **schnuppern.**

schnodd(e)rig ['ʃnɔd(ə)rıç], *adj.* (*coll.*) pert, saucy, (*coll.*) cheeky; insolent, (*sl.*) snotty. **Schnodd(e)rigkeit,** *f.* pertness, sauce, insolence, cheek.

schnöd(e) ['ʃnø:t (–də)], *adj.* base, mean, vile, shameful, disgraceful, despicable, shameless, iniquitous, (*coll.*) shabby; disdainful, contemptuous, scornful; inconsiderate, unfriendly; ***–es Geld,*** filthy lucre; ***–er Gewinn,*** shameless profit; ***–er Undank,*** base ingratitude.

Schnorchel ['ʃnɔrçəl], *m.* air-inlet, breathing-tube, (*sl.*) snort, snorkel (*on submarines*).

Schnörkel ['ʃnœrkəl], *m.* florid ornament, (*coll.*) frills (*also fig.*); (*handwriting*) flourish, (*coll.*) squiggle, (*signature*) paraph; (*Archit.*) scroll, volute. **schnörkelhaft, schnörkelig,** *adj.* full of flourishes, loaded with ornament; (*fig.*) capricious, whimsical. **schnörkeln, 1.** *v.i.* make flourishes. **2.** *v.t.* adorn with scrolls *etc.*

schnorren ['ʃnɔrən], *v.t., v.i.* (*coll.*) scrounge, cadge. **Schnorrer,** *m.* scrounger, cadger; tramp, (*Am.*) bum.

schnorz [ʃnɔrts], *adj.* (*dial.*) ***das ist mir ganz –,*** *see* **schnuppe.**

Schnucke [ˈʃnukə], *f.* (*dial.*) (moorland) sheep. **Schnuckelchen,** *n.* (*coll.*), **Schnuckeli,** *n.* (*dial.*) darling, pet. **schnuckelig,** *adj.* (*coll.*) cuddly.

schnüffeln [ˈʃnyfəln], *v.i.* sniff (*an* (*Dat.*), at), snuffle; (*fig.*) snoop (around *or* about). **Schnüffler,** *m.* sniffer, snuffler; snooper.

schnullen [ˈʃnulən], *v.i.*, *v.t.* (*coll.*) suck (*an* (*Dat.*), at *or* on). **Schnuller,** *m.* rubber teat, dummy, comforter.

Schnulze [ˈʃnultsə], *f.* sentimental ditty, (*sl.*) tear-jerker.

[1]**Schnupfen** [ˈʃnupfən], *n.* snuff-taking.

[2]**Schnupfen,** *m.* cold (in the head), catarrh; ***den – bekommen, sich*** (*Dat.*) ***einen – holen,*** catch (a) cold.

schnupfen, 1. *v.t.* sniff up. **2.** *v.i.* take snuff. **Schnupf|tabak,** *m.* snuff. **–tuch,** *n.* (*dial.*) (pocket-)handkerchief.

Schnuppe [ˈʃnupə], *f.* 1. snuff (*of a candle*); 2. shooting-star. **schnuppe,** *adj.* (*coll.*) ***das ist mir*** (***ganz*** or ***total***) ***–!*** it's all the same to me, I don't care a rap *or* damn.

[1]**Schnur** [ʃnu:r], *f.* (-, *pl.* **⸚e** *or* **-en**) string, cord, twine; (*Elec.*) cord, flex; string of beads; braid, piping; (*fig.*) ***nach der –,*** straight as a die; ***nach der – leben,*** be strictly methodical; ***mit Schnüren besetzen,*** braid, pipe, trim with lace; (*fig.*) ***über die – hauen,*** overstep the line *or* mark, kick over the traces.

[2]**Schnur,** *f.* (-, *pl.* **-en** *or* **⸚e**) (*B.*) daughter-in-law.

Schnürband [ˈʃny:rbant], *n.* string with a tag; stays-lace; bootlace.

Schnurbesatz [ˈʃnu:rbəzats], *m.* braid, piping, (lace) trimming.

Schnür|boden, *m.* rigging-loft, (*Theat.*) gridiron. **–brust,** *f. See* **–leib. –bund,** *m.* (*Naut.*) lashing (*of spars*).

Schnürchen [ˈʃny:rçən], *n.* (*coll.*) ***wie nach dem*** or ***am – gehen,*** go like clockwork; (***wie***) ***am – haben,*** (*a th.*) have at one's fingers' ends, (*a p.*) have under one's thumb, have on a bit of string.

schnüren [ˈʃny:rən], **1.** *v.t.* tie, tie up, tie with string, string, cord, lace, strap, fasten; (*coll.*) ***sein Bündel –,*** pack up (one's traps *or* things). **2.** *v.r.* wear stays.

schnurgerade [ˈʃnu:rgəra:də], *adv.* in a straight line, dead-straight, as the crow flies, in a bee-line.

Schnür|latz, *m.* (*Hist.*) stomacher. **–leib,** *m.*, **–leibchen,** *n.* (pair of) stays, corset. **–loch,** *n.* eyelet. **–nadel,** *f.* bodkin; tag.

schnurpsen [ˈʃnurpsən], *v.i.* (*dial.*) munch noisily, chomp.

Schnurrant [ʃnuˈrant], *m.* (**-en,** *pl.* **-en**) street-musician.

Schnurrbart [ˈʃnurba:rt], *m.* moustache. **schnurrbärtig,** *adj.* moustached, with a moustache.

Schnurre [ˈʃnurə], *f.* 1. funny tale, joke, quip; piece of nonsense; 2. humming-top, rattle; 3. old hag. **schnurren, 1.** *v.i.* (*aux.* h. *&* s.) hum, buzz, whirr, whizz, purr; *see also* **schnorren**; ***Katzen –,*** cats purr. **2.** *v.t.* cadge; ***Vorlesungen –,*** gate-crash lectures. **Schnurrer,** *m. See* **Schnorrer.**

Schnür|riemen, *m. See* **–senkel.**

schnurrig [ˈʃnurıç], *adj.* droll, funny, quaint, queer, odd.

Schnurschalter [ˈʃnu:rʃaltər], *m.* (*Elec.*) pendant switch.

Schnür|schuh, *m.* laced shoe. **–senkel,** *m.* boot *or* shoe-lace.

schnurstracks [ˈʃnu:rʃtraks], *adv.* straight(way), at once, immediately, on the spot; directly; ***– zuwider,*** directly *or* diametrically opposed.

schnurz [ʃnurts], *adj.* (*dial.*) *see* **schnorz, schnuppe.**

Schnute [ˈʃnu:tə], *f.* (*dial.*, *coll.*) *see* **Schnauze.**

schob [ʃo:p], **schöbe** [ˈʃø:bə], *see* **schieben.**

Schober [ˈʃo:bər], *m.* stack, rick; barn, shed; measure (= *60 bundles or bottles*) (*of straw etc.*). **schobern** (*also* **schöbern**), *v.t.* stack, pile (*hay*).

[1]**Schock** [ʃɔk], *n.* (**-(e)s,** *pl.* **-e** *or* -) heap, shock; three-score; a (large) quantity; mass, lot; ***zwei –,*** six-score.

[2]**Schock,** *m.* (**-(e)s,** *pl.* **-e** *or* **-s**) (*Med.*) shock; shell-shock.

schockant [ʃɔˈkant], *adj.* shocking, disgraceful, improper, scandalous.

Schockbehandlung [ˈʃɔkbəhandluŋ], *f.* (*Med.*) shock-therapy.

schocken [ˈʃɔkən], **1.** *v.t.* count by sixties; place in heaps of sixty. **2.** *v.i.* yield in abundance.

schockieren [ʃɔˈki:rən], *v.t.* shock, scandalize, offend. **schockschwerenot!** *int.* damn and blast! **Schocktruppen,** *f.pl.* shock troops, commandos. **schockweise,** *adv.* by threescores; in bundles, in heaps *or* masses.

Schofel [ˈʃo:fəl], *m.* trash, refuse, rubbish. **schofel,** *adj.* paltry, worthless, mean, shabby.

Schöffe [ˈʃœfə], *m.* (**-n,** *pl.* **-n**) (*obs.*) juror, juryman. **Schöffengericht,** *n.* lay assessor's court; court of jurors, judge and jury.

schoflig [ˈʃo:flıç], *adj. See* **schofel.**

Schokolade [ʃokoˈla:də], *f.* chocolate. **schokoladen,** *adj.* chocolate. **schokoladenfarben,** *adj.* chocolate-coloured. **Schokoladentafel,** *f.* slab *or* bar of chocolate.

Scholar [ʃoˈla:r], *m.* (**-en,** *pl.* **-en**) scholar, medi(a)eval student. **Scholarch,** *m.* (**-en,** *pl.* **-en**) (*obs.*) school-inspector; headmaster. **Scholastie** [–ˈsti:], *f. See* **Scholastion. Scholastik,** *f.* scholasticism; (*collect.*) the Schoolmen. **Scholastiker,** *m.* (*Hist.*) schoolman, scholastic. **Scholastion,** *n.* (**-s,** *pl.* **-tien**) (*obs.*) scholium, comment, annotation.

scholl [ʃɔl], **schölle** [ˈʃœlə], *see* **schallen.**

[1]**Scholle** [ˈʃɔlə], *f.* clod, sod; floe (*of ice*); (*fig.*) soil, homeland; ***an der – haften,*** be tied *or* bound to the soil.

[2]**Scholle,** *f.* flat fish (*Pleuronectidae*), flounder, plaice.

Schöllkraut [ˈʃœlkraut], *n. See* **Schellkraut.**

schölte [ˈʃœltə], *see* **schelten.**

schon [ʃo:n], *adv.* 1. (*temporal*) already, by this time, as yet, even, as far, (*in questions*) yet; ***ich habe mein Ei – gegessen,*** I have already eaten my egg; ***hast du dein Ei – gegessen?*** have you eaten your egg yet? ***er wollte – gehen,*** he was ready *or* about to go; ***willst du – gehen?*** are you going already? must you go so soon? (**a**) (*with other adv.*) ***– damals,*** even then; ***– einmal,*** once so far; ***hast du es – einmal gesehen?*** have you ever seen it (before)? ***ich habe es – einmal gesehen,*** I have seen it before; ***– früher,*** before this, earlier on; ***– ganz müde,*** (already) quite tired; ***– immer,*** all the time, all along; ***– jetzt,*** even now; ***– lange,*** long ago; ***– längst,*** see ***– immer***; ***– oft,*** often enough; ***– wieder,*** again already, yet again; ***was gibt's da – wieder?*** what is it now? (**b**) (*with prep. phrases*) ***– am nächsten Tag,*** the very next day; ***– im 6. Jahrhundert,*** as far back as *or* as early as the 6th century; ***– seit zwei Jahren,*** these past two years, for as long as two years; ***– um 5 Uhr,*** as early as 5 o'clock;

2. (*assurance*) surely, certainly, indeed, after all, no doubt, (*coll.*) for sure, sure enough; ***er wird – wissen,*** he will doubtless know, he is sure to know; ***es wird – gehen,*** (I am sure) it will be all right; ***ich mach es –,*** leave it to me! I'll manage all right; ***es ist – möglich,*** it's quite *or* indeed possible; ***du kannst – hier bleiben,*** you can certainly stay here; ***– gut!*** that's all right, that will do, (*Am.*) okay! ***es ist – so,*** there's nothing can be done *or* nothing we (you *etc.*) can do about it, that's how it is;

3. (*reservation*) ***– der Name,*** the bare *or* very name; ***– der Gedanke,*** the mere *or* very idea; ***– weil,*** if only because, just because; ***– wegen,*** merely on account of, if only because of; ***– deswegen,*** for that reason alone, if only for that reason; (*coll.*) ***wenn –, denn –,*** one might as well be hanged for a sheep as for a lamb; (*coll.*) ***wenn –!*** what of it! (*sl.*) so what! ***wenn –, dann gründlich,*** what is worth doing at all is worth doing well;

4. (*concession*) ***es gibt des Elends so – genug,*** there's enough misery in the world as it is; ***er gibt – zu,*** he cannot but admit; ***das ist – wahr,*** that's all very well, that's true enough; ***ich verstehe –!*** I dare say! ***das kennen wir –!*** it's the same old story!

schön [ʃø:n], **1.** *adj.* beautiful, (*also of women*) fair, (*of men*) handsome, good-looking; fine, lovely, splendid; pretty, nice; ***–e Augen machen,*** make sheep's eyes; (*coll.*) (*iron.*) ***eine –e Bescherung,*** a nice mess, a pretty kettle of fish, a fine business *or* how-do-you-do; ***–en Dank!*** many thanks; ***das –e Geschlecht,*** the fair sex; ***die –en Künste,*** the fine arts; ***–e Literatur,*** belles-lettres; ***manch –es Mal,*** many a time; ***in –ster Ordnung,*** in perfect *or* (*coll.*) apple-pie order; (*iron.*) ***das sind (mir) –e Sachen!*** fine goings-on indeed! ***–e Seele,*** sentimentalist; enthusiastic devotee; ***das ist alles recht –,*** that's all very well; ***das ist – von dir,*** that's very nice *or* kind of you; ***eines –en Tages,*** one of these (fine) days; ***die –e Welt,*** the fashionable world; ***–es Wetter,*** fine weather; ***die –en Wissenschaften,*** literature and the arts; ***–e Worte,*** fair *or* fine words; (*iron.*) ***das wäre ja noch –er,*** that would be the limit *or* would beat everything; impossible! out of the question! certainly not! **2.** *adv.* (*often iron.*) very, exceedingly, nicely, beautifully; ***halte dich – warm!*** keep yourself nice and warm; ***grüßen Sie ihn –stens von mir!*** give him my kindest regards; ***bitte –,*** (*offering*) if you please, (*receiving*) yes, please; ***danke –,*** no, thank you; ***sei – brav!*** be a good child! ***da sind wir – daran!*** we're in a nice mess *or* fix; ***das werde ich – bleiben lassen,*** I shall take good care to do nothing of the sort, (*coll.*) catch me doing that! ***du hast – lachen,*** it's all very well for you to laugh, (*coll.*) you can laugh; ***er wird sich – erschrecken,*** he will get quite a shock; ***bleib – sitzen!*** don't (you) budge from your seat! ***ich habe mich – gewundert,*** I got the surprise of my life.

Schonbezug ['ʃo:nbətsu:k], *m.* (protective) covering, seat cover.

Schöndruck ['ʃø:ndruk], *m.* (*Typ.*) primer.

Schöne ['ʃø:nə], *f.* beautiful woman, beauty, belle.

schonen ['ʃo:nən], **1.** *v.t.*, (*obs.*) *v.i.* (*Gen.*) treat with consideration *or* indulgence, respect, spare (*a p., his feelings etc.*); be sparing of, save, conserve, husband; take (good) care of, protect, preserve, care for. **2.** *v.r.* take care of *or* look after o.s.; save one's strength, (*coll.*) take it easy.

schönen ['ʃø:nən], *v.t.* (re)fine, clarify (*liquids*), beautify, brighten, gloss.

schonend ['ʃo:nənt], **1.** *adj.* careful, considerate, indulgent, gentle. **2.** *adv.* ***– beibringen*** (*Dat.*), break (*news*) gently to; ***– umgehen mit,*** use sparingly, (*coll.*) go easy with.

[1]**Schoner** ['ʃo:nər], *m.* (protective) covering, protector; antimacassar.

[2]**Schoner,** *m.* (*Naut.*) schooner. **Schoner|bark,** *f.* barque, barquentine. **–brigg,** *f.* brigantine.

Schöne(s) ['ʃø:nə(s)], *n.* ***das Schöne,*** the beautiful; ***Sie werden was Schönes von mir denken,*** you will have a nice opinion of me; ***da hast du was Schönes angerichtet!*** a fine mess you've made of it!

schönfärben ['ʃø:nfɛrbən], *v.t.* (*fig.*) gloss over, put in a favourable light, (*coll.*) whitewash. **Schön|färber,** *m.* (*fig.*) apologist; optimist. **–färberei,** *f.* (*fig.*) palliation, embellishment, (*coll.*) whitewashing; optimism.

Schongang ['ʃo:ngaŋ], *m.* (*Motor.*) overdrive.

Schön|geist, *m.* bel esprit, aesthete. **–geisterei,** *f.* pretension to wit *or* to culture. **schöngeistig,** *adj.* aesthetic; literary, belletristic.

Schönheit ['ʃø:nhaɪt], *f.* beauty, fineness; *see* **Schöne**; ***–en der Natur,*** beauties of nature. **Schönheits|fehler,** *m.* blemish, disfigurement. **–königin,** *f.* beauty queen. **–konkurrenz,** *f.* beauty contest. **–lehre,** *f.* (*obs.*) aesthetics. **–mittel,** *n.* cosmetic. **–pflästerchen,** *n.* beauty-patch *or* -spot. **–pflege,** *f.* beauty treatment *or* culture. **–pflegerin,** *f.* beautician. **–salon,** *m.* beauty parlour. **–sinn,** *m.* sense of beauty, good taste. **–wasser,** *n.* complexion wash, skin lotion.

Schonkost ['ʃo:nkɔst], *f.* (*Med.*) diet.

schön|machen, 1. *v.i.* (*of a dog*) sit up, beg. **2.** *v.r.* smarten *or* (*coll.*) get o.s. up. **–redend,** *adj.* fine-spoken, flattering, fulsome, unctuous, (*coll.*) mealy-mouthed. **Schönredner,** *m.* (*coll.*) speechifier, spouter, (*iron.*) fine talker. **schönrednerisch,** *adj.* rhetorical, grandiloquent, magniloquent, pretentious, pompous, high-sounding. **Schön|-schreibekunst,** *f.*, **–schreiben,** *n.*, **–schrift,** *f.* calligraphy. **–tuer,** *m.* flatterer, flunky, toady, lickspittle, (*coll.*) back-scratcher. **–tuerei,** *f.* flattery, blandishment, cajolery, fawning, flunkeyism; honeyed words, (*coll.*) soft soap, blarney; flirtatiousness, coquetry. **schöntun,** *irr.v.i.* (*Dat.*) coax, cajole, flatter, (*coll.*) soft-soap, play up to; flirt with.

Schonung ['ʃo:nuŋ], *f.* 1. consideration, regard, forbearance, indulgence; 2. care, careful treatment, protection, preservation; ***sich (Dat.) – auferlegen,*** relax, take a rest, (*coll.*) take it easy; 3. mercy; 4. (*Hort.*) nursery, (young) plantation, (*Hunt.*) preserve. **schonungsbedürftig,** *adj.* in need of rest, ailing, indisposed, unwell, sickly, (*coll.*) poorly, seedy, off colour, out of sorts. **schonungslos,** *adj.* merciless, pitiless, relentless; unsparing, unrelenting (***gegen,*** towards); (*of utterance*) blunt, brutal.

Schönungsmittel ['ʃø:nuŋsmɪtəl], *n.* fining agent, gloss.

schonungsvoll ['ʃo:nuŋsfɔl], *adj. See* **schonend.**

schönwissenschaftlich ['ʃø:nvɪsənʃaftlɪç], *adj.* literary, belletristic; artistic.

Schonzeit ['ʃo:ntsaɪt], *f.* (*Hunt.*) close *or* (*Am.*) closed season.

Schopf [ʃɔpf], *m.* **(-(e)s,** *pl.* **¨-e)** 1. crown, top of the head; tuft of hair, shock *or* mop of hair; (*of birds*) tuft, crest; ***ihn beim –e fassen*** or ***packen,*** seize him by the scruff of the neck; ***die Gelegenheit beim –e fassen*** or ***nehmen,*** seize an opportunity, take time by the forelock; 2. tree-top, (*Bot.*) coma; 3. (*dial.*) shed, shelter. **Schopfalk,** *m.* (*Orn.*) crested auklet (*Aethia cristatella*).

Schöpf|brunnen ['ʃœpf–], *m.* draw-well. **–bütte,** *f.* (*Paperm.*) pulp-vat. **–eimer,** *m.* (well-)bucket, pail.

schöpfen ['ʃœpfən], *v.t., v.i.* scoop, ladle; draw (*water from a well*); (*fig.*) ***Atem –,*** draw *or* take breath; ***wieder Atem –,*** recover one's breath, get one's breath back; ***tief Atem –,*** take a deep breath; (*fig.*) ***Erfahrungen –,*** obtain *or* derive experience; (*fig.*) ***neue Hoffnung –,*** gather fresh hope; (*fig.*) ***frische Luft –,*** get a breath of fresh air; (*fig.*) ***Mut –,*** take courage; (*fig.*) ***Verdacht –,*** harbour suspicion(s), become suspicious, (*coll.*) smell a rat.

Schöpfer ['ʃœpfər], *m.* 1. creator, maker, author, originator; 2. drawer (*of water*); scoop, ladle, dipper. **Schöpfer|geist,** *m.* creative genius. **–hand,** *f.* hand of the creator, creative touch. **schöpferisch,** *adj.* creative, productive, fertile. **Schöpferkraft,** *f.* creative power *or* energy.

Schöpf|gefäß, *n.*, **–gelte,** *f.*, **–kelle,** *f.*, **–löffel,** *m.* scoop, dipper, bailer, basting ladle. **–rad,** *n.* bucket *or* well-wheel.

Schöpfung ['ʃœpfuŋ], *f.* creation; the universe, created things; production, work; (*iron.*) ***die Herren der –,*** the lords of creation. **Schöpfungs|-geschichte,** *f.* (**–sage,** *f.*) history (myth) of (the) creation, genesis.

Schöpfwerk ['ʃœpfvɛrk], *n.* bucket-elevator, water-engine.

Schöppe ['ʃœpə], *m.* **(-n,** *pl.* **-n)** (*dial.*) *see* **Schöffe.**

schöppeln ['ʃœpəln], *v.i.* (*coll.*) tipple; ***er schöppelt gern,*** he likes his little drink.

[1]**Schoppen** ['ʃɔpən], *m.* half a pint; ***ein – Bier,*** a glass of beer.

[2]**Schoppen,** *m.* (*dial.*) *see* **Schuppen.**

Schöps [ʃœps], *m.* **(-es,** *pl.* **-e)** 1. wether, (*Cul.*) mutton; 2. (*fig.*) simpleton.

schor [ʃo:r], **schöre** ['ʃø:rə], *see* **scheren.**

Schore ['ʃo:rə], *f.* (*Naut.*) prop, support, shore; (*dial.*) spade.

Schorf [ʃɔrf], *m.* (**-(e)s,** *pl.* **-e**) scab, scurf. **schorfig,** *adj.* scabby, scurfy.

Schörl [ʃœrl], *m.* (**-(e)s,** *pl.* **-e**) schorl, black tourmaline.

Schorlemorle [ʃɔrlə'mɔrlə], *n.* (**-s,** *pl.* **-e**) *or f.* wine and water mixed.

Schornstein ['ʃɔrnʃtaɪn], *m.* chimney, flue; funnel, smoke-stack; (*coll.*) ***in den – schreiben,*** consider as lost, dismiss as a bad debt, write off. **Schornstein|aufsatz,** *m. See* **–kappe. –brand,** *m.* chimney (on) fire. **–feger,** *m.* chimney-sweep. **–kappe,** *f.* chimney-pot. **–kasten,** *m.* chimney-stack.

1**Schoß** [ʃɔs], *m.* (**-(ss)es,** *pl.* **-(ss)e**) (*Bot.*) sprig, shoot, sprout, scion.

2**Schoß** [ʃɔs], *m.* (**-(ss)es,** *pl.* **-(ss)e(n)** *or* **¨-(ss)e(r)**) (*obs.*) tax, impost.

3**Schoß** [ʃo:s], *m.* (**-es,** *pl.* **¨-e**) lap; (*Poet.*) womb; (*fig.*) bosom; ***es ist ihm in den – gefallen,*** it fell right into his lap; ***die Hände in den – legen,*** fold one's arms, twiddle one's thumbs, do nothing, be idle; ***in Abrahams –e sein,*** be as safe as houses; ***im –e der Erde,*** in the bowels of the earth; ***im –e seiner Familie,*** in the bosom of his family; ***im –e der Kirche,*** within the pale *or* bosom of the Church; ***das ruht im –e der Götter,*** that lies in the lap of the gods; ***das liegt noch im –e der Zukunft,*** only time will tell.

4**Schoß** [ʃo:s], *f.* (-, *pl.* **-en** *or* **¨-e**) (*Austr.*) skirt; coat-tail.

schoß [ʃɔs], *see* **schießen.**

Schoßbein ['ʃo:sbaɪn], *n.* (*Anat.*) os pubis.

schösse ['ʃœsə], *see* **schießen.**

Schoß|hund, *m.* lapdog, pet dog. **–kind,** *n.* pet, darling, spoiled child. **–kissenfallschirm,** *m.* lap-pack *or* -type parachute.

Schößling ['ʃœslɪŋ], *m.* (**-s,** *pl.* **-e**) shoot, sprig, sprout, scion; sucker; stripling.

Schot [ʃo:t], *f.* (-, *pl.* **-e**) (*Naut.*) sheet.

1**Schote** ['ʃo:tə], *f. See* **Schot.**

2**Schote,** *f.* pod, husk, shell, cod; (*pl.*) green peas.

3**Schote,** *m.* (**-n,** *pl.* **-n**) (*coll.*) fool.

Schoten|dorn, *m.* acacia. **–erbsen,** *f.pl.* peas in the pod. **schotenförmig,** *adj.* pod-shaped. **Schoten|frucht,** *f.* legume, pod. **–gewächse,** *n.pl.* leguminous plants. **–pfeffer,** *m.* capsicum, red pepper.

Schothorn ['ʃo:thɔrn], *n.* clew (*of sail*).

Schott [ʃɔt], *n.* (**-(e)s,** *pl.* **-e**) (*Naut.*) bulkhead.

1**Schotte** ['ʃɔtə], *f. See* **Schott.**

2**Schotte,** *f.* (*dial.*) whey.

3**Schotte,** *m.* (**-n,** *pl.* **-n**) Scot, Scotsman, (*coll.*) Scotchman.

Schotten ['ʃɔtən], *m.* (*dial.*) *see* 2**Schotte.**

Schotter ['ʃɔtər], *m.* road-metal; (*Railw.*) ballast; broken stone, rubble, gravel. **Schotterbahn,** *f.* macadamized *or* metalled road. **schottern,** *v.t.* metal (*road*); macadamize. **Schotter|straße,** *f. See* **–bahn.**

Schottin ['ʃɔtɪn], *f.* Scotswoman, (*coll.*) Scotchwoman. **schottisch,** *adj.* Scottish (*history etc.*), Scots (*law*), Scotch (*whisky*). **Schottland,** *n.* Scotland.

Schraffe ['ʃrafə], *f.* (*usu. pl.*) *see* **Schraffur. Schraffen,** *m.* (*dial.*) *see* **Schramme. schraffieren** [–'fi:rən], *v.t., v.i.* hatch, hachure. **Schraff(ier)ung, Schraffur,** *f.* (-, *pl.* **-en**) hachures, hatching (*in drawing etc.*).

schräg [ʃrɛ:k], *adj.* slanting, inclined, sloping; diagonal, oblique, transverse; (*Tech.*) chamfered, bevelled; ***der –e Durchschnitt eines Kegels,*** the oblique conic section; ***–e Ebene,*** inclined plane; ***– gegenüber von,*** diagonally across from; (*sl.*) ***–e Musik,*** hot *or* heavy music. **Schräg|aufnahme,** *f.* oblique view. **–balken,** *m.* (*Her.*) bar, bend. **Schräge,** *f.* incline, slope, (*Tech.*) bevel, chamfer; *see* **Schrägheit.**

Schragen ['ʃra:gən], *m.* trestle, frame, jack; stack (*of wood*). **schragen,** *v.t.* joint (*beams*) slantwise.

schrägen ['ʃrɛ:gən], *v.t.* slant, slope, bevel, chamfer.

Schräg|entfernung, *f.* slant range. **–feuer,** *n.* (*Mil.*) oblique *or* flanking fire, enfilade. **Schrägheit,** *f.* obliquity, inclination, slope, slant. **Schräg|kante,** *f.* chamfer, bevel. **–kreuz,** *n.* (*Her.*) saltire. **–lage,** *f.* sloping position, (*Av.*) bank(ing), (*Med.*) (*of birth*) oblique presentation. **schräglaufend,** *adj.* diagonal, oblique. **Schräg|linie,** *f.* diagonal. **–schrift,** *f.* sloping writing *or* hand, (*Typ.*) italics. **schräg|stellen,** *v.t.* incline, tilt. **–über,** *adv.* diagonally across, almost opposite.

schrak [ʃra:k], *see* **schrecken.**

schral [ʃra:l], *adj.* (*Naut.*) weak, unfavourable (*of wind*).

Schram [ʃra:m], *m.* (**-(e)s,** *pl.* **¨-e**) (*Min.*) holing. **schramen,** *v.t.* (*Min.*) hole, cut through.

Schramme ['ʃramə], *f.* scratch, graze, abrasion, scar.

Schrammel|musik ['ʃraməl–], *f.* popular Viennese music. **–quartett,** *n.* tavern band (*two violins, guitar, and accordion*).

schrammen ['ʃramən], *v.t.* scratch, graze, scar. **schrammig,** *adj.* scratched, abraded, grazed, scarred, marred. **Schrammstein,** *m.* kerb- *or* curb-(stone).

Schrank [ʃraŋk], *m.* (**-(e)s,** *pl.* **¨-e**) 1. cupboard, locker, cabinet, bookcase, (linen-)press, wardrobe; 2. (*Hunt.*) lateral spacing of footprints; 3. set (*of a saw*).

Schranke ['ʃraŋkə], *f.* barrier; level-crossing gate; fence, rail(ing), grating, grid, (*Hist.*) turnpike, toll-bar; (*fig.*) boundary, bounds, limits, arena, enclosure; *pl.* (*Hist.*) lists, (*Law*) bar; ***die –n überschreiten,*** go beyond (all) bounds; ***die –n einhalten, in den –n bleiben,*** keep within bounds; ***sich in –n halten,*** restrain o.s., keep within bounds; ***–n setzen,*** set bounds *or* limits (*Dat.*, to), check, restrain; ***in die –n treten,*** enter the lists; ***in die –n fordern,*** throw down the gauntlet to, defy, challenge; ***–n ziehen,*** draw a line, set limits.

schränken ['ʃrɛŋkən], *v.t.* 1. put crosswise, cross (*one's legs*); fold (*one's arms*); 2. set (*a saw*); ***geschränkte Zähne,*** crosscut teeth (*of a saw*).

schrankenlos ['ʃraŋkənlo:s], *adj.* unbounded, boundless, unlimited; (*fig.*) unbridled, unrestrained. **Schrankenlosigkeit,** *f.* boundlessness; (*fig.*) lack of restraint, licentiousness. **Schrankenwärter,** *m.* gate-man, signalman.

Schrankfach ['ʃraŋkfax], *n.* partition, compartment; pigeon-hole (*for letters*); safe-deposit box. **schrankfertig,** *adj.* (*of laundry*) ironed and ready for use. **Schrankkoffer,** *m.* wardrobe-trunk.

Schränkung ['ʃrɛŋkuŋ], *f.* setting (*of a saw*); offset; (*Av.*) variation in angle of incidence.

Schranne ['ʃranə], *f.* (*obs.*) (*dial.*) baker's *or* butcher's stall; corn-market. **Schrannenhalle,** *f.* market-hall.

Schranze ['ʃrantsə], *m.* (**-n,** *pl.* **-n**) *or f.* toady, sycophant, lickspittle; *see* **Hofschranze. schranzen,** *v.i.* be servile, toady, (*sl.*) crawl, creep.

Schrape ['ʃra:pə], *f.* (*dial.*) scraper. **schrapen,** *v.t.* scrape.

Schrapnell [ʃrap'nɛl], *n.* (**-s,** *pl.* **-e** (*Austr.* **-s**)) shrapnel.

schrappen ['ʃrapən], *v.t., v.i.* (*dial.*) *see* **schrapen. Schrapper,** *m.* scraper; (*fig.*) niggard, skinflint.

schrat [ʃra:t], *adj.* (*dial.*) *see* **schräg. Schratsegel,** *n.* (*Naut.*) loose-footed sail.

Schrat(t) [ʃra:t (ʃrat)], *m.* (**-(e)s,** *pl.* **-e**) hobgoblin, imp.

Schraubdeckel ['ʃraupdɛkəl], *m.* screw-cap, screwed lid.

Schraube ['ʃraubə], *f.* (screw-)bolt, (wood-)screw; (*Naut.*) screw, propeller, (*Av.*) air-screw, propeller, (*Spt.*) spin, screw (*on a ball*); (*coll.*) ***alte –,*** old frump, gushing female; ***linksgängige –,*** left-handed screw; ***eingelassene –,*** countersunk screw; ***– ohne Ende,*** endless screw; (*fig.*) vicious circle; (*coll.*) ***bei ihm ist eine – los,*** he has a screw loose; ***die – anziehen,*** tighten the screw; (*fig.*) put on the screw, (*sl.*) turn on the heat.

schrauben [ˈʃraubən], *reg. & irr.v.t.* screw; (*coll.*) *ihn –*, mock *or* quiz *or* tease him; (*coll.*) *ihn um sein Geld –*, cheat him out of his money; *seine Hoffnungen niedriger –*, scale down one's expectations, come down a peg; *den Preis in die Höhe –*, push up *or* raise the price. *See* **geschraubt.**

Schrauben|achse, *f. See* **–welle. –bakterie,** *f.* spirillum. **–bohrer,** *m.* auger, twist-drill. **–bolzen,** *m.* (screw-)bolt. **–drehbank,** *f.* screw-cutting lathe. **–feder,** *f.* coil-spring. **–flasche,** *f.* screw-topped bottle. **–flügel,** *m.* blade (*of propeller*). **–förderer,** *m.* screw-conveyor. **schraubenförmig,** *adj.* screw-shaped, spiral, helical. **Schrauben|gang,** *m.*, **–gewinde,** *n.* screw-thread. **–kopf,** *m.* screw-head. **–mutter,** *f.* female screw, nut. **–schlüssel,** *m.* spanner, wrench; *englischer –*, adjustable spanner, monkey-wrench. **–spindel,** *f.* male screw. **–strahl,** *m.* (*Av.*) slip-stream. **–welle,** *f.* propeller-shaft. **–winde,** *f.* jack-screw. **–windung,** *f.* spiral turn. **–zieher,** *m.* screwdriver.

Schraub|lehre, *f.* micrometer. **–stock,** *m.* (bench) vice. **–verschluß,** *m. See* **–deckel. –zwinge,** *f.* hand-vice, screw-clamp, cramp.

Schreber|garten [ˈʃre:bər–], *m.* allotment (garden). **–gärtner,** *m.* allotment holder.

Schreck [ʃrɛk], *m.* **(-(e)s,** *pl.* **-e)** fright, scare, shock; fear, alarm, terror, panic, dread, horror; dismay, consternation; *einen – bekommen* or *erleben,* get a fright *or* shock, be frightened *or* scared; *ihm einen – versetzen* or *einflößen* or *einjagen,* give him a fright *or* shock, frighten *or* scare him (out of his wits); *ich bin mit dem (bloßen) – davongekommen,* it just gave me a fright *or* shock, it did no more than frighten me; *vor – wie gelähmt,* paralysed with fear, (*coll.*) stiff with fright; *vor – aufschreien,* cry out in alarm; *see* **Schrecken. Schreckbild,** *n.* bog(e)y, fright, bugbear, (*nursery talk*) bog(e)y-man.

schrecken [ˈʃrɛkən], *v.t.* 1. frighten, scare, startle, alarm, dismay, terrify; deter, frighten away; 2. (*Tech.*) chill; 3. (*dial.*) crack. **Schrecken,** *m.* 1. *ihn in – setzen* or *halten,* put him in fear, strike terror in him, excite his fears, alarm *or* terrify him; *– verbreiten* or *hervorrufen unter* (*Dat.*), bring terror to, strike with terror, terrorize; *die – des Krieges,* the horrors of war; *die – des Meeres,* the terrors of the sea; 2. (*dial.*) crack (*in glass etc.*). *See* **Schreck.**

schreckensbleich [ˈʃrɛkənsblaiç], *adj.* pale with fright. **Schreckens|bote,** *m.* bearer of evil tidings. **–botschaft,** *f.* terrible *or* alarming news. **–herrschaft,** *f.* reign of terror. **–kammer,** *f.* Chamber of Horrors. **–kind,** *n.* enfant terrible. **–nachricht,** *f. See* **–botschaft. –tat,** *f.* atrocity.

schreckerregend [ˈʃrɛkˀɛrre:gənt], *adj.* terrifying, alarming; *see* **schrecklich. Schreckgespenst,** *n.* (terrible *or* frightening) apparition, phantom, (*fig.*) nightmare; *see* **Schreckbild. schreckhaft,** *adj.* frightened, nervous, timid. **Schreckladung,** *f.* (*Mil.*) booby-trap.

schrecklich [ˈʃrɛkliç], **1.** *adj.* frightful, fearful, dreadful, terrible, horrible, hideous, ghastly, awful, atrocious. **2.** *adv.* (*coll.*) terribly, awfully, frightfully. **Schrecklichkeit,** *f.* frightfulness, horror.

Schreckmittel [ˈʃrɛkmitəl], *n.* bog(e)y, scarecrow. **Schrecknis,** *n.* **(-ses,** *pl.* **-se)** horror, atrocity; *see* **Schrecken. Schreck|schuß,** *m.* warning shot, shot fired in the air; (*fig.*) false alarm. **–sekunde,** *f.* (*Motor.*) reaction time (*of driver*).

Schrei [ʃrai], *m.* **(-(e)s,** *pl.* **-e)** cry, shout, yell, howl, wail, scream, shriek; *einen – tun* or *ausstoßen,* utter a cry, give a shout *or* yell; (*coll.*) *der letzte –*, the latest rage. **Schreiadler,** *m.* (*Orn.*) lesser spotted eagle (*Aquila pomarina*); *großer –*, *see* **Schelladler.**

Schreib|arbeit [ˈʃraip–], *f.* clerical work, paper-work. **–art,** *f.* manner of writing, (written) style; handwriting; (*of a word*) spelling. **–bedarf,** *m.* stationery, writing materials. **–block,** *m.* writing- *or* scribbling-pad. **–buch,** *n.* writing- *or* copy-book. **–büro,** *n.* copying office, typing agency.

schreiben [ˈʃraibən], **1.** *irr.v.t., v.i.* write (*über* (*Acc.*), on *or* about); write down, record; *ihm* or *an ihn –*, write to him; *groß –*, write with a capital letter; *ins Konzept –*, jot down, make a rough copy *or* draft of; *zur Last –*, debit with; *mit Bleistift –*, write in pencil; *mit der Maschine –*, type; *seinen Namen darunter –*, subscribe to *or* put one's name to it; *noch einmal –*, rewrite, write out once more; (*coll.*) *– Sie sich das hinter die Ohren* or *hinters Ohr,* make a special note of it, take it to heart; *es auf Rechnung meiner Dummheit –*, put it down to my stupidity; *ins Reine –*, write out neatly, make a fair copy of; (*coll.*) *sage und schreibe,* believe it or believe it not; *den wievielten – wir heute?* what is the date today? *ein Wort richtig –*, spell a word correctly; *ein Wort falsch –*, spell a word wrong, misspell a word; *die Zeitung schreibt,* the newspaper says, according to the newspaper. **2.** *irr.v.r. wie – Sie sich?* how do you spell your name? *auf diesem Papier schreibt es sich schlecht,* this paper is no good for writing on. **Schreiben,** *n.* 1. writing; *das – fällt mir schwer,* I find it difficult to write; 2. (*Comm.*) letter; *Ihr (geehrtes) – vom 10. Mai,* yours (*or* your esteemed favour) of 10th May; (*on letter-heads*) *Ihr –*, your reference.

Schreiber [ˈʃraibər], *m.* 1. writer; clerk, secretary; copyist; (*of a newspaper*) correspondent; *– dieses Briefs,* the undersigned; 2. (*Tech.*) recorder, recording mechanism. **Schreiberei** [–ˈrai], *f.* scribbling, (endless) paperwork. **Schreiberling,** *m.* **(-s,** *pl.* **-e), Schreiberseele,** *f.* pen-pusher, quill-driver, scribe, pedant.

schreibfaul [ˈʃraipfaul], *adj.* lazy about writing (letters); *– sein,* be a bad correspondent. **Schreib|feder,** *f.* pen, (pen-)nib; (*obs.*) quill (pen). **–fehler,** *m.* slip of the pen, typing *or* clerical error. **–fertigkeit,** *f.* penmanship. **–gebühr,** *f.* copying-fee. **–gerät,** *n.* recording instrument. **–heft,** *n.* scribbling-jotter, exercise-book, copybook. **–hilfe,** *f.* clerical *or* secretarial assistance. **–kalender,** *m.* diary, memorandum-book. **–kräfte,** *f.pl.* clerical *or* secretarial staff. **–krampf,** *m.* writer's cramp. **–mappe,** *f.* writing-case; blotter. **–maschine,** *f.* typewriter. **–maschinenschrift,** *f.* typescript. **–material(ien),** *n.(pl.) see* **–waren. –papier,** *n.* writing- *or* note-paper. **–pult,** *n.* (writing-)desk. **–schrift,** *f.* handwriting, script. **schreibselig,** *adj.* fond of writing. **Schreib|stift,** *m.* stylus. **–stube,** *f.* office; (*Mil.*) orderly-room. **–stunde,** *f.* writing-lesson. **–tafel,** *f.* slate. **–tinte,** *f.* writing-ink. **–tisch,** *m.* desk, office table.

Schreibung [ˈʃraibuŋ], *f.* spelling, orthography; *phonetische –*, phonetic script *or* transcription.

Schreib|unterlage, *f.* blotting-pad, desk-pad. **–vorlage,** *f.* copy. **–waren,** *f.pl.* writing materials, stationery. **–warenhändler,** *m.* stationer. **–warenhandlung,** *f.* stationer's (shop). **–weise,** *f. See* **–art. –zeug,** *n.* pen and ink.

schreien [ˈʃraiən], *irr.v.t., v.i.* cry (out), shout, yell, howl, scream, shriek; (*of donkey*) bray, (*of owl*) hoot, screech, (*of stag*) bell, (*of cock*) crow; *aus vollem Halse –*, cry out *or* call out at the top of one's voice; *ihm in die Ohren –*, din in his ears; *– nach,* clamour for; *um Hilfe –*, shout for help; *zum Himmel –*, be scandalous, be a crying shame. **Schreien,** *n.* crying, shouting *etc.*, cries, screams *etc.*; (*coll.*) *es ist zum –*, it's screamingly funny, it's a scream. **schreiend,** *adj.* crying, clamorous, shrill; (*of colour*) loud, glaring, gaudy; (*fig.*) flagrant, monstrous (*as injustice*); *–er Gegensatz,* flagrant *or* glaring contradiction. **Schreier,** *m.* crier, bawler; cry-baby, squalling child. **Schrei|hals,** *m.* (*coll.*) *see* **Schreier. –vögel,** *pl.* (*Orn.*) Clamatores.

Schrein [ʃrain], *m.* **(-(e)s,** *pl.* **-e)** cupboard; chest, case, cabinet, casket, coffer; shrine; *etwas im – des Herzens* or *der Seele bewahren,* enshrine s.th. in one's heart *or* soul. **Schreiner,** *m.* joiner, cabinet-maker. **Schreinerei** [–ˈrai], *f.* joinery, cabinet making; carpenter's shop. **schreinern,** *v.i.* do joinery; work as a joiner.

schreiten ['ʃraɪtən], *irr.v.i.* (*aux.* s.) 1. stride, step, stalk, strut; ***im Zimmer auf und ab –,*** pace (up and down) the room; 2. (*fig.*) – ***zu,*** proceed to (*do*); set about (*doing*); progress *or* advance to; ***zur Abstimmung –,*** proceed to a division, come to the vote; ***die Erzählung schritt rasch zum Schluß,*** the narrative advanced to its close; ***zum Äußersten –,*** take extreme measures; ***zu Werk –,*** set to work.

schricken ['ʃrɪkən], *v.i.* (*Naut.*) ease away.

schrie [ʃri:], *see* **schreien.**

Schrieb [ʃri:p], *m.* **(-s,** *pl.* **-e)** (*coll.*) screed.

schrieb, schriebe, *see* **schreiben.**

schriee ['ʃri:ə], *see* **schreien.**

Schrift [ʃrɪft], *f.* (-, *pl.* **-en**) writing, handwriting, hand; letters, script, character(s), (*Typ.*) type, fount; book, work, publication; paper, document, pamphlet; (*on coins etc.*) text, inscription, legend, (*coll.*) tails; *pl.* works, writings; (*Typ.*) ***Abdruck vor der –,*** proof before letters; (*Typ.*) ***falsche –,*** wrong fount; ***die Heilige –,*** the Holy Scriptures; ***Kopf oder –?*** heads or tails? ***in lateinischer –,*** in Roman characters; ***phonetische –,*** phonetic script; ***sämtliche –en,*** collected (edition of the) works; ***vermischte –en,*** miscellaneous writings.

Schrift|art, *f.* type, fount. **–auslegung,** *f.* interpretation of the Scriptures, exegesis. **–beweis,** *m.* Scriptural proof *or* evidence. **–bild,** *n.* (*Typ.*) face. **–deutsch,** *n.* literary German. **–forschung,** *f.* Scriptural research. **–führer,** *m.* secretary. **–gelehrte(r),** *m.* (*B.*) scribe. **–gießer,** *m.* type-founder. **–gießerei,** *f.* type-foundry. **–grad,** *m.* size of type. **–guß,** *m.* type-casting; fount of type. **–kasten,** *m.* (*Typ.*) letter-case. **–kegel,** *m.* (*Typ.*) body *or* depth of a letter. **–leiter,** *m.* editor. **–leitung,** *f.* editorship; editorial staff; newspaper-office.

schriftlich ['ʃrɪftlɪç], **1.** *adj.* written, in writing, by letter; ***–e Arbeit,*** written exercise; ***–er (Gerichts)-befehl,*** writ; ***–e Prüfung,*** written examination; ***–e Überlieferung,*** written records; ***–es Zeugnis,*** certificate, testimonial. **2.** *adv.* in writing, in black and white; – ***abfassen*** or ***niederlegen,*** put in writing *or* on record; – ***mitteilen,*** inform by letter *or* post. **Schriftlichkeit,** *f.* proper legal form.

Schrift|material, *n.* stock of type. **–metall,** *n.* type-metal. **–probe,** *f.* specimen of writing *or* type. **–rolle,** *f.* scroll. **–sachverständige(r),** *m., f.* handwriting expert. **–satz,** *m.* (*Typ.*) composition. **–seite,** *f.* page of print; reverse (*of a coin*). **-setzer,** *m.* compositor, type-setter. **–sprache,** *f.* written *or* literary language. **–steller,** *m.* (**–stellerin,** *f.*) author, (authoress), writer. **schrift|-stellerisch,** *adj.* literary. **–stellern,** *v.i.* write, do literary work. **Schrift|stellername,** *m.* nom de plume, pen-name. **–stück,** *n.* 1. document, paper, deed, written deposition; 2. (*Typ.*) packet.

Schrifttum, *n.* literature.

Schrift|verkehr, *m.* correspondence, (*Pol.*) exchange of notes. **–wart,** *m.* secretary (*to a society*). **–wechsel,** *m.* exchange of letters, correspondence. **–zeichen,** *n.* letter, character. **–zeug, 1.** *m.* type-metal. **2.** *n.* worn type. **–zug,** *m.* written character; flourish.

schrill [ʃrɪl], *adj.* shrill, piercing. **schrillen,** *v.i.* sound shrilly, screech.

schrinden ['ʃrɪndən], *irr.v.i.* (*dial.*) chap, get chapped, split, crack.

schrinnen ['ʃrɪnən], *irr.v.i.* (*aux.* h. & s.) (*dial.*) smart, itch.

Schrippe ['ʃrɪpə], *f.* (*dial.*) breakfast-roll.

Schritt ['ʃrɪt], *m.* **(-(e)s,** *pl.* **-e)** step, stride, pace; (*audible*) footstep, footfall; walk, gait; (*fig.*) step, measure; ***diplomatischer –,*** démarche; ***einen entscheidenden – tun,*** take a decisive step, (*coll.*) take the plunge; ***den ersten – tun,*** take the initiative, make the first move; (*Motor.*) – ***fahren!*** 5 m.p.h. max.! dead slow! at a walking pace; – ***für –,*** step by step; ***im – gehen,*** walk, pace (*of horses*); – ***halten,*** keep in step; – ***halten mit,*** keep pace with, keep up with, (*fig.*) keep abreast of; ***keinen – aus dem Hause tun,*** not put one's foot out of doors; ***aus dem – kommen,*** get out of step; ***drei – vom Leibe!*** keep your distance! ***die nötigen –e tun,*** take all necessary steps; ***ein paar –e von,*** within a stone's throw of; ***auf – und Tritt,*** at every step *or* turn, constantly; ***ihm auf – und Tritt folgen,*** dog his footsteps; – ***um –,*** a step at a time; (*Mil.*) – ***wechseln,*** change step; ***den zweiten – vor dem ersten tun,*** go about it in the wrong way, put the cart before the horse.

schritt, *see* **schreiten.**

Schrittanz ['ʃrɪttants], *m.* step-dance.

Schritt|gänger, *m.* pacing horse. **–länge,** *f.* length of stride. **schrittlings,** *adv.* pacing, step by step; straddled, astride; – ***im Sattel sitzen,*** sit astride the saddle. **Schritt|macher,** *m.* pace-maker, pacer; (*fig.*) harbinger. **–schuh,** *m.* (*obs.*) skate. **–stein,** *m.* stepping-stone. **–wechsel,** *m.* (*Mil.*) change of step. **schrittweise,** *adv.* step by step, by steps, progressively, gradually. **Schritt|weite,** *f.* (length of) stride. **–zähler,** *m.* pedometer.

schrob [ʃro:p], **schröbe** ['ʃrø:bə], *see* **schrauben.**

Schrof [ʃro:f], *m.* **(-(e)s** *or* **-en,** *pl.* **-en), Schrofe,** *f.*, **Schrofen,** *m.* (*Austr.*), **Schroff,** *m.* **(-(e)s,** *pl.* **-en)** *see* **Schroffen.**

schroff [ʃrɔf], *adj.* rough, rugged, jagged; steep, precipitous; (*fig.*) rough, uncouth, gruff, blunt, brusque, abrupt, harsh; ***–er Widerspruch,*** glaring contradiction; ***–er Gegensatz,*** absolute opposite *or* contrary; ***–er Übergang,*** abrupt transition; ***–e Absage,*** flat refusal.

Schroffen ['ʃrɔfən], *m.* crag.

Schroffheit ['ʃrɔfhaɪt], *f.* steepness, ruggedness; roughness, gruffness, uncouthness; abruptness.

schröpfen ['ʃrœpfən], *v.t.* (*Med.*) cup, bleed; scarify; (*fig.*) fleece, overcharge. **Schröpf|glas,** *n.*, **–kopf,** *m.* cupping-glass. **–schnäpper,** *m.* cupping-instrument, scarifier.

Schropphobel ['ʃrɔpho:bəl], *m.* *See* **Schrupphobel.**

Schrot [ʃro:t], *m. or n.* **(-(e)s,** *pl.* **-e)** 1. small shot, buckshot, slugs; 2. block *or* log (of wood); ***von gleichem*** or ***vom selben –,*** a chip of the old block; 3. groats, grist, bruised grain; 4. due weight (*of coin*); ***von echtem*** or ***gutem (altem) – und Korn,*** of standard weight and alloy, (*usu. fig.*) of the good old type, of sterling worth; 4. *See* **Schrott.**

Schrot|axt, *f.* woodcutter's axe. **–blatt,** *n.* 15th-century engraving in white on stippled background. **–brot,** *n.* wholemeal bread. **–büchse,** *f.* fowling-piece, shotgun. **–effekt,** *m.* (*Rad.*) shot-effect. **–eisen,** *n.* blacksmith's chisel.

schroten ['ʃro:tən], *v.t.* 1. (*p.p. also* **geschroten**) rough-grind (*corn*); crush, bruise (*malt*); saw up (*logs*); gnaw, nibble, eat (*of rats etc*); 2. lower, roll down, load *or* unload (*heavy articles*); (*Naut.*) parbuckle.

Schröter ['ʃrø:tər], *m.* stag-beetle; brewer's van-man, drayman.

Schrot|flinte, *f.* *See* **–büchse. –hammer,** *m.* blacksmith's hammer. **–käfer,** *m.* stag-beetle. **–kleie,** *f.* coarse bran. **–korn,** *n.* pellet (of shot), single shot. **-lauf,** *m.* smooth barrel. **–leiter,** *f.* drayman's ladder.

Schrötling ['ʃrø:tlɪŋ], *m.* **(-s,** *pl.* **-e)** cutting, piece cut off; *see* **Schrotstück.**

Schrot|mehl, *n.* groats, coarse meal. **–meißel,** *m.* *See* **–eisen. –mühle,** *f.* grist-mill. **–patrone,** *f.* shotgun cartridge. **–säge,** *f.* crosscut saw. **schrot-sägeförmig,** *adj.* runcinate. **Schrot|schere,** *f.* plate-shears, tin-snips. **–seil,** *n.* (*Naut.*) parbuckle. **–stück,** *n.* minting blank, planchet.

Schrott [ʃrɔt], *m.* **(-(e)s,** *pl.* **-e)** scrap-metal. **Schrott|eisen,** *n.* scrap-iron. **–entfall,** *m.* manufacturing loss, scrap. **–händler,** *m.* scrap dealer.

schrubben ['ʃrubən], *v.t.* scrub, scour. **Schrubber,** *m.* scrubber, scourer; swab; scrubbing brush.

Schrulle ['ʃrulə], *f.* whim, fad, crotchet; (*fig.*) crotchety old woman, crone; ***–n haben,*** be faddy, have a kink. **schrullenhaft, schrullig,** *adj.* crotchety, cranky, whimsical.

schrumm! [ʃrum], *int.* (*coll.*) done! finished! stop! enough!

Schrumpel [ˈʃrumpəl], *f.* (-, *pl.* **-n**) (*dial.*) fold, wrinkle; ***alte –,*** withered old crone. **schrump(e)lig,** *adj.* crumpled, creased, wrinkled, shrivelled. **schrumpeln,** *v.i.* (*aux.* s.) (*dial.*) *see* **schrumpfen.**

Schrumpf [ʃrumpf], *m.* (loss by) shrinkage. **Schrumpfel,** *f.* (*dial.*) *see* **Schrumpel. schrumpf(e)lig,** *adj.* wrinkled, shrivelled, creased, crumpled. **schrumpfen,** *v.i.* (*aux.* s.) shrivel, shrink, contract; crumple, wrinkle, become wrinkled. **schrumpfig,** *adj. See* **schrumpf(e)lig. Schrumpf|niere,** *f.* (*Med.*) cirrhosis. **–sitz,** *m.* (*Tech.*) shrink-fit. **Schrumpfung,** *f.* shrinking, shrinkage, contraction, shrivelling, wrinkling; (*Med.*) stricture.

Schrund [ʃrunt], *m.* **(-(e)s,** *pl.* **⸚e** *or* **-e), Schrunde,** *f.* cleft, crack, chink, crevice, crevasse; *pl.* chaps. **schrundig,** *adj.* cracked, chapped.

schruppen [ˈʃrupən], *v.t.* 1. (*dial.*) *see* **schrubben**; 2. (*Carp.*) rough-plane. **Schrupp|feile,** *f.* rasp. **–hobel,** *m.* jack-plane.

Schub [ʃu:p], *m.* **(-(e)s,** *pl.* **⸚e)** 1. shove, push, thrust; throw (*at skittles etc.*); 2. (*of bread and fig.*) batch; ***ich kam mit dem ersten – hinein,*** I entered with the first wave *or* batch; 3. compulsory conveyance (*of vagrants etc.*) by the police; ***auf den – bringen,*** pass (*paupers etc.*) to their parish; (*coll.*) give (*a p.*) the push; 4. thrust (*of a propeller*); (*Mech.*) shear(ing force).

Schubbeanspruchung [ˈʃu:pbəanʃpru:xuŋ], *f.* shear-stress.

Schubbejack [ˈʃubəjak], *m.* **(-s** *or* **-en,** *pl.* **-s** *or* **-e(n))** ragamuffin, rapscallion.

schubbe(r)n [ˈʃubə(r)n], *v.t.* (*dial.*) *see* **schrubben.**

Schub|fach, *n.* drawer. **–fenster,** *n.* sash-window. **–festigkeit,** *f.* shear-strength. **–karre,** *f.*, **–karren,** *m.* wheelbarrow. **–kasten,** *m. See* **–lade. –kraft,** *f.* thrust, shearing force. **–lade,** *f.* drawer. **–lehre,** *f.* sliding callipers. **–leistung,** *f.* thrust (horse-power). **–riegel,** *m.* (sliding) bolt.

Schubs [ʃups], *m.* **(-es,** *pl.* **-e)** (*coll.*) push, shove, nudge, dig in the ribs.

Schubschraube [ˈʃu:pʃraubə], *f.* (*Av.*) pusher-screw.

schubsen [ˈʃupsən], *v.t.* (*coll.*) push, shove, nudge, dig (*s.o.*) in the ribs. **Schubser,** *m.* (*coll.*) *see* **Schubs.**

Schub|stange, *f.* push-rod. **–ventil,** *n.* slide-valve. **schubweise,** *adv.* gradually, little by little, by degrees; in batches.

schüchtern [ˈʃyçtərn], *adj.* shy, timid, diffident, bashful, coy. **Schüchternheit,** *f.* shyness, diffidence, bashfulness, timidity.

Schüdderump [ˈʃydərump], *m.* (*dial.*) rickety cart, boneshaker.

schuf [ʃu:f], **schüfe** [ˈʃy:fə], *see* **schaffen.**

Schuft [ʃuft], *m.* **(-(e)s,** *pl.* **-e)** rogue, scamp, scoundrel, blackguard; ***ein – wer Böses dabei denkt,*** honi soit qui mal y pense.

schuften [ˈʃuftən], *v.i.* (*coll.*) toil, drudge, slave, work like a navvy. **Schufterei** [–ˈraɪ], *f.* knavery, rascality, villainy, treachery, meanness; toil, drudgery, slavery, (*coll.*) grind. **schuftig,** *adj.* shabby, rascally, blackguardly, base, mean, vile.

Schuh [ʃu:], *m.* **(-(e)s,** *pl.* **-e)** shoe, boot; (*as measure, inv.*) foot; shoeing, ferrule, socket; (*fig.*) ***ihm etwas in die –e schieben,*** lay a th. at his door, put the blame on him for s.th.; (*Prov.*) ***umgekehrt wird ein – daraus,*** you are beginning at the wrong end, you are setting about it in just the wrong way; (*fig.*) ***Sie wissen nicht, wo mich der – drückt,*** you do not know where the shoe pinches.

Schuh|absatz, *m.* heel. **–anzieher,** *m. See* **–löffel. –band,** *n.* boot- *or* shoe-lace. **–bürste,** *f.* boot-brush. **–flicker,** *m.* cobbler. **–größe,** *f.* size of shoe. **–knöpfer,** *m.* button-hook. **–kratzer,** *m.* (door-) scraper. **–krem,** *f.* boot-polish, shoe-cream. **–leisten,** *m.* last. **–löffel,** *m.* shoe-horn. **–macher,** *m.* shoemaker, bootmaker. **–macherpech,** *n. See* **–wachs. –plattler,** *m.* (Bavarian) clog dance. **–putzer,** *m.* bootblack; ***wie einen – behandeln,*** treat like dirt. **–riemen,** *m. See* **–band**; (*B.*) latchet; ***er ist nicht wert, ihr die – zu lösen,*** he isn't fit to lick her boots. **–schmiere,** *f.* dubbin(g). **–schwärze,** *f.* blacking. **–sohle,** *f.* sole; ***sich*** (*Dat.*) ***etwas an den –n abgelaufen haben,*** know a th. full well, have a th. at one's finger-tips *or* -ends; ***sich*** (*Dat.*) ***die –n ablaufen nach,*** run one's legs off for *or* in search of. **–spanner,** *m.* boot- *or* shoe-tree. **–wachs,** *n.* cobbler's wax. **–waren,** *f.pl.*, **–werk,** *n.* footwear, boots and shoes. **–wichse,** *f. See* **–krem. –wichser,** *m. See* **–putzer**; boots (*servant in an hotel*). **–zeug,** *n. See* **–werk.**

Schuhu [ˈʃu:hu], *m.* **(-s,** *pl.* **-e)** (*dial.*) owl.

Schul|amt [ˈʃu:l–], *n.* school board, (local authority) education department; teaching post. **–anstalt,** *f.* educational establishment. **–arbeit,** *f.* school-work, lesson; homework. **–arzt,** *m.* school medical officer. **–ausgabe,** *f.* school edition. **–bank,** *f.* (*coll.*) ***die – drücken,*** go to *or* be at school. **–behörde,** *f.* education authority. **–beispiel,** *n.* typical example, test-case, model, pattern. **–besuch,** *m.* school attendance. **–bildung,** *f.* (statutory) education. **–bube,** *m.* (little) schoolboy. **–buch,** *n.* schoolbook, textbook. **–bücherverlag,** *m.* (firm of) educational publishers.

Schuld [ʃult], *f.* (-, *pl.* **-en**) debt, indebtedness, liability, obligation; guilt, sin, wrong, offence; fault, cause, blame; responsibility; *pl.* debts, liabilities; ***eine – abtragen,*** pay off a debt; ***ihm die – geben,*** lay the blame on him, blame him (***an*** (*Dat.*), for); ***in –en geraten,*** run into debt; ***–en haben,*** be in debt; ***–en machen,*** incur *or* contract debts, run into debt; ***die – auf sich nehmen,*** take the blame; ***ohne deine –,*** through no fault of yours; ***in –en stecken,*** be up to the ears in debt; ***ich bin*** or ***stehe in Ihrer –,*** I am in your debt, I am under an obligation to you, I am indebted to you; ***sich in –en stürzen,*** see ***–en machen***; ***– tragen an*** (*Dat.*), be guilty of; ***die Sühnung der tragischen – in einem Stücke,*** the Nemesis of a play; ***ihn trifft die –,*** he is to blame; ***vergib uns unsere –(en),*** forgive us our trespasses.

schuld, *adj.* ***– haben,*** be guilty, be responsible; ***du hast – daran, daß*** . . ., it is your fault that . . .; ***– sein an*** (*Dat.*), be to blame, be responsible (for); ***wer ist – daran?*** whose fault is it? who is to blame for it?

Schuld|abzahlung, *f.* liquidation of debts. **–anerkenntnis,** *f.* (*Law*) recognizance, (*Scots*) bond of caution; *see also* **–schein, –versprechen. –bekenntnis,** *n.* admission of guilt. **schuldbeladen,** *adj.* laden *or* burdened with guilt. **Schuldbeweis,** *m.* proof of guilt. **schuldbewußt,** *adj.* guilty, conscience-stricken. **Schuld|bewußtsein,** *n.* guilty conscience, acknowledgement of sin. **–brief,** *m. See* **–schein. –buch,** *n.* journal, ledger, account-book; (*coll.*) ***unser – sei vernichtet!*** let all old scores be forgotten.

schulden [ˈʃuldən], *v.t.* (*esp. fig.*) ***ihm etwas –,*** owe him s.th., be indebted to him for s.th. **schulden|belastet,** *adj.* burdened *or* crippled with debts, deep in debt. **–frei,** *adj.* free from debt, unencumbered. **–halber,** *adv.* on account of debts. **Schulden|last,** *f.* burden of debt, liabilities. **–masse,** *f.* aggregate liabilities. **–tilgung,** *f.* liquidation of debt. **–tilgungskasse,** *f.* sinking-fund.

Schuld|erlaß, *m.* remission of a debt. **–forderung,** *f.* active debt, demand for payment. **–frage,** *f.* question of guilt *or* responsibility. **schuldfrei,** *adj. See* **schuldlos. Schuld|gefängnis,** *n.* (*Hist.*) debtor's prison. **–gefühl,** *n.* sense of guilt, guilty conscience. **–haft,** *f.* imprisonment for debt. **schuldhaft,** *adj.* (*Swiss*) *see* **schuldig.**

Schul|diener, *m.* school porter *or* janitor. **–dienst,** *m.* teaching (profession).

schuldig [ˈʃuldɪç], *adj.* 1. guilty (*Gen.*, of), responsible (for), culpable; (*Law*) ***ihn für – erklären,*** convict him, find him guilty (*Gen.*, of (*a crime*), on (*a* *charge*)); (*Law*) ***ihn – sprechen,*** pronounce judgement against him, pronounce him guilty; (*Law*) ***sich – bekennen,*** plead guilty; – ***geschieden,*** divorced as the guilty partner; 2. (*money*) owing, due; (*fig.*) indebted (*Dat.*, to; *Acc.*, for); (*fig.*) ***ihm die Antwort – bleiben,*** make *or* vouchsafe no reply; (*fig.*) ***er bleibt ihr nichts –,*** with her he gives as good as he gets, he gives her tit for tat; (*fig.*) ***ihm eine Erklärung – sein,*** owe him an explanation. **Schuldige(r),** *m., f.* guilty person *or* party, culprit, person responsible *or* answerable. **Schuldiger,** *m.* (*B.*) ***wie wir vergeben unsern –n,*** as we forgive them that trespass against us. **schuldigermaßen,** *adv.* as in duty bound. **Schuldigkeit,** *f.* duty, obligation; ***verdammte Pflicht und –,*** bounden duty. **Schuldigsprechung,** *f.* conviction, condemnation, verdict of guilty. **schuldigst,** *adv.* most duly, as is right and proper.

Schul|direktor, *m.* headmaster, principal. **–direktorin,** *f.* headmistress.

Schuldklage, *f.* (*Law*) action for debt. **schuldlos,** *adj.* innocent, guiltless, blameless, irreproachable. **Schuldlosigkeit,** *f.* innocence, blamelessness. **Schuldner(in),** *m.* (*f.*) debtor. **Schuldposten,** *m.* amount owing *or* due.

Schuldrama [ˈʃuːldraːma], *n.* Latin play (*of Humanists*).

Schuld|schein, *m.* promissory note; (mortgage) bond; debenture (stock). **–turm,** *m.* (*Hist.*) debtor's prison. **–verhältnis,** *n.* obligation. **–verschreibung,** *f. See* **–schein. –versprechen,** *n.* acknowledgement of liabilities.

Schule [ˈʃuːlə], *f.* school, college, academy; school of thought; school (*of whales*); school(-house); ***Hohe –,*** manège, haute école; ***Hohe – reiten,*** put a horse through its places; ***höhere –,*** secondary school; (*esp. Am.*) high school; ***konfessionelle –,*** church school; ***städtische –,*** municipal school; ***auf*** or ***in der –,*** at school; ***aus der – schwatzen*** or ***plaudern,*** tell tales out of school; ***durch eine harte – gehen,*** learn it the hard way; ***hinter die – gehen*** or ***laufen,*** play truant; ***in die – gehen,*** see ***zur – gehen;*** ***in die – kommen,*** start school; (*fig.*) ***ihn in die – nehmen,*** take him in hand; ***in die – tun,*** send to school; – ***machen,*** set a precedent, be imitated, find followers *or* adherents; ***ein Pferd die – machen lassen,*** put a horse through its paces; ***die – schwänzen,*** play truant; ***zur – gehen,*** go to school.

schulen [ˈʃuːlən], **1.** *v.t.* teach, instruct; train, school, discipline; (*Pol.*) indoctrinate; break in, train (*horses*). **2.** *v.r.* undergo (a course of) training; ***geschult,*** (well-)trained.

schulentlassen [ˈʃuːlʔɛntlasən], *adj.* having left school. **Schulentlassungs|feier,** *f.* speech-day. **–zeugnis,** *n.* school-leaving certificate.

Schüler [ˈʃyːlər], *m.* schoolboy, pupil, (*obs. or Am.*) student; (*B. etc.*) disciple, follower; (*fig.*) tyro, novice; (*Hist.*) ***fahrender –,*** itinerant scholar. **Schüler|ausschuß,** *m.* pupils' committee. **–austausch,** *m.* pupils' exchange (visits). **schülerhaft,** *adj.* schoolboyish, (*fig.*) immature, juvenile, callow. **Schülerin,** *f.* schoolgirl. **Schüler|lotsendienst,** *m.* (system of) traffic wardens. **–mütze,** *f.* school-cap. **–sprache,** *f.* schoolboys' slang. **–zeitung,** *f.* school magazine.

Schul|fach, *n.* school subject. **–fall,** *m. See* **–beispiel. –ferien,** *pl.* (school) holidays, vacation. **–film,** *m.* educational film. **–flugzeug,** *n.* training plane. **–frage,** *f.* educational problem. **schulfrei,** *adj.* ***–er Tag,*** day's holiday; ***–er Nachmittag,*** half-holiday; – ***haben,*** have a holiday from school. **Schul|freund,** *m.* classmate, schoolfellow, pal. **–fuchs,** *m.* pedant. **–funk,** *m.* schools' broadcasts. **–gebrauch,** *m.* ***für den –,*** for use in schools, for class use. **–gelände,** *n.* school fields *or* grounds. **–geld,** *n.* school fees. **–gelehrsamkeit,** *f. See* **–weisheit. schulgerecht,** *adj.* according to rule, methodical; well-trained (*of horses*). **Schul|gesetz,** *n.* education act. **–haus,** *n.* school premises. **–heft,** *n.* exercise-book. **–hof,** *m.* playground.

schulisch [ˈʃuːlɪç], *adj.* scholastic, academic, collegiate. **Schul|jahr,** *n.* scholastic year; *pl.* schooldays. **–jugend,** *f.* school-children, juveniles. **–junge,** *m.* schoolboy. **–kamerad,** *m. See* **–freund. –kenntnisse,** *f.pl.* scholastic *or* classroom knowledge; rudiments. **–kind,** *n.* school-age child. **–klasse,** *f.* class, form, (*Am.*) grade. **–lehrer,** *m.* teacher, schoolmaster. **–lehrerin,** *f.* schoolmistress, (lady) teacher. **–leiter,** *m.* principal, headmaster. **–mädchen,** *n.* schoolgirl. **–mann,** *m.* (*pl.* **¨–er**) educationalist, experienced teacher, pedagogue. **–mappe,** *f.* satchel, schoolbag. **schulmäßig,** *adj.* orthodox. **Schulmeister,** *m.* (*derogatory*) schoolmaster, pedagogue. **schul|meisterlich,** *adj.* pedantic. **–meistern, 1.** *v.i.* keep a school; teach (pedantically), be pedantic, be censorious, dogmatize; (*coll.*) always know better. **2.** *v.t.* censure. **Schulordnung,** *f.* school regulations; school discipline.

Schulp [ʃulp], *m.* (**-(e)s,** *pl.* **-e**), **Schulpe,** *f.* cuttle-bone.

Schul|pferd, *n.* trained horse; riding-school horse. **–pflicht,** *f. See* **–zwang. schulpflichtig,** *adj.* of school age. **Schul|programm,** *n.* school's annual report. **–ranzen,** *m. See* **–mappe. –rat,** *m.* education authority; school inspector. **–reform,** *f.* educational reform. **–reiter,** *m.* manège rider. **–sattel,** *m.* manège-saddle. **–schießstand,** *m.* practice rifle-range. **–schiff,** *n.* training-ship. **–schluß,** *m.* end of term, breaking-up. **–schritt,** *m.* short pace (*of a horse*). **–schwänzer,** *m.* truant. **–speisung,** *f.* school meals. **–sprache,** *f.* official language of instruction. **–system,** *n.* educational system. **–tasche,** *f. See* **–mappe.**

Schulter [ˈʃultər], *f.* (-, *pl.* **-n**) shoulder; – ***an –,*** shoulder to shoulder, side by side, (*racing*) neck and neck; ***ihn über die – ansehen,*** look down one's nose at him; ***die –n hochziehen,*** shrug one's shoulders; ***ihm die kalte – zeigen,*** give him the cold shoulder; ***etwas auf die leichte – nehmen,*** take a th. lightly; ***Wasser auf beiden –n tragen,*** blow hot and cold; *see also* **Achsel.**

Schulter|band, *n.* humeral ligament. **–bein,** *n.,* **–blatt,** *n.* shoulder-bone, shoulder-blade, scapula. **–breite,** *f.* breadth of shoulders. **schulterfrei,** *adj.* off-the-shoulder, strapless (*dress*). **Schulter|gelenk,** *n.* shoulder-joint. **–gurt,** *m.* shoulder-strap. **–klappe,** *f.* (*Mil.*) shoulder-strap. **schultern,** *v.t.* shoulder. **Schulter|riemen,** *m.* (*Mil.*) cross-strap, cross-belt. **–stück,** *n.* epaulette; (*Anat.*) episternum. **–tuch,** *n.* scapulary (*of monks*). **–wehr,** *f.* (*Fort.*) epaulement, breastwork.

Schultheiß [ˈʃulthaɪs], *m.* (**-en,** *pl.* **-en**) (*obs.*) village mayor.

Schulung [ˈʃuːluŋ], *f.* training, practice, schooling, (*Pol.*) indoctrination. **Schulungs|brief,** *m.* (*Pol.*) party directive. **–kurs(us),** *m.* training *or* refresher course. **–lager,** *n.* training camp. **–woche,** *f.* short course of instruction, refresher course.

Schul|unterricht, *m.* school-teaching. **–versäumnis,** *n.* absence from school, non-attendance. **–vorstand,** *m.* school governors. **–wanderung,** *f.* school excursion. **–weg,** *m.* way to school. **–weisheit,** *f.* book-learning, erudition. **–wesen,** *n.* educational system; ***das höhere –,*** secondary education. **–zahnpflege,** *f.* school dental service. **–zeit,** *f.* school-time; school-days. **–zeugnis,** *n.* school-report. **–zimmer,** *n.* classroom, school-room. **–zucht,** *f.* school discipline. **–zwang,** *m.* compulsory education.

Schulze [ˈʃultsə], *m.* (**-n,** *pl.* **-n**) (*dial.*) *see* **Schultheiß.**

Schum [ʃuːm], *m.* (*coll.*) (*only in*) ***im –,*** tipsy, tiddly, fuddled, in one's cups.

schummeln [ˈʃuməln], *v.i.* (*coll.*) diddle, swindle.

Schummer [ˈʃumər], *m.* (*dial.*) twilight, dusk, gloaming. **schummerig,** *adj.* dusky, dim. **schummern, 1.** *v.i.* grow *or* be dim. **2.** *v.t.* shade, hatch (*maps*). **Schummerung,** *f.* hatching (*of maps*), hachures.

schund [ʃunt], *see* **schinden.**

Schund, *m.* trash, rubbish. **Schund|blatt,** *n.* rag.

–literatur, *f.* rubbishy *or* trashy literature. **–waren,** *f.pl.* shoddy *or* trashy goods.

schunkeln ['ʃuŋkəln], *v.i.* (*coll.*) see-saw, rock.

Schupf [ʃupf], *m.* (**-(e)s,** *pl.* **-e**) (*Austr., Swiss*) push, shove. **schupfen,** *v.t.* push, shove.

Schupo ['ʃu:po], (*coll.*) **1.** *f.* the police. **2.** *m.* (**-s,** *pl.* **-s**) policeman, bobby; *see* **Schutzpolizei, Schutzpolizist.**

Schupp [ʃup], *m.* (*dial.*) *see* **Schupf.**

Schuppe ['ʃupə], *f.* scale; scurf, dandruff; flake, (*Bot., Zool.*) squama; ***es fielen ihm wie –n von den Augen,*** the scales have fallen from his eyes, his eyes were opened.

Schüppe ['ʃypə], *f.* (*dial.*) shovel, scoop.

Schuppen ['ʃupən], *m.* shed, barn; coach-house, (*Railw.*) engine-house, (*Motor.*) garage, (*Av.*) hangar.

1**schuppen,** *v.t.* (*dial.*) *see* **schupfen.**

2**schuppen, 1.** *v.t.* scale (*fish etc.*), scrape, scratch. **2.** *v.r.* scale *or* peel off, slough, desquamate.

schuppenartig ['ʃupənʔartıç], *adj.* scaly, squamous. **Schuppen|baum,** *m.* lepidodendron. **–bildung,** *f.* flaking. **–eidechse,** *f.* scaly lizard. **–flechte,** *f.* (*Med.*) psoriasis. **schuppenförmig,** *adj.* scaly, (*Med.*) squamiform. **Schuppen|kette,** *f.* chin-strap (*of helmets*). **–naht,** *f.* (*Anat.*) scaly suture. **–panzer,** *m.* coat of mail. **–tanne,** *f.* (*Bot.*) monkey-puzzle (*Araucaria imbricata*). **–tier,** *n.* (*Zool.*) scaly ant-eater, pangolin (*Pholidota*). **schuppenweise,** *adv.* in scales, flake by flake. **Schuppenwurz,** *f.* (*Bot.*) toothwort (*Lathraea squamaria*).

schuppig ['ʃupıç], *adj.* scaly, scaled; squamous; scurfy.

Schup(p)s, *m.*, **schup(p)sen,** *v.t.* *See* **Schubs, schubsen.**

Schur [ʃu:r], *f.* (-, *pl.* **-en**) 1. (sheep-)shearing; mowing, clipping; fleece; swath(e); clippings; 2. (*coll.*) teasing, raillery.

Schüreisen ['ʃy:rʔaızən], *n.* poker.

schüren ['ʃy:rən], *v.t.* stir, poke, rake (*the fire*); (*fig.*) stir up, foment, fan, incite. **Schürer,** *n.* stoker; instigator.

Schurf [ʃurf], *m.* (**-es,** *pl.* **⸚e**) 1. opening, pit, hole (*in the ground*); 2. scratch, abrasion; 3. prospector's claim.

Schürfarbeit ['ʃyrfʔarbaıt], *f.* prospecting. **schürfen, 1.** *v.t.* scratch, scrape, graze. **2.** *v.i.* prospect, dig (*for ore*); (*fig.*) ***tief –,*** dig beneath the surface, get to the bottom. **Schürfer,** *m.* prospector. **Schürf|recht,** *n.*, **–schein,** *m.* prospecting licence. **–stelle,** *f.* prospect, digging. **Schürfung,** *f.* prospecting, digging; mining claim; abrasion, graze. **Schürfwunde,** *f.* abrasion, graze.

Schür|haken, *m.* *See* **–eisen.**

schurigeln ['ʃu:ri:gəln], *v.t.* torment, harass, pester, plague.

Schurke ['ʃurkə], *m.* (**-n,** *pl.* **-n**) scoundrel, rogue, knave, rascal, blackguard, villain. **Schurkenstreich,** *m.*, **Schurkerei** [–'raı], *f.* rascally *or* (*coll.*) dirty trick, rascality, knavery, villainy. **schurkisch,** *adj.* villainous, rascally, knavish, base, vile.

Schürloch ['ʃy:rlɔx], *n.* stoke-hole.

Schurre ['ʃurə], *f.* slide, chute. **schurren,** *v.i.* (*aux.* s. & h.) glide, slide.

Schurz [ʃurts], *m.* (**-es,** *pl.* **-e** *or* **⸚e**) apron, loin-cloth.

Schürze ['ʃyrtsə], *f.* 1. apron, pinafore; 2. (*sl.*) wench, skirt, petticoat, bit of stuff; ***hinter jeder – herlaufen,*** run after every skirt.

schürzen ['ʃyrtsən], **1.** *v.t.* tie (*a knot etc.*); tuck *or* fasten up (*one's skirt*); purse (*one's lips*). **2.** *v.r.* tuck up one's dress, pick up one's skirts; (*B.*) gird up one's loins; ***sich – zu,*** make *or* get (o.s.) ready for, (*fig.*) roll up one's sleeves (in readiness for); ***der Knoten schürzt sich,*** the plot thickens. **Schürzen|band,** *n.* (**-(e)s,** *pl.* **⸚er**) apron-string; ***ans – gebunden sein,*** be kept in leading-strings, be tied to (one's mother's) apron-strings. **–jäger,** *m.* rip, rake, (*sl.*) wolf. **–regiment,** *n.* petticoat government.

Schurzfell ['ʃurtsfɛl], *n.* leather apron.

Schuß [ʃus], *m.* (**-(ss)es,** *pl.* **⸚(ss)e**) (live) round; gunshot *or* bullet wound; shot, report (*of a gun*); (*Footb.*) shot; rapid movement, rush (*of water etc.*), swing, swoop; dash; (*skiing*) downhill run; rapid growth; (*Min.*) blasting charge; (*Weav.*) woof, weft; (*pl.* -) batch (*of bread*), dash, swig (*of brandy etc.*); ***einen – abfeuern*** *or* ***abgeben*** or ***tun,*** fire a shot *or* round; ***es fiel ein –,*** a shot was fired, there was a shot; ***sich zum – fertig machen,*** make ready to fire; ***– ins Blaue,*** random shot; (*fig.*) ***er kam mir gerade vor den –,*** he popped up just at the right moment; (*fig.*) ***in – bringen,*** get (*s.th.*) going *or* started, get into working order; (*fig.*) ***in – kommen,*** get going, get into one's stride, get under way; (*fig.*) ***(gut) in – sein,*** be in full swing, be going (on) well; be running well (*of an engine*); ***– ins Schwarze,*** bull's-eye; ***weit vom –,*** (well) out of harm's way; ***er ist keinen – Pulver wert,*** he is not worth a rap.

Schuß|bahn, *f.* line of fire. **–beobachtung,** *f.* (*Artil.*) spotting. **–bereich,** *m.* zone of fire, (effective) range. **schußbereit,** *adj.* ready to fire. **Schußbremse,** *f.* recoil-brake.

Schussel ['ʃusəl], *f.* (-, *pl.* **-n**) *or m.* (*dial.*) fidgety *or* restless p.

Schüssel ['ʃysəl], *f.* (-, *pl.* **-n**) dish, bowl, basin; (*for soup*) tureen, (*for gravy*) sauce- *or* gravy-boat; (*of a meal*) dish, course. **Schüssel|brett,** *n.* plate-rack. **–gestell,** *n.* (kitchen-)dresser; *see also* **–brett.**

schusselig ['ʃusəlıç], *adj.* (*dial.*) restless, fidgety. **schusseln,** *v.i.* (*dial.*) slide, go sledging.

Schüsselwärmer ['ʃysəlvɛrmər], *m.* plate-warmer.

Schusser ['ʃusər], *m.* (*dial.*) marble, taw. **schussern,** *v.i.* play marbles.

Schuß|faden, *m.* *See* **–garn. –fahrt,** *f.* (*skiing*) downhill run. **–feld,** *n.* field of fire. **schuß|fertig,** *adj.* *See* **–bereit**; (*of gun*) cocked. **–fest,** *adj.* bullet-proof, shell-proof; (*fig.*) ***er ist –,*** he bears a charmed life. **Schuß|folge,** *f.* rate of fire. **–garbe,** *f.* cone of fire. **–garn,** *n.* (*Weav.*) woof, weft. **schußgerecht,** *adj.* steady under fire (*of horses*); true (*of guns*); within range (*of game*). **Schuß|linie,** *f.* line of fire, line of sight. **–loch,** *n.* bullet-hole. **–richtung,** *f.* line *or* direction of fire. **schuß|scheu,** *adj.* gun-shy (*of horses*). **–sicher,** *adj.* *See* **–fest**; (*Av.*) ***–er Brennstoffbehälter,*** self-sealing fuel-tank. **Schuß|tafel,** *f.* range-table. **–träger,** *m.* (*Weav.*) shuttle-carrier. **–verbesserung,** *f.* (*Artil.*) correction. **–waffe,** *f.* firearm. **–weite,** *f.* (effective) range; ***in –,*** within range. **–werte,** *m.pl.* firing-data. **–wunde,** *f.* gunshot wound, bullet wound. **–zahl,** *f.* number of rounds.

Schuster ['ʃu:stər], *m.* shoemaker, cobbler; (*Prov.*) ***– bleib' bei deinem Leisten!*** cobbler, stick to your last! (*coll.*) ***auf –s Rappen,*** on Shanks's pony, on foot. **Schuster|ahle,** *f.* awl. **–draht,** *m.* waxed thread, shoemaker's thread. **schustern, 1.** *v.t.* make, mend (*shoes*), cobble. **2.** *v.i.* (*fig.*) work clumsily, bungle; (*coll.*) chum up (***mit,*** with). **Schuster|pech,** *n.* cobbler's wax, heel-ball. **–pfriem,** *m.* *See* **–ahle.**

Schute ['ʃu:tə], *f.* 1. (*Naut.*) barge, lighter; 2. (*coll.*) bonnet. **Schutengeld,** *n.* lighterage.

Schutt [ʃut], *m.* ruins; rubble, debris; refuse, rubbish; trash; (*B.*) bank of earth; ***in – und Asche legen,*** lay in ruins, raze to the ground. **Schutt|abladeplatz,** *m.* refuse-dump. **–ablagerung,** *f.* (*Geol.*) detritus.

Schüttboden ['ʃytbo:dən], *m.* granary, corn-loft.

Schütte ['ʃytə], *f.* 1. (*dial.*) heap, pile (*of straw etc.*); (*dial.*) truss (*of straw*); (*dial.*) granary; 2. blight (*which attacks pines*).

Schüttel|frost ['ʃytəl–], *m.* shivering fit, shivers, chill. **–lähmung,** *f.* shaking palsy.

schütteln ['ʃytəln], *v.t.* shake, agitate, (make) vibrate; jolt, (*coll.*) joggle; ***aus dem Ärmel –,*** improvise, do on the spur of the moment, produce from one's sleeve, do off the cuff; ***ihm die Hand*** or

Hände –, shake him by the hand, shake hands with him, shake his hand; *es schüttelt mich,* I shudder (*with disgust etc.*), I shake (*with laughter*); *den Kopf* (or *die Faust*) –, shake one's head (*or* fist). **Schüttel|reim,** *m.* Spoonerism. **–rinne,** *f.* shaking-trough, chute. **–rost,** *m.* rocker-grating, raker (*in furnace*). **–rutsche,** *f. See* **–rinne.**

schütten [ˈʃytən], **1.** *v.t.* pour (out), cast, shed, spill, shoot; *leer* –, empty out; *voll* –, fill up; *auf einen Haufen* –, pile up; *Öl auf die Wogen* –, pour oil on troubled waters. **2.** *v.i.* shed leaves (*of pines*); litter, whelp; (*imp.*) pour (with rain). **Schütten-abwurf,** *m. See* **Schüttwurf.**

schütter [ˈʃytər], *adj.* (*of hair*) thin, sparse.

schüttern [ˈʃytərn], **1.** *v.i.* tremble, quake, shake. **2.** *v.t.* shake, rattle.

Schütt|gewicht, *n.* loose weight. **–gut,** *n.* loose goods, bulk goods.

Schutt|halde, *f.* (*Geol.*) scree(-slope). **–haufen,** *m.* rubbish-heap *or* -dump; pile of rubble; *in einen – verwandeln,* see *in Schutt und Asche legen.*

Schütt|ofen, *m.* self-feeding stove. **–stein,** *m.* (*Swiss*) sink, gutter. **–stroh,** *n.* litter. **–wurf,** *m.* (*Av.*) salvo *or* random bombing.

Schutz [ʃuts], *m.* shelter, refuge, cover, shield, screen; defence, protection, safeguard (*vor* (*Dat.*) *or gegen,* against *or* from); care, custody, keeping; patronage; – *und Schirm,* protection; *im – der Dunkelheit,* under cover of darkness; *unter dem –e der Kanonen,* under cover of the guns; *sich in seinen – begeben,* seek shelter *or* take refuge with him; *zu – und Trutz,* defensive(ly) and offensive(ly); – *suchen,* take shelter (*vor* (*Dat.*), from), seek refuge (*bei,* with); *in – nehmen,* take under one's protection *or* (*coll.*) wing; (*fig.*) defend, come to (*s.o.'s*) defence, (*coll.*) stand up for (*a p.*), back (*a p.*) up; (*Comm.*) honour (*a bill*).

[1]**Schütz** [ʃyts], *m.* **(-en,** *pl.* **-en)** *see* [2]**Schütze.**

[2]**Schütz,** *n.* **(-es,** *pl.* **-e)** 1. (*Elec.*) remote-controlled switch, relay, contactor; 2. (*Weav.*) shuttle; 3. sluice-board, sluice-gate.

Schutz|anstrich, *m.* protective coat(ing); (*Mil.*) dazzle *or* camouflage paint. **–anzug,** *m.* protective clothes. **–ärmel,** *m.pl.* sleeve-protectors. **schutz-bedürftig,** *adj.* needing protection, in distress. **Schutz|befohlene(r),** *m., f.* charge, protégé(e); ward. **–blech,** *n.* (*Motor.*) mudguard, wing, (*Am.*) fender; (*Mech.*) guard(-plate). **–brief,** *m.* (letter of) safe-conduct. **–brille,** *f.* (safety) goggles. **–bündnis,** *n.* defensive alliance. **–dach,** *n.* shed, lean-to, (*fig.*) shelter, protection. **–decke,** *f.* cover(ing). **–deckel,** *m.* cardboard box, case, carton.

[1]**Schütze** [ˈʃytsə], *f. See* [2]**Schütz,** 3.

[2]**Schütze,** *m.* **(-n,** *pl.* **-n)** marksman, huntsman, (good) shot; sharpshooter, rifleman; private (*infantry*); (*Hist.*) archer; (*Astr.*) Sagittarius.

schützen [ˈʃytsən], *v.t.* protect, guard, defend (*gegen,* against; *vor* (*Dat.*), from); shelter, secure; shield, screen (*vor,* from); (*Comm.*) honour (*a bill*); dam up; *in dem Besitze* –, maintain in possession of; *gesetzlich* or *patentrechtlich geschützt,* patented; *urheberrechtlich geschützt,* protected by copyright.

Schützen|abzeichen, *n.* marksman's badge. **–auftritt,** *m.* fire-step. **–bataillon,** *n.* light-infantry *or* rifle battalion. **–brigade,** *f.* rifle brigade. **–bruder,** *m.* fellow member of a rifle-club. **–fest,** *n.* shooting match. **–feuer,** *n.* independent fire. **–gefecht,** *n.* skirmish.

Schutzengel [ˈʃutsˀɛŋəl], *m.* guardian angel.

Schützen|gilde, *f.* rifle-club. **–graben,** *m.* (*Mil.*) trench. **–grabenkrieg,** *m.* trench-warfare. **–kette,** *f.* skirmishing order, extended order, line of skirmishers. **–könig,** *m.* champion shot. **–linie,** *f. See* **–kette.** **–loch,** *n.* (*Mil.*) fox-hole. **–nest,** *n.* rifle-pit. **–schleier,** *m.* covering party, infantry screen. **–stand,** *m.* firing position, (*Av.*) gun-turret. **–steuerung,** *f.* (*Elec.*) contactor control, remote-control switching. **–übung,** *f.* firing *or* rifle-practice. **–verein,** *m.* rifle-club. **–zug,** *m.* infantry platoon.

Schutz|farbe, *f.* protective paint, (*Mil.*) camouflage (paint). **–färbung,** *f.* protective colouring. **–frist,** *f.* term of copyright. **–gebiet,** *n.* (*Pol.*) protectorate; reservation, nature reserve, sanctuary. **–geist,** *m.* guardian spirit, (tutelary) genius. **–geländer,** *n.* railing, balustrade, guard-rail. **–geleit,** *n.* safe-conduct, (*Av.*) escort, (*Naut.*) convoy. **–gerät,** *n.* safety appliances. **–gift,** *n. See* **–(pocken)gift.** **–gitter,** *n.* fireguard; safety *or* protecting screen; (*Rad.*) screen grid, (*Motor.*) radiator grille. **–glas,** *n.* glass shield. **–glocke,** *f.* bell-jar. **–gott,** *m.* (**–göttin,** *f.*) tutelary god(dess). **–haft,** *f.* protective custody, preventive arrest. **–haube,** *f.* (protective) cover, hood. **–heilige(r),** *m., f.* patron saint. **–heiligtum,** *n.* palladium. **–herr,** *m.* (**–herrin,** *f.*) patron(ess), protector (protectress). **–herrschaft,** *f.* protectorate. **–hülle,** *f.* casing, armour (*of a cable*); dust-cover, jacket (*of book*). **–hütte,** *f.* shelter, refuge (*in the Alps*). **–impfung,** *f.* vaccination, immunization, protective inoculation. **–insel,** *f.* island, refuge (*in the street*).

Schützling [ˈʃytslɪŋ], *m* **(-s,** *pl.* **-e)** protégé(e), charge.

schutzlos [ˈʃutsloːs], *adj.* defenceless, unprotected.

Schutz|macht, *f.* (*Pol.*) protecting power. **–mann,** *m.* (*pl.* **–̈er** *or* **-leute)** policeman, constable. **–marke,** *f.* trade-mark. **–masse,** *f.* resist (*of fabrics*). **–maßnahme, –maßregel,** *f.* protective *or* safety *or* precautionary measure, precaution, preventative. **–mauer,** *f.* rampart, bulwark. **–mittel,** *n.* preservative, preventative, prophylactic. **–patron,** *m.,* **–patronin,** *f.* patron saint. **–pocken,** *f.pl.* cowpox. **–(pocken)gift,** *n.* vaccine lymph *or* virus. **–pockenimpfung,** *f.* vaccination. **–polizei,** *f.* (municipal) police. **–polizist,** *m. See* **–mann.** **–raum,** *m.* (air-raid) shelter. **–salbe,** *f.* barrier cream. **–scheibe,** *f.* (*Motor.*) windscreen, (*Am.*) windshield. **–schicht,** *f.* protective layer. **–schiene,** *f.* (*Railw.*) guard-rail. **–schild,** *m.* (*Mil.*) armoured shield; blast-wall. **–staffel,** *f.* (*Nat. Soc.*) S.S., Blackshirts. **–stoff,** *m.* antidote, alexin, antibody, vaccine. **–truppe,** *f.* colonial troops. **–umschlag,** *m.* dust-cover, jacket (*of book*). **–vorrichtung,** *f.* safety device. **–wache,** *f.* escort. **–waffen,** *f.pl.* defensive arms; means of defence. **–wand,** *f.* safety wall, protective screen. **–wehr,** *f.* dike; (*Mil.*) bulwark, defence work, rampart, mantlet. **–zoll,** *m.* protective duty *or* tariff. **–zöllner,** *m.* protectionist. **–zollsystem,** *n.* protectionism.

schwabbelig [ˈʃvabəlɪç], *adj.* wobbly, flabby. **schwabbeln, 1.** *v.i.* wobble, flop about; (*of liquid*) swill, slop *or* spill over; (*dial.*) prattle, prate, babble. **2.** *v.t.* (*Tech.*) buff. **Schwabbelscheibe,** *f.* buffing wheel.

Schwabber [ˈʃvabər], *m.* (*Naut.*) swab, mop. **schwabbern,** *v.t.* swab (*the deck*); *see also* **schwabbeln.**

[1]**Schwabe** [ˈʃvaːbə], *f.* cockroach; *see* [1]**Schabe.**

[2]**Schwabe,** *m.* **(-n,** *pl.* **-n)** Swabian.

schwäbeln [ˈʃvɛːbəln], *v.i.* speak in the Swabian dialect. **Schwaben** [ˈʃvaːbən], *n.* Swabia. **Schwäbin,** *f. See* [2]**Schwabe.** **schwäbisch,** *adj.* Swabian.

schwach [ʃvax], *adj.* (*comp. schwächer, sup. schwächst*) weak, feeble, infirm, frail, delicate; mild, slight, flimsy, thin, poor, meagre, sparse, scanty; faint, dim, dull, low (*of sound, light*); *–e Ähnlichkeit,* faint *or* slight resemblance; *–er Besuch,* poor attendance; *–e Bevölkerung,* sparse population; *–e Erinnerung,* dim *or* faint recollection; *–es Gedächtnis,* poor *or* bad memory; *das –e Geschlecht,* the weaker sex; *–e Hoffnung,* faint hope; *–es Lächeln,* faint *or* feeble smile; *–er Motor,* low-powered engine; *–e Seite,* weak point; *–e Stelle,* vulnerable spot; *–e Stunde,* moment of weakness, unguarded moment; *–e Stimme,* feeble voice; *–er Versuch,* feeble attempt; *–es Zeitwort,* weak verb; *es wurde ihr –,* she felt faint; *sich – zeigen,* betray weakness; (*coll.*) *das macht mich –,* it's enough to drive one dotty.

schwach|bevölkert, *adj.* thinly *or* sparsely populated. **–gläubig,** *adj.* weak in faith.

Schwäche [ˈʃvɛçə], *f.* weakness, faintness, debility, feebleness, frailty, infirmity; foible, failing, weakness, shortcoming, weak point *or* side; ***menschliche* –**, frailty of human nature, human failing; (*männliche*) –, impotence; ***eine – haben für,*** have a weakness *or* (*coll.*) a soft spot for. **Schwäche|anfall,** *m.* attack of faintness. **–gefühl,** *n.* faintness, fatigue, (*coll.*) sinking feeling.

schwächen [ˈʃvɛçən], *v.t.* 1. weaken, enfeeble, debilitate, enervate; impair, sap, undermine (*health*); lessen, diminish, dilute, qualify, (*coll.*) tone down; 2. (*obs.*) seduce, ravish. **Schwächezustand,** *m.* feeble condition, asthenia, debility.

Schwachheit [ˈʃvaxhaɪt], *f.* weakness, feebleness, frailty, debility, debilitated condition; fainting turn *or* fit; weak will; ***moralische* –**, frailty; ***sich*** (*Dat.*) ***–en einbilden,*** get silly notions into one's head, indulge in *or* cherish false hopes; cherish illusions, deceive *or* (*coll.*) fool o.s.

schwach|herzig, *adj.* faint-hearted. **–kochen,** *v.t.* boil gently, simmer. **Schwachkopf,** *m.* idiot, nincompoop, simpleton, imbecile. **schwachköpfig,** *adj.* weak-minded, brainless, silly.

schwächlich [ˈʃvɛçlɪç], *adj.* feeble, weakly, sickly, delicate, frail, infirm. **Schwächlichkeit,** *f.* sickliness, delicacy, infirmity, frailty.

Schwächling [ˈʃvɛçlɪŋ], *m.* (**-s,** *pl.* **-e**) weakling.

Schwachmatikus [ʃvaxˈmatikus], *m.* (-, *pl.* **-se** *or* **-ker**) (*hum.*) *see* **Schwächling. schwachsichtig,** *adj.* with poor vision, amblyopic. **Schwach|sichtigkeit,** *f.* dimness of vision, poor sight, amblyopia. **–sinn,** *m.* feeble-mindedness. **schwachsinnig,** *adj.* feeble-minded, moronic. **Schwach|sinnige(r),** *m., f.* moron, imbecile, half-wit. **–strom,** *m.* low-tension current.

Schwächung [ˈʃvɛçuŋ], *f.* 1. weakening, debilitation; *see* **Abschwächung**; 2. (*obs.*) defloration.

Schwad [ʃva:d], *m.* (**-en,** *pl.* **-en**), **Schwade,** *f. See* [1]**Schwaden.**

[1]**Schwaden** [ˈʃva:dən], *m.* swath(e).

[2]**Schwaden,** *m.* suffocating vapour, exhalation, cloud of gas, (*Min.*) firedamp.

Schwadron [ʃvaˈdro:n], *f.* (-, *pl.* **-en**) squadron, troop (of cavalry). **Schwadroneur** [-ˈnø:r], *m.* (**-s,** *pl.* **-e**) braggart, blusterer, (*coll.*) gas-bag. **schwadronieren,** *v.i.* brag, boast, swagger, draw the long bow.

Schwafelei [ʃva:fəˈlaɪ], *f.* (-, *pl.* **-en**) (*coll.*) drivel, tosh, piffle. **schwafeln** [ˈʃva:fəln], *v.i.* talk piffle, drivel on.

Schwager [ˈʃva:gər], *m.* (**-s,** *pl.* ¨) 1. brother-in-law; 2. (*obs.*) postilion, coachman.

Schwägerin [ˈʃvɛ:gərɪn], *f.* sister-in-law. **Schwägerschaft,** *f.* relationship by marriage; brothers- and sisters-in-law, relations by marriage.

Schwäher [ˈʃvɛ:ər], *m.* (*obs., Poet.*) father-in-law; (*rare*) brother-in-law.

schwaien [ˈʃvaɪən], **1.** *v.i.* (*Naut.*) swing (at anchor). **2.** *v.t.* swing (*the ship*) round.

Schwaige [ˈʃvaɪgə], *f.* (*dial.*) dairy-farm. **schwaigen,** *v.i.* make cheese. **Schwaiger,** *m.* Alpine herdsman.

schwajen, *v.t., v.i. See* **schwaien.**

Schwalbe [ˈʃvalbə], *f.* swallow (*see* **Mehlschwalbe, Rauchschwalbe, Uferschwalbe**). **Schwalben|möwe,** *f.* (*Orn.*) Sabine's gull (*Xema sabini*). **–nest,** *n.* swallow's nest; (*Av.*) (*sl.*) blister (*for gunner*). **–schwanz,** *m.* swallow-tail; swallow-tail coat; (*Carp.*) dovetail; (*Ent.*) swallowtail (butterfly) (*Papilio machaon*); split-trail (*of gun*).

Schwalch [ʃvalç], *m.* (**-(e)s,** *pl.* **-e**) gullet (*of a furnace*). **schwalchen,** *v.i.* smoulder.

schwälen [ˈʃvɛ:lən], *v.i., v.t.* (*dial.*) *see* **schwelen.**

Schwall [ʃval], *m.* swell, surge, undulation; deluge, flood (*of water*), sheet (*of flame*); torrent (*of words*); throng (*of people*). **Schwallblech,** *n.* baffle(-plate).

Schwalm [ʃvalm], *m.* (**-(e)s,** *pl.* **-e**) (*Swiss*) *see* **Schwall.**

Schwamm [ʃvam], *m.* (**-(e)s,** *pl.* **¨e**) sponge; (*Bot.*) fungus, mushroom, toadstool; (*Path.*) morbid growth; dry-rot; tinder; (*sl.*) ***– drüber!*** no more of it! forget it! let bygones be bygones!

schwamm, *see* **schwimmen.**

Schwamm|gewächs, *n.* fungoid growth. **–gummi,** *m.* sponge-rubber, latex foam. **schwammig,** *adj.* spongy, porous; fungous, fungoid; bloated, (*coll.*) puffy. **Schwammigkeit,** *f.* sponginess.

Schwan [ʃva:n], *m.* (**-(e)s,** *pl.* **¨e**) (*dial.* **-en,** *pl.* **-en**) swan (*see* **Höckerschwan, Singschwan**).

schwand [ʃvant], *see* **schwinden.**

schwanen [ˈʃva:nən], *v.i.* ***es schwant mir,*** I have an inkling *or* a vague feeling *or* a presentiment; ***mir schwant nichts Gutes,*** I have my misgivings, I have dark forebodings.

Schwanen|gans, *f.* (*Orn.*) swan-goose (*Cygnopsis cygnoides*). **–gesang,** *m.* swan-song. **–hals,** *m.* 1. swan's neck; 2. (*Naut.*) goose-neck. **–teich,** *m.* swannery.

Schwang [ʃvaŋ], *m.* (*only in*) ***im –e sein,*** be in full swing, be customary *or* in vogue, be (all) the fashion *or* (*coll.*) the rage; ***in – kommen,*** come into fashion *or* vogue, become the fashion *or* (*coll.*) the rage.

schwang, *see* **schwingen.**

schwanger [ˈʃvaŋər], *adj.* pregnant, with child, (*coll.*) expectant, in the family way; (*fig.*) ***mit großen Plänen – gehen,*** be full of great ideas. **Schwangere,** *f.* pregnant woman, expectant mother. **Schwangerenfürsorge,** *f.* pre-natal care.

schwängern [ˈʃvɛŋərn], *v.t.* get with child, (*coll.*) put in the family way; (*fig.*) fecundate, impregnate, (*Chem.*) saturate.

Schwangerschaft [ˈʃvaŋərʃaft], *f.* pregnancy. **Schwangerschaftsunterbrechung,** *f.* interruption of pregnancy, abortion. **schwangerschaftsverhütend,** *adj.* contraceptive.

Schwängerung [ˈʃvɛŋəruŋ], *f.* getting with child, (*usu. fig.*) fecundation, impregnation, (*Chem.*) saturation; conception.

schwank [ʃvaŋk], *adj.* pliable, flexible, supple, lithe, slender; faltering, shaky, wavering, unsteady; (*B.*) ***ein –es Rohr im Winde,*** a reed shaken by the wind; ***–es Seil,*** slack rope.

Schwank, *m.* (**-(e)s,** *pl.* **¨e**) prank, hoax; funny story, anecdote; (*Theat.*) farce.

schwanken [ˈʃvaŋkən], *v.i.* swing *or* wave to and fro, rock, sway, shake, (*coll.*) wobble; (*as a ship*) roll, toss; totter, stagger, reel, oscillate, fluctuate, alternate, vary; (*usu. fig.*) be irresolute, waver, vacillate, falter, hesitate, (*coll.*) shilly-shally. **Schwanken,** *n.* swaying, rocking, shaking; staggering, tottering; fluctuation, variation, oscillation, (*Astr.*) nutation; (*fig.*) wavering, vacillation, inconstancy. **schwankend,** *adj.* staggering, tottering, unsteady; unstable, precarious, uncertain, unsettled, fluctuating; (*fig.*) vacillating, wavering, faltering, undecided, fickle, unreliable. **Schwankung,** *f.* variation, deviation, (*Astr.*) nutation; *see* **Schwanken**; *pl.* (*coll.*) ups and downs. **Schwankungs|bereich,** *m.* range (of variation). **–grenze,** *f.* limit of variability.

Schwanz [ʃvants], *m.* (**-es,** *pl.* **¨e**) tail; trail (*of a gun*); flourish (*of writing*), (*dial.*) train (*of dress*); (*sl.*) penis, (*vulg.*) cock, prick; ***das Pferd beim – aufzäumen,*** place the cart before the horse; (*fig.*) ***den – einziehen,*** draw in one's horns, climb down; (*Studs. sl.*) ***einen – machen,*** fail in one subject; (*fig.*) ***den – zwischen die Beine nehmen,*** take to one's heels, slink *or* sneak away, (*coll.*) slope off, make tracks; (*fig.*) ***ihm den – streichen,*** butter him up; (*fig.*) ***ihm auf den – treten,*** tread on his toes *or* corns; (*coll.*) ***kein –,*** not a living soul.

Schwanz|abschnitt, *m.* caudal segment. **–blech,** *n.* (*Artil.*) trail-spade.

schwänzeln [ˈʃvɛntsəln], *v.i.* wag the tail; (*coll. of a p.*) wiggle one's bottom; (*fig.*) ***– um,*** fawn upon, wheedle, flatter. **schwänzen, 1.** *v.t.* provide with a tail; ***geschwänzt,*** with a tail, tailed, caudate. **2.** *v.t., v.i.* (*coll.*) ***die Schule –,*** play hooky *or* truant; ***die Kirche*** (or ***eine Stunde***) ***–,*** cut church (*or* a lesson); (*Mus.*) *Noten –,* miss out *or* skip notes.

Schwanz|ende, *n.* tip of a tail, (*fig.*) tail-end. **–feder,** *f.* tail-feather. **–fläche,** *f.* (*Av.*) tail-plane *or* -fin. **–flosse,** *f.* caudal fin, tail-fin. **–fortsatz,** *m.* (*Zool.*) coccyx. **schwanzlastig,** *adj.* (*Av.*) tail-heavy. **Schwanz|meise,** *f.* (*Orn.*) long-tailed titmouse (*Aegithalos caudatus*). **–riegel,** *m.* (*Artil.*) trail-transom. **–riemen,** *m.* crupper. **–säge,** *f.* whip-saw. **–spitze,** *f. See* **–ende.** **–sporn,** *m.* (*Av.*) tail-skid; *see* **–blech.** **–stern,** *m.* comet. **–steuer,** *n.* (*Av.*) rudder. **–stück,** *n.* tail-piece (*of fish*); rump (*of beef*); (*Artil.*) trail. **–wirbel,** *m.* caudal vertebra.

schwapp! [ʃvap], *int.* splash! smack! slap! whack! **schwapp(e)lig,** *adj.* flabby, wobbly. **schwappeln,** *v.i.* be flabby, wobble; *see also* **schwappen.** **schwappen, schwappern,** *v.i.* splash, spill, splash over; ***schwappend voll,*** full to overflowing.

schwaps! [ʃvaps], *int. See* **schwapp.**

Schwär [ʃvɛ:r], *m.* **(-(e)s,** *pl.* **-e), Schwäre,** *f.*, **Schwären,** *m.* abscess, ulcer. **schwären,** *irr.v.i.* (*aux.* h. *&* s.) suppurate, ulcerate, fester, (*fig.*) fester, rankle. **schwärig,** *adj.* covered with sores *or* ulcers.

Schwarm [ʃvarm], *m.* **(-(e)s,** *pl.* **¨-e)** 1. swarm, cluster, colony; (*of animals*) pack, flock, herd; (*of birds*) flight, flock, covey; (*of fish*) shoal, school; (*of people*) host, throng, multitude, crowd; 2. (*coll.*) (*of a p.*) hero, idol, pet, (*of a th.*) craze, fancy, ideal.

schwärmen [ˈʃvɛrmən], *v.i.* (*aux.* h. *&* s.) 1. swarm, sprawl; revel, riot, (*Mil.*) skirmish; rove, wander, stray; migrate; (*Mil.*) ***– lassen,*** deploy; ***es schwärmt von Menschen auf der Straße,*** the streets are swarming *or* thronged with people; 2. ***– von*** or ***für,*** be enthusiastic about, (*coll.*) enthuse *or* rave over *or* about, gush over; ***– für,*** be crazy *or* mad *or* wild about (*a th.*), have a crush on, be smitten *or* (*sl.*) gone on (*a p.*); ***alles schwärmt für sie,*** everyone is in raptures about her.

Schwärmer [ˈʃvɛrmər], *m.* 1. enthusiast, dreamer, visionary, (*coll.*) crank, (*Eccl.*) fanatic, zealot; 2. (*Ent.*) hawk-moth (*Sphingidae*); 3. (*Mil.*) skirmisher, sharpshooter; 4. (fire-)cracker, squib. **Schwärmerei** [–ˈraɪ], *f.* 1. revelry, riotous behaviour; 2. enthusiasm (***für,*** for *or* over *or* about), rapture, ecstasy (over), (*coll.*) gush(ing) (over); worship, idolization (of); (*Eccl.*) fanaticism. **schwärmerisch,** *adj.* visionary, fanciful; (*Eccl.*) fanatical; enthusiastic, rapturous, enraptured, entranced, (*coll.*) gushing, raving, wild (***für,*** over). **Schwärm|spore,** *f.* (*Bot.*) swarm-cell. **–zeit,** *f.* swarming time (*of bees*).

Schwarte [ˈʃva:rtə], *f.* (bacon) rind, skin, (pork) crackling; outside plank; (*coll.*) hide; ***alte –,*** old tome; (*coll.*) ***daß die – knackt,*** like blazes, till the pips squeak. **schwarten, 1.** *v.t.* (*coll.*) pummel, pommel, trounce. **2.** *v.i.* pore over books. **Schwartenmagen,** *m.* collared pork, smoked brawn. **schwartig,** *adj.* thick-skinned.

schwarz [ʃvarts], *adj.* (*comp.* *schwärzer, sup. schwärzest*) black; dark, swarthy; (*Her.*) sable; (*fig.*) gloomy, dismal; ***bei ihm – angeschrieben sein,*** be in his bad books; ***sich – ärgern,*** foam with rage, see red, (*coll.*) blow one's top; ***–es Brett,*** notice-board; ***–es Brot,*** brown bread; ***der –e Erdteil,*** the dark continent; ***–e Gedanken,*** dismal *or* gloomy thoughts; ***–e Kunst,*** black magic, the black art, necromancy, sorcery, witchcraft; ***–e Liste,*** black list; ***auf die –e Liste setzen,*** black-list; ***–er Markt,*** black market; ***Schwarzes Meer,*** Black Sea; ***– sehen,*** be pessimistic, look on the black side; ***ich sehe – (für ihn),*** things look black (for him); ***mir wurde – vor den Augen,*** everything went black, I blacked out; (*Med.*) ***–er Star,*** amaurosis; ***der –e Tod,*** the Black Death, (bubonic) plague; ***– auf weiß,*** in black and white; ***warten bis man – wird,*** wait till one is blue in the face.

Schwarz, *n.* black (colour), blackness; ***– tragen, in – gekleidet sein,*** wear black, be in mourning; ***ins –e treffen,*** hit the bull's-eye, (*fig.*) pull it off, come off with flying colours, score a success.

Schwarzarbeit [ˈʃvartsʔarbaɪt], *f.* non-union *or* blackleg labour; illicit employment (*i.e. while drawing unemployment benefit*). **schwarzäugig,** *adj.* dark-eyed. **Schwarz|beere,** *f.* (*dial.*) elderberry. **–blech,** *n.* sheet-iron. **–blei,** *n.* blacklead. **–brenner,** *m.* illicit distiller. **–brot,** *n.* brown *or* rye bread. **–dorn,** *m.* (*dial.*) sloe, blackthorn (*Prunus spinosa*). **–drossel,** *f. See* **Amsel.**

Schwärze [ˈʃvɛrtsə], *f.* 1. blackness, darkness, swarthiness; 2. blacking; 3. printer's ink.

Schwarze(r) [ˈʃvartsə(r)], *m., f.* black ((wo)man), Negro (Negress); (*coll.*) parson, cleric; ***die Schwarzen,*** the black race(s); (*coll.*) the clerical party.

schwärzen [ˈʃvɛrtsən], *v.t.* 1. blacken, (make) black, darken; blacklead, (*Typ.*) ink; (*fig.*) blacken, defame, vilify; 2. (*dial.*) smuggle (in).

schwarz|fahren, *irr.v.i.* drive without a licence; travel without a ticket; go for a joy-ride (*in a stolen vehicle*). **–gallig,** *adj.* melancholic, atrabilious. **–gar,** *adj.* tanned black. **–gestreift,** *adj.* with black stripes. **–haarig,** *adj.* dark-haired. **Schwarz|halstaucher,** *m.* (*Orn.*) black-necked *or* (*Am.*) -eared grebe (*Podiceps nigricollis*). **–handel,** *m.* black market(eering); ***im –,*** on the black market. **–hemden,** *n.pl.* (Italian) fascists. **schwarzhören,** *v.i.* listen-in illegally. **Schwarz|hörer,** *m.* owner of an unlicensed wireless set, secret listener to forbidden radio. **–kauf,** *m.* illicit sale. **–kehlchen,** *n.* (*Orn.*) stonechat (*Saxicola torquata*). **–kehldrossel,** *f.* (*Orn.*) black-throated thrush (*Turdus atrogularis*). **–kiefer,** *f.* Austrian pine (*Pinus nigricans*). **–kopfgrasmücke,** *f.* (*Orn.*) Sardinian warbler (*Sylvia melanocephala*). **–kopfmöwe,** *f.* (*Orn.*) Mediterranean black-headed gull (*Larus melanocephalus*). **–kunst,** *f.* black magic, the black art, sorcery, necromancy. **–künstler,** *m.* necromancer, sorcerer, magician.

schwärzlich [ˈʃvɛrtslɪç], *adj.* blackish, darkish, swarthy, tawny.

Schwarz|markt, *m.* black market. **–markthändler,** *m.* black-marketeer. **–pappel,** *f.* black poplar (*Populus nigra*). **–plättchen,** *n. See* **Mönchsgrasmücke.** **schwarzrotgold,** *adj.* (German) Republican. **Schwarz|scheck,** *m.*, **–schecke,** *f.* piebald horse. **–schimmel,** *m.* iron-grey horse. **–schlachtung,** *f.* illicit slaughter(ing) (*of cattle*). **–schnabelkuckuck,** *m.* (*Orn.*) black-billed cuckoo (*Coccyzus erythrophthalmus*). **–schnabel-Sturmtaucher,** *m.* (*Orn.*) Manx shearwater (*Puffinus puffinus*). **–seher,** *m.* alarmist, pessimist. **–seherei,** *f.* pessimism, defeatism. **–sender,** *m.* illegal transmitter, radio pirate. **–specht,** *m.* (*Orn.*) black woodpecker (*Dryocopus martius*). **–stirnwürger,** *m.* (*Orn.*) lesser grey shrike (*Lanius minor*). **–storch,** *m.* (*Orn.*) black stork (*Ciconia nigra*).

Schwärzung [ˈʃvɛrtsuŋ], *f.* (*Phot.*) density.

Schwarzwald, *m.* Black Forest. **schwarz|weiß,** *adj.* black and white. **–weißrot,** *adj.* (German) Nationalist. **Schwarz|weißzeichnung,** *f.* black-and-white drawing. **–wild,** *n.* wild boars. **–wurz,** *f.* (*Bot.*) comfrey (*Symphytum officinale*). **–wurzel,** *f.* (*Bot.*) viper's grass (*Scorzonera*).

Schwatz [ʃvats], *m.* (*coll.*) talk, chatter, twaddle, blether. **Schwatzbase,** *f.* chatterbox, gossip. **schwatzen, schwätzen** [ˈʃvɛtsən], *v.i.* chatter, chat, prattle, gossip; ***ins Blaue hinein –,*** talk at random *or* foolishly. **Schwätzer,** *m.* bletherer, babbler, (*coll.*) gas-bag. **Schwätzerei** [–ˈraɪ], *f.* gossip, prattle, tittle-tattle. **schwatzhaft,** *adj.* talkative, chatty, garrulous. **Schwatzhaftigkeit,** *f.* chattiness, talkativeness, loquacity. **Schwatz|maul,** *n.* (*coll.*) *see* **–base.**

Schwebe [ˈʃve:bə], *f.* (state of) suspense; (*Chem.*) suspension; ***in der – sein,*** (*of a p.*) be in suspense, be unsettled *or* undecided; (*of an issue*) be in abeyance, hang in the balance, (*Law*) be pending; ***in der – lassen,*** leave unsettled *or* undecided. **Schwebe|bahn,** *f.* suspension-railway. **–baum,** *m.* horizontal bar. **–flug,** *m.* soaring, hovering.

schweben [ˈʃve:bən], *v.i.* soar, float (through the air); hover, hang (in the air); be poised *or* suspended, (*fig.*) be pending, be in suspense, be undecided; (*B.*) move; ***in Gefahr –,*** be in danger; ***in Ungewißheit –,*** be (kept) in suspense; ***auf der Zunge –,*** be on the tip of one's tongue; ***über den Wolken –,*** live in the clouds; ***sein Bild schwebt mir immer vor Augen,*** his image is always before my eyes *or* always in my mind's eye; ***zwischen Leben und Tod –,*** hover between life and death. **schwebend,** *adj.* floating, hovering, suspended, (*Chem.*) in suspension; (*fig.*) undecided; pending; (*Phonet.*) ***–e Betonung,*** level stress; ***–e Frage,*** unsettled *or* moot question; ***–e Gärten,*** hanging-gardens; (*Poet.*) ***–e Pein,*** agony of suspense; ***–e Schuld,*** floating debt; ***–er Schritt,*** light *or* elastic step.

Schwebe|reck, *n.* trapeze. **–schritt,** *m.* (*Mil.*) balance-step. **–stange,** *f.* tightrope-walker's pole. **–stoff,** *m.* suspended matter.

Schwebfliege [ˈʃveːpfliːɡə], *f.* (*Ent.*) hovering fly (*Syrphidae*).

Schwebung [ˈʃveːbuŋ], *f.* (*Rad.*) beat, surge; ***–en bilden mit,*** beat with (*of oscillations*); ***um eine – hinaufgehen,*** rise a shade *or* fraction.

Schwede [ˈʃveːdə], *m.* Swede. **Schweden,** *n.* Sweden. **Schwedin,** *f.* *See* **Schwede. schwedisch,** *adj.* Swedish; (*coll.*) ***hinter –en Gardinen,*** behind bars, in clink.

Schwefel [ˈʃveːfəl], *m.* sulphur (*Am.* sulfur); brimstone; ***plastischer –,*** amorphous sulphur. **schwefelartig,** *adj.* sulphurous. **Schwefel|äther,** *m.* sulphuric ether. **–bad,** *n.* (*Chem.*) sulphur-bath; (*Med.*) sulphurous springs. **–bande,** *f.* (*coll.*) band of hooligans. **–blei,** *n.* sulphide of lead. **–blumen,** *f.pl.*, **–blüte,** *f.* flowers of sulphur. **–eisen,** *n.* ferrous sulphide. **–holz, –hölzchen,** *n.* (*obs.*) lucifer, match.

schwef(e)lig [ˈʃveːf(ə)lɪç], *adj.* sulphurous; ***–es Salz,*** sulphite; ***–e Säure,*** sulphur dioxide, sulphurous acid. **schwef(e)ligsauer,** *adj.* sulphurous, sulphide of.

Schwefel|kies, *m.* iron pyrites. **–kohlenstoff,** *m.* carbon disulphide. **–leber,** *f.* potassium sulphide. **–milch,** *f.* milk of sulphur. **schwefeln,** *v.t.* impregnate with sulphur, sulphurate; treat *or* fumigate with sulphur; vulcanize (*rubber*); ***geschwefelt,*** sulphuretted. **schwefelsauer,** *adj.* ***–es Salz,*** sulphate; ***–er Kalk,*** calcium sulphate. **Schwefel|säure,** *f.* sulphuric acid, oil of vitriol. **–wasserstoff,** *m.* sulphuretted hydrogen, hydrogen sulphide.

schweflig, *adj.* *See* **schwef(e)lig.**

Schweif [ʃvaɪf], *m.* **(–(e)s,** *pl.* **–e)** tail; train (*of a dress*); trail. **schweifen, 1.** *v.i.* (*aux.* s.) wander *or* roam about, rove, stray; (*aux.* h.) wander, ramble (*of thoughts etc.*). **2.** *v.t.* provide with a tail; curve, cut on the curve, scallop; rinse (out); ***schön geschweift,*** with a handsome tail; finely arched *or* curved.

Schweif|haar, *n.* tail-hair, horsehair. **–riemen,** *m.* crupper. **–säge,** *f.* bow-saw, fretsaw, compass-saw. **–stern,** *m.* comet. **Schweifung,** *f.* curve, bend, sweep, rounding, swell. **Schweifwedeln,** *n.* fawning, servility. **schweifwedeln,** *v.i.* (*coll.*) wag the tail; fawn (*vor* (*Dat.*) upon).

Schweige|geld, *n.* hush-money. **–kegel,** *m.* (*Rad. etc.*) cone of silence. **–marsch,** *m.* (silent) protest march.

schweigen [ˈʃvaɪɡən], *irr.v.i.* keep *or* be silent, keep silence, say nothing, hold one's tongue *or* peace, be quiet (*über* (*Acc.*), about); ***schweig(e)!*** be quiet! silence! ***auf eine Frage –,*** not answer a question; ***ganz zu – von,*** to say nothing of, not to speak of, let alone; ***– Sie mir davon,*** do not speak to me about it; ***zu etwas –,*** pass s.th. over in silence, make no reply to *or* offer no comment on a th. **Schweigen,** *n.* silence; ***zum – bringen,*** silence, reduce to silence; ***– gebieten,*** order *or* impose silence. **schweigend,** *adj.* silent; ***– zuhören,*** listen in silence; ***sich – verhalten,*** keep silent, hold one's peace; ***– darüber hinweggehen,*** pass over in silence.

Schweigepflicht [ˈʃvaɪɡəpflɪçt], *f.* professional discretion, pledge of secrecy. **Schweiger,** *m.* taciturn person, man of few words. **schweigsam,** *adj.* silent, taciturn; reserved, discreet. **Schweigsamkeit,** *f.* taciturnity, discretion.

Schwein [ʃvaɪn], *n.* **(–(e)s,** *pl.* **–e) 1.** hog, pig; swine; (*fig.*) filthy wretch; ***wildes –,*** wild boar; **2.** (*coll.*) good luck, stroke of luck; lucky chance, (*sl.*) fluke; (*coll.*) ***– haben,*** be in luck, fall on one's feet, strike it lucky, strike oil.

Schweine|braten, *m.* roast pork. **–fett,** *n.* lard. **–fleisch,** *n.* pork. **–hirt,** *m.* swineherd. **–hund,** *m.* (*coll.*) dirty dog, cur, skunk, son of a gun; ***der innere –,*** cowardice, faint-heartedness, funk. **–koben, –kofen,** *m.* *See* **–stall. –mast,** *f.* mast for swine. **–metzger,** *m.* *See* **–schlächter. –pest,** *f.* swine-fever. **–pökelfleisch,** *n.* salt-pork. **Schweinerei** [–ˈraɪ], *f.* filth(iness), obscenity, disgusting behaviour; smut, smutty *or* dirty joke; (*coll.*) dirty trick; (*coll.*) awful mess, shocking state. **Schweinerne(s),** *n.* (*dial.*) pork. **Schweine|schlächter,** *m.* pork-butcher. **–schmalz, –schmer,** *n.* lard. **–stall,** *m.* pigsty. **–treiber,** *m.* *See* **–hirt. –wirtschaft,** *f.* dirty mess, disgusting state of affairs. **–zucht,** *f.* pig-breeding.

Schwein|hund, *m.* *See* **Schweinehund. –igel,** *m.* (*fig.*) dirty pig *or* swine. **schweinigeln,** *v.i.* behave in a beastly way; talk smut. **schweinisch,** *adj.* piggish, swinish, filthy, beastly; smutty.

Schweins|blase, *f.* pig's bladder. **–borste,** *f.* hog's bristle. **–füße,** *m.pl.* (pig's) trotters. **–keule,** *f.* leg of pork. **–kopf,** *m.* hog's (*or* boar's) head. **–kotelett,** *n.* pork chop. **–leder,** *n.* pigskin, hogskin. **–rippchen,** *n.* *See* **–kotelett. –rücken,** *m.* loin of pork.

Schweiß [ʃvaɪs], *m.* **(–es,** *pl.* **–e)** sweat, perspiration; moisture, exudation, (*on windows*) steam; sebaceous secretion, (*of wool*) yolk, suint; (*Hunt.*) blood; (*fig.*) sweat of one's brow; (*Prov.*) ***ohne – kein Preis,*** no gains without pains; ***in – geraten,*** break out in perspiration; ***das ist mein saurer –,*** that is the fruit of my labours; (*of wool*) ***im –,*** in the greasy state.

Schweiß|apparat, *m.* welding equipment. **–arbeit,** *f.* welding. **–ausbruch,** *m.* profuse perspiration. **–band,** *n.* sweatband (*in hats*). **schweißbar,** *adj.* weldable. **Schweiß|blatt,** *n.* dress-shield *or* -preserver. **–brenner,** *m.* welding torch. **–drüse,** *f.* sweat-gland. **–eisen,** *n.* wrought iron.

schweißen [ˈʃvaɪsən], **1.** *v.i.* (*aux.* h. & s.) (*Hunt.*) bleed; leak, (*dial.*) sweat. **2.** *v.t.* weld. **Schweißen,** *n.* welding. **Schweißer,** *m.* welder. **Schweißerei** [–ˈraɪ], *f.* (–, *pl.* **–en**) welding shop.

Schweiß|fuchs, *m.* sorrel *or* dark chestnut horse. **–gang,** *m.* sweat *or* sebaceous duct. **schweißgebadet,** *adj.* bathed in perspiration, dripping with sweat. **Schweiß|geruch,** *m.* body-odour. **–hund,** *m.* bloodhound. **schweißig,** *adj.* perspiring, sweaty. **Schweiß|leder,** *n.* *See* **–band. –mittel,** *n.* (*Med.*) sudorific, (*Mech.*) welding flux. **–naht,** *f.* welded joint *or* seam. **–perle,** *f.* bead of perspiration, drop of sweat. **–stahl,** *m.* weld steel. **–stelle,** *f.* weld. **schweiß|treibend,** *adj.* sudorific, diaphoretic. **–triefend,** *adj.* *See* **–gebadet. Schweiß|tropfen,** *m.* *See* **–perle. –tuch,** *n.* sweat-rag; ***das – Christi,*** sudarium. **–tüchlein,** *n.* (*B.*) kerchief, napkin. **Schweißung,** *f.* welding; weld. **Schweißwolle,** *f.* untreated *or* unscoured wool.

Schweiz [ʃvaɪts], *f.* ***die –,*** Switzerland. **Schweizer,** *m.*, *inv. adj.* Swiss. **Schweizerdeutsch,** *n.*, **schweizerdeutsch,** *adj.* Swiss German (language). **Schweizerei,** *f.* dairy. **Schweizerin,** *f.*, **schweizerisch,** *adj.* *See* **Schweizer.**

schwelen [ˈʃveːlən], **1.** *v.i.* smoulder. **2.** *v.t.* burn slowly, carbonize at low temperature; ***Teer –,*** extract *or* distil tar.

schwelgen [ˈʃvɛlɡən], *v.i.* feast, carouse; lead a life of luxury, (*coll.*) live on the fat of the land; indulge, luxuriate, revel, (*coll.*) wallow (*in* (*Dat.*), in). **Schwelger,** *m.* sybarite, reveller, epicure, glutton. **Schwelgerei** [–ˈraɪ], *f.* revelry, gluttony, feasting, debauchery. **schwelgerisch,** *adj.* luxurious, voluptuous, debauched; gluttonous.

Schwelkoks [ˈʃve:lko:ks], *m.* low-temperature coke.

Schwelle [ˈʃvɛlə], *f.* threshold, doorstep, sill; (*Railw.*) sleeper, tie; crossbar, ledge, architrave, joist; (*fig.*) brink.

schwellen [ˈʃvɛlən], **1.** *irr.v.i.* (*aux.* s.) swell, rise, increase, expand, grow (fat), grow bigger, (*Mus.*) swell. **2.** *reg.v.t.* swell, inflate, distend, fill.

Schwellenwert [ˈʃvɛlənve:rt], *m.* threshold value.

Schweller [ˈʃvɛlər], *m.* (*Mus.*) swell. **Schwell|gewebe,** *n.* erectile tissue. **–körper,** *m.* erectile organ. **–ton,** *m.* crescendo. **Schwellung,** *f.* swelling, growth, tumour; tumefaction, tumescence. **Schwellwerk,** *n.* (*Mus.*) *see* **Schweller.**

Schwel|ofen, *m.* low-temperature carbonizing furnace; distilling oven (*for tar*). **–teer,** *m.* low-temperature tar. **Schwelung,** *f.* low-temperature carbonization. **Schwelwasser,** *n.* water of distillation.

Schwemme [ˈʃvɛmə], *f.* **1.** horse-pond, watering-place (*for cattle*); ***ein Pferd in die – reiten,*** ride a horse to water; ***Vieh in die – treiben,*** water cattle; 2. tavern, taproom; 3. (*fig.*) glut (***an*** (*Dat.*), of). **schwemmen,** *v.t.* float (*timber*), soak (*hides*), wash *or* sluice down, flush; water (*cattle etc.*). **Schwemm|land,** *n.* alluvial land. **–system,** *n.* flushing-system. **–wiese,** *f.* irrigation-meadow.

Schwengel [ˈʃvɛŋəl], *m.* 1. clapper (*of a bell*), handle (*of a pump*), swingle (*of a flail*), swingletree, swing-bar (*of a wagon*; 2. (*coll.*) lout.

Schwenk [ˈʃvɛŋk], *m.* **(-(e)s,** *pl.* **-e)** (*Films*) pan-shot. **Schwenk|achse,** *f.* axis of swivel. **–arm,** *m.* swivel-arm. **schwenkbar,** *adj.* swivel-mounted, swivelling, revolving, rotatable, slewing, traversable. **Schwenkbereich,** *m.* (*Artil.*) field of traverse.

schwenken [ˈʃvɛŋkən], **1.** *v.t.* swing, pivot, slew round, swivel; (*Artil.*) traverse, (*Films*) pan; shake about, wave to and fro, flourish, brandish, (*Cul.*) toss; rinse (out) (*a glass etc.*). **2.** *v.r., v.i.* turn *or* swivel (round), (*Artil.*) traverse; (*Mil.*) wheel; (*fig.*) change one's mind, change sides; ***links schwenkt, marsch!*** left wheel, quick march!

Schwenker [ˈʃvɛŋker], *m.* (*dial.*) tail-coat.

Schwenk|kran, *m.* slewing crane. **–lafette,** *f.* swivelled gun-mounting. **–rad,** *n.* swivel wheel.

Schwenkung [ˈʃvɛŋkuŋ], *f.* turning movement, swivelling, slewing, (*Mil.*) wheeling, (*Artil.*) traversing; (*fig.*) change of mind; change of front, (*coll.*) about-face. **Schwenkungs|punkt,** *m.* pivot. **–winkel,** *m.* angle of traverse.

schwer [ʃve:r], **1.** *adj.* heavy, weighty, ponderous; clumsy, heavy-handed; difficult, hard, (*coll.*) tough; onerous, burdensome, arduous, severe, oppressive; grave, bad, serious, grievous; strong (*of wine, cigars*); heavy, rich, indigestible, (*coll.*) stodgy (*of food*); ***–er Angriff,*** heavy attack; ***–e Angst,*** great anxiety; ***–e Arbeit,*** difficult (piece of) work; ***–e Artillerie,*** medium artillery; ***–ste Artillerie,*** heavy artillery; ***–er Atem,*** shortness of breath; ***– von Begriff,*** slow *or* dull of comprehension, (*coll.*) slow on the uptake; ***–er Boden,*** heavy *or* rich soil; ***–e Entscheidung,*** difficult decision; ***ein –es Geld kosten,*** cost a lot of money; ***–es Geld verdienen,*** earn big money; ***–es Geschütz,*** heavy guns; ***–es Gewitter,*** violent storm; ***–en Herzens,*** reluctantly, with a heavy heart; ***–er Irrtum,*** gross error; (*coll.*) ***–er Junge,*** tough customer, hard case; ***–er Kampf,*** hard fight; ***–es Leben,*** hard life; (*coll.*) ***–e Menge,*** an awful lot; ***–e Pflicht,*** onerous duty; ***–es Schicksal,*** hard lot; ***–e See,*** heavy *or* rough sea; ***–e Strafe,*** severe punishment, heavy fine; ***–e Stunde,*** hour of trial; (*Naut.*) ***–er Sturm,*** whole gale; ***–e Verantwortung,*** grave responsibility; ***–es Verbrechen,*** serious crime; ***–er Wein,*** full-bodied wine; ***–e Wunde,*** grave *or* serious wound; ***–e Zeit,*** hard times; ***–e Zunge,*** sluggish tongue. **2.** *adv.* heavily *etc.*; very (much), (*coll.*) badly, awfully; ***– arbeiten,*** work hard; ***– beleidigen,*** deeply offend; ***– betrunken,*** helplessly drunk; ***– büßen,*** pay dearly for; ***– eingehen,*** be understood only with difficulty (*Dat.*, by); ***– enttäuscht,*** bitterly disappointed; ***– hören,*** be hard of hearing; ***sich – hüten,*** take good care (***zu tun,*** not to do; ***daß,*** lest); (*coll.*) ***– reich sein,*** be rolling in wealth, be made of money; ***sich – täuschen,*** be very much mistaken; ***– verwundet,*** seriously *or* dangerously wounded.

Schwer|arbeiter, *m.* manual labourer, navvy. **–athletik,** *f.* strenuous athletics (*boxing, wrestling*). **schwer|atmig,** *adj.* asthmatic. **–beschädigt,** *adj.* badly damaged (*of a th.*), seriously disabled (*of a p.*). **–bewaffnet,** *adj.* heavily armed. **–blütig,** *adj.* phlegmatic.

Schwere [ˈʃve:rə], *f.* heaviness, weight, (*Phys.*) gravity; (*fig.*) seriousness, gravity, severity, difficulty, rigour; body (*of wine*); full weight, import (*of a word*). **schwerelos,** *adj.* weightless; ethereal. **Schwerelosigkeit,** *f.* weightlessness. **Schwere|–not,** *f.* ***es ist um die – zu kriegen,*** it's enough to sicken one; (*vulg.*) ***– noch einmal!*** damn your eyes! **–nöter,** *m.* lady-killer, ladies' man.

Schwerverbrecher [ˈʃve:rfɛrbrɛçər], *m.* felon, criminal, gangster.

schwer|errungen, –erworben, *adj.* hard-earned, hard-won. **–erziehbar,** *adj.* recalcitrant; ***–es Kind,*** problem child. **–fallen,** *irr.v.i.* (*Dat.*) be difficult (for) *or* a burden (to *or* on). **–fällig,** *adj.* heavy, ponderous, cumbersome, unwieldy; (*of a p.*) dull, slow, sluggish; clumsy, awkward. **Schwerfälligkeit,** *f.* heaviness, clumsiness, awkwardness, slowness, dullness. **schwerflüssig,** *adj.* (*of solids*) difficult to fuse, refractory, (*of liquids*) viscous, viscid. **Schwer|gewicht,** *n.* 1. (*Boxing*) heavyweight (class); 2. (*fig.*) main stress, emphasis. **–gewichtler,** *m.* heavyweight (*boxer*) (*over 80 kg.*).

schwer|halten, *irr.v.i.* be a hard task; ***es wird –, daß ich komme,*** it will be difficult for me to come. **–hörig,** *adj.* hard of hearing, rather deaf. **Schwer|–hörigkeit,** *f.* defective hearing, deafness. **–industrie,** *f.* heavy industry, mining and iron and steel industries. **–kraft,** *f.* gravitation, (force of) gravity. **–kraftsbeschleunigung,** *f.* acceleration of a falling body. **–kriegsbeschädigte(r),** *m.* disabled soldier *or* ex-serviceman.

schwerlich [ˈʃve:rlɪç], *adv.* hardly, scarcely, with difficulty. **Schwermut,** *f.* melancholy, sadness, depression. **schwer|mütig,** *adj.* dejected, depressed, sad, melancholy, mournful. **–nehmen,** *irr.v.t.* take to heart, be upset by. **Schwer|–ölmotor,** *m.* diesel engine. **–punkt,** *m.* centre of gravity; (*Mil.*) point of main effort; (*fig.*) stress, emphasis, focal *or* crucial point. **–punktbildung,** *f.* (*Mil.*) concentration of forces. **–spat,** *m.* heavy spar, barytes.

Schwert [ʃve:rt], *n.* **(-(e)s,** *pl.* **-er)** 1. sword; ***zum –e greifen,*** draw one's sword; 2. (*Naut.*) centre-board, lee-board, drop-keel; 3. (*fig.*) force of arms, military force.

Schwert|adel, *m.* military nobility. **–boot,** *n.* centre-board boat. **Schwertel,** *m.* (*Bot.*) sword-lily, gladiolus. **Schwertertanz,** *m.* sword-dance. **Schwertfisch,** *m.* (*Ichth.*) swordfish (*Xiphias gladius*). **schwertförmig,** *adj.* sword-shaped, ensiform. **Schwert|leite,** *f.* (*Hist.*) inauguration into knighthood. **–lilie,** *f.* (*Bot.*) iris. **–schwanz,** *m.* king- *or* horseshoe-crab. **–streich,** *m.* ***ohne –,*** without striking a blow, without bloodshed. **–tanz,** *m.* *See* **Schwertertanz.**

schwer|verdaulich *adj.* indigestible, (*coll.*) heavy, stodgy. **–verdient,** *adj.* hard-earned. **–verletzt,** *adj.* seriously injured. disabled **Schwerverletzte(r),** *m., f.* stretcher case. **schwer|verständlich,** *adj.* difficult (to understand), abstruse, (*coll.*) hard to grasp. **–verwundet,** *adj.* seriously *or* (*coll.*) badly wounded. **Schwerverwundete(r),** *m., f.* (*Mil.*) major casualty. **schwerwiegend,** *adj.* (*fig.*) weighty, grave, serious, important, momentous.

Schwester [ˈʃvɛstər], *f.* **(-,** *pl.* **-n)** 1. sister; ***leibliche –,*** full sister; 2. (hospital) nurse; 3. nun; ***barmherzige –,*** sister of mercy. **Schwester|art,** *f.* (*Biol.*) sister-species. **–kind,** *n.* sister's child. **schwesterlich,** *adj.* sisterly; sororal. **Schwester|liebe,** *f.* sisterly love. **–(n)paar,** *n.* two sisters. **–(n)schaft,** *f.* sisterhood. **–ntracht,** *f.* nurse's uniform.

Schwibbogen [ˈʃvɪpbo:gən], *m.* flying-buttress.

schwichten ['ʃvɪçtən], *v.t.* (*Naut.*) rope together.
schwieg [ʃvi:k], **schwiege** ['ʃvi:gə], *see* **schweigen.**
Schwieger ['ʃvi:gər], *f.* (-, *pl.* **-n**) (*obs., Poet.*) mother-in-law. **Schwieger|eltern,** *pl.* parents-in-law. **–mutter,** *f.* mother-in-law. **–sohn,** *m.* son-in-law. **–tochter,** *f.* daughter-in-law. **–vater,** *m.* father-in-law.
Schwiele ['ʃvi:lə], *f.* callosity, callus; weal, welt. **schwielig,** *adj.* callous, horny; marked with weals.
Schwiemel ['ʃvi:məl], *m.* (*dial.*) giddiness, fainting fit. **Schwiemelei** [–'laɪ], *f.* dissolute behaviour. **schwiem(e)lig,** *adj.* dizzy, giddy, (*fig.*) dissolute. **schwiemeln,** *v.i.* (*aux.* h. *&* s.) (*coll., dial.*) reel, get dizzy *or* giddy, (*fig.*) lead a dissolute life.
schwierig ['ʃvi:rɪç], *adj.* difficult, hard, (*coll.*) tough; onerous, arduous, irksome, troublesome, awkward, (*coll.*) tricky; intricate, complicated, delicate, (*coll.*) ticklish; precarious, critical, (*coll.*) trying; (*of a p.*) exacting, fastidious, particular, fractious, rebellious, (*coll.*) difficult; ***–e Frage,*** puzzling *or* vexed question; ***–e Lage*** or ***Verhältnisse,*** trying circumstances, awkward *or* critical position, predicament, dilemma; ***–e Sache,*** knotty *or* thorny point; ***das –ste haben wir hinter uns,*** the worst is over. **Schwierigkeit,** *f.* difficulty, awkwardness, irksomeness; intricacy, delicacy; crux (of the problem), critical situation, crisis; obstacle, stumbling-block, (*coll.*) snag, hitch; predicament, dilemma, (*coll.*) fix; ***–en machen,*** raise *or* present difficulties; raise objections; ***ihm –en machen,*** put obstacles in his way, give *or* cause him trouble; ***auf –en stoßen,*** meet with *or* encounter difficulties, (*coll.*) come up against a snag; ***in –en geraten,*** get into trouble *or* (*coll.*) hot water; ***nicht ohne –en,*** not without some difficulty.
schwiert [ʃvi:rt], *see* **schwären.**
schwill ['ʃvɪl], **schwillst, schwillt,** *see* **schwellen.**
Schwimm|anstalt ['ʃvɪm–], *f.* swimming-pool *or* baths. **–art,** *f.* style of swimming. **–bad,** *n. See* **–anstalt. –bewegung,** *f.* (*Biol.*) ciliary movement. **–blase,** *f.* 1. water-wings; 2. (*Ichth.*) air-bladder, sound. **–dock,** *n.* floating dock.
schwimmen ['ʃvimən], *irr.v.i.* (*aux.* h. *&* s.) swim; float; (*fig.*) flounder, be at sea; ***– in*** (*Dat.*), be bathed in *or* flooded with, overflow with; ***im Gelde –,*** be rolling in money; ***im Glück –,*** be in clover, be in ecstasies, be in the seventh heaven, ride on air; ***im Blute (in Tränen) –,*** be bathed in blood (in tears); ***mit dem Strom –,*** go *or* swim with the stream; ***der Schauspieler schwimmt,*** the actor relies on the prompter. **Schwimmen,** *n.* swimming. **schwimmend,** *adj.* floating, swimming; ***–es Strandgut,*** flotsam; ***–er Tank,*** amphibian tank; ***–e Waren,*** goods afloat *or* carried by water, goods in transit. **Schwimmer,** *m.* 1. swimmer; 2. (*Mech., Av., Motor., fishing*) float. **Schwimmergestell,** *n.* (*Av.*) float undercarriage *or* landing-gear.
schwimmfähig ['ʃvɪmfɛ:ɪç], *adj.* buoyant. **Schwimm|fähigkeit,** *f.* buoyancy. **–fest,** *n.* swimming-gala. **–flosse,** *f.* fin. **–fuß,** *m.* webbed *or* palmated foot. **–füßer,** *m.* palmiped. **–gürtel,** *m.* life-belt, water-wings. **–haut,** *f.* web, membrane. **–hose,** *f.* bathing-trunks. **–kampfwagen,** *m.* amphibian tank. **–kasten,** *m.* caisson. **–körper,** *m.* float. **–kraft,** *f.* buoyancy. **–lehrer,** *m.* swimming-instructor. **–sport,** *m.* swimming. **–stoß,** *m.* stroke. **–vogel,** *m.* web-footed bird, palmiped. **–werk,** *n.* (*Av.*) float landing-gear. **–weste,** *f.* life-jacket, buoyancy-aid.
Schwindel ['ʃvɪndəl], *m.* 1. giddiness, dizziness, vertigo, (*Vet.*) staggers; 2. (*fig.*) swindle, fraud, trick(ery), (*coll.*) humbug, skulduggery, (*sl.*) eyewash; (*coll.*) ***den – kenn' ich,*** I know that trick, I am up to that dodge; (*coll.*) ***der ganze –,*** the whole bag of tricks *or* (*sl.*) shemozzle. **Schwindelanfall,** *m.* attack of giddiness. **Schwindelei** [–'laɪ], *f. See* **Schwindel,** 2. **schwindelfrei.** *adj.* free from giddiness. **Schwindel|gefühl,** *n.* vertigo. **–gesellschaft,** *f.* bogus *or* (*Am.*) wildcat company. **schwindelhaft,** *adj.* fraudulent, swindling, bogus; *see also* **schwind(e)lig. schwind(e)lig,** *adj.* giddy, dizzy; (*fig.*) staggering (*as prices etc.*). **Schwindelkopf,** *m.* hare-brained *or* giddy person, harum-scarum. **schwindelköpfig,** *adj.* hare-brained.
schwindeln ['ʃvɪndəln], **1.** *v.i.* tell a (white) lie *or* (*coll.*) a fib, tell lies *or* (*coll.*) fibs; swindle, cheat. **2.** *v.imp.* (*Dat.*) be *or* feel giddy *or* dizzy; ***mir schwindelt,*** my head swims, my brain is reeling; I feel *or* am giddy; ***–de Höhe,*** dizzy height.
Schwindel|preis, *m.* fraudulent *or* scandalous price. **–unternehmen,** *n. See* **–gesellschaft.**
schwinden ['ʃvɪndən], *irr.v.i.* (*aux.* s.) become less, decline, shrink, contract, dwindle, (*coll.*) fall off, go down; wane, ebb; wither, wilt, decay, waste away; disappear, vanish, fade (away), die away; ***die Geschwulst schwindet,*** the swelling is going down; ***ihm schwindet der Mut,*** his courage is dwindling, he is losing courage, his heart sinks. **Schwinden,** *n.* shrinking, shrinkage, contraction; wastage, atrophy; disappearance, dwindling.
Schwindler ['ʃvɪndlər], *m.*, **Schwindlerin,** *f.* swindler, cheat, humbug, fraud, liar, imposter, confidence-trickster, (*sl.*) crook, shark. **schwindlerisch,** *adj.* fraudulent, bogus. **schwindlig,** *adj. See* **schwind(e)lig.**
Schwind|maß, *n.* (amount of) shrinkage. **–maßstab,** *m.* scale, reduction factor (*for models*). **–risse,** *m.pl.* shrinkage cracks. **–sucht,** *f.* consumption, phthisis. **schwindsüchtig,** *adj.* consumptive. **Schwindsüchtige(r),** *m., f.* consumptive.
Schwing|achse ['ʃvɪŋ–], *f.* (*Motor.*) independent axle. **–brett,** *n.* swingle (*for flax*).
Schwinge ['ʃvɪŋə], *f.* 1. wing (*of bird*), (*Poet.*) pinion; 2. swingle (*for flax*); winnow, fan (*for corn*); 3. (*Mech.*) rocker arm.
Schwingel(gras) ['ʃvɪŋəl(gra:s)], *m.* (*n.*) (*Bot.*) fescue(-grass) (*Festuca pratensis*).
schwingen ['ʃvɪŋən], **1.** *irr.v.t.* swing, flourish, brandish, wield, wave; (*Swiss*) wrestle; swingle, winnow, scutch (*grain*); hydro-extract, centrifuge; (*coll.*) ***das Tanzbein –,*** foot it, do the light fantastic; (*coll.*) ***eine Rede –,*** make a speech, hold forth; (*coll.*) ***sie schwingt den Pantoffel,*** she wears the trousers; (*Swiss*) ***den Nidel –,*** whip cream. **2.** *irr.v.r.* swing o.s., spring, bound, vault, leap; soar, rise, ascend; ***sich in den Sattel –,*** vault *or* jump into the saddle; ***sich auf den Thron –,*** usurp the throne. **3.** *irr.v.i.* swing, sway, oscillate, vibrate; ***geschwungen,*** sweeping, curved, bowed, arched. **Schwinger,** *m.* 1. (*Boxing*) swing, swinging blow; 2. (*Swiss*) wrestler. **Schwing|fest,** *n.* (*Swiss*) wrestling competition. **–gerät,** *n.* (*Gymn.*) trapeze, swing. **–kolben,** *m.* (*Ent.*) balancer, poiser. **–maschine,** *f. See* **–brett. –messer,** *n.pl.* scutching blades. **–seil,** *n.* slack rope, swing. **–spule,** *f.* (*Elec.*) moving-coil. **–stock,** *m.* flail, swingle.
Schwingung ['ʃvɪŋuŋ], *f.* swinging; oscillation, wave, vibration; (*Rad. etc.*) cycle (of oscillation); ***in – versetzen,*** cause to vibrate, set oscillating. **Schwingungs|achse,** *f.* axis of oscillation, nodal line. **–dämpfung,** *f.* attenuation. **–dauer,** *f.* period of oscillation, cycle. **–knoten,** *m.* node. **–kreis,** *m.* (*Rad.*) oscillator circuit. **–weite,** *f.* amplitude. **–welle,** *f.* undulation, travelling wave. **–zahl,** *f.* frequency (of oscillations). **–zeit,** *f. See* **–dauer.**
schwipp! [ʃvɪp], **1.** *int.* crack! (*as a whip*), splash! **2.** *adj.* (*dial.*) nimble, agile; pliant, flexible. **Schwippe,** *f.* (*dial.*) whip-lash, switch. **schwippen** (*dial.*), **1.** *v.t.* jerk, throw, fling; lash, (*coll.*) swipe. **2.** *v.i.* (*aux.* h. *&* s.) overflow, spill (over). **Schwipp|schwager,** *m.* (**–schwägerin,** *f.*) (*coll.*) brother- (sister-)in-law of one's wife *or* husband; father (mother) of one's son- *or* daughter-in-law.
schwips! [ʃvɪps], *int.* smack! slap! **Schwips,** *m.* (**-es,** *pl.* **-e**) cut, lash, flip (*with a whip etc.*); (*sl.*) ***einen – haben,*** be tight *or* tipsy *or* fuddled.
Schwirl [ʃvɪrl], *m.* (**-(e)s,** *pl.* **-e**) (*Orn.*) warbler (*Locustella*).
schwirren ['ʃvɪrən], *v.i.* (*aux.* h. *&* s.), *imp.* whiz(z), whir; buzz, hum (*as insects*), fly (about) (*of rum-*

ours); (*coll.*) buzz off; ***es schwirrt mir in den Ohren*** (***vor den Augen***), I have a buzzing in my ears (a mist before my eyes). **Schwirren,** *n.* whizzing, whir(ring), buzz(ing).

Schwitzbad ['ʃvɪtsba:d], *n.* Turkish *or* steam bath.

Schwitze ['ʃvɪtsə], *f.* thickening (*for soups etc.*); ***in die – bringen,*** sweat (*hides*). **schwitzen, 1.** *v.i.* sweat, perspire. **2.** *v.t.* (cause to) sweat (*hides*); (*fig.*) ***Blut –,*** sweat blood. **Schwitzen,** *n.* sweating, perspiration. **Schwitz|kasten,** *m.* 1. sweating-box; 2. (*Wrestling*) headlock. **–mittel,** *n.* sudorific, diaphoretic. **–wasser,** *n.* condensation.

Schwof ['ʃvo:f], *m.* **(-(e)s,** *pl.* **-e)** (*coll.*) (public) dance, (*sl.*) hop. **schwofen,** *v.i.* go dancing *or* to a dance.

schwoien ['ʃvɔyən], *v.i., v.t.* (*Naut.*) *see* **schwaien.**

schwoll [ʃvɔl], **schwölle** ['ʃvœlə], *see* **schwellen.**

schwor [ʃvo:r], **schwöre** ['ʃvø:rə], *see* **schwären** *or* **schwören.**

schwören ['ʃvø:rən], *irr.v.t., v.i.* swear (on oath); take an oath; (*B.*) swear, curse; ***auf ihn –,*** have absolute confidence in him, (*coll.*) swear by him; ***ich könnte fast darauf –,*** I could almost swear to it; ***bei meiner Ehre –,*** swear on my honour; ***bei Gott –,*** swear to God; (*Hist.*) ***Huld und Treue –,*** take the oath of allegiance; ***ihm Rache –,*** vow vengeance against him; ***vor Gericht –,*** take the oath; ***zur Fahne –,*** take the military oath.

schwude! ['ʃvu:də], *int.* (*dial.*) (to the) left!

schwul ['ʃvu:l], *adj.* (*vulg.*) homosexual, (*coll.*) gay, kinky.

schwül [ʃvy:l], *adj.* sultry, close, oppressive, stifling, (*coll.*) muggy; (*fig.*) ***mir ist – zu Mute, mir wird's – ums Herz,*** I feel very uneasy *or* ill at ease. **Schwüle,** *f.* sultriness, closeness.

Schwule(r) ['ʃvu:lə(r)], *m., f.* homosexual, (*coll.*) homo, queer.

Schwulität [ʃvuli'tɛ:t], *f.* (*sl.*) trouble, scrape, fix, hot water.

Schwulst [ʃvulst], *m.* **(-es,** *pl.* **⸚e)** *or f.* (-, *pl.* **⸚e)** swelling, tumour; (*usu. fig.*) pomposity, bombast, turgidity. **schwulstig,** *adj.* swollen, puffed up (*not fig.*).

schwülstig ['ʃvylstɪç], *adj.* (*fig.*) bombastic, high-flown, pompous, inflated, turgid. **Schwülstigkeit,** *f.* bombastic style, pomposity, grandiloquence.

schwummerig ['ʃvumərɪç], *adj.* (*coll.*) *see* **schwind(e)lig.**

Schwund ['ʃvunt], *m.* withering, contraction, shrinkage, (*Med.*) atrophy; disappearance, dwindling, (*coll.*) falling off; loss (*of hair etc.*), dropping (*of a vowel etc.*); (*Rad. etc.*) fading. **Schwund|ausgleich,** *m.,* **–regelung,** *f.* (*Rad.*) automatic volume-control. **–stufe,** *f.* (*Philol.*) null-grade. **–zone,** *f.* (*Rad.*) area of no reception.

Schwung [ʃvuŋ], *m.* **(-(e)s,** *pl.* **⸚e)** swing, bound, spring, vault; soaring, flight, play (*of imagination etc.*); stream (*of traffic*); energy, speed, impetus, momentum, headway; (*fig.*) vitality, verve, vivacity, life, animation, warmth, ardour; (*coll.*) drive, punch, go, dash, (*sl.*) vim, pep; ***ihn auf – bringen,*** goad him into activity; ***keinen – haben,*** fall flat; ***in – bringen,*** set going; ***in – kommen,*** get going, get into one's stride; ***in – sein,*** be on *or* in form; ***im – sein,*** be in full swing.

Schwung|feder, *f.* pinion (*of birds*). **–flachs,** *m.* scutched flax. **–gewicht,** *n.* pendulum. **schwunghaft,** *adj.* *See* **schwungvoll;** (*Comm.*) lively, flourishing, brisk, roaring (*trade*). **Schwungkraft,** *f.* centrifugal force; momentum; (*fig.*) *see* **Schwung** (*fig.*). **schwunglos,** *adj.* dull, commonplace, unimaginative. **Schwung|rad,** *n.* (*Mech.*) flywheel, (*of clock*) balance-wheel. **–riemen,** *m.pl.* main-braces, check-braces (*of a carriage*). **–seil,** *n.* slack rope. **schwungvoll,** *adj.* lofty, stirring, full of fire *or* enthusiasm *or* (*coll.*) go, enterprising, spirited, animated, energetic, sparkling, (*coll.*) bold, racy, (*sl.*) snappy.

schwupp [ʃvup], *adv., int.* presto, like a shot, no sooner said than done. **Schwupp,** *m.* **(-es,** *pl.* **-e)** push, shove, jolt, splash. **schwuppdiwupp!** *int.* *See* **schwupp. schwups!** *int.,* **Schwups,** *m.* *See* **schwupp, Schwupp.**

schwur ['ʃvu:r], *see* **schwören.**

Schwur, *m.* **(-s,** *pl.* **⸚e)** oath, vow; ***einen – leisten*** or ***tun,*** make a vow, take an oath. **Schwur|finger,** *m.pl.* fingers raised in swearing. **–formel,** *f.* wording of an oath. **–gericht,** *n.* assize court. **–gerichtsverfahren,** *n.* trial by jury.

Sech [zɛç], *n.* **(-(e)s,** *pl.* **-e)** ploughshare, coulter.

sechs [zɛks], *num.adj.* six; ***mit –en fahren,*** drive a coach and six, drive six in hand; ***viertel –,*** a quarter past five; ***halb –,*** half-past five; ***drei Viertel –,*** (***ein***) ***Viertel vor*** or ***auf –,*** a quarter to six; (*sl.*) ***meiner –!*** *see* **Six. Sechs,** *f.* (-, *pl.* **-en)** number 6.

Sechsachteltakt ['zɛksˀaxtəltakt], *m.* (*Mus.*) six-eight time. **sechsblätt(e)rig,** *adj.* hexaphyllous; hexapetalous. **sechse,** (*coll.*) *see* **sechs** (*only used when not followed by anything*); ***wir –,*** we six, the six of us. **Sechseck,** *n.* hexagon. **sechseckig,** *adj.* hexagonal. **sechs|einhalb,** *see* **–(und)einhalb. Sechsender,** *m.* stag with 6 points.

Sechser ['zɛksər], *m.* number 6; soldier of the 6th regiment; coin (*denomination varies according to locality: 5, 10 or 20 Pfennig*); ***nicht Verstand für einen – haben,*** not have a ha'porth of sense. **sechserlei,** *indecl.adj.* of 6 kinds, 6 kinds of.

sechs|fach, *adj.* six-fold, sextuple; ***das Sechsfache,*** 6 times the amount. **–fältig,** *adj.* *See* **–fach. Sechs|flach,** *n.,* **–flächner,** *m.* hexahedron. **sechs|gliedrig,** *adj.* of 6 digits. **–hebig,** *adj.* containing 6 accented syllables (*a verse*). **–hundert,** *num.adj.* six hundred. **–jährig,** *adj.* 6 years old, sexennial. **Sechs|kant,** *n.* hexagon. **–kanteisen,** *n.* hexagonal-section bar. **sechs|mal,** *adv.* 6 times over. **–malig,** *adj.* 6 times repeated. **–monatig,** *adj.* six-month, lasting 6 months. **–monatlich, 1.** *adj.* six-monthly, half-yearly, bi-annual. **2.** *adv.* every 6 months. **–motorig,** *adj.* six-engined. **Sechspolröhre,** *f.* (*Rad.*) hexode. **sechs|schüssig,** *adj.* ***–er Revolver,*** six-shooter. **–seitig,** *adj.* hexagonal. **–silbig,** *adj.* of 6 syllables. **–spännig,** *adj.* six-horse, with 6 horses. **–stellig,** *adj.* *See* **–gliedrig. Sechsstern,** *m.* hexagram, six-pointed star. **sechs|stimmig,** *adj.* (*Mus.*) for 6 voices. **–stündig,** *adj.* six-hour, lasting 6 hours.

sechst [zɛkst], *adj.* sixth; ***am –n,*** on the 6th (of the month); ***zum –n,*** *see* **sechstens.**

sechs|tägig, *adj.* of *or* lasting 6 days. **–tausend,** *num.adj.* six thousand.

sechst(e)halb ['zɛkst(ə)halp], *num.adj.* five and a half. **Sechstel,** *n.* (*Swiss m.*) one-sixth, sixth part. **sechstens,** *adv.* sixthly, in the sixth place.

sechs|(und)einhalb, *num.adj.* six-and-a-half. **–undsechzig,** *num.adj.* sixty-six. **Sechsundsechzig,** *n.* (a kind of) German card game. **sechswöchentlich, 1.** *adj.* six-weekly. **2.** *adv.* every sixth week, every six weeks. **Sechszylindermotor,** *m.* six-cylinder engine.

sechzehn ['zɛçtse:n], *num.adj.* sixteen. **Sechzehn,** *f.* the number sixteen. **sechzehn|jährig,** *adj.* 16 year old. **–lötig,** *adj.* weighing 8 ounces; (*fig.*) pure (*silver*). **–zehnt,** *num.adj.* sixteenth.

Sechzehntel [zɛçtse:ntəl], *n.* sixteenth part; *see* **Sechzehntelnote. Sechzehntel|format,** *n.* *See* **Sedez. –note,** *f.* (*Mus.*) semiquaver. **–pause,** *f.* (*Mus.*) semiquaver rest.

sechzig ['zɛçtsɪç], *num.adj.* sixty. **Sechzig,** *f.* (-, *pl.* **-e)** the number sixty. **Sechziger,** *m.* 1. sexagenarian; 2. (*Cards*) pique. **sechziger,** *indecl.adj.* ***die – Jahre,*** the sixties; ***er ist hoch in den Sechzigern,*** he is well into his sixties. **Sechzigerin,** *f.* *See* **Sechziger,** 1. **sechzigst,** *num. adj.* sixtieth. **Sechzigstel,** *n.* sixtieth (part).

Sedez [ze'de:ts], *n.* **(-es,** *pl.* **-e), Sedezformat,** *n.* (*Typ.*) sixteens, sextodecimo, 16mo.

Sediment [zedi'mɛnt], *n.* **(-s,** *pl.* **-e)** sediment, deposit, settlings. **sedimentär** [–'tɛ:r], *adj.* sedimentary. **Sedimentgestein,** *n.* sedimentary rock.

[1]**See** [ze:], *m.* **(-s,** *pl.* **-n)** lake, pond, pool.

[2]**See,** *f.* (-, *pl.* **-n)** sea; ocean; ***an der –,*** by the sea-

(side); ***an die – gehen,*** go to the seaside; ***auf (der) –,*** at sea; ***auf hoher –,*** on the high seas, out at sea; ***die – ging hoch,*** the sea ran high; ***in – gehen*** or ***stechen,*** put (out) to sea, set sail; ***zur –,*** by sea; ***zur – gehen,*** go to sea, become a sailor; ***Kapitän zur –,*** naval captain.

See|adler, *m.* (*Orn.*) white-tailed (*Am.* gray sea) eagle (*Haliaetus albicilla*). **–alpen,** *m.pl.* maritime Alps. **–amt,** *n.* maritime court, (German) Admiralty Court. **–bad,** *n.* seaside resort. **–bär,** *m.* (*coll.*) old salt, old seadog. **–beben,** *n.* submarine earthquake. **–beute,** *f.* (*Naut.*) prize (ship). **–brief,** *m.* sea-letter, ship's passport. **–dienst,** *m.* service afloat. **seefähig,** *adj.* seaworthy, sea-going.

seefahrend ['ze:fa:rənt], *adj.* seafaring, maritime. **Seefahrer,** *m.* mariner, sailor; seafarer. **Seefahrt,** *f.* seafaring, navigation (at sea); sea voyage *or* passage, cruise. **Seefahrt|buch,** *n.* seaman's registration book. **–schule,** *f.* merchant marine school.

seefest ['ze:fest], *adj.* seaworthy; (*coll.*) not subject to seasickness; ***– werden,*** get *or* find one's sea-legs; (***nicht***) ***– sein,*** be a good (*or* bad) sailor.

See|festung, *f.* fortified naval base. **–fisch,** *m.* salt-water fish. **–fischerei,** *f.* deep-sea fishing. **–flieger,** *m.* naval airman. **–fliegerhorst,** *m.*, **–flugstation,** *f.* seaplane base. **–flugzeug,** *n.* seaplane. **–frachtbrief,** *m.* bill of lading. **–gang,** *m.* heavy sea(s), swell, seaway; ***der – nimmt zu,*** the sea is getting up. **–gebiet,** *n.* waters. **–gefahr,** *n.* sea-risk; ***Versicherung gegen –,*** marine insurance. **–gefecht,** *n.* naval engagement *or* action **.–gefrörne,** *f.* (*Swiss*) closure by ice, state of being ice-bound. **–geltung,** *f.* naval prestige. **–gemälde,** *n.* sea-piece. **–gericht,** *n.* maritime *or* naval court; Court of Admiralty. **–gesetz,** *n.* maritime law. **–gras,** *n.* (*Bot.*) grass-weed (*Zostera marina*). **–gurke,** *f.* *See* **–walze. –hafen,** *m.* seaport. **–hahn,** *m.* sea-cock. **–handel,** *m.* maritime *or* overseas trade. **–herrschaft,** *f.* naval supremacy, command of the sea. **–hoheitsgebiet,** *n.* territorial waters. **–hund,** *m.* (*Zool.*) seal (*Phocidae*). **–hundsfell,** *n.* sealskin. **–igel,** *m.* (*Zool.*) sea-urchin (*Echinoidea*). **–jungfer,** *f.* mermaid; (*Zool.*) dugong, halicore. **–kabel,** *n.* submarine cable. **–kadett,** *m.* naval cadet. **–karte,** *f.* (hydrographic) chart. **seeklar,** *adj.* ready for sea, ready to sail. **See|klima,** *n.* maritime climate. **–kohl,** *m.* (*Bot.*) sea-kale (*Crambe maritima*). **–kompaß,** *m.* mariner's compass. **seekrank,** *adj.* seasick. **See|krankheit,** *f.* seasickness. **–krebs,** *m.* (*Zool.*) lobster (*Decapoda*). **–krieg,** *m.* naval warfare. **–kuh,** *f.* (*Zool.*) sea-cow (*Sirenia*). **–küste,** *f.* sea-coast, seashore, seaboard. **–lachs,** *m.* sea-salmon.

Seele ['ze:lə], *f.* 1. soul; mind, spirit, heart; (*fig.*) human being; ***die – aushauchen,*** breathe one's last; ***er ist die – des Ganzen,*** he is the very life and soul of it all; ***sie ist eine – von einem Mädchen,*** she is a dear good soul; ***es war keine*** (***menschliche***) ***– da,*** there was not a (living) soul there; ***ihm etwas auf die – binden,*** enjoin s.th. upon him very earnestly; ***das liegt*** or ***brennt mir auf der –,*** that weighs heavily upon me, that preys on my mind; ***sich*** (*Dat.*) ***die – aus dem Leib reden,*** talk o.s. hoarse; ***Sie sprechen mir aus der –,*** you have read *or* guessed my (inmost) thoughts, those are exactly my sentiments; (***bei***) ***meiner Seel***(***e***)***!*** upon my soul! ***zwei –n und ein Gedanke,*** two minds with but a single thought; ***ein Herz und eine – sein,*** be of one heart and mind; ***mit ganzer – dabei sein,*** be heart and soul in it; ***das ist mir in tiefster – zuwider,*** I detest that from the the bottom of my heart; ***das tut mir in der – weh,*** that cuts me to the quick; ***von ganzer –,*** with all one's heart, from the bottom of one's heart; 2. pith (*of quill*); bore (*of gun*); 3. sounding-post (*of violin*); 4. bladder (*of herring*); 5. central strand (*of shroud-laid rope*); core (*of cable*).

Seelen|achse, *f.* axis of the bore. **–adel,** *m.* nobility of soul *or* mind. **–amt,** *n.* office for the dead, requiem. **–angst,** *f.* anguish of mind, mental agony. **–braut,** *f.* (*Poet.*) mystical bride of Christ, the Church. **–bräutigam,** *m.* (*Poet.*) Christ. **–freund,** *m.* bosom friend, soul-mate. **–friede(n),** *m.* peace of mind. **seelenfroh,** *adj.* very glad indeed, heartily pleased. **Seelengröße,** *f.* magnanimity. **seelengut,** *adj.* kind-hearted. **Seelen|heil,** *n.* salvation, spiritual welfare. **–heilkunde,** *f.* psychotherapy. **–hirt,** *m.* pastor. **–kunde,** *f.* psychology. **–leben,** *n.* inner *or* spiritual life, psyche. **–leiden,** *n.* mental suffering.

seelenlos ['ze:lənlo:s], *adj.* soulless, heartless.

Seelen|messe, *f.* *See* **–amt. –not, –pein, –qual,** *f.* *See* **–angst. –rohr,** *n.* (*Artil.*) liner. **–ruhe,** *f.* peace of mind, equanimity, tranquillity. **seelenruhig,** *adv.* (*coll.*) as cool as you please. **Seelenstärke,** *f.* equanimity, composure, long-sufferance, fortitude. **seelen|vergnügt,** *adj.* *See* **–froh. Seelenverkäufer,** *m.* 1. (*obs.*) kidnapper, slave-dealer; 2. (*coll.*) cranky boat, cockle-shell. **seelenverwandt,** *adj.* congenial, sympathetic. **Seelenverwandte,** *pl.* kindred spirits. **–verwandtschaft,** *f.* congeniality, amity, understanding, harmony. **seelenvoll,** *adj.* soulful, sentimental, tender. **Seelen|wanderung,** *f.* transmigration of souls, metempsychosis, palingenesis, reincarnation. **–wärmer,** *m.* (*coll.*) woolly, cardigan. **–weite,** *f.* (*Artil.*) calibre. **–zustand,** *m.* spiritual condition, psychic state, state *or* frame of mind.

Seeleute ['ze:lɔytə], *pl.* sailors, seamen, mariners.

seelisch ['ze:lɪʃ], *adj.* mental, spiritual, psychic(al); emotional.

Seelöwe ['ze:lø:və], *m.* (*Zool.*) sea-lion (*Zalophus*).

Seel|sorge, *f.* care *or* cure of souls; ministerial duties, spiritual charge, (*Mil.*) chaplaincy; pastoral *or* spiritual care. **–sorger,** *m.* spiritual adviser, pastor, minister, clergyman. **seelsorgerisch,** *adj.* pastoral, ministerial; ***–e Betreuung,*** religious *or* spiritual welfare (work).

Seemacht ['ze:maxt], *f.* naval *or* sea-power, naval forces.

Seemann ['ze:man], *m.* (*pl.* **-leute**) seaman, mariner, sailor. **seemännisch,** *adj.* seamanlike, nautical. **Seemanns|amt,** *n.* seamen's registration-office. **–amtskommissar, –amtsleiter,** *m.* shipping master *or* (*Am.*) commissioner. **–ausdruck,** *m.* nautical term. **–heim,** *n.* seamen's hostel. **–sprache,** *f.* nautical language.

See|marke, *f.* (marker) buoy. **–meile,** *f.* nautical mile (*1853 metres*); ***– pro Stunde,*** knot. **–not,** *f.* distress at sea. **–notdienst,** *m.* air-sea rescue service. **–notzeichen,** *n.* SOS, mayday.

Seenplatte ['ze:ənplatə], *f.* (*Geog.*) flat country covered with lakes.

See|offizier, *m.* naval officer. **–pferdchen,** *n.* (*Zool.*) sea-horse (*Hippocampus*). **–pflanze,** *f.* marine plant. **–polyp,** *m.* octopus. **–ratte, –ratze,** *f.* (*coll.*) old salt, old sea-dog. **–räuber,** *m.* pirate, (*Hist.*) buccaneer, corsair. **–räuberei,** *f.* piracy. **–raum,** *m.* sea-room, offing. **–recht,** *n.* maritime law. **–regenpfeifer,** *m.* (*Orn.*) Kentish (*Am.* snowy) plover (*Charadrius alexandrinus*). **–reise,** *f.* (sea) voyage, cruise. **–rose,** *f.* (*Bot.*) water-lily (*Nymphaea*). **–rüstung,** *f.* naval armament. **–sack,** *m.* kitbag. **–schaden,** *m.* loss suffered at sea, average. **–schiff,** *n.* sea-going vessel. **–schiffahrt,** *f.* merchant shipping. **–schildkröte,** *f.* (*Zool.*) turtle (*Cheloniidae*). **–schlacht,** *f.* naval engagement *or* battle. **–schlange,** *f.* 1. (*Zool.*) sea-serpent (*Hydrophiinae*); 2. (*fig.*) mare's nest. **–schule,** *f.* naval academy. **–schwalbe,** *f.* (*Orn.*) ***Kaspische –,*** *see* **Raubseeschwalbe;** ***Rüppelsche –,*** lesser crested tern (*Thalasseus bengalensis*); ***rußbraune –,*** *see* **Rußseeschwalbe;** ***weißbärtige –,*** *see* **Weißbartseeschwalbe. –soldat,** *m.* marine. **–sprache,** *f.* nautical language. **–staat,** *m.* maritime nation. **–stern,** *m.* (*Zool.*) starfish (*Asteroidea*). **–strand,** *m.* seashore, beach. **–strandläufer,** *m.* (*Orn.*) *see* **Meerstrandläufer. –streitkräfte,** *f.pl.* naval forces. **–stück,** *n.* *See* **–gemälde. –sturm,** *m.* storm at sea. **–stützpunkt,** *m.* naval base.

See|tang, *m.* seaweed, brown alga. **–treffen,** *n.* *See* **–schlacht. –trift,** *f.* flotsam and jetsam, jettisoned goods. **seetüchtig,** *adj.* seaworthy. **See|ufer,** *n.*

lakeside. **verbindung,** *f.* sea-route. **–verkehr,** *m.* sea-borne *or* ocean traffic. **–versicherung,** *f.* marine insurance. **–volk,** *n.* maritime nation, seafaring people; ship's crews, seamen, seafaring men. **–walze,** *f.* (*Zool.*) sea-slug, sea-cucumber (*Holothuria*). **–warte,** *f.* marine observatory. **seewärts,** *adv.* out to sea, seawards. **See|wasser,** *n.* seawater, salt-water, (*Poet.*) brine. **–weg,** *m.* searoute; ***auf dem –,*** by sea. **–wesen,** *n.* maritime affairs. **–wind,** *m.* sea-breeze. **–wurf(gut),** *m.* (*n.*) jetsam. **–zeichen,** *n.* (marker) buoy, navigational aid. **–zunge,** *f.* (*Ichth.*) sole (*Solea vulgaris*).

Segel ['ze:gəl], *n.* sail, canvas; (*Bot., Zool., Anat.*) ala, velum; ***alle – aufspannen*** or ***beisetzen,*** crowd all sail; ***– bergen*** or ***einziehen,*** shorten sail; ***das war Wind in seine –,*** that was grist to his mill; ***lose –,*** spare sails; ***die – streichen,*** strike sail; (*fig.*) give in, climb down, throw up the sponge; ***unter – gehen,*** set sail.

Segelboot ['ze:gəlbo:t], *n.* sailing boat. **segelfertig,** *adj.* ready for sea, ready to sail. **Segel|fliegen,** *n.* gliding. **–flieger,** *m.* glider-pilot. **–flug,** *m.* glide, gliding flight. **–flugzeug,** *n.* glider, sailplane. **–garn,** *n.* sailmaker's thread. **segel|klar,** *adj. See* **–fertig. Segel|klasse,** *f.* rating (*yacht racing*). **–klub,** *m.* sailing *or* yachting club. **–macher,** *m.* sail-maker.

segeln ['ze:gəln], *v.t., v.i.* (*aux.* h. *&* s.) sail; soar (*of glider*), (*coll.*) speed, dash, dart, scoot; sweep, flounce. **Segeln,** *n.* sailing, yachting.

Segel|schiff, *n.* sailing ship *or* vessel. **–schlitten,** *m.* ice-yacht. **–sport,** *m.* yachting. **–tuch,** *n.* sailcloth, canvas. **–werk,** *n.* (suit of) sails.

Segen ['ze:gən], *m.* blessing, benediction; grace (*at mealtimes*); (*fig.*) prosperity, abundance, yield, proceeds; (good) luck, boon, godsend; sign of the cross; (*coll.*) ***der ganze –,*** the whole shoot *or* boiling; ***den – geben*** or ***erteilen,*** pronounce the benediction, give one's blessing; ***im Grunde ein –,*** a blessing in disguise; ***den – sprechen,*** say grace; ***das bringt keinen –,*** no good will come of it. **Segenerteilung,** *f.* (*Eccl.*) benediction. **segensreich,** *adj.* lucky, beneficial. **Segens|spruch,** *m.* benediction. **–wunsch,** *m.* good wishes.

Segge ['zɛgə], *f.* (*Bot.*) sedge, rush (*Carex*). **Seggen(rohr)sänger,** *m.* (*Orn.*) aquatic warbler (*Acrocephalus paludicola*).

Segler ['ze:glər], *m.* 1. yachtsman; 2. sailing vessel, sailer; glider, sailplane; 3. (*Orn.*) *see* **Manersegler.**

segnen ['ze:gnən], **1.** *v.t.* bless, give benediction to, make the sign of the cross over, consecrate; ***das Zeitliche –,*** depart this life; ***gesegnet mit,*** blessed *or* blest *or* endowed with; ***gesegneten Andenkens,*** of blessed memory; ***gesegnete Mahlzeit,*** *see* **Mahlzeit**; ***gesegneten Leibes, in gesegneten Umständen,*** in the family way, pregnant. **2.** *v.r.* cross o.s. **Segnung,** *f.* blessing, benediction.

Sehe ['ze:ə], *f.* (*obs.*) eyesight; (*dial.*) pupil (*of the eye*); (*Hunt.*) eye.

sehen ['ze:ən], **1.** *irr.v.t.* see, perceive, (*Poet.*) behold; look at, watch, observe; realize, discern, distinguish, notice, (*coll.*) spot, spy; ***flüchtig –,*** glimpse, catch a glimpse of; ***gern –,*** be pleased with, like; ***gern gesehen sein bei,*** be popular with, be a welcome visitor *or* guest at; ***– lassen,*** show, display, exhibit; ***sich – lassen,*** show o.s., appear, put in an appearance, (*coll.*) turn up; ***du hast dich lange nicht – lassen,*** you are quite a stranger; (*coll.*) ***er kann sich – lassen,*** he's quite a good-looking fellow; (*coll.*) ***ich kann mich mit dem Kleid nicht – lassen,*** I can't possibly wear this dress *or* be seen in this dress, this dress is just impossible; ***zu – sein,*** be on exhibition *or* show; be visible *or* seen, show; ***dein Unterrock ist zu –,*** your slip is showing; ***niemand ist zu –,*** no one is in sight; ***ich sah ihn sterben,*** I saw him die; ***ich habe es kommen –,*** I knew it would happen, (*coll.*) I saw it coming; (*coll.*) ***ich kann sie nicht –,*** I can't bear *or* stand the sight of her, I can't stand her. **2.** *irr.v.r.* ***sich – als,*** see *or* picture *or* imagine o.s. as; ***sich gegenüber einer Aufgabe –,*** be faced with a problem; ***sich gezwungen –,*** find o.s. compelled; ***sich satt – an*** (*Dat.*), feast one's eyes on; ***ich kann mich daran nicht satt –,*** I never get tired of looking at it. **3.** *irr.v.i.* see, look; ***sieh nur!*** just look! (*Poet.*) ***siehe da!*** lo! behold! – ***Sie mal!*** look here! ***sieh doch,*** would you believe it! (*coll.*) look you now! ***siehe oben*** (***unten***) (*abbr.* ***s.o., s.u.***), see above (below); (*coll.*) ***na siehst du!*** I told you so! there you are! what did I say! ***ihm ähnlich –,*** resemble him, look (very much) like him; (*coll.*) ***das sieht ihm ähnlich!*** that is just like him! that is just what you would expect of him! (*coll.*) ***hast du nicht gesehen,*** like a shot, in a flash *or* jiffy; ***gut*** (or ***schlecht***) –, have good (*or* bad *or* poor) eyesight; ***– auf*** (*Acc.*), look out on *or* over, face (*as windows*); (*of a p.*) look at, watch; take care, mind, (*coll.*) look *or* see to (it) (***daß,*** that); set great store by, be particular about; ***ihm auf die Finger –,*** watch him closely, keep a sharp eye *or* keep one's eyes on him; ***auf Gehalt wird nicht gesehen,*** salary is no object; ***nur auf seinen Vorteil –,*** have eyes only for one's own advantage, (*coll.*) have an eye to the main chance; ***daraus ist zu –,*** hence it appears, this shows; ***ihm sieht der Schelm aus den Augen,*** he looks a rogue; ***durch die Finger –,*** pretend not to see, close one's eyes (*Dat.*, to), turn a blind eye (on); (*coll.*) ***ihm in die Karten –,*** see through his game, be wise to his tricks; ***– nach,*** look for; look after; ***nach dem Rechten –,*** see that *or* make sure that everything is in order *or* is done properly; ***nach der Uhr –,*** look at the clock.

Sehen, *n.* seeing, (eye)sight, vision; ***nur vom – kennen***, know only by sight; ***ihm verging Hören und –,*** he lost all consciousness. **sehend,** *adj.* ***mit –en Augen,*** with one's eyes open; ***wieder – werden,*** regain one's sight.

sehens|wert, –würdig, *adj.* worth seeing, remarkable. **Sehenswürdigkeit,** *f.* object of interest, thing *or* place worth seeing, curiosity, spectacle; *pl.* sights; ***die –en besichtigen,*** go sight-seeing, see *or* (*coll.*) do the sights.

Seher ['ze:ər], *m.* seer, prophet. **Seher|blick,** *m.*, **–gabe,** *f.* prophetic eye *or* vision, gift of prophecy. **Seherin,** *f.* prophetess. **seherisch,** *adj.* prophetic.

Seh|fehler, *m.* visual defect, defective vision. **–feld,** *n.* field of vision. **–grübchen,** *n.* optic pit. **–hügel,** *m.* optic thalamus. **–klappe,** *f. See* **–schlitz. –kraft,** *f.* eyesight. **–linie,** *f.* line of sight. **–loch,** *n.* pupil, optic foramen.

Sehne ['ze:nə], *f.* sinew, tendon, fibre; string (*of a bow*); chord (*of an arc*).

sehnen ['ze:nən], *v.r.* long, yearn, crave, (*coll.*) hanker (***nach,*** for); pine (for), grieve (for *or* over); ***sich nach Hause –,*** long for home, be homesick; ***ich sehne mich danach, ihn zu sehen,*** I long *or* am longing to see him. **Sehnen,** *n.* longing, yearning, (ardent) desire, nostalgia.

Sehnen|band, *n.* (*Anat.*) ligament, tendon. **–klapp,** *m.* (*Vet.*) sprain. **–scheide,** *f.* tendon-sheath. **–schmiere,** *f.* synovial fluid. **–schnitt,** *m.* tenotomy. **–zerrung,** *f.* pulled tendon, strain(ed ligament).

Sehnerv ['ze:nɛrf], *m.* optic nerve.

sehnig ['ze:nɪç], *adj.* sinewy, (*of meat*) stringy, gristly, (*of a p.*) wiry, muscular, brawny.

sehnlich ['ze:nlɪç], *adj.* longing, ardent, passionate; ***–ster Wunsch,*** fondest wish.

Sehnsucht ['ze:nzuxt], *f.* longing, yearning, ardent desire, (*coll.*) hankering (***nach,*** for); pining, nostalgia. **sehnsuchtsvoll, sehnsüchtig,** *adj.* longing, wistful, yearning, pining; *see* **sehnlich.**

Seh|organ, *n.* organ of sight. **–probe, prüfung,** *f.* vision *or* eyesight test. **–purpur,** *m.* visual purple.

sehr [ze:r], *adv.* very, most; (*with vb*) (very) much, greatly; ***– gern,*** most willingly; ***– im Rückstand,*** very much behind; ***– mit Unrecht,*** quite wrongly; ***recht –,*** very much indeed; ***wenn er es auch noch so – verlangen sollte,*** however much he may wish for it; ***– vermissen,*** miss badly *or* (*Poet.*) sorely; ***– vermissen lassen,*** be sadly lacking in; ***– viel,*** very much, (*coll.*) a lot; ***– viele,*** a great many, (*coll.*) plenty of; ***wie – auch . . .,*** however much . . ., much as . . .; ***zu – verbittert,***

too much embittered; ***bitte –***, don't mention it! certainly! willingly! you're (very) welcome!

sehren ['ze:rən], *v.t.* (*obs., dial.*) hurt, injure.

Seh|rohr, *n.* telescope; periscope. **–rohrtiefe,** *f.* periscope depth (*of submarine*). **–schärfe,** *f.* focus; clearness of vision, keen eyesight; ***auf – einstellen,*** focus. **–schlitz,** *m.* visor, observation port *or* slit (*of a tank*), peep-hole. **–störung,** *f.* disturbance of vision. **–vermögen,** *n.* visual faculty. **–weite,** *f.* visual range; ***in –,*** within sight; ***außer –,*** out of sight. **–werkzeug,** *n.* organ of sight. **–winkel,** *m.* visual angle. **–zeichen,** *n.* visual signal.

sei [zaɪ], *see* [2]**sein.**

Seiber ['zaɪbər], *m.* (*dial.*) dribble. **seibern,** *v.i.* dribble, slobber.

Seich [zaɪç], *m.* 1. (*vulg.*) piss; 2. (*coll.*) twaddle, bosh. **Seiche,** *f.* (*dial.*) urine. **seichen,** *v.i.* 1. urinate, (*vulg.*) piss; 2. talk bosh.

seicht ['zaɪçt], *adj.* shallow; low, flat; (*fig.*) shallow, trivial, banal, superficial; insipid; ***–e Stelle,*** shoal; ***–e Redensarten,*** empty phrases, banalities, platitudes. **Seichtheit, Seichtigkeit,** *f.* shallowness, insipidity, superficiality.

seid [zaɪt], *see* [2]**sein.**

Seide ['zaɪdə], *f.* silk; ***dabei wird er keine – spinnen,*** he will not get much out of that.

Seidel ['zaɪdəl], *n.* half-litre, pint; mug, tankard.

Seidelbast ['zaɪdəlbast], *m.* (*Bot.*) spurge-laurel (*Daphne mezereon*).

seiden ['zaɪdən], *adj.* silk, silken; ***an einem –en Faden hängen,*** hang by a thread.

Seiden|abfall, *m.* waste silk. **–affe,** *m.* (*Zool.*) marmoset. **–arbeiter,** *m.* silk-weaver. **seidenartig,** *adj.* silk-like, silky. **Seiden|atlas,** *m.* silk-satin. **–bast,** *m.* tusser- *or* tussore- *or* tussur-silk. **–bau,** *m.* rearing of silkworms, seri(ci)culture. **–fabrik,** *f.* silk-mill. **–faden,** *m.* silk thread. **–fadennaht,** *f.* (*Surg.*) silk suture. **–garn,** *n.* silk yarn, spun silk. **–gespinst,** *n.* cocoon of the silkworm. **–glanz,** *m.* silky lustre *or* sheen, (*of fabric*) silk-finish. **–holz,** *n.* satinwood. **–papier,** *n.* tissue paper. **–raupe,** *f.* silkworm. **–raupenzucht,** *f.* seri(ci)culture. **–reiher,** *m.* (*Orn.*) little egret (*Egretta garzetta*). **–sänger,** *m.* (*Orn.*) Cetti's warbler (*Cettia cetti*). **–schwanz,** *m.* (*Orn.*) waxwing (*Bombycilla garrulus*). **–spinner,** *m.* (*Ent.*) silk-moth; silk-spinner *or* -throw(st)er. **–stickerei,** *f.* embroidery in silk. **–stoffe,** *m.pl.* silks. **seidenumsponnen,** *adj.* (*Elec.*) silk-covered (*wire*). **Seiden|waren,** *f.pl.* *See* **–stoffe. –wurm,** *m. See* **–raupe. –züchter,** *m.* rearer of silkworms, silk-grower. **–zwirnen,** *n.* silk-throwing.

seidig ['zaɪdɪç], *adj.* silky; silken.

seiet ['zaɪət], *see* [2]**sein.**

Seife ['zaɪfə], *f.* 1. soap; ***grüne*** or ***weiche –,*** soft soap; ***Stück –,*** cake of soap; 2. (*Geol.*) placer, alluvial deposit, silt; ***– sieden,*** boil *or* make soap. **seifen,** *v.t.* 1. soap, lather; 2. wash (*alluvial deposits*).

Seifen|bad, *n.* soap-suds. **–becken,** *n.*, **–behälter,** *m.* soap-dish. **–bereitung,** *f.* soap-making. **–bildung,** *f.* saponification. **–blase,** *f.* soap-bubble; ***–n machen,*** blow bubbles. **–brühe,** *f.* soap-suds. **–erz,** *n.* alluvial ore. **–flocken,** *f.pl.* soap-flakes. **–gold,** *n.* alluvial *or* placer gold. **–kraut,** *n.* (*Bot.*) soapwort (*Saponaria officinalis*). **–lauge,** *f. See* **–bad. –napf,** *m. See* **–becken**; shaving-mug. **–pulver,** *n.* soap-powder. **–riegel,** *m.* bar of soap. **–schale,** *f. See* **–becken. –schaum,** *m.* lather. **–sieder,** *m.* soap-boiler; (*coll.*) ***mir geht ein – auf,*** a light dawns, the penny drops. **–siederei,** *f.* soap-works. **–stein,** *m.* soapstone, saponite, steatite. **–stoff,** *m.* (*Chem.*) saponine. **–ton,** *m.* fuller's earth, saponaceous clay. **–wasser,** *n.* soapy water, soap-suds. **–zäpfchen,** *n.* (*Med.*) suppository.

Seifer ['zaɪfər], *m. See* **Seiber. seifig,** *adj.* soapy, saponaceous. **Seifner,** *m.* (*Min.*) ore-washer.

Seige ['zaɪgə], *f.* (*Min.*) sump. **seigen,** *v.t. See* **seihen.**

Seiger ['zaɪgər], *m.* plumb-line; hour-glass; (*dial.*) pendulum, clock. **seiger,** *adj.* (*Min.*) perpendicular. **Seiger|blei,** *n.* liquation lead. **–herd,** *m.* refining-hearth. **–hütte,** *f.* liquation plant. **–krätze,** *f.* liquation slag. **seigern, 1.** *v.t.* 1. (*Min.*) sink a shaft; make perpendicular; 2. (*Metall.*) refine, segregate, liquate. **2.** *v.i.* (*aux.* s.) drip, trickle. **Seigern,** *n.* liquation. **Seiger|riß,** *m.* vertical section of mine. **–schacht,** *m.* (*Min.*) vertical shaft. **–teufe,** *f.* (*Min.*) perpendicular depth (*of shaft*). **Seigerung,** *f. See* **Seigern.**

Seihe ['zaɪə], *f.* strainer, filter; dregs. **seihen,** *v.t.* filter, strain, sieve; (*B.*) ***Mücken – und Kamele verschlucken,*** strain at a gnat and swallow a camel. **Seiher,** *m.* filter, strainer, colander. **Seih(e)tuch,** *n.* straining-cloth, strainer. **Seihsack,** *m.* filter- *or* straining-bag.

Seil [zaɪl], *n.* **(-(e)s,** *pl.* **-e)** rope, cord, line; cable; (*Naut.*) ***– und Treil,*** rigging; ***sich am –e führen lassen,*** let o.s. be led by the nose; (*coll.*) ***an einem –e ziehen,*** be in the same boat. **Seil|bahn,** *f.* cable-railway, funicular. **–bremse,** *f.* cable-brake. **seilen,** *v.t.* (*Weav.*) warp (*the yarns*); rig; fasten with rope.

Seiler ['zaɪlər], *m.* rope-maker. **Seiler|arbeit,** *f.* rope-making. **–bahn,** *f.* rope-walk. **–waren,** *f.pl.* cordage.

Seil|hüpfen, *n. See* **–springen. Seilschaft,** *f.* (*Mount.*) roped party. **Seil|scheibe,** *f.* rope-pulley. **–springen,** *n.* skipping. **–tanzen,** *n.* tightrope-walking. **–tänzer,** *m.* tightrope-walker. **–trommel,** *f.* cable-drum. **–waren,** *f.pl.* cordage. **–werk,** *n.* rope-work; rigging. **–ziehen,** *n.* tug-of-war. **–zug,** *m.* tackle, tow-rope.

Seim [zaɪm], *m.* **(-(e)s,** *pl.* **-e)** 1. mucilage; 2. strained honey. **seimen, 1.** *v.t.* strain (*honey*). **2.** *v.i.* yield a glutinous liquid. **seimig,** *adj.* viscous, glutinous; mucilaginous.

[1]**sein** [zaɪn], **1.** *poss.adj. referring to 3rd pers. sing. m. and n. antecedents (declined as def. art.)* his, its, her; one's; ***das Mädchen hat –en Schatz verloren,*** the girl has lost her sweetheart; ***alles zu –er Zeit,*** all in good time, all in due course; ***– Glück machen,*** make one's fortune; ***für –e Zwecke,*** for his purposes; ***einer –er Freunde,*** one of his friends; (*coll.*) ***dem Vater – Stock,*** father's stick; (*sl.*) ***wem – Hund ist das?*** whose dog is that? **2.** (*obs. and Poet.*) = ***seiner*** (*Gen. sing. of pers. pron. er and es*) of him, of it; ***–(er) nicht mehr mächtig sein,*** have lost control of o.s.; ***ich erinnere mich –(er),*** I remember him. **3.** *pers.pron. (standing alone when antecedent is m. or n. nom. or n.acc.)* ***das Haus ist –,*** the house is his; ***alles was – ist,*** everything that is his. **4.** *poss. pron.* 1. (*when standing alone*) ***wessen Frau ist das? Seine,*** whose wife is that? his; (*but when the antecedent is m. or n. nom. or n. acc.* ***sein*** *remains undeclined, see* **3.**); 2. (*after def. art. declined as adj.*) ***die Seinen,*** his family *or* folks; ***das Seine,*** what is his; his property *or* belongings; ***jedem das Seine,*** to everyone his due; ***er machte sie zu der Seinen,*** he made her his wife *or* his own.

[2]**sein,** *irr.v.i.* (*aux.* s.) 1. be (there), exist, be alive; happen, occur, take place; ***ich bin's,*** it is I, (*coll.*) it's me; ***sind Sie es?*** is it you? ***es ist ein Gott,*** there is a God; (*Math.*) ***3 und 4 ist 7,*** 3 and 4 is *or* are *or* make 7; (*Math.*) ***3 mal 4 ist 12,*** 3 times 4 is *or* equals 12; ***es sei! es kann*** or ***mag –!*** perhaps! maybe! that's possible! so be it! granted! let it pass! ***es sei denn daß,*** unless; ***sei es . . . oder . . .,*** whether . . . or . . .; (*Math.*) ***x sei 10,*** let x be *or* equal 10; ***muß das –?*** is that really necessary? ***laß das –!*** stop that! ***was soll das –?*** what might that be? what does that mean? ***etwas (gut) –lassen,*** leave *or* let a th. (well) alone; 2. (*with Gen.*) ***der Ansicht –,*** hold the view, be of the opinion; ***des Glaubens –,*** believe, hold firmly; ***der Meinung –,*** be of the opinion; ***guten Mutes –,*** be of good courage;
3. (*with Dat. referring to physical condition, health etc.*) ***es ist mir als ob,*** I feel as if, it seems to me that; ***mir ist warm,*** I am *or* feel warm; ***wie ist Ihnen?*** how do you feel? ***mir ist schlecht,*** I feel unwell; ***was ist Ihnen?*** what is the matter with you? what ails you? ***ihm gut –,*** like him, feel

friendly towards him; ***ihm ist es nur ums Geld,*** he is only concerned about the money;
4. (*as aux. with comp. verbs indicating change of position or change of state*) ***er ist eben abgereist,*** he has just left; ***er ist vom Dach gesprungen,*** he jumped off the roof; ***ich bin Schlittschuh gelaufen,*** I have been skating; ***er ist nach London gereist,*** he (has) travelled to London; ***er ist viel gereist,*** he has been travelling a great deal (N.B. ***er hat viel gereist,*** he has travelled a great deal); ***er ist erkrankt*** (***genesen, verarmt, eingeschlafen***), he has fallen ill (recovered, become poor, fallen asleep *or* (*coll.*) gone to sleep); ***ich bin gewesen*** (***geworden***), I have been (become); (*dial.*) ***er ist gesessen,*** he (has) sat down;
5. (*with inf. giving pass. construction*) ***das Haus ist zu verkaufen,*** the house is for sale; ***das Stück ist nicht zu spielen,*** the piece is unplayable; ***er ist nicht zu sprechen,*** he cannot be seen, he is engaged *or* busy; ***die Blumen sind an meine Mutter zu schicken,*** the flowers are to be sent to my mother.

Sein, *n.* being, existence; entity, essence, true nature; – ***oder Nicht–,*** to be or not to be.

seiner|seits, *adv.* on his side, as far as he is concerned, for *or* on his part; ***er –,*** he for one. **–zeit,** *adv.* 1. in his *or* its time, at the *or* at that *or* at one time, in those days, formerly; 2. in due course, one day, in its proper time.

seinesgleichen ['zaɪnəsglaɪçən], *indecl.adj., pron.* of his *or* its kind, such as he, people like him, his *or* its equal; ***ihn wie – behandeln,*** treat him as one's equal; ***nicht – haben,*** have no equal *or* parallel.

seinet|halben, –wegen, –willen, *adv.* on his account *or* behalf, for his sake, because of him; for all he cares, so far as he is concerned.

seinig ['zaɪnɪg], *poss.pron.* (*declined as adj.*) *see* **sein, 4,** 2; ***das Seinige tun,*** do one's duty *or* one's share *or* one's best *or* (*coll.*) one's bit, play one's part.

Seising ['zaɪsɪŋ], *n.* (**-s,** *pl.* **-e**) (*Naut.*) seizing, lashing, tie.

Seismik ['zaɪsmɪk], *f.* seismology. **seismisch,** *adj.* seismic; ***–e Störung,*** earthquake. **Seismologe,** *m.* (**-n,** *pl.* **-n**) seismologist.

seit [zaɪt], **1.** *prep.* (*Dat.*) since; for; – ***alters her,*** for ages; – ***damals,*** since then; – ***kurzem,*** of late, lately; – ***langem,*** for some *or* a long time; – ***Menschengedenken,*** within living memory; – ***wann?*** how long (ago)? – ***drei Wochen,*** for the last *or* past three weeks; – ***einiger Zeit,*** for some time past; – ***undenklicher Zeit,*** from time immemorial. **2.** *conj. See* **seitdem, 2.**

seitdem [zaɪt'de:m], **1.** *adv.* since (then *or* that time), from that time on, ever since. **2.** *conj.* since; ***es ist lange her, – ich ihn zum letzten Mal gesehen habe,*** it is a long time (now) since I saw him (last).

Seite ['zaɪtə], *f.* side, (*of a book*) page, (*Mil.*) flank, (*Geom.*) face, (*Math.*) member (*of equations*); (*Pol. etc.*) side, party, faction, camp; (*fig.*) side, facet, aspect, feature; – ***an –,*** side by side; ***ihn dem andern an die – stellen,*** compare him with the other one; ***dem ist nichts an die – zu stellen,*** nothing bears comparison with it, (*coll.*) there's nothing to touch it; ***auf der einen –,*** on the one side *or* (*fig.*) hand; ***es auf die – bringen*** or ***schaffen,*** remove it, get it out of the way, make off *or* away with it; (*coll.*) ***ihn auf die – bringen*** or ***schaffen,*** remove him, get rid of him, finish him off, put him out of the way; ***ihn auf meine – bringen,*** bring him over to my side; ***auf*** or ***an die – gehen,*** step aside; ***auf die – legen,*** put on one side; save, put by (for a rainy day); ***sich auf die – legen,*** turn on one's side (*in bed and of ships*); ***sich auf die faule – legen,*** lounge about, while away the time, take it easy, (*vulg.*) sit on one's bottom; ***ihn auf die – nehmen,*** take him aside; ***auf meiner – stehen,*** be on my side *or* of my opinion; ***nach allen –n,*** in all directions; ***nach allen –n hin,*** from all points of view; ***seine schwache –,*** his weakness *or* foible *or* weak point; ***von –n*** (*Gen.*), on behalf of, on the part of; ***von allen –n,*** from all sides, from every quarter; ***ich habe es von anderer –,*** I have it from another quarter *or* source; ***ein Blick von der –,*** a sidelong glance; ***von der – angreifen,*** make a flank attack on; (*fig.*) ***von der – ansehen,*** look askance at; ***sie kommen mir nicht von der –,*** they never leave my side *or* leave me; ***von dieser – gesehen,*** from this point of view, seen from this angle *or* in this light; ***sich von der besten – zeigen,*** show o.s. *or* show up to advantage; (*Theat.*) ***zur –,*** aside; ***zur – legen,*** see ***auf die – legen; zur – treten,*** step aside, make room; ***zur – stehen*** (*Dat.*), support, stand by, help, assist.

Seiten|abstand, *m.* lateral displacement. **–abweichung,** *f.* lateral deviation, deflexion; error. **–achse,** *f.* lateral axis. **–änderung,** *f.* deflexion; correction. **–angriff,** *m.* (*Mil.*) flank attack. **–ansicht,** *f.* side-view; side-elevation; profile. **–band,** *n.* (*Rad.*) side-band. **–begrenzer,** *m.* (*Artil. etc.*) traversing-stop. **–blick,** *m.* side-glance; scornful glance, leer, sneer. **–deckung,** *f.* (*Mil.*) flank guard. **–druck,** *m.* lateral pressure. **–erbe,** *m.* collateral heir. **–feuer,** *n.* (*Mil.*) enfilading fire. **–flosse,** *f.* (*Av.*) vertical fin. **–flügel,** *m.* (*Archit.*) side-aisle; transept. **–gang,** *m.* side-path *or* -passage; (*Theat.*) slip. **–gebäude,** *n.* wing (*of a building*). **–gewehr,** *n.* side-arm, bayonet. **–gleis,** *n.* (*Railw.*) siding. **–hieb,** *m.* side-cut; (*fig.*) sarcastic remark, taunt, innuendo, home-thrust, passing shot. **–holm,** *m.* (*Artil.*) outrigger. **–hut,** *f. See* **–deckung. –hüter,** *m.* (*Typ.*) catchword. **–kraft,** *f.* component (force). **–lähmung,** *f.* (*Med.*) hemiplegia. **–lampe,** *f.* (*Motor.*) sidelight. **seitenlang,** *adj.* pages long, voluminous. **Seiten|lehne,** *f.* side-rail; arm (*of a chair etc.*). **–leitwerk,** *n.* (*Av.*) rudder-assembly. **–linie,** *f.* (*Geom.*) side; collateral line (*of family*); (*Spt.*) side-line, touch(-line); (*Railw.*) branch line. **–rand,** *m.* margin. **–richttrieb,** *m.* (*Artil.*) traversing-mechanism. **–riß,** *m. See* **–ansicht. –ruder,** *n. See* **–steuer. –rutsch,** *m.* (*Av.*) side-slip.

seitens ['zaɪtəns], *prep.* (*Gen.*) on *or* from the side (of); (*fig.*) on the part of.

Seiten|schiff, *n.* aisle. **–schlag,** *m.* (*Min.*) branch gallery. **–schritt,** *m.* side-step. **–schwimmen,** *n.* side-stroke. **–sicherung,** *f. See* **–deckung. –sprung,** *m.* 1. leap to one side, caper; (*fig.*) evasion; 2. (amorous) escapade. **–stechen,** *n.* stitch in the side, (*Med.*) pleuralgia. **–steuer,** *n.* (*Av.*) rudder. **–straße,** *f.* side-street. **–streuung,** *f.* (*Artil.*) lateral error. **–stück,** *n.* side-piece; counterpart, pendant. **–trieb,** *m.* (*Hort.*) lateral shoot. **–verhältnis,** *n.* (*Av.*) aspect ratio. **–verschiebung,** *f. See* **–abweichung. –verwandschaft,** *f.* collateral relationship. **–vorhalt,** *m.* deflexion lead (*in anti-aircraft gunnery*). **–wagen,** *m.* (*Motor.*) sidecar. **–wahl,** *f.* (*Spt.*) choice of ends. **–wand,** *f.* side (-wall); cheek (*of press, of gun-carriage*); *pl.* (*Theat.*) side-scenes. **–wandbein,** *n.* (*Anat.*) parietal bone. **–wechsel,** *m.* (*Spt.*) change of ends. **–weg,** *m.* side-road; (*fig.*) side-track, round-about way; ***–e gehen,*** act surreptitiously. **–wind,** *m.* cross-wind, side-wind, beam-wind. **–winkel,** *m.* horizontal *or* lateral angle. **–zahl,** *f.* number of a page; number of pages; ***mit –en versehen,*** paginate; (*Geom.*) ***Vieleck von ungerader –,*** inequilateral polygon.

seither [zaɪt'he:r], *adv.* since (then), since *or* from that time; (up) till now, up to now; ***ich habe ihn – nicht gesehen,*** I haven't seen him since. **seitherig,** *adj.* subsequent; former; present, current.

–seitig ['zaɪtɪç], *adj.suff.* -sided.

seitlich ['zaɪtlɪç], **1.** *adj.* side, lateral. **2.** *adv.* at *or* to the side. **seitlichgleich,** *adj.* equilateral, symmetrical.

seitwärts ['zaɪtvɛrts], *adv.* aside; sideward(s), sideways, edgeways, laterally, on one side.

Sekans ['ze:kans], *m.* (-, *pl.* **-kanten**) (*Math.*) secant. **Sekante** [–'kantə], *f.* (*Math.*) secant line.

sekkant [zɛ'kant], *adj.* (*Austr.*) vexing, irritating. **Sekkatur** [–'tu:r], *f.* (-, *pl.* **-en**) (*Austr.*) teasing, annoyance. **sekkieren,** *v.t.* (*Austr.*) tease, plague, torment.

Sekret [ze'kreːt], *n.* (**-(e)s,** *pl.* **-e**) secretion.

Sekretär [zekre'tɛːr], *m.* (**-s,** *pl.* **-e**) 1. secretary; 2. bureau, writing-desk. **Sekretariat** [–tari'aːt], *n.* (**-(e)s,** *pl.* **-e**) secretary's office.

Sekretion [zekretsi'oːn], *f.* (act of) secretion. **Sekretionsstoff,** *m. See* **Sekret.**

Sekt ['zɛkt], *m.* (**-(e)s,** *pl.* **-e**) champagne.

Sekte ['zɛktə], *f.* sect. **Sektenwesen,** *n.* sectarianism. **Sektierer** [–'tiːrər], *m.* sectarian. **sektiererisch,** *adj.* sectarian.

Sektion [zɛktsi'oːn], *f.* 1. section, department; 2. (*Surg.*) dissection; autopsy, post-mortem examination. **Sektions|befund,** *m.* findings of post-mortem examination. **–chef,** *m.* departmental head. **–saal,** *m.* dissecting room.

Sektkühler, *m.* ice-pail.

Sektor ['zɛktɔr], *m.* (**-s,** *pl.* **-en**) (*Geom., Mil.*) sector; (*fig.*) branch, field.

Sekunda [ze'kunda], *f.* (-, *pl.* **-den**) fifth form; (*Austr.*) second form. **Sekundaner** [–'daːnər], *m.* fifth-form boy, (*Austr.*) second-form boy.

Sekundant [zekun'dant], *m.* (**-en,** *pl.* **-en**) second (*in duels, boxing etc.*).

sekundär [zekun'dɛːr], *adj.* secondary, subordinate. **Sekundär|arzt,** *m.* (*Austr.*) assistant physician. **–bahn,** *f.* branch-line. **–element,** *n.* (*Elec.*) secondary cell, storage battery. **–kreis,** *m.* secondary circuit.

Sekundarschule [zekun'daːrʃuːlə], *f.* (*Swiss*) intermediate school.

Sekundawechsel [ze'kundavɛksəl], *m.* second (bill) of exchange.

Sekunde [ze'kundə], *f.* (*Mus., Fenc., Chron., Geom.*) second; (*coll.*) ***auf die –,*** on the dot. **Sekunden|-bruchteil,** *m.* split second. **–meter,** *m.pl.* meters per second. **–zeiger,** *m.* second(s)-hand.

sekundieren [zekun'diːrən], *v.t.* act as second to (*duel*); second (*a motion*); (*Mus.*) accompany.

sela! ['zeːla], *int.* (*B., coll.*) all right! done! settled! agreed!

selb [zɛlp], *adj.* same (*now only in Dat. after certain preps.*); ***zur –en Stunde,*** at that very hour; ***unter –em Dach,*** under the same roof. **selb|ander,** *adv.* (*obs.*) with *or* and another, we two; (*dial.*) with child. **–dritt,** *adv.* (*obs.*) with two others, three together. **selber,** *indecl.adj., pron. See* **selbst, 1. selbig,** *adj.* the same, the selfsame.

selbst [zɛlpst], **1.** *indecl.adj., pron.* self; in person; by o.s., unaided, without assistance; ***ich –,*** I myself; ***er –,*** he himself; ***du –,*** you yourself; ***er ist es –,*** it is he himself; ***aus sich –,*** of oneself; ***sie ist die Güte –,*** she is kindness itself; ***mit sich – reden,*** talk to o.s.; (*Prov.*) ***jeder ist sich – der Nächste,*** charity begins at home; ***– getan ist wohl getan,*** what one does oneself is well done; ***von –,*** (*of a p.*) of one's own accord, voluntarily; (*of a th.*) of itself, spontaneously, automatically; ***das versteht sich von –,*** that goes without saying; ***zu sich – kommen,*** come to o.s. *or* to one's senses. **2.** *adv.* even; ***– seine Freunde*** or ***seine Freunde –,*** his very friends, even his friends; ***– wenn,*** even if, even though. **Selbst,** *n.* (*indecl.*) (one's own) self, individuality, ego. **selbstabdichtend,** *adj.* self-sealing. **Selbstachtung,** *f.* self-respect, self-esteem.

selbständig ['zɛlpʃtɛndɪç], **1.** *adj.* (*of a p.*) self-supporting; self-reliant, self-dependent, responsible; (*of one's livelihood*) independent, established; (*of activities*) independent, unaided, without assistance; (*for tax purposes*) self-employed; (*of a th.*) separate, self-contained; (*Pol.*) independent, autonomous; ***–e Forschung,*** original research; (*Elec.*) ***–e Stromleitung,*** (ionization-, spark- *or* corona-)discharge. **2.** *adv.* independently; ***– handeln,*** act on one's own initiative; ***sich – machen,*** (*of a p.*) set up for o.s. (*in business*), (*of a th.*) move by itself, (*as a vehicle*) (start to) run away. **Selbständigkeit,** *f.* independence, self-reliance, (*Pol.*) independence, autonomy, sovereignty.

Selbst|anklage, *f.* self-accusation, self-recrimination. **–anlasser,** *m.* self-starter. **–anschluß,** *m.* automatic dialling (*of telephone*). **–anschlußamt,** *n.* automatic exchange. **–anschlußgerät,** *n.* dial-telephone. **–ansteckung,** *f.* self-infection. **–antrieb,** *m.* automatic drive; self-propulsion. **–auslöser,** *m.* (*Phot.*) automatic release, self-timer. **–bedarf,** *m.* personal requirements. **–bedienung,** *f.* self-service (*restaurant*). **–befleckung, –befriedigung,** *f.* onanism, self-abuse, masturbation. **–beherrschung,** *f.* self-control. **–bemitleidung,** *f.* self-pity. **–beobachtung,** *f.* introspection. **–besinnung,** *f.* self-examination, self-communing. **–bespiegelung,** *f.* self-conceit, self-importance, self-admiration, self-esteem. **–bestäubung,** *f.* self-pollination. **–bestimmung,** *f.* self-determination. **–bestimmungsrecht,** *n.* (*Pol.*) sovereign right. **–betrug,** *m.* self-deception. **selbstbewußt,** *adj.* self-assured, self-confident; proud, conceited. **Selbst|bewußtsein,** *n.* self-assurance, self-confidence. **–bezichtigung,** *f. See* **–anklage. –bildnis,** *n.* self-portrait. **–binder,** *m.* 1. open-end tie; 2. (*Agr.*) reaper-binder. **–biographie,** *f.* autobiography.

selbst|dichtend, *adj. See* **–abdichtend. –eigen,** *adj.* one's very own. **Selbst|einschätzung,** *f.* self-assessment; statement of income. **–entzündlichkeit,** *f.* spontaneous combustibility. **–entzündung,** *f.* spontaneous combustion, self-ignition. **–erhaltung,** *f.* self-preservation. **–erkenntnis,** *f.* self-knowledge, awareness of one's limitations. **–erniedrigung,** *f.* self-abasement. **selbsterregend,** *adj.* (*Rad.*) self-excited (*of oscillators*). **Selbst|fahrartillerie,** *f.* self-propelled artillery. **–fahrer,** *m.* owner-driver. **–fahrerdienst,** *m.* drive-yourself car-hire service. **–gärung,** *f.* spontaneous fermentation. **selbst|gebacken,** *adj.* home-baked. **–gefällig,** *adj.* self-satisfied, complacent, smug. **Selbst|gefälligkeit,** *f.* complacency, smugness, self-satisfaction. **–gefühl,** *n.* self-reliance, self-confidence, self-esteem, amour-propre; ***– haben,*** know one's worth. **selbst|gemacht,** *adj.* home-made. **–genügsam,** *adj.* self-sufficient; self-contained, self-satisfied. **Selbstgenügsamkeit,** *f.* self-sufficiency, self-contentment, self-satisfaction. **selbstgerecht,** *adj.* self-righteous. **Selbstgespräch,** *n.* monologue, soliloquy; ***ein – führen,*** soliloquize. **selbst|gezogen, –gezüchtet,** *adj.* home-grown, home-bred. **Selbstgift,** *n.* autotoxin. **selbstherrlich,** *adj.* authoritarian, arbitrary, (*coll.*) high-handed. **Selbst|herrscher,** *m.* autocrat. **–hilfe,** *f.* self-help, co-operative enterprise; self-defence; ***zur – schreiten,*** take the law into one's own hands. **–induktion,** *f.* (*Elec.*) self-induction.

selbstisch ['zɛlpstɪʃ], *adj.* selfish, egotistic, self-seeking.

Selbst|kostenpreis, *m.* prime cost, cost price. **–kritik,** *f.* self-criticism. **–ladepistole,** *f.*, **–lader,** *m.* automatic (pistol). **–laut(er),** *m.* vowel. **–lob,** *m.* self-praise.

selbstlos ['zɛlpstloːs], *adj.* unselfish, distinterested; self-sacrificing. **Selbstlosigkeit,** *f.* unselfishness, distinterestedness; self-sacrifice.

Selbst|mord, *m.* suicide; ***– begehen,*** commit suicide. **–mörder,** *m.* suicide; (*Law*) felo-de-se. **selbstmörderisch,** *adj.* suicidal. **Selbst|mordversuch,** *m.* attempted suicide. **–öler,** *m.* automatic lubricator. **–ordner,** *m.* card-index. **selbst|quälerisch,** *adj.* self-tormenting. **–redend,** *adj. See* **–verständlich. Selbst|reflektant,** *m.* (*Comm.*) prospective buyer *or* customer. **–regierung,** *f.* self-government, autonomy. **selbst|regulierend,** *adj.* self-regulating, self-adjusting. **–schmierend,** *adj.* self-lubricating. **Selbst|schreiber,** *m.* self-recording instrument. **–schuldner,** *m.* debtor on one's own account. **–schuß,** *m.* spring-gun. **–schutz,** *m.* self-defence, self-protection. **selbstsicher,** *adj.* self-assured, self-confident, self-opinionated. **Selbst|sicherheit,** *f.* self-confidence, self-assurance, aplomb. **–steuergerät,** *n.* (*Av.*) automatic pilot. **–steuerung,** *f.* automatic control. **–studium,** *n.* private study. **–sucht,** *f.* egoism, selfishness. **selbst|süchtig,** *adj.* egoistic, selfish.

–tätig, *adj.* self-acting, automatic; spontaneous. **Selbst|täuschung,** *f.* self-deception. **–überhebung, –überschätzung,** *f.* overweening opinion of o.s., self-importance, conceit; pretention, presumption. **–überwindung,** *f.* self-conquest. **–unterbrecher,** *m.* automatic circuit-breaker. **–unterricht,** *m.* self-instruction.

Selbst|verblendung, *f. See* **–täuschung. selbstvergessen,** *adj.* self-forgetful, unselfish. **Selbst|-vergiftung,** *f.* auto-intoxication. **–vergötterung,** *f.* self-adulation, self-regard. **–verlag,** *m. im –,* published by the author. **–verleger,** *m.* author and publisher. **–verleugnung,** *f.* self-abnegation, self-denial. **–verschluß,** *m. mit –,* self-locking. **selbstverschuldet,** *adj.* brought about by one's own fault. **Selbst|versenkung,** *f.* (*Naut.*) scuttling. **–versorger,** *m.* self-supporter, farmer living on his own produce. **–versorgung,** *f.* self-support, self-sufficiency. **selbstverständlich, 1.** *adj.* self-evident, obvious; *das ist –,* that goes without saying, that is a matter of course; *es für – halten,* take it for granted. **2.** *adv. –!* of course! naturally! **Selbst|verständlichkeit,** *f.* matter of course, foregone conclusion, truism. **–verstümmelung,** *f.* self-mutilation, mayhem. **–verteidigung,** *f. See* **–schutz. –vertrauen,** *n. See* **–gefühl. –verwaltung,** *f. See* **–regierung. –wahlbetrieb,** *m. See* **–anschluß. –wähler,** *m.* (*Tele.*) dial; *see* **–anschlußgerät. –wählerfernverkehr,** *m.* subscriber trunk dialling, (*Am.*) direct distance dialling. **selbst|wirkend,** *adj. See* **–tätig. Selbstzucht,** *f.* self-discipline. **selbst|-zufrieden,** *adj. See* **–gefällig. –zündend,** *adj.* self-igniting, pyrophorous. **Selbst|zünder,** *m.* (*Chem.*) pyrophorus. **–zweck,** *m.* end in itself, absence of ulterior motive.

selchen ['zɛlçən], *v.t., v.i.* (*dial.*) smoke, cure (*meats etc.*); *Geselchtes, or* **Selchfleisch,** *n.* smoked meat.

Selekta [ze'lɛkta], *f.* (-, *pl.* **-ten**) class of senior pupils, special class (of chosen pupils). **Selektivität** [–ivi'tɛ:t], *f.* (*Rad.*) selectivity.

Selen [ze'le:n], *n.* (*Chem.*) selenium. **Selenit** [–'ni:t], **1.** *n.* (**-s,** *pl.* **-e**) (*Min.*) calcium sulphate, selenite. **2.** *m.* (**-en,** *pl.* **-en**) moon-dweller. **Selen|salz,** *n.* selenide. **–säure,** *f.* selenic acid. **–zelle,** *f.* selenium cell.

selig ['ze:lɪç], *adj.* 1. blessed, happy, blissful, blest; ***Gott habe ihn –!*** God rest his soul! ***eines –en Todes sterben,*** go to one's rest; ***–en Andenkens,*** of blessed memory; ***– werden,*** go to heaven, (*fig.*) find salvation; ***–e Tage,*** blissful days; ***die Gefilde der Seligen,*** Elysium; 2. deceased, late; ***meine –e Mutter*** or ***meine Mutter –,*** my deceased *or* late mother; (*coll.*) ***meine Selige,*** my late wife, my wife of blessed memory; (*coll.*) ***ihr Seliger,*** her late husband; 3. (*coll.*) fuddled, tipsy. **Seligkeit,** *f.* happiness, bliss; ***ewige –,*** everlasting bliss, salvation. **seligmachend,** *adj.* beatific. **Selig|machung,** *f.* salvation; sanctification. **–preisung,** *f.* (*B.*) Beatitude. **seligsprechen,** *irr.v.t.* canonize, beatify. **Seligsprechung,** *f.* beatification.

Sellerie ['zɛləri], *m.* (**-s,** *pl.* **-(s)**) *or f.* (-, *pl.* - (*Austr.* **-n**)) (*Bot.*) celeriac (*Apium graveolens*). **Selleriestangen,** *f.pl.* celery.

selten ['zɛltən], **1.** *adj.* rare, unusual, exceptional; infrequent, scarce; ***das ist nichts Seltenes,*** that is nothing extraordinary, that happens pretty often. **2.** *adv.* rarely, seldom; ***nicht eben –,*** not infrequently pretty often; ***höchst –,*** very rarely, most infrequently; ***– billig,*** exceptionally cheap. **Seltenheit,** *f.* rarity, scarcity; curiosity.

Selterswasser ['zɛltərsvasər], *n.* soda-water.

seltsam ['zɛltza:m], *adj.* strange, peculiar, curious, queer, unusual, odd, singular. **seltsamerweise,** *adv.* oddly (enough), strange to say, paradoxically. **Seltsamkeit,** *f.* strangeness, peculiarity, queerness, oddness; oddity, curiosity.

Semantik [ze'mantɪk], *f.* semantics, science of meanings.

Semaphor [zema'fo:r], *n.* (*Austr. m.*) (**-s,** *pl.* **-e**) semaphore.

Semasiologie [zemaziolo'gi:], *f. See* **Semantik.**

Semester [ze'mɛstər], *n.* half-year; university term, session, semester. **Semesterschluß,** *m.* end of term.

Seminar [zemi'na:r], *n.* (**-s,** *pl.* **-e** *or* **-ien**) training-college (*for teachers*), (*Eccl.*) seminary; (*Univ.*) advanced tutorial class. **Seminar|arbeit,** *f. See* **–übung. –bibliothek,** *f.* (*Univ.*) class *or* departmental library. **–jahr,** *n.* post-graduate teachers' training course. **–übung,** *f.* tutorial exercise.

Semit [ze'mi:t], *m.* (**-en,** *pl.* **-en**) Semite. **semitisch,** *adj.* Semitic.

Semmel ['zɛməl], *f.* (-, *pl.* **-n**) breakfast roll; (*coll.*) ***wie warme –n abgehen,*** sell like hot cakes. **semmelblond,** *adj.* flaxen-haired. **Semmel|kloß,** *m.* bread dumpling. **–mehl,** *n.* white *or* wheat flour.

Senat [ze'na:t], *m.* (**-(e)s,** *pl.* **-e**) (*Pol.*) senate; (*Law*) panel; (*Univ.*) university court *or* council (N.B. *not* senate). **Senator,** *m.* (**-s,** *pl.* **-en**) senator. **senatorisch** [–'to:rɪʃ], *adj.* senatorial.

Send [zɛnt], *m.* (**-(e)s,** *pl.* **-e**) (*Hist.*) synod; (*dial.*) fair.

Send|bote, *m.* envoy, emissary. **–brief,** *m.* open letter, circular (letter); epistle.

Sende|antenne ['zɛndə–], *f.* (*Rad.*) transmitting aerial. **–bereich,** *m.* (*Rad.*) service area. **–folge,** *f.* (broadcast) programme, radio feature. **–leistung,** *f.* transmitting power. **–leiter,** *m.* radio producer.

senden ['zɛndən], *irr. & reg.v.t.* 1. send (***nach,*** for); forward, dispatch; 2. (*only reg.*) (*Rad.*) broadcast, transmit. **Sender,** *m.* 1. sender; 2. (*Rad.*) broadcasting station, transmitter.

Senderaum ['zɛndəraum], *m.* broadcasting studio.

Sender|empfänger, *m.* combined transmitter and receiver, transceiver. **–gruppe,** *f.* transmitter network.

Senderöhre ['zɛndərø:rə], *f.* transmitter-valve.

Senderwelle ['zɛndərvɛlə], *f.* (*Rad.*) carrier-wave.

Sende|spiel, *n.* radio drama *or* play. **–stärke,** *f. See* **–leistung. –station, –stelle,** *f.* broadcasting *or* transmitting station. **–zeichen,** *n.* (*Rad.*) call-sign.

Sendling ['zɛntlɪŋ], *m.* (**-s,** *pl.* **-e**) *see* **Sendbote.**

Send|schreiben, *n. See* **–brief.**

Sendung ['zɛnduŋ], *f.* 1. sending; package, parcel, consignment, shipment; 2. (*Rad.*) transmission, broadcast; 3. (*fig.*) mission.

Senf [zɛnf], *m.* mustard; (*coll.*) ***einen langen – machen über*** (*Acc.*), hold forth about, spin a long yarn about; (*coll.*) ***seinen – dazu geben,*** have a word to say, have one's say. **Senf|brühe,** *f.* mustard-sauce. **–büchse,** *f.* mustard-pot. **–gas,** *n.* mustard-gas. **–gurke,** *f.* gherkin in piccalilli. **–korn,** *n.* grain of mustard-seed. **–mehl,** *n.* ground mustard. **–öl,** *n.* oil of mustard. **–packung,** *f.,* **–papier, –pflaster,** *n.* mustard-plaster. **–säure,** *f.* sinapic acid. **–topf,** *m. See* **–büchse. –tunke,** *f. See* **–brühe. –umschlag,** *m. See* **–packung.**

Senge ['zɛŋə], *pl.* (*dial.*) sound thrashing.

sengen ['zɛŋən], **1.** *v.t.* singe, scorch; burn; ***– und brennen,*** burn and ravage, lay waste (*a country*). **2.** *v.i.* burn, singe, be singed *or* scorched. **seng(e)rig,** *adj.* (smelling *or* tasting) burnt; (*fig.*) suspect, precarious, (*coll.*) ticklish, tricky, fishy.

senil [ze'ni:l], *adj.* senile. **Senilität** [–i'tɛ:t], *f.* senility.

Senior ['ze:niɔr], *m.* (**-s,** *pl.* **-en**) chairman, spokesman.

Senk|blei ['zɛŋk–], *n.* plummet, plumb-line; (*Naut.*) sounding-lead. **–brunnen,** *m.* (*Build.*) sunken well.

Senke ['zɛŋkə], *f.* 1. layering of vines; 2. low ground, hollow, depression; 3. (*Mech.*) countersink; 4. visor (*of helmet*).

Senkel ['zɛŋkəl], *m.* 1. (boot)lace, string with a tag; 2. (*dial.*) *see* **Senkblei. senkeln,** *v.t.* lace. **Senkelstift,** *m.* tag.

senken ['zɛŋkən], **1.** *v.t.* sink (*a shaft etc.*); let down, lower; ***Preise –,*** reduce *or* lower *or* (*coll.*) cut prices; ***den Blick –,*** lower *or* cast down one's eyes; ***die Fahne –,*** dip the colours; ***das Haupt –,*** bow one's head. **2.** *v.r.* settle, sink, subside, sag; ***die Straße***

senkt sich, the road dips *or* drops *or* falls; *die Nacht senkt sich,* night falls. **Senker,** *m.* 1. (*Hort.*) layer, shoot; 2. (*Mech.*) countersink-bit.

Senk|fuß, *m.* flat foot, fallen arch (*of foot*). **–fußeinlage,** *f.* arch support. **–grube,** *f.* cesspool, drain, sump. **–kasten,** *m.* caisson. **–lot,** *n. See* **–blei. –niete,** *f.* countersunk *or* flush rivet. **–pfahl,** *m.* prop (*for a young vine*). **–rebe,** *f.* vine-layer.

senkrecht ['zɛŋkrɛçt], *adj.* perpendicular, vertical; *nicht – stehen,* be out of the perpendicular; (*coll.*) *das einzig Senkrechte,* the only one that is proper *or* right *or* correct. **Senkrechte,** *f.* perpendicular, vertical; *eine – fällen* or *ziehen,* let fall a perpendicular, raise *or* draw a perpendicular.

Senk|reis, *n.* layer, shoot. **–rücken,** *m.* (*Vet.*) sway-back. **–schacht,** *m.* (*Min.*) vertical shaft. **–schnur,** *f.* plumb-line. **–schraube,** *f.* countersunk screw. **–spindel,** *f.* hydrometer.

Senkung ['zɛŋkuŋ], *f.* sinking, settling, subsidence, sag; dip, depression, hollow, incline, slope, declivity; (*fig.*) (*Metr.*) unaccented syllable, thesis; (*Med.*) prolapsus.

Senk|waage, *f.* aerometer; hydrometer. **–werk,** *n.* sunken fascine dam.

Senn [zɛn], *m.* (**-(e)s,** *pl.* **-e**) 1. Alpine cowherd; 2. cheese-maker.

[1]**Senne** ['zɛnə], *m.* (**-n,** *pl.* **-n**) *see* **Senn.**

[2]**Senne,** *f.* Alpine pasture.

sennen ['zɛnən], *v.i.* make cheese. **Senner,** *m.* (*dial.*) *see* **Senn. Sennerei** [–'raɪ], *f.* Alpine dairy-farm. **Sennerin,** *f.* (*dial.*) *see* **Sennin.**

Sennesblätter ['zɛnəsblɛtər], *n.pl.* (*Pharm.*) senna leaves.

Sennhütte ['zɛnhytə], *f.* chalet; Alpine dairy. **Sennin,** *f.* dairymaid. **Senntum,** *n.* (**-s,** *pl.* **⸚er**) (*Swiss*) (Alpine) dairy-herd. **Sennwirtschaft,** *f. See* **Sennerei.**

Sensal [zɛn'za:l], *m.* (**-s,** *pl.* **-e**) licensed broker, agent. **Sensalgebühr, Sensalie,** *f.* brokerage.

Sensarie [zɛnza'ri:], *f.* (*Austr.*) *see* **Sensalie.**

Sensation [zɛnzatsi'o:n], *f.* sensation, thrill; stunt; *– machen,* create a sensation, (*coll.*) make a (big) splash. **sensationell** [–'nɛl], *adj.* sensational, exciting, spectacular, thrilling. **Sensations|hascherei, –lust, –sucht,** *f.* sensationalism.

Sense ['zɛnzə], *f.* scythe. **Sensen|mann,** *m.* (*fig.*) Death. **–wagen,** *m.* scythed war-chariot. **–wurf,** *m.* handle of a scythe.

sensibel [zɛn'zi:bəl], *adj.* sensitive. **sensibilisieren** [–bili'zi:rən], *v.t.* (*Phot.*) sensitize. **Sensibilität** [–'tɛ:t], *f.* sensitiveness, sensibility, feeling. **sensitiv** [–'ti:f], *adj.* (super- *or* hyper-) sensitive; (*coll.*) touchy. **Sensitivität** [–vi'tɛ:t], *f.* (super-)sensitiveness.

Sente ['zɛntə], *f.* 1. (*Naut.*) centre line; 2. (*dial.*) thin lath.

Sentenz [zɛn'tɛnts], *f.* (-, *pl.* **-en**) aphorism, maxim. **sentenziös** [–i'ø:s], *adj.* sententious.

sentimental [zɛntimɛn'ta:l], *adj.* sentimental. **sentimentalisch,** *adj.* (*Lit.*) subjective, reflective. **Sentimentalität** [–i'tɛ:t], *f.* sentimentalism.

separat [zepa'ra:t], *adj.* separate, detached, special, particular. **Separat|abdruck, –abzug,** *m.* special impression, off-print; reprint. **–eingang,** *m.* private entrance.

Separatismus [zepara'tɪsmus], *m.* (*Pol.*) separatism, secessionism. **Separatist,** *m.* (**-en,** *pl.* **-en**) sectarian, seceder, separatist. **separatistisch,** *adj.* separatist.

Separatkonto [zepa'ra:tkɔnto], *n.* special account.

separieren, **1.** *v.t.* separate. **2.** *v.r.* (*Comm.*) dissolve the partnership.

Sepia ['ze:pia], *f.* (-, *pl.* **-pien**) (*Zool.*) cuttlefish; sepia. **Sepia|schale,** *f.* cuttle-bone. **–zeichnung,** *f.* sepia-drawing.

September [zɛp'tɛmbər], *m.* September.

septennal [zɛptɛ'na:l], *adj.* septennial. **Septennat,** *n.* (**-s,** *pl.* **-e**) seven-year period. **Septett** [–'tɛt], *n.* (**-s,** *pl.* **-e**) (*Mus.*) septet. **Septime** [–'ti:mə], *f.* (*Mus.*) seventh, leading note.

Sequenz [ze'kvɛnts], *f.* (-, *pl.* **-en**) (*Cards, Mus.*) sequence.

Sequester [ze'kvɛstər], **1.** *n.* 1. (*Law*) sequestration, confiscation, compulsory administration (*of a debtor's estate*); 2. (*Med.*) sequestrum. **2.** *m.* (*Law*) sequestrator. **sequestrieren** [–'tri:rən], *v.t.* sequester; (*Law*) sequestrate, confiscate.

Serail [ze'raɪl], *n.* (**-s,** *pl.* **-s**) seraglio.

Seraph ['ze:raf], *m.* (**-s,** *pl.* **-e** *or* **-im**) seraph, angel. **seraphisch** [–'ra:fɪʃ], *adj.* seraphic, angelic, ecstatic.

Serbe ['zɛrbə], *m.* (**-n,** *pl.* **-n**) Serbian. **Serbien,** *n.* Serbia. **Serbin,** *f. See* **Serbe. serbisch,** *adj.* Serbian.

Serenissimus [zere'nɪsimus], *m.* (-, *pl.* **-mi**) (*Hist.*) (His) Serene Highness; (*coll.*) petty prince.

Sergeant [zɛr'ʃant], *m.* (**-en,** *pl.* **-en**) sergeant.

Serie ['ze:riə], *f.* series; (*Comm.*) issue; set (*of periodicals etc.*), (*Bill.*) break. **Serien|arbeit,** *f.* serial work. **–artikel,** *m.* mass-produced article. **–erzeugung, –fabrikation, –fertigung, –herstellung,** *f.* mass-production. **serienmäßig,** **1.** *adj.* mass-produced. **2.** *adv.* *– herstellen,* mass-produce. **Serien|schaltung,** *f.* (*Elec.*) series-connection. **–wagen,** *m.* mass-produced *or* production-line *or* standard-model car.

seriös [zeri'ø:s], *adj.* serious, responsible, (*Comm.*) sound, reliable.

Sermon [zɛr'mo:n], *m.* (**-s,** *pl.* **-e**) diatribe.

serös [ze'rø:s], *adj.* serous, watery.

Serpentin [zɛrpɛn'ti:n], *m.* (**-s,** *pl.* **-e**) (*Min.*) serpentine(-stone), ophite.

Serpentine [zɛrpɛn'ti:nə], *f.* double bend (*in road*), winding road.

Serum ['ze:rum], *n.* (**-s,** *pl.* **-ren** *or* **-ra**) (blood) serum. **Serum|behandlung,** *f.* inoculation. **–eiweiß,** *n.* blood protein.

Service [zɛr'vi:s], **1.** *n.* (**-s,** *pl.* -) service, set (*of crockery etc.*). **2.** *m. or n.* (-, *pl.* **-s**) 1. service (*e.g. for cars*), attendance; 2. (*Austr., Swiss*) *see* **Servis.**

Servierbrett [zɛr'vi:rbrɛt], *n.* tray, salver. **servieren,** *v.t., v.i.* serve (*a meal*), wait (*at table*); *es ist serviert,* dinner *etc.* is on the table *or* is served. **Serviererin,** *f.,* **Servier|mädchen,** *n.* waitress. **–tisch,** *m.* side-table, sideboard. **–wagen,** dinner-waggon, tea-trolley.

Serviette [zɛrvi'ɛtə], *f.* table-napkin, serviette.

servil [zɛr'vi:l], *adj.* servile, obsequious.

Servis [zɛr'vi:s], *m.* (-, *pl.* **-gelder**) (*Mil.*) billeting allowance.

Servitut [zɛrvi'tu:t], *f.* (*Austr. n.*) (*Hist.*) compulsory service; easement, charge upon an estate.

servus! ['zɛrvus], *int.* (*Austr.*) hello! greetings!

Sessel ['zɛsəl], *m.* seat; armchair, easy-chair; (*Austr.*) chair. **Sessel|lift,** *m.* chair-lift. **–recht,** *n.* right to remain seated in the presence of the sovereign. **–rolle,** *f.* caster. **–träger,** *m.* sedan-chair bearer.

seßhaft ['zɛshaft], *adj.* settled, established, sedentary, stationary; resident; *– werden,* settle (down).

Sestine [zɛs'ti:nə], *f.* (*Metr.*) sextain.

Setz|art ['zɛtsʔa:rt], *f.* (*Typ.*) composition. **–bord,** *m.* (*Naut.*) washboard. **–bottich,** *m.* settling-vat. **–brett,** *n.* (*Typ.*) composing board. **–ei,** *n.* fried *or* poached egg.

setzen ['zɛtsən], **1.** *v.t.* place, set, put; fix, erect, put up; (*Hort.*) set, plant; wager, stake, lay (*a bet*) (*auf* (*Acc.*), on); (*Mus.*) compose, set (to music); (*Typ.*) compose, set (up in type); *den Fall –,* suppose, put the case; *ihm eine Frist –,* impose a time limit on him; *Grenzen –,* set a limit (*Dat.,* to); *seine Hoffnung – auf* (*Acc.*), pin one's hopes on; (*Zool.*) *Junge –,* bring forth young, breed, (*of fish*) spawn; *sein Leben daran –,* risk one's life for it, (*fig.*) stake everything on it; *matt –,* (*Chess*) check, (*fig.*) hold in check; *Satzzeichen –,* punctuate, put

in punctuation marks; *seine Unterschrift – unter* (*Acc.*), put *or* affix one's signature to.
(*with preps.*) **an**: *alles daran –*, leave no stone unturned, move heaven and earth, do one's utmost; *einen Topf ans Feuer –*, put a pot on the fire; *ihm das Messer an die Kehle –*, see *ihm die Pistole auf die Brust –*; *an Land –*, land, disembark, put ashore; *an die Lippen –*, put *or* raise to one's lips; (*coll.*) *ihm an die (frische) Luft –*, fling *or* sling *or* kick him out; *an die Stelle – von*, put in the place of, substitute for; **auf**: *ihm die Pistole auf die Brust –*, hold a pistol to his head; *ihn auf freien Fuß –*, set him free; *alles auf eine Karte –*, stake everything on one throw, put all one's eggs in one basket; (*coll.*) *sein Alles auf ein Pferd –*, put one's shirt on a horse; *auf seine Rechnung –*, charge to his account; *aufs Spiel –*, risk; *auf die Straße –*, turn out of the house; *auf den Thron –*, place on the throne; **außer**: *außer Gebrauch –*, supersede, discard; *außer Gefecht –*, put out of action; *außer Kraft –*, invalidate, repeal; *außer Stand –*, disable; **in**: *in Angst –*, terrify; *in Bewegung –*, move, set in motion; *Himmel und Hölle in Bewegung –*, move heaven and earth; *in Brand* or *Flammen –*, set on fire, set fire to; *in Freiheit –*, set free, set at liberty; *in Gang –*, start, set *or* get going, set in motion, (*fig.*) set on foot, launch; *sich* (*Dat.*) *in den Kopf –*, take *or* get into one's head; *ein Pferd in Galopp –*, put one's horse to a gallop; *in Marsch –*, give orders to march; *in Noten –*, set to music; *ein Stück in Szene –*, put a play on the stage; *Kinder in die Welt –*, bring children into the world; *in die Zeitung –*, insert *or* advertise in the newspaper; **über**: *den Punkt über das i –*, dot the i; *keinen Fuß über die Schwelle –*, not cross the threshold, not put a foot inside the door; *übers Wasser –*, take *or* put across the water, ferry across; **unter**: *unter Wasser –*, submerge; flood; **vor**: *ihm den Stuhl* or *ihn vor die Tür –*, turn him out, show him the door; *keinen Fuß vor die Tür –*, not step (a foot) outside the house; **zu**: (*Prov.*) *den Bock zum Gärtner –*, set the fox to keep the geese; *zum Pfande –*, give as a pledge; pawn; *zum Richter –*, appoint *or* constitute as judge; *ihn zur Ruhe –*, pension him off; *gesetzter Herr*, stout middle-aged man; *in gesetzten Jahren*, middle-aged; *gesetzten Falls*, in the given case, suppose; *gesetzt, es wäre so*, supposing it were so, granted that it is so.
2. *v.r.* seat o.s., sit down, take a seat; (*of bird*) perch; (*of soil etc.*) sink, subside, settle; precipitate, clarify, be deposited; (*fig.*) calm down, become pacified; *sich auf die Hinterbeine –*, dig one's heels in; (*coll.*) *sich auf die Hosen –*, work hard; (*fig.*) *sich aufs hohe Pferd –*, ride the high horse; *sich bequem –*, make o.s. comfortable; *sich gerade –*, sit up; *eine Geschwulst setzt sich*, a swelling goes down; *sich in Besitz –*, put o.s. in possession of; *sich bei ihm in Gunst –*, ingratiate o.s. *or* curry favour with him; *sich mit ihm in Verbindung –*, get into communication with him; *sich zu ihm –*, sit down by him; *sich zur Ruhe –*, retire from business; *sich zu Tische –*, sit down to a meal; *sich zur Wehr –*, defend o.s.
3. *v.i.* (*aux.* h. & s.) *an den Feind –*, fall upon the enemy; *– auf* (*Acc.*), (place a) bet on, back; *auf die falsche Karte –*, back the wrong horse; *der Gang setzt durch das Gebirge*, the lode strikes into the rock; *– über* (*Acc.*), leap over, clear, take (*a fence etc.*); *über einen Fluß –*, cross a river; *über einen Graben –*, jump (across) a ditch.
4. *v.imp.* (*coll.*) *es wird Schläge –*, there will be a fight, it will come to blows; you will get into trouble, you will catch it; (*coll.*) *was hat es gesetzt?* what is afoot? what's doing?

Setzer ['zɛtsər], *m.* compositor, type-setter. **Setzerei** [–'raɪ], *f.* composing-room, compositor's room. **Setzer|junge,** *m.* printer's devil. **–saal,** *m. See* **Setzerei.**

Setz|fehler, *m.* typographical *or* printer's error, misprint. **–hase,** *m.* doe hare. **–holz,** *n.* (*Hort.*) dibble. **–kartoffel,** *f.* seed-potato. **–kasten,** *m.* (*Typ.*) type- *or* letter-case; settling-tank. **–kopf,** *m.* round- *or* cheese-head (*of screw*).

Setzling ['zɛtslɪŋ], *m.* (**-s,** *pl.* **-e**) 1. (*Hort.*) cuttings slip, layer, sapling; 2. (*Ichth.*) fry, spawn.

Setz|linie, *f.* (*Typ.*) reglet, composing- *or* spacing-rule. **–maschine,** *f.* (*Typ.*) typesetting machine; (*Mech.*) machine-jigger. **–rebe,** *f.* vine-layer. **–reis,** *n.* (*Hort.*) slip, layer, shoot. **–schiff,** *n.* (*Typ.*) galley. **–teich,** *m.* fish(-breeding) pond. **–tisch,** *m.* (*Typ.*) composing-table. **–waage,** *f.* (mason's) level. **–zapfen,** *m.* suppository. **–zeit,** *f.* planting time, breeding time, spawning time.

Seuche ['zɔyçə], *f.* contagious disease, epidemic; pestilence. **seuchen|artig,** *adj.* epidemic; contagious, infectious. **–fest, –frei,** *adj.* immune. **Seuchen|gebiet,** *n.* infested area. **–herd,** *m.* centre of contagion. **–lazarett,** *n.* hospital for infectious diseases, isolation hospital.

seufzen ['zɔyftsən], *v.i.* sigh, heave a sigh. **Seufzen,** *n.* sighing, groaning. **seufzend,** *adv.* with a sigh *or* groan. **Seufzer,** *m.* sigh, groan. **Seufzer|brücke,** *f.* Bridge of Sighs. **–spalte,** *f.* (*coll.*) agony-column.

Sexta ['zɛksta], *f.* (-, *pl.* **-ten**) first form (*school*), (*Austr.*) sixth form. **Sextaner** [–'ta:nər], *m.* first-(*or Austr.* sixth-)form boy.

Sextant [zɛks'tant], *m.* (**-en,** *pl.* **-en**) sextant.

Sexte ['zɛkstə], *f.* (*Mus.*) sixth, (*Cards*) sequence of six; *kleine (große) –*, minor (major) sixth. **Sextett** [–'tɛt], *n.* (**-(e)s,** *pl.* **-e**) (*Mus.*) sextet.

sexual [zɛksu'a:l], *adj.* sexual. **Sexualhormon,** *n.* sex-hormone. **Sexualität** [–i'tɛ:t], *f.* sexuality. **Sexual|leben,** *n.* sex-life. **–pädagogik,** *f.* sex-education. **–verbrechen,** *n.* sex-crime. **–wissenschaft,** *f.* psychology of sex. **sexuell,** *adj. See* **sexual**; (*coll.*) sexy; *–e Aufklärung, see* **Sexualpädagogik,** (*coll.*) education about the facts of life.

Sexus ['zɛksus], *m.* sex, libido.

Sezession [zetsɛsi'o:n], *f.* secession. **Sezessionskrieg,** *m.* war of secession.

sezieren [ze'tsi:rən], *v.t.* dissect. **Seziermesser,** *n.* scalpel.

Sibirer [zi'bi:rər], *m.,* **Sibirerin,** *f.* Siberian. **Sibirien,** *n.* Siberia. **sibirisch,** *adj.* Siberian.

sich [zɪç] (*3rd pers. sing. or pl., m., f. or n. Dat. or Acc. of refl. pron.*) himself, herself, itself, themselves; (*where 3rd pers. is used in address*) yourself, yourselves; (*with imp. subj. or inf.*) oneself; (*reciprocal*) one another, each other; (*after preps.*) him, her, it, them; *an (und für) –*, in itself, on its own, properly considered, in the abstract; *es hat wenig auf –*, it is of little concern *or* consequence *or* importance, it matters little; *was hat das auf –?* what is the point of it? *sie ist nicht bei –*, she is unconscious; (*fig.*) she is out of her mind; *Geld bei – haben*, have money in one's pocket; *das findet –* or *wird – finden*, that will be settled later, that will turn *or* work out all right; *es fragt – ob*, it is a question whether; *eine S. für –*, a separate matter, a matter apart, (*coll.*) another story; *ihn zu – laden*, invite him home; *– etwas zum Muster nehmen*, take s.th. as a model; *das schickt – nicht*, that is not proper *or* nice; *das versteht – (von selbst)*, that goes without saying, that is self-evident; *– die Hände waschen*, wash one's hands; *sie lieben –*, they love one another *or* each other; (*Prov.*) *jeder ist – selbst der Nächste*, charity begins at home.

Sichel ['zɪçəl], *f.* (-, *pl.* **-n**) sickle; (*fig.*) crescent. **Sichelente,** *f.* (*Orn.*) falcated teal (*Anas falcata*). **sichelförmig,** *adj.* crescent- *or* sickle-shaped. **Sichelfrone,** *f.* (*Hist.*) statute-reaping. **sicheln,** *v.t.* cut with a sickle, reap. **Sichel|strandläufer,** *m.* (*Orn.*) curlew-sandpiper (*Calidris ferrugineus*). **–wagen,** *m.* (*Hist.*) chariot armed with wheel-blades.

sicher ['zɪçər], 1. *adj.* secure, safe (*vor* (*Dat.*), from), proof (against); sure, certain, definite, positive, confident, assured, trusty, trustworthy, reliable, steady; (*St. Exch.*) gilt-edged; *–es Auftreten*, self-assured presence *or* bearing, poise; *–er Beweis*, positive *or* sure proof, proof positive; *–e Existenz*, established position, assured means of livelihood; *–es Geleit*, safe-conduct; *–er Griff*, firm hold *or* grip; *-er Halt,* secure *or* sure *or* firm foothold; *-e Hand,* sure *or* steady hand; *aus* or *von -er Hand,* on good authority; *-e Nachricht,* trustworthy *or* reliable report, definite *or* firm news; (*coll.*) *er sitzt auf Nummer Sicher,* he is safely locked up *or* behind bars; *seiner S. - sein,* know what one is about, be sure of one's facts *or* (*coll.*) one's ground; *-er Tod,* certain death; *-es Urteil,* sound *or* reliable judgement. **2.** *adv. See* **sicherlich**; *um - zu gehen,* to make sure, to be on the safe side; *- glauben,* believe confidently; *- rechnen auf* (*Acc.*), have complete confidence in, count confidently upon, be quite sure of; *- ist -!* better be safe than sorry! keep on the safe side! *- wissen,* know for certain, be certain *or* positive.

Sicherheit ['zɪçərhaɪt], *f.* certainty; reliability, trustworthiness; confidence, assurance; (*Comm.*) cover, guarantee, guaranty, safeguard; security, safety; *mit -,* safely, confidently, reliably; *- im Auftreten,* (self-)assurance, self-possession, poise; *- leisten,* act as *or* stand surety, furnish cover *or* security; *in - bringen,* place in safety, secure; (*Law*) *- leisten,* offer *or* become *or* (*coll.*) go bail.

Sicherheits|ausschuß, *m.* committee of public safety. **-bestimmungen,** *f.pl.* safety regulations. **-dienst,** *m.* secret service, security services. **-faktor,** *m.* safety factor. **-fonds,** *m.* (*Comm.*) guarantee fund. **-glas,** *n.* safety glass. **-gurt,** *m.* (*Motor.*) safety belt. **sicherheitshalber,** *adv.* for safety('s sake), (*coll.*) to be on the safe side. **Sicherheits|klausel,** *f.* safeguard. **-lampe,** *f.* (*Min.*) safety lamp. **-leistung,** *f.* (*Comm.*) security, (*Law*) bail. **-maßnahme,** *f.* precaution(ary measure), (safety) precaution, safeguard. **-nadel,** *f.* safety pin. **-pakt,** *m.* (*Pol.*) security pact. **-polizei,** *f.* security police. **-rat,** *m.* (*Pol.*) Security Council. **-regel,** *f. See* **-maßnahme. -schloß,** *m.* safety lock. **-stift,** *m.* shearing pin. **-ventil,** *n.* safety valve. **-wechsel,** *m.* (*Comm.*) bill deposited as collateral. **-zündholz,** *n.* safety match.

sicherlich ['zɪçərlɪç], *adv.* surely, certainly, assuredly, undoubtedly, doubtless, without doubt, no doubt, (*coll.*) for sure, (*Am.*) sure; *-!* to be sure! rather! (*coll.*) you bet! (*Am.*) sure (thing)! *er kommt -,* I am sure he will come, (*coll.*) he is sure to come.

sichern ['zɪçərn], **1.** *v.t.* secure, make safe, (*Mount.*) belay, (*Mech.*) lock, (*Mil.*) protect, cover; (*of firearms*) put at 'safe'; (*fig.*) ensure, safeguard, (*Comm.*) guarantee, cover, give security for. **2.** *v.i.* be watchful *or* on the alert, (*Hunt.*) wind, scent.

sicherstellen ['zɪçərʃtɛlən], *v.t.* secure, put in safe keeping; place *or* take in custody; make safe, guarantee. **Sicherstellung,** *f.* safeguard(ing), guarantee.

Sicherung ['zɪçəruŋ], *f.* securing; ensuring; assurance, safeguard, guarantee, (*Comm.*) cover, security, (*Mil.*) protection, defence; (*Elec.*) fuse, cut-out; (*Mech.*) safety device, (*on firearms*) safety catch; (*Mount.*) belay. **Sicherungs|draht,** *m.* (*Elec.*) fuse wire. **-fahrzeug,** *n.* (*Naut.*) escort vessel. **-flügel,** *m.* 1. (*Mil.*) protective flank; 2. (*on firearms*) safety catch. **-fonds,** *m. See* **Sicherheitsfonds. -geschäft,** *n.* covering transaction. **-kasten,** *m.* (*Elec.*) fuse box. **-patrone,** *f. See* **-stöpsel. -posten,** *m.* (*Mil.*) outpost. **-schalter,** *m.* safety switch. **-stöpsel,** *m.* (*Elec.*) cartridge fuse. **-verwahrung,** *f.* (*Law*) preventive detention.

Sichler ['zɪçlər], *m.* (*Orn.*) *brauner -,* glossy ibis (*Plegadis falcinellus*).

Sicht [zɪçt], *f.* sight, view, visibility; *auf* or *bei -,* at sight; *auf lange* (or *kurze*) *-,* at long (*or* short) sight, long- (*or* short-)dated (*bill*); (*fig.*) *auf weite -,* on a long-term basis, with a view to the future, (*coll.*) in the long run; *in -,* in sight, within view; *in - kommen,* come in(to) sight *or* view, come within view; *ihm die - nehmen,* obstruct *or* block his view *or* the view for him; (*Comm.*) *7 Tage nach -,* 7 days after sight, at 7 days' sight.

sichtbar ['zɪçtba:r], *adj.* visible, noticeable, perceptible, evident, obvious, conspicuous, marked; (*coll.*) *ich bin noch nicht -,* I am not ready yet (to receive visitors); *ohne -en Erfolg,* without appreciable success; *- werden,* appear, (*Naut.*) heave into sight; (*fig.*) become manifest, manifest itself. **Sichtbarkeit,** *f.* visibility. **sichtbarlich,** *adv.* visibly, obviously, evidently.

[1]**sichten** ['zɪçtən], *v.t.* sight (*a ship, the enemy*).

[2]**sichten,** *v.t.* sift, winnow; (*fig.*) sort (out *or* over), screen.

Sicht|feld, *n.* field of vision. **-flug,** *m.* (*Av.*) visual flight. **-geschäft,** *n.* (*St. Exch.*) forward transaction; *pl.* futures. **sichtig,** *adj.* (*Meteor.*) clear (visibility); (*as suff.*) -sighted. **Sichtigkeit,** *f.* (*Meteor.*) visibility. **sichtlich,** *adj. See* **sichtbar(lich). Sicht|note,** *f. See* **-wechsel. -tage,** *m.pl.* days of grace. **Sichtung,** *f.* 1. sighting; 2. sifting, (*fig.*) sorting, screening. **Sicht|verhältnisse,** *pl. See* **Sichtigkeit. -vermerk,** *m.* endorsement; visa (*on passports*). **-wechsel,** *m.* sight-bill, bill payable at sight. **-weite,** *f.* range of sight; *in* (or *außer*) *-,* within (*or* out of) sight. **-zeichen,** *n.* (*Av.*) ground-signal *or* -panel.

sickern ['zɪkərn], *v.i.* (*aux.* h. & s.) trickle, drip, seep, ooze, percolate.

siderisch [zi'de:rɪʃ], *adj.* siderial.

sie [zi:], *pers. pron.* 1. (*3rd sing. f. Nom. and Acc.*) she; her; it; 2. (*3rd pl. m., f. and n. Nom. and Acc.*) they; them. **Sie, 1.** *pers. pron.* (*2nd pl. Nom. and Acc.*) you. **2.** *f.* (*coll.*) she, female (*usu. of birds*); *dieser Vogel ist eine -,* this bird is a she.

Sieb [zi:p], *n.* (**-es,** *pl.* **-e**) sieve, filter, strainer, colander, riddle, screen. **Sieb|band,** *n.* travelling screen. **-boden,** *m.* perforated bottom.

[1]**sieben** ['zi:bən], *v.t.* sift, strain, filter, (pass through a) sieve, riddle, screen, bolt (*flour*); (*fig.*) sift, screen; pick *or* weed out; (*Rad. etc.*) filter.

[2]**sieben, 1.** *num.adj.* seven; *halb -,* half-past six; *ein Buch mit - Siegeln,* a sealed book, a complete mystery. **Sieben,** *f.* number 7; *böse -,* vixen, shrew.

Sieben|bürgen, *n.* (*Geog.*) Transylvania. **-eck,** *n.* heptagon. **siebeneckig,** *adj.* heptagonal. **siebenerlei,** *indecl.adj.* of 7 different kinds, 7 sorts of. **siebenfach, -fältig,** *adj.* sevenfold. **-gescheit,** *adj.* (*coll.*) too clever by half. **Sieben|gestirn,** *n.* Pleiades. **-herrschaft,** *f.* heptarchy. **sieben|hundert,** *num.adj.* seven hundred. **-jährig, 1.** *adj.* 7 years old; *der -e Krieg,* the Seven Years' War. **2.** *adv.* lasting 7 years. **-jährlich,** *adj.* septennial, occurring every 7 years. **-mal,** *adv.* 7 times. **-malig,** *adj.* 7 times repeated. **Sieben|meilenschritte,** *m.pl.* giant strides. **-meilenstiefel,** *m.pl.* seven-league boots. **-monatskind,** *n.* premature child. **-punkt,** *m.* (*Ent.*) ladybird. **-sachen,** *f.pl.* (*coll.*) odds and ends, goods and chattels, things, belongings. **-schläfer,** *m.* sluggard, lie-abed, lazy-bones; (*Zool.*) dormouse (*Myoxus glis*).

siebent ['si:bənt], *num.adj. See* **siebt.**

sieben|tausend, *num.adj.* seven thousand. **-undzwanzig,** *num.adj.* twenty-seven. **-wertig,** *adj.* (*Chem.*) heptavalent.

siebförmig ['zi:pfœrmɪç], *adj.* cribiform. **Sieb|kette,** *f.* (*Rad.*) band-pass filter. **-korb,** *m.* wire basket. **-maschine,** *f.* sifting *or* screening machine. **-mehl,** *n.* coarse flour, siftings.

siebt [zi:pt], *num.adi.* seventh. **Siebtel,** *n.* (*Swiss m.*) seventh (part). **siebtens,** *adv.* seventh(ly), in the seventh place.

Sieb|trommel, *f.* revolving screen. **-tuch,** *n.* straining *or* bolting cloth.

siebzehn ['zi:ptse:n], *num.adj.* seventeen. **siebzehnt,** *adj.* seventeenth. **Siebzehntel,** *n.* (*Swiss m.*) seventeenth (part). **siebzehntens,** *adv.* (in the) seventeenth (place).

siebzig ['zi:ptsɪç], *num.adj.* seventy; *die siebziger Jahre,* the seventies (*e.g.* 1970–80). **Siebziger(in),** *m.* (*f.*) septuagenarian. **siebzigjährig, 1.** *adj.* 70 year-old, septuagenarian. **2.** *adv.* lasting 70 years.

siebzigst, *num.adj.* seventieth. **Siebzigstel,** *n.* (*Swiss m.*) seventieth (part).

siech [ziːç], *adj.* ailing, invalid, sickly, infirm. **siechen,** *v.i.* be a confirmed invalid; waste away, languish, pine away. **Siechenhaus,** *n.* hospital for incurables. **Siechtum,** *n.* chronic ill health, (permanent) infirmity, long illness, invalidism.

Siede [ˈziːdə], *f.* 1. boiling; ***in der – sein,*** be boiling *or* seething; 2. (*dial.*) mash (*for cattle*). **Siede|grad,** *m.* *See* **–punkt. siedeheiß,** *adj.* boiling *or* scalding hot. **Siede|hitze,** *f.* boiling temperature. **–kessel,** *m.* boiler, boiling- *or* evaporating-pan.

siedeln [ˈziːdəln], *v.i.* settle, colonize.

sieden [ˈziːdən], **1.** *reg. & irr.v.i.* boil; simmer; ***mein Blut siedete,*** my blood was boiling, I was seething. **2.** *v.t.* boil, refine (*sugar*); make (*soap*); ***hart gesottene Eier,*** hard-boiled eggs. **siedend,** *adj.* boiling, (*fig.*) seething.

Siedepunkt [ˈziːdəpuŋkt], *m.* boiling-point. **Siederei** [–ˈraɪ], *f.* refinery.

Siedler [ˈziːdlər], *m.* settler, colonist. **Siedlung,** *f.* settlement, colony; housing estate. **Siedlungs|bau,** *m.* (suburban) housing development. **–gelände,** *n.* development area. **–gesellschaft,** *f.* building-and-loan association. **–politik,** *f.* housing policy.

Sieg [ziːk], *m.* (**-(e)s,** *pl.* **-e**) victory, triumph (*über* (*Acc.*), over), conquest (of), (*Spt.*) win (over); ***den – davontragen,*** carry *or* win the day; ***schließlich den – behaupten,*** win through; ***den – behalten,*** be victorious; (*Nat. Soc.*) ***– Heil!*** hurrah!

Siegel [ˈziːɡəl], *n.* seal; ***unter – legen,*** seal; ***Brief und – haben über*** (*Acc.*), have under sign (*or* hand) and seal; ***unter dem – der Verschwiegenheit,*** under the seal of secrecy, in strict confidence; (*fig.*) ***ein Buch mit sieben –n,*** a sealed book. **Siegel|bewahrer,** *m.* keeper of the seal; Lord Privy Seal. **–erde,** *f.* sealed *or* Lemnian earth. **–gebühr,** *f.* fee paid for affixing a seal. **–lack,** *m.* sealing-wax. **siegeln,** *v.t.* seal; affix a seal to. **Siegel|ring,** *m.* signet-ring. **–stecher,** *m.* seal-engraver.

siegen [ˈziːɡən], *v.i.* be victorious, triumph, gain a victory (*über* (*Acc.*), over); ***– über,*** conquer; (*Spt.*) win. **Sieger,** *m.* conqueror, victor, (*Spt.*) winner; (*Spt.*) ***zweiter –,*** runner-up. **Sieger|ehrung,** *f.* distribution of trophies. **–kranz,** *m.* victor's crown. **–staat,** *m.* (*usu. pl.*) victorious country.

Siegesbahn [ˈziːɡəsbaːn], *f.* career of victory. **sieges|bewußt,** *adj.* *See* **–gewiß. Sieges|bogen,** *m.* triumphal arch. **–feier,** *f.*, **–fest,** *n.* victory celebration. **siegesgewiß,** *adj.* sure *or* certain *or* confident of victory. **Sieges|lauf,** *m.* *See* **–bahn. –pokal,** *m.* (*Spt.*) challenge-cup. **–säule,** *f.* triumphal column. **–taumel,** *m.* flush of victory. **siegestrunken,** *adj.* drunk with success, flushed with victory. **Sieges|wagen,** *m.* triumphal car. **–wille(n),** *m.* will to win. **–zeichen,** *n.* trophy. **–zug,** *m.* triumphal procession; (*fig.*) triumphant progress, victorious advance.

sieggekrönt [ˈziːkɡəkrøːnt], **sieghaft,** *adj.* triumphant. **siegreich,** *adj.* victorious (*über* (*Acc.*), over), conquering, successful.

sieht [ziːt], *see* **sehen.**

Siel [ziːl], *m.*, *n.* (**-(e)s,** *pl.* **-e**) (*dial.*) sluice, culvert, drain, sewer.

Siele [ˈziːlə], *f.* breast-piece (*of harness*), towing-belt (*of barrow-man*); (*fig.*) ***in den –n sterben,*** die in harness. **Sielengeschirr,** *n.* breast-harness.

Sielwasser [ˈziːlvasər], *n.* sewage, drainage.

siezen [ˈziːtsən], *v.t.* be on formal terms with (*a p.*), address (*a p.*) formally with '***Sie***' (*and not with* '***Du***').

Sigel [ˈziːɡəl], *n.* logogram, grammalogue; sign, symbol.

Sigill [ziˈɡɪl], *n.* (*Poet., obs.*) *see* **Siegel.**

Sigle [ˈziːɡəl], *f.* *See* **Sigel.**

Signal [zɪɡˈnaːl], *n.* (**-s,** *pl.* **-e**) signal; bugle-call; (*Motor.*) ***– geben,*** sound the horn. **Signal|anlage,** *f.* signalling system. **–apparat,** *m.* signalling apparatus. **–bombe,** *f.* signal-flare. **–buch,** *n.* code of signals.

Signalement [zɪɡnal(ə)mã], *n.* (**-s,** *pl.* **-s**) description (*of a p.*).

Signal|feuer, *n.* beacon. **–flagge,** *f.* signalling flag. **–gast,** *m.* naval signaller. **–glocke,** *f.* warning-bell. **–hupe,** *f.* klaxon horn, siren. **signalisieren** [–iˈziːrən], *v.t.* signal; give a summary description of. **Signal|lampe. –laterne,** *f.* signal-light, signalling lamp. **–leine,** *f.* bell-rope, communication cord. **–leuchtkugel,** *f.* (*Artil.*) star-shell. **–mast,** *m.* (*Railw.*) signal-post, semaphore. **–pfeife,** *f.* whistle signal. **–rakete,** *f.* rocket-flare. **–ruf,** *m.* warning cry; bugle-call. **–schuß,** *m.* signal-gun, maroon. **–wärter,** *m.* (*Railw.*) signalman.

Signatar [zɪɡnaˈtaːr], *m.* (**-s,** *pl.* **-e**) signatory. **Signatarmacht,** *f.* signatory power (*to treaty*).

Signatur [zɪɡnaˈtuːr], *f.* (-, *pl.* **-en**) signature (*also Typ.*); (*Comm.*) mark; stamp, brand; label (*on a medicine bottle etc.*); conventional sign (*on maps*); catalogue number (*library books*).

Signet [zɪɡˈneːt], *n.* (**-(e)s,** *pl.* **-e**) (*Typ.*) colophon.

signieren [zɪɡˈniːrən], *v.t.* sign, initial; designate, mark, brand.

Sigrist [ˈziːɡrɪst, ziˈɡrɪst], *m.* (**-en,** *pl.* **-en**) (*Swiss*) sacristan, sexton.

Silbe [ˈzɪlbə], *f.* syllable; ***keine – davon sagen,*** not say a word about it; ***–n verschlucken,*** swallow one's words; ***keine – verstehen,*** not understand a word; ***–n stechen,*** quibble, split hairs.

Silben|maß, *n.* metre, quantity. **–messung,** *f.* prosody. **–rätsel,** *n.* charade. **–stecher,** *m.* stickler, hair-splitter, quibbler. **–stecherei,** *f.* hair-splitting; quibbling, **–trennung,** *f.* hyphenation. **silbenweise,** *adv.* syllable by syllable.

Silber [ˈzɪlbər], *n.* silver. **Silberarbeiter,** *m.* silversmith. **silberartig,** *adj.* silvery, argentine. **Silber|ätzstein,** *m.* *See* **–nitrat. –barren,** *m.* bar *or* ingot of silver. **–blei,** *n.* argentiferous lead. **–blende,** *f.* galena of silver, pyrargyrite, proustite. **–blick,** *m.* gleam of silver (*in refining process*); (*fig.*) bright moment, lucky chance; (*coll.*) slight squint. **–brenner,** *m.* silver-refiner. **–buche,** *f.* (*Bot.*) white beech (*Fagus americana*). **–distel,** *f.* (*Bot.*) carline thistle (*Carlina acaulis*). **–erz,** *n.* silver-ore. **silber|farben, –farbig,** *adj.* silvery (*in colour*), silver-coloured. **Silber|fischchen,** *n.* (*Ent.*) sugar-mite. **–gehalt,** *m.* silver content (*of an alloy*). **–geld,** *n.* silver (money). **–geschirr,** *n.* silver(-plate), silverware. **–glanz,** *m.* 1. silvery lustre; 2. (*Min.*) argentine, silver-glance. **–glätte,** *f.* litharge. **–glimmer,** *m.* common mica. **–gold,** *n.* electrum, argentiferous gold. **silber|grau,** *adj.* silver-grey. **–haltig,** *adj.* argentiferous. **–hell,** *adj.* (as) bright as silver; ***–e Stimme,*** silvery voice. **Silberhochzeit,** *f.* silver wedding. **silberig,** *adj.* (of) silver. **Silber|kammer,** *f.* plate-room. **–klang,** *m.* clear *or* silvery sound. **–korn,** *n.* grain of silver.

Silberling [ˈzɪlbərlɪŋ], *m.* (**-s,** *pl.* **-e**) (*B.*) piece of silver, shekel.

Silber|lot, *n.* silver solder. **–löwe,** *m.* puma, cougar. **–medaillenträger,** *m.* (*Spt.*) silver-medallist. **–möwe,** *f.* (*Orn.*) herring-gull (*Larus argentatus*). **silbern,** *adj.* (of) silver; ***–e Hochzeit,*** silver wedding. **Silber|nitrat,** *n.* nitrate of silver; lunar caustic. **–papier,** *n.* silver-paper, tinfoil. **–pappel,** *f.* (*Bot.*) white poplar (*Populus alba*). **–reiher,** *m.* (*Orn.*) large egret, (*Am.*) egret (*Egretta alba*). **–scheider,** *m.* silver refiner. **–schimmel,** *m.* silver-grey horse. **–schmied,** *m.* silversmith. **–schrank,** *m.* plate-cupboard. **–stift,** *m.* (*Engr.*) silverpoint. **–stoff,** *m.* silver brocade; silver cloth *or* tissue. **–streif(en),** *m.* (*fig.*) silver lining, gleam of hope. **–tanne,** *f.* silver-fir. **–tresse,** *f.* silver lace. **–währung,** *f.* silver currency; ***Anhänger der –,*** bimetallist, (*Am.*) silverite. **–waren,** *f.pl.* silverware. **–weide,** *f.* (*Bot.*) white willow (*Salix alba*). **silberweiß,** *adj.* silvery white. **Silber|zeug,** *n.* *See* **-geschirr.**

silbrig [ˈzɪlbrɪç], *adj.* *See* **silberig.**

Silikat [ziliˈkaːt], *n.* (**-(e)s,** *pl.* **-e**) (*Chem.*) silicate. **Silikose,** *f.* (*Med.*) silicosis.

Silizium [zi'li:tsium], *n.* silicon.

Sill [zɪl], *n.* (*dial.*) *see* **Siele.**

Silvester(abend) [zɪl'vɛstər(a:bənt)], *m.* New Year's Eve, (*Scots*) Hogmanay.

Similistein ['zi:miliʃtaɪn], *m.* artificial gem, paste (diamond).

Simonie [zimo'ni:], *f.* simony. **simonisch** [–'mo:nɪʃ], *adj.* simoniacal. **Simonist,** *m.* (**-en,** *pl.* **-en**) simoniac.

simpel ['zɪmpəl], *adj.* plain, simple, stupid. **Simpel,** *m.* (*coll.*) nincompoop, simpleton. **simpelhaft,** *adj.* simple, silly. **simpeln,** *v.i.* be thoughtless *or* absent-minded.

Sims [zɪms], *m.* (*Austr. n.*) (**-es,** *pl.* **-e**) 1. cornice, moulding; 2. mantelpiece, shelf, ledge, (window) sill. **Sims|hobel,** *m.* moulding-plane. **–werk,** *n.* mouldings.

Simulant [zimu'lant], *m.* (**-en,** *pl.* **-en**) (*Mil.*) malingerer; (*sl.*) leadswinger. **simulieren,** *v.t., v.i.* feign, sham (*illness*), (*Mil.*) malinger; (*sl.*) swing the lead; (*v.t. only*) simulate; ***simulierte Rechnung,*** pro forma account; (*dial.*) – ***über*** (*Acc.*), brood over, ponder.

simultan [zimul'ta:n], *adj.* simultaneous; joint. **Simultanschule,** *f.* undenominational school.

sind [zɪnt], *see* **sein.**

Sinfonie [zɪnfo'ni:], *f.* symphony.

Singakademie ['zɪŋʔakademi:], *f.* singing academy.

Singapur ['zɪŋgapu:r], *n.* Singapore.

singbar ['zɪŋba:r], *adj.* singable. **Singdrossel,** *f.* (*Orn.*) song-thrush (*Turdus philomelos*).

singen ['zɪŋən], **1.** *irr.v.t., v.i.* sing, chant, (*Poet.*) carol (*of birds*); ***vom Blatte –,*** sing at sight; ***immer dasselbe Lied –,*** be always harping on the same subject; ***falsch –,*** sing out of tune; ***davon weiß ich ein Lied zu –,*** I can say s.th. about that; ***sein eignes Lob –,*** sing one's own praises, (*coll.*) blow one's own trumpet; ***mehrstimmig –,*** sing part-songs, sing in parts; ***nach Noten –,*** sing from music; ***in Schlaf –,*** sing to sleep; ***Sopran –,*** have a soprano voice; sing the soprano part; (*coll.*) ***das war(d) ihm an der Wiege nicht gesungen,*** no one thought he would come to this. **2.** *irr.v.r., imp.* ***das Lied singt sich leicht,*** this song is easy to sing; ***es singt sich schön im Bade,*** it is pleasant to sing in the bath; ***es singt mir in den Ohren,*** there is a singing *or* ringing in my ears; ***singende Säge,*** musical saw.

Singrün ['zɪngry:n], *n.* (*Bot.*) periwinkle.

Sing|sang, *m.* sing-song. **–schwan,** *m.* (*Orn.*) whooper-swan (*Cygnus cygnus*). **–spiel,** *n.* operetta; musical (comedy). **–stimme,** *f.* 1. singing voice; 2. (*Mus.*) vocal part; ***Lied für eine –,*** song for a single voice, solo song. **–stunde,** *f.* singing lesson.

Singular ['zɪŋgula:r], *m.* (**-s,** *pl.* **-e**) (*Gram.*) singular (number).

Sing|vogel, *m.* singing-bird, song-bird, songster; (*Poet.*) warbler. **–weise,** *f.* 1. style of singing; 2. tune, melody, air.

sinken ['zɪŋkən], *irr.v.i.* (*aux.* s.) sink, subside, give way (*as ground*), go down, founder, sink (*as a ship*), sink, set (*as the sun*), go down, drop, fall (*as prices*), (*fig.*) go down, decrease, abate, diminish, decline; ***in Ohnmacht –,*** faint, swoon; ***die Stimme – lassen,*** lower *or* drop one's voice; ***ihm in die Arme –,*** fall *or* sink into his arms; ***in die Knie –,*** fall *or* drop to one's knees; ***den Kopf – lassen,*** hang one's head; ***den Mut – lassen,*** lose heart *or* courage; ***der Mut sank ihm,*** his courage failed; ***bis in die –de Nacht,*** till nightfall. **Sinken,** *n.* sinking, subsidence; setting (*of the sun*), drop, fall (*of prices*), decrease, decline, lowering, abatement. **Sink|kasten,** *m.* street-drain. **–körper,** *m.* sinker. **–stoff,** *m.* sediment, deposit, precipitate.

Sinn [zɪn], *m.* (**-(e)s,** *pl.* **-e**) 1. sense, organ of perception, faculty, mind; ***andern –es werden,*** change one's mind; ***sich*** (*Dat.*) ***etwas aus dem –e schlagen,*** put *or* get s.th. out of one's mind, dismiss a th. from one's mind; ***bei –en sein,*** be in one's right mind, have one's wits about one; ***es fuhr ihm durch den –,*** it suddenly struck him; ***eines –es sein,*** agree, be of the same mind, be of *or* have the same opinion; ***seine fünf –e beisammen haben,*** have one's wits about one; ***im –e haben,*** have in mind, intend; ***in seinem –e handeln,*** act as he would, act according to his ideas *or* wishes; ***es kam mir in den –, daß,*** it occurred to me that; ***es will mir nicht in den –,*** I cannot grasp it *or* make head or tail of it; it does not appeal to me at all; (*Prov.*) ***viel Köpfe, viel –e,*** many men, many minds; ***von –en kommen,*** lose consciousness; go out of one's mind; ***von –en sein,*** be out of one's mind *or* senses, be crazy; 2. taste, liking, feeling (***für,*** for), disposition, inclination (for *or* towards), tendency (towards), flair, instinct (for); – ***haben für,*** have a taste for, be susceptible to, take an interest in; ***sein – steht nicht nach lauten Freuden,*** he has no liking *or* inclination for noisy *or* boisterous pleasures; – ***für Humor,*** sense of humour; – ***für Literatur,*** interest in literature; – ***für Musik,*** ear for music; – ***für Natur,*** appreciation of nature; – ***für Schönheit,*** eye for beauty, sense of beauty; ***hoher –,*** high-mindedness, magnanimity; 3. (basic) idea, meaning, significance, purport, import, gist, sense, interpretation, construction; sense, direction; ***keinen – haben,*** make no sense, have no point; ***im bildlichen –e,*** figuratively; ***im eigentlichen –e,*** literally, verbally; ***in gewissem –e,*** in a sense *or* way; ***im gleichen –e,*** to the same effect, likewise, similarly; ***im –e des Gesetzes,*** within the meaning of the act; ***im übertragenen –e,*** metaphorically; ***im wahrsten*** or ***tiefsten –e des Wortes,*** in the true *or* fullest sense of the word; ***im –e wie,*** in the way that, just as; ***dem –e nach,*** in spirit (*rather than according to the letter*); ***weder – noch Verstand,*** neither rhyme nor reason; ***– und Zweck einer S.,*** essence and purpose of a th.

Sinnbild ['zɪnbɪlt], *n.* symbol, emblem; allegory. **sinnbildlich,** *adj.* symbolic(al), emblematic; allegorical; ***–e Darstellung,*** allegory, symbolization; – ***darstellen,*** symbolize.

sinnen ['zɪnən], *irr.v.t., v.i.* (*aux.* h. & s.) think, brood (***über*** (*Acc.*), about *or* over), meditate, muse, reflect, speculate (about *or* upon); ponder; – ***auf*** (*Acc.*), scheme, plan, contrive, contemplate, devise, plot; ***auf Mittel und Wege –,*** devise ways and means; (***auf***) ***Rache –,*** plot revenge; ***er sinnt nichts Gutes,*** he harbours evil intentions; ***gesonnen sein,*** be inclined, have a mind (*to do*), intend, purpose; ***gesinnt,*** minded, inclined, disposed; ***er war protestantisch gesinnt,*** he had Protestant sympathies. **Sinnen,** *n.* thinking, planning; thoughts, aspirations. **sinnend,** *adj.* musing, pensive, thoughtful, contemplative, reflective.

Sinnen|freude, *f. See* **–genuß. sinnenfreudig,** *adj.* sensuous. **Sinnen|genuß,** *m.,* **–lust,** *f.* sensual pleasure, voluptuousness, sensuality. **–mensch,** *m.* sensualist. **–rausch,** *m.* sensual orgy. **–reiz,** *m.* sense-stimulus, titillation. **–taumel,** *m. See* **–rausch.**

sinnentstellend ['zɪnʔɛntʃtɛlənt], *adj.* falsifying, distorting (*meaning*).

Sinnenwelt ['zɪnənvɛlt], ˙ . material *or* external world.

Sinnes|änderung, *f.* change of mind; recantation. **–art,** *f.* way of thinking, mentality, character, disposition. **–eindruck,** *m.* sense-impression, sensation. **–nerv,** *m.* sensory nerve. **–organ,** *n.* sense-organ. **–täuschung,** *f.* illusion, hallucination. **–wahrnehmung,** *f.* sensory perception. **–werkzeug,** *n. See* **–organ.**

sinnfällig ['zɪnfɛlɪç], *adj.* obvious, apparent, manifest, palpable, conspicuous, striking. **Sinngedicht,** *n.* epigram. **sinn|gemäß, 1.** *adj.* corresponding, analogous. **2.** *adv.* analogously, accordingly, mutatis mutandis. **–getreu,** *adj.* faithful (*rendering*).

sinnieren [zɪ'ni:rən], *v.i.* be lost in thought, brood, ponder, muse, ruminate.

sinnig ['zɪnɪç], *adj.* sensible, judicious; thoughtful; ingenious; ***–es Mädchen,*** sensible girl; ***–es Geschenk,*** apt *or* appropriate *or* fitting present.

–sinnig, *adj.suff.* -minded. **Sinnigkeit,** *f.* thoughtfulness, ingenuity, aptness.

sinnlich ['zɪnlɪç], *adj.* 1. sensual, carnal: voluptuous; *–e Liebe,* sensual love; *–er Mensch,* sensualist, voluptuary; 2. (*Phil.*) sentient, sensuous, perceptible, physical, material; *–e Wahrnehmung,* sense, perception. **Sinnlichkeit,** *f.* 1. sensuality; 2. sentience, sensuousness, perceptibility.

sinnlos ['zɪnlo:s], *adj.* senseless, meaningless, pointless, futile; absurd, foolish, crazy; *– betrunken,* helplessly *or* (*coll.*) dead *or* blind drunk. **Sinnlosigkeit,** *f.* senselessness, futility; absurdity, foolishness. **sinnreich,** *adj.* witty, ingenious, clever. **Sinnspruch,** *m.* motto, maxim, epigram, aphorism. **sinn|verwandt,** *adj.* synonymous; *–es Wort,* synonym. **–verwirrend,** *adj.* bewildering, confusing, (*coll.*) staggering. **–voll,** *adj.* 1. significant, suggestive; pregnant *or* fraught with meaning; 2. sensible. **–widrig,** *adj.* nonsensical, absurd, preposterous.

sintemal [zɪntə'ma:l], *conj.* (*obs.*) since, whereas, inasmuch as.

Sinter ['zɪntər], *m.* sinter, stalactite; (*dial.*) iron-dross. **sintern,** *v.i.* (*aux.* s.) trickle, drip, ooze, percolate; form a deposit, frit together, slag, cake, clinker.

Sintflut ['zɪntflu:t], *f.* (*B.*) flood, deluge.

Sinus ['zi:nus], *m.* (-, *pl.* - *or* **-se**) (*Math.*) sine. **sinusförmig,** *adj.* sinusoidal. **Sinus|kurve,** *f.* (*Math.*) sine-curve. **–satz,** *m.* (*Math.*) sine theorem. **–strom,** *m.* (*Elec.*) sinusoidal current.

Sippe ['zɪpə], *f.* kin(ship), consanguinity; family, relatives, relations, kith and kin, kindred; (*Zool.*) genus, tribe; (*coll.*) clan, gang, clique, set, pack, crew, lot. **Sippenforschung,** *f.* genealogical research. **Sippschaft,** *f.* *See* **Sippe**; (*coll.*) *die ganze –,* the whole caboodle.

Sirene [zi're:nə], *f.* siren (*also Myth.*). **Sirenengeheul,** *n.* wail of sirens. **sirenenhaft,** *adj.* seductive, captivating, bewitching.

Sirup ['zi:rup], *m.* (**-s,** *pl.* **-e**) syrup, treacle, molasses. **sirupartig,** *adj.* syrupy.

Sisalhanf ['zi:zalhanf], *m.* sisal.

sistieren [zɪs'ti:rən], *v.t.* stop, check, inhibit; (*Law*) stay, suspend; arrest, take into custody. **Sistierung,** *f.* inhibition, stay, suspension, (*Law*) arrest, detention.

Sitte ['zɪtə], *f.* custom, habit, usage, tradition; practice, fashion, mode, way; propriety, etiquette; *pl.* morals, manners; *–n und Gebräuche,* manners and customs; *das ist bei uns nicht –,* that is not our custom *or* the custom with us; *das ist so seine –,* that is his way *or* habit; *feine –n,* good breeding; *lockere –n,* loose morals; *es ist –,* it is customary (*daß man tut,* to do).

Sitten|bild, –gemälde, *n.* genre-painting. **–gesetz,** *n.* moral law. **–kodex,** *m.* moral code. **–lehre,** *f.* ethics, moral philosophy. **–lehrer,** *m.* moral philosopher; moralist. **sittenlos,** *adj.* immoral, licentious, profligate, dissolute. **Sittenlosigkeit,** *f.* immorality, licentiousness, profligacy. **Sitten|polizei,** *f.* control of prostitutes, police surveillance of brothels, (*Am.*) vice-squad. **–prediger,** *m.* *See* **–richter. –predigt.** *f.* moralizing sermon; (*coll.*) *ihm eine – halten,* lay down the law to him. **–regel,** *f.* moral precept, rule of conduct. **sittenrein,** *adj.* (morally) pure, chaste. **Sitten|reinheit,** *f.* purity (of morals), chastity. **–richter,** *m.* moralizer, censor. **sitten|richterlich,** *adj.* censorious. **–streng,** *adj.* puritanical, austere. **Sitten|strenge,** *f.* austerity. **–verderbnis,** *f.*, **–verfall,** *m.* demoralization, depravity, corruption. **sittenwidrig,** *adj.* (*Law*) immoral, shameless, scandalous, contra bonos mores.

Sittich ['zɪtɪç], *m.* (**-(e)s,** *pl.* **-e**) parakeet.

sittig ['zɪtɪç], *adj.* 1. modest, virtuous, chaste; 2. well-bred, well-mannered, polite.

sittlich ['zɪtlɪç], *adj.* moral, ethical. **Sittlichkeit,** *f.* morality, morals. **Sittlichkeits|gefühl,** *n.* moral sense. **–verbrechen, –vergehen,** *n.* sex-offence, indecent assault.

sittsam ['zɪtza:m], *adj.* modest, demure, bashful, coy; virtuous, chaste; well-behaved, decent, proper. **Sittsamkeit,** *f.* modesty, demureness, bashfulness, coyness; good manners, decency.

Situation [zɪtuatsi'o:n], *f.* situation, position; state of affairs; *sich der – gewachsen fühlen,* be equal to the occasion; *sich der – gewachsen zeigen,* rise to the occasion; *wir sind in derselbcn –,* we are in the same situation *or* (*coll.*) same boat; *die – retten,* save the situation; *eine – ausnutzen,* make the most of an opportunity. **Situationskomik,** *f.* (*Theat.*) comedy of situation, slapstick (comedy).

situiert [zitu'i:rt], *adj.* placed; *wohl* or *gut –,* well off, well-to-do.

Sitz [zɪts], *m.* (**-es,** *pl.* **-e**) 1. seat, chair; perch; 2. (place of) residence, domicile; place of business, headquarters (*of a firm*); place, spot; (episcopal) see; *– und Stimme haben,* have a seat and vote; *seinen – an einem Orte aufschlagen,* establish o.s. *or* take up residence *or* settle in a place; *London ist der – der Regierung,* London is the seat of government; 3. fit (*of a garment*); (*Mech.*) seat(ing) (*of valve*). **Sitz|arbeit,** *f.* sedentary work. **–bad,** *n.* hip-bath. **–bank,** *f.* bench, seat, settee. **–bein,** *n.* (*Anat.*) ischium.

sitzen ['zɪtsən], *irr.v.i.* (*aux.* h. & (*dial.*) s.) 1. sit, be seated; perch (*of bird*); stay, be situated, remain, be; (*of a firm*) have its place of business (*in* (*Dat.*), at); (*of a conference*) be in session; *es sitzt sich gut hier,* here is a comfortable place to sit, (*Theat. etc.*) this is a good seat; *die Truppen – am Ufer,* the troops are established on *or* occupy the bank; *ihm auf dem Nacken –,* be a pest *or* (*sl.*) be a pain in the neck to him; *beim Tanze –,* sit out (a dance); *da – wir!* now we're in a mess; (*Fenc., fig.*) *der Hieb sitzt!* that's a home thrust! (*coll.*) *in Butter –,* be fine and dandy; *im Ausschuß –,* sit on the committee; *ihm sitzt der Schelm im Nacken,* he is a scamp *or* rascal; *im Rate –,* have a seat on the council; (*coll.*) *in der Tinte* or *Patsche –,* be in an awful mess *or* jam *or* fix; *fest im Sattel –,* have a firm seat, (*fig.*) be firmly in the saddle, be firmly established in power; *da sitzt der Knoten!* there's the rub! (*einem Maler*) *–,* sit for a portrait, give a sitting; 2. stick fast, adhere; (*coll.*) (*of a blow, remark*) tell, go home; *der Nagel sitzt fest,* the nail holds firm; *das Schiff sitzt fest* (*auf dem Grunde*), the ship is fast aground; *der Schuß saß,* the shot hit the mark; 3. fit (*of clothes*); 4. (*sl.*) be doing time, be in clink *or* jug; *im Gefängnis –,* be in prison.

sitzenbleiben ['zɪtsənblaɪbən], *irr.v.i.*, 1. remain seated, keep one's seat; (*fig.*) be a wallflower, be on the shelf; 2. stay down (*at school*); 3. (*coll.*) not rise (*of dough*). **sitzend,** *adj.* seated, perched; sedentary; (*Bot.*) sessile; *–e Lebensweise,* sedentary (mode of) life. **sitzenlassen,** *irr.v.t.* (*coll.*) leave in the lurch, let down; jilt; (*coll.*) walk out on, throw over; *auf sich* (*Dat.*) *–,* put up with *or* pocket (*an affront*).

–sitzer [zɪtsər], *m.suff.* -seater.

Sitz|fläche, *f.* seat (*of chair*), (*coll.*) backside, sit-upon. **–fleisch,** *n.* (*coll.*) ham, buttock; (*fig.*) perseverance; (*coll.*) *er hat kein –,* he cannot stick at a job. **–fuß,** *m.* (*Orn.*) insessorial foot. **–füßler,** *m.pl.* (*Orn.*) perchers, insessores. **–gelegenheit,** *f.* seating-accommodation, (number of) seats (available).

–sitzig [zɪtsɪç], *adj.suff.* -seater.

Sitz|ordnung, *f.* seating arrangements. **–platz,** *m.* seat. **–reihe,** *f.* (*Theat.*) row (of seats). **–stange,** *f.* perch. **–streik,** *m.* sit-down strike.

Sitzung ['zɪtsuŋ], *f.* sitting (*also for a portrait*); session; meeting; conference; (*coll.*) *eine lange – halten,* sit a long time over one's drink, have a long session (in the pub); *öffentliche –,* public session *or* hearing. **Sitzungs|bericht,** *m.* report of a meeting, proceedings, minutes. **–dauer, –periode,** *f.* session, term. **–saal,** *m.*, **–zimmer,** *n.* council-room, committee-room, conference-room, board-room, (*Parl.*) chamber.

Six! [zɪks], *int.* (*coll.*) *meiner –! mein Sixchen!* upon my soul! upon my word!

Sizilien [zi'tsi:liən], *n.* Sicily. **Sizilier,** *m.*, **sizilisch,** *adj.* Sicilian.

skabiös [skabi'ø:s], *adj.* (*Med.*) scabious. **Skabiose,** *f.* (*Bot.*) scabious.

Skala ['ska:la], *f.* (-, *pl.* **-len**) gamut; scale, graduation. **Skalen|ablesung,** *f.* direct *or* scale reading. **-einteilung,** *f.* graduation. **-meßgerät,** *n.* (*Elec. etc.*) direct-reading instrument. **-ring,** *m.* graduated ring. **-scheibe,** *f.* graduated dial, (*Rad.*) tuning-dial.

Skalde ['skaldə], *m.* (**-n,** *pl.* **-n**) scald, ancient bard. **Skalden|dichtung, -poesie,** *f.* old Norse poetry.

Skalp [skalp], *m.* (**-s,** *pl.* **-e**) scalp.

Skalpell [skal'pɛl], *n.* (**-s,** *pl.* **-e**) scalpel.

skalpieren [skal'pi:rən], *v.t.* scalp.

Skandal [skan'da:l], *m.* (**-s,** *pl.* **-e**) scandal; row, uproar, (*coll.*) racket; – ***machen*** or ***schlagen,*** *see* **skandalieren. Skandalgeschichte,** *f.* (piece of) scandal. **skandalieren** [–'li:rən], *v.i.* make a din, kick up a row. **skandalisieren** [–li'zi:rən], *v.r.* be shocked *or* scandalized (*über* (*Acc.*), at). **skandalös** [–'lø:s], *adj.* scandalous, shocking, disgraceful. **Skandalpresse,** *f.* gutter press.

skandieren [skan'di:rən], *v.t.* scan (*verses*).

Skandinavien [skandi'na:viən], *n.* Scandinavia. **Skandinavier,** *m.*, **skandinavisch,** *adj.* Scandinavian.

Skat [ska:t], *m.* (**-(e)s,** *pl.* **-e**) skat (*a German card game*).

Skelett [ske'lɛt], *n.* (**-(e)s,** *pl.* **-e**) skeleton. **skelettartig,** *adj.* skeleton-like; reduced to a skeleton, all skin and bones.

Skepsis ['skɛpsɪs], *f.* scepticism, doubt. **Skeptiker,** *m.* sceptic. **skeptisch,** *adj.* sceptical. **Skeptizismus** [–'tsɪsmus], *m.* (*Phil.*) scepticism.

Ski [ʃi:], *m.* (**-s,** *pl.* **-er**) ski; – ***laufen*** or ***fahren,*** ski, go skiing. **Ski|fahren,** *n. See* **-laufen. -fahrer,** *see* **-läufer. -hütte,** *f.* ski-hut. **-laufen,** *n.* skiing. **-läufer,** *m.* skier. **-lehrer,** *m.* ski(ing) instructor. **-springen,** *n.* ski-jumping.

Skizze ['skɪtsə], *f.* sketch, outline, rough draft. **skizzenhaft,** *adj.* sketchy. **skizzieren** [–'tsi:rən], *v.t.* sketch, outline, make a rough draft.

Sklave ['skla:və], *m.* (**-n,** *pl.* **-n**) slave. **Sklaven|arbeit,** *f.* slave-work; (*fig.*) drudgery. **-befreiung,** *f.* emancipation of slaves. **-dienst,** *m.* slavery; drudgery. **-halter,** *m.* slave-owner. **-handel,** *m.* slave-trade. **-händler,** *m.* slave-dealer. **-seele,** *f.* slavish mind, servile disposition. **-staaten,** *m.pl.* slave-states (*of America*). **Sklaventum,** *n. See* **Sklaverei.**

Sklaverei [skla:və'raɪ], *f.* slavery, (*fig.*) servitude, bondage, thraldom. **Sklavin,** *f.* slave (girl), female slave. **sklavisch,** *adj.* slavish, servile.

skontieren [skɔn'ti:rən], *v.t.* deduct, allow discount on. **Skonto,** *m.* (*Austr. n.*) discount. **skontrieren,** *v.t.* check (*cash*), collate. **Skontrierung,** *f.* settling, balancing, clearing, checking, collating. **Skontro,** *n.* settlement, balance. **Skontro|buch,** *n.* account-current book. **-tag,** *m.* settling-day.

Skorbut [skɔr'bu:t], *m.* scurvy. **skorbutisch,** *adj.* scorbutic.

Skribent [skri'bɛnt], *m.* (**-en,** *pl.* **-en**) (*obs.*) writer; (*coll*) scribbler, pen-pusher, quill-driver, literary hack.

Skripturen [skrip'tu:rən], *f.pl.* (*obs.*) papers, documents.

Skrofel(n) ['skro:fəl(n)], *f.*(*pl.*) scrofula. **skrofulös** [–u'lø:s], *adj.* scrofulous, strumous. **Skrofulose** [–u'lo:zə], *f.* scrofula.

Skrupel ['skru:pəl], *m.* scruple; ***sich*** (*Dat.*) ***– machen über*** (*Acc.*), have one's scruples about. **skrupellos,** *adj.* unscrupulous. **Skrupellosigkeit,** *f.* unscrupulousness, lack of scruples. **skrupulös** [–u'lø:s], *adj.* scrupulous.

skullen ['skulən], *v.t., v.i.* scull, row.

Skulptur [skulp'tu:r], *f.* (-, *pl.* **-en**) (piece of) sculpture.

skurril [sku'ri:l], *adj.* scurrilous, ludicrous.

Slawe ['sla:və], *m.* (**-n,** *pl.* **-n**), **Slawin,** *f.* Slav. **slawisch,** *adj.* Slav, Slavic, Slavonian.

Slowake [slo'va:kə], *m.* (**-n,** *pl.* **-n**), **Slowakin,** *f.* Slovakian. **Slowakei** [–'kaɪ], *f.* Slovakia. **slowakisch,** *adj.* Slovakian.

Slowene [slo've:nə], *m.* (**-n,** *pl.* **-n**) Slovenian. **Slowenien,** *n.* Slovenia. **Slowenier,** *m. See* **Slowene. Slowenierin, Slowenin,** *f.*, **slowenisch,** *adj.* Slovenian.

Smaragd [sma'rakt], *m.* (**-(e)s,** *pl.* **-e**) emerald. **smaragden, smaragd|farben, -grün,** *adj.* emerald (green). **Smaragdhuhn,** *n.* (*Orn.*) green-backed gallinule (*Porphyrio madagascariensis*).

Smoking ['smo:kɪŋ], *m.* (**-s,** *pl.* **-s**) dinner-jacket, (*Am.*) tuxedo.

so [zo:], **1.** *adv.* so, thus, in this *or* that way *or* manner, in such a way *or* manner, like this *or* that; (*in comparison*) as; ***er spricht bald –, bald –,*** he says now this, now that; ***sein Betragen war –, daß,*** his conduct was such as (to); ***– ein,*** such a; ***– . . . auch,*** however; ***– groß er auch sein mag,*** however great he may be; ***– etwas,*** such a thing, that sort of thing; ***– etwas!*** the very idea! would you believe it! well, I never! ***er hat nicht – ganz Unrecht,*** he is not so far wrong; ***ich summte – vor mich hin,*** I was just humming to myself; ***– lange*** (***daß***), so long that; ***Sie sagen das nur –,*** you are only saying that, you do not really mean it; ***das reicht nur – eben,*** that is barely sufficient *or* only just enough and no more; ***– oder –,*** one way or another, by hook or by crook; ***– recht!*** or ***recht –!*** quite right! just so! ***er ist – schon böse,*** he is angry anyhow; ***– sehr,*** so much, to such a degree; ***– ist es,*** that is right, that is so; ***– ist das Leben,*** such is life; ***wenn dem – ist,*** if that is so; ***es ist mir –, als könnte ich fliegen,*** I feel as if *or* though I could fly; ***das ist nun einmal –,*** that is the way things are; ***– bin ich nun einmal,*** that is my nature *or* way; ***um – besser,*** all the better, so much the better; ***– und – oft,*** every so often, time and again; ***es waren nicht – viele,*** there were not so very many (of them); ***– wahr ich lebe!*** as (sure as) I live! ***– . . . wie . . .,*** as . . . as . . .; ***nicht – groß wie,*** not as *or* so big as; ***machen Sie es – wie ich,*** do as I do; ***– gut wie keine,*** practically none; ***– gut wie nichts,*** next to nothing; ***– ziemlich,*** pretty well, pretty good. **2.** *conj.* therefore, for that reason, consequently, so, then; if, in case; ***er war nicht zu Hause, – war mein Besuch vergebens,*** he was not at home, consequently my visit was in vain; ***er ist krank, – daß er nicht kommen kann,*** he is too ill to come; ***– Gott will,*** if it please God; ***– lasset uns gehen,*** let us go then; (*in consecutive clause frequently untranslated*) ***da du nicht kannst,*** (–) ***werde ich selbst hingehen,*** since you cannot go, (then) I will go myself; ***kaum warst du fort,*** (–) ***kam er zurück,*** you were scarcely gone, when he returned. **3.** *int.* indeed! really! ***ach –!*** Oh! I see. **4.** (*B., obs.*) *rel. pron.* who, that, which; ***diejenigen, – mich lieben,*** those who love me.

sobald [zo'balt], *conj.* as soon as; – (***als***) ***es Ihnen bequem ist,*** at your earliest convenience.

Söckchen ['zœkçən], anklet, ankle-sock.

Socke ['zɔkə], *f.* sock; (*coll.*) ***sich auf die -n machen,*** make off, take to one's heels.

Sockel ['zɔkəl], *m.* base, pedestal, stand, foot, socle, socket. **Sockelplatte,** *f.* plinth.

Sockenhalter ['zɔkənhaltər], *m.* (sock-)suspender, garter.

Sod [zo:t], *m.* (**-(e)s,** *pl.* **-e**) 1. boil, boiling, brew; 2. heartburn; 3. (*dial.*) spring, well.

Soda ['zo:da], *f. or n.* (carbonate of) soda.

sodann [zo'dan], *adv.* then, thereafter, thereupon, after that.

Sodawasser ['zo:davasər], *n.* soda-water, aerated *or* mineral water.

Sodbrennen ['zo:tbrɛnən], *n.* heartburn, (*Med.*) pyrosis.

soeben [zo'e:bən], *adv.* just (now), a moment ago.

Sofa ['zo:fa], *n.* (**-s,** *pl.* **-s**) sofa, couch, settee.

sofern [zo'fɛrn], *conj.* inasmuch as, (in) so far as; – *nur,* as long as, if only; – *nicht,* unless.
Soff [zɔf], *m. See* **Suff.**
soff, söffe ['zœfə], *see* **saufen.**
Soffitte [zɔ'fɪtə], *f.* (*Archit.*) soffit; *pl.* (*Theat.*) flies. **Sofittenlampe,** *f.* strip-light(ing).
sofort [zo'fɔrt], *adv.* immediately, instantly, forthwith, at once, (*coll.*) straight away, on the spot, (*sl.*) right away. **sofortig,** *adj.* immediate, prompt, instantaneous; *–e Kasse,* ready *or* spot cash. **Sofortmaßnahme,** *f.* prompt *or* urgent measure.
Sog [zo:k], *m.* **(-(e)s,** *pl.* **-e)** undertow; (*Av.*) suction; (*Naut.*) wake, (*fig.*) whirl(pool), maelstrom, hurly-burly (*of events*).
sog, *see* **saugen.**
sogar [zo'ga:r], *adv.* even; *ja –,* yes, and what is more.
söge ['zø:gə], *see* **saugen.**
sogenannt ['zo:gənant], *adj.* so-called; pretended, self-styled, would-be.
soggen ['zɔgən], *v.i.* crystallize out. **Soggepfanne,** *f.* crystallizing pan.
sogleich [zo'glaɪç], *adv. See* **sofort.**
Sohle ['zo:lə], *f.* **1.** sole (*of foot or shoe*); (*coll.*) *sich* (*Dat.*) *etwas an den –n abgelaufen haben,* have known s.th. long ago; *mir brennt es auf* or *unter den –n,* it is getting too hot for me; *auf leisen –n,* (treading) softly *or* gently, on tip-toe; (*coll.*) *mach dich auf die –n!* beat it! *sich die –n wund laufen,* run one's legs off (*nach,* after); *vom Scheitel bis zur –,* from head to foot, from top to toe. **2.** face (*of a plane*); bottom (*of a valley*); floor (*of a mine*); **3.** (*coll.*) lie, fib. **sohlen, 1.** *v.t.* sole. **2.** *v.i.* (*coll.*) tell fibs.
Sohlen|band, *n.* (*Anat.*) plantar ligament. **–gänger,** *m.* (*Zool.*) plantigrade (animal). **–platte,** *f.* bedplate foundation.
söhlig ['zø:lɪç], *adj.* (*Min.*) level, horizontal.
Sohlleder ['zo:lle:dər], *n.* sole-leather.
Sohn [zo:n], *m.* **(-(e)s,** *pl.* **⸚e)** son; *Schmidt –,* Schmidt junior; *Ihr Herr –,* your son; (*B.*) *des Menschen –,* the Son of Man; (*B.*) *der verlorene –,* the prodigal son.
Söhnerin ['zø:nərɪn], *f.* (*dial.*) daughter-in-law.
Sohnes|liebe, *f.* filial affection. **–pflicht,** *f.* filial duty.
Soiree [zwa're:], *f.* (-, *pl.* **-n**) soirée, dinner-party; (*Theat.*) evening performance.
Soja ['zo:ja], **Sojabohne,** *f.* soya-bean, soybean.
solang(e) [zo'laŋ(ə)], *conj.* – (*als*), as *or* so long as, while, whilst.
Solawechsel ['zo:lavɛksəl], *m.* bill (of exchange), promissory note.
Solbad ['zo:lba:t], *n.* brine bath.
solch [zɔlç], **1.** *adj., dem.pron.* such; *ein –er Mensch, – ein Mensch, – einer,* a man like that, such a one, such a man; *ich habe –e,* I have some like that *or* these. **2.** *adv. in – schlechter* or *in – einer schlechten Lage,* in such a bad position *or* state. **solcher|art,** *adv.* of this sort, of such a kind, (*coll.*) along these lines. **–gestalt,** *adv.* in such a way *or* manner, so, thus, to such a degree. **solcherlei,** *indecl.adj.* of such a kind, such; (*coll.*) suchlike. **solcher|maßen, –weise,** *adv.* in such a way *or* manner.
Sold [zɔlt], *m.* (soldier's) pay; (*fig.*) wages; *halber –,* half-pay; (*Poet.*) *der Minne –,* reward *or* guerdon of love; (*B.*) *der Tod ist der Sünde –,* the wages of sin is death; (*fig.*) *in seinem –e stehen,* be in his pay, be one of his hirelings.
Soldat [zɔl'da:t], *m.* **(-en,** *pl.* **-en)** soldier; *abgedankter –,* discharged soldier; *aktiver –,* regular (soldier); *alter* or *erfahrener –,* old campaigner, veteran; *– zu Fuß,* infantryman, foot-soldier; *gedienter –,* time-expired man, ex-serviceman; *gemeiner –,* private; *gemeine –en,* rank and file; *– zu Pferde,* cavalryman, trooper; *–en spielen,* play at soldiers; *– werden,* enlist, join the army, (*coll.*) join up.
Soldaten|bund, *m.* ex-servicemen's *or* (*Am.*) veteran's association. **–eid,** *m.* military oath. **–friedhof,** *m.* war cemetery. **–geist,** *m.* military *or* martial spirit. **–grab,** *m.* war grave. **soldatenhaft,** *adj. See* **soldatisch. Soldaten|heim,** *n.* leave-centre. **–leben,** *n.* military life. **–lied,** *n.* soldier's song, marching song. **–mütze,** *f.* forage cap. **–rock,** *m.* uniform; tunic; (*coll.*) *den – anziehen,* enlist; *den – ausziehen,* be demobilized *or* discharged. **–schenke,** *f.* tavern frequented by soldiers, troops' canteen. **-sprache,** *f.* military jargon, soldiers' slang. **Soldatentum,** *n.* soldiery; soldierliness, soldierly spirit, military tradition.
Soldateska [zɔlda'tɛska], *f.* (coarse *or* licentious) soldiery, rabble of soldiers.
soldatisch [zɔl'da:tɪʃ], *adj.* soldier-like, soldierly; military, martial.
Soldbuch ['zɔldbu:x], *n.* (soldier's) pay-book.
Söldling ['zœltlɪŋ], *m.* **(-s,** *pl.* **-e), Söldner,** *m.* hired soldier, mercenary, (*fig.*) hireling. **Söldner|-heer,** *n.* (army of) mercenaries. **–truppen, Sold-truppen,** *f.pl.* mercenary troops.
Sole ['zo:lə], *f.* brine, salt-spring. **Solei** ['zo:lʔaɪ], *n.* pickled egg.
solenn [zo'lɛn], *adj.* solemn. **Solennität** [–i'tɛ:t], *f.* solemnity.
solfeggieren [zɔlfɛ'dʒi:rən], *v.i.* sing sol-fa.
solid [zo'li:t], *adj.* solid, substantial, strong, robust, durable, hard-wearing; (*Comm.*) (*of a firm*) safe, sound, reliable; solvent; (*of prices*) fair, reasonable, moderate; (*fig.*) respectable, steady; *–er Mieter,* steady *or* respectable tenant.
Solidar|bürgschaft [zoli'da:r–], **–haftung,** *f.* joint security *or* surety. **solidarisch, 1.** *adj.* joint, jointly (and severally) liable; unanimous. **2.** *adv.* solidly, in a body, (*Comm., Law*) jointly and severally; *sich – erklären mit,* declare one's solidarity with. **Solidarität** [–i'tɛ:t], *f.* joint liability, unanimity, solidarity. **Solidarschuldner,** *m.* joint debtor.
solide [zo'li:də], *adj. See* **solid. Solidität** [–i'tɛ:t], *f.* solidity, (*Comm.*) soundness, stability, trustworthiness; respectability, steadiness.
Solist [zo'lɪst], *m.* **(-en,** *pl.* **-en), Solistin,** *f.* soloist.
Solitär [zoli'tɛ:r], *m.* **(-s,** *pl.* **-e)** brilliant, solitaire; (*Astr.*) single star.
Soll [zɔl], *n.* **(-(s),** *pl.* **-(s))** **1.** debit (side); (*das*) *– und Haben,* debit and credit; **2.** quota, (production *or* delivery) target, (*fig.*) obligation; *ins – eintragen,* debit (*a p.'s account*); *das – und das Muß,* obligation and necessity; *ein Mehr gegenüber dem –,* a surplus over and above estimated revenue; *in jedem – sieht er ein Muß,* he accepts every obligation as binding.
Soll|ausgaben, *f.pl.* estimated expenditure. **–bestand,** *m.* presumed *or* calculated assets *or* stock, (*Mil.*) establishment. **–bruchlast,** *f.* breaking load. **–durchmesser,** *m.* (*Tech.*) nominal diameter. **–einnahme,** *f.* estimated receipts *or* revenue, receipts due.
Solleistung ['zɔllaɪstuŋ], *f.* rated *or* nominal output.
sollen [zɔlən], *irr.v.i.* **1.** be obliged *or* bound to, have to, must; **2.** be said to, be supposed to, pass for; **3.** shall, should, ought to, am (is, are *etc.*) to; *nicht –,* must not; *was soll ich?* what am I (expected) to do? *was soll das (heißen)?* what is the meaning *or* use *or* purpose of this? *was soll mir das alles?* what is all that to me? *wir tun nicht immer was wir –,* we do not always do what we ought; *ich weiß nicht was ich tun soll,* I do not know what to do; *wie soll man da nicht lachen?* how can one help laughing? *er soll gelehrt sein,* he is reputed to be very learned; *er soll recht haben!* let him have his own way! granted that he is right! *der soll erst geboren werden, der . . .,* the man is not yet born who . . .; *er soll es getan haben,* he is said to have done it; (*B.*) *du sollst nicht töten,* thou shalt not kill; *was soll ich sagen?* what ought I to *or* shall I say? *er sollte König werden,* he was (destined) to be king; *Ihr Kinder sollt etwas warten,* you children

are *or* have to wait a little; ***was sollte ich dagegen machen?*** how could I help it? ***man sollte meinen,*** one would think; ***es sollte ein Witz sein,*** it was meant for a joke; ***wenn es regnen sollte,*** if it should rain; ***sollte es die Katze gewesen sein?*** could it have been the cat? ***ich hätte es nicht tun –,*** I ought not to have done it. **sollend,** *adj.* ***sein –,*** would-be.

Söller ['zœlər], *m.* balcony; loft, garret.

Soll|posten, *m.* (*Comm.*) debit item *or* entry. **–seite,** *f.* (*Comm.*) debit side. **–stärke,** *f.* (*Mil.*) establishment. **–wert,** *m.* rated *or* nominal value.

solmisieren [zɔlmi'zi:rən], *v.i.* sing sol-fa.

solo ['zo:lo], *adv.* alone. **Solo,** *n.* (**-s,** *pl.* **-s** *or* **Soli**) solo. **Solo|geiger,** *m.* solo violinist. **–gesang,** *m.* solo (singing). **–partie,** *f.* solo (part). **–sänger,** *m.* solo singer, soloist. **–spieler,** *m.* solo player, soloist. **–stimme,** *f.* solo part. **–tanz,** *m.* pas seul. **–tänzer,** *m.* principal dancer.

Solözismus [zolø'tsɪsmus], *m.* (-, *pl.* **-men**) solecism.

Solquelle ['zo:lkvɛlə], *f.* salt-spring *or* -well.

somit [zo'mɪt], *adv.* so, then, consequently, accordingly, thus.

Sommer ['zɔmər], *m.* summer; *pl.* (*Poet.*) years; ***fliegender –,*** *see* **Sommerfäden.**

Sommer|fäden, *m.pl.* gossamer. **–fahrplan,** *m.* summer time-table. **–ferien,** *pl.* summer vacation. **–fleck,** *m.* freckle. **–frische,** *f.* holiday resort, health resort. **–frischler,** *m.* summer visitor, holidaymaker. **–getreide,** *n.* spring wheat. **–goldhähnchen,** *n.* (*Orn.*) firecrest (*Regulus ignicapillus*). **–haus,** *n.* summer-house; holiday cottage. **–hitze,** *f.* heat of summer. **–kartoffel,** *f.* early potato. **–kleid,** *n.* summer coat (*of animals and birds*). **–kleidung,** *f.* summer wear. **–leutnant,** *m.* (*sl.*) reserve officer.

sommerlich ['zɔmərlɪç], *adj.* summer-like, summery; ***sich – kleiden,*** put on summer clothes. **sommern, 1.** *v.i., imp.* ***es sommert,*** summer is drawing on; ***der Baum sommert,*** the tree is sprouting. **2.** *v.t.* (*also* **sömmern**) 1. expose to the sun; turn out (*cattle*) to graze; 2. lop, prune (*trees*); 3. sow (*a field*) for early crop. **3.** *v.r.* ***die Hühner – sich,*** the hens bask in the sun.

Sommer|nachtstraum, *m.* Midsummer Night's Dream. **–obst,** *n.* early fruit. **–saat,** *f.* spring corn. **–schlaf,** *m.* (*Zool.*) (a)estivation. **–semester,** *n.* summer term. **–sitz,** *m.* summer residence. **–sonnenwende,** *f.* summer solstice. **–sprosse,** *f.* freckle. **sommersprossig,** *adj.* freckled. **Sommer|theater,** *n.* open-air theatre. **–tracht,** *f.* (*beekeeping*) summer flow of honey. **–vogel,** *m.* (*dial.*) butterfly. **–weg,** *m.* fine-weather road, seasonal road. **–weizen,** *m.* spring(-sown) wheat. **–wohnung,** *f. See* **–haus. –zeit,** *f.* summertime, summer season; daylight-saving *or* summer time.

sonach [zo'na:x], *adv. See* **somit.**

Sonde ['zɔndə], *f.* (*Med.*) probe; (*Naut.*) sounding-lead, plummet; (*Rad., Meteor.*) sonde, sounding balloon.

sonder ['zɔndər], *prep.* (*obs.*) (*Acc.*) without; ***– Zweifel,*** without doubt, undoubtedly; ***– Zahl,*** countless.

Sonder|abdruck, –abzug, *m.* separate impression; offprint. **–anfertigung,** *f.* special design *or* model. **–angebot,** *n.* special offer, bargain. **–auftrag,** *m.* special mission. **–ausbildung,** *f.* special training. **–ausführung,** *f. See* **–anfertigung. –ausgabe,** *f.* 1. special edition; 2. (*Comm.*) special expenditure. **–ausschuß,** *m.* special *or* select committee.

sonderbar ['zɔndərba:r], *adj.* singular, peculiar, extraordinary, queer, strange, odd, curious, droll. **sonderbarerweise,** *adv.* oddly enough, strange to say.

Sonder|beauftragte(r), *m., f.* minister with special responsibilities. **–beilage,** *f.* (special) supplement. **–berichterstatter,** *m.* special correspondent (*to a newspaper*). **–bestimmungen,** *f.pl.* special regulations, exceptional provisions. **–bestrebung,** *f.* (*Pol.*) separatism, particularism. **–bündler,** *m.* separatist. **–druck,** *m. See* **–abdruck. –fall,** *m.* special *or* particular case, exception. **–friede(n),** *m.* separate peace. **sondergleichen,** *indecl.adj.* unequalled, unparalleled, unprecedented, incomparable, matchless, peerless, unique. **Sonderkonto,** *n.* separate account.

sonderlich ['zɔnderlɪç], *adj.* special, peculiar, particular, remarkable; ***nichts –es,*** nothing out of the ordinary; ***kein –er Gelehrter,*** no great scholar; ***nicht –,*** not very, not specially, not much. **Sonderling,** *m.* (**-s,** *pl.* **-e**) odd *or* queer *or* eccentric p., oddity, crank, original. **Sondermeldung,** *f.* special announcement.

[1]**sondern** ['zɔndərn], *v.t.* separate, segregate, (set a)sunder, part, sever; sift, sort; distinguish.

[2]**sondern,** *conj.* but, on the contrary; ***nicht nur . . . –,*** not only . . . but (moreover *or* on the contrary).

Sonder|nummer, *f.* special edition (*of a paper etc.*). **–preis,** *m.* preferential *or* special price. **–recht,** *n.* (special) privilege. **sonders,** *adv.* (*only in*) ***samt und –,*** one and all, altogether, (*coll.*) the whole lot. **Sonderstellung,** *f.* special *or* exceptional position. **Sonderung,** *f.* separation, division, segregation; ***völlige –,*** isolation. **Sonder|urlaub,** *m.* (*Mil.*) special leave; ***– aus Familiengründen,*** compassionate *or* (*Am.*) emergency leave. **–verband,** *m.* (*Mil.*) task-force. **–vorführung,** *f.* special performance. **–zug,** *m.* special train. **–zulage,** *f.* special bonus.

sondieren [zɔn'di:rən], *v.t., v.i.* (*Med.*) probe, (*Naut., Meteor.*) sound; (*fig.*) probe, sound, (*v.i. only*) explore the ground.

Sonett [zo'nɛt], *n.* (**-(e)s,** *pl.* **-e**) sonnet. **Sonettist** [–'tɪst], *m.* (**-en,** *pl.* **-en**) sonnet-writer, sonneteer.

Sonnabend ['zɔnˀa:bənt], *m.* Saturday. **sonnabends,** *adv.* on Saturdays, on a Saturday.

Sonne ['zɔnə], *f.* sun, sunshine; ***Platz an der –,*** place in the sun; ***die – meint es gut,*** the sun is trying to shine; ***die – schießen,*** take bearings on the sun. **sonnen, 1.** *v.t.* expose to the sun, air (*beds etc.*). **2.** *v.r.* bask (in the sun); (*fig.*) ***sich – an*** or ***in*** (*Dat.*), bask *or* revel in.

Sonnen|aufgang, *m.* sunrise. **–bad,** *n.* sun-bath. **–bahn,** *f.* ecliptic; orbit of the sun. **–belichtung,** *f.* exposure to sunlight. **–beobachtung,** *f.* bearings on the sun. **sonnenbeschienen,** *adj.* sunlit, sunny. **Sonnen|bestrahlung,** *f.* solar irradiation, insolation; *see* **–belichtung. –blende,** *f.* sunblind, (*Phot.*) lens shade. **–blume,** *f.* (*Bot.*) sunflower (*Helianthus annuus*). **–brand,** *m.* sunburn. **–bräune,** *f.* (sun)tan. **–dach,** *n.* awning, sunblind, (*Motor.*) sunshine-roof. **–deck,** *n.* (*Naut.*) awning. **–ferne,** *f.* aphelion. **–finsternis,** *f.* solar eclipse. **–fleck,** *m.* sunspot. **–geflecht,** *n.* (*Anat.*) solar plexus. **–glut,** *f.* blazing sun. **sonnenhaft,** *adj.* sunny, radiant. **sonnenhell,** *adj.* bright as day, sunny. **Sonnen|hof,** *m.* halo round the sun. **–höhe,** *f.* sun's altitude. **–jahr,** *n.* solar *or* astronomical year. **–käfer,** *m.*, **–kälbchen,** *n.* (*Ent.*) ladybird. **sonnenklar,** *adj.* (*fig.*) (plainly) obvious, clear as daylight, evident. **Sonnen|licht,** *n.* sunlight. **–nähe,** *f.* perihelion. **–protuberanzen,** *f.pl.* (*Astr.*) solar prominences. **–rose,** *f. See* **–blume.**

Sonnen|scheibe, *f.* solar disk. **–schein,** *m.* sunshine. **–scheinsdauer,** *f.* (*Meteor.*) hours of sunshine. **sonnenscheu,** *adj.* (*Bot.*) heliophobic. **Sonnen|schirm,** *m.* sunshade, parasol. **–segel,** *n.* awning. **–seite,** *f.* sunny side, southern aspect. **–spektrum,** *n.* solar spectrum. **–spiegel,** *m.* (*Bot.*) turnsole. **–stand,** *m.* position of the sun. **–stich,** *m.* sunstroke. **–strahl,** *m.* sunbeam, ray of sunshine. **–strahlung,** *f.* solar radiation. **–system,** *n.* solar system. **–tau,** *m.* (*Bot.*) sundew (*Drosera*). **–tierchen,** *n.* (*Zool.*) sun-animalcule (*Heliozoa*). **–uhr,** *f.* sundial. **–untergang,** *m.* sunset. **sonnenverbrannt,** *adj.* sunburnt, tanned. **Sonnen|wende,** *f.* 1. solstice; 2. (*Bot.*) heliotrope. **–wendfeier,** *f. See* **Sonnwendfeier. –zeit,** *f.* solar time. **–zelt,** *n.* awning; (*Poet.*) canopy of the sky.

sonnig ['zɔnɪç], *adj.* sunny, bright, radiant.

Sonntag ['zɔnta:k], *m.* Sunday; ***am –,*** on Sunday. **sonntägig,** *adj.* Sunday, on Sunday. **sonntäg-**

lich, *adv.* every Sunday; ***sich – anziehen,*** put on one's Sunday best. **sonntags,** *adv.* on Sundays, on a Sunday.

Sonntags|anzug, *m.* Sunday suit *or* (*coll.*) best. **–ausflug,** *m.* week-end excursion. **–beilage,** *f.* Sunday supplement (*of a newspaper*). **–blatt,** *n.* Sunday paper. **–entheiliger,** *m.* Sabbath-breaker. **–fahrer,** *m.* week-end driver. **–fahrkarte,** *f.* week-end ticket. **–feier,** *f.* day of rest. **–heiligung,** *f.* keeping the Sabbath. **–jäger,** *m.* holiday *or* week-end sportsman. **–karte,** *f. See* **–fahrkarte. –kind,** *n.* Sunday's child; ***er ist ein –,*** he was born under a lucky star *or* with a silver spoon in his mouth. **–ruhe,** *f.* Sabbath rest, observance of the Sabbath. **–schule,** *f.* Sunday school. **–staat,** *m. See* **–anzug.**

Sonn|wende, *f.* solstice. **–wendfeier,** *f.* mid-summer festival.

sonor [zo'no:r], *adj.* sonorous.

sonst [zɔnst], *adv.* else, otherwise; besides, moreover, in other respects; at other times, at any other time, as a rule, usually, normally, formerly; ***– sind wir gesund,*** otherwise we are all well; ***– etwas,*** something else *or* besides, anything else; ***– jemand,*** anybody *or* somebody else; ***– keiner,*** see ***– niemand***; ***– nichts,*** nothing more *or* else; ***– niemand,*** no one else; ***– nirgendwo,*** nowhere else, in no other place; ***– habe ich noch zu berichten,*** in addition I have to report; ***– noch Neues,*** any news apart from this, any other *or* further news; ***wenn –,*** if on the other hand, provided; ***– wer,*** see ***– jemand***; ***wie –?*** how else? ***wie –,*** as usual; ***sie kommen nicht mehr so häufig wie –,*** they no longer come so frequently as they used to.

sonstig ['zɔnstɪç], *adj.* other, remaining; former. **sonst|wie,** *adv.* in some other way. **–wo,** *adv.* elsewhere, somewhere (else). **–woher,** *adv.* from some other place. **–wohin,** *adj.* to another place, somewhere else.

sooft [zo'ɔft], *conj.* as often as, whenever.

Sophist [zo'fɪst], *m.* (**-en,** *pl.* **-en**) sophist. **Sophisterei** [–'raɪ], *f.* sophistry, (*coll.*) hair-splitting. **Sophistin,** *f. See* **Sophist. sophistisch,** *adj.* sophistical.

Sopran [zo'pra:n], *m.* (**-s,** *pl.* **-e**) treble, soprano. **Sopranistin** [–'nɪstɪn], *f.* soprano (singer).

Sorge ['zɔrgə], *f.* grief, sorrow; worry, apprehension, anxiety, care, trouble, uneasiness, concern; ***Borgen macht –n,*** borrowing brings sorrowing; ***die – ertränken*** or ***ersäufen,*** drown one's sorrows (in drink); ***sei*** (***darum***) ***ohne –,*** do not let that worry you; (*coll.*) ***keine –!*** don't worry! never fear! ***laß das meine – sein!*** leave that to me! ***das ist meine –,*** that is my worry *or* problem *or* (*coll.*) headache; ***das ist meine geringste –,*** that is the least of my worries; ***– tragen für,*** ensure, take care of, make (*s.th*) one's business, see to; ***du hast dafür – zu tragen, daß . . .,*** it is your responsibility to see to it that . . .; ***– um die Zukunft,*** concern for the future; ***sich*** (*Dat.*) ***–n machen, in –*(*n*) *sein,*** be worried *or* concerned (***um,*** about); ***ihm –n machen,*** worry him, give *or* cause him trouble.

sorgen ['zɔrgən], **1.** *v.r.* be anxious *or* apprehensive *or* concerned *or* troubled, worry (***um,*** about). **2.** *v.i.* ***– für,*** care *or* provide for; look after, take care of; ***dafür – daß,*** take care that, see to it that, ensure that; ***dafür laß mich –!*** leave that to me, let me see to that; ***dafür hat er zu –,*** that's his look-out.

Sorgenbrecher ['zɔrgənbrɛçər], *m.* (*Poet.*) dispeller of cares, wine. **sorgenfrei,** *adj.* free from care(s), untroubled. **Sorgenkind,** *n.* difficult *or* problem child, (*coll.*) handful. **sorgenlos,** *adj. See* **sorgenfrei. Sorgenstuhl,** *m.* easy-chair. **sorgenvoll,** *adj.* full of care, careworn; anxious, troubled, worried, uneasy.

Sorgfalt ['zɔrkfalt], *f.* carefulness, diligence; care, solicitude, attention; accuracy, neatness, conscientiousness, circumspection. **sorgfältig,** *adj.* careful, attentive; diligent, painstaking, conscientious, scrupulous, precise, accurate.

sorglich ['zɔrklɪç], *adj.* careful, anxious; solicitous. **sorglos,** *adj.* carefree, light-hearted, (*coll.*) happy-go-lucky, devil-may-care; thoughtless, indifferent, unconcerned, negligent, careless. **Sorglosigkeit,** *f.* light-heartedness, thoughtlessness; unconcern, negligence, carelessness. **sorgsam,** *adj.* careful, attentive; provident; cautious. **Sorgsamkeit,** *f.* care(fulness), caution, providence.

sorren ['zɔrən], *v.t.* (*Naut.*) lash, seize.

Sorte ['zɔrtə], *f.* **1.** kind, sort, type, description, species, quality, grade, variety, brand; **2.** *pl.* (*Comm.*) foreign currency. **Sorten|abteilung,** *f.* foreign-exchange department. **–geschäft,** *n.* exchange transactions.

sortieren [zɔr'ti:rən], *v.t.* classify, arrange, put in order, (*coll.*) sort out; sort, sift, grade. **Sortierung,** *f.* sorting, classifying, grading.

Sortiment [zɔrti'mɛnt], *n.* (**-s,** *pl.* **-e**) **1.** assortment, collection, miscellaneous stock; range, set; **2.** retail book-trade *or* -shop. **Sortimenter,** *m.* bookseller.

sosehr [zo'ze:r], *conj.* – (***auch***), however much, no matter how much.

soso [zo'zo:], *adv.* (*coll.*) tolerably well, middling, so-so, not bad.

Soße ['zo:sə], *f.* sauce, gravy (*from meat*), dressing (*for salad*). **Soßenschüssel,** *f.* sauce-boat.

sott [zɔt], **sötte** ['zœtə], *see* **sieden.**

Souffleur [zu'flø:r], *m.* (**-s,** *pl.* **-e**) prompter. **Souffleurkasten,** *m.* prompt(er's) box. **Souffleuse,** *f. See* **Souffleur. soufflieren,** *v.i.* (*Dat.*), *v.t.* prompt.

soundso ['zo:untzo:], *adv.* ***– viel,*** a certain amount (of), so much; (*coll.*) ***– viele,*** umpteen; ***– oft,*** over and over again, again and again. **Soundso,** *s.* ***Herr*** (or ***Frau***) ***–,*** Mr. (*or* Mrs.) What's his (her) name.

Soutane [zu'ta:nə], *f.* cassock, soutane.

Souterrain [zutɛ'rɛ̃], *n.* (**-s,** *pl.* **-s**) basement.

Souverän [zuvə'rɛ:n], *m.* (**-s,** *pl.* **-e**) sovereign. **souverän,** *adj.* sovereign, (*fig.*) superior; (*fig.*) ***– beherrschen,*** have complete *or* absolute command of. **Souveränität** [–i'tɛ:t], *f.* sovereignty. **Souveränitätsrechte,** *n.pl.* sovereign rights.

so|viel, 1. *conj.* as *or* so far as; ***– ich gehört habe,*** from what I have heard. **2.** *adv.* as *or* so much; ***– wie ein Eid,*** as good as *or* much the same as an oath; ***doppelt –,*** twice as much; ***doppelt –e,*** twice as many. **–weit, 1.** *conj.* as *or* so far as; *see also* **–fern. 2.** *adv.* so far; ***– ganz gut,*** good as far as it goes, (*coll.*) not at all bad; ***– wie*** or ***als möglich,*** as much *or* far as possible. **–wenig,** *conj.* (just) as little (***wie,*** as), no more (than). **–wie,** *conj.* as soon as, just as, (at) the moment (when); as well as, as also. **–wieso,** *adv.* anyway, anyhow, in any case, as it is.

Sowjet [zɔ'vjɛt], *m.* (**-s,** *pl.* **-s**) Soviet. **sowjetisch,** *adj.* soviet. **Sowjet|rußland,** *n.* Soviet Russia. **–union,** *f.* Union of Soviet Socialist Republics, (*coll.*) Soviet Union.

sowohl [zo'vo:l], *conj.* ***– . . . als auch,*** both . . . and, both . . . as well as, as well . . . as, not only . . . but also.

Soz ['zo:ts], *m.* (**-en,** *pl.* **-en**), **Sozi,** *m.* (**-s,** *pl.* **-s**) *or* *f.* (-, *pl.* **-s**) (*sl.*) Red, commie, bolshie.

sozial [zotsi'a:l], *adj.* social; ***–e Fürsorge,*** (social) welfare work; ***–e Wohlfahrt,*** social welfare; ***–er Wohnungsbau,*** public authority housing, (*coll.*) council housing.

Sozial|abgaben, *f.pl.* national insurance contributions. **–beamte(r),** *m.*, **–beamtin,** *f.* welfare-worker, social worker. **–demokrat,** *m.* (German) Socialist. **sozial|demokratisch,** *adj.* socialist(ic). **–denkend,** *adj.* public-spirited. **Sozial|einrichtungen,** *f.pl.* social services. **–fürsorge,** *f.* (social) welfare work. **–gericht,** *n.* Social Court.

Sozialisierung [zotsiali'zi:ruŋ], *f.* socialization, nationalization. **Sozialismus** [–'lɪsmus], *m.* socialism. **Sozialist** [–'list], *m.* (**-en,** *pl.* **-en**) socialist. **Sozialistengesetz,** *n.* (*Hist.*) (Bismarck's) law against socialists. **sozialistisch,** *adj.* socialist(ic).

Sozial|lasten, *f.pl.* employer's (national insurance) contributions; expenditure on the social services. **–politik,** *f.* social legislation. **sozialpolitisch,** *adj.* social(-security). **Sozial|produkt,** *n.* gross national product. **–rentner(in),** *m.* (*f.*) national insurance *or* (*coll.*) old-age pensioner. **–unterstützung,** *f.* national assistance. **–versicherung,** *f.* social insurance. **–wissenschaft,** *f.* sociology, *pl.* social sciences. **–zulage,** *f.* *See* **–unterstützung.**

Sozietät [zotsie'tɛ:t], *f.* society; partnership, company. **Sozietätsvertrag,** *m.* deed of partnership.

Soziologe [zotsio'lo:gə], *m.* (**-n,** *pl.* **-n**) sociologist. **Soziologie** [–'gi:], *f.* sociology. **soziologisch,** *adj.* sociological.

Sozius ['zo:tsius], *m.* (-, *pl.* **-se**) 1. (*Comm.*) partner, joint-owner; ***stiller* –**, sleeping *or* (*Am.*) silent partner; 2. (*Motor.*) pillion-rider. **Soziussitz,** *m.* pillion (seat).

sozusagen [zotsu'za:gən], *adv.* so to speak, as it were.

Spachtel ['ʃpaxtəl] *m.* (*Austr. f.* (-, *pl.* **-n**)) spatula. **Spachtel|kitt,** *m.* plastic wood. **–masse,** *f.* primer, filler. **–messer,** *n.* putty-knife. **spachteln,** **1.** *v.t.* fill (*cracks*), smooth (*a surface*). **2.** *v.i.* (*coll.*) gorge o.s., tuck in.

[1]**Spagat** [ʃpa'ga:t], *m.* (**-s,** *pl.* **-e**) (*Austr.*) cord, string.

[2]**Spagat,** *m. or n.* (*Gymn.*) splits; – ***machen,*** do the splits.

spähen ['ʃpɛ:ən], *v.i.* (*Mil.*) scout, reconnoitre; (*coll.*) watch, (be on the) look out (***nach,*** for); peer. **Späher,** *m.* scout, look-out. **Späherblick,** *m.* (*fig.*) furtive glance. **Späh|trupp,** *m.* (*Mil.*) patrol. **–(trupp)wagen,** *m.* reconnaissance (*or coll.*) recce car.

Spakat [ʃpa'ka:t], *m. or n. See* [2]**Spagat.**

Spalier [ʃpa'li:r], *n.* (**-s,** *pl.* **-e**) 1. espalier, trellis; 2. (*fig.*) lane (*formed by people*); – ***bilden*** or ***stehen,*** form a lane. **Spalier|obst,** *n.* wall-fruit. **–werk,** *n.* trellis-work.

Spalt [ʃpalt], *m.* (**-(e)s,** *pl.* **-e**) cleft, chink, slot, slit, split, crack, aperture, fissure, gap, rift, crevice, (*of glacier*) crevasse. **spaltbar,** *adj.* cleavable, divisible, fissile. **Spalte,** *f.* 1. *See* **Spalt**; 2. (*Typ.*) column.

spalten ['ʃpaltən], (*p.p.* ***gespalten*** *or* ***gespaltet***) **1.** *v.t.* 1. split, cleave, slit, cut open; rend, divide; ***Haare*** or ***Begriffe* –**, split hairs; 2. (*Chem. etc.*) decompose. **2.** *v.r., v.i.* (*aux.* s.) split, crack; (*fig.*) split *or* break up; open, divide, branch off; (*of skin*) chap, (*of oil*) crack.

Spaltenbreite ['ʃpaltənbraɪtə], *f.* (*Typ.*) column-width. **spalten|lang,** *adj.* (*Typ.*) running to several columns. **–reich,** *adj.* fissured. **Spaltensteller,** *m.* (*typewriter*) tabulator. **spaltenweise,** *adv.* in columns.

Spalt|fläche, *f.* plane of cleavage. **–flügel,** *m.* (*Av.*) slotted wing. **–frucht,** *f.* (*Bot.*) dehiscent fruit, schizocarp. **spaltfrüchtig,** *adj.* schizocarpous. **Spalt|fußkrebs,** *m.* (*Zool.*) schizopod. **–glimmer,** *m.* (*Min.*) muscovite. **–holz,** *n.* split logs, firewood. **–hufer,** *m.* (*Zool.*) ruminant. **–leder,** *n.* skiver. **–messer,** *n.* grafting-knife; cleaver. **–pfropfung,** *f.* stock-grafting. **–pilz,** *m.* fission-fungus, schizomycete. **–produkt,** *n.* product of (atomic) fission. **–ring,** *m.* split-ring.

Spaltung ['ʃpaltuŋ], *f.* fissure, split, crack, cleavage; splitting, division, fission; (*Chem.*) separation, decomposition; (*fig.*) dissension, rupture, split, rift, (*Eccl.*) schism. **Spaltungsprodukt,** *n. See* **Spaltprodukt.**

Span [ʃpa:n], *m.* (**-(e)s,** *pl.* **⸚e**) 1. chip, shaving, shred, splinter; *pl.* chippings, shavings, cuttings, turnings, swarf; (*coll.*) ***wo gehobelt wird, fallen Späne,*** you can't make an omelet without breaking eggs; (*coll.*) ***nicht ein* –**, not a thing *or* (*sl.*) sausage; (*coll.*) ***er hat einen* –**, he's off his head, he's daft *or* dotty *or* cracked; (*sl.*) ***der hat Späne,*** he's got money to burn; (*coll.*) ***das geht übern* –**, that's really too much, that's going too far; (*coll.*) ***mach keine Späne,*** don't make a fuss; 2. (*dial.*) quarrel, squabble; 3. (*dial.*) dug, nipple.

spänen ['ʃpɛ:nən], *v.t.* 1. suckle (*animals*); wean; 2. (*Tech.*) scour.

Spanferkel ['ʃpa:nfɛrkəl], *n.* sucking-pig.

Spange ['ʃpaŋə], *f.* clasp, brooch; clip, hair-slide; buckle; bar (*military decorations*). **Spangenschuh,** *n.* buckled shoe, strap-shoe.

Spanien ['ʃpa:niən], *n.* Spain. **Spanier(in),** *m.* (*f.*) Spaniard. **spanisch,** *adj.* Spanish; ***das kommt mir – vor,*** that's all Greek *or* (double) Dutch to me; ***–e Fliege,*** Spanish fly, cantharis; ***–er Pfeffer,*** red *or* cayenne pepper; ***–er Reiter,*** chevaux-de-frise; ***–es Rohr,*** Bengal cane; ***–er Stiefel,*** boot (*torture*); ***–e Wand,*** folding screen.

Spankorb ['ʃpa:nkɔrp], *m.* chip-basket.

Spann [ʃpan], *m.* (**-(e)s,** *pl.* **-e**) instep.

spann, *see* **spinnen.**

Spann|ader, *f.* (*obs.*) sinew. **–balken,** *m.* tie-beam. **–beton,** *m.* pre-stressed concrete. **–dienst,** *m.* (*Hist.*) statute-labour with teams. **–draht,** *m.* tension *or* guy wire.

Spanne ['ʃpanə], *f.* 1. (*time*) short space of time, span, stretch; (*space*) short distance, span; 2. (*fig.*) margin (*of profit*).

spannen ['ʃpanən], **1.** *v.t.* strain, stretch, brace, bend, flex; tighten, (make) tense, subject to tension; clamp, grip, hold (*in a chuck*); bend, draw (*a bow*); cock (*a gun*); harness (***an*** *or* ***vor*** (*Acc.*), to); fetter (*grazing cattle*); ***Dampf* –**, superheat steam, build up the steam pressure; ***auf die Folter* –**, put to the rack; (*fig.*) rouse intense curiosity in, keep in suspense; ***die Forderungen zu hoch* –**, demand too much, be exorbitant in one's demands, make excessive demands, pitch one's demands too high; ***Gardinen* –**, put up *or* hang curtains; ***Neugier aufs höchste* –**, excite the liveliest curiosity, rouse curiosity to white heat; ***die Oktave – können,*** be able to stretch an octave; (*Prov.*) ***das Pferd hinter den Wagen* –**, put the cart before the horse; ***in den Schraubstock* –**, put in the vice; (*fig.*) ***ich bin sehr gespannt,*** I am very anxious *or* curious; ***jede Muskel gespannt,*** all muscles tense; ***ich stehe mit ihm auf gespanntem Fuße,*** the relations between us are strained. **2.** *v.i.* be (too) tight, pinch, (*fig.*) be exciting, absorbing, gripping, thrilling *or* breath-taking. **spannend,** *adj.* exciting, tense, gripping, absorbing, thrilling, breath-taking.

Spanner ['ʃpanər], *m.* 1. stretcher, press (*for trousers, tennis racket etc.*); last, boot-tree; tenter (*for cloth*); trigger, gaffle (*of a crossbow*); 2. (*Ent.*) looper (*Geometridae*).

Spann|feder, *f.* tension-spring. **–futter,** *n.* mandrel, chuck. **–haken,** *m.* tenter-hook. **–hebel,** *m.* cocking-handle (*of gun*). **–kabel,** *n. See* **–draht.** **–kette,** *f.* tether. **–kloben,** *m.* jaw (*of vice*). **–kraft,** *f.* elasticity, spring; (*Phys.*) strain, tension; (*fig.*) vigour, tone. **spannkräftig,** *adj.* elastic. **Spann|lack,** *m.* stiffening varnish, dope. **–muskel,** *m. or f.* (*Anat.*) extensor (muscle). **–rahmen,** *m.* tenter(frame); stretcher. **–säge,** *f.* frame-saw. **–schloß,** *n.* turnbuckle, rigging-screw. **–seil,** *n.* guy-rope; fetter, tether. **–seite,** *f.* hypotenuse.

Spannung ['ʃpanuŋ], *f.* 1. stretching, straining, bracing, tightening; tension, stress, strain; span (*of an arch*); pressure, head (*of steam*); 2. (*Elec.*) voltage, potential (difference); ***effektive* –**, root mean square (*abbr.* R.M.S.) voltage; ***innere* –**, electromotive force; 3. (*fig.*) tenseness, eager expectation, suspense, close attention, interest, excitement; discord, strained relations, tension.

Spannungs|abfall, *m.* voltage- *or* potential-drop. **–apparat,** *m.* (*Sew.-mach.*) tension-regulator. **–differenz,** *f.* potential difference. **spannungs|führend,** *adj.* (*Elec.*) live. **–geladen,** *adj.* (*fig.*) *See* **spannend.** **spannungslos,** *adj.* (*fig.*) unexciting, dull, dead. **Spannungs|messer,** *m.* voltmeter. **–regler,** *m.* voltage regulator. **–teiler,** *m.* potentiometer. **–wandler,** *m.* voltage transformer.

Spann|weite, *f.* span, spread; (*Av.*) wingspread; (*fig.*) range. **–wirbel,** *m. See* **–schloß.**

Spant [ʃpant], *n.* (**-(e)s,** *pl.* **-en**) rib (*of a ship*), (*Av.*) transverse frame.

Spar|anleihe, *f.* savings certificate. **-brenner,** *m.* pilot light. **-buch,** *n.* bank-book, pass-book. **-büchse,** *f.* money-box. **-einlagen,** *f.pl.* savings (-bank deposits).

sparen [ˈʃpa:rən], **1.** *v.t., v.i.* economize, cut down expenses; save, lay by, put by; be thrifty; use sparingly, be sparing *or* (*fig.*) chary of. **Sparer,** *m.* saver, investor, depositor.

Spar|flamme, *f. See* **-brenner. -flug,** *m.* (*Av.*) economical cruising. **-fonds,** *m. See* **-guthaben.**

Spargel [ˈʃpargəl], *m.* asparagus. **Spargel|kohl,** *m.* (*Bot.*) broccoli (*Brassica oleracea*). **-stecher,** *m.* asparagus-knife.

Spar|gelder, *n.pl. See* **-guthaben. -gemisch,** *n.* (*Motor.*) lean mixture. **-groschen,** *n. See* **-pfennig. -guthaben,** *n.* savings account *or* deposits. **-herd,** *m.* slow-combustion stove. **-kasse,** *f.* savings-bank. **-kassenbuch,** *n. See* **-buch.**

spärlich [ˈʃpɛ:rlɪç], *adj.* scanty, sparse; poor, bare, meagre, scant, scarce; – ***bevölkert,*** thinly *or* sparsely populated. **Spärlichkeit,** *f.* scantiness, sparseness, meagreness; scarcity.

Spar|marke, *f.* savings stamp. **-maßnahme,** *f.* economy measure, *pl.* economies. **-pfennig,** *m.* (small) savings, nest-egg, money put by (for a rainy day). **-prämienlos,** *n.* premium bond.

Sparren [ˈʃparən], *m.* spar, rafter; (*Her.*) chevron; (*coll.*) ***einen – (zuviel) haben,*** have a screw loose. **Sparren|kopf,** *m.* (*Archit.*) modillion, mutule; rafter-end. **-werk,** *n.* rafters.

sparsam [ˈʃpa:rza:m], **1.** *adj.* economical (***mit,*** with *or* of), thrifty, parsimonious, frugal (with), (*fig.*) chary (of). **2.** *adv.* sparingly; – ***leben,*** live frugally; – ***umgehen mit,*** use sparingly, (*fig.*) be chary of. **Sparsamkeit,** *f.* economy, thrift(iness), parsimony; frugality.

Sparsinn [ˈʃpa:rzɪn], *m.* thrift, parsimony.

Spartaner [ʃparˈta:nər], *m.* (*Hist.*) Spartan. **spartanisch,** *adj.* Spartan, (*fig.*) spartan, austere.

Sparte [ˈʃpartə], *f.* subject, branch, line, field.

Spar|verein, *m.* savings group. **-zwang,** *m.* compulsory *or* enforced saving.

Spaß [ʃpa:s], *m.* (**-es,** *pl.* **¨-e**) jest, joke; fun, amusement, pastime; prank, merry antic, (*coll.*) lark; ***handgreiflicher –,*** practical joke; ***rauher –,*** horseplay; – ***haben an*** (*Dat.*), enjoy; – ***beiseite!*** joking apart! – ***machen,*** *see* **spaßen**; ***es macht mir –,*** I think it is good fun, it amuses me; ***seinen – treiben mit,*** play tricks on, make fun *or* sport of; ***das geht über den –,*** that is beyond a joke; ***keinen – verstehen,*** not understand *or* appreciate *or* (*coll.*) take a joke; ***viel –!*** have a good time! enjoy yourself! ***aus*** or ***im*** or ***zum –,*** for *or* in fun, for the fun of it, in jest.

spaßen [ˈʃpa:sən], *v.i.* joke, jest, make fun; ***Sie – wohl,*** you are surely joking; ***damit*** or ***darüber ist nicht zu –,*** that is no joking matter, (*coll.*) it's no joke; ***mit ihm ist nicht zu –,*** he is not to be trifled with; ***Sie belieben zu –,*** you are pleased to be facetious.

spaßhaft [ˈʃpa:shaft], **spaßig,** *adj.* facetious, jocular, joking, jocose, waggish; comical, funny, amusing, droll. **Spaß|macher,** *m.* wag, joker, clown, buffoon. **-verderber,** *m.* spoil-sport, kill-joy. **-vogel,** *m. See* **-macher.**

Spastiker(in) [ˈspastikər(ɪn)], *m.* (*f.*) spastic.

spat [ʃpa:t], *adv.* (*obs.*) *see* **spät.**

Spat, *m.* (**-(e)s,** *pl.* **-e** *or* **¨-e**) 1. (*Min.*) spar; 2. (*no pl.*) (*Vet.*) spavin.

spät [ʃpɛ:t], *adj., adv.* late, belated, behindhand, tardy, backward, slow; ***von früh bis –,*** from morning till night; (*coll.*) ***-es Mädchen,*** old maid; – ***in der Nacht*** or ***bei -er Nacht,*** late at night; ***wie – ist es?*** what time is it?

Spatel [ˈʃpa:təl], *m. See* **Spachtel. Spatelraubmöwe,** *f.* (*Orn.*) *see* ***mittlere Raubmöwe.***

Spaten [ˈʃpa:tən], *m.* spade. **Spatenstich,** *m.* cut with a spade; ***den ersten – tun,*** turn the first sod, (*fig.*) break ground.

später [ˈʃpɛ:tər], **1.** *comp.adj.* later, subsequent. **2.** *adv.* afterwards, later on, subsequently, at a later date; ***-e Jahreszeit,*** end of the season, latter part of the year; ***in -en Jahren,*** in after years, in later life; ***in -en Zeiten,*** at a later period, in the future. **späterhin,** *adv. See* **später, 2. spätestens,** *adv.* at the latest, not later than.

Spät|fährte, *f.* (*Hunt.*) cold scent. **-geburt,** *f.* delayed birth. **-herbst,** *m.* end of the season, late autumn.

spatiieren [ʃpatsiˈi:rən], **spatinieren, spationieren,** *v.t.* (*Typ.*) space. **spatiös,** *adj.* spaced, roomy, spacious. **Spatium** [ˈʃpa:tsium], *n.* (**-s,** *pl.* **-tien**) (*Typ.*) space; ***die Spatien einsetzen*** or ***mit Spatien durchschießen,*** space.

Spätjahr [ˈʃpɛ:tja:r], *n.* autumn, (*Am.*) fall. **Spätling,** *m.* (**-s,** *pl.* **-e**) late arrival; animal born late in the year; late fruit; (*dial.*) autumn. **spätreif,** *adj.* delayed, backward, retarded. **Spätsommer,** *m.* Indian summer.

Spatz [ʃpats], *m.* (**-en** *or* **-es,** *pl.* **-en**) (*Austr.* **-es,** *pl.* **-en**) (*coll.*) *see* **Haussperling**; ***das pfeifen die -en von allen Dächern,*** that is all over the town, that is notorious; ***mit Kanonen nach -en schießen,*** break butterflies on the wheel; (*Prov.*) ***besser ein – in der Hand als eine Taube auf dem Dach,*** a bird in the hand is worth two in the bush. **spatzenhaft,** *adj.* cheeky, cocky.

Spätzle [ˈʃpɛtslə], *n.* (*dial.*) (Swabian) dumpling.

Spätzündung [ˈʃpɛ:ttsyndʊŋ], *f.* (*Motor.*) retarded ignition; (*coll.*) slowness on the uptake.

spazieren [ʃpaˈtsi:rən], *v.i.* (*aux.* s.) go for *or* take a walk *or* stroll. **spazieren|fahren, 1.** *irr.v.i.* go for a drive; go (out) in a boat. **2.** *irr.v.t.* take for a drive. **-führen,** *v.t.* take for a walk; walk (out) (*a dog*); push *or* take (*child*) out (in the perambulator). **-gehen,** *irr.v.i. See* **spazieren.**

Spazier|fahrt, *f.* drive; pleasure trip. **-gang,** *m.* walk, stroll; ***einen – machen,*** take a walk; 2. (*coll.*) (*Spt.*) walkover. **-gänger,** *m.* walker, stroller. **-ritt,** *m.* ride. **-stock,** *m.* walking-stick. **-weg,** *m.* walk, promenade, footpath.

Specht [ʃpɛçt], *m.* (**-(e)s,** *pl.* **-e**) woodpecker. **Spechtmeise,** *f.* (*Orn.*) *see* **Kleiber.**

Speck [ʃpɛk], *m.* (**-(e)s,** *pl.* **-e**) bacon; (*whales*) blubber; (*coll.*) fat; – ***auf den Rippen haben,*** be well off; – ***ansetzen,*** put on fat; ***den – spicken,*** gild the lily; ***den – riechen,*** be drawn towards a th.; ***im – sitzen,*** be in clover; (*Prov.*) ***mit – fängt man Mäuse,*** good bait catches fine fish.

Speck|bauch, *m.* (*coll.*) fat belly, big paunch. **-geschwulst,** *f.* steatoma. **-glanz,** *m.* greasy lustre. **-hals,** *m.* (*coll.*) thick(set) neck, bull-neck. **speckig,** *adj.* fat, greasy, fatty; (*coll.*) spotted with grease. **Speck|kuchen,** *m.* lardy cake. **-scheibe,** *f. See* **-schnitte. -schneider,** *m.* blubber-cutter. **-schnitte,** *f.* rasher of bacon. **-schwarte,** *f.* bacon-rind. **-seite,** *f.* side *or* flitch of bacon; ***die Wurst nach der – werfen,*** throw a sprat to catch a mackerel. **-stein,** *m.* soapstone, talc, steatite.

spedieren [ʃpeˈdi:rən], *v.t.* forward, dispatch, send (on), ship. **Spediteur** [–ˈtø:r], *m.* (**-s,** *pl.* **-e**) forwarding agent, shipping agent, haulage contractor, carrier; furniture-remover. **Spedition** [–tsiˈo:n], *f.* dispatch, delivery, forwarding; haulage, carrying, shipping; forwarding *or* shipping department. **Speditions|gebühren,** *f.pl.* delivery charge(s). **-geschäft,** *n.* forwarding agency, carriers; furniture-removal business.

Speer [ʃpe:r], *m.* (**-(e)s,** *pl.* **-e**) spear, lance, javelin. **speeren,** *v.t.* spear, pierce, impale. **speerförmig,** *adj.* (*Bot.*) lanceolate. **Speer|träger,** *m.* spearman. **-werfen,** *n.* (*Spt.*) throwing the javelin. **-wurf,** *m.* throw of the spear, spear-thrust.

Speiche [ˈʃpaɪçə], *f.* spoke (*of a wheel*); (*Anat.*) radius, spokebone; (*fig.*) ***ihm in die -n fallen,*** put a spoke in his wheel; (*fig.*) ***mit in die -n greifen,*** put one's shoulder to the wheel.

Speichel [ˈʃpaɪçəl], *m.* spittle, saliva, (*coll.*) spit, dribble. **Speichel|bildung,** *f.* salivation. **–drüse,** *f.* salivary gland. **–fluß,** *m.* flow of saliva, salivation. **–gang,** *m.* salivary duct. **–lecker,** *m.* (*fig.*) toady, sycophant, lickspittle. **–leckerei,** *f.* toadyism. **speichelleckerisch,** *adj.* toadying, fawning. **speicheln,** *v.i.* (*dial.*) spit.

speichen ['ʃpaɪçən], *v.t.* spoke, fit spokes to (*a wheel*). **Speichen|blatt,** *n.* inner end of spoke. **–nerv,** *m.* (*Anat.*) radial nerve. **–rad,** *n.* spoke(d) wheel. **–schlagader,** *f.* (*Anat.*) radial artery. **–zapfen,** *m.* outer end of spoke.

Speicher ['ʃpaɪçər], *m.* 1. granary, silo, (grain) elevator; reservoir, warehouse; (*dial.*) store (room), storage place, garret, attic, loft; 2. (*Elec.*) storage-battery, (*Am.*) accumulator; 3. hot-water tank; 4. (*computers*) data bank.

Speicher|anlage, *f. See* **–becken. –batterie,** *f. See* **Speicher,** 2. **–becken,** *n.* storage basin, impounding reservoir. **–geld,** *n.* warehouse *or* storage charges. **–kondensator,** *m.* (*Elec.*) reservoir condenser. **–kraftwerk,** *n.* hydro-electric scheme *or* power-station.

speichern ['ʃpaɪçərn], *v.t.* store (up); accumulate; warehouse; (*fig.*) hoard, treasure up. **Speicherung,** *f.* storage, accumulation.

speien ['ʃpaɪən], *irr.v.t., v.i.* spit; (*dial.*) spew, vomit; (*fig.*) belch forth (*fire*); discharge (*water*); ***Feuer und Flamme –,*** fret and fume; ***Gift und Galle –,*** vent one's spleen; ***es ist mir alles zum Speien,*** it makes me sick *or* fills me with loathing. **Speigatt,** *n.* **(-(e)s,** *pl.* **-s** *or* **-en)** (*Naut.*) scupper.

Speik [ʃpaɪk], *m. See* **Spiek.**

Speil [ʃpaɪl], *m.* **(-(e)s,** *pl.* **-e), Speile,** *f.* skewer. **speilen,** *v.t.* skewer. **Speiler,** *m.* (*Austr.*) *see* **Speil. speilern,** *v.t.* (*Austr.*) *see* **speilen.**

Speis [ʃpaɪs], *m.* (*dial.*) mortar.

Speise ['ʃpaɪzə], *f.* 1. food, nourishment, eatables, victuals, meal, dish; ***– und Trank,*** meat and drink; (*Prov.*) ***dem einen ist's –, dem andern Gift,*** one man's meat is another man's poison; (*Prov.*) ***verbotene – schmeckt am besten,*** forbidden fruit tastes sweetest; 2. (bell- *or* gun-)metal; 3. mortar.

Speise|anstalt, *f.* eating-house. **–aufzug,** *m.* service lift, dumb-waiter. **–brei,** *m.* chyme. **–eis,** *n.* ice-cream, ices. **–fett,** *n.* edible *or* cooking fat. **–gang,** *m.* alimentary canal, digestive tract. **–graben,** *m.* feeder (trench). **–hahn,** *m.* feed-cock. **–haus,** *n. See* **–anstalt. –kammer,** *f.* larder, pantry. **–karte,** *f.* bill of fare, menu; ***nach der – essen,*** dine à la carte. **–korb,** *m.* luncheon basket, hamper. **–leitung,** *f.* feed-pipe, (*Elec.*) power lead, (*Rad.*) feeder.

speisen ['ʃpaɪzən], **1.** *v.t.* feed; board, entertain; supply (*a mill or boiler with water, a mill with corn etc.*); (*Elec.*) charge (*a battery*); (*fig.*) ***ihn mit leeren Hoffnungen –,*** fill him with vain hopes; ***durch mehrere Bäche gespeist,*** fed by many streams. **2.** *v.i.* eat, take food, have a meal, take one's meals; ***zu Mittag –,*** lunch, dine, have lunch *or* dinner *or* one's midday meal; ***zu Abend –,*** have supper *or* (late) dinner *or* one's evening meal; ***auswärts –,*** dine *or* eat out; ***in diesem Gasthof speist man gut,*** the food is good in this inn; ***wohl zu –!*** good appetite! ***wünsche wohl gespeist zu haben,*** I hope you enjoyed your dinner. **Speisenfolge,** *f.* menu (*at a banquet*).

Speise|öl, *n.* salad-oil, olive oil. **–opfer,** *n.* (*Eccl.*) oblation (*of first fruits etc.*). **–pumpe,** *f.* feed- *or* supply-pump. **–punkt,** *m.* (*Rad.*) input terminals. **–reste,** *m.pl.* particles *or* remains of food, (*coll.*) leftovers. **–rohr,** *n.* feed-pipe. **–röhre,** *f.* (*Anat.*) gullet, oesophagus. **–saal,** *m.* dining-room, banqueting- *or* dining-hall; dining-saloon (*on steamers*); refectory (*in monasteries, hostels etc.*), (*Mil.*) mess. **–saft,** *m.* chyle. **–salz,** *n.* table-salt. **–schrank,** *m.* pantry, food-cupboard, meat-safe. **–strom,** *m.* (*Elec.*) feed-current. **–trichter,** *m.* hopper. **–ventil,** *n.* feed-valve. **–wagen,** *m.* (*Railw.*) restaurant-car, dining-car. **–walze,** *f.* feed-roll(er). **–wasser,** *n.* feed-water (*steam engines*). **–wirtschaft,** *f.* (unlicensed) restaurant. **–würze,** *f.* condiments. **–zettel,** *m. See* **–karte. –zimmer,** *n.* dining-room.

Speisung ['ʃpaɪzuŋ], *f.* feeding, (*Elec.*) supply, feed; (*B.*) – ***der Fünftausend,*** feeding of the five thousand.

Spektakel [ʃpɛk'ta:kəl], **1.** *m.* (*Austr. n.*) noise, uproar, row, din, shindy, racket. **2.** *n.* (*obs.*) show, display. **spektakeln,** *v.i.* (*coll.*) make a din, kick up a row. **Spektakelstück,** *n.* (*Theat.*) lavish *or* spectacular show.

Spektralanalyse [spɛk'tra:lˀanaly:zə], *f.* spectrum analysis. **specktralanalytisch,** *adj.* spectroscopic. **Specktrum** ['spɛktrum], *n.* **(-s,** *pl.* **-tren** (*Austr.* **-tra**)) spectrum.

Spekulant [ʃpeku'lant], *m.* **(-en,** *pl.* **-en)** speculator, stock-exchange operator. **Spekulation** [–tsi'o:n], *f.* (*Phil.*) speculation, deliberation, contemplation; 2. (*Comm.*) speculation, gamble, venture; (*coll.*) ***auf –,*** on spec. **Spekulations|geist,** *m.* gambling spirit. **–geschäft,** *n.* speculative transaction, gamble. **–papier,** *n.* speculative *or* (*Am.*) fancy stock.

Spekulatius [ʃpeku'la:tsius], *m.* (-, *pl.* -) almond biscuit.

spekulativ [ʃpekula'ti:f], *adj.* speculative, venturesome, risky. **spekulieren** [–'li:rən], *v.i.* meditate, reflect (***über*** (*Acc.*), on), speculate (about), ponder, contemplate; (*Comm.*) speculate, gamble (***in*** (*Dat.*), in); – ***auf*** (*Acc.*), count *or* reckon on, (*Comm.*) speculate *or* gamble on.

spellen ['ʃpɛlən], *v.t.* (*obs.*) split, cleave.

Spelt [ʃpɛlt], *m.* **(-(e)s,** *pl.* **-e)** spelt.

Spelunke [ʃpe'luŋkə], *f.* low tavern, den, (*sl.*) dive, joint.

Spelz [ʃpɛlts], *m.* **(-es,** *pl.* **-e)** spelt. **Spelze,** *f.* glume, husk, beard, awn. **spelzenartig, spelzig,** *adj.* glumaceous.

spendabel [ʃpɛn'da:bəl], *adj.* (*coll.*) open-handed, free with one's money.

Spende ['ʃpɛndə], *f.* gift, donation, present, benefaction, contribution; alms, charity, bounty. **spenden,** *v.t.* dispense, distribute; (*Eccl.*) administer (*sacrament*); donate, give, contribute (*Dat.*, to), bestow (on); ***Beifall –,*** clap, cheer, applaud. **Spender,** *m.* distributor, dispenser; donor, contributor, benefactor.

spendieren [ʃpɛn'di:rən], *v.t.* give freely *or* lavishly, make a gift of; ***ihm etwas –,*** treat him to s.th., pay for s.th. for him, (*coll.*) stand him a th.; ***sich*** (*Dat.*) ***etwas –,*** treat o.s. to s.th., (*coll.*) stand o.s. a th. **Spendierhosen,** *pl.* (*coll.*) ***die – anhaben,*** be in a generous mood.

Spendung ['ʃpɛnduŋ], *f.* 1. *See* **Spende**; 2. (*Eccl.*) administration (*of the sacrament*).

Spengler ['ʃpɛŋlər], *m.* (*dial.*) tinsmith, sheet-metal worker, plumber.

Sperber ['ʃpɛrbər], *m.* (*Orn.*) sparrow-hawk (*Accipiter nisus*). **Sperber|baum,** *m.* service-tree. **–eule,** *f.* (*Orn.*) hawk-owl (*Surnia ulula*). **–grasmücke,** *f.* (*Orn.*) barred warbler (*Sylvia nisoria*). **sperbern.** *v.i.* (*Swiss*) observe closely.

Sperenzchen [ʃpe'rɛntsçən], **Sperenzien,** *pl.* (*coll.*) ***machen Sie keine –!*** don't make a fuss! no ceremony, please!

Sperling ['ʃpɛrlɪŋ], *m.* **(-s,** *pl.* **-e)** sparrow. **Sperlings|beine,** *n.pl.* (*coll.*) spindle-shanks. **–kauz,** *m.* (*Orn.*). pygmy-owl (*Glaucidium passerinum*). **–männchen,** *n.* cock sparrow. **–papagei,** *m.* (*Orn.*) love-bird (*Agapornis pullaria*). **–schrot,** *n.* small shot. **–vogel,** *m.* passerine (bird); *pl.* passerines. **–weibchen,** *n.* hen sparrow.

Sperma ['ʃpɛrma], *n.* **(-s,** *pl.* **-men** *or* **-mata)** sperm, semen. **Spermakern,** *m.* sperm-nucleus.

Spermazet [ʃpɛrma'tse:t], *n.* spermaceti. **Spermazetöl,** *n.* sperm oil, whale oil.

Sperrad ['ʃpɛrˀra:t], *n.* ratchet-wheel.

sperrangelweit ['ʃpɛrˀaŋəlvaɪt], *adv.* – ***offen,*** wide open, gaping. **Sperr|ballon,** *m.* (*Mil.*) barrage balloon. **–baum,** *m.* barrier, turnpike, (*Naut.*) boom. **–druck,** *m.* (*Typ.*) spaced type.

Sperre [ˈʃpɛrə], *f.* shutting, closing (*of gates*); closure, stoppage, blocking, blockage; barricade, obstruction, bar, barrier, obstacle; roadblock; (*Naut.*) boom; (*fig.*) blockade, embargo, ban, prohibition, (*health*) quarantine; (*Spt. etc.*) suspension; power cut; (*Mech.*) lock(ing device), detent, catch, stop; drag, skid, shoe (*of a wheel*); ***eine – verhängen über*** (*Acc.*), ban, block, impose a ban on, (*Parl.*) (apply) closure (to), (*Comm.*) place an embargo on; (*Av.*) – ***fliegen,*** fly on defensive patrol.

sperren [ˈʃpɛrən], **1.** *v.t.* 1. spread *or* stretch out, straddle; (*Typ.*) space (*a word*); ***gesperrte Schrift,*** spaced type; 2. bar, barricade, obstruct, block, close, cordon off; blockade, place an embargo on; cut off (*electricity etc.*), stop, freeze (*payments*); (*Spt.*) disqualify, suspend; lock, trig (*wheels*); (*dial.*) shut, close, lock, bolt; ***einen Scheck –,*** stop (payment on) a cheque; ***ins Gefängnis –,*** put in prison, (*coll.*) lock up; ***ihn aus dem Hause –,*** shut the door in his face, lock him out; ***den Seehandel –,*** blockade ports, lay an embargo on commerce; ***Straße gesperrt!*** road closed! **2.** *v.i.* (*of a door*) not able to be shut, be stuck *or* jammed open; ***die Tür sperrt,*** the door will not shut. **3.** *v.r.* ***sich – gegen,*** struggle against, balk at, resist, oppose.

Sperr|feder, *f.* retaining-spring. **–feuer,** *n.* (*Mil.*) barrage, curtain-fire; – ***legen,*** lay down a barrage. **–filter,** *m.* (*Rad.*) rejector circuit. **–flieger,** *m.* interceptor plane, patrol aircraft. **–frist,** *f.* period of closure. **–gebiet,** *n.* prohibited area, blockade zone. **–geld,** *n.* toll, entrance-money; (*coll.*) tip to the porter for opening the door late at night. **–getriebe,** *n.* trip-gear. **–gürtel,** *n.* fortified lines, (*Artil.*) barrage. **–gut,** *n.* bulky goods, bulk freight. **–guthaben,** *n.* blocked account. **–hahn,** *m.* stopcock. **–haken,** *m.* (safety-)catch; skeleton key, pick-lock. **–hebel,** *m.* locking-lever. **–holz,** *n.* plywood.

Sperriegel [ˈʃpɛrri:gəl], *m.* bolt (*of a door*), (*Artil.*) barrage.

sperrig [ˈʃpɛrɪç], *adj.* stretched out, spreading, widespread; wide open; loose, unwieldy, cumbersome, bulky.

Sperr|kette, *f.* 1. door-chain; drag-chain (*on wheel*); 2. (*fig.*) (police) cordon. **–klinke,** *f.* safety-catch, ratchet, pawl. **–kreis,** *m.* (*Rad.*) rejector circuit, interference filter. **–mark,** *f.* blocked mark (*currency*). **–maßregeln,** *f.pl.* prohibitive measures. **–schicht,** *f.* insulating layer. **–schiff,** *n.* blockship. **–sitz,** *m.* (*Theat.*) stall, reserved seat; – ***im Parkett,*** orchestra-stall.

Sperrung [ˈʃpɛruŋ], *f.* 1. spreading out, interspacing; 2. blocking, barring, closing; obstruction, barricade; stoppage, ban, prohibition, embargo, blockade; *see* **Sperre.**

Sperr|ventil, *n.* check-valve. **–vermerk,** *m.* non-negotiability notice. **–vorrichtung,** *f.* ratchet-wheel, stop, catch, locking device. **–wirkung,** *f.* (*Rad.*) rectifying effect. **–zeit,** *f.* closing time; restriction hours. **–zoll,** *m.* prohibitory duty.

Spesen [ˈʃpe:zən], *f.pl.* charges. expenses, costs. **spesenfrei,** *adj.* expenses paid, free of costs. **Spesen|konto,** *n.* expense account. **–nachnahme,** *f.* charges to follow, expenses (to be) paid on delivery. **–rechnung,** *f.* bill for expenses. **–vergütung,** *f.* reimbursement of expenses.

Spezereien [ʃpe:tsəˈraɪən], *f.pl.* spices; (*dial.*) groceries. **Spezerei|händler,** *m.* (*dial.*) grocer. **–handlung,** *f.* (*dial.*) grocer's shop.

Spezi [ˈʃpe:tsi], *m.* **(-s,** *pl.* **-(e)s)** (*dial.*), **Spezial,** *m.* **(-s,** *pl.* **-e)** 1. (*dial.*) bosom friend *or* pal, (*coll.*) crony, buddy; 2. (*dial.*) choice wine.

Spezial|arzt, *m.* (medical) specialist. **–bericht,** *m.* detailed report, particulars. **–erfahrung,** *f.* specialized experience. **–fach,** *n.* special(i)ty, specialism, special subject *or* line. **–fahrzeug,** *n.* special-purpose vehicle. **–fall,** *m.* special case. **–gebiet,** *n.* *See* **–fach. –geschäft,** *n.* one-line shop, (*Am.*) specialty store.

spezialisieren [ʃpetsialiˈzi:rən], **1.** *v.t.* specify, particularize. **2.** *v.r.* specialize (*auf* (*Acc.*), in).

Spezialität, *f.* speciality, special interest, (*coll.*) strong point.

Spezial|karte, *f.* local map, large-scale map. **–kräfte,** *f.pl.* specialists, skilled workers. **–truppen,** *f.pl.* technical *or* special-service troops.

speziell [ʃpetsiˈɛl], *adj.* special, specific, particular; – ***angeben,*** specify; ***–er Freund,*** particular friend; ***auf Ihr Spezielles!*** your health!

Spezies [ˈʃpe:tsiɛs], *f.* species; ***die 4 –,*** the 4 first rules of arithmetic. **spezies|fremd,** *adj.* of a different species. **–gleich,** *adj.* of the same species. **Speziestaler,** *m.* (*Hist.*) specie dollar.

spezifisch [ʃpeˈtsi:fɪʃ], *adj.* specific; (*Biol.*) ***–er Bildungstrieb,*** automorphosis; ***–es Gewicht,*** specific gravity; ***–e Wärme,*** specific heat. **spezifizieren** [–fiˈtsi:rən], *v.t.* specify, particularize.

Sphäre [ˈsfɛ:rə], *f.* 1. sphere, range, domain, province; 2. globe. **Sphärenmusik,** *f.* music of the spheres. **sphärisch,** *adj.* spherical; celestial.

Spickaal [ˈʃpɪkˀa:l], *m.* (*dial.*) smoked eel.

spicken [ˈʃpɪkən], *v.t.* lard; (*fig.*) garnish; (*dial.*) smoke; (*coll.*) cheat, copy (*in school*); ***den Beutel –,*** line one's pocket; (*coll.*) ***ihn –,*** grease his palm; ***seine Rede mit Zitaten –,*** interlard one's discourse with quotations. **Spicknadel,** *f.* larding-pin.

spie, spiee [ʃpi:(ə)], *see* **speien.**

Spiegel [ˈʃpi:gəl], *m.* 1. looking-glass, mirror; reflector, (reflecting) surface (*of water etc*), (*Surg.*) speculum; ***das stecke ich mir hinter den –,*** I shall not forget that in a hurry, I will keep that in mind; ***ihm einen – vorhalten,*** hold a mirror up to him, let him see himself as he is; (*fig.*) ***im –*** (*Gen.*), as reflected in; ***das Bild ist wie aus dem – gestohlen,*** the picture is a wonderful likeness; 2. panel (*of door etc.*), bull's-eye (*of target*), (*Typ.*) type-area, (*Mil.*) tab (*on collar*), silk facing (*on evening dress*); 3. (*Bot.*) medullary rays; 4. (*Naut.*) square stern; 5. (*Hunt.*) escutcheon.

Spiegel|achse, *f.* axis of symmetry. **–bild,** *n.* mirror-image, (*fig.*) reflection. **spiegelblank,** *adj.* mirror-like, highly polished, glassy. **Spiegel|ei,** *n.* fried egg. **–eisen,** *n.* specular iron. **–erz,** *n.* specular iron-ore. **–fechterei,** *f.* shadow-boxing, sham fight; (*fig.*) dissimulation, pretence, (*coll.*) humbug, (*sl.*) eyewash. **–fenster,** *n.* plate-glass window. **–fläche,** *f.* smooth *or* glassy surface. **–folie,** *f.* mirror-foil, silvering. **–frequenz,** *f.* (*Rad.*) image *or* second-channel frequency. **–glanz,** *m.* reflecting lustre. **–glas,** *n.* plate-glass. **spiegel|glatt,** *adj.* (as) smooth as a mirror, mirror-like, (*of water*) unrippled, glassy, (*of ice*) slippery. **–gleich,** *adj.* (*Geom.*) symmetrical. **Spiegelgleichheit,** *f.* (exact) symmetry. **spiegelig,** *adj. See* **spiegelgleich.**

spiegeln [ˈʃpi:gəln], **1.** *v.i.* sparkle, glitter, shine. **2.** *v.t.* reflect, mirror; ***das Auge spiegelt Freude,*** the eye lights up *or* gleams with joy; ***gespiegeltes Pferd,*** dappled horse. **3.** *v.r.* be reflected *or* mirrored, reflect, (*fig.*) be revealed.

Spiegel|pfeiler, *m.* (*Archit.*) pier. **–reflexkamera,** *f.* reflex camera. **–saal,** *m.* hall of mirrors. **–scheibe,** *f.* pane of plate-glass. **–schiefer,** *m.* specular schist. **–schrank,** *m.* wardrobe with mirror. **–schrift,** *f.* mirror-writing. **–telegraph,** *m.* heliograph. **–tisch,** *m.* glass-topped table. **–tür,** *f.* plate-glass door. **Spiegelung,** *f.* reflection; mirage. **Spiegelvisier,** *n.* mirror *or* reflecting sight.

spieglig, *adj.,* **Spieglung,** *f.* *See* **spiegelig, Spiegelung.**

Spiek [ʃpi:k], *m.,* **Spieke,** *f.* (*Bot.*) lavender (*Lavandula officinalis*); spikenard (*Valeriana spica*).

Spieker [ˈʃpi:kər], *m.* (*Naut.*) large nail, spike, brad, peg, tack.

Spieköl [ˈʃpi:kˀø:l], *n.* oil of lavender, spike-oil.

Spiel [ʃpi:l], *n.* **(-(e)s,** *pl.* **-e)** 1. play(ing), sport; match, game; (*Theat.*) playing, acting, performance; gambling, gaming; (*Mus.*) manner of playing, execution, touch; ***ich bin am –,*** it is my turn to play; ***aufs – setzen,*** risk, hazard, stake; ***auf dem – stehen,*** be at stake; (*fig.*) ***das – ist aus,*** the game is up; ***aus dem – bleiben,*** take no part in *or* have nothing to do with it; ***ihn aus dem – lassen,*** leave him out of it; ***gute Miene zum bösen – machen,*** make the best of a bad job, put a good face on the matter; ***dem – ergeben,*** addicted to gambling; ***ihm freies – lassen,*** leave the field clear for him, give him a free hand; ***gewagtes –,*** gamble, risky game; ***gewonnenes – haben,*** have gained the day *or* gained one's point; ***Glück im –, Pech in der Liebe,*** lucky at cards, unlucky in love; ***die Hand im – haben*** (***bei***), have a finger in the pie; ***sich ins – mischen,*** have a hand in it; ***ihm ins – sehen,*** look at *or* see his cards *or* hand; (*fig.*) see through his game; (***mit***) ***im – sein,*** be implicated *or* involved (***bei***, in), be at the bottom (of); ***mit klingendem –e,*** with drums beating and trumpets sounding; ***– der Kräfte,*** interplay of forces; ***leichtes – haben,*** win hands down, (*coll.*) have a walkover, (*fig.*) have little *or* no trouble, have an easy task *or* job; ***– der Muskeln,*** action of the muscles; ***– der Natur,*** freak of nature; ***sein – mit ihm treiben,*** make fun *or* game of him; ***das – verloren geben,*** throw up the sponge, throw in one's hand; ***ein – der Wellen sein,*** be at the mercy of the waves; ***das – hat sich gewandt,*** the tables are turned; ***es wird ihm zum –*** or ***ist ihm ein –,*** it's child's play to him; 2. (*Mech.*) clearance, play, allowance, looseness, slackness, backlash; 3. set (*of knitting needles etc.*), pack, deck (*of cards*); 4. (*fig.*) child's play.

Spiel|anzug, *m.* playsuit, rompers. **–art,** *f.* style of play; (*Zool., Bot. etc.*) variety, sport. **–automat,** *m.* gambling machine. **–ball,** *m.* (*Tenn.*) game ball, (*Bill.*) ball in play; (*fig.*) sport, plaything; ***ein – der Winde und Wellen,*** at the mercy of the winds and waves. **–bank,** *f.* (gambling) casino. **–brett,** *n.* board (*for chess, draughts etc.*). **–dauer,** *f.* playing time, (*of film*) running time. **–dose,** *f.* musical box.

spielen [ˈʃpi:lən], *v.t., v.i.* play; play (at) (*cards etc.*), play (on) (*musical instrument*); gamble; act, perform (*a play*), take the part of, play (*a character*); toy (***mit***, with) (*a th.*), trifle, dally, coquet (with) (*a p.*); feign, simulate, pretend; (*of colours*) flash, glitter, sparkle; ***vom Blatte –,*** play (*music*) at sight; ***falsch –,*** cheat; (*Mus.*) play wrong notes; ***eine klägliche Figur –,*** cut a sorry *or* poor figure; ***mit dem Gedanken –,*** toy *or* flirt with the idea; ***nach Gehör –,*** play (*music*) from ear; ***ihm etwas in die Hände –,*** slip a th. into his hand; ***einander in die Hände –,*** play into one another's hands, have a secret understanding; ***hoch –,*** play for high stakes; ***das Stück spielt in . . .,*** the scene is laid in . . .; (*Bill.*) ***ins Loch –,*** pocket (*a ball*); ***ins Rote –,*** incline to red, have a reddish tinge; ***im Winde –,*** flutter in the wind; ***mit offenen Karten –,*** be open and above board; ***mit verdeckten Karten –,*** have underhand dealings, behave in an underhand manner; ***– lassen,*** bring into play; ***seine Beziehungen – lassen,*** pull strings; ***er läßt nicht mit sich –,*** he is not to be trifled with; ***keine Rolle –,*** count for nothing, carry no weight; ***um Geld –,*** play for money.

spielend [ˈʃpi:lənt], *adv.* easily, with the greatest (of) ease, effortlessly. **Spieler,** *m.* player; actor, performer; gambler. **Spielerei** [–ˈraɪ], *f.* play, sport, pastime, childish amusement; dalliance, frivolity; trifle.

Spielergebnis [ˈʃpi:lʔɛrge:pnɪs], *n.* score.

spielerisch [ˈʃpi:lərɪʃ], *adj.* perfunctory, frivolous; playful.

Spiel|feld, *n.* playing-field, sports ground, (tennis) court. **–film,** *m.* feature (film). **–gefährte,** *m.* playfellow, playmate. **–gehilfe,** *m.* croupier. **–geld,** *n.* stake(s), pool, card-money. **–gesellschaft,** *f.* card-party. **–gewinn,** *m.* winnings (*at play*). **–grenze,** *f.* (*Footb.*) (dead-ball) line. **–gruppe,** *f.* (*Theat.*) amateur company *or* players. **–hälfte,** *f.* (*Footb.*) half. **–hölle,** *f.* gambling-den. **–kamerad,** *m. See* **–gefährte**; (*Spt.*) team-mate. **–karte,** *f.* playing-card. **–leiter,** *m.* (*Theat.*) stage-manager, (*Films*) producer, (*Spt.*) referee. **–mann,** *m.* (*pl.* **-leute**) (*Mil.*) bandsman; (*Hist.*) troubadour, minstrel. **–mannschaft,** *f.* (*Spt.*) team. **–mannsdichtung,** *f.* minstrel poesy, minstrelsy. **–mannszug,** *m.* (military) band. **–marke,** *f.* counter, chip. **–oper,** *f.* comic opera. **–plan,** *m.* (*Theat.*) (season's) programme; repertory, repertoire. **–platz,** *m.* playground; *see* **–feld. –ratte,** *f.* (*coll.*) gambler. **–raum,** *m.* room to move, (*coll.*) elbow-room; (*fig.*) (free) play, full scope; margin, latitude; (*Tech.*) play, clearance; (*Artil.*) windage. **–regeln,** *f.pl.* rules (of the game) (*also fig.*); (*fig.*) ***sich an die – halten,*** play the game. **–sache,** *f.* plaything, toy. **–schuld,** *f.* gambling debt. **–schule,** *f.* kindergarten. **–sitz,** *m.* (*Tech.*) clearance fit. **–tisch,** *m.* gaming-table. **–trieb,** *m.* play instinct. **–uhr,** *f.* musical box, musical clock. **–verbot,** *m.* (*Spt.*) suspension. **–verderber,** *m.* spoil-sport, kill-joy, wet-blanket. **–verlängerung,** *f.* (*Spt.*) extra time. **–waren,** *f.pl.* toys. **–werk,** *n.* chime (*of clock*), peal (*of bells*). **–wut,** *f.* passion for gambling. **–zeit,** *f.* playtime; (*Theat., Spt.*) season; (*Films*) run, (*Mus., Spt.*) playing time. **–zeug,** *n.* plaything, toy. **–zimmer,** *n.* play-room, (day-) nursery.

Spier [ʃpi:r], *m. or n.* (**-s,** *pl.* **-e**) (*Bot.*) spiraea; thin stalk, blade of grass. **Spierchen,** *n.* (*dial.*) ***kein –,*** not a bit, not in the very least. **Spiere,** *f.* (*Naut.*) spar, boom; (*Av.*) rib; (*Bot.*) spiraea. **Spier|staude,** *f.*, **–strauch,** *m.* (*Bot.*) spiraea.

Spieß [ʃpi:s], *m.* (**-es,** *pl.* **-e**) spear, lance, pike, javelin, harpoon; (*Cul.*) spit; (*Typ.*) blot, pick; first year's antlers; (*sl.*) sergeant-major; ***den – umkehren,*** turn the tables. **Spieß|bock,** *m.* (*Hunt.*) pricket, brocket. **–braten,** *m.* meat roasted on a spit.

Spießbürger [ˈʃpi:sbyrgər], *m.* narrow-minded p., bourgeois, commonplace fellow, philistine. **spießbürgerlich,** *adj.* bourgeois, narrow-minded, commonplace, humdrum, (*coll.*) stodgy.

spießen [ˈʃpi:sən], *v.t.* pierce, spear, impale, run through, transfix.

Spießente [ˈʃpi:sʔɛntə], *f.* (*Orn.*) pintail (*Anas acuta*).

Spießer [ˈʃpi:sər], *m.* (*coll.*) 1. *See* **Spießbürger**; 2. *See* **Spießbock. spießerisch,** *adj. See* **spießbürgerlich.**

Spieß|flughuhn, *n.* (*Orn.*) pintailed sandgrouse (*Pterocles alchata*). **–gesell(e),** *m.* accomplice. **–glanz,** *m.* antimony. **–hirsch,** *m. See* **–bock. spießig,** *adj.* (*coll.*) *see* **spießbürgerlich. Spieß|rute,** *f.* rod, switch; ***–n laufen,*** run the gauntlet. **–träger,** *m.* spearman, pikeman, halberdier.

Spill [ʃpɪl], *n.* (**-(e)s,** *pl.* **-e**) capstan, windlass, winch. **Spillbaum,** *m.* capstan-bar; (*dial.*) *see* **Spindelbaum. Spille,** *f.* (*dial.*) *see* **Spindel. spillerig,** *adj.* (*dial.*) thin as a rake. **Spillgelder,** *n.pl.* (*dial.*) pin-money.

Spilling [ˈʃpɪlɪŋ], *m.* (**-s,** *pl.* **-e**) small yellow plum.

Spinat [ʃpiˈna:t], *m.* (**-(e)s,** *pl.* **-e**) spinach.

Spind [ʃpɪnt], *n.* (*dial. m.*) (**-(e)s,** *pl.* **-e**), **Spinde,** *f.* locker, cupboard, wardrobe, press.

Spindel [ˈʃpɪndəl], *f.* (-, *pl.* **-n**) 1. distaff; 2. spindle, shaft, pin, peg, pinion, pivot, arbor, mandrel, axis, axle; 3. (*Chem.*) hydrometer; 4. (*Archit.*) newel. **Spindel|baum,** *m.* (*Bot.*) spindle-tree (*Euonymus*). **–beine,** *n.pl.* spindle-shanks. **spindeldürr,** *adj.* thin as a rake, spindly. **Spindel|presse,** *f.* screw-press. **–waage,** *f.* hydrometer. **–welle,** *f.* bobbin. **–zapfen,** *m.* pivot, axis, spindle.

Spinett [ʃpiˈnɛt], *n.* (**-(e)s,** *pl.* **-e**) spinet.

Spinne [ˈʃpɪnə], *f.* spider; (*coll.*) ***pfui –!*** disgusting! shocking! **spinnefeind** [–ˈfaɪnt], *pred.adj.* bitterly hostile; ***ihm – sein,*** hate him like poison.

spinnen [ˈʃpɪnən], **1.** *irr.v.t.* spin, twist; (*coll.*) ***Hanf –,*** be on bread and water; ***Ränke –,*** hatch plots; ***Verrat –,*** plot treason. **2.** *irr.v.i.* 1. spin (round); 2. (*of cats*) purr; 3. (*coll.*) be crazy; (*coll.*) ***du spinnst wohl!*** you must be crazy! you're off your head! 4. (*sl.*) be in clink, do a stretch. **Spinnengewebe,** *n. See* **Spinngewebe. Spinner,** *m.* spinner; (*Ent.*) bombycid. **Spinnerei** [–ˈraɪ], *f.* spinning; spinning-mill. **Spinnerin,** *f.* spinner.

Spinn|faden, *m.* spider's thread, gossamer. **–faser,**

f. spun *or* synthetic fibre. **-gewebe,** *n.* spider's web, cobweb. **-haus,** *n.* (*obs.*) workhouse. **-maschine,** *f.* spinning-machine. **-rad,** *n.* spinning-wheel. **-rocken,** *m.* distaff. **-stoff-(waren),** *m.* (*f.pl.*) textiles. **-stube,** *f.* spinning-room. **-warze,** *f.* spinning-orifice (*of spiders*), spinneret. **-web,** *n.* (**-(e)s,** *pl.* **-e**) (*Austr.*) *see* **-gewebe.**

spinös [ʃpi'nø:s], *adj.* spiny; (*fig.*) pernickety.

[1] **Spint** [ʃpɪnt], *n.* (**-(e)s,** *pl.* **-e**) (*obs.*) a dry measure (*local variations from ½ gallon to 1½ gallons*).

[2] **Spint,** *m.* (*Orn.*) *see* **Bienenfresser.**

spintisieren [ʃpɪnti'zi:rən], *v.i.* brood, ruminate (*über* (*Acc.*), over), meditate, muse (on).

Spion [ʃpi'o:n], *m.* (**-s,** *pl.* **-e**) 1. spy; 2. window-mirror. **Spionage** [-'na:ʒə], *f.* spying, espionage. **Spionage|abwehr,** *f.* counter-espionage. **-ring,** *m.* spy-ring. **spionieren,** *v.i.* engage in espionage, spy; pry, play the spy.

Spiralbohrer [ʃpi'ra:lbo:rər], *m.* twist-drill. **Spirale,** *f.* spiral, helix; coil; clock-spring. **Spiralfeder,** *f.* helical *or* spiral spring; main-spring (*of a watch*). **spiralförmig,** *adj.* spiral, helical; (*Bot.*) convolute. **Spiral|linie,** *f.* spiral. **-nebel,** *m.* spiral nebula.

Spiritismus [ʃpiri'tɪsmus], *m.* spiritualism. **Spiritist,** *m.* spiritualist. **spiritistisch,** *adj.* spiritualist(ic).

spiritual [ʃpiritu'a:l]. *adj.* spiritual. **Spiritualismus,** *m.* (*Philos.*) spiritualism.

spirituell [ʃpiritu'ɛl], *adj.* intellectual, mental.

Spirituosen [ʃpiritu'o:zən], *pl.* spirits, spirituous liquors.

Spiritus ['ʃpi:ritus], *m.* (-, *pl.* - *or* **-se**) 1. alcohol, spirit, spirits; methylated spirit; ***denaturierter* –,** methylated spirit; ***normalstarker* –,** proof-spirit; 2. (*Metr.*) breath(ing); 3. (*fig.*) mettle. **Spiritus|-brennerei,** *f.* distillery. **-kocher,** *m.* spirit-stove. **-lack,** *m.* spirit-varnish. **-lampe,** *f.* spirit-lamp.

Spital [ʃpi'ta:l], *n.* (**-s,** *pl.* **¨-er**) hospital; old-people's *or* pauper's home. **Spital|schiff,** *n.* hospital-ship. **-zug,** *m.* ambulance train.

Spittel ['ʃpɪtəl], *n.* (*dial. m.*) *see* **Spital.**

spitz [ʃpɪts], *adj.* pointed, peaked, sharp, tapering, (*Geom.*) acute; (*fig.*) sarcastic, caustic, biting; ***–er Wein,*** thin *or* sharp *or* acid wine; ***–er Winkel,*** acute angle; ***–e Zunge,*** sharp tongue; ***mit –en Fingern angreifen,*** handle cautiously; ***– zulaufen,*** taper to a point; (*coll.*) ***ich kann es nicht – kriegen,*** I can't make it out.

Spitz, *m.* (**-es,** *pl.* **-e**) 1. Pomeranian dog; 2. (*Swiss*) *see* **Spitze**; (*coll.*) ***einen* (*kleinen*) *– haben,*** be (somewhat) tipsy.

Spitz|ahorn, *m.* (*Bot.*) Norway maple (*Acer platanoides*). **-bart,** *m.* goatee, pointed beard. **-bauch,** *m.* paunch. **-beutel,** *m.* triangular filter-bag. **-bogen,** *m.* Gothic *or* pointed arch. **-bogen-stil,** *m.* (*Archit.*) Gothic style. **-bohrer,** *m.* centre-bit. **-bub(e),** *m.* rascal, rogue; swindler, thief; (*coll.*) little rogue *or* rascal. **-bubengesicht,** *n.* roguish *or* impish face. **-bubenstreich,** *m.*, **-büberei,** *f.* rascality, roguery, (*of children*) roguish trick. **-bübin,** *f.* *See* **-bub(e). spitz-bübisch,** *adj.* rascally, knavish, (*of children*) impish, roguish.

Spitze ['ʃpɪtsə], *f.* 1. point, peak; prong, spike; extremity, tip; nib (*of pen*); mouthpiece (*of a pipe*); (cigarette-)holder; top, summit, peak (*of mountain*), top (*of tree*), spire (*of tower*); vertex (*of triangle*), apex (*of pyramid*); head (*of enterprise, marching column*), (*Mil.*) spearhead (*of attack*), (*Spt.*) leaders, leading group (*in race*); (*Anat., Astr.*) cusp; ***die – nehmen*** or ***abbrechen*** (*Dat.*), take the edge off; ***die –n der Behörden,*** the heads of the administration, the authorities; ***ihm die – bieten,*** defy him; ***die –n der Gesellschaft,*** the leaders *or* cream of society; (*Spt.*) ***an der – liegen,*** be among the leaders, be in the lead; ***an der – stehen,*** be at the head (*of affairs*); ***auf die – treiben,*** carry to extremes, carry too far; 2. (*fig.*) sarcastic *or* cutting *or* pointed remark, (*coll.*) cut; 3. *pl.* lace; ***–n klöppeln,*** make (pillow-)lace.

Spitzel ['ʃpɪtsəl], *m.* police spy, informer, (*sl.*) stool-pigeon, nark, snout; (*fig., coll.*) snooper. **spitzeln,** *v.i.* spy, inform, (*coll.*) snoop around.

spitzen ['ʃpɪtsən], **1.** *v.t.* point, tip, sharpen; ***einen Bleistift –,*** sharpen a pencil; ***seine Antwort –,*** make a cutting reply; ***das ist auf mich gespitzt,*** that is aimed at me; ***den Mund –,*** purse one's lips; ***die Ohren –,*** prick up one's ears, sit up and take notice. **2.** *v.i.* (*dial.*) pay attention, look out. **3.** *v.r.* (*coll.*) look forward (***auf*** (*Acc.*) to), count (on), set one's heart (upon), hope (for).

Spitzen|abstand, *m.* distance between centres. **-arbeit,** *f.* lace-work. **-belastung,** *f.* (*Elec.*) peak load. **-besatz,** *m.* lace-trimming. **-entladung,** *f.* (*Elec.*) point-discharge. **-fahrzeug,** *n.* leading vehicle (*of a column*). **-film,** *m.* star production. **-flieger,** *m.* flying-ace. **-geschwindigkeit,** *f.* top speed, peak velocity. **-kleid,** *n.* dress trimmed with *or* made of lace. **-klöppel,** *m.* lace-bobbin. **-klöppelei,** *f.* pillow-lace (making). **-klöppler(in),** *m.* (*f.*) lace-maker. **-kompagnie,** *f.* (*Mil.*) advance party. **-leistung,** *f.* first-class *or* outstanding *or* masterly performance, (*Spt.*) record; (*Tech.*) maximum efficiency, peak output; (*Elec.*) peak-power. **-lohn,** *m.* wage ceiling. **-spieler,** *m.* top-ranking player. **-strom,** *m.* (*Elec.*) peak current. **-tanz,** *m.* toe dance. **-verband,** *m.* head *or* central organization; (*Mil.*) *see* **-kompagnie. -wachstum,** *n.* (*Bot.*) apical growth. **-wert,** *m.* peak value. **-wirkung,** *f.* (*Elec.*) needle-effect.

Spitzer ['ʃpɪtsər], *m.* (pencil- *etc.*) sharpener.

spitzfindig ['ʃpɪtsfɪndɪç], *adj.* subtle, crafty, sharp, shrewd, ingenious; cavilling, captious, hyper-critical, hair-splitting. **Spitzfindigkeit,** *f.* subtlety, craftiness, captiousness, hair-splitting, sophistry. **Spitz|geschoß,** *n.* pointed bullet *or* shell. **-glas,** *n.* conical glass. **-hacke,** *f.* pickaxe.

spitzig ['ʃpɪtsɪç], *adj.* *See* **spitz.**

Spitz|kant, *m.* (**-es,** *pl.* **-e**) pyramid. **-knospe,** *f.* terminal bud. **-kolumne,** *f.* (*Typ.*) head-piece. **-marke,** *f.* (*Typ.*) heading. **-maus,** *f.* (*Zool.*) shrew (*Sorex*). **-name,** *m.* nickname. **-nase,** *f.* pointed nose. **-pfeiler,** *m.* obelisk. **-pocken,** *f.pl.* (*Med.*) chicken-pox. **-säule,** *f.* *See* **-pfeiler. -wegerich,** *m.* (*Bot.*) ribwort (*Plantago lanceolata*). **spitzwink(e)lig,** *adj.* (*Geom.*) acute-angled.

Spleiß [ʃplaɪs], *m.* (**-es,** *pl.* **-e**) (*Naut.*) splice. **Spleiße,** *f.* (*dial.*) splinter; scale (*of iron*). **spleißen,** *irr.v.t., v.i.* (*aux.* s.) (*Naut.*) splice; (*rare*) split, splinter, cleave. **spleißig,** *adj.* friable, easily split.

splendid [ʃplɛn'di:t], *adj.* 1. splendid, magnificent; open-handed, liberal, generous; 2. (*Typ.*) wide, spaced.

Spließ [ʃpli:s], *m.* (**-es,** *pl.* **-e**) (*dial.*) shingle, wooden tile.

Splint [ʃplɪnt], *m.* (**-(e)s,** *pl.* **-e**) 1. (*Bot.*) sapwood, alburnum; 2. (*Mech.*) securing pin, cotter, split-pin. **Splintbolzen,** *m.* keyed bolt.

spliß [ʃplɪs], *see* **spleißen.**

Spliß, *m.* (**-(ss)es,** *pl.* **-(ss)e**) 1. (*Naut.*) splice; 2. *See* **Splitter. splissen,** *v.t.* (*Naut.*) splice.

Splitt [ʃplɪt], *m.* stone chip(ping)s, crushed stone, gravel. **Splitter,** *m.* splinter, chip, fragment; scale (*of metal etc.*); (*B.*) mote. **Splitterbombe,** *f.* fragmentation *or* anti-personnel bomb. **splitter|-dicht,** *adj.* splinter-proof. **-(faser)nackt,** *adj.* stark naked. **-frei,** *adj.* non-splintering (*glass*). **Splittergraben,** *m.* slit-trench. **splitterig,** *adj.* splintery, brittle. **splittern,** *v.t., v.i.* (*aux.* s.) shatter, shiver, splinter, split (to pieces). **Splitter|-partei,** *f.* (*Pol.*) splinter-party. **-richter,** *m.* hair-splitter, caviller, carper, fault-finder. **splitter|-sicher,** *adj.* *See* **-dicht, -frei**; ***–es Glas,*** safety-glass. **Splitterwirkung,** *f.* (*Mil.*) fragmentation.

Spodium ['ʃpo:dium], *n.* bone-black.

Spolien ['ʃpo:liən], *n.pl.* spoils, booty.

spondeisch [ʃpɔn'de:ɪʃ], *adj.* spondaic. **Spondeus,** *m.* (-, *pl.* **-deen**) spondee.

spönne ['ʃpœnə], *see* **spinnen.**

Sponsalien [ʃpɔn'za:liən], *pl.* (*Law*) betrothal; betrothal celebrations. **sponsieren,** *v.i.* (*obs.*) court, woo.

spontan [ʃpɔn'ta:n], *adj.* spontaneous, autogenous; *–e Änderung* or *Variation,* mutation.

Spor [ʃpo:r], *m.* **(-(e)s,** *pl.* **-e)** (*dial.*) mildew, mouldiness.

sporadisch [ʃpo'ra:dɪʃ], *adj.* sporadic.

Spore ['ʃpo:rə], *f.* spore, sporule. **sporen,** *v.i.* (*dial.*) get mouldy, dry up, rot.

Sporen ['ʃpo:rən], *pl. of* **Sporn.**

sporenbildend ['ʃpo:rənbɪldənt], *adj.* sporular, sporogenous. **Sporen|bildung,** *f.* sporogenesis, sporulation. **–kapsel,** *f.* spore-capsule, sporangium. **–pflanzen,** *f.pl.* acotyledons, sporophytes, cryptogamous plants. **–tiere,** *n.pl.* sporozoa.

sporig ['ʃpo:rɪç], *adj.* mildewed, mouldy.

Sporn [ʃpɔrn], *m.* 1. **(-(e)s,** *pl.* **Sporen)** spur; (*Av.*) tail-skid, (*Naut.*) ram, (*Artil.*) trail-spade; ***dem Pferde die Sporen geben,*** set spurs to one's horse; ***sich*** (*Dat.*) ***die Sporen verdienen,*** win one's spurs; 2. (*pl.* **-e**) (*Bot.*) thorn, spine. **Sporn|ammer,** *f.* (*Orn.*) Lapland bunting (*Calcarius lapponicus*). **–blume,** *f.* (*Bot.*) larkspur (*Centranthus*).

spornen ['ʃpɔrnən], *v.t.* spur, set spurs to.

Sporn|halter, *m.* heel-plate. **–kiebitz,** *m.* (*Orn.*) spur-winged plover (*Hoplopterus spinosus*). **–pieper,** *m.* (*Orn.*) Richard's pipit (*Anthus richardi*). **–rad,** *n.* (*Av.*) tail-wheel. **–rädchen,** *n.* rowel; spur-wheel; (*Her.*) mullet. **sporn|stätisch,** *adj.* restive. **–streichs,** *adv.* posthaste, with all speed, at once, immediately, (*coll.*) straight away.

Sport [ʃpɔrt], *m.* **(-(e)s,** *pl.* (*rare*) **-e)** sport, athletics; *– treiben,* go in for sport. **Sport|abzeichen,** *n.* (official German) sports badge. **–anlage,** *f.* sports facilities. **–anzug,** *m.* sportswear. **–art,** *f.* branch of athletics, form of sport. **–ausrüstung,** *f.* sports kit. **–bericht,** *m.* sports *or* sporting news.

sporteln ['ʃpɔrtəln], *v.i.* (*coll.*) go in for sport.

Sporteln, *f.pl.* fees, perquisites.

Sport|feld, *n.* athletics ground, sports field *or* ground, playing field. **–fest,** *n.* sports day *or* meeting. **–fex,** *m.* (*coll.*) *see* **–freund. –flugzeug,** *n.* sports plane. **–freund,** *m.* sports fan. **–funk,** *m.* (radio) sports news *or* commentary. **–geist,** *m.* sportsmanship. **–gelände,** *m. See* **–feld. –gerät,** *n. See* **–ausrüstung. –geschäft,** *n.* sport-shop. **–halle,** *f.* gymnasium. **–hemd,** *n.* sports shirt; running vest, strip. **–herz,** *n.* athlete's heart. **–hochschule,** *f.* college of physical education. **–hose,** *f.* shorts. **–jacke,** *f.* sports jacket. **–kabriolett,** *n.* (*Motor.*) roadster, sports car. **–kleidung,** *f.* sportswear. **–lehrer,** *m.* physical training instructor; trainer, coach.

Sportler(in) ['ʃpɔrtlər(ɪn)], *m.* (*f.*) sportsman (sportswoman), (woman) athlete. **sportlich,** *adj.* sporting, athletic; sportsmanlike, (*coll.*) sporting; *–e Veranstaltung,* sporting event. **Sportlichkeit,** *f.* sportsmanship, (*coll.*) sporting behaviour.

Sport|platz, *m. See* **–feld.**

Sports|kanone, *f,* (*coll.*) top-ranking athlete, star performer. **–mann,** *m.* (*pl.* **⸚er** *or* **-leute**) sportsman. **sportsmäßig,** *adj.* sportsmanlike.

sporttreibend ['ʃpɔrttraɪbənt], *adj.* sporting, actively engaged in sport. **Sport|veranstaltung,** *f. See* **–fest. –verband,** *m.* athletics association. **–verein,** *m.* athletics club, sports club. **–wagen,** *m.* 1. *See* **–kabriolett**; 2. push-chair, folding pram. **–welt,** *f.* world of sport. **–zeitung,** *f.* sporting paper, sports magazine.

Spott [ʃpɔt], *m.* mockery, ridicule, scorn, derision, contumely; sarcasm, irony; banter, raillery; butt, laughing-stock; ***beißender –,*** biting sarcasm; ***Schande und –,*** shame and disgrace; (*Prov.*) ***wer den Schaden hat, braucht für den – nicht zu sorgen,*** the laugh is always on the loser; ***seinen – treiben mit,*** make fun of, turn to ridicule, mock (at), scoff at; ***Zielscheibe des –es,*** butt, laughing-stock; ***zum – werden,*** become the laughing-stock. **Spottbild,** *n.* caricature. **spottbillig,** 1. *adj.* dirt-cheap. 2. *adv.* for a song. **Spottdrossel,** *f.* (*Orn.*) mocking-bird (*Mimus polyglottus and Dumetella carolinensis*).

Spöttelei [ʃpœtə'laɪ], *f.* sarcasm, irony; banter, raillery, persiflage, gibes, jibes. **spötteln** ['ʃpœtəln], *v.i.* scoff, jeer, sneer (***über*** (*Acc.*), at), pass sarcastic remarks (about).

spotten ['ʃpɔtən], *v.i.* 1. mock, scoff, sneer, jeer, laugh (***über*** (*Acc.*), at); *–* ***über*** (*Acc.*), ridicule, deride, mock, taunt, chaff; make fun *or* game of; 2. (*fig.*) – (*Gen.*) defy; ***es spottet jeder Beschreibung,*** it defies *or* beggars description.

Spötter ['ʃpœtər], *m.* mocker, scoffer, cynic; (*Eccl.*) blasphemer. **Spötterei** [–'raɪ], *f.* jeering, scoffing, mocking, derision, mockery, sarcasm; *see* **Spott.**

Spott|gebot, *n.* ridiculous(ly low) offer. **–geburt,** *f.* monstrosity, abortion. **–gedicht,** *n.* satirical poem, lampoon. **–gelächter,** *n.* derisive laughter. **–geld,** *n.* trifling sum, ridiculously small figure, (*coll.*) a mere song; *see* **–preis.**

spöttisch ['ʃpœtɪʃ], *adj.* mocking, scoffing, jeering, sneering; scornful, derisive; ironical, sarcastic, caustic, biting.

Spott|lied, *n.* satirical *or* derisive song. **–lust,** *f.* love of sarcasm. **spottlustig,** *adj.* satirical, sarcastic. **Spott|name,** *m.* abusive name. **–preis,** *m.* ridiculously low price. **–rede,** *f.* gibe, sneer, taunt. **–schrift,** *f.* lampoon, satire. **–vogel,** *m.* mocking-bird; (*fig.*) mocker, wag.

sprach [ʃpra:x], *see* **sprechen.**

Sprach|bau, *m.* structure of a language. **–beherrschung,** *f.* command of a language. **–denkmal,** *n.* literary document *or* text.

Sprache ['ʃpra:xə], *f.* speech, diction, parlance, delivery, articulation, style; language, tongue, idiom, vernacular, dialect; voice, accent; ***alte –n,*** classical languages; ***– der Bibel,*** biblical language; ***– der Diebe,*** thieves' cant; ***– der Kanzel,*** pulpit oratory; ***neuere –n,*** modern languages; ***– der Vernunft,*** language of common sense; ***ich erkenne ihn an der –,*** I know him by his voice *or* accent; ***der – beraubt sein,*** be bereft of speech; ***blumenreiche –,*** flowery style; ***eine derbe – führen,*** use strong language; ***eine dreiste – führen,*** make impudent remarks; ***gehobene –,*** elevated diction; ***heraus mit der –!*** out with it! speak out! ***mit der – nicht recht herauswollen,*** be reluctant to speak, be unwilling to explain o.s. *or* to speak out; ***mit der – herausrücken,*** speak freely, (*coll.*) come out with it; ***das redet eine deutliche –,*** that speaks for itself; ***die – wiederbekommen,*** find one's voice; ***die – wiedergewinnen,*** recover one's speech; ***zur – bringen,*** bring (*a matter*) up, broach (*a subject*); ***zur – kommen,*** come up (for discussion), be mentioned, be touched on.

spräche ['ʃprɛ:çə], *see* **sprechen.**

Sprach|eigenheit, –eigentümlichkeit, *f.* idiomatic peculiarity, idiom; ***deutsche*** (***englische, amerikanische, französische, lateinische***) *–,* Germanism (Anglicism, Americanism, Gallicism, Latinism). **Sprachengewirr,** *n.* confusion of tongues, babel. **Sprach|fähigkeit,** *f.* faculty of speech. **–fehler,** *m.* (*Med.*) impediment of *or* in speech, speech defect, (*Gram.*) solecism, grammatical mistake. **–fertigkeit,** *f.* fluency, (*coll.*) gift of the gab; proficiency in (foreign) languages. **–forscher,** *m.* linguist, philologist. **–forschung,** *f.* philology, linguistics. **–führer,** *m.* elementary guide (*to a language*), phrase-book. **–gebiet,** *n.* area where a language is spoken; ***das gesamte deutsche –,*** all German-speaking countries; ***englisches –,*** English-speaking world. **–gebrauch,** *m.* linguistic usage. **–gefüge,** *n.* connected speech. **–gefühl,** *n.* feeling for correct idiom, feeling for a language. **–gelehrte(r),** *m., f. See* **–forscher. –gesellschaft,** *f.* society for promoting the vernacular. **–gesetz,** *n.* linguistic law. **sprachgewandt,** *adj.* fluent. **Sprach|grenze,** *f.* linguistic frontier. **–gut,** *n.* resources of a language. **–insel,** *f.* district dialectically isolated from its surroundings, linguistic enclave, isolated dialect. **–kenner,** *m.*

linguist. **–kenntnis,** *f.* knowledge of *or* proficiency in a language. **sprachkundig,** *adj.* proficient in languages. **Sprach|lehre,** *f.* grammar, language primer. **–lehrer,** *m.* teacher of languages.

sprachlich [ˈʃpraːxlɪç], *adj.* linguistic; grammatical. **sprachlos,** *adj.* speechless, (*coll.*) dumbfounded, flabbergasted.

Sprach|neuerer, *m.* language reformer. **–organ,** *n.* organ of speech. **–pflege,** *f.* fostering the mother tongue. **–regel,** *f.* grammatical rule. **–reinheit,** *f.* purity of speech; purity of a language. **–reiniger,** *m.* purist. **–reinigung,** *f.* elimination of foreign elements from a language. **sprachrichtig,** *adj.* correct, grammatical. **Sprach|rohr,** *n.* speaking-tube, megaphone; (*fig.*) mouthpiece; – ***der öffentlichen Meinung,*** organ of public opinion. **–schatz,** *m.* vocabulary. **–schnitzer,** *m.* grammatical mistake *or* blunder, solecism, (*coll.*) howler. **sprachschöpferisch,** *adj.* creative in the use of language, influential on style *or* vocabulary. **Sprach|spötter,** *m.* (*Orn.*) *see* **Orpheusspötter.** **–störung,** *f. See* **–fehler** (*Med.*). **–studium,** *n.* language study. **–stunde,** *f.* lesson in a (foreign) language; ***deutsche –,*** German lesson. **–sünde,** *f. See* **–schnitzer.** **–talent,** *n.* linguistic talent. **–unterricht,** *m.* language teaching, teaching of languages; ***deutschen – erteilen,*** give German lessons. **–verbesserung,** *f.* language reform. **–verderber,** *m.* corrupter of a language. **–verein,** *m.* philological society. **–vergleichung,** *f.* comparative philology. **–vermögen,** *n. See* **–fähigkeit.** **–verschandelung,** *f.* corruption of a language. **–verstärker,** *m.* public-address system, speech amplifier. **–werkzeug,** *n. See* **–organ.** **sprachwidrig,** *adj.* ungrammatical, incorrect. **Sprach|wissenschaft,** *f. See* **–forschung.** **sprachwissenschaftlich,** *adj.* philological. **Sprachzentrum,** *n.* (*Anat.*) speech centre.

sprang [ʃpraŋ], **spränge** [ˈʃprɛŋə], *see* **springen.**

Sprech|art [ˈʃprɛç–], *f.* diction, style of speech, manner of speaking. **–band,** *n.* (*Films etc.*) soundtrack. **–bühne,** *f.* (*Theat.*) living stage. **–chor,** *m.* speaking chorus; ***im – rufen,*** chorus.

sprechen [ˈʃprɛːçən], *irr.v.t., v.i.* speak, talk (*mit,* to *or* with (*a p.*); *von, über* (*Acc.*), about *or* of (*a th.*)), discourse, converse (with (*a p.*), about *or* on (*a th.*)), discuss, talk over ((*a th.*) with (*a p.*)); (*only v.t.*) say, pronounce, declare, utter; ***ich möchte ihn –,*** I would like a word with him *or* like to speak to him *or* like to meet *or* see him; ***es spricht dir aus dem Gesicht,*** it is written on *or* in your face; ***aus seinen Worten spricht Begeisterung,*** his words express enthusiasm, enthusiasm is evident from his words; ***– für,*** speak on behalf of, speak for (*a p.*); advocate, argue in favour of, plead for (*a th.*); put in a good word for (*a p. or th.*); (*fig.*) speak well for, tell in favour of; ***alles spricht dafür*** (***daß*** . . .), there is every reason to believe (that . . .), there is everything to be said for it; ***das spricht für sich selbst,*** it tells its own tale; ***ich bin heute für niemand zu –,*** I cannot see *or* I am not free *or* available to see anyone today; ***nicht zu – sein,*** be engaged *or* busy; ***auf ihn gut zu – sein,*** be well *or* kindly disposed towards him; ***auf ihn nicht gut zu – sein,*** be ill-disposed towards him, not have a good word to say about him, (*coll.*) have it in for him; ***es spricht sich herum,*** it is the talk of the town; ***zu – kommen auf*** (*Acc.*), touch upon, bring up, come to speak of; ***er läßt nicht mit sich –,*** he will not listen to reason, it is no use talking to him; ***nicht mehr miteinander –,*** be no longer on speaking terms; ***– wie dir der Schnabel gewachsen ist,*** say what you think, give rein to your tongue, not mince matters; ***wir – uns noch darüber,*** we shall see about that; ***unter uns gesprochen,*** between ourselves; ***das Urteil –,*** pronounce judgement; ***man spricht davon,*** it is much talked about *or* of; ***von etwas anderem –,*** change the subject; ***– wir nicht davon,*** don't talk about it, the less said about it the better; ***ganz allgemein gesprochen,*** speaking quite generally.

Sprechen, *n.* speaking, talking. **sprechend,** *adj.* (*fig.*) life-like, speaking, expressive, eloquent; striking, telling, convincing, conclusive. **Sprecher,** *m.* speaker; spokesman, foreman (*of a jury*); (*Rad.*) broadcaster, announcer.

Sprech|fehler, *m.* slip of the tongue. **–film,** *m.* talking-picture, (*coll.*) talkie. **–funk,** *m.* radiotelephony. **–funkgerät,** *n.* radiotelephone, (*Mil., coll.*) walkie-talkie. **–gesang,** *m.* (*Mus.*) recitative. **–melodie,** *f.* intonation. **–muschel,** *f.* (*Tele.*) mouthpiece. **–probe,** *f.* (*Theat. etc.*) audition. **–rolle,** *f.* (*Theat.*) speaking part. **–stelle,** *f.* telephone extension, call-station. **–stunde,** *f.* time set apart for interviewing, (*Med.*) consulting-hour, surgery-hour; (*Comm.*) office-hour. **–stundenhilfe,** *f.* (*Med.*) receptionist. **–trichter,** *m. See* **–muschel.** **–übung,** *f.* elocution exercise. **–verständigung,** *f.* (*Tele.*) quality of reception. **–weise,** *f. See* **–art.** **–zimmer,** *n.* office, (*Med.*) surgery, consulting-room.

Spreißel [ˈʃpraɪsəl], *m.* (*Austr. n.*) (*dial.*) splinter.

Spreitdecke [ˈʃpraɪtdɛkə], **Spreite,** *f.* cover, counterpane, bedspread.

Spreize [ˈʃpraɪtsə], *f.* 1. stay, spreader, prop, strut; (*Gymn.*) straddle, splits; 2. (*sl.*) fag. **spreizen, 1.** *v.t.* spread, stretch out, force apart, straddle, spread wide (*the legs, wings etc.*); prop up, support. **2.** *v.r.* swagger, strut; ***sich – gegen,*** resist; strive *or* struggle against; ***sich – mit,*** boast of, plume o.s. on. **Spreiz|fuß,** *m.* (*Med.*) splay-foot. **–klappe,** *f.* spreader. **–lafette,** *f.* (*Artil.*) split-trail.

Spreng|arbeit [ˈʃprɛŋ–], *f.* blasting operations. **–bombe,** *f.* high-explosive bomb. **–büchse,** *f.* blasting charge.

Sprengel [ˈʃprɛŋəl], *m.* 1. diocese, bishopric; 2. sprinkling brush (*for holy water*).

sprengen [ˈʃprɛŋən], **1.** *v.t.* 1. sprinkle, spray, water; ***den Garten –,*** water the garden; 2. spring, burst, explode, blow up, blast, (*fig.*) break up (*a meeting*), disperse, scatter (*a crowd*); burst open, force (open); rupture (*a blood-vessel*); ***die Bank –,*** break the bank (*gambling*); ***die Fesseln –,*** burst one's chains; (*fig.*) break loose, throw over restrictions; ***in die Luft –,*** blow up; ***den Rahmen dieses Aufsatzes –,*** be outside the scope of this essay; ***ein Tor –,*** break open *or* force a gate. **2.** *v.i.* (*aux.* s.) gallop, ride hard *or* at full speed; ***auf den Feind –,*** charge (at) the enemy. **Sprenger,** *m.* 1. sprinkler, spray; 2. blaster; 3. (*Hunt.*) started game; 4. (*Bill.*) ***einen – machen,*** spring a ball.

Spreng|falle, *f.* (*Mil.*) booby-trap. **–geschoß,** *n.* projectile, shell. **–granate,** *f.* high-explosive shell. **–höhe,** *f.* height of burst (*of a shell*). **–kanne,** *f.* watering-can. **–kapsel,** *f.* detonator, primer, cap. **–kommando,** *n.* (*Mil.*) demolition squad, bomb-disposal unit. **–kopf,** *m.* warhead. **–körper,** *m.* explosive. **–kraft,** *f.* disruptive force. **–ladung,** *f.* explosive *or* demolition charge. **–laut,** *m.* (*Phonet.*) plosive, tenuis. **–loch,** *n.* (*Min.*) blast-hole. **–mittel,** *n.pl.* explosives. **–öl,** *n.* nitroglycerine. **–patrone,** *f.* blasting-cartridge. **–pulver,** *n.* blasting-powder. **–ring,** *m.* (*Tech.*) snap-ring. **–stoff,** *m.* explosive. **–trichter,** *m.* (*Mil.*) bomb-crater. **–trupp,** *m. See* **–kommando.**

Sprengung [ˈʃprɛŋuŋ], *f.* 1. blasting, blowing-up, explosion; (*fig.*) dispersal, dispersion; 2. sprinkling, spraying.

Spreng|wagen, *m.* watering-cart. **–wedel,** *m.* (*Eccl.*) sprinkler. **–weite,** *f.* range of burst. **–werk,** *n.* (*Build.*) strut-frame. **–wirkung,** *f.* blast-effect.

Sprenkel [ˈʃprɛŋkəl], *m.* 1. gin, snare, noose; 2. speck, speckle, spot. **sprenkeln,** *v.t.* speckle, spot, mottle, dapple.

sprenzen [ˈʃprɛntsən], *v.t.* (*dial.*) spray, sprinkle, water.

Spreu [ʃprɔy], *f.* chaff. **spreuartig,** *adj.* (*Bot.*) paleaceous. **Spreu|blättchen,** *n.* (*Bot.*) palea. **–regen,** *m.* drizzling rain.

sprich [ʃprɪç], **sprichst, spricht,** *see* **sprechen.**

Sprichwort [ˈʃprɪçvɔrt], *n.* **(-(e)s,** *pl.* **¨er)** (proverbial) saying, proverb, maxim, adage; ***zum – werden,*** become a byword, become proverbial. **sprichwörtlich,** *adj.* proverbial.

Spriegel [ˈʃpriːgəl], *m.* (*dial.*) hoop, strut (*of wagon hood*); frame, rack.

Sprieße [ˈʃpriːsə], *f.* 1. (*dial.*) strut, support; 2. (*dial.*) *see* **Sproß.**

sprießen [ʃpriːsən], **1.** *reg.v.t.* (*dial.*) prop, support. **2.** *irr.v.i.* (*aux.* s.) sprout, germinate, bud, shoot.

Spriet [ʃpriːt], *n.* **(-(e)s,** *pl.* **-e)** (*Naut.*) sprit, spar.

Spring [ʃprɪŋ], **1.** *m.* **(-(e)s,** *pl.* **-e)** spring, source (*of water*). **2.** *f.* (-, *pl.* **-e**) (*Naut.*) anchor-rope *or* cable. **Spring|bein,** *n.* (*Ent.*) saltatorial leg. **-bock,** *m.* springbok, Cape antelope. **-bohne,** *f.* jumping-bean. **-brett,** *n.* *See* **Sprungbrett. -brunnen,** *m.* fountain.

springen [ˈʃprɪŋən], *irr.v.i.* (*aux.* h. & s.) 1. leap, spring, jump, vault, bound, hop, skip, bounce; (*Swimming*) dive; (*dial.*) run; ***auf die Seite –,*** leap aside; ***aus dem Stand –,*** make a standing jump; ***das springt in die Augen,*** that leaps to *or* strikes the eye, that is evident *or* obvious; ***mit Anlauf –,*** make *or* take a running jump; ***über einen Graben –,*** leap *or* clear a ditch; ***über die Klinge – lassen,*** put to the sword; ***über die Zunge – lassen,*** let (*a rash statement*) slip out; 2. gush, spout, play (*of fountains*); crack, burst, split, break, explode; (*coll.*) ***etwas – lassen,*** spend one's money freely, stand a treat; (*coll.*) ***– lassen,*** stand, treat (*s.o.*) to; ***eine Mine – lassen,*** spring *or* detonate a mine; ***eine Saite ist gesprungen,*** a string has snapped (*violin etc.*); 3. copulate (*of animals*).

Springen, *n.* jumping, vaulting, (*Swimming*) diving. **springend,** *adj.* ***der -e Punkt,*** the (essential *or* crucial *or* salient) point. **Springer,** *m.* jumper, leaper, vaulter, (*Swimming*) diver; (*Chess*) knight.

Spring|feder, *f.* spring. **-federmatratze,** *f.* spring-mattress. **-flut,** *f.* spring-tide. **-hengst,** *m.* stallion, stud-horse. **-insfeld,** *m.* harum-scarum, madcap, (*of a girl*) tomboy, romp. **-konkurrenz,** *f.* show-jumping. **-kraft,** *f.* elasticity, resilience, springiness. **-kraut,** *n.* (*Bot.*) touch-me-not (*Impatiens noli-me-tangere*). **springlebendig,** *adj.* (*coll.*) full of beans. **Spring|maus,** *f.* (*Zool.*) jerboa (*Dipodidae*). **-mine,** *f.* (*Mil.*) anti-personnel mine. **-quell,** *m.*, **-quelle,** *f.* spring; geyser. **-schloß,** *n.* snap-lock. **-seil,** *n.* skipping-rope. **-stange,** *f.* vaulting- *or* jumping-pole. **-welle,** *f.* tidal wave, bore. **-wettkampf,** *m.* (*Swimming*) diving contest. **-wurzel,** *f.* (*Bot.*) mandrake (*Mandragora*).

Sprit [ʃprɪt], *m.* **(-s,** *pl.* **-e)** spirit(s), alcohol, (*Motor.*) (*coll.*) gas, (*sl.*) juice. **spritig,** *adj.* alcoholic. **Spritlack,** *m.* spirit-varnish.

Spritz|apparat [ˈʃprɪts–], *m.* spray-gun, spray(er). **-bad,** *n.* shower-bath, douche. **-bewurf,** *m.* rough-cast. **-brett,** *n.* splashboard, (*of a coach*) dashboard. **-düse,** *f.* spray-nozzle, (*Motor etc.*) injection nozzle.

Spritze [ˈʃprɪtsə], *f.* syringe, sprayer, squirt; (*Med.*) injection, (*coll.*) shot, jab, (*fig.*) shot in the arm; fire-engine; (*coll.*) trip; ***bei der – sein,*** be at one's post; (*coll.*) ***erster Mann bei der – sein,*** be cock of the walk.

spritzen [ˈʃprɪtsən], **1.** *v.i.* (*aux.* h. & s.) gush (forth), spout, spurt, splash; splutter (*as a pen*), (*fig.*) dash, flit. **2.** *v.t.* squirt, syringe; (*Med.*) inject; splash, spray, sprinkle, spatter.

Spritzen|haus, *n.* fire-station. **-leute,** *pl.* firemen. **-röhre,** *f.*, **-schlauch,** *m.* fire-hose.

Spritzer [ˈʃprɪtsər], *m.* splash, squirt, blob, blot; (*dial.*) shower (*of rain*); (*coll.*) fizzy drink.

Spritz|fahrt, *f.* (*coll.*) excursion, trip, (*Motor.*) run, spin; flying visit. **-färbung,** *f.* colour-spraying. **-flasche,** *f.* (*Chem.*) wash-bottle. **-guß,** *m.* pressure die-casting, (*plastics*) injection moulding.

spritzig [ˈʃprɪtsɪç], *adj.* prickling, fizzy, lively; (*dial.*) impetuous, hot-headed.

Spritz|kanne, *f.* (*Swiss*) watering-can. **-kuchen,** *m.* fritter. **-leder,** *n.* splash-leather (*on carriages*). **-mittel,** *n.* (*Med.*) injection, (*Hort.*) spray, insecticide. **-nudeln,** *f.pl.* vermicelli. **-pistole,** *f.* spray-gun. **-regen,** *m.* drizzle. **-tour,** *f.* (*coll.*) *see* **-fahrt. -vergaser,** *m.* (*Motor.*) spray-carburettor. **-wasser,** *n.* spray.

spröde [ˈʃprøːdə], **1.** *adj.* 1. brittle, friable, short; hard, inflexible, unyielding, dry, rough, chapped (*of the skin*); ***-r Stoff,*** difficult material; 2. (*fig.*) prim, reserved, shy, (*of girls*) coy, demure, prudish; ***– tun,*** affect shyness, be coy, play the prude; ***– Tugend,*** prim virtue. **Spröde,** *f.* prude. **Sprödigkeit,** *f.* 1. brittleness, friability, hardness, shortness, dryness; 2. (*fig.*) reserve, shyness, demureness, primness, coyness; prudishness, prudery.

sproß [ʃprɔs], *see* **sprießen, 2.**

Sproß, *m.* **(-(ss)es,** *pl.* **-(ss)e)** shoot, sprout, spray, sprig; (*fig.*) descendant, offspring, scion; tine, branch (*of antlers*); ***sein erster –,*** his first-born (child).

[1]**Sprosse** [ˈʃprɔsə], *m.* **(-n,** *pl.* **-n)** *see* **Sproß.**

[2]**Sprosse,** *f.* 1. rung (*of ladder*); 2. freckle.

sprösse [ˈʃprœsə], **sprossen** [ˈʃprɔsən], *see* **sprießen.**

sprossen|tragend, -treibend, *adj.* proliferous, prolific. **Sprossenwand,** *f.* (*Gymn.*) wall-bars.

Sprosser [ˈʃprɔsər], *m.* (*Orn.*) thrush-nightingale (*Luscinia luscinia*).

Sprößling [ˈʃprœslɪŋ], *m.* **(-s,** *pl.* **-e)** *see* **Sproß;** (*coll.*) son (and heir).

Sprotte [ˈʃprɔtə], *f.* (*Ichth.*) sprat (*Clupea sprattus*).

Spruch [ʃprux], *m.* **(-(e)s,** *pl.* **⸚e)** 1. sentence, verdict, decision, decree, judgement, award, ruling; 2. saying, motto, maxim, dictum, aphorism, epigram; passage (from the Bible), (scriptural) text; ***Sprüche Salomonis,*** Proverbs of Solomon; (*coll.*) ***große ⸚e machen,*** talk big, draw the long bow. **spruchartig,** *adj.* aphoristic, epigrammatic. **Spruch|band,** *n.* (*pl.* **⸚er**) banner (*in procession*); (*Archit.*) banderol, scroll. **-dichter,** *m.* epigrammatic poet. **-dichtung,** *f.* epigrammatic poetry. **spruch|fertig,** *adj.* *See* **-reif. spruchhaft,** *adj.* *See* **spruchartig. Spruchkammer,** *f.* (*Pol.*) (denazification) tribunal. **spruchreif,** *adj.* ripe for decision; ***die S. ist noch nicht –,*** the matter is still under investigation, no decision can yet be reached. **Spruch|weiser,** *m.* concordance (*to the Bible*). **-weisheit,** *f.* epigrammatic saying *or* truth.

Sprudel [ˈʃpruːdəl], *m.* bubbling source, spring, well; hot spring; (*coll.*) soda-water; (*fig.*) overflow. **Sprudelkopf,** *m.* spitfire, hothead. **sprudeln,** *v.i.* 1. (*aux.* s.) bubble, effervesce; 2. (*aux.* h.) bubble *or* boil up, gush, spout, (*of speech*) splutter, (*fig.*) bubble *or* brim over (***vor*** (*Dat.*), with). **sprudelnd,** *adj.* purling, murmuring; ***in -er Laune,*** brimming over with good humour. **Sprudel|salz,** *n.* mineral salt. **-wasser,** *n.* mineral water. **Sprudler,** *m.* (*Austr.*) whisk, (egg) beater.

Sprüh|apparat [ˈʃpryː–], *m.* atomizer. **-elektrode,** *f.* ionizing electrode.

sprühen [ˈʃpryːən], **1.** *v.t.* spray, sprinkle, scatter, shower, spit, send forth, emit (*sparks etc.*). **2.** *v.i.* spark, sparkle, scintillate; (*fig.*) flash (***vor,*** with); (*imp.*) shower (*with rain*).

Sprüh|entladung, *f.* (*Elec.*) corona (discharge). **-feuer,** *n.* shower of sparks. **-regen,** *m.* drizzling rain, drizzle; spray.

Sprung [ʃpruŋ], *m.* **(-es,** *pl.* **⸚e)** 1. crack, fissure, fault, flaw, break, split, chink; 2. spring, leap, jump, bound, vault, (*Swimming*) dive; bounce, skip, (forward) dash; (*Hunt.*) herd of deer; (*Zool.*) copulation; (*coll.*) short distance, short time; ***auf dem – sein zu . . .,*** be on the point of . . .; ***auf einen – zu dir kommen,*** pay you a flying visit, drop in on you (in passing); ***ihm auf die Sprünge helfen,*** help him out, put him right; ***wieder auf seine alten Sprünge kommen,*** fall back into one's old ways; ***– aus dem Stand,*** standing jump; ***es ist nur ein – bis dahin,*** it is only a stone's throw from here; ***er kann keine großen Sprünge machen,*** he cannot do much on his income, he cannot afford much, he has no money to burn; ***ihm auf die Sprünge kommen,*** find him out, be wise to his tricks; ***– ins Ungewisse,*** leap in the dark; ***mit einem -e,*** at a bound; ***– mit Anlauf,***

running jump, flying leap; ***in vollem -e,*** at full speed.

Sprung|balken, *m.* (*Spt.*) springboard. **-bein,** *n.* (*Zool.*) saltatorial leg; (*Anat.*) astragalus, ankle-bone; (*Spt.*) take-off leg. **sprungbereit,** *adj.* ready to jump. **Sprung|brett,** *n.* *See* **-balken**; (*Swimming*) diving-board; (*fig.*) jumping-off place, stepping-stone. **-feder,** *f.* compression-spring. **-federmatratze,** *f.* spring-mattress. **-geld,** *n.* stud-fee. **-gelenk,** *n.* ankle-joint, hock (*of horses*). **-grube,** *f.* (*Spt.*) (landing) pit.

sprunghaft ['ʃprʊŋhaft], **1.** *adj.* (*fig.*) desultory, disconnected, erratic, spasmodic, jerky, unsteady. **2.** *adv.* (*fig.*) by leaps and bounds, by fits and starts.

Sprung|kasten, *m.* (*Gymn.*) vaulting-horse. **-latte, -leine,** *f.* (*Spt.*) cross-bar, lath. **-netz,** *n.* safety-net. **-revision,** *f.* (*Law*) direct appeal. **-riemen,** *m.* (*harness*) martingale. **-schalter,** *m.* (*Elec.*) quick-release *or* snap-switch. **-schanze,** *f.* ski-jump. **-tuch,** *n.* safety *or* jumping sheet. **-turm,** *m.* high-diving board; parachute practice tower. **sprungweise,** *adv.* by leaps *or* bounds; (*fig.*) *see* **sprunghaft, 2. Sprung|weite,** *f.* length of jump. **-wellenprobe,** *f.* (*Tech.*) surge pressure test.

Spucke ['ʃpukə], *f.* (*coll.*) spit, spittle, saliva; (*coll.*) ***ihm bleibt die - weg,*** he is dumbfounded *or* flabbergasted; (*Prov.*) ***mit Geduld und - fängt man manche Mucke,*** softlee, softlee, catchee monkey. **spucken,** *v.t., v.i.* spit (out), expectorate; (*of an engine*) splutter. **Spuck|napf,** *m.,* **-schale,** *f.* spittoon, cuspidor.

Spuk [ʃpu:k], *m.* **(-(e)s,** *pl.* **-e)** ghost, apparition, spectre, phantom, (*coll.*) spook; uproar, hubbub; spookiness, nightmare; ***mach keinen -,*** don't make a fuss; ***es ist - dabei,*** there's s.th. eerie *or* uncanny about it. **spuken,** *v.i., imp.* haunt (*in* (*Dat.*), *a place*), be haunted; ***der Wein spukt in seinem Kopf,*** the wine has gone to his head; ***es spukt bei ihm*** (***im Kopfe***), it haunts his mind, it is haunting him, he is obsessed with it. **Spuk|geist,** *m.* imp, hobgoblin. **-geschichte,** *f.* ghost-story. **spukhaft,** *adj.* ghost-like, ghostly, weird, (*coll.*) spooky.

Spül|bad ['ʃpy:l-], *n.* rinsing bath. **-becken,** *n.* (flush) pan (*of W.C.*).

Spule ['ʃpu:lə], *f.* **1.** spool, bobbin, reel, drum, (*Elec.*) coil; 2. quill (*of feather*).

Spüleimer ['ʃpy:lʔaɪmər], *m.* slop-pail.

spulen ['ʃpu:lən], *v.t.* wind, reel, spool, coil.

spülen ['ʃpy:lən], **1.** *v.t.* wash, rinse *or* swill (out), flush (*W.C.*), flush out (*an engine*); ***die Wogen - Trümmer ans Land,*** the waves wash up debris on the shore *or* wash debris ashore. **2.** *v.i.* wash (*an* (*Acc.*), ***gegen,*** against), lap.

Spulen|kern, *m.* (*Elec.*) core. **-wicklung,** *f.* (*Elec.*) (coil) winding.

Spül|faß, *n.* wash-tub. **-frau,** *f.* scullery maid, (*coll.*) washer-up. **Spülicht,** *n.* dish-water, slops; spent water. **Spül|klosett,** *n.* water-closet. **-küche,** *f.* scullery. **-lappen,** *m.* dish-cloth. **-napf,** *m.* slop-basin. **-stein,** *m.* sink. **Spülung,** *f.* rinsing, washing, flushing, (*Med.*) irrigation, lavage. **Spülwasser,** *n.* washing-up water; *see also* **Spülicht.**

Spulwurm ['ʃpu:lvurm], *m.* maw-worm.

Spund [ʃpunt], *m.* **(-(e)s,** *pl.* **¨-e)** bung, plug, stopper, spigot; (*Artil.*) tampion, tompion; (*Carp.*) feather, tongue. **Spund|brett,** *n.* tongued board. **spunden, spünden** ['ʃpyndən], *v.t.* bung (*casks*); tongue and groove (*planks*). **Spund|hobel,** *m.* tonguing *or* grooving plane. **spundig, spündig,** *adj.* doughy, soggy, sad. **Spund|loch,** *n.* bung-hole. **-messer,** *n.* cooper's hatchet. **-tiefe,** *f.* centre measurement (*of a cask*). **spundvoll,** *adj.* brimful, (*sl.*) bung-full.

Spur [ʃpu:r], *f.* (-, *pl.* **-en**) (*Chem., radar etc.*) trace; (*Hunt.*) track, trail, scent; footprint, footmark, footstep; (*of wheel*) rut, track; (*of ship*) wake; channel, groove, mark; (*fig.*) mark, trace, sign, vestige; *see also* **Spurweite**; ***auf die richtige - bringen,*** put on the right track *or* scent, give (*s.o.*) a clue; ***auf die - kommen*** (*Dat.*), be *or* get on the track of, track down, find out, trace; (***scharf***) ***auf der - sein*** (*Dat.*), be (hot) on the trail of; ***auf der falschen - sein,*** be on the wrong track, (*coll.*) be barking up the wrong tree; ***keine - von,*** not the least *or* not a trace *or* sign *or* vestige of; (*coll.*) ***keine -!*** by no means! not in the least! not a bit of it! ***eine - Salz,*** a touch *or* dash of salt; ***von der - abbringen,*** put *or* throw off the scent.

spürbar ['ʃpy:rba:r], *adj.* perceptible, noticeable; considerable, distinct, marked; ***- sein,*** be (much) in evidence, be felt.

spuren ['ʃpu:rən], *v.i.* keep to *or* follow the track, (*fig., coll.*) do one's job (properly), (*esp. Pol.*) toe the line; (*esp. skiing*) make the track, lead the way; (*coll.*) ***nicht -,*** be a slacker.

spüren ['ʃpy:rən], **1.** *v.t.* feel, perceive, be conscious of, notice, sense, experience; detect, scent (out). **2.** *v.i.* (***nach***) follow the trail *or* track (of), (*Hunt.*) track, (*fig.*) track (down), search (for), go in search *or* quest (of), trace.

Spurgeschoß ['ʃpu:rgəʃɔs], *n.* tracer (bullet).

Spürhaar ['ʃpy:rha:r], *n.* tactile hair.

Spurhaltigkeit ['ʃpu:rhaltɪçkaɪt], *f.* (*Motor.*) steering stability.

Spürhund ['ʃpy:rhunt], *m.* tracker (dog), (*fig.*) sleuth, bloodhound.

Spurkranz ['ʃpu:rkrants], *m.* flange (*of wheel*). **spurlos, 1.** *adj.* trackless. **2.** *adv.* without leaving a trace; ***- verschwinden,*** disappear completely *or* without leaving a trace, vanish from sight *or* into thin air; (*fig.*) ***nicht - an ihm vorbeigehen,*** leave its mark on him, tell on him.

Spür|nase, *f.* keen sense of smell, good nose; (*coll.*) snooper. **-sinn,** *m.* shrewdness, penetration; flair *or* eye *or* (*coll.*) nose (***für,*** for).

Spurt [ʃpurt], *m.* **(-s,** *pl.* **-s** *or* **-e)** (*Spt.*) spurt. **spurten,** *v.i.* spurt.

Spurweite ['ʃpu:rvaɪtə], *f.* (*Railw.*) gauge, (*Motor.*) track.

sputen ['ʃpu:tən], *v.r.* make haste, hurry (up).

st! [st], *int.* sh! hush!

Staat [ʃta:t], *m.* **(-(e)s,** *pl.* **-en)** 1. state, nation, country, government; (*Zool.*) colony (*bees etc.*); (*fig.*) ***von -s wegen,*** as a matter of policy; 2. (*no pl.*) pomp, splendour, state, show, finery; ***in vollem -,*** in full dress; ***großen - machen,*** live in great *or* grand style, (*coll.*) cut a dash; ***- machen mit,*** make a show *or* parade of, parade, show off with; ***damit kannst du keinen - machen,*** that's nothing to boast about *or* (*coll.*) to write home about.

Staatenbund ['ʃta:tənbunt], *m.* federal union, confederacy, confederation. **staatenlos,** *adj.* stateless.

staatlich ['ʃta:tlɪç], *adj.* government(al), state, national; public; ***-e Unterstützung,*** state subsidy; ***-e Einrichtung,*** public institution; ***- anerkannt,*** certified, recognized.

Staats|akt, *m.* act of state; state ceremony. **-akten,** *f.pl.* state papers, state records. **-aktien,** *f.pl.* government bonds *or* securities. **-aktion,** *f.* government undertaking; (*fig.*) great fuss *or* to-do. **-amt,** *n.* government *or* civil-service appointment, public office. **-angehörige(r),** *m., f.* subject, citizen, national. **-angehörigkeit,** *f.* citizenship, nationality; ***- erwerben,*** become naturalized; ***- aufgeben,*** repudiate one's nationality; ***- aberkennen,*** deprive of citizenship. **-angestellte(r),** *m., f.* public servant. **-anleihe,** *f.* government loan, stocks, bonds *or* securities. **-anstellung,** *f.* public appointment *or* office. **-anwalt,** *m.* public prosecutor, (*Am.*) district attorney. **-anwaltschaft,** *f.* (*Brit.*) Director of Public Prosecutions, (*Am.*) Office of the District Attorney. **-anzeiger,** *m.* official gazette. **-archiv,** *n.* public-record office. **-aufsicht,** *f.* state *or* government control. **-auftrag,** *m.* government contract. **-ausgaben,** *f.pl.* government spending, public expenditure. **-bank,** *f.* national bank. **-beamte(r),** *m., f.* civil servant, government official. **-begräbnis,** *n.* public funeral. **-behörde,** *f.* public authorities. **-besitz,**

m. state *or* government property; *in* –, publicly *or* state-owned. **–besuch,** *m.* state visit. **–bürger,** *m.* citizen, subject. **–bürgerkunde,** *f.* civics, citizenship. **staatsbürgerlich,** *adj.* civic, civil; *–e Erziehung,* training in citizenship.

Staats|chef, *m.* chief of state. **–dienst,** *m.* civil *or* (*Am.*) public service. **staatseigen,** *adj.* state-owned. **Staats|eigentum,** *n.* government property. **–eingriff,** *m.* state intervention. **–einkünfte,** *f.pl.* public revenue. **–examen,** *n.* civil-service examination. **–feind,** *m.* public enemy. **staatsfeindlich,** *adj.* subversive. **Staats|form,** *f.* form of government. **–gebäude,** *n.* public building. **–gefangene(r),** *m., f.* state prisoner. **–geheimnis,** *n.* official *or* state secret. **–gelder,** *n.pl.* public funds. **–gesetz,** *n.* law of the land. **–gewalt,** *f.* supreme *or* executive power. **–haushalt,** *m.* national budget. **–hoheit,** *f.* sovereignty. **–kanzlei,** *f.* (*Hist.*) chancery. **–karosse,** *f.* *See* **–kutsche.** **–kasse,** *f.* public exchequer, treasury. **–kerl,** *m.* (*coll.*) fine fellow. **–kirche,** *f.* established church; *Englische* –, Church of England. **staatsklug,** *adj.* politic; diplomatic. **Staats|klugheit,** *f.* political shrewdness: statesmanship, statecraft. **–körper,** *m.* body politic. **–kosten,** *f.pl. auf* –, at the public expense. **–kunde,** *f.* *See* **–wissenschaft.** **–kunst,** *f.* politics, statecraft. **–kutsche,** *f.* state coach. **–mann,** *m.* (*pl.* ¨er) statesman. **staatsmännisch,** *adj.* statesmanlike. **Staats|-minister,** *m.* minister (of state), Secretary of State. **–mittel,** *n.pl.* *See* **–gelder.** **–monopol,** *n.* government *or* state monopoly. **–oberhaupt,** *n.* head of the state; sovereign, president.

Staats|papiere, *n.pl.* *See* **–aktien.** **–polizei,** *f.* state police; (*Nat. Soc.*) *Geheime* –, Gestapo. **–prüfung,** *f.* *See* **–examen.** **–rat,** *m.* 1. privy council; 2. privy councillor. **–recht,** *n.* constitutional law. **staatsrechtlich,** *adj.* constitutional. **Staats|rente,** *f.* government annuity. **–schatz,** *m.* *See* **–kasse.** **–schiff,** *n.* (*fig.*) ship of state. **–schuld,** *f.* national debt; *fundierte* –, consols, consolidated annuities. **–schuldschein,** *m.* *See* **–anleihe.** **–sekretär,** *m.* secretary of state, (*Brit.*) Permanent Secretary. **–siegel,** *n.* official seal; *großes* –, Great Seal. **–streich,** *m.* coup d'état. **–umwälzung,** *f.* (political) upheaval, revolution. **–unterstützung,** *f.* government subsidy, state aid, grant-in-aid. **–verbrechen,** *n.* political crime, sedition. **–verfassung,** *f.* constitution. **–vertrag,** *m.* international treaty. **–verwaltung,** *f.* public administration. **–wesen,** *n.* state, commonwealth; political system; public affairs. **–wirtschaft,** *f.* political economy. **–wissenschaft,** *f.* political science. **–wohl,** *n.* common weal. **–zuschuß,** *m.* *See* **–unterstützung.**

Stab [ʃta:p], *m.* **(-(e)s,** *pl.* ¨**e)** staff, stick, rod; bar (*of metal*); mace, (*Eccl.*) crosier; (*Spt., Mus.*) baton; (magic) wand, (shepherd's) crook; (*Mil.*) staff, headquarters; *hinter Stäben,* behind bars; *seinen – weiter setzen,* continue one's journey; *den – über ihn brechen,* condemn him (to death); *ich stehe nicht unter Ihrem –e,* I am not under your authority *or* jurisdiction.

Stab|antenne, *f.* (*Rad.*) dipole. **–bakterie,** *f.* bacillus. **–batterie,** *f.* torch battery.

Stäbchen ['ʃtɛ:pçən], *n.* 1. rod; 2. bacillus; 3. (*crochet*) long stitch; 4. (*coll.*) fag. **Stäbchen|-bakterie,** *f.* *See* **Stabbakterie.** **–zelle,** *f.* (*Anat.*) rod-cell (*of the eye*).

Stabeisen ['ʃta:pˀaɪzən], *n.* wrought iron.

Stabelle [ʃta'bɛlə], *f.* (*Swiss*) wooden stool *or* chair.

Stab|führung, *f.* (*Mus.*) conducting. **–heuschrecke,** *f.* (*Ent.*) (walking-)stick insect. **–hochsprung,** *m.* pole-vault.

stabil [ʃta'bi:l], *adj.* stable, steady, solid, sturdy, robust, rugged. **stabilieren** [–'li:rən], *v.t., v.r.* *See* **stabalisieren.** **Stabilisator** [–i'za:tɔr], *m.* **(-s,** *pl.* **-en)** stabilizer. **stabilisieren, 1.** *v.t.* stabilize. **2.** *v.r.* become steadier *or* stabilized *or* (more) stable. **Stabilisierungsfläche,** *f.* (*Av.*) stabilizer. **Stabilität,** *f.* stability, sturdiness.

Stab|magnet, *m.* bar-magnet. **–reim,** *m.* alliteration. **stabreimend,** *adj.* alliterative.

Stabs|arzt, *m.* (*Mil.*) medical officer; (*Naut.*) staff-surgeon. **–chef,** *m.* (*Mil.*) chief of staff. **–feldwebel,** *m.* (*Mil.*) warrant officer, regimental sergeant-major, (*Am.*) master serjeant.

stabsichtig ['ʃta:pzɪçtɪç], *adj.* astigmatic. **Stabsichtigkeit,** *f.* astigmatism.

Stabs|kompagnie, *f.* (*Mil.*) headquarters company. **–offizier,** *m.* (*major and colonel*) field-officer, (*above colonel*) staff-officer.

Stab|sprung, *m.* *See* **–hochsprung.**

Stabs|quartier, *n.* headquarters. **–wagen,** *m.* (*Mil.*) staff car.

Stab|tierchen, *n.* bacillus. **–träger,** *m.* mace-bearer, beadle, sergeant-at-arms. **–wechsel,** *m.* (*Spt.*) baton change (*in relay races*).

stach [ʃta:x], **stäche** ['ʃtɛ:çə], *see* **stechen.**

Stachel ['ʃtaxəl], *m.* **(-s,** *pl.* **-n)** thorn, prickle; prick, sting; spine, quill, spike, prong, goad; (*fig.*) sting, spur, prodding, stimulus; *ein – im Auge sein,* be a thorn in the flesh; *– des Fleisches,* lusts of the flesh; (*B.*) *wider den – lecken* (or *löcken*), kick against the pricks.

Stachel|beere, *f.* (*Bot.*) gooseberry (*Ribes grossularia*). **–beerspanner,** *m.* (*Ent.*) magpie-moth (*Abraxus grossulariata*). **–draht,** *m.* barbed wire. **–flosse,** *f.* spinous dorsal fin. **–flosser,** *m.pl.* (*Ichth.*) acanthopterygians. **stachelfrüchtig,** *adj.* (*Bot.*) acanthocarpus. **Stachel|halsband,** *n.* spiked dog-collar. **–häuter,** *m.pl.* (*Zool.*) echinodermata.

stach(e)lig ['ʃtax(ə)lɪç], *adj.* prickly, thorny, spinous, bristly; (*fig.*) stinging, biting, caustic, poignant. **stacheln,** *v.t.* prick, sting; (*fig.*) stimulate, spur on, prod, goad.

Stachel|raupe, *f.* prickly caterpillar. **–rede,** *f.* satirical *or* caustic speech; sharp words. **–roche,** *m.* (*Ichth.*) thorn-back. **–schwanzsegler,** *m.* (*Orn.*) needle-tailed swift (*Chaetura caudacuta*). **–schwein,** *n.* (*Zool.*) porcupine (*Hystrix*). **–stock,** *m.* prod, goad. **–zaun,** *m.* barbed-wire fence.

Stadel ['ʃta:dəl], *m.* (*dial.*) stall, barn, shed.

Staden ['ʃta:dən], *m.* (*dial.*) river-side walk.

Stadion ['ʃta:diɔn], *n.* **(-s,** *pl.* **-dien)** (*Spt.*) stadium, arena.

Stadium ['ʃta:dium], *n.* **(-s,** *pl.* **-dien)** phase, state, stage (*of development*).

Stadt [ʃtat], *f.* (-, *pl.* ¨**e**) town, city; *die Ewige –,* the Eternal City (*Rome*); *die Heilige –,* the Holy City (*Jerusalem*); *in der – aufgewachsen,* town-bred; *das weiß die ganze –,* that is all over the town.

Stadt|adel, *m.* patricians. **–amt,** *n.* municipal office. **–anleihe,** *f.* municipal *or* corporation loan. **–bahn,** *f.* metropolitan railway. **–bank,** *f.* municipal bank. **–bau,** *m.* **(-s,** *pl.* **-ten)** municipal building. **–baumeister,** *m.* city architect. **–bauplan,** *m.* municipal development plan *or* building programme. **–behörde,** *f.* municipal authorities. **stadtbekannt,** *adj.* generally known, notorious; *die Geschichte ist –,* the story is the talk of the town. **Stadt|bewohner,** *m.* townsman, city-dweller. **–bezirk,** *m.* ward, urban district. **–bild,** *n.* general aspect *or* character of a town. **–brief,** *m.* local letter.

Städtchen ['ʃtɛ:tçən], *n.* small *or* market town.

Stadtdirektor ['ʃtatdirɛktɔr], *m.* town clerk, (*esp. Am.*) city manager.

Städte|bau ['ʃtɛ:tə–], *m.* town-planning. **–bund,** *m.* (*Hist.*) league of cities. **–ordnung,** *f.* municipal ordinances; Municipal Corporation Act. **–planung,** *f.* *See* **–bau.**

Städter(in) ['ʃtɛ:tər(ɪn)], *m.* (*f.*) city-dweller, townsman (townswoman); *pl.* townspeople.

Stadt|gas, *n.* municipal gas (supply). **–gebiet,** *n.* area under municipal control, city limits. **–gemeinde,** *f.* urban community; township, municipality, city borough. **–gespräch,** *n.* talk of the town; (*Tele.*) local call. **–graben,** *m.* (*Hist.*) town-moat. **–grenze,** *f.* city boundary. **–haus,** *n.* town-hall, guildhall.

städtisch ['ʃtɛ:tɪʃ], *adj.* town-, city-, municipal,

urban, metropolitan; *–e Bevölkerung,* urban population; *–er Beamter,* municipal officer, civic official; *–e Schule,* council *or* corporation school.

Stadt|kasse, *f.* city treasurer's office. **–kern,** *m. See* **–mitte. –kind,** *n.* townsman, confirmed city-dweller, (*coll.*) towny. **–klatsch,** *m. See* **–gespräch. –koffer,** *m.* attaché-case. **–kommandant,** *m.* (*Mil.*) town major. **–kreis,** *m.* urban district. **–leute,** *pl.* townspeople, townsfolk, city-dwellers. **–mauer,** *f.* town wall. **–miliz,** *f.* civic guard. **–mitte,** *f.* town- *or* city-centre, (*Am.*) mid-town. **–neuigkeit,** *f.* local news. **–park,** *m.* municipal park. **–plan,** *m.* street-map. **–planung,** *f. See* **Städtebau. –rand,** *m.* outskirts of the town, suburban fringe. **–randsiedlung,** *f.* (suburban) housing estate. **–rat,** *m.* municipal *or* town-council; town-councillor, alderman. **–recht,** *n.* municipal law(s); civic rights. **–richter,** *m.* recorder. **–schreiber,** *m.* (*obs.*) *see* **–syndikus. –schule,** *f.* council *or* corporation school. **–schulkommission,** *f.* local education committee. **–schulrat,** *m.* local school inspector. **–staat,** *m.* (*Hist.*) city-state. **–steuer,** *f.* municipal rates. **–syndikus,** *m.* town-clerk. **–teil,** *m. See* **–bezirk. –theater,** *n.* municipal theatre. **–tor,** *n.* town gate. **–väter,** *m.pl.* city-fathers. **–verordnete(r),** *m., f.* town-councillor. **–verwaltung,** *f.* municipality, municipal government. **–viertel,** *n. See* **–bezirk. –wappen,** *n.* town's *or* city's coat-of-arms. **–wohnung,** *f.* town residence.

Stafel [ˈʃta:fəl], *m.* (**-s,** *pl.* ¨-) (*Swiss*) Alpine pasture.

Stafette [ʃtaˈfɛtə], *f.* 1. relay(-race); 2. (*obs.*) courier, dispatch-rider. **Stafettenlauf,** *m.* (*Spt.*) relay race.

Staffage [ʃtaˈfa:ʒə], *f.* figures (in a landscape), accessories; decoration, ornamental details; (*fig.*) mere *or* empty show.

Staffel [ˈʃtafəl], *f.* (-, *pl.* **-n**) rung (*of a ladder*); step (*of a gable etc.*); (*fig.*) step, stage, degree; (*Spt.*) relay, lap (*of a race*); (*Mil.*) echelon, detachment; (*Av.*) squadron. **Staffelei** [–ˈlaɪ], *f.* (-, *pl.* **-en**) easel. **staffelförmig,** *adj.* in steps; in echelon. **Staffel|kapitän,** *m.* (*Av.*) squadron leader. **–lauf,** *m.* relay race. **staffeln,** *v.t., v.r.* graduate, differentiate; raise in steps, stagger. **Staffeltarif,** *m.* sliding tariff.

staffieren [ʃtaˈfi:rən], *v.t.* garnish, dress, trim, decorate; furnish, equip. **Staffierer,** *m.* trimmer, dresser; decorator. **Staffiernaht,** *f.* garnish-seam.

Stag [ʃta:k], *n.* **-(e)s,** *pl.* **-e(n)**) (*Naut.*) stay. **Stagfock,** *f.* staysail.

stagnieren [ʃtaˈgni:rən], *v.i.* stagnate. **stagnierend,** *adj.* stagnant.

Stag|segel, *n. See* **–fock.**

stahl [ʃta:l], *see* **stehlen.**

Stahl, *m.* (**-s,** *pl.* ¨**e** (*Austr.* **-e**)) steel; (*Poet.*) sword, dagger; tool; heater-bolt (*of a flat iron*). **Stahl|bad,** *n.* chalybeate bath *or* spa. **–band,** *n.* strip steel. **–bandmaß,** *n.* steel tape-measure. **–bau,** *m.* steel-girder construction. **–beton,** *m.* ferro-concrete. **stahlblau,** *adj.* steel(y) blue. **Stahl|blech,** *n.* sheet-steel. **–brunnen,** *m.* chalybeate spring. **–bürste,** *f.* wire *or* steel brush.

stählen [ˈʃtɛ:lən], *v.t.* convert into steel, temper (*iron*), (*fig.*) harden, steel (*the courage, one's heart*). **stählern,** *adj.* (of) steel, steely.

Stahl|fach, *n.* safe-deposit box, strong-box. **–feder,** *f.* 1. pen-nib; 2. steel spring. **–frischen,** *n.* steel-fining (process). **–gewinnung,** *f.* production of steel. **–guß,** *m.* steel casting; cast-steel. **stahl|haltig,** *adj.* chalybeate. **–hart,** *adj.* (as) hard as steel. **Stahl|helm,** *m.* steel helmet, (*coll.*) tin hat; (*Hist.*) German Association of ex-servicemen (*cf.* British Legion). **–hütte,** *f. See* **–werk. –kammer,** *f.* strong-room. **–kassette,** *f. See* **–fach. –kerngeschoß,** *n.* armour-piercing shell. **–panzerung,** *f.* armour-plating. **–quelle,** *f. See* **–brunnen. –rohrmöbel,** *n.* tubular-steel furniture. **–roß,** *n.* (*hum.*) (*Railw.*) iron horse; bike. **–stecher,** *m.* steel-engraver. **–stich,** *m.* steel-engraving. **–waren,** *f.pl.* cutlery, hardware. **–werk,** *n.* steel-works *or* mill.

stak [ʃta:k], *see* **stecken.**

Stake [ˈʃta:kə], *f.*, **Staken,** *m.* (*dial.*) 1. stake; boat-hook; punt(ing)-pole; 2. wicker-fence; 3. sheaf, stook (*of corn*). **staken, 1.** *v.t.* (*dial.*) 1. punt, pole (*a boat*); 2. turn (*sheaves*) with a fork. **2.** *v.i.* (*dial.*) stalk, strut. **Staket** [–ˈke:t], *n.* (**-s,** *pl.* **-e**) paling, palisade, fence, rail, railing. **Stakete,** *f.* (*Austr.*) pale, stake. **Staketenzaun,** *m.* (*Austr.*) *see* **Staket. staksig,** *adj.* (*dial.*) stiff, wooden, awkward.

Stall [ʃtal], *m.* (**-es,** *pl.* ¨**e**) stall, stable, (cow)shed, (pig)sty, (sheep-)pen, kennel, hen-house, chicken-run, shed, barn. **Stalldienst,** *m.* stable-work, stable-duty. **Stalleine,** *f.* (*Mil.*) picket-line. **stallen, 1.** *v.i.* 1. stale, urinate (*of animals*); 2. (*dial.*) clean out a stable *etc.* **2.** *v.t.* stall, stable (*animals*).

Stall|feind, *m.* (*Swiss*) foot-and-mouth disease. **–gefährte,** *m.* (*Spt.*) stable-mate. **–geld,** *n.* stallage; stabling-money. **–hase,** *m.* domestic rabbit. **–hengst,** *m.* stallion. **–junge, –knecht,** *m.* stable-hand *or* boy, ostler, groom. **–meister,** *m.* equerry, master of the horse; riding-master. **–miete,** *f. See* **–geld.**

Stallung [ˈʃtaluŋ], *f.* stabling, stables, *pl.* mews.

Stamm [ʃtam], *m.* (**-es,** *pl.* ¨**e**) 1. (*Bot.*) stem, trunk, bole; ***Holz auf dem –,*** standing timber; ***einen – Kegel schieben,*** play a game of skittles; (*Prov.*) ***der Apfel fällt nicht weit vom –,*** like father, like son. 2. (*Biol.*) phylum, (*coll.*) family, clan, line, tribe, race, stock, breed, strain; ***die zwölf Stämme,*** the twelve tribes; ***von königlichem –,*** of royal blood; ***männlicher –,*** male line; 3. (*fig.*) stem, root (*of words*); cadre, main body (*of an army, customers etc.*); nucleus, core, backbone; ***– von Kunden,*** regular customers, **Stammaktie,** *f.* original *or* ordinary share, (*Am.*) common stock.

Stammannschaft [ˈʃtammanʃaft], *f.* cadre, nucleus.

Stamm|baum, *m.* genealogical *or* family tree, pedigree, (*Biol.*) phylogenetic tree, (*Tech.*) flow sheet. **–besatzung,** *f.* skeleton crew. **–buch,** *n.* album; (*Zool.*) herd-book. **–burg,** *f.* ancestral castle, family seat. **–einheit,** *f.* (*Mil.*) parent unit.

stammeln [ˈʃtaməln], *v.i., v.t.* stammer, stutter.

Stammeltern, *pl.* progenitors, first parents.

stammen [ˈʃtamən], *v.i.* (*aux.* s.) be descended, spring, originate, stem, proceed, come, hail, (*Gram.*) be derived, (*in time*) date (***von, aus,*** from).

Stammes|bewußtsein, *n.* clan spirit, clannishness. **–geschichte,** *f.* tribal history, (*Biol.*) phylogeny. **–häuptling,** *m.* chieftain.

Stamm|folge, *f.* line of descent. **–form,** *f.* primitive form (*of a word*); *pl.* principal parts (*of a verb*). **–gast,** *m.* regular (guest) (*at an inn etc.*), habitué; regular customer. **–gericht,** *n.* speciality of the house. **–gut,** *n.* family estate, (*Law*) entail. **–halter,** *m.* eldest son of the family, son and heir. **–haus,** *n.* (*Comm.*) parent firm. **–holz,** *n.* standing timber.

stämmig [ˈʃtɛmɪç], *adj.* full-grown; sturdy, burly, (*coll.*) hefty, brawny; stalwart, vigorous; stocky. **Stämmigkeit,** *f.* sturdiness, robustness *etc.*

Stamm|kapital, *n.* original *or* (ordinary) share capital, (*Am.*) (common) capital stock. **–kneipe,** *f.* regular haunt, favourite pub. **–kunde,** *m.* regular customer, patron. **–kundschaft,** *f.* clientele. **–lehen,** *n.* (*Hist.*) family fief, fee-simple. **–linie,** *f.* line, lineage. **–lokal,** *n. See* **–kneipe. –lösung,** *f.* standard *or* stock solution. **–personal,** *n.* (*Mil.*) cadre, (*Comm.*) permanent staff. **–rolle,** *f.* (*Mil.*) nominal roll. **–schloß,** *n. See* **–burg. –silbe,** *f.* radical *or* root syllable. **–sitz,** *m.* ancestral seat, (*Theat. etc.*) regular seat. **–tafel,** *f.* genealogical table, (*Tech.*) flow chart, flow sheet. **–tisch,** *m.* table reserved for regular customers; regular circle of cronies.

Stammutter [ˈʃtammutər], *f.* ancestress.

Stamm|vater, *m.* progenitor, ancestor. **–vermächtnis,** *n.* entail. **stammverwandt,** *adj.*

kindred, cognate. **Stamm|verwandtschaft,** *f.* kinship, affinity. **–vokal,** *m.* root vowel. **–volk,** *n.* aborigines, primitive race *or* people. **–wappen,** *n.pl.* family arms. **–wort,** *n.* root-word, stem. **–zeiten,** *f.pl.* principal parts (of verbs). **–zuchtbuch,** *n.* herd-book.

Stampe ['ʃtampə], *f.* (*dial.*) tavern. **Stamperl,** *n.* (**-s,** *pl.* **-(n)**) (*dial.*) small wine- *or* spirits-glass.

Stampfbeton ['ʃtampfbeto:n], *m.* tamped concrete. **Stampfe,** *f.* stamp, punch; pestle, beetle, beater, rammer. **stampfen,** **1.** *v.i.* 1. stamp, trample; trudge, tramp; ***mit dem Fuß –,*** stamp one's foot, (*of horse*) paw (the ground); 2. (*of a ship*) pitch. **2.** *v.t.* pound, crush, stamp, beat, tamp, ram; mash (*potatoes*), bruise (*corn*), express (*oil*); press (*grapes*); (*fig.*) ***aus dem Boden –,*** conjure up, produce by magic. **Stampfer,** *m.* 1. *See* **Stampfe**; 2. potato-mash; 3. pawing *or* stamping horse; 4. pitching ship. **Stampf|kartoffeln,** *f.pl.* mashed potatoes. **–klotz,** *m.* pile-driver, rammer. **–mühle,** *f.*, **–werk,** *n.* crushing-mill, stamping-mill.

Stampiglie [ʃtam'pɪljə], *f.* (*Austr.*) stamp, seal.

Stand [ʃtant], *m.* (**-es,** *pl.* **-e**) 1. (*no pl.*) place to stand, foothold, footing; ***Sprung aus dem –,*** standing jump; ***seinen – einnehmen,*** take up one's stand; ***einen guten – bei ihm haben,*** be well thought of by him; ***bei ihm einen harten – haben,*** have a great deal of trouble with him; ***einen schweren – haben,*** be in a difficult position, be badly placed, be awkwardly situated, have very limited opportunities, have a hard time of it, (*coll.*) be faced with a tough job; 2. standing *or* upright position, situation, position, station, stand, standing; standard, level, height, state, condition; strength (*of army etc.*); reading (*of thermometer etc.*); ***– der Aktien,*** value of shares; ***– der Dinge,*** state of affairs; ***gut im – sein,*** be in good condition; ***auf den neuesten – bringen,*** bring up to date; ***ihn in den – bringen, es zu tun,*** enable him to do it; ***in den vorigen – setzen,*** restore to the former condition; ***– der Sterne,*** position of the stars; ***– des Wassers,*** level of the water; *see* **außerstande, imstande, instand, zustande**; 3. (*no pl.*) social position *or* standing, status, station; ***ehelicher –,*** married state; 4. (*with pl.*) class, ranks, caste; profession, trade; (*Pol.*) estate of the realm; ***er ist seines –es Advokat,*** he is a lawyer by profession; (*Hist.*) ***die Stände,*** the Diet; ***aus allen Ständen,*** from all walks of life; ***geistlicher –,*** clergy; ***gelehrte Stände,*** learned professions; ***die höheren Stände,*** the upper classes; ***Leute von –,*** men of rank; ***weltlicher –,*** laity; 5. (*with pl.*) stand, stall, pitch, booth.

stand, *see* **stehen.**

Standanzeiger ['ʃtantˀantsaɪgər], *m.* level-indicator.

Standard ['ʃtandart], *m.* (**-s,** *pl.* **-s**) standard, norm; pattern, sample. **standardisieren** [–di'zi:rən], *v.t.* standardize.

Standarte [ʃtan'dartə], *f.* 1. standard, banner; 2. (*Nat. Soc.*) unit, regiment (*of S.S. etc.*); 3. (*Hunt.*) brush (*of fox*).

Stand|bein, *n.* (*sculpture*) supporting leg. **–bild,** *n.* statue, (*Phot.*) still.

Ständchen ['ʃtɛntçən], *n.* serenade; ***ihr ein – bringen,*** serenade her.

Stande ['ʃtandə], *f.* (*dial.*) vat, butt.

Stände ['ʃtɛndə], *pl. of* **Stand.**

Stander ['ʃtandər], *m.* (*Naut., Motor.*) pennant.

Ständer ['ʃtɛndər], *m.* stand, rack; post, pillar, pedestal, mount, upright; stator (*of dynamo*); (*dial.*) *see* **Stande.**

Ständerat ['ʃtɛndəra:t], *m.* (*Swiss*) representative federal body of the cantons.

Standesamt ['ʃtandesˀamt], *n.* registry office. **standesamtlich,** *adj.* ***–e Trauung,*** civil marriage. **Standes|beamte(r),** *m.* registrar of births, marriages and deaths. **–bewußtsein,** *n.* class-consciousness; caste-allegiance *or* feeling. **–dünkel,** *m.* pride of place. **–ehe,** *f.* marriage for position *or* rank. **–ehre,** *f.* professional honour. **–gebühr,** *f.* ***nach –,*** with due honour, according to one's rank. **standesgemäß,** *adj.* in accordance with *or* appropriate to one's class *or* rank. **Standes|genosse,** *m.* one's equal in station, compeer; ***meine –n,*** people of my own class. **–interesse,** *n.* class interest. **standes|mäßig,** *adj. See* **–gemäß. Standes|person,** *f.* person of rank *or* quality. **–rücksichten,** *f.pl.* considerations of rank. **–unterschied,** *m.* difference of rank, class distinction. **–vorurteil,** *n.* class prejudice. **standeswidrig,** *adj.* unprofessional, unethical (*behaviour*). **Standeswürde,** *f.* dignity of rank *or* position. **standes|würdig,** *adj. See* **–gemäß.**

standfest ['ʃtantfɛst], *adj.* firmly placed, firm, rigid, stable, steady. **Stand|geld,** *n.* stall-rent, (*Naut.*) demurrage. **–gericht,** *n.* summary court of justice, (*Mil.*) drumhead court-martial. **–glas,** *n.* level-gauge.

standhaft ['ʃtanthaft], *adj.* (*fig.*) steady, steadfast, constant, staunch, unflinching, unyielding, resolute. **Standhaftigkeit,** *f.* steadiness, steadfastness, constancy, staunchness, resoluteness, firmness, resolution.

standhalten ['ʃtanthaltən], *irr.v.i.* (*Dat.*) hold one's ground *or* one's own, stand firm, (*coll.*) hold out (against), withstand, resist; ***der Prüfung –,*** stand the test; ***einer näheren Prüfung nicht –,*** not bear closer examination.

ständig ['ʃtɛndɪç], *adj.* fixed, permanent, established; constant, continuous; ***–er Ausschuß,*** standing committee; ***–er Begleiter,*** constant *or* inseparable companion; ***–es Einkommen,*** regular *or* fixed income; ***–e Wohnung,*** permanent residence.

Stand|licht, *n.* (*Motor.*) parking light. **–motor,** *m.* stationary engine. **–ort,** *m.* site, location, (*Naut.*) position, (*Mil.*) post, station, garrison, (*Bot., Zool. Orn.*) habitat. **–ortbestimmung,** *f.* (*Naut.*) position-finding *or* -fixing. **–ortlazarett,** *n.* (*Mil.*) station hospital. **–platz,** *m.* stand, station, (*for taxis*) rank. **–pauke,** *f.* (*coll.*) severe reprimand, dressing-down, telling-off. **–punkt,** *m.* point of view, viewpoint, standpoint; ***überwundener –,*** out-of-date view, discarded idea, exploded notion; ***den – vertreten, auf dem – stehen, sich auf den – stellen,*** be of the opinion, hold *or* take the view; ***ihm den – klarmachen,*** give him a piece of one's mind. **–quartier,** *n.* (*Mil.*) cantonment, fixed quarters, base-camp, base (for operations). **–recht,** *n.* summary jurisdiction, (*Mil.*) martial law. **standrechtlich,** *adj.* summary, (*Mil.*) according to martial law. **Stand|rede,** *f.* harangue; *see* **–pauke. –rohr,** *n.* standpipe. **–scheibe,** *f.* fixed target. **standsicher,** *adj.* firm, steady, stable. **Stand|spiegel,** *m.* full-length mirror, cheval-glass. **–uhr,** *f.* grandfather('s) clock. **–visier,** *n.* (*Mil.*) fixed sight. **–vogel,** *m.* resident (bird). **–wild,** *n.* sedentary game.

Stange ['ʃtaŋə], *f.* pole, post, stake, (*for flag*) pole, staff; (*of shaving soap etc.*) stick; (*for birds*) perch, roost; (*of harness*) bridle-bit; (*of antlers*) branch; (*Metall.*) bar, rod, ingot; (*coll.*) ***eine – Geld,*** a mint of money, a tidy penny, (*sl.*) quite a packet; (*fig.*) ***bei der – bleiben,*** (*in argument*) stick to the point, (*in attitudes*) stick to one's guns; (*fig.*) ***ihn bei der – halten,*** keep him up to scratch, make him toe the line; (*fig.*) ***ihm die – halten,*** take his part, stand by him, (*coll.*) back him up; (*as opponent*) be a match for him; ***ein Anzug von der –,*** a ready-made suit, a suit off the peg.

Stangen|besen, *m.* long-handled *or* sweeping broom. **–bohne,** *f.* runner- *or* string-bean. **–eisen,** *n.* bar iron, rod iron; trap (*for foxes etc.*). **–gebiß,** *n.* bridle-bit. **–gold,** *n.* gold ingots. **–pferd,** *n.* wheeler, pole-horse. **–seife,** *f.* bar-soap. **–sellerie,** *m.* sticks of celery. **–spargel,** *m.* whole asparagus. **–tabak,** *m.* twist.

Stanitzel [ʃta'nɪtsəl], *n.* (*Austr.*) paper bag.

Stank [ʃtaŋk], *m.* (*dial.*) stench, stink, (*coll.*) dissension, discord.

stank, stänke ['ʃtɛŋkə], *see* **stinken.**

Stänker ['ʃtɛŋkər], *m.* (*coll.*) quarrelsome *or* cantankerous p., trouble-maker, mischief-maker, (*sl.*) stinker. **Stänkerei** [–'raɪ], *f.* quarrelling, bickering, squabbling, wrangling; quarrel, wrangle, squabble, (*coll.*) row; (*dial.*) stink. **stänkern,** *v.i.* have an offensive smell, smell, stink; (*fig.*) quarrel, make trouble, wrangle, bicker, squabble.

Stanniol [ʃtani'o:l], *n.* (**-s,** *pl.* **-e**) tinfoil, silver paper.

Stanze ['ʃtantsə], *f.* 1. (*Metr.*) (eight-lined) stanza; 2. (*Tech.*) metal stamp, die, punch, matrix; stamping machine, press. **stanzen,** *v.t.* stamp, punch.

Stapel ['ʃta:pəl], *m.* pile, stack, heap; (*Naut.*) stocks, slips; marketing centre, mart; depot, stockpile, (*cotton etc.*) staple; (*Naut.*) ***auf – legen,*** lay down; (*Naut., fig.*) ***vom – laufen,*** be launched; (*Naut., fig.*) ***vom*** or ***von – lassen,*** launch, (*coll.*) bring out, release, publish; deliver, make, give, hold (*a speech*). **Stapel|faser,** *f.* staple fibre, rayon. **–holz,** *n.* stacked wood. **–lauf,** *m.* (*Naut.*) launch, launching. **stapeln, 1.** *v.t.* pile up, stack, accumulate, store. **2.** *v.r.* pile up, accumulate. **Stapelplatz,** *m.* depot, dump; staple market, mart, trading centre.

Stapf [ʃtapf], *m.* (**-en,** *pl.* **-en**), **Stapfe,** *f.*, **Stapfen,** *m.* footstep. **stapfen,** *v.t.* (*aux.* h. & s.) trudge, plod.

1**Star** [ʃta:r], *m.* (**-(e)s,** *pl.* **-e**) (*Orn.*) starling (*Sturnus vulgaris*).

2**Star,** *m.* (**-s,** *pl.* **-s**) (*Theat. etc.*) star.

3**Star,** *m.* (**-(e)s,** *pl.* **-e**) (*Med.*) (***grauer –***) cataract; ***grüner –,*** glaucoma; ***schwarzer –,*** amaurosis; ***ihm den – stechen,*** operate on him for cataract; (*fig.*) open his eyes.

Stär [ʃtɛ:r], *m.* (**-(e)s,** *pl.* **-e**) ram.

starb [ʃtarp], *see* **sterben.**

Starbesetzung ['ʃta:rbəzɛtsuŋ], *f.* star cast.

starblind [ʃta:rblɪnt], *adj.* blind from a cataract.

stark [ʃtark], **1.** *adj.* (*comp.* ***stärker,*** *sup.* ***stärkst***) (*of physique*) strong, sturdy, robust, vigorous; (*of figure*) thick, thickset, stout, portly, corpulent; (*of an engine, telescope etc.*) powerful, (*size of a th.*) thick, fat, (*coll.*) mighty, (*quantity*) large, numerous, considerable, (*degree*) intense, violent, severe, heavy; hearty (*appetite*); ***–e Auflage,*** large edition; ***–er Band,*** big *or* fat volume; ***–e Beugung,*** strong *or* irregular conjugation; ***–e Erkältung,*** bad *or* heavy cold; ***–er Esser,*** hearty eater; ***–es Fieber,*** high temperature; ***–er Frost,*** hard frost; ***–es Gedächtnis,*** good memory; ***das –e Geschlecht,*** the stronger sex; ***–er Hirsch,*** warrantable stag; ***–e Kälte,*** severe *or* intense cold; ***–e Leidenschaften,*** violent emotions; ***eine –e Meile,*** rather more than a mile, a good mile; ***–e Nachfrage,*** great *or* keen *or* good demand (***nach,*** for) (*goods*), (*coll.*) heavy run (on); ***–er Regen*** heavy rain; ***–er Schachspieler,*** good chess player; (*fig.*) ***–e Seite,*** strong point, forte; (*coll.*) ***ein –es Stück,*** a piece of impudence, (*coll.*) a bit thick; (*coll.*) ***das ist –er Tabak,*** that is rather near the knuckle; ***–er Trinker*** heavy *or* hard drinker; ***–er Verkehr,*** heavy traffic; ***–e Zeitwörter,*** strong *or* irregular verbs; ***stärkere Damen,*** stout(ish) ladies; ***stärker werden,*** put on weight *or* flesh; ***wie – ist Ihre Familie?*** how large is your family? (*coll.*) ***das ist etwas –! das ist aber*** (***zu***) ***–!*** that is the limit! that is a bit thick! that is rather too much! that's too bad! ***in –en Tagemärschen,*** by forced marches; ***darin ist er –,*** he is great at that; (*Prov.*) ***Einigkeit macht –,*** union is strength. **2.** *adv.* greatly, very much, strongly, heavily, hard, (*Mus.*) forte; (*coll.*) ***– auftragen,*** exaggerate, boast, (*sl.*) pile it on thick; ***– benachteiligt,*** severely *or* seriously *or* (*coll.*) badly handicapped; ***– besetzt,*** well attended, (*coll.*) crowded, packed; ***– erkältet sein,*** have a severe *or* (*coll.*) bad cold; ***– gefragt*** or ***gesucht,*** in great demand; ***– übertrieben,*** grossly *or* greatly exaggerated.

Stärke ['ʃtɛrkə], *f.* 1. strength, sturdiness, robustness; stoutness, portliness, corpulence; (*Tech.*) size, thickness, gauge, diameter; vigour, energy; force, power; violence, intensity, (*Chem.*) concentration, (*Med.*) potency; magnitude, greatness, (large) number, (*Mil.*) strength; (*fig.*) strong point, forte; 2. (*Chem.*) starch.

Stärke|fabrik, *f.* starch-factory. **–grad** *m.* degree of strength, intensity. **stärkehaltig,** *adj.* containing starch, starchy, amylaceous. **Stärke|kleister,** *m.* starch-paste. **–mehl,** *n.* starch-flour. **–meldung,** *f.* (*Mil.*) strength-return, **stärken, 1.** *v.t.* 1. strengthen, fortify, brace, invigorate; 2. starch. **2.** *v.r.* take refreshment; (*hum.*) have a quick one. **Stärkezucker,** *m.* glucose.

stark|gliedrig, *adj.* strong-limbed. **–knochig,** *adj.* big-boned. **–leibig,** *adj.* stout, corpulent. **Stark|strom,** *m.* (*Elec.*) power *or* high-voltage current. **–stromkabel,** *n.* power cable. **–stromleitung,** *f.* high-voltage line, power circuit. **–stromtechnik,** *f.* power engineering.

Stärkung ['ʃtɛrkuŋ], *f.* 1. strengthening, invigoration; (*fig.*) comfort, refreshment; (*coll.*) pick-me-up; 2. starching. **Stärkungsmittel,** *n.* tonic, restorative, (*coll.*) pick-me-up.

starkwirkend ['ʃtarkvɪrkənt], *adj.* (*Med.*) potent, efficacious, powerful, drastic.

starr [ʃtar], *adj.* stiff, motionless, rigid, fixed; (*of eyes*) fixed, staring, glassy; (*fig.*) inflexible, unbending, obstinate, stubborn; ***– vor Erstaunen,*** dumbfounded, thunderstruck, transfixed with amazement; ***– vor Kälte,*** numb with cold; ***– ansehen,*** look at fixedly, stare at. **Starre,** *f. See* **Starrheit.**

starren ['ʃtarən], *v.i.* 1. stare, look fixedly (***auf*** (*Acc.*), at); ***ins Leere –,*** stare into space, gaze vacantly; 2. stiffen, be benumbed *or* rigid; ***die Finger – mir vor Kälte,*** my fingers are numb with cold; ***seine Hände—vor Schmutz,*** his hands are covered *or* caked with mud; 3. stand out, tower up, project; bristle, stand on end; ***von Bajonetten –*** bristle with bayonets.

Starrheit ['ʃtarhaɪt], *f.* stiffness, rigidity; numbness; inflexibility, obstinacy, stubbornness. **Starrkopf,** *m.* stubborn *or* headstrong p., (*coll.*) mule. **starrköpfig,** *adj.* stubborn, obstinate, headstrong, (*coll.*) mulish, pig-headed. **Starr|köpfigkeit,** *f. See* **–sinn. –krampf,** *m.* tetanus, lockjaw. **–sinn,** *m.* obstinacy, stubbornness, inflexibility, obduracy, contumacy, self-will. **starr|sinnig,** *adj. See* **–köpfig. Starrsucht,** *f.* catalepsy.

Start [ʃtart], *m.* (**-(e)s,** *pl.* **-e** *or* **-s**) (*Spt.*) start; (*Av.*) take-off. **Startbahn,** *f.* (*Av.*) runway. **start|berechtigt,** *adj.* (*Spt.*) eligible; ***nicht –,*** disqualified. **–bereit,** *adj.* ready to start *or* (*Av.*) to take off. **Startblock,** *m.* (*Spt.*) starting-block.

starten ['ʃtartən], **1.** *v.i.* (*Spt.*) start, (*coll.*) get away; (*Av.*) take off, take the air; ***– zu,*** participate in, take part in, have entered for (*a contest*); (*Spt.*) ***zu früh –,*** make a false start, (*coll.*) jump the gun. **2.** *v.t.* (*Spt.*) start (*a race*); (*fig.*) launch (*an undertaking*), get (*s.th.*) started *or* going. **Starter,** *m.* (*Spt., Motor.*) starter. **Starterklappe,** *f.* (*Motor.*) choke.

Start|geld, *n.* (*Spt.*) entry-fee. **–hilfe,** *f.* (*Av.*) assisted take-off. **Start|knopf,** *m.* (*Motor.*) starter-button. **–kommando,** *n.* (*Spt.*) starter's order. **–nummer,** *f.* starting number. **–pistole,** *f.* starter's pistol. **–platz,** *m.* (*Spt.*) starting-line, (*Av.*) take-off point. **–rakete,** *f.* (*Av.*) launching rocket. **–schleuder,** *m.* (*Av.*) catapult launching device. **–schuß,** *m.* (*Spt.*) starting-signal, starter's gun. **–strecke,** *f.* (*Av.*) take-off run. **–verbot,** *n.* (*Spt.*) disqualification, suspension; (*Av.*) grounding.

statarisch [ʃta'ta:rɪʃ], *adj.* standing, progressing slowly; ***–e Lektüre,*** careful and slow reading.

Statik ['ʃta:tɪk], *f.* statics.

Station [ʃtatsi'o:n], *f.* station, stop; ward (*of hospital*); ***freie – haben,*** have board and lodging free *or* found; ***– machen,*** make a halt, break one's journey; ***die –en des Kreuzwegs,*** the Stations of the Cross.

stationär [ʃtatsio'nɛ:r], *adj.* stationary; steady, constant. **Stationärbehandlung,** *f.* hospitalization, in-patient treatment. **stationieren,** *v.t.* station. **Stations|arzt,** *m.* house physician, resident physician. **–schwester,** *f.* ward nurse.

–skala, *f.* (*Rad.*) turning dial. **–vorsteher,** *m.* (*Railw.*) station-master.

statisch ['ʃta:tɪʃ], *adj.* static.

stätisch ['ʃtɛ:tɪʃ], *adj.* restive (*of horses*).

Statist [ʃta'tɪst], *m.* (**-en,** *pl.* **-en**), **Statistin,** *f.* (*Theat.*) supernumerary, walker-on, (*Films*) extra.

Statistik [ʃta'tɪstɪk], *f.* (-, *pl.* **-en**) statistics. **Statistiker,** *m.* statistician. **statistisch,** *adj.* statistical.

Stativ [ʃta'ti:f], *n.* (**-s,** *pl.* **-e**) tripod, stand, foot, base, support.

Statt [ʃtat], *f.* (-, *pl.* **⸚e**) place, stead, lieu; ***an Vaters –,*** in the place of a father; ***an Kindes – annehmen,*** adopt (*a child*); ***an Eides –,*** in lieu of oath.

statt, 1. *prep.* (*Gen.*) (*dial. also Dat.*) instead of, in lieu of, in the place of; – ***meiner,*** instead of me, in my place; – ***dessen,*** in place of *or* instead of which; **2.** *conj* – ***rechts ging er links,*** he went to the left instead of the right; – ***mitzuhelfen ging er nach Hause,*** he went home instead of helping us; *see also* **anstatt.**

Stätte ['ʃtɛtə], *f.* place, spot; abode; ***keine bleibende – haben,*** have no fixed abode; ***eine – des Grauens,*** a scene of horror.

statt|finden, *irr.v.i.* (*sep.*) (*oft. imp.*) take place, happen, occur, (*coll.*) come off; be held *or* staged; ***eine Bitte – lassen,*** grant a request. **–geben,** *irr.v.i.* (*sep.*) (*Dat.*) allow, grant (*a request*); be swayed by, give way to. **–haben,** *irr.v.i. See* **–finden.**

statthaft ['ʃtathaft], *adj.* admissible, allowable, permissible, valid, legal, legitimate.

Statthalter ['ʃtathaltər], *m.* viceroy, governor. **Statthalterschaft,** *f.* governorship.

stattlich ['ʃtatlɪç], *adj.* stately, imposing, impressive, distinguished; splendid, magnificent, grand, (*coll.*) fine; considerable, ample, handsome, (*coll.*) goodly, respectable, decent (*sum*); (*coll.*) handsome; (*coll.*) portly. **Stattlichkeit,** *f.* magnificence, splendour, grandeur, impressiveness, stateliness; (*coll.*) portliness.

Statue ['ʃta:tuə], *f.* statue; (*pl.*) statuary. **statuenhaft,** *adj.* statuesque.

statuieren [ʃtatu'i:rən], *v.t.* decree, ordain, enact, establish, affirm, (*coll.*) lay down; ***ein Exempel –,*** serve as an example, be a warning.

Statur [ʃta'tu:r], *f.* figure; stature, height, size.

Status ['ʃta:tus], *m.* state, status, (*Comm.*) statement, financial state *or* condition; ***die Dinge im – quo belassen,*** leave things as they are; – ***quo ante,*** as things were.

Statut [ʃta'tu:t], *n.* (**-(e)s,** *pl.* **-en**) regulation, statute; *pl.* articles (of association). **statutarisch** [–'ta:rɪʃ], **statutenmäßig,** *adj.* statutory, legal.

Stau [ʃtau], *m.* (**-(e)s,** *pl.* **-e**) slack water; ***im –,*** at the turn of the tide.

Staub [ʃtaup], *m.* dust; powder; (*Bot.*) pollen; (*fig.*) – ***aufwirbeln,*** create a sensation, cause *or* make quite a stir; ***sich aus dem – machen,*** abscond, decamp, (*coll.*) make off, make tracks, (*sl.*) do a bunk *or* bolt; (*fig.*) ***in den – ziehen,*** drag through the mire *or* mud; ***den – löschen,*** lay the dust; ***in – zerfallen,*** crumble into dust.

Staubbach ['ʃtaupbax], *m.* high alpine waterfall (falling as spray). **staubbedeckt,** *adj.* dusty, thick with dust. **Staub|besen,** *m.* soft broom, dusting mop. **–beutel,** *m.* (*Bot.*) anther. **staubbeuteltragend,** *adj.* (*Bot.*) antheriferous. **Staub|blatt,** *n.* (*Bot.*) stamen. **–blüte,** *f.* (*Bot.*) male flower.

Stäubchen ['ʃtɔʏpçən], *n.* (tiny) particle of dust, mote.

staubdicht ['ʃtaupdɪçt], *adj.* dustproof.

Staubecken ['ʃtaubɛkən], *n.* reservoir, catchment basin.

stauben ['ʃtaubən], *v.i.* make (a) dust, raise (clouds of) dust; give off dust, rise as dust, (*of water*) fall as spray; (*imp.*) ***es staubt,*** it is dusty.

stäuben ['ʃtɔʏbən], **1.** *v.i. See* **stauben;** (*of birds*) take a dust-bath. **2.** *v.t.* (*usu. with pref.* ***ab–, aus–*** *etc.*) dust, (spray *or* strew with) powder.

Staub|fach, *n.* (*Bot.*) pollen-sac. **–faden,** *m.* (*Bot.*) filament. **staub|fadenlos,** *adj.* (*Bot.*) anandrous. **–frei,** *adj.* dust-free. **–geboren,** *adj.* (*B.*) earth-born. **Staub|gefäß,** *n. See* **–blatt. –gehalt,** *m.* pollution (*of atmosphere*). **staubhaltig,** *adj.* dust-laden.

staubig ['ʃtaubɪç], *adj.* dusty, powdery.

Staub|kittel, *m.* dust-coat, smock. **–lappen,** *m. See* **–tuch. –lawine,** *f.* avalanche of dry snow. **–luft,** *f.* dust-laden atmosphere. **–lunge,** *f.* (*Med.*) pneumoconiosis. **–mantel,** *m. See* **–kittel. –regen,** *m.* fine rain, drizzle; spray. **–sand,** *m.* fine sand. **–sauger,** *m.* vacuum cleaner. **staubtrocken,** *adj.* bone-dry. **Staub|tuch,** *n.* duster. **–wedel,** *m.* feather-duster. **–wolke,** *f.* cloud of dust, dust cloud. **–zucker,** *m.* castor sugar.

Stauche ['ʃtauxə], *m.* (**-ns,** *pl.* **-n**) *or f.* **1.** bundle (of flax); **2.** (*coll.*) blow, jolt, thrust; **3.** (*dial. usu. pl.*) mitten, muff. **stauchen,** *v.t.* **1.** jolt, thrust, ram together; (*Metall.*) compress, upset, shorten by forging; **2.** (*sl.*) pinch, swipe. **Staucher,** *m.* blow, jolt, thrust, (*coll.*) telling-off, dressing-down.

Staudamm ['ʃtaudam], *m.* coffer-dam, dike.

Staude ['ʃtaudə], *f.* bush, shrub, perennial (plant). **stauden,** *v.i.* (*aux.* h. & s.), *v.r.* grow bushy, form a head (*as lettuce*). **Staudengewächs,** *n. See* **Staude.**

Staudruckmesser ['ʃtaudrukmɛsər], *m.* pressure gauge, airspeed indicator.

stauen ['ʃtauən], **1.** *v.t.* stow (away) (*goods*); dam up (*water*). **2.** *v.r.* pile up, accumulate (*of goods*); be dammed up, rise (*of water*), (*fig.*) be choked *or* blocked *or* jammed *or* obstructed *or* congested. **Stauer,** *m.* (*Naut.*) stevedore.

Stauf ['ʃtauf], *m.* (**-(e)s,** *pl.* **-e**) (*dial.*) tankard.

Stauffer|büchse ['ʃtaufər–], *f.* (*Mech.*) grease-cup. **–fett,** *n.* axle-grease.

Stau|höhe, *f.* overflow level. **–mauer,** *f.* earth *or* stone dam, retaining wall.

staunen ['ʃtaunən], *v.i.* be surprised *or* astonished *or* astounded *or* amazed (***über*** (*Acc.*), at), marvel (at). **Staunen,** *n.* surprise, astonishment, amazement; wonder, awe; ***in – versetzen,*** amaze, astound; ***voll –,*** lost in wonder *or* amazement, (*coll.*) open-mouthed (with astonishment). **staunenswert,** *adj.* astonishing, astounding, amazing; marvellous, wonderful.

Staupe ['ʃtaupə], *f.* **1.** (public) flogging; **2.** (*Vet.*) distemper.

Stäupe ['ʃtɔʏpə], *f. See* **Staupe. stäupen,** *v.t.* flog publicly, scourge.

Stau|see, *m.* reservoir. **–stufe,** *f. See* **–wehr. Stauung,** *f.* (*Naut.*) stowage; (*of water*) damming (up); (*fig.*) accumulation, piling up; stoppage, blockage, obstruction, (*Med., traffic*) congestion; bottleneck, block. **Stau|wasser,** *n.* backwater; static *or* dammed-up water. **–wehr,** *n.* weir, (river-)dam. **–werk,** *n.* barrage.

Stearin [ʃtea'ri:n], *n.* (**-s,** *pl.* **-e**) (*Chem.*) stearin(e). **Stearinsäure,** *f.* stearic acid.

Stech|apfel ['ʃtɛç–], *m.* thorn-apple. **–bahn,** *f.* (*Hist.*) tilt(ing)-yard. **–becken,** *n.* bed-pan. **–beitel,** *m.* chisel. **–eisen,** *n.* awl, pricker.

stechen ['ʃtɛçən], *irr.v.t., v.i.* prick, pierce, (*of insects*) sting, bite, (*as hot sun*) scorch, burn, (*with a weapon*) stab, (*Med.*) puncture, couch (*a cataract*); (*Hist.*) tilt, joust; stick (*pigs*); cut (*turf, peat*); (*Spt.*) play off a tie; clock in (*at work*); (*Dressm.*) stitch; tap, draw *or* rack off (*wine, molten metal etc.*); engrave; (*Cards*) trump (*a card*), take (*a trick*); ***sich in den Finger –,*** prick one's finger; ***der Hafer sticht ihn,*** success has gone to his head, (*coll.*) he's getting cocky; ***ins Rote –,*** incline to red; ***das sticht mir in die Augen,*** that takes my fancy *or* takes my eye; ***es sticht mich in der Seite,*** I've got a stitch; ***in See –*** (*aux.* s.), put to sea; ***wie ein gestochenes Kalb,*** like a stuck pig; ***die Kontrolluhr –,*** clock in; ***in ein Wespennest –,*** raise a hornet's nest; (*Cards*) – ***müssen,*** be forced; ***nach dem Ringe –,*** tilt; ***Silben –,*** split hairs, (*coll.*) pick holes *or* flies (in); ***um eine S. –,*** cast lots for a th.; ***schreiben wie gestochen,*** write a copperplate hand.

Stechen, *n.* 1. casting lots; 2. shooting pains, stitch; 3. (*Spt.*) running *or* jumping off (*a tie*); 4. engraving. **stechend,** *adj.* piercing, penetrating (*glance*), biting, pungent (*smell*), shooting, stabbing (*pain*). **Stecher,** *m.* 1. pricker; engraver; proof-stick; 2. binoculars; 3. hair-trigger (*of a gun*).

Stech|fliege, *f.* horse- *or* stable-fly, gadfly, cleg. **-ginster,** *m.* furze, gorse, whin. **-heber,** *m.* pipette. **-kahn,** *m.* punt. **-karte,** *f.* winning card, trump(-card). **-kunst,** *f.* engraving. **-mücke,** *f.* gnat, midge. **-nelke,** *f.* (*Bot.*) rose-campion. **-palme,** *f.* (*Bot.*) holly (*Ilex aquifolium*). **-ring,** *m.* tilting-ring. **-rüssel,** *m.* (*Zool.*) proboscis. **-sattel,** *m.* jousting-saddle. **-schritt,** *m.* (*Mil.*) goose-step. **-uhr,** *f.* control-clock. **-zirkel,** *m.* dividers.

Steck|becken ['ʃtɛk-], *n.* See **Stechbecken.** **-brief,** *m.* warrant of arrest. **steckbrieflich,** *adv.* ***ihn – verfolgen,*** take out a warrant against him *or* for his arrest; ***– verfolgt werden,*** be under warrant of arrest. **Steckdose,** *f.* (*Elec.*) wall-socket.

stecken ['ʃtɛkən], **1.** *reg.* (*& irr.*) *v.t.* put, place; insert, (*Elec.*) plug (*in* (*Acc.*), into); (*Hort.*) set, plant; stick, fix, pin; (*coll.*) ***es ihm gehörig –,*** give him a good ticking-off; ***Grenzen –,*** set bounds *or* limits (*Dat.*, to); ***sich etwas hinter den Spiegel –,*** not forget s.th. in a hurry; ***in Brand –,*** set fire to, set on fire; ***Geld in ein Geschäft –,*** put money into a business; (*coll.*) ***ins Loch –,*** put in prison; ***die Nase in alles –,*** poke one's nose into everything; ***den Degen in die Scheide –,*** sheath one's sword; (*fig.*) ***das Geld in die Tasche –,*** pocket the money, put the money in one's pocket; ***zu sich –,*** put in one's pocket. **2.** *reg.v.r.* ***sich hinter eine S. –,*** get behind a th.; work at a th. secretly; ***sich hinter ihn –,*** make a tool of him, let him do one's dirty work. **3.** *reg.* (*& irr.*) *v.i.* be, stay, remain; stick fast, be fixed *or* stuck; be involved (*in* (*Dat.*), in); hide, be hiding *or* hidden (away), lie hidden; ***da steckt er,*** there he is; ***da steckt's!*** there's the rub! ***es steckt etwas dahinter,*** there is more in it than meets the eye, there is something at the bottom of it; (*coll.*) ***in dem Kerl steckt etwas,*** that chap will go a long way, there is something in that fellow; ***in seiner Haut –,*** be in his shoes; (*fig.*) ***noch in den Kinderschuhen –,*** be still in the early stages; ***tief in Schulden –,*** be up to the eyes in debt; ***der Schlüssel steckt,*** the key is left in the door; ***mit ihm unter einer Decke –,*** be hand in glove with him; ***voll – von,*** be full of; ***gesteckt voll,*** crammed (full).

Stecken, *m.* stick, staff, rod; (*B.*) ***dein – und dein Stab,*** thy rod and thy staff.

stecken|bleiben, *irr.v.i.* stick fast, be *or* get stuck, (*fig.*) come to a standstill; (*in a speech*) break down, (*coll.*) get stuck; (*fig.*) ***im Halse –,*** stick in one's throat *or* gorge. **-lassen,** *irr.v.t.* leave (where it is); ***den Schlüssel –,*** leave the key in the lock *or* door; ***ihn –,*** leave him in the lurch.

Steckenpferd ['ʃtɛkənpfe:rt], *n.* hobby-horse; hobby; fad, whim.

Stecker ['ʃtɛkər], *m.* (*Elec.*) plug. **Stecker|buchse,** *f.* plug adapter. **-schnur,** *f.* (supply) lead.

Steck|kartoffeln, *f.pl.* seed-potatoes. **-kissen,** *n.* baby's pillow. **-kontakt,** *m.* (*Elec.*) plug and socket, plug connection.

Steckling ['ʃtɛklɪŋ], *m.* (**-s,** *pl.* **-e**) (*Hort.*) slip, cutting, layer, shoot.

Steck|nadel, *f.* pin; ***wie eine – suchen,*** look *or* hunt for like a needle in a haystack, search for high and low; ***eine – fallen hören,*** hear a pin drop. **-nadelkissen,** *n.* pin-cushion. **-reis,** *n.* See **Steckling.** **-rübe,** *f.* turnip. **-schlüssel,** *m.* box-spanner. **-schuß,** *m.* retained bullet. **-zwiebel,** *f.* planting-out bulb.

Steg [ʃte:k], *m.* (**-(e)s,** *pl.* **-e**) footpath, (narrow) path; footbridge, plank bridge; (*Naut.*) gangplank, gangway, (*on machinery*) catwalk; (*Mech.*) crosspiece, (metal) strap, bar, flange, stay; bridge (*violin, spectacles*); (*Archit.*) fillet; (*Typ.*) stick, *pl.* furniture; ***Weg und – kennen,*** know (a place) like the back of one's hand; (*fig.*) know all the ins and outs.

Stegreif ['ʃte:kraɪf], *m.* (*obs.*) stirrup; ***aus dem –,*** extempore, impromptu, on the spur of the moment, without preparation, (*coll.*) ad lib.; ***aus dem – sprechen,*** extemporize, (*coll.*) ad lib. **Stegreif|-dichter,** *m.* improvisator, extempore poet. **-gedicht,** *n.* impromptu poem.

Steh|auf ['ʃte:-], *m.*, **-aufmännchen,** *n.* tumbler-doll, kelly. **-bierhalle,** *f.* bar, taproom. **-bild,** *n.* (*Phot.*) still.

stehen ['ʃte:ən], **1.** *irr.v.i.* (*aux.* h. *&* s.) 1. stand, be upright; be (situated); 2. (*of language*) be used *or* written; 3. stand still, stop; 4. (*Dat.*) suit, become (*of clothes etc.*).

(a) (*with preps.*) (*coll.*) ***da – die Ochsen* am *Berge,*** that's the difficulty, here's the snag; ***die Aktien* – auf *200%,*** the shares are at 200 per cent.; ***das Thermometer steht auf 20,*** the thermometer stands at *or* reads 20; ***auf dem Kopf –,*** be topsy-turvy; ***es steht der Kopf darauf,*** it is a capital crime; ***auf einer Liste –,*** appear *or* figure in a list; ***auf seine Seite –,*** be on his side, side with him; (*Gram.*) ***auf 'um' steht der Akkusativ,*** 'um' is followed by the accusative; ***es steht vieles auf dem Spiele,*** there is a lot at stake; ***es steht* bei *Ihnen,*** it rests with you, it is in your power, it is for you (*to decide etc.*); ***bei seiner Meinung –,*** hold to one's opinion; ***Geld bei ihm – haben,*** have money deposited *or* lying with him; (*fig.*) **– für,** guarantee, stand security for, vouch *or* answer for; ***ich mußte selbst für alles –,*** I had to look after everything myself, I was responsible for everything; **in** ***einem Amte –,*** hold *or* fill an office; ***bei ihm in Arbeit –,*** be employed by him, be in his employ; ***in einem Gesetz –,*** be embodied *or* laid down in a law; ***im fünften Jahre –,*** be in one's fifth year; ***es steht in seinen Kräften,*** it lies in his power; ***es steht ganz in Ihrer Macht,*** the matter rests solely with you; ***im Verdacht –,*** be suspected, be under suspicion; ***was steht in den Zeitungen?*** what do the papers (have to) say? ***ich stehe gut* mit *ihm,*** I am on good terms with him; ***ich stehe nicht allein mit meiner Meinung,*** I am not alone in my opinion *or* in thinking so; ***ihm* nach *dem Leben –,*** make an attempt on his life; ***sein Sinn steht nach Geld*** money is his aim; ***er steht* über *mir,*** he is my superior, he is over me; ***es steht schlecht* um *ihn,*** things go badly with him, he is in a bad way; ***er steht* unter *mir,*** he is my subordinate, he is under me; ***die Felder – unter Wasser,*** the fields are *or* lie under water; ***es steht mir immer* vor *Augen,*** I cannot get it out of my mind; ***im Rang steht er vor mir,*** he ranks above *or* (*coll.*) comes before me; ***vor einer vollendeten Tatsache –,*** be faced with a fait accompli; ***vor etwas Unangehmem –,*** be in for s.th. unpleasant; **zu** ***ihm –,*** give him one's help *or* support, stand by him; ***wie – Sie dazu?*** what is your view *or* opinion (of it) *or* attitude (to it)? ***es – mir die Haare zu Berge,*** my hair stands on end; ***zur Debatte –,*** be at issue; ***ich stehe zu Ihren Diensten,*** I am at your service; ***ihm zur Seite –,*** help him; ***ihm zur Verfügung –,*** be at his disposal; ***zu seinem Versprechen –,*** stand by *or* (*coll.*) stick to one's word.

(b) (*other idioms*) ***wie ich gehe und stehe,*** just as I am, without changing *or* bothering to change (my clothes); ***ich weiß nicht, wo mir der Kopf steht,*** I don't know which way to turn, I am beside myself; ***und wie steht's mit dir?*** and what do you think (about it)? what's your view *or* attitude? (*coll.*) and what about you? ***wie steht's zu Hause?*** how is everyone at home? ***es kam ihm teuer zu –,*** he had to pay dearly for it, it cost him dear(ly); ***es steht zu hoffen,*** it is to be hoped.

2. *irr.v.t.* ***der Hund steht das Wild,*** the hound points (the game); ***seinen Mann –,*** stand one's ground, hold one's own, stand the test; ***ihm Modell –,*** pose for him, (*fig.*) serve as a model for him; ***Posten –,*** be on guard (duty); ***ihm Rede –,*** answer his questions; ***Rede und Antwort –,*** justify o.s., give an account (of o.s.); ***Schlange –,*** stand in *or* form a queue, queue up.

3. *irr.v.r.* ***hier steht es sich besser,*** here is a better place to stand; ***sich müde –,*** tire o.s. out with standing; (*coll.*) ***ich stehe mich gut dabei,*** I'm doing very nicely, I don't do so badly, I'm in easy-street; ***er steht sich im Monat auf 3,000 Mark,*** he has an income of *or* he gets *or* makes 3,000 marks a month; *see* **dahin–, fest–, frei–** *etc.*

Stehen, *n.* 1. standing; ***das – fällt ihm schwer,*** he cannot stand for long; ***im – schlafen,*** sleep on one's feet; ***Mahlzeit im –,*** stand-up meal; 2. stopping, halting; ***zum – bringen,*** bring to a stop *or* standstill, (*fig.*) stop, stay, arrest; ***das Blut zum – bringen,*** staunch the blood, arrest the bleeding; ***zum – kommen,*** come to a stop *or* halt.

stehenbleiben ['ʃte:ənblaɪbən], *irr.v.i.* 1. remain standing, remain on one's feet, (*of a th.*) remain upright *or* erect; 2. stand still, stop (short), (*also of a th.*) come to a standstill; (*of clocks*) stop, (*of engines*) stall, (*as the market*) remain stationary, (*as mistakes*) be overlooked, be left (uncorrected); ***nicht –!*** keep moving! move on! ***das Wort muß jetzt –,*** the word will have to stand now; ***wo bist du gestern (beim Lesen) stehengeblieben?*** where did you leave off (reading) yesterday?

stehend ['ʃte:ənt], *adj.* standing, upright, erect, vertical; fixed, permanent, stationary, (*of water*) stagnant; ***–e Bühne,*** permanent theatre; ***–en Fußes,*** at once, straight *or* right away, on the spot; (*Naut.*) ***–es Gut,*** standing rigging; ***–es Heer,*** standing *or* regular army; ***–e Redensart,*** common expression, hackneyed *or* stock phrase; (*Rad.*) ***–e Welle,*** standing wave; ***–er Wind,*** settled wind.

stehenlassen ['ʃte:ənlasən], *irr.v.t.* (*of a p.*) keep standing, make stand, (*fig.*) turn one's back on, ignore; (*of a th.*) leave there *or* in its place; leave (behind), forget (*umbrella etc.*), leave (untouched), not eat (*food*), leave in (the bank), not withdraw (*money*), leave (uncorrected), overlook, miss (*mistakes*); (*Chem. etc.*) allow *or* leave to stand *or* settle; (*Spt.*) ***ihn glatt –,*** leave him standing; ***sich (Dat.) einen Bart –,*** grow a beard; ***alles stehen– und liegenlassen,*** drop everything.

Steher ['ʃte:ər], *m.* (*Spt.*) stayer, long-distance racer. **Steherrennen,** *n.* long-distance *or* endurance race (*esp. cycling*).

Steh|imbiß, *m.* stand-up snack. **–kragen,** *m.* stand-up collar. **–lampe,** *f.* standard *or* (*Am.*) floor lamp. **–leiter,** *f.* (pair of) steps, step-ladder.

stehlen ['ʃte:lən], **1.** *irr.v.i.* steal, pilfer, thieve, (*Law*) commit larceny. **2.** *irr.v.t.* steal, purloin, pilfer (*Dat.*, from); ***es ihm –,*** steal it from him, rob him of it; ***er hat mir die Zeit gestohlen,*** he has wasted *or* has been wasting my time; (*coll.*) ***dem lieben Gott die Zeit*** or ***den Tag –,*** idle away one's time; (*coll.*) ***das kann mir gestohlen bleiben,*** that leaves me cold, to hell with it! (*coll.*) ***er kann mir gestohlen bleiben,*** he can go and drown himself *or* (*sl.*) go and fry his face. **3.** *irr.v.r.* steal, slink (into, out from, away *etc.*). **Stehlen,** *n.* stealing, thieving, theft, robbery, larceny. **Stehler,** *m.* (*only in*) ***der Hehler ist so schlimm wie der –,*** the receiver is no better than the thief. **Stehl|sucht,** *f.* kleptomania. **–süchtige(r),** *m., f.* kleptomaniac.

Steh|platz, *m.* standing-room. **–pult,** *m.* standing *or* high desk. **–vermögen,** *n.* (*Spt.*) staying-power, stamina.

Steierin ['ʃtaɪərɪn], *f. See* **Steirer(in). Steier|-mark,** *f.* (*Geog.*) Styria. **–märker(in),** *m.,* (*f.*), **steiermärkisch,** *adj. See* **Steirer(in), steirisch.**

steif [ʃtaɪf], **1.** *adj.* stiff, rigid (*vor* (*Dat.*), with), inflexible, (*of limbs*) stiff, muscle-bound; numb (*vor Kälte,* with cold); (*of semi-liquids*) firm, thick; (*of laundry*) starched; (*fig.*) clumsy, awkward, stiff, wooden; pedantic, formal, strait-laced, (*coll.*) starchy; (*Naut.*) (*of ropes*) taut; ***–er Grog,*** strong *or* (*coll.*) stiff grog; ***–er Hut,*** bowler hat, (*Am.*) derby; (*Naut.*) ***–er Wind,*** strong breeze. **2.** *adv.* ***– und fest behaupten,*** maintain obstinately *or* stubbornly, be absolutely positive about; ***die Ohren – halten,*** keep a stiff upper lip.

Steife ['ʃtaɪfə], *f.* 1. starch, dressing, stiffening, size; 2. strut, prop, stay, support, buttress; 3. *See* **Steifheit. steifen,** *v.t.* stiffen; starch; prop, support, stay, shore up; ***ihm den Nacken –,*** stiffen his resistance. **Steifheit,** *f.* stiffness, rigidity, stability; inflexibility; awkwardness, formality. **Steifigkeit,** *f.* (*Tech.*) rigidity, stability. **steifleinen,** *adj.* strait-laced, (*coll.*) starchy; dull, (*coll.*) stodgy. **Steif|leinen,** *n.,* **–leinwand,** *f.* buckram.

Steig [ʃtaɪk], *m.* **(-(e)s,** *pl.* **-e)** (foot-)path, mountain track. **Steig|brunnen,** *m.* artesian well. **–bügel,** *m.* stirrup, (*Anat.*) stirrup-bone. **Steige,** *f. See* **Stiege. Steigeisen,** *n.* climbing-irons, crampons.

steigen ['ʃtaɪgən], *irr.v.i.* (*aux.* s.) 1. climb (up), mount, ascend, go up; (*in the air*) climb, rise, soar, (*Av.*) zoom; (*of horse*) rear, prance, rise on its hindlegs; (*fig.*) increase, rise; (*Comm.*) advance, improve, move upwards, (*coll.*) rise, go up; ***an Land –,*** land, disembark, go ashore; ***auf einen Baum –,*** climb (up) a tree; (*coll.*) ***ihm aufs Dach –,*** come down on him (like a ton of bricks); ***auf ein Pferd –,*** mount a horse; ***auf den Thron –,*** ascend the throne; ***aus dem Bett –,*** get out of bed; (*coll.*) ***ins Examen –,*** go in for *or* sit an examination; ***das Blut steigt mir in den Kopf,*** the blood goes *or* rushes to my head; ***Tränen stiegen ihr in die Augen,*** tears came into her eyes; (*coll.*) ***in die Schüssel –,*** help o.s. to more; ***Waren – im Preise,*** the price of goods is rising; ***vom Pferde –,*** dismount; ***zu Pferde –,*** mount (one's horse); ***die Haare stiegen ihm zu Berge,*** his hair stood on end; ***– lassen,*** fly (*a kite*); 2. take place, be held *or* staged, (*coll.*) come off; (*coll.*) ***ein Lied – lassen,*** sing *or* render a song; ***eine Rede – lassen,*** make *or* deliver *or* give a speech; (*Studs. sl.*) ***der Cantus steigt!*** open your mouths and sing (the following song)! ***das Endspiel steigt nächste Woche,*** the final takes *or* will take place next week.

Steigen, *n.* rise, ascent, climb(ing); (*fig.*) rise, advance, increase, (*of the market*) improvement, upward movement *or* trend. **steigend,** *adj.* rising, increasing, advancing, growing; ***mit –em Alter,*** with increasing years; (*Her.*) ***–er Löwe,*** lion rampant; ***–e Tendenz,*** upward trend *or* tendency. **Steiger,** *m.* (*Min.*) pit foreman, (*Am.*) overman.

steigern ['ʃtaɪgərn], **1.** *v.t.* 1. raise, increase, augment, heighten, enhance, intensify, (*coll.*) step up (*production*); ***die Miete –,*** raise *or* increase the rent; ***ihn mit der Miete –,*** raise *or* increase his rent; 2. (*Gram.*) compare; 3. (*at auctions*) (make a) bid for. **2.** *v.r.* become greater *or* intensified, increase, rise, mount. **Steigerung,** *f.* increase, rise, raising, augmentation, enhancement, intensification; climax; (*Gram.*) gradation, comparison. **Steigerungs|gegenstände,** *m.pl.* articles sold by auction. **–grad,** *m.,* **–stufe,** *f.* (*Gram.*) degree of comparison.

Steig|fähigkeit, *f.* (*Motor., Av.*) climbing-power. **–flug,** *m.* (*Av.*) climb, zooming. **–geschwindigkeit,** *f.* (*Av.*) rate of climb. **–höhe,** *f.* (*Av.*) ceiling, (*Tech.*) pitch (*of a screw*). **–riemen,** *m.* stirrup leather. **–rohr,** *n.* ascending pipe, overflow pipe, standpipe. **–röhre,** *f.* suction pipe (*of a pump*).

Steigung ['ʃtaɪguŋ], *f.* rise, increase; incline, slope, ascent, gradient, (*Am.*) (up)grade; pitch (*of a screw*), lead (*of a propeller*). **Steigungswinkel,** *m.* angle of gradient *or* (*Av.*) of climb.

steil [ʃtaɪl], *adj.* steep, precipitous, sheer. **Steile,** *f.* steepness; steep place, precipice, declivity. **Steil|feuer,** *n.* (*Artil.*) high-angle fire. **–flug,** *m.* (*Av.*) vertical flight. **–hang,** *m.* steep slope, precipice. **Steilheit,** *f.* steepness; (*Elec.*) mutual conductance; (*Phot.*) contrast. **Steil|kurve,** *f.* (*Av.*) steep turn. **–küste,** *f.* sheer *or* steeply shelving coast, (*Naut.*) steep-to shore. **–schrift,** *f.* vertical writing.

Stein [ʃtaɪn], *m.* **(-(e)s,** *pl.* **-e)** stone, rock; precious stone, gem, (*of watch*) jewel, (*of lighter*) flint; monument, gravestone; (*Draughts*) man, piece; (*of fruit*) stone, kernel; (*Med.*) concretion, calculus; beer-mug; ***– des Anstoßes,*** stumbling-block; ***keinen – auf dem andern lassen,*** raze to the ground; ***behauener –,*** hewn stone; ***– und Bein frieren,*** freeze hard; ***– und Bein schwören,*** swear by all that is holy *or* all the gods; ***bei ihm, einen – im Brett haben,*** be in his good books; ***es hätte einen – erbarmen können,*** it was enough to melt a (heart of) stone;

geschnittener* –,** gem, intaglio; ***ein – fällt mir vom Herzen, that is a load *or* weight off my mind; ***den – ins Rollen bringen,*** start the ball rolling; ***über Stock und –,*** through thick and thin; ***ihm –e in den Weg legen,*** put obstacles in his way; ***– der Weisen,*** philosopher's stone; ***zu – machen*** *(v.t.) or* ***werden*** *(v.i.)*, petrify.

Stein|abdruck, *m.* lithograph(ic print). **–abfälle,** *m.pl.* stone chips *or* chippings. **–acker,** *m.* stony field. **–adler,** *m.* *(Orn.)* golden eagle *(Aquila chrysaëtos)*. **steinalt,** *adj.* (as) old as the hills. **Steinart,** *f.* species of stone, mineral. **steinartig,** *adj.* rock-like, stony. **Stein|bau,** *m.* stone building. **–beil,** *n.* flint axe. **–beschwerde,** *f.* *(Med.)* calculus, the stone. **–beißer,** *m.* *(Ichth.)* loach *(Cobitis taenia)*. **–bild,** *n.* statue. **–bildung,** *f.* formation of stone; *(Med.)* lithiasis. **–bock,** *m.* *(Zool.)* ibex *(Capra ibex)*; *(Astr.)* Capricorn. **–boden,** *m.* stony soil; stone floor. **–bohrer,** *m.* *(Min.)* rock-drill, *(Build.)* masonry drill. **–brand,** *m.* stinking smut *(on corn)*. **–brech,** *m.* *(Bot.)* saxifrage. **–brecher,** *m.* quarryman, *(machine)* stone-crusher. **–bruch,** *m.* quarry. **–butt,** *m.* *(Ichth.)* turbot *(Rhombus maximus)*. **–damm,** *m.* paved road, *(Naut.)* mole, pier. **–drossel,** *f.* *(Orn.)* *see* **–rötel.** **–druck,** *m.* lithography; lithograph(ic print). **–drucker,** *m.* lithographic printer. **–eiche,** *f.* *(Bot.)* oak *(Quercus sessiliflora)*. **–erbarmen,** *n.* ***das ist zum –,*** it is enough to melt a heart of stone.

steinern ['ʃtaɪnərn], *adj.* of stone, stony *(also fig.)*.

Stein|erweichen, *n.* *See* **–erbarmen. –flechte,** *f.* rock lichen. **–fliese,** *f.* *See* **–platte. –frucht,** *f.* stone-fruit. **–galle,** *f.* *(Vet.)* windgall. **–garten,** *m.* rock-garden, rockery. **–geröll,** *n.* scree, shingle. **–grube,** *f.* quarry. **–grund,** *m.* stony ground; stony bottom *(of a river)*. **–gut,** *n.* stoneware, earthenware, pottery. **–hagel,** *m.* hail *or* shower of stones. **steinhart,** *adj.* hard as stone *or* brick. **Stein|hauer,** *m.* *See* **–metz. –holz,** *n.* xylolith. **–huhn,** *n.* *(Orn.)* rock partridge, *(Am.)* chukar *(Alectoris graeca)*. **steinig,** *adj.* stony; full of stones, rocky.

steinigen ['ʃtaɪnɪgən], *v.t.* stone. **Steinigung,** *f.* (death by) stoning.

Stein|kauz, *m.* *(Orn.)* little owl *(Athene noctua)*. **–kern,** *m.* stone *(of fruit)*. **–klee,** *m.* *(Bot.)* melilot *(Melilotus officinalis)*. **–kohle,** *f.* coal, pit-coal, bituminous coal. **–kohlenflöz,** *n.* coal-bed *or* -seam. **–kohlengas,** *n.* coal-gas. **–kohlenlager,** *n.* *See* **–kohlenflöz. –kohlenteer,** *m.* coal-tar. **–kolik,** *f.* *See* **–krankheit. –krähe,** *f.* *(Orn.)* *see* **Alpenkrähe. steinkrank,** *adj.* suffering from stone. **Stein|krankheit,** *f.* *(Med.)* stone. **–kunde,** *f.* mineralogy; lithology. **–leiden,** *n.* *See* **–krankheit. –lerche,** *f.* *(Orn.)* *see* **Sandlerche. –mann,** *m.* cairn *(on mountain)*. **–marder,** *m.* *(Zool.)* beech marten *(Martes foina)*. **–meißel,** *m.* stone-mason's chisel. **–metz,** *m.* **(-en,** *pl.* **-en)** stone-mason. **–nelke,** *f.* *(Bot.)* wood pink. **–nuß,** *f.* vegetable ivory, corozo nut. **–obst,** *n.* *See* **–frucht. –öl,** *n.* petroleum, mineral oil, rock oil. **–operation,** *f.* *(Surg.)* lithotomy. **–pflaster,** *n.* stone pavement. **–pilz,** *m.* edible mushroom *(Boletus edulis)*. **–platte,** *f.* stone slab, flagstone. **–reich,** *n.* mineral kingdom. **steinreich,** *adj.* *(fig.)* enormously rich, *(pred.)* rolling in money. **Stein|rötel,** *m.* *(Orn.)* rock-thrush *(Monticola saxatilis)*. **–salz,** *n.* rock-salt. **–sarg,** *m.* sarcophagus. **–säure,** *f.* lithic acid. **–schlag,** *m.* broken stones, metalling *(for roads)*; falling stones, rock-fall. **–schleifer,** *m.* lapidary, gem-polisher. **–schleuder,** *m.* *(Hist.)* sling(shot). **–schloß(gewehr),** *n.* flintlock (musket). **–schmätzer,** *m.* *(Orn.)* wheatear *(Oenanthe oenanthe)*. **–schneiden,** *n.* 1. gem-carving; 2. engraving on stone; *(Surg.)* lithotomy. **–schneider,** *m.* gem cutter, lapidary; stone engraver. **–schnitt,** *m.* *(Surg.)* lithotomy. **–setzer,** *m.* paver, paviour. **–sperling,** *m.* *(Orn.)* rock-sparrow *(Petronia petronia)*. **–waffen,** *f.pl.* flint weapons. **–wälzer,** *m.* *(Orn.)* *(Am.* European) turnstone *(Arenaria interpres)*. **–ware,** *f.* *See* **–gut. –werkzeug,** *n.* eolith. **–wurf,** *m.* stone's throw. **–zeichnung,** *f.* lithographic design. **–zeit,** *f.* Stone Age; ***ältere –,*** Palaeolithic period; ***jüngere –,*** Neolithic period. **–zeug,** *n.* *See* **–gut.**

Steiper ['ʃtaɪpər], *m.* *(dial.)* *see* **Stieper.**

Steirer(in) ['ʃtaɪrər(ɪn)], *m.* *(f.)*, **steirisch,** *adj.* Styrian.

Steiß [ʃtaɪs], *m.* **(-es,** *pl.* **-e)** rump, buttocks *(usu. of birds)*; *(coll.)* backside. **Steiß|bein,** *n.* *(Anat.)* coccyx. **–flosse,** *f.* anal fin. **–lage,** *f.* breech presentation.

Stellage [ʃtɛ'la:ʒə], *f.* stand, frame, rack. **Stellagengeschäft,** *n.* *(Comm.)* put and call, dealing in futures, *(Am.)* spread.

stellbar ['ʃtɛlba:r], *adj.* adjustable, moveable.

Stelldichein ['ʃtɛldɪçˀaɪn], *n.* **(-(s),** *pl.* **-(s))** meeting, assignation, appointment, rendezvous, *(obs.)* tryst, *(coll.)* date; ***ihm ein – geben*** arrange to meet him, *(coll.)* make a date with him; ***sich*** *(Dat. pl.)* ***ein – geben,*** arrange a meeting, fix an appointment, *(coll.)* have a date.

Stelle ['ʃtɛlə], *f.* place, position, situation, site, spot, point; post, position, *(coll.)* job; office, agency; authority, passage *(in a book)*; *(Math.)* figure, digit, (decimal) place; ***an meiner –,*** in my place, in place *or* instead of me; ***wenn ich an Ihrer – wäre,*** if I were you, if I were in your place; ***an seine – treten,*** take his place, act as his substitute, replace him, *(coll.)* stand in for him; ***an Ort und – sein,*** be on the spot; be delivered *(of goods)*; ***auf der –,*** on the spot, there and then, forthwith, immediately; *(Mil.)* ***auf der – treten,*** mark time; ***eine – bekleiden,*** hold a post *or* position; ***er bewirbt sich um die –,*** he is applying for the post; ***freie*** or ***offene –,*** vacancy, opening; ***nicht von der –!*** don't move *or* *(coll.)* budge! ***nicht von der – kommen,*** make no progress, not get ahead *or* on, be at a deadlock; ***sich nicht von der – rühren,*** not move *or* stir *or* *(coll.)* budge (an inch); ***zur –!*** here! ***zur – sein,*** be at hand, be on call, be available, be present; ***sich zur – melden,*** report (o.s. present) (***bei,*** to); ***zur – schaffen,*** produce, make available; ***zuständige –,*** proper authority.

stellen ['ʃtɛlən], **1.** *v.t.* 1. put, place, set, lay, stand, position, post, station; *(fig.)* impose *(conditions etc.)*, set *(task, problem)*; 2. provide, supply, furnish, contribute, make available; produce *(witnesses, evidence)*; 3. adjust, regulate, set *(clock, spring, trap etc.)*; 4. intercept, challenge, *(coll.)* corner, buttonhole; *(Hunt.)* bring to *or* hold at bay. **(a)** *(with nouns)* *(Parl.)* ***einen Antrag –,*** bring forward a motion, move a resolution; ***Antrag – auf*** *(Acc.)*, apply for *or* make *or* file an application for; ***Bedingungen –,*** impose conditions; ***ihm ein Bein –,*** trip him up; ***den Feind –,*** engage the enemy; ***Forderungen –,*** make claims *or* demands; ***eine Frage –,*** ask *or* put a question; ***ein Gesuch –,*** submit *or* file a petition, submit *or* make an application; ***ihm das Horoskop –,*** cast his horoscope; ***den Hirsch –,*** hold the stag at bay; ***seinen Mann –,*** *(obs.)* arrange for *or* find *or* supply a substitute; *(coll.)* play one's part, do one's share *or* bit, pull one's weight; ***eine Uhr –,*** regulate a clock; ***die Uhr auf 12 –,*** set the clock to 12 o'clock; ***den Verbrecher –,*** apprehend the criminal; ***Zeugen –,*** produce witnesses. **(b)** *(with preps.)* **an** ***den Pranger –,*** pillory, *(fig.)* expose; **auf** ***den Kopf –,*** turn upside down, upset, bring into disorder, disarrange; ***auf die Probe –,*** (put to the) test; ***er ist ganz auf sich*** *(Acc.)* ***selbst gestellt,*** he is entirely dependent upon himself, he can look for no one's support, *(coll.)* he is all on his own; ***etwas* in *Abrede –,*** question *or* deny a th., dispute (the validity of) a th.; ***etwas in Aussicht –,*** promise a th., hold out the prospect of s.th.; *(Naut.)* ***in Dienst –,*** commission, put into service *(a ship)*; ***es in sein Belieben*** or ***Ermessen –,*** leave it to him *or* to his discretion; ***in Frage –,*** see ***in Zweifel –***; jeopardize; ***ihm in Rechnung –,*** charge *or* place *or* debit to his account; ***in den Schatten –,*** put into the shade, eclipse, excel by far, surpass; ***in Zweifel –,*** doubt, (call in) question, have (one's) doubts about, question the advisability of; **unter** ***Beweis –,*** *see* **beweisen**; *(B.)* ***sein Licht unter den Scheffel –,*** hide one's light under a bushel; **zur** ***Diskussion –,*** throw open to discussion; ***ihn zur***

Rede* –,** call him to account, take him to task (wegen,*** for), demand an explanation from him (of *or* about); ***ihm etwas zur Verfügung* –,** place s.th. at his disposal.
(c) (*with adjs.*) ***gut*** (or ***schlecht***) ***gestellt sein,*** be well (*or* badly) off; ***kalt* –,** put into cold storage, keep in a cool place, (*wine*) put on ice; ***warm* –,** keep (*food*) warm, put (*food*) to keep warm.
2. *v.r.* **1.** place *or* post *or* position *or* station o.s.; (*fig.*) appear (*Dat.*, before), present o.s. (to *or* before), surrender, give o.s. up (to); (*Mil.*) enlist, (*coll.*) join up; **2.** pretend to be, feign, sham, affect; **3.** ***sich – auf*** (*Acc.*), (turn out *or* prove to) be.
(a) (*with preps.*) ***der Preis stellt sich* auf *8 Mark,*** the price is 8 marks; ***es stellt sich (im Preis) auf 8 Mark,*** it is priced at *or* it works out at *or* it amounts *or* comes to *or* it costs 8 marks; ***sich auf eig(e)ne Füße* –,** support o.s., (*coll.*) stand on one's own feet; (*coll.*) ***sich auf die Hinterbeine* –,** dig one's heels in; ***sich auf den Kopf* –,** go to any length, set one's mind on it; (*sl.*) do one's damnedest; ***sich mit ihm auf eine Stufe* –,** put o.s. on the same footing as him; ***sich* – gegen,** oppose, set one's face against (*a th.*), take up a hostile attitude towards (*a p.*), (*Hunt.*) stand at bay; ***sich gut* mit *ihm* –,** get on good terms with him; ***ich kann mich mit ihm nicht* –,** I cannot get on with him; ***sich* vor *Augen* –,** imagine, visualize; ***sich* zum *Kampfe* –,** accept battle, (*fig.*) enter the lists; ***wie – Sie sich dazu?*** what is your view of *or* attitude to the matter? what do you think *or* say?
(b) (*with Dat. nouns*) ***sich einem Gegner* –,** face up to an opponent; ***sich dem Gericht* –,** appear before the court; ***sich der Polizei* –,** give o.s. up to the police; ***sich seinen Verfolgern* –,** keep one's pursuers at bay, stand one's ground against one's pursuers; ***die Probleme, die sich allen Wissenschaftlern* –,** the problems facing *or* confronting all scholars, (*coll.*) the problems that all scholars are up against. **(c)** (*with adjs.*) ***sich dumm* –,** act as if *or* pretend that one knows nothing, pretend ignorance; ***sich krank* –,** pretend that one is ill, feign *or* sham illness, malinger; (*Comm.*) ***die Preise – sich niedrig,*** prices rule low; ***er stellt sich nur so,*** he is only pretending *or* shamming, (*coll.*) he's putting on an act, he's just putting it on.

Stellen|angebot, *n.* vacancy, offer of a post, *pl.* situations vacant. **–bewerber,** *m.* applicant (for a post). **–gesuch,** *n.* application for a post, *pl.* situations wanted. **–inhaber,** *m.* incumbent. **–jäger,** *m.* place-hunter. **stellenlos,** *adj.* unemployed. **Stellen|nachweis,** *m.* employment agency. **–suche,** *f.* job-hunting. **–vermittlung(s-büro),** *f.* (*n.*) Labour Exchange; *see* **–nachweis. stellenweise,** *adv.* here and there, in places, sporadically.

Stell|geld, *n.* (*Comm.*) premium for put and call *or* (*Am.*) for spread. **–geschäft,** *n. See* **Stellage. –hebel,** *m.* adjusting *or* adjustment lever.

–stellig [ʃtɛlɪç], *adj.suff.* of (*so many*) digits *or* figures.

Stelling ['ʃtɛlɪŋ], *m.* (**-s,** *pl.* **-e**) (*Naut.*) gangway.

Stell|jagd, *f.* (*Hunt.*) netting. **–macher,** *m.* wheelwright. **–mutter,** *f.* adjusting nut, lock-nut. **–ring,** *m.* setting-ring (*of fuse*), damping-collar. **–schlüssel,** *m.* adjustable spanner; *see* **–ring. –schraube,** *f.* adjusting screw, set-screw.

Stellung ['ʃtɛluŋ], *f.* **1.** position, situation (*in space*), position, attitude, posture (*of body*); placing, setting, disposition, arrangement; (*fig.*) **– *nehmen zu,*** give one's opinion on, express one's view(s) about *or* attitude to; come to a decision about; (*fig.*) **– *nehmen gegen,*** express one's disapproval of, repudiate, reject, blackball, (*coll.*) turn down, draw the line at; **2.** post, position, situation, employment, (*coll.*) job; ***eine einflußreiche – bekleiden*** or ***innehaben,*** hold *or* occupy an influential position *or* post; **3.** social position, rank, station, standing, (legal) status; **4.** supply, provision, furnishing; production (*of witnesses etc.*); **5.** (*Mil.*) position, line(s), trenches, fieldworks, (*of guns*) emplacement; (*Mil.*) ***eine – behaupten,*** hold a position.

Stellungnahme ['ʃtɛluŋna:mə], *f.* opinion (expressed) (***zu,*** about *or* on), comment (on), attitude (to), point of view.

Stellungs|bau, *m.* (*Mil.*) construction of defences. **–befehl,** *m.* calling-up papers, enlistment *or* induction order, (*coll.*) call-up. **–kampf, –krieg,** *m.* static *or* positional *or* trench warfare. **stellungslos,** *adj. See* **stellenlos. stellungspflichtig,** *adj.* liable for military service. **Stellungs|suchende(r),** *m., f. See* **Stellenbewerber. –spiel,** *n.* (*Footb.*) positional play. **–wechsel,** *m.* change of position *or* job.

stellvertretend ['ʃtɛlfɛrtre:tənt], *adj.* vicarious; delegated, acting, deputy; ***–er Geschäftsführer,*** assistant general manager; ***–er Vorsitzender,*** vice-chairman. **Stell|vertreter,** *m.* deputy, representative, delegate, proxy, substitute, (*Med.*) locum tenens, (*Am.*) executive officer. **–vertretung,** *f.* representation, substitution, proxy; agency; ***in* –,** by proxy, per pro(curation).

Stell|vorrichtung, *f.* adjusting mechanism, regulator. **–wagen,** *m.* (*Austr.*) coach, motor-bus. **–werk,** *n.* (*Railw.*) signal-box. **–zirkel,** *m.* adjustable bezel.

Stelzbein ['ʃtɛltsbaɪn], *n.* wooden *or* (*coll.*) peg leg. **stelzbeinig,** *adj.* (*fig.*) stiff, stilted, affected. **Stelze,** *f.* stilt; (*Min.*) prop, shore; ***–n laufen, auf –n gehen,*** walk on stilts; (*fig.*) be bombastic *or* affected *or* stilted. **stelzen,** *v.i.* strut. **Stelzenläufer,** *m.* (*Orn.*) black-winged stilt (*Himantopus himantopus*). **Stelz|fuß,** *m. See* **–bein. –vögel,** *m.pl.* wading birds, grallatores. **–wurzel,** *f.* adventitious root.

Stemm|bogen, *m.* (*skiing*) stem-turn. **–eisen,** *n.* crowbar; paring-chisel.

Stemmeißel ['ʃtɛmmaɪsəl], *m.* caulking-chisel.

stemmen ['ʃtɛmən], **1.** *v.t.* stem; dam up (*water etc.*); prop, support; lift (*heavy weights*), prize *or* lever up; (*Carp.*) mortise, chisel (out); cut down, fell (*trees*); **– *gegen,*** push *or* press against; ***die Arme in die Seiten* –,** put one's hands on one's hips, (*coll.*) set one's arms akimbo; ***die Arme auf den Tisch* –,** prop one's arms on the table; ***die Füße gegen die Wand* –,** plant one's feet firmly against the wall. **2.** *v.r.* lean heavily *or* push one's weight against; (*fig.*) oppose, resist, make headway against. **Stemmen,** *n.* (*Spt.*) weight-lifting. **Stemmtor,** *n.* sluice-gate.

Stempel ['ʃtɛmpəl], *m.* **1.** rubber stamp; seal, stamp, (*on metals*) hallmark, (*on goods*) trade-mark, brand, (*on letters*) postmark, cancellation; (*fig.*) mark, stamp, imprint, impress, seal, hallmark; **2.** (*Min.*) prop, shore, stemple; **3.** pestle, pounder; **4.** (*Mech.*) punch, stamp, die; **5.** (*of a pump*) piston; **6.** (*Bot.*) pistil.

Stempel|abgabe, *f.* stamp-duty. **–eisen,** *n.* stamp; punch. **–farbe,** *f.* stamping *or* marking ink. **stempelfrei,** *adj.* free from stamp-duty. **Stempel|gebühr,** *f.*, **–geld,** *n. See* **–abgabe. –kissen,** *n.* ink-pad. **stempellos,** *adj.* (*Bot.*) without pistils, male.

stempeln ['ʃtɛmpəln], **1.** *v.t.* stamp, mark, brand, hallmark (*silver etc.*); cancel (*postage stamps*); (*Min.*) shore up, prop (up); (*fig.*) label, mark, brand, stamp (*a p. or th.*) (***zu,*** as); (*coll.*) ***ihn* –,** prepare *or* prime him. **2.** *v.i.* have one's (dole-)card stamped; (*sl.*) **– *gehen,*** go on *or* draw the dole. **stempelpflichtig,** *adj.* liable to stamp-duty. **Stempel|presse,** *f.* stamping-press. **–schneider,** *m.* stamp-cutter, die-sinker. **–steuer,** *f. See* **–abgabe. –träger,** *m.* (*Bot.*) gynophore. **–uhr,** *f.* (factory) control-clock.

Stenge ['ʃtɛŋə], *f.* topmast.

Stengel ['ʃtɛŋəl], *m.* stalk, stem; (*coll.*) ***vom – fallen,*** come a cropper. **Stengel|bohne,** *f.* climbing-bean. **–glas,** *n.* wine-glass (*with stem*). **–knolle,** *f.* tuber. **stengellos,** *adj.* stemless, acaulose. **stengeln,** *v.i.* run to stalk.

Stenogramm [ʃteno'gram], *n.* (**-s,** *pl.* **-e**) shorthand notes *or* report. **Stenograph,** *m.* (**-en,** *pl.* **-en**) stenographer, shorthand-writer. **Stenographie** [–'fi:], *f.* stenography, shorthand. **stenographie-**

ren [–'fi:rən], *v.t., v.i.* write shorthand, take down in shorthand. **stenographisch,** *adj.* stenographic(al), (in) shorthand. **Stenotypist** [–ty'pɪst], *m.* (**-en,** *pl.* **-en**), **Stenotypistin,** *f.* shorthand-typist.

Stentorstimme ['ʃtɛntɔrʃtɪmə], *f.* stentorian voice, very loud voice.

Steppdecke ['ʃtɛpdɛkə], *f.* quilt.

Steppe ['ʃtɛpə], *f.* steppe, prairie, savannah, grassland.

[1]**steppen** ['ʃtɛpən], *v.t.* quilt.

[2]**steppen,** *v.i.* (do a) tap-dance.

Steppen|adler, *m.* (*Orn.*) steppe eagle (*Aquila nipalensis*). **–fuchs,** *m.* (*Zool.*) corsac; caragan. **–huhn,** *n.* (*Orn.*) Pallas's sandgrouse (*Syrrhaptes paradoxus*). **-kiebitz,** *m.* (*Orn.*) sociable plover (*Chettusia gregaria*). **–regenpfeifer,** *m.* (*Orn.*) Caspian plover (*Charadrius asiaticus*). **–weiher,** *m.* (*Orn.*) pallid harrier (*Circus macrourus*). **–wolf,** *m.* (*Zool.*) prairie wolf, coyote.

Stepper ['ʃtɛpər], *m.* tap-dancer.

Stepp|naht, *f.* quilting-seam, closing-seam. **–stich,** *m.* back-stitch, lock-stitch. **Step(p)tanz,** *m.* tap-dance.

Ster [ʃte:r], *f. See* [2]**Stör.**

Sterbe|alter ['ʃtɛrbə–], *m.* age of death *or* decease. **–bett,** *n.* death-bed. **–fall,** *m.* (case of) death, decease. **–fallversicherung,** *f.* life assurance. **–geld,** *n.* death benefit. **–glocke,** *f.* funeral bell. **–hemd,** *n.* shroud, winding-sheet. **–hilfe,** *f.* (*Med.*) mercy killing, euthanasia. **–kasse,** *f.* burial fund. **–lager,** *n. See* **–bett. –liste,** *f.* register of deaths.

sterben ['ʃtɛrbən], *irr.v.i., v.t.* die (*an* (*Dat.*), of); be killed, lose one's life; ***als Martyrer –,*** die a martyr; ***an der Pest –,*** die of the plague; ***am Schlage –,*** die as a result of a stroke; ***aus Gram –,*** die of grief; ***durch Mißachtung der Sicherheitsmaßregeln –,*** die through neglect of the safety precautions; ***durch Mörderhand –,*** die at the hand of an assassin; ***durch das Schwert –,*** die by the sword; ***den Heldentod –,*** die (the death of) a hero; ***– für,*** die for (the sake of), give one's life for, sacrifice o.s. for; ***für das Vaterland –,*** make the supreme sacrifice; ***eines natürlichen Todes*** or ***einen natürlichen Tod –,*** die a natural death; ***über seinen Plänen –,*** die before one's plans are carried out; (*fig.*) ***vor Lachen –,*** die with laughter, kill o.s. laughing; (*fig.*) ***vor Lange(r)weile –,*** be bored to death; ***vor Hunger –,*** be starving to death *or* dying of hunger *or* starvation.

Sterben, *n.* dying; death; ***im – liegen,*** be dying *or* at the point of death; ***es geht um Leben und –,*** it is a matter of life and death; ***das große –,*** the plague, the Black Death; ***zum – langweilig,*** intolerably boring; ***zum – zuviel und zum Leben zuwenig,*** barely enough to keep body and soul together.

Sterbensangst ['ʃtɛrbəns'aŋst], *f.* mortal fear. **sterbens|bange,** *adj.* mortally afraid. **–krank,** *adj.* dangerously ill; (*B.*) sick unto death. **–matt, –müde,** *adj.* (*coll.*) tired to death, (*sl.*) dead-beat. **Sterbens|seele,** *f.* ***keine –,*** not a living soul. **–wort,** *n.* ***kein –,*** not a (single) word *or* syllable.

Sterbe|sakramente, *n.pl.* last sacraments *or* unction. **–stunde,** *f.* dying hour. **–urkunde,** *f.* death certificate. **–ziffer,** *f.* number of deaths.

sterblich ['ʃtɛrplɪç], *adj.* mortal; (*coll.*) ***– verliebt,*** hopelessly *or* head over heels in love. **Sterbliche(r),** *m., f.* mortal. **Sterblichkeit,** *f.* mortality; mortality figures, death-rate; ***aus dieser – abgefordert*** or ***abberufen werden,*** be called to other realms. **Sterblichkeitsziffer,** *f.* mortality *or* death-rate.

Stereoaufnahme ['stereo'aufna:mə], *f.* stereoscopic photograph. **Stereographie,** *f.* descriptive geometry. **Stereokamera,** *f.* stereoscopic camera. **Stereometrie** [–me'tri:], *f.* solid geometry, stereometry. **Stereophonie** [–fo'ni:], *f.* stereoscopic recording. **Stereoplatte,** *f.* stereo(phonic) (gramophone) record. **Stereoskop** [–'sko:p], *n.* (**-(e)s,** *pl.* **-e**) stereoscope. **stereoskopisch,** *adj.* stereoscopic. **Stereoton,** *m.* stereophony. **stereotyp** [–'ty:p], *adj.* stereotype, (*fig.*) stereotyped, hackneyed. **Stereotypausgabe,** *f.* stereotype *or* offset edition. **Stereotypie** [–'pi:], *f.* stereotype *or* offset printing, stereotyping. **stereotypieren,** *v.t.* stereotype.

steril [ʃte'ri:l], *adj.* barren, sterile; sterilized, antiseptic. **sterilisieren** [–i'zi:rən], *v.t.* sterilize. **Sterilität** [–i'tɛ:t], *f.* sterility, barrenness.

Sterke ['ʃtɛrkə], *f.* heifer.

Stern [ʃtɛrn], *m.* (**-(e)s,** *pl.* **-e**) star; (*Typ.*) asterisk; white mark (*on horse's face*); ***– der Londoner Theaterwelt,*** star of the London theatre; ***er hat weder Glück noch –,*** the fates are against him; ***nach den –en greifen,*** reach for the stars; ***– erster Größe,*** star of the first magnitude; ***ein*** or ***sein guter –,*** his lucky star; ***der Hoffnung letzte –e,*** the last rays *or* gleam of hope.

sternartig ['ʃtɛrn'artɪç], *adj.* starlike, astral, asteroid. **Stern|bild,** *n.* constellation. **–blume.** *f.* star-shaped *or* stellate flower, (*pl.*) Asteraceae. **Sternchen,** *n.* 1. asterisk; 2. (*Theat.*) minor star, starlet. **Stern|deuter,** *m.* astrologer. **–deutung,** *f.* astrology.

Sternen|bahn, *f.* orbit of a star. **–banner,** *m.* Stars and Stripes, star-spangled banner. **–himmel,** *m. See* **Sternhimmel. sternenklar,** *adj. See* **sternhell. Sternenzelt,** *n.* (*Poet.*) *see* **Sternhimmel.**

Sternfahrt ['ʃtɛrnfa:rt], *f.* motor-rally. **sternförmig,** *adj.* star-shaped, stellar, (*Bot.*) stellate, (*Mech.*) radial. **Stern|gucker,** *m.* star-gazer. **–guckerei,** *f.* star-gazing. **sternhagelvoll,** *adj.* (*coll.*) dead *or* rolling drunk. **Sternhaufen,** *m.* star-cluster, multiple star. **sternhell,** *adj.* starry, starlit, starlight. **Stern|himmel,** *m.* starry sky, firmament. **–jahr,** *n.* sidereal year. **–karte,** *f.* astronomical chart. **stern|klar,** *adj. See* **–hell. Stern|-kreuzung,** *f.* (*on roads*) multiple crossing. **–kunde,** *f.* astronomy. **–leuchtpatrone,** *f.* (*Mil.*) star-shell. **–miere,** *f.* (*Bot.*) stitchwort, starwort (*Stellaria*). **–motor,** *m.* radial engine. **–physik,** *f.* astrophysics. **–schnuppe,** *f.* shooting star, asteroid. **–schreiber,** *m.* (*radar*) plan-position indicator. **–stunde,** *f.* sidereal hour, (*fig.*) fateful *or* auspicious hour. **–tafel,** *f.* astronomical table. **–tag,** *m.* sidereal day. **–taucher,** *m.* (*Orn.*) red-throated diver *or* (*Am.*) loon (*Gavia stellata*). **–warte,** *f.* observatory. **–wolke,** *f.* nebula. **–zeit,** *f.* sidereal time.

Sterz [ʃtɛrts], *m.* (**-es,** *pl.* **-e**) plough-handle, plough-tail; (*dial.*) tail, rump.

stet [ʃte:t], **stetig,** *adj.* constant, continual, continuous, persistent, perpetual; steady, stable. **Stetigkeit,** *f.* constancy, continuity, persistence, steadiness. **stets,** *adv.* regularly, steadily, constantly, continually, (for) ever, at all times, always. **stetsfort,** *adv.* (*Swiss*) incessantly, perpetually, continuously.

[1]**Steuer** ['ʃtɔyər], *n.* (*Naut.*) rudder, helm; (*Motor.*) steering-wheel; (*Av.*) control-surface; ***am –,*** (*Naut.*) at the helm, (*Motor.*) at the wheel (*both also fig.*); ***das – führen,*** be at the helm; ***das – an Backbord!*** port the helm! ***das – herumwerfen,*** put the helm over.

[2]**Steuer,** *f* (**-,** *pl.* **-n**) 1. tax, duty, (local) rate(s) (***auf*** (*Dat.*), on); ***indirekte –n,*** duties; ***städtische –n,*** local rates; ***die gesamten –n,*** rates and taxes; 2. (*obs.*) redress, defence, aid; ***zur – der Wahrheit,*** for the sake of *or* in the interests of truth.

Steuer|abzug, *m.* deduction for (income-)tax. **–amt,** *n.* inland-revenue office. **–anlage,** *f.* (*Mech.*) control gear. **–anschlag,** *m.* tax assessment. **–aufkommen,** *n.* tax yield, internal *or* inland revenue. **–aufschlag,** *m.* supplementary tax.

steuerbar ['ʃtɔyərba:r], *adj.* 1. steerable, controllable, manoeuvrable; 2. taxable, assessable, rat(e)able, (*of goods*) dutiable, (*of a p.*) liable for tax. **Steuerbarkeit,** *f.* tax liability.

Steuer|beamte(r), *m.* inland-revenue officer, tax collector. **–befreiung,** *f.* tax exemption. **–behörde,**

f. inland-revenue department. **-belastung,** *f. See* **-druck. -berater,** *m.* accountant. **-bescheid,** *m. See* **-anschlag. -bord,** *n.* (*Naut.*) starboard. **-delikt,** *n.* tax offence. **-druck,** *m.* burden of taxation. **-einnehmer,** *m.* tax collector. **-erhebung,** *f.* tax collection, levy of taxes. **-erklärung,** *f.* (income-)tax return. **-erlaß,** *m.* tax exemption. **-fähigkeit,** *f.* manœuvrability. **-fläche,** *f.* (*Av.*) control-surface. **-flosse,** *f.* (*Av.*) fin. **-flügel,** *m.* fin (*of a bomb*). **-freiheit,** *f. See* **-erlaß. -gerät,** *n.* steering-gear. **-gitter,** *n.* (*Rad.*) control grid. **-hebel,** *m.* control lever. **-hinterziehung,** *f.* tax evasion. **-knüppel,** *m.* (*Av.*) control stick *or* column, (*coll.*) joystick. **-kurs,** *m.* (*Naut.*) compass course, heading. **steuerlastig,** *adj.* (*Naut.*) trimmed by the stern. **Steuer|mann,** *m.* (*pl.* **⸗er** *or* **-leute**) helmsman, man at the wheel, coxswain, mate. **-mannsmaat,** *m.* (*Naut.*) second mate. **-marke,** *f.* revenue stamp. **-meßzahl,** *f.* (income-tax) code number *or* coding.

steuern [ˈʃtɔyərn], **1.** *v.t.* (*Naut.*) steer; navigate; (*also Av.*) pilot; (*Motor.*) drive, steer; (*Mech., Rad. etc.*) control; (*fig.*) control, direct. **2.** *v.i.* (*aux.* s.) 1. (*Naut.*) steer (a course), head, make, be bound (***nach***, for), stand (towards); 2. (*fig.*) (*Dat.*) check, curb, put a check on, put a stop to, obviate, ward off, find a remedy for.

Steuer|nachlaß, *m.* tax relief. **-nocken,** *m.* (*Mech.*) cam. **steuerpflichtig,** *adj.* taxable (*income*), (*of goods*) dutiable, (*of a p.*) liable for tax, subject to taxation. **Steuer|politik,** *f.* fiscal policy. **-rad,** *n.* (*Motor.*) (steering-)wheel, (*Av.*) control wheel. **-recht,** *n.* fiscal law. **-ruder,** *n.* (*Naut.*) helm, rudder; (*Av.*) control surface. **-satz,** *m.* rate of assessment, coding. **-säule,** *f.* (*Motor.*) steering column; (*Av.*) *see* **-knüppel. -schätzung,** *f.* (notice of) assessment. **-schein,** *m.* tax-collector's receipt. **-schraube,** *f.* oppressive taxation. **-schuld,** *f.* tax due *or* underpaid. **-tabelle,** *f.* list of codes.

Steuerung [ˈʃtɔyəruŋ], *f.* 1. steering, piloting, (*Mech., Rad.*) control; (*Motor.*) steering mechanism, (*Av.*) controls, (*Mech.*) valve-gear; (*fig.*) control, direction, regulation; 2. prevention, relief, redress.

Steuer|veranlagung, *f. See* **-schätzung. -vergünstigung,** *f.* tax concession. **-verwaltung,** *f.* inland-revenue department. **-welle,** *f.* (*Mech.*) camshaft. **-wert,** *m.* rat(e)able value. **-wesen,** *n.* taxes, taxation, fiscal matters. **-zahler,** *m.* taxpayer, ratepayer. **-zettel,** *m.* notice to pay, tax-demand, notice of coding. **-zuschlag,** *m.* surtax, supertax.

Steven [ˈʃteːvən], *m.* stem; (*Naut.*) stern-post.

Stewardeß [ˈstjuːərdɛs], *f.* (-, *pl.* **-(ss)en**) stewardess, (*Av.*) air-hostess.

stibitzen [ʃtiˈbɪtsən], *v.t., v.i.* (*coll.*) pilfer, filch, (*sl.*) swipe.

stich, *see* **stechen.**

Stich [ʃtɪç], *m.* (**-(e)s,** *pl.* **-e**) 1. prick, puncture, (*with a weapon*) stab, thrust, (*with a spade*) cut, (*of an insect*) sting, bite; shooting pain, twinge, stitch (in the side), (*fig.*) gibe, taunt; ***das ist mir ein – durch die Seele***, that cuts me to the quick; ***– halten***, stand the test, hold good, (*coll.*) hold water; ***Hieb und –***, cut and thrust; ***im – lassen***, desert, forsake, abandon, (*coll.*) let down, leave in the lurch; 2. (*Dressm.*) stitch; 3. (*Art*) engraving, print; 4. (*Cards*) trick; 5. (*Naut.*) knot, hitch, bend; 6. (*fig.*) touch, streak, shade, tinge; ***einen – haben***, be turning sour *or* going bad, be no longer fresh, (*coll.*) be (slightly) off; (*fig.*) (*of a p.*) be touched *or* cracked, have a screw loose; ***– ins Blaue***, tinge *or* shade *or* touch of blue.

Stich|bahn, *f.* (*Railw.*) dead-end line. **-balken,** *m.* half-beam. **-blatt,** *n.* 1. guard (*of a sword*), hilt; 2. (*Cards*) winning card, trump.

Stichel [ˈʃtɪçəl], *m.* style, graver, graving tool; burin. **Stichelei** [–ˈlaɪ], *f.* (-, *pl.* **-en**) taunt, gibe. **sticheln,** *v.t., v.i.* grave, engrave (*in metal*); stitch, sew; prick, puncture; (*fig.*) taunt, jeer, sneer, gibe; tease. **Stichel|name,** *m.* nickname. **-rede,** *f.* sarcasm, taunt, gibe.

Stichentscheid [ˈʃtɪçʔɛntʃaɪt], *m.* casting vote. **stichfest,** *adj.* inviolable, unassailable, dependable; ***hieb- und –***, invulnerable, proof against all danger, immune against all attack. **Stich|flamme,** *f.* jet of flame; pilot-light. **-graben,** *m.* (*Mil.*) communication trench. **stich|halten,** *irr.v.i.* (*Austr.*) *see* ***Stich halten***. **-haltig,** *adj.* (*Austr.* **-hältig**) sound, valid, proof, lasting. **Stich|haltigkeit,** *f.* soundness, validity. **-heber,** *m.* pipette.

Stichling [ˈʃtɪçlɪŋ], *m.* (**-s,** *pl.* **-e**) (*Ichth.*) stickleback (*Gasterosteus aculeatus*).

Stich|loch, *n.* (*Metall.*) tapping-hole. **-ofen,** *m.* blast-furnace. **-platte,** *f.* (*Sew.-mach.*) needle plate. **-probe,** *f.* spot-check, random sample. **-säge,** *f.* keyhole-saw. **-tag,** *m.* fixed day, key-date, (*coll.*) deadline. **-torf,** *m.* cut peat. **-waffe,** *f.* pointed weapon, foil. **-wahl,** *f.* second *or* final ballot. **-wort,** *n.* (*pl* **⸗er**) catchword, keyword, caption; (*pl.* **-e**) (*Theat.*) cue; (*Pol.*) party-cry. **-wortverzeichnis,** *n.* subject-index. **-wunde,** *f.* stab.

Stickarbeit [ˈʃtɪkʔarbaɪt], *f.* (piece of) embroidery. **sticken,** *v.t., v.i.* embroider. **Stickerei** [–ˈraɪ], *f. See* **Stickarbeit. Stickerin,** *f.* embroiderer. **Stick|garn,** *n.* embroidery cotton. **-gas,** *n.* carbon dioxide, suffocating *or* asphyxiating gas. **-gaze,** *f.*, **-grund,** *m.* embroidery canvas *or* material. **-husten,** *m.* choking cough. **stickig,** *adj.* stifling, suffocating, close, stuffy. **Stick|luft,** *f.* close *or* stuffy air, (*fig.*) oppressive atmosphere. **-muster,** *n.* embroidery pattern. **-oxyd,** *n. See* **-stoffoxyd. -oxydul,** *n. See* **-stoffoxydul. -rahmen,** *m.* embroidery frame.

Stickstoff [ˈʃtɪkʃtɔf], *n.* nitrogen. **Stickstoffdünger,** *m.* nitrogenous fertilizer. **stickstoff|-frei,** *adj.* non-nitrogenous. **-haltig** (*Austr.* **-hältig**), *adj.* nitrogenous. **Stickstoff|oxyd,** *n.* nitric oxide. **-oxydul,** *n.* nitrous oxide, laughing-gas. **-wasserstoff,** *n.* hydrogen nitride.

stieben [ˈʃtiːbən], *irr. or reg.v.i.* (*aux.* h. *&* s.) fly about (like dust), rise up, scatter; (*of liquids*) spray.

Stiefbruder [ˈʃtiːfbruːdər], *m.* stepbrother.

Stiefel [ˈʃtiːfəl], *m.* boot; large tankard; barrel (*of a pump*); (*dial.*) prop, support; (*sl.*) ***seinen – arbeiten***, work on in the same old way; (*coll.*) ***den alten – weitertragen***, carry on as usual; (*coll.*) ***er kann einen guten – vertragen***, he carries his drink well; ***hoher –***, knee-boot; (*coll.*) ***einen – zusammenreden***, talk through one's hat.

Stiefel|anzieher, *m.* shoe-horn. **-appell,** *m.* (*Mil.*) boot inspection. **-holz,** *n.* boot-tree, last; spreader (*on fishing nets*). **-knecht,** *m.* boot-jack. **stiefeln, 1.** *v.t.* provide with boots; ***gestiefelt und gespornt***, booted and spurred; ***der gestiefelte Kater***, Puss-in-Boots. **2.** *v.i.* (*aux.* s.) (*coll.*) walk, march, stride *or* stalk along. **Stiefel|putzer,** *m.* boots (*at hotels*); shoe-black (*in the streets*). **-schaft,** *m.* leg of a boot. **-schwärze,** *f.* boot-blacking. **-spanner,** *m.* (boot-)tree.

Stiefeltern [ˈʃtiːfʔɛltərn], *pl.* step-parents.

Stiefel|wichse, *f. See* **-schwärze.**

Stief|geschwister, *pl.* stepbrothers and stepsisters. **-kind,** *n.* stepchild; (*usu. fig.*) neglected child; ***das – der Künste***, the Cinderella of the arts. **-mutter,** *f.* stepmother. **-mütterchen,** *n.* (*Bot.*) pansy (*Viola tricolor*). **stiefmütterlich,** *adj.* like a stepmother; perfunctory, inconsiderate, slighting, unkind, (*coll.*) shabby; ***– behandeln***, neglect, treat shabbily. **Stief|schwester,** *f.* stepsister. **-sohn,** *m.* stepson. **-tochter,** *f.* stepdaughter. **-vater,** *m.* stepfather.

Stieg [ʃtiːk], *m.* (**-(e)s,** *pl.* **-e**) (*dial.*) *see* **Steig.**

stieg, stiege, *see* **steigen.**

Stiege [ˈʃtiːgə], *f.* 1. staircase, (flight of) stairs *or* steps; crate, hen-house; stile; 2. score (= *20*). **Stiegenhaus,** *n.* stair-well.

Stieglitz [ˈʃtiːklɪts], *m.* (**-es,** *pl.* **-e**) (*Orn.*) (*Am.* European) goldfinch (*Carduelis carduelis*).

stiehl [ʃtiːl], **stiehlst, stiehlt,** *see* **stehlen.**

Stiel [ʃtiːl], *m.* (**-(e)s,** *pl.* **-e**) haft, handle, stick (*of a broom*); stem (*of a pipe*); post, strut; (*Bot.*) stem, stalk, peduncle, petiole; ***mit Stumpf und – ausrotten***, destroy *or* eliminate root and branch.

Stiel|augen, *n.pl.* protruding eyes; *er machte* or *bekam –,* his eyes popped out of his head, he made big eyes. **–brille,** *f.* lorgnette. **–eiche,** *f.* pedunculate oak. **–handgranate,** *f.* stick-grenade. **–loch,** *n.* eye (*of a hatchet etc.*), foramen. **stiellos,** *adj.* without a handle; sessile, stalkless. **Stielrippe,** *f.* main rib (*of a leaf*). **stielständig,** *adj.* growing on the stem, pedunculate. **Stielstich,** *m.* stem stitch.

Stieper [ˈʃtiːpər], *m.* short prop, strut, stanchion.

stier [ʃtiːr], *adj.* fixed, staring; *–er Blick,* fixed stare, vacant look.

Stier, *m.* **(-(e)s,** *pl.* **-e)** bull; (*Astr.*) Taurus; *den – an* or *bei den Hörnern fassen* or *packen,* take the bull by the horns. **Stierauge,** *n. See* **Stierenauge.**

stieren [ˈʃtiːrən], *v.i.* stare, gaze fixedly, glare (*auf* (*Acc.*), at).

Stierenauge [ˈʃtiːrənˀaugə], *n.* (*Swiss*) fried egg.

Stier|fechter, *m.* bullfighter. **–gefecht,** *n. See* **–kampf. –gespann,** *n.* team *or* span of oxen. **–kampf,** *m.* bullfight. **–kämpfer,** *m. See* **–fechter. stier|köpfig,** *adj.* obstinate, stiff-necked, self-willed. **–nackig,** *adj.* bull-necked; *see also* **–köpfig.**

Stiesel [ˈʃtiːzəl], *m. See* **Stießel.**

stieß [ʃtiːs], **stieße,** *see* **stoßen.**

Stießel [ˈʃtiːsəl], *m.* (*coll.*) boor, clod.

[1]**Stift** [ʃtɪft], *m.* **(-(e)s,** *pl.* **-e)** 1. pin, peg, stud, brad, tack; quid, plug (*of tobacco*); 2. pencil, crayon; 3. (*coll.*) apprentice, stripling, youngster, chap.

[2]**Stift,** *n.* **(-(e)s,** *pl.* **-e(r))** foundation; charitable institution, home (for old people); religious establishment, seminary, training-college (*for clergymen*); (*dial.*) convent, monastery; (*obs.*) chapter, bishopric.

stiften [ˈʃtɪftən], *v.t.* found, establish, institute; (*coll.*) give, endow, donate, make a present of; bring about, originate, cause, make; *Brand –,* set on fire, set fire to; *Freundschaft –,* promote a friendship; *Frieden –,* make peace; *Gutes –,* do good; *Ordnung –,* put in order; *Unfrieden –,* make trouble, sow discord; *Unheil –,* cause mischief. **Stifter,** *m.* founder, sponsor, donor; author, originator.

Stifts|dame, *f.*, **–fräulein,** *n.* canoness. **–gebäude,** *n.* chapter-house. **–gemeinde,** *f.* congregation of a cathedral. **–gut,** *n.* chapter property; ecclesiastical endowment. **–herr,** *m.* canon, prebendary. **–hütte,** *f.* (*B.*) (Jewish) tabernacle. **–kirche,** *f.* collegiate church. **–pfründe,** *f.* prebend. **–schule,** *f.* school attached to the chapters of collegiate churches. **–versammlung,** *f.* meeting of a chapter.

Stiftung [ˈʃtɪftuŋ], *f.* 1. establishment; foundation, institution; 2. endowment, bequest, donation, gift, grant; 3. originating, causing, making. **Stiftungs|-fest,** *n.* commemoration *or* founder's day. **–urkunde,** *f.* deed of foundation.

Stiftzahn [ˈʃtɪfttsaːn], *m.* pivot-tooth.

Stigma [ˈstɪgma], *n.* **(-s,** *pl.* **-ta** *or* **-men)** mark, stigma; scar (*of plants*); spiracle, stigma (*of insects*). **stigmatisieren** [–tiˈziːrən], *v.t.* stigmatize, brand.

Stil [ʃtiːl], *m.* **(-(e)s,** *pl.* **-e)** style; manner, way, kind; *im großen –,* on a large scale, in the grand manner. **Stil|art,** *f.* genre. **–blüte,** *f.* pun, bull, spoonerism. **stilecht,** *adj.* true to style.

Stilett [ʃtiˈlɛt], *n.* **(-(e)s,** *pl.* **-e)** stiletto.

Stilgefühl [ˈʃtiːlgəfyːl], *n.* stylistic sense, feeling for style. **stil|gerecht,** *adj. See* **–voll. stilisieren** [–liˈziːrən], *v.t.* compose, word; *gut stilisiert,* written in good style, well written. **Stilist** [–ˈlɪst], *m.* **(-en,** *pl.* **-en)** writer with a good style, elegant writer. **Stilistik,** *f.* art of composition. **stilistisch,** *adj.* stylistic; *in –er Hinsicht,* stylistically, as regards style. **Stil|kleid,** *n.* period costume. **–kunde,** *f. See* **Stilistik.**

still [ʃtɪl], *adj.* silent, quiet, hushed, soft; still, motionless, stagnant, dull, lifeless, inanimate; calm, peaceful, tranquil; tacit, secret; *–es Beileid,* unspoken sympathy; *wir bitten um –es Beileid,* no visits of condolence desired (*in announcement of a death*); *Stiller Freitag,* Good Friday; *–es Gebet,* silent prayer; *–er Gesellschafter,* see *–er Teilhaber*; *–es Glück,* quiet contentment; *–e Hoffnung,* secret *or* unspoken hopes; *im –en,* quietly, in silence, secretly, privately; in one's *or* at heart, (*coll.*) on the quiet; *–e Jahreszeit,* slack season; *–e Liebe,* secret *or* unavowed love; *–e Messe,* low mass; *Stille Nacht,* Christmas Eve; *bei –er Nacht,* at dead of night; *Stiller Ozean,* Pacific (Ocean); *–e Reserven,* hidden reserves; *–er Teilhaber,* sleeping *or* (*Am.*) silent partner; *dem –en Trunk ergeben,* addicted to secret drinking; *–e Übereinkunft,* tacit agreement *or* understanding; *sich – verhalten,* not stir *or* move, keep still *or* quiet, (*fig.*) bide one's time, (*coll.*) lie low; *–er Vorbehalt,* mental reservation; *–er Vorwurf,* silent reproach; (*Prov.*) *–e Wasser sind* or *gründen tief,* still waters run deep; *Stille Woche,* Passion Week; *–e Wut,* dumb rage; paralytic rabies.

still|beglückt, *adj.* secretly happy. **–bleiben,** *irr.v.i.* be still, keep quiet.

Stille [ˈʃtɪlə], *f.* quiet, stillness, silence; calm, tranquillity, repose, peace; *in der* or *aller –,* silently, quietly; secretly, furtively, (*coll.*) on the quiet; *in der – abziehen,* slink *or* steal away; *in der – leben,* lead a secluded life; *die – vor dem Sturm,* the lull before the storm.

stille, *adj.* (*coll.*) *see* **still.**

Stilleben [ˈʃtɪlleːbən], *n.* (*Art*) still-life. **stillegen,** *v.t.* bring to a standstill, stop; immobilize (*fractured limb*), lay up, put out of commission (*a ship etc.*), shut down (*a business*).

Stil|lehre, *f. See* **–kunde.**

stillen [ˈʃtɪlən], *v.t.* quiet, hush, silence, calm; still, appease, soothe, mitigate, allay (*pain etc.*); stay, quench (*thirst etc.*); staunch (*blood*); gratify, satisfy (*desires*); nurse, suckle (*a child*). **stillend,** *adj.* soothing, sedative, lenitive; *–e Mutter,* nursing mother.

Still|geld, *n.* insurance payment for nursing mothers. **–halteabkommen,** *n.* standstill agreement, moratorium. **still|halten,** *irr.v.i., v.t.* keep quiet *or* still; pause, stop. **Stillhaltung,** *f.* (*Comm.*) respite, delay in payments, moratorium.

stilliegen [ˈʃtɪlliːgən], *irr.v.i.* lie quiet; lie down; lie to (*as a ship*); (*fig.*) lie dormant; (*of business*) be at a standstill; (*of traffic*) be suspended.

stillos [ˈʃtiːlloːs], *adj.* without style, in bad taste.

stillschweigen [ˈʃtɪlʃvaɪgən], *irr.v.i.* be silent; *zu etwas –,* pass a th. over in silence, close one's eyes to a th. **Stillschweigen,** *n.* silence, secrecy. **still-schweigend,** *adj.* silent; tacit, implied, implicit.

Stillstand [ˈʃtɪlʃtant], *m.* standstill, stop, stoppage; cessation, suspension; (*fig.*) inaction, stagnation, inactivity; deadlock; (*Astr.*) station; *zum – bringen,* stop, halt, arrest, bring to a standstill; *zum – kommen,* come to a standstill, (*fig.*) reach a deadlock. **still|stehen,** *irr.v.i.* stop, stand still; (*Mil.*) stand at attention; (*fig.*) (*of machinery*) be idle, (*of business*) be at a standstill; *da steht mir der Verstand still,* my mind reels, I am staggered *or* (*coll.*) flabbergasted (*bei,* at); (*Mil.*) *stillgestanden!* (stand at) attention! **–stehend,** *adj.* stationary, motionless; at a standstill, idle, inactive, stagnant.

Stillung [ˈʃtɪluŋ], *f.* stilling, appeasing; gratification; quenching; staunching; nursing, breastfeeding, suckling, lactation.

stillvergnügt [ˈʃtɪlfɛrgnyːkt], *adj.* quietly contented, placid, calm and serene. **Stillzeit,** *f.* lactation period.

Stil|möbel, *n.pl.* period furniture. **–übung,** *f.* exercise in writing, practice in composition. **stil|voll,** *adj.* stylish. **–widrig,** *adj.* in bad taste.

Stimm|abgabe [ˈʃtɪm–], *f.* voting, polling, vote. **–band,** *n.* (*pl.* **¨-er**) vocal c(h)ord. **stimmberechtigt,** *adj.* entitled to vote, enfranchised. **Stimm|-berechtigung,** *f. See* **–recht. –bildung,** *f.* voice production. **–bruch,** *m.* breaking of the voice. **–bürger,** *m.* (*Swiss*) elector.

Stimme [ˈʃtɪmə], *f.* voice; vote; opinion; (*Mus.*) part; sound-post (*of a violin*); stop (*of an organ*); –

–abgeben, (cast one's) vote; (*Mus.*) ***die –n austeilen,*** distribute the parts; (***gut***) ***bei –,*** in (good) voice; ***nicht bei –,*** not in voice; ***ohne eine – dagegen,*** without a (single) dissentient voice; ***sich der – enthalten,*** withhold one's opinion, abstain from voting; ***entscheidende –,*** casting vote; (*Mus.*) ***erste –,*** soprano; ***ihm seine – geben,*** give him one's vote, vote for him; ***keine – haben,*** have no say *or* no voice in the matter; ***– der Presse,*** press comment; ***die –n sammeln,*** put the matter to the vote; ***–n werben,*** canvass; ***Sitz und – haben,*** have a seat and vote.

stimmen [ˈʃtɪmən], **1.** *v.t.* tune (*an instrument*) (***nach,*** to); (*fig.*) dispose, incline (*a p.*) (***für,*** towards), prejudice (*a p.*) (***für,*** in favour of; ***gegen,*** against); ***ihn fröhlich –,*** put him in a good humour; ***die Nachricht hat mich traurig gestimmt,*** the news has saddened *or* depressed me *or* has made me (feel) sad; ***seine Forderungen hoch –,*** pitch one's demands high; ***er ist schlecht gestimmt,*** he is in low spirits *or* in a bad mood. **2.** *v.i.* 1. agree, tally, correspond; be true *or* right *or* correct; be in order, be all right; accord, be in tune, be in keeping, harmonize; tone, (*coll.*) go, fit in (***zu,*** with); 2. vote (***für,*** for; ***gegen,*** against); (***das***) ***stimmt,*** (that is) all right *or* (*sl.*) OK *or* okay.

Stimmen|einheit, *f.* unanimity; ***mit –,*** unanimously, with no dissentient vote, nem. con. **–fang,** *m.* canvassing; ***auf – ausgehen,*** go round canvassing. **–gewirr,** *n.* confused voices, din *or* babel of voices. **–gleichheit,** *f.* equality of votes (for and against); ***bei – den Ausschlag geben,*** give the casting vote. **–mehrheit,** *f.* majority (*of votes*); ***einfache –,*** bare majority. **–minderheit,** *f.* minority (*of votes*). **–prüfung,** *f.* scrutiny *or* recounting of votes.

Stimmenthaltung [ˈʃtɪmˀɛnthaltuŋ], *f.* abstention from voting.

Stimmen|werber, *m.* canvasser. **–zähler,** *m.* (*Parl.*) teller.

Stimmer [ˈʃtɪmər], *m.* (*Mus.*) tuner. **stimm|fähig,** *adj. See* **–berechtigt. Stimm|führer,** *m.* spokesman. **–gabel,** *f.* tuning-fork. **stimmhaft,** *adj.* (*Phonet.*) voiced. **Stimmlage,** *f.* register, pitch. **stimmlich,** *adj.* vocal. **stimmlos,** *adj.* (*Phonet.*) voiceless. **Stimm|recht,** *n.* right to vote, franchise, suffrage. **–rechtlerin,** *f.* suffragette. **–ritze,** *f.* (*Anat.*) glottis. **–ritzendeckel,** *m.* (*Anat.*) epiglottis. **–ritzenverschluß(laut),** *m.* (*Phonet.*) glottal stop. **–stock,** *m.* sound-post (*of a violin*).

Stimmung [ˈʃtɪmuŋ], *f.* (*Mus.*) tuning, key, pitch; (*fig.*) mood, humour, temper, disposition, sentiment, feeling; state *or* frame of mind, (*Mil. etc.*) morale; (*Comm. etc.*) tendency, tone; impression, atmosphere; (*coll.*) high spirits; ***– machen für,*** canvass, make propaganda for, (*coll.*) plug; ***bei –,*** (*Mus.*) in tune, (*fig.*) in good humour, in good spirits; ***in –,*** in the mood; ***– halten,*** stay in *or* keep tune (*of an instrument*).

Stimmungs|bericht, *m.* opinion poll. **–bild,** *n.* impressionistic picture. **–kanone,** *f.* (*coll.*) life (and soul) of the party. **–mache,** *f.* propaganda, boost(ing). **–mensch,** *m.* moody fellow. **–musik,** *f.* background music. **–umschwung,** *m.* change of attitude *or* mood. **stimmungsvoll,** *adj.* appealing to the emotions; moving, impressive; full of genuine feeling.

Stimm|vieh, *n.* (*coll.*) the fatuous electorate. **–wechsel,** *m. See* **–bruch. –werkzeug,** *n.* vocal organs. **–zettel,** *m.* ballot- *or* voting-paper.

Stimulans [ˈʃti:mulans], *n.* (-, *pl.* **-ntia**) (*Med.*) stimulant. **stimulieren** [–ˈli:rən], *v.t.* stimulate.

Stink|apparat, *m.* (*Zool.*) stink-gland. **–bombe,** *f.* stink-bomb. **–drüse,** *f. See* **–apparat.**

stinken [ˈʃtɪŋkən], *irr.v.i.* stink (***nach,*** of), be fetid, smell foul; (*fig.*) (*coll.*) be fishy; (*Prov.*) ***Eigenlob stinkt,*** self-praise is no recommendation; ***er stinkt nach*** or ***vor Geld,*** he is lousy *or* stiff with money; ***der Junge stinkt vor Faulheit,*** that boy is bone-idle. **stinkend,** *adj. See* **stinkig. stinkfaul,** *adj.* bone-idle. **stinkig,** *adj.* evil-smelling, stinking, fetid, (*fig.*) foul. **Stink|tier,** *n.* skunk. **–wut,** *f.* (*coll.*) filthy temper, towering rage.

Stint [ʃtɪnt], *m.* (**-(e)s,** *pl.* **-e**) (*Ichth.*) smelt (*Osmerus eperlanus*).

Stipendiat [ʃtipɛndiˈa:t], *Austr.*) **Stipendist** [–ˈdɪst], *m.* (**-en,** *pl.* **-en**) scholarship holder, exhibitioner. **Stipendium** [–ˈpɛndium], *n.* (**-s,** *pl.* **-dien**) scholarship, exhibition.

Stippangriff [ˈʃtɪpˀangrɪf], *m.* (*Mil.*) hit-and-run raid.

Stippe [ˈʃtɪpə], *f.* (*dial.*) 1. stigma, mark; pimple, speck, freckle; 2. gravy, sauce. **Stippel,** *m.* (*dial.*) ladle. **stippen,** *v.t.* (*dial.*) steep, dip. **Stippvisite,** *f.* (*coll.*) flying visit, short call.

stipulieren [ʃtipuˈli:rən], *v.t.* stipulate.

stirb [ʃtɪrp], **stirbst, stirbt,** *see* **sterben.**

Stirn [ʃtɪrn], *f.* (-, *pl.* **-en**) forehead, brow; (*Archit.*) front; (*fig.*) impudence, cheek, face; ***ihm etwas an der – ansehen,*** read s.th. in his face; ***ihm auf der – geschrieben stehen,*** be written in his face; ***ihm die – bieten,*** show a bold front to him, defy him; ***sich vor der – schlagen,*** stand aghast; (*fig.*) ***eiserne*** or ***eherne –,*** bold front, brazen-faced impudence; ***mit erhobener –,*** holding one's head high; ***er hatte die –,*** he had the cheek; ***die – runzeln,*** wrinkle one's brow.

Stirn|ader, *f.* frontal vein. **–ansicht,** *f.* front view. **–band,** *n.* head-band; fillet, frontlet. **–bein,** *n.* frontal bone. **–beinhöhle,** *f.* frontal sinus. **–binde,** *f. See* **–band.**

Stirne [ˈʃtɪrnə], *f. See* **Stirn.**

Stirn|falte, *f.* wrinkle of the brow, furrow. **–fläche,** *f.* face (*of an arch*), front, end-surface. **–höhle,** *f.* frontal cavity, frontal sinus. **–holz,** *n.* end-grained wood. **–lage,** *f.* frontal presentation (*of foetus*). **–lappen,** *m.* frontal lobe. **–locke,** *f.* forelock. **–rad,** *n.* spur-gear. **–radgetriebe,** *n.* spur-gearing. **–riemen,** *m.* frontlet, head-piece (*of a bridle*). **–runzeln,** *n.* frown(ing). **–seite,** *f.* (*Archit.*) façade, front.

stob [ʃtob], **stöbe** [ˈʃtø:bə], *see* **stieben.**

stoben [ˈʃto:bən], *v.t.* (*dial.*) stew.

Stöberei [ʃtø:bəˈraɪ], *f.* (*dial.*) spring-clean(ing). **stöbern** [ˈʃtø:bərn], *v.i.* 1. hunt about, search everywhere, rummage; (*dial.*) do spring-cleaning; ***in einem Buch –,*** turn over the leaves of a book; 2. drift, blow about (*of snow*); drizzle (*of rain*).

Stocher [ˈʃtɔxər], *m.* poker; toothpick. **stochern** *v.t., v.i.* (***in*** (*Dat.*)) poke about (in); pick (*one's teeth*); poke, rake, stir (*the fire*).

Stock [ʃtɔk], *m.* 1. (**-(e)s,** *pl.* **¨-e**) stick, staff, rod, pole, wand, cane, walking-stick; stem (*of a plant*), trunk, stump (*of a tree, tooth etc.*); (*Mus.*) baton, (*Bill.*) cue; stock, block, body (*of an anvil etc.*); stocks (*for culprits*); (bee)hive; mountain-mass, massif, mass (*of rocks etc.*); pot plant; (vine-)stock; ***in den – legen,*** put in the stocks; ***im – sitzen,*** be (put) in the stocks; ***einen Hut über den – schlagen,*** put a hat on the block; ***über – und Stein,*** up hill and down dale; ***am – gehen,*** walk with (the help of) a stick; ***Regiment des –es,*** rule of the rod; 2. (**-s,** *pl.* **-s**) (*Comm.*) capital, stocks, funds; 3. (**-(e)s,** *pl.* **-(e)** *or* **-werke**) storey (*of a house*), floor (*above ground-floor*); ***wie viel – hat es?*** how many storeys has it? ***im ersten –,*** on the first (*or Am.* second) floor.

stockblind [ˈʃtɔkblɪnt], *adj.* stone-blind. **Stockdegen,** *m.* sword-cane. **stock|dumm,** *adj.* utterly stupid, blockheaded. **–dunkel,** *adj.* pitch-dark.

Stöckel [ˈʃtœkəl], *m.* (*dial.*) heel (*of shoe*). **Stöckelschuh,** *m.* high-heeled shoe.

stocken [ˈʃtɔkən], *v.i.* (*aux.* h. *&* s.) 1. stop (short), come to *or* be at a standstill; (*fig.*) make no progress, stagnate, (*coll.*) hang fire; halt, hesitate, falter, (*fig.*) reach a deadlock; stop running *or* flowing *or* circulating, stagnate; (*fig.*) (*as conversation*) flag, (*as trade*) be slack; ***im Reden –,*** break down, falter, hesitate, (*coll.*) get stuck; 2. (*dial.*) curdle, coagulate, cake, thicken; turn mouldy *or* fusty, decay, spoil; (*dial.*) ***gestockte Milch,*** curdled milk. **Stocken,** *n.* stopping, cessation; stagnation, interruption; ***ins – geraten,*** come to a standstill; ***– der Zähne,*** dental caries.

Stock|engländer, *m.* true-blue *or* typical Englishman, John Bull. **–ente,** *f.* (*Orn.*) mallard (*Anas platyrhynchos*).

Stockerl [ˈʃtɔkərl], *n.* (**-s,** *pl.* **-(n)**) (*Austr.*) stool.

stock|finster, *adj.* *See* **–dunkel. Stock|fisch,** *m.* stockfish, dried cod; (*fig.*) insufferable bore. **–fleck,** *m.* damp-stain; (*Bot.*) mildew. **stock|fleckig,** *adj.* stained by damp, mouldy; foxed, spotted (*of paper*). **–fremd,** *adj.* utterly strange. **–gelehrt,** *adj.* pedantic. **Stock|griff,** *m.* walking-stick handle. **–haus,** *n.* (*obs.*) jail.

stockig [ˈʃtɔkɪç], *adj.* mildewed, mouldy, musty, fusty; obstinate, stubborn; stocky, stumpy; ***–e Zähne,*** decayed teeth.

–stöckig [–ˈʃtœkɪç], *adj.suff.* -storied, -floor.

Stock|laterne, *f.* cresset. **–makler,** *m.* stockjobber, stock broker. **–meister,** *m.* (*obs.*) jailer. **–prügel,** *pl.* flogging, caning, beating. **–punkt,** *m.* solidifying point. **–rose,** *f.* (*Bot.*) hollyhock (*Althaea rosea*). **–schirm,** *m.* walking-stick umbrella. **–schläge,** *pl.* *See* **–prügel. –schnupfen,** *m.* chronic cold, thick cold. **stock|steif,** *adj.* (as) stiff as a poker. **–still,** *adj.* stock-still. **–taub,** *adj.* stone-deaf, (as) deaf as a post.

Stockung [ˈʃtɔkuŋ], *f.* stopping, stoppage, standstill, cessation; interruption, pause, delay, (*coll.*) hold-up; (*Med.*) stasis; stagnation; congestion, (traffic) block *or* jam.

Stock|werk, *n.* storey, floor, tier. **–zahn,** *m.* (*dial.*) molar.

Stoff [ʃtɔf], *m.* (**-(e)s,** *pl.* **-e**) matter, substance, body; subject, subject-matter, theme, topic; material, stuff, textile, cloth, fabric; (paper) pulp; (*Studs. sl.*) beer; ***– zum Lesen,*** reading matter; ***– zum Nachdenken,*** food for thought. **Stoffbahn,** *f.* web of cloth. **stoff|bespannt,** *adj.* fabric-covered. **–bildend,** *adj.* tissue-forming.

Stoffel [ˈʃtɔfəl], *m.* boor, yokel, dolt, lout, booby. **stoff(e)lig,** *adj.* uncouth, loutish, stupid.

Stoffetzen [ˈʃtɔffɛtsən], *m.* scrap of material.

Stoff|gebiet, *n.* range of subjects. **–gewicht,** *n.* specific gravity. **–halter,** *m.* (*Sew.-mach.*) foot. **stofflich,** *adj.* material; with regard to the subject-matter. **Stoff|muster,** *n.* pattern (of fabric). **–puppe,** *f.* stuffed doll. **–teilchen,** *n.* particle of matter.

Stoffülle [ˈʃtɔffylə], *f.* wealth of material.

Stoff|umsatz, *m.* *See* **–wechsel. –verwandtschaft,** *f.* chemical affinity. **–wahl,** *f.* choice of subject. **–wechsel,** *m,* metabolism. **–wechselgleichgewicht,** *n.* nutritive equilibrium. **–wechselgröße,** *f.* metabolic rate. **–zerfall,** *m.* decay, decomposition.

stöhle [ˈʃtøːlə], *see* **stehlen.**

stöhnen [ˈʃtøːnən], *v.i.* groan, moan (***über*** (*Acc.*), at; ***vor*** (*Dat.*), with). **Stöhnen,** *n.* groaning, moaning.

Stola [ˈʃtoːla], *f.* (-, *pl.* **-len**), **Stole,** *f.* stole, (*R.C.*) surplice.

Stolle [ˈʃtɔlə], *f.* (*Austr.*) *see* **¹Stollen.**

¹Stollen [ˈʃtɔlən], *m.* fruit-loaf.

²Stollen, *m.* post, prop, support; (*Mil.*) dugout; (*Min.*) adit, gallery, tunnel; calkin (*of horseshoe*). **Stollen|arbeit,** *f.*, **–bau,** *m.* tunnelling. **–hauer, –häuer,** *m.* tunneller. **–holz,** *n.* pit props.

Stolper [ˈʃtɔlpər], *m.* (*dial.*) stumble; blunder. **Stolperdraht,** *m.* trip-wire. **stolperig,** *adj.* stumbling, blundering; uneven, rough, bumpy (*as a road*). **stolpern,** *v.i.* (*aux.* h. & s.) stumble, trip (***über*** (*Acc.*), over); blunder.

stolz [ʃtɔltz], *adj.* proud (***auf*** (*Acc.*), of); haughty, arrogant, conceited, vain (about); (*fig.*) fine, noble, majestic, splendid, stately; ***– sein auf*** (*Acc.*), be proud of, take pride in. **Stolz,** *m.* pride (***auf*** (*Acc.*), in); conceit, vanity, haughtiness, arrogance; ***seinen – in eine S. setzen,*** pride o.s. on a th., make a th. one's boast. **stolzieren** [–ˈtsiːrən], *v.i.* (*aux.* s.) flaunt, swagger, strut, (*as a horse*) prance.

Stopf|büchse, *f.* (*Mech.*) stuffing-box. **–ei,** *n.* darning-ball *or* mushroom.

Stöpfel [ˈʃtœpfəl], *m.* (*dial.*) *see* **Stöpsel.**

stopfen [ˈʃtɔpfən], **1.** *v.t.* fill (*a pipe etc.*), stuff, cram; darn, mend (*stockings*); plug, close, stop up, mute (*a wind instrument*); (*dial.*) cork; caulk (*a ship*); (*Mil.*) cease fire; (*coll.*) ***ihm den Mund*** (or ***das Maul***) **–**, shut his mouth, make him shut up; ***gestopft voll,*** crammed full; ***gestopfte Trompete,*** muted trumpet. **2.** *v.i.* (*coll.*) be filling; bind, cause constipation; ***Eier –,*** eggs are binding. **3.** *v.r.* stuff o.s., gorge; become blocked *or* jammed.

¹Stopfen, *n.* stuffing, cramming.

²Stopfen, *m.* (*dial.*) *see* **Stöpsel.**

Stopf|garn, *n.* darning-wool. **–mittel,** *n.* astringent, styptic. **–nadel,** *f.* darning-needle. **–naht,** *f.* darn. **–pilz,** *m.* *See* **–ei. –werg,** *n.* oakum (*for caulking*).

Stopp [ʃtɔp], *m.* ban, prohibition; freeze (*prices, incomes*).

¹Stoppel [ˈʃtɔpəl], *m.* (*Austr.*) *see* **Stöpsel.**

²Stoppel, *f.* (-, *pl.* **-n**) stubble; *pl.* pin-feathers, bristles (*of beard*). **Stoppel|bart,** *m.* bristly *or* stubbly beard. **–feder,** *f.* pin-feather. **–feld,** *n.* stubble-field, field of stubble. **stoppelig,** *adj.* stubbly, bristly. **Stoppelmast,** *f.* stubble-grazing. **stoppeln,** *v.t., v.i.* glean. **Stoppel|vers,** *m.* halting verse. **–weide,** *f.* stubble-pasture. **–werk,** *n.* patchwork, compilation.

stoppen [ˈʃtɔpən], *v.t., v.i.* 1. stop; 2. time (with a stop-watch). **Stopp|licht,** *n.* (*Motor.*) stop and tail lamp. **–preis,** *m.* ceiling-price, price limit. **–schild,** *m.* (*Motor.*) halt sign. **–uhr,** *f.* stop-watch.

Stöpsel [ˈʃtœpsəl], *m.* stopper, cork, bung, plug; (*coll.*) little runt. **Stöpsel|automat,** *m.* (*Elec.*) automatic cut-out. **–glas,** *n.* glass-stoppered bottle. **stöpseln,** *v.t.* cork, stopper, plug. **Stöpselschnur,** *f.* (*Elec.*) lead with plug.

¹Stör [ʃtøːr], *m.* (**-s,** *pl.* **-e**) (*Ichth.*) sturgeon (*Acipensidae*).

²Stör, *f.* (*Austr., Swiss*) ***in*** or ***auf die – gehen, auf der – arbeiten,*** work at a customer's house, do job-work.

störanfällig [ˈʃtøːrˀanfɛlɪç], *adj.* (*Mech.*) prone to trouble, (*Rad.*) susceptible to interference. **Stör|-angriff,** *m.* (*Mil.*) nuisance raid. **–anzeigelampe,** *f.* (*Motor. etc.*) warning light, fault indicator lamp. **–befreiung,** *f.* (*Rad.*) elimination of interference.

Storch [ʃtɔrç], *m.* (**-(e)s,** *pl.* **¨-e**) stork; (*Orn.*) ***schwarzer –,*** *see* **Schwarzstorch**; ***weißer –,*** *see* **Weißstorch**; (*coll.*) ***da brat' mir einer einen –!*** did you ever hear anything like it! that beats everything! (*sl.*) that's the giddy limit! **storchbeinig,** *adj.* spindle-shanked. **Storch(en)nest,** *n.* stork's nest. **Storchschnabel,** *m.* stork's bill, (*Bot.*) geranium, (*Surg.*) cranesbill, (*drawing*) pantograph.

Store [stɔr], *m.* (**-s,** *pl.* **-s**) (window) curtain.

Stör|einsatz, *m.* (*Av.*) *see* **–angriff.**

stören [ˈʃtøːrən], **1.** *v.t.* interrupt, disturb, inconvenience, trouble, bother, irritate, vex, annoy, harass (*the enemy*); upset, interfere with, disarrange, disorder, derange, (*Rad.*) jam; (*dial.*) scratch, scrape (*as hens*); ***laß dich nicht –!*** do not let me disturb you! ***stört Sie mein Rauchen?*** or ***stört es Sie, daß*** or ***wenn ich rauche?*** do you mind my smoking *or* mind if I smoke? ***geistig gestört,*** mentally deranged; ***gestörter Schlaf,*** broken sleep; (*Tele.*) ***gestörte Leitung,*** faulty line, fault on the line. **2.** *v.i.* intrude, be in the way, be awkward *or* inconvenient; be obtrusive, spoil the effect *or* the picture, be disturbing. **störend,** *adj.* interfering, troublesome, annoying, harassing, inconvenient, awkward; disturbing, obtrusive. **Störenfried,** *m.* (**-(e)s,** *pl.* **-e**) intruder, troublemaker, mischief-maker. **Störer,** *m.* troublesome p., meddler, kill-joy, intruder; *see also* **Störsender.**

Stör|feuer, *n.* (*Mil.*) harassing fire. **–flecke,** *m.pl.* (*radar*) clutter. **–flieger,** *m.* (*Av.*) nuisance *or* sneak raider. **–flug,** *m.* (*Av.*) *see* **–angriff. störfrei,** *adj.* (*of elec. apparatus*) causing no interference, interference-suppressed; *see also* **störungsfrei. Störfunk,** *m.* (*Rad.*) jamming.

Storger [ˈʃtɔrgər], *m.* (*dial.*) vagabond, tramp.

Störgeräusch [ˈʃtø:rgərɔyʃ], *n.* (*Rad.*) background noise, interference, static, atmospherics.

stornieren [ʃtɔrˈni:rən], *v.t.* (*Comm.*) cancel, annul, rescind; reverse, delete (*an entry*). **Stornierung,** *f.*, **Storno** [ˈʃtɔrno], *n.* (**-s,** *pl.* **-ni**) cancellation.

störrig [ˈʃtœrıç], *adj.* stubborn, obstinate, headstrong, (*coll.*) pigheaded, mulish; refractory, unmanageable, (*of horse*) restive. **Störrigkeit,** *f.* stubbornness, obstinacy, (*coll.*) pig-headedness; refractoriness, restiveness. **störrisch** *See* **störrig.**

Stör|schutz, *m.* (*Rad.*) interference *or* noise suppressor, screening. **–sender,** *m.* (*Rad.*) jamming station. **–sendung,** *f.* jamming.

Störung [ˈʃtø:ruŋ], *f.* disturbance; trouble, inconvenience, bother, upset, intrusion, interruption, interference; disorder, disarrangement, derangement, obstruction, (*coll.*) hitch, (*of traffic*) dislocation, (*Mech. etc.*) breakdown, fault, failure, (*coll.*) trouble; (*Rad.*) (*natural*) atmospherics, static, (*artificial*) interference, jamming; (*Astr., Magnet.*) perturbation; ***geistige –,*** mental derangement; ***verzeihen Sie die –!*** excuse the interruption! pardon the intrusion!

Störungs|dienst, *m.* (*Rad., Tele.*) faults section, servicing. **–feuer,** *n. See* **Störfeuer. störungsfrei,** *adj.* undisturbed, uninterrupted; (*Rad.*) free from interference (*of reception*). **Störungs|-stelle,** *f.* (*Tele.*) fault; *see also* **–dienst. –sucher,** *m.* (*Tele.*) lineman. **–trupp,** *m.* (*Tele.*) repair gang.

Stoß [ʃto:s], *m.* (**-es,** *pl.* **⸗e**) 1. push, shove, thrust, (*swimming, Bill.*) stroke, (*Fenc.*) thrust, pass; (*of bird of prey*) swoop; knock, blow, hit, (*with fist*) punch, (*with foot*) kick, (*with head*) butt, (*with stick*) poke, (*with elbow*) nudge, dig; bump, jolt, jerk, jog; collision, crash, shock, impact, (*of firearms*) recoil, kick, (*explosion*) blast, (*of trumpet*) flourish, (*Elec.*) surge; ***ihm einen – versetzen,*** give him a push, (*fig.*) come as *or* be a blow to him; (*fig.*) ***seinem Glauben einen – versetzen,*** shake his faith; (*fig.*) ***seiner Gesundheit einen – versetzen,*** affect *or* damage his health; (*fig.*) ***einen – erleiden,*** suffer a setback, be impaired; (*coll.*) ***ich kann einen – vertragen,*** I can take it; (*coll.*) ***gib deinem Herzen einen –!*** be a sport! 2. (*of papers*) bundle, pile, heap, stack, sheaf, (*coll.*.) wad; 3. (*Dressm.*) seam, hem, (*Mech.*) butt-joint.

Stoßarbeiter [ˈʃtosʔarbaıtər], *m.* shock-worker. **stoßartig,** *adj.* sporadic, abrupt, intermittent. **Stoß|balken,** *m.* abutment beam. **–bedarf,** *m.* emergency requirements. **–brigade,** *f. See* **–truppen. –dämpfer,** *m.* shock absorber. **–degen,** *m.* rapier, foil. **–druck,** *m.* impact pressure.

Stößel [ˈʃtø:səl], *m.* pestle; rammer, pounder, beetle, ramming *or* tamping tool; plunger, (*Motor.*) tappet.

stoßen [ˈʃto:sən], **1.** *irr.v.t.* push, shove, thrust; strike, knock, hit, (*with fist*) punch, (*with foot*) kick, (*with stick*) poke, (*with head*) butt, ram, (*with elbow*) nudge; buffet, jab, jog, jostle; (*with implement*) pound, crush, bruise, bray, powder, pulverize; (*fig.*) drive out (***aus,*** of *or* from), turn out (of), expel, oust (from); ***ihm den Degen in die Brust –,*** plunge the dagger into his breast; ***ich habe mir den Kopf gestoßen,*** I have banged *or* bumped my head; ***ich habe mir den Kopf am Stuhl gestoßen,*** I have banged my head on the chair; ***ihn über den Haufen –,*** knock *or* bowl him over, knock him to the ground, run him down; (*fig.*) ***ihn vor den Kopf –,*** offend *or* antagonize him; (*fig.*) ***ihn mit der Nase auf etwas –,*** shove s.th. under his nose, rub his nose in s.th.; (*fig.*) ***ihn vom Throne –,*** topple him from the throne; ***von sich –,*** push away *or* aside, (*fig.*) discard, reject, repudiate. **2.** *irr.v.r.* knock *or* bang *or* hurt o.s.; ***sich am Stuhl –,*** bump *or* bang o.s. on the chair; (*fig.*) ***sich – an*** (*Dat.*), take offence at *or* exception to, take amiss; object to, disapprove of, be shocked at *or* by. **3.** *irr.v.i.* 1. push, shove, thrust, kick (***nach,*** against); (*of goats etc.*) butt, (*of guns*) kick, recoil; jostle, jolt, run, bump (***an*** (*Acc.*), against), (*Mech.*) butt (against), (*fig.*) border, abut (on), touch, adjoin; ***auf eine Klippe –,*** run on to a reef; ***ans Land –,*** run ashore; ***vom Lande –,*** put (out) to sea; ***ins Horn –,*** blow *or* sound (a blast on) the horn; (*fig.*) ***ins gleiche Horn –,*** sing the same tune (***mit,*** as); 2. (*aux.* s.) swoop down, pounce (***auf*** (*Acc.*), upon), (*fig.*) come *or* stumble (upon *or* across), encounter, (happen to) meet (with), chance (upon); ***auf Hindernisse –,*** run *or* come up against difficulties; ***– zu,*** join up with; 3. (*aux.* h. *&* s.) bump, bang, knock (***gegen, an*** (*Acc.*), against); ***mit dem Bein gegen den Tisch –,*** bang *or* knock *or* bump one's leg on the table; ***mit den Zehen – an*** (*Acc.*), stub one's toes on.

Stoß|fänger, *m.* buffer, bumper; *see also* **–dämpfer. stoß|fest,** *adj.* shock-proof, shock-resistant. **–frei,** *adj.* free, smooth (*of movement*). **Stoß|fuge,** *f.* butt-joint. **–gebet,** *n.* short fervent prayer.

Stößig [ˈʃtø:sıç], *adj.* butting, vicious, (*as goats etc.*).

Stoß|keil, *m.* (*Mil.*) spearhead. **–kissen,** *n. See* **–scheibe. –kraft,** *f.* (*Mech.*) impact, impetus, (*coll.*) thrust, drive, force. **–kugel,** *f.* (*Spt.*) shot, weight. **–platte,** *f.* butt-plate (*covering a butt-joint*). **–polster,** *n. See* **–scheibe. –punkt,** *m.* point of impact. **–riemen,** *m.* check-brace (*of a coach*). **–scheibe,** *f.* buffer. **–seufzer,** *m.* deep heartfelt sigh. **stoß|sicher,** *adj. See* **–fest. Stoß|-stange,** *f.* (*Motor.*) bumper, (*Am.*) fender. **–taktik,** *f.* (*Mil.*) shock tactics. **–trupp,** *m.* assault detachment, raiding party, *pl.* shock troops. **–verkehr,** *m.* rush-hour traffic. **–waffe,** *f.* stabbing weapon. **stoßweise,** *adv.* by jerks, by fits and starts, jerkily, sporadically, intermittently, in waves. **Stoß|welle,** *f.* percussion wave, shock-wave. **–wind,** *m.* gust (of wind), squall. **–zahn,** *m.* tusk.

Stotterer [ˈʃtɔtərər], *m.* stutterer, stammerer. **stottern,** *v.i.* stammer, stutter; (*Motor.*) splutter. **Stottern,** *n.* stuttering, stammering; (*coll.*) ***auf – kaufen,*** buy on the instalment plan *or* (*coll.*) on the never-never.

stowen [ˈʃto:vən], *v.t.* (*dial.*) steam, stew.

stracks [ʃtraks], *adv.* straightway, directly, (*coll.*) right away, on the spot; direct, straight (ahead); exactly.

Straf|änderung [ˈʃtra:f–], *f.* commutation of sentence. **–androhung,** *f.* ***unter –,*** prohibited under penalty. **–anstalt,** *f.* penal institution, penitentiary, prison, jail, gaol, (*Mil.*) detention barracks. **–antrag,** *m.* sentence proposed *or* demanded (by the public prosecutor). **–anzeige,** *f.* ***– erstatten gegen,*** bring a charge against. **–arbeit, –aufgabe,** *f.* (*school*) imposition, lines. **–aufschub,** *m.* reprieve. **–aussetzung,** *f.* suspension of sentence.

strafbar [ˈʃtra:fba:r], *adj.* punishable, criminal (*offence*), culpable, liable to punishment (*a p.*); ***– sein,*** be punishable, be an offence (***nach,*** under); ***sich – machen,*** be liable to prosecution, incur a penalty. **Strafbarkeit,** *f.* criminal nature (*of an act*), culpability, guilt (*of a p.*).

Straf|befehl, *m.* penal order. **–befugnis,** *f.* penal authority. **–bestimmungen,** *f.pl.* penal laws, penalties. **–dienst,** *m.* (*Mil.*) extra duties.

Strafe [ˈʃtra:fə], *f.* punishment, penalty, fine; judgement, sentence; chastisement, (*fig.*) retribution; ***bei – des Todes,*** on pain *or* penalty of death; ***er hat seine –,*** he got what he deserved *or* (*coll.*) what was coming to him; ***ihm zur –,*** in order to punish him, as a punishment for him.

strafen [ˈʃtra:fən], *v.t.* punish, (*Spt. etc.*) penalize; chastise; (*B.*) blame, reprove, rebuke, censure; ***ihn an Geld (und Gut) –,*** fine him, inflict a fine on him; ***mit der Rute –,*** inflict corporal punishment; ***ihn Lügen –,*** give the lie to him; ***solche Fehler – sich selbst,*** such faults bring their own punishment. **strafend,** *adj.* punishing, punitive; avenging; (*Law*) penal; (*fig.*) reproachful (*glance*).

Straf|entlassene(r), *m.* ex-convict. **–erkenntnis,** *n.* sentence passed on *or* judgement pronounced against a p. **–erlaß,** *m.* remission of punishment; ***allgemeiner –,*** amnesty. **–erleichterung,** *f.* mitigation of punishment. **–exerzieren,** *n.* (*Mil.*) punishment drill. **–expedition,** *f.* punitive expedition.

straff [ʃtraf], **1.** *adj.* stretched, tense, taut, tight; erect, straight; (*fig.*) austere, stern, strict, rigid; ***–er Beutel,*** well-filled *or* well-lined purse; ***–er Busen,*** firm *or* shapely breasts; ***–e Haltung,*** erect bearing, (*fig.*) stern *or* rigid attitude; ***–e Zucht,*** strict *or* rigid discipline. **2.** *adv.* ***– anliegen,*** fit close *or* tightly *or* snugly; ***– anziehen,*** pull tight; tighten, screw up tightly; ***sich – halten,*** stand erect, stand bolt upright.

Straffall ['ʃtra:ffal], *m.* criminal case, punishable offence. **straffällig,** *adj. See* **strafbar.**

straffen ['ʃtrafən], *v.t., v.r.* tighten, stretch, tauten; (*fig.*) make tighter *or* more concise, tighten up. **Straffheit,** *f.* tightness, tension, tautness; tenseness; conciseness; rigidity, rigour, strictness, severity.

straffrei ['ʃtra:ffraɪ], *adj. See* **straflos. Straffreiheit,** *f. See* **Straflosigkeit.**

Straf|gebühr, *f.* fine; *see also* **–zuschlag. –gefangene(r),** *m.* convict. **–geld,** *n. See* **–gebühr. –gericht,** *n.* criminal court; (*fig.*) punishment, vengeance; ***göttliche*** or ***des Himmels –,*** judgement of God. **–gerichtsbarkeit,** *f.* criminal jurisdiction *or* justice. **–gesetz,** *n.* penal law. **–gesetzbuch,** *n.* penal code. **–gesetzgebung,** *f.* penal legislation. **–gewalt,** *f.* disciplinary power *or* authority. **–kammer,** *f.* criminal division. **–kolonie,** *f.* penal *or* convict settlement. **–lager,** *n.* concentration camp.

sträflich ['ʃtrɛ:flɪç], **1.** *adj.* punishable, criminal; culpable, blamable; unpardonable, inexcusable, reprehensible. **2.** *adv.* (*coll.*) severely, enormously, awfully; ***das tut – weh,*** that's excruciatingly painful; ***er ist – faul,*** he's incredibly lazy.

Sträfling ['ʃtrɛ:flɪŋ], *m.* (**-s,** *pl.* **-e**) convict. **Sträflings|fürsorge,** *f.* prison welfare work. **–kleidung,** *f.* prison clothes.

straflos ['ʃtra:flo:s], **1.** *adj.* exempt from punishment. **2.** *adv.* with impunity; ***– ausgehen,*** go unpunished, get off scot-free. **Straflosigkeit,** *f.* impunity, immunity (from criminal proceedings).

Straf|mandat, *n. See* **–befehl. –maß,** *n.* ***höchstes –,*** maximum penalty. **–maßnahme,** *f.* sanction. **strafmildernd,** *adj.* mitigating, extenuating. **Straf|milderung,** *f.* mitigation (*of a penalty*), commutation (*of a sentence*). **–milderungsgrund,** *m.* extenuating circumstance. **strafmündig,** *adj.* of a responsible age. **Straf|mündigkeit,** *f.* age of discretion. **–porto,** *n.* surcharge, postage due, excess postage. **–predigt,** *f.* severe reprimand. **–prozeß,** *m.* criminal case. **–prozeßordnung,** *f.* criminal procedure. **–punkt,** *m.* (*Spt.*) penalty, point deducted. **–raum,** *m.* (*Spt.*) penalty area. **–recht,** *n.* criminal law. **strafrechtlich,** *adj.* penal, criminal; ***– verfolgen,*** prosecute. **Straf|richter,** *m.* criminal-court judge. **–sache,** *f. See* **–fall. –stoß,** *m.* (*Footb.*) penalty (kick). **–tat,** *f.* punishable offence, criminal act, crime, felony. **–verfahren,** *n.* criminal procedure *or* proceedings. **–versetzung,** *f.* transfer for disciplinary reasons. **–verteidiger,** *m.* counsel for the defence. **–vollstreckung,** *f.*, **–vollzug,** *m.* infliction of punishment, execution of sentence; ***sich der*** (or ***dem***) ***– entziehen,*** evade justice. **straf|weise,** *adv.* as a punishment. **–würdig,** *adj. See* **sträflich. Strafzuschlag,** *m.* surcharge.

Strahl [ʃtra:l], *m.* (**-(e)s,** *pl.* **-en**) ray, beam; (*of water*) stream, jet; (*Geom.*) radius, straight line; (*Vet.*) frog (*of hoof*); ***– von Hoffnung,*** gleam *or* glimmer of hope; ***kosmische –en,*** cosmic rays.

Strähl [ʃtrɛ:l], *m.* (**-(s),** *pl.* **-e**) (*dial.*) comb.

Strahl|antrieb, *m.* jet-propulsion. **–düse,** *f.* jet, nozzle.

Strähle ['ʃtrɛ:lə], *f.* (*dial.*) *see* **Strähl.**

strahlen ['ʃtra:lən], **1.** *v.i.* radiate, emit rays; shine, gleam; (*fig.*) be radiant, shine, beam (***vor*** (*Dat.*), with); ***vor Gesundheit –,*** radiate *or* be radiant with health. **2.** *v.t.* radiate, beam (forth), (*Rad.*) beam.

strählen ['ʃtrɛ:lən], *v.t.* (*dial.*) comb.

Strahlenbehandlung ['ʃtra:lənbəhandluŋ], *f.* radio-therapy; ray-treatment. **strahlenbrechend,** *adj.* refracting, refractive. **Strahlen|brechung,** *f.* refraction, diffraction. **–brechungsmesser,** *m.* refractometer. **–bündel, –büschel,** *n.* pencil of rays, beam.

strahlend ['ʃtra:lənt], *adj.* radiating; (*fig.*) radiant, beaming, shining.

Strahlen|dosis, *f.* radiation dosage. **–einfall,** *m.* incidence of rays. **strahlenförmig,** *adj. See* **strahlig**; (*Biol.*) actinomorphic, actinomorphous. **Strahlen|forschung,** *f.* radiology. **–glanz,** *m.* radiancy, brilliance, lustre. **–kegel,** *m.* cone of rays. **–krone,** *f.* halo, nimbus, aureole, (*fig.*) glory. **–messer,** *m.* actinometer, radiometer. **–pilz,** *m.* (*Bot.*) ray fungus. **–schädigung,** *f.* radiation damage. **–schutz,** *m.* protection against radiation. **strahlensicher,** *adj.* safe from radiation.

Strahler ['ʃtra:lər], *m.* emitter, radiator, heater, (*Rad.*) aerial array, directional *or* beam aerial *or* (*Am.*) antenna. **strahlig,** *adj.* radiating, radiate.

Strahl|motor, *m.* jet-engine. **–ofen,** *m.* radiator. **–sender,** *m.* (*Rad.*) directional *or* beam transmitter. **–triebwerk,** *n. See* **–motor. –turbine,** *f.* turbo-jet (engine).

Strahlung ['ʃtra:luŋ], *f.* radiation, rays. **Strahlungs|messer,** *m. See* **Strahlenmesser. –quant,** *n.* photon. **–schäden,** *m.pl. See* **Strahlenschädigung. –wärme,** *f.* radiant heat.

Strähn [ʃtrɛ:n], *m.* (**-(e)s,** *pl.* **-e**) (*Austr.*), **Strähne,** *f.* strand, (*of hair*) lock, (*of thread*) skein, hank. **strähnig,** *adj.* in strands; wispy, stringy.

strakeln ['ʃtra:kəln], *v.r.* stretch o.s.

Stramin [ʃtra'mi:n], *m.* (**-s,** *pl.* **-e**) embroidery canvas.

stramm [ʃtram], **1.** *adj.* tight, taut; (*of bearing*) erect, (*of constitution*) robust, sturdy, (*coll.*) strapping, (*of manner*) smart, (*coll.*) snappy, (*sl.*) nifty; (*fig.*) severe, rigid, strict; ***–er Bursche,*** strapping youngster; ***–es Mädel,*** comely lass; ***–er Soldat,*** smart soldier. **2.** *adv.* ***– arbeiten,*** work hard, put one's back into it; (*coll.*) ***ihm die Hosen – ziehen,*** dust the seat of his pants; ***– stehen,*** stand at attention.

Strampelhöschen ['ʃtrampəlhø:sçən], *n.* rompers. **strampeln,** *v.i.* kick, struggle; (*coll.*) pedal hard (*cycle*); ***sich bloß –,*** kick the bed-clothes off.

strampfen ['ʃtrampfən], *v.t.* (*Austr.*) *see* **stampfen.**

Strand [ʃtrant], *m.* (**-(e)s,** *pl.* **-e**) (sea)shore, beach, foreshore, (*Poet.*) strand; ***auf*** (***den***) ***– laufen,*** run aground, be stranded; ***auf*** (***den***) ***– setzen,*** beach. **Strand|ablagerung,** *f.* littoral deposit. **–anzug,** *m.* beach-wear. **–bad,** *n.* open-air swimming bath; lido, seaside resort. **–batterie,** *f.* (*Mil.*) shore battery.

stranden ['ʃtrandən], *v.i.* (*aux.* s. & h.) be stranded, run aground, be (ship)wrecked *or* beached; (*fig.*) founder, fail, (*coll.*) come unstuck; ***gestrandetes Mädchen,*** girl that has gone to the bad.

Strand|fischerei, *f.* fishing from the foreshore. **–gerechtigkeit,** *f.* prescriptive right over the foreshore. **–gewächse,** *n.pl.* littoral plants. **–gut,** *n.* flotsam, jetsam, wreckage. **–hafer,** *n.* (*Bot.*) lyme *or* dune grass, bent (*Amnophila arundinacea*). **–kanone,** *f.* (*coll.*) ***geladen wie eine –,*** half-seas over, three sheets in the wind, lit-up. **–korb,** *m.* beach chair. **–läufer,** *m.* (*Orn.*) sandpiper, stint (*Calidris*); ***bogenschnabliger –,*** *see* **Sichelstrandläufer**; ***isländischer –,*** *see* **Knutt**; ***kleiner –,*** *see* **Zwergstrandläufer**; ***spitzschwänziger –,*** Siberian pectoral sandpiper, (*Am.*) sharp-tailed sandpiper (*Calidris acuminata*). **–linie,** *f.* high-water mark. **–pieper,** *m.* (*Orn.*) rock pipit (*Anthus spinoletta spinoletta*). **–raub,** *m.* wrecking. **–räuber,** *m.* wrecker. **–recht,** *n.* right of salvage. **–schuhe,** *m.pl.* beach- *or* sand-shoes.

Strandung ['ʃtranduŋ], *f.* stranding, shipwreck.

Strand|wache, *f.*, **–wächter,** *m.* coastguard. **–weg,** *m.* promenade.

Strang [ʃtraŋ], *m.* **(-(e)s,** *pl.* **¨e)** rope, cord, line; hank, skein; (*of harness*) halter, trace; (*Railw.*) rail, track; ***wenn alle ¨e reißen,*** if the worst comes to the worst, if all else fails, as a last resort; ***über den –*** or ***die ¨e schlagen,*** kick over the traces; ***er verdient den –,*** he deserves hanging; ***an einem – ziehen,*** pull together, act in concert; ***alle am gleichen*** or ***selben – ziehen,*** be all in the same boat. **strangfarbig,** *adj.* dyed in the yarn. **Stranggewebe,** *n.* (*Anat.*) vascular tissue. **strangpressen,** *v.t.*, *v.i.* (*Metall.*) extrude.

strangulieren [ʃtraŋgu'li:rən], *v.t.* strangle. **Strangulierung,** *f.* strangling, strangulation.

Strapaz– [ʃtra'pa:ts], *pref.* (*Austr.*) *see* **Strapazier–. Strapaze,** *f.* fatigue, exertion, strain; toil, hardship, drudgery. **Strapazier–** [–'tsi:r], *pref.* hard-wearing. **strapazieren, 1.** *v.t.* strain, fatigue, exhaust, tire. **2.** *v.r.* exert o.s., wear o.s. out, (*coll.*) do o.s. up. **strapazierfähig,** *adj*, hard-wearing, durable. **strapaziös** [–i'ø:s], *adj.* tiring, exhausting, fatiguing.

Straßburg ['ʃtra:sburk], *n.* Strasbourg.

Straße ['ʃtra:sə], *f.* street, road, thoroughfare, highway; strait(s), waterway; route; ***an der –,*** by the wayside *or* roadside; ***auf der –,*** in the street, on the road, (*of prostitutes*) on the streets; ***auf offener –,*** in a public place, in broad daylight; ***der Mann auf der –,*** the man in the street; (*fig.*) ***auf der – liegen,*** be there all around us, be there for the asking; ***auf die – setzen,*** turn out, send packing; ***sein Geld auf die – werfen,*** throw one's money down the drain; ***die breit(getreten)e – des Herkommens,*** the well-trodden path of custom; ***von der – aufgelesen,*** picked up in the gutter; ***– von Gibraltar,*** Straits of Gibraltar.

Straßen|anzug, *m.* lounge suit. **–arbeit,** *f.* roadwork(s). **–arbeiter,** *m.* roadman, navvy. **–bahn,** *f.* tramway; tram(car), (*Am.*) streetcar. **–bahner,** *m.* tramways employee. **–bahnhaltestelle,** *f.* tram stop. **–bahnwagen,** *m.* tramcar. **–bau,** *m.* road-building *or* construction. **–belag,** *m.* road metal; road surface. **–beleuchtung,** *f.* street-lighting. **–beschaffenheit,** *f.* road conditions. **–brücke,** *f.* road bridge. **–damm,** *m.* roadway, causeway. **–decke,** *f. See* **–belag. –dirne,** *f.* streetwalker, prostitute. **–disziplin,** *f.* road-sense. **–dorf,** *n.* village built along a single street. **–einmündung,** *f.* road junction. **–feger,** *m.* road-sweeper, (*Am.*) scavenger. **–graben,** *m.* roadside ditch. **–händler,** *m.* street vendor, costermonger, hawker. **–junge,** *m.* street arab, urchin, ragamuffin, guttersnipe. **–kampf,** *m.* street-fighting. **–kehrer,** *m. See* **–feger. –kehricht,** *m.* street-sweepings. **–kleid,** *n.* outdoor dress. **–kot,** *m.* mud (from the street). **–kreuzung,** *f.* crossroads, intersection. **–lage,** *f.* (*Motor.*) road-holding qualities. **–laterne,** *f.* street-lamp. **–mädchen,** *n. See* **–dirne. –netz,** *n.* highway system, network of roads. **–ordnung,** *f.* traffic regulations, rules of the road, Highway Code.

Straßen|pflaster, *n.* pavement. **–planum,** *n.* street-level. **–raub,** *m.* highway robbery. **–räuber,** *m.* highway robber, highwayman, footpad. **–reinigung,** *f.* street-cleaning, scaveng(er)ing. **–renner,** *m.* (*Cycl.*) road-racer. **–rinne,** *f.* gutter. **–sammlung,** *f.* street-collection. **–schild,** *n.* street- *or* road-sign. **–schreck,** *m.*, **–schwein,** *n.* (*coll.*) road-hog. **–sperre,** *f.* road-block. **–spinne,** *f.* multiple intersection *or* road junction. **–transport,** *m.* road-haulage. **–tür,** *f.* front *or* street door. **–überführung,** *f.* viaduct, overpass. **–übergang,** *m.* pedestrian crossing. **–umleitung,** *f.* detour. **–unfall,** *m.* road *or* street *or* traffic accident. **–unterführung,** *f.* subway, underpass. **–verengung,** *f.* bottleneck. **–verhältnisse,** *pl. See* **–beschaffenheit. –verkäufer,** *m. See* **–händler. –verkehr,** *m.* (road) traffic. **–verkehrsordnung,** *f. See* **–ordnung. –verstopfung,** *f.* traffic congestion *or* (*coll.*) jam. **–walze,** *f.* road-roller.

Stratege [ʃtra'te:gə], *m.* **(-n,** *pl.* **-n)** strategist.

Strategie [–'gi:], *f.* strategy. **strategisch,** *adj.* strategic.

sträuben ['ʃtrɔybən], **1.** *v.t.* ruffle (up). **2.** *v.r.* stand on end, bristle (up); boggle (***bei,*** at); (*fig.*) ***sich – gegen,*** struggle against, resist, oppose. **Sträuben,** *n.* struggling, resistance, opposition; reluctance. **sträubig, straubig,** *adj.* bristling, stiff, rough, coarse; (*fig.*) obstinate, stubborn, cross-grained, rebellious.

Strauch [ʃtraux], *m.* **(-(e)s,** *pl.* **¨e(r))** shrub, bush. **strauchartig,** *adj.* bushy, shrub-like. **Strauchdieb,** *m.* highwayman, footpad.

straucheln ['ʃtrauxəln], *v.i.* (*aux.* h. & s.) stumble, trip, slip (***über*** (*Acc.*), over), (*fig.*) make *or* take a false step, (make a) blunder.

Strauchen ['ʃtrauxən], *m.* (*Austr.*) cold in the head.

strauchig ['ʃtrauxıç], *adj.* bushy; covered with shrubs. **Strauch|ritter,** *m.* robber knight. **–werk,** *n.* shrubbery, shrubs; brushwood, undergrowth.

Strauken ['ʃtraukən], *m. See* **Strauchen.**

[1]**Strauß** [ʃtraus], *m.* **(-es,** *pl.* **¨e) 1.** bunch (of flowers), nosegay, bouquet; (*Bot.*) thyrsus; (*dial.*) crest, tuft, bush, top-knot; 2. (*Poet.*) strife, struggle, feud, combat, conflict.

[2]**Strauß,** *m.* **(-es,** *pl.* **-e)** ostrich; ***der Vogel –,*** the ostrich; ***Vogel–-Politik,*** head-in-the-sand policy. **Straußen|ei,** *n.* ostrich-egg. **–feder,** *f.* ostrich feather. **–züchterei,** *f.* ostrich-farming.

Strauß|kuckuck, *m.* (*Orn.*) *see* **Häherkuckuck. –wirtschaft,** *f.* inn kept by a vintner (who sells his own wine).

Strazze ['ʃtratsə], *f.* (*Comm.*) scrap-book, rough note-book; day book.

Strebe ['ʃtre:bə], *f.* support, stay, buttress, prop; strut, brace, crosspiece, crossbeam, traverse. **Strebe|balken,** *m.* prop, shore, buttress, brace. **–bogen,** *m.* flying-buttress. **–mauer,** *f.* retaining wall.

streben ['ʃtre:bən], *v.i.* strive, strain (***nach,*** after), struggle (for), press (towards), aspire (to), aim (at), endeavour (to get), seek, pursue; make an effort, exert o.s., (*school sl.*) (be a) swot; tend, gravitate (towards). **Streben,** *n.* striving, endeavour, effort, aim, aspiration; tendency.

Strebepfeiler ['ʃtre:bəpfaılər], *m.* buttress, abutment-pier.

Streber ['ʃtre:bər], *m.* pushing fellow, place-hunter, careerist, (*school sl.*) swot. **Strebertum,** *n.* place-hunting.

strebsam ['ʃtre:pza:m], *adj.* assiduous, industrious, ambitious, zealous, aspiring, eager, (*coll.*) pushing. **Strebsamkeit,** *f.* industry, assiduity, perseverance, zeal, (*coll.*) push.

streckbar ['ʃtrɛkba:r], *adj.* extensible; ductile, malleable. **Streckbarkeit,** *f.* extensibility; ductility, tensility.

Streck|balken, *m.* strut, stretcher, stringer, crossbeam, road-bearer (*of bridges*). **–bett,** *n.* orthopaedic bed.

Strecke ['ʃtrɛkə], *f.* extent, span, distance; stretch, tract (*of land*), route (*of a journey*), length (*of trench*), section (*of railw. line*), stage (*of public transport*), reach (*of a river*); (*Min.*) gallery, roadway; (*Geom.*) straight line; (*Spt.*) course, distance; (*Hunt.*) bag; ***auf freie –,*** on the road; (*Railw.*) on the open track; ***auf der – bleiben,*** break down, succumb, perish, come to grief; ***meine – betrug 20 Hasen,*** my bag consisted of 20 hares; ***zur – bringen,*** (*Hunt.*) kill, shoot, bag; (*fig.*) destroy, hunt down, (*coll.*) do for; ***in einer –,*** at a stretch; ***eine gute – Weges,*** a good piece of the way, some distance; ***eine – zurücklegen,*** cover a distance.

strecken ['ʃtrɛkən], **1.** *v.t.* stretch, extend, elongate; spread *or* flatten *or* draw *or* roll *or* beat out; make (*a th.*) go a long way, make (*a th.*) spin out *or* last, eke *or* spin (*a th.*) out; dilute, adulterate, reduce, thin; ***Arbeit –,*** go slow (*at work*); ***die Hände zum Himmel –,*** raise one's hands towards heaven; ***alle viere von sich –,*** drop down dead, give up the ghost, turn up one's toes; ***die Waffen –,*** lay down one's arms, surrender; *zu Boden* –, fell to the ground; *in gestrecktem Galopp,* at full speed, (at) full tilt; *gestreckter Winkel,* rectilinear angle. **2.** *v.r.* stretch o.s.; *sich ins Gras* –, stretch out on the grass; *sich nach der Decke* –, cut one's coat according to one's cloth, make the best of it.

Strecken|arbeiter, *m.* (*Railw.*) plate-layer. **–bau,** *m.* railway construction, track-laying. **–block,** *m.* (*Railw.*) (signalling) section. **–dienst,** *m.* (*Railw.*) supervision of permanent way. **–flug,** *m.* long-distance flight. **–förderung,** *f.* (*Min.*) underground transport. **–führung,** *f.* routing. **–geschwindigkeit,** *f.* (*Railw., Av. etc.*) speed of run. **–netz,** *n.* airlines network. **–rekord,** *m.* (*Spt.*) track record. **–signal,** *n.* (*Railw.*) block signal. **–tauchen,** *n.* underwater swimming. **–wärter,** *m.* (*Railw.*) linesman, permanent way inspector. **streckenweise,** *adv.* here and there, in parts.

Streck|grenze, *f.* elastic limit. **–lage,** *f.* (*Gymn.*) extended position. **–mittel,** *n.* adulterant, thinner, diluting medium *or* agent. **–muskel,** *m. or f.* extensor (muscle). **–probe,** *f.* tensile test. **–sessel,** *m.* deck-chair. **–stahl,** *m.* rolled steel. **–stütz,** *m.* (*Gymn.*) resting on one's hands.

Streckung [ˈʃtrɛkuŋ], *f.* stretching, extension, lengthening, elongation, (*Metall.*) rolling; spread; adulteration, dilution. **Streck|verband,** *m.* (*Surg.*) Thomas splint appliance. **–walze,** *f.* (*Metall.*) rolling press. **–werk,** *n.* rolling-mill; plate-rollers.

Streich [ʃtraɪç], *m.* (**-(e)s,** *pl.* **-e**) stroke, blow, (*with whip*) lash; (*fig.*) stroke (*of business*), escapade, trick, prank, joke; *auf einen* –, at one blow; *ihm einen (bösen)* – *spielen,* play a mean *or* shabby *or* (*coll.*) dirty trick on him; *dummer* –, silly trick, stupid th. to do, piece of folly; *ihm einen* – *versetzen,* deal him a blow; (*Prov.*) *von einem –e fällt keine Eiche,* Rome was not built in a day.

Streiche [ˈʃtraɪçə], *f.* 1. spatula; 2. (*Geol.*) direct on of strata.

streicheln [ˈʃtraɪçəln], *v.t.* stroke; caress, fondle.

streichen [ˈʃtraɪçən], **1.** *irr.v.i.* 1. (*aux.* s.) extend, stretch, reach, run, sweep; roam, ramble, stroll, (*predatory*) prowl, (*of birds*) migrate; – *an* (*Acc.*), graze, brush; touch *or* rub in passing; – *über* (*Acc.*), skim over; 2. (*aux.* h.) *mit der Hand – über* (*Acc.*), pass one's hand over. **2.** *irr.v.t.* 1. stroke, touch gently; spread (*bread*); whet (*a knife*), strop (*a razor*); card (*wool*), strike (*a match*) (*an* (*Dat.*), on); *den Bogen* –, resin the bow; *Brot mit Butter* –, spread butter on the bread; (*coll.*) *die Geige* – scrape on the fiddle; *sich* (*Dat.*) *die Haare aus dem Gesichte* –, push one's hair out of one's eyes *or* off one's face; *Lerchen* –, snare larks; (*obs.*) *mit Ruten* –, cane, flog; *die Riemen* or *Ruder* –, back water; *den Schweiß von der Stirn* –, wipe the perspiration from one's brow; *Ziegel* –, make *or* mould tiles; 2. strike out, cross out *or* off, delete, erase, (*fig.*) expunge, cancel, (*Spt.*) scratch; strike, haul down (*a flag*), furl, lower (*sails*); (*coll.*) *er ließ einen* –, he broke wind; 3. paint, stain, varnish, brush, coat; *frisch gestrichen!* wet paint! *gestrichene Note,* ledger-line note; *gestrichen voll,* full to the brim.

Streicher [ˈʃtraɪçər], *m.* 1. migratory bird; 2. wool-carder; 3. *pl.* (*Mus.*) strings (section) (*of an orchestra*).

Streich|garn, *n.* worsted yarn. **–holz,** *n.* match. **–holzschachtel,** *f.* matchbox. **–instrument,** *n.* string(ed) instrument; *pl.* strings (*in an orchestra*). **–kamm,** *m.* carding-comb. **–käse,** *m.* spreading *or* soft cheese. **–masse,** *f.* plastic compound, filler, coating. **–musik,** *f.* string-music. **–netz,** *n.* drag-net, draw-net, seine. **–ofen,** *m.* reverberating furnace. **–orchester,** *n.* string orchestra. **–papier,** *n.* coated paper. **–quartett,** *n.* string quartet. **–riemen,** *m.* (razor) strop. **–teich,** *m.* breeding pond.

Streichung [ˈʃtraɪçuŋ], *f.* deletion, erasure; cancellation, deleted *or* suppressed passage, (*coll.*) cut. **Streich|vogel,** *m.* bird of passage. **–wolle,** *f.* carding wool. **–zeit,** *f.* migrating *or* spawning season.

Streif [ʃtraɪf], *m.* (**-(e)s,** *pl.* **-e**) stripe, streak. **Streif|band,** *n.* (postal) wrapper; *unter* –, by book post, (*Comm.*) (held) in safe custody. **–blick,** *m.* fleeting glance.

Streife [ˈʃtraɪfə], *f.* patrol, (*police*) beat; raid, sweep, razzia.

Streifen [ˈʃtraɪfən], *m.* stripe, streak, (*in marble etc.*) vein, marking, (*Anat. etc.*) stria; strip, tract (*of land*), (*Mil.*) sector, lane; (*Archit.*) fillet, band; shred, strip, slip (*of paper*); braid; (*Astr.*) belt; (*Tele.*) tape, ribbon; (*coll.*) *in den – passen* or *hauen* (*Dat.*), see eye to eye with.

[1]**streifen,** *v.t.* streak, stripe, striate; (*Archit. etc.*) channel, flute, rib.

[2]**streifen, 1.** *v.t., v.i.* (*an* (*Acc.*)), touch (lightly); brush (against), graze, skim; (*fig.*) touch (up)on; verge *or* border on, skirt; take *or* strip *or* slip off; – *über* (*Acc.*), skim *or* glide over; *die Ärmel in die Höhe* –, turn *or* roll up one's sleeves; *einen Hasen* –, skin a hare. **2.** *v.i.* (*aux.* s.) wander, roam, range, prowl; ramble, stroll, rove, (*Mil.*) patrol, reconnoitre.

Streifen|dienst, *m.* (*Mil.*) patrolling. **–gans,** *f.* (*Orn.*) bar-headed goose (*Eulabeia indica*). **–karte,** *f.* sector map. **–reiher,** *m.* (*Orn.*) green-backed *or* (*Am.*) green heron (*Butorides striatus*). **–saat,** *f.* strip-sowing. **–schwirl,** *m.* (*Orn.*) Pallas's grasshopper-warbler (*Locustella certhiola*). **–wagen,** *m.* (police) patrol *or* squad car. **streifenweise,** *adv.* in strips.

Streifhieb [ˈʃtraɪfhi:p], *m.* glancing blow. **streifig,** *adj.* striped, streaked, streaky, striated. **Streif|jagd,** *f.* battue, coursing. **–kolonne,** *f.,* **–kommando, –korps,** *n.* flying column, raiding party. **–licht,** *n.* side-light, spotlight. **–schuß,** *m.* grazing *or* glancing shot.

Streifung [ˈʃtraɪfuŋ], *f.* streaking, striation. **Streif|wunde,** *f.* (mere) scratch, superficial *or* skin wound. **–zug,** *m.* expedition; incursion, raid.

Streik [ʃtraɪk], *m.* (**-(e)s,** *pl.* **-e** *or* **-s**) strike; *sich im – befinden,* be on strike; *in den – treten,* go on strike; *wilder* –, unauthorized *or* (*coll.*) wildcat strike. **Streikbrecher,** *m.* strike-breaker; (*coll.*) blackleg, scab. **streiken,** *v.i.* strike (*work*), go on strike, be on strike. **Streikende(r),** *m., f.* striker. **Streik|kasse,** *f.* strike-fund. **–lohn,** *m.* strike-pay. **–posten,** *m.* picket.

Streit [ʃtraɪt], *m.* (**-(e)s,** *pl.* **-e** *or* **-igkeiten**) dispute, quarrel, wrangling, argument, altercation, (*coll.*) squabble, row (*über* (*Acc.*), about); strife, struggle, conflict, battle, fight, clash, brawl, feud, controversy, contest, difference (over); lawsuit, litigation (over); *in – geraten,* (have a) quarrel, clash, (*coll.*) fall out; *in – liegen,* be at loggerheads *or* variance; – *suchen,* pick a quarrel. **Streitaxt,** *f.* battle-axe; (*fig.*) *die – begraben,* bury the hatchet. **streitbar,** *adj.* warlike, militant, belligerent, fighting, combatant, combative, valiant; quarrelsome, pugnacious, disputatious.

streiten [ˈʃtraɪtən], **1.** *irr.v.i.* quarrel, disagree, be at loggerheads, (*coll.*) squabble, bicker, wrangle (*um,* about *or* over); dispute, argue, (*coll.*) have words (about); fight, struggle, contend (for); go to law (about *or* over); (*of a th.*) be at variance, clash (*mit,* with), be contrary (*gegen,* to); *darüber läßt sich* –, that is a moot *or* debatable point, that is open to question. **2.** *v.r.* quarrel (with one another); *sich um des Kaisers Bart* –, squabble over trifles. **streitend,** *adj.* *–e Kirche,* Church Militant; *–e Mächte,* belligerent powers; *–e Parteien,* litigants, opposing parties. **Streiter,** *m.* fighter, combatant; champion, disputant.

Streit|fall, *m.,* **–frage,** *f.* controversy, point *or* question at issue, matter in question *or* dispute; conflict, dispute, difference; (*Law*) case (at law). **–hammel,** *m.* (*coll.*) quarrelsome p. **–hammer,** *m.* (*Hist.*) club, mace. **–handel,** *m.* quarrel, dispute. **–hans(e)l,** *m.* (**-s,** *pl.* **-n**) (*Austr.*) *see* **–hammel.**

streitig [ˈʃtraɪtɪç], *adj.* disputable, contestable, debatable, controversial, (*Law*) sub judice; (*pred.*) at issue, in dispute; *–er Punkt,* (point at) issue, matter in dispute; *ihm etwas – machen,* contest *or* dispute his right to s.th.; ***ihm den Rang – machen,*** rival him, compete *or* vie with him. **Streitigkeit,** *f. See* **Streit.**

Streit|kolben, *m. See* **–hammer. –kräfte,** *f.pl.* troops, (armed *or* military) forces, armed services. **–lust,** *f.* quarrelsomeness, pugnacity, aggressiveness. **streitlustig,** *adj.* quarrelsome, pugnacious, aggressive, belligerent; disputatious, litigious. **Streit|macht,** *f. See* **–kräfte. –objekt,** *n.* (*coll.*) bone of contention, (*Law*) matter in dispute. **–punkt,** *m.* (point *or* question at) issue, (matter in) question, controversial *or* moot point. **–roß,** *n.* (*Hist.*) warhorse, charger. **–sache,** *f.* controversial matter, (*Law*) lawsuit, litigation. **–schrift,** *f.* polemic. **–sucht,** *f.* disputatiousness, quarrelsome *or* contentious disposition. **streitsüchtig,** *adj.* quarrelsome, disputatious, contentious, argumentative, cantankerous. **Streit|wagen,** *m.* (*Hist.*) war-chariot. **–wert,** *m.* (*Law*) sum in dispute.

streng(e) [ˈʃtrɛŋ(ə)], **1.** *adj.* severe, strict, rigorous, stringent, rigid; severe, stern, austere; (*as weather*) harsh, inclement; (*of flavour*) astringent, acrid, tart, sharp; ***–er Arrest,*** close confinement; ***–e Kälte,*** bitter cold; ***–e Kritik,*** severe *or* harsh criticism; ***–e Maßregel,*** strict *or* rigorous measure; ***–e Prüfung,*** severe *or* (*coll.*) stiff examination; ***ein –es Regiment führen,*** rule with a rod of iron *or* with a heavy hand; ***–e Sitten,*** strict morals; ***– sein gegen,*** be strict *or* severe with. **2.** *adv.* ***– geheim,*** top secret; ***sich – halten an*** (*Acc.*), adhere strictly to; ***– verboten,*** strictly forbidden; ***– verfahren mit,*** deal severely *or* harshly with; ***– vertraulich,*** in strict confidence, strictly confidential; ***– nach Vorschrift,*** in strict accordance with *or* strictly according to the regulations.

Strenge, *f.* severity, rigour, stringency; strictness, sternness, austerity; harshness, inclemency; astringency, tartness. **streng|flüssig,** *adj.* (*Metall.*) refractory. **–genommen,** *adv.* in the strict sense, strictly speaking. **–gläubig,** *adj.* orthodox. **Strenggläubigkeit,** *f.* orthodoxy.

Streu [ʃtrɔy], *f.* litter, layer *or* bed of straw, (*coll.*) shakedown. **Streubüchse,** *f.* castor, dredger, sprinkler. **streuen,** *v.t., v.i.* strew, litter, scatter, spread; (*fig.*) ***ihm Sand in die Augen –,*** throw dust in his eyes. **Streuer,** *m. See* **Streubüchse. Streu|feuer,** *n.* (*Mil.*) scattered *or* sweeping fire. **–garbe,** *f.* cone of dispersion. **–gold,** *n.* gold-dust.

streunen [ˈʃtrɔynən], *v.i.* roam about, stray. **Streuner,** *m.* (*dial.*) tramp, vagrant.

Streu|pulver, *n.* dusting powder. **–sand,** *m.* dry sand, (*Hist.*) blotting- *or* writing-sand.

Streusel [ˈʃtrɔyzəl], *n.* dust, sprinklings; (*Cul.*) (bread)crumbs. **Streuselkuchen,** *m.* (kind of) cake sprinkled with ground almonds.

Streustrahlung [ˈʃtrɔyʃtra:luŋ], *f.* radiation scatter. **Streuung,** *f.* strewing, scattering *etc.*; deviation, variation; (*Artil. etc.*) dispersion, spread, (*Stat.*) scatter, deviation. **Streu(ungs)winkel,** *m.* angle of spread *or* scatter. **Streuzucker,** *m.* caster *or* castor sugar.

Strich [ʃtrɪç], *m.* **(-(e)s,** *pl.* **-e)** stroke, line, dash, streak, stripe, (*Paint.*) stroke (of the brush); hairline, graticule; (*Geog.*) region, district, tract, zone, climate, (*Geol.*) trend; (*no pl.*) compass-point; migration, (*of birds*) flight, covey (*of partridge etc.*); grain (*of wood etc.*); (*Mus.*) bowing, touch; (*Swiss*) teat, nipple, dug; (*sl.*) ***auf den – gehen,*** walk the streets; ***ihn auf dem – haben,*** bear him a grudge, (*coll.*) have it in for him; ***einen – machen durch,*** cross out, delete, run one's pen through; (*fig.*) ***einen – durch die Rechnung machen,*** upset one's plans *or* calculations; (*coll.*) ***keinen – machen*** or ***tun,*** not do a stroke of work *or* a hand's turn; ***– fliegen,*** fly on a compass course; ***das Schiff hält einen guten –,*** the ship holds its course well; ***in einem –,*** at one stroke, without a break; ***nach – und Faden,*** properly, thoroughly; ***einen – machen unter*** (*Acc.*), underline; (*fig.*) make a clean break with; (*coll.*) ***– darunter!*** forget it! ***unter dem –,*** in the feuilleton; ***– von Eitelkeit,*** touch of vanity; ***wider*** or ***gegen den –,*** against the grain.

strich, *see* **streichen.**

Strich|ätzung, *f.* line-etching. **–einteilung,** *f.* graduation (*of a scale*).

stricheln [ˈʃtrɪçəln], *v.t.* shade, hatch, dot, mark with little lines; ***gestrichelte Linie,*** dotted line. **Strichelschwirl,** *m.* (*Orn.*) Temminck's grasshopper-warbler (*Locustella lanceolata*).

Strichgitter [ˈʃtrɪçgɪtər], *n.* reticle.

strichlieren [ʃtrɪçˈli:rən], *v.t.* (*Austr.*) *see* **stricheln.**

Strich|mädchen, *n.* (*coll.*) streetwalker. **–platte,** *f.* graduated dial. **–punkt,** *m.* semicolon. **–regen,** *m.* local shower. **–scheibe,** *f. See* **–platte. –vogel,** *m.* (*Orn.*) local migrant. **strichweise,** *adv.* in certain places, here and there; ***– Regen,*** scattered showers. **Strichzeit,** *f.* 1. time of migration (*of birds*); 2. spawning time (*of fishes*).

Strick [ʃtrɪk], *m.* **(-(e)s,** *pl.* **-e)** 1. cord, rope, line, string; (*fig.*) ***ihm einen – drehen*** or ***legen,*** lay a trap for him, catch in him out, trip him up; ***wenn alle –e reißen,*** if all else fails, if the worst comes to the worst, as a last resort; 2. (*coll.*) scapegrace; good-for-nothing, young rascal, scamp.

Strick|arbeit, *f.* knitting. **–beutel,** *m.* knitting-bag. **stricken,** *v.t., v.i.* knit. **Stricken,** *n.* knitting. **Strickerei** [–ˈraɪ], *f.* (piece of) knitting. **Strickerin,** *f.* knitter. **Strick|garn,** *n.* knitting-wool. **–jacke,** *f.* knitted jacket, cardigan, (*coll.*) woolly. **–leiter,** *f.* rope-ladder. **–masche,** *f.* knitting stitch, stitch of knitting. **–maschine,** *f.* knitting-machine. **–muster,** *n.* knitting pattern. **–nadel,** *f.* knitting-needle. **–naht,** *f.* knitted seam; back seam (*of stockings*). **–strumpf,** *m.* stocking being knitted. **–waren,** *f.pl. See* **–zeug. –weste,** *f. See* **–jacke. –zeug,** *n.* knitted wear *or* goods *or* clothing.

Striegel [ˈʃtri:gəl], *m.* (*also f.* (-, *pl.* **-n**)) curry-comb. **striegeln,** *v.t.* curry, comb; (*fig.*) take to task; ***gestriegelt und gebügelt,*** spick and span.

Strieme [ˈʃtri:mə], *f.*, **Striemen,** *m.* weal. **striemig,** *adj.* striped, streaked; covered with weals.

[1]**Striezel** [ˈʃtri:tsəl], *f.* (-, *pl.* **-n**) *or m.* (*dial.*) (form of) white loaf.

[2]**Striezel,** *m.* (*Austr.*) little devil, young rascal.

striezen [ˈʃtri:tsən], *v.t.* (*coll.*) torment, plague (*a p.*), filch, pinch, lift, swipe (*a th.*).

strikt [strɪkt], *adj.* strict, exact. **strikt(e),** *adv.* strictly. **Striktur** [–ˈtu:r], *f.* (-, *pl.* **-en**) (*Med.*) stricture.

Strippe [ˈʃtrɪpə], *f.* (*coll.*) (piece of) string, strap, band; (*coll.*) ***dauernd an der – hängen,*** be everlastingly on the phone.

stritt [ʃtrɪt], **stritte,** *see* **streiten.**

strittig [ˈʃtrɪtɪç], *adj.* questionable, contested, debatable, moot; in dispute.

Strizzi [ˈʃtrɪtsi], *m.* **(-s,** *pl.* **-s)** (*Austr.*) idler, lounger, gad-about; pimp.

Strobel [ˈʃtro:bəl], *m.* mop of hair. **strob(e)lig,** *adj. See* **struppig.**

Stroh [ʃtro:], *n.* **(-s,** *no pl.*) straw; thatch; ***eine Schütte –,*** a load of straw; ***– im Kopfe haben,*** be empty-headed; ***wie – schmecken,*** taste of nothing; (*fig.*) (***leeres***) ***– dreschen,*** beat the air, flog a dead horse.

Strohbedeckung [ˈʃtrɔ:bədɛkuŋ], *f.* mulch. **strohblond,** *adj.* flaxen-haired, ash-blond(e). **Stroh|blume,** *f.* artificial flower; (*Bot.*) immortelle. **–bund,** *n.* truss of straw. **–dach,** *n.* thatched roof. **–decker,** *m.* thatcher. **strohern,** *adj.* of straw; insipid, jejune, dry as dust. **stroh|farben, –farbig,** *adj.* straw-coloured, beige. **Stroh|feuer,** *n.* passing enthusiasm, transient ardour; ***– der Liebe,*** short-lived passion. **–futter,** *n.* straw fodder. **stroh|gelb,** *adj. See* **–farben. Stroh|häcksel,** *m.* chaff, chopped straw. **–halm,** *m.* (single) straw; ***sich an einen – klammern,*** clutch at a straw. **–hut,** *m.* straw hat. **–hütte,** *f.* thatched cottage. **–kopf,** *m.* (*coll.*) numskull, simpleton, blockhead. **–lager,** *n.* straw bed. **–mann,** *m.* (*pl.* **⸚er**) scarecrow; man of straw; dummy (*at whist*); lay-figure. **–matte,** *f.* rush mat; *see also* **–bedeckung. –pappe,** *f.* strawboard. **–puppe,** *f. See*

–mann. –sack, *m.* paillasse, straw mattress; (*coll.*) ***ach du gerechter –!*** good gracious! dear me! **–stoff,** *m.* straw pulp. **–wein,** *m.* vin de paille. **–wisch,** *m.* wisp of straw. **–witwe,** *f.* grass-widow. **–witwer,** *m.* grass-widower. **–zeug,** *n.* *See* **–stoff.**

Strolch [ʃtrɔlç], *m.* **(-(e)s,** *pl.* **-e)** idler, lounger; tramp, vagrant, vagabond. **strolchen,** *v.i.* (*aux.* h. & s.) stroll *or* roam about, idle away one's time. **Strolchfahrt,** *f.* (*Swiss*) journey without paying one's fare.

Strom [ʃtro:m], *m.* **(-(e)s,** *pl.* **¨e)** large *or* broad river, stream, current (*also Elec.*); flow, flood, torrent (*of words etc.*); crowd, throng (*of people*); ***in Strömen gießen (fließen),*** pour (flow) in torrents; ***gegen den –,*** against the current, (*fig.*) against the tide; (*Elec.*) ***den – öffnen,*** break the circuit; ***Ströme von Tränen,*** flood of tears; (*Elec.*) ***unter –,*** live; ***– der Welt,*** hurly-burly of life; ***– der Zeit,*** passage of time *or* the years.

stromab [ʃtro:m'ap], *adv.* downstream. **Strom|-abgabe,** *f.* current-output. **–abnehmer,** *m.* (*Elec.*) brush (contact). **strom|abwärts,** *adv.* *See* **–ab. Strom|anker,** *m.* current-anchor (*bridge-building*). **–atlas,** *m.* hydrographic atlas. **stromauf** [–'auf], *adv.* upstream. **Stromaufnahme,** *f.* current-consumption, charging rate. **strom|-aufwärts,** *adv.* *See* **–auf. Strom|bett,** *n.* river bed. **–einheit,** *f.* unit of current, ampere.

strömen ['ʃtrø:mən], *v.i.* (*aux.* s. & h.) stream, flow, run, pour, gush; ***ihm strömt das Blut in den Kopf,*** the blood rushes to his head.

Strom|enge, *f.* narrows (*of a river*). **–entnahme,** *f.* (*Elec.*) current-consumption.

Stromer ['ʃtro:mər], *m.* (*coll.*), **stromern,** *v.i.* *See* **Strolch, strolchen.**

Strom|erzeuger, *m.* dynamo, generator. **–erzeu-gung,** *f.* generation of current. **stromführend,** *adj.* current-carrying, live. **Strom|gebiet,** *n.* river-basin. **–gleichrichter,** *m.* *See* **–richter. –kreis,** *m.* electric circuit. **–leiter,** *m.* (*Elec.*) conductor. **–linienform,** *f.* streamline shape. **stromlinienförmig,** *adj.* streamlined. **Strom|-menge,** *f.* (*Elec.*) quantity of current, coulombs. **–messer,** *m.* ammeter. **–netz,** *n.* power supply. **–polizei,** *f.* river police. **–quelle,** *f.* (*Elec.*) source of current. **–richter,** *m.* (*Elec.*) rectifier, D.C. converter. **–sammler,** *m.* storage battery, (*Am.*) accumulator. **–schiene,** *f.* bus-bar, (*Railw.*) live *or* contact rail. **–schnellen,** *f.pl.* rapids. **–schwan-kung,** *f.* (*Elec.*) current fluctuation. **–spannung,** *f.* circuit voltage. **–sperre,** *f.* power cut. **–spule,** *f.* solenoid. **–stärke,** *f.* (*Elec.*) intensity of current. **–stoß,** *m.* (*Elec.*) surge of current.

Strömung ['ʃtrø:muŋ], *f.* current, stream; flow, flux; (*fig.*) current, stream, movement, drift, trend. **Strömungs|getriebe,** *n.* (*Mech.*) fluid drive, hydraulic gear. **–lehre,** *f.* aerodynamics, hydrodynamics, fluid mechanics.

Strom|unterbrecher, *m.* (*Elec.*) contact *or* circuit-breaker, cut-out. **–verbrauch,** *m.* current consumption. **–versorgung,** *f.* electricity supply. **–wache,** *f.* *See* **–polizei. –wandler,** *m.* current transformer. **–wechsel,** *m.* alternation of current. **–wechsler, –wender,** *m.* (*Elec.*) commutator.

Strontian ['strɔntsian], *m.* strontium salt; ***kohlen-saurer –,*** strontium carbonate, strontianite. **Strontium,** *n.* strontium.

Strophe ['ʃtro:fə], *f.* stanza, verse. **Strophen|bau,** *m.* verse structure. **–form,** *f.* type of stanza. **strophig,** *adj. suff.* of . . . stanzas. **strophisch,** *adj.* strophic; divided into stanzas.

Strosse ['ʃtrɔsə], *f.* (*Min.*) stope. **Strossenbau,** *m.* stoping.

strotzen ['ʃtrɔtsən], *v.i.* be puffed *or* swelled up, be distended *or* swollen (***vor*** (*Dat.*), with); (*fig.*) be brimming *or* bursting, bristle (with), be full (of), abound (in), be covered *or* teeming *or* swarming, teem, swarm (with). **strotzend,** *adj.* swollen, distended, turgid, puffed up; (*fig.*) bursting, overflowing, abundant, exuberant (***von, vor*** (*Dat.*), with).

strub [ʃtru:p], *adj.* (*Swiss*) *see* **struppig.**

strubbelig ['ʃtrubəlɪç], *adj.* tousled, shock-headed, shaggy; dishevelled, unkempt.

Strudel ['ʃtru:dəl], *m.* eddy, whirlpool, vortex; (type of) flaky pastry; ***– der Vergnügungen,*** round *or* whirl of pleasure. **Strudelkopf,** *m.* (*coll.*) hothead. **strudelköpfig,** *adj.* hotheaded. **stru-deln,** *v.i.* whirl, swirl, eddy; boil, bubble, spout, gush.

Struktur [ʃtruk'tu:r], *f.* structure; texture (*of metals*). **strukturell** [–'rɛl], *adj.* structural. **strukturidentisch,** *adj.* structurally identical. **structurlos,** *adj.* (*Metall. etc.*) amorphous.

Strumpf [ʃtrumpf], *m.* **(-(e)s,** *pl.* **¨e)** 1. stocking, sock, *pl.* hose; (*coll.*) ***sich auf die Strümpfe machen,*** beat it, skedaddle, make off; 2. gas-mantle.

Strumpf|band, *n.* garter. **–halter,** *m.* suspender, (*Am.*) garter. **–haltergürtel,** *m.* suspender belt, girdle. **–waren,** *pl.* hosiery. **–weber, –wirker,** *m.* stocking-weaver. **–wirkerei,** *f.* stocking manufacture. **–wirkerstuhl,** *m.* stocking-loom.

Strunk [ʃtruŋk], *m.* **(-(e)s,** *pl.* **¨e)** trunk, stump, stalk, stem; core (*of apple etc.*).

Strunze ['ʃtruntsə], *f.* (*dial.*) slut, slattern.

struppiert [ʃtru'pi:rt], *adj.* (*dial.*) worn out, done in, knocked up.

struppig ['ʃtrupɪç], *adj.* rough, bristly; unkempt, dishevelled, (*of dog*) shaggy.

Struw(w)el|bart ['ʃtruvəl–], *m.* bristly *or* scrubby beard. **–kopf,** *m.* shaggy *or* unkempt hair, mane; shock- *or* shaggy-headed person.

Strychnin ['stryçni:n], *n.* strychnine.

Stubbe ['ʃtubə], *f.,* **Stubben,** *m.* tree-stump.

Stube ['ʃtu:bə], *f.* room, chamber, apartment; (*Mil.*) barrack-room; ***gute –,*** drawing-room, best room, parlour; ***in der – hocken,*** hug the fireplace.

Stuben|älteste(r), *m.* senior soldier (*in a barrack-room*). **–appell,** *m.* (*Mil.*) barrack-room inspection. **–arbeit,** *f.* indoor work. **–arrest,** *m.* (*Mil.*) confinement to quarters. **–dienst,** *m.* (*Mil.*) cleaning barracks. **–farbe,** *f.* (*coll.*) ***er hat –,*** he is pasty-faced. **–fliege,** *f.* common house-fly. **–gelehr-samkeit,** *f.* book-learning. **–gelehrte(r),** *m., f.* bookworm. **–genosse,** *m.* *See* **–kamerad. –hocker,** *m.* stay-at-home. **–kamerad,** *m.* roommate, fellow-lodger. **–luft,** *f.* close *or* stuffy atmosphere. **–mädchen,** *n.* housemaid, parlourmaid. **–maler,** *m.* interior decorator. **stubenrein,** *adj.* house-trained (*of dogs*). **Stuben|uhr,** *f.* mantelpiece clock. **–vogel,** *m.* cage-bird.

Stüber ['ʃty:bər], *m.* stiver (*old coin*); fillip; (*coll.*) biff on the nose.

Stubsnase, *f.* *See* **Stupsnase.**

Stuck [ʃtuk], *m.* stucco.

Stück [ʃtyk], *n.* **(-(e)s,** *pl.* **-e)** 1. piece, bit, part, portion, fragment, morsel; (*Theat.*) play; piece of music; number (*of a magazine*); passage, extract (*from a book*); (*no pl.*) pat (*of butter*); slice (*of bread*); lump (*of sugar*); cake, tablet (*of soap*); lot, plot, patch (*of land*); head (*of cattle*); ***6 – Eier,*** 6 eggs; ***20 – Vieh,*** 20 head of cattle; ***ein gut(es) – Arbeit,*** a hard task *or* (*coll.*) tough job; ***aus einem –,*** in one piece, all of a piece; ***aus freien –en,*** of one's own accord *or* own free will, voluntarily, spontaneously; ***– für –,*** piece by piece, each piece individually; ***man hält große –e auf ihn,*** people have a high opinion of him *or* think highly *or* a lot of him *or* make much of him; ***sich*** (*Dat.*) ***große –e einbilden,*** think a lot of o.s.; ***ein hübsches – Geld,*** a nice little sum, a tidy penny; ***in allen –en,*** in every respect, in all respects; ***in diesem –,*** in this respect; ***in vielen –en,*** in many ways *or* respects; ***in einem –e (fort),*** continuously, uninterruptedly, the whole (night, day *etc.*) through; ***in –e gehen,*** break in *or* fall to pieces; (*coll.*) ***ein starkes –,*** a bit thick, really too bad *or* much, going too far; ***Stoff vom – kaufen,*** buy cloth from the piece; 2. butt (*approx. 1200 l. of wine*) (*see* **Stückfaß**); 3. (*obs.*) field-piece, gun, cannon; 4. *pl.* stocks, securities.

Stuckarbeit ['ʃtukarbaɪt], *f.* stucco-work.

Stück|arbeit, *f.* piecework. **–arbeiter,** *m.* piece-worker. **Stückchen,** *n.* little piece, particle, morsel, bit, scrap; *ihm ein – spielen,* play a trick on him.

stückeln [ˈʃtykəln], *v.t.* cut into pieces, cut up; piece together, patch. **Stück(e)lung,** *f.* dismemberment, distintegration, subdivision.

stucken [ˈʃtukən], *v.i.* (*Austr.*) swot.

stücken [ˈʃtykən], *v.t. See* **stückeln. Stückenzucker,** *m.* lump-sugar.

stuckern [ˈʃtukərn], *v.i.* (*dial.*) curdle, congeal.

stückfarbig [ˈʃtykfarbɪç], *adj.* dyed in the piece. **Stück|faß,** *n.* butt, large cask (*of about 8 hogsheads*). **–fracht,** *f.* baled *or* parcelled freight.

Stuckgips [ˈʃtukgɪps], *m.* plaster of Paris.

Stück|größe, *f.* size of piece. **–gut,** *n.* 1. piece-goods, parcelled goods; 2. *obs.*) gunmetal. **–gutladung,** *f.* mixed cargo. **–holz,** *n.* chopped wood, billets of wood. **–kohle,** *f.* lump-coal. **–liste,** *f.* inventory, specification, parts list. **–lohn,** *m.* wages for piecework. **–metall,** *n.* gun-metal. **–pforte,** *f.* (*obs.*) gunport. **–preis,** *m.* price by the piece. **–waren,** *f.pl. See* **–gut. stückweise,** *adv.* piece by piece, piecemeal. **Stück|werk,** *n.* patchwork; ***unser Wissen ist –,*** our knowledge is scrappy, (*B.*) we know in part. **–zahl,** *f.* number of pieces *or* shares. **–zinsen,** *m.pl.* accrued interest.

Student [ʃtuˈdɛnt], *m.* (**-en,** *pl.* **-en**) (university) student, undergraduate; (*Austr.*) secondary-school pupil; – ***der alten Sprachen,*** student of classics, classical student.

Studenten|ausschuß, *m.* students' committee. **–bund,** *m.* students' association. **–haus,** *n.* students' club. **–heim,** *n.* students' hostel. **–hilfe,** *f.* students' welfare organization. **–leben,** *n.* university life, college life. **Studentenschaft,** *f.* students, undergraduates, the student body. **Studenten|sprache,** *f.* students' slang. **–verbindung,** *f.* (German) students' club.

Studentin [ʃtuˈdɛntɪn], *f.* woman student. **studentisch,** *adj.* student(-like), academic, collegiate.

Studie [ˈʃtu:diə], *f.* (preparatory) study, sketch, essay.

Studien|anstalt, *f.* girls' secondary school. **–assessor,** *m.* probationary schoolmaster. **–direktor,** *m.* secondary-school headmaster, (*Am.*) high-school principal. **–fach,** *n.* subject, branch of study. **–fahrt,** *f.* educational journey, study trip. **–freund,** *m.* fellow-student, friend at college. **–gang,** *m.* course of study *or* studies. **–gebühr,** *f.* university fees. **–genosse,** *m. See* **–freund. studienhalber,** *adv.* for the purpose of studying. **Studien|jahre,** *n.pl.* college days, student days. **–plan,** *m.* syllabus, curriculum, scheme of work. **–rat,** *m.* assistant master (*secondary school*); (*Mil.*) instructor. **–rätin,** *f.* assistant mistress. **–referendar,** *m.* assistant master on probation. **–reise,** *f. See* **–fahrt. –zeit,** *f. See* **–jahre.**

studieren [ʃtuˈdi:rən], *v.t., v.i.* study; be at the university *or* at college; ***er läßt seinen Sohn –,*** he is sending his son to the university; ***die Rechte –,*** study law, be a law-student, read for the bar; ***wir – zusammen,*** we are at college together. **Studierende(r),** *m., f.* (university) student. **studiert,** *adj.* studied; premeditated; affected; ***ein –er Mann,*** (*coll.*) ***ein Studierter,*** a man with a university education, a graduate. **Studierzimmer,** *n.* study.

Studio [ˈʃtu:dio], **1.** *n.* (**-s,** *pl.* **-s**) (artist's) studio; broadcasting studio. **2.** *m.* (**-s,** *pl.* **-s**), **Studiosus,** *m.* (-, *pl.* **-iosen** (*Austr.* **-iosi**)) (*obs.*) student.

Studium [ˈʃtu:dium], *n.* (**-s,** *pl.* **-dien**) study, attendance at a university; university *or* college education.

Stufe [ˈʃtu:fə], *f.* (door)step; rung (*of ladder*); tuck (*in a dress*); (*Mus.*) interval; (*Gram.*) degree (of comparison); gradation, shade, nuance; (*fig.*) standard, level, degree, rank, grade; stage, phase; ***Achtung –!*** mind the step! ***auf gleicher – mit,*** on a level *or* par with, on the same footing as; ***die höchste – des Glücks,*** the height of happiness, the pinnacle of good fortune.

stufenartig [ˈʃtu:fənˀa:rtɪç], *adj.* step-like; (*fig.*) graduated, gradual. **Stufenfolge,** *f.* gradation; sequence *or* succession of steps *or* stages; gradual development. **stufenförmig,** *adj.* graduated, graded, by steps. **Stufenleiter,** *f.* step-ladder; (*Mus.*) scale, gamut, (*fig.*) graduation, gradation. **stufenlos,** *adj.* (*Mech.*) infinitely variable. **Stufen|rakete,** *f.* multi-stage rocket. **–schalter,** *m.* (*Elec.*) step-up switch. **–scheibe,** *f.* step-pulley. **–transformator,** *m.* (*Elec.*) step-up *or* step-down transformer. **stufenweise,** *adv.* by steps, by degrees, in stages, gradually.

–stufig [ʃtu:fɪç], *adj.suff.* with . . . steps, (*fig*) in. . . stages.

Stuhl [ʃtu:l], *m.* (**-(e)s,** *pl.* **⸚e**) 1. chair; stool; seat; pew (*in church*); close- *or* night-stool; ***Gottes –,*** God's judgement seat; ***Heiliger –,*** Holy See; ***Meister vom –,*** Master of the Lodge; ***ihm den – vor die Tür setzen,*** turn him out, show him the door; ***sich zwischen zwei Stühle setzen,*** fall between two stools; 2. (*Weav.*) loom, frame; 3. (*Med.*) stool, evacuation of the bowels; faeces; ***keinen – haben,*** be constipated, not have been moved.

Stuhl|abgang, *m. See* **–gang. –bein,** *n.* chair leg. **–drang,** *m.* need to relieve the bowels. **–feier,** *f.* St. Peter's day. **–flechtarbeit,** *f.* cane seating of chairs. **stuhlfördernd,** *adj.* laxative, aperient. **Stuhl|gang,** *m.* stool, excrement, faeces; defaecation; evacuation *or* action *or* movement of the bowels. **–geld,** *n.* pew-rent. **–lehne,** *f.* chair back. **–richter,** *m.* (*obs.*) presiding judge. **–sitz,** *m.* seat of a chair, chair bottom. **–verhaltung, –verstopfung,** *f.* constipation. **–zäpfchen,** *n.* anal suppository. **–zwang,** *m.* (*Med.*) tenesmus.

Stukkateur [ʃtukaˈtø:r], *m.* (**-s,** *pl.* **-e**) stucco-worker. **Stukkatur,** *f.* (-, *pl.* **-en**) stucco-work.

Stulle [ˈʃtulə], *f.* (*dial.*) slice of bread and butter.

Stulp [ˈʃtulp], **Stülp** [ʃtylp], *m.* (**-es,** *pl.* **-e**) turned-back *or* -up flap; sheath, shield, cover, guard. **Stulpe,** *f. See* **Stulp**; boot-top; pot-lid; cuff (*of sleeve*). **stülpen,** *v.t.* turn upside down *or* inside out; turn (up), invert; put *or* clap the lid on; ***den Hut auf den Kopf –,*** cram one's hat on one's head. **Stulpenstiefel,** *m.pl.* top-boots. **Stulphandschuh,** *m.* gauntlet (glove). **Stülpnase,** *f.* turned-up *or* snub *or* retroussé nose.

stumm [ʃtum], *adj.* dumb, mute; silent, speechless; ***–er Buchstabe,*** silent letter; ***–er Diener,*** dinner wagon; (*Theat.*) ***–e Rolle,*** non-speaking *or* walking-on part; ***–es Spiel,*** dumb-show, by-play.

Stummel [ˈʃtuməl], *m.* stump; stub, butt, (fag-)end. **Stummel|füße,** *m.pl.* parapodia, prolegs. **–lerche,** *f.* (*Orn.*) lesser short-toed lark (*Calandrella rufescens*). **–möwe,** *f.* (*Orn.*) (*Am.* black-legged) kittiwake (*Rissa tridactyla*). **–pfeife,** *f.* short-stemmed pipe.

Stumme(r) [ˈʃtumə(r)], *m., f.* mute (p.). **Stummfilm,** *m.* silent film. **Stummheit,** *f.* dumbness; silence.

Stumpen [ˈʃtumpən], *m.* 1. felt hat; 2. (*dial.*) stump; (*Swiss*) cheroot, small cigar.

Stümper [ˈʃtympər], *m.* bungler, blunderer, dabbler. **Stümperei** [–ˈraɪ], *f.* bungling, shoddy work, incompetence. **stümperhaft,** *adj.* clumsy, bungling, incompetent. **stümpern,** *v.t., v.i.* bungle, botch.

stumpf [ʃtumpf], *adj.* blunt, obtuse; (*fig.*) dull, dead, flat; stolid, insensible, indifferent, apathetic; ***–er Kegel,*** truncated cone; ***–e Nase,*** snub nose; ***–er Reim,*** masculine rhyme; ***–es Schwert,*** blunt sword; ***–e Stoßrapiere,*** buttoned foils; ***für eine S. ganz – sein,*** be quite indifferent *or* apathetic to a matter; ***–er Winkel,*** obtuse angle; ***die Zähne – machen,*** set the teeth on edge.

Stumpf, *m.* (**-(e)s,** *pl.* **⸚e**) stump, stub; (*Geom.*) frustrum; ***mit – und Stiel,*** root and branch; lock, stock and barrel. **stumpfeckig,** *adj.* obtuse-angled, blunt-cornered. **Stumpfheit,** *f.* bluntness, dullness, flatness; obtuseness, apathy, indifference. **stumpfkantig,** *adj.* blunt-edged. **Stumpf|kegel,** *m.* truncated cone. **–naht,** *f.* butt-seam. **–nase,** *f. See* **Stülpnase. –schwanz,** *m.* docked tail. **–sinn,** *m.* stupidity, dullness.

stumpf|sinnig, *adj.* dull, stupid; (*coll.*) thick- *or* bone-headed. **–wink(e)lig,** *adj. See* **–eckig.**

stund [ʃtynt], **stünde** ['ʃtyndə], (*Poet.*) *see* **stehen.**

Stunde ['ʃtundə], *f.* hour; period, lesson; distance covered in an hour; ***bis auf diese*** or ***bis zur –,*** till now, as yet, up till this moment; ***–n geben,*** give lessons; ***– halten,*** have a class; ***–n nehmen,*** have lessons (***bei,*** with), take lessons (from); ***in letzter –,*** in the nick of time, at the eleventh hour; ***in einer schwachen –,*** in a weak moment; ***freie –,*** free period; ***eine – lang,*** a whole hour, for an hour; ***seine – hat geschlagen*** or ***ist gekommen,*** his hour *or* time has come, his time is up, his sands are running out; ***von Stund' an,*** from that very hour, ever since then; (*dial.*) ***was ist die –?*** what is the time? (*Prov.*) ***Zeit und – warten nicht,*** time and tide wait for no man; ***– X,*** zero hour; ***zur Stund(e),*** now, at once; ***zu guter –,*** in good time; ***zu jeder –,*** at any time; ***zur rechten –,*** at the right moment.

stunden ['ʃtundən], *v.t.* (*Comm.*) grant a respite for, allow time to pay, extend the term of.

Stunden|buch, *n.* breviary. **–durchschnitt,** *m.* (average) speed per hour. **–gebete,** *n.pl.* (*R.C.*) the hours. **–geld,** *n.* fee for instruction. **–geschwindigkeit,** *f. See* **–durchschnitt. –glas,** *n.* hour-glass. **–kilometer,** *m.pl.* kilometres per hour. **–kreis,** *m.* (*Astr.*) horary circle. **stundenlang, 1.** *adj.* lasting (for) hours *or* more than an hour. **2.** *adv.* for hours (and hours), for hours together. **Stunden|leistung,** *f.* output per hour, hourly output. **–lohn,** *m.* payment by the hour. **–plan,** *m.* time-table, schedule. **–satz,** *m.* hourly rate. **–schlag,** *m.* (*clocks*) striking of the hour; ***mit dem –,*** on the stroke. **–tafel,** *f.* gnomonic table. **stundenweise,** *adv.* by the hour. **Stunden|winkel,** *m.* (*Astr.*) horary angle. **–zeiger,** *m.* hour-hand.

–stündig [ʃtyndɪç], *adj.suff.* lasting . . . hours. **Stündlein,** *n.* short hour; ***wenn sein – kommt,*** when his last hour draws nigh; ***Gott gebe ihm ein seliges –,*** God grant him an easy passing. **stündlich, 1.** *adj.* hourly. **2.** *adv.* from hour to hour, hour by hour, every hour, per hour.

Stundung ['ʃtunduŋ], *f.* delay, respite, extension (of time). **Stundungsfrist,** *f.* days of grace.

Stunk [ʃtuŋk], *m.* (*coll.*) squabble, row; ***– machen,*** kick up a row, (*sl.*) make a stink.

Stupf [ʃtupf], *m.*, **stupfen,** *v.t.* (*dial.*) *see* **Stups, stupsen.**

stupid(e) [ʃtu'pi:t (–i:də)], *adj.* half-witted, vacuous, fatuous, idiotic (*N.B. stronger than* stupid).

stuprieren [ʃtu'pri:rən], *v.t.* rape, violate. **Stuprum** ['ʃtu:prum], *n.* (**-s,** *pl.* **-ra**) rape, violation.

Stups [ʃtups], *m.* (**-es,** *pl.* **-e**) (*coll.*) nudge, push, shove, jolt. **stupsen,** *v.t.* nudge, jog. **Stupsnase,** *f. See* **Stülpnase.**

stur [ʃtu:r], *adj.* stubborn, obdurate, (*Scots*) dour; ***–er Blick,*** fixed *or* staring gaze. **Sturheit,** *f.* stubbornness. **Sturkurs,** *m.* (*coll.*) ***– fliegen,*** not budge an inch, stick to one's guns.

Sturm [ʃturm], *m.* (**-(e)s,** *pl.* **⸚e**) storm, (*Poet.*) tempest; gale, (*Naut.*) strong gale; (*fig.*) rush, tumult, turmoil, fury; (*Mil.*) charge, onset, attack, assault; (*Footb.*) forward-line, forwards; (*Nat. Soc.*) company, unit; (*Comm.*) ***– auf*** (*Acc.*), rush on (*goods*), run on (*a book, bank*); ***– blasen,*** sound the alarm; ***– und Drang,*** Storm and Stress; ***im – erobern,*** take by assault *or* (*fig.*) by storm; ***– laufen auf*** (*Acc.*), charge, attack, (*also fig.*) assail, assault, storm; ***sie kamen – gelaufen,*** they advanced at the charge; ***– läuten,*** ring the alarm-bell, (*coll.*) bring the house down; (*Naut.*) ***schwerer –,*** storm; (*Naut.*) ***voller –,*** whole gale; ***– im Wasserglas,*** storm in a teacup; (*Mil.*) ***zum – auf!*** charge!

Sturm|abteilung, *f.* (*Nat. Soc.*) storm troops *or* detachment, S.A. **–angriff,** *m.* charge, assault. **–band,** *n.* chin-strap (*on helmet*). **–bann,** *m.* (*Nat. Soc.*) battalion of S.A. **–bock,** *m.* (*Hist.*) battering-ram. **–boot,** *n.* assault boat, landing craft. **–dach,** *n.* (*Hist.*) testudo. **–deck,** *n.* (*Naut.*) hurricane-deck.

stürmen ['ʃtyrmən], **1.** *v.t.* storm, take by storm, force; ***den Himmel –,*** reach for the stars. **2.** *v.i.* be stormy, be violent, (*fig.*) storm, rage; (*Mil.*) charge, make an assault, advance to the attack, (*Footb.*) attack; (*aux.* s.) dash, rush along. **stürmend,** *adj.* attacking; impetuous; violent; ***mit –er Hand erobern,*** take by assault. **Stürmer,** *m.* 1. assailant; dare-devil, hothead; ***– und Dränger,*** poets of the German Storm and Stress period; 2. (*Footb.*) forward; 3. student's cap.

Sturmfahne ['ʃturmfa:nə], *f.* banner, battle standard. **sturmfest,** *adj.* storm-proof. **Sturmflut,** *f.* tidal wave. **sturmfrei,** *adj.* unassailable; (*Studs. sl.*) ***–e Bude,*** furnished room where there is no objection to lady visitors. **Sturm|führer,** *m.* (*Nat. Soc.*) company commander of S.S. **–gasse,** *f.* assault lane. **–geschütz,** *n.* assault gun. **–gewehr,** *n.* automatic rifle. **–glocke,** *f.* tocsin, alarm-bell. **–haube,** *f.* (*Hist.*) morion. **–hut,** *m.* (*Bot.*) monkshood, wolf's-bane (*Aconitum napellus*).

stürmisch ['ʃtyrmɪʃ], *adj.* stormy, tempestuous; turbulent, violent, tumultuous, passionate, impetuous; ***–er Beifall,*** tumultuous *or* uproarious applause; ***–e Entrüstung,*** storm of indignation, indignant outcry.

Sturm|kegel, *m.* (storm) cone. **–laterne,** *f.* storm lantern. **–leiter,** *f.* scaling-ladder. **–möwe,** *f.* (*Orn.*) common *or* (*Am.*) mew gull (*Larus canus*). **–pforten,** *f.pl.* (*Naut.*) dead-lights. **sturmreif,** *adj.* easily assailable; ***– machen,*** soften up (*a position*). **Sturm|riemen,** *m. See* **–band. –schaden,** *m.* storm damage. **–schritt,** *m.* double-quick step *or* march; ***im –,*** at the double. **–schwalbe,** *f.* (*Orn.*) storm-petrel (*Hydrobates pelagicus*), (*coll.*) Mother Carey's chicken. **–taucher,** *m.* (*Orn.*) ***dunkler –,*** sooty shearwater (*Puffinus griseus*); ***großer –,*** great shearwater (*Puffinus gravis*); ***kleiner –,*** little shearwater (*Puffinus baroli*). **–trupp,** *m.* storming party, shock *or* assault troops. **–vögel,** *m.pl.* procellarians, oceanic birds. **–warnung,** *f.* gale warning. **–welle,** *f.* (*Mil.*) assault wave. **–wetter,** *n.* stormy weather; storm. **–wind,** *m.* heavy gale, high wind.

Sturz [ʃturts], *m.* 1. (**-es,** *pl.* **⸚e**) (sudden) fall, tumble, (*coll.*) cropper; crash, drop, plunge, dive; precipice; waterfall, cataract; (*fig.*) downfall, overthrow (*of government etc.*); collapse, slump (*of prices*), failure, ruin, (*coll.*) crash (*of a firm*), audit (*of accounts*); ***ein Glas auf einen – austrinken*** empty a glass at one draught; ***zum – bringen,*** overthrow; 2. (*pl.* **-e**) lintel (*of doors, windows etc.*); 3. *See* **Stürze.**

Sturz|acker, *m.* newly-ploughed land. **–angriff,** *m.* (*Av.*) dive-bombing attack. **–bach,** *m.* torrent, waterfall. **–bett,** *n.* spillway (*of a dam*). **–bomber,** *m.* (*Av.*) dive-bomber. **–bügel,** *m.* safety-stirrup.

Stürze ['ʃtyrtsə], *f.* dish-cover, lid.

Stürzel ['ʃtyrtsəl], *m.* stub(-end), (tree-)stump.

stürzen ['ʃtyrtsən], **1.** *v.i.* (*aux.* s.) fall *or* tumble (down), have a fall; rush, dash, crash, plunge, (*Av.*) dive; (*of ground*) fall *or* drop *or* descend steeply, (*of prices*) collapse; ***ins Zimmer –,*** rush *or* burst into the room; ***vom Pferde –,*** fall off one's horse, (*coll.*) come a cropper. **2.** *v.t.* throw *or* hurl down, plunge, precipitate; overturn, upset; dump, tip (*rubbish*); plough up, turn over (*ground*); (*fig.*) overthrow (*government etc.*); ***in einen Krieg –,*** plunge into a war; ***ins Elend*** or ***Verderben –,*** (bring to) ruin, bring ruin upon; ***nicht –!*** with care! do not drop! **3.** *v.r.* rush, plunge; ***sich – auf*** (*Acc.*), rush at, plunge upon; ***sich auf die Arbeit –,*** throw o.s. into one's work; ***sich ins Wasser –,*** throw o.s. *or* jump into the water; drown o.s.; ***sich in Unkosten –,*** go to a great deal of expense; ***sich in Schulden –,*** get hopelessly in debt; ***sich in sein Schwert –,*** fall upon one's sword.

Sturz|flug, *m.* (*Av.*) (nose-)dive. **–güter,** *n.pl.* bulk goods. **–helm,** *m.* crash-helmet. **–kampfflugzeug,** *n. See* **–bomber. –pflug,** *m.* fallow-plough. **–regen,** *m.* torrential downpour. **–see,** *f.* heavy sea; ***eine – bekommen,*** ship a sea. **–spirale,** *f.* (*Av.*) spiral dive. **–wellen,** *f.pl.* breakers; ***– bekommen,*** ship heavy seas.

Stuß [ʃtus], *m.* (*coll.*) stuff and nonsense, rubbish, balderdash.

Stute [ˈʃtuːtə], *f.* mare.

Stuten [ˈʃtuːtən], *m.* (*dial.*) breakfast-roll. **Stutenbäcker,** *m.* pastrycook.

Stuten|fohlen, –füllen, *n.* foal, filly. **–knecht,** *m.* stud-groom. **Stuterei** [–ˈraɪ], *f.* stud.

Stutz [ʃtuts], *m.* (**-es,** *pl.* **-e**) 1. (*dial.*) shove, jolt; ***auf den –, auf – und Blutz,*** all of a sudden; 2. plume (*on hats*); 3. (*Swiss*) steep slope.

Stütz [ʃtyts], *m.* (*Gymn.*) rest(ing) position, (straight-arm) rest.

Stutzärmel [ˈʃtutsˀɛrməl], *m.* short sleeve; sleeve protector.

Stützbalken [ˈʃtytsbalkən], *m.* supporting beam, wooden support *or* stay, prop, joist, shore, brace.

Stutz|bart, *m.* close-cropped beard. **–büchse,** *f.* carbine. **–degen,** *m.* short sword.

Stütze [ˈʃtytsə], *f.* support, post, pillar, prop, stay, leg, shore; (*fig.*) mainstay, support, backing; (*coll.*) lady-help; ***im Gesetz keine – finden,*** have no case in law.

stutzen [ˈʃtutsən], **1.** *v.i.* stop short, be startled, start (***bei,*** at), be taken aback (by); be puzzled, become suspicious, boggle (at); (*of horse*) prick up its ears (at). **2.** *v.t.* cut (short), shorten, curtail, (*tree*) prune, lop, (*tail*) dock, (*ears*) crop, (*beard*) crop, trim, (*wings, hedge*) clip.

Stutzen, *m.* 1. carbine; 2. (*Mech.*) connecting-piece, connection, union; 3. footless stocking.

stützen [ˈʃtytsən], **1.** *v.t.* support, prop (up), stay, shore up, buttress; (*fig.*) support, uphold, (*coll.*) back (up), (*Comm.*) peg (*prices etc.*); rest, lean (*arms etc.*) (*auf* (*Acc.*), on), (*fig.*) base, found, rest (*one's argument*) (*auf* (*Acc.*), on); ***auf seine Ellbogen gestützt,*** propped on his elbows; ***auf sein Recht gestützt,*** relying on the justice of his cause. **2.** *v.r.* (*auf* (*Acc.*)) rest, lean (on), (*fig.*) rely, depend, be based *or* founded (on).

Stutzer [ˈʃtutsər], *m.* 1. fop, dandy, (*coll.*) swell; 2. (*Swiss*) carbine. **stutzerhaft,** *adj.* foppish, dandified. **Stutzertum,** *n.* foppishness.

Stützfläche [ˈʃtytsflɛçə], *f.* supporting *or* bearing surface.

Stutz|flügel, *m.* baby-grand (piano). **–glas,** *n.* short-stemmed glass, squat tumbler. **–handschuh,** *m.* mitten.

stutzig [ˈʃtutsɪç], (*dial.*) **stützig,** *adj.* startled, surprised, taken aback, disconcerted; puzzled, perplexed, nonplussed; – ***machen,*** startle, surprise, perplex, puzzle; – ***werden,*** be taken aback, be puzzled *or* startled, prick up one's ears, become suspicious, begin to wonder.

Stutzkopf [ˈʃtutskɔpf], *m.* (*coll.*) regulation haircut.

Stützmauer [ˈʃtytsmauər], *f.* retaining *or* supporting wall.

Stutzperücke [ˈʃtutsperykə], *f.* bobtail wig.

Stütz|pfeiler, *m.* (supporting) pillar, column, buttress, abutment, support. **–punkt,** *m.* point of support, fulcrum, (*Mil.*) base, (*fig.*) foothold, footing. **–punktlinie,** *f.* (*Mil.*) line of strongpoints.

Stutz|schwanz, *m.* bobtail, docked tail. **–uhr,** *f.* shelf *or* mantelpiece clock.

Stützung [ˈʃtytsuŋ], *f.* (*Comm.*) pegging, support (*of the market*). **Stützungsaktion,** *f.* pegging the market. **Stützweite,** *f.* span (*of an arch*).

Suada [zuˈaːda], **Suade,** *f.* (*coll.*) gift of the gab, blarney.

subaltern [zupˀalˈtɛrn], *adj.* subordinate, (*Mil.*) subaltern; ***–er Geist,*** second-rate mind; ***–e Gesinnung,*** servile attitude. **Subalternbeamte(r),** *m.* subordinate (official). **Subalterne(r),** *m.* underling. **Subalternoffizier,** *m.* (*Mil.*) subaltern.

Subhastation [zuphastatsiˈoːn], *f.* public auction *or* (*Scots*) roup. **subhastieren** [–ˈtiːrən], *v.t.* sell by auction, bring under the hammer.

Subjekt [zupˈjɛkt], *n.* (**-(e)s,** *pl.* **-e**) 1. (*Gram., Log.*) subject, (*Mus.*) theme; 2. (*coll.*) fellow, creature; ***übles*** or ***verkommenes –,*** blackguard, bad lot.

subjektiv [–ˈtiːf], *adj.* subjective; personal, biased. **Subjektivität** [–tiviˈtɛːt], *f.* subjectivity, personal attitude.

subkutan [zupkuˈtaːn], *adj.* subcutaneous; ***–e Einspritzung,*** hypodermic injection. **Subkutanspritze,** *f.* hypodermic syringe.

sublim [zuˈbliːm], *adj.* sublime. **Sublimat** [–ˈmaːt], *n.* (**-(e)s,** *pl.* **-e**) mercuric chloride, (corrosive) sublimate. **sublimieren,** *v.t.* sublimate.

submiß [zupˈmɪs], *adj.* submissive, humble(d), deferential, respectful. **Submission** [–iˈoːn], *f.* 1. submissiveness, submission, deference, humility; 2. (*Comm.*) invitation for tenders; ***in – geben,*** invite tenders for. **Submissions|angebot,** *n.* tender. **–strich,** *m.* (*Hist.*) line drawn lengthwise from the foot of a petition down to the signature(s).

Subsidien [zupˈziːdiən], *n.pl.* subsidies; ***durch – unterstützen,*** subsidize.

Subskribent [zupskriˈbɛnt], *m.* (**-en,** *pl.* **-en**) subscriber (***auf*** (*Acc.*), to). **subskribieren,** *v.i.* subscribe (***auf*** (*Acc.*), to). **Subskription** [–skrɪptsiˈoːn], *f.* subscription. **Subskriptionsanzeige,** *f.* prospectus.

substantiell [zupstantsiˈɛl], *adj.* substantial, material.

Substantiv [zupstanˈtiːf], *n.* (**-s,** *pl.* **-e**) substantive, noun. **substantivisch,** *adj.* (*Gram.*) substantival. **Substantivum,** *n.* (**-s,** *pl.* **-va**) *see* **Substantiv.**

Substanz [zupˈstants], *f.* (–, *pl.* **-en**) substance, matter, stuff; (*Comm.*) principal, capital. **substanzieren** [–tsiːrən], *v.t.* (*Law*) particularize (*a claim*).

substituieren [zupstituˈiːrən], *v.t.* substitute (***durch,*** for).

Substrat [zupˈstraːt], *n.* (**-(e)s,** *pl.* **-e**) base, precipitate; substratum, foundation.

subsumieren [zupzuˈmiːrən], *v.t.* ascribe (***unter*** (*Dat.*), to), impute (to), include (with, among), comprise (within). **Subsumtion** [–tsiˈoːn], *f.* inclusion, imputation. **subsumtiv** [–ˈtiːf], *adj.* presumptive, presumed, imputed, insinuated.

subtil [zupˈtiːl], *adj.* subtle, cunning; delicate, fine; ***–e Behandlung,*** minute and careful treatment; ***mit ihm sehr – umgehen,*** treat him with great circumspection, (*coll.*) treat *or* handle him gently. **Subtilität** [–iˈtɛːt], *f.* subtlety.

subtrahieren [zuptraˈhiːrən], *v.t.* subtract, deduct. **Subtraktion** [–traktsiˈoːn], *f.* subtraction.

subvenieren [zupveˈniːrən], *v.t.* help, assist, support. **Subvention** [–vɛntsiˈoːn], *f.* subvention, subsidy. **subventionieren,** *v.t.* subsidize.

Such|aktion [ˈzuːx–], *f.* search. **–anzeige,** *f.* wanted advertisement. **–büro,** *n.* department for tracing missing persons.

Suche [ˈzuːxə], *f.* search, hunt, quest; scent (*of dogs*); ***auf die – gehen, sich auf die – machen,*** go in search (***nach,*** of), search (for); ***auf der – sein,*** be on the look-out (***nach,*** for).

suchen [ˈzuːxən], *v.t., v.i.* seek, desire, want; – ***nach,*** search *or* hunt *or* look for, seek; ***– zu tun,*** seek *or* endeavour *or* try to do; ***Abenteuer –,*** seek adventure, go in quest of adventure; ***seinesgleichen –,*** be unrivalled, have no equal, stand alone; ***Streit –,*** pick a quarrel; ***seinen Vorteil –,*** seek one's own advantage, (*coll.*) have an eye to the main chance; ***das Weite –,*** beat a (hasty) retreat, (*coll.*) make o.s. scarce; ***nach Worten –,*** grope for words, be at a loss for words; ***was hast du hier zu –?*** what do you want here? what business have you here? (*sl.*) what are you nosing about here for? *See* **gesucht.**

Sucher [ˈzuːxər], *m.* seeker, searcher; (*Phot.*) viewfinder; (*Med.*) probe. **Such|gerät,** *n.* (*Mil.*) sound-detector, (*radar*) scanner. **–mannschaft,** *f.* search-party. **–stelle,** *f.* *See* **–büro.**

Sucht [zuxt], *f.* (–, *pl.* (*rare*) **¨-e**) 1. passion, mania, rage, craze (***nach,*** for), (*Med.*) addiction (for); 2. (*obs.*) sickness, disease, epidemic; ***fallende –,*** falling sickness, epilepsy.

süchtig [ˈzyçtɪç], *adj.* 1. having a mania (***nach,*** for), craving (for), (*coll.*) crazy (for), (*Med.*) addicted (to), (*sl.*) hooked (on); 2. (*obs.*) sickly, diseased. **Süchtige(r),** *m., f.* addict.

Such|trupp, *m. See* **–mannschaft.**

suckeln ['zukəln], *v.i.* (*dial.*) suck (*an* (*Dat.*), at).

Sud [zu:t], *m.* (**-(e)s,** *pl.* **-e**) boiling, brewing; decoction, brew.

Süd [zy:t], *m.* south; south wind.

Süd|afrika, *n.* South Africa. **–afrikaner(in),** *m.* (*f.*), **südafrikanisch,** *adj.* South African; ***Südafrikanische Union,*** Union of South Africa. **Süd|amerika,** *n.* South *or* Latin America. **–amerikaner(in),** *m.,* (*f.*) South American. **südamerikanisch,** *adj.* South *or* Latin American.

Sudan [zu'da:n], *m.* the Sudan. **Sudanese,** *m.,* **Sudanesin,** *f.,* **sudanesisch,** *adj.* Sudanese.

Sudel ['zu:dəl], *m.* (*dial.*) 1. pool, puddle; dirt; 2. rough draft. **Sudelarbeit, Sudelei** [–'laɪ], *f.* dirty *or* slovenly work, (*coll.*) mess; daub(ing); scrawl(ing), scribble, scribbling; obscene *or* (*coll.*) dirty picture(s). **sud(e)lig,** *adj.* dirty, slovenly, messy; (*fig.*) obscene, filthy. **Sudelkoch,** *m.* (*fig.*) bungler, botcher, messy worker. **sudeln,** *v.i., v.t.* work *or* do in a slovenly manner, bungle, botch, make a mess of; scribble, scrawl; daub; (*Typ.*) soil, slur. **Sudelwetter,** *n.* dirty weather.

Süden ['zy:dən], *m.* south; ***im –,*** in the South; ***im – der Stadt,*** to the south of the town; ***nach –,*** southward(s); ***Kreuz des –s,*** Southern Cross.

Süd|früchte, *f.pl.* (semi-)tropical fruit. **–küste,** *f.* south(ern) coast. **–lage,** *f.* southern exposure. **–länder(in),** *m.* (*f.*) southerner.

Sudler ['zu:dlər], *m. See* **Sudelkoch.**

südlich ['zy:tlɪç], **1.** *adj.* south, southern, southerly; ***–e Breite,*** south latitude; ***–e Halbkugel,*** southern hemisphere; ***–e Richtung,*** southerly direction, southward(s). **2.** *adv.* ***– von,*** (to the) south of, southward(s) of *or* from.

Süd|licht, *n.* southern lights, Aurora australis. **–ost(en),** *m.* south-east; (*wind*) southeaster. **süd|östlich,** *adj.* south-east(ern), south-easterly. **–ostwärts,** *adv.* south-eastward(s), south-easterly. **Süd|pol,** *m.* South Pole. **–polarforschung,** *f.* antarctic exploration. **–polarländer,** *n.pl.* antarctic regions. **–see,** *f.* (southern) Pacific (Ocean). **–seeinseln,** *f.pl.* South-Sea Islands. **–seeinsulaner,** *m.* South-Sea Islander. **–seeländer,** *n.pl. See* **–seeinseln. –seite,** *f.* south *or* sunny side. **–slawe,** *m.* Yugoslav. **–slawien,** *n.* Yugoslavia. **südslawisch,** *adj.* Yugoslav. **Südstaaten,** *m.pl.* southern states. **südwärts,** *adv.* southward(s), (to the) south. **Süd|west(en),** *m.* south-west; (*wind*) southwester. **–wester,** *m.* (*hat*) southwester, sou'wester. **südwestlich,** *adj.* south-west(ern). **Süd|westwind,** *m.* southwester. **–wind,** *m.* south wind, southerly breeze.

Suff [zuf], *m.* (*coll.*) boozing, tippling; booze; ***sich dem – ergeben,*** take to drink, (*sl.*) hit the bottle; ***sich dem stillen – ergeben,*** be a secret drinker.

Süffel ['zyfəl], *m.* (*coll.*) drunkard, toper, tippler. **süffeln,** *v.i.* (*coll.*) booze, tipple. **süffig,** *adj.* palatable, delicious, tasty.

süffisant [syfi'zant], *adj.* self-satisfied, smug.

suggerieren [zuge'ri:rən], *v.t.* suggest; influence (*a p.'s mind*) by suggestion. **Suggestivfrage,** *f.* leading question.

Suhle ['zu:lə], *f.* muddy puddle, wallow, slough. **suhlen, sühlen,** *v.i., v.r.* wallow in mire.

sühnbar ['zy:nbar], *adj.* expiable, atonable.

Sühne ['zy:nə], *f.* atonement, expiation; reconciliation; propitiation. **sühnen,** *v.t.* expiate, atone for. **sühnend,** *adj.* expiatory, propitiatory. **Sühne|termin,** *m.* (*Law*) conciliation hearing. **–versuch,** *m.* attempt at reconciliation. **Sühnopfer,** *n.* propitiatory sacrifice, (*fig.*) atonement. **Sühnung,** *f. See* **Sühne.**

Suite ['svi:tə], *f.* 1. suite (*also Mus.*), train, retinue; 2. (*coll.*) prank, lark, trick; ***–n reißen,*** play tricks.

Sukkurs [zu'kurs], *m.* support, succour; (*Mil.*) reinforcement.

sukzedieren [zuktse'di:rən], *v.i.* succeed (to), inherit. **Sukzession** [–tsɛsi'o:n], *f.* (legal) succession. **Sukzessionsakte,** *f.* (*Pol.*) act of settlement. **sukzessions|berechtigt, –fähig,** *adj.* legally entitled to the succession.

sukzessiv [zuktsɛ'si:f], *adj.* gradual, successive. **sukzessive,** *adv.* gradually, little by little, (*coll.*) bit by bit.

Sulfat [zul'fa:t], *n.* (**-(e)s,** *pl.* **-e**) sulphate. **Sulf|hydrat, –hydrid,** *n.* hydrosulphide. **Sulfid,** *n.* (**-(e)s,** *pl.* **-e**) sulphide. **sulfieren,** *v.t.* sulphurize, sulphonate. **Sulfit,** *n.* (**-(e)s,** *pl.* **-e**) sulphite.

Sülf|meister ['zylf–], *m.* (*Hist.*) master of salt-works; (*dial.*) bungler.

Sulfo|base ['zulfo–], *f.* sulphur base. **–gruppe,** *f.* sulphonic group. **–hydrat,** *n. See* **Sulfhydrat. –namid,** *n.* sulphonamide. **sulfonieren** [–'ni:rən], *v.t. See* **sulfieren. Sulfur,** *n. See* **Sulfid. sulfurieren,** *v.t. See* **sulfieren. sulfurös** [–'rø:s], *adj.* sulphurous.

Sulph–, *see* **Sulf–.**

Sultan ['zulta:n], *m.* (**-s,** *pl.* **-e**) sultan. **Sultanat** [–'na:t], *n.* (**-(e)s,** *pl.* **-e**) sultanate. **Sultanin,** *f.* sultana.

Sultanine [zulta'ni:nə], *f.* sultana (*raisin*).

Sulz [zults], **Sulze** (*Austr.*), **Sülze** ['zyltsə], *f.* aspic; (*dial.*) brine; pickled (jellied) meat; brawn; deer-lick. **sülzen,** *v.t.* pickle in jelly. **Sülzfleisch,** *n.* meat in aspic.

Summa ['zuma], *f.* (**-,** *pl.* **-men**) *see* **Summe**; ***in –,*** in short, to sum up; ***– summarum,*** (taking) all in all, in a nutshell. **Summand** [–'mant], *m.* (**-en,** *pl.* **-en**) (*Math.*) term of a sum, (*Comm.*) item. **summarisch** [–'ma:rɪʃ], *adj.* summary, succinct; (*Law*) ***–es Verfahren,*** summary proceedings.

Sümmchen ['zymçən], *n.* (*coll.*) ***nettes –,*** tidy little sum, pretty penny, (*sl.*) (quite) a packet.

Summe ['zumə], *f.* sum, (sum) total, amount; ***die – ziehen,*** sum up; ***fehlende –,*** deficit; ***höchste –,*** maximum; ***– der Bewegung,*** momentum.

summen ['zumən], **1.** *v.i.* buzz. **2.** *v.t.* hum, drone. **Summen,** *n.* buzz(ing), hum(ming), drone, droning.

Summen|gleichung, *f.* (*Math.*) summation equation. **–wirkung,** *f.* combined effect.

Summer ['zumər], *m.* buzzer; (*coll.*) bluebottle. **Summer|ton,** *m.,* **–zeichen,** *n.* (*Tele.*) dialling tone.

summieren [zu'mi:rən], **1.** *v.t.* add *or* (*coll.*) tot up. **2.** *v.r.* amount to, come to; total *or* (*coll.*) run up. **Summierung,** *f.* summing up, summarizing; addition; accumulation.

Sumpf [zumpf], *m.* (**-(e)s,** *pl.* **¨-e**) swamp, bog, marsh, fen; morass, quagmire; (*Min., Motor.*) sump; ***– der Schändlichkeit,*** sink of corruption, den of iniquity. **Sumpf|blüte,** *f.* deplorable exhibition, outrage, indignity, monstrosity, eyesore, vulgarism. **–boden,** *m.* marshy ground. **–dotterblume,** *f.* (*Bot.*) marsh-marigold (*Caltha palustris*).

sumpfen ['zumpfən], *v.i.* (*coll.*) go on the binge; lead a dissolute life.

sümpfen ['zympfən], *v.t.* 1. drain (*a mine*); 2. knead (*potter's clay*).

Sumpf|eule, *f. See* **–ohreule. –fieber,** *n.* malaria, marsh-fever. **–gas,** *n.* marsh gas, methane. **–huhn,** *n.* (*sl.*) rake, dissolute wretch; (*Orn.*) ***kleines –,*** little crake (*Porzana parva*). **sumpfig,** *adj.* marshy, swampy, boggy. **Sumpf|läufer,** *m.* (*Orn.*) broad-billed sandpiper (*Limicola falcinellus*). **–meise,** *f.* (*Orn.*) marsh-titmouse (*Parus palustris*). **–ohreule,** *f.* (*Orn.*) short-eared owl (*Asio flammeus*). **–pflanze,** *f.* marsh-plant, uliginose *or* limnodophilous plant. **–rohrsänger,** *m.* (*Orn.*) marsh-warbler (*Acrocephalus palustris*). **–schildkröte,** *f.* (*Zool.*) marsh-turtle (*Emydes*). **–schnepfe,** *f.* (*Orn.*) ***gemeine –,*** common *or* (*Am.*) European snipe (*Gallinago gallinago*); ***große –,*** great snipe (*Gallinago media*); ***kleine –,*** jack snipe, (*Am.*) European jacksnipe (*Lymnocryptes minimus*). **–vogel,** *m.* wading-bird, wader. **–wasser,** *n.* stagnant water, marshy pool. **–wiese,** *f.* swampy meadow.

Sums [zums], *m.* (*dial.*) buzzing noise; (*coll.*) empty chatter; (*coll.*) ***einen großen – machen,*** make a great fuss. **sumsen,** *v.i. See* **summen.**

Sund [zunt], *m.* (–**(e)s,** *pl.* –**e**) sound, straits.

Sünde ['zyndə], *f.* sin; transgression, trespass, offence; ***Gott verzeih' mir die –!*** Heaven forgive me! ***ich hasse ihn wie die –,*** I hate him like poison; ***eine – und Schande,*** a sin and a shame, a wicked shame; ***der Tod ist der – Sold,*** the wages of sin is death.

Sünden|babel, *n.* hotbed of vice, sink of iniquity. **–bahn,** *f.* road to perdition. **–bekenntnis,** *n.* confession (of sin). **–bock,** *m.* scapegoat. **–erlaß,** *m.* remission of sins, absolution. **–fall,** *m.* the Fall (of Man). **–geld,** *n.* ill-gotten gain; (*coll.*) enormous sum, mint of money. **–leben,** *n.* sinful *or* wicked life, life of sin. **–lohn,** *m.* wages of sin. **–pfuhl,** *m.* sink of corruption. **–register,** *n.,* **–schuld,** *f.* list of trangressions. **–vergebung,** *f.* **–erlaß.**

Sünder ['zyndər], *m.* sinner; culprit; delinquent; (*fig.*) ***armer –,*** poor devil *or* wretch; ***verstockter –,*** unrepentant sinner; ***Gott sei mir – gnädig!*** God forgive me, sinner that I am! **Sünderin,** *f. See* **Sunder. Sünderschemel,** *m.* stool of repentance.

Sündflut ['zyntflu:t], *f.* (*coll.*) *see* **Sintflut.**

sündhaft ['zynthaft], **1.** *adj.* sinful; erring, wicked. **2.** *adv.* (*coll.*) awfully, shockingly; ***– viel,*** a mighty lot. **Sündhaftigkeit,** *f.* wickedness, sinfulness.

sündig ['zyndɪç], *adj.* sinful, wicked; guilty. **sündigen,** *v.i.* (commit a) sin, trespass, transgress; ***was habe ich gesündigt?*** what (wrong) have I done? ***an ihm –,*** wrong him, do him a wrong. **sündlich,** *adj.* sinful, unlawful, impious, infamous, nefarious. **sündlos,** *adj.* innocent, blameless, righteous. **Sündwasser,** *n.* water of purification.

superarbitrieren [zupɛrˀarbi'tri:rən], *v.t.* (*Austr.*) review, revise, reconsider (*a judgement*). **Super|-azidität,** *f.* hyperacidity. **–dividende,** *f.* extra dividend, (cash) bonus. **–intendent,** *m.* (Protestant) senior minister. **Superiorin** [–i'o:rɪn], *f.* Mother Superior. **Superiorität** [–'tɛ:t], *f.* superiority, preponderance. **superklug,** *adj.* too clever by half, (*coll.*) cocky. **Superlativ** [–la'ti:f], *m.* superlative. **superlativisch,** *adj.* superlative. **Super|oxyd,** *n.* peroxide. **–revision,** *f.* final revision.

Suppe ['zupə], *f.* soup, broth; (*fig.*) ***die – ausessen*** or ***auslöffeln müssen,*** have to abide by the consequences, have to face the music; ***ihm eine schöne – einbrocken,*** make things awkward for him, get him into hot water; (*coll.*) ***das macht die – nicht fett,*** that won't do much good, that won't help; (*fig.*) ***ein Haar in der –,*** a fly in the ointment; ***ihn auf einen Löffel – einladen,*** invite him to drop in for a meal; ***ihm die – versalzen,*** (*vulg.*) ***ihm in die – spucken,*** spoil his fun *or* pleasure, spoil things for him.

Suppen|einlage, *f.* things added to soup. **–fleisch,** *n.* gravy-beef. **–kaspar,** *m.* (*coll.*) child without appetite, difficult eater. **–kelle,** *f.* soup-ladle. **–kräuter,** *n.pl.* pot-herbs. **–löffel,** *m.* soup-spoon. **–schüssel,** *f.* soup-bowl. **–teller,** *m.* soup-plate *or* dish. **–terrine,** *f.* soup-tureen. **–topf,** *m.* stock-pot. **–würfel,** *m.* soup-cube. **–würze,** *f.* seasoning.

Supplement [zuple'mɛnt], *n.* (**-(e)s,** *pl.* **-e**) supplement, (*Geom.*) supplementary angle.

Supplent [zu'plɛnt], *m.* (**-en,** *pl.* **-en**) (*Austr.*) assistant master.

Supplik [zu'pli:k], *f.* (-, *pl.* **-en**) petition, plea. **Supplikant** [–'kant], *m.* (**-en,** *pl.* **-en**) supplicant, petitioner. **supplizieren** [–'tsi:rən], *v.t.* supplicate, plead, sue.

supponieren [zupo'ni:rən], *v.t.* assume, surmise, presume, suppose, presuppose, impute (to).

Suppositorium [zupozi'to:rium], *n.* (**-s,** *pl.* **-rien**) (*Med.*) suppository.

Suppositum [zu'pɔzitum], *n.* (**-s,** *pl.* **-ita**) assumption, surmise, (pre-)supposition, imputation.

Supremat [zupre'ma:t], *n.* supremacy.

Sur [zu:r], *f.* (*Austr.*) brine, pickle.

surren ['zurən], *v.i.* hum, buzz, whizz, whirr. **Surren,** *n.* hum(ming), buzz(ing), whirring.

Surrogat [zuro'ga:t], *n.* (**-(e)s,** *pl.* **-e**) substitute; makeshift. **Surrogation** [–tsi'o:n], *f.* substitution, replacement.

suspendieren [zuspɛn'di:rən], *v.t.* suspend. **Suspendierung, Suspension** [–zi'o:n], *f.* suspension. **Suspensorium** [–'zo:rium], *n.* (**-s,** *pl.* **-rien**) (*Surg.*) suspensor(y).

süß [zy:s], *adj.* sweet, sweetened; fresh; (*fig.*) sweet, lovely, charming, dear, delightful; ***–e Milch,*** fresh milk; ***–e Tränen,*** tears of joy; ***–e Worte,*** soft *or* honeyed *or* winning words. **Süße,** *f.* sweetness; (*fig.*) darling, honey, sweetie. **süßen,** *v.t.* sweeten. **Süßholz,** *n.* (*Bot.*) liquorice; (*fig.*) ***– raspeln,*** pay compliments, say sweet nothings; flirt.

Süßigkeit ['zy:sɪçkaɪt], *f.* sweetness; (*fig.*) suavity; sweetmeat; (*pl.*) sweets.

süßlich ['zy:slɪç], *adj.* sweetish; (*fig. of a p.*) mawkish, fulsome, (*sl.*) soppy, smarmy. **Süßling,** *m.* (**-s,** *pl.* **-e**) mawkish *or* wishy-washy *or* namby-pamby p., milksop, (*coll.*) drip.

Süß|mandelöl, *n.* oil of sweet almonds. **–maul,** *n.* sweet-tooth. **–most,** *m.* unfermented wine; (*Swiss*) fruit drink. **süßsauer,** *adj.* bitter-sweet. **Süß|speise,** *f.* sweet, pudding, dessert. **–stoff,** *m.* saccharin, sweetening agent. **–waren,** *f.pl.* sweets, sweetmeats. **–wasser,** *n.* fresh water. **–wasserfisch,** *m.* freshwater fish. **–wein,** *m.* dessert wine.

Sust ['zust], *f.* (-, *pl.* **-en**) (*Swiss*) shed, shelter.

Suszeption [zustsɛptsi'o:n], *f.* acceptance, taking in hand. **suszipieren** [–tsi'pi:rən], *v.t.* accept, undertake, take in hand.

Suzerän [zutse'rɛ:n], *m.* (**-s,** *pl.* **-e**) suzerain, paramount ruler. **suzerän,** *adj.* paramount, sovereign. **Suzeränität** [–i'tɛ:t], *f.* suzerainty.

Sykomore [zyko'mo:rə], *f.* (*Bot.*) Egyptian sycamore (*Ficus sycomorus*).

Sylphe ['zylfə], *m.* (**-n,** *pl.* **-n**), *Austr. f.,* **Sylphide** [–'fi:də], *f.* sylph.

Sylvesterabend, *m. See* **Silvesterabend.**

Symbasis [zym'ba:zɪs], *f.* agreement, parallelism.

Symbiose [zymbi'o:zə], *f.* symbiosis.

Symbol [zym'bo:l], *n.* (**-s,** *pl.* **-e**) symbol, (*Her.*) emblem, (*Geog.*) conventional sign. **Symbolik,** *f.* symbolism. **symbolisch,** *adj.* symbolic(al). **symbolisieren** [–i'zi:rən], *v.t.* symbolize. **Symbolismus** [–'lɪsmus], *m.* symbolism (*in art*).

Symmetrie [zyme'tri:], *f.* symmetry. **symmetrisch** [–'me:trɪʃ], *adj.* symmetric(al).

sympathetisch [zympa'te:tɪʃ], *adj.* **1.** sympathetic; **2.** mysterious, miraculous; ***–e Kur,*** faith-healing. **Sympathie,** *f.* sympathy, fellow-feeling, congeniality; inclination, fondness. **Sympathiestreik,** *m.* strike in sympathy (with).

sympathisch [zym'pa:tɪʃ], *adj.* congenial, likeable; ***sie ist mir –,*** she sppeals to me, I like her; ***–es Nervensystem,*** sympathetic nerve-ganglia *or* nervous system. **sympathisieren** [–'zi:rən], *v.i.* sympathize, agree, be in agreement (***mit,*** with).

Symphonie [zymfo'ni:], *f. See* **Sinfonie.**

Symptom [zymp'to:m], *n.* (**-s,** *pl.* **-e**) symptom. **symptomatisch** [–'ma:tɪʃ], *adj.* symptomatic, characteristic (***für,*** of).

Synagoge [zyna'go:gə], *f.* synagogue.

synchron [zyn'kro:n], *adj.* synchronous, simultaneous. **Synchrongetriebe,** *n.* (*Motor.*) synchromesh gear. **synchronisieren** [–ni'zi:rən], *v.t.* synchronize, (*Films*) dub. **Synchronisierung,** *f.* synchronization, (*Films*) dubbing. **Synchronismus** [–'nɪsmus], *m.* synchronism. **synchronistisch,** *adj.* concurrent, coincident, isochronous. **Synchronmotor,** *m.* synchronous motor.

Syndikalismus [zyndɪka'lɪsmus], *m.* trade(s)-union movement, working-class radicalism. **Syndikat** [–'ka:t], *n.* (**-(e)s,** *pl.* **-e**) syndicate, cartel, combine, trust. **Syndikus** ['zyndikus], *m.* (-, *pl.* **-ken** *or* **Syndizi**) syndic, trustee, legal representative, (*Am.*) corporation lawyer.

Synkope, *f.* 1. ['zynkope] (*no pl.*) (*Metr., Med.*) syncope; 2. [zyn'ko:pə] (*Mus.*) syncope. **synkopieren** [–'pi:rən], *v.t.* (*Metr., Mus.*) syncopate.

Synode [zy'no:də], *f.* synod, church council. **synodisch,** *adj.* synodal; (*Astr.*) synodic(al).

synonym [zyno'ny:m], *adj.* synonymous, synonymic. **Synonym,** *n.* (**-s,** *pl.* **-e**) synonym. **Synonymik,** *f.* study of synonyms. **synonymisch,** *adj. See* **synonym**; ***–es Wörterbuch,*** dictionary of synonyms.

synoptisch [zy'nɔptɪʃ], *adj.* synoptic(al); ***die –en Evangelien,*** the synoptic gospels.

syntaktisch [zyn'taktɪʃ], *adj.* syntactical.

Synthese [zyn'te:zə], *f.* synthesis. **synthetisch,** *adj.* synthetic, artificial. **synthetisieren** [–ti'zi:rən], *v.t.* synthesize.

Syrien ['zy:riən], *n.* Syria. **Syr(i)er(in),** *m.* (*f.*), Syrian.

Syringe [zy'rɪŋgə], *f.* (*Bot.*) lilac.

syrisch, *adj.* Syrian.

System [zys'te:m], *n.* (**-s,** *pl.* **-e**) system, plan, scheme; method, doctrine, school; (*Nat. Soc. term of reproach*) formal principle (*particularly of the constitution, legal system etc.*); ***in ein – bringen,*** systematize.

Systematik [zyste'ma:tɪk], *f.* systematic representation, taxonomy. **Systematiker,** *m.* systematic *or* methodical *or* dogmatic person. **systematisch,** *adj.* systematic, methodic(al). **systematisieren** [–'zi:rən], *v.t., v.i.* systematize, deal with systematically *or* methodically.

systemlos [zys'te:mlo:s], *adj.* unsystematic, unmethodical. **System|zeit,** *f.* (*Nat. Soc.*) Weimar Republic (1918–33). **–zwang,** *m.* force of association, analogy.

Szenar [stse'na:r], *n.* (**-s,** *pl.* **-e**), **Szenario,** *n.* (**-s,** *pl.* **-s**), **Szenarium,** *n.* (**-s,** *pl.* **-rien**) scenario.

Szene ['stse:nə], *f.* (*Theat., fig.*) scene; (*Films*) shot, sequence; ***eine – machen,*** make a scene *or* fuss, (*coll.*) have a show-down (*Dat.*, with); ***in – setzen,*** stage, put on the stage; ***bei offener –,*** before the curtain falls; ***hinter der –,*** behind the scenes (*also fig.*), backstage; (*fig.*) ***sich in – setzen,*** show off, make a show, put o.s. in the limelight. **Szenen|aufnahme,** *f.* (*Films*) shot; shooting. **–wechsel,** *m.* change of scenes *or* (*fig.*) of scene. **Szenerie** [–'ri:], *f.* scenery, decor. **szenisch,** *adj.* scenic.

Szepter ['stsɛptər], *n. See* **Zepter.**

T

Many words were formerly spelt with **Th.** This is now obsolete, except in some foreign words and proper names.

T, t [te:], *n.* T, t. *See List of Abbreviations.*

Tabak ['ta(:)bak, (*Austr.*) ta'bak], *m.* (**-s,** *pl.* **-e**) tobacco; (*coll.*) ***das ist starker –,*** that's a bit thick, that is hard to swallow, that is really too bad. **Tabak|bau,** *m.* tobacco growing *or* cultivation. **–händler,** *m.* tobacconist. **–pflanzung,** *f.* tobacco-plantation. **–regie,** *f.* state tobacco-monopoly. **Tabaks|beutel,** *m.* tobacco-pouch. **–dose,** *f.* tobacco-jar; snuff-box. **–pfeife,** *f.* (tobacco-)pipe. **Tabaksteuer,** *f.* duty on tobacco.

Tabatiere [tabati'e:rə], *f.* snuff-box.

tabellarisch [tabɛ'la:rɪʃ], **1.** *adj.* tabulated, tabular. **2.** *adv.* in tabular form. **tabellarisieren** [–'zi:rən], *v.t.* tabulate. **Tabelle** [–'bɛlə], *f.* table, list, tabulation, index, chart, schedule. **tabellenförmig,** *adj.* tabular.

Tabernakel [tabər'na:kəl], *n. or m.* tabernacle.

Tabes ['ta:bɛs], *f.* (*Med.*) tabes, locomotor ataxia. **Tabeszenz** [–'tsɛnts], *f.* emaciation.

Tablett [ta'blɛt], *n.* (**-s,** *pl.* **-e**) tray, salver.

Tablette [ta'blɛtə], *f.* tablet, pill, lozenge.

Tabu [ta'bu:], *n.* (**-s,** *pl.* **-s**) taboo. **tabu,** *pred.adj.* taboo.

Tabulator [tabu'la:tɔr], *m.* (**-s,** *pl.* **-en**) tabulator (rack) (*of typewriter*). **Tabulatur** [–'tu:r], *f.* (*Mus.*) tabulature.

Tabulett [tabu'lɛt], *n.* (**-es,** *pl.* **-e**) hawker's *or* pedlar's stand. **Tabulettkrämer,** *m.* pedlar.

Taburett [tabu'rɛt], *n.* (**-(e)s,** *pl.* **-e**) stool, pouffe.

tachinieren [taxi'ni:rən], *v.i.* (*Austr.*) shirk, (*sl.*) scrimshank; laze, be lazy.

Tachometer [taxo'me:tər], *n. or m.* (*Motor.*) speedometer, (*Mech.*) tachometer.

Tachygraphie [taxygra'fi:], *f.* (*Hist.*) shorthand.

Tadel ['ta:dəl], *m.* blame, censure, disapproval; reproof, rebuke, reproach, reprimand, admonition; bad mark (*in schools*); fault, flaw, blemish, shortcoming; ***ohne –,*** blameless, faultless; ***Ritter ohne Furcht und –,*** knight without fear or reproach (*Bayard*); ***über jeden – erhaben,*** beyond reproach; ***sich*** (*Dat.*) ***einen – zuziehen,*** lay o.s. open to criticism. **tadelfrei, tadellos,** *adj.* irreproachable, beyond *or* above reproach, blameless; flawless, faultless, perfect; (*coll.*) splendid, excellent, first-class, first-rate.

tadeln ['ta:dəln], *v.t.* blame, rebuke, admonish, scold, reprove, reprimand, find fault with, criticize, disapprove of, censure (***wegen,*** for); ***an allem etwas zu – finden,*** find fault with everything. **tadelns|wert, –würdig,** *adj.* blameworthy, blameable, reprehensible, objectionable. **Tadelsucht,** *f.* censoriousness. **tadelsüchtig,** *adj.* censorious, fault-finding, nagging.

Tadler ['ta:dlər], *m.* fault-finder, carper, carping critic.

Tafel ['ta:fəl], *f.* (**-,** *pl.* **-n**) (notice) board, blackboard; (school) slate; tablet, slab, cake, bar (*of chocolate etc.*); plaque, panel, (stone) slab; plate (*book illustration*), table, chart, diagram; lamina, lamella; (dinner) table, meal, banquet; ***die – aufheben,*** rise from table; ***bei –,*** at table, at dinner; ***die – decken,*** lay the cloth *or* the table; ***freie – haben bei . . .,*** have free board with . . .; ***große – bei Hofe,*** court banquet; ***mit –n,*** with plates (*in books*); ***offene – halten,*** keep open house; ***sich zur – setzen,*** sit down to a meal.

tafelartig ['ta:fəlʔa:rtɪç], *adj.* tabular; laminar, lamellar. **Tafel|aufsatz,** *m.* table-centre, centrepiece. **–besteck,** *n.* knife, fork and spoon. **–birne,** *f.* dessert pear. **–blei,** *n.* sheet-lead. **–butter,** *f.* best butter. **–diener,** *m.* waiter (*at table*), footman. **–druck,** *m.* hand-printing. **–ente,** *f.* (*Orn.*) pochard, (*Am.*) common pochard (*Aythya ferina*). **tafel|fertig,** *adj.* ready-to-eat *or* to-serve. **–förmig,** *adj. See* **–artig. Tafel|gedeck,** *n.* (set of) table-linen. **–gelder,** *n.pl.* living *or* subsistence allowance. **–geschirr,** *n.* tableware, dinner-service, plate. **–glas,** *n.* plate-glass. **–land,** *n.* plateau, tableland. **–leim,** *m.* carpenter's *or* cake glue. **–musik,** *f.* lunch- (tea- *etc.*) time music.

tafeln ['ta:fəln], *v.i.* dine, feast, banquet.

täfeln ['tɛ:fəln], *v.t.* panel, wainscot (*walls*), inlay, board (*floor*).

Tafel|obst, *n.* dessert fruit. **–öl,** *n.* salad oil. **–runde,** *f.* guests, party (*at table*); (*Hist.*) (King Arthur's) Round Table. **–salz,** *n.* table salt. **–schiefer,** *m.* slate slabs. **–service,** *n. See* **–geschirr. –tuch,** *n.* tablecloth.

Täfelung ['tɛ:fəluŋ], *f.* panelling, wainscot(ing); inlaying (*of floors*).

Tafel|waage, *f.* platform scales. **–wasser,** *n.* table-water, mineral water. **–wein,** *m.* table wine. **–werk,** *n.* 1. *See* **Täfelung**; 2. book with plates. **–zeug,** *n. See* **–gedeck.**

Täfer ['tɛ:fər], *n.*, **Täf(e)rung,** *f.* (*Swiss*) *see* **Täfelung.**

Taf(fe)t [taf(ə)t], *m.* (**-(e)s,** *pl.* **-e**) taffeta. **Taftpapier,** *n.* satin paper.

Tag [ta:k], *m.* (**-(e)s,** *pl.* **-e**) day, daylight; ***alle –e,*** every day; (*coll.*) (***all***) ***mein –,*** in all my life, ever; ***am –e,*** by day; ***am –e nach,*** (on) the day after; ***früh am –e,*** early (in the day); (*fig.*) ***am –e liegen,*** be clear *or* manifest; (*fig.*) ***an den – bringen,*** bring to light, disclose, unearth, make manifest; (*fig.*) ***an den – kommen,*** come to light; (*fig.*) ***an den – legen,*** show, display, exhibit; ***auf den –,*** to a day; ***bis auf den heutigen –,*** to this day; ***auf seine alten –e,*** in his old age; ***binnen acht –en,*** within a *or* the week; ***bei –e,*** in the daytime, during the day; by day(light); ***zweimal des –s,*** twice a day; ***dieser –e,*** (*past*) recently, lately; the other day; (*future*) one of these days; (*coll.*) ***er hat heute seinen dummen –,*** he's in a bad mood today, it's just not one of his days; ***einen – um den andern,*** every other *or* second day; ***eines –es,*** one (fine) day, some day (or other); ***freier –,*** day off; ***– für –,*** day by *or* after day; ***den ganzen –,*** the whole day (long), all day (long); (*coll.*) ***er hat seinen guten –,*** he's in good form; (*coll.*) ***sich*** (*Dat.*) ***einen guten – machen,*** enjoy o.s., make a day of it; ***am hellen*** or ***lichten*** or ***hellichten –,*** in broad daylight; ***in acht –en,*** in a week, this day week; ***in den – hinein leben,*** live for the present, live from hand to mouth; ***in den – hinein reden,*** talk at random; ***in den nächsten –en,*** in a day or two *or* day or so, one of these days, shortly; ***vor Jahr und –,*** a long time ago, ages ago; ***der Jüngste –,*** Doomsday, the Last Judgement; ***den lieben langen –,*** the livelong day; (*Prov.*) ***man soll den – nicht vor dem Abend loben,*** don't count your chickens before they're hatched, don't halloo till you're out of the wood, don't crow too soon; (*Min.*) ***über –,*** above ground, on the surface; ***heute über acht –e,*** this day week, in a week's time; (*Min.*) ***unter –e,*** underground; ***vor acht –en,*** a week ago; ***es wird –,*** day is breaking *or* dawning, (*fig.*) I see (daylight), now it's beginning to become clear; ***jeden zweiten –,*** every other *or* second day.

Tag|arbeit, *f.* day-labour; daily task. **–arbeiter,** *m.* day-labourer. **tagaus** [–'aus], *adv.* ***– tagein,*** day in day out. **Tag|bau, –blatt, –dieb,** (*Austr.*) *see under* **Tage–.**

Tage|bau, *m.* (*Min.*) open-cast working. **–blatt,** *n.* daily (paper). **–buch,** *n.* diary, journal; (*Comm.*) daybook, order-book; (*Naut.*) log. **–dieb,** *m.* idler, sluggard, loafer, (*coll.*) lazybones. **–geld(er),** *n.* (*pl.*) subsistence *or* travelling allowance.

tag|ein, *adv. See* **–aus.**

tagelang ['ta:gəlaŋ], *adj., adv.* for days (on end), day after day; all day long. **Tage|licht,** *n.* (*dial.*) skylight. **–lied,** *n.* morning song, alba (*of the Minnesingers*). **–lohn,** *m.* day's wages, daily wages. **–löhner,** *m.* day-labourer. **–marsch,** *m.* day's march.

tagen ['ta:gən], **1.** *v.i.* (*imp.*) ***es tagt,*** it is getting light, day is breaking *or* dawning; (*fig.*) ***es tagt bei ihm,*** it dawns on him, he is beginning to see daylight *or* the light. **2.** *v.i.* meet, hold a meeting; be in conference *or* in session; confer, deliberate.

Tages|ablauf, *m.* daily routine. **–anbruch,** *m.* break of day, daybreak, dawn. **–angriff,** *m.* daylight raid. **–arbeit,** *f.* day's work. **–ausflug,** *m.* day trip. **–befehl,** *m.* routine order, order of the day. **–bericht,** *m.* daily report, bulletin. **–einnahme,** *f.* day's *or* daily takings. **–ereignis,** *n.* event of the day, *pl.* current events. **–fragen,** *f.pl.* questions of the day. **–gespräch,** *n.* topic of the day; ***das – bilden,*** be in the news. **–grauen,** *n.* dawn. **–karte,** *f.* day-ticket. **–kasse,** *f.* (*Theat.*) box-office (*for today's performance*); (*Comm.*) petty cash; *see also* **–einnahme. –krem,** *f.* vanishing cream. **–kurs,** *m.* current rate of exchange, quotation of the day. **–leistung,** *f.* daily output. **–licht,** *n.* daylight; ***ans – kommen,*** come to light, become known; ***ans – bringen,*** bring to light, disclose, unearth, make manifest; (*fig.*) ***das – scheuen,*** shun the light of day. **–literatur,** *f.* current literature. **–mädchen,** *n.* daily (help). **–marsch,** *m.* day's march. **–neuigkeiten,** *f.pl.* news of the day. **–ordnung,** *f.* day's programme; agenda; (*fig.*) ***an der – sein,*** be an everyday occurrence, be the order of the day. **–preis,** *m.* current price. **–presse,** *f.* daily press. **–satz,** *m.* daily rate; (*Comm.*) today's *or* current rate; (*of food*) daily ration, one day's supply. **–schicht,** *f.* day-shift. **–stempel,** *m.* date-stamp. **–zeit,** *f.* time of day, hour of the day; daytime; ***zu jeder –,*** at any hour *or* time (of the day); ***bei guter – ankommen,*** arrive while it is still light. **–zeitung,** *f.* daily (paper).

Tagewerk ['ta:gəvɛrk], *n.* day's work, (*as measure of output*) man-day; daily task; (*dial.*) measure of land.

Tagfalter ['ta:kfaltər], *m.* butterfly. **taghell,** *adj.* clear as day. **Taghemd,** *n.* shirt (*for men*), chemise (*for women*).

–tägig [tɛ:gɪç], *adj.suff.* lasting *or* of . . . days; . . .-day. **täglich, 1.** *adj.* daily, (*Astr.*) diurnal, (*Med.*) quotidian; ordinary, everyday; (*Comm.*) ***–es Geld,*** call-money; ***auf –e Kündigung,*** at call. **2.** *adv.* daily, every day, (*Comm.*) per diem; ***dreimal –,*** three times a day.

Tag|lohn, –raum, (*Austr., Swiss*) *see* **Tagelohn, Tagesraum.**

tags [ta:ks], *adv.* ***– darauf,*** the day after, (on) the following day, next day; ***– zuvor,*** the day before, (on) the previous day.

Tag|satzung, *f.* (*Swiss*) Diet; (*Austr.*) term, fixed day *or* date. **–schicht,** *f. See* **Tagesschicht.**

tagsüber ['ta:ksʔy:bər], *adv.* in the daytime, during the day.

tagtäglich [ta:k'tɛ:klɪç], *adv.* daily, every day, day in day out.

Tag- und Nachtgleiche [ta:kʔunt'naxtglaɪçə], *f.* equinox.

Tagung ['ta:guŋ], *f.* meeting, conference, congress, convention, (*Parl.*) session.

Tag|wache, –wacht, *f.* (*Swiss*) (*Mil.*) reveille. **–wasser,** *n.* surface water. **tagweise,** *adv.* by the day.

Taifun [taɪ'fu:n], *m.* (**-s,** *pl.* **-e**) typhoon.

Taille ['taljə], *f.* waist, waist-line; (*of dress*) bodice. **Taillenweite,** *f.* waist measurement. **tailliert** [ta'ji:rt], *adj.* close-fitting, fitted to the waist.

Takel ['ta:kəl], *n.* (*Naut.*) block and tackle. **Takelage** [–'la:ʒə], *f. See* **Takelung. Takeling,** *f.* (*Naut.*) whipping. **takeln,** *v.t.* rig (*a ship*). **Takelung,** *f.*, **Takelwerk,** *n.* rigging, tackle.

Takt [takt], *m.* (**-(e)s,** *pl.* **-e**) (*Mus.*) time, beat, measure; (*Metr.*) rhythm; (*Mech.*) stroke, cycle; (*fig.*) tact; ***den – halten,*** keep time; ***aus dem – bringen,*** disconcert, (*coll.*) put out *or* off; ***aus dem – kommen,*** lose the beat, (*fig.*) be put off one's stroke; ***im –,*** in time, in step; ***den – angeben*** or ***schlagen,*** beat time; $\frac{3}{4}$-(***dreiviertel***)–, three-four time. **Takt|art,** *f.* (*Mus.*) measure, time. **–bezeichnung,** *f.* time-signature. **taktfest,** *adj.* keeping good time; (*coll.*) reliable, sound, firm, consistent. **Taktgefühl,** *n.* tact, tactfulness, delicacy.

taktieren [tak'ti:rən], *v.i.* (*Mus.*) beat time. **Taktierstock,** *m.* (conductor's) baton.

Taktik ['taktɪk], *f.* (**-,** *pl.* **-en**) tactics. **Taktiker,** *m.* tactician. **taktisch,** *adj.* tactical.

taktlos ['taktlo:s], *adj.* tactless, indiscreet, injudicious, ill-advised, in bad taste. **Taktlosigkeit,** *f.* tactlessness, want of tact, bad taste; ***eine – begehen,*** commit an indiscretion, (*coll.*) put one's foot in it.

taktmäßig ['taktmɛ:sɪç], *adj.* rhythmical, measured. **Takt|messer,** *m.* metronome. **–note,** *f.* semibreve. **–pause,** *f.* bar-rest. **–schritt,** *m.* measured (*or* dance-)step. **–stock,** *m. See* **Taktierstock. –strich,** *m.* (*Mus.*) bar.

taktvoll ['taktfɔl], *adj.* tactful, discreet, judicious.

Tal [ta:l], *n.* (**-s,** *pl.* **¨-er** (*Poet.* **-e**)) valley, vale, dale, glen; ***zu – fahren,*** go downstream *or* downhill. **talabwärts,** *adv.* downstream, downhill.

Talar [ta'la:r], *m.* (**-s,** *pl.* **-e**) (*Law*) robe, (*Eccl., Univ.*) gown.

talaufwärts [ta:l'aufvɛrts], *adv.* upstream, uphill. **Tal|bewohner,** *m.* valley-dweller. **–enge,** *f.* narrow (part of a) valley; (*coll.*) bottle-neck.

Talent [ta'lɛnt], *n.* (**-(e)s,** *pl.* **-e**) talent, (natural) gift, aptitude, capacity (***für*** for), *pl.* talent, ability; talented *or* gifted *or* able p. **talentiert** [–'ti:rt], *adj.* talented, gifted. **talentlos,** *adj.* without talent *or* ability, not gifted. **talentvoll,** *adj. See* **talentiert.**

Talfahrt ['ta:lfa:rt], *f.* descent; downhill run.

Talg [talk], *m.* (**-(e)s,** *pl.* **-e**) tallow, grease, suet; (*Med.*) sebum. **talgartig,** *adj.* tallowy, suety; (*Med.*) sebaceous. **Talg|drüse,** *f.* sebaceous gland. **–fett,** *n.* stearin. **talgig,** *adj. See* **talgartig. Talg|kerze,** *f.*, **–licht,** *n.* tallow candle.

Talhang ['ta:lhaŋ], *m.* valley-slope.

Talje ['ta:ljə], *f.* (*Naut.*) light tackle, reef, line, halyard.

Talk [talk], *m.* (*Min.*) talc(um), magnesium silicate. **Talkerde,** *f.* talcite.

Talkessel ['ta:lkɛsəl], *m.* (valley-)basin, hollow.

talkig ['talkɪç], *adj.* talcose, talcous; (*dial.*) soggy, sad (*of pastry*). **Talk|puder,** *m.* talcum powder. **–säure,** *f.* stearic acid. **–schiefer,** *m.* talc-schist. **–stein,** *m.* steatite, soapstone.

Talmi ['talmi], *n.* pinchbeck; (*fig.*) counterfeit, sham.

Tal|mulde, *f. See* **–kessel. –schlucht,** *f.* glen, gorge, canyon. **–senke,** *f. See* **–kessel. –sohle,** *f.* valley-bottom. **–sperre,** *f.* barrage, dam. **tal|wärts,** *adv. See* **–abwärts. Talweg,** *m.* road through *or* along a valley, valley-road.

Tambour ['tambu:r], *m.* (**-s,** *pl.* **-e** (*Swiss* **-en**)) drummer; (*Archit.*) tambour; small drum; *see* **Tambur. Tambourstab,** *m.* drum-major's baton.

Tambur ['tambur], *m.* (**-s,** *pl.* **-e**) embroidery frame. **tamburieren,** *v.t.* tambour (*embroidery*). **Tamburin** [–'ri:n], *n.* (**-s,** *pl.* **-e**) (*Mus.*) tambourine.

Tamp [tamp], *m.* (**-s,** *pl.* **-e**) (*Naut.*) rope's end.

Tampon ['tampɔn, tã'pɔ̃], *m.* (**-s,** *pl.* **-s**) (*Med.*) swab. **tamponieren** [–'ni:rən], *v.t.* plug (*a wound*).

Tamtam [tam'tam, 'tamtam], *m.* (**-s,** *pl.* **-s**) gong, tom-tom; (*fig.*) fuss, pother, to-do, palaver ballyhoo.

Tand [tant], *m.* bauble, gewgaw, trumpery; trifles, trinkets, (k)nick-(k)nacks; tinsel, finery.

Tändelei [tɛndə'laɪ], *f.* (-, *pl.* **-en**) trifling, dallying, flirting, philandering; flirtation. **Tändel|kram,** *m. See* **Tand. –markt,** (*dial.*) **Tandelmarkt,** *m.* rag-fair, jumble-sale. **tändeln,** *v.i.* 1. dally, trifle; flirt, philander; dally, dawdle; 2. (*dial.*) deal in second-hand goods. **Tändelschürze,** *f.* fancy apron. **Tändler,** *m.* 1. trifler, philanderer, flirt; 2. dawdler, (*coll.*) slow-coach; 3. (*dial.*) (*also* **Tandler**) second-hand dealer.

Tang [taŋ], *m.* (**-(e)s,** *pl.* **-e**) seaweed. **Tangasche,** *f.* kelp.

Tangens ['taŋgɛns], *m.* (-, *pl.* -) (*Trigonometry*) tangent. **Tangent** [–'gɛnt], *m.* (**-s,** *pl.* **-e**) jack (*of a harpsichord*), plectrum. **Tangente,** *f.* (*Geom.*) tangent. **Tangentialebene** [–tsi'a:lˀe:bənə], *f.* tangent plane. **tangieren** [–'gi:rən], *v.t.* be tangent to, (*fig.*) touch (upon), affect.

Tank [taŋk], *m.* (**-(e)s,** *pl.* **-e** (*Austr.* **-s**)) tank (*for liquids, Mil.*). **Tankabwehr,** *f.* anti-tank defence. **tanken,** *v.i.* refuel, (*coll.*) fill up. **Tanker,** *m. See* **Tankschiff. Tank|falle,** *f.* (*Mil.*) tank-trap. **–säule,** *f.* petrol pump. **–schiff,** *n.* tanker. **–stelle,** *f.* petrol *or* service *or* filling station. **–wagen,** *m.* (*Railw.*) tank-car; (*Motor.*) tank-lorry, petrol tanker. **–wart,** *m.* petrol-pump attendant.

Tann [tan], *m.* (**-(e)s,** *pl.* **-e**) (*Poet.*) pine forest. **Tanne,** *f.* (*Bot.*) (silver) fir (*Abies*). **tannen,** *adj.* fir. **Tannen|apfel,** *m.* fir-cone. **–baum,** *m.* fir-tree. **–häher,** *m.* (*Orn.*) nutcracker (*Nucifraga caryocatactes*). **–harz,** *n.* resin from fir-trees. **–holz,** *n.* fir-wood, deal. **–meise,** *f.* (*Orn.*) coal-titmouse (*Parus ater*). **–nadel,** *f.* fir-needle. **–zapfen,** *m.* fir-cone. **Tannicht,** *n.* (**-s,** *pl.* **-e**) (*dial.*) fir plantation.

Tannin [ta'ni:n], *n.* tannin, tannic acid.

Tantal ['tantal], *n.* tantalum. **Tantalsäure,** *f.* tantalic acid.

Tantalusqualen ['tantaluskva:lən], *f.pl.* torments of hell.

Tante ['tantə], *f.* aunt; (*Cards, roulette*) ***meine –, deine –,*** game of hazard; (*coll.*) ***bei – Meier,*** at the lavatory.

Tantieme [tãti'ɛ:mə], *f.* share of profits, bonus, percentage; (author's) royalty; fee(s), commission.

Tanz [tants], *m.* (**-es,** *pl.* **⸚e**) dance, dancing, ball; (*coll.*) shindy, brawl; ***einen – mit ihm wagen,*** let o.s. in for trouble with him; (*coll.*) ***da ging der – los,*** then the fun *or* the row began; ***zum – auffordern,*** request the pleasure of a dance.

Tanz|abend, *m.* ball, dance, evening's dancing. **–bär,** *m.* performing bear. **–bein,** *n.* (*coll.*) ***das – schwingen,*** go dancing, shake a leg, do the light fantastic. **–diele,** *f.* dance-hall; wine cellar with dancing.

tänzeln ['tɛntsəln], *v.i.* frisk, skip, caper, hop, trip, dance, (*of horse*) amble.

tanzen ['tantsən], **1.** *v.i.* (*aux.* h. & s.) dance; (*fig.*) be rocked (*on the waves*); (*Prov.*) ***– wollen, wenn die Musik aufhört,*** come a day after the fair; ***nach seiner Pfeife –,*** be at his beck and call. **2.** *v.t.* dance (*a waltz etc.*). **Tanzen,** *n.* dancing. **Tänzer,** *m.* dancer. **Tänzerin,** *f.* dancer, (*ballet*) danseuse.

Tanz|fest, *n.* ball, dance. **–kapelle,** *f.* dance-band. **–kunst,** *f.* dancing. **–lehrer(in),** *m.* (*f.*) dancing-master (mistress). **–lied,** *n.* choral dance. **–lokal,** *n.* dance-hall. **tanzlustig,** *adj.* fond of dancing. **Tanz|meister,** *m.* dancing instructor. **–musik,** *f.* dance-music. **–platz,** *m.* dance-floor. **–schritt,** *m.* dancing-step. **–schule,** *f.* dancing-school. **–stunde,** *f.* dancing-lesson. **–tee,** *m.* thé-dansant. **–unterricht,** *m.* dancing-lessons. **–wut,** *f.* dancing-mania.

taperig ['ta:pərɪç], *adj. See* **täppisch.**

Tapet [ta'pe:t], *n.* ***aufs – bringen,*** broach *or* introduce (*a subject*), (*coll.*) bring (*a subject*) up; ***aufs – kommen,*** come under discussion, (*coll.*) come up.

Tapete [ta'pe:tə], *f.* wallpaper; tapestry. **Tapeten|bahn,** *f.* roll of wallpaper. **–tür,** *f.* concealed door.

Tapezier [tape'tsi:r], *m.* (**-s,** *pl.* **-e**) paperhanger, decorator; upholsterer. **tapezieren,** *v.t.* paper (*walls*), hang with tapestry. **Tapezierer,** *m. See* **Tapezier. Tapeziernagel,** *m.* upholstery brad *or* tack. **Tapezierung,** *f.* paperhanging, papering (*of walls*). **Tapezierware,** *f.* upholstery.

tapfer ['tapfər], *adj.* brave, gallant, valiant, heroic; bold, courageous, fearless, dauntless, intrepid, (*coll.*) plucky; ***– arbeiten,*** work with a will, work doggedly *or* manfully, (*coll.*) work like blazes; ***halte dich –!*** be firm! don't flinch! ***sich – wehren,*** make a bold stand. **Tapferkeit,** *f.* bravery, gallantry, valour, courage, heroism, (*coll.*) pluck. **Tapferkeitsmedaille,** *f.* award for gallantry.

Tapisserie [tapɪsə'ri:], *f.* tapestry-work, embroidery.

Tappe ['tapə], *f.* paw; paw-mark. **tappen,** *v.i.* (*aux.* s. & h.) grope (about), fumble.

täppisch ['tɛpɪʃ], *adj.* awkward, clumsy, (*coll.*) gawkish, ham-fisted.

taprig ['ta:prɪç], *adj.* (*dial.*) *see* **täppisch. Taps,** *m.* (**-es,** *pl.* **-e**) (*coll.*) awkward fellow, clumsy lout, hobbledehoy. **tapsen,** *v.i.* be awkward, walk clumsily, plod.

Tara ['ta:ra], *f.* (*Comm.*) tare, weight of packing.

Tarantel [ta'rantəl], *f.* (-, *pl.* **-n**) (*Ent.*) tarantula; ***wie von der – gestochen,*** like one possessed.

tarieren [ta'ri:rən], *v.t.* (ascertain the *or* allow for the) tare (of).

Tarif [ta'ri:f], *m.* (**-s,** *pl.* **-e**) price list, (table of) rates, (scale of) prices *or* charges; tariff, rate; postal rates; wage-scale; (*Railw.*) list of fares; ***gleitender –,*** sliding scale. **Tarifabkommen,** *n.* wage agreement. **tariflich, 1.** *adj.* agreed, contractual, negotiated, regulation, standard. **2.** *adv.* according to scale. **Tariflohn,** *m.* standard wage. **tarifmäßig,** *adj. See* **tariflich. Tarif|ordnung,** *f.* wage-scale. **–satz,** *m.* tariff rate. **–verhandlungen,** *f.pl.* collective bargaining. **–vertrag,** *m. See* **–abkommen.**

Tarn|anstrich ['tarn–], *m.* camouflage *or* dazzle

painting. **–anzug,** *m.* camouflage suit. **–bezeichnung,** *f.* code-word.

tarnen ['tarnən], *v.t.* camouflage, mask, screen, (*fig.*) disguise, mask, cloak. **Tarn|farbe,** *f.* camouflage *or* dazzle paint. **–kappe,** *f.* cloak of invisibility. **–netz,** *n.* camouflage net. **Tarnung,** *f.* camouflage, masking, screen(ing).

Tartsche ['tartʃə], *f.* (*Hist.*) (small) round shield, targe, target.

Tasche ['taʃə], *f.* pocket; purse, (hand)bag, case, (school) satchel, wallet, pouch, (*Anat.*) ventricle, (*Zool.*) bursa; ***ihm auf der – liegen,*** be a (financial) drain on him; ***aus seiner – leben,*** live at his expense, (*coll.*) live on him; ***in die eigene – arbeiten,*** line one's pocket; (*fig. coll.*) ***etwas schon in der – haben,*** have s.th. in one's pocket *or* in the bag; ***etwas in die – stecken,*** pocket a th.; (*fig.*) ***ihn in die – stecken,*** be more than a match for him.

Taschen|apotheke, *f.* pocket first-aid kit. **–ausgabe,** *f.* pocket edition. **–buch,** *n.* pocket-book, notebook. **–dieb,** *m.* pickpocket. **–format,** *n.* pocket-size. **–geld,** *n.* pocket-money **–kalender,** *m.* pocket diary. **–krebs,** *m.* common crab. **–lampe,** *f.* electric torch, flashlight. **–messer,** *n.* pocket-knife, penknife, clasp-knife. **–spieler,** *m.* juggler, conjurer. **–spielerei,** *f.* conjuring, legerdemain, sleight of hand. **–tuch,** *n.* (pocket-) handkerchief. **–uhr,** *f.* pocket-watch.

Taschner ['taʃnər], **Täschner** ['tɛʃnər], *m.* (*Austr.*) bag maker, dealer in leather goods.

Tasse ['tasə], *f.* **1.** cup; **2.** (*Austr.*) saucer; tray, salver. **Tassenkopf,** *m.* (*dial.*) cup.

Tastatur [tasta'tu:r], *f.* (-, *pl.* **-en**) keys, keyboard, fingerboard (*of piano etc.*).

tastbar ['tastba:r], *adj.* palpable, tangible. **Tastborste,** *f.* tactile bristle. **Taste,** *f.* key (*of piano etc.*), push-button; ***eine falsche – anschlagen,*** play a wrong note (*piano*), strike a wrong key *or* letter (*typewriter*).

tasten ['tastən], **1.** *v.i.* touch, feel; grope (about), fumble (***nach,*** for); ***–d gehen,*** grope *or* feel one's way, grope about. **2.** *v.r.* grope *or* feel one's way, grope about. **3.** *v.t.* tap out (*a message*). **Tastenbrett,** *n. See* **Tastatur. tastend,** *adj.* (*fig.*) groping, tentative, hesitant. **Tast|feld,** *n.* (typewriter) keyboard. **–instrument,** *n.* (*Mus.*) keyed instrument.

Taster ['tastər], *m.* (*Ent.*) feeler, antenna; (*Mech.*) calliper(s); (*typewriter*) keyboard; bell-push.

Tast|haar, *n.* tactile hair. **–organ,** *n. See* **–werkzeug. –reiz,** *m.* contact stimulus. **–sinn,** *m.* sense of touch. **–spitze,** *f.* palp. **–versuch,** *m.* tentative experiment, preliminary trial. **–werkzeug,** *n.* organ of touch, (*Ent.*) feeler.

Tat [ta:t], *f.* (-, *pl.* **-en**) deed, act, action; feat, achievement, exploit; ***auf frischer – ertappen,*** catch red-handed *or* in the (very) act; ***den guten Willen*** or ***die gute Absicht für die – nehmen,*** take the will for the deed; ***in der –,*** in reality, actually, indeed, really, in fact, in point of fact, as a matter of fact; ***ein Mann der –,*** a man of action; ***mit Rat und –,*** in every possible way, in all ways possible; ***zur – schreiten,*** proceed to act(ion).

tat, *see* **tun.**

Tatar [ta'ta:r], *m.* (**-en,** *pl.* **-en**) Tartar. **Tatarei** [–'raɪ], *f.* Tartary. **Tatarennachricht,** *f.* canard, alarmist report.

Tat|bericht, *m.* circumstantial report, (*Law*) summary of evidence. **–bestand,** *m.* facts (of the case), factual findings, state of affairs. **–einheit,** *f.* (*Law*) coincidence.

Taten|drang, –durst, *m.* zest *or* thirst for action, enterprise. **tatenlos,** *adj.* idle, inactive. **tatenreich,** *adj.* active, eventful.

Täter(in) ['tɛ:tər(ɪn)], *m.* (*f.*) doer, author, perpetrator; committer (*of crime*), culprit, wrongdoer. **Täterschaft,** *f.* guilt; ***die – ableugnen,*** plead not guilty.

Tatform ['ta:tfɔrm], *f. See* **Tätigkeitsform.**

tätig ['tɛ:tɪç], *adj.* active, busy, hard at work, engaged, employed; energetic; effective, efficacious; ***als Arzt – sein,*** practise as a doctor, practise medicine; ***– sein für,*** be active for, work for (*charity etc.*); ***– sein bei,*** be employed with, be in the employ of, work for (*an employer*).

tätigen ['tɛ:tɪgən], *v.t.* (*Comm.*) transact, effect (*a sale*), conclude (*a transaction*), undertake (*a project*); carry out, bring off; ***in Goldwährung getätigte Käufe,*** purchases paid for *or* effected in gold.

Tätigkeit ['tɛ:tɪçkaɪt], *f.* activity, action, function; business, occupation, profession, vocation, (*coll.*) job; ***in – setzen,*** set *or* get going, put into action, activate; ***außer – setzen,*** suspend (*a p.*) (from duty), stop, bring to a standstill, put out of action (*a th.*). **Tätigkeits|bereich,** *m.* field of activity. **–bericht,** *m.* progress report. **–form,** *f.* (*Gram.*) active voice. **–gebiet,** *n. See* **–bereich. –wort,** *n.* verb.

Tätigung ['tɛ:tɪguŋ], *f.* conclusion, transaction; undertaking, effecting.

Tatkraft ['ta:tkraft], *f.* energy, enterprise. **tatkräftig,** *adj.* energetic, active, enterprising.

tätlich ['tɛ:tlɪç], *adj.* violent; (*Law*) ***–e Beleidigung,*** assault and battery; ***– angreifen*** or ***– werden gegen,*** (commit an) assault (on); ***– werden,*** become violent, come to blows. **Tätlichkeit,** *f.* physical violence, (act of) violence; (*Law*) assault (and battery).

Tatort ['ta:tˀɔrt], *m.* scene of the crime.

tätowieren [tɛto'vi:rən], *v.t.* tattoo. **Tätowierung,** *f.* tattoo(ing).

Tatsache ['ta:tzaxə], *f.* fact, matter of fact, fact of the matter; *pl.* (established) facts, data; ***nackte –n,*** plain *or* hard facts; ***verbürgte –,*** matter of record, established fact; ***vollendete –,*** fait accompli; ***sich auf den Boden der –n stellen,*** face the facts, be realistic, come to terms with reality; ***als – hinstellen,*** aver; ***–n sind stärker als Worte,*** facts speak louder than words. **Tatsachen|bericht,** *m.* factual *or* documentary *or* first-hand account. **–film,** *m.* documentary (film). **–frage,** *f.* (*Law*) issue in fact. **–irrtum,** *m.* (*Law*) error of fact.

tatsächlich ['ta:tzɛçlɪç], **1.** *adj.* real, actual, factual, matter-of-fact; (*Mil.*) ***–e Schußweite,*** effective range. **2.** *adv.* in fact *or* reality, really, actually, (*Law*) de facto; (*coll.*) the fact is that, believe it or (believe it) not; (*Law*) ***rechtlich und –,*** in fact and in law.

Tätschen ['tɛtʃçən], *n.* (*coll.*) slap. **Tatsche** ['tatʃə], *f.* (*dial.*) podgy hand. **tätscheln,** *v.t.* caress, fondle, pet, stroke. **tatschen,** (*coll.*) **1.** *v.t.* slap. **2.** *v.i.* talk baby-language.

Tatterich ['tatərɪç], *m.* (*coll.*) ***den – haben,*** (*with age*) be doddering, be an old dodderer, (*with fear*) be all of a dither.

Tat|umstände, *m.pl.* circumstances surrounding the case. **–verdacht,** *m.* suspicion (of being the culprit).

Tatze ['tatsə], *f.* paw, (*Mech.*) claw; (*coll.*) ***ihm eine – geben,*** give him a stroke with the cane. **Tatzenhieb,** *m.* blow with the paw.

[1]**Tau** [tau], *m.* dew; ***vor – und Tag,*** in the dewy morn; (*coll.*) ***er hört den – fallen,*** he thinks he's pretty clever.

[2]**Tau,** *n.* (**-(e) s,** *pl.* **-e**) rope, cable; (*Naut.*) line, hawser.

taub [taup], *adj.* deaf; (*fig.*) (*limbs*) numb, benumbed, (*seed, soil etc.*) unfruitful, barren, sterile, (*egg*) addled, (*nuts etc.*) empty; (*of a p.*) oblivious, deaf (***für, gegen,*** to); ***auf einem Ohre –,*** deaf in one ear; ***–en Ohren predigen,*** cry in the wilderness; ***– machen,*** deafen; ***–e Flut,*** slack tide *or* water; ***–es Gestein,*** unproductive rock, rubble, deads; ***–er Gang,*** exhausted lode.

Täubchen ['tɔypçən], *n.* (*coll.*) pet, poppet, sweetie, duckie.

Taube ['taubə], *f.* pigeon, dove; ***sanft wie eine –,*** gentle as a dove *or* lamb; ***Land der gebratenen –n,*** Cockaigne, fool's paradise; ***ihm fliegen die gebratenen –n in den Mund,*** everything falls into his lap; (*Prov.*) ***besser ein Sperling in der Hand als eine – auf dem Dach,*** a bird in the hand is worth two in the bush; ***wo –n sind, fliegen –n hin,*** to him who hath shall be given.

tauben|farbig, -grau, *adj.* dove-grey. **Tauben|-haus,** *n.*, (*Austr.*) **-kobel,** *m. See* **-schlag. -post,** *f.* pigeon-post. **-schlag,** *m.* dovecot, pigeon loft; (*fig.*) ***wie in einem* -,** with continual coming and going. **-zucht,** *f.* pigeon breeding. **-züchter,** *m.* pigeon fancier.

Tauber ['taubər], **Täuber** ['tɔybər], **Tauberich, Täuberich,** *m.* cock pigeon.

Taubheit ['tauphaɪt], *f.* deafness; numbness; barrenness, emptiness. **Taubnessel,** *f.* (*Bot.*) dead-nettle (*Lamium*). **taubstumm,** *adj.* deaf and dumb. **Taubstumme(r),** *m., f.* deaf mute.

tauchen ['tauçən], **1.** *v.i.* (*aux.* s. & h.) dive, plunge (*into water*); remain *or* swim under water; (*submarine*) submerge; (*as the sun etc.*) dip, (*Boxing*) (*coll.*) duck. **2.** *v.t.* dip, immerse, (*coll.*) duck, soak, steep, (*fig. as in light*) bathe. **Tauchen,** *n.* diving *etc.*

Taucher ['tauçər], *m.* diver. **Taucher|anzug,** *m.* diving-suit. **-glocke,** *f.* diving-bell. **-helm,** *m.* diver's helmet. **-kolben,** *m.* (*Mech.*) plunger.

tauch|fähig, *adj.* submersible. **-klar,** *adj.* (*submarine*) ready to submerge. **Tauch|kolben,** *m.* plunger. **-retter,** *m.* escape gear *or* apparatus (*from submarines*). **-sieder,** *m.* (*Elec.*) immersion heater.

[1]**tauen** ['tauən], **1.** *v.i.* (*aux.* h. & s.) thaw, melt. **2.** *v.i.* (*imp.*) (*aux.* h.) ***es taut,*** it is thawing; dew is falling.

[2]**tauen,** *v.t.* (*Naut.*) tow.

Tauende ['tauˀɛndə], *n.* ***das - kosten,*** get a taste of the rope's end.

Tauf|akt ['tauf-], *m.* baptism, christening (ceremony). **-becken,** *n.* (baptismal) font. **-buch,** *n.* church *or* parish register.

Taufe ['taufə], *f.* baptism, christening; (*of ships etc.*) christening, naming ceremony; ***aus der - heben,*** be godparent to, (*fig.*) stand sponsor to, inaugurate, initiate, call into being, originate, launch, start, get going, set on its feet; ***die - empfangen,*** be baptized *or* christened. **taufen,** *v.t.* baptize, christen; christen, name (*ship etc.*); (*coll.*) adulterate, water (*wine*); ***getaufter Jude,*** converted Jew.

Täufer ['tɔyfər], *m.* (*B.*) ***Johannes der* -,** John the Baptist.

taufeucht ['tauˀfɔyçt], *adj.* wet with dew, bedewed, dewy.

Tauf|formel, *f.* form of baptism. **-geschenk,** *n.* christening present. **-handlung,** *f. See* **-akt. -kind,** *n.* infant to be baptized.

Täufling ['tɔyflɪŋ], *m.* (**-s,** *pl.* **-e**) infant to be baptized, (*adult*) candidate for baptism; (*fig.*) neophyte.

Tauf|name, *m.* Christian *or* (*Am.*) given name. **-pate, 1.** *m.* godfather. **2. -patin,** *f.* godmother.

taufrisch ['taufrɪʃ], *adj.* dewy, fresh as a daisy.

Tauf|schein, *m.* certificate of baptism. **-stein,** *m. See* **-becken. -wasser,** *n.* baptismal water. **-zeuge,** *m.* godparent, sponsor.

taugen ['taugən], *v.i.* be good *or* fit *or* of use (*zu,* for); (*zu*) ***nichts* -,** be worthless, be of no use, be no good, be good for nothing; ***wozu taugt das?*** what use *or* good is that? what is the use *or* good of that? ***taugt es was?*** is it any good? is it of any use? ***es taugt nicht viel,*** it is not worth much, it is not much good *or* use, (*coll.*) it's not up to much. **Taugenichts,** *m.*(*-or*-**es,** *pl.*-**e**) good-for-nothing, ne'er-do-well.

tauglich ['tauklɪç], *adj.* good, useful, fit, suitable, qualified, adapted (***für, zu,*** for), capable (of); (*Mil.*) fit for active service; (*Naut.*) (*of ship*) seaworthy. **Tauglichkeit,** *f.* usefulness, fitness, suitability, qualification; military fitness; seaworthiness. **Tauglichkeitsgrad,** *m.* (*Mil.*) medical category.

tauig ['tauɪç], *adj.* dewy.

Tau|kranz, *m.* (*Naut.*) coir fender. **-länge,** *f.* (*Naut.*) cable's length.

Taumel ['tauməl], *m.* **1.** reeling, staggering; giddiness; **2.** (*fig.*) whirl; rapture, ecstasy, frenzy, transport, delirium. **taumelig,** *adj.* reeling, giddy. **Taumelkäfer,** *m.* (*Ent.*) whirligig beetle (*Gyrinidae*). **taumeln,** *v.i.* (*aux.* s. & h.) reel, totter, stagger; be giddy; ***er kam in das Zimmer getaumelt,*** he staggered *or* tottered into the room; ***er taumelte von diesem unverhofften Glück,*** this unexpected good fortune made him reel.

Tauner ['taunər], *m.* (*Swiss*) day-labourer.

Tau|perle, *f. See* **-tropfen. -punkt,** *m.* dew-point. **-regen,** *m.* mild and gentle rain.

Tausch [tauʃ], *m.* (**-es,** *pl.* **-e**) exchange, barter, (*obs.*) truck; ***in - nehmen,*** take in exchange; ***im - gegen,*** in exchange for. **tauschbar,** *adj.* exchangeable. **tauschen,** *v.t., v.i.* exchange, barter, (*sl.*) swap, swop (***gegen,*** for); ***ich möchte nicht mit Ihnen* -,** I would not change places with you, I should not like to be in your place *or* (*coll.*) in your shoes.

täuschen ['tɔyʃən], **1.** *v.t., v.i.* deceive, delude, mislead, lead astray, dupe, hoax, trick, hoodwink; cheat, defraud, impose upon; (*of a th.*) be deceptive, disappoint; ***der Schein täuscht,*** appearances are deceptive; ***in der Liebe getäuscht werden,*** be disappointed in love. **2.** *v.r.* deceive o.s., be mistaken *or* wrong. **täuschend,** *adj.* deceptive, illusory; ***- ähnlich,*** indistinguishable, practically identical, (*coll.*) as like as two peas; ***-e Ähnlichkeit,*** striking resemblance; ***- nachgeahmt,*** copied to perfection *or* to the life. **Täuscher,** *m.* (*obs.*) (horse-)dealer.

Tauscherei [tauʃə'raɪ], *f.* (*coll.*) chopping and changing. **Tausch|geschäft,** *n.* barter (transaction), exchange, (*sl.*) swap, swop. **-handel,** *m.* barter, exchange-trade.

tauschieren [tau'ʃi:rən], *v.t.* inlay (*metal*), damascene.

Tauschlag ['tauʃla:k], *m.* track (*of game*) in the dew.

Tausch|mittel, *n.* medium of exchange. **-objekt,** *n.* object of value in exchange.

Täuschung ['tɔyʃuŋ], *f.* deception, fraud; hoax, trick, mystification, delusion; illusion, error, mistake, fallacy; ***optische* -,** optical illusion; ***sich einer - hingeben,*** deceive o.s., labour under a delusion (***über*** (*Acc.*), about). **Täuschungs|absicht,** *f.* (*Law*) intent to defraud. **-angriff,** *m.* (*Mil.*) feint attack. **-manöver,** *n.* (*Mil.*) feint, diversion. **-versuch,** *m.* attempt to deceive *or* defraud.

tauschweise ['tauʃvaɪzə], *adv.* in exchange, by way of exchange. **Tauschwert,** *m.* exchange value.

tausend ['tauzənt], *num.adj.* thousand; ***- und aber -,*** thousands and *or* (up)on thousands; ***nicht einer unter -,*** not one in a thousand; (*Mil.*) ***- Mann,*** a thousand men; ***an die - Mann,*** getting on for a thousand men; - (*Austr.* ***-e***) ***Menschen,*** a thousand people; ***- und eine Nacht,*** Arabian Nights (Entertainments). **Tausend, 1.** *n.* (**-s,** *pl.* **-e**) thousand; ***zu -en,*** in (their) thousands, by the thousand; ***es geht in die -e,*** it runs to thousands; ***-e und aber -e*** (*Austr.* ***Abertausende***) ***von,*** thousands and *or* (up)on thousands of; ***der Beifall! Tausender von Zuschauern,*** the applause of thousands of spectators; ***ein paar - or einige -(e),*** a few thousand; ***neun vom -,*** nine pro mille, 0.9 per cent. **2.** *f.* (-, *pl.* **-en**) (figure *or* number) thousand. **3.** *m.* (*obs.*) (***ei***) ***der -! potz -!*** the (very) deuce!

Tausender ['tauzəndər], *m.* (*digit*) thousand; thousand (mark *etc.*) note. **tausenderlei,** *indecl. adj.* of a thousand kinds; ***- Dinge,*** thousands of *or* ever so many things. **tausend|fach, -fältig, 1.** *adj.* a thousand times, thousandfold. **2.** *adv.* in a thousand ways. **Tausend|fuß, -füß(l)er,** *m.* (*Ent.*) wireworm, centipede (*Myriapoda*). **-güldenkraut,** *n.* (*Bot.*) centaury (*Erythraea*). **tausendjährig,** *adj.* a thousand years old; millennial; ***-es Reich,*** millennium. **Tausendkünstler,** *m.* wizard; Jack of all trades. **tausend|mal,** *adv.* a thousand times. **-sackerment!** *int.* the deuce! devil take it! **Tausend|sappermenter, -sasa,** (*Austr.*) **-sassa,** *m.* (**-s,** *pl.* -) (*coll.*) devil of a fellow. **-schön,** *n.* (**-s,** *pl.* **-e**) (*Bot.*) daisy (*Bellis perennis*). **tausendst,**

num.adj. thousandth; ***das weiß der Tausendste nicht,*** not one in a thousand knows that; ***vom Hundertsten ins Tausendste kommen,*** not stick to the point, be led from one thing to another. **Tausendstel,** *n.* (*Swiss m.*) thousandth (part).

Tautologie [tautolo'ɡi:], *f.* tautology. **tautologisch** [–'lo:ɡɪʃ], *adj.* tautological.

Tau|tropfen, *m.* dewdrop. **–werk,** *n.* (*Naut.*) rigging; ropes, cordage. **–wetter,** *n.* thaw. **–wind,** *m.* mild *or* warm breeze. **–ziehen,** *n.* tug-of-war.

Taxameter [taksa'me:tər], *m.* 1. taximeter, (*coll.*) clock; 2. (*obs.*) *see* **Taxi.**

Taxator [tak'sa:tɔr], *m.* (**-s,** *pl.* **-en**) tax assessor; appraiser, valuer.

Taxe ['taksə], *f.* 1. rate, charge, fee; tax, duty; valuation, assessment, appraisal; 2. *See* **Taxi.**

Taxi ['taksi], *n.* (*Swiss m.*) (**-(s),** *pl.* **-(s)**) taxi(-cab).

taxieren [tak'si:rən], *v.t.* appraise, value, estimate, assess, rate, tax, fix the price (***auf*** (*Acc.*), at). **Taxierer,** *m. See* **Taxator. Taxierung,** *f.* appraisal, valuation, estimate, assessment.

Taxifahrer ['taksifa:rər], *m.* taxi-driver.

Tax|ordnung, *f.* tariff, scale of fees *or* costs. **–uhr,** *f. See* **Taxameter.**

Taxus ['taksus], *m.* (-, *pl.* -) (*Bot.*) yew(-tree) (*Taxus baccata*).

Taxwert, *m.* assessed value.

Technik ['tɛçnɪk], *f.* (-, *pl.* **-en**) 1. technique, skill, (*Mus.*) execution; 2. technical *or* applied science, engineering, technology. **Techniker,** *m.* technician; engineer, technologist. **Technikum,** *n.* (**-s,** *pl.* **-ken**) technical school *or* college.

technisch ['tɛçnɪʃ], *adj.* technical; ***–er Ausdruck,*** technical term; ***–e Chemie,*** applied *or* industrial chemistry; ***–er Chemiker,*** chemical engineer, industrial chemist; ***–er Direktor,*** engineering manager; ***–e Einzelheiten,*** technical details, technicalities; ***–e Hochschule,*** college of technology, polytechnic; ***–e Nothilfe,*** emergency repair service; ***–er Offizier,*** technical *or* specialist officer; ***–e Reinheit,*** commercial grade *or* quality (*of a product*); ***–e Schwierigkeiten,*** technical difficulties; ***–e Störung,*** technical fault *or* (*coll.*) hitch, mechanical failure *or* breakdown; ***–e Wunder,*** marvels of science *or* technology.

Technisierung [tɛçni'zi:ruŋ], *f.* mechanization.

Technologe [tɛçno'lo:ɡə], *m.* (**-n,** *pl.* **-n**) technologist; engineer. **Technologie** [–'ɡi:], *f.* technology; engineering. **technologisch,** *adj.* technological.

Techtelmechtel ['tɛçtəlmɛçtəl], *n.* (*coll.*) flirtation, entanglement, (*coll.*) affair; (*coll.*) goings-on.

Teckel ['tɛkəl], *m.* dachshund.

Teddybär ['tɛdibɛ:r], *m.* Teddy bear.

Tee [te:], *m.* 1. (**-s,** *pl.* **-sorten**) tea; infusion; ***wollen Sie bei uns – trinken?*** will you have *or* take tea with us? (*dial.*) ***im – sein,*** be drunk; be well in with the teacher; (*dial.*) ***seinen – kriegen,*** get one's marching orders, be flung *or* kicked out; (*coll.*) ***abwarten und – trinken,*** wait and see; 2. (*pl.* **-s**) tea-party.

Tee|bau, *m.* tea-growing *or* -planting. **–brett,** *n.* tea-tray. **–büchse, –dose,** *f.* tea-caddy. **--Ei,** *n.* tea-infuser. **--Ernte,** *f.* tea-harvest. **–gebäck,** *n.* cakes, (*Am.*) cookies. **–geschirr,** *n.* tea-service *or* -set. **–haube,** *f.* tea-cosy. **–kanne,** *f.* teapot. **–kessel,** *m.* tea-urn, (*coll.*) blockhead, dolt. **–kiste,** *f.* tea-chest. **–kräuter,** *n.pl.* herbs used for infusion. **–löffel,** *m.* teaspoon. **–löffelvoll,** *m.* teaspoonful. **–maschine,** *f.* tea-urn. **–mischung,** *f.* blend of tea. **–mütze,** *f. See* **–haube.**

Teer [te:r], *m.* (**-s,** *pl.* **-e**) (coal-)tar, pitch. **Teer|-decke,** *f. See* **–leinwand. teeren,** *v.t.* (spread *or* impregnate with) tar. **Teer|farbe,** *f.*, **–farbstoff,** *m.* coal-tar *or* aniline dye. **–faß,** *n.* tar-barrel. **–hütte,** *f.* tar-factory. **teerig,** *adj.* tarred, tarry. **Teer|jacke,** *f.* (*coll.*) Jack Tar. **–leinwand,** *f.* tarpaulin.

Teerose ['te:ʔro:zə], *f.* (*Bot.*) tea-rose (*Rosa indica*).

Teer|pappe, *f.* tarred paper, roofing felt. **–schwelerei,** *f.* distillation of tar; tar-distilling plant. **–seife,** *f.* coal-tar soap. **–straße,** *f.* tarred *or* asphalt road. **–tuch,** *n. See* **–decke. Teerung,** *f.* tarring.

Tee|service, *n. See* **–geschirr. –sieb,** *n.* tea-strainer. **–stoff,** *m.* theine. **–strauch,** *m.* tea-plant. **–tasse,** *f.* teacup. **–topf,** *m. See* **–kanne. –wagen,** *m.* tea-trolley. **–zeug,** *n.* tea-things.

Teich [taɪç], *m.* (**-(e)s,** *pl.* **-e**) pond, pool; (*coll.*) ***der große –,*** the Pond (*Atlantic Ocean*). **Teich|binse,** *f.* bulrush. **–huhn,** *n.* (*Orn.*) moorhen, (*Am.*) gallinule (*Gallinula chloropus*). **–rohr,** *n. See* **–schilf. –rohrsänger,** *m.* (*Orn.*) reed-warbler (*Acrocephalus scirpaceus*). **–rose,** *f.* (*Bot.*) (yellow) waterlily (*Nuphar luteum*). **–schilf,** *n.* reed(s). **–wasserläufer,** *m.* (*Orn.*) marsh-sandpiper (*Tringa stagnatilis*).

Teig [taɪk], *m.* (**-(e)s,** *pl.* **-e**) dough, batter, paste; pulp, plastic mass. **teig,** *adj.* (*dial.*) (*of fruit*) mellow, over-ripe, (*of pastry*) soggy, sad.

Teig|decke, *f.* covering *or* crust of pastry. **–holz,** *n. See* **–rolle.**

teigig ['taɪɡɪç], *adj.* doughy, pasty; *see also* **teig.**

Teig|klöpfel, *m. See* **–rolle. –kratze,** *f.*, **–kratzer,** *m. See* **–scharre. –mulde,** *f.* baker's trough. **–rolle,** *f.* rolling-pin. **–scharre,** *f.* baker's scraper. **–schüssel,** *f.* mixing-bowl, kneading-trough. **–waren,** *f.pl.* cereals, farinaceous food(stuff).

Teil [taɪl], **1.** *m.* (**-s,** *pl.* **-e**) part, portion, piece, member, component, element, section; ***edle –e,*** vital parts. **2.** (*also n.*) share, portion, division, (*Law*) party; ***beide –e,*** both sides *or* parties; ***er hat seinen – bekommen,*** he has got his due; ***sich*** (*Dat.*) ***seinen – denken,*** have one's own ideas; ***ich für meinen –,*** I for my part, I for one, as for me; ***der größte – der Menschen,*** most people, the majority of (the) people, (*coll.*) the bulk of the people; ***ein gut – davon,*** a good deal *or* share *or* (*coll.*) bit of it; ***ich halte es mit keinem –,*** I side with neither party; ***zum –,*** in part, partly, to some extent; ***zum großen –,*** largely, to a great extent; ***zum größten –,*** mostly, for the most part.

Teilansicht ['taɪl'anzɪçt], *f.* partial view. **teilbar,** *adj.* divisible, separable. **Teilbarkeit,** *f.* divisibility. **Teil|beschäftigte(r),** *m., f.* part-time worker. **–beschäftigung,** *f.* part-time employment *or* occupation. **–besitzer,** *m.* part-owner. **–betrag,** *m.* part-payment, instalment. **–bild,** *n.* (*T.V.*) frame, (*Am.*) field. **–bruch,** *m.* partial fraction. **Teilchen,** *n.* particle.

teilen ['taɪlən], **1.** *v.t.* divide, separate, partition (off); split, dismember; portion *or* share (out), divide, distribute, deal out, (*coll.*) split; (*fig.*) *see* **teilhaben**; ***Ansichten*** (***Gefühle*** *etc.*) **–**, share views (feelings *etc.*); ***geteilte Gefühle,*** mixed feelings; ***geteilte Meinungen,*** divided opinions; ***geteilter Meinung sein,*** be of a different opinion, hold a different view. **2.** *v.r.* divide, part, diverge, branch (off), fork; ***sich – in*** (*Acc.*), share (in), (*coll.*) go shares (in), (*fig.*) participate in (***mit,*** with); (*Math.*) ***sich – lassen,*** be divisible (***durch,*** by). **Teiler,** *m.* divider, sharer, (*Math.*) divisor; (*Math.*) ***größter gemeinschaftlicher –,*** greatest common measure.

Teil|erfolg, *m.* partial success. **–gebiet,** *n.* branch, department, section.

teilhaben ['taɪlha:bən], *irr.v.i.* share, participate, take part (***an*** (*Dat.*), in), partake, have a share (of). **Teil|haber(in),** *m.* (*f.*) sharer, participator, participant; joint-owner, partner, associate; ***stiller –,*** sleeping *or* (*Am.*) silent partner. **–haberschaft,** *f.* partnership, joint-ownership. **teilhaft(ig),** *adj.* (*Gen.*) partaking of, sharing *or* participating in; ***– werden*** (*Gen.*), partake of, share *or* participate in.

–teilig [taɪlɪç], *adj.suff.* in . . . parts, . . .-part *or* -piece. **Teil|kraft,** *f.* component force. **–lieferung,** *f.* part-delivery, instalment. **–lösung,** *f.* partial solution.

Teilnahme ['taɪlna:mə], *f.* participation, share (***an*** (*Dat.*), in), (*Law*) complicity (in); co-operation, collaboration (in); interest (in), sympathy, compassion (for *or* with); ***seine – ausdrücken*** (*Dat.*), condole with, offer (*s.o.*) one's condolences *or* sympathy. **teilnahmslos,** *adj.* unconcerned, indifferent; apathetic, impassive. **Teilnahmslosigkeit,** *f.* indifference, unconcern, apathy, lack of sympathy. **teilnahm(s)voll,** *adj.* sympathetic, solicitous.

teil|nehmen, *irr. v.i.* take (an active) part, participate, join, share, co-operate, collaborate, take an interest, interest o.s. (***an*** (*Dat.*), in), sympathize (with); be present (at), attend; contribute (to). **–nehmend,** *adj.* sympathetic (towards), solicitous (about), interested (in). **Teilnehmer,** *m.* participant, participator, partner, sharer, part-owner, member, (*Spt.*) entrant, contestant, competitor, (*Tele.*) subscriber; those present; (*Tele.*) ***– antwortet nicht,*** there is no reply.

teils [taɪls], *adv.* partly, in part. **Teil|schaden,** *m.* partial loss *or* damage. **–staat,** *m.* constituent state. **–strecke,** *f.* (*Railw.*) section (of line), (*fig.*) stage, leg. **–streckengrenze,** *f.* fare-stage. **–strich,** *m.* division, graduation (mark) (*on a scale*). **–stück,** *n.* fragment.

Teilung [ˈtaɪluŋ], *f.* division, separation, partition, (*Biol*). segmentation (*of cells*); distribution, sharing, (*of land*) parcelling out; (*of a scale*) graduation; (*of roads etc.*) fork(ing), bifurcation. **Teilungs|artikel,** *m.* (*Gram.*) partitive article. **–bruch,** *m.* (*Math.*) partial fraction. **–linie,** *f.* dividing line. **–punkt,** *m.* point of division. **–vertrag,** *m.* partition treaty. **–zahl,** *f.* (*Math.*) dividend. **–zeichen,** *n.* (*Math.*) division sign.

teilweise [ˈtaɪlvaɪzə], **1.** *adj.* partial. **2.** *adv. See* **teils**; (*fig.*) to some extent, in some cases. **Teil|zahl,** *f.* (*Math.*) quotient. **–zahlung,** *f.* part-payment, instalment. **–zeichnung,** *f.* (*Tech., Archit.*) detail (drawing); ***–en machen,*** (draw in) detail. **–zieher,** *m.* (*Orn.*) partial migrant.

Tein [teˈi:n], *n.* (*Chem.*) theine.

Teint [tɛ̃], *m.* (**-s,** *pl.* **-s**) complexion.

tektonisch [tɛkˈto:nɪʃ], *adj.* tectonic, structural.

Tele|fon, *n. See* **–phon. –graf,** *m. See* **–graph.**

Telegramm [teleˈgram], *n.* (**-s,** *pl.* **-e**) telegram, (*coll.*) wire. **Telegramm|adresse, –anschrift,** *f.* telegraphic address. **–formular,** *n.* telegraph-form.

Telegraph [teleˈgra:f], *m.* (**-en,** *pl.* **-en**) telegraph; ***optischer –,*** semaphore. **Telegraphen|amt,** *n.* telegraph-office. **–bote,** *m.* telegraph-boy. **–draht,** *m.* telegraph-wire. **–mast,** *m. See* **–stange. –netz,** *n.* telegraph-system. **–stange,** *f.* telegraph-pole. **–wesen,** *n. See* **Telegraphie.**

Telegraphie [telegraˈfi:], *f.* telegraphy; ***drahtlose –,*** wireless *or* radio telegraphy. **telegraphieren,** *v.t., v.i.* telegraph, cable, (*coll.*) wire. **telegraphisch** [–ˈgra:fɪʃ], *adj.* telegraphic, by telegram.

Teleobjektiv [ˈteleˀɔpiɛkti:f], *n.* telephoto lens.

Telepathie [telepaˈti:], *f.* telepathy.

Telephon [teleˈfo:n], *n.* (**-s,** *pl.* **-e**) telephone, (*coll.*) phone; ***– haben,*** be on the (tele)phone; ***ans – gehen,*** answer the (tele)phone. **Telephon|anruf,** *m.* (tele)phone call. **–anschluß,** *m.* telephone extension; ***– haben,*** be on the telephone. **–buch,** *n.* telephone directory. **telephonieren** [–ˈni:rən], *v.t., v.i.* telephone, (*coll.*) phone. **telephonisch, 1.** *adj.* telephonic. **2.** *adv.* over the *or* by (tele)phone; ***– (nicht) erreichbar,*** (not) on the phone. **Telephonist** [–ˈnɪst], *m.* (**-en,** *pl.* **-en**) telephone operator; telephonist. **Telephon|leitung,** *f.* telephone circuit. **–verbindung,** *f.* telephone connection. **–zelle,** *f.* call-box, phone-box. **–zentrale,** *f.* telephone exchange.

Telephotographie [telefotograˈfi:], *f.* long-distance photography. **Teleskop** [–ˈsko:p], *n.* (**-s,** *pl.* **-e**) telescope.

Teller [ˈtɛlər], *m.* (*dial. n.*) plate, dish; trencher; (*Mech.*) disk, disc, (*of valve*) seat; (*rare*) palm of the hand. **Teller|bord, –brett,** *n.* plate-drainer. **–mütze,** *f.* flat-peaked cap. **–rost,** *m.* plate-rack. **–schrank,** *m.* cupboard, sideboard. **–tuch,** *n.* dish-cloth. **–ventil,** *n.* disc valve. **–wärmer,** *m.* plate-warmer.

Tellur [tɛˈlu:r], *n.* tellurium. **Tellur|blei,** *n.* lead telluride. **–säure,** *f.* telluric acid.

Tempel [ˈtɛmpəl], *m.* temple, place of worship, sanctuary. **Tempel|diener,** *m.* officer of the temple, priest. **–herr,** *m.* Knight Templar. **–orden,** *m.* Order of Knights Templar. **–raub,** *m.* sacrilege. **–ritter,** *m. See* **–herr. –schändung,** *f. See* **–raub. –weihe,** *f.* ***Fest der –,*** (Jewish) Feast of Dedication.

Tempera [ˈtɛmpera], *f.* distemper, tempera.

Temperament [tɛmperaˈmɛnt], *n.* (**-(e)s,** *pl.* **-e**) temperament; character, disposition, constitution, humour; temper, mettle, (high) spirits, vivacity, liveliness, (*coll.*) life; ***seinem – die Zügel schießen lassen,*** have no control over one's feelings, be carried away by one's high spirits. **temperamentlos,** *adj.* spiritless. **temperamentvoll,** *adj.* lively, vivacious, (high-)spirited, full of spirits, ebullient, impetuous, passionate.

Temperatur [tɛmperaˈtu:r], *f.* temperature (*also Med.*); ***– im Freien,*** outdoor temperature. **Temperatur|abfall,** *m. See* **–sturz. –anstieg,** *m.* rise in temperature. **–bereich,** *m.* range of temperature. **temperaturbeständig,** *adj.* unaffected by temperature changes. **Temperatur|erhöhung,** *f. See* **–anstieg. –grad,** *m.* degree of temperature. **–konstanz,** *f.* constant temperature. **–mittel,** *n.* mean temperature. **–regler,** *m.* thermostat. **–schwankung,** *f.* change of *or* in temperature. **–sturz,** *m.* fall in temperature.

Temperenzler [tɛmpeˈrɛntslər], *m.* teetotaller.

Temperguß [ˈtɛmpərgus], *m.* malleable iron casting, malleable cast-iron. **temperieren** [–ˈri:rən], *v.t.* temper, moderate, soften; control the temperature of; cool down; ***temperiertes Wasser,*** lukewarm water. **tempern,** *v.t.* (*Metall.*) temper, anneal. **Temperofen,** *m.* tempering *or* annealing furnace.

Templer [ˈtɛmplər], *m. See* **Tempelherr.**

Tempo [ˈtɛmpo], *n.* (**-s,** *pl.* **-s** *or* **-pi**) time, tempo, measure, pace, rate, speed; ***– des Angriffs,*** pace of the attack; (*Motor.*) (*coll.*) ***– fahren,*** scorch along; ***er gab das – an,*** he set the pace; ***in rasendem –,*** at a breakneck speed; ***in langsamem –,*** at a slow pace; (*coll.*) ***–!*** get a move on! (*sl.*) step on it!

Temporalien [tɛmpoˈra:liən], *pl.* temporalities, secular possessions; (clerical) living.

temporär [tɛmpoˈrɛ:r], *adj.* temporary. **temporisieren** [–riˈzi:rən], *v.i.* temporize; delay.

Tempus [ˈtɛmpus], *n.* (-, *pl.* **Tempora**) (*Gram.*) tense.

Tenakel [teˈna:kəl], *n.* (**-s,** *pl.* **-e**) (*Typ.*) copy-holder; (*Surg.*) tenaculum; filtering-frame.

Tendenz [tɛnˈdɛnts], *f.* (-, *pl.* **-en**) tendency, propensity, inclination, trend, intention. **tendenziös** [–iˈø:s], *adj.* tendentious, partisan, biased, prejudiced. **Tendenz|meldung,** *f.* tendentious information. **–roman,** *m.,* **–stück,** *n.* novel (drama) with a purpose.

tendieren [tɛnˈdi:rən], *v.i.* tend, show a tendency, be inclined, incline (***nach,*** to(wards)).

Tenne [ˈtɛnə], *f.* threshing-floor, floor of a barn.

Tennis [ˈtɛnɪs], *n.* (lawn) tennis. **Tennis|platz,** *m.* tennis-court. **–schläger,** *m.* tennis-racket. **–turnier,** *n.* tennis tournament.

Tenor, *m.* 1. [teˈno:r] (**-s,** *pl.* **-e** *or* **¨-e**) (*Mus.*) tenor; 2. [ˈte:nɔr] (*no pl.*) purport, purpose, intent, tenor. **Tenorist** [–ˈrɪst], *m.* (**-en,** *pl.* **-en**) (*Mus.*) tenor. **Tenorstimme,** *f.* tenor voice *or* part.

Tentamen [tɛnˈta:mən], *n.* (**-s,** *pl.* **-mina**) preliminary examination. **Tentamenphysikum,** *n.* pre-medical.

Tenuis [ˈte:nuɪs], *f.* (-, *pl.* **-ues**) (*Phonet.*) voiceless stop.

Tepp [tɛp], *m.* (**-s** *or* **-en,** *pl.* **-e** *or* **-en**) (*dial., coll.*) dunce, nincompoop.

Teppich [ˈtɛpɪç], *m.* (**-s,** *pl.* **-e**) carpet, rug; tapestry; ***mit einem – überziehen*** or ***belegen,*** carpet. **Teppich|arbeit,** *f.* tapestry-work. **–kehrmaschine,** *f.* carpet-sweeper. **–pflanzen,** *f.pl.* small plants suited for carpet-gardening. **–schoner,** *m.*

drugget. **–sticker,** *m.* tapestry-worker. **–weber, –wirker,** *m.* carpet-manufacturer.

Termin [tɛr'mi:n], *m.* (**-s,** *pl.* **-e**) (appointed *or* fixed) time *or* term *or* date *or* day; closing date; date for completion, target-date, time-limit; (*Spt.*) fixture; (*Law*) summons; ***ich habe morgen –,*** I am (summoned) to appear (in court) tomorrow; ***in vier –en zahlbar,*** payable in four instalments; ***seine Miete noch zwei –e schuldig sein,*** be two quarters in arrears with one's rent; ***äußerster –,*** final date, (*coll.*) deadline. **termin|gemäß, –gerecht,** *adv.* on the appointed day, (*coll.*) to schedule, on time. **Termin|geschäft,** *n.* forward transactions, futures. **–handel,** *m.* time-bargain. **–kalender,** *m.*, **–liste,** *f.* (*Law*) cause list.

Terminologie [tɛrminolo'gi:], *f.* terminology, nomenclature; technical language.

Termin|tag, *m.* quarter-day. **–verkauf,** *m.* forward *or* future sale. **–verlängerung,** *f.* extension (of the time-limit), postponement (of the closing date). **–versicherung,** *f.* term-policy (*life assurance*). **terminweise,** *adv.* at fixed times, (*payment*) by instalments. **Terminzahlung,** *f.* (payment by) instalment.

Terpentin [tɛrpɛn'ti:n], *n.* (*Austr. m.*) turpentine. **Terpentinöl,** *n.* spirits (*or* oil) of turpentine.

Terrain [tɛ'rɛ̃], *n.* (**-s,** *pl.* **-s**) ground, terrain; building site, plot of land; (*fig.*) ***– aufholen,*** make up leeway. **Terrainaufnahme,** *f.* surveying.

Terrasse [tɛ'rasə], *f.* terrace; platform, balcony. **terrassieren** [–'si:rən], *v.t.* terrace, step.

Terrine [tɛ'ri:nə], *f.* tureen, soup-bowl.

Territorial|gewalt [tɛritori'a:l–], *f.* (*Hist.*) absolute authority. **–staaten,** *m.pl.* (medieval) independent states. **Territorium** [–'to:rium], *n.* (**-s,** *pl.* **-rien**) territory.

terrorisieren [tɛrori'zi:rən], *v.t.* terrorize, browbeat. **Terrorismus** [–'rɪsmus], *m.* terrorism. **Terrorist,** *m.* (**-en,** *pl.* **-en**) terrorist.

Tertia ['tɛrtsia], *f.* (-, *pl.* **-tien**) **1.** fourth form (*school*); (*Austr.*) third form; **2.** (*Typ.*) great primer. **Tertianer,** *m.* fourth- (*Austr.* third-)form boy. **Tertianfieber** [–'a:nfi:bər], *n.* tertian fever (*malaria*). **tertiär** [–'ɛ:r], *adj.* tertiary (*also Geol.*). **Tertiaschrift,** *f.* (*Typ.*) great primer.

Terz [tɛrts], *f.* (-, *pl.* **-en**) **1.** (*Mus.*) third; ***kleine –,*** minor third; ***große –,*** major third; **2.** (*Fenc.*) tierce.

Terzerol [tɛrtsə'rɔl], *n.* (**-s,** *pl.* **-e**) pocket pistol.

Terzerone [tɛrtsə'ro:nə], *m.* (**-n,** *pl.* **-n**) offspring of a white and a mulatto.

Terzett [tɛr'tsɛt], *n.* (**-s,** *pl.* **-e**) vocal trio.

Terzhieb ['tɛrtshi:p], *m.* (*Fenc.*) thrust in tierce.

Terzine [tɛr'tsi:nə], *f.* (*Metr.*) terza-rima.

Tesching ['tɛʃɪŋ], *n.* (**-s,** *pl.* **-s**) sub-calibre rifle.

Test [tɛst], *m.* (**-(e)s,** *pl.* **-e** *or* **-s**) (*Psych.*) test, investigation; (*Chem.*) cupel.

Testament [tɛsta'mɛnt], *n.* (**-(e)s,** *pl.* **-e**) testament, will; (*Law*) last will and testament; ***Altes*** (***Neues***) –, Old (New) Testament; ***ohne*** (***Hinterlassung eines***) –(*s*) ***sterben,*** die intestate *or* without leaving a will; ***Anerkennung des –s,*** probate; ***Anhang zu einem –,*** codicil to a will. **testamentarisch** [–'ta:rɪʃ], **1.** *adj.* testamentary. **2.** *adv.* by will; ***– hinterlassen*** or ***vermachen,*** leave by will, bequeath. **Testaments|bestätigung,** *f.* probate. **–eröffnung,** *f.* opening *or* reading of the will. **–vollstrecker,** *m.* executor. **–vollstreckerin,** *f.* executrix. **–zusatz,** *m.* codicil.

Testat [tɛs'ta:t], *n.* (**-(e)s,** *pl.* **-e**) certificate, attestation. **Testator,** *m.* (**-s,** *pl.* **-en**) testator.

testen ['tɛstən], *v.t.* (submit to a) test, submit to investigation.

testieren [tɛs'ti:rən], **1.** *v.t.* bequeath, dispose of by will; certify, testify, attest. **2.** *v.i.* make a will.

Tetraeder [tɛtra'e:dər], *n.* tetrahedron. **tetraedrisch,** *adj.* tetrahedral.

teuer ['tɔyər], *adj., adv.* dear, costly, expensive; precious, valuable; (*fig.*) dear, beloved, cherished; ***ich habe es – bezahlt,*** I have paid dearly for it; ***– kaufen,*** buy at a high price; ***–e Preise,*** high prices; ***hier ist guter Rat –,*** there's not much we can do; ***hoch und – schwören,*** swear solemnly, take a solemn oath; ***das soll ihm – zu stehen kommen,*** that will cost him dear, he shall pay *or* smart for that; ***– verkaufen,*** sell for a high price, (*fig.*) (*as one's life*) sell dearly; ***wie – ist es?*** how much is it? what does it cost? what price is it?

Teuerung ['tɔyəruŋ], *f.* dearth, scarcity, famine; rising prices, high cost of living. **Teuerungs|-zulage,** *f.* cost-of-living bonus. **–zuschlag,** *m.* price rise due to rising costs. **–zuwachs,** *m.* price increment.

Teufe ['tɔyfə], *f.* (*Min.*) depth.

Teufel ['tɔyfəl], *m.* devil, demon, fiend; (*coll.*) deuce, dickens, Old Nick; (*fig.*) ***armer –,*** poor devil *or* wretch, luckless beggar; ***eingefleischter –,*** devil incarnate; ***er fragt den – danach,*** he does not care a rap about it; ***in –s Küche kommen,*** get into a devil *or* a hell of a mess; ***er hat den – im Leibe,*** he is a devil of a fellow; ***der – ist los!*** now the fat's in the fire; ***das müßte mit dem – zugehen,*** the devil must have his hand in it; ***pfui –!*** ugh! disgusting! ***bist du des –s?*** are you crazy? ***den – an die Wand malen,*** talk of the devil; ***der – mag wissen warum,*** devil only knows; ***er weiß den – davon,*** he knows damn all about it; ***was zum –!*** what the hell *or* devil *or* dickens! hang it! ***zum – gehen,*** go to the devil *or* the dogs *or* (*sl.*) to pot; ***scher dich zum –!*** go to hell *or* blazes! **Teufelei** [–'laɪ], *f.* devilry, (*Am.*) deviltry; devilment; devilishness, devilish *or* diabolical trick.

Teufels|abbiß, *m.* (*Bot.*) devil's-bit (*Succisa pratensis*). **–arbeit,** *f.* devilishly *or* tremendously hard work. **–austreibung,** *f.*, **–bann,** *m.*, **–beschwörung,** *f.* exorcism. **–braten,** *m.* (*coll.*) villain, rake, thorough scamp. **–braut,** *f.* witch. **–brut,** *f.* hellish crew, bad lot. **–dreck,** *m.* asafoetida. **–finger,** *m.* (*Mollusc.*) belemnite. **–gestank,** *m.* (*coll.*) infernal stench. **–glück,** *n.* (*coll.*) devil's own luck. **–junge,** *m.* (*coll.*) young imp *or* scamp; (*Irish*) broth of a boy. **–kerl,** *m.* (*coll.*) devil of a fellow. **–kind,** *n.* hardened sinner. **–kirsche,** *f.* (*Bot.*) deadly-nightshade, belladonna (*Atropa belladonna*). **–kreis,** *n.* vicious circle. **–lärm,** *m.* (*coll.*) infernal noise. **–list,** *f.* diabolical cunning. **–sturmschwalbe,** *f.* (*Orn.*) black-capped petrel (*Pterodroma hasitata*). **–weib,** *n.* (*coll.*) she-devil, shrew. **–werk,** *n.* (*coll.*) piece of devilry.

teufen ['tɔyfən], *v.t.* (*Min.*) bore (deeper).

teuflisch ['tɔyflɪʃ], *adj.* devilish, diabolical, satanic, fiendish, infernal.

Text [tɛkst], **1.** *m.* (**-es,** *pl.* **-e**) text, letterpress; wording, (*of a song*) words, lyric, (*of an opera*) libretto, (Bible) text; (*coll.*) ***weiter im –!*** come to the point! (*coll.*) ***ihm den – lesen,*** give him a good talking to, lecture him; ***aus dem – kommen,*** lose the thread, be put out, break down (*in a speech*). **2.** *f.* (*Typ.*) double pica. **Text|abbildung,** *f.* illustration in the text. **–ausgabe,** *f.* plain text, edition without notes. **–buch,** *n.* (*Theat.*) book, words, lines, (*Mus.*) libretto. **–dichter,** *m.* librettist. **Texter,** *m.* copywriter.

textil [tɛks'ti:l], *adj.* textile. **Textilien,** *pl.*, **Textilwaren,** *f.pl.* textile goods, textiles.

Textkritik ['tɛkstkriti:k], *f.* textual criticism. **textlich,** *adj.* textual. **Text|schreiber,** *m. See* **Texter.** **⌐schrift,** *f.* (*Typ.*) *see* **Text, 2.**

Textur [tɛks'tu:r], *f.* (-, *pl.* **-en**) texture; (*Geol.*) structure.

Theater [te'a:tər], *n.* theatre; stage; (*coll.*) hullaballoo, fuss; ***ans – gehen,*** see ***zum – gehen***; ***ins – gehen,*** go to the theatre; ***heute ist kein –,*** there is no performance today; (*coll.*) ***– machen,*** make believe, feign, (*sl.*) put it on, put on an act; ***mach kein –!*** don't make (such) a fuss! ***– spielen,*** go in for amateur theatricals, put on an amateur show; (*coll.*) ***das reinste –,*** a complete sham, utter humbug; ***zum – gehen,*** go on the stage, become an actor (actress), take up acting.

Theater|agentur, *f.* theatrical agency. **–besuch,** *m.*

playgoing, theatre-going. **–besucher,** *m.* playgoer, theatre-goer. **–coup,** *m. See* **–streich. –dichter,** *m.* dramatist, playwright. **–direktor,** *m.* theatre manager. **–karte,** *f.* theatre ticket. **–kasse,** *f.* box-office. **–maler,** *m.* scene-painter. **–mantel,** *m.* opera-cloak. **–manuskript,** *n.* acting-copy. **–maschinist,** *m.* scene-shifter, stage technician. **–streich,** *m.* stage-trick, coup de théâtre. **–stück,** *n.* stage-play, drama. **–vorstellung,** *f.* theatrical *or* stage performance. **–wesen,** *n.* the stage. **–zensur,** *f.* stage censorship. **–zettel,** *m.* play-bill.

Theatralik [tea'tra:lɪk], *f.* staginess, theatricality. **theatralisch,** *adj.* dramatic, scenic, histrionic, theatrical; stagy, unnatural.

Theismus [te'ɪsmus], *m.* theism.

Theke ['te:kə], *f.* 1. counter (*in a shop*), bar (*in a tavern*); 2. (*Austr.*) notebook.

Thema ['te:ma:], *n.* (**-s,** *pl.* **-ta** *or* **-men**) theme, topic, subject; (*coll.*) ***beim – bleiben,*** stick to the subject *or* point. **thematisch** [–'ma:tɪʃ], *adj.* thematic.

Themse ['tɛmzə], *f.* (River) Thames.

Theokratie [teokra'ti:], *f.* theocracy.

Theologe [teo'lo:gə], *m.* (**-n,** *pl.* **-n**) theologian. **Theologie** [–'gi:], *f.* theology, divinity; *– **studieren,*** read for holy orders, study for the ministry; ***Professor der –,*** professor of divinity. **theologisch,** *adj.* theological.

Theoretiker [teo're:tikər], *m.* theorist. **theoretisch, 1.** *adj.* theoretic(al), hypothetical, speculative, academic. **2.** *adv.* theoretically, in theory. **theoretisieren** [–'zi:rən], *v.i.* theorize. **Theorie,** *f.* theory, hypothesis; ***eine – aufstellen,*** evolve *or* (*coll.*) put forward a theory; ***die – ist aufgegeben,*** the theory is exploded *or* holds good no longer.

Theosoph [teo'zo:f], *m.* (**-en,** *pl.* **-en**) theosophist. **Theosophie** [–'fi:], *f.* theosophy.

Therapeutik [tera'pɔytɪk], *f.* therapeutics. **Therapie,** *f.* therapy.

Thermalquellen [tɛr'ma:lkvɛlən], **Thermen** ['tɛrmən], *f.pl.* hot springs. **Thermik,** *f.* thermal, warm up-current of air. **thermisch,** *adj.* thermal, thermic; ***–e Behandlung,*** heat treatment.

Thermo|dynamik ['tɛrmo–], *f.* thermodynamics. **–element,** *n.* (*Elec.*) thermo-couple.

Thermometer [tɛrmo'me:tər], *n.* thermometer; ***feuchtes –,*** wet-bulb thermometer. **Thermometerstand,** *m.* thermometer reading.

Thermo|paar, *n. See* **–element.**

Thermophor [tɛrmo'fo:r], *m.* (**-s,** *pl.* **-e**) hot-water bottle.

Thermo|säule, *f.*, **–stat,** *m.* (**-(e)s** *or* **-en,** *pl.* **-e(n)**) thermostat. **–syphonkühlung,** *f.* (*Motor.*) gravity-system cooling.

thesaurieren [tezau'ri:rən], *v.t.* lay up, store, hoard.

These ['te:zə], *f.* thesis, postulate, assertion, proposition. **Thesis,** *f.* (**–,** *pl.* **Thesen**) 1. *See* **These**; 2. (*Metr.*) unaccented syllable, (*Mus.*) down-beat.

Thing [tɪŋ], *n.* (**-(e)s,** *pl.* **-e**) (*obs.*) assembly. **Thing|platz,** *m.*, **–stätte,** *f.* (*Nat. Soc.*) festival arena.

Thomas|eisen ['to:mas–], *n.* basic (low-carbon) steel. **–mehl,** *n.* artificial fertilizer. **–prozeß,** *m.* (*Metall.*) Bessemer process. **–schiene,** *f.* (*Surg.*) (Thomas) extension splint. **–stahl,** *m.* basic (Bessemer) steel.

Thorshühnchen ['to:rshy:nçən], *n.* (*Orn.*) grey *or* (*Am.*) red phalarope (*Phalaropus fulicarius*).

Thrombose [trɔm'bo:zə], *f.* thrombosis.

Thron [tro:n], *m.* (**-(e)s,** *pl.* **-e**) throne; ***den – besteigen,*** ascend the throne; ***vom –e stoßen,*** dethrone, depose; ***auf den – erheben,*** raise to the throne; ***auf den – verzichten,*** renounce the succession. **Thron|anwärter,** *m.* heir apparent. **–besteigung,** *f.* accession (to the throne). **–bewerber,** *m.* pretender to the throne. **thronen,** *v.i.* be enthroned; reign; (*coll.*) lord it. **Thron|-entsagung,** *f.* abdication. **–erbe,** *m.* heir (to the throne), heir apparent. **–folge,** *f.* succession (to the throne). **–folger,** *m.* successor to the throne. **–himmel,** *m.* canopy. **–räuber,** *m.* usurper. **–rede,** *f.* (*Parl.*) King's (Queen's) speech. **–saal,** *m.* throne-room, presence-chamber. **–sessel,** *m.* chair of state. **–verzicht,** *m.* abdication. **–wechsel,** *m.* change of sovereign.

Thunfisch ['tu:nfɪʃ], *m.* (*Ichth.*) tunny (*Thynnus*).

Thüringen ['ty:rɪŋən], *n.* (*Geog.*) Thuringia.

Thymian ['ty:mia:n], *m.* (**-s,** *pl.* **-e**) (*Bot.*) thyme (*Thymus*).

Tibetaner(in) [tɪbe'ta:nər(ɪn)], *m.* (*f.*), **tibetanisch,** *adj.* Tibetan.

Tick [tɪk], *m.* (**-s,** *pl.* **-s**) wince; (*coll.*) whim, fancy, fad, crotchet; ***einen – haben,*** be cracked *or* dotty; be conceited; ***einen – auf ihn haben,*** have a grudge against him. **ticken,** *v.i.* tick (*as a clock*).

tief [ti:f], **1.** *adj.* deep, profound, low, dark; far; (*Mus.*) low-pitched, bass; (*fig.*) innermost, utmost, extreme, utter; ***–e Einsicht,*** profound insight; ***im –sten Elend,*** in utter misery, in extreme poverty; ***aus –stem Herzen,*** from the bottom of the heart; ***– in der Nacht, in –er Nacht,*** at dead of night; ***bis – in die Nacht,*** far into the night; ***im –sten Norden,*** in the extreme north; ***in –em Schlaf,*** in a deep sleep, deep in sleep; ***in –stem Vertrauen,*** in the utmost confidence; ***im –en Walde,*** in the depths of the wood; ***im –sten Winter,*** in the depth(s) *or* dead of winter. **2.** *adv.* deep, low; (*fig.*) deeply, profoundly; ***– atmen,*** breath deeply, take a deep breath; ***den Hut – in die Augen drücken,*** pull one's hat low over one's eyes; ***–er begründen,*** substantiate more fully; ***das läßt – blicken,*** that gives (much) food for thought, that speaks volumes; (*coll.*) ***zu – ins Glas gucken,*** drink more than is good for one; ***der Grund liegt –er,*** the reason is not apparent, there's more to it than meets the eye; (*coll.*) ***– in der Patsche sitzen,*** be well and truly in a mess; ***– seufzen,*** give a deep sigh; (*Mus.*) ***–er stimmen,*** lower the pitch; ***zu – singen,*** sing flat; ***– in seiner Schuld,*** deep in debt to him, (*fig.*) deeply indebted to him; ***sich – verbeugen,*** bow low.

Tief, *n.* (**-(e)s,** *pl.* **-s**) 1. deep channel of water; 2. (barometric) depression; 3. (*Rad.*) bass distortion.

Tief|angriff, *m.* (*Av.*) low-level attack, (*coll.*) strafing. **–aufschlag,** *m.* (*Tenn.*) underarm service. **–bahn,** *f.* underground railway. **–bau,** *m.* excavation, site-preparation, underground workings. **tief|beleidigt,** *adj.* stung to the quick. **–betrübt,** *adj.* deeply grieved. **–bewegt,** *adj.* deeply agitated *or* moved. **–blau,** *adj.* dark blue. **Tief|blick,** *m.* penetration, deep *or* keen insight. **–bohrer,** *m.* auger. **–bunker,** *m.* deep *or* underground shelter. **–decker,** *m.* low-wing monoplane. **–druck,** *m.* photogravure printing, heliogravure, intaglio. **–druckgebiet,** *n.* (*Meteor.*) low-pressure area.

Tiefe ['ti:fə], *f.* 1. depth, deepness; profundity; deep, abyss, gorge; ***– des Herzens,*** depth *or* bottom of the heart, innermost heart; ***– des Gedankens,*** profundity (of thought); 2. disposition in depth (*of troops*); 3. *pl.* (*Mus.*) bass notes, (*Naut.*) soundings.

Tiefebene ['ti:fʔebənə], *f.* (low-lying) plain, lowland(s). **tief|eindringend, –eingreifend,** *adj.* penetrating.

Tiefen|anzeiger, *m.* depth gauge. **–ausdehnung,** *f.* (*Mil.*) extension in depth. **–feuer,** *n.* (*Mil.*) searching fire. **–gestein,** *n.* (*Geol.*) plutonic rock. **–gliederung,** *f.* (*Mil.*) distribution *or* disposition in depth. **–lot,** *n.* (*Naut.*) sounding-lead. **–messung,** *f.* bathymetry. **–psychologie,** *f.* psychology of the subconscious. **–ruder,** *n.* elevator, hydroplane (*submarines*). **–schärfe,** *f.* (*Phot.*) depth of focus. **–staffelung,** *f. See* **–gliederung. –steuerung,** *f.* hydroplane gear (*submarines*). **–wirkung,** *f.* effect in depth, (*of sound*) stereophonic effect, (*of pictures*) stereoscopic effect.

tiefernst ['ti:fʔɛrnst], *adj.* deadly serious, very grave. **Tief|flieger,** *m.* low-flying aircraft. **–flug,** *m.* low-level flight, (*coll.*) hedge-hopping. **–gang,** *m.* draught (*of vessels*); ***ein Schiff von 8 Fuß –,*** a ship drawing 8 feet of water. **tief|gebeugt,** *adj.* bowed down, deeply afflicted. **–gefühlt,** *adj.* heartfelt. **–gegliedert,** *adj.* organized in depth (*defences*). **–gehend,** *adj.* deep, profound, intense, far-reaching, penetrating, thoroughgoing; (*Naut.*) deep-drawing. **–gekühlt,** *adj.* deep-frozen. **–greifend,** *adj.* far-reaching, thoroughgoing; deep-seated, penetrating; fundamental, profound, radical. **–gründig,** *adj.* deep, profound. **Tief|kühltruhe,** *f.* deep-freeze (tray *or* compartment). **–kultur,** *f.* subsoil ploughing. **–ladelinie,** *f.* (*Naut.*) load-line. **–land,** *n. See* **–ebene. tiefliegend,** *adj.* low-lying; deep-seated; (*of eyes*) sunken, deep-set. **Tief|punkt,** *m.* lowest point, nadir; (*fig.*) low ebb, rock-bottom. **–schlag,** *m.* (*Boxing*) blow below the belt. **tief|schürfend,** *adj.* (*fig.*) profound, exhaustive, thorough. **–schwarz,** *adj.* jet-black. **–seekunde,** *f.* oceanology. **–seelotung,** *f.* deep-sea soundings, bathymetry. **–seetauch(er)kugel,** *f.* bathysphere. **–sinn,** *m.* thoughtfulness, pensiveness, reverie; melancholy. **tiefsinnig,** *adj.* thoughtful, pensive, meditative, serious; melancholy, melancholic. **Tiefstand,** *m.* lowest level, nadir; low-water mark. **tief|stehend,** *adj.* low-lying, low; (*fig.*) inferior. **–stimmig,** *adj.* deep-voiced, deep-mouthed. **–wurzelnd,** *adj.* deep-rooted.

Tiegel ['ti:gəl], *m.* 1. (*Cul.*) saucepan, stew-pan, (*Metall.*) melting-pot, crucible; 2. (*Typ.*) platen. **Tiegel|druck,** *m.* platen-printing. **–gußstahl,** *m.* crucible cast steel. **–ofen,** *m.* crucible furnace.

Tiekholz ['ti:khɔlts], *n.* teak.

Tiene ['ti:nə], *f.* (*dial.*) little tub *or* cask.

Tier [ti:r], *n.* (**-(e)s,** *pl.* **-e**) animal, beast, (*fig.*) brute; doe, hind; ***das – in uns,*** the animal side of our nature, the beast in us; (*coll.*) ***ein großes*** or ***hohes –,*** a big bug *or* shot, a bigwig.

Tier|art, *f.* species of animals. **–arzt,** *m.* veterinary surgeon. **tierärztlich,** *adj.* veterinary. **Tier|ausstopfer,** *m.* taxidermist. **–bändiger,** *m.* wild-beast tamer. **Tierchen,** *n.* animalcule; (*Prov.*) ***jedes – hat sein Pläsierchen,*** every man to his taste, there is no accounting for tastes. **Tier|epos,** *n.* beast epic. **–fabel,** *f.* animal fable. **–freund,** *m.* animal-lover. **–garten,** *m.* zoological gardens. **–gattung,** *f.* genus of animal. **tierhaft,** *adj.* animal-like. **Tier|handel,** *m.* trade in livestock. **–handlung,** *f.* pet-shop. **–haut,** *f.* hide, pelt. **–heilkunde,** *f.* veterinary science.

tierisch ['ti:rɪʃ], *adj.* animal; (*fig.*) bestial, brutish, beastly; (*fig.*) *–er Ernst,* deadly seriousness. **Tier|kohle,** *f.* animal charcoal. **–kreis,** *m.* (*Astrol.*) zodiac. **–kreiszeichen,** *n.* sign of the zodiac. **–kunde,** *f.* zoology. **–park,** *m. See* **–garten. –pflanze,** *f.* zoophyte. **–quälerei,** *f.* cruelty to animals. **–reich,** *n.* animal kingdom. **–schau,** *f.* menagerie; cattle (horse *etc.*) show. **–schutzgebiet,** *n.* game (p)reserve. **–schutzverein,** *m.* society for the prevention of cruelty to animals. **–versteinerung,** *f.* zoolite. **–wärter,** *m.* keeper (*of animals*). **–welt,** *f.* animal kingdom, fauna. **–zucht,** *f.* animal-husbandry, livestock-breeding.

Tiger ['ti:gər], *m.* tiger. **Tiger|decke,** *f.*, **–fell,** *n.* tiger-skin (rug). **Tigerin,** *f.* tigress. **Tigerkatze,** *f.* (*Zool.*) (African) tiger-cat, serval (*Felis serval*). **tigern,** *v.t.* spot, speckle; ***getigert,*** speckled, mottled; tabby (*of cats*). **Tiger|pferd,** *n.* (*obs.*) zebra. **–schlange,** *f.* (*Zool.*) Indian python (*Python molurus*). **–tier,** *n.* (*Poet.*) tiger. **–weibchen,** *n. See* **Tigerin.**

Tilde ['tɪldə], *f.* (*Typ.*) swung dash, (*in Spanish*) tilde.

tilgbar ['tɪlkba:r], *adj.* extinguishable, effaceable; (*Comm.*) redeemable; ***nicht –,*** irredeemable.

tilgen ['tɪlgən], *v.t.* extinguish, blot out, abolish, eradicate, expunge, obliterate, efface, delete, erase; extirpate, destroy, exterminate; cancel, annul; amortize, redeem, discharge (*debt*), (*coll.*) pay *or* clear *or* write off (*debt*), expiate, (*coll.*) wipe out (*disgrace etc.*). **Tilgung,** *f.* extermination, extinction, obliteration, destruction, eradication; effacement, deletion, erasure, cancellation; liquidation, annulment, settlement, discharge, repayment, amortization, redemption, expiation.

Tilgungs|anleihe, *f.* amortization loan. **–fonds,** *m.*, **–kasse,** *f.* sinking-fund. **–schein,** *m.* bill of amortization. **–zeichen,** *n.* (*Typ.*) delete.

Tingeltangel ['tɪŋəltaŋəl], *m. or n.* (*coll.*) low music-hall, (*sl.*) honky-tonk.

Tinktur [tɪŋk'tu:r], *f.* (-, *pl.* **-en**) tincture, infusion; dye.

Tinte ['tɪntə], *f.* ink; (*Paint.*) tint; (*fig.*) ***in der – sitzen,*** be in the soup; (*sl.*) ***er muß – gesoffen haben,*** he must be cracked; (*coll.*) ***klar wie dicke –,*** clear as mud. **Tinten|faß,** *n.* ink-well, inkstand. **–fisch,** *m.* (*Ichth.*) cuttlefish, squid, sepia (*Cephalopodae*). **–fleck,** *m. See* **–klecks. –gummi,** *m.* ink-eraser. **–klecks,** *m.* ink-stain, ink-spot, blot. **–kleckser,** *m.* pen-pusher, scribbler. **–stift,** *m.* copying-ink *or* indelible pencil. **–wischer,** *m.* pen-wiper.

Tip [tɪp], *m.* (**-s,** *pl.* **-s**) hint, warning, (*Spt.*) tip; ***ihm einen – geben,*** tip him off.

Tippel ['tɪpəl], *m.* (*coll.*) tittle; dot; ***bis aufs –chen wissen,*** know down to the last detail.

Tippelbruder ['tɪpəlbru:dər], *m.* (*coll.*) tramp, beggar.

[1]**tippeln** ['tɪpəln], *v.t.* dot, stipple.

[2]**tippeln,** *v.i.* (*aux.* s.) tramp, trudge.

tippen ['tɪpən], *v.t.* 1. touch gently, tap; (*coll.*) type; 2. (*coll.*) place a bet; ***– auf*** (*Acc.*), tip (*a winner*). **Tipp|fehler,** *m.* typing error. **–fräulein,** *n.* typist.

tipptopp ['tɪptɔp], *adj.* (*coll.*) tip-top, first-class *or* -rate, (*sl.*) posh, swell.

Tirailleur [tira'jø:r], *m.* (**-s,** *pl.* **-s** *or* **-e**) (*obs.*) skirmisher. **tiraillieren,** *v.i.* skirmish.

tirilieren [tiri'li:rən], *v.i.* warble, chirrup (*of birds*).

Tirol [ti'ro:l], *n.* the Tyrol. **Tiroler(in),** *m.* (*f.*), **tirolerisch,** *adj.* Tyrolese, Tyrolean.

Tisch [tɪʃ], *m.* (**-(e)s,** *pl.* **-e**) table, board; meal; ***den – abdecken,*** clear the table; ***am – sitzen,*** sit at the table; ***Scheidung von – und Bett,*** judicial separation; ***bei –,*** at table; during the meal; ***den – decken,*** lay the cloth *or* table; ***freien – haben,*** have free board; ***am grünen –,*** in official quarters, at an official level; ***vom grünen – aus,*** bureaucratic, red-tape (*decisions*), armchair (*strategy*); ***zum – des Herrn gehen,*** partake of the Lord's Supper; ***nach –,*** after dinner *or* supper; (*fig.*) ***reinen – machen,*** make a clean sweep (***mit,*** of); (*fig.*) ***unter den – fallen,*** be pushed on one side, come to nothing, (*coll.*) fall flat; (*fig.*) ***unter den – fallen lassen,*** ignore, (*coll.*) let drop; ***sich zu – setzen,*** sit down to a meal *or* to dinner (*etc.*); ***zu – bitten,*** invite *or* ask to dinner *or* to a meal; ***bitte zu –!*** dinner (*etc.*) is served *or* ready.

Tisch|aufsatz, *m.* centre-piece, table-centre. **–bein,** *n.* table leg. **–besen,** *m.* crumb-brush. **–blatt,** *n.* table-top; leaf of a table. **–dame,** *f.* lady taken in to dinner. **–decke,** *f.* table-cloth. **–ende,** *n.* ***oberes*** (***unteres***) **–,** head (foot) of the table. **tischfertig,** *adj.* ready-to-serve, ready-prepared. **Tisch|gänger,** *m.* boarder; regular diner. **–gast,** *m.* guest (at dinner). **–gebet,** *n.* grace; ***das – sprechen,*** say grace. **–geld,** *n.* board-wages (*of servants*); (*Mil.*) messing-allowance. **–genosse,** *m.* fellow-boarder; messmate. **–gerät, –geschirr,** *n.* tableware. **–gesellschaft,** *f.* company at table, dinner party. **–gespräch,** *n.* table-talk. **–glocke,** *f.* dinner-bell *or* -gong. **–herr,** *m.* gentleman taking a lady in to dinner. **–karte,** *f.* place-card. **–klopfen,** *n.* table-rapping. **–lade,** *f.* table-drawer. **–läufer,** *m.* table-centre *or* runner. **–leindeckdich,** *n.* magic table.

Tischler ['tɪʃlər], *m.* joiner, carpenter, cabinet-maker. **Tischlerarbeit,** *f.* carpentry, joinery. **Tischlerei** [–'raɪ], *f.* joiner's *or* carpenter's (work)-shop; *see also* **Tischlerarbeit. Tischler|leim,** *m.* carpenter's glue. **–meister,** *m.* master joiner. **tischlern, 1.** *v.i.* do carpentry *or* woodwork. **2.** *v.t.* make, (*coll.*) knock together. **Tischler|werkstatt,** *f.* carpenter's shop. **–werkzeug,** *n.* woodworking tools.

Tisch|nachbar, *m.* neighbour at table. **–platte,** *f.*

table-top; stage plate (*of microscope*). **–rede,** *f.* after-dinner speech. **–rücken,** *n.* table-turning. **–tennis,** *n.* table-tennis, (*coll.*) ping-pong. **–tuch,** *n.* tablecloth; ***das – zwischen sich und ihm zerschneiden,*** have nothing more to do with him, break (off all contact) with him. **–wäsche,** *f.* table-linen. **–wein,** *m.* table-wine, dinner-wine. **–zeug,** *n.* table-linen and cutlery.

Titan [ti'ta:n], **1.** *m.* (**-en,** *pl.* **-en**) (*Myth.*) Titan. **2.** *n.* (*Chem.*) titanium. **Titane,** *m.* (**-n,** *pl.* **-n**) *see* **Titan, 1. Titaneisenerz,** *n.* titaniferous *or* titanic iron-ore, ilmenite. **titanisch,** *adj.* titanic. **titansauer,** *adj.* titanite of.

Titel ['ti:təl], *m.* title, heading; claim, (*Law*) title (-deed); ***bloßer –,*** mere *or* empty title; ***den größten – auf etwas haben,*** have the greatest *or* best claim to a th.; ***Buch mit aufgedrucktem –,*** lettered book; ***den – Graf*** or ***eines Grafen führen,*** have *or* bear the title of count.

Titel|auflage, –ausgabe, *f.* edition having merely a new title-page. **–bewerber,** *m.* (*Spt.*) challenger for the title. **–bild,** *n.* frontispiece. **–blatt,** *n.* title-page. **–halter,** *m.* (*Spt.*) title holder. **–kopf,** *m.* heading (*of an article*). **–kupfer,** *n. See* **–bild. –rolle,** *f.* title-role, name-part. **–sucht,** *f.* craze for titles, tuft-hunting. **–träger, –verteidiger,** *m. See* **–halter. –vignette,** *f.* head-piece. **–wort,** *n.* head-word, caption. **–zeile,** *f.* headline, rubric.

Titer ['ti:tər], *m.* (*Chem.*) standard strength of solution.

Titrier|analyse [ti'tri:r–], *f.* volumetric analysis. **–apparat,** *m.* volumetric *or* titrating apparatus. **titrieren,** *v.t.* titrate. **Titrier|flüssigkeit,** *f.* standard solution. **–methode,** *f.* titration, volumetric method.

Titsche ['tɪtʃə], *f.* (*dial.*) sauce. **titschen,** *v.t.* (*dial.*) dip, soak, sop.

Titte ['tɪtə], *f.* (*dial.*) tit, dug.

titular [titu'la:r], *adj.* titular, nominal, honorary; (*Mil.*) brevet. **Titulatur** [–'tu:r], *f.* styling; full title(s). **titulieren,** *v.t.* style; call, give the title of, address as.

Tjost [tjo:st], *m.* (**-es,** *pl.* **-e**) *or f.* (-, *pl.* **-en**) (*obs.*) joust.

Toast [to:st], *m.* (**-es,** *pl.* **-e**) 1. toast, health; ***einen – auf ihn ausbringen,*** toast him, propose a toast to him; ***auf einen – antworten,*** respond to a toast; 2. toast(ed bread). **toasten,** (*Austr.* **toastieren** [–'ti:rən]), *v.i.* – ***auf*** (*Acc.*), toast, propose *or* drink a toast to.

Tobak ['to:bak], *m.* (*obs.*) *see* **Tabak**; (*coll.*) ***Anno –,*** the year dot.

Tobel ['to:bəl], *n.* (*Austr. m.*) (*dial.*) wooded gorge, ravine, gully.

toben ['to:bən], *v.i.* storm, rage, rave, bluster, fume, foam, (*as battles*) rage, (*as wind, waves*) rage, roar; (*of children*) romp, be wild. **tobend,** *adj.* raging, raving, frantic, furious; tempestuous; boisterous. **Tobsucht,** *f.* frenzy, mania, raving madness. **tobsüchtig,** *adj.* raving mad, frenzied, frantic. **Tobsuchtsanfall,** *m.* (*coll.*) ***einen – bekommen,*** have the tantrums, throw a tantrum, (*sl.*) blow one's top.

Tochter ['tɔxtər], *f.* (-, *pl.* ¨-) daughter; (*Swiss*) girl, servant, waitress. **Tochter|anstalt,** *f.* branch *or* affiliated establishment. **–gesellschaft,** *f.* subsidiary company. **–kind,** *n.* (*dial.*) daughter's child, grandchild. **–kirche,** *f.* branch *or* filial church. **–kompaß,** *m.* (*Naut.*) repeater compass.

töchterlich ['tœctərlɪç], *adj.* daughterly, filial.

Tochter|liebe, *f.* filial *or* daughter's love. **–mann,** *m.* (*dial.*) son-in-law.

Töchterschule ['tœçtərʃu:lə], *f.* ***höhere –,*** high school for girls.

Tochter|sprache, *f.* derived *or* derivative language. **–staat,** *m.* colony. **–stadt,** *f.* overspill town.

Tod [to:t], *m.* (**-(e)s,** *pl.* **-e** (*rare*) *or* **-esfälle**) death; decease; ***auf den – liegen,*** be mortally ill; ***auf den – verwundet,*** mortally wounded; ***bürgerlicher –,*** loss of civil rights; ***den – finden,*** meet one's death; (*fig.*) ***sich*** (*Dat.*) ***den – holen,*** catch one's death (of cold); ***du bist*** (***ein Kind***) ***des –es, wenn . . .,*** you're doomed *or* you are a dead man if . . .; (*Prov.*) ***gegen den – ist kein Kraut gewachsen,*** there is no remedy against death; ***Kampf auf Leben und –,*** mortal combat, fight to the death, (*fig.*) life-and-death struggle; (*coll.*) ***für den – nicht leiden können,*** hate like poison; ***nach dem –e,*** after death, posthumously; ***nahe am –e*** or ***dem –e nahe sein,*** be at death's door; ***eines natürlichen –es sterben,*** die a natural death; (*fig.*) ***das wird noch mein – sein,*** that will be the death of me; ***es geht um Leben und –,*** it is a matter of life and death; (*Prov.*) ***umsonst ist nur der –,*** everything costs money; (*fig.*) ***sich zu –e ärgern,*** fret o.s. to death; (*fig.*) ***zu –e betrübt,*** mortally grieved; ***zu –e hetzen,*** (*Hunt.*) run down, (*fig.*) run (*a th.*) to death; ***sich zu –e lachen,*** kill o.s. laughing; ***zu –e langweilen,*** bore stiff *or* to death.

tod|ähnlich, *adj.* deathlike, deathly. **–bang,** *adj.* mortally afraid, frightened to death. **–blaß, –bleich,** *adj.* deathly pale, pale as death. **–bringend,** *adj.* deadly, fatal, lethal, mortal. **–elend,** *adj.* (*coll.*) utterly wretched *or* miserable. **–ernst, 1.** *adj.* deadly serious. **2.** *adv.* in dead earnest.

Todes|ahnung, *f.* foreboding *or* presentiment of death. **–angst,** *f.* mortal terror. **–anzeige,** *f.* obituary (notice). **–art,** *f.* manner of death. **–becher,** *m.* (*Poet.*) fatal cup. **–blässe,** *f.* deathly pallor. **–engel,** *m.* Angel of Death. **–erklärung,** *f.* (official) notification of death. **–fall,** *m.* (case of) death; casualty (*in war*); *pl.* deaths (*used as a pl. of* **Tod**). **–furcht,** *f.* fear of death. **–gefahr,** *f.* deadly peril, peril of one's life; ***in – schweben,*** be in imminent danger *or* deadly peril; ***ihn aus – retten,*** rescue him from (certain) death. **–kampf,** *m.* death-agony, throes of death. **–kandidat,** *m.* doomed *or* dying man, (*sl.*) goner. **–keim,** *m.* seeds of death. **todesmutig,** *adj.* fearless unto death *or* in the face of death.

Todes|nachweis, *m.* proof of death. **–not,** *f.* peril of death, deadly peril; *pl. See* **–qual. –opfer,** *n.* death, casualty; ***Zahl der –,*** death-toll. **–patrouille,** *f.* 'death or glory' squad, suicide squad. **–pein,** *f.* (*Poet.*), **–qual,** *f.* (*usu. pl.*) pangs of death, death-throes. **–röcheln,** *n.* death-rattle. **–schlaf,** *m.* sleep of the dead; deathlike *or* profound sleep. **–schrecken,** *m. See* **–furcht. –schweiß,** *m.* cold sweat of death. **–stoß,** *m.* death-blow, coup-de-grâce. **–strafe,** *f.* death penalty, capital punishment; ***bei –,*** on penalty *or* pain of death. **–strahl,** *m.* death-ray. **–streich,** *m. See* **–stoß. –stunde,** *f.* hour of death; last *or* fatal *or* supreme hour. **–sturz,** *m.* (*climbing*) fatal fall, (*Av.*) fatal crash; fall to one's death. **–tag,** *m.* day of death; anniversary of (*a p.'s*) death. **–ursache,** *f.* cause of death. **–urteil,** *n.* death sentence, sentence of death, (*fig.*) death warrant. **–verachtung,** *f.* defiance of death; ***mit –,*** recklessly, without thought for one's own safety. **–wunde,** *f.* mortal *or* fatal wound.

Tod|fall, *m.* (*Law*) *see* **Todesfall. –feind(in),** *m.* (*f.*) deadly *or* mortal enemy. **todfeind,** *adj.* (*Dat.*) bitterly hostile. **Todfeindschaft,** *f.* deadly *or* bitter enmity. **tod|geweiht,** *adj.* doomed. **–krank,** *adj.* dangerously *or* critically ill, (*B.*) sick unto death.

tödlich ['tø:tlɪç], **1.** *adj.* fatal, deadly, mortal, lethal; murderous; ***–er Unfall*** or ***Unfall mit –em Ausgang,*** fatal accident; ***mit –er Sicherheit,*** with infallible *or* (*coll.*) dead certainty; ***–es Schweigen,*** deathly silence. **2.** *adv.* ***– hassen,*** hate like poison; (*fig.*) ***sich – langweilen,*** be bored stiff *or* to death; ***– treffen,*** strike a mortal blow to; ***– verunglücken,*** be killed in an accident, meet with a fatal accident.

tod|müde, *adj.* dead-tired, tired to death, (*coll.*) worn out, knocked up, (*sl.*) dead-beat. **–schick,** *adj.* (*coll.*) dressed up to the nines, (*sl.*) classy. **–sicher, 1.** *adj.* (*coll.*) dead-certain, sure as fate; ***–e Sache,*** sure th., (*sl.*) cinch. **2.** *adv.* without any doubt, (*coll.*) for sure. **Todsünde,** *f.* mortal sin. **tod|unglücklich,** *adj.* miserably unhappy, (*Poet.*) sick at heart. **–wund,** *adj.* mortally wounded.

Tohuwabohu [tohuwa'bo:hu], *n.* hubbub, confusion, hullabaloo, (*sl.*) racket.

Toilette [twa'lɛtə], *f.* toilet; dressing-table; lavatory, W.C., toilet, convenience; – *machen,* dress, get dressed, make one's toilet; *auf die – gehen,* go to the lavatory; *in großer –,* in evening-dress. **Toiletten|artikel,** *m.pl.* toilet requisites. **–garnitur,** *f.* toilet-set, dressing-case. **–papier,** *n.* toilet-paper. **–seife,** *f.* toilet-soap. **–tisch,** *m.* dressing-table. **–zimmer,** *n.* dressing-room.

Töle ['tø:lə], *f.* (*dial.*) bitch.

tolerant [tɔle'rant], *adj.* tolerant (*gegen,* of), broad-minded. **Toleranz,** *f.* toleration, tolerance, broad-mindedness; (*Mech.*) tolerance, clearance, allowance. **tolerieren,** *v.t.* tolerate.

toll [tɔl], **1.** *adj.* (raving) mad, raving, insane; crazy, frenzied, frantic, furious, wild; grotesque, bizarre, extravagant, eccentric, absurd, senseless, nonsensical; (*coll.*) fantastic, incredible, terrific, great, frightful, awful, breathtaking, stupendous, too funny for words; *–es Gerücht,* wild rumour; *–er Hund,* mad dog; (*coll.*) *–er Kerl,* devil of a fellow; (*coll.*) *–e Sache,* fantastic show, (*sl.*) wow, humdinger; a perfect scream; (*coll.*) *–e Wirtschaft,* awful *or* shocking mess; *–es Zeug,* crazy ideas, extravagant views *or* notions, ravings. **2.** *adv. es ging – her,* it was a wild affair, things got out of hand; *es zu – treiben,* go too far, overdo it; *wie –,* like mad.

Tolle ['tɔlə], *f.* (*dial.*) tuft, topknot, crest, frill. **Tolleisen,** *n.* crimping-iron.

[1]**tollen** ['tɔlən], *v.t.* crimp, goffer.

[2]**tollen,** *v.i.* (*aux.* h. & s.) romp, frolic, fool about, be wild.

Toll|haus, *n.* lunatic asylum, (*fig.*) madhouse, bedlam. **–häusler,** *m.* madman, maniac, lunatic. **Tollheit,** *f.* madness, frenzy, fury; mad trick, crazy escapade, piece of folly. **Toll|kirsche,** *f.* (*Bot.*) deadly-nightshade (*Atropa belladonna*). **–kopf,** *m.* madcap. **toll|köpfig,** *adj.* hot-headed, hare-brained. **–kühn,** *adj.* foolhardy, rash, reckless, dare-devil. **Toll|kühnheit,** *f.* foolhardiness, rashness, recklessness. **–wut,** *f.* rabies, hydrophobia. **tollwütig,** *adj.* rabid.

Tolpatsch ['tɔlpatʃ], *m.* (**-es,** *pl.* **-e**), **tolpatschig,** *adj. See* **Tölpel, tölpelhaft.**

Tölpel ['tœlpəl], *m.* 1. blockhead, duffer, booby; lout, boor, oaf; 2. (*Orn.*) gannet (*Morus bassanus*). **Tölpelei** [-'laɪ], *f.* awkwardness, clumsiness; loutishness, boorishness. **tölpelhaft,** *adj.* awkward, clumsy, doltish, loutish, boorish. **Tölpelhaftigkeit,** *f. See* **Tölpelei. tölpeln,** *v.i.* be awkward *or* clumsy. **tölpisch,** *adj. See* **tölpelhaft.**

Tomate [to'ma:tə], *f.* tomato. **Tomatenmark,** *f.* tomato pulp.

Tombak ['tɔmbak], *m.* tombac, pinchbeck.

[1]**Ton** [to:n], *m.* (**-(e)s,** *pl.* **-e** *or* **-sorten**) (potter's) clay, kaolin; *feuerfester –,* fire-clay.

[2]**Ton,** *m.* (**-(e)s,** *pl.* **⸚e**) sound; (*Mus.*) note; (*Mus.*) timbre, (*Metr.*) accent, stress, emphasis, (*Art*) tone, tint, shade; *den – angeben,* (*Mus.*) give the note, (*fig.*) set the tone *or* fashion, call the tune; *einen anderen – anschlagen,* change one's tune *or* tone; *einfacher –,* (*Mus.*) simple note, (*Phys.*) sinusoidal sound wave; *keinen – von sich geben,* not utter a sound; *keinen – mehr!* not another sound *or* word! *zum guten – gehören,* be a mark of good breeding; (*Mus.*) *halber –,* semitone; (*coll.*) *hast du Töne!* you don't say! well I never! can you beat it?

Ton|abnehmer, *m.* (gramophone) pick-up. **–abstand,** *m.* (*Mus.*) interval. **tonangebend,** *adj.* setting the fashion; *–e Kreise,* leading *or* fashionable circles. **Ton|angeber,** *m.* leader of fashion. **–arm,** *m.* (*gramophone*) tone-arm. **–art,** *f.* 1. kind of clay; 2. (*Mus.*) key; (*fig.*) tone, strain; (*fig.*) *eine andere – anschlagen,* change one's tune *or* tone. **–aufnahme,** *f.* sound-recording. **–bad,** *n.* (*Phot.*) toning solution. **–band,** *n.* (recording) tape. **–bandaufnahme,** *f.* tape-recording. **–bandgerät,** *n.* tape-recorder. **–bereich,** *m.* (*Rad.*) audio-range. **–blende,** *f.* (*Rad.*) tone control. **–boden,** *m.* clayey soil. **–dichter,** *m.* (musical) composer. **–dichtung,** *f.* (musical) composition, symphonic poem.

tonen ['to:nən], *v.t.* (*Phot.*) tone.

[1]**tönen** ['tø:nən], *v.t.* tint, colour, tone, shade.

[2]**tönen,** *v.i.* sound, resound, ring; (*coll.*) hold forth.

Tonerde ['to:nˀe:rdə], *f.* argillaceous earth; alumina, aluminium oxide; *essigsaure –,* aluminium acetate.

tönern ['tø:nərn], *adj.* (of) clay, clayey, argillaceous, earthen, earthenware; (*fig. of sound*) dull, hollow; *–e Füße,* feet of clay.

Ton|fall, *m.* (*Mus.*) cadence, modulation; (*of speech*) inflexion, intonation, accent. **–farbe,** *f.* (*Mus.*) timbre. **–film,** *m.* talking *or* sound-film, (*coll.*) talkie. **–fixierbad,** *n.* (*Phot.*) toning and fixing bath. **–folge,** *f.* (*Mus.*) succession of notes, scale; melodic line, melody, strain(s). **–frequenz,** *f.* (*Rad.*) audio-frequency. **–führung,** *f.* (*Mus.*) tonal quality. **–fülle,** *f.* volume (of sound), sonority. **–gebung,** *f.* (*Mus.*) tone (production). **–gefäß,** *n.* earthen(ware) vessel. **–geschirr,** *n.* pottery, earthenware. **–grube,** *f.* clay-pit. **–gut,** *n. See* **–geschirr. –halle,** *f.* concert hall.

tonhaltig ['to:nhaltɪç], *adj.* argillaceous, clayey.

Tonhöhe ['to:nhø:ə], *f.* (musical) pitch.

tonig ['to:nɪç], *adj. See* **tonhaltig. -tonig,** *adj.suff.* -toned. **Tonika,** *f.* (-, *pl.* **-ken**) (*Mus.*) tonic, keynote. **Toningenieur,** *m.* sound-engineer. **tonisch,** *adj.* (*Med.*) tonic. **Ton|kalk,** *m.* argillaceous limestone. **–kunst,** *f.* music, musical art. **–künstler(in),** *m.* (*f.*) musician. **–lage,** *f.* (*Mus.*) pitch, compass. **–lager,** *n.* clay-bed *or* stratum. **–leiter,** *f.* (*Mus.*) scale, gamut. **tonlos,** *adj.* soundless, voiceless; unstressed, unaccented; (*fig.*) toneless. **Tonmalerei,** *f.* onomatopœia.

Tonnage [to'na:ʒə], *f.* (*Naut.*) tonnage.

Tonne ['tɔnə], *f.* cask, barrel, butt, tun; (*Naut.*) buoy; (*weight*) (metric) ton (= *1,000 kg or 2,205 lbs.*). **tonnenförmig,** *adj.* barrel-shaped. **Tonnen|fracht,** *f.* freight (charged) by the ton. **–gehalt,** *m.* (*Naut.*) tonnage. **–gewölbe,** *n.* (*Archit.*) barrel-vault. **tonnenweise,** *adv.* by the barrel; by the ton, in tons.

Ton|papier, *n.* tinted paper. **–pfeife,** *f.* clay pipe. **–rohr,** *n.,* **–röhre,** *f.* clay *or* earthenware piping *or* conduit. **–schwund,** *m.* (*Rad.*) fading. **–setzer,** *m.* (musical) composer. **–silbe,** *f.* (*Metr.*) accented *or* stressed syllable. **–stärke,** *f.* intensity *or* volume of sound, (*Metr.*) degree of stress. **–streifen,** *m.* (*Films*) sound-track. **–stück,** *n.* piece of music. **–stufe,** *f.* (*Mus.*) pitch (*of a note*), note (*of a scale*).

Tonsur [tɔn'zu:r], *f.* (-, *pl.* **-en**) tonsure.

Ton|taube, *f.* clay pigeon. **–techniker,** *m. See* **–ingenieur. –übergang,** *m.* change of key, modulation. **–umfang,** *m.* compass, range (*of voice or instrument*).

Tönung ['tø:nʊŋ], *f.* shade, tint, tone, tinge; tinting, shading.

Ton|veränderung, *f.* (*fig.*) change of tone. **–verschiebung,** *f.* (*Metr.*) shifting of stress. **–verstärker,** *m.* (*Rad.*) audio-amplifier. **–verstärkung,** *f.* (*Rad.*) amplification. **–waren,** *f.pl. See* **–gut. –wiedergabe,** *f.* (*Rad.*) sound reproduction; fidelity. **–zeichen,** *n.* (*Mus.*) note, (*Metr.*) stress mark, accent.

Topas [to'pa:s, (*Austr.* 'to:pas)], *m.* (**-es,** *pl.* **-e**) topaz.

Topf [tɔpf], *m.* (**-es,** *pl.* **⸚e**) pot, jar, vessel; (*Cul.*) saucepan; *in Töpfe setzen,* pot (*plants*); *alles in einen – werfen,* lump everything together, make no distinction, treat (them) all alike.

Töpfchen ['tœpfçən], *n.* gallipot; (*coll.*) chamber (pot); (*nursery talk*) *aufs – gehen,* go on the pot, do pottie.

Topfen ['tɔpfən], *m.* (*dial.*) curds.

Töpfer ['tœpfər], *m.* potter; stove-fitter. **Töpferarbeit,** *f.* pottery, ceramics. **Töpferei** [–'raɪ], *f.*

pottery trade, ceramic art; potter's workshop; *see also* **Töpferarbeit. Töpfer|erde,** *f.* potter's clay. **-gut,** *n. See* **-ware. töpfern,** *adj.* earthen(ware), pottery. **Töpfer|scheibe,** *f.* potter's wheel. **-ton,** *m. See* **-erde. -ware,** *f.* pottery, crockery, earthenware.

Topf|gucker, *m.* (*coll.*) Nosy Parker. **-haken,** *m.* pot-hook. **-hut,** *m.* cloche (hat). **-kieker,** *m.* (*dial.*) *see* **-gucker. -kuchen,** *m.* large cake. **-lappen,** *m.* kettle-holder, oven-cloth. **-pflanze,** *f.* pot(ted) plant. **-scherbe,** *f.* piece of broken crockery, potsherd.

Topik ['to:pɪk], *f.* thematic organization, arrangement of material, treatment of the subject.

topisch ['to:pɪʃ], *adj.* local, (*Med.*) topical. **Topographie** [-ogra'fi:], *f.* topography. **topographisch** [-'gra:fɪʃ], *adj.* topographical.

topp! [tɔp], *int.* done! agreed! (*coll.*) right oh! OK!

Topp, *m.* (**-s,** *pl.* **-e**) (*Naut.*) (mast-)head, topmast; (*sl. Theat.*) the gods; ***vor – und Takel treiben,*** sail under the bare poles. **Topp(e)nant,** *f.* (-, *pl.* **-en**) (*Naut.*) topping-lift. **Topp|laterne,** *f.*, **-licht,** *n.* masthead light. **-reep,** *n.* guy-line, stay. **-segel,** *n.* topsail.

[1]**Tor** [to:r], *m.* (**-en,** *pl.* **-en**) fool.

[2]**Tor,** *n.* (**-(e)s,** *pl.* **-e**) gate, gateway, door, portal; (*Footb.*) goal; (*skiing*) (slalom) gate; ***ein – machen*** or ***schießen,*** score *or* shoot a goal. **Tor|bogen,** *m.* archway. **-chance,** *f.* (*Footb.*) scoring chance.

Tordalk ['to:rtˀalk], *m.* (*Orn.*) razorbill (*Alca torda*).

Tor(ein)fahrt ['to:r(aɪn)fa:rt], *f.* gateway.

Torf [tɔrf], *m.* (**-(e)s,** *pl.* **⸚e** (*Austr.* **-e**)) peat; **–** ***graben*** or ***stechen,*** cut peat. **torfartig,** *adj.* peaty. **Torf|boden,** *m.* peat-bed. **-bruch,** *m.* peat-bog. **-erde,** *f. See* **-boden. -gewinnung,** *f.* peat-cutting. **-gräber,** *m.* peat-cutter. **-grube,** *f.* peat-hole. **-lager,** *n. See* **-bruch.**

Torflügel ['to:rfly:gəl], *m.* wing of a gate.

Torf|moor, *n. See* **-bruch. -mull,** *m.* peaty mould. **-stecher,** *m. See* **-gräber. -stich,** *m. See* **-gewinnung.**

Tor|halle, *f.* porch. **-höhe,** *f.* clearance of an archway.

Torheit ['to:rhaɪt], *f.* folly, foolishness; piece of silliness.

Torhüter ['to:rhy:tər], *m.* gatekeeper, porter; (*Spt.*) goalkeeper.

töricht ['tø:rɪçt], *adj.* foolish, unwise, silly. **törichterweise,** *adv.* foolishly, like a fool.

Törin ['tø:rɪn], *f.* foolish woman.

Torkel ['tɔrkəl], *f.* (-, *pl.* **-n**) *or m.* 1. (*dial.*) wine press; 2. (*m. only*) (*coll.*) gift from the gods. **torkeln,** *v.i.* (*aux.* s.) reel, stagger, totter.

Törl [tœrl], *n.* (**-s,** *pl.* -) (*Austr.*) gorge.

Tor|latte, *f.* (*Footb.*) crossbar. **-lauf,** *m.* (*skiing*) slalom race. **-linie,** *f.* (*Footb.*) goal-line. **-mann,** *m. See* **-wart.**

Tornister [tɔr'nɪstər], *m. or n.* knapsack, pack, rucksack; (*dial.*) school-bag, satchel. **Tornisterfunkgerät,** *n.* (*Mil.*) portable radio equipment, (*coll.*) walkie-talkie.

torpedieren [tɔrpe'di:rən], *v.t.* torpedo. **Torpedo** [-'pe:do], *m. or n.* (**-s,** *pl.* **-s**) torpedo. **Torpedo|bahn,** *f.* torpedo wake *or* track. **-bomber,** *m.* torpedo-carrying aircraft. **-boot,** *n.* torpedo boat. **-rohr,** *n.* torpedo tube. **-spur,** *f. See* **-bahn.**

Tor|pfosten, *m.* gate-post, (*Footb.*) goal-post. **-raum,** *m.* (*Footb.*) goal area. **-schluß,** *m.* closing of the gates; closing-time; (*fig.*) ***kurz vor –,*** at the eleventh hour, at the last minute. **-schlußpanik,** *f.* (*coll.*) last-minute panic. **-schuß,** *m.* kick *or* shot at goal; goal. **-schütze,** *m.* (goal) scorer.

Torsion [tɔrsi'o:n], *f.* torsion, twist(ing), torque. **Torsions|beanspruchung,** *f.* torsional stress. **-feder,** *f.* torsion spring. **-festigkeit,** *f.* torsional strength, torque. **-stab,** *m.* torsion bar. **-waage,** *f.* torsion balance. **-winkel,** *m.* angle of torque.

Torso ['tɔrzo], *m.* (**-s,** *pl.* **-s**) torso.

Tor|steher, *m. See* **-wart. -stoß,** *m.* goal-kick.

Tort [tɔrt], *m.* wrong, injury; ***ihm einen – antun,*** play a trick *or* (*coll.*) a dirty trick on him; ***ihm zum –,*** to spite him.

Torte ['tɔrtə], *f.* tart, pie, flan, flat cake. **Torten|bäcker,** *m.* pastrycook. **-form,** *f.* cake- *or* baking-tin. **-heber,** *m.* cake-server, cake-slice.

Tortur [tɔr'tu:r], *f.* (-, *pl.* **-en**) torture, (*fig.*) ordeal.

Tor|wächter, *m.* gate-keeper, doorman, porter. **-wart,** *m.* (*Footb.*) goalkeeper. **-weg,** *m.* gateway, archway.

tosen ['to:zən], *v.i.* (*aux.* h. & s.) rage, roar; ***-der Beifall,*** uproarious *or* thunderous applause.

tot [to:t], *adj.* dead, defunct, deceased; lifeless, extinct, inanimate; (*fig.*) deserted, desolate, dead, dull, stagnant; (*Spt.*) ***-er Ball,*** dead ball; (*Med.*) ***-es Fleisch,*** proud flesh; (*Mech.*) ***-er Gang,*** dead travel, lost motion, backlash, (*coll.*) play, slop; (*Min.*) ***-es Gebirge,*** exhausted workings; ***aufs -e Gleis*** or ***Geleise kommen*** or ***geraten,*** come to a dead end, reach a deadlock; (*Law*) ***-e Hand,*** mortmain; (*Law*) ***an die -e Hand veräußern,*** amortize; ***-es Kapital,*** unemployed *or* uninvested capital; (*Min. coll.*) ***-er Mann,*** exhausted working; ***das Tote Meer,*** the Dead Sea; (*Mech.*) ***-er Punkt,*** dead-centre; (*fig.*) deadlock, impasse; (*Spt.*) ***-es Rennen,*** dead-heat; ***-e Sprache,*** dead language; (*Mil.*) ***-er Winkel,*** dead ground, dead arc; ***-es Wissen,*** useless *or* unprofitable knowledge; ***-e Zeit,*** dead *or* (*coll.*) silly season; (*Rad.*) ***-e Zone,*** skip distance, (*coll.*) blind spot.

total [to'ta:l], **1.** *adj.* total, whole, entire, complete; ***-er Krieg,*** total *or* (*coll.*) all-out war(fare); ***-er Staat,*** totalitarian state. **2.** *adv.* totally, completely, entirely, wholly, (*coll.*) utterly, absolutely, altogether. **Total|ausverkauf,** *m.* clearance sale. **-betrag,** *m.* aggregate. **-bilanz,** *f.* final balance. **-finsternis,** *f.* total eclipse. **Totalisator** [-i'za:tɔr], *m.* (**-s,** *pl.* **-en**) totalizer, (*sl.*) tote. **totalitär** [-'tɛ:r], *adj.* totalitarian. **Totalität,** *f.* totality, entirety.

tot|arbeiten, *v.r.* kill o.s. with work, work o.s. to death. **-ärgern,** **1.** *v.t.* worry the life out of. **2.** *v.r.* worry o.s. to death.

töten ['tø:tən], **1.** *v.t.* kill, slay, put to death; destroy; deaden, soften (*colours*); mortify (*the body*). **2.** *v.r.* kill o.s., take one's own life, commit suicide.

Toten|acker, *m.* (*dial., Poet.*) burying-ground, graveyard. **-amt,** *n.* burial service, mass for the dead, requiem. **-bahre,** *f.* bier. **-baum,** *m.* (*Swiss*) coffin. **-bett,** *n.* death-bed. **totenblaß,** *adj.* pale as death, deathly pale, (as) white as a sheet. **Totenblässe,** *f.* deathly pallor. **toten|bleich,** *adj. See* **-blaß. Toten|blume,** *f.* (*Bot.*) marigold (*Calendula officinalis*). **-feier,** *f.* funeral rites, obsequies, exequies. **-geläut(e),** *n.* knell, passing-bell. **-geleit,** *n.* funeral cortège. **-gerippe,** *n.* skeleton. **-geruch,** *m.* cadaverous smell. **-gerüst,** *n.* catafalque. **-glocke,** *f. See* **-geläut(e). -gräber,** *m.* grave-digger; (*Ent.*) burying-beetle (*Necrophorus*). **-gruft,** *f.* vault, sepulchre. **-hemd,** *n.* shroud, winding sheet. **-klage,** *f.* dirge, wake. **-kopf,** *m.* death's-head; skull; (*Ent.*) death's-head moth (*Acherontia atropos*). **-kranz,** *m.* funeral wreath. **-liste,** *f.* list of casualties, death roll. **-marsch,** *m.* funeral march. **-maske,** *f.* death-mask. **-messe,** *f. See* **-amt. -reich,** *n.* Hades, the Underworld. **-schädel,** *m. See* **-kopf. -schau,** *f.* coroner's inquest, post-mortem examination. **-schein,** *m.* death-certificate. **-sonntag,** *m.* All Souls' Day. **-starre,** *f.* rigor mortis. **totenstill,** *adj.* as silent as the grave, deathly silent. **Toten|stille,** *f.* silence of the grave, deathly *or* dead silence. **-tanz,** *m.* dance of death, danse macabre. **-uhr,** *f.* (*Ent.*) death-watch beetle (*Anobium*). **-urne,** *f.* funeral *or* sepulchral urn. **-wache,** *f.* wake, death-watch. **-wagen,** *m.* hearse.

Tote(r) ['to:tə(r)], *m., f.* dead man (*or* woman), dead person, (dead) body, corpse; *pl.* the dead, (*Mil.*) fatal casualties.

tot|fahren, *irr.v.t.* kill by running down. **-gar,** *adj.* (*Metall.*) over-refined. **-geboren,** *adj.* stillborn, (*fig.*) abortive. **-gebrannt,** *adj.* overburnt (*lime etc.*). **Totgeburt,** *f.* still-birth; still-born child. **tot|geglaubt,** *adj.* presumed dead. **-gemahlen,** *adj.* overshort (*paper pulp*). **-gesagt,** *adj.* reported dead. **-gewalzt,** *adj.* rolled to death (*rubber*). **-hetzen,** *v.t.* work to death. **-küssen,** *v.t.* smother with kisses. **-lachen,** *v.r.* split one's sides (with laughter); ***sie wollten sich –,*** they were tickled to death, they nearly died with laughter. **Tot|lachen,** *n.* ***es ist zum –,*** it's a perfect scream, it's too funny for words; ***Geschichte zum –,*** screamingly funny story. **-lauf,** *m.* (*Mech.*) dead travel. **tot|laufen,** *irr.v.r.* come to a standstill *or* deadlock, (*coll.*) peter out. **-machen,** *v.t.* (*coll.*) scotch, hush up, (*sl.*) *see* **töten.**

Toto ['to:to], *m. or* (*coll.*) *n.* (**-s,** *pl.* **-s**) football pools; ***im – spielen,*** bet on *or* (*coll.*) do the pools; ***im – gewinnen,*** win on the pools. **Toto|gewinn,** *m.* win on the pools; pools premium. **-zettel,** *m.* pools coupon.

Totpunkt ['to:tpuŋkt], *m.* (*Tech.*) dead-centre. **totschießen, 1.** *irr.v.t.* shoot dead. **2.** *irr.v.r.* blow one's brains out. **Totschlag,** *m.* homicide, manslaughter. **totschlagen,** *irr.v.t.* kill, slay; (*fig.*) ***die Zeit –,*** kill time. **Totschläger,** *m.* cudgel, life-preserver. **tot|schweigen,** *irr.v.t.* hush up, pass over in silence. **-stellen,** *v.r.* feign death, (*sl.*) play possum. **-treten,** *irr.v.t.* crush (*beetle etc.*) underfoot, stamp one's foot on.

Tötung ['tø:tuŋ], *f.* killing, slaying, (*Law*) homicide; (*Law*) *fahrlässige –,* manslaughter; (*Med.*) ***– der Leibesfrucht,*** termination of pregnancy.

Tour [tu:r], *f.* (-, *pl.* **-en**) 1. tour, trip, excursion; (*coll.*) ***in einer –,*** at a stretch, without stopping, (*coll.*) in *or* at one go; 2. (*dancing*) set, figure; (*Tech.*) revolution; (*knitting*) round, row; (*coll.*) trick, dodge; ***außer der –,*** out of one's turn, (*Mil.*) not according to seniority; (*Mech.*) ***auf -en,*** at speed; ***auf -en kommen,*** (*Motor.*) pick up, gather speed, (*coll.*) rev up; (*fig.*) get into one's stride; (*fig.*) ***auf vollen -en laufen,*** be in full swing, (*coll.*) be going full blast.

Touren|fahrt, *f.* (*Motor.*) reliability trial. **-rad,** *n.* (*Cycl.*) roadster. **-wagen,** *m.* touring-car, tourer. **-zahl,** *f.* number of revolutions, revolutions per minute. **-zähler,** *m.* revolution *or* (*coll.*) rev counter, tachometer, speed indicator.

Tourist [tu'rɪst], *m.* (**-en,** *pl.* **-en**) tourist, excursionist, (*coll.*) tripper; hiker. **Touristen|(fahr)-karte,** *f.* excursion ticket. **-klasse,** *f.* (*Naut.*) tourist *or* third class. **-verkehr,** *m.* tourist traffic, tourism.

Tournee [tur'ne:], *f.* (-, *pl.* **-s** *or* **-n**) (*Theat.*) tour.

Trab [tra:p], *m.* trot; ***im -e,*** at a trot, (*fig.*) on the run *or* (*coll.*) trot; ***in – setzen,*** put (*a horse*) into a trot; (*coll.*) ***ihn auf – bringen,*** make him get a move on.

Trabant [tra'bant], *m.* (**-en,** *pl.* **-en**) satellite; (*fig.*) follower, (*coll.*) hanger-on; (*obs.*) gentleman-at-arms, footman. **Trabantenstaat,** *m.* (*Pol.*) satellite (state).

traben ['tra:bən], *v.i.* (*aux.* h. & s.) trot; jog along; (*of horse*) ***hoch –,*** be a high-stepper. **Traber,** *m.* trotting-horse, trotter. **Traberwagen,** *m.* sulky. **Trabrennen,** *n.* trotting-race.

Tracht [traxt], *f.* (-, *pl.* **-en**) 1. dress, attire, garb; costume, uniform; national *or* peasant costume; fashion, style; 2. load (*as much as one can carry*), (*of puppies*) litter, (*of honey etc.*) yield; (*coll.*) ***eine – Prügel,*** a sound thrashing; 3. (*bees*) swarming-time.

trachten ['traxtən], *v.i.* ***– nach,*** strive after *or* for, endeavour *or* try to get, aspire to, seek, covet, (*coll.*) have an *or* one's eye on; ***ihm nach dem Leben –,*** make an attempt on his life, seek his life. **Trachten,** *n.* endeavour, aim; aspiration, striving.

Trachtenfest ['traxtənfɛst], *n.* display *or* festival of national costumes.

trächtig ['trɛçtɪç], *adj.* (*of animals*) with young. **Trächtigkeit,** *f.* pregnancy, gestation.

traditionell [traditsio'nɛl], *adj.* traditional.

traf [tra:f], *see* **treffen.**

träf [trɛ:f], *adj.* (*Swiss*) pertinent, to the point.

Trafik [tra'fɪk], *m.* (**-s,** *pl.* **-s**) *or* (*Austr.*) *f.* (-, *pl.* **-en**) tobacconists' (shop). **Trafikant** [-'kant], *m.* (**-en,** *pl.* **-en**) tobacconist.

Trafo ['tra:fo], *m.* (**-s,** *pl.* **-s**) (*Elec. coll.*) transformer.

Tragant [tra'gant], *m.* (**-(e)s,** *pl.* **-e**) tragacanth (*Astralagus*).

Trag|bahre, *f.* stretcher, litter. **-balken,** *m.* (supporting) beam, girder, stringer, transom, balk. **-band,** *n.* carrying-strap, brace, (*Tech.*) conveyor-belt. **tragbar,** *adj.* 1. portable, (*of clothes*) wearable; 2. (*fig.*) bearable, supportable, endurable, tolerable, acceptable, reasonable; ***im Rahmen des Tragbaren,*** as far as is possible, within reason. **Tragbinde,** *f.* (*Surg.*) suspensory (bandage), suspensor.

Trage ['tra:gə], *f.* carrying-frame, carrier; hand-barrow; *see also* **Tragbahre.**

träg(e) ['trɛ:k (-gə)], *adj.* lazy, idle, indolent; slothful, sluggish, slow, dull; inactive, inert.

tragen ['tra:gən], **1.** *irr.v.t.* carry, bear, convey, transport, take; (*clothes*) wear, have on; (*load*) carry, bear, support, (*fig.*) (up)hold, sustain; (*fig.*) bear, endure, suffer; (*Bot.*) bear, produce, yield; (*Geom.*) subtend; ***schwer – an*** (*Dat.*), be weighed down by; ***ihn auf den Händen –,*** treat him with great consideration; ***Bedenken –,*** have one's doubts *or* scruples (***wegen,*** about); ***bei sich –,*** have about one, have on one's person; ***die Folgen –,*** accept *or* take *or* bear the consequences; ***seine Haut zu Markte –,*** risk one's neck; ***ein Herz im Busen –,*** have one's heart in the right place; ***das Herz auf der Zunge –,*** wear one's heart on one's sleeve; ***seine Hoffnung zu Grabe –,*** bury one's hopes, abandon all hope; ***ein Kind*** (***unterm Herzen***) ***–,*** be with child, be pregnant, (*coll.*) be expecting, be in the family way; ***die Kosten –,*** bear *or* defray the cost, meet the expenses; ***den Namen –,*** bear the name; ***Rechnung –*** (*Dat.*), take into account, make allowance for; accommodate o.s. to; ***Sorge – für,*** attend *or* (*coll.*) see to, ensure, take care (that); ***die Verantwortung – für,*** be responsible for, bear the responsibility for; ***Verlangen – nach,*** long for, have a longing for, (*coll.*) hanker for *or* after; ***den Verlust –,*** bear *or* suffer the loss; ***Waffen –,*** bear *or* carry arms; ***Zinsen –,*** bear interest; ***zur Schau –,*** display, exhibit, flaunt, show off, parade.
2. *irr.v.r.* (*of clothes*) ***sich gut –,*** wear well; ***sich – mit,*** have on one's mind, not be able to get out of one's mind, be preoccupied with, brood over; ***sich mit der Absicht –,*** intend, have the intention, have in mind, be mindful (***zu tun,*** to do), entertain the idea, (*coll.*) toy with the idea (of doing); ***sich mit der Hoffnung –,*** cherish the hope; ***sich nach der letzten Mode –,*** dress in the latest fashion; ***das Unternehmen trägt sich*** (***selbst***), the enterprise is self-supporting *or* pays its way; ***es trägt sich unbequem,*** it is awkward to carry *or* uncomfortable to wear.
3. *irr.v.i.* (*Bot.*) bear fruit, (*Zool.*) be with young; carry, reach; ***das Eis trägt noch nicht,*** the ice is not bearing yet; ***soweit das Auge trägt,*** as far as the eye can reach; ***das Geschütz trägt . . .,*** the gun has a range of . . .; ***seine Stimme trägt gut,*** his voice carries well *or* carries a long way; ***der Baum trägt noch nicht,*** the tree is not bearing (fruit) yet; ***die Kuh trägt,*** the cow is in calf; ***schwer zu – haben,*** be heavily laden, be burdened; ***die -de Rolle,*** the leading rôle; ***getragene Kleider,*** worn *or* second-hand clothes; ***von den Gedanken getragen sein,*** (*of argument*) based on the idea, (*of a p.*) inspired *or* governed by the idea; ***in einer getragenen Stimmung,*** in a solemn frame of mind; ***getragene Töne*** sustained *or* measured tones.

Träger ['trɛ:gər], *m.* 1. carrier, porter; stretcher-bearer; bearer, holder; 2. responsible body; champion, representative, supporter; 3. wearer; 4. support, bracket, truss, trestle, girder, (supporting) beam; base, post, pillar, prop; (*of underclothes*) (shoulder) strap; (*Bot.*) stamen, (*Anat.*) atlas,

(*Rad., Med.*) carrier, (*Chem.*) vehicle. **Träger|-flugzeug,** *n.* carrier-based aircraft. **-frequenz,** *f.* (*Rad.*) carrier-frequency. **-lohn,** *m.* porterage, carriage. **trägerlos,** *adj.* strapless (*dress*). **Träger-welle,** *f.* carrier-wave.

tragfähig ['tra:kfɛ:ɪç], *adj.* 1. capable of supporting *or* (*coll.*) standing the load; 2. productive, (*fig.*) sound. **Trag|fähigkeit,** *f.* 1. carrying *or* load *or* load-carrying capacity, (*of crane*) lifting capacity, (*of bridge*) safe load, load-limit, (*in water*) buoyancy, (*Naut.*) dead-weight tonnage; 2. productivity, (*fig.*) soundness. **-feder,** *f.* (*Motor.*) frame *or* main spring. **-fläche,** *f. See* **-flügel**; bearing-surface. **-flügel,** *m.* (*Av.*) wing, airfoil. **-gurt,** *m.* carrying-strap.

Trägheit ['trɛ:khaɪt], *f.* laziness, idleness, indolence; sluggishness, dullness; inactivity, inertia. **Träg-heits|gesetz,** *n.* law of inertia. **-moment,** *n.* moment of inertia.

Trag|himmel, *m.* canopy. **-holz,** *n.* yoke, bearer, stringer.

Tragik ['tra:gɪk], *f.* tragic art, tragedy; tragic nature. **Tragiker,** *m.* tragedian, tragic poet. **tragisch,** 1. *adj.* tragic(al); *-e Muse,* tragic muse, muse of tragedy. 2. *adv.* tragically; *– nehmen,* take to heart.

Trag|kleidchen, *n.pl.* long clothes (*of baby*). **-korb,** *m.* hamper, basket, pannier. **-kraft,** *f.* transverse strength; *see also* **-fähigkeit.** **-last,** *f.* peak *or* maximum working-load.

Tragöde [tra'gø:də], *m.* (**-n,** *pl.* **-n**) tragic actor, tragedian. **Tragödie,** *f.* tragedy, tragic drama; tragic event, calamity. **Tragödiendichter,** *m. See* **Tragiker.** **Tragödin,** *f.* tragic actress, tragedienne.

Trag|pfeiler, *m.* (supporting) pillar. **-rad,** *n.* trailing-wheel. **-riemen,** *m.* carrying-strap, (*Mil.*) sling; *pl.* main braces (*of a coach*). **-sattel,** *m.* pack-saddle. **-schrauber,** *m.* gyroplane, autogiro. **-seil,** *n.* supporting-rope. **-sessel, -stuhl,** *m.* sedan chair. **-tier,** *n.* pack-animal. **-vermögen,** *n.* buoyancy. **-weite,** *f.* range, (*fig.*) bearing, consequence; import(ance), significance. **-werk,** *n.* (*Av.*) wing assembly, (*Archit.*) supporting-structure. **-zeit,** *f.* period *or* duration of gestation.

Train [trɛ̃ (*Austr.* tre:n)], *m.* (**-s,** *pl.* **-s**) vehicle train, army service corps.

Trainer ['tre:nər], *m.* trainer, coach. **trainieren** [-'ni:rən], 1. *v.t., v.i.* train; *eine Stunde lang –,* do an hour's training. 2. *v.r. sich – für* or *auf* (*Acc.*), train for, go into training for. **Training,** *n.* training. **Trainingsanzug,** *m.* track-suit.

Train|kolonne, *f.* (*Mil.*) supply column. **-soldat,** *m.* soldier of a service unit. **-wagen,** *m.* supply-truck, ration-lorry, baggage-wagon.

Trajekt [tra'jɛkt], *n.* (*Austr. m.*) (**-(e)s,** *pl.* **-e**) train-ferry.

Trakt [trakt], *m.* (**-(e)s,** *pl.* **-e**) tract (*of land*), stretch (*of road*), wing (*of a building*).

Traktament [trakta'mɛnt], *n.* (**-(e)s,** *pl.* **-e**) treating, entertainment; treatment; (*obs.*) (military) pay. **Traktandum** [-'tandum], *n.* (**-s,** *pl.* **-den**) (*Swiss*) subject under discussion *or* of negotiation, object of a transaction. **Traktat** [-'ta:t], *m. or n.* (**-(e)s,** *pl.* **-e**) treatise, tract; treaty; *pl.* negotiations. **traktieren,** *v.t., v.i.* treat (*mit,* to); negotiate (*mit,* with); treat badly *or* roughly; *ihn mit dem Stock –,* give him a dose of the stick.

Traktor ['traktɔr], *m.* (**-s,** *pl.* **-en**) tractor.

Tralje ['tra:ljə], *f.* (*Naut., dial.*) bar (*of grating*); rail, banister.

trällern ['trɛlərn], *v.t., v.i.* hum, trill, warble.

[1]**Tram** [tra:m], *m.* (**-(e)s,** *pl.* **-e** *or* **¨-e**) girder.

[2]**Tram** [tram], *f.* (-, *pl.* **-s**) *or* (*Swiss*) *n.* (*coll.*) tramway; tramcar. **Trambahn,** *f.* tramway.

Tramen ['tra:mən], *m.* (*Swiss*) *see* [1]**Tram.**

Trampel ['trampəl], *n.* (*Austr. m.*) (**-s,** *pl.* -) *or f.* (-, *pl.* **-n**) oaf, clumsy lout. **trampeln,** *v.i.* trample, stamp (one's feet). **Trampel|pfad,** *m. See* **-weg.** **-tier,** *n.* 1. Bactrian camel; 2. (*coll.*) *see* **Trampel.** **-weg,** *m.* beaten track.

trampen ['trampən], *v.i.* (*coll.*) hike; hitch-hike, thumb a lift.

Trampolin [trampo'li:n], *n.* (**-s,** *pl.* **-e**) (*Austr.*), **Trampoline,** *f.* trampoline, spring-board.

trampsen ['trampsən], *v.i.* (*coll.*) *see* **trampeln.**

Tramway ['træmwei], *f.* (-, *pl.* **-s**) *or m.* (**-s,** *pl.* **-s**) tramway; tramcar.

Tran [tra:n], *m.* (**-s,** *pl.* **-e** *or* **-sorten**) train-oil, fish oil, whale oil, blubber; (*sl.*) *im – sein,* be dopey.

Tranchierbesteck [trã'ʃi:rbəʃtɛk], *n.* (pair of) carvers. **tranchieren,** *v.t., v.i.* carve, cut up. **Tranchiermesser,** *n.* carving-knife.

Träne ['trɛ:nə], *f.* tear, teardrop; ***in -n schwimmen*** or ***zerfließen,*** burst into tears; ***in -n aufgelöst sein,*** bathed in tears; ***ihm keine – nachweinen,*** not shed a tear of regret for him; ***den -n nahe,*** on the verge of tears; ***unter -n,*** amid tears; ***-n vergießen,*** shed tears, weep. **tränen,** *v.i.* be filled with tears, water (*of eyes*), (*fig.*) ooze, weep; ***die Augen – ihm,*** his eyes are running *or* watering; ***mit -den Augen,*** with tears in his (her *etc.*) eyes; (*Bot.*) ***-des Herz,*** bleeding heart (*Dicentra spectabilis*).

Tränen|drüse, *f.* lachrymal gland. **-feuchtigkeit,** *f.* lachrymal fluid. **-fluß,** *m.* flow *or* flood of tears. **-gang,** *m.* lachrymal duct. **-gas,** *n.* tear-gas. **-grube,** *f.* lachrymal fossa. **tränenlos,** *adj.* tearless, dry-eyed. **tränenreich,** *adj.* tearful, lachrymose. **Tränen|sack,** *m.* lachrymatory sac. **-strom,** *m. See* **-fluß.** **-tal,** *n.* (*fig.*) vale of tears *or* of woe.

tränieren, *see* **trainieren.**

tranig ['tra:nɪç], *adj.* smelling *or* tasting of oil, oily, greasy; (*fig., coll.*) dopey.

Trank [traŋk], *m.* (**-(e)s,** *pl.* **¨-e**) drink, potion, beverage, draught; ***Speise und –,*** meat *or* food and drink.

trank, *see* **trinken.**

Tränke ['trɛŋkə], *f.* watering-place, drinking-trough, horse-pond; ***zur – führen,*** water (*cattle*). **tränken,** *v.t.* give to drink, water (*cattle, the ground*); soak, saturate, steep, impregnate; (*fig.*) imbue. **Tränkfaß,** *n.* drinking-tub (*for horses*); pig's trough.

Trank|opfer, *n.* libation. **-same,** *f.* (*Swiss*) drink, beverage.

Tränk|stoff, *m.* liquor, dip, bath. **-trog,** *m. See* **-faß.**

transatlantisch [trans?at'la:ntɪʃ], *adj.* transatlantic.

transferierbar [transfe'ri:rba:r], *adj.* transferable. **transferieren,** *v.t.* transfer (*an* or *auf* (*Acc.*), to).

Transformator [transfɔr'ma:tɔr], *m.* (**-s,** *pl.* **-en**) (*Elec.*) transformer (station).

transfundieren [transfun'di:rən], *v.t., v.i.* decant.

Transgression [transgrɛsi'o:n], *f.* submergence, flooding (*by the sea*).

transigieren [tranzi'gi:rən], *v.i.* come to an understanding.

transitiv ['tranziti:f], *adj.* (*Gram.*) transitive.

Transit|lager ['tranzɪt-], *n.* bonded warehouse. **-verkehr,** *m.* transit trade, through traffic.

Transjordanien [transjɔr'da:niən], *n.* (*Geog.*) Trans-Jordan.

Transkription [transkrɪptsi'o:n], *f.* transcription (*into other characters, or* (*Mus.*) *for another instrument*).

Translation [translatsi'o:n], *f.* transposition.

Transmission [transmɪsi'o:n], *f.* (belt) transmission. **Transmissions|kette,** *f.* driving-chain. **-welle,** *f.* connecting-rod *or* -shaft.

transozeanisch [trans?o:tse'a:nɪʃ], *adj.* transoceanic.

Transparent [transpa'rɛnt], *n.* 1. transparency; 2. banner, streamer.

Transpiration [transpiratsi'o:n], *f.* perspiration. **transpirieren,** *v.i.* perspire.

transponieren [transpo'ni:rən], *v.t.* (*Mus.*) transpose (*into another key*).

Transport [trans'pɔrt], *m.* (**-(e)s,** *pl.* **-e**) 1. transport(ation), carriage, haulage, conveyance, shipment; 2. (*Comm.*) carrying forward, amount brought forward. **transportabel** [–ˈta:bəl], *adj. See* **transportfähig. Transportband,** *n.* conveyor(-belt). **Transporter,** *m. See* **Transportschiff. Transporteur** [–ˈtø:r], *m.* **(-s,** *pl.* **-e)** (*Geom.*) protractor, (*sewing-machine*) feed-dog. **transportfähig,** *adj.* transportable, portable, moveable. **Transport|flugzeug,** *n.* troop-carrying *or* transport plane. **–geschäft,** *n.* carrying-trade, forwarding-business. **transportieren** [–ˈti:rən], *v.t.* 1. transport, convey, carry, ship; 2. (*Comm.*) carry *or* bring forward, transfer. **Transport|-kolonne,** *f.* (*Mil.*) motor convoy. **–kosten,** *f.pl.* transport(ation) charges, carriage, (*Naut.*) freight charges. **–makler,** *m.* forwarding *or* delivery agent. **–schiff,** *n.* troopship, (troop) transport. **–schnecke,** *f.* (*Mech.*) screw-conveyor. **–schwimmen,** *n.* life-saving. **–unternehmen,** *n.* haulage contractor, carrier. **–versicherung,** *f.* insurance against damage *or* loss in transit. **–wesen,** *n.* transport(ation) (system).

transversal [transfɛrˈza:l], *adj.* transverse, transversal. **Transversale,** *f.* (*Geom.*) transverse (line).

transzendent [transtsɛnˈdɛnt], *adj.* transcendental.

Transzendenz, *f.* transcendence, transcendency.

Trapez [traˈpe:ts], *n.* **(-es,** *pl.* **-e)** 1. trapezoid, trapezium; 2. (*Gymn.*) trapeze. **trapezförmig,** *adj.* trapezoid(al), quadrilateral. **Trapez|gewinde,** *n.* (*Mech.*) acme thread. **–künstler,** *m.* trapeze artist.

trapp! [trap], *int.* clop, clump.

1**Trappe** [ˈtrapə], *f.* (*dial.*) footstep, (dirty) footmark, track.

2**Trappe,** *m.* **(-n,** *pl.* **-n)** *or f.* bustard; *see* **Groß-trappe, Zwergtrappe.**

trappeln [ˈtrapəln], *v.i.* trot, toddle, patter, trip. **trappen,** *v.i.* (*aux.* h. *&* s.), **trap(p)sen,** *v.i.*(*coll.*) walk heavily, stride, trudge, stamp, tramp, trample.

Trara [traˈra:], *n.* (*coll.*) fuss, hullabaloo; bunkum, hanky-panky, flapdoodle.

Trassant [traˈsant], *m.* **(-en,** *pl.* **-en)** (*Comm.*) drawer (*of a bill*). **Trassat,** *m.* **(-en,** *pl.* **-en)** (*Comm.*) drawee. **Trasse,** *f.*, (*Swiss*) **Trassee,** *n.* **(-s,** *pl.* **-s)** (*Surv.*) line, alignment. **trassieren,** *v.t., v.i.* 1. draw (*a bill*) (*auf* (*Acc.*), on); 2. mark out, stake out.

trat [tra:t], *see* **treten.**

Tratsch [tratʃ], *m.* (*coll.*) tittle-tattle, gossip; twaddle. **tratschen,** *v.t., v.i.* chatter, gossip, blether.

trätschen [ˈtrɛtʃən], *v.i.* (*dial.*) splash, drip; rain cats and dogs.

Tratte [ˈtratə], *f.* draft, bill of exchange.

Traualtar [ˈtrauˀaltar], *m.* marriage-altar.

Traube [ˈtraubə], *f.* grape; bunch of grapes; cluster, raceme. **Trauben|abfall,** *m.* husks of grapes. **–beere,** *f.* grape. **–blut,** *n.* (*Poet.*) wine. **traubenförmig,** *adj.* grape-like, in clusters, racemose. **Trauben|geländer,** *n.* vine-trellis. **–kamm,** *m.* vine-stalk. **–kirsche,** *f.* (*Bot.*) bird-cherry (*Prunus padus*). **–lese,** *f.* grape *or* vine harvest, vintage. **–most,** *m.* grape juice, new wine, must. **–presse,** *f.* wine-press. **–saft,** *m.* grape juice; (*Poet.*) wine. **traubensauer,** *adj. –er Zucker, see* **Traubenzucker. Trauben|säure,** *f.* racemic acid. **–stock,** *m.* vine. **–zucker,** *m.* grape-sugar, glucose.

1**trauen** [ˈtrauən], **1.** *v.i.* (*Dat.*) ***ihm –,*** trust (in) him, confide in *or* put one's trust in *or* have confidence in *or* rely on him; ***ihm nicht über den Weg –,*** not trust him out of one's sight; ***den Augen kaum –,*** hardly believe one's eyes; (*fig.*) ***dem Frieden traue ich nicht,*** I have my doubts *or* suspicions; ***dem Glück ist nicht zu –,*** fortune is fickle; ***restlos –,*** trust implicitly, have absolute confidence in; (*Prov.*) ***trau, schau, wem!*** look before you leap! **2.** *v.r.* venture, dare, be so bold as (to do), risk (doing).

2**trauen,** *v.t.* marry, give in marriage, join in wedlock; ***sich – lassen,*** get married.

Trauer [ˈtrauər], *f.* mourning, grief, sorrow (***um, über,*** for); ***– haben,*** be in mourning; ***– anlegen*** or ***tragen,*** wear black, go into mourning.

Trauer|anzeige, *f.* obituary *or* in memoriam notice. **–bachstelze,** *f.* (*Orn.*) pied wagtail (*Motacilla alba yarrelli*). **–binde,** *f.* black crape. **–birke,** *f.* (*Bot.*) weeping birch (*Betula pendula*). **–botschaft,** *f.* sad news, mournful tidings; news of a death. **–decke,** *f.* mourning-housings (*on horses*). **–ente,** *f.* (*Orn.*) common scotar (*Melanitta nigra*). **–fahne,** *f.* half-mast flag. **–fall,** *m.* death, bereavement. **–feier,** *f.* exequies, obsequies. **–fliegenfänger,** *m. See* **–schnäpper. –flor,** *m.* mourning-crape. **–geleit,** *n.* funeral procession. **–gesang,** *m.* funeral hymn, dirge. **–gestalt,** *f.* doleful figure. **–gottesdienst,** *m.* funeral service. **–haus,** *n.* house of mourning. **–jahr,** *n.* year of mourning. **–kleid,** *n.*, **–kleidung,** *f.* mourning-dress; widow's weeds. **–kloß,** *m.* (*coll.*) spoil-sport, wet blanket. **–leute,** *pl.* mourners. **–mahl,** *n.* funeral repast. **–mantel,** *m.* 1. mourning-cloak; 2. (*Ent.*) Camberwell Beauty (*Vanessa antiopa*). **–marsch,** *m.* funeral march. **–meise,** *f.* (*Orn.*) sombre tit (*Parus lugubris*).

trauern [ˈtrauərn], *v.i.* mourn, grieve (***um,*** for); ***über den Tod seines Vaters –,*** lament the loss of his father, mourn his father's death; ***Trauernde(r),*** mourner.

Trauer|nachricht, *f. See* **–botschaft. –rand,** *m.* black edge (*on notepaper*); (*coll.*) dirty fingernails. **–rede,** *f.* funeral oration *or* sermon. **–schleier,** *m.* mourning-veil. **–schnäpper,** *m.* (*Orn.*) pied flycatcher (*Ficedula hypoleuca*). **–seeschwalbe,** *f.* (*Orn.*) black tern (*Chlidonias niger*). **–spiel,** *n.* (*Theat.*) tragedy. **–steinschmätzer,** *m.* (*Orn.*) black wheatear (*Oenanthe leucura*). **trauervoll,** *adj.* sad, mournful. **Trauer|weide,** *f.* (*Bot.*) weeping willow (*Salix babylonica*). **–zeit,** *f.* time of mourning. **–zug,** *m.* funeral procession.

Traufe [ˈtraufə], *f.* drippings (from the roof); gutter, eaves; ***aus dem*** or ***vom Regen in die – kommen,*** jump out of the frying-pan into the fire. **traufen,** *v.i.* (*dial.*), **träufeln** [ˈtrɔyfəln], **1.** *v.i.* (*aux.* h. *&* s.) drip, trickle, fall in drops. **2.** *v.t.* let fall in drops, drop, drip; (*fig.*) ***Balsam in*** or ***auf die Wunde –,*** pour balm on a wound. **Trauf|rinne,** *f.* gutter (*of roof*). **–röhre,** *f.* down-pipe, spouting. **–wasser,** *n.* rain-water.

traulich [ˈtraulɪç], *adj.* intimate, snug, cosy. **Traulichkeit,** *f.* intimacy, cosiness.

Traum [traum], *m.* **(-(e)s,** *pl.* **⸚e)** dream; vision, fancy, illusion; reverie, day-dream; ***böser –,*** bad dream, nightmare; ***ich denke im – nicht daran, das fällt mir im – nicht ein,*** I would never dream of it; ***alle meine Träume haben sich erfüllt,*** all my dreams have come true; ***ihm aus dem – helfen,*** bring him to his senses; ***das Kleid ist ein –,*** it is a dream of a dress. **Traum|bild,** *n.* vision, phantom, illusion. **–buch,** *n.* dream-book, fortune-book. **–deuter,** *m.* interpreter of dreams, fortune-teller. **–deutung,** *f.* interpretation of dreams.

träumen [ˈtrɔymən], *v.t., v.i., v. imp.* dream (***von,*** of), be lost in thought, day-dream; believe, imagine; ***ich*** or ***mir träumte,*** I dreamed *or* dreamt; ***wachend –,*** go about in a dream *or* daze, be given to day-dreaming; ***das hätte ich mir nie – lassen,*** I should never have dreamt of such a thing. **Träumen,** *n.* dreams, dreaming. **Träumer,** *m.* dreamer, visionary. **Träumerei** [–ˈraɪ], *f.* dreaming, musing, fancy, reverie (*also Mus.*), day-dream, brown study. **träumerisch,** *adj.* dreamy, dreaming, musing.

Traum|gesicht, *n. See* **–bild. –gestalt,** *f.* vision. **traumhaft,** *adj.* dreamlike, unreal, illusory. **Traumland,** *n.* dreamland, land of dreams. **traum|verloren, –versunken,** *adj.* lost in dreams. **–wach,** *adj.* in a trance. **Traum|welt,** *f.* dream-world, world of fancy. **–zustand,** *m.* trance.

traun! [traun], *int.* indeed! to be sure! surely! upon my word! (*obs.*) faith! forsooth!

traurig [ˈtraurɪç], *adj.* sad, melancholy, mournful, sorrowful, unhappy, grieved; depressed, wretched, gloomy (***über*** (*Acc.*), about); ***–er Anblick,*** dismal *or* sorry *or* deplorable sight; ***Ritter von der –en Gestalt,*** Knight of the Doleful Countenance; ***–stimmen,*** sadden, depress. **Traurigkeit,** *f.* sadness, sorrow, grief; depression, melancholy, wretchedness.

Trau|ring, *m.* wedding-ring. **–schein,** *m.* marriage certificate *or* (*coll.*) lines.

traut [traut], *adj.* dear, beloved; *see also* **traulich. Traute,** *f.* (*coll.*) confidence, courage.

Trauung ['trauuŋ], *f.* marriage ceremony, wedding. **Trauzeuge,** *m.* witness to a marriage.

Traverse [tra'vɛrsə], *f.* (cross-)girder.

Travestie [travɛs'ti:], *f.* travesty, parody, skit. **travestieren,** *v.t.* travesty, parody, make ridiculous.

Treber ['tre:bər], *pl.* (*Austr.* **Trebern**) husks *or* skins (of grapes); draff, brewer's grains. **Treberwein,** *m.* after-wine.

trecken ['trɛkən], *v.t.* (*dial.*) drag, pull, haul, tow. **Trecker,** *m.* tractor. **Treck|schute,** *f.* canal-boat, barge. **–seil,** *n.* tow-rope. **–weg,** *m.* tow(ing)-path.

Treff [trɛf], **1.** *m.* **(-(e)s,** *pl.* **-e)** blow, knock, nudge; winning hit; shrewd *or* cutting remark; (*coll.*) ***er hat einen –,*** he is cracked *or* dotty. **2.** *n.* **(-s,** *pl.* **-s)** (*Cards*) club. **Treffas,** *n.* ace of clubs.

treffen ['trɛfən], **1.** *irr.v.t.* hit, strike; (*fig.*) affect, touch, concern; befall, fall in with, come upon, meet (with), encounter, find, light upon, hit upon; ***Anstalten –,*** arrange, make arrangements (***zu,*** for); ***ihn –,*** meet with *or* encounter him; ***Auslese*** or ***Auswahl –,*** make a selection; ***vom Blitze getroffen,*** struck by lightning; (*fig.*) thunderstruck; ***eine Entscheidung –,*** make *or* take a *or* come to a decision, decide; ***sich getroffen fühlen,*** feel hurt, take to heart, be cut to the quick; ***wer sich getroffen fühlt, nehme sich bei der Nase,*** if the cap fits wear it; (*coll.*) ***es gut –,*** strike it lucky; ***er trifft gut,*** he is a good shot; ***zu Hause –,*** find at home; ***das Los traf ihn,*** it fell to his lot; ***der Maler hat Sie gut getroffen,*** the painter has hit you off well; ***Maßnahmen*** or ***Maßregeln –,*** take action *or* steps *or* measures (***gegen,*** against); (*fig.*) ***den Nagel auf den Kopf –,*** hit the nail on the head; ***nicht –,*** miss; ***wen trifft die Schuld?*** who is to blame? who is responsible *or* answerable? ***die Reihe trifft dich,*** it is your turn; ***ein Übereinkommen mit ihm –,*** come to an agreement with him; ***das Unglück traf mich,*** I had the misfortune; ***die Verantwortung trifft ihn,*** the responsibility rests with him; ***Vorkehrungen –,*** take precautions *or* measures (***gegen,*** against), arrange, make arrangements *or* provision *or* preparations (***für,*** for); ***Vorsorge –,*** take precautions, make provision, provide (***gegen,*** against); ***der Vorwurf trifft ihn,*** he comes in for the blame; he is responsible, the reproach applies to him; ***eine Wahl –,*** choose, make a choice. **2.** *irr.v.r.* (*of persons*) meet; ***sich mit ihm –,*** have an appointment with him; (*of events*) happen; ***es traf sich, daß,*** it so happened that; ***sich gut –,*** be lucky. **3.** *irr.v.i.* hit, find its (*etc.*) mark, (*coll., fig.*) go home, (*Boxing, coll.*) land, connect; ***nicht –,*** miss (the mark); ***– auf*** (*Acc.*), come upon *or* across, meet with, (*coll.*) light *or* stumble on; (*Mil.*) encounter, fall in with; ***tödlich –,*** strike a mortal blow; ***getroffen!*** good shot! right on the mark! (*Fenc.*) touché, (*fig.*) right! you've got it! that's just it!

Treffen, *n.* encounter, rendezvous, meeting; meeting, gathering, assembly, rally; (*Mil.*) encounter, engagement, action combat, battle; (*fig.*) ***ins – führern,*** bring to bear; ***ein – liefern,*** give battle; ***mittleres –,*** centre of an order of battle; (*fig.*) ***als es zum – kam,*** when it came to the point.

treffend ['trɛfənt], *adj.* well-aimed, striking, apt, pertinent, suitable, appropriate; ***das –e Wort,*** the right word; ***seine Bemerkungen waren –,*** his remarks were to the point.

Treffer ['trɛfər], *m.* (direct) hit, good shot, (*Footb.*) goal, (*fig.*) lucky shot; winning ticket, prize; (*Theat., coll.*) smash hit, (*book*) bestseller. **Trefferbild,** *n.* (*target shooting*) group (*of hits*).

trefflich ['trɛflɪç], *adj.* excellent, choice, exquisite, first-rate, admirable. **Trefflichkeit,** *f.* excellence, perfection.

Treffpunkt ['trɛfpuŋkt], *m.* 1. rendezvous, meeting-place; 2. (*Artil.*) point of impact. **treffsicher,** *adj.* well-aimed, unerring, accurate, sound; ***–e Bemerkungen,*** pertinent remarks; ***–es Urteil,*** sound *or* unerring judgement. **Treffsicherheit,** *f.* accuracy of fire, unerring aim.

Treib|anker, *m.* sea-anchor, drag-anchor. **–eis,** *n.* drift-ice.

treiben ['traɪbən], **1.** *irr.v.t.* 1. drive, push, force; set in motion, propel; work, operate, drive (*machines*), force (*plants*); ***etwas aufs Äußerste*** or ***zum Äußersten –*** or ***auf die Spitze –,*** push s.th. to extremes; (*Golf*) ***den Ball –,*** drive the ball; ***der Fluß treibt Eis,*** the river is bringing down *or* carrying ice; ***ihn in die Enge –,*** drive him into a corner; ***in die Flucht –,*** put to flight, rout; ***Preise in die Höhe –,*** force up prices; ***Kreisel –,*** play whip and top; ***Kühe auf die Weide –,*** drive cattle to pasture; ***einen Nagel –,*** drive a nail (***in*** (*Acc.*), in); ***Pflanzen –,*** force plants (*in hothouse*); ***Reifen –,*** bowl a hoop; ***den Teig –,*** roll out the dough; ***über das Ziel hinaus –,*** carry *or* push too far; ***vor sich her –,*** sweep before one; (*Footb.*) dribble; ***das Wild –,*** beat game; ***zur Verzweiflung –,*** drive to despair; 2. hammer, emboss, chase (*metal*), refine, cupel (*precious metals*); ***getriebene Arbeit,*** embossed *or* raised work; 3. (*of plants*) put forth, sprout (*leaves, buds etc.*); ***Knospen –,*** bud, come into bud; 4. (*fig.*) impel, induce, urge, prompt, press, force, move, bring, drive (*a p. to do s.th.*); promote, stimulate, produce (*activity*); ***Schweiß –,*** promote perspiration; ***ihn zur Eile –,*** hurry him (up), urge him on; 5. (*of a p.*) work at, occupy o.s. with, pursue, follow, practise, cultivate, (*coll.*) carry on (*some line of activity*); ***was treibst du da?*** what are you doing *or* (*coll.*) are you up to there? ***er treibt es zu arg*** or ***zu bunt,*** he goes too far; ***Aufwand –,*** live in grand style, (*coll.*) do o.s. well; ***Blutschande –,*** commit incest; ***Deutsch –,*** go in for German, study German; ***es gemütlich –,*** take things comfortably; ***Handel –,*** carry on trade; ***ein Handwerk –,*** follow a trade *or* craft; ***Musik –,*** devote o.s. to music, study music; ***eine Politik –,*** pursue a policy; ***Schindluder mit ihm –,*** treat *or* use him badly; ***seinen Spaß*** or ***sein Spiel*** or ***seinen Spott mit ihm –,*** make fun *or* game of him; ***Sport –,*** engage in *or* go in for sport; ***es toll –,*** carry on like a fool, act madly; ***Unfug*** (***Unsinn***) ***–,*** play the fool, be *or* get up to mischief; ***ich lasse keinen Unsinn mit mir –,*** I will stand no nonsense; ***sein Unwesen –,*** be up to one's tricks; ***Unzucht –,*** fornicate. **2.** *irr.v.i.* (*aux.* h. *&* s.) 1. drift, float; ***vor Anker –,*** drag the anchor; ***ans Land –,*** drift *or* be driven ashore; (*fig.*) ***sich – lassen,*** let o.s. drift, take things as they come; ***die Dinge – lassen,*** let things drift, let things go their own way; 2. (*of plants*) germinate, shoot, sprout, blossom forth; ferment; ***das Bier treibt,*** the beer works; ***der Saft treibt im Holze,*** the sap rises in the wood.

Treiben, *n.* driving; drifting; (*of plants*) sprouting, (*of buds*) bursting, germination, gemmation; activities, goings-on, doings; bustle, activity, stir; ***das ganze Tun und –,*** all these goings-on; ***ein wüstes –,*** riotous scenes. **treibend,** *adj.* (*Mech., fig.*) ***–e Kraft,*** driving force, prime mover. **Treiber,** *m.* driver, drover, (*Hunt.*) beater; (*Mech.*) driving-wheel, propeller; (*fig.*) oppressor, (*coll.*) slave-driver. **Treiberei** [–'raɪ], *f.* hurry, rush(ing), bustle.

Treib|fäustel, *m.* sledge-hammer. **–gas,** *n.* power gas. **–hammer,** *m.* chasing-hammer. **–haus,** *n.* hothouse, greenhouse, conservatory. **–hauspflanze,** *f.* hothouse plant; (*fig.*) mollycoddle. **–herd,** *m.* cupelling furnace, cupel. **–holz,** *n.* driftwood. **–jagd,** *f.* battue. **–kapelle,** *f.* cupel. **–kasten,** *m.* forcing-frame. **–kraft,** *f.* propellant, motive power, driving force. **–ladung,** *f.* propellant, propellent charge. **–mine,** *f.* floating mine. **–mittel,** *n.* (*Mech.*) propellant; (*Med.*) purgative; (*Cul.*) raising agent. **–netz,** *n.* drift-net. **–öl,** *n.* fuel oil. **–pflanze,** *f.* hothouse plant. **–prozeß,** *m.* cupellation. **–rad,** *n.* driving-wheel. **–riemen,** *m.*

driving-belt. **-sand,** *m.* shifting sand. **-stock,** *m.* embossing anvil. **-stoff,** *m.* (motor) fuel, (rocket) fuel, propellant.

Treidel ['traɪdəl], *m.* towline, tow-rope. **treideln,** *v.i.* (*Naut.*) tow. **Treidel|pfad, -weg,** *m.* tow(ing)-path.

Trekker, *m.* *See* **Trecker.**

Trema ['tre:ma], *n.* (**-s, or** *pl.* **-s** *or* **-ta**) diæresis.

tremolieren [tremo'li:rən], *v.i.* quaver, shake. **Tremolo** ['tre:molo], *n.* (**-s,** *pl.* **-s**) shake, trill, tremolo.

Tremse ['trɛmzə], *f.* (*dial.*) cornflower.

Tremulant [tremu'lant], *m.* (**-en,** *pl.* **-en**) trill, shake, (*Org.*) tremolo-stop. **tremulieren,** *v.i.* (*Mus.*) shake, play *or* sing vibrato *or* with a tremolo.

trendeln ['trɛndəln], *v.i.* dawdle, loiter, temporize.

trennbar ['trɛnba:r], *adj.* separable, detachable; divisible. **Trennbarkeit,** *f.* separability, detachability; divisibility.

trennen ['trɛnən], **1.** *v.t.* separate, divide, part, sever, detach; (*Elec. etc.*) disconnect, (*coll.*) cut off; segregate, isolate, divorce; undo (*seam etc.*); break up, dissolve (*partnership, a marriage*). **2.** *v.r.* part, separate (***von,*** from), sever one's connection, (*coll.*) break (with); (*of married couple*) be(come) separated; (*as roads*) branch off. **Trennpunkt,** *m.* point of separation. **trennscharf,** *adj.* (*Rad.*) selective. **Trennschärfe,** *f.* selectivity.

Trennung ['trɛnuŋ], *f.* separation, parting, disconnection, severance, partition, division, segregation, dissociation, dissolution; (*fig.*) divorce; (*Law*) ***eheliche –,*** judicial separation.

Trennungs|festigkeit, *f.* (*Mech.*) breaking-strength. **-fläche,** *f.* cleavage (*in crystals*). **-linie,** *f.* dividing line, line of demarcation. **-partikel,** *f.* (*Gram.*) disjunctive particle. **-schmerz,** *m.* pain of separation. **-strich,** *m.* dash, stroke. **-wand,** *f.* partition (wall). **-zeichen,** *n.* hyphen. **-zulage,** *f.* separation allowance.

Trennwand ['trɛnvant], *f.* *See* **Trennungswand.**

Trense ['trɛnzə], *f.* snaffle, bridoon (*of horses*).

trepanieren [trepa'ni:rən], *v.t.* (*Surg.*) trepan.

trepp|ab, *adv.* downstairs. **-auf,** *adv.* upstairs.

Treppe ['trɛpə], *f.* staircase, (flight of) stairs, stairway, steps; ***die – hinab*** (***hinauf***), downstairs (upstairs); ***zwei -n hoch,*** in the second storey, on the second floor.

Treppen|absatz, *m.* landing. **-flucht,** *f.* flight of stairs. **treppen|förmig,** *adj.* rising in steps, stepped, terraced; scalariform. **-geländer,** *n.* railing, banister. **-haus,** *n.* hall, (well of a) staircase. **-läufer,** *m.* stair-carpet. **-stufe,** *f.* step, stair. **-witz,** *m.* afterthought, wisdom after the event, esprit de l'escalier.

Tresor [tre'zo:r], *m.* (**-s,** *pl.* **-e**) treasury; safe, vault, strongroom. **Tresorfach,** *n.* safe-deposit (box).

Trespe ['trɛspə], *f.* brome-grass.

Tresse ['trɛsə], *f.* lace, braid, galloon; (*Mil.*) stripe. **tressieren** [-'si:rən], *v.t.* plait, braid (*hair*).

Trester ['trɛstər], *pl.* residue (*of fruit*); grape-skins, husks. **Tresterwein,** *m.* after-wine, poor wine.

Tret|anlasser ['tre:t-], *m.* (*Motor.*) kick-starter. **-eimer,** *m.* pedal-bin.

treten ['tre:tən], **1.** *irr.v.i.* (*aux.* h. *&* s.) tread, walk, step, stride; (*Cycl.*) pedal; treadle; ***ans Licht –,*** come to light, appear, become known; ***an die Spitze –,*** assume the leadership, (take the) lead; ***an seine Stelle –,*** take his place, supersede *or* replace him; substitute for *or* (*coll.*) stand in for him; ***auf seine Seite –,*** take his part, side with him; (*Mil.*) ***auf der Stelle –,*** mark time; ***kalter Schweiß trat ihm auf die Stirn,*** cold perspiration broke out on his brow; ***aus dem Dienste –,*** retire from (active) service; ***der Mond tritt hinter eine Wolke,*** the moon went behind a cloud; (*fig.*) ***in ein Amt –,*** take up a post; ***Tränen traten ihm in die Augen,*** the tears came into his eyes; ***ins Dasein –,*** come into being *or* existence; ***in den Ehestand –,*** marry, get married; ***in Erscheinung –,*** appear, become apparent *or* visible; (*fig.*) ***in seine Fuß(s) tapfen –,*** follow his example *or* in his footsteps; ***ins Haus –,*** enter the house; ***in den Hintergrund –,*** retire into the background; ***sie ist in ihr zehntes Jahr getreten,*** she has entered her tenth year; ***in Kraft –,*** come into force *or* operation *or* effect, become effective; ***die Sonne tritt in den Löwen,*** the sun enters Leo; ***mit ihm in Verbindung –,*** enter into communication *or* correspondence *or* association with him, communicate *or* correspond with him; ***in den Vordergrund –,*** come into the foreground *or* limelight; ***ihm in den Weg –,*** oppose *or* obstruct him, stand in *or* block his way; ***in Wirksamkeit –,*** take effect; ***leise –,*** go gently, tread softly; be artful; ***ihm zu nahe –,*** offend him, hurt his feelings; ***ohne der Wahrheit zu nahe zu –,*** without any violation of truth; ***ohne ihrer Bescheidenheit zu nahe zu –,*** without offence to her modesty; ***– Sie näher!*** come in, step this way; ***über die Ufer –,*** overflow its banks; ***tritt mir nie wieder unter die Augen!*** never show your face again! ***vor den Richterstuhl Gottes –,*** appear before the judgement-seat of God; ***zu ihm –,*** go *or* walk *or* step up to him; ***zur Seite –,*** step aside, make room, get out of the way; ***zutage –,*** appear, become evident.
2. *irr.v.t.* tread, walk upon; kick; (*Sew.-mach. etc.*) treadle, work (*a treadle*), push (*a pedal*); (*sl.*) dun; ***die Bälge –,*** work *or* treadle the bellows; ***sich*** (*Dat.*) ***einen Dorn in den Fuß –,*** run a thorn into one's foot; (*vulg.*) ***ihn in den Hintern –,*** kick his backside *or* bottom; ***mit Füßen –,*** trample underfoot; (*fig.*) ride roughshod over; ***sein Glück mit Füßen –,*** act against one's own interest, spurn one's good fortune; ***das Pflaster –,*** wander *or* traipse the streets; ***seine Schuhe schief –,*** wear one's shoes down at heel; ***den Takt –,*** beat time with one's foot; ***Wasser –,*** tread water.

Treter ['tre:tər], *m.* treader; bellows-blower; fuller (*of cloth*); *pl.* (*coll.*) boots.

Tret|hebel, *m.*, **-kurbel,** *f.* treadle, pedal. **-lager,** *n.* (*Cycl.*) pedal-bearing. **-mine,** *f.* contact mine. **-mühle,** *f.* treadmill; ***die alte – des Beruf(e)s,*** the humdrum daily round. **-rad,** *n.* tread-wheel; (*coll.*) push-bike. **-schalter,** *m.* foot- *or* floor-switch. **-schemel,** *m.* *See* **-kurbel. -werk,** *n.* *See* **-mühle.**

treu [trɔy], *adj.* (*Dat.*) faithful, loyal, devoted (to); constant; staunch, trusty, upright, sincere; accurate, true; (*dial.*) generous; ***seinem Charakter – bleiben,*** be true to one's character; ***seinem Vorsatz – bleiben,*** stick to one's purpose; ***-es Gedächtnis,*** reliable *or* retentive memory; (*B.*) ***Du -er Gott,*** Lord God of Truth; ***zu -en Händen,*** in trust; ***es mit ihm – meinen,*** mean well by him; ***sein -es Schwert,*** his trusty sword; ***-e Übersetzung,*** close *or* faithful translation. **Treu,** *f.* *See* **Treue**; ***– und Glauben halten,*** keep one's word; ***auf – und Glauben,*** (*Swiss*) ***in guten -en,*** in good faith; (***bei***) ***meiner –!*** upon my honour!

Treubruch ['trɔybrux], *m.* breach of trust *or* faith; disloyalty, perfidy. **treubrüchig,** *adj.* faithless, disloyal, perfidious. **Treue,** *f.* fidelity, faithfulness, constancy, loyalty; sincerity, honesty; accuracy; ***– brechen*** or ***verletzen*** (*Dat.*), break (one's) faith with; betray; ***die – halten*** or ***bewahren*** (*Dat.*), keep faith with, remain loyal to; ***den Eid der – ablegen,*** take the oath of allegiance. **Treueid,** *m.* oath of allegiance. **treu|ergeben, -gesinnt,** *adj.* loyal (*Dat.*, to).

Treu|hand, *f.* trust. **-händer,** *m.* trustee, official receiver, fiduciary. **treuhänderisch,** **1.** *adj.* fiduciary. **2.** *adv.* in trust. **Treuhänderschaft,** *f.* trusteeship. **Treuhandgesellschaft,** *f.* trust-company.

treuherzig ['trɔyhɛrtsɪç], *adj.* frank, trusting, candid; simple, ingenuous, naïve, guileless. **Treuherzigkeit,** *f.* frankness, ingenuousness, naïvety. **treulich,** *adv.* truly, faithfully, loyally, conscientiously, reliably. **treulos,** *adj.* faithless, disloyal (***gegen,*** to), perfidious, treacherous, traitorous. **Treulosigkeit,** *f.* faithlessness, perfidy, treachery, (*marital*) infidelity. **Treu|pflicht,** *f.* conscientious duty, matter of conscience; *Verletzung der –*, breach of faith. **–schwur,** *m.* (*obs.*) plighting of troth.

Triangel ['tri:aŋgəl], *m.* (*Mus., Math.*) triangle. **triangulieren** [–u'li:rən], *v.t.* triangulate, survey by trigonometry.

Trias ['tri:as], *f.* (*Math.*) triad; (*Geol.*) trias.

Tribun [tri'bu:n], *m.* (**-s,** *pl.* **-e,** (*Austr.*) **-en,** *pl.* **-en**) tribune. **Tribunal** [–'na:l], *n.* (**-s,** *pl.* **-e**) tribunal, high court of justice.

Tribüne [tri'by:nə], *f.* platform, rostrum, (*Spt.*) (grand)stand; spectators, audience.

Tribut [tri'bu:t], *m.* (**-(e)s,** *pl.* **-e**) tribute, reparations; ***seinen – zollen*** or ***entrichten,*** pay tribute (*Dat.*, to). **tributär** [–'tɛ:r], **tributpflichtig,** *adj.* tributary.

Trichine [tri'çi:nə], *f.* (*Zool.*) trichina (*Trichinella spiralis*). **trichinös** [–'nø:s], *adj.* trichinous, trichinosed. **Trichinose** [–'no:zə], *f.* trichinosis.

Trichter ['trɪçtər], *m.* 1. funnel, cone, hopper; (*fig.*) ***ihn auf den – bringen,*** put him on the right way *or* track; 2. crater, shell-hole; 3. horn (*of a gramophone*). **Trichterfeld,** *n.* shell-scarred *or* bombarded area. **trichterförmig,** *adj.* funnel-shaped, infundibular. **Trichterfortsatz,** *m.* (*Anat.*) infundibulum. **trichtern,** *v.t.* pour through a funnel. **Trichterwagen,** *m.* hopper-truck.

Trick [trɪk], *m.* (**-s,** *pl.* **-e** *or* **-s**) trick, stunt, dodge; (*Cards*) trick. **Trick|aufnahme,** *f.* faked *or* trick photo. **–film,** *m.* cartoon. **–track,** *n.* backgammon.

Trieb [tri:p], *m.* (**-(e)s,** *pl.* **-e**) 1. (*Hort.*) sprout, young shoot; germinating power; 2. (*Mech.*) driving force, motive power; instinct, impulse, urge, bent, propensity, inclination, desire; ***aus eignem –e,*** instinctively, of one's own accord; ***– zum Studieren,*** studious bent; ***sinnlicher –,*** carnal instinct *or* desire, sexual urge; 3. (*dial.*) flock, herd.

trieb, *see* **treiben.**

Triebel ['tri:bəl], *m.* (*dial.*) mallet, crank (handle).

Triebfeder ['tri:pfe:dər], *f.* mainspring (*of clock*); (*fig.*) mainspring, motive; ***die – einer S. sein,*** be at the bottom of a th. **triebhaft,** *adj.* instinctive, impulsive; carnal. **Trieb|knospe,** *f.* leaf-bud. **–kraft,** *f.* motive power, motivating *or* driving force, impetus.

Triebling ['tri:plɪŋ], *m.* (**-s,** *pl.* **-e**) (*Mech.*) pinion.

Trieb|malz, *n.* leavening malt. **–rad,** *n.* driving-wheel; pinion. **–sand,** *m.* shifting sand, quicksand. **–stange,** *f.* (*Motor.*) push-rod. **–wagen,** *m.* diesel train, rail-car. **–welle,** *f.* drive-shaft. **–werk,** *n.* (driving) mechanism; power unit *or* plant, engine, motor; transmission (machinery), drive-gear.

Triefauge ['tri:fʔaugə], *n.* bleary eye. **triefäugig,** *adj.* blear-eyed, bleary.

triefen ['tri:fən], *irr.v.i.* (*aux.* h. *&* s.) drip, trickle, run (***von,*** with), (*of candle*) gutter; (*fig.*) overflow (with); ***die Augen – ihm,*** his eyes are watering *or* running. **triefend,** *adj.* dripping. **trief|nasig,** *adj.* snivelling. **–naß,** *adj.* sopping *or* dripping wet.

Triel [tri:l], *m.* (**-s,** *pl.* **-e**) 1. (*Orn.*) stone-curlew, (*Am.*) thick-knee (*Burhinus oedicnemus*); 2. (*dial.*) mouth, maw, muzzle; dewlap. **trielen,** *v.i.* (*dial.*) dribble, slaver, slobber. **Trieler,** *m.* (*dial.*) bib.

Trier [tri:r], *n.* Trèves.

triezen ['tri:tsən], *v.t.* (*coll.*) vex, worry, pester, bother, plague.

triffst [trɪfst], **trifft,** *see* **treffen.**

Trift [trɪft], *f.* (-, *pl.* **-en**) 1. right of pasturage, pasture, common; (*Poet.*) meadow, sward; cattle-track; 2. drove, flock, herd; 3. floating, drift (*of timber*); (*Naut.*) current, drift. **triften,** *v.t.* 1. float, drift (*timber*); 2. pasture.

triftig ['trɪftɪç], *adj.* 1. cogent, forcible, weighty, strong, conclusive, convincing, plausible, sound, valid; ***–er Grund,*** good *or* valid reason; 2. (*dial.*) drifting, (*only pred.*) adrift. **Triftigkeit,** *f.* plausibility, cogency (*of arguments*), validity, soundness.

Triftströmung ['trɪftʃtrø:muŋ], *f.* glacial current.

Trigonometrie [trigonome'tri:], *f.* trigonometry.

trigonometrisch [–'me:trɪʃ], *adj.* trigonometrical; ***–er Punkt,*** triangulation point.

Trikot [tri'ko:, 'trɪko], (**-s,** *pl.* **-s**) 1. *m.* tricot, stockinet, knitted fabric; 2. *n.* (*Spt.*) vest, slip, strip; *pl.* tights. **Trikotage** [–'ta:ʒə], *f.*, **Trikotwaren,** *f.pl.* knitted goods, woollens.

Triller ['trɪlər], *m.* (*Mus.*) trill, shake; ***einen – schlagen,*** shake, trill; (*coll.*) ***mit einem – über die S. hinweggehen,*** pass the matter off with a shrug (of the shoulders). **trillern,** *v.t., v.i.* shake, trill; (*of birds*) warble, twitter.

Trinität [trini'tɛ:t], *f.* trinity.

trinkbar ['trɪŋkba:r], *adj.* drinkable, potable. **Trinkbecher,** *m.* drinking-cup.

trinken ['trɪŋkən], **1.** *irr.v.t.* drink; (*fig.*) drink in, imbibe, absorb; ***– auf*** (*Acc.*), drink to, toast; ***mit ihm Brüderschaft –,*** pledge one's close friendship with him; ***sich*** (*Dat.*) ***einen Rausch –,*** get drunk; ***der Wein läßt sich –,*** the wine is quite drinkable; ***ein Glas leer –,*** empty a glass; ***gern einen über den Durst –,*** be fond of the bottle. **2.** *irr.v.i.* (take a) drink, tipple, carouse. **Trinken,** *n.* drinking; ***sich*** (*Dat.*) ***das – angewöhnen,*** take to drink. **Trinker,** *m.* heavy drinker, toper, drunkard, alcoholic. **Trinkerheilanstalt,** *f.* hospital for inebriates.

trinkfest ['trɪŋkfɛst], *adj.* able to carry one's drink *or* to hold one's liquor. **Trink|gefäß,** *n.* drinking-vessel. **–gelage,** *n.* drinking-bout, carouse, carousal. **–geld,** *n.* gratuity; (*coll.*) tip; (*coll.*) ***ihm ein – geben,*** tip him. **–halle,** *f.* pump-room (*of a spa*). **–halm,** *m.* drinking-straw. **–lied,** *n.* drinking-song. **–schale,** *f.* goblet. **–spruch,** *m.* toast. **–wasser,** *n.* drinking-water.

Trinom [tri'no:m], *n.* (**-s,** *pl.* **-e**) (*Math., Biol.*) trinomial. **trinomisch,** *adj.* (*Math.*) trinomial.

Triole [tri'o:lə], *f.* (*Mus.*) triplet.

Tripel ['tri:pəl], *m.* rottenstone.

Triplik [tri'pli:k], *f.* (-, *pl.* **-en**) (*Law*) surrejoinder.

trippeln ['trɪpəln], *v.i.* trip, patter.

Tripper ['trɪpər], *m.* (*Med.*) gonorrhoea.

Triptik ['trɪptɪk], **Triptyk,** *n.* (**-s,** *pl.* **-s**) triptych.

Tripus ['tri:pus], *m.* (-, *pl.* - *or* **-poden**) (*Myth.*) tripod.

Trischübel ['tri:ʃybəl], *m.* (*Swiss*) lintel.

Tritt [trɪt], *m.* (**-(e)s,** *pl.* **-e**) 1. step, pace; (*visible*) footstep, footprint, track, (*audible*) footstep, footfall, tread; kick; ***einen falschen – tun,*** miss one's step; ***ihm auf Schritt und – folgen,*** follow in his footsteps; ***ihm einen – versetzen,*** give him a kick, kick him; ***ihm den – geben,*** give him the push; (*Mil.*) ***ohne –!*** break step! march at ease! ***im –,*** in step; ***in falschem –,*** out of step; ***– fassen,*** fall *or* get in step; ***– wechseln!*** change step! ***– halten,*** keep in step; keep pace (***mit,*** with); 2. carriage-step; step-ladder, pair of steps; treadle; 3. (*climbing etc.*) foothold.

tritt, *see* **treten.**

Tritt|brett, *n.* treadle (*of a loom*); pedal (*of an organ*); (*Motor., Railw.*) footboard, running-board. **–fläche,** *f.* tread (*protective surface of steps etc.*). **–klinke,** *f.* foot-release. **–leiter,** *f.* (pair of) steps, step-ladder. **–wechsel,** *m.* change of step.

Triumph [tri'umf], *m.* (**-(e)s,** *pl.* **-e**) triumph, victory; ***im –,*** triumphantly; ***ihm den – gönnen,*** not grudge him his victory. **Triumphator** [–'fa:tɔr], *m.*(**-s,** *pl.* **-en**) conquering hero, victor. **Triumphbogen,** *m.* triumphal arch. **triumphieren** [–'fi:rən], *v.i.* triumph (***über*** (*Acc.*), over), vanquish, conquer; (*fig.*) exult *or* (*coll.*) gloat *or* crow (over), (*coll.*) score (off); ***zu früh –,*** count one's chickens before they are hatched. **Triumph|wagen,** *m.* triumphal car. **–zug,** *m.* triumphal procession.

trivial [trivi'a:l], *adj.* trivial, trite, hackneyed. **Trivialität** [–i'tɛ:t], *f.* triviality.

trochäisch [trɔ'xɛ:ɪʃ], *adj.* trochaic. **Trochäus,** *m.* (-, *pl.* **-äen**) trochee.

trocken ['trɔkən], **1.** *adj.* dry, dried up, arid, parched, barren; (*fig.*) dull, uninteresting, tedious, boring; ***auf dem Trockenen,*** high and dry, stranded; (*fig.*) ***auf dem trocknen sitzen,*** be on one's beam-ends *or* on the rocks, be in low water, be at the end of one's tether, not know which way to turn; ***-er Empfang,*** cool reception; ***-er Frost,*** black ice; ***-en Fußes,*** dry-shod; ***-es Gedeck,*** dinner without wine; ***noch nicht – hinter den Ohren,*** still wet behind the ears; ***im Trockenen,*** under cover, (*coll.*) in the dry; (*fig.*) ***im trocknen,*** in safety, safe; ***ins trockne bringen,*** rescue, save, bring into safety; ***sein Schäfchen ins trockne bringen,*** line one's pocket, feather one's nest; ***-er Mensch,*** prosaic fellow, (*coll.*) dry stick; ***-e Messe,*** mass without the Sacrament; ***-er Wechsel,*** promissory note. **2.** *adv.* (*fig.*) dryly, drily.

Trocken|anlage, *f.* drying-plant. **-apparat,** *m.* drying-apparatus *or* -frame, drier. **-bagger,** *m.* excavator. **-boden,** *m.* drying-room *or* -loft. **-dampf,** *m.* dry steam. **-dock,** *n.* graving-dock, dry-dock. **-ei,** *n.* dehydrated *or* dried egg. **-element,** *n.* dry cell, dry battery. **-fäule,** *f.* dry-rot. **-futter,** *n.* fodder, provender. **-fütterung,** *f.* dry-feeding *or* fodder. **-gehalt,** *m.* amount of solid matter. **-gemüse,** *n.* dehydrated *or* dried vegetables. **-gestell,** *n.* drying-frame, clothes-horse. **-gewicht,** *n.* dry weight.

Trockenheit ['trɔkənhaɪt], *f.* dryness, drought, aridity; (*fig.*) dullness. **Trockenkammer,** *f.* drying-room. **trockenlegen,** *v.t.* drain (*a marsh*); change (*a baby's nappies*). **Trocken|legung,** *f.* draining, drainage. **-maß,** *n.* dry measure. **-milch,** *f.* milk-powder, dried *or* dehydrated *or* powdered milk. **-mittel,** *n.* drier, drying agent, siccative. **-obst,** *n.* dried fruit. **-ofen,** *m.* drying-kiln. **-periode,** *f.* dry spell (*weather*). **-pflanze,** *f.* xerophyte. **-platte,** *f.* (*Phot.*) dry-plate. **-platz,** *m.* drying-ground. **-rahmen,** *m.* drying-frame, stenter. **-rasierer,** *m.* electric razor. **trockenreiben,** *irr.v.t.* rub (till) dry. **Trocken|reinigung,** *f.* dry-cleaning. **-rückstand,** *m.* dry residue. **-schleuder,** *f.* spin-drier. **-schwund,** *m.* shrinkage through drying. **-ständer,** *m.* *See* **-gestell. -stempel,** *m.* embossed seal. **-verfahren,** *n.* drying-process. **-wäsche,** *f.* dried laundry.

trocknen ['trɔknən], **1.** *v.i.* (*aux.* s.) dry, dry up, become dry. **2.** *v.t.* dry, wipe *or* rub dry; (hang out to) dry, air (*laundry*); desiccate, dehydrate; season (*timber*), drain (*land*). **Trockner,** *m.* drier, desiccator. **Trocknung,** *f.* drying; desiccation, dehydration; seasoning.

Troddel ['trɔdəl], *f.* (-, *pl.* **-n**) tassel, bob; sword-knot.

Trödel ['trøːdəl], *m.* rubbish, lumber, junk, trash; second-hand goods, bric-à-brac; (*rare*) fun, pleasantry; (*coll.*) lark, spree. **Trödelei** [–'laɪ], *f.* dawdling, loitering, negligence. **Trödel|kram,** *m.* lumber, old clothes, second-hand goods. **-markt,** *m.* second-hand market, rag-fair. **trödeln,** *v.i.* 1. deal in second-hand goods; 2. (*fig.*) dawdle, loiter, waste one's time; (*coll.*) go slow (*at work*). **Trödel|waren,** *f.pl.* *See* **-kram. Trödler,** *m.* 1. second-hand *or* old-clothes dealer, rag-and-bone man; 2. (*fig.*) loiterer, dawdler, (*coll.*) slow-coach.

troff [trɔf], **tröffe** ['trœfə], *see* **triefen.**

Trog [troːk], *m.* (**-(e)s,** *pl.* **⸚e**) trough, vat; (builder's) hod; ***schwingender –,*** cradle (*for washing ore*).

trog, tröge, *see* **trügen.**

Troja ['troːja], *n.* Troy. **Trojaner,** *m.*, **trojanisch,** *adj.* Trojan.

Troll [trɔl], *m.* (**-(e)s,** *pl.* **-e**) hobgoblin, gnome. **Trollblume,** *f.* (*Bot.*) globe-flower (*Trollius europaeus*).

trollen ['trɔlən], **1.** *v.i.* (*aux.* s.) trot, toddle. **2.** *v.r.* toddle off; ***trolle dich!*** be off! away with you!

Trommel ['trɔməl], *f.* (-, *pl.* **-n**) drum; (*Anat.*) tympanum, eardrum; (*Mech.*) cylinder, barrel; (tin) canister; ***die – rühren,*** play the drum, (*fig.*) beat the big drum; ***auf der – wirbeln,*** give a roll on the drum. **Trommelfell,** *n.* drumskin, drumhead; (*Anat.*) eardrum, tympanic membrane. **trommelfellerschütternd,** *adj.* deafening, ear-splitting. **Trommel|feuer,** *n.* drumfire, (*also fig.*) barrage, intense *or* heavy bombardment. **-klöppel,** *m.* *See* **-schlegel.**

trommeln ['trɔməln], *v.t., v.i.* drum, beat the drum; (*with the fists*) pommel; ***es trommelt,*** the drum is beating; ***einen Marsch –,*** beat a march on the drum; ***mit den Fingern –,*** beat a devil's tattoo, drum with one's fingers; ***ich lasse nicht auf mir –,*** I will not stand for it, I will not allow myself to be walked over. **Trommel|revolver,** *m.* revolver, (*coll.*) six-shooter. **-schlag,** *m.* beat on the drum; ***unter –,*** with drums beating; ***bei gedämpftem –,*** with muffled drums. **-schläger,** *m.* tympanist, drummer. **-schlegel, -stock,** *m.* drumstick. **-wirbel,** *m.* roll of the drum.

Trommler ['trɔmlər], *m.* drummer.

Trompete [trɔm'peːtə], *f.* trumpet; (*Anat.*) Fallopian (*or* Eustachian) tube; ***die –*** or ***auf der – blasen, in die – stoßen,*** blow *or* sound the trumpet. **trompeten,** *v.i.* blow *or* sound the trumpet, (*of elephant*) trumpet; (*fig.*) trumpet forth.

Trompeten|bläser, *m.* trumpeter. **-geschmetter,** *n.* blare *or* flourish of trumpets. **-register,** *n.* *See* **-zug. -schall,** *m.* sound of trumpets; ***unter – bekannt machen,*** announce with a flourish of trumpets. **-stoß,** *m.* trumpet-blast, flourish of trumpets. **-zug,** *m.* trumpet-stop (*of an organ*).

Trompeter [trɔm'peːtər], *m.* trumpeter.

Trope ['troːpə], *f.* trope.

Tropen ['troːpən], *pl.* the tropics. **Tropen|ausführung,** *f.* model, version, design, pattern *etc.* tested under tropical conditions. **-ausrüstung,** *f.* tropical kit. **tropen|beständig, -fest,** *adj.* suitable for the tropics, tested under tropical conditions. **Tropen|festigkeit,** *f.* resistance to tropical conditions, suitability for the tropics. **-helm,** *m.* pith *or* sun-helmet, topee. **-kleidung,** *f.* *See* **-ausrüstung. -koller,** *m.* tropical frenzy. **-krankheit,** *f.* tropical disease.

Tropf [trɔpf], *m.* (**-(e)s,** *pl.* **⸚e**) simpleton, ninny, booby; ***armer –,*** poor wretch.

tropfbar ['trɔpfbaːr], *adj.* liquid. **Tropf|bernstein,** *m.* liquid amber. **-brett,** *n.* draining board.

tröpfeln ['trœpfəln], **1.** *v.i.* (*aux.* h. *&* s.) drop, drip, trickle, fall in drops, (*of a tap*) leak, run; (*coll.*) ***es tröpfelt,*** it is spotting with rain. **2.** *v.t.* drip, drop, pour drop by drop.

Tropfen ['trɔpfən], *m.* drop, spot, tear, bead (*of perspiration*); *pl.* (*Med.*) drops; ***haben Sie einen – Milch?*** have you a drop *or* spot of milk? ***ein – auf den heißen Stein,*** a drop in the bucket *or* ocean; ***er trinkt gern seinen –,*** he is fond of his drink.

tropfen, *v.t., v.i.* *See* **tröpfeln**; (*of a candle*) gutter; ***steter Tropfen höhlt den Stein,*** constant dripping wears the stone.

Tropfenfänger ['trɔpfənfɛŋər], *m.* drip-catcher. **tropfen|förmig,** *adj.* bead-like. **-weise,** *adv.* in drops, drop by drop.

Tropfflasche ['trɔpfflaʃə], *f.* dropping-bottle. **tropfflüssig,** *adj.* *See* **tropfbar. tropfnaß,** *adj.* dripping wet. **Tropf|ölung,** *f.* drip-feed lubrication. **-pfanne,** *f.* drip-pan. **-rinne,** *f.* gutter. **-stein,** *m.* stalactite.

Trophäe [tro'fɛːə], *f.* trophy.

tropisch ['troːpɪʃ], *adj.* 1. tropical (*see* **Tropen**); 2. metaphorical, figurative (*see* **Trope**). **Tropus,** *m.* (-, *pl.* **-pen**) (*Austr.*) *see* **Trope.**

Troß [trɔs], *m.* (**-(ss)es,** *pl.* **-(ss)e**) (*Mil.*) supply lines, baggage train; camp followers; (*fig.*) crowd, followers, hangers-on.

Trosse ['trɔsə], *f.* cable, hawser, warp.

Trost [troːst], *m.* comfort, consolation, solace; ***– zusprechen*** (*Dat.*), *see* **trösten**; ***schlechter –,*** cold *or* poor comfort; ***– schöpfen aus,*** take comfort from, find solace in; (*coll.*) ***du bist wohl nicht bei –e?*** you are off your head *or* (*sl.*) rocker, you must be out of your mind. **trost|bedürftig,** *adj.* in need of consolation. **-bringend,** *adj.* comforting, consolatory.

trösten ['trøːstən], **1.** *v.t.* comfort, console, solace; ***ihn über eine S.*** or ***wegen einer S. –,*** console him for a thing. **2.** *v.r.* ***sich* – *mit,*** take comfort *or* find consolation in, console o.s. with, be consoled *or* comforted by. **Tröster,** *m.* comforter, consoler; child's comforter *or* dummy; (*coll.*) cane; consolation of the bottle; favourite book. **tröstlich,** *adj.* consoling, comforting; cheering; (*dial.*) cheerful, merry, gay.

trostlos ['tro:stlo:s], *adj.* (*of a p.*) disconsolate, despondent, inconsolable; wretched, miserable; (*fig. of a th.*) cheerless, desolate, bleak, dreary, (*coll.*) hopeless. **Trostlosigkeit,** *f.* despair, despondency, hopelessness; (*fig.*) bleakness, desolation, wretchedness, cheerlessness, dreariness. **Trostpreis,** *m.* consolation prize, (*coll.*) booby prize. **trost|reich,** *adj. See* **–bringend.**

Tröstung ['trø:stuŋ], *f.* consolation, cheering *or* comforting words, comfort; ***die letzten –en,*** the last unction.

Trott [trɔt], *m.* (**-(e)s,** *pl.* **-e**) trot, jog-trot; ***der gewöhnliche –,*** the daily round *or* routine.

Trottel ['trɔtəl], *m.* cretin, idiot, fool, (*coll.*) nincompoop, sap. **trottelhaft,** *adj.* imbecile, idiotic, half-witted, block-headed, fatuous. **Trottellumme,** *f.* (*Orn.*) guillemot, (*Am.*) Atlantic murre (*Uria aalge*).

trotten ['trɔtən], *v.i.* (*aux.* s.) trot *or* jog along.

Trottoir [trɔto'a:r], *n.* (**-s,** *pl.* **-e** (*Austr.* **-s**)) pavement, footpath, (*Am.*) sidewalk.

Trotz [trɔts], *m.* defiance, insolence; stubbornness, obstinacy (***gegen,*** in the face of); – ***bieten*** (*Dat.*), defy; weather (*a storm*); ***ihm zum –,*** in defiance of him, to spite him; ***aus –,*** from spite.

trotz, *prep.* (*Gen. or Dat.*) in spite of, despite, notwithstanding; – ***allem*** or ***alledem,*** for all that, notwithstanding everything.

trotzdem [trɔts'de:m], **1.** *adv.* in spite of it, nevertheless, notwithstanding, all the same. **2.** *conj.* notwithstanding that, although, even though, albeit.

trotzen ['trɔtsən], *v.i.* (*Dat.*) bid defiance to, defy, dare, brave, oppose, resist; be obstinate *or* sulky. **trotzig,** *adj.* defiant, refractory, obstinate; sulky. **Trotzkopf,** *m.* stubborn *or* pig-headed person; sulky child. **trotzköpfig,** *adj. See* **trotzig.**

trüb(e) [try:p ('try:bə)], *adj.* muddy, cloudy, turbid, thick; (*fig.*) gloomy, dreary, bleak, (*as thoughts*) dismal, cheerless, sad, melancholy; (*of weather*) overcast, dull, (*of gems etc.*) clouded, (*of metal*) tarnished; ***die Lampe brennt –,*** the lamp burns dimly; ***im trüben fischen,*** fish in troubled waters; ***es sieht – damit aus,*** things are looking black, (*coll.*) the outlook is pretty dim.

Trubel ['tru:bəl], *m.* confusion, turmoil, turbulence; bustle, hubbub, hurly-burly; milling throng.

trüben ['try:bən], **1.** *v.t.* make thick *or* muddy, darken, dull, dim, tarnish (*metal*), cloud, blur (*vision etc.*); disturb, ruffle, upset, trouble; sadden, cast a gloom over; spoil, mar (*pleasure*), cloud, poison (*relationship*); ***er sieht aus, als ob er kein Wässerchen – könnte,*** he looks the picture of innocence, he looks as if butter would not melt in his mouth. **2.** *v.r.* become thick *or* muddy *or* cloudy *or* turbid; (*of weather*) become overcast; (*of relations*) become strained.

Trübheit ['try:phaɪt], *f.* muddiness, cloudiness, turbidity, dimness; (*fig.*) dreariness, gloom. **Trübnis,** *f.* (-, *pl.* **-se**), **Trübsal,** *f.* (-, *pl.* **-e**), also *n.* (**-s,** *pl.* **-e**) affliction, distress, misery, sorrow, grief, woe; (*coll.*) ***Trübsal blasen,*** mope, be in the dumps. **trübselig,** *adj.* (*of a p.*) troubled, afflicted, forlorn, dejected, woeful; (*of a th.*) bleak, dreary; (*of a p. or th.*) sad, melancholy, gloomy, miserable, wretched. **Trüb|seligkeit,** *f.* sadness, despondency, melancholy. **–sinn,** *m.* melancholy, dejection, depression, gloom, low spirits. **trübsinnig,** *adj.* low-spirited, dejected, gloomy, sad, melancholy. **Trübung,** *f.* darkening, cloudiness, turbidity, dimness.

Truchseß ['truxzɛs], *m.* ((**ss)es,** *pl.* **-(ss)e**) (*obs.*) lord high steward.

trudeln ['tru:dəln], *v.i.* (*aux.* s.) saunter, amble, drift; (*Av.*) go into a spin. **Trudeln,** *n.* ambling, sauntering; ***ins – kommen*** or ***geraten,*** develop a spin.

Trüffel ['tryfəl], *f.* (-, *pl.* **-n**) truffle.

trug [tru:k], *see* **tragen.**

Trug, *m.* deceit, imposture, fraud; deception, delusion, illusion; ***ohne –,*** open and above board, straightforward, upright; ***Lug und –,*** deceit and lying. **Trug|bild,** *n.* phantom, vision, hallucination, mirage, optical illusion. **–dolde,** *f.* (*Bot.*) cyme.

trüge ['try:gə], *see* **tragen.**

trügen ['try:gən], **1.** *irr.v.t.* deceive, delude, mislead; ***wenn mein Gedächtnis mich nicht trügt,*** if my memory serves me right. **2.** *irr.v.i.* (*of a p.*) be deceitful, (*of a th.*) be deceptive, prove fallacious; ***Gottes Wort kann nicht –,*** the word of God cannot fail; (*Prov.*) ***der Schein trügt,*** appearances are deceptive. **trügerisch,** *adj.* (*of a p.*) deceitful; (*of a th.*) deceptive, misleading; false, fallacious; illusory, delusive, (*as ice*) treacherous.

Trugschluß ['tru:kʃlus], *m.* sophism, false conclusion, fallacy.

Truhe ['tru:ə], *f.* trunk, chest; (*Rad. etc.*) cabinet, console; (clothes-)press; (*dial.*) coffin.

Trulle ['trulə], *f.* (*dial.*) trollop, wench, hussy.

Trumm [trum], *n.* (**-(e)s,** *pl.* **¨-er**) (*dial.*) (stub-)end, stump, lump, clod; (*Weav.*) thrum; ***ein – Arbeit,*** a pile of work; ***ein – von einem Kerl,*** a great lump of a fellow; ***den – verlieren,*** unthread one's needle, lose the end (*of thread*).

Trümmer ['trymər], *pl.* wreckage, ruins, remains, remnants, broken pieces, fragments, debris, rubble; ***in – legen,*** lay in ruins; ***zu –n*** or ***in – gehen,*** be shattered, go to pieces *or* (*fig.*) to rack and ruin; ***zu –n*** or ***in – schlagen,*** smash to pieces, wreck. **Trümmer|feld,** *n.* expanse of ruins, (*fig.*) shambles. **–gestein,** *n.* (*Geol.*) breccia, rubble. **–grundstück,** *n.* bomb-site. **–haufe(n),** *m.* heap of ruins *or* rubble.

Trumpf [trumpf], *m.* (**-(e)s,** *pl.* **¨-e**) trumps, trump-card; ***was ist –?*** what are trumps? ***Herz ist –,*** hearts are trumps; ***einen – darauf setzen,*** play one's trump-card (*also fig.*), (*fig.*) make it one's special business *or* concern; (*fig.*) ***den letzten – ausspielen,*** play one's last card; (*fig.*) ***seine Trümpfe ausspielen,*** push home one's advantage; ***ihm zeigen, was – ist,*** show him what is what; ***kariert ist jetzt –,*** checks are now the last word. **trumpfen,** *v.t., v.i.* trump, play trumps; (*fig.*) – ***auf*** (*Acc.*), pride o.s. on. **Trumpf|farbe,** *f.* trump(-suit). **–karte,** *f.* trump-card.

Trunk [truŋk], *m.* (**-(e)s,** *pl.* **¨-e**) drink, potion; draught, gulp; drinking, drunkenness, alcoholism; ***dem – ergeben,*** addicted to drink; ***auf einen –,*** at one draught *or* gulp *or* (*sl.*) swig; ***im –,*** when drunk *or* intoxicated, (*coll.*) while under the influence (of drink).

trunken ['truŋkən], *adj.* inebriated, drunken, (*pred.*) drunk, (*also fig.*) intoxicated; ***sie waren – vor Freude,*** they were wild *or* elated with joy. **Trunkenbold,** *m.* drunkard. **Trunkenheit,** *f.* drunkenness, intoxication, inebriation.

Trunksucht ['truŋkzuxt], *f.* drunkenness, dipsomania, alcoholism. **trunksüchtig,** *adj.* addicted to drink, dipsomaniac. **Trunksüchtige(r),** *m., f.* alcoholic, dipsomaniac.

Trupp [trup], *m.* (**-s,** *pl.* **-s**) troop; (*of workers*) band, gang, crew, team, group, (*of animals*) flock, drove, herd; (*Mil.*) section, party, squad, detachment, detail.

Truppe ['trupə], *f.* (*Mil.*) unit; (*Theat.*) troupe, company; *pl.* troops, the army, the (armed) forces, the services, military forces, soldiers.

Truppen|abteilung, *f.* unit, detachment. **–ansammlung,** *f.* concentration of forces, massing of troops. **–aushebung,** *f.* levy (of troops). **–betreuung,** *f.* army welfare services, (*Am.*) special services. **–bewegung,** *f.* troop movements *or* manœuvres. **–einteilung,** *f.* disposition of forces. **–führer,** *m.* military leader, commander. **–gat-**

tung, *f.* arm of the service. **–schau,** *f.* military review, parade. **–teil,** *m.* formation, unit; ***vom – zurückbleiben,*** lose contact with one's unit, straggle. **–transport,** *m.* movement of troops. **–transporter,** *m.* (*Naut.*) troopship, (*Av.*) troop carrier. **–übung,** *f.* manœuvres, field exercise. **–übungsplatz,** *m.* training area. **–verbandplatz,** *m.* advanced *or* field dressing-station. **–verschiebung,** *f.* change in disposition of troops.

Truppführer ['trupfy:rər], *m.* section leader. **truppweise,** *adv.* in troops, in bands.

Trut|hahn ['tru:t–], *m.* turkey(-cock). **–henne,** *f.*, **–huhn,** *n.* turkey-hen. **–hühner,** *n.pl.* turkeys.

Trutschel ['trutʃəl], *f.* (-, *pl.* **-n**) (*dial.*) buxom wench *or* lass; fat woman.

Trutz [truts], *m.* (*obs.*) defiance; offensive; *see* **Trotz**; ***zu Schutz und –,*** offensively and defensively. **Trutzbündnis,** *n.* offensive alliance. **trutzen,** *v.i.*, **trutzig,** *adj.* (*obs.*) *see* **trotzen, trotzig. Trutzwaffen,** *f.pl.* offensive weapons.

Tschako ['tʃa:ko], *m.* (**-s,** *pl.* **-s**) shako.

Tschapka ['tʃapka], *f.* (-, *pl.* **-s**) lancer's helmet.

Tscheche ['tʃɛçə], *m.* (**-n,** *pl.* **-n**), **Tschechin,** *f.*, **tschechisch,** *adj.* Czech. **Tschechoslowakei [–oslova'kaɪ],** *f.* Czechoslovakia.

Tuba ['tu:ba], *f.* (-, *pl.* **-ben**) (*Mus.*) tuba; (*Anat.*) Eustachian *or* Fallopian tube. **Tube,** *f.* tube (*paint, tooth-paste etc.*); *see also* **Tuba** (*Anat.*); (*sl.*) (*Motor.*) ***auf die – drücken,*** step on the gas *or* on it.

Tuberkel [tu'bɛrkəl], *f.* (-, *pl.* **-n**) *or* (*Austr.*) *m.* tubercle. **tuberkulös** [–u'lø:s], *adj.* tubercular, tuberculous. **Tuberkulose,** *f.* tuberculosis.

Tuch [tu:x], *n.* **1.** (**-(e)s,** *pl.* **-e**) cloth, fabric, stuff, material; 2. (**-(e)s,** *pl.* **⸗er**) kerchief, shawl, scarf; ***das bunte –,*** soldiers, the military; ***die Herren von zweierlei –,*** the officers; ***das wirkt wie ein rotes –,*** that is like (a) red rag to a bull. **tuchen,** *adj.* (of) cloth *or* fabric.

Tuch|fühlung, *f.* ***in –,*** shoulder to shoulder, (*fig.*) in close touch *or* contact, (*coll.*) rubbing shoulders. **–halle,** *f.* drapers' hall. **–händler,** *m.* draper. **–handlung,** *f.*, **–laden,** *m.* draper's (shop). **–nadel,** *f.* shawl-pin, breast-pin, brooch. **–rahmen,** *m.* tenter. **–rauhmaschine,** *f.* cloth-dressing machine. **–rest,** *m.* remnant (*of cloth*). **–schrot,** *n.*, **–streifen,** *m.* list (*of cloth*).

tüchtig ['tyçtɪç], **1.** *adj.* fit, able, capable, qualified, competent, proficient, efficient, experienced, sound, strong, hearty, good, excellent, thorough; clever, skilful; ***– in*** (*Dat.*), proficient *or* good at. **2.** *adv.* well, thoroughly, vigorously, (*coll.*) with a vengeance, (*sl.*) like blazes, like nobody's business; ***– arbeiten,*** work hard; ***er wurde – geneckt,*** he was teased unmercifully; ***er wurde – geprügelt,*** he got a sound thrashing; ***– essen,*** eat heartily. **Tüchtigkeit,** *f.* ability, prowess, fitness; soundness, excellence; proficiency, efficiency.

Tuch|walker, *m.* fuller. **–waren,** *f.pl.* drapery. **–zeichen,** *n.* (*Av.*) ground-strip *or* -panel.

Tuck [tuk], *m.* (**-(e)s,** *pl.* **⸗e**) (*dial.*) spiteful trick.

Tücke ['tykə], *f.* prank, trick; malice, spite, perfidy, treachery. **tückisch,** *adj.* malicious, spiteful; insidious, treacherous; ***–e Krankheit,*** malignant disease; ***–er Hund,*** vicious dog.

Tuder ['tu:dər], **Tüder** ['ty:dər], *m.* tether, hobble.

Tuerei [tu:ə'raɪ], *f.* humbug, make-believe, lip-service, dissimulation, dissembling.

Tuff [tuf], *m.* (**-s,** *pl.* **-e**) tufa, tuff; volcanic rock. **Tuff|kalk, –stein,** *m.* tufaceous *or* volcanic limestone.

Tüfte ['ty:ftə], *f.* (*dial.*) potato.

Tüftelei [tyftə'laɪ], *f.* (-, *pl.* **-en**) hair-splitting, subtlety. **Tüft(e)ler** ['tyft(ə)lər], *m.* (*coll.*) (old) fuss-pot **tüft(e)lig,** *adj.* punctilious, very fussy, pernickety. **tüfteln,** *v.i.* split hairs, draw overnice distinctions; go in for subtleties, subtilize; ***– an*** (*Dat.*), fuss over.

Tugend ['tu:gənt], *f.* (-, *pl.* **-en**) virtue; female virtue, chastity, purity; ***aus der Not eine – machen,*** make a virtue of necessity; ***arme – ist besser als reiche Schande,*** virtuous poverty is better than shameful riches; (*Prov.*) ***Jugend hat keine –,*** boys will be boys. **Tugendbold,** *m.* paragon of virtue. **tugendhaft,** *adj.* virtuous. **Tugendhaftigkeit,** *f.* respectability, righteousness, rectitude. **Tugend|held,** *m. See* **–bold. –pfad,** *m.* path of virtue. **–richter,** *m.* moralist, censor. **tugendsam,** *adj.* virtuous, chaste.

Tukan ['tu:kan], *m.* (**-s,** *pl.* **-e**) (*Orn.*) toucan (*Rhamphastidae*).

tulich ['tu:lɪç], *adj.* (*obs.*) *see* **tunlich.**

Tulipane [tu:li'pa:nə], *f.* (*obs.*) *see* **Tulpe.**

Tüll [tyl], *m.* (**-(e)s,** *pl.* **-e**) tulle; net.

Tülle ['tylə], *f.* spout, nozzle; socket.

Tulpe ['tulpə], *f.* 1. tulip; 2. beer-glass. **Tulpen|baum,** *m.* (*Bot.*) tulip-tree (*Liriodendron tulipifera*). **–zucht,** *f.* tulip-growing. **–zwiebel,** *f.* tulip-bulb.

tummeln ['tuməln], **1.** *v.t.* exercise (*horse etc.*), keep (*a p.*) moving. **2.** *v.r.* move, keep moving, disport o.s., frisk about, romp; hurry (up), bestir o.s., make haste, hustle. **Tummelplatz,** *m.* exercise-ground; riding-school; playground; (*fig.*) scene, arena, hotbed.

Tümmler ['tymlər], *m.* 1. (*Orn.*) tumbler-pigeon; 2. (*Zool.*) dolphin, porpoise.

Tümpel ['tympəl], (*Austr. also*) **Tümpfel,** *m.* pond, pool; puddle.

Tumult [tu'mult], *m.* (**-(e)s,** *pl.* **-e**) uproar, tumult, turmoil, hubbub, commotion, riot, disturbance. **Tumultuant** [–u'ant], *m.* (**-en,** *pl.* **-en**) rioter. **tumultuarisch,** *adj.* riotous, tumultuous, noisy, excited. **tumultuieren,** *v.i.* create a disturbance *or* commotion, (*sl.*) kick up a row *or* racket.

tun [tu:n], **1.** *irr.v.t.* do, perform, execute; make; put; ***eine Bitte –,*** make a request; ***einen Blick – (in*** (*Acc.*)), cast a glance (at); ***einen Eid –,*** take an oath; ***eine Frage –,*** put *or* ask a question; ***in die Schule –,*** put *or* send to school; ***mein möglichstes –,*** do all I can, do whatever is in my power; ***das tut man nicht,*** it isn't done; ***tue ihm nichts!*** do not hurt him! ***er tut nichts,*** he does nothing, he is idle; he does no harm; (*of a dog*) it does not bite; ***es tut nichts,*** it does not matter, it is of no consequence, (*coll.*) never mind; ***das tut nichts zur S.,*** that does not advance matters *or* alter things, that is of no significance, (*coll.*) that is neither here nor there; ***es tut not,*** it is necessary, there is need; ***einen Schluck –,*** take a drink *or* (*sl.*) a swig; ***einen Schritt –,*** take a step; ***das Seinige –,*** play one's part, (*coll.*) do one's bit; ***einen Sprung –,*** take a jump; ***ein Übriges –,*** do more than necessary; ***von sich –,*** put away; ***was habe ich dir getan?*** what harm have I done you? ***dazu –,*** add (to it), contribute; ***er kann nichts dazu –,*** he cannot help it; ***des Guten zu viel –,*** go too far, overdo a th.
2. *irr.v.i.* act, do; ***so – als ob,*** do *or* act as if, pretend (*with inf.*); ***– Sie, als ob Sie zu Hause wären,*** make yourself at home; ***ich habe zu –,*** I am busy; ***gut daran –,*** act wisely, do well (*with inf.*); ***das tut gut,*** that is a relief *or* comfort; ***das tut nicht gut,*** no good can come of it; (*obs.*) ***kund und zu wissen –,*** give notice of, make known; ***es tut mir leid,*** I am sorry, I regret; ***mit ihm zu – haben,*** have dealings *or* business with him; ***das hat damit nichts zu –,*** that has nothing to do with it; ***was habe ich damit zu –?*** what has that to do with me? how does that affect me? ***du wirst es mit mir zu – bekommen,*** you will have to answer to me, (*coll.*) I shall be down on you; ***es mit der Angst zu – bekommen,*** be overcome with fear; ***es ist damit nicht getan,*** that is not enough, the matter does not end there, that does not settle it; ***Sie haben recht getan,*** you did well *or* right; ***das will getan sein,*** that needs *or* (*coll.*) wants doing; ***er tut nur so,*** he is making a fuss, (*coll.*) he's putting it on; ***spröde –,*** play the prude; ***es ist mir sehr darum zu –,*** I attach great importance to it, it is of great consequence to me; ***es ist mir nur darum zu –,*** my only concern is, I am only concerned *or* anxious about; ***mir ist nur um das Geld zu –,*** I am only

interested in *or* anxious about the money; ***das läßt sich –,*** that may *or* can be done, that is possible *or* practicable *or* feasible; ***alle Hände voll zu – haben,*** have one's hands full; ***Sie täten besser zu gehen,*** you had better go, it would be better if you went; (*coll.*) (*pres. and imperf.*) (*oft. Poet. tät with inf. instead of simple verb*) ***rechnen tue ich gut,*** I am good at figures; ***lesen tat*** (or ***tät***) ***er das nicht,*** he did not read it; (*Poet.*) ***die Augen täten ihm sinken,*** he lowered his eyes.
3. *v.r.* ***es tut sich etwas,*** there's s.th. going on *or* s.th. afoot *or* brewing *or* s.th. in the wind; (*coll.*) ***sich dicke – mit etwas,*** brag *or* boast of *or* give o.s. airs about a th.; ***sich gütlich –,*** eat heartily, enjoy *or* relish one's food, (*coll.*) do o.s. well; (*coll.*) ***das tut sich leicht,*** that's easy; (*coll.*) ***man tut sich leicht daran,*** that won't give much trouble; ***er tut sich schwer damit,*** he is trying very hard, (*coll.*) he's making heavy weather of it.

Tun, *n.* doings, activities, proceedings; conduct, dealings, action; ***sein – und Treiben,*** everything he does, his entire behaviour; ***Sagen und – ist zweierlei,*** promise and performance are two different things.

Tünche [ˈtynçə], *f.* lime-wash, whitewash, distemper, (*fig.*) varnish, veneer. **tünchen,** *v.t.* whitewash, distemper. **Tünch|farbe,** *f.* distemper. **–pinsel,** *m.* whitewash-brush.

Tunesien [tuˈne:siən], *n.* Tunisia. **Tunes(i)er(in),** *m.* (*f.*), **tunesisch,** *adj.* Tunisian.

Tunichtgut [ˈtu:nɪçtgu:t], *m.* (**-(e)s,** *pl.* **-**) ne'er-do-well, good-for-nothing.

Tunke [ˈtuŋkə], *f.* sauce, gravy. **tunken,** *v.t.* dip, soak, steep, (*bread etc.*) sop.

tunlich [ˈtu:nlɪç], *adj.* feasible, practicable, possible, advisable, expedient, convenient. **Tunlichkeit,** *f.* feasibility, practicability, expediency, convenience. **tunlichst,** *adv.* as far as possible, if possible, as far as (is) *or* wherever practicable.

Tunnel [ˈtunəl], *m.* (**-s,** *pl.* **-s** (*Austr.* **-**)) tunnel, (*Min.*) gallery, (*Railw. etc.*) subway. **Tunnelbau,** *m.* tunnelling. **tunnelieren** [–ˈli:rən], *v.t., v.i.* tunnel, excavate.

Tupf [tupf], *m.* (**-es,** *pl.* **-e**) (*Austr.*) *see* **Tupfen.**

Tüpfel [ˈtypfəl], *m.* (*Austr. n.*) dot, spot, speck. **Tüpfelchen,** *n.* ***bis aufs –,*** to a T. **Tüpfel|farn,** *m.* (*Bot.*) polypodium. **–gewebe,** *n.* pitted tissue. **tüpf(e)lig,** *adj.* spotted, speckled. **tüpfeln,** *v.t.* dot, spot, speckle, mottle, stipple. **Tüpfelsumpfhuhn,** *n.* (*Orn.*) spotted crake (*Porzana porzana*).

Tupfen [ˈtupfən], *m.* dot, spot. **tupfen,** *v.t.* dab, touch lightly, (*Med.*) swab. **Tupfer,** *m.* (*Med.*) swab, tampon.

Tür [ty:r], *f.* (**-,** *pl.* **-en**) door; ***offene –en einrennen,*** assert the obvious, carry coals to Newcastle; ***mit der – ins Haus fallen,*** blurt it out; ***die – fiel ins Schloß,*** the door slammed (to); ***vor seiner eigenen – kehren,*** mind one's own business; ***ihn vor die – setzen,*** show him the door, turn him out (of the house); (*fig.*) ***vor der – stehen,*** be forthcoming *or* imminent *or* near at hand, (*coll.*) be just round the corner; ***ihm die – vor der Nase zuschlagen,*** slam the door in his face; ***zwei –en von hier,*** next door but one, two doors away; ***zwischen – und Angel,*** on the point of leaving, (*fig.*) as an aside, in an offhand manner.

Türangel [ˈty:rˀaŋəl], *f.* door-hinge.

Turbine [turˈbi:nə], *f.* turbine. **Turbinen|flugzeug,** *n.* turbo-jet plane. **–pumpe,** *f.* turbo-pump. **–schaufel,** *f.* turbine blade. **–strahltriebwerk,** *n.* turbo-jet engine.

turbulent [turbuˈlɛnt], *adj.* turbulent, (*fig.*) hectic.

Türe [ˈty:rə], *f.* (*dial.*) *see* **Tür.**

Tür|einfassung, *f.* door-frame. **–eingang,** *m.* doorway. **–falle,** *f.* (*Swiss*) *see* **–griff. –feld,** *n.* *See* **–füllung. –flügel,** *m.* leaf *or* wing of a door. **–füllung,** *f.* door-panel. **–giebel,** *m.* pediment (of a door). **–griff,** *m.* doorknob, door-handle. **–hüter,** *m.* 1. doorkeeper, porter, doorman; 2. (*Anat.*) pylorus.

Türke [ˈty:rkə], *m.* (**-n,** *pl.* **-n**) Turk. **Türkei** [–ˈkaɪ], *f.* ***die –,*** Turkey. **Türken|bund,** *m.* (*Bot.*) Turk's-cap (lily) (*Lilium martagon*). **–taube,** *f.* (*Orn.*) collared dove (*Streptopelia decaocto*). **Türkin,** *f.* Turkish woman.

Türkis [tyrˈki:s], *m.* (**-es,** *pl.* **-e**) turquoise. **türkisblau,** *adj.* turquoise (blue).

türkisch [ˈty:rkɪʃ], *adj.* Turkish; ***–e Bohne,*** scarlet-runner (bean); ***–er Honig,*** Turkish delight; ***–er Weizen,*** Indian corn. **türkischrot,** *adj.* Turkey red.

Tür|klinke, *f.* latch, door-handle. **–klopfer,** *m.* (door-)knocker.

Turkmene [turkˈme:nə], *m.* (**-n,** *pl.* **-n**) Turkoman. **turkmenisch,** *adj.* Turkoman, Turkmenian.

Turm [turm], *m.* (**-(e)s,** *pl.* **⸚e**) tower, spire, steeple, belfry; (*of tank*) turret, (*of submarine*) conning-tower; (*Hist.*) dungeon; (*Chess*) castle, rook.

Turmalin [turmaˈli:n], *m.* (**-s,** *pl.* **-e**) (*Min.*) tourmaline.

turmartig [ˈturmˀa:rtɪç], *adj.* tower-like, turreted; (*fig.*) towering. **Turmbau,** *m.* building of a tower; tower-like structure.

Türmchen [ˈtyrmçən], *n.* turret.

türmen [ˈtyrmən], **1.** *v.t.* pile (up). **2.** *v.r.* pile up, be piled high, tower (up), rise high. **3.** *v.i.* (*sl.*) bolt, clear off, do a bunk, skedaddle, vamose, sling one's hook. **Türmer,** *m.* (*Hist.*) watchman, look-out; jailer, gaoler, warder.

Turm|fahne, *f.* (weather-)vane. **–falke,** *m.* (*Orn.*) kestrel (*Falco tinnunculus*). **–geschütz,** *n.* turret-gun. **turmhoch, 1.** *adj.* towering, very high, lofty. **2.** *adv.* ***– überlegen sein*** (*Dat.*), tower above, be head and shoulders above, be vastly superior to. **Turm|lafette,** *f.* turret-mounting. **–schwalbe,** *f.* (*Orn.*) *see* **Mauersegler. –spitze,** *f.* spire. **–springen,** *n.* (*swimming*) high-diving. **–uhr,** *f.* tower-clock, church-clock. **–verlies,** *n.* dungeon, keep. **–wächter,** *m.* *See* **Türmer. –wagen,** *m.* tramways-department servicing vehicle. **–wart,** *m.* *See* **Türmer. –zinne,** *f.* battlement(s) of a tower.

Turn [turn], *m.* (*obs.*) *see* **Turm.**

Turnanzug [ˈturnˀantsu:k], *m.* P.T. *or* gym-dress.

Turnei [turˈnaɪ], *m. or n.* (**-(e)s,** *pl.* **-e**) (*obs.*) *see* **Turnier.**

turnen [turnən], *v.i.* 1. do gymnastics *or* P.T. *or* drill; 2. (*coll.*) wriggle out of a difficulty, wangle through. **Turnen,** *n.* gymnastics, drill, physical training (P.T.), callisthenics. **Turner,** *m.* gymnast. **turnerisch,** *adj.* gymnastic. **Turnerschaft,** *f.* group *or* squad of gymnasts, gymnastics club.

Turn|fest, *n.* gymnastic display. **–gerät,** *n.* gymnastic apparatus. **–halle,** *f.* gymnasium. **–hemd,** *n.* singlet, P.T. vest, gym-slip. **–hose,** *f.* P.T. shorts.

Turnier [turˈni:r], *n.* (**-s,** *pl.* **-e**) tournament, contest, (*Hist.*) jousting. **Turnier|bahn,** *f.,* **–platz,** *m.* the lists, tilt-yard. **–reiter,** *m.* competition rider. **–richter,** *m.* marshal of the lists. **–schranken,** *f.pl.* *See* **–bahn.**

Turn|lehrer, *m.* gym(nastic) instructor. **–platz,** *m.* open-air gymnasium, athletic grounds. **–riege,** *f.* *See* **Turnerschaft. –schuh,** *m.* gym(nasium) shoe, pump. **–spiele,** *n.pl.* indoor games. **–übung,** *f.* gymnastic exercise. **–unterricht,** *m.* P.T. lesson.

Turnüre [turˈny:rə], *f.* 1. bustle (*of dress*); 2. deportment.

Turnus [ˈturnus], *m.* (**-,** *pl.* **-se**) turn, cycle, rotation, sequence; ***im –,*** in rotation, by turns.

Turn|vater, *m.* the Old Man of gymnastics (Ludwig Jahn). **–verein,** *m.* gymnastics *or* athletic club. **–wart,** *m.* squad leader, gymnastics supervisor.

Tür|pfosten, *m.* door-post. **–rahmen,** *m.* door-frame. **–riegel,** *m.* bolt. **–schild,** *m.* door-plate, brass-plate. **–schließer,** *m.* 1. door-keeper; 2. door-spring. **–schwelle,** *f.* threshold. **–steher,** *m.* doorman, door-keeper, (*Law*) usher. **–sturz,** *m.* lintel.

Turteltaube [ˈturtəltaubə], *f.* (*Orn.*) turtle-dove (*Streptopelia turtur*).

Tusch [tuʃ], *m.* (**-(e)s,** *pl.* **-e**) 1. fanfare, flourish (of trumpets); 2. (*Studs. sl.*) challenge, affront.
Tusche ['tuʃə], *f.* watercolour; (water-proof) drawing-ink; ***schwarze*** or ***chinesische* –,** Indian ink.
tuscheln ['tuʃəln], *v.i., v.t.* mutter, whisper.
tuschen ['tuʃən], *v.t.* draw in Indian ink; colour-wash, paint in watercolours. **Tusch|farbe,** *f. See* **Tusche. –kasten,** *m.* paint-box. **–zeichnung,** *f.* watercolour drawing; sketch in Indian ink.
Tute ['tu:tə], *f.* (*dial.*) 1. *See* **Tüte**; 2. *See* **Tuthorn.**
Tüte ['ty:tə], *f.* paper bag; (*coll.*) (ice-cream) cone; candle extinguisher; (*coll.*) ***er muß –n kleben,*** he is doing time; (*coll.*) ***kommt nicht in die –!*** not on your life! nothing doing!
Tutel [tu'te:l], *f.* guardianship.
tuten ['tu:tən], *v.i., v.t.* blow one's horn, (*coll.*) toot(le), honk; (*coll.*) ***von Tuten und Blasen hat er keine Ahnung,*** he doesn't know the first thing about it, he hasn't the least idea, he doesn't know a hawk from a handsaw. **Tuthorn,** *n.* (*obs.*) bugle.
Tütte ['tytə], **Tutte** ['tutə], *f.* (*dial.*) nipple, teat, pap, dug; (*sl.*) tit.
Tuttel ['tytəl], *m.,* **Tüttelchen,** *n.* dot; tittle, jot.
Twiete ['tvi:tə], *f.* (*dial.*) narrow side-street, alley.
Twing(er) ['tvɪŋər], *m.* (*dial.*) *see* **Zwing, Zwinger.**
[1]**Twist** [tvɪst], *m.* (**-es,** *pl.* **-e**) darning-thread.
[2]**Twist,** *m.,* **twisten,** *v.i.* (*dancing*) twist.
Typ [ty:p], *m.* (**-s,** *pl.* **-en**) type, standard, model, prototype. **Type,** *f.* 1. (*Typ.*) type; 2. (*Tech.*) *see* **Typ;** 3. (*coll.*) crank, eccentric, (queer) card, character; ***finstere* –,** ugly customer. **Typen|druck,** *m.* type-printing. **–hebel,** *m.* type-bar (*typewriter*). **–muster,** *n.* standard sample.
typhös [ty'fø:z], *adj.* typhoid. **Typhus** ['ty:fus], *m.* typhoid (fever). **Typhus|impfung,** *f.* anti-typhoid inoculation. **–kranke(r),** *m., f.* typhoid patient.
typisch ['ty:pɪʃ], *adj.* typical (*für,* of); **– *sein für,*** typify, be typical of; (*coll.*) ***das ist – Molly,*** that's Molly all over; ***das Typische,*** the typical character *or* feature. **typisieren** [–'zi:rən], *v.t.* typify; (*Tech.*) standardize.
Typograph [typo'gra:f], *m.* (**-en,** *pl.* **-en**) typographer. **typographisch,** *adj.* typographic(al).
Typus ['ty:pus], *m.* (-, *pl.* **-pen**) *see* **Typ.**
Tyrann [ty'ran], *m.* (**-en,** *pl.* **-en**) tyrant, despot. **Tyrannei** [–'naɪ], *f.* tyranny, despotism.
Tyrannen|mord, *m.* (*act*), **–mörder,** *m.* (*p.*) tyrannicide. **tyrannisch,** *adj.* tyrannical, despotic, power-loving, domineering. **tyrannisieren** [–i'zi:rən], *v.t.* tyrannize over, oppress, enslave.

U

U, u [u:], *n.* U, u; ***ihm ein X für ein U machen,*** deceive *or* humbug *or* cheat *or* dupe him, (*coll.*) take him in, pull his leg. *See List of Abbreviations.*
U-bahn, *f. See* **Untergrundbahn.**
übel ['y:bəl], **1.** *adj.* (*üble(r, –s)*; *comp.* ***übler,*** *sup.* ***übelst***) evil, bad, wrong; sick, ill; ***ihm einen üblen Dienst erweisen,*** do him a bad turn, treat him badly *or* shabbily, (*coll.*) play a dirty trick on him; ***übler Kerl,*** ugly customer, (*coll.*) bad lot; ***kein übler Kerl,*** not a bad sort; ***in einer üblen Lage,*** in a fix *or* mess; ***üble Laune,*** bad temper *or* humour; ***nicht – Lust haben,*** have a (good) mind, be inclined (*with inf.*); ***ihn in üble Nachrede bringen,*** slander him, speak ill of him, give him a bad name; ***nicht* –,** rather nice, not bad, (*coll.*) pretty good; ***in üblem Ruf stehen,*** have a bad name, be in bad odour; ***mir ist*** or ***wird* –,** I do not feel well, I feel sick; ***auf ihn – zu sprechen sein,*** not have a good word to say of him; ***übler Streich,*** nasty *or* (*coll.*) dirty trick; ***dabei kann einem – werden,*** it is enough to make one sick, it is sickening. **2.** *adv.* badly, ill; **– *angebracht,*** misplaced, inappropriate; **– *ankommen,*** catch a Tartar; ***bei ihm – angeschrieben sein,*** be in his bad books; **– *aufnehmen,*** take in bad part, take amiss; **– *aufgenommen werden,*** be ill received; **– *auslegen,*** put a wrong construction on, misconstrue; ***es bekam ihm* –,** he came off badly, he paid (dearly) for it; (*Med.*) it did not agree with him; **– *beraten,*** ill advised; **– *daran sein,*** be in a bad way; **– *deuten,*** see **– *auslegen***; ***es gefällt ihm nicht* –,** he rather likes it; **– *gelaunt,*** in a bad mood, cross; ***ihm – mitspielen,*** use him ill, play a nasty *or* (*coll.*) dirty trick on him; **– *riechen,*** smell bad(ly), have an unpleasant *or* offensive smell; ***wohl oder* –,** willy-nilly, come what may, cost what it may, at all costs, in any case; **– *zumute,*** ill at ease, uncomfortable.
Übel, *n.* evil; complaint, ailment, malady, disease; inconvenience, nuisance, (*coll.*) pest; misfortune, calamity; grievance, abuse; ***das kleinere* –,** the lesser of two evils; ***vom* –,** harmful, no good; (*B.*) ***was darüber ist, das ist vom* –,** whatsoever is more cometh of evil.
Übelbefinden ['y:bəlbəfɪndən], *n.* indisposition.
übel|beraten, *adj.* ill-advised. **–berüchtigt,** *adj.* ill-famed. **–gelaunt,** *adj.* ill-humoured, bad-tempered cross, grumpy. **–gesinnt,** *adj.* ill-disposed (*Dat.,* towards); ***ihm – sein,*** bear him a grudge.
Übelkeit ['y:bəlkaɪt], *f.* sickness, nausea; (*fig.*) disgust; **– *verursachen,*** be sickening, make one feel sick, turn one's stomach.
übel|nehmen, *irr.v.t.* take amiss *or* ill *or* in bad part, take offence at, resent. **–nehmend, –nehm(er)isch,** *adj.* easily offended, touchy. **–riechend,** *adj.* evil-smelling, smelly, fetid, foul, offensive, malodorous. **Übel|stand,** *m.* defect, disadvantage, drawback, nuisance, inconvenience, *pl.* abuses. **–tat,** *f.* misdeed, misdemeanour. **–täter,** *m.* wrongdoer, evil-doer, miscreant, malefactor. **–wollen,** *n.* ill-will, malevolence, enmity. **übel|-wollen,** *irr.v.i.* ***ihm* –,** bear him a grudge, bear a grudge against him, bear him ill-will, wish him ill, wish ill to him, (*coll.*) have it in for him. **–wollend,** *adj.* hostile, malevolent, ill-disposed, spiteful.
üben ['y:bən], **1.** *v.t., v.i.* exercise, (*Mil.*) drill, (*Mil., Spt.*) train; practise (*also Mus.*); ***Barmherzigkeit* –,** show mercy (***an*** (*Dat.*), to); ***Geduld* –,** have patience, be patient; ***Gerechtigkeit* –,** exercise justice; do justice (***gegen,*** to); ***Gewalt* –,** use violence; ***ein Handwerk* –,** pursue *or* carry on a trade; ***Nachsicht* –,** show consideration, bear and forbear, (*coll.*) stretch a point; ***Rache* –,** take vengeance *or* revenge (***an*** (*Dat.*), on). **2.** *v.r.* do training; ***sich im Schwimmen* –,** practise swimming, do swimming practice; ***geübt,*** skilled, skilful, practised, experienced, well versed (***in*** (*Dat.*), in); ***mit geübter Hand,*** skilfully, deftly, with a cunning *or* skilful hand; ***geübtes Auge,*** trained *or* practised eye.
über ['y:bər], **1.** *prep. with Dat. when implying rest or limited motion; with Acc. when implying transfer or motion across, to, past or over, and in figurative uses without reference to motion*; over, above, on top of, higher than; superior to, more than, exceeding; in the process of, during, while; across, beyond, over, on the other side of; by way of, via; through *or* by the agency of; on account of, about, concerning, with regard to, relating to, as to, dealing with, (up)on. (*The many idiomatic expressions using* ***über*** *should be sought under the more characteristic word notably in the case of verbal constructions with –, e.g.* ***herfallen –, herrschen –, hinauswachsen –, klagen –, nachdenken –, reden –, verfügen –, sich entrüsten –, sich freuen –, sich hermachen –, sich hinwegsetzen –,*** *etc.*; *here follows only a sample illustrating more difficult usages.*)
(a) (*place, fig.*) ***das geht – alles,*** there's nothing to

equal *or* nothing like this, that beats everything; ***das geht mir – alles andere,*** I prize that above *or* prefer that to everything else; ***ein Mal – das andere,*** time upon *or* after time, time and again, again and again; – ***der Arbeit sein,*** be at work; – ***alle Begriffe sein,*** pass comprehension, be beyond all conception; – ***alle Berge sein,*** be gone, be far away; – ***Berg und Tal,*** up hill and down dale; ***Briefe – Brief,*** letter after *or* upon letter, one letter after another; ***eins – den Durst trinken,*** have one over the eight; – ***alles Erwarten,*** beyond (all) expectation; – ***die Neugierde hinaus sein,*** be past *or* above curiosity; – ***das Maß des Erlaubten gehen,*** go beyond what is permissible, exceed the permitted limits, (*coll.*) go too far; ***man vergaß den Dichter – dem Menschen,*** one forgot the poet in the man; – ***die Straße verkaufen,*** sell (*alcohol*) outdoor.

(b) (*time or quantity*) ***heute – acht Tage,*** this day week; ***heute –s Jahr,*** a year from today; – ***eine Woche her,*** over a *or* more than a week (ago); – ***kurz oder lang,*** sooner or later; ***5 minuten – 2,*** 5 minutes past 2; – ***Mittag,*** during the lunch-hour; – ***Nacht,*** overnight, during the night; – ***dem Essen,*** during the meal, while eating; – ***den Sommer,*** over the *or* in the course of the summer, the whole summer; – ***100 Studenten,*** more than 100 students.

2. *adv.* over, above, too much, in excess; – ***und –,*** through and through, out and out, completely, thoroughly, entirely; ***die ganze Zeit –,*** all along; (*Mil.*) ***Gewehr –!*** shoulder arms! (*coll.*) ***es ist mir –,*** I'm sick (and tired) of it; ***ihm darin – sein,*** surpass *or* outdo him in it, have the better of him there.

Über–, über–, *pref. to nouns and adjs.* over-, super-, supra-, per-, hyper-; *see the alphabetical list following.*

über–, *verb pref. In compound v.i. the pref. is generally insep.; with most compound v.t. the pref. may be both sep. and insep.; when sep. the pref. carries the accent and its meaning is more or less literal; when insep. and unstressed the meaning is more or less figurative. See the alphabetical list following.*

überall [y:bər'al], *adv.* everywhere; all over, throughout; – ***wo,*** wherever. **überallher** [–'he:r], *adv.* ***von –,*** from all sides *or* quarters. **überallhin** [–'hɪn], *adv.* everywhere, in every direction, in all directions.

überaltert [y:bər'altərt], *adj.* grown too old, superannuated.

Überangebot ['y:bərˀangəbo:t], *n.* **(-(e)s,** *pl.* **-e)** excessive supply.

überanstrengen [y:bər'anʃtrɛŋən], *v.t., v.r.* (*insep.*) (*p.p.* ***überanstrengt***) overwork, over-exert, (over)-strain. **Überanstrengung,** *f.* over-exertion, overstrain.

überantworten [y:bər'antvɔrtən], *v.t.* (*insep.*) deliver up, surrender, consign (*Dat.*, to).

überarbeiten [y:bərˀarbaɪtən], **1.** *v.i.* (*sep.*) work overtime. **2.** *v.t.* revise, go over, retouch, touch up. **3.** *v.r.* (*insep.*) overwork, work too hard. **überarbeitet,** *adj.* overworked; overwrought. **Überarbeitung,** *f.* revision, retouching, touching up; overwork, (nervous) exhaustion.

Überärmel ['y:bərˀɛrməl], *m.* sleeve protector.

überaus ['y:bərˀaus], *adv.* exceedingly, extremely.

Überbau ['y:bərbau], *m.* **(-(e)s,** *pl.* **-e** *or* **-ten)** superstructure; projecting part. **überbauen, 1.** *v.t.* (*insep.*) build over *or* on top of. **2.** *v.i.* (*sep.*) build a projection (*over another building*); build above; build higher.

überbeanspruchen ['y:bərbəˀanʃpruxən], *v.t.* (*insep.*) overload, overstress; (*fig.*) overtax, overstrain.

Überbein ['y:bərbaɪn], *n.* **(-s,** *pl.* **-e)** (*Surg.*) exostosis; ganglion (*in the sinews*); node; (*Vet.*) bone-spavin.

überbelasten [y:bərbə'lastən], *v.t.* (*insep.*) overload. **Überbelastung,** *f.* overloading.

überbelichten [y:bərbə'lɪçtən], *v.t.* (*insep.*) (*Phot.*) over-expose. **Überbelichtung,** *f.* over-exposure.

Überbett ['y:bərbɛt], *n.* quilt, coverlet.

überbewerten [y:bərbə've:rtən], *v.t.* (*insep.*) overestimate, overvalue.

überbieten [y:bər'bi:tən], (*insep.*) **1.** *irr.v.t.* outbid; (*fig.*) outdo, excel, beat, surpass; ***den Rekord –,*** break the record. **2.** *irr.v.r.* ***sie – sich in Höflichkeit,*** they vie with each other in civilities.

überbinden [y:bər'bɪndən], *irr.v.t.* (*insep.*) (*Swiss*) impose (*Dat.*, on).

überbleiben ['y:bərblaɪbən], *irr.v.i.* (*aux.* s.) (*sep. p.p.* ***übergeblieben***) remain (over), be left over; (*insep.*) (*only in p.p.*) ***überblieben,*** surviving. **Überbleibsel,** *n.* remainder, remains, relic, residue; vestige, remnant, (*coll. of meal*) left-overs.

Überblick ['y:bərblɪk], *m.* survey, view, prospect; (*fig.*) general view, conspectus, review, synopsis, summary (***über*** (*Acc.*), of); ***an – fehlen,*** lack perspective. **überblicken** [–'blɪkən], *v.t.* (*insep.*) glance over, survey, take in at a glance; assess.

Überbliebene(r) [y:bər'bli:bənə(r)], *m., f.* survivor (*see* **überbleiben**).

überborden [y:bər'bɔrdən], *v.i.* (*aux.* h. *or* s.) (*insep.*) (*Swiss*) deteriorate, degenerate; go too far.

Überbrettl ['y:bərbrɛtl], *n.* **(-s,** *pl.* **-)** cabaret, variety theatre.

überbringen [y:bər'brɪŋən], *irr.v.t.* (*insep.*) bring, take, deliver, convey, carry (*Dat.*, to). **Überbringer,** *m.* bearer. **Überbringung,** *f.* delivery, transmission, conveyance.

überbrücken [y:bər'brykən], *v.t.* (*insep.*) bridge-span; (*fig.*) bridge over, reconcile, settle (*a difference*). **Überbrückung,** *f.* spanning; settlement. **Überbrückungs|hilfe,** *f.* resettlement allowance, stop-gap relief. **–kredit,** *m.* short-term *or* bridging loan.

überbürden [y:bər'by:rdən], *v.t.* (*insep.*) overload, overburden. **Überbürdung,** *f.* overburdening, overwork, pressure of work.

überchlorsauer ['y:bərklo:rzauər], *adj.* (*Chem.*) perchlorate of.

überdachen [y:bər'daxən], *v.t.* (*insep.*) roof (over *or* in).

überdauern [y:bər'dauərn], *v.t.* (*insep.*) outlast, outlive, survive.

überdecken ['y:bərdɛkən], *v.t.* (*sep.*) stretch over, spread out over; (*insep.*) cover up *or* over, conceal, veil, shroud, mask; overlap.

überdem [y:bər'de:m], *adv. See* **überdies.**

überdenken [y:bər'dɛŋkən], *irr.v.t.* (*insep.*) think over, reflect *or* meditate on, consider.

überdies [y:bər'di:s], *adv.* besides, moreover, what is more.

Überdosis ['y:bərdo:sɪs], *f.* overdose.

überdrehen [y:bər'dre:ən], *v.t.* (*insep.*) overwind (*a watch*); strip (*thread of screw*).

Überdruck ['y:bərdruk], *m.* **(-(e)s,** *pl.* **-e)** overprint; surcharge (*postage stamps*); excess pressure; transfer, transfer printing. **Überdruckanzug,** *m.* high-pressure suit. **überdrucken** [–'drukən], *v.t.* (*insep.*) overprint. **Überdruckkabine,** *f.* (*Av.*) pressurized cabin.

Überdruß ['y:bərdrus], *m.* boredom, ennui; satiety, disgust; ***zum – werden,*** become boring *or* a bore; ***bis zum –,*** to the point of satiety; ***Überfluß bringt –,*** abundance begets indifference. **überdrüssig,** *adj.* (*Acc. or Gen.*) sick *or* tired *or* weary of; satiated *or* disgusted *or* bored with.

überdurchschnittlich ['y:bərdurçʃnɪtlɪç], *adj.* above-average, outstanding, exceptional.

übereck [y:bər'ɛk], *adv.* (*dial.*) across, crosswise, diagonally.

Übereifer ['y:bərˀaɪfər], *m.* excessive zeal. **übereifrig,** *adj.* over-zealous.

übereignen [y:bər'aɪgnən], *v.t.* (*insep.*) transfer, assign, convey, make over (*Dat.*, to). **Übereignung,** *f.* (*Law*) transfer, assignment, conveyance.

übereilen [y:bər'aɪlən], (*insep.*) **1.** *v.t.* precipitate, (*coll.*) rush (*a decision etc.*), scamp (*work*); ***die Nacht übereilte uns,*** night overtook us. **2.** *v.t.* be in too much of *or* too great a hurry, be precipitate, act rashly *or* inconsiderately, (*coll.*) overshoot the mark. **übereilt,** *adj.* premature, rash, precipitate, over-hasty, unguarded, thoughtless. **Übereilung,** *f.* precipitancy, hastiness, rashness; overhaste, heedlessness.

übereinander [y:bərˀaɪn'andər], *adv.* one upon the other *or* another, superimposed. **übereinander|-greifen,** *irr.v.i.* overlap. **–lagern,** *v.t.* superimpose. **–legen,** *v.t.* lay one upon another, pile up. **–schlagen,** 1. *irr.v.t.* cross (*legs*), fold (*arms*). 2. *irr.v.i. See* **–greifen. –setzen,** *v.t. See* **–lagern.**

übereinkommen [y:bər'aɪnkɔmən], *irr.v.i.* (*sep.*) (*aux.* s.) (*p.p.* ***übereingekommen***) come to an agreement *or* to terms, reach an agreement (***über*** (*Acc.*), on *or* about). **Übereinkommen,** *n.*, **Übereinkunft,** *f.* agreement, understanding, arrangement, settlement, compromise; contract, pact, treaty; ***ein(e) – treffen,*** come to *or* make *or* reach an agreement; ***laut –,*** by agreement, as agreed (upon) *or* arranged; ***stillschweigende(s) –,*** tacit agreement.

übereinstimmen [y:bər'aɪnʃtɪmən], *v.i.* (*sep.*) (*p.p.* ***übereingestimmt***) (*of a p.*) ***mit ihm über*** or ***in*** (*Acc.*) **–**, agree *or* be in agreement with him on *or* about, concur with him in, share his opinion of; (*coll.*) see eye to eye with him about; (*of a th.*) accord, harmonize, be in agreement *or* (*coll.*) keeping, tally, coincide, (*coll.*) square (***mit,*** with), correspond (to *or* with). **übereinstimmend,** 1. *adj.* agreeing, harmonious; (*fig.*) corresponding, conformable, consistent, concurring, congruous; identical. 2. *adv.* **– *mit,*** in conformity *or* accordance *or* (*coll.*) keeping *or* line with. **Übereinstimmung,** *f.* agreement, conformity, accord, concord, harmony, unison, correspondence, concurrence; ***in – bringen,*** reconcile; synchronize.

überempfindlich ['y:bərˀɛmpfɪntlɪç], *adj.* hypersensitive, (*Med.*) allergic.

überessen [y:bərˀɛsən], 1. *irr.v.r.* (*insep.*) (*p.p.* ***übergessen***) overeat. 2. *irr.v.t.* (*sep.*) (*p.p.* ***übergegessen***) ***sich*** (*Dat.*) ***etwas –,*** have a surfeit of a th.

überfahren [y:bərfa:rən], 1. *irr.v.i.* (*sep.*) (*aux.* s.) pass over, cross. 2. *irr.v.t.* (*insep.*) traverse, cross (*river etc.*); pass over, stroke, rub (*surface with s.th.*); run over (*a p.*); pass, overrun (*a certain point*); (*fig.*) ride roughshod over, (*coll.*) walk all over, (*Spt.*) trounce, (*sl.*) lick; (*sep.*) convey *or* ferry across. **Überfahrt,** *f.* passage, crossing (*by ship*).

Überfall ['y:bərfal], *m.* surprise attack, raid; inroad, invasion; hold-up; overfall, weir. **überfallen,** (*insep.*) 1. *irr.v.t.* fall upon suddenly, attack without warning, surprise; invade, raid; assault, hold up; overtake (*as nightfall, illness etc.*); ***vom Regen –,*** caught in the rain; ***der Schlaf überfiel mich,*** sleep stole up on me; ***Schrecken überfiel uns,*** we were seized with terror. 2. *irr.v.imp.* (*fig.*) ***plötzlich überfiel es ihn,*** suddenly he fancied, it came to him suddenly. 3. ['y:bər–] *irr.v.i.* (*sep.*) (*aux.* s.) fall over (*to the other side*).

überfällig ['y:bərfɛlɪç], *adj.* overdue.

Überfall|kommando, *n.* raiding party, flying *or* (*Am.*) riot squad. **–krieg,** *m.* undeclared war. **–rohr,** *n.* overflow pipe.

überfein ['y:bərfaɪn], *adj.* over-refined, superfine; (*fig.*) fastidious. **überfeinern** [–'faɪnərn], *v.t.* (*insep.*) over-refine. **Überfeinerung,** *f.* over-refinement, fastidiousness.

überfliegen 1. ['y:bərfli:gən], *irr.v.i.* (*sep.*) (*aux.* s.) fly over *or* across. 2. [–'fli:gən] *irr.v.t.* (*insep.*) fly over, pass, swiftly across; (*with the eyes*) run *or* glance over, skim through; ***den Kanal –,*** fly (over) the Channel; ***ihr Antlitz überflog ein roter Schein,*** the colour rose to her face.

überfließen 1. ['y:bərfli:sən], *irr.v.i.* (*sep.*) (*aux.* s.) flow over, overflow; be overflowing (***vor Freude, u.s.w.,*** with joy *etc.*). 2. [–'fli:sən] *irr.v.t.* (*insep.*) inundate, submerge, flood.

überflügeln [y:bər'fly:gəln], *v.t.* (*insep.*) (*Mil.*) outflank; (*fig.*) surpass, outstrip, outdo.

Überfluß ['y:bərflus], *m.* profusion, plenty, (super)-abundance, surplus, excess, wealth, superfluity, (*Comm.*) glut (***an*** (*Dat.*), of); ***im – haben, – haben an,*** have plenty of, abound in; ***zum –,*** unnecessarily, needlessly; (*Prov.*) ***– bringt Überdruß,*** abundance begets indifference. **überflüssig,** *adj.* superfluous, unnecessary, uncalled-for; excess, surplus, left over; (*B.*) running over; ***– machen,*** render unnecessary *or* superfluous.

überfluten 1. ['y:bərflu:tən], *v.i.* (*sep.*) (*aux.* s.) over flow. 2. [–'flu:tən], *v.t.* (*insep.*) inundate, flood, swamp. **überflutet,** *adj.* (*Naut.*) awash. **Überflutung,** *f.* flooding, inundation, overflow.

überfordern [y:bər'fɔrdərn], *v.t., v.i.* (*insep.*) demand too much, overcharge; (*fig.*) overstrain, overtax. **Überforderung,** *f.* exorbitant demand, excessive charge, overcharge; (*fig.*) overstrain, overwork.

Überfracht ['y:bərfraxt], *f.* overweight, overload; (charge for) excess luggage.

überfragen [y:bər'fra:gən], *v.t., v.i.* (*insep.*) (*Swiss*) overwhelm with questions; ***da bin ich überfragt,*** I'm afraid I don't know.

Überfremdung [y:bər'frɛmduŋ], *f.* foreign influence *or* penetration, infiltration of foreigners *or* foreign goods.

Überfuhr ['y:bərfu:r], *f.* (*Austr.*) ferry.

überführen [y:bərfy:rən], *irr.v.t.* (*sep. or insep.*) conduct *or* lead across, transport, ferry across; convert, bring over (*to an opinion*); (*Chem.*) convert, transform (***in*** (*Acc.*), into); (*insep.*) convey; transport (*a corpse*) in state; (*Comm.*) transfer (*money*); (*Law*) convict, find guilty (*Gen.*, of), (*fig.*) convince (*Gen.*, of). **Überführung** [–'fy:ruŋ], *f.* transport(ation), conveyance, ferrying; (*Law*) conviction; crossing, viaduct, roadbridge, (*Am.*) overpass.

Überfülle ['y:bərfylə], *f.* superabundance, profusion, excess, repletion, plethora; exuberance (*of spirits etc.*). **überfüllen** [–'fylən], *v.t.* (*insep.*) overfill, overload, surfeit, overstock, glut (*a market*); crowd, cram. **Überfüllung,** *f.* overfilling, overloading, overcrowding; cramming, surfeit, repletion; (*traffic*) congestion; (*Comm.*) overstocking, oversupply, glut.

überfüttern [y:bər'fytərn], *v.t.* (*insep.*) overfeed, gorge.

Übergabe ['y:bərga:bə], *f.* delivery, conveyance, transfer, submission, handing over, (*Mil.*) surrender, capitulation.

Übergang ['y:bərgaŋ], *m.* (**-s,** *pl.* **⸚e**) 1. passage, crossing, (*Railw.*) level *or* (*Am.*) grade crossing; 2. transition, change(-over), conversion; (*Law*) assignment, devolution; desertion, going over (*to the enemy*); 3. *pl.* (*Paint., Mus.*) shades, nuances, blending.

Übergangs|bestimmungen, *f.pl.* provisional *or* transitional *or* temporary arrangements. **–farbe,** *f.* half-tone, intermediate shade. **–gebirge,** *n.* (*Geol.*) transition *or* secondary rocks. **–kleidung,** *f.* between-seasons wear. **–stadium,** *n.* transition stage. **–stelle,** *f.* crossing place. **–zeit,** *f.* transition period. **–zustand,** *m.* state of transition; temporary arrangement.

übergeben [y:bər'ge:bən], 1. *irr.v.t.* (*insep.*) give *or* deliver up, hand over, remit, present (*Dat.*, to), place in the hands (of), entrust, consign, commit (to); surrender; ***dem Druck –,*** have printed; ***eigenhändig –,*** deliver personally; ***den Flammen –,*** consign to the flames; ***dem Gericht –,*** take to court; ***dem Verkehr –,*** open to traffic. 2. *irr.v.r.* (*insep.*) 1. surrender, capitulate; 2. vomit, be sick.

Übergebot ['y:bərgəbo:t], *n.* higher bid.

übergehen ['y:bərge:ən], 1. *irr.v.i.* (*sep.*) (*aux.* s.) flow *or* run over, overflow; cross *or* go *or* pass over (***zu,*** to), devolve (***auf*** (*Acc.*), upon); desert; change, turn, (*of colours*) merge, fade (***in*** (*Acc.*), into); turn, proceed, (*coll.*) switch over (***zu,*** to); ***die Augen gingen ihm über,*** his eyes filled with tears; ***in seinen Besitz –,*** pass to him, pass into his possession; ***in Fäulnis –,*** become rotten; ***in andere Hände –,*** change hands; ***der Druckfehler ist in alle folgenden Ausgaben übergegangen,*** the misprint has been perpetuated in all subsequent editions;

zum Angriff –, take the offensive; *zur Gegenpartei* –, change sides. **2.** [–'ge:ən], *irr.v.t.* (*insep.*) pass over, pass by, neglect, omit, leave out, overlook, ignore, (*coll.*) skip; *mit Stillschweigen* –, pass over in silence.

Übergehung [y:bər'ge:uŋ], *f.* omission, neglect; passing over (*in silence*); (*Rhet.*) pretermission.

übergenug ['y:bərgənu:k], *adv.* more than enough, ample; – *haben,* have enough and to spare.

übergeordnet ['y:bərgəordnət], *adj.* superior, higher.

Übergewicht ['y:bərgəvıçt], *n.* overweight, excess weight; (*fig.*) preponderance, predominance, ascendancy, superiority; *das – bekommen,* lose its balance, become top-heavy; (*fig.*) get the upper hand, prevail; *das – haben,* predominate.

übergießen 1. ['y:bərgi:sən], *irr.v.t.* (*sep.*) pour carelessly, spill; 2. [–gi:sən], (*insep.*) pour (*a liquid*) on *or* over; water, sprinkle, douche, douse; baste (*meat*), ice, glaze (*cake*); (*Chem.*) transfuse; (*fig.*) suffuse; *mit Licht* –, bathe in light; *es übergoß ihm purpurrot,* he flushed crimson.

überglasen [y:bər'gla:zən], *v.t.* (*insep.*) ice, glaze (*cake*).

überglücklich ['y:bərglyklıç], *adj.* extremely happy, delighted, overjoyed.

übergreifen ['y:bərgraıfən], *irr.v.i.* (*sep.*) overlap; (*Mus.*) shift (*on violin etc.*); (*fig.*) spread (***auf*** or ***in*** (*Acc.*), to), encroach, infringe (upon). **Übergriff,** *m.* encroachment, infringement, inroad (***auf*** (*Acc.*), on).

übergroß ['y:bərgro:s], *adj.* oversize, outsize, immense, huge, enormous, colossal.

Überguß ['y:bərgus], *m.* crust, covering, (*on cakes*) icing, topping.

überhaben ['y:bərha:bən], *irr.v.t.* (*sep.*) have on (*over other clothes*); have left over, have remaining; (*coll.*) be sick (and tired) of, be fed up with.

überhalten [y:bər'haltən], *irr.v.t.* (*insep.*) (*Austr.*) overcharge.

Überhand ['y:bər'hant], *f.* (*obs.*) the upper hand. **Überhand|nahme** [y:bər'hant–], *f. See* **–nehmen. überhandnehmen,** *irr.v.i.* (*sep.*) *p.p. überhandgenommen*) prevail, gain ground, get *or* gain the upper hand; spread, increase. **Überhandnehmen,** *n.* prevalence; growth, increase, spread.

Überhang ['y:bərhaŋ], *m.* 1. (*Archit.*) projection; curtain, hangings; (*of rocks*) cornice, overhang; 2. (*fig.*) excess, surplus (*money etc.*), residue, backlog, carry-over (*work etc.*). **überhangen,** *irr.v.i.* (*sep.*) hang over, overhang, project, jut out.

überhängen, **1.** *reg.v.t.* 1. ['y:bərhɛŋən], (*sep.*) hang (*s.th.*) over; (*as a cloak*) put on, throw round one's shoulders, (*as a bag or rifle*) sling over one's shoulder; 2. [–'hɛŋən], (*insep.*) cover, drape. **2.** *irr.v.i.* (*sep.*) *see* **überhangen.**

überhapps ['y:bərhaps], *adv.* (*Austr.*) approximately, roughly, about.

überhasten [y:bər'hastən], *v.t.*, *v.i.* (*insep.*) hurry *or* race through, (*Mus. etc.*) take too quickly. **überhastet,** **1.** *adj.* overhasty, precipitate. **2.** *adv.* overhastily.

überhäufen [y:bər'hɔyfən], *v.t.* (*insep.*) load, overwhelm, (*coll.*) swamp (***mit,*** with); overload, overstock, glut (*the market*).

überhaupt [y:bər'haupt], *adv.* generally (speaking), in general, on the whole, after all, altogether; actually, really, at all; – ***nicht,*** not . . . at all; – ***kein,*** no . . . whatever; – ***keine,*** none at all, none whatever; ***gibt es – eine Möglichkeit?*** is there any chance (at all *or* whatever)? ***wenn –,*** if at all; ***was willst du –?*** what are you getting at?

überheben [y:bər'he:bən], **1.** *irr.v.t.* (*insep.*) exempt, excuse (*Gen.*, from); spare, save (*trouble etc.*). **2.** *irr.v.r.* (*insep.*) strain o.s.; (*fig.*) be overbearing *or* overweening, presume too much. **überheblich,** *adj.* overbearing, overweening, presumptuous, arrogant. **Überheblichkeit, Überhebung,** *f.* arrogance, presumption.

überheizen [y:bər'haıtsən], *v.t.* (*insep.*) overheat (*a room*), (*Tech.*) superheat.

überhin [y:bər'hın], *adv.* superficially, sketchily; ***ein Buch nur – lesen,*** skim (through) a book; (*dial.*) *see* **überdies.**

überhitzen [y:bər'hıtsən], *v.t.* (*insep.*) *see* **überheizen**; (*fig.*) ***überhitztes Gemüt,*** fiery temperament.

überhöhen [y:bər'hø:ən], *v.t.* (*insep.*) surmount, command; put up *or* raise (*prices*) excessively, make (*prices*) prohibitive; (*Geom.*) increase. **überhöht,** *adj.* banked, cambered (*road*), (*Railw.*) superelevated; (*of prices*) excessive, exorbitant, prohibitive. **Überhöhung,** *f.* banking, camber (*of road*), (*Railw.*) superelevation; (*of prices*) exorbitant rise *or* increase.

überholen **1.** *v.t.* ['y:bərho:lən], 1. (*sep.*) take *or* bring over to *or* fetch over from the other side; ferry across; bring across (*sails*); 2. [–'ho:lən] (*insep.*) overtake, pass, overhaul, out-distance, out-pace, (*fig.*) outstrip, surpass; (*Tech.*) overhaul, recondition, service, put in order. **2.** ['y:bər–] *v.i.* (*sep.*) (*Naut.*) heel (over). **Überholen,** *n.* (*Motor etc.*) overtaking, passing. **überholt,** *adj.* antiquated, out of date, outmoded; (*Tech.*) overhauled, reconditioned; – ***durch,*** superseded by. **Überholung,** *f.* (*Tech.*) overhaul, reconditioning, servicing.

überhören [y:bər'hø:rən], *v.t.* (*insep.*) not pay attention to, not hear *or* (*coll.*) catch, miss, (*intentionally*) ignore, turn a deaf ear to; (*coll.*) ***das will ich überhört haben!*** don't ever say that again!

überirdisch ['y:bərˀırdıʃ], *adj.* super-terrestrial, unworldly, spiritual, celestial, heavenly, divine; supernatural, unearthly.

überjährig ['y:bərjɛ:rıç], *adj.* more than a year old, last year's; (*fig.*) too old, superannuated.

überkippen ['y:bərkıpən], *v.t.*, *v.i.* (*aux.* s.) (*sep.*) tip *or* topple *or* (*v.i. only*) fall over, overturn, upset; (*of a p.*) (*v.i. only*) lose one's balance.

Überkleid ['y:bərklaıt], *n.* outer garment; tunic, overall. **Überkleidung,** *f.* top clothes.

überklug ['y:bərklu:k], *adj.* too clever (by half), conceited, pert, cheeky.

überkochen **1.** *v.i.* ['y:bərkɔxən], (*sep.*) (*aux.* s.) boil over, (*fig.*) boil, seethe (*with rage etc.*). **2.** [–'kɔxən] *v.t.* (*insep.*) bring up to the boil once more.

überkommen [y:bər'kɔmən], **1.** *irr.v.i.* (*aux.* s.) (*insep.*) come down, be handed down (*Dat.*, to). **2.** *irr.v.t.* (*insep.*) receive, have handed down; be overcome by; ***Angst überkam sie,*** they were overcome *or* seized *or* gripped by fear. **3.** *adj.* traditional, conventional, accepted.

überladen, **1.** *irr.v.t.* ['y:bərla:dən], 1. (*sep.*) tranship, trans-ship; 2. [–'la:dən], (*insep.*) overload, overburden; overcharge, surfeit. **2.** [–'la:dən] *adj.* florid, ornate, flamboyant, pretentious, bombastic.

überlagern [y:bər'la:gərn], *v.t.* (*insep.*) superimpose, overlap, overlie, overlay, (*Rad.*) heterodyne. **Überlagerung,** *f.* overlaying, superimposition, (*Rad.*) heterodyning, jamming. **Überlagerungs|empfänger,** *m.* (*Rad.*) superheterodyne receiver, (*coll.*) superhet. **–röhre,** *f.* (*Rad.*) baretter.

Überland|bahn ['y:bərlant–], *f.* inter-city tramway. **–flug,** *m.* cross-country flight. **–leitung,** *f.* (*Elec.*) overhead cables. **–zentrale,** *f.* power station supplying the grid.

überlassen, **1.** *irr.v.t.* ['y:bərlasən], 1. (*sep.*) leave (over *or* remaining); 2. (*insep.*) [–'lasən] (*Dat.*) give up, relinquish, abandon, cede, make over, leave, entrust (to), let (*a p.*) have; ***zur Miete –,*** let; ***käuflich –,*** sell; – ***Sie das mir,*** leave that to me; ***es ist ihm –, was er tun will,*** it is left to him to do *or* he is at liberty to do as he pleases; ***ihn sich*** (*Dat.*) ***selbst –,*** leave him to himself *or* to his own resources *or* devices. **2.** [–'lasən] *irr.v.r.* (*insep.*) give way, give o.s. up, abandon o.s. (*Dat.*, to). **Überlassung** *f.* leaving, abandonment, yielding up, cession.

Überlast ['y:bərlast], *f.* overload, overweight. **überlasten** [–'lastən], *v.t.* (*insep.*) overload; (*fig.*) overtax, overburden, overstrain. **Überlastung,** *f.* overload, (*fig.*) overstrain, overwork, severe pressure of work.

Überlauf ['y:bərlauf], *m.* 1. overflow, spillway; 2. (*Elec.*) flash-over; 3. (*Comm.*) net profit.

überlaufen, 1. [y:bər'laufən], *irr.v.t.* (*insep.*) run all over, spread over, overrun; (*fig.*) overwhelm, deluge, besiege, pester, importune; ***die Gegend ist* –,** the district is overrun *or* overcrowded; ***es überläuft mich,*** I shudder, my blood runs cold; ***es überlief ihn ein kalter Schauer,*** a cold shudder seized him. **2.** ['y:bər–] *irr.v.i.* (*sep.*) (*aux.* s.) run *or* flow over, overflow; boil over; (*Mil.*) desert, go over (***zu,*** to); ***die Augen laufen ihm über,*** the tears run down his cheeks; ***die Galle läuft ihm über,*** his blood boils; ***die Farben laufen ineinander über,*** the colours run (into one another).

Überläufer ['y:bərlɔyfər], *m.* (*Mil.*) deserter; (*Eccl.*) apostate; (*Pol.*) turncoat.

Überlauf|rohr ['y:bərlauf–], *n.* overflow pipe. **–ventil,** *n.* overflow trap.

überlaut ['y:bərlaut], *adj.* too loud; (too) noisy, uproarious, deafening.

überleben [y:bər'le:bən], (*insep.*) **1.** *v.t.* outlive, survive; ***das überlebe ich nicht,*** that will be the death of me. **2.** *v.r.* (*insep.*) become out-of-date, be antiquated; ***das hat sich überlebt,*** that has had its day, that has gone out of fashion. **Überlebende(r),** *m., f.* survivor. **überlebensgroß** ['y:bər–], *adj.* more than life-size; larger than life. **Überlebensrente,** *f.* reversionary *or* survivorship annuity.

überlebt [y:bər'le:pt], *adj.* antiquated, obsolete, out of date *or* of fashion, outmoded.

[1]**überlegen** ['y:bərle:gən], **1.** (*sep.*) *v.t.* lay over, cover with; (*coll.*) ***ein Kind* –,** put a child over one's knee. **2.** *v.r.* (*sep.*) lean *or* bend over, heel over (*of a ship*). **3.** [–'le:gən], *v.t.* (*insep.*) reflect on, think *or* ponder over, weigh, consider; ***noch einmal* –,** reconsider; ***es sich*** (*Dat.*) ***wieder*** or ***anders* –,** change one's mind; ***ich werde es mir* –,** I shall think the matter over, I shall think about it; ***wenn ich es mir recht überlege,*** on second thoughts; ***das würde ich mir zweimal* –,** I should think twice about that.

[2]**überlegen** [y:bər'le:gən], *adj.* (*Dat.*) superior to, excelling, surpassing, more than a match for (***an*** (*Dat.*), in). **Überlegenheit,** *f.* superiority, dominance, ascendancy, preponderance.

überlegt [y:bər'le:kt], *adj.* premeditated, considered, deliberate; prudent, circumspect, judicious, discreet, guarded; ***alles wohl* –,** taking everything into account. **Überlegtheit,** *f.* deliberation, care, premeditation, circumspection, discretion, studied demeanour, guarded manner.

Überlegung [y:bər'le:guŋ], *f.* reflection, thought, consideration, deliberation; ***nach reiflicher* –,** upon mature consideration; ***bei näherer*** or ***nochmaliger* –,** on second thoughts; ***mit* –,** deliberately, intentionally, with premeditation; ***ohne* –,** inconsiderately, unpremeditatedly, blindly, (*coll.*) on the spur of the moment, without giving it a second thought.

überlei [y:bər'laɪ], *adv.* (*dial.*) *see* **übrig.**

überleiten ['y:bərlaɪtən], (*sep.*) **1.** *v.t.* lead *or* conduct over *or* across; (*Med.*) transfuse (*blood*). **2.** *v.i.* lead over, transfer, form a transition (***zu,*** to).

überlesen [y:bər'le:zən], *irr.v.t.* (*insep.*) 1. read *or* run through *or* over; 2. overlook in reading.

überliefern [y:bər'li:fərn], *v.t.* (*insep.*) deliver, hand over; transmit, hand down, pass on, (*Mil.*) surrender (*Dat.*, to). **überliefert,** *adj.* traditional. **Überlieferung,** *f.* 1. delivery; (*Mil.*) surrender; 2. (*fig.*) tradition.

Überliege|geld ['y:bərli:gə–], *n.* demurrage. **–tage,** *m. pl.,* **–zeit,** *f.* (days of) demurrage.

überlisten [y:bər'lɪstən], *v.t.* (*insep.*) outwit; deceive, dupe, (*coll.*) outsmart.

überm ['y:bərm] = ***über dem.***

übermachen [y:bər'maxən], *v.t.* (*insep.*) make *or* hand over, bequeath; consign, (*money*) remit (*Dat.*, to).

Übermacht ['y:bərmaxt], *f.* superior strength *or* force, superiority, (*fig.*) predominance. **übermächtig,** *adj.* overwhelming, too powerful, (*fig.*) predominant, paramount.

übermalen [y:bər'ma:lən], *v.t.* (*usu. insep.*) paint over *or* out, cover up with paint.

übermangansauer ['y:bərmaŋga:nzauər], *adj.* (*Chem.*) permanganate of.

übermannen [y:bər'manən], *v.t.* (*insep.*) overcome, overpower, overwhelm, subdue.

Übermantel ['y:bərmantəl], *m.* overcoat, greatcoat.

Übermaß ['y:bərma:s], *n.* excess; abundance, superfluity; ***im* –** or ***bis zum* –,** to excess, excessively. **übermäßig, 1.** *adj.* excessive, extreme, immoderate, undue. **2.** *adv.* too much, excessively, immoderately, unduly.

Übermensch ['y:bərmɛnʃ], *m.* superman, demigod. **übermenschlich,** *adj.* superhuman; godlike; (*coll.*) excessive, enormous; ***sich* – *anstrengen,*** make superhuman efforts.

übermitteln [y:bər'mɪtəln], *v.t.* (*insep.*) convey; deliver, hand over, transmit (*Dat.*, to). **Übermitt(e)lung,** *f.* conveyance; delivery, transmission.

übermodern ['y:bərmodɛrn], *adj.* ultra-modern.

übermorgen ['y:bərmɔrgən], *adv.* the day after tomorrow; ***morgen oder* –,** tomorrow or the day after.

übermüdet [y:bər'my:dət], *adj.* overtired, tired out. **Übermüdung,** *f.* overfatigue, great weariness.

Übermut ['y:bərmu:t], *m.* high spirits; wantonness; arrogance, insolence, presumption; bravado; (*Prov.*) **– *tut selten gut,*** look before you leap. **übermütig,** *adj.* high-spirited, frolicsome, playful, wanton; arrogant, insolent, presumptuous, (*coll.*) cocky.

übern ['y:bərn], (*Poet.*) = ***über den.***

übernächst ['y:bərnɛ:çst], *adj.* the next but one; ***–e Woche,*** the week after next; ***am –en Tag,*** the day after tomorrow.

übernachten [y:bər'naxtən], (*insep.*) **1.** *v.i.* stay overnight, pass *or* spend the night. **2.** *v.t.* (*obs.*) take in for the night, give a night's lodging to. **übernächtig(t)** ['y:bərnɛçtɪç(t)], *adj.* tired out, fatigued (from lack of sleep), worn out, haggard, heavy- *or* bleary-eyed, (*coll.*) with the bed on one's back; (*coll.*) ***aussehen,*** look tired to death.

Übernachtung [y:bər'naxtuŋ], *f.* spending *or* staying the night; lodging for the night, overnight lodging *or* accommodation. **Übernachtungs|geld,** *n.* lodging allowance. **–möglichkeit,** *f.* (facilities for) overnight accommodation.

Übernahme ['y:bərna:mə], *f.* taking over, acceptance, taking possession *or* charge of, taking in hand, undertaking, taking upon o.s.; (*Comm.*) take-over; assumption, adoption, acceptance; ***– eines Amtes,*** entering upon *or* succession to an office; ***– einer Arbeit,*** undertaking a task; ***– einer Erbschaft,*** succession to a legacy, entering upon an inheritance. **Übernahme|angebot,** *n.* take-over bid. **–bedingungen,** *f.pl.* conditions of acceptance. **Übernahmsstelle,** *f.* (*Austr.*) *see* **Annahmestelle.**

Übername ['y:bərna:mə], *m.* (*dial.*) nickname.

übernatürlich ['y:bərnaty:rlɪç], *adj.* supernatural, miraculous.

übernehmen [y:bər'ne:mən], **1.** *irr.v.t.* (*insep.*) take possession of, accept, receive; take over, take charge of; take upon o.s., undertake (*work*); assume (*responsibility*), enter upon, succeed to (*an office*); ***sich vom Zorne – lassen,*** allow o.s. to be overcome with rage; ***Bürgschaft* –,** stand security; (*Comm.*) ***übernommene Gefahr,*** risk subscribed; (*Rad.*) ***übernommene Sendung,*** outside broadcast, (*Am.*) hook-up. **2.** *irr.v.r.* (*insep.*) over-exert *or* overstrain o.s., overwork; overeat; (*fig.*) undertake too much, overreach o.s., (*coll.*) bite off more than one can chew. **3.** ['y:bər–], *irr.v.t.* (*sep.*) take over *or* across, transfer; cover over with; ship (*a sea*); ***ein Gewehr* –,** shoulder a rifle. **Übernehmer** [–'ne:mər], *m.* receiver; contractor; (*Comm.*) acceptor, drawee; (*Law*) assign, transferee.

überordnen ['y:bərˀɔrdnən], *v.t.* (*sep.*) place, set (*Dat.*, above *or* over).

überort [y:bər'ɔrt], *adv.* (*dial.*) *see* **übereck.**
Überoxyd ['y:bər'ɔksy:t], *n.* (*Chem.*) (su)peroxide.
überparteilich ['y:bərpartaılıç], *adj.* (*Pol.*) non-party.
Überpflanzung [y:bər'pflantsuŋ], *f.* (*Surg.*) graft(ing), transplantation.
Überproduktion ['y:bərproduktsio:n], *f.* over-production.
überprüfen [y:bər'pry:fən], *v.t.* (*insep.*) examine, test, scrutinize, investigate, inspect, study; (*Pol.*) screen; check, verify, review, revise. **Überprüfung,** *f.* examination, investigation, inspection, scrutiny, test, check, review, revision; audit, verification; (*Pol.*) screening.
überquellen ['y:bərkvɛlən], *irr.v.i.* (*sep.*) overflow (*also fig.*).
überquer [y:bər'kve:r], *adv.* (*obs.*) across, crosswise, crossways, diagonally; ***es geht mir –,*** all my efforts come to nothing, everything goes wrong. **überqueren,** *v.t.* cross, traverse. **Überquerung,** *f.* crossing.
überragen [y:bər'ra:gən], *v.t.* (*insep.*) overtop, rise *or* tower above; extend beyond; overlook; (*fig.*) tower above, surpass, transcend, (*also v.i.*) excel. **überragend,** *adj.* (*fig.*) outstanding, surpassing, paramount.
überraschen [y:bər'raʃən], *v.t.* (*insep.*) (take by) surprise, take unawares; startle; ***vom Sturm überrascht,*** caught in the storm. **überraschend,** *adj.* astonishing, amazing, surprising, unexpected, startling. **Überraschung,** *f.* surprise. **Überraschungs|angriff,** *m.* surprise attack. **–moment,** *n.* element of surprise.
überrechnen [y:bər'rɛçnən], *v.t.* (*insep.*) calculate, reckon up; compute; run through, check (*an account*).
überreden [y:bər're:dən], *v.t.* (*insep.*) persuade, (*coll.*) talk round; ***ihn – etwas zu tun, ihn zu etwas –,*** persuade him to do a th., talk him into (doing) a th.; ***sich – lassen,*** allow o.s. to be persuaded *or* (*coll.*) to be talked round *or* talked into (*doing*). **überredend** *adj.* persuasive. **Überredung,** *f.* persuasion. **Überredungs|gabe,** *f.* (*of a p.*), **–kraft,** *f.* (*of a th.*) persuasiveness, power of persuasion.
überreich ['y:bərraıç], *adj.* too rich; extremely rich; (*fig.*) – ***an*** (*Dat.*), abounding in, teeming *or* overflowing with.
überreichen [y:bər'raıçən], *v.t.* (*insep.*) hand over, submit, present, deliver (*Dat.*, to).
überreichlich ['y:bərraıçlıç], **1.** *adj.* superabundant. **2.** *adv.* amply, in profusion.
Überreichung [y:bər'raıçuŋ], *f.* presentation, handing over, submission, delivery.
überreif ['y:bərraıf], *adj.* overripe.
überreizen [y:bər'raıtsən], *v.t.* (*insep.*) overexcite, overstimulate; overstrain; (*Cards*) outbid. **überreizt,** *adj.* over-excited, overwrought, (*coll.*) on edge. **Überreiztheit, Überreizung,** *f.* overexcitement, overwrought state, overstrain, nervous excitement.
überrennen [y:bər'rɛnən], *irr.v.t.* (*insep.*) run over, run down; (*Mil.*) overrun; (*fig.*) pester, importune.
Überrest ['y:bərrɛst], *m.* **(-(e)s,** *pl.* **-e)** rest, remains, remnant; residue, remainder; *pl.* remains, ruins, relics; ***sterbliche –e,*** mortal remains, (*Poet.*) ashes.
überrieseln 1. ['y:bərri:zəln], *v.i.* (*sep.*) trickle over. **2.** [–'ri:zəln] *v.t.* (*insep.*) irrigate.
Überrock ['y:bərrɔk], *m.* overcoat, top-coat; frock coat; top skirt.
überrumpeln [y:bər'rumpəln], *v.t.* (*insep.*) (take by) surprise, take *or* catch unawares; ***sich – lassen,*** be caught by surprise, be caught unawares *or* (*coll.*) napping. **Überrump(e)lung,** *f.* surprise, (*Mil.*) surprise attack.
überrunden [y:bər'rundən], *v.t.* (*insep.*) (*Spt.*) lap.
übers ['y:bərs] = ***über das.***
übersät [y:bər'zɛ:t], *adj.* littered, strewn, dotted, studded.
übersatt ['y:bərzat], *adj.* surfeited, gorged (*Gen. or* ***von,*** with). **übersättigen** [–'zɛtıgən], *v.t.* (*insep.*) surfeit, satiate; (*Chem.*) supersaturate, (*Tech.*) superheat (*steam*); (*fig.*) (*coll.*) ***übersättigt von,*** fed up with, sick (and tired) of. **Übersättigung,** *f.* (*Chem.*) supersaturation; satiation, surfeit, satiety.
übersäuern [y:bər'zɔyərn], *v.t.* (*insep.*) make too acid, over-acidify. **Übersäuerung,** *f.* hyper-acidity.
Überschall– ['y:bərʃal], *pref.* supersonic.
überschatten [y:bər'ʃatən], *v.t.* (*insep.*) over-shadow (*also fig.*), (*fig.*) throw into the shade.
überschätzen [y:bər'ʃɛtsən], *v.t.* (*insep.*) think too highly of, overrate, overestimate; assess too heavily (*a house*). **Überschätzung,** *f.* over-estimate; over-estimation.
Überschau ['y:bərʃau], *f. See* **Übersicht** *or* **Überblick. überschauen** [–'ʃauən], *v.t.* (*insep.*) over-look, survey, command a view of; (*fig.*) comprehend, grasp.
überschäumen ['y:bərʃɔymən], *v.i.* (*aux.* s.) (*sep.*) froth over; (*fig.*) brim *or* bubble over (***vor*** (*Dat.*), with). **überschäumend,** *adj.* (*fig.*) ebullient, exuberant.
Überschicht ['y:bərʃıçt], *f.* overtime *or* extra shift.
überschießen, 1. [y:bər'ʃi:sən], *irr.v.t.* (*insep.*) fire across *or* over; shoot too high; overshoot (*the mark*); outshoot, shoot better than. **2.** ['y:bərʃi:sən], *irr.v.i.* (*sep.*) (*aux.* s.) shoot *or* fly *or* gush *or* fall over; (*as milk*) boil over; (*fig.*) be surplus *or* in excess. **überschießend,** *adj.* (*Naut.*) shifting (*of ballast*), (*fig.*) surplus, left over.
überschlächtig ['y:bərʃlɛçtıç], *adj.* overshot (*of a water-wheel*).
überschlafen [y:bər'ʃla:fən], *irr.v.t.* (*insep.*) sleep on (*an idea*).
Überschlag ['y:bərʃla:k], *m.* somersault, (*Gymn.*) handspring, (*Av.*) loop; (*Dressm.*) facing; (*Elec.*) flashover; turn (*of the scale*); (*fig.*) rough calculation, estimate; (*Av.*) – ***über den Flügel,*** barrel roll.
überschlagen, 1. ['y:bərʃla:gən], *irr.v.t.* **1.** (*sep.*) throw *or* lay *or* spread over; fold over; cross (*one's legs*). **2.** [–'ʃla:gən] *v.t.* (*insep.*) skip, miss, pass over, omit, leave out; calculate roughly, estimate; drown (*a sound*). **3.** *v.i.* (*aux.* s.) (*sep.*) 1. turn over; tumble over; (*Elec.*) (*of spark*) flash across; 2. (*of the voice*) crack, break. **4.** *v.r.* (*insep.*) go head over heels, (turn a) somersault; tumble over, (*Motor.*) overturn, (*Naut.*) capsize, (*Av.*) loop the loop; (*of events*) follow hot on the heels of each other; (*fig.*) ***sich vor Hilfsbereitschaft*** (***fast***) –, fall over o.s. to be helpful. **5.** *adj.* lukewarm, tepid.
über|schlägig, *adj. See* **–schläglich.**
Überschlaglaken ['y:bərʃla:kla:kən], *n.* top sheet.
überschläglich ['y:bərʃlɛ:klıç], *adj.* approximate, rough, estimated.
Überschlagrechnung ['y:bərʃla:krɛçnuŋ], *f.* rough estimate, rough calculation.
überschnappen ['y:bərʃnapən], *v.i.* (*sep.*) (*aux.* s.) snap *or* slip *or* jerk over; (*fig.*) go crazy, lose one's head; ***die Stimme schnappte über,*** (his *etc.*) voice cracked; (*coll.*) ***übergeschnappt,*** cracked, off one's head, dotty, crazy.
überschneiden [y:bər'ʃnaıdən], *irr.v.t., v.r.* (*insep.*) intersect, cross, cut (each other); overlap. **Überschneidung,** *f.* (point of) intersection; overlap(ping).
überschreiben [y:bər'ʃraıbən], *irr.v.t.* (*insep.*) 1. entitle, label, head, mark, address; dedicate; superscribe, inscribe; 2. (*Comm.*) make *or* sign over, transfer, remit (*Dat.*, to), (*in the books*) carry over.
überschreien [y:bər'ʃraıən], (*insep.*) **1.** *irr.v.t.* shout louder than, shout *or* cry down. **2.** *irr.v.r.* shout o.s. hoarse, strain one's voice.
überschreiten [y:bər'ʃraıtən], *irr.v.t.* (*insep.*) go across, step *or* stride *or* pass over, cross; ford (*a stream*); (*fig.*) overstep, overrun, transcend, go beyond, exceed; fail to meet (*a time limit*), trans-

gress, infringe (*laws*), overdraw (*one's account*); ***das überschreitet alles Maß,*** that oversteps all bounds, that goes too far; ***sein Einkommen –,*** spend beyond one's means, overspend. **Überschreitung,** *f.* crossing; transgression, infringement; exceeding, overrunning, transcending.

Überschrift ['y:bərʃrɪft], *f.* superscription, inscription, heading, title, (*newspapers*) headline.

Überschuh ['y:bərʃu:], *m.* overshoe, golosh (*usu. pl.*).

überschuldet [y:bər'ʃuldət], *adj.* involved in debt, heavily encumbered. **Überschuldung,** *f.* heavy indebtedness *or* encumbrance.

Überschuß ['y:bərʃus], *m.* surplus, excess; (*Comm.*) balance, (profit) margin, profit. **überschüssig,** *adj.* surplus, excess.

überschütten ['y:bərʃytən], *v.t.* (*sep.*) upset, spill; [–'ʃytən] (*insep.*) pour over *or* on, cover, (*fig.*) shower, load, overwhelm.

Überschwang ['y:bərʃvaŋ], *m.* superabundance, excess, (*fig.*) ebullience, rapture, exuberance.

überschwappen ['y:bərʃvapən], (*sep.*) **1.** *v.i.* spill; slop *or* splash over. **2.** *v.t.* (*coll.*) *see* **überschütten.**

überschwemmen [y:bər'ʃvɛmən], *v.t.* (*insep.*) inundate, flood, submerge; (*fig.*) flood, swamp, deluge; (*Comm.*) overstock, flood, glut (*the market*). **Überschwemmung,** *f.* inundation, flooding, flood. **Überschwemmungskatastrophe,** *f.* flood disaster.

überschwenglich ['y:bərʃvɛŋlɪç], *adj.* superabundant, boundless, excessive; exuberant, effusive, high-flown, rapturous, extravagant, (*coll.*) gushing. **Überschwenglichkeit,** *f.* excess, exuberance, effusiveness, extravagance, (*coll.*) gush.

Übersee ['y:bərze:], *f.* overseas; ***nach – gehen,*** go overseas; ***Bestellungen aus –,*** oversea(s) orders. **Übersee|dampfer,** *m.* ocean liner. **–handel,** *m.* overseas trade. **überseeisch,** *adj.* oversea(s), transoceanic; colonial, foreign (*markets*).

übersegeln [y:bər'ze:gəln], *v.t.* (*insep.*) sail faster than; run foul of, run down (*a ship*).

übersehbar [y:bər'ze:ba:r], *adj.* visible at a glance, in full view.

übersehen [y:bər'ze:ən], *irr.v.t.* (*insep.*) 1. take in at a glance, survey, run the eye over, glance over; 2. overlook, omit, miss, fail to *or* not see *or* notice, take no notice of, disregard, ignore, (*coll.*) wink at, shut one's eyes to, make allowances for (*failings etc.*); ***von ihm – werden,*** escape his notice. *See* **überblicken.**

überselig ['y:bərze:lɪç], *adj.* overjoyed, transported *or* delirious with joy.

übersenden [y:bər'zɛndən], *irr.v.t.* (*insep.*) send, transmit, forward; consign, ship (*freight*); remit (*money*). **Übersender,** *m.* consignor, sender, remitter; forwarding agent. **Übersendung,** *f.* transmission, sending; consignment, shipment; remittance.

übersetzbar [y:bər'zɛtsba:r], *adj.* translatable.

übersetzen, 1. ['y:bərzɛtsən], *v.t.* (*sep.*) carry *or* ferry across, transport. **2.** [–'zɛtsən] *v.t.* (*insep.*) translate, render (*in* (*Acc.*), into), interpret; adapt (*for the stage etc.*); (*Tech.*) gear; ***wörtlich*** or ***wortgetreu –,*** translate literally; ***frei –,*** give a free rendering; ***falsch –,*** mistranslate. **Übersetzer,** *m.* translator, interpreter. **Übersetzung,** *f.* 1. crossing (*by ferry*); 2. translation (***aus,*** from; ***in*** (*Acc.*), into); version; 3. (*Tech.*) gear(ing), transmission; ***kleine –,*** bottom gear; ***doppelte –,*** two-speed gear; ***größte –,*** top gear. **Übersetzungs|fehler,** *m.* mistranslation, faulty rendering. **–getriebe,** *n.* transmission gearing. **–verhältnis,** *n.* gear-ratio.

Übersicht ['y:bərzɪçt], *f.* view, sight, prospect; (*fig.*) survey, review; outline, abstract, summary, synopsis, digest; control, supervision. **übersichtig,** *adj.* (*obs.*) *see* **weitsichtig. Übersichtigkeit,** *f.* (*obs.*) *see* **Weitsichtigkeit. übersichtlich,** *adj.* easy to take in at a glance, (*of terrain*) open; (*fig.*) clear, distinct, lucid, clearly arranged, synoptic(al). **Übersichtlichkeit,** *f.* clearness, clarity, lucidity; perspicuity. **Übersichts|karte,** *f.* general map, index map. **–tabelle, –tafel,** *f.* synoptical table, tabular summary.

übersiedeln [y:bərzi:dəln], *v.i.* (*sep. or insep.*) (*aux.* s.) emigrate; remove, move (***nach,*** to). **Übersied(e)lung,** *f.* emigration; removal.

übersinnlich ['y:bərzɪnlɪç], *adj.* supernatural, spiritual, immaterial; supersensual; transcendental.

übersommern [y:bər'zɔmərn], (*insep.*) **1.** *v.t.* keep through the summer. **2.** *v.i.* (*aux.* s.) spend *or* pass the summer (*in a place*).

überspannen, 1. ['y:bərʃpanən], *v.t.* (*sep.*) stretch over. **2.** [–'ʃpanən] *v.t.* (*insep.*) spread over, cover; overstretch, overstrain, (*fig.*) overexcite; exaggerate, carry *or* push too far (*one's demands etc.*); (*fig.*) ***den Bogen –,*** go too far, force the issue, overdo it. **überspannt,** *adj.* overstrained, exaggerated, extravagant, high-flown, fantastic, crazy, eccentric. **Überspanntheit,** *f.* exaltation, excitement, excitability; extravagance, eccentricity. **Überspannung,** *f.* over-tension, overstrain(ing), (*Elec.*) excess voltage, (*fig.*) exaggeration.

überspielen [y:bər'ʃpi:lən], *v.t.* (*insep.*) outmanœuvre (*also Spt. and fig.*), (*Theat.*) over-play, over-act. **überspielt,** *adj.* (*Spt.*) out of form, played out; (*Austr.*) (*as a piano*) overplayed, played to death.

überspinnen [y:bər'ʃpɪnən], *irr.v.t.* (*insep.*) wind over *or* round, enclose (*as in a cocoon*), cover; ***übersponnene Saiten,*** silver (covered) strings; ***übersponnener Kupferdraht,*** covered copper wire.

überspitzen [y:bər'ʃpɪtsən], *v.t.* (*insep.*) exaggerate, overdo. **überspitzt,** *adj.* over-subtle, exaggerated, (*coll.*) footling.

überspringen, 1. [y:bər'ʃprɪŋən], *irr.v.t.* (*insep.*) 1. leap (across), jump over, clear (*an obstacle*), (*fig.*) omit, miss, skip; ***ihn im Amte –,*** be promoted over his head; 2. (*dial.*) strain, sprain (*an ankle etc.*). **2.** ['y:bərʃprɪŋən] *irr.v.i.* (*sep.*) (*aux.* s.) leap over; pass over (to); (*Elec.*) flash across *or* over; (*fig.*) ***– von . . . zu,*** dart *or* flit from . . . to; (*Med.*) ***– auf*** (*Acc.*), spread to.

übersprudeln ['y:bərʃpru:dəln], *v.i.* (*sep.*) (*aux.* s.) bubble *or* gush over. **übersprudelnd,** *adj.* (*fig.*) exuberant, sparkling.

überstaatlich ['y:bərʃta:tlɪç], *adj.* international, cosmopolitan.

Überständer ['y:bərʃtɛndər], *m.* (*For.*) old tree, *pl.* old standing. **überständig,** *adj.* outworn, stale, flat, vapid, decrepit; ***–e Frucht,*** over-ripe fruit.

überstechen [y:bər'ʃtɛçən], *irr.v.t., v.i.* (*insep.*) play a higher card, trump higher.

überstehen, 1. [y:bər'ʃte:ən], *irr.v.t.* (*insep.*) endure, overcome, surmount, stand; weather, survive, go through, get over; ***er hat*** (***es***) ***überstanden,*** he is gone to rest, he has died. **2.** ['y:bərʃte:ən] *irr.v.i.* (*sep.*) stand *or* jut out, project, hang over; overlap.

übersteigen, 1. [y:bər'ʃtaɪgən], *irr.v.t.* (*insep.*) step *or* climb *or* get over; cross, traverse; (*fig.*) surmount, overcome (*difficulties*), exceed, surpass, go beyond, pass (*expectations, understanding etc.*), be too much for (*one's strength*). **2.** ['y:bərʃtaɪgən] *v.i.* (*aux.* s.) (*sep.*) step over *or* across, climb over, cross.

übersteigern [y:bər'ʃtaɪgərn], *v.t.* (*insep.*) push *or* force up (*prices*); outbid (*a p.*); (*fig.*) overdo, exaggerate. **übersteigert,** *adj.* excessive, exaggerated.

überstellen [y:bər'ʃtɛlən], *v.t.* (*insep.*) (*Austr.*) transfer (*an official to another post*).

überstimmen [y:bər'ʃtɪmən], *v.t.* (*insep.*) (*Mus.*) tune too high *or* above concert-pitch; out-vote, vote down, overrule.

überstrahlen [y:bər'ʃtra:lən], *v.t.* (*insep.*) shine upon, irradiate; (*fig.*) outshine, eclipse, put into the shade.

überstreichen [y:bər'ʃtraɪçən], *irr.v.t.* (*insep.*) paint over; ***mit Firnis –,*** varnish; (***mit***) ***schwarz –,*** black(en) out.

überstreifen ['y:bərʃtraɪfən], *v.t.* (*sep.*) slip over.

überströmen [y:bər'ʃtrø:mən], **1.** *v.t.* (*insep.*) inundate, deluge, flood. **2.** *v.i.* (*sep.*) (*aux.* s.) flow *or* run over, overflow; (*fig.*) overflow, abound (*vor* (*Dat.*), with); ***vor Freude –,*** exult.

Überstrumpf ['y:bərʃtrumpf], *m.* legging (*usu. pl.*).

überstülpen ['y:bərʃtylpən], *v.t.* (*sep.*) put on, cover over with.

Überstunden ['y:bərʃtundən], *f.pl.* overtime; ***– machen,*** work overtime. **Überstundengelder,** *n.pl.* overtime pay.

überstürzen [y:bər'ʃtyrtsən], (*insep.*) **1.** *v.t.* precipitate, hurry, rush, do rashly *or* in a hurry. **2.** *v.r.* act hastily *or* rashly *or* precipitately; follow in rapid succession, press on each other. **überstürzt,** *adj.* rash, hasty, precipitate; headlong. **Überstürzung,** *f.* hurry, rush, precipitancy, rashness; ***nur keine –!*** do not act rashly! there's no hurry! take it easy! take your time!

übertäuben [y:bər'tɔybən], *v.t.* (*insep.*) stun, deafen; stifle.

überteuern [y:bər'tɔyərn], *v.t.* (*insep.*) charge too much for; raise, push up (*price*). **Überteu(e)rung,** *f.* rise in prices, overcharging.

übertölpeln [y:bər'tœlpəln], *v.t.* (*insep.*) deceive, cheat, dupe, (*coll.*) take (*a p.*) in, bamboozle. **Übertölp(e)lung,** *f.* imposition, duplicity, double-dealing, trickery.

übertönen [y:bər'tø:nən], *v.t.* (*insep.*) drown, rise above, be louder than (*a sound*).

Übertrag ['y:bərtra:k], *m.* **(-(e)s,** *pl.* **¨-e)** (*Comm.*) amount brought *or* carried forward, balance. **übertragbar** [–'tra:kba:r], *adj.* (*Comm.*) transferable, negotiable; (*Med.*) infectious, contagious, communicable, (*coll.*) catching; translatable. **Übertragbarkeit,** *f.* (*Comm.*) transferability, negotiability; (*Med.*) infectiousness, contagiousness.

übertragen [y:bər'tra:gən], **1.** *irr.v.t.* (*insep.*) (*Comm.*) transfer, carry over, bring *or* carry forward; (*Med.*) transmit, communicate, infect with; (*Rad.*) transmit, broadcast, relay; translate, render, transcribe (*in* (*Acc.*), into); ***– auf*** (*Acc.*), transfer *or* assign *or* convey *or* make over to, confer upon, entrust *or* delegate to; charge *or* commission *or* vest (*a p.*) with; ***Blut –,*** transfuse blood; ***Haut –,*** graft *or* transplant skin. **2.** *irr.v.r.* (*insep.*) (*Med.*) be infectious *or* (*coll.*) catching; (*fig.*) communicate itself (***auf*** (*Acc.*), to) (*as panic etc.*); ***die Krankheit übertrug sich auf ihn,*** he caught the disease. **3.** *adj.* ***–e Bedeutung,*** figurative sense, metaphorical meaning; (*Austr.*) ***–e Kleider,*** worn(-out) *or* second-hand clothes.

Übertragung [y:bər'tra:guŋ], *f.* transference, carrying over; (*Comm.*) transfer (*of book-debts*); conveyance (*of real estate*), endorsement (*of a bill of exchange*); cession, delegation (*of powers*), assignment, transfer (*of rights*), conferring (*of an office*); translating, translation, transcription, (*Med.*) communication, spreading, infection, (*Rad.*) transmission, broadcast (programme), relay(ing); transfusion (*of blood*), graft(ing), transplantation (*of skin, kidney etc.*). **Übertragungsurkunde,** *f.* (*real estate*) deed of conveyance, (*shares*) transfer deed.

übertreffen [y:bər'trɛfən], (*insep.*) **1.** *irr.v.t.* surpass, excel, outdo, outstrip (*a p.*), exceed, beat, surpass (*a th.*) (***an*** or ***in*** (*Dat.*), in); ***alle Erwartungen –,*** exceed *or* surpass all expectations. **2.** *irr.v.r.* do better than usual, surpass *or* excel o.s.

übertreiben [y:bər'traɪbən], (*insep.*) **1.** *irr.v.t.* carry too far, carry to excess; exaggerate, overstate (*a case*), overact, overdo (*a part*). **2.** *irr.v.i.* (*insep.*) exaggerate, be given to exaggeration, (*coll.*) draw the long bow, lay it on thick; ***see*** **übertrieben. Übertreibung,** *f.* exaggeration, over-statement; excess, extravagance.

übertreten, 1. [y:bər'tre:tən], *irr.v.t.* (*insep.*) overstep, transgress, violate, infringe, trespass against, break (*the law*); ***sich*** (*Dat.*) ***den Fuß –*** or ***sich*** (*Acc.*) ***–,*** strain one's ankle. **2.** ['y:bərtre:tən] *irr.v.i.* (*sep.*) (*aux.* s.) (*Spt.*) step over; overflow (its banks) (*of rivers*); ***– zu*** or ***in*** (*Acc.*), go *or* change over to, join (*a party etc.*); ***er ist zum Katholizismus übergetreten,*** he has become a *or* turned Catholic.

Übertreter [y:bər'tre:tər], *m.* trespasser, offender, transgressor. **Übertretung,** *f.* transgression, trespass; offence, misdemeanour; infringement, breach, violation (*of a law*).

übertrieben [y:bər'tri:bən], *adj.* exaggerated, excessive, extreme, overdone, boundless, extravagant, immoderate, unreasonable, exorbitant; ***leicht –,*** mildly *or* slightly exaggerated; ***in –em Maße,*** to an exaggerated degree, excessively; ***aus –em Eifer,*** through excessive zeal.

Übertritt ['y:bərtrɪt], *m.* **(-(e)s,** *pl.* **-e)** going over (***zu*** or ***in*** (*Acc.*), to), joining (*a party*); change (*of religion*), conversion.

übertrumpfen [y:bər'trumpfən], *v.t.* (*insep.*) trump higher; (*fig.*) surpass, outdo, (*coll.*) go one better than.

übertünchen [y:bər'tynçən], *v.t.* (*insep.*) whitewash; (*fig.*) whitewash, varnish, gloss over; ***die Wahrheit –,*** veil the truth; ***übertünchte Höflichkeit,*** veneer of civility.

übervölkern [y:bər'fœlkərn], *v.t.* (*insep.*) over-populate. **Übervölkerung,** *f.* over-population.

übervoll ['y:bərfɔl], *adj.* brimful; overcrowded; ***– von,*** bursting *or* brimming with.

übervorteilen [y:bər'fo:rtaɪlən], *v.t.* (*insep.*) take advantage of, cheat, (*coll.*) do (down), take in.

überwachen [y:bər'vaxən], *v.t.* (*insep.*) watch over, control, inspect, supervise, superintend; (*Rad.*) monitor; (*Law*) keep under surveillance, (*coll.*) shadow. **Überwachung,** *f.* control, inspection, supervision, surveillance, (*Rad.*) monitoring. **Überwachungs|ausschuß,** *m.* control commission. **–stelle,** *f.* control board; control *or* check point.

überwachsen [y:bər'vaxsən], *irr.v.t.* (*insep.*) overgrow.

überwallen ['y:bərvalən], *v.i.* (*sep.*) (*aux.* s.) boil over.

überwältigen [y:bər'vɛltɪgən], *v.t.* (*insep.*) overcome, subdue, defeat, vanquish, conquer, subjugate, overpower, overwhelm. **überwältigend,** *adj.* imposing, overwhelming; (*iron.*) (*coll.*) ***nicht –,*** nothing to write home about, not so hot. **Überwältigung,** *f.* overwhelming defeat, subjugation.

Überwasser|fahrt ['y:bərvasər–], *f.* travelling on the surface (*submarines*). **–fahrzeug,** *n.* surface craft.

überweisen [y:bər'vaɪzən], *irr.v.t.* (*insep.*) assign transfer, make over, remit (*money*), refer (*decision*), send (*Dat. or* ***an*** (*Acc.*), to); (*Austr.*) convict (*criminal*); (*dial.*) ***ihn seines Irrtums –,*** convince him of his error. **Überweisung,** *f.* assignment, transfer, remittance (*of money*), (*Parl.*) reference (***an*** (*Acc.*), to), devolution (upon), (*Law*) committal. **Überweisungs|auftrag,** *m.* remittance order. **–formular,** *n.* transfer-form. **–scheck,** *m.* transfer-cheque. **–verkekr,** *m.* giro business.

überwendlich [y:bər'vɛntlɪç], **1.** *adj.* (*Dressm.*) whipped, overcast; ***–e Naht,*** overhand seam. **2.** *adv.* ***– nähen,*** oversew. **überwendlings,** *adv.* *See* **überwendlich, 2.**

überwerfen, 1. ['y:bərvɛrfən], *irr.v.t.* (*sep.*) throw over; ***einen Mantel –,*** throw a coat round one's shoulders, slip a coat on. **2.** [–'vɛrfən] *irr.v.r.* (*insep.*) fall out *or* quarrel (***mit,*** with).

überwiegen, 1. [y:bər'vi:gən], *irr.v.t.* (*insep.*) outweigh, weigh down. **2.** *irr.v.i.* (*insep.*) preponderate, prevail, predominate. **3.** ['y:bərvi:gən] *irr.v.i.* (*sep.*) be over-weight. **überwiegend, 1.** *adj.* predominant, preponderant, dominant, prevailing, dominating, paramount; ***–er Teil,*** majority, bulk; ***–e Mehrzahl,*** vast *or* overwhelming majority. **2.** *adv.* mainly, chiefly, predominantly.

überwindeln [y:bər'vɪndəln], *v.t.* (*insep.*) hem.

überwinden [y:bər'vɪndən], (*insep.*) **1.** *irr.v.t.* overcome, prevail over, overpower, conquer; subdue, vanquish, surmount, (*coll.*) get over (*obstacles*); ***überwundener Standpunkt,*** antiquated *or* outmoded *or* obsolete viewpoint, exploded idea. **2.** *irr.v.r.* ***ich kann mich nicht –,*** I cannot prevail on myself *or* bring myself (*to do*). **Überwinder,** *m.* conqueror. **Überwindung,** *f.* surmounting, overcoming; conquest, victory; self-control; ***das hat mich – gekostet,*** it cost me an effort; ***nur mit –,*** with great reluctance.

überwintern [y:bər'vɪntərn], (*insep.*) **1.** *v.t.* keep through the winter. **2.** *v.i.* winter, pass the winter; (*of animals*) hibernate. **Überwinterung,** *f.* wintering; hibernation.

überwölben [y:bər'vœlbən], *v.t.* (*insep.*) arch *or* vault over.

überwuchern, 1. [y:bər'vuxərn], *v.t.* (*insep.*) overgrow, overrun; (*fig.*) stifle. **2.** *v.i.* (*sep. & insep.*) (*aux.* s. & h.) grow luxuriantly. **Überwucherung,** *f.* hypertrophy.

Überwurf ['y:bərvurf], *m.* cloak, shawl, wrap; (bed- *or* divan-)cover; (*Tech.*) hasp. **Überwurfmutter,** *f.* screw-cap.

Überzahl ['y:bərtsa:l], *f.* superior numbers *or* (*Mil.*) forces, numerical superiority; ***große*** or ***starke –,*** heavy odds.

überzählen [y:bər'tsɛ:lən], *v.t.* (*insep.*) count over, recount, check. **überzählig** ['y:bər–], *adj.* surplus, spare, left over, supernumerary.

überzeichnen [y:bər'tsaɪçnən], *v.t.* (*insep.*) oversubscribe. **Überzeichnung,** *f.* over-subscription.

Überzeitarbeit ['y:bərtsaɪtˀarbaɪt], *f.* (*Swiss*) overtime.

überzeugen [y:bər'tsɔygən], (*insep.*) **1.** *v.t.* convince (***von,*** of), persuade (as to). **2.** *v.r.* satisfy o.s. (***von,*** about), make sure (of); – ***Sie sich selbst!*** go *or* come and see for yourself! **3.** *v.i.* be convincing, carry conviction. **überzeugend,** *adj.* convincing, compelling (*a p.*), conclusive, telling (*argument*); – ***wirken,*** be convincing, carry conviction. **überzeugt,** *adj.* assured, convinced, certain, sure, positive; firm, strong, unshakable (*believer etc.*). **Überzeugung,** *f.* persuasion; conviction, belief, assurance, certainty; ***der festen – sein,*** be thoroughly convinced; ***seiner – treu bleiben,*** hold firm to one's convictions. **Überzeugungskraft,** *f.* persuasive power.

überziehen, 1. ['y:bərtsi:ən], *irr.v.t.* 1. (*sep.*) put *or* draw over; put on; ***ihm eins –,*** give him a blow, (*sl.*) swipe him one; 2. [–'tsi:ən] (*insep.*) cover (over with), overlay, spread over; (*Comm.*) overdraw (*an account*); ***das Bett –,*** change the bed-clothes; ***Ihr Konto ist um . . . überzogen,*** your account is overdrawn by . . .; ***mit Zucker –,*** ice (*a cake*); ***mit Gips –,*** plaster; ***einen Stuhl –,*** cover a chair; ***ein Land mit Krieg –,*** invade *or* overrun a country, carry war into a country. **2.** *v.r.* (*insep.*) ***der Himmel überzieht sich mit Wolken,*** the sky becomes overcast. **3.** *v.i.* (*sep.*) (*aux.* s.) move, remove (*into a new house etc.*) (***nach,*** to). **Überziehen,** *n.* covering; plating; overlaying; (*Av.*) stall. **Überzieher,** *m.* overcoat, greatcoat, top-coat; sweater, jersey. **Überziehung,** *f.* (*Comm.*) overdraft.

überzuckern [y:bər'tsukərn], *v.t.* (*insep.*) (cover with) sugar, sugar (over); candy (*fruit*); ice (*cakes*).

Überzug ['y:bərtsu:k], *m.* cover; coverlet, pillow-case, pillow-slip, cushion-cover, bed-tick; (protective) coat *or* coating; film, plating; (*Min.*) crust.

überzwerch ['y:bərtsvɛrç], *adv.* (*dial.*) awry; athwart, across, aslant, crosswise, crossways.

üble(r, -s *etc.*) *see* **übel.**

üblich ['y:plɪç], *adj.* usual, customary, conventional, normal, ordinary, common, (*pred.*) in normal *or* ordinary *or* common use; ***wie –,*** as is (was *etc.*) the custom; ***allgemein –,*** normal *or* (a) common practice; ***nicht mehr –,*** no longer in (common) use, (gone) out of use, antiquated, out-moded. **Üblichkeit,** *f.* customariness, common *or* normal usage.

U-Boot, *n. See* **Unterseeboot.**

übrig ['y:brɪç], *adj.* (left) over, remaining, residual; superfluous, (*pred.*) to spare; ***mein -es Geld,*** the rest *or* remainder of my money, the money I have left; – ***haben,*** have over *or* left; (*coll.*) ***nichts – haben für,*** not care for, think little of, not think much of, (*coll.*) have no time for; ***keine Zeit – haben,*** have no time to spare; ***ein -es tun,*** do more than is necessary; go out of one's way to be helpful; ***die -en,*** the others, the rest; ***im -en,*** *see* **übrigens.**

übrigbleiben ['y:brɪçblaɪbən], *irr.v.i.* (*sep.*) (*Dat.*) be left (to), remain (for) (*a p. to do*); ***es bleibt mir nichts*** (***anderes***) –, I have no choice *or* no (other) alternative (***als,*** but).

übrigens ['y:brɪgəns], *adv.* (as) for the rest, in other respects, otherwise; after all, by the way, moreover, furthermore, besides, however.

übriglassen ['y:brɪçlasən], *irr.v.t.* (*sep.*) leave (over *or* behind), (*Math.*) leave over, leave a remainder; ***viel*** (***wenig***) ***zu wünschen –,*** leave much (little) to be desired.

Übung ['y:buŋ], *f.* exercise, practice, (*Mil. etc.*) training, drill(ing); use, practice; (*Mus.*) study, exercise; (*Prov.*) – ***macht der Meister,*** practice makes perfect; ***aus der – kommen,*** get out of practice; ***aus der –*** or ***nicht in – sein,*** be out of practice; ***in – bleiben,*** keep in practice *or* training, (*coll.*) keep one's hand in; ***außer – sein,*** have fallen into disuse.

Übungs|buch, *n.* exercise-book. **-flug,** *m.* practice flight. **-flugzeug,** *n.* training-plane, (*coll.*) trainer. **-gelände,** *n.* training ground. **-hang,** *m.* (*skiing*) practice *or* nursery slope. **-heft,** *n. See* **-buch. -lager,** *n.* practice *or* training camp. **-marsch,** *m.* (*Mil.*) route-march. **-munition,** *f.* practice ammunition. **-platz,** *m.* (*Mil.*) drill-ground, barrack square. **-schießen,** *n.* practice-firing, firing *or* target practice. **-stück,** *n.* (*Mus.*) exercise, study.

Ufer ['u:fər], *n.* bank (*of river*), beach, shore (*of sea*), edge, shore (*of lake*); ***ans – gehen,*** go ashore; ***am – sein,*** be ashore; ***über die – treten,*** overflow (its banks).

Ufer|bau, *m.* embankment construction *or* repairs. **-bewohner,** *m.* riparian (dweller). **-damm,** *m.* embankment. **-land,** *n.* shoreland (*sea*), lakeside, riverside. **-läufer,** *m.* (*Orn.*) ***amerikanischer –,*** spotted sandpiper (*Tringa macularia*); ***Bartrams –*** Bartram's sandpiper, (*Am.*) upland plover (*Bartramia longicauda*); ***rötlicher –,*** *see* **Grasläufer.**

uferlos ['u:fərlo:s], *adj.* (*fig.*) boundless; extravagant, wild (*as plans*); ***ins Uferlose führen,*** lead nowhere. **Ufer|mauer,** *f.* quay. **-schnepfe,** *f.* (*Orn.*) (*also* ***schwarzschwänzige*** –) black-tailed godwit (*Limosa limosa*); ***rostrote –,*** *see* **Pfuhlschnepfe. -schutzbauten,** *m.pl.* embankment, dikes, sea-walls. **-schwalbe,** *f.* (*Orn.*) sandmartin, (*Am.*) bank swallow (*Riparia riparia*). **-staat,** *m.* riparian state.

Uhr [u:r], *f.* (-, *pl.* **-en**) clock, watch; timepiece; time (of the day), o'clock, hour; (*Tech.*) meter; (*Poet.*) ***seine – ist abgelaufen,*** his time has come, his sands have run; ***nach der – sehen,*** have one's eye on the clock; ***wie nach der –,*** like clockwork; ***um drei –,*** at three o'clock; ***um wieviel –?*** what time? when? ***wieviel – ist es?*** what is the time? what time is it? ***können Sie mir sagen, wieviel – es ist?*** can you tell me the time? ***es ist halb drei –,*** it is half-past two. **Uhrarmband,** *n.* watch strap *or* bracelet.

Uhren|fabrikation, *f.* watch (*or* clock-) making. **-geschäft,** *n.* watch-maker's (shop). **-industrie,** *f.* watch and clock-making industry.

Uhr|feder, *f.* watch- *or* clock-spring. **-gehänge,** *n.* trinkets on a watch-chain. **-gehäuse,** *n.* clock- *or* watch-case. **-gewicht,** *n.* clock-weight. **-glas,** *n.* watch-glass. **-kette,** *f.* watch-chain. **-macher,** *m.* watch- *or* clock-maker. **-stempel,** *m.* time-stamp. **-tasche,** *f.* watch-pocket. **-werk,** *n.* clockwork, clockwork motor; works (*of a clock*). **-zeiger,** *m.* hand of a watch *or* clock. **-zeigersinn,** *m.* clockwise direction; ***im –,*** clockwise; ***entgegen dem –,*** counter- *or* anti-clockwise. **-zeit,** *f.* time by the clock.

Uhu ['u:hu:], *m.* (**-s,** *pl.* **-s** (*rare* **-e**)) (*Orn.*) eagle owl (*Bubo bubo*).

Ukas ['u:kas], *m.* (**-es,** *pl.* **-e**) decree, ukase.

Ukraine [u'krainə], *f. die –,* the Ukraine. **ukrainisch,** *adj.* Ukrainian.

Ulan [u'la:n], *m.* (**-en,** *pl.* **-en**) uhlan, lancer.

Ule ['u:lə], *f.* (*dial.*) hair-broom. **ulen,** *v.t., v.i.* (*dial.*) sweep.

Ulk [ulk], *m.* (**-(e)s,** *pl.* **-e**) fun, trick, hoax, (practical) joke, lark, spree; *– treiben, see* **ulken**; *– treiben mit,* make fun of, have one's joke with. **Ulkbild,** *n.* caricature. **ulken,** *v.i.* skylark, lark (about), play practical jokes. **ulkig,** *adj.* funny, amusing, comical, droll.

Ulme ['ulmə], *f.* (*Bot.*) elm (*Ulmus*). **ulmen,** *adj.* (made of) elm(-wood).

Ultimo ['ultimo], *m.* (**-s,** *pl.* **-s**) (*Comm.*) last day of the month, end of the month; *per –,* for the monthly settlement; *ultimo August,* at the end of August. **Ultimo|abrechnung,** *f.,* **–abschluß,** *m.* monthly settlement. **–geld,** *n.* money due at end of this month. **–geschäft,** *n.* business (done) for the (monthly) settlement.

Ultra|kurzwelle ['ultra–], *f.* ultra-short wave, very high frequency. **–lampe,** *f.* ultra-violet lamp. **–marin,** *n.* ultramarine, lazulite blue. **ultra|-montan,** *adj.* ultramontane. **–rot,** *adj.* infra-red. **Ultra|schall,** *m.* supersonics. **–schallwelle,** *f.* supersonic wave. **–strahlung,** *f.* cosmic radiation. **ultraviolett,** *adj.* ultra-violet.

um [um], **1.** *prep.* (*with Acc.*) 1. (*place*) about, round, around (*see – . . . herum*); 2. (*time and degree*) round, about, round about, near, toward(s), approximately, (*clock-time*) at (*see – . . . herum*); 3. (*cause*) for, because of; (in exchange) for (*see – . . . willen*); 4. (*manner*) by (*so much*); alternately with; 5. (*many idiomatic phrases, for which see the significant word, e.g. bringen –, drehen –, – sich greifen, handeln –, kommen –, schade –, stehen –, wissen – etc.*); *– alles in der Welt nicht,* not for (all) the world; *– ein bedeutendes* or *beträchtliches* or *erkleckliches,* by a great deal, very much, considerably; *– bares Geld kaufen,* buy for cash; *– einen Kopf größer,* taller by a head, a head taller; *– ein Haar,* by a hair's breadth; *– die Hälfte mehr,* half as much again; *– uns herum,* round about us; *– 100 Mark herum,* roughly, approximately *or* in the neighbourhood of 100 marks, round (about) 100 marks; *Sie wissen nicht, wie mir –s Herz ist,* you have no idea how deeply I am affected; *– Lohn arbeiten,* work for money; *– ein Mehrfaches,* many times over; *– nichts gebessert,* no better in any way, showing no improvement; *– so besser!* all the *or* so much the better! *– so mehr,* all the *or* so much the more; *– so weniger darf ich es tun,* all the more reason why I mustn't do it; *je mehr . . . – so . . .,* the more . . . the . . .; *– die sechste Stunde,* about the sixth hour; *einen Tag – den andern,* every other *or* alternate day; *– 6 Uhr,* at 6 o'clock; *– die Wette,* for a wager; *– Gottes willen!* for God's sake! *– der Partei willen,* for the sake of *or* on behalf of the party; *– meinetwillen,* for my sake; *Woche – Woche,* week by *or* after week; *– die Zeit (herum),* (round) about that time. **2.** *conj. – zu* (*with inf.*), so as to, in order to, to. **3.** *adv.* 1. around, round about; *– und –,* round about, everywhere, from *or* on all sides; *rechts –!* (*Mil.*) right turn! 2. *– sein,* be over *or* gone, be past *or* (*coll.*) up, have come to a close; *das Jahr ist –,* the year has come to an end; *seine Zeit ist –,* his time is up.

um–, *verb pref., either sep. or insep. implying* (*a*) round, round about; (*b*) over again, repeatedly; (*c*) in another way; (*d*) to the ground, down, over. *When sep. the pref. is stressed, when insep. the root is stressed. See alphabetical entries below.*

umackern ['umˀakərn], *v.t.* (*sep.*) plough up.

umadressieren ['umˀadrɛ'si:rən], *v.t.* (*sep.*) redirect (*letters*).

umändern ['umˀɛndərn], *v.t.* (*sep.*) alter, change, modify, rearrange, transform. **Umänderung,** *f.* alteration, change, modification, rearrangement, transformation.

umarbeiten ['umˀarbaɪtən], *v.t.* (*sep.*) do over again, work over; modify, adapt, remodel, recast, rewrite, revise. **Umarbeitung,** *f.* modification, adaptation, remodelling, recasting, revision.

umarmen [um'armən], *v.t.* (*insep.*) embrace, hug. **Umarmung,** *f.* embrace, hug.

Umbau ['umbau], *m.* (**-s,** *pl.* **-ten**) rebuilding, reconstruction, building alterations, conversion; (*fig.*) reorganization. **umbauen,** *v.t.* 1. [um'bauən] (*insep.*) surround with buildings, enclose; 2. ['umbauɛn] (*sep.*) rebuild, reconstruct; make alterations (in), modify, convert, remodel.

umbehalten ['umbəhaltən], *irr.v.t.* (*sep.*) keep on (*a wrap, shawl etc.*).

umbenennen ['umbənɛnən], *irr.v.t.* (*sep.*) rename, redesignate.

[1]**Umber** ['umbər], *m. See* **Umbererde.**

[2]**Umber,** *m.* (**-s,** *pl.* **-n**) *see* **Umberfisch.**

Umber|erde, *f.* umber. **–fisch,** *m.* (*Ichth.*) grayling (*Sciaenidae*).

umbetten ['umbɛtən], *v.t.* (*sep.*) put into a fresh *or* another bed; (*fig.*) put on a new foundation, reseat; change the course of (*a river*).

umbiegen ['umbi:gən], *irr.v.t.* (*sep.*) bend back *or* over, turn *or* double back *or* down *or* up.

umbilden ['umbɪldən], *v.t.* (*sep.*) remould; remodel, recast, transform; reform, reconstruct, (*Parl.*) reshuffle. **Umbildung,** *f.* change, reconstruction, transformation; modification, reorganization, reform, (*Parl.*) reshuffle.

umbinden ['umbɪndən], *irr.v.t.* (*sep.*) tie *or* bind round; *sich* (*Dat.*) *eine Schürze –,* put on an apron.

umblasen, *irr.v.t.* 1. ['umbla:zən], (*sep.*) blow down *or* over; 2. [–'bla:zən] (*insep.*) *von den Winden –,* exposed to every wind that blows.

umblättern ['umblɛtərn], *v.t., v.i.* (*sep.*) turn over the pages (*of a book*).

Umblick ['umblɪk], *m.* panorama, survey. **umblicken** ['umblɪkən], *v.r., v.i.* (*sep.*) look about one; look back *or* round.

Umbra ['umbra], *f. See* **Umbererde.**

umbrechen, *irr.v.t.* 1. ['umbrɛçən], (*sep.*) break down *or* up; plough up, turn (*a field*); 2. [–brɛçən] (*insep.*) (*Typ.*) make up into pages.

umbringen ['umbrɪŋən], (*sep.*) **1.** *irr.v.t.* kill, murder, destroy, make away with, slay. **2.** *irr.v.r.* commit suicide, do away with o.s.; (*coll., iron.*) *bring dich bloß nicht um!* mind you don't strain yourself!

Umbruch ['umbrux], *m.* (**-s,** *pl.* **¨-e**) 1. revolutionary *or* radical change, complete changeover *or* reorganization, (*coll.*) upheaval, landslide; 2. (*Typ.*) page-proof; (*Typ.*) making up into pages.

umbuchen ['umbu:xən], *v.t.* (*sep.*) (*Comm.*) transfer to another account. **Umbuchung,** *f.* book-transfer.

umdenken ['umdɛŋkən], (*sep.*) **1.** *irr.v.t.* rethink, reconsider. **2.** *irr.v.i.* change one's attitude *or* views.

umdeuten ['umdɔytən], *v.t.* (*sep.*) give a new interpretation *or* meaning to.

umdisponieren ['umdɪsponi:rən], (*sep.*) **1.** *v.t.* rearrange, redispose. **2.** *v.i.* change one's plans, make new arrangements.

umdrängen [um'drɛŋən], *v.t.* (*insep.*) press *or* throng round.

umdrehen ['umdre:ən], (*sep.*) **1.** *v.t.* turn *or* twist round; turn, rotate, revolve, spin; (*coll.*) *ihm den Hals –,* wring his neck; *ihm das Wort im Munde –,* twist his words; *wie man die Hand umdreht,* in a twinkling; *den Spieß –,* turn the tables (*gegen,* on). **2.** *v.r.* turn round, rotate, revolve; *sich im Grabe –,* turn (over) in one's grave. **Umdrehung,** *f.* turning round; turn, rotation, revolution; *–en pro Minute,* revolutions per minute.

Umdrehungs|achse, *f.* axis of rotation. **–bewegung,** *f.* rotary *or* rotatory motion. **–geschwindigkeit,** *f.* rotary velocity. **–zähler,** *m.* revolution counter, tachometer. **–zeit,** *f.* period of revolution.

Umdruck ['umdruk], *m.* reprint, transfer(-printing), manifolding. **umdrucken,** *v.t.* (*sep.*)

reprint, transfer. **Umdruckpapier,** *n.* transfer-paper.

umdüstert [um'dystərt], *adj.* gloomy, overshadowed.

Umerziehung ['umɛrtsi:uŋ], *f.* re-education, indoctrinization.

umfahren, 1. *irr.v.t.* 1. ['umfa:rən], (*sep.*) run down *or* over; 2. [–'fa:rən] (*insep.*) drive round; (sail) round, double (*a headland etc.*). **2.** ['umfa:rən] *irr.v.i.* (*sep.*) (*aux.* s.) drive a round-about way, make a detour. **Umfahrt,** *f.* circular tour, round trip; ***eine – halten,*** go on circuit (*of judges*); make the round (*of a parish etc.*). **Umfahrung,** *f.* journey round; (*Naut.*) rounding, doubling.

Umfall ['umfal], *m.* (*fig.*) sudden change of opinion *or* mind, (*Pol.*) defection. **umfallen** ['umfalən], *irr.v.i.* (*sep.*) (*aux.* s.) fall *or* (*coll.*) tumble down *or* over, (*of a p.*) collapse, (*of a th.*) overturn, be overturned *or* upset; (*fig.*) capitulate, (*coll.*) give in, give way; (*Pol.*) defect, change sides, (*sl.*) rat.

Umfang ['umfaŋ], *m.* **(-(e)s,** *pl.* **¨-e)** circumference, circuit, periphery, perimeter; girth, bulk, size, (*Dressm.*) width; volume (*of sound*); compass (*of instruments*); scope, extent (*of a business*); range (*of interests*); radius, sphere (*of activity*); ***in großem –,*** on a large *or* wide scale, (*coll.*) wholesale; ***in vollem –,*** in its entirety; ***– des Körpers,*** girth. **umfangen** [–'faŋən], *irr.v.t.* (*insep.*) enclose, surround, encircle, encompass. **umfangreich,** *adj.* extensive, comprehensive; bulky, voluminous, spacious. **Umfangskreis,** *m.* periphery.

umfassen, *v.t.* 1. [um'fasən], (*insep.*) put one's arm round, embrace, clasp; enclose, surround; (*Mil.*) encircle, envelop, outflank, (*fig.*) include, comprise, cover; ***in einem Blick –,*** take in at a glance; 2. ['umfasən] (*sep.*) reset (*jewels*). **umfassend,** *adj.* far-reaching; sweeping, drastic, complete, full, extensive, broad, comprehensive. **Umfassung,** *f.* (*Fort.*) enclosure, enceinte; (*Mil.*) encirclement, out-flanking movement, investment, envelopment, (*fig.*) encompassing, embracing. **Umfassungs|bewegung,** *f.* (*Mil.*) outflanking movement. **–mauer,** *f.* enclosing wall.

umflattern [um'flatərn], *v.t.* (*insep.*) flutter round, flow loosely round.

umflechten [um'flɛçtən], *irr.v.t.* (*insep.*) weave round; cover with wickerwork; cover, braid (*wire*).

umfliegen, 1. [um'fli:gən], *irr.v.t.* (*insep.*) fly round. **2.** ['umfli:gən] *irr.v.i.* (*sep.*) (*aux.* s.) (*Av.*) fly in a detour; (*coll.*) *see* **umfallen.**

umfließen [um'fli:sən], *irr.v.t.* (*insep.*) flow (a)round, encircle; ***von Licht umflossen,*** bathed in light.

umfloren [um'flo:rən], *v.t.* (*insep.*) cover with crape; veil; ***umflort,*** (*eyes*) dim with tears, (*voice*) muffled.

umfluten [um'flu:tən], *v.t.* (*insep.*) *see* **umfließen.**

umformen ['umfɔrmən], *v.t.* (*sep.*) remodel, recast, reshape, re-design, transform; (*Elec.*) transform, convert. **Umformer,** *m.* (*Elec.*) rotary converter.

Umfrage ['umfra:gə], *f.* general inquiry, opinion poll; ***– halten,*** inquire everywhere, make general inquiries.

umfried(ig)en [um'fri:d(ɪg)ən], *v.t.* (*insep.*) enclose, fence in. **Umfried(ig)ung,** *f.* enclosure, fence.

umfüllen ['umfylən], *v.t.* (*sep.*) transfuse, decant.

Umgang ['umgaŋ], *m.* (social) intercourse, intimate acquaintance, intimacy, connection, (business *etc.*) relations, association; society, company, acquaintances, (circle of) friends; procession, round, circuit; rotation, loop, turn (*of a spiral*), (con)volution (*of a shell*); (*Archit.*) passage, gallery, ambulatory; breeching (*harness*); ***– haben,*** be on visiting terms (***mit,*** with), see a great deal (of), be friendly, associate (with); ***durch vielen –,*** by mixing much with people; ***wenig – haben,*** have few acquaintances, not see many people; ***geschlechtlicher –,*** sexual intercourse; ***guten (schlechten) – haben*** or ***pflegen,*** keep good (bad) company.

umgänglich ['umgɛŋlɪç], *adj.* sociable, companionable; affable, (*coll.*) easy to get on with. **Umgänglichkeit,** *f.* sociability, pleasant ways, affability.

Umgangs|formen, *f.pl.* (good) manners, deportment, (*coll.*) good form. **–sprache,** *f.* colloquial speech; ***deutsche –,*** colloquial German; ***Ausdruck der –,*** colloquialism. **umgangssprachlich,** *adj.* colloquial.

umgarnen [um'ga:rnən], *v.t.* (*insep.*) ensnare, enmesh, trap.

umgaukeln [um'gaukəln], *v.t.* (*insep.*) hover *or* flit *or* flutter around.

umgeben, *irr.v.t.* 1. [umge:bən], (*sep.*) put on (*a cloak*); 2. [–'ge:bən] (*insep.*) surround, encircle.

Umgebung [um'ge:buŋ], *f.* surroundings, environs, neighbourhood, vicinity; (*fig.*) environment, background; acquaintances, associates, company, society. **Umgebungstemperatur,** *f.* ambient temperature.

Umgegend ['umge:gənt], *f.* surroundings, vicinity, environs, neighbourhood.

umgehen, 1. *irr.v.i.* ['umge:ən], (*aux.* s.) (*sep.*) go round, revolve, circulate; make a circuit *or* detour, go a roundabout way; (*fig.*) associate, have to do, keep company (***mit,*** with); deal *or* be occupied *or* have dealings (with); (*ideas, plans*) have in mind, be thinking of, contemplate, turn over in one's mind; (*tools, machines etc.*) use, handle, operate; (*people, animals etc.*) handle, manage, (*coll.*) have a way with; ***– in*** (*Dat.*), haunt (*of ghosts*); ***einen Brief – lassen,*** let a letter circulate, pass a letter round; ***gern mit ihm –,*** be fond of *or* like his company; ***er weiß mit Menschen umzugehen,*** he knows how to get on with people, he knows the (ways of the) world; ***hart – mit,*** treat harshly; ***schonend*** or ***sparsam – mit,*** use sparingly, (*coll.*) go easy on; ***du gehst nicht recht damit um,*** you set about it the wrong way, you are not handling it the right way; ***mit Betrug –,*** practise deceit; ***mit Verrat –,*** contemplate treachery; ***damit –, sich zu verheiraten,*** contemplate marriage, (*coll.*) toy with the idea of marrying; (*Prov.*) ***sage mir, mit wem du umgehst, und ich will dir sagen, wer du bist,*** a man is known by the company he keeps. **2.** *irr.v.t.* [–'ge:ən] (*insep.*) walk round; (*of traffic*) by-pass; (*fig.*) avoid, elude, evade, (*coll.*) dodge; (*Mil.*) envelop, outflank. **umgehend,** *adj.* ***mit –er Post,*** by return (of post); ***– antworten,*** reply immediately. **Umgehung,** *f.* by-passing, detour; avoidance, evasion; (*Mil.*) turning *or* flanking movement, envelopment. **Umgehungsstraße,** *f.* by-pass; detour.

umgekehrt ['umgəke:rt], **1.** *adj.* opposite, contrary, reverse, inverted, inverse; *see* **umkehren, 2.** *adv.* on the other hand, conversely, vice versa.

umgestalten ['umgəʃtaltən], *v.t.* (*sep.*) transform, alter, change completely, remodel, recast, reshape, (*fig.*) reorganize, reform. **Umgestaltung,** *f.* alteration, transformation, reshaping, reorganization.

umgießen ['umgi:sən], *irr.v.t.* (*sep.*) pour from one vessel into another, decant; (*Metall.*) recast.

umgliedern ['umgli:dərn], *v.t.* (*sep.*) reorganize, regroup, redistribute.

umgraben ['umgra:bən], *irr.v.t.* (*sep.*) dig (up), dig over (*a field*), break up (*soil*).

umgrenzen [um'grɛntsən], *v.t.* (*insep.*) encrcle, enclose, bound; (*fig.*) circumscribe, limit, define. **Umgrenzung,** *f.* boundary; enclosure; circumscription, limitation.

umgruppieren ['umgrupi:rən], *v.t.* (*sep.*) (*Mil.*) regroup, redistribute, (*Pol.*) reshuffle.

umgucken ['umgukən], *v.r.* (*sep.*) (*coll.*) glance round, look around one.

umgürten, *v.t.* 1. ['umgyrtən], (*sep.*) gird, gird o.s. with; buckle on (*a sword*); 2. [–'gyrtən] (*insep.*) ***seine Lenden –,*** gird up one's loins; (*fig.*) ***– mit,*** gird *or* encircle with.

Umguß ['umgus], *m.* transfusion, decanting; (*Metall.*) recasting; recast.

umhaben ['umha:bən], *irr.v.t.* (*sep.*) have round (one), have (*a cloak etc.*) on.

umhalsen [umˈhalzən], *v.t.* (*insep.*) embrace, hug. **Umhalsung,** *f.* embrace.

Umhang [ˈumhaŋ], *m.* (**-(e)s,** *pl.* **⸚e**) wrap, shawl, cloak, mantle, cape.

umhängen, *v.t.* 1. [ˈumhɛŋən], (*sep.*) put on (*a shawl etc.*); sling (*a rifle*); re-hang (*a picture*); ***der Katze die Schelle* –,** bell the cat, call a spade a spade; (*fig.*) ***ein Mäntelchen* –** (*Dat.*), wrap up in fine words, conceal the truth about; 2. [–ˈhɛŋən] (*insep.*) hang round (***mit,*** with). **Umhänge|tasche,** *f.* shoulder-bag. **–tuch,** *n.* shawl, wrap.

umhauen [ˈumhauən], *irr.v.t.* (*sep.*) hew *or* cut down, fell (*trees etc.*), (*coll.*) knock down, bowl over.

umher [umˈhe:r], *adv.* about, around, up and down, all round, here and there, on all sides; *see also* **herum.**

umher–, *sep.pref.* **–blicken,** *v.i.* look *or* glance round; look around, look about one, have *or* take a look round. **–fahren,** *irr.v.i.* (*aux.* s.) drive about; ***mit der Hand* –,** gesticulate. **–führen,** *v.t.* lead *or* conduct round (*a building etc.*). **–gehen,** *irr.v.i.* (*aux.* s.) stroll about. **–irren,** *v.i.* (*aux.* s.) be lost, wander *or* roam about. **–laufen,** *irr.v.i.* (*aux.* s.) rush around, run about, (*coll.*) chase about. **–liegen,** *irr.v.i.* lie about. **–schweifen,** *v.i.* (*aux.* s.) *see* **–irren;** ***seine Blicke* – *lassen,*** let one's eyes wander. **–streifen,** *v.i.* (*aux.* s.) *see* **–gehen. –treiben,** *irr.v.i.* wander *or* loaf about. **–ziehen,** *irr.v.i.* (*aux.* s.) *see* **–gehen. –ziehend,** *adj.* wandering, strolling, itinerant.

umhinkönnen [umˈhınkø:nən], *irr.v.i.* (*sep.*) (*Austr. p.p.* ***umhinkönnen***) ***ich kann nicht umhin, zu . . .,*** I cannot help (*doing*), I have no choice but (*to do*), I cannot but (*do*), I cannot refrain from (*doing*).

umhören [ˈumhø:rən], *v.r.* (*sep.*) inquire *or* make inquiries (***nach,*** about), (*coll.*) keep one's ear to the ground.

umhüllen, *v.t.* 1. [umˈhylən], (*insep.*) envelop, cover (***mit,*** with), wrap up (in), (*fig.*) veil, clothe (in), (*Tech.*) sheathe; 2. [ˈumhylən] (*sep.*) wrap (*Dat.*, round). **Umhüllung,** *f.* 1. veiling, concealment, envelopment; 2. cover, covering, wrapping, envelope, case, casing, sheathing, jacket.

Umkehr [ˈumke:r], *f.* turning back, return; change, (*Pol.*) change of front; revulsion (*of feeling*); conversion, (*coll.*) fresh start; (*Elec.*) reversal. **umkehren** [ˈumke:rən], (*sep.*) **1.** *v.i.* (*aux.* s.) turn back, turn round, return, retrace one's steps, (*fig.*) reform, make a fresh start, change one's ways, (*coll.*) turn over a new leaf. **2.** *v.t.* turn (round, about, back, over, up, inside out, upside down *etc.*); overturn, upset, (*Elec.*) reverse, (*Mus., Math., Gram.*) invert; ***wie man die Hand umkehrt,*** in a twinkling; ***mit umgekehrter Hand,*** with the back of the hand; ***den Spieß* – (*gegen*),** turn the tables (on); ***die Taschen* –,** turn one's pockets inside out; *see* **umgekehrt. 3.** *v.r.* turn round, turn over in bed; ***mir kehrt sich das Herz um,*** it makes my heart bleed; ***bei dem Anblick kehrt sich der Magen um,*** the sight turns one's stomach.

Umkehr|feld, *n.* (*Elec.*) reversing field. **–motor,** *m.* reversible engine. **Umkehrung,** *f.* overturning; inversion, reversion; reversal, (*fig.*) subversion.

umkippen [ˈumkıpən], (*sep.*) **1.** *v.i.* (*aux.* s.) tip over, upset, overturn, (*of a p.*) topple over, lose one's balance; (*Naut.*) capsize. **2.** *v.t.* upset, overturn, tip over.

umklammern [umˈklamərn], *v.t.* (*insep.*) clasp, clutch (at), cling to; embrace; (*Boxing*) clinch; (*Mil.*) encircle. **Umklammerung,** *f.* embrace, (*Boxing*) clinch, (*Mil.*) pincer-movement.

umklappen [ˈumklapən], (*sep.*) **1.** *v.t.* turn *or* fold back. **2.** *v.i.* (fall down in a) faint.

umkleiden, 1. *v.t.* 1. [ˈumklaıdən], (*sep.*) change the dress of; 2. [–ˈklaıdən] (*insep.*) clothe, cover, drape, adorn; (*fig.*) surround, invest. **2.** *v.r.* (*sep.*) change (one's clothes *or* dress). **Umkleideraum,** *m.* changing- *or* dressing-room. **Umkleidung,** *f.* 1. [ˈum–] changing (one's *or* s.o.'s) clothes; 2. [–ˈklaıduŋ] clothing, draping, covering.

umknicken [ˈumknıkən], *v.i., v.t.* (*sep.*) (*aux.* s.) snap off; ***der Fuß ist mir umgeknickt,*** I have twisted my foot.

umkommen [ˈumkɔmən], *irr.v.i.* (*sep.*) (*aux.* s.) perish, die, be killed, succumb; fall (*in battle*); (*of a th.*) spoil, go bad, go to waste, be lost *or* wasted; ***vor Langweile* –,** die of boredom, be bored to death.

Umkreis [ˈumkraıs], *m.* circumference; circuit, periphery; area, vicinity; (*fig.*) extent, range; (*Geom.*) circumscribed circle; ***im* – *von,*** within a radius of. **umkreisen** [–ˈkraızən], *v.t.* (*insep.*) revolve, turn *or* circle round, encircle. **Umkreisung,** *f.* encirclement.

umkrempeln [ˈumkrɛmpəln], *v.t.* (*sep.*) turn *or* tuck up; (*fig.*) turn upside down, turn topsy-turvy.

umladen [ˈumla:dən], *irr.v.t.* (*sep.*) reload, transfer a load of; (*Naut.*) tranship. **Umladung,** *f.* reloading, transhipment.

Umlage [ˈumla:gə], *f.* assessment (*of taxes*), rating, apportionment; special fee, contribution.

umlagern, *v.t.* 1., [umˈla:gərn], (*insep.*) enclose, surround closely, besiege; (*fig.*) beleaguer, assail, beset; 2. [ˈumla:gərn] (*sep.*) transpose, rearrange; re-store (*goods*); move camp. **Umlagerung,** *f.* transposition, rearrangement.

Umlauf [ˈumlauf], *m.* turn, cycle, revolution, rotation, circulation, (*money*) circulation, (*Comm.*) circular (letter); (*Med.*) whitlow; ***in* – *bringen*** or ***setzen,*** put into circulation, issue, circulate; start, spread (*a rumour*); ***außer* – *setzen,*** withdraw from circulation, call in; ***im* – *sein,*** circulate. **umlaufen, 1.** *irr.v.t.* (*sep.*) run over, run *or* knock down. **2.** *irr.v.i.* (*aux.* s.) (*sep.*) rotate, revolve; circulate (*as blood, reports, money etc.*); (*Typ.*) run on. **3.** *irr.v.t.* (*insep.*) move *or* run round (*a circuit*).

Umlauf|getriebe, *n.* planetary gear. **–motor,** *m.* rotary engine. **–schreiben,** *n.* circular letter.

Umlaufs|kapital, *n.* floating capital. **–mittel,** *n.* currency. **–schreiben,** *n.* *See* **Umlaufschreiben. –zeit,** *f.* time of rotation, (circulation) period.

Umlaut [ˈumlaut], *m.* (**-(e)s,** *pl.* **-e**) (*Phonet.*) modification (*of a vowel*), vowel mutation; modified *or* mutated vowel. **umlauten,** (*sep.*) **1.** *v.t.* modify (*the vowel*), cause modification. **2.** *v.i.* (*aux.* s.) modify, become modified, take modification; ***die Plurale auf „. . . er" lauten gewöhnlich um,*** plurals in '. . . er' usually modify; ***dieser Diphthong lautet um,*** this diphthong is modified.

Umlegekragen [ˈumle:gəkra:gən], *m.* turn-down collar.

umlegen, 1. *v.t.* 1. [umˈle:gən], (*insep.*) surround, garnish (***mit,*** with); 2. [ˈumle:gən] (*sep.*) lay (down), (*of storm*) beat down (*crops*); put on (*a collar etc.*), apply (*a bandage*); shift, change the position of, place differently, (*Mil.*) remove to other quarters; careen (*a ship*), throw (over) (*a switch*), re-lay (*rails*), divert (*traffic*), transfer (*telephone call*), dip, lower (*a funnel on passing bridges*); turn down (*an edge*), tuck (in) (*a seam*); divide, apportion (*charges etc.*); (*sl.*) do in, bump off. **2.** *v.r.* (*sep.*) tilt (over), tip over, (*of wind*) veer (round). **Umlegung,** *f.* division, allocation, apportionment; shifting, transfer, diversion.

umleiten [ˈumlaıtən], *v.t.* (*sep.*) divert, re-route (*traffic etc.*). **Umleitung,** *f.* (traffic) diversion, by-pass.

umlenken [ˈumlɛŋkən], *v.t.* (*sep.*) turn back *or* round.

umlernen [ˈumlɛrnən], (*sep.*) **1.** *v.t.* learn afresh. **2.** *v.i.* change one's views, readjust one's ideas.

umliegend [ˈumli:gənt], *adj.* surrounding, neighbouring; circumjacent.

ummauern *v.t.* 1. [umˈmauərn], (*insep.*) wall in *or* round; 2. [ˈum–] (*sep.*) rebuild (the brickwork of).

ummodeln [ˈummo:dəln], *v.t.* (*sep.*) remodel, reshape, alter; (*fig.*) ***gänzlich* –,** put into the melting-pot.

umnachten [umˈnaxtən], *v.t.* (*insep.*) shroud in darkness. **umnachtet,** *adj.* (*fig.*) clouded, demented, benighted, deranged. **Umnachtung,** *f.* (mental) derangement.

umnebeln [um'ne:bəln], *v.t.* (*insep.*) wreathe in clouds; (*fig.*) cloud, confuse, obfuscate, (be)fog, (*with drink*) (be)fuddle.

umnehmen ['umne:mən], *irr.v.t.* (*sep.*) put on, wrap round o.s., wrap o.s. up in.

umordnen ['umˀɔrdnən], *v.t.* (*sep.*) rearrange.

umpacken ['umpakən], *v.t.* (*sep.*) repack.

umpflanzen, *v.t.* 1. ['umpflantsən], (*sep.*) transplant, replant; 2. [–'pflantsən] (*insep.*) – ***mit,*** plant all round with.

umpflügen *v.t.* 1. ['umpfly:gən], (*sep.*) plough up, turn (*soil*); 2. [–'pflygən] (*insep.*) encircle with furrows; plough round (*a tree etc.*).

umpolen ['umpo:lən], *v.t.* (*sep.*) (*Elec.*) reverse the polarity of. **Umpolung,** *f.* reversion of polarity.

umquartieren ['umkvarti:rən], *v.t.* (*sep.*) (*p.p.* ***umquartiert***) remove to other quarters, re-billet (*troops*), evacuate (*civilians*).

umrahmen, *v.t.* 1. [um'ra:mən], (*insep.*) frame, (*fig.*) surround (***von,*** with), place in a setting (of); 2. ['um–] (*sep.*) re-frame, change the frame of.

umranden [um'randən], **umrändern** [um'rɛndərn], *v.t.* (*insep.*) put a border round, border, edge. **Umrandung,** *f.* edge, border, rim. **Umrandungsfeuer,** *n.* (*Av.*) boundary *or* perimeter lights.

umranken [um'raŋkən], *v.t.* (*insep.*) twine (itself) round, cling to, (*fig.*) entwine.

umräumen ['umrɔymən], *v.t.* (*sep.*) rearrange, (re)-move.

umrechnen ['umrɛçnən], *v.t.* (*sep.*) reduce (***in*** (*Acc.*), to), convert (into), express in terms (of). **Umrechnung,** *f.* reduction, conversion. **Umrechnungs|größen,** *f.pl.* conversion data. **–kurs,** *m.* rate of exchange. **–tabelle, –tafel,** *f.* conversion table. **–wert,** *m.* exchange value.

umreißen, *irr.v.t.* 1. ['umraɪsən], (*sep.*) pull, tear, knock *or* throw down; blow down (*trees etc.*); demolish; 2. [–'raɪsən] (*insep.*) outline, sketch in (*usu. fig.*).

umreiten *irr.v.t.* 1. [um'raɪtən], (*insep.*) ride round (*the track*); 2. ['um–] (*sep.*) ride down.

umrennen ['umrɛnən], **1.** *irr.v.t.* (*sep.*) run down, knock down *or* over (*an obstacle*). **2.** *irr.v.i.* (*insep.*) rush *or* race round.

Umrichter ['umrɪçtər], *m.* (*Rad.*) frequency-changer.

umringen [um'rɪŋən], *reg.v.t.* (*insep.*) encircle, enclose, crowd *or* throng round, close in on, surround, (*fig.*) encompass, beset.

Umriß ['umrɪs], *m.* (**-(ss)es,** *pl.* **-(ss)e**) outline, contour; ***in kräftigen Umrissen,*** in bold outlines; ***in groben Umrissen,*** in broad outline. **umrissen** [–'rɪsən], *adj. See* **umreißen**; ***scharf –,*** sharply *or* clearly defined, clear-cut. **Umriß|karte,** *f.* outline map. **–zeichnung,** *f.* sketch, outline drawing.

umrühren ['umry:rən], *v.t.* (*sep.*) stir (up), agitate; (*Metall.*) puddle, rake.

ums [ums] = ***um das***; **um's** (*coll.*) = ***um des.***

umsatteln ['umzatəln], (*sep.*) **1.** *v.t.* resaddle (*a horse*). **2.** *v.i.* (*aux.* h. & s.) (*coll.*) change one's studies *or* profession; change one's ideas *or* opinion; (*coll.*) – ***auf*** (*Acc.*), switch to.

Umsatz ['umzats], *m.* (**-es,** *pl.* **⸚e**) (*Comm.*) turnover, returns, sales, business; ***geringer –,*** small turnover, slow returns; (*Comm.*) ***rascher –,*** quick returns; ***großer –, kleiner Nutzen,*** small profits and quick returns. **Umsatz|betrag,** *m.* total turnover. **–kapital,** *n.* working capital. **–steuer,** *f.* value-added tax. **–ziffer,** *f.* turnover rate.

umsäumen [um'zɔymən], *v.t.* (*insep.*) (*Dressm.*) hem (round), (*fig.*) surround, hem in, line (*street with trees etc.*).

umschalten ['umʃaltən], *v.t.* (*sep.*) switch *or* change over; (*Elec.*) reverse the current. **Umschalter,** *m.* change-over switch, commutator; shift-key (*typewriter*). **Umschalt|hebel,** *m.* switch-lever. **–stöpsel,** *m.* switch-plug. **Umschaltung,** *f.* (change-over) switching, commutation.

umschatten [um'ʃatən], *v.t.* (*insep.*) shade, overshadow.

Umschau ['umʃau], *f.* survey, review; (*coll.*) look round; – ***halten,*** look out *or* round, be on the look-out (***nach,*** for). **umschauen,** *v.r.* (*sep.*) look round, take a look around; look *or* glance back.

umschaufeln ['umʃaufəln], *v.t.* (*sep.*) turn (over) with a shovel, dig over.

umschichten ['umʃɪçtən], *v.t.* (*sep.*) turn over (*hay etc.*), pile anew, rearrange in layers; (*fig.*) shift, regroup. **Umschichtung,** *f.* shifting, regrouping, reshuffle; ***soziale –,*** social upheaval.

umschiffen, *v.t.* 1. [um'ʃɪfən], (*insep.*) sail round, circumnavigate; round *or* double (*a cape*); 2. ['um–] (*sep.*) tranship (*cargo*), transfer (*passengers*). **Umschiffung,** *f.* 1. circumnavigation; – ***der Erde,*** circumnavigation of the globe; 2. transhipment.

Umschlag ['umʃla:k], *m.* (**-(e)s,** *pl.* **⸚e**) 1. revulsion, (sudden) change (*of the weather, of opinions*), turn, alteration; 2. cover, covering, wrapper, jacket (*of a book*), envelope; (*of sleeve*) cuff, (*of trousers*) turn-up; 3. (*Med.*) compress, poultice; 4. (*Comm.*) reshipment, transfer (*of goods*); sale, turnover. **umschlagen,** (*sep.*) **1.** *irr.v.t.* knock down *or* over, fell (*a tree*), turn over (*a page etc.*), turn up (*a hem, cuff*), turn down (*a collar*), roll up (*sleeves*); wrap round o.s., put on (*a shawl*). **2.** *irr.v.i.* (*aux.* s.) turn over, overturn, upset, fall over *or* down, topple over, (*Naut.*) capsize; (*Swiss aux.* h.) turn, change (abruptly) (***in*** (*Acc.*), into), turn (to); (*of wind*) shift, veer (round), (*of weather*) change, grow worse, (*of milk*) go sour; (*of the voice*) break; ***zum Guten –,*** take a favourable turn. **Umschlag(e)-tuch,** *n.* shawl, wrap.

Umschlag|hafen, *m.* port of transhipment. **–platz,** *m.*, **–stelle,** *f.* reloading point.

umschleichen [um'ʃlaɪçən], *irr.v.t.* (*insep.*) prowl round, spy on.

umschließen [um'ʃli:sən], *irr.v.t.* (*insep.*) enclose, surround; (*Mil.*) invest, besiege; (*fig.*) include, comprise, encompass; ***mit seinen Armen –,*** clasp in one's arms.

umschlingen, *irr.v.t.* 1. [um'ʃlɪŋən], (*insep.*) embrace; enclose tightly, cling to, clasp, entangle; 2. ['um–] (*sep.*) coil (up) (*rope*).

umschmeicheln, *v.t.* (*insep.*) *see* **schmeicheln.**

umschmeißen ['umʃmaɪsən], *irr.v.t.* (*sep.*) (*coll.*) *see* **umwerfen.**

umschmelzen ['umʃmɛltsən], *irr.v.t.* (*sep.*) re-melt, recast, refound; (*fig.*) alter completely.

umschnallen ['umʃnalən], *v.t.* (*sep.*) buckle on (*a sword*), put on (*a belt*).

umschreiben, *irr.v.t.* 1. ['umʃraɪbən], (*sep.*) rewrite, transcribe; (*Comm.*) transfer, make over (***rights, property etc.***) (***auf*** (*Acc.*), to); ***einen Wechsel –,*** reindorse a bill; 2. [–'ʃraɪbən] (*insep.*) (*Geom.*) circumscribe; (*fig.*) (*usu. p.p. only*) (*Med.*) localize; re-word, paraphrase; ***ein Dreieck mit einem Kreise –,*** describe a circle round a triangle. **umschreibend,** *adj.* periphrastic. **Umschreibung,** *f.* 1. transcription, transcript; 2. paraphrase; (*Geom.*) circumscription. **umschrieben,** *adj.* (*Geom.*) circumscribed, (*Med.*) localized; paraphrased.

Umschrift ['umʃrɪft], *f.* (-, *pl.* **-en**) (phonetic) transcription; circular legend, circumscription (*on a medal*).

umschulen ['umʃu:lən], *v.t.* (*sep.*) remove from one school to another, (re-)train (*black-coated workers for industry etc.*). **Umschulung,** *f.* re-training (programme).

umschütten ['umʃytən], *v.t.* (*sep.*) spill, upset; pour into another vessel, decant.

umschwärmen [um'ʃvɛrmən], *v.t.* (*insep.*) swarm *or* buzz *or* crowd round, beset; (*fig.*) *see* **schwärmen.**

Umschweife ['umʃvaɪfə], *m. pl.* circumlocution, digression; (*coll.*) falderal; ***ohne –,*** bluntly, point-blank, without further *or* more ado; – ***machen,*** digress, beat about the bush.

umschwenken [ˈumʃvɛŋkən], *v.t., v.i.* (*sep.*) turn *or* wheel round; (*fig.*) change one's mind, come round (*to a point of view*).
umschwirren [umˈʃvɪrən], *v.t.* (*insep.*) buzz *or* whizz round.
Umschwung [ˈumʃvuŋ], *m.* (**-s,** *pl.* **–̈e**) **1.** rotation, revolution, turn, wheeling; (*fig.*) reversal, sudden change, reaction, revulsion (*of feeling etc.*); reverse (*of fortune*); (*Gymn.*) swing (*round the bar*); *pl.* vicissitudes (of fortune); 2. (*Swiss, sing. only*) land round *or* immediate surroundings of a house.
umsegeln [umˈzeːɡəln], *v.t.* (*insep.*) sail round, circumnavigate (*the world*); double (*a cape*).
umsehen [ˈumzeːən], *irr.v.r.* (*sep.*) look back, look round (***nach,*** at); look about one; (*fig.*) look round, (be on the) look out (***nach,*** for); ***im Umsehen,*** in a twinkling *or* flash; ***sich in der Stadt –,*** have *or* take a look round the town; ***er hat sich viel in der Welt umgesehen,*** he has seen a great deal of the world.
umseitig [ˈumzaɪtɪç], *adj., adv.* on the next page, (*adv. only*) overleaf.
umsetzbar [ˈumzɛtsbaːr], *adj.* (*Comm.*) realizable, convertible, negotiable; saleable, marketable; exchangeable.
umsetzen [ˈumzɛtsən], **1.** *v.t.* (*sep.*) transfer, shift, (*Hort.*) transplant, (*Mus.*) transpose, (*Typ.*) reset, (*Math.*) permutate, (*Elec.*) convert, transform, (*Mech.*) change (*gear*), (*Comm.*) sell, realize, dispose of, convert (into cash); ***in die Tat –,*** carry out (*plans*), translate (*ideas*) into action. **2.** *v.r.* (*sep.*) change, be converted (*in* (*Acc.*), into). **Umsetzung,** *f.* change of place; transposition; conversion, transformation, (*Math.*) permutation, (*Chem.*) reaction, (*Comm.*) sale, realization, (*Hort.*) transplantation; *see* **Umsatz.**
Umsichgreifen [ˈumzɪçɡraɪfən], *n.* progress, spread(ing).
Umsicht [ˈumzɪçt], *f.* circumspection, discretion, caution, wariness, prudence. **umsichtig,** *adj.* circumspect, prudent, cautious, open-eyed.
umsiedeln [ˈumziːdəln], (*sep.*) **1.** *v.i.* settle somewhere else, (re)move to another place, move (house), change one's quarters. **2.** *v.t.* resettle. **Umsiedlung,** *f.* resettlement, evacuation (*from danger area*).
umsinken [ˈumzɪŋkən], *irr.v.i.* (*sep.*) (*aux.* s.) sink down, drop, fall to the ground, (fall into a) swoon.
umso [ˈumzo], (*Austr.*) = ***um so.*** **umsomehr,** (*Austr.*) = ***um so mehr.***
umsonst [umˈzɔnst], *adv.* for nothing, without pay(ment), gratis, free of charge, gratuitously; to no purpose, in vain, uselessly; ***nicht –,*** not for nothing, not without (good) reason; (*Prov.*) ***– ist nur der Tod,*** nothing for nothing; no pay no work.
umsoweniger [umzoˈveːnɪɡər], (*Austr.*) = ***um so weniger.***
umspannen [ˈumʃpanən], **1.** *v.i.* (*sep.*) change horses. **2.** *v.t.* 1. (*sep.*) (*Elec.*) transform; 2. [ˈʃpanən] (*insep.*) span, encompass, (*fig.*) embrace, comprise. **Umspanner,** *m.* (*Elec.*) transformer. **Umspannwerk,** *n.* transformer station.
umspielen [umˈʃpiːlən], *v.t.* (*insep.*) (*Footb.*) dribble round.
umspinnen [umˈʃpɪnən], *irr.v.t.* (*insep.*) spin a web round; cover, braid (*wire etc.*); (*fig.*) entwine, entangle. **umsponnen,** *adj.* covered, braided (*wire*).
umspringen, **1.** *v.t.* [umˈʃprɪŋən], (*insep.*) jump *or* skip round. **2.** [ˈum–] *v.i.* (*sep.*) (*aux.* s.) change, shift, veer (*of wind*); ***mit ihm umzuspringen wissen,*** know how to handle *or* manage *or* treat him *or* deal with *or* (*coll.*) cope with him.
umspulen [ˈumʃpuːlən], *v.t.* (*sep.*) rewind.
umspülen [umˈʃpyːlən], *v.t.* (*insep.*) wash round (*a rock etc.*).
Umstand [ˈumʃtant], *m.* (**-(e)s,** *pl.* **–̈e**) **1.** circumstance, case, fact; condition, situation; *pl.* details, particulars, circumstances, position, state of affairs; ***mildernder –,*** redeeming feature, extenuating circumstance; (*coll.*) ***in andern*** or ***gesegneten –̈en,*** in the family way, expecting (a child); ***günstige –̈e,*** favourable circumstances; ***in guten –̈en,*** well-to-do, well off; ***nähere –̈e,*** further particulars; ***unter –̈en,*** in certain cases, under certain circumstances, if need be; circumstances permitting, possibly, perhaps; ***unter allen –̈en,*** in any case, at all events; by hook or by crook; ***unter diesen –̈en,*** as matters stand; ***unter keinen –̈en,*** under no circumstances, not on any *or* on no account; 2. formalities, ceremony, fuss, bother, trouble, difficulty; ***–̈e machen,*** (*of a th.*) cause trouble, be inconvenient *or* a nuisance; (*of a p.*) make a fuss, go to a lot of *or* to great trouble; ***machen Sie (meinetwegen) keine –̈e!*** do not put yourself out (for me), do not go to any trouble (on my account); ***ohne (viel) –̈e,*** without (standing on) ceremony, without much ado; ***nicht viel –̈e machen mit,*** make short work of.
umständehalber [ˈumʃtɛndəhalbər], *adv.* owing to circumstances, in view of the position.
umständlich [ˈumʃtɛntlɪç], *adj.* circumstantial, detailed, minute, (*coll.*) long-winded; complicated, involved, intricate; ceremonious, formal, (*coll.*) fussy; troublesome, laborious; ***das ist mir viel zu –,*** that is far too much bother *or* trouble (for me); ***– erzählen,*** narrate at great length, go into all the details of, (*coll.*) be long-winded about; particularize. **Umständlichkeit,** *f.* circumstantiality; ceremoniousness, formality, (*coll.*) fuss(iness); *pl.* formalities.
umstandshalber [ˈumʃtantshalbər], *adv.* *See* **umständehalber. Umstands|kleid,** *n.* maternity dress. **–krämer, —meier,** *m.* punctilious *or* (*coll.*) fussy p., (*coll.*) fuss-pot. **–satz,** *m.* adverbial clause. **–wort,** *n.* adverb.
umstehen, *irr.v.i.* 1. [ˈumʃteːən], (*sep.*) (*of animal*) perish, come to grief; (*of liquid*) become stale *or* stagnant; 2. [–ˈʃteːən] (*insep.*) stand around; ***umstanden von,*** surrounded by.
umstehend [ˈumʃteːənt], **1.** *adj.* ***–e Seite,*** next page; ***die Umstehenden,*** the bystanders. **2.** *adv.* on the next page, as stated overleaf.
Umsteig(e)|billet [ˈumʃtaɪɡə–], *n.*, **–fahrschein,** *m.*, **–karte,** *f.* through-ticket, transfer ticket. **umsteigen,** *irr.v.i.* (*sep.*) (*aux.* s.) (*Railw. etc.*) change (***nach,*** for). **Umsteiger,** *m.* *See* **Umsteigekarte.**
umstellen, **1.** *v.t.* 1. [ˈumʃtɛlən], (*sep.*) place differently, put in a different place, shift, move, rearrange, (*Gram.*) transpose, invert; convert, switch, change over (***auf*** (*Acc.*), to); ***auf Kraft(fahr)betrieb –,*** motorize; ***auf Maschinenbetrieb –,*** mechanize; 2. [–ˈʃtɛlən] (*insep.*) surround, encompass. **2.** *v.r.* (*sep.*) adapt *or* readjust *or* accommodate o.s. (***auf*** (*Acc.*), to), change one's attitude; change over, switch (to). **Umstellung,** *f.* 1. change of position, inversion, transposition; change-over, conversion; (*fig.*) adaptation, readjustment; change of face; ***politische –,*** change of political attitude; 2. encompassment, encompassing, surrounding.
umstimmen [ˈumʃtɪmən], *v.t.* (*sep.*) (*Mus.*) retune, tune to another pitch; ***ihn –,*** (make him) change his opinion *or* mind, bring *or* talk him round. **Umstimmung,** *f.* conversion, change of mind.
umstoßen [ˈumʃtoːsən], *irr.v.t.* (*sep.*) overturn, upset, overthrow, knock down *or* over, (*fig.*) abrogate, overrule, cancel, revoke, annul (*a decision*), set aside, reverse, void, quash, invalidate (*a verdict*), change (*a will*); upset, change (*plans*).
umstrahlen [umˈʃtraːlən], *v.t.* (*insep.*) irradiate, bathe in light.
umstricken, *v.t.* 1. [umˈʃtrɪkən], (*insep.*) (*fig.*) ensnare, entangle; 2. [ˈum–] (*sep.*) re-knit.
umstritten [umˈʃtrɪtən], *adj.* controversial, disputed, contested.
umstülpen [ˈumʃtylpən], *v.t.* (*sep.*) turn upside down, invert, overturn; turn inside out.
Umsturz [ˈumʃturts], *m.* (**-es,** *pl.* **–̈e**) downfall, ruin, overthrow; (*fig.*) upheaval, revolution, subversion. **Umsturzbestrebungen,** *f.pl.* revolutionary aims.
umstürzen [ˈumʃtyrtsən], (*sep.*) **1.** *v.t.* throw down, overthrow, upset, overturn; (*fig.*) subvert. **2.** *v.i.* (*aux.* s.) fall down *or* over, collapse, overturn.

Umsturzideen ['umʃturts?ide:ən], *f.pl.* subversive ideas.

Umstürzler ['umʃtyrtslər], *m.* revolutionary, anarchist. **umstürzlerisch,** *adj.* revolutionary, subversive.

umtaufen ['umtaufən], *v.t.* (*sep.*) rechristen, rename.

Umtausch ['umtauʃ], *m.* (**-es,** *pl.* **-e**) exchange, barter, (*of money*) conversion. **umtauschen,** *v.t.* (*sep.*) exchange, change (***gegen,*** for).

umtippen ['umtɪpən], *v.t.* (*sep.*) (*coll.*) re-type.

umtoben [um'to:bən], *v.t.* (*insep*). roar *or* rage round.

umtreiben ['umtraɪbən], (*sep.*) **1.** *irr.v.i.* (*aux.* s.) drift *or* wander round (aimlessly). **2.** *irr.v.t.* (*fig.*) be *or* prey on (*a p.'s*) mind. **Umtreiber,** *m.* (*Anat.*) rotator muscle.

Umtrieb ['umtri:p], *m.* (**-(e)s,** *pl.* **-e**) cycle, circulation, (*For.*) cycle of cultivation; (*coll.*) bustle, activity; (*usu. pl.*) intrigues, subversive activity, machinations.

umtun ['umtu:n], (*sep.*) **1.** *irr.v.t.* put on (*a shawl etc.*). **2.** *irr.v.r.* bestir o.s.; ***sich – nach,*** look around *or* about *or* out for, make inquiries about.

umwachsen [um'vaksən], *adj.* overgrown.

umwälzen ['umvɛltsən], *v.t.* (*sep.*) rotate, revolve, roll over *or* round, (*usu. fig.*) overturn, overthrow, revolutionize. **umwälzend,** *adj.* revolutionary, epoch-making. **Umwälzung,** *f.* upheaval; revolution.

umwandeln, 1. *v.t.* 1. ['umvandəln], (*sep.*) change, turn, metamorphose, transform, convert (***in*** (*Acc.*) *or* ***zu,*** into), commute (*punishment*), (*Gram.*) conjugate, inflect; ***er ist wie umgewandelt,*** he is a changed man; 2. [–'vandəln] (*insep.*) wander *or* stroll round. **2.** *v.r.* (*sep.*) (*Chem.*) be converted (***in*** (*Acc.*), into). **Umwandler,** *m.* (*Elec.*) transformer, converter. **Umwandlung,** *f.* change, transformation, metamorphosis; (*Physiol.*) metabolism, (*Law*) commutation, (*Comm.*) conversion.

umwechseln ['umvɛksəln], *v.t.* (*sep.*) exchange (for), change (*money*).

Umweg ['umve:k], *m.* (**-(e)s,** *pl.* **-e**) roundabout way, detour; (*fig.*) subterfuge, wile, ruse, (*coll.*) dodge; (*fig.*) ***auf –en,*** indirectly, in a roundabout way, by devious *or* underhand means, stealthily, by subterfuge; ***einen – machen,*** go a roundabout way, take a circuitous route; ***ohne –e,*** straightforwardly, plain-spoken; without mincing matters, in plain English, point-blank, bluntly, straight to the point.

umwehen, *v.t.* 1. ['umve:ən], (*sep.*) blow down; 2. [–'ve:ən] (*insep.*) blow *or* waft around, fan (*with breezes*).

Umwelt ['umvɛlt], *f.* world around us, (social) surroundings, milieu, environment. **umweltbedingt,** *adj.* environmental. **Umwelt|einflüsse,** *m.pl.* environmental factors. **–verschmutzung,** *f.* pollution of the environment.

umwenden ['umvɛndən], (*sep.*) **1.** *reg. & irr.v.t., v.r.* turn, turn round *or* over; reverse, invert; ***wie man eine Hand umwendet,*** in a twinkling; ***mit umgewandter Hand,*** with the back of the hand; ***es wendet mir das Herz um,*** it wrings my heart; ***umgewandte Seite,*** wrong side (*of cloth etc.*); ***bitte umwenden!*** please turn over! **2.** *irr.v.i.* (*aux.* h. & s.) *see* **umkehren.**

umwerben [um'vɛrbən], *irr.v.t.* (*insep.*) court, woo; ***sie ist viel umworben,*** she has many suitors, she is much sought after.

umwerfen ['umvɛrfən], (*sep.*) *irr.v.t.* knock down, overturn, upset, overthrow, subvert; throw round (one's shoulders), throw *or* put on; *see* **umstoßen.**

umwerten ['umve:rtən], *v.t.* (*sep.*) ascribe a different value to, revalue, reassess. **Umwertung,** *f.* revaluation.

umwickeln, *v.t.* 1. [um'vɪkəln], (*insep.*) wrap round, bind, cover (***mit,*** with), wrap up (in); 2. ['um–] (*sep.*) rewind, rewrap.

umwinden [um'vɪndən], *irr.v.t.* (*insep.*) twine *or* wind around, encircle.

umwittern [um'vɪtərn], *v.t.* (*insep.*) (*fig.*) surround.

umwohnend ['umvo:nənt], *adj.* neighbouring. **Umwohner,** *m.pl.* inhabitants of the neighbourhood, neighbours.

umwölken [um'vœlkən], *v.t., v.r.* (*insep.*) cloud (over), become overcast, darken.

umwühlen ['umvy:lən], *v.t.* (*sep.*) (*of pigs*) root (up) (*the ground*), (*fig.*) turn upside down, ransack (*a drawer etc.*).

umzäunen [um'tsɔynən], *v.t.* (*insep.*) enclose, hedge round, fence in. **Umzäunung,** *f.* enclosure, fence.

umziehen, 1. *irr.v.t.* 1. ['umtsi:ən], (*sep.*) change (*clothes*), put fresh clothes on (*a child etc.*); ***die Schuhe –,*** change one's shoes; 2. [–'tsi:ən] (*insep.*) surround; cover, hang with, envelop. **2.** *irr.v.r.* 1. (*sep.*) change (one's clothes); 2. (*insep.*) ***der Himmel hat sich umzogen,*** the sky has become overcast. **3.** *irr.v.i.* (*sep.*) (*aux.* s.) remove, move, move house, change one's residence (***nach,*** to); (*Prov.*) ***dreimal umgezogen ist einmal abgebrannt,*** three removals are as bad as a fire.

umzingeln [um'tsɪŋəln], *v.t.* (*insep.*) surround, encompass, encircle, envelop, (*Mil.*) invest. **Umzing(e)lung,** *f.* investment, encirclement.

Umzug ['umtsu:k], *m.* (**-(e)s,** *pl.* **¨-e**) 1. change of residence, removal, (*coll.*) move; 2. procession. **umzugshalber,** *adv.* owing to change of address. **Umzugskosten,** *f.pl.* cost of removal, moving expenses.

umzüngeln [um'tsyŋəln], *v.t.* (*insep.*) play *or* lick around, surround, envelop (*as flames*).

un– [un], *negative pref.* = un-, in-, im-, dis-, ir-, not, non-. *The principal meanings of* **un–** *are*: 1. *absolute negative, e.g.* **Unglück, unwahr**; 2. *a bad sort of, e.g.* **Unmensch, Untier**; 3. *excessive amount, e.g.* **Unmenge, Unsumme.** *Of the numberless compounds with* **un–** *only those are given in which the English equivalent is not also merely un-. In the case of compounds from nouns and of adjs. formed from them, and of negative adjs., the stress is usu. on the pref. In the case of verbal and participal negatives the position of stress may vary, depending on the emphasis desired on the negation.*

unabänderlich [un?ap'ɛndərlɪç], *adj.* unalterable, unchangeable, irrevocable, immutable; ***sich ins Unabänderliche fügen,*** bow to *or* resign o.s. to the inevitable, accept (with a good grace) what cannot be changed.

unabdingbar [un?ap'dɪŋba:r], *adj.* unalterable, irrevocable, final; inalienable (*rights*).

unabhängig ['un?aphɛŋɪç], *adj.* independent (***von,*** of), autonomous; (*Mech.*) self-contained; (*Gram.*) unrelated, absolute; freelance (*journalist etc.*); (*fig.*) ***– von,*** irrespective of. **Unabhängige(r),** *m., f.* (*Pol.*) independent. **Unabhängigkeit,** *f.* independence, autonomy.

unabkömmlich ['un?apkœmlɪç], *adj.* indispensable, irreplaceable, essential; (*Mil.*) (in a) reserved (occupation); (*coll.*) busy, occupied, engaged.

unablässig ['un?aplɛsɪç], *adj.* incessant, uninterrupted, unrelenting, unremitting, unceasing, interminable.

unablöslich [un?ap'lø:slɪç], *adj.* irredeemable (*mortgage*), perpetual (*loan*); ***–e Anleihe,*** consolidated fund.

unabsehbar ['un?apze:ba:r], *adj.* immense, vast, unbounded, boundless, incalculable, immeasurable, unlimited, limitless, unfathomable; ***in –er Ferne,*** in the distant *or* unforeseeable future.

unabsetzbar ['un?apzɛtsba:r], *adj.* irremovable, immutable.

unabsichtlich ['un?apzɪçtlɪç], *adj.* unintentional, accidental, fortuitous, adventitious; involuntary, unintended, inadvertent.

unabweisbar [un?ap'vaɪzba:r], **unabweislich,** *adj.* pressing, urgent, imperative, peremptory; *see also* **unabwendbar.**

unabwendbar [un?ap'vɛntba:r], *adj.* unavoidable, inescapable, inevitable, irrevocable.

unachtsam ['un?axtza:m], *adj.* inattentive, careless, negligent, heedless; absent-minded, thoughtless, unmindful. **Unachtsamkeit,** *f.* inattention, carelessness, heedlessness, negligence, inadvertence, inadvertency.

unähnlich ['un?ɛ:nlɪç], *adj.* dissimilar (*Dat.*, to), unlike. **Unähnlichkeit,** *f.* unlikeness, dissimilarity, diversity.

unanfechtbar ['un?anfɛçtba:r], *adj.* incontestable, indisputable, unchallengeable, unimpeachable, undeniable, incontrovertible.

unangebracht ['unangəbraxt], *adj.* unsuitable, inapt, inappropriate, inopportune, inexpedient, unseemly, out of place.

unangefochten ['un?angəfɔxtən], *adj.* undisputed, unchallenged, undoubted, indubitable; unhampered, unhindered, unmolested; ***laß mich –!*** let me alone! let me be!

unangemeldet ['un?angəmɛldət], **1.** *adj.* unannounced. **2.** *adv.* without being previously announced, (*Comm.*) in the absence of advice, without previous notice.

unangemessen ['un?angəmɛsən], *adj.* inadequate, unfit, unfitting, unsuited, unsuitable, unseemly, improper, incompatible, incongruous.

unangenehm ['un?angəne:m], *adj.* unpleasant, disagreeable, distasteful, displeasing, unwelcome, troublesome, irksome, awkward, annoying.

unangesehen ['un?angəze:ən], **1.** *adj.* undistinguished, inglorious. **2.** *prep.* (*Comm., Law*) (*Acc. or Gen.*) irrespective of, without regard for.

unangreifbar ['un?angraɪfba:r], *adj.* unassailable, unimpeachable; impregnable, secure, safe (*from attack*).

Unannehmlichkeit ['un?anne:mlɪçkaɪt], *f.* unpleasantness, disagreeableness, vexatiousness, irksomeness, inconvenience, drawback, annoyance, trouble, nuisance, difficulty.

unansehnlich ['un?anze:nlɪç], *adj.* mean-looking, plain, unattractive, unsightly, ill-favoured, unprepossessing, (*Am.*) homely; inconsiderable, paltry, insignificant, trifling. **Unansehnlichkeit,** *f.* plainness, (*Am.*) homeliness; unsightliness; paltriness, insignificance.

unanständig ['un?anʃtɛndɪç], *adj.* improper, indecent, indecorous, immodest, unseemly, indelicate, unmannerly; obscene, coarse, shocking. **Unanständigkeit,** *f.* impropriety, immodesty, indelicacy, indecency, obscenity, coarseness, unmannerliness.

unanstellig ['un?anʃtɛlɪç], *adj.* awkward, clumsy, unskilful, unhandy, bungling, maladroit.

unanstößig ['un?anʃtø:sɪç], *adj.* inoffensive, harmless, innocuous, unobjectionable.

unantastbar ['un?antastba:r], *adj.* inviolable, incontestable, unassailable, inalienable, unimpeachable, prescriptive, sacrosanct, taboo.

unanwendbar ['un?anvɛntba:r], *adj.* inapplicable; inapposite, unsuitable, unbefitting, unadapted.

unappetitlich ['un?apeti:tlɪç], *adj.* unappetizing; uninviting; unsavoury, disgusting, repellent.

Unart ['un?a:rt], **1.** *f.* ill-breeding, bad manners, rudeness, incivility; bad habit; bad behaviour, naughtiness (*of children*). **2.** *m.* (**-s,** *pl.* **-e**) (*coll.*) naughty child. **unartig,** *adj.* badly behaved, ill-bred, uncivil, rude; vicious (*of horses*), naughty (*of child*).

unartikuliert ['un?artikuli:rt], *adj.* inarticulate.

unästhetisch ['un?ɛste:tɪʃ], *adj.* repellent, odious, horrid, offensive, nasty; unrefined, coarse, vulgar.

unauffällig ['un?auffɛlɪç], *adj.* unobtrusive, inconspicuous.

unauffindbar ['un?auffɪntba:r], *adj.* not to be found, undiscoverable, untraceable, impenetrable.

unaufgefordert ['un?aufgəfɔrdərt], **1.** *adj.* uncalled for, unasked, unbidden. **2.** *adv.* of one's own accord, voluntarily, freely, spontaneously.

unaufgeklärt ['un?aufgəklɛ:rt], *adj.* unsolved, unexplained, mysterious (*problem*), (*of a p.*) unenlightened.

unaufgeschlossen ['un?aufgəʃlɔsən], *adj.* reserved; narrow-minded, (*coll.*) blinkered.

unaufgeschnitten ['un?aufgəʃnɪtən], *adj.* uncut (*of books*).

unaufhaltbar ['un?aufhaltba:r], **unaufhaltsam, 1.** *adj.* incessant; irresistible; impetuous. **2.** *adv.* without stopping.

unaufhörlich ['un?aufhø:rlɪç], *adj.* incessant, constant, continuous, unceasing, unending, perpetual, endless, interminable.

unauflösbar ['un?auflø:sba:r], **unauflöslich,** *adj.* indissoluble; (*Math., Chem.*) insoluble, (*fig.*) impenetrable, inscrutable, undecipherable; inexplicable.

unaufmerksam ['un?aufmɛrkza:m], *adj.* inattentive; absent-minded, distracted; careless, thoughtless. **Unaufmerksamkeit,** *f.* inattention, absent-mindedness, thoughtlessness, (*coll.*) day-dreaming, wool-gathering.

unaufrichtig ['un?aufrɪçtɪç], *adj.* insincere, deceitful, disingenuous, underhand, two-faced, shady, shifty. **Unaufrichtigkeit,** *f.* insincerity, underhandedness.

unaufschiebbar ['un?aufʃi:pba:r], *adj.* pressing, urgent, vital, imperative.

unausbleiblich ['un?ausblaɪplɪç], *adj.* unfailing, certain; inevitable, inexorable, ineluctable.

unausführbar ['un?ausfy:rba:r], *adj.* impracticable, impossible; (*pred. only*) not feasible.

unausgebildet ['un?ausgəbɪldət], *adj.* not fully developed, (*Bot., Zool.*) rudimentary, (*Mil.*) untrained.

unausgeglichen ['un?ausgəglɪçən], *adj.* unbalanced.

unausgemacht ['un?ausgəmaxt], *adj.* undecided, uncertain, questionable; (*pred only*) not settled.

unausgesetzt ['un?ausgəzɛtst], **1.** *adj.* continual, perpetual, uninterrupted, incessant, unending, constant. **2.** *adv.* continually, without interruption, incessantly.

unausgesprochen ['un?ausgəʃprɔxən], *adj.* unspoken, tacit; (*fig.*) implied, inferred, implicit.

unauslöschlich ['un?auslœʃlɪç], *adj.* inextinguishable, indelible, unquenchable, imperishable, indestructible, lasting; ***–e Dankbarkeit,*** undying gratitude; ***–e Tinte,*** indelible ink; ***–e Erinnerung,*** ineffaceable memory.

unaussprechbar ['un?ausʃprɛçba:r], *adj.* unpronounceable. **unaussprechlich,** *adj.* inexpressible, indescribable, unspeakable, unutterable, ineffable.

unausstehlich ['un?ausʃte:lɪç], *adj.* insufferable, unbearable, unendurable, insupportable, intolerable; hateful, detestable, loathsome, odious.

unausweichlich ['un?ausvaɪçlɪç], *adj.* inevitable, unavoidable, inescapable.

Unband ['unbant], *m.* (**-(e)s,** *pl.* **⸚e** *or* **-e**) (*Austr.*) unruly child. **unbändig** [–bɛndɪç], *adj.* unruly, intractable, wayward, headstrong, refractory; (*coll.*) tremendous, whopping, mighty.

unbarmherzig ['unbarmhɛrtsɪç], *adj.* unmerciful, merciless, pitiless, relentless, unrelenting, ruthless. **Unbarmherzigkeit,** *f.* harshness, cruelty, ruthlessness.

unbeabsichtigt ['unbəapzɪçtɪçt], *adj.* unintentional, unwitting, inadvertent.

unbeachtet ['unbəaxtət], *adj.* unnoticed, neglected, unheeded, disregarded; ***– lassen,*** ignore, disregard, pay no regard to, take no notice of, not take into account.

unbeanstandet ['unbəanʃtandət], *adj.* unexceptionable, unopposed, uncontested; not objected to.

unbearbeitet ['unbəarbaɪtət], *adj.* unwrought, undressed, unformed, in the raw *or* native state; unfinished, rough, crude, raw; not previously treated (*of a subject*).

unbeaufsichtigt ['unbəaufzɪçtɪçt], *adj.* without supervision.

unbedacht ['unbədaxt], **unbedachtsam,** *adj.* inconsiderate, unthinking, remiss, thoughtless, careless, imprudent, improvident, indiscreet, rash.

unbedeckt ['unbədɛkt], *adj.* uncovered, bare; ***–en Hauptes,*** bare-headed.

unbedenklich ['unbədɛŋklɪç], **1.** *adj.* (*of a p.*) unhesitating, unswerving; (*of a th.*) unobjectionable, harmless, inoffensive. **2.** *adv.* unhesitatingly, without hesitation *or* scruples. **Unbedenklichkeitsbescheinigung,** *f.* clearance (certificate).

unbedeutend ['unbədɔytənt], *adj.* insignificant, unimportant, immaterial, of no account *or* consequence, negligible, paltry, trifling, trivial.

unbedingt ['unbədɪŋt], **1.** *adj.* unconditional, unquestioning, unqualified, positive, absolute; implicit (*obedience etc.*). **2.** *adv.* in any case, under any circumstances, whatever happens, without fail; by all means.

unbefähigt ['unbəfɛ:ɪçt], *adj.* incompetent, ill-qualified, unqualified.

unbefahrbar ['unbəfa:rba:r], *adj.* impracticable, impassable. **unbefahren,** *adj.* untraversed, untrodden, pathless, trackless; ***–es Volk,*** inexperienced sailors; green hands.

unbefangen ['unbəfaŋən], *adj.* unprejudiced, unbiased, impartial, disinterested; calm, dispassionate, unembarrassed, unabashed; unconstrained, free and easy; artless, natural, unaffected, ingenuous. **Unbefangenheit,** *f.* impartiality, freedom from bias; ease, unaffectedness, unreservedness, ingenuousness, openness, simplicity, naivety, naïveté, candour.

unbefestigt ['unbəfɛstɪçt], *adj.* unfortified, open (*town etc.*), unsurfaced (*road*).

unbefiedert ['unbəfi:dərt], *adj.* without feathers, unfledged.

unbefleckt ['unbəflɛkt], *adj.* spotless, undefiled, unblemished, unsullied, blameless; (*Eccl.*) ***–e Empfängnis,*** Immaculate Conception.

unbefrachtet ['unbəfraxtət], *adj.* unfreighted, empty.

unbefriedigend ['unbəfri:dɪgənt], *adj.* unsatisfying, unsatisfactory, disappointing, insufficient. **unbefriedigt,** *adj.* unsatisfied, dissatisfied, discontented, disappointed; unappeased (*appetite*).

unbefristet ['unbəfrɪstət], **1.** *adj.* unlimited. **2.** *adv.* for an unlimited period.

unbefugt ['unbəfu:kt], *adj.* unauthorized, unwarranted, incompetent. **Unbefugte(r),** *m., f.* trespasser, unauthorized p.; ***Unbefugten ist der Eintritt verboten!*** no admittance except on business! **unbefugterweise,** *adv.* without authority *or* permission.

unbegabt ['unbəga:pt], *adj.* not gifted *or* clever, untalented. **Unbegabtheit,** *f.* lack of talent.

unbeglichen ['unbəglɪçən], *adj.* unpaid, outstanding (*debt*).

unbegreiflich ['unbəgraɪflɪç], *adj.* inconceivable, incredible, incomprehensible; inexplicable. **Unbegreiflichkeit,** *f.* incomprehensibility, incredibility; inconceivability.

unbegrenzbar ['unbəgrɛntsba:r], *adj.* illimitable. **unbegrenzt,** *adj.* boundless, unbounded, limitless, unlimited, infinite. **Unbegrenztheit,** *f.* boundlessness, infinitude.

unbegründet ['unbəgryndət], *adj.* unfounded, groundless; spurious, factitious.

unbegütert ['unbəgy:tərt], *adj.* without landed property; not rich, not well off, badly off.

unbehaart ['unbəha:rt], *adj.* hairless, bald; (*Zool.*) smooth; (*Bot.*) smooth-leaved; (*Anat.*) glabrous.

Unbehagen ['unbəha:gən], *n.* discomfort; uneasiness, malaise, disquiet. **unbehaglich,** *adj.* unpleasant, uncomfortable; (*fig.*) uneasy, (*pred.*) ill at ease. **Unbehaglichkeit,** *f.* uneasiness.

unbehelligt ['unbəhɛlɪçt], *adj.* unmolested, undisturbed.

unbehindert ['unbəhɪndərt], *adj.* unrestrained, unimpeded, unencumbered, untrammelled, unhindered, unhampered.

unbeholfen ['unbəhɔlfən], *adj.* clumsy, awkward, bungling, fumbling; ungainly, brusque, blunt, bluff, (*coll.*) heavy-handed; embarrassed. **Unbeholfenheit,** *f.* clumsiness, awkwardness, brusqueness, ungraciousness.

unbeirrbar ['unbəɪrba:r], *adj.* unwavering, imperturbable, unruffled, composed. **unbeirrt,** *adj.* unperturbed, unflinching, unswerving, staunch; unflustered, unconcerned.

unbekannt ['unbəkant], *adj.* (*of a th.*) unknown, unfamiliar, unheard of, obscure; (*of a p.*) ignorant, unaware (***mit,*** of); unacquainted, unfamiliar, unconversant (with), a stranger (to), unversed (in); ***er ist mir –,*** I do not know him; ***es wird dir nicht – sein, daß*** . . ., you know, of course, that . . .; ***ich bin hier –,*** I am a stranger here; (*Math.*) ***–e Größe,*** unknown quantity. **Unbekannt,** *n.* (*Law*) person or persons unknown. **unbekannterweise,** *adv.* unwittingly, without personal knowledge. **Unbekanntheit,** *f.* unfamiliarity, unawareness.

unbekehrbar ['unbəke:rba:r], *adj.* inconvertible, confirmed, callous.

unbekümmert ['unbəkymərt], *adj.* untroubled, carefree; careless (***von,*** of), unconcerned, reckless. **Unbekümmertheit,** *f.* unconcern, carelessness.

unbelastet ['unbəlastət], *adj.* unencumbered; (*of a p.*) carefree, light-hearted, (*Law*) with a clean record, not incriminated, (*Pol.*) uncompromised; (*Elec.*) with no load; ***– von,*** free of, unencumbered by.

unbelaubt ['unbəlaupt], *adj.* leafless, bare, without foliage, aphyllous.

unbelebt ['unbəle:pt], *adj.* lifeless, inanimate; (*Comm.*) dull, dead, slack, inactive, torpid, sluggish; unfrequented, empty (*streets*). **Unbelebtheit,** *f.* lifelessness; dullness, torpidity.

unbeleckt ['unbəlɛkt], *adj.* (*coll.*) ***von der Kultur –,*** without any trace of culture, uncultured, uncivilized.

unbelehrbar ['unbəle:rba:r], *adj.* unteachable, not open to reason.

unbelesen ['unbəle:zən], *adj.* unlettered, unread, illiterate.

unbeliebt ['unbəli:pt], *adj.* disliked (***von,*** by), unpopular (with). **Unbeliebtheit,** *f.* unpopularity.

unbemerkbar ['unbəmɛrkba:r], *adj.* imperceptible, undiscernible, unapparent. **unbemerkt,** *adj.* unperceived, unnoticed, unobserved, unseen.

unbemittelt ['unbəmɪtəlt], *adj.* impecunious, needy, poverty-stricken.

unbenannt ['unbənant], *adj.* nameless, unnamed, anonymous; ***–e Zahl,*** abstract number.

unbenommen ['unbənɔmən], *adj.* ***es ist*** (or ***bleibt***) ***Ihnen – zu*** . . ., you are (still) free *or* at liberty to. . . .

unbenutzt ['unbənutst], *adj.* unused, unemployed; idle (*of money*); unoccupied (*of buildings*); ***das wird er nicht – lassen,*** he will make good use of it.

unbequem ['unbəkve:m], *adj.* uncomfortable, inconvenient, irksome, troublesome, (*of a p.*) disagreeable. **Unbequemlichkeit,** *f.* inconvenience, discomfort.

unberechenbar ['unbərɛçənba:r], *adj.* unpredictable, incalculable, unfathomable, imponderable; ***er ist ganz –,*** there is no telling what he will do.

unberechtigt ['unbərɛçtɪçt], *adj.* unauthorized, unjustified, unfounded, unlawful, unwarranted, without authority; unreasonable, unfair; unqualified. **unberechtigterweise,** *adv.* without good *or* valid *or* sufficient reason; without authority.

unberitten ['unbərɪtən], *adj.* 1. not broken in (*of horses*); 2. unmounted (*of cavalry*).

unberücksichtigt ['unbərykzɪçtɪçt], *adj.* unconsidered, unheeded, disregarded, overlooked, not taken into account; ***– lassen,*** make no allowance for.

unberufen ['unbəru:fən], *adj.* unauthorized, unjustified, uncalled for, unwarrantable, gratuitous, officious; (*coll.*) ***–!*** touch wood!

unberührt ['unbəry:rt], *adj.* untouched, unused, intact; virgin (*forest, soil*); unaffected; ***– bleiben von,*** lie outside the scope of.

unbeschadet ['unbəʃa:dət], *prep.* (*Gen.*) without detriment *or* prejudice to.

unbeschädigt [ˈunbəʃɛːdɪçt], *adj.* uninjured, unhurt, intact, safe and sound; (*Comm.*) undamaged, in good condition.

unbeschaffen [ˈunbəʃafən], *adj.* (*dial.*) sickly, poorly, ailing.

unbescheiden [ˈunbəʃaɪdən], *adj.* unblushing, self-opinionated, presumptuous, impudent, bumptious, overweening, forward; (*coll.*) stuck up, cocky; unreasonable, exorbitant (*demands*). **Unbescheidenheit,** *f.* presumption, presumptuousness, bumptiousness, impudence, effrontery; (*coll.*) brass, cheek, lip, side, nerve.

unbeschnitten [ˈunbəʃnɪtən], *adj.* uncircumcised; unshorn, untrimmed; unclipped (*of coin*); uncut (*of books*).

unbescholten [ˈunbəʃɔltən], *adj.* irreproachable, blameless; of good character *or* reputation. **Unbescholtenheit,** *f.* integrity, good name, blamelessness. **Unbescholtenheitszeugnis,** *n.* certificate of good behaviour.

unbeschränkt [ˈunbəʃrɛŋkt], *adj.* boundless, unlimited, unrestricted; (*of power*) absolute, unconditional, uncontrolled, discretionary.

unbeschreiblich [ˈunbəʃraɪplɪç], *adj.* indescribable, inexpressible, unspeakable, unutterable; stupendous, prodigious, wondrous, monstrous, beggaring *or* past (all) description.

unbeschrieben [ˈunbəʃriːbən], *adj.* blank (*paper*); (*fig.*) ***–es Blatt,*** unknown quantity, dark horse.

unbeschwert [ˈunbəʃvɛrt], *adj.* unburdened, unencumbered; free and easy, light-hearted; easy (*conscience*). **Unbeschwertheit,** *f.* light-heartedness, carefree nature.

unbeseelt [ˈunbəzeːlt], *adj.* spiritless, lifeless, inanimate.

unbesehen [ˈunbəzeːən], **1.** *adj.* unexamined, unseen; just as it is; ***etwas – kaufen,*** buy a pig in a poke. **2.** *adv.* (*dial.*) suddenly.

unbesetzt [ˈunbəzɛtst], *adj.* unoccupied, empty, free, vacant, disengaged.

unbesiegbar [ˈunbəziːkbaːr], **unbesieglich,** *adj.* invincible, unconquerable.

unbesonnen [ˈunbəzɔnən], *adj.* thoughtless, inconsiderate, ill-advised, heedless, reckless, rash; indiscreet, imprudent. **Unbesonnenheit,** *f.* imprudence, thoughtlessness, indiscretion, rashness, recklessness.

unbesorgt [ˈunbəzɔrkt], *adj.* unconcerned; carefree; ***seien Sie*** (***deswegen***) ***–!*** don't let it worry you! set your mind at rest!

Unbestand [ˈunbəʃtant], *m. See* **Unbeständigkeit. unbeständig,** *adj.* unstable, unsteady, fluctuating, variable, inconstant, shifting, labile, (*as weather*) changeable, unsettled; (*of a p.*) erratic, fickle. **Unbeständigkeit,** *f.* inconstancy, impermanence, instability, variability, changeableness, fickleness.

unbestechlich [ˈunbəʃtɛçlɪç], *adj.* incorruptible; (*fig.*) unerring. **Unbestechlichkeit,** *f.* incorruptibility, integrity.

unbestellbar [ˈunbeʃtɛlbaːr], *adj.* 'addressee unknown', dead (*letter*).

unbestimmbar [ˈunbəʃtɪmbaːr], *adj.* indeterminable, indefinable; equivocal, problematic, vague, nondescript. **unbestimmt,** *adj.* indeterminate, indefinite, vague, indecisive, ambiguous; undetermined, undefined, uncertain, undecided, doubtful; ***–es Zahlwort,*** indefinite numeral; ***auf –e Zeit,*** for an indefinite time, indefinitely, (*Law*) sine die. **Unbestimmtheit,** *f.* indefiniteness, uncertainty, vagueness; indecision, lack of determination.

unbestreitbar [ˈunbəʃtraɪtbaːr], *adj.* incontestable, indisputable, undeniable, unquestionable, acknowledged.

unbestritten [ˈunbəʃtrɪtən], *adj.* undisputed, uncontested; absolutely certain, positive, categorical.

unbeteiligt [ˈunbətaɪlɪçt], *adj.* not interested *or* involved *or* participating *or* concerned (***bei,*** in), indifferent (to), detached (from). **Unbeteiligte(r),** *m., f.* disinterested party, outsider.

unbeträchtlich [ˈunbətrɛçtlɪç], *adj.* trifling, trivial, scant, insignificant, inconsiderable, inappreciable, of little importance.

unbeugsam [ˈunbɔykzaːm], *adj.* (*fig.*) inflexible, unbending, uncompromising, adamant; stubborn, obstinate, firm.

unbewaffnet [ˈunbəvafnət], *adj.* unarmed, defenceless; (*Bot.*) thornless; ***mit –em Auge,*** with the unaided *or* naked eye.

unbewandert [ˈunbəvandərt], *adj.* inexperienced; unskilled, unversed (***in*** (*Dat.*), in).

unbeweglich [ˈunbəveːklɪç], *adj.* immovable, immutable, fixed, rigid, stationary, motionless; real (*property*); (*fig.*) apathetic, impassive, unimpressionable, unresponsive; *see also* **unbeugsam**; ***–es Eigentum,*** realty, real estate; ***–e Güter,*** immovables; ***– machen,*** immobilize. **Unbeweglichkeit,** *f.* immutability, stability, permanence, fixedness, inflexibility. **unbewegt,** *adj.* motionless; (*fig.*) unflinching, unwavering, unmoved, unshaken, inflexible.

unbeweibt [ˈunbəvaɪpt], *adj.* unmarried, single, bachelor.

unbewirtschaftet [ˈunbəvɪrtʃaftət], *adj.* non-rationed, not subject to control.

unbewohnbar [ˈunbəvoːnbaːr], *adj.* uninhabitable. **unbewohnt,** *adj.* uninhabited, unoccupied, deserted, vacant.

unbewölkt [ˈunbəvœlkt], *adj.* cloudless.

unbewußt [ˈunbəvust], *adj.* unconscious, unaware (*Gen.*, of), involuntary, instinctive; ***mir –,*** without my knowledge; ***Philosophie des Unbewußten,*** philosophy of the unconscious.

unbezahlbar [ˈunbətsaːlbaːr], *adj.* priceless, invaluable.

unbezähmbar [ˈunbətsɛːmbaːr], *adj.* untamable; (*fig.*) unyielding, indomitable.

unbezwingbar [ˈunbətsvɪŋbaːr], **unbezwinglich,** *adj.* invincible, indomitable, unconquerable, (*as a fortress*) unassailable, impregnable. **unbezwungen,** *adj.* unconquered (*peak*).

unbiegsam [ˈunbiːkzaːm], *adj.* inflexible, stiff, rigid.

Unbilden [ˈunbɪldən], *f.pl.* injury, hardship; wrong, injustice; *see* **Unbill**; ***– der Witterung,*** inclemency of the weather; ***– des Winters,*** rigours of winter.

Unbildung [ˈunbɪlduŋ], *f.* lack of education *or* culture.

Unbill [ˈunbɪl], *f.* (-, *pl.* **Unbilden**) wrong, injury; inequity, injustice; inclemency (*of weather*). **unbillig,** *adj.* unfair, unjust, inequitable; undue, unreasonable; iniquitous. **Unbilligkeit,** *f.* injustice, unfairness, inequity.

unblutig [ˈunbluːtɪç], **1.** *adj.* bloodless. **2.** *adv.* without bloodshed.

unbotmäßig [ˈunboːtmɛːsɪç], *adj.* insubordinate, unruly, refractory, contumacious. **Unbotmäßigkeit,** *f.* insubordination, unruliness, contumacy.

unbrauchbar [ˈunbrauxbaːr], *adj.* useless, unserviceable, (*pred.*) of no use; (*fig.*) unworkable, impracticable (*ideas*). **Unbrauchbarkeit,** *f.* uselessness.

unbußfertig [ˈunbuːsfɛrtɪç], *adj.* impenitent, unrepentant. **Unbußfertigkeit,** *f.* impenitence.

unchristlich [ˈunkrɪstlɪç], *adj.* unchristian, uncharitable.

und [unt], *conj.* and; ***an dem – dem Platze,*** at such-and-such a place; ***–?*** what then? and after that? (*coll.*) so what? ***er – Furcht haben!*** he afraid! ***– wenn*** (***auch***), even if; ***– ich auch nicht,*** nor I either; ***er tanzt nicht, – sie auch nicht,*** he does not dance, neither does she; ***für – für,*** on and on, continually, incessantly; ***– zwar,*** that is; ***– andere(s)*** or ***desgleichen*** (***mehr***), and so forth.

Undank [ˈundaŋk], *m.* ingratitude, ungratefulness; ***– ernten,*** get small thanks for it, (*coll.*) get more kicks than ha'pence. **undankbar,** *adj.* ungrateful (***gegen,*** to), thankless (*task*). **Undankbarkeit,** *f.* ingratitude.

undefinierbar [ˈundefiniːrbaːr], *adj.* indefinable.

undehnbar ['unde:nba:r], *adj.* inextensible; inelastic, nonductile.
undeklinierbar ['undeklini:rba:r], *adj.* indeclinable.
undenkbar ['undɛŋkba:r], *adj.* inconceivable, incredible, unthinkable, (*pred.*) out of the question. **undenklich,** *adj.* ***seit –er Zeit,*** for ages, from time immemorial, from time out of mind.
undeutlich ['undɔytlɪç], *adj.* (*visual*) indistinct, blurred, hazy; (*of meaning*) obscure, vague, confused; (*of speech*) inarticulate. **Undeutlichkeit,** *f.* indistinctness, haziness, vagueness; obscurity, confusion, lack of clarity.
undicht ['undɪçt], *adj.* not watertight, leaking, leaky, unsound, porous, pervious; not airtight.
Unding ['undɪŋ], *n.* **(-(e)s,** *pl.* **-e)** impossibility, absurdity, nonsense; monstrosity.
unduldsam ['undultza:m], *adj.* intolerant, impatient. **Unduldsamkeit,** *f.* intolerance.
undurchdringlich ['undurçdrɪŋlɪç], *adj.* impenetrable, impermeable, impervious (***für,*** to), watertight, waterproof; (*fig.*) inscrutable.
undurchführbar ['undurçfy:rba:r], *adj.* impracticable, not feasible, unworkable.
undurchlässig ['undurçlɛsɪç], *adj.* impermeable, impervious (***für,*** to), waterproof, watertight.
undurchsichtig ['undurçzɪçtɪç], *adj.* non-transparent, opaque, (*fig.*) impenetrable, unfathomable. **Undurchsichtigkeit,** *f.* opaqueness, opacity.
Und-Zeichen, *n.* ampersand, &; (*Math.*) addition *or* plus sign.
uneben ['unˀe:bən], *adj.* uneven, rough, rugged; (*coll.*) ***nicht –,*** not bad, not so dusty. **unebenbürtig,** *adj.* (of) inferior (rank). **Unebenheit,** *f.* unevenness, irregularity, roughness, ruggedness.
unecht ['unˀɛçt], *adj.* not genuine, false, sham, fake(d), spurious, counterfeit(ed), (*sl.*) phon(e)y, (*attrib. only*) imitation, artificial; not fast (*of colours*), affected (***gegen,*** by), fugitive (to) (*light etc.*); (*Math.*) improper.
unedel ['unˀedəl], *adj.* ignoble, (*also of metals*) base; inert, electro-negative.
unehelich ['unˀe:əlɪç], *adj.* illegitimate, natural (*child*), unmarried (*mother*). **Unehelichkeit,** *f.* illegitimacy.
Unehre ['unˀe:rə], *f.* dishonour, disgrace, discredit. **unehrenhaft,** *adj.* dishonourable, discreditable. **unehrerbietig,** *adj.* disrespectful, irreverent. **Unehrerbietigkeit,** *f.* disrespect(fulness), irreverence, want of respect. **unehrlich,** *adj.* dishonest, insincere, underhand, false, (*coll.*) shady, shifty, double-faced. **Unehrlichkeit,** *f.* dishonesty, insincerity, duplicity, double-dealing.
uneigennützig ['unˀaɪgənnytsɪç], *adj.* disinterested, unselfish, magnanimous, altruistic.
uneigentlich ['unˀaɪgəntlɪç], *adj.* not real *or* proper; not literal, figurative.
uneinbringlich ['unˀaɪnbrɪŋlɪç], *adj.* irretrievable, irrecoverable. **Uneinbringlichkeit,** *f.* ***im Falle der –,*** in default of payment.
uneingedenk ['unˀaɪngədɛŋk], *adj.* (*Gen.*) forgetful *or* unmindful of; regardless of.
uneingeschränkt ['unˀaɪngəʃrɛŋkt], *adj.* unlimited, unrestricted, uncontrolled; (*fig.*) unqualified.
uneinheitlich ['unˀaɪnhaɪtlɪç], *adj.* irregular, non-uniform.
uneinig ['unˀaɪnɪç], *adj.* disunited, disagreeing, divided, discordant; ***– sein,*** disagree, be at variance *or* odds *or* loggerheads, differ; ***– werden,*** quarrel, wrangle, squabble, (*coll.*) fall out; ***ich bin mit mir selber noch –,*** I have not quite made up my mind yet. **Uneinigkeit,** *f.* disagreement, dissension, discord; misunderstanding, dispute.
uneinnehmbar ['unˀaɪnne:mba:r], *adj.* impregnable, invulnerable.
uneins ['unˀaɪns], *adj.* ***– sein,*** *see* **uneinig.**
unelegant ['unˀelegant], *adj.* inelegant.
unempfänglich ['unˀɛmpfɛŋlɪç], *adj.* unreceptive, insusceptible (***für,*** to), unimpressionable.
unempfindlich ['unˀɛmpfɪntlɪç], *adj.* insensible (***gegen,*** to), insensitive (to), unaffected (by), inured, resistant (to); (*fig.*) indifferent (to), apathetic (towards). **Unempfindlichkeit,** *f.* indifference, insensibility, (*Chem.*) stability.
unendlich [un'ɛntlɪç], **1.** *adj.* infinite, endless, boundless, unlimited, illimitable; ***ins Unendliche,*** ad infinitum; ***das geht ins Unendliche,*** there is no end to it. **2.** *adv.* ***– klein,*** infinitesimal; ***– lang,*** endless; ***– viel,*** no end of. **Unendlichkeit,** *f.* infinity, endlessness.
unentbehrlich ['unˀɛntbe:rlɪç], *adj.* indispensable, essential, absolutely necessary; ***es ist ihm –,*** he cannot do without it. **Unentbehrlichkeit,** *f.* absolute necessity.
unentgeltlich [unˀɛnt'gɛltlɪç], *adj.* free (of charge), for nothing, gratis, gratuitous, (*sl.*) buckshee.
unenthaltsam ['unˀɛnthaltza:m], *adj.* incontinent, intemperate, self-indulgent.
unentrinnbar [unˀɛnt'rɪnba:r], *adj.* inescapable, ineluctable.
unentschieden ['unˀɛntʃi:dən], **1.** *adj.* undecided, not settled, open, pending, in dispute, uncertain, indecisive, (*of a game*) drawn, (*of a p.*) undecided, irresolute; ***–e Frage,*** open question; ***–es Rennen,*** tie, dead heat; ***–es Spiel,*** tie, draw. **2.** *adv.* ***– spielen,*** tie, draw; ***– enden,*** be a tie, finish as a draw *or* dead heat. **Unentschieden,** *n.* (*Spt.*) tie, draw. **Unentschiedenheit,** *f.* indecision, uncertainty.
unentschlossen ['unˀɛntʃlɔsən], *adj.* undecided, irresolute; ***– sein,*** waver, vacillate, hesitate, (*coll.*) sit on the fence. **Unentschlossenheit,** *f.* indecision, irresolution, vacillation.
unentschuldbar ['unˀɛntʃultba:r], *adj.* inexcusable, unpardonable, indefensible. **unentschuldigt,** *adj.* without excuse.
unentwegt ['unˀɛntve:kt], *adj.* firm, steadfast, unflinching, unswerving, staunch. **Unentwegte(r),** *m., f.* (*Pol.*) die-hard.
unentwickelt ['unˀɛntvɪkəlt], *adj.* undeveloped, immature, in embryo.
unentwirrbar ['unˀɛntvɪrba:r], *adj.* inextricable, involved, tangled.
unentzifferbar ['unˀɛnttsɪfərba:r], *adj.* indecipherable, incrutable.
unentzündbar ['unˀɛnttsyntba:r], *adj.* non-inflammable.
unerachtet ['unˀɛrˀaxtət], *prep.* (*obs.*) *see* **ungeachtet, 2.**
unerbittlich ['unˀɛrbɪtlɪç], *adj.* inexorable, relentless, unrelenting, inflexible, unbending, pitiless.
unerbrochen ['unˀɛrbrɔxən], *adj.* unopened (*letter*), unbroken (*seal*).
unerfahren ['unˀɛrfa:rən], *adj.* inexperienced; inexpert, unskilled (***in*** (*Dat.*), in), (*coll.*) raw, green.
unerfindlich ['unˀɛrfɪntlɪç], *adj.* undiscoverable, incomprehensible, impenetrable; ***es ist mir –,*** it is a mystery to me, it baffles me; ***aus –en Gründen,*** for obscure reasons.
unerforschlich ['unˀɛrfɔrʃlɪç], *adj.* impenetrable, inexplicable, inscrutable.
unerfreulich ['unˀɛrfrɔylɪç], *adj.* unpleasant, displeasing, unwelcome, distasteful, vexatious, unsatisfactory, thankless, tiresome, irksome.
unerfüllbar ['unˀɛrfylba:r], *adj.* unrealizable, unattainable, impossible of fulfilment.
unergiebig ['unˀɛrgi:bɪç], *adj.* unproductive, unfruitful, unprofitable; sterile, barren.
unergründlich ['unˀɛrgryntlɪç], *adj.* unfathomable, bottomless; (*fig.*) inscrutable, impenetrable.
unerheblich ['unˀɛrhe:plɪç], *adj.* insignificant, unimportant, inconsiderable, trivial, trifling; (*Law*) immaterial, irrelevant (***für,*** to).
unerhört ['unˀɛrhø:rt], *adj.* 1. unheard, not granted, disallowed, turned down; 2. unheard of, unprecedented; outrageous, shocking, scandalous; exorbitant (*price*), (*coll.*) tremendous, terrific.
unerkenntlich ['unˀɛrkɛntlɪç], *adj.* ungrateful, unmindful. **Unerkenntlichkeit,** *f.* ingratitude, thanklessness.

unerklärbar ['un?ɛrklɛ:rba:r], **unerklärlich,** *adj.* inexplicable, unaccountable, mysterious, puzzling, enigmatical, abstruse, obscure.

unerläßlich ['un?ɛrlɛslɪç], *adj.* indispensable; essential, requisite.

unerlaubt ['un?ɛrlaupt], *adj.* unlawful, illicit, forbidden, prohibited, unauthorized, (*Spt.*) foul; (*Mil.*) ***-e Entfernung von der Truppe,*** absence without leave; (*Law*) ***-e Handlung,*** tort.

unerledigt ['un?ɛrle:dɪçt], *adj.* unfinished, unaccomplished; (*pred.*) left undone, not disposed of, (*Law*) pending.

unermeßlich ['un?ɛrmɛslɪç], *adj.* immense, immeasurable, boundless, unbounded; vast, huge, untold. **Unermeßlichkeit,** *f.* immensity, vastness, boundlessness.

unermüdlich ['un?ɛrmy:tlɪç], *adj.* indefatigable, unflagging, untiring, unremitting.

unerquicklich ['un?ɛrkvɪklɪç], *adj.* unpleasant, unedifying; uncomfortable, disagreeable.

unerreichbar ['un?ɛrraɪçba:r], *adj.* unattainable, inaccessible, unprocurable, unobtainable, impracticable, (*pred.*) out of *or* beyond reach. **unerreicht,** *adj.* unequalled, unrivalled, unparalleled, record (*performance*).

unersättlich ['un?ɛrzɛtlɪç], *adj.* insatiable, ravenous, rapacious, avid.

unerschlossen ['un?ɛrʃlɔsən], *adj.* undeveloped (*of territory etc.*), untapped (*resources etc.*), (*pred.*) not opened up.

unerschöpflich ['un?ɛrʃœpflɪç], *adj.* inexhaustible.

unerschrocken ['un?ɛrʃrɔkən], *adj.* fearless, intrepid, undaunted, undismayed. **Unerschrockenheit,** *f.* fearlessness, intrepidity.

unerschütterlich ['un?ɛrʃytərlɪç], *adj.* immovable, unshakeable; imperturbable, stolid; unflinching, (*pred.*) (as) firm as a rock.

unerschwinglich ['un?ɛrʃvɪŋlɪç], *adj.* unattainable; (*of price*) prohibitive, exorbitant, (*pred.*) beyond one's means; ***das ist mir* –,** I cannot afford it, it is too dear for me.

unersetzlich ['un?ɛrzɛtslɪç], *adj.* irreplaceable, irretrievable, irrecoverable, irreparable.

unersprießlich ['un?ɛrʃpri:slɪç], *adj.* unpleasant, displeasing, distasteful; unprofitable, fruitless.

unerträglich ['un?ɛrtrɛ:klɪç], *adj.* intolerable, unbearable, insupportable, insufferable, overpowering (*heat etc.*).

unerwähnt ['un?ɛrvɛ:nt], *adj.* unmentioned; ***– lassen,*** make no mention of, pass over (in silence).

unerwartet ['un?ɛrvartət], *adj.* unexpected, unlooked for, unforeseen; sudden, abrupt, (*of attack, visitors etc.*) surprise.

unerweislich ['un?ɛrvaɪslɪç], *adj.* indemonstrable.

unerwidert ['un?ɛrvi:dərt], *adj.* unanswered (*letter*); unreturned, unrequited (*love*).

unerwiesen ['un?ɛrvi:zən], *adj.* not proved, unconfirmed; (*Scottish Law*) not proven.

unerzogen ['un?ɛrtso:gən], *adj.* unmannerly, ill-bred.

unfähig ['unfɛ:ɪç], *adj.* incapable (*Gen.*, of), unable (to), unfit (for); incompetent, inefficient; (*Law*) ***für – erklären,*** incapacitate. **Unfähigkeit,** *f.* unfitness, incapacity, inability; incompetence, inefficiency.

unfahrbar ['unfa:rba:r], *adj.* impassable, impracticable, (*Naut.*) not navigable.

unfair ['unfɛ:r], *adj.* unsporting.

Unfall ['unfal], *m.* (**-(e)s,** *pl.* **⸚e**) accident, mishap, misadventure, mischance; disaster, calamity, catastrophe; ***– mit tödlichem Ausgang,*** fatal accident; ***Tod durch* –,** accidental death. **Unfallflucht,** *f.* (*Motor.*) failure to report an accident. **Unfalliste,** *f.* list of casualties. **Unfall|station,** *f.* first-aid post. **–stelle,** *f.* scene of an *or* the accident. **–verhütung(s)vorschrift(en),** *f.*(*pl.*) safety precautions. **-verluste,** *m.pl.* casualties. **–versicherung,** *f.* accident insurance. **–wagen,** *m.* motor ambulance, (*Av.*) crash tender. **–ziffer,** *f.* accident rate, casualty figures, (*Motor.*) toll of the road.

unfaßbar ['unfasba:r], **unfaßlich,** *adj.* unintelligible, inconceivable, incomprehensible.

unfehlbar ['unfe:lba:r], **1.** *adj.* unfailing, infallible, unerring. **2.** *adv.* certainly, without fail, infallibly, inevitably. **Unfehlbarkeit,** *f.* infallibility.

unfein ['unfaɪn], *adj.* coarse, indelicate, unmannerly, ungentlemanly, unladylike, (*pred.*) not nice, bad form.

unfern ['unfɛrn], **1.** *adv.* not far off, near (at hand). **2.** *prep.* (*Gen., Dat.,* ***von***) near, not far from.

unfertig ['unfɛrtɪç], *adj.* unfinished, incomplete, (*fig.*) immature, (*coll.*) half-baked.

Unflat ['unfla:t], *m.* filth, dirt; riff-raff. **unflätig,** *adj.* filthy, dirty; beastly, lewd.

unfolgsam ['unfɔlkza:m], *adj.* disobedient, unruly, wilful, wayward (*of children*).

unförmig ['unfœrmɪç], *adj.* misshapen, deformed; shapeless, unwieldy, clumsy, bulky. **Unförmigkeit,** *f.* shapelessness, unwieldiness, clumsiness, bulkiness.

unförmlich ['unfœrmlɪç], *adj.* informal, unceremonious.

unfrankiert ['unfraŋki:rt], *adj.* not prepaid, carriage forward; unstamped (*letter*).

unfrei ['unfraɪ], *adj.* dependent, subject, feudatory, subjugated; (*pred.*) not free, in bondage *or* thrall to, (*fig.*) constrained, embarrassed, self-conscious. **Unfreiheit,** *f.* bondage, serfdom, thraldom, (*fig.*) constraint.

unfreiwillig ['unfraɪvɪlɪç], *adj.* involuntary, compulsory, (*Av.*) forced (*landing*).

unfreundlich ['unfrɔyntlɪç], *adj.* (*of a p.*) unfriendly, unkind, disobliging, ungracious, uncharitable; ill-disposed, spiteful, churlish (***zu, gegen,*** to); cheerless (*as a room*), inclement (*weather*). **Unfreundlichkeit,** *f.* unfriendliness, unkindness, ill will, churlishness; cheerlessness (*of a room*); inclemency (*of the weather*).

Unfriede(n) ['unfri:də(n)], *m.* discord, dissension, strife, enmity, friction.

unfruchtbar ['unfruxtba:r], *adj.* unfruitful, unprofitable, unproductive; barren, sterile; ***auf –en Boden fallen,*** fall upon stony ground; ***bei ihm auf –en Boden fallen,*** have no effect on him, be lost on him. **Unfruchtbarkeit,** *f.* barrenness, sterility. **Unfruchtbarmachung,** *f.* sterilization.

Unfug ['unfu:k], *m.* misdemeanour, misconduct; nuisance; mischief; (*Law*) ***grober* –,** gross misconduct, public nuisance; ***großer* –,** sheer nonsense; ***– treiben,*** be up to mischief.

unfügsam ['unfy:kza:m], *adj.* intractable, unmanageable.

unfühlbar ['unfy:lba:r], *adj.* impalpable, intangible, imperceptible.

ungalant ['ungalant], *adj.* discourteous.

ungangbar ['unganba:r], *adj.* impassable, impracticable; not current (*of coins*); unsaleable (*of wares*).

Ungar ['uŋga:r], *m.* (**-n,** *pl.* **-n**), **Ungarin,** *f.*, **ungarisch,** *adj.* Hungarian. **Ungarn,** *n.* Hungary.

ungastlich ['ungastlɪç], *adj.* inhospitable, unsociable. **Ungastlichkeit,** *f.* inhospitality.

ungattlich ['ungatlɪç], *adj.* (*Swiss*) clumsy, bulky, massive, misshapen.

ungeachtet ['ungəaxtət], **1.** *adj.* despised, snubbed, (*pred.*) not esteemed. **2.** *prep.* (*Gen. or rarely Dat.*) notwithstanding, in spite of, regardless of, irrespective of, despite.

ungeahndet ['ungəa:ndət], **1.** *adj.* unpunished. **2.** *adv.* with impunity.

ungeahnt ['ungəa:nt], *adj.* *See* **unvorhergesehen.**

ungebärdig ['ungəbɛ:rdɪç], *adj.* wild, unruly, boisterous, rowdy.

ungebeten ['ungəbe:tən], *adj.* uninvited; unasked, unbidden; ***–er Gast,*** intruder; (*sl.*) gate-crasher.

ungebildet ['ungəbɪldət], *adj.* ill-bred, uncivilized, unmannerly; uneducated, uncultured, unrefined.

Ungebühr ['ungəby:r], *f.* indecency, impropriety, unseemliness; abuse, excess; ***zur* –,** unduly, to excess. **ungebührend, ungebührlich,** *adj.* undue, excessive, unwarrantable, unbecoming, unseemly, improper, indecorous, indecent. **Ungebührlichkeit,** *f. See* **Ungebühr.**

ungebunden ['ungəbundən], *adj.* unbound, (*pred.*) in sheets; (*fig.*) free and easy, unrestrained, unbridled; licentious, dissolute, (*coll.*) loose; free, unlinked, uncombined; ***–e Rede,*** prose. **Ungebundenheit,** *f.* freedom, liberty; lack of restraint, licence.

ungedeckt ['ungədɛkt], *adj.* uncovered (*also Spt., Comm.* (*cheque*)), open, exposed, unprotected; (*Spt.*) unmarked, (*Comm.*) unsecured (*credit*); ***der Tisch ist noch –,*** the table is not yet laid.

Ungedeih ['ungədaɪ], *m.* ***auf Gedeih und –,*** in success or failure, in sickness or in health.

Ungeduld ['ungədult], *f.* impatience. **ungeduldig,** *adj.* impatient.

ungeeignet ['ungəaɪknət], *adj.* unsuitable, unsuited, unfit (***zu,*** for), inappropriate, incongruous, inopportune; (*of a p.*) unqualified.

ungefähr ['ungəfɛ:r], **1.** *adj.* casual, chance, accidental; approximate, rough. **2.** *adv.* casually, sketchily; about, around, approximately, in the neighbourhood *or* region of; ***vor – einem Monat,*** about *or* around a month ago; ***das war –, was er mir sagte,*** that was pretty much what he said to me; ***wenn ich – wüßte,*** if I had the slightest *or* faintest *or* had some idea; ***– wie,*** much as; ***– wo,*** more or less where; ***wie – hast du es gemeint?*** what roughly did you have in mind? ***wo –?*** whereabouts? ***von –,*** by chance, by accident, out of the blue.

ungefährdet ['ungəfɛ:rdət], *adj.* safe, secure, (*pred.*) out of danger, out of harm's way, in safety. **ungefährlich,** *adj.* harmless, safe, innocuous, (*pred.*) not dangerous.

ungefällig ['ungəfɛlɪç], *adj.* (*of a p.*) discourteous, ungracious, uncivil, churlish, unaccommodating, disobliging, (*of a th.*) unpleasant, disagreeable; ungraceful, ungainly.

ungeflügelt ['ungəfly:gəlt], *adj.* wingless, apterous.

ungefragt ['ungəfra:kt], *adv.* without being asked.

ungefrierbar ['ungəfri:rba:r], *adj.* non-freezing, uncongealable.

ungefrühstückt ['ungəfry:ʃtykt], *adv.* (*coll.*) without breakfast, on an empty stomach.

ungefüge ['ungəfy:gə], *adj.* misshapen, clumsy, bulky, massive, (*coll.*) hulking. **ungefügig,** *adj.* inflexible, unbending, unyielding; unwieldy, unmanageable; disobedient, recalcitrant.

ungehalten ['ungəhaltən], *adj.* indignant, annoyed, displeased (***über*** (*Acc.*), at).

ungeheißen ['ungəhaɪsən], **1.** *adj.* unbidden, unasked, uninvited. **2.** *adv.* voluntarily, of one's own accord, spontaneously.

ungeheuer ['ungəhɔyər], **1.** *adj.* huge, vast, immense, colossal, enormous, monstrous. **2.** *adv.* exceedingly, tremendously, (*coll.*) awfully, mighty, mightily. **Ungeheuer,** *n.* monster. **ungeheuerlich,** *adj.* monstrous, atrocious, frightful. **Ungeheuerlichkeit,** *f.* monstrosity, atrocity, enormity.

ungehobelt ['ungəho:bəlt], *adj.* unplaned, (*fig.*) rude, rough, uncouth, boorish.

ungehörig ['ungəhø:rɪç], *adj.* undue, unmerited; unseemly, improper; impertinent, impudent. **Ungehörigkeit,** *f.* impropriety, unseemliness; (piece of) impudence, impertinence; incongruity.

ungehorsam ['ungəho:rza:m], *adj.* disobedient, refractory, intractable; (*Mil*) insubordinate. **Ungehorsam,** *m.* disobedience, insubordination, (*Law*) non-compliance; default.

ungekocht ['ungəkɔxt], *adj.* uncooked, raw.

ungekränkt ['ungəkrɛŋkt], *adj.* unhurt, unimpaired; ***der Vorwurf läßt mich –,*** that reproach leaves me cold.

ungekünstelt ['ungəkynstəlt], *adj.* unaffected, unstudied, artless, naïve, ingenuous, simple, natural, frank.

ungeladen ['ungəla:dən], *adj.* (*firearms*) unloaded, (*visitor*) uninvited, (*Elec.*) uncharged.

Ungeld ['ungɛlt], *n.* (*dial.*) a mint of money.

ungelegen ['ungəle:gən], *adj.* inconvenient, inopportune, untimely, unseasonable, (*coll.*) awkward; inexpedient, unwelcome, unsuitable. **Ungelegenheit,** *f.* inconvenience, trouble; ***ihm –en machen,*** inconvenience him, put him to inconvenience, give him trouble.

ungelegt ['ungəle:kt], *adj.* (*Prov.*) ***kümmere dich nicht um –e Eier!*** don't count your chickens before they're hatched.

ungelehrig ['ungəle:rɪç], *adj.* unteachable, dull, unintelligent, incapable of learning, (*pred.*) **ungelehrt,** *adj.* uneducated, uncultured.

ungelenk(ig) ['ungəlɛŋk(ɪç)], *adj.* stiff, ungainly, uncouth, awkward, clumsy.

ungelernt ['ungəlɛrnt], *adj.* unskilled (*workman*).

ungelogen ['ungəlo:gən], *adv.* (*coll.*) without a word of a lie.

ungelöscht ['ungəlœʃt], *adj.* unquenched; ***–er Kalk,*** unslaked lime, quicklime.

Ungemach ['ungəma:x], *n.* discomfort, privation, hardship, adversity, trouble. **ungemächlich** [–mɛçlɪç], *adj.* unpleasant, disagreeable, uncomfortable; troublesome, tiresome, irksome.

ungemein ['ungəmaɪn], **1.** *adj.* extraordinary, unusual, uncommon. **2.** *adv.* greatly, extremely, exceedingly, intensely, acutely, inordinately, extraordinarily, particularly, remarkably, singularly, profoundly.

ungemessen ['ungəmɛsən], *adj.* boundless, immense, unlimited; ***ins Ungemessene gehen*** or ***wachsen,*** go beyond all limits, know no bounds.

ungemünzt ['ungəmyntst], *adj.* ***–es Gold*** or ***Silber,*** bullion.

ungemütlich ['ungəmy:tlɪç], *adj.* cheerless, uncomfortable, unpleasant; (*coll.*) ***– werden,*** get awkward, turn nasty.

ungenannt ['ungənant], *adj.* anonymous; nameless, unnamed.

ungenau ['ungənau], *adj.* inaccurate, inexact. **Ungenauigkeit,** *f.* inaccuracy, inexactitude.

ungeneigt ['ungənaɪkt], *adj.* disinclined, unwilling, reluctant (to), averse (from). **Ungeneigtheit,** *f.* unwillingness, disinclination, reluctance.

ungeniert ['unʒəni:rt], **1.** *adj.* unembarrassed, undisturbed, unabashed; nonchalant, free and easy. **2.** *adv.* freely, unhesitatingly, nonchalantly, without misgivings, without let or hindrance. **Ungeniertheit,** *f.* lack of constraint, free and easy way(s); unceremoniousness, nonchalance.

ungenießbar ['ungəni:sba:r], *adj.* unpalatable, uneatable, undrinkable, (*pred.*) not fit to eat *or* drink; (*fig.*) dull, tedious, boring, (*of a p.*) sullen, surly, unbearable, (*coll.*) grumpy, (*pred.*) in a bad humour.

ungenügend ['ungəny:gənt], **1.** *adj.* insufficient, inadequate; below standard, poor, unsatisfactory. **2.** *adv.* under-.

ungenügsam ['ungəny:gsa:m], *adj.* insatiable, greedy, avid. **Ungenügsamkeit,** *f.* greediness, avidity, insatiability.

ungenutzt ['ungənutst], **ungenützt,** *adj.* not made use of, not taken advantage of; ***see*** **unbenutzt.**

ungeordnet ['ungəɔrdnət], *adj.* disorganized, disorderly, disarranged; unregulated, incoherent; ***–er Lebenswandel,*** dissolute life.

ungepflegt ['ungəpfle:kt], *adj.* untidy, neglected, uncared for, (*of a p.*) unkempt.

ungerade ['ungəra:də], *adj.* (*pred.*) not straight, out of line; uneven, odd (*number*).

ungeraten ['ungəra:tən], *adj.* stultified, unavailing, ineffectual, unsuccessful; (*dial.*) dirty; ***–e Kinder,*** spoiled *or* undutiful children.

ungerechnet ['ungərɛçnət], **1.** (*pred.*) *adj.* not counted; not included, not taken into account. **2.** *adv.* not counting *or* including, apart from.

ungerecht ['ungərɛçt], *adj.* unjust, unfair, inequitable (***gegen,*** to).

ungerechtfertigt ['ungərɛçtfɛrtɪçt], *adj.* unjustified, unwarranted.

Ungerechtigkeit ['ungərɛçtıçkaıt], *f.* injustice, unfairness.
ungeregelt ['ungəre:gəlt], *adj.* not regulated; irregular, disorderly.
ungereimt ['ungəraımt], *adj.* unrhymed; (*fig.*) nonsensical, absurd. **Ungereimtheit,** *f.* absurdity, nonsense.
ungern ['ungərn], *adv.* unwillingly, reluctantly, regretfully, grudgingly, perforce, (*coll.*) against the grain; ***ich sehe –,*** I am sorry to see; ***gern oder –,*** willy-nilly, whether you like it or not.
ungerupft ['ungərupft], *adj.* unplucked; (*fig.*) – ***davonkommen,*** get off lightly, not be fleeced.
ungesäuert ['ungəzɔyərt], *adj.* unleavened, azymous.
ungesäumt ['ungəzɔymt], **1.** *adj.* 1. seamless; 2. prompt, immediate. **2.** *adv.* without delay, at once, immediately, straightway, forthwith, right away.
ungeschehen ['ungəʃe:ən], *adj.* undone; rectified, redressed, remedied; ***man kann das nicht – machen,*** it cannot be undone.
ungescheut ['ungəʃɔyt], *adj.* fearless, undaunted, unabashed.
Ungeschick ['ungəʃık], *n.* incompetence, ineptitude, gaucherie, bungling, awkwardness, clumsiness; – ***läßt grüßen!*** clumsy fool! (*iron.*) that's clever! **Ungeschicklichkeit,** *f. See* **Ungeschick. ungeschickt,** *adj.* awkward, clumsy, unskilful; gauche, inept, maladroit.
ungeschlacht ['ungəʃlaxt], *adj.* uncouth, ungainly, bulky, (*coll.*) hulking; boorish, lubberly.
ungeschlechtlich ['ungəʃlɛçtlıç], *adj.* asexual, agamic, neuter, unsexed.
ungeschliffen ['ungəʃlıfən], *adj.* unpolished, uncut (*gems*), unground, blunt (*knives*); (*fig.*) ill-bred, uncivil, uncouth, crude, rude, coarse, unrefined.
Ungeschmack ['ungəʃmak], *m.* (*obs.*) tastelessness; bad taste.
ungeschmälert ['ungəʃmɛ:lərt], *adj.* undiminished, unimpaired, whole, intact, (*pred.*) in full.
ungeschmeidig ['ungəʃmaıdıç], *adj.* rigid, firm, inflexible; (*fig.*) unbending, unyielding, obdurate, self-opinionated, intractable, (*coll.*) stiff-necked.
ungeschminkt ['ungəʃmıŋkt], *adj.* without make-up, (*fig.*) unadorned, unvarnished, plain (*truth*).
ungeschoren ['ungəʃo:rən], *adj.* unshorn; (*fig.*) unmolested; ***lassen Sie mich –!*** let me alone! leave me in peace!
ungesellig ['ungəzɛlıç], *adj.* unsociable, (*coll.*) stand-offish.
ungesetzlich ['ungəzɛtslıç], *adj.* illegal, unlawful, illicit. **Ungesetzlichkeit,** *adj.* illegality, unlawfulness.
ungesittet ['ungəzıtət], *adj.* unmannerly, uncivil, ungracious, ungenteel, ill-bred; rude, uncivilized, uncultured.
ungestalt ['ungəʃtalt], *adj.* shapeless, misshapen, deformed. **ungestaltet,** *adj.* defaced, disfigured, mutilated, distorted.
ungestört ['ungəʃtø:rt], *adj.* untroubled, undisturbed, uninterrupted, peaceful, tranquil.
ungestraft ['ungəʃtra:ft], **1.** *adj.* unpunished. **2.** *adv.* with impunity; – ***davonkommen,*** get off scot-free.
ungestüm ['ungəʃty:m], *adj.* stormy, turbulent, tumultuous, furious, violent, vehement, boisterous, obstreperous, impetuous. **Ungestüm,** *n.* impetuosity, violence, vehemence, turbulence.
ungesucht ['ungəzuxt], *adj.* (*fig.*) unstudied, unsought, unaffected, natural, spontaneous, artless.
ungesund ['ungəzunt], *adj.* (*of a p.*) unhealthy, unsound in health, sickly, poorly, (*coll.*) seedy; (*of a th.*) unwholesome, deleterious, injurious to health, (*fig.*) unsound.
ungeteilt ['ungətaılt], *adj.* undivided, integral; unanimous (*opinion*), ungraduated (*as a dial*).
ungetrübt ['ungətry:pt], *adj.* clear, unclouded, (*fig.*) untroubled, unruffled, serene, placid.
Ungetüm ['ungəty:m], *n.* (**-(e)s,** *pl.* **-e**) monster, monstrosity.
ungeübt ['ungəy:pt], *adj.* unpractised; untrained, inexperienced.
ungewaschen ['ungəvaʃən], *adj.* unwashed, unclean, soiled, dirty; ***–es Zeug!*** stuff and nonsense! cock-and-bull story; ***–es Maul,*** scurrilous *or* foul tongue.
ungewiß ['ungəvıs], *adj.* uncertain, doubtful, dubious, undecided, indecisive; hazardous, precarious, problematic, (*coll.*) chancy; depending on circumstances; ***ihn im Ungewissen lassen,*** leave him in the dark, keep him in suspense; ***ins Ungewisse leben,*** live from hand to mouth; ***Sprung ins Ungewisse,*** leap in the dark. **Ungewißheit,** *f.* doubt, suspense, uncertainty; perplexity, hesitation, misgiving, qualm.
Ungewitter ['ungəvıtər], *n.* storm, thunder-storm, cloudburst.
ungewöhnlich ['ungəvø:nlıç], *adj.* unusual, uncommon, exceptional, abnormal, odd, extraordinary, rare, strange.
ungewohnt ['ungəvo:nt], *adj.* (*of a th.*) unusual, unaccustomed, unfamiliar, unwonted; (*of a p.*) unaccustomed, unused (*Gen.*, to). **Ungewohntheit,** *f.* strangeness, unfamiliarity, novelty.
ungewollt ['ungəvɔlt], *adj.* unintentional, involuntary.
ungezählt ['ungətsɛ:lt], *adj.* unnumbered, uncounted; untold, countless, innumerable, unlimited, endless.
ungezähnt ['ungətsɛ:nt], *adj.* imperforate (*of postage stamps*).
Ungeziefer ['ungətsi:fər], *n.* vermin.
ungeziemend ['ungətsi:mənt], *adj.* unseemly, improper.
ungezogen ['ungətso:gən], *adj.* ill-bred, ill-mannered, rude, uncivil; ***–es Kind,*** naughty *or* disobedient child. **Ungezogenheit,** *f.* naughtiness; rudeness, impertinence, piece of impudence.
ungezwungen ['ungətsvuŋən], *adj.* unconstrained, free, spontaneous; natural, unaffected, unforced, easy. **Ungezwungenheit,** *f.* naturalness, spontaneity, ease, unconstraint, lack of constraint.
ungiftig ['ungıftıç], *adj.* non-poisonous, non-toxic, innocuous.
Unglaube(n) ['unglaubə(n)], *m.* incredulity, unbelief, disbelief. **unglaubhaft,** *adj.* unconvincing, implausible, incredible.
ungläubig ['unglɔybıç], *adj.* incredulous, sceptical, disbelieving, doubting; (*Eccl.*) unbelieving, irreligious, undevout, infidel. **Ungläubige(r),** *m., f.* unbeliever, infidel.
unglaublich ['unglauplıç], *adj.* incredible, unbelievable, unheard of, (*coll.*) staggering; (*coll.*) ***–er Kerl,*** astonishing *or* incredible *or* impossible fellow. **unglaubwürdig,** *adj.* (*of a p.*) untrustworthy, unreliable; (*of a th.*) incredible, fantastic, unbelievable; unauthenticated.
ungleich ['unglaıç], **1.** *adj.* unequal, unlike, different, dissimilar, disparate, varying; (*of numbers*) uneven, odd. **2.** *adv.* incomparably, a great deal, (by) far, much; – ***besser,*** far better; – ***schöner,*** much more beautiful.
ungleich|artig, *adj.* different, dissimilar, diverse, multifarious, polymorphic, heterogeneous. **–erbig,** *adj.* heterozygous. **–förmig,** *adj.* not uniform, irregular, unequal, dissimilar.
Ungleichheit ['unglaıçhaıt], *f.* inequality, disparity, dissimilarity, diversity; variation, difference, disproportion.
ungleich|mäßig, *adj.* uneven, unbalanced, disproportionate; unsymmetrical, asymmetrical; non-uniform, erratic. **–seitig,** *adj.* scalene (*of triangles*). **–stoffig,** *adj.* (*Chem.*) inhomogeneous.
Unglimpf ['unglımpf], *m.* rigour, stringency, sternness, harshness; wrong, injustice, unfairness; insult, affront, indignity, outrage. **unglimpflich,** *adj.* unfair; harsh.
Unglück ['unglyk], *n.* (**-s,** *no pl.*) misfortune, ill *or* bad luck; distress, misery; (*pl.* **Unglücksfälle**) accident, mishap, piece of ill luck, misadventure,

mischance, calamity, catastrophe, disaster; ***zum –,*** as (ill) luck would have it, unfortunately; (*Prov.*) ***kein – so groß, es hat ein Glück im Schoß,*** it is an ill wind that blows no one any good; (*Prov.*) ***ein – kommt selten allein,*** it never rains but it pours.

unglücklich ['unglyklıç], *adj.* unfortunate, unlucky, luckless, hapless, ill-fated, ill-starred; unsuccessful, disastrous, calamitous; unhappy, miserable, sad, wretched, woebegone; ***–e Liebe,*** unrequited love; ***– enden*** or ***ablaufen,*** turn out badly, miscarry, end disastrously, come to nothing. **unglücklicherweise,** *adv.* unluckily, unfortunately, as (ill) luck would have it.

Unglücksbote ['unglyksbo:tə], *m.* bringer of bad tidings, bird of ill omen.

unglückselig ['unglykze:klıç], *adj.* unhappy, miserable; unfortunate, distressing, grievous, lamentable, deplorable, disastrous, calamitous. **Unglückseligkeit,** *f.* unhappiness, misery, wretchedness.

Unglücks|fall, *m.* accident, misadventure, mishap. **–gefährte,** *m.* companion in misfortune. **–häher,** *m.* (*Orn.*) Siberian jay (*Cractes infaustus*). **–kind,** *n.*, **–mensch,** *m.* victim of misfortune, child of woe. **–rabe,** *m.* croaker, prophet of evil, Jeremiah, (*coll.*) dismal Jimmy. **–stern,** *m.* ***unter einem – stehen,*** be ill-fated *or* ill-starred. **–stunde,** *f.* unlucky hour. **–tag,** *m.* fatal *or* black day. **–vogel,** *m. See* **–rabe. –wurm,** *m. or n.* wretched *or* miserable creature.

Ungnade ['ungna:də], *f.* disgrace, disfavour, displeasure; ***in – fallen,*** fall into disgrace, incur displeasure, fall out of favour; ***bei ihm in – fallen,*** incur his displeasure, get into his bad books; ***auf Gnade und*** or ***oder –,*** unconditionally.

ungnädig ['ungnɛ:dıç], **1.** *adj.* ungracious, uncivil, unaccommodating, churlish, unkind, ill-humoured, cross. **2.** *adv.* ungraciously, with disfavour, adversely, amiss.

Ungrund ['ungrunt], *m.* (*obs.*) *see* **Abgrund.**

ungültig ['ungyltıç], *adj.* invalid, invalidated, inoperative, inadmissable, refuted, rebutted, disproved; void, worthless, not current, cancelled; not available (*as a ticket*); ***für – erklären,*** render void, invalidate, abrogate, repudiate, set aside, disallow, annul, revoke, rescind, repeal, quash, declare null and void; ***– machen,*** cancel, countermand, nullify. **Ungültigkeit,** *f.* invalidity, nullity. **Ungültigkeitserklärung, Ungültigmachung,** *f.* invalidation, abrogation, cancellation, repudiation, revocation, annulment, nullification, repeal.

Ungunst ['ungunst], *f.* disfavour, ill-will; malice, unkindness; inauspiciousness, unpropitiousness; ***– des Wetters,*** inclemency of the weather; ***zu seinen –en,*** to his disadvantage; ***es fiel zu seinen –en aus,*** it went against him.

ungünstig ['ungynstıç], *adj.* unfavourable, adverse, untoward, disadvantageous, detrimental, deleterious.

ungut ['ungu:t], *adj.* ***–es Gefühl,*** misgivings; ***für – nehmen,*** take amiss *or* ill; ***nichts für –!*** no offence! no harm meant! no hard feelings!

unhaltbar ['unhaltba:r], *adj.* (*fig.*) untenable, indefensible (*of a position*); that cannot be kept (*of promises*); (*Footb.*) unstoppable.

unhandlich ['unhantlıç], *adj.* unwieldy, clumsy, bulky.

unharmonisch ['unharmo:nıʃ], *adj.* inharmonious, discordant.

Unheil ['unhaıl], *n.* harm, mischief, trouble; ruin, havoc, disaster, calamity; ***– stiften*** or ***anrichten,*** cause mischief, do harm, bring trouble, (*of storm*) create *or* wreak havoc.

unheilbar ['unhaılba:r], *adj.* incurable, (*fig.*) irreparable.

unheil|bringend, *adj.* baneful, baleful, hurtful; unlucky, fatal. **–drohend,** *adj.* boding ill, ominous, portentous. **–schwanger,** *adj.* fraught with danger. **Unheilstifter,** *m.* mischief-maker. **unheil|verkündend,** *adj. See* **–drohend. –voll,** *adj.* disastrous, calamitous, sinister.

unheilig ['unhaılıç], *adj.* unholy, unhallowed, profane.

unheimlich ['unhaımlıç], **1.** *adj.* uncanny, weird, unearthly, sinister. **2.** *adv.* (*coll.*) awfully, tremendously, mighty; (*coll.*) ***– viel,*** an awful lot of, heaps *or* piles of.

unhöflich ['unhø:flıç], *adj.* rude, impolite, uncivil, unmannerly, discourteous. **Unhöflichkeit** *f.* rudeness, discourtesy, bad manners, incivility, impoliteness.

unhold ['unhɔlt], *adj.* unfriendly, disobliging, unkind, ungracious, ill-disposed (*Dat.*, to).

Unhold, *m.* **(-(e)s,** *pl.* **-e)** monster, demon, fiend.

unhörbar ['unhø:rba:r], *adj.* inaudible, imperceptible.

unhygienisch ['unhygie:nıʃ], *adj.* insanitary, unhygienic.

Uni ['u:ni:], *f.* (*coll.*) varsity.

uni [y'ni:], *adj.* of one colour, plain, self-coloured.

unieren [u'ni:rən], *v.t.* unite; ***die Unierten,*** United Protestants; Greek Catholics.

uniform [uni'fɔrm], *adj.* uniform, homogeneous. **Uniform,** *f.* (-, *pl.* **-en**) uniform, regimentals; livery. **uniformiert** [–'mi:rt], *adj.* uniform, reduced to uniformity; uniformed, in uniform. **Uniformierung,** *f.* levelling. **Uniformität,** *f.* uniformity, homogeneity, regularity, conformity.

Unikum ['u:nikum], *n.* **(-s,** *pl.* **-s** *or* **-ka)** unique instance, unique example; (*of a p.*) original, (*coll.*) character.

uninteressant ['unˀıntərɛsant], *adj.* uninteresting, dull, boring, tedious, devoid of interest, unattractive. **uninteressiert,** *adj.* uninterested, disinterested (*an* (*Dat.*), in), impartial (about), indifferent (to), with no personal interest (in). **Uninteressiertheit,** *f.* indifference, lack of interest.

Universal|erbe [univɛr'za:l–], *m.* sole heir, residuary legatee. **–mittel,** *m.* sovereign *or* universal remedy, panacea, cure-all. **–schraubenschlüssel,** *m.* monkey-wrench. **–werkzeug,** *n.* all-purpose tool.

universell [univɛr'zɛl], *adj.* universal.

Universität [univɛrzi'tɛ:t], *f.* university. **Universitäts|dozent,** *m.* university lecturer. **–rektor,** *m.* vice-chancellor of the university. **–studium,** *n.* study at a university. **–vorlesung,** *f.* university lecture.

Universum [uni'vɛrzum], *n.* universe.

Unke ['uŋkə], *f.* 1. (*Zool.*) orange-speckled toad (*Bombinator*); 2. (*coll.*) croaker, grumbler, prophet of evil, Jeremiah. **unken,** *v.i.* (*fig.*) grumble, complain, (*coll.*) grouse, groan, croak, (*sl.*) bellyache.

unkenntlich ['unkɛntlıç], *adj.* unrecognizable, irrecognizable, indiscernible; ***– machen,*** disguise, obliterate, deface. **Unkenntlichkeit,** *f.* irrecognizable condition; ***bis zur –,*** past recognition. **Unkenntnis,** *f.* ignorance, unawareness, incognizance; ***in – sein über*** (*Acc.*), be unaware of; ***in – (er)halten*** or ***lassen über*** (*Acc.*), keep in the dark about; ***– schützt vor Strafe nicht,*** ignorance of the law is no excuse.

unkeusch ['unkɔyʃ], *adj.* unchaste, impure. **Unkeuschheit,** *f.* unchastity, impurity.

unklar ['unkla:r], *adj.* not clear, muddy, thick, turbid; hazy, misty, foggy, indistinct; (*fig.*) unintelligible, obscure, abstruse; vague, confused, uncertain, muddled, (*coll.*) woolly; (*Naut. etc.*) fouled, not ready, out of action; ***im –en sein,*** be in the dark (***über*** (*Acc.*), about); ***ihm im –en lassen,*** keep him guessing. **Unklarheit,** *f.* obscurity, vagueness, confusion.

unklug ['unklu:k], *adj.* thoughtless, silly, senseless, idiotic; unwise, misguided, imprudent, ill-advised, impolitic. **Unklugheit,** *f.* imprudence, indiscretion, silliness.

unkollegial ['unkɔle:gia:l], *adj.* unfriendly, disobliging, unaccommodating, unneighbourly, stand-offish, uncooperative.

unkontrollierbar ['unkɔntrɔli:rba:r], *adj.* uncontrollable, (*fig.*) unverifiable, unable to be vouched for.

unkonvertierbar ['unkɔnvɛrti:rba:r], *adj.* inconvertible.

unkörperlich ['unkœrpərlɪç], *adj.* incorporeal, disembodied, immaterial; spiritual.

Unkosten ['unkɔstən], *pl.* expense(s), costs, charges; (*Comm.*) overheads; ***auf meine* –**, at my expense; ***sich in – stürzen***, go to great expense. **Unkosten|-berechnung,** *f.* cost accounting. **-konto,** *n.* expense account. **-rechnung,** *f.* charge account.

Unkraut ['unkraut], *n.* (**-(e)s,** *pl.* **¨-er**) weed, weeds; (*Prov.*) **–** ***vergeht*** or ***verdirbt nicht***, ill weeds grow apace.

unkristallinisch ['unkrɪstali:nɪʃ], *adj.* non-crystalline, amorphous.

unkündbar ['unkyntba:r], *adj.* irredeemable, irreclaimable, irreversible, irrevocable, incommutable, immutable; permanent (*post*); ***-e Papiere***, irredeemable stock; ***-e Rente***, perpetual annuity; ***-er Vertrag***, binding agreement.

unkundig ['unkundɪç], *adj.* (*Gen.*) ignorant *or* unaware *or* incognizant of; unacquainted *or* not conversant with, uninformed about; unversed in; a stranger to; ***des Griechischen –***, knowing *or* having no Greek.

unkünstlerisch ['unkynstlərɪʃ], *adj.* inartistic, (*of a p.*) unartistic.

unlängst ['unlɛŋst], *adv.* not long ago, recently, latterly, lately, the other day, of late.

unlauter ['unlautər], *adj.* impure; (*fig.*) mean, sordid, self-seeking, self-interested; ***-er Wettbewerb***, unfair competition.

unleidig ['unlaɪdɪç], *adj.* irritable, impatient, moody. **unleidlich,** *adj.* intolerable, insufferable, unbearable; (*dial.*) *see* **unleidig.**

unlenksam ['unlɛŋkza:m], *adj.* unruly, unmanageable, intractable.

unlesbar ['unle:zba:r], **unleserlich,** *adj.* illegible, unreadable. **Unleserlichkeit,** *f.* illegibility.

unleugbar ['unlɔykba:r], *adj.* undeniable, unquestionable, indisputable.

unlieb ['unli:p], *adj.* (*only with* **zu** *and inf.*) displeasing, disagreeable; ***es ist mir nicht – zu hören***, I am rather glad to hear that. **unliebenswürdig,** *adj.* unfriendly, unkind, disobliging, churlish, surly. **unliebsam,** *adj.* disagreeable, unpleasant.

unliniert ['unlini:rt], *adj.* without lines, unruled.

unlogisch ['unlo:gɪʃ], *adj.* illogical.

unlösbar ['unlø:zba:r], *adj.* indissoluble, inseparable, inextricable; (*fig.*) (*of problems*) unsolvable, (*pred.*) not admitting solution. **unlöslich,** *adj.* (*Chem.*) insoluble.

Unlust ['unlust], *f.* dislike, disinclination (***zu***, for), aversion (to), repugnance, disgust (at); listlessness; (*Comm.*) dullness, slackness. **unlustig,** *adj.* listless; disinclined (***zu***, for), averse, reluctant (to).

Unmacht ['unmaxt], *f.* (*dial.*) *see* **Ohnmacht.**

Unmanier ['unmani:r], *f. See* **Unart, 1. unmanierlich,** *adj.* unmannerly, ill- *or* badly behaved, ill-bred; ***sich – aufführen***, behave abominably.

unmännlich ['unmɛnlɪç], *adj.* unmanly, effeminate.

Unmaß ['unma:s], *n. See* **Unmasse**; ***im –***, *see* **unmäßig, 2.**

Unmasse ['unmasə], *f.* enormous number, vast quantity, no end, a host *or* sea, (*coll.*) heaps, piles, (*sl.*) oodles (***von*** *or Gen.*, of); ***in -n***, *see* **unmäßig, 2.**

unmaßgeblich ['unma:sge:plɪç], *adj.* (*pred.*) not authoritative, open to correction; ***nach meiner -en Meinung***, speaking without authority *or* subject to correction, in my humble opinion.

unmäßig ['unmɛ:sɪç], **1.** *adj.* immoderate, intemperate, excessive, inordinate. **2.** *adv.* to excess, excessively, extremely. **Unmäßigkeit,** *f.* excess, intemperance, lack of moderation.

Unmenge ['unmɛŋə], *f. See* **Unmasse.**

Unmensch ['unmɛnʃ], *m.* (**-en,** *pl.* **-en**) inhuman creature, hard-hearted wretch, monster, brute; (*coll.*) ***sei kein –!*** have a heart! (*coll.*) ***ich bin kein –***, I will not say no, I am open to persuasion. **unmenschlich,** *adj.* inhuman, brutal, barbarous, fiendish; (*coll.*) vast, prodigious, tremendous, exorbitant; ***-e Kraft***, superhuman strength; ***-e Verhältnisse***, degrading conditions. **Unmenschlichkeit,** *f.* inhumanity, cruelty, brutality, barbarity, ferocity.

unmerklich ['unmɛrklɪç], *adj.* imperceptible, inappreciable.

unmeßbar ['unmɛsba:r], *adj.* immeasurable, incommensurable.

unmitteilbar ['unmɪttaɪlba:r], *adj.* incommunicable; (*pred.*) unfit for publication. **unmitteilsam,** *adj.* uncommunicative, secretive, close, reserved, taciturn.

unmittelbar ['unmɪtəlba:r], **1.** *adj.* immediate, direct; ***-e Kenntnis***, first-hand knowledge; ***-er Sinn***, literal sense (*of a passage*). **2.** *adv.* directly; ***sich – wenden an*** (*Acc.*), apply direct(ly) to; **–** ***vor*** (*Dat.*), right *or* straight *or* directly in front of; **–** ***bevorstehen***, be imminent, (*coll.*) be just round the corner; **–** ***darauf***, immediately afterwards. **Unmittelbarkeit,** *f.* directness; immediacy.

unmodern ['unmodɛrn], *adj.* old-fashioned, out of date, outmoded, antiquated. **unmodisch,** *adj.* unfashionable.

unmöglich ['unmø:klɪç], **1.** *adj.* impossible. **2.** *adv.* not possibly; ***ich kann es – tun***, it is out of the question *or* impossible for me to do that, I cannot possibly do it; (*fig.*) ***sich – machen***, compromise o.s., (*coll.*) put one's foot in it. **Unmöglichkeit,** *f.* impossibility; ***es ist ein Ding der –***, it's an impossibility, it is out of the question, that can never be.

unmoralisch ['unmora:lɪʃ], *adj.* immoral.

unmotiviert ['unmotivi:rt], *adj.* without motive *or* reason, unmotivated, unfounded, groundless.

unmündig ['unmyndɪç], *adj.* (*pred.*) under age, not of age; ***-es Kind***, dependent child. **Unmündige(r),** *m., f.* minor. **Unmündigkeit,** *f.* minority.

Unmut ['unmu:t], *m.* ill humour, bad temper; displeasure, annoyance (***über*** (*Acc.*), at). **unmutig,** *adj.* displeased, annoyed, indignant, angry. **unmutsvoll,** *adj.* disgruntled.

unnachahmlich ['unnaxʔa:mlɪç], *adj.* inimitable, matchless.

unnachgiebig ['unnaxgi:bɪç], *adj.* inflexible, unyielding, uncompromising; stubborn, relentless, (*pred.*) adamant.

unnachsichtig ['unnaxzɪçtɪç], *adj.* unrelenting, strict, severe.

unnahbar ['unna:ba:r], *adj.* inaccessible, unapproachable.

Unnatur ['unnatu:r], *f.* unnaturalness, abnormality; abnormity, monstrosity.

unnatürlich ['unnaty:rlɪç], *adj.* unnatural, abnormal; outlandish, monstrous, grotesque, out of the ordinary; affected, precious, stilted, pretentious, forced.

unnennbar ['unnɛnba:r], *adj.* unutterable, inexpressible; ineffable.

unnötig ['unnø:tɪç], *adj.* unnecessary, needless, superfluous. **unnötigerweise,** *adv.* unnecessarily, needlessly.

unnütz ['unnyts], *adj.* useless, unprofitable, vain, idle, superfluous; (*coll.*) good-for-nothing, naughty; ***-es Geschwätz***, idle talk; ***-es Zeug***, trash, nonsense; ***den Namen Gottes – im Munde führen***, take the name of God in vain; ***sich – machen***, make o.s. a nuisance, make a nuisance of o.s.

unoperierbar ['unʔopəri:rba:r], *adj.* (*Med.*) inoperable.

unordentlich ['unʔɔrdəntlɪç], *adj.* disorderly; untidy; unkempt, (*coll.*) slovenly, slipshod. **Unordentlichkeit,** *f.* disorderliness, untidiness. **Unordnung,** *f.* disorder, disarray, confusion; litter, untidiness; ***in – bringen***, throw into disorder *or* confusion, disarrange, disorganize.

unorganisch ['unʔɔrga:nɪʃ], *adj.* inorganic.

unorthographisch ['un?ɔrtoɡra:fɪʃ], *adj.* wrongly spelt, misspelt.

unpaar ['unpa:r], *adj.* not even, odd (*number*); not paired, odd, without a fellow (*gloves etc.*); (*Bot. etc.*) azygous. **Unpaar|hufer,** *m. See* **–zeher. unpaarwertig,** *adj.* (*Chem.*) (*pred.*) of odd valence. **Unpaarzeher,** *m.* (*Zool.*) perissodactyl.

unparteiisch ['unpartaɪɪʃ], *adj.* impartial, disinterested, unprejudiced, unbiased, neutral. **Unparteiische(r),** *m., f.* umpire. **unparteilich,** *adj. See* **unparteiisch. Unparteilichkeit,** *f.* impartiality, neutrality.

unpaß ['unpas], **1.** *adv.* inopportunely. **2.** *pred.adj. See* **unpäßlich.**

unpassend ['unpasənt], *adj.* unsuitable, inappropriate; (*pred.*) out of place; unbecoming, improper, indiscreet; misplaced, inopportune, untimely, unseasonable.

unpassierbar ['unpasi:rba:r], *adj.* impracticable, impassable; unfordable (*of rivers*).

unpäßlich ['unpɛslɪç], *adj.* ailing, indisposed, (*pred.*) unwell, poorly, (*coll.*) out of sorts, off colour. **Unpäßlichkeit,** *f.* indisposition.

unpersönlich ['unpɛrzø:nlɪç], *adj.* impersonal (*also Gram.*), objective.

unpolitisch ['unpoli:tɪʃ], *adj.* non-political, unpolitical; (*fig.*) impolitic, injudicious, ill-advised, ill-judged.

unpraktisch ['unpraktɪʃ], *adj.* unpractical, inexpert, unskilful; impracticable, unmanageable.

unproportioniert ['unprɔpɔrtsioni:rt], *adj.* ill-proportioned, unshapely; disproportionate, (*pred.*) out of proportion.

unqualifizierbar ['unkvalifitsi:rba:r], *adj.* unspeakable, indescribable (*esp. of behaviour*).

Unrast ['unrast], **1.** *f.* restlessness. **2.** *m.* (**-es,** *pl.* **-e**) (*coll.*) restless *or* fidgety child.

Unrat ['unra:t], *m.* rubbish, refuse, garbage; ordure, excrement, filth; (*coll.*) – ***merken*** or ***wittern,*** smell a rat.

unrationell ['unratsionɛl], *adj.* wasteful, extravagant; misapplied, inefficient.

unrätlich ['unrɛ:tlɪç], **unratsam** [–ra:tza:m], *adj.* unadvisable, inadvisable, inexpedient.

unrecht ['unrɛçt], *adj.* wrong, false, incorrect, not right; unsuitable, inopportune, improper; unjust, unfair; ***das geht mit –en Dingen zu,*** there is s.th. uncanny *or* queer about it; (*Prov.*) ***– Gut gedeiht nicht,*** ill-gotten gain never thrives; ***in –e Hände kommen,*** fall into the wrong hands; (*coll.*) ***in die –e Kehle kommen,*** go down the wrong way; ***komme ich –?*** have I come at the wrong *or* at a bad time? ***an den Unrechten kommen,*** catch a Tartar; (*fig.*) ***am –en Ort*** or ***Platz sein,*** be misplaced, be out of place (*as remarks*); ***–e Seite,*** wrong *or* reverse side (*of stuff*); ***zur –en Zeit,*** inopportunely.

Unrecht, *n.* wrong, injustice; error, fault; ***bei dir bekommt er nie –,*** in your opinion he is never wrong; ***ihm – geben,*** decide against him, disagree with him; ***es geschieht ihm –,*** he has been wronged; ***– haben, im – sein,*** be (in the) wrong, be mistaken; ***du hast nicht so ganz –,*** there is s.th. in what you say, you are not so far wrong; ***mit –,*** wrongly, wrongfully, unjustly; ***ihm – tun,*** wrong him, do him an injustice; ***zu –,*** see ***mit –.***

unrechtmäßig ['unrɛçtmɛ:sɪç], *adj.* unlawful, illegal. **unrechtmäßigerweise,** *adv.* unlawfully, illegally. **Unrechtmäßigkeit,** *f.* illegality, unlawfulness.

unredlich ['unre:tlɪç], *adj.* dishonest. **Unredlichkeit,** *f.* dishonesty.

unreell ['unreɛl], *adj.* (*Comm.*) dishonest, fraudulent; unfair (*dealings*), unsound, unreliable (*firm*).

unregelmäßig ['unre:ɡəlmɛ:sɪç], *adj.* irregular, anomalous, abnormal; erratic; aperiodic. **Unregelmäßigkeit,** *f.* irregularity; anomaly.

unreif ['unraɪf], *adj.* unripe, raw, green; (*fig.*) immature, callow, (*coll.*) raw. **Unreife,** *f.* unripeness, immaturity.

unrein ['unraɪn], *adj.* unclean, dirty, impure, polluted, foul; (*of gems*) flawed, (*Mus.*) out of tune; ***ins –e schreiben,*** jot down, make a rough copy of; ***–e Luft,*** foul air; ***–er Stil,*** bad style; ***–er Ton,*** false note. **Unreinheit,** *f.* uncleanness; impurity, foulness, pollution. **Unreinigkeiten,** *f.pl.* impurities, pollution, dross, dirt. **unreinlich,** *adj.* unclean, dirty, unwashed, unkempt, squalid. **Unreinlichkeit,** *f.* dirtiness, uncleanliness, slovenliness, squalor.

unrentabel ['unrɛnta:bəl], *adj.* unprofitable, unremunerative, (*pred.*) not paying *or* able to pay its way.

unrettbar ['unrɛtba:r], **1.** *adj.* irrecoverable, irretrievable, (*pred.*) past help *or* saving *or* recovery. **2.** *adv.* infallibly, definitely; – ***verloren,*** irretrievably lost, lost for good

unrichtig ['unrɪçtɪç], *adj.* false, wrong, incorrect, erroneous; ***–e Angaben,*** false return, misrepresentation; ***diese Uhr geht –,*** this watch does not keep time. **Unrichtigkeit,** *f.* incorrectness, falsity, error, inaccuracy.

Unruh ['unru:], *f.* (-, *pl.* **-en**) balance wheel (*of watch*).

Unruhe ['unru:ə], *f.* unrest, commotion, disturbance, tumult; unrest, restlessness, uneasiness, disquiet, anxiety, alarm, trouble, agitation; (*coll.*) *see* **Unruh**; *pl.* disturbances, riots, rioting, outbreaks of violence. **unruhig,** *adj.* (*of a p.*) restless, agitated, nervous, (*coll.*) fidgety; (*fig.*) uneasy, worried; (*as times*) unsettled, troubled; (*as sea*) choppy, rough, turbulent, (*as sleep*) broken, fitful; (*of horses*) restive.

unrühmlich ['unry:mlɪç], *adj.* inglorious, shameful, infamous, discreditable, reprehensible.

Unruhstifter ['unru:ʃtɪftər], *m.* trouble-maker, (*Law*) disturber of the peace, (*Pol.*) agitator.

uns [unz], *pers.pron.* (*Acc. and Dat. of* **wir**) us; to us; ourselves; to ourselves; ***ein Freund von –,*** a friend of ours, one of our friends; ***er gehört zu –,*** he is one of us; ***unter – gesagt,*** between ourselves; ***von – beiden,*** from both of us; ***wir sehen – nie,*** we never see each other.

unsachgemäß ['unzaxɡəmɛ:s], *adj.* improper, inappropriate, unapt; inexpert, faulty (*work*).

unsachlich ['unzaxlɪç], *adj.* subjective, personal; irrelevant, (*pred.*) not pertinent, off the point, not to the point.

unsagbar ['unza:kba:r], **unsäglich, 1.** *adj.* unspeakable, unutterable. **2.** *adv.* immensely, beyond (all) words.

unsanft ['unzanft], *adj.* harsh, rough, violent.

unsauber ['unzaubər], *adj.* unclean, dirty, filthy; unfair, (*coll.*) shady; ***–e Mittel,*** underhand dealings.

unschädlich ['unʃɛ:tlɪç], *adj.* harmless, safe, innocuous; ***– machen,*** render harmless *or* innocuous, prevent from doing harm; (*coll.*) hamstring; clip the wings of; disarm (*a mine*), neutralize (*a poison*).

unscharf ['unʃarf], *adj.* blurred, hazy, poorly defined, (*pred.*) out of focus, not sharp; (*Rad.*) ***–e Trennung,*** poor selectivity.

unschätzbar ['unʃɛtsba:r], *adj.* invaluable, inestimable.

unscheinbar ['unʃaɪnba:r], *adj.* insignificant, inconspicuous, inconsiderable; plain, (*Am.*) homely; unpretentious.

unschicklich ['unʃɪklɪç], *adj.* unbecoming, improper, unseemly, indecent; out of place, inapt, inadmissible. **Unschicklichkeit,** *f.* impropriety, unseemliness, unsuitability, inappropriateness.

Unschlitt ['unʃlɪt], *n.* tallow, suet.

unschlüssig ['unʃlysɪç], *adj.* wavering, irresolute, undecided, vacillating, indecisive. **Unschlüssigkeit,** *f.* indecision, irresolution, lack of resolution, vacillation, hesitancy.

unschmackhaft ['unʃmakha:ft], *adj.* unpalatable, (*also fig.*) tasteless, insipid.

unschön ['unʃø:n], *adj.* unlovely, unsightly, plain, ugly; (*fig.*) unfair, (*pred.*) not nice.

Unschuld ['unʃult], *f.* innocence; purity; virginity,

chastity; ***ich wasche meine Hände in –,*** I wash my hands of it; ***in aller –,*** quite innocently, with no evil intent; (*coll.*) ***– vom Lande,*** simple innocent country girl; ***gekränkte –,*** injured innocence. **unschuldig,** *adj.* innocent (***an*** (*Dat.*), of), guileless; pure, virgin, chaste (*girl*); harmless (*remark*). **Unschulds|engel,** *m.* little innocent. **–miene,** *f.* air of innocence.

unschwer ['unʃveːr], **1.** *adj.* not difficult, easy. **2.** *adv.* without difficulty.

Unsegen ['unzeːgən], *m.* adversity, misfortune; evil genius.

unselbständig ['unzɛlpʃtɛndɪç], *adj.* dependent (on others), helpless; unoriginal; (*Law*) ***–e Erwerbsperson,*** employed person; (*Law*) ***Einkommen aus –er Arbeit,*** earned income. **Unselbständigkeit,** *f.* dependence (on others), lack of independence, helplessness; lack of originality.

unselig ['unzeːlɪç], *adj.* unhappy, unlucky, wretched, unfortunate; fatal, accursed.

unser ['unzər], **1.** *pers.pron.* (*Gen. of* ***wir***) of us; ***wir*** (or ***es***) ***waren – vier,*** there were four of us; (*B.*) ***Vater –, der Du bist im Himmel,*** Our Father which art in heaven; ***– aller Wunsch,*** the wish of all of us. **2.** *poss.adj.* (***unser, uns(e)re, unser***) our; ***die Schriftsteller –er Zeit,*** the writers of our time. **3.** *poss.pron.* (***der, die, das unsere*** or ***uns(e)rige***) ours; our property; our duty; ***die Unsrigen,*** our people, our men.

unsereiner ['unzərʔaɪnər], *pron.*, **unsereins,** *indecl. pron.* one of us; such as we, people like us. **uns(e)re** (**-r,** *pl.* **-s**), *see* **unser, 2. unser(er)seits,** *adv.* as for us, for our part. **unser(e)sgleichen,** *adj.* the like of us, people like us, our equals. **unserthalben unsertwegen, unsertwillen,** *adv.* for our sake, on our behalf, because *or* on account of us.

unsicher ['unzɪçər], *adj.* unsafe, insecure, unstable, unsteady, precarious; uncertain, doubtful, dubious; ***– auf den Beinen,*** unsteady on one's legs, shaky on one's feet; (*coll.*) ***ihn – machen,*** shake *or* rattle him; ***–es Gedächtnis,*** unreliable *or* (*coll.*) shaky memory. **Unsicherheit,** *f.* insecurity, precariousness, unsteadiness, uncertainty.

unsichtbar ['unzɪçtbaːr], *adj.* invisible, imperceptible, (*pred.*) lost to sight *or* view; (*coll.*) ***sich – machen,*** make o.s. scarce, vanish. **Unsichtbarkeit,** *f.* invisibility.

unsichtig ['unzɪçtɪç], *adj.* hazy, misty (*of the atmosphere*).

Unsinn ['unzɪn], *m.* nonsense, absurdity, (*coll.*) rubbish, rot, rigmarole, twaddle, piffle; ***barer*** or ***blühender –,*** utter *or* downright nonsense; ***– machen*** or ***treiben,*** play the fool, fool about. **unsinnig,** *adj.* nonsensical, absurd, senseless, foolish; crazy, insane; ***– verliebt,*** madly in love.

unsinnlich ['unzɪnlɪç], *adj.* spiritual, supersensual; ***–e Liebe,*** platonic love.

Unsitte ['unzɪtə], *f.* bad habit; abuse. **unsittlich,** *adj.* immoral; indecent. **Unsittlichkeit,** *f.* immorality; indecency.

unsolid(e) ['unzoliːt (–iːdə)], *adj.* (*Comm.*) unreliable, unstable; fickle; loose, dissipated.

unsozial ['unzoːtsiaːl], *adj.* anti-social; unsociable.

unsre, unsrige *etc. See* **unser.**

unständig ['unʃtɛndɪç], *adv.* ***– Beschäftigte(r),*** casual worker.

unstarr ['unʃtaːr], *adj.* non-rigid (*of airships*).

unstät, *adj.* (*dial.*) *see* **unstet.**

unstatthaft ['unʃtathaft], *adj.* inadmissible; forbidden, illicit, (*Spt.*) foul, contrary to the rules.

unsterblich ['unʃtɛrplɪç], **1.** *adj.* immortal; undying (*love*). **2.** *adv.* (*coll.*) ***sich – blamieren,*** make a complete *or* an utter ass of o.s.; ***– machen,*** immortalize; ***sich – machen,*** gain immortality. **Unsterblichkeit,** *f.* immortality.

Unstern ['unʃtɛrn], *m.* unlucky star, evil genius; misfortune, ill-luck, adversity.

unstet ['unʃteːt], *adj.* changeable, inconstant; unsteady, fluctuating, variable; restless, unsettled, wandering, not fixed. **unstetig,** *adj.* (*Math.*) ***–e Größe,*** discrete quantity. **Unstetigkeit,** *f.* unsteadiness, instability, inconstancy, changeableness; unsettled condition, restlessness.

unstillbar ['unʃtɪlbaːr], *adj.* insatiable, unappeasable, unquenchable.

Unstimmigkeit ['unʃtɪmɪçkaɪt], *f.* discrepancy, inconsistency; difference of opinion, disagreement, dissension, friction.

unstörbar ['unʃtøːrbaːr], *adj.* imperturbable, impassive; (*Law*) ***– im Besitze,*** in incommutable possession.

unsträflich ['unʃtrɛːflɪç], *adj.* irreproachable, blameless, impeccable.

unstreckbar ['unʃtrɛkbaːr], *adj.* non-ductile.

unstreitig ['unʃtraɪtɪç], **1.** *adj.* incontestable, indisputable, unquestionable. **2.** *adv.* doubtless, certainly.

unsühnbar ['unzyːnbaːr], *adj.* inexpiable.

Unsumme ['unzumə], *f.* enormous *or* immense sum.

unsymmetrisch ['unzymetrɪʃ], *adj.* asymmetrical, unsymmetrical.

unsympathisch ['unzympaːtɪʃ], *adj.* unpleasant, disagreeable, distasteful; ***er ist mir –,*** I do not like him.

untadelhaft ['untaːdəlhaft], **untad(e)lig,** *adj.* irreproachable, blameless; flawless, unexceptionable.

Untat ['untaːt], *f.* (monstrous) crime, outrage.

untätig ['untɛːtɪç], *adj.* inactive, indolent, idle; unemployed, non-productive; indifferent, inert, dormant. **Untätigkeit,** *f.* inactivity, inaction, idleness, indolence; inertness.

untauglich ['untauklɪç], *adj.* unfit, unserviceable, disabled, useless, unsuitable. **Untauglichkeit,** *f.* uselessness, unfitness, unsuitability.

unteilbar ['untaɪlbaːr], *adj.* indivisible. **Unteilbarkeit,** *f.* indivisibility. **unteilhaftig,** *adj.* non-participating.

unten ['untən], *adv.* below, beneath, under(neath); at the bottom *or* foot; downstairs; ***– am Berge,*** at the foot of the hill; ***– am See,*** down by the lake; ***– an der Seite,*** at the foot *or* bottom of the page; ***– auf der Erde,*** here below; down on the ground; ***da*** or ***dort –,*** down there; (*coll.*) ***– durch sein,*** be fit for nothing, be found wanting, be despised, count for nothing; (*coll.*) ***bei ihm – durch sein,*** be in his bad books; ***– im Wasser,*** at the bottom of the water; ***nach –,*** downwards; ***tief –,*** right down below, far below; ***von oben bis –,*** from top to bottom; (*coll.*) ***– wie oben sein,*** be much of a muchness, be no great shakes; ***kaum noch wissen was oben und was – ist,*** not know whether one is coming or going; ***siehe –!*** see below; ***von – an*** or ***auf,*** right from the bottom, right up from below; (*Mil.*) ***von – auf dienen,*** rise from the ranks; ***weiter –,*** farther down; farther on, later on (*in the text*). **untenstehend,** *adj.* undermentioned, mentioned below.

unter ['untər], **1.** *prep.* (*Acc. or Dat.*) (*Dat. in answer to* **wo**? where? in which place? *Acc. in answer to* **wohin**? whither? to which place?) under, below, beneath, underneath; among, amongst; (*Dat. only*) during.
(a) (*with Dat.*) ***– anderem,*** among other things, (*Law*) inclusive of but not confined to; ***– dieser Bedingung,*** on this condition; ***– dem 30. Breitengrade,*** latitude 30°; (*Comm.*) ***– dem heutigen Datum,*** under today's date; ***– einer Decke stecken mit,*** be hand in glove with; ***– Gelächter,*** amid laughter; ***– dem Gesetze stehen,*** be subject to the law; ***– diesem Gesichtspunkt,*** from this point of view; ***– Glockengeläute,*** with bells ringing; ***– der Hand,*** secretly, on the quiet; ***etwas – den Händen*** or ***der Hand haben,*** have a th. in hand; ***ein Kind – dem Herzen haben,*** be pregnant, be in the family way; ***– freiem Himmel,*** in the open air; ***Kinder – 12 Jahren,*** children under the age of 12; (*coll.*) ***– aller Kanone*** or ***Kritik,*** beneath contempt; ***nicht – 50 Mark,*** not less than 50 marks; ***– dem Namen bekannt sein,*** be known by the name of; ***– Null,***

below zero; – ***seinen Papieren,*** amongst his papers; – ***pari,*** below par; – ***der Presse,*** in the press; – ***Quarantäne,*** in quarantine; – ***der Regierung von,*** in *or* during the reign of; – ***seinem Stande heiraten,*** marry beneath o.s.; – ***dem Strich,*** in the feuilleton; (*Min.*) – ***Tage,*** below ground; – ***Tränen,*** with tears in (his, her *etc.*) eyes, weeping; – ***zwei Übeln das kleinere wählen,*** choose the less of two evils; – ***Umständen,*** under certain conditions, in certain circumstances; – ***allen Umständen,*** in any case; – ***diesen*** or ***solchen Umständen,*** in these circumstances, this being the case, in this case; – ***uns,*** among *or* between ourselves; ***der Größte – uns,*** the tallest of us; – ***uns gesagt,*** between ourselves, between you and me; ***was verstehst du – diesem Ausdruck?*** what do you mean *or* understand by this expression? – ***vier Augen,*** face to face, tête à tête, in private; – ***Vorbehalt aller Rechte,*** all rights reserved; – ***üblichem Vorbehalt,*** with the usual reservations; – ***Waffen,*** under arms, in the field; ***er wohnt – mir,*** he lives in the room below mine; – ***meiner Würde,*** beneath my dignity.
(b) (*with Acc.*) ***ihm – die Augen treten,*** come into his sight, be seen by him; ***bis – das Dach voll,*** full right up to the roof; ***ihn – die Erde bringen,*** be the death of him; – ***die Haube kommen,*** find a husband; ***alle – einen Hut bringen,*** make them all agree upon the same thing, reconcile conflicting opinions; ***wenn es – die Leute kommt,*** if it is talked about, if it gets around *or* about; (*fig.*) ***ihm etwas – die Nase halten*** or ***reiben,*** rub his nose in a th.; – ***die Räuber geraten,*** fall among thieves; – ***die Soldaten gehen,*** enlist; – ***Strafe stellen,*** impose a penalty on; – ***den Tisch fallen,*** fall under the table; (*fig.*) be pushed on one side, be set aside; be forgotten; – ***Wasser setzen,*** flood, inundate.
2. *adj.* under, underneath; lower, inferior; ***–st,*** lowest, undermost, bottom, last; ***zu –st,*** at the bottom; ***das Unterste zuoberst kehren,*** turn everything topsy-turvy *or* upside down, upset everything.
3. *adv.* ***Kinder, die unter 12 Jahre alt sind,*** children who are less than *or* under 12 years of age; ***Städte von unter 10 000 Einwohnern,*** towns of less *or* fewer than 10,000 inhabitants.

Unter, *m.* (*Cards*) knave.

Unter–, *noun pref.*, **unter–,** *sep. and insep. pref.* (*In general, when the pref. has a literal meaning it is sep. and carries the accent; when it has a figurative meaning it is insep. and the accent is on the root of the verb. See entries below, from which in most cases the obvious literal (sep.) meanings are omitted.*)

Unterabsatz ['untərˀapzats], *m.* sub-paragraph.

Unterabteilung ['untərˀaptaɪluŋ], *f.* subdivision; (*Comm.*) branch, department.

Unterarm ['untərˀarm], *m.* forearm.

Unterart ['untərˀa:rt], *f.* subspecies, variety.

Unterarzt ['untərˀa:rtst], *m.* junior surgeon; (*Navy*) surgeon ensign, (*Mil.*) medical N.C.O.

Unterbau ['untərbau], *m.* substructure; foundation, base; (*Railw.*) formation level; (*fig.*) ***gemeinsamer –,*** common basis.

Unterbauch ['untərbaux], *m.* (*Anat.*) hypogastrium.

unterbauen [untər'bauən], *v.t.* (*insep.*) undermine; lay a foundation for; found, establish, underpin.

Unterbeamte(r) ['untərbəamtə(r)], *m.* subordinate official.

Unterbefehlshaber ['untərbəfe:lzha:bər], *m.* (*Mil.*) second in command.

Unterbeinkleider ['untərbaɪnklaɪdər], *n.pl.* knickers, pants.

unterbelichten ['untərbəlɪçtən], *v.t.* (*insep.*) (*Phot.*) under-expose. **Unterbelichtung,** *f.* under-exposure.

unterbesetzt ['untərbəzɛtst], *adj.* understaffed, shorthanded.

Unterbett ['untərbɛt], *n.* feather bed, mattress.

unterbevölkert ['untərbəfœlkərt], *adj.* underpopulated.

unterbewußt ['untərbəvust], *adj.* subconscious. **Unterbewußtsein,** *n.* subconsciousness; ***im –,*** subconsciously, (*coll.*) at the back of one's mind.

unterbieten [untər'bi:tən], *irr.v.t.* (*insep.*) undercut, undersell; lower (*a record*).

Unterbilanz ['untərbilants], *f.* deficit, adverse balance.

unterbinden, *irr.v.t.* **1.** ['untərbɪndən], (*sep.*) tie underneath; **2.** [–'bɪndən] (*insep.*) tie up *or* off; apply a ligature to (*a vein*); neutralize (*an attack*); (*fig.*) cut off, check, thwart, stop, call a halt to; forestall, obviate.

unterbleiben [untər'blaɪbən], *irr.v.i.* (*insep.*) not take place, not occur, not be forthcoming, be left undone, be omitted; cease, be discontinued. **Unterbleiben,** *n.* cessation, discontinuance; omission.

Unterboden ['untərbo:dən], *m.* subsoil; base plate (*of a watch*), base.

unterbrechen [untər'brɛçən], *irr.v.t.* (*insep.*) interrupt; discontinue, suspend, cut short, stop; ***die Reise –,*** break one's journey, (*Am.*) stop over. **Unterbrecher,** *m.* (*Elec.*) circuit-breaker, contact-breaker, cut-out. **Unterbrechung,** *f.* interruption, intermission, cessation, suspension, break, disconnection; ***mit –en,*** intermittently; ***ohne –,*** without a pause *or* break.

unterbreiten, *v.t.* **1.** ['untərbraɪtən], (*sep.*) spread underneath; **2.** (*insep.*) [–'braɪtən] (*Dat.*) lay before, present *or* submit *or* refer to. **Unterbreitung,** *f.* submission.

unterbringen ['untərbrɪŋən], *irr.v.t.* (*sep.*) shelter, house, accommodate, lodge; billet, quarter (*troops*); provide *or* arrange (*a place*) for; store (*goods*); dispose of, sell; invest (*money*); negotiate (*bills*); (*Tech.*) install, fit; ***Pferde –,*** stable horses; (*coll.*) ***ich kann ihn nirgends –,*** I cannot place him. **Unterbringung,** *f.* accommodation, lodging, quarters; placing, placement; storage; disposal, investment. **Unterbringungsmöglichkeit(en),** *f.*(*pl.*) accommodation.

unterbrochen [untər'brɔxən], *adj.* intermittent, interrupted, broken. *See* **unterbrechen.**

Unterbruch ['untərbrux], *m.* (*Swiss*) *see* **Unterbrechung.**

unterchlorigsauer ['untərklo:rɪçzauər], *adj.* (*Chem.*) hypochlorite of.

Unterdeck ['untərdɛk], *n.* lower deck, below decks.

unterderhand [untərdɛr'hant], *adv.* secretly, in secret, on the quiet.

unterdes(sen) [untər'dɛs(ən)], *adv.* meanwhile, in the meantime, by that time.

Unterdruck ['untərdruk], *m.* partial vacuum, negative pressure, sub-atmospheric pressure.

unterdrücken [untər'drykən], *v.t.* (*insep.*) oppress; suppress, crush, quell, put down (*opposition*); repress, restrain, stifle (*smile, yawn etc.*). **Unterdrücker,** *m.* oppressor, tyrant. **Unterdrückung,** *f.* oppression; suppression, repression.

unterdurchschnittlich ['untərdurçʃnɪtlɪç], *adj.* below normal, sub-average.

untereinander [untərˀaɪn'andər], *adv.* **1.** between *or* with each other, one with another, among themselves; together, mutually; – ***heiraten,*** intermarry; **2.** one beneath *or* underneath the other; ***alles –,*** higgledy-piggledy, topsy-turvy. **Untereinander,** *n. See* **Durcheinander.**

Untereinheit ['untərˀaɪnhaɪt], *f.* sub-unit.

Untereinteilung ['untərˀaɪntaɪluŋ], *f.* subdivision.

unterentwickelt ['untərˀɛntvɪkəlt], *adj.* under-developed (*region, also Phot.*), backward, emergent (*country*); subnormal (*intelligence*).

unterernährt ['untərˀɛrnɛ:rt], *adj.* underfed, undernourished. **Unterernährung,** *f.* under-nourishment, malnutrition.

unterfangen [untər'faŋən], **1.** (*insep.*) *irr.v.r.* (*Gen.*) attempt, venture on; dare *or* presume to undertake; (*zu with inf.*) presume, venture (to). **2.** *irr.v.t.* strengthen the foundations of. **Unterfangen,** *n.* risky enterprise *or* undertaking, bold venture.

unterfassen ['untərfasən], (*sep.*) **1.** *v.t.* put one's hand under, hold up; (*coll.*) ***sie gehen untergefaßt,*** they go arm in arm. **2.** *v.r.* link arms, go arm in arm.

Unterfeldwebel ['untərfɛltve:bəl], *m.* sergeant.

unterfertigen [untər'fɛrtɪgən], *v.t.* (*insep.*) (*Comm.*) (under)sign. **Unterfertigte(r),** *m.* the undersigned.

unterführen [untər'fy:rən], *v.t.* (*insep.*) (*Typ.*) carry down (*a word etc.*) with the ditto mark. **Unterführer,** *m.* (*Mil.*) noncommissioned officer. **Unterführung,** *f.* subway, underpass. **Unterführungszeichen,** *n.* (*Typ.*) ditto mark.

Unterfunktion ['untərfuŋktsio:n], *f.* subnormal functioning.

Unterfutter ['untərfutər], *n.* inner lining.

Untergang ['untərgaŋ], *m.* going down, setting, sinking (*of sun etc.*), (*Naut.*) sinking, shipwreck; (*fig.*) decline, end, (down)fall, ruin, destruction.

Untergärung ['untərgɛ:ruŋ], *f.* bottom fermentation.

Untergattung ['untərgatuŋ], *f.* subspecies.

untergeben [untər'ge:bən], **1.** *irr.v.t.* (*insep.*) (*Poet.*) (*Dat.*) commit *or* submit *or* entrust to; subordinate (to). **2.** *adj.* inferior, subordinate, subject. **Untergebene(r),** *m., f.* subordinate, inferior, underling; subject. **Untergebenheit,** *f.* subordination, subjection.

untergehen ['untərge:ən], *irr.v.i.* (*sep.*) (*aux.* s.) set (*of sun etc.*), (*Naut.*) sink, be wrecked, founder; (*fig.*) be ruined, go to ruin, perish; be lost *or* drowned *or* submerged *or* annihilated; become extinct; ***mit Mann und Maus –,*** go down with all hands.

untergeordnet ['untərgəɔrdnət], *adj.* (*Dat.*) subordinate, inferior, secondary, ancillary (to), minor.

Untergeschoß ['untərgəʃɔs], *n.* ground-floor (*Am.* first floor); basement.

Untergestell ['untərgəʃtɛl], *n.* (*Motor., Av.*) undercarriage; (*Mech.*) base, trestle.

Untergewicht ['untərgəvɪçt], *n.* short weight.

untergraben, *irr.v.t.* ['untərgra:bən], (*sep.*) dig in (*as manure*); [–'gra:bən] (*insep.*) undermine, sap; (*fig.*) undermine, sap, destroy, ruin, corrupt.

Untergrund ['untərgrunt], *m.* subsoil, lower stratum; ground (coat), undercoat (*of paint*). **Untergrund|bahn,** *f.* underground (railway), (*coll.*) tube, (*Am.*) subway. **–bewegung,** *f.* (*Pol.*) underground (movement). **untergründig,** *adj.* (*fig.*) underlying, deep-seated.

Untergruppe ['untərgrupə], *f.* sub-group.

unterhaken ['untərha:kən], *v.t.* (*sep.*) (*coll.*) take (*a p.'s*) arm.

unterhalb ['untərhalp], *prep.* (*Gen.*) below, under(neath); downstream from.

Unterhalt ['untərhalt], *m.* maintenance, support, upkeep, sustenance; livelihood, subsistence, living; (*Law*) maintenance, alimony; ***seinen – verdienen,*** earn one's living *or* livelihood, make a living (***durch,*** by). **unterhalten** [–'haltən], (*insep.*) **1.** *irr.v.t.* 1. sustain, support, maintain, keep; keep up (*a correspondence*); run, operate (*a business*), feed, keep (*a fire*) stoked, keep (*buildings*) in repair; 2. entertain, amuse. **2.** *irr.v.r.* ***sich mit ihm*** (***über eine S.***) –, converse with him (about a th.); ***sich mit etwas –,*** enjoy *or* amuse o.s. with s.th., pass the time with s.th.; ***sich gut –,*** enjoy o.s., have a good time. **unterhaltend, unterhaltsam,** *adj.* amusing, entertaining.

Unterhalts|anspruch, *m.* right to alimony. **–beihilfe** *f.*, **–beitrag,** *m.* subsistence allowance, maintenance grant. **–berechtigte(r),** *m., f.* dependant. **–kosten,** *pl.* (*Law*) alimony. **unterhalts|pflichtig,** *adj.* responsible for maintenance. **–verpflichtet,** *adj.* liable for maintenance.

Unterhaltung [untər'haltuŋ], *f.* 1. (*no pl.*) maintenance, upkeep, support, keep; 2. (*with pl.*) conversation; entertainment, amusement. **Unterhaltungs|beilage,** *f.* recreational *or* literary supplement (*of newspaper*). **–kosten,** *pl.* cost of maintenance *or* upkeep. **–lektüre, –literatur,** *f.* light reading. **–musik,** *f.* light music. **–programm,** *n.* (*Rad.*) light programme. **–ton,** *m.* conversational tone.

unterhandeln [untər'handəln], *v.i.* (*insep.*) negotiate; treat (with), parley; ***mit ihm wegen einer S.*** or ***über eine S. –,*** confer with him about s.th., discuss a th. with him. **Unterhändler,** *m.* negotiator, mediator, intermediary, agent, (*coll.*) contact-man, go-between; (*Mil.*) parlementaire. **Unterhandlung,** *f.* negotiation, mediation; (*Mil.*) parley; ***in – stehen*** (***mit***), carry on negotiations (with); ***in – treten,*** enter into negotiations.

Unterhaus ['untərhaus], *n.* lower part of a house, ground floor; (*Pol.*) Lower Chamber *or* House, House of Commons.

Unterhautgewebe ['untərhautgəve:bə], *n.* hypoderm(a), hypodermis.

Unterhemd ['untərhɛmt], *n.* vest, undershirt.

unterhöhlen [untər'hø:lən], *v.t.* (*insep.*) undermine, hollow out.

Unterholz ['untərhɔlts], *n.* undergrowth, brushwood; copse.

Unterhose(n) ['untərho:zə(n)], *f.* (*pl.*) (under) pants (*men*), drawers, knickers, panties (*women*).

unterirdisch ['untərˀɪrdɪʃ], *adj.* underground, subterraneous, subterranean.

Unterjacke ['untərjakə], *f.* waistcoat, (*Am.*) vest.

unterjochen [untər'jɔxən], *v.t.* (*insep.*) subjugate, subdue; enslave. **Unterjochung,** *f.* subjugation, subdual, enslavement.

unterkellern [untər'kɛlərn], *v.t.* (*insep.*) excavate for a cellar.

Unterkiefer ['untərki:fər], *m.* lower jaw, mandible.

Unterkiefergebiß, *n.* the lower teeth.

Unterkinnlade ['untərkɪnla:də], *f.* (*Anat.*) inferior maxilla.

Unterklassen ['untərklasən], *f.pl.* lower school.

Unterkleid ['untərklaɪt], *n.* undergarment. **Unterkleidung,** *f.* underwear, underclothing.

unterkommen ['untərkɔmən], *irr.v.i.* (*sep.*) (*aux.* s.) find shelter *or* refuge *or* accommodation, (*coll.*) be taken in; find employment *or* a situation, (*coll.*) be taken on. **Unterkommen,** *n.* 1. shelter, lodging(s), accommodation; (*Mil.*) billet, quarters; 2. employment, situation, place; *see* **Unterkunft.**

Unterkörper ['untərkœrpər], *m.* lower part of the body, abdomen.

unterkötig ['untərkø:tɪç], *adj.* (*dial.*) festering.

unterkriegen ['untərkri:gən], *v.t.* (*sep.*) (*coll.*) get the better of; bring (*a p.*) to his knees; (*coll.*) ***laß dich nicht –!*** hold your ground! don't give in! don't let it get you down! never say die!

unterkühlen [untər'ky:lən], *v.t.* (*insep.*) supercool.

Unterkunft ['untərkunft], *f.* (-, *pl.* **⁻e**) *see* **Unterkommen,** 1.; ***– und Verpflegung,*** board and lodging. **Unterkunfts|hütte,** *f.* (mountain) refuge, chalet. **–lager,** *n.* (*Mil.*) rest camp.

Unterlage ['untərla:gə], *f.* 1. support, stand, rest, bed, base (plate); (*Railw.*) groundwork, foundation; (*Geol.*) substratum, subsoil; backing, foil; blotting-pad; (waterproof) drawsheet, underblanket; 2. (*fig.*) proof, evidence, voucher, record, (supporting) document; *pl.* particulars, data, source material, sources, references.

Unterland ['untərlant], *n.* lowland(s), low-lying *or* flat country.

Unterlaß ['untərlas], *m.* ***ohne –,*** without intermission *or* (*coll.*) let-up, unceasingly, incessantly, continuously. **unterlassen** [–'lasən], *irr.v.t.* (*insep.*) leave off, discontinue, stop (*doing*); fail, omit (*to do*), neglect (*doing*), refrain, forbear, abstain (*from doing*); ***nichts –,*** leave nothing undone. **Unterlassung,** *f.* failure, omission, neglect, oversight; (*Law*) default; (*Law*) ***auf – klagen,*** apply for an injunction (order). **Unterlassungs|klage,** *f.* action for default. **–sünde,** *f.* sin of omission, lapse.

Unterlauf ['untərlauf], *m.* lower course (*of a river*).

unterlaufen [untər'laufən], **1.** *irr.v.i.* (*insep.*) (*aux.*

s.) (*of mistakes*) slip *or* creep in, occur; ***mir ist ein Fehler –*** (*also coll.* ***untergelaufen***), I made a mistake. **2.** *irr.v.t.* (*insep.*) run *or* get in under (*a p.'s*) guard. **3.** *adj.* suffused; ***mit Blut –***, bloodshot.

Unterleder [ˈuntərleːdər], *n.* sole leather.

unterlegen, 1. *v.t.* 1. [ˈuntərleːgən], (*sep.*) put *or* lay underneath; (*fig.*) attribute *or* impute (*to a p.*); credit (*a p.*) with; ***einem Kinde frische Windeln –***, change a baby's napkin; ***einer Melodie Worte –***, put (new) words to a tune; ***einem Worte einen anderen Sinn –***, put a new construction upon *or* give *or* attach another meaning to a word; 2. [–ˈleːgən] (*insep.*) back, stiffen, underlay, line (***mit***, with). **2.** [–ˈleːgən] *adj.* inferior (*Dat.*, to); *see* **unterliegen. Unterlegene(r),** *m., f.* loser, victim, sufferer. **Unterlegenheit,** *f.* inferiority. **Unterlegscheibe,** *f.* (*Tech.*) washer.

Unterleib [ˈuntərlaɪp], *m.* abdomen, belly. **Unterleibs|beschwerde,** *f.* abdominal trouble *or* complaint. **–höhle,** *f.* abdominal cavity. **–schmerzen,** *m.pl.* abdominal pains. **–typhus,** *m.* enteric *or* typhoid (fever).

Unterlieferant [ˈuntərliːfərant], *m.* sub-contractor.

unterliegen [untərˈliːgən], *irr.v.i.* (*insep.*) (*aux.* s.) (*Dat.*) succumb (to), be overcome *or* overthrown *or* defeated *or* (*coll.*) worsted (by); (*fig.*) (*also aux.* h.) be subject *or* liable (to), be governed (by); ***es unterliegt einem Rabatt,*** it is subject to discount; ***das unterliegt keinem Zweifel,*** that admits of no doubt, that is not open to doubt; ***dem Zoll –***, be dutiable, be subject to duty. *See* **unterlegen, 2.**

Unterlippe [ˈuntərlɪpə], *f.* lower lip.

unterm [ˈuntərm] = ***unter dem.***

untermalen [untərˈmaːlən], *v.t.* (*insep.*) prepare the canvas, apply the ground colour to, prime; (*Mus.*) supply the background to *or* for; (*fig.*) make clear the underlying motives of.

untermauern [untərˈmauərn], *v.t.* (*insep.*) underpin; (*fig.*) corroborate, (*coll.*) bolster (up).

untermengen [untərmɛŋən], *v.t.* (*sep. or insep.*) (inter)mingle, intermix.

Untermensch [ˈuntərmɛnʃ], *m.* gangster, thug, hoodlum.

Untermiete [ˈuntərmiːtə], *f.* sub-tenancy; ***in – wohnen,*** be a lodger. **Untermieter,** *m.* subtenant, lodger.

untermischen [untərmɪʃən], *v.t.* (*sep. or insep.*) *see* **untermengen.**

untern [ˈuntərn], (*coll.*) = **unter den.**

unternehmen [untərˈneːmən], *irr.v.t.* (*insep.*) undertake, attempt, venture upon; ***nichts –***, take no action. **Unternehmen,** *n.* firm, business, undertaking, enterprise; *see also* **Unternehmung. unternehmend,** *adj.* enterprising, venturesome. **Unternehmer,** *m.* entrepreneur, contractor, (*Am.*) undertaker. **Unternehmertum,** *n.* employers, industrialists; ***freies –***, free enterprise; ***– und Arbeiter,*** industry and labour. **Unternehmerverband,** *m.* employers' association. **Unternehmung,** *f.* undertaking, project, enterprise, venture. **Unternehmungsgeist,** *m.* (spirit of) enterprise, initiative. **unternehmungslustig,** *adj.* enterprising, venturesome, (*coll.*) go-ahead.

Unteroffizier [ˈuntərˀɔfitsiːr], *m.* (*Mil.*) noncommissioned officer, (*Navy*) petty officer.

unterordnen [ˈuntərˀɔrdnən], **1.** *v.t.* subordinate. **2.** *v.r.* submit. **Unterordnung,** *f.* subordination.

Unterpfand [ˈuntərpfant], *n.* pledge, security.

Unterprima [untərˈpriːma], *f.* lower sixth (form).

unterreden [untərˈreːdən], *v.r.* (*insep.*) converse, confer. **Unterredung,** *f.* conversation, talk, discussion, (press) interview; conference; (*Mil.*) parley.

Unterricht [ˈuntərrɪçt], *m.* instruction, teaching, tuition, lessons, classes; ***– geben,*** teach, give lessons, hold classes. **unterrichten** [–ˈrɪçtən], (*insep.*) **1.** *v.t.* teach, instruct, train; (*fig.*) inform, advise, apprise (***über*** (*Acc.*), ***von,*** of), acquaint (with); ***unterrichtete Kreise,*** informed circles; ***unterrichtet sein,*** be (well) informed (***über*** (*Acc.*), about), be conversant (with). **2.** *v.r.* inform o.s., obtain information (***über*** (*Acc.*), about), acquaint o.s. (with).

Unterrichts|briefe, *m.pl.* correspondence course. **–fach,** *n.* special subject, subject one is qualified to teach. **–film,** *m.* educational *or* instructional film. **–gegenstand,** *m.* subject of instruction. **–methode,** *f.* teaching-method. **–minister,** *m.* Minister of *or* (*Am.*) Secretary for Education. **–ministerium,** *n.* Ministry *or* (*Am.*) Office of Education. **–programm,** *n.* syllabus of instruction. **–stoff,** *m.* subject-matter. **–wesen,** *n.* education, educational affairs, public instruction.

Unterrichtung [untərˈrɪçtuŋ], *f.* instruction, apprisal, briefing.

Unterrock [ˈuntərrɔk], *m.* petticoat, slip; (*sl. of a woman*) petticoat, skirt.

unters [ˈuntərs] = ***unter das.***

untersagen [untərˈzaːgən], *v.t.* (*insep.*) forbid (***ihm etwas,*** him to do s.th.), tell (him) not (to do s.th.), prohibit *or* (*Law*) restrain (him from doing s.th.). **Untersagung,** *f.* prohibition, interdiction.

Untersatz [ˈuntərzats], *m.* saucer; table-mat; (*Tech.*) support, base, stand, (*Archit.*) socle; (*Log.*) minor proposition.

unterschätzen [untərˈʃɛtsən], *v.t.* (*insep.*) undervalue, underrate, underestimate. **Unterschätzung,** *f.* undervaluation, underestimate.

unterscheidbar [untərˈʃaɪtbaːr], *adj.* distinguishable, discernible.

unterscheiden [untərˈʃaɪdən], (*insep.*) **1.** *irr.v.t.* distinguish, discern, discriminate, differentiate, separate, make a distinction, (*coll.*) tell. **2.** *irr.v.r.* differ (*von*, from). **unterscheidend,** *adj.* distinctive, characteristic. **Unterscheidung,** *f.* distinction, discrimination; difference.

Unterscheidungs|fähigkeit, *f.* distinctiveness. **–merkmal,** *n.* distinctive mark *or* feature, characteristic, criterion. **–vermögen,** *n.* discernment, (power of) discrimination. **–zeichen,** *n.* *See* **–merkmal.**

Unterschenkel [ˈuntəˌʃɛŋkəl], *m.* lower leg, shin(bone), (*Anat.*) tibia; shank.

Unterschicht [ˈuntərʃɪçt], *f.* substratum.

unterschieben [untərʃiːbən], *irr.v.t.* (*sep.*) (*Austr. also insep.*) push under; (*fig.*) (*also insep., esp. Austr.*) substitute; attribute falsely, impute (*Dat.*, to), foist, father ((up)on); ***den Worten einen falschen Sinn –***, put a wrong construction on the words; *see* **untergeschoben. Unterschiebung,** *f.* substitution; imputation, false attribution.

Unterschied [ˈuntərʃiːt], *m.* (**-s** *pl.* **-e**) difference, distinction; ***einen – machen,*** make *or* draw a distinction, discriminate; ***zum – von,*** unlike, as opposed to, as distinguished *or* distinct from, in contradistinction to; ***ohne –***, without distinction, indiscriminately; irrespective of.

unterschieden [untərˈʃiːdən], *adj.* *See* **unterscheiden.**

unterschiedlich [ˈuntərʃiːtlɪç], *adj.* different, distinct; differing, differential, varied, variable; ***– behandeln,*** discriminate between. **unterschiedslos, 1.** *adj.* indiscriminate. **2.** *adv.* indiscriminately, without exception.

unterschlächtig [ˈuntərʃlɛçtɪç], *adj.* undershot (*of waterwheel*); (*Bot.*) succubous.

unterschlagen [untərˈʃlaːgən], *irr.v.t.* (*insep.*) embezzle (*money*), intercept (*a letter*), suppress, hold back, keep silent about (*information etc.*). **Unterschlagung,** *f.* embezzlement; interception; suppression.

Unterschleif [ˈuntərʃlaɪf], *m.* (**-(e)s,** *pl.* **-e**) embezzlement, fraud, (*Law*) peculation.

Unterschlupf [ˈuntərʃlupf], *m.* (**-(e)s,** *pl.* **¨e** *or* **-e**) shelter, dug-out, refuge; hiding-place, (*coll.*) hideout. **unterschlupfen, unterschlüpfen,** *v.i.* (*aux.* s.) (*sep.*) seek shelter.

unterschreiben [untərˈʃraɪbən], *irr.v.t.* (*insep.*) sign; affix one's signature to; (*fig.*) subscribe to, approve of.

unterschreiten [untər'ʃraɪtən], *v.t.* (*insep.*) not come up to, fall short of, work out cheaper than.
Unterschrift ['untərʃrɪft], *f.* signature; inscription, caption (*under a picture etc.*). **unterschriftsberechtigt,** *adj.* with power to sign.
unterschwefelsauer ['unterʃve:fəlzauər], *adj.* hyposulphate of. **unterschwefligsauer,** *adj.* hyposulphite of.
unterschwellig ['untərʃvɛlɪç], *adj.* (*Psych.*) subliminal.
Unterseeboot ['untərze:bo:t], *n.* submarine, (*German*) U-boat. **unterseeisch,** *adj.* submarine. **Unterseekabel,** *n.* submarine cable.
Untersekunda ['untərsekunda], *f.* lower fifth (form).
untersetzen, *v.t.* [untər'zɛtsən], (*insep.*) mix (***mit,*** with), intermix; (*Mech.*) gear down; ['untər–] (*sep.*) place underneath. **Untersetzer,** *m. See* **Untersatz. untersetzt,** [–'zɛtst] *adj.* square-built, stocky, thick-set, squat. **Untersetztheit,** *f.* stockiness. **Untersetzung,** *f.* (gear) reduction. **Untersetzungsgetriebe,** *n.* reduction gear.
unterst ['untərst], *adj. See* **unter.**
Unterstaatssekretär ['untərʃta:tssɛkrətɛ:r], *m.* Under-Secretary of State.
Unterstand ['untərʃtant], *m.* (*Mil.*) dug-out, foxhole. **Unterständer,** *m.* supporting beam; (*Her.*) foot.
Unterstatthalter ['untərʃtathaltər], *m.* lieutenant-governor (*of a colony*).
unterstehen, **1.** ['untərʃte:ən], *irr.v.i.* (*sep.*) (*aux.* h. & s.) take *or* find shelter. **2.** [–'ʃte:ən] *irr.v.r.* (*insep.*) dare, presume, venture, be so bold as, have the impudence *or* (*coll.*) cheek (***zu tun,*** to do); ***was – Sie sich!*** how dare you! **3.** *irr.v.i.* (*insep.*) (*Dat.*) be (placed) under, be subordinate to, be subject to (*control*), come under (*a law etc.*).
unterstellen ['untərʃtɛlən], **1.** *v.t.* (*sep.*) put *or* place under; put under cover *or* shelter; (*Motor.*) park, garage. **2.** *v.r.* (*sep.*) take shelter (***vor*** (*Dat.*), from). **3.** [–'ʃtɛlən] *v.t.* (*insep.*) 1. impute (*Dat.*, to), (pre)-suppose, assume, grant; 2. (*Dat.*) (*Mil. etc.*) put under the command of, attach *or* assign to. **4.** *v.r.* (*insep.*) acknowledge the authority (*Dat.*, of). **Unterstellung,** *f.* imputation, supposition; (*Mil.*) assignment, attachment.
unterstreichen [untər'ʃtraɪçən], *irr.v.t.* (*insep.*) underline; (*fig.*) emphasize.
Unterstufe ['untərʃtu:fə], *f.* lower grade; lower (forms of a) school.
unterstützen [untər'ʃtytsən], *v.t.* (*insep.*) prop (up), support; (*fig.*) support, aid, assist; (*Law*) abet; (*fig.*) corroborate (*proof*), endorse (*views*); (*debating*) second. **Unterstützung,** *f.* propping; support, help, aid, assistance; relief (*of the poor etc.*), (*from insurance*) benefit, (*by the state*) subsidy; ***zur –,*** in support (*of a claim*), in corroboration (*of evidence*), for the guidance (*of a p.*) (*Gen.*, of).
Unterstützungs|beihilfe, *f.* grant-in-aid. **–berechtigte(r),** *m., f.* one who qualifies for public assistance. **–empfänger,** *m.* one who receives benefits under the social security scheme. **–geld,** *n.* (*usu. pl.*) subsidy. **–gesuch,** *n.* application for relief. **–kasse,** *f.* benevolent fund, friendly-society. **–leistungen,** *f.pl.* (social security) benefits.
Untersuch ['untərzu:x], *m.* (*Swiss*) *see* **Untersuchung. untersuchen** [–'zu:xən], *v.t.* (*insep.*) inquire *or* (*coll.*) look into, examine (*also Med.*), inspect, scrutinize, test (***auf*** (*Acc.*), for), (*Law*) investigate, (*Chem.*) analyse, (*Mech.*) overhaul; explore, probe. **Untersuchung,** *f.* examination (*also Med.*), scrutiny, inquiry, investigation, inspection, test, analysis. **Untersuchungs|-ausschuß,** *m.* committee of inquiry, fact-finding committee. **–gericht,** *n.* court of inquiry, magistrate's court. **–haft,** *f.* imprisonment on remand, detention pending trial; ***in – nehmen*** (***wegen***), commit for trial (on a charge of). **–richter,** *m.* examining magistrate.
Untertagearbeiter [untər'ta:gəˀarbaɪtər], *m.* miner, mine-worker, pitman.
Untertaille ['untərtaljə], *f.* bodice.
untertan ['untərta:n], *pred.adj.* (*Dat.*) subject (to). **Untertan,** *m.* (**-s** *or* **-en,** *pl.* **-en**) subject, vassal. **Untertanen|eid,** *m.* oath of allegiance. **–pflicht,** *f.* allegiance. **–treue,** *f.* loyalty, fealty. **–verstand,** *m.* servile spirit, subservience.
untertänig ['untərtɛ:nɪç], *adj.* subject, (*fig.*) submissive, humble; ***–ster Diener,*** (your) most humble and obedient servant. **Untertänigkeit,** *f.* submission; submissiveness, humility, servility.
Untertasse ['untərtasə], *f.* saucer.
untertauchen ['untərtauxən], (*sep.*) **1.** *v.i.* (*aux.* h. & s.) dive, submerge (*of submarines*); (*coll.*) duck; (*fig.*) disappear, be lost. **2.** *v.t.* immerse, dip, (*coll.*) duck.
Unterteil ['untərtaɪl], *m. or n.* lower part, base.
unterteilen, *v.t.* ['untərtaɪlən], (*sep.*) split up, break down; [–'taɪlən] (*insep.*) subdivide, classify. **Unterteilung,** *f.* subdivision, classification.
Untertertia ['untərtɛrtsia], *f.* lower fourth (form).
Untertitel ['untərti:təl], *m.* subtitle, subhead(ing) (*of a book*).
untertreten ['untərtre:tən], *irr.v.i.* (*sep.*) (*aux.* s.) take shelter.
untertunneln [untər'tunəln], *v.t.* (*insep.*) tunnel through.
untervermieten ['untərfɛrmi:tən], *v.t.* (*insep.*) sublet. **Untervermieter,** *m.* subletter, sublessor.
unterwandern ['untərvandərn], *v.t.* (*insep.*) infiltrate. **Unterwanderung,** *f.* infiltration.
unterwärts ['untərvɛ:rts], *adv.* (*dial.*) downwards, underneath.
Unterwäsche ['untərvɛʃə], *f.* underclothing, underclothes, underwear.
Unterwasser ['untərvasər], *n.* subsoil water; tailrace (*of a mill*). **Unterwasser|bombe,** *f.* depth charge. **–horchgerät,** *n.* hydrophone. **–wende,** *f.* (*swimming*) underwater turn.
unterwegen [untər've:gən], *adv.* (*Swiss*) *see* ***unterwegs lassen.*** **unterwegs,** *adv.* on the way, en route; (*Comm.*) in transit; (*dial.*) ***– lassen,*** leave undone *or* alone; (*dial.*) ***– bleiben,*** be passed over; not take place; ***immer –,*** always on the move.
unterweilen [untər'vaɪlən], **1.** *adv.* (*dial.*) from time to time. **2.** *conj.* meanwhile, in the meantime.
unterweisen [untər'vaɪzən], *irr.v.t.* (*insep.*) (***in*** (*Dat.*)) instruct, teach. **Unterweisung,** *f.* instruction; (*Swiss*) preparation for confirmation; ***– abwarten,*** await instructions.
Unterwelt ['untərvɛlt], *f.* underworld (*also fig. of criminals*); lower regions, Hades.
unterwerfen [untər'vɛrfən], (*insep.*) **1.** *irr.v.t.* subdue, subjugate; submit, subject (*Dat.*, to); ***einer S. unterworfen sein,*** be subject *or* exposed to s.th. **2.** *irr.v.r.* submit, yield, resign o.s. (*Dat.*, to), acquiesce (in), accept. **Unterwerfung,** *f.* subjection, subjugation (***unter*** (*Acc.*), to); (*fig.*) submission, resignation (to), acquiescence (in).
unterwertig ['untərve:rtɪç], *adj.* below value; ***–e Qualität,*** inferior quality.
unterwinden [untər'vɪndən], *irr.v.r.* (*insep.*) *see* **unterfangen.**
unterwühlen [untər'vy:lən], *v.t.* (*insep.*) undermine.
unterwürfig [untər'vyrfɪç ('untər–)], *adj.* submissive; obsequious, subservient, servile. **Unterwürfigkeit,** *f.* subservience, obsequiousness, servility.
unterzeichnen [untər'tsaɪçnən], **1.** *v.t.* (*insep.*) sign; ratify, underwrite. **2.** *v.r.* sign one's name. **Unterzeichner,** *m.* signatory (*of a treaty*). **Unterzeichnete(r),** *m., f.* undersigned. **Unterzeichnung,** *f.* signing; signature, ratification.
Unterzeug ['untərtsɔyk], *n.* (*coll.*) underclothes, underclothing, underwear, (*coll.*) smalls.
unterziehen, **1.** ['untərtsi:ən], *irr.v.t.* (*sep.*) draw *or* pull under; put on (underneath) (*as a petticoat*). **2.** [–'tsi:ən] *irr.v.t.* (*insep.*) submit, subject (*Dat.*, to). **3.** *irr.v.r.* (*insep.*) (*Dat.*) submit to, undergo (*an operation*), sit for, go in for (*an examination*); ***sich der***

Mühe –, take the trouble (*zu tun*, to do), take it upon o.s. (to do). **Unterziehstrumpf,** *m.* undersock.

Unterzug ['untərtsu:k], *m.* support, prop, beam, girder; (*of bed*) underlay.

untief ['unti:f], *adj.* shallow. **Untiefe,** *f.* shallow (water), shoal, (*fig. coll.*) bottomless pit, abyss.

Untier ['unti:r], *n.* (**-(e)s,** *pl.* **-e**) monster, brute.

untilgbar ['untılkba:r], *adj.* inextinguishable; indelible; indestructible; (*Comm.*) irredeemable (*loan*).

untragbar ['untra:kba:r], *adj.* (*fig.*) unbearable, intolerable, insufferable, (*pred.*) past endurance; (*prices*) prohibitive.

untrennbar ['untrɛnba:r], *adj.* inseparable.

untreu ['untrɔy], *adj.* unfaithful; faithless, disloyal; ***ihn seiner Pflicht – machen,*** turn him from the path of duty; – ***werden*** (*Dat.*), break (*an oath*), desert (*a cause*), deviate from (*a course of action*). **Untreue,** *f.* unfaithfulness, faithlessness, disloyalty; inconstancy, infidelity; (*Law*) breach of trust, malfeasance, fraudulent conversion; (*Prov.*) – ***schlägt ihren eignen Herrn,*** treachery comes back on the traitor.

untröstlich ['untrø:stlıç], *adj.* disconsolate, inconsolable.

untrüglich ['untry:klıç], *adj.* unerring, unfailing, infallible, certain, sure; unmistakable, indubitable. **Untrüglichkeit,** *f.* infallibility, certainty.

untüchtig ['untyçtıç], *adj.* unfit (*zu*, for), incapable, incompetent, inefficient; (*coll.*) good-for-nothing; (*Naut.*) unseaworthy. **Untüchtigkeit,** *f.* unfitness, incapacity, incompetence, inefficiency.

Untugend ['untu:gənt], *f.* vice, bad habit.

untunlich ['untu:nlıç], *adj.* impracticable, (*pred.*) not feasible.

unüberbrückbar [unˀy:bər'brykba:r], *adj.* unbridgeable, (*fig.*) insurmountable, irreconcilable.

unüberlegt ['unˀy:bərle:kt], *adj.* ill-advised, ill-considered, unwise, unthinking, heedless, rash; inconsiderate, thoughtless.

unüberschreitbar [unˀy:bər'ʃraıtba:r], *adj.* insurmountable, insuperable.

unübersehbar [unˀy:bər'ze:ba:r], *adj.* immense, vast; incalculable, illimitable, boundless, unbounded.

unübersichtlich ['unˀy:bərzıçtlıç], *adj.* obscure, unintelligible; badly arranged, unmethodical; complex, involved, tortuous; (*Motor.*) blind (*corner*); ***–e Fahrbahn!*** concealed drive!

unübersteigbar [unˀy:bər'ʃtaıkba:r], *adj.* insurmountable, insuperable.

unübertragbar [unˀy:bər'tra:kba:r], *adj.* incommunicable (*of diseases*); (*Comm.*) non-negotiable, not transferable, unassignable; untranslatable.

unübertrefflich [unˀy:bər'trɛflıç], *adj.* unequalled, unrivalled, unsurpassed, incomparable, matchless, peerless.

unübertroffen ['unˀy:bərtrɔfən], *adj.* unsurpassed, unexcelled, unparalleled.

unüberwindlich [unˀy:bər'vıntlıç], *adj.* unconquerable, invincible; impregnable (*fortress*), (*fig.*) insurmountable, insuperable (*difficulties*).

unumgänglich [unˀum'gɛŋlıç], *adj.* indispensable, absolutely necessary, unavoidable, inevitable, ineluctable; ***–e Notwendigkeit,*** absolute necessity.

unumschränkt ['unˀumʃrɛŋkt], *adj.* unlimited; unconditional; absolute, despotic, autocratic, arbitrary.

unumstößlich [unˀumʃtø:slıç], *adj.* irrefutable, indisputable, incontestable, unanswerable; irrevocable, incontrovertible, irrefragable.

unumwunden ['unˀumvundən], **1.** *adj.* plain, flat, blunt, candid, frank, unreserved. **2.** *adv.* point-blank, (*coll.*) in so many words.

ununterbrochen ['unˀuntərbrɔxən], *adj.* uninterrupted, unbroken, consecutive, continuous; incessant, unremitting.

ununterscheidbar ['unˀuntərʃaıtba:r], *adj.* indistinguishable.

unveränderlich ['unfɛrˀɛndərlıç], *adj.* unchangeable, unalterable, constant, stable, invariable, immutable. **Unveränderliche,** *f.* (*Math. etc.*) constant. **Unveränderlichkeit,** *f.* constancy, immutability. **unverändert,** *adj.* unchanged, unaltered, (*coll.*) (just) as it was, the same as ever *or* as before.

unverantwortlich ['unfɛrˀantvɔrtlıç], *adj.* irresponsible; unjustifiable, unwarranted, inexcusable. **Unverantwortlichkeit,** *f.* irresponsibility; inexcusable action.

unverarbeitet ['unfɛrˀarbaıtət], *adj.* unfinished, unwrought, unprocessed, raw, (*pred.*) in the native state; (*fig.*) undigested (*facts etc.*).

unverausgabt ['unfɛrˀausga:pt], *adj.* (*Comm.*) unexpended.

unveräußerlich ['unfɛrˀɔysərlıç], *adj.* inalienable, unsaleable.

unverbesserlich ['unfɛrbɛsərlıç], *adj.* incorrigible, irredeemable, irreclaimable; inveterate; ***–er Junggeselle,*** confirmed bachelor.

unverbindlich ['unfɛrbıntlıç], *adj.* not binding *or* obligatory, informal; without guarantee; without obligation, non-committal; disobliging; ***Preise –,*** prices subject to change.

unverblümt ['unfɛrblymt], *adj.* plain, blunt, direct, point-blank.

unverbrennbar ['unfɛrbrɛnba:r], *adj.* fire-proof, incombustible.

unverbrüchlich ['unfɛrbryçlıç], *adj.* inviolable, absolute; (*fig.*) staunch, firm, steadfast, unswerving.

unverbürgt ['unfɛrbyrkt], *adj.* unwarranted, unconfirmed, not authenticated.

unverdaulich ['unfɛrdaulıç], *adj.* indigestible, heavy (*of food*). **unverdaut,** *adj.* undigested; crude.

unverderblich ['unfɛrdɛrplıç], *adj.* incorruptible, unspoilable. **unverderbt,** *adj.* unspoilt, uncorrupted, pure, innocent.

unverdichtbar ['unfɛrdıçtba:r], *adj.* incompressible.

unverdorben ['unvərdɔrbən], *adj. See* **unverderbt.**

unverdrossen ['unfɛrdrɔsən], *adj.* indefatigable, untiring, unflagging, unwearied, persistent, persevering, unremitting, assiduous; patient.

unverehelicht ['unvɛrˀe:əlıçt], *adj. See* **unverheiratet.**

unvereinbar ['unfɛraınba:r], *adj.* incompatible, irreconcilable, incongruous, inconsistent (*mit*, with), repugnant (to). **Unvereinbarkeit,** *f.* incompatibility, incongruity, inconsistency.

unverfälscht ['unfɛrfɛlʃt], *adj.* unadulterated, pure; (*fig.*) real, genuine. **Unverfälschtheit,** *f.* genuineness.

unverfänglich ['unfɛrfɛŋlıç], *adj.* natural, simple; harmless.

unverfroren ['unfɛrfro:rən], *adj.* unabashed, (*coll.*) brazen(-faced), impertinent, impudent, (*coll.*) cheeky. **Unverfrorenheit,** *f.* imperturbability; impertinence, impudence, (*coll.*) cheek, face.

unvergänglich ['unfɛrgɛŋlıç], *adj.* imperishable, everlasting, ageless, deathless, undying, immortal.

unvergeßlich ['unfɛrgɛslıç], *adj.* unforgettable, memorable; ***das wird mir – bleiben,*** I shall never forget that.

unvergleichlich ['unfɛrglaıçlıç], *adj.* incomparable, inimitable, unrivalled, matchless, peerless, unique.

unverhältnismäßig ['unfɛrhɛltnısmɛ:sıç], *adj.* disproportionate, incongruous; – ***hohe Preise,*** unreasonable *or* excessive prices.

unverheiratet ['unfɛrhaıra:tət], *adj.* unmarried, single.

unverhofft ['unfɛrhɔft], *adj.* unhoped (for), unexpected, unforeseen; (*Prov.*) – ***kommt oft,*** the unexpected always happens.

unverhohlen ['unfɛrho:lən], *adj.* unconcealed, open, frank, candid, unreserved.

unverjährbar ['unfɛrjɛ:rba:r], *adj.* (*Law*) not subject to prescription, imprescriptible; not subject to a period of limitation.
unverkäuflich ['unfɛrkɔyflɪç], *adj.* unsaleable, unmarketable, not negotiable; (*pred.*) not for sale; *–e Ware,* dead stock, (*coll.*) a drug on the market, white elephant.
unverkennbar ['unfɛrkɛnba:r], *adj.* unmistakable, unambiguous, unequivocal; obvious, evident, manifest, palpable; (*coll.*) glaring, (*pred.*) plain as a pikestaff, clear as day.
unverletzbar ['unfɛrlɛtsba:r], *adj.* invulnerable; unassailable, inviolable (*rights*); (*fig.*) sacred, sacrosanct. **Unverletzbarkeit,** *f.* invulnerability, inviolability, immunity, (*fig.*) sanctity. **unverletzlich,** *adj. See* **unverletzbar. unverletzt,** *adj.* unhurt, uninjured, unharmed, intact, unimpaired, (*pred.*) safe (and sound).
unverlierbar ['unfɛrli:rba:r], *adj.* safe; unforgettable, (*pred.*) in safe keeping.
unvermählt ['unfɛrmɛ:lt], *adj. See* **unverheiratet.**
unvermeidlich ['unfɛrmaɪtlɪç], *adj.* inevitable, unavoidable, unfailing, inexorable, ineluctable, irresistible.
unvermittelt ['unfɛrmɪtəlt], *adj.* sudden, abrupt, unexpected, unheralded.
Unvermögen ['unfɛrmø:gən], *n.* powerlessness, inability, incapacity, ineptitude, impotence; *– zu zahlen,* insolvency. **unvermögend,** *adj.* unable, powerless (*zu tun,* to do), incapable (of doing); incompetent, inept, feeble, impotent; penniless, impecunious, (*pred.*) without means.
unvermutet ['unfɛrmu:tət], *adj.* unthought (of), unlooked (for), unexpected, unforeseen.
unvernehmlich ['unfɛrne:mlɪç], *adj.* inaudible; indiscernible, indistinct.
Unvernunft ['unfɛrnunft], *f.* unreasonableness, irrationality, senselessness, absurdity, folly, silliness; *das ist die höhere –!* that is the height of absurdity! **unvernünftig,** *adj.* irrational, unreasonable, senseless, foolish, silly, nonsensical, ridiculous, absurd; *–e Tiere,* dumb animals.
unverpfändbar ['unfɛrpfɛntba:r], *adj.* (*Law*) not subject to distraint.
unverrichtet ['unfɛrrɪçtət], *adj.* unaccomplished, (*pred.*) left undone, not completed; *–erdinge, –ersache,* (*Austr.*) *–er Dinge* or *Sache,* unsuccessfully, without having achieved one's purpose *or* object, (*coll.*) empty-handed.
unverrückbar ['unfɛrrykba:r], *adj.* irremovable, immovable, fixed; (*fig.*) unshakable, steadfast, (*pred.*) adamant. **unverrückt, 1.** *adj.* unmoved, (*pred.*) (still) in its place; steady, fixed. **2.** *adv.* fixedly, immovably; uninterruptedly, steadily.
unverschämt ['unfɛrʃɛ:mt], *adj.* shameless, brazen; insolent, impudent, impertinent, (*coll.*) cheeky, saucy; (*of price*) exorbitant, (*of demands*) unconscionable; *–e Lüge,* bare-faced lie. **Unverschämtheit,** *f.* impudence, impertinence, insolence, effrontery; (*coll.*) cheek, face, sauce.
unverschuldet ['unfɛrʃuldət], *adj.* 1. unmerited, undeserved; 2. (*of a p.*) not in debt, (*of an estate*) unencumbered. **unverschuldeter|maßen, –weise,** *adv.* undeservedly, innocently, (arising) through no fault of (mine, his *etc.*).
unversehens ['unfɛrze:əns], *adv.* 1. unexpectedly, suddenly, unawares, (*coll.*) all of a sudden, in less than no time; 2. unintentionally, accidentally, fortuitously, casually, by chance.
unversehrt ['unfɛrze:rt], *adj.* undamaged, uninjured, intact, entire. **Unversehrtheit,** *f.* entirety.
unversiegbar ['unfɛrzi:kba:r], *adj.* inexhaustible; ever-flowing.
unversöhnlich ['unfɛrzø:nlɪç], *adj.* irreconcilable; implacable, intransigent.
unversorgt ['unfɛrzɔrkt], *adj.* destitute, (*pred.*) unprovided (for), without means.
Unverstand ['unfɛrʃtant], *m.* lack of understanding *or* judgement, injudiciousness, imprudence; stupidity, senselessness, folly. **unverstanden,** *adj.* not understood; misunderstood, misinterpreted, misconstrued. **unverständig,** *adj.* unwise, injudicious, imprudent, foolish, silly, stupid. **unverständlich,** *adj.* unintelligible, incomprehensible, inconceivable, inexplicable, inscrutable, impenetrable; obscure, enigmatic, recondite. **Unverständlichkeit,** *f.* unintelligibility, incomprehensibility; obscurity.
unverstellbar ['unfɛrʃtɛlba:r], *adj.* fixed, non-adjustable.
unversucht ['unfɛrzu:xt], *adj.* untried, unattempted; *nichts – lassen,* try everything, leave no stone unturned.
unvertilgbar ['unfɛrtɪlkba:r], *adj.* indelible, ineffaceable, ineradicable, indestructible, imperishable.
unverträglich ['unfɛrtrɛ:klɪç], *adj.* irreconcilable, incompatible (*mit,* with); unsociable, quarrelsome, irritable, cantankerous. **Unverträglichkeit,** *f.* incompatibility, unsociability, quarrelsomeness, irritability.
unverwandt ['unfɛrvandt], *adj.* fixed, resolute, unswerving, steadfast, unflinching, unwavering, undeterred.
unverwehrt ['unfɛrve:rt], *adj.* permitted, vouchsafed; *es ist Ihnen – zu . . .,* you are quite free *or* at liberty to. . . .
unverweilt ['unfɛrvaɪlt], *adv.* without delay, directly, promptly, immediately, at once, forthwith.
unverweslich ['unfɛrve:slɪç], *adj.* incorruptible.
unverwischbar ['unfɛrvɪʃba:r], *adj.* ineffaceable, ineradicable, indelible.
unverwundbar ['unfɛrvuntba:r], *adj.* invulnerable.
unverwüstlich ['unfɛrvystlɪç], *adj.* indestructible, imperishable; (*fig.*) inexhaustible, irrepressible (*as good spirits*).
unverzagt ['unfɛrtsa:kt], *adj.* undaunted, undismayed, unabashed; fearless, intrepid, indomitable.
unverzeihlich ['unfɛrtsaɪlɪç], *adj.* unpardonable, inexcusable, indefensible.
unverzinslich ['unfɛrtsɪnslɪç], *adj.* bearing no interest; *–es Darlehen,* free loan.
unverzollt ['unfɛrtsɔlt], *adj.* duty unpaid, in bond.
unverzüglich ['unfɛrtsy:klɪç], **1.** *adj.* immediate, instant, prompt. **2.** *adv.* without delay, at once, promptly, instantly, immediately, straightway, forthwith, at short notice, (*coll.*) on the spot, right away.
unvollendet ['unfɔlˀɛndət], *adj.* unfinished, incomplete; *etwas – lassen,* leave a th. half finished.
unvollkommen ['unfɔlkɔmən], *adj.* imperfect, defective, wanting. **Unvollkommenheit,** *f.* imperfection, defectiveness; defect.
unvollständig ['unfɔlʃtɛndɪç], *adj.* incomplete, deficient. **Unvollständigkeit,** *f.* incompleteness; deficiency.
unvollzählig ['unfɔltsɛ:lɪç], *adj.* incomplete.
unvorbereitet ['unfo:rbəraɪtət], *adj.* unprepared, unready, not ready; unpremeditated, extemporaneous, extempore; *–e Übersetzung,* unseen (translation); *– sprechen,* extemporize, (*coll.*) ad-lib.
unvordenklich ['unfo:rdɛŋklɪç], *adj. seit –er Zeit,* from time immemorial, time out of mind.
unvoreingenommen ['unfo:raɪngənɔmən], *adj.* impartial, unbiased, unprejudiced.
unvorgreiflich ['unfo:rgraɪflɪç], *adj.* disinterested, impartial; with diffidence, subject to correction.
unvorhergesehen ['unfo:rhe:rgəze:ən], *adj.* unforeseen, unexpected; *–er Schicksalsschlag,* bolt from the blue.
unvorschriftsmäßig ['unfo:rʃrɪftsmɛ:sɪç], *adj.* irregular, improper, (*pred.*) contrary to regulations.
unvorsichtig ['unfo:rsɪçtɪç], *adj.* careless, negligent; unwary, incautious; inconsiderate, improvident, unwise, imprudent. **Unvorsichtigkeit,** *f.* lack of foresight, improvidence, imprudence; carelessness, negligence; *aus –,* inadvertently, by mistake, through negligence.

unvorstellbar ['unfo:rʃtɛlba:r], *adj.* unimaginable, incredible.

unvorteilhaft ['unfo:rtaɪlhaft], *adj.* unfavourable, disadvantageous, (*as dress*) unbecoming; inexpedient; unprofitable, unremunerative.

unwägbar ['unvɛ:kba:r], *adj.* imponderable.

unwahr ['unva:r], *adj.* false, untrue, fictitious. **unwahrhaftig,** *adj.* untruthful, insincere, disingenuous. **Unwahrhaftigkeit,** *f.* insincerity, untruthfulness, dissimulation, falseness, mendacity. **Unwahrheit,** *f.* falsehood, untruth, inaccuracy, falsity, misstatement, misrepresentation. **unwahrscheinlich,** *adj.* unlikely, improbable; incredible, fantastic. **Unwahrscheinlichkeit,** *f.* unlikelihood, improbability.

unwandelbar ['unvandəlba:r], *adj.* immutable, invariable, unchangeable; unshakable, undeviating, constant. **Unwandelbarkeit,** *f.* immutability, permanence, constancy.

unwegsam ['unve:kza:m], *adj.* impracticable, impassable, pathless.

Unweib ['unvaɪp], *n.* virago, shrew, vixen, termagant. **unweiblich,** *adj.* unwomanly.

unweigerlich ['unvaɪgərlɪç], **1.** *adj.* unhesitating, unquestioning; *-er Gehorsam,* unquestioning *or* implicit obedience. **2.** *adv.* without fail.

unweit ['unvaɪt], *adv.* **1.** not far off, near, close by. **2.** *prep.* (*Gen. or von*) not far from, close to, near; *– von hier,* in the immediate vicinity *or* neighbourhood, close by, close at hand.

Unwesen ['unve:zən], *n.* disorder, confusion, excesses; mischief, nuisance, abuse; *sein – treiben,* be up to mischief *or* to one's tricks; haunt (*an einem Ort,* a place).

unwesentlich ['unve:zəntlɪç], *adj.* unessential, non-essential, immaterial (*für,* to), negligible, unimportant, insignificant (for), (*pred.*) beside the point, of no consequence.

Unwetter ['unvɛtər], *n.* stormy weather; violent storm.

unwichtig ['unvɪçtɪç], *adj.* unimportant, insignificant, trifling, trivial, (*coll.*) footling, fiddling, piffling. **Unwichtigkeit,** *f.* insignificance, unimportance, triviality, paltriness; trifle, bagatelle; (*coll.*) flea-bite, brass farthing, fig, *pl.* trivialities, trifles.

unwiderlegbar ['unvi:dərle:kba:r], **unwiderleglich,** *adj.* unanswerable, irrefutable, conclusive.

unwiderruflich ['unvi:dərru:flɪç], *adj.* irrevocable, irretrievable, irreversible; definite, positive; (*pred.*) beyond *or* past recall; *– letzte Aufführung,* positively the last performance.

unwidersprechlich ['unvi:dərʃprɛçlɪç], *adj.* incontestable, incontrovertible, undeniable.

unwiderstehlich ['unvi:dərʃte:lɪç], *adj.* irresistible, overpowering.

unwiederbringlich ['unvi:dərbrɪŋlɪç], *adj.* irreparable, irremediable, irretrievable, irrecoverable, irredeemable; *– dahin* or *verloren,* irretrievably lost, gone for ever *or* (*coll.*) for good.

Unwille(n) ['unvɪlə(n)], *m.* (**-ns,** *pl.* **-n**) resentment, displeasure; indignation, anger, annoyance, vexation, bitterness, animosity.

urwillfährig ['unvɪlfɛ:rɪç], *adj.* disobliging, uncomplying, grudging, contumacious. **Unwillfährigkeit,** *f.* contumacy, insubordination, noncompliance.

unwillig ['unvɪlɪç], *adj.* indignant, resentful, annoyed, exasperated, angry (*über* (*Acc.*), at *or* about); (*coll.*) nettled, riled, sore; reluctant, unwilling.

unwillkommen ['unvɪlkɔmən], *adj.* unwelcome; unpleasant, disagreeable; troublesome.

unwillkürlich ['unvɪlky:rlɪç], *adj.* involuntary, unintentional, unintended; instinctive, automatic.

unwirklich ['unvɪrklɪç], *adj.* unreal, non-existent.

unwirksam ['unvɪrkza:m], *adj.* ineffectual, ineffective, inoperative, (*Law*) void; inefficient, inefficacious; (*Chem.*) inactive, neutral, inert. **Unwirksamkeit,** *f.* inefficacy, futility; (*Law*) invalidity; inefficiency; (*Chem.*) inactivity, inertness.

unwirsch ['unvɪrʃ], *adj.* morose, surly, churlish, brusque. uncivil; (*coll.*) cross, grumpy.

unwirtlich ['unvɪrtlɪç], *adj.* uninhabited, desolate, waste, barren; dreary, uninviting, inhospitable.

unwissend ['unvɪsənt], *adj.* ignorant, unaware (of), unacquainted, unconversant (with), ill informed (about); uninformed, ignorant, stupid. **Unwissenheit,** *f.* ignorance, incomprehension; inexperience. **unwissentlich,** *adv.* unwittingly, unknowingly, unconsciously, unawares.

unwohl ['unvo:l], (*pred.*) *adj.* unwell, indisposed; (*coll.*) poorly, off colour, out of sorts, seedy; *mir ist –, ich bin –, ich fühle mich –,* I don't feel well; I feel unwell; *sie ist –,* she has her period. **Unwohlsein,** *n.* **1.** indisposition; **2.** monthly period.

unwohnlich ['unvo:nlɪç], *adj.* cheerless, uncomfortable.

unwürdig ['unvy:rdɪç], *adj.* unworthy (*Gen.,* of); discreditable, disgraceful; despicable, disreputable, shameful, degrading, (*coll.*) shabby. **Unwürdigkeit,** *f.* unworthiness; discredit, disgrace.

Unzahl ['untsa:l], *f.* immense number. **unzählbar, unzählig,** *adj.* innumerable, countless, numberless. **unzähligemal,** *adv.* times without number.

unzart ['untsa:rt], *adj.* ungracious, rough, rude, indelicate, tactless. **Unzartheit,** *f.* indelicacy, tactlessness, ungraciousness.

[1]**Unze** ['untsə], *f.* ounce (= *approx. 30 gr.*).

[2]**Unze,** *f.* (*Zool.*) jaguar (*Felis uncia*).

Unzeit ['untsaɪt], *f. zur –,* unseasonably, at the wrong time, inopportunely; prematurely. **unzeitgemäß,** *adj.* out-of-date, behind the times, old-fashioned, unfashionable; unseasonable, inopportune. **unzeitig,** *adj.* untimely, ill-timed, inopportune; premature; unseasonable; out of season; (*of fruit*) unripe.

unzerbrechlich ['untsɛrbrɛçlɪç], *adj.* unbreakable, infrangible.

unzerlegbar ['untsɛrle:kba:r], **unzersetzbar,** *adj.* indivisible, elementary, simple.

unzerstörbar ['untsɛrʃtø:rba:r], *adj.* indestructible, imperishable.

unzertrennlich ['untsɛrtrɛnlɪç], *adj.* inseparable; *-e Eigenschaften,* inherent qualities.

unziemend ['untsi:mənt], **unziemlich,** *adj.* unbecoming, unseemly, improper, indecorous, indecent, unmentionable. **Unziemlichkeit,** *f.* impropriety, indecorum, unseemliness, indecency, immodesty, indelicacy.

Unzucht ['untsuxt], *f.* lechery, lewdness; incontinence, fornication; (*Law*) sexual offence; *gewerbsmäßige –,* prostitution. **unzüchtig,** *adj.* lewd, lecherous, lascivious; obscene, bawdy, salacious, meretricious. **Unzüchtigkeit,** *f.* immodesty, concupiscence; obscenity, bawdiness, lewdness.

unzufrieden ['untsu:fri:dən], *adj.* dissatisfied, discontented. **Unzufriedenheit,** *f.* discontent, dissatisfaction.

unzugänglich ['untsu:gɛŋlɪç], *adj.* inaccessible, unapproachable; (*of a p.*) reserved, (*coll.*) stand-offish; *– für,* impervious *or* (*coll.*) deaf to.

unzukömmlich ['untsu:kœmlɪç], *adj.* (*Austr.*) *see* **unzulänglich. Unzukömmlichkeit,** *f.* (*usu. pl.*) (*Austr.*) incongruity, impropriety, unseemliness; nuisance, abuses.

unzulänglich ['untsu:lɛŋlɪç], *adj.* insufficient, inadequate; unavailing. **Unzulänglichkeit,** *f.* insufficiency, inadequacy; deficiency, shortcoming.

unzulässig ['untsu:lɛsɪç], *adj.* inadmissible, forbidden; (*as influence*) undue; *für – erklären,* rule out of order.

unzurechnungsfähig ['untsu:rəçnuŋsfɛ:ɪç], *adj.* not responsible (for one's actions), insane, certifiable, feeble-minded, imbecile, (*pred.*) of unsound mind. **Unzurechnungsfähigkeit,** *f.* feeble-mindedness; irresponsibility, (*Law*) diminished responsibility; (*Law*) *Einrede der –,* plea of insanity.

unzureichend ['untsu:raɪçənt], *adj.* insufficient, inadequate.

unzusammenhängend ['untsu:zamənhɛŋənt], *adj.* unconnected, disconnected, disjointed; incoherent (*speech*).

unzuständig ['untsu:ʃtɛndɪç], *adj.* (*Law*) incompetent, with no jurisdiction (*für*, over).

unzuträglich ['untsu:trɛ:klɪç], *adj.* disadvantageous, prejudicial (*Dat.*, to), (*pred.*) not good (for); unhealthy, unwholesome. **Unzuträglichkeit,** *f.* unwholesomeness.

unzutreffend ['untsu:trɛfənt], *adj.* inapplicable, incorrect, erroneous; unfounded, groundless (*of news*); ***das ist gänzlich –,*** nothing could be further from the truth.

unzuverlässig ['untsu:fɛrlɛsɪç], *adj.* unreliable, untrustworthy; (*as ice*) treacherous, (*as memory*) uncertain, fallible. **Unzuverlässigkeit,** *f.* untrustworthiness, unreliability.

unzweckmäßig ['untsvɛkmɛ:sɪç], *adj.* unsuitable, inopportune, inexpedient; inappropriate, inapt, inapposite, not pertinent. **Unzweckmäßigkeit,** *f.* unsuitableness, inappropriateness, inexpediency.

unzweideutig ['untsvaɪdɔytɪç], *adj.* unequivocal, unambiguous, explicit, clear, precise.

unzweifelhaft ['untsvaɪfəlhaft], **1.** *adj.* undoubted, indubitable, unquestionable; ***–e Tatsache,*** established fact, certainty. **2.** *adv.* without doubt, doubtless; ***es ist – (wahr),*** it is beyond question, there is no doubt about it, (*coll.*) sure as fate, depend upon it.

üppig ['ypɪç], *adj.* 1. abundant, plentiful, rich, opulent, sumptuous; (*as vegetation*) luxuriant, rank, lush, (*of health*) exuberant, (*woman's figure*) voluptuous, well-developed; ***–er Haarwuchs,*** exuberant growth of hair; ***– leben,*** live on the fat of the land; ***–es Mahl,*** sumptuous repast; 2. (*of a p.*) presumptuous, supercilious, pompous, arrogant, lordly, (*coll.*) uppish, uppity, high and mighty, cocky, (*Am.*) chesty; (*coll.*) ***er wird zu –,*** he's getting too big for his boots. **Üppigkeit,** *f.* 1. luxuriant growth, exuberance; opulence, luxury, plenty, richness; voluptuousness; 2. presumption, arrogance, uppishness.

Ur [u:r], *m.* **(-(e)s,** *pl.* **-e)** (*Zool.*) aurochs (*Bos primigenius*).

Ur–, ur–, *pref. to many nouns and adjs. indicating*: (1) origin, source; (2) very old, primitive; (3) thorough, extremely, very. *See examples below.*

Ur|ahn, *m.* great-grandfather; ancestor. **–ahne,** *f.* great-grandmother; ancestress.

uralt ['u:rˀalt], *adj.* very old, aged; ancient, primeval, (*coll.*) as old as the hills. **uralters,** *adv.* in ancient times; ***von – her,*** from time immemorial.

Uran [u'ra:n], *n.* uranium.

Uranfang ['u:rˀanfaŋ], *m.* the very beginning, prime origin. **uranfänglich, 1.** *adj.* primordial, primeval, original. **2.** *adv.* in the very beginning.

Uranlage ['u:rˀanla:gə], *f.* original disposition; rudiment, vestige, primordium.

Uranpech|blende, *f.*, **–erz,** *n.* pitchblende.

uraufführen ['u:rˀauffy:rən], *v.t.* (*only inf. or p.p.* ***uraufgeführt***) play *or* perform for the first time, (*Films*) release. **Uraufführung,** *f.* world première, (*Films*) release.

urban [ur'ba:n], *adj.* urbane, suave, bland. **Urbanität** [–i'tɛ:t], *f.* urbanity, suavity.

urbar ['u:rba:r], *adj.* cleared, arable, capable of cultivation; ***– machen,*** reclaim, clear (*land*). **Urbar,** *n.* (*Hist.*) cadastral register. **Urbarisierung** [–ri'zi:ruŋ], *f.* (*Swiss*), **Urbarmachung,** *f.* clearing, reclamation.

Urbedeutung ['u:rbədɔytuŋ], *f.* original meaning.

Urbestandteil ['u:rbəʃtanttaɪl], *m.* ultimate constituent.

Urbewohner ['u:rbəvo:nər], *m. See* **Ureinwohner.**

Urbild ['u:rbɪlt], *n.* original; archetype, prototype; (*fig.*) ideal. **urbildlich,** *adj.* original, archetypal.

Urblatt ['u:rblat], *n.* primordial leaf.

Urboden ['u:rbo:dən], *m.* virgin soil.

urchig ['u:rçɪç], *adj.* (*Swiss*) genuine, primitive.

Urchrist ['u:rkrɪst], *m.* early Christian. **Urchristentum,** *n.* primitive Christianity, the early Church.

urdeutsch ['u:rdɔytʃ], *adj.* thoroughly German, German to the core.

Urei ['u:rˀaɪ], *n.* primitive ovum.

ureigen ['u:rˀaɪgən], *adj.* innate, inherent, peculiar (to); (one's) very own. **Ureigenheit,** *f.* characteristic, particularity, specific peculiarity.

Ureinwohner ['u:rˀaɪnvo:nər], *m.* original inhabitant, aborigine.

Ureltern ['u:rˀɛltərn], *pl.* ancestors; first-parents.

Urenkel ['u:rˀɛŋkəl], *m.* great-grandson, great-grandchild. **Urenkelin,** *f.* great-granddaughter.

Urfehde ['u:rfe:də], *f.* (*Hist.*) oath to keep the peace, oath of truce.

urfidel ['ur:fide:l], *adj.* (*coll.*) very jolly.

Urform ['u:rfɔrm], *f.* original form, prototype, archetype.

Urgebirge ['u:rgəbɪrgə], *n. See* **Urgestein.**

urgemütlich ['u:rgəmy:tlɪç], *adj.* in the lap of comfort.

Urgeschichte ['u:rgəʃɪçtə], *f.* early history, prehistory. **urgeschichtlich,** *adj.* prehistoric.

Urgestalt ['u:rgəʃtalt], *f. See* **Urform.**

Urgestein ['u:rgəʃtaɪn], *n.* (*Geol.*) basement complex.

urgieren [u:r'gi:rən], *v.t.* (*Austr.*) entreat, press.

Urgroß|eltern ['u:rgro:s–], *pl.* great-grandparents. **–mutter,** *f.* great-grandmother. **–vater,** *m.* great-grandfather.

Urheber ['u:rhe:bər], *m.* author, creator, founder, originator. **Urheberrecht,** *n.* copyright; ***Inhaber des –s,*** copyright holder. **Urheberschaft,** *f.* authorship.

urig ['u:rɪç], *adj.* (*dial.*) original, odd, eccentric, whimsical, ludicrous.

Urin [u'ri:n], *m.* urine. **Urin|flasche,** *f.*, **–glas,** *n.* urinal. **urinieren** [–'ni:rən], *v.i.* urinate, pass *or* make water. **Urinstein,** *m.* urinary calculus. **urintreibend,** *adj.* diuretic.

Urkirche ['u:rkɪrçə], *f.* primitive *or* early church.

Urkoks ['u:rkɔks], *m.* low-temperature coke.

urkomisch ['u:rko:mɪʃ], *adj.* very *or* (*coll.*) screamingly *or* excruciatingly funny.

Urkraft ['u:rkraft], *f.* primitive strength, original force, elementary power; moving principle.

Urkunde ['u:rkundə], *f.* deed, document, charter, title (deed), legal instrument; voucher, record, attestation; (*obs.*) ***zu Urkund dessen,*** in witness whereof. **Urkunden|beweis,** *m.* documentary evidence *or* proof. **–buch,** *n.* record (book), register. **–sammelstelle, –sammlung,** *f.* archives.

urkundlich ['u:rkuntlɪç], *adj.* documentary; authentic; ***– belegt,*** documented, authenticated; (*Law*) ***– dessen,*** in witness whereof. **Urkundsbeamte(r),** *m.* clerk of the court, registrar.

Urlaub ['u:rlaup], *m.* **(-(e)s,** *pl.* **-e)** leave (of absence), furlough, vacation; ***wilder –,*** absence without leave; ***in*** or ***im*** or ***auf –,*** on vacation. **Urlauber,** *m.* holiday-maker, (*Mil.*) soldier on leave. **Urlaubs|gesuch,** *n.* application for leave. **–schein,** *m.* (leave-)pass. **–verlängerung,** *f.* extension of leave. **-zeit,** *f.* vacation, holiday-time.

Ur|lehre, *f.*, **–maß,** *n.* standard *or* master gauge.

Urmensch ['u:rmɛnʃ], *m.* primitive *or* prehistoric man.

Urne ['u:rnə], *f.* urn, casket; ballot-box.

Urning ['u:rnɪŋ], *m.* **(-s,** *pl.* **-e)** homosexual.

Urochs ['u:rˀɔks], *m. See* **Ur.**

urplötzlich ['u:rplœtslɪç], **1.** *adj.* very sudden, totally unexpected. **2.** *adv.* abruptly, quite suddenly, (*coll.*) all of a sudden.

Urquell ['u:rkvɛl], *m.* **(-(e)s,** *pl.* **-e)** fountain-head; primary source, origin.

Ursache ['u:rzaxə], *f.* cause, reason, origin, motive,

ground, occasion; ***keine –!*** don't mention it! you are welcome! ***man hat – zu glauben,*** there is reason to believe; ***gleiche –n, gleiche Wirkungen,*** like causes produce like effects; (*Prov.*) ***kleine –n, große Wirkungen,*** great oaks from little acorns grow.

ursächlich ['u:rzɛçlɪç], *adj.* causal, (*Gram.*) causative. **Ursächlichkeit,** *f.* causality.

Urschleim ['u:rʃlaɪm], *m.* protoplasm.

Urschrift ['u:rʃrɪft], *f.* original (text). **urschriftlich,** *adj.* orthographic, (in the) original.

Ursprache ['u:rʃpra:xə], *f.* primitive language; (*of translation*) original.

Ursprung ['u:rʃpruŋ], *m.* source, origin, inception, provenance, starting-point, beginning, cause; ***seinen – haben in*** (*Dat.*), originate in *or* from, take its rise from, descend from; ***deutschen –s,*** (*of a p.*) of German extraction, native of Germany; (*of goods*) made in Germany.

ursprünglich ['u:rʃprʏŋlɪç], *adj.* primitive, primordial; initial, primary, original. **Ursprünglichkeit,** *f.* primitiveness; originality.

Ursprungs|land, *n.* country of origin. **–zeugnis,** *n.* certificate of origin.

Urstier ['u:rʃti:r], *m. See* **Ur.**

Urstoff ['u:rʃtɔf], *m.* original substance, primary matter; (*Chem.*) element.

Urteer ['u:rte:r], *m.* low-temperature tar.

Urteil ['urtaɪl], *n.* (**-s,** *pl.* **-e**) judg(e)ment, decision; opinion, view; (*Law*) judgement, finding, sentence, verdict; ***sich*** (*Dat.*) ***ein – bilden über*** (*Acc.*), form an opinion about, have one's views on; ***ein – fällen über*** (*Acc.*), (*Law*) pronounce *or* pass sentence on, (*fig.*) pass judgement on, express a considered opinion about; ***meinem – nach,*** in my judgement *or* opinion; ***darüber enthalte ich mich jedes –s,*** I refuse to express any opinion about it, I have no views on the subject.

urteilen ['urtaɪlən], *v.i.* judge, pass judgement (***über*** (*Acc.*), on), give one's opinion, form an opinion (on *or* about); ***nach seinen Reden*** or ***seiner Sprache nach zu –,*** judging *or* to judge by *or* from what he says; ***darüber kann er nicht –,*** he is no judge (of such matters); ***dem Schein nach –,*** judge by *or* from appearances.

Urteils|aufhebung, *f.* reversal of judgement. **–eröffnung,** *f.* publication of a judgement, pronouncement *or* proclamation of sentence. **urteilsfähig,** *adj.* competent to judge, judicious; discerning, discriminating. **Urteils|fällung,** *f.* passing of judgement. **–kraft,** *f.* (power of) judgement; discernment, discrimination. **–spruch,** *m.* judg(e)ment, finding, sentence, verdict. **–verkündung,** *f. See* **–eröffnung. –vollstreckung,** *f.* execution of a sentence.

Urtel ['urtəl], *m. dial. & Poet. for* **Urteil.**

Urtext ['u:rtɛkst], *m.* original text.

Urtier ['u:rti:r], *n.* primitive *or* prehistoric animal. **Urtierchen,** *n.* protozoon, *pl.* protozoa.

urtümlich ['u:rty:mlɪç], *adj.* original, native.

Urur|ahn ['u:rʔu:r–], *m.* progenitor, great-great-grandfather. **–eltern,** *pl.* forefathers, first parents, early ancestors. **–enkel,** *m.* great-great-grandson, great-great-grandchild. **–enkelin,** *f.* great-great-granddaughter. **–großmutter,** *f.* great-great-grandmother. **–großvater,** *m.* great-great-grandfather.

Urvater ['u:rfa:tər], *m.* first parent, forefather. **urväterlich,** *adj.* primitive; ancestral. **Urväterzeit,** *f.* olden times, days of yore.

urverwandt ['u:rfɛrvant], *adj.* of the same origin; (*of words*) cognate.

Urvolk ['u:rfɔlk], *n.* primitive people, aborigines.

Urwahl ['u:rva:l], *f.* preliminary election (*of electors*).

Urwald ['u:rvalt], *m.* primeval *or* virgin forest; tropical forest, jungle.

Urwelt ['u:rvɛlt], *f.* primeval world. **urweltlich,** *adj.* primeval, antediluvian.

urwüchsig ['u:rvy:ksɪç], *adj.* original, native; (*fig.*) racy; earthy, blunt, rough.

Urzeit ['u:rtsaɪt], *f.* primitive times, prehistory, dawn of history. **urzeitlich,** *adj.* prehistoric, primeval, primordial.

Urzelle ['u:rtsɛlə], *f.* primitive cell.

Urzeugung ['u:rtsɔyguŋ], *f.* spontaneous generation, abiogenesis.

Urzustand ['u:rtsu:ʃtant], *m.* primitive state, original condition.

Usance [y'zãs(ə)], *f.* (*Comm.*) usage, custom, practice; ***nach –,*** as is customary (in the trade), according to (stock exchange) practice.

Uso ['u:zo:], *m.* (*Comm.*) usance. **Usowechsel,** *m.* bill at usance.

usuell [u:zu'ɛl], *adj.* usual, customary; ***nicht –,*** not the custom *or* practice.

Usurpator [u:zur'pa:tɔr], *m.* (**-s** *pl.* **-en**) usurper. **usurpieren,** *v.t.* usurp.

Usus ['u:zus], *m.* usage, custom, habit, rule, practice.

Utensilien [u:tɛn'si:liən], *pl.* utensils, implements.

Utilitarier [u:tili'ta:riər], *m.* utilitarian. **Utilitarismus** [–'rɪsmus], *m.* utilitarianism. **utilitaristisch,** *adj.* utilitarian.

Utopie [u:to'pi:], *f.*, **Utopien** [–'to:piən], *n.* Utopia. **utopisch,** *adj.* utopian.

UV|-Licht ['u:fau–], *n.* ultra-violet light. **–Strahlen,** *pl.* ultra-violet rays.

Uz [u:ts], *m.* (**-es,** *pl.* **-e**) chaffing, leg-pulling, teasing, (*coll.*) kidding. **uzen,** *v.t.* tease, chaff, (*coll.*) kid.

V

V, v [fau], *n.* V, v; *see Index of Abbreviations.*

vag [va:k], *adj.* vague, indeterminate.

Vagabund [vaga'bunt], *m.* (**-en,** *pl.* **-en**) vagabond, vagrant, tramp, (*Am.*) bum, hobo. **vagabundieren** [–di:rən], *v.i.* (*aux.* h *&* s.) wander *or* roam (about), lead a vagabond life; ***wegen Vagabundierens angeklagt sein,*** be on a vagrancy charge; (*Elec.*) ***–der Strom,*** stray current.

Vagant [va'gant], *m.* (**-en,** *pl.* **-en**) (*Hist.*) itinerant scholar.

Vagheit ['va:khaɪt], *f.* vagueness.

vagieren [va'gi:rən], *v.i. See* **vagabundieren.**

vakant [va'kant], *adj.* vacant, void, unoccupied. **Vakanz,** *f.* (-, *pl.* **-en**) 1. vacancy, vacant post; 2. (*Law*) vacation, recess.

Vaku-Blitz ['va:kublɪts], *m.* (*Phot.*) flashlight, photo-flash.

Vakuum ['va:kuum], *n.* (**-s,** *pl.* **-kua** *or* **-kuen**) vacuum. **Vakuum|pumpe,** *f.* air suction pump. **–röhre,** *f.* vacuum-tube.

Vakzination [vaktsinatsi'o:n], *f.* vaccination. **vakzinieren** [–'ni:rən], *v.t.* vaccinate.

Valand ['fa:lant], *m.* (*dial.*) devil, evil fiend.

Valenz [va'lɛnts], *f.* valence, valency.

Valet [va'lɛt, –'le:t], *n.* (**-s,** *pl.* **-s**) farewell, adieu, valediction; ***– geben*** (*Dat.*), dismiss; ***– sagen,*** bid farewell *or* adieu (*Dat.*, to), take leave (of). **Valetschmaus,** *m.* farewell banquet, valedictory celebration.

validieren [vali'di:rən], *v.t.* (*Comm.*) make valid; validate, effect (*an insurance etc.*); ***eine Summe – lassen gegen,*** credit a sum against. **Validierung,** *f.* validation, ratification.

Valorisation [valorizatsi'o:n], *f.* (*Comm.*) price-pegging. **valorisieren** [–'zi:rən], *v.t.* maintain *or* peg the price of. **Valorisierung,** *f. See* **Valorisation.**

Valuta [va'lu:ta], *f.* (-, *pl.* **-ten**) value, rate (of exchange), currency, monetary standard. **Valutanotierung,** *f.* foreign-exchange quotation. **valuta|schwach,** (–**stark**), *adj.* with a low (high) rate of exchange. **valutieren** [–'ti:rən], *v.t.* value, valuate.

valvieren [val'vi:rən], *v.t.* (*obs.*) *see* **valutieren.**

Vampir ['vampi:r, (*Austr.*) –'pi:r], *m.* (**-s,** *pl.* **-e**) vampire.

Vanadin [vana'di:n], *n.* vanadium.

Vandale [van'da:lə], *m.* (**-n,** *pl.* **-n**), **vandalisch,** *adj.* (*Hist., also fig.*) Vandal. **Vandalismus** [–'lɪsmus], *m.* (*fig.*) vandalism.

Vanille [va'ni:ljə], *f.* vanilla.

Varia ['va:ria], *pl.* sundries, odds and ends, miscellaneous items. **variabel** [–'a:bəl], *adj.* variable; (*Math.*) ***variable Größe,*** variable.

Variante [vari'antə], *f.* 1. variant (reading); 2. (*Biol.*) sport. **Variantenapparat,** *m.* synopsis of all the variants.

variationsfähig [variatsi'o:nsfɛ:ɪç], *adj.* variable.

Varietät [varie'tɛ:t], *f.* variety. **Varieté(theater),** *n.* variety theatre, music-hall, vaudeville.

variieren [vari'i:rən], *v.t., v.i.* vary; ***ein Thema –*** compose *or* play variations of an air.

Varizen [va'ri:tsən], *pl.* varicose veins.

Vasall [va'sal], *m.* (**-en,** *pl.* **-en**) vassal, retainer. **Vasallenstaat,** *m.* dependent *or* vassal *or* tributary state.

Vaselin [va:ze'li:n], *n.* (-, *pl.* **-s**), **Vaseline,** *f.* (*registered trade mark*) vaseline.

Vater ['fa:tər], *m.* (**-s,** *pl.* ⸚) father; (male) parent; (*Poet., Zool.*) sire; ***unsre Väter,*** our forefathers *or* ancestors; ***die Väter der Stadt,*** the civic dignitaries. **Vater|haus,** *n.* paternal home *or* roof, home (of one's childhood). **–land,** *n.* native country *or* land, mother-country, fatherland; ***fürs – sterben,*** die for one's country; ***für König und –,*** for king and country; ***der Prophet gilt nichts in seinem –,*** a prophet is without honour in his own country. **vaterländisch,** *adj.* native, national; patriotic. **Vaterlandsliebe,** *f.* patriotism. **vaterlandslos,** *adj.* unpatriotic. **Vaterlandsverräter,** *m.* traitor (to one's country).

väterlich ['fɛ:tərlɪç], *adj.* paternal, fatherly; ***er hat sich meiner – angenommen,*** he has taken a fatherly interest in me; ***–es Erbteil,*** patrimony. **väterlicherseits,** *adv.* on the father's side.

Vaterliebe ['fa:tərli:bə], *f.* paternal *or* fatherly love. **vaterlos,** *adj.* fatherless. **Vater|mord,** *m.* parricide. **–mörder,** *m.* 1. parricide; 2. (*obs.*) (old-fashioned) stand-up collar. **–name,** *m. See* **Vatersname. –pflicht,** *f.* paternal duty. **Vatersbruder,** *m.* paternal uncle.

Vaterschaft ['fa:tərʃaft], *f.* paternity, fatherhood; (*Law*) ***Nachforschung über die –,*** affiliation case; (*Law*) ***Feststellung der –,*** affiliation order. **Vaterschaftsklage,** *f.* paternity suit, affiliation case.

Vaters|name, *m.* family name, surname. **–schwester,** *f.* paternal aunt.

Vater|stadt, *f.* home *or* native town. **–stelle,** *f.* – ***vertreten bei,*** be a father to. **–unser,** *m.* the Lord's Prayer; (*R.C.*) paternoster.

Vegetabilien [vegeta'biliən], *pl.* vegetables, herbs, greenstuff. **vegetabilisch,** *adj.* vegetable. **Vegetarier** [–'ta:riər], *m.* vegetarian. **vegetarisch,** *adj.* vegetarian; ***–e Diät,*** vegetarianism. **vegetativ** [–'ti:f], *adj.* vegetative. **vegetieren** [–'ti:rən], *v.i.* vegetate.

Vehemenz [vehe'mɛnts], *f.* vehemence, impetuosity.

Vehikel [ve'h:ikəl], *n.* vehicle; medium.

Veilchen ['faɪlçən], *n.* (*Bot.*) violet. **veilchenblau,** *adj.* violet. **Veilchenfresser,** *m.* (*dial.*) lady-killer, ladies' man.

Veitstanz ['faitstants], *m.* St. Vitus's dance.

Velin [ve'li:n], **Velinpapier,** *n.* vellum.

Velo ['ve:lo], *n.* (**-s,** *pl.* **-s**) (*Swiss*) bicycle.

Vene ['ve:nə], *f.* vein.

Venedig [ve'ne:dɪç], *n.* Venice.

Venenentzündung ['ve:nən?ɛnttsyndʊŋ], *f.* phlebitis.

Venerabile [vene'ra:bile:], *n.* (*R.C.*) the consecrated wafer, the host.

venerisch [ve'ne:rɪʃ], *adj.* venereal, syphilitic.

Venezianer [venetsi'a:nər], *m.,* **Venezianerin,** *f.,* **venezianisch,** *adj.* Venetian.

Venisektion [venisɛktsi'o:n], *f.* phlebotomy.

venös [ve'nø:s], *adj.* venous.

Ventil [vɛn'ti:l], *n.* (**-s,** *pl.* **-e**) valve, air-valve, vent; (*Mus.*) stop; (*fig.*) outlet, safety-valve. **Ventilation** [–latsi'o:n], *f.* ventilation, airing, weathering. **Ventilator** [–'la:tɔr], *m.* (**-s,** *pl.* **-en**) ventilator; fan, blower. **Ventilführung,** *f.* valve-guide. **ventilieren** [–'li:rən], *v.t.* ventilate, air (*also fig. a grievance etc.*).

Ventil|klappe, *f.* flap, valve. **–kolben,** *m.* valve piston. **–sitz,** *m.* valve seating. **–steuerung,** *f.* valve timing *or* mechanism *or* gear. **–stößel,** *m.* valve rocker. **–teller,** *m.* valve face. **–trompete,** *f.* key bugle.

ver–, Ver– [fɛr–], *insep. and unstressed pref. to verbs and to nouns and adjs. derived from them, with the idea of* (1) removal, loss; (2) stoppage, reversal, opposite; (3) using up, expenditure, continuation to the end; (4) alteration (*usu.* deterioration); (5) *to form verbs from nouns or adjs. without any change of the root meaning. See entries below.*

verabfolgen [fɛr'apfɔlgən], *v.t.* deliver, consign, remit; give, hand over; (*Med.*) administer; provide, serve (*food*); ***ihm etwas – lassen,*** let him have a th.; ***nicht –*** (***lassen***), retain, keep back. **Verabfolgung,** *f.* delivery, consignment; provision, (*Med.*) administration.

verabreden [fɛr'apre:dən], **1.** *v.t.* agree upon, arrange, fix, appoint, stipulate; (*Law*) conspire; ***anderweitig verabredet sein,*** have a previous engagement; ***verabredete Sache,*** pre-arranged affair, (*coll.*) put-up job; ***wie verabredet,*** *see* **verabredetermaßen. 2.** *v.r.* make an appointment. **verabredetermaßen,** *adv.* according to arrangement, as agreed (upon), as arranged. **Verabredung,** *f.* agreement, arrangement, appointment; (*Law*) conspiracy; ***nach –,*** by appointment.

verabreichen [fɛr'apraɪçən], *v.t. See* **verabfolgen.**

verabsäumen [fɛr'apzɔymən], *v.t.* (*usu. used negatively*) neglect, omit, fail (to do).

verabscheuen [fɛr'apʃɔyən], *v.t.* abhor, abominate, detest, loathe. **verabscheuenswert, verabscheuungswürdig,** *adj.* abominable, detestable, loathsome, execrable.

verabschieden [fɛr'apʃi:dən], **1.** *v.t.* dismiss, discharge, send away; (*Mil.*) retire (*an officer*), disband (*troops*); ***ein Gesetz –,*** pass a bill. **2.** *v.r.* take leave (***von,*** of), take one's leave (from), say good-bye (to); retire (*from service*). **Verabschiedung,** *f.* dismissal; discharge.

verachten [fɛr'axtən], *v.t.* despise, scorn, (hold in) contempt *or* disdain, (*coll.*) look down on; (*coll.*) ***nicht zu –,*** not to be sneezed at. **verachtenswert,** *adj.* despicable, contemptible.

Verächter [fɛr'ɛçtər], *m.* scorner, despiser. **verächtlich,** *adj.* (*of a p.*) contemptuous, scornful, disdainful; (*of a th.*) despicable, contemptible.

Verachtung [fɛr'axtʊŋ], *f.* disdain, scorn, contempt.

veralbern [fɛr'albərn], *v.t.* (hold to) ridicule, mock, poke fun at, make a fool of.

verallgemeinern [fɛr'algəmaɪnərn], *v.t., v.i.* generalize. **Verallgemeinerung,** *f.* generalization.

veralten [fɛr'altən], *v.i.* (*aux.* s.) go out of date *or* fashion *or* use, become obsolete *or* antiquated. **veraltet,** *adj.* antiquated, obsolete; out-of-date, out-moded; (*Med.*) inveterate; ***–er Ausdruck,*** archaism.

Veranda [ve'randa], *f.* (-, *pl.* **-den**) veranda.

veränderlich [fɛr'ɛndərlɪç], *adj.* changing, changeable, variable; unsettled, unstable, fluctuating. **Veränderlichkeit,** *f.* variability, changeableness; instability. **verändern, 1.** *v.t.* change, alter, vary. **2.** *v.r.* change, alter, vary; take another situation (*of servants*); ***er hat sich zu seinem Vorteil verändert,*** he has changed for the better. **Veränderung,** *f.* change, alteration; variation, fluctuation.

verängstigt [fɛr'ɛŋstɪçt], *adj.* cowed, intimidated.

verankern [fɛr'aŋkərn], *v.t.* anchor, moor; (*fig.*) embody, establish. **Verankerung,** *f.* anchorage, mooring.

veranlagen [fɛr'anla:gən], *v.t.* assess (***für, zu,*** for). **veranlagt,** *adj.* (*fig.*) talented, (*coll.*) cut out (***für,*** for), (*Med.*) predisposed (***zu,*** to); ***künstlerisch –,*** artistically gifted. **Veranlagung,** *f.* assessment; (*fig.*) disposition, inclination, bent, turn of mind, talent, gift, (*Med.*) predisposition.

veranlassen [fɛr'anlasən], *v.t.* cause, occasion, bring about, effect, call forth, give rise to; ***ihn – zu tun,*** induce *or* (*coll.*) get him to do, prevail (up)on him to do, make him do; ***sich veranlaßt fühlen zu tun,*** feel bound *or* obliged to do; ***das Nötige –,*** take (all) the necessary steps; ***das hat mich zu dem Glauben veranlaßt,*** that has led me to believe. **Veranlassung,** *f.* cause, occasion; motive, reason; instigation, suggestion, inducement, order, request; ***– geben zu,*** give rise to, cause, occasion; ***auf –*** (*Gen.*) *or* ***von,*** at the instance *or* instigation of; on the initiative *or* recommendation of, at the suggestion *or* request of; ***ohne jede –,*** without any provocation; ***zur weiteren –,*** for further action; ***aus dienstlicher –,*** in line of duty.

veranschaulichen [fɛr'anʃaulɪçən], *v.t.* make clear, illustrate, be illustrative of; ***sich*** (*Dat.*) ***–,*** visualize. **Veranschaulichung,** *f.* demonstration, illustration.

veranschlagen [fɛr'anʃla:gən], *v.t.* value, rate, estimate, appraise, assess (***auf*** (*Acc.*), at), (*Pol.*) appropriate. **Veranschlagung,** *f.* valuation, estimate, assessment, appraisal, (*Pol.*) appropriation.

veranstalten [fɛr'anʃtaltən], *v.t.* arrange, organize, bring about; (*coll.*) stage, get up. **Veranstalter,** *m.* organizer. **Veranstaltung,** *f.* arrangement, organization; performance, show, fête, (sporting) event, meeting.

verantworten [fɛr'antvɔrtən], **1.** *v.t.* answer for, account for, be responsible for; ***das kann ich schon –,*** I can explain that. **2.** *v.r.* justify o.s. (***vor ihm,*** with him). **verantwortlich,** *adj.* responsible, accountable, answerable (***für,*** for); ***ihn – machen für,*** blame him for, hold him responsible for. **Verantwortlichkeit,** *f.* accountability, responsibility.

Verantwortung [fɛr'antvɔrtuŋ], *f.* responsibility; justification, vindication, excuse; ***die – auf sich laden,*** incur the responsibility; ***auf seine –,*** at his (own) peril *or* risk, on his own responsibility; ***zur – ziehen,*** call to account. **verantwortungsbewußt,** *adj.* responsible. **Verantwortungsbewußtsein,** *n.* sense of duty *or* responsibility. **verantwortungs|freudig,** *adj.* willing to accept *or* ready to take responsibility. **-los,** *adj.* irresponsible. **-voll,** *adj.* involving great responsibility; responsible.

veräppeln [fɛr'ɛpəln], *v.t.* (*coll.*) tease, pull (*a p.'s*) leg, (*sl.*) kid.

verarbeiten [fɛr'arbaɪtən], *v.t.* manufacture, work up, process, treat, machine; (*fig.*) ponder over, assimilate, digest; (*coll.*) ***ihn gehörig –,*** pitch into him, pull him to pieces; ***verarbeitete Hände,*** hands worn with work; ***verarbeitetes Silber,*** wrought silver. **Verarbeitung,** *f.* treatment, processing, working up, manufacture; workmanship, finish; (*fig.*) digestion, thorough study.

verargen [fɛr'argən], *v.t.* ***ihm etwas –,*** blame him for a th.; ***ich verarge es Ihnen nicht,*** I do not hold it against you; ***das kann mir niemand –,*** no one can take me up about that.

verärgern [fɛr'ɛrgərn], *v.t.* anger, vex, irritate, annoy, exasperate. **Verärgerung,** *f.* vexation, irritation, annoyance, exasperation.

verarmen [fɛr'armən], **1.** *v.i.* (*aux.* s.) become poor *or* impoverished, be reduced to poverty. **2.** *v.t.* impoverish; ***verarmter Boden,*** impoverished *or* depleted soil. **Verarmung,** *f.* impoverishment, pauperization.

verarzten [fɛr'artstən], *v.t.* (*coll.*) doctor, treat.

verästeln [fɛr'ɛstəln], *v.r.* branch out, ramify. **Verästelung,** *f.* ramification.

verauktionieren [fɛrˀauktsio'ni:rən], *v.t.* put up for sale, sell by auction; ***verauktioniert werden,*** come under the hammer, be sold by auction.

verausgaben [fɛr'ausga:bən], **1.** *v.t.* spend, expend, pay out. **2.** *v.r.* spend all one's money, run short of money; (*fig.*) spend o.s., wear o.s. out. **Verausgabung,** *f.* spending, payment; ***– falschen Geldes,*** passing *or* uttering counterfeit money.

verauslagen [fɛr'ausla:gən], *v.t.* disburse, advance, lay out (*money*).

veräußerlich [fɛr'ɔysərlɪç], *adj.* alienable, saleable, negotiable. **veräußern,** *v.t.* 1. sell, dispose of, transfer (***an*** (*Acc.*), to); 2. alienate. **Veräußerung,** *f.* 1. alienation; 2. sale, disposal, transfer.

Verb [vɛrp], *n.* (**-s,** *pl.* **-en**) verb. **verbal** [-'ba:l], *adj.* verbal; terminological. **Verbalinjurie,** *f.* insult, slander.

verballhornen [fɛr'balhɔrnən], *v.t.* bowdlerize.

Verband [fɛr'bant], *m.* (**-(e)s,** *pl.* **¨-e**) 1. binding, bracing, bonding, bond, joint; (*Med.*) bandage, (surgical) dressing; 2. union, association, federation, league, alliance; (*Mil.*) unit, formation. **Verband|kasten,** *m.* medicine chest. **-päckchen,** *n.* field-dressing, first-aid kit. **-platz,** *m.* (*Mil.*) (field) dressing-station. **-schere,** *f.* surgical scissors.

Verbands|fliegen, *n.* (*Av.*) formation flying. **-kasse,** *f.* funds of a society. **-mitglied,** *n.* member of a society *or* an association.

Verband|stelle, *f.* first-aid post. **-stoff,** *m.* *See* **-zeug. -watte,** *f.* surgical cotton wool. **-zeug,** *n.* dressing, bandage.

verbannen [fɛr'banən], *v.t.* banish, exile, deport, (*Hist.*) outlaw; (*fig.*) dispel, banish. **Verbannte(r),** *m., f.* exile, (*Hist.*) outlaw. **Verbannung,** *f.* banishment, exile, deportation. **Verbannungsort,** *m.* place of exile.

verbarrikadieren [fɛrbarika'di:rən], **1.** *v.t.* barricade; block. **2.** *v.r.* entrench *or* intrench o.s.

verbauen [fɛr'bauən], *v.t.* 1. shut out, obstruct, block up; ***einem Hause die Aussicht –,*** block the view from a house; ***sich*** (*Dat.*) ***den Weg –,*** bar one's way (***zu,*** to), cut o.s. off (from); (*fig. coll.*) prevent, thwart, preclude; (*a p., Dat.*) debar from; 2. build up; 3. use up in building (*materials*); spend in building (*money*); 4. build badly. **Verbauung,** *f.* 1. obstruction (*of view*); 2. building up.

verbauern [fɛr'bauərn], *v.i.* (*aux.* s.) become countrified.

verbeißen [fɛr'baɪsən], **1.** *irr.v.t.* clench one's teeth on; (*fig.*) swallow, stifle, suppress; ***sich*** (*Dat.*) ***das Lachen –,*** stifle (one's) laughter; ***seinen Ärger –,*** conceal one's annoyance; ***mit schlecht verbissenem Grimm,*** with ill-concealed wrath. **2.** *irr.v.r.* stick obstinately (***in*** (*Acc.*), to), be set (on).

Verbene [vɛ́r'be:nə], *f.* (*Bot.*) verbena.

verbergen [fɛr'bɛrgən], **1.** *irr.v.t.* hide, conceal (***vor*** (*Dat.*), from). **2.** *irr.v.r.* hide.

Verbesserer [fɛr'bɛsərər], *m.* improver; reformer. **verbessern, 1.** *v.t.* improve, ameliorate, amend, revise, correct, rectify. **2.** *v.r.* improve, reform; (*in speaking*) correct o.s.; (*financially*) better o.s. **Verbesserung,** *f.* improvement, amelioration, reform; amendment, correction, rectification, emendation. **Verbesserungsantrag,** *m.* amendment. **verbesserungs|bedürftig,** *adj.* in need of improvement. **-fähig,** *adj.* capable of improvement.

verbeten [fɛr'be:tən], *see* **verbitten.**

verbeugen [fɛr'bɔygən], *v.r.* bow, make a bow (***vor***

(*Dat.*), to). **Verbeugung,** *f.* bow, reverence, obeisance.

verbeulen [fɛr'bɔylən], *v.t.* dent, batter. **Verbeulung,** *f.* dent.

verbiegen [fɛr'bi:gən], **1.** *irr.v.t.* bend, twist; bend out of shape, distort. **2.** *irr.v.r.* twist, warp, get bent.

verbiestern [fɛr'bi:stərn], *v.r.* (*coll., dial.*) become confused *or* annoyed.

verbieten [fɛr'bi:tən], *irr.v.t.* forbid (***ihm etwas (zu tun***), him (to do) s.th.), prohibit (him (from doing) s.th.); ***das verbietet sich von selbst,*** that obviously cannot be allowed; ***du hast mir nichts zu –,*** you have no authority *or* (*coll.*) no say over me; ***streng verboten,*** strictly prohibited.

verbilden [fɛr'bɪldən], *v.t.* spoil, deform, shape *or* form wrongly; train *or* educate badly. **Verbildung,** *f.* malformation; bad training.

verbilligen [fɛr'bɪlɪgən], *v.t.* cheapen, make cheaper, bring down the price of, reduce in price. **Verbilligung,** *f.* reduction in price, cheapening.

verbinden [fɛr'bɪndən], **1.** *irr.v.t.* unite, join, combine (***mit,*** with), connect (with *or* to), bind, link, couple (to); bandage, dress (*wounds*), tie (together), bind up; ***ihn zu etwas –,*** bind *or* pledge him to s.th.; ***eng verbunden mit,*** closely bound up with; ***mit verbundenen Augen,*** blindfolded; ***durch Heirat verbunden,*** connected by marriage; ***mit Gefahr*** or ***Risiko verbunden,*** involving danger *or* risk; ***mit einander verbunden,*** united; ***ich bin Ihnen sehr verbunden,*** I am greatly obliged *or* indebted to you; ***die damit verbundenen Bedingungen,*** the conditions attaching thereto; ***die damit verbundenen Unkosten,*** the incidental expenses. **2.** *irr.v.r.* join, unite, combine; ***sich – mit,*** (*Comm.*) go into partnership with; (*Chem.*) combine; (*for some purpose*) join forces with; ***sich ehelich – (mit einem Mädchen***), marry (a girl).

verbindlich [fɛr'bɪntlɪç], *adj.* binding, obligatory, compulsory; obliging, courteous; ***sich – machen zu tun,*** bind o.s. *or* undertake *or* engage to do; ***sich gerichtlich – machen,*** enter into recognizances; ***das ist für mich nicht –,*** that does not bind me; ***danke –st!*** my sincerest thanks! very much obliged! **Verbindlichkeit,** *f.* 1. binding force (*of treaties*); obligation, commitment, liability; ***mit gegenseitiger –,*** mutually binding; ***mündliche –,*** verbal promise; ***seinen –en nachkommen,*** fulfil one's engagements, meet one's liabilities; ***ohne –,*** without liability *or* obligation; 2. civility, courtesy, readiness to oblige; favour, kindness, compliment; ***die –, mit der er es sagte,*** the polite way in which he said it.

Verbindung [fɛr'bɪnduŋ], *f.* binding, joining, connecting; blending, combination; union. association, league, alliance; relation(s), relationship; connection (*also Tele.*); (*Tech.*) union, bond, joint, junction; (*Chem.*) compound; (*Surg.*) bandaging, dressing; (*Anat.*) inosculation; (*Mil.*) communication, contact, liaison; ***– aufnehmen,*** establish contact *or* communications; (*Tele.*) ***– bekommen,*** be connected, (*coll.*) get through; be put through; ***in – bleiben,*** keep in touch; ***in – bringen,*** connect, link up, associate; ***in eine – eintreten,*** join a students' association, become a member of a students' club; ***in – mit,*** in connection *or* conjunction with, combined with; (*Mil.*) ***rückwärtige –en,*** lines of communication; ***in – stehen,*** be connected; correspond, be in touch *or* communication (***mit,*** with); ***sich in – setzen mit,*** get into touch with; ***schlagende –,*** duelling association (*of students*); ***studentische –,*** students' corporation; ***in – treten,*** get in touch, enter into correspondence (***mit,*** with); ***– herstellen,*** (make) contact, establish communication, (*Tele.*) get a connection.

Verbindings|bahn, *f.* branch- *or* junction-line. **–gang,** *m.* connecting passage *or* duct. **–glied,** *n.* copula. **–graben,** *m.* communication trench. **–hülse,** *f.* (*Tech.*) union (coupling). **–linie,** *f.* line of communication. **–mann,** *m.* contact (man), mediator, go-between. **–mittel,** *n.* *See* **–glied.** **–offizier,** *m.* liaison officer. **–rohr,** *n.*, **–röhre,** *f.* connecting tube *or* pipe. **–stange,** *f.* connecting rod. **–straße,** *f.* communication *or* feeder road. **–stück,** *n.* tie, brace, joint, coupling, connecting piece, (*Elec.*) connector; *see also* **–hülse.** **–tür,** *f.* communication door. **–weg,** *m.* *See* **–linie.**

verbissen [fɛr'bɪsən], *adj.* 1. obstinate, dogged, grim; 2. morose, sullen; *see* **verbeißen. Verbissenheit,** *f.* 1. obstinacy, doggedness; 2. sullenness, moroseness, sour temper.

verbitten [fɛr'bɪtən], *irr.v.t.* refuse to tolerate, not permit, object to, decline, (*coll.*) not stand for, not put up with; ***das verbitte ich mir,*** I will not stand (for) that; ***ich verbitte mir die Ehre,*** I beg to decline the honour; ***solche Bemerkungen verbitte ich mir,*** I will not tolerate such remarks; ***Beileid dankend verbeten,*** no cards *or* flowers by request.

verbittern [fɛr'bɪtərn], *v.t.* embitter; ***ihm das Leben –,*** make life miserable for him; ***sich – lassen,*** become soured *or* embittered. **Verbitterung,** *f.* embitterment, bitterness (*of heart*).

verblassen [fɛr'blasən], *v.i.* (*aux.* s.) grow *or* turn pale, lose colour, fade; (*fig.*) ***– gegenüber,*** pale into insignificance beside.

Verbleib [fɛr'blaɪp], *m.* abode, whereabouts; ***dabei muß es sein – haben,*** that must be the end of the matter. **verbleiben,** *irr.v.i.* (*aux.* s.) remain, continue, stay the same; ***bei seiner Meinung –,*** persist in *or* hold *or* (*coll.*) stick to one's opinion; ***lassen wir es dabei –,*** let the matter rest there; ***ich verbleibe hochachtungsvoll,*** Yours faithfully.

verbleichen [fɛr'blaɪçən], *irr.v.i.* (*aux.* s.) *see* **verblassen.**

verbleien [fɛr'blaɪən], *v.t.* line *or* coat with lead, affix a lead seal to.

verblenden [fɛr'blɛndən], *v.t.* 1. blind, dazzle; delude; beguile, infatuate; 2. (*Build.*) face (*a wall*) with brick *or* plaster *or* roughcast; 3. (*Mil. etc.*) mask, screen (*a light*). **Verblender, Verblendklinker,** *m.* facing brick *or* tile. **Verblendung,** *f.* 1. (*Build.*) facing; 2. (*fig.*) blindness, delusion.

verbleuen [fɛr'blɔyən], *v.t.* (*coll.*) beat (*a p.*) black and blue.

verblichen [fɛr'blɪçən], *adj.* ashy-pale, faded; (*fig.*) dead, deceased; *see* **verbleichen. Verblichene(r),** *m., f.* deceased (person).

verblöden [fɛr'blø:dən], *v.i.* (*aux.* s.) become feeble-minded *or* puerile. **Verblödung,** *f.* imbecility, idiocy. vacuity, hebetude.

verblüffen [fɛr'blyfən], *v.t.* amaze, perplex, stupefy, dumbfound, nonplus, disconcert, bewilder, stagger, stun, flabbergast. **verblüfft,** *adj.* amazed *etc.*, nonplussed, dumbfounded, flabbergasted, taken aback. **Verblüffung,** *f.* stupefaction, bewilderment, amazement, perplexity.

verblühen [fɛr'bly:ən], *v.i.* (*aux.* h. & s.) fade, wither; (*fig.*) ***verblühte Schönheit,*** faded beauty; ***verblühe!*** be off! clear off!

verblümt [fɛr'bly:mt], *adj.* figurative, allusive, veiled, covert, indirect; ***etwas – zu verstehen geben*** hint at a th., make insinuations.

verbluten [fɛr'blu:tən], *v.r., v.i.* (*aux.* s.) bleed to death; ***– lassen,*** allow to bleed (to death). **Verblutung,** *f.* bleeding to death, severe haemorrhage.

verbocken [fɛr'bɔkən], *v.t.* (*coll.*) bungle, botch, make a hash of.

verbogen [fɛr'bo:gən], *see* **verbiegen.**

verbohren [fɛr'bo:rən], *v.r.* ***sich – in*** (*Acc.*), be opinionated *or* (*coll.*) pig-headed about, be wedded to (*an opinion*). **verbohrt,** *adj.* stubborn, obstinate, pig-headed. **Verbohrtheit,** *f.* obstinacy, stubbornness, pig-headedness.

verbolzen [fɛr'bɔltsən], *v.t.* bolt together.

[1]**verborgen** [fɛr'bɔrgən], *v.t.* lend (out), make a loan of.

[2]**verborgen,** *adj.* hidden, concealed, secret, clandestine; (*Phys.*) latent; ***im –en,*** in secret, in obscurity, secretly, unnoticed; ***–e Befruchtung,*** cryptogamy; ***–e Wärme,*** latent heat. **Verborgenheit,** *f.* concealment, secrecy; retirement, seclusion, obscurity.

Verbot [fɛr'bo:t], *n.* (**-(e)s,** *pl.* **-e**) prohibition; (*Law*) inhibition; suppression (*of a book etc.*); veto, ban. **verboten,** *adj.* forbidden, prohibited, illicit; *see* **verbieten**; *-e Waren,* contraband goods.

verbracht [fɛr'braxt], **verbrachte,** *see* **verbringen.**

verbrämen [fɛr'brɛ:mən], *v.t.* border, edge, trim, garnish, embellish. **Verbrämung,** *f.* border, edging, trimming.

verbrannt [fɛr'brant], *see* **verbrennen.**

Verbrauch [fɛr'braux], *m.* consumption, expenditure (*an* (*Dat.*), of). **verbrauchen,** *v.t.* use (up), consume, spend, expend; wear out, exhaust; *verbrauchte Batterie,* run down *or* flat *or* empty battery; *verbrauchte Luft,* stale air. **Verbraucher,** *m.* consumer, user.

Verbraucher|gas, *n.* generator gas. **-genossenschaft,** *f.* co-operative society. **-kreis,** *n.* (*Elec.*) output *or* load circuit. **-waren,** *f.pl. See* **Verbrauchsgüter.**

Verbrauchs|artikel, -gegenstand, *m.* article of consumption, commodity. **-güter,** *n.pl.* commodities, consumer goods. **-satz,** *m.* rate of consumption. **-skala,** *f.* maintenance scale, vitamin requirements. **-steuer,** *f.* indirect tax, excise duty.

verbrechen [fɛr'brɛçən], *irr.v.t.* commit (*a crime or an offence*), perpetrate (*a joke etc.*); *was habe ich verbrochen?* what have I done wrong? **Verbrechen,** *n.* crime, felony, criminal offence; *leichtes –,* venial offence. **Verbrecher,** *m.* criminal, felon; *überführter –,* convicted felon. **Verbrecher|-album,** *n.* rogues' gallery. **-bande,** *f.* gang. **-gesicht,** *n.* guilty look. **verbrecherisch,** *adj.* criminal. **Verbrecher|kneipe,** *f.* thieves' kitchen. **-kolonie,** *f.* convict *or* penal settlement.

verbreiten [fɛr'braɪtən], **1.** *v.t., v.r.* spread, disperse, distribute (*über* (*Acc.*), over), (*light etc.*) diffuse, shed; (*news etc.*) circulate, spread abroad, disseminate, propagate; *weit verbreitet,* widespread, very common, widely held (*views*), customary, popular, general. **2.** *v.r.* expatiate, enlarge, hold forth (*über* (*Acc.*), on).

verbreitern [fɛr'braɪtərn], *v.t., v.r.* broaden, widen. **Verbreiterung,** *f.* widening, broadening.

Verbreitung [fɛr'braɪtuŋ], *f.* spreading, diffusion, propagation, dissemination, dispersal, circulation; distribution, range, spread.

verbrennbar [fɛr'brɛnba:r], *adj.* combustible.

verbrennen [fɛr'brɛnən], **1.** *irr.v.t.* burn, scorch, singe; scald; cremate (*the dead*); *zu Asche –,* reduce to ashes; (*fig.*) *sich* (*Dat.*) *die Finger –,* burn one's fingers; *verbrannte Erde,* scorched earth. **2.** *irr.v.i.* (*aux.* s.) burn, be scorched, be burnt up; be burnt to death.

Verbrennung [fɛr'brɛnuŋ], *f.* burning, combustion, incineration; cremation (*of the dead*); burn, scald; death by fire, death at the stake. **Verbrennungs|-halle,** *f.* crematorium. **-kammer,** *f.* (*Motor.*) combustion chamber. **-maschine,** *f.,* **-motor,** *m.* internal-combustion engine. **-narbe,** *f.* burn scar. **-ofen,** *m.* incinerator. **-probe,** *f.* ignition test. **-produkt,** *n.* combustion product. **-raum,** *m. See* **-kammer. -vorgang,** *m.* (process of) combustion.

verbriefen [fɛr'bri:fən], **1.** *v.t.* acknowledge *or* confirm in writing; mortgage *or* pledge by documents, secure by charter. **2.** *v.r.* give a written undertaking, bind o.s. by deed. **verbrieft,** *adj.* chartered, documented; *-e Rechte,* vested rights; *-e Schulden,* obligations, bonded debts; *versiegelt und –,* positive, categorical, indisputable. **Verbriefung,** *f.* written acknowledgement *or* pledge, confirmation in writing, charter, bond.

verbringen [fɛr'brɪŋən], *irr.v.t.* spend, pass (*time*).

verbrüdern [fɛr'bry:dərn], *v.r.* become intimate, fraternize, get on good terms (*mit,* with). **Verbrüderung,** *f.* fraternization.

verbrühen [fɛr'bry:ən], *v.t.* scald. **Verbrühung,** *f.* scald.

verbuchen [fɛr'bu:xən], *v.t.* (*Comm.*) book (*an order etc.*); (*fig.*) register.

verbuhlt [fɛr'bu:lt], *adj.* amorous, wanton, debauched. **Verbuhltheit,** *f.* debauchery, wantonness.

Verbum ['vɛrbum], *n.* (**-s,** *pl.* **Verba**) *see* **Verb.**

verbumfeien [fɛr'bumfaɪən], **verbumfiedeln** [-fi:dəln], *v.t.* (*sl.*) *see* **verbocken.**

verbummeln [fɛr'buməln], **1.** *v.t.* waste, squander, idle *or* fritter away (*time*), (*sl.*) blue; (*coll.*) completely forget. **2.** *v.i.* (*aux.* s.) come down in the world. **verbummelt,** *adj.* idle, slothful, lackadaisical, dawdling; *-er Kerl,* wastrel, good-for-nothing, loafer.

Verbund [fɛr'bunt], *m.* (**-(e)s,** *pl.* **⸚e**) (*Tech.*) compound. **verbunden,** *see* **verbinden.**

verbünden [fɛr'byndən], *v.r.* ally o.s. (*mit,* to *or* with); enter into *or* form an alliance (with).

Verbundenheit [fɛr'bundənhaɪt], *f.* community, association, relationship, connection, bonds, ties, solidarity.

Verbündete(r) [fɛr'byndətə(r)], *m., f.* ally, confederate.

Verbund|glas, *n.* laminated glass. **-maschine,** *f.* compound engine. **-motor,** *m.* (*Elec.*) compound motor. **-wirtschaft,** *f.* collective economy.

verbürgen [fɛr'byrgən], *v.t., v.r.* guarantee, vouch for, answer for. **verbürgt,** *adj.* established, authentic(ated), well-founded.

verbüßen [fɛr'by:sən], *v.t.* atone for, pay the penalty of; *seine Strafzeit –,* serve one's sentence, (*coll.*) do one's time.

verbutten [fɛr'butən], *v.i.* (*dial.*) become dwarfed *or* stunted.

verbuttern [fɛr'butərn], *v.t.* (*coll.*) bungle, botch; waste, squander.

verchromen [fɛr'kro:mən], *v.t., v.i.* plate with chromium. **verchromt,** *adj.* chromium-plated. **Verchromung,** *f.* chromium plating.

Verdacht [fɛr'daxt], *m.* suspicion, distrust; *in – bringen,* bring under suspicion; *in – haben,* suspect; *in – kommen,* be suspected, incur suspicion; *– schöpfen* or *hegen,* become suspicious, (*coll.*) smell a rat.

verdächtig [fɛr'dɛçtɪç], *adj.* suspected; (*pred. only*) suspect (*Gen.,* of); suspicious, questionable, doubtful, (*sl.*) fishy; *sich – machen,* arouse suspicion. **verdächtigen,** *v.t.* cast *or* throw suspicion on, be suspicious of, distrust; suspect (*Gen.,* of), impute (to). **Verdächtigung,** *f.* suspicion, imputation, insinuation.

Verdachts|grund, *m.* grounds for suspicion. **-moment,** *n.* suspicious fact. **-person,** *f.* suspect.

verdammen [fɛr'damən], *v.t.* condemn; damn, curse, anathematize. **verdammenswert,** *adj.* damnable, execrable. **Verdammnis,** *f.* damnation, perdition. **verdammt,** *adj.* condemned, damned, accursed; (*coll.*) *–!* damn it! damnation! (*sl.*) *es ist – kalt,* it is damnably cold; *seine -e Schuldigkeit,* his bounden duty. **Verdammung,** *f.* condemnation, (*Eccl.*) damnation.

verdampfen [fɛr'dampfən], *v.t., v.i.* (*aux.* s.) vaporize; evaporate. **Verdampfer,** *m.* vaporizer. **Verdampfung,** *f.* evaporation, vaporization.

verdanken [fɛr'daŋkən], *v.t.* **1.** owe (*ihm etwas,* s.th. to him), be indebted *or* obliged (to him for a th.); *seinem Rate ist es zu –, daß . . .,* it is owing *or* due to his advice that . . .; **2.** (*Swiss*) give *or* return thanks for; *wir – Ihren Brief,* we thank you for your letter.

verdarb [fɛr'darp], *see* **verderben.**

verdattert [fɛr'datərt], *adj.* (*coll.*) flabbergasted.

verdauen [fɛr'dauən], **1.** *v.t.* digest; (*fig.*) tolerate, (*coll.*) stand, swallow, get over. **2.** *v.r.* be digested *or* digestible. **verdaulich,** *adj.* digestible; *schwer –,* indigestible, rich, heavy (*of food*). **Verdaulichkeit,** *f.* digestibility. **Verdauung,** *f.* digestion.

Verdauungs|beschwerden, *f.pl.* indigestion, digestive trouble. **-ferment,** *n.* pepsin. **-flüssigkeit,** *f. See* **-saft. -kanal,** *m.* alimentary canal, digestive tract. **-mittel,** *n.* stomachic, digestive remedy. **-saft,** *m.* gastric juice. **-schwäche,** *f.* weak digestion, dyspepsia. **-spaziergang,** *m.* (*coll.*) constitutional. **–stoff,** *m. See* **–ferment. –störung,** *f.* indigestion; bilious attack.

Verdeck [fɛrˈdɛk], *n.* **(-(e)s,** *pl.* **-e)** covering, awning; hood, canopy, roof (*of a car*), tilt (*of a carriage*); (*Naut.*) deck. **verdecken,** *v.t.* cover (up), hide, conceal; (*Mil. etc.*) camouflage, mask, veil, screen, cloak. **verdeckt,** *adj.* hidden, concealed, covered; covert; camouflaged, screened, masked; (*Naut.*) – ***werden,*** occult; ***mit –en Karten spielen,*** not show one's hand. **Verdeckung,** *f.* covering, concealment; (*Naut.*) occultation.

verdenken [fɛrˈdɛŋkən], *v.t. See* **verargen.**

Verderb [fɛrˈdɛrp], *m.* ruin, destruction; decay, deterioration; waste; ***auf Gedeih und –,*** in success or adversity, come what may.

verderben [fɛrˈdɛrbən], **1.** *irr.v.t.* spoil, damage, ruin, destroy, (*coll.*) make a mess *or* hash of; (*fig.*) deprave, corrupt, demoralize, drag down; ***sich*** (*Dat.*) ***die Augen –,*** ruin one's eyes; ***ihm die Freude –,*** spoil *or* mar his pleasure; ***ihm das Konzept –,*** put a spoke in his wheel; ***ihm die Laune –,*** upset him, put him out of temper; ***sich*** (*Dat.*) ***den Magen –,*** upset one's stomach; ***es mit ihm –,*** fall out *or* quarrel with him, incur his displeasure, (*coll.*) get into his bad books; ***er will es mit keinem –,*** he tries to please everybody, he wishes to keep in with everybody; (*Prov.*) ***böse Beispiele – gute Sitten,*** evil communications corrupt good manners. **2.** *irr.v.i.* (*aux.* s.) spoil, get *or* be spoilt, decay, deteriorate, go bad, rot, perish; ***an ihm ist ein guter Schauspieler verdorben,*** a good actor is lost in him.

Verderben, *n.* corruption, destruction, ruin; doom, perdition; ***ihn ins – stürzen,*** ruin him, bring him to ruin; ***ins – rennen*** or ***stürzen,*** rush (headlong) into destruction; ***der Weg des –s,*** the road to ruin; ***es wird noch mein – sein,*** it will be my undoing. **verderbenbringend,** *adj.* ruinous, disastrous, fatal.

verderblich [fɛrˈdɛrplɪç], *adj.* easily spoiled, perishable; pernicious, destructive, injurious; deadly, fatal (*für,* to). **Verderblichkeit,** *f.* perishableness; perniciousness, destructiveness. **Verderbnis,** *f.* corruption, decay, deterioration; depravity, perversion.

verderbt [fɛrˈdɛrpt], *adj.* corrupt(ed), depraved, vicious, dissolute, dissipated. **Verderbtheit,** *f.* corruption, corruptness, depravity, vice.

verdeutlichen [fɛrˈdɔytlɪçən], *v.t.* elucidate, make clear *or* plain, illustrate.

verdeutschen [fɛrˈdɔytʃən], *v.t.* translate into German.

verdichten [fɛrˈdɪçtən], **1.** *v.t.* condense, compress, solidify; thicken, concentrate; liquefy (*a gas*). **2.** *v.r.* become thick *or* condensed *or* concentrated *or* solid (*of a liquid*) *or* liquid (*of a gas*); (*fig.*) consolidate, grow stronger, take shape (*in one's mind*). **Verdichter,** *m.* condensor, compressor. **Verdichtung,** *f.* compression, condensation, solidification, liquefaction; (*fig.*) consolidation, concentration. **Verdichtungs|hub,** *m.* (*Motor.*) compression stroke. **–zahl,** *f.* compression ratio.

verdicken [fɛrˈdɪkən], *v.t.* thicken, boil down, (*Chem. etc.*) inspissate; coagulate, congeal, clot, curdle. **Verdickung,** *f.* thickening; thickening agent, thickener.

verdienen [fɛrˈdiːnən], *v.t.* earn; gain, get, make (*money*), (*fig.*) deserve, merit; ***mehr Glück – als haben,*** be more deserving than lucky; ***etwas daran –,*** make s.th. out of it; ***daran ist nichts zu –,*** there is no money in it; ***man verdient dabei nicht das Salz zur Suppe,*** that brings in next to nothing; ***das habe ich um Sie nicht verdient,*** I did not deserve that from you; ***sich verdient machen um,*** deserve well of.

Verdienst [fɛrˈdiːnst], **1.** *m.* gain, profit; earnings, wages; ***das ist mein ganzer – dabei,*** that is all I get out of it. **2.** *n.* merit, deserts; ***das – wird selten belohnt,*** merit seldom receives its due reward; ***sich*** (*Dat.*) ***–e erwerben um,*** deserve well of; ***die –e dieses Mannes,*** the services which this man has rendered; ***nach –,*** deservedly, according to one's deserts; ***wie das –, so der Ruhm,*** honour (is given) to whom honour is due; ***es ist sein –, daß . . .,*** it is owing *or* due to him that . . ., to him the credit is due that . . .; ***sich*** (*Dat.*) ***etwas zum –e anrechnen,*** take credit for s.th.

Verdienst|ausfall, *m.* loss of wages *or* earnings. **–kreuz,** *n.* distinguished service medal, order of merit. **verdienstlich,** *adj. See* **verdienstvoll. Verdienst|möglichkeit,** *f.* chance to earn money, money-making opportunity. **–spanne,** *f.* profit margin. **verdienstvoll,** *adj.* meritorious, deserving, creditable.

verdient [fɛrˈdiːnt], *adj.* (*of a th.*) deserved, well-earned; well-deserved (*punishment*); (*of a p.*) deserving; ***sein –er Lohn,*** no more than he deserves. **verdienter|maßen, –weise,** *adv.* deservedly, according to one's deserts.

Verdikt [vɛrˈdɪkt], *n.* **(-(e)s,** *pl.* **-e)** verdict, decision, judgement.

Verding [fɛrˈdɪŋ], *n.* **(-(e)s,** *pl.* **-e)** *see* **Verdingung;** ***auf – übernehmen,*** contract for. **verdingen, 1.** *v.t.* (*p.p. usu.* ***verdungen***) hire out, contract for; ***sie als Dienerin bei ihm –,*** put her into service with him; ***Arbeiten –,*** let out work under contract; ***den Bau eines Hauses –,*** contract for the building of a house. **2.** *v.r.* ***sich*** (***als Diener***) ***bei ihm –,*** go into service with him. **Verdingung,** *f.* 1. hiring out; 2. agreement, contract.

verdirb [fɛrˈdɪrp], **verdirbst, verdirbt,** *see* **verderben.**

verdolmetschen [fɛrˈdɔlmɛtʃən], *v.t.* translate, interpret, expound.

verdonnern [fɛrˈdɔnərn], *v.t.* (*coll.*) scold, condemn. **verdonnert,** *adj.* thunderstruck, dumbfounded.

verdoppeln [fɛrˈdɔpəln], *v.t., v.r.* double, duplicate; redouble (*one's steps*). **Verdoppelung,** *f.* doubling, duplication.

verdorben [fɛrˈdɔrbən], *adj.* tainted, spoilt, rotten; foul (*air*), disordered, upset (*stomach*); (*fig.*) corrupt, depraved; *see* **verderben, verderbt. Verdorbenheit,** *f.* spoiled *or* ruined condition; rottenness, corruption, depravity.

verdorren [fɛrˈdɔrən], *v.i.* (*aux.* s.) dry up, wither.

verdrängen [fɛrˈdrɛŋən], *reg.v.t.* drive out *or* away, dislodge, displace, supersede, supplant, oust, push *or* thrust aside, expel, crowd out; (*Psych. etc.*) suppress, repress; ***verdrängte Bevölkerung,*** displaced population. **Verdrängung,** *f.* removal, ousting, dispossession, displacement (*also Naut.*); (*Psych.*) suppression, repression.

verdrehen [fɛrˈdreːən], *v.t.* twist; roll (*one's eyes*), contort (*one's limbs*); wrench, sprain, dislocate; force, distort, misrepresent, warp, pervert; ***sich*** (*Dat.*) ***den Arm –,*** sprain one's arm; ***das Gesicht –,*** (make a) grimace; (***sich***) ***den Hals –,*** crane one's neck; ***ihm den Kopf –,*** turn his head; ***das Recht –,*** pervert justice; ***den Sinn –,*** twist *or* force the meaning; ***die Tatsachen –,*** misrepresent the facts; ***seine Worte –,*** twist his words. **verdreht,** *adj.* twisted, distorted; forced; (*fig.*) cracked, crazy, (*coll.*) dotty, barmy, screwy. **Verdrehtheit,** *f.* craziness.

Verdrehung [fɛrˈdreːuŋ], *f.* twist(ing), (*Tech.*) torsion; sprain; contortion; distortion, misrepresentation. **Verdrehungs|festigkeit,** *f.* torsional strength. **–versuch,** *m.* torsion test.

verdreifachen [fɛrˈdraɪfaxən], *v.t.* treble.

verdreschen [fɛrˈdrɛʃən], *irr.v.t.* (*coll.*) thrash, give (*a p.*) a good thrashing.

verdrießen [fɛrˈdriːsən], *irr.v.t.* vex, annoy, displease; ***sich etwas nicht – lassen,*** not shrink from, not be discouraged by, (*coll.*) not be put off by; ***sich keine Mühe – lassen,*** spare no pains. **verdrießlich,** *adj.* (*of a p.*) vexed, annoyed; sulky, disagreeable, peevish, cross, bad-tempered, out of humour; (*of a th.*) vexatious, annoying, irksome, tiresome, disagreeable. **Verdrießlichkeit,** *f.* bad temper, sulkiness, peevishness, crossness; irksomeness, vexation, annoyance.

verdroß [fɛr'drɔs], **verdrösse** [–'drœsə], *see* **verdrießen.**
verdrossen [fɛr'drɔsən], *adj.* cross, peevish, vexed; listless, sulky, sullen; *see* **verdrießen. Verdrossenheit,** *f.* peevishness, crossness; listlessness, sulkiness.
verdrucken [fɛr'drukən], *v.t.* misprint.
verdrücken [fɛr'drykən], **1.** *v.t.* 1. (*dial.*) *see* **zerdrücken**; 2. (*sl.*) stow away, polish off (*food*). **2.** *v.r.* (*sl.*) slink *or* slip away.
Verdruß [fɛr'drus], *m.* displeasure, annoyance, discontent, dismay, chagrin, vexation; ***ihm etwas zum – tun,*** do a th. to spite him; ***allen Menschen zum –,*** to everyone's annoyance; ***ihm – bereiten*** or ***machen,*** vex *or* annoy *or* irritate him, give him trouble; ***zu meinem – finde ich,*** I am annoyed to find; (*sl.*) ***einen – haben,*** be humpbacked.
verduften [fɛr'duftən], *v.i.* (*aux.* s.) evaporate; lose its scent; (*coll.*) make off, vamoose, hop it, beat it.
verdummen [fɛr'dumən], **1.** *v.t.* make stupid, stupefy, stultify. **2.** *v.i.* become stupid.
verdunkeln [fɛr'duŋkəln], **1.** *v.t.* darken, black out, obscure, cloud; eclipse, throw into the shade. **2.** *v.r.* grow dim; ***der Himmel verdunkelt sich,*** the sky becomes clouded *or* overcast. **Verdunk(e)lung,** *f.* 1. darkening; eclipse; black-out; 2. (*Law*) prejudicing the course of justice.
verdünnen [fɛr'dynən], *v.t.* thin, weaken, dilute; attenuate, rarefy; reduce, temper (*colours*); (*Chem.*) ***verdünnte Lösung,*** dilute solution. **Verdünnung,** *f.* thinning, dilution, rarefaction, attenuation. **Verdünnungsmittel,** *n.* diluting agent, thinner, reducer.
verdunsten [fɛr'dunstən], *v.i.* (*aux.* s.) evaporate, vaporize, volatilize.
verdünsten [fɛr'dynstən], *v.t.* evaporate.
Verdunstung [fɛr'dunstuŋ], *f.* evaporation, vaporization, volatilization. **Verdunstungs|druck,** *m.* vapour pressure. **–kälte,** *f.* heat lost by evaporation.
verdürbe [fɛr'dyrbə], *see* **verderben.**
verdursten [fɛr'durstən], *v.i.* (*aux.* s.) die of thirst.
verdüstern [fɛr'dy:stərn], **1.** *v.t.* darken, cloud, wrap in gloom. **2.** *v.r., v.i.* (*aux.* s.) grow dark *or* gloomy.
verdutzen [fɛr'dutsən], *v.t.* startle, bewilder, nonplus, disconcert. **verdutzt,** *adj.* startled, bewildered, stupefied, disconcerted, nonplussed, (*pred.*) taken aback.
verebben [fɛr'ɛbən], *v.i.* ebb (away), subside, die down *or* away.
veredeln [fɛr'e:dəln], *v.t.* 1. ennoble; improve, enrich; refine, purify; 2. (*Hort.*) cultivate, graft; 3. finish (*goods*). **Vered(e)lung,** *f.* 1. ennobling; improvement; refinement, cultivation; 2. finishing (*of goods*); 3. budding, grafting. **Veredelungsindustrie,** *f.* finishing trade.
verehelichen [fɛr'e:alıçən], *v.t., v.r.* marry; ***eine Tochter –,*** give one's daughter in marriage.
verehren [fɛr'e:rən], *v.t.* revere, worship, venerate, reverence; (*fig.*) admire, adore, (*coll.*) look up to; ***ihm etwas –,*** present him with a th., make a present of a th. to him. **Verehrer,** *m.* reverer; devoted admirer, adorer; ***er ist ein großer – Schillers,*** he is a great admirer of Schiller. **verehrlich,** *adj.* honoured, estimable, esteemed. **Verehrung,** *f.* respect, veneration, reverence, worship, adoration. **verehrungswürdig,** *adj.* respected, worthy, honourable, venerable, illustrious.
vereidigen [fɛr'aıdıgən], *v.t.* put on *or* under oath, administer an oath to, swear in. **Vereidigung,** *f.* attestation, swearing-in, taking the oath.
Verein [fɛr'aın], *m.* (**-s,** *pl.* **-e**) association, society, club, union; ***im – mit,*** in conjunction with, together *or* jointly with; ***– für neuere Sprachen,*** modern language association.
vereinbar [fɛr'aınba:r], *adj.* reconcilable, compatible, consistent. **vereinbaren,** *v.t.* agree upon, come to an understanding about, arrange; make compatible, reconcile; ***im voraus –,*** pre-arrange. **vereinbart,** *adj.* agreed, arranged; ***–es Vorgehen,*** concerted action; ***–e Regelungen,*** agreed ruling; ***zu –em Lohn,*** for *or* at a negotiated wage. **vereinbartermaßen,** *adv.* as agreed (upon), according to the terms of the agreement. **Vereinbarung,** *f.* agreement, arrangement; ***laut –,*** as agreed (upon); ***nach –,*** by appointment; ***eine – treffen mit,*** come to an agreement *or* arrangement with.
vereinen [fɛr'aınən], *v.t.* (*obs., Poet.*) *see* **vereinigen, vereint.**
vereinfachen [fɛr'aınfaxən], *v.t.* simplify, (*Math.*) reduce. **Vereinfachung,** *f.* simplification, reduction; ***zur –,*** to simplify matters.
vereinheitlichen [fɛr'aınhaıtlıçən], *v.t.* unify, standardize. **Vereinheitlichung,** *f.* unification, standardization.
vereinigen [fɛr'aınıgən], **1.** *v.t.* unite, join, combine; pool (*resources*), co-ordinate (*efforts*); (*Mil. etc.*) gather, assemble, concentrate, rally; (*Comm.*) consolidate, amalgamate, merge (***zu,*** into); (*fig.*) reconcile; ***Vereinigte Staaten,*** United States; ***in sich –,*** unite, combine; ***sich – lassen,*** be compatible *or* consistent. **2.** *v.r.* unite, join, combine, (*as rivers etc.*) meet, merge; (*of a p.*) ally o.s.; (*Mil. etc.*) gather, assemble, rally; (*Comm.*) amalgamate, merge, associate o.s. with. **Vereinigung,** *f.* union, combination; alliance, coalition, confederacy; (*of persons*) *see* **Verein**; (*Mil.*) concentration; (*Comm.*) amalgamation, incorporation, merger; meeting, gathering, assembly; (*of rivers etc.*) junction, confluence. **Vereinigungs|ort,** *m.* meeting place, place of assembly. **–punkt,** *m.* junction, meeting point, point of union, focus; (*Mil.*) rallying point, rendezvous. **–recht,** *n.* right of assembly.
vereinnahmen [fɛr'aınna:mən], *v.t.* take (in), receive, collect (*money*), (*coll.*) pocket.
vereinsamen [fɛr'aınza:mən], *v.i.* (*aux.* s.) grow lonely, become isolated *or* solitary, become (more and more) cut off from society. **vereinsamt,** *adj.* lonely, solitary, isolated. **Vereinsamung,** *f.* isolation.
Vereins|bruder, *m. See* **–kamarad. –freiheit,** *f.* freedom of association. **–gesetz,** *n.* law relating to societies. **–haus,** *n. See* **–lokal. –kamarad,** *m.* fellow-member (of a society). **–kampf,** *m.* inter-club contest. **–kasse,** *f.* funds of a society. **–leitung**. *f.* executive committee of a society. **–lokal,** *n.* club rooms, club(-house). **--und-Versammlungsrecht,** *n. See* **Vereinigungsrecht. –wesen,** *n.* club activities.
vereint [fɛr'aınt], *adj.* united; ***Vereinte Nationen,*** United Nations; ***mit –en Kräften,*** with (all our, your *etc.*) united strength, with a combined effort.
vereinzeln [fɛr'aıntsəln], *v.t.* isolate, separate, segregate; take separately; ***Zusammengehöriges –,*** separate *or* break up a pair *or* set. **vereinzelt, 1.** *adj.* single, solitary, isolated; scattered, sporadic. **2.** *adv.* singly, individually; sporadically, now and then, here and there.
vereisen [fɛr'aızən], *v.i.* turn to ice, freeze (*of rivers*), be covered with ice (*of roads*), ice up (*of aircraft*). **vereist,** *adj.* frozen, covered *or* coated with ice, iced over, (*Av.*) iced up, (*Geol.*) glaciated. **Vereisung,** *f.* freezing, (*Av.*) icing(-up), (*Geol.*) ice-formation, glaciation.
vereiteln [fɛr'aıtəln], *v.t.* thwart, frustrate, balk, foil, bring to naught; ***Hoffnungen –,*** disappoint *or* shatter hopes; ***eine Absicht –,*** defeat a purpose; ***das Unternehmen ist vereitelt,*** the undertaking has miscarried. **Vereit(e)lung,** *f.* frustration, disappointment, defeat.
vereitern [fɛr'aıtərn], *v.i.* (*aux.* s.) fester, suppurate. **Vereiterung,** *f.* suppuration.
verekeln [fɛr'e:kəln], *v.t.* (*coll.*) make loathsome to (***ihm,*** him), spoil for (him), disgust (him) with.
verelenden [fɛr'e:ləndən], *v.i.* become wretched *or* miserable, sink into *or* be reduced to poverty. **Verelendung,** *f.* progressive deterioration; pauperization, reduction to poverty.
verenden [fɛr'ɛndən], *v.i.* (*aux.* h. *&* s.) die, perish (*of animals*).
verenge(r)n [fɛr'ɛŋə(r)n], *v.t., v.r.* narrow, contract,

become narrow(er). **Vereng(er)ung,** *f.* narrowing, contraction.

vererben [fɛr'ɛrbən], **1.** *v.t.* (***ihm etwas*** (*legally*) or ***etwas auf ihn*** (*genetically*)) leave, bequeath, hand down (s.th. to him); transmit (*diseases etc.*). **2.** *v.r.* devolve (***auf*** (*Acc.*), upon), descend *or* (*coll.*) come down (to); be hereditary, run in the family. **vererblich,** *adj.* (in)heritable; hereditary. **vererbt,** *adj.* hereditary, inherited, bequeathed, handed down. **Vererbung,** *f.* heredity, transmission. **Vererbungs|forschung,** *f.* genetics. **–gesetz,** *n.* law of heredity. **–lehre,** *f.* theory of heredity.

verewigen [fɛr'e:vɪgən], **1.** *v.t.* perpetuate, immortalize. **2.** *v.r.* perpetuate one's memory (***in*** (*Dat.*), in), (*coll.*) carve *or* scratch one's name (on) (*benches, stones etc.*). **verewigt,** *adj.* (*Poet.*) deceased, departed, late.

verfahren [fɛr'fa:rən], **1.** *irr.v.i.* (*aux.* h. & s.) act, behave, proceed (***nach,*** on); deal (***mit,*** with), handle, manage, use; ***redlich –,*** deal honestly; ***mit Nachsicht –,*** act with leniency, be indulgent; ***gerichtlich gegen ihn –,*** take (legal) proceedings against him; (*Comm.*) ***womit Sie nach Bericht zu – belieben,*** of which you will dispose according to advices. **2.** *irr.v.t.* 1. spend (*time or money*) driving *or* travelling about; 2. (*Min.*) ***einen Gang –,*** work a lode; 3. (*coll.*) bungle, botch, make a hash of. **3.** *irr.v.r.* lose one's way, take the wrong road, (*fig.*) be on the wrong tack *or* track, get into a hopeless muddle, be barking up the wrong tree. **4.** *adj.* muddled, bungled, botched; ***– sein,*** be in a hopeless muddle *or* mess.

Verfahren, *n.* proceedings; procedure, treatment, method, process, technique; system, policy, scheme; ***gerichtliches –,*** legal proceedings; ***das – einleiten,*** institute *or* take proceedings (***gegen,*** against); ***das – einstellen,*** quash proceedings. **verfahrensrechtlich,** *adj.* procedural. **Verfahrens|vorschrift,** *f.* rule of procedure. **–weise,** *f.* procedure.

Verfall [fɛr'fal], *m.* 1. decay, dilapidation, deterioration, degeneration; degeneracy, decadence; decline, fall, downfall, ruin; ***in – geraten*** or ***kommen,*** go to ruin, (fall into) decay, become dilapidated; decline, deteriorate; ***– der Kräfte,*** decline of vital powers; ***– der Sitten,*** corruption of morals, moral decay, depravity; ***– des Reichs,*** downfall of the empire; 2. (*Comm.*) expiration, lapse (*of a claim*), maturity (*of a bill*), foreclosure (*of a mortgage*); (*Comm.*) ***bei –,*** when due, at *or* on maturity, upon expiration; (*Comm.*) ***bis –,*** till due, till maturity; 3. forfeiture (***an*** (*Acc.*), to); (*Law*) ***– einer Klage,*** nonsuit; ***– eines Rechtes,*** forfeiture *or* loss of a right. **Verfall|buch,** *n.* (*Comm.*) bill-book. **–datum,** *n.* (*Comm.*) expiry date, date of maturity, due date.

verfallen [fɛr'falən], **1.** *irr.v.i.* (*aux.* s.) 1. (fall into) decay, decline, deteriorate, go to ruin, become dilapidated, fall into disrepair; 2. expire, fall due, be forfeited, lapse; 3. fall (*Dat.*, to), come into the power *or* possession (of), become the property (of); ***einem Laster –,*** become addicted to a vice; ***dem Staate –,*** become the property of the state; ***dem Teufel –,*** fall into the hands of the devil; 4. ***– auf*** (*Acc.*), hit *or* chance upon; ***auf ihn wäre ich nicht –,*** I should never have thought of him; 5. ***– in*** (*Acc.*), (re)lapse into, fall *or* slip back into; ***in eine Geldstrafe –,*** incur a fine; ***in eine Krankheit –,*** fall ill. **2.** *adj.* 1. ruinous, decayed, dilapidated, (*coll.*) tumbledown; (*of features*) worn, wasted, sunken; 2. (*Law, Comm.*) confiscated; forfeited; lapsed, expired; ***–e Güter,*** confiscated property; ***die Klage ist –,*** the plaintiff has been nonsuited; ***das Pfand ist –,*** the pledge is forfeited *or* has lapsed; ***für – erklären,*** foreclose (*a mortgage*); 3. addicted (*Dat.*, to) (*a drug*), (*sl.*) hooked (on).

Verfall|erklärung, *f.* confiscation order, foreclosure. **–frist,** *f.* *See* **–zeit. Verfallserscheinung,** *f.* symptom of decay. **Verfall|tag,** *m.*, **–termin,** *m.*, **–zeit,** *f.* day of payment, expiry date, due date; ***zur Verfallzeit,*** when due; ***bis zur Verfallzeit,*** till due, until maturity.

verfälschen [fɛr'fɛlʃən], *v.t.* falsify; adulterate (*foodstuffs*); *see* **fälschen. Verfälscher,** *m.* adulterator; falsifier. **Verfälschung,** *f.* falsification; adulteration. **Verfälschungsmittel,** *n.* adulterant.

verfangen [fɛr'faŋən], **1.** *irr.v.i.* take effect, operate, be of avail, (*coll.*) tell (***bei,*** on), go down (with); ***nicht –,*** be of no avail, avail nothing, (*coll.*) cut no ice (***bei,*** with), be thrown away *or* lost (on). **2.** *irr. v.r.* be caught, become entangled, (*fig.*) become confused, contradict o.s.

verfänglich [fɛr'fɛŋlɪç], *adj.* insidious, captious; (*situation*) awkward, risky, (*coll.*) tricky; (*joke*) risqué, embarrassing.

verfärben [fɛr'fɛrbən], **1.** *v.t.* discolour. **2.** *v.r.* discolour, become discoloured, (*of a p.*) lose *or* change colour.

verfassen [fɛr'fasən], *v.t.* compose, write (*a book*), draw up (*a document*). **Verfasser,** *m.* author, writer. **Verfasserin,** *f.* authoress, lady writer. **Verfasserschaft,** *f.* authorship.

Verfassung [fɛr'fasuŋ], *f.* 1. writing, composition (*of a book*); 2. (*of a th.*) condition, state, (*of a p.*) disposition, state *or* frame of mind; 3. (*Pol.*) system (of government), constitution. **verfassunggebend,** *adj.* ***–e Versammlung,*** constituent assembly.

Verfassungs|änderung, *f.* amendment of the constitution. **–bruch,** *m.* violation of the constitution. **verfassungsmäßig,** *adj.* constitutional. **Verfassungsrecht,** *n.* constitutional law. **verfassungsrechtlich,** *adj.* (under) constitutional (law). **Verfassungsurkunde,** *f.* charter of the constitution. **verfassungswidrig,** *adj.* unconstitutional.

verfaulen [fɛr'faulən], *v.i.* (*aux.* s.) rot, decay, decompose, putrefy, moulder.

verfechten [fɛr'fɛçtən], *irr.v.t.* fight for, defend, champion (*a cause*), assert, maintain, argue (*a point of view*), (*coll.*) stand up for. **Verfechter(in),** *m.(f.)* defender, champion, advocate. **Verfechtung,** *f.* defence, advocacy.

verfehlen [fɛr'fe:lən], **1.** *v.t.* miss, fail (to do *or* achieve); ***nicht –,*** not fail, be sure (to do); ***seine Wirkung –,*** be of no avail, produce no effect, fail to carry any weight, (*coll.*) miss fire, not come off; ***den Zug –,*** miss the train; ***seinen Zweck –,*** fail in its object, (*coll.*) miss the mark. **2.** *v.r.* ***sich*** or ***einander –,*** miss each other, fail to meet. **verfehlt,** *adj.* unsuccessful, misplaced, misguided, wrong, false; misspent (*life*). **Verfehlung,** *f.* offence, lapse, mistake, (*coll.*) slip.

verfeinden [fɛr'faɪndən], **1.** *v.t.* ***mich mit ihm –,*** set *or* turn me against him. **2.** *v.r.* make an enemy (***mit,*** of), fall out (with).

verfeinern [fɛr'faɪnərn], **1.** *v.t.* refine, improve, polish, purify, bolt (*flour*). **2.** *v.r.* become *or* grow (more) refined, become (more) polished, improve. **Verfeinerung,** *f.* refinement; improvement; polish.

verfemen [fɛr'fe:mən], *v.t.* proscribe, outlaw, ostracize, (*coll.*) send to Coventry.

verfertigen [fɛr'fɛrtɪgən], *v.t.* make, manufacture, construct, fabricate. **Verfertiger,** *m.* maker, manufacturer. **Verfertigung,** *f.* making, manufacture, preparation, fabrication.

verfestigen [fɛr'fɛstɪgən], *v.t., v.i.* harden, solidify, strengthen, stabilize, consolidate.

Verfettung [fɛr'fɛtuŋ], *f.* (*Med.*) fatty degeneration, adiposis.

verfeuern [fɛr'fɔyərn], *v.t.* burn, use as fuel; use up (*powder or ammunition*); burn up, consume, waste (*coal etc.*).

verfilmen [fɛr'fɪlmən], *v.t.* film, make a film of, (put on the) screen.

verfilzen [fɛr'fɪltsən], **1.** *v.t.* clog up, mat (together). **2.** *v.r.* get matted *or* clogged. **verfilzt,** *adj.* matted, clogged.

verfinstern [fɛr'fɪnstərn], *v.r.* *See* **verdunkeln.**

verfitzen [fɛr'fɪtsən], **1.** *v.t.* entangle. **2.** *v.r.* get tangled up.

verflachen [fɛr'flaxən], **1.** *v.t.* flatten, level. **2.** *v.r., v.i.* (*aux.* s.) become flat, level *or* flatten off; become shallow; become superficial (*mentally*).

verflechten [fɛr'flɛçtən], *irr.v.t.* entwine, interlace, interweave; (*fig.*) involve, implicate (*in* (*Acc.*), in). **Verflechtung,** *f.* interlacing, interweaving; (*fig.*) entanglement, involvement; – ***von Umständen,*** (strange) coincidence.

verfliegen [fɛr'fli:gən], **1.** *irr.v.i.* (*aux.* s.) fly away; evaporate, volatilize; (*fig.*) vanish, disappear, pass (by), (*coll.*) blow over; ***die Zeit*** or ***Stunde verfliegt,*** time flies. **2.** *irr.v.r.* get lost (*in flight*), (*Av.*) lose one's bearings; ***verflogene Tauben*** or ***Bienen,*** stray pigeons *or* bees. **verfliegend,** *adj.* volatile, evanescent.

verfließen [fɛr'fli:sən], *irr.v.i.* (*aux.* s.) flow away; (*of colours*) blend, run into each other, (*as ink*) run, (*of time*) pass *or* slip by, elapse; ***das verflossene Jahr,*** the past year; ***in der verflossenen Woche,*** last week.

verflixt [fɛr'flɪkst], *adj.* (*coll.*) confounded; ***–e Geschichte,*** nice mess, pretty kettle of fish; ***–er Kerl,*** devil of a fellow.

verflogen [fɛr'flo:gən], *see* **verfliegen.**

verflossen [fɛr'flɔsən], *see* **verfließen.**

verfluchen [fɛr'flu:xən], *v.t.* curse, damn, execrate. **verflucht,** *adj.* accursed, confounded; *–!* confound it! curse it! (*coll.*) ***seine –e Schuldigkeit,*** no more than his duty, his bounden duty.

verflüchtigen [fɛr'fly:çtɪgən], *v.t., v.r.* volatilize, evaporate; (*coll.*) make o.s. scarce. **Verflüchtigung,** *f.* volatilization, evaporation, sublimation.

verflüssigen [fɛr'flysɪgən], *v.t., v.r.* liquefy (*by condensation*), fuse (*by heat*); dilute, thin. **Verflüssigung,** *f.* liquefaction.

Verfolg [fɛr'fɔlk], *m.* course, progress; sequel; ***in*** or ***im – der Arbeit,*** in the course of the work; ***im – Befehls,*** in pursuance of orders; (*Comm.*) ***im – unseres Briefs,*** reverting to our letter. **verfolgen,** *v.t.* pursue, follow, trail, track; persecute, prosecute; (*as thoughts etc.*) haunt; (*fig.*) follow up (*an idea*); ***eine Anklage –,*** proceed with a charge; ***heimlich –,*** trail, shadow. **Verfolger,** *m.* pursuer; persecutor.

Verfolgung [fɛr'fɔlgʊŋ], *f.* pursuit, chase; persecution; pursuance, continuation; ***strafrechtliche –,*** prosecution. **Verfolgungs|jäger,** *m.* (*Av.*) pursuit plane. **–kampf,** *m.* (*Mil.*) rearguard engagement. **–wahn,** *m.* persecution mania.

Verformung [fɛr'fɔrmʊŋ], *f.* 1. working, shaping; 2. distortion, deformation.

verfrachten [fɛr'fraxtən], *v.t.* charter (*a ship*), hire out; pay the freight *or* carriage; load *or* ship (*goods*). **Verfrachter,** *m.* consigner, shipper, carrier, forwarding-agent. **Verfrachtung,** *f.* chartering, freighting, shipping, transport; shipment, consignment.

verfranzen [fɛr'frantsən], *v.r.* (*sl.*) (*Av.*) get *or* wander off course, lose one's way.

verfressen [fɛr'frɛsən], *adj.* (*coll.*) greedy, gluttonous.

verfroren [fɛr'fro:rən], *adj.* frozen, chilly, icy; chilled through; ***–er Mensch,*** p. sensitive to cold.

verfrühen [fɛr'fry:ən], *v.t.* precipitate, anticipate. **verfrüht,** *adj.* premature.

verfügbar [fɛr'fy:kba:r], *adj.* available, (*pred.*) at one's disposal; ***–es Geld,*** cash in hand; ***–es Kapital,*** funds available, uninvested capital; ***frei –,*** freely usable; (*Tech.*) ***–e Pferdestärke,*** actual horsepower. **Verfügbarkeit,** *f.* availability.

verfügen [fɛr'fy:gən], **1.** *v.t.* dispose, order, arrange; provide, prescribe, ordain, decree, enact. **2.** *v.r.* proceed, betake o.s. (***nach,*** to). **3.** *v.i.* – ***über*** (*Acc.*), dispose of, have at one's disposal, be provided *or* equipped with; make use of; – ***Sie über mich!*** I am at your disposal.

Verfügung [fɛr'fy:gʊŋ], *f.* disposal, disposition; order, instruction, decree, enactment; ***–en treffen über*** (*Acc.*), take steps about, give orders with regard to; (*Mil.*) ***zur besonderen –,*** seconded for special duty; ***sich zur – halten,*** hold o.s. in readiness, (*coll.*) stand by; ***ihm zur – stehen,*** be at his disposal, be available to him; ***ihm zur – stellen,*** place at his disposal, make available to him; ***sich zur – stellen,*** volunteer (one's services); ***sein Amt zur – stellen,*** tender one's resignation. **verfügungsberechtigt,** *adj.* authorized to make dispositions. **Verfügungs|freiheit,** *f.* discretion. **–gewalt,** *f.* discretionary power, control, authority. **–recht,** *n.* right to give orders.

verführen [fɛr'fy:rən], *v.t.* lead astray, entice, tempt, seduce (*also sexually*), prevail upon; (*coll.*) ***einen fürchterlichen Lärm –,*** make a fearful din, kick up an awful row. **Verführer,** *m.* tempter; seducer. **verführerisch,** *adj.* tempting, seductive, enticing, bewitching. **Verführung,** *f.* temptation, enticement; seduction. **Verführungskünste,** *f.pl.* art of deception, wiles, artifice.

verfuhrwerken [fɛr'fu:rvɛrkən], *v.t.* (*Swiss*) botch, bungle, make a hash of.

verfünffachen [fɛr'fynffaxən], *v.t.* increase fivefold.

verfuttern [fɛr'futərn], *v.t.* use as fodder; overfeed (*cattle*).

Vergabe [fɛr'ga:bə], *f.* (*Comm.*) placing (*of orders*), allocation (*of funds*); (*Swiss*) gift. **vergaben,** *v.t.* (*Swiss*) present, give away, bequeath. **Vergabung,** *f.* gift, donation, bequest, legacy.

vergaffen [fɛr'gafən], *v.r.* fall in love, (*coll.*) be smitten (***in*** (*Acc.*), with).

vergällen [fɛr'gɛlən], *v.t.* embitter, mar, (turn) sour; (*Chem.*) denature, methylate (*alcohol*); ***sich*** (*Dat.*) ***das Leben –,*** make one's life a burden, become embittered *or* soured.

vergallopieren [fɛrgalo'pi:rən], *v.r.* (*coll.*) put one's foot in it, overshoot the mark.

vergangen [fɛr'gaŋən], *adj.* past, gone, bygone; ***–e Woche,*** last week; *see* **vergehen. Vergangenheit,** *f.* past; (*Gram.*) past *or* preterite tense; ***dunkle –,*** shady past *or* antecedents; ***der – angehören,*** be a th. of the past, belong to the past; ***eine – haben,*** (*of a th.*) have a history, (*of a p.*) have a past; ***laß die – ruhen!*** let bygones be bygones.

vergänglich [fɛr'gɛŋlɪç], *adj.* fleeting, fugitive, passing, transitory, transient, ephemeral. **Vergänglichkeit,** *f.* transitoriness, transience, transiency.

verganten [fɛr'gantən], *v.t.* (*dial.*) sell by auction.

vergasen [fɛr'ga:zən], *v.t.* vaporize, (*Motor.*) carburet; (*Mil. etc.*) gas. **Vergaser,** *m.* (*Motor.*) carburettor.

vergaß [fɛr'ga:s], **vergäße** [fɛr'gɛ:sə], *see* **vergessen.**

Vergasung [fɛr'ga:zʊŋ], *f.* vaporization, (*Motor.*) carburetion, (*Mil. etc.*) gassing; (*sl.*) ***bis zur –,*** like blazes.

vergattern [fɛr'gatərn], *v.t.* 1. enclose with trellis-work *or* with a grating; 2. (*Mil.*) assemble (*troops*). **Vergatterung,** *f.* 1. lattice-work, grating; 2. (*Mil.*) changing of the *or* mounting the guard; ***die*** or ***zur – schlagen,*** call out the guard.

vergeben [fɛr'ge:bən], **1.** *irr.v.t.* 1. give away, dispose of (*an* (*Acc.*), to), confer, bestow (on), distribute, give out (to); cede, relinquish (*rights*) (to); ***ein Amt an ihn –,*** appoint him to an office, bestow an office on him; ***einen Auftrag –,*** place an order (*an* (*Acc.*), with); ***die Stelle ist noch nicht –,*** the place is still vacant; ***die Hand seiner Tochter –,*** give one's daughter in marriage; ***ihre Hand ist schon –,*** she is engaged (to be married); ***ich habe den nächsten Tanz schon –,*** I have already promised the next dance; ***ich bin schon –,*** I have a previous engagement; 2. (*Dat.*) forgive, pardon; ***sich*** (*Dat.*) ***etwas –,*** forget o.s., compromise o.s.; ***sich*** (*Dat.*) or ***seiner Ehre nichts –,*** be jealous of one's honour, maintain one's dignity; ***sich*** (*Dat.*) ***von seinem Rechte etwas –,*** allow one's rights to be infringed. **2.** *irr.v.t., v.r.* (*Cards*) misdeal. **3.** *adj.* *See* **vergeblich, 1**; ***–e Liebesmüh,*** wasted effort, much ado about nothing; ***–es Hoffen,*** vain hopes. **vergebens,** *adv.* in vain, vainly, to no purpose *or* avail, of no avail.

vergeblich [fɛrˈgeːplɪç], **1.** *adj.* vain, idle, fruitless, useless, needless, wasted, futile, (*pred.*) of no use *or* avail; ***sich*** (*Dat.*) ***-e Mühe machen,*** go to a lot of trouble for nothing. **2.** *adv. See* **vergebens. Vergeblichkeit,** *f.* uselessness, fruitlessness, futility.

Vergebung [fɛrˈgeːbʊŋ], *f.* **1.** giving, granting (*an* (*Acc.*), to), bestowal, conferment (on), distribution (to *or* among); collation (*to a benefice*), allocation (*of work, funds etc.*), placing (*of an order*); 2. forgiveness, pardon, (*of sins*) remission; ***ihn um – bitten,*** ask his forgiveness; ***bitte um –!*** excuse *or* forgive *or* pardon me! 3. (*Cards*) misdeal(ing).

vergegenwärtigen [fɛrgeːgənˈvɛrtɪgən], *v.t.* represent, bring to mind, (*coll.*) bring home (*Dat.*, to); ***sich*** (*Dat.*) ***etwas –,*** realize *or* visualize s.th., picture a th. to o.s. **Vergegenwärtigung,** *f.* representation, realization, visualization.

vergehen [fɛrˈgeːən], **1.** *irr.v.i.* (*aux.* s.) pass *or* fade away, pass off *or* over, vanish, disappear, be lost; (*fig.*) die (***vor*** (*Dat.*), of); ***vor Angst –,*** be scared to death; ***vor Gram –,*** pine away; ***vor Scham –,*** die of shame; ***vor Ungeduld –,*** be dying with impatience; (*B.*) ***meine Tage sind vergangen wie ein Rauch,*** my days are consumed like smoke; (*Prov.*) ***Unkraut vergeht nicht,*** ill weeds grow apace; ***es verging ihm Hören und Sehen,*** it took his breath away; ***der Appetit ist mir vergangen,*** I have lost my appetite. **2.** *irr.v.r.* err, offend, transgress, commit an offence; ***sich wider*** or ***gegen das Gesetz –,*** offend *or* transgress against *or* infringe *or* violate the law; ***sich tätlich an ihm –,*** assault him; ***sich an dem Mädchen –,*** commit an indecent assault on *or* violate the girl. **Vergehen,** *n.* 1. disappearance, passing, lapse (*of time*); 2. offence, petty crime, misdemeanour, fault, transgression, trespass, sin.

vergeistigen [fɛrˈgaɪstɪgən], *v.t.* spiritualize, etherealize. **Vergeistigung,** *f.* spiritualization.

vergelten [fɛrˈgɛltən], *irr.v.t.* requite, repay, reward, recompense (***ihm etwas,*** him for s.th.), pay (him) back (for s.th.), retaliate; ***Gott vergelte es Ihnen*** or ***vergelt's Gott!*** Heaven bless you! ***Gleiches mit Gleichem –,*** give tit for tat; ***Böses mit Gutem –,*** return good for evil. **Vergeltung,** *f.* requital, retribution; reward, recompense; retaliation, reprisal; ***– üben,*** retaliate (***an*** (*Dat.*), on); ***zur – für,*** in return for. **Vergeltungs|feuer,** *n.* (*Mil.*) retaliating fire. **–maßregel,** *f.* retaliatory measure, reprisal. **–recht,** *n.* right of reprisal *or* retaliation, lex talionis. **–tag,** *m.* day of retribution.

vergesellschaften [fɛrgəˈzɛlʃaftən], *v.t., v.r.* associate, combine, unite with, (*Comm.*) form into a public company *or* (*Am.*) corporation, (*Pol.*) socialize, nationalize. **Vergesellschaftung,** *f.* socialization, nationalization.

vergessen [fɛrˈgɛsən], **1.** *irr.v.t.* forget; neglect; omit; leave (behind); ***ja, daß ich nicht vergesse . . .,*** oh! in case I should forget . . .; ***etwas bei ihm –,*** leave a th. (behind) at his house; ***vergiß mich nicht,*** (*B., Poet.*) ***vergiß mein nicht,*** do not forget me! **2.** *irr.v.i.* (*Austr.*) ***– auf*** (*Acc.*), *see* **1. 3.** *irr.v.r.* forget o.s., lose one's head; ***so etwas vergißt sich leicht,*** such things are easily forgotten. **4.** *adj.* forgotten, neglected, omitted. **Vergessenheit,** *f.* oblivion; ***in – geraten,*** fall (*or* sink) into oblivion.

vergeßlich [fɛrˈgɛslɪç], *adj.* forgetful. **Vergeßlichkeit,** *f.* forgetfulness.

vergeuden [fɛrˈgɔydən], *v.t.* squander, dissipate, waste, fritter away. **Vergeuder,** *m.* spendthrift. **Vergeudung,** *f.* squandering, waste, wastefulness, extravagance.

vergewaltigen [fɛrgəˈvaltɪgən], *v.t.* use force on, do *or* offer violence to, (*sexually*) ravish, rape, violate. **Vergewältiger,** *m.* rapist. **Vergewaltigung,** *f.* violation, rape.

vergewissern [fɛrgəˈvɪsərn], *v.r.* make sure (*Gen.*, of), confirm, ascertain; (re)assure o.s. **Vergewisserung,** *f.* confirmation; assurance.

vergießen [fɛrˈgiːsən], *irr.v.t.* spill, shed; (*Metall.*) cast; (*coll.*) drown (*plants by watering too much*). **Vergießen,** *n.*, **Vergießung,** *f.* spilling, shedding (*of blood etc.*).

vergiften [fɛrˈgɪftən], **1.** *v.t.* poison, contaminate; (*fig.*) taint, infect; embitter (*one's life*). **2.** *v.r.* take poison. **Vergiftung,** *f.* poisoning, contamination.

vergilben [fɛrˈgɪlbən], *v.i.* turn yellow.

vergiß [fɛrˈgɪs], **vergissest,** *see* **vergessen.**

Vergißmeinnicht [fɛrˈgɪsmaɪnnɪçt], *n.* (**-(e)s,** *pl.* **-e** (*Austr.* -)) (*Bot.*) forget-me-not (*Myosotis*).

vergißt [fɛrˈgɪst], *see* **vergessen.**

vergittern [fɛrˈgɪtərn], *v.t.* enclose with latticework *or* a trellis *or* bars, grate (up), wire in.

verglasen [fɛrˈglaːzən], **1.** *v.t.* vitrify; glaze (*a window*), glass in (*a veranda etc.*). **2.** *v.i.* turn into glass; (*fig.*) become glazed. **verglast,** *adj.* glazed (*also fig. of eyes*).

Vergleich [fɛrˈglaɪç], *m.* (**-(e)s,** *pl.* **-e**) comparison, parallel; (*Rhet.*) simile; agreement, arrangement, settlement, compromise; composition (*with creditors*); ***einen – schließen,*** conclude an agreement, come to terms; ***gütlicher –,*** amicable arrangement *or* settlement; ***über allen –,*** beyond comparison, incomparably; ***im – mit*** or ***zu,*** compared to *or* with, in comparison with; ***einen – anstellen*** or ***machen,*** make a comparison, draw a parallel; ***einen – eingehen,*** enter into an agreement, come to an arrangement; ***den – aushalten,*** bear comparison. **vergleichbar,** *adj.* comparable (***mit,*** to *or* with).

vergleichen [fɛrˈglaɪçən], **1.** *irr.v.t.* **1.** compare (***mit,*** with *or* to), liken (to); draw *or* make a comparison (*between things or with a th.*); (*figures*) check (against), (*text*) collate (with *or* against), (*clocks etc.*) synchronize (with); 2. settle (*disputes*), reconcile (*opposing views*); adjust (*discrepancies*); ***etwas Strittiges –,*** settle a quarrel, compose a difference. **2.** *irr.v.r.* come to an arrangement *or* agreement *or* to terms, become reconciled, reach a settlement (***mit,*** with), settle, compound (*with creditors*); ***verglichen mit,*** compared to *or* with, in comparison with, as against. **vergleichend,** *adj.* comparative.

Vergleichs|lösung, *f.* standard solution. **–maßstab,** *m.* standard of comparison. **–summe,** *f.* compensation, indemnity. **–unterlage,** *f.* basis of comparison. **–verfahren,** *n.* negotiations, attempts to reach a settlement. **vergleichsweise,** *adv.* comparatively, by way of comparison. **Vergleichs|wert,** *m.* relative value. **–zahlen,** *f.pl.* comparative figures.

Vergleichung [fɛrˈglaɪçʊŋ], *f. See* **Vergleich. Vergleichungs|punkt,** *m.* point of comparison. **–versuch,** *m.* comparative test.

vergletschern [fɛrˈglɛtʃərn], *v.i.* (*aux.* s.) form a glacier. **Vergletscherung,** *f.* glacier formation, glaciation.

verglichen [fɛrˈglɪçən], *see* **vergleichen.**

verglimmen [fɛrˈglɪmən], *irr.v.i.* (*aux.* s.) die out *or* away, go *or* burn out.

verglühen [fɛrˈglyːən], **1.** *v.i.* (*aux.* s.) *see* **verglimmen. 2.** *v.t.* fire, bake (*porcelain*).

vergnügen [fɛrˈgnyːgən], **1.** *v.t.* amuse, delight; (*dial.*) content, satisfy, gratify. **2.** *v.r.* amuse *or* enjoy o.s. **Vergnügen,** *n.* pleasure, fun, joy, delight, enjoyment; amusement, diversion, entertainment; ***– finden an*** (*Dat.*), find pleasure in; ***sein – haben an*** (*Dat.*), delight in; ***mit –!*** with pleasure, willingly, gladly; ***viel –!*** enjoy yourself! have a good time! (*iron.*) I wish you joy! (*coll.*) ***es war kein –,*** it was no picnic; ***es war mir ein –,*** it was a pleasure; ***zu meinem –,*** to my delight; ***etwas zum – tun,*** do a thing for pleasure *or* for fun.

vergnüglich [fɛrˈgnyːklɪç], *adj.* amusing, diverting, enjoyable, pleasurable. **vergnügt,** *adj.* pleased (***über*** (*Acc.*), with), glad (about), happy, delighted (at); merry, joyous, cheerful, gay, (*pred.*) in high spirits. **Vergnügung,** *f.* (*usu. pl.*) pleasure, amusement, recreation, entertainment, pastime, diversion.

Vergnügungs|dampfer, *m.* pleasure steamer. **–lokal,** *n.* fun-fair, amusement-arcade. **–park,** *m.* amusement-park. **–reise,** *f.* pleasure-trip, excursion. **–reisende(r),** *m., f.* tourist, excursionist, (*coll.*)

tripper. **–stätte,** *f. See* **–lokal. –steuer,** *f.* entertainment-tax. **–sucht,** *f.* (inordinate) love of pleasure, craze for amusement. **vergnügungssüchtig,** *adj.* pleasure-seeking *or* -loving.

vergolden [fɛr'gɔldən], *v.t.* gild. **Vergolder,** *m.* gilder. **vergoldet,** *adj.* gilt, gilded, gold-plated. **Vergoldung,** *f.* gilding, gold-plating; ***trockene –,*** leaf-gilding; ***nasse –,*** water-gilding; ***galvanische –,*** electro-gilding.

vergönnen [fɛr'gœnən], *v.t.* (*Dat.*) permit, allow, grant, not grudge *or* (*coll.*) begrudge.

vergossen [fɛr'gɔsən], *see* **vergießen.**

vergöttern [fɛr'gœtərn], *v.t.* deify; (*fig.*) idolize, worship, adore. **Vergötterung,** *f.* deification, apotheosis; adoration, worship, idolatry.

vergraben [fɛr'gra:bən], **1.** *irr.v.t.* bury, hide (in the ground). **2.** *irr.v.r.* burrow (*of animals*); (*fig.*) hide o.s.; bury o.s. (*in books*).

vergrämen [fɛr'grɛ:mən], *v.t.* grieve, vex, anger (*a p.*), (*Hunt.*) start (*game*). **vergrämt,** *adj.* careworn, woebegone, grief-stricken.

vergrasen [fɛr'gra:zən], *v.i.* (*aux.* s.) be overgrown *or* covered with grass.

vergreifen [fɛr'graɪfən], **1.** *irr.v.t.* ***sich*** (*Dat.*) ***die Hand*** (***den Finger***) ***–,*** sprain one's hand (finger). **2.** *irr.v.r.* make a mistake; (*fig.*) go about a th. in the wrong way, (*Mus.*) play the wrong note; ***sich – an*** (*Dat.*), assault, attack, lay (violent) hands on (*a p.*), commit an indecent assault on, violate (*a woman*); appropriate, (*coll.*) make off with (*a th.*), encroach on (*s.o.'s rights*); misappropriate, embezzle (*money*); ***sich an den Gesetzen –,*** violate *or* infringe the law; ***sich an dem Namen Gottes –,*** take the name of God in vain; ***sich an geheiligten Sachen –,*** profane holy things.

vergreisen [fɛr'graɪzən], *v.i.* (*aux.* s.) become senile; (*of population*) age. **Vergreisung,** *f.* senility, senescence.

vergriffen [fɛr'grɪfən], *adj.* sold out, (*books*) out of print.

vergröbern [fɛr'grø:bərn], **1.** *v.t.* make coarse(r) *or* crude(r), coarsen. **2.** *v.r.* become coarse(r) *or* crude(r).

vergrößern [fɛr'grø:sərn], **1.** *v.t.* enlarge, magnify; increase, expand, augment, widen, extend; (*fig.*) aggravate, exaggerate; ***in vergrößertem Maßstab,*** on a larger scale. **2.** *v.r.* grow larger, increase, expand, extend, (*fig.*) become aggravated, aggrandize o.s., extend one's power. **Vergrößerung,** *f.* enlargement (*also Phot.*), increase, augmentation, expansion, extension, (*Opt.*) magnification, (*fig.*) aggravation, exaggeration. **Vergrößerungs|apparat,** *m.* (*Phot.*) enlarger. **–glas,** *n.* magnifying glass. **–kraft,** *f.* magnification power. **–plan,** *m.* (*fig.*) programme of aggrandizement.

vergucken [fɛr'gukən], *v.r.* (*coll.*) make a mistake, see wrong; (*coll.*) ***sich in ihn –,*** be smitten by him.

vergülden [fɛr'gyldən], *v.t.* (*Poet.*) *see* **vergolden.**

Vergunst [fɛr'gunst], *f.* ***mit –,*** by your leave.

Vergünstigung [fɛr'gynstɪguŋ], *f.* privilege, favour, concession, preferential treatment, (*Comm.*) (price) reduction, discount, deduction, rebate, allowance.

vergüten [fɛr'gy:tən], *v.t.* 1. (***ihm etwas***) make amends (to him for s.th.), reimburse, indemnify, compensate (him for s.th.), refund (s.th. to him), make good (*a loss*), allow (*discount*); 2. (*Metall.*) harden, temper, heat-treat, refine (*metals*); ***ich werde Ihnen Ihre Mühe –,*** I shall make it worth your while. **Vergütung,** *f.* 1. compensation, indemnification, reimbursement; allowance; consideration; 2. (*Metall.*) hardening, refining, heat treatment.

Verhack [fɛr'hak], *m.* **(-(e)s,** *pl.* **-e)** (*Fort.*) abatis.

Verhaft [fɛr'haft], *m.* ***in –,*** under arrest, in custody; ***in – nehmen,*** seize, arrest, take into custody; ***– legen auf*** (*Acc.*), lay an embargo on. **Verhaft|befehl, –brief,** *m. See* **Verhaftungs|befehl, –brief.**

verhaften [fɛr'haftən], *v.t.* arrest, apprehend, take into custody (***wegen,*** on a charge of). **verhaftet,** *adj.* (*fig.*) closely bound up (*Dat.,* ***mit,*** with), bound (to), rooted (in), dependent (on), dominated (by); ***der Scholle –,*** bound to the soil; ***einer Idee –,*** dominated by an idea. **Verhaftung,** *f.* arrest, apprehension, capture. **Verhaftungs|befehl, –brief,** *m.* warrant of arrest.

verhageln [fɛr'ha:gəln], *v.i.* (*aux.* s.) be destroyed *or* damaged by hail; (*coll.*) ***ihm ist die Petersilie verhagelt,*** he has had (a stroke of) bad luck, his plan did not come off.

verhallen [fɛr'halən], *v.i.* (*aux.* s.) die *or* fade away, (*of sounds*) become attenuated, become fainter and fainter.

Verhalt [fɛr'halt], *m.* state of affairs, condition; behaviour.

verhalten [fɛr'haltən], **1.** *irr.v.t.* keep *or* hold back; hold (*one's breath*); retain (*urine*); repress, suppress, check, restrain; (*Mil.*) ***Schritte –,*** check one's step, shorten step. **2.** *irr.v.r.* (*of a th.*) be, be the case; (*of a p.*) act, behave; conduct *or* comport *or* demean o.s.; ***die S. verhält sich so,*** the matter stands thus, the facts of the matter are; ***wenn es sich so verhält,*** if that be *or* that is the case; ***a verhält sich zu b, wie 5 zu 2,*** a is to b as 5 is to 2; ***sich umgekehrt – zu,*** be in inverse ratio to; ***sich anders –,*** be different; ***sich ruhig –,*** hold one's peace, keep quiet; ***sich passiv –,*** maintain a passive attitude; ***verhaltet Euch brav!*** behave yourselves! be good! **3** *adj.* ***mit –em Atem,*** with bated breath; ***mit –em Gähnen*** (***Lächeln***), suppressing a yawn (smile); ***–e Stimmung,*** tense atmosphere, suppressed excitement; ***–er Zorn,*** pent-up anger; ***– spielen,*** play a waiting game, hold back; (*Theat.*) underact. **Verhalten,** *n.* conduct, behaviour, demeanour; attitude, approach (*to a problem*), policy, procedure; (*Chem.*) reaction, (*Tech.*) characteristics.

Verhältnis [fɛr'hɛltnɪs], *n.* **(-ses,** *pl.* **-se)** 1. relation, proportion, rate, ratio; ***außer – zu,*** disproportionate to; ***außer jedem – stehen,*** be out of all proportion; ***im entsprechenden –,*** proportionately; ***in umgekehrtem –,*** in inverse ratio; ***im – von 2 zu 4,*** in the ratio of 2 to 4; ***im – zu,*** in proportion to, compared with, in comparison with; ***nach – der Bevölkerung,*** in proportion to the population; 2. (*usu. pl.*) (economic) situation, (financial) state; conditions, circumstances; relation(s) (***zu,*** with); love-affair, liaison; (*Law*) illicit intercourse; (*coll.*) mistress; ***in angenehmen –sen,*** in easy circumstances, comfortably off; ***in freundschaftlichem – zu ihm stehen,*** be on a friendly footing *or* on friendly terms with him; ***aus kleinen –sen,*** of lowly origin; ***über seine –sen leben,*** live beyond one's means; ***unter solchen –sen,*** such being the case, in the(se) circumstances.

Verhältnisanteil [fɛr'hɛltnɪsˀantaɪl], *m.* quota, share; dividend. **verhältnismäßig, 1.** *adj.* proportionate, proportional, relative, commensurate, pro rata. **2.** *adv.* in proportion, comparatively (speaking). **Verhältnis|regel,** *f.* (*Math.*) rule of three *or* proportion. **–wahl,** *f.* proportional representation. **verhältniswidrig,** *adj.* disproportionate, (*pred.*) out of all proportion. **Verhältnis|wort,** *n.* preposition. **–zahl,** *f.* proportional number, ratio, coefficient, factor.

Verhaltungsmaßregeln [fɛr'haltuŋsma:sre:gəln], *f.pl.* rules of conduct; instructions, directions, rules, precautions.

verhandeln [fɛr'handəln], **1.** *v.i.* negotiate, treat (***über*** (*Acc.*), ***wegen,*** for), (*Mil.*) parley; confer, deliberate (about), discuss, debate; (*Law*) dispose of, try (*a case*). **2.** *v.t.* 1. discuss, debate; 2. sell, dispose of.

Verhandlung [fɛr'handluŋ], *f.* negotiation, discussion, deliberation, (*Mil.*) parley, (*Pol. etc.*) talks, conference; (*Law*) proceedings, trial, hearing. **Verhandlungs|bericht,** *m.* record of proceedings, minutes; minute-book. **–friede,** *m.* negotiated peace. **–führer,** *m.* (*Law*) clerk of sessions. **–gegenstand,** *m.* (item of) business, (point at) issue. **–partner,** *m.* party to a deal. **–saal,** *m.* court(-room); chamber, debating hall. **–tag, –termin,** *m.* day fixed for trial. **–tisch,** *m.* conference table. **-weg,** *m.* ***auf dem -e,*** by negotiation, (*coll.*) round the table.

verhängen [fɛr'hɛŋən], *v.t.* 1. cover, hang, drape (*mit,* with); veil, conceal; ***einem Pferde den Zügel -,*** give a horse his head; ***mit verhängtem Zügel,*** with reins flying, at full gallop; 2. hang up in a wrong way *or* place; 3. (*fig.*) decree, ordain, pronounce (*judgement*); inflict, impose (*a penalty*) (*über* (*Acc.*), on); ***den Belagerungszustand -,*** proclaim martial law; ***wie es Gott verhängt,*** as God ordains.

Verhängnis [fɛr'hɛŋnɪs], *n.* fate, destiny; doom; ***durch ein sonderbares -,*** by strange ill luck; ***ihm zum - werden,*** be his doom *or* undoing. **verhängnisvoll,** *adj.* fatal, fateful, disastrous, ominous, portentous.

verhärmt [fɛr'hɛrmt], *adj.* care-worn, woebegone.

verharren [fɛr'harən], *v.i.* (*aux.* h. & s.) abide (***bei, auf*** or ***in*** (*Dat.*), by), continue, persist (in), (*coll.*) stick (to); persevere, (*coll.*) hold out, see it *etc.* through.

verharschen [fɛr'harʃən], *v.i.* (*aux.* s.) form a scab; cicatrice, heal (up), close (*of wounds*); form a crust (*of snow*). **Verharschung,** *f.* scabbing over (*of wounds*); crusting (*of snow etc.*).

verhärten [fɛr'hɛrtən], **1.** *v.t.* harden (*also fig. one's heart*), make hard; indurate. **2.** *v.i.* (*aux.* s.) harden, grow hard. **3** *v.r.* harden, grow hard, (*fig.*) become obdurate, harden one's heart. **verhärtet,** *adj.* (*fig.*) obdurate, callous. **Verhärtung,** *f.* hardening; induration, callosity; obduracy.

verharzen [fɛr'hartsən], **1.** *v.t.* impregnate with resin. **2.** *v.r., v.i.* (*aux.* s.) become resinous, turn to resin.

verhaspeln [fɛr'haspəln], **1.** *v.t.* entangle, get (*thread*) into a tangle. **2.** *v.r.* become tangled (up); (*coll.*) become confused, get in a muddle. **Verhasp(e)lung,** *f.* entanglement, tangle; muddle.

verhaßt [fɛr'hast], *adj.* detested, hated; (*coll.*) hateful, odious.

verhätscheln [fɛr'hɛ:tʃəln], *v.t.* over-indulge, coddle, pamper, (*coll.*) spoil.

Verhau [fɛr'hau], *m.* (**-(e)s,** *pl.* **-e**) (*Fort.*) abatis, entanglement.

verhauen [fɛr'hauən], **1.** *irr.v.t.* flog, thrash, spank (*a child*), (*coll.*) beat up; (*fig.*) bungle, botch, make a mess *or* hash of, muff; squander, run through (*one's money*); ***ihm den Weg -,*** put obstacles in his way; (*coll.*) ***das Spiel -,*** spoil the game. **2.** *irr.v.r.* make a false cut, chop in the wrong place; (*coll.*) make an awful blunder *or* boob, perpetrate a howler.

verheben [fɛr'he:bən], *irr.v.r.* strain o.s. in lifting.

verheddern [fɛr'hɛdərn], *v.r.* (*coll., dial.*) get muddled *or* confused.

verheeren [fɛr'he:rən], *v.t.* ravage, devastate, lay waste. **verheerend,** *adj.* (*fig.*) disastrous, devastating, catastrophic; (*coll.*) awful. **Verheerung,** *f.* devastation, havoc.

verhehlen [fɛr'he:lən], *v.t.* hide, conceal, keep a secret (*Dat.*, from), keep (*a p.*) in the dark about. **Verhehlung,** *f.* hiding, concealment, (*fig.*) suppression, dissimulation.

verheilen [fɛr'haɪlən], *v.i.* heal (up). **Verheilung,** *f.* healing process.

verheimlichen [fɛr'haɪmlɪçən], *v.t. See* **verhehlen. Verheimlichung,** *f. See* **Verhehlung.**

verheiraten [fɛr'haɪra:tən], **1.** *v.t.* marry, give in marriage (***mit, an*** (*Acc.*), to); perform the marriage ceremony. **2.** *v.r.* marry, get married; ***sich günstig -,*** make a good match; ***sich untereinander -,*** intermarry. **Verheiratung,** *f.* marriage; ***- unter verschiedenen Rassen,*** racial intermarriage.

verheißen [fɛr'haɪsən], *irr.v.t.* promise. **Verheißung,** *f.* promise; ***Land der -,*** Promised Land. **verheißungsvoll,** *adj.* promising, auspicious.

verhelfen [fɛr'hɛlfən], *irr.v.i.* ***ihm zu einer S. -,*** help him to (get) a th., procure a th. for him.

verherrlichen [fɛr'hɛrlɪçən], *v.t.* glorify, extol, exalt. **Verherrlichung,** *f.* glorification.

verhetzen [fɛr'hɛtsən], *v.t.* instigate, incite, stir up; goad on, exasperate, irritate. **Verhetzung,** *f.* incitement, instigation.

verheuern [fɛr'hɔyərn], *v.t.* (*Naut.*) sign on (*ship's crew*).

verhexen [fɛr'hɛksən], *v.t.* bewitch, enchant, (*sl.*) put the jinx on.

verhimmeln [fɛr'hɪməln], *v.t.* praise *or* laud to the skies, worship; ***verhimmelt sein,*** be in raptures. **Verhimm(e)lung,** *f.* extravagant praise, adulation; rapture, ecstasy.

verhindern [fɛr'hɪndərn], *v.t.* hinder, prevent, stop, impede (*an* (*Dat.*), from); ***ich kann es nicht -,*** I cannot prevent *or* (*coll.*) help it; ***am Kommen verhindert,*** prevented from coming; ***verhinderter Dichter,*** would-be poet; ***den Umlauf des Blutes -,*** stop the circulation of the blood. **Verhinderung,** *f.* hindrance, prevention; obstacle, impediment.

verhoffen [fɛr'hɔfən], *v.i.* 1. (*obs.*) *see* **hoffen**; 2. (*Hunt.*) scent the air (*of game*). **Verhoffen,** *n.* ***wider alles -,*** contrary to all expectations.

verhohlen [fɛr'ho:lən], *adj.* hidden, concealed, secret; surreptitious, secretive, underhand, clandestine.

verhöhnen [fɛr'hø:nən], *v.t.* scoff *or* jibe *or* jeer *or* laugh at, snap one's fingers at, mock, taunt, deride, make game of, expose to ridicule. **Verhöhnung,** *f.* scoffing, taunting, jeering, derision, mockery.

verholen [fɛr'ho:lən], *v.t.* (*Naut.*) tow, haul.

Verhör [fɛr'hø:r], *n.* (**-(e)s,** *pl.* **-e**) cross-examination, interrogation; hearing, trial; ***ein - anstellen,*** institute an inquiry; ***ihn zum - ziehen,*** bring him up for cross-examination; ***ins - nehmen,*** question closely, cross-examine, (*sl.*) grill; (*fig.*) take to task. **verhören, 1.** *v.t.* 1. question, interrogate, examine (*an accused p.*); 2. hear say *or* repeat (*lessons of school-children*); 3. not hear. **2.** *v.r.* hear wrong, mishear, misunderstand his *etc.* words.

verhudeln [fɛr'hu:dəln], *v.t.* (*coll.*) bungle, botch.

verhüllen [fɛr'hylən], *v.t.* cover, veil, drape, wrap up; (*fig.*) disguise, cloak, veil, (*coll.*) wrap up; ***in verhüllten Worten,*** in veiled language, euphemistically; ***in Dunkelheit verhüllt,*** shrouded *or* wrapped in obscurity. **Verhüllung,** *f.* cover(ing), wrapping; (*fig.*) veil, disguise.

verhundertfachen [fɛr'hundərtfaxən], *v.t., v.r.* multiply a hundredfold, centuple.

verhungern [fɛr'huŋərn], *v.i.* (*aux.* s.) die of hunger, starve (to death); ***- lassen,*** starve to death; (*fig.*) ***verhungert aussehen,*** look wretched *or* famished *or* half-starved.

verhunzen [fɛr'huntsən], *v.t.* spoil, bungle, botch, make a botch *or* mess *or* hash of; ***die englische Sprache -,*** murder the Queen's English.

verhüten [fɛr'hy:tən], *v.t.* prevent, obviate, avert, ward off, preserve (from); (***das***) ***verhüte Gott!*** God forbid! **verhütend,** *adj.* preventive, (*Med.*) prophylactic. **Verhütung,** *f.* prevention, (*Med.*) prophylaxis. **Verhütungs|maßregel,** *f.* preventive measure. **-mittel,** *n.* preventive, prophylactic; contraceptive.

verhütten [fɛr'hytən], *v.t.* work, smelt (*ore*).

verhutzelt [fɛr'hutsəlt], *adj.* shrivelled (up), wizened.

verinnerlichen [fɛr'ɪnərlɪçən], *v.t., v.i.* (*aux.* s.) intensify, deepen, spiritualize. **Verinnerlichung,** *f.* intensification, spiritualization; introversion.

verirren [fɛr'ɪrən], *v.r.* go astray, lose one's way; ***verirrte Kugel,*** stray bullet. **Verirrung,** *f.* aberration, error, mistake.

verjagen [fɛr'ja:gən], *v.t.* drive away *or* out, chase away, put to flight, (*fig.*) banish, dispel.

verjährbar [fɛr'jɛ:rba:r], *adj.* (*Law*) prescriptible. **verjähren,** *v.i.* (*aux.* s.) grow old, become superannuated; go out of date *or* fashion, become obsolete; become rooted *or* inveterate; (*also v.r.*) (*Law*) fall under the statute of limitations, lapse, become null and void. **verjährt,** *adj.* inveterate, deep-rooted; (*Law*) prescriptive, statute-barred, (*pred.*) barred under the statute of limitations; obsolete, superannuated. **Verjährung,** *f.* (*Law*) (negative) prescription, limitation. **Verjährungs|frist,** *f.* term of limitation *or* prescription. **–gesetz, –recht,** *n.* statute of limitations.

verjubeln [fɛr'ju:bəln], *v.t.* pass, waste (*one's time etc.*), squander, (*sl.*) blue (*one's money*); (*coll.*) frivol away.

verjuden [fɛr'ju:dən], *v.t., v.i.* (*aux.* s.) become *or* make Jewish, come *or* bring under Jewish influence. **Verjudung,** *f.* increasing Jewish influence.

verjüngen [fɛr'jyŋən], **1.** *v.t.* rejuvenate, renovate, regenerate; (*Tech.*) reduce to a smaller scale; narrow, taper; ***in verjüngtem Maßstabe,*** on a small(er) *or* reduced scale, in miniature; (*Metall.*) ***verjüngte Probe,*** small assay. **2.** *v.r.* be restored to youth, be rejuvenated *or* regenerated; (*Tech.*) taper (off). **Verjüngung,** *f.* 1. rejuvenation, regeneration; 2. (*Tech.*) reduction, tapering. **Verjüngungs|kur,** *f.* rejuvenation treatment. **–maßstab,** *m.* reduction scale. **–quelle,** *f.* fountain of youth.

verjuxen [fɛr'juksən], *v.t.* (*coll.*) *see* **verjubeln.**

verkalben [fɛr'kalbən], *v.i.* calve prematurely.

verkalken [fɛr'kalkən], *v.r., v.i.* (*aux.* s.), *v.t.* calcine, calcify, turn to chalk; (*coll.*) grow old, become decrepit, ossify. **Verkalkung,** *f.* calcination, calcification, (*Med.*) arteriosclerosis.

verkannt [fɛr'kant], *adj.* mistaken, misunderstood. *See* **verkennen.**

verkappen [fɛr'kapən], **1.** *v.t.* muffle up, envelop, (*Hunt.*) hoodwink (*a hawk*), (*fig.*) cloak, mask, disguise. **verkappt,** *adj.* masked, veiled, disguised; secret, surreptitious, (*pred.*) in disguise; ***verkappter Schriftsteller,*** writer under an assumed name.

verkapseln [fɛr'kapsəln], *v.r.* (*Med.*) become encysted. **Verkaps(e)lung,** *f.* encystation.

verkatert [fɛr'ka:tərt], *adj.* (*coll.*) with a hangover, (*sl.*) hungover, morning-afterish.

Verkauf [fɛr'kauf], *m.* (**-(e)s,** *pl.* **-̈e**) sale; selling, disposal, realization; ***zum –,*** on sale, for sale. **verkaufen, 1.** *v.t.* sell, dispose of (*Dat.*, ***an*** (*Acc.*), to), realize (*assets*); ***mit Schaden –,*** sell at a loss; ***zu –,*** for sale, to be sold; (*coll.*) ***verraten und verkauft,*** sold down the river; ***sein Leben teuer –,*** sell one's life dearly. **2.** *v.r.* sell o.s. (*of prostitutes or traitors*); ***es verkauft sich leicht,*** it sells well *or* readily, has a ready sale *or* finds a ready market; ***das verkauft sich schwer,*** that finds no sale *or* is unsaleable *or* is a drug on the market *or* is difficult to dispose of.

Verkäufer [fɛr'kɔyfər], *m.* 1. seller, vendor, salesman, retailer; 2. shop-assistant, (*Am.*) (sales)clerk. **Verkäuferin,** *f.* shop-assistant, shop-girl, saleswoman, (*Am.*) salesgirl.

verkäuflich [fɛr'kɔyflıç], *adj.* for sale; saleable, marketable; negotiable (*of bills*); ***leicht –,*** readily saleable, easy to dispose of, commanding a ready sale; ***schwer –,*** unsaleable, difficult to dispose of, drug on the market. **Verkäuflichkeit,** *f.* saleableness.

Verkaufs|abteilung, *f.* sales department. **–automat,** *m.* vending *or* penny-in-the-slot machine. **–bedingungen,** *f.pl.* terms *or* conditions of sale. **–bude,** *f.* stall, kiosk. **–büro,** *n.* distribution centre. **–förderung,** *f.* sales promotion. **–leiter,** *m.* sales manager. **–personal,** *n.* selling *or* counter staff. **–preis,** *m.* selling-price, market-value. **–raum,** *m.* saleroom. **–schlager,** *m.* popular line. **–stand,** *m.* stall, stand, booth. **–stelle,** *f.* (retail) outlet, retail shop. **–vertretung,** *f.* selling agency. **–werbung,** *f. See* **–förderung. –wert,** *m.* market-value.

Verkehr [fɛr'ke:r], *m.* traffic; transport, (train *etc.*) service, communication; commerce, trade, business; (sexual *or* social) intercourse; circulation (*of money*); communion (*of ideas*); ***bargeldloser –,*** transfer business, clearing trade; ***brieflicher –,*** correspondence; ***freier –,*** unrestricted communication *or* trade; ***geselliger*** or ***gesellschaftlicher –,*** social intercourse; ***Handel und –,*** trade and commerce; ***inniger – mit der Natur,*** communings with nature; ***das ist kein – für dich,*** that is poor company for you; ***mit ihm – haben, in – mit ihm stehen,*** have dealings with him; ***in – bringen,*** market, offer for sale, issue; ***dem – übergehen,*** open for traffic; ***aus dem – ziehen,*** withdraw (*vehicle*) from service or (*money*) from circulation.

verkehren [fɛr'ke:rən], **1.** *v.t.* 1. turn the wrong way, reverse; turn upside down, invert; turn topsy-turvy; 2. turn, change, convert, transform (***in*** (*Acc.*), into), (*fig.*) pervert; ***seine Worte –,*** put a wrong construction on his words, (*coll.*) twist his words. **2.** *v.r.* turn, change, be changed (***in*** (*Acc.*), into). **3.** *v.i.* (come and) go, frequent, visit; (*of traffic*) run, ply; ***mit ihm –,*** have (sexual) intercourse with *or* cohabit with him; associate with *or* mix with *or* see a good *or* great deal of him; ***bei ihm*** or ***in seinem Haus –,*** be a frequent visitor to *or* at his house.

Verkehrs|ader, *f.* arterial road. **–ampeln,** *f.pl.* traffic lights. **–andrang,** *m.* rush of traffic. **–büro,** *n.* travel agency. **–disziplin,** *f.* road-sense. **–einrichtungen,** *f.pl.* communications, traffic arrangements. **–erziehung,** *f.* road-safety campaign. **–flugzeug,** *n.* airliner, civil aircraft. **–insel,** *f.* island, refuge. **–karte,** *f.* road *or* rail map. **–knotenpunkt,** *m.* (railway) junction. **–luftfahrt,** *f.* civil aviation. **–minister,** *m.* Minister of Transport. **–mittel,** *n.pl.* 1. means of communication *or* transport; (public) conveyance, passenger vehicle; 2. (*money*) currency. **–netz,** *n.* communications network. **–ordnung,** *f.* traffic regulations. **–polizist,** *m. See* **–schutzmann. –regelung,** *f.* traffic control. **verkehrsreich,** *adj.* busy, crowded, congested (*streets*). **Verkehrs|schild,** *n.* road *or* traffic sign. **–schutzmann,** *m.* traffic *or* point-duty policeman. **verkehrsschwach,** *adj.* slack (*period*). **Verkehrs|sicherheit,** *f.* road safety. **–spitze,** *f.* rush-hour, peak-traffic period. **verkehrsstark,** *adj.* busy, rush (*period*). **Verkehrs|stauung, –stockung,** *f.* traffic jam, congestion, block. **–störung,** *f.* interruption of traffic, (service) breakdown. **–straße,** *f.* main road, highway, thoroughfare; (*Hist., Naut.*) trade route. **–sünder,** *m.* traffic offender, (*pedestrian*) jay-walker. **–tafel,** *f. See* **–schild. –teilnehmer,** *m.* road user. **–turm,** *m.* traffic control tower. **–unfall,** *m.* road *or* traffic accident. **–unternehmen,** *n.* (public) transport body. **–verein,** *m.* tourist board. **–vorschrift,** *f.* traffic regulation. **–werbung,** *f.* tourist-traffic propaganda. **–wesen,** *n.* traffic, transport system. **–zeichen,** *n. See* **–schild.**

verkehrt [fɛr'ke:rt], *adj.* reversed, inside out; inverted, upside down; wrong, perverted, absurd, preposterous; (*of a p.*) perverse, wrong-headed; ***–e Seite,*** wrong side (*of cloth*); (*Mil.*) ***mit –em Gewehr,*** arms reversed; ***Kaffee –,*** white coffee, (*coll.*) coffee dash; ***–e Welt,*** crazy *or* topsy-turvy world; ***– anfangen,*** set about (*a th.*) the wrong way, put the cart before the horse. **Verkehrtheit,** *f.* perversity, wrongheadedness, absurdity, folly.

verkeilen [fɛr'kaılən], *v.t.* 1. wedge (tight), fasten with a wedge, (*Typ.*) quoin; 2. (*sl.*) thrash (*a p.*); (*sl.*) flog (*a th.*).

verkennen [fɛr'kɛnən], *irr.v.t.* (*a p.*) mistake, fail to recognize, take for s.o. else; (*a th.*) misunderstand, misjudge, misconstrue, have *or* get a false idea of, fail to appreciate, undervalue; ***nicht –,*** be aware of, not be unaware of; ***nicht zu –,*** unmistakable; ***verkanntes Genie,*** unappreciated *or* unrecognized genius. **Verkennung,** *f.* (*of a p.*) mistaken identity, lack of recognition, failure to recognize; (*of a th.*) lack of appreciation, misunderstanding, misjudgement.

verketten [fɛr'kɛtən], *v.t.* chain up *or* together, (*Elec. etc.*) interconnect; (*fig.*) link up, connect, unite. **verkettet,** *adj.* interlinked. **Verkettung,** *f.* chaining, linking; linkage, connection, interlinkage; chain, concatenation, coincidence.

verketzern [fɛr'kɛtsərn], *v.t.* accuse of heresy, (*fig.*) abuse, disparage, calumniate. **Verketzerung,** *f.* charge of heresy, (*fig.*) abuse, disparagement, calumniation.

verkirchlichen [fɛr'kırçlıçən], *v.t.* bring under ecclesiastical control.

verkitten [fɛr'kɪtən], *v.t.* cement, putty (up), lute.

verklagbar [fɛr'kla:kba:r], *adj.* actionable, indictable. **verklagen,** *v.t.* 1. (*Law*) bring an action against, take legal proceedings against, sue (***wegen,*** (*obs.*) *Gen.*, ***auf*** (*Acc.*), for); ***ihn des Hochverrats –,*** arraign *or* indict him on a charge of high treason; 2. (*coll.*) accuse, inform against, (*sl.*) squeal on. **Verklagte(r),** *m., f.* accused, (*Law*) defendant; respondent (*in divorce proceedings*).

verklammern [fɛr'klamərn], *v.t.* clamp, fasten with cramp-irons.

verklären [fɛr'klɛ:rən], *v.t.* transfigure; (*fig.*) illumine. **verklärt,** *adj.* transfigured; (*fig.*) radiant, effulgent; ***die Verklärten,*** the blessed ones, the blest. **Verklärung,** *f.* transfiguration; (*fig.*) radiance, effulgence, ecstasy.

Verklarung [fɛr'kla:ruŋ], *f.* (*Law*) sea-protest.

verklatschen [fɛr'klatʃən], *v.t.* 1. waste (*time*) gossiping, gossip away (*time*); 2. slander, backbite, tell tales about (*a p.*).

verklauseln [fɛr'klauzəln], **verklausulieren** [–u-'li:rən], *v.t.* stipulate; safeguard *or* limit by *or* (*coll.*) hedge with provisos.

verkleben [fɛr'kle:bən], *v.t.* paste over, plaster up; glue, cement, gum up, stick together; (*Med.*) apply a plaster to.

verklecksen [fɛr'klɛksən], *v.t.* cover with blots *or* smudges, make a mess of (*book, tablecloth etc.*), spill ink on.

verkleiden [fɛr'klaɪdən], **1.** *v.t.* 1. cover, face, (en)case, revet, plank, panel, board; 2. disguise, (*Theat.*) dress *or* make up, (*Mil.*) camouflage, (*fig.*) veil (*an insult etc.*). **2.** *v.r.* (*Theat.*) disguise o.s., dress *or* make (o.s.) up. **Verkleidung,** *f.* 1. covering, facing, lining, casing, cowling, wainscoting, panelling, (*Fort.*) revetment, (*Av.*) fairing; 2. disguise, (*Theat.*) make-up.

verkleinern [fɛr'klaɪnərn], *v.t.* make smaller, diminish, lessen, reduce (in size), scale down; (*fig.*) disparage, depreciate, belittle; detract from; ***einen Bruch –,*** reduce a fraction; ***den Wert –,*** depreciate the value; ***ihn –,*** belittle him; ***sein Verdienst –,*** disparage his services. **Verkleinerung,** *f.* diminution, reduction, lessening; (*fig.*) detraction, depreciation, disparagement, belittling. **Verkleinerungs|maßstab,** *m.* reduction scale. **–silbe,** *f.* diminutive ending *or* suffix. **–wort,** *n.* diminutive.

verkleistern [fɛr'klaɪstərn], *v.t.* paste up; (*fig.*) patch up (*a difference*); cover up (*faults, mistakes*).

Verklicker [fɛr'klɪkər], *m.* (*Naut.*) burgee.

verklingen [fɛr'klɪŋən], *irr.v.i.* (*aux.* s.) die *or* fade away (*of sounds*).

verklopfen [fɛr'klɔpfən], (*dial.*) **verkloppen**, *v.t.* 1. (*coll.*) beat soundly, thrash; 2. (*Studs. sl.*) sell, flog.

verknacken [fɛr'knakən], *v.t.* (*coll.*) sentence (*a p.*); play a trick on (*a p.*), pull (*a p.'s*) leg.

verknacksen [fɛr'knaksən], *v.t.* (*coll.*) ***sich*** (*Dat.*) ***den Fuß –,*** sprain one's foot.

verknallen [fɛr'knalən], **1.** *v.i.* (*aux.* s.) explode, go off with a bang; (*sl.*) ***verknallt sein in*** (*Acc.*), be badly smitten with, be gone on, have a crush on. **2.** *v.t.* fire off, use up (*all one's ammunition*). **3.** *v.r.* (*coll.*) fall violently in love (***in*** (*Acc.*), with).

verknappen [fɛr'knapən], *v.r.* become scarce, (*coll.*) get tight, run short. **Verknappung,** *f.* scarcity, shortage.

verkneifen [fɛr'knaɪfən], *irr.v.t.* (*coll.*) ***sich*** (*Dat.*) ***etwas –,*** deny o.s. a th., forgo s.th.; (*coll.*) ***ich kann mir nicht –*** (***zu tun***), I cannot resist the temptation (to do), I cannot help (doing); ***verkniffenes Gesicht,*** pinched *or* hardbitten *or* grim expression.

verknistern [fɛr'knɪstərn], *v.i.* decrepitate.

verknittern [fɛr'knɪtərn], *v.t.* crumple, crease.

verknöchern [fɛr'knœçərn], **1.** *v.t.* ossify. **2.** *v.i.* (*aux.* s.) ossify, (*coll.*) become fossilized, grow narrow-minded *or* pedantic; (*coll.*) ***verknöcherter Kerl,*** pedantic old fossil. **Verknöcherung,** *f.* ossification; fossilization.

verknorpeln [fɛr'knɔrpəln], *v.r., v.i.* (*aux.* s.) become cartilaginous.

verknoten [fɛr'kno:tən], *v.t.* knot; tie up (in knots), entangle.

verknüllen [fɛr'knylən], *v.t.* *See* **verknittern.**

verknüpfen [fɛr'knypfən], *v.t.* knot, tie *or* bind (together); (*fig.*) link, connect, combine (***mit,*** with), join, attach (to). **verknüpft,** *adj.* (*fig.*) attended (***mit,*** with), involving, entailing; ***logisch -e Ideen,*** logically connected ideas; ***mit wenig Kosten –,*** involving *or* entailing little expense. **Verknüpfung,** *f.* knotting *or* tying together; combination, connection, bond, link, nexus.

verknusen [fɛr'knu:zən], *v.t.* (*coll.*) (*usu. neg.*) stomach, put up with, stand; ***ich kann ihn nicht –,*** I can't stand *or* stick him.

verkochen [fɛr'kɔxən], *v.t., v.i.* (*aux.* s.) overboil, boil into the water; boil down *or* away; (*fig.*) ***sein Zorn verkochte bald,*** his anger soon cooled down *or* blew over.

verkohlen [fɛr'ko:lən], *v.t., v.i.* (*aux.* s.) char, carbonize; (*coll.*) hoax, pull (*a p.'s*) leg, pull the wool over (*a p.'s*) eyes. **Verkohlung,** *f.* carbonization.

verkoken [fɛr'ko:kən], *v.t.* coke, carbonize. **Verkokung,** *f.* coking, carbonization.

verkommen [fɛr'kɔmən], **1.** *irr.v.i.* (*aux.* s.) decay, go bad, (*fig.*) be ruined, (*coll.*) go to seed, go to wrack and ruin, (*of a p.*) come down in the world, (*coll.*) go to the dogs. **2.** *adj.* decayed, (*fig.*) ruined, (*of a p.*) corrupt, degenerate, depraved. **Verkommenheit,** *f.* depravity, degeneracy.

Verkommnis [fɛr'kɔmnɪs], *n.* (**-ses,** *pl.* **-se**) (*Swiss*) agreement, treaty.

verkoppeln [fɛr'kɔpəln], *v.t.* couple, link, join (together), combine.

verkorken [fɛr'kɔrkən], *v.t.* cork (up).

verkorksen [fɛr'kɔrksən], *v.t.* (*coll.*) make a mess *or* hash *or* (*sl.*) muck of, bungle, botch, (*sl.*) muck up; ***sich*** (*Dat.*) ***den Magen –,*** upset one's stomach.

verkörpern [fɛr'kœrpərn], *v.t.* embody, personify, (*fig.*) typify, represent, (*Theat.*) impersonate. **Verkörperung,** *f.* embodiment, personification; incarnation; impersonation.

verkosten [fɛr'kɔstən], *v.t.* taste, test, try (*food*).

verkostgelden [fɛr'kɔstgɛldən], *v.t.* (*Swiss*) put out to board.

verköstigen [fɛr'kœstɪgən], *v.t.* feed, board. **Verköstigung,** *f.* board, food.

Verköterung [fɛr'kø:təruŋ], *f.* mongrelization, racial degeneration.

verkrachen [fɛr'kraxən], **1.** *v.i.* (*coll.*) go bankrupt, go bust *or* broke; ***verkrachte Existenz,*** ne'er-do-well, failure. **2.** *v.r.* fall out (***mit,*** with).

verkraften [fɛr'kraftən], *v.t.* supply electricity to; (*coll.*) cope *or* deal with, handle, bear.

verkrampft [fɛr'krampft], *adj.* cramped, clenched; (*fig.*) tense, rigid; unnatural (*style*).

verkriechen [fɛr'kri:çən], *irr.v.r.* crawl away, sneak off, hide o.s.; ***sich in das Bett –,*** creep into one's bed; ***er verkriecht sich vor jedem,*** he shuns everyone; ***er muß sich vor Wilhelm –,*** he is no match for William.

verkrümeln [fɛr'kry:məln], **1.** *v.t., v.i.* (*aux.* s.) crumble away, fritter away; ***sein Geld –,*** fritter away one's money. **2.** *v.r.* (*coll.*) slink away, make off, (*sl.*) make tracks; ***das Geld verkrümelt sich,*** the money trickles away.

verkrümmen [fɛr'krymən], **1.** *v.t.* make crooked, bend; spoil by bending. **2.** *v.r.* grow crooked, (*of wood*) warp. **Verkrümmung,** *f.* distortion, warping, crookedness, curvature; ***– der Wirbelsäule,*** curvature of the spine.

verkrüppeln [fɛr'krypəln], **1.** *v.t.* stunt, deform, cripple, mutilate. **2.** *v.i.* (*aux.* s.) become deformed *or* mutilated *or* stunted.

verkrusten [fɛr'krustən], *v.r.* become caked *or* encrusted; ***von Schmutz verkrustet,*** caked with mud.

verkühlen [fɛr'ky:lən], *v.r.* (*dial.*) catch (a) cold.

verkümmern [fɛr'kymərn], **1.** *v.t.* spoil; ***ihm die Freude –,*** spoil his pleasure; ***seine Rechte –,*** encroach *or* infringe upon *or* curtail his rights. **2.** *v.i.* (*aux.* s.) become stunted, atrophy, waste away, shrink, shrivel up; (*fig.*) pine away, languish. **verkümmert,** *adj.* stunted, rudimentary, vestigial. **Verkümmerung,** *f.* stunted growth, atrophy; curtailment, encroachment.

verkünd(ig)en [fɛr'kynd(ɪg)ən], *v.t.* announce, make known, publish, proclaim; promulgate (*a law*), preach (*the Gospel*), pronounce (*a judgement*); ***im voraus –,*** foretell, prophesy, predict, forewarn of; ***Schlimmes –,*** bode ill; ***eine neue Zeit –,*** herald a new epoch; (*dial.*) ***ein Brautpaar –,*** publish the banns. **Verkünd(ig)er,** *m.* messenger, harbinger, herald, prophet. **Verkünd(ig)ung,** *f.* announcement, publication, promulgation, proclamation; preaching (*of the Gospel*); prophecy, prediction; pronouncement (*of a sentence*); ***Mariä –,*** the Annunciation, Lady Day.

verkünstelt [fɛrkynstəlt], *adj.* over-refined.

verkupfern [fɛr'kupfərn], *v.t.* plate *or* line with copper, copperplate, (*Typ.*) copper-face. **verkupfert,** *adj.* copper-sheathed *or* -bottomed (*of ships*); copper-plate(d).

verkuppeln [fɛr'kupəln], *v.t.* 1. couple, connect (*coaches, shafts etc.*); bring together, pair off; 2. pander, procure.

verkürzen [fɛr'ky:rtsən], **1.** *v.t.* shorten, abridge, curtail, cut (down), lessen, diminish, (*Paint. etc.*) foreshorten; ***ihn –,*** encroach upon *or* curtail his rights; ***die Zeit –,*** while away *or* beguile the time. **2.** *v.r.* become shorter, diminish, contract, shrink; ***verkürzte Arbeitszeit,*** short time. **Verkürzung,** *f.* shortening, abridgement, curtailment; retrenchment, cut, cutting down; (*Paint. etc.*) foreshortening; (*Gram.*) abbreviation, contraction.

verlachen [fɛr'laxən], *v.t.* laugh at, deride.

Verlad [fɛr'la:t], *m.* **(-s,** *no pl.*) (*Swiss*) *see* **Verladung. Verladehafen,** *m.* port of embarkation.

verladen [fɛr'la:dən], *irr.v.t.* load, ship, consign, dispatch, forward (*goods*); (*Mil.*) embark, entrain (*troops*); ***lose –,*** ship in bulk. **Verlader,** *m.* shipping-agent; carrier. **Verlade|rampe,** *f.* loading bay *or* platform. **–stelle,** *f.* loading point, entraining point, point of embarkation. **Verladung,** *f.* loading, entraining, embarkation; shipping, shipment; carriage, forwarding.

Verlag [fɛr'la:k], *m.* **(-s,** *pl.* **-e** (*Austr.* **-̈e**)) publication (*of a book*); publishing house, (firm of) publishers; ***in – nehmen,*** undertake the publication of, publish; ***im – von,*** published by.

Verläge [fɛr'lɛ:gə], *pl.* outlay, estimated expenses, advance.

verlagern [fɛr'la:gərn], **1.** *v.t.* shift, displace; (*for reasons of security*) remove, transfer, evacuate. **2.** *v.r.* shift, be switched (over). **Verlagerung,** *f.* (*Geol. etc.*) shifting, displacement; removal, transfer, evacuation; (*fig.*) shift, switch.

Verlags|anstalt, *f.* publishing house. **–artikel,** *m.pl.* publications, books published. **–(buch)handel,** *m.* publishing business *or* trade. **–(buch)handlung,** *f. See* **–anstalt. –katalog,** *m.* publisher's catalogue. **–recht,** *n.* copyright. **verlagsrechtlich,** *adj.* (pertaining to) copyright; ***–e Ausgabe,*** copyright edition.

verlangen [fɛr'laŋən], **1.** *v.t.* demand, claim, ask for, desire; insist on, call for, require; ***Genugtuung –,*** demand satisfaction; ***was – Sie von mir?*** what do you want of me? ***wieviel – Sie dafür?*** how much do you want for it? ***man verlangt zu wissen,*** information is desired; ***du hast gar nichts zu –,*** you are in no position to make demands; ***das ist zu viel verlangt,*** that is asking too much; ***mehr kann man nicht –!*** one cannot wish for more; (*imp.*) ***mich verlangt zu wissen,*** I am anxious *or* I want to know. **2.** *v.i.* ***– nach,*** desire, wish for, long for, hanker after, crave.

Verlangen, *n.* desire, wish, craving, longing (***nach,*** for); request, demand, (*Law*) claim; ***auf –,*** on demand, by request; (*Comm.*) at call; ***auf – von,*** at the request of.

verlängern [fɛr'lɛŋərn], **1.** *v.t.* lengthen, elongate; (*time*) extend, prolong; protract, (*coll.*) hold over, spin out; renew (*contract etc.*); (*Geom.*) produce; eke out, dilute (*paint, soup etc.*). **2.** *v.r.* grow longer, lengthen, stretch. **Verlängerung,** *f.* lengthening, elongation; prolongation; extension, renewal; (*Geom.*) production; projection; (*Anat.*) process; (*Spt.*) extra time. **verlängerungsfähig,** *adj.* extensible, extensile, protractile. **Verlängerungs|punkt,** *m.* (*Mus.*) dot. **–schnur,** *f.* (*Elec.*) extension lead *or* wire. **–stück,** *n.* 1. extension piece; 2. (*Comm.*) rider, allonge (*of a bill*). **–trieb,** *m.* (*Bot.*) terminal shoot. **–zettel,** *m. See* **–stück,** 2.

verlangsamen [fɛr'laŋza:mən], **1.** *v.t.* slacken, slow down, retard, impede, delay. **2.** *v.r.* slacken, slow down. **Verlangsamung,** *f.* delay(ing); slackening, retardation, (*Motor. etc.*) deceleration.

verläppern [fɛr'lɛpərn], *v.t.* (*coll.*) waste (*money*) on trifles, squander, trifle *or* fritter away.

Verlaß [fɛr'las], *m.* trustworthiness, dependence, reliance; ***auf den ist kein –,*** there is no relying on him, there is no dependence on him, he cannot be trusted, he cannot be relied on.

verlassen [fɛr'lasən], **1.** *irr.v.t.* leave, quit, relinquish, leave behind, forsake, (*coll.*) give up; abandon, desert, (*coll.*) leave in the lurch; ***seine Kräfte – ihn,*** his strength fails him. **2.** *irr.v.r.* rely, depend, count (***auf*** (*Acc.*), on), trust (to), (*coll.*) bank, figure (on); ***darauf kannst du dich –,*** you may depend *or* rely on it, you can rest assured, (*sl.*) you can bet your bottom dollar on it; ***– Sie sich darauf!*** take it from me! (*sl.*) (you can) bank on it! you bet! **3.** *adj.* (*of a p. or place*) deserted, forsaken, abandoned, (*of a p.*) forlorn, (*of a place*) lonely, isolated. **Verlassen,** *n.* (*Law*) ***böswilliges –,*** desertion. **Verlassenheit,** *f.* loneliness, solitude, isolation; abandonment. **Verlassenschaft,** *f.* (*dial.*) bequest, legacy.

verläßlich [fɛr'lɛslɪç], *adj.* reliable, trustworthy, (*pred.*) to be depended on. **Verläßlichkeit,** *f.* dependability, reliability, trustworthiness.

verlasten [fɛr'lastən], *v.t.* (*Mil.*) load on lorries *or* trucks.

verlästern [fɛr'lɛstərn], *v.t.* slander, defame, malign, calumniate, traduce.

verlastet [fɛr'lastət], *adj.* lorry-borne, (*Am.*) trucked (*troops*).

Verlaub [fɛr'laup], *m.* ***mit –,*** with your permission, by your leave; ***mit – zu sagen,*** if I may (be permitted to) say so.

Verlauf [fɛr'lauf], *m.* lapse, expiration; course, process (*of time*); progress, development (*of a matter*); ***nach – einiger Tage,*** in the course of a few days, after (the lapse of) some days; ***– einer Krankheit,*** course of a disease; ***der ganze – der S.,*** the whole trend *or* history of the affair; ***einen schlimmen – nehmen,*** take a turn for the worse; ***im weiteren –,*** later on, in the sequel *or* outcome *or* (*coll.*) upshot.

verlaufen [fɛr'laufən], **1.** *irr.v.i.* (*aux.* s.) 1. pass, elapse, proceed, take its course, turn out, develop; ***die Zeit verläuft,*** time passes quickly, time flies; ***die Krankheit verläuft normal,*** the disease is taking its normal course; ***wie ist die S. –?*** how has the affair turned out? ***alles ist gut –,*** everything has gone off well; 2. (*as crowd*) scatter, disperse, (*coll.*) drift away; (*as water*) flow away *or* off, subside; (*as colours*) run, blend! (*fig.*) ***im Sand –,*** come to nothing, (*coll.*) peter *or* fizzle out. **2.** *irr.v.r.* lose one's way, get lost, go astray. **3.** *adj.* stray (*animal*), lost (*child*).

verlaust [fɛr'laust], *adj.* full of lice, (*coll.*) bug-ridden.

verlautbaren [fɛr'lautba:rən], **1.** *v.t.* make known, disclose, divulge, publish, notify. **2.** *v.i.* become *or* be made known *or* public. **Verlautbarung,** *f.* announcement, disclosure, notification; report, bulletin, (press) release.

verlauten [fɛr'lautən], *v.i.* (*aux.* h. & s.) be said *or* rumoured, be reported *or* disclosed, transpire; (*Swiss*) *see* **verlautbaren**; – ***lassen,*** give to understand, be heard to say; ***nichts von der S. – lassen,*** let nothing leak out, not breathe a word; ***wie verlautet,*** according to report, as the story goes.

verleben [fɛr'le:bən], *v.t.* pass, spend (*time*). **verlebt,** *adj.* worn out, spent, debilitated, jaded, decrepit. **Verlebtheit,** *f.* debility, exhaustion, decrepitude.

[1]**verlegen** [fɛr'le:gən], **1.** *v.t.* 1. transfer, shift, remove to another place; 2. misplace, mislay, put in the wrong place; 3. delay, postpone, adjourn, put off (***auf*** (*Acc.*), to *or* till); 4. lay (*pipes, cables etc.*); lay, locate (*the scene of a story*); 5. stop, hinder, obstruct, bar; ***ihm den Rückzug –,*** block his retreat; 6. publish, bring out (*a book*). **2.** *v.r.* apply *or* devote o.s. to, resort to, (*coll.*) turn to, go in for, take (*a th.*) up; ***er verlegte sich aufs Leugnen,*** he resorted to denials.

[2]**verlegen,** *adj.* embarrassed, confused, self-conscious, disconcerted, ill at ease; – ***sein um,*** be at a loss for; ***um Geld – sein,*** be short of cash, be financially embarrassed. **Verlegenheit,** *f.* embarrassment, difficulty, dilemma, predicament, straits; ***in – bringen*** or (***ver***)***setzen,*** embarrass, make (*s.o.*) embarrassed; ***ihm aus der – helfen,*** help him over his embarrassment; ***in – kommen,*** get embarrassed, be put in an awkward position, get into trouble; ***in – sein um,*** be at a loss for; ***sich aus der – ziehen,*** get out of a difficulty.

Verleger [fɛr'le:gər], *m.* publisher; (*dial.*) retailer, distributor (*liquor trade particularly*).

Verlegung [fɛr'le:guŋ], *f.* 1. shift, change of position, transfer, removal; postponement, adjournment; 2. mislaying, temporary loss; 3. publication, publishing; 4. laying (*of cables*).

verleiden [fɛr'laɪdən], *v.t.* spoil (***ihm etwas,*** a th. for him), disgust (him with a th.); ***das Landleben war ihm verleidet,*** he had taken a dislike to life in the country; ***es ist mir alles verleidet,*** I am sick of everything.

Verleih [fɛr'laɪ], *m.* (**-s,** *pl.* **-e**) lending department (*of a library etc.*); hire service; (*Films*) distribution; (film) distributors. **verleihen,** *irr.v.t.* 1. lend (out), loan, let out, hire out; 2. award, grant (*Dat.*, to), bestow, confer (on), endow *or* invest (*him*) with, vest (in); ***ihm eine Pfründe –,*** endow him in a living; ***ihm ein Amt –,*** appoint him to an office; ***ihm Hilfe –,*** render him assistance; ***Gott verleihe uns seinen Segen!*** may God grant us His blessing! **Verleihung,** *f.* lending (out), loan; investiture, conferment, bestowal, grant, award.

verleiten [fɛr'laɪtən], *v.t.* lead astray, mislead, lure, seduce, suborn; ***einen Soldaten zur Fahnenflucht –,*** induce a soldier to desert; ***sich – lassen,*** be lead *or* induced, be carried away (*to do*). **Verleitung,** *f.* misleading; temptation, seduction, subornation (*of witnesses*); – ***zum Bösen,*** incitement *or* instigation to wrong(-doing); – ***zum Meineid,*** inducement to perjury.

verlernen [fɛr'lɛrnən], *v.t.* unlearn, forget (*what one has learnt*).

verlesen [fɛr'le:zən], **1.** *irr.v.t.* read out, call out (*names*), call (*a register*); (*dial.*) pick (out), select. **2.** *irr.v.r.* make a mistake in reading, misread. **Verlesung,** *f.* roll-call.

verletzbar [fɛr'lɛtsba:r], *adj.* *See* **verletzlich.**

verletzen [fɛr'lɛtsən], *v.t.* hurt, wound; damage, injure; insult, offend; offend (against), violate; encroach upon (*rights*), infringe (*laws*); ***seinen guten Namen –,*** injure *or* damage his reputation; ***eine Regel –,*** break a rule; ***seine Ehre –,*** wound his honour; ***seine Interessen –,*** wrong him, damage his interest(s); ***seine Pflicht –,*** fail in his duty; ***er fühlte sich verletzt,*** he felt (himself) aggrieved. **verletzend,** *adj.* offensive, insulting. **verletzlich,** *adj.* vulnerable, easily damaged; (over-)sensitive, susceptible, (*coll.*) touchy. **Verletzte(r),** *m., f.* injured p., victim, casualty. **Verletzung,** *f.* hurt, damage, injury, wound; violation, infringement, breach, encroachment; offence, insult.

verleugnen [fɛr'lɔyknən], **1.** *v.t.* deny, disown, disclaim, disavow, renounce; (*Cards*) not follow suit, revoke; act contrary to, act against; ***seinen Glauben –,*** renounce *or* disclaim one's belief; ***sich – lassen,*** refuse to see visitors, not be at home (***vor*** (*Dat.*), to). **2.** *v.r.* (*fig.*) (*of a th.*) ***sich nicht –,*** show *or* reveal itself, become clear; (*of a p.*) ***sich selbst –,*** belie o.s., be untrue to o.s., give a wrong impression of o.s. **Verleugnung,** *f.* denial, disavowal, renunciation; (*Cards*) revoking.

verleumden [fɛr'lɔymdən], *v.t.* calumniate, slander, defame, traduce, accuse wrongfully. **Verleumder,** *m.* calumniator, slanderer, libeller. **verleumderisch,** *adj.* slanderous, libellous, defamatory. **Verleumdung,** *f.* libel, calumny, slander, defamation (of character), wrongful accusation. **Verleumdungsprozeß,** *m.* action for defamation of character, action for libel *or* slander.

verlieben [fɛr'li:bən], *v.r.* fall in love (***in*** (*Acc.*), with). **verliebt,** *adj.* in love (with), enamoured (of); (*as glances etc.*) amorous, love-sick; ***närrisch –,*** madly in love, infatuated. **Verliebtheit,** *f.* amorousness (*of disposition*).

verlieren [fɛr'li:rən], **1.** *irr.v.t.* lose; ***Sie haben an ihm einen guten Freund verloren,*** you have lost a good friend in him; ***an ihm ist Hopfen und Malz verloren,*** he is incorrigible, one might as well give him up as a bad job; ***aus den Augen –,*** lose sight of; ***alle Bitten waren bei ihm verloren,*** all entreaties were lost on him; ***Blätter –,*** shed leaves; ***den Boden unter den Füßen –,*** get out of one's depth; ***eine Gewohnheit –,*** outgrow a habit; ***Hoffnung –,*** give up *or* lose hope; ***den Kopf –,*** lose all self-control, lose one's head; ***kein Wort –,*** not waste a word; ***Zeit –,*** waste time; ***da ist keine Zeit zu –,*** there is no time to lose *or* be lost; *see* **verloren. 2.** *irr.v.i.* – ***gegen,*** lose to; – ***an*** (*Dat.*), go *or* fall off *or* decline in (*value etc.*), suffer loss of; ***die Blume hat etwas an Duft verloren,*** the flower has lost something of its fragrance; (*fig.*) ***bei ihm –,*** sink in his estimation. **3.** *irr.v.r.* get lost, lose o.s., lose one's way, go astray; (*of a crowd*) disperse; (*of a sight*) fade, disappear; (*of sound*) die away; (*of pain*) subside, go down; ***diese Farbe verliert sich ins Grüne,*** this colour melts into green; ***sich in Gedanken –,*** be lost in thought. **Verlierer,** *m.* loser.

Verlies [fɛr'li:s], (*Austr.*) **Verließ,** *n.* (**-es,** *pl.* **-e**) dungeon, keep.

verloben [fɛr'lo:bən], **1.** *v.t.* engage, betroth (***mit,*** to). **2.** *v.r.* become engaged (***mit,*** to).

Verlöbnis [fɛr'lø:pnɪs], *n.* (**-ses,** *pl.* **-se**) *see* **Verlobung. Verlöbnisbruch,** *m.* breach of promise.

Verlobte [fɛr'lo:ptə], *f.* fiancée. **Verlobter,** *m.* fiancé; ***die Verlobten,*** the engaged couple.

Verlobung [fɛr'lo:buŋ], *f.* engagement, betrothal; ***eine – aufheben,*** break off an engagement. **Verlobungs|anzeige,** *f.* announcement of an engagement. **–ring,** *m.* engagement ring.

verlocken [fɛr'lɔkən], *v.t.* entice, tempt, inveigle; allure, seduce. **verlockend,** *adj.* tempting, enticing, alluring, seductive. **Verlockung,** *f.* enticement, allurement, temptation, lure.

verlogen [fɛr'lo:gən], *adj.* (given to) lying, untruthful, mendacious. **Verlogenheit,** *f.* habitual lying, untruthfulness, mendacity.

verlohnen [fɛr'lo:nən], *v.imp.* (*Gen.*) ***es verlohnt sich der Mühe,*** it is worth the trouble, it is worth while.

verlor [fɛr'lo:r], **verlöre** [fɛr'lø:rə], *see* **verlieren.**

verloren [fɛr'lo:rən], *adj.* lost, forlorn; ***–e Arbeit,*** wasted labour; ***–es Ei,*** poached egg; ***– geben,*** give up for lost, (*fig.*) give up as a bad job; ***das Spiel – geben,*** throw one's hand in, acknowledge defeat, (*coll.*) give in; ***–e Hoffnung,*** vain hope; (*Metall.*) ***–er Kopf,*** dead-head; ***das Verlorene Paradies,*** Paradise Lost; ***–er Posten,*** forlorn hope; ***auf –em Posten stehen,*** fight a losing battle; ***–er Schuß,*** random shot, stray bullet; (*B.*) ***der Verlorene Sohn,*** the Prodigal Son.

verlorengehen [fɛr'lo:rənge:ən], *irr.v.i.* (*aux.* s.) be *or* get lost; (*of post*) go astray, miscarry, (*of ships*)

be lost, go down, founder; ***an ihm ist ein Diplomat verlorengegangen,*** he would have made a good diplomat.
verlöschen [fɛr'lœʃən], **1.** *reg.v.t.* extinguish; obliterate, efface. **2.** *irr.v.i.* (*aux.* s.) be extinguished; become extinct; expire, die *or* go out; ***verloschene Kohlen,*** dead coals; ***verloschene Inschriften,*** obliterated inscriptions. **Verlöschung,** *f.* extinction; obliteration, effacement.
verlosen [fɛr'lo:zən], *v.t.* raffle, cast lots for. **Verlosung,** *f.* raffle, lottery.
verlöten [fɛr'lø:tən], *v.t.* solder; ***hart –,*** braze; (*sl.*) ***einen –,*** have a snifter.
verlottern [fɛr'lɔtərn], **verlumpen** [fɛr'lumpən], **verlundern** [fɛr'lundərn], **1.** *v.t.* (*coll.*) waste in riotous living, squander. **2.** *v.i.* (*of a p.*) come down in the world, go to the dogs; (*of a th.*) go to rack and ruin.
Verlust [fɛr'lust], *m.* (**-es,** *pl.* **-e**) loss (*an* (*Dat.*), of); damage, detriment; bereavement; *pl.* casualties (*in war*), losses (*in gambling*); ***bei – von,*** with loss of, with forfeiture of, under pain of; ***in – geraten,*** (*of a th.*) get lost; ***mit – verkaufen,*** sell at a loss *or* a sacrifice. **verlustbringend,** *adj.* involving loss; detrimental, prejudicial. **verlustig,** *adv.* (*Gen.*) ***einer S. – gehen,*** incur the loss of s.th., lose *or* forfeit s.th.; ***ihn einer S. für – erklären,*** declare him to have forfeited all *or* to be devoid of all claims to a th.
Verlust|konto, *n.* loss account. **–liste,** *f.* (*Mil.*) list of casualties, casualty returns. **–meldung,** *f.* report of a loss, (*Mil.*) casualty report. **–rechnung,** *f. See* **–konto.** **–träger,** *m.* loser. **–vortrag,** *m.* (*Comm.*) debit balance, debit carried forward.
vermachen [fɛr'maxən], *v.t.* bequeath, will, leave (*Dat.*, to).
Vermächtnis [fɛr'mɛçtnɪs], *n.* (**-ses,** *pl.* **-se**) will, testament; legacy, bequest; ***ohne – sterben,*** die intestate. **Vermächtnis|erbe,** *m. See* **–nehmer.** **–geber,** *m.* legator. **–nehmer,** *m.* legatee.
vermag [fɛr'ma:k], *see* **vermögen.**
vermahlen [fɛr'ma:lən], *irr.v.t.* grind (up *or* down).
vermählen [fɛr'mɛ:lən], **1.** *v.t.* marry, give in marriage (***mit,*** to); (*fig.*) unite (to *or* with). **2.** *v.r.* get married (***mit,*** to), marry, wed; ***die Vermählten,*** the newly-married couple, the bridal pair, the bride and bridegroom. **Vermählung,** *f.* marriage (ceremony), wedding.
vermahnen [fɛr'ma:nən], *v.t.* warn, admonish, exhort. **Vermahnung,** *f.* warning, admonition, exhortation.
vermaledeien [fɛrma:lə'daɪən], *v.t.* curse, execrate.
vermanschen [fɛr'manʃən], *v.t.* (*coll.*) mess *or* (*sl.*) muck up.
vermasseln [fɛr'masəln], *v.t.* (*sl.*) bungle, botch, make a botch *or* hash of, play the deuce with.
vermauern [fɛr'mauərn], *v.t.* wall in *or* up.
vermehren [fɛr'me:rən], *v.t., v.r.* increase, enlarge, augment, (*in number*) multiply (***um,*** by); (*Zool.*) breed, propagate; ***dies vermehrt meinen Kummer,*** this adds to my grief; ***vermehrte Auflage,*** enlarged edition. **Vermehrung,** *f.* increase (*Gen.*, in *or* of), multiplication, augmentation (of), addition (to); (*Zool.*) propagation, procreation, reproduction. **Vermehrungs|organe,** *n.pl.* reproductive organs. **–trieb,** *m.* procreative instinct.
vermeiden [fɛr'maɪdən], *irr.v.t.* avoid, shun; evade, elude, escape from, (*coll.*) dodge, shirk; ***es läßt sich nicht –,*** it is unavoidable, it cannot be helped. **vermeidlich,** *adj.* avoidable. **Vermeidung,** *f.* avoidance, evasion; ***bei – unserer Ungnade,*** under pain of (incurring) our displeasure.
vermeinen [fɛr'maɪnən], *v.t.* think, believe, consider, be of the opinion; imagine, suppose, presume, deem. **vermeintlich,** *adj.* supposed, presumed, alleged; putative, presumptive, would-be, pretended, imaginary.
vermelden [fɛr'mɛldən], *v.t.* announce, mention, send word (*Dat.*, to), notify, inform (*a p.*); ***mit Respekt zu –,*** with all due deference to you, saving your presence.
vermengen [fɛr'mɛŋən], **1.** *v.t.* mingle, mix, blend; mix up, confuse; ***vermengt werden in*** (*Acc.*), be involved in *or* mixed up with. **2.** *v.r.* (*of a th.*) mix, blend (***mit,*** with), (*of a p.*) meddle (with), be *or* get mixed up (with).
vermenschlichen [fɛr'mɛnʃlɪçən], *v.t.* represent in a human form, humanize; ***die Gottheit –,*** clothe Divinity with a human form.
Vermerk [fɛr'mɛrk], *m.* (**-(e)s,** *pl.* **-e**) observation, notice, note, entry, endorsement. **vermerken,** *v.t.* observe, remark; note down, record, enter, make *or* take a note of; ***etwas übel –,*** take a th. amiss, take offence *or* umbrage at a th.
vermessen [fɛr'mɛsən], **1.** *irr.v.t.* measure, take the measurement of; survey (*land*). **2.** *irr.v.r.* 1. make a mistake in measuring, measure wrong; 2. (*with Gen., or inf. with zu*) presume, venture, dare, have the audacity *or* impudence (to); ***sich zu viel –,*** be cocksure, take too much upon oneself. **3.** *adj.* daring, presumptuous; insolent, arrogant, impudent. **Vermessenheit,** *f.* daring, audacity, presumption, presumptuousness, arrogance, impudence, insolence.
Vermesser [fɛr'mɛsər], *m.* surveyor. **Vermessung,** *f.* 1. measuring; measurement; survey; 2. mistake in measuring. **Vermessungs|amt,** *n.* survey-office. **–ingenieur,** *m.* land surveyor. **–karte,** *f.* ordnance-survey map. **–kunde,** *f.* geodesy. **–punkt,** *m.* bench-mark.
vermieten [fɛr'mi:tən], *v.t.* let, lease, hire out; ***Haus zu –,*** house to let; ***Boot zu –,*** boat for hire. **Vermieter,** *m.* landlord; hirer, (*Law*) lessor. **Vermietung,** *f.* letting, leasing, hiring(-out).
vermindern [fɛr'mɪndərn], **1.** *v.t.* lessen, diminish (*also Mus.*), decrease, reduce, curtail, (*coll.*) cut down; abate; ***an Zahl –,*** reduce *or* decrease in number; ***um die Hälfte –,*** reduce by half; ***seine Kräfte –,*** impair one's strength. **2.** *v.r.* grow less, diminish, decrease, decline, abate; (*coll.*) fall off. **Verminderung,** *f.* lessening, diminution, decrease, reduction, abatement, (*coll.*) cut; decrement, depreciation.
verminen [fɛr'mi:nən], *v.t.* lay mines in, mine (*a harbour etc.*).
vermischen [fɛr'mɪʃən], **1.** *v.t.* mix, mingle, blend; cross, interbreed; adulterate, alloy. **2.** *v.r.* mix, mingle, blend, (*coll.*) go well together; interbreed. **vermischt,** *adj.* mixed, miscellaneous. **Vermischung,** *f.* mixture, blend; intermixture, adulteration, alloy(ing) (*of metals*); crossing *or* interbreeding (*of races*); (*fig.*) medley, jumble.
vermissen [fɛr'mɪsən], *v.t.* miss, fail to see, (*fig.*) regret; ***man vermißt ihn,*** he is missing; (*fig.*) he is missed, his absence is (greatly) felt. **Vermissen,** *n.* ***schmerzliches –,*** deep regret. **vermißt,** *adj.* missing. **Vermißte(r),** *m., f.* missing person.
vermitteln [fɛr'mɪtəln], **1.** *v.i.* mediate, intervene, intercede, act as mediator (***bei,*** in). **2.** *v.t.* 1. adjust, arrange, settle (*a difference etc.*); negotiate (*a peace, a loan etc.*); establish; ***widerstreitende Ideen –,*** reconcile conflicting ideas; 2. arrange, bring about, facilitate, obtain, get, secure, procure (*Dat.*, for), supply with; (*fig.*) impart (*knowledge*), convey, give (*impression*) (*Dat.*, to). **vermittelnd,** *adj.* intermediary, conciliatory; ***– eintreten,*** intercede. **vermittels,** (*Austr.*) **vermittelst,** *prep.* (*Gen.*) by means *or* by dint of, with the help of, through.
Vermittler(in) [fɛr'mɪtlər(ɪn)], *m.* (*f.*) mediator, arbiter, (*coll.*) go-between; (*Comm.*) agent, middleman. **Vermittlung,** *f.* mediation, agency, intercession, intervention; negotiation, settlement, arrangement, adjustment (*of differences*); conveyance, transmission (*of sound*); procuring, supplying, providing; (*Tele.*) exchange; ***durch seine freundliche –,*** by his good offices *or* kind intervention. **Vermittlungs|amt,** *n.* telephone exchange. **–ausschuß,** *m.* mediation board. **–gebühr,** *f.* commission, brokerage. **–geschäft,** *n.* (commission-)agency. **–provision,** *f. See* **–gebühr.** **–schrank,** *m.* (*Tele.*) switchboard. **–vorschlag,** *m.* offer of mediation; proposal for a settlement.
vermöbeln [fɛr'mø:bəln], *v.t.* (*coll.*) sell, turn into

cash; sell at any price, (*sl.*) flog; *see also* **verprügeln.**

vermodern [fɛr'mo:dərn], *v.i.* (*aux.* s.) moulder, (fall into) decay, rot.

vermöge [fɛr'mø:gə], *prep.* (*Gen.*) in *or* by virtue of, by dint of; owing to, on the strength of, according to, in pursuance of.

vermögen [fɛr'mø:gən], *irr.v.t.* be able to do, be capable of doing; be able (***zu tun,*** to do), be capable (of doing), have the power *or* capacity, be in a position (to do); ***ich will tun, was ich vermag,*** I will do all that lies in my power; ***viel bei ihm –,*** have influence with him; ***wenn er es über sich vermag,*** if he can bring himself to do it; ***ihn zu etwas –,*** induce him *or* prevail upon him to do s.th.

Vermögen, *n.* 1. ability, capacity, power; ***alles was in meinem – steht,*** all that lies in my power; ***nach bestem –,*** to the best of one's ability; ***das geht über mein –,*** that is beyond me *or* outside my power; 2. fortune, property, wealth, riches, means; ***ein – verdienen,*** make a fortune; ***zu – kommen,*** come into a fortune. **vermögend,** *adj.* 1. rich, well-to-do, wealthy, affluent, propertied, (*pred.*) well off; 2. powerful, influential.

Vermögens|abgabe, *f.* capital levy. **–anfall,** *m.* succession to property. **–anlage,** *f.* capital asset. **–aufstellung,** *f.* financial statement. **–bestand,** *m.* amount of property, assets. **–bilanz,** *f. See* **–aufstellung. –gegenstand,** *m.* asset. **–masse,** *f.* estate. **–recht,** *n.* law of property. **vermögensrechtlich,** *adj.* under the law of property; ***–e Ansprüche,*** action for recovery of one's property. **Vermögens|steuer,** *f.* property tax. **–umstände,** *m.pl.*, **–verhältnisse,** *n.pl.* financial position, means, resources; ***in angenehmen –n,*** in easy circumstances. **–verwalter,** *n.* administrator of an estate, trustee. **–werte,** *n.pl. See* **–bestand. –zuwachssteuer,** *f.* capital gains tax.

vermorscht [fɛr'mɔrʃt], *adj.* mouldering, mouldy, rotten.

vermottet [fɛr'mɔtət], *adj.* moth-eaten.

vermummen [fɛr'mumən], *v.t.* wrap *or* muffle up; mask, disguise. **Vermummung,** *f.* masquerade, mummery.

vermuten [fɛr'mu:tən], *v.t.* suppose, surmise, presume, assume, (*coll.*) gather; expect, imagine, conjecture, suspect, (*coll.*) have an idea *or* (*Am.*) hunch that, (*Am.*) guess; ***nichts Arges –,*** suspect no harm *or* nothing wrong. **Vermuten,** *n.* supposition, expectation; ***meinem – nach,*** in my opinion, as I imagine, (*coll.*) my guess is.

vermutlich [fɛr'mu:tlɪç], **1.** *adj.* presumable, supposed, (*Law*) presumptive; probable, likely. **2.** *adv.* presumably, supposedly, probably, (*coll.*) likely; I suppose.

Vermutung [fɛr'mu:tuŋ], *f.* presumption, supposition, conjecture, surmise, expectation; speculation, guess(work), (*sl.*) hunch; ***gegen alle –,*** contrary to all expectation(s); ***aller – nach,*** to all appearances; ***das brachte ihn auf die –,*** that gave him the idea; ***–en anstellen über*** (*Acc.*), speculate about.

vernachlässigen [fɛr'naxlɛsɪgən], *v.t.* neglect, be negligent about *or* neglectful of *or* in. **Vernachlässigung,** *f.* negligence; neglect, dereliction (*of duty*).

vernageln [fɛr'na:gəln], *v.t.* nail, nail up (*a crate*), nail down (*a lid*); (*Mil.*) ***eine Kanone –,*** spike a gun. **vernagelt,** *adj.* (*coll.*) thick- *or* block-headed, dense; ***ich bin wie –,*** my mind is a blank.

vernähen [fɛr'nɛ:ən], *v.t.* sew up.

vernarben [fɛr'narbən], *v.r.*, *v.i.* (*aux.* s.) heal up, scar over.

vernarren [fɛr'narən], *v.r.* become infatuated, fall madly in love (***in*** (*Acc.*), with), be crazy (about), (*sl.*) be gone *or* nuts (on); ***in das Kind vernarrt sein,*** dote on the child.

vernaschen [fɛr'naʃən], *v.t.* ***sein Geld –,*** spend all *or* waste one's money on sweets.

vernebeln [fɛr'ne:bəln], **1.** *v.t.* (*Mil.*) cover with a smoke-screen, screen with smoke. **2.** *v.i.* (*aux.* s.) become obscured, become wreathed in mist. **Vernebelung,** *f.* (*Mil.*) (laying a) smoke-screen.

vernehmbar [fɛr'ne:mba:r], *adj. See* **vernehmlich. vernehmen,** *irr.v.t.* 1. perceive, become aware of; hear, learn, understand; (*Eccl.*) ***vernimm mein Gebet!*** hearken to my prayer! ***– lassen,*** express one's opinion about, declare, intimate; ***sich – lassen,*** make o.s. heard, obtain a hearing; 2. (*Law*) question, interrogate, examine.

Vernehmen [fɛr'ne:mən], *n.* ***dem – nach,*** according to report, from what one hears, rumour has it that; ***gutem*** or ***sicherem – nach,*** we have it on good authority; ***gutes –,*** friendly terms, good understanding; ***im – mit,*** in agreement with.

Vernehmlassung [fɛr'ne:mlasuŋ], *f.* (*Swiss*) notification, promulgation.

vernehmlich [fɛr'ne:mlɪç], *adj.* audible, perceptible, (*pred.*) within ear-shot; distinct, clear.

Vernehmung [fɛr'ne:muŋ], *f.* questioning, interrogation, examination. **Vernehmungsbeamte(r),** *m.* interrogator. **vernehmungsfähig,** *adj.* (*Law*) fit to plead. **Vernehmungsoffizier,** *m.* interrogating officer.

verneigen [fɛr'naɪgən], *v.r.* bow, curtsy (***vor*** (*Dat.*), to). **Verneigung,** *f.* bow, curts(e)y, obeisance.

verneinen [fɛr'naɪnən], **1.** *v.t.* deny, disavow; answer (*a question*) in the negative, say no to. **2.** *v.i.* reply in the negative, say no; ***er verneinte,*** his answer was no. **verneinend,** *adj.* negative. **Verneinung,** *f.* denial, negation; (*Gram.*) negative. **Verneinungs|satz,** *m.* negative clause. **–wort,** *n.* negative.

vernichten [fɛr'nɪçtən], *v.t.* annihilate, exterminate, eradicate; destroy; dash, shatter, disappoint (*hopes*). **vernichtend,** *adj.* destructive, devastating; (*fig.*) devastating, crushing (*blow, defeat etc.*), withering (*glance*), scathing (*reply, criticism*). **Vernichtung,** *f.* destruction, annihilation, extermination, eradication. **Vernichtungs|feuer,** *n.* annihilating fire. **–krieg,** *m.* war of extermination. **–lager,** *n.* (*Nat. Soc.*) extermination camp. **–mittel,** *n.* weed-killer.

vernickeln [fɛr'nɪkəln], *v.t.* nickel-plate.

verniedlichen [fɛr'ni:tlɪçən], *v.t.* minimize, (*coll.*) play down, prettify.

vernieten [fɛr'ni:tən], *v.t.* rivet (together).

Vernunft [fɛr'nunft], *f.* reason; understanding, judgement, common- *or* good sense; ***– annehmen,*** listen to reason; ***bei guter – sein,*** be in one's senses; ***die Jahre der – erreichen,*** arrive at years of discretion; ***gesunde –,*** common-sense; ***ihm – predigen,*** plead with him to be reasonable; ***das geht über die*** or ***alle –,*** that goes beyond the bounds of reason; ***ihn zur – bringen,*** bring him to his senses, make him listen to reason; ***zur – kommen,*** come to one's senses. **vernunftbegabt,** *adj.* reasonable, sensible. **Vernunft|beweis,** *m.* rational proof. **–ehe,** *f.* prudential match, marriage of convenience.

Vernünftelei [fɛrnynftə'laɪ], *f.* (-, *pl.* **-en**) sophistry, chicanery, casuistry, subtlety, quibbling, hair-splitting. **vernünfteln** [–'nynftəln], *v.i.* reason speciously, subtilize, (*coll.*) split hairs.

vernunftgemäß [fɛr'nunftgəmɛ:s], *adj.* reasonable, rational, logical. **Vernunft|glaube,** *m.* rationalism, rational belief. **–grund,** *m.* rational argument; ***aus Vernunftgründen,*** a priori.

vernünftig [fɛr'nynftɪç], *adj.* reasonable, sensible, rational, level-headed, wise, judicious; ***–e Wesen,*** rational beings; ***–er Mann,*** sensible *or* reasonable man; ***– handeln,*** act sensibly *or* reasonably *or* judiciously *or* wisely; ***– reden,*** talk sense. **vernünftigerweise,** *adv.* from a rational point of view; ***– kommt er nicht,*** he has the good sense not to come.

vernunftlos [fɛrnunftlo:s], *adj.* irrational, unreasonable, senseless, unreasoning. **vernunft|mäßig,** *adj. See* **–gemäß. Vernunft|schluß,** *m.* syllogism. **–wesen,** *n.* rational being. **vernunftwidrig,** *adj.* contrary to reason, unreasonable, irrational, illogical.

veröden [fɛr'ø:dən], **1.** *v.t.* lay waste, devastate; depopulate. **2.** *v.i.* (*aux.* s.) become desolate *or* deserted *or* depopulated. **Verödung,** *f.* desolation; devastation; depopulation; – *des Verkehrs,* stagnation of the market.

veröffentlichen [fɛr'œfəntlɪçən], *v.t.* publish, announce, advertise, make public; *ein Gesetz –,* promulgate a law. **Veröffentlichung,** *f.* publication; (public) announcement, promulgation.

verordnen [fɛr'ɔrdnən], *v.t.* order, prescribe (*Dat.*, for); decree, enact; ordain, establish, institute; *ihm Ruhe –,* order him to rest *or* to take things easy, prescribe rest for him. **Verordnung,** *f.* (*Med.*) prescription; (*Pol. etc.*) decree, ordinance, regulation, order. **Verordnungsblatt,** *n.* official list, gazette. **verordnungs|gemäß, –mäßig,** *adj.* as decreed *or* prescribed, by order *or* appointment. **Verordnungsweg,** *m. auf dem –,* by decree.

verpachten [fɛr'paxtən], *v.t.* let, lease, farm out. **Verpächter,** *m.* lessor. **Verpachtung,** *f.* leasing, farming out, letting (out) on lease.

verpacken [fɛr'pakən], *v.t.* pack (up), wrap (up), (*Comm.*) package; (*coll.*) *hart verpackt,* dull of comprehension, slow on the uptake. **Verpacker,** *m.* packer. **Verpackung,** *f.* packing, wrapping, packaging; packing (material), wrapping (paper). **Verpackungsgewicht,** *n.* tare, dead weight.

verpäppeln [fɛr'pɛpəln], *v.t.* pamper, spoil (*a child*), (*coll.*) (molly)coddle.

verpassen [fɛr'pasən], *v.t.* let slip (*an opportunity*), miss (*a train*), pass (*cards etc.*); try on, fit on (*clothes etc.*); (*sl.*) *ihm eine* (*Ohrfeige*) or *eins –,* give *or* land *or* dot *or* paste him one.

verpatzen [fɛr'patsən], *v.t.* (*sl.*) spoil, bungle, botch, make a hash *or* mess of.

verpesten [fɛr'pɛstən], *v.t.* pollute, taint, defile, infect, poison. **Verpestung,** *f.* pollution, defilement, infection.

verpetzen [fɛr'pɛtsən], *v.t.* inform against, tell tales about.

verpfänden [fɛr'pfɛndən], *v.t.* pledge, pawn, mortgage; (*Naut.*) raise money by bottomry; *sein Wort –,* give *or* pledge one's word, promise faithfully. **Verpfändung,** *f.* pawning, mortgaging, pledging.

verpfeifen [fɛr'pfaɪfən], *irr.v.t.* (*coll.*) squeal *or* peach *or* grass on, shop.

verpflanzen [fɛr'pflantsən], *v.t.* transplant. **Verpflanzung,** *f.* transplanting, (*also Med.*) transplantation.

verpflegen [fɛr'pfle:gən], *v.t.* feed, cater for, provide for, board (*a p.*), provision (*an army*); tend, nurse (*an invalid*). **Verpflegung,** *f.* feeding, catering, food-supply; (*Mil.*) provisioning, messing; maintenance, support, alimentation; board, food, provisions, (*Mil.*) rations; (*Med.*) nursing; *gute –,* good table *or* food; *Wohnung mit –,* board and lodging.

Verpflegungs|amt, *n.* food office; (*Mil.*) commissariat. **–entschädigung,** *f.* maintenance allowance, board-wages (*of domestic staff*). **–geld,** *n.pl.* cost of maintenance, charge for board; maintenance *or* subsistence *or* (*Mil.*) ration allowance. **–kolonne,** *f.* (*Mil.*) supply-column. **–mittel,** *n.pl.* victuals, provisions. **–offizier,** *m.* messing officer. **–satz,** *m.* ration (scale), daily ration. **–stärke,** *f.* (*Mil.*) ration strength. **–unteroffizier,** *m.* mess sergeant.

verpflichten [fɛr'pflɪçtən], **1.** *v.t.* bind, pledge, engage, oblige; *ihn eidlich –,* bind him on oath; *zu Dank –,* place *or* lay under an obligation; *wir sind Ihnen sehr zu Dank verpflichtet,* we are greatly indebted *or* obliged to you; *zu pünktlicher Zahlung verpflichtet,* liable for prompt payment; *sich verpflichtet fühlen,* feel bound, feel under an obligation. **2.** *v.r.* bind *or* commit o.s., engage, undertake, (*Law*) covenant (*zu etwas,* to do a th.). **verpflichtend,** *adj.* binding, obligatory. **Verpflichtung,** *f.* obligation, duty, responsibility; undertaking, engagement, commitment; pledge, liability; *seinen –en nachkommen,* fulfil one's obligations, (*Comm.*) meet one's liabilities; *–(en) haben gegen,* be under an obligation to; *eine – eingehen,* undertake an obligation, assume *or* incur liability.

verpfuschen [fɛr'pfuʃən], *v.t.* bungle, botch, make a mess of, wreck (*one's life etc.*).

verpichen [fɛr'pɪçən], *v.t.* (coat with) pitch *or* tar, stop with pitch.

verpimpeln [fɛr'pɪmpəln], *v.t.*, (*v.r.*) (*coll.*) coddle (o.s.), pamper (o.s.), muffle (o.s.) up (*in too many clothes*).

verplanen [fɛr'pla:nən], *v.t.* plan *or* budget for.

verplappern [fɛr'plapərn], *v.r.* (*coll.*) give o.s. away, blab, let the cat out of the bag.

verplaudern [fɛr'plaudərn], **1.** *v.t.* chatter (*time etc.*) away. **2.** *v.r. See* **verplappern.**

verplempern [fɛr'plɛmpərn], **1.** *v.t.* fritter away, squander, waste foolishly. **2.** *v.r.* fritter away one's energies; waste one's opportunities, make a mess of one's life; throw o.s. away on a (*socially inferior or worthless*) woman, marry beneath o.s.

verpönen [fɛr'pø:nən], *v.t.* (*obs.*) forbid, prohibit. **verpönt** *adj.* prohibited, taboo(ed); despised, in bad taste.

verprassen [fɛr'prasən], *v.t.* waste in riotous living, dissipate, (*coll.*) get through (*one's money*).

verproviantieren [fɛrprovian'ti:rən], *v.t.* supply, victual, provision.

verprügeln [fɛr'pry:gəln], *v.t.* thrash soundly, trounce, (*coll.*) beat up.

verpuffen [fɛr'pufən], **1.** *v.t.* throw away, scatter to the winds, waste. **2.** *v.i.* (*aux.* s.) detonate, explode, fulminate, deflagrate, decrepitate; (*coll.*) peter *or* fizzle out, go up in smoke, fall flat (*as a joke*).

verpulvern [fɛr'pulvərn], *v.t.* (*coll.*) squander, blue.

verpumpen [fɛr'pumpən], *v.t.* (*sl.*) give on tick.

verpuppen [fɛr'pupən], *v.r.*, *v.i.* pupate, change into a chrysalis; (*coll.*) retire into one's shell. **Verpuppung,** *f.* pupation.

verpusten [fɛr'pustən], *v.r.* (*coll.*) recover one's breath, get one's wind back.

Verputz [fɛr'puts], *m.* plaster, roughcast. **verputzen,** *v.t.* plaster, rough-cast; (*coll.*) squander, blue; (*coll.*) gobble up, polish off; *das kann ich nicht –,* I cannot stomach *or* stand that.

verqualmt [fɛr'kvalmt], *adj.* smoky, smoke-filled, (*pred.*) filled *or* thick with smoke.

verquasen [fɛr'kva:zən], *v.t.* (*dial.*) squander.

verquer [fɛr'kve:r], *adv.* (*coll.*) *mir geht das –,* that upsets my plans *or* puts a spoke in my wheel.

verquicken [fɛr'kvɪkən], *v.t.* amalgamate (*mit* with); mix up (with). **Verquickung,** *f.* amalgamation, fusion.

verquisten [fɛr'kvɪstən], *v.t.* (*dial.*) *see* **verquasen.**

verquollen [fɛr'kvɔlən], *adj.* swollen, bloated (*of a face*), warped (*of wood*).

verramme(l)n [fɛr'ramə(l)n], *v.t.* ram tight; bar, barricade, block (up).

verramschen [fɛr'ramʃən], *v.t.* (*coll.*) sell at a loss, sell dirt-cheap.

verrannt [fɛr'rant], *adj.* – *sein in* (*Acc.*), be enamoured *or* wedded to *or* stubbornly attached to *or* (*sl.*) stuck on (*an idea*). **Verranntheit,** *f.* stubborn attachment, wrongheadedness, bigotry.

Verrat [fɛr'ra:t], *m.* betrayal (*an* (*Dat.*), of), treachery, (*Pol.*) treason (to); – *an ihm begehen,* betray him; – *militärischer Geheimnisse,* disclosure of military secrets. **verraten, 1.** *irr.v.t.* betray, divulge, disclose, (*coll.*) give away; (*fig.*) reveal, show, give evidence of, manifest, betray, bespeak; *das Vaterland dem Feind –,* betray one's country to the enemy; (*coll.*) *alles –,* give the show away; *ein Geheimnis –,* betray *or* divulge a secret. **2.** *irr.v.r.* betray o.s., (*coll.*) give o.s. away.

Verräter [fɛr'rɛ:tər], *m.* traitor; betrayer, informer; *er ist ein – an seinem Vaterlande,* he is a traitor to his country; *er ist an mir zum – geworden,* he has betrayed me *or* has behaved treacherously towards me. **Verräterei** [–'raɪ], *f.* treachery. **Verräterin,** *f.* traitress. **verräterisch,** *adj.* treacherous, treasonable, traitorous; faithless, perfidious; (*fig.*) revealing, (*coll.*) tell-tale.

verrauchen [fɛr'rauxən], **1.** *v.t.* spend (*time etc.*) in smoking *or* (*money*) on tobacco. **2.** *v.i.* (*aux.* s.) evaporate, go up in smoke; (*fig.*) subside, pass *or* (*coll.*) blow over (*as anger*).

verräuchern [fɛr'rɔyçərn], *v.t.* fill *or* blacken with smoke. **verräuchert,** *adj.* smoke-blackened, (*pred.*) thick with smoke.

verraucht [fɛr'rauxt], *adj.* smoke-dried, (*pred.*) black with smoke.

verrauschen [fɛr'rauʃən], *v.i.* (*aux.* s.) (*fig.*) die away, subside; pass away, roll on (*of time*).

verrechnen [fɛr'rɛçnən], **1.** *v.t.* reckon up, charge (to account); balance, set off (*mit,* against). **2.** *v.r.* make a mistake in one's accounts, miscalculate; (*fig.*) be mistaken, (*coll.*) be out in one's reckoning; ***er hat sich um 20 Mark verrechnet,*** he is 20 marks out (in his accounts). **Verrechnung,** *f.* 1. charging to account, settlement (of an account), settling; reckoning up, calculation; (*on cheques*) ***nur zur –,*** not negotiable; 2. error in calculation, miscalculation.

Verrechnungs|abkommen, *n.* clearing (agreement). **–konto,** *n.* offset-account. **–scheck,** *m.* crossed cheque, non-negotiable cheque. **–stelle,** *f.* clearing-house. **–verkehr,** *m.* clearing(-business).

verrecken [fɛr'rɛkən], *v.i.* (*aux.* s.) (*of animals*) die, perish; (*sl.*) croak, turn up one's toes, kick the bucket, snuff it; (*sl.*) ***nicht ums Verrecken,*** not on your life.

verregnen [fɛr're:gnən], *v.t.* spoil by rain. **verregnet,** *adj.* rainy, (*coll.*) washed out.

verreiben [fɛr'raɪbən], *irr.v.t.* rub well, rub in (*ointment*); rub away; rub *or* grind down, triturate.

verreisen [fɛr'raɪzən], **1.** *v.i.* (*aux.* s.) go on a journey; set out, leave (*nach,* for); ***wie lange ist er verreist?*** how long has he been away (from home)? **2.** *v.t.* spend (*money or time*) travelling.

verreißen [fɛr'raɪsən], *irr.v.t.* (*coll.*) pull to pieces, run down (*with criticism*).

verrenken [fɛr'rɛŋkən], *v.t.* dislocate, sprain, put out of joint, (*Med.*) luxate; (*coll.*) ***sich*** (*Dat.*) ***den Hals –,*** crane one's neck. **Verrenkung,** *f.* dislocation, sprain, (*Med.*) luxation.

verrennen [fɛr'rɛnən], *irr.v.r.* ***sich – in*** (*Acc.*), *see under* **verrannt**; ***sich in eine Sackgasse –,*** run one's head against a brick wall.

verrichten [fɛr'rɪçtən], *v.t.* do, perform, carry out, execute; achieve, accomplish, acquit o.s. of; ***seine Andacht –,*** be at prayer, perform one's devotions; ***einen Auftrag –,*** execute *or* carry out a commission; ***seine Dienste –,*** (*of a p.*) officiate, be on duty; (*of a th.*) work well, answer the purpose; ***sein Gebet –,*** say one's prayers; ***Geschäfte –,*** transact business; ***seine Notdurft –,*** ease nature, relieve o.s. **Verrichtung,** *f.* performance, execution; accomplishment, achievement, discharge (*of business*); work, action, business, function; ***tägliche –en,*** daily work, routine jobs; ***ich wünsche Ihnen gute –,*** I wish you much success, I hope everything goes off well; ***ich bin mit seiner – zufrieden,*** I am satisfied with his achievement.

verriegeln [fɛr'ri:gəln], *v.t.* bolt, bar; (*Mil.*) cut off, encircle.

verringern [fɛr'rɪŋərn], **1.** *v.t.* diminish, lessen, decrease, reduce, attenuate, (*fig.*) extenuate; (*coll.*) cut down. **2.** *v.r.* diminish, decrease, grow less. **Verringerung,** *f.* decrease, reduction, diminution, attenuation.

verrinnen [fɛr'rɪnən], *irr.v.i.* (*aux.* s.) run off *or* away *or* out, (*fig.*) pass away, elapse, fly (*of time*).

verröcheln [fɛr'rœçəln], *v.i.* breathe one's last.

verrohen [fɛr'ro:ən], **1.** *v.t.* brutalize. **2.** *v.i.* become brutal *or* savage. **Verrohung,** *f.* brutalization.

verrollen [fɛr'rɔlən], **1.** *v.i.* (*aux.* s.) roll away, die away. **2.** *v.r.* (*coll.*) toddle off.

verrosten [fɛr'rɔstən], *v.i.* (*aux.* s.) rust, get rusty, corrode.

verrotten [fɛr'rɔtən], *v.i.* (*aux.* s.) rot, decay. **verrottet,** *adj.* rotten.

verrucht [fɛr'ru:xt], *adj.* infamous, vile, heinous, wicked, nefarious. **Verruchtheit,** *f.* infamy, wickedness, villainy.

verrücken [fɛr'rykən], *v.t.* displace, move (out of place), shift, remove; disarrange, derange, disturb, confuse, unsettle; ***seinen Plan*** or ***ihm den Plan –,*** upset *or* frustrate his plan; ***ihm den Kopf –,*** turn his head. **verrückt,** *adj.* mad, deranged, crazy, (*coll.*) cracked, barmy, batty, potty, nuts (***auf*** (*Acc.*), about); ***– nach,*** mad on, crazy for; ***du bist wohl –,*** you're off your head *or* (*sl.*) chump, you're crazy; ***wie –,*** like mad. **Verrückte(r),** *m., f.* lunatic, madman. **Verrücktheit,** *f.* mental derangement, madness; crazy *or* mad *or* foolish action *or* craze.

Verruf [fɛr'ru:f], *m.* (**-(e)s,** *pl.* **-e**) obloquy, disparagement; ill repute; ***in – bringen,*** bring into discredit *or* disrepute; ***in – sein,*** be notorious, be under a cloud, (*coll.*) be in bad odour; ***in – kommen,*** fall into disrepute *or* discredit; ***in – tun,*** boycott, taboo. **verrufen, 1.** *irr.v.t.* decry, disparage, condemn; give a bad name to, (*coll.*) bring into bad odour, cry down; withdraw (*coin*) from circulation. **2.** *adj.* notorious, infamous, ill-famed; discredited, (*pred.*) in disrepute.

verrühren [fɛr'ry:rən], *v.t.* mix, stir, whip, whisk, beat up (*eggs etc.*).

verrußen [fɛr'rusən], **1.** *v.t.* cover with soot, make sooty. **2.** *v.i.* (*aux.* s.) become sooty *or* sooted *or* smoked.

verrutschen [fɛr'rutʃən], *v.i.* (*aux.* s.) slip; get *or* slip out of place, become displaced.

Vers [fɛrs], *m.* (**-es,** *pl.* **-e**) verse, poetry; line (*of verse*); strophe, stanza; verse (*of the Bible*); ***in -e bringen,*** put into verse; ***ich kann mir keinen – daraus*** (or ***darauf***) ***machen,*** I cannot make head or tail of it; ***-e schmieden,*** hammer out verses, versify.

versacken [fɛr'zakən], *v.i.* (*aux.* s.) sink, go down (*of a ship*); (*fig.*) become blocked, make no headway, (*coll.*) be ditched, get bogged down.

versagen [fɛr'za:gən], **1.** *v.t.* deny, refuse; ***versagt haben,*** have already promised; ***versagt sein,*** be engaged; (*of a th.*) ***den Dienst –,*** fail to work *or* function; ***die Beine – mir den Dienst,*** my legs fail me *or* refuse to carry me; ***dieses Glück ist mir versagt,*** this happiness is denied to me; ***sich*** (*Dat.*) ***etwas –,*** deny o.s. a th., deprive o.s. of a th., forgo a th.; ***sie ist*** (***bereits***) ***versagt,*** she is (already) promised in marriage, she is engaged (to be married). **2.** *v.i.* fail, fail to work, break down, miss fire; ***sie haben versagt,*** they have failed *or* disappointed, they have not come up to expectations.

Versagen, *n.* failure, breakdown. **Versager,** *m.* 1. misfire, (*coll.*) dud; stoppage, breakdown; 2. (*of a p.*) failure, (*coll.*) wash-out, flop; 3. blank (*lottery ticket*). **Versagung,** *f.* refusal, denial.

Versalbuchstabe [fɛr'za:lbu:xʃta:bə], *m.* (**-n,** *pl.* **-n** *or* **Versalien**) (*Typ.*) capital letter, initial.

versalzen [fɛr'zaltsən], *v.t.* (*p.p.* ***versalzt***) oversalt; (*fig.*) (*p.p.* ***versalzen***) ***ihm ein Vergnügen –,*** spoil *or* mar his pleasure; (*coll.*) ***ihm die Suppe –,*** make it hot for him, give him what for *or* what's what.

versammeln [fɛr'zaməln], **1.** *v.t.* assemble, bring together, gather, collect; convoke, convene; ***die Truppen –,*** rally the troops; ***zu seinen Vätern versammelt werden,*** be gathered to one's fathers. **2.** *v.r.* meet, assemble, hold a meeting, gather, come together. **Versammlung,** *f.* assembly, gathering, meeting, congress, convention, convocation, congregation, concourse; ***eine – sprengen,*** break up a meeting; ***gesetzgebende –,*** legislative assembly.

Versammlungs|freiheit, *f.* right of assembly. **–haus,** *n.* assembly rooms, meeting-house. **–ort, –platz,** *m.* meeting-place, rendezvous, (*Mil.*) rallying *or* assembly point. **–raum,** *m.* (*Mil.*) assembly area. **–recht,** *n. See* **–freiheit. –zimmer,** *n.* 1. assembly hall; 2. (*Theat.*) greenroom.

Versand [fɛr'zant], *m.* dispatch, forwarding, mailing, delivery, conveyance; shipment, export(ation).

Versand|abteilung, *f.* dispatch *or* forwarding department. **–anweisung,** *f.* forwarding *or* shipping instructions. **–anzeige,** *f.* dispatch note. **–artikel,** *m.* article for export, *pl.* export goods, exports. **versandbereit,** *adj.* ready for dispatch. **Versandbier,** *n.* export beer.

versanden [fɛr'zandən], **1.** *v.t.* cover *or* fill up *or* choke with sand. **2.** *v.i.* (*aux.* s.) become covered *or* choked with sand, silt up; (*fig.*) get stuck, get bogged down, make no headway, reach a deadlock.

versand|fertig, *adj.* *See* **–bereit. Versand|geschäft,** *n.* mail-order business. **–kosten,** *f.pl.* forwarding costs, delivery charges. **–rechnung,** *f.* bill for delivery. **–spesen,** *f.pl.* *See* **–kosten. –wechsel,** *m.* foreign bill.

Versart ['fɛrsˀa:rt], *f.* verse form, metre.

Versatz [fɛr'zats], *m.* 1. pledging, pawning; ***in – geben,*** pledge, pawn; 2. (*Min.*) rubble, refuse. **Versatz|amt, –haus,** *n.* pawn-shop, loan-bank. **–mauer,** *f.* (*Min.*) partition-wall, embankment. **–stück,** *n.* (*Theat.*) movable scenery, set.

versauen [fɛr'zauən], *v.t.* (*sl.*) make a mess *or* muck of, mess *or* muck up.

versauern [fɛr'zauərn], **1.** *v.i.* (*aux.* s.) turn sour; (*fig.*) get rusty *or* stale (*of the mind*), vegetate; become moody *or* morose.

versäuern [fɛr'zɔyərn], *v.t.* acidify, sour; (*fig.*) spoil, embitter.

versaufen [fɛr'saufən], **1.** *irr.v.t.* (*sl.*) waste (*time etc.*) drinking, squander (*money*) on drink. **2.** *irr.v.i.* (*aux.* s.) (*coll.*) *see* **ersaufen.**

versäumen [fɛr'zɔymən], *v.t.* neglect (*one's duty*), miss, let slip (*opportunity*); omit, fail (***zu tun,*** to do); ***den Appell –,*** be absent at roll-call; ***den Zug –,*** miss the train; ***Versäumtes nachholen,*** recover lost ground, make up leeway, (*coll.*) catch up. **Versäumnis,** *n.* **(-ses,** *pl.* **-se)** neglect, (sin of) omission; failure (to appear), late arrival; loss of time, delay. **Versäumnisurteil,** *n.* (*Law*) judgement by default.

Versbau ['fɛrsbau], *m.* metrical structure, versification.

verschachern [fɛr'ʃaxərn], *v.t.* sell off, barter away.

verschachteln [fɛr'ʃaxtəln], *v.t.* interlock; (*Gram.*) ***verschachtelter Satz,*** involved period.

verschaffen [fɛr'ʃafən], *v.t.* get, obtain, secure, procure (*Dat.,* for); supply, provide, furnish (with); ***sich*** (*Dat.*) ***Arbeit –,*** find work; ***was verschafft mir die Ehre Ihres Besuches?*** to what do I owe the pleasure of your visit? ***sich*** (*Dat.*) ***Gehör –,*** obtain a hearing; ***sich*** (*Dat.*) ***Geld –,*** raise money; ***sich*** (*Dat.*) ***Geltung –,*** secure recognition; ***sich*** (*Dat.*) ***Genugtuung –,*** obtain satisfaction; ***sich*** (*Dat.*) ***Gewißheit –,*** reassure o.s.; ***dies wird Ihnen Linderung –,*** this will give you relief; ***ihm Recht –,*** see that justice is done to him; ***sich*** (*Dat.*) (***selbst***) ***Recht –,*** take the law into one's own hands; ***er verschafft sich*** (*Dat.*) ***Respekt,*** he ensures that proper respect is shown to him; ***sich*** (*Dat.*) ***einen Vorteil –,*** gain an advantage. **Verschaffung,** *f.* supply, provision.

verschalen [fɛr'ʃa:lən], *v.t.* case (in); board *or* plank *or* box in; (*Naut.*) fish (*a mast*), cover with boards *or* planks.

verschallen [fɛr'ʃalən], *irr.v.i.* (*aux.* s.) die away (*of sound*); be forgotten, sink into oblivion; *see* **verschollen.**

Verschalung [fɛr'ʃa:luŋ], *f.* planking, boarding, (*Mil.*) revetment; covering, casing, (*Build.*) form, mould (*for concrete*); (*Av.*) fairing, cowling.

verschämt [fɛr'ʃɛ:mt], *adj.* bashful, modest; shamefaced, abashed; ***–e Arme,*** deserving poor; ***– tun,*** put on a bashful air. **Verschämtheit,** *f.* bashfulness, modesty; shamefacedness.

verschandeln [fɛr'ʃandəln], *v.t.* (*coll.*) ruin, disfigure; murder (*language*).

verschanzen [fɛr'ʃantsən], **1.** *v.t.* entrench, fortify. **2.** *v.r.* entrench o.s., (*fig.*) (take) shelter (***hinter*** (*Dat.*), behind). **verschanzt,** *adj.* entrenched, sheltered, secure, dug in. **Verschanzung,** *f.* entrenchment, fortification, earthworks, trenches; (*fig.*) sheltered *or* secure position.

verschärfen [fɛr'ʃɛrfən], *v.t.* heighten, sharpen, intensify, add to, aggravate, make worse; tighten up (*regulations etc.*); ***das Tempo –,*** increase the pace. **Verschärfung,** *f.* increase, intensification, sharpening, heightening, aggravation, tightening up.

verscharren [fɛr'ʃarən], *v.t.* bury secretly *or* hurriedly, cover with earth.

verschätzen [fɛr'ʃɛtsən], *v.r.* be out in one's reckoning, miscalculate.

verschäumen [fɛr'ʃɔymən], *v.i.* (*aux.* s.) turn into froth, vanish in spray.

verscheiden [fɛr'ʃaɪdən], *irr.v.i.* (*aux.* s.) (*Poet.*) pass away, expire. **Verscheiden,** *n.* decease, passing; ***am – sein, im – liegen,*** be on the point of death.

verschenken [fɛr'ʃɛŋkən], *v.t.* give away, make a present of; (*coll.*) ***den Sieg –,*** throw away the victory; ***sein Herz –,*** give one's heart, bestow one's affections; ***Bier –,*** sell *or* serve beer.

verscherzen [fɛr'ʃɛrtsən], *v.t.* ***den Abend –,*** spend the evening frivolously; ***sich*** (*Dat.*) ***etwas –,*** lose *or* forfeit a th. (frivolously); ***sein Glück –,*** frivolously throw away one's chance of happiness; ***verscherzte Jugend,*** youth spent in frivolity. **Verscherzen,** *n.,* **Verscherzung,** *f.* loss, forfeiture.

verscheuchen [fɛr'ʃɔyçən], *v.t.* chase *or* drive *or* (*coll.*) shoo off, scare away; (*fig.*) banish (*care etc.*).

verschicken [fɛr'ʃɪkən], *v.t.* send out (*invitations etc.*); evacuate, send away (*children etc. into the country*); forward, dispatch, send away (*goods*); deport (*a criminal*). **Verschickung,** *f.* evacuation; forwarding, dispatch; transportation, deportation.

verschiebbar [fɛr'ʃi:pba:r], *adj.* movable, sliding, adjustable. **Verschiebebahnhof,** *m.* (*Railw.*) shunting *or* marshalling yard.

verschieben [fɛr'ʃi:bən], **1.** *irr.v.i.* move (out of place), remove, shift, displace, disarrange; postpone, defer, delay, adjourn, (*coll.*) put off; (*Railw.*) shunt; sell on *or* through the black-market; (*Math.*) ***verschobenes Viereck,*** lozenge. **2.** *irr.v.r.* get out of place, shift. **Verschiebung,** *f.* displacement, shifting; slip, shift, fluctuation; (*Geol.*) dislocation; delay, postponement, adjournment; (*Comm.*) illicit sale; (*Psych.*) transference. **Verschiebungsstrom,** *m.* (*Elec.*) displacement current.

[1]**verschieden** [fɛr'ʃi:dən], *p.p.* (*Poet.*) deceased, departed; *see* **verscheiden.**

[2]**verschieden,** *adj.* different, differing, distinct (***von,*** from); diverse, varied; dissimilar, unlike; *pl.* sundry, several, various, divers; ***himmelweit –,*** as different as day from night *or* as chalk from cheese; ***die Anlagen sind –,*** dispositions differ; ***–es zu tun haben,*** have sundry *or* various jobs to do; (*coll.*) ***da hört doch –es auf!*** that is really too much!

verschiedenartig [fɛr'ʃi:dənˀartɪç], *adj.* varied, various; heterogeneous, dissimilar, different, (*pred.*) of a different kind. **Verschiedenartigkeit,** *f.* difference; variety, heterogeneity. **verschiedenerlei,** *indecl.adj.* of various kinds, sundry, divers. **verschiedenfarbig,** *adj.* of a different colour, of different colours; variegated, varicoloured. **Verschiedenheit,** *f.* difference, diversity, variety; difference, disparity, variation, dissimilarity, discrepancy. **verschiedentlich, 1.** *adj.* several, repeated. **2.** *adv.* at (different) times, repeatedly, more than once, occasionally, now and then.

verschießen [fɛr'ʃi:sən], **1.** *irr.v.t.* 1. fire off, discharge, use up, expend (*ammunition*); (*fig.*) ***sein Pulver verschossen haben,*** have shot one's bolt, have come to the end of one's tether; 2. (*dial.*) forget, do wrong. **2.** *irr.v.r.* run out of ammunition; (*coll.*) ***sich in ihn –,*** fall madly in love with him. **3.** *irr.v.i.* (*aux.* s.) fade, discolour, become discoloured, lose colour; ***nicht –d,*** non-fading, fast (*of colour*); *see* **verschossen.**

verschiffen [fɛr'ʃɪfən], *v.t.* ship, send *or* transport by water; export (overseas). **Verschiffung,** *f.* shipment, exportation (overseas).

verschimmeln [fɛr'ʃɪməln], *v.i.* (*aux.* s.) get *or* go mouldy. **Verschimmelung,** *f.* mould, mouldiness.

verschimpfieren [fɛrʃɪmp'fi:rən], *v.t.* (*coll.*) call (*a p.*) names, pull (*a p.*) to pieces, throw mud at (*a p.*).

Verschiß [fɛr'ʃɪs], *m.* (*Studs. sl.*) disapproval, odium, bad odour.

verschlacken [fɛr'ʃlakən], *v.r., v.i.* (*aux.* s.) scorify, be reduced to dross *or* slag.

verschlafen [fɛr'ʃla:fən], **1.** *irr.v.t.* sleep away, spend *or* pass (*the time*) in sleeping; miss *or* lose by sleeping; sleep off (*effects of alcohol etc.*). **2.** *irr.v.r.* oversleep (o.s.). **3.** *adj.* sleepy, drowsy. **Verschlafenheit,** *f.* sleepiness, drowsiness.

Verschlag [fɛr'ʃla:k], *m.* (wooden) partition; compartment, room partitioned off, shed; (*dial.*) crate, box.

[1]**verschlagen** [fɛr'ʃla:gən], **1.** *irr.v.t.* 1. fasten with nails, nail up, board up, board off, partition off; ***mit Nägeln –,*** stud with nails, nail; ***mit Brettern –,*** board (up); ***ein Zimmer –,*** partition off a room; ***es verschlägt mir die Rede*** or ***Sprache,*** words fail me, I am dumbfounded; ***es verschlug mir die Luft*** or ***den Atem,*** it took my breath away; 2. nail badly, spoil with hammering; ***viele Nägel –,*** waste many nails; ***ein Pferd –,*** shoe a horse badly; 3. (*a ball*) mis-hit, knock too far; drive (*a ship*) off *or* out of its course *or* ashore *or* on to the shore; (*s.th. cold*) take the chill off; ***den Ball –,*** lose a ball, knock a ball out of bounds; ***der Sturm verschlug uns auf eine Insel,*** the storm drove us on to an island; (*Naut.*) ***– werden,*** be driven off course; ***in ein Dorf unter dummen Bauern – werden,*** find o.s. in a village among stupid peasants; ***die Seite im Buch –,*** lose one's place in a book; ***sich*** (*Dat.*) ***die Kunden –,*** drive away customers. **2.** *irr.v.imp.* (*Dat.*) (*only in neg. and inter. sentences*) avail, be of use, matter; ***was verschlägt's?*** what does it matter? ***das verschlägt nichts,*** that does not matter (at all *or* in the least); ***was verschlägt Ihnen das?*** what is that to you? ***nichts will bei ihm –,*** nothing has any effect on him; ***es will nichts –,*** it will be no good, it will be of no use, it will not do.

[2]**verschlagen,** *adj.* 1. (*of a p.*) cunning, crafty, sly, wily; (*of appearance*) shifty; 2. (*of water etc.*) tepid, lukewarm. **Verschlagenheit,** *f,* slyness, craftiness, cunning.

Verschlagwagen [fɛr'ʃla:kva:gən], *m.* crate car, cattle truck.

verschlammen [fɛr'ʃlamən], *v.i.* (*aux.* s.) get filled *or* choked with mud, silt up, become muddy.

verschlämmen [fɛr'ʃlɛmən], **1.** *v.t.* fill *or* choke *or* cover with mud. **2.** *v.r.* *See* **verschlammen.**

verschlampen [fɛr'ʃlampən], **1.** *v.t.* (*coll.*) lose *or* forget *or* ruin through neglect, take no care of. **2.** *v.i.* become slovenly, neglect o.s.

verschlechtern [fɛr'ʃlɛçtərn], **1.** *v.t.* impair, debase, spoil, make worse, change for the worse. **2.** *v.r.* get worse, worsen, (take a) change for the worse, deteriorate, degenerate, become debased, (*coll.*) fall off. **Verschlechterung,** *f.* worsening, change for the worse, deterioration, degeneration, debasement.

verschleiern [fɛr'ʃlaɪərn], *v.t.* veil, mask, conceal, (*Mil.*) screen (*an attack*); (*coll.*) fake, doctor, cook (*accounts*). **verschleiert,** *adj.* veiled; (*of sky*) hazy, overcast, (*of voice*) husky. **Verschleierung,** *f.* veiling, masking, screening, camouflage, concealment; (*coll.*) eyewash, window-dressing.

Verschleif [fɛr'ʃlaɪf], *m.* 1. (*Comm.*) disposal, sale (*of goods*); 2. (*Tech.*) abrasion, wear (and tear). **verschleifen, 1.** *reg.v.t.* 1. slur (*notes, syllables*); 2. (*Comm.*) dispose of, sell (*goods*). **2.** *irr.v.t.* rub away *or* off, scour, abrade.

verschleimen [fɛr'ʃlaɪmən], **1.** *v.t.* choke with phlegm *or* mucus; coat, fur (*tongue*), foul (*gun*). **2.** *v.r., v.i.* (*aux.* s.) be choked with phlegm *or* slime, become congested *or* slimy, (*of a gun*) get foul. **verschleimt,** *adj.* congested, slimy; coated, furred (*tongue*), fouled (*gun*).

Verschleiß [fɛr'ʃlaɪs], *m.* (**-es,** *pl.* **-e**) 1. abrasion, wear (and tear); corrosion; (*from water*) erosion; (*fig.*) attrition, wastage; 2. (*Austr.*) retail trade; general stores. **verschleißen, 1.** *irr.v.i.* (*aux.* s.), *v.r.* become worn, wear out; get wasted. **2.** *irr.v.t.* 1. use up; 2. (*Austr.*) sell, retail. **Verschleißer(in),** *m.*(*f.*) (*Austr.*) retail dealer, retailer. **Verschleiß|festigkeit,** *f.* abrasion resistance, resistance to wear and tear. **–spanne,** *f.* margin of profit, retail profit. **–stelle,** *f.* retail shop, (*usu.*) newspaper *or* tobacco kiosk.

verschlemmen [fɛr'ʃlɛmən], *v.t.* squander on food and drink *or* on riotous living.

verschleppen [fɛr'ʃlɛpən], **1.** *v.t.* 1. carry off, kidnap, abduct, (*Pol.*) deport, (*whole population*) displace; (*disease, infection*) carry, spread; 2. (*fig.*) delay, protract, (*coll.*) draw *or* drag out, (*Pol.*) obstruct. **2.** *v.r.* be protracted *or* (*coll.*) drawn out, (*coll.*) drag on and on. **Verschleppte(r),** *m., f.* (*Pol.*) displaced p. **Verschleppung,** *f.* 1. removal, carrying off; abduction; (*Pol.*) deportation, (*of population*) displacement; (*of disease etc.*) spread(ing), carrying; 2. (*fig.*) delay, procrastination, (*Pol.*) obstruction. **Verschleppungs|politik, –taktik,** *f.* (*Pol.*) obstructionism, (*Am.*) filibuster.

verschleudern [fɛr'ʃlɔydərn], *v.t.* waste, squander, dissipate, (*coll.*) throw away; (*Comm.*) sell below cost, sell at a loss, sell off (dirt) cheap; flood the market with, (*abroad*) dump. **Verschleuderung,** *f.* squandering, dissipation; (*Comm.*) underselling, (*abroad*) dumping.

verschließbar [fɛr'ʃli:sba:r], *adj.* lockable, (provided) with lock and key. **verschließen, 1.** *irr.v.t.* close, shut (up); lock (up), put under lock and key; bolt; (*fig.*) seal (*a letter*); block (up), obstruct; blockade (*a port etc.*); ***das Geheimnis in sich –,*** keep the secret to o.s.; ***sein Herz –,*** hide one's feelings (***gegen,*** from), steel one's heart (against); (*fig.*) ***die Augen –,*** shut one's eyes (***vor*** (*Dat.*), to), (*coll.*) wink (at). **2.** *irr.v.r.* shut o.s. off, remain aloof (*Dat.*, from), refuse to have anything to do (with), close one's mind (to); ***sich in sich selbst –,*** turn in on o.s., become wrapped up in o.s.

verschlimmbessern [fɛr'ʃlɪmbɛsərn], *v.t.* make worse instead of better.

verschlimmern [fɛr'ʃlɪmərn], **1.** *v.t.* make worse, aggravate, exacerbate. **2.** *v.r.* get worse, worsen, (take a) change for the worse, go from bad to worse, deteriorate. **Verschlimmerung,** *f.* worsening, change for the worse, deterioration; aggravation, exacerbation.

[1]**verschlingen** [fɛr'ʃlɪŋən], *irr.v.t.* devour, swallow *or* (*coll.*) gobble up, swallow *or* gulp down, (*coll.*) bolt, wolf (*one's food*); (*fig.*) engulf; ***viel Geld –,*** run away with a lot of money; (*fig.*) ***ein Buch –,*** devour a book (greedily); (*fig.*) ***mit den Augen –,*** stare at hungrily *or* open-mouthed.

[2]**verschlingen, 1.** *irr.v.t.* twist, interlace, (inter-) twine, entwine, entangle. **2.** *irr.v.r.* intertwine, become interlaced *or* entangled, get tangled up, be inextricably mixed; *see* **verschlungen. Verschlingung,** *f.* entwining, interlacing; festoon; intricacy, maze.

verschlissen [fɛr'ʃlɪsən], *adj.* worn (out), threadbare; *see* **verschleißen.**

verschlossen [fɛr'ʃlɔsən], *adj.* locked (up), closed, shut; (*fig.*) reserved, uncommunicative, close, taciturn; ***das bleibt mir –,*** that remains a mystery to me; ***–er Brief,*** sealed letter; ***hinter –en Türen,*** behind closed doors. **Verschlossenheit,** *f.* reserve, taciturnity.

verschlucken [fɛr'ʃlukən], **1.** *v.t.* swallow, (*Chem.*) absorb, (*fig.*) slur over (*one's words*). **2.** *v.r.* swallow the wrong way, choke; ***ich habe mich verschluckt,*** something has gone down the wrong way.

verschlungen [fɛr'ʃluŋən], *adj.* winding, tortuous (*path*), interwoven, intertwined; (*fig.*) complex, intricate; *see* **verschlingen.**

Verschluß [fɛr'ʃlus], *m.* lock, catch, clasp; seal, stopper, plug; fastener, fastening; (*Artil.*) breech (mechanism), lock; locker, cover; (*Phot.*) shutter; ***unter –,*** under lock and key; (*merchandise*) in bond;

Waren in – legen, bond goods; *aus dem – nehmen,* take out of bond. **Verschluß|auslösung,** *f.* (*Phot.*) shutter release. **–block,** *m.* (*Artil.*) breech-block. **–hahn,** *m.* stop-cock. **–laut,** *m.* (*Phonet.*) stop, plosive. **–mutter,** *f.* lock nut. **–schraube,** *f.* locking screw. **–stück,** *n.* plug, stopper, lid, (*Artil.*) breech-block. **–vorrichtung,** *f.* locking device.

verschlüsseln [fɛrˈʃlysəln], *v.t.* encode, encipher.

verschmachten [fɛrˈʃmaxtən], *v.i.* (*aux.* s.) languish, pine away; *vor Durst –,* be parched with *or* dying of thirst; *vor Hitze –,* be suffocated with (the) heat; *ihn – lassen,* let him die of thirst.

verschmähen [fɛrˈʃmɛ:ən], *v.t.* disdain, scorn, spurn, despise, reject; *verschmähte Liebe,* unrequited love.

verschmelzen [fɛrˈʃmɛltsən], **1.** *reg. & irr.v.t.* melt, smelt, fuse; blend, merge, amalgamate; *gut verschmolzene Farben,* well-blended colours. **2.** *irr.v.i.* (*aux.* s.) melt, fuse; blend, coalesce, merge. **Verschmelzung,** *f.* melting, fusion, smelting; blending, coalescence, (*fig.*) merger, amalgamation.

verschmerzen [fɛrˈʃmɛrtsən], *v.t.* console o.s. for, get over (the loss of), put up with, make the best of; *längst verschmerzt,* all over and forgotten.

verschmieren [fɛrˈʃmi:rən], **1.** *v.t.* smear (over), daub, stop up. **2.** *v.r.* become blurred, get misted over.

verschmitzt [fɛrˈʃmɪtst], *adj.* wily, artful, cunning, crafty, sly. **Verschmitztheit,** *f.* craftiness, cunning, slyness, wiliness.

verschmutzen [fɛrˈʃmutsən], **1.** *v.t.* dirty, soil, pollute. **2.** *v.i.* (*aux.* s.) get dirty *or* soiled, become foul *or* polluted.

verschnappen [fɛrˈʃnapən], *v.r.* (*coll.*) make a slip of the tongue, say a word too many, let the cat out of the bag, give the show away, spill the beans.

verschnauben [fɛrˈʃnaubən], **verschnaufen,** *v.r.* recover one's breath, stop for breath, (*coll. also fig.*) have a breather.

verschneiden [fɛrˈʃnaɪdən], *irr.v.t.* cut away, cut off, cut down; cut wrong *or* badly, spoil in cutting; clip, prune, lop; (*animals*) castrate, geld; (*wine etc.*) dilute, adulterate, blend; (*fig.*) *ihm die Flügel –,* clip his wings; *6 Meter Stoff zu einem Kleide –,* use *or* cut up 6 metres of material for a dress; *see* **verschnitten.**

verschneit [fɛrˈʃnaɪt], *adj.* snow-bound, (*pred.*) covered with snow, snowed up, (*roads etc.*), snow-covered, snow-capped (*peaks*).

Verschnitt [fɛrˈʃnɪt], *m.* blend, adulteration. **verschnitten,** *adj.* 1. castrated; *–er Hahn,* capon; *–er Stier,* bullock; *–es Tier,* gelding; 2. badly cut; *–es Kleidungsstück,* misfit (*article of clothing*); 3. blended; *–es Öl,* blended oil. **Verschnittene(r),** *m.* eunuch. **Verschnitt|mittel,** *n.* adulterant, diluent, reducing agent. **–wein,** *m.* blended *or* adulterated wine.

verschnörkeln [fɛrˈʃnœrkəln], *v.t.* adorn *or* disfigure with flourishes. **verschnörkelt,** *adj.* ornate, ornamented, flamboyant, florid.

verschnupfen [fɛrˈʃnupfən], *v.t.* (*coll.*) annoy, rattle, rile, nettle, pique, huff; (*coll.*) *das hat mich verschnupft,* I was put out by it. **verschnupft,** *adj.* *– sein,* have a cold (in the head), be stuffed up with (a) cold.

verschnüren [fɛrˈʃny:rən], *v.t.* lace *or* tie up.

verschollen [fɛrˈʃɔlən], *adj.* not heard of again, forgotten; (*of a p. or ship*) lost, missing; (*Law*) presumed dead; *er ist –,* he has disappeared *or* has never been heard of again, (*Law*) he is (missing and) presumed dead; *in –en Jahrhunderten,* in times of long ago *or* (*Poet.*) of yore. **Verschollene(r),** *m., f.* missing p. **Verschollenheit,** *f.* disappearance; prolonged absence; (*Law*) presumption of death.

verschonen [fɛrˈʃo:nən], *v.t.* spare, exempt (*mit,* from); *verschont bleiben mit,* be spared (*s.th.*), be exempt *or* exempted from.

verschönen [fɛrˈʃø:nən], (*usu.*) **verschönern,** *v.t.* beautify, embellish, adorn. **Verschönerung,** *f.* embellishment, (*coll.*) face-lift. **Verschönerungsverein,** *m.* society for the preservation of local amenities.

verschossen [fɛrˈʃɔsən], *adj.* faded, discoloured; (*coll.*) *– sein in* (*Acc.*), madly in love with, smitten with.

Verschränkbarkeit [fɛrˈʃrɛŋkba:rkaɪt], *f.* lock (*of steering axle*). **verschränken,** *v.t.* cross (*legs*), fold (*arms*), (*Tech.*) stagger; set (*teeth of a saw*).

verschrauben [fɛrˈʃraubən], *reg. & irr.v.t.* screw up *or* on *or* in; *miteinander –,* screw together. **Verschraubung,** *f.* screw cap, screw joint.

verschreiben [fɛrˈʃraɪbən], **1.** *irr.v.t.* 1. use up in writing; spend (*time*) in writing; 2. order, write, (*Med.*) prescribe (*Dat.,* for), (*Law*) assign, make over (to); 3. write incorrectly; miswrite (*a word*). **2.** *v.r.* 1. make a mistake in writing, make a slip of the pen; 2. give a written pledge; *sich dem Teufel –,* sell o.s. to the devil. **Verschreibung,** *f.* order, prescription; assignment; written promise *or* undertaking, bond.

verschreien [fɛrˈʃraɪən], *irr.v.t.* decry, cry down, give a bad name to, cast a slur on. **verschrien,** *adj.* in ill repute, in bad odour; *– sein,* be branded *or* notorious.

verschroben [fɛrˈʃro:bən], *adj.* eccentric, odd, queer, (*coll.*) cranky; wrong-headed, perverse; *see* **verschrauben. Verschrobenheit,** *f.* perverseness, wrong-headedness; eccentricity, oddity.

verschroten [fɛrˈʃro:tən], *v.t.* grind coarsely.

verschrotten [fɛrˈʃrɔtən], *v.t.* break up, scrap. **Verschrottung,** *f.* scrapping.

verschrumpeln [fɛrˈʃrumpəln] (*coll.*), **verschrumpfen** [fɛrˈʃrumpfən], *v.t., v.i.* (*aux.* s.) shrink, shrivel (up), wither.

verschüchtern [fɛrˈʃyçtərn], *v.t.* intimidate, scare.

verschulden [fɛrˈʃuldən], *v.t.* 1. be guilty of, be to blame for, be the cause of; 2. encumber with debt(s). **Verschulden,** *n.* fault, blame, responsibility; wrong, guilt; cause; *ohne mein –,* through no fault of mine. **verschuldet,** *adj.* (*of a p.*) indebted, in debt, (*of property*) encumbered. **Verschuldung,** *f.* indebtedness; encumbering, mortgaging.

verschütt [fɛrˈʃyt], *adv.* *– gehen,* (*sl.*) be nicked, be run in; (*coll.*) go off the rails, come unstuck. **verschütten,** *v.t.* 1. fill (up) *or* block with earth *or* rubble; 2. spill, upset; (*coll.*) *sie hat es bei ihm verschüttet,* she has got into his bad books *or* has fallen out with him; (*coll.*) *sich* (*Dat.*) *alles –,* make a complete mess of everything; 3. bury (alive).

verschwägern [fɛrˈʃvɛ:gərn], *v.r.* become related by marriage (*mit,* to). **verschwägert,** *adj.* related by marriage, (*fig., coll.*) hand in glove (*mit,* with). **Verschwägerung,** *f.* relationship by marriage.

verschwatzen [fɛrˈʃvatsən], **verschwätzen** [–ˈʃvɛtsən], *v.r. See* **verplappern.**

verschweigen [fɛrˈʃvaɪgən], *irr.v.t.* keep secret, withhold, hide, conceal (*Dat.,* from); pass over in silence, suppress; *ich habe nichts zu –,* I have nothing to conceal *or* to hide; *see* **verschwiegen. Verschweigen,** *n.,* **Verschweigung,** *f.* silence (*regarding a th.*), suppression, concealment.

verschwenden [fɛrˈʃvɛndən], *v.t.* waste, squander, lavish (*an* (*Acc.*), on). **Verschwender,** *m.* spendthrift. **verschwenderisch,** *adj.* wasteful, extravagant (*mit,* with), lavish, prodigal (of). **Verschwendung,** *f.* waste; extravagance. **Verschwendungssucht,** *f.* extravagance, prodigality, wastefulness, (*coll.*) squandermania.

verschwiegen [fɛrˈʃvi:gən], *adj.* discreet, reticent; taciturn, reserved, (*coll.*) close; (*of a place*) quiet, secluded; *– wie das Grab,* silent as the grave; *see* **verschweigen. Verschwiegenheit,** *f.* secrecy, discretion, reticence, reserve; *unter dem Siegel der –,* under the seal of secrecy; *zur – verpflichtet,* sworn to secrecy.

verschwimmen [fɛrˈʃvɪmən], *irr.v.i.* (*aux.* s.) grow hazy, become indistinct *or* blurred; dissolve, merge *or* melt into one another, blend, mingle; *see* **verschwommen.**

verschwinden [fɛr'ʃvɪndən], *irr.v.i.* (*aux.* s.) vanish, disappear; pass *or* fade away; (*coll.*) make o.s. scarce; – ***neben*** (*Dat.*) or ***gegen,*** sink into insignificance by the side of; ***auf Nimmerwiedersehen –,*** disappear never to be seen again; (*coll.*) ***verschwinde!*** beat it! get lost! **Verschwinden,** *n.* disappearance. **verschwindend,** *adv.* – ***klein,*** negligible, infinitely small, infinitesimal.

verschwistert [fɛr'ʃvɪstərt], *adj.* like brothers *or* sisters; like brother and sister; (*fig.*) closely united, intimately connected; ***–e Seelen,*** congenial souls, kindred spirits. **Verschwisterung,** *f.* brotherly *or* sisterly union, close relationship, intimate connection.

verschwitzen [fɛr'ʃvɪtsən], *v.t.* 1. wet through *or* soak with perspiration; 2. (*coll.*) forget.

verschwommen [fɛr'ʃvɔmən], *adj.* indistinct, hazy, blurred (*also Phot.*), indefinite, vague, (*coll.*) foggy (*recollection*), woolly (*as ideas*); *see* **verschwimmen. Verschwommenheit,** *f.* haziness, vagueness, indistinctness, uncertainty.

verschwören [fɛr'ʃvøːrən], **1.** *irr.v.t.* forswear, abjure, renounce. **2.** *irr.v.r.* conspire, form a conspiracy, plot (***mit,*** with; ***gegen,*** against); ***sich zu einer S. –,*** plot s.th. **verschworen,** *adj.* pledged, sworn; ***–e Gemeinschaft,*** blood brotherhood. **Verschworene(r), Verschwörer,** *m.* conspirator, plotter. **Verschwörung,** *f.* conspiracy, plot.

versehen [fɛr'zeːən], **1.** *irr.v.t.* 1. provide, furnish, equip, supply (***mit,*** with); (*Comm.*) ***mit Akzept –,*** accept, honour; (*Comm.*) ***mit Giro –,*** endorse; ***sich – lassen,*** receive the Last Sacrament; ***einen Sterbenden –,*** administer the Last Sacrament to s.o.; ***mit Unterschrift –,*** affix *or* append one's signature to; ***mit Vollmacht –,*** invest with full power(s), authorize; 2. discharge, perform (*a duty*); ***er versah das Amt des Lehrers,*** he filled the post as *or* acted as teacher; ***den Dienst eines andern –,*** discharge another man's duties; take another man's place, (*coll.*) stand in for s.o. else; ***Geschäfte –,*** look after the business; ***den Gottesdienst –,*** hold divine service; ***den Haushalt –,*** keep house, do the housekeeping, look after the house; ***die Küche –,*** do the cooking. **2.** *irr.v.r.* 1. equip *or* supply *or* furnish *or* provide o.s. (***mit,*** with); 2. make a mistake *or* (*coll.*) slip, be mistaken, be in error, be *or* go wrong (***in*** (*Dat.*), about); (*Prov.*) – ***ist auch verspielt,*** a miss is as good as a mile; 3. (*Gen.*) expect, look for, look forward to, be prepared for; ***ich versehe mich eines Bessern zu euch,*** I expect better things of you; ***wes*** or ***wessen soll man sich zu euch –?*** what is one to expect from you? ***ehe er sich's*** or ***sich dessen versah,*** before he was aware of it, before he could turn round; ***ehe man sich's versieht,*** suddenly, unexpectedly, all of a sudden, (*coll.*) in the twinkling of an eye, before you can say Jack Robinson; ***wer hätte sich das –,*** who would have looked for *or* expected *or* anticipated that; 4. (*of pregnant women*) be scared *or* frightened (***an*** (*Dat.*), by). **3.** *adj.* ***wohl –es Lager,*** good stock, ample supply, well equipped store; ***reichlich – sein mit,*** be amply supplied with, have ample supplies of, have plenty of.

Versehen, *n.* oversight, error, mistake, blunder, slip; ***aus –,*** through oversight *or* inadvertence, in error, by mistake. **versehentlich,** *adv.* inadvertently, through oversight, in error, by mistake, erroneously.

versehren [fɛr'zeːrən], *v.t.* (*Poet.*) wound, hurt, injure, damage, disable. **Versehrte(r),** *m.* disabled soldier. **Versehrten|geld,** *n.*, **–rente,** *f.* disability pension.

verseifen [fɛr'zaɪfən], *v.t.* saponify; soap (all over), lather thoroughly; (*sl.*) thrash.

Verseinschnitt ['fɛrsˀaɪnʃnɪt], *m.* (*Metr.*) caesura.

verselbständigen [fɛr'zɛlpʃtɛndɪgən], *v.t.* render independent, grant autonomy to.

Versemacher ['fɛrsəmaxər], *m.* versifier, rhymester, poetaster.

versenden [fɛr'zɛndən], *reg. & irr.v.t.* send out *or* off *or* away, dispatch, forward, transmit; ***ins Ausland –,*** export, ship. **Versendung,** *f.* consignment, conveyance, forwarding, dispatch, transport, transmission, exportation, shipment.

versengen [fɛr'zɛŋən], *v.t.* singe, scorch.

versenken [fɛr'zɛŋkən], **1.** *v.t.* sink, lower, let down; (*ship*) sink, send to the bottom, (*Tech.*) countersink (*screws*); ***ein Schiff selbst –,*** scuttle a ship; ***die Hände in die Taschen –,*** stick *or* thrust one's hands in one's pockets; ***tief in Gedanken versenkt,*** deeply absorbed *or* deep in thought. **2.** *v.r.* immerse o.s., become absorbed (***in*** (*Acc.*), in). **Versenker,** *m.* (*Tech.*) countersink *or* rose bit. **Versenkung,** *f.* sinking; lowering, dropping; (*Theat.*) trap-door; (*fig.*) ***spurlos in der – verschwinden,*** drop completely out of *or* disappear from sight, disappear off the face of the earth.

versessen [fɛr'zɛsən], *adj.* (*coll.*) – ***auf*** (*Acc.*), bent on, mad *or* crazy about. **Versessenheit,** *f.* craze.

versetzen [fɛr'zɛtsən], **1.** *v.t.* 1. transfer, remove, displace, (*plants*) transplant, (*at school*) move up, promote, (*in rank*) advance, promote, (*in place of employment*) transfer; (*letters, words etc.*) transpose; ***versetzte Betonung,*** shifting of the accentuation; ***versetzter Rhythmus,*** transposed rhythm; ***in den Ruhestand –,*** pension off; ***das versetzt mich in die Notwendigkeit,*** that reduces me to the necessity (***zu tun,*** of doing); ***in Angst –,*** alarm, terrify; ***in Schwingungen –,*** set vibrating; ***der Glaube versetzt Berge,*** faith removes mountains; 2. put, place (*into a certain condition*); give, deal (*a blow etc.*); ***ihm einem Schlag –,*** give him a blow; 3. pledge, mortgage, pawn; ***seine Uhr –,*** pawn one's watch; 4. compound, mix, temper, alloy (***mit,*** with); ***den Wein mit Wasser –,*** add water to the wine, mix water with the wine; 5. answer, (say in) reply; ***auf meine Frage versetzte er folgendes,*** to my question he made the following reply; 6. (*coll.*) leave in the lurch; 7. block; ***das versetzt mir den Atem,*** that takes my breath away; ***den Eingang mit Steinen –,*** block up the entrance with stones. **2.** *v.r.* 1. change its place, shift; – ***Sie sich in meine Lage*** or ***an meine Stelle,*** put *or* place *or* imagine yourself in my position; 2. curdle.

Versetzung [fɛr'zɛtsuŋ], *f.* 1. removal, transference; transfer; promotion, moving up; transplantation; transposition, inversion (*of words*), (*Math.*) permutation; (*Naut., Av.*) drift, deviation from course; ***– eines Bischofs,*** translation of a bishop; 2. pawning, pledging; 3. mixing, dilution, alloy. **Versetzungs|prüfung,** *f.* examination for promotion (*to a higher form*). **–zeichen,** *n.* (*Mus.*) accidental.

verseuchen [fɛr'zɔyçən], *v.t.* infect, infest; (*Mil.*) contaminate (*with gas*). **Verseuchung,** *f.* infection, contamination.

Versfuß ['fɛrsfus], *m.* (*Metr.*) (metrical) foot.

versicherbar [fɛr'zɪçərbaːr], *adj.* insurable. **Versicherer,** *m.* insurer, underwriter. **versichern,** **1.** *v.t.* insure (*property*), assure (*one's life*); (*fig.*) assure, certify; protest, affirm, aver, assert; ***ihm etwas*** or ***ihn einer S.*** (*Gen.*) –, assure *or* convince him of a th.; ***ich versichere dir*** or (*coll.*) ***dich,*** I assure you; ***er versicherte mir das Gegenteil*** or ***mich des Gegenteils,*** he assured me of *or* to the contrary; ***seien Sie versichert, daß,*** you may depend *or* rely upon it *or* you may rest assured that; ***eidesstattlich –,*** make a statutory declaration, pledge one's word. **2.** *v.r.* make sure, assure o.s. (*Gen.*, of), ascertain; insure o.s. (***gegen,*** against; ***bei,*** with), assure *or* (*coll.*) insure one's life; ***sich seiner*** (*Gen.*) –, make sure of him, get him under one's control, secure him, take him into one's custody.

Versicherung [fɛr'zɪçəruŋ], *f.* insurance (*of property*), assurance (*of life*); (*fig.*) assurance, affirmation, protestation; guarantee, security; ***eine – abschließen,*** effect an insurance, take out a policy. **Versicherungs|anspruch,** *m.* insurance claim. **–anstalt,** *f.* insurance company. **–beitrag,** *m.* (insurance) premium. **–betrag,** *m.* amount insured. **versicherungsfähig,** *adj. See* **versicherbar.**

Versicherungs|fall, *m. See* **–anspruch. –fonds,** *m.* benefit fund. **–höhe,** *f. See* **–betrag. –mathematik,** *f.* actuarial theory. **–mathematiker,** *m.* actuary. **versicherungsmathematisch,** *adj.* actuarial. **Versicherungsnehmer,** *m.* insured *or* assured p., policy holder. **versicherungspflichtig,** *adj.* compulsorily insured. **Versicherungs|police,** *f. See* **–schein. –prämie,** *f. See* **–beitrag. –schein,** *m.* (insurance) policy. **–schutz,** *m.* insurance cover. **–statistik,** *f.* actuarial practice. **–statistiker,** *m.* actuary. **versicherungsstatistisch,** *adj.* actuarial. **Versicherungs|summe,** *f. See* **–betrag. –träger,** *m. See* **Versicherer. –wesen,** *n.* insurance (business). **–zwang,** *m.* compulsory insurance.

versickern [fɛrˈzɪkərn], *v.i.* (*aux.* s.) ooze *or* seep *or* trickle away, percolate.

versiegeln [fɛrˈzi:gəln], *v.t.* seal (up), affix one's seal to; (*coll.*) pawn.

versiegen [fɛrˈzi:gən], *v.i.* (*aux.* s.) dry up, run dry, be exhausted.

versiert [fɛrˈzi:rt], *adj.* versed (*in* (*Dat.*), in).

versifizieren [fɛrzifiˈtsi:rən], *v.t.* versify, put into verse.

versilbern [fɛrˈzɪlbərn], *v.t.* silver-plate; (*coll.*) realize, turn into cash; (*coll.*) pawn; ***galvanisch* –,** electro-plate; (*fig.*) ***ihm die Hände* –,** cross his palm with silver. **Versilberung,** *f.* silvering, silver-plating; (*coll.*) selling, realization.

versimpeln [fɛrˈzɪmpəln], *v.i.* (*aux.* s.) become childish *or* simple. **versimpelt,** *adj.* half-witted, fatuous, drivelling, addle-pated, (*sl.*) half-baked, dim.

versinken [fɛrˈzɪŋkən], *irr.v.i.* (*aux.* s.) sink; become engulfed, be swallowed up; (*of ships*) sink, founder, go down; (*fig.*) lapse (***in*** (*Acc.*), into); *see* **versunken.**

versinnbildlichen [fɛrˈzɪnbɪltlɪçən], *v.t.* symbolize, represent. **Versinnbildlichung,** *f.* symbolization, symbolic representation.

versintern [fɛrˈzɪntərn], *v.t.* incrust, sinter. **Versinterung,** *f.* incrustation.

versippt [fɛrˈzɪpt], *adj.* closely related.

versittlichen [fɛrˈzɪtlɪçən], *v.t.* improve the morals of, civilize.

versklaven [fɛrˈskla:vən], *v.t.* enslave.

Vers|kunst, *f.* versification, poetic art. **–lehre,** *f.* metrics, prosody. **–macher,** *m. See* **Versemacher. –maß,** *n.* metre.

verso [ˈvɛrzo], *adv.* overleaf. **Verso,** *n.* **(-s,** *pl.* **-s)** reverse (*of the sheet*).

versoffen [fɛrˈzɔfən], *adj.* (*sl.*) drunk, drunken, tight, sozzled; (*of nose, voice*) beery; ***–er Kerl,*** drunkard, boozer.

versohlen [fɛrˈzo:lən], *v.t.* (*coll.*) thrash, beat the hide off, tan.

versöhnen [fɛrˈzø:nən], **1.** *v.t.* reconcile (***mit,*** to *or* with); conciliate, propitiate, appease, placate. **2.** *v.r.* become reconciled (***mit,*** to *or* with), make one's peace (with), (*coll.*) make it up (with), bury the hatchet. **versöhnlich,** *adj.* forgiving, conciliatory; **–** ***stimmen,*** placate, conciliate. **Versöhnung,** *f.* reconciliation, propitiation, appeasement.

Versöhnungs|bund, *m.* covenant of peace. **–fest,** *n. See* **–tag. –lehre,** *f.* doctrine of atonement. **–opfer,** *n.* expiatory sacrifice; scapegoat. **–politik,** *f.* appeasement policy. **–tag,** *m.* Day of Atonement, (*Jew.*) Yom Kippur.

versonnen [fɛrˈzɔnən], *adj.* lost in thought, daydreaming, dreamy; thoughtful, meditative, pensive.

versorgen [fɛrˈzɔrgən], *v.t.* provide, supply, furnish (***mit,*** with); provide for, support, maintain (*family*); take care of, look after, care for, nurse; tend (*cattle*), dress (*wound*); ***er ist lebenslänglich versorgt,*** he is provided for for the rest of his life. **Versorger,** *m.* mainstay, support, supporter, breadwinner. **versorgt,** *adj.* careworn. **Versorgung,** *f.* maintenance, support; providing (for); provision, supply; providing, supplying (with); living, subsistence; appointment, post, situation; public assistance; ***ärztliche* –,** medical care *or* attention; **–** ***auf dem Luftwege*** or ***aus der Luft,*** airlift.

Versorgungs|anspruch, *m.* claim to maintenance. **–betrieb,** *m.* public utility. **–lage,** *f.* supply position, food situation. **–truppen,** *f.pl.* army service corps, supply services. **–weg,** *m.* supply line. **–wesen,** *n.* public assistance, poor-relief.

verspannen [fɛrˈʃpanən], *v.t.* stay, guy, brace. **Verspannung,** *f.* stays, struts, bracing.

versparen [fɛrˈʃpa:rən], *v.t.* ***sich*** (*Dat.*) ***etwas* –,** postpone *or* defer *or* (*coll.*) put off (s.th.).

verspäten [fɛrˈʃpɛ:tən], *v.r.* be late, come too late, be behind time. **verspätet,** *adj.* late, behind time, belated, delayed, overdue. **Verspätung,** *f.* delay, lateness; ***der Zug hat 20 Minuten* –,** the train is 20 minutes late *or* overdue; **–** ***aufholen,*** make up (for) lost time, (*coll.*) catch up.

verspeisen [fɛrˈʃpaɪzən], *v.t.* eat up, consume.

verspekulieren [fɛrʃpekuˈli:rən], *v.r.* make a bad speculation, lose by speculation; (*fig.*) be out in one's reckoning.

versperren [fɛrˈʃpɛrən], *v.t.* bar, barricade, obstruct, block (up); shut, close, lock up; ***ihm die Aussicht* –,** obstruct *or* block his view.

verspielen [fɛrˈʃpi:lən], **1.** *v.t.* lose (*money*) (at cards *or* gambling), gamble away (*an evening etc.*). **2.** *v.i.* play wrong; (*Cards*) lead badly; ***du hast verspielt,*** you have lost your chance; ***er hat bei ihr verspielt,*** he has got into her bad books, (*coll.*) he has blotted his copybook with her. **verspielt,** *adj.* playful.

Verspillern [fɛrˈʃpɪlərn], *n.* (*Bot.*) etiolation.

verspinnen [fɛrˈʃpɪnən], **1.** *irr.v.t.* use up in spinning. **2.** *irr.v.r.* get wrapped up (***in*** (*Acc.*), in) (*an idea*), get mixed up (in) (*an affair*). **versponnen,** *adj.* wrapped *or* mixed up (***in*** (*Acc.*), in).

verspotten [fɛrˈʃpɔtən], *v.t.* scoff *or* sneer *or* jeer at, deride, taunt, mock, ridicule. **Verspottung,** *f.* scoffing, derision, ridicule.

versprechen [fɛrˈʃprɛçən], **1.** *irr.v.t.* promise (***ihm etwas,*** him s.th. *or* s.th. to him); give promise of (*s.th.*), bid fair (*to do*); ***sich*** (*Dat.*) ***etwas – von,*** expect much of, have hopes of; ***sich*** (*Dat.*) ***nicht viel – von,*** have no great hopes of, set no great hopes *or* (*coll.*) store by; ***ich versprach ihm, es zu tun*** or ***daß ich es tun wollte,*** I promised him I would do it; ***er war ein junger Mensch, der viel versprach,*** he was a very promising youth; ***er verspricht ein großer Maler zu werden,*** he has the makings of a *or* he promises to be a great painter; ***das Unternehmen verspricht etwas,*** the undertaking shows promise; ***hoch und teuer* –,** promise faithfully; ***auf Treu und Glauben* –,** pledge one's word; ***das Blaue vom Himmel* –,** promise the earth. **2.** *irr.v.r.* 1. make a slip of the tongue, say the wrong thing; 2. be *or* become engaged; ***ich habe mich schon für den nächsten Tanz versprochen,*** I am already engaged for the next dance.

Versprechen, *n.* 1. promise; ***ihm ein – abnehmen,*** exact a promise from him; ***schriftliches* –,** written promise, promissory note; ***ihn seines –s entbinden,*** release him from his promise; ***auf dein – hin,*** on the strength of your promise; (*Prov.*) ***gebrochenes –, gesprochenes Verbrechen,*** a promise broken is a bad deed spoken; 2. slip of the tongue. **Versprechung,** *f.* promise, undertaking; ***ihm große –en machen,*** hold out great hopes to him, promise him the earth.

versprengen [fɛrˈʃprɛŋən], *v.t.* scatter, disperse; (*Bill.*) strike (*a ball*) off the table; ***versprengte Truppen,*** troops cut off from the main body. **Versprengte(r),** *m.* (*Mil.*) straggler.

verspritzen [fɛrˈʃprɪtsən], *v.t.* spatter, splash, squirt, spray; spill, shed; (*Metall.*) die-cast; ***sein Blut* –,** shed one's blood.

versprochen [fɛrˈʃprɔxən], *adj.* promised; engaged; ***sie sind miteinander* –,** they are engaged to be married. **versprochenermaßen,** *adv.* as promised.

Verspruch [fɛrˈʃprux], *m.* (*obs.*) betrothal.

verspunden [fɛrˈʃpundən], (*Austr.*) **verspünden** [fɛrˈʃpyndən], *v.t.* bung up (*a cask*).

verspüren [fɛrˈʃpy:rən], *v.t.* feel, perceive, notice, sense, be *or* become conscious *or* aware of.

verstaatlichen [fɛrˈʃta:tlɪçən], *v.t.* nationalize, bring under government control *or* under state *or* public ownership. **Verstaatlichung,** *f.* nationalization, public *or* state ownership.

verstädtern [fɛrˈʃtɛ:tərn], **1.** *v.t.* urbanize. **2.** *v.i.* become urbanized. **Verstädterung,** *f.* urbanization.

verstadtlichen [fɛrˈʃtatlɪçən], *v.t.* take over by the municipality, bring under municipal control.

Verstand [fɛrˈʃtant], *m.* mind, intellect, intelligence, (*coll.*) wits, brains; understanding, (common)-sense, discernment, judgement; (*obs.*) sense, meaning; ***er ist nicht (recht) bei –,*** he is not in his right mind, (*coll.*) he is not all there; (*Med.*) ***bei – bleiben,*** retain one's (mental) faculties; ***gesunder –,*** common- *or* good sense; ***klarer*** or ***kühler –,*** cool *or* clear head; ***nach meinem geringen –e,*** in my humble opinion; ***ohne Sinn und –,*** without rhyme or reason; ***scharfer –,*** keen intellect *or* mind; ***ihm steht der – still,*** his mind boggles at it, he is at his wits' end; ***das geht über meinen –,*** that is over my head *or* beyond me; ***ihn um den – bringen,*** drive him out of his senses *or* wits; ***den – verlieren,*** go out of one's mind; ***zu – kommen,*** arrive at the age of discretion; ***wieder zu – kommen,*** come to one's senses; (*coll.*) ***seinen – zusammennehmen,*** have *or* keep all one's wits about one; ***im eigentlichen –,*** in its literal meaning, in the true sense; ***in jedem –,*** in every sense *or* respect.

verstanden [fɛrˈʃtandən], *adj.* understood; *see* **verstehen**; ***–?*** is that understood *or* clear? (*coll.*) you get me? do you follow me? ***wohl –,*** let it be understood.

verstandes|gemäß, *adj. See* **–mäßig. Verstandeskraft,** *f.* intellectual power. **verstandesmäßig,** *adj.* rational, reasonable, sensible. **Verstandes|-mensch,** *m.* matter-of-fact p. **–schärfe,** *f.* (intellectual) penetration, acumen, sagacity, sound judgement. **–wesen,** *n.* rational *or* intelligent being.

verständig [fɛrˈʃtɛndɪç], *adj.* intelligent; rational, reasonable, sensible; prudent, judicious; ***–es Alter,*** age *or* years of discretion; ***–er Einfall,*** sensible idea. **verständigen, 1.** *v.t.* inform, notify, advise, give notice (***von,*** of), acquaint (with). **2.** *v.r.* come to an understanding (***mit,*** with; ***über*** (*Acc.*), about); ***sich mit Deutschen – können,*** be able to make o.s. understood with Germans. **Verständigkeit,** *f.* good sense, prudence, wisdom.

Verständigung [fɛrˈʃtɛndɪguŋ], *f.* agreement, understanding, arrangement; information; (*Rad. etc.*) communication, (quality of) reception. **Verständigungs|friede,** *m.* negotiated peace. **–politik,** *f.* policy of appeasement.

verständlich [fɛrˈʃtɛntlɪç], *adj.* intelligible, clear, distinct; understandable, comprehensible; ***allgemein –,*** within everybody's grasp; ***schwer –,*** abstruse, difficult (to grasp); ***es ist –, daß . . .,*** one can (easily) understand why . . .; ***sich – machen,*** make o.s. understood (*Dat.*, by); ***ihm etwas – machen,*** make s.th. clear to him. **Verständlichkeit,** *f.* intelligibility, clarity, clearness, lucidity.

Verständnis [fɛrˈʃtɛntnɪs], *n.* comprehension, understanding, appreciation (***für,*** of), sympathy (for), insight (into); ***– haben für,*** understand, appreciate, sympathize with; ***ich habe kein – für solche Dummheit,*** I have no sympathy with such stupidity; ***ihm – entgegenbringen,*** show understanding *or* sympathy for him. **verständnisinnig,** *adj.* meaningful; ***–er Blick,*** knowing glance; ***–e Worte,*** appreciative words. **verständnislos,** *adj.* unsympathetic, unappreciative, uncomprehending. **Verständnislosigkeit,** *f.* lack of comprehension *or* understanding *or* sympathy. **verständnisvoll,** *adj.* understanding, sympathetic, appreciative; knowing (*glance etc.*).

verstänkern [fɛrˈʃtɛŋkərn], *v.t.* fill with stench, (*coll.*) stink (*a room etc.*) out.

verstärken [fɛrˈʃtɛrkən], **1.** *v.t.* strengthen, fortify, (*Tech., Mil.*) reinforce; augment, increase, intensify, (*Elec., coll.*) boost, (*Rad. etc.*) amplify. **2.** *v.r.* increase, intensify, strengthen, grow stronger. **Verstärker,** *m.* (*Rad.*) amplifier, (*Tele.*) repeater, (*Phot.*) intensifier; activator, reinforcing agent. **Verstärker|röhre,** *f.* amplifying valve. **–stufe,** *f.* amplification stage.

Verstärkung [fɛrˈʃtɛrkuŋ], *f.* strengthening, intensification, (*Tech., Mil.*) reinforcement, (*Rad.*) amplification, gain; (*Rad.*) ***– pro Stufe,*** stage-gain.

verstatten [fɛrˈʃtatən], *v.t.* (*obs.*) *see* **gestatten.**

verstauben [fɛrˈʃtaubən], *v.i.* (*aux.* s.) become covered with dust, get dusty.

verstäuben [fɛrˈʃtɔybən], **1.** *v.t.* reduce to dust *or* powder, atomize; (cover with) dust *or* powder. **2.** *v.i.* (*aux.* s.) fly off as dust. **Verstäuber,** *m.* atomizer, spray(er).

verstaubt [fɛrˈʃtaupt], *adj.* dusty; (*fig.*) dry-as-dust, antiquated, moth-eaten.

verstauchen [fɛrˈʃtauxən], *v.t.* sprain, strain; ***sich*** (*Dat.*) ***die Hand –,*** sprain one's hand. **Verstauchung,** *f.* sprain, strain.

verstauen [fɛrˈʃtauən], *v.t.* stow away.

verstechen [fɛrˈʃtɛçən], *irr.v.t.* 1. (*Dressm.*) fine-draw; 2. adulterate (*wine*).

Versteck [fɛrˈʃtɛk], *n.* **(-(e)s,** *pl.* **-e)** hiding-place, (*coll.*) hide-out; ambush, (*Mil.*) ambuscade; (*dial.*) hide-and-seek. **verstecken, 1.** *v.t.* hide, conceal, secrete. **2.** *v.r.* hide (o.s.); ***sich versteckt halten,*** be in hiding; (*fig.*) ***sich vor ihm – müssen,*** not be a match for him, (*coll.*) not be able to hold a candle to him. **Versteckspiel,** *n.* hide-and-seek. **versteckt,** *adj.* hidden, concealed; (*fig.*) covert, veiled; ***–e Anspielung,*** veiled *or* indirect hint; ***–e Absicht,*** ulterior motive.

verstehen [fɛrˈʃte:ən], **1.** *irr.v.t.* understand, comprehend, (*coll.*) grasp; (*a language*) know (well); ***falsch –,*** misunderstand, (*coll.*) get wrong; ***ihm zu – geben,*** give him to understand, intimate to him; ***von Grund aus –,*** know thoroughly; (*Prov.*) ***jeder macht's wie er's versteht,*** everyone (acts) according to his lights; (*sl.*) ***den Rummel –,*** know what's what; ***Spaß –,*** see *or* take a joke; ***was – Sie darunter?*** what do you mean by it? what do you understand by *or* from it? what does it mean to you? ***etwas davon –,*** know s.th. *or* know a th. or two about it; ***nichts davon –,*** not know the first th. about it. **2.** *irr.v.r.* understand one another, be in agreement *or* accord; ***sich – auf*** (*Acc.*), know well, be skilled *or* (*coll.*) at home in, be an expert at, be a (sound) judge of; ***sich auf seinen Vorteil –,*** know where one's (own) interests lie, (*coll.*) know which side one's bread is buttered; ***sich mit ihm –,*** get on well with him; ***das versteht sich (von selbst),*** that goes without saying, of course; that is obvious; ***sich zu einer S. –,*** agree *or* consent *or* accede to a th., bring o.s. to do s.th.; *see* **verstanden.**

versteifen [fɛrˈʃtaɪfən], **1.** *v.t.* prop, strut, brace, stay; stiffen, reinforce. **2.** *v.r.* stiffen, harden (*also Comm. as prices*); (*fig.*) ***sich – auf*** (*Acc.*), insist upon, make a point of, stick obstinately to.

versteigen [fɛrˈʃtaɪgən], *irr.v.r.* lose one's way in the mountains; (*fig.*) ***sich – zu*** (*Dat.*), go so far as to, have the presumption to (*inf.*).

Versteigerer [fɛrˈʃtaɪgərər], *m.* auctioneer. **versteigern,** *v.t.* (sell by *or* (*Am.*) at) auction, put up for auction. **Versteigerung,** *f.* auction (sale).

versteinern [fɛrˈʃtaɪnərn], *v.t., v.i.* (*aux.* s.) turn (in)to stone, petrify. **versteinert,** *adj.* (*fig.*) petrified, transfixed, thunderstruck. **Versteinerung,** *f.* petrification, fossilization; fossil, petrifaction. **Versteinerungskunde,** *f.* palaeontology.

verstellbar [fɛrˈʃtɛlba:r], *adj.* movable, variable, adjustable. **verstellen, 1.** *v.t.* 1. shift, transpose, adjust; change the position *or* order of; 2. misplace, disarrange, put in the wrong place; 3. obstruct, block, bar; 4. disguise (*one's voice etc.*). **2.** *v.r.* dissemble, feign, pretend, play a part. **Verstelluftschraube,** *f.* (*Av.*) variable pitch propeller. **Verstellung,** *f.* (*Mech.*) adjustment;

(*fig.*) pretence, dissembling, dissimulation, disguise, make-believe, play-acting.

versteuerbar [fɛr'ʃtɔyərba:r], *adj.* taxable, dutiable. **versteuern,** *v.t.* pay tax *or* duty on; *zu -de Einkünfte,* taxable income. **versteuert,** *adj.* duty-paid. **Versteuerung,** *f.* payment of duty. **Versteuerungswert,** *m.* taxable value.

verstiegen [fɛr'ʃti:gən], *adj.* (*fig.*) eccentric; extravagant, high-flown; *see* **versteigen. Verstiegenheit,** *f.* eccentricity; extravagance.

verstimmen [fɛr'ʃtɪmən], *v.t.* put out of tune, detune; (*fig.*) put out of humour, upset, irritate, annoy, put into a bad temper *or* humour. **verstimmt,** *adj.* out of tune; (*fig.*) in a bad temper *or* mood, disgruntled, cross, upset (*über* (*Acc.*), about), annoyed, irritated (at *or* about); (*digestion*) disordered, upset. **Verstimmung,** *f.* ill humour, bad temper, irritation, annoyance; (*between two people*) ill feeling, resentment, disagreement, discord; (*of digestion*) disorder, upset.

verstockt [fɛr'ʃtɔkt], *adj.* hardened, callous; obdurate, stubborn; impenitent. **Verstocktheit,** *f.* callousness, hardness of heart; obduracy, stubbornness; impenitence.

verstofflichen [fɛr'ʃtɔflɪçən], *v.t.* materialize.

verstohlen [fɛr'ʃto:lən], **1.** *adj.* stealthy, furtive, surreptitious, clandestine. **2.** *adv. also* by stealth, (*coll.*) on the sly; *– lachen,* laugh in *or* up one's sleeve; *– anblicken,* steal a glance at.

verstopfen [fɛr'ʃtɔpfən], *v.t.* plug, stop up, block, clog, obstruct, choke (up), (*Tech.*) tamp, (*Med.*) constipate. **Verstopfung,** *f.* obstruction, clogging, blocking, choking, stoppage; congestion, (*coll.*) jam; (*Med.*) constipation.

verstorben [fɛr'ʃtɔrbən], *adj.* deceased, defunct, late. **Verstorbene(r),** *m., f.* deceased; *die Verstorbenen,* the dead *or* departed.

verstört [fɛr'ʃtø:rt], *adj.* troubled, agitated, disconcerted, bewildered, distracted; haggard, stricken. **Verstörtheit,** *f.* agitation, bewilderment, consternation, distraction.

Verstoß [fɛr'ʃto:s], *m.* mistake, error, fault, blunder, slip; offence (*gegen,* against), infringement, violation (of). **verstoßen, 1.** *irr.v.i.* – *gegen,* give offence to, offend against, contravene, infringe, transgress, violate (*a regulation etc.*). **2.** *irr.v.t.* push away, repel, repulse, reject, repudiate; divorce (*a wife*), disown, disinherit, cast off (*a son etc.*); cast out, expel (*aus,* from). **Verstoßene(r),** *m., f.* outcast. **Verstoßung,** *f.* expulsion, banishment, rejection, repudiation.

verstreben [fɛr'ʃtre:bən], *v.t.* brace, support, strut.

verstreichen [fɛr'ʃtraɪçən], **1.** *irr.v.t.* spread, smear with; fill in (*cracks*), grout (*joints*); *eine Mauer mit Mörtel –,* plaster up *or* parget a wall; *verstrichene Fugen,* filled joints. **2.** *irr.v.i.* (*aux.* s.) slip by, pass (*of time*); elapse; *der Termin ist verstrichen,* the term has expired.

verstreuen [fɛr'ʃtrɔyən], *v.t.* scatter, disperse, strew about, litter.

verstricken [fɛr'ʃtrɪkən], *v.t.* use up (*wool etc.*) in knitting; ensnare, entangle; *verstrickt sein in* (*Acc.*), be *or* get involved in, be *or* get mixed up (with *or* in).

verstümmeln [fɛr'ʃtyməln], *v.t.* mutilate, maim, mangle; (*fig.*) garble. **Verstümm(e)lung,** *f.* mutilation, maiming; garbling.

verstummen [fɛr'ʃtumən], *v.i.* (*aux.* s.) grow dumb; become silent; (*of sounds*) cease, die away; *vor Erstaunen –,* be struck dumb with astonishment; *– machen,* silence. **Verstummung,** *f.* loss of speech.

Versüberschreitung, *f.* enjambement.

Versuch [fɛr'zu:x], *m.* (**-(e)s,** *pl.* **-e**) attempt, trial, (*coll.*) try, try-out; effort, endeavour; test, experiment; (*Metall.*) assay; *es kommt auf einen – an,* it could be tried; *einen – anstellen mit,* (make an) experiment on, give (*s.th.*) a trial, (*coll.*) try (*s.th.*) out; *einen – machen mit,* try one's hand at, (*coll.*) have a go *or* shot at; *ein – kann nicht schaden,* it can do no harm to try; *strafbarer –,* attempted felony.

versuchen, *v.t.* attempt, try; endeavour, make an effort; (*a p.*) tempt, entice; (*food*) sample, taste, (*coll.*) try; *alles –,* try everything; *sein Glück –,* try one's luck; *es – mit,* give (*s.th.*) a trial, try one's hand at; *es mit ihm –,* try him, (*sl.*) see if he will play. **Versucher,** *m.* tempter.

Versuchs|anstalt, *f.* research institute, experimental station. **-ballon,** *m.* (*fig.*) attempt to gauge public opinion, kite. **-bedingungen,** *f.pl.* test *or* experimental conditions. **-bohrung,** *f.* test drilling. **-fahrt,** *f.* trial run. **-fehler,** *m.* experimental error. **-feld,** *n.* proving ground. **-flug,** *m.* test flight. **-gut,** *n.* experimental farm. **-kaninchen,** *n.* (*fig.*) (experimental) guinea-pig. **-labor(atorium),** *n.* research laboratory. **-ladung,** *f.* (*Artil.*) proof-charge. **-modell,** *n.* working model. **-muster,** *n.* experimental type. **-raum,** *m.* test room, laboratory. **-reihe,** *f.* series of tests. **-rennen,** *n.* trial stakes. **-stadium,** *n.* experimental stage. **-stand,** *m.* testing-stand. **-station,** *f.* experimental station. **-tier,** *n.* laboratory *or* test animal. **versuchsweise,** *adv.* by way of (an) experiment, as an experiment, tentatively; *– nehmen,* take on trial *or* on approval. **Versuchszweck,** *m. zu -en,* for experimental purposes.

Versuchung [fɛr'zu:xuŋ], *f.* temptation; *in – führen,* lead into temptation; *in – kommen,* be tempted, fall into temptation.

versumpfen [fɛr'zumpfən], *v.i.* (*aux.* s.) become marshy *or* boggy; (*fig.*) come down in the world, become dissolute, (*coll.*) go to the bad *or* the dogs.

versündigen [fɛr'zyndɪgən], *v.r. sich – an* (*Dat.*), sin against; do wrong to, wrong (*a p.*). **Versündigung,** *f.* sin; *– an Gott,* sin against God.

versunken [fɛr'zuŋkən], *adj.* sunk, submerged; (*fig.*) engrossed, absorbed, (*coll.*) lost (*in* (*Acc.*), in); *see* **versinken. Versunkenheit,** *f.* (*fig.*) absorption (*in thought*), preoccupation, reverie.

versüßen [fɛr'zy:sən], *v.t.* (over)sweeten, sugar.

versweise, ['fɛrsvaɪzə], *adv.* in verse; verse by verse. **Verszeile,** *f.* metrical line, line of poetry, verse.

vertagen [fɛr'ta:gən], **1.** *v.t.* adjourn, prorogue (*parliament*). **2.** *v.r.* adjourn. **Vertagung,** *f.* adjournment, prorogation.

vertändeln [fɛr'tɛndəln], *v.t.* fritter *or* trifle away.

vertäuen [fɛr'tɔyən], *v.t.* moor (*a boat*).

vertauschen [fɛr'tauʃən], *v.t.* exchange (*gegen, mit, für, um,* for), interchange (with), change (*places*); (*Math.*) substitute; mistake, take *or* leave by mistake *or* in mistake for (*umbrella, hat etc.*). **Vertauschung,** *f.* (*Math.*) exchange, substitution.

vertausendfachen [fɛr'tauzəntfaxən], *v.t., v.r.* increase a thousandfold; multiply by a thousand.

verteidigen [fɛr'taɪdɪgən], **1.** *v.t.* defend; justify, vindicate, uphold, support, (*coll.*) stand up for; *einen Satz –,* maintain a proposition. **2.** *v.r.* defend *or* justify *or* vindicate o.s. **Verteidiger,** *m.* **1.** defender; (*fig.*) champion, (*Law*) advocate, counsel for the defence; 2. (*Footb.*) full back. **Verteidigung,** *f.* defence; vindication, advocacy, justification; (*Law*) case for the defence; (*Mil.*) defensive; (*Footb.*) defence; *in die – gedrängt,* forced on to the defensive, compelled to adopt a defensive attitude.

Verteidigungs|anlagen, *f.pl.* defence works, defences. **-bündnis,** *n.* defensive alliance. **-grund,** *m.* ground for defence, justification. **-krieg,** *m.* defensive war. **-minister,** *m.* Minister *or* (*Am.*) Secretary of Defence. **-ministerium,** *n.* Ministry *or* (*Am.*) Department of Defence. **-rede,** *f.* plea, counsel's speech, speech for the defence. **-schrift,** *f.* vindication in writing, written defence. **-stand,** *m.* state of defence. **-stellung,** *f.* (*Mil.*) defensive position. **-waffe,** *f.* defensive weapon. **-zustand,** *m. See* **-stand.**

verteien [fɛr'taɪən], *v.t. See* **vertäuen.**

verteilen [fɛr'taɪlən], **1.** *v.t.* distribute, disperse, disseminate, divide, share (*auf* or *unter* (*Acc.*), among), allocate, assign, apportion, allot (to); *die Farbe –,* spread the paint; *milde Gaben an die Armen –,* distribute alms *or* dispense charity among the poor; (*Theat.*) *die Rollen –,* assign *or* allot the parts. **2.** *v.r.* be distributed; spread (out), (*as clouds etc.*) disperse; (*Mil.*) deploy; ***die Kosten – sich auf alle,*** the cost is spread among everyone, everyone shares the cost; ***die Zahlungen – sich über sechs Monate,*** the payments are spread over six months.

Verteiler [fɛr'taɪlər], *m.* retailer, distributor; distribution list; (*Tech.*) distributor. **Verteiler|dose,** *f.* *See* **–kasten. –finger,** *m.* distributor arm. **–kasten,** *m.* junction box.

Verteilung [fɛr'taɪluŋ], *f.* distribution, dispersion, dissemination, diffusion, (*Mil.*) deployment; division, apportionment, allotment, allocation. **Verteilungs|kurve,** *f.* (*Stat.*) distribution curve. **–schlüssel,** *m.* ratio of distribution.

verteuen [fɛr'tɔyən], *v.t. See* **vertäuen.**

verteuern [fɛr'tɔyərn], *v.t.* raise *or* increase the price of, raise in price, make dearer. **Verteuerung,** *f.* rise *or* increase in price.

verteufelt [fɛr'tɔyfəlt], **1.** *adj.* devilish, fiendish, confounded; ***–er Kerl,*** devil of a fellow. **2.** *adv.* (*coll.*) deuced, infernally, awfully; ***ihm – mitspielen,*** play the very devil with him.

vertiefen [fɛr'ti:fən], **1.** *v.t.* deepen, sink deeper; hollow out; ***den Eindruck –,*** heighten the impression; ***in Gedanken vertieft,*** lost *or* absorbed in thought; ***der vertiefte halbe Ton zu C,*** the half-tone lower than C. **2.** *v.r.* become deeper, deepen; (*fig.*) ***sich – in*** (*Acc.*), become absorbed *or* engrossed in; ***sich in seine Gedanken –,*** be wrapped up in one's thoughts. **Vertiefung,** *f.* 1. deepening; cavity, hollow, indentation, depression, recess, niche; 2. (*fig.*) absorption, preoccupation.

vertiert [fɛr'ti:rt], *adj.* brutish, bestial.

vertikal [vɛrti'ka:l], *adj.* vertical. **Vertikale,** *f.* vertical (line).

vertilgen [fɛr'tɪlgən], *v.t.* destroy, annihilate, extirpate, exterminate, eradicate, uproot, efface, wipe *or* blot out, extinguish; (*coll.*) (*food*) devour, consume, (*sl.*) finish *or* polish off. **Vertilgung,** *f.* extermination, extirpation, destruction. **Vertilgungskrieg,** *m.* war of extermination, war to the death.

vertippen [fɛr'tɪpən], (*coll.*) **1.** *v.t.* type wrongly. **2.** *v.r.* make a typing error.

vertonen [fɛr'to:nən], *v.t.* set to music, compose. **Vertonung,** *f.* musical setting *or* arrangement; (musical) composition; (*Naut.*) coastal outline (*on charts*).

vertrackt [fɛr'trakt], *adj.* (*coll.*) confounded, deuced.

Vertrag [fɛr'tra:k], *m.* **(-(e)s,** *pl.* **⸚e)** (*Pol.*) treaty, pact; (*Comm.*) contract, agreement, covenant, settlement, compact; ***leoninischer –,*** one-sided bargain; ***mündlicher –,*** verbal agreement, (*Law*) parol contract.

vertragen [fɛr'tra:gən], **1.** *irr.v.t.* 1. carry away *or* off; 2. (*fig.*) endure, tolerate, bear, suffer, (*Poet.*) brook, (*coll.*) stand, put up with; ***das kann ich nicht –,*** I cannot bear *or* stand it, (*of food*) it does not agree with me; ***er kann einen Puff –,*** he has a thick skin; ***einen Spaß –,*** take a joke; ***er kann keinen Widerspruch –,*** he cannot tolerate contradiction. **2.** *irr.v.r.* (*of persons*) get on well together, be compatible, agree; (*of things*) go well together, harmonize; ***sich wieder –,*** be reconciled, settle one's differences, (*coll.*) make it up (***mit,*** with); ***sie – sich wie Hund und Katze,*** they live a cat-and-dog life; ***Grün und Blau – sich nicht,*** green and blue do not go well together, (*coll.*) green and blue clash; ***es verträgt sich nicht mit meiner Pflicht,*** it is incompatible with my duty; (*Prov.*) ***Pack schlägt sich, Pack verträgt sich,*** thieves may quarrel but they stick together.

vertraglich [fɛr'tra:klɪç], **1.** *adj.* contractual, stipulated. **2.** *adv.* as stipulated, under the (terms of the) contract *or* (*Pol.*) treaty, by contract; ***sich – verpflichten,*** contract; ***– verpflichtet sein,*** be under contract.

verträglich [fɛr'trɛ:klɪç], *adj.* (*of persons*) peaceable, friendly, good-natured, sociable; tractable, conciliatory, accommodating; (*of things*) compatible, consistent. **Verträglichkeit,** *f.* (*of persons*) good nature, easy temper, peaceable disposition, conciliatory *or* accommodating spirit, tolerant attitude; sociability; (*of things*) compatibility.

Vertrags|bedingungen, *f.pl.* terms of contract. **–bruch,** *m.* breach of contract. **vertragsbrüchig,** *adj.* defaulting. **vertragschließend,** *adj.* contracting (*party*). **Vertragschließende(r),** *m., f.* party to a contract. **Vertrags|dauer,** *f.* term of a contract. **–entwurf,** *m.* draft agreement. **vertrags|fähig,** *adj.* competent to negotiate an agreement. **–gemäß,** *adv. See* **vertraglich, 2. Vertrags|-hafen,** *m.* treaty port. **–hilfe,** *f.* (*Law*) judicial assistance. **–macht,** *f.* treaty power. **vertragsmäßig,** *adj. See* **vertraglich, 1. Vertrags|-nehmer,** *m.* contractor. **–partei,** *f.,* **–partner,** *m. See* **Vertragschließende(r). –pflicht,** *f.* contractual obligation. **–preis,** *m.* contract price. **–recht,** *n.* 1. law of contract; 2. contractual right. **–strafe,** *f.* penalty for breach of contract. **–verhältnis,** *n.* contractual relationship. **vertragswidrig,** *adj.* contrary to the (terms of the) agreement *or* (*Pol.*) to the (provisions of the) treaty.

vertrauen [fɛr'trauən], **1.** *v.t.* (*rare*) *see* **anvertrauen. 2.** *v.i.* (*Dat.*) trust (*a p.*); ***– auf*** (*Acc.*), trust *or* confide in, put one's trust in, rely (up)on, have confidence in. **Vertrauen,** *n.* trust, confidence (***in*** (*Acc.*), ***zu,*** in); ***im –,*** in confidence, confidentially, (*coll.*) between ourselves; ***im – auf*** (*Acc.*), relying on, trusting to, confiding in; ***ihm sein – schenken, sein – in ihn setzen,*** have confidence *or* place one's trust in him; ***ihn ins – ziehen,*** take him into one's confidence, confide in him; ***– zu ihm haben,*** trust him, have confidence *or* put one's trust *or* faith in him; ***das – zu ihm verlieren,*** lose (one's) faith *or* lose confidence in him. **vertrauenerweckend,** *adj.* inspiring confidence *or* trust, promising; ***wenig –,*** suspicious, unpromising.

Vertrauens|bruch, *m.* breach of trust *or* confidence, indiscretion. **–frage,** *f.* (*Pol.*) ***die – stellen,*** call for a vote of confidence. **–mann,** *m.* **(⸚er** *or* **-leute)** confidential agent, informant; confidant, trusted person; spokesman, (*in industry*) shop-steward. **–posten,** *m.* position of trust. **–sache,** *f.* confidential matter. **–schüler(in),** *m.(f.)* prefect, monitor. **vertrauensselig,** *adj.* gullible, too confiding. **Vertrauens|seligkeit,** *f.* gullibility, blind faith. **–stellung,** *f. See* **–posten. vertrauensvoll,** *adj.* trusting, trustful. **Vertrauensvotum,** *n.* (*Pol.*) vote of confidence. **vertrauenswürdig,** *adj.* trustworthy, reliable.

vertrauern [fɛr'trauərn], *v.t.* pass (*period of time*) in mourning.

vertraulich [fɛr'traulɪç], *adj.* private, confidential; (*of relationship*) familiar, intimate; ***– behandeln,*** treat confidentially, deal with in confidence; ***streng –,*** in strict confidence, strictly confidential; (*coll.*) ***er kommt mir plump –,*** he's very pally with me. **Vertraulichkeit,** *f.* familiarity, intimacy; confidence; ***sich*** (*Dat.*) ***–en herausnehmen,*** take liberties, become too familiar.

verträumen [fɛr'trɔymən], *v.t.* dream away. **verträumt,** *adj.* dreamy (*as eyes*), sleepy (*as a village*).

vertraut [fɛr'traut], *adj.* intimate, familiar (*with a p.*), well acquainted, (fully) conversant (*with a th.*), (well) versed, (*coll.*) (thoroughly) at home (*in a th.*); ***sich – machen mit,*** make o.s. (thoroughly) familiar with, familiarize *or* acquaint o.s. with; ***sich mit dem Gedanken – machen,*** get used to the idea. **Vertraute(r),** *m., f.* confidant (*f.* confidante), intimate friend. **Vertrautheit,** *f.* intimacy, familiarity (***mit,*** with), thorough *or* intimate knowledge (of).

vertreiben [fɛr'traɪbən], *irr.v.t.* 1. drive away, expel (***aus,*** from); disperse, scatter, dislodge (*enemy*), (*fig.*) dispel, banish (*care*), kill, beguile, (*coll.*) while away (*time*); ***ihn aus seinem Besitz –,*** dispossess *or* evict him; ***ihn aus dem Lande –,*** banish *or* exile him; ***ihn aus dem Hause –,*** turn him out of the house, (*coll.*) throw him out; ***Gewalt mit Gewalt –,*** repel force by force; (*coll.*) ***ihm den Kitzel –,*** knock the nonsense out of him; 2. sell, retail, distribute (*goods*); 3. soften, blend, shade down (*colours etc.*); ***die Umrisse –,*** soften the outlines. **Vertreibung,** *f.* 1. expulsion, banishment; dispersion, dispersal; eviction, dispossession; 2. sale, disposal; 3. softening, blending.

vertretbar [fɛr'tre:tba:r], *adj.* justifiable, defendable (*point of view*), (*Law*) fungible. **vertreten,** *irr.v.t.* 1. ***sich*** (*Dat.*) ***den Fuß –,*** sprain one's foot; (*coll.*) ***sich*** (*Dat.*) ***die Beine –,*** stretch one's legs; ***ihm den Weg –,*** stand in *or* bar *or* block his way, stop him; 2. replace, represent; act, substitute *or* deputize for, act on behalf of; (*Law*) appear *or* plead for (*a p.*), plead (*a cause*); champion, hold a brief for (*a p. or th.*), advocate (*a th.*); ***eine Ansicht –,*** hold *or* take *or* adopt a view; ***seine Interessen –,*** look after *or* safeguard his interests; ***einen Wahlbezirk –,*** represent a constituency. **Vertreter,** *m.* representative, agent, substitute, proxy, deputy, (*of a doctor*) locum (tenens); advocate, champion, exponent.

Vertretung [fɛr'tre:tuŋ], *f.* representation, (*Comm.*) agency; substitution; advocacy; (*Comm.*) ***in –,*** by proxy, acting *or* signed for; ***seine – übernehmen,*** take his place, deputize for him. **Vertretungs|macht,** *f.* (agents') authority. **–vollmacht,** *f.* power of attorney. **vertretungsweise,** *adv.* by proxy, as a representative *or* substitute, (*Comm.*) per pro.

Vertrieb [fɛr'tri:p], *m.* sale, distribution, marketing.

vertrieben [fɛr'tri:bən], *see* **vertreiben. Vertriebene(r),** *m., f.* expellee, displaced p., refugee.

Vertriebs|abkommen, *m.* marketing agreement. **–abteilung,** *f.* sales department. **–genossenschaft, –gesellschaft,** *f.* trading company. **–kosten,** *pl.* distribution costs. **–leiter,** *m.* sales manager.

vertrinken [fɛr'trɪŋkən], *irr.v.t.* spend *or* squander on drink.

vertrocknen [fɛr'trɔknən], *v.i.* wither, shrivel, dry up.

vertrödeln [fɛr'trø:dəln], *v.i.* 1. waste; fritter *or* idle away; 2. (*obs.*) hawk, peddle.

vertrösten [fɛr'trø:stən], *v.t.* console (***auf*** (*Acc.*), with *or* with the prospect of), give hope, feed with hope (of); ***von einem Tag zum anderen –,*** put off (*creditors etc.*) from one day to the next; ***ihn auf morgen –,*** put him off till tomorrow. **Vertröstung,** *f.* (poor) consolation, vain *or* empty promise(s), fair words.

vertrusten [fɛr'trustən], *v.t.* (*Comm.*) corner, pool.

vertun [fɛr'tu:n], **1.** *irr.v.t.* spend, squander, waste; ***Zeit – mit,*** waste time on. **2.** *irr.v.r.* (*coll.*) go wrong, miss one's aim, come a cropper.

vertuscheln [fɛr'tuʃəln], **vertuschen,** *v.t.* suppress, hush up, keep dark; gloss over.

verübeln [fɛr'y:bəln], *v.t.* take amiss; ***ihm etwas –,*** blame him for s.th.

verüben [fɛr'y:bən], *v.t.* commit, perpetrate; ***einen Streich –,*** play a trick. **Verübung,** *f.* perpetration, commission (*of a crime*).

verulken [fɛr'ulkən], *v.t.* make fun of, tease, (*coll.*) kid, rag, pull (*s.o.'s*) leg.

Verumständung [fɛr'umʃtɛnduŋ], *f.* (*Swiss*) *see* **Umstand.**

verunehren [fɛr'unˀe:rən], *v.t.* dishonour, disgrace, discredit, profane.

veruneinigen [fɛr'unˀaɪnɪgən], **1.** *v.t.* set at variance. **2.** *v.r.* fall out, quarrel. **Veruneinigung,** *f.* disunion, discord.

verunglimpfen [fɛr'unglɪmpfən], *v.t.* bring into discredit, defame, disparage, blacken, calumniate, traduce. **Verunglimpfung,** *f.* defamation, disparagement, calumny.

verunglücken [fɛr'unglykən], *v.i.* (*aux.* s.) meet with an accident; perish, be killed in an accident; (*of a th.*) fail, miscarry, come to grief, go wrong; ***er ist tödlich verunglückt,*** he has met with a fatal accident; ***verunglückter Versuch,*** abortive attempt. **Verunglückte(r),** *m., f.* victim, casualty.

verunmöglichen [fɛr'unmø:glɪçən], *v.t.* (*Swiss*) render *or* make impossible.

verunreinigen [fɛr'unraɪnɪgən], *v.t.* dirty, soil, contaminate, infect, pollute, taint. **Verunreinigung,** *f.* soiling, contamination, pollution; impurity, impurities.

verunschicken [fɛr'unʃɪkən], *v.t.* (*Swiss*) lose *or* forfeit through one's own fault *or* by one's own mistake.

verunstalten [fɛr'unʃtaltən], *v.t.* disfigure, deface, deform. **verunstaltet,** *adj.* misshapen, deformed, disfigured, defaced. **Verunstaltung,** *f.* deformity, disfigurement.

veruntreuen [fɛr'untrɔyən], *v.t.* embezzle, misappropriate; ***Gelder –,*** embezzle funds, defalcate. **Veruntreuung,** *f.* embezzlement, misappropriation.

verunzieren [fɛr'untsi:rən], *v.t.* disfigure, deface, mar.

verursachen [fɛr'u:rzaxən], *v.t.* cause, occasion, bring about, create, produce, give rise to, entail.

verurteilen [fɛr'turtaɪlən], *v.t.* condemn, sentence (***zu,*** to), convict; ***ihn zu einer Geldstrafe von 20 Mark –,*** fine him 20 marks, impose a fine of 20 marks on him. **Verurteilte(r),** *m., f.* condemned p. **Verurteilung,** *f.* condemnation, conviction, sentence.

vervielfachen [fɛr'fi:lfaxən], *v.t.* multiply. **Vervielfachung,** *f.* multiplication.

vervielfältigen [fɛr'fi:lfɛltɪgən], *v.t.* copy, reproduce, duplicate, manifold, mimeograph; *see also* **vervielfachen. Vervielfältigung,** *f.* reproduction, duplication, copying, manifolding; duplicate, (mimeographed) copy. **Vervielfältigungs|apparat,** *m.* duplicator, hectograph, mimeograph. **–papier,** *n.* duplicating paper. **–recht,** *n.* right of reproduction. **–verfahren.** *n.* copying process, duplication.

vervierfachen [fər'fi:rfaxən], **1.** *v.t.* quadruple. **2.** *v.r.* increase *or* multiply fourfold.

vervollkommnen [fɛr'fɔlkɔmnən], *v.t.* perfect, improve (upon). **Vervollkommnung,** *f.* perfection, improvement, completion. **vervollkommnungsfähig,** *adj.* perfectible.

vervollständigen [fɛr'fɔlʃtɛndɪgən], *v.t.* complete; replenish. **Vervollständigung,** *f.* completion.

verwachsen [fɛr'vaksən], **1.** *irr.v.i.* (*aux.* s.) close, heal up, grow over, fill up, grow together, coalesce; become overgrown. **2.** *adj.* 1. grown together, healed up; 2. deformed, crooked, misshapen; 3. (*of plants*) thick, dense, overgrown; 4. (*fig.*) ***– mit,*** intimately bound up with, deeply rooted in, closely attached to, engrossed in; ***innig – sein mit,*** be as one with. **Verwachsung,** *f.* 1. fusion, coalescence, concrescence; healing up, cicatrization; 2. defective growth, deformity.

verwackeln [fɛr'vakəln], *v.t.* (*Phot.*) ***eine Aufnahme –,*** move the camera.

Verwahr [fɛr'va:r], *m.* (**-(e)s,** *pl.* **-e**) ***in – geben (nehmen),*** give (take) into custody; *see* **Verwahrung. verwahren, 1.** *v.t.* keep, preserve, guard (***vor*** (*Dat.*), from), secure (against); put away safely. have in safe-keeping, hold in trust; ***ihm zu – geben,*** give into his safe-keeping, entrust to his care; ***trocken –,*** keep dry. **2.** *v.r.* take precautions, secure o.s. (***gegen,*** against); (make *or* enter a) protest (against), resist; ***sein Recht*** or ***sich –,*** reserve the right (to). **Verwahrer,** *m.* keeper, guardian, trustee.

verwahrlosen [fɛr'va:rlo:zən], **1.** *v.t.* neglect. **2.** *v.i.* be neglected, be spoiled by neglect, degenerate, (*coll.*) go to seed; (*of a p.*) go to the bad, (*of children*) run wild. **verwahrlost,** *adj.* neglected, uncared-for; (*appearance*) ragged, unkempt; degenerate, depraved; (*of children*) wayward, wild. **Verwahrlosung,** *f.* neglect; degeneration, demoralization.

Verwahrsam [fɛr'va:rza:m], *m.,* (*usu.*) **Verwahrung,** *f.* charge, guard, care, (safe-)keeping *or* custody; preservation (***vor*** (*Dat.*), from); ***in – haben,*** *see* **verwahren;** ***in – nehmen,*** (*a th.*) take charge of, take under one's care; (*a p.*) take into custody; ***ihm in – geben,*** give into his charge, give him to look after; ***in – liegen,*** be deposited, be well looked after, be in safe-keeping; ***Verwahrung einlegen,*** protest, make *or* enter a protest (***gegen,*** against). **Verwahrungs|konto,** *n.* suspense account. **-ort,** *m.* place of safe-keeping, repository.

verwaisen [fɛr'vaɪzən], *v.i.* (*aux.* s.) become an orphan, lose one's parent(s); (*fig.*) be deserted, be abandoned. **verwaist,** *adj.* orphan(ed); fatherless; (*fig.*) deserted, destitute.

verwalken [fɛr'valkən], *v.t.* (*coll.*) beat, thrash.

verwalten [fɛr'valtən], *v.t.* administer, manage, conduct, superintend, supervise; fill (*a post*), hold (*an office*); ***übel –,*** mismanage, maladminister, misgovern; ***sein Vermögen –,*** act as trustee to his property *or* estate. **Verwalter,** *m.* administrator, manager, superintendent, (*of estates*) steward, (*Law*) trustee; custodian, curator.

Verwaltung [fɛr'valtuŋ], *f.* administration, management, stewardship, governing body, (administrative) authority, Civil Service. **Verwaltungs|-abteilung,** *f.* administrative branch. **-apparat,** *m.* administrative machinery. **-ausschuß,** *m.* committee of management, management committee. **-beamte(r),** *m.* administrative officer, official, Civil Servant. **-behörde,** *f.* the administration; government office; board of management. **-bezirk,** *m.* administrative area. **-dienst,** *m.* Civil Service. **-gericht,** *n.* Administrative Court. **-gerichtshof,** *m.* Higher Administrative Court. **-kosten,** *pl.* administrative expenses. **-rat,** *m.* board of directors *or* managers *or* trustees, management committee; managing director. **-weg,** *m.* ***auf dem –,*** administratively, through administrative channels. **-wesen,** *n.* (public) administration. **-zweig,** *m.* administrative department, branch of the administration.

verwamsen [fɛr'vamzən], *v.t.* (*coll.*) beat, thrash.

verwandelbar [fɛr'vandəlba:r], *adj.* transformable, convertible, transmutable. **verwandeln, 1.** *v.t.* change, convert, turn, transform (***in*** (*Acc.*), into), transmute, metamorphose; commute (*penalties etc.*); (*Math.*) reduce; ***in einen Trümmerhaufen –,*** reduce to (a heap of) rubble; ***in Geld –,*** turn into money, realize; ***in den Leib und das Blut Christi –,*** change into the body and blood of Christ; (*Footb.*) ***den Strafstoß –,*** score from the penalty (kick). **2.** *v.r.* change, turn; be changed *or* turned *or* converted *or* transformed (***in*** (*Acc.*), into).

Verwandlung [fɛr'vandluŋ], *f.* alteration, change, conversion, transformation, transmutation, metamorphosis; (*Eccl.*) transubstantiation; (*Law*) commutation; (*Theat.*) change of scenes. **Verwandlungs|künstler,** *m.* quick-change artist. **-szene,** *f.* (*Theat.*) transformation scene.

verwandt [fɛr'vant], *adj.* related (***mit,*** to), (*word*) cognate (with), connected (with), allied (to); analogous, similar (to), kindred, like, congenial; ***er ist mit mir –,*** he is a relation of mine; ***wir sind nahe –,*** we are near relations; ***wie sind Sie mit ihm –?*** in what way are you related to him? ***Malerei und Dichtkunst sind miteinander –,*** painting and poetry are kindred arts. **Verwandte(r),** *m., f.* relative, relation; ***der nächste –,*** the next of kin. **Verwandtenehe,** *f.* consanguineous marriage.

Verwandtschaft [fɛr'vantʃaft], *f.* relationship, kinship, consanguinity; (*fig.*) congeniality; connection; (chemical) affinity; (*coll.*) relations, relatives; ***– der Stämme und Sprachen,*** affinity of race and language. **verwandtschaftlich,** *adj.* kindred, allied, as among relatives; congenial. **Verwandtschafts|-grad,** *m.* degree of relationship, affinity. **-kraft,** *f.* (*Chem.*) force of affinity. **-kreis,** *m.* family, relations. **-linie,** *f.* line of descent. **-verhältnis,** *n.* hereditary *or* family relationship.

verwanzt [fɛr'vantst], *adj.* bug-ridden, (*coll.*) buggy.

verwarnen [fɛr'varnən], *v.t.* warn, caution, admonish. **Verwarnung,** *f.* warning, admonition, reprimand, caution.

verwaschen [fɛr'vaʃən], **1.** *irr.v.t.* wash away *or* wash out (*stains etc.*); wear out *or* spoil through washing. **2.** *adj.* washed-out, faded; (*fig.*) vapid, pale, vague, characterless, (*coll.*) wishy-washy.

verwässern [fɛr'vɛsərn], *v.t.* water, dilute, weaken; (*fig.*) water down; ***verwässerte Schreibart,*** vapid *or* (*coll.*) wishy-washy style.

verweben [fɛr've:bən], *reg. & irr.v.t.* interweave, intertwine, (inter)mingle; ***Wahrheit mit Dichtung –,*** mingle truth inextricably with fiction.

verwechseln [fɛr'vɛksəln], *v.t.* confuse, mix up (***mit,*** with), take, mistake (for); change by mistake; ***er verwechselt stets die Namen,*** he is always mixing up *or* confusing names; ***wir haben unsere Hüte verwechselt,*** we have taken the wrong hats; ***zum Verwechseln ähnlich,*** as like as two peas, confusingly alike. **Verwechs(e)lung,** *f.* confusion, mistake, (*coll.*) mix-up.

verwegen [fɛr've:gən], *adj.* bold, daring, audacious; rash, foolhardy. **Verwegenheit,** *f.* boldness, daring, audacity, temerity, rashness, foolhardiness, dare-devilry. **verwegentlich,** *adj.* (*rare*) *see* **verwegen.**

verwehen [fɛr've:ən], **1.** *v.t.* blow away *or* about, scatter; ***der Wind hat den Weg mit Schnee verweht,*** the wind has covered the path with snow. **2.** *v.i.* (*aux.* s.) blow about *or* away, drift, be scattered; ***seine Hoffnungen sind verweht,*** his hopes are dead *or* are blighted.

verwehren [fɛr've:rən], *v.t.* ***ihm etwas –,*** debar *or* stop *or* keep *or* hinder *or* prevent him from; ***ihm Zutritt –,*** refuse him admittance, forbid him to enter, prohibit him from entering.

Verwehung [fɛr've:uŋ], *f.* snow-drift.

verweiblicht [fɛr'vaɪplɪçt], *adj.* effeminate.

verweichlichen [fɛr'vaɪçlɪçən], **1.** *v.t.* (molly) coddle, pamper. **2.** *v.i.* become effeminate *or* flabby *or* soft. **verweichlicht,** *adj.* pampered, (molly)coddled, effeminate. **Verweichlichung,** *f.* (molly)coddling, pampering; effeminacy.

verweigern [fɛr'vaɪgərn], *v.t.* refuse, deny, decline; ***Annahme –,*** refuse acceptance, decline to accept; ***Auslieferung –,*** withhold delivery; ***Dienst –,*** refuse *or* withhold one's service; ***ihm den Gehorsam –,*** refuse *or* decline to obey him. **Verweigerung,** *f.* denial, refusal; ***– der Annahme,*** non-acceptance. **Verweigerungsfall,** *m.* ***im –,*** in case of refusal, if refused.

verweilen [fɛr'vaɪlən], *v.i.* stay, tarry, linger (***bei,*** with); (*fig.*) ***bei einem Gegenstande –,*** dwell *or* enlarge on a subject.

verweint [fɛr'vaɪnt], *adj.* (*eyes*) red with tears, (*face*) tear-stained.

Verweis [fɛr'vaɪs], *m.* (**-es,** *pl.* **-e**) 1. reprimand, rebuke, reproof, censure; ***einen – erteilen*** (*Dat.*), reprimand, upbraid, reprove, rebuke, censure (*a p.*) (***wegen,*** for); 2. reference (*to a book*). **verweisen,** *irr.v.t.* 1. ***etwas –*** (*Dat.*), *see* ***einen Verweis erteilen*** (*Dat.*); 2. refer (***an*** (*Acc.*), to (*a p.*); ***auf*** (*Acc.*), to (*a th.*)); 3. banish, exile, (*school*) expel (***aus, Gen.,*** from); (*Spt.*) send *or* order off (the field).

Verweisung [fɛr'vaɪzuŋ], *f.* 1. reference (***auf*** or ***an*** (*Acc.*), to); 2. banishment, exile; expulsion, proscription; relegation. **Verweisungszeichen,** *n.* reference mark.

verwelken [fɛr'vɛlkən], *v.i.* (*aux.* s.) fade, wither, wilt, droop.

verwelschen [fɛr'vɛlʃən], *v.t.* frenchify, italianize.

verweltlichen [fɛr'vɛltlɪçən], **1.** *v.t.* secularize. **2.** *v.i.* (*aux.* s.) become worldly. **Verweltlichung,** *f.* secularization.

verwendbar [fɛr'vɛntba:r], *adj.* applicable, adapted (***auf*** (*Acc.*), ***für,*** to), suitable, usable, serviceable, available (for). **Verwendbarkeit,** *f.* applicability, adaptability, suitability, serviceableness, availability.

verwenden [fɛr'vɛndən], **1.** *reg. & irr.v.t.* 1. use, make use of, employ, utilize (***auf*** (*Acc.*), ***für,*** in *or* for); apply (to); bestow, spend, expend (upon), devote (to); ***Sorgfalt – auf,*** bestow care upon; ***zu einem besonderen Gebrauch –,*** assign to a particular use; ***Zeit* – *auf,*** devote time to; ***etwas nützlich* –,** utilize s.th. to the full, turn s.th. to account; 2. (*irr. only*; *usu. neg.*) turn aside *or* away; ***er verwandte kein Auge von ihr,*** he never moved *or* turned his eyes from her. **2.** *reg. & irr.v.r.* use one's influence (***für,*** on behalf of), intercede (for *or* on behalf of).

Verwendung [fɛr'vɛnduŋ], *f.* use, utilization, application, employment; expenditure, appropriation; intercession; ***auf seine* – *hin,*** as a result of *or* following his intervention; ***keine* – *haben für,*** have *or* find no use for; ***vielseitige* –,** versatility; (*Law*) ***widerrechtliche* –,** conversion; ***zur* – *kommen,*** come into use, be used; (*Mil.*) ***zur besonderen* –,** (seconded) for special duty. **Verwendungs|gebiet,** *n.* field of application. **–zweck,** *m.* intended use, purpose.

verwerfen [fɛr'vɛrfən], **1.** *irr.v.t.* throw away, discard; (*usu. fig.*) reject, repudiate, disallow, (*coll.*) turn down; spurn; (*Law*) ***eine Klage* –,** dismiss a summons; (*Law*) ***eine Anklage* –,** quash an indictment; ***eine Einwendung* –,** overrule an objection. **2.** *irr.v.r.* (*of wood*) warp, become warped, (*Geol.*) (show a) fault, dislocate. **verwerflich,** *adj.* objectionable, reprehensible, thoroughly bad, abominable. **Verwerfung,** *f.* 1. rejection, repudiation; (*Law*) dismissal, quashing; 2. (*Geol.*) dislocation, fault.

verwertbar [fɛr've:rtba:r], *adj.* usable, utilizable; (*Comm.*) realizable, negotiable, convertible. **verwerten,** *v.t.* utilize, turn to (good) account, make use of; realize, turn into cash; ***Papiere* –,** convert stock; ***ein Patent* –,** exploit a patent; ***sich gut* – *lassen,*** fetch a good price; be most useful, come in handy. **Verwertung,** *f.* utilization, exploitation, (*Comm.*) disposal, realization; ***ich habe keine* – *dafür,*** I have no use for it, I cannot use it *or* do anything with it *or* make any use of it.

[1]**verwesen** [fɛr've:zən], *v.t.* administer, manage, deal with on his *etc.* behalf.

[2]**verwesen,** *v.i.* (*aux.* s.) putrefy, decompose, decay, moulder, rot.

Verweser [fɛr've:zər], *m.* administrator, manager; (*Pol.*) (vice-)regent.

verweslich [fɛr've:slıç], *adj.* perishable, corruptible, liable to decay.

[1]**Verwesung** [fɛr've:zuŋ], *f.* decay, decomposition, putrefaction.

[2]**Verwesung,** *f.* management, administration.

verwetten [fɛr'vɛtən], *v.t.* gamble away; stake, bet, wager (***für,*** on).

verwichen [fɛr'vıçən], *adj.* (*obs.*) former, past, late; ***–es Jahr,*** last year.

verwickeln [fɛr'vıkəln], **1.** *v.t.* entangle, implicate, involve, embroil (***in*** (*Acc.*), in). **2.** *v.r.* get entangled, be involved *or* implicated, (*coll.*) get mixed up (***in*** (*Acc.*), in). **verwickelt,** *adj.* complicated, intricate, involved. **Verwick(e)lung,** *f.* complication, complexity, intricacy; implication, involvement; embarrassment, entanglement, imbroglio; confusion, tangle.

verwiesen [fɛr'vi:zən], *see* **verweisen**; ***es sei* – *auf*** (*Acc.*), reference should be made to.

verwildern [fɛr'vıldərn], *v.r., v.i.* (*aux.* s.) (*of a p.*) grow wild *or* savage, become depraved *or* brutalized, degenerate; (*of plants*) run wild, run to seed; (*of a garden*) be neglected, (*coll.*) become a wilderness; **–** ***lassen,*** let run wild, neglect. **verwildert,** *adj.* (*of a p.*) wild, unruly, brutal; (*of a garden*) neglected, uncultivated, overgrown with weeds. **Verwilderung,** *f.* return to a wild *or* savage state; degeneration; wildness, unruliness, barbarism.

verwilligen [fɛr'vılıgən], *v.t.* (*obs.*) *see* **einwilligen.**

verwinden [fɛr'vındən], *irr.v.t.* 1. overcome, get the better of; get over, recover from; ***er wird es nie* –,** he will never get over it; 2. (*Tech.*) distort, twist. **Verwindung,** *f.* distortion.

verwirken [fɛr'vırkən], *v.t.* 1. forfeit, lose (*through one's own fault*); 2. be liable to, merit, incur (*a punishment*).

verwirklichen [fɛr'vırklıçən], **1.** *v.t.* realize, embody; put into action, translate into reality. **2.** *v.r.* be realized, come true, materialize. **Verwirklichung,** *f.* realization, materialization.

Verwirkung [fɛr'vırkuŋ], *f.* loss, forfeiture.

verwirren [fɛr'vırən], *irr.v.t.* tangle, entangle, disarrange; complicate, make involved *or* intricate; (*fig.*) confuse, bewilder, perplex, confound; disconcert, embarrass; ***ihm den Kopf* –,** make him quite confused, make his head spin. **verwirrt,** *adj.* (*of a p.*) confused, perplexed, bewildered, (*coll.*) dazed, (*as hair*) tousled, dishevelled. **Verwirrung,** *f.* entanglement, complication; confusion, disorder, muddle, (*coll.*) mix-up; embarrassment, perplexity, bewilderment; ***in* – *bringen,*** (*a th.*) throw into disorder, (*a p.*) throw into confusion, confuse; ***in* – *geraten,*** become confused, (*coll.*) get mixed up.

verwirtschaften [fɛr'vırtʃaftən], *v.t.* squander, dissipate.

verwischen [fɛr'vıʃən], **1.** *v.t.* wipe away, efface, blot out; blur, smear; stump, soften (*an outline*). **2.** *v.r.* become effaced *or* blurred.

verwittern [fɛr'vıtərn], *v.i.* (*aux.* s.) weather, crumble away, disintegrate, decay; (*Chem.*) effloresce. **verwittert,** *adj.* weather-beaten *or* -worn, weathered, crumbled, dilapidated; ***verwitterter Kalk,*** air-slaked lime. **Verwitterung,** *f.* weathering, decomposition, decay, crumbling, disintegration; (*Chem.*) efflorescence.

verwitwet [fɛr'vıtvət], *adj.* widowed; ***–e Königin,*** Queen dowager, dowager queen.

verwogen [fɛr'vo:gən], *adj.* (*obs. or dial.*) bold, audacious, rash, foolhardy; *see* **verwegen.**

verwöhnen [fɛr'vø:nən], **1.** *v.t.* spoil, pamper, coddle. **2.** *v.r.* (over)indulge o.s., allow o.s. to be pampered. **verwöhnt,** *adj.* 1. spoiled, spoilt, pampered; 2. fastidious. **Verwöhntheit,** *f.* 1. bad habits, evil results of pampering; 2. fastidiousness. **Verwöhnung,** *f.* pampering, spoiling, indulgence; *see also* **Verwöhntheit.**

verworfen [fɛr'vɔrfən], *adj.* depraved, base, vile, infamous; reprobate; *see* **verwerfen. Verworfenheit,** *f.* depravity, baseness, vileness, infamy.

verworren [fɛr'vɔrən], *adj.* entangled, intricate, confused, muddled; ***der –e Bericht eines verwirrten Menschen,*** the confused *or* muddled account of a bewildered *or* muddle-headed person. **Verworrenheit,** *f.* intricacy, confusion, muddled state, disorder.

verwundbar [fɛr'vuntba:r], *adj.* vulnerable; (*fig.*) ***–e Stelle,*** weak *or* sore point.

[1]**verwunden** [fɛr'vundən], *v.t.* wound, injure, hurt; ***auf das schmerzlichste* –,** cut to the quick.

[2]**verwunden,** *see* **verwinden.**

verwunderlich [fɛr'vundərlıç], *adj.* astonishing, surprising, odd, remarkable, strange, (*Poet.*) wondrous; ***es ist nicht* – *daß*** . . ., it is small wonder that. . . .

verwundern [fɛr'vundərn], **1.** *v.t.* surprise, astonish, amaze. **2.** *v.r.* be amazed *or* astonished *or* surprised, wonder (***über*** (*Acc.*), at); ***sich verwundert stellen,*** feign *or* affect surprise; ***es ist nicht zu* –,** it is small wonder, it is not to be wondered at. **Verwunderung,** *f.* astonishment, surprise, amazement. **Verwunderungs|ausruf,** *m.* exclamation of surprise. **–brille,** *f.* (*coll.*) ***die* – *aufsetzen,*** affect astonishment, pretend to be surprised.

verwundet [fɛr'vundət], *adj.* wounded, injured, hurt. **Verwundeten|abschub,** *m.* evacuation of wounded. **–abzeichen,** *n.* (*Mil.*) wound-stripe, (*Am.*) Purple Heart. **–sammelstelle,** *f.* casualty clearing-station. **Verwundete(r),** *m., f.* injured person, wounded soldier, casualty. **Verwundung,** *f.* wound, injury.

verwunschen [fɛr'vunʃən], *adj.* (*Poet.*) bewitched, enchanted; haunted (*house*).

verwünschen [fɛr'vynʃən], *v.t.* deplore (*a th.*), wish (*a p.*) ill, curse, execrate; bewitch, cast a spell on. **verwünscht,** *adj.* (ac)cursed, confounded, damned, execrable; ***das –e Geld,*** that confounded money;

-er Spaß, joke in bad taste; (*coll.*) – ***gescheit***, confoundedly *or* damned clever; *–!* confound it! curse! damn! **Verwünschung,** *f.* curse, imprecation, malediction; ***–en ausstoßen gegen***, curse, hurl imprecations at.

verwurzeln [fɛr'vurtsəln], *v.i.*, *v.r.* be *or* become rooted. **verwurzelt,** *adj.* deeply *or* firmly rooted (***in*** (*Dat.*), in). **Verwurz(e)lung,** *f.* close attachment (***mit, in*** (*Dat.*), to), intimate contact (with).

verwüsten [fɛr'vy:stən], *v.t.* lay waste, devastate, ravage, ruin, destroy. **Verwüstung,** *f.* devastation, destruction, ravages.

verzagen [fɛr'tsa:gən], *v.i.* (*aux.* s.) despair (***an*** (*Dat.*), of), give up hope, lose heart *or* courage, despond, be despondent. **verzagt,** *adj.* discouraged, despondent, dejected, disheartened; faint-hearted, timorous, pusillanimous; – ***machen,*** dishearten, discourage; – ***werden,*** despond, lose heart, give up hope. **Verzagtheit,** *f.* despair, despondency, faint-heartedness.

verzählen [fɛr'tsɛ:lən], *v.r.* make a mistake (in counting), count (up) wrong, miscount.

verzahnen [fɛr'tsa:nən], **1.** *v.t.* tooth, cog (*a wheel*), dovetail (*a joint*); (*fig.*) link together, make cross-connections between, supply with cross-references. **2.** *v.r.* engage, mesh (*as gears*); (*usu. fig.*) interlock, interconnect, dovetail. **Verzahnung,** *f.* indentation, notch; gear, gearing; (*fig.*) interconnection, dovetailing.

verzapfen [fɛr'tsapfən], *v.t.* 1. sell (*beer etc.*) on draught; 2. join by mortise and tenon; 3. (*sl.*) dish out; ***Unsinn –***, spout rubbish.

verzärteln [fɛr'tsɛ:rtəln], *v.t.* spoil, pamper, coddle, pet. **verzärtelt,** *adj.* spoiled, spoilt, pampered. **Verzärtelung,** *f.* over-indulgence, pampering, coddling; effeminacy.

verzaubern [fɛr'tsaubərn], *v.t.* charm, bewitch, put *or* cast a spell on; transform, change, turn (***in*** (*Acc.*), into); ***verzauberter Prinz,*** enchanted prince; ***verzauberte Insel,*** magic island.

verzehnfachen [fɛr'tse:nfaxən], *v.t.* increase *or* multiply tenfold. **verzehnten,** *v.t.* (*Hist.*) pay tithe on.

Verzehr [fɛr'tse:r], *m.* consumption (*of food etc.*). **verzehren, 1.** *v.t.* consume, eat (up); use up. **2.** *v.r.* be consumed (***vor*** (*Dat.*), with); waste *or* pine away. **verzehrend,** *adj.* (all-)consuming, burning (*passion etc.*). **Verzehrung,** *f.* consumption. **Verzehrzwang,** *m.* obligation to order (*food, drink etc. at an inn*).

verzeichnen [fɛr'tsaɪçnən], *v.t.* 1. write *or* note down, record, register, enter; specify, (make a) list (of); 2. draw badly *or* incorrectly, (*fig.*) distort, misrepresent; (*Comm.*) ***zu dem verzeichneten Kurs,*** at the price quoted; ***auf der Liste verzeichnet sein,*** be recorded *or* listed, figure in *or* on the list.

Verzeichnis [fɛr'tsaɪçnɪs], *n.* (**-ses,** *pl.* **-se**) list, table, schedule, catalogue, inventory, roll; index, register; statement, specification, invoice, price-list; – ***der Anmerkungen,*** index of notes; – ***der Druckfehler,*** list of errata; – ***der Einkünfte,*** rent-roll; – ***des Inhalts,*** table of contents; – ***der Verstorbenen,*** obituary, necrology.

Verzeichnung [fɛr'tsaɪçnuŋ], *f.* error in drawing; (*Opt.*) distortion. **verzeichnungsfrei,** *adj.* (*Opt.*) orthoscopic.

verzeigen [fɛr'tsaɪgən], *v.t.* (*Swiss*) *see* **anzeigen.**

verzeihen [fɛr'tsaɪən], *irr.v.t.* forgive, pardon, excuse (***ihm etwas,*** him s.th.), remit (*sins*), condone (*a fault*); – ***Sie!*** excuse me! pardon me! I beg your pardon! ***nicht zu –***, inexcusable. **verzeihlich,** *adj.* pardonable, excusable, (*of sins*) venial. **Verzeihung,** *f.* pardon, forgiveness; (*of sins*) remission; ***ihn um – bitten,*** beg his pardon; *–!* excuse me! (please) forgive me! I beg your pardon!

verzerren [fɛr'tsɛrən], **1.** *v.t.* distort, deform; twist *or* pull out of shape; (*fig.*) caricature; ***das Gesicht –***, grimace, (*coll.*) pull a face; ***sich*** (*Dat.*) ***den Knöchel –***, strain one's ankle; ***etwas ins Lächerliche –***, make s.th. look ridiculous; ***verzerrt darstellen,*** caricature, give a distorted picture of. **2.** *v.r.* get out of shape, become distorted. **Verzerrung,** *f.* distortion; contortion, grimace.

verzetteln [fɛr'tsɛtəln], **1.** *v.t.* 1. scatter, disperse, dissipate, fritter away; 2. make a card-index of, enter on cards, catalogue. **2.** *v.r.* dissipate one's energies.

Verzicht [fɛr'tsɪçt], *m.* renunciation, abandonment (***auf*** (*Acc.*), of); (*Law*) disclaimer, waiver; – ***leisten,*** *see* **verzichten. verzichten,** *v.i.* – ***auf*** (*Acc.*), renounce, relinquish, abandon, forgo, dispense with, (*coll.*) do without; give up all claim to, (*Law*) waive, disclaim. **Verzicht|erklärung,** *f.* (*Law*) waiver, disclaimer. **–leistung,** *f. See* **Verzicht.**

verziehen [fɛr'tsi:ən], **1.** *irr.v.t.* distort, twist; ***das Gesicht –***, grimace, make a wry face, (*coll.*) pull a face; ***keine Miene –***, not move a muscle, (*sl.*) not bat an eyelid; ***den Mund –***, screw up one's mouth; (*fig.*) ***ein Kind –***, bring up a child badly, spoil a child; ***einen Stein –***, move the wrong piece, make a wrong move (*in draughts etc.*). **2.** *irr.v.r.* 1. (*as mist*) dissolve, (*as clouds, a crowd etc.*) disperse, (*as a storm*) pass *or* blow over, (*as pain*) subside, pass away, (*of a p.*) vanish, disappear, (*coll.*) make off; 2. (*of wood*) warp, become warped, (*of clothes*) hang badly, pucker; ***sein Mund verzog sich zu einem Grinsen,*** his mouth twisted into a grin. **3.** *irr.v.i.* 1. (*aux.* s.) (re)move, go away; ***in die Stadt –***, move into (the) town; ***von M. nach O. –***, (re)move from M. to O.; ***falls verzogen,*** in case of change of address; 2. (*aux.* h.) (*obs.*) linger, hesitate.

verzieren [fɛr'tsi:rən], *v.t.* adorn, ornament, decorate, trim, embellish; ***verzierter Kontrapunkt,*** figured counterpoint. **Verzierung,** *f.* decoration, ornamentation, ornament, embellishment, (*Mus.*) flourish, grace-note, (*coll.*) frills.

verzinken [fɛr'tsɪŋkən], *v.t.* coat *or* line with zinc, galvanize; (*coll.*) inform against, (*sl.*) split on.

verzinnen [fɛr'tsɪnən], *v.t.* tin, tin-plate, coat *or* line with tin; ***verzinntes Eisenblech,*** tin-plate.

verzinsen [fɛr'tsɪnzən], **1.** *v.t.* pay interest on; ***ihm das Geld zu 3% –***, pay him 3% interest on the money; ***zu 5% verzinst,*** bearing 5% interest. **2.** *v.r.* yield *or* bear interest; ***es verzinst sich nicht,*** it yields no interest. **verzinslich,** *adj.* bearing interest; – ***anlegen,*** put out at interest, invest; ***–es Darlehen,*** loan on interest; – ***mit 5%,*** bearing interest at 5%, bearing 5% interest; – ***vom 1. Oktober,*** interest payable from October 1. **Verzinsung,** *f.* interest rate; return *or* payment of interest; ***zur – ausleihen,*** put out at interest.

verzogen [fɛr'tso:gən], *adj.* warped, distorted; spoiled (*of a child*); *see* **verziehen.**

verzögern [fɛr'tsø:gərn], **1.** *v.t.* defer, delay; retard, slow down, protract, (*coll.*) spin out. **2.** *v.r.* (*of a p.*) be delayed, come late, be a long time coming; (*of a th.*) be protracted *or* deferred; slow down. **Verzögerung,** *f.* delay, postponement, adjournment; retardation, time-lag, delay(ed)-action. **Verzögerungs|spannung,** *f.* (*Elec.*) threshold voltage. **–taktik,** *f.* delaying action. **–zünder,** *m.* delayed-action fuse.

verzollbar [fɛr'tsɔlba:r], *adj.* dutiable, subject *or* liable to duty. **verzollen,** *v.t.* pay duty on; ***haben Sie etwas zu –?*** have you anything to declare? ***Waren –***, clear goods at the customs. **verzollt,** *adj.* duty-paid. **Verzollung,** *f.* payment of duty, clearance.

verzücken [fɛr'tsykən], *v.t.* enrapture.

verzuckern [fɛr'tsukərn], *v.t.* sweeten, sugar (over), ice; (*fig.*) ***die Pille –***, sugar the pill.

verzückt, *adj.* enraptured, ecstatic, rapt, in raptures, in transports (of delight), in ecstasy, (*coll.*) beside o.s. (with enthusiasm).

Verzückung [fɛr'zykuŋ], *f.* ecstasy, rapture, transport.

Verzug [fɛr'tsu:k], *m.* (**-(e)s,** *pl.* **¨-e**) 1. delay, postponement; ***bei – der Zahlung,*** in the case of arrears of *or* in payment; ***bei – neue Anschrift angeben!*** notify any change of address; ***es ist Gefahr im –e,*** there is danger imminent *or* ahead; ***in –***, in arrears, in default; ***ohne –***, without delay, at once, immediately, forthwith; 2. (*dial.*) darling, pet, spoilt child.

Verzugs|aktien, *f.pl.* deferred shares. **–klausel,** *f.* clause relating to default. **–strafe,** *f.* penalty for delay *or* default. **–tage,** *m.pl.* days of grace. **–zinsen,** *m.pl.* interest payable on arrears.

verzwatzeln [fɛr'tsvatsəln], *v.i.* (*dial.*) despair, lose one's patience.

verzweifeln [fɛr'tsvaɪfəln], *v.i.* (*aux.* s. & h.) despair (***an ihm,*** of him; ***über eine S.,*** of a th.); give up *or* abandon hope (for), be despondent *or* in despair (about); ***es ist zum –,*** it is enough to drive one to despair; ***nur nicht –!*** never say die! **verzweifelt,** *adj.* despairing, desperate; ***eine –e Geschichte,*** a desperate *or* hopeless case, (*coll.*) a dreadful business. **Verzweiflung,** *f.* despair, desperation; ***zur – bringen,*** drive to despair; ***in – geraten,*** become despondent, (give way to) despair; ***aus*** or ***in*** or ***vor – tun,*** do in desperation; ***die Kraft der –,*** the strength of despair; ***– an Gott,*** despair about *or* over (the existence of) God.

verzweigen [fɛr'tsvaɪgən], *v.r.* branch (out), ramify. **Verzweigung,** *f.* branching, ramification.

verzwergen [fɛr'tsvɛrgən], *v.i.* (*aux.* s.) become dwarfed, grow stunted. **verzwergt,** *adj.* dwarf, dwarfed, dwarfish, stunted.

verzwicken [fɛr'tsvɪkən], *v.t.* 1. entangle, confuse; 2. (*Build.*) fill up with rubble *or* packing; ***den Weinstock –,*** prune the vine. **verzwickt,** *adj.* (*coll.*) puzzling, confused; awkward, complicated, intricate, (*coll.*) ticklish, tricky.

Vesper ['fɛspər], *f.* (-, *pl.* **-n**) vespers, evensong; afternoon tea; ***die – schlägt,*** the evening bell tolls. **Vesper|bild,** *n.* pietà, Virgin with dead body of Christ. **–brot,** *n.* afternoon tea. **–glocke,** *f.* vesper-bell. **vespern,** *v.i.* take afternoon-tea.

Vestalin [ve'sta:lɪn], *f.* vestal (virgin).

Vestibül [vɛsti'by:l], *n.* (**-s,** *pl.* **-e**) vestibule, hall.

Veteran [vete'ra:n], *m.* (**-en,** *pl.* **-en**) ex-serviceman, (*Am.*) veteran, (*sl.*) old sweat; (*fig.*) veteran.

Veterinär [veteri'nɛ:r], *m.* (**-s,** *pl.* **-e**) veterinary surgeon, (*coll.*) vet. **veterinär,** *adj.* veterinary.

Veto ['ve:to], *n.* (**-s,** *pl.* **-s**) veto; ***aufschiebendes –*** suspensive veto; ***gegen eine S. sein – einlegen,*** veto a th., put a veto on a th.

Vettel ['fɛtəl], *f.* (-, *pl.* **-n**) slut, slattern, trollop, drab.

Vetter ['fɛtər], *m.* (**-s,** *pl.* **-n**) (male) cousin. **vetterlich,** *adj.* cousinly, cousin-like. **Vetterliwirtschaft,** *f.* (*Swiss*), **Vetternwirtschaft,** *f.* nepotism.

Vexierbild [vɛk'si:rbɪlt], *n.* picture puzzle. **vexieren,** *v.t.* vex, tease, trick, puzzle, mystify, hoax, (*coll.*) take in. **Vexier|schloß,** *n.* puzzle- *or* combination-lock. **–spiegel,** *m.* distorting mirror. **–spiel,** *n.* Chinese puzzle.

Vezier [ve'tsi:r], *m.* (**-s,** *pl.* **-e**) vizier.

Viatikum [vi'a:tikum], *n.* (**-s,** *pl.* **-ka** *or* **-ken**) viaticum, alms; (*R.C.*) extreme unction.

Vibration [vibratsi'o:n], *f.* vibration. **Vibrationsmassage,** *f.* vibro-massage. **vibrieren** [–'bri:rən], *v.i.* vibrate.

vidimieren [vidi'mi:rən], *v.t.* pass for press, sign as correct.

Viech [fi:ç], *n.* (**-s,** *pl.* **-er**) (*dial.*) *see* **Vieh**; (*vulg.*) beast, swine, cow (*as abuse*).

Vieh [fi:], *n.* cattle, livestock; dumb animal, beast; (*fig.*) beast, brute; ***zwei Stück –,*** two head of cattle; ***eine Herde*** or ***Trift –,*** a drove of cattle; ***Menschen und –,*** men and beasts.

Vieh|bestand, *m.* cattle population, livestock. **–bremse,** *f.* gadfly. **–diebstahl,** *m.* cattle-stealing. **–dünger,** *m.* stable manure. **–futter,** *n.* fodder, forage. **–händler,** *m.* cattle-dealer. **–hof,** *m.* stockyard. **–hürde,** *f.* cattle-pen. **viehisch,** *adj.* brutal, beastly, bestial. **Vieh|knecht,** *m.* farmhand, cattlehand, herdsman. **–magd,** *f.* farmservant, dairyhand, dairymaid. **–markt,** *m.* cattle- *or* stock-market. **–schlag,** *m.* breed of cattle. **–seuche,** *f.* cattle-pest, murrain. **–stall,** *m.* cowhouse, cattle-shed, stable. **–stamm,** *m.* *See* **–schlag. –stand, –stapel,** *m.* *See* **–bestand. –treiber,** *m.* drover. **–trift,** *f.* cattle-run, pasturage. **–wagen,** *m.* cattle-truck; (*Am.*) stock-car. **–weide,** *f.* *See* **–trift. –zählung,** *f.* cattle-census. **–zeug,** *n.* (*coll.*) animals. **–zucht,** *f.* stock-farming, cattle-breeding. **–züchter,** *m.* stock-farmer, cattle-breeder.

viel [fi:l], *adj., adv.* (*comp.* ***mehr,*** *sup.* ***meist***) much, a great deal of, (*coll.*) a lot, lots of; *pl.* many, *see* **viele**; ***–es andere,*** many other things; ***– Geld,*** much money, a lot of money; ***das –e Geld,*** all that money; ***trotz seines –en Geldes,*** in spite of all his wealth; ***ein bißchen –, etwas –,*** rather *or* a little too much; ***gar –,*** a great deal; ***wir haben gleich –,*** we have equal amounts, we have each the same amount, (*coll.*) we have just as much as each other; ***in –em,*** in many respects; (*Prov.*) ***mit Vielem hält man Haus, mit Wenigem kommt man aus,*** the more you have, the more you want; ***er hat – gelesen,*** he has read a great deal, he is widely read; ***– mehr als,*** much *or* far more than; ***nicht –,*** not much; ***nicht –es, sondern –,*** non multa, sed multum; ***es hätte nicht – gefehlt, so hätte er . . .,*** a little more and he would have . . .; ***recht –,*** see ***sehr –***; ***das will – sagen,*** that is saying a great deal; ***sehr –,*** very much, a great deal; ***eben so –,*** just as much; ***noch einmal so –,*** as much again; ***so – weiß ich,*** this *or* that much I know; ***soundso –,*** so much (and no more), neither more nor less; ***um –es größer,*** a great deal larger, much *or* far larger, larger by far; ***ziemlich –,*** a good deal; ***einer zu –,*** one too many; ***– zu –,*** much *or* far too much; ***mehr als zu –,*** more than enough.

viel|adrig, *adj.* multi-core (*cable*). **–artig,** *adj.* manifold, multifarious, various. **–bändig,** *adj.* of many volumes. **–bedeutend,** *adj.* very significant. **–beschäftigt,** *adj.* much occupied, very busy. **–deutig,** *adj.* ambiguous. **Vieldeutigkeit,** *f.* ambiguity.

viele ['fi:lə], *adj.pl.* many; ***die –n,*** the many; ***es kamen ihrer –,*** many of them came; ***gar –,*** very many; ***sehr –,*** very many, a great many.

Vieleck ['fi:lʔɛk], *n.* polygon. **vieleckig,** *adj.* many-cornered, polygonal. **Vielehe,** *f.* polygamy.

vielerlei ['fi:lərlaɪ], *indecl.adj.* various, divers, multifarious, many kinds of, (*pred.*) of many kinds. **Vielerlei,** *n.* great variety. **vielerorts,** *adv.* in many places.

vielfach ['fi:lfax], **1.** *adj.* multiple, repeated, reiterated. **2.** *adv.* often, frequently; in many cases *or* ways. **Vielfache(s),** *n.* the multiple; ***um ein Vielfaches,*** many times over. **Vielfach|schalter,** *m.* multiple switch. **–schaltung,** *f.* (*Elec.*) multiple connection.

vielfältig ['fi:lfɛltɪç], *adj.* multifarious, manifold, various. **Vielfältigkeit,** *f.* diversity, variety, multiplicity. **vielfarbig,** *adj.* many-coloured, multicoloured, variegated, polychromatic. **Viel|flach,** *n.*, **–flächner,** *m.* polyhedron. **viel|flüg(e)lig,** *adj.* (*Ent.*) polypterous. **–förmig,** *adj.* multiform, polymorphous. **Vielfraß,** *m.* (*Zool.*) wolverine; (*fig.*) glutton, voracious eater. **vielfrüchtig,** *adj.* (*Bot.*) polycarpous. **Vielfuß,** *m.* polypod, centipede, millepede.

viel|gebraucht, *adj.* much *or* constantly used. **–geliebt,** *adj.* well-beloved. **–genannt,** *adj.* oftenmentioned, much discussed. **–gereist,** *adj.* widely travelled. **–gerühmt.** *adj.* much praised. **–geschmäht,** *adj.* much abused. **–gestaltig,** *adj.* of many shapes, polymorphic, multiform. **–gliede(e)rig,** *adj.* with *or* of many members, (*Math.*) polynomial. **Vielgötterei,** *f.* polytheism.

Vielheit ['fi:lhaɪt], *f.* plurality, multiplicity; multitude, large *or* great number *or* quantity. **viel|jährig,** *adj.* many years old; ***–er Freund,*** friend of many years standing. **–kantig,** *adj.* many-sided, polygonal. **–köpfig,** *adj.* many-headed, polycephalous, (*fig.*) numerous.

vielleicht [fi'laɪçt], *adv.* perhaps, maybe, possibly, perchance; ***du hast – recht,*** you may be right; (*coll.*) ***das war – eine Bescherung!*** that was a mess if you like! ***wenn er – kommen sollte,*** if he should chance to come.

Vielliebchen ['fi:lli:pçən], *n.* 1. darling, sweetheart; 2. philippina.

viel|linig, *adj.* multilinear. **–malig,** *adj.* often-repeated, reiterated, frequent. **–mal(s),** *adv.* often, frequently, many times, (*obs.*) often-times; ***ich danke Ihnen –,*** I thank you very much, many thanks; ***ihn – grüßen lassen,*** send one's kind regards to him; ***ich bitte – um Entschuldigung,*** I am very sorry. **Vielmännerei,** *f.* polyandry (*also Bot.*). **viel|mehr,** *adv.* rather, on the contrary. **–motorig,** *adj.* multi-engined. **–phasig,** *adj.* (*Elec.*) polyphase. **–sagend,** *adj.* expressive, significant, highly suggestive, eloquent. **–saitig,** *adj.* many-stringed. **–schichtig,** *adj.* many-layered, stratified. **Vielschreiber,** *m.* prolific writer, quill-driver, scribbler.

vielseitig ['fi:lzaɪtɪç], *adj.* (*as a treaty*) multilateral; (*Math.*) polygonal, polyhedral; (*fig.*) (*of a p.*) many-sided, all-round, versatile; ***auf –en Wunsch,*** by popular request. **Vielseitigkeit,** *f.* many-sidedness, versatility.

viel|silbig, *adj.* polysyllabic. **–sprachig,** *adj.* polyglot. **–stimmig,** *adj.* for many voices, many-voiced, polyphonic. **–teilig,** *adj.* multipartite; multinominal (quantity); (*Bot., Zool.*) multifid, multisect, polytomous. **–umfassend,** *adj.* vast, comprehensive. **–umstritten,** *adj.* much discussed, widely disputed. **–verheißend, –versprechend,** *adj.* very promising, of great promise, (*coll.*) up-and-coming. **Vielweiberei,** *f.* polygamy. **vielweibig,** *adj.* (*Bot.*) polygynous. **Vielweibigkeit,** *f.* (*Bot.*) polygyny. **vielwertig,** *adj.* polyvalent, multivalent. **Vielwisser,** *m.* erudite man, man of great learning, (*coll.*) pundit, walking encyclopaedia. **vielzellig,** *adj.* multicellular.

vier [fi:r], *num.adj.* (*coll. when used pred. Nom. and Acc.* **-e**; *Dat.* **-en**) four; ***auf allen –en gehen,*** go on all fours; ***alle –e von sich strecken,*** stretch o.s. out, lie sprawling, (*coll.*) turn up one's toes, give up the ghost; ***unter – Augen,*** tête-à-tête, privately, confidentially; (*coll.*) ***setz dich auf deine – Buchstaben!*** find somewhere to sit; ***sich in seine – Ecken*** or ***Pfähle begeben,*** be off home; ***um halb –,*** at half-past three; ***mit –en fahren,*** drive four-in-hand; ***in seinen – Wänden,*** at home; ***in alle – Winde,*** to the four winds; ***wir waren zu –en*** or ***zu –t,*** there were four of us; ***zu je –en,*** in fours. **Vier,** *f.* (-, *pl.* **-en**) the number 4, the figure 4.

vier|basisch, *adj.* (*Chem.*) tetrabasic. **–beinig,** *adj.* four-legged. **–bindig,** *adj.* (*Chem.*) quaternary. **Vierblatt,** *n.* 1. four comrades; 2. (*Archit.*) quatrefoil; (*Bot.*) quadrifolium. **vier|blätt(e)rig,** *adj.* four-leaved, tetrapetalous. **–dimensional,** *adj.* fourth-dimensional; (*coll.*) unreal, spooky. **Viereck,** *n.* square, rectangle, quadrilateral. **vier|eckig,** *adj.* square, quadrilateral, rectangular, quadrate, four-cornered. **–einhalb,** *num.adj.* four and a half.

Vierer ['fi:rər], *m.* one of four; soldier of the fourth regiment; wine of the year '04; (*Rowing*) four, (*Golf*) foursome. **Vierer|bob,** *m.* four-man bob-sleigh. **–kreis,** *m.* (*Elec.*) phantom circuit. **viererlei,** *indecl.adj.* four (different) kinds of, of four different kinds. **Viererl|reihe,** *f.* (*Gymn.*) column of four. **–rennen,** *n.* four-man relay-race. **–spiel,** *n.* (*Golf*) foursome.

vier|fach, *adj.* quadruple, fourfold; ***um das Vierfache vermehren,*** multiply by four, quadruple. **–fältig,** *adj. See* **–fach**; ***–e Ausfertigung,*** four copies, (in) quadruplicate. **Vier|farbendruck,** *m.* four-colour print(ing). **–felderwirtschaft,** *f.* four-strip cultivation. **–flach,** *n. See* **–flächner. vierflächig,** *adj.* tetrahedral. **Vier|flächner,** *m.* tetrahedron. **–fürst,** *m.* tetrarch. **–füßer,** *m.* quadruped, tetrapod. **vierfüßig,** *adj.* four-footed, (*Metr.*) tetrameter. **Vier|füßler,** *m. See* **–füßer. –gesang,** *m.* four-part song, quartet. **–gespann,** *n.* four-in-hand, carriage and four, (*Hist.*) quadriga; (*coll.*) foursome. **vier|gestrichen,** *adj.* four-tailed (note); (note) in altissimo; ***–es F,*** F in altissimo, F of the sixth octave; ***das Klavier geht bis ins –e F,*** it is a six-octaved piano. **–gliederig,** *adj.* with 4 members *or* parts; (*Math.*) quadrinomial. **–händig,** *adj.* four-handed; ***–es Tonstück,*** piece arranged as a piano duet *or* for four hands; ***– spielen,*** play a duet. **–hundert,** *adj.* four hundred. **Vierhundertjahrfeier,** *f.* quatercentenary. **vier|jährig,** *adj.* four years old, lasting four years, quadrennial; ***–es Kind,*** four-year-old child. **–jährlich,** *adj.* recurring every fourth year, occurring once every four years; quadrennial.

Vierkant ['fi:rkant], *n.* square. **vierkant,** *adj.* (*Naut.*) level, on an even keel. **Vierkantholz,** *n.* squared timber. **vierkantig,** *adj.* square, four-sided. **Vierkantstange,** *f.* bar of rectangular section.

Vierling ['fi:rlɪŋ], *m.* (**-s,** *pl.* **-e**) four-barrelled gun. **Vierlinge,** *m.pl.* quadruplets, (*coll.*) quads. **Vierlingsturm,** *m.* four-gun turret.

vier|mal, *adv.* four times. **–malig,** *adj.* repeated four times. **–mals,** *adv. See* **–mal. Vier|paß,** *m.* (*Archit.*) quatrefoil. **–pfünder,** *m.* four-pounder. **–plätzer,** *m.* (*Swiss*) *see* **–sitzer. –pol,** *m. See* **–polschaltung. –polröhre,** *f.* tetrode. **–polschaltung,** *f.* (*Elec.*) four-terminal network. **–radantrieb,** *m.* four-wheel drive. **–radbremse,** *f.* four-wheel brake. **–röhrenverstärker,** *m.* four-valve amplifier.

vier|schrötig, *adj.* square-built; thick-set, stocky, (*coll.*) hulking. **–seitig,** *adj.* four-sided, quadrilateral, rectangular. **–silbig,** *adj.* four-syllabled, tetrasyllabic. **Vier|sitzer,** *m.* four-seater (*car*). **–spänner,** *m.* carriage and four, four-in-hand. **vier|spännig,** *adj.* ***– fahren,*** drive a carriage and four, drive four-in-hand. **–stellig,** *adj.* (*Math.*) of four places *or* digits. **–stimmig,** *adj.* for four voices *or* parts; ***–es Stück,*** four-part song; quartet. **–stöckig,** *adj.* four-storied. **–stufig,** *adj.* four-stage. **–stündig,** *adj.* lasting four hours. **–stündlich,** *adj.* every four hours. **–tägig,** *adj.* four-day, four days old, of *or* lasting four days; ***–es Fieber,*** quartan ague. **–täglich,** *adj.* recurring *or* happening every fourth day. **viert** [fi:rt], *num. adj.* fourth. **Vier|takt,** *m.* (*Motor.*) four-stroke cycle. **–taktmotor,** *m.* four-stroke engine.

viert(e)halb, *num. adj.* three and a half.

vier|teilen, *v.t.* (*p.p.* ***gevierteilt***) divide into four parts; (*Hist.*) draw and quarter. **–teilig,** *adj.* quadripartite; quadrinomial; (*Her.*) quartered.

Viertel ['fi:rtəl], *n.* (*Swiss m.*) fourth (part), quarter; ward (*of a town*), district; ***ein – (auf) vier,*** a quarter past three; ***drei – (auf) vier,*** a quarter to four; ***fünf Minuten vor drei –,*** twenty minutes to; ***ein – Wein,*** a quarter (of a litre) of wine; ***akademisches –,*** (*Univ.*) 15 minutes after the time announced.

Viertel|jahr, *n.* quarter (of a year); three months. **–jahr(es)schrift,** *f.* quarterly (*journal*). **–jahrhundert,** *n.* quarter century. **viertel|jährig,** *adj.* three months old, lasting *or* of three months, three-month. **–jährlich,** *adj.* every three months, once in three months, quarterly; ***–e Kündigung,*** three months' notice. **Viertel|jahrschrift,** *f. See* **–jahr(es)schrift. –jahrsgehalt,** *n.* quarter's salary. **–kreis,** *m.* quadrant.

vierteln ['fi:rtəln], *v.t.* quarter (*also Her.*).

Viertel|note, *f.* (*Mus.*) crotchet. **–pause,** *f.* (*Mus.*) crotchet-rest. **–stunde,** *f.* quarter of an hour; ***drei –n,*** three-quarters of an hour. **viertel|-stündig,** *adj.* lasting a quarter of an hour, fifteen-minute (*break etc.*). **–stündlich,** *adj.* every quarter of an hour, every 15 minutes. **Viertelton,** *m.* half a semitone.

viertens ['fi:rtəns], *adv.* fourthly, in the fourth place. **viert|halb,** *num.adj. See* **viert(e)halb. –letzt,** *adj.* last but three, fourth from the end.

vier|undeinhalb, *num.adj. See* **–einhalb. Vier|-undsechzigstel,** *n.* one sixty-fourth. **–undsechzigstelnote,** *f.* hemidemisemiquaver.

Vierung ['fi:ruŋ], *f.* (*Archit.*) intersection of the nave. **Vierungskuppel,** *f.* central cupola.

Viervierteltakt [fi:r'fi:rtəltakt], *m.* (*Mus.*) common time.

Vierwaldstätter See ['fi:rvaltʃtɛtər], *m.* Lake of Lucerne.

vierwertig ['fi:rve:rtɪç], *adj.* (*Chem.*) tetravalent, quadrivalent. **Vierzahl,** *f.* quaternion.

vierzehn ['fi:rtse:n], *num.adj.* fourteen; – ***Tage,*** a fortnight; ***alle – Tage,*** every fortnight; ***heute über – Tage*** or ***in – Tagen,*** this day fortnight; ***vor – Tagen,*** a fortnight ago. **vierzehnt,** *adj.* fourteenth. **vierzehn|tägig,** *adj.* lasting a fortnight, fortnightly. **–täglich,** *adj.* (recurring) every fortnight, fortnightly. **Vierzehntel,** *n.* fourteenth part.

Vierzeiler ['fi:rtsaɪlər], *m.* quatrain, four-lined stanza. **vierzeilig,** *adj.* four-lined.

vierzig ['fi:rtsɪç], *num.adj.* forty. **Vierzig,** *f.* (-, *pl.* **-en**) the number 40. **Vierziger(in),** *m.*,(*f.*) man (woman) in his (her) forties; ***in den Vierzigern,*** in the forties. **vierzigst,** *num.adj.* fortieth. **Vierzigstel,** *n.* fortieth part.

vigilant [vigi'lant], *adj.* (*coll.*) quick-witted, crafty. **Vigilant,** *m.* (**-en,** *pl.* **-en**) (police) spy *or* agent.

Vigilie [vi'gi:liə], *f.* 1. vigil; 2. (*R.C.*) eve (*of a feast*). **vigilieren** [–'li:rən], *v.i.* (*dial.*) watch out (***auf*** (*Acc.*), for), keep an eye (on) *or* open (for).

Vignette [vi'njɛtə], *f.* vignette.

Vikar [vi'ka:r], *m.* (**-s,** *pl.* **-e**) curate; substitute. **Vikariat** [–i'a:t], *n.* (**-(e)s,** *pl.* **-e**) curacy; temporary office.

Viktoria [vik'to:ria], *f.* acclamation of victory; – ***rufen,*** acclaim victory; – ***schießen,*** fire a victory salute.

Viktualien [viktu'a:liən], *pl.* victuals, provisions.

Villa ['vɪla], *f.* (-, *pl.* **Villen**) villa, house (in its own grounds), detached house. **Villen|besitzer,** *m.* house-owner, owner-occupier. **–bewohner,** *m.* suburban dweller, (*coll.*) suburbanite. **–kolonie,** *f.* residential suburb, garden-city. **–viertel,** *n.* residential area *or* district.

vindizieren [vɪndi'tsi:rən], *v.t.* claim, lay claim to, assert *or* vindicate one's right to.

[1]**Viola** ['vi:ola], *f.* (-, *pl.* **-len**) *see* **Viole.**

[2]**Viola** [vi'o:la], *f.* (-, *pl.* **-len**) (*Mus.*) viola.

Viole [vi'o:lə], *f.* (*Bot.*) violet, viola.

violett [vio'lɛt], *adj.*, **Violett,** *n.* (**-s,** *pl.* - (*coll.* **-s**)) violet.

Violine [vio'li:nə], *f.* violin. **Violinist** [–'nɪst], *m.* (**-en,** *pl.* **-en**), **Violinistin,** *f.* violinist. **Violin|kasten,** *m.* violin-case. **–schlüssel,** *m.* treble clef. **–stimme,** *f.* violin-part.

Violoncello [violɔn'tʃɛlo], *n.* (**-s,** *pl.* **-s**) (violon)-cello.

Viper ['vi:pər], *f.* (-, *pl.* **-n**) viper, adder.

virtuell [vɪrtu'ɛl], *adj.* virtual.

virtuos [vɪrtu'o:z], *adj.* masterly. **Virtuose,** *m.* (**-n,** *pl.* **-n**) virtuoso, outstanding *or* masterly (*usu.* musical) performer; (*Theat.*) star. **virtuosenhaft,** *adj.* masterly, technically perfect (*often implying superficiality*). **Virtuosentum,** *n.* professional skill; (*oft.*) superficial finesse, airs of a virtuoso; (*collect.*) virtuosi. **Virtuosin,** *f. See* **Virtuose. Virtuosität** [–i'tɛ:t], *f.* virtuosity, masterly skill.

Visage [vi'za:ʒə], *f.* (*vulg.*) face, dial, mug.

Visier [vi'zi:r], *n.* (**-s,** *pl.* **-e**) visor (*of helmet*); sight (*of a gun*); ***im – anpeilen,*** sight, get a fix on; ***das – aufschlagen,*** lift one's visor; ***das – stellen,*** set the sights; (*fig.*) ***mit offnem –,*** fearlessly, openly, in the face of the world. **visieren, 1.** *v.t.* 1. adjust, gauge; 2. examine (*passport*), endorse, visé. **2.** *v.i.* take a sight (***auf*** (*Acc.*), on), sight; (take) aim (at); (*coll.*) look out (for). **Visier|fernrohr,** *n.* telescopic sight. **–kimme,** *f.* notch of back-sight. **–korn,** *n.* (bead of) fore-sight. **–linie,** *f. See* **–(schuß)linie. –schuß,** *m.* sighting shot. **–(schuß)linie,** *f.* line of sight. **–stab,** *m.* (*Surv.*) ranging-pole.

Vision [vizi'o:n], *f.* dream, vision. **Visionär** [–'nɛ:r], *m.* (**-s,** *pl.* **-e**), **visionär,** *adj.* visionary.

Visitation [vizitatsi'o:n], *f.* (visit of) inspection, search, examination. **Visitationsrecht,** *n.* right of search. **Visitator** [–'ta:tɔr], *m.* (**-s,** *pl.* **-en**) inspector, excise-officer.

Visite [vi'zi:tə], *f.* visit, (social) call. **Visiten|karte,** *f.* visiting *or* (*Am.*) calling card. **–tag,** *m.* at-home day; visiting day. **–zimmer,** *n.* drawing-room, reception-room.

visitieren [vizi'ti:rən], *v.t.* inspect, search; ***eine Wunde –,*** probe a wound.

viskos [vis'ko:z], *adj.* viscous, viscid. **Viskose,** *f.* artificial silk, rayon. **Viskosität** [–i'tɛ:t], *f.* viscosity.

Vista ['vɪsta], *f.* (-, *pl.* **Visten**) view, vista; (*Mus.*) sight; (*Comm.*) ***a vista,*** at sight. **Vistawechsel,** *m.* sight-bill.

visuell [vizu'ɛl], *adj.* visual.

Visum ['vi:zum], *n.* (**-s,** *pl.* **Visen** *or* **Visa**) visa, endorsement.

Vitalität [vitali'tɛ:t], *f.* vitality, vigour.

Vitamin [vita'mi:n], *n.* (**-s,** *pl.* **-e**) vitamin. **vitaminarm,** *adj.* deficient in vitamins. **Vitaminmangel,** *m.* vitamin deficiency.

Vitrine [vi'tri:nə], *f.* glass case, show *or* display case. **Vitrinenpuppe,** *f.* display model, tailor's dummy.

Vitriol [vitri'o:l], *m.*, (*coll., Austr. n.*) (**-s,** *pl.* **-e**) vitriol. **vitriolartig,** *adj.* vitriolic. **Vitriolflasche,** *f.* carboy. **vitriolhaltig,** *adj.* vitriolated. **Vitriolöl,** *n.* oil of vitriol, sulphuric acid. **vitriolsauer,** *adj.* sulphuric; ***vitriolsaures Salz,*** sulphate. **Vitriol|säure,** *f. See* **–öl.**

Vivat ['vi:vat], *n.* (**-s** (*Austr.* -), *pl.* **-s**) cheer, shout of acclamation; ***ihm ein – bringen,*** give three cheers for him. **vivat,** *int.* hurrah! – ***der König!*** long live the king!

Vize|admiral ['vi:tsə–, 'fi:tsə–], *m.* vice-admiral. **–kanzler,** *m.* vice-chancellor. **–könig,** *m.* viceroy, lord-lieutenant. **–präsident,** *m.* vice-president.

Vizinal|bahn [vitsi'na:l–], *f.* branch *or* local line. **–straße,** *f.* country road.

Vlies [fli:s], (*Austr.*) **Vließ,** *n.* (**-es,** *pl.* **-e**) fleece; ***goldenes –,*** (*Hist.*) golden fleece, (*Her.*) toison d'or.

Vogel ['fo:gəl], *m.* (**-s,** *pl.* **¨-**) bird; (*coll.*) fellow, chap, customer; (*coll.*) ***den – abschießen,*** take the cake, steal the show; (*dial.*) – ***Bülow,*** golden oriole; (*Prov.*) ***friß – oder stirb!*** sink or swim; devil take the hindmost; (*Prov.*) ***einem jeden – gefällt sein Nest,*** there is no place like home; (*coll.*) ***einen – haben,*** have a bee in one's bonnet, have bats in the belfry, be off one's head; ***es ist ihm so wohl, wie dem – im Hanfsamen,*** he is in clover; (*coll.*) ***komischer –,*** queer fish *or* customer; (*coll.*) ***lockerer*** or ***loser –,*** loose fish, good-for-nothing scamp; (*coll.*) ***lustiger –,*** gay dog; (*Prov.*) ***ein schlechter –, der sein eigen Nest beschmutzt,*** it is an ill bird that fouls its own nest; (*Prov.*) ***jeder – singt wie ihm der Schnabel gewachsen ist,*** every bird is known by its song; – ***Strauß,*** ostrich; (*coll.*) queer fish.

Vogelart ['fo:gəlʔa:rt], *f.* species of bird. **vogelartig,** *adj.* birdlike. **Vogel|bauer,** *n.* bird-cage. **–beerbaum,** *m.* (*Bot.*) mountain-ash, rowan (*Sorbus aucuparia*). **–beere,** *f.* mountain-ash berry. **–beize,** *f.* falconry. **–beobachtung,** *f.* bird-watching. **–deuter,** *m.* augur. **–deuterei,** *f.* divination by the flight of birds, augury. **–dunst,** *m.* small shot. **–ei,** *n.* bird's egg. **–fang,** *m.* fowling, bird-catching. **–fänger,** *m. See* **–steller. –flinte,** *f.* fowling-piece. **–flug,** *m.* flight *or* flock of birds. **vogelfrei,** *adj.* outlawed; ***für – erklären,*** outlaw. **Vogel|freund,** *m.* bird lover. **–fuß,** *m.* (*Bot.*) bird's-foot (*Ornithopus*). **–futter,** *n.* bird-seed. **–garn,** *n.* fowler's net. **–(ge)sang,** *m.* bird-song. **–händler,** *m.* bird-dealer. **–haus,** *n.* aviary. **–hecke,** *f.* breeding-cage *or* -place. **–kenner,** *m.* ornithologist, bird-fancier. **–kirsche,** *f.* bird-cherry; (*Bot.*) common wild cherry (*Prunus avium*). **–kunde,** *f.* ornithology. **–kundige(r),** *m. See* **–kenner. –leim,** *m.* bird-lime. **–liebhaber,** *m. See* **–kenner. –miere,** *f.* (*Bot.*) chickweed (*Stellaria*). **–mist,** *m.* bird's droppings, guano.

vogeln ['fo:gəln], **vögeln** ['fø:gəln], *v.i.* mate (*of birds*); (*vulg.*) fornicate.

Vogel|napf, *m.* seed-box *or* drawer. **–nest,** *n.* bird's nest. **–perspektive,** *f.* bird's-eye view. **–sang,** *m.*

See **–gesang.** **–schau,** *f. See* **–perspektive.** **–schauer,** *m. See* **–deuter.** **–scheuche,** *f.* scarecrow. **vogelschlecht,** *adj.* (*dial.*) horizontal, level. **Vogel|schutzgebiet,** *n.* bird sanctuary. **–stange,** *f.* perch (*in a bird-cage*). **–steller,** *m.* bird-catcher, fowler. **––Strauß-Politik,** *f.* ostrich-like attitude; *– treiben,* shut one's eyes to the facts, hide one's head in the sand. **–tränke,** *f.* bird-bath. **–wahrsager,** *m. See* **–deuter.** **–warte,** *f.* ornithological station. **–weibchen,** *n.* hen bird. **–welt,** *f.* feathered world. **–wicke,** *f.* (*Bot.*) bird's-tares (*Vicia cracca*). **–zug,** *m.* (bird) migration.

Vogesen [vo'ge:zən], *pl.* (the) Vosges Mountains.

Vöglein ['fø:glaın], *n.* little bird, (*coll.*) birdie; (*coll.*) *ich habe ein – singen hören,* a little bird told me.

Vogler ['fo:glər], *m.* fowler, bird-catcher.

Vogt [fo:kt], *m.* (**-(e)s,** *pl.* **⸚e**) overseer, bailiff, steward, warden; prefect, governor, administrator; (*obs.*) provost, constable, beadle; (*Swiss*) guardian. **Vogtei** [–'taı], *f.* (-, *pl.* **-en**) 1. office *or* duties *or* jurisdiction *or* residence *or* income of a Vogt; prefecture, bailiwick; 2. (*dial.*) prison. **vogten,** *v.t.* (*Swiss*) act as guardian to.

Vokabel [vo'ka:bəl], *f.* (-, *pl.* **-n**) word, vocable. **Vokabelschatz,** *m.* vocabulary (*of a p.*). **Vokabular** [–'la:r], *n.* (**-s,** *pl.* **-e**), **Vokabularium,** *n.* (**-s,** -, *pl.* **-rien**) vocabulary.

Vokal [vo'ka:l], *m.* (**-s,** *pl.* **-e**) vowel. **Vokal|ablaut,** *m.* (vowel) gradation. **–anlaut,** *m.* initial vowel. **–auslaut,** *m.* final vowel. **–inlaut,** *m.* medial vowel. **vokalisch,** *adj.* vocalic; *–er Laut,* vowel sound; *–er Auslaut,* vowel ending, word *or* syllable ending with a vowel. **vokalisieren** [–i'zi:rən], *v.i.* vocalize. **Vokalisierung,** *f.* vocalization. **Vokalismus** [–'lısmus], *m.* vowel-system. **Vokal|merkmale,** *n.pl.* (*Stenography*) vowel points. **–musik,** *f.* vocal music. **–partie,** *f.* vocal *or* voice part. **–schwund,** *m.* vowel atrophy. **–umlaut,** *m.* (vowel) mutation.

Vokation [vokatsi'o:n], *f.* nomination to an office, call.

Vokativ [voka'ti:f], *m.* (**-s,** *pl.* **-e**) (*Gram.*) vocative.

Vokativus [voka'ti:vus], *m.* (*coll.*) sly dog, rogue.

Voland ['fo:lant], *m.* (*Poet.*) evil fiend.

Volant [vo'lã], *m.* (**-s,** *pl.* **-s**) 1. flounce, frill; 2. (*obs.*) (*Motor.*) steering-wheel.

Volk [fɔlk], *n.* (**-(e)s,** *pl.* **⸚er**) people, nation, tribe, race; soldiery, troops, men, crew; herd (*of beasts*), flock (*of birds*), covey (*of partridges etc.*), swarm (*of bees*); the common people, the lower classes; the populace *or* crowd, the common herd, rabble; *das arbeitende –,* the working classes; *das junge –,* young people, youngsters; *das kleine –,* little folk, children; *der Mann aus dem –,* the man in the street; *er ist ein Mann aus dem –,* he is a man of the people; *viel –,* a swarm *or* crowd of people, a large crowd; *ein – Wachteln,* a bevy of quails.

volkarm ['fɔlkˀarm], *adj.* thinly peopled *or* populated.

Völkchen ['fœlkçən], *n.* (*coll.*) *lustiges –,* merry crowd *or* throng; (*coll.*) *mein –,* my little ones.

Völker|beschreibung, *f.* ethnography. **–bund,** *m.* League of Nations. **–kunde,** *f.* ethnology. **völkerkundlich,** *adj.* ethnological. **Völker|mord,** *m.* genocide. **–recht,** *n.* international law. **völkerrechtlich,** **1.** *adj.* (relating to) international (law). **2.** *adv.* under international law. **Völkerschaft,** *f.* people, tribe, nation. **Völker|schlacht,** *f.* the Battle of Leipzig (1815). **–verständigung,** *f.* international understanding. **–wanderung,** *f.* mass migration.

volkhaft ['fɔlkhaft], **völkisch** ['fœlkıʃ], *adj.* racial, national, (*Nat. Soc.*) anti-Semitic.

volkreich ['fɔlkraıç], *adj.* populous, thickly populated.

Volks|abstimmung, *f.* plebiscite, referendum. **–aufklärung,** *f.* education of the masses. **–aufruhr, –aufstand,** *m.* popular rising, insurrection. **–aufwiegler,** *m.* agitator, demagogue. **–ausdruck,** *m.* popular expression. **–ausgabe,** *f.* popular edition. **–befragung,** *f.* public-opinion poll. **–begehren,** *n. See* **–abstimmung.** **–beglücker,** *m.* public benefactor. **–beschluß,** *m. See* **–abstimmung.** **–bewegung,** *f.* national movement. **–bewußtsein,** *n.* national consciousness. **–bibliothek,** *f.* public library, free library. **–bildung,** *f.* popular education. **–bildungswerk,** *n.* (*Nat. Soc.*) adult education programme. **–brauch,** *m.* national custom. **–buch,** *n.* popular prose romance; chapbook. **–bücherei,** *f. See* **–bibliothek.** **–charakter,** *m.* national character. **–demokratie,** *f.* people's democracy. **–deutsche,** *m.pl.* (members of the) German ethnic group, Germans abroad. **–dichte,** *f.* density of population. **–dichter,** *m.* popular poet; national poet. **–dichtung,** *f.* popular poetry; national poetry. **volkseigen,** *adj.* publicly owned, nationalized. **Volks|eigentum,** *n.* public property; *im –,* in public ownership; *ins – überführen,* nationalize. **–einkommen,** *n.* national income. **–empfänger,** *m.* utility radio set. **–entscheid,** *m. See* **–abstimmung.** **–epos,** *n.* national epic. **–erhebung,** *f. See* **–aufstand.** **–etymologie,** *f.* popular etymology. **–feind,** *m.* public enemy. **volksfeindlich,** *adj.* inimical to the national interests, subversive, unpatriotic. **Volks|fest,** *n.* fair, popular fête. **–front,** *f.* (*Pol.*) People's *or* Popular Front. **–führer,** *m.* popular leader, demagogue.

Volks|ganze, *n.* the whole nation, all the people. **–gebrauch,** *m.* popular usage. **–geist,** *m.* national spirit. **–genosse,** *m.* (fellow) countryman, (*Nat. Soc.*) fellow German. **–gericht,** *n.* (*Nat. Soc.*) people's court. **–gesundheit,** *f.* the nation's health. **–glaube,** *m.* popular belief. **–gruppe,** *f.* ethnic group. **–gunst,** *f.* popularity. **–haufe,** *m.* mob, crowd. **–heer,** *n.* conscript army, people's army. **–herrschaft,** *f.* democracy. **–hochschule,** *f.* adult education classes, extramural studies, university extension. **–hymne,** *f.* national anthem. **–justiz,** *f.* mob-justice; lynch-law. **–klasse,** *f.* class of people, social stratum; *die höheren –n,* the upper classes. **–küche,** *f.* soup-kitchen, feeding centre. **–kunde,** *f.* folklore. **–kundler,** *m.* folklorist. **volkskundlich,** *adj.* regarding folklore. **Volks|lied,** *n.* folksong. **–märchen,** *n.* popular legend, fairy story. **volksmäßig,** *adj.* popular; *– machen,* popularize. **Volks|meinung,** *f.* public opinion *or* feeling. **–melodie,** *f.* popular air. **–menge,** *f.* crowd (of people), multitude, throng; mob. **–mund,** *m.* vernacular. **volksnah,** *adj.* rooted in *or* responsive to popular sentiment, popular.

Volks|partei, *f.* National Liberal Party, People's Party, the Moderates. **–poesie,** *f. See* **–dichtung.** **–polizei,** *f.* people's police. **–redner,** *m.* popular speaker, soap-box *or* mob orator, agitator. **–regierung,** *f.* popular government; democracy. **–sage,** *f.* national legend, popular tradition, folk-tale. **–schädling,** *m.* (*Nat. Soc.*) anti-social parasite. **–schicht,** *f.* social class, social stratum. **–schlag,** *m.* race, racial group. **–schule,** *f.* elementary *or* primary school. **–schüler,** *m.* elementary school pupil. **–schullehrer,** *m.* primary teacher, elementary teacher. **–schulwesen,** *n.* primary education. **–sprache,** *f.* vernacular, popular speech. **–staat,** *m.* republic. **–stamm,** *m.* tribe, race. **–stimme,** *f.* public opinion. **–stimmung,** *f.* public temper, popular feeling. **–tanz,** *m.* folk-dance. **–tracht,** *f.* national costume *or* dress. **–trauertag,** *m.* day of national mourning.

Volkstum ['fɔlkstu:m], *n.* nationality, nationhood, national characteristics; *sein – bewahren,* preserve one's national characteristics. **volkstümeln,** *v.i.* court popularity. **volkstümlich,** *adj.* national; popular; *–e Dichtung,* popular national poetry. **Volkstümlichkeit,** *f.* nationality; national trait *or* characteristic; popularity.

Volks|überlieferung, *f.* popular tradition. **–unterricht,** *m.* national system of education. **volksverbunden,** *adj.* rooted in one's national soil. **Volks|verbundenheit,** *f.* national solidarity. **–vermögen,** *n. See* **–einkommen.** **–versammlung,** *f.* national assembly. **–vertreter,** *m.* deputy, people's (elected) representative. **–vertretung,** *f.* representation of the people. **–wirt,** *m.* political economist. **–wirtschaft,** *f.* political economy. **–wirtschaftler,** *m. See* **–wirt. volkswirtschaftlich,** *adj.* relating to political economy, economic. **Volks|wirtschaftslehre,** *f. See* **–wirtschaft. –wohl,** *n.* common weal *or* good. **Volks|wohlfahrt,** *f.* (*Nat. Soc.*) social *or* public welfare. **–wohlstand,** *m.* standard of living of the masses, national wealth. **–zählung,** *f.* census.

voll [fɔl], **1.** *adj.* (*comp.* *–er, sup.* *–st*) (*with Gen. or* *von*) full, filled, replete; complete, whole, entire; (*coll.*) (*of figure*) well-developed, buxom, rounded; (*sl.*) drunk; ***der Saal ist –*** or ***–er*** or ***– mit*** or ***– von Menschen,*** the hall is full of *or* filled with people; ***des Lobes –,*** full of praise; ***ein Glas – Wein,*** a glassful of wine; ***ihn für – ansehen,*** take him seriously; ***in –er Arbeit,*** in the midst of work; ***mit –en Backen sprechen,*** speak with one's mouth full; ***–e Beschäftigung,*** full(-time) employment; ***bei –er Besinnung,*** fully conscious; ***–e Börse,*** well-filled purse; ***zum Brechen –,*** enough to make one sick; ***aus –er Brust,*** heartily, lustily; (*coll.*) ***ihm den Buckel – schlagen,*** thrash him soundly; ***in –em Ernst,*** quite seriously, in dead earnest; ***in –er Fahrt,*** at full *or* top speed; ***–es Gesicht,*** round *or* chubby face; ***mit –en Händen,*** lavishly; ***das Herz ist –,*** the heart is overflowing; ***aus –em Herzen,*** from the bottom of one's heart, heartily; ***–e 40 Jahr(e alt),*** quite 40 years (old); ***aus –er Kehle,*** at the top of one's voice; ***im –en leben,*** live in the lap of luxury; (*coll.*) ***das Kind macht sich –,*** the child soils itself (its trousers, napkin *etc.*); ***das Maß ist –,*** that is the limit; ***ihm die Ohren – schreien,*** din (s.th.) in his ears; ***mit –em Recht,*** with perfect right; ***aus dem –en schöpfen,*** draw on lavish resources, (*coll.*) have plenty; ***die –e Summe,*** the entire sum; ***eine –e Stunde,*** a full *or* (*coll.*) solid hour; ***um das Unglück – zu machen,*** to crown everything, as the last straw; ***–es Vertrauen,*** complete confidence; ***die –e Wahrheit,*** the whole truth; ***in –en Zügen trinken,*** drink off at a gulp. **2.** *adv.* fully, entirely, in full; ***– eingezahlt,*** fully paid up; ***alle Hände – zu tun haben,*** have one's hands full; (*of clock*) ***– schlagen,*** strike the (full) hour.

voll–, *vb. pref. signifying completion, accomplishment etc.* (a) *more figurative use, insep. and unstressed,* (b) *more literal meanings, sep. and stressed* = full, to the top *etc. Particularly in the latter case, words should be sought under the stem inf. if not found here.* (*N.B. When the following element begins with l, one of the three letters is dropped, except if the word is hyphenated.*)

Voll|aktie, *f.* fully paid-up share. **–anstalt,** *f.* secondary school with sixth form.

vollauf ['fɔlʔauf], *adv.* abundantly, plentifully, amply; ***– zu tun haben,*** have one's hands full, have plenty to do.

vollaufen ['fɔllaufən], *irr.v.i.* (*sep.*) (*aux.* s.) be filled to overflowing; (*sl.*) ***sich – lassen,*** drink too much, get tanked up.

vollautend ['fɔllautənt], *adj.* sonorous.

vollautomatisch ['fɔlʔautomaːtɪʃ], *adj.* fully automatic.

Voll|bad, *n.* bath, plunge-bath. **–bahn,** *f.* standard gauge railway. **–bart,** *m.* beard.

voll|berechtigt, *adj.* fully entitled *or* authorized. **–beschäftigt,** *adj.* fully employed, in full-time employment. **Vollbeschäftigung,** *f.* full(-time) employment.

Voll|besitz, *m.* full possession. **–bild,** *n.* full-page illustration. **–bildfrequenz,** *f.* (*T.V.*) picture frequency. **–blut,** *n.*, **–blüter,** *m.* thoroughbred (horse).

vollblütig ['fɔlblyːtɪç], *adj.* full-blooded, plethoric; sanguine. **Vollblütigkeit,** *f.* full-bloodedness, plethora.

Voll|blutpferd, *n. See* **–blut.**

vollbringen [fɔl'brɪŋən], *irr.v.t.* (*insep.*) accomplish, achieve; do, perform, execute, fulfil, carry out, complete, consummate; perpetrate; ***es ist vollbracht,*** it is finished *or* completed *or* carried out. **Vollbringung,** *f.* accomplishment, achievement; performance, fulfilment, completion, execution; consummation, perpetration.

voll|bürtig, *adj.* of the same parents, whole-blood; ***–e Geschwister,*** full brothers and sisters. **–busig,** *adj.* full-bosomed, (*coll.*) bosomy. **Voll|dampf,** *m.* full (steam) pressure; ***– voraus!*** full steam ahead! (*fig., coll.*) ***mit –,*** at full blast. **–draht,** *m.* solid wire.

volleibig ['fɔllaɪbɪç], *adj.* corpulent, stout. **Volleibigkeit,** *f.* stoutness, corpulence, obesity.

Voll|eigentümer, *m.* (*Law*) owner in one's own right. **–einzahlung,** *f.* payment in full.

vollelektrisch ['fɔlʔelɛktrɪʃ], *adj.* all-electric.

vollenden [fɔl'ɛndən], (*insep.*) **1.** *v.t.* bring to a close, finish, terminate; achieve, accomplish, complete, perfect. **2.** *v.r., v.i.* pass away, die. **vollendet,** *adj.* finished, accomplished, consummate, perfect; ***die früh Vollendeten,*** those who died young; (*coll.*) ***–er Blödsinn,*** sheer *or* perfect *or* utter nonsense; ***–e Tatsache,*** accomplished fact, fait accompli.

vollends ['fɔlɛnts], *adv.* wholly, completely, entirely; altogether, quite; finally, moreover.

Vollendung [fɔl'ɛndʊŋ], *f.* completion, finishing, termination, ending; perfecting, consummation, perfection.

voller ['fɔlər], **1.** *comp. adj.* fuller. **2.** *indecl. adj.* (*Gen.*) full of; *see* **voll.**

Vollerbe ['fɔlʔɛrbə], *m.* sole heir.

Völlerei [fœlə'raɪ], *f.* intemperance, gluttony.

vollführen [fɔl'fyːrən], *v.t.* (*insep.*) carry out, execute. **Vollführung,** *f. See* **Vollendung.**

vollfüllen ['fɔlfylən], *v.t.* (*sep.*) fill up.

Vollgas ['fɔlgaːs], *n.* (*Motor.*) open *or* full throttle; ***– geben,*** open the throttle, (*coll.*) put one's foot down, step on it.

vollgefahren ['fɔlgəfaːrən], *adj.* able-bodied (*seaman*).

Voll|gefühl, *n.* (full) consciousness; ***im – von,*** fully conscious of. **–gehalt,** *m.* good alloy, full weight and value. **vollgehaltig,** *adj.* of good alloy, of full weight and value; of sterling value, standard. **Vollgenuß,** *m.* full enjoyment.

voll|gepackt, –gepfropft, –gestopft, *adj.* crammed (full), packed (tight), crowded.

Voll|gewalt, *f.* full power, absolute power; power of attorney. **–gewicht,** *n.* full weight.

voll|gießen, *irr.v.t.* (*sep.*) *see* **-füllen. –gültig,** *adj.* of full value, sterling; valid, unexceptionable.

Vollgummireifen ['fɔlgumiraɪfən], *m.* solid (rubber) tyre (*Am.* tire).

voll|haben, *irr.v.t.* (*coll.*) ***die Nase –,*** be fed up to the (back) teeth, (*vulg.*) have had a bellyful. **–haltig,** *adj. See* **–gehaltig. –hauen,** *v.t.* (*coll.*) ***ihm die Jacke –,*** give him a good hiding.

Vollholz ['fɔlhɔlts], *n.* log.

völlig ['fœlɪç], **1.** *adj.* full, total, entire, complete; absolute, thorough, downright, out-and-out; (*Tech.*) circular (*of cross-section*); ***–er Ablaß,*** plenary indulgence; ***–e Gewißheit,*** absolute *or* dead certainty; ***–er Narr,*** perfect *or* downright fool; ***–e Unwahrheit,*** utter *or* out-and-out falsehood. **2.** *adv.* fully, entirely, totally, completely, thoroughly, quite; ***– abschlagen,*** give a flat refusal; ***– falsch,*** utterly wrong; ***ich bin nicht – Ihrer Meinung,*** I cannot quite share your opinion; ***– verrückt,*** quite mad, (*coll.*) plain dotty; ***– verschwunden,*** completely disappeared, (*coll.*) clean gone. **Völligkeit,** *f.* circular cross-section.

volljährig ['fɔljɛːrɪç], *adj.* of (full) age; ***– werden,*** come of age, attain one's majority. **Volljährigkeit,** *f.* majority, full age.

Vollkettenfahrzeug ['fɔlkɛtənfaːrtsɔyk], *n.* (*Mil.*) full-track vehicle.

vollkommen ['fɔlkɔmən], *adj.* perfect, consummate; complete, entire, finished; full; ***–e Gewalt,*** absolute power; ***–e Zahl,*** perfect number. **Vollkommenheit,** *f.* perfection, completeness.

Voll|kornbrot, *n.* wholemeal bread. **–kraft,** *f.* full strength *or* vigour, energy, prime (*of life*). **–kugel,** *f.* round shot.

vollmachen ['fɔlmaxən], (*sep.*) **1.** *v.t.* fill up, complete; ***die Summe* –,** pay the remainder *or* deficit; ***um sein Unglück vollzumachen,*** to crown his misfortune. **2.** *v.r.* (*coll.*) dirty *or* soil o.s., get dirty.

Vollmacht ['fɔlmaxt], *f.* full power(s), authority; fullness of power; power of attorney; proxy; (*Comm.*) ***in* –,** per pro; ***ihm – erteilen,*** give him (full) authority, empower *or* authorize him; ***unbeschränkte* –,** plenary powers. **Vollmacht|-brief,** *m.* warrant, (written) authority, permit; procuration. **–geber,** *m.* mandator. **–haber, –träger,** *m.* mandatary, mandatory; proxy, procurator.

Voll|matrose, *m.* able-bodied seaman. **–milch,** *f.* full-cream milk. **–mond,** *m.* full moon; ***wir haben* –,** the moon is full.

voll|mundig, *adj.* strong, full-bodied (*of beer*). **–nehmen,** *irr.v.t.* (*sep.*) ***den Mund* –,** brag, boast, blow one's own trumpet, draw the long bow, (*coll.*) talk big. **–packen, –pfropfen,** (*sep.*) *see* **–stopfen.**

Voll|reifen, *m.* solid tyre (*Am.* tire). **–rohr,** *n.* one-piece barrel (*of gun*).

vollsaftig ['fɔlzaftɪç], *adj.* very juicy, succulent.

Vollschiff ['fɔlʃɪf], *n.* full-rigged ship.

voll|schlank, *adj.* (*coll.*) not-so-slim. **–schwenkbar,** *adj.* fully *or* completely traversable.

Voll|sein, *n.* (*coll.*) drunkenness, tipsiness. **–sicht,** *f.* (*Av.*) all-round visibility. **–sitzung,** *f.* plenary session. **–spurbahn,** *f. See* **–bahn. vollspurig,** *adj.* (*Railw.*) standard gauge.

vollst [fɔlst], *sup. of* **voll.**

vollständig ['fɔlʃtɛndɪç], **1.** *adj.* complete, entire, whole, total, integral. **2.** *adv.* fully, wholly, entirely, completely, totally, quite, utterly; ***– machen,*** complete; ***das Unglück – machen,*** crown everything, (*coll.*) put the lid on it. **Vollständigkeit,** *f.* completeness, entirety, totality, integrity.

Vollstange ['fɔlʃtaŋə], *f.* (solid) bar.

vollstimmig ['fɔlʃtɪmɪç], *adj.* for full orchestra *or* chorus.

vollstopfen ['fɔlʃtɔpfən], (*sep.*) **1.** *v.t.* stuff, cram, pack full. **2.** *v.r.* (*coll.*) stuff o.s.

voll|streckbar, *adj.* executable, dischargeable, enforceable. **–strecken,** *v.t.* (*insep.*) execute, discharge, enforce; put into effect, carry out. **Voll|-strecker,** *m.* executor. **–streckerin,** *f.* executrix. **–streckung,** *f.* execution, discharge. **Voll-streckungs|aufschub,** *m.* stay of execution. **–beamte(r),** *m.* (*Law*) executory officer. **–befehl,** *m.* writ of execution, warrant.

voll|tönend, –tönig, *adj.* full-sounding, full-toned, sonorous, rich.

Voll|traghöhe, *f.* (*Av.*) ceiling with full load. **–treffer,** *m.* (*Artil.*) direct hit. **–versammlung,** *f.* plenary session, full assembly *or* meeting. **–waise,** *f.* orphan.

voll|wertig, *adj.* of full value, sterling, up to standard, of high quality; valid. **–wichtig,** *adj.* of full weight, weighty, forcible, very important. **–wüchsig,** *adj.* full(y)-grown. **–zählig,** *adj.* complete, in full strength. **Vollzähligkeit,** *f.* completeness, fullness.

vollziehen [fɔl'tsiːən], (*insep.*) **1.** *irr.v.t. See* **voll-strecken;** ***ein Urteil* –,** execute a sentence; ***–de Gewalt,*** executive (power); ***eine Heirat* –,** consummate a marriage. **2.** *irr.v.r.* be effected, take place, come to pass. **Vollziehung,** *f.*, **Vollzug,** *m.* execution, discharge, accomplishment, fulfilment. **Vollzugsgewalt,** *f.* executive power.

Volontär [vɔlɔn'tɛːr], *m.* (**-s,** *pl.* **-e**) volunteer, voluntary helper, unsalaried clerk, unpaid assistant. **volontieren,** *v.i.* volunteer, give voluntary help, do voluntary work for *or* on.

Volt [vɔlt], *n.* (**-(s),** *pl.* **-**) (*Elec.*) volt. **voltaisch** [–'taːɪʃ], *adj.* galvanic, voltaic. **Voltampere** [–am'pɛːr], *n.* (*Elec.*) watt.

Volte ['vɔltə], *f.* (*Fenc., Equestrianism*) volte; sleight of hand; (*Cards*) ***die – schlagen*** make the pass.

Volt|messer, *m.*, **–meter,** *n.* voltmeter. **–spannung, –zahl,** *f.* voltage.

Voltigeur [vɔlti'ʒøːr], *m.* (**-s,** *pl.* **-e**) vaulter, tumbler, equestrian acrobat. **voltigieren,** *v.i.* perform equestrian acrobatics. **Voltigierkunst,** *f.* equestrian acrobatics, vaulting.

Volubilität [vɔlubili'tɛːt], *f.* volubility.

Volumen [vɔ'luːmən], *n.* (**-s,** *pl.* **-** (*Austr.* **-mina**)) **1.** volume; content, capacity; size, bulk; (*fig.*) (*as of sound, traffic etc.*) volume, total amount; **2.** volume (= *book*). **Volumeneinheit,** *f.* unit of volume. **volumetrisch** [–'meːtrɪʃ], *adj.* volumetric. **voluminös** [–'nøːz], *adj.* bulky, voluminous.

vom [fɔm] = ***von dem.***

vomieren [vo'miːrən], *v.i., v.t.* vomit. **Vomitiv** [–'tiːf], *n.* (**-s,** *pl.* **-e**) (*Austr.*), **Vomitorium** [–'toːrium], *n.* (**-s,** *pl.* **-rien**) emetic.

von [fɔn], *prep.* (*Dat.*)
1. = of; 1. *possession or instead of genitive*; ***die Ausfuhr – Kohlen,*** the export of coal; ***der Bau – Häusern,*** the erection of houses; ***die Belagerung – Paris,*** the siege of Paris; ***ein Freund – mir,*** a friend of mine; ***der Herr vom Hause,*** the master of the house; ***das Unglück – Millionen,*** the misfortune of millions; 2. *partitive genitive*; ***zwei – uns,*** two of us; ***– allem nichts mehr übrig,*** nothing left of it all; ***trinken Sie – diesem Weine,*** drink some of this wine; ***er kann – Glück sagen,*** he can consider himself lucky, he can thank his lucky stars; ***ich weiß etwas – der Sache,*** I know s.th. of *or* about the affair; 3. *to denote quantity, measure, quality or material*; ***ein Urlaub – 3 Wochen,*** a three weeks' holiday; ***9 – 10 Leuten,*** 9 out of 10 people; ***ein Kind – 6 Jahren,*** a child of six; ***ein Betrag – 150 Pfund,*** a sum of £150; ***ein Mann – edlem Sinne,*** a man of noble mind; ***ein Geschäft – Wichtigkeit,*** an affair of importance; ***Lehre – der Buße,*** doctrine of atonement; ***klein – Gestalt,*** small of stature; ***ein Engel – einem Weibe,*** an angel of a woman; ***– gutem Schrot und Korn,*** of sterling worth; ***ein Denkmal – Marmor,*** a monument (made) of marble; ***– großem Vorteil,*** of great advantage; 4. *before a proper name which is part of a title*; ***Königin – England,*** Queen of England; ***Herzog Johann – Schwaben,*** Duke John of Swabia. *Before family names* **von** *is part of title and should be left unchanged or rendered by* **de.** (N.B. *a capital V* (***Von Bismarck***) *is commonly used by British writers but is incorrect.*) 5. *to denote the subject treated of*; ***– wem sprechen Sie?*** of whom are you speaking? *also to denote various other relations*; ***es ist nicht recht – ihm,*** it is not right of him.
2. = from; 1. *used with an adv. or prep. following*; ***– heute an,*** as from today, from this day on *or* forward; ***– nun an,*** henceforth; ***– klein auf,*** from childhood upwards *or* onwards, from earliest childhood; ***– Hause aus,*** originally, in its origins; ***– mir aus,*** I do not mind *or* care if; from my point of view; (*placed afterwards*) as far as I am concerned, for all I care, if you like; ***– wo aus,*** whence, from where; ***– außen,*** from without; ***– alters her,*** from time immemorial; ***– oben herab,*** down from above, from on high; ***– hinnen,*** hence; ***– hinten,*** from behind; ***– jeher,*** at all times, from time immemorial; ***– neuem,*** afresh, anew, all over again; ***– oben,*** from above; ***– seiten,*** on the part (*Gen.*, of); ***– vornherein,*** from the outset, from the first, from the beginning; ***– weitem,*** from afar; 2. *to denote motion or separation from*; ***– Berlin kommen,*** come from Berlin; ***etwas – seinem Gehalt abziehen,*** deduct something from his salary; ***was wollen Sie – mir?*** what do you want with *or* of *or* from me? ***– wem haben Sie das Geld geliehen?*** from whom did you borrow that money? ***etwas – einem Original abschreiben,*** copy s.th. from the original; ***– allen Seiten,*** from all sides, from every side; ***– Sinnen sein,*** be off one's head; ***– der Arbeit ruhen,*** rest from work; ***keinen Ton – sich geben,*** not utter a sound.
3. = by; *expressing origin, including use with agent of passive verb*; ***– Gottes Gnaden,*** by the grace of God; ***– allen geliebt,*** beloved of *or* by all; ***ein Werk – Goethe,*** a work by Goethe; ***– ganzem Herzen,*** with all one's heart; ***– Person kennen,*** know personally, know at first hand; ***– selbst,*** automatically, of

its own accord, of *or* by itself, spontaneously; ***Kinder – der zweiten Frau,*** children by the second wife; ***gedruckt und im Verlage –,*** printed and published by; ***ein Deutscher – Geburt,*** a German by birth; ***– deutschen Eltern geboren,*** born of German parents; ***– seinen Einkünften leben,*** live on one's income; ***er ist nicht – heute,*** he was not born yesterday.

voneinander [fɔn'ʔaɪn'andər], *adv.* apart, separate, asunder; from *or* of each other. **voneinander-gehen,** *irr.v.i.* part (company), separate.

vonnöten [fɔn'nøːtən], *adv.* ***– haben,*** be *or* stand in need of; ***– sein,*** be needful *or* necessary; ***ich habe es –,*** I need it badly.

vonstatten [fɔn'ʃtatən], *adv.* ***– gehen,*** proceed, progress, (*coll.*) come off; ***gut – gehen,*** go (well), prove a success.

vonwegen [fɔn've:gən], *prep.* (*obs. or coll.*) because, on account of, for the sake of.

vor [foːr], **1.** *prep.* **(a)** (*Dat.*) 1. (*referring to place only when it indicates condition or rest (if it answers the question* 'where?')) before, in front of, ahead of, in the presence of, opposite; 2. (*referring to time*) before, previous *or* prior to, in advance of, preparatory *or* antecedent to, (*Poet.*) ere; 3. (*fig.*) on account of, through, because of, with (*joy etc.*); from, against (*with verbs of protection, warning, concealment etc.*); in preference to, more than, above; (*Prov.*) ***man soll den Tag nicht – dem Abend loben,*** don't count your chickens until they are hatched, don't halloo till you're out of the wood, (*coll.*) don't speak too soon; ***– allem,*** above all; ***– alters,*** of yore; ***– Angst,*** with fear; ***– Anker gehen,*** ride at anchor; ***– Augen haben,*** have before one's eyes, have in view, intend, propose; ***– seinen Augen,*** before his very eyes; ***– allen Augen verborgen,*** hidden from all eyes; ***er steht – dem Bankerott,*** he is on the verge of bankruptcy; (*Prov.*) ***er sieht den Wald – lauter Bäumen nicht,*** he cannot see the wood for trees; ***– sich hin brummen,*** mutter to o.s.; ***– Christi Geburt,*** B(efore) C(hrist); ***– allen Dingen,*** above all; ***– Freude,*** with joy; ***sich – ihm fürchten,*** be afraid of *or* fear him; ***ich habe keine Geheimnisse – Ihnen,*** I have no secrets from you; ***– sich gehen,*** occur, take place, proceed, (*coll.*) pass off; ***Achtung – dem Gesetz,*** respect for the law; ***– Gott,*** in the presence of God, in the eyes of God; ***– sich*** (*Dat.*) ***haben,*** be face to face with, (*fig.*) have s.th. clearly in mind; ***– dem Hintergrund,*** against the background; ***heute – einem Jahr,*** a year ago today; ***– vielen Jahren,*** many years ago; ***– Kälte zittern,*** shiver with cold; ***– kurzem,*** recently; ***ihm die Tür – der Nase zuschlagen,*** shut the door in his face; (*Prov.*) ***Gewalt geht – Recht,*** might is stronger than right; ***Gnade – Recht ergehen lassen,*** be moved by compassion rather than by justice; ***Schritt – Schritt,*** step by step; ***Schutz – dem Winde,*** shelter from the wind; ***– ihm sicher*** or ***in Sicherheit sein,*** be safe from him; ***– Hunger sterben,*** die of hunger *or* starvation; ***der Tag – dem Feste,*** the day before the festival; ***– dem Tore wohnen,*** live outside the gates; ***– der Tür stehen,*** be at the door, (*fig.*) be close at hand; ***– dem Untergang stehen,*** be on the verge of ruin; ***sein Herz – einer S. verschließen,*** shut one's heart to *or* against s.th.; ***sich – ihm verstecken,*** hide from him; ***sie hat – ihrer Schwester den Vorrang,*** she takes precedence over her sister; ***– der Zeit,*** prematurely, too early, (*of payment*) in advance; ***– Zeiten,*** formerly, in former times, in times gone by; ***– alten Zeiten,*** in olden times, in times of old *or* (*Poet.*) of yore; ***das Subjekt steht – dem Zeitwort,*** the subject precedes the verb. **(b)** (*Acc.*) *referring to place it indicates movement or change of condition (if it answers the question* 'whither?'); ***das Subjekt stellt man – das Zeitwort,*** the subject is placed before the verb; ***sich*** (*Dat.*) ***eine Kugel – den Kopf schießen,*** put a bullet through one's head, blow one's brains out; ***– das Tor gehen,*** go out from the gate; ***ihn – die Tür werfen,*** throw *or* fling *or* kick him out.
2. *adv.* (*only in*) ***nach wie –,*** as always, as ever, still, now as before.

vor–, *sep.pref. See verbs listed below.*

vorab [foːr'ap], *adv.* first of all, to begin with, beforehand; tentatively; (*rare*) above all, especially.

Vorabend ['foːrʔaːbənt], *m.* eve, evening before.

vorahnen ['forʔaːnən], *v.t.* have a presentiment *or* foreboding of. **Vorahnung,** *f.* presentiment, foreboding, premonition.

Voralarm ['foːrʔalarm], *m.* preliminary *or* early warning.

Voralpen ['foːrʔalpən], *pl.* Lower Alps.

voran [for'an], *adv.* before; at the head, in front (*Dat.*, of); (***mit dem***) ***Kopf –,*** head first *or* foremost; ***nur –!*** go on *or* ahead! on you go! **voran|eilen,** *v.i.* hurry on ahead, run on in front (*Dat.*, of). **–gehen,** *irr.v.i.* go ahead *or* in front, lead the way, go *or* walk in front *or* at the head (*Dat.*, of); (*also in time*) precede; (*also fig.*) take the lead; ***die Arbeit geht gut voran,*** the work is making good progress *or* headway *or* is getting on nicely; ***mit gutem Beispiel –,*** set a good example. **–gehend,** *adj.* preceding, foregoing. **–kommen,** *irr.v.i.* get on *or* ahead, advance, make headway, (make) progress.

Vor|ankündigung, *f. See* **–anzeige. –anschlag,** *m.* preliminary *or* rough estimate, estimated cost.

voran|schreiten, *irr.v.i. See* **–gehen**; stride ahead (*Dat.*, of). **–stellen,** *v.t.* place in front (*Dat.*, of). **–treiben,** *irr.v.t.* hasten, advance, push on ahead with.

Vor|anzeige, *f.* preliminary announcement, advance notice, (*Films*) trailer. **–arbeit,** *f.* preliminary *or* preparatory work, preparation(s); *pl.* preliminary studies; (*coll.*) spade-work. **vorarbeiten,** **1.** *v.t.* do in advance, prepare. **2.** *v.i.* prepare one's work, work in preparation; (*fig.*) prepare the ground, pave the way (*Dat.*, for). **3.** *v.r.* work one's way forward *or* up, (*coll.*) forge ahead. **Vorarbeiter,** *m.* foreman, ganger. **Vorarbeiterin,** *f.* forewoman.

vorauf [for'auf], *adv.* (*obs.*) *see* **voran.**

voraus [for'aus], *adv.* in advance, in front, ahead (*Dat.*, of); ***er ist seinem Alter –,*** he is in advance of his years, he is forward for his age; ***im*** or ***zum –,*** in advance, beforehand; ***vielen Dank im –,*** many thanks in anticipation.

Vorausbildung [for'ausbɪlduŋ], *f.* preparatory training.

vorausbedingen [for'ausbədɪŋən], *reg. & irr.v.t.* stipulate beforehand *or* in advance; ***sich*** (*Dat.*) ***etwas –,*** reserve to o.s. (*a right etc.*). **Voraus|-bedingung,** *f.* stipulation, understanding. **–berechnung,** *f.* advance calculation, preliminary estimate. **voraus|bestellen,** *v.t. See* **vorbestellen. –bestimmen,** *v.t.* predetermine. **–bezahlen,** *v.t.* pay in advance, prepay. **–datieren,** *v.t.* antedate. **–eilen,** *v.i. See* **voraneilen. –gegangen,** *adj.* previous, preliminary. **–gehen,** *irr.v.i. See* **vorangehen. –heben,** *irr.v.t.* ***ihm etwas –,*** have an advantage over him *or* be superior to him *or* excel him in s.th.

Voraussage [for'auszaːgə], *f.* prediction, prophecy, prognosis, (*weather*) forecast; (*horse racing*) selections, (*coll.*) tip. **voraussagen,** *v.t.* predict, prophesy, foretell, forecast. **Voraus|sagung,** *f. See* **–sage. voraus|schauen,** *v.i.* look forward, anticipate. **–schauend,** *adj.* prospective; far-sighted. **–schicken,** *v.t.* send (on) in advance, send on ahead, forward; (*fig.*) mention beforehand, premise. **–sehen,** *irr.v.t.* foresee. **–setzen,** *v.t.* presuppose, suppose, assume, surmise, presume; ***vorausgesetzt daß,*** provided that; ***als bekannt –,*** take for granted. **Voraussetzung,** *f.* supposition, presupposition, assumption, surmise, postulate, hypothesis; requirement, provision, pre-condition, prerequisite; ***unter der – daß,*** on condition *or* on the understanding that; ***zur – haben,*** presuppose; ***zur – machen,*** take for granted, make the basis of. **voraussetzungslos,** *adj.* unconditional, unqualified, absolute. **Voraussicht,** *f.* foresight; ***in der – daß,*** on the assumption that; ***aller – nach,*** in all probability. **voraussichtlich,** *adj.* probable, presumable, expected, prospective. **Vorauszahlung,** *f.* advance (payment).

Vorbau ['f:orbau], *m.* (**-s,** *pl.* **-ten**) front (of building); projecting structure; porch. **vorbauen,** **1.** *v.t.* build in front of; build out beyond *or* from. **2.** *v.i.* (*fig.*) (*Dat.*) obviate, preclude, guard against, take precautions against; provide for (*the future*).

Vorbedacht ['fo:rbədaxt], *m.* forethought, premeditation; ***mit* –,** advisedly, deliberately, on purpose. **vorbedacht,** *adj.* premeditated, (*after noun*) aforethought.

vorbedeuten ['fo:rbədɔytən], *v.t.* forebode, presage, augur. **Vorbedeutung,** *f.* foreboding, portent, omen, augury.

Vor|bedingung, *f.* prerequisite, basic necessity, necessary condition (***zu,*** of *or* for). **–befehl,** *m.* (*Mil.*) warning order.

Vorbehalt ['fo:rbəhalt], *m.* reservation, proviso; ***mit – meiner Rechte,*** without prejudice to my rights; ***unter – aller Rechte,*** all rights reserved; ***ohne* –,** without reserve *or* restriction, unconditionally; ***unter dem üblichen* –,** with the usual proviso; ***geistiger*** or ***innerer*** or ***stiller* –,** mental reservation. **vorbehalten, 1.** *irr.v.t.* (hold *or* keep in) reserve (*Dat.*, for); ***Änderungen* –,** subject to alteration; ***Irrtümer* –,** errors excepted; ***es bleibt der Zukunft* –,** it remains to be seen, time will tell. **2.** *irr.v.r.* reserve to *or* for o.s. **vorbehaltlich,** *prep.* (*Gen.*) with the proviso *or* reservation that, subject to (the provisions of), except as provided in; ***– abweichender Vorschriften,*** unless otherwise provided for. **vorbehaltlos,** *adj.* without reservation, unreserved, unconditional. **Vorbehaltsklausel,** *f.* proviso (clause).

Vorbehandlung ['fo:rbəhandluŋ], *f.* preliminary treatment, pre-treatment.

vorbei [fo:r'baɪ], *adv.* (*place*) along, by, past; (*time*) past, over, done (with), gone; ***es ist mit ihm* –,** it is all over *or* (*coll.*) up with him; ***– ist* –,** what is done is done, it is no good crying over spilt milk; ***4 Uhr* –,** past 4 o'clock; ***an ihm* –,** past him, beyond him, (*fig.*) over his head; ***–!*** missed!

vorbei|drücken, *v.r.* squeeze by *or* past (***an ihm,*** him). **–gehen,** *irr.v.i.* (*aux.* s.) go *or* pass by, go past (***an ihm,*** him); ***daran* –,** fail to see it, take no notice of it, overlook *or* ignore it, pass it over, pass over it in silence; ***im Vorbeigehen,*** in passing. **–gelingen,** *irr.v.i.* (*coll.*) not be successful, miss the mark, go wrong, miscarry, not come off, come unstuck. **–kommen,** *irr.v.i.* (*aux.* s.) get past *or* round, pass by (***an ihm,*** him); (*coll.*) pay a call, drop in (***bei,*** on). **–lassen,** *irr.v.t.* let pass, let get past.

Vorbeimarsch [fo:r'baɪmarʃ], *m.* march past, review. **vorbei|marschieren,** *v.i.* (*aux.* s.) march *or* file past (***an ihm,*** him). **–reden,** *v.i.* be at cross-purposes (***an*** (*Dat.*), with); ***aneinander* –,** be at cross-purposes; ***an den Dingen* –,** talk round the subject, evade the issue, not get to grips with the matter. **–schießen,** *irr.v.i.* 1. (*aux.* s.) shoot *or* dart past (***an ihm,*** him); 2. (*aux.* h.) miss (the mark), (*fig.*) miss the point. **–ziehen,** *irr.v.i.* march past; pass (***an ihm,*** him).

Vorbemerkung ['fo:rbəmɛrkuŋ], *f.* preliminary remark(s), prefatory notice, preamble.

vorbenannt ['fo:rbənant], *adj.* above-mentioned, (afore)said.

Vorbenutzung ['fo:rbənutsuŋ], *f.* prior use.

vorbereiten ['for:bəraɪtən], **1.** *v.t.* prepare, get *or* make ready (***auf*** (*Acc.*), ***für,*** for); ***darauf vorbereitet sein,*** be prepared *or* ready for it. **2.** *v.r.* prepare o.s., make one's preparations, get ready, (*Spt. etc.*) train, get into training (***auf*** (*Acc.*), ***für, zu,*** for); ***es bereitet sich etwas vor,*** there's s.th. brewing *or* (*sl.*) cooking, there's s.th. in the wind *or* air. **vorbereitend** *adj.* preparatory, preliminary; predisposing. **Vorbereitung,** *f.* preparation (***auf*** (*Acc.*), ***für, zu,*** for); ***als – zu,*** preparatory to; *pl.* preparations, preliminaries.

Vor|berg, *m.* mountain spur, foothill. **–bericht,** *m.* introduction, preface; preliminary *or* advance report. **–bescheid,** *m.* preliminary decree, (*Law*) interlocutory judgement. **–besprechung,** *f.* preliminary discussion.

vorbestellen ['fo:rbəʃtɛlən], *v.t.* order in advance, (*books etc.*) subscribe to, (*rooms, seats etc.*) book (in advance), make reservations for. **Vorbestellung,** *f.* advance order, (*books*) subscription, (*rooms etc.*) booking, reservation.

vorbestraft ['fo:rbəʃtra:ft], *adj.* having a previous conviction. **Vorbestrafte(r),** *m., f.* s.o. with a criminal record; ***nicht* –,** first offender.

vorbeten ['fo:rbe:tən], **1.** *v.t.* repeat *or* recite (a prayer) (*Dat.*, to). **2.** *v.i.* lead in prayer. **Vorbeter,** *m.* prayer leader.

vorbeugen ['fo:rbɔygən], **1.** *v.t., v.r.* bend forward. **2.** *v.i.* (*fig.*) (*Dat.*) prevent, obviate, (safe)guard against. **vorbeugend,** *adj.* preventive, (*Med.*) prophylactic. **Vorbeugung,** *f.* prevention; prophylaxis. **Vorbeugungs|maßregel,** *f.* preventive measure. **–mittel,** *n.* preventive, (*Med.*) prophylactic.

Vorbild ['fo:rbɪlt], *n.* model, example, pattern, standard, prototype. **vorbildlich,** *adj.* typical, representative (***für,*** of); model, ideal, exemplary.

Vorbildung ['fo:rbɪlduŋ], *f.* preparation, preparatory training, preliminary instruction; basic education *or* training; ***allgemeine* –,** educational background.

vorbinden ['fo:rbɪndən], *irr.v.t.* tie *or* put on (*a tie etc.*).

vorbohren ['fo:rbo:rən], *v.t.* drill *or* bore *or* make a hole first, pre-drill. **Vorbohrer,** *m.* gimlet, bradawl, auger.

Vorbote ['fo:rbo:tə], *m.* (**-n,** *pl.* **-n**) precursor, forerunner, harbinger, herald; early sign, indication, symptom.

Vorbramsegel ['fo:rbra:mze:gəl], *n.* fore-top-gallant-sail.

vorbringen ['fo:rbrɪŋən], *irr.v.t.* bring forward, produce, (*coll.*) bring up (*reasons, proofs etc.*), prefer (*a charge*), make, offer (*excuses*), propose (*a plan*), advance, put forward (*an opinion*), allege, state, utter; ***er konnte kein Wort* –,** he could not utter *or* say a word.

vorbuchstabieren ['fo:rbu:xʃtabi:rən], *v.t.* spell out (*Dat.*, for *or* to).

Vorbühne ['fo:rby:nə], *f.* (*Theat.*) proscenium.

vor|christlich, *adj.* pre-Christian. **–datieren,** *v.t.* antedate.

vordem [fo:r'de:m], *adv.* (*obs.*) formerly, in former times, of old.

vorder ['fɔrdər], *adj.* fore, forward, anterior, front, foremost.

Vorder|achsantrieb, *m.* front-wheel drive. **–achse,** *f.* front axle. **–ansicht,** *f.* front view, (*Archit.*) front elevation. **–antrieb,** *m. See* **–achsantrieb. –arm,** *m.* forearm. **–asien,** *n.* the Near East. **–bauch,** *m.* epigastrium. **–bein,** *n.* foreleg, front leg. **–deck,** *n.* fore-deck. **–decke,** *f.* front cover (*of books*). **–fläche,** *f.* anterior surface. **–fuß,** *m.* fore-foot; front part of the foot. **–gaumen,** *m.* hard palate. **–gaumenlaut,** *m.* palatal sound. **–glied,** *n.* 1. forelimb, anterior member; 2. front rank; 3. (*Math.*) antecedent, first term. **–grund,** *m.* foreground, (*fig.*) forefront; ***in den – rücken*** or ***stellen,*** place in the foreground *or* forefront, put first, emphasize, throw into relief; ***im – stehen,*** be in the forefront *or* limelight, be well to the fore; ***in den – treten,*** come into the forefront, come to the fore. **–hand,** *f.* 1. fore-part of the hand; forepaw (*of animals*); 2. (*Cards*) lead.

vorderhand ['fɔrdərhant], *adv.* for the present, in the meantime, for the time being, just now.

Vorder|hang, *m.* (*Mil.*) forward slope. **–haupt,** *n.*, **–kopf,** *m.* fore-part of the head, forehead, (*Anat.*) sinciput. **–lader,** *m.* muzzle-loader. **–lage,** *f.* anterior position. **vorderlastig,** *adj.* (*Naut., Av.*) nose-heavy. **Vorder|lauf,** *m.* fore-leg (*of game*), fore-end (*of the barrel*). **–leute,** *pl.* front-rank men.

vorderlich ['fɔrdərlɪç], *adj.* (*Naut.*) ***–e See,*** head-sea.

Vorder|mann, *m.* front-rank man, man ahead *or* in front; (*fig.*) superior; (*Comm.*) previous *or* prior endorser; (*Mil.*) *–!* cover (off)! (*Mil.*) ***auf – stehen,*** be covered; (*coll.*) ***ihn auf – bringen,*** make him toe the line. **–mast,** *m.* foremast. **–pferd,** *n.* leader, leading horse. **–pfote,** *f.* forepaw. **–radantrieb,** *m. See* **–achsantrieb. –radgabel,** *f.* (*Cycl.*) front fork. **–radschutzblech,** *n.* front mudguard. **–reihe,** *f.* front rank *or* row. **–satz,** *m.* (*Gram.*) protasis; (*Log.*) antecedent, premise. **–seite,** *f.* (*Archit.*) front, façade; obverse; face (*of a coin*); recto (*in manuscripts*). **–sitz,** *m.* front seat.

vorderst ['fɔrdərst], *sup.adj.* first, foremost; (*Mil.*) ***–e Linie,*** front line.

Vorder|steven, *m.* (*Naut.*) stem, prow, cutwater. **–stich,** *m.* running stitch. **–teil,** *n.* front; prow (*of a ship*). **–tür,** *f.* house-door, front door. **–wand,** *f.* front wall. **–zahn,** *m.* front tooth.

vor|drängen, *v.t., v.r.* press *or* push forward, (*also v.r.*) thrust o.s. forward. **–dringen,** *irr.v.i.* (*aux.* s.) push on, press forward, advance, make headway, forge ahead, gain ground. **Vordringen,** *n.* (*Mil.*) advance. **vordringlich,** *adj.* urgent, pressing; ***– behandelt werden,*** be given priority, be treated as urgent *or* as a matter of urgency. **Vordringlichkeit,** *f.* urgent nature, priority. **Vordringlichkeitsliste,** *f.* list of priorities.

Vordruck ['fo:rdruk], *m.* (*Typ.*) first *or* original impression; (printed) form.

vor|ehelich, *adj.* premarital, prenuptial. **–eilig,** *adj.* hasty, precipitate, rash; premature; ***–e Schlüsse ziehen,*** jump *or* rush to conclusions. **Voreiligkeit,** *f.* precipitancy, rashness, overhaste.

voreingenommen ['fo:rʔaıngənɔmən], *adj.* prejudiced, biased, prepossessed (***für,*** in favour of; ***gegen,*** against). **Voreingenommenheit,** *f.* prejudice, bias, prepossession.

Vor|eltern, *pl.* ancestors, forefathers, progenitors. **–empfindung,** *f.* presentiment, foreboding.

vorenthalten ['fo:rʔɛnthaltən], *irr.v.t.* (*sep. and insep.*) (*p.p. only*) withhold, keep back (*Dat.*, from), deny (to); (*Law*) detain. **Vorenthaltung,** *f.* withholding, denial, retention, (*Law*) detention.

Vorentscheidung ['fo:rʔɛntʃaıduŋ], *f.* provisional decision, previous judgement, precedent.

vorerst ['fo:rʔe:rst], *adv.* first of all; *see also* **vorderhand.**

vor|erwähnt, *adj.* before-mentioned, (afore)said, above. **–erzählen,** *v.t.* relate, recount (*Dat.*, to). **–essen,** *irr.v.t.* ***das ist vorgegessenes Brot,*** that is counting one's chickens before they are hatched.

Vorfahr ['fo:rfa:r], *m.* (**-en,** (*obs.*) **-s,** *pl.* **-en**) ancestor, forefather, predecessor, progenitor.

vorfahren ['fo:rfa:rən], *irr.v.i.* (*aux.* s.) drive up (***an*** (*Dat.*), ***bei,*** to), stop (at); pass, overtake (*in traffic*); ***den Wagen – lassen,*** have the car brought round. **Vorfahrt,** *f.* (*coll.*), **Vorfahrt(s)recht,** *n.* (*Motor.*) right of way.

Vorfall ['fo:rfal], *m.* **1.** occurrence, event, incident; **2.** (*Med.*) prolapsus; **3.** detent (*of a clock*). **vorfallen,** *irr.v.i.* (*aux.* s.) **1.** happen, occur, come to pass, take place; **2.** (*Med.*) prolapse.

vorfärben ['fo:rfɛrbən], *v.t.* pre-dye, ground, bottom.

Vor|fechter, *m.* pioneer, champion, advocate. **–feier,** *f.* preliminary celebration, eve of a festival. **–feld,** *n.* approaches, perimeter.

vor|finden, 1. *irr.v.t.* find, meet with, come *or* light upon. **2.** *irr.v.r.* be found, be met with; be forthcoming. **–flunkern,** *v.t.* (*coll.*) tell a fib (*Dat.*, to).

Vorfluter ['fo:rflu:tər], *m.* main drainage channel.

vorfordern ['fo:rfɔrdərn], *v.t. See* **vorladen.**

Vor|frage, *f.* preliminary *or* previous question. **–freude,** *f.* pleasure of anticipation. **–frucht,** *f.* early crop; preceding crop (*in rotation*). **–frühling,** *m.* early spring.

vorfühlen ['fo:rfy:lən], *v.i.* (*Mil.*) seek (to establish) contact; (*fig.*) feel one's way forward, put out feelers.

Vorführdame ['fo:rfy:rda:mə], *f.* mannequin. **vorführen,** *v.t.* bring forward, bring to the front; produce (*witnesses*); show, display, exhibit, demonstrate; present, show, project (*film*); ***dem Richter –,*** bring before the court. **Vorführer,** *m.* demonstrator; (*Films*) operator, projectionist. **Vorführraum,** *m.* (*Films*) projection room. **Vorführung,** *f.* production, performance; presentation, showing; projection (*of films*); demonstration, display; production (*of witnesses*). **Vorführungs|befehl,** *m. See* **Vorladung. –raum,** *m.* demonstration room.

Vorgabe ['fo:rga:bə], *f.* points *or* odds given *or* allowed; (*Spt.*) handicap. **Vorgaberennen,** *n.* handicap (race).

Vorgang ['fo:rgaŋ], *m.* proceedings, procedure; process, operation; facts, occurrence, incident, event; (*Comm.*) previous correspondence, record (of a transaction).

Vorgänger ['fo:rgɛŋər], *m.* forerunner, predecessor.

Vorgarten ['fo:rgartən], *m.* front garden.

vorgaukeln ['fo:rgaukəln], *v.t.* (*Dat.*) buoy up *or* deceive with false promises *or* hopes, mislead, lead to believe, (*coll.*) lead up the garden path.

vorgeben ['fo:rge:bən], *irr.v.t.* (*Dat.*) **1.** (*Spt. etc.*) give handicap, give points to, allow points; **2.** assert, allege, pretend. **Vorgeben,** *n.* pretence, pretext.

vorgebildet ['fo:rgəbıldət], *adj.* trained.

Vorgebirge ['fo:rgəbırgə], *n.* promontory, cape, headland; mountain spur, foothills.

vorgeblich ['fo:rge:plıç], *adj.* pretended, ostensible, alleged, so-called, would-be.

vor|geburtlich, *adj.* prenatal. **–gedacht,** *adj. See* **–erwähnt. –gefaßt,** *adj.* preconceived; ***–e Meinung,*** preconceived idea, prejudice, bias.

Vorgefühl ['fo:rgəfy:l], *n.* presentiment; ***banges –,*** misgivings, foreboding.

vorgehen ['fo:rge:ən], *irr.v.i.* (*aux.* s.) **1.** gain, be fast (*of watches*); go first *or* before, precede, lead the way, take the lead; advance, go forward; ***gehen Sie vor, ich folge,*** lead the way, I will follow; **2.** (*fig.*) have *or* take precedence (*Dat.*, over), have priority (over), be more important (than), transcend; ***deine Schularbeiten gehen jetzt allem andern vor,*** your homework is more important than anything else, your homework must come first; **3.** act, take action *or* steps, proceed; (*Law*) proceed, take proceedings (***gegen,*** against); ***rücksichtslos –,*** act ruthlessly; **4.** happen, occur, go on, take place; ***was geht hier vor?*** what is going on here? ***ich weiß nicht, was in mir vorging,*** I do not know what came over me *or* what I was thinking of. **Vorgehen,** *n.* **1.** advance; **2.** procedure, proceedings; **3.** (concerted) action.

Vorgelege ['fo:rgəle:gə], *n.* (*Mech.*) reduction gear. **Vorgelegewelle,** *f.* (*Mech.*) counter-shaft.

vorgenannt ['fo:rgənant], *adj.* aforementioned, (afore)said.

Vor|genuß, *m.* pleasure in anticipation, foretaste of pleasure. **–gericht,** *n. See* **–speise.**

vorgerückt ['fo:rgərykt], *adj.* advanced (*in time*), late; ***ein Mann –en Alters,*** an elderly man, a man of advancing *or* advanced years; ***in –em Alter,*** at an advanced age; ***wegen der –en Stunde,*** owing to the lateness of the hour; ***zu einer –en Stunde,*** at a late hour. *See* **vorrücken.**

Vorgeschichte ['fo:rgəʃıçtə], *f.* prehistory, early history, prehistoric times; (*of an event*) past *or* previous history; (*of a p.*) antecedents. **vorgeschichtlich,** *adj.* prehistoric.

Vorgeschmack ['fo:rgəʃmak], *m.* foretaste.

vorgeschoben ['fo:rgəʃo:bən], *adj.* (*Mil.*) forward, advanced (*sentries etc.*).

Vorgesetztenverhältnis ['fo:rgəzɛtstənfɛrhɛltnıs], *n.* (*Mil.*) authority. **Vorgesetzte(r),** *m., f.* superior, senior; chief, employer, master.

vorgestern ['fo:rgɛstərn], *adv.* the day before yesterday. **vorgestrig,** *adj.* of two days ago.

Vorgraben ['fo:rgra:bən], *m.* avant-fosse, outer *or* forward trench.

vorgreifen ['fo:rgraıfən], *irr.v.i.* (*Dat.*) anticipate, forestall; ***den Ereignissen –,*** anticipate (the) events;

einer Frage –, prejudge a matter. **vorgreiflich,** *adv.* in anticipation. **Vorgriff,** *m.* anticipation.

vorhaben [ˈfoːrhaːbən], *irr.v.t.* 1. have before one; have on, wear (*as an apron*); 2. have in mind *or* in view, design, propose, intend, mean, (*coll.*) plan; ***er hat etwas Böses vor,*** he is plotting some mischief; ***was hast du mit ihm vor?*** what do you intend to do with him? what are your plans with him? 3. be engaged on *or* in, be busy *or* occupied with, (*coll.*) be about, have on; ***was hat er vor?*** what is he about *or* after? ***haben Sie für morgen etwas vor?*** have you anything on tomorrow? 4. (*coll.*) call to account, take to task, haul over the coals, have on the carpet. **Vorhaben,** *n.* intention, purpose, (*Law*) intent; design, project, scheme, plan.

Vor|hafen, *m.* outer harbour. **–halle,** *f.* vestibule, (entrance) hall, lobby (*also Parl.*), (*hotel, theatre etc.*) lounge.

Vorhalt [ˈfoːrhalt], *m.* 1. (*Swiss*) *see* **Vorhaltung**; 2. (*Mus.*) suspended note; 3. (*Av., Artil.*) lead, allowance for speed.

vorhalten [ˈfoːrhaltən], **1.** *irr.v.t.* 1. hold up *or* out (*Dat.*, to) *or* out (for) *or* out in front (of) *or* out (before); 2. (*fig.*) ***ihm etwas*** –, charge *or* reproach him with s.th., remonstrate with him about s.th. **2.** *irr.v.i.* 1. hold out, last; ***solange das Geld vorhält,*** as long as the money holds out; 2. (*Av., Artil.*) apply (a) lead. **Vorhaltewinkel,** *m.* (*Artil.*) angle of lead, (*Av.*) dropping *or* bombing angle.

Vorhaltung [ˈfoːrhaltuŋ], *f.* representation, remonstrance; ***ihm –en machen,*** make representations to him, remonstrate with him (***über*** (*Acc.*), about).

Vorhand [ˈfoːrhant], *f.* (*Comm.*) first option *or* claim; (*Tenn.*) forehand; (*Cards, fig.*) lead; ***ihm die – lassen*** or ***geben,*** give him the lead; ***wer hat die –?*** who has the lead?

vorhanden [foːrˈhandən], *adj.* (*Comm.*) on hand, in stock; available, present, at hand; existing, existent, extant; – ***sein,*** be, exist, be on hand, be in stock; ***davon ist nichts mehr –,*** there is no more of it (left). **Vorhandensein,** *n.* existence, presence, availability.

Vor|hang, *m.* curtain; ***eiserner –,*** (*Theat.*) fire-proof curtain, (*Pol.*) Iron Curtain. **–hängeschloß,** *n.* padlock. **–haut,** *f.* foreskin, prepuce. **–hemd,** *n.* shirt-front; (*coll.*) dickey.

vorher [foːrˈheːr], *adv.* before, previously; ***am Abend –,*** (on) the previous evening; ***kurz –,*** a short *or* little time *or* while before.

vorher–, *sep. pref.* in advance, beforehand. *See examples below.*

Vorher|bestellen, *v.t. See* **vorbestellen. –bestimmen,** *v.t.* determine *or* settle beforehand, predetermine, (*as fate*) preordain; (*Eccl.*) predestine. **Vorherbestimmung,** *f.* predetermination, (*Eccl.*) predestination. **vorher|gehen,** *irr.v.i.* (*aux.* s.) (*Dat.*) precede; ***ohne vorhergegangene Warnung,*** without previous warning. **–gehend,** *adj.* preceding, foregoing, previous, prior; ***aus dem Vorhergehenden,*** from the foregoing, from what has already been said; ***die –en Seiten,*** the foregoing pages.

vorherig [foːrˈheːrɪç], *adj.* previous, preceding, foregoing; former, antecedent.

Vorherrschaft [ˈfoːrhɛrʃaft], *f.* predominance, superiority, ascendancy. **vorherrschen,** *v.i.* prevail, dominate, predominate. **vorherrschend,** *adj.* dominant, predominant, prevailing, prevalent.

Vorhersage [foːrˈheːrzaːgə], *f. See* **Voraussage. vorhersagen,** *v.t. See* **voraussagen. Vorhersagung,** *f. See* **Voraussage. vorher|sehen,** *irr.v.t.* foresee. **–wissen,** *irr.v.t.* know beforehand *or* already. **Vorherwissen,** *n.* foreknowledge.

vorhin [foːrˈhɪn], *adv.* before, heretofore; a short time ago, just now; ***erst –,*** only just now. **vorhinein** [ˈfoːrhɪnaɪn], *adv.* (*Austr.*) (*only in*) ***im –,*** from the beginning *or* outset.

Vorhof [ˈfoːrhoːf], *m.* outer court, forecourt, vestibule, porch; (*Anat.*) auricle (*of the heart*).

vorholen [ˈfoːrhoːlən], *v.t.* (*Naut.*) haul home.

Vor|holer, *m.* (*Artil.*) counter-recoil mechanism. **–hölle,** *f.* limbo, purgatory. **–hut,** *f.* (*Mil.*) advance guard, vanguard

vorig [ˈfoːrɪç], *adj.* former, preceding, previous, last; ***die –en,*** the same (*in stage directions*); ***–en Monats,*** of last month, (*Comm.*) ult(imo).

Vor|instanz, *f.* (*Law*) lower court. **–jahr,** *n.* preceding *or* previous *or* last year. **vorjährig,** *adj.* of last year, last year's; ***–e Kartoffeln,*** old potatoes.

vorjammern [ˈfoːrjamərn], **1.** *v.i.* pour forth a tale of woe, (*sl.*) bellyache (*Dat.*, to). **2.** *v.t.* pour forth a tale of woe about, (*sl.*) bellyache about.

Vor|kammer, *f. See* **–hof** (*Anat.*). **–kampf,** *m.* (*Spt.*) semi-final, (*Boxing*) preliminary bout. **–kämpfer(in),** *m.* (*f.*) protagonist, champion; pioneer.

vorkauen [ˈfoːrkauən], *v.t.* chew previously (*Dat.*, for); (*usu. fig.*) spell out (for), (*coll.*) spoon-feed.

Vorkauf [ˈfoːrkauf], *m.* pre-emption, option on purchase, first refusal. **vorkaufen,** *v.t.* buy before others, forestall, buy for future delivery. **Vorkäufer,** *m.* pre-emptor, (*St. Exch.*) dealer in futures. **Vorkaufs|preis,** *m.* pre-emption price. **–recht,** *n.* right of pre-emption; ***das – haben,*** have the (first) refusal (***für, auf*** (*Acc.*), of), have the option (on).

Vorkehr [ˈfoːrkeːr], *f.* (-, *pl.* **-en**) (*Swiss*), **Vorkehrung,** *f.* provision, precaution, (preventive *or* precautionary) measure; ***–en treffen,*** make arrangements *or* provision (***für,*** for), take precautions *or* measures (***gegen,*** against).

Vor|kenntnis, *f.* previous knowledge; basic knowledge, necessary grounding, rudiments. **–kiefrigkeit,** *f.* prognathism.

vor|klönen, *v.t.* (*dial., coll.*) blether about, unburden o.s. of (*Dat.*, to). **–knöpfen,** *v.t.* (*coll.*) ***sich*** (*Dat.*) ***ihn –,*** take him to task, haul him over the coals, give him a dressing-down.

vorkommen [ˈfoːrkɔmən], *irr.v.i.* (*aux.* s.) 1. be found, be met with, present itself, happen, occur, take place, (*coll.*) crop up; ***dergleichen kommt nicht alle Tage vor,*** such things do not occur every day; ***so etwas ist mir noch nicht vorgekommen,*** I have never heard of such a thing; 2. call, look in, (*coll.*) drop in (***bei,*** on), visit; ***kommen Sie nächsten Sonntag bei mir vor,*** give me a call *or* look in on me *or* drop in next Sunday; 3. (*Dat.*) seem, appear; ***er kommt sich*** (*Dat.*) ***recht gelehrt vor,*** he fancies himself as a great scholar, he believes himself to be *or* thinks he is very learned; ***es kam mir seltsam vor,*** it seemed strange to me, I thought it was *or* it struck me as (being) odd; ***sich*** (*Dat.*) ***dumm –,*** feel silly; ***das kommt dir nur so vor,*** you are just imagining it; (*coll.*) ***wie kommst du mir eigentlich vor?*** who do you think you are? ***das kommt mir spanisch vor,*** that's all Greek to me; there's s.th. fishy about it; ***ich weiß nicht, wie du mir heute vorkommst,*** I do not know what to make of you *or* I cannot make you out today.

Vorkommen, *n.* 1. occurrence, incidence; 2. (*Geol.*) deposit. **vorkommendenfalls,** *adv.* should the case arise, in the eventuality. **Vorkommnis,** *n.* (**-ses,** *pl.* **-se**) incident, occurrence, happening, event.

Vorkriegs– [ˈfoːrkriːks–], *pref.* pre-war.

vorladen [ˈfoːrlaːdən], *irr.v.t.* summon (to appear), serve a summons on, cite, subpoena. **Vorladung,** *f.* summons, warrant, citation, subpoena.

Vorlage [ˈfoːrlaːgə], *f.* 1. submission, presentation, production (*of documents etc.*); (*Comm.*) ***zahlbar bei –,*** payable on demand *or* at sight; 2. proposal, subject, matter (*for discussion*), (*Parl.*) bill; 3. copy, model, pattern; 4. advance (*of credit*); 5. rug, mat, (carpet) runner; 6. (*Chem. etc.*) condenser, receiver, receiving vessel; 7. (*Artil.*) flash reducer; 8. (*Footb.*) forward pass; 9. (*Skiing*) (correct) stance leaning forward.

vorlagern [ˈfoːrlaːgərn], *v.i.* stretch out *or* extend in front (*Dat.*, of).

Vorland [ˈfoːrlant], *n.* foreland; foreshore, mud-flat; land outside a dike.

vorlängst ['fo:rlɛŋst], *adv.* (*obs.*) long ago *or* since.

vorlassen ['fo:rlasən], *irr.v.t.* let come forward, let pass *or* allow to pass (in front); admit, show in; ***vorgelassen werden,*** be shown in *or* admitted (***bei,*** to). **Vorlassung,** *f.* admittance, admission.

Vorlauf ['fo:rlauf], *m.* 1. (*Spt.*) (elimination) heat; 2. (*Distilling*) first runnings, heads.

Vorläufer(in) ['fo:rlɔyfər(ɪn)], *m.* (*f.*) forerunner, precursor; (*fig.*) harbinger.

vorläufig ['fo:rlɔyfɪç], **1.** *adj.* preliminary, tentative, provisional, temporary, interim. **2.** *adv.* for the present, for the time being, temporarily, provisionally, in the meantime.

vorlaut ['fo:rlaut], *adj.* forward, cheeky, saucy, pert, brash; (*of dogs*) – ***sein,*** be badly trained.

vorleben ['fo:rle:bən], *v.t.* hold up as *or* set as an example (*Dat.*, to). **Vorleben,** *n.* former life, past (life), previous career *or* history, early life, antecedents; ***sie hat kein einwandfreies –,*** she has a doubtful past.

Vorlege|besteck ['fo:rle:gə–], *n.* (pair of) carvers. **–gabel,** *f.* carving-fork. **–löffel,** *m.* soup ladle. **–messer,** *n.* carving-knife.

vorlegen ['fo:rle:gən], **1.** *v.t.* 1. put *or* lay out; serve (*food*), put on (*a padlock*), produce, submit, tender (*documents etc.*), present (*a bill, cheque etc.*), propose, put forward (*an idea*); ***Waren zum Verkauf –,*** expose goods for sale; (*coll.*) ***ein Tempo –,*** show a turn of speed, put on a spurt; ***Schloß und Riegel –,*** secure *or* barricade o.s. against intrusion; 2. lay *or* place *or* put before (***ihm,*** him), show, display, exhibit (to him), submit, refer (*a suggestion*) (to him), (*at table*) help (him) to; ***dem Vieh Heu –,*** give the cattle hay. **2.** *v.r.* lean forward. **Vorleger,** *m.* (carpet) runner, rug, mat.

Vorlege|schloß, *n.* padlock. **–welle,** *f.* (*Mech.*) countershaft. **Vorlegung,** *f. See* **Vorlage.**

Vorlese ['fo:rle:zə], *f.* early vintage.

vorlesen ['fo:rle:zən], *irr.v.t.* read aloud *or* out (*Dat.*, to). **Vorlesung,** *f.* reading (aloud), recital; (university) lecture; ***–en halten,*** lecture, give a course of *or* hold lectures (***über*** (*Acc.*), on); ***–en hören,*** attend lectures; ***–en schwänzen,*** cut lectures. **Vorlesungs|gebühr,** *f.* lecture-fee. **–verzeichnis,** *n.* university prospectus *or* calendar *or* (*Am.*) catalog.

vorletzt ['fo:rlɛtst], *adj.* last but one, penultimate; ***am –en Abend,*** on the evening before last.

Vorliebe ['fo:rli:bə], *f.* predilection, preference, partiality, special liking (***für,*** for); ***eine – haben für,*** be partial to.

vorliebnehmen [fo:r'li:pne:mən], *irr.v.i.* put up (***mit,*** with), make do (with), have to be satisfied (with); (*coll.*) (*of an unexpected guest*) take potluck.

vorliegen ['fo:rli:gən], *irr.v.i.* (*Dat.*) lie *or* be in front of; be put forward *or* submitted; be in hand, be under discussion *or* consideration; be (present *or* there), exist; ***es liegt heute nichts vor,*** there is nothing planned *or* on the programme (for) today, (*coll.*) there's nothing doing today; ***hier muß ein Irrtum –,*** there must be some mistake here. **vorliegend,** *adj.* present, existing; at issue, in hand *or* question.

vorlügen ['fo:rly:gən], *irr.v.t.* tell lies, lie (*Dat.*, to; ***über*** (*Acc.*), about).

Vorluke ['fo:rlu:kə], *f.* (*Naut.*) fore *or* forward hatch.

vorm [fo:rm] = ***vor dem.***

vormachen ['fo:rmaxən], *v.t.* put *or* place before *or* in front; (*fig.*) ***ihm etwas –,*** demonstrate s.th. to him, show him how to do s.th.; impose upon him, hoodwink *or* humbug him, (*coll.*) take him in; ***sich*** (*Dat.*) (***selbst***) ***etwas –,*** fool o.s.; ***ihm ein X für ein U –*** or ***ihm*** (***einen***) ***blauen Dunst –,*** pull the wool over his eyes, throw dust in his eyes; ***ihm kannst du nichts –,*** he's nobody's fool; ***mir kannst du nichts –,*** go and teach your grandmother to suck eggs!

Vormacht ['fo:rmaxt], *f.* predominance, supremacy. **Vormachtstellung,** *f.* hegemony.

Vormagen ['fo:rma:gən], *m.* (*Zool.*) omasum, crop.

vormalig ['fo:rma:lɪç], *adj.* former. **vormals,** *adv.* formerly, erstwhile, once upon a time.

Vor|mann, *m. See* **Vordermann. –mars,** *m. or f.* (*Naut.*) foretop. **–marsch,** *m.* (*Mil.*) advance, push. **vormarschieren,** *v.i.* (*aux.* s.) advance, push forward.

vormärzlich ['fo:rmɛrtslɪç], *adj.* reactionary, obscurantist, (*characterizing political attitude*) before 1848 (revolution).

Vor|mast, *m.* foremast. **–mauer,** *f.* outer wall, bulwark; claustrum. **–meldung,** *f.* preliminary report.

vormerken ['fo:rmɛrkən], *v.t.* note *or* take down, make *or* take a note of; book, reserve, earmark, bespeak; ***seine Fahrkarte – lassen,*** book one's ticket; ***sich – lassen*** (***für***), put one's name down (for). **Vormerk|gebühr,** *f.* booking *or* registration fee. **–liste,** *f.* waiting list. **Vormerkung,** *f.* note, entry, memorandum; reservation, booking.

Vor|milch, *f.* colostrum. **–mittag,** *m.* (**-s,** *pl.* **-e**) morning, forenoon. **vormittags,** *adv.* in the morning. **Vormonat,** *m.* previous month.

Vormund ['fo:rmunt], *m.* (**-(e)s,** *pl.* **¨-er**) guardian, trustee; (*coll.*) ***ich brauche keinen –,*** I will not stand any interference. **Vormundschaft,** *f.* guardianship, trusteeship, tutelage; ***unter – stehen*** (***stellen***), be (place) under the care of a guardian. **vormundschaftlich,** *adj.* tutelary. **Vormundschafts|gelder,** *n.pl.* trust-money, property of a ward. **–gericht,** *n.* Court of Chancery.

[1]**vorn** [fɔrn], *adv.* (*place*) in (the) front, ahead, at the head *or* front; (*time*) at the beginning; ***ganz –,*** right at the *or* in front; ***nach –,*** forward, to(wards) the front; ***– und hinten,*** before and behind, fore and aft; ***er ist überall, hinten und –,*** he is here, there and everywhere; ***von –,*** from the front; ***ich sah sie von –,*** I saw her face; ***von – anfangen,*** make a fresh start, start afresh *or* anew, begin at the beginning; ***noch einmal von –,*** all over again.

[2]**vorn** [fo:rn], (*coll.*) = ***vor den.***

vornächtig ['fo:rnɛçtɪç], *adj.* last night's.

Vorname ['fo:rna:mə], *m.* Christian *or* first *or* (*Am.*) given name.

vornan [fɔrn'an], *adv.* in front, at the front. **vorne,** *adv. See* [1]**vorn.**

vornehm ['fo:rne:m], **1.** *adj.* of high *or* superior rank, aristocratic, noble; grand, elegant, stylish, fashionable, genteel, refined; distinguished, eminent, exclusive, high-class; chief, principal, first and foremost; ***–er Anstrich, –es Äußere,*** distinguished appearance; ***–er Besuch,*** distinguished visitor(s); ***dies ist das –ste und größte Gebot,*** this is the first and greatest commandment; ***–e Gesinnung,*** high-mindedness; ***die Vornehmen,*** people of rank *or* quality, distinguished people; ***die –e Welt,*** fashionable circles, high society; ***–es Wesen,*** air of superiority. **2.** *adv.* – ***denken,*** be high-minded *or* high-principled, (*coll.*) behave very decently; – ***tun,*** put on *or* give o.s. airs.

vornehmen ['fo:rne:mən], *irr.v.t.* 1. put on (*as an apron*); 2. (*fig.*) take in hand, undertake, deal with, (*coll.*) take up; ***sich*** (*Dat.*) ***etwas –*** or ***vorgenommen haben,*** make up one's mind *or* be determined *or* intend *or* resolve *or* propose to do a th.; occupy *or* busy o.s. with a th.; ***sich*** (*Dat.*) ***ihn –,*** call him to account, take him to task, (*coll.*) take him up (***wegen,*** about).

Vornehmheit ['fo:rne:mhaɪt], *f.* (high *or* superior) rank; distinction, refinement, elegance.

vornehmlich ['forne:mlɪç], *adv.* chiefly, mainly, largely, principally, particularly, (e)specially, above all, in the main.

Vornehmtuerei ['fo:rne:mtu:əraɪ], *f.* airs and graces, snobbery, (*coll.*) swank, side.

vorneweg ['fɔrnəvɛk], *adv.* (*coll.*) *see* [1]**vorn, vornan**; (*sl.*) ***mit dem Mundwerk –,*** shooting off one's mouth.

vorn|herein, *adv.* ***von –,*** from the start *or* first *or* beginning, to start *or* begin with. **–über,** *adv.*

forward; head first *or* foremost. **-weg,** *adv. See* **vorneweg.**

Vorort ['fo:rʔɔrt], *m.* 1. suburb; 2. administrative headquarters, central office (*of an association*). **Vorort(s)|verkehr,** *m.* suburban traffic. **-zug,** *m.* suburban *or* local train.

Vor|platz, *m.* forecourt, esplanade; (*of a staircase*) landing. **-posten,** *m.* (*Mil.*) outpost, advance post; ***auf* –,** on outpost duty. **-postenboot,** *n.* patrol vessel. **-postenkette,** *f.* line of outposts. **-prüfung,** *f.* preliminary examination, (*Spt.*) trial.

vor|pumpen, *v.t.* prime (*a pump*). **-quellen,** *irr.v.i.* (*aux.* s.) ooze out *or* forth; bulge (out). **-ragen,** *v.i.* project, protrude, jut out.

Vorrang ['fo:rraŋ], *m.* pre-eminence, precedence, priority; ***den* – *haben,*** have *or* take precedence (***vor*** (*Dat.*), over), (*of a th.*) have priority (over).

Vorrat ['fo:rra:t], *m.* **(-(e)s,** *pl.* **⸚e)** store, stock, supply, reserve (***an*** (*Dat.*), of); **– *auf Lager,*** stock in hand; ***auf* – *kaufen,*** buy in(to) stock, (*coll.*) stock up; ***im* –,** in stock; in store *or* reserve; ***solange der* – *reicht,*** as long as supplies last.

vorrätig ['fo:rrɛ:tɪç], *adj.* in stock, on hand, available; **– *haben,*** (have *or* keep in) stock; ***nicht* (*mehr*) –,** out of stock; ***nicht mehr* – *haben,*** be out of (*s.th.*).

Vorrats|ansammlung, *f.* overstocking, stockpiling. **-behälter,** *m.* storage container. **-kammer,** *f.* storeroom; (*for food*) pantry, larder. **-lager,** *n.* store. **-schrank,** *m.* store-cupboard. **-verzeichnis,** *n.* inventory, stock-list.

Vorraum ['fo:rraum], *m.* anteroom, lobby; (entrance-)hall, vestibule.

vorrechnen ['fo:rrɛçnən], *v.t.* reckon up, calculate; enumerate.

Vorrecht ['fo:rrɛçt], *n.* special right, privilege, prerogative; priority.

Vorrede ['fo:rre:də], *f.* (*verbal*) words of introduction, opening speech; (*written*) introduction, preface, preamble; (*Prov.*) **– *spart Nachrede,*** a word before is worth two after. **vorreden,** *v.t.* ***ihm etwas* –,** tell him a (plausible) tale, (*sl.*) hand him a line (***über*** (*Acc.*), about); ***sich*** (*Dat.*) ***etwas* – *lassen,*** let o.s. be talked into a th. *or* round, let the wool be pulled over one's eyes. **Vorredner,** *m.* last *or* previous speaker.

Vorreiber ['fo:rraɪbər], *m.* window catch.

vorreiten ['fo:rraɪtən], **1.** *irr.v.t.* put (*a horse*) through its paces; (*fig.*) ***ihm etwas* –,** parade a th. *or* show a th. off before him. **2.** *v.i.* (*aux.* s.) (*Dat.*) ride before; ride forward; show (*a p.*) how to ride. **Vorreiter,** *m.* outrider.

vorrichten ['fo:rrɪçtən], *v.t.* prepare, make *or* get ready, put in order, fit up; put on, advance (*a watch etc.*). **Vorrichtung,** *f.* preparation, arrangement; apparatus, contrivance, appliance, device, (*coll.*) gadget.

vorrücken ['fo:rrykən], **1.** *v.t.* move *or* push forward, put (*a clock*) on. **2.** *v.i.* (*aux.* s.) advance, move forward, progress, move *or* push on; ***Truppen* – *lassen,*** order troops to advance, push troops forward; ***die Zeit rückt vor,*** time is getting on. *See* **vorgerückt.**

Vorrunde ['fo:rrundə], *f.* (*Spt.*) preliminary *or* elimination round, heat.

vors [fo:rs] = ***vor das.***

Vorsaal ['fo:rza:l], *m.* entrance hall, vestibule, anteroom, antechamber, waiting-room.

vorsagen ['fo:rza:gən], *v.t.* say to, tell (*Dat.*, a p.), prompt, dictate to; recite, rehearse (*what one has to say*); ***du sagst mir das wohl nur so vor,*** you are only saying that, there is not a word of truth in it, I do not believe a word of it; ***ihr viel Schönes* –,** make pretty speeches to her.

Vorsänger ['fo:rzɛŋər], *m.* leader of a choir, precentor, officiating minister (*in a synagogue*).

Vorsatz ['fo:rzats], *m.* 1. design, project, purpose, resolution, plan, intention; (*Law*) malice aforethought, criminal intent, premeditation. **2.** (*also n.*) *see* **-blatt**; ***aus*** or ***mit* –,** on purpose, purposely, deliberately, intentionally, (*Law*) with malice aforethought, with premeditation; ***mit* – *lügen,*** tell a deliberate lie; (*Prov.*) ***der Weg zur Hölle ist mit guten Vorsätzen gepflastert,*** the road to hell is paved with good intentions.

Vorsatz|blatt, *n.* (*Bookb.*) end-paper. **-gerät,** *n.* attachment, (*Elec.*) adapter.

vorsätzlich ['fo:rzɛtslɪç], **1.** *adj.* intentional, deliberate, wilful, premeditated. **2.** *adv.* purposely, on purpose, designedly, deliberately, (*Law*) with malice aforethought, with criminal intent.

vorschalten ['fo:rʃaltən], *v.t.* (*Elec.*) connect in series. **Vorschaltwiderstand,** *m.* series resistance.

Vorschau ['fo:rʃau], *f.* forecast, preview (***auf*** (*Acc.*), of), (*Films etc.*) trailer.

Vorschein ['fo:rʃaɪn], *m.* (*only in*) ***zum* – *bringen,*** bring to light, produce; ***zum* – *kommen,*** come to light, appear, (*coll.*) turn up.

vorschicken ['fo:rʃɪkən], *v.t.* send forward *or* to the front.

vorschieben ['fo:rʃi:bən], *irr.v.t.* push *or* shove forward; (*fig.*) pretend, plead as an excuse; ***den Riegel* –,** shoot *or* slip the bolt; (*fig.*) ***einen Riegel*** – (*Dat.*), put a stop to; ***vorgeschobene Befestigungen,*** advanced forts, outlying fortifications; ***vorgeschobene Person,*** man of straw. **Vorschiebung,** *f.* (*Sew.-mach.*) feed.

vorschießen ['fo:rʃi:sən], **1.** *irr.v.t.* 1. advance, provide with, loan, lend (*money*); 2. ***einen Saum* –,** turn up *or* make a hem. **2.** *irr.v.i.* (*aux.* s.) shoot *or* dart forth; (*aux.* h.) (*Dat.*) show how to shoot; shoot first.

Vorschiff ['fo:rʃɪf], *n.* forecastle.

Vorschlag ['fo:rʃla:k], *m.* 1. proposition, proposal, recommendation, suggestion, (*Parl.*) motion, (*Comm.*) offer; nomination (*a candidate*); ***in* – *bringen,*** propose, move; ***auf* – *von,*** at the suggestion *or* on the proposal *or* recommendation of; ***auf einen* – *eingehen,*** agree to a proposal; **– *zur Güte,*** conciliatory proposal; good way out of the difficulty; 2. (*Mus.*) appoggiatura, grace-note; (*Metr.*) anacrusis; 3. (*Typ.*) blank space on the first page; 4. (*Tech.*) flux. **vorschlagen,** *irr.v.t.* put forward, propose, nominate (*a candidate*), suggest, propose, propound, move (*a resolution*); recommend (*Dat.*, to), (*Mus.*) beat (*time*) (for), give (*the note*); ***auf eine Ware 3 Mark* –,** put 3 marks on the price of s.th. **Vorschlaghammer,** *m.* sledge hammer. **Vorschlags|note,** *f.* (*Mus.*) appoggiatura. **-recht,** *n.* right of nominating (*to an office*). **-silbe,** *f.* (*Metr.*) anacrusis.

Vorschlußrunde ['fo:rʃlusrundə], *f.* (*Spt.*) semifinal.

Vorschmack ['fo:rʃmak], *m.* (*obs.*) foretaste, foreboding.

Vorschneide|brett ['fo:rʃnaɪdə-], *n.* trencher. **-messer,** *n.* carving-knife. **vorschneiden,** *irr.v.t.* carve (*at table*). **Vorschneider,** *m.* carver; (*Tech.*) taper tap (*for screws*).

vorschnell ['fo:rʃnɛl], *adj. See* **voreilig.**

vorschreiben ['fo:rʃraɪbən], *irr.v.t.* set as a copy, write out (*Dat.*, for); (*fig.*) dictate, prescribe (to), lay down (for), command, order, direct; ***ich lasse mir nichts* –,** I will not be dictated to; ***Sie haben mir nichts vorzuschreiben,*** you have no say over me.

vorschreiten ['fo:rʃraɪtən], *irr.v.i.* (*aux.* s.) step forth *or* forward, advance; ***vorgeschrittenes Stadium,*** advanced stage; ***vorgeschrittene Jahreszeit,*** advanced season, late in the year *or* season.

Vorschrift ['fo:rʃrɪft], *f.* specification, (*also Med.*) prescription; direction, instruction, order, precept, rule(s), regulation(s); ***nach* –,** as prescribed. **Vorschriftenbuch,** *n.* manual of instructions. **vorschrifts|gemäß, -mäßig,** *adj.* according to instructions *or* regulations, as ordered, as prescribed. **-widrig,** *adj.* contrary to instructions, against orders, against the rules.

Vorschub ['fo:rʃup], *m.* (unfair) help *or* assistance *or* aid *or* support, furtherance; (*Tech.*) feed; ***ihm* – *leisten,*** help *or* support *or* abet him, afford him assistance; ***einer S. – leisten*** or ***tun,*** further *or* promote a matter, support a th. **Vorschubleistung,** *f.* (*Law*) aiding and abetting.

Vorschuh ['fo:rʃu:], *m.* vamp, upper leather (*of a boot*). **vorschuhen,** *v.t.* new-foot, re-vamp (*shoes*).

Vorschule ['fo:rʃu:lə], *f.* preparatory department *or* school; elementary course.

Vorschuß ['fo:rʃus], *m.* advance (of money), payment in advance, (*coll.*) loan; (*Law*) retaining fee, retainer. **Vorschuß|dividende,** *f.* interim dividend. **–kasse,** *f.* loan-fund. **vorschußweise,** *adv.* as an advance, by way of a loan.

vorschützen ['fo:rʃytsən], *v.t.* shelter behind; plead as an excuse, pretend; ***Unwissenheit* –,** plead ignorance. **Vorschützung,** *f.* pretext, excuse; (hollow) pretence.

vorschweben ['fo:rʃve:bən], *v.i. imp.* ***es schwebt mir vor,*** I have it in mind, I have a (vague) notion of it, I have a (dim) recollection of it.

vorschwindeln ['fo:rʃvɪndəln], *v.t.* ***es ihm* –,** try to make him believe it, humbug him, tell him (a pack of) lies about it.

Vorsegel ['fo:rze:gəl], *n.* foresail.

vorsehen ['fo:rze:ən], **1.** *irr.v.t.* 1. provide for; ***der Fall ist im Gesetze nicht vorgesehen,*** this case is not provided for by the law; 2. assign, earmark (*für*, for) (*a purpose*). **2.** *irr.v.r.* take care, be cautious *or* careful; be mindful (***vor*** (*Dat.*), of), be on one's guard (against), beware (of), (*coll.*) mind; ***vorgesehen!*** look out! take care! (*Prov.*) ***vorgesehen ist besser als nachgesehen,*** better safe than sorry, prevention is better than cure. **Vorsehung,** *f.* providence.

vorsetzen ['fo:rzɛtsən], *v.t.* set, place, put (*Dat.*, before); serve (*food*); offer; (*Gram.*) prefix; ***darf ich Ihnen etwas –?*** may I offer you anything (to eat)? ***sich*** (*Dat.*) ***etwas* –,** propose to do s.th., aim at s.th., intend *or* resolve *or* determine to do a th., determine upon s.th.; ***ihn einem andern* –,** set him over another, prefer him to another; (*Mus.*) ***einer Note ein Kreuz (ein B)* –,** mark *or* prefix a note with a sharp (a flat); ***vorgesetzte Behörde,*** appointed authorities, those in authority; ***seine Vorgesetzten,*** his superior officers, his superiors. **Vorsetzer,** *m.* fire-screen, fireguard, fender. **Vorsetz|fenster,** *n.* outer window (*of double windows*). **–zeichen,** *n.* (*Mus.*) accidental.

Vorsicht ['fo:rzɪçt], *f.* caution, care, prudence; discretion, circumspection; (*obs.*) providence; ***–!*** look out! have a care! take care! (*on notices*) caution! danger! beware! (*on parcels*) with care! (*Prov.*) ***– ist besser als Nachsicht,*** prevention is better than cure; (*Prov.*) ***– ist die Mutter der Weisheit*** or (*coll.*) ***der Porzellanschüssel,*** caution is the mother of wit; ***– Stufe!*** mind the step! ***mit* –,** cautiously; ***mit – zu Werke gehen,*** proceed with caution, (*coll.*) play it safe. **vorsichtig,** *adj.* cautious, careful, prudent, wary, chary, guarded, circumspect, discreet; ***– sein,*** be cautious, take care, go carefully; ***–e Schätzung,*** conservative esimate. **vorsichtshalber,** *adv.* as a precaution. **Vorsichts|maßnahme, –maßregel,** *f.* precautionary measure; ***–n treffen,*** take precautions.

Vorsilbe ['fo:rzɪlbə], *f.* prefix.

vorsingen ['fo:rzɪŋən], **1.** *irr.v.t.* sing (*Dat.*, to). **2.** *v.i.* lead the singing.

vorsintflutlich ['fo:rzɪntflu:tlɪç], *adj.* antediluvian.

Vorsitz ['fo:rzɪts], *m.* presidency, chairmanship; the chair; ***den – haben*** or ***führen,*** preside (***bei***, over), be in the chair (at); ***den – übernehmen,*** take the chair, act as chairman; ***unter dem – von,*** under the chairmanship of, with . . . in the chair. **Vorsitzende(r),** *m., f.* president, chairman.

vorsohlen ['fo:rzo:lən], *v.t.* (*coll.*) *see* **vorlügen.**

Vorsorge ['fo:rzɔrgə], *f.* foresight, care, precaution, provision; ***– tragen*** or ***treffen,*** make provision, take precautions, (*coll.*) see to it. **vorsorgen,** *v.i.* take precautions; provide for the future. **vorsorglich, 1.** *adj.* provident, careful. **2.** *adv.* as a precaution, (*coll.*) just in case.

Vorspann ['fo:rʃpan], *m.* (extra) team of horses; (*fig.*) ***– leisten*** or ***stellen,*** help, give a hand. **vorspannen,** *v.t.* harness to. **Vorspannpferd,** *n.* relay-horse, additional horse.

Vorspannung ['fo:rʃpanuŋ], *f.* (*Rad.*) bias, grid potential.

Vorspeise ['fo:rʃpaɪzə], *f.* hors-d'œuvre.

vorspiegeln ['fo:rʃpi:gəln], *v.t.* deceive *or* delude (***ihm,*** him) with, try to make (him) believe, raise false hopes (in (his) mind). **Vorspiegelung,** *f.* delusion, pretence, make-believe, sham, shamming; misrepresentation; ***unter – falscher Tatsachen,*** under false pretences.

Vorspiel ['fo:rʃpi:l], *n.* (*Mus.*) prelude, overture, (*Theat.*) curtain-raiser; prologue, (*Spt.*) preliminary match. **vorspielen,** *v.t.* (*Dat.*) play before *or* to.

Vorspinnen ['fo:rʃpɪnən], *n.* roving. **Vorspinnmaschine,** *f.* roving-frame.

vorsprechen ['fo:rʃprɛçən], **1.** *irr.v.t.* (*Dat.*) pronounce to *or* for, demonstrate how to pronounce. **2.** *irr.v.i.* (*aux.* h. & s.) call, (*coll.*) drop in (***bei***, on).

vorspringen ['fo:rʃprɪŋən], *irr.v.i.* (*aux.* s.) leap forward; jut out, project. **vorspringend,** *adj.* projecting, prominent; ***–es Fenster,*** bay window; ***–er Winkel,*** salient.

Vorsprung ['fo:rʃpruŋ], *m.* projection, prominence, protrusion; ledge; salient; (*fig.*) lead (***vor*** (*Dat.*), on *or* over), advantage (over); ***mit großem* –,** by a wide margin.

Vorstadt ['fo:rʃtat], *f.* suburb. **Vorstädter,** *m.* suburban dweller, (*coll.*) suburbanite. **vorstädtisch,** *adj.* suburban.

Vorstand ['fo:rʃtant], *m.* board of directors, directorate, executive committee, board of governors, governing body. **Vorstands|mitglied,** *n.* director, manager; member of the board *or* the executive *or* the governing body. **–sitzung,** *f.* board meeting.

vorstechen ['fo:rʃtɛçən], **1.** *irr.v.t.* prick the outline of, mark out with holes. **2.** *irr.v.i.* stand out, be prominent, catch the eye.

vorstecken ['fo:rʃtɛkən], *reg.* & *irr.v.t.* pin *or* fasten on; poke *or* stick out; ***den Kopf* –,** stick *or* poke out one's head; ***sich*** (*Dat.*) ***ein Ziel* –,** set o.s. a goal *or* object; ***das vorgesteckte Ziel erreichen,*** attain *or* achieve one's object, reach one's goal.

Vorstecker ['fo:rʃtɛkər], *m.* (*Tech.*) cotter-pin, (*Mil.*) safety pin (*of bomb etc.*). **Vorsteck|keil,** *m.* *See* **Vorstecker. –latz,** *m.*, **–lätzchen,** *n.* bib, pinafore. **–nadel,** *f.* scarf *or* breast pin. **–schlips,** *m.* bow.

vorstehen ['fo:rʃte:ən], *irr.v.i.* 1. jut out, project, protrude, overhang; 2. (*fig.*) (*Dat.*) superintend, preside over, be at the head of, be in charge of, manage, direct, administer. **vorstehend,** *adj.* 1. projecting, protruding; 2. (*fig.*) foregoing, aforesaid, above; ***wie* –,** as above. **Vorsteher,** *m.* principal, chief, head; director, manager, superintendent, supervisor; headmaster (*of school*), superior (*of convent*), governor (*of prison*), warden, master (*of college*). **Vorsteherdrüse,** *f.* (*Anat.*) prostate gland. **Vorsteherin,** *f.* manageress, forewoman; mother-superior (*of convent*). **Vorstehhund,** *m.* pointer, setter.

vorstellen ['fo:rʃtɛlən], **1.** *v.t.* 1. place before, put in front of; (*clocks*) put forward *or* on; 2. present, introduce (*a p.*) (*Dat.*, to); ***darf ich Sie meiner Schwester –?*** may I introduce you to my sister? 3. represent, personate (*a character*), (*Theat.*) play (*a part*); 4. stand for, mean, signify; ***was soll das –?*** what is that supposed to be? what is the meaning of that? 5. point out, make clear, explain (*Dat.*, to), remonstrate *or* expostulate about (with), protest about (to); 6. ***sich*** (*Dat.*) **–,** imagine, fancy, suppose, conceive, envisage, visualize, picture to o.s.; (*iron.*) ***so habe ich mir das vorgestellt!*** I couldn't have done better myself! ***so stelle ich es mir vor,*** that is my idea of it; (*coll.*) ***stell dir vor!*** fancy that! ***stellen Sie sich*** (*Dat.*) ***meine Freude vor!*** imagine my delight! ***ich kann mir nichts Besseres* –,** I can think of nothing better. **2.** *v.r.* 1.

stand in front, go *or* come forward *or* to the front; 2. present *or* introduce o.s., make o.s. known.

vorstellig ['fo:rʃtɛlɪç], *adj.* (*only in*) – ***werden,*** present a case *or* petition, make representations (***bei,*** to), protest (to), lodge a complaint (with).

Vorstellung ['fo:rʃtɛlʊŋ], *f.* 1. introduction, presentation (*at court etc.*); 2. performance, representation; ***erste –,*** first performance; 3. complaint, remonstrance, expostulation; ***ihm –en machen,*** make representations to him, take up a point *or* lodge a complaint with him; 4. imagination, idea, notion, conception, mental image; ***das geht über alle –,*** the mind boggles at it; ***sich*** (*Dat.*) ***eine – machen von,*** get *or* form an idea of *or* some notion of; ***Sie machen sich*** (*Dat.*) ***keine –!*** you have no idea! you would scarcely believe it! **Vorstellungs|-fähigkeit, –kraft,** *f.*, **–vermögen,** *n.* (power of) imagination. **–weise,** *f.* way of looking at things, attitude of mind.

Vorstoß ['fo:rʃto:s], *m.* 1. push forward, forward movement, (*Mil.*) attack, advance, thrust, drive, (*Spt.*) forward rush; 2. piping, edging, braid, binding, raised seam. **vorstoßen, 1.** *irr.v.t.* push *or* thrust forward; ***einen Saum –,*** make a raised seam. **2.** *irr.v.i.* (*aux.* s.) push *or* thrust forward, advance, attack; project, protrude.

Vorstrafe ['fo:rʃtra:fə], *f.* previous conviction. **Vorstrafen(register),** *pl.* (*n.*) (criminal) record.

vorstrecken ['fo:rʃtrɛkən], *v.t.* stretch forward *or* out, stick out, poke out, extend; advance, lend (*money*).

vorstreichen ['fo:rʃtraɪçən], *irr.v.t., v.i.* apply an undercoat (to). **Vorstreichfarbe,** *f.* undercoat, primer, priming colour.

Vorstufe ['fo:rʃtu:fə], *f.* first step, first *or* preliminary stage; (*Rad.*) input stage; *pl.* rudiments, elements.

vortanzen ['fo:rtantsən], **1.** *v.t.* demonstrate (*a dance*). **2.** *v.i.* lead the dance. **Vortänzer(in),** *m.* (*f.*) leading dancer; leader of a dance; dancing demonstrator.

vortäuschen ['fo:rtɔyʃən], *v.t.* feign, simulate; ***einen Schlag –,*** feint.

Vorteil ['fɔrtaɪl], *m.* **(-(e)s,** *pl.* **-e)** advantage, benefit, profit, gain, (*coll.*) main chance; (*Tenn.*) (ad)-vantage; ***die Vor- und Nachteile,*** the pros and cons; ***ihm den – abgewinnen,*** get the better of him; ***sich auf seinen – verstehen,*** know on which side one's bread is buttered; ***auf seinen – bedacht sein,*** have one's own interests at heart, (*coll.*) have an eye to the main chance; ***seinen – ausnützen,*** exploit one's advantage; ***– bringen,*** be advantageous *or* of advantage; (*Prov.*) ***jeder – gilt,*** all's fair in love and war; ***ihm zum – gereichen,*** be of benefit to him, turn out to his advantage; ***– haben von,*** (derive) benefit from; ***einer S. einen – herausholen*** or ***herausschlagen,*** turn a th. to (one's) advantage; ***im – sein,*** be at an advantage, have the odds on one's side; have the advantage (***vor*** (*Dat.*), of *or* over); ***mit – verkaufen,*** sell at a profit; ***sich*** (*Dat.*) ***einen unerlaubten – verschaffen,*** take an unfair advantage; ***von*** or ***aus einer S. – ziehen,*** derive benefit *or* advantage from a th., turn s.th. to account; ***zu meinem eignen –,*** in my own interest, to my advantage; ***sich zu seinem – unterscheiden,*** show up to advantage; ***zu seinem – benützen,*** turn to account; ***sich zu seinem – verändern,*** change for the better. **vorteilhaft,** *adj.* profitable, beneficial, advantageous, favourable (***für,*** to), lucrative, remunerative (for); ***– aussehen.*** look one's best; ***–e Gelegenheit,*** favourable opportunity; ***–es Geschäft,*** (good) bargain.

Vortrab ['fo:rtra:p], *m.* vanguard, advance guard.

Vortrag ['fo:rtra:k], *m.* **(-(e)s,** *pl.* **⸚e)** 1. diction, delivery, utterance, enunciation; elocution; (*Mus.*) execution; ***er hat einen deutlichen –,*** his diction *or* enunciation is good, he has a clear delivery; ***zum – bringen,*** sing (*a song*), play (*a piece of music*), recite (*a poem*), deliver (*a speech*), express (*one's views*); 2. lecture, address, talk, discourse, (*Mus.*) recital, (*poetry*) recitation; report, statement; ***einen – halten über*** (*Acc.*), (give a) lecture *or* read a paper on; 3. (*Comm.*) balance carried forward; (*Comm.*) – ***auf neue Rechnung,*** balance carried forward.

vortragen ['fo:rtra:gən], *irr.v.t.* 1. carry *or* bring forward (*also Comm.*); ***den Saldo auf neue Rechnung –,*** carry forward the balance; 2. explain, expound, report on; recite, declaim (*poetry*), perform, execute, play (*piece of music*), state, express (*one's opinion*), propose, submit (*a suggestion*), discourse, lecture (***über*** (*Acc.*), on); give, deliver (*a speech etc.*); ***eine Bitte –,*** make a request, solicit a favour. **Vortragende(r),** *m., f.* speaker, lecturer; performer.

Vortrags|folge, *f.* series of lectures. **–kunst,** *f.* declamation, elocution. **–künstler,** *m.* elocutionist; (*Mus.*) executant, performer. **–recht,** *n.* ***direktes –,*** direct access (***bei,*** to). **–saal,** *m.* lecture hall.

vortrefflich [fo:r'trɛflɪç], *adj.* excellent, splendid, superb, fine, capital. **Vortrefflichkeit,** *f.* excellence.

vortreten ['fo:rtre:tən], *irr.v.i.* come *or* step forward; project, protrude, stick *or* jut out.

Vortrieb ['fo:rtri:p], *m.* forward thrust, propulsion.

Vortritt ['fo:rtrɪt], *m.* precedence; ***den – haben,*** take precedence (***vor*** (*Dat.*), over); ***den – lassen*** or ***geben,*** give precedence (*Dat.*, to); ***unter –*** (*Gen.*), preceded by.

vortrocknen ['fo:rtrɔknən], *v.t.* pre-dry.

Vortrupp ['fo:rtrup], *m.* vanguard, advance party.

Vortuch ['fo:rtu:x], *n.* (*dial.*) apron, bib.

vortun ['fo:rtu:n], *irr.v.t.* do rashly *or* prematurely; (*only in*) (*Prov.*) ***vorgetan und nachgedacht, hat manchem schon groß Leid gebracht,*** it's no use shutting the stable door after the horse is gone; look before you leap.

Vorturner ['fo:rturnər], *m.* (*Gymn.*) squad leader, gymnastics demonstrator.

vorüber [for'y:bər], *adv.* (*space*) along, by, past, gone (by); (*time*) over, finished, done with; ***der Regen ist –,*** the rain is over; ***sein Ruhm war schnell –,*** his fame soon passed away; ***er ging an mir –,*** he went past me, he passed me (by).

vorübergehen [for'y:bərge:ən], *irr.v.i.* (*aux.* s.) (*space*) pass (by), go past *or* by; (*time*) pass (away), pass *or* (*coll.*) blow over; (*fig.*) pass over; – ***an*** (*Dat.*), pass over (in silence), ignore; ***eine Gelegenheit – lassen,*** miss a chance, let a chance slip by. **Vorübergehen,** *n.* ***im –,*** in passing (*also fig.*); by the way, incidentally, **vorübergehend,** *adj.* passing, temporary, transient, transitory; ***sich – aufhalten,*** make a short stay, stay for the time being.

vorüberziehen [for'y:bərtsi:ən], *irr.v.i.* (*aux* s.) march past; pass (by).

Vorübung ['fo:rˀy:buŋ], *f.* preliminary practice; preparatory exercise.

Voruntersuchung ['fo:rˀuntərzu:xuŋ], *f.* preliminary examination *or* inquiry *or* investigation.

Vorurteil ['fo:rˀurtaɪl], *n.* **(-s,** *pl.* **-e)** prejudice, bias, prepossession; ***ihm –e einflößen,*** prejudice him. **vorurteilsfrei, vorurteilslos,** *adj.* unprejudiced, unbiased. **Vorurteilslosigkeit,** *f.* freedom from prejudice, open-mindedness, impartiality.

Vor|vater, *m.* forefather, ancestor, progenitor. **–verdichter,** *m.* (*Mech.*) supercharger. **–vergangenheit,** *f.* (*Gram.*) pluperfect. **–verkauf,** *m.* advance sale *or* (*Theat.*) booking; ***im – zu haben,*** bookable (in advance). **–verkaufskasse,** *f.* advance booking office.

vorverlegen ['fo:rfɛrle:gən], *v.t.* 1. (*Artil.*) lift (*a barrage*); increase range; 2. (*time or date*) advance.

Vor|versicherung, *f.* previous insurance. **–verstärker,** *m.* (*Rad.*) pre-amplifier. **–versuch,** *m.* pilot test.

vor|vorgestern, *adv.* three days ago. **–vorig,** *adj.* last but one, penultimate. **-vorletzt,** *adj.* last but two, antepenultimate.

Vor|wahl, *f.* 1. preliminary *or* (*Am.*) primary election; 2. (*Rad.*) preselection. **–wähler,** *m.* preselector. **–wählnummer,** *f.* (*Tele.*) dialling prefix. **–wählschalter,** *m.* (*Motor.*) preselector gearchange. **–wall,** *m.* outer rampart.

vorwalten ['fo:rvaltən], *v.i.* predominate, prevail; (*obs.*) be, exist.
Vorwand ['fo:rvant], *m.* (**-(e)s,** *pl.* **⸚e**) pretext, pretence, subterfuge, excuse; ***unter dem –,*** on the pretext, with the plea; ***einen – suchen,*** look for an excuse.
vorwärmen ['fo:rvɛrmən], *v.t.* preheat, warm up.
Vorwarnung ['fo:rvarnuŋ], *f.* preliminary *or* early warning.
vorwärts ['fɔrvɛrts], *adv.* forward, onward, (further) on; forwards; *–!* forward! march! move on! go on! get on! go ahead! ***sich – bewegen,*** move forward, advance; ***– gehen,*** go forward(s); *see* **vorwärtsgehen**; ***sich*** (*Dat.*) ***– helfen,*** make one's way in the world; ***– kommen,*** come forward(s) *or* to the front; *see* **vorwärtskommen**; (*Prov.*) ***langsam kommt man auch –,*** slow and steady wins the race; more haste less speed.
Vorwärts|beuge, *f.* (*Gymn.*) forwards bend. **-bewegung,** *f.* forward movement.
vorwärtsbringen ['fɔrvɛrtsbrɪŋən], *irr.v.t.* promote, advance, further, foster, abet, expedite.
Vorwärtsgang ['fɔrvɛrtsgaŋ], *m.* (*Motor.*) forward speed.
vorwärts|gehen, *irr.v.i.* (*aux.* s.) go ahead, advance, progress; improve, get on; ***es will*** (***mit ihm***) ***nicht –,*** he makes no headway *or* progress. **-kommen,** *irr.v.i.* proceed, get on, make headway; (*fig.*) prosper, get on in the world, make one's way in the world, improve one's position. **Vorwärtsschreiten,** *n.* progress, advance. **vorwärtstreiben,** *irr.v.t.* propel.
vorweg [fɔr'vɛk], *adv.* before, beforehand, to begin with, from the beginning; ***– genießen,*** enjoy in anticipation; (*coll.*) ***–*** (***mit der Zunge***) ***sein,*** be too free with one's tongue, let one's tongue run away with one. **Vorwegnahme,** *f.* anticipation, forestalling. **vorwegnehmen,** *irr.v.t.* anticipate, forestall.
vorweisen ['fo:rvaɪzən], *irr.v.t.* show, produce (for inspection), display, exhibit.
Vorwelt [fo:rvɛlt], *f.* former ages, antiquity, primitive *or* prehistoric world *or* times. **vorweltlich,** *adj.* primeval, prehistoric, (*fig.*) antediluvian.
vorwerfen ['fo:rvɛrfən], *irr.v.t.* (*Dat.*) cast before, throw to; (*fig.*) ***ihm etwas –,*** reproach him with s.th., cast a th. in his teeth; ***du hast dir nichts vorzuwerfen,*** you have nothing to reproach yourself with; ***sie haben einander nichts vorzuwerfen,*** the one is as bad as the other, six of one and half-a-dozen of the other.
Vor|werk, *n.* (*Agr.*) steading; (*Mil.*) outworks. **-widerstand,** *m.* (*Elec.*) series resistance, (*Rad.*) dropping resistor.
vorwiegen ['fo:rvi:gən], *irr.v.i.* outweigh, preponderate, prevail, predominate, dominate. **vorwiegend,** **1.** *adj.* preponderant, (pre)dominant, prevailing. **2.** *adv.* predominantly, largely, mostly, mainly, chiefly, principally.
Vor|wind, *m.* head wind. **-wissen,** *n.* foreknowledge, prescience, (previous) knowledge; ***es geschah mit meinem –,*** it happened with my full knowledge and consent; ***ohne mein –,*** without my knowledge, unknown to me. **-witz,** *m.* curiosity, inquisitiveness; forwardness, impertinence, pertness. **vorwitzig,** *adj.* inquisitive, prying; forward, pert, impertinent. **Vor|wort,** *n.* 1. (*pl.* **-e**) foreword, preface, preamble, introduction; 2. (*pl.* **⸚er**) preposition. **-wurf,** *m.* 1. reproach, reproof, rebuke, remonstrance; blame; ***sich Vorwürfe machen,*** reproach o.s.; 2. subject, theme, motif. **vorwurfs|frei,** *adj.* irreproachable, blameless. **-voll,** *adj.* reproachful.
vorzählen ['fo:rtsɛ:lən], *v.t.* count out, enumerate.
Vorzeichen ['fo:rtsaɪçən], *n.* previous indication, (*Med.*) early symptom; omen, prognostic; (*Math.*) sign; (*Mus.*) signature (*of the stave*), accidental (*with a note*); (*fig.*) ***mit umgekehrten –,*** with a complete reversal of the premises *or* (*coll.*) complete change of ground. **Vorzeichenwechsel,** *m.* (*Math.*) change of sign.
vorzeichnen ['fo:rtsaɪçnən], *v.t.* draw, sketch (*Dat.*, for), show how to draw; mark *or* trace out, sketch; indicate, prescribe. **Vorzeichnung,** *f.* indication; pattern, copy, design; (*Mus.*) signature.
vorzeigen ['fo:rtsaɪgən], *v.t.* show, display, exhibit; produce, present (*a bill*). **Vorzeiger,** *m.* bearer (*of a bill*). **Vorzeigung,** *f.* production, exhibition, display.
Vorzeit ['fo:rtsaɪt], *f.* antiquity, past ages, olden times; ***die graue –,*** remote antiquity, days of yore. **vorzeiten** [–'tsaɪtən], *adv.* (*Poet.*) formerly, in former times, once upon a time. **vorzeitig,** *adj.* premature, untimely, all too soon. **vorzeitlich,** *adj.* prehistoric. **Vorzeitmensch,** *m.* prehistoric man.
vorziehen ['fo:rtsi:ən], **1.** *irr.v.t.* 1. draw forth; draw (*curtains*); move *or* draw up (*a car*), move up (*troops*); 2. (*fig.*) prefer (*Dat.*, to), give preference to (*Dat.*, over), like better (*Dat.*, than). **2.** *irr.v.i.* (*aus.* s.) (*Mil.*) advance, move up, move to the front.
Vorzimmer ['fo:rtsɪmər], *n.* anteroom, antechamber.
Vorzug ['fo:rtsu:k], *m.* (**-(e)s,** *pl.* **⸚e**) 1. preference, precedence, priority (***vor*** (*Dat.*), over); excellence, superiority; prerogative, privilege; *pl.* good qualities, merit(s), advantage; ***den – haben,*** have the advantage (***vor*** (*Dat.*), over), be superior (to), surpass, excel; ***den – geben*** (*Dat.*), *see* **vorziehen,** 1. 2; 2. (*Railw.*) pilot train.
vorzüglich [fo:r'tsy:klɪç], **1.** *adj.* superior, excellent, choice, exquisite, first-rate; (*obs.*) chief, principal, pre-eminent. **2.** *adv.* above all, particularly, especially. **Vorzüglichkeit,** *f.* superiority, excellence, (superior) quality.
Vorzugs|aktien, *f.pl.* preference shares. **-behandlung,** *f.* preferential treatment. **-druck,** *m.* de-luxe edition. **-milch,** *f.* grade-A milk. **-pfandrecht,** *n.* (*Law*) prior lien. **-preis,** *m.* special (reduced) price. **-recht,** *n.* privilege. **vorzugsweise,** *adv.* preferably, by preference, pre-eminently, chiefly. **Vorzugszoll,** *m.* preferential duty.
Vorzündung ['fo:rtsynduŋ], *f.* (*Motor.*) premature ignition.
votieren [vo'ti:rən], *v.i.* vote.
Votiv|bild [vo'ti:f–], **-gemälde,** *n.* votive picture. **-tafel,** *f.* votive tablet.
Votum ['vo:tum], *n.* (**-s,** *pl.* **Voten** *or* **Vota**) vote, suffrage.
vulgär [vul'gɛ:r], *adj.* vulgar, common, coarse.
Vulgata [vul'ga:ta], *f.* Vulgate.
vulgo ['vulgo], *adv.* commonly, usually, normally.
Vulkan [vul'ka:n], *m.* (**-s,** *pl.* **-e**) volcano; ***auf einem – tanzen,*** sit on a volcano. **Vulkanfiber,** *f.* vulcanized fibre. **vulkanisch,** *adj.* volcanic; Plutonic. **vulkanisieren** [–i'zi:rən], *v.t.* vulcanize (*india-rubber*).

W

W, w [ve:], *n.* W, w; *see Index of Abbreviations.*
Waage ['va:gə], *f.* (pair of) scales, balance, weighing-machine; (*Astrol.*) Libra; (spirit) level, levelling bubble; (*Gymn.*) lever; (*fig.*) ***in die – fallen,*** be of weight *or* import *or* importance; ***die – halten*** (*Dat.*), counterbalance; (*fig.*) ***ihm die – halten,*** be a match for him; ***in der – halten,*** hold in equilibrium; ***das Zünglein an der – bilden,*** turn *or* tip the scale.

Waage|amt, *n.* public weighbridge. **–balken,** *m.* beam of a balance. **–geld,** *n.* weighbridge-toll *or* -fee. **–meister,** *m.* official in charge of a weighbridge, inspector of weights and measures. **waag(e)recht,** *adj.* horizontal, level.

Waagschale ['va:kʃa:lə], *f.* pan of the scales; scale; (*fig.*) ***schwer in die – fallen,*** weigh heavily, be of *or* carry great weight, be of great importance; ***seine Worte auf die – legen,*** weigh one's words; (*fig.*) ***in die – werfen,*** tip the scales with, bring to bear.

wabb(e)lig ['vab(ə)lıç], *adj.* flabby, wobbly.

Wabe ['va:bə], *f.* honeycomb. **wabenartig,** *adj.* honeycombed, alveolar. **Wabenhonig,** *m.* honey in the comb.

Waberlohe ['va:bərlo:ə], *f.* (*Poet.*) flickering flame, magic fire. **wabern,** *v.i.* flicker.

wach ['vax], *adj.* (*attrib.*) waking (*state*), (*pred.*) awake; (*fig.*) wide-awake, alert; (*interests etc.*) live(ly) (*attrib.*), alive (*pred.*); – ***werden,*** awake(n), wake up; ***ganz –,*** wide awake.

Wachbataillon ['vaxbataljo:n], *n.* battalion of guards.

Wache ['vaxə], *f.* (*Mil.*) guard, (*Naut.*) watch; watchman, guard, sentry, sentinel; guard-house, guard-room; police station; ***die – ablösen,*** relieve the guard, change guard *or* (*Naut.*) the watch; – ***haben,*** – ***stehen,*** ***auf – sein,*** (*sl.*) – ***schieben,*** be on guard; ***auf – ziehen,*** mount guard; – ***halten,*** keep guard, be on the watch *or* look-out.

wachen ['vaxən], *v.i.* be awake; ***bei ihm –,*** sit up with him; – ***über*** (*Acc.*), guard, watch over, keep an eye on.

Wach|gänger, *m.* look-out (man). **–mann,** *m.* (*dial.*) policeman.

Wacholder [va'xɔldər], *m.* juniper. **Wacholder|-branntwein,** *m.* geneva gin. **–drossel,** *f.* (*Orn.*) fieldfare (*Turdus pilaris*). **–geist,** *m. See* **–branntwein. –harz,** *n.* gum-juniper.

Wachposten ['vaxpɔstən], *m.* guard; sentry. **wach|-rufen,** *irr.v.t.* (*fig.*) rouse, call forth, evoke, bring back (*memories etc.*). **–rütteln,** *v.t.* rouse from sleep, (*fig.*) open (his *etc.*) eyes.

Wachs [vaks], *n.* (**-es,** *pl.* **-e**) wax. **Wachsabdruck,** *m.* wax impression.

wachsam ['vaxza:m], *adj.* watchful, vigilant; wide-awake, alert, attentive; ***ein –es Auge haben,*** keep a sharp *or* watchful eye (***auf*** (*Acc.*), on). **Wachsamkeit,** *f.* watchfulness, vigilance.

Wachs|blume ['vaksblu:mə], *f.* wax flower; (*Bot.*) honey-wort (*Cerinthe minor*). **–bohner,** *m.* floor polish.

wachseln ['vaksəln], *v.t.* (*Austr.*) wax (*skis*).

[1]**wachsen** ['vaksən], *v.t.* (*Austr.*) *see* **wächsen.**

[2]**wachsen,** *irr.v.i.* (*aux.* s.) grow; (*fig.*) grow, increase (***an*** (*Dat.*), in), extend, expand, develop, thrive; ***einer S. gewachsen sein,*** be equal to a th., be able to cope with a th.; ***ihm nicht gewachsen sein,*** be no match for him; ***sie ist mir ans Herz gewachsen,*** I have become attached to her, I have grown fond of her; ***an Weisheit –,*** grow in wisdom; ***er ist aus den Kleidern gewachsen,*** he has outgrown his clothes; ***in die Höhe –,*** grow tall, shoot up; ***sehr ins Kraut –,*** run to leaf; ***der Mond wächst,*** the moon is on the increase *or* is waxing; ***darüber keine grauen Haare – lassen,*** not get grey hairs on that account; (*fig.*) ***ihm über den Kopf –,*** get too much for him, get beyond him; ***das Wasser wächst,*** the water is rising. **Wachsen,** *n.* growing, growth, increase, development, expansion, extension, spread.

wächsen ['vɛksən], *v.t.* (coat *or* smear with) wax.

wachsend ['vaksənt], *adj.* growing, increasing, (*Mus.*) crescendo; ***mit –er Spannung,*** with growing *or* mounting suspense.

wächsern ['vɛksərn], *adj.* wax; waxen, waxy, wax-like, wax-coloured.

Wachsfigurenkabinett ['vaksfigu:rənkabinɛt], *n.* waxworks. **wachsgelb,** *adj.* wax-coloured, waxen. **Wachs|haut,** *f.* cere. **–kerze,** *f.* wax candle. **–leinen,** *n.*, **–leinwand,** *f. See* **–tuch. –licht,** *n. See* **–kerze. –papier,** *n.* grease-proof paper. **–salbe,** *f.* cerate. **–sonde,** *f.* bougie. **–stock,** *m.* taper. **–streichholz,** *n.* wax vesta.

wächst [vɛkst], *see* **wachsen, wächsen.**

Wachs|tafel, *f.* cake of beeswax; (*ancient writing*) wax tablet. **–tuch,** *n.* oilcloth, American cloth.

Wachstum ['vakstu:m], *n.* growth; increase, expansion, development; ***im – hemmen,*** stunt; ***der Wein ist mein eignes –,*** the wine is of my own growing. **Wachstums|ring,** *m.* growth ring (*of trees*). **–spitze,** *f.* growing-point.

wachsweich ['vaksvaıç], *adj.* (as) soft as wax; (*of eggs*) medium boiled. **Wachszieher,** *m.* wax-chandler.

Wacht [vaxt], *f.* (-, *pl.* **-en**) (*Mil.*) guard, (*Naut.*) watch; ***die – am Rhein,*** the watch on the Rhine. **Wacht|boot,** *n.* patrol boat. **–dienst,** *m.* guard duty, (*Naut.*) watch.

Wächte ['vɛçtə], *f.* snow-cornice.

Wachtel ['vaxtəl], *f.* (-, *pl.* **-n**) (*Orn.*) quail (*Coturnix coturnix*). **Wachtel|hund,** *m.* spaniel. **–könig,** *m.* (*Orn.*) corncrake, landrail (*Crex crex*). **–weizen,** *m.* (*Bot.*) (meadow) cow-wheat (*Melampyrum pratense*).

Wachter ['vɛçtər], *m.* watchman, guard, guardian, caretaker, keeper, warder, attendant, (*Naut.*) look-out(man), (*Elec.*) automatic control gear. **Wächter|lied,** *n.* aubade. **–ruf,** *m.* (night)watchman's call.

Wachtfeuer ['vaxtfɔyər], *n.* watch-fire. **wachthabend,** *adj.* (*pred.*) on duty, on guard *or* watch. **Wacht|habende(r),** *m.* (*Mil.*) guard commander, (*Naut.*) officer of the watch. **–haus,** *n.* guard-house. **–hund,** *m.* watchdog. **–mannschaft,** *f.* guard, picket, sentries. **–meister,** *m.* sergeant-major (*of artillery or cavalry*); police sergeant. **–parade,** *f.* changing of *or* mounting the guard.

Wachtraum ['vaxtraum], *m.* waking dream, day-dream, reverie.

Wacht|stube, *f.* guardroom. **–turm,** *m.* watch-tower. **–vergehen,** *n.* neglect of duty *or* negligence while on guard.

Wachzustand ['vaxtsu:ʃtant], *m.* waking state.

wack(e)lig ['vak(ə)lıç], *adj.* shaky, unsteady, tottering; loose, wobbly, rickety, ramshackle; (*coll.*) on the verge of bankruptcy, tottering on the brink. **Wackelkontakt,** *m.* (*Elec.*) loose connection. **wackeln,** *v.i.* shake, rock; (*of a p.*) stagger, reel, totter; (*of a th.*) wobble, be loose; ***mit dem Kopf –,*** shake *or* wag one's head; (*coll.*) ***es wackelt mit seiner Gesundheit,*** his health is rather shaky.

wacker ['vakər], **1.** *adj.* valiant, brave, gallant, stout (-hearted), (*fig.*) upright, honest, worthy. **2.** *adv.* soundly, thoroughly, heartily, lustily.

wacklig, *adj. See* **wack(e)lig.**

Wade ['va:də], *f.* calf (*of the leg*). **Waden|bein,** *n.* fibula; splint-bone. **–krampf,** *m.* cramp in the leg. **–strumpf,** *m.* long *or* knee-length stocking.

Waffe ['vafə], *f.* weapon, arm; ***bei welcher – hast du gedient?*** which branch of the service were you in? ***ihn mit seinen eigenen –n schlagen,*** beat him at his own game; ***die –n strecken,*** lay down one's arms, surrender; ***unter den –n stehen,*** be under arms; ***zu den –n greifen,*** take up arms.

Waffel ['vafəl], *f.* (-, *pl.* **-n**) wafer, waffle, (*dial.*) chatterbox. **Waffeleisen,** *n.* waffle-iron.

Waffen|amt, *n.* ordnance department. **–appell,** *m.* arms inspection. **–ausbildung,** *f.* weapon training. **–beistand,** *m.* armed support *or* assistance. **–bruder,** *m.* comrade in arms. **–dienst,** *m.* military service. **–fabrik,** *f.* munitions factory. **waffenfähig,** *adj.* capable of bearing arms. **Waffen|gang,** *m.* passage of arms; armed conflict. **–gattung,** *f.* branch *or* arm of the service. **–gewalt,** *f.* force of arms, armed force. **–kammer,** *f.* armoury. **waffenkundig,** *adj.* skilled in the use of arms. **Waffenlager,** *n.* ordnance depot; (*surreptitious*) cache. **waffenlos,** *adj.* unarmed.

Waffen|meister, *m.* armourer. **–pflege,** *f.* care and maintenance of weapons. **–platz,** *m.* (*Swiss*) garrison town. **–rock,** *m.* tunic, battledress. **–ruf,**

m. call to arms. **-ruhe,** *f.* cease-fire, truce, suspension of hostilities. **-ruhm,** *m.* military glory. **-rüstung,** *f.* armour; armament; warlike preparations. **-schein,** *m.* gun-licence. **-schmied,** *m.* armourer. **-schmuck,** *m.* full armour, warlike accoutrements; (*hum.*) full war-paint. **-schmuggel,** *m.* gun-running. **-stillstand,** *m.* armistice, (*fig.*) truce. **-streckung,** *f.* capitulation, surrender. **-tat,** *f.* feat of arms, military exploit, warlike achievement. **-träger,** *m.* (*Hist.*) armour-bearer, esquire. **-übung,** *f.* military exercise.

waffnen ['vafnən], **1.** *v.t.* arm; ***mit gewaffneter Hand,*** by force of arms. **2.** *v.r.* take up arms.

wäg [vɛ:k], *adj.* (*Swiss*) good, fine, splendid; ***die Wägsten und Besten,*** the élite, the cream.

wägbar ['vɛ:kba:r], *adj.* weighable, (*fig.*) ponderable.

Wage, *f.* (*obs.*) *see* **Waage.**

Wagehals ['va:ɡəhals], *m.* dare-devil. **wagehalsig,** *adj.* daring, reckless, rash, foolhardy, (*only attrib.*) daredevil, breakneck (*speed*). **Wagehalsigkeit,** *f.* daring, recklessness, rashness, foolhardiness; daredevilry.

Wägelchen ['vɛ:ɡəlçən], *n.* (supermarket) trolley.

Wagemut ['va:ɡəmu:t], *m.* gallantry, daring; spirit of adventure.

wagen ['va:ɡən], **1.** *v.t.* venture, risk, hazard; dare to do; ***es mit ihm* –,** cross swords with *or* measure one's strength with him; ***ich wage (es) nicht, dies zu behaupten,*** I do not *or* would not venture *or* presume to assert this; ***alles* –,** risk *or* stake everything, take a chance, take the plunge; ***frisch gewagt!*** take a chance! (*Prov.*) ***frisch gewagt ist halb gewonnen,*** well begun is half done; fortune favours the brave; nothing venture nothing gain; *see* **gewagt. 2.** *v.r.* ***sich an eine S.* –,** venture upon s.th.; ***sich auf das Eis* –,** trust o.s. to the ice, venture on the ice; ***sich unter die Leute* –,** venture into society.

Wagen, *m.* (**-s,** *pl.* - (*dial.* ¨-)) van, truck, car, lorry; wagon, cart, carriage (*also of typewriters*), coach, chariot; (*Astr.*) ***der Große* –,** the Great Bear, the Plough, Charles's Wain; ***die Pferde hinter den – spannen,*** put the cart before the horse; (*Railw.*) ***– erster Klasse,*** first-class carriage; (*coll.*) ***ihm an den – fahren,*** tread on his toes *or* corns; (*coll.*) ***unter den – kommen,*** be worsted.

wägen ['vɛ:ɡən], *irr.v.t.* weigh, balance, (*fig.*) ponder, consider; ***er wog das Schwert in der Hand,*** he poised the sword in his hand; ***seine Worte wohl* –,** weigh *or* consider one's words well; (*Prov.*) ***erst – dann wagen,*** look before you leap.

Wagen|abteil, *n.* (*Railw.*) compartment. **-aufbau,** *m.* coachwork, (*Motor.*) car body. **-bauer,** *m.* coachbuilder, cartwright. **-burg,** *f.* laager, barricade of wagons. **-führer,** *m.* coachman, wagoner, (*Hist.*) charioteer; tram driver, (*Am.*) motorman. **-haltung,** *f. See* **-pflege. -heber,** *m.* (lifting-) jack; (*typewriter*) carriage lever. **-kasten,** *m.* car body. **-ladung,** *f.* cartload, wagon-load. **-park,** *m.* (*Railw.*) rolling-stock, (*Mil.*) vehicle pool. **-pferd,** *n.* coach-horse. **-pflege,** *f.* car maintenance, servicing. **-rennen,** *n.* (*Hist.*) chariot race. **-schlag,** *m.* carriage *or* car door. **-schmiere,** *f.* cart-grease, axle-grease. **-schuppen,** *m.* coach-house. **-spur,** *f.* wheel-rut *or* track. **-verkehr,** *m.* vehicular traffic. **-winde,** *f. See* **-heber.**

Wage|spiel, *n.* game of chance. **-stück,** *n.* daring *or* venturesome exploit, rash act.

Waggon [va'ɡõ], *m.* (**-s,** *pl.* **-s** *or* **-e**) railway carriage, (*Am.*) railroad car; luggage *or* goods van, (*Am.*) freight car; (*Comm.*) ***frei* –,** free on rail. **waggonweise,** *adv.* by the truck-load.

waghalsig ['va:khalzɪç], *adj. See* **wagehalsig.**

Wagner ['va:knər], *m.* (*dial.*) *see* **Wagenbauer.**

Wagnis [va:knɪs], *n.* (**-ses,** *pl.* **-se**) risk, hazard, (bold) venture, hazardous undertaking. **Wagniszuschlag,** *m.* danger money.

Wahl [va:l], *f.* (-, *pl.* **-en**) choice, selection; option, alternative; (*Pol.*) election, poll(ing); ***-en abhalten,*** hold elections; ***sich zur – aufstellen lassen,*** put up for election; ***mir bleibt keine (andere)* –,** I have no alternative *or* no (other) choice, it is Hobson's choice; ***in (die) engere – kommen,*** be *or* get on the short list; ***die – fällt mir schwer,*** I find it hard to choose, it is a difficult choice for me to make; ***aus freier* –,** of one's own (free) choice; ***ihm die – lassen,*** leave the choice to him, leave him to please himself; ***zur – schreiten,*** go to the polls; ***ihn vor die – stellen,*** let him choose, give him the choice *or* option, leave the decision *or* choice to him; ***seine – treffen,*** make one's choice, come to one's decision; (*Comm.*) ***Waren erster* –,** top-quality goods; ***Waren zweiter* –,** seconds, rejects.

Wahl|agitation *f.* electioneering. **-akt,** *m.* election (proceedings), poll(ing). **-akten,** *f.pl. See* **-bericht. -alter,** *n.* age of enfranchisement, (*coll.*) voting age.

Wählamt ['vɛ:lˀamt], *n.* (*Tele.*) automatic exchange.

Wahlaufruf ['va:lˀaufru:f], *m.* election manifesto.

wählbar ['vɛ:lba:r], *adj.* eligible; ***nicht* –,** ineligible. **Wählbarkeit,** *f.* eligibility.

wahlberechtigt ['va:lbərɛçtɪçt], *adj.* enfranchised, entitled to vote. **Wahl|berechtigung,** *f. See* **-recht. -bericht,** *m.* election returns. **-beteiligung,** *f.* percentage of votes cast, (*coll.*) turnout. **-bezirk,** *m.* ward, constituency. **-bude,** *f.* polling-booth. **-bühne,** *f.* (*Hist.*) hustings. **-eltern,** *pl.* (*Austr.*) foster parents.

wählen ['vɛ:lən], *v.t.* choose, select (***zu,*** as *or* for), (*coll.*) pick (out); (*Pol.*) elect, vote for; (*Tele.*) dial; ***– Sie!*** take your choice! (*Tele.*) dial your number! ***ihn ins Parlament* –,** return him to parliament; ***das kleinere Übel* –,** choose the lesser of two evils; ***ihn zum Präsidenten* –,** elect him (as) president; ***– (gehen),*** go to the polls. **Wähler,** *m.* 1. elector, voter; 2. (*Elec.*) selector. **Wählerbetrieb,** *m.* (*Tele.*) automatic dialling (system).

Wahlergebnis ['va:lˀɛrɡe:pnɪs], *n.* election result(s).

wählerisch ['vɛ:lərɪʃ], *adj.* fastidious, particular, (*coll.*) fussy, choosy (***in*** (*Dat.*), about), (*pred.*) difficult to please; ***nicht gerade* –,** not over-particular *or* over-scrupulous.

Wählerliste ['vɛ:lərlɪstə], *f.* register of electors. **Wählerschaft,** *f.* body of electors, enfranchised population; constituency.

Wahlfach ['va:lfax], *n.* optional subject. **wahl|fähig,** *adj.* eligible (for election); *see also* **-berechtigt. Wahlfeldzug,** *m.* election campaign. **wahlfrei,** *adj.* optional, elective. **Wahl|gang,** *m.* ballot, poll. **-gesetz,** *n.* electoral law. **-handlung,** *f. See* **-gang. -heimat,** *f.* adopted country. **-kampf,** *m. See* **-feldzug. -kind,** *n.* (*Austr.*) adopted child, foster-child. **-kommissar,** *m.* returning officer. **-kreis,** *m. See* **-bezirk. -liste,** *f.* (*Am.*) party ticket. **-lokal,** *n.* polling-centre.

wahllos ['va:llo:s], **1.** *adj.* indiscriminate. **2.** *adv.* indiscriminately, at random, haphazardly, without consideration.

Wahl|mann, *m.* (*pl.* ¨**er**) delegate, (*Am.*) (secondary) elector (*at presidential election*). **-männerwahl,** *f.* election of delegates. **-prüfung,** *f.* scrutiny of the poll. **-recht,** *n.* right to vote, franchise, suffrage; eligibility (for election); ***allgemeines* –,** universal suffrage; ***Entziehung des -s,*** disfranchisement. **-rede,** *f.* election address. **-reform,** *f.* electoral reform.

Wählscheibe ['vɛ:lʃaɪbə], *f.* (*Tele.*) dial.

Wahl|schlacht, *f. See* **-feldzug. -spruch,** *m.* motto, device; slogan. **-stimme,** *f.* vote. **-tag,** *m.* election day. **-umtriebe,** *m.pl. See* **-agitation. -urne,** *f.* ballot-box; ***zur – schreiten,*** go to the polls. **-verfahren,** *n.* system of voting, electoral system. **-versammlung,** *f.* election meeting. **-verwandtschaft,** *f.* (*Chem.*) elective affinity, (*fig.*) congeniality. **wahlweise,** *adv.* by *or* from choice; alternatively. **Wahl|zelle,** *f. See* **-bude. -zettel,** *m.* voting- *or* ballot-paper.

Wahn [va:n], *m.* illusion; delusion, erroneous impression; madness, mania; ***in einem – befangen sein,*** labour under a delusion. **Wahnbild,** *n.* hallucination, chimera, vision, phantom.

wähnen ['vɛ:nən], *v.t.* imagine, fancy, believe, presume, suppose.

Wahn|idee, *f.* delusion, mania, (*coll.*) crazy idea *or* notion. **-korn,** *n.* (*dial.*) empty ear of corn. **wahnschaffen,** *adj.* (*dial.*) misshapen, deformed.

Wahnsinn ['va:nzɪn], *m.* madness, insanity; ***dichterischer –,*** poetic frenzy; ***religiöser –,*** religious mania. **wahnsinnig,** *adj.* mad (***vor*** (*Dat.*), with), insane; (*coll.*) terrible, awful (*pain, fright etc.*); ***es ist zum – werden,*** it is enough to drive one mad; (*coll.*) ***– viel zu tun,*** an awful lot to do. **Wahnsinnige(r),** *m., f.* madman, lunatic.

Wahn|vorstellung, *f.* delusion, fixed idea, idée fixe; hallucination. **-witz,** *m.* madness, absurdity. **wahn|witzig,** *adj.* mad, senseless, reckless, irresponsible; (*obs.*) *see* **-sinnig.**

wahr [va:r], *adj.* true, real, genuine, veritable, proper; sincere, frank; ***sein -es Gesicht zeigen,*** show one's true face, drop the mask; ***-er Gesichtskreis,*** rational horizon; ***etwas für – halten,*** believe a th. to be true, believe in a th.; ***so – mir Gott helfe!*** so help me God! ***der -e Jakob,*** just the man; ***so – ich lebe!*** as sure as I stand here *or* live! ***etwas – machen,*** make s.th. come true, go ahead with s.th., translate a th. into action, carry a th. out, bring a th. about, realize *or* fulfil a th.; ***nicht –?*** isn't it? don't you think? ***eine -e Null,*** a mere cipher; ***– werden,*** come true; ***eine -e Wohltat,*** a real comfort; ***es ist kein -es Wort daran,*** there is not a word of truth in it; ***das Wahre an der S.,*** the fact *or* truth of the matter; ***Wahres wird schon daran sein,*** there's no smoke without fire, there must be some truth in it.

wahren ['va:rən], *v.t.* watch over, look after, take care of, safeguard; keep up, maintain, preserve; ***ein Geheimnis –,*** keep a secret; ***seine Interessen –,*** look after one's interests; ***seine Würde –,*** maintain one's dignity.

währen ['vɛ:rən], *v.i.* continue, endure, last; (*Prov.*) ***ehrlich währt am längsten,*** honesty is the best policy; ***es währte nicht lange, so brach der Lärm wieder aus,*** it was not long before the noise broke out again. **währschaft,** *adj.* (*Swiss*) lasting, enduring; permanent; sound, genuine. **Währschaft,** *f.* guarantee, surety, security, bail.

während ['vɛ:rənt], **1.** *prep.* (*Gen. or* (*Austr.*) *Dat.*) during, in the course of, (*Law*) pending; ***– eines Jahres,*** for a year. **2.** *conj.* while, whilst; whereas. **währendǀdem** [-'de:m], *adv.* (*Austr.*), **-dessen,** *adv.* meanwhile.

wahrhaben ['va:rha:bən], *irr.v.t.* admit, accept, acknowledge (the truth of); ***etwas nicht – wollen,*** not (be ready to) admit s.th.

wahrhaft(ig) ['va:rhaft (va:r'haftɪç)], **1.** *adj.* true, actual, genuine, veritable, real; truthful, veracious. **2.** *adv.* truly, really, surely, actually, indeed. **Wahrhaftigkeit,** *f.* truthfulness, veracity.

Wahrheit ['va:rhaɪt], *f.* truth; reality, fact; ***in –,*** truly, in truth *or* fact *or* reality; (*coll.*) ***ihm die – sagen,*** tell him the plain truth, speak plainly to him, give him a piece of one's mind; ***der – gemäß*** faithfully, in accordance with the facts *or* truth. **Wahrheitsbeweis,** *m.* factual evidence. **wahrheits|gemäß, -getreu, 1.** *adj.* faithful, true, truthful. **2.** *adv.* truly, in accordance with the facts *or* truth. **Wahrheitsliebe,** *f.* love of truth, veracity. **wahrheitsliebend,** *adj.* truthful, veracious. **Wahrheitssucher,** *m.* seeker after truth.

wahrlich ['va:rlɪç], *adv.* truly, surely, verily, indeed.

wahrnehmbar ['va:rne:mba:r], *adj.* perceptible, noticeable, visible, audible. **wahrnehmen,** *irr.v.t.* (*sep.*) notice, observe, perceive, become aware of; make use of, avail o.s. of, profit by *or* from; look after, protect, safeguard; ***die Gelegenheit –,*** take *or* seize the opportunity, make the most of the chance; ***den Termin –,*** observe the closing date, appear on the appointed day; ***seinen Vorteil –,*** look after one's interests. **Wahrnehmung,** *f.* perception, observation; safeguarding, care, protection. **Wahrnehmungs|bild,** *n.* perceptual image. **-kraft,** *f.*, **-vermögen,** *n.* power of perception *or* observation.

wahrsagen ['va:rza:gən], *v.t., v.i.* (*sep. and insep.*) (*Dat.*) prophesy, predict, foretell; tell fortunes; ***aus Kaffeesatz –,*** tell fortunes in coffee-grounds (*usu.* tea leaves); ***sich*** (*Dat.*) ***– lassen,*** have one's fortune told. **Wahrsager(in),** *m.* (*f.*) soothsayer, fortune-teller. **Wahrsagerei** [-'raɪ], *f.* soothsaying, divination; fortune-telling.

wahrscheinlich [va:r'ʃaɪnlɪç], **1.** *adj.* probable, likely, plausible. **2.** *adv.* probably, in all likelihood; ***er kommt –,*** he will probably come, he is likely to come. **Wahrscheinlichkeit,** *f.* probability, likelihood, plausibility; ***aller – nach,*** in all probability, very probably. **Wahrscheinlichkeitsrechnung,** *f.* theory of probabilities.

Wahr|spruch, *m.* verdict (*of a jury*). **-traum,** *m.* prophetic dream, dream destined to come true.

Wahrung ['va:ruŋ], *f.* maintenance; preservation, safeguarding, protection.

Währung ['vɛ:ruŋ], *f.* currency; standard; ***harte –,*** hard currency. **Währungs|abkommen,** *n.* monetary agreement. **-ausgleich,** *m.* exchange equalization. **-bank,** *f.* bank of issue, issuing bank. **-einheit,** *f.* monetary unit. **-krise,** *f.* monetary crisis. **-politik,** *f.* monetary *or* currency policy. **währungspolitisch,** *adj.* monetary, currency. **Währungsreform,** *m.* currency reform.

Wahrzeichen ['va:rtsaɪçən], *n.* (distinctive) mark *or* sign, token; (*topographical*) landmark.

Waid [vaɪt], *m.* **(-(e)s,** *pl.* **-e)** (*Bot.*) woad (*Isatis tinctoria*).

Waid|mann, *m.*, **-werk,** *n.* (*obs.*) *see* **Weid|mann, -werk.**

Waise ['vaɪzə], *f.* orphan; ***zum -n machen,*** orphan. **Waisen haus,** *n.* orphanage. **-kind,** *n.* *See* **Waise. -knabe,** *m.* orphan boy; (*coll., fig.*) ***ein – sein gegen,*** not to be compared with, not able to hold a candle to. **-mutter,** *f.* matron of an orphanage. **-vater,** *m.* superintendent of an orphanage.

Wake ['va:kə], *f.* hole in the ice.

[1]**Wal** [va:l], *m.* **(-s,** *pl.* **-e)** whale.

[2]**Wal,** *f.* (-, *pl.* -) (*obs., Poet.*) battlefield.

Wald [valt], *m.* **(-(e)s,** *pl.* **:-er)** wood, forest, woodland; (*Prov.*) ***wie man in den – hinein ruft, so schallt's heraus,*** as you make your bed, so you must lie in it; (*coll.*) ***er sieht den – vor*** (***lauter***) ***Bäumen nicht,*** he cannot see the wood for trees.

Wald|ahorn, *m.* (*Bot.*) sycamore (*Acer pseudoplatanus*). **-ameise,** *f.* red ant. **-ammer,** *f.* (*Orn.*) rustic bunting (*Emberiza rustica*). **waldarm,** *adj.* sparsely wooded. **Wald|bau,** *m.* afforestation, silviculture. **-baum,** *m.* woodland tree. **-baumläufer,** *m.* (*Orn.*) tree- *or* (*Am.*) brown creeper (*Certhia familiaris*). **-baumschule,** *f.* young plantation. **-bauschule,** *f.* school of forestry. **waldbedeckt,** *adj.* well-wooded. **Wald|beere,** *f.* (*Bot.*) cranberry (*Vaccinium myrtillus*). **-blume,** *f.* woodland flower. **-brand,** *m.* forest fire. **-einsamkeit,** *f.* sylvan solitude. **-erdbeere,** *f.* (*Bot.*) wild strawberry (*Fragaria vesca*). **-erholungsstätte,** *f.* woodland sanatorium.

Waldesdunkel ['valdəsduŋkəl], *n.* forest gloom.

Wald|frevel, *m.* violation of the forestry regulations, wanton damage (*to trees*). **-gebirge,** *n.* wooded mountains. **-gegend,** *f.* woodland, wooded country. **-gehege,** *n.* plantation, forest-preserve. **-geist, -gott,** *m.* sylvan deity, woodland spirit; faun, satyr. **-göttin,** *f.* wood-nymph, dryad. **-grenze,** *f.* timber line. **-horn,** *n.* French horn; (*Poet.*) bugle, hunting horn. **-hüter,** *m.* keeper, forest-ranger.

waldig ['valdɪç], *adj.* wooded, woody.

Wald|kauz, *m.* (*Orn.*) brown *or* tawny owl (*Strix aluco*). **-kultur,** *f.* *See* **-bau. -landschaft,** *f.* woodland scenery. **-laubsänger,** *m.* (*Orn.*) wood-warbler (*Phylloscopus sibilatrix*). **-lauf,** *m.* cross-country run. **-männchen,** *n.* sprite, goblin; *see* **-geist. -meister,** *m.* (*Bot.*) woodruff (*Asperula odorata*). **-mensch,** *m.* wild man of the woods. **-ohreule,** *f.* (*Orn.*) long-eared owl (*Asio otus*). **-ordnung,** *f.* forest laws. **-rand,** *m.* *See* **-saum. -rebe,** *f.* (*Bot.*) traveller's joy

(*Clematis vitalba*). **wald|reich,** *adj. See* **–bedeckt. Wald|revier,** *n.* preserve. **–rotschwanz,** *m.* (*Orn.*) *see* **Gartenrotschwanz. –sänger,** *m.* (*Orn.*) ***grüner –,*** black-throated green warbler (*Dendroica virens*). **–saum,** *m.* forest fringe. **–schaden,** *m. See* **–frevel. –schnepfe,** *f.* (*Orn.*) (*Am.* European) woodcock (*Scolopax rusticola*). **–schrat,** *m. See* **–männchen. –schule,** *f.* open-air school, children's sanatorium. **–schütze,** *m.* forest-ranger. **–schwirrvogel,** *m.* (*Orn.*) *see* **–laubsänger. –stätte,** *pl.* (*Swiss*) Forest Cantons.

Waldung ['valduŋ], *f.* wood; woodland, wooded expanse.

Wald|wasserläufer, *m.* (*Orn.*) green sandpiper (*Tringa ochropus*). **–weg,** *m.* woodland path. **–wiese,** *f.* forest *or* woodland glade. **–wirtschaft,** *f.* forestry. **–wolle,** *f.* pine-needle wool.

Wal|fahrer, *m. See* **–fänger. –fang,** *m.* whaling. **–fänger,** *m.* whaler (*ship and man*).

Walfeld ['va:lfɛlt], *n. See* **²Wal.**

Wal|fisch, *m.* (*coll.*) *see* **¹Wal. –fischbarte,** *f.*, **–fischbein,** *n.* whalebone. **–fischtran,** *m. See* **–öl.**

Wälgerholz ['vɛlgərhɔlts], *n.* rolling-pin. **wälgern,** *v.t.* (*dial.*) roll (*pastry*).

Walke ['valkə], *f.* fulling; fulling machine. **walken,** *v.t.* full (*cloth*); felt (*hats*); (*coll.*) pummel, cudgel. **Walker,** *m.* fuller. **Walker|distel,** *f.* fuller's teazle *or* teasel. **–erde,** *f.* fuller's earth. **Walk|mühle,** *f.* fulling-mill. **–müller,** *m.* fuller.

Walküre [val'ky:rə], *f.* (*Poet.*) Valkyrie.

¹Wall [val], *m.* **(-(e)s,** *pl.* **¨-e)** rampart, bulwark, bank, embankment, dam, dike.

²Wall, *m.* fourscore (*of fish*).

Wallach ['valax], *m.* **(-(e)s** *or* **-en,** *pl.* **-e** (*Austr.* **-en))** gelding.

Wall|beine, *pl.* (*dial.*) bandy *or* bow legs. **–bruch,** *m.* breach in a dike.

¹wallen ['valən], *v.i.* 1. undulate, float, flutter, flow, wave; 2. bubble, simmer, (*fig.*) boil, seethe; ***ihm wallt das Blut,*** his blood boils, his blood is up.

²wallen, *v.i.* (*aux.* s.) (*Poet.*) travel, wander; go on a pilgrimage.

wällen ['vɛlən], *v.t.* (*dial.*) boil, steam, simmer.

Waller ['valər], *m.* (*obs.*) pilgrim, (*Poet.*) wanderer. **wallfahren,** *reg.v.i. See* **wallfahrten. Wall|fahrer,** *m.* pilgrim. **–fahrt,** *f.* pilgrimage. **wallfahrten,** *v.i.* (*insep.*) (*aux.* s.) go on *or* make a pilgrimage. **Wallfahrtsort,** *m.* place of pilgrimage.

Wall|gang, *m.* path along the ramparts. **–graben,** *m.* moat.

Wallung ['valuŋ], *f.* ebullition, bubbling; (*fig.*) ***ihn in – bringen,*** enrage him, make his blood boil; ***in – geraten,*** fly into a rage *or* temper, (*sl.*) blow one's top.

Walm [valm], *m.* **(-(e)s,** *pl.* **-e)** (*Archit.*) slope (*of roof*), hip. **Walmdach,** *n.* hip-roof.

Walnuß ['valnus], *f.* (*Bot.*) walnut (*Juglans regia*).

Wal|öl, *n.* train-oil, sperm oil. **–rat,** *n.* (*Austr. m.*), **–ratfett, –ratöl,** *n.* spermaceti. **–roß,** *n.* walrus.

Walstatt ['va:lʃtat], *f. See* **²Wal.**

walten ['valtən], *v.i.* 1. rule, govern, hold sway, hold the reins of government; ***schalten und –,*** have complete control *or* authority, do exactly as one pleases; ***ihn – lassen,*** give him a free hand, let him do as he pleases; ***Gnade – lassen,*** show mercy; ***Sorgfalt – lassen,*** exercise due *or* proper care; 2. (*Gen.*) carry out, execute; ***walte deines Amtes!*** attend to your duties! discharge the duties of your office! (*coll.*) get on with the job! ***walte das Gott!*** amen! God grant it! **Walten,** *n.* rule, control; ***das – Gottes,*** the hand of God.

Waltier ['va:lti:r], *n.* cetacean.

Walz|blech ['valts–], *n. See* **–eisen. Walze,** *f.* roll, roller, barrel, drum, cylinder, (*of typewriter*) platen, (*Typ., Phot.*) squeegee; (*coll.*) ***immer die alte –,*** the same old story, the usual complaint; (*coll.*) ***auf der – sein,*** be on the road; (*coll.*) ***auf die – gehen,*** take to the road. **walzen, 1.** *v.t.* roll, roll out (*dough*). **2.** *v.i.* (dance the) waltz; (*coll.*) tramp, (*sl.*) foot it.

wälzen ['vɛltsən], **1.** *v.t.* roll, rotate, turn about, trundle; ***Bücher –,*** pore over books; ***Gedanken –,*** turn ideas over in one's mind; ***von sich –,*** exonerate o.s. from, shift (*blame*) from o.s.; ***die Schuld auf ihn –,*** throw the blame on to him. **2.** *v.r.* roll, wallow, welter; ***er wälzt sich vor Lachen,*** he is rolling *or* shaking *or* is convulsed with laughter. **Wälzen,** *n.* (*coll.*) ***das ist zum –,*** it's a real scream, it's enough to make a cat laugh.

Walzendruck ['valtsəndruk], *m.* cylinder printing. **walzenförmig,** *adj.* cylindrical.

Walzer ['valtsər], *m.* waltz.

Wälzer ['vɛltsər], *m.* (*coll.*) bulky volume, ponderous tome.

Walzgold ['valtsgɔlt], *n.* rolled gold.

Wälzlager ['vɛltsla:gər], *n.* roller bearing.

Walz|stahl, *m.* rolled steel. **–werk,** *n.* rolling-mill.

Wamme ['vamə], *f.* dewlap; (*dial.*) belly, paunch.

Wams [vams], *n. or m.* **(-es,** *pl.* **¨-er** *or* **-e)** (*Hist.*) doublet; jacket, jerkin, jersey. **wamsen,** *v.t.* (*coll.*) thrash, give a good hiding (to).

Wand [vant], *f.* **(-,** *pl.* **¨-e)** wall (*of a room*), partition, screen; (*Bot., Anat.*) septum; side, cheek; (rock)-face; (*fig.*) ***ihn an die – drücken,*** push him on one side *or* to the wall; (*fig.*) ***an die – gedrückt werden,*** go to the wall; ***an die – stellen,*** put against the wall; (*coll.*) ***es ist um an den Wänden hochzugehen,*** it's enough to drive you up the wall; (*Prov.*) ***der Horcher an der – hört seine eigne Schand,*** listeners never hear good of themselves; (*Prov.*) ***man soll den Teufel nicht an die – malen,*** talk of the devil and he will appear; (*coll.*) ***mit dem Kopf durch die – wollen,*** run one's head against a (brick) wall; (*fig.*) ***in seinen vier Wänden,*** at home, by one's own fireside; ***Wände haben Ohren,*** walls have ears; ***spanische –,*** folding screen; (***zu***) ***leeren Wänden reden,*** waste one's breath, beat the air.

wand, *see* **winden.**

Wand|arm, *m.* (wall) bracket. **–bein,** *n.* (*Anat.*) parietal bone. **–bekleidung,** *f.* panelling, wainscot(ing). **–bewurf,** *m.* plastering, parget(ing).

Wandel ['vandəl], *m.* 1. change; mutation; ***– schaffen,*** bring about a change (*in* (*Dat.*), in); ***– der Zeiten,*** changing times; (*B.*) ***Gottes Wege sind ohne –,*** God's way is perfect; 2. mode of life, conduct, behaviour, habits; ***Handel und –,*** trade, commerce; ***einen tugendhaften – führen,*** lead a virtuous life. **Wandelanleihe,** *f.* convertible loan. **wandelbar,** *adj.* changeable, variable, inconstant, fickle. **Wandelbarkeit,** *f.* changeableness, changeability, inconstancy, fickleness. **Wandel|gang,** *m.*, **–halle,** *f.* (*Parl. etc.*) lobby, (*Theat.*) foyer, (*spa*) pump-room.

wandeln ['vandəln], **1.** *v.t., v.r.* change, turn, convert (*in* (*Acc.*), into). **2.** *v.i.* (*aux.* h. & s.) (*Poet.*) go (on foot), walk, amble, saunter; wander, travel; (*B.*) live; ***handeln und –,*** trade, traffic; ***unsträflich –,*** lead an irreproachable life; (*coll.*) ***–des Lexikon,*** walking encyclopaedia.

Wandel|obligation, *f.* convertible bond. **–stern,** *m.* planet.

Wander|arbeiter, *m.* itinerant workman. **–ausrüstung,** *f.* hiking equipment. **–ausstellung,** *f.* touring exhibition. **–bühne,** *f.* travelling theatre; touring company. **–bursche,** *m.* travelling *or* itinerant journeyman, (*coll.*) tramp. **–drossel,** *f.* (*Orn.*) American robin (*Am.* robin) (*Turdus migratorius*). **Wanderer,** *m.* traveller (on foot), foot-traveller; hiker; wanderer, vagrant. **Wander|falke,** *m.* (*Orn.*) peregrine falcon (*Falco peregrinus*). **–geselle,** *m. See* **–bursche. –gewerbe,** *n.* itinerant trade, hawking, peddling. **–gewerbeschein,** *m.* pedlar's licence. **–heuschrecke,** *f.* migratory locust. **–jahre,** *n.pl.* journeyman's time of travel. **–laubsänger,** *m.* (*Orn.*) *see* ***nordischer Laubsänger.*** **–leben,** *n.* vagrant *or* nomadic life, nomadism. **–lust,** *f.* call of the open (air).

wandern ['vandərn], *v.i.* (*aux.* s.) travel (on foot), go (on foot), walk; wander, roam; ramble, hike; (*of birds etc.*) migrate; (*of ghosts*) walk; (*of sand etc.*) shift; (*Metall.*) creep; (*Chem.*) diffuse; (*coll.*) ***ins Gefängnis –,*** go to prison; ***seines Weges –,*** go (on) one's way; (*coll.*) ***seine Uhr wanderte aufs Leihhaus,*** his watch found its way to the pawnshop. **wandernd,** *adj.* travelling, itinerant; strolling; nomadic; migratory; (*as a library etc.*) touring; (*as kidney*) floating; (*as sand*) shifting; (*Geol.*) erratic.

Wander|niere, *f.* floating kidney. **–prediger,** *m.* itinerant preacher, evangelist. **–preis,** *m.* challenge trophy. **–ratte,** *f.* (*Zool.*) brown *or* sewer rat (*Epimys norvegicus*). **Wanderschaft,** *f.* travelling, travel(s); migration; ***auf die – gehen,*** set out *or* go on one's travels; ***auf der – sein,*** be on one's travels (*of journeymen*). **Wandersmann,** *m.* (-, *pl.* **-leute**) (*Poet.*) *see* **Wanderer. Wander|stab,** *m.* pilgrim's staff, (*coll.*) walking-stick; (*fig.*) ***den – ergreifen, zum – greifen,*** set out, leave home; ***den – weiter setzen,*** continue on one's way. **–trieb,** *m.* migratory instinct, (*coll.*) roving spirit, restlessness. **–truppe,** *f.* (*Theat.*) strolling players. **Wanderung,** *f.* trip, excursion, (walking) tour, hike; migration; (*coll.*) peregrinations. **Wandervogel,** *m.* bird of passage (*also fig.*); rambler, hiker; *pl.* German youth movement.

wandfest ['vantfεst], *adj.* fixed to the wall. **Wand|-fliese,** *f.* wall-tile. **–gemälde,** *n.* mural (painting). **–karte,** *f.* wall-map. **–konsole,** *f. See* **–arm.**

Wandler ['vandlər], *m.* (*Elec.*) transformer, converter, transducer.

Wandleuchter ['vantlɔyçtər], *m.* lamp-bracket, sconce.

Wandlung ['vandluŋ], *f.* change, alteration, (*also Elec.*) transformation; mutation, metamorphosis; (*Comm.*) conversion; (*Eccl.*) transubstantiation.

Wand|malerei, *f.* mural painting. **–pfeiler,** *m.* pilaster. **–putz,** *m.* parget(ing), plaster.

Wandrer, *m. See* **Wanderer.**

Wand|schirm, *m.* folding screen. **–schoner,** *m.* splash-back. **–schrank,** *m.* closet, built-in cupboard. **–spiegel,** *m.* wall-mirror, pier-glass. **wandständig,** *adj.* (*Anat., Bot.*) parietal. **Wand|-stärke,** *f.* thickness of wall. **–stecker,** *m.* wall-plug. **–tafel,** *f.* blackboard; wall-chart.

wandte ['vantə], *see* **wenden.**

Wand|teppich, *m.* tapestry, wall-hanging. **–uhr,** *f.* wall-clock, hanging clock. **–verkleidung,** *f.* wall-facing, panelling, wainscot(ing). **–zelle,** *f.* (*Bot.*) parietal cell.

Wange ['vaŋə], *f.* cheek, (*Mech.*) side-piece. **Wangenbein,** *n.* cheek-bone. **–wangig,** *adj.suff.* -cheeked.

Wank [vaŋk], *m.* (*only in*) ***ohne –,*** unwavering(ly), unflinchingly, steadfastly. **wank,** (*dial.*) **wankel,** *adj. See* **wankend. Wankelmut,** *m.* inconstancy, vacillation, fickleness, inconsistency. **wankelmütig,** *adj.* changeable, inconstant, irresolute, vacillating, fickle; inconsistent.

wanken ['vaŋkən], *v.i.* (*aux.* h. *&* s.) (*of a p.*) stagger, reel, totter; (*of a th.*) rock, sway; (*fig.*) falter, waver, be irresolute, vacillate, hesitate, flinch; ***mir – die Knie,*** my knees give way beneath me; ***den Feind zum Wanken bringen,*** break the enemy's ranks; ***nicht weichen und nicht –,*** stand firm, be as firm as a rock, not budge (an inch), not falter *or* waver *or* flinch. **wankend,** *adj.* unsteady, irresolute, wavering, vacillating, hesitant.

wann [van], **1.** *adv.* when; ***seit –?*** since when? how long? ***dann und –,*** now and then. **2.** *conj.* (*dial.*) when; ***es sei – es wolle,*** whatever time *or* whenever it may be; ***– immer,*** whenever.

Wanne ['vanə], *f.* **1.** tub, vat, tank, bath; trough; (*Motor.*) (oil-)sump; (*Mil.*) hull (*of a tank*); 2. (*dial.*) winnow, swingle.

[1]**wannen** ['vanən], **1.** *v.t.* (*dial.*) winnow. **2.** *v.i.* (*dial.*) hover (*of birds*).

[2]**wannen,** *adv.* (*dial.*) ***von –,*** whence.

Wannenbad ['vanənba:t], *n.* (full-length) bath.

Wanst [vanst], *m.* (**-es,** *pl.* **¨-e**) belly, paunch.

Wante ['vantə], *f.* (*Naut.*) shroud.

Wanze ['vantsə], *f.* (*Ent.*) bug (*Heteroptera*). **wanzig,** *adj.* bug-ridden *or* infested, (*coll.*) buggy.

Wappen ['vapən], *n.* (coat of) arms, escutcheon, armorial bearings; ***– ohne Beizeichen,*** plain coat of arms; ***– im Siegel,*** crest, signet; ***im – führen,*** bear. **Wappen|ausleger,** *m.* herald. **–balken,** *m.* fesse. **–bild,** *n.* heraldic figure. **–buch,** *n.* book of heraldry. **–erklärung,** *f. See* **–kunde. –feld,** *n.* field, quarter. **–halter,** *m.* supporter. **–könig,** *m.* king-at-arms. **–kunde,** *f.* heraldry. **–mantel,** *m.* mantling. **–schild,** *n.* escutcheon. **–schmuck,** *m.* blazonry. **–spruch,** *m.* heraldic motto, device. **–zierde,** *f.* accompaniment.

wappnen ['vapnən], *v.t.* (*Poet. or fig.*) arm.

war [va:r], *see* **sein.**

warb [varb], *see* **werben.**

ward [vart], *see* **werden.**

Wardein [var'daın], *m.* (**-s,** *pl.* **-e**) assayer, mint warden. **wardieren,** *v.t.* (*dial.*) value, test, check.

Ware ['va:rə], *f.* article, commodity, product; *pl.* goods, wares, merchandise; ***grüne –,*** vegetables, greenstuff, greens; ***gute – lobt sich selbst,*** good wine needs no bush; ***irdene –,*** pottery, crockery; ***kurze –,*** small wares; hardware; ***schwimmende –,*** flotsam; ***verbotene –,*** contraband goods; ***das ist teure –,*** that is a luxury.

wäre ['vε:rə], *see* **sein;** (*coll.*) ***wie – es mit einer Kleinigkeit zu essen?*** how about s.th. to eat? ***wie – es, wenn er käme?*** what if he should come?

Waren|absatz, *m.* sale of goods. **–abschluß,** *m.* contract in goods. **–aufzug,** *m.* hoist. **–ausfuhr,** *f.* export. **–ausgangsbuch,** *n.* sales ledger. **–bedarf,** *m.* demand. **–bestand,** *m.* stock on hand. **–bezieher,** *m.* importer. **–börse,** *f.* commodity exchange. **–eingang,** *m.* goods received. **–einsender,** *m.* consigner. **–empfänger,** *m.* consignee. **–haus,** *n.* department store. **–konto,** *n.* current-account book, goods account. **–kredit,** *m.* credit (allowed) on goods. **–kunde,** *f.* market research. **–lager,** *n.* stock in trade; warehouse. **–lieferant,** *m.* contractor, purveyor of goods. **–markt,** *m.* produce-market. **–niederlage,** *f.* warehouse, magazine. **–preis,** *m.* current price of goods. **–probe,** *f.* sample, pattern. **–sendung,** *f.* consignment *or* shipment of goods. **–speicher,** *m. See* **–niederlage. –stempel,** *m.* trade-mark, manufacturer's *or* factory mark. **–umsatz,** *m.* turnover of goods. **–umsatzsteuer,** *f.* purchase tax. **–umschlag,** *m.* movement of goods. **–verzeichnis,** *n.* list of goods; specification; inventory. **–vorrat,** *m. See* **–bestand. –zeichen,** *n. See* **–stempel.**

warf [varf], *see* **werfen.**

warm [varm], *adj.* (*comp.* ***wärmer,*** *sup.* ***wärmst***) warm; hot; ***– auftragen,*** serve up hot; ***– baden,*** take hot baths; (*coll.*) ***–er Bruder,*** homo(sexual); (*Prov.*) ***man muß das Eisen schmieden, solang es noch – ist,*** strike while the iron is hot; ***– essen,*** have a hot meal; ***sich – halten,*** keep (o.s.) warm, dress warmly; ***nicht – nicht kalt,*** neither one thing nor the other; ***ihm den Kopf – machen,*** provoke him, stir him up; ***mir ist –,*** I am warm; ***wie –e Semmeln abgehen,*** go *or* sell like hot cakes; ***– stellen,*** keep (*food*) hot; ***– sitzen,*** be in easy circumstances; (*fig.*) ***– werden,*** get excited (***für,*** about *or* over), warm up (to); get into a passion (about); ***bei ihm – werden,*** feel at home *or* at one's ease with him; ***mit –en Worten,*** with kindly *or* cordial words.

Warmbad ['varmba:t], *n.* thermal springs. **warmbehandelt,** *adj.* (*Tech.*) heat-treated. **Warmblüter,** *m.* warm-blooded animal. **warmblütig,** *adj.* warm-blooded. **Warmbrunnen,** *m.* hot spring.

Wärme ['vεrmə], *f.* warmth, heat, temperature, (*fig.*) warmth, ardour; ***– durchlassen,*** transmit heat; (*Phys.*) ***freie –,*** sensible heat; ***gebundene –,*** latent heat; ***12 Grad –,*** temperature of 12 degrees; ***strahlende –,*** radiant heat. **Wärme|abgabe,** *f.* loss *or* emission of heat. **–äquator,** *m.* thermal equator. **–aufnahme,** *f.* absorption of heat. **–ausdehnung,**

f. thermal expansion. **-ausstrahlung,** *f.* heat radiation. **-behandlung,** *f.* heat treatment. **wärmebeständig,** *adj.* heat-proof, heat-resistant. **Wärmebeständigkeit,** *f.* high-temperature stability, resistance to heat. **wärmedurchlässig,** *adj.* heat conducting, diathermic. **Wärme|einheit,** *f.* thermal unit, unit of heat, calorie. **-elektrizität,** *f.* thermo-electricity. **wärmeerzeugend,** *adj.* calorific. **Wärme|grad,** *m.* degree of heat; temperature. **-isolierung,** *f.* heat insulation. **-jahresmittel,** *n.* mean annual temperature. **-konstanz,** *f.* constant heat. **-kraftmaschine,** *f.* heat-engine. **-lehre,** *f.* theory of heat. **-leiter,** *m.* conductor of heat. **-leitfähigkeit,** *f.* heat conductivity. **-leitung,** *f.* heat conduction. **-mechanik,** *f.* thermodynamics. **-menge,** *f.* quantity of heat. **-messer,** *m.* thermometer, calorimeter. **-messung,** *f.* calorimetry.

wärmen ['vɛrmən], **1.** *v.t.* warm, heat; make warm *or* hot; ***sich*** (*Dat.*) ***die Hände –,*** warm one's hands. **2.** *v.r.* warm o.s., bask.

Wärme|quelle, *f.* source of heat, heat supply. **-regler,** *m.* thermostat. **-schutz,** *m.* lagging (*of pipes etc.*). **-speicher,** *m.* storage-heater. **-strahl,** *m.* heat-ray. **-strahler,** *m.* radiator. **-strahlung,** *f.* heat radiation. **-technik,** *f.* heat technology. **-übertragung,** *f.* heat convection. **-vergütung,** *f.* artificial ageing (*of metals*). **-wert,** *m.* calorific value. **-wirkungsgrad,** *m.* thermal efficiency.

warmfest ['varmfɛst], *adj.* heat-resistant, high-temperature.

Wärmflasche ['vɛrmflaʃə], *f.* hot-water bottle.

warmhalten ['varmhaltən], *irr.v.t.* keep warm; (*fig.*) ***sich*** (*Dat.*) ***ihn –,*** keep in with him, keep in his good books. **Warmhalter,** *m.* hot-plate, plate warmer. **warm|herzig,** *adj.* warm-hearted. **-laufen,** *irr.v.i.* (*Mech.*) run hot; (*Motor.*) ***– lassen,*** warm up. **Warm|luftfront,** *f.* (*Meteor.*) warm front. **-luftheizung,** *f.* hot-air heating (installation).

Wärmplatte ['vɛrmplatə], *f.* warming-pan; chafing-dish.

warnen ['varnən], *v.t.* warn (***vor*** (*Dat.*), of *or* against), caution (against); ***vor . . . wird gewarnt!*** beware of . . .! **Warn|ruf,** *m.* warning cry. **-streik,** *m.* token strike. **Warnung,** *f.* warning; caution, admonition; ***laßt euch das zur – dienen,*** let this be a warning to you. **Warnungs|laterne,** *f.* danger light. **-signal,** *n.* danger signal. **-tafel,** *f.* danger notice. **-zeichen,** *n. See* **-signal.**

Warp [varp], *m. or n.* (**-s,** *pl.* **-e**) warp. **Warpanker,** *m.* kedge (anchor). **warpen,** *v.t.* (*Naut.*) tow, kedge.

Warschau ['varʃau], *n.* Warsaw.

Wart [vart], *m.* (**-(e)s,** *pl.* **-e**) (*obs.*) keeper, warder; *now only in compounds, e.g.* ***Kassen–, Schrift–, Turn–.*** **Warte,** *f.* look-out, watch-tower; (*fig.*) ***alles von hoher – sehen,*** adopt a lofty attitude towards everything. **Warte|frau,** *f.* nurse, attendant. **-geld,** *n.* (*Mil.*) half-pay, (*Naut.*) demurrage. **-liste,** *f.* waiting-list.

warten ['vartən], **1.** *v.i.* wait, stay, bide; ***– auf*** (*Acc.*) *or rarely* (*Gen.*), await, wait for, wait on; (*coll.*) ***da können Sie lange –,*** you will wait till the cows come home, you may whistle for it; (*coll.*) ***warte nur!*** you just wait! ***er läßt auf sich –,*** he is a long time coming; ***ihn – lassen,*** keep him waiting; ***mit dem Essen auf ihn –,*** keep dinner waiting for him; (*obs.*) ***seines Amtes –,*** discharge one's duties; ***seiner Arbeit –,*** attend to one's work. **2.** *v.t.* attend to, look after, tend, nurse; mind (*children*); groom (*horses*), maintain, service (*machines*). **Warten,** *n.* waiting; tending; ***ich bin des –s müde,*** I am tired of waiting.

Wärter ['vɛrtər], *m.* keeper, caretaker, (prison) warder, attendant, male nurse; signalman.

Warte|raum, *m. See* **-saal, -zimmer.**

Wärterin ['vɛrtərɪn], *f. See* **Wartefrau.**

Warte|saal, *m.* (*Railw.*) waiting-room. **-stand,** *m.* provisional retirement. **-turm,** *m.* watch *or* look-out tower. **-zeit,** *f.* demurrage, time of waiting; (*Insur.*) gap. **-zimmer,** *n.* (doctor's) waiting room.

Wartung ['vartuŋ], *f.* nursing, tending; attendance, (*Tech.*) maintenance, servicing; (*of animals*) grooming.

warum [va'rum], *adv., conj.* why, for what reason? on what grounds? wherefore; ***– nicht gar?*** you don't say so! surely not! what next!

Warze ['vartsə], *f.* wart; (*Anat., Zool.*) nipple, teat; (*Bot.*) tubercle; (*Mech.*) stud, lug, pin. **Warzen|bein,** *n.* mastoid bone. **-fortsatz,** *m.* papillary tubercle; mastoid process. **-gewebe,** *n.* papillary tissue. **-hof, -ring,** *m.* (*Anat.*) areola of the nipple. **-schwein,** *n.* (*Zool.*) wart-hog (*Phacochoerus aethiopicus*). **warzig,** *adj.* warty, (*Mech.*) studded, nodular.

was [vas], **1.** *inter.pron.* what; whatever; ***ach –!*** rubbish! stuff and nonsense! ***– bekommen Sie?*** how much is it? the bill, please; ***– dann?*** what then? is that all? ***– für ein?*** what sort of a? ***– für ein Unglück!*** what a misfortune! ***– haben wir gelacht!*** how we laughed! ***– Sie nicht sagen!*** you don't say so! really! **2.** *rel.pron.* what, that which; whatever; (*referring to entire previous clause*) ***– mich völlig kalt läßt,*** which leaves me quite cold; ***alles, – du siehst,*** all that you can see; ***nimm dir, – du willst,*** take whatever you want; ***er läuft – er*** (***nur***) ***kann,*** he runs as hard as he can; ***– mich anlangt*** or ***betrifft,*** as for me; ***– auch immer,*** whatever, no matter what. **3.** (*coll.*) = ***etwas; ich will dir mal – sagen,*** I will tell you something; ***das ist auch – Rechtes!*** I do not think much of that! ***nein, so –!*** well, I never! ***so – lebt nicht!*** such a thing has never been heard of; ***zu – Besserm sind wir geboren,*** man is born for better things. **4.** (*coll.*) isn't it? eh? ***ein bißchen kalt heute, –?*** rather cold today, don't you think?

Waschanstalt ['vaʃʔanʃtalt], *f.* laundry. **waschbar,** *adj.* washable; (*of colours*) fast. **Wasch|bär,** *m.* (*Zool.*) raccoon (*Procyon lotor*). **-becken,** *n.* hand- *or* wash-basin. **-blau,** *n.* washing-blue. **-brett,** *n.* washboard. **-bütte,** *f.* wash(ing)-tub.

Wäsche ['vɛʃə], *f.* washing, wash, laundry; linen, underwear, underclothes, underclothing; ***morgen haben wir (große) –,*** tomorrow is washing-day; ***das Hemd ist in der –,*** the shirt is being washed *or* is in the wash; ***in die – geben*** or ***tun*** or ***schicken,*** send to the laundry; ***schmutzige –,*** dirty linen (*also fig.*); ***die – wechseln,*** change one's underclothes. **Wäschebeutel,** *m.* soiled-linen *or* dirty clothes bag.

waschecht ['vaʃʔɛçt], *adj.* (*of colours*) fast; (*fig., coll.*) dyed-in-the-wool, true-blue, genuine, real, thorough, true.

Wäsche|geschäft, *n.* lingerie *or* draper's shop. **-gestell,** *n.* clothes-horse. **-klammer,** *f.* clothes-peg. **-korb,** *m.* dirty clothes basket. **-leine,** *f.* clothes line.

Wascheln ['vaʃəln], *f.pl.* (*dial.*) ears, (*sl.*) lugs.

waschen ['vaʃən], *irr.v.t., irr.v.i.* wash, launder; shampoo (*hair*); (*coll., dial.*) gossip, chatter; (*Prov.*) ***eine Hand wäscht die andere,*** one good turn deserves another; ***sich – lassen,*** bear *or* stand washing, wash well; ***sich*** (*Dat.*) ***das Gesicht*** or ***die Hände –,*** wash one's face *or* hands; ***ich wasche meine Hände in Unschuld,*** I wash my hands of it; (*coll., fig.*) ***ihm den Kopf –,*** give him a dressing down; (*coll.*) ***das hat sich gewaschen!*** that was very effective! ***er ist mit allen Wassern gewaschen,*** he is a smooth *or* slippery customer.

Wäscherei [vɛʃə'raɪ], *f.* laundry. **Wäscherin** ['vɛʃərɪn], *f.* washerwoman, laundress.

Wäsche|rolle, *f.* mangle, wringer. **-schleuder,** *m.* spin-drier. **-schrank,** *m.* linen-cupboard, linen-press. **-ständer,** *m. See* **-gestell. -tinte,** *f.* marking-ink.

Wasch|faß, *n. See* **-bütte. -flasche,** *f.* (*Chem.*) washing bottle. **-frau,** *f. See* **Wäscherin. -gelegenheit,** *f.* lavatory, toilet. **-geschirr,** *n.* washstand set. **-gold,** *n.* placer gold. **-handschuhe,** *m.pl.* wash-leather gloves. **-haus,** *n.* wash-house. **-kessel,** *m.* copper, boiler. **-kleid,** *n.* washable dress, cotton frock. **-korb,** *m.* clothes-basket. **-küche,** *f. See* **-haus;** (*sl.*) pea-soup (*fog*).

-lappen, *m.* face-cloth; (*for crockery*) dish-cloth; (*fig.*) milksop, sissy. **-leder,** *n.* wash-leather, chamois, (*coll.*) shammy. **-maschine,** *f.* washing-machine. **-mittel, -pulver,** *n.* washing-powder, detergent. **-raum,** *m. See* **-gelegenheit. -schüssel,** *f. See* **-becken. -seife,** *f.* washing soap. **-tag,** *m.* washing-day. **-tisch,** *m.*, **-toilette,** *f.* wash-stand. **-topf,** *m.* washing-up bowl. **-trog,** *m. See* **-bütte**; (*Min.*) standing-buddle, wash-cradle.

Waschung ['vaʃuŋ], *f.* washing, ablution, lavation; wash, lotion.

Wasch|wasser, *n.* washing water; wash, cosmetic lotion; dish-water. **-weib,** *n.* (*fig.*) washerwoman, gossip, chatterbox (*also used of men*). **-zettel,** *m.* laundry list; (*sl.*) publisher's blurb. **-zuber,** *m. See* **-bütte.**

Wasen ['vazən], *m.* 1. sod, turf, grass; lawn; (*dial.*) bundle of brushwood; 2. (*dial.*) steam, vapour.

Wasser ['vasər], *n.* (**-s,** *pl.* - *or* (**Mineral**)⸚) water; ***voll* –,** (*of ships etc.*) waterlogged; ***fließendes* –,** running water; ***stehendes* –,** stagnant water; (*fig.*) ***er ist mit allen -n gewaschen,*** he is a smooth *or* slippery customer; (*Prov.*) ***– hat keine Balken,*** water is a treacherous element; ***bei Brot und – sitzen,*** be on bread and water; (*fig.*) ***ins – fallen,*** see ***zu – werden***; (*coll.*) ***ein Schlag ins –,*** a flop; ***– lassen,*** make *or* pass water; ***das – läuft ihm im Munde zusammen,*** his mouth waters; ***das ist – auf seine Mühle,*** that is grist to his mill; ***ihm das – nicht reichen können,*** be far inferior to him, not to be compared with him, (*coll.*) not be a patch on him, not be fit to hold a candle to him; ***von reinstem –,*** of the first water; (*fig.*) ***– auf beiden Schultern tragen,*** blow hot and cold; (*Prov.*) ***stille – sind tief,*** still waters run deep; ***sich über – halten,*** keep one's head above water (*also fig.*); ***unter – setzen,*** flood, inundate, submerge; ***– ziehen,*** let in water, leak; ***zu – und zu Lande,*** by land and sea; ***zu – werden,*** come to nothing *or* naught, end in smoke, (*coll.*) not come off, flop.

Wasser|abfluß, *m.* drain, scupper. **-abfuhr,** *m.* draining, drainage. **-abgabe,** *f.* elimination of water, transpiration. **-ablaß,** *m. See* **-abfluß. -ablaufrinne,** *f.* gutter. **-abspaltung,** *f.* dehydration. **wasserabstoßend,** *adj.* water-repellent. **Wasserader,** *f.* underground watercourse. **wasser|ähnlich,** *adj. See* **-artig. Wasser|amsel,** *f.* (*Orn.*) dipper (*Cinclus cinclus*). **-anlage,** *f. See* **-werk. wasser|anziehend,** *adj.* hygroscopic. **-arm,** *adj.* parched, arid. **Wasserarmut,** *f.* shortage *or* scarcity of water. **wasserartig,** *adj.* aqueous. **Wasser|auslaß, -austritt,** *m. See* **-abfluß. -ball,** *m.* water-polo. **-bau,** *m.* dike construction *or* maintenance. **-baukunst,** *f.* hydraulic engineering. **-becken,** *n.* (natural) reservoir, basin. **-behälter,** *m.* tank, cistern, reservoir. **wasser|beständig,** *adj. See* **-fest. Wasser|bewohner,** *m.* aquatic animal *or* plant. **-blase,** *f.* water-blister, vesicle, pustule; bubble. **wasserblau,** *adj.* sea-blue. **Wasser|blume,** *f.* aquatic flower. **-bombe,** *f.* (*Mil.*) depth-charge. **-bruch,** *m.* (*Med.*) hydrocele.

Wässerchen ['vɛsərçən], *n.* rivulet; (*coll.*) ***er sieht aus, als könne er kein – trüben,*** he looks as if butter wouldn't melt in his mouth.

Wasserdampf ['vasərdampf], *m.* water vapour, steam. **wasser|dicht,** *adj.* watertight; *see also* **-fest**; ***– sein,*** hold water. **Wasser|druck,** *m.* hydrostatic *or* hydraulic pressure. **-dunst,** *m.* water vapour. **-enthärtung,** *f.* water softening. **-entziehung,** *f.* dehydration. **-fahrt,** *f.* boating (trip), trip by water. **-fahrzeug,** *n.* vessel, craft. **-fall,** *m.* waterfall, cataract, cascade; (*coll.*) ***wie ein – reden,*** talk the hind-leg(s) off a donkey. **-fang,** *m.* reservoir, catchment; cistern. **-farbe,** *f.* water-colour, distemper. **wasserfest,** *adj.* waterproof. **Wasser|fläche,** *f.* surface of the water; sheet of water. **-flasche,** *f.* water-bottle, carafe. **-flugzeug,** *n.* seaplane, hydroplane. **wasserfrei,** *adj.* free from water, anhydrous; ***-er Alkohol,*** absolute alcohol.

Wasser|gang, *m.* canal, aqueduct; drain, scupper. **-geflügel,** *n.* waterfowl. **-gehalt,** *m.* water *or* moisture content. **-geist,** *m.* water-sprite. **-geschwulst,** *f.* (*Med.*) oedema. **-gewächs,** *n.* aquatic plant. **-glas,** *n.* drinking-glass, tumbler; (*Chem.*) waterglass, sodium silicate; (*coll.*) ***Sturm im* –,** storm in a teacup. **-graben,** *m.* ditch, moat, (*Spt.*) water-jump. **-hahn,** *m.* water-tap, water-cock, (*Am.*) faucet. **wasser|haltig,** *adj.* watery, containing water, (*Chem.*) aqeuous, hydrous, hydrated. **-hart,** *adj.* (*of pottery*) air-dried. **Wasser|-haushalt,** *m.* water conservation. **-heilanstalt,** *f.* hydropathic establishment. **-heilkunde,** *f.* hydropathy. **-heizung,** *f.* (hot-water) central heating. **wasserhell,** *adj.* clear as crystal. **Wasser|hose,** *f.* waterspout. **-huhn,** *n.* (*Orn.*) ***schwarzes* –,** *see* **Bläßhuhn.**

wässerig ['vɛsərɪç], *adj.* watery, aqueous, (*Chem.*) hydrous, (*Med.*) serous; diluted, weak; (*fig.*) insipid, (*coll.*) wishy-washy; ***ihm den Mund – machen,*** make his mouth water (***nach,*** for).

Wasser|jungfer, *f.* (*Ent.*) dragonfly (*Odonata*); water-nymph, mermaid. **-käfer,** *m.* water-beetle (*Hydrophilidae*). **-kanne,** *f.* water-jug, ewer. **-kante,** *f.* (North German) seaboard. **-karte,** *f.* hydrographic chart. **-kasten,** *m.* water-tank, (*Motor.*) header tank. **-kessel,** *m.* kettle, cauldron, copper, boiler. **-kitt,** *m.* hydraulic cement. **-kläranlage,** *f.* water purifying plant. **-klee,** *m.* (*Bot.*) marsh trefoil (*Menyantus trifoliata*). **-klosett,** *n.* water-closet, W.C. **-kopf,** *m.* (*Med.*) hydrocephalus. **-kraft,** *f.* water- *or* hydraulic power. **-kraftwerk,** *n.* hydro-electric power-station. **-krug,** *m. See* **-kanne. -kühlung,** *f.* water cooling(-system). **-kunde,** *f.* hydrology. **-kunst,** *f.* fountain; hydraulic engine. **-kur,** *f.* hydropathic treatment. **-landflugzeug,** *n.* amphibian plane. **-lauf,** *m.* watercourse. **-läufer,** *m.* (*Ent.*) pond skater (*Gerridae*); (*Orn.*) ***dunkler* –,** spotted redshank (*Tringa erythropus*); ***einsamer* –,** solitary sandpiper (*Tringa solitaria*); ***heller* –,** *see* **Grünschenkel.**

Wasser|leitung, *f.* water pipe(s) *or* piping, water main, conduit; aqueduct. **-leitungsrohr,** *n.* water-pipe, conduit. **-leitungswasser,** *n.* tap water. **-lilie,** *f.* (*Bot.*) waterlily (*Nymphaea alba*). **-linie,** *f.* water mark; (*Naut.*) waterline, load line. **-linse,** *f.* (*Bot.*) duckweed (*Lemna minor*). **-loch,** *n.* drain hole. **wasserlöslich,** *adj.* water-soluble. **Wasser|mangel,** *m.* water shortage, drought. **-mann,** *m.* (*Astr.*) water-carrier, Aquarius. **-mantel,** *m.* water-jacket. **-menge,** *f.* amount of water; plenty of water. **-messer,** *m.* hydrometer, water-gauge. **-meßkunst,** *f.* hydrometry. **-mine,** *f. See* **-bombe. -mühle,** *f.* watermill.

wassern ['vasərn], *v.i.* (*aux.* h. *&* s.) (*Av.*) alight on water.

wässern ['vɛsərn], *v.t.* water, irrigate (*land*), soak, steep, macerate (*materials*), (*Phot.*) wash, (*Chem.*) hydrate.

Wasser|nixe, *f.* water-nymph *or* sprite, naiad. **-not,** *f. See* **-mangel. -nymphe,** *f. See* **-nixe. -partie,** *f. See* **-fahrt. wasserpaß,** *adj.* level with the water; horizontal. **Wasser|paß,** *m.* level of the water. **-perle,** *f.* imitation pearl. **-pest,** *f.* (*Bot.*) water-thyme (*Elodea canadensis*). **-pfeife,** *f.* narghile, hookah. **-pflanze,** *f.* aquatic plant, hydrophyte. **-pieper,** *m.* (*Orn.*) water-pipit (*Anthus spinoletta spinoletta*). **-pocken,** *f.pl.* chickenpox. **-polizei,** *f.* river *or* harbour police. **-rad,** *n.* waterwheel; ***ober–*** (or ***unter***)***schlägiges* –,** overshot (undershot) waterwheel. **-ralle,** *f.* (*Orn.*) water-rail (*Rallus aquaticus*). **-ratte,** *f.* (*Zool.*) water-rat (*Arvicola scherman*); (*coll.*) good swimmer; old salt, seadog. **wasserreich,** *adj.* well watered; of high humidity. **Wasser|rinne,** *f.* (*Build.*) gutter. **-rohr,** *n.*, **-röhre,** *f.* water-pipe. **-rutschbahn,** *f.* water-chute. **-sack,** *m.* watery cyst; water trap (*of pipe*); canvas bucket. **-schacht,** *m.* draining-shaft (*in a mine*). **-schaden,** *m.* flood damage. **-scheide,** *f.* watershed, (*Am.*) divide. **wasserscheu,** *adj.* afraid of water. **Wasser|-scheu,** *f.* hydrophobia. **-schlange,** *f.* sea-serpent; (*Astr.*) Hydra. **-schlauch,** *m.* water-hose; (*Bot.*) bladder wort (*Utricularia*). **-schmätzer,** *m.* (*Orn.*)

see **-amsel. -schwebegesellschaften,** *f.pl.* plankton. **-schwere,** *f.* specific gravity of water. **-semmel,** *f.* plain roll. **Wassersnot,** *f.* floods, inundation. **Wasser|speicher,** *m.* tank, reservoir. **-speier,** *m.* gargoyle. **-sperre,** *f.* water obstacle. **-spiegel,** *m.* surface of the water; water level; expanse of water. **-sport,** *m.* aquatic sports. **-spülung,** *f.* flushing. **-stand,** *m.* state of the tide, water-level. **-standsanzeiger,** *m.*, **-standsglas,** *n.*, **-standsmesser,** *m.* water-level indicator. **-star,** *m.* (*Orn.*) *see* **-amsel. -staub,** *m.* spray. **-stein,** *m.* incrustation, scale. **-stiefel,** *m.pl.* waders, gum-boots.

Wasserstoff ['vasərʃtɔf], *m.* hydrogen; ***schwerer* –,** heavy hydrogen, deuterium. **wasserstoffblond,** *adj.* peroxide blond, bleached. **Wasserstoffbombe,** *f.* hydrogen *or* H-bomb. **wasserstoffhaltig,** *adj.* hydrogenous. **Wasserstoffsuperoxyd,** *n.* hydrogen peroxide.

Wasser|strahl, *m.* jet of water; (*fig.*) ***kalter* –,** cold water. **-straße,** *f.* channel (*of a river*), navigable river, waterway, canal; ocean highway. **-sucht,** *f.* dropsy. **wassersüchtig,** *adj.* dropsical, hydropic. **Wasser|suppe,** *f.* gruel. **-tier,** *n.* aquatic animal. **-tor,** *n.* flood-gate. **-träger,** *m.* water-carrier. **-transport,** *m.* carriage *or* transportation *or* conveyance by water. **-treten,** *n.* (*Swimming*) treading water. **-treter,** *m.* (*Orn.*) ***Halsband*--** or ***schmalschnäbeliger* –,** *see* **Odinshühnchen;** ***plattschnäbeliger*** or ***rostroter* –,** *see* **Thorshühnchen. -trog,** *m.* water-trough. **-tropfen,** *m.* drop of water. **-turm,** *m.* water-tower. **-uhr,** *f.* water-gauge. **-umschlag,** *m.* cold-water compress.

Wässerung ['vɛsəruŋ], *f.* watering, irrigation; soaking, steeping, maceration, (*Phot.*) washing, (*Chem.*) hydration.

wasserunlöslich ['vasərˀunlø:zlɪç], *adj.* insoluble in water. **Wasser|verdrängung,** *f.* displacement (*of water*). **-versorgung,** *f.* water-supply. **-vögel,** *m.pl.* waterfowl, aquatic birds. **-wa(a)ge,** *f.* spirit-level. **-weg,** *m.* waterway; ***Verkehr auf dem* –,** waterborne traffic, traffic by water. **-welle,** *f.* (*Hairdressing*) water-wave. **-werk,** *n.* waterworks. **-wirtschaft,** *f.* water conservation, water-supply. **-wüste,** *f.* watery waste. **-zeichen,** *n.* watermark (*in paper*); ***mit* –,** watermarked. **-zement,** *m. or n.* hydraulic cement. **-zins,** *m.* water-rate.

wäßrig, *adj. See* **wässerig.**

Wat [va:t], *f.* (-, *no pl.*) (*obs., Poet.*) garment, garb, raiment.

Wate ['va:tə], *f.* (*dial.*) drag-net.

waten ['va:tən], *v.i.* (*aux.* h. & s.) wade, paddle.

Watsche ['vatʃə], *f.* (*dial.*) box on the ear, (*sl.*) clout.

watschelig ['vatʃəlɪç], *adj.* (*coll.*) waddling. **watscheln,** *v.i.* (*aux.* h. & s.) (*coll.*) waddle.

[1]**Watt** [vat], *n.* **(-(e)s,** *pl.* **-e)** (*usu. pl.*) sandbank, shoal, mud-flat, shallows.

[2]**Watt,** *n.* **(-s,** *pl.* **-)** (*Elec.*) watt.

[1]**Watte** ['vatə], *f. See* [1]**Watt.**

[2]**Watte,** *f.* wadding, cotton-wool. **Wattebausch,** *m.* wad *or* swab of cotton-wool.

Watten|fahrer, *m.* shallow-draught coasting vessel. **-fischerei,** *f.* inshore *or* shoal fishing. **-meer,** *n.* shoals, shallows, mud-flats.

Watte|pfropfen, *m. See* **-bausch.**

wattieren [va'ti:rən], *v.t.* wad, line with wadding, pad; (*coll.*) ***ihm die Backen* –,** slap his face.

Watt|leistung, *f.*, **-verbrauch,** *m.*, **-zahl,** *f.* (*Elec.*) wattage.

Watvogel ['va:tfo:gəl], *m.* wading bird, wader (*Limicolae*).

Wau [vau], *m.* **(-(e)s,** *pl.* **-e)** (*Bot.*) dyer's weed (*Reseda luteola*). **Waugelb,** *n.* luteolin.

wauwau ['vauvau], *int.* (*nursery talk*) bow-wow. **Wauwau,** *m.* **(-s,** *pl.* **-s)** bow-wow, doggie.

Webe ['ve:bə], *f.* piece of weaving, web, tissue. **Webe|kante,** *f.* selvage. **-leine,** *f.* (*Naut.*) ratline. **weben, 1.** *reg.v.t., v.i.* (*Poet., Swiss irr.v.t., v.i.*) weave. **2.** *reg.v.i.* (*Poet.*) move, be active; wave, float; (*B.*) ***in Ihm leben, – und sind wir,*** in Him we live and move and have our being; ***alles lebt und webt,*** everything is full of life *or* activity.

Weber ['ve:bər], *m.* weaver. **Weber|baum,** *m.* weaver's beam, warp-beam, yarn-roller. **-distel,** *f.* (*Bot.*) fuller's teasel (*Dipsacus fullonum*). **Weberei** [–'raɪ], *f.* weaving; woven material; weaving-mill. **Weber|einschlag, -eintrag,** *m.* woof, weft. **-gesell,** *m.* journeyman weaver. **Weberin,** *f. See* **Weber. Weber|kamm,** *m.* weaver's reed. **-knecht,** *m.* (*Ent.*) daddy-long-legs (*Phalangium*). **-knoten,** *m.* reef knot. **-lade,** *f.* batten, lathe of the loom. **-schiffchen,** *n.* shuttle.

Web|fehler, *m.* flaw in the weaving. **-stoff,** *m.* textile, fabric, woven material. **-stuhl,** *m.* (weaver's) loom. **-waren,** *f.pl.* woven *or* textile goods, textiles.

Wechsel ['vɛksəl], *m.* 1. change, alteration, turn; succession, alternation, rotation (*of crops etc.*); variation, fluctuation, vicissitude, reverse; relay (*of horses*); ***keinen – in Kleidern haben,*** have no change of clothes; 2. (*Comm.*) bill (of exchange), draft; ***einen – ausstellen,*** draw a bill (***auf*** (*Acc.*), on); ***eigener* –,** note of hand, promissory note; ***gezogener* –,** drawn bill, draft; ***indossierter* –,** endorsed bill (of exchange); ***kurzer* –,** bill at short date, short bill; ***langer* –,** long-dated *or* -sighted bill of exchange; ***offener* –,** letter of credit; ***– auf Sicht,*** sight bill, bill payable at sight; 3. (*Studs. sl.*) allowance; 4. (*Hunt.*) run, runway, haunt; 5. (*dial.*) (*Railw.*) points.

Wechsel|abrechnung, *f.* discount liquidation. **-agent,** *m.* bill-broker. **-agio,** *n.* exchange. **-akzept,** *n.* acceptance of a bill. **-balg,** *m.* changeling. **-beanspruchung,** *f.* alternating stress. **-bestand,** *m.* bill holdings, bills in hand. **-beziehung,** *f.* correlation, interrelation. **-brief,** *m.* (*obs.*) bill of exchange. **-bürge,** *m.* guarantor of a bill. **-bürgschaft,** *f.* collateral acceptance on a bill. **-diskont,** *m.* bill-discount. **-diskontierung,** *f.* discounting of bills. **wechselfähig,** *adj.* authorized to draw bills of exchange. **Wechsel|fall,** *m.* alternative (case). **-fälle,** *m.pl.* vicissitudes, (*coll.*) ups and downs. **wechselfarbig,** *adj.* iridescent. **Wechsel|fieber,** *n.* intermittent fever, malaria. **-folge,** *f.* alternation, rotation, succession. **-frist,** *f.* usance. **-geber,** *m.* drawer (of a bill). **-geld,** *n.* (*Comm.*) exchange, agio, (*coll.*) (small) change. **-gesang,** *m.* antiphony. **-gespräch,** *n.* dialogue. **-getriebe,** *n.* variable gear. **-giro,** *n.* endorsement (on a bill of exchange). **-gläubiger,** *m.* holder of a bill of exchange. **-handel,** *m.* bill-broking. **-händler,** *m. See* **-agent. -inhaber,** *m. See* **-gläubiger. -inkassogeschäft,** *n.* collection of bills of exchange. **-jahre,** *n.pl.* menopause, climacteric, change of life. **-konto,** *n.* account of exchange, bill account. **-kredit,** *m.* acceptance *or* discount credit. **-kurs,** *m.* rate of exchange, foreign exchange rate. **-lager,** *n.* (*Mech.*) double-thrust bearing. **-laufzeit,** *f.* currency of a bill. **-makler,** *m. See* **-agent.**

wechseln ['vɛksəln], **1.** *v.t., v.i.* (*aux.* h. & s.) change, vary; alternate, change places (***mit,*** with). **2.** *v.t.* exchange, interchange; ***Worte mit ihm* –,** bandy words with him; ***Briefe mit ihm* –,** exchange letters *or* correspond *or* be in correspondence with him; ***– Sie mir diese Note!*** give me change for this note; ***den Besitzer* –,** change hands; ***die Farbe* –,** change colour, (*fig.*) change sides; ***die Kleider* –,** change (one's clothes); ***seinen Wohnort* –,** move (house); ***die Zähne* –,** cut one's new *or* second teeth.

Wechsel|nehmer, *m.* payee, taker *or* buyer of a bill of exchange. **-pari,** *n.* par of exchange. **-pfennig,** *m.* nest-egg. **-protest,** *m.* bill-protest; ***– einlegen,*** have a bill protested. **-rechnung,** *f.* exchange account. **-recht,** *n.* law relating to bills of exchange. **-rede,** *f.* dialogue, discussion. **-reiten,** *n.*, **-reiterei,** *f.* bill-jobbing; speculation in accommodation bills, (*sl.*) kite-flying. **-richter,** *m.* (*Elec.*) inverter. **-satz,** *m.* (*Math., Log.*) converse. **-schalter,** *m.* (*Elec.*) change-over switch. **-schaltung,** *f.* (*Elec.*) alternate switching. **wechselseitig,** *adj.* mutual, reciprocal. **Wechsel|-**

seitigkeit, *f.* reciprocity. **–spiel,** *n.* interplay. **wechselständig,** *adj.* (*Bot.*) alternate. **Wechsel|strom,** *m.* (*Elec.*) alternating current. **–stube,** *f.* (currency) exchange-office. **–tierchen,** *n.* amoeba. **–verbindlichkeiten,** *f.pl.* bills payable. **–verjährung,** *f.* prescription of a bill of exchange. **–verkehr,** *m.* (*Tele.*) two-way communication. **wechselvoll,** *adj.* changeable, eventful. **Wechselweide,** *f.* temporary pasture. **wechselweise,** *adv.* mutually, reciprocally, alternately. **Wechsel|wild,** *n.* migratory game. **–winkel,** *m.pl.* (*Geom.*) alternate angles. **–wirkung,** *f.* reciprocal action, interaction, mutual effect. **–wirtschaft,** *f.* rotation-system in farming. **–zahn,** *m.* milk-tooth. **–zersetzung,** *f.* double decomposition.

Wechsler ['vɛkslər], *m.* money-changer.

Weck [vɛk], *m.* (**-(e)s,** *pl.* **-e**), **Wecke,** *f.*, **Wecken,** *m.* (*dial.*) (breakfast-)roll.

wecken ['vɛkən], *v.t.* wake, waken, awaken, rouse; ***Bedarf –,*** create a need; *see* **geweckt. Wecken,** *n.* waking, awakening, (*Mil.*) reveille. **Wecker,** *m.* 1. knocker-up; 2. alarm clock; 3. buzzer. **Weckerruf,** *m.* (*Mil.*) reveille.

Wedel ['ve:dəl], *m.* fan; whisk, feather-duster; tail, brush (*of foxes etc.*); (*Bot.*) frond. **wedeln,** *v.t.*, *v.i.* fan; ***mit dem Schwanz –,*** wag its tail.

weder ['ve:dər], *conj.* neither; ***– er noch ich,*** neither he nor I.

Weg [ve:k], *m.* (**-(e)s,** *pl.* **-e**) way, road, path, course, direction, route, passage; (*Mech.*) travel; way, manner, method, means; walk, errand, business; ***am –e,*** by the roadside *or* wayside; ***auf dem –e,*** on the way; (*fig.*) in a fair way; ***auf dem –e über*** (*Acc.*), by way of, via, (*fig.*) through (the channel of); ***auf diplomatischem –e,*** through diplomatic channels; ***sich auf den – machen*** or ***begeben,*** set off *or* out, start; ***Glück auf den –!*** good luck! a pleasant journey to you! ***die S. ist auf gutem –e,*** the matter is making satisfactory progress; ***auf gütlichem –e,*** amicably; ***auf halbem –e stehenbleiben,*** stop halfway; ***ihm auf halbem –e entgegenkommen,*** meet him half-way; ***auf den rechten – bringen,*** put in the right way; ***auf dem richtigen –e sein,*** be on the right track; ***aus dem –e gehen*** (*Dat.*), get out of the way of, stand aside from, (*fig.*) avoid, evade, steer clear of, dodge, shirk; ***aus dem –e räumen,*** remove, kill, liquidate, (*sl.*) bump off; ***bedeckter –,*** covert-way; ***den – bereiten,*** pave the way (*Dat.*, for); ***neue –e beschreiten,*** apply *or* adopt new methods, take new steps; ***geht Eures –es!*** be off! go your way! mind your own business! ***lassen Sie ihn seiner –e gehen!*** let him alone! let him go his own way; (*Prov.*) ***der gerade – ist der beste,*** honesty is the best policy; ***es hat damit gute –e!*** there is no hurry for that! there is plenty of time; ***ihm in den – laufen*** or ***kommen,*** get in his way; ***in die –e leiten,*** prepare, pave the way for, initiate, set on foot; ***im –e Rechtens,*** by law; ***ihm im –e stehen,*** be *or* stand in his way; ***sich*** (*Dat.*) ***selbst im –e stehen,*** stand in one's own light; ***ihm in den – treten, sich ihm in den – stellen,*** thwart *or* oppose him; ***–(e) und Steg(e) kennen,*** know one's way (about), know all the ins and outs; ***–e machen,*** go errands, do the shopping; ***die Mitte des –es,*** midway; ***er weiß Mittel und –e,*** he has ways and means; ***seinen ruhigen – fortgehen,*** go on in one's own quiet way; ***ich traue ihm nicht über den –,*** I do not trust him out of my sight; ***verbotener –!*** no thoroughfare; ***woher des –s?*** where do you come from? (*Poet.*) whence do you come? ***wohin des –s?*** where are you off to? (*Poet.*) whither are you going? ***der – zum Erfolg,*** the road to success; *see* **zuwege.**

weg [vɛk], *adv.* away, gone, (far) off; lost; ***ich muß –,*** I must be off; ***Hände –!*** hands off! ***– damit!*** away with it! take it away! ***– da!*** be *or* clear off! ***das Haus liegt weit – von der Straße,*** the house stands *or* lies far (back) from the road; (*coll.*) ***ganz*** or ***rein – sein,*** be quite beside o.s. (***vor*** (*Dat.*), with), be in raptures *or* ecstasies (***über*** (*Acc.*), over *or* about); ***– wie der Blitz,*** off like a shot; (*coll.*) ***frisch von der Leber –,*** straight out, without frills.

wegbekommen ['vɛkbəkɔmən], *irr.v.t.* succeed in removing, (*coll.*) (*fig.*) get the knack *or* hang of; (*sl.*) ***eins –,*** stop one.

Wegbereiter ['ve:kbəraɪtər], *m.* pioneer, forerunner; ***der – sein für,*** pave the way for.

weg|blasen ['vɛk–], *irr.v.t.* blow away *or* off; (*coll.*) ***wie weggeblasen,*** without leaving a trace, clean gone. **–bleiben,** *irr.v.i.* (*aux.* s.) stay away; be left out *or* omitted; ***bleiben Sie davon weg!*** do not meddle with it! leave it alone! (*coll.*) ***ihm blieb die Spucke weg,*** he was flabbergasted. **–blicken,** *v.i.* look away. **–bringen,** *irr.v.t.* take away, remove; take out (*stains*). **–denken,** *irr.v.t.* imagine as absent *or* non-existent; ***aus dem Leben ist das Fernsehen kaum wegzudenken,*** life is almost unthinkable without the T.V., one can scarcely imagine life without T.V.

Wege|abgabe ['ve:gə–], *f.* (highway) toll. **–bau,** *m.* road construction. **–dorn,** *m.* (*Bot.*) buckthorn (*Rhamnus catharticus*). **–gabel,** *f.* fork in the road. **–geld,** *n.* travelling *or* mileage allowance; *see also* **–abgabe. –lagerer,** *m.* highwayman. **–macher,** *m.* roadman, road mender.

wegen ['ve:gən], *prep.* (*preceding or following Gen.* (*dial. Dat.*)) (*coll. also* ***von –***) because of, by reason of, on account of; in consequence of, as a result of, due *or* owing to; for (the sake of), on behalf of; in consideration of, with regard to, regarding; ***der Kürze –,*** for brevity's sake, to be brief; ***von Amts –,*** by virtue of one's office, ex officio; ***von Rechts –,*** by right.

Wege|netz ['ve:gə–], *n.* road network *or* system. **–recht,** *n.* right of way.

Wegerich ['ve:gərɪç], *m.* (**-s,** *pl.* **-e**) (*Bot.*) plantain (*Plantago major*).

weg|essen ['vɛk–], *irr.v.t.* eat up, (*sl.*) polish off. **–fahren, 1.** *irr.v.t.* cart away. **2.** *v.i.* (*aux.* s.) drive away *or* off, sail away, depart, set off *or* out.

Wegfall ['vɛkfal], *m.* omission, suppression; cessation, abolition; (*Law*) lapse; ***in – bringen,*** suppress, abolish; ***in – kommen,*** be omitted *or* suppressed *or* abolished. **wegfallen,** *irr.v.i.* (*aux.* s.) fall away *or* off; be omitted *or* suppressed *or* (*coll.*) dropped; be abolished *or* cancelled, become void, lapse; cease, come to nothing, not take place; ***– lassen,*** suppress, omit, leave out, (*coll.*) drop; abolish, cancel, discard.

weg|fieren ['vɛk–], *v.i.* (*Naut.*) lower away the boats. **–fischen,** *v.t.* (*coll.*) ***ihm etwas –,*** snatch s.th. from under his nose. **–führen,** *v.t.* lead *or* take away, carry off. **–führend,** *adj.* (*Med.*) efferent.

Weggang ['vɛkgaŋ], *m.* departure, leaving.

weg|geben ['vɛk–], *irr.v.t.* give away, dispose of; send away (*to school etc.*). **–gehen,** *irr.v.i.* (*aux.* s.) go away, depart; ***wie warme Semmeln –,*** sell like hot cakes; (*fig.*) ***– über*** (*Acc.*), pass over; ***geh mir weg damit!*** drop the subject! **–haben,** *irr.v.t.* have received (one's share of); (*coll.*) have got the knack *or* hang of; ***er hat es gleich weg,*** he sees it *or* the point at once; (*sl.*) ***der hat aber einen weg,*** he's had one over the eight. **–helfen,** *irr.v.i.* (*Dat.*) help (*s.o.*) to get away. **–jagen, 1.** *v.t.* drive *or* chase away *or* off, expel. **2.** *v.i.* (*aux.* s.) gallop off. **–kapern,** *v.t.* (*coll.*) *see* **–fischen. –kommen,** *irr.v.i.* (*aux.* s.) get away *or* off; be *or* get lost, be missing; ***gut*** (***schlecht***) ***–,*** come off well (badly); ***am schlimmsten –,*** get the worst of it; (*fig.*) ***– über*** (*Acc.*), get over. **–lassen,** *irr.v.t.* (*a th.*) leave out, omit; (*a p.*) let go. **Weglassung,** *f.* omission. **weglegen,** *v.t.* put away *or* aside, lay down *or* aside.

Wegleitung ['ve:klaɪtuŋ], *f.* (*Swiss*) direction, instruction.

wegmachen ['vɛkmaxən], **1.** *v.t.* take away, remove, take out (*stains etc.*), obliterate. **2.** *v.r.* (*coll.*) make off, make o.s. scarce.

Weg|markierung ['ve:k–], *f.* route marker *or* indicator. **–messer,** *m.* odometer, mileage indicator.

wegmüssen ['vɛkmysən], *irr.v.i.* be obliged to leave, (*coll.*) have to be off *or* to go; ***das muß weg,*** that must go.

Wegnahme ['vɛkna:mə], *f.* taking (away), elimination; seizure, capture, confiscation. **wegnehmen,** *irr.v.t.* take away, remove (*Dat.*, from); carry off, confiscate; (*space etc.*) occupy, take up; ***ihm etwas*** –, rob him of a th.; (*Motor.*) ***Gas*** –, throttle down, reduce speed, (*coll.*) take one's foot off (the gas).

weg|packen ['vɛk–], **1.** *v.t.* pack *or* put away. **2.** *v.r.* (*coll.*) pack off, make o.s. scarce, (*sl.*) scram. **–putzen,** *v.t.* brush *or* wipe off; (*sl.*) pick off, drop (*with a shot*). **–radieren,** *v.t.* erase, rub out. **–raffen,** *v.t.* carry off (*as disease*). **–räumen,** *v.t.* remove, clear away, tidy up. **–reisen,** *v.i.* (*aux.* s.) depart, set out *or* off (on a journey). **–reißen,** *irr.v.t.* tear *or* snatch *or* pull off *or* away; (*of a storm*) carry *or* sweep away; (*house etc.*) demolish, pull down. **–rücken, 1.** *v.t.* move away, remove. **2.** *v.i.* (*aux.* s.) make way, move *or* edge away *or* aside. **–schaffen,** *reg.v.t.* clear away, carry off, remove, get rid of, do away with; (*Math.*) eliminate.

Weg|scheid ['ve:k–], *m.* **(-s,** *pl.* **-e)** *or* (*Austr.*) *f.* (-, *pl.* **-en**), **–scheide,** *f.* fork in the road.

weg|scheren ['vɛk–], *reg.v.r.* (*imper. only*) (*coll.*) be off, vamoose, (*sl.*) do a bunk, scram. **–schicken,** *v.t.* send off *or* away, dispatch, (*coll.*) (*a p.*) send packing. **–schleichen,** *irr.v.i.* (*aux.* s.) steal away, sneak off. **–schließen,** *irr.v.t.* lock up *or* away, put under lock and key. **–schmeißen,** *irr.v.t.* throw *or* fling *or* toss away. **–schnappen,** *v.t.* snatch away (*Dat.*, from).

Wegschnecke ['vɛkʃnɛkə], *f.* (*Zool.*) slug (*Arionidae*).

weg|schütten ['vɛk–], *v.t.* pour away (*liquids*), throw away, jettison, (*coll.*) dump. **–sehen,** *irr.v.i.* look away; – ***über*** (*Acc.*), overlook, shut one's eyes to, (*coll.*) wink at. **–sein,** *irr.v.i.* be absent *or* away, be gone; not be at home, not be in, be out; (*of a th.*) be lost *or* gone; – ***über*** (*Acc.*), be past, have passed. **–setzen, 1.** *v.t.* lay aside, put away. **2.** *v.r.* ***sich*** – ***über*** (*Acc.*), disregard, ignore, not trouble about. **3.** *v.i.* (*aux.* s.) – ***über*** (*Acc.*), jump over, clear. **–spülen,** *v.t.* wash *or* rinse *or* swill away. **–stecken,** *v.t.* put away, hide. **–sterben,** *irr.v.i.* die off. **–stoßen,** *irr.v.t.* push *or* thrust away *or* aside. **–streben,** *v.i.* tend (away) (***von,*** from).

Wegstrecke ['ve:kʃtrɛkə], *f.* stretch of road; distance (covered), mileage.

weg|streichen ['vɛk-], **1.** *irr.v.t.* smooth away *or* off; erase, cancel, strike out. **2.** *irr,v.i.* (*aux.* s.) fly away, depart (*of birds*). **–treiben, 1.** *irr.v.t.* drive away *or* off. **2.** *irr.v.i.* (*aux.* s.) drift away *or* off. **–treten,** *irr.v.i.* (*aux.* s.) step aside; (*Mil.*) dismiss, fall out; ***weggetreten!*** dismiss! **–tun,** *irr.v.t.* put away *or* aside, set *or* lay aside; remove; ***tu die Hände weg!*** (keep your) hands off!

Wegweiser ['ve:kvaɪzər], *m.* signpost, road sign; guide (book).

weg|wenden ['vɛk–], *irr.v.t.* turn away *or* aside; ***mit weggewandtem Gesicht,*** with averted face. **–werfen, 1.** *irr.v.t.* throw away, cast off, jettison, reject; (*Cards*) throw down *or* away. **2.** *irr.v.r.* (*fig.*) throw o.s. away (***an*** (*Acc.*), on), degrade o.s. **–werfend,** *adj.* disparaging, disdainful, contemptuous, deprecatory. **–wischen,** *v.t.* wipe away *or* off, efface. **–zaubern,** *v.t.* spirit away.

Wegzehrung ['ve:ktse:ruŋ], *f.* food *or* provisions for the journey; (*R.C.*) ***letzte*** –, viaticum.

wegziehen ['vɛktsi:ən], **1.** *irr.v.t.* draw *or* pull away *or* off, draw aside, withdraw. **2.** *irr.v.i.* (*aux.* s.) withdraw, depart; march off *or* away; move (house), change one's address *or* residence; go somewhere else. **Wegzug,** *m.* move, removal; departure; migration.

weh [ve:], **1.** *int.* alas! oh dear! – ***mir!*** woe is me! – ***ihm, wenn . . .!*** woe betide him if . . .! **2.** *adj.* painful, sore, aching; ***–er Finger,*** sore finger; ***–es Gefühl,*** pangs of sorrow; ***mit –em Herzen,*** with heavy *or* aching heart; ***es ist mir – zumute*** or ***– ums Herz,*** my heart aches; ***sich – tun,*** hurt o.s.; ***mir tut der Kopf –,*** my head hurts; ***ihm – tun,*** hurt him, cause him pain, (*fig.*) grieve *or* wound *or* offend him; ***ihm tut kein Zahn mehr –,*** he is beyond the reach of pain. **Weh,** *n.* **(-s,** *pl.* **-e)** pain, ache, (*fig.*) grief, woe; ***Ach und –,*** plaint, lament; ***Wohl und –,*** weal and woe.

Wehe ['ve:ə], *f.* snowdrift; sand-drift.

Wehen ['ve:ən], *pl.* labour(-pains) (*childbirth*).

wehen, 1. *v.t.* blow *or* waft away *or* along. **2.** *v.i.* wave, flutter; drift; (*fig.*) ***wissen woher der Wind weht,*** know which way the wind blows.

Weh|geschrei, *n.* wail(ing), howl(ing), cries of pain. **–klage,** *f.* lament(ation). **weh|klagen,** *v.i.* (*insep.*) lament (*über* (*Acc.*), over); – ***um,*** bewail. **–leidig,** *adj.* plaintive, tearful, woebegone, (*coll.*) snivelling; (*pred.*) sorry for o.s. **Wehmut,** *f.* sadness, melancholy, wistfulness. **weh|mütig, –mutsvoll,** *adj.* sad, melancholy, wistful. **Wehmutter,** *f.* midwife.

[1]**Wehr** [ve:r], *n.* **(-(e)s,** *pl.* **-e)** weir, spillway; dam, dike, barrage.

[2]**Wehr,** *f.* defence, resistance; bulwark; weapon, arm, armour, military equipment; ***sich zur – setzen*** or ***stellen,*** struggle, offer resistance, show fight, (*coll.*) put up a fight; ***mit – und Waffen,*** fully armed; (*Poet.*) ***schimmernde –,*** shining armour.

Wehr|auftrag, *m.* defence contract. **–bereich,** *m.* military district. **–bereitschaft,** *f.* military preparedness. **–bezirk,** *m.* military sub-area. **–dienst,** *m.* military service. **–dienstbeschädigung,** *f.* disability due to military service. **–drüse,** *f.* (*Zool.*) defensive scent-gland.

wehren ['ve:rən], **1.** *v.i.* (*Dat.*) restrain, check, control, arrest; ***dem Feuer –,*** arrest the spread of the fire. **2.** *v.t.* ***ihm etwas –,*** hinder *or* prevent *or* keep him from doing s.th., forbid him to do a th.; ***wer will es –?*** who will prevent it? **3.** *v.r.* defend o.s.(***gegen,*** against), offer resistance (to); ***sich mit Händen und Füßen –,*** fight tooth and nail, put up a fierce resistance.

Wehrertüchtigung ['ve:rˀɛrtyçtɪguŋ], *f.* premilitary training. **wehr|fähig,** *adj.* able-bodied, fit for military service. **–fliegertauglich,** *adj.* (*Av.*) fit for flying duties. **–freudig,** *adj.* military-minded. **Wehr|gehänge, –gehenk,** *n.* sword-belt. **–gesetz,** *n.* national defence regulations. **wehrhaft,** *adj.* militant, valiant; *see* **wehrfähig. Wehr|-hoheit,** *f.* military sovereignty. **–kraft,** *f.* military strength *or* potential. **wehrlos,** *adj.* unarmed, defenceless; weak, helpless; – ***machen,*** disarm. **Wehr|macht,** *f.* armed services *or* forces. **–machtsbericht,** *m.* army communiqué. **–machtseigentum,** *n.* property of the War Department. **–meldeamt,** *n.* recruiting station. **–ordnung,** *f.* army regulations. **–paß,** *m.* serviceman's papers, service record book. **–pflicht,** *f.* compulsory military service. **wehrpflichtig,** *adj.* liable for military service. **Wehr|pflichtige(r),** *m.* conscript. **–politik,** *f.* national defence policy. **–sold,** *m.* basic (service-)pay. **–sport,** *m.* paramilitary physical training. **–vorlage,** *f.* (*Parl.*) defence bill. **–wissenschaft,** *f.* military science.

Weib [vaɪp], *n.* **(-(e)s,** *pl.* **-er)** woman; (*Poet., dial.*) wife; ***er nimmt sie sich*** (*Dat.*) ***zum –e,*** he takes her for his wife. **Weibchen,** *n.* female (animal), hen (bird); (*coll.*) wifie.

Weibel ['vaɪbəl], *m.* (*dial.*) bailiff, (*obs.*) sergeant. **weibeln,** *v.i.* (*Swiss*) make propaganda.

Weiber|art ['vaɪbər–], *f.* woman's (silly) ways. **–feind,** *m.* woman-hater, misogynist. **–geschwätz, –gewäsch,** *n.* women's gossip *or* cackle. **–held,** *m.* lady-killer, ladies' man. **–herrschaft,** *f.* petticoat government. **–list,** *f.* woman's wiles. **–narr,** *m.* *See* **–held. –regiment,** *n.* *See* **–herrschaft. –stamm,** *m.* female line. **–volk,** *n.* women(folk).

–weibig ['vaɪbɪç], *adj.suff.* (*Bot.*) -pistilled, *e.g.* ***drei–,*** having three pistils. **weibisch,** *adj.* womanish, effeminate.

weiblich ['vaɪplɪç], *adj.* female, (*also Gram.*) feminine, womanly; (*Bot.*) pistillate; ***–e Keimzelle,*** megaspore; ***–er Vorkern,*** egg nucleus. **weiblicherseits,** *adv.* on the female side, in the female line. **Weiblichkeit.** *f.* womanhood, womanliness; feminine nature *or* ways *or* weakness; ***die holde –,*** the fair sex.

Weibsbild ['vaɪpsbɪlt], (*dial.*) **Weibsen,** *n.* female, (*sl.*) skirt. **Weibs|leute,** *pl.* (*coll.*) womenfolk, females. **–person,** *f.*, **–stück,** *n.* (*vulg.*) *see* **–bild.**

weich [vaɪç], *adj.* soft, smooth, mellow; gentle, mild, tender (*also of meat*); effeminate, weak, yielding, pliant; sensitive, impressible, soft(-hearted); ductile, pliable, supple; *– **gesottenes*** or ***gekochtes Ei,*** soft-boiled egg; ***Fleisch – kochen,*** boil meat until tender; ***mir wird ganz – ums Herz,*** I feel deeply touched *or* moved; (*fig.*) *–* ***werden,*** relent, yield, give way, be moved.

Weichbild ['vaɪçbɪlt], *n.* municipal area, city boundaries; outskirts, precincts.

Weich|blei, *n.* refined lead. **–bottich,** *m.* steeping vat.

[1]**Weiche** ['vaɪçə], *f.* (*Poet.*) softness; (*Anat.*) flank, side; *pl.* groin.

[2]**Weiche,** *f.* (*Railw.*) points, (*Am.*) switch; ***die –n stellen,*** move the points, (*Am.*) shift the switch.

[1]**weichen** ['vaɪçən], **1.** *v.t.* make soft, soften, steep, soak. **2.** *v.i.* (*aux.* h. *&* s.) become soft, grow tender *or* mellow.

[2]**weichen,** *irr.v.i.* (*aux.* s.) yield, give in; give way, give ground (*Dat.*, to); (*Mil.*) fall back, withdraw, retire, retreat (*Dat.*, before); (*Comm.*) recede, fall, sag, ease off (*of prices*); ***nicht von der Stelle –,*** not budge an inch; ***von ihm –,*** leave *or* abandon *or* desert him.

Weichen|band, *n.* inguinal ligament. **–gegend,** *f.* groin. **–signal,** *n.* points (*Am.* switch) signal. **–steller,** *m.* pointsman, (*Am.*) switchman.

weich|geglüht, *adj.* (*Metall.*) soft-annealed. **–haarig,** *adj.* soft-haired, pilose, pubescent. **Weichheit,** *f.* softness, smoothness, suppleness, plasticity; tenderness, mellowness, mildness, gentleness, sensibility; permeability. **weichherzig,** *adj.* soft- *or* tender-hearted. **Weichkäse,** *m.* cream-cheese. **weichlich,** *adj.* soft, flabby, weak, feeble, effeminate, (*sl.*) sloppy; indolent, tame, spiritless, insipid. **Weichling,** *m.* (**-s,** *pl.* **-e**) weakling, milksop, (*sl.*) sissy, sap. **weichlöten,** *v.t.* (*sep.*) soft-solder. **Weichmacher,** *m.* softener, softening agent, plasticizer.

[1]**Weichsel** ['vaɪksəl], *f.* River Vistula.

[2]**Weichsel,** *f.* (-, *pl.* **-n**), **Weichsel|kirsche,** *f.* (*Bot.*) morello *or* mahaleb *or* perfumed cherry (*Prunus cerasus*). **–rohr,** *n.* cherry-wood pipe. **–zopf,** *m.* elf-lock, Polish plait.

Weich|teile, *m.pl.* (*Anat.*) abdomen, belly, underside. **–tier,** *n.* mollusc.

Weid [vaɪt], *f.* (*obs.*) hunt, chase (*only in compounds see below*).

[1]**Weide** ['vaɪdə], *f.* pasture, pasturage, meadow; ***auf die – treiben,*** turn out to grass, drive to pasture.

[2]**Weide,** *f.* (*Bot.*) willow, osier (*Salix*).

Weide|koppel, *f.* grazing paddock. **–land,** *n.* pasture(land). **weiden, 1.** *v.i.* graze. **2.** *v.t.* lead *or* drive to pasture, turn out to grass; tend, feed (*a flock*). **3.** *v.r.* (*fig.*) feast one's eyes (***an*** (*Dat.*), on), delight *or* revel (in), gloat (over).

Weiden|ammer, *f.* (*Orn.*) yellow-breasted bunting (*Emberiza aureola*). **–geflecht,** *n.* wickerwork. **–gerte,** *f.* willow twig, osier-switch. **–kätzchen,** *n.* willow catkin. **–korb,** *m.* wicker basket. **–laubsänger,** *m.* (*Orn.*) *see* **Zilpzalp. –meise,** *f.* (*Orn.*) willow-tit, (*Am.*) black-capped chickadee (*Parus atricapillus*). **–röschen,** *n.* (*Bot.*) ***zottiges –,*** willow-herb (*Epilobium hirsutum*). **–rute,** *f. See* **–gerte. –sperling,** *m.* (*Orn.*) Spanish sparrow (*Passer hispaniolensis*).

Weide|platz, *m.* pasture ground, pasturage, grazing place. **–recht,** *n.* pasture rights.

Weiderich ['vaɪdərɪç], *m.* (*Bot.*) purple loosestrife (*Lythrum salicaria*).

weidgerecht ['vaɪtgərɛçt], *adj.* skilled in hunting *or* woodcraft; (*of animals*) trained to the chase.

weidlich ['vaɪtlɪç], *adv.* thoroughly, properly, to one's heart's content.

Weid|loch, *n.* anus (*of game*). **–mann,** *m.* (*pl.* ¨**er**) huntsman, sportsman. **weidmännisch,** *adj.* sporting. **Weid|mannsheil!** *int.* good hunting! **–mannssprache,** *f.* language of the chase. **–messer,** *n.* hunting-knife. **–ruf,** *m.* tally-ho, hue and cry. **–sack,** *m.*, **–tasche,** *f.* game-bag. **–werk,** *n.* hunt(ing), woodcraft, (*obs.*) venery; ***niederes –,*** small game. **weidwund,** *adj.* shot in the belly.

Weife ['vaɪfə], *f.* reel, spool. **weifen,** *v.t.*, *v.i.* wind, reel (*yarn*).

weigern ['vaɪgərn], **1.** *v.r.* refuse, decline, be unwilling. **2.** *v.t.* (*obs.*) *see* **verweigern. Weigerung,** *f.* refusal. **Weigerungsfall,** *m.* ***im –,*** in case of refusal *or* (*Comm.*) non-acceptance.

Weih [vaɪ], *m.* (**-en,** *pl.* **-en**) *see* [1]**Weihe.**

Weih|altar, *m.* consecrated altar. **–becken,** *n. See* **–wasserbecken. –bischof,** *m.* suffragan (bishop). **–brot,** *n.* consecrated bread.

[1]**Weihe** ['vaɪə], *m.* (**-n,** *pl.* **-n**) *or f.* (*Orn.*) kite (*Milvus*).

[2]**Weihe,** *f.* 1. consecration, dedication, inauguration; (*of a priest*) ordination, (*of a monk*) initiation; ***ihm die – erteilen,*** consecrate him in holy orders, ordain him; 2. solemn mood, solemnity. **weihen, 1.** *v.t.* consecrate; ***ihn zum Priester –,*** ordain him as a priest; ***sich – lassen,*** take holy orders; (*fig.*) ***dem Untergang geweiht,*** doomed to destruction. **2.** *v.r.* (*fig.*) devote o.s. (*Dat.*, to).

Weiher ['vaɪər], *m.* fishpond.

Weihe|stätte, *f.* shrine, sacred place. **–stunde,** *f.* hour of commemoration. **weihevoll,** *adj.* solemn.

Weih|gabe, *f.*, **–geschenk,** *n.* votive offering, oblation.

Weihnachten ['vaɪnaxtən], *f.pl.* Christmas. **Weihnachts|abend,** *m.* Christmas Eve. **–baum,** *m.* Christmas tree. **–fest,** *n. See* **Weihnachten. –geschenk,** *n.* Christmas present *or* gift *or* box. **–lied,** *n.* Christmas carol. **–mann,** *m.* Father Christmas, Santa Claus. **–rose,** *f.* (*Bot.*) Christmas *or* Lenten rose (*Helleborus niger*). **–spiel,** *n.* nativity play. **–tag,** *m.* ***erster –,*** Christmas Day; ***zweiter –,*** Boxing Day. **–zeit,** *f.* Christmas time, Yuletide.

Weih|rauch, *m.* incense, (*B.*) frankincense; (*fig.*) ***ihm – streuen,*** laud him to the skies, overwhelm him with flattery. **–rauchfaß,** *n.* censer. **–wasser,** *n.* holy water. **–wasserbecken,** *n.* font, aspersorium. **–wedel,** *m.* aspergillum.

weil [vaɪl], *conj.* 1. because, since; 2. (*obs., dial.*) while, as long as; ***freut euch des Lebens, weil noch das Lämpchen glüht,*** enjoy life while you may.

weiland ['vaɪlant], *adv.* (*obs.*) formerly, of old, erstwhile, quondam; (*of a p.*) late, deceased.

Weilchen ['vaɪlçən], *n.* (*coll.*) ***ein –,*** a little while, a bit. **Weile,** *f.* a (space of) time, a while; leisure; ***geraume –,*** a long time; ***damit hat es gute –,*** there is no hurry, we shall see; (*Prov.*) ***eile mit –,*** more haste less speed; (*Prov.*) ***gut Ding will – haben,*** nothing good is done in a hurry, haste makes waste; (*Poet.*) (***bei***) ***nächtlicher –,*** during the night. **weilen,** *v.i.* (*Poet.*) stay, stop, abide, sojourn; tarry, linger; ***er weilt nicht mehr unter uns,*** he is no longer with us, he has passed away.

Weiler ['vaɪlər], *m.* hamlet.

Weimutskiefer ['vaɪmu:tski:fər], *f.* (-, *pl.* **-n**) (*Bot.*) Weymouth pine.

Wein [vaɪn], *m.* (**-(e)s,** *pl.* **-e**) wine; vine; (*coll.*) ***ihm klaren*** or ***reinen – einschenken,*** tell him the whole *or* plain truth, speak plainly; ***beim – sitzen,*** sit over one's wine; ***Wasser in seinen – gießen,*** pour cold water on his enthusiasm; ***Wasser predigen und – trinken,*** not practise what one preaches; (*Bot.*) ***wilder –,*** Virginia creeper (*Parthenocissus quinquefolia*).

weinartig ['vaɪnˀa:rtɪç], *adj.* vinous, vinaceous. **Wein|bau,** *m.* wine-growing, viniculture. **–bauer,** *m.* wine-grower. **–beere,** *f.* grape. **–berg,** *m.* vineyard. **–bergschnecke,** *f.* edible snail. **–blatt,** *n.* vine-leaf. **–blattlaus,** *f.* phylloxera. **–brand,** *m.* brandy, cognac. **–drossel,** *f.* (*Orn.*) *see* **Rotdrossel.**

weinen ['vaɪnən], *v.t.*, *v.i.* weep, cry; ***um ihn –,*** shed tears over him; ***über etwas –,*** weep about *or* lament s.th.; ***vor Freude –***, weep for joy; ***sich*** (*Dat.*) ***die Augen rot –***, make one's eyes red with weeping; ***sich*** (*Acc.*) ***blind –, sich*** (*Dat.*) ***die Augen aus dem Kopfe –***, cry one's eyes out. **Weinen,** *n.* weeping, tears; ***zum – bringen,*** move to tears; ***dem – nahe,*** on the verge of tears; ***ihr war das – näher als das Lachen,*** she was nearer to tears than to laughter; (*coll.*) ***es ist zum –,*** it's a crying shame. **weinerlich,** *adj.* (*pred.*) inclined to weep, given to tears, (*attrib.*) lachrymose, tearful; whining, crying; (*coll.*) weepy; ***ihm ist – zu Mute,*** he is in a crying mood; ***in –em Tone,*** in a whimpering *or* whining tone; ***–es Lustspiel,*** comédie larmoyante, (*coll.*) sob-stuff drama.

Wein|ernte, *f.* vintage. **–erzeuger,** *m. See* **–bauer. –essig,** *m.* wine vinegar. **–faß,** *n.* wine-cask; (*fig.*) wine-bibber, toper. **–flasche,** *f.* wine-bottle. **–garten,** *m.* vineyard. **–gärtner,** *m.* vine-dresser. **–gegend,** *f.* wine-growing district. **–geist,** *m.* spirits of wine; ethyl alcohol. **–glas,** *n.* wine glass. **–händler,** *m.* vintner, wine-merchant. **–hauer,** *m.* (*Austr.*) *see* **–bauer. –hefe,** *f.* dregs *or* lees of wine, wine yeast. **–jahr,** *n.* year's wine crop, vintage. **–karaffe,** *f.* decanter. **–karte,** *f.* wine-list. **–keller,** *m.* wine-cellar, vaults. **–kelter,** *f.* wine-press. **–kenner,** *m.* connoisseur of wine.

Weinkrampf ['vaınkrampf], *m.* convulsive sobbing, (*coll.*) crying fit; *see* **Weinen.**

Wein|laub, *n.* vine-leaves. **–laune,** *f.* expansive mood; ***in*** (***einer***) ***–***, in one's cups. **–lese,** *f.* vintage; ***– halten,*** gather the grapes. **–leser,** *m.* vintager. **–met,** *m.* vinous hydromel. **–monat, –mond,** *m.* (*obs.*) October. **–most,** *m.* must. **–probe,** *f.* tasting of wine; sample of wine. **–ranke,** *f.* vine-branch *or* tendril. **–rebe,** *f.* grapevine. **–reisende(r),** *m.* traveller for a wine-firm. **–rose,** *f.* (*Bot.*) eglantine, sweet-brier (*Rosa rubiginosa*). **wein|rot,** *adj.* ruby-*or* claret-coloured. **–sauer,** *adj.* (*Chem.*) tartrate of. **Wein|säure,** *f.* tartaric acid. **–schank,** *m. See* **–keller. –schenk,** *m.* (*Hist.*) cup-bearer, butler. **–schenke,** *f. See* **–keller. –schlauch,** *m.* wine-skin; (*fig.*) wine-bibber. **weinselig,** *adj.* in one's cups, tipsy. **Weinstein,** *m.* (cream of) tartar, potassium bitartrate. **wein|steinsauer,** *adj. See* **–sauer. Wein|steinsäure,** *f. See* **–säure. –stock,** *m.* grapevine. **–stube,** *f.* tavern, wine-cellar. **–traube,** *f.* grape; bunch of grapes. **–treber, –trester,** *pl.* skins *or* husks of pressed grapes. **–waage,** *f.* wine-gauge. **–wirtschaft,** *f.* licensed house. **–zeche,** *f.* wine-bill. **–zierl,** *m.* (*Austr.*) *see* **–bauer. –zoll,** *m.* duty on wine. **–zwang,** *m.* obligation to take wine with one's meal.

weise ['vaızə], *adj.* wise; prudent, judicious; (*obs.*) ***– Frau,*** midwife; fortune-teller; ***– anordnen,*** make sensible arrangements; ***Weise(r),*** wise man, sage, philospher; ***Stein der Weisen,*** philosopher's stone; ***die Weisen aus dem Morgenlande,*** the (three) wise men from the East.

Weise, *f.* manner, way, method; style, fashion, mode, habit, custom; (*Gram.*) mood; (*Mus.*) melody, air, tune; ***Art und –,*** way, manner; ***das ist doch keine Art und –,*** that is no way to behave; ***in der – daß,*** in such a way that, so that; ***in derselben –,*** likewise, similarly; ***auf diese –, in dieser –,*** in this way, like this, by this means; ***auf folgende –,*** as follows; ***auf jede*** (or ***alle***) ***–,*** in every way; in any case; ***auf keine –, in keiner –,*** in no way, by no means, not at all; ***jeder nach seiner*** or ***auf seine –,*** everyone in his own way; ***auf welche –?*** in what way? (*Mus.*) ***Wort und –,*** words and melody.

–weise, *adv.suff.* 1. *to adv., e.g.* ***glücklicher–,*** happily, fortunately; ***irrtümlicher–,*** by mistake; ***natürlicher–,*** naturally, of course; 2. *to noun, e.g.* ***haufen–,*** in heaps; ***kreuz–,*** in the form of a cross, crosswise; ***massen–,*** in large numbers, plentifully; ***teil–,*** partly, partially, in part.

Weisel ['vaızəl], *m.* queen bee. **Weiselwiege,** *f.* queen cell.

weisen ['vaızən], 1. *irr.v.t.* show, point out, indicate; ***– an*** or ***auf*** (*Acc.*), refer to; ***– aus,*** expel, banish; ***aus dem Lande –,*** exile; ***– nach,*** direct to; ***von sich*** or ***von der Hand –,*** decline, refuse, reject, dismiss, set aside; (*Footb. etc.*) ***vom Felde –,*** order *or* send off (the field); ***ihm die Tür –,*** show him the door. 2. *irr.v.i.* point (***auf*** (*Acc.*), at *or* to). **Weiser.** *m.* pointer, indicator; finger, hand (*of a clock etc.*).

Weisheit ['vaıshaıt], *f.* wisdom; ***– Salomos,*** Psalms of Solomon; ***er denkt, er hat die – mit Löffeln gegessen,*** he thinks he is very *or* (*coll.*) pretty clever; ***behalte deine – für dich!*** keep your remarks to yourself, mind your own business; ***mit seiner – am Ende sein,*** be at one's wits' end; ***der – letzter Schluß,*** the last resort. **Weisheits|krämer,** *m.* wiseacre. **–zahn,** *m.* wisdom-tooth. **weislich,** *adv.* wisely, prudently.

weismachen ['vaısmaxən], *v.t.* (*sep.*) ***ihm etwas –,*** make him believe a th., hoax him about a th., (*sl.*) pull a fast one on him; ***laß dir nichts –!*** don't be taken in *or* fooled! ***das machen Sie einem andern weis!*** don't try that one on me! tell that to the marines!

[1]**weiß** [vaıs], *adj.* white; clean, blank; (*Her.*) argent; ***– lassen,*** leave blank; ***– machen,*** whiten; blanch, bleach; ***ein –es Blatt Papier,*** a clean sheet of paper; ***sich – brennen,*** clear o.s., assert one's innocence; ***–er Fluß,*** leucorrhoea; ***die –e Frau,*** the Woman in White; ***–e Kohle,*** water power; ***–er Leim,*** gelatine; ***ein –er Rabe,*** a white crow; ***etwas schwarz auf – haben,*** have a th. in black and white; ***–er Sonntag,*** Sunday after Easter, Low Sunday; ***der –e Tod,*** freezing to death; ***–er Ton,*** china clay, kaolin; ***die –e Wand,*** the screen (*cinema*); (*fig.*) ***ihn – waschen,*** whitewash him; ***– werden,*** turn white; ***eine –e Weste haben,*** be entirely blameless, have clean hands; ***–e Woche,*** white sale (*in large stores*); ***das Weiße,*** the white (*of the eye; of an egg*).

[2]**weiß,** *see* **wissen.**

Weiß|augenente, *f.* (*Orn.*) *see* **Moorente. –bäcker,** *m.* baker and confectioner. **–bartseeschwalbe,** *f.* (*Orn.*) whiskered tern (*Chlidonias hybrida*). **–bier,** *n.* light *or* pale ale. **–binden-Seeadler,** *m.* (*Orn.*) Pallas's sea eagle (*Haliaeetus leucoryphus*). **–binder,** *m.* (*dial.*) cooper, decorator, house-painter. **–birke,** *f.* (*Bot.*) silver birch (*Betula alba*). **–blech,** *n.* tin-plate. **–blechwaren,** *f.pl.* tinware. **–bleiche,** *f.* full bleaching. **–bluten,** *n.* last extremity; ***eine Firma zum – bringen,*** bring a business to the verge of ruin; ***ihn zum – auspressen,*** extort the last penny from him, bleed him white, (*sl.*) squeeze him till the pips squeak. **–blütigkeit,** *f.* leukæmia. **–brauendrossel,** *f.* (*Orn.*) eyebrowed thrush (*Turdus obscurus*). **–brennen,** *n.* blanching, bleaching. **–brot,** *n.* white bread *or* loaf. **–buch,** *n.* (*Pol.*) white paper. **–buche,** *f.* (*Bot.*) hornbeam (*Carpinus betulus*) **–bürzelsegler,** *m.* (*Orn.*) white-rumped swift (*Apus affinis*). **–bürzelsteinschmätzer,** *m.* (*Orn.*) white-rumped black wheatear (*Oenanthe leucopyga*). **–bürzelstrandläufer,** *m.* (*Orn.*) Bonaparte's *or* (*Am.*) white-rumped sandpiper (*Caldiris fuscicollis*). **–dorn,** *m.* (*Bot.*) hawthorn, may (*Crataegus oxyacantha*).

Weiße ['vaısə], *f.* whiteness; whitewash; (*dial.*) ***eine*** (***Berliner***) ***–***, a (glass of) wheaten ale.

weißen ['vaısən], *v.t.* whiten; whitewash; blanch; (*Metall.*) refine. **Weiße(r),** *m., f.* white man *or* woman (*also fig.*); ***die Weißen,*** the white races.

Weiß|fichte, *f.* (*Bot.*) white spruce (*Picea canadensis*). **–fisch,** *m.* silver-scaled fish (*e.g.* bleak (*Alburnus lucidus*), bream (*Sparus pagrus*), chub (*Leuciscus rutilus*), dace (*Leuciscus leuciscus*), roach (*Leuciscus cephalus*), whiting (*Gadus merlangus*)). **–flügellerche,** *f.* (*Orn.*) white-winged lark (*Melanocorypha leucoptera*). **–flügelseeschwalbe,** *f.* (*Orn.*) white-winged black tern (*Chlidonias leucoptera*). **–fluß,** *m.* (*Med.*) leucorrhoea. **–fuchs,** *m.* (*Zool.*) silver fox (*Vulpes lagopus*); light sorrel horse. **weiß|gar,** *adj.* tawed. **–gekleidet,** *adj.* dressed *or* (*Poet.*) clad in white. **–gelb,** *adj.* pale yellow. **–gerben,** *v.t.* (*sep.*) taw. **–glühend,** *adj.* white-hot, incandescent. **Weiß|glühhitze, –glut,** *f.* white heat, incandescence. **–gold,** *n.* artificial platinum. **weißgrau,** *adj.* light grey. **Weiß|güldenerz, –guldigerz,** *n.* (*Chem.*) argentiferous tetrahedrite. **weißhaarig,** *adj.* white-haired. **Weiß|käse,** *m.* cream cheese. **–kehlammer,** *f.*

(*Orn.*) white-throated sparrow (*Zonotrichia albicollis*). **-kohl,** *m.*, **-kraut,** *n.* white cabbage. **-kupfer,** *n.* German silver. **weißlich,** *adj.* whitish.

Weißling ['vaɪslɪŋ], *m.* (**-s,** *pl.* **-e**) (*Ent.*) Pieridae.

Weiß|lot, *n.* soft solder. **-mehl,** *n.* wheat(en) flour. **-nähen,** *n.*, **-näherei,** *f.* plain needlework. **-näherin,** *f.* needlewoman, seamstress. **-ofen,** *m.* refining furnace. **-papp,** *m.* (*Paperm.*) white resist. **-rückenspecht,** *m.* (*Orn.*) white-backed woodpecker (*Dendrocopus leucotos*). **-schwanzsteppenkiebitz,** *m.* (*Orn.*) white-tailed plover (*Chettusia leucura*). **weißsieden,** *v.t.* (*sep.*) blanch, whiten. **Weiß|spießglanzerz,** *n.* antimony. **-storch,** *m.* (*Orn.*) white stork (*Ciconia ciconia*). **-sucht,** *f.* albinism. **-sud,** *m.* blanching solution. **-tanne,** *f.* (*Bot.*) silver fir (*Abies alba*). **-tüncher,** *m.* whitewasher. **-wangengans,** *f.* (*Orn.*) barnacle goose (*Branta leucopsis*). **-waren,** *f.pl.* linen goods, linens, drapery, cottons. **-warenhändler,** *m.* draper. **-wäsche,** *f.* (household) linen. **-wein,** *m.* white wine, hock. **-wurz,** *f.* (*Bot.*) Solomon's seal (*Polygonatum multiflora*). **-zeug,** *n.* *See* **-wäsche. -zügelente,** *f.* (*Orn.*) see **Blauflügelente.**

Weisung ['vaɪzuŋ], *f.* direction, instruction, order. **weisungs|gebunden,** *adj.* subject to instructions. **-gemäß,** *adv.* as instructed *or* directed.

weit [vaɪt], **1.** *adj.* wide, broad; large, vast, extensive, spacious, ample, capacious, loose (*of clothes*); far, distant, remote; (*fig.*) ***-e Auslegung,*** broad interpretation; ***-er Begriff,*** all-embracing *or* comprehensive concept; ***das steht noch in -em Felde,*** that is still a very remote possibility; ***-es Gewissen,*** elastic conscience; ***-e Hosen,*** baggy trousers; ***-e Reise,*** long journey; ***im -esten Sinne,*** in the broadest sense; ***-er Umweg,*** long way round; ***-er Unterschied,*** vast difference; ***ein -er Weg,*** a long way; ***in die -e Welt gehen,*** go out into the world. **2.** *adv.* far (off), widely, greatly, by far; ***- aus-*** (or ***von)einander,*** far apart, widely separated, at long intervals; ***bei -em nicht,*** by no means, not by a long way *or* (*coll.*) long chalk; ***bei -em nicht so gut,*** not nearly so good; - or ***bei -em besser,*** much *or* far better; ***- und breit,*** far and wide; ***es - bringen,*** get on (well), (*coll.*) go far; ***- entfernt,*** far away; ***- entfernt von,*** a long distance from, (*fig.*) far from, a far cry from; ***- gefehlt!*** far from it! not at all! ***- nach Hause haben,*** be a long way from home; ***nicht - her sein,*** be of little value, not be worth much, (*coll.*) not be up to much, (*sl.*) be not so hot; (*Prov.*) ***mit der Zeit kommt man auch -,*** many a little makes a mickle; ***die Zeit ist nicht mehr -,*** the time is drawing near; ***eine Meile -,*** a mile off; ***wenn es so - ist,*** if *or* when it is ready; ***ist es so - gekommen?*** is it reduced *or* has it come to this? ***es ist noch nicht so —,*** the moment has not yet arrived, it has not come to that yet; ***ich bin so -,*** I am ready; ***- über 80,*** well over 80; ***von -em,*** from afar, from a distance; ***4 Fuß - von der Wand,*** 4 feet (away) from the wall; (*Prov.*) ***- davon ist gut vorm Schuß,*** prudence is the better part of valour; ***wie - sind Sie mit Ihrer Arbeit?*** how far have you got with your work? ***zu - gehen, es zu - treiben,*** go too far, overshoot the mark, overplay one's hand.

Weit, *n.* (**-(e)s,** *pl.* **-e**) (*Naut.*) beam.

weit|ab, *adv.* far away *or* off (*von*, from). **-ästig,** *adj.* with spreading branches. **-aus,** *adv.* by far, much. **-ausgebreitet,** *adj.* expanded, widespread, effuse. **-bekannt,** *adj.* widely *or* well-known, far-famed. **Weitblick,** *m.* far-sightedness, foresight, vision. **weitblickend,** *adj.* far-seeing, far-sighted.

Weite ['vaɪtə], **1.** *f.* width, breadth, wideness; size, expanse, extent; diameter, (*Astr.*) amplitude; distance; (*fig.*) scope, range; ***lichte -,*** width in the clear, inside *or* internal diameter, bore; ***in die - ziehen,*** go out into the world. **2.** *n.* ***das - suchen,*** take to one's heels, make o.s. scarce, decamp, (*coll.*) cut and run, skedaddle, do a bunk; ***des -n und Breiten erzählen,*** relate at length *or* in detail; ***es liegt noch ganz im -n,*** it is still quite undecided.

weiten ['vaɪtən], **1.** *v.t.* widen, broaden, expand, enlarge, extend; stretch (*shoes etc.*). **2.** *v.r.* become broader, widen, expand, broaden out.

weiter ['vaɪtər], **1.** *comp.adj.* farther, further, more distant; broader, wider; additional. **2.** *adv.* farther, furthermore, moreover; on, forward; ***bis auf -es,*** for the present, for the time being, until further notice; ***- entfernt,*** more distant, farther off *or* away; ***hören Sie -!*** hear what follows! ***immer -,*** on and on; ***immer -!*** see ***nur -!*** ***in -en Kreisen bekannt,*** widely known, known widely; ***- hat es keinen Zweck,*** it serves no other purpose, that is all it is good for; ***nicht -,*** not any further, no further; ***nichts -, - nichts,*** nothing else *or* more *or* further, that is all; ***das hat - nichts zu sagen,*** that is not very important *or* significant, that (after all) carries no weight *or* is of no consequence; ***- niemand,*** no one else; ***nur -!*** continue! go on! proceed! ***ohne -es*** (*Austr.* ***ohneweiters***), without further ceremony, without further *or* more ado; immediately, directly, readily, easily; ***ohne -en Aufschub,*** without further delay; ***ohne -e Umstände,*** see ***ohne -eres; und -?*** and then? ***und so -,*** and so forth, and so on; ***das Weitere,*** what follows, the remainder *or* rest; further particulars *or* details; ***Weiteres mündlich,*** further details by word of mouth, more when I see you.

weiter- ['vaɪtər], *sep.pref.* **weiterbefördern,** *v.t.* forward (on), send on, post on, redirect. **Weiterbeförderung,** *f.* forwarding, redirection; ***zur -,*** to be forwarded (***an*** (*Acc.*), to). **weiterbegeben,** *irr. v.t.* negotiate (*bills*). **Weiterbestand,** *m.* continued existence. **weiter|bestehen,** *irr.v.i.* continue to exist, survive. **-bewegen,** *v.i.* move forward, advance, proceed. **Weiterbildung,** *f.* development, improvement; further education; (*Gram.*) derivation. **weiterbringen,** *irr.v.t.* promote, help on; ***das bringt mich nicht weiter,*** that is not much help; ***es -,*** make progress, get on. **Weiterentwicklung,** *f.* further development. **weiter|erzählen,** *v.t.* *See* **-sagen. -führen,** *v.t.* carry on, continue, extend. **Weitergabe,** *f,* transmission, passing on. **weiter|geben,** *irr.v.t.* pass on, transmit. **-gehen,** *irr.v.i.* walk *or* move *or* go *or* pass on, (*fig.*) go on, continue.

weiterhin ['vaɪtər'hɪn], *adv.* for the *or* in future, from now on; furthermore, moreover; ***es - tun,*** continue to do it, go on *or* continue doing it, (*coll.*) keep (on) doing it.

weiter|kommen, *irr.v.i.* get on, progress, advance; ***nicht -,*** make no headway; ***er kommt so nicht weiter,*** this won't get him anywhere. **-können,** *irr.v.i.* ***nicht -,*** be brought to a standstill, be forced to stop; (*coll.*) get stuck. **-leben,** *v.i.* survive, live on. **-leiten,** *v.t.* *See* **-befördern. -lesen,** *irr.v.t., v.i.* go on *or* continue reading, read on. **-machen,** *v.t., v.i.* continue, carry on; (*Mil.*) ***-!*** as you were!

weitern ['vaɪtərn], *v.t., v.r.* (*rare*) *see* **erweiten.**

Weiterreise ['vaɪtərraɪzə], *f.* continuation of the journey. **weiter|sagen,** *v.t.* tell others, repeat (*what one has heard*). **-schreiten,** *irr.v.i.* advance.

Weiterungen ['vaɪtəruŋən], *f.pl.* difficulties, complications, formalities.

weiter|verbreiten, *v.t.* *See* **-sagen. -verfolgen,** *v.t.* follow up. **-vermieten,** *v.t.* sub-let. **-wursteln,** *v.i.* (*coll.*) muddle along.

weit|gehend, **1.** *adj.* (*sup.* ***-st*** or ***weitestgehend***) vast, far-reaching, extensive; (*of statements*) sweeping, (*of powers*) wide, exceptional. **2.** *adv.* largely. **-gereist,** *adj.* widely travelled. **-greifend,** *adj.* far-reaching. **-her,** *adv.* from afar. **-hergeholt,** *adj.* far-fetched. **-herzig,** *adj.* broad-minded. **-läuf(t)ig,** **1.** *adj.* spacious, roomy; vast, widespread, extensive, wide; scattered, straggling, rambling; (*fig.*) diffuse, prolix, long-winded, lengthy, detailed, circumstantial; ***sie sind - verwandt,*** they are distantly related; ***die S. ist sehr -,*** the matter is very complicated. **2.** *adv.* at great length, in great detail. **Weitläuf(t)igkeit,** *f.* vast extent, spaciousness; (*fig.*) diffuseness, prolixity. **weit|maschig,** *adj.* wide-meshed. **-reichend,** *adj.* far-reaching, very extensive. **-schichtig,** *adj.* widely spaced, far apart; extensive, large, vast. **-schweifig,** *adj.* detailed, circumstantial, diffuse, verbose, prolix, (*coll.*) long-winded. **Weitschweifigkeit,** *f,* verbosity, prolixity. **weit-**

sichtig, *adj.* long-sighted; (*fig.*) far-seeing, far-sighted, clear-sighted. **Weit|sichtigkeit,** *f.* long-sightedness; perspicacity. **–sprung,** *m.* (*Spt.*) long *or* broad jump. **weit|spurig,** *adj.* wide-tracked, broad-gauged. **–tragend,** *adj.* long-range (*of firearms*); (*fig.*) far-reaching. **–umfassend,** *adj.* comprehensive, extensive.

Weitung ['vaɪtuŋ], *f.* **1.** enlargement, extension, widening; distance, space, width; – ***einer Treppe,*** room under a staircase; *pl.* (*Min.*) hollows, excavations.

weit|verbreitet, *adj.* widespread, prevalent, widely known *or* held. **–verzweigt,** *adj.* widely ramified *or* spread, very extensive.

Weizen ['vaɪtsən], *m.* wheat; corn; ***türkischer* –,** maize, Indian corn; (*coll.*) ***mein – blüht,*** I am in luck's way, I am in clover; (*coll.*) ***mein – blüht nicht,*** my ship has not come home. **Weizen|-brand,** *m.* black rust. **–brot,** *n.* white bread. **–flugbrand,** *m.* loose smut. **–grieß,** *m.* wheat grits *or* middlings. **–mehl,** *n.* wheaten flour. **–stein-brand, –stinkbrand,** *m.* bunt.

welch [vɛlç], **1.** *indecl.pron.* – ***ein Mann!*** what a man! ***da sieht man, – (ein) großer Tor er gewesen ist,*** you see what a fool he has been. **2.** *inter.adj.* which? ***–er Mann?*** which man? ***–e Frau?*** which woman? **3.** *inter.pron.* which? who? ***–e von euch Damen?*** which of you ladies? ***einer meiner Brüder; –er?*** one of my brothers; which one? ***–es sind ihre Kinder?*** which are her children? **4.** *rel.pron.* (*Gen. sing. m. and n.* ***dessen***; *Gen. sing. f.* ***deren***; *Gen. pl.* ***deren,*** *Dat. pl.* ***denen***) which, what, that, who, whom; ***derjenige –er,*** he who; ***die Dame, –er wir geschrieben haben,*** the lady to whom we wrote; ***die Bücher, ohne –e ich meine Arbeit nicht vollenden kann,*** the books, without which I cannot finish my work; ***–er auch (immer),*** who(so)ever, whichever; ***–es auch immer Ihre Ansprüche sein mögen,*** whatever (*all-embracing*) *or* whichever (*selective*) your claims may be. **5.** *rel.adj.* ***100 Mark, –e Summe Sie einliegend finden,*** 100 marks, which (sum) you will find enclosed; ***–e Tugenden er auch haben mag,*** whatever virtues he may possess; ***von –er Art auch (immer),*** of whichever *or* whatever kind (whatsoever). **6.** *indef.pron.* (*coll.*) some, any; ***haben Sie Zucker? ich habe –en,*** have you sugar? yes, I have some; ***ich brauche Zucker, haben Sie –en?*** I need some sugar, have you any? ***es sind schon –e da,*** there are some (people) here already; ***eine Menge Menschen, –e zu Pferde und –e zu Fuß,*** a lot of people, some on horseback and some on foot.

welcherlei ['vɛlçər'laɪ], *indecl.adj.* of whatever kind, whatever sort; ***– Gründe er auch haben mag, – Art seine Gründe auch sein mögen,*** whatever reasons he may have, whatever his reasons may be.

Welf [vɛlf], *n.* **(-(e)s,** *pl.* **-er)** *or m.* **(-(e)s,** *pl.* **-e)** (*Hunt.*) whelp, cub.

Welfe ['vɛlfə], *m.* **(-n,** *pl.* **-n)** (*Hist.*) Guelph.

welfen ['vɛlfən], *v.i.* cub, have young.

welk [vɛlk], *adj.* withered, faded; shrivelled, wrinkled; limp, flabby, flaccid. **welken,** *v.i.* (*aux.* s.) wilt, wither, fade (away), shrivel (up). **Welk-heit,** *f.* faded *or* withered state; flabbiness, flaccidity.

Wellblech ['vɛlblɛç], *n.* corrugated (sheet) iron; (*sl.*) ***– reden,*** talk rot *or* bilge. **Wellblechbaracke,** *f.* (*Mil.*) Nissen hut.

Welle ['vɛlə], *f.* **1.** wave (*also Opt., Elec., hairdressing and fig.*); billow, ripple; surge; oscillation, undulation; (*Rad.*) wavelength; ***gedämpfte* –,** damped wave; ***ungedämpfte* –,** undamped oscillation; ***–n schlagen,*** rise in waves, surge; ***die –n durchschneiden,*** plough the waves; ***eine – der Begeisterung,*** a wave *or* upsurge of enthusiasm; 2. axle(-tree), shaft, (*Mech.*) spindle, arbor; ***liegende* –,** horizontal shaft; ***gekröpfte* –,** crankshaft; ***stehende* –,** vertical shaft, capstan; (*Elec.*) stationary *or* standing wave; 3. (*dial.*) faggot, bundle of brushwood; bottle (*of straw*); 4. (*Gymn.*) circle *or* revolution round the horizontal bar, (*coll.*) grinder. **wellen, 1.** *v.t.* wave (*hair*); corrugate (*iron*). **2.** *v.r.* wave, undulate.

Wellenantrieb ['vɛlənˀantri:p], *m.* shaft drive. **wellenartig,** *adj.* waved, wavy, wave-like, undulating, undulatory. **Wellen|ausbreitung,** *f.* wave propagation. **–bad,** *n.* sea-bath, swimming-bath with artificial waves. **–band,** *n.* (*Rad.*) wave-band. **–bereich,** *m.* (*Rad.*) wave-range *or* band. **–bewe-gung,** *f.* undulatory motion, undulation. **–bre-cher,** *m.* breakwater, groyne. **–echo,** *n.* (*Rad.*) second-channel interference. **wellen|förmig,** *adj.* *See* **–artig. Wellen|holz,** *n.* (*dial.*) brushwood. **–lager,** *n.* shaft-bearing. **–länge,** *f.* (*Rad. etc.*) wave-length. **–läufer,** *m.* (*Orn.*) Leach's petrel (*Oceanodroma leucorrhoa*). **–linie,** *f.* wavy line. **–messer,** *m.* (*Rad.*) wavemeter. **–reiten,** *n.* surf-riding. **–schaltung,** *f.* (*Rad.*) wave-change switch. **–schlag,** *m.* breaking of the waves; ***kurzer* –,** choppy sea. **–schlucker,** *m.* (*Rad.*) wave-trap, interference filter. **–sittich,** *m.* (*Orn.*) budgerigar, (*coll.*) lovebird (*Melopsittacus undulatus*). **–tal,** *n.* wave trough, trough of the sea. **–theorie,** *f.* wave theory (*of light etc.*). **–übertragung,** *f.* (*Mech.*) shaft transmission. **–verteilung,** *f.* (*Rad.*) allocation of frequencies. **–widerstand,** *m.* (*Elec.*) surge resistance. **–zapfen,** *m.* (*Mech.*) pivot, journal.

Weller ['vɛlər], *m.* daub. **wellern,** *v.t.* build with wattle and daub.

wellig ['vɛlɪç], *adj.* wavy (*hair*), undulating, rolling (*ground*).

Well|papier, *n.,* **–pappe,** *f.* corrugated paper. **–zapfen,** *m.* *See* **Wellenzapfen.**

Welpe ['vɛlpə], *m.* **(-n,** *pl.* **-n)** *see* **Welf.**

Wels [vɛls], *m.* **(-es,** *pl.* **-e)** (*Ichth.*) catfish (*Silurus glanis*).

welsch [vɛlʃ], *adj.* Latin, Romance, French, Italian, (*coll.*) foreign; (*Swiss*) French-speaking; ***–e Bohne,*** French bean.

Welt [vɛlt], *f.* (-, *pl.* **-en**) world; ***alle* –,** all the world, everyone, everybody; ***auf der* –,** in the world, on earth; ***aus der – schaffen,*** (*a p.*) put out of the way, do away with; (*problems etc.*) settle; (*coll.*) ***nicht aus der – sein,*** not be all that far away; ***bis ans Ende der* –,** to the world's end, till doomsday; (*coll.*) ***da ist die – mit Brettern vernagelt,*** that is beyond the wit of man; ***sich durch die – schlagen,*** make one's way in the world; ***die große* –,** high society, the upper ten *or* crust; ***warum in aller –?*** why on earth? why in the world? ***das wird die – kosten,*** that will cost the earth *or* a fortune; ***das geht mich in aller – nichts an,*** that is no earthly concern of mine; ***um alles in der –!*** for goodness sake! ***nicht um alles in der* –,** not for all the world, (*coll.*) not on my *or* your life; ***so geht es in der* –,** that is the way of the world.

welt|abgeschieden, *adj.* *See* **–entrückt. –abge-wandt,** *adj.* detached from the world, remote from reality. **Welt|all,** *n.* universe, cosmos. **–alter,** *n.* age, period (of history). **weltanschaulich,** *adj.* ideological. **Welt|anschauung,** *f.* philosophy of life, outlook, view, creed, ideology. **–ausstellung,** *f.* international exhibition, world fair. **–bank,** *f.* world bank. **welt|bekannt, –berühmt,** *adj.* world-famous, world-renowned, notorious, (*pred.*) generally known, known everywhere, known all over the world, of world-wide fame *or* renown. **Welt|berühmtheit,** *f.* p. of world-wide renown, world-famous p. **–beschreibung,** *f.* cosmography. **–bestleistung,** *f.* *See* **–rekord. welt|bewegend,** *adj.* *See* **–erschütternd. Welt|bild,** *n.* view *or* theory of life. **–bummler,** *m.* (*coll.*) *see* **–reisen-de(r). –bund,** *m.* international union. **–bürger,** *m.* cosmopolitan; (*coll.*) ***ein kleiner – ist angekommen,*** a little visitor has arrived. **weltbürger-lich,** *adj.* cosmopolitan. **Welt|bürgersinn,** *m.,* **–bürgertum,** *n.* cosmopolitanism. **–dame,** *f.* woman of the world, lady of fashion. **–eislehre,** *f.* glacial cosmology. **–ende,** *n.* end of the world.

weltenfern ['vɛltənfɛrn], *adj.* *See* **weltfern. Welten|lehre,** *f.* cosmology. **–raum,** *m.* (immensity *or* infinity of) space.

weltentrückt ['vɛltˀɛntrykt], *adj.* secluded, isolated. **Welt|entstehung,** *f.* origin of the universe, creation of the world. **–ereignis,** *n.* event of world-wide importance, international sensation. **welt|-erfahren,** *adj. See* **–klug. Welterfahrung,** *f.* experience of the world *or* of life. **welterschütternd,** *adj.* world-shaking *or* -shattering. **Welt|-firma,** *f.* firm of international importance. **–flucht,** *f.* withdrawal from life *or* society, seclusion; escapism. **–flug,** *m.* round-the-world flight. **weltfremd,** *adj.* unworldly, innocent, naïve, (*coll.*) starry-eyed; (*pred.*) ignorant of the world. **Welt|friede(n),** *m.* universal peace. **–gebäude,** *n.* cosmic system. **–geistliche(r),** *m.* secular priest. **–geistlichkeit,** *f.* secular clergy. **–geltung,** *f.* international reputation *or* standing. **–gericht,** *n.* Last Judgement. **–geschehen,** *n.* world affairs. **–geschichte,** *f.* universal history. **welt|gewandt,** *adj. See* **–klug. Welt|handel,** *m.* international trade, world commerce. **–herrschaft,** *f.* world dominion. **–karte,** *f.* map of the world. **–kenntnis,** *f.* knowledge of the world, savoir-vivre. **–kind,** *n.* worldling; opportunist. **weltklug,** *adj.* worldly-wise, politic, prudent, astute. **Welt|-klugheit,** *f.* worldly wisdom, astuteness, prudence. **–körper,** *m.* heavenly body. **–krieg,** *m.* world war. **–kugel,** *f.* globe. **–lage,** *f.* international situation. **–lauf,** *m.* way of the world.

weltlich ['vɛltlɪç], *adj.* worldly, mundane; secular, profane, temporal, lay; ***–e Freuden,*** worldly pleasures; ***–e Güter,*** worldly *or* temporal possessions, temporalities; ***– gesinnt,*** worldly(-minded); ***– Gesinnte(r),*** worldling; ***–e Schule,*** independent *or* undenominational school. **Weltlichkeit,** *f.* worldliness, worldly-mindedness; secular state, secular *or* civil power; *pl.* temporal rights *or* possessions, temporalities.

Welt|macht, *f.* world power. **–mann,** *m.* (*pl.* **¨er**) man of the world; *see also* **–kind. welt|männisch,** *adj.* urbane, man-of-the-world (*attitude etc.*); *see also* **–klug. Welt|markt,** *m.* world market, international trade. **–meer,** *n.* ocean. **–meister,** *m.* world champion. **–meisterschaft,** *f.* world championship. **–politik,** *f.* world policy; international politics. **–postverein,** *m.* Postal Union. **–rätsel,** *n.* riddle of the universe. **–raum,** *m.* (outer) space. **–raumflug,** *m.* space travel. **–reich,** *n.* empire. **–reise,** *f.* journey *or* voyage round the world, world tour. **–reisende(r),** *m., f.* globe-trotter. **–rekord,** *m.* world record. **–rekordler, –rekordmann,** *m.* world-record holder. **–ruf,** *m.* international *or* world-wide reputation. **–schmerz,** *m.* weariness of life, pessimistic outlook, romantic discontent. **–sprache,** *f.* international *or* world language. **–stadt,** *f.* metropolis. **weltstädtisch,** *adj.* metropolitan. **Weltteil,** *m.* continent; quarter of the globe. **weltumfassend,** *adj.* world-wide, universal. **Welt|umseglung,** *f.* circumnavigation of the globe; journey round the world. **–untergang,** *m.* end of the world. **welt|-vergessen, –verlassen, –verloren,** *adj.* lonely, isolated, solitary, (*pred.*) cut off from the world. **Welt|weise(r),** *m., f.* philosopher. **–weisheit,** *f.* philosophy (of life). **–wende,** *f.* turning-point in history. **–wirtschaft,** *f.* international economic relations, world commerce. **–wunder,** *n.* wonder of the world, (*of a p.*) prodigy.

wem [ve:m], *Dat. of* **wer**; (to) whom. **Wemfall,** *m.* (*Gram.*) dative case.

wen [ve:n], *Acc. of* **wer**; whom; (*coll.*) ***ich höre – rufen,*** I hear someone calling.

Wende ['vɛndə], *f.* turning, turn, (*Gymn.*) face-vault; (*fig.*) turning-point. **Wende|getriebe,** *n.* (*Mech.*) reversing gear. **–hals,** *m.* (*Orn.*) wryneck (*Jynx torquilla*). **–kreis,** *m.* 1. (*Geog.*) tropic; 2. (*Motor.*) turning-circle.

Wendel ['vɛndəl], *f.* (-, *pl.* **-n**) coil, spiral, helix. **Wendel|baum,** *m.* axle-tree; winch. **–treppe,** *f.* 1. spiral staircase, winding stairs; 2. (*Mollusc.*) *Scalaria pretiosa.*

wenden ['vɛndən], **1.** *reg. & irr.v.t., v.i.* turn (round *or* about), turn over (*a page, hay*), turn up (*soil*); (*Naut.*) put (*v.t.*) *or* go (*v.i.*) about; ***Geld – an*** (*Acc.*), spend money on; ***Zeit – an*** (*Acc.*), devote time to; ***seine Kräfte – auf*** (*Acc.*), apply one's strength *or* direct one's energies to; ***die Augen – auf*** (*Acc.*), turn one's eyes to, glance at; ***kein Auge – von,*** not take one's eyes off; ***bitte –!*** please turn over! ***ein Schiff –,*** put a ship about; ***das Schiff wendet,*** the ship goes about; ***mit –der Post,*** by return of post; ***ein gewendetes Kleidungsstück,*** a garment that has been turned; *see* **gewandt. 2.** *reg. & irr.v.r.* turn (round); (*fig.*) change; ***sich an ihn –,*** address o.s. *or* appeal to him; turn *or* apply to him; have recourse to him; ***um nähere Auskunft wende man sich an*** (*Acc.*), for further particulars apply to; ***das Gespräch wendete*** or ***wandte sich auf*** (*Acc.*), the conversation turned upon *or* came round to; ***sich gegen ihn –,*** turn against *or* on him, set one's face against him; ***sich gegen etwas –,*** object to a th.; ***sich – von,*** turn away from, turn one's back on; ***sich zum Guten*** or ***Besseren –,*** take a turn for the better; ***sich zum besten –,*** turn out for the best.

Wende|pflug, *m.* swivel-plough. **–pol,** *m.* (*Elec.*) reversing pole. **–punkt,** *m.* turning-point; crisis; (*Astr.*) solstitial point; (*Gram.*) point of inflexion.

wendig ['vɛndɪç], *adj.* manœuvrable, manageable, (*pred.*) easily managed *or* steered; (*of a p.*) agile, nimble, (*fig.*) versatile, adaptable, resourceful, flexible; ***ein –es Boot,*** a handy boat. **Wendigkeit,** *f.* manœuvrability, flexibility; agility, nimbleness; versatility, resourcefulness.

wendisch ['vɛndɪʃ], *adj.* (*Geog.*) Wendish.

Wendung ['vɛndʊŋ], *f.* 1. turn, turning; (*Fenc.*) volte; (*Mil.*) wheeling; (*Naut.*) going about; (*fig.*) change, turn, turning-point; ***eine andere*** or ***neue – geben,*** give a new turn *or* twist (*Dat.,* to); ***glückliche –,*** favourable turn; ***– zum Besseren,*** change *or* turn for the better; 2. (turn of) expression, phrase, saying, figure of speech, idiomatic expression.

Wenfall ['ve:nfal], *m.* (*Gram.*) accusative case.

wenig ['ve:nɪç], *adj., adv.* little, not much; slightly; (*pl.*) a few; (*usu. indecl. in sing.*; *may be even in pl. when not preceded by art. or pron., esp. when governed by prep.*) ***ein –,*** a little; ***mit ein – Geduld,*** with a little patience; ***mit ein – gutem Willen,*** with a little good will; ***ein klein –,*** just a little, a tiny bit; ***mein –es*** or ***das –e, was ich habe,*** the little (that) I have; ***– Gutes,*** little that *or* not much that is good; ***– Geld,*** little money, not much money; ***ein – Geld,*** some money, (just) a little money; ***sein –(es) Geld,*** the little money (that) he has; ***die –en,*** the few; ***die –en Male, daß . . .,*** the few occasions when . . .; ***in –(en) Worten,*** in a few words; ***in diesen –en Worten,*** in those few words; ***in nicht –(en) andern Ländern,*** in not a few *or* in quite a few *or* in (a good) many other countries; ***in den –en andern Ländern,*** in (the) few remaining countries; ***einige –e,*** a *or* some few, a small quantity of; ***um einiges –e,*** by a small amount; ***ein – schnell(er),*** a little *or* a bit *or* slightly *or* somewhat quick(er); ***eine – bekannte Tatsache,*** a little-known fact; ***es fehlte –, so wäre ich . . .,*** I was nearly . . .; ***eben so – als,*** just as little as; ***so – auch,*** however little; ***– gut,*** not very good; ***ich war nicht – überrascht,*** I was not a little surprised; ***er ist so – arm, daß . . .,*** so far from (him) being poor. . . .

weniger ['ve:nɪgər], *comp.adj.* less, fewer; *pl.* fewer; (*Math.*) less, minus; ***nicht – als,*** no less *or* no(t) fewer than; ***nichts – als,*** nothing less than, anything but; ***um so –,*** all the less; ***6 – 2,*** 6 minus *or* less 2.

Wenigkeit ['ve:nɪçkaɪt], *f.* little, small quantity; littleness, smallness, trifle; ***meine –,*** my humble self, your humble servant, (*coll.*) yours truly.

wenigst ['ve:nɪçst], *sup. adj.* least, fewest; ***am –en,*** least of all; ***nicht zum –en,*** last but not least; ***die –en,*** only very few. **wenigstens,** *adv.* at least, at all events; ***wenn . . . –,*** if only. . . .

wenn [vɛn], *conj.* 1. (*time*) when, whenever; as long as; as soon as; 2. (*condition*) if, in case, provided (that), (*Law*) if and when; ***– die Zeit da ist, müssen wir fort,*** when the time comes we must be off; ***– Fritz vor mir stirbt, so wird das Haas mir gehören,*** if F. dies *or* should die before me, the house will be mine; ***– ich es wüßte,*** if I knew it; ***– ich es***

gewußt hätte, had I *or* if I had known it; – *man danach urteilt,* judging by *or* from this; – *man ihn hört, sollte man glauben,* to hear him one would think; – *ich die Wahrheit sagen soll,* to tell the truth; *allemal* –, whenever; *als* –, as if; *nicht als – das nicht häufig vorkäme,* it is not as if it were a rare occurrence; – . . . *auch,* (al)though, even if *or* though, supposing (that), granted that; – *es auch noch so wenig ist,* little though it (may) be, if *or* though it be ever so little, however little it may be; *außer* –, unless, if . . . not, except when *or* if; – *bloß* or *doch,* if only; – *etwa,* if by chance; – *man kein Narr ist,* if one is not *or* unless one is a fool; – *nicht,* if not, unless, except when *or* if; – . . . *nur,* see – . . . *bloß*; (*coll.*) – *schon!* even so! what of it! (*sl.*) so what! – . . . *schon,* see – . . . *auch*; – *er schon nicht viel gelernt hat,* even if he has not learned much; (*coll.*) – *schon, denn schon,* what must be, must be; it cannot be helped; in for a penny, in for a pound; one may as well be hanged for a sheep as for a lamb; *selbst* – or *und* –, see – . . . *auch*; *wie* –, see *als* –.

Wenn, *n. ohne – und Aber,* without 'ifs' or 'buts', without shilly-shally; unreservedly.

wenn|gleich, –schon, *adv.* (al)though.

Wenzel ['vɛntsəl], *m.* (*Cards*) knave, jack.

wer [ve:r], **1.** *inter.pron.* who? which? – *ist da?* who is there? (*Mil.*) – *da?* who goes there? – *anders als?* who else but? – *von euch beiden?* which of you two? – *ist größer, er oder sein Bruder?* who *or* which is the taller, he or his brother? **2.** *rel.pron.* (he) who, he that; – *auch* (*immer*), who(so)ever; – *es auch sei,* whoever it may be. **3.** *indef.pron.* (*coll.*) someone, sombody; anyone, anybody.

Werbe|abteilung ['vɛrbə–], *f.* advertising *or* publicity department. **–agent,** *m.* canvasser, sales-promotion agent. **–aktion,** *f. See* **–feldzug. –artikel,** *m.* (free) advertising offer. **–berater,** *m.* advertising *or* publicity agent. **–blatt,** *n.* advertising leaflet. **–brief,** *m.* sales *or* publicity letter. **–büro,** *n.* advertising agency, (*Mil.*) recruiting office. **–dienst,** *m.* advertising service. **–fachmann,** *m. See* **–berater. –feldzug,** *m.* publicity *or* advertising campaign *or* (*coll.*) drive. **–film,** *m.* advertisement film. **–fläche,** *f.* advertising space. **–gewohnheit,** *f.* (*Zool., Orn.*) courting habit. **–graphik,** *f.* commercial art. **–kosten,** *pl.* advertising expenses. **–kraft,** *f.* publicity value. **werbekräftig,** *adj.* of great publicity value; effective in appealing to the customer. **Werbe|leiter,** *m.* advertising *or* publicity manager, public-relations officer. **–mittel,** *n.* advertising medium; appropriation for publicity *or* propaganda purposes. **–muster,** *n.* trial *or* free sample.

werben ['vɛrbən], **1.** *irr.v.t.* enrol, enlist (*members, customers*), canvass (*votes*), (*Mil.*) recruit, enlist; (*fig.*) win over (*für,* to). **2.** *irr.v.i.* – *für,* make propaganda for, canvass for; (*Comm.*) publicize, advertise, (*coll.*) push, boost, (*sl.*) plug; – *um,* sue for, court, woo; (*Comm.*) *–des Kapital,* working capital. **Werben,** *n. See* **Werbung.**

Werbeoffizier ['vɛrbəɔfɪtsi:r], *m.* (*Mil.*) recruiting officer.

Werber ['vɛrbər], *m.* suitor, wooer; canvasser; *see also* **Werbeoffizier.**

Werbe|schrift, *f.* advertising pamphlet, brochure, prospectus; *see also* **–blatt. –sendung,** *f.* (*Rad.*) commercial (radio *or* T.V. programme). **–sergeant,** *m.* recruiting sergeant. **–trommel,** *f.* (*fig.*) *die – rühren,* make propaganda, rouse enthusiasm, (*coll.*) beat the big drum.

Werbung ['vɛrbuŋ], *f.* courtship, courting, wooing; canvassing, solicitation; propaganda, publicity (campaign), advertising, sales-promotion. **Werbungskosten,** *pl.* (*on tax-returns*) business expenses, professional outlay; *see also* **Werbekosten.**

Werdegang ['ve:rdəgaŋ], *m.* development, growth, evolution; (*of a p.*) career, background; (*Tech.*) process of manufacture.

werden ['ve:rdən], **1.** *irr.v.i.* (*aux.* s.) become; come to be, grow, turn, get, turn out *or* prove (to be); arise, come into existence; *alt* –, grow old; *es muß anders* –, there must be a change, we cannot go on like this; *Arzt* –, become a doctor; *daraus wird nichts,* nothing will come of it, it will come to nothing, (*coll.*) nothing doing! that's out! *aus ihm wird nichts,* he will not amount *or* (*coll.*) come to much, he will come to no good; *aus nichts wird nichts,* nothing comes from nothing; *was soll aus ihm –?* what will become of him? *was ist aus ihm geworden?* what has become of him? (*coll.*) *wird's bald?* will you soon be done? will it soon be ready? hurry up, I am waiting; *mir wurde bange,* I began to feel afraid; *mit ihm bekannt* –, make his acquaintance; *blind* –, go blind; *böse* –, grow *or* get angry; *einig* –, agree, come to an understanding; *wie wird die Ernte –?* how will the harvest turn out? *frech* –, get cheeky; *gesund* –, get well, recover; *gewahr* –, become aware of; *es wird hell,* it is getting light; *er ist katholisch geworden,* he has turned Catholic; *was nicht ist, kann noch* –, what is not yet may yet be; *krank* –, fall ill; *alle Tage, die Gott – läßt,* every day which God grants us; (*B.*) *es werde Licht! und es ward Licht,* let there be light! and there was light; *man weiß nicht, was noch – soll,* there is no knowing what might happen; *Mutter* –, be going to have a child; *Recht soll euch* –, justice shall be done you; *satt* –, eat one's fill; *es wird mir schwach,* I feel faint; *mir wird schwer ums Herz,* my heart grows heavy; *die Tage – länger,* the days grow longer; *man möchte des Teufels* –, it is enough to drive one mad; *es wird schon* –, it will turn out all right; *das Wetter wird kalt,* the weather turns cold; (*coll.*) *der Kranke wird wieder* –, the patient will recover; *was will er –?* what is he going to be *or* does he want to be? *es wird Zeit,* the time is drawing near, it will soon be time; *die Zeit wird mir lang,* time hangs heavy with *or* on me; – *zu,* change *or* turn into; *zum Gelächter* –, become a laughing-stock; *es wird mir zur Last,* it becomes a burden to me; *zum Mann* –, grow into a man; *die Ausnahme wird zur Regel,* the exception is becoming the rule; *es wird mir zum Rätsel,* it begins to puzzle me; *ein* or *zum Verräter* –, turn traitor; *der Schnee wird zu Wasser,* the snow is turning to water; *alle seine Pläne sind zu Wasser geworden,* all his plans have fallen through *or* gone up in smoke *or* come to nothing.

2. *irr.v.aux.* **(a)** (*with inf. forming the future and conditional tenses*) shall, will; should, would; *wir – es ihm gleich sagen,* we shall tell him at once; *er würde es mir gesagt haben,* he would have told me; *es wird ihm doch nichts passiert sein?* I hope nothing has happened to him, he surely will not have come to any harm; (*coll.*) *euch werd' ich* (*kommen*)! you will catch it! **(b)** (*with p.p. forming the passive voice. N.B. in compound tenses p.p. worden*) be, is, are *etc.*; *geliebt* –, be loved; *ich bin geliebt worden,* I have been loved; *das Haus wird gebaut,* the house is being built; *die Glocke wurde geläutet,* the bell was rung; *es wurde gesungen und getanzt,* there was singing and dancing.

Werden, *n.* growing, developing; development, growth, formation, rise, progress; evolution, genesis; *Afrika im* –, Africa in the making; *noch im – sein,* be in embryo, be in the process of development; *große Dinge sind im* –, great things are in preparation *or* are on their way. **werdend,** *adj.* growing, developing, nascent; *–e Mutter,* expectant mother.

Werder ['vɛrdər], *m.* river island, islet, eyot, ait, holm.

Werfall ['ve:rfal], *m.* (*Gram.*) nominative case.

werfen ['vɛrfən], **1.** *irr.v.t., v.i.* throw, cast, fling, toss, pitch, hurl, project (*nach,* at); (*of animals*) bring forth young; *Anker* –, cast anchor; *die Augen – auf* (*Acc.*), cast one's eyes *or* a glance at; *beiseite* –, toss *or* fling aside; *Blasen* –, give off bubbles; *einen Blick* –, see *Augen* –; *Bomben* –, drop bombs; *Falten* –, wrinkle, pucker, hang in folds; *Ferkel* –, litter; *ein Füllen* –, foal; *den Gegner* –, throw *or* unhorse one's opponent; *über den Haufen* –, overthrow (*enemy*); (*fig.*) overthrow, upset (*plans*), cast aside, throw overboard, throw to the winds (*scruples etc.*); (*of animals*) ***Junge –,*** bring forth young; ***ein Kalb –,*** calve; ***ihm etwas an den Kopf –,*** fling s.th. in his teeth; ***die Flinte ins Korn –,*** throw in the towel, throw up the sponge, lose heart; ***das Los –,*** cast lots (*über* (*Acc.*), for); ***aufs Papier –,*** jot down; ***Schatten –,*** cast a shadow; ***mit dem Schinken*** or ***der Wurst nach der Speckseite –,*** throw good money after bad; ***Strahlen –,*** emit rays, beam forth; ***alles in einen Topf –,*** treat everything alike, make no distinctions; ***mit Geld um sich –,*** throw one's money about, be lavish of *or* with one's money; ***mit Beleidigungen um sich –,*** insult people right and left; ***mit französischen Brocken um sich –,*** show off by using scraps of French; ***Wellen –,*** break in waves; (*dice*) ***Sie – zuerst,*** you have the first throw. **2.** *irr.v.r.* (*of wood*) warp, become warped, (*of a wheel etc.*) buckle, get buckled; become distorted; (*fig.*) (*of a p.*) throw o.s. (***auf*** (*Acc.*), into), apply o.s. (energetically) (to), give o.s. up (to), (*coll.*) take up (with enthusiasm); ***sich ihm an den Hals –,*** throw o.s. at his head; ***sich in die Brust –,*** swagger, strut, give o.s. airs; bridle up; (*coll.*) ***sich ins Zeug –,*** exert o.s., throw one's weight about; ***sich im Bett hin und her –,*** toss and turn in bed. **Werfer,** *m.* (*Crick.*) bowler, (*Baseball*) pitcher; (*Mil.*) mortar, rocket projector *or* launcher.

[1]**Werft** [vɛrft], *f.* (-, *pl.* **-en**) *or* (*Austr.*) *n.* (**-(e)s,** *pl.* **-e**) docks, dockyard; ship(-building) yard; (*Av.*) *see* **Werfthalle.**

[2]**Werft,** *m.* (**-(e)s,** *pl.* **-e**) (*Weav.*) warp.

Werft|arbeiter, *m.* docker, dock labourer; shipyard worker. **–halle,** *f.* (*Av.*) aerodrome workshops, repair hangar.

Werg [vɛrk], *n.* tow, oakum. **wergen,** *adj.* hempen.

Werk [vɛrk], *n.* (**-(e)s,** *pl.* **-e**) 1. act, action, deed, performance, achievement; ***das ist sein –,*** that is his doing; ***ein gutes – tun,*** do a good deed, perform an act of kindness (***an*** (*Dat.*), to); 2. undertaking, enterprise, (*coll.*) job; ***es ist das – weniger Augenblicke,*** it will only take a moment or two, (*coll.*) that's soon done; ***am – sein,*** be at work, (*coll.*) be on the job; (*coll.*) ***ans –!*** let's begin, now for it! ***ans – gehen*** or ***sich ans – machen,*** set to work, (*coll.*) go to it; ***Hand ans – legen,*** take a job in hand, set one's hand to *or* set about a job; ***es ist etwas im –e,*** there is s.th. afoot *or* s.th. in the wind *or* s.th. going on; ***ins – setzen,*** set going, set on foot, bring about, effect, accomplish, engineer; ***zu –e gehen,*** proceed, go *or* set about it; 3. work, labour, production, workmanship; 4. mechanism, works, clockwork; 5. workshop, works, factory, (manufacturing *or* industrial) plant; (*Comm.*) ***ab –,*** ex works; 6. publication, book, work, (*esp. Mus.*) opus; ***das – lobt den Meister,*** a man is known by his work; 7. *pl.* (*Mil.*) forts, fortifications, works.

Werk|abteilung, *f.* bay, shop (*in a factory*). **–anlage,** *f.* works, manufacturing *or* industrial plant. **–bank,** *f.* workbench. **–blei,** *n.* crude lead.

Werkeltag ['vɛrkəlta:k], *m.* (*obs.*) *see* **Werktag.**

werken [vɛrkən], *v.i.* work perfunctorily, (*coll.*) potter about. **Werk|führer,** *m.* foreman, overseer. **–halle,** *f. See* **–abteilung. –heilige(r),** *m., f.* doer of good works, sanctimonious p., hypocrite. **–heiligkeit,** *f.* outward piety, sanctimoniousness, hypocrisy. **–küche,** *f.* factory canteen. **–leute,** *pl.* workmen, workpeople, (*coll.*) hands. **–meister,** *m.* 1. *See* **–führer**; 2. (*dial.*) master builder. **–nummer,** *f.* production (serial) number.

Werks|angehörige(r), *m., f.* employee of the firm. **–anlage,** *f. See* **Werkanlage.**

Werk|satz, *m.* (*Typ.*) set of type for book-work. **–seide,** *f.* floss silk.

Werks|kantine, *f. See* **Werkküche. –leiter,** *m.* factory *or* works manager. **–norm,** *f.* standard specification.

Werk|spionage, *f.* industrial espionage. **–statt, –stätte,** *f.* workshop. **–stattschreiber,** *m.* time recorder. **–stattwagen,** *m.* mobile workshop, repair *or* maintenance truck. **–stattzeichnung,** *f.* workshop drawing. **–stein,** *m.* freestone. **–stelle,** *f.* place of work; *see also* **–statt. –stoff,** *m.* raw material. **–stoffermüdung,** *f.* material fatigue. **–stoffprüfung,** *f.* material testing. **–stück,** *n.* (*Mech.*) working part, component; worked article; dressed stone. **–stückzeichnung,** *f.* component drawing. **–student,** *m.* part-time student. **–tag,** *m.* working-day, weekday. **werk|täglich,** *adj.* weekday; (*fig.*) workaday, everyday, commonplace. **–tags,** *adv.* on weekdays *or* working days. **–tätig,** *adj.* working; practical; ***–e Bevölkerung,*** working population; ***–e Liebe,*** charity; ***–e Unterstützung,*** active support, practical assistance; ***die Werktätigen,*** the working classes, the workers. **Werk|tisch,** *m.* work-table. **–wohnung,** *f.* company-owned house. **–zeichnung,** *f.* working drawing. **–zeug,** *n.* tool, implement, instrument, (*fig.*) instrument, tool, passive agent. **–zeugmaschine,** *f.* machine-tool. **–zeugschlosser,** *m.* toolmaker.

Wermut ['ve:rmu:t], *m.* (*Bot.*) wormwood; (*wine*) vermouth; (*fig.*) bitterness, gall.

Werre ['vɛrə], *f.* (*dial.*) (*Ent.*) mole-cricket (*Grillotalpa*); sty(e) (*in the eye*).

wert [ve:rt], *adj.* 1. (*Dat.*) dear (to), valued, esteemed (by); ***Sie und Ihre –e Frau,*** you and your dear wife; ***Sie und Ihre –e Familie,*** you and your esteemed family; ***wie ist Ihr –er Name?*** to whom have I the honour of speaking? (*Comm.*) ***Ihr –es Schreiben,*** your esteemed letter *or* favour; 2. (*Gen.*) worth (*s.th.*), worthy (of); ***nicht viel –,*** of no great value, (*coll.*) not up to much; ***nicht der Mühe –,*** not worth the trouble; ***nicht der Rede –,*** not worth speaking of *or* mentioning; ***nichts –,*** of no value, valueless, worth nothing, (*coll.*) no good, good for nothing; ***das ist schon viel –,*** that's a good point in its favour, (*coll.*) there's s.th. to be said for that; ***du bist es nicht –, daß ich mir Mühe gebe,*** you do not deserve that I put myself to any trouble; ***keinen Schuß Pulver –*** or ***keinen (roten) Heller –,*** not worth a straw *or* a pin *or* a fig; (*coll.*) ***er ist 100,000 Pfund –,*** he is worth £100,000.

Wert, *m.* (**-(e)s,** *pl.* **-e**) value, worth; price, rate, standard (*of coin*); (*Phys., Math. etc.*) factor, coefficient; (*Chem.*) valence; (*Comm.*) asset; (*fig.*) value, merit, use; *pl.* (*Phys. etc.*) data, (*Comm.*) assets, securities; ***äußerer –,*** face value; (*Math.*) ***fester –,*** fixed quantity; ***von geringem –,*** of little value; (*Comm.*) ***greifbare –e,*** tangible assets; ***großen – legen auf*** (*Acc.*), set a high value on, set great store by, attach great importance to; make a point of, insist on; ***im –e von,*** to the value of, valued at; ***innerer –,*** intrinsic value; ***im – sinken,*** depreciate; (*Math.*) ***veränderlicher –,*** variable quantity.

Wert|angabe, *f.* declared value; declaration of value. **–arbeit,** *f.* high-class work(manship). **–berichtigung,** *f.* adjustment of value. **wertbeständig,** *adj.* stable, of fixed value. **Wert|-beständigkeit,** *f.* stability. **–bestimmung,** *f.* determination of value *or* (*Chem.*) valence; (e)valuation, estimate, appraisal, assessment. **–brief,** *m.* letter containing valuables, registered letter.

werten ['ve:rtən], *v.t.* value, evaluate, estimate, appraise; classify, rate, judge; (*Footb.*) ***ein Tor nicht –,*** disallow a goal.

Wertgegenstand ['ve:rtge:gənʃtant], *m.* article of value, *pl.* valuables. **wertgeschätzt,** *adj.* valued, esteemed. **–wertig,** *adj.suff.* of . . . value, (*Chem.*) -valent; *e.g.* ***gleich–,*** of equal value, equivalent; ***minder–,*** inferior; (*Chem.*) ***drei–,*** trivalent. **Wertigkeit,** *f.* (*Chem.*) valence. **Wertigkeitsstufe,** *f.* (*Chem.*) valency. **wertlos,** *adj.* worthless, valueless, useless, futile. **wertmäßig,** *adj., adv.* (*Comm.*) ad valorem. **Wert|maßstab, –messer,** *m.* standard of value, criterion. **–minderung,** *f.* depreciation, deterioration in value. **–paket,** *n.* insured parcel. **–papier,** *n.* (*Comm.*) bond, security; scrip. **–sachen,** *f.pl.* valuables. **wertschätzen,** *v.t.* (*sep.*) appreciate *or* value *or* esteem highly. **Wert|schätzung,** *f.* esteem, regard (*Gen.*, for), estimation, appreciation (of). **–schrift,** *f.* (*Swiss*) *see* **–papier. –sendung,** *f.* remittance (*of money*), consignment of valuables.

Wertung ['ve:rtuŋ], *f.* valuing, appraising, rating, judging, evaluation; valuation, appraisal, estimate; estimation, appreciation.

Wert|urteil, *n.* value judgement. **–verhältnis,** *n.* comparative *or* relative value, ratio of values. **–verringerung,** *f. See* **–minderung. wertvoll,** *adj.* valuable, precious. **Wert|zeichen,** *n.* (postage) stamp. **–zoll,** *m.* ad valorem duty. **–zuwachs,** *m.* increment value.

Werwolf ['ve:rvɔlf], *m.* werewolf.

wes [vɛs], (*obs.*) *see* **wessen**; (*B.*) – ***das Herz voll ist, des gehet der Mund über,*** out of the abundance of the heart the mouth speaketh.

wesen ['ve:zən], *v.i.* (*Poet.*) live, be, (be at) work.

Wesen, *n.* 1. essence, substance; ***das gehört zum – der S.,*** that is the essence of the th.; 2. entity, being, creature, living thing, organism; ***das höchste –,*** the Supreme Being; 3. state, condition, nature, character, (*of a p. only*) personality; 4. conduct, demeanour, air, ways, bearing, attitude; ***gesetztes –,*** quiet bearing; ***gekünsteltes*** or ***gezwungenes –,*** affected air; ***mürrisches –,*** disgruntled air, morose demeanour; ***sein – mißfällt mir,*** his manner *or* his whole attitude displeases me; 5. (*coll.*) fuss, bother, bustle, noise; (*coll.*) ***sein – treiben,*** go on in one's own way; be up to one's mischief; (*coll.*) ***viel –s machen von,*** make a fuss about; (*coll.*) ***nicht viel –s mit ihm machen,*** treat him unceremoniously *or* with scant ceremony; 6. (*oft. in compounds*) organization, system; affairs, matters, concerns, *e.g.* ***Bank–,*** banking; ***Finanz–,*** financial affairs *or* matters; ***Rettungs–,*** rescue service.

wesenhaft ['ve:zənhaft], *adj.* real, substantial; characteristic. **Wesenheit,** *f.* spirit, essence, substance, decisive *or* significant factors; (*Phil.*) substantiality. **wesenlos,** *adj.* incorporeal, unsubstantial; unreal, shadowy; insignificant, trivial.

Wesensart ['ve:zənsʔa:rt], *f.* character, nature, personality, temperament, mentality. **wesenseigen,** *adj.* characteristic. **Wesenseinheit,** *f.* (*Eccl.*) consubstantiality. **wesens|eins,** *pred.adj. See* **–gleich. –fremd,** *adj.* incompatible, (*pred.*) foreign to one's nature. **–gleich,** *adj.* homogeneous, identical (in character); (*Eccl.*) consubstantial. **Wesens|gleichheit,** *f.* identity (of character); *see also* **–einheit. –lehre,** *f.* ontology. **–zug,** *m.* characteristic gesture *or* trait.

wesentlich ['ve:zəntlɪç], *adj.* essential, substantial, material, vital, fundamental, intrinsic (***für,*** to); ***das Wesentliche,*** that which is essential, the vital point, the essential point *or* thing *or* factor; ***–er Inhalt eines Buchs,*** substance of a book; ***im –en,*** in the main, essentially.

Wesfall ['vɛsfal], *m.* (*Gram.*) genitive case.

weshalb ['vɛs'halp], **1.** *inter.pron.* why? for what reason? wherefore? **2.** *conj.* on account of which, and so, and therefore, (*coll.*) and that's why.

Wesir [ve'zi:r], *m.* (**-s,** *pl.* **-e**) vizier.

Wespe ['vɛspə], *f.* wasp. **Wespen|bussard,** *m.* (*Orn.*) honey-buzzard (*Pernis apivorus*). **–nest,** *n.* (*coll.*) ***in ein – greifen*** or ***stechen,*** stir up a hornet's nest, put one's foot in it. **–stich,** *m.* wasp sting. **–taille,** *f.* (*fig.*) wasp-waist.

wessen ['vɛsən], 1. *Gen. of* **wer,** whose; ***in – Hause wohnst du?*** in whose house do you live? 2. *Gen. of* **was,** of which, of what; ***– klagt man dich an?*** what are you charged with? ***– er mich anklagt,*** what he accused me of.

West [vɛst], *m.* 1. west; 2. (*Poet.*) (**-s,** *pl.* **-e**) west wind.

Weste ['vɛstə], *f.* waistcoat, vest; ***er hat eine reine*** or ***saubere*** or ***weiße –,*** he has not a blot on his scutcheon; (*coll.*) ***feste auf die –!*** let him have it!

Westen ['vɛstən], *m.* the west, the Occident; ***nach*** or ***gegen –,*** westward, towards the west.

Westentasche ['vɛstəntaʃə], *f.* waistcoat *or* vest pocket. **Westentaschenformat,** *n.* ***im –,*** (vest-) pocket-size.

Westeuropa ['vɛstʔɔyro:pa], *n.* Western Europe. **westeuropäisch,** *adj.* Western European; ***–e Zeit,*** Greenwich (mean) time.

Westfale [vɛst'fa:lə], *m.* (**-n** *pl.* **-n**). Westphalian. **Westfalen,** *n.* Westphalia. **westfälisch** [vɛst'fɛ:lɪʃ], *adj.* Westphalian.

Westindien [vɛst'ɪndiən], *n.* the West Indies. **Westindienfahrer,** *m.* West-Indiaman (*ship*).

westisch ['vɛstɪʃ], *adj.* (*Ethn.*) Mediterranean. **westlich, 1.** *adj.* west(ern), westerly, occidental. **2.** *adv.* westward; ***– von,*** (to the) west(ward) of. **West|mächte,** *f.pl.* Western powers. **–mark,** *f.* West-German mark. **–wind,** *m.* west(erly) wind.

weswegen [vɛs've:gən], *inter.pron. See* **weshalb.**

wett [vɛt], *adj.* (*only with* ***sein*** or ***werden***) equal, even; (*coll.*) ***nun sind wir –,*** now we are quits.

Wett|annahme(stelle), *f. See* **–büro. –bewerb,** *m.* competition, contest; (*Comm.*) ***freier –,*** free enterprise *or* competition; (*Comm.*) ***unlauterer –,*** unfair competition. **–bewerber,** *m.* competitor, contestant. **wettbewerbsfähig,** *adj.* competitive. **Wettbüro,** *n.* betting office.

Wette ['vɛtə], *f.* bet, wager; (*fig.*) rivalry; (*fig.*) ***ich gehe jede – ein,*** I bet you ten to one; ***was gilt die –?*** what do you bet? ***um*** or (*Austr.*) ***in die – laufen,*** race (against), run a race; ***sie boten mir um die – ihre Dienste an,*** they vied with each other in their offers of assistance.

Wetteifer ['vɛtʔaɪfər], *m.* rivalry, emulation. **wetteifern,** *v.i.* (*insep.*) (***mit***) compete, contend, vie (with) (***um,*** for); rival, emulate.

wetten ['vɛtən], *v.t., v.i.* bet, wager (***mit ihm,*** him; ***um es,*** it), stake; ***– auf*** (*Acc.*), bet on, back (*horse etc.*); ***es läßt sich Hundert gegen Eins – daß . . .,*** it's a 100 to 1 that . . .; (*fig.*) ***so haben wir nicht gewettet,*** we did not bargain for that. **Wetten,** *n.* betting. **Wettende(r),** *m., f.* better, bettor, backer, punter.

[1]**Wetter** ['vɛtər], *m. See* **Wettende(r).**

[2]**Wetter,** *n.* weather; bad weather, storm; ***ein – zieht sich zusammen,*** a storm is gathering; ***es ist schönes –,*** it is a fine day, the weather is fine; (*coll.*) ***alle –!*** good gracious! good heavens! dear me! gee! golly! my word! good Lord! (*coll.*) ***– noch (ein)-mal!*** hang *or* confound it! damnation! ***falls das – mitmacht,*** weather permitting; (*Min.*) ***schlagende –,*** firedamp.

Wetter|ansage, *f. See* **–bericht. –aussichten,** *f.pl.* weather prospects. **–beobachter,** *m.* meteorologist. **–bericht,** *m.* meteorological report; weather report *or* forecast. **–dach,** *n.* canopy, eaves, shelter. **–dienst,** *m.* meteorological *or* weather service. **–fahne,** *f.* weather-vane. **wetterfest,** *adj.* weatherproof. **Wetter|führung,** *f.* ventilation of mines. **–funk,** *m.* radio weather-forecasts. **–glas,** *n.* barometer. **–hahn,** *m.* weather-cock. **wetterhart,** *adj.* weather-beaten. **Wetter|karte,** *f.* weather chart. **–kunde,** *f.* meteorology. **–lage,** *f.* weather conditions. **wetterleuchten,** *v.i.* (*insep.*) ***es wetterleuchtet,*** it lightens, there is sheet-lightning. **Wetter|leuchten,** *n.* sheet-lightning. **–mantel,** *m.* cape, raincoat. **–meldung,** *f.*, **–nachrichten,** *f.pl. See* **–bericht.**

wettern ['vɛtərn], *v.i.* (*aux.* h. & s.), *imp.* be stormy; (*fig.*) curse and swear, storm, bluster, thunder; (*fig.*) ***– gegen,*** inveigh against.

Wetter|schacht, *m.* (*Min.*) air-shaft. **–schaden,** *m.* storm damage; damage from exposure. **–schutz,** *m.* protection from the weather *or* against exposure. **–seite,** *f.* weather-side. **–stelle,** *f.* weather centre *or* bureau. **–sturz,** *m.* sudden fall of temperature. **–tür,** *f.* (*Min.*) ventilation trap. **–umschlag,** *m.* sudden change in the weather. **–voraussage, –vorhersage,** *f.* weather-forecast. **–wart,** *m.* meteorological observer, (*coll.*) weatherman. **–warte,** *f.* meteorological *or* weather station. **–wechsel,** *m.* change of weather. **wetterwendisch,** *adj.* fickle, capricious, changeable. **Wetter|wolke,** *f.* storm-cloud, thunder-cloud. **–zeichen,** *n.* sign of approaching storm.

Wett|fahrt, *f.* motor- *or* cycle- *or* boat-race. **–fliegen,** *n.*, **–flug,** *m.* air-race. **–kampf,** *m.* competition, contest, match. **–kämpfer,** *m.* competitor, contestant. **–kurs,** *m.* (betting) odds. **–lauf,** *m.* (foot-) race, skiing-race. **–läufer,** *m.* runner. **wett-**

machen, *v.t.* (*sep.*) *es –,* make amends *or* (*coll.*) up for it, make it good (*bei,* with), (*coll.*) make it up (to), square it (with). **Wett|rennen,** *n.* race; racing. **–rudern,** *n.* boat-race. **–rüsten,** *n.* armaments race. **–schwimmen,** *n.* swimming contest. **–segeln,** *n.* regatta. **–spiel,** *n.* match. **–springen,** *n.* ski-jumping competition. **–steuer,** *f.* betting tax. **–streit,** *m.* (*usu. fig.*) contest, competition, emulation. **–zettel,** *m.* betting slip.

wetzen ['vɛtsən], **1.** *v.t.* whet, grind, sharpen. **2.** *v.i.* rub, brush (against). **Wetz|stahl,** *m.* honing steel. **–stein,** *m.* whetstone, none.

wich [vɪç], **wiche,** *see* **weichen.**

Wichs [vɪks], *m.* (**-es,** *pl.* **-e**) (German) students' gala dress; (*sl.*) glad rags; ***sich in – werfen,*** deck o.s. out; ***in vollem (höchstem) –,*** decked out, in full dress, in one's best clothes.

Wichsbürste ['vɪksby:rstə], *f.* blacking-brush. **Wichse,** *f.* blacking, boot-polish; (*sl.*) thrashing, tanning. **wichsen,** *v.t.* black, polish (*boots etc.*); (*dial.*) wax (*thread, a floor etc.*); (*sl.*) thrash, tan; *see* **gewichst. Wichser,** *m.* bootblack; (*coll.*) awkward situation, jam, hole. **Wichsier** [–'si:r], *m.* (*coll.*) bootblack. **Wichs|lappen,** *m.* polishing cloth. **–zeug,** *n.* shoe-cleaning utensils.

Wicht [vɪçt], *m.* (**-(e)s,** *pl.* **-e**) creature, little child, urchin, brat, chit, wight; ***armer –,*** poor wretch; ***grober –,*** rough customer; ***kleiner –,*** whipper-snapper.

Wichte ['vɪçtə], *f.* specific gravity.

Wichtel ['vɪçtəl], *m. or n.,* **Wichtelmännchen,** *n.* brownie, pixie, goblin.

wichtig ['vɪctɪc], *adj.* weighty, essential; important, significant, vital, momentous, serious; ***– tun, sich – machen,*** give o.s. airs. **Wichtigkeit,** *f.* importance, significance, seriousness, import, moment, consequence. **Wichtig|tuer,** *m.* pompous ass, busybody, Jack-in-office. **–tuerei,** *f.* self-importance, pomposity. **wichtigtuerisch,** *adj.* pompous, bumbling.

Wicke ['vɪkə], *f.* (*Bot.*) vetch (*Vicia*); (*coll.*) ***in die –n gehen,*** get lost; come down in the world.

Wickel ['vɪkəl], *f.* (-, *pl.* **-n**) *or m.* roll; packing, wrapping, wrapper; curl-paper; ***feuchter –,*** wet compress; ***heißer –,*** hot fomentation; (*coll.*) ***beim – kriegen,*** take *or* seize by the scruff of the neck, collar, get one's hands on. **Wickel|band,** *n.* baby's binder, swaddling-band. **–bär,** *m.* (*Zool.*) kinkajou (*Potus flavus*). **–blatt,** *n.* wrapper, outside leaf (*of cigar*). **–gamasche,** *f.* puttee. **–kind,** *n.* baby in arms, baby in long *or* swaddling clothes. **–maschine,** *f.* automatic winder, lap-machine.

wickeln ['vɪkəln], **1.** *v.t.* roll (up), coil (up), wind (up), wrap (up); put (*hair*) in curlers; dress, swathe, swaddle (*a baby*); roll, make (*cigarettes*); ***in ein*** or ***zu einem Knäuel –,*** roll into a ball; ***man kann ihn um den Finger –,*** you can twist him round your little finger. **2.** *v.r.* wind, coil, twist (*um,* round); ***sich in eine Decke –,*** wrap o.s. in a blanket, wrap a blanket round o.s.; (*fig.*) ***sich aus dem Handel –,*** wriggle out of the difficulty; (*sl.*) ***schief gewickelt sein,*** be wildly mistaken, have got hold of the wrong end of the stick.

Wickel|puppe, *f.* baby-doll. **–ranke,** *f.* tendril, runner, cirrus. **wickelrankig,** *adj.* (*Bot.*) cirrate. **Wickel|schwanz,** *m.* (*Zool.*) prehensile tail. **–tuch,** *n.* wrapper; *see also* **–band. –zeug,** *n.* baby-clothes, swaddling-clothes.

Wickler ['vɪklər], *m.* (*Ent.*) (leaf-)roller moth (*Tortricidae*). **Wicklung,** *f.* (*Elec.*) winding.

Widder ['vɪdər], *m.* ram; (*Mil.*) battering-ram; (*Astr.*) Aries. **Widderchen,** *n.,* **Widderschwärmer,** *m.* (*Ent.*) burnet-moth (*Zygaenidae*).

wider ['vi:dər], *prep.* (*Acc.*) against, contrary to, in opposition to, in the face of, versus; ***– Willen,*** against one's will, unwillingly; ***das Für und Wider,*** the pros and cons.

Wider–, wider–, *sep. or insep. pref.* counter-, contra-, anti–, re–, with–; *see examples below.*

widerborstig ['vi:dərbɔrstɪç], *adj.* obstinate, stubborn, perverse, refractory, cross-grained.

widerfahren [vi:dər'fa:rən], *irr.v.i.* (*insep.*) (*3rd p. only with Dat.*) (*aux.* s.) happen *or* occur *or* fall to, befall; ***mir ist viel Ehre –,*** great honour has been done to me; ***ihm ist ein Unglück –,*** he has met with an accident; ***ihm – lassen,*** mete out to him; ***ihm Gerechtigkeit – lassen,*** do justice to him, give him his due.

wider|haarig, *adj. See* **–borstig. Wider|haken,** *m.* barb. **–hall,** *m.* (**-(e)s,** *pl.* **-e**) echo, reverberation, resonance; (*fig.*) response. **widerhallen,** *v.i.* (*usu. sep. also insep.*) (re-)echo, resound (***von,*** with). **Wider|halt,** *m.* support, backing. **–handlung,** *f.* (*Swiss*) contravention. **–klage,** *f.* counter-plea, counter-claim. **–lager,** *n.* abutment, buttress, pier.

widerlegbar [vi:dərle:kba:r], *adj.* refutable. **widerlegen,** *v.t.* (*insep.*) refute, confute, rebut, disprove, negative; ***seine eignen Worte –,*** give the lie to one's own words. **Widerlegung,** *f.* refutation, confutation, (*Law*) rebuttal.

widerlich ['vi:dərlɪç], *adj.* loathsome, sickening, distasteful, unsavoury, nauseous, nauseating, obnoxious, offensive, disgusting, repugnant, repulsive; *see also* **widerwärtig. Widerlichkeit,** *f.* loathsomeness, distastefulness, offensiveness, repulsiveness. **widern,** *v.t.* sicken, disgust, be repugnant *or* distasteful *or* obnoxious to.

widernatürlich ['vi:dərnaty:rlɪç], *adj.* unnatural, perverse; ***–e Unzucht,*** sodomy. **Widernatürlichkeit,** *f.* perversity.

Widerpart ['vi:dərpart], *m.* (**-(e)s,** *pl.* **-e**) adversary, opponent; ***– halten*** (*Dat.*), oppose.

widerraten [vi:dər'ra:tən], *irr.v.t.* (*insep.*) ***es ihm –,*** dissuade him from it, persuade him against it.

widerrechtlich ['vi:dərrɛçtlɪç], *adj.* wrongful, unjust; unlawful, illegal; ***sich*** (*Dat.*) ***– aneignen,*** misappropriate, usurp; ***– betreten,*** trespass on. **Widerrechtlichkeit,** *f.* unlawfulness, illegality.

Widerrede ['vi:dərre:də], *f.* contradiction, objection; ***ohne –,*** unquestioning(ly); (*coll.*) unquestionably.

Widerrist ['vi:dərrɪst], *m.* (**-es,** *pl.* **-e**) (*Vet.*) withers.

Widerruf ['vi:dərru:f], *m.* recantation, retraction, disavowal; countermand, cancellation, revocation, (*Law*) disclaimer; ***bis auf –,*** until recalled *or* countermanded *or* cancelled. **wider|rufbar,** *see* **–ruflich. –rufen** [–'ru:fən], *irr.v.t.* (*insep.*) revoke, repeal; disavow, recant, retract; withdraw, countermand, cancel. **–ruflich, 1.** *adj.* revocable. **2.** *adv.* revocably; on probation, at will *or* pleasure.

Widersacher ['vi:dərzaxər], *m.* antagonist, adversary, opponent.

Widerschein ['vi:dərʃaɪn], *m.* reflection.

wider|setzen [vi:dər'zɛtsən], *v.r.* (*insep.*) (*Dat.*) oppose, resist, combat, set one's face against; disobey (*the law*). **–setzlich,** *adj.* obstructive, refractory, insubordinate. **Widersetzlichkeit,** *f.* insubordination, recalcitrance, obstructiveness.

Widersinn ['vi:dərzɪn], *m.* nonsense, absurdity, paradox. **widersinnig,** *adj.* nonsensical, absurd, paradoxical, preposterous; (*pred.*) contrary to common-sense, flying in the face of reason.

widerspenstig ['vi:dərʃpɛnstɪç], *adj.* rebellious, unmanageable, refractory, recalcitrant, obstinate, stubborn, (*of horses*) restive, unruly, (*as hair*) unruly; ***der Widerspenstigen Zähmung,*** The Taming of the Shrew. **Widerspenstigkeit,** *f.* obstinacy, stubbornness, recalcitrance, refractoriness, unruliness.

widerspiegeln ['vi:dərʃpi:gəln], *v.r.* (*sep.*) be reflected. **Widerspieg(e)lung,** *f.* reflexion.

Widerspiel ['vi:dərʃpi:l], *n.* opposite, reverse, contrary; counterpart; ***ihm das – halten,*** act in opposition to him.

wider|sprechen [vi:dər'ʃprɛçən], **1.** *irr.v.i.* (*insep.*) (*Dat.*) contradict; be at variance with, conflict with; oppose, gainsay; ***diese Sätze – einander,*** these propositions are contradictory. **2.** *irr.v.r.* (*insep.*) (*of a p.*) contradict o.s.; (*of ideas etc.*) be (self-) contradictory. **–sprechend,** *adj.* contradictory, conflicting. **Widerspruch,** *m.* contradiction; opposition, disagreement, conflict; ***einen – beseitigen,*** reconcile a contradiction; – ***in sich selbst,*** contradiction in terms; ***innerer –,*** inconsistency; ***im – stehen zu,*** be incompatible *or* at variance with. **Widerspruchsgeist,** *m.* contradictoriness, (*coll.*) contrariness. **widerspruchslos, 1.** *adj.* uncontradicted. **2.** *adv.* without contradiction, meekly. **widerspruchsvoll,** *adj.* (self-)contradictory, inconsistent.

Widerstand ['vi:dərʃtant], *m.* opposition, (*also Elec.*) resistance; (*Rad.*) resistor, (*Elec.*) rheostat, (*Tech.*) strength, stability; – ***leisten,*** offer *or* (*coll.*) put up resistance, resist; (*Mil.*) ***hinhaltender –,*** delaying action; (*Av.*) ***induzierter –,*** induced drag; (*Av.*) ***schädlicher –,*** parasitic drag; (*Law*) – ***gegen die Staatsgewalt,*** resisting an officer in the execution of his duty. **Widerstandsbewegung,** *f.* (*Pol.*) resistance movement. **widerstandsfähig,** *adj.* resistant, robust, rugged. **Widerstands|fähigkeit,** *f.* (power of) resistance, strength, stability, ruggedness, robustness; load-bearing capacity. **–herd, –kern, –kessel,** *m.* (*Mil.*) centre *or* pocket of resistance. **–kraft,** *f. See* **–fähigkeit. widerstandslos, 1.** *adj.* unresisting. **2.** *adv.* without resistance, meekly. **Widerstands|messer,** *m.* (*Elec.*) ohmmeter, (*coll.*) megger. **–nest,** *n. See* **–herd. –wert,** *m.* coefficient of resistance.

widerstehen [vi:dər'ʃte:ən], *irr.v.i.* (*insep.*) (*Dat.*) resist, withstand; be repugnant to, (*coll.*) go against the grain; (*of food*) disagree with; ***nicht –,*** succumb to.

widerstreben [vi:dər'ʃtre:bən], *v.i.* (*insep.*) (*Dat.*) resist, oppose; struggle *or* strive against; be repugnant to; ***es widerstrebt mir,*** it goes against the grain (with me). **Widerstreben,** *n.* opposition, resistance; reluctance; ***mit –,*** reluctantly, with reluctance; ***ohne –,*** readily, with a good grace. **widerstrebend,** *adv.* reluctantly, with reluctance.

Widerstreit ['vi:dərʃtraɪt], *m.* opposition, antagonism, (*coll.*) clash, conflict. **wider|streiten** [–'ʃtraɪtən], *irr.v.i.* (*insep.*) conflict *or* (*coll.*) clash (*Dat.*, with), be antagonistic *or* contrary (to), militate (against). **–streitend,** *adj.* antagonistic, conflicting.

widerwärtig ['vi:dərvɛrtɪç], *adj.* unpleasant, disagreeable, nasty; repulsive, loathsome, offensive, repugnant, disgusting, hateful, odious. **Widerwärtigkeit,** *f.* nastiness, disagreeableness, loathsomeness, repulsiveness, offensiveness; nuisance, unpleasantness, bother; adversity, calamity untoward happening.

Widerwille ['vi:dərvɪlə], *m.* dislike (***gegen,*** for), aversion, antipathy (to), disgust (for), loathing (of), repugnance, reluctance. **widerwillig, 1.** *adj.* reluctant, unwilling, grudging. **2.** *adv.* reluctantly, unwillingly, grudgingly, with reluctance.

widmen ['vɪdmən], **1.** *v.t.* dedicate, inscribe (*a book etc.*) (*Dat.*, to). **2.** *v.r.* devote o.s., (*coll.*) give o.s. up; devote one's time *or* attention *or* care, give up one's time (*Dat.*, to). **Widmung,** *f.* dedication. **Widmungsexemplar,** *n.* presentation copy.

widrig ['vi:drɪç], *adj.* adverse, contrary; inimical, unfavourable, hostile; *see also* **widerwärtig**; ***–e Umstände,*** adverse *or* unfavourable circumstances. **widrigenfalls,** *adv.* (*Comm.*) failing which, in default whereof. **Widrigkeit,** *f.* unpleasantness, untoward event, adversity; *see also* **Widerwärtigkeit**; ***allerlei –en,*** all sorts of unpleasantness(es).

wie [vi:], **1.** *adv.* **(a)** (*question*) how? in what way? to what extent? – ***geht's?*** how are you (getting on)? – ***bitte?*** what did you say? (I beg your) pardon! – ***wäre es, wenn . . .?*** what if . . .? – ***wäre es mit . . .?*** what about . . .? – ***denn anders?*** how could it be otherwise? how else? **(b)** (*exclamation*) how! (*coll.*) ***und –!*** and how! (*sl.*) not half! – ***leicht man sich täuscht!*** how easily one is deceived! **(c)** (*manner*) – ***schwer es mir auch ankommt,*** however hard it may be for me, cost what it may; – ***sie alle heißen mögen,*** whatever their names might be; – ***dem auch sei,*** be that as it may, however that may be. **2.** *conj.* **(a)** (*comparison*) as, like, such as; ***er ist – ein Freund,*** he is as *or* like a friend; ***ein Mann – er,*** a man such as *or* such a man as he (is); ***so – ich bin,*** such *or* just as I am; – ***sehr ich mich bemühe,*** however hard I try, try as I will; – ***sich's gehört,*** as is (right and) proper; – ***gesagt,*** as I have *or* as has been stated; – ***oben,*** as above; ***schön – ein Engel,*** beautiful as an angel; – ***du mir, so ich dir,*** as you treat me, so I shall treat you; (*coll.*) tit for tat; ***so groß –,*** as big as; ***nicht so groß –,*** not as *or* so big as; (*Prov.*) – ***man's treibt, so geht's,*** as you make your bed, so you must lie; (*Prov.*) – ***die Saat, so die Ernte,*** like father like son; **(b)** (*time*) (just) as; – ***ich vorbeiging, kam er heraus,*** he came out just as I was passing; – ***er dies hörte, ging er fort,*** on hearing this he left; ***ich sah, – die Tränen ihr in die Augen traten,*** I saw the tears coming to her eyes; – ***gesagt, so getan,*** no sooner said than done.

Wie, *n.* ***das – und Warum,*** the why and the wherefore; ***auf das – kommt es an,*** it all depends on the way *or* on how it's done.

Wiede ['vi:də], *f.* (*dial.*) withe, willow-twig. **Wiedehopf,** *m.* **(-(e)s,** *pl.* **-e)** (*Orn.*) hoopoe (*Upupa epos*).

wieder ['vi:dər], *adv.* again, afresh, once more, anew; back (again); in return; – ***und*** – or ***immer –,*** again and again, time and again, over and over again; ***hin und –,*** now and then, now and again, from time to time.

Wieder–, wieder–, *pref.* (*v. pref. sep. except where specifically mentioned below*) re–, back (again), in return (for).

Wieder|abdruck, *m.* reprint, new impression. **–anfang,** *m.* recommencement, (*of school etc.*) reopening.

wieder|anknüpfen, *v.t.* (*fig.*) renew. **–anstellen,** *v.t.* re-appoint, re-install. **Wiederanstellung,** *f.* re-appointment.

Wiederaufbau [vi:dər'aufbau], *m.* reconstruction, rebuilding; (*fig.*) rehabilitation. **wiederaufbauen,** *v.t.* reconstruct, rebuild; (*fig.*) rehabilitate.

wieder|aufblühen, *v.i. See* **–aufleben.**

wiederauferstehen [vi:dər'aufˀɛrʃte:ən], *irr.v.i.* (*aux.* s.) rise from the dead, be resurrected. **Wiederauferstehung,** *f.* resurrection.

wiederaufkommen [vi:dər'aufkɔmən], *irr.v.i.* (*aux.* s.) (*of a patient*) recover, get well again; (*of fashions*) revive, be revived. **Wiederaufkommen,** *n.* recovery; revival.

wiederaufladen [vi:dər'aufla:dən], *irr.v.t.* recharge (*battery*).

wiederaufleben [vi:dər'aufle:bən], *v.i.* revive; – ***lassen,*** revive, resuscitate; re-instate. **Wiederaufleben,** *n.* revival, rebirth.

Wiederaufnahme [vi:dər'aufna:mə], *f.* resumption. **Wiederaufnahmeverfahren,** *n* (*Law*) re-trial, new hearing. **wiederaufnehmen,** *irr.v.t.* resume.

wiederaufrüsten [vi:dər'aufrystən], *v.t., v.i.* re-arm. **Wiederaufrüstung,** *f.* rearmament, re-arming.

wiederauftauchen [vi:dər'auftauxən], *v.i.* (*aux.* s.) (*of submarine*) re-surface; (*fig.*) reappear, come to light again, (*coll.*) turn up again.

wiederauftreten [vi:dər'auftre:tən], *irr.v.i.* (*aux.* s.) reappear. **Wiederauftreten,** *n.* reappearance.

Wieder|beginn, *m. See* **–anfang.**

wiederbekommen ['vi:dərbəkɔmən], *irr.v.t.* get back, recover.

wiederbeleben ['vi:dərbəle:bən], *v.t.* revive, reactivate, resuscitate, re-animate, revitalize, put new life into. **Wiederbelebung,** *f.* revival, resuscitation, re-animation. **Wiederbelebungsversuch,** *m.* artificial respiration.

wiederbeschaffen ['vi:dərbəʃafən], *v.t.* replace. **Wiederbeschaffungspreis,** *m.* cost of replacement.

wiederbringen ['vi:dərbrɪŋən], *irr.v.t.* return, restore, bring back (*Dat.*, to).

wiedereinfinden [vi:dər'aɪnfɪndən], *irr.v.r.* turn up again.

Wiedereinfuhr [vi:dər'aɪnfu:r], *f.* re-importation. **wiedereinführen,** *v.t.* re-introduce, re-establish; (*Comm.*) re-import.

Wiedereingliederung [vi:dər'aɪngli:dəruŋ], *f.* re-integration; (*of workers*) resettlement.

wiedereinlösen [vi:dər'aɪnlø:zən], *v.t.* redeem. **Wiedereinlösung,** *f.* redemption.

Wiedereinnahme [vi:dər'aɪnna:mə], *f.* recapture. **wiedereinnehmen,** *irr.v.t.* recapture (*prisoner*); resume (*one's seat*).

Wiedereinreiseerlaubnis [vi:dər'aɪnraɪzəɛrlaupnɪs], *f.* re-entry permit.

wiedereinsetzen [vi:dər'aɪnzɛtsən], *v.t.* replace; reinstate, reinstall (*in* (*Acc.*), in), restore (to). **Wiedereinsetzung,** *f.* replacement, restitution; reinstatement, restoration.

wiedereinstellen [vi:dər'aɪnʃtɛlən], *v.t.* re-employ, re-engage; (*Mil.*) re-enlist. **Wiedereinstellung,** *f.* re-employment; re-enlistment.

wieder|erhalten, *irr.v.i. See* **–bekommen.**

wiedererkennen ['vi:dərˀɛrkɛnən], *irr.v.t.* recognize; ***nicht wiederzuerkennen,*** past recognition, totally changed. **Wiedererkennung,** *f.* recognition.

wieder|erlangen, *v.t. See* **–bekommen**; be restored to (*a lost position*). **–ernennen,** *irr.v.t.* reappoint. **–erobern,** *v.t.* reconquer, recapture.

Wiedereröffnung ['vi:dərˀɛrœfnuŋ], *f.* re-opening; resumption (*of hostilities*).

wieder|erscheinen, *irr.v.i.* (*aux.* s.) reappear; resume publication. **–erstatten,** *v.t. See* **–bringen**; (*expenses*) reimburse, refund, repay. **Wiedererstattung,** *f.* restitution; repayment, reimbursement, refund.

wiederfinden ['vi:dərfɪndən], **1.** *irr.v.t.* find once more. **2.** *irr.v.r.* return to normal, come to one's senses.

Wiedergabe ['vi:dərga:bə], *f.* 1. return, restitution; 2. (*Mus.*) rendering, (*Art*) reproduction. **Wiedergabe|güte,** *f.* (*Rad.*) fidelity, quality of reproduction. **–röhre,** *f.* (*T.V.*) (picture-)tube. **–treue,** *f.* fidelity of reproduction.

wiedergeben ['vi:dərge:bən], *irr.v.t.* 1. give back, return, restore (*Dat.*, to); 2. (*Art*) reproduce, (*Mus.*) render, interpret; (*from text*) quote.

wiedergeboren ['vi:dərgəbo:rən], *adj.* reborn, regenerated. **Wiedergeburt,** *f.* rebirth, regeneration, palingenesis.

wiedergewinnen ['vi:dərgəvɪnən], *irr.v.t.* recover, regain; reclaim (*used material*). **Wiedergewinnung,** *f.* recovery, reclamation, salvage.

wiedergutmachen [vi:dər'gu:tmaxən], *v.t.* make good, repair, cure (*a fault*); (*fig.*) make reparation *or* amends (*Dat.*, to); ***nicht wiedergutzumachen(d),*** irreparable. **Wiedergutmachung,** *f.* reparation, amends.

wiederherstellen [vi:dər'he:rʃtɛlən], *v.t.* restore, (*Med.*) cure; (*fig.*) re-establish. **Wiederherstellung,** *f.* restoration, (*Med.*) recovery, (*Law*) restitution; re-establishment.

wieder|holen, **1.** *v.t.* 1. (*sep.*) bring *or* fetch back; 2. (*insep.*) repeat, reiterate, say *or* do (over) again; ***kurz –,*** recapitulate, sum up. **2.** *v.r.* (*insep.*) (*of a p.*) repeat o.s.; (*of events*) happen (over and over) again, recur. **–holt** [–'ho:lt], **1.** *adj.* repeated, recurring. **2.** *adv.* repeatedly, (over) again, over and over again, again and again. **Wiederholung** [–'ho:luŋ], *f.* repetition, reiteration; repeat; ***kurze –,*** recapitulation, summing up. **Wiederholungs|fall,** *m.* ***im –,*** if it should occur again, in case of recurrence. **–kurs,** *m.* 1. revision course; 2. (*Swiss*) annual military training. **–spiel,** *n.* (*Spt.*) re-play. **–zeichen,** *n.* (*Mus.*) repeat; (*Typ.*) ditto marks.

Wiederhören ['vi:dərhø:rən], *n.* (*Tele.*) ***auf –!*** good-bye!

wiederinstandsetzen [vi:dərˀɪn'ʃtantzɛtsən], *v.t.* overhaul, repair, re-condition. **Wiederinstandsetzung,** *f.* overhaul, repair(s), re-conditioning.

wiederkäuen ['vi:dərkɔyən], **1.** *v.i.* ruminate, chew the cud. **2.** *v.t.* (*coll.*) repeat over and over again. **Wiederkäuer,** *m.* (*Zool.*) ruminant.

Wiederkauf ['vi:dərkauf], *m.* re-purchase; redemption (*of a pledge*).

Wiederkehr ['vi:dərke:r], *f.* return, reappearance; repetition, recurrence; ***25jährige –,*** 25th anniversary. **wieder|kehren,** *v.i.* (*aux.* s.) come back, return; reappear, recur, repeat itself. **–kehrend,** *adj.* recurring, periodical.

wiederkommen ['vi:dərkɔmən], *irr.v.i.* (*aux.* s.) come again *or* back, return. **Wiederkunft,** *f.* return.

wiedersehen ['vi:dərze:ən], **1.** *irr.v.t.* see *or* meet again. **2.** *irr.v.r.* see one another *or* see each other again, meet again. **Wiedersehen,** *n.* subsequent meeting, reunion; ***auf –!*** good-bye! au revoir! (*coll.*) so long!

Wiedertäufer ['vi:dərtɔyfər], *m.* (*Eccl.*) anabaptist.

wiederum ['vi:dərum], *adv.* (over) again, anew, afresh; on the other hand, on the contrary; in return, in (his, her, their *etc.*) turn.

wiedervereinigen ['vi:dərfɛrˀaɪnɪgən], *v.t.*, *v.r.* re-unite. **Wiedervereinigung,** *f.* reunion, (*Pol.*) reunification.

wiedervergelten ['vi:dərfɛrgɛltən], *irr.v.t.* requite, retaliate for, (*coll.*) pay back for. **Wiedervergeltung,** *f.* retaliation, reprisal, requital.

wiederverheiraten ['vi:dərfɛrhaɪra:tən], *v.t.*, *v.r.* re-marry. **Wiederverheiratung,** *f.* remarriage.

wiederverkaufen ['vi:dərfɛrkaufən], *v.t.* resell, retail. **Wiederverkäufer,** *m.* retailer. **Wiederverkaufspreis,** *m.* retail price.

wiederverpflichten ['vi:dərfɛrpflɪçtən], *v.t.*, *v.r.* (*Mil.*) re-enlist.

Wiederwahl ['vi:dərva:l], *f.* re-election. **wieder|wählbar,** *adj.* eligible for re-election. **–wählen,** *v.t.* re-elect.

Wiege ['vi:gə], *f.* cradle (*also Artil.*); ***von der – bis zur Bahre*** or ***zum Grabe,*** from (the) cradle to (the) grave.

Wiege|brett, *n.* chopping-board. **–brücke,** *f.* weigh-bridge. **–messer,** *n.* chopping-knife.

[1]**wiegen** ['vi:gən], **1.** *irr.v.t.* weigh. **2.** *irr.v.i.* weigh, have a weight of; (*fig.*) carry weight; ***was*** or ***wieviel – Sie?*** how heavy are you? what is your weight? (*fig.*) ***schwer –,*** carry (much) weight; ***schwerer – als,*** be heavier *or* weigh more than, outweigh.

[2]**wiegen,** **1.** *v.t.* rock (*a cradle, a child*); ***in (den) Schlaf –,*** rock to sleep; ***den Kopf –,*** sway one's head. **2.** *v.r.* sway, seesaw; (*fig.*) lull o.s. (*in* (*Acc.*), into), delude o.s. (with); ***–der Gang,*** rolling gait.

[3]**wiegen,** *v.t.* (*Cul.*) chop, mince.

Wiegen|druck, *m.* incunabulum, early printed book. **–fest,** *n.* birthday celebrations. **–kind,** *n.* baby, infant (in the cradle). **–korb,** *m.* bassinet. **–lied,** *n.* cradle-song, lullaby.

wiehern ['vi:ərn], *v.i.* neigh; (*fig.*) guffaw; ***–des Gelächter,*** guffaw, horse-laugh, (*sl.*) belly-laugh. **Wiehern,** *n.* neighing.

Wiek [vi:k], *f.* (-, *pl.* **-en**) (*dial.*) creek, cove, bay.

Wieling ['vi:lɪŋ], *m.* (**-s,** *pl.* **-e**) (*Naut.*) fender.

Wiemen ['vi:mən], *m.* (*dial.*) perch, roost; drying-frame.

Wien [vi:n], *n.* (*Geog.*) Vienna. **Wiener(in),** *m.* (*f.*), **wienerisch,** *adj.* Viennese.

Wiepe ['vi:pə], *f.* (*dial.*) wisp (*of straw etc.*).

wies [vi:s], *see* **weisen.**

Wiese ['vi:zə], *f.* meadow, field; pasture(-land); lawn, (*Poet.*) greensward, mead.

Wiesel ['vi:zəl], *n.* (*Zool.*) weasel (*Mustela vulgaris*).

Wiesen|ammer, *f.* (*Orn.*) meadow bunting (*Emberiza cioides*). **–bau,** *m.* cultivation of pasture *or* grassland. **–gras,** *n.* meadow-grass. **–grund,** *m.* grassy hollow. **–klee,** *m.* (*Bot.*) red clover (*Trifolium pratense*). **–knarrer,** *m.* (*Orn.*) *see* **Wachtelkönig.** **–knopf,** *m.* (*Bot.*) great burnet (*Sanguisorba*). **–pieper,** *m.* (*Orn.*) meadow pipit (*Anthus* *pratensis*). **-ralle,** *f.* (*Orn.*) *see* **Wachtelkönig. -schaumkraut,** *n.* (*Bot.*) cuckoo-flower, lady's smock (*Cardamine pratensis*). **-schmätzer,** *m.* (*Orn.*) *braunkehliger –, see* **Braunkehlchen**; *schwarzkehliger –, see* **Schwarzkehlchen. -weihe,** *m.* (*Orn.*) Montagu's harrier (*Circus pygargus*).

wie|so [–'zo:], *adv.* why? but why? – *weißt du das?* how is it you know that? **-viel,** *adv.* how much, *pl.* how many; – *Uhr ist es?* what time is it? **-vielt,** *adj.* which? what number? *den -en haben wir heute?* what is the date today? *den -en ist er in der Klasse?* what is his position in class? **-wohl,** *conj.* (al)though.

wild [vılt], *adj.* wild, savage, uncivilized, fierce, ferocious; enraged, furious, tempestuous, impetuous, unruly, turbulent, uproarious, unmanageable; wild, uncultured, (*pred.*) in the natural state, growing naturally; (*as hair*) unkempt, dishevelled; *-er Boden,* virgin soil; *-e Ehe,* concubinage; *-es Fleisch,* proud flesh; *-e Flucht,* headlong flight, rout; *-e Gegend,* rough *or* rugged country; (*Min.*) *-es Gestein,* dead rock; *-e Jagd,* (*Myth.*) Wotan's horde; (*coll.*) wild chase; *-es Leben,* disorderly life; *-es Mädchen,* tomboy; (*coll.*) *den -en Mann machen,* go wild *or* beserk; *-er Streik,* wildcat strike; *-es Volk,* savage tribe(s); (*Bot.*) *-er Wein,* Virginia creeper; *– machen,* enrage, infuriate, exasperate, (*coll.*) drive mad; *ein Tier – machen,* scare *or* frighten an animal; (*coll.*) *– sein auf* (*Acc.*), be mad *or* crazy about; (*coll.*) *sei nicht so –!* don't make such a noise *or* so much noise! *– wachsen,* grow wild; *– werden,* turn wild; (*of animals*) take fright, shy; (*coll.*) get wild, see red, (*sl.*) blow one's top.

Wild, *n.* **(-(e)s,** *no pl.*) (head of) game, deer; (*Cul.*) game, venison.

Wild|bach, *m.* (mountain) torrent. **-bad,** *n.* natural springs, hotsprings, thermal baths. **-bahn,** *f.* hunting-ground. **-braten,** *m.* roast venison. **-bret,** *n.* game, venison. **-dieb,** *m.* poacher. **-dieberei,** *f.* poaching.

Wilde ['vıldə], *f. See* **Wildnis. Wilde(r),** *m., f.* savage; (*Parl.*) freelance, independent; (*coll.*) *wie ein Wilder,* like mad. **Wilderer,** *m. See* **Wilddieb. wildern,** *v.i.* poach. **Wilde(s),** *n.* wildness.

Wild|fang, *m.* madcap, romp; (*of girls*) tomboy. **-fleisch,** *n. See* **-bret. wildfremd,** *adj.* utterly strange; *ein -er Mensch,* a complete *or* perfect *or* an utter stranger. **Wild|frevel,** *m. See* **-dieberei. -geschmack,** *m.* gamy taste. **Wild|heit,** *f.* wildness, savagery, barbarity, ferocity; anger, fury. **-hüter,** *m.* gamekeeper. **-leder,** *n.* deerskin, buckskin, doeskin, suede.

Wildling ['vıltlıŋ], *m.* **(-s,** *pl.* **-e)** parent stock, wild seedling *or* tree; wild beast; animal in the wild state; *see also* **Wildfang.**

Wildnis ['vıltnıs], *f.* (-, *pl.* **-se**) wilderness; wild, jungle.

Wild|park, *m.* deer-park, game-preserve. **-pret,** *n.* (*obs.*) *see* **-bret. -schaden,** *m.* damage done by game. **-schur,** *f.* heavy fur, travelling cloak. **-schütz(e),** *m.* poacher. **-schutzgebiet,** *n.* game-preserve. **-schwein,** *n.* (*Zool.*) wild boar (*Sus scrofa*). **wildwachsend,** *adj.* (growing) wild, self-sown. **Wildwasser,** *n.* torrent.

will [vıl], *see* **wollen.**

Wille ['vılə], *m.* **(-ns,** *pl.* **-n)** will, volition, determination; design, purpose, intent, intention, wish, inclination; *beim besten -n,* much as I would like to; *böser –,* ill-will; *aus freiem -n,* voluntarily, of one's own free will *or* own accord; *gegen seinen -n,* against his will, despite himself; *guter –,* good intention; *mit dem guten -n vorlieb nehmen,* take the will for the deed; *ich ließ ihm seinen -n,* I let him have his (own) way; *letzter –,* last will and testament; *mit -n,* on purpose, expressly, intentionally; *es ging ihm nach -n,* he had his wish *or* his (own) way; *ohne meinen -n,* without my consent, against my will; *wider -n,* unwillingly, involuntarily, unintentionally, in spite of o.s.; *ihm zu -n sein,* humour *or* oblige him, comply with his wishes; *das Mädchen war ihm zu -n,* the girl gave herself to him.

Willen ['vılən], *m.* (*Austr.*) *see* **Wille. willen,** *prep.* (*Gen.*) (*always preceded by um*) *um meinet–,* for my sake; *um Gottes* (*Himmels*) *–,* for God's (Heaven's) sake. **willenlos,** *adj.* irresolute, weak-minded, characterless, (*pred.*) lacking will-power, having no will of one's own. **Willenlosigkeit,** *f.* lack of will-power, indecision.

willens ['vıləns], *adv.* – *sein,* be willing *or* ready *or* disposed (to), have a mind *or* the intention (to).

Willens|akt, *m.* act of volition, voluntary action. **-änderung,** *f.* change of mind. **-anstrengung,** *f.* effort of will. **-äußerung,** *f.* expression of one's intention. **-erklärung,** *f.* (*Law*) declaratory act. **-freiheit,** *f.* free will, freedom of will. **-kraft,** *f.* will-power, strength of will *or* mind. **willensschwach,** *adj.* weak-willed. **Willensschwäche,** *f.* weak will, lack of will-power. **willensstark,** *adj.* strong-willed *or* -minded. **Willens|stärke,** *f. See* **-kraft.**

willentlich ['vıləntlıç], *adj.* intentional; *wissentlich und –,* consciously and deliberately.

willfahren ['vıl'fa:rən], *v.i.* (*p.p. willfahrt* or *gewillfahrt*) (*Dat.*) accede to, comply with, gratify, grant (*a wish*); humour, please (*a p.*). **willfährig,** *adj.* (*Dat.*) obliging, accommodating, complaisant, compliant. **Willfährigkeit,** *f.* compliancy, complaisance.

willig ['vılıç], *adj.* willing; ready; docile. **willigen,** *v.i. See* **einwilligen.**

Willkomm ['vılkɔm], *m.* **(-s,** *pl.* **-e)** (*Austr.*), **Willkommen,** *n. or m.* welcome, reception. **willkommen,** *adj.* (*Dat.*) welcome, acceptable, opportune, gratifying; *seien Sie –!* welcome! *ihn – heißen,* bid him welcome, welcome him.

Willkür ['vılky:r], *f.* option, choice; (*Law*) decree; discretion; arbitrariness, caprice; *ich lasse das in Ihre – gestellt,* I leave that to your (own) discretion; *nach –,* at will, as one pleases; in an arbitrary manner; *er ist ihrer – preisgegeben,* he is at their mercy. **Willkür|akt,** *m.* arbitrary action. **-herrschaft,** *f.* arbitrary rule, despotism. **willkürlich, 1.** *adj.* arbitrary, (*coll.*) high-handed; (*of choice*) random. **2.** *adv.* in an arbitrary manner, high-handedly, at will; at random. **Willkürlichkeit,** *f.* arbitrariness; arbitrary act.

willst [vılst], *see* **wollen.**

wimmeln ['vıməln], *v.i.* (*aux.* h. & s.) swarm, be crowded *or* (*coll.*) alive *or* crawling, abound, teem (*von,* with).

wimmen ['vımən], *v.i.* (*Swiss*) harvest grapes.

[1]**Wimmer** ['vımər], **1.** *f.* (-, *pl.* **-n**) vintage. **2.** *m.* vintager.

[2]**Wimmer, 1.** *m.* gnarled branch, tree-stump. **2.** *n.*, **Wimmerchen,** (*dial.*) **Wimmerl,** *n.* birthmark, mole.

wimmern ['vımərn], *v.i.* whimper, whine, moan, (*coll.*) grizzle.

Wimpel ['vımpəl], *m.* pennant, streamer, pennon, (*Naut.*) burgee. **Wimpelfall,** *m.* (*Naut.*) burgee halyard.

Wimper ['vımpər], *f.* (-, *pl.* **-n**) eyelash; *pl.* (*Bot., Zool.*) cilia; *ohne mit der – zu zucken,* without flinching *or* wincing; (*fig.*) without turning a hair *or* (*coll.*) batting an eyelid.

Wimperg ['vımpɛrk], *m.* **(-(e)s,** *pl.* **-e), Wimperge,** *f.* (*Archit.*) Gothic gable.

wimperig ['vımpərıç], *adj.* (*Bot., Zool.*) ciliate. **Wimperntusche,** *f.* mascara.

Wind [vınt], *m.* **(-(e)s,** *pl.* **-e)** wind; (*Med.*) flatulence, (*coll.*) wind; (*Hunt.*) scent; (*fig.*) humbug, bombast; *einen – abgehen lassen,* break wind; *beim –* or *hart* or *dicht am – segeln,* sail close-hauled, hug the wind; *bei – und Wetter,* in all weathers; (*fig.*) *– haben* or *bekommen von,* get wind of; (*Naut.*) *frischer –,* fresh breeze (Beaufort 5); *gegen den –,* into the wind; *guten – haben,* have a fair wind; *halber –,* side *or* beam wind; (*Naut.*) *harter –,* near gale (Beaufort 7); (*fig.*) *in dem*

– ***reden,*** talk in vain, beat the air; (*fig.*) ***in den – schlagen,*** disregard, ignore, pay no heed to, set at naught, make light of, throw to the winds; ***in alle –e zerstreut,*** scattered to the four winds; (*fig.*) ***– machen,*** bluster, (*coll.*) talk hot air; (*Naut.*) ***mäßiger –,*** moderate breeze (Beaufort 4); (*fig.*) ***den Mantel nach dem – hängen,*** trim one's sails to the wind; (*Naut.*) ***schwacher –,*** gentle breeze (Beaufort 3); ***das ist – in seine Segel,*** that is grist to his mill; ***starker –,*** high wind; (*Naut.*) ***steifer –,*** strong breeze (Beaufort 6); (*Naut.*) ***stürmischer –,*** fresh gale (Beaufort 8); ***unter dem –,*** under the lee; (*Geog.*) ***Inseln unter dem –e,*** Leeward Islands; ***vom – abkommen,*** fall to leeward; (*fig.*) ***wissen woher der – weht,*** know which way the wind is blowing; ***sich*** (*Dat.*) ***den – um die Nase wehen lassen,*** see the world; ***zwischen – und Wasser,*** awash.

Wind|beutel, *m.* (*Cul.*) cream-puff, éclair; (*fig.*) braggart, windbag. **–beutelei,** *f.* humbug, bombast, (*coll.*) hot air. **–blattern,** *f.pl. See* **–pocken. –blume,** *f. See* **–röschen. –blütler,** *m.* (*Bot.*) anemophilae. **–bruch,** *m.* 1. windfall, woodfallen wood; 2. (*Med.*) pneumatocele. **–büchse,** *f.* air-gun.

Winde ['vɪndə], *f.* 1. winch, (lifting-)jack, hoist; (*Naut.*) capstan, windlass; (*Weav.*) reel, spool, winder; 2. (*Bot.*) bindweed, wild convolvulus; 3. (*Swiss*) attic, loft.

Windei ['vɪntˀaɪ], *n.* addled egg, wind-egg; soft shelled egg.

Windel ['vɪndəl], *f.* (-, *pl.* **-n**) baby's napkin, (*coll.*) nappy, (*Am.*) diaper; (*fig.*) ***noch in den –n stecken,*** be still in its infancy *or* its early stages. **windeln,** *v.t.* swathe, swaddle. **windelweich,** *adj.* (*fig.*) ***– schlagen,*** beat to a jelly.

[1]**winden** ['vɪndən], *v.i.* 1. (*imp.*) ***es windet,*** there's a wind blowing, it is windy; 2. (*Hunt.*) catch the scent.

[2]**winden, 1.** *irr.v.t.* wind, reel, coil; twist, twine, twirl; ***in die Höhe –,*** hoist, wind up; ***ihm aus den Händen –,*** twist *or* wrest *or* wrench out of his hands; ***einen Kranz –,*** make *or* bind a wreath. **2.** *irr.v.r.* (*of a p.*) writhe, squirm (*vor* (*Dat.*), with), (*as a worm*) wriggle, (*as a stream*) wind its way, meander; (*fig.*) ***sich – und drehen,*** wriggle (like an eel).

Windenschwärmer ['vɪndənʃvɛrmər], *m.* (*Ent.*) convolvulus hawk-moth (*Protopare convolvuli*).

Windeseile ['vɪndəsˀaɪlə], *f.* ***mit –,*** in no time, at lightning-speed, like wildfire.

Wind|fahne, *f.* weather-vane. **–fang,** *m.* wind-break, draught-screen, (*Archit.*) porch. **–flügel,** *m.* fan-blade. **wind|frei, –geschützt,** *adj.* sheltered. **Wind|geschwulst,** *f.* (*Med.*) emphysema. **–hafer,** *m.* (*Bot.*) wild oats (*Avena fatua*). **–harfe,** *f.* Aeolian harp. **–hauch,** *m.* breath of wind. **–hose,** *f.* whirlwind, cyclone, tornado. **–hund,** *m.* greyhound, (*fig.*) harum-scarum.

windig ['vɪndɪç], *adj.* windy, breezy; wind-swept; (*fig.*) (*of a p.*) frivolous, light-hearted, giddy, (*of a th.*) precarious, shaky, (*of excuses*) empty, lame.

Wind|jacke, *f.* windproof jacket *or* jerkin, anorak. **–kanal,** *m.* wind-tunnel. **–klappe,** *f.* air-valve. **–licht,** *n.* storm-lantern. **–messer,** *m.* anemometer, wind-gauge. **–mühle,** *f.* windmill. **–mühlenflugzeug,** *n.* autogyro, gyroplane. **–pocken,** *f.pl.* (*Med.*) chickenpox. **–richtung,** *f.* wind direction, direction of the wind. **–röschen,** *n.* (*Bot.*) wood-anemone (*Anemone silvestris*). **–rose,** *f.* compass *or* rhumb-card. **–sack,** *m.* (*Av.*) wind-sleeve.

Windsbraut ['vɪntsbraut], *f.* gale, hurricane, whirlwind.

Wind|schacht, *m.* (*Min.*) air-shaft. **–schatten,** *m.* lee(side). **windschief,** *adj.* (*usu. fig.*) warped, twisted, skew, awry, (*sl.*) cock-eyed. **Windschirm,** *m.* wind-break, draught-screen. **wind|schlüpfrig,** *See* **–schnittig. –schnell,** *adj.* (as) quick as lightning. **–schnittig,** *adj.* streamlined, aerodynamic. **Wind|(schutz)scheibe,** *f.* (*Motor.*) windscreen. **–seite,** *f.* windward *or* weather *or* exposed side. **–spiel,** *n.* whippet. **–stärke,** *f.* strength *or* velocity of the wind; (*Naut.*) – 2, Beaufort scale 2. **wind-still,** *adj.* calm, windless. **Wind|stille,** *f.* (*Naut.*) calm (Beaufort 0). **–stoß,** *m.* gust of wind, squall. **–strich,** *m.* direction of the wind; point of the compass, rhumb. **–strom,** *m.*, **–strömung,** *f.* current of air, blast. **–sucht,** *f.* flatulence, tympanitis. **–tür,** *f.* (*Min.*) ventilation door *or* trap.

Windung ['vɪnduŋ], *f.* winding, turn, twist, convolution, (*of rope etc.*) coil, (*of shell*) whorl, (*of screw*) thread; sinuosity, meandering.

Wind|wehe, *f.* snowdrift. **–winkel,** *m.* (*Av.*) angle of drift. **–zug,** *m.* draught, current of air.

Wingert ['vɪŋɛrt], *m.* (**-s,** *pl.* **-e**) (*dial.*) vineyard.

Wink [vɪŋk], *m.* (**-(e)s,** *pl.* **-e**) sign, (*with the hand*) wave, (*with the eye*) wink, (*with the head*) nod; (*fig.*) hint, suggestion, pointer, (*coll.*) tip, (*sl.*) tip-off; (*dial.*) twinkling, jiffy; ***ihm einen – geben,*** drop him a hint; ***einen – verstehen,*** take a hint; ***– mit dem Laternenpfahl*** or ***Zaunpfahl,*** broad hint.

Winkel ['vɪŋkəl], *m.* (*Geom.*) angle; corner, nook; (*Mil.*) stripe, chevron; (*Fort.*) ***ausspringender –,*** salient; (*Fort.*) ***einspringender –,*** re-entrant; ***rechter –,*** right angle; ***spitzer*** (***stumpfer***) ***–,*** acute (obtuse) angle; ***vorspringender*** or ***vorstehender –,*** see ***ausspringender –.***

Winkel|abstand, *m.* angular distance. **–advokat,** *m.* shady *or* unqualified lawyer, (*sl.*) shyster. **–blatt,** *n.* (*coll.*) local rag. **–bogen,** *m.* arc subtending an angle. **–börse,** *f.* outside broker's business, (*coll.*) bucket-shop. **–eisen,** *n.* angle-iron. **winkelförmig,** *adj.* angular. **Winkel|funktion,** *f.* trigonometrical ratio. **–gasse,** *f.* back lane. **–geschwindigkeit,** *f.* angular velocity. **–größe,** *f.* size of an angle. **–haken,** *m.* (*Typ.*) justifier; composing-stick. **–halbierende,** *f.* bisector of an angle.

winkelig ['vɪŋkəlɪç], *adj.* angular; full of angles *or* corners, bent, crooked, twisted. **–winkelig,** *adj.suff.* (*Geom.*) -angled.

Winkel|kneipe, *f.* back-street pub, low haunt. **–lineal,** *n.* set-square. **–linie,** *f.* diagonal. **–makler,** *m.* outside broker. **–maß,** *n.* set- *or* T-square. **–messer,** *m.* (*Geom.*) protractor, (*Surv.*) goniometer, clinometer, theodolite. **winkelrecht, 1.** *adj.* rectangular, right-angled. **2.** *adv.* at right angles. **Winkel|schenke,** *f. See* **–kneipe. –schule,** *f.* unrecognized school, dame-school. **–stück,** *n.* angle-plate. **–stütze,** *f.* bracket. **–zug,** *m.* (*usu. pl.*) subterfuge, evasion, shift, pretext, dodge, trick.

winken ['vɪŋkən], *v.i.* (make a) sign, signal, (*with hand*) wave, beckon, motion, (*with head*) nod (*Dat.*, to), (*with eye*) wink (at); (*Mil., Naut.*) semaphore; (*coll.*) ***eine Belohnung winkt dir,*** there's some reward in store for you. **Winker,** *m.* (*Mil., Naut.*) signaller; (*Motor.*) direction indicator, trafficator, (*coll.*) winker. **Winker|flagge,** *f.* signalling flag. **–spruch,** *m.* semaphore message. **–zeichen,** *n.pl.* manual signals, semaphore.

winklig, *adj. See* **winkelig.**

winseln ['vɪnzəln], *v.i.* whine, whimper, moan, pule, (*coll.*) grizzle.

Winter ['vɪntər], *m.* winter; ***mitten im –,*** in the depth of winter. **Winter|ammer,** *f.* (*Orn.*) slate-coloured junco (*Junco hyematis*). **–festigkeit,** *f.* winter hardiness. **–frische,** *f.* winter resort. **–frucht,** *f.* winter *or* spring crop. **–garten,** *m.* conservatory. **–getreide,** *n. See* **–frucht. –goldhähnchen,** *n.* (*Orn.*) goldcrest (*Regulus regulus*). **–grün,** *n.* (*Bot.*) wintergreen (*Pirola*); periwinkle (*Vinca*). **winterhart,** *adj.* hardy (*of plants*). **Winter|hilfswerk,** *n.* (*Nat. Soc.*) compulsory charity (*ostensibly for relieving hardship during cold weather*). **–kleid,** *n.* winter coat *or* plumage. **–kleidung,** *f.* winter clothes *or* clothing. **–kohl,** *m.* spring cabbage. **–korn,** *n. See* **–frucht, –kurort,** *m. See* **–frische. –lagerung,** *f.* winter storage.

winterlich ['vɪntərlɪç], *adj.* wintry. **Winterling,** *m.* (*Bot.*) winter aconite (*Eranthus hiemalis*). **wintern, 1.** *v.i.* (*imp.*) ***es wintert,*** winter is coming (on), it grows wintry. **2.** *v.t.* lay by for the winter.

Winter|öl, *n.* non-freezing oil. **-ort,** *m. See* **-frische. -saat,** *f.* (seed for) autumn sowing. **-schlaf,** *m.* hibernation; – ***halten,*** hibernate. **-schläfer,** *m.* hibernating animal. **-seite,** *f.* northern aspect. **-semester,** *n.* winter term (*October till March*). **-sonnenwende,** *f.* winter solstice. **-sport,** *m.* winter sport(s). **-sportler,** *m.* winter sport enthusiast. **-vorrat,** *m.* winter stocks.

Winzer ['vɪntsər], *m.* vine-grower *or* -dresser; vintager. **Winzer|fest,** *n.* vintage festival. **-lied,** *n.* vintager's song.

winzig ['vɪntsɪç], *adj.* tiny, minute, diminutive, microscopic, infinitesimal; petty, scanty, paltry, trifling. **Winzigkeit,** *f.* diminutive size, tininess, minuteness, pettiness. **Winzigposten,** *pl.* (*Comm.*) petty account.

Wipfel ['vɪpfəl], *m.* (tree-)top. **wipfeln,** *v.t.* lop (*trees*).

Wippchen ['vɪpçən], *n.* (*coll.*) trick, shift; ***mach mir keine – vor!*** don't try your tricks on me! none of your nonsense!

Wippe ['vɪpə], *f.* seesaw, (*fig.*) brink, critical point; (*Hist.*) strappado; (*Gymn.*) balancing (exercise); (*dial.*) whip; (*dial.*) tip-wagon; (*coll.*) ***auf der – sein*** or ***stehen,*** be on the point of falling *or* of turning back. **wippen, 1.** *v.i.* move up and down, rock, sway, seesaw. **2.** *v.t.* (*Hist.*) strappado (*criminals*). **Wipp|galgen,** *m.* strappado. **-säge,** *f.* jig-saw.

wir [vi:r], *pers.pron.* (*1st pers. pl.*) we; – ***alle,*** all of us; – ***beide,*** both of us.

wirb [vɪrp], *see* **werben.**

Wirbel ['vɪrbəl], *m.* 1. whirl, swirl; whirlpool, eddy, vortex; whirlwind; (*of smoke*) wreathe, curl; 2. crown (of the head); vertebra; ***vom – bis zur Zehe,*** from top to toe; 3. swivel (*on chain*); window-catch; peg (*of violins etc.*); 4. drum roll; warbling, trill(ing) (*of birds*); (*fig.*) turmoil, hurly-burly; whirl (*of pleasures*), (*coll.*) racket; (*coll.*) ***einen – machen,*** make a fuss *or* to-do; ***einen – schlagen,*** sound a roll (on the drum).

Wirbel|balken, *m.* screw-plate (*of piano*). **-bildung,** *f.* (*Av. etc.*) turbulence. **wirbel|förmig,** *adj.* vertebral; spindle-shaped. **-frei,** *adj.* non-rotating. **Wirbelgelenk,** *n.* swivel-joint. **wirbelig,** *adj.* whirling, swirling, eddying; (*fig.*) giddy, wild, harum-scarum. **Wirbel|kasten,** *m.* neck for the pegs (*violin*). **-knochen,** *m.* vertebra. **wirbellos,** *adj.* invertebrate, spineless.

wirbeln ['vɪrbəln], *v.i.* (*aux.* h. & s.) swirl, whirl, eddy, whirl *or* swirl round; (*of birds*) warble, trill, (*of drum*) roll; ***der Kopf wirbelt mir,*** my head is in a whirl *or* is swimming.

Wirbel|säule, *f.* spine, spinal *or* vertebral column. **-stock,** *m. See* **-balken. -strom,** *m.* (*Elec.*) eddy-current. **-sturm,** *m.* cyclone, tornado, typhoon, hurricane. **-tier,** *n.* vertebrate (animal). **-wind,** *m.* whirlwind.

wird [vɪrd], *see* **werden.**

wirf [vɪrf], *see* **werfen.**

wirken ['vɪrkən], **1.** *v.t.* 1. cause, bring about, produce, work (*miracles*); 2. weave, knit; 3. knead (*dough*). **2.** *v.i.* work, operate, be active, take (effect), have an effect; – ***als,*** act *or* function as; ***an einer Schule –,*** teach in a school, be employed as a teacher; – ***auf*** (*Acc.*), have an effect *or* influence on, produce *or* make an impression on, influence, impress; ***auf die Sinne –,*** affect the senses; ***dahin – daß,*** bring one's influence to bear so that, see (to it) that; ***jedes Wort wirkte,*** every word told *or* counted. **Wirken,** *n.* work, functioning, activity, action; influence, effect. **wirkend,** *adj.* acting, active, operating; effective, operative, efficacious, (*coll.*) telling; ***stark –,*** highly effective *or* efficacious, drastic.

Wirker ['vɪrkər], *m.* knitter, weaver, stocking-maker. **Wirkerei** [–'raɪ], *f.* weaving, knitting.

Wirkleistung ['vɪrklaɪstuŋ], *f.* (*Tech.*) output, over-all efficiency.

wirklich ['vɪrklɪç], **1.** *adj.* actual, real, substantial; true, genuine; (*Mil.*) ***-er Bestand,*** effective strength; (*Hist.*) ***-er Geheimer Rat,*** (a title in Imperial times bestowed on Under Secretaries *etc.* and carrying the form of address 'Excellency'.) **2.** *adv.* actually, really, truly, in truth, in fact, indeed; (*Mil.*) – ***vorhanden,*** effective.

Wirklichkeit ['vɪrklɪçkaɪt], *f.* reality, actuality, actual fact, truth; ***in –,*** in reality; ***rauhe –,*** harsh reality, hard facts. **Wirklichkeitsform,** *f.* (*Gram.*) indicative mood. **wirklichkeits|fremd,** *adj.* unrealistic, (*coll*) starry-eyed **-nah,** *adj.* realistic, (*coll.*) down-to-earth. **Wirklichkeitssinn,** *m.* sense of reality, realistic *or* matter-of-fact outlook.

wirklichmachen ['vɪrklɪcmaxən], *v.t.* (*sep.*) *see* **verwirklichen.**

Wirkmaschine ['vɪrkmaʃi:nə], *f.* knitting-machine.

wirksam ['vɪrkza:m], *adj.* effective, efficacious, (*coll.*) telling; active, operative; (*of a p.*) efficient; (*esp. Med.*) – ***gegen,*** effective *or* efficacious against, good for; – ***werden,*** take effect, become effective, come into effect *or* force. **Wirksamkeit,** *f.* effectiveness, efficacy, efficiency; ***in – sein,*** be in force *or* operation; ***außer – setzen,*** suspend (*a law*); ***in – setzen,*** put into force *or* operation; ***in – treten,*** come into force *or* effect *or* operation, take effect.

Wirk|stoff, *m.* active agent, (*Med.*) hormone. **-stuhl,** *m.* loom, knitting-frame.

Wirkung ['vɪrkuŋ], *f.* operation, action, reaction; result, effect, consequence; impression, influence; impact, appeal; ***mit – von,*** as *or* effective from, with effect from; ***mit sofortiger –,*** effective *or* taking effect immediately, (*coll.*) as from now; ***seine – verfehlen*** or ***ohne – bleiben,*** produce no effect, prove ineffectual, (*coll.*) fail to work; (*Prov.*) ***keine – ohne Ursache,*** no effect without cause, no smoke without a fire.

Wirkungs|bereich, *m.* radius of action, (*Artil.*) effective range, zone of fire. **-dauer,** *f.* effective duration, persistency. **wirkungsfähig,** *adj.* effective, efficient. **Wirkungs|grad,** *m.* (*Mech.*) efficiency. **-kraft,** *f.* efficiency, efficacy. **-kreis,** *m.* field *or* sphere of action *or* activity, sphere of effective influence; province, domain. **wirkungslos,** *adj.* ineffectual, inefficacious, ineffective, futile, (*pred.*) without effect; – ***bleiben,*** produce no effect, (*coll.*) fall flat; ***bei ihm – bleiben,*** be lost on him. **Wirkungslosigkeit,** *f.* ineffectiveness, inefficacy; inefficiency; inactivity. **wirkungsvoll,** *adj.* effective, efficacious, (*coll.*) striking, telling. **Wirkungsweise,** *f.* mode of action *or* operation, manner of working.

Wirk|waren, *f.pl.* knitted goods, knitwear. **-widerstand,** *m.* (*Elec.*) effective resistance. **-zeit,** *f.* (*Chem.*) reaction time.

wirr [vɪr], *adj.* (*of a p.*) confused, bewildered, (*coll.*) muddle-headed, (*of a th.*) tangled, disorderly, chaotic, (*of speech*) incoherent, (*of hair*) dishevelled; ***-es Durcheinander,*** chaos, confusion. **Wirren,** *pl.* disorders, disturbances, troubles. **wirren,** *v.t.* (*obs.*) *see* **verwirren. Wirrkopf,** *m.* muddle-headed fellow, scatterbrain. **Wirrnis,** *f.* (-, *pl.* **-se**), **Wirrsal,** *n.* (**-s,** *pl.* **-e**) entanglement, confusion, disorder, chaos. **Wirrwarr,** *m.* welter, jumble, muddle, mess; disorder, confusion, chaos; (*noise*) hurly-burly, hubbub.

wirsch [vɪrʃ], *adj.* gruff, abrupt, disobliging.

Wirsing(kohl) ['vɪrzɪŋ(ko:l)], *m.* savoy cabbage.

wirst [vɪrst], *see* **werden.**

Wirt [vɪrt], *m.* **(-(e)s,** *pl.* **-e)** host, landlord, innkeeper, hotel *or* restaurant proprietor, lodging-house keeper; (*dial.*) head of the household; ***den – machen,*** do the honours; ***die Rechnung ohne den – machen,*** overlook the most vital factor.

Wirtel ['vɪrtəl], *m.* distaff; fly-wheel; whorl; (*Bot.*) verticil. **wirtelig,** *adj.* (*Bot.*) verticilate.

Wirtin ['vɪrtɪn], *f.* hostess, landlady, innkeeper's wife, proprietress; (*dial.*) mistress of the household.

wirtlich ['vɪrtlɪç], *adj.* hospitable, (*of dwelling*) habitable.

Wirtschaft ['vɪrtʃaft], *f.* 1. housekeeping, domestic economy, (*obs.*) husbandry; *die – führen,* keep house, look after *or* manage things; 2. economic system, economy; economics, industry and trade, economic activity; *freie –,* free enterprise; *polnische –,* shocking state of affairs, terrible mess; 3. household; farm; establishment, inn, public house, restaurant, refreshment room; 4. (*coll.*) doings, goings-on, bustle, to-do, mess, row, racket; (*coll.*) *was ist das für eine –?* how do you explain this mess *or* these goings-on? (*coll.*) *die ganze –,* the whole shoot *or* boiling; (*iron.*) *eine schöne –!* a fine state of affairs! fine goings-on!

wirtschaften ['vɪrtʃaftən], *v.i.* 1. run the household, keep house; manage, run (*business, farm etc.*); *arg* or *schlecht* or *übel – mit,* mismanage, play havoc with; *gut –,* manage well, be a good manager; *zugrunde –,* wreck *or* ruin by bad management; 2. economize, (*obs.*) husband; *gut – mit,* economize with, husband; *toll –,* make a fearful pother *or* to-do; 3. (*coll.*) rummage about. **Wirtschafter,** *m.* manager; steward. **Wirtschafterin,** *f.* manageress; housekeeper. **Wirtschaftler,** *m.* (political) economist, economic expert.

wirtschaftlich ['vɪrtʃaftlɪç], *adj.* 1. economic, financial, commercial, business; 2. economical, thrifty; 3. efficient, self-supporting, profitable, paying; *– gestalten,* rationalize. **Wirtschaftlichkeit,** *f.* economy, thriftiness; good management, efficiency, profitability.

Wirtschafts|abkommen, *n.* economic *or* trade agreement. **–berater,** *m.* business consultant. **–betrieb,** *m.* *See* **–unternehmen**; (*Railw. etc.*) buffet service; *Gasthaus mit –,* fully licensed inn. **–buch,** *n.* housekeeping book. **–einheit,** *f.* economic unit. **–führer,** *m.* captain of industry, (*coll.*) business tycoon. **–gebäude,** *n.* farm buildings; (*Law*) domestic offices. **–geld,** *n.* housekeeping money. **–gemeinschaft,** *f.* *Europäische –,* European Economic Community, Common Market. **–hilfe,** *f.* economic aid. **–jahr,** *n.* financial year. **–kraft,** *f.* economic resources. **–krieg,** *m.* economic warfare. **–krise,** *f.* economic crisis, (business) depression, (*coll.*) slump. **–lage,** *f.* economic situation. **–lenkung,** *f.* government control (of trade and industry). **–minister,** *m.* Minister for Economic Affairs. **–plan,** *m.* budget. **–politik,** *f.* economic policy. **wirtschaftspolitisch,** *adj.* economic. **Wirtschafts|prüfer,** *m.* chartered accountant. **–rat,** *m.* (advisory) economic council. **–stelle,** *f.* economic planning board. **–teil,** *m.* business *or* city pages (*of newspaper*). **–unternehmen,** *n.* business undertaking *or* enterprise, commercial firm. **–verband,** *m.* trade association. **–wunder,** *n.* economic miracle. **–zweig,** *m.* sector of the economy.

Wirts|haus, *n.* inn, tavern, public house, (*coll.*) pub, (*Am.*) saloon. **–leute,** *pl.* innkeeper *or* publican and his wife, landlord and landlady, host and hostess. **–pflanze,** *f.* (*Bot.*) host plant, plant attacked by a parasite. **–stube,** *f.* inn parlour, private bar.

Wisch [vɪʃ], *m.* **(-e(e)s,** *pl.* **-e)** wisp (of straw *etc.*), rag, wiper; (*coll.*) scrap of paper, note, chit. **wischen,** *v.t.* wipe; *sich* (*Dat.*) *den Mund –,* wipe one's mouth; *sich* (*Dat.*) *die Stirn –,* mop one's brow. **Wischer,** *m.* wiper, (*Motor.*) windscreen wiper, (*Art*) stump; (*coll.*) telling-off, wigging. **wischfest,** *adj.* spongeable (*wallpaper etc.*). **Wisch|lappen,** *m.* cleaning-rag, duster; dishcloth; floor-cloth. **–stock,** *m.* (*Artil.*) cleaning-rod. **–tuch,** *n.* *See* **–lappen. –wasch,** *m.* (*coll.*) twaddle, bosh.

Wisent ['vi:zənt], *m.* **(-(e)s,** *pl.* **-e)** (*Zool.*) bison.

Wismut ['vɪsmu:t], *n.* (*Austr. m.*) (*Chem.*) bismuth. **Wismut|butter,** *f.* bismuth trichloride. **–oxyd,** *n.* bismuth trioxide. **–säureanhydrid,** *n.* bismuth pentoxide.

Wispel ['vɪspəl], *m.* (*obs.*) corn measure (*approx. 24 bushels*).

wispeln ['vɪspəln], **wispern** ['vɪspərn], *v.t., v.i.* whisper.

Wißbegier(de) ['vɪsbəgi:r(də)], *f.* thirst for knowledge, (intellectual) curiosity. **wißbegierig,** *adj.* anxious to know *or* learn, curious, inquisitive.

wissen ['vɪsən], **1.** *irr.v.t.* know, be acquainted with, understand; *see also – von* (*under* **2**); *Bescheid – (über* (*Acc.*) *or in* (*Dat.*)), know for certain (about), be well aware *or* fully informed (of), be well acquainted *or* fully conversant (with), (*coll.*) be in the know (about); *ihm Dank –,* be grateful *or* feel obliged to him; *ihn – lassen,* give him to understand (that), let him know, send him word (of), acquaint him (with), tell him; *nichts – von,* know nothing of *or* about, have no idea of, be quite in the dark about; *ich will davon nichts –,* I'll have nothing *or* I'll not have anything to do with it; *er will nichts davon –,* he won't hear of it; *– Sie noch?* do you remember? *sich* (*Dat.*) *Rat –,* know what to do; *sich* (*Dat.*) *keinen Rat mehr –,* be at a loss (what to do), be at one's wits' end; *ihm* (*kund und*) *zu – tun,* see *– lassen*; (*coll.*) *– Sie was!* I'll tell you s.th.; (*sl.*) *was weiß ich!* search me! (*coll.*) *als wäre er wer weiß was,* as if he were the Lord Almighty; (*coll.*) *er kann mir wer weiß was sagen,* I shan't believe a word he says; *und was weiß ich noch alles,* and all the rest *or* the other things; (*Prov.*) *was ich nicht weiß, macht mich nicht heiß,* what the eye doesn't see, the heart doesn't grieve about.
2. *irr.v.i.* *– um,* know of *or* about; *– von,* be informed *or* aware of, have knowledge of, be acquainted with; *– zu tun,* be able to do, know how to do; *ich weiß nicht anders als . . .,* all I know is that . . .; *genau –,* know for certain, be positive; *weiß Gott!* God (only) knows! (*obs.*) *kund und zu – sei hiermit,* be it known by these presents; *ich möchte – ob . . .,* I wonder whether . . .; *nicht aus noch ein –,* not know which way to turn; *nicht daß ich wüßte,* not that I am aware of; *ich weiß nicht recht,* I don't rightly know; I am not very sure; *man kann nie –,* you never know, you never can tell; *so viel ich weiß,* so *or* as far as I know, for all I know.

Wissen, *n.* knowledge; learning, scholarship, erudition; *meines –s,* to (the best of) my knowledge, as far as I know, (*coll.*) for all I know; *nach bestem – und Gewissen,* to the best of one's knowledge and belief, (*coll.*) 'cross my heart'; *ohne mein –,* without my knowledge, unknown to me; *technisches –,* technical knowledge *or* (*coll.*) know-how; *wider besseres –,* against one's better judgement. **wissend,** *adj.* knowing, initiated. **Wissende(r),** *m., f.* party to a secret, s.o. in the know.

Wissenschaft ['vɪsənʃaft], *f.* science, knowledge; *die schönen –en,* belles-lettres; *die philologisch-historischen –en,* the arts, the humanities. **Wissenschaftler,** *m.* scientist, man of science; scholar. **wissenschaftlich,** *adj.* scholarly, scientific, learned; *– gebildet,* academically trained. **Wissenschaftlichkeit,** *f.* scholarly method, scientific character.

Wissens|drang. –durst, *m.* urge *or* thirst for knowledge. **–gebiet,** *n.* field *or* branch of knowledge. **–trieb,** *m.* *See* **–drang. wissenswert,** *adj.* worth knowing; *–e Einzelheiten,* interesting details.

wissentlich ['vɪsəntlɪç], **1.** *adj.* conscious, deliberate, wilful. **2.** *adv.* knowingly, wittingly, deliberately, on purpose.

Witfrau [vɪtfrau], (*obs.*) **Witib** ['vi:tɪp], *f.* *See* **Witwe.**

wittern ['vɪtərn], *v.t.* scent, smell, (*fig.*) suspect; (*coll.*) get wind of; *Unrat –,* smell a rat; *Gefahr –,* see danger *or* rocks ahead.

Witterung ['vɪtərʊŋ], *f.* weather, atmospheric conditions; (*Hunt.*) scent; *bei günstiger –,* weather permitting; *bei jeder –,* in all weathers; *eine feine –,* a good nose. **witterungsbeständig,** *adj.* weatherproof, resistant to exposure. **Witterungs|kunde,** *f.* meteorology. **–umschlag,** *m.* sudden change in the weather. **–verhältnisse,** *n.pl.* atmospheric conditions. **–versuch,** *m.* (*Metall.*) weathering test.

Wittib ['vɪtɪp], *f.* (*Austr.*) *see* **Witwe. Wittum** ['vɪttu:m], *n.* (**-s,** *pl.* **¨-er** (*Austr.* **-e**)) widow's estate, dower, (*Law*) jointure.

Witwe ['vɪtvə], *f.* widow, (*of royalty etc.*) dowager; ***zur – geworden*** or ***gemacht,*** widowed. **Witwen|geld,** *n.* widow's pension *or* allowance. **–jahr,** *n.* year of mourning. **-kasse,** *f.* widow's pension fund. **–kleid,** *n.* *See* **–tracht. –rente,** *f.* *See* **–geld. –schaft,** *f.* *See* **–stand. –sitz,** *m.* dowager's estate. **–stand,** *m.* widowhood. **–tracht, –trauer,** *f.* widow's weeds. **Witwentum,** *n.* *See* **Witwen|stand. –verbrennung,** *f.* suttee.

Witwer ['vɪtvər], *m.* widower.

Witz [vɪts], *m.* (**-es,** *pl.* **-e**) wit, wittiness; joke, witticism, pleasantry; (*obs.*) esprit, mother wit; ***alter –,*** stale joke, (*coll.*) chestnut; ***beißender –,*** caustic wit, sarcasm; ***fauler –,*** weak joke, practical joke; (*coll.*) ***das ist*** (***ja eben***) ***der –,*** that's the whole point, that's just the point; ***das ist der – an der Sache,*** that's the funny part of it; (*coll.*) ***mach keine –e!*** you don't say! no kidding? ***weder – noch Verstand,*** neither rhyme nor reason.

Witz|blatt, *n.* comic (paper). **–bold,** *m.* (**-(e)s,** *pl.* **-e**) witty fellow, wit, wag, joker.

Witzelei [vɪtsə'laɪ], *f.* (-, *pl.* **-en**) witticism, wise-crack, joking, chaffing, leg-pulling. **witzeln,** *v.i.* ***– über*** (*Acc.*), poke fun at, mock, ridicule, be witty at (*s.o.'s*) expense.

witzig ['vɪtsɪç], *adj.* witty, facetious, funny; ***–er Einfall,*** smart *or* clever idea. **witzigen,** *v.t.* (*obs.*) teach, drive home. **Witzigung,** *f.* (*obs.*) warning, example, lesson.

wo [vo:], **1.** *inter.* where? ***– wohnt er?*** where does he live? **2.** *rel.* where, in which; ***das Haus, – ich wohnte,*** the house in which I lived. **3.** *conj.* 1. (*place*) ***– auch nur*** or ***immer,*** wherever; (*abbr. for* **irgendwo**) ***– anders,*** somewhere else; 2. (*time*) when, while; ***es gab Zeiten, – . . .,*** there were times when . . .; 3. (*condition*) ***– nicht . . ., so doch . . .,*** unless . . . *or* if not . . ., then certainly . . . **4.** *int.* (*coll.*) ***i –!*** or ***ach –!*** what rubbish *or* nonsense! what can you be thinking of? (*sl.*) not on your life!

wob [vo:p], *see* **weben.**

wobei [vo:'baɪ], *rel.adv.* (= ***bei welchem***) through which, in *or* by doing which, whereby; in the course of which, during which, whereat; in connection with which, as well as which; ***es geschieht nichts, – sein Name nicht genannt wird,*** nothing is done without his name appearing; ***– mir einfällt,*** and that brings to my mind; ***– es sein Bewenden hatte,*** and there the matter ended.

Woche ['vɔxə], *f.* 1. week; ***von – zu –,*** week in week out; ***– für*** or ***um –,*** week by week; ***heute in*** or ***über eine –,*** today *or* this day week, a week today; ***heute vor einer –,*** a week ago today; ***Stille –,*** Passion Week; ***Weiße –,*** white sale; 2. *pl.* childbed, confinement, lying-in period; ***in den –n sein*** or ***liegen,*** be confined, be in childbed.

Wochen|ausgabe, *f.* weekly edition. **–beihilfe,** maternity benefit. **–bett,** *n.* childbed. **–bettfieber,** *n.* *See* **–fieber. –blatt,** *n.* weekly paper. **–ende,** *n.* weekend. **–fieber,** *n.* puerperal fever. **–fluß,** *m.* (*Med.*) lochia. **–geld,** *n.* weekly allowance; *see also* **–beihilfe. –hilfe,** *f.* *See* **–beihilfe. –kleid,** *n.* everyday dress. **wochenlang, 1.** *adj.* lasting for weeks; ***nach –er Unsicherheit,*** after (many) weeks of uncertainty. **2.** *adv.* for weeks (on end). **Wochen|lohn,** *m.* weekly wage. **–schau,** *f.* (*Films*) newsreel. **–schrift,** *f.* weekly (magazine). **–tag,** *m.* weekday. **wochentags,** *adv.* on weekdays.

wöchentlich ['vœçəntlɪç], **1.** *adj.* weekly, week-by-week. **2.** *adv.* weekly, every week; by the week.

wochenweise ['vɔxənvaɪzə], *adv.* *See* **wöchentlich, 2.**

Wöchnerin ['vœçnərɪn], *f.* maternity case, woman in childbed. **Wöchnerinnenheim,** *n.* maternity home, lying-in hospital.

Wocken ['vɔkən], *m.* (*dial.*) distaff.

Wodka ['vɔdka], *m.* vodka.

wodurch [vo:'durç], **1.** *rel.adv.* (= ***durch welches*** or ***was***), by (means of) *or* through which, whereby. **2.** *inter.adv.* by which *or* what means? how?

wofern [vo:'fɛrn], *conj.* provided that, (in) so far as; in case, if; ***– nicht,*** unless.

wofür [vo:'fy:r], **1.** *rel.adv.* (= ***für welches*** or ***was***), in return for which; ***er ist das nicht, – er angesehen sein wird,*** he is not what he pretends to be. **2.** *inter.adv.* for what? what? what . . . for? wherefore? ***– ist das gut?*** what is it good for?

wog ['vo:k], *see* **wägen, wiegen.**

Woge ['vo:gə], *f.* wave, billow, (*fig.*) wave, (up)-surge; (*fig.*) ***die –n glätten,*** pour oil on troubled waters.

wogegen [vo:'ge:gən], **1.** *rel.adv.* (= ***gegen welches*** or ***was***) against which, in return *or* exchange for which. **2.** *inter.adv.* against what? **3.** *conj.* whilst, whereas, on the other hand.

wogen ['vo:gən], *v.i.* surge, billow, heave, roll; wave, undulate; (*fig.*) fluctuate, seesaw (*as a struggle*). **wogig,** *adj.* wavy, rolling, billowing, surging.

woher [vo:'he:r], *rel. and inter. adv.* from where, where . . . from, from what *or* which place, whence; ***– weißt du das?*** how do you know that? (*coll.*) where do you get that from? ***er sagt nicht, – er gekommen ist,*** he won't say where he has come from; (*coll.*) ***ach –!*** tell that to the marines! nothing of the sort!

wohin [vo:'hɪn], **1.** *rel. and inter. adv.* where, where . . . to, whither; ***– gehst du?*** where are you going to? ***er sagt nicht, – er geht,*** he won't say where he is going. **2.** *indef.adv.* somewhere, (*coll.*) some place; (*coll.*) ***ich muß –,*** I must disappear (*to the lavatory*). **wohingegen** [–'ge:gən], *conj.* whilst, whereas.

wohl [vo:l], *pred. adj. and adv.*
1. (*stressed*) (*comp.* ***–er*** and ***besser***; *sup.* ***am –sten*** and ***am besten***) well; ***sich – fühlen,*** be *or* feel well; be contented *or* at (one's) ease, be in good spirits; feel at home (***bei,*** with); ***sich nicht – fühlen,*** be *or* feel unwell *or* (*coll.*) poorly *or* out of sorts; feel ill at ease; be out of one's element; ***–er habe ich mich nie gefühlt,*** I never felt better; ***ich fühle mich hier am –sten,*** it suits me best here; (*Naut.*) ***–!*** aye, aye sir! ***– ihm, daß . . .,*** good for him that . . .; ***– dem, der . . .,*** happy (is) he who . . .; ***– bekomm's*** (***Ihnen***)***!*** your health! (*coll.*) cheers! (*iron.*) I wish you joy! ***ich bin mir dessen – bewußt,*** I am (quite) well aware *or* am fully conscious of the fact; ***leben Sie –!*** farewell! goodbye! ***– und munter,*** alive and kicking; ***sich's*** (*Dat.*) ***– sein lassen,*** enjoy o.s., have a good time; ***du tust –, daran zu schweigen,*** you will do well to keep silent; *see* **wohltun**; ***– oder übel,*** come what may, willy-nilly; ***er muß – oder übel bleiben,*** he has no choice but to stay, (*coll.*) he can't help staying; ***er weiß das sehr –,*** he knows that well enough *or* that all right; ***ich wünsche, – geruht zu haben,*** I hope you slept well *or* you had a good night; ***ich wünsche*** (***Ihnen***) ***– zu schlafen,*** (I hope you will) sleep well, I wish you a good night; ***ich wünsche, – gespeist zu haben,*** I hope the meal was to your satisfaction, I hope you enjoyed your meal.
2. (*unstressed*) (*a*) (*little doubt*) doubtless, no doubt, to be sure, indeed, it is true, (*obs.*) forsooth; (*b*) (*some doubt*) possibly, probably, perhaps, maybe; (*c*) (*more doubt*) I suppose, I presume, I daresay, I (should) think, I should say, I shouldn't wonder; ***er ist – gescheit, aber . . .,*** he is clever enough, but . . .; ***heute nicht, – aber morgen,*** not today but perhaps tomorrow; ***er hat – Geld, aber . . .,*** it is true that he has *or* to be sure he has money *or* he has money all right, but . . .; ***das habe ich mir – gedacht,*** I thought as much; ***er kommt – kaum,*** he will hardly come now, there is little chance that he will come now; ***er wird – noch kommen,*** to be sure he may come yet *or* yet come, I daresay he will probably come; ***du hättest – kommen können,*** I should think you might have come, you might very well have come; ***ich möchte – wissen,*** I should indeed like to know; ***das ist – möglich,*** I suppose that is possible; ***es ist – mög-***

lich, daß . . ., quite possibly, I shouldn't wonder; I should say it's possible that . . .; ***das darf ich – nicht tun,*** I cannot very well do that; ***ob er mich – noch kennt!*** I wonder whether he still knows me; ***es sind – drei Jahre, daß*** . . ., I suppose it's three years since . . .; – ***hundertmal,*** at least a hundred times; a hundred times, to be sure.

Wohl, *n.* welfare, well-being, prosperity, (*obs.*) weal; ***auf Ihr –! zum –!*** your health! here's to you! ***das gemeine –,*** the common good *or* weal; – ***und Wehe,*** weal and woe.

wohlan! [vo:l'an], *int.* well! now then! all right! good!

wohl|angebracht, *adj.* (very) apt, well-timed, opportune. **–anständig,** *adj.* decent, proper, decorous.

wohlauf [vo:l'auf], **1.** *pred.adj.* well, in good health, (*coll.*) full of beans. **2.** *int.* cheer up! come on now! now then!

wohlbedacht ['vo:lbədaxt], *adj.* deliberate, well-considered. **Wohl|bedacht,** *m.* ***mit –,*** after *or* on mature consideration. **–befinden,** *n.* good health, well-being. **–behagen,** *n.* comfort, ease; ***mit –,*** with relish. **wohl|behalten,** *adj.* (*of a p.*) safe and sound, (*of a th.*) in good condition. **–bekannt,** *adj.* well-known, familiar; notorious. **–beleibt,** *adj.* stout, portly, corpulent. **–beschaffen,** *adj.* in good condition *or* (*coll.*) shape. **–bestallt, –bestellt,** *adj.* duly installed *or* appointed. **Wohlergehen,** *n.* well-being, welfare, health and happiness, prosperity. **wohl|erwogen,** *adj.* well-weighed *or* -considered. **–erworben,** *adj.* duly acquired, well-established, vested (*rights etc.*). **–erzogen,** *adj.* well-bred, well brought up.

Wohlfahrt ['vo:lfa:rt], *f.* welfare, (*obs.*) weal; ***öffentliche –,*** public assistance, (public) relief; ***der – zur Last fallen,*** be a burden on the rates. **Wohlfahrts|amt,** *n.* welfare centre. **–ausschuß,** *m.* (*Hist.*) Committee of Public Safety. **–beamte(r),** *m.* welfare officer. **–fonds,** *m.* benefit fund. **–pflege,** *f.* welfare work. **–pflegerin,** *f.* woman welfare-worker. **–staat,** *m.* welfare state. **–unterstützung,** *f.* public assistance.

wohlfeil ['vo:lfaɪl], *adj.* cheap, low-priced. **Wohlfeilheit,** *f.* cheapness, low price.

wohl|geartet, *adj.* well-disposed; *see also* **–erzogen. Wohl|geboren,** *adj.* (*Hist.*) *Ew. –,* Sir *or* Madam, (*following name*) Esquire. **–gefallen,** *n.* pleasure, satisfaction (***über*** (*Acc.*), at), delight (in); ***sein – finden an*** (*Dat.*), take delight in, be well pleased with; ***sich in – auflösen,*** be settled to everyone's satisfaction; (*B.*) ***Friede auf Erden und den Menschen ein –,*** peace on earth and goodwill to all men. **wohlgefällig,** *adj.* pleasant, agreeable, satisfactory; (*of character*) complacent. **Wohl|gefälligkeit,** *f.* pleasantness; complacency. **–gefühl,** *n.* pleasant feeling *or* sensation, sense of well-being. **wohl|gelitten,** *adj.* well *or* much liked, popular. **–gemeint,** *adj.* well-meant *or* -intentioned. **–gemerkt!** *int. See* **–verstanden, 2. –gemut,** *adj.* cheerful, gay, joyous, cheery. **–genährt,** *adj.* well-fed *or* -nourished. **–geneigt,** *adj.* well-disposed, favourably inclined (*Dat.*, towards), affectionate (to(wards)). **–geraten,** *adj.* (*of a child*) good, well-behaved, (*of a th.*) (*pred.*) well done. **Wohl|geruch,** *m.* pleasant odour, scent, fragrance, perfume, aroma. **–geschmack,** *m.* pleasant taste *or* flavour. **wohl|gesetzt,** *adj.* well-chosen (*words*), well-worded *or* -turned (*speech*). **–gesinnt,** *adj.* well-meaning; *see also* **–geneigt. –gesittet,** *adj.* well-mannered. **Wohlgestalt,** *f.* shapeliness. **wohl|gestaltet,** *adj.* shapely, well-shaped *or* -turned. **–habend,** *adj.* well-to-do, wealthy, moneyed (*classes*), (*pred.*) well off, (*coll.*) well fixed. **Wohlhabenheit,** *f.* wealth, affluence, prosperity, easy circumstances.

wohlig ['vo:lɪç], *adj.* comfortable, pleasant, nice, (*coll.*) cosy, snug; (*of a p.*) cheerful, content(ed).

Wohlklang ['vo:lklaŋ], *m.* pleasant *or* pleasing *or* melodious sound; harmony, euphony. **wohlklingend,** *adj.* harmonious, melodious, musical, euphonious, sonorous, (*pred.*) pleasing to the ear.

Wohl|laut, *m. See* **–klang. –leben,** *n.* life of pleasure; luxury, good living. **wohl|meinend,** *adj.* well-meaning, friendly. **–riechend,** *adj.* (sweet) scented, fragrant, perfumed, aromatic; (*Bot.*) ***–e Wicke,*** sweet pea (*Lathyrus odoratus*). **–schmeckend,** *adj.* tasty, savoury, palatable, (*coll.*) nice. **Wohl|sein,** *n. See* **–befinden**; ***auf Ihr –! zum –!*** your health! **–stand,** *m. See* **–habenheit.**

Wohl|tat, *f.* benefit, boon, blessing; kindness, favour; good deed, benefaction; charity; (*coll.*) ***eine wahre –,*** a real treat, quite a comfort. **–täter,** *m.* benefactor. **–täterin,** *f.* benefactress. **wohltätig,** *adj.* beneficent, salutary; charitable. **Wohltätigkeit,** *f.* charity, beneficence. **Wohltätigkeits|veranstaltung,** *f.* charity performance. **–verein,** *m.* charitable organization, charity. **–zweck,** *m.* charity, charitable use.

wohl|tuend, *adj.* beneficial; pleasant, comforting; – ***berührt,*** gratified, pleasantly surprised. **–tun,** *irr.v.i.* (*sep.*) do good, give pleasure, be pleasing (*Dat.*, to), (*B.*) dispense charity; ***Wohltun bringt Zinsen,*** he who gives to the poor lends to the Lord. **–überlegt,** *adj. See* **–bedacht**; ***–e Rede,*** well-prepared speech. **–unterrichtet,** *adj.* well-informed. **–verdient,** *adj.* just, merited, well-earned *or* -deserved; (*of a p.*) deserving. **Wohl|verhalten,** *n.* good conduct. **–verleih,** *m.* (*Bot.*) arnica. **wohl|verstanden, 1.** *adj.* well-known, generally understood. **2.** *int.* mark my words! mind you! **–weislich,** *adv.* prudently, wisely, circumspectly; – ***tun,*** be careful to do. **–wollen,** *irr.v.i.* (*sep.*) (*Dat.*) wish well; be well-disposed (towards). **Wohlwollen,** *n.* goodwill, benevolence, kind feeling(s); favour, kindness. **wohlwollend,** *adj.* kind, benevolent; – ***gegenüberstehen*** (*Dat.*), take a favourable view of.

Wohn|bau ['vo:n–], *m.* domestic architecture; (*pl.* **-ten**) *see* **–gebäude. –bedarf,** *m.* domestic requirements, household necessities. **–bevölkerung,** *f.* resident population. **–bezirk,** *m.* residential district. **–block,** *m.* block of (residential) flats.

wohnen ['vo:nən], *v.i.* live, dwell, reside, (*Scots*) stay (***bei,*** with); ***zur Miete –,*** lodge; ***so wahr ein Gott im Himmel wohnt,*** as sure as there is a God in Heaven *or* God above.

Wohn|gebäude, *n.* residential premises, dwelling-house, block of flats, apartment house. **–gebiet,** *n.* residential area, (*Bot., Zool., Orn.*) habitat. **–grube,** *f.* cave dwelling. **wohnhaft,** *adj.* living, resident (***in*** (*Dat.*), at); ***sich – niederlassen,*** take up residence, settle (***in*** or ***an*** (*Dat.*), in). **Wohn|haus,** *n. See* **–gebäude. –haushalt,** *m.* ecology. **–küche,** *f.* living-room-cum-kitchen, kitchen-breakfast room. **–kultur,** *f.* style of living. **wohnlich,** *adj.* habitable; comfortable, convenient, (*coll.*) cosy, snug, (*pred.*) pleasant to live in; ***in –em Zustand,*** ready for occupation. **Wohn|ort,** *m.* (place of) residence, dwelling-place, (*coll.*) home, (*Law*) domicile. **–partei,** *f.* tenant(s). **–raum,** *m. See* **–stube**; (*Mil., Naut.*) quarters. **--Schlafzimmer,** *n.* bed-sitting room, (*coll.*) bed-sitter. **–siedlung,** *f.* housing estate. **–sitz,** *m. See* **–ort**; ***mit – in,*** resident in. **–stätte,** *f. See* **–ort. –straße,** *f.* residential street. **–stube,** *f.* living- *or* sitting-room.

Wohnung ['vo:nuŋ], *f.* dwelling, residence, habitation; house, flat; lodgings, apartments, rooms, accommodation; home; ***Kost und –,*** board and lodging. **Wohnungs|amt,** *n.* housing department, (*for students etc.*) lodgings office. **–bau,** *m.* house-building. **–baugenossenschaft,** *f.* building-cooperative. **–bauprogramm,** *n.* building *or* housing programme. **–frage,** *f.* housing problem. **wohnungslos,** *adj.* homeless; (*Law*) (*pred.*) of no fixed abode. **Wohnungs|mangel,** *m. See* **–not. –nachweis,** *m.* house agency. **–not,** *f.* housing shortage. **–suche,** *f.* house-hunting. **–wechsel,** *m.* change of address. **–wesen,** *n.* housing. **–zwecke,** *m.pl.* habitation.

Wohn|verhältnisse, *n.pl.* housing conditions. **–viertel,** *n.* residential quarter *or* suburb. **–wagen,** *n.* caravan. **–zimmer,** *n. See* **–stube.**

Woilach ['vɔylax], *m.* (**-s,** *pl.* **-e**) saddle-blanket.

wölben ['vœlbən], *v.t., v.r.* curve, arch, vault; camber; ***gewölbter Gang,*** arched *or* vaulted passage; ***gewölbter Keller,*** vault. **Wölbgerüst,** *n.* (*Archit.*) cent(e)ring. **Wölbung,** *f.* (*Archit.*) arch, vault, dome; bow, curve, curvature, camber. **Wölbungsfläche,** *f.* (*Archit.*) ***innere –,*** intrados; ***äußere –,*** extrados.

Wolf [vɔlf], *m.* (**-(e)s,** *pl.* **¨-e**) **1.** (*Zool.*) wolf; (*Prov.*) ***man muß mit den Wölfen heulen,*** do in Rome as the Romans do; (*Prov.*) ***wenn man den – nennt, so kommt er gerennt*** or ***wenn man vom – spricht, so ist er weit nicht,*** speak *or* talk of the devil and he appears; ***reißende Wölfe,*** ravening wolves; ***– und Schaf,*** fox and geese (*game*); ***ein – im Schafspelz,*** a wolf in sheep's clothing; **2.** (*Cul.*) mincing-machine, mincer; (*Spin.*) willow; (*Paperm.*) devil; **3.** (*Med.*) chafe, chafing, soreness; (*Metall.*) pig, bloom; ***sich*** (*Dat.*) ***einen – laufen,*** get sore *or* develop sores through walking. **wolfen, 1.** *v.i.* (*of wolves*) whelp; (*dial.*) (*of children*) cut teeth. **2.** *v.t.* willow (*cotton*).

Wölfin ['vœlfɪn], *f.* she-wolf. **wölfisch,** *adj.* wolfish, lupine.

Wolfram ['vɔlfram], *n.* (*Chem.*) tungsten, wolframite. **wolframsauer,** *adj.* tungstate of. **Wolframsäure,** *f.* tungstic acid.

Wolfs|bohne, *f.* (*Bot.*) lupin(e). **-eisen,** *n.* wolf-trap, caltrop; (*Metall.*) bloom-iron. **-grube,** *f.* pitfall; (*Mil.*) covered pit, tank-trap. **-hund,** *m.* wolfhound, Alsatian (dog). **-hunger,** *m.* ravenous appetite, rapacious hunger. **-milch,** *f.* (*Bot.*) spurge (*Euphorbia*). **-rachen,** *m.* (*Med.*) cleft palate. **-rudel,** *n.* pack of wolves. **-sucht,** *f.* lycanthropy.

Wolke ['vɔlkə], *f.* cloud; (*in gems*) flaw; (***wie***) ***aus den*** or ***allen -n fallen,*** be thunderstruck; (*fig.*) ***in die -n erheben,*** exalt to the skies; ***über den -n schweben,*** live in the clouds.

wölken ['vœlkən], *see* **bewölken.**

Wolken|achat, *m.* clouded agate. **-bildung,** *f.* cloud formation. **-bruch,** *m.* cloudburst, torrential downpour. **wolkenbruchartig,** *adj.* torrential. **Wolken|decke,** *f.* cloud cover, pall of cloud. **-himmel,** *m.* cloudy sky, (*Poet.*) welkin. **-höhe,** *f.* (*Av.*) (cloud) ceiling. **-kratzer,** *m.* skyscraper. **-kuckucksheim,** *n.* Cloud-Cuckoo-Land, fools' paradise. **-kunde,** *f.* nephology. **wolkenlos,** *adj.* cloudless, clear. **Wolken|schicht,** *f.* cloud layer *or* stratum. **-schieber,** *m.* (*Theat., coll.*) scene-shifter. **-wand,** *f.* bank of clouds.

wolkig ['vɔlkɪç], *adj.* cloudy, clouded, overcast.

Woll|abfall, -abgang, *m.* wool-waste. **-arbeiter,** *m.* wool-dresser. **-atlas,** *m.* worsted satin. **-baum,** *m.* silk-cotton tree (*Bombacaceae*). **-bereiter,** *m.* *See* **-arbeiter. -decke,** *f.* (woollen) blanket.

Wolle ['vɔlə], *f.* (-, *pl.* **-n** *or* **Wollarten**) wool; down; (*of rabbits, goats, camels etc.*) hair; (*coll.*) ***ihn in die – bringen,*** enrage *or* nettle him, (*sl.*) get his goat; ***in der – gefärbt,*** dyed in the wool (*also fig.*); (*coll.*) ***in die – geraten,*** be enraged, lose one's temper *or* (*sl.*) wool, (*sl.*) blow one's top; (*coll.*) ***sich in die – geraten mit,*** have a row with; (*fig.*) ***– lassen müssen,*** come off a *or* the loser, be fleeced; (*fig.*) ***in der – sitzen,*** be on velvet *or* in clover, be on a bed of roses; (*fig.*) ***– spinnen,*** make a nice *or* tidy profit; (*Prov.*) ***viel Geschrei und wenig –,*** great boast small roast, much ado about nothing.

wollen ['vɔlən], **1.** *irr.v.i.* **(a)** be willing, will, ordain; ***machen Sie, was Sie –!*** please yourself (what you do)! do your worst! ***Gott will es,*** it is God's will; ***so Gott will!*** please God! ***er mag – oder nicht,*** whether he likes it or not; **(b)** wish, want, desire; ***was – Sie von mir?*** what do you want (of me)? ***was – Sie mit dem Hammer?*** what do you want the hammer for? ***Sie wissen nicht, was Sie –,*** you don't know what you want, you don't know your own mind; ***wie Sie –,*** just as you like *or* please, suit *or* please yourself; ***hier ist nichts zu –,*** there's nothing to be had here, (*coll.*) there's nothing doing here; ***mit ihm ist nichts zu –,*** there's nothing to be done with him, (*coll.*) he's hopeless; ***Sie haben's so gewollt,*** you (have) asked for it; ***ohne es zu –,*** involuntarily, unintentionally, in spite of o.s.
2. *irr.v.aux.* **(a)** will (*tun,* do), be willing (to do); ***nicht –,*** be unwilling, refuse (to do); **(b)** wish, want, desire (to do); ***lieber –,*** prefer (to do); ***ich wollte lieber,*** I would rather (do), I should prefer (to do); ***nicht –,*** not want *or* wish; ***unbedingt –,*** insist on (doing); **(c)** mean, intend, have a mind (to do); ***was – Sie damit sagen?*** what do you mean (by that)? ***ich will nur hoffen, daß er . . .,*** I do hope he . . .; ***ich will nicht hoffen, daß er . . .,*** I do hope he won't . . .; ***ich will nichts gesagt haben,*** I take back my words *or* what I said; ***das will ich nicht gehört haben,*** you mind your tongue! be careful what you say! **(d)** be about *or* (*coll.*) going (to do), be on the point (of doing); ***wir – gehen!*** let's go! ***ich wollte eben weggehen,*** I was (just) about to leave, I was on the point of leaving; ***es wollte Nacht werden,*** night was just coming on; **(e)** claim, require, demand; ***er will alles wissen,*** he claims he knows *or* claims to know everything; ***das will ich meinen,*** I should think so indeed; ***das will was heißen,*** that's saying a great deal, there's something in that, that's indeed something; ***das will nicht viel heißen,*** that doesn't count for *or* mean much, that's of little consequence *or* account, (*coll.*) that's nothing to write home about; **(f)** (= **mögen**) ***ich will mich gern geirrt haben,*** I should like to think *or* should be glad to think I am mistaken; ***ich will gern glauben daß . . .,*** I am ready to believe that . . .; ***es geschehe, was da wolle,*** whatever happens *or* may happen, come what may; ***dem sei wie ihm wolle,*** be that as it may; ***es sei wo es wolle,*** wherever it may be; **(g)** (= **müssen**; *with neg.* = **dürfen**) ***was – wir sagen, wenn . . .,*** what are we (going) to say if . . .; ***die Arbeit will Zeit haben,*** the job must take time; ***weitere Auskunft wolle man einholen bei . . .,*** for further information (you should) apply to . . .; ***er wolle sofort kommen,*** he is to come immediately; ***das will überlegt werden,*** that needs thinking about; **(h)** (*ellipt.*) (*usu. with meanings as under* **(b)** *and an omitted inf. implying movement*) ***wo willst du hin?*** where do you wish to go? where are you making for? ***zu wem – Sie?*** whom do you wish to see? ***hoch hinaus –,*** have extravagant aims, (*coll.*) fly high; ***es will mir nicht in den Sinn,*** I can't understand it, (*coll.*) I can't make head or tail of it; ***es will mir nicht aus dem Sinn,*** I can't forget it, I can't get it out of my mind; ***die S. will nicht vorwärts,*** the affair makes no headway; ***der Deckel will nicht ab,*** the lid won't come off; ***der Baum will fetten Boden,*** the tree needs a rich soil; **(i)** (*as p.p.* = **gewollt** *after inf. in compound tense*) ***er hat nicht kommen –,*** he didn't want to come; ***ich habe nur scherzen –,*** I was only joking, I only intended it as a joke.

Wollen, *n.* will, volition; inclination(s), intention(s), wish(es), aspiration(s).

Woll|faden, *m.* *See* **-haar. -färber,** *m.* wool-dyer. **-fett,** *n.* lanolin(e). **-garn,** *n.* woollen yarn, worsted. **-gras,** *n.* (*Bot.*) cotton-grass (*Eriophorum*). **-haar,** *n.* strand of wool, (*coll.*) woolly hair. **-handel,** *m.* wool trade. **wollig,** *adj.* woolly, downy, fleecy; lanate, laniferous, lanigerous. **Woll|industrie,** *f.* woollen industry. **-jacke,** *f.* cardigan, (*coll.*) woolly. **-kamm,** *m.* carding-comb. **-kämmerer,** *m.* wool-carder. **-kleidung,** *f.* woollen clothing, woollens. **-kraut,** *n.* (*Bot.*) mullein (*Verbascum*). **-markt,** *m.* wool mart. **-pulver,** *n.* flock. **-sachen,** *f.pl.* *See* **-kleidung. -schaf,** *n.* sheep reared for its wool. **-schur,** *f.* sheep-shearing. **-schweiß,** *m.* suint. **-stoff,** *m.* woollen material.

Wollust ['vɔlust], *f.* (-, *pl.* **¨-e**) sensual pleasure, voluptuousness; lust, lasciviousness, pleasures of the flesh; (*obs.*) delight, bliss. **wollüstig,** *adj.* sensual, voluptuous, lascivious, lustful, lecherous. **Wollüstling,** *m.* (**-s,** *pl.* **-e**) voluptuary, sensualist, debauchee, libertine.

Woll|waren, *f.pl.* woollen goods, woollens. **-zeug,** *n.* *See* **-stoff.**

womit [vo:'mɪt], **1.** *rel.adv.* (= ***mit welchem***) with *or* by which, wherewith, whereby; ***das ist's, – ich nicht zufrieden bin,*** that is what I'm not satisfied with; ***– ich nicht sagen will,*** by which I do not mean to say. **2.** *inter. adv.* with what? what . . . with? by what means? – ***kann ich dienen?*** what can I do for you? can I be of any help?

womöglich [vo:'mø:klɪç], *adv.* if possible, possibly, perhaps; (*coll.*) if anything.

wonach [vo:'na:x], **1.** *rel.adv.* (= ***nach welchem***) after which, whereupon; according to which. **2.** *inter. adv.* after *or* for *or* about what? what . . . about *or* for? – ***fragt er?*** what is he asking for *or* about?

Wonne ['vɔnə], *f.* delight, bliss, joy, rapture, ecstasy; ***in eitel – schweben*** or ***schwimmen,*** be in raptures *or* ecstasies, be enraptured, (*coll.*) be riding on air; (*coll.*) ***mit –,*** with relish. **Wonne|-gefühl,** *n.* thrill of delight, delightful sensation. **–monat, –mond,** *m.* (*obs.*) month of May. **–rausch,** *m.* transport of delight, ecstasy, rapture. **–schauer,** *m.* thrill of delight. **–taumel,** *m. See* **–rausch. –tränen,** *f.pl.* tears of joy. **wonnetrun-ken,** *adj.* blissful, enraptured, in raptures *or* ecstasies.

wonnig ['vɔnɪç], (*Poet.*) **wonniglich,** *adj.* delightful, blissful; delicious, lovely, sweet.

woran [vo:'ran], **1.** *rel.adv.* (= ***an welchem***) at *or* by *or* against which; ***ich weiß, – es liegt,*** I know the reason for it; ***weißt du, – er mich erkannt hat?*** do you know how he recognized me? ***ich weiß nicht, – ich bin,*** I don't know where I stand; . . . ***– ich mit ihm bin,*** . . . where I stand with him, . . . what to make of him. **2.** *inter.adv.* at *or* by *or* against what? ***– liegt es, daß . . .?*** how is it that . . .? what is the reason for . . .? ***– hat er mich erkannt?*** how did he recognize me? ***– bin ich?*** where did I get to? how far did I get *or* reach? where did I leave off? ***– denkst du?*** what are you thinking of? (*coll.*) a penny for your thoughts.

worauf [vo:'rauf], **1.** *rel.adv.* (= ***auf welchem***) on which; upon *or* after which, whereupon. **2.** *inter. adv.* on what? what . . . on? ***– warten Sie?*** what are you waiting for? ***– sinnst du?*** what have you in mind? what are you meditating on *or* brooding over?

woraus [vo:'raus], **1.** *rel.adv.* (= ***aus welchem***) from which, out of which, whence. **2.** *inter.adv.* from what? what . . . from? out of what?

worden ['vɔrdən], *p.p. of* **werden** *in compound tenses.*

worein [vo:'raɪn], (*rare*) **1.** *rel.adv.* (*in welch|en, –e, –es* (*Acc.*)) into which; ***das ist etwas, – ich mich nicht mische,*** that is s.th. I don't meddle in. **2.** *inter.adv.* into what *or* where?

Worfel ['vɔrfəl], *f.* (-, *pl.* **-n**) (*dial.*) winnowing-shovel. **Worfelmaschine,** *f. See* **Worfler. worfeln,** *v.t.* winnow, fan. **Worfler,** *m.* winnowing-machine.

worin [vo:'rɪn], **1.** *rel.adv.* (= ***in welchem***) in which, wherein. **2.** *inter.adv.* in what? what . . . in? wherein?

wornach [vo:r'na:x], (*Austr.*) *see* **wonach.**

Wort [vɔrt], *n.* **(-(e)s,** *pl.* **¨er** = *unconnected words, vocables; in all other cases* **–e**) word, vocable, term; expression, saying; promise, pledge, word of honour; ***ihm die –e vom Munde ablesen,*** take the words out of his mouth; ***ihm das – abschneiden,*** see ***ins – fallen***; ***am –e sein,*** have leave to speak, (*Parl.*) have the ear of the House, (*Am.*) have *or* hold the floor; ***aufs –,*** to the letter, implicitly; ***auf ein –!*** just a word (with you)! ***auf mein –,*** on my word of honour; ***auf seine –e hin,*** on the strength of his remarks; ***ich komme nur auf ein paar –e,*** may I have a few words; ***er hielt mich beim –,*** he held me to my word; ***er nahm mich beim –e,*** he took me at my word; ***in – und Bild,*** with text and illustrations; ***dein – in Ehren,*** with all deference to you; ***man kann sein eignes – nicht verstehen,*** one cannot hear o.s. speak *or* hear one's own voice; ***ihm das – entziehen,*** refuse him permission to continue (speaking), (*Parl.*) rule him out of order; ***das – ergreifen,*** (begin to) speak, (*Parl.*) rise to speak, (*Am.*) take the floor; ***das – erhalten,*** be allowed to speak, (*Parl.*) catch the Speaker's eye, (*Am.*) get the floor; ***ihm das – erteilen,*** see ***ihm das – geben***; ***nicht das leiseste – fallen lassen,*** not drop *or* let fall the slightest hint; ***das – führen,*** be the spokesman, (*coll.*) do the talking; ***das große – führen,*** brag, boast, draw the long bow; lay down the law, (*coll.*) talk big; do all the talking; ***ihm das – geben,*** allow him to speak; ***ein – gab das andere,*** one word led to another; ***geflügelte –e,*** household words, familiar quotations; ***mit wenig –en,*** in a few words, briefly; ***ein gutes – einlegen für,*** intercede for, (*coll.*) put in a good word for; ***nicht für Geld und gute –e zu haben,*** not to be had for love or money; ***das – haben,*** see ***am –e sein***; (*coll.*) ***hast du –e!*** my word! well I never! goodness gracious! ***das letzte – haben,*** have the last word *or* the final say; ***– halten,*** keep one's word; ***nicht – halten,*** break one's word; ***ihm ins – fallen,*** interrupt him, cut him short; ***in –e fassen,*** put into words, express (in words), formulate; ***kein – mehr!*** not another word! ***er läßt ein – mit sich reden,*** he listens to reason; ***jedes – auf die Goldwaage legen,*** weigh every word; ***seinen Gedanken –e leihen,*** clothe one's thoughts in words; ***ein Mann, ein –!*** word of honour! honour bright! ***mit anderen –en,*** in other words; ***mit einem –,*** in a word; ***es war mit keinem – davon die Rede,*** not a word of it was mentioned; (*Prov.*) ***ein gutes – findet eine gute Statt,*** a good (*or* kind) word is never out of place; ***ihm*** (or ***einer S.***) ***das – reden,*** speak for *or* in favour of *or* hold a brief for him (*or* a th.), take his part, support *or* defend *or* (*coll.*) back him (*or* a th.); ***spare dir deine –e,*** save your breath; ***ums – bitten,*** beg permission *or* ask leave to speak; ***ihm das – im Munde umdrehen,*** twist his words; ***er macht nicht viele –e,*** he is a man of few words; ***ohne viel –e zu machen,*** without more *or* further ado, (*in narration*) to cut a long story short; ***er ist ein Mann von –,*** he is as good as his word *or* is a man of his word; ***– und Weise,*** words and music; ***zu –e kommen,*** get a hearing, get a chance to speak; (*coll.*) ***nicht zu –e kommen,*** not get a word in edgeways; ***ihn zu –e kommen lassen,*** let him have his say; ***sich zum –e melden,*** see ***ums – bitten***; ***ein – zu seiner Zeit,*** a word spoken in season.

Wort|akzent, *m.* word-stress. **–armut,** *f.* deficiency in vocabulary, poverty of language. **–art,** *f.* (*Gram.*) part of speech. **–aufwand,** *m.* verbosity. **–bedeutungslehre,** *f.* semantics. **–biegung,** *f.* inflection. **–biegungslehre,** *f.* accidence. **–bil-dung,** *f.* word-formation. **–bruch,** *m.* treachery, breach of faith. **wortbrüchig,** *adj.* treacherous, false; ***– werden,*** break one's word.

Wörtchen ['vœrtçən], *n. See* **Wörtlein.**

Wörterbuch ['vœrtərbu:x], *n.* dictionary.

Worterklärung ['vɔrtˀɛrklɛ:ruŋ], *f.* verbal explanation; definition.

Wörterverzeichnis ['vœrtərfɛrtsaɪçnɪs], *n.* word list, vocabulary, glossary.

Wort|folge, *f.* word order. **–fügung,** *f.* sentence structure *or* construction. **–fügungslehre,** *f.* syntax. **–führer,** *m.* spokesman; (*of a jury*) foreman. **–fülle,** *f.* verbosity. **–gefecht,** *n. See* **–streit, –gepränge,** *n.* bombast. **wort|getreu,** *adj.* word for word, literal. **–gewandt,** *adj.* glib, eloquent. **–habend,** *adj.* presiding. **–karg,** *adj.* laconic, taciturn. **Wort|kargheit,** *f.* taciturnity. **–klasse,** *f. See* **–art. –klauber,** *m.* quibbler, hair-splitter. **–klauberei,** *f.* quibble; quibbling, hair-splitting. **–kram,** *m.* verbiage, idle talk. **–krämer,** *m.* phrase-monger. **–laut,** *m.* wording, text; . . . ***hat folgenden –,*** . . . runs as follows.

Wörtlein ['vœrtlaɪn], *n.* ***ein –*** (***ein gewichtiges –***) ***mitzureden haben,*** have some say (quite a say) in the matter.

wörtlich ['vœrtlɪç], *adj.* literal, verbal, word for word, verbatim; ***–e Beleidigung,*** verbal insult, slander. **Wörtlichkeit,** *f.* literalness, literal character.

Wort|rätsel, *n.* rebus. **–reichtum,** *m.* verbosity; wordiness, verbiage. **–reiz,** *m.* verbal stimulus.

–**schatz,** *m.* vocabulary, words in use. –**schwall,** *m.* flood *or* torrent of words, rigmarole; verbosity, bombast, fustian. –**sinn,** *m.* literal sense. –**spiel,** *n.* play (up)on words, pun. –**stamm,** *m.* root, radical. –**stammkunde,** *f.* etymology. –**stellung,** *f.* *See* –**folge.** –**streit,** *m.* altercation, squabble, dispute, controversy. –**stummheit,** *f.* motor aphasia. –**tarif,** *m.* (*telegrams*) charge per word. –**taubheit,** *f.* sensory aphasia. –**treue,** *f.* fidelity to the text. –**verdrehung,** *f.* distortion of the meaning, equivocation. –**versetzung,** *f.* transposition of words, inversion. –**wechsel,** *m.* *See* –**streit**; ***ein – haben mit,*** have words with. –**witz,** *m.* *See* –**spiel. wortwörtlich,** *adj.* *See* **wörtlich.**

worüber [vo:'ry:bər], **1.** *rel.adv.* (= ***über welchem***) upon *or* over *or* about which; ***– ich sehr ärgerlich war,*** which annoyed me, at which I was very annoyed; ***das ist es, – ich mich wundere,*** that is what astonishes me. **2.** *inter.adv.* at *or* over *or* about which *or* what? what . . . at *or* about? ***– lachst du?*** what are you laughing at *or* about?

worum [vo:'rum], **1.** *rel.adv.* (= ***um welches*** or ***was***) for *or* about which; ***erzähle mir – es sich handelt,*** tell me what it's all about. **2.** *inter.adv.* about what *or* which? what . . . about? ***– handelt es sich?*** what is it about? (*coll.*) what's the trouble *or* matter?

worunter [vo:'runtər], **1.** *rel.adv.* (= ***unter welchem***) under *or* among which; ***die verbotenen Bücher, – dieses gehört,*** the prohibited books, of which this is one. **2.** *inter.adv.* under *or* among which *or* what? what . . . under *or* among? ***– hatte er sich versteckt?*** under what was he hiding? what was he hiding under?

woselbst [vo:'zɛlpst], *adv.* where, in the very place where *or* that.

wovon [vo:'fɔn], **1.** *rel.adv.* (= ***von welchem***) from *or* of *or* about *or* concerning which, whereof. **2.** *inter.adv.* of *or* from *or* about which *or* what? what . . . about *or* of *or* from? ***– lebt er?*** what does he live on? what does he make his living by?

wovor [vo:'fo:r], **1.** *rel.adv.* (= ***vor welchem***) of *or* from *or* before which. **2.** *inter.adv.* of *or* from which *or* what? what . . . of *or* from? ***– fürchtest du dich?*** what are you afraid of?

wozu [vo:'tsu:], **1.** *rel.adv.* (= ***zu welchem***) to which *or* what end *or* purpose; why; to *or* for *or* at *or* in addition to which; ***– kommt noch,*** to which must be added; ***– man Lust hat,*** what one is inclined for. **2.** *inter. adv.* to what end? for what purpose? for what? what . . . for? why? ***– das?*** what is that for? why that?

wrack [vrak], *adj.* (*Naut.*) wrecked, derelict; unserviceable, beyond repair; (*Comm.*) unusable, discarded. **Wrack,** *n.* **(-(e)s,** *pl.* **-e** *or* **-s)** (*Naut.*) wreck (*also fig.*), wreckage, derelict, hulk. **Wrackgut,** *n.* jetsam; ***treibendes –,*** flotsam.

Wrasen ['vra:zən], *m.* (*dial.*) steam, vapour, hot exhalation.

wricken ['vrɪkən], **wriggen** ['vrɪgən], *v.t.* scull (*a boat over the stern*).

wringen ['vrɪŋən], *irr.v.t.* twist; wring. **Wringmaschine,** *f.* wringer, mangle.

Wruke ['vru:kə], *f.* (*dial.*) Swedish turnip.

Wucher ['vu:xər], *m.* usury; profiteering, (*B., dial.*) gain, profit; interest; ***– treiben,*** practise usury, make excessive profit; ***mit – vergelten,*** repay *or* return with interest. **Wucherblume,** *f.* (*Bot.*) (ox-eye) daisy (*Chrysanthemum leucanthemum*). **Wucherer,** *m.* money-lender, usurer; profiteer. **Wuchergewinn,** *m.* inordinate profit. **wucherhaft, wucherisch,** *adj.* usurious, profiteering. **Wuchermiete,** *f.* rack-rent.

wuchern ['vu:xərn], *v.i.* grow luxuriantly *or* rankly, (*fig.*) be rampant, proliferate, produce abundantly; profiteer, practise usury; ***mit dem Gelde –,*** lend money at usurious interest; (*fig.*) ***mit seinem Pfunde –,*** make the most of one's opportunities, exploit one's resources. **wuchernd,** *adj.* rank (*growth*), (*fig.*) prolific, rampant.

Wucher|preis, *m.* exorbitant *or* (*coll.*) cut-throat price. –**stier,** *m.* (*dial.*) bull. **Wucherung,** *f.* rank growth, proliferation, exuberance; (*Med.*) growth, excrescence, proud flesh. **Wucherzins(en),** *m.*(*pl.*) usurious *or* extortionate interest.

Wuchs [vu:ks], *m.* **(-es,** *pl.* **¨-e)** growth, development; figure, form, shape; physique, build, stature, height.

wuchs, *see* **wachsen.**

–**wüchsig** ['vy:ksɪç], *adj.suff.* of . . . growth *or* stature; *e.g.* ***hoch–,*** tall-growing.

Wucht [vuxt], *f.* weight, pressure, impact; force, impetus; (*Phys.*) momentum, kinetic energy; ***die volle – des Angriffs,*** the (full) brunt of the attack; (*coll.*) ***eine ganze –*** (*Gen.*), a load of; (*sl.*) ***das ist eine –!*** it's a wow! **wuchten, 1.** *v.i.* weigh heavy, lie *or* press heavily (***auf*** (*Acc.*), upon); (*coll.*) work like a horse *or* slave. **2.** *v.t.* lift with difficulty, lever *or* prise up. **wuchtig,** *adj.* weighty, ponderous, heavy; (*of a blow*) powerful, vigorous.

Wühlarbeit ['vy:lˀarbaɪt], *f.* subversive *or* underground activity, (insidious) agitation. **wühlen,** *v.i.* root, grub, turn up the ground; (*also v.r.*) dig, burrow (***in*** (*Dat.*), into), (*fig.*) rummage, rake about (in); ***im Gelde –,*** wallow *or* be rolling in money; ***sich*** (*Dat.*) ***in den Haaren –,*** run one's hands through one's hair; (*fig.*) ***in eine Wunde –,*** turn the knife in the wound; ***Schmerz wühlt mir in den Eingeweiden,*** pain is gnawing at my vitals; ***Haß wühlt in ihm,*** hatred rankles in his heart. **Wühler,** *m.* 1. agitator; 2. *pl.* (*Zool.*) rooting animals. **wühlerisch,** *adj.* subversive, inflammatory, (*coll.*) rabble-raising. **Wühl|gang,** *m.* (*of mole etc.*) burrow, run. –**maus,** *f.* (*Zool.*) vole (*Microtus*).

Wuhne, *f.* (*Austr.*) *see* **Wune.**

Wulst [vulst], *m.* **(-es,** *pl.* **¨-e)** *or f.* **(-,** *pl.* **¨-e)** swelling, tuberosity, bulge, lump, hump; fold, roll, pad; (*for hair*) chignon; (*Archit.*) torus. **wulstig,** *adj.* padded, stuffed; bulging; lumpy; swollen, puffed up; (*as lips*) thick, protruding, pouting, puffy.

wummern ['vumərn], *v.i.* (*coll.*) boom.

wund [vunt], *adj.* sore, chafed, galled, chapped; wounded, injured; ***sich*** (*Dat.*) ***die Füße – laufen,*** get sore feet, become footsore; ***sich – liegen,*** get bedsores; (*fig.*) ***–er Punkt,*** sore point; ***– reiben,*** chafe, rub sore; ***–e Stelle,*** sore *or* tender spot *or* place, sore. **Wund|arzneikunst,** *f.* (*obs.*) surgery. –**arzt,** *m.* (*obs.*) surgeon. –**balsam,** *m.* vulnerary balsam. –**benzin,** *n.* surgical spirit. –**brand,** *m.* gangrene.

Wunde ['vundə], *f.* wound, injury; sore; (*fig.*) hurt; (*fig.*) ***alte –n wieder aufreißen,*** open old wounds; (*fig.*) ***seine Finger in eine offene – legen,*** put one's finger on a tender spot; ***die Zeit heilt alle –n,*** time is a great healer.

Wunder ['vundər], *n.* miracle, marvel, wonder; (*coll.*) ***sein blaues – erleben,*** get the shock *or* surprise of one's life (***an, bei, mit,*** with); ***das ist kein –,*** that is not at all surprising; (***es ist***) ***kein – daß*** . . ., (it is) no *or* small wonder that . . .; ***– verrichten,*** perform miracles; (*fig.*) ***– tun*** or ***wirken,*** work wonders *or* miracles; ***er denkt*** or ***glaubt, wunder was getan zu haben,*** he thinks the world of what he has done, he thinks he has done s.th. wonderful; ***ich dachte wunder, was das wäre,*** I expected s.th. wonderful, I expected far more; ***er bildet sich wunder was ein,*** he thinks a lot *or* no end of himself; ***er bildet sich wunder was darauf ein,*** he prides himself on it no end; ***wunder was halten von,*** think the world of.

wunderbar ['vundərba:r], *adj.* amazing, astounding, marvellous, miraculous, wondrous, magic; (*coll.*) wonderful, splendid, great, (*sl.*) fabulous. **wunderbarerweise,** *adv.* strange to relate *or* say.

Wunder|baum, *m.* (*Bot.*) castor-oil plant (*Riccinus communis*). –**baumöl,** *n.* castor-oil. –**bild,** *n.* wonder-working image. –**ding,** *n.* wonder(ful thing), marvel, prodigy, phenomenon. –**doktor,** *m.* quack (doctor), faith-healer. –**erscheinung,** *f.* miraculous phenomenon. –**glaube,** *m.* belief in miracles. –**horn,** *n.* magic horn. **wunderhübsch,** *adj.* wonderfully pretty, (*coll.*) awfully sweet.

Wunder|kerze, *f.* sparkler. **-kind,** *n.* infant prodigy. **-kraft,** *f.* magic *or* miraculous power. **-kur,** *f.* miraculous cure. **-land,** *n.* wonderland, fairyland.

wunderlich ['vundərlıç], *adj.* strange, odd, singular, peculiar, quaint, queer, curious; whimsical, wayward, eccentric; *-er Kauz,* odd fish, queer chap; ***es ist ihm – ergangen,*** strange things happened to him; ***mir wurde – zu Mute,*** I felt very queer. **Wunderlichkeit,** *f.* oddness, strangeness; queerness; oddity, whimsicality; eccentricity.

Wunder|märe, *f.* wonderful *or* wondrous news, fantastic story. **-mittel,** *n.* panacea.

wundern ['vundərn], **1.** *v.t., imp.* surprise, astonish; ***das wundert mich,*** I am astonished at it; ***es wundert mich daß*** . . ., I am surprised that . . .; ***es soll mich doch –, ob*** . . ., I wonder if. . . . **2.** *v.r.* be surprised *or* astonished (***über*** (*Acc.*), at).

wundernehmen ['vundərne:mən], *irr.v.t.* (*sep.*) astonish, surprise; ***es sollte mich nicht –, wenn*** . . ., I should not be at all surprised if. . . . **wundersam,** *adj.* (*Poet.*) *see* **wunderbar. wunderschön,** *adj.* very beautiful, lovely, exquisite. **Wunder|spiegel,** *m.* magic mirror. **-tat,** *f.* miracle; wonderful exploit, (*Poet.*) doughty deed. **-täter,** *m.* miracle-worker. **wundertätig,** *adj.* wonder-working, miraculous. **Wundertier,** *n.* monster; (*coll.*) prodigy; ***ihn wie ein – anstaunen,*** stare at him as if he were a strange animal. **wundervoll,** *adj.* wonderful, marvellous; splendid, admirable. **Wunder|werk,** *n.* phenomenal achievement, wonder, miracle. **-zeichen,** *n.* miraculous sign, portent.

Wundfieber ['vuntfi:bər], *n.* wound-fever. **wundgelaufen,** *adj.* footsore. **Wund|klammer,** *f.* (*Med.*) suture clip. **-klee,** *m.* (*Bot.*) kidney vetch (*Anthyllis vulneraria*). **wund|laufen,** *irr.v.r. See under* **wund. -liegen,** *irr.v.r. See under* **wund. Wund|mal,** *n.* scar, (*Eccl.*) stigma (*pl.* stigmata). **-mittel,** *n.* vulnerary. **-pflaster,** *n.* adhesive plaster *or* dressing. **-rose,** *f.* erysipelas. **-salbe,** *f.* ointment, salve. **-schere,** *f.* probe-scissors. **-schorf,** *m.* scab. **-sein,** *n.* soreness, excoriation. **-starrkrampf,** *m.* tetanus.

Wune ['vu:nə], *f.* (*dial.*) vent-hole in ice, ice-hole.

Wunsch [vunʃ], *m.* (**-es,** *pl.* **⸚e**) wish, desire, request; desideratum (*pl.* desiderata), felt want; *pl.* good wishes, congratulations; ***ihm jeden – von den Augen ablesen,*** anticipate his every wish; ***auf –,*** if desired; on *or* by request; ***auf allgemeinen –,*** by popular request; ***hätten Sie noch einen –?*** is there anything else I can do for you *or* else you require? (***je***) ***nach –,*** as desired *or* required; ***mir geht alles nach –,*** everything is going on as well as I could wish; ***mein sehnlichster –,*** my dearest wish.

wünschbar ['vynʃba:r], *adj.* (*Swiss*) *see* **wünschenswert.**

Wunsch|bild, *n.* ideal. **-denken,** *n.* wishful thinking.

Wünschelrute ['vynʃəlru:tə], *f.* wishing-wand; divining-rod, dowser's rod. **Wünschelrutengänger,** *m.* diviner, dowser.

wünschen ['vynʃən], *v.t.* wish, desire, want, request (***ihm etwas,*** s.th. for him); ***sich*** (*Dat.*) ***–,*** long for, wish for; ***ich wünsche*** (***Ihnen***) ***alles Gute,*** I wish you well *or* (*coll.*) I wish you all the best; ***ihm*** (***zu etwas***) ***Glück –,*** congratulate him (on a th.), wish him luck (with a th.); ***nichts sehnlicher – als,*** wish nothing better than; ***es läßt*** (***viel***) ***zu – übrig,*** it is not satisfactory, it leaves much to be desired; (***ich***) ***wünsche wohl geruht zu haben,*** I hope you have slept well; ***wie Sie –,*** as you wish *or* please, (*coll.*) suit yourself. **wünschenswert,** *adj.* desirable (*Dat.*, for).

Wunschform ['vunʃfɔrm], *f.* (*Gram.*) optative (form). **wunschgemäß,** *adv.* as desired *or* requested, according to one's wishes. **Wunschkonzert,** *n.* (musical) request programme. **wunschlos, 1.** *adj.* contented, satisfied, unrepining; resigned, blasé. **2.** *adv.* ***– glücklich,*** blissfully happy. **Wunsch|maid,** *f.* (*Poet.*) Valkyrie. **-programm,** *n.* request programme. **-satz,** *m.* (*Gram.*) optative clause. **-traum,** *m.* wish-fulfilment, wishful thinking, (*coll.*) pipe-dream. **-zettel,** *m.* list of desiderata; (child's) letter to Santa Claus.

wupp [vup], **1.** *adv.* like a shot, in a flash. **2.** *int.* here goes! pop! **Wuppdich,** *m.* (**-s,** *pl.* **-s**) (*coll.*) flip, jerk; (*dial.*) noggin, shot (*of brandy etc.*). **wupps,** *see* **wupp. Wupptizität** [-tıtsi'tɛ:t], *f.* (*sl.*) speed, agility.

würbe ['vyrbə], *see* **werben.**

wurde ['vurdə], **würde** ['vyrdə], *see* **werden.**

Würde, *f.* dignity, propriety; position *or* post (of honour), rank, office, title; ***akademische –,*** academic degree; ***in Amt und –n,*** holding (high) office; ***nach –n,*** worthily; ***unter aller –,*** beneath contempt; ***unter meiner –,*** beneath my dignity; ***seiner – etwas vergeben,*** compromise one's dignity. **würdelos,** *adj.* undignified. **Würde(n)träger,** *m.* high official, dignitary. **würdevoll, 1.** *adj.* dignified, grave, solemn. **2.** *adv.* with dignity.

würdig ['vyrdıç], *adj.* worthy, deserving (*Gen.*, of); estimable, respectable, dignified; ***er ist dessen nicht –,*** he does not deserve it.

würdigen ['vyrdıgən], *v.t.* deem worthy (*Gen.*, of), deign, vouchsafe; value, appreciate, rate, estimate; ***ihn eines Blickes*** (***Wortes***) ***–,*** deign to look at (speak to) him; ***ihn keines Blickes –,*** ignore him completely; ***er würdigte mich seiner Freundschaft,*** he honoured me with his friendship; ***nach seinem Werte –,*** rate at its true value, value at its true worth; ***er würdigte mich keiner Antwort,*** he vouchsafed no reply; ***zu – wissen,*** know how to appreciate, have a proper appreciation of. **Würdigung,** *f.* appreciation, estimation, assessment, valuation; ***in – seiner Verdienste,*** in appreciation of his services.

Wurf [vurf], *m.* (**-(e)s,** *pl.* **⸚e**) **1.** throw, pitch, cast, projection, (*of bombs*) release; (*fig.*) ***auf den ersten –,*** at the first shot; (*fig.*) ***alles auf einen – setzen,*** stake all on a single throw *or* card, put all one's eggs in one basket; ***der – der Falten,*** the way the folds hang; (*fig.*) ***großer –,*** bold plan *or* design; (*fig.*) ***glücklicher –,*** lucky shot; (*fig.*) ***einen guten – tun,*** have a stroke of luck, (*coll.*) hit the jackpot; (*fig.*) ***das kommt ihm in den –,*** that just suits him, (*sl.*) that's right up his street; ***das kommt ihm nicht in den –,*** that doesn't suit him at all, (*sl.*) that's not his cup of tea; ***zum – ausholen,*** make *or* get ready to throw; 2. (*of animals*) brood, litter.

Wurf|anker, *m.* kedge (anchor). **-bahn,** *f.* trajectory.

würfe ['vyrfə], *see* **werfen.**

Würfel ['vyrfəl], *m.* **1.** cube, hexahedron; **2.** die (*usu. pl.* dice); ***die – sind gefallen,*** the die is cast; ***falsche –,*** loaded dice; ***– spielen,*** play at dice, (*sl.*) play the bones. **Würfel|becher,** *m.* dice-box. **-bein,** *n.* (*Anat.*) cuboid (bone). **würfelförmig,** *adj.* cubic(al), cube-shaped, cubiform. **würfelig,** *adj.* cubic(al), (*pattern*) chequered. **Würfelmuster,** *n.* chequered design. **würfeln, 1.** *v.i.* play at *or* throw dice; ***– um,*** throw dice (*or usu.*) toss for. **2.** *v.t.* chequer; (*dial.*) throw *or* toss about; winnow (*grain*); ***gewürfelt,*** *see* **würfelig**; *also* (*pavement*) tessellated. **Würfel|spat,** *m.* (*Chem.*) boracite. **-spiel,** *n.* game of dice. **-zucker,** *m.* lump-sugar.

Wurf|gerät, *n.* (*Mil.*) projector, (rocket) launcher. **-geschoß,** *n.* projectile, missile. **-granate,** *f.* mortar shell. **-größe,** *f.* size of litter. **-höhe,** *f.* height of projection. **-kraft,** *f.* projectile force. **-lehre,** *f.* ballistics. **-leine,** *f.* (*Naut.*) heaving-line. **-linie,** *f.* line of projection; *see also* **-bahn. -messer,** *n.* throwing-knife. **-netz,** *n.* casting-net. **-pfeil,** *m.* dart. **-riemen,** *m.* (falcon's) leash. **-schaufel,** *f.* winnowing-shovel. **-scheibe,** *f.* quoit, discus. **-sendung,** *f.* house-to-house distribution (of pamphlets). **-speer, -spieß,** *m.* javelin. **-taube,** *f.* clay pigeon. **-weite,** *f.* distance one can throw, (*Mil.*) mortar range, (*Av.*) forward travel (*of bombs*), (*fig.*) stone's throw.

Würgegriff ['vyrgəgrıf], *m.* stranglehold. **würgen, 1.** *v.t.* strangle, choke, throttle; take by the throat; (*Poet.*) slaughter, slay, massacre; (*of food*) stick in one's throat. **2.** *v.i., v.r.* choke, retch, gulp; (*fig.*) ***an einer Arbeit –,*** sweat over a task; (*coll.*) ***mit***

Hängen und Würgen, with blood and sweat, with no end of trouble.

Würgengel ['vyrkʔɛŋəl], *m.* (*B.*) angel of death *or* destruction. **Würger,** *m.* (*Poet.*) murderer, slayer, butcher; (*Orn.*) *grauer* or *kleiner –, see* **Schwarzstirnwürger**; *großer –, see* **Raubwürger**; *rotrückiger –, see* **Neuntöter. Würgfalke,** *m.* (*Orn.*) Saker falcon (*Falco cherrug*).

Wurm [vurm], **1.** *m.* (**-(e)s,** *pl.* **¨-er**) worm, grub, maggot; (*Poet.*) (*pl. also* **¨-e**) serpent, dragon, reptile; (*fig.*) fancy, whim, crotchet; (*Med.*) whitlow; (*Vet.*) farcy; *auch der – krümmt sich,* even a worm will turn; (*coll.*) *ihm die Würmer aus der Nase ziehen,* worm secrets out of him, draw him out; (*Hort.*) *den – haben,* be maggoty. **2.** *n.* (*coll.*) little mite, poor little creature; *du armes –!* poor little mite!

wurm|abtreibend, *adj.* anthelmintic; *–es Mittel,* vermifuge, worm-powder. **–ähnlich, –artig,** *adj.* vermicular, vermiculate.

Würmchen ['vyrmçən], *n.* little worm, grub; (*coll.*) (*fig.*) little mite; *see* **Wurm, 2.**

wurmen ['vurmən], *v.t.* (*usu. imp.*) *es wurmt mich,* it rankles, I am vexed at it; *das wurmt und frißt so weiter,* that keeps on eating at me.

wurmförmig ['vurmfœrmıç], *adj.* vermicular, vermiform, worm-like. **Wurm|fortsatz,** *m.* (*Anat.*) appendix. **–fraß,** *m.* damage by maggots; *das Holz hat –,* the wood is worm-eaten. **wurmig,** *adj.* worm-eaten; wormy, maggoty; (*coll.*) annoyed, vexed. **wurmkrank,** *adj.* suffering from worms. **Wurm|krankheit,** *f.* (intestinal) worms. **–kraut,** *n.* anthelmintic herb. **–loch,** *n. See* **–stich. –mehl,** *n.* worm(-hole) dust. **–mittel,** *n.* vermifuge, anthelmintic, worm-medicine. **–same,** *m.* (*Bot.*) worm-seed (*Artemsia and Chenopodium*). **–stich,** *m.* worm-hole. **wurmstichig,** *adj.* worm-eaten, maggoty; (*fig.*) rotten, corrupt.

Wurst [vurst], *f.* (-, *pl.* **¨-e**) sausage; *die – nach dem Manne braten,* treat a p. according to his deserts; (*Prov.*) *bratst du mir die –, so lösch' ich dir den Durst,* one good turn deserves another, (*coll.*) you scratch my back and I'll scratch yours; (*sl.*) *das ist mir* (*ganz*) *–,* it is all one *or* all the same to me, it leaves me cold, I don't care (a rap), (*sl.*) I don't give a damn; (*coll.*) *es geht um die –,* it's do or die *or* now or never; *mit der – nach der Speckseite werfen,* risk a sprat to catch a mackerel; (*coll.*) *– wider –,* tit for tat.

Würstchen ['vyrstçən], *n.* small sausage, chippolata; (*sl.*) *kleines –,* small fry, pip-squeak; (*coll.*) *warmes –,* hot dog.

Wurstdarm ['vurstdarm], *m.* sausage skin.

Wurstelei [vurstə'laı], *f.* (*coll.*) muddle, muddling. **wursteln** ['vurstəln], *v.i.* (*coll.*) muddle through *or* along; *es wird so weiter gewurstelt,* the same old muddle goes on. **Wurstel|prater,** *m.* (*Austr.*) amusement park, fun-fair (*Prater in Vienna*). **–theater,** *n.* (*Austr.*) Punch and Judy show.

wursten ['vurstən], *v.i.* make sausages. **Wurstfleisch,** *n.* sausage-meat. **wurstförmig,** *adj.* sausage-shaped. **Wursthändler,** *m.* pork-butcher.

wurstig ['vurstıç], *adj.* (*sl.*) quite indifferent, devil-may-care. **Wurstigkeit,** *f.* unconcern, nonchalance, utter indifference.

Wurst|kessel, *m.* (*coll.*) *jetzt sitze ich im –,* now I am in the soup. **–laden,** *m.* pork-butcher's shop. **–vergiftung,** *f.* sausage-poisoning, botulism, allantiasis. **–waren,** *f.pl.* sausages. **–warenhandlung,** *f. See* **–laden.**

Würze ['vyrtsə], *f.* spice, condiment, seasoning, flavouring, dressing; (*Brew.*) wort; (*fig.*) fragrance; zest; (*Prov.*) *in der Kürze liegt die –,* brevity is the soul of wit; *– des Lebens,* salt of life.

Wurzel ['vurtsəl], *f.* (-, *pl.* **-n**) root (*also Math.*); (*Gram.*) root, stem; (*dial.*) carrot; *mit der – ausreißen,* uproot, pull up by the root(s); (*fig.*) *mit der – ausrotten,* eradicate; *die – aus einer Zahl ziehen,* find *or* extract the (square) root of a number; *– schlagen* or *treiben* or *fassen,* take *or* strike root; *gelbe –,* carrot; (*Math.*) *zweite –,* square root; *dritte –,* cube root. **Wurzel|ausläufer,** *m.* stolon. **–ausschlag,** *m. See* **–schößling. –auszieher,** *m.* (*dentistry*) stump-forceps. **–brand,** *m.* root-rot (*of sugar beet etc.*).

Würzelchen ['vyrtsəlçən], *n.* radicle, rootlet.

wurzelecht ['vurtsəlʔɛçt], *adj.* (*Hort.*) own-rooted, ungrafted; (*fig.*) genuine. **Wurzel|exponent,** *m.* (*Math.*) radical index. **–faser,** *f.* root fibril. **–fäule,** *f. See* **–brand. –füß(l)er,** *m.pl.* (*Zool.*) rhizopoda. **–gemüse,** *n.* root vegetable. **–gewächse,** *n.pl.* root crops. **–größe,** *f.* (*Math.*) radical quantity. **wurzelhaft,** *adj.* rooted, radical. **wurzelig,** *adj.* rooty, full of roots (*of the ground*). **Wurzel|keim,** *m.* radicle. **–knollen,** *m.* root nodule, tubercle, tuber. **–knospe,** *f.* (*Bot.*) turion. **wurzellos,** *adj.* rootless, without roots.

wurzeln ['vurtsəln], **1.** *v.i.* (*aux.* h. *&* s.) take *or* strike root, become rooted, send out roots; (*fig.*) *– in* (*Dat.*), have its root *or* origin in, be rooted *or* grounded in. **2.** *v.r.* (*fig.*) *sich fest –,* become firmly established, be deep-rooted.

Wurzel|ranke, *f.*, **–schößling,** *m.* sobole, sucker, runner, layer. **–silbe,** *f.* (*Gram.*) root syllable, stem. **–sprosse,** *f. See* **–schößling. wurzel|sprossend,** *adj.* putting forth suckers, soboliferous. **–ständig,** *adj.* radical; growing from the root. **Wurzel|-stock,** *m.* rootstock, rhizome. **–trieb,** *m. See* **–schößling. –werk,** *n.* roots, root-system. **–zahl,** *f.* (*Math.*) root. **–zeichen,** *n.* (*Math.*) radical *or* root sign.

würzen ['vyrtsən], *v.t.* spice, season, flavour, (*fig.*) add spice to, give zest to, (*coll.*) ginger up. **Würzfleisch,** *n.* spiced meat. **würzig,** *adj.* spicy, (well-) seasoned, piquant; aromatic, fragrant. **Würzkräuter,** *n.pl.* aromatic herbs. **würzlos,** *adj.* unspiced, unseasoned, flavourless, insipid, (*fig.*) insipid, flat, jejune. **Würz|näg(e)lein,** *n.*, **–nelke,** *f.* (*Bot.*) clove (*Eugenica aromatica*). **–stoff,** *m.* seasoning, condiments; aromatic essence. **–wein,** *m.* spiced *or* mulled wine; medicated wine.

wusch [vuʃ], *see* **waschen.**

wuschelig ['vuʃəlıç], *adj.* tousled. **Wuschelkopf,** *m.* mop of hair.

wuseln ['vu:zəln], *v.i.* (*coll.*) swarm, crawl, be swarming *or* crawling (*von,* with).

wußte ['vustə], *see* **wissen.**

[1]**Wust** [vu:st], *m.* (chaotic) mess, jumble, confusion; rubbish, trash, lumber. **2.** *f.* (*Austr., Swiss*) (*abbr. for* **Warenumsatzsteuer**) purchase-tax.

wüst [vy:st], *adj.* 1. desert, waste, desolate; (*dial.*) uncultivated, fallow; (*dial.*) *– liegen* or *stehen,* lie fallow; *– und leer,* waste and desolate; 2. (*fig.*) confused; disorderly, wild, depraved, dissolute; vulgar, coarse, vile, filthy; (*coll.*) awful; *– durcheinander liegen,* lie around in utter confusion; *der Kopf ist mir ganz –,* my head is quite muddled; *ein –es Leben,* a depraved *or* dissolute life.

Wüste ['vy:stə], *f.* desert, wilderness, waste; *der Prediger* or *Rufer in der –,* a voice crying in the wilderness; (*fig.*) *in die – schicken,* send into the wilderness, (*coll.*) send to Coventry.

wüsten ['vy:stən], *v.i.* *– mit,* waste, squander, ruin, spoil, play havoc with.

Wüstenei [vy:stə'naı], *f.* (-, *pl.* **-en**) (*Poet.*) *see* **Wüste.**

Wüsten|gimpel, *m.* (*Orn.*) trumpeter bullfinch (*Bucanetes githagineus*). **–grasmücke,** *f.* (*Orn.*) desert warbler (*Sylvia nana*). **–läuferlerche,** *f.* (*Orn.*) bifasciated lark (*Alaemon alaudipes*). **–regenpfeifer,** *m.* (*Orn.*) greater sand plover (*Charadrius leschenaultii*). **–schiff,** *n.* ship of the desert, camel. **–steinschmätzer,** *m.* (*Orn.*) desert wheatear (*Oenanthe deserti*). **–trompete,** *m.* (*Orn.*) *see* **–gimpel.**

Wüstling ['vy:stlıŋ], *m.* (**-(e)s,** *pl.* **-e**) libertine, rake, lecher, debauchee, dissolute p.

Wut [vu:t], *f.* rage, fury, wrath; frenzy, madness, mania; *in –, in* a rage; *in – geraten,* fly into a rage, (*coll.*) see red; *in – bringen* or *setzen,* enrage, infuriate, incense; *seine – auslassen,* vent one's fury (*an* (*Dat.*), on), (*coll.*) take it out (on);

vor – kochen, fume, boil with rage, (*coll.*) foam at the mouth; ***vor – platzen,*** lose one's temper, (*sl.*) blow one's top. **Wut|anfall,** *m.* fit of rage. **–ausbruch,** *m.* outburst of fury, (*of children*) tantrum.

wüten ['vy:tən], *v.i.* storm, rave, be furious, rage (*also of storms*). **wütend,** *adj.* enraged, infuriated, furious, fuming (with rage), convulsed with rage; frenzied, raving, rabid, fanatical; (*of storms*) raging, (*of attack*) fierce, savage; (*coll.*) mad (***auf*** (*Acc.*), at (*a p.*); ***über*** (*Acc.*), at (*a th.*)).

wutentbrannt ['vu:tʔɛntbrant], *adj. See* **wütend** (*only of p.*).

Wüterich ['vy:tərɪç], *m.* bloodthirsty villain, ruthless tyrant, maniac.

wütig ['vy:tɪç], *adj. See* **wutend**; (*of dogs*) rabid.

Wutkrankheit ['vu:tkraŋkhaɪt], *f.* rabies, hydrophobia. **wut|schäumend, –schnaubend,** *pred. adj.* fuming, foaming with rage, in a towering rage, breathing vengeance. **Wutschrei,** *m.* cry *or* yell of rage.

X

X, x [ɪks], *n.* X, x; ***Herr X,*** Mr. what's-his-name; ***ihm ein X für ein U vormachen,*** throw dust in his eyes, bamboozle *or* dupe him, (*coll.*) take him in; ***ich lasse mir kein X für ein U vormachen,*** I wasn't born yesterday, I'm nobody's fool.

x-Achse, *f.* (*Math.*) x-axis, axis of the abscissa.

Xanthippe [ksan'tɪpə], *f.* (*coll.*) shrewish wife, (*sl.*) 'trouble and strife'.

X-Beine, *n.pl.* knock-knees. **X-beinig,** *adj.* knock-kneed.

x-beliebig, *adj.* any (. . . whatever *or* at all), any *or* whatever *or* whichever . . . you please; ***eine –e Person,*** anyone you please *or* like, anyone at all.

Xenie ['kse:njə], *f.* (*Poet.*) satirical epigram.

Xereswein ['kse:rəsvaɪn], *m.* sherry.

x-Koordinate, *f.* (*Math.*) x-coordinate, coordinate of the abscissa.

x-mal ['ɪksma:l], *adv.* (*coll.*) any number of times, (ever so) many times, time without number, ever so often, over and over again, I don't know how many times, (*sl.*) umpteen times.

x-te(r, -s) ['ɪkstə(r, -s)], *adj.* (*Math.*) ***die x-te Potenz,*** the nth power; (*coll.*) ***zum x-ten Male,*** for the umpteenth time.

Xylograph [ksylo'gra:f], *m.* (**-en,** *pl.* **-en**) wood-engraver, xylographer. **Xylographie** [–'fi:], *f.* wood-engraving, xylography. **xylographisch,** *adj.* xylographic.

Xylol [ksy'lo:l], *n.* (*Chem.*) xylene.

Xylophon [ksylo'fo:n], *n.* (**-s,** *pl.* **-e**) (*Mus.*) xylophone.

Y

Y, y ['ypsilɔn], *n.* Y, y.

y-Achse, *f.* (*Math.*) y-axis, axis of the ordinate.

Yacht, *f. See* **Jacht.**

Yperit [ypə'ri:t], *n.* (*Mil.*) mustard gas.

Ypsiloneule ['ypsilɔnʔɔylə], *f.* (*Ent.*) *Agrotis ypsilon.*

Ysop ['i:zɔp], *m.* (**-s,** *pl.* **-e**) (*Bot.*) hyssop (*Hyssopus officinalis*).

Ytterbin(erde) ['ytərbɪn(e:rdə)], *n.*(*f.*) (*Chem.*) yetterbia, ytterbium oxide. **Ytterbium** [y'tɛrbium], *n.* ytterbium.

Ytter|erde ['ytər–], *f.* (*Chem.*) yttria, yttrium oxide. **–flußspat,** *m.* yttrocerite. **ytterhaltig,** *adj.* yttric, yttrious, yttriferous. **Ytterspat,** *m.* xenotime.

Yttrium ['ytrium], *n.* yttrium.

Z

See also under C.

Z, z [tsɛt], *n.* Z, z; ***von A bis Z,*** from beginning to end; *see Index of Abbreviations.*

Zabel ['tsa:bəl], *m.* (*obs.*) chess-board.

Zäckchen ['tsɛkçən], *n.* small prong, denticle; (*lace*) purl.

Zacke ['tsakə], *f.*, **Zacken,** *m.* (sharp) point, peak, jag; spike; prong, tine (*of a fork*); tooth (*of saw or comb*); notch, indent(ation), (*Dressm.*) scallop, (*Bot.*) crenature. **zacken,** *v.t.* tooth, notch, indent, (*Dressm.*) scallop, pink. **Zackenborte,** *f.* purl edging. **zackenförmig,** *adj.* notched, indented, serrated; jagged. **Zacken|krone,** *f.* indented crown. **–linie,** *f.* notched *or* serrated line; (*Fort.*) line of a redan; (*Geog.*) line of peaks. **–muster,** *n.* toothed pattern. **–schere,** *f.* pinking-scissors. **–walze,** *f.* notched roller, clod-crusher. **–werk,** *n.* scalloping, pinking; (*Fort.*) redan.

zackern ['tsakərn], *v.t.* (*dial.*) plough.

zackig ['tsakɪç], *adj.* 1. pointed, jagged, toothed, pronged; notched, indented, scalloped; (*Bot.*) crenate, dentated, serrate(d); 2. (*coll.*) smart, snappy, glamorous, (*sl.*) snazzy.

zaddrig ['tsadrɪç], *adj.* sinewy, stringy (*as meat*).

zag(e) [tsa:k (–gə)], *adj. See* **zaghaft.**

Zagel ['tsa:gəl], *m.* (*dial.*) 1. tail, pigtail; 2. penis.

zagen ['tsa:gən], *v.i.* be afraid, be faint-hearted *or* timorous, hesitate, waver, shrink, flinch, quail; ***mit Zittern und Zagen,*** with great trepidation, (*coll.*) quaking in one's shoes. **zaghaft,** *adj.* faint-hearted, fearful, timorous, timid, cautious, irresolute. **Zaghaftigkeit,** *f.* timidity, timorousness, faint-heartedness, irresolution.

zäh(e) [tsɛ:(ə)], *adj.* tough, tenacious; stubborn, dogged; (*of liquid*) ropy, viscous, sticky, glutinous, gluey; (*of meat*) tough, stringy, (*of metal*) ductile; ***–e Beharrlichkeit,*** stubborn perseverance; ***–er Bursche,*** tough customer, hard case; ***ein –es Leben haben,*** be tenacious of life. **Zäh|festigkeit,** *f.* tenacity. **–flüssigkeit,** *f.* viscosity, sluggishness. **Zähigkeit,** *f.* toughness, tenacity, doggedness; ropiness, viscosity; ductility.

Zahl [tsa:l], *f.* (-, *pl.* **-en**) number, numeral, figure, digit, cipher; ***wenig an der –,*** few in number; ***benannte –,*** denominate quantity, concrete number; ***ganze –,*** whole *or* integral number; ***gebrochene –,*** fraction; ***gerade –,*** even number; ***in großer –,*** in large numbers; ***ohne –,*** numberless, countless, innumerable; ***runde –,*** round number; ***–en sprechen,*** numbers talk; ***an – übertreffen,*** outnumber; ***unbenannte –,*** abstract number; ***ungerade –,*** odd number; ***vierstellige –,*** number of four digits; ***die volle –,*** the full number, the total, all of them.

Zählapparat [ˈtsɛːlˀaparaːt], *m. See* **Zähler** (*Tech.*).
zahlbar [ˈtsaːlbaːr], *adj.* payable, due (*an* (*Acc.*), to); – ***sein*** or ***werden,*** fall due; – ***bei Lieferung,*** cash on delivery; – ***auf*** or ***bei Sicht,*** a vista, payable at sight.
zählbar [ˈtsɛːlbaːr], *adj.* countable, computable, assessable.
zählebig [ˈtsɛːleːbɪç], *adj.* tenacious of life, difficult to kill.
zahlen [ˈtsaːlən], *v.t., v.i.* pay; pay for, settle (*also fig.*), (*fig.*) atone for; ***Kinder – die Hälfte,*** children half-price; ***Kellner, –!*** waiter! the bill, please! ***einen Wechsel –,*** settle *or* meet a bill.
zählen [ˈtsɛːlən], *v.t., v.i.* count, reckon, number; (*Spt., Cards*) (keep the) score; (*Mech.*) register, integrate; ***die Bevölkerung –,*** take the census; ***ihm die Bissen in den Mund –,*** grudge him every mortal thing; ***die Stadt zählt 100,000 Einwohner,*** the town numbers 100,000 inhabitants; ***er zählte bloß 16 Jahre,*** he was only 16 (years old); ***meine Tage sind gezählt,*** my days are numbered; ***das zählt nicht,*** that doesn't count; ***er sieht aus, als könnte er nicht bis drei –,*** he looks as if he couldn't say bo to a goose, *or* as if butter wouldn't melt in his mouth; – ***auf*** (*Acc.*), count *or* rely on; – ***unter*** (*Acc.*) *or* ***zu,*** (*v.t.*) rank with, number among; (*v.i.*) be classed with, be reckoned among, be considered one of.
Zahlen|akrobatik, *f.* juggling with figures. **–angaben,** *f.pl.* figures, numerical data. **–beispiel,** *n.* numerical example. **–bruch,** *m.* numerical fraction. **–folge,** *f.* numerical order. **–größe,** *f.* number, numerical quantity. **–lotterie,** *f.* lottery, lotto. **zahlenmäßig,** *adj.* numerical; – ***überlegen sein*** (*Dat.*), outnumber. **Zahlen|material,** *n. See* **–angaben. –mystik,** *f.* magic of numbers. **–reihe,** *f.* numerical series *or* progression. **–schloß,** *n.* combination lock. **–sinn,** *m.* head for figures. **–theorie,** *f.* theory of numbers. **–verhältnis,** *n.* numerical proportion. **–wert,** *m.* numerical value.
Zahler [ˈtsaːlər], *m.* payer; ***säumiger –,*** one who is behind(hand) in his payments; ***schlechter –,*** defaulter, bad customer.
Zähler [ˈtsɛːlər], *m.* counter, (*Parl., banks*) teller; (*Math.*) numerator; (*Tech.*) automatic counter, integrating meter, (*Elec., gas etc.*) meter. **Zählerablesung,** *f.* meter reading.
Zahl|grenze, *f.* fare-stage. **–karte,** *f.* paying-in slip *or* form.
Zählkarte [ˈtsɛːlkartə], *f.* census form; (*Spt.*) score *or* scoring card.
Zahlkellner [ˈtsaːlkɛlnər], *m.* head waiter. **zahllos,** *adj.* numberless, innumerable, countless. **Zahl|meister,** *m.* (*Mil.*) paymaster, (*Naut.*) purser. **–meisterei,** *f.* paymaster's *or* purser's office. **–pfennig,** *m.* counter (*for indoor games*). **zahlreich, 1.** *adj.* numerous, a great number of. **2.** *adv.* – ***vertreten,*** present in great *or* large numbers.
Zählrohr [ˈtsɛːlroːr], *n.* Geiger counter.
Zahlstelle [ˈtsaːlʃtɛlə], *f.* cash-desk; paying office, cashier's office; (*banks*) sub-branch.
Zählstrich [ˈtsɛːlʃtrɪç], *m.* tally.
Zahltag [ˈtsaːltaːk], *m.* pay day, (*St. Exch.*) settling day.
Zahlung [ˈtsaːlʊŋ], *f.* payment, acquittance, disbursement; settlement, clearance (*of debts*); (*Comm.*) – ***erhalten,*** paid, settled (*at foot of bills*); ***die – einstellen,*** suspend payment; – ***leisten,*** make *or* effect (a) payment; ***mangels –,*** in default of payment; ***etwas in – geben,*** trade s.th. in; ***in – nehmen,*** take in part-payment; ***an –s Statt,*** in lieu of payment *or* of cash.
Zählung [ˈtsɛːlʊŋ], *f.* counting, enumeration, computation; registering, metering; count, (*of population*) census.
Zahlungs|anweisung, *f.* order (to pay), draft; postal *or* money order. **–aufschub,** *m.* respite, moratorium, extension of time (to pay). **–bedingungen,** *f.pl.* terms of settlement *or* payment. **–befehl,** *m.* writ of execution. **–beleg,** *m.* voucher, receipt. **–bilanz,** *f.* balance of payments. **–einstellung,** *f.* suspension of payment. **–empfänger,** *m.* payee. **–erleichterungen,** *f.pl.* credit facilities, deferred terms. **zahlungsfähig,** *adj.* solvent, able to pay. **Zahlungs|fähigkeit,** *f.* solvency, ability to pay. **–frist,** *f.* time *or* term for payment. **–mittel,** *n.* (legal) tender; ***bargeldloses –,*** credit instrument. **–plan,** *m.* instalment plan, deferred payment; (*of debt*) terms of redemption. **–schwierigkeiten,** *f.pl.* financial difficulties, (*coll.*) pecuniary embarrassment. **–sperre,** *f.* stoppage *or* blocking of payments. **–termin,** *m.* date for *or* of payment; *see* **–frist. zahlungsunfähig,** *adj.* insolvent, unable to pay. **Zahlungs|unfähigkeit,** *f.* insolvency, inability to pay. **–verbindlichkeit,** *f. See* **–verpflichtung. –verkehr,** *m.* transfers, financial transactions; ***bargeldloser –,*** clearance. **–verpflichtung,** *f.* liability. **–versprechen,** *n.* promissory note. **–verweigerung,** *f.* non-payment, refusal to pay. **–verzug,** *m.* default. **–weise,** *f.* mode of payment.
Zahl|wort, *n.* (*Gram.*) numeral. **–zeichen,** *n.* numerical symbol, figure.
zahm [tsaːm], *adj.* tame, domestic(ated); cultivated; (*fig.*) docile, tractable, peaceable, gentle, mild; (*fig.*) ***ihn – machen*** or ***kriegen,*** bring him to heel.
zähmbar [ˈtsɛːmbaːr], *adj.* tamable, controllable, restrainable. **zähmen,** *v.t.* tame, domesticate, break in (*horse*); subdue, control, restrain, check.
Zahmheit [ˈtsaːmhaɪt], *f.* tameness; gentleness, mildness, docility.
Zähmung [ˈtsɛːmʊŋ], *f.* taming, domestication.
Zahn [tsaːn], *m.* **(-(e)s,** ***pl.*** **⁼e)** tooth, (*beasts of prey*) fang, (*elephant etc.*) tusk; (*Mech.*) tooth, cog; (*fig.*) ***ihm auf den – fühlen,*** sound him, (*coll.*) try him out; ***Haare auf den ⁼en haben,*** be well able to look after o.s.; be a (real) Tartar; ***bis an die ⁼e bewaffnet,*** armed to the teeth; ***sich*** (*Dat.*) ***einen – ausbeißen,*** break a tooth (*an* (*Dat.*), on); ***⁼e bekommen,*** cut one's teeth; ***die ⁼e fletschen,*** show *or* bare one's teeth; (*coll.*) ***etwas für den hohlen –,*** precious *or* mighty little, (*sl.*) damn all; ***die ⁼e klappern*** (*mir*), ***ich klappere mit den ⁼en,*** my teeth are chattering; ***mit den ⁼en knirschen,*** gnash one's teeth; ***die ⁼e stumpf machen,*** set one's teeth on edge; (*sl.*) ***mit einem tollen –,*** at breakneck speed; (*fig.*) ***die ⁼e zeigen,*** show one's teeth, show fight; ***der – der Zeit,*** the ravages of time; ***die ⁼e zusammenbeißen,*** clench *or* grit *or* set one's teeth.
Zahnarzt [ˈtsaːnˀaːrtst], *m.* dentist, dental surgeon. **zahnärztlich,** *adj.* dental. **Zahn|behandlung,** *f.* dental treatment. **–bein,** *n.* dentine. **–belag,** *m.* film (*on teeth*), tartar. **–bogen,** *m.* dental arch. **–bürste,** *f.* tooth-brush. **–chirurgie,** *f.* dental surgery. **–durchbruch,** *m.* dentition.
Zähne|fletschen, *n.* showing *or* baring one's teeth. **–klappern,** *n.* chattering of teeth; ***mit –,*** with chattering teeth. **–knirschen,** *n.* grinding *or* gritting *or* gnashing of teeth.
zahnen [ˈtsaːnən], **1.** *v.i.* teethe, be teething, cut one's teeth. **2.** *v.t.* (*Mech.*) notch, tooth, cog. **Zahnen,** *n.* dentition, teething.
zähnen [ˈtsɛːnən], *v.t.* notch, indent, denticulate.
Zahn|ersatz, *m.* artificial teeth, denture. **–fach,** *n.* alveolus. **–fäule,** *f.* (tooth-)decay, dental caries. **–fistel,** *f.* fistula in the gum. **–fleisch,** *n.* gum(s). **–fleischentzündung,** *f.* gingivitis. **–füllung,** *f. See* **–plombe. –geschwür,** *n.* gumboil, abscess. **–heilkunde,** *f.* dentistry, odontology. **–höhle,** *f.* socket of a tooth, dental cavity. **–kranz,** *m.* (*Tech.*) teeth, cogs, toothed rim (*of gear*). **–krem,** *f. See* **–paste. –krone,** *f.* crown of a tooth. **–laut,** *m.* (*Phonet.*) dental (consonant). **–lippenlaut,** *m.* (*Phonet.*) labiodental (sound). **zahnlos,** *adj.* toothless; ***–e Tiere,*** edentata. **Zahn|lücke,** *f.* gap between teeth. **–paste,** *f.* dental cream, toothpaste, dentifrice. **–pflege,** *f.* dental care, care of the teeth. **–plombe,** *f.* stopping, filling. **–prothese,** *f. See* **–ersatz. –pulver,** *n.* tooth *or* dental powder; dentifrice.
Zahnrad [ˈtsaːnraːt], *n.* cogged *or* toothed wheel; cog-wheel, gear(-wheel). **Zahnrad|antrieb,** *m.*

gear-drive. **-bahn,** *f.* rack-railway. **-fräser,** *m.* gear-cutting machine. **-getriebe,** *n.* pinion gear. **-übersetzung,** *f.* gear transmission, gearing.

Zahn|reinigung, *f.* cleaning of teeth. **-schmelz,** *m.* dental enamel. **-schmerz,** *m.* toothache. **-schnitt,** *m.* denticulation; (*Archit.*) row of dentils. **-schutz,** *m.* (*Spt.*) gum-shield. **-stange,** *f.* rack; cog-rail. **-stangengetriebe,** *n.* rack and pinion. **-stein,** *m.* tartar. **-steinansatz,** *m.* tartar deposit. **-stocher,** *m.* toothpick. **-techniker,** *m.* dental mechanic.

Zähnung ['tsɛ:nuŋ], *f.* serration.

Zahn|wasser, *n.* mouth-wash, dental lotion. **-wechsel,** *m.* second dentition. **-weh,** *n.* *See* **-schmerz. -wurzel,** *f.* root of a tooth. **-zange,** *f.* dentist's forceps. **-zerfall,** *m.* *See* **-fäule. -ziehen,** *n.* extraction of teeth *or* of a tooth.

Zähre ['tsɛ:rə], *f.* (*Poet.*) tear.

Zain [tsaɪn], *m.* **(-(e)s,** *pl.* **-e)** 1. (*minting*) ingot, bar, fillet, slip; 2. (*dial.*) willow switch. **Zaine,** *f.* (*dial.*) basketwork, wickerwork; wicker basket.

Zander ['tsandər], *m.* (*Ichth.*) pike-perch.

Zange ['tsaŋə], *f.* pliers, tongs, pincers; tweezers, forceps; (*Ent.*) palp; (*Zool.*) maxilla, forcipated claw; (*fig.*) ***ihn in die – nehmen,*** corner him, get (at) him from both sides; (*Spt.*) sandwich him, box him in.

zängen ['tsɛŋən], *v.t.* (*Metall.*) shingle.

Zangen|bewegung, *f.* (*Mil.*) pincer-movement. **-entbindung, -geburt,** *f.* forceps delivery. **-schanze,** *f.*, **-werk,** *n.* (*Fort.*) tenail. **-winkel,** *m.* flanking angle.

Zank [tsaŋk], *m.* **(-es,** *pl.* (*rare*) **⸚e)** quarrel, wrangle, bickering, squabble, (*coll.*) row; ***einen – vom Zaune brechen,*** go out of one's way to pick a quarrel; ***– suchen,*** pick a quarrel. **Zankapfel,** *m.* bone of contention. **zanken,** *v.r., v.i.* quarrel, wrangle, bicker, squabble (*um*, over); ***sie – sich über*** (*Acc.*) ***Kleinigkeiten*** or ***um des Kaisers Bart,*** they quarrel over trifles.

Zänker(in) ['tsɛŋkər(ɪn)], *m.(f.)* quarrelsome p.; (*only f.*) shrew, scold, termagant. **Zänkerei** [-'raɪ] **(Zankerei),** *f.* wrangling, bickering. **zankhaft, zänkisch, zanklustig,** *adj.* quarrelsome, bickering, (*of a wife*) nagging, shrewish. **Zanksucht,** *f.* quarrelsomeness, contentiousness. **zanksüchtig,** *adj.* *See* **zankhaft.**

Zapf [tsapf], *m.* 1. (*dial.*) *see* **Zapfen**; 2. tap-room; 3. hydrant; 4. (*coll.*) toper.

Zäpfchen ['tsɛpfçən], *n.* 1. (*Anat.*) uvula, (*of the eye*) cone; 2. (*Med.*) suppository. **Zäpfchen-,** *pref.* uvular, guttural. **Zäpfchenschnitt,** *m.* (*Med.*) staphylotomy.

Zapfen ['tsapfən], *m.* plug, bung, spigot, cock, tap; peg, pin, pivot, gudgeon, journal, trunnion; (*Carp.*) tenon; fir-cone; fruit of the hop. **zapfen,** *v.t.* tap (*a cask*); join (*timber*) with mortise and tenon.

Zapfenbohrer ['tsapfənbo:rər], *m.* tap-borer. **zapfenförmig,** *adj.* cone-shaped, plug-like. **Zapfen|lager,** *n.* bush, socket, trunnion seat, pivot *or* journal bearing. **-loch,** *n.* bung-hole; (*Mech.*) pivot socket, (*Carp.*) mortise. **-lochmaschine,** *f.* mortising-machine. **-streich,** *m.* (*Mil.*) tattoo, retreat; ***den – schlagen,*** beat the tattoo. **zapfentragend,** *adj.* coniferous. **Zapfen|träger,** *m.pl.* conifers. **-zieher,** *m.* (*dial.*) corkscrew.

Zapfer ['tsapfər], *m.* 1. tapster; 2. (*Tech.*) feeder. **Zapf|hahn,** *m.* tap, (*Am.*) faucet. **-säule,** *f.* petrol-pump. **-stelle,** *f.* (petrol-)filling station, (*Elec.*) mains output. **-wart,** *m.* petrol-pump attendant.

Zappelfritze ['tsapəlfrɪtsə], *m.* (*coll.*) fidget. **zappelig,** *adj.* restless, fidgety, nervous. **Zappel|-liese,** *f.* *See* **-fritze. zappeln,** *v.i.* struggle, wriggle, fidget (about); ***ihn – lassen,*** keep him in suspense *or* on tenterhooks, tantalize him, (*coll.*) keep him dangling.

Zar [tsa:r], *m.* **(-en,** *pl.* **-en)** tsar, czar. **Zarentum,** *n.* tsardom.

Zarge ['tsargə], *f.* top rail (*of chairs, tables etc.*); surround (*of doors, windows etc.*); side (*of a flat box or case*), ribs (*of a violin etc.*).

Zarin ['tsa:rɪn], *f.* tsarina, czarina.

zart [tsa:rt], *adj.* (*comp.* ***-er,*** *sup.* ***-est***) delicate, fragile, frail; slender, slight; tender, soft, gentle, fine, sensitive; subdued, pale (*of colours*); ***–es Fleisch,*** tender meat; ***das –e Geschlecht,*** the gentle sex; ***–e Gesichtsfarbe,*** delicate complexion; ***–e Gesundheit,*** delicate health; ***–er Wink,*** gentle hint. **zart|besaitet,** *adj.* sensitive, impressible, (*pred.*) with fine feelings. **-fühlend,** *adj.* tactful, considerate. **Zartgefühl,** *n.* delicacy of feeling, tactfulness, considerateness, good sense. **Zartheit,** *f.* tenderness, gentleness, delicacy, softness; weakness, delicateness, frailty; (*Paint.*) morbidezza.

zärtlich ['tsɛrtlɪç], *adj.* affectionate, tender, loving, amorous, fond; ***–es Geflüster*** or ***Getue,*** billing and cooing, sweet nothings. **Zärtlichkeit,** *f.* affection, tenderness, fondness; caress. **Zärtling,** *m.* **(-s,** *pl.* **-e)** weakling, milksop, (*sl.*) pansy, cissy.

zart|rosa, *adj.* pale pink. **-sinnig,** *adj.* *See* **-fühlend.**

Zaser ['tsa:zər], *f.*, **zaserig,** *adj.* (*dial.*) *see* **Faser, faserig.**

Zaspel ['tsaspəl], *f.* (-, *pl.* **-n**) skein, hank.

Zaster ['tsastər], *m.* (*sl.*) cash, lolly, tin, brass, dough, bread.

Zäsur [tsɛ'zu:r], *f.* (-, *pl.* **-en**) caesura; ***klingende –,*** feminine caesura; ***stumpfe –,*** masculine caesura.

Zauber ['tsaubər], *m.* spell, charm; magic, enchantment, glamour, lure, fascination; (*coll.*) ***fauler –,*** lame excuse, tall story, humbug; (*coll.*) ***der ganze –,*** the whole concern; (*coll.*) ***den – kennen wir,*** we are up to those tricks; ***den – lösen*** or ***bannen,*** break the spell. **Zauber|bann,** *m.* spell, magic charm, incantation. **-buch,** *n.* book of charms.

Zauberei [tsaubə'raɪ], *f.* magic, sorcery, witchcraft; conjuring, sleight-of-hand.

Zauberer ['tsaubərər], *m.* magician, sorcerer, wizard (*also fig.*); *see also* **Zauberkünstler. Zauber|flöte,** *f.* magic flute. **-formel,** *f.* *See* **-bann. -garten,** *m.* enchanted garden. **zauberhaft,** *adj.* magical, enchanted; bewitching, enchanting. **Zauberin,** *f.* sorceress, (*fig.*) enchantress. **Zauberinsel,** *f.* enchanted isle. **zauberisch,** *adj.* *See* **zauberhaft. Zauber|kraft,** *f.* magic power. **-kunst,** *f.* magic art, black magic, witchcraft, sorcery; *pl.* conjuring, sleight-of-hand. **-künstler,** *m.* conjurer, illusionist, juggler. **-kunststück,** *n.* conjuring trick. **-land,** *n.* fairyland. **-laterne,** *f.* (*obs.*) magic lantern. **-mittel,** *n.* *See* **-bann.**

zaubern ['tsaubərn], **1.** *v.t.* conjure up, produce by magic; charm, cast a spell on *or* over. **2.** *v.i.* practise magic *or* witchcraft, do by magic, do conjuring tricks; (*coll.*) ***ich kann doch nicht –,*** I can't work miracles.

Zauber|spiegel, *m.* magic mirror. **-spruch,** *m.* *See* **-bann. -stab,** *m.* magic wand. **-trank,** *m.* magic potion, philtre. **-wald,** *m.* enchanted forest. **-werk,** *n.* *See* **Zauberei. -wort,** *n.* magic word; *see* **-bann.**

Zauderer ['tsaudərər], *m.* dilatory *or* irresolute p., temporizer, procrastinator. **zauderhaft,** *adj.* hesitating, vacillating, irresolute, dilatory. **zaudern,** *v.i.* hesitate, linger, delay, procrastinate; temporize, waver, dally, (*coll.*) shilly-shally (***mit,*** over). **Zaudern,** *n.* hesitation, lingering, dallying, wavering, procrastination, delay.

Zaum [tsaum], *m.* **(-(e)s,** *pl.* **⸚e)** bridle, rein; ***ihm den – anlegen, ihn im –e halten,*** keep a curb *or* a tight rein on him, keep him in check, curb *or* restrain him. **zäumen** ['tsɔymən], *v.t.* bridle, curb, restrain, keep in check. **Zaum|pfad,** *m.* bridle-path. **-zeug,** *n.* (horse's) bridle.

Zaun [tsaun], *m.* **(-(e)s,** *pl.* **⸚e)** fence, railing; hedge; ***lebendiger –,*** quickset hedge; ***eine Gelegenheit vom –e brechen,*** make an opportunity; ***einen Streit vom –e brechen,*** pick a quarrel; ***hinter jedem – zu finden,*** to be found at every street corner; ***das ist nicht hinter jedem – zu finden,*** one does not meet with that sort of thing every day; (*fig.*) ***ihm über den – helfen,*** help him over a stile; ***hinterm –e sterben,*** die in a ditch.

Zaun|ammer, *f.* (*Orn.*) cirl bunting (*Emberiza cirlus*). **–gast,** *m.* looker-on, intruder. **–grasmücke,** *f.* (*Orn.*) *see* **Klappergrasmücke. –könig,** *m.* (*Orn.*) wren (*Am.* winter wren) (*Troglodytes troglodytes*). **–latte,** *f. See* **–pfahl. –lilie,** *f.* (*Bot.*) St. Bernard's lily, spiderwort (*Anthericum liliago*). **–pfahl,** *m.* stake, pale; ***ihm einen Wink mit dem – geben,*** give him a broad hint. **–rebe,** *f.* (*Bot.*) Virginia creeper (*Parthenocissus quinquefolia*). **–rübe,** *f.* (*Bot.*) bryony (*Bryonia*). **–tritt,** *m.* stile.

zausen ['tsauzən], *v.t.* pull (about), tug; tousle, ruffle.

Zebra ['tse:bra], *n.* (**-s,** *pl.* **-s**) zebra. **Zebrastreifen,** *m.* (*traffic*) zebra crossing.

Zebu ['tse:bu:], *m. or n.* (**-s,** *pl.* **-s**) Indian bull, zebu.

Zechbruder ['tsɛçbru:dər], *m.* boon companion; tippler, toper, (*sl.*) boozer. **Zeche,** *f.* 1. bill, score, reckoning (*at an inn*); ***die – bezahlen,*** foot the bill, (*fig.*) pay the piper, suffer the consequences; ***die – ohne den Wirt machen,*** overlook the most important factor; ***die – prellen,*** leave without paying the bill; 2. mine, colliery, (coal-)pit; mining company. **zechen,** *v.i.* drink, tipple, carouse, (*sl.*) booze; run up a bill at an inn.

Zechen|kohle, *f.* pit-coal. **–koks,** *m.* foundry *or* furnace coke. **–preis,** *m.* pithead price. **–revier,** *n.* mining district *or* area.

Zecher ['tsɛçər], *m.* (hard) drinker, (*sl.*) boozer; toper; reveller. **zechfrei,** *adj.* free of expense, scot-free; ***ihn – halten,*** stand his drinks. **Zech|-gelage,** *n.* drinking bout, spree. **–genosse, –kumpan,** *m. See* **–bruder. –preller,** *m.* one who evades paying his bill. **–prellerei,** *f.* evading payment of one's bill, bilking.

Zechine [tse'ci:nə], *f.* sequin.

Zeck [tsɛk], *n.* (*dial.*) tick, tag (*game*).

Zecke ['tsɛkə], *f.* (*Ent.*) tick (*Ixodes*).

Zedent [tse'dɛnt], *m.* (**-en,** *pl.* **-en**) (*Comm.*) assigner, transferrer.

Zeder ['tse:dər], *f.* (**-,** *pl.* **-n**) (*Bot.*) cedar (*Pinus cedrus*). **zedern,** *adj.* of cedar. **Zedernholz,** *n.* cedar-wood.

zedieren [tse'di:rən], *v.t.* (*Comm.*) cede, surrender, transfer, assign (*Dat.*, to).

Zedrat [tse'dra:t], *n.* candied (lemon) peel.

Zeh [tse:], *m.* (**-(e)s,** *pl.* **-en**), (*usu.*) **Zehe,** *f.* 1. toe; ***auf den –n gehen,*** walk on tiptoe *or* on one's toes; ***sich auf die –n stellen,*** stand on one's toes *or* on tiptoe; (*fig.*) ***ihm auf die –n treten,*** tread on his toes *or* corns; ***vom Wirbel bis zur –,*** from top to toe; 2. root (*of ginger*), stick (*of celery*), clove (*of garlic*).

Zehen|gänger, *m.pl.* (*Zool.*) digitigrades (*Ungulata*). **–nagel,** *m.* toe-nail. **–spitze,** *f.* tip of the toe, tiptoe; ***auf den –n,*** on tiptoe, on one's toes. **–stand,** *m.* (*Gymn.*) standing on tiptoe.

zehn [tse:n], *num.adj.* ten; ***es ist halb –,*** it is half-past nine. **Zehn(e),** *f.* the figure 10; the number 10, the ten (*at cards*). **Zehneck,** *n.* decagon. **zehn|eckig,** *adj.* decagonal. **–einhalb,** *num.adj.* ten-and-a-half. **Zehnender,** *m.* stag of ten points.

Zehner ['tse:nər], *m.* a ten, half a score; a ten-pfennig piece; wine of the year 1910; soldier of the tenth regiment; (*coll.*) ***der – fällt,*** the penny drops. **zehnerlei,** *adv.* of ten (different) sorts *or* kinds. **Zehner|reihe,** *f.* (*Math.*) column of tens. **–stelle,** *f.* (*Math.*) decimal place.

zehn|fach, –fältig, *adj.* tenfold. **Zehn|finger-system,** *n.* touch-typing. **–flach,** *n.*, **–flächner,** *m.* (*Geom.*) decahedron. **–füßer,** *m.* (*Zool.*) decapod. **zehnjährig,** *adj.* 10-year(-old), (*pred.*) of *or* lasting 10 years, decennial. **Zehnkampf,** *m.* (*Spt.*) decathlon. **zehn|mal,** *adv.* 10 times. **–malig,** *adj.* 10 times repeated. **–silbig,** *adj.* decasyllabic.

zehnt [tse:nt], *adj.* tenth; ***der –e August,*** August 10th, the tenth of August; ***die –e Muse,*** variety (stage); ***das kann der –e nicht vertragen,*** not one in ten can stand it; ***das weiß der –e nicht,*** nine out of ten don't know it.

zehn|tägig, *adj.* of *or* lasting 10 days, 10 days', 10-day. **–tausend,** *adj.* 10 thousand; ***Zehntausende von,*** tens of thousands of.

Zehnte ['tse:ntə], *m.* (**-n,** *pl.* **-n**) tithe; ***mit –n belegen,*** tithe; ***den –n entrichten,*** pay tithe (***von,*** on). **zehnt(e)halb,** *num.adj.* nine-and-a-half. **Zehntel,** *n.* (*Swiss m.*) tenth (part). **zehnten,** *v.t.* tithe; pay tithe on; decimate. **zehntens,** *adv.* tenthly, in the tenth place. **zehnt|frei,** *adj.* exempt from paying tithe. **–pflichtig,** *adj.* tithable, subject to pay tithe.

zehren ['tse:rən], *v.i.* ***– von,*** live *or* exist *or* feed on; (*fig.*) draw on, live off (*supplies, capital etc.*); ***von der Erinnerung –,*** recall wistfully; (*fig.*) ***– an*** (*Dat.*), gnaw at, prey upon; undermine; ***Seeluft zehrt,*** sea air gives you an appetite; ***Kummer zehrt an ihr,*** she wastes away with worry. **zehrend,** *adj.* wasting, consumptive.

Zehr|fieber, *n.* hectic fever. **–geld,** *n.*, **–pfennig,** *m.* travelling expenses *or* allowance, subsistence. **Zehrung,** *f.* 1. living expenses; 2. provisions, victuals; (*Eccl.*) ***letzte –,*** viaticum, extreme unction; 3. waste, loss through shrinkage.

Zeichen ['tsaiçən], *n.* sign, symbol, mark, token; badge; (*fig.*) sign, signal, indication, evidence, portent, omen, (*Med.*) symptom; (*Comm.*) trademark, brand, stamp, (*Rad. etc.*) call-sign; ***ich bin meines –s ein Tischler,*** I am a joiner by trade; ***als*** or ***zum – der Freundschaft,*** as a token *or* mark of friendship; ***ein – geben,*** (give a) signal, (make a) sign; ***ein – geben für,*** give the word for; ***im –*** (. . . *Gen.*) ***stehen,*** (*Astr.*) be in . . ., (*fig.*) be marked *or* governed *or* affected by, be under the banner of; ***das – des Kreuzes,*** the sign of the cross; ***ein – sein für,*** be a sign *or* mark of, be indicative of; ***– setzen,*** punctuate, put in punctuation marks; ***wenn nicht alle – trügen,*** if all the indications are correct; ***unter einem glücklichen – geboren,*** born under a lucky star; (*Comm.*) ***unser –,*** our reference; (*coll.*) ***es geschehen – und Wunder,*** wonders will never cease; ***die – der Zeit,*** the signs of the times; ***zum –, daß*** . . ., as a proof that . . .; ***zum –*** (*Gen.*), as a mark *or* indication of.

Zeichen|block, *m.* sketching block, sketch book. **–brett,** *n.* drawing-board. **–büro,** *n.* drawing office, (*Am.*) drafting room. **–deuter,** *m.* astrologer. **–deutung,** *f.* divination, astrology. **–dreieck,** *n.* set-square. **–erklärung,** *f.* list of conventional signs, key to the symbols used. **–film,** *m.* animated cartoon. **–heft,** *n. See* **–block. –kreide,** *f.* crayon. **–kunst,** *f.* drawing, designing, sketching. **–lehrer,** *m.* art master. **–mappe,** *f.* portfolio. **–papier,** *n.* drawing-paper. **–rolle,** *f.* register of trade-marks. **–saal,** *m.* art room (*at school*); *see also* **–büro. –setzung,** *f.* punctuation. **–sprache,** *f.* sign language. **–stift,** *m. See* **–kreide. –stunde,** *f. See* **–unterricht. –system,** *n.* code. **–trickfilm,** *m. See* **–film. –unterricht,** *m.* drawing lesson, art (*at school*). **–tinte,** *f.* marking-ink.

zeichnen ['tsaiçnən], *v.t., v.i.* draw, sketch, delineate (***nach,*** from), draft, draught, design; mark; sign, put one's signature to; ***– für,*** subscribe towards, underwrite; ***nach dem Leben –,*** draw from life; ***Wäsche –,*** mark the laundry; ***der Hund zeichnet die Fährte,*** the dog draws on the scent; ***das Wild zeichnet,*** the quarry leaves a trail; ***ich zeichne hochachtungsvoll*** or ***ergebenst,*** I have the honour to remain, Sir (*or* Madam), your obedient servant *or* yours faithfully; ***vom Tode gezeichnet,*** touched *or* marked with the hand of death; ***vom Schicksal gezeichnet,*** marked out by fate. **Zeichnen,** *n.* drawing, sketching, designing, (*at school*) art; ***– aus freier Hand,*** freehand drawing. **Zeichner,** *m.* 1. designer, draughtsman, (*Am.*) draftsman; 2. signatory, subscriber (*Gen.*, to).

zeichnerisch ['tsaiçnərɪʃ], *adj.* graphic, diagrammatic; ***–e Begabung,*** gift for drawing. **Zeichnung,** *f.* drawing, design, sketch; figure, diagram; signature, subscription (*Gen.*, to); marking, pattern, (*of wood*) grain. **zeichnungsberechtigt,** *adj.* authorized to sign, with signatory power. **Zeichnungs|grenze,** *f.* (*Insur.*) limit of liability. **–liste,**

f. subscription list. **–vollmacht,** *f.* signatory power, authority to sign.

Zeidel|bär [ˈtsaɪdəl–], *m.* (*Zool.*) black *or* sloth *or* honey bear (*Melursus ursinus*). **–meister,** *m.* (*obs.*) *see* **Zeidler. zeideln,** *v.i.* cut honeycombs (from the hives). **Zeidler,** *m.* (*obs.*) bee-keeper.

Zeigefinger [ˈtsaɪgəfɪŋər], *m.* forefinger, index finger.

zeigen [ˈtsaɪgən], **1.** *v.t.* show, display, exhibit, manifest, demonstrate, (*Theat.*) present, show; point at *or* out, indicate; ***ihm den Herrn –,*** show him who is master *or* (*coll.*) the boss; ***ihm den Rücken –,*** turn one's back on him; ***ihm die kalte Schulter –,*** give him the cold shoulder; ***das Thermometer zeigt 20 Grad,*** the thermometer stands at 20°; ***die Uhr zeigt (auf) 12,*** the clock points to 12; (*coll.*) ***ihm – was eine Harke ist,*** show him where he gets off; (*coll.*) ***ich werde dir – wo der Zimmermann das Loch gelassen hat,*** you'll get thrown out on your neck. **2.** *v.r.* (*of a p.*) show o.s., appear, make one's appearance, (*coll.*) show *or* turn up; (*of a th.*) show (itself), appear, become apparent *or* evident, emerge, come to light, be found to be, turn out, prove to be; ***das wird sich –,*** time will tell, we shall see; ***es zeigt sich, daß . . .,*** it appears that . . .; we see that . . .; ***sich freundlich –,*** be friendly; ***er hat sich recht gezeigt,*** he has shown what he can do; ***er will sich mit seinen Kenntnissen –,*** he is trying to show off his knowledge.

Zeiger [ˈtsaɪgər], *m.* pointer, needle, indicator; finger, (*of clocks*) hand, (*of sundial*) style, gnomen, (*Math.*) index; (*Comm.*) ***– dieses,*** the bearer of this (note, paper). **Zeiger|ausschlag,** *m.* needle deflexion. **–galvanometer,** *n.* needle galvanometer. **Zeigestock,** *m.* pointer.

zeihen [ˈtsaɪən], *irr.v.t.* (*high style*) accuse (*Gen.*, of), charge (with).

Zeile [ˈtsaɪlə], *f.* line (*also Typ.*), row; ***– für –,*** line by line; ***ein paar –n,*** a short note; ***zwischen den –n lesen,*** read between the lines; ***zwischen zwei –n geschrieben,*** interlinear. **Zeilen|breite,** *f.* (*Typ.*) measure. **–gießmaschine,** *f.* linotype machine. **–honorar,** *n.* rate per line. **–länge,** *f.* length of line; justification. **–schalter,** *m.* (*typewriter*) (line) spacer. **–schreiber,** *m.* (*coll.*) penny-a-liner. **zeilenweise,** *adv.* in lines, line by line.

Zein, *m. See* **Zain.**

zeise(l)n [ˈtsaɪzə(l)n], **1.** *v.t.* (*dial.*) lure, entice. **2.** *v.i.* (*dial.*) hurry.

Zeisig [ˈtsaɪzɪç], *m.* (**-s,** *pl.* **-e**) (*Orn.*) siskin (*Carduelis spinus*); (*coll.*) ***lockerer –,*** dissolute fellow, loose fish. **zeisiggrün,** *adj.* canary-green.

Zeising [ˈtsaɪzɪŋ], *n.* (*Naut.*) seizing, lashing.

Zeit [tsaɪt], *f.* (-, *pl.* **-en**) time; epoch, age, era; period, season, term, space of time, duration; stage, phase; (*Gram.*) tense; *pl.* (*dial.*) tides; ***seine – abwarten,*** bide one's time; ***aller –en,*** of all time; ***für alle –en,*** for all time, for ever *or* (*coll.*) good; ***es ist an der –,*** it is time, the moment has come; ***es ist früh an der –,*** it is too early; (*Prov.*) ***andre –en, andre Sitten,*** manners change with the times; ***die – arbeitet für uns,*** time is on our side; (*Comm.*) ***auf –,*** on account, on credit; (*Comm.*) ***auf – kaufen,*** make a forward purchase; (*Spt.*) ***auf – laufen,*** run against the clock; ***auf ewige –en,*** for ever and ever, in perpetuity; ***auf einige –,*** for a short *or* certain time; ***außer der –,*** out of season; ***freie –,*** spare time, leisure hours; (*Boxing*) ***für die – zu Boden gehen,*** go down for the count; ***die (ganze) – her*** or ***durch*** or ***über,*** all along, ever since; ***ich gebe dir – bis morgen,*** I'll give you till tomorrow; ***gegen die – arbeiten etc.,*** work *etc.* against time *or* the clock; ***hast du –?*** have you time? can you spare the time? ***hast du genaue –?*** have you the right *or* exact time? ***sie hat ihre –,*** she has her (monthly) period; ***alles hat seine –,*** there's a right time for everything; ***das hat –, damit hat es –,*** there is plenty of time, there is no hurry, that can wait; ***es ist die höchste –,*** it is high time; ***in – von acht Tagen,*** within a week; ***in früherer –,*** formerly; ***in jüngster*** or ***neuester –,*** quite recently; ***in kürzester –,*** in no time (at all); ***in letzter –,*** lately, recently, of late; (*Prov.*) ***spare in der –, so hast du in der Not,*** waste not, want not; ***in der nächsten –,*** in the near future; ***in alten –en*** in days gone by; (*Prov.*) ***kommt –, kommt Rat,*** time brings wisdom; ***seine – ist gekommen,*** he is about to die; ***ihre – ist nahe,*** she is near her time; ***ihre – ist gekommen,*** her child is due; ***das kostet –,*** that takes time; ***lange – vorher,*** long before this; ***eine – lang,*** for a time *or* a little while *or* a short space of time; ***längere –,*** for a fairly long time; ***laß dir nur –*** give yourself time, take your time; ***die – wird es lehren,*** time will tell; (*coll.*) ***O du liebe –!*** good heavens! ***mit der –,*** in (the course of) time, in the end, gradually; ***mit der – gehen,*** march *or* keep pace with the times; ***mit der – geizen,*** not waste a minute *or* second; ***nach einiger –,*** after some time, some time afterwards; (*Spt.*) ***die – nehmen*** (*Gen.*), time (*a race*); ***wo nimmst du die – her?*** where do you find the time? ***die – nutzen,*** take time by the forelock, not let the grass grow under one's feet; ***die – ist noch nicht reif,*** the time has not come; ***– schinden,*** play for time, temporize; ***er hat bessere –en gesehen,*** he has seen better days; ***er war seiner – . . .,*** he was . . . in his day; ***seit längerer*** or ***langer –,*** for a long time; (*coll.*) ***dem lieben Gott die – stehlen,*** idle one's time away; ***vor der –,*** prematurely; ***vor –en,*** once upon a time, formerly, in former *or* olden times; ***vor grauen –en,*** in days of yore; ***vor kurzer –,*** a short time ago; ***vor langer –,*** long ago, a long time ago; ***von – zu –,*** from time to time, now and then; (*Prov.*) ***jedes Ding währt seine –,*** every dog has his day; ***mir wird die – lang,*** time hangs heavy on my hands; ***der Zahn der –,*** the ravages of time; ***zur –,*** at present, at the moment, for the time being; ***zu meiner –,*** in my time *or* day; ***alles zu seiner –,*** all in due course *or* in good time; ***zur – der Römer,*** in the age of the Romans; ***zu gleicher –,*** at the same time; ***zu rechter –,*** at the right time *or* moment; à propos; ***zur rechten –,*** in (the nick of) time; (*Prov.*) ***wer nicht kommt zur rechten –, der muß essen was übrig bleibt,*** first come, first served; ***zu –en,*** now and then, at times; ***zu allen –en, zu jeder –,*** at any time, always; ***zu –en Schillers, zu Schillers –en,*** in the time of Schiller, in Schiller's day.

zeit, *prep.* (*Gen.*) ***– seines Lebens,*** during his lifetime, as *or* so long as he lives.

Zeit|ablauf, *m.* lapse of time. **–abschnitt,** *m.* period, epoch. **–abstand,** *m.* time interval; ***in regelmäßigen –en,*** periodically. **–alter,** *n.* age, epoch, era; generation. **–angabe,** *f.* date, day and hour; ***ohne –,*** undated. **–ansage,** *f.* (*Rad.*) time signal. **–aufnahme,** *f.* (*Phot.*) time exposure. **–aufwand,** *m.* sacrifice *or* loss of time, time spent (*on s.th.*). **–ball,** *m.* time indicator (*in harbours*). **zeitbedingt,** *adj.* under the current circumstances. **Zeit|bedürfnis,** *n.* needs of the time. **–behelf,** *m.* temporary expedient. **–dauer,** *f.* length *or* space of time, duration, period. **–dehner,** *m. See* **–lupe. –dokument,** *n.* document of our time. **–einheit,** *f.* unit of time.

Zeit|enfolge [ˈtsaɪtənfɔlgə], *f. See* **–folge.**

Zeit|ersparnis, *f.* saving of time. **–folge,** *f.* chronological order; (*Gram.*) sequence of tenses. **–form,** *f.* (*Gram.*) tense. **–frage,** *f.* **1.** question of time; **2.** topic of the day. **–geist,** *m.* spirit of the age. **zeitgemäß,** *adj.* timely, seasonable, opportune; up to date, modern. **Zeit|genosse,** *m.*, **–genossin,** *f.*, **zeit|genössisch,** *adj.* contemporary. **–gerecht, 1.** *adj.* timely. **2.** *adv.* in *or* on time, according to schedule. **Zeit|geschäft,** *n.* time-bargain; option business; *pl.* forward transactions, futures. **–geschichte,** *f.* contemporary history. **–geschmack,** *m.* prevailing taste, current fashion. **–gewinn,** *m. See* **–ersparnis.**

zeitig [ˈtsaɪtɪç], **1.** *adj.* early; ripe, mature. **2.** *adv.* early, in *or* on time, in good time. **zeitigen,** *v.t.* mature, ripen, bring to maturity; bring to a head, effect, produce, call forth.

Zeit|karte, *f.* season-ticket. **–kauf,** *m.* credit sale, sale on account. **–kontrollwesen,** *n.* time and motion study. **–lage,** *f.* juncture, state of affairs. **–lang,** *f.* ***eine –,*** for a while, for a *or* some time.

-lauf, *m.* course of time *or* events; lapse of time. **-läuf(t)e,** *m.pl.* times, conjunctures. **zeitlebens,** *adv.* for life, during life; all his (her) life, all their lives.

zeitlich ['tsaɪtlɪç], **1.** *adj.* 1. temporal, secular, earthly; ***das Zeitliche segnen,*** depart this life; 2. chronological, time; ***-e Abstimmung,*** timing; ***-er Verlauf,*** progress in time. **2.** *adv.* with respect to time, within a given time, per unit time; ***– zusammenfallen,*** coincide. **Zeitlichkeit,** *f.* this life, earthly life, life on earth; temporal state; *pl.* temporalities

Zeitlohn ['tsaɪtlo:n], *m.* payment by the hour. **zeitlos,** *adj.* lasting, timeless, (*pred.*) valid at all times. **Zeit|lose,** *f.* (*Bot.*) meadow saffron (*Colchicum autumnale*). **-lupe,** *f.* slow-motion camera. **-lupentempo,** *n.* slow-motion. **-mangel,** *m.* lack *or* shortage of time. **-maß,** *n.* measure of time; (*Mus.*) tempo; (*Metr.*) measure, quantity. **-messer,** *m.* chronometer; (*Mus.*) metronome. **-messung,** *f.* measurement of time; timing; (*Metr.*) prosody. **zeitnah(e),** *adj.* topical, current, up-to-date, (*pred.*) with contemporary appeal. **Zeit|nehmer,** *m.* (*Spt.*) time-keeper. **-ordnung,** *f.* chronological order. **-plan,** *m.* timing, phasing; time-table, schedule. **-punkt,** *m.* moment, instant, (point of) time; juncture; ***von dem – an,*** from that point on. **-raffer,** *m.* quick-motion camera. **zeitraubend,** *adj.* time-wasting *or* consuming. **Zeit|raum,** *m.* period, interval, space of time. **-rechnung,** *f.* chronology; ***christliche –,*** Christian era; ***neue –,*** new style. **-schrift,** *f.* periodical (publication), journal, magazine. **-schriftenwesen,** *n.* periodical literature. **-sichtwechsel,** *m.* (*Comm.*) after-sight bill. **-sinn,** *m.* sense of time *or* timing. **-spanne,** *f.* space *or* period of time, interval. **zeitsparend,** *adj.* time-saving. **Zeit|stil,** *m.* ***Tracht im –,*** period costume. **-stück,** *n.* (*Theat.*) period piece. **-studienwesen,** *n. See* **-kontrollwesen. -tafel,** *f.* chronological table. **-umstände,** *m.pl.* circumstances (of the time), times, juncture(s); ***bei den augenblicklichen –,*** in the present state of affairs.

Zeitung ['tsaɪtʊŋ], *f.* newspaper, (*obs.*) tidings, news, intelligence; (***sich*** (*Dat.*)) ***eine – halten,*** take a newspaper; ***in die – setzen,*** insert in a newspaper, advertise.

Zeitungs|abonnement, *n.* subscription to a paper. **-anzeige,** *f.* newspaper advertisement, announcement in the press. **-artikel,** *m.* newspaper article. **-ausschnitt,** *m.* press-cutting. **-beilage,** *f.* supplement. **-deutsch,** *n.* journalese. **-ente,** *f.* canard, newspaper hoax. **-expedition,** *f.* newspaper office. **-händler,** *m.* newsagent. **-inserat,** *n. See* **-anzeige. -junge,** *m.* news(paper) vendor, paper-boy. **-kiosk,** *m.* newspaper stall, (*Am.*) news stand. **-mache,** *f.* puff. **-papier,** *n.* old newspapers. **-reklame,** *f.* newspaper advertising; *see also* **-mache. -schreiber,** *m.* columnist, journalist. **-stand,** *m. See* **-kiosk. -stil,** *m. See* **-deutsch. -verkäufer,** *m. See* **-händler, -junge. -werbung,** *f. See* **-reklame. -wesen,** *n.* journalism; the press.

Zeit|vergeudung, *See* **-verschwendung. -verlust,** *m.* loss of time. **-verschwendung,** *f.* waste of time. **-vertreib,** *m.* pastime, amusement, diversion; ***zum –,*** to pass the time, for amusement. **zeit|weilig, 1.** *adj.* temporary. **2.** *adv.* for a time, for the time being, from time to time, at times, occasionally. **-weise,** *adv. See* **-weilig, 2. Zeit|wert,** *m.* (*Comm.*) current value. **-wort,** *n.* (*Gram.*) verb. **-zeichen,** *n. See* **-ansage. -zünder,** *m.* time-fuse, delayed action fuse.

zekeln ['tse:kəln], *v.i.* (*coll.*) stand on tiptoe *or* on one's toes.

Zelebrant [tsele'brant], *m.* **(-en,** *pl.* **-en)** officiating priest (*at Mass*); celebrant. **zelebrieren,** *v.t.* celebrate, officiate at.

Zelle ['tsɛlə], *f.* cell, segment, compartment, (*Anat.*) vesicle, alveolus; bucket (*of water-wheels*); phone-box; (*Av.*) air-frame, (*Naut.*) tank. **Zellen|atmung,** *f.* vesicular breathing. **-aufbau,** *m.* cell structure. **-bildung,** *f.* cell-formation. **zellenförmig,** *adj.* cellular, alveolate. **Zellen|gang,** *m.* (*Anat.*) cellular duct; corridor (*in prisons etc.*). **-gefangene(r),** *m., f.* prisoner in solitary confinement. **-gewebe,** *n.* (*Anat.*) cellular tissue. **-kunde, -lehre,** *f.* cytology. **-pflanzen,** *f.pl.* vascular plants.

Zell|faser, *f.* cellular fibre. **-faserstoff,** *m.* cellulose. **-haut,** *f.* cellophane. **-horn,** *n.* celluloid. **zellig,** *adj.* cellular, vesicular, honeycombed. **Zell|kern,** *m.* cell-nucleus, cytoplast. **-masse,** *f.* cellular substance.

Zellophan(papier) [tsɛlo'fa:n–], *n. See* **Zellhaut.**

Zellstoff ['tsɛlʃtɔf], *m.* cellulose, wood pulp *or* fibre.

Zelluloid [tsɛlu'lɔyt], *n. See* **Zellhorn.**

Zellulose [tsɛlu'lo:zə], *f. See* **Zellstoff.**

Zellwolle ['tsɛlvɔlə], *f.* rayon.

Zelot [tse'lo:t], *m.* **(-en,** *pl.* **-en)** zealot, fanatic. **zelotisch,** *adj.* fanatical.

[1]**Zelt** [tsɛlt], *n.* **(-(e)s,** *pl.* **-e)** tent; marquee; awning; (*B.*) tabernacle; (*Poet., fig.*) vault *or* canopy (of heaven).

[2]**Zelt,** *m. See* **Zeltgang.**

Zelt|bahn *f.* ground-sheet. **-bett,** *n.* canopy bed.

Zeltchen ['tsɛltçən], *n.* (*dial.*) lozenge, pastille.

Zelt|dach, *n.* (*Build.*) pavilion-roof; *see also* **-decke. -decke,** *f.* awning, tilt.

Zelte ['tsɛltə], *f. See* [1]**Zelten.**

[1]**Zelten** ['tsɛltən], *m.* (*dial.*) small flat.

[2]**Zelten,** *n.* camping.

[1]**zelten,** *v.i.* camp (out), sleep under canvas.

[2]**zelten,** *v.i.* amble, pace. **Zelter,** *m.* palfrey.

Zeltfahrt ['tsɛltfa:rt], *f.* camping trip.

Zeltgang ['tsɛltgaŋ], *m.* amble, ambling pace.

Zelt|hering, *m. See* **-pflock. -lager,** *n.* camp, encampment. **-leben,** *n.* camping (out), living under canvas. **-leine,** *f.* guy-rope. **-leinwand,** *f.* tent-cloth. **-pflock,** *m.* tent-peg. **-platz,** *m.* camp(ing) site. **-schnur,** *f. See* **-leine. -stange,** *f.*, **-stock,** *m.* tent-pole.

Zement [tse'mɛnt], *m. or n.* **(-s,** *pl.* **-e)** cement. **Zement|beton,** *m.* concrete. **-formstück,** *n.* concrete block. **-fußboden,** *m.* cement *or* concrete floor. **zementieren** [–'ti:rən], *v.t.* cement (*also fig.*); (*Metall.*) convert (*iron*) into steel; case-harden, carburize. **Zementier|ofen,** *m.* converting furnace. **-stahl,** *m.* converted *or* cementation steel. **Zementierung,** *f.* cementation.

Zenit [tse'ni:t] (*Austr.* **Zenith**), *m. or n.* zenith (*also fig.*), vertical point; (*fig.*) height, climax; ***im –,*** at the zenith.

zensieren [tsɛn'zi:rən], *v.t.* censor, (*fig.*) censure, criticize; (*at school*) mark, give marks, (*Am.*) grade. **Zensor** ['tsɛnzɔr], *m.* **(-s,** *pl.* **-en)** censor. **Zensur** [–'zu:r], *f.* (-, *pl.* **-en)** censorship; (*at school*) mark(s), (*Am.*) point(s); report, certificate, (*Am.*) grade, credit.

Zent [tsɛnt], *f.* (-, *pl.* **-en)** (*Hist.*) hundred.

Zentenarfeier [tsɛntə'na:rfaɪər], *f.* centenary.

zentesimal [tsɛntezi'ma:l], *adj.* hundredth, centesimal.

Zenti|folie [tsɛnti'fo:ljə], *f.* centifolious rose, cabbage-rose. **-gramm,** *n.* **(-(e)s,** *pl.* **-e)** centigram(me). **-meter,** *n.* (*Swiss, coll. m.*) centimetre. **-meterwelle,** *f.* (*Rad.*) ultra-high frequency (wave).

Zentner ['tsɛntnər], *m.* hundredweight; (*metric*) quintal, 50 kg. **Zentnerlast,** *f.* (*fig.*) heavy burden; ***eine – fiel mir vom Herzen,*** that was a load off my mind. **zentnerschwer,** *adj.* (*fig.*) very heavy, burdensome, crushing.

zentral [tsɛn'tra:l], *adj.* central. **Zentral|amt,** *n.* directorate. **-bahnhof,** *m.* central *or* main station. **-bank,** *f.* central bank. **Zentrale,** *f.* 1. central *or* head office, headquarters; (*Tech.*) control-room; (telephone) exchange; (electric) power station; 2. (*Geom.*) line joining two (or more) centres. **Zentral|gewalt,** *f.* central authority, federal government. **-heizung,** *f.* central heating.

zentralisieren [tsɛntrali'zi:rən], *v.t.* centralize. **Zentralisierung,** *f.* centralization.

Zentral|kartei, *f.* master-file. **-mächte,** *f.pl.* (*Hist.*) Central Powers (*Germany and Austria-Hungary*). **-nervensystem,** *n.* central nervous system. **-stelle,** *f.* coordinating office. **-verband,** *m.* federation of industry.

Zentrierbohrer [tsɛn'tri:rbo:rər], *m.* centre-bit. **zentrieren,** *v.t.* centre.

zentrifugal [tsɛntrifu'ga:l], *adj.* centrifugal. **Zentrifuge** [-'fu:gə], *f.* centrifuge, separator, hydro-extractor.

zentripetal [tsɛntripe'ta:l], *adj.* centripetal.

zentrisch ['tsɛntrɪʃ], *adj.* (con)centric.

Zentrum ['tsɛntrum], *n.* (**-s,** *pl.* **-ren**) 1. centre, bull's-eye; 2. (*Pol.*) Centre Party. **Zentrumbohrer,** *m.* *See* **Zentrierbohrer.**

Zephir ['tsɛfi:r], *m.* (**-s,** *pl.* **-e**) zephyr.

Zepter ['tsɛptər], *n. or m.* sceptre, mace; ***das* – *tragen*** or ***führen*** or ***schwingen,*** wield the sceptre.

Zer [tse:r], *n.* (*Chem.*) cerium.

zer- [tsɛr], *insep. v. pref. with meanings*: asunder, to pieces, (*fig.*) spoil by. (*For verbs not listed below see the simple v.*)

zerbeißen [tsɛr'baɪsən], *irr.v.t.* bite through, break with the teeth *or* beak; crunch, bite to pieces.

zerbersten [tsɛr'bɛrstən], *irr.v.i.* burst apart *or* asunder.

zerbeulen [tsɛr'bɔylən], *v.t.* dent, crumple.

zerbleuen [tsɛr'blɔyən], *v.t.* (*coll.*) thrash soundly, (*coll.*) tan the hide off.

zerbombt [tsɛr'bɔmpt], *adj.* bombed, devastated by bombing.

zerbrechen [tsɛr'brɛçən], *irr.v.t., v.i.* break to *or* in pieces, smash, shatter; (*fig.*) – ***an*** (*Dat.*), be broken by, break under; (*fig.*) ***sich*** (*Dat.*) ***den Kopf* –,** rack one's brain(s) (***über*** (*Acc.*), over). **zerbrechlich,** *adj.* breakable, brittle, fragile. **Zerbrechlichkeit,** *f.* brittleness, fragility.

zerbröckeln [tsɛr'brœkəln], *v.t., v.i.* crumble (away *or* to pieces).

zerdrücken [tsɛr'drykən], *v.t.* crush, squeeze flat, squash; mash (*potatoes*); crease, crumple, wrinkle, crush (*clothes*).

Zerealien [tsere'a:liən], *f.pl.* cereals.

zerebral [tsere'bra:l], *adj.* cerebral.

Zeremonie [tseremo'ni:], *f.* ceremony; formality. **zeremoniell** [-i'ɛl], *adj.* ceremonial, formal. **Zeremoniell,** *n.* (**-s,** *pl.* **-e**) ceremonial. **Zeremonienmeister** [-'mo:niən-], *m.* master of ceremonies. **zeremoniös** [-i'ø:s], *adj.* ceremonious, punctilious.

zerfahren [tsɛr'fa:rən], 1. *irr.v.t.* cut to pieces, ruin (*road surface*). 2. *irr.v.i.* (*aux.* s.) burst, fly asunder. 3. *adj.* (*of road*) cut to pieces, rutted; (*fig.*) inattentive, distracted, absent-minded; scatter-brained, harum-scarum, flighty, giddy; (*as replies*) irrelevant, inconsistent. **Zerfahrenheit,** *f.* absent-mindedness, inattentiveness; thoughtlessness, giddiness, flightiness; irrelevance, inconsistency.

Zerfall [tsɛr'fal], *m.* ruin, decay, (*Chem.*) decomposition, (*Phys.*) disintegration, dissociation; (*fig.*) decadence. **zerfallen,** 1. *irr.v.i.* (*aux.* s.) fall apart *or* to pieces, crumble away, fall into ruin, decay, (*Chem.*) decompose, (*Phys.*) disintegrate, dissociate; ***in zwei Teile* –,** fall under two heads; ***in Stücke* –,** fall to pieces; ***mit ihm* –,** fall out *or* quarrel with him, be at variance with him. 2. *adj.* in ruins, dilapidated; (*fig.*) on bad terms *or* at variance (***mit,*** with). **Zerfalls|produkt,** *n.* (*Phys.*) dissociated constituent, (*Chem.*) product of decomposition. **-reihe,** *f.* stage of radio-active disintegration.

zerfasern [tsɛr'fa:zərn], *v.t.* (reduce to) pulp, break up; unravel, fray (out).

zerfetzen [tsɛr'fɛtsən], *v.t.* tear up, tear to *or* in pieces, tear to rags, shred, slash, hack to pieces. **zerfetzt,** *adj.* ragged, tattered, in rags.

zerflattern [tsɛr'flatərn], *v.i.* (*aux.* s.) be scattered, flutter away, (*fig.*) be ineffective.

zerfleischen [tsɛr'flaɪʃən], *v.t.* lacerate; tear *or* rend to pieces, mangle.

zerfließen [tsɛr'fli:sən], *irr.v.i.* (*aux.* s.) melt, dissolve, (*Chem.*) liquefy, deliquesce, (*as paint*) run; (*fig.*) (*as hopes*) melt away; ***in Tränen* –,** dissolve into tears.

zerfressen [tsɛr'frɛsən], *irr.v.t.* eat *or* gnaw away; (*Chem.*) corrode. **Zerfressung,** *f.* corrosion.

zerfurcht [tsɛr'furçt], *adj.* furrowed, wrinkled.

zergehen [tsɛr'ge:ən], *irr.v.i.* (*aux.* s.) melt, dissolve, (*fig.*) dwindle (away), vanish; ***der Nebel zergeht,*** the mist dissolves *or* disperses; ***in nichts* –,** dwindle to nothing.

zergen ['tsɛrgən], *v.t.* (*dial.*) tease, pester.

zergliedern [tsɛr'gli:dərn], *v.t.* dismember, cut up; (*Anat.*) dissect; (*fig., Gram.*) analyse. **Zergliederung,** *f.* dismemberment; dissection; analysis.

zerhacken [tsɛr'haken], *v.t.* hack *or* chop *or* cut in pieces; slash; (*Cul.*) mince.

zerhauen [tsɛr'hauən], *irr.v.t* cut in pieces; cut asunder; ***den* (*gordischen*) *Knoten* –,** cut the Gordian knot.

zerkauen [tsɛr'kauən], *v.t.* masticate *or* chew thoroughly.

zerkleinern [tsɛr'klaɪnərn], *v.t.* break up, reduce to small pieces, shred; crush, grind, pulverize, triturate, comminute.

zerklopfen [tsɛr'klɔpfən], *v.t.* beat, pound, knock to pieces, smash.

zerklüftet [tsɛr'klyftət], *adj.* cleft, fissured, rugged. **Zerklüftung,** *f.* cleft, cleavage, fissure; disruption, fragmentation.

zerknallen [tsɛr'knalən], *v.i.* blow up, explode, detonate.

zerknautschen [tsɛr'knautʃən], *v.t.* (*coll.*) crush, crumple.

zerknicken [tsɛr'knɪkən], *v.t.* break, crack, snap (in two).

zerknirscht [tsɛr'knɪrʃt], *adj.* contrite. **Zerknirschung,** *f.* broken-heartedness, remorse, contrition.

zerknistern [tsɛr'knɪstərn], *v.t., v.i.* decrepitate.

zerknittern [tsɛr'knɪtərn], *v.t.* crumple, rumple, crease, wrinkle. **zerknittert,** *adj.* (*also fig. coll.*) crestfallen.

zerknüllen [tsɛr'knylən], *v.t.* *See* **zerknautschen.**

zerkochen [tsɛr'kɔxən], *v.t.* spoil by over-cooking, boil (*potatoes etc.*) into the water.

zerkratzen [tsɛr'kratsən], *v.t.* scratch to pieces.

zerkrümeln [tsɛr'kry:məln], *v.t., v.i.* *See* **zerbröckeln.**

zerlassen [tsɛr'lasən], *irr.v.t.* melt, dissolve.

zerlegbar [tsɛr'le:kba:r], *adj.* divisible, (*Chem.*) decomposable, (*Mech.*) collapsible, capable of being dismantled. **zerlegen,** *v.t.* cut up, (*Anat.*) dissect, (*Cul.*) carve; (*Chem.*) decompose, (*Math., Mus.*) resolve, (*Gram. also fig.*) analyse; (*Mech.*) dismantle, take apart *or* to pieces, strip (*a weapon*); disperse, (*Mil.*) (*sl.*) shoot up; ***in zwei Teile* –,** divide in two. **Zerlegung,** *f.* dismantling; dissection; decomposition; analysis; (*Phys.*) – ***der Kräfte,*** resolution of forces.

zerlesen [tsɛr'le:zən], *adj.* well-thumbed (*of a book*).

zerlöchert [tsɛr'lœçərt], *adj.* full of holes.

zerlumpt [tsɛr'lumpt], *adj.* *See* **zerfetzt**; ***-er Kerl,*** ragamuffin, scruff.

zermahlen [tsɛr'ma:lən], *irr.v.t.* grind (down), crush, pulverize.

zermalmen [tsɛr'malmən], *v.t.* bruise, crush, dash in pieces; grind, crunch, powder, pulverize; (*fig.*) cast down, depress.

zermartern [tsɛr'martərn], *v.t.* torment, torture; ***sich*** (*Dat.*) ***den Kopf* –,** rack one's brains.

zermürben [tsɛr'myrbən], *v.t.* grind down, wear down (*also the enemy*). **zermürbend,** *adj.* (*fig.*) wearing, punishing. **zermürbt,** *adj.* broken (-down), exhausted, worn-out. **Zermürbung,** *f.* attrition. **Zermürbungskrieg,** *m.* war of attrition.

zernagen [tsɛr'na:gən], *v.t.* gnaw *or* eat away; (*Chem.*) corrode; erode (*also fig.*).

zernieren [tsɛr'ni:rən], *v.t.* invest, besiege, encircle, blockade. **Zernierung,** *f.* investment, siege.
zerpflücken [tsɛr'pflykən], *v.t.* pluck to pieces, pull apart.
zerplatzen [tsɛr'platsən], *v.i. See* **zerbersten.**
zerquetschen [tsɛr'kvɛtʃən], *v.t.* crush, bruise, squash, pulp, mash.
Zerrbild ['tsɛrbɪlt], *n.* caricature, (*fig. also*) distorted picture.
zerreiben [tsɛr'raɪbən], *irr.v.t.* rub away; grind down; pulverize, (*Chem.*) triturate.
Zerreißdiagramm [tsɛr'raɪsdiagram], *n.* (*Metall.*) stress-strain diagram.
zerreißen [tsɛr'raɪsən], **1.** *irr.v.t.* tear *or* rip up, tear *or* rip to pieces, tear *or* rip apart, rend; break up, disrupt, sever, rupture, dismember; shred, lacerate; (*fig.*) break (*an alliance, a p.'s heart etc.*); ***ich werde mich nicht darum –,*** I shan't break my neck over it; ***ich kann mich nicht –,*** I cannot do two things *or* be in two places at once. **2.** *v.i.* (*aux.* s.) break, snap, tear, split.
Zerreiß|festigkeit, *f.* tensile strength. **–probe,** *f. See* **–versuch**; (*fig.*) test of nerves. **Zerreißung,** *f.* rending, breaking, tearing, dismemberment; (*Med.*) laceration, rupture. **Zerreißversuch,** *m.* tensile test.
zerren ['tsɛrən], *v.t., v.i.* pull, tug, drag; haul; ***– an*** (*Dat.*), pull *or* tug at; (*fig.*) ***durch den Schmutz*** or ***Kot –,*** drag through the mud; ***eine Muskel –,*** pull *or* strain a muscle.
zerrinnen [tsɛr'rɪnən], *irr.v.i.* (*aux.* s.) *see* **zergehen**; ***Geld zerrinnt ihm unter*** or ***zwischen den Fingern,*** money runs through his fingers like water; ***in nichts –,*** come to nothing, go up in smoke; (*Prov.*) ***wie gewonnen, so zerronnen,*** easy come, easy go.
zerrissen [tsɛr'rɪsən], *see* **zerreißen. Zerrissenheit,** *f.* raggedness, (*fig.*) confusion, disruption, inner strife.
Zerrspiegel ['tsɛrʃpi:gəl], *m.* distorting mirror. **Zerrung,** *f.* tugging, hauling; (*of muscle etc.*) strain.
zerrupfen [tsɛr'rupfən], *v.t. See* **zerpflücken.**
zerrütten [tsɛr'rytən], *v.t.* disarrange, derange, unsettle, disturb, disorganize, throw into confusion; ruin, destroy; (*fig.*) shatter (*nerves*), unhinge (*the mind*); wreck, disrupt (*a marriage*). **Zerrüttung,** *f.* disruption, derangement, disorganization; disorder, confusion.
Zerrwanst ['tsɛrvanst], *m.* (*sl.*) squeeze-box.
zerschellen [tsɛr'ʃɛlən], **1.** *v.t.* dash in pieces, smash (to pieces), shatter, shiver. **2.** *v.i.* (*aux.* s.) go to pieces, be dashed to pieces, be shattered *or* smashed, (*Naut.*) be wrecked, (*Av.*) crash.
zerschießen [tsɛr'ʃi:sən], *irr.v.t.* shoot to pieces; riddle with bullets.
zerschlagen [tsɛr'ʃla:gən], **1.** *irr.v.t.* 1. knock *or* break to pieces, smash *or* batter (to pieces); 2. parcel out (*an estate*). **2.** *irr.v.r.* (*fig.*) be broken off (*as an engagement*), come to nothing, be disappointed (*hopes etc.*). **3.** *adj.* smashed, shattered, battered; (*fig.*) (***wie***) –, knocked up, (*coll.*) all in, all washed up.
zerschlissen [tsɛr'ʃlɪsən], *adj.* worn to shreds *or* into holes, tattered, ragged, threadbare.
zerschmettern [tsɛr'ʃmɛtərn], *v.t., v.i. See* **zerschellen.**
zerschneiden [tsɛr'ʃnaɪdən], *irr.v.t.* cut in two, cut to pieces, cut into shreds; slice, cut up, carve; ***ihm das Herz –,*** break his heart; ***das (Tisch) tuch ist (zwischen ihnen) zerschnitten,*** it is all over between them.
zersetzen [tsɛr'zɛtsən], *v.t., v.r.* decompose, disintegrate, (*fig.*) disintegrate, undermine, demoralize. **zersetzend,** *adj.* destructive, deleterious; demoralizing. **Zersetzung,** *f.* decay, decomposition; disintegration, dissolution; (*fig.*) demoralization, subversion. **Zersetzungs|gase,** *n.pl.* gases of decomposition. **–literatur,** *f.* seditious *or* subversive literature.

zerspalten [tsɛr'ʃpaltən], *v.t.* cleave, split (up).
zersplittern [tsɛr'ʃplɪtərn], **1.** *v.t., v.i.* (*aux.* s.) splinter, split (up), split into pieces. **2.** *v.t.* disperse, split *or* break up (*crowd etc.*), (*fig.*) dissipate, fritter away (*time, energy*). **3.** *v.r.* disperse; split *or* break up (*of a crowd*), fritter away one's time, dissipate one's energies, have too many irons in the fire (*of a p.*). **zersplittert,** *adj.* splintered, (*Med.*) comminuted, (*fig.*) disunited. **Zersplitterung,** *f.* dispersal, fragmentation, splintering, (*Med.*) comminuted fracture, (*fig.*) dissipation, waste of time *or* energy, (*Pol.*) disunion.
zersprengen [tsɛr'ʃprɛŋən], *v.t.* burst *or* break open, blow up; rout, disperse, scatter; ***zersprengende Kraft,*** disruptive force.
zerspringen [tsɛr'ʃprɪŋən], *irr.v.i.* (*aux.* s.) fly to pieces, break, burst, split, crack; explode; ***der Kopf will mir –,*** my head is splitting; ***das Herz wollte ihr (vor Aufregung) –,*** she was beside herself *or* (*coll.*) was bursting (with excitement).
zerstampfen [tsɛr'ʃtampfən], *v.t.* trample underfoot; stamp *or* trample *or* tread down; pound; crush; ***zu Pulver –,*** reduce to powder.
zerstäuben [tsɛr'ʃtɔybən], **1.** *v.t.* pulverize, atomize, reduce to dust *or* spray; (*fig.*) disperse, scatter. **2.** *v.i.* (*aux.* s.) turn *or* fall to dust, be scattered (as dust). **Zerstäuber,** *m.* pulverizer, atomizer, scent-spray, spray-diffuser, spray-gun.
zerstieben [tsɛr'ʃti:bən], *irr.v.i.* (*aux.* s.) turn to dust; be scattered as dust, disperse, scatter; vanish.
zerstörbar [tsɛr'ʃtø:rba:r], *adj.* destructible. **zerstören,** *v.t.* destroy, demolish, ruin, lay in ruins, wreck, devastate, ravage; ***zerstörte Ehe,*** wrecked marriage; ***zerstörte Gesundheit,*** broken *or* ruined *or* shattered health; ***zerstörte Gebiete,*** devastated areas; ***zerstörte Hoffnungen,*** blighted hopes. **zerstörend,** *adj.* destructive, devastating, ruinous. **Zerstörer,** *m.* destroyer (*also Naut.*), (*Av.*) fighter-bomber, interceptor (plane), long-range fighter. **zerstörerisch,** *adj. See* **zerstörend. zerstörlich,** *adj.* (*Swiss*) unconditional, absolute, final. **Zerstörung,** *f.* destruction, demolition; devastation, ruin. **Zerstörungs|feuer,** *n.* (*Mil.*) devastating fire. **–kraft,** *f.* destructive power. **–lust,** *f.*, **–trieb,** *m.* destructiveness. **–werk,** *n.* work of destruction. **–wut,** *f.* vandalism.
zerstoßen [tsɛr'ʃto:sən], *irr.v.t.* knock *or* beat to pieces; bruise, pound, crush, pulverize, levigate.
zerstreuen [tsɛr'ʃtrɔyən], **1.** *v.t.* disperse, dissipate, diffuse, scatter, disseminate, (*fig.*) dissipate, dispel, banish (*fear etc.*); distract, divert, amuse. **2.** *v.r.* disperse, scatter, (*fig.*) amuse o.s.; ***sich – lassen,*** allow one's attention to wander. **zerstreut,** *adj.* dispersed, scattered; diffused (*light*); (*fig.*) distracted, preoccupied, absent-minded. **Zerstreutheit,** *f.* absent-mindedness, preoccupation. **Zerstreuung,** *f.* scatter(ing), dispersion, diffusion, dissipation, dissemination; (*fig.*) distraction, diversion, amusement; *see also* **Zerstreutheit. Zerstreuungs|linse,** *f.* diverging *or* dispersing lens. **–punkt,** *m.* point of dispersion, focus of divergence. **–spiegel,** *m.* convex mirror.
zerstückeln [tsɛr'ʃtykəln], *v.t.* cut into little pieces, cut *or* chop up, dismember; (*land*) divide, parcel out, partition. **Zerstück(e)lung,** *f.* dismemberment; parcelling out, partition.
zerteilen [tsɛr'taɪlən], *v.t., v.r.* divide, separate; split (up); disperse; (*Math.*) resolve. **Zerteilung,** *f.* division, separation; dispersion, dissolution; (*Math.*) resolution.
zertrampeln [tsɛr'trampəln], *v.t.,* **zertreten** [–'tre:ten], *irr.v.t.* trample underfoot; stamp *or* tread *or* trample down, stamp out (*fire, also fig.*).
zertrümmern [tsɛr'trymərn], *v.t. See* **zerstören**; smash (to pieces), shatter; split (*the atom*). **Zertrümmerung,** *f.* destruction, smashing, disintegration, demolition, (*of atoms*) splitting.
Zervelatwurst [(t)sɛrvə'la:tvurst], *f.* smoked sausage; saveloy.
zerwühlen [tsɛr'vy:lən], *v.t. See* **zerzausen.**

Zerwürfnis [tsɛr'vyrfnɪs], *n.* (**-ses,** *pl.* **-se**) difference (of opinion), disagreement, discord, dissension, quarrel, dispute, strife.

zerzausen [tsɛr'tsauzən], *v.t.* crumple; tousle, dishevel (*hair*); pull about; ***ihn tüchtig* –,** treat him roughly *or* (*coll.*) rough, (*sl.*) rough him up.

zerzupfen [tsɛr'tsupfən], *v.t.* pull *or* pick to pieces.

Zession [tsɛsi'o:n], *f.* (*Law*) cession, transfer, assignment, conveyance (*of land*). **Zessionar** [–'na:r], *m.* (**-s,** *pl.* **-e**) assignee, transferee, (*Am.*) assign.

Zeter ['tse:tər], *n.* (*obs.*) – ***schreien,*** cry murder, cry for help, raise a hue and cry. **Zeter|geschrei, –mordio,** *n.* shout for help; outcry, clamour, hue and cry. **zetern,** *v.i.* clamour, (*dial.*) scold, nag.

Zettel ['tsɛtəl], *m.* 1. (scrap of) paper; slip (of paper), note; leaflet, (hand-)bill, poster, placard; ticket, label, tag, docket, (*coll.*) sticker; 2. (*Weav.*) warp, chain. **Zettel|ankleben,** *n.* – ***verboten!*** stick no bills! **–ankleber,** *m.* bill-sticker, bill-poster. **–anschlagen,** *n. See* **–ankleben. –bank,** *f.* bank of issue. **–kartei,** *f.*, **–kasten,** *m.* filing-cabinet, card-index. **–katalog,** *m.* card-index. **–wahl,** *f.* card-vote.

zeuch [tsɔyç], **zeuchst, zeucht,** (*obs., Poet.*) *see* **ziehen.**

Zeug [tsɔyk], *n.* (**-(e)s,** *pl.* **-e**) stuff, material; cloth, fabric, textiles, textile goods; clothes; implements, tools, equipment; utensils, (*coll.*) things; type-metal; (paper) pulp; (*obs.*) arms, ordnance; (*coll.*) rubbish, trash, junk; ***ihm am – flicken,*** find fault with him, pick holes *or* a hole in him, pull him to pieces; ***dummes* –,** (stuff and) nonsense; rubbish, (*coll.*) tosh, bosh, (*sl.*) bilge; ***mach' kein dummes –!*** no nonsense! don't play the fool! ***das – haben zu,*** have it in one (to), be cut out (for), have the makings (of); (*coll.*) ***er hat das – dazu,*** he's got what it takes; (*coll.*) ***was das – hält*** or (***nur***) ***halten will,*** with might and main, for all it is worth, (*coll.*) hell for leather; ***ins – gehen, sich ins – legen,*** set to work with a will, make a tremendous effort, (*coll.*) put one's back into it, put one's shoulder to the wheel.

Zeug|amt, *n.* (*obs.*) arsenal, ordnance department. **–bütte,** *f.* pulp-vat. **–druck,** *m.* calico printing.

Zeuge ['tsɔygə], *m.* (**-n,** *pl.* **-n**) witness; ***einen –n stellen,*** produce evidence *or* a witness; ***als – vorgeladen werden,*** be called as a witness; ***zum –n anrufen,*** call to witness.

[1]**zeugen** ['tsɔygən], *v.i.* (bear) witness, testify, give evidence; (*fig.*) – ***von,*** testify to, be evidence of, prove, bespeak.

[2]**zeugen, 1.** *v.t.* beget, procreate; engender; (*fig.*) generate, produce, create. **2.** *v.i.* produce offspring.

Zeugen|aussage, *f.* evidence, deposition, testimony. **–bank,** *f.* witness-box *or* (*Am.*) -stand. **–beeinflussung, –bestechung,** *f.* suborning of witnesses. **–beweis,** *m.* first-hand proof. **–eid,** *m.* oath administered to witnesses. **–verhör,** *n.*, **–vernehmung,** *f.* hearing of witnesses.

Zeug|haus, *n.* (*obs.*) *see* **–amt.**

Zeugin ['tsɔygɪn], *f.* (female) witness.

Zeugmeister ['tsɔykmaɪstər], *m.* (*obs.*) master of ordnance.

Zeugnis ['tsɔyknɪs], *n.* (**-ses,** *pl.* **-se**) 1. (*Law*) testimony, evidence, deposition; – ***ablegen,*** bear witness (***für,*** to), give evidence *or* proof (of), testify (to), vouch (for); (*B.*) ***Du sollst kein falsch – reden wider Deinen Nächsten,*** thou shalt not bear false witness against thy neighbour; (*Law*) ***zum – dessen,*** in witness whereof; 2. attestation, certificate; testimonial; character; (school-)report, (*Am.*) credit, grade; ***ein – ausstellen,*** write a testimonial. **Zeugnis|ablegung,** *f.* deposition. **–abschrift,** *f.* copy of testimonials. **–verweigerung,** *f.* refusal to give evidence. **–zwang,** *m.* obligation to give evidence.

Zeug|schmied, *m.* (*obs.*) armourer, toolsmith. **–schuhe,** *m.pl.* canvas shoes.

Zeugung ['tsɔyguŋ], *f.* generation, procreation, reproduction. **Zeugungs|fähigkeit, –kraft,** *f.* potency, seminal power, virility. **–organe,** *n.pl.* reproductive *or* sexual *or* genital organs. **–trieb,** *m.* procreative instinct. **–unfähigkeit,** *f.* impotence. **–vermögen,** *n. See* **–fähigkeit.**

Zibbe ['tsɪbə], *f.* (*dial.*) ewe (*of rabbit, hare, goat*).

Zibebe [tsi'be:bə], *f.* (*dial.*) raisin.

Zibet ['tsi:bɛt], *m.* civet (*secretion*). **Zibet|katze,** *f.*, **–tier,** *n.* (*Zool.*) civet cat (*Viverra civetta*).

Zichorie [tsɪ'ço:riə], *f.* (*Bot.*) chicory, succory (*Cichorium intybus*).

Zicke ['tsɪkə], *f.* (*coll.*) *see* **Ziege;** (*sl.*) ***mach' keine –n!*** don't be funny! **Zickel,** *n.* (*dial.*), **Zicklein,** *n.* kid.

Zickzack ['tsɪktsak], *m.* (**-s,** *pl.* **-e**), **zickzack,** *adv.* zigzag; ***zickzack*** or ***im Zickzack fahren,*** zigzag, follow a zigzag course. **zickzackförmig,** *adj.* zigzag.

Zieche ['tsi:çə], *f.* (*dial.*) coverlet, quilt.

Ziege ['tsi:gə], *f.* 1. goat; she-goat, (*coll.*) nanny-goat; 2. (*Ichth.*) *Pelecus cultratus.*

Ziegel ['tsi:gəl], *m.* brick; tile; – ***brennen,*** bake *or* fire bricks; ***mit –n decken,*** tile, roof with tiles. **Ziegel|bau,** *m.* bricklaying; brick structure. **–brenner,** *m.* brickmaker. **–brennerei,** *f.* brick-works, brickyard. **–dach,** *n.* tiled roof. **–decker,** *m.* tiler, roofer. **Ziegelei** [–'laɪ], *f. See* **Ziegelbrennerei. Ziegelerde,** *f.* brick-clay. **ziegelfarbig,** *adj.* brick red. **Ziegel|hütte,** *f.* brick-kiln. **–mehl,** *n.* brick-dust. **–ofen,** *m. See* **–hütte. ziegel|rot,** *adj. See* **–farbig. Ziegel|stein,** *m.* brick. **–streicher,** *m. See* **–brenner.**

Ziegen|bart ['tsi:gən–], *m.* goat's beard, (*of a p.*) goatee. **–bock,** *m.* he-goat, (*coll.*) billy-goat. **–fell,** *n.* goat-skin. **–hainer,** *m.* knobkerrie. **–hirt,** *m.* goatherd. **–käse,** *m.* goat's milk cheese. **–lamm,** *n.* kid. **–leder,** *n.* kid (*leather*). **–melker,** *m.* (*Orn.*) nightjar (*Caprimulgus europaeus*). **–milch,** *f.* goat's milk. **–peter,** *m.* (*Med.*) mumps.

Zieger(käse) ['tsi:gər(kɛ:zə)], *m.* (*dial.*) soft *or* milk *or* cream cheese.

Ziegler ['tsi:glər], *m.* brickmaker.

zieh [tsi:], *see* **zeihen.**

Ziehbank ['tsi:baŋk], *f.* draw-bench, (wire-)drawing frame. **ziehbar,** *adj.* ductile. **Ziehbarkeit,** *f.* ductility. **Zieh|brücke,** *f.* drawbridge. **–brunnen,** *m.* draw-well, bucket-well.

Ziehe ['tsi:ə], *f.* (*dial.*) rearing, nursing; ***in die – geben,*** put (*a child*) with foster-parents.

ziehen ['tsi:ən], **1.** *irr.v.t.* 1. draw, pull, drag, haul, tug; tow (*a boat etc.*); take off *or* raise (*one's hat*); move (*at draughts etc.*); pull out, extract (*teeth*); 2. cultivate, grow (*plants*), breed, rear (*animals*); 3. drop, erect (*a perpendicular*); describe (*a circle etc.*); 4. rifle (*a gun*); 5. build, erect (*a wall*); cut, dig (*a trench*); ***an sich*** (*Acc.*) –, attract, draw to o.s., win over to one's side; engross, monopolize; ***ihn am Ärmel* –,** pluck him by the sleeve; ***ihn an den Haaren* –,** pull his hair; ***ein Boot ans Land* –,** haul a boat ashore; ***ans Licht*** or ***Tageslicht* –,** bring to light, make known; ***Perlen auf einen Faden* –,** string *or* thread pearls; ***Wein auf Flaschen* –,** bottle wine; ***alle*** or ***aller Augen*** or ***Aufmerksamkeit auf sich* –,** attract universal attention; ***auf die Seite* –,** draw aside; ***auf seine Seite* –,** win over to one's side; (*Comm.*) ***einen Wechsel auf ihn* –,** draw a bill on him; ***eine Lehre – aus,*** learn a lesson from; ***ihm Würmer aus der Nase* –,** worm secrets out of him; ***Nutzen*** or ***Gewinn – aus,*** derive profit *or* advantage *or* benefit from; turn to one's own account; (*fig.*) ***den Kopf aus der Schlinge* –,** make one's escape, extricate o.s.; ***Schlüsse – aus,*** draw conclusions from; ***Öl aus Samen* –,** extract oil from seeds; ***die Wurzel aus einer Zahl* –,** extract the root of a number; ***die Bilanz* –,** draw up the balance-sheet; ***Blasen* –,** raise blisters; ***ihn durch den Schmutz*** or (*coll.*) ***Kakao* –,** drag his name in the dirt; ***Flachs* –,** pull flax; ***Flachs durch die Hechel* –,** hackle flax; (*coll.*) ***einen Flunsch*** or ***Fratze* –,** see ***ein Gesicht* –; *Folgerungen* –,** see ***Schlüsse* –; *einen Gewinn* –,** draw a winner; ***ein Gesicht* –,** make faces, pull a face; ***ein schiefes***

Gesicht –, pull a long face; ***Grenzen –***, set limits; ***den Hut vor ihm –***, raise one's hat to him (*also fig.*); ***in Betracht*** or ***Erwägung –***, take into consideration; ***die Stirn in Falten –***, frown, wrinkle one's brow; ***ins Geheimnis –***, take *or* let into the secret; ***in die Höhe –***, pull up, raise, hoist; ***etwas ins Lächerliche –***, make s.th. look ridiculous; ***in die Länge –***, draw *or* drag out, protract (*discussion*), spin out (*a story*); ***in Verdacht –***, suspect; ***ihn ins Vertrauen –***, take him into one's confidence; ***in Zweifel –***, (call in) question, doubt; ***den kürzeren –***, come off a loser, get the worst of it; ***das Los –***, draw lots; ***ein schiefes Maul –***, make a wry face; ***nach sich –***, entail, involve, be attended with, have as a consequence; ***eine Niete –***, draw a blank; (*fig.*) ***alle Register –***, pull out all the stops; ***einen Strich –***, draw a line; ***ihm das Fell über die Ohren –***, fleece him; ***Vergleiche –***, draw *or* make a comparison; ***vor Gericht –***, summon before a magistrate, bring to justice; ***Wasser –***, leak; ***sich*** (*Dat.*) ***etwas zu Gemüte –***, take a th. seriously; ***zu Rate –***, consult, (*coll.*) call in; ***zur Rechenschaft*** or ***Verantwortung –***, call to account (***wegen***, for); ***zur Strafe –***, punish, inflict a penalty on.
2. *irr.v.i.* **(a)** (*aux.* h.) 1. prove attractive, make an impression, have a strong appeal, go down well, attract (custom), draw (an audience), (*coll.*) catch on; 2. (*imp.*) be draughty; 3. (*of pains*) twinge, ache; ***der neue Professor zieht***, the new professor draws large audiences; ***dieser Grund zieht bei mir nicht***, this reason does not weigh with me *or* (*coll.*) cuts no ice with me; ***vom Leder –***, draw one's sword; ***es zieht hier***, there is a draught here; ***der Tee hat jetzt genug gezogen***, the tea has infused *or* (*coll.*) stood long enough; ***der Ofen zieht gut***, the stove draws well; ***die Bremse zieht nicht***, the brake does not hold; ***– an*** (*Dat.*), pull *or* tug at; (*fig.*) ***an einem Stricke*** or ***am gleichen Strange –***, have the same aim, play the same game; ***an einer Zigarre –***, have a puff of a cigar, puff at a cigar; ***an der Glocke –***, pull *or* ring the bell; ***mit dem König –***, move *or* play the king; (*Chess*) ***du mußt –***, your move; ***– lassen***, (*tea etc.*) allow to draw *or* infuse *or* (*coll.*) stand. **(b)** (*aux.* s.) move, go, pass, march, advance; grow (*of plants*); change one's residence, move, remove (***nach***, to), (*of servant*) leave one's post, quit, (*of birds*) migrate; ***das Gewitter ist südwärts gezogen***, the storm has passed over to the south; ***gezogen kommen***, come along, arrive; ***auf Wache –***, mount guard; ***in ein anderes Zimmer –***, change one's room; ***in den Krieg –***, go to war; ***in die Stadt –***, move to *or* go and live in the town; ***der Rauch zieht ins Zimmer***, the smoke is coming *or* drifting into the room; ***durch die Stadt –***, pass through the town; ***in die Fremde –***, go abroad; ***übers Meer –***, cross the sea; ***zu ihm –***, go to live with *or* take lodgings with him; (*Mil.*) ***zu Felde*** or ***ins Feld –***, take the field.
3. *irr.v.r.* stretch, extend; run; distort, become distorted, (*of wood*) warp, (*coll.*) give; (*of liquids*) become ropy *or* tacky; ***sich geschickt aus der Affäre –***, back *or* wriggle out of the affair, rise to the occasion; ***das Gebirge zieht sich weit ins Meer***, the mountains extend *or* stretch *or* run far out into the sea; ***die Strümpfe – sich nach dem Fuße***, the stockings give to the feet; ***sich in die Länge –***, go on and on, drag on interminably; ***sich ins Blaue –***, have a tinge of blue.

Ziehen, *n.* 1. drawing, pulling, hauling, draught, traction; 2. cultivation (*of plants*), rearing, breeding (*of animals*); 3. removal, move, (*of birds*) migration; 4. attraction, appeal; 5. rheumatic pain, twinge, ache. **Zieher,** *m.* (*Comm.*) drawer (*of a bill*).

Zieh|harmonika, *f.* accordion, concertina. **–kind,** *n.* foster-child. **–kraft,** *f. See* **Zugkraft. –maschine,** *f.* wire-drawing machine; stretcher. **–mutter,** *f.* (*dial.*) foster-mother. **–pflaster,** *n. See* **Zugpflaster. –schnur,** *f. See* **Zugschnur. –topf,** *m.* steeping *or* infusing vessel.

Ziehung ['tsi:uŋ], *f.* drawing (*of bills*), draw (*of lots etc.*). **Ziehungs|liste,** *f.* list of prizewinners (*in a lottery*). **–tag,** *m.* day of the draw (*lottery*).

Ziel [tsi:l], *n.* **(-(e)s,** *pl.* **-e)** aim; goal, end, object, objective, purpose, (*of a journey*) destination, (*Spt.*) finish, winning-post; target, mark; (*Comm.*) term; (*Mil.*) ***das – ansprechen***, aim at the target; ***am – seines Lebens***, at the end of his life; ***am – seiner Wünsche anlangen***, attain *or* reach the object of one's desire; (*Comm.*) ***auf kurzes –***, at short date; (*Comm.*) ***gegen*** or ***auf 3 Monate –***, with 3 months to pay *or* to run, with 3 months' grace *or* credit; ***das – aufsitzen lassen***, aim low; ***begrenztes –***, limited objective; (*Spt.*) ***durchs – gehen***, reach the finishing post, breast the tape; ***als Sieger durch – gehen***, be the winner, come in *or* finish first; (*fig.*) ***sein – erreichen***, reach one's goal, attain *or* gain one's end, achieve one's object *or* purpose; ***Maß und – halten***, keep within reasonable limits *or* bounds; ***ohne Zweck und –***, without aim or purpose; ***ein – setzen*** (*Dat.*), set bounds *or* limits to, put a stop to; ***sich*** (*Dat.*) ***ein – setzen***, aim at *or* for, have as one's aim; ***sich*** (*Dat.*) ***ein hohes – setzen***, aim high; ***das – treffen***, hit the mark; ***über das – hinausschießen***, overshoot *or* (*only fig.*) overstep the mark, (*fig.*) go too far; (*fig.*) ***er ist weit vom –***, he is quite beside the mark; ***weitgestecktes –***, unlimited objective; ***zum – führen***, succeed, be successful, (*coll.*) come off; ***nicht zum – führen***, fail, be unsuccessful, (*coll.*) not come off.

Ziel|anflug, *m.* (*Av.*) homing *or* bombing run. **–ansprache,** *f.* (*Mil.*) fire-order. **–aufnahme,** *f.* reconnaissance photograph. **–band,** *n.* (*Spt.*) tape; ***das – durchreißen***, break *or* breast the tape. **–beleuchter,** *m.* (*Av.*) pathfinder. **ziel|bewußt,** *adj.* 1. systematic, methodical; 2. *See* **–strebig. Ziel|bezeichnung,** *f.* target designation. **–bild,** *n.* pattern, model, ideal, (*Mil.*) target-image.

zielen ['tsi:lən], *v.i.* (take) aim (***auf*** (*Acc.*), ***nach***, at); (*fig.*) ***– auf*** (*Acc.*), aim at, tend to(wards); allude *or* refer to, (*coll.*) drive at; (*Gram.*) ***–des Zeitwort***, transitive verb.

Ziel|fernrohr, *n.* telescopic sight, sighting telescope. **–flug,** *m.* (*Av.*) homing (flight). **–gelände,** *n.* (*Av.*) target area. **–genauigkeit,** *f.* accuracy of aim. **–gerade,** *n.* (*Spt.*) home stretch, the straight. **–gerät,** *n.* sighting *or* aiming mechanism, (*Av.*) bomb-sight. **–hafen,** *m.* port of destination. **–kamera,** *f.* (*Spt.*) photo-finish camera. **–landung,** *f.* (*Av.*) precision landing. **–linie,** *f.* line of sight, (*Spt.*) finishing line. **ziellos,** *adj.* aimless, purposeless. **Ziel|peilung,** *f.* (*Av.*) homing. **–photographie,** *f.* (*Spt.*) photo-finish. **–punkt,** *m.* aiming point, aim, mark, (*fig.*) goal, objective, aim in view. **–reaktion,** *f.* (*Psych.*) purposive behaviour. **–richter,** *m.* (*Spt.*) judge. **–scheibe,** *f.* (practice) target; ***– des Spottes***, laughing-stock, butt. **–schiff,** *n.* target-ship. **–setzung,** *f.* (*fig.*) fixing one's aim; objective, target, aim *or* object in view. **ziel|sicher,** *adj.* unerring, sure of one's aim. **–strebig,** *adj.* purposeful, single-minded, clear-sighted, resolute, steadfast, (*pred.*) with an aim *or* purpose in view. **Zielstrebigkeit,** *f.* singleness *or* steadfastness of purpose, determination, resoluteness; purposeful behaviour.

Ziem [tsi:m], *m.* **(-(e)s,** *pl.* **-e)** rump (steak).

ziemen ['tsi:mən], *v.i.*, *v.r. See* **geziemen.**

Ziemer ['tsi:mər], *m.* buttock, hind quarter (*of animals*), haunch (*of venison*); penis (*of large animals*), pizzle.

ziemlich ['tsi:mlıç], **1.** *adj.* considerable, tolerable, passable, (*coll.*) middling, fair; (*obs.*) suitable, fit(ting), becoming; ***eine –e Anzahl***, a good *or* fair *or* (*coll.*) goodly number; ***eine –e Strecke***, a considerable *or* good *or* (*coll.*) fair distance, quite a distance, rather a long way. **2.** *adv.* tolerably, rather, fairly, (*coll.*) pretty; ***– alles***, practically everything; ***– ausführlich***, at some length; ***– gleich***, very nearly the same, (pretty) much the same; ***– gut***, pretty good, fair; ***– spät***, rather late; ***– viel***, rather *or* quite a lot, a good deal; ***– viel Menschen***, a good many *or* quite a few people.

ziepen ['tsi:pən], **1.** *v.t.* (*coll.*) pull, tug, pluck, tweak. **2.** *v.i.* 1. squeak, tweet, cheep; 2. (*imp.*) twinge, itch.

Zier [tsi:r], *f.* (-, *pl.* **-en**) ornament, embellishment; *see* **Zierde. Zieraffe,** *m.* fop, coxcomb; dressy woman.

Zierat ['tsi:ra:t], *m.* (**-(e)s,** *pl.* **-e**) decoration, adornment, finery, ornament(ation).

Zierde ['tsi:rdə], *f.* ornament, decoration, (*fig.*) ornament, credit (*für*, to).

zieren ['tsi:rən], **1.** *v.t.* adorn, ornament, embellish, decorate; garnish; be an ornament to, grace. **2.** *v.r.* (*fig.*) be affected, behave affectedly, put on airs, give o.s. airs; be prim *or* prudish; stand on ceremony, refuse out of politeness, (*coll.*) need pressing. **Ziererei** [–'raɪ], *f.* affection, airs (and graces).

Zier|garten, *m.* ornamental garden. **–kappe,** *f.* (*Motor.*) hub cap, wheel-trim. **–leiste,** *f.* (ornamental *or* decorative) edging, moulding, border, frieze, (*Typ.*) vignette, tail-piece.

zierlich ['tsi:rlɪç], *adj.* graceful, dainty, neat, elegant; slight, delicate. **Zierlichkeit,** *f.* grace, gracefulness, daintiness, neatness, elegance; delicacy.

Zier|nagel, *m.* (upholstery) stud. **–pflanze,** *f.* ornamental plant. **–puppe,** *f.* dressy woman. **–schrift,** *f.* ornate type, (*coll.*) fancy letters. **–vogel,** *m.* cage-bird.

Ziesel ['tsi:zəl], *m.* (*Zool.*) ground squirrel, souslik, (*Am.*) gopher (*Citellus*).

Ziest [tsi:st], *m.* (**-es,** *pl.* **-e**) (*Bot.*) hedge-nettle (*Stachys*).

Ziestig ['tsi:stɪç], *m.* (*dial.*) Tuesday.

Ziffer ['tsɪfər], *f.* (-, *pl.* **-n**) figure, numeral, digit, number; cipher; (*Typ.*) sub-paragraph, item. **Zifferblatt,** *n.* clock-face, face, dial. **ziffernmäßig,** *adj.* numerical, in figures. **Ziffer(n)-schrift,** *f.* cipher, code. **Ziffersystem,** *n.* numerical notation.

Zigarette [tsiga'rɛtə], *f.* cigarette. **Zigaretten|automat,** *m.* cigarette (slot-)machine. **–etui,** *n.* cigarette-case. **–marke,** *f.* brand of cigarettes. **–schachtel,** *f.* cigarette-packet. **–spitze,** *f.* cigarette-holder. **–stummel,** *m.* cigarette-end, (*coll.*) fag-end, stub, butt.

Zigarre [tsi'garə], *f.* cigar; (*coll.*) ***ihm eine – verpassen,*** give him a wigging *or* a dressing down, blow him up. **Zigarren|abschneider,** *m.* cigar-cutter. **–deckblatt,** *n.* wrapper. **–händler,** *m.* tobacconist. **–kiste,** *f.* cigar-box. **–laden,** *m.* tobacconist's (shop). **–spitze,** *f.* cigar-holder. **–stummel,** *m.* cigar-end. **–tasche,** *f.* cigar-case.

Ziger, *m.* (*Swiss*) *see* **Zieger(käse).**

Zigeuner(in) [tsi'gɔynər(ɪn)], *m.* (*f.*) gipsy (woman *or* girl). **Zigeuner|kapelle,** *f.* gipsy *or* Tzigane band. **–leben,** *n.* Bohemianism, roaming *or* vagrant life. **zigeunern,** *v.i.* (*dial.*) rove, roam *or* wander about; lead a vagrant life. **Zigeunersprache,** *f.* Romany. **Zigeunertum,** *n. See* **Zigeunerleben. Zigeuner|volk,** *n.* the gipsies. **–wagen,** *m.* gipsy caravan.

Zikade [tsi'ka:də], *f.* grasshopper.

Zille ['tsɪlə], *f.* barge.

Zilpzalp ['tsɪlptsalp], *m.* (*Orn.*) chiffchaff (*Phylloscopus collybita*).

Zimbel ['tsɪmbəl], *f.* (-, *pl.* **-n**) cymbal.

Zimmer ['tsɪmər], *n.* room, apartment, chamber; – ***mit zwei Betten, zweibettiges*** –, double-bedded room; ***Haus mit elf –n,*** eleven-roomed house; ***das – hüten,*** keep to one's room; ***möblierte –,*** furnished apartments. **Zimmer|antenne,** *f.* indoor aerial *or* (*Am.*) antenna. **–arbeit,** *f.* carpentry, timber-work. **–axt,** *f.*, **–beil,** *n.* carpenter's axe, hatchet. **–bekleidung,** *f.* wainscoting, panelling. **–bock,** *m.* joiner's trestle. **–decke,** *f.* ceiling. **–einrichtung,** *f.* furnishings, furniture; interior decoration.

Zimmerer ['tsɪmərər], *m. See* **Zimmermann.**

Zimmer|flucht, *f.* suite of rooms *or* apartments. **–genosse,** *m.* room-mate. **–gesell(e),** *m.* journeyman carpenter. **–gymnastik,** *f.* indoor exercises. **–handwerk,** *n.* carpentry; carpenter's trade. **–herr,** *m.* gentleman lodger. **–holz,** *n.* timber, building material. **–kamerad,** *m. See* **–genosse. –mädchen,** *n.* chambermaid, housemaid. **–mann,** *m.* (*pl.* **¨–er** *or* **-leute**) carpenter, joiner; (*Naut.*) shipwright; (*coll.*) ***ihm zeigen, wo der – das Loch gelassen hat,*** show him the door.

zimmern ['tsɪmərn], *v.t.* timber; frame, joint; build, make, construct, (*fig.*) frame, fabricate.

Zimmer|nachweis, *m.* letting agency, lodgings bureau. **–pflanze,** *f.* pot- *or* indoor plant. **–platz,** *m.* timber *or* lumber yard. **–polier, –polierer,** *m.* foreman carpenter. **–spiel,** *n.* indoor game, parlour-game. **–tanne,** *f.* (*Bot.*) Norfolk Island pine (*Araucaria excelsa*). **–temperatur,** *f.* room temperature. **–vermieter,** *m.* landlord, lodging-house keeper. **–vermieterin,** *f.* landlady. **–werk,** *n. See* **–arbeit.**

Zimmet ['tsɪmət], *m.* (*obs.*) *see* **Zimt.**

zimperlich ['tsɪmpərlɪç], *adj.* prim, prudish; affected; super- *or* hypersensitive, squeamish. **Zimperlichkeit,** *f.* primness, prudery; affectation, super-sensitiveness, squeamishness.

Zimt [tsɪmt], *m.* cinnamon; (*coll.*) bosh, tosh, piffle; (*coll.*) ***der ganze –,*** the whole caboodle. **Zimt|blüte,** *f.* cinnamon-flower, cassia bud. **–säure,** *f.* cinnamic acid.

Zindel(taft) ['tsɪndəl(taft)], *m.* light taffeta.

Zingulum ['tsɪŋgulum], *n.* (**-s,** *pl.* **-la** *or* **-s**) girdle (*of a R.C. priest*).

Zink [tsɪŋk], *n.* (*Austr. m.*) zinc; spelter. **Zink|asche,** *f.* dross of zinc. **–ätzung,** *f.* zinc etching, zincography. **–blech,** *n.* sheet-zinc. **–blumen,** *f.pl* zinc bloom, hydrozincile.

Zinke ['tsɪŋkə], *f.* 1. prong, tine; spike; tooth (*of a comb*); (*Carp.*) tenon, dovetail; 2. (*Mus.*) cornet; 3. card-sharper's *or* beggar's secret mark. **Zinken,** *m. See* **Zink**; (*sl.*) beak, boko.

[1]**zinken** ['tsɪŋkən], **1.** *v.t.* (*Cards*) mark (secretly); (*Carp.*) join with mortise and tenon; furnish with spikes *or* prongs. **2.** *v.i.* play the cornet.

[2]**zinken,** *adj.* (of) zinc.

Zinkenbläser ['tsɪŋkənblɛ:zər], **Zinkenist,** *m.* (**-en,** *pl.* **-en**) (*dial.*) cornet player. **Zinken|register,** *n.*, **–zug,** *m.* (*organ*) cornet register *or* stop.

zinkhaltig ['tsɪŋkhaltɪç], *adj.* zincic, zinciferous.

–zinkig ['tsɪŋkɪç], *adj.suff.* -spiked, -pronged.

Zink|kalk, *m. See* **–asche. –salbe,** *f.* zinc ointment. **–vitriol,** *m. or n.* sulphate of zinc, white copperas. **–wasser,** *n.* zinc lotion.

Zinn [tsɪn], *n.* tin; pewter, tinware.

Zinne ['tsɪnə], *f.* pinnacle, battlement.

zinnen ['tsɪnən], *adj. See* **zinnern.**

zinnen|artig, –förmig, *adj.* crenel(l)ated. **Zinnen|lücke,** *f.* crenelle, loophole. **–werk,** *n.* crenel(l)ated wall, embattled work.

zinnern ['tsɪnərn], *adj.* (of) tin, pewter; (*Chem.*) stannic. **Zinn|folie,** *f.* tinfoil. **–geschirr,** *n.* pewter vessel. **–gießer,** *m.* tinfounder. **zinnhaltig,** *adj.* stanniferous. **Zinn|kies,** *m.* tin pyrites, sulphuret of tin. **–kraut,** *n.* (*Bot.*) horse-tail, Dutch rush (*Equisetum hyemale*). **–krug,** *m.* pewter mug. **–lot,** *n.* soft solder.

Zinnober [tsɪ'no:bər], *m.* (*Austr. n.*) 1. cinnabar, red mercury sulphide; 2. (*sl.*) piffle, poppycock. **zinnober|farbig, –rot,** *adj.* vermilion.

Zinn|oxyd, *n.* stannic oxide. **–oxydul,** *n.* stannous oxide. **–säure,** *f.* stannic acid. **–soldat,** *m.* tin soldier. **–stufe,** *f.* tin-ore. **–waren,** *f.pl.* pewter, tinware.

Zins [tsɪns], *m.* 1. (**-es,** *pl.* **-e**) tax, duty, (*B.*) tribute; 2. (**-es,** *pl.* **-en**) (ground-)rent; ***mit – und Zinseszinsen,*** in full measure; *see* **Zinsen. zinsbar,** *adj. See* **zins|bringend, –pflichtig. Zins|bauer,** *m.* (*Hist.*) copyholder, tenant farmer. **–brief,** *m.* (*Hist.*) copyhold deeds. **zinsbringend,** *adj.* interest-bearing, (*pred.*) bearing *or* yielding interest; – ***anlegen,*** put out at interest, invest. **Zins|darlehen,** *n.* interest-bearing loan. **–einkommen,** *n.* income from interest *or* investments.

Zinsen ['tsɪnsən], *pl.* (*see* **Zins,** 2.) interest; ***aufgelaufene –,*** accumulated interest; – ***berechnen,***

charge interest; *die – zum Kapital schlagen,* allow the interest to accumulate; *– tragen,* bear interest; (*fig.*) *mit – heimzahlen* return with interest.

Zinserhöhung ['zɪnsˀɛrhø:uŋ], *f.* increase in the interest-rate.

Zinseszins ['tsɪnsəstsɪns], *m.* compound interest; *see under* **Zins.**

zinsfrei ['tsɪnsfraɪ], *adj.* free of interest; rent-free, freehold. **Zins|fuß,** *m.* rate of interest. **–groschen,** *n.* (*B.*) tribute-money. **–gut,** *n.* leasehold. **–herabsetzung,** *f.* reduction in the rate of interest. **–herr,** *m.* (*Hist.*) lord of the manor. **–knechtschaft,** *f.* (*Nat. Soc.*) capitalist exploitation of the economy. **–lehen,** *n.* (*Hist.*) copyhold fief. **zinslos,** *adj. See* **zinsfrei. Zins|mann,** *m.* (*pl.* **-leute**) (*obs.*) *see* **–bauer. –mehraufwand,** *m.* net interest paid. **–mehrertrag,** *m.* net interest earned. **Zinsner,** *m.* (*obs.*), **Zins|pächter,** *m. See* **–bauer. zinspflichtig,** *adj.* subject to tax *or* rent, tributary. **Zins|rechnung,** *f.* interest-account; calculation of interest. **–satz,** *m. See* **–fuß. –schein,** *m.* dividend-warrant, coupon. **zins|tragend,** *adj. See* **–bringend. Zinswucher,** *m.* usury.

Zionismus [tsio'nɪsmus], *m.* Zionism. **Zionist(in),** *m.*(*f.*), **zionistisch,** *adj.* Zionist.

Zipfel ['tsɪpfəl], *m.* tip, point, end, (*of handkerchief*) corner, (*of coat*) lappet; (*Anat.*) lobe, tongue; (*fig.*) *am rechten – anfassen,* tackle in the right way *or* from the right angle; (*fig.*) *bei allen vier –n anfassen,* get a good *or* firm hold of. **zipfelig,** *adj.* pointed, peaked. **Zipfel|klappen,** *f.pl.* (*Anat.*) tricuspid and mitral valves (*of the heart*). **–mütze,** *f.* nightcap, peaked cap.

Zipolle [tsi'pɔlə], *f.* (*dial.*) onion, shallot, scallion.

Zippammer ['tsɪpˀamər], *f.* (*Orn.*) rock-bunting (*Emberiza cia*). **Zippe,** *f.* (*Orn.*) *see* **Singdrossel.**

Zipperlein ['tsɪpərlaɪn], *n.* (*coll.*) gout.

Zirbe ['tsɪrbə], *f.*, **Zirbel,** *f.* (-, *pl.* **-n**) *or m.* (*Bot.*) stone-pine (*Pinus cembra*). **Zirbel|drüse,** *f.* (*Anat.*) pineal gland. **–kiefer,** *f. See* **Zirbe.**

zirka ['tsɪrka], *adv.* about, approximately, roughly, in the neighbourhood of, (*following*) or thereabouts.

Zirkel ['tsɪrkəl], *m.* (pair of) compasses *or* dividers; (*fig.*) circle, group, coterie, gathering, company; (*Poet.*) *der goldene –,* the crown; (*fig.*) *alles mit dem – abmessen,* be precise *or* painstaking in everything one does. **zirkeln, 1.** *v.t.* (*usu. fig.*) measure off, mark out. **2.** *v.i.* move in a circle. **Zirkelschluß,** *m.* vicious circle.

Zirkon [tsɪr'ko:n], *m.* (**-s,** *pl.* **-e**) (*Chem.*) zircon, zirconium silicate. **Zirkon|erde,** *f.* zirconia. **–lampe,** *f.* zirconium lamp.

Zirkular [tsɪrku'la:r], *n.* (**-s,** *pl.* **-e**) circular, pamphlet, brochure, broad-sheet. **zirkulieren,** *v.i.* circulate; *– lassen,* pass *or* send round, circulate.

Zirkus ['tsɪrkus], *m.* (-, *pl.* **-se**) circus; (*coll.*) hurly-burly.

Zirpe ['tsɪrpə], *f.* cricket, grasshopper, *pl.* Cicadidae. **zirpen,** *v.i.* chirp, cheep, chirrup.

Zirruswolke ['tsɪrusvɔlkə], *f.* cirrus cloud.

zischeln ['tsɪʃəln], *v.t., v.i.* whisper, say (*v.t.*) *or* speak (*v.i.*) in an undertone *or* under one's breath.

zischen ['tsɪʃən], *v.t., v.i.* (*of a p., animals*) hiss, (*v.i. only*) (*of liquids*) fizzle, sizzle, (*of flying objects*) whiz; (*sl.*) *einen –,* knock one back. **Zischen,** *n.* hiss(ing), fizz(ing), sizzling, whizzing, (*Theat.*) hissing, hisses. **Zischlaut,** *m.* hissing noise, (*Phonet.*) sibilant.

Ziselierarbeit [tsizə'li:rˀarbaɪt], *f.* chased work. **ziselieren,** *v.t.* chase, chisel, engrave.

Zisterne [tsɪs'tɛrnə], *f.* cistern, (water-)tank.

Zitadelle [tsita'dɛlə], *f.* citadel.

Zitat [tsi'ta:t], *n.* (**-(e)s,** *pl.* **-e**) quotation; *falsches –,* misquotation.

Zither ['tsɪtər], *f.* (-, *pl.* **-n**) zither, (*in antiquity*) cithara.

zitieren [tsi'ti:rən], *v.t.* **1.** quote, cite; **2.** (*Law*) summon, cite; invoke (*spirits*).

Zitronat [tsitro'na:t], *n.* candied (lemon-)peel.

Zitrone [tsi'tro:nə], *f.* lemon.

Zitronellengras [tsɪtro'nɛləngra:s], *n. See* **Zitronengras.**

Zitronen|falter, *m.* brimstone butterfly (*Gonopteryx rhamni*). **–fink,** *m.* (*Orn.*) *see* **–zeisig. zitronengelb,** *adj.* lemon-yellow, citrine. **Zitronen|gras,** *n.* (*Bot.*) citonella (*Andropogon nardus*). **–limonade,** *f.* (still) lemonade, lemon squash. **–presse,** *f.* lemon squeezer. **zitronensauer,** *adj.* (*Chem.*) citrate of. **Zitronen|säure,** *f.* citric acid. **–scheibe,** *f.* slice of lemon. **–stelze,** *f.* (*Orn.*) yellow-headed wagtail (*Motacilla citreola*). **–wasser,** *n. See* **–limonade. –zeisig,** *m.* (*Orn.*) citril finch (*Carduelis citrinella*).

Zitter|aal ['tsɪtər–], *m.* (*Ichth.*) electric eel (*Gymnotus electricus*). **–gras,** *n.* (*Bot.*) quaking-grass (*Briza media*). **zitterig,** *adj.* trembling, shaky, shivery, (*coll.*) trembly, (*of voice*) faltering, tremulous, (*old age*) doddering, (*coll.*) doddery.

zittern ['tsɪtərn], *v.i.* tremble, shiver, shake, quiver, quake (*vor* (*Dat.*), with); vibrate; *mir – alle Glieder,* I am shaking in every limb; *an allen Gliedern –,* be quaking in one's shoes, be trembling *or* shaking all over. **Zittern,** *n.* trembling, shaking, shiver(s); vibration(s); *mit – und Zagen,* with fear and trembling, shaking with fear.

Zitter|pappel, *f.* (*Bot.*) aspen (*Populus tremula*). **–rochen,** *m.* (*Ichth.*) torpedo-fish, electric ray. **–spiel,** *n.* spillikins. **–stimme,** *f.* quaking *or* tremulous voice. **–wels,** *m.* (*Ichth.*) thunder-fish, electric catfish.

Zitwer ['tsɪtvər], *m.* (*Bot.*) zedoary (*Curcuma zedoaria*).

Zitz [tsɪts], *m.* (**-es,** *pl.* **-e**) chintz, printed calico.

Zitze ['tsɪtsə], *f.* nipple, teat, dug, (*vulg.*) tit.

zivil [tsi'vi:l], *adj.* civil; civilian; (*coll.*) (*of prices*) moderate, reasonable; *–e Verteidigung,* civil defence. **Zivil,** *n.* **1.** civil body, civil population, civilians; **2.** civilian *or* plain clothes, (*coll.*) civvies, mufti.

Zivil|angestellte(r), *m., f.* civilian employee. **–bevölkerung,** *f.* civilian population, civilians; non-combatants. **–courage,** *f.* courage of one's convictions. **–dienst,** *m.* Civil Service. **–ehe,** *f.* civil marriage. **–gerichtsbarkeit,** *f.* civil justice.

Zivilisation [tsivilizatsi'o:n], *f.* civilization. **zivilisatorisch** [–a'to:rɪʃ], *adj.* civilizing. **zivilisieren** [–'zi:rən], *v.t.* civilize.

Zivilist [tsivi'lɪst], *m.* (**-en,** *pl.* **-en**) civilian, non-combatant.

Zivil|klage, *f. See* **–prozeß. –kleidung,** *f. See* **Zivil,** 2. **–leben,** *n.* civilian life, (*sl.*) civvy-street. **–liste,** *f.* Civil List. **–luftfahrt,** *f.* civil aviation. **–person,** *f. See* **Zivilist. –prozeß,** *m.* civil suit *or* action. **–recht,** *n.* civil law. **zivilrechtlich,** *adj., adv.* under *or* according to civil law; *– verfolgen,* bring a civil action against, sue. **Zivil|rechtsfall,** *m.,* **–sache,** *f. See* **–prozeß. –standsamt,** *n.* (*Swiss*) registry office. **–standsbeamte(r),** *m.* (*Swiss*) registrar for births, marriages and deaths. **–trauung,** *f. See* **–ehe. –versorgung,** *f.* guarantee of civil employment for ex-servicemen. **–verwaltung,** *f.* civil government *or* administration; *see* **–dienst.**

Zobel ['tso:bəl], *m.* **1.** (*Zool.*) sable (*Mustela zibellina*); **2.** (*also* **Zobelpelz**) sable-fur.

Zober ['tso:bər], *m.* (two-handled) tub; (*for butter*) firkin.

zockeln ['tsɔkəln], *v.i.* (*aux.* s.) (*dial.*) dawdle, saunter, amble. **zocken,** *v.i.* (*aux.* s.) (*dial.*) toddle.

Zodiakus [tso'di:akus], *m.* zodiac.

Zofe ['tso:fə], *f.* (lady's) maid.

zog [tso:k], *see* **ziehen.**

zögern ['tsø:gərn], *v.i.* hesitate, linger, waver, (*coll.*) shilly-shally; delay, tarry, linger, lag; *– mit,* delay, defer; *er zögerte nicht, zu kommen,* he lost no time in coming. **Zögern,** *n.* hesitancy; hesitation, delay; wavering, (*coll.*) shilly-shallying; *ohne –,* without delay *or* (a moment's) hesitation, unhesitatingly. **zögernd,** *adj.* hesitant, hesitating, dilatory; (*of a th.*) slow, gradual.

Zögling ['tsø:klɪŋ], *m.* (**-s,** *pl.* **-e**) inmate of an approved school; (*obs.*) pupil in a boarding-school, pupil under a private tutor; (*fig., obs.*) disciple, follower.

Zohe ['tso:ə], *f.* (*dial.*) bitch.

Zölestin [tsø:lɛs'ti:n], *m.* celestine, celestite, strontium sulphate.

Zölibat [tsøli'ba:t], *n. or m.* celibacy; bachelordom.

[1]**Zoll** [tsɔl], *m.* (**-(e)s,** *pl.* -) inch; (*Astr.*) digit; ***jeder – ein König,*** every inch a king; ***auf – und Linie,*** in every respect, (*coll.*) to a T.

[2]**Zoll,** *m.* (**-(e)s,** *pl.* **⸚e**) custom(s), duty, (*roads, bridges etc.*) toll, dues; (*fig.*) tribute; ***beim – angeben,*** declare at the customs, enter at the custom-house; (*fig.*) ***den – der Dankbarkeit entrichten,*** pay one's debt of gratitude; (*fig.*) ***der Natur den – entrichten,*** pay one's debt to nature; (*fig.*) ***seinen – fordern,*** take its toll.

Zoll|abfertigung, *f.* custom(s) clearance. **-abfertigungsstelle,** *f.* custom-barrier.

Zollager ['tsɔlla:gər], *n.* bonded warehouse.

Zollamt ['tsɔlˀamt], *n.* custom-house. **zollamtlich,** *adj.* ***-e Untersuchung,*** customs examination; ***unter -em Verschluß,*** in bond. **Zoll|angabe,** *f.* customs declaration. **-aufschlag,** *m.* additional duty. **-aufseher,** *m.* customs inspector. **-ausschließzone,** *f.* free territory. **-beamte(r),** *m.* customs officer. **-begleitschein,** *m.* bond-warrant. **-behörde,** *f.* customs and excise *or* inland revenue department. **-breit,** *n.* ***kein – Landes,*** not an inch of territory. **-einfuhrschein,** *m.* bill of entry. **-einnehmer,** *m.* toll-collector.

zollen ['tsɔlən], *v.t.* render (*what is due*) (*Dat.*, to); ***Achtung –,*** show (due) respect; ***Anerkennung –,*** pay tribute; ***Beifall –,*** applaud; ***Dank –,*** thank, express one's gratitude; ***Tränen –,*** shed tears (*Dat.*, for).

Zoll|erklärung, *f. See* **-angabe. -fahndungsbeamte(r),** *m.* preventive officer. **zollfrei,** *adj.* duty-free; (*Prov.*) ***Gedanken sind –,*** thought is free. **Zoll|freiheit,** *f.* exemption from duty. **-gebühr,** *f.* duty, customs dues. **-gefälle,** *n.* inland revenue. **-gesetz,** *n.* tariff law. **-haus,** *n.* custom-house, (*Hist.*) toll-booth. **-hinterziehung,** *f.* evasion of duty.

zollig ['tsɔlɪç], *adj.* inch-thick. **-zöllig, -zollig,** *adj. suff.* (*with numbers*) -inch.

Zoll|kontrolle, *f.* customs examination. **-krieg,** *m.* tariff war.

Zöllner ['tsœlnər], *m.* customs *or* (*Hist.*) toll collector; (*B.*) publican.

zollpflichtig ['tsɔlpflɪçtɪç], *adj.* liable to duty, dutiable. **Zoll|politik,** *f.* customs policy. **-revision,** *f. See* **-kontrolle. -satz,** *m.* rate of duty, tariff. **-schein,** *m.* certificate of clearance. **-schiff,** *n.* revenue-cutter. **-schranke,** *f.* customs-barrier. **-schutz,** *m.* (tariff-)protection. **-speicher,** *m. See* **Zollager. -stock,** *m.* foot-rule. **-straße,** *f.* turnpike *or* toll-road. **-tarif,** *m.* tariff, schedule of dues; *see also* **-satz. -union,** *f.*, **-verein,** *m.* customs-union. **-vergünstigung,** *f.* preferential tariff. **-verschluß,** *m.* customs seal, leads, bond; ***unter – lassen,*** leave in bond; ***Waren unter –,*** bonded goods. **-verwaltung,** *f. See* **-behörde. -vorschriften,** *f.pl.* customs regulations. **zollweise,** *adv.* inch by inch, by inches.

Zönakel [tsø'na:kəl], *n.* monastery refectory.

Zone ['tso:nə], *f.* zone, region; ***die heiße (kalte) (gemäßigte) –,*** the torrid (frigid) (temperate) zone; (*Rad.*) ***tote –,*** area of poor reception. **Zonen|grenze,** *f.* zone boundary (*usu. the frontier between Federal Germany and the Democratic Republic*). **-karte,** *f.* unrestricted-travel ticket (*valid within prescribed limits*). **-linse,** *f.* (*lighthouse*) echelon-lens.

Zoologe [tso:o'lo:gə], *m.* (**-n,** *pl.* **-n**) zoologist. **Zoologie** [–'gi:], *f.* zoology. **zoologisch,** *adj.* zoological.

Zopf [tsɔpf], *m.* (**-(e)s,** *pl.* **⸚e**) pigtail, plait, tress; (*fig.*) antiquated tradition, obsolete custom; pedantry; pettifoggery; (*coll.*) ***ihm auf den – spucken,*** give him a wigging. **Zopf|band,** *n.* hair-ribbon. **-holz,** *n.* (*dial.*) top branches. **zopfig,** *adj.* (*fig.*) antiquated, old-fashioned; pedantic, pettifogging. **Zopfstil,** *m.* (*Art*) late Rococo (style).

Zorn [tsɔrn], *m.* anger, rage, wrath, (*Poet.*) ire, choler; passion, temper; ***seinen – an ihm auslassen, die Schale seines -s über ihn ausgießen,*** vent one's anger *or* rage *or* pour out the vials of one's wrath on him; ***ihn in – bringen,*** enrage *or* anger *or* infuriate him. **zornentbrannt,** *adj.* furious, fuming, incensed; boiling *or* fuming with rage. **Zorn(es)|ader,** *f.* frontal vein. **-anfall, -ausbruch,** *m.* fit of anger *or* rage. **-röte,** *f.* flush of anger. **zornig,** *adj.* angry (***auf*** (*Acc.*), at (*a th.*), with (*a p.*)), irate, (*pred.*) in a temper *or* rage *or* passion; ***– werden,*** get angry, fly into a rage *or* temper.

Zote ['tso:tə], *f.* obscenity; obscene *or* ribald *or* (*coll.*) dirty *or* smutty joke; ***-n reißen,*** make obscene jokes, tell dirty stories, (*coll.*) talk smut. **zotenhaft,** *adj.* obscene, lewd, indecent, bawdy, (*coll.*) filthy, smutty. **Zotenreißer,** *m.* obscene *or* bawdy talker, retailer of dirty jokes. **zotig,** *adj. See* **zotenhaft.**

Zotte ['tsɔtə], *f.* lock, tuft (of hair), (*Anat.*) villus; (*dial.*) spout, rose (*of watering-can*); (*dial.*) tassel.

Zottel ['tsɔtəl], *f.* (-, *pl.* **-n**) (*dial.*) tuft, tassel. **zotteln,** *v.i.* (*aux.* s.) shuffle along, dawdle. **Zottelwicke,** *f.* (*Bot.*) hairy vetch (*Vicia villosa*).

Zotten|anhang, *m.* (*Anat.*) villous appendage. **-haut,** *f.* (*Anat.*) chorion. **zottig,** *adj.* shaggy, matted, tufted; downy, hairy, (*Anat., Bot.*) villous.

Zötus ['tsø:tus], *m.* (-, *pl.* **Zöten**) division (*of a class in school*), (parallel) set *or* form.

zu [tsu:], **I.** *prep.* (*Dat.*)
I. (*direction*) to, towards, up to, (*Poet.*) unto; **(a)** (*of movement*) ***– ihm gehen,*** go to (see) him; ***– Berg fahren,*** go uphill *or* upstream *or* against the stream; ***– Bett gehen,*** go to bed; ***– Boden stürzen,*** fall to the ground, fall down; ***-m Essen gehen,*** go to dinner *etc.*, (*coll.*) go and eat; ***– Felde ziehen,*** go to war, take the field, (*also fig.*) take up arms; ***-m Fenster hinaus,*** out of *or* (out) through the window; ***von Kopf – Fuß,*** from head to foot, from top to toe; ***ihm – Füßen fallen,*** throw o.s. *or* fall at his feet; ***das Blut*** (*or fig.* ***Erfolg*** *etc.*) ***steigt mir – Kopfe,*** the blood (*or* success *etc.*) goes to my head; ***– Tal fahren,*** go downhill *or* downstream *or* with the stream; ***– Tisch gehen,*** go in to dinner; ***-r Tür herein,*** in at *or* by *or* through the door; **(b)** (*fig. of development*) ***die Haare stehen mir – Berge,*** my hair rises; ***es kam mir – Bewußtsein,*** I became aware; ***-m Dichter geboren,*** born (to be) a poet; ***-r Bühne gehen,*** go on the stage; ***– Ende bringen (gehen),*** bring (come) to an end; ***ihm -r Ehre gereichen,*** redound to his honour; ***sich*** (*Dat.*) ***ihn -m Feind machen,*** make an enemy of him; ***-r Folge haben,*** have as a result *or* consequence; ***sie -r Frau nehmen,*** take her as one's wife; ***mir – Gefallen,*** to please me, for my sake; ***ihm etwas – Gemüte führen,*** impress s.th. on him; ***– Gesicht bekommen,*** catch sight *or* a glimpse of; ***-m Glück,*** fortunately, happily; ***sich -m Guten wenden,*** take a turn for the better; ***– Grunde gehen,*** *see* **zugrunde**; ***es geht mir – Herzen,*** it touches *or* moves me deeply; ***– Herzen nehmen,*** take to heart; ***– Kreuze kriechen,*** humble o.s., eat humble pie, (*coll.*) climb down; ***es ist -m Lachen,*** it is laughable; ***mir ist nicht -m Lachen,*** I am in no laughing mood; ***ihm – Leibe gehen,*** attack, tackle (*a p.*), grapple with, tackle (*a problem*); ***-m König machen,*** put on the throne; ***sich*** (*Dat.*) ***-m Muster nehmen,*** take as a model; ***es kommt mir – Ohren,*** I hear, it comes to my ears; ***-r Ordnung rufen,*** call to order; ***– Paaren treiben,*** put to flight, rout; ***– Papier bringen,*** put (down) in writing *or* in black and white; ***mit sich – Rate gehen,*** think things over; ***– Rate ziehen,*** consult, (*coll.*) call in; ***-r Rede stellen,*** call to account, take to task; ***-r Ruhe***

gehen, retire for the night; – ***Schaden kommen,*** (*of a p.*) meet with an accident, sustain *or* suffer injury, be injured, (*of p. or th.*) come to harm, (*of a th.*) be harmed *or* damaged; ***–r Schau tragen,*** make a show of, display, parade, flaunt; ***–r Schau stellen,*** (put on) display, exhibit; ***nur –r Schau,*** only for show; – ***Staub werden,*** turn to dust; – ***Tage bringen,*** *see* **zutage**; – ***nichts taugen,*** be good for nothing, be no use at all; ***–m Theater gehen,*** go on the stage; ***–r Verantwortung ziehen,*** hold responsible, call to account; ***–r Verfügung stehen,*** be available, be at (*Dat.*, his) disposal; ***–r Verfügung stellen,*** make available, place at (*Dat.*, his) disposal; (*fig.*) – ***Wasser werden,*** come to naught, go up in smoke; – ***Werke gehen,*** set to work; – ***welchem Zweck?*** to *or* for what purpose? to what end?
2. (*place*) **(a)** at, on, in; – ***Berlin,*** in Berlin; – ***ebener Erde,*** on the ground floor; ***ihm – Fußen,*** at his feet; – ***Gericht sitzen,*** sit in *or* pass judgement (***über*** (*Acc.*), on); – ***ihm halten,*** stand *or* (*coll.*) stick by him; ***–r Hand,*** at hand; ***–r rechten Hand,*** *see* ***–r Rechten***; ***–r linken Hand heiraten,*** marry morganatically; – ***Hause,*** at home; ***–r Not,*** in case of need *or* necessity, if necessary, if need be; – ***Paaren,*** in couples; ***–r Rechten,*** on *or* at the right hand *or* the right-hand side; ***–r See,*** at sea; ***ihm –r Seite,*** at his side; – ***Wasser und Lande,*** by land and sea; **(b)** by (the side of), beside, next to, with; ***er setzte sich – mir,*** he sat down beside *or* (*coll.*) by me *or* at my side; ***Milch –m Kaffee,*** milk with one's coffee; ***im Vergleich –,*** in comparison with; ***im Verhältnis –,*** in proportion to; – ***meiner Verteidigung,*** in my defence;
3. (*time*) – ***Abend,*** in the evening; – ***Anfang,*** in *or* at the beginning; ***–m ersten,*** in the first place; – ***guter Letzt,*** finally, last of all, to finish up with; ***–m letzten Male,*** for the last time; – ***Nacht,*** at *or* by night, in the night(-time); ***–r Unzeit,*** at an unsuitable *or* inconvenient time, inopportunely, unseasonably, prematurely; ***–r Zeit,*** at the time; at the present time; – ***rechter*** or ***–r rechten Zeit,*** at the right time, opportunely; – ***Zeiten,*** at times; – ***Zeiten*** (*Gen.*), in the time *or* days of;
4. (*relation*) ***ihm – Liebe, aus Liebe – ihm,*** out of love for him; ***Bananen – 60 Pf. das Stück,*** bananas at 60 Pf. each; ***das Pfund – 60 Pf.,*** a pound for 60 Pf., 60 Pf. a pound; (*Spt.*) ***5 – 3,*** (*score*) 5 to *or* against 3; ***–m besten,*** for the best; (*fig.*) ***–m besten haben,*** make fun of, pull (*s.o.'s*) leg; – ***Dutzenden (Hunderten),*** in (their) dozens (hundreds), by the dozen (hundred); – ***Fuß,*** on foot; ***–r Hälfte fertig,*** half finished; ***–m Lohne für,*** as a reward for, in return for; ***ihn –m Narren haben*** or ***halten,*** make a fool of him; – ***Recht bestehen,*** be true *or* valid; ***–m Scherz,*** as a joke, in *or* for fun; – ***Schiff,*** by ship; ***–m Teil,*** in part, partly, partially; ***–m größten Teil,*** for the most part; ***ihm –m Trotz,*** to spite him, in defiance of him; ***–m wenigsten*** or ***mindesten,*** at (the very) least; – ***zweien,*** in twos, two at a time; – ***zweit (dritt),*** in pairs (threes).
2. *adv.* 1. (*before adj. or adv.*) too; ***gar – viel,*** (all *or* far) too much; ***sich – sehr anstrengen,*** over-strain o.s.; – ***neugierig,*** over-inquisitive; – ***schön um wahr zu sein,*** too good to be true; 2. (*ellipt. for* **zumachen, zuschließen**) closed, shut; (***mach' die***) ***Tür –!*** shut the door! ***die Tür ist nicht –,*** the door is not shut *or* closed *or* (*coll.*) to; 3. (*ellipt. for* **zufahren, zugehen**) on(wards); ***der Küste*** or ***auf die Küste –,*** towards the shore, shorewards; ***geh –! nur*** or ***immer –!*** go ahead! go on! get on! keep on! ***Glück –!*** good luck (to you)! ***schreibe nur –!*** keep on writing; 4. ***ab und –,*** now and then, from time to time, at times.
3. *part.* 1. (*with inf.*) ***ich habe – arbeiten,*** I have work to do, I have to work; ***um mich – täuschen,*** in order to deceive me; ***anstatt selbst – gehen,*** instead of going oneself; ***ohne es – wissen,*** without knowing (it); ***ich erinnere mich, ihn gesehen – haben,*** I remember seeing *or* having seen him; 2. (*inf. used passively after sein*) ***es ist*** or ***steht – hoffen,*** it is to be hoped, it may be hoped for; ***was ist – tun?*** what is to be done? ***das ist – erwarten,*** that is to be expected; ***er ist nicht – sprechen,*** he is not available, he cannot see anyone; ***es ist – unterscheiden,*** a distinction must be made; ***das ist – kaufen,*** that is for sale, that may be purchased; ***Haus – verkaufen,*** house for sale; 3. (*with pres. p. as attrib. adj.*) ***ein – verbessernder Fehler,*** an error to be corrected *or* requiring correction; ***ein – erwartendes Ereignis,*** an event that may be expected; ***ein sorgfältig – erwägender Plan,*** a plan requiring careful consideration; ***eine nicht – ertragende Hitze,*** unendurable heat.

zualler|erst [–'alərʔe:rst], *adv.* first of all. **–letzt,** *adv.* last of all.

zuballern ['tsu:balərn], *v.t.* (*coll.*) slam (shut *or* to).

Zubau ['tsu:bau], *m.* annex(e); extension, addition (*to a building*). **zubauen, 1.** *v.t.* 1. build *or* wall in *or* up, block (*the view*); 2. build (*an extension*) (**an** (*Acc.*), on to). **2.** *v.i.* – **an** (*Acc.*), extend, make extensions to (*a building*); *see* **anbauen.**

Zubehör ['tsu:bəhø:r], *n. or m.* (**-s.** *pl.* **-e** (*Swiss* **-den**)) appurtenances, accessories, attachments, fittings; ***Wohnung von 6 Zimmern mit –,*** 6-roomed apartment with offices *or* with all conveniences; – ***zu den Speisen,*** dressing, seasoning. **Zubehörteil,** *m.* accessory, fitting, attachment.

zubeißen ['tsu:baɪsən], *irr.v.i.* (have *or* take a) bite, (*of dog*) bite, snap; (*coll.*) ***tüchtig –,*** eat heartily, (*sl.*) tuck in.

zubekommen ['tsu:bəkɔmən], *irr.v.t.* 1. get in addition *or* into the bargain; 2. (*coll.*) (manage to) get (*door etc.*) shut.

zubenam(s)t ['tsu:bənam(s)t], **zubenannt,** *adj.* (sur)named.

Zuber ['tsu:bər], *m. See* **Zober.**

zubereiten ['tsu:bəraɪtən], *v.t.* prepare, finish; dress (*hides, salads*), dispense (*medicine*), mix (*a drink*). **Zubereitung,** *f.* preparation; dressing.

zubilligen ['tsu:bɪlɪgən], *v.t.* grant, allow, concede. **Zubilligung,** *f.* acknowledgement, acquiescence, compliance; – ***mildernder Umstände,*** allowing for extenuating circumstances, making allowances.

zubinden ['tsu:bɪndən], *irr.v.t.* bind *or* tie up, bandage; ***ihm die Augen –,*** blindfold him.

zubleiben ['tsu:blaɪbən], *irr.v.i.* (*aux.* s.) remain shut *or* closed.

zublinzeln ['tsu:blɪntsəln], *v.i.* (*Dat.*) wink at; make a sign to.

zubringen ['tsu:brɪŋən], *irr.v.t.* 1. bring, carry, convey, take (*Dat.*, to), (*Mech.*) feed; ***sie hat 3 Jahre damit zugebracht,*** she has spent 3 years at it, it has taken her 3 years to do it; 2. pass, spend (*time*); ***ihm eins*** or ***einen Trunk –,*** drink his health, drink a toast to him; ***das Zugebrachte,*** separate personal estate, dowry; ***zugebrachte Kinder,*** children by a previous marriage. **Zubringer,** *m.* (*Mech.*) feeder, feed mechanism, (*gun*) follower; (*coll.*) pander. **Zubringer|dienst,** *m.* feeder *or* ferry service. **–linie,** *f.* (*Railw.*) auxiliary *or* feeder line.

Zubuße ['tsu:bu:sə], *f.* (additional) contribution, allowance; additional payment. **zubüßen,** *v.t.* contribute, pay (*one's share*); spend *or* lose over and above (*one's estimate*).

Züchen ['tsy:çən], *m.* (*dial.*) ticking, tick (*for bedding*).

Zucht [tsuxt], *f.* (-, *pl.* **-en**) 1. *See* **Züchtung**; breed, stock, race, brood; ***auf*** or ***zur – halten,*** keep at stud *or* for breeding; ***eine – Schweine,*** a stud of pigs; 2. education, training; discipline, drill; decency, propriety, decorum, good breeding *or* manners, modesty; ***in – halten (nehmen),*** keep (take) in hand; ***ihn an – und Ordnung gewöhnen,*** accustom him to discipline; ***er nimmt keine – an,*** he is not amenable to discipline, (*coll.*) you can do nothing with him; ***in – und Ehre(n)*** or ***in allen Züchten,*** with due propriety, in all modesty; (*coll.*) ***das ist ja eine nette –!*** a fine way to go on, fine goings-on! ***was ist das für eine –?*** what sort of behaviour is this?

Zucht|buch, *n.* (*cattle*) herdbook, (*horses, dogs*)

stud-book, (*dogs etc.*) pedigree. **-bulle,** *m.* pure-bred sire.

züchten ['tsyçtən], *v.t.* breed, rear, raise (*animals*), (*coll.*) keep; cultivate, grow (*plants*); culture (*bacteria, pearls*). **Züchter,** *m.* breeder; cultivator, grower; keeper (*of bees*).

Zucht|haus, *n.* convict prison, penitentiary; ***10 Jahre* –,** 10 years' penal servitude. **-hausarbeit,** *f.* convict labour. **-häusler,** *m.* convict. **-hausstrafe,** *f.* penal servitude. **-hengst,** *m.* stallion. **-henne,** *f.*, **-huhn,** *n.* brood-hen.

züchtig ['tsyçtıç], *adj.* chaste, modest, bashful, coy; demure.

züchtigen ['tsyçtıgən], *v.t.* chastise, punish; discipline, correct; ***körperlich* –,** flog, thrash; ***mit Worten* –,** lash with one's tongue; ***sein Fleisch* –** mortify one's flesh.

Züchtigkeit ['tsyçtıçkaıt], *f.* chastity, modesty; coyness, bashfulness.

Züchtigung ['tsyctıguŋ], *f.* (corporal) punishment, flogging, chastisement, correction.

zuchtlos ['tsuxtlo:s], *adj.* undisciplined; unruly, wild; dissolute, licentious. **Zuchtlosigkeit,** *f.* want of discipline; disorderly behaviour, unruliness; licentiousness, loose-living.

Zucht|meister, *m.* taskmaster; disciplinarian. **-mittel,** *n.* disciplinary measure, corrective. **-perle,** *f.* culture pearl. **-rasse,** *f.* improved breed. **-rute,** *f.* (*fig.*) scourge, punishment. **-sau,** *f.* brood-sow. **-schaf,** *n.* breeding ewe. **-stier,** *m.* *See* **-bulle. -stute,** *f.* brood-mare. **-tiere,** *n.pl.* *See* **-vieh.**

Züchtung ['tsyçtuŋ], *f.* breeding, rearing (*animals*); growing, cultivation (*plants*); culture (*of bacteria*); ***neue* –,** variety.

Zucht|vieh, *n.* registered *or* breeding-cattle. **-wahl,** *f.* ***natürliche* –,** natural selection.

Zuck [tsuk], *m.* **(-(e)s,** *pl.* **-e)** jerk, twitch, start; ***in einem* (*Ruck und*) –,** in one jerk, in one rush, all at once, in a trice. **zuckeln,** *v.i.* (*aux.* s.) (*coll.*) move on in fits and starts; meander, dawdle, jog along. **zucken, 1.** *v.i.* move convulsively, jerk, start, twitch; quiver, thrill; wince (*with pain*), (*of light*) flicker; ***der Blitz zuckte,*** the lightning flashed; ***mit den Achseln* –,** *see* **2**; ***er zuckt mit den Augenlidern,*** his eyelids quiver; ***ohne mit der Wimper zu* –,** without turning a hair *or* batting an eyelid; ***das zuckte ihm in allen Gliedern,*** he was itching to do it. **2.** *v.t.* ***die Achseln* –,** shrug one's shoulders.

zücken ['tsykən], *v.t.* draw (*one's sword*); (*coll.*) ***den Geldbeutel* –,** put one's hand in one's pocket.

Zucker ['tsukər], *m.* sugar; ***ein Stück* –,** a lump of sugar; ***in – einmachen,*** preserve, candy; ***er hat* –,** he is diabetic *or* has diabetes; ***seinem Affen – geben,*** pander (to) his whims.

Zucker|abbau, *m.* breaking down of sugar. **-ahorn,** *m.* (*Bot.*) sugar maple (*Acer saccharum*). **zuckerartig,** *adj.* sugary. **Zucker|bäcker,** *m.* confectioner. **-bäckerei,** *f.* confectioner's shop. **-bau,** *m.* cultivation of the sugar-cane. **-bildung,** *f.* formation of sugar, saccharification, (*Biol.*) glycogenesis. **-bonbon,** *n.* sweet. **-büchse,** *f.* sugar-basin *or* bowl. **-couleur,** *f.* caramel. **-dose,** *f.* *See* **-büchse. -erbse,** *f.* small green pea (*Pisum sativum*). **-fabrik,** *f.* sugar-refinery. **-früchte,** *f.pl.* candied fruit. **-gärung,** *f.* saccharine fermentation. **-gast,** *m.* (*Ent.*) sugar-mite. **-gebäck, -geback(e)ne(s),** *n.* *See* **-werk. -gehalt,** *m.* sugar content. **-gewinnung,** *f.* extraction of sugar. **-guß,** *m.* icing. **zuckerhaltig,** *adj.* containing sugar, sugary, saccharated. **Zucker|harnruhr,** *f.* *See* **-krankheit. -hut,** *m.* sugar-loaf. **zuckerig,** *adj.* sugary. **zuckerkrank,** *adj.*, **Zucker|kranke(r),** *m.*, *f.* diabetic. **-krankheit,** *f.* diabetes (mellitus).

Zuckerl ['tsukərl], *n.* **(-s,** *pl.* **-)** (*Austr.*) sweet, bonbon. **Zucker|mandel,** *f.* sugared almond. **-mäulchen,** *n.* sweet-tooth. **-melone,** *f.* sweet melon. **-messung,** *f.* saccharometry.

zuckern ['tsukərn], *v.t.* sugar, sweeten. **Zucker|pflanzung,** *f.* sugar-plantation. **-plätzchen,** *n.* sweet. **-puppe,** *f.* (*coll.*) honey-child, sweetie. **-rohr,** *n.* sugar-cane. **-rübe,** *f.* sugar-beet. **-ruhr,** *f.* *See* **-krankheit. -saft,** *m.* syrup, molasses. **zuckersauer,** *adj.* (*Chem.*) saccharic; ***zuckersaures Salz,*** saccharate. **Zucker|säure,** *f.* saccharic acid. **-schale,** *f.* *See* **-büchse. -schote,** *f.* *See* **-erbse. -sieder,** *m.* sugar-refiner. **-siederei,** *f.* *See* **-fabrik. -sirup,** *m.* molasses, treacle. **zuckersüß,** *adj.* sweet as sugar, sugary; (*fig.*) honeyed. **Zucker|überzug,** *m.* *See* **-guß. -umwandlung,** *f.* sugar metabolism. **-verbindung,** *f.* saccharate, sucrate. **-waren,** *f.pl.*, **-werk,** *n.* confectionery, sweetmeats, sweets, (*Am.*) candy. **-zange,** *f.* sugar-tongs. **-zeltchen,** *n.* (*Austr.*) *see* **Zuckerl.**

Zuckung ['tsukuŋ], *f.* spasm, convulsion; convulsive movement, twitch, jerk; quiver, thrill; ***letzte -en,*** death throes.

zudämmen ['tsu:dɛmən], *v.t.* dam up.

zudecken ['tsu:dɛkən], *v.t.* cover (up); put a lid on; cover up, hide, conceal; ***durch Artillerie zugedeckt,*** pinned *or* held down by artillery fire; (*coll.*) ***mit Schlägen* –,** rain blows on.

zudem [tsu'de:m], *adv.* besides, moreover, in addition.

zudenken ['tsu:dɛŋkən], *irr.v.t.* (*usu. p.p. only*) destine, intend (*Dat.*, for); ***dies hatte ich dir zum Geschenk zugedacht,*** I had intended this as a present for you.

Zudrang ['tsu:draŋ], *m.* crowding; throng, press; rush, run (***zu***, on). **zudrängen,** *v.r.* throng, crowd, push *or* press forward (***zu***, to).

zudrehen ['tsu:dre:ən], *v.t.* shut *or* turn off (*a tap*); ***ihm den Rücken* –,** turn one's back on him.

zudringlich ['tsu:drıŋlıç], *adj.* importunate, intruding, forward, obtrusive, (*coll.*) pushing. **Zudringlichkeit,** *f.* importunity, forwardness, obtrusiveness.

zudrücken ['tsu:drykən], *v.t.* shut, close; ***ein Auge – bei,*** turn a blind eye to, connive *or* wink at, overlook, let pass.

zueignen ['tsu:aıgnən], *v.t.* dedicate (*a book*) (*Dat.*, to); ***sich*** (*Dat.*) **–,** appropriate (to o.s.), claim as one's own; ***sich*** (*Dat.*) ***widerrechtlich* –,** misappropriate, arrogate to o.s., convert unlawfully to one's use, usurp. **Zueignung,** *f.* dedication; appropriation; ***rechtswidrige* –,** misappropriation. **Zueignungsschrift,** *f.* dedicatory epistle.

zueilen ['tsu:aılən], *v.i.* (*aux.* s.) (*Dat. or* ***auf*** (*Acc.*)) run towards *or* up to, hasten towards; ***seinem Verderben* –,** rush headlong into ruin *or* to destruction.

zueinander ['tsu:aın'andər], *adv.* to each other.

zuerkennen ['tsu:ɛrkɛnən], *irr.v.t.* grant, award (*Dat.*, to), confer (on), adjudge, adjudicate (to); ***ihm den Vorzug* –,** give the preference to him; ***ihm das Recht* –,** acknowledge *or* admit his right. **Zuerkennung,** *f.* award, adjudication, acknowledgement.

zuerst [tsu'e:rst], *adv.* 1. (*sequence*) first; (*Prov.*) ***wer – kommt, mahlt* –,** first come, first served; 2. (*time*) at first, in *or* at the beginning; ***gleich* –,** at the very beginning; 3. (*importance*) first (of all), firstly, in the first place, above all, especially.

zu|erteilen, *v.t.* *See* **-teilen, -erkennen.**

zufächeln ['tsu:fɛçəln], *v.t.* fan, waft (*Dat.*, towards); ***sich*** (*Dat.*) ***Luft* –,** fan o.s.

zufahren ['tsu:fa:rən], *irr.v.i.* (*aux.* h. & s.) drive *or* go on; **– *auf*** (*Acc.*), approach, drive up to; drive towards *or* in the direction of, make *or* head for; ***fahr zu, Kutscher!*** drive on, coachman! (*fig.*) ***auf ihn* –,** fly *or* rush at *or* fall upon *or* (*coll.*) pitch into him; ***gut* –,** drive at a brisk pace; ***die Tür ist zugefahren,*** the door has slammed. **Zufahrt,** *f.* drive(way), approach. **Zufahrtsstraße,** *f.* approach road.

Zufall ['tsu:fal], *m.* **(-(e)s,** *pl.* **⸚e)** chance, accident; contingency; ***der – fügte es*** or ***wollte, daß . . .,*** as luck would have it . . ., as it happened . . .; ***es hängt vom – ab,*** it is a matter of chance; ***bloßer* –,** mere chance; ***durch* –,** by chance *or* accident, accidentally; ***glücklicher* –,** lucky chance *or* (*sl.*) break;

piece of good luck; ***unglücklicher*** or ***widriger* –**, misfortune, piece of ill-luck, mischance, unfortunate accident.

zufallen ['tsu:falən], *irr.v.i.* (*aux.* s.) 1. close (of) itself, fall to; ***die Augen fallen ihm zu,*** he cannot keep his eyes open; 2. (*Dat.*) fall to ((one's) lot), devolve (up)on; ***die Schuld fällt ihm zu,*** the blame rests with him; ***der Beweis hiervon fällt ihm zu,*** the burden of proof is his; ***viel Geld ist ihm zugefallen,*** he has come in for a lot of money; ***ihm ist eine Erbschaft zugefallen,*** an inheritance has devolved upon him.

zufällig ['tsu:fɛlɪç], *adj.* accidental, fortuitous, (*attrib. only*) chance; random, casual, contingent, incidental; ***–e Ausgaben,*** incidental expenses; ***–er Kunde,*** chance customer; ***wir waren – da,*** we chanced *or* happened to be there. **zufällig(erweise),** *adv.* by chance *or* accident, accidentally, as chance would have it, as it happened; ***ich traf ihn –,*** I chanced to meet him, I met him accidentally *or* by chance. **Zufälligkeit,** *f.* fortuitousness, contingency, chance; *pl.* coincidences, contingencies.

Zufalls|auswahl, *f.* random sample. **–gesetz,** *n.* law of probability. **–kurve,** *f.* probability curve. **–moment,** *n.* chance factor. **–treffer,** *m.* chance *or* lucky hit, (*coll.*) fluke.

zufassen ['tsu:fasən], *v.i.* seize, grasp, catch, grab, clutch, (*coll.*) make a grab; set to work, give *or* lend a (helping) hand.

zufertigen ['tsu:fɛrtɪgən], *v.t.* forward, deliver, send (*Dat.*, to).

zufliegen ['tsu:fli:gən], *irr.v.i.* (*aux.* s.) (*Dat. or* ***auf*** (*Acc.*)) fly to *or* towards; ***die Tür flog zu,*** the door slammed *or* shut with a bang; ***ihm fliegt alles zu,*** things come easily to him, he picks things up without difficulty.

zufließen ['tsu:fli:sən], *irr.v.i.* (*aux.* s.) (*Dat.*) flow to *or* towards, flow into; ***ihm – lassen,*** bestow upon him, give *or* grant to him, let him have; ***die Worte fließen ihm (nur so) zu,*** words come readily to him, he is never at a loss for words; ***ein Gewinn fließt ihm zu aus . . .,*** he derives (a) profit *or* profit accrues to him from. . . .

Zuflucht ['tsu:fluxt], *f.* (-, *pl.* **-en**) refuge, shelter; recourse; ***seine – nehmen zu,*** resort to, have recourse to; ***seine – nehmen bei,*** take refuge with; ***seine – zu den Waffen nehmen,*** appeal to arms. **Zufluchts|ort,** *m.* (**-s,** *pl.* **-e** *or* **¨-er**), **–stätte,** *f.* place of refuge, retreat, asylum, sanctuary; (*Fort.*) retirade.

Zufluß ['tsu:flus], *m.* (**-(ss)es,** *pl.* **¨-(ss)e**) influx, inflow; afflux; (*Mech.*) feed; (*river*) tributary, affluent; (*of goods*) flow, supply; ***– von Blut nach dem Kopf,*** flow of blood to the head; ***– von Fremden,*** influx of foreigners. **Zufluß|behälter,** *m.* feed-tank. **–gebiet,** *n.* (*Geol.*) basin. **–graben,** *m.* feeder, intake (*of a pond*). **–rohr,** *n.* feed- *or* supply-pipe.

zuflüstern ['tsu:flystərn], *v.t.* (*Dat.*) whisper to, prompt.

zufolge [tsu'fɔlgə], *prep.* (*preceded by Dat. or followed by Gen.*) in consequence of, as a result of, due *or* owing to; on the strength of, by *or* in virtue of, in pursuance of.

zufrieden [tsu'fri:dən], *adj.* contented, pleased, satisfied, gratified, (*pred. only*) content; ***sich – geben,*** be *or* rest content (***mit,*** with), acquiesce (in), (*coll.*) put up (with); ***ich bin damit –,*** I am satisfied with it; ***ich bin es –,*** that is very gratifying, well and good, I have no objection; ***laß ihn –!*** leave him in peace! let him alone! (*coll.*) let him be! **Zufriedenheit,** *f.* contentment, contentedness; satisfaction, gratification. **zufrieden|stellen,** *v.t.* (*sep.*) content, satisfy, give satisfaction to (*a p.*), satisfy, gratify (*wishes*). **–stellend,** *adj.* satisfactory, gratifying.

zufrieren ['tsu:fri:rən], *irr.v.i.* (*aux.* s.) freeze up *or* over, become *or* get frozen, be *or* become covered with ice.

zufügen ['tsu:fy:gən], *v.t.* add to; do, cause (*harm etc.*) (*Dat.*, to), inflict (*injury*) (on); ***ihm Schaden –,*** harm *or* injure him; ***sich selbst zugefügt,*** self-inflicted.

Zufuhr ['tsu:fu:r], *f.* conveying, conveyance, supply, delivery, bringing up (*of supplies*); importation; imports; (*Meteor.*) influx; ***die – abschneiden,*** cut off supplies.

zuführen ['tsu:fy:rən], *v.t.* conduct, lead, bring (*Dat.*, to); supply, deliver, convey, transport; introduce (*customers etc.*); (*Elec.*) lead in, (*Mech.*) feed; ***ihm künstlich Nahrungsmittel –,*** feed him artificially; ***eine S. ihrer Bestimmung –,*** devote s.th. to its proper purpose; ***ihm eine Braut –,*** procure a bride for him; ***ihn seinem Untergang –,*** lead him to ruin, be the cause of his ruin; ***einem Heere Lebensmittel –,*** provision an army. **Zuführung,** *f.* conveyance, delivery, provision, supply; importation; (*Elec.*) lead, (*Mech.*) feed; ***– von Lebensmitteln,*** provisioning, victualling; food-supply. **Zuführungs|draht,** *m.* (*Elec.*) lead. **–rohr,** *n.* feed- *or* supply-pipe. **–schnur,** *f.* (*Elec.*) flexible lead, (*coll.*) flex. **–walze,** *f.* (*Mech.*) feed(ing)-roller.

zufüllen ['tsu:fylən], *v.t.* fill up *or* in.

Zug [tsu:k], *m.* (**-(e)s,** *pl.* **¨-e**) 1. traction, draught; tension, stretch; suction; grip; 2. pull, tug, jerk; ***– des Herzens,*** inner voice, promptings of one's heart; ***– der Zeit,*** trend *or* sign of the times; ***in einem –e,*** at one pull *or* stroke *or* (*coll.*) go, straight off; in one stretch, without a break; 3. (railway) train; ***abgehender (ankommender) –,*** train departing (arriving); ***durchgehender –,*** through *or* non-stop train; ***im –e,*** in *or* on the train; 4. course, progress; march, drift (*of clouds etc.*); migration (*of birds*); ***– der Ereignisse,*** course *or* train of events; ***im –e,*** in train *or* progress, in the course (*Gen.*, of); 5. draught, current (*of air*); ***es ist kein – darin,*** there is no life in it, it is very dull *or* slow; ***gut im –e, im besten –e,*** well under way, in full swing, (*coll.*) going strong; ***in – bringen,*** give an impetus to, set *or* get going; ***im –e stehen,*** stand in a draught; 6. train, retinue; band, gang, team; span, yoke, team (*of oxen etc.*); flight (*of birds*), flock (*of birds, sheep*), herd (*of animals*), shoal, school (*of fish*), range (*of mountains*), row (*of horses*); (*Mil.*) file, column; squad, section, platoon, troop; 7. stroke (*of a pen*), line, outline; feature, trait, characteristic, lineament; ***ein – seines Charakters,*** a trait *or* feature of his character; ***in großen Zügen,*** along general lines, in broad outline; ***in kurzen Zügen,*** in a few strokes, in brief outline; ***in kräftigen Zügen,*** in bold outlines; 8. (*fig.*) disposition, inclination, impulse; trend, tendency, bias (***nach,*** towards), bent (for); 9. gulp, draught (*Am.* draft), (*coll.*) swig (*of drink*); whiff, puff (*of smoke*); ***in den letzten Zügen liegen,*** (*of a p.*) be breathing one's last, (*coll.*) be at one's last gasp; (*of a th.*) be in its death-throes, be petering out; ***in vollen Zügen,*** fully, deeply, thoroughly, to the full; 10. draw-thread, strap; grip (*for pulling*), bell-pull; hoist, pulley; 11. (*of gun-barrel*) groove, *pl.* rifling; 12. (*Chess etc.*) ***wer ist am –e?*** whose move is it? who has the next move? ***einen – tun,*** (make a) move; ***– um –,*** without delay, without a break, uninterruptedly, in rapid succession; concurrently, pari passu; (*Comm.*) against delivery.

Zugabe ['tsu:ga:bə], *f.* addition, extra; bonus, premium; makeweight; (*Theat.*) encore; (*fig.*) ***als –,*** into the bargain.

Zugang ['tsu:gaŋ], *m.* admittance, entry, access; gate(way), entrance; entry, approach(-road), access-road; (*Comm.*) increase, accrual; receipts, credit-entries; (*of goods*) accessions, arrivals, incoming stock; ***– zum Meere,*** access to the sea.

zugängig ['tsu:gɛŋɪc], *pred.adj.* (*only with* ***sein, werden, machen***) accessible, available. **zugänglich,** *adj.* accessible, amenable, (*coll.*) open (***für,*** to); approachable, (*coll.*) get-at-able; (*Psych.*) responsive, susceptible (to); ***– machen,*** render accessible, make available, (*coll.*) throw open; ***der Öffentlichkeit – machen,*** popularize. **Zugänglich-**

keit, *f.* accessibility, availability; response, susceptibility.

Zugangsweg ['tsu:gaŋsve:k], *m.* approach, access-road.

Zug|artikel, *m.* popular *or* much-sought-after commodity, *(coll.)* draw. **-band,** *n.* tie-rod. **-beanspruchung,** *f.* tensile stress. **-(begleit)-personal,** *n.* train-crew. **-brücke,** *f.* drawbridge. **-brunnen,** *m.* draw-well, bucket-well.

zugeben ['tsu:ge:bən], *irr.v.t.* 1. add, give into the bargain, *(coll.)* throw in; 2. grant, concede, confess, admit, allow, own, acknowledge; ***zugegeben*** or ***man muß –, daß er nicht reich ist,*** granted that *or* (it is) true (that) he is not wealthy; 3. *(Cards)* follow suit; ***klein –,*** follow suit with a low card. **zugegebenermaßen,** *adv.* as already acknowledged, admittedly, avowedly.

zugegen [tsu'ge:gən], *pred.adj.* present, in attendance (***bei,*** at).

zugehen ['tsu:ge:ən], *irr.v.i.* *(aux.* s.) 1. close, shut *(as door)*, meet, fasten *(as belt)*; 2. go, move (***auf*** *(Acc.)*, towards *or* up to); go on *or* faster; ***ihm –,*** reach him, come to his hand *(letter etc.)*, *(Law)* be served on him; ***ihm etwas – lassen,*** forward s.th. to him, let him have s.th.; ***auf Ostern –,*** be getting near Easter; ***geraden Wegs auf ihn –,*** make *or* head straight for him; make a beeline for him; ***spitz –,*** end in a point, taper (off) to a point; 3. happen, take place, come to pass; ***wie geht es zu, daß . . .?*** how is that . . .? how does it come about that . . .? ***es müßte komisch*** or ***seltsam*** or ***mit dem Teufel –, wenn . . .,*** it would be strange if . . .; ***mit rechten Dingen –,*** come about naturally; ***es geht nicht mit rechten Dingen zu,*** there is s.th. uncanny about it, *(coll.)* there's s.th. fishy here; ***bunt*** or ***lustig –,*** *see* **hergehen.**

Zugeherin ['tsu:ge:ərɪn], **Zugehfrau,** *f.* *(dial.)* charwoman, daily help.

Zugehör ['tsu:gəhø:r], *n.* *(Austr., Swiss)* *see* **Zubehör. zugehören,** *v.i.* *(Dat.)* belong to *(a p.)*, appertain to *(a th.)*. **zugehörig,** *adj.* belonging to *(a p.)* *(pred. only)*, proper, pertinent, *(pred.)* appertaining to *(a th.)*; accompanying, matching; ***–e Briefumschläge,*** envelopes to match. **Zugehörigkeit,** *f.* membership (***zu,*** of), affiliation (to *or* with), relationship (with).

zugeknöpft ['tsu:gəknœpft], *adj.* *(fig.)* uncommunicative, reserved, taciturn.

Zügel ['tsy:gəl], *m.* rein(s), *(fig.)* bridle, curb, check, restraint; ***ihn an die – nehmen,*** take him in hand; ***sich an die – nehmen,*** get a grip on o.s.; ***ihm die*** or ***den – kurz halten,*** keep a tight rein on *or* a firm hold over him, keep him under one's thumb; ***die – der Regierung,*** the reins of government; ***einem Pferd die – schießen lassen,*** give a horse his head; *(fig.)* ***ihn den – (schießen) lassen,*** let him do as he likes, give him his head; ***seinen Leidenschaften die – schießen lassen,*** give full rein *or* free vent to one's feelings, let one's feelings get out of hand; ***mit verhängtem –,*** at full gallop.

zugelassen ['tsu:gəlasən], *see* **zulassen.**

zügellos ['tsu:gəllo:s], *adj.* *(fig.)* unbridled, unrestrained, inordinate *(desires)*; licentious, dissolute. **Zügellosigkeit,** *f.* lack of restraint; licentiousness, loose living. **zügeln, 1.** *v.t.* rein (in), *(fig.)* bridle, curb, check, restrain. **2.** *v.i.* *(Swiss)* move house, change one's quarters. **Zügelseeschwalbe,** *f.* *(Orn.)* bridled tern *(Sterna anaethetus)*.

Zugemüse ['tsu:gəmy:zə], *n.* side dish of vegetables.

zugenannt ['tsu:gənant], *adj.* surnamed.

Zugereiste(r) ['tsu:gəraɪstə(r)], *m., f.* newcomer.

zugesellen ['tsu:gəzɛlən], *v.t., v.r.* *(Dat.)* associate with, join.

zugestandenermaßen, *adv. See* **zugebenermaßen.**

Zugeständnis ['tsu:gəʃtɛntnɪs], *n.* **(-ses,** *pl.* **-se)** concession, admission; compromise; ***–se machen,*** make concessions, compromise, *(fig.)* make allowances. **zugestehen,** *irr.v.t.* concede, grant, admit, acknowledge.

zugetan ['tsu:gəta:n], *pred.adj.* *(Dat.)* attached *or* devoted to, fond of.

Zugewanderte(r) ['tsu:gəvandərtə(r)], *m., f. See* **Zugereiste(r).**

zugewandt ['tsu:gəvant], *pred.adj.* *(Dat.)* interested in, sympathetic towards; *(Hist.)* ***die –en Orte,*** cantons affiliated to the old Swiss Confederation.

Zug|feder, *f.* tension spring, *(clocks)* mainspring. **-festigkeit,** *f.* tensile strength. **-fisch,** *m.* migratory fish. **-führer,** *m.* *(Railw.)* guard, *(Am.)* conductor; *(Mil.)* platoon *or* section commander. **-griff,** *m.* handle, grip.

zugießen ['tsu:gi:sən], **1.** *irr.v.t.* *(liquid)* add, pour more in; *(vessel)* fill up, top up (***mit,*** with). **2.** *irr. v.i.* keep on pouring.

zugig ['tsu:gɪç], *adj.* draughty *(Am.* drafty).

zügig ['tsy:gɪç], *adj.* speedy; uninterrupted, unbroken; efficient, smooth, easy; *(Swiss) see* **zugkräftig**; *(Motor.)* ***– schalten,*** change gear smoothly; *(Comm.)* ***– beliefern,*** supply freely. **Zügigkeit,** *f.* efficiency, uninterrupted *or* smooth flow.

Zug|klappe, *f.* damper. **-knopf,** *m.* pull-button. **-kraft,** *f.* tractive *or* pulling power; suction; *(of propeller)* thrust; *(fig.)* (force of) attraction, appeal. **zugkräftig,** *adj.* *(fig.)* attractive, popular, *(pred.)* in vogue, with strong appeal; ***– sein,*** *(coll.)* be a draw.

zugleich [tsu'glaɪç], *adv.* at the same time (as), conjointly (with), *(coll.)* together (with), along with.

Zug|leine, *f.* tow(ing) rope. **-leistung,** *f.* traction, tractive power. **-luft,** *f.* draught *(Am.* draft), current of air. **-maschine,** *f.* traction engine, tractor; prime mover. **-meldewesen,** *n.* *(Railw.)* signalling system. **-mittel,** *n.* *(fig.)* attraction, draw. **-ochse,** *m.* draught-ox. **-personal,** *n.* train-crew. **-pferd,** *n.* draught-horse. **-pflaster,** *n.* blistering plaster, vesicatory, vesicant.

zugreifen ['tsu:graɪfən], *irr.v.i.* 1. (make a) grab, take hold; *(at meals)* help o.s., *(coll.)* fall to, tuck in; 2. take *or* lend a hand, *(coll.)* put one's back into it; 3. *(fig.)* seize the opportunity; ***er braucht nur zuzugreifen,*** he can have it for the asking.

Zugrichtung ['tsu:krɪçtuŋ], *f.* *(Railw.)* facing the engine.

Zugriff ['tsu:grɪf], *m.* grip, clutches; ***es seinem – entziehen,*** remove it from his reach.

zugrunde [tsu'grundə], *adv.* ***– gehen,*** perish, be ruined; ***– legen,*** take as a basis *(Dat.,* for); ***er legte seiner Stellungnahme eine Reihe von Tatsachen –,*** he based his attitude on a series of facts; ***– liegen*** *(Dat.)*, underlie, be at the root *or* bottom of, *(coll.)* be *or* lie behind; ***der Predigt liegt eine Bibelstelle –,*** the sermon is based on a text from the Bible; ***– richten,*** wreck, ruin, destroy. **Zugrunde|gehen,** *n.* ruin, destruction. **-legung,** *f.* ***unter –*** *(Gen. or* ***von***), taking . . . as a basis. **zugrundeliegend,** *adj.* underlying, basic, fundamental.

Zug|salbe, *f.* vesicant ointment. **-schaffner,** *m. See* **-führer. -schalter,** *m.* *(Elec.)* hanging *or* cord switch. **-seil,** *n.* hoisting *or* haulage rope, towrope, towing-line, *(Mech.)* control cable. **-stange,** *f.* drawbar, tie-rod, *(of a pump)* swipe. **-stiefel,** *m.* elastic-sided boot. **-stück,** *n. See* **-mittel**; *(Theat. coll.)* hit. **-tier,** *n.* draught *(Am.* draft) animal.

zugucken ['tsu:gukən], *(coll.) see* **zuschauen.**

Zugunglück ['tsu:kʔunglyk], *n.* railway accident, train disaster *or* *(coll.)* crash.

zugunsten [tsu'gunstən], *prep.* *(Gen.)* for the benefit of, in favour of, to the credit of.

zugute [tsu'gu:tə], *adv.* ***ihm etwas – halten,*** give him credit for s.th.; make allowance for his . . . *(youth, inexperience etc.)*, excuse *or* pardon him *or* take a lenient view *or* be forebearing *or* *(coll.)* let him off lightly on account of his . . .; ***– kommen*** *(Dat.)*, be an advantage to, be to the benefit *or* advantage of, stand *(s.o.)* in good stead; ***sich*** *(Dat.)* ***etwas – tun auf*** *(Acc.)*, be proud of, take pride in, pride o.s. on.

Zug|verkehr, *m.* train *or* railway service, railway

traffic. **–vieh,** *n.* draught (*Am.* draft) cattle. **–vogel,** *m.* migrant. **zugweise,** *adv.* in herds *or* flocks, (*Mil.*) in squads, by platoons. **Zug|welle,** *f.* (*Mech.*) feed-screw. **–wind,** *m. See* **–luft.**

zuhalten ['tsu:haltən], **1.** *irr.v.t.* keep shut; close (*eyes*), clench (*fist*), stop (*ears*); ***sich*** (*Dat.*) ***die Nase –,*** hold one's nose. **2.** *irr.v.i.* – ***auf*** (*Acc.*), go straight for, proceed towards, make for; ***mit ihm –,*** have an understanding *or* (illicit) relations with him. **3.** *irr.v.r.* hurry (up), make haste, bestir o.s.

Zuhälter ['tsu:hɛltər], *m.* souteneur, (*coll.*) pimp. **Zuhälterei** [–'raɪ], *f.* procuration, living on the proceeds of prostitution.

Zuhaltung ['tsu:haltuŋ], *f.* tumbler (*of a lock*).

zuhanden [tsu'handən], *prep.* (*Gen.*) (*on letters*) for the attention of.

zuhängen ['tsu:hɛŋən], *v.t.* cover with drapery *or* a curtain, hang, drape.

zuhauen ['tsu:hauən], **1.** *irr.v.t.* rough-hew; dress, trim, (cut to) shape; cut up (*meat*). **2.** *irr.v.i.* lay about one; ***auf ihn –,*** lay hands on him.

zuhauf [tsu'hauf], *adv.* (*Poet.*) together.

Zuhause [tsu'hauzə], *n.* home.

zuheften ['tsu:hɛftən], *v.t.* stitch up.

zuheilen ['tsu:haɪlən], *v.i.* (*aux.* s.) heal up *or* over, cicatrize.

Zuhilfenahme [tsu'hɪlfəna:mə], *f.* ***unter*** (***ohne***) – ***von,*** by *or* with (without) the aid *or* help of, with (without having) recourse to.

zuhinterst [tsu'hɪntərst], *adv.* at the very end, last of all.

zuhöchst [tsu'hœçst], *adv.* topmost, uppermost, highest of all.

zuhorchen ['tsu:hɔrçən], *v.i.* (*Dat.*) listen secretly (to), eavesdrop (on).

zuhören ['tsu:hø:rən], *v.i.* (*Dat.*) listen (to); attend (to); ***hör mal zu!*** mark my words! **Zuhörer(in),** *m.*(*f.*) listener, auditor; member of the audience; *pl.* (members of the) audience. **Zuhörerraum,** *m.* auditorium, lecture-room *or* -hall. **Zuhörerschaft,** *f.* audience.

zuinnerst [tsu'ɪnərst], *adv.* innermost, in the very heart, right inside, (*fig.*) in one's heart (of hearts), deeply.

zu|jauchzen, –jubeln, *v.i.* (*Dat.*) cheer, hail, shout to.

zukaufen ['tsu:kaufən], *v.t.* buy in addition *or* as an afterthought.

zukehren ['tsu:ke:rən], *v.t.* (*Dat.*) turn to(wards), face; ***ihm das Gesicht –,*** turn one's face towards him, face him; ***ihm den Rücken –,*** turn one's back on him.

zuklappen ['tsu:klapən], **1.** *v.t.* close, slam, bang. **2.** *v.i.* (*aux.* s.) close with a snap, slam to.

zuklatschen ['tsu:klatʃən], *v.i.* (*Dat.*) applaud, clap.

zu|kleben, –kleistern, *v.t.* paste *or* glue up (*a hole*); fasten, gum down, seal (*envelope*).

zu|klemmen, *v.t. See* **–kneifen.**

zuklinken ['tsu:klɪŋkən], *v.t., v.i.* latch.

zuknallen ['tsu:knalən], *v.t., v.i.* shut with a bang, slam.

zukneifen ['tsu:knaɪfən], *irr.v.t.* squeeze together, press *or* squeeze shut.

zuknöpfen ['tsu:knœpfən], *v.t.* button (up); *see* **zugeknöpft.**

zuknüpfen ['tsu:knypfən], *v.t.* tie (up), knot, fasten with a knot.

zukommen ['tsu:kɔmən], *irr.v.i.* (*aux.* s.) – ***auf*** (*Acc.*), come up to, approach; ***ihm –,*** reach him (*as a letter*), be due to him, fall to his share, (*fig.*) befit him; ***ihm etwas – lassen,*** let him have a th., supply *or* furnish him with a th., pass *or* send s.th. to him; ***ihm ärztliche Behandlung – lassen,*** see (to it) that he receives medical attention; ***es kommt dir nicht zu, so zu sprechen,*** it is not for you *or* you have no right *or* no business to speak like that; ***das kommt ihm nicht zu,*** he has no right to that; ***es kommt mir nicht zu,*** it is not within my province; ***jedem, was ihm zukommt,*** to everyone his due.

zukorken ['tsu:kɔrkən], *v.t.* cork (up).

Zukost ['tsu:kɔst], *f.* something eaten with bread *or* served with meat.

Zukunft ['tsu:kunft], *f.* future, time to come, life hereafter; (*Gram.*) future tense; ***in –,*** in future, henceforth, from this time onwards, from now on; ***in naher –,*** in the near future; ***in nächster –,*** in the immediate future; ***das muß die – lehren, das ist der – vorbehalten,*** time will tell, that remains to be seen; ***Mann der –,*** coming man.

zukünftig ['tsu:kynftɪç], **1.** *adj.* future; ***–e Zeit,*** time to come; future times; ***mein Zukünftiger*** (***meine Zukünftige***), my prospective *or* future husband (*or* wife), (*coll.*) my intended, my husband (*or* wife) to be. **2.** *adv.* in future, for the future.

zukunftsfreudig ['tsu:kunftsfrɔydɪç], *adj.* optimistic. **Zukunfts|hoffnung,** *f.* hopes for the future. **–musik,** *f.* (*fig.*) future aims, plans for the future; castles in the air, dreams of the future, (*coll.*) pipe-dreams. **–pläne,** *m.pl.* future plans, plans for the future. **–roman,** *m.* science fiction.

zulächeln ['tsu:lɛçəln], *v.i.* (*Dat.*) smile at; (*fig.*) smile on.

Zuladung ['tsu:la:duŋ], *f.* additional load.

Zulage ['tsu:la:gə], *f.* increase (of salary), extra pay, (*coll.*) rise; additional payment, allowance.

zulande [tsu'landə], *adv.* ***bei uns –,*** in my country; ***hier –,*** in this country.

zulangen ['tsu:laŋən], **1.** *v.t. See* **zureichen.** **2.** *v.i.* 1. stretch out the hand for, reach out for, (*at meals*) help o.s.; 2. (*fig.*) suffice, be sufficient *or* enough, (*coll.*) do; reach (far enough).

zulänglich ['tsu:lɛŋlɪç], *adj.* sufficient, adequate. **Zulänglichkeit,** *f.* sufficiency, adequacy.

Zulaß ['tsu:las], *m. See* **Zulassung.**

zulassen ['tsu:lasən], **1.** *irr.v.t.* 1. leave closed, not open; 2. grant, concede, allow, permit, tolerate, suffer, (*of doubt etc.*) admit of; ***diese Erklärung läßt zwei Deutungen zu,*** this explanation admits of two interpretations; 3. (*Law*) grant (permission for), authorize, approve, license; ***Kaution –,*** grant bail; ***als Rechtsanwalt –,*** call (*or Am.* admit) to the Bar; ***sie sind zugelassen,*** they are admitted *or* accepted.

zulässig ['tsu:lɛsɪç], *adj.* permissible, allowable, admissable, approved, authorized; ***nicht –,*** inadmissable, not allowed *or* authorized *or* approved; (*Mech.*) ***–e Abweichung,*** tolerance, allowance, permissible deviation *or* variation; ***–e Belastung,*** permitted load.

Zulassung ['tsu:lasuŋ], *f.* admission; permission, concession; ***um – zum Examen nachsuchen,*** make application for admission to an examination. **Zulassungs|gesuch,** *n.* application for admission. **–nummer,** *f.* (*Motor.*) licence number. **–papiere,** *n.pl.* registration papers. **–prüfung,** *f.* entrance *or* admission *or* qualifying examination; (*Motor.*) driving-test, (*Av.*) examination for pilot's certificate. **–schein,** *m.* permit, licence.

Zulauf ['tsu:lauf], *m.* throng (of people); ***einen – von Kunden haben,*** have a rush of customers; ***großen – haben,*** be much sought after, be in great demand, be popular *or* in vogue, (*of a speaker or play*) draw large crowds *or* audiences, (*of a doctor etc.*) have an extensive practice. **zulaufen,** *irr.v.i.* (*aux.* s.) run on, go on running; – ***auf*** (*Acc.*), run in the direction of, run towards, run up to; ***ihm –,*** run *or* crowd *or* flock to him; ***lauf zu!*** be quick! hurry! ***spitz –,*** come *or* run to a point, taper (off) (to a point); ***zugelaufener Hund,*** stray dog.

zulegen ['tsu:le:gən], **1.** *v.t.* 1. close, cover up (***mit,*** with); 2. ***etwas –*** (*Dat.*), add s.th. (to), put more of s.th. (to), increase *or* raise (*salary*) by . . ., (*Artil.*) increase the range by . . ., (*bargaining*) raise one's offer by . . .; (*coll.*) ***sich*** (*Dat.*) ***etwas –,*** buy *or* get for o.s., treat o.s. to; (*coll.*) ***sich*** (*Dat.*) ***eine Frau –,*** find o.s. a wife, get o.s. married. **2.** *v.i.* 1. raise one's offer; 2. lose money (***bei,*** on); 3. get fatter, put on weight *or* flesh.

zuleid [tsu'laɪt], *adv.* (*Austr.*), **zuleide** [–'laɪdə], *adv.* ***ihm etwas – tun,*** do him harm, harm *or* hurt him; ***was hat er dir – getan?*** what harm has he done you? what has he done to you? *See* **zuliebe.**

zuleiten ['tsu:laɪtən], *v.t.* lead *or* feed in, supply (*water etc*), conduct, direct, lead (*Dat.*, to); (*information*) transmit, impart, (*coll.*) pass on (to). **Zuleitung,** *f.* supply, conduction, transmission; (*Mech.*) feed, (*Elec.*) lead. **Zuleitungs|draht,** *m.* (*Elec.*) lead-in wire, input lead. **–rohr,** *n.* inlet *or* feed *or* supply pipe.

zulernen ['tsu:lɛrnən], *v.t., v.i.* learn (*s.th.*) (in addition), add (*s.th.*) to one's (stock of) knowledge.

zuletzt [tsu'lɛtst], *adv.* finally, ultimately, eventually, in the end, after all, at last; last, for the last time; ***bis – bleiben,*** stay till the end; ***als er uns – sah,*** when he last saw us, the last time he saw us, when he saw us for the last time; ***nicht –,*** (last but) not least; ***du kommst immer –,*** you are always the last to arrive; (*Prov.*) ***wer – lacht, lacht am besten,*** who laughs last laughs longest.

zulieb [tsu'li:p], *adv.* (*Austr.*), **zuliebe** [–'li:bə], *adv.* ***ihm –,*** for his sake, to please *or* oblige him; ***niemandem –, niemandem zuleide,*** without fear or favour.

Zulieferer ['tsu:li:fərər], *m.* supplier, purveyor; sub-contractor. **Zulieferungs|industrie,** *f.* ancillary *or* supply industry. **–teile,** *m.pl.* manufactured components.

Zulk [tsulk], **Zuller** ['tsulər], **Zulp(er)** [tsulp(ər)], *m.* (*dial.*) (baby's) dummy, comforter.

zum [tsum] = ***zu dem.***

zumachen ['tsu:maxən], **1.** *v.t.* close, shut, fasten; stop (up) (*a hole*), button *or* do up (*a coat*), seal (*an envelope*), put down (*an umbrella*); ***kein Auge –,*** not sleep a wink; (*coll.*) ***die Bude –,*** *see* **2. 2.** *v.i.* close down (*a business*), (*also fig. coll.*) shut up shop; (*coll.*) ***da können wir –,*** we might as well pack up *or* (*sl.*) pack it in; (*coll.*) ***mach zu!*** get a move on! (*sl.*) step on it!

zumal [tsu'ma:l], *adv.* above all, especially; (*used as conj.*) – (***da*** or ***weil***), especially since, particularly because, (*positive*) (all) the more so as, (*negative*) the less so since; – ***es eine*** (***keine***) ***Erklärung enthält,*** including (lacking), as it does, an explanation.

zumauern ['tsu:mauərn], *v.t.* wall up (*a space*), brick up (*a hole*).

zumeist [tsu'maɪst], *adv.* mostly, in most cases, for the most part, generally.

zumessen ['tsu:mɛsən], *irr.v.t.* measure out, allot, apportion, allocate, assign (*Dat.*, to), (*fig.*) mete out (*punishment etc.*).

zumindest [tsu'mɪndəst], *adv.* at (the very) least.

zumischen ['tsu:mɪʃən], *v.t.* add, admix. **Zumischung,** *f.* admixture.

zumute [tsu'mu:tə], *adv.* (*imp. subject with Dat. of p.*) ***schlecht – sein,*** be in low spirits, be dispirited; ***gut – sein,*** be in good spirits, (*coll.*) feel fine; ***sonderbar – sein,*** feel strange *or* (*coll.*) funny; ***nicht danach – sein,*** be in no mood for it; ***nicht lächerlich –,*** in no joking mood.

zumuten ['tsu:mu:tən], *v.t.* expect, ask (*Dat.*, of), demand (of *or* from); ***sich*** (*Dat.*) ***zuviel –,*** attempt *or* undertake *or* (*coll.*) take on too much, (*coll.*) bite off more than one can chew; (*physically only*) overtask one's strength *or* o.s. **Zumutung,** *f.* unreasonable *or* exacting demand, unwarranted expectation; (piece of) impudence; (*coll.*) ***das ist eine starke –,*** that's a tall order, that's a bit thick.

zunächst [tsu'nɛçst], **1.** *adv.* 1. first (of all), in the first place *or* instance, to begin with, above all; 2. for the present, for the time being. **2.** *prep.* (*Dat.*) next *or* close to. **Zunächstliegende(s),** *n.* the obvious (thing).

zunageln ['tsu:na:gəln], *v.t.* nail up (*hole, gap*), nail down (*lid, box*).

zunähen ['tsu:nɛ:ən], *v.t.* sew *or* stitch up.

Zunahme ['tsu:na:mə], *f.* increase, growth, rise, augmentation, (*in quality*) improvement, advancement, (*in value*) increment.

Zuname(n) ['tsu:na:mə(n)], *m.* surname, family name.

Zünd|anlage ['tsynt–], *f.* (*Motor.*) ignition (system). **–bolzen,** *m.* (*Artil.*) percussion pin. **–einstellung,** *f.* (*Motor.*) (ignition) timing, (*diesel engine*) injection timing.

Zundel ['tsundəl], *m.* *See* **Zunder.**

zünden ['tsyndən], **1.** *v.i.* catch fire, kindle, ignite, (*Motor.*) fire; (*fig.*) ***bei ihm –,*** catch his attention, electrify him, arouse *or* fire his enthusiasm. **2.** *v.t.* kindle, set fire to, set alight, set on fire, ignite, (*explosive charge*) detonate, fire. **zündend,** *adj.* (*fig.*) inflammatory, stirring, rousing, electrifying.

Zunder ['tsundər], *m.* 1. tinder, touchwood, punk; (*Metall.*) dross, scale; 2. (*Mil.*) heavy punishment.

Zünder ['tsyndər], *m.* fuse, detonator. **zündfertig,** *adj.* primed. **Zünd|flamme,** *f.* pilot light. **–folge,** *f.* order of firing (*of engines*). **–funke,** *m.* (*Motor.*) (ignition) spark. **–holz, –hölzchen,** *n.* match. **–holzmasse,** *f.* match-head. **–holzschachtel,** *f.* matchbox. **–hütchen,** *n.* percussion-cap. **–kapsel,** *f.* detonator. **–kerze,** *f.* (*Motor.*) spark(ing) plug. **–ladung,** *f.* detonating- *or* firing-charge. **–loch,** *n.* (*Min.*) touch-hole; (*Artil.*) flash-vent. **–magnet,** *m.* magneto. **–masse,** *f.* *See* **–holzmasse. –nadel,** *f.* priming needle. **–nadelgewehr,** *n.* needle-gun. **–papier,** *n.* slow-match, touch-paper. **–patrone,** *f.* priming-cartridge. **–pfanne,** *f.* touch-pan. **–punkt,** *m.* ignition point. **–punkteinstellung,** *f.* (*Motor.*) magneto timing. **–satz,** *m.* detonating- *or* priming-charge. **–schalter,** *m.* (*Motor.*) ignition switch. **–schlüssel,** *m.* (*Motor.*) ignition key. **–schnur,** *f.* (-, *pl.* **-en** *or* **¨-e**) match, fuse. **–schwamm,** *m.* tinder. **–stoff,** *m.* inflammable matter; fuel; (*fig.*) seeds of discontent, (*coll.*) dynamite.

Zündung ['tsyndʊŋ], *f.* kindling; priming, detonation; (*Motor.*) ignition. **Zündverteiler,** *m.* (*Motor.*) (ignition) distributor.

zunehmen ['tsu:ne:mən], *irr.v.i.* increase, grow, gain (***an*** (*Dat.*), in), get *or* grow (larger, longer, stronger, heavier *etc.*); rise, swell; improve, advance, thrive, prosper; grow *or* get worse (*of an evil*); get stouter, put on weight *or* flesh *or* fat; grow *or* get longer (*of the days*); ***an Kräften –,*** grow stronger; ***an Jahren –,*** advance in years; ***an Wert –,*** increase *or* improve in value; ***an Zahl –,*** increase in number; get more. **zunehmend, 1.** *adj.* increasing, growing; progressive; ***–e Geschwindigkeit,*** rising speed; ***bei –en Jahren,*** with advancing years, as one gets older; ***in –em Maße,*** *see* **2**; ***–er Mond,*** waxing moon. **2.** *adv.* increasingly, progressively, more and more.

zuneigen ['tsu:naɪgən], *v.t., v.r.* (*Dat.*) lean towards; incline to; ***sich dem Ende –,*** draw to a close. **Zuneigung,** *f.* liking, affection (***für, zu,*** for), attachment (to), partiality (for), inclination (for *or* towards); – ***zu ihm fassen,*** take a liking *or* (*coll.*) fancy to him.

Zunft [tsunft], *f.* (-, *pl.* **¨-e**) guild, corporation; (*iron.*) fraternity, clique, gang, band, tribe; ***die – der Gelehrten,*** the learned fraternity; – ***der Handwerker,*** craft guild. **Zunft|brief,** *m.* charter of a guild or city company. **–geist,** *m.* party-spirit, sectarianism, (*coll.*) clannishness. **zunftgemäß,** *adj.* according to the statutes *or* practice of the guild. **Zunfthaus,** *n.* guildhall.

zünftig ['tsynftɪç], *adj.* *See* **zunftgemäß**; (*fig.*) expert, skilled; competent; (*coll.*) proper, thorough, real; (*Footb.*) ***– spielen,*** play scientifically; – ***werden,*** receive the freedom of a company.

Zunft|meister, *m.* master of a guild. **–wesen,** *n.* system of guilds, guild matters *or* affairs.

Zunge ['tsuŋə], *f.* tongue; (*Poet.*) language; tongue (*of shoe*); languet (*of organ*); reed (*of wind instruments*); (*Railw.*) switch-tongue; catch (*of a buckle etc.*); slide (*of slide rule*); blade (*of T-square*), pointer, finger (*of scales*); (*Ichth.*) sole (*Soleidae*); ***mit der – anstoßen,*** lisp; ***sich auf die – beißen,*** bite one's tongue; ***belegte –,*** coated *or* dirty tongue; ***eine geläufige – haben,*** have the gift of the gab;

eine feine* – *haben, be a gourmet; ***ihm die* – *herausstrecken,*** put one's tongue out at him; ***das Herz auf der* – *tragen,*** wear one's heart on one's sleeve; ***die* – *klebt mir am Gaumen,*** my tongue cleaves to the roof of my mouth; ***der* – *freien Lauf lassen,*** let one's tongue run away with one; ***ihm das Wort von der* – *nehmen,*** take the words out of his mouth; ***es liegt*** or ***schwebt mir auf der* –,** I have it on the tip of my tongue; ***eine schwere* – *haben,*** have an impediment in one's speech; ***auf der* – *zergehen,*** melt in the mouth.

züngeln ['tsyŋəln], *v.i.* dart, leap up, shoot out, lick (*as flames*); ***Schlangen* –,** snakes hiss.

Zungen|band, *n.* (*Anat.*) frenulum of the tongue. **–bein,** *n.* (*Anat.*) hyoid bone. **–belag,** *m.* fur *or* coating on the tongue. **–blüte,** *f.* lingulate flower. **zungenblütig,** *adj.* (*Bot.*) lingulate. **Zungen|-brecher,** *m.* (*fig.*) jaw-breaker, tongue-twister. **–drescher,** *m.* (*coll.*) chatterer, babbler, chatterbox, windbag. **–drescherei,** *f.* (*coll.*) jabber, prattle, gab, clap-trap. **–drüse,** *f.* lingual gland. **–fehler,** *m.* speech defect, impediment in one's speech. **zungenfertig,** *adj.* fluent, voluble; glib, flippant. **Zungen|fertigkeit,** *f.* verbosity, garrulity, glibness, (*coll.*) gift of the gab. **–haut,** *f.* (*Anat.*) epithelium of the tongue. **–hieb,** *m.* bitter *or* harsh remark. **–krebs,** *m.* cancer of the tongue, glossanthrax. **–laut,** *m.* (*Phonet.*) lingual (sound). **–pfeife,** *f.* (*organ*) reed-pipe. **–-R,** *n.* (*Phonet.*) lingual *or* trilled r. **–rücken,** *m.* dorsal surface *or* (*coll.*) back of the tongue. **–schiene,** *f.* (*Railw.*) switch-point. **–schlag,** *m.* stammering, (*when drunk*) thick speech. **–spitze,** *f.* tip of the tongue. **–(spitzen)-R,** *n. See* **–-R.** **–vorfall,** *m.* (*Med.*) glossocele. **–wurzel,** *f.* root *or* base of the tongue.

Zünglein ['tsyŋlaɪn], *n.* (*fig.*) ***das* – *an der Waage sein*** or ***bilden,*** hold the balance, tip the scale.

zunicht [tsu'nɪçt] (*Austr.*), **zunichte,** *adv.* **–** ***machen,*** ruin, destroy; frustrate, thwart, undo; explode (*theory*), blight (*hopes*); **–** ***werden,*** come to nothing, be ruined, frustrated *etc.*

zunicken ['tsu:nɪkən], *v.i.* nod (*Dat.*, to).

zunutze [tsu'nutsə], *adv.* ***sich*** (*Dat.*) ***etwas* – *machen,*** make use *or* the most of a th., make capital out of a th., put s.th. to good use, turn s.th. to account, avail o.s. *or* take advantage of a th.

zuoberst [tsu'o:bərst], *adv.* at the (very) top, uppermost.

zuordnen ['tsu:ɔrdnən], *v.t.* adjoin, coordinate; associate (*Dat.*, with), assign, appoint, attach (to). **Zuordnung,** *f.* coordination, association, assignment.

zupacken ['tsu:pakən], *v.i. See* **zugreifen. zupackend,** *adj.* (*fig.*) gripping, arresting, powerful.

zupaß [tsu'pas], **zupasse,** *adv.* **–** ***kommen,*** come at the right time *or* moment, come in the nick of time (*Dat.*, for), come in handy (for), suit admirably.

zupfen ['tsupfən], *v.t.* (*v.i.* – ***an*** (*Dat.*)) pull, tug, pluck; (*v.t. only*) pick, unravel; (*coll.*) – ***Sie sich doch an Ihrer eignen Nase!*** sweep before your own door! consider your own shortcomings! **Zupf|instrument,** *n.* (*Mus.*) plucking instrument. **–leinwand,** *f.* (*Med.*) lint.

zupfropfen ['tsu:pfrɔpfən], *v.t.* cork *or* bung *or* stopper up.

zur [tsu:r] = ***zu der.***

zuraten ['tsu:ra:tən], *irr.v.i.* (*Dat.*) advise, recommend, persuade; ***ich will dir weder zu- noch abraten,*** I don't wish to advise *or* persuade you one way or the other. **Zuraten,** *n.* ***auf sein* – (*hin*),** on his advice, at his suggestion.

zu|raunen, *see* **–flüstern.**

Zürcher ['tsyrçər], **zürcherisch,** *adj.* (*Swiss*) *see* **Züricher, züricherisch.**

zurechnen ['tsu:rɛçnən], *v.t.* add (*Dat.*, to), number, reckon (among), include, class (with); (*fig.*) ascribe, attribute, impute (to). **Zurechnung,** *f.* addition, inclusion, attribution; ***mit* – *aller Kosten,*** including all charges. **zurechnungsfähig,** *adj.* (*fig.*) accountable *or* responsible (for one's actions), sane, (*pred.*) of sound mind. **Zurechnungsfähigkeit,** *f.* accountability (for one's actions), soundness of mind, sanity, (*Law*) responsibility before the law; (*Law*) ***verminderte* –,** diminished responsibility.

zurecht [tsu'rɛçt], *adv.* right, in (good) order, in the right place; rightly, to rights, with reason; in (good) time; as it ought to be.

zurecht|basteln, *v.t.* (*coll.*) rig up, knock together. **–bringen,** *irr.v.t.* set right, put to rights; bring about, contrive. **–finden,** *irr.v.r.* find one's way (about), (*usu. fig.*) see one's way, manage (all right). **–hämmern,** *v.t.* knock into shape. **–kommen,** *irr.v.i.* arrive in (good) time; (*usu. fig.*) – ***mit,*** get on well with (*a p.*); succeed in doing, manage to do, (*coll.*) cope with (*a th.*). **–legen,** *v.t.* arrange, get *or* put ready; place *or* put in order; ***sich*** (*Dat.*) ***etwas* –,** explain s.th. to o.s., account for s.th., (*coll.*) figure out a th., figure s.th. out. **–machen,** **1.** *v.t.* get ready, prepare; ***das Bett* –,** make the bed; ***den Salat* –,** dress the salad; ***er hat sich*** (*Dat.*) ***eine schöne Ausrede* –,** he has concocted a fine excuse. **2.** *v.r.* dress, get dressed, get (o.s.) ready; (*of women*) make (o.s.) up, (*coll.*) put on one's face. **–rücken,** *v.t.* put right *or* straight *or* in order, set right, set *or* put in the right place; (*fig.*) ***ihm den Kopf* –,** bring him to his senses, make him see reason. **–schneiden,** *irr.v.t.* cut *or* trim to size *or* shape. **–setzen,** *v.t. See* **–rücken. –stellen,** *v.t.* set up, put in the right position; *see also* **–rücken. –stutzen,** *v.t. See* **–schneiden. –weisen,** *irr.v.t.* (*fig.*) reprimand, rebuke, set right. **Zurechtweisung,** *f.* reprimand, rebuke, reproof, correction. **zurecht|zimmern,** *v.t.* knock into shape; *see also* **–basteln.**

zureden ['tsu:re:dən], *v.i.* (*Dat.*) (try to) persuade, coax, encourage, urge, exhort; ***er läßt sich*** (*Dat.*) ***nicht* –,** he is not to be persuaded, (*coll.*) he will not listen. **Zureden,** *n.* persuasion, encouragement, coaxing, urging, exhortation, entreaty; ***auf unser* – (*hin*),** at our urgent request.

zureichen ['tsu:raɪçən], **1.** *v.i.* suffice, be sufficient, (*coll.*) do, be enough; reach; (*coll.*) ***es reicht nicht zu,*** it's not enough, it won't do. **2.** *v.t.* pass, hand (over), hold out (*Dat.*, to). **zureichend,** *adj.* adequate, (just) sufficient *or* enough; ***–er Grund,*** sufficient reason.

zureiten ['tsu:raɪtən], **1.** *irr.v.t.* break in (*a horse*); ***nicht zugeritten,*** unbroken. **2.** *irr.v.i.* (*aux.* s.) ride on, press on; – ***auf*** (*Acc.*), ride up to. **Zureiter,** *m.* horse-breaker.

Züricher ['tsy:rɪçər], **züricherisch,** *adj.* of Zurich. **Zürichsee,** *m.* Lake of Zurich.

Zurichte|bogen ['tsu:rɪçtər–], *m.* (*Typ.*) register-sheet. **–hammer,** *m.* dressing-hammer.

zurichten ['tsu:rɪçtən], *v.t.* prepare; make *or* get ready, (*coll.*) do up; (*cloth*) finish, (*leather*) dress, (*dough*) leaven, (*timber, stone*) shape, trim, square, dress, (*Typ.*) prepare for press; ***übel*** or ***arg* –,** use badly, ill-use, ill-treat, maltreat, maul, handle roughly, (*coll.*) make a mess of, knock about. **Zurichter,** *m.* (*Typ.*) feeder; dresser, finisher, (*leather*) currier. **Zurichtung,** *f.* preparation; trimming, dressing, (*of fabrics*) finish.

zürnen ['tsyrnən], *v.i.* be annoyed *or* angry (***über*** (*Acc.*), about (*a th.*); ***mit, auf*** (*Acc.*), with (*a p.*)).

zurren ['tsurən], *v.t.* (*Naut.*) lash, seize.

Zurschaustellung [tsur'ʃauʃtɛluŋ], *f.* exhibition, display, (*fig.*) parading.

zurück [tsu'ryk], **1.** *adv.* back, backward(s); behind, in the rear; (*fig.*) behindhand, in arrears; (*Spt.*) ***2 Punkte* –,** 2 points down; ***–!*** stand back! go back! ***an den Absender* –,** return to sender. **2.** *sep. pref. See below.*

zurück|arten, *v.i.* revert to type. **–beben,** *v.i.* (*aux.* s.) start *or* shrink back, recoil (***vor*** (*Dat.*), from). **–begeben,** *irr.v.r.* return (***an*** (*Acc.*), to).

zurückbehalten [tsu'rykbəhaltən], *irr.v.t.* keep back, detain (*a p.*), keep back, retain, withhold (*a th.*). **Zurückbehaltung,** *f.* detention; retention. **Zurückbehaltungsrecht,** *n.* (*Law*) lien (***an*** (*Dat*), on).

zurück|bekommen, *irr.v.t.* get back, recover. **-bezahlen,** *v.t.* pay back, repay, reimburse, refund. **-bleiben,** *irr.v.i.* (*aux.* s.) remain *or* stay behind; fall *or* lag behind; be left behind, (*Spt.*) drop back; (*fig.*) (*of a p.*) survive, (*of a th.*) be left (over *or* behind), (*of clock*) lose, be slow, (*at school*) stay *or* be kept down; – ***hinter*** (*Dat.*), fall short of *or* not come up to (*expectations*), drop off from (*previous level*); ***geistig zurückgeblieben,*** backward, mentally retarded. **zurückbleibend,** *adj.* (*of a p.*) surviving, (*of a th.*) residual.

zurück|blenden, *v.i.* (*Films*) flash back. **-blicken,** *v.i.* look back; ***auf*** or ***in die Vergangenheit*** **–,** recall *or* review the past. **-blickend,** *adj.* retrospective. **-bringen,** *irr.v.t.* bring back, restore, (*Math.*) reduce (***auf*** (*Acc.*), to); ***zum Gehorsam*** **–,** reduce to obedience; ***ins Leben*** **–,** bring back *or* recall *or* restore to life; ***diese Verluste haben ihn sehr zurückgebracht,*** these losses have set *or* put him back a great deal.

zurück|datieren, *v.t.* antedate. **-denken, 1.** *irr.v.i.* reflect (***an*** (*Acc.*), on), think back (to *or* on), recall (to memory). **2.** *irr.v.r.* cast one's thoughts *or* mind back (***in*** (*Acc.*), to). **-drängen,** *v.t.* push back, (*Mil.*) force *or* drive *or* roll back, repel, repulse, (*fig.*) repress.

zurück|erhalten, *irr.v.t. See* **-bekommen. -erinnern,** *v.r.* ***sich – an*** (*Acc.*), recall, remember, recollect; *see* **-denken. -erobern,** *v.t.* reconquer. **-erstatten,** *v.t.* hand back, return, restore; *see also* **-bezahlen.**

zurück|fahren, 1. *irr.v.i.* (*aux.* s.) drive *or* go *or* come *or* travel back, return; (*of projectile*) fly back, rebound, recoil; (*fig.*) start back (in surprise). **2.** *irr. v.t.* drive (*a vehicle*) back. **-fallen,** *irr.v.i.* (*aux.* s.) fall back, (*Spt.*) fall behind, drop back; (*of rays*) be reflected; (*fig.*) revert (***an*** (*Acc.*), to), relapse (***in*** (*Acc.*), into); ***die Schande ist auf ihn zurückgefallen,*** the disgrace redounds upon him. **-finden,** *irr.v.r.* find one's *or* the way back. **-fließen,** *irr.v.i.* (*aux.* s.) flow back, recede; ***die Wohltat fließt auf den Wohltäter zurück,*** a good deed comes home to the benefactor. **-fordern,** *v.t.* demand *or* claim back, reclaim. **Zurückforderung,** *f.* reclamation.

zurückführen [tsu'rykfy:rən], *v.t.* 1. lead *or* conduct back, (*Mech.*) feed back; ***in die Heimat*** **–,** repatriate; ***in die Haft*** **–,** remand into custody; 2. (*fig.*) trace (back) (***auf*** (*Acc.*), to), attribute (to), explain (by); (*Math.*) ***auf einen Nenner*** **–,** reduce to a denominator; ***zurückzuführen auf*** (*Acc.*), traceable to, explainable by, due to. **Zurückführung,** *f.* reduction; – ***auf das Unmögliche,*** reductio ad absurdum; – ***des Heeres auf den Friedenstand,*** reduction of the army to a peace footing.

Zurückgabe [tsu'rykga:bə], *f.* return(ing), restoration, restitution; surrender. **zurück|geben,** *irr.v.t.* give back, return, restore; surrender, deliver up; (*Footb.*) pass back; (*discourse*) retort. **-gebogen,** *adj.* reflexed.

zurückgehen [tsu'rykge:ən], *irr.v.i.* go *or* walk back, return, retrace one's steps; (*Mil.*) fall back, retreat, retire; (*fig.*) decrease, diminish, get smaller, decline, recede, subside, abate; (*coll.*) fall off; be cancelled, not take place, come to nothing, (*as engagement*) be broken off, (*coll.*) be off; – ***auf*** (*Acc.*), trace (back) to; be traced back to, originate in (*a th.*) *or* with *or* from (*a p.*), have its origin in (*a th.*) *or* with (*a p.*); ***Waren – lassen,*** return goods, send goods back; ***auf die Ursache des Streits*** **–,** trace the quarrel back to its beginnings; ***der Streit geht auf eine lächerliche Kleinigkeit zurück,*** the quarrel has its origin in a ridiculously trifling matter; ***das Geschäft geht zurück,*** business is declining *or* (*coll.*) falling off; ***die Verlobung ist zurückgegangen,*** the engagement has been broken off *or* (*coll.*) is off.

zurück|geleiten, *v.t.* lead *or* conduct *or* escort back. **-gewinnen,** *irr.v.t.* win back, regain, recover, recuperate (*one's losses*). **-gezogen,** *adj.* retired, secluded; – ***leben,*** live in seclusion, lead a retired life. **Zurückgezogenheit,** *f.* seclusion, privacy, retirement.

zurück|greifen, *irr.v.i.* – ***auf*** (*Acc.*), fall back (up)on, have recourse to, (*fig.*) refer to; ***in der Erzählung weiter*** **–,** pick up the story at an earlier point. **-halten, 1.** *irr.v.t.* hold *or* keep back, retain, withhold; delay, retard; suppress, restrain (*tears, outcry etc.*), repress, keep to o.s. (*feelings*); ***ihn*** **–,** keep him (back), prevent him (***von,*** from). **2.** *irr.v.r.* restrain o.s., hold back, keep a rein *or* check on o.s.; keep aloof *or* to o.s., be reserved. **3.** *irr.v.i.* – ***mit,*** keep *or* hold back, conceal; ***mit seiner Meinung*** **–,** suspend *or* reserve one's opinion, keep one's opinion to o.s. **-haltend,** *adj.* reserved, uncommunicative, guarded, cautious, discreet, (*coll.*) cool, distant, stand-offish; (*coll.*) ***nicht – sein,*** not be bashful; (*coll.*) ***mit seinem Lob nicht – sein,*** be unsparing in his praise. **Zurückhaltung,** *f.* retention; (*fig.*) reserve, caution, discretion; ***sich*** (*Dat.*) – ***auferlegen,*** exercise restraint; ***mit*** **–,** cautiously, discreetly, guardedly.

zurück|hängen, *v.i.* (*coll.*) hang back, lag behind, trail. **-holen,** *v.t.* (*a th.*) fetch back, (*a p.*) call *or* fetch back. **-kaufen,** *v.t.* buy back, repurchase; redeem (*a pledge*). **-kehren,** *v.i.* (*aux.* s.) come *or* go back, return. **-kommen,** *irr.v.i.* (*aux.* s.) come back, return; become reduced in circumstances, come down in the world; get behindhand (with one's work); ***von seiner Meinung*** **–,** change *or* alter one's opinion *or* mind; (*fig.*) – ***auf*** (*Acc.*), return *or* revert *or* refer to, (*coll.*) come back to. **Zurückkunft,** *f.* return.

zurück|lassen, *irr.v.t.* 1. permit to return; 2. leave (behind), abandon; 3. leave (far) behind, outdistance, outstrip. **-laufen,** *irr.v.i.* (*aux.* s.) run back; flow back; recoil. **-legen, 1.** *v.t.* 1. put back; 2. (*fig.*) put *or* lay aside, hold in reserve, (*coll.*) put by (*Dat.*, for); (*money*) save, put by (for a rainy day); 3. travel, traverse, complete, cover (*a distance*); ***zurückgelegte Strecke,*** distance covered, (*Motor.*) mileage; ***nach zurückgelegtem 70. Lebensjahr,*** on completion of *or* having completed one's 70th year. **2.** *v.r.* lie back, recline.

zurück|leiten, *v.t.* lead back, return; trace back; (*Mech.*) feed back. **-lenken,** *v.t.* ***seine Schritte*** **–,** retrace one's steps. **-liegen,** *irr.v.i.* belong to the past, date back. **-melden,** *v.r.* report back.

Zurücknahme [tsu'rykna:mə], *f.* 1. reacceptance; resumption; ***ich hoffe, Sie beanstanden die – nicht,*** I hope you won't object to taking it back; 2. withdrawal, recantation, revocation; (*Law*) – ***einer Klage,*** non-suit. **zurücknehmen,** *irr.v.t.* 1. take back; 2. withdraw, retract, (*statement*) revoke, (*Law*) cancel, countermand (*order*), (*Law*) withdraw, (*coll.*) drop (*a charge*); ***sein Wort*** **–,** go back on one's word *or* promise; ***das Gesagte*** **–,** withdraw what one has said, (*coll.*) eat one's words.

zurück|prallen, *v.i.* (*aux.* s.) rebound, recoil, bounce back; (*projectile*) ricochet, (*rays*) reverberate, be reflected; (*fig.*) recoil, start back (***vor*** (*Dat.*), from). **-rechnen,** *v.i.* count back. **-reichen, 1.** *v.t.* hand *or* give back, return. **2.** *v.i.* (*in time*) reach *or* go back (***bis,*** (*Dat.*) *or* ***bis in*** (*Acc.*), ***auf*** (*Acc.*), to). **-reisen,** *v.i.* (*aux.* s.) travel back, return. **-rufen,** *irr.v.t.* call back, (*Comm.*) withdraw (*a bill*); ***ins Gedächtnis*** **–,** recall, call to mind.

zurück|sagen, *v.t.* reply; – ***lassen,*** send a reply, send word back. **-schallen,** *v.i.* (*aux.* s.) resound, re-echo. **-schalten,** *v.i.* (*Motor.*) change down. **-schaudern,** *v.i.* (*aux.* s.) recoil, shrink back (in horror) (***vor*** (*Dat.*), from). **-schauen,** *v.i.* look back. **-scheuen,** *v.i.* shrink (back), flinch (***vor*** (*Dat.*), from), balk (at); ***vor nichts*** **–,** stop *or* stick at nothing. **-schicken,** *v.t.* send back, return; ***in die Haft*** **–,** remand in(to) custody.

zurück|schlagen, 1. *irr.v.t.* beat *or* drive back, repel, repulse, beat *or* throw off; ***die Decke*** **–,** fold back the cover; ***den Mantel*** **–,** throw open one's coat; (*Tenn.*) ***den Ball*** **–,** return the ball. **2.** *irr.v.i.* hit *or* strike back; (*as flames*) blow *or* flash back, back-fire. **-schnellen, 1.** *v.i.* (*aux.* s.) (*of a p.*) jump back; (*of a th.*) fly back, rebound, recoil. **2.** *v.t.* fling back. **-schrecken, 1.** *irr.v.i. See* **-scheuen. 2.** *reg.v.t.* frighten away, scare off, deter. **-sehnen,** *v.r.* long to be back *or* to return. **-senden,** *irr.v.t. See* **-schicken. -setzen,** *v.t.* put *or* place back, replace; (*fig.*) reduce, lower (*price*); neglect, slight, snub, (*coll.*) push into the background (*a p.*); ***zurückgesetzte Waren,*** rejects, seconds, reduced-price goods. **Zurücksetzung,** *f.* reduction (*in price*); slight, snub; neglect, discrimination.

zurück|sinken, *irr.v.i.* (*aux.* s.) sink *or* fall back, (*fig.*) relapse (***in*** (*Acc.*), into). **–spiegeln,** *v.t.* reflect. **–spielen,** *v.t., v.i.* (*Footb.*) pass back. **–springen,** *irr.v.i.* (*aux.* s.) leap *or* jump *or* spring back; rebound, recoil, (*Geom.*) re-enter (*as an angle*); (*Archit.*) recede (*of frontage*). **–stecken, 1.** *v.t.* put *or* push (further) back. **2.** *v.i.* (*fig.*) come down a peg (or two), come off one's high horse. **–stehen,** *irr.v.i.* (*aux.* s.) stand back; (*fig.*) – ***hinter*** (*Dat.*), be inferior to; not come up to (*expectations etc.*); – ***müssen,*** have to wait *or* to stand down, be passed over, be pushed into the background. **–stellen,** *v.t.* put back (in its place), replace; postpone, defer, (*coll.*) hold over (*a decision*), (*Mil.*) defer (*enlistment*), exempt (from service); (*Comm.*) reserve, put *or* lay aside, keep on one side; (*Mech.*) reset; put back (*a clock*); ***die eigenen Interessen –,*** sink one's own interest. **Zurückstellung,** *f.* (*Mil.*) deferment, exemption.

zurück|stoßen, *irr.v.t. See* **–drängen. –stoßend,** *adj.* repellent. **–strahlen, 1.** *v.t.* reflect (*light, sound*). **2.** *v.i.* (*light*) reflect, be reflected, (*sound*) reverberate. **Zurückstrahlung,** *f.* reflection, reverberation.

zurück|streifen, *v.t.* turn *or* roll *or* tuck up, turn *or* roll back (*sleeves*). **–taumeln,** *v.i.* (*aux.* s.) reel back. **–treiben,** *irr.v.t.* drive back (*flock*); (*Mil.*) *see* **–drängen. –treten,** *irr.v.i.* (*aux.* s.) step *or* stand back, (*Mil.*) fall back into line; (*of floods*) recede, subside; (*fig.*) withdraw (***von,*** from) (*an undertaking*), (*coll.*) back out (of); resign, retire (from) (*a post*); be unimportant *or* insignificant (***gegenüber,*** in comparison with); – ***von,*** cancel, terminate (*an agreement*); ***ins Privatleben –,*** retire into *or* return to private life; – ***lassen,*** push into the background, throw into the shade. **–tun,** *irr.v.t.* put back, replace; ***einen Schritt –,*** (take a) step back.

zurück|übersetzen, *v.t.* retranslate, translate back (***in*** (*Acc.*), into). **–verfolgen,** *v.t.* retrace (*a route*), (*fig.*) trace back (***zu,*** to). **–vergüten,** *v.t.* refund, reimburse. **–verlegen,** *v.t.* (*Artil.*) shorten (*range*). **–versetzen, 1.** *v.t.* put back, restore (to its former condition), (*Mil.*) demote, (*at school*) relegate to a lower class, (*coll.*) put down. **2.** *v.r.* ***sich in eine frühere Zeit –,*** go back (in one's mind *or* in imagination) *or* think back to a former time; ***sich in seine Kindheit zurückversetzt fühlen,*** feel that one has stepped back into one's childhood. **–verwandeln, 1.** *v.t.* transform *or* change back (***in*** (*Acc.*), into). **2.** *v.r.* change back (into), revert (to). **–verweisen,** *irr.v.t.* refer back (***an*** (*Acc.*), to).

zurück|weichen, *irr.v.i.* (*aux.* s.) fall back, give way (under pressure), give ground, withdraw, retreat, yield (***vor*** (*Dat.*), before); (*fig.*) shrink (back) (***vor*** (*Dat.*), from); submit, give in, give way (to). **–weisen,** *irr.v.t.* turn *or* send back; (*fig.*) decline, reject, refuse (to accept), (*Law*) dismiss (*a charge*), (*Comm.*) dishonour (*a bill*), (*Mil.*) repulse, repel (*an attack*), rebuff (*an opponent*); – ***auf*** (*Acc.*), *see* **–verweisen**; ***als unberechtigt –,*** repudiate. **Zurückweisung,** *f.* refusal, rejection; dismissal, rebuff; repudiation; repulse. **zurück|werfen,** *irr. v.t.* throw back; (*fig.*) repel, repulse, throw back (*enemy*), reflect, throw back (*light, sound*), inflict a setback on (*a p.*). **–wirken,** *v.i.* react (***auf*** (*Acc.*), on); be retrospective (*as laws*).

zurückzahlen [tsuˈryktsa:lən], *v.t.* pay back, repay, refund; (*a debt*) pay back *or* off, redeem. **Zurückzahlung,** *f.* repayment, refund.

zurück|ziehen, 1. *irr.v.t.* draw back, withdraw, (*Comm.*) call in (*money*); (*fig.*) retract, recant. **2.** *irr.v.r.* retreat, retire, withdraw, fall back; retire (for the night); ***sich – auf*** (*Acc.*), fall back on; ***sich – von,*** give up, quit, retire from, take no more part in; ***sich vom Geschäft –,*** retire from business; ***sich in sich selbst –,*** withdraw *or* retire into o.s., become self-absorbed. **3.** *irr.v.i.* (*aux.* s.) move *or* march back. **–ziehend,** *adj.* retractive. **Zurück|ziehen,** *n.,* **–ziehung,** *f.* withdrawal, retraction.

Zuruf [ˈtsu:ru:f], *m.* shout, call; cheer, acclamation; ***durch –,*** by acclamation. **zurufen,** *irr.v.t., v.i.* (*Dat.*) call (out) *or* shout to; cheer, acclaim; ***ihm Beifall –,*** cheer *or* applaud him.

zurüsten [ˈtsu:rystən], *v.t.* fit out, equip; make *or* get ready, prepare. **Zurüstung,** *f.* preparation, fitting out, equipment; ***–en treffen,*** make preparations.

Zusage [ˈtsu:za:gə], *f.* promise, word, pledge, undertaking; assent, acceptance, approval. **zusagen, 1.** *v.t.* promise, pledge; ***es ihm auf den Kopf –,*** tell it him to his face. **2.** *v.i.* 1. promise *or* undertake to come, accept (*an invitation*); ***–de Antwort,*** acceptance; 2. (*Dat.*) suit, please, appeal to, be to one's taste *or* liking, meet one's wishes, (*of food, climate etc.*) agree with.

zusammen [tsuˈzamən], **1.** *adv.* together, (con)jointly; at the same time; ***alle –,*** all of them, all in a body, (*coll.*) the whole bunch; (*of speech*) (all of them) in chorus; ***alles –,*** all together, (all) in all, (*coll.*) the whole lot; – ***mit,*** in company with, together *or* (*coll.*) along with; in conjunction with, at the same time as. **2.** *sep.pref. See below.*

Zusammenarbeit [tsuˈzamənˀarbaɪt], *f.* co-operation, team-work; collaboration (*also Pol. with the enemy*). **zusammenarbeiten,** *v.i.* work together, collaborate, co-operate.

zusammen|backen, *v.i.* cake (together), stick together. **–ballen, 1.** *v.t.* form *or* roll into a ball, agglomerate, conglomerate, (*fig.*) mass, concentrate. **2.** *v.r.* agglomerate, conglomerate, bunch (together), (*as clouds*) mass, gather. **Zusammen|ballung,** *f.* concentration, massing, agglomeration, conglomeration; bunching, congestion. **–bau,** *m.* assembly, montage. **zusammenbauen,** *v.t.* assemble, (*coll.*) rig up.

zusammen|beißen, *irr.v.t.* ***die Zähne –,*** clench *or* set one's teeth. **–bekommen,** *irr.v.t.* (*coll.*) manage to join, get together, (*money*) scrape together, raise. **–berufen,** *irr.v.t.* call together, summon, convoke. **–binden,** *irr.v.t.* tie *or* bind together; tie up. **–brauen, 1.** *v.t.* concoct (*also fig.*). **2.** *v.r.* (*fig.*) be brewing. **–brechen,** *irr.v.i.* (*aux.* s.) collapse, break down, (*fig. of a p.*) go to pieces, (*Comm.*) fail, (*coll.*) go smash; ***seine Knie brechen unter ihm zusammen,*** his knees give way under him. **–bringen,** *irr.v.t.* bring *or* get together, join, unite; collect, gather together, raise (*money*), amass (*a fortune*), rally (*troops*); (*coll.*) ***es –,*** manage it, cope with it; ***seine Gedanken –,*** collect one's thoughts; ***die Parteien (wieder) –,*** reconcile the parties; ***keine drei Sätze –,*** not have a sensible word to say; ***zusammengebrachtes Vermögen,*** joint property; ***zusammengebrachte Kinder,*** half-brothers and sisters. **Zusammenbruch,** *m.* collapse, débâcle, failure, breakdown, (*coll.*) crack-up.

zusammen|drängen, 1. *v.t.* crowd *or* press together; compress, concentrate, condense. **2.** *v.r.* crowd *or* huddle together. **–drückbar,** *adj.* compressible. **–drücken,** *v.t.* compress; press *or* squeeze together.

zusammen|fahren, *irr.v.i.* (*aux.* s.) 1. come into collision, collide (***mit,*** with), crash (into); 2. (*fig.*) start back (***vor*** (*Dat.*), with *or* in), wince (with). **–fallen,** *irr.v.i.* 1. fall down, collapse; shrink, crumble away; (*of a p.*) waste away, lose strength; 2. (*in time or place*) coincide (***mit,*** with). **–fallend,** *adj.* coincident. **–falten,** *v.t.* fold (up); furl (*sails*).

zusammen|fassen, *v.t.* embrace, combine, comprise, comprehend, unite; collect (*one's thoughts etc.*); mass (*troops*), concentrate (*fire*), pool (*resources*); summarize, condense, sum up, recapitulate; ***um es kurz zusammenzufassen,*** to sum up. **–fassend,** *adj.* comprehensive, summary. **Zusammenfassung,** *f.* summary, summing up, recapitulation, synopsis, résumé; collection, concentration, pooling; condensation.

zusammen|finden, *irr.v.r.* come together, meet. **–flicken,** *v.t.* patch up. **–fließen,** *irr.v.i.* flow together, (*of rivers*) join, meet. **Zusammenfluß,** *m.* confluence, junction (*of two rivers*). **zusammen|fügen, 1.** *v.t.* join (together), unite, combine: (*Mech.*) fit together, assemble. **2.** *v.r.* join, unite, (*Mech.*) fit into one another, articulate. **–führen,** *v.t.* bring together.

zusammen|geben, *irr.v.t.* join in marriage *or* wedlock. **–gehen,** *irr.v.i.* (*aux.* s.) 1. go together; be accompanied *or* attended (***mit,*** by); 2. suit one another, match; 3. shrink, get smaller, diminish; 4. close up, fold down *or* together.

zusammen|gehören, *v.i.* belong together, be correlated, match, be fellows, form a pair. **–gehörig,** *adj.* belonging together, related, allied, correlated, congruous, homogeneous, homologous. **Zusammengehörigkeit,** *f.* correlation, congruity, intimate connection, unity; solidarity (*of persons*), (*coll.*) togetherness. **Zusammengehörigkeitsgefühl,** *n.* (feeling of) solidarity *or* togetherness, team-spirit.

zusammen|genommen, *adj.* combined. **–geraten,** *irr.v.i.* (*fig.*) clash, quarrel, (*coll.*) fall out, have words (***mit,*** with). **–gerollt,** *adj.* convolute(d). **–gesetzt,** *adj.* composed, consisting (***aus,*** of), compounded (from); composite, compound, complex; ***–er Satz,*** complex sentence; ***–es Wort,*** compound (word). **–gewürfelt,** *adj.* motley, (*Spt.*) scratch (*team*).

Zusammenhalt [tsu'zamənhalt], *m.* holding together; consistence, consistency, coherence, cohesion, cohesiveness, unity; tie, bond, solidarity, team-spirit. **zusammen|halten, 1.** *irr.v.t.* hold together; compare; maintain, keep going, support. **2.** *irr.v.i.* hold *or* stick together; be firm friends; cohere. **–haltend,** *adj.* cohesive.

Zusammenhang [tsu'zamənhaŋ], *m.* connection (connexion), association; relationship, relation, correlation; cohesion, continuity, coherence; context; ***Mangel an –,*** incoherence; ***aus dem – kommen,*** lose the thread (of one's discourse); ***aus dem – gerissene Wörter,*** words separated *or* divorced from their context; ***– der Begriffe,*** association of ideas; ***der ganze – der S.,*** the whole story, the ins and outs of the matter; ***in – bringen mit,*** link *or* connect with; ***im – stehen mit,*** be connected with; ***nicht im – stehen mit . . .,*** have no connection with . . .; ***ohne –,*** incoherent, disconnected. **zusammen|hangen, –hängen,** *irr.v.i.* hang together, cohere; (*fig.*) be connected; ***das hängt damit nicht zusammen,*** that has nothing to do with it. **–hängend,** *adj.* connected, continuous, uninterrupted, (*fig.*) coherent; connected, related, allied, interdependent. **zusammenhang(s)los,** *adj.* disconnected, incoherent, inconsistent, disjointed, loose, rambling. **Zusammenhang(s)losigkeit,** *f.* incoherence, lack of connection, inconsistency.

zusammen|hauen, *irr.v.t.* cut *or* smash *or* dash to pieces; thrash soundly, (*coll.*) beat up; (*coll.*) knock together. **–haufen,** *v.t.* heap *or* pile up, accumulate. **–heften,** *v.t.* stitch together, (*Dressm.*) tack. **–heilen,** *v.i.* (*aux.* s.) heal up *or* over. **–holen,** *v.t.* collect, bring together, gather (together).

zusammen|kauern, *v.r.* cower; squat down, squat on one's haunches. **–kaufen,** *v.t.* buy up.

Zusammenklang [tsu'zamənklaŋ], *m.* accord, consonance, harmony.

zusammen|klappbar, *adj.* folding, collapsible. **–klappen, 1.** *v.t.* fold up; close (*a knife, fan etc.*); ***die Hacken –,*** click one's heels. **2.** *v.i.* (*aux.* s.) (*coll.*) collapse, go to pieces, break down, have a (nervous) breakdown. **–knüllen,** *v.t.* crumple (up). **–kommen,** *irr.v.i.* (*aux.* s.) come together; assemble; meet. **–krachen,** *v.i.* (*aux.* s.) crash down, come crashing down. **Zusammenkunft,** *f.* meeting, gathering, reunion, conference, assembly, convention; (*of two people*) interview, rendezvous; (*Astr.*) conjunction.

zusammen|läppern, *v.r.* (*coll.*) (*of expenses*) add *or* mount up, run into money, cost a lot. **–laufen,** *irr.v.i.* (*aux.* s.) run together; congregate, collect, gather; (*as lines, streets etc.*) converge, (tend to) meet; (*of colours*) blend, run (into one another); (*as milk*) curdle, coagulate; (*coll.*) (*of fabrics*) shrink; ***auf*** or ***in einen Punkt –,*** meet in a point; ***das Wasser lief ihm im Munde zusammen,*** his mouth watered. **–leben,** *v.i.* live together; cohabit; ***– mit,*** live with. **Zusammenleben,** *n.* living together, association; companionship; social *or* corporate life; (*Law*) ***außereheliches –,*** cohabitation. **zusammen|legbar,** *adj. See* **–klappbar. –legen,** *v.t.* place *or* lay *or* put together; fold (*one's arms*), fold up, close (*a penknife*); collect, pool, club together (*money*), (*Comm.*) combine, consolidate, unite, fuse, merge; integrate, centralize; ***auf einen Haufen –,*** put into a pile, make a heap of. **Zusammenlegung,** *f.* consolidation, merger, fusion; integration, centralization.

zusammennehmen [tsu'zamənne:mən], **1.** *irr.v.t.* take together, gather (up *or* together), husband (*one's strength etc.*); ***seine Gedanken –,*** collect one's thoughts; ***seine Kräfte –,*** summon all one's strength, brace o.s.; ***alles zusammengenommen,*** all in all, all things considered; ***alle Umstände –,*** take all the circumstances into consideration. **2.** *irr.v.r.* collect o.s., control o.s.; make an effort, pull o.s. together, pluck up courage; be on one's best behaviour.

zusammen|packen, *v.t.* pack up. **–passen, 1.** *v.i.* be well matched, go well together; agree, harmonize, (*of a couple*) be a good match. **2.** *v.t.* fit (into one another *or* together); adapt *or* adjust (to fit), (*colours, shapes etc.*) match. **–pferchen,** *v.t.* pack *or* crowd *or* squeeze together, (*coll.*) pack like sardines; pen up (*cattle*). **Zusammenprall,** *m.* collision, impact, (*fig.*) clash. **zusammen|prallen,** *v.i.* (*aux.* s.) collide, (*coll.*) crash; (*fig.*) clash; ***– mit,*** bump into *or* against. **–pressen,** *v.t.* press *or* squeeze together, compress, condense; ***die Zähne –,*** set *or* clench one's teeth.

zusammen|raffen, 1. *v.t.* seize; sweep *or* snatch up; collect hurriedly, amass (*a fortune*). **2.** *v.r.* pull o.s. together, make an effort. **–rechnen,** *v.t.* reckon up; add up, total; ***alles zusammengerechnet,*** taking everything into account, all in all. **–reimen, 1.** *v.t.* (*coll.*) make out, make sense of, put two and two together; ***ich kann es mir nicht –,*** I cannot make head or tail of it. **2.** *v.r. See* **–passen, 1**; ***wie reimt sich das zusammen?*** how can that be reconciled? how can *or* do you account for that? **–reißen,** *irr.v.r. See* **–raffen. –rollen,** *v.t.* roll *or* coil up. **–rotten,** *v.r.* band *or* flock together, form a gang; ***sich – mit,*** plot *or* conspire *or* (*coll.*) gang up with. **Zusammenrottung,** *f.* unlawful assembly. **zusammen|rücken, 1.** *v.t.* move (closer) together. **2.** *v.i.* move up, make room; sit *or* move *or* draw closer together; (*Mil.*) ***nach rechts –,*** move to the right. **–rufen,** *irr.v.t.* call together, convoke, convene, summon. **–rühren,** *v.t.* stir *or* mix up.

Zusammenschau [tsu'zamənʃau], *f.* synoptic presentation. **zusammen|schieben, 1.** *irr.v.t.* push together, telescope. **2.** *irr.v.r.* telescope. **–schießen, 1.** *irr.v.t.* shoot down *or* to pieces; (*fig.*) ***eine Summe –,*** club together to raise a sum. **2.** *irr.v.i.* (*aux.* s.) crystallize.

zusammenschlagen [tsu'zamənʃla:gən], **1.** *irr.v.i.* (*aux.* s.) strike against one another, crash together; close with a bang *or* crash; ***die Wellen schlugen über ihm zusammen,*** the waves dashed *or* closed over *or* engulfed him. **2.** *irr.v.t.* strike *or* beat together; clap (*one's hands*); click (*one's heels*); smash (up) (*a hostile force*); (*newspapers etc.*) fold (up); gather; (*coll.*) throw together, knock up (*a makeshift construction*); (*coll.*) ***ihn –,*** beat him up, (*sl.*) give him a going-over *or* the works; ***vor Verwunderung die Hände über dem Kopf –,*** throw up one's hands in astonishment.

zusammen|schließen, 1. *irr.v.t.* join *or* link (together), unite, (*Comm.*) amalgamate, pool, merge (***zu,*** with), integrate (with *or* into), consolidate. **2.** *irr.v.r.* combine, unite, join forces, amalgamate; (*Pol.*) form an alliance, (*Mil.*) close ranks; *see also* **–rotten. Zusammenschluß,** *m.* union, association, combination, integration, consolidation, federation, (*Comm.*) amalgamation, merger, (*Pol.*) alliance, coalition.

zusammen|schmelzen, 1. *irr.v.i.* (*aux.* s.) melt, dissolve, fuse; melt away (*also fig.*). **2.** *irr.v.t.* melt down, fuse. **–schmieden,** *v.t.* (*fig.*) weld together, forge. **–schmieren,** *v.t.* (*coll.*) scribble, jot down hurriedly. **–schnüren,** *v.t.* lace *or* tie up; (*fig.*) ***ihm die Kehle –,*** take his breath away; ***ihm das Herz –,*** wring his heart. **–schrecken,** *irr.v.i.* (give a) start (***bei,*** at). **–schreiben,** *irr.v.t.* compile; write in *or* as one word; ***sich*** (*Dat.*) ***ein Vermögen –,*** make a fortune by one's pen *or* with one's books *or* out of writing. **–schrumpfen,** *v.i.* (*aux.* s.) shrivel (up), shrink, contract; (*fig.*) dwindle (away), (*coll.*) run short. **–schütteln,** *v.t.* shake up well. **–schweißen,** *v.t.* weld (together) (***zu,*** into) (*also fig.*; *see also* **–schmieden**). **Zusammensein,** *n.* meeting, gathering.

zusammensetzen [tsu'zamənzɛtsən], **1.** *v.t.* put together, pile (up), stack; compose, make up, piece together; compound, combine, (*Mech.*) construct, assemble; ***die Gewehre –,*** pile arms; ***zusammengesetztes Wort,*** compound (word). **2.** *v.r.* (*persons*) sit (down) together; (*fig.*) (*coll.*) get together, (*sl.*) go into a huddle; (*things*) be composed, consist (***aus,*** of). **Zusammensetzspiel,** *n.* jigsaw puzzle. **Zusammensetzung,** *f.* composition, ingredients; construction, assembly, formation; (*Chem., Gram.*) compound; structure, synthesis.

zusammen|sinken, *irr.v.i.* (*aux.* s.) sink down, collapse. **–sparen,** *v.t.* save up, accumulate, amass by saving. **Zusammenspiel,** *n.* co-operation, acting in unison, interplay (*of forces*); (*Mus., Theat.*) ensemble; (*Theat., Spt.*) teamwork.

zusammen|stecken, 1. *v.t.* stick *or* put together, join *or* fasten *or* pin together; ***die Köpfe –,*** put one's heads together. **2.** *v.i.* (*coll.*) conspire together, be hand in (*or* and) glove with one another; ***immer –,*** be constantly together, be inseparable. **–stehen,** *irr.v.i.* stand together *or* side by side, stand shoulder to shoulder; (*fig.*) unite for a common cause, (*coll.*) stick together. **–stellen,** *v.t.* place *or* put together; (*fig.*) arrange, assort, classify, group; compile, make up (*a list*), assemble (*troops, a train*). **Zusammenstellung,** *f.* arrangement, grouping, juxtaposition, combination, assembly (*of troops, a train*), compilation; list, table, synopsis, summary, survey, inventory, classification.

zusammen|stimmen, *v.i.* agree, accord, match, tally, harmonize; be congruous. **–stoppeln,** *v.t.* patch up, piece together.

Zusammenstoß [tsu'zamənʃto:s], *m.* collision, (*Motor.*) (*coll.*) crash; impact, shock; (*fig.*) hostile encounter, engagement, conflict, clash; (*Motor.*) ***frontaler –,*** head-on collision. **zusammenstoßen, 1.** *irr.v.t.* bang *or* knock against one another; ***die Gläser –,*** clink *or* touch glasses. **2.** *irr.v.i.* (*aux.* h. & s.) **– *mit,*** collide with, run *or* smash into; (*fig.*) encounter, meet (with), clash with, abut on, adjoin.

zusammen|strömen, *v.i.* (*aux.* s.) flow together; (*people*) flock *or* crowd together, assemble. **–stücke(l)n,** *v.t. See* **–stoppeln. –stürzen,** *v.i.* (*aux.* s.) collapse, fall to the ground, (*coll.*) cave in. **–suchen,** *v.t.* gather up *or* together, collect.

zusammen|tragen, *irr.v.t.* gather, collect, bring together, (*fig.*) compile. **–treffen,** *irr.v.i.* (*aux.* s.) meet (one another); (*of events*) concur, coincide; ***nicht mit unseren Erwartungen –,*** not meet *or* answer our expectation(s). **Zusammentreffen,** *n.* meeting, gathering; (*Mil.*) engagement, (hostile) encounter; (*of events*) concurrence, coincidence. **zusammen|treiben,** *irr.v.t.* drive together; beat up (*game*); (*coll.*) round *or* drum up (*people*), get hold of, raise (*money*). **–treten,** *irr.v.i.* (*aux.* s.) meet, come together, (*Parl.*) convene, assemble. **Zusammentritt,** *m.* meeting, assembly. **zusammen|trommeln,** *v.t. See* **–treiben** (*coll.*). **–tun, 1.** *irr.v.t.* put together, join; mix. **2.** *irr.v.r.* come together, join forces, combine, associate, (*coll.*) team up (***mit,*** with), (*sl.*) gang up (***gegen,*** on).

zusammen|wachsen, *irr.v.i.* (*aux.* s.) grow together, coalesce. **–werfen,** *irr.v.t.* throw together, throw into a heap, (*fig.*) lump together; mix *or* jumble up, confuse, confound. **–wickeln,** *v.t.* roll *or* wrap up. **–wirken,** *v.i.* act *or* work together, collaborate, co-operate, (*of events*) combine, concur. **Zusammenwirken,** *n.* combined efforts *or* action, collaboration, co-operation, (*of circumstances*) combination, concurrence. **zusammen|würfeln,** *v.t. See* **–werfen.**

zusammen|zählen, *v.t.* count *or* add up, total, (*coll.*) tot up. **–ziehbar,** *adj.* contractile, contractible. **–ziehen, 1.** *irr.v.t.* draw together, gather, assemble; contract, (*fig.*) condense, abridge, epitomize; ***Zahlen –,*** add up figures, reduce figures to a total; ***die Augenbrauen –,*** knit one's brows; ***die Lippen –,*** purse one's lips; ***Truppen –,*** mass *or* concentrate troops; ***zusammengezogene*** (***Wort***)-***formen,*** contracted forms, contractions. **2.** *irr.v.r.* gather, be brewing, draw to a head; contract, shrink; ***es zieht sich ein Gewitter zusammen,*** a storm is brewing. **3.** *irr.v.i.* (*aux.* s.) move into the same house *or* rooms, share rooms. **–ziehend,** *adj.* (*Med.*) astringent. **Zusammenziehung,** *f.* contraction, constriction, shrinking, shrinkage; condensation; mustering, concentration (*of troops etc.*), contracted (form of) word, contraction.

Zusatz ['tsu:zats], *m.* (**-es,** *pl.* **¨-e**) addition, adjunct, admixture; (*Metall.*) alloy, (*Chem.*) additive; (*to writing*) addendum, appendix, postscript, supplement; corollary, rider (*to a clause*), codicil (*to a will*).

Zusatz|abkommen, *n.* supplementary agreement. **–antrag,** *m.* (*Parl.*) amendment. **–ausrüstung,** *f.* auxiliary equipment. **–batterie,** *f.* booster battery. **–behälter,** *m.* (*Motor.*) spare tank. **–gerät,** *n.* auxilliary *or* ancillary apparatus, attachment, adaptor. **–ladung,** *f.* booster (charge). **–last,** *f.* (*Elec.*) additional load. **–legierung,** *f.* (*Metall.*) hardener.

zusätzlich ['tsu:zɛtslɪç], **1.** *adj.* additional, added, extra, supplementary, complementary; auxiliary. **2.** *adv.* in addition, besides, (*coll.*) on top of that, into the bargain.

Zusatz|steuer, *f.* supplementary tax. **–versicherung,** *f.* supplementary *or* complementary insurance.

zuschanden [tsu'ʃandən], *adv.* ***sich – arbeiten,*** wear o.s. out *or* kill o.s. with work; ***– gehen,*** go to rack and ruin; ***– machen,*** spoil, ruin, blight, destroy; foil, thwart, defeat, frustrate; ***– reiten,*** override, founder (*a horse*); ***– werden,*** come to nothing, be ruined *or* foiled *or* frustrated.

zu|schanzen, *v.t.* (*coll.*) get, secure, (*sl.*) wangle (*Dat.*, for). **–scharren,** *v.t.* cover (up), fill (in *or* up).

zuschauen ['tsu:ʃauən], *v.i.* (*Dat.*) look at *or* on, watch. **Zuschauer(in),** *m.*(*f.*) spectator, onlooker; looker-on, bystander; observer, (eye-)witness; *pl.* spectators, audience, the public. **Zuschauerraum,** *m.* auditorium.

zu|schaufeln, *v.t.* shovel *or* fill up *or* in. **–schicken,** *v.t.* send (on), forward; post, mail (*letters, parcels*), consign (*goods*), transmit, remit (*money*) (*Dat.*, to).

zuschieben ['tsu:ʃi:bən], *irr.v.t.* 1. shove *or* push (*Dat.*, towards); shut (*a drawer*), shoot, put on (*a bolt*); 2. (*fig.*) impute (*Dat.*, to), put the blame for (on); ***ihm die Schuld –,*** put the blame on him, lay the blame at his door; ***ihm die Verantwortung –,*** saddle him with the responsibility, saddle the responsibility on him; (*Law*) ***ihm den Eid –,*** put him on oath; administer the oath to him.

zuschießen ['tsu:ʃi:sən], **1.** *irr.v.i.* (*aux.* s.) ***– auf*** (*Acc.*), rush at, rush up to. **2.** *irr.v.t.* (*Dat.*) add *or* supply (to), furnish (*s.o.*) with; contribute (to), subsidize; ***ihm einen Blick –,*** give *or* throw him a rapid *or* fleeting glance, dart a glance at him.

Zuschlag ['tsu:ʃla:k], *m.* 1. addition; extra *or* additional charge, surcharge, increase (in price); bonus; surtax; 2. knocking down (*to a bidder*); award of contract, acceptance of tender; ***der – erfolgte an . . .,*** it was knocked down to (*at auctions*), the contract was awarded to, the tender of . . . was accepted; ***den – erhalten,*** have one's tender accepted, obtain the contract; 3. (*Metall.*) flux.

zuschlagen, 1. *irr.v.t.* 1. close, shut (*a book*), slam (*a door*); 2. knock down (*Dat.*, to) (*a bidder*); 3. give as bonus; put on, add (*surcharge*). **2.** *irr.v.i.* strike, hit hard; strike away, hit out, lay on; (*aux.* s.) bang, slam (to). **Zuschlagporto,** *n.* excess postage, surcharge, postage due. **Zuschlag(s)|gebühr,** *f.* surcharge, extra charge, excess fare, additional fee. **–karte,** *f.* additional ticket, excess fare ticket. **zuschlag(s)pflichtig,** *adj.* liable to surcharge. **Zuschlagsteuer,** *f.* surtax.

zuschließen ['tsu:ʃli:sən], *irr.v.t.* lock (up).

zuschmeißen ['tsu:ʃmaɪsən], *irr.v.t.* (*coll.*) throw to; slam, bang (to).

zuschmieren ['tsu:ʃmi:rən], *v.t.* smear *or* daub up *or* over.

zuschnallen ['tsu:ʃnalən], *v.t.* buckle (up) (*a strap*), fasten, strap up (*a bundle*).

zuschnappen ['tsu:ʃnapən], *v.i.* 1. (*aux.* s.) close with a snap, snap to *or* shut; 2. (*aux.* h.) snap (***nach,*** at) (*as a dog*).

Zuschneide|kunst ['tsu:ʃnaɪdə–], *f.* art of cutting out. **–maschine,** *f.* cutting-out machine.

zuschneiden ['tsu:ʃnaɪdən], *irr.v.t.* cut up; cut out (*a dress etc.*); (*fig.*) ***ihm das Brot (kärglich) –,*** keep him on short rations; (*fig.*) ***zugeschnitten auf*** (*Acc.*), tailored *or* styled for; (*Theat.*) ***eine Rolle auf ihn –,*** write a part for him. **Zuschneider,** *m.* tailor's cutter. **Zuschneiderei** [–'raɪ], *f.* cutting-out room.

Zuschnitt ['tsu:ʃnɪt], *m.* cut (*of clothes*); style (*also fig.*); ***der häusliche –,*** style of living, household arrangements; ***der – seines Lebens,*** his way of life; (*fig.*) ***es schon im – versehen,*** go wrong *or* make a mistake at the very outset, (*coll.*) start off on the wrong foot.

zuschnüren ['tsu:ʃny:rən], *v.t.* lace (up); tie up (*a parcel*); ***ihm die Kehle –,*** strangle *or* choke *or* (*coll.*) throttle him; ***mir war die Kehle wie zugeschnürt,*** I could not speak, I choked, a lump came into my throat.

zuschrauben ['tsu:ʃraubən], *v.t.* screw tight *or* up.

zuschreiben ['tsu:ʃraɪbən], *irr.v.t.* ascribe, assign, attribute, impute, (*coll.*) put down (*Dat.*, to), blame (on), (*Comm.*) place to (*a p.'s*) credit; (*obs.*) dedicate, inscribe (*Dat.*, to); ***ihm eine Summe –,*** credit him with an amount, place a sum to his credit; ***das hast du dir selbst zuzuschreiben,*** you have yourself to blame *or* thank for this, it is your own fault; ***das schreibe ich seiner Unwissenheit zu,*** I attribute that *or* (*coll.*) put that down to his ignorance.

zuschreien ['tsu:ʃraɪən], *irr.v.t., v.i.* cry *or* shout *or* call out (*Dat.*, to).

zuschreiten ['tsu:ʃraɪtən], *irr.v.i.* (*aux.* s.) step up (***auf*** (*Acc.*), to); step out, walk on briskly.

Zuschrift ['tsu:ʃrɪft], *f.* letter, communication; (*obs.*) address, dedication, inscription. **zuschriftlich,** *adv.* by letter, in writing.

zuschulden [tsu'ʃuldən], *adv.* ***sich etwas – kommen lassen,*** be guilty of a th., do s.th. wrong, misbehave, be guilty of misconduct.

Zuschuß ['tsu:ʃus], *m.* allowance, subsidy, contribution, grant(-in-aid). **Zuschuß|betrieb,** *m.* subsidized undertaking. **–bogen,** *m.* (*Typ.*) extra sheet. **–gebiet,** *n.* area receiving economic aid, depressed area. **–steuer,** *f.* surtax. **–summe,** *f.* additional sum. **–tage,** *m.pl.* (*Astr.*) epact. **–wirtschaft,** *f.* policy of (economic) subsidies.

zuschütten ['tsu:ʃytən], *v.t.* fill up *or* in (*a hole*); pour on in addition.

zuschwören ['tsu:ʃvø:rən], *irr.v.t.* ***es ihm –,*** swear it to him, give him a solemn assurance about *or* on it.

zusehen ['tsu:ze:ən], *irr.v.i.* look on (***bei,*** at); (*Dat.*) watch, witness (***bei,*** doing); (*fig.*) wait and see, stand by, be patient; tolerate, (*coll.*) stomach, stand for; ***– daß . . .,*** see (to it) that, take care that *or* take care (*inf.*); ***einer S. ruhig –,*** look on at a th. unmoved, connive at *or* (*coll.*) wink at a th.; ***da kann ich nicht länger –,*** I cannot put up with *or* stand this any longer; ***sieh zu, daß du nicht fällst,*** take care not to fall; ***da muß er –,*** that is his look-out. **Zusehen,** *n.* ***bei genauerem –,*** on closer examination *or* inspection; (*fig.*) ***das – haben,*** get nothing for one's trouble, (*coll.*) be left out in the cold, get no change. **zusehends,** *adv.* visibly, obviously, noticeably.

zusenden, *irr.v.t. See* **zuschicken.**

zusetzen ['tsu:zɛtsən], **1.** *v.t.* 1. add (***zu,*** to), mix, admix, alloy (***zu,*** with); 2. raise one's stake, lose, sacrifice (*money etc.*); ***er hat bei dem Geschäft (viel Geld) zugesetzt,*** he lost (a lot of money) on the deal; ***er hat sein Vermögen dabei zugesetzt,*** he lost everything by it; ***er hat dabei zugesetzt,*** he was the loser by it. **2.** *v.i.* (*Dat.*) press, importune, pester, (*coll.*) plague; ***ihm mit Bitten –,*** overwhelm him with entreaties; ***ihm mit Fragen –,*** ply him with questions; ***die Hitze setzte ihm zu,*** the heat affected him *or* (*coll.*) told on him.

zusichern ['tsu:zɪçərn], *v.t.* ***ihm etwas –,*** guarantee s.th. to him, assure him of a th., promise him s.th. **Zusicherung,** *f.* guarantee, pledge, assurance, promise.

zusiegeln ['tsu:zi:gəln], *v.t.* seal (up).

Zuspeise ['tsu:ʃpaɪzə], *f.* (*dial.*) side dish, vegetables served with meat.

zusperren ['tsu:ʃpɛrən], *v.t.* block (up), close, bar, lock.

Zuspiel ['tsu:ʃpi:l], *n.* (*Footb.*) pass(ing). **zuspielen,** *v.t.* play, pass (*the ball*) (*Dat.*, to), (*fig.*) play into (*s.o.'s*) hands.

zuspitzen ['tsu:ʃpɪtsən], **1.** *v.t.* point, sharpen, taper; toe off, graft (*a stocking in knitting*); ***epigrammatisch –,*** give an epigrammatic turn to. **2.** *v.r.* taper (off); (*fig.*) come to a crisis *or* head, get critical. **Zuspitzung,** *f.* pointing, sharpening; tapering off; point (*of an epigram*); ***die – der Lage,*** the increasing gravity of the situation.

Zusprache ['tsu:ʃpraxə], *f.* consolation, encouragement.

zusprechen ['tsu:ʃprɛçən], **1.** *irr.v.t.* convey by word of mouth (*Dat.*, to), award, grant, adjudge (*a prize*) (to); ***ihm Mut –,*** cheer him up, encourage him; ***ihm Trost –,*** comfort *or* console him; ***ein Telegramm –,*** phone a telegram. **2.** *v.i.* (*Dat.*) address, accost; exhort, encourage, console, comfort; ***ihm gut –,*** reason with him; ***der Flasche fleißig –,*** partake freely of the bottle; ***einer Speise wacker –,*** do ample justice to a dish, eat heartily of a dish; ***sprich zu!*** go *or* carry on speaking! speak away!

zuspringen ['tsu:ʃprɪŋən], *irr.v.i.* (*aux.* s.) 1. spring *or* leap (***auf*** (*Acc.*), towards), rush *or* jump (at); 2. snap *or* spring to (*of locks*).

Zuspruch ['tsu:ʃprux], *m.* 1. exhortation, (*coll.*) lecture, (*sl.*) pep-talk; praise, encouragement; consolation, words of comfort; 2. (run of) customers, custom, clientele; ***– finden, sich (eines) großen –s erfreuen,*** be in (great) demand, be much sought after, (*coll.*) go down well.

Zustand ['tsu:ʃtant], *m.* condition, state, situation, position; circumstances, state of affairs; ***in betrunkenem –,*** while under the influence of drink; ***in elendem –,*** in a wretched condition *or* plight; (*coll.*) in poor shape; ***in gutem –,*** in good condition *or* order; in good repair (*of buildings*); ***– des Gemüts,*** frame of mind; ***mobiler –,*** war footing.

zustande [tsu'ʃtandə], *adv.* ***– bringen,*** achieve, accomplish, bring about *or* (*coll.*) off, realize, manage, get done, (*coll.*) wangle; ***– kommen,*** occur, happen, come about *or* (*coll.*) off, come to pass, take place, be realized, materialize; ***nicht – kommen,*** not come to pass, fail to materialize, (*coll.*) not come off, come to nothing. **Zustandekommen,** *n.* realization, accomplishment, occurrence; ***das – des Vertrags ist gesichert,*** the treaty is sure to be signed, the agreement is sure to be reached.

zuständig ['tsu:ʃtendɪç], *adj.* proper, appropriate; duly qualified, authorized, responsible, competent; ***– für,*** with jurisdiction over; ***dafür bin ich nicht –,*** that's not in my province; ***von –er Seite hören wir,*** we are informed from a responsible quarter; ***–e***

Stelle or *Behörde*, competent authority; (*dial.*) *mir* –, belonging to me, mine. **Zuständigkeit,** *f.* competence; power(s); jurisdiction (*für*, over), responsibilty (for).

zustatten [tsu'ʃtatən], *adv.* *ihm* – *kommen,* prove *or* be useful to him, stand him in good stead, (*coll.*) come in handy for him.

zustecken ['tsu:ʃtɛkən], *v.t.* pin up, fix with pins; *ihm etwas* –, slip s.th. into his hand(s).

zustehen ['tsu:ʃte:ən], *irr.v.i.* (*Dat.*) belong to, befit, behove, be vested in, be due to, be incumbent upon; become, suit; *das steht dir nicht zu,* it is not for you, that is none of your business, you have no right to (do) this, it is not yours by right, you are not entitled to it.

zustellen ['tsu:ʃtɛlən], *v.t.* hand over, forward, deliver (*Dat.*, to); *ihm eine Klage* –, serve a writ on him, serve him a writ. **Zustellpostamt,** *n.* district post-office. **Zustellung,** *f.* delivery, forwarding; (*Law*) service of legal process. **Zustellungs|gebühr,** *f.* charge for delivery. **-urkunde,** *f.* writ.

zusteuern ['tsu:ʃtɔyərn], **1.** *v.t.* contribute, make a contribution (*Dat.*, to). **2.** *v.i.* – *auf* (*Acc.*), set a course for, steer *or* make for, (*fig.*) aim at, be headed for.

zustimmen ['tsu:ʃtɪmən], *v.i.* (*Dat.*) agree (with) (*a p.*); agree (to), (give one's) assent *or* consent (to), approve (of), concur (with), acquiesce (in), subscribe (to), endorse (*a th.*). **zustimmend,** **1.** *adj.* affirmative; *-e Antwort,* answer in the affirmative, consent, agreement. **2.** *adv.* – *nicken,* nod approvingly, nod assent. **Zustimmung,** *f.* agreement, assent, consent, approval, acquiescence, concurrence; – *finden,* meet with approval; *unter* – *von,* with the consent *or* approval of.

zustopfen ['tsu:ʃtɔpfən], *v.t.* stop *or* fill up, plug (up), stuff (up); close, stop (*one's ears*); darn, mend (*hole in a sock etc.*).

zustöpseln ['tsu:ʃtœpsəln], *v.t.* cork *or* stopper up.

zustoßen ['tsu:ʃto:sən], **1.** *irr.v.t.* push shut *or* to (*a door*). **2.** *irr.v.i.* 1. push *or* thrust forward *or* on; (*Fenc.*) lunge, thrust; 2. (*aux.* s.) (*Dat.*) befall, happen to; *mir ist ein Unglück zugestoßen,* I had a *or* I met with misfortune; *falls mir etwas* – *sollte,* in case anything should happen to me.

zustreben ['tsu:ʃtre:bən], *v.i.* (*Dat.*) strive for *or* after, aim at, try to reach; hurry towards, (*coll.*) make for; (*of a th.*) tend towards.

Zustrom ['tsu:ʃtro:m], *m.* influx; infiltration; flow, rush (*of ideas*), run (*on the bank etc.*). **zuströmen,** *v.i.* (*aux.* s.) (*Dat.*) pour *or* flood *or* stream towards, (*fig. of crowd*) pour *or* throng to(wards), mill towards.

zustürzen ['tsu:ʃtyrtsən], *v.i.* (*aux.* s.) – *auf* (*Acc.*), rush up to, rush towards.

zustutzen ['tsu:ʃtutsən], *v.t.* fashion, adapt, trim, cut to size, (*coll., fig.*) lick into shape; *für die Bühne* –, adapt for the stage.

zutage [tsu'ta:gə], *adv.* open to view, to light; (*fig.*) – *bringen,* bring to light, unearth; – *fördern,* (*Min.*) bring to the surface, extract, (*fig.*) *see* – *bringen*; – *liegen,* (*Min.*) be *or* lie on the surface, (*Geol.*) *see* – *treten*; (*fig.*) be evident *or* manifest; (*fig.*) – *kommen,* come to light, become evident *or* manifest, manifest itself; – *treten,* (*Geol.*) crop out, (*fig.*) *see* – *kommen.* **Zutage|liegen, -treten,** *n.* outcrop(ping).

Zutat ['tsu:ta:t], *f.* (*usu. pl.* **-en**) (*on dress*) trimming, ornament, (*Cul.*) seasoning, garnishing; (*fig.*) addition.

zuteil [tsu'taɪl], *adv.* *ihm* – *werden,* fall to his share *or* lot; *ihm etwas* – *werden lassen,* allot *or* grant s.th. to him, bestow s.th. on him.

zuteilen ['tsu:taɪlən], *v.t.* issue, distribute (*Dat.*, to); grant, allow (to); delegate, assign, allot, allocate, apportion (to); (*Mil.*) attach, post (to); *in reichem Maße* –, lavish (up)on. **Zuteilung,** *f.* issue, distribution; apportioning, allocation, assignment, allotment; (*Mil.*) attachment, posting; ration, quota.

zutiefst [tsu'ti:fst], *adv.* at bottom, deeply.

zutragen ['tsu:tra:gən], **1.** *irr.v.t.* carry, bring (*Dat.*, to), (*fig.*) report, repeat (*rumour*), carry (*tales*). **2.** *irr.v.r.* happen, occur, take place, come to pass. **Zuträger,** *m.* talebearer, gossip, scandal-monger; informer, tell-tale. **Zuträgerei** [–'raɪ], *f.* talebearing, gossip, tittle-tattle.

zuträglich ['tsu:trɛ:klɪç], *adj.* conducive, beneficial, salutary, advantageous (*für or Dat.*, to), wholesome (*food*), salubrious (*climate*); *es ist mir* (*nicht*) –, it (dis)agrees with me (*of food or climate*). **Zuträglichkeit,** *f.* conduciveness, advantageousness; wholesomeness, salubrity.

zutrauen ['tsu:trauən], *v.t.* *ihm etwas* –, believe him capable of, credit him with, give him credit for; *ihm nicht viel* –, not expect much of him, give him credit for very little; *sich* (*Dat.*) *zuviel* –, overrate *or* overestimate o.s., be over-confident, take too much on o.s.; *ich traue es mir nicht zu,* I don't think I can do *or* manage it; (*coll.*) *ich traue es ihm glatt zu,* I wouldn't put it past him; *ich hätte es ihm nie zugetraut,* I didn't think he had it in him. **Zutrauen,** *n.* confidence (*zu*, in). **zutraulich,** *adj.* trusting, confiding, (*of animals*) tame, friendly. **Zutraulichkeit,** *f.* trust, confidingness, (*of animals*) tameness.

zutreffen ['tsu:trɛfən], *irr.v.i.* (*aux.* s.) be right *or* true *or* correct (*bei*, of), be the case (with), prove right *or* correct, come *or* hold true (in the case of); – *auf* (*Acc.*) *or für,* apply to, be true of, be in keeping with; *auf ein Haar* –, be exactly correct, be right to a T; *es trifft nicht immer zu,* it does not always hold true *or* good *or* always follow. **zutreffend,** *adj.* right, true, correct; applicable; (*of remarks*) apt, pertinent, (*pred.*) to the point. **zutreffendenfalls,** *adv.* if this should be the case, if *or* where applicable; if true *or* correct *or* so.

zutreten ['tsu:tre:tən], *irr.v.i.* (*aux.* s.) – *auf* (*Acc.*), come *or* step up to, approach.

zutrinken ['tsu:trɪŋkən], *irr.v.i.* (*Dat.*) drink to, raise one's glass to.

Zutritt ['tsu:trɪt], *m.* access, entrance, admittance, admission; – *haben zu,* have access to, (*coll.*) have the run of; – *frei,* admission free; – *verboten,* no admittance, no entry, (*Mil. etc.*) out of bounds; (*Am.*) off limits.

zutulich ['tsu:tu:lɪç], *adj.* *See* **zutunlich.**

zutun ['tsu:tu:n], *irr.v.t.* 1. add (*Dat.*, to); 2. close, shut; *ich habe kein Auge zugetan,* I have not slept a wink. **Zutun,** *n.* assistance, help, co-operation; *es geschah ohne mein* –, I had nothing to do with it, it was none of my doing, it was through no fault of mine.

zutunlich ['tsu:tu:nlɪç], *adj.* confiding, trusting; obliging, helpful.

zuungunsten [tsu'ungunstən], *prep.* (*Gen.*) to the detriment *or* disadvantage of.

zuunterst [tsu'untərst], *adv.* right at the bottom, below all the others.

zuverlässig ['tsu:fɛrlɛsɪç], *adj.* reliable, trustworthy, dependable; certain, sure, authentic; *aus -er Quelle* or *von -er Seite,* from a reliable source, on good authority. **Zuverlässigkeit,** *f.* reliability, dependability; trustworthiness; certainty, authenticity. **Zuverlässigkeits|fahrt,** *f.* (*Motor.*) reliability trial. **-überprüfung,** *f.* (*Pol.*) screening, security clearance.

Zuversicht ['tsu:fɛrzɪçt], *f.* confidence, trust, faith (*auf* (*Acc.*), in); confident expectation, conviction; – *zu Gott,* trust in God; *er hat die feste* or *ist der festen* –, he confidently expects, he is confident; *mit* –, confidently. **zuversichtlich,** *adj.* confident, assured, hopeful, optimistic. **Zuversichtlichkeit,** *f.* confidence, assurance; self-assurance.

zuviel [tsu'fi:l], *adv.* too much; *einer* –, one too many; *mehr als* –, more than enough; – *des Guten,* more than is good for one, too much of a good thing; *des Guten* – *tun,* go too far; *viel* –, much *or* far too much; (*Prov.*) *was* – *ist, ist* –, more than enough is too much, (*coll.*) that's really too much! **Zuviel,** *n.* excess.

zuvor [tsu'fo:r], *adv.* before, previously; beforehand, first, formerly; (*coll.*) ***so klug als wie –,*** none the wiser (for it).

zuvorderst [tsu'fɔrdərst], **zuvörderst** [–'fœrdərst], *adv.* first of all, in the first place, first and foremost, to begin with.

zuvor|kommen, *irr.v.i.* (*aux.* s.) (*sep.*) (*Dat.*) (*a p.*) forestall, anticipate, (*coll.*) steal a march on, (*sl.*) beat (*s.o.*) to it; (*a th.*) forestall, prevent, obviate. **–kommend,** *adj.* obliging, polite, charming, courteous, civil. **Zuvorkommenheit,** *f.* politeness, civility, courtesy, kindness.

zuvortun [tsu'fo:rtu:n], *irr.v.t.* (*sep.*) ***es ihm –,*** surpass *or* excel *or* outdo him, (*coll.*) go one better than him (***in*** *Dat.*), in).

Zuwaage ['tsu:va:gə], *f.* (*dial.*) makeweight.

Zuwachs ['tsu:vaks], *m.* increase, expansion, increment, accretion, accession, augmentation; ***– in der Familie bekommen,*** have an addition to the family; (*coll.*) ***einen Rock auf – machen,*** make a coat allowing for growth. **zuwachsen,** *irr.v.i.* 1. heal up *or* over, close (*as wounds*); grow together; become overgrown; 2. (*Dat.*) accrue (to). **Zuwachs|ring,** *m.* (*Bot.*) growth ring. **–steuer,** *f.* increment-tax.

Zuwahl ['tsu:va:l], *f.* co-option.

zuwandern ['tsu:vandərn], *v.i.* (*aux.* s.) immigrate.

zuwarten ['tsu:vartən], *v.i.* wait patiently, wait and see.

zuwege [tsu've:gə], *adv.* ***– bringen,*** bring about, bring to pass, accomplish, effect, succeed in doing, get done, (*coll.*) put across; (*dial.*) ***gut –,*** (*of a th.*) in good condition; (*of a p.*) quite well.

zuweilen [tsu'vaɪlən], *adv.* sometimes, at times, occasionally, now and then.

zuweisen ['tsu:vaɪzən], *irr.v.t.* attribute, assign, allocate, allot (*Dat.*, to); ***ihm einen Kunden –,*** send *or* recommend a customer to him. **Zuweisung,** *f.* assignment, allocation, allotment.

zuwenden ['tsu:vɛndən], **1.** *reg. & irr.v.t.* (*Dat.*) 1. turn to(wards); ***ihm das Gesicht –,*** (turn one's) face towards him; 2. bestow (upon), make a present of, present, give (to), let (*s.o.*) have; (*fig. attention, effort etc.*) bestow (upon), devote (to); ***seine Freundlichkeit wandte ihm alle Herzen zu,*** his kindliness won him all hearts. **2.** *reg. & irr.v.r.* (*Dat.*) devote *or* apply o.s. (to); (*coll.*) switch over (to); ***sich einer anderen Arbeit –,*** change *or* (*coll.*) switch (over) to other employment. **Zuwendung,** *f.* allocation, grant, allowance; bequest, gift, donation.

zuwerfen ['tsu:vɛrfən], *irr.v.t.* 1. fill up (*a hole*); slam, bang (*a door*); 2. (*Dat.*) throw *or* toss to(wards); ***ihm einen Blick –,*** cast a glance at *or* towards him; ***ihr eine Kußhand –,*** throw her a kiss.

zuwider [tsu'vi:dər], **1.** *prep.* (*Dat. following*) contrary *or* opposed to, against. **2.** *adv.* (*with sein and Dat. of p.*) hateful, distasteful, repugnant, odious, offensive (to); ***Gefühle, die ihrer Pflicht – waren,*** feelings which conflicted with her duty; ***er ist mir in den Tod –,*** the very sight of him offends me; ***es wird Ihnen nicht – sein, wenn . . .,*** you will have no objection if. . . .

zuwiderhandeln [tsu'vi:dərhandəln], *v.i.* (*sep.*) (*Dat.*) offend against, contravene, infringe, violate, disobey (*regulations*), act contrary to, counteract, oppose (*another action*). **Zuwider|handelnde(r),** *m., f.* offender, trespasser. **–handlung,** *f.* contravention, infringement, violation (of), offence (against). **zuwiderlaufen,** *irr.v.i.* (*sep.*) (*aux.* s.) (*Dat.*) run counter *or* be contrary to.

zuwinken ['tsu:vɪŋkən], *v.i.* (*Dat.*) wave, motion, nod, beckon, make a sign (to).

Zuwuchs ['tsu:vu:ks], *m. See* **Zuwachs.**

zuzahlen ['tsu:tsa:lən], *v.t.* pay . . . in addition, pay an additional . . ., make an extra *or* further payment of. . . .

zuzählen ['tsu:tsɛ:lən], *v.t.* (*Dat.*) add (to), include; count out (to) (*a p.*).

zuzeiten [tsu'tsaɪtən], *adv.* at times.

zuziehen ['tsu:tsi:ən], **1.** *irr.v.t.* 1. draw together, draw tight, (*screw, noose etc.*) tighten, (*curtains etc.*) draw; ***einen Knoten –,*** pull a knot tight; 2. (*fig.*) (*doctor etc.*) call in, consult; ***zur Beratung –,*** bring in for consultation; ***ihn als Zeugen –,*** call him as a witness; 3. ***sich*** (*Dat.*) **–,** incur, involve o.s. in, contract; ***sich*** (*Dat.*) ***einen Tadel –,*** incur blame, expose o.s. to criticism; ***sich*** (*Dat.*) ***eine Krankheit –,*** contract *or* (*coll.*) catch *or* get a disease; ***sich*** (*Dat.*) ***Unannehmlichkeiten –,*** involve o.s. in difficulties, get into trouble; ***sich*** (*Dat.*) ***einen Verdacht –,*** bring suspicion on o.s., lay o.s. open to suspicion. **2.** *irr.v.i.* 1. (*aux,* s.) (*Dat.*) move in (*a house*), move *or* come into (*a district*); immigrate; 2. (*aux.* h.) ***kräftig –,*** pull hard, pull away. **Zuziehung,** *f.* consultation; inclusion; aid, assistance; ***mit*** or ***unter – eines Arztes,*** a doctor having been called; ***unter – Ihrer Spesen,*** including your expenses; ***unter – der Umstehenden,*** with the assistance of the bystanders.

Zuzug ['tsu:tsu:k], *m.* 1. immigration; 2. increase in population; (*Mil.*) reinforcements. **Zuzüger,** *m.* (*Swiss*), **Zuzügler,** *m.* newcomer, recent arrival *or* settler. **zuzüglich,** *prep.* (*Gen.*) including, in addition to, with the addition of, plus. **Zuzugsgenehmigung,** *f.* residence permit.

zwacken ['tsvakən], *v.t.* pinch, (*fig.*) tease, pester, torment.

Zwang [tsvaŋ], *m.* force, coercion, compulsion, constraint, (*Law*) duress; control, restraint; (moral) obligation, pressure; (*Med.*) constriction, tenesmus; ***– antun*** (*Dat.*), do violence to; ***einem Text – antun,*** twist the meaning of a passage; ***sich*** (*Dat.*) ***– antun*** or ***auferlegen,*** check *or* restrain o.s.; ***sich*** (*Dat.*) ***keinen – antun,*** not stand on ceremony, be quite free and easy, make o.s. at home; ***dem Gesetz – antun,*** pervert the law; ***unter –,*** under coercion *or* duress.

zwang, *see* **zwingen.**

zwängen ['tsvɛŋən], *v.t.* force, constrain, press.

Zwangläufigkeit ['tsvaŋlɔyfɪçkaɪt], *f.* (*Mech.*) direct *or* fixed drive.

zwanglos ['tsvaŋlo:s], *adj.* unconstrained, unrestricted; unceremonious, informal. free and easy; random, occasional, irregular; ***in –er Folge,*** in irregular sequence, as a random series; ***in –en Heften,*** (*publication*) appearing in occasional numbers and at no fixed date. **Zwanglosigkeit,** *f.* freedom, lack of constraint, unconstraint, informality; lack of regularity.

Zwangs|anleihe, *f.* forced loan. **–arbeit,** *f.* forced labour, (*in prison*) hard labour. **–bewirtschaftung,** *f.* economic control. **–enteignung,** *f.* compulsory expropriation. **–ernährung,** *f.* forcible feeding. **–erscheinung,** *f. See* **–neurose. –erziehungsanstalt,** *f.* approved school, Borstal institution, reformatory. **zwangsgestellt,** *adj.* in custody. **Zwangs|gestellung,** *f.* custody, arrest, detention. **–handlung,** *f.* compulsive act(ion). **–herrschaft,** *f.* despotism, absolute rule. **–jacke,** *f.* strait-jacket. **–kauf,** *m.* compulsory purchase. **–kurs,** *m.* legal rate. **–lage,** *f.* exigency, position of constraint; embarrassing situation, quandary, (*coll.*) fix, jam; ***in einer –,*** hard pressed.

zwangsläufig ['tsvaŋslɔyfɪc], **1.** *adj.* obligatory, compulsory, enforced; unavoidable, necessary. **2.** *adv.* necessarily, unavoidably, inevitably, automatically.

Zwangs|lieferung, *f.* enforced delivery. **–liquidation,** *f.* compulsory liquidation *or* (*coll.*) winding-up. **zwangsmäßig,** *adj.* forced, compulsory. **Zwangs|maßregel,** *f.* coercive measure, (*Pol.*) sanction, reprisal; ***–n anwenden, zu –n ergreifen,*** employ *or* use force, resort to force *or* compulsion. **–mittel,** *n.* violent means, means of coercion. **–neurose,** *f.* obsession, compulsion. **–preis,** *m.* fixed *or* controlled price. **–räumung,** *f.* compulsory evacuation. **–schlaf,** *m.* hypnosis. **–verfahren,** *n.* coercive measures. **–vergleich,** *m.* enforced settlement. **–versteigerung,** *f.* compulsory *or* bankrupt sale. **–verwalter,** *m.* (official) receiver. **–verwaltung,** *f.* sequestration. **zwangsvollstrecken,** *v.t.* (*insep.*) foreclose. **Zwangs|-**

vollstreckung, *f.* distraint, legal execution. **–vorstellung,** *f.* obsession, hallucination. **zwangsweise,** *adv.* compulsorily, forcibly, by (main) force. **Zwangswirtschaft,** *f.* government *or* economic control; controlled economy.

zwanzig ['tsvantsɪç], *num.adj.* twenty; ***in den –er Jahren,*** in the (19)20s. **Zwanzig,** *f.* (-, *pl.* **-en**) (the number) twenty, a score; ***in den –en, see* Zwanziger**; ***sie ist über die – hinaus,*** she is over *or* turned 20. **Zwanziger,** *m.* man in his twenties; wine of the year '20; ***in den –n sein,*** be in one's twenties. **zwanzigerlei,** *indecl.adj.* of 20 different kinds; ***auf – Art,*** in a score of (different) ways. **zwanzig|fach, –fältig,** *adj.* twentyfold. **–flächig,** *adj.* icosahedral. **zwanzigst,** *num.adj.* twentieth. **Zwanzigstel,** *n.* (*Swiss m.*) twentieth (part); ***drei –,*** three-twentieths. **zwanzigstens,** *adv.* in the 20th place.

zwar [tsva:r], *adv.* indeed, certainly, to be sure, of course, I admit (*with* ***aber*** *or* ***doch*** *in the following clause*); ***und –,*** that is, namely, in fact; ***er ist – alt, aber noch sehr rüstig,*** he is certainly old but still very active; ***er ist sehr alt, und – über 90,*** he is very old, in fact over 90.

Zweck [tsvɛk], *m.* **(-(e)s,** *pl.* **-e)** aim, end, object, goal, objective; intent(ion), purpose, design, (*coll.*) point; function, application, (intended) use; (*of a th.*) ***seinen – erfüllen,*** fulfil *or* serve *or* answer its purpose; (*of a p.*) ***seinen – erreichen,*** attain one's goal *or* object, carry one's point; ***das Mittel zum –,*** the means to an end; ***der – heiligt die Mittel,*** the end justifies the means; ***keinen – haben,*** be pointless, be (of) no use, have no point; (*coll.*) ***das ist (gerade) der – der Übung,*** that is the whole point *or* just the point; (*of a th.*) ***seinen – verfehlen,*** fail in its object *or* purpose, (*coll.*) miss the point *or* its mark; (*of a p.*) ***einen – verfolgen,*** pursue an aim, (*coll.*) have s.th. in view, be after *or* be out for s.th.; ***– und Ziel,*** aim and purpose; ***zu dem –*** (*Gen.*), with the purpose of; ***zu dem – (zu tun),*** with a view to *or* with the object of (doing); ***zu diesem –,*** to this end; ***zu welchem –?*** to *or* for what purpose? what . . . for? why?

Zweckbau ['tsvɛkbau], *m.* **(-s,** *pl.* **-ten)** functional building. **zweckbestimmt,** *adj.* purposive, functional; (*writings etc.*) tendentious. **Zweckbestimmung,** *f.* (*of money*) appropriation (*for a purpose*), application (*to an end*). **zweck|betont,** *adj. See* **–bestimmt. –bewußt,** *adj.* purposeful, clear-sighted. **–dienlich,** *adj.* appropriate, suitable, expedient, relevant, pertinent, (*pred.*) to the point; useful, serviceable, efficient.

Zwecke ['tsvɛkə], *f.* tack, brad; (*of wood*) peg; drawing-pin, (*Am.*) thumb tack. **zwecken,** *v.t.* tack, peg, pin.

zweck|entfremdet, *adj.* used for purposes other than originally intended. **–entsprechend,** *adj. See* **–dienlich. Zweckessen,** *n.* banquet to celebrate a special occasion. **zweckgebunden,** *adj.* appropriated, earmarked. **zwecklos,** *adj.* aimless, purposeless, pointless, useless, (*pred.*) to no purpose *or* point, of no use; ***es ist –, zu gehen,*** there is no point in going. **zweckmäßig,** *adj.* appropriate, expedient, suitable, proper, advisable; practical, functional; ***es für – halten, zu gehen,*** think fit *or* think it proper *or* advisable to go. **Zweck|mäßigkeit,** *f.* appropriateness, expediency, suitability, advisability; practicality, functionalism. **–mäßigkeitserwägung,** *f.* considerations of expediency, practical considerations. **–mäßigkeitslehre,** *f.* teleology. **–möbel,** *pl.* functional furniture.

zwecks [tsvɛks], *prep.* (*Gen.*) for the purpose of, by way of, with a view to.

zweckwidrig ['tsvɛkvi:drɪç], *adj.* inappropriate, inexpedient, unsuitable, injudicious.

Zwehle ['tsve:lə], *f.* (*dial.*) towel.

zwei [tsvaɪ], *num.adj.* (*Gen. –er, Dat. –en*) two; ***halb –,*** half-past one; ***zu –en,*** in twos, two by two; ***das Spiel läßt sich zu –en spielen,*** two can play at that game. **Zwei,** *f.* (-, *pl.* **-en**) (the number) two.

zwei|achsig, *adj.* biaxial, (*Motor.*) four-wheeled. **–atomig,** *adj.* diatomic. **–bändig,** *adj.* two-volume, (*pred.*) in two volumes. **–basisch,** *adj.* dibasic. **–beinig,** *adj.* two-legged. **–bettig,** *adj.* double-bedded. **–blätt(e)rig,** *adj.* two-leaved, bifoliate. **–brüderig,** *adj.* (*Bot.*) diadelphous. **Zwei|bund,** *m.* (*Pol.*) dual alliance. **–decker,** *m.* (*Av.*) biplane. **zweideutig,** *adj.* ambiguous, equivocal, (*coll.*) (*of jokes*) doubtful, risqué, suggestive; ***– reden,*** equivocate. **Zweideutigkeit,** *f.* ambiguity, equivocality, equivocalness; equivocation; suggestiveness, suggestive remark, risqué joke.

zweien ['tsvaɪən], *v.r.* (*Poet.*) go together in pairs, pair off; select a partner. **Zweier,** *m.* the figure 2; a two (mark *etc.*) piece; a two (pfennig *etc.*) stamp; two-seater, two-man sledge; two-oared boat, pair; ***– mit Steuermann,*** coxed pair. **Zweierbob,** *m.* two-man bobsleigh.

zweierlei ['tsvaɪərlaɪ], *indecl.adj.* two sorts of, of two kinds, two different (kinds of); ***das ist –,*** those are two very different things. **zwei|fach,** *adj.* double, twofold, dual; ***in –er Ausführung,*** in duplicate. **–fächerig,** *adj.* (*Bot.*) two-celled, biloculate, bilocular. **–fältig,** *adj. See* **–fach.**

Zweifarbendruck ['tsvaɪfarbəndruk], *m.* two-colour print(ing). **zweifarbig,** *adj.* two-coloured, two-tone, dichromatic.

Zweifel ['tsvaɪfəl], *m.* doubt, uncertainty; hesitation, misgiving(s); suspicion; ***außer –,*** beyond (a) doubt; ***im – sein,*** be doubtful *or* in doubt, (*coll.*) be in two minds (***über*** (*Acc.*), about); ***in – stellen*** or ***ziehen,*** have one's doubts about, doubt, (call in) question; ***ohne –,*** without doubt, doubtless, no doubt, undoubtedly, unquestionably, indubitably; ***über allen*** or ***jeden – erhaben,*** beyond all doubt.

Zweifelderwirtschaft ['tsvaɪfɛldərvɪrtʃaft], *f.* two-crop rotation.

zweifelhaft ['tsvaɪfəlhaft], *adj.* doubtful, uncertain, questionable, dubious; ***– machen,*** cast (a) doubt on, call in question, throw suspicion on. **zweifellos,** *adv.* undoubted, unquestionable, indubitable. **zweifeln,** *v.i.* have doubts, be in doubt; ***– an*** (*Dat.*), doubt, question, have (one's) doubts *or* be in doubt about; ***ich zweifle nicht daran,*** I do not doubt it. **Zweifelsfall,** *m.* ***im –,*** in case of doubt. **zweifelsohne,** *adv.* undoubtedly, unquestionably, indubitably, without doubt, doubtless, no doubt, beyond all doubt. **Zweifelsucht,** *f.* scepticism. **zweifelsüchtig,** *adj.* sceptical, doubting.

Zweifler ['tsvaɪflər], *m.* doubter, sceptic.

zweiflügelig ['tsvaɪfly:gəlɪç], *adj.* two-winged, (*propeller*) two-bladed, (*Bot., Ent.*) dipterous. **Zwei|flügler,** *m.pl* (*Ent*) diptera. **–frontenkrieg,** *m.* war on two fronts. **zweifüßig,** *adj.* biped. **Zweifüß(l)er,** *m.* biped.

Zweig [tsvaɪk], *m.* **(-(e)s,** *pl.* **-e)** branch (*also fig.*), bough; twig; (*coll.*) ***er kommt auf keinen*** or ***kommt nie auf einen grünen –,*** he will never get on *or* ahead in the world, he will never amount to much *or* never come to anything, he'll never make the grade.

Zweiganggetriebe ['tsvaɪgaŋgətri:bə], *n.* two-speed gear. **zweigängig,** *adj.* double-threaded (*screw*).

Zweig|anstalt, *f.* branch (establishment). **–bahn,** *f.* branch line.

zweigeschlechtig ['tsvaɪgəʃlɛçtɪç], *adj.* bisexual, androgynal, androgynous, hermaphrodite. **Zweigespann,** *n.* carriage and pair. **zwei|gestaltig,** *adj.* dimorphic, dimorphous. **–gestrichen,** *adj.* (*Mus.*) ***–e Note,*** semiquaver. **–geteilt,** *adj.* divided, split, bipartite.

Zweig|geschäft, *n.* branch (office). **–gesellschaft,** *f.* affiliated company, subsidiary (company).

Zweigitterröhre ['tsvaɪgɪtərrø:rə], *f.* (*Rad.*) tetrode, screen-grid valve *or* (*Am.*) tube. **zweigleisig,** *adj.* (*Railw.*) double-track.

Zweig|leitung, *f.* branch pipe (*for water, gas*) *or* line *or* wire (*electricity*). **–niederlassung, –stelle,** *f. See* **–geschäft.**

Zweihänder ['tsvaɪhɛndər], *m.* two-handed sword. **zwei|händig,** *adj.* two-handed; (*Mus.*) for two hands. **–häusig,** *adj.* (*Bot.*) diœcious. **Zweiheit,** *f.*

duality, dualism. **zweihöckerig,** *adj.* two-humped; *-es Kamel,* Bactrian camel. **Zweihufer,** *m.* cloven-footed animal. **zwei|hufig,** *adj.* cloven-footed, bisulcate. **–hundert,** *num.adj.* two hundred. **Zweihundertjahrfeier,** *f.* bicentenary. **zwei|hundertjährig,** *adj.* bicentennial. **–jährig,** *adj.* of 2 years, 2 years', two-year-old, of *or* lasting 2 years, biennial. **–jährlich,** *adj.* occurring every 2 years, biennial. **Zwei|kammersystem,** *n.* (legislative) system with upper and lower houses *or* chambers. **–kampf,** *m.* duel, single combat. **zwei|keimblättrig,** *adj.* (*Bot.*) dicotyledonous; *-e Pflanze,* dicotyledon. **–klappig,** *adj.* (*Bot.*) bivalve. **–köpfig,** *adj.* *-er Muskel,* biceps. **Zweileiterkabel,** *n.* (*Elec.*) two-core cable. **zweimächtig,** *adj.* (*Bot.*) didynamian.

zweimal ['tsvaɪma:l], *adv.* twice; double; *er wird sich* (*Dat.*) *das nicht – sagen lassen,* he will need no second telling, he won't wait to be told twice, (*coll.*) he'll jump at it; *es sich* (*Dat.*) *– überlegen,* think twice; *– die Woche,* twice a week. **zweimalig,** *adj.* done twice, repeated.

zwei|männig, *adj.* (*Bot.*) diandrous. **–monatig,** *adj.* lasting 2 months; *-er Urlaub,* 2 months' leave. **–monatlich,** *adj.* occurring every 2 months; *-e Lieferung,* delivery every second month. **–motorig,** *adj.* twin-engined. **Zwei|pasch,** *m.* double-two (*dominoes*). **–pfünder,** *m.* (*Artil.*) two-pounder. **zwei|phasig,** *adj.* (*Elec.*) two-phase. **–polig,** *adj.* bipolar, two-pole; two-pin (*plug*). **Zwei|polröhre,** *f.* (*Rad.*) diode. **–rad,** *n.* bicycle. **zwei|räd(e)rig,** *adj.* two-wheeled. **–reihig,** *adj.* having two rows; (*Bot.*) bifarious, distichous; double-breasted (*jacket*). **–schalig,** *adj.* (*Mollusc.*) bivalve. **–schenk(e)lig,** *adj.* branched, forked. **–schläfrig,** *adj.* *-es Bett,* double bed. **–schneidig,** *adj.* two- *or* double-edged; *die Bemerkung ist –,* that observation cuts both ways. **–schürig,** *adj.* *-e Wiese,* meadow for second mowing; *-e Wolle,* wool of the second shearing. **–seitig,** *adj.* bilateral, bipartite; double-sided, two-sided, (*cloth*) reversible. **–silbig,** *adj.* two-syllabled, disyllabic. **Zweisitzer,** *m.* two-seater (*plane, car*); tandem (*bicycle*). **zweispaltig,** *adj.* (*Bot.*) bifid; (*Typ.*) in double columns. **Zwei|spänner,** *m.* *See* **–gespann. zwei|spännig,** *adj.* drawn by two horses. **–sprachig,** *adj.* bilingual. **–spurig,** *adj.* *See* **–gleisig. Zweistärkenglas,** *n.* bifocal lens. **zwei|stellig,** *adj.* *-e Zahl,* two-figure number; *-e Dezimalzahl,* decimal to two places. **–stimmig,** *adj.* for two voices; *-er Gesang,* vocal duet. **–stöckig,** *adj.* two-storied. **–stufig,** *adj.* two-stage. **–stündig,** *adj.* lasting 2 hours; 2 hours old. **–stündlich,** *adj.* every second hour.

zweit [tsvaɪt], *num.adj.* second; next; *der -e Mai,* May 2nd; *den -en Tag darauf,* the next day but one; *mein -es Ich,* my other self, my alter ego; (*fig.*) *die -e Geige spielen,* play second fiddle; *-es Gesicht,* second-sight; *aus -er Hand kaufen,* buy second-hand; *zu –,* two of (us, them *etc.*); *zum -en,* in the second place, secondly.

zweitägig ['tsvaɪtɛ:gɪç], *adj.* lasting 2 days, 2 days old, two-day. **Zweitaktmotor,** *m.* two-stroke engine.

Zweitälteste(r) ['tsvaɪtˀɛltəstə(r)], *m., f.* second-eldest, eldest but one.

zweitausend ['tsvaɪtauzənt], *num.adj.* two thousand.

Zweit|ausfertigung, *f.* *See* **–schrift. zweitbest,** *adj.* second-best.

zweiteilig ['tsvaɪtaɪlɪc], *adj.* bipartite; two-piece (*suit*). **Zweiteilung,** *f.* bisection, binary fission, dichotomy, bifurcation.

zweitens ['tsvaɪtəns], *adv.* secondly, in the second place. **zweit|geboren,** *adj.* second, younger. **–jüngst,** *adj.* youngest but one. **–klassig,** *adj.* second-class, second-rate. **Zweit|klasswagen,** *m.* (*Swiss*) second-class compartment. **–kommandierende(r),** *m., f.* second-in-command. **zweit|-letzt,** *adj.* last but one, penultimate. **–nächst,** *adj.* next but one. **–rangig,** *adj.* secondary, of secondary importance. **Zweitschrift,** *f.* second copy, duplicate.

Zwei|unddreißigstelformat, *n.* (*Typ.*) 32mo. **–unddreißigstelnote,** *f.* demisemiquaver. **–unddreißigstelpause,** *f.* demisemiquaver rest. **–viertelnote,** *f.* minim. **–viertelpause,** *f.* minim rest. **–vierteltakt,** *m.* (*Mus.*) two-four time. **–wegantenne,** *f.* (*Rad.*) duplex aerial *or* (*Am.*) antenna. **–wegehahn,** *m.* two-way cock. **–weggleichrichter,** *m.* (*Rad.*) full-wave rectifier. **zwei|wellig,** *adj.* *See* **–phasig. –wertig,** *adj.* (*Chem.*) bivalent, divalent; *-es Element,* dyad. **–wöchentlich,** *adj.* fortnightly. **–wöchig,** *adj.* 2 weeks old; lasting 2 weeks. **–zackig,** *adj.* two-pronged. **Zwei|zahn,** *m.* (*Bot.*) bur marigold (*Bidens cernua*). **–zeiler,** *m.* couplet, distich. **zwei|zeilig,** *adj.* two-lined, (*typewriter*) double-spaced; *-e Gerste,* two-rowed barley. **–zinkig,** *adj.* *See* **–zackig. –zipfelig,** *adj.* bicuspid(ate). **Zweizweck–,** *pref.* double-purpose.

zwerch ['tsvɛrç], *adj.* (*dial.*) athwart, across. **Zwerchfell,** *n.* diaphragm, midriff. **zwerchfellerschütternd,** *adj.* (*fig.*) side-splitting.

Zwerg [tsvɛrk], *m.* **(-(e)s,** *pl.* **-e)** dwarf, gnome, pygmy, (*fig.*) midget.

Zwerg|adler, *m.* (*Orn.*) booted eagle (*Hieraëtus pennatus*). **–ahorn,** *m.* (*Bot.*) dwarf maple (*Acer glabrum*). **–ammer,** *f.* (*Orn.*) little bunting (*Emberiza pusilla*). **–apfel,** *m.* dwarf apple. **–apfelsine,** *f.* tangerine, mandarin (orange). **–birke,** *f.* (*Bot.*) dwarf birch (*Betula nana*). **–drossel,** *f.* (*Orn.*) olive-backed *or* (*Am.*) Swainson's thrush (*Hylocichla ustulata*).

zwergenhaft ['tsvɛrgənhaft], *adj.* dwarfish, pygmy, diminutive, tiny, minute, undersized, stunted. **Zwergenhaftigkeit,** *f.* dwarfishness, diminutiveness, minuteness, undersize, stunted growth.

Zwerg|falke, *m.* (*Orn.*) merlin, (*Am.*) pigeon hawk (*Falco columbarius*). **–fliegenfänger,** *m.* *See* **–schnäpper. –gans,** *f.* (*Orn.*) lesser white-fronted goose (*Anser erythropus*). **–habicht,** *m.* *See* **Kurzfangsperber. –heidelbeere,** *f.* (*Bot.*) dwarf bilberry (*Vaccinium caespitosum*). **–holunder,** *m.* (*Bot.*) dwarf elder (*Sambucus ebulus*). **–huhn,** *n.* bantam. **–hund,** *m.* lapdog, toy dog.

zwergig ['tsvɛrgɪç], *adj.* *See* **zwergenhaft. Zwergling,** *m.* **(-s,** *pl.* **-e)** *see* **Zwergmensch.**

Zwerg|maus, *f.* (*Zool.*) harvest-mouse (*Micromys domesticus*). **–mensch,** *m.* pygmy. **–möwe,** *f.* (*Orn.*) little gull (*Larus minutus*). **–ohreule,** *f.* (*Orn.*) scops owl (*Otus scops*). **–pferd,** *n.* pony (*under 1.36 metres*). **–pflanze,** *f.* dwarf plant. **–rohrdommel,** *f.* (*Orn.*) little bittern (*Ixobrychus minutus*). **–säger,** *m.* (*Orn.*) smew (*Mergus albellus*). **–scharbe,** *f.* (*Orn.*) pygmy cormorant (*Phalacrocorax pygmeus*). **–schnäpper,** *m.* (*Orn.*) red-breasted flycatcher (*Siphia parva*). **–schnepfe,** *f.* (*Orn.*) jack-snipe, (*Am.*) European jacksnipe (*Lymnocryptes minimus*). **–schwan,** *m.* (*Orn.*) Bewick's swan (*Cygnus bewickii*). **–seeschwalbe,** *f.* (*Orn.*) little *or* (*Am.*) least tern (*Sterna albifrons*). **–specht,** *m.* *See* **Kleinspecht. –stamm,** *m.* pygmy race, tribe of pygmies. **–steißfuß,** *m.* *See* **–taucher. –strandläufer,** *m.* (*Orn.*) little stint (*Calidris minuta*); *amerikanischer –,* American stint, (*Am.*) least sandpiper (*Calidris minutilla*). **–sumpfhuhn,** *n.* (*Orn.*) Baillon's crake (*Porzana pusilla*). **–taucher,** *m.* (*Orn.*) little grebe (*Podiceps ruficollis*). **–trappe,** *f.* (*Orn.*) little bustard (*Otis tetrax*). **–wuchs,** *m.* stunted growth, nanism. **zwergwüchsig,** *adj.* dwarfish, stunted.

Zwetsch(g)e ['tsvɛtʃ(g)ə], (*Austr.*) **Zwetschke,** *f.* plum; *gedorrte –,* prune.

Zwick [tsvɪk], *m.* **(-(e)s,** *pl.* **-e)** pinch, nip; twinge (*of pain*); cut (*with a whip*), whiplash.

Zwickel ['tsvɪkəl], *m.* wedge, (*Archit.*) spandrel, (*Dressm.*) gusset, gore; (*of stockings*) clock. **zwickeln,** *v.t.* (*Dressm.*) put a gore *or* gusset in.

zwicken ['tsvɪkən], *v.t., v.imp.* pinch, nip, (*coll.*) tweak; (*coll.*) *es zwickt mich im Bauch* or *Leib,* I have the gripes. **Zwicken,** *n.* twinge (*of pain*), gripes, (*coll.*) collywobbles.

Zwicker ['tsvɪkər], *m.* eye-glasses, pince-nez.

Zwick|mühle, *f.* (*fig.*) dilemma, predicament, quandary, (*coll.*) fix, jam; ***in einer –***, on the horns of a dilemma, in a quandary *or* fix *or* jam. **–zange,** *f.* pincers, nippers.

Zwieback ['tsvi:bak], *m.* **(-(e)s,** *pl.* **-e** *or* **⸚e)** rusk, (*Am.*) biscuit.

Zwiebel ['tsvi:bəl], *f.* (-, *pl.* **-n)** onion; (*of flowers*) bulb; (*coll.*) turnip (= *watch*). **zwiebel|artig,** *adj. See* **–förmig. Zwiebelfische,** *m.pl.* (*Typ.*) (printer's) pie. **zwiebelförmig,** *adj.* bulbous. **Zwiebel|-gewächs,** *n.* bulbous plant. **–knollen,** *m.* bulbous tuber. **zwiebeln,** *v.t.* (*coll.*) ***ihn –***, plague *or* torment him, give him a bad time, give it him hot, let him have it. **Zwiebel|schale,** *f.* onion skin. **–turm,** *m.* bulbous spire (*of S. German churches*).

Zwiebrache ['tsvi:braxə], *f.* double ploughing. **zwiebrachen,** *v.t.* (*insep.*) plough a second time, twifallow.

zwie|fach, –fältig, *adj.* double, twofold. **Zwie|-gespräch,** *n.* dialogue, colloquy; private talk. **–licht,** *n.* twilight, (*Poet.*) gloaming. **zwielichtig,** *adj.* (*fig.*) shady (*character etc.*).

Zwiesel ['tsvi:zəl], *f.* (-, *pl.* **-n)** fork, bifurcation; forked branch.

Zwiespalt ['tsvi:ʃpalt], *m.* dispute, conflict, (*Eccl.*) schism; strife, discord, dissension, disunion; (*fig.*) discrepancy; ***innerer –***, inner conflict; ***im – mit,*** at variance with. **zwiespältig,** *adj.* divided, disunited, discordant; conflicting, ambivalent.

Zwie|sprache, *f.* discussion, conversation, dialogue; ***– halten mit,*** have a heart-to-heart talk with. **–tracht,** *f.* strife, feud; discord, dissension; ***– säen,*** sow the seeds of discord. **zwieträchtig,** *adj.* discordant, (*pred.*) at variance.

Zwilch [tsvɪlç], **Zwillich** ['tsvɪlɪç], *m.* **(-s,** *pl.* **-e)** ticking, drill.

Zwilling ['tsvɪlɪŋ], *m.* **(-s,** *pl.* **-e)** twin; double-barrelled gun; *pl.* (*Astr.*) Gemini.

Zwillings|bereifung, *f.* (*Motor.*) double *or* dual tyres. **–bildung,** *f.* twinning, congemination. **–bruder,** *m.* twin brother. **–fenster,** *n.* (*Archit.*) gemel window. **–geburt,** *f.* birth of twins, twin birth. **–geschwister,** *pl. See* **–paar. –gestirn,** *n.* (*Astr.*) Gemini, Castor and Pollux. **–kristalle,** *m.pl.* twinned crystals. **–paar,** *n.* twins. **–schwester,** *f.* twin sister.

Zwingburg ['tsvɪŋburk], *f.* fortified castle, fortress, (tyrant's) stronghold.

Zwinge ['tsvɪŋə], *f.* clamp, cramp, (hand-)vise *or* vice; (*of sticks*) ferrule.

zwingen ['tsvɪŋən], **1.** *irr.v.t.* force, compel, constrain, oblige, (*coll.*) make; overcome, master, conquer, get the better of; (*coll.*) cope with. **2.** *irr. v.r.* ***sich dazu –***, force o.s. to (do) it, make o.s. do it, do it with an effort, make an effort to do it; ***das läßt sich nicht –***, force won't do any good; ***er läßt sich nicht –***, force won't move him, he won't give way to force. **zwingend,** *adj.* forcible, coercive; (*fig.*) compelling, cogent (*reasons*), convincing (*argument*), conclusive (*proof*), imperative (*necessity*), peremptory (*demands*).

Zwinger ['tsvɪŋər], *m.* (*Hist.*) bailey, outer courtyard; bear-pit, den; cage (*for wild animals*), (dog) kennel. **Zwing|herr,** *m.* despot, tyrant. **–herrschaft,** *f.* despotism, tyranny.

zwinke(r)n ['tsvɪŋkə(r)n], *v.i.* wink, blink, twinkle.

zwirbelig ['tsvɪrbəlɪç], *adj.* (*Swiss*) giddy, dizzy. **zwirbeln,** *v.t.* (*coll.*) twirl, twist.

Zwirn [tsvɪrn], *m.* **(-(e)s,** *pl.* **-e)** thread, (sewing) cotton; twine; (*Weav.*) (twisted) yarn; (*sl.*) ideas, notions, fancies; (*coll.*) ***sie hat – im Kopfe,*** she's no fool; (*coll.*) ***der – ging ihm aus,*** he came to the end of what he had to say, he had nothing more to say. **zwirnen, 1.** *adj.* (of) thread. **2.** *v.t.* (double and) twist (*yarn*), twine (*thread*); throw (*silk*); ***gezwirnte Seide,*** silk twist.

Zwirn|handschuh, *m.* string glove. **–knäuel,** *n. or m.* ball of thread. **–maschine,** *f.* twisting-frame, doubler; spinning-mill. **–seide,** *f.* thrown silk. **Zwirnsfaden,** *m.* piece of cotton *or* thread; ***über einen – stolpern,*** strain at gnats. **Zwirnspitze,** *f.* thread-lace. **Zwirnsrolle,** *f.* reel of cotton *or* thread.

zwischen ['tsvɪʃən], *prep.* (*Dat. for position, Acc. for passage or movement*) (*with reference to two things*) between, (*Poet.*) betwixt; (*with reference to more than two things*) among, amongst; ***– Himmel und Erde,*** between *or* (*Poet.*) 'twixt heaven and earth; ***Unkraut – den Weizen säen,*** sow tares among the wheat; ***er setzte sich – sie und mich,*** he seated himself between her and me; ***sich – zwei Stühle setzen,*** fall between two stools; ***er saß – ihr und mir,*** he sat between her and me; ***– mir und dir soll kein anderer stehen,*** no one shall come between us; ***– Tür und Angel sagen,*** say hurriedly when leaving, add as a final word; ***Wettrudern – den Universitäten,*** inter-university boat-race; ***wählen Sie – diesen Büchern,*** choose from among these books.

Zwischen|abschluß, *m.* interim balance. **–akt,** *m.* (*Theat.*) entr'acte; ***im –***, as an entr'acte, between the acts. **–aktsmusik,** *f.* musical entr'acte. **–aufenthalt,** *m.* intermediate stop, (*coll.*) stop-over. **–ausweis,** *m.* (*Comm.*) interim return. **–bahnhof,** *m.* intermediate station. **–balken,** *m.* mid-beam. **–bemerkung,** *f.* incidental remark, interruption, digression, aside. **–bescheid,** *m.* provisional decree. **–bilanz,** *f. See* **–abschluß. –blatt,** *n.* interleaved sheet *or* page. **–deck,** *n.* (*Naut.*) lower deck, steerage. **–ding,** *n.* combination, mixture, cross, hybrid, (*coll.*) a bit of both.

zwischen|drein [–'draɪn], *adv.* (*coll.*) in among; ***– legen,*** lay in among. **–drin** [–'drɪn], *adv.* (*coll.*) *see* **–drein**; ***– liegen,*** be *or* lie (in) among. **–durch** [–'durç], *adv.* through, in the midst (of), in between; at times, occasionally, between whiles, at intervals; for *or* as a change.

Zwischen|entscheidung, *f.* (*Law*) interlocutory decree. **–ergebnis,** *n.* provisional result. **–fall,** *m.* (untoward) incident, unforeseen event *or* episode; ***ohne –***, without incident, (*coll.*) without a hitch. **–farbe,** *f.* half-tint, secondary colour, intermediate shade. **–frage,** *f.* interpolated question. **–gas,** *n.* (*Motor.*) (*coll.*) ***– geben,*** double-declutch. **–gelände,** *n.* (*Mil.*) ***neutrales –***, No-Man's-Land. **–gericht,** *n.* side-dish, entremets. **–geschäft,** *n.* incidental business. **–geschoß,** *n. See* **–stock. –gewinn,** *m.* middleman's profit. **–glied,** *n.* connecting link. **–glühung,** *f.* intermediate annealing. **–handel,** *m.* middleman's business, carrying *or* transit trade; commission business. **–händler,** *m.* (commission-)agent, intermediary, middleman. **–handlung,** *f.* episode, incident.

zwischen|her [–'he:r], *adv.* (*coll.*) in the interval *or* meantime, meanwhile. **–hin** [–'hɪn], *adv.* (*coll.*) right in(to) the *or* their midst.

Zwischenhirn ['tsvɪʃənhɪrn], *n.* mid(le)-brain, diencephalon, thalamencephalon.

zwischeninne [tsvɪʃən'ɪnə], *adv.* (*coll.*) in the midst of, right among.

Zwischen|kiefer(knochen), *m.* intermaxillary bone. **–konto,** *n.* suspense account. **–kreis,** *m.* (*Rad.*) aerial *or* input circuit. **–lage,** *f.* intermediate position. **–landung,** *f.* (*Av.*) touch-down, intermediate landing, (*coll.*) stop-over; ***Flug ohne –***, non-stop flight. **zwischenliegend,** *adj.* intermediate, intervening. **Zwischen|lösung,** *f.* interim solution; (*fig.*) makeshift, stopgap. **–mauer,** *f.* partition wall. **–pause,** *f.* intermission, interval, interlude, break. **–person,** *f.* agent, intermediary, middleman; go-between. **–prüfung,** *f.* intermediate examination. **–raum,** *m.* (intermediate) space, clearance, gap, interstice, (*Typ.*) space, spacing; (intervening) distance; (*time*) interval. **–raumtaste,** *f.* (*typewriter*) space-bar. **–regierung,** *f.* interregnum, interim government. **–rippenraum,** *m.* (*Anat.*) intercostal space. **–ruf,** *m.* interruption, *pl.* heckling. **–runde,** *f.* (*Spt.*) semi-final.

Zwischen|satz, *m.* insertion; interpolation, parenthesis. **–schaltung,** *f.* (*Elec.*) intermediate switch position, (*Typ.*) insertion, interlineation. **–sender,** *m.* (*Rad.*) relay station. **–spiel,** *n.* intermezzo, interlude; (*fig.*) incident. **–staat,** *m.* buffer state. **zwischenstaatlich,** *adj.* international, inter-state.

Zwischen|stadium, *n.* intermediate stage *or* phase. **–station,** *f.* intermediate station. **–stecker,** *m.* (*Elec.*) adapter (plug). **–stock,** *m.* (*Archit.*) mezzanine, entresol. **–streifen,** *m.* (*Dressm.*) insertion, inserted piece. **–stück,** *n.* inset, insertion; connecting piece, connection, (*Elec.*) adapter; (*Theat.*) interlude, entr'acte; *see* **–spiel. –stufe,** *f.* intermediate stage. **–stunde,** *f.* interval, intermission, (*at school*) break, recreation. **–ton,** *m.* intermediate note (*sound*) *or* shade (*colour*), (*fig.*) overtone. **–träger,** *m.* informant, go-between; talebearer, scandalmonger, (*coll.*) tell-tale. **–trägerei,** *f.* tale-bearing. **–urteil,** *n.* (*Law*) interlocutory decree. **–verkauf,** *m.* (*Comm.*) – ***vorbehalten,*** subject to prior sale. **–vorhang,** *m.* (*Theat.*) drop-scene, drop-curtain. **–wand,** *f.* partition (wall). **–zaun,** *m.* dividing fence. **–zeile,** *f.* (*Typ.*) space-line. **–zeit,** *f.* intervening time *or* period, interim (period), interval; ***in der –,*** meanwhile, in the meantime. **–ziel,** *n.* (*Mil.*) intermediate objective. **–zustand,** *m.* intermediate state.

Zwist [tsvɪst], *m.* (**-es,** *pl.* **-e**) dissension, discord; dispute, quarrel, feud. **zwistig,** *adj.* dissentient, discordant. **Zwistigkeit,** *f.* discordance, discordancy; *see also* **Zwist.**

zwitschern ['tsvɪtʃərn], *v.t., v.i.* twitter, chirp, (*coll.*) chirrup; ***wie die Alten singen, so – die Jungen,*** like father like son.

Zwitter ['tsvɪtər], *m.* hermaphrodite, androgyne; hybrid, cross. **zwitterartig,** *adj.* hermaphrodite, androgynous, bisexual; hybrid. **Zwitter|bildung,** *f.* hybridization, hermaphroditism, androgyny, androgynism. **–blüte,** *f.* hermaphrodite flower, androgyne. **–geschlecht,** *n.* hybrid stock; mongrel *or* bastard race. **zwitterhaft,** *adj. See* **zwitterartig. Zwitterhaftigkeit,** *f.* hybrid character. **zwitt(e)rig,** *adj.* (*Bot.*) *see* **zwitterartig. Zwitter|stellung,** *f.* (*fig.*) ambiguous position. **–wort,** *n.* hybrid *or* bastard word.

zwo [tsvo:], (*obs.*) *see* **zwei** (*though nowadays used on the telephone etc. to avoid confusion with* ***drei***).

zwölf [tsvœlf], *num.adj.* twelve; ***fünf Minuten vor –,*** five minutes to twelve, eleven fifty-five; (*fig.*) at the eleventh hour; (*coll.*) ***nun hat es aber – geschlagen,*** that's really the limit, that's really too much, that's going too far. **Zwölf,** *f.* (-, *pl.* **-en**) (the number) twelve.

Zwölfeck ['tsvœlfʔɛk], *n.* (*Geom.*) dodecagon. **zwölfeckig,** *adj.* dodecagonal, twelve-cornered. **Zwölfender,** *m.* stag of twelve points. **zwölferlei,** *indecl.adj.* twelve (different) kinds *or* sorts of, twelve different, of twelve different kinds. **zwölffach,** *adj.* twelvefold. **Zwölf|fingerdarm,** *m.* (*Anat.*) duodenum. **–flach,** *n.* (*Geom.*) dodecahedron. **zwölf|flächig,** *adj.* dodecahedral, twelve-sided. **–jährig,** *adj.* twelve-year-old (*child*), twelve-year, twelve years', lasting twelve years. **–malig,** *adj.* repeated twelve times, twelve times repeated. **–seitig,** *adj. See* **–flächig. –stündig,** *adj.* twelve-hour, of *or* lasting twelve hours; (*instruction*) in *or* for twelve lessons.

zwölft [tsvœlft], *num.adj.* twelfth; (*fig.*) ***in -er Stunde,*** at the eleventh hour. **Zwölftel,** *n.* (*Swiss m.*) twelfth (part). **zwölftens,** *adv.* in the twelfth place.

zwot [tsvo:t], *num.adj. See* **zweit.**

Zyan [tsy'a:n], *n.* (*Chem.*) cyanogen. **Zyan|kali(um),** *n.* cyanide of potassium, potassium cyanide. **–wasserstoff(säure),** *m.(f.)* hydrocyanic *or* prussic acid.

Zyane [tsy'a:nə], *f.* (*Bot.*) cornflower, bachelor's button (*Centaurea cyanus*).

zyklisch ['tsy:klɪʃ], *adj.* cyclic(al).

Zyklon [tsy'klo:n], *m.* (**-s,** *pl.* **-e**) cyclone, tornado. **Zyklone,** *f.* (*Meteor.*) cyclone, depression.

Zyklop [tsy'klɔp], *m.* (**-en,** *pl.* **-en**) (*Myth.*) Cyclops. **zyklopisch,** *adj.* cyclopean, gigantic, gargantuan.

Zyklotron ['tsy:klotro:n], *n.* (**-s,** *pl.* **-e**) cyclotron.

Zyklus ['tsy:klus], *m.* (-, *pl.* **-len**) cycle; (*of lectures etc.*) series, course.

Zylinder [tsi'lɪndər], *m.* (*Geom., Mech.*) cylinder; (*of oil lamp*) chimney; (*coll.*) silk hat, top-hat. **Zylinder|bohrung,** *f.* (*Mech.*) cylinder bore. **–büro,** *n.* roll-top desk. **–hemmung,** *f.* (*Horol.*) cylinder escapement. **–hub,** *m.* (*Mech.*) (piston) stroke. **–inhalt,** *m.* (*Mech.*) cylinder capacity, piston displacement. **–presse,** *f.* roller-press, revolving press. **–reihe,** *f.* (*Mech.*) bank of cylinders. **–schreibtisch,** *m. See* **–büro. –uhr,** *f.* lever-watch. **–zahl,** *f.* number of cylinders. **zylindrisch,** *adj.* cylindrical.

Zyniker ['tsy:nɪkər], *m.* cynic. **zynisch,** *adj.* cynical. **Zynismus** [–'nɪsmus], *m.* cynicism.

Zypern ['tsy:pərn], *n.* (*Geog.*) Cyprus. **Zyperwein,** *m.* Cypress *or* Cyprian wine. **Zyprer,** *m.* Cypriot.

Zypresse [tsy'prɛsə], *f.* (*Bot.*) cypress(-tree). **Zypressen|hain,** *m.* cypress-grove. **--Wolfsmilch,** *f.* (*Bot.*) cypress spurge (*Euphorbia cyparissias*).

zyprisch ['tsy:prɪʃ], *adj.* Cypriot.

zyrillisch [tsy'rɪlɪʃ], *adj.* Cyrillic.

Zyste ['tsystə], *f.* (*Med.*) cyst.

Weights and Measures
Maße und Gewichte

1 mm (Millimeter)	=	0·04 in. (inch)
1 cm (Zentimeter)	=	0·39 in.
1 cm^2 (Quadratzentimeter)	=	0·155 sq. in. (square inch)
1 cm^3 (Kubikzentimeter)	=	0·06 cu. in. (cubic inch)
1 m (Meter)	=	39·5 in. (= 1·09 yd. (yards))
1 m^2 (Quadratmeter)	=	1·196 sq. yd. (square yards)
1 m^3 (Kubikmeter)	=	35·3 cu. ft. (cubic feet) (= 1·3 cu. yd. (cubic yards))
1 km (Kilometer)	=	0·62 mile
1 km^2 (Quadratkilometer)	=	247 acres (= 0·39 sq. mile)
1 ha (Hektar)	=	2·5 acres (*approx.*)

1 g (Gramm)	=	0·04 oz. (ounce)
1 dkg (Dekagramm)	=	0.35 oz.
1 kg (Kilogramm)	=	2·2 lb. (pounds)
1 Zentner (= 50 kg)	=	0·98 cwt. (hundredweight) (*Am.* 1·1 cwt.)
(*Austr.* = 100 kg)	=	1·97 cwt. (*Am.* 2·2 cwt.)
1 Tonne	=	2,200 lb. (= 0·98 ton, *i.e.* 40 lb. less than 1 ton) (*Am.* = 1·1 ton)

1 l (Liter)	=	1·76 pints (*Am.* 2·1 pint)
10 l (Liter)	=	2·2 gallons (*Am.* 2·64 gallons)
50 l (Liter)	=	11 gallons (*approx.*) (*Am.* 13 gallons (*approx.*))

1 in. (inch)	=	2·54 cm (Zentimeter)
1 sq. in. (square inch)	=	6·5 cm^2 (Quadratzentimeter)
1 cu. in. (cubic inch)	=	16·39 cm^3 (Kubikzentimeter)
1 ft. (foot)	=	0·3 m (Meter)
1 sq. ft. (square foot)	=	930 cm^2
1 cu. ft. (cubic foot)	=	0·029 m^3 (Kubikmeter)
1 yd. (yard)	=	0·9 m
1 sq. yd. (square yard)	=	0·836 m^2 (Quadratmeter)
1 cu. yd. (cubic yard)	=	0·76 m^3
1 furlong	=	201 m
1 mile	=	1,609 m
1 acre	=	0.4 ha (Hektar) (= 4047 m^2)
1 sq. mile (square mile)	=	259 ha (= 2·59 km^2 (Quadratkilometer))

1 oz. (ounce)	=	28·35 g (Gramm)
1 lb. (pound)	=	453·6 g
1 stone	=	6·35 kg (Kilogramm)
1 cwt. (hundredweight)	=	50·8 kg (*Am.* 45·36 kg)
1 ton	=	1016 kg (*Am.* 907 kg)

1 pint	=	0·57 l (Liter) (*Am.* 0·47 l)
1 quart	=	1·14 l (*Am.* 0·95 l)
1 gallon	=	4·55 l (*Am.* 3·79 l)
5 gallons	=	23 l (*approx.*) (*Am.* 19 l (*approx.*))
10 gallons	=	45 l (*approx.*) (*Am.* 39 l (*approx.*))

Clothing Sizes
Kleidergrößen

(approx. equivalents)

Shoes/Schuhe

Deutsch	36	37	38	39	40	41	42	43	44	45	46	47
British	3½	4	5	6	6½	7	8	9	9½	10½	11	12
American	5	5¾	6½	7¼	8	8¾	9½	10¼	11	11¾	12½	13¼

Collars/Kragen

Deutsch	35–36	37	38	39	40–41	42	43
British & American	14	14½	15	15½	16	16½	17

Stockings/Strümpfe

Deutsch	35	36	37	38	39	40	41
British & American	8	8½	9	9½	10	10½	11

Vehicle Performance
Benzinverbrauch

In Germany this is measured differently—not the number of miles travelled on each gallon, but the number of litres required for each 100 kilometres.

The ratio of 1 gallon to 1 mile gives 282·49 litres to 100 kilometres. Thus the factor by which the miles are multiplied must divide the number of litres, giving the following table of equivalents.

To find the equivalent of e.g. 23 miles per gallon, follow the 20 line to its intersection with the +3 column, to give 12·3 litres per 100 kilometres.

Miles per gallon/Litres per 100 kilometres

		+1	+2	+3	+4	+5	+6	+7	+8	+9
10	28·3	25·7	23·5	21·7	20·2	18·8	17·7	16·6	15·7	14·9
20	14·1	13·5	12·8	12·3	11·8	11·3	10·9	10·5	10·1	9·7
30	9·4	9·1	8·8	8·6	8·3	8·1	7·8	7·6	7·4	7·25
40	7·1	6·9	6·7	6·6	6·4	6·3	6·1	6·0	5·9	5·8
50	5·7									

Since the Imperial gallon is larger than the U.S. gallon, the factor of 223·95 is necessary to give equivalents appropriate to American usage.

U.S. miles per gallon/Litres per 100 kilometres

		+1	+2	+3	+4	+5	+6	+7	+8	+9
10	22·4	20·4	18·7	17·2	16·0	14·9	14·0	13·2	12·4	11·8
20	11·2	10·7	10·2	9·7	9·3	9·0	8·6	8·3	8·0	7·7
30	7·5	7·2	7·0	6·8	6·6	6·3	6·2	6·1	5·9	5·7
40	5·6	5·5	5·3	5·2	5·1	5·0	4·9	4·8	4·7	4·6
50	4·5									

Specialist Dictionaries
Spezialwörterbücher

Chemistry and Chemical Technology
Chemie, Chemische Technologie

Carriere, G. *Lexicon of Detergents, Cosmetics and Toiletries*. Amsterdam, Elsevier, 1966
Clason, W. E. *Dictionary of Chemical Engineering in six languages*. Amsterdam, Elsevier, 1968
Dorian, A. F. *Dictionary of Industrial Chemistry in six languages*. Amsterdam, Elsevier, 1964
Dorian, A. F. *Six-language Dictionary of Plastics and Rubber Technology*. London, Iliffe, 1965
Technological Dictionary for Industries concerning Dyestuffs and Textile Auxiliaries. Farbw. Hoechst, 1967
Ernst, R. *Fachwörterbuch der Chemie* . . . Wiesbaden, Brandstetter, 1961–63
Also as: *Dictionary of Chemistry*. London, Pitman, 1961–63
Fischer, W. *Fachwörterbuch für Brauerei und Mälzerei*. Nuremberg, Carl, 2nd ed. 1955
Fouchier, J., Billet, F. and Epstein, H. *Dictionnaire de Chimie. Fachwörterbuch für Chemie. Chemical Dictionary*. Baden-Baden, Wervereín, 1953
Also as: *Chemical Dictionary*. Nijmegen, Netherlands Univ. Press, 1970
Hartong, B. D. *Dictionary of Barley, Malting and Brewing*. Amsterdam, Elsevier, 1961
Lueck, E. *Fachwörterbuch des Lebensmittelwesens. Dictionary of Food Technology. Englisch–Deutsch*. Wiesbaden, Brandstetter, 1963
Merz, O. *Deutsch–Englisches und Englisch–Deutsches Fachwörterbuch für Fachausdrücke aus dem Lack- und Farbengebiet*. Stuttgart, Wissenschaftlicher Verlag, 2nd ed. 1954
Mohrberg, W. *Technisches Wörterbuch Zellstoff und Papier*. Darmstadt, Roether, 1955
Neville, H. H., Johnstone, N. C. and Boyd, G. V. *A New German–English Dictionary for Chemists*. London/Glasgow, Blackie, 1964
The Van Nostrand Chemists' Dictionary. New York, Van Nostrand, 1953
Patterson, C. *German–English Dictionary for Chemists*. New York, Wiley; London, Chapman & Hall, 1954
Sobecka, Z. *Dictionary of Chemistry and Chemical Technology in six languages*. Oxford, Pergamon, 1966
Stechl, G. *Der Brauer in 9 Sprachen: Italienisch, Portugiesisch, Spanisch, Französisch, Deutsch, Englisch, Holländisch, Schwedisch, Tschechisch*. Nuremberg, Carl, 1960
Vries, L. de and Kolb, H. *Dictionary of Chemistry and Chemical Engineering*. Weinheim, Verlag Chemie; New York/London, Academic Press, 1970
Wittfoht, A. *Kunststofftechnisches Wörterbuch . . . Plastics Technical Dictionary*. Munich/New York, Hanser, 1959–61

Commerce, Law, Politics etc.
Handel, Rechtswissenschaft, Politik, etc.

Back, H., Cirullies, H. and Marquard, G. *POLEC Dictionary of Politics and Economics: English, French, German*. Berlin, de Gruyter, 1967
Banking Terms: French, German, Italian, Spanish, Swedish. Stockholm, Skand. Banken, 1964
Basedow, K. H. *Wörterbuch der Rechtssprache: Deutsch–Englisch und Englisch–Deutsch*. Hamburg, Heldt, 1947–48
Becker, U. *Rechtswörterbuch für die gewerbliche Wirtschaft*. Frankfurt, Knapp, 1966
Eichborn, R. von. *Wirtschaftswörterbuch: Deutsch–Englisch und Englisch–Deutsch*. Düsseldorf, Econ. Verlag, 3rd ed. 1969–70.
Also as: *Business Dictionary*. Englewood Cliffs, N.J., Prentice-Hall, 1962
Erdsiek, G. and Deill, C. E. *Wörterbuch für Recht, Wirtschaft, Politik*. Hamburg, Meissner, 1964–68
Feldbausch, F. K. *Bankwesen: Deutsch–Englisch, Englisch–Deutsch*. Munich, Verlag Moderne Industrie, 1972
Freudenberg, W. *Internationales Wörterbuch der Lederwirtschaft*. Berlin/Göttingen/Heidelberg, Springer, 1951
Freyd, H. T. *Englisches Wirtschafts-ABC. English Economic Terms with definitions and German vocabulary*. Stuttgart, Grossmann, 1967
Grohmann, H. W. 750 *Werbefachwörter*. Essen, Wirtschaft und Werbung Verlag, 1960
Gunston, C. A. *Deutsch–Englisches Glossarium finanzieller und wirtschaftlicher Fachausdrücke*. Frankfurt, Knapp, 6th ed. 1972
Haensch, G. *Dictionary of International Relations and Politics*. Amsterdam, Elsevier, 1965
Heinze, S. *Fachwörterbuch des Versicherungswesens*. Wiesbaden, Brandstetter, 1961
Herbst, R. *Dictionary of Commercial, Financial and Legal Terms: English, French, German*. Zug, Translegal Ltd., 1966–68
Klaften, B. and Allison, F. C. *Wörterbuch der Patentfachsprache*. Munich, Wila Verlag für Wirtschaftswerbung, 1959
Klaus, H. *Englisch/Amerikanische Fachausdrücke im Bankgeschäft*. Bern/Stuttgart, Haupt, 3rd ed. 1970
Kniepkamp, H. P. *Rechtswörterbuch*. Berlin, Colloquium-Verlag; New York, Oceana Publ.,1954
Glossary of Technical Terms for Market Researchers. Brussels, European Society for Opinion and Marketing Research, 1969
Orne, J. *The Language of the Foreign Book Trade*. Chicago, American Library Assoc., 2nd ed. 1962
Renner, R., Sachs, R. and Fosburg, J. *Deutsch–Englische Wirtschaftssprache*. Munich, Hueber, 1965
Also as: *German–English Economic Terminology*. London, Macmillan, 1965
Renner, R. and Tooth, J. *Rechtssprache Englisch–Deutsch . . .* Munich, Hueber, 1971
Sachs, W. and Drude, G. *Lebensversicherungstechnisches Wörterbuch: Deutsch–Englisch–Französisch–Italienisch–Spanisch*. Karlsruhe, Verlag Versicherungswirtschaft, 1964
Scharf, T. *Dictionary of Development Economics*. Amsterdam, Elsevier, 1969
Scharf, T. and Shetty, M. C. *Dictionary of Development Banking*. Amsterdam, Elsevier, 1965
Sommer, W. and Schönfeld, H.-M. *Management Dictionary: Fachwörterbuch für Betriebswirtschaft, Wirtschafts- und Steuerrecht und Datenverarbeitung*. Berlin/New York, de Gruyter, 4th ed. 1972
Steneberg, W. *Handwörterbuch des Finanzwesens in deutscher und englischer Sprache* . . . Berlin, Siemens, 2nd ed. 1947
Thole, B. L. M. *Lexicon of Stock Market Terms*. Amsterdam, Elsevier, 1965
Waschke, H. *Juristisches Taschenwörterbuch in deutscher und englischer Sprache*. Berlin, Siemens, 1948
Wolf, F., Haensch, G. and Lawatsch, E. *Taschenwörterbuch des Fremdenverkehrs*. Munich, Hueber, 1970

Zahn, H. E. *Euro Wirtschafts-Wörterbuch: Deutsch, Englisch, Französisch.* Frankfurt, Knapp, 1973
Zavada, D. *Satzlexikon der Handelskorrespondenz. New Commercial Dictionary.* Wiesbaden, Brandstetter; London, Pitman, 1969

Electricity, Electronics, Radio
Elektrizität, Elektronik, Rundfunk

Arnoldt, H. *Funktechnik. Technisches Fachwörterbuch in deutscher und englischer Sprache.* Berlin, Siemens, 1947–48
Bindemann, W. *Dictionary of Semiconductor Physics and Electronics.* Berlin, VEB Verlag Technik; Oxford, Pergamon, 1965
Bogenschütz, A. F., *Fachwörterbuch für Batterien und Energie-Direktumwandlung.* Wiesbaden, Brandstetter, 1968
Broadbent, D. T. *Multilingual Dictionary of Automatic Control Terminology.* Pittsburgh, Instrument Society of America, 1967
Clason, W. E. *Dictionary of Amplification, Modulation, Reception and Transmission in six languages.* Amsterdam, Elsevier, 1960
Clason, W. E. *Dictionary of Television, Radar and Antennas.* Amsterdam, Elsevier, 1964
Clason, W. E. *Electrotechnical Dictionary in six languages.* Amsterdam, Elsevier, 1965
Clason, W. E. *Dictionary of Electronics and Waveguides in six languages.* Amsterdam, Elsevier, 1966
Cook, N. and Marcus, J. *Electronics Dictionary.* New York, McGraw-Hill, 1945
Dorian, A. F. *Six-language Dictionary of Automation, Electronics and Scientific Instruments.* London, Iliffe; Englewood Cliffs, N.J., Prentice-Hall, 1962
Fachwörterbuch für das Fernmeldewesen. Deutsch–Englisch, Englisch–Deutsch. Brunswick/Berlin/Hamburg, Westermann, 1948–49
Freeman, H. G. *Elektrotechnisches Englisch: Deutsch–Englisch, Englisch–Deutsch.* Essen, Girardet, 5th ed. 1956
Goedecke, W. *Wörterbuch der Elektrotechnik, Fernmeldetechnik und Elektronik.* Wiesbaden, Brandstetter, 1964–67
Also as: *Dictionary of Electrical Engineering, Telecommunications and Electronics.* London, Pitman, 1966–67
Höhn, E. *Wörterbuch der Elektroindustrie.* Düsseldorf/Vienna, Econ. Verlag, 1966
Neidhardt, P. *Dictionary of Telecommunications Engineering, Television, Electronics.* Berlin, VEB Verlag Technik; Oxford, Pergamon, 1964
Rint, C. *Lexikon der Hochfrequenz-, Nachrichten-, und Elektrotechnik.* Berlin, VEB Verlag Technik; Munich, Porta-Verlag, 1957–61
Schwenkhagen, H. F. *Fachwörterbuch Elektrotechnik.* Essen, Girardet, 1959
Also as: *Dictionary of Electrical Engineering.* London, Pitman, 1959
Semiconductors: International Dictionary in seven languages. Milan, Angeli; London, Business Books Ltd., 1971
Thali, H. *Technisches Wörterbuch über Elektrotechnik, Radio, Fernsehen und Fernmeldetechnik: Deutsch–Englisch–Französisch.* Hitzkirch, Thali, 1948
Visser, A. *Telecommunications Dictionary in six languages.* Amsterdam, Elsevier, 1960
Wernicke, H. *Lexikon der Elektronik, Nachrichten- und Elektrotechnik. Dictionary of Electronics, Communications and Electrical Engineering.* Munich, Wernicke, 1962–64

Engineering and Allied Fields
Ingenieurwissenschaft und verwandte Fächer

Breuer, K. *Technisch-wissenschaftliches Taschen-Wörterbuch. In deutscher und englischer Sprache.* Berlin, Siemens, 6th ed. 1971
Brielmaier, A. A. *German–English Glossary of Civil Engineering.* Univ. of Illinois Engineering Experimental Station, Circular Series 40, 1940
Bucksch, H. *Wörterbuch für Bautechnik und Baumaschinen. Dictionary of Civil Engineering and Construction Machinery and Equipment.* Wiesbaden/Berlin, Bauverlag; London, Contractors' Record Ltd., 5th ed. 1971
Courtauld's Vocabulary of Textile Terms: English, French, Spanish, German, Russian. London, Courtaulds Ltd. Marketing Division, 1964
Darcy, L. *Luftfahrttechnisches Wörterbuch.* Berlin, de Gruyter, 1960
Dettner, H. W. *Dictionary of Metal Finishing and Corrosion in five languages.* Amsterdam, Elsevier, 1971
Didier-Kogag-Hinselmann G.m.b.H. *Wörterbuch der Kokereitechnik.* Essen, Vulkan-Verlag Classen, 1954
Elmer, T. H. *German–English Dictionary of Glass, Ceramics and allied Sciences.* New York/London, Interscience Publications, 1963
Ernst, R. *Wörterbuch der industriellen Technik, einschließlich Hilfswissenschaften und Bauwesen.* Wiesbaden, Brandstetter, 3rd ed. 1971
Also as: *Dictionary of Industrial Technology including related fields of Science and Civil Engineering: German-English, English-German.* London, Pitman, 1962
Freeman, H. G. *Taschenwörterbuch Kraftfahrzeugtechnik.* Munich, Hueber, 1968
Freeman, H. G. *Spezial-Wörterbuch für das Maschinenwesen.* Essen, Girardet, 1958
Freeman, H. G. *Fachwörterbuch: Werkzeuge.* Essen, Girardet, 1950–52
Freeman. H. G. *Enzyklopädisches Fachwörterbuch: Spanende Werkzeugmaschinen. Dictionary of Metal-cutting machine tools.* Essen, Girardet, 1963–65
Frenot, G. H. and Holloway, A. H. *AGARD Aeronautic Multilingual Dictionary.* Oxford, Pergamon, 1960; 1st supplement 1963
Goebel, E. H. and Dürbeck, A. *Technisches Taschenwörterbuch in deutscher und englischer Sprache.* Berlin, Siemens, 5th ed. 1963
Gros, E. and Singer, L. *Russian–English–French–German Constructional Engineering Dictionary.* London, Scientific Information Consultants Ltd., 1965
Heiler, T. *Illustrated Technical Dictionary of Metal-Cutting Tools in five languages.* London/Glasgow, Blackie, 1964
Also as: *Technisches Bildwörterbuch für spanende Werkzeuge zur Metallbearbeitung in fünf Sprachen.* Munich, Hanser, 1964
Hoffmann, E. *Fachwörterbuch für die Glasindustrie.* Berlin/Göttingen/Heidelberg, Springer, 1963
Holmström, J. E. and Fickelson, M. *Trilingual Dictionary for Materials and Structures.* Oxford, Pergamon, 1971
Horten, H. E. *Numerical Control of Machine Tools Dictionary in four languages.* London, Hinkel, 1969
Köhler, E. L. *English–German and German–English Dictionary for the Iron and Steel Industries.* Vienna, Springer, 1955
Korner, R. *Technical Dictionary of Textile Finishing.* Berlin, VEB Verlag Technik; Oxford, Pergamon, 1966
Leuk, G. and Börner, H. *Technisches Fachwörterbuch der Grundstoff-Industrien, Bergbau, Steine, und Erdenindustrie, Aufbereitung, Hüttenwesen, Metallverarbeitung* ... Göttingen, Vandenhoeck & Ruprecht, 1962

Lindeke, W. *Technical Dictionary of Heating, Ventilation and Sanitary Engineering.* Berlin, VEB Verlag Technik; Oxford, Pergamon, 1970
Mansum, C. J. van. *Dictionary of Building Construction.* Amsterdam, Elsevier, 1959
Meink, F. and Möhle, H. *Wörterbuch für das Wasser- und Abwasserfach. Dictionary of water and sewage engineering.* Munich/Vienna, Oldenbourg, 1963
Michelson, D. O. *Fachwörterbuch Textil.* Frankfurt, Deutscher Fachverlag, 1967
Oppermann, A. *Technisches Taschenwörter- und Handbuch der Luftfahrt.* Munich, Aeronautik Verlag, 1970
Oppermann, A. *Wörterbuch der modernen Technik.* Munich, Aeronautik Verlag, 1965–68
Polanyi, M. *Technical and Trade Dictionary of Textile Terms.* Oxford, Pergamon, 2nd ed. 1967
Rahlenbeck, W. D. *Fachwörterbuch der Ölhydraulik und Servotechnik.* Mainz, Krausskopf, 1967
Schlomann, A. *Hoyer-Kreuter Technologisches Wörterbuch: Deutsch–Englisch–Französisch.* New York, Unger, 1944
Schwicker, A. C. *International Dictionary of Construction.* Milan, Technoprint International, 1972
Stahleisen-Wörterbuch. Iron and Steel Dictionary. Düsseldorf, Verlag Stahleisen, 2nd ed. 1962
Stekhoven, G. S. and Valk, W. B. *Dictionary of Metal-Cutting Tools in seven languages.* Amsterdam, Elsevier, 1970 ff.
Multilingual Glossary of Textile Terminology. Cambridge, Mass., Massachusetts Institute of Technology, 1972
Vollmer, E. *Lexikon für Wasserwesen, Erd- und Grundbau. Deutsch–Englisch.* Stuttgart, Fischer, 1967
Vries, L. de and Jörgensen, O. M. *Fachwörterbuch des Kraftfahrzeugwesens und verwandter Gebiete.* Wiesbaden, Brandstetter, 1962
Vries, L. de and Luken, O. H. *Wörterbuch der Textilindustrie.* Wiesbaden, Brandstetter, 1959–60
Walther, R. *Polytechnical Dictionary: German–English, English–German.* Berlin, VEB Verlag Technik, 1967
Wüster, E. *The Machine Tool—An Interlingual Dictionary of Basic Concepts.* London, Technical Press, 1968

Geography, Geology etc.
Geographie, Geologie etc.

Amstutz, G. C. *Glossary of Mining Geology in English, Spanish, French and German.* Stuttgart, Emke, 1971
Backhaus, K. O. *Kristallographie: Englisch, Deutsch, Französisch, Russisch.* Berlin, VEB Verlag Technik, 1972
Cagnacci-Schwicker, A. *International Dictionary of Metallurgy, Mineralogy, Geology, Mining and Oil Industries in four languages.* Milan, Technoprint International; New York, McGraw-Hill, 1968
Clason, W. E. *Dictionary of Metallurgy in six languages.* Amsterdam, Elsevier, 1967
Fischer, E. and Elliott, F. E. *A German and English Glossary of Geographical Terms.* New York, American Geographical Soc., 1950
Schieferdecker, A. A. G. *Geological Nomenclature.* Royal Geological and Mining Society of the Netherlands, 1959
Singer, T. E. R. *German–English Dictionary of Metallurgy.* New York/London, McGraw-Hill, 1945
Zylka, R. *Geological Dictionary: English, Polish, Russian, French, German.* Warsaw, Wydawnictwa Geologiczne, 1970

Mathematical Sciences
Mathematische Wissenschaften

Alsleben, K. *Lexikon der kybernetischen Pädagogik und der programmierten Instruktion.* Quickborn, Schnelle, 1966
Amkreutz, C. *Wörterbuch der Datenverarbeitung.* Bergisch-Gladbach, Fachbuchverlag, 1972
Clason, W. E. *Dictionary of Computers, Automatic Control and Data Processing in six languages.* Amsterdam, Elsevier, 1971
Clason, W. E. *Dictionary of General Physics in six languages.* Amsterdam, Elsevier, 1962
Clason, W. E. *Dictionary of Nuclear Science and Technology.* Amsterdam, Elsevier, 1955
Data Processing Dictionary. Berlin, Siemens, 1970
Herland, L. *Wörterbuch der mathematischen Wissenschaften.* Wiesbaden, Brandstetter, 1951–54; 2nd ed. 1965
Also: *Dictionary of Mathematical Sciences: German–English, English–German.* London, Harrap, 1965
Hofmann, E. *Wörterbuch Datenverarbeitung.* Berlin, Verlag der Wirtschaft, 3rd ed. 1971
Hyman, C. J. and Idlin, R. *Wörterbuch der Physik und verwandter Wissenschaften. Dictionary of Physics and Allied Sciences.* London, Owen, 1958–62
James, G. *Mathematical Dictionary.* Princeton/London, Van Nostrand, 3rd mutilingual ed. 1968
Klaften, B. *Mathematisches Vokabular. Englisch–Deutsch, Deutsch–Englisch.* Munich, Wila Verlag für Wirtschaftswerbung, 1961
Krüger, K. H. *Wörterbuch der Datenverarbeitung.* Munich, Verlag Dokumentation, 1968
Lettenmeyer, L. *Atomterminologie, Atomic Terminology . . . Englisch, Deutsch, Französisch, Italienisch.* Munich, Isar-Verlag, 1958
MacIntyre, S. and Witte, E. *German–English Mathematical Vocabulary.* Edinburgh, Oliver & Boyd, 1956
Oppermann, A. *Wörterbuch Kybernetik.* Munich, Verlag Dokumentation, 1969
Rau, H. *Wörterbuch der Kernphysik und Kernchemie.* Wiesbaden, Brandstetter, 1964
Also: *Dictionary of Nuclear Physics and Nuclear Chemistry.* London, Pitman, 2nd ed. 1965
Sube, R. *Dictionary of Physics and Technology: English, German, French, Russian.* Oxford, Pergamon, 1962
Trollhann, L. and Wittmann, A. *Dictionary of Data Processing.* Amsterdam, Elsevier, 1964

Medicine
Medizin

Arnandov, G. *Terminologia Medica Polyglotta.* Sofia, Medicina et Physcultura, 1964
Branconi, L. R. *Hematology: a Glossary of Terms in English/American, French, Spanish, Italian, German, Russian.* Amsterdam, Elsevier, 1964
Féderation dentaire internationale. *Dental Lexicon.* Hague, Sijthoff, 1966
Lejeune, F. and Bunjes, W. E. *German–English, English–German Dictionary for Physicians.* Stuttgart, Thieme, 2nd ed. 1968
Schoenewald, F. S. *German–English Medical Dictionary.* London, Lewis, 1949
Sliosberg, A. *Dictionary of Pharmaceutical Science and Techniques in five languages.* Amsterdam, Elsevier, 1968
Sliosberg, A. *Medical Dictionary in five languages.* Amsterdam, Elsevier, 1964
Unseld, D. W. *Medizinisches Wörterbuch der deutschen und englischen Sprache.* Stuttgart, Wissenschaftliche Verlagsanstalt, 6th ed. 1971
Veillon, E. and Nobel, A. *Medizinisches Wörterbuch, Medical Dictionary, Dictionnaire médical.* Berne, Huber, 5th ed. 1969

Miscellaneous
Verschiedenes

Lexicon of Archive Terminology. Amsterdam, Elsevier, 1964

Beigel, H. G. *Dictionary of Psychology and Related Fields: German–English.* London, Harrap, 1971

Bucksch, H. *Holz-Wörterbuch. Dictionary of Wood and Wood-working Practice.* Wiesbaden, Bauverlag; London, Pitman, 1966

Carsten, L. von. *English–German, German–English Military Dictionary.* Stuttgart, Francke, 1944

Cescotti, R. *Luftfahrt-Wörterbuch.* Munich, Reich, 1954

Clason, W. E. *Dictionary of Library Science, Information and Documentation in six languages.* Amsterdam, Elsevier, 1973

Craeybeckx, A. S. H. *Dictionary of Photography in three languages.* Amsterdam, Elsevier, 1965

Dietel, W. *Seefahrts-Wörterbuch. Seafaring Dictionary.* Munich, Lehmann, 1954

Dorian, A. F. *Dictionary of Science and Technology: English–German, German–English.* Amsterdam, Elsevier, 1967

Dorian, A. F. and Oseton, J. *Dictionary of Aeronautics in six languages.* Amsterdam, Elsevier, 1964

Eitzen, K. H. *Deutsches Militärwörterbuch.* Bonn, Verlag WEU Offene Worte, 4th ed. 1957

Grau, W. *Dictionary of Photography and Motion Picture Engineering and related topics. English, German, French.* Berlin, Verlag für Radio-, Foto-, Kinotechnik, 1958

Haensch, G. and Haberkamp, G. *Dictionary of Agriculture in four languages.* Amsterdam, Elsevier, 3rd ed. 1966

Heinze, S. and Engelen-Weybridge, V. *Fachwörterbuch des gesamten Transportwesens . . .* Wiesbaden, Brandstetter, 1961

Hepp, F. and Katona, L. *Sportwörterbuch in sieben Sprachen, Englisch, Deutsch, Spanisch, Italienisch, Französisch, Ungarisch, Russisch.* Budapest, Terra; Berlin, Sportverlag, 1962

Kaupert, W. *Dictionary of Waste Disposal and Public Cleansing in three languages.* Amsterdam, Elsevier, 1966

King, M. K. *Photographic Dictionary. Photo-Fachwörterbuch.* Düsseldorf, Bach, 1956

Krollmann, F. *Langenscheidts Fachwörterbuch Wehrwesen.* Berlin, Langenscheidt, 1957

International Lighting Vocabulary: French, English, German, Russian. Paris, Bureau Central de la Commission Internationale de l'Eclairage, 3rd ed. 1970

Leibiger, J. S. *German–English and English–German Dictionary for Scientists.* Ann Arbor, Mich., Edwards Bros., 1950

Leuchtmann, H. and Schick, P. *Langenscheidts Fachwörterbuch Musik.* Berlin, Langenscheidt, 1964

Lingemann, E. *Glossary of Social Work Terms in English, French, German.* Cologne/Berlin, Heymann, 1958

Litschauer, R. von. *Vocabularium polyglottum vitae silvarum. Waldbiologisches Fachwörterbuch . . . Latein, Deutsch, Englisch, Französisch, Spanisch, Russisch.* Hamburg/Berlin, Parey, 1955

Meyer-Jenin, F. W. *Taschenwörterbuch für den Strassenverkehr.* Berlin / Bielefeld / Detmold, Schmidt, 1948

Moor, L. *Lexique Français–Anglais–Allemand des Termes Usuels en Psychiatrie, Neuro-Psychiatrie Infantile et Psychologie Pathologique.* Paris, L'Expansion Scientifique Française, 2nd ed. 1965–69

Philipp, H. *Deutsch–Englisches Wörterbuch für Architekten, Baubehörden, Bauwirtschaft.* Hamburg, Sachse, 1946

Rae, K. and Southern, R. *An International Vocabulary of Technical Theatre Terms.* London, Reinhardt, 1959

Glossary of Terms used in Quality Control. Rotterdam, European Organization for Quality Control, 2nd ed. 1969

International Dictionary of Refrigeration. Paris, International Institute of Refrigeration; Oxford, Pergamon, 1962

Richter, G. *Dictionary of Optics, Photography and Photogrammetry.* Amsterdam, Elsevier, 1966

Ruttkowski, W. V. and Blake, R. E. *Literaturwörterbuch, Glossary of Literary Terms. German, English, French.* Berne/Munich, Francke, 1969

Schlemminger, J. *Fachwörterbuch des Buchwesens.* Darmstadt / Nuremberg / Düsseldorf / Berlin, Stoytscheff, 2nd ed. 1954

Schmitz, W. *Englisches Wörterbuch für Eisenbahnsignalwesen und Fernmeldetechnik.* Frankfurt/Berlin, Tetzlaff, 1954

Schreyer, R., Maurer, S. and Wolter, F. W. *Dictionary of Photography and Cinematography.* Halle, Fotokinoverlag; London/New York, Focal Press, 1961

Schulz, E. *Wörterbuch der Optik und Feinmechanik.* Wiesbaden, Brandstetter, 1960

Schulz, M. R. *Polygraph-Wörterbuch der graphischen Industrie in sechs Sprachen . . .* Frankfurt, Polygraph-Verlag, 1967

Schuurman Stekhoven, G. *Automobile Dictionary in eight languages.* Amsterdam, Elsevier, 1966

Segditsas, P. E. *Nautical Dictionary.* Amsterdam, Elsevier, 1965–66

Trondt, L. *Polygraph Dictionary. Fachausdrücke der graphischen Industrie.* Frankfurt, Polygraph-Verlag, 1959

Visser, A. D. *Dictionary of Soil Mechanics.* Amsterdam, Elsevier, 1965

Vries, L. de. *German–English Science Dictionary for Students in Chemistry, Physics, Biology, Agriculture and Related Sciences.* New York/London, McGraw-Hill, 3rd ed. 1959

Wijnekus, F. J. M. *Dictionary of the Printing and Allied Industries.* Amsterdam, Elsevier, 1967

Common German Abbreviations

1. There is a modern tendency to omit stops or periods after abbreviations, but it should be understood that forms both with and without stops are current.
2. Certain abbreviations may be found with either capital or small letters.
3. The notes in **square** brackets are NOT translations of the German words preceding them, but indicate the corresponding English phrase or organization, the expansion of which can be found in the list of English abbreviations.

A

A. Ampere
a Ar (= *100 sq. m.*)
a. am (*before names of rivers*)
A.A. Auswärtiges Amt
a.a.O. am angeführten Orte [= *loc. cit.*]
A.B. Augsburger Bekenntnis
Abb. Abbildung
A.B.C.-Waffen atomare, biologische und chemische Waffen
abds. abends
A.B.F. Arbeiter- und Bauernfakultät (*E. Germany*)
Abf. Abfahrt
Abg. Abgeordnete(r)
A.B.G.B. Allgemeines Bürgerliches Gesetzbuch (*Austria*)
Abh. Abhandlung
Abk. Abkürzung
Abs. Absender; Absatz
Abschn. Abschnitt
Abt. Abteilung
A. Ch.(n.) *ante Christum* (*natum*) (= vor Christi Geburt) [= *B.C.*]
a d. *a dato* (= *after date*)
a.d. an der (*before names of rivers*)
a.D. (*Mil.*) außer Dienst
A.D.A.C. Allgemeiner Deutscher Automobil-Club
A.D.B. Allgemeine Deutsche Biographie
A.D.G.B. Allgemeiner Deutscher Gewerkschaftsbund
A.D.N. Allgemeiner Deutscher Nachrichtendienst (*E. Germany*)
Adr. Adresse
AdW Akademie der Wissenschaften
AG Aktiengesellschaft
a.G. auf Gegenseitigkeit; (*Theat.*) als Gast
Agfa Aktiengesellschaft für Anilinfabrikation
A.H. alter Herr
ahd. althochdeutsch
A.K. Aktienkapital; Armeekorps
Aki (*coll.*) Aktualitätenkino
Akk. Akkusativ
Akku (*coll.*) Akkumulator
allg. allgemein
Angekl. Angeklagte(r)
Anh. Anhang
Ank. Ankunft
Anm. Anmerkung
Antw. Antwort
Anw. Anweisung
Anz. Anzeiger; Anzeigen
A.O.K. Allgemeine Ortskrankenkasse
a.o. Prof. außerordentlicher Professor
apl. außerplanmäßig
A.R.D. Arbeitsgemeinschaft der (öffentlichen rechtlichen) Rundfunkanstalten (der Bundesrepublik) Deutschland
Art. Artikel
a. St. alten Stils (*of dates*)
ASTA Allgemeine Studentenausschuß
A.T. Altes Testament
at Atmosphäre
ata absolute Atmosphäre
Atm. Atmosphäre
atü Atmosphärenüberdruck
Aufl. Auflage
Ausg. Ausgabe
Aussch. Ausschuß
A.v.D. Automobilclub von Deutschland
A.V.G. Angestelltenversicherungsgesetz
a.Z. (*Comm.*) auf Zeit

B

B (*Comm.*) Brief
b. bei(m) (*with persons* [= *c/o*])
-b. (*as suffix*) -bar, *e.g.* lieferb(ar); -bau, *e.g.* Bergb(au)
Bd. Band
Bde. Bände
Bearb. Bearbeiter; Bearbeitung
beif. beifolgend
beil. beiliegend
Bem. Bemerkung
Ber. Bericht
bes. besonders
Betr. Betreff
betr. betreffend; betreffs
Bez. Bezirk; Bezeichnung
bez. bezahlt; bezüglich
Bf. Brief
Bg. Bogen
B.G.B. Bürgerliches Gesetzbuch
B.G.Bl. Bundesgesetzblatt
B.H.E. Bund der Heimatvertriebenen und Entrechteten
Bhf. Bahnhof
bisw. bisweilen
B.I.Z. Bank für internationalen Zahlungsausgleich
Bl. Blatt
Bln. Berlin
B.M.W. Bayerische Motorenwerke
Br. Bruder; (*Geog.*) Breite
br. breit; broschiert
B.R.D. Bundesrepublik Deutschland
B.R.T. Bruttoregistertonnen
btto. brutto
b.w. bitte wenden! [= *P.T.O.*, over]
Bz. Bezirk
bz. bezahlt
bzw. beziehungsweise

C

cal. Kalorie
cand. Kandidat
cbm Kubikmeter
ccm Kubikzentimeter
C.D.U. Christlich-Demokratische Union
cg Zentigramm
Chr. Christus
cm Zentimeter
cmm Kubikmillimeter
cr(t). (*Comm.*) *currentis*
C.S.U. Christlich-Soziale Union
c.t. (*Univ.*) *cum tempore*
C.V.J.M. Christlicher Verein Junger Männer (= *Y.M.C.A.*)

D

D. Dichte
d. der; das; die; den; des; dem
d.Ä. der Ältere
D.A.B. Deutsches Arzneibuch
D.A.G. Deutsche Angestelltengewerkschaft
Dat. Dativ
D.B. Deutsche Bundesbahn
db Dezibel
D.B.B. Deutscher Beamtenbund
D.B.D. Deutsche Bauernpartei Deutschlands (*E. Germany*)
D.B.G.M. Deutsches Bundes-Gebrauchsmuster
d. Bl. dieses Blattes
D.B.P. Deutsche Bundespost: Deutsches Bundespatent
d.d. (*Comm.*) *de dato*
D.D.R. Deutsche Demokratische Republik
DEFA Deutsche Film Aktiengesellschaft (*E. Germany*)
D.F.B. Deutscher Fußballbund
Dg Dekagramm
dg Dezigramm
D.G.B. Deutscher Gewerkschaftsbund
dgl. dergleichen
d. Gr. der Große
d.h. das heißt [= *viz.* or *i.e.*]
d.i. das ist [= *i.e.*]
D.I.N. Deutsche Industrie-Norm
Dipl.-Chem. Diplomchemiker
Dipl.-Ing. Diplomingenieur
Dipl.-Kfm. Diplomkaufmann
Diss. Dissertation
d. J. der Jüngere; dieses Jahres
D.J.H. Deutsche Jugendherberge
Dkfm. Diplomkaufmann (*Austria*)
dkg Dekagramm (*Austria*)
D.K.W. Deutsche Kraftwagen-Werke
D.M. Deutsche Mark
d.M. dieses Monats [= *inst.*]
D.N.B. Deutsches Nachrichtenbüro
d.O. der Obige
D.P. Deutsche Partei
d.p.a. Deutsche Presse-Agentur
Dr. E.h. Doktor ehrenhalber, Ehrendoktor
Dr. h.c. *Doctor honoris causa, see* Dr. E.h.
Dr.-Ing. Doktor der Ingenieurwissenschaft
Dr. j.u. *Doctor juris utriusque* (= Doktor beider Rechte) [= *LL.D.*]
Dr. jur. *Doctor juris* (= Doktor der Rechte) [= *LL.D.*]
D.R.K. Deutsches Rotes Kreuz
Dr. med. Doktor der Medizin [= *M.D.*]
Dr. phil. Doktor der Philosophie [= *Ph.D.*]
Dr. phil. nat. *Doctor philosophiæ naturalis* (= Doktor der Naturwissenschaften) [= *D.Sc.*]
Dr. rer. nat. *Doctor rerum naturalium* (= Doktor der Naturwissenschaften) [= *D.Sc.*]
Dr. rer. pol. *Doctor rerum politicarum* (= Doktor der Staatswissenschaften)
Dr. techn. (*Austria*) *see* Dr.-Ing.
Dr. theol. Doktor der Theologie [= *D.D.*]
D.S.G. Deutsche Schlafwagen- und Speisewagen-Gesellschaft
dt. deutsch
D.T.B. Deutscher Turnerbund
Dtzd. Dutzend
d.u. (*Mil.*) dienstuntauglich [= *C3*]
Durchl. Durchlaucht
d. Verf. der (*or* des) Verfasser(s)
D.V.O. Durchführungsverordnung
D.-Wagen Durchgangswagen
dz Doppelzentner
dz. derzeit
D-Zug Durchgangszug

E

E Eilzug
ebd. ebenda(selbst)
edul. entgegengesetzt dem Uhrzeiger laufend
E.G.m.b.H. eingetragene Genossenschaft mit beschränkter Haftpflicht
E.h. Ehren halber [= *h.c.* (*honoris causa*)]
Ehape Einheitspreisgeschäft
eidg. eidgenössisch (*Switzerland*)
eigtl. eigentlich
E.K. Eisernes Kreuz
E.K.D. Evangelische Kirche in Deutschland
E.K.G. Elektrokardiogramm
E-Lok. elektrische Lokomotive
em. emeritiert
entspr. entsprechend
entw. entweder
Erdg. Erdgeschoß
erg. ergänze!
Erg.-Bd. Ergänzungsband
E.T.H. Eidgenössische Technische Hochschule
etw. etwas
Ev. Evangelium
E.V. eingetragener Verein
eV Elektronenvolt
ev. evangelisch
E.V.G. Europäische Verteidigungs-Gemeinschaft (= *EDC*)
ev.-luth. evangelisch-lutherisch
ev.-ref. evangelisch-reformiert
evtl. eventuell
Ew. Euer (Eure, Eurer) (*in titles*)
E.W.G. Europäische Wirtschafts-Gemeinschaft (= *EEC*)
exkl. exklusive
Expl. Exemplar
E.Z.U. Europäische Zahlungsunion
E-Zug Eilzug

F

F. Fahrenheit; (*Elec.*) Farad
f. für; folgende (*Seite*)
Fa. Firma [= *Messrs.*]
f.d.D. (*Mil.*) für den Dienstgebrauch
F.D.G.B. Freier Deutscher Gewerkschaftsbund (*E. Germany*)
F.D.J. Freie Deutsche Jugend (*E. Germany*)
F.D.P. Freie Demokratische Partei
FD-Zug Fernschnellzug
ff. folgende (*Seiten*)
F.K.K. Freikörperkultur
Fl., fl. Florin, Gulden
Flak Flugzeugabwehrkanone; Flugabwehrartillerie
fm Festmeter
F.O. (*Mil.*) Felddienstordnung
Fr. Frau
fr. frei
frdl. freundlich
Frhr. Freiherr
Frl. Fräulein
Frzbd. Franzband
F.U. Freie Universität

G

g Gramm
G.D.P. Gesamtdeutsche Partei
geb. geboren(e); gebunden
Gebr. Gebrüder [= *Bros.*]
gef. (*Mil.*) gefallen
gefl. gefällig(st)
gegr. gegründet
geh. geheftet

Gen.	Genitiv
gen.	genannt
gesch.	geschieden
geschr.	geschrieben
ges. gesch.	gesetzlich geschützt
gest.	gestorben
get.	getauft
Gew.O.	Gewerbeordnung
gez.	gezeichnet
G.G.	Grundgesetz
ggf.	gegebenenfalls
G.m.b.H.	Gesellschaft mit beschränkter Haftung [Ltd. *or* Co.]
gr.-kath.	griechisch-katholisch

H

-h.	(*as suffix*) –handwerk, *e.g.* Schmiedeh(andwerk); –hütte, *e.g.* Eisenh(ütte)
ha	Hektar
Hapag	Hamburg-Amerikanische Paketfahrt-Aktiengesellschaft
Hbf.	Hauptbahnhof
Hg.	Herausgeber
hg	Hektogramm
hg.	herausgegeben
H.G.B.	Handelsgesetzbuch
hl	Hektoliter
hl.	heilig
H.O.	Handelsorganisation (*E. Germany*)
Hpt.	Haupt
Hr.	Herr
Hrn.	Herrn
hrsg.	*see* **hg.**
Hsg.	*see* **Hg.**
Hz.	Hertz

I

i.	in; im (*in place-names*)
i.A.	(*Comm.*) im Auftrag
i. allg.	im allgemeinen
ib(d).	*ibidem*
i. Durchschn.	im Durchschnitt
I.G.	Interessengemeinschaft
I.H.K.	Industrie- und Handelskammer
i. J.	im Jahre
I.M.	Ihre Majestät
imp(r).	imprimatur
Ind.	Indikativ
Ing.	Ingenieur
inkl.	inklusive
I.O.K.	Internationales Olympisches Komitee
I.R.	Infanterieregiment
i.R.	im Ruhestand
I.R.K.	Internationales Rotes Kreuz
i.T.	in der Trockenmasse
i.V.	in Vertretung; in Vollmacht

J

J.	(*Elec.*) Joule
Jg.	Jahrgang
Jh.	Jahrhundert
J.-Nr.	(*Comm.*) Journalnummer
jr., jun.	junior

K

-k.	(*as suffix*) –keit, *e.g.* Ewigk(eit); –kunst, *e.g.* Bauk(unst); –kunde, *e.g.* Heilk(unde)
Kap.	Kapitel
kart.	kartoniert
kath.	katholisch
kcal	Kilo(gramm)kalorie
Kfz.	Kraftfahrzeug
kg	Kilogramm
K.G.(a.A.)	Kommanditgesellschaft (auf Aktien)
kgl.	königlich
k.H.	kurzerhand
kHz	Kilohertz
k.J.	künftigen Jahres
Kl.	Klasse
k.M.	künftigen Monats
km	Kilometer
kn	(*Naut.*) Knoten
Komp.	Kompanie
Konj.	Konjunktiv
kp	Kilopond
K.P.D.	Kommunistische Partei Deutschlands
kpm	Kilopondmeter
kr.	Krone (*coinage*)
Kr(s).	Kreis
Kripo	Kriminalpolizei
Kt.	Kanton
K.V.	(*Mus.*) Köchelverzeichnis
K.Z.	Konzentrationslager

L

-l.	-(*as suffix*) –lich, *e.g.* freundl(ich); –lung, *e.g.* Handl(ung)
l.	Liter
l.	lies!; links
L.A.(G.)	Lastenausgleich(gesetz)
L.D.P.	Liberal-Demokratische Partei (*E. Germany*)
lfd.	laufend
L.G.	Landgericht
l.J.	laufenden Jahres
L.K.W.	Lastkraftwagen
L.P.G.	Landwirtschaftliche Produktionsgenossenschaft (*E. Germany*)
lt.	laut
Lt.	Leutnant
L.V.A.	Landesversicherungsanstalt
L.Z.B.	Landeszentralbank

M

m	Meter
m.	männlich
MA.	Mittelalter
Ma.	Mach-Zahl
mA	Milliampere
ma.	mittelalterlich
Mag.	Magister
m.A.n.	meiner Ansicht nach
Math.	Mathematik
m.a.W.	mit anderen Worten
mb	Millibar
m.b.H.	mit beschränkter Haftung
Md.	*see* **Mrd.**
M.d.B.	Mitglied des Bundestages
M.d.L.	Mitglied des Landtages
M.E.	Mache-Einheit
m.E.	meines Erachtens
MeV	1 Million Elektronenvolt [= *mc/s*]
M.E.Z.	Mitteleuropäische Zeit
M.G.	Maschinengewehr
mg	Milligramm
mhd.	mittelhochdeutsch
MHz	Megahertz
Mill.	Million(en)
Mio.	*see* **Mill.**
mkg	Meterkilogramm
mks	Meter-Kilogramm-Sekunde
mlat.	mittellatein
mm	Millimeter
Mrd.	Milliarde
Mskr.	Manuskript [= *MS.*]
MW	Megawatt
m.W.	meines Wissens

N

N.	Nord(en)
Nachf.	Nachfolger(in)
nachm.	nachmittags [= *p.m.*]
n. Br.	nördliche Breite
Nchf.	*see* **Nachf.**
n.Chr.G.	nach Christi Geburt [= *A.D.*]
nd.	niederdeutsch
N.F.	neue Folge
N.H.	Normalhöhenpunkt
nhd.	neuhochdeutsch
n.J.	nächsten Jahres
n.M.	nächsten Monats
nm.	*see* **nachm.**
N.N.	Normalnull
N.O.K.	Nationales Olympisches Komitee
Nom.	Nominativ
N.P.D.	Nationaldemokratische Partei Deutschlands
Nr(n).	Nummer(n)
N.R.T.	Nettoregistertonne(n)
N.S.	Nachschrift [= *P.S.*]; (*Comm.*) nach Sicht
n. St.	neuen Stils (*in dates*)
N.T.	Neues Testament

O

O.	Ost(en)
o.ä.	oder ähnliche(s)
O.B.	Oberbürgermeister
o.B.	ohne Befund
Ö.B.B.	Österreichische Bundesbahn
Oblt.	Oberleutnant
Obus	Oberleitungsomnibus
od.	oder
O.E.Z.	osteuropäische Zeit
O.H.G.	offene Handelsgesellschaft
o.J.	ohne Jahr [= *n.d.*]
ö.L.	östliche Länge
O.L.G.	Oberlandsgericht
o.O.	ohne Ort
o.O.u.J.	ohne Ort und Jahr
OP.	Operationssaal
o.P.	ordentlicher Professor
O.P.D.	Oberpostdirektion
O.R.	Obligationsrecht

P

P.	Pastor; (*R.C.*) Pater
p.A.	per Adresse [= *c/o*]
Pak	Panzerabwehrkanone
Part.	Parterre
Pf.	Pfennig
Pfd.	Pfund
P.H.	Pädagogische Hochschule
ph	Photographie
Pkt.	Punkt
P.K.W.	Personenkraftwagen
p.p(a).	(*Comm.*) per procura
Pp(bd).	Pappband
prot.	protestantisch
Prov.	Provinz
P.S.	Pferdestärke
P.Sch.A.	Postscheckamt
P.T.T.	Post, Telephon, Telegraph (*Switzerland*)

Q

qcm	Quadratzentimeter
qkm	Quadratkilometer
qm	Quadratmeter
qmm	Quadratmillimeter

R

r.	rechts
rd.	rund
Reg.-Bez.	Regierungsbezirk
Reg.-Rat	Regierungsrat
Reg(t).	*see* **Rgt.**
resp.	respektive
Rgt.	Regiment
Rhld.	Rheinland
R.I.A.S.	Rundfunk im amerikanischen Sektor
Rp.	Rappen (*Swiss centime*)
R.T.	Registertonne(n)
R.V.O.	Reichsversicherungsordnung

S

S.	Süd(en); Schilling (*Austria*); Seite [= *p.*]
s.	siehe!
Sa.	Sachsen
San.-Rat	Sanitätsrat
S.-Bahn	Schnellbahn
S.B.B.	Schweizerische Bundesbahnen
s. Br.	südliche Breite
Schupo	Schutzpolizist; Schutzpolizei
s.d.	siehe dies!
S.E.D.	Sozialistische Einheitspartei Deutschlands (*E. Germany*)
Sek.	Sekunde
sel.	selig
sen.	senior
S.F.B.	(*Rad.*) Sender Freies Berlin
sFr., sfr.	Schweizer Franken
S.M.	Seine Majestät
sm	Seemeile
s.o.	siehe oben!
sog.	sogenannt
Sp.	Spalte
S.P.D.	Sozialdemokratische Partei Deutschlands
S.S.D.	Staatssicherheitsdienst (*E. Germany*)
St.	Sankt; Stück; *see* **Std.**
Std.	Stunde
St.G.B.	Strafgesetzbuch
St.P.O.	Strafprozeßordnung
Str.	Straße
stud.	*studiosus* (= Student)
Stuka	Sturzkampfflugzeug
St.V.O.	Straßenverkehrsordnung
St.V.Z.O.	Straßenverkehrs-Zulassungs-Ordnung
s.u.	siehe unten!
S.V.	Sportverein
sva.	soviel als
svw.	soviel wie
s.Z.	seinerzeit

T

t	Tonne (= *1,000 kg*)
Tb(c).	Tuberkulose
T.E.E.	Trans-Europ-Expreß
Tgb.-Nr.	(*Comm.*) Tagebuchnummer
T.H.	Technische Hochschule
T.H.W.	Technisches Hilfswerk
Tit.	Titel
tkm	Tonnenkilometer
Trafo	Transformator
Transp.	Transport
Tsd.	Tausend
T.U.	Technische Universität
T.u.S.	Turn- und Sportverein
T.Ü.V.	Technischer Überwachungs-verein
T.V.	Turnverein

U

u.	und
u.a.	und andere(s); unter anderem *or* anderen
u.ä.	und ähnliche(s)
u.a.m.	und andere(s) mehr
u.A.w.g.	um Antwort wird gebeten [= *R.S.V.P.*]
U-Bahn	Untergrundbahn
U-Boot	Unterseeboot
u.d.ä.	und dem ähnliche(s)
u.desgl.(m.)	und desgleichen (mehr)
u.dgl.(m.)	und dergleichen (mehr)
u.d.M.	unter dem Meeresspiegel
ü.d.M.	über dem Meeresspiegel
U.d.S.S.R.	Union der Sozialistischen Sowjetrepubliken (= *U.S.S.R.*)
u.ff.	und folgende (*Seiten*)
Uffz.	Unteroffizier
U.K.W.	Ultrakurzwellen
u.R.	unter Rückerbittung
urspr.	ursprünglich
usf.	und so fort [= *etc.*]
usw.	und so weiter [= *etc.*]
u.U.	unter Umständen
u.ü.V.	unter üblichem Vorbehalt
U.V.	ultraviolett
u.v.a.(m.)	und viele(s) andere (mehr)
u.W.	unseres Wissens
u.zw.	und zwar

V

V.	Volumen; (*Elec.*) Volt; Vers
v.	von, vom
V.A.	Voltampere
V.A.R.	Vereinigte Arabische Republik
v.Chr.G.	vor Christi Geburt [= *B.C.*]
V.D.S.	Verband deutscher Studentenschaften
V.E.B.	Volkseigener Betrieb (*E. Germany*)
verh.	verheiratet
verm.	vermählt
Verm.-Ing.	Vermessungs-Ingenieur
Ver.St.(v.A.)	Vereinigte Staaten (von Amerika) (= *U.S.(A.)*)
verw.	verwitwet
vgl.	vergleiche!
v.,g.,u.	vorgelesen, genehmigt, unterschrieben
v.H.	vom Hundert
v.J.	vorigen Jahres
v.M.	vorigen Monats [= *ult.*]
V.N.	Vereinigte Nationen (= *U.N.*)
v.o.	von oben
vorm.	vormals; vormittags [= *a.m.*]
Vors.	Vorsitzende(r)
V.P.	Volkspolizei (*E. Germany*)
Vp.	Versuchsperson
v.R.w.	von Rechts wegen
v.T.	vom Tausend
v.u.	von unten
V.W.	Volkswagen

W

W.	West(en); (*Elect.*) Watt
-w.	(*suffix*) –weise, *e.g.* teilw(eise); –wesen, *e.g.* Finanzw(esen); –wort, *e.g.* Bindew(ort)
weil.	weiland
W.E.U.	Westeuropäische Union
W.E.Z.	westeuropäische Zeit
W.G.	Wechselgesetz
W.K.	(*Mil.*) Wiederholungskurs (*Switzerland*)
w.L.	westliche Länge
W.O.	Wechselordnung
w.o.	wie oben
W.P.V.	Weltpostverein (= *U.P.U.*)
Ws	Wattsekunde
WUSt.	Warenumsatzsteuer
Wwe.	Witwe

Z

Z.	Zeile; Zahl
z.B.	zum Beispiel [= *e.g.*]
z.b.V.	zur besonderen Verwendung
z.D.	zur Disposition
z.d.A.	zu den Akten
Z.D.F.	Zweites Deutsches Fernsehen
z.E.	zum Exempel [= *e.g.*]
Z.G.B.	Zivilgesetzbuch (*Switzerland*)
z.H.	zu Händen
Ziff.	Ziffer
Z.K.	Zentralkomitee
Z.P.O.	Zivilprozeßordnung
z.T.	zum Teil
Ztr.	Zentner (*50 kg*)
Z.Wv.	zur Wiedervorlage
z.w.V.	zur weiteren Veranlassung
Zz.	Zinszahl
z.Z.	zur Zeit

Auswahl englischer Abkürzungen

(Siehe auch *Cassell's Dictionary of Abbreviations*, J. W. Gurnett and C. H. J. Kyte (eds.), second edition 1972.)

A

A	adult (*of films suitable for adults*); (*cards*) ace
A.	Associate; (*Elec.*) ampère
a	are (*metric*)
a.	acre(s)
AA	(*of films*) children under 14 not admitted
A.A.	Automobile Association; Alcoholics Anonymous; Anti-Aircraft
A.A.A.	Amateur Athletic Association; American Automobile Association
A.A.M.	air-to-air missile
a.a.r.	(*Comm.*) against all risks
A.B.	Able-Bodied Seaman; *Artium Baccalaureus* (= Bachelor of Arts) (*U.S.A.*)
A.B.A.	Amateur Boxing Association
abbr(ev).	abbreviation
A.B.C.	American Broadcasting Company; Australian Broadcasting Commission
abl.	(*Gram.*) ablative
Abp.	archbishop
abs(ol).	absolute
abs(tr).	abstract
A.C.	(*Elec.*) Alternating Current; Aircraftman; Alpine Club
a/c	(*Comm.*) account
A.C.A.	Associate of the Institute of Chartered Accountants
acc(t).	(*Comm.*) account
A.C.G.B.	Arts Council of Great Britain
act.	(*Gram.*) active
A.C.W.	Aircraftwoman
A.D.	*Anno Domini* (= in the year of Our Lord)
a.d.	(*Comm.*) after date
A.D.C.	aide-de-camp
Adjt.	Adjutant
Adm.	admiral
Admin.	administration
A.D.P.	automatic data processing
adv.	adverb; advisory
ad val.	(*Comm.*) *ad valorem* (= to the value of)
A.E.A.	Atomic Energy Authority (*Gt. Britain*)
A.E.C.	Association of Education Committees; Atomic Energy Commission (*U.S.A.*); (*Mil.*) (*see* **R.A.E.C.**)
A.F.	Associate Fellow; (*Rad.*) audio frequency
A.F.A.	Amateur Football Association
A.F.L.-C.I.O.	American Federation of Labor and Congress of Industrial Organizations (*U.S.A.*)
A.F.N.	(*Rad.*) American Forces Network
A.F.V.	(*Mil.*) armoured fighting vehicle
A.G.	Adjutant-General
A.-G.	Attorney-General
A.g.	air gunner
A.G.M.	Annual General Meeting
Agr(ic).	Agriculture
Agt.	(*Comm.*) agent
A.I.D.	Artificial Insemination Donor
AK	Alaska
AL	Alabama
Al(a).	*see* **AL**
Ald.	alderman
alt.	altitude
A.M.	Associate Member; *Artium Magister* (= Master of Arts) (*U.S.A.*); (*Rad.*) amplitude modulation
a.m.	*ante meridiem* (= before noon)
Am(er).	America(n)
ammo	(*coll.*) ammunition
amp.	(*Elec.*) ampère
amt.	amount
a.m.t.	air-mail transfer
A.M.U.	Atomic Mass Unit
anc.	ancient
angl.	*anglice* (= in English)
ann.	annual
anon.	anonymous
ans.	answer
Anzac.	Austrialian and New Zealand Army Corps
aor.	(*Gram.*) aorist
Ap.	Apostle
A.P.B.	all points bulletin (*U.S.A.*)
app.	appendix; apparent(ly); appointed; apprentice
appro.	approval
approx.	approximate(ly)
AR	Arkansas
A.R.C.	American Red Cross
arch.	archaic
Ariz.	*see* **AZ**
Ark.	*see* **AR**
arr.	arranged; arrival
arty.	artillery
A.-S.	Anglo-Saxon
A.S.A.	Amateur Swimming Association
A.S.E.	Amalgamated Society of Engineers
ASLEF	Amalgamated Society of Locomotive Engineers and Firemen
A.S.M.	air-to-surface missile
Assoc.	Association
Asst.	Assistant
A.S.T.	Atlantic Standard Time
A.T.	air temperature; (*Mil.*) anti-tank
A.T.C.	Air Training Corps
atm.	atmosphere(s)
at. no.	atomic number
A.T.V.	Associated Television
at. wt.	atomic weight
A.U.E.W.	Amalgamated Union of Engineering Workers
A.U.T.	Association of University Teachers
aux.	auxiliary
A.V.	Authorized Version
avdp.	avoirdupois
Ave.	Avenue
AZ	Arizona
Az.	azimuth

B

B	(*on pencils*) soft; (*chess*) bishop
b.	born; (*cricket*) bowled
B.A.	Bachelor of Arts; British Association (for the Advancement of Science); British Academy; British Airways
bact.	bacteriology
bal.	(*Comm.*) balance
B.A.L.P.A.	British Airline Pilots' Association
b. & b.	bed and breakfast
B.A.O.R.	British Army of the Rhine
Bapt.	Baptist
bap(t).	baptized

Barr.	barrister
Bart.	baronet
BB	(*on pencils*) double black
B.B.C.	British Broadcasting Corporation
B.C.	Before Christ; British Columbia
B.Ch.	*Baccalaureus Chirugiae* (= Bachelor of Surgery)
B.Com(m).	Bachelor of Commerce
B.D.	Bachelor of Divinity
B/E	(*Comm.*) bill of exchange
B.Ed.	Bachelor of Education
Benelux	Belgium, Netherlands and Luxembourg
B.Eng.	Bachelor of Engineering
b/f	(*Comm.*) brought forward
B.F.B.S.	British and Foreign Bible Society
B.F.N.	(*Rad.*) British Forces Network
B.F.O.	(*Rad.*) beat-frequency oscillator
b.h.p.	brake horse-power
Bib.	Bible
Bibl.	Biblical
bibl(iog).	bibliography
B.I.S.	Bank for International Settlements
bk.	book
B.L.	Bachelor of Law
B/L	(*Comm.*) bill of lading
bldg(s)	building(s)
B.Lit(t).	*Baccalaureus Litterarum* (= Bachelor of Letters)
B.L.	Bachelor of Law
B.M.	Bachelor of Medicine; British Museum; (*Mil.*) Brigade Major; (*Surv.*) bench mark
B.M.A.	British Medical Association
B.M.E.W.S.	Ballistic Missile Early Warning System
B.Mus.	Bachelor of Music
B/O	branch office
b.o.	(*Comm.*) buyer's option
b/o	(*Comm.*) brought over; back order
bor(o).	borough
bos'n	boatswain
Bp.	bishop
B.P.	British Pharmacopoeia; British Petroleum
b.p.	boiling point; below proof
b/p	(*Comm.*) bills payable; blueprint
bpl.	birthplace
B.R.	British Rail
b.r.	bank rate
b/r	(*Comm.*) bills receivable
B.R.C.S.	British Red Cross Society
b.rec.	*see* **b/r**
Brev.	(*Mil.*) brevet
Brig.	(*Mil.*) Brigadier; brigade
Brit.	Britain; British
Bros.	(*Comm.*) Brothers
B.R.S.	British Road Services
B.S.	Bachelor of Surgery; Bachelor of Science (*U.S.A.*)
B/S	(*Comm.*) bill of sale; balance sheet
b.s.	(*Theat.*) back-stage
B.Sc.	Bachelor of Science
B.S.C.	British Steel Corporation
B.S.T.	British Summer Time; British Standard Time
Bt.	baronet
bt.	beat; (*Comm.*) bought
B. Th. U.	British Thermal Unit(s)
Btu.	*see* **B. Th. U.**
B.T.U.	Board of Trade Unit(s)
B.U.A.	British United Airways
B.U.P.	British United Press
Bur. St.	Bureau of Standards (*U.S.A.*)
B.V.M.	Blessed Virgin Mary
B.V.M.S.	Bachelor of Veterinary Medicine and Surgery
B.W.B.	British Waterways Board
B.W.G.	Birmingham Wire Gauge

C

C.	Centigrade; (*Geog.*) Cape
c.	cent(s); cubic; (*cricket*) caught; *circa* (= approximately)
CA	California
C.A.	Chartered Accountant
C.A.B.	Citizens' Advice Bureau; Civil Aeronautics Board (*U.S.A.*)
Cal(if).	*see* **CA**
c. & b.	(*cricket*) caught and bowled
c. & f.	(*Comm.*) cost and freight
Cantab.	of Cambridge University
cap(s).	capital letter(s)
Capt.	captain
Card.	cardinal
Cath.	Catholic; cathedral
cath.	(*Rad.*) cathode
C.B.	Companion of the Order of the Bath; (*Mil.*) confined to barracks
C.B.C.	Canadian Broadcasting Corporation
C.B.E.	Commander of the Order of the British Empire
C.B.I.	Confederation of British Industry
C.B.S.	Columbia Broadcasting System (*U.S.A.*)
C.C.	Cricket Club; Cycling Club; (*Rad.*) closed circuit (transmission)
cc	cubic centimetre(s)
c.c.	carbon copy
C.D.	Civil Defence
Cdr.	Commander
Cdre.	Commodore
C.E.	Council of Europe; Civil Engineer
C.E.B.	Central Electricity Board
C.E.G.B.	Central Electricity Generating Board
Celt.	Celtic
Cent.	Centigrade; central
cent.	century
cert.	certificate; certified
C.E.T.	Central European Time
cf.	*confer* (= compare)
c/f	(*Comm.*) carried forward
c.f.i.	(*Comm.*) cost, freight, insurance
cg	centigram(me)(s)
c.g.	centre of gravity
c.g.s.	centimetre-gram(me)-second(s)
Ch.	church
ch.	chapter; chain (*measure*)
C.H.	Companion of Honour
c.h.	central heating
chap.	chapter
Chas.	Charles
Ch.B.	*Chirurgiae Baccalaureus* (= Bachelor of Surgery)
Ch.M.	*Chirurgiae Magister* (= Master of Surgery)
C.I.	Channel Islands
C.I.A.	Central Intelligence Agency (*U.S.A.*)
C.I.D.	Criminal Investigation Department
c.i.f.c.(i.)	(*Comm.*) cost, insurance, freight, commission (and interest)
C.I.G.S.	Chief of the Imperial General Staff
C.-in-C.	Commander-in-Chief
C.I.O.	*see* **A.F.L.-C.I.O.**
cit.	citation; cited
civ.	civil(ian)
ckw.	clockwise
cl	centilitre(s)
cl.	class; clause
c.l.	*cum laude* (= with commendation)
cm	centimetre(s)
C.M.	Corresponding Member; (*Naut.*) Certificated Master; *Chirurgiae Magister* (= Master of Surgery)

Cmdr.	Commander
Cmdt.	Commandant
C.M.G.	Companion of the Order of Saint Michael and Saint George
C.M.H.	Congressional Medal of Honor (*U.S.A.*)
C.M.S.	Church Missionary Society
C.N.D.	Campaign for Nuclear Disarmament
CO	Colorado
Co.	company; county (*in Ireland*)
C.O.	Commanding Officer; Conscientious Objector; (*see* **F.C.O.**)
c/o	care of
C.O.D.	cash on delivery
C. of A.	certificate of airworthiness
C. of C.	coefficient of correlation
C. of E.	Church of England
C. of I.	Church of Ireland
C. of S.	Church of Scotland
C.O.I.	Central Office of Information
Col.	colonel
col.	column
Coll.	college
coll.	colloquial; collection; collective(ly)
Colo.	*see* **CO**
Comdr.	Commander
COMECON	Council for Mutual Economic Assistance
comm.	commerce
comp.	compare; comparative; comparison; compound(ed)
cond.	condition(al)
Conf.	conference
Cong.	Congress; Congregation(al)
conj.	conjunction; conjunctive
Conn.	*see* **CT**
Cons.	Conservative
constr.	constructed; construction
cont(d).	continue(d); contain(ed)
Co-op	(*coll.*) Co-operative (Stores)
Corp.	corporation; (*Mil.*) corporal
cox	(*coll.*) coxswain
cp.	compare
C.P.	(Court of) Common Pleas; Clerk of the Peace; Communist Party
c.p.	candle-power; (*Comm.*) carriage paid
Cpl.	corporal
C.P.R.	Canadian Pacific Railway
c.p.s.	cycles per second
Cr.	(*Comm.*) credit
Cres.	Crescent
C.R.M.P.	Corps of Royal Military Police
C.R.O.	cathode-ray oscilloscope; Criminal Records Office
C.R.T.	cathode-ray tube
C.S.	Civil Service; Court of Session; Christian Science
c/s	cycles per second
C.S.E.	Certificate of Secondary Education
C.S.T.	Central Standard Time
CT	Connecticut
ct.	carat; cent; (*cricket*) caught
C.T.C.	Cyclists' Touring Club
cu., cub.	cubic
Cum. Pref.	(*Comm.*) cumulative preference (shares)
C.V.O.	Commander of the Royal Victorian Order
C.W.	chemical warfare
c.w.	(*Rad.*) continuous *or* carrier wave
c.w.o.	(*Comm.*) cash with order
C.W.S.	Co-operative Wholesale Society
cwt.	hundredweight
Cym.	Cymric
CZ	Canal Zone (*Panama*)

D

d.	died; daughter; (*before 1971*) penny, pence
D.A.	District Attorney (*U.S.A.*)
dat.	dative
dB	decibel(s)
D.B.E.	Dame Commander of the Order of the British Empire
DC	District of Columbia
D.C.	(*Elec.*) Direct Current
d.c.	(*Mech.*) dead centre
D.C.L.	Doctor of Civil Law
D.C.M.	Distinguished Conduct Medal
D.D.	Doctor of Divinity
d.d.	(*Comm.*) days after date
D.D.T.	dichlorodiphenyltrichlorethane (*insecticide*)
DE	Delaware
D.E.A.	Department of Economic Affairs
dec.	deceased
decl.	(*Gram.*) declension
Del.	*see* **DE**
Dem.	Democrat
Dep.	deputy
dep.	departure
D.E.P.	Department of Employment and Productivity
Dept.	department
D.E.R.V.	diesel-engined road vehicle
D.E.S.	Department of Education and Science
Det.	detective
D.F.	Defender of the Faith; Dean of Faculty
D/F	(*Rad.*) direction finding
dg	decigram(me)(s)
D.H.S.S.	Department of Health and Social Security
D.I.H.	Diploma in Industrial Health
Dip.	diploma
Dir.	director
dis(c).	discount
Dist.	district
Div.	(*Mil.*) Division
div.	divide, division; (*Comm.*) dividend; divorced
D.I.Y.	do-it-yourself
dl	decilitre(s)
D.L.	Deputy Lieutenant; Doctor of Law
D.Lit(t).	*Doctor Litterarum* (= Doctor of Letters)
D.L.O.	*see* **R.L.O.**
D.N.B.	*Dictionary of National Biography*
D. o. E.	Department of the Environment
Dom. Sci.	Domestic Science
Dor.	Doric
doz.	dozen(s)
D.P.	displaced person; data processing
D.P.H.	Diploma in Public Health
D.Ph(il).	Doctor of Philosophy
Dr.	Doctor; (*Comm.*) debit
dr.	dram
dram.	drama(tic)
D/S	(*Comm.*) days after sight
D.Sc.	Doctor of Science
d.s.c.	(*Theat.*) down stage centre
D.S.O.	Distinguished Service Order
D.T.	data transmission; delirium tremens
D.T.I.	Department of Trade and Industry
dup.	duplicate
D.V.	(*coll.*) God willing
D.V.S(c).	Doctor of Veterinary Science
dwt.	pennyweight

E

E.	East(ern)
E. & O.E.	(*Comm.*) errors and omissions excepted
E.C.G.	electrocardiogram
econ.	economics
E.C.S.C.	European Coal and Steel Community
E.C.U.	English Church Union
ed.	edition, editor, edited; educated, education
Ed.B.	Bachelor of Education
E.D.C.	European Defence Community; (*Med.*) expected date of confinement
Edin.	Edinburgh
E.E.	(*Comm.*) errors excepted
E.E.C.	European Economic Community
EFTA	European Free Trade Association
e.g.	*exempli gratia* (= for example)
E.H.L.	(*Phys.*) effective half-life
e.h.p.	effective horse-power
E.I.S.	Educational Institute of Scotland
elec.	electric(al), electricity
elem.	elementary
elev.	elevation
ellipt.	elliptical
E. long.	east longitude
E.M.F.	electromotive force
e.m.u.	electromagnetic unit(s)
enc(l).	enclosed, enclosure
engr.	engineer; engraver, engraving
E.N.T.	ear, nose and throat
ent(om).	entomology
Ent. Sta. Hall	Entered at Stationers' Hall
Env. Extr.	Envoy-Extraordinary
EP	extended play (*gramophone record*)
E.P.	electroplate(d)
Episc.	Episcopal(ian)
E.P.N.S.	electroplated nickel silver; English Place-Name Society
E.P.T.	excess profits tax
eq.	equal
equiv.	equivalent
ERNIE	electronic random number indicating equipment
esp.	especially
E.S.P.	extra-sensory perception
Esq(r).	Esquire
E.S.T.	Eastern Standard Time
est(ab).	established
est(d).	estimated
E.S.U.	English-Speaking Union
e.s.u.	electrostatic unit(s)
E.T.A.	estimated time of arrival
et al.	*et alii* (= and others)
etc.	*et cetera* (= and so on, and so forth)
et seq.	*et sequentia* (= and what follows)
E.T.U.	Electrical Trades Union
E.U.	Evangelical Union
EURATOM	European Atomic Energy Community
ex.	example
Exc.	Excellency
Exch.	exchange
Exch.	Exchequer
exch.	exchange
excl.	exclusive, excluding
ex div.	(*Comm.*) without dividend
Exec.	executive
exes	(*coll.*) expenses
ex int.	(*Comm.*) without interest
Exp.	express
exs.	*see* **exes**
ext.	external(ly); extension; extinct

F

F.	Fellow; Fahrenheit; (*Elec.*) farad; (*Opt.*) focal length
f.	foot, feet; fathom(s); frequency; feminine; following
F.A.	Football Association
f.a.	(*Comm.*) free alongside
Fac.	faculty
f.a.s.	(*Comm.*) free alongside ship
F.B.I.	Federal Bureau of Investigation (*U.S.A.*)
F.C.	Football Club; Free Church (of Scotland)
fcap.	foolscap
F.C.O.	Foreign and Commonwealth Office
fcp.	*see* **fcap.**
fd.	forward
ff.	following
F.H.	fire hydrant
fig.	figure; figurative(ly)
fin.	the end
FL	Florida
fl.	florin(s), guilder(s); flourished
Fla.	*see* **FL**
fm.	fathom(s)
F.M.	Field Marshal; (*Rad.*) frequency modulation
F.M.D.	foot-and-mouth disease
F.O.	Field Officer; (*see* **F.C.O.**)
F/O	Flying Officer
f.o.b.	(*Comm.*) free on board
foll.	follow(ing)
f.o.r.	(*Comm.*) free on rail
F.P.A.	Family Planning Association
f.p.s.	foot-pound-second
Fr.	France, French; friar; Friday
fs.	facsimile
ft.	foot, feet
fthm.	fathom(s)
F.U.	Farmers' Union
fur.	furlong(s)
fut.	future
f.w.b.	four wheel brake
fwd.	forward
f.w.d.	four wheel drive

G

g	gram(me)(s)
GA	Georgia (*U.S.A.*)
Ga.	*see* **GA**
G.A.	General Assembly
Gael.	Gaelic
gal.	gallon
G.B.	Great Britain; Gas Board
g.b.h.	grievous bodily harm
G.B.S.	George Bernard Shaw
G.C.	George Cross; Gas Council; Golf Club
G.C.D.	(*Naut.*) great circle distance
G.C.E.	General Certificate of Education
g.c.f.	(*Math.*) greatest common factor
G.C.M.	general court-martial
g.c.m.	(*Math.*) greatest common multiple
Gdn(s).	Garden(s)
Gen.	(*Mil.*) General; (*B.*) Genesis
gen.	general(ly); (*Gram.*) gender; genitive
Geo.	George
ger.	gerund(ive)
G.G.	Girl Guide(s)
G.H.Q.	General Headquarters
G.I.	government issue (*U.S.A.*); (*coll.*) American soldier
G.L.C.	Greater London Council
gm	gram(me)
G.M.	George Medal
G.M.C.	General Medical Council
G.M.T.	Greenwich Mean Time
Gnr.	gunner
gns.	guineas
G.O.C.(in C.)	General Officer Commanding (in Chief)
Gov.	Governor

Govt.	Government
Gp.	Group
G.P.	(*Med.*) General Practitioner
G.P.O.	General Post Office
gr.	grain; gross
G.R.T.	gross register tonnage
G.S.	(*Mil.*) General Staff; (*Av.*) ground speed
G.S.O.	General Staff Officer
G.T.C.	government training centre; (*Scots*) General Teaching Council
GU	Guam
guar.	guarantee(d)

H

H	(*on pencils*) hard
H.	hydrant
h.	hour(s)
ha	hectare(s)
Ha.	*see* **HI**
hab.	habitat(ion)
h. & c.	hot and cold (*water*)
HB	(*on pencils*) hard black
h.c.	*honoris causa* (= honorary)
h.c.f.	(*Math.*) highest common factor
hdbk.	handbook
hdqrs.	headquarters
H.E.	His Excellency *or* Eminence; high explosive
h.e.	horizontal equivalent
Heb.	Hebrew; (*B.*) Hebrews
Hebr.	Hebrides
H.F.	high frequency
H.G.	His *or* Her Grace
H.G.V.	heavy goods vehicle
HH	(*on pencils*) double hard
H.H.	His Holiness
HI	Hawaii
Hi-fi	(*coll.*) high fidelity
hl	hectolitre(s)
H.M.	His *or* Her Majesty
H.M.I.	His *or* Her Majesty's Inspector (of Schools)
H.M.S.	His *or* Her Majesty's Ship
H.M.S.O.	His *or* Her Majesty's Stationery Office
H.M.V.	(*reg. trade name*) His Master's Voice
H.N.C.	Higher National Certificate
H.N.D.	Higher National Diploma
ho.	house
Hon.	honorary; (*in titles*) Honourable
Hons.	honours
hor.	horizon(tal)
H.P.	horsepower; (*Mil.*) half pay; (*Comm.*) hire purchase
H.Q.	headquarters
hr.	hour
H.R.H.	His *or* Her Royal Highness
H.T.	(*Elec.*) high tension
H.V.	high velocity
h.w.	(*cricket*) hit wicket
H.W.M.	high-water mark
hydr.	hydraulics
Hz	(*Rad.*) hertz, cycles per second

I

I.	island; (*see* **ID**)
IA	Iowa
Ia.	*see* **IA**
I.A.	Institute of Actuaries
I.B.	Institute of Bankers
i.b.	(*Comm.*) in bond
ib(id).	*ibidem* (= in the same place)
i/c	in command *or* charge
I.C.B.M.	intercontinental ballistic missile
I.C.E.	Institution of Civil Engineers
I.Chem.E.	Institution of Chemical Engineers
I.C.I.	Imperial Chemical Industries
icon.	iconography
ID	Idaho
Id.	*see* **ID**
id.	*idem* (= the same)
i.d.	inside diameter
i.e.	*id est* (= that is (to say))
I.E.E.	Institution of Electrical Engineers
I.F.	(*Rad.*) intermediate frequency
i.h.p.	indicated horsepower
IL	Illinois
I.L.E.A.	Inner London Education Authority
Ill.	*see* **IL**
I.L.O.	International Labour Organization
I.Mech.E.	Institution of Mechanical Engineers
I.M.F.	International Monetary Fund
imit.	imitative
imp.	(*Gram.*) imperative; impersonal
imperf.	(*Gram.*) imperfect
IN	Indiana
in.	inch(es)
inc.	incorporated
incl.	including, included, inclusive
incog.	incognito
Ind.	(*Pol.*) Independent; (*see* **IN**)
indecl.	indeclinable
indic.	(*Gram.*) indicative
indiv.	individual
Inf.	infantry
inf.	*infra* (= below)
inorg.	inorganic
ins.	inches
inscr.	inscription
Insp.	inspector; inspection
Inst.	institute, institution
inst.	(*Comm.*) instant (*the present month*)
int.	interior; internal; (*Comm.*) interest
Inter.	intermediate
intercom	(*coll.*) intercommunication
internat.	international
INTERPOL	International Criminal Police Organization
interrog.	(*Gram.*) interrogative(ly)
intr(ans).	(*Gram.*) intransitive
in trans.	(*Comm.*) in transit
introd.	introduced, introduction
inv.	invented, inventor; (*Comm.*) invoice
Io.	*see* **IA**
I.O.M.	Isle of Man
I.O.U.	(*coll.*) I owe you
I.o.W.	Isle of Wight
I.Q.	intelligence quotient
I.R.A.	Irish Republican Army
I.R.B.M.	intermediate range ballistic missile
I.R.O.	industrial relations officer; International Refugee Organization
Is.	islands
I.S.S.	International Student Service
isth.	isthmus
I.T.A.	Independent Television Authority
i.t.a.	initial teaching alphabet
Ital.	Italian
ital.	italic(s)
I.W.	*see* **I.o.W.**

J

J	(*Elec.*) joule; (*cards*) jack, knave
Jas.	James
J.C.	Jockey Club
Jnr.	junior
J.P.	Justice of the Peace
Jr.	*see* **Jnr.**
Jun.	*see* **Jnr.**
junc.	junction
jurisp.	jurisprudence

K

N.B. See under Q for titles in which 'Queen' may vary to 'King'.

K	(*chess, cards*) king
Kan.	*see* **KS**
K.B.	Knight of the Order of the Bath
K.B.E.	Knight Commander of the Order of the British Empire
kc	kilocycle(s)
K.C.	King's College (*London University*)
K.C.B.	Knight Commander of the Order of the Bath
K.C.C.	King's College, Cambridge
K.C.M.G.	Knight Commander of the Order of Saint Michael and Saint George
K.C.V.O.	Knight Commander of the Royal Victorian Order
Ken.	*see* **KY**
kg	kilogram(me)(s)
K.G.	Knight of the Order of the Garter
kHz	kilohertz
K.K.K.	Ku-Klux-Klan
km	kilometre(s)
K.M.	Knight of Malta
kn.	(*Naut.*) knot(s)
KS	Kansas
Kt.	Knight
kW	kilowatt(s)
kWh	kilowatt-hour(s)
KY	Kentucky
Ky.	*see* **KY**

L

L	Learner (*driver or motor-cyclist*)
l	litre(s)
L.	lake; Latin
l.	long, length; left; latitude; line
LA	Louisiana
La.	*see* **LA**
L.A.	Law Agent; Library Association; Los Angeles
Lab.	Labrador; (*Pol.*) Labour (*Party*)
lang.	language(s)
Lat.	Latin
lat.	latitude
lb(s)	pound(s) (*weight*)
l.b.w.	(*cricket*) leg before wicket
L.C.	Library of Congress (*U.S.A.*)
L/C	(*Comm.*) letter of credit
l.c.	(*Typ.*) lower case; left centre (*of stage*)
L.C.C.	*see* **G.L.C.**
l.c.f.	(*Math.*) lowest common factor
l.c.m.	(*Math.*) lowest common multiple
Ldn.	London
L.D.S.	Licentiate in Dental Surgery
L.E.A.	Local Education Authority
L.F.	low frequency
l.h.	left hand
L.H.A.	Local Health Authority
L.I.	Light Infantry
Lib.	Liberal (*Party*); library; (*coll.*) Liberation
Lieut.	lieutenant
liq.	liquid
lit.	literally
Lit(t).D.	*Litterarum Doctor* (= Doctor of Letters)
ll.	lines
LL.B.	*Legum Baccalaureus* (= Bachelor of Laws)
L.L.C.M.	Licentiate of the London College of Music
LL.D.	*Legum Doctor* (= Doctor of Laws)
L.O.	(*Rad.*) local oscillator
l.o.a.	length over all
loc. cit.	*loco citato* (= in the place mentioned)
log.	logarithm
long.	longitude
Lou.	*see* **LA**
LP	long-playing (*record*)
L.P.	(*Scots*) Lord Provost
l.p.	(*Meteor.*) low pressure
L.P.O.	London Philharmonic Orchestra
L.R.A.M.	Licentiate of the Royal Academy of Music
L.S.D.	lysergic acid diethylamide
L.S.E.	London School of Economics and Political Science
L.S.O.	London Symphony Orchestra
L.T.	(*Elec.*) low tension
L.T.A.	Lawn Tennis Association
Ltd.	limited
L.T.E.	London Transport Executive
L.W.L.	load waterline

M

M	Motorway
m	mass; metre(s)
M.	Master
m.	mile(s); minute(s); male, masculine; married
MA	Massachusetts
M.A.	Master of Arts
Maj.	major
March.	Marchioness
marit.	maritime
Marq.	Marquis, Marquess
masc.	masculine
Mass.	*see* **MA**
math(s)	mathematics
matric	(*coll.*) matriculation
Matt.	Matthew
max.	maximum
mb.	millibar(s)
M.B.	Bachelor of Medicine
M.C.	Member of Congress (*U.S.A.*); Military Cross; Master of Ceremonies
M.C.C.	Marylebone Cricket Club
M.C.C.C.	Middlesex County Cricket Club
M.Ch.	*Magister Chirurgiae* (= Master of Surgery)
mc/s	megacycles per second
MD	Maryland
Md.	*see* **MD**
M.D.	*Medicinae Doctor* (= Doctor of Medicine); mentally deficient
ME	Maine
Me.	*see* **ME**
M.E.	Middle English
mech.	mechanical
med.	medical, medicine; medium
memo	memorandum
Met.	Metropolitan
met(eor).	meteorology
Meth.	Methodist
meths	(*coll.*) methylated spirits
mF	(*Elec.*) microfarad(s)
mfr(s).	manufacturer(s)
M.F.V.	motor fleet vessel
mg	milligram(me)(s)
m.g.	machine gun
Mgr.	Monsignor; manager
M.H.	Master of Horse
M.H.G.	Middle High German
MI	Michigan
Mi.	*see* **MS**
M.I.	Military Intelligence
Mich.	*see* **MI**
mil.	military
Min.	ministry
min.	minute (*time*); minimum
Minn.	*see* **MN**
Mis.	*see* **MO**
misc.	miscellaneous
Miss.	*see* **MS**

M.I.T.	Massachusetts Institute of Technology
m.k.s.(a.)	metre-kilogram(me)-second(s)-(ampère(s))
ml	millilitre(s)
mm	millimetre(s)
MN	Minnesota
M.N.	Merchant Navy
MO	Missouri
Mo.	*see* **MO**
mo.	month
M.O.	medical officer
M.O.D.	Ministry of Defence
M.O.H.	Medical Officer of Health
mol. wt.	molecular weight
Mon.	*see* **MT**
M.O.T.	Ministry of Transport
M.P.	Member of Parliament; Military Police
m.p.	melting point
m.p.g.	miles per gallon
Mr.	Mister
M.R.	map reference
M.R.A.	Moral Rearmament
M.R.C.	Medical Research Council
Mrs.	Missis; Mistress
MS	Mississippi
MS.	manuscript
Ms.	Miss/Mrs.
M.Sc.	Master of Science
msec	millisecond(s)
MT	Montana
Mt.	Mount
mtg.	meeting
mth.	month
Mus.B.	*Musicae Baccalaureus* (= Bachelor of Music)
Mus.D.	*Musicae Doctor* (= Doctor of Music)
M.V.O.	Member of the Royal Victorian Order
M.W.	(*Rad.*) medium wave

N

N.	north(ern)
n.	noun; neuter
N.A.	North America; Nautical Almanac
NAAFI	Navy, Army and Air Force Institute
NALGO	National and Local Government Officers' Association
NASA	National Aeronautics and Space Administration (*U.S.A.*)
Nat.	National(ist)
nat. hist.	natural history
NATO	North Atlantic Treaty Organization
nat. phil.	(*esp. Scots*) natural philosophy
NATSOPA	National Society of Operative Printers and Assistants
nav.	navy, naval
navig.	navigation
N.B.	*nota bene* (= note particularly); New Brunswick; North Britain
n.b.	(*cricket*) no ball
N.B.C.	National Broadcasting Company (*U.S.A.*)
N.B.L.	National Book League
N.B.S.	National Bureau of Standards (*U.S.A.*)
NC	North Carolina
N.C.	*see* **NC**
N.C.B.	National Coal Board
N.C.C.L.	National Council for Civil Liberties
N.C.L.	National Central Library
N.C.O.	non-commissioned officer
N.C.U.	National Cyclists' Union
n.c.v.	no commercial value
N.C.W.	National Council of Women
ND	North Dakota
n.d.	no date
N. Dak.	*see* **ND**
NE	Nebraska
Neb(r).	*see* **NE**
N.E.D.C.	National Economic Development Council
neg.	negative(ly)
neut.	neuter
Nev.	*see* **NV**
N.F.	Newfoundland
N/F	(*Comm.*) no funds
N.F.S.	National Fire Service
N.F.U.	National Farmers' Union
NH	New Hampshire
N.H.	*see* **NH**
N.H.G.	New High German
N.H.I.	National Health Insurance
N.H.S.	National Health Service
N.I.	Northern Ireland
N.I.C.	National Incomes Commission
NJ	New Jersey
N.J.	*see* **NJ**
N.J.C.	National Joint Council
N.L.R.B.	National Labor Relations Board (*U.S.A.*)
NM	New Mexico
N.Mex.	*see* **NM**
no.	number
N.O.	New Orleans
n.o.	(*Cricket*) not out
nom.	nominative
Noncon.	Nonconformist
non seq.	*non sequitur* (= it does not follow)
N.P.	Notary Public
n.p.	new paragraph; no place (*of publication*)
N.P.F.A.	National Playing Fields Association
N.P.L.	National Physical Laboratory
n.p.t.	normal pressure and temperature
nr.	near
N.S.	Nova Scotia; New Style (*in dates*)
N.S.P.C.C.	National Society for the Prevention of Cruelty to Children
N.S.W.	New South Wales
N.T.	New Testament; Northern Territory; (*cards*) no trumps
n.u.	name unknown
N.U.G.M.W.	National Union of General and Municipal Workers
N.U.I.	National Union of Ireland
N.U.M.	National Union of Mineworkers
N.U.R.	National Union of Railwaymen
N.U.S.	National Union of Students
N.U.T.	National Union of Teachers
NV	Nevada
N.V.	new version
N.W.T.	Northwest Territories (*of Canada*)
NY	New York (*State*)
NYC	New York City
N.Z.	New Zealand

O

O.	*see* **OH**
O/A	on account of
O.A.P.	old-age pension(er)
O.A.S.	Organization of American States
O.A.U.	Organization of African Unity
O.B.E.	Officer of the Order of the British Empire
obj.	object(ive)
obs.	obsolete; observation
O.C.	Officer Commanding
o/c	(*Comm.*) overcharge
occ.	occasional(ly)
oct.	octavo
O.C.T.U.	Officer Cadets' Training Unit
O.D.	Ordnance datum *or* data
o/d	(*Comm.*) on demand

O.E. Old English
O.E.C.D. Organization for Economic Cooperation and Development
O.F. Old French; Oddfellow
off. official; officinal
O.Fr. Old French
O. Fris. Old Frisian
OH Ohio
O.H.G. Old High German
O.H.M.S. On (His *or*) Her Majesty's Service
O.i/c. officer in charge
O. Icel. Old Icelandic
OK Oklahoma
Okla. *see* **OK**
O.M. Member of the Order of Merit
O.N. Old Norse
O.N.C. Ordinary National Certificate
O.N.D. Ordinary National Diploma
o.n.o. (*Comm.*) or near(est) offer
Ont. Ontario
Op. opus
O/P out of print
o.p. overproof (*of spirits*); (*Theat.*) opposite the prompter's side
op. cit. *opere citato* (= in the work cited)
O.P.E.C. Organization of Petroleum Exporting Countries
ophth. ophthalmic
opp. opposite; opposed
ops (*coll. Mil.*) operations (room *or* officer)
opt. optics, optical; (*Gram.*) optative
OR Oregon
Or. *see* **OR**
O.R. (*Mil.*) other ranks
o.r. (*Comm.*) owner's risk
Ord. ordnance
ord. ordinary; order; ordinal
Oreg. *see* **OR**
O.S. Old Saxon; Old Style (*of dates*); Ordnance Survey; outsize
O. Slav. Old Slavonic
O.T. Old Testament
O.T.C. Officers' Training Corps
oz(s). ounce(s)

P

P (*Motor.*) parking; (*chess*) pawn
p (new) penny *or* pence
p. page; (*Gram.*) person; participle
PA Pennsylvania
Pa. *see* **PA**
P.A. Press Association; Publishers' Association; personal assistant
p.a. *per annum* (= yearly)
P.A.A. Pan-American Airways
P. & O. Peninsular and Oriental (Steam Navigation Company)
pa. p. past participle
par. parallel; parish
par(a). paragraph
parl. parliament(ary)
part. (*Gram.*) participle
pass. (*Gram.*) passive
pat. patent(ed)
path. pathology
Pat. Off. Patent Office
P.A.Y.E. pay as you earn (*income tax*)
P.C. Privy Council(lor); police constable
p.c. postcard; per cent
pd. paid
P.D. (*Elec.*) potential difference
-pdr. -pounder (*gun*)
P.D.S.A. People's Dispensary for Sick Animals
P.E. physical education
P.E.C. photo-electric cell
P.E.N. Poets, Playwrights, Editors, Essayists and Novelists
Penn. *see* **PA**
Pent. Pentateuch; Pentecost
P.E.P. Political and Economic Planning
per. period; (*Gram.*) person(al)
perf. (*Gram.*) perfect; perforated
perh. perhaps
per pro. *per procurationem* (= by proxy)
pers. person(s)
P.G. paying guest
P.G.A. Professional Golfers' Association
P.H. Purple Heart (*U.S.A.*)
Ph.D. *Philosophiae Doctor* (= Doctor of Philosophy)
Phil. Philadelphia
phil. philosophy
philol. philology
phys. physics, physical
physiol. physiology
P.I. Philippine Islands
Pk. park
pkg. packing, package
pkt. packet; pocket
pl. place; (*Gram.*) plural
P.L. (*Naut.*) Plimsoll Line
P.L.A. Port of London Authority
Plen. Plenipotentiary
plup. (*Gram.*) pluperfect
Pm. (*Comm.*) premium
P.M. Prime Minister; post mortem (examination)
p.m. *post meridiem* (= after noon)
P/N (*Comm.*) promissory note
P.O. Post Office; Postal Order; (*Navy*) Petty Officer; (*Av.*) Pilot Officer
pol. politics, political
pop. population
P.O.P. Post-Office-Preferred; (*Phot.*) printing-out paper
pos. position; positive
P.O.S.B. Post-Office Savings Bank
P.O.W. prisoner of war
pp. pages
p.p. (*Gram.*) past participle; (*Comm.*) by authority of
p.pd. prepaid, postage paid
P.P.E. Philosophy, Politics and Economics
P.P.I. plan position indicator
P.P.S. Parliamentary Private Secretary; *post postscriptum* (= additional postscript)
PR Puerto Rico
pr. price; pair; pronoun
P.R. proportional representation; public relations; (*see also* **PR**)
Preb. prebend(ary)
pred. (*Gram.*) predicative(ly)
Pref. (*Comm.*) preference; preface
pref. (*Gram.*) prefix; preferred, preferably
prelim. preliminary, preliminaries; (*coll.*) preliminary examination
prelims (*Typ.*) preliminary matter; (*coll.*) preliminary examinations
prem. premium
prep. (*Gram.*) preposition; (*coll., in schools*) preparation
Pres. president
pres. (*Gram.*) present
pret. (*Gram.*) preterite
prev. previous
Prin(c). principal
pro (*coll.*) professional
P.R.O. Public Record Office; Public Relations Officer
prob. probably
proc. proceedings
Prof. professor
Prom(s) (*coll.*) Promenade Concert(s)
pron. (*Gram.*) pronoun; pronounced, pronunciation
prop. proposition; proper(ly); (*coll.*) propellor
propr. proprietary, proprietor

props (*coll., Theat.*) properties
pros. prosody
Prot. Protestant
Prov. Province; Provençal
prov. provincial; proverbial; provisional
prox. (*Comm.*) *proximo* (*mense*) (= next (month))
prox. acc. *proxime accessit* (= next in order (of merit))
P.S. postscript
p.s. (*Theat.*) prompt side
P.S.A. Property Services Agency
P.S.T. Pacific Standard Time
P.S.V. public service vehicle
Pt. (*Geog.*) point
pt. pint(s); part
P.T.A. Parent Teacher Association
Pte. (*Mil.*) Private
P.T.I. physical training instructor
P.T.O. please turn over
P.U. pick-up (*gramophone*)
pub (*coll.*) public house
pub. public
publ. published; publication
punc(t). punctuation
P.V.C. polyvinyl-chloride
P.X. Post Exchange (*U.S.A.*)

Q

N.B. Titles with 'Queen' vary to 'King' according to reign.

Q (*Elec.*) coulomb; (*chess, cards*) queen
Q. Queen; question
Q.B.D. Queen's Bench Division
Q.C. Queen's Counsel
qr. quarter; quire
Q.S. Quarter Sessions
qt. quantity; quart(s)
q.t. (*coll.*) quiet
Qu. Queen; question
quad. quadrant; (*coll.*) quadrangle
qual. quality; qualified
Que. Quebec
Queensl. Queensland
quot. (*Comm.*) quotation
q.v. *quod vide* (= which see)

R

R (*chess*) rook
R. River; Railway; Réaumur
r. right; recto (*of page*); (*cricket*) runs
R.A. Royal Academy *or* Academician; Royal Artillery; Regular Army (*U.S.A.*)
R.A.A.F. Royal Australian Air Force
R.A.C. Royal Automobile Club; (*Mil.*) Royal Armoured Corps
R.A.D.A. Royal Academy of Dramatic Art
R.A.E.C. Royal Army Educational Corps
R.A.F. Royal Air Force
R.A.M. Royal Academy of Music
R.A.M.C. Royal Army Medical Corps
R.A.N. Royal Australian Navy
R.A.O.C. Royal Army Ordnance Corps
R.B.A. Royal Society of British Artists
R.B.L. Royal British Legion
R.C. Roman Catholic; Red Cross
R.C.A. Royal College of Art; Radio Corporation of America
R.C.A.F. Royal Canadian Air Force
R.C.M.P. Royal Canadian Mounted Police
R.C.N. Royal Canadian Navy; Royal College of Nursing
R.C.O. Royal College of Organists
R.C.P. Royal College of Physicians
rcpt. (*Comm.*) receipt
R.C.S. Royal College of Surgeons; (*Mil.*) Royal Corps of Signals
R.C.T. (*Mil.*) Royal Corps of Transport
R.C.V.S. Royal College of Veterinary Surgeons
Rd. road
rd. round
R.D. Rural Dean
R/D (*Comm.*) refer to drawer
R.E. Royal Engineers
recce (*coll.*) reconnaissance
redup(l). reduplicated
ref (*coll.*) referee
ref. reference; reformed
refd. referred
refl. reflex; (*Gram.*) reflexive
reg. regular(ly); regulation; region
regd. registered
Reg.-Gen. Registrar-General
Reg. Prof. Regius Professor
Regs. regulations
Regt. regiment
Reg.T.M. registered trade mark
rel. (*Gram.*) relative; religion
R.E.M.E. Royal Electrical and Mechanical Engineers
Rep (*coll.*) repertory (theatre)
rep (*coll.*) representative
Rep. Republic; Republican
rep. repeat
repr. reprinted
resp. respectively; (*Law*) respondent
ret(d). returned; retired
retnr. (*Law*) retainer
Rev. Reverend
rev. revised
revs (*coll., Tech.*) revolutions
R.F. radio frequency
R.F.C. rugby football club
R.G.N. Registered General Nurse
R.G.S. Royal Geographical Society
Rgt. *see* **Regt.**
Rgtl. regimental
Rh rhesus
r.h. right hand
R.H.A. Royal Horse Artillery
rhet. rhetoric(al)
R. Hist. S. Royal Historical Society
R.H.S. Royal Horticultural Society; Royal Humane Society
RI Rhode Island
R.I. Religious Instruction; (*see* **RI**)
R.I.B.A. Royal Institute of British Architects
R.I.P. *requiescat in pace* (= may he *or* she rest in peace)
R.L.O. returned letter office
Rly. railway
R.M. Royal Mail; Royal Marines; Resident Magistrate
R.M.A. Royal Military Academy
R.N. Royal Navy; Registered Nurse
R.N.I.B. Royal National Institute for the Blind
R.N.L.I. Royal National Lifeboat Institution
R.N.R. Royal Naval Reserve
R.N.V.R. Royal Naval Volunteer Reserve
R.N.V.S.R. Royal Naval Volunteer Supplementary Reserve
R.N.Z.A.F. Royal New Zealand Air Force
R.N.Z.N. Royal New Zealand Navy
rom. roman type
Rospa *see* **R.S.P.A.**
r.p. reply paid
r.p.m. revolutions per minute
R.P.S. Royal Photographic Society
rpt. report; repeat; reprint
R.S. Royal Society
R.S.A. Royal Society of Arts; Royal Scottish Academy *or* Academician
R.S.L. Royal Society of Literature
R.S.M. Royal School of Mines; Royal Society of Medicine; Regimental Sergeant Major

R.S.P.A.	Royal Society for the Prevention of Accidents
R.S.P.B.	Royal Society for the Protection of Birds
R.S.P.C.A.	Royal Society for the Prevention of Cruelty to Animals
R.S.V.	(*B.*) Revised Standard Version
R.S.V.P.	*répondez s'il vous plait* (= please reply)
rt.	right
R.T.	radio telephony *or* telegraphy
Rt. Hon.	Right Honourable
Rt. Rev.	Right Reverend
R.U.	Rugby Union
R.V.	(*B.*) Revised Version
Ry.	railway
R.Z.S.	Royal Zoological Society

S

S.	south(ern); society; saint
s.	second(s); son; see; (*Gram.*) singular; (*obs.*) shilling(s)
S.A.	Salvation Army; South Africa; South America; sex appeal
S.A.A.	South African Airways
S.A.A.A.	Scottish Amateur Athletic Association
S.A.A.F.	South African Air Force
s.a.e.	stamped addressed envelope
Salop	Shropshire
S.A.L.T.	Strategic Arms Limitation Talks
Sam.	Samuel
S. Am.	South America(n)
S.A.M.	surface-to-air missile
san.	sanitary
S.A.S.	Scandinavian Airlines System; Special Air Service Regiment
Sask.	Saskatchewan
SC	South Carolina
Sc.	Scotland, Scottish; (*Theat.*) scene
S.C.	*see* **SC**
Scand.	Scandinavia(n)
s. cap(s).	small capital(s)
Sc.D.	*Scientiae Doctor* (= Doctor of Science)
S.C.E.	Scottish Certificate of Education
sch.	school
sched.	schedule
sci-fi	science fiction
S.C.M.	Student Christian Movement; State Certified Midwife
Scot.	Scotland, Scottish
Scrip(t).	scripture
sculp(t).	sculpture, sculptor
SD	South Dakota
S.D.	standard deviation; State Department (*U.S.A.*)
s.d.	*sine die* (= indefinitely adjourned)
S. Dak.	*see* **SD**
Sec.	secretary
sec(s).	second(s)
Sect.	section
Secy.	secretary
S.E.D.	Scottish Education Department
Sem.	Semitic; seminary
Sen.	Senate; Senator; Senior
S.E.N.	State Enrolled Nurse
seq.	*sequens* (= the following)
ser.	series
Serg(t).	(*Mil.*) sergeant
Serjt.	(*Law*) serjeant
S.E.T.	Selective Employment Tax
S.F.	(*Rad.*) signal frequency; (*see also* **sci-fi**)
S.F.A.	Scottish Football Association
S.G.	Solicitor-General
s.g.	specific gravity
Sgt.	(*Mil.*) sergeant
sh.	(*obs.*) shilling(s)
sig(n).	signature
sing.	singular
S.J.	Society of Jesus
S.J.C.	Supreme Judicial Court (*U.S.A.*)
S.L.	Solicitor-at-Law
S/L	searchlight
S. lat.	south latitude
Smith. Inst.	Smithsonian Institution (*U.S.A.*)
S.N.O.	Scottish National Orchestra
S.N.P.	Scottish National Party
Snr.	Senior
S.O.	Stationery Office; Standing Order(s); (*Mil.*) Staff Officer; Signals Officer
s.o.	(*Comm.*) seller's option
Soc.	Society; Socialist
SOGAT	Society of Graphical and Allied Trades
sop.	soprano
Soton.	Southampton
S.P.C.K.	Society for Promoting Christian Knowledge
spec.	(*coll.*) speculation
sp. gr.	specific gravity
sq.	square
Sq(d)n.	squadron
Sr.	Senior
S.R.	self-raising (*flour*)
S.R.C.	Students' Representative Council
S.R.N.	State Registered Nurse
S.R.U.	Scottish Rugby Union
SS.	Saints
S.S.	Steamship
S/Sgt.	staff sergeant
S.S.M.	surface-to-surface missile
S.S.R.C.	Social Science Research Council
St.	saint; street
st.	stanza; stone(s); (*cricket*) stumped
Sta.	station
stat.	statistics
Stat. Hall	Stationers' Hall
std.	standard; started
S.T.D.	subscriber trunk dialling
stereo	(*coll.*) stereophonic
stereo.	stereotype
St. Ex.	stock exchange
stg.	sterling
stn.	station
s.t.p.	standard temperature and pressure
str.	(*Gram.*) strong; stroke (oar)
S.T.U.C.	Scottish Trades Union Congress
S.T.V.	Scottish Television
sub	(*coll.*) subscription; (*coll.*) submarine
sub.	(*Mil.*) subaltern
subj.	subject; subjunctive
subst.	substantive
suff.	suffix; sufficient
Suff(r).	suffragan
super.	superintendent; supernumerary
superl.	(*Gram.*) superlative
suppl.	supplement(ary)
Supt.	Superintendent
surg.	surgery, surgical
surv.	surveying; surviving
S.U.S.	Scottish Union of Students
S.W.G.	standard wire gauge
S.Y.H.A.	Scottish Youth Hostels Association
syn.	synonym(ous); synthetic

T

t.	troy (*weight*)
T.A.	telegraphic address; (*see also* **T. & A.V.R.**)
T. & A.V.R.	Territorial and Auxiliary Army Reserve
T. & G.W.U.	*see* **T.G.W.U.**
Tasm.	Tasmania(n)
T.B.	tuberculosis
tech.	technical(ly)
tel.	telephone

telecom.	telecommunications
temp.	temperature; temporary; *tempore* (= in the time of)
Tenn.	*see* **TN**
Ter(r).	Terrace
Terr.	territory
Teut.	Teutonic
Tex.	*see* **TX**
T.G.W.U.	Transport and General Workers' Union
thou.	(*coll. Tech.*) thousandth(s); thousand
tks.	thanks
T.L.S.	*The Times Literary Supplement*
t.m.	trade mark
TN	Tennessee
T.N.T.	trinitrotoluene
T.O.	transport officer
tonn.	tonnage
Tp.	troop
Tr.	(*Comm.*) trustee
tr.	transaction; (*Typ.*) transpose
trans.	translation; (*Gram.*) transitive
transf.	transfer(red)
transl.	translated, translation
Treas.	treasurer
T.R.F.	(*Rad.*) tuned radio frequency
Trin.	Trinity; Trinidad
Trs.	(*Comm.*) trustees
trs.	(*Typ.*) transpose
T.S.A.	Training Services Agency
tsp.	teaspoonful
T.T.	Tourist Trophy; teetotaller; tuberculin tested (*milk*)
T.U.C.	Trades Union Congress
T.V.	television
TX	Texas
typ.	typography, typographical

U

U	universal (*of films suitable for children*)
U.	Unionist; (*see* **UT**)
U.A.M.	underwater-to-air missile
U.A.R.	United Arab Republic
u.c.	(*Typ.*) upper case
U.C.C.A.	Universities' Central Council on Admissions
U.D.I.	Unilateral Declaration of Independence
U.F.	United Free Church (of Scotland)
U.F.O.	unidentified flying object
U.G.C.	University Grants Committee
U.H.F.	ultra-high frequency
U.K.	United Kingdom (of Great Britain and Northern Ireland)
ult.	*ultimo* (= of last month)
U.N.	United Nations
UNESCO	United Nations Educational, Scientific and Cultural Organization
UNICEF	United Nations (International) Children's (Emergency) Fund
Unit.	Unitarian
Univ.	university
unm.	unmarried
U.N.O.	United Nations Organization
U.N.R.R.A.	United Nations Relief and Rehabilitation Administration
U.P.	United Press
U.P.U.	Universal Postal Union
u/s	unserviceable
U.S.(A.)	United States (of America)
U.S.A.F.	United States Air Force
U.S.C.L.	United Society for Christian Literature
U.S.M.C.	United States Marine Corps
U.S.N.	United States Navy
U.S.P.G.	United Society for the Propagation of the Gospel
U.S.S.	United States Ship
U.S.S.R.	Union of Soviet Socialist Republics
usu.	usual(ly)
UT	Utah
U.U.	Ulster Unionist

V

V	(*Elec.*) volt(s)
v.	verse; *vide* (= see); *versus*; (*Gram.*) verb
VA	Virginia
Va.	*see* **VA**
V.A.	Vicar Apostolic
V.A.D.	Voluntary Aid Detachment
V. Adm.	Vice-Admiral
V. & A.	Victoria and Albert Museum; Royal Order of Victoria and Albert
var.	variety, variant, variation
V.A.T.	Value Added Tax
v. aux.	auxiliary verb
vb(l).	verb(al)
V.C.	(*Mil.*) Victoria Cross
V.D.	venereal disease
v.d.	various dates
vel.	velocity
Ven.	Venerable
Verm.	*see* **VT**
vet	(*coll.*) veterinary surgeon
V.F.	video frequency
V.G.	Vicar General
V.H.F.	very high frequency
VI	Virgin Islands (*U.S.*)
V.I.	*see* **VI**
v.i.	intransitive verb
Vict.	Victoria (*Australia*)
vil(l).	village
V.I.P.	very important person
v.irr.	irregular verb
viz.	*videlicet* (= namely)
V.O.A.	(*Rad.*) Voice of America
voc.	(*Gram.*) vocative
Vol.	volunteer
vol.	volume
v.r.	reflexive verb
vs.	*versus*
v.s.	*vide supra* (= see above); variable speed
V.S.O.	Voluntary Service Overseas
VT	Vermont
Vt.	*see* **VT**
v.t.	transitive verb
V.T.O.	vertical take-off
Vulg.	Vulgate

W

W.	West(ern); (*Elec.*) watt(s); Women's (*size*)
w.	with; wide; (*cricket*) wicket
WA	Washington (*State*)
W.A.	Western Australia
Wash.	*see* **WA**
W.C.	water closet
W.-Cdr.	Wing-Commander
W.D.	War Department
W.E.A.	Workers' Educational Association
w.e.f.	with effect from
Wes.	Wesleyan
w.f.	(*Typ.*) wrong fount
W.F.T.U.	World Federation of Trade Unions
Wh.	(*Elec.*) watt-hour(s)
wh.	which
W.H.O.	World Health Organization
WI	Wisconsin
W.I.	West Indies; Women's Institute
Wis(c).	*see* **WI**
wk(ly)	week(ly)
wkt(s).	(*cricket*) wicket(s)
W.L.	(*Rad.*) wave-length

W. long.	West longitude
Wm.	William
W.O.	War Office; (*Mil.*) Warrant Officer; wireless operator; welfare officer
w.p.b.	waste-paper basket
w.p.m.	words per minute
W.R.A.C.	Women's Royal Army Corps
W.R.A.F.	Women's Royal Air Force
W.R.N.S.	Women's Royal Naval Service
W.R.V.S.	Women's Royal Voluntary Service
W.S.	(*Scots*) Writer to the Signet
W.S.C.F.	World Student Christian Federation
W/T, W.T.	wireless telegraphy
wt.	weight
WV	West Virginia
W.Va.	*see* **WV**
WX	Women's Extra (*size*)
WY	Wyoming
Wy(o).	*see* **WY**

X

X	(*film*) to which those under 18 are not admitted
x-d(iv).	without (right to) dividend
x-i(nt).	without (right to) interest
Xn.	*see* **Xtian.**
XOS	extra outsize
Xt(ian).	Christ(ian)

Y

yd(s).	yard(s)
Y.H.(A.)	Youth Hostel(s Association)
Y.M.C.A.	Young Men's Christian Association
yr(s).	year(s); your(s)
Y.W.C.A.	Young Women's Christian Association

Z

z.(d.)	zenith distance
Zod.	zodiac

Advice to the User

- Gender
- Homographs
- Keyword
- Pronunciation in international phonetic alphabet
- Parts of speech
- Stylistic level
- Optional forms
- Appropriate context
- Idiomatic usage
- Stress marks
- Examples of use
- Genitive and plural forms
- Regional usage
- Grammatical information
- Figurative expressions
- Specialized vocabulary
- Cross-reference to irregular verb tables
- Mode of verb
- Different meanings
- Auxiliary verb

[1]**Gehalt** [gə'halt], *m.* (**-s,** *pl.* **-e**) contents; capacity; strength, body, concentration; content, substance, intrinsic value, merit; – ***an Säure,*** acid content, proportion *or* percentage of acid.

[2]**Gehalt,** *n.* (*Austr. and Bav. m.*) (**-(e)s,** *pl.* **¨er** *or* **-e**) pay, wages, salary, stipend; allowance.

glatt [glat], **1.** *adj.* (*comp.* *–er, sup. –est, better than* ***glätter, glättest,*** *which also occur*) 1. smooth, even, level, unruffled, flat, flush; sleek; ***–es Geschäft,*** even business; ***–es Gesicht,*** smooth *or* sleek face; ***–es Kinn,*** smooth *or* clean-shaven chin; ***–e Stirn,*** unruffled brow; 2. polished, slippery, glossy; ***es ist zu – zum Gehen,*** it is too slippery for walking; 3. plain, clear, obvious; downright, outright, absolute; ***–e Absage,*** flat refusal; ***–e Lüge,*** barefaced lie; ***–er Sieg,*** clear win *or* victory; ***–er Unsinn,*** sheer nonsense; 4. round (*number etc.*); ***–e 10 Pfund,*** all of £10; 5. (*fig.*) smooth, bland, oily, flattering; ***–e Worte,*** smooth *or* oily words; ***–e Zunge,*** smooth tongue; 6. (*Swiss*) splendid, capital. **2.** *adv.* 1. smoothly; – ***anliegen,*** fit tightly *or* closely; be *or* lie flush (***an*** (*Dat.*), with); ***die S. ging ganz –,*** the affair went (off) smoothly *or* without the slightest hitch, it was all plain sailing; 2. quite, entirely, thoroughly, (*coll.*) clean, plainly; unhesitatingly; – ***abschlagen,*** flatly refuse; – ***durchschneiden,*** cut clean through; – ***gewinnen,*** win hands down, win easily; – ***heraussagen,*** tell bluntly *or* plainly *or* frankly; ***ihm – ins Gesicht,*** to his face; (*coll.*) – ***vergessen,*** clean forget.

krätzig ['krɛtsɪç], *adj.* (*Med.*) scabious, psoric; itchy.

Kratz|maschine, *f.* carding-machine. **–wunde,** *f.* surface wound, scratch.

krauchen ['krauxən], *v.i.* (*coll.*) *see* **kriechen.**

kraue(l)n ['krauə(l)n], *v.t.* rub *or* scratch gently, stroke.

kraul(schwimm)en ['kraul(ʃvɪm)ən], *irr.v.i.* swim the crawl.

passen ['pasən], **1.** *v.i.* 1. (*Dat.*) fit, suit, be suited to, become; be suitable *or* convenient for (*a p.*); – ***auf*** (*Acc.*) or ***für*** or ***zu,*** fit, fit in with, be suited to *or* suitable for (*a th.*), (*coll.*) go with (*a th.*); agree, harmonize, tally, (*esp. of colours*) match; ***nicht –,*** (*esp. of colours*) clash; ***gut zueinander –,*** be well-matched, (*coll.*) go well together; ***nur wenn es mir (in den Kram) paßt,*** only if I feel like it *or* if it suits me *or* suits my purpose; ***das paßt wie die Faust aufs Auge,*** that's entirely out of place; 2. – ***auf*** (*Acc.*), wait *or* watch for, be attentive *or* pay attention to; 3. (*Cards*) pass. **2.** *v.r.* be proper *or* seemly *or* becoming; ***es paßt sich einfach nicht,*** it just isn't done, it's just bad form; ***es paßt sich nicht für mich,*** it ill befits *or* becomes me.

Perle ['pɛrlə], *f.* pearl; bead; sparkling bubble; (*fig.*) gem, jewel; ***–n vor die Säue werfen,*** cast pearls before swine.

perlen ['pɛrlən], *v.i.* sparkle, glisten; ripple (*laughter*); form bubbles, effervesce; (*aux.* s.) appear in drops *or* beads; ***die Träne perlte aus ihrem Auge,*** the tear-drop rolled from her eye.

Perlen|fischer, *m.* pearl-fisher *or* diver. **–glanz,** *m.* pearly *or* nacrous lustre. **–kette, –schnur,** *f.* string of pearls, pearl necklace *or* necklet. **–stickerei,** *f.* beading.

Hinweise für den Benutzer

Betonung — **Stichwort** — **Aussprache** — **Beispiel** — **Fachgebiet** — **übertragener Sinn**

dislocate ['dislokeit], *v.t.* 1. (*Med.*) verrenken, ausrenken; – ***one's shoulder***, sich (*Dat.*) die Schulter verrenken; 2. (*Tech.*) verschieben, verrücken; 3. (*Geol.*) verwerfen, versetzen; 4. (*fig.*) in Verwirrung bringen. **dislocation** [–'keiʃən], *s.* (*Med.*) die Verrenkung; (*Tech.*) Verrückung, Verschiebung; (*Geol.*) Verwerfung; (*fig.*) Verwirrung.

Homonyme — **Stilschicht** — **idiomatische Wendung** — **Sprachgebiet** — **Erklärung**

[1]**nip** [nip], **1.** *v.t.* 1. kneifen, kneipen, zwicken, klemmen; – ***off***, abzwicken, abkneifen; 2. durch Frost beschädigen *or* zerstören *or* töten; – ***in the bud***, im Keime ersticken; 3. (*coll.*) klauen. **2.** *v.i.* 1. zwicken; 2. schneiden, beißen (*as wind*); 3. (*sl.*) sich schnell bewegen, flitzen; (*sl.*) – ***in***, hineinschlüpfen, sich hineindrängen *or* hineinschieben. **3.** *s.* 1. das Kneifen, Zwicken; 2. der Zwick, Biß, Knick (*of a rope*); 3. Frostbrand; – ***in the air***, frostige Luft; 4. (*coll.*) (*Am.*) – ***and tuck***, in schnellem Wechsel, in hartem Kampf.

[2]**nip, 1.** *s.* das Schlückchen (*of brandy etc.*). **2.** *v.i.* (*v.t.*) nippen (an (*Dat.*)).

verschiedene Bedeutungen — **grammatischer Hinweis** — **Trennung der Wortarten**

wing [wiŋ], **1.** *s.* 1. der Flügel (*also Archit.*, *Pol.*, *Spt.*); (*Poet.*) Fittich, die Schwinge (*of bird*); (*fig.*) ***clip his –s***, die Flügel stutzen; (*fig.*) ***lend –s to***, beschleunigen, beflügeln; ***on the –***, im Fluge; (*Poet.*) ***on the –s of love***, auf Fittichen der Liebe; ***on the –s of the wind***, mit Windeseile; ***take –***, aufsteigen, davonfliegen; (*fig.*) ***take under one's –***, unter seine Fittiche *or* seinen Schutz nehmen; 2. die Federfahne (*of an arrow*); 3. (*Av.*) (Flieger)-gruppe, (*Am.*) das Geschwader; *pl.* das Fliegerabzeichen (*Air Force*); 4. (*Footb. etc.*) (*coll.*) der Außenstürmer; ***left –***, das Linksaußen (*position*), der Linksaußen (*player*); 5. (*Motor.*) Kotflügel; 6. (*Av.*) die Tragfläche; 7. (*Theat.*) (*usu. pl.*) die Kulisse; ***in the –s***, an der Bühnenseite; (*fig.*) in Reserve. **2.** *v.t.* 1. mit Federn versehen, befiedern (*an arrow*); 2. durchfliegen, im Flug zurücklegen (*one's way*); 3. (*fig.*) (*Poet.*) beflügeln, beschwingen, beschleunigen; 4. (*Hunt.*) flügeln, flügellahm schießen; (*coll.*) leicht (*or* am Arm *or* an der Schulter) verwunden, treffen.

Wortart — **Übersetzung**

wing|-area, *s.* (*Av.*) tragende Fläche. **--beat,** *s.* der Flügelschlag. **--case,** *s.* (*Ent.*) der Deckflügel. **--chair,** *s.* der Ohrensessel. **--collar,** *s.* der Eckenkragen. **--commander,** *s.* der Oberstleutnant (der Luftwaffe); (*Am.*) Geschwaderkommodore. **--covert,** *s.* (*Orn.*) die Deckfeder.

Unregelmäßige englische Verben

Infinitiv	Präteritum	Partizip Perfekt
abide	abode *oder* abided	abode *oder* abided
arise	(*siehe* rise)	
awake(n)	(*siehe* wake)	
be { S. I am, II are, III is; P. are	S. was; P. were	been
bear	bore	borne[1]
beat	beat	beaten[2]
become	(*siehe* come)	
befall	(*siehe* fall)	
beget	begot	begotten
begin	began	begun
behold	(*siehe* hold)	
bend	bent[3]	bent[3]
bereave	bereft *oder* bereaved[4]	bereft *oder* bereaved[4]
beseech	besought *oder* beseeched	besought *oder* beseeched
bestride	(*siehe* stride)	
bet	bet *oder* betted[5]	bet *oder* betted[5]
bid	bid *oder* bade	bid *oder* bidden
bide[6]	bided *oder* bode	bided
bind	bound	bound[7]
bite	bit	bitten[8]
bleed	bled	bled
blow	blew	blown[9]
break	broke	broken[10]
breed	bred	bred
bring	brought	brought
build	built	built
burn	burnt *oder* burned[11]	burnt *oder* burned[11]
burst	burst	burst
buy	bought	bought
Präs. can[12]	could[13]	—[14]
cast	cast	cast
catch	caught	caught
chide	chided[15]	chided[16]
choose	chose	chosen
cleave[17]	cleft *oder* clove	cleft *oder* cloven[18]
cling	clung	clung
clothe	clothed *oder* clad[19]	clothed *oder* clad[19]
come	came	come
cost[20]	cost	cost
creep	crept	crept
crow	crowed *oder* crew	crowed
cut	cut	cut
dare[21]	dared[22]	dared
deal	dealt	dealt
dig	dug	dug
dive	dived[23]	dived
do[24]	did[25]	done
draw	drew	drawn
dream	dreamt *oder* dreamed[11]	dreamt *oder* dreamed[11]
drink	drank	drunk[26]
drive	drove	driven
dwell	dwelt *oder* dwelled[11]	dwelt *oder* dwelled[11]
eat	ate[27]	eaten
fall	fell	fallen
feed	fed	fed

1 Jedoch adjektivisch: ***born*** im Sinne von 'geboren sein'; auch attributiv, z.B. ***born fool, in all my born days.***
2 Adjektivisch: ***dead beat.***
3 Schlechter: ***bended***; vgl. aber: ***on bended knee.***
4 Zweite Form findet nur bei Todesfall Verwendung.
5 Zweite Form nur gelegentlich, nur britisch.
6 Veraltet oder schottisch.
7 Ungebräuchlich: ***bounden***; besteht weiterhin als Adjektiv (= obligatorisch).
8 Ungebräuchlich: ***bit***; besteht weiterhin in: ***the biter bit.***
9 Salopp, in Verwünschungen: ***blowed.***
10 Vulgär: ***broke***; jedoch als Adjektiv in der Umgangssprache (= pleite).
11 Zweite Form vor allem amerikanisch.
12 Verneinung: ***cannot***; umgangssprachlich: ***can't.***
13 Verneinung umgangssprachlich: ***couldn't.***
14 Fehlende Verbformen entsprechen: ***be able to.***
15 Gelegentlich noch: ***chid.***
16 Gelegentlich noch: ***chid*** oder ***chidden.***
17 Transitiv (= spalten). Intransitiv (= kleben, haften) ist das Verb regelmäßig.
18 Adjektivisch: ***cleft stick, cleft palate***; ***cloven hoof.***
19 Die zweite Form (die als gehobener Stil gilt) hat in technischer Sprache im Infinitiv eine neue Bedeutung angenommen (= ein Material mit einem anderen überziehen); in dieser Bedeutung ist es regelmäßig.
20 Transitiv (= Kosten berechnen) regelmäßig.
21 (1) (= wagen) 3. Person singular Präsens: ***dare*** vor einem Infinitiv mit ***to*** oder: ***dares*** vor einem Infinitiv mit oder ohne ***to.***
(2) (= herausfordern) regelmäßig.
22 Im Sinne von (1) (vgl. Note 21) in gehobenem Stil oder scherzhaft auch: ***durst*** mit ***to.***
23 Selten gebrauchte amerikanische Form: ***dove.***
24 Verneinung umgangssprachlich: ***don't***; für 3. Person singular: ***does not,*** umgangssprachlich: ***doesn't*** (***don't*** in dieser Person gilt als vulgär).
25 Verneinung umgangssprachlich: ***didn't.***
26 Auch adjektivisch (= betrunken) als Aussage über eine Person; sonst: ***drunken,*** z.B. ***drunken orgy.***
27 Aussprache: et; oder amerikanisch: eit.

Infinitiv	Präteritum	Partizip Perfekt
feel	felt	felt
fight	fought	fought
find	found	found
flee	fled	fled
fling	flung	flung
fly	flew	flown
forbear	(*siehe* bear)	
forbid	forbad(e)	forbidden
forecast	forecast(ed)	forecast(ed)
forget	forgot	forgotten
forgive	(*siehe* give)	
forsake	forsook	forsaken
forswear	(*siehe* swear)	
freeze	froze	frozen
get	got	got[28]
gird	girded *oder* girt	girded *oder* girt
give	gave	given
go	went	gone
grind	ground	ground
grow	grew	grown
hang[29]	hung	hung
have[30]	had[31]	had
hear	heard	heard
heave	heaved *oder* hove[32]	heaved *oder* hove[32]
hew	hewed	hewn *oder* hewed
hide	hid	hidden[33]
hit	hit	hit
hold	held	held[34]
hurt	hurt	hurt
keep	kept	kept
kneel	knelt *oder* kneeled[11]	knelt *oder* kneeled[11]
knit	knitted *oder* knit[35]	knitted *oder* knit[35]
know	knew	known
lade[36]	laded	laded *oder* laden
lay	laid	laid
lead	led	led
lean	leant *oder* leaned[11]	leant *oder* leaned[11]
leap	leapt *oder* leaped[11]	leapt *oder* leaped[11]
learn	learnt *oder* learned[11]	learnt *oder* learned[37]
leave	left	left
lend	lent	lent
let	let	let
lie[38]	lay	lain
light	lit *oder* lighted	lit *oder* lighted[39]
lose	lost	lost
make	made	made
Präs. may[40]	might	—
mean	meant	meant
meet	met	met
melt	melted	melted[41]
mislead	(*siehe* lead)	
mistake	(*siehe* take)	
misunderstand	(*siehe* stand)	
mow	mowed	mowed *oder* mown
Präs. must[42]	—	—
outdo	(*siehe* do)	
outgrow	(*siehe* grow)	
overcome	(*siehe* come)	
overdo	(*siehe* do)	
overtake	(*siehe* take)	
overthrow	(*siehe* throw)	
pay	paid[43]	paid[43]
prove	proved	proved[44]
put	put	put
quit	quit *oder* quitted	quit *oder* quitted
—	quoth[45]	—
read	read[46]	read[46]
rend	rent	rent
rid	rid *oder* ridded	rid *oder* ridded

28 Ungebräuchlich oder schottisch, auch in den einfachen Bedeutungen (z.B. = erhalten; = bewegen; = erlangen); amerikanisch: ***gotten***; vgl. ***ill-gotten gains***.

29 Im Sinne von Tod am Strang (erhängen) wird das Verb transitiv und intransitiv regelmäßig konjugiert.

30 Verneinung umgangssprachlich: ***haven't***; für 3. Person singular: ***has not***, umgangssprachlich: ***hasn't***.

31 Verneinung umgangssprachlich: ***hadn't***.

32 Zweite Form gehört zur Seemannssprache.

33 Gelegentlich: ***hid***; jedoch nie adjektivisch.

34 Ungebräuchlich: ***holden***; besteht weiterhin in: ***beholden***.

35 Zweite Form nur gelegentlich. Als figuratives Adjektiv, z.B. ***well-knit***.

36 Selten, außer: ***laden***. Gewöhnlich adjektivisch.

37 Zweite Form vor allem amerikanisch. Als Adjektiv jedoch nur: ***learned*** (Aussprache: . . . nid).

38 =ruhen. ***Lie*** = lügen ist regelmäßig.

39 Zweite Form wird gewöhnlich als attributives Adjektiv verwandt.

40 Verneinung im Sinne von 'erlauben': ***must not*** oder ***cannot***.

41 Ungebräuchlich: ***molten***; besteht weiterhin als attributives Adjektiv.

42 Verneinung, wenn Zwang oder Notwendigkeit ausgedrückt werden soll: ***need not***.

43 Ungebräuchlich: ***payed***; besteht weiterhin in der Seemannssprache.

44 Ungebräuchlich oder amerikanisch (findet jedoch zunehmend in England Aufnahme): ***proven*** (Aussprache: pru:vn). Auch in schottischer Gerichtssprache (Aussprache: prouvn).

45 Nur die 1. und 3. Person bestehen weiterhin in gehobener poetischer Sprache, mit nachgestelltem Subjekt, z.B. ***quoth he***.

46 Aussprache: red.

Infinitiv	**Präteritum**	**Partizip Perfekt**
ride	rode	ridden
ring	rang[47]	rung
rise	rose	risen
rive[48]	rived	rived *oder* riven
run	ran	run
saw	sawed	sawn *oder* sawed
say[49]	said	said
see	saw	seen
seek	sought	sought
sell	sold	sold
send	sent	sent
set	set	set
sew	sewed	sewn *oder* sewed
shake	shook	shaken
Präs. shall[50]	should[51]	—
shape	shaped	shaped[52]
shave	shaved	shaved[53]
shear	sheared	sheared *oder* shorn[54]
shed	shed	shed
shew	(*siehe*	show)
shine	shone[55]	shone[55]
shoe	shod[56]	shod[56]
shoot	shot	shot
show	showed	shown[57]
shrink	shrank[58]	shrunk[59]
shrive[60]	shrived *oder* shrove	shrived *oder* shriven
shut	shut	shut
sing	sang[61]	sung
sink	sank[62]	sunk[63]
sit	sat	sat
slay	slew	slain
sleep	slept	slept
slide	slid	slid
sling	slung	slung
slink	slunk	slunk
slit	slit	slit
smell	smelt *oder* smelled[11]	smelt *oder* smelled[11]
smite[64]	smote	smitten
sow	sowed	sown *oder* sowed
speak	spoke	spoken
speed	sped *oder* speeded[65]	sped *oder* speeded[65]
spell	spelt *oder* spelled[11]	spelt *oder* spelled[11]
spend	spent	spent
spill	spilt *oder* spilled[11]	spilt *oder* spilled[11]
spin	spun	spun
spit	spat[66]	spat
split	split	split
spoil	spoilt *oder* spoiled[67]	spoilt *oder* spoiled[67]
spread	spread	spread
spring	sprang[68]	sprung
stand	stood	stood
stave	staved *oder* stove[69]	staved *oder* stove[69]
steal	stole	stolen
stick	stuck	stuck
sting	stung	stung
stink	stank[70]	stunk
strew	strewed	strewed *oder* strewn
stride	strode	stridden
strike[71]	struck	struck[72]
string	strung	strung
strive	strived *oder* strove	strived *oder* striven
swear	swore	sworn
sweat	sweat *oder* sweated	sweat *oder* sweated
sweep	swept	swept
swell	swelled	swelled *oder* swollen[73]
swim	swam[74]	swum

47 Selten: ***rung***; hat heute vulgären Anklang.
48 Nur adjektivischer Gebrauch von: ***riven***; sonst selten.
49 3. Person singular: ***says*** (Aussprache: sez).
50 Verneinung umgangssprachlich: ***shan't.***
51 Verneinung umgangssprachlich: ***shouldn't.***
52 Ungebräuchlich: ***shapen***; besteht weiterhin als Adjektiv, z.B. ***ill-shapen***, ***misshapen.***
53 Ungebräuchlich: ***shaven***; besteht weiterhin als Adjektiv.
54 Zweite Form gebräuchlicher in den einfachen — buchstäblichen und figurativen — Bedeutungen. In der Metallverarbeitung jedoch: ***sheared***; ebenso überall dort, wo die Idee einer Verformung vermittelt werden soll.
55 Transitiv (= polieren) auch: ***shined***; besonders im Amerikanischen.
56 Selten: ***shoed.***
57 Die gelegentlich verwendete Form: ***showed*** gilt als vulgär.
58 Die gelegentlich verwendete Form: ***shrunk*** gilt als vulgär.
59 Nur adjektivisch: ***shrunken*** (= eingeschrumpft, eingefallen).
60 Selten.
61 Heute nur vulgär: ***sung.***
62 Heute nur vulgär: ***sunk.***
63 Ungebräuchlich: ***sunken***; besteht weiterhin als Adjektiv.
64 Veraltet, außer: ***smitten*** bei figurativer Verwendung.
65 In technischer Sprache (= Geschwindigkeit regulieren) nur die zweite Form.
66 Ungebräuchlich und amerikanisch: ***spit.***
67 Die jeweils zweite Form ist vor allem amerikanisch. Nur diese Formen im Sinne von: plündern, berauben.
68 Heute nur vulgär oder amerikanisch: ***sprung.***
69 Nur die jeweils erste Form kann figurativ verwendet werden, z.B. ***it (has) staved off the evil day.***
70 Gelegentlich auch: ***stunk.***
71 Intransitiv (= streiken) auch regelmäßig.
72 Ungebräuchlich: ***stricken***; wird noch figurativ und als Adjektiv (= ergriffen) verwandt.
73 ***Swollen head*** (= von einem Zusammenprall); ***swelled head*** (= eingebildet, überheblich).
74 Heute nur vulgär: ***swum.***

Infinitiv	Präteritum	Partizip Perfekt
swing	swung[75]	swung
take	took	taken
teach	taught	taught
tear	tore	torn
tell	told	told
think	thought	thought
thrive	thrived *oder* throve[76]	thrived *oder* thriven[76]
throw	threw	thrown
thrust	thrust	thrust
tread	trod	trodden[77]
undergo	(*siehe* go)	
understand	(*siehe* stand)	
undertake	(*siehe* take)	
undo	(*siehe* do)	
uphold	(*siehe* hold)	
upset	(*siehe* set)	
wake(n)	wak(en)ed *oder* woke	wak(en)ed *oder* woken
wear	wore	worn
weave	wove[78]	woven[79]
wed	wed *oder* wedded	wed *oder* wedded
weep	wept	wept
wet	wet *oder* wetted	wet *oder* wetted
Präs. will[80]	would[81]	—
win	won	won
wind	wound	wound
withdraw	(*siehe* draw)	
withhold	(*siehe* hold)	
withstand	(*siehe* stand)	
work	worked[82]	worked[82]
wring	wrung	wrung
write	wrote[83]	written[83]

75 Heute nur vulgär: ***swang.***

76 Die jeweils zweite Form stirbt aus.

77 Die Form: ***trod*** gilt heute als vulgär.

78 Selten: ***weaved***; besonders figurativ, z.B. ***he weaved in and out through the crowd.***

79 N.B.: ***wove paper.***

80 Verneinung umgangssprachlich: ***won't.***

81 Verneinung umgangssprachlich: ***wouldn't.***

82 Ungebräuchlich: ***wrought***; wird weiterhin verwandt zur Beschreibung von Kunsthandwerk: ***wrought in brass***, ***wrought-iron.*** Umgangssprachlich: ***wrought-up*** (= aufgewühlt).

83 Ungebräuchlich: ***writ***; jedoch in fester Verbindung: ***writ large.***

Erläuterung der englischen Aussprache

Ein Doppelpunkt (:) bezeichnet die Länge des vorhergehenden Vokals. Das Zeichen (') steht vor der Silbe mit Hauptton.

Vokale

Einige aus dem Französischen entlehnte Wörter enthalten nasale Vokale, die durch eine Tilde über dem Vokal bezeichnet werden (z.B. ã). Sie werden gleichzeitig durch Mund und Nase ausgesprochen.

Deutsch		**Englisch**
[ɑ:]	wie *aa* in S*aa*l	half, father, harbour
[æ]	zwischen *a* in h*a*t und *ä* in n*ä*chste	man, marry
[ʌ]	ähnlich wie *a* in h*a*t	but, son, flood, come
[e]	wie *e* in f*e*st	very, head, said
[ə:]	eher wie *ö* in l*ö*sen, aber mit gedehnten Lippen (ungerundet)	sir, her, fur, word, earn, adjourn
[ə]	wie *e* in hab*e*n, aber mit gedehnten Lippen (ungerundet)	perhaps, idea, mother, honour, horror, about, bishop
[i:]	wie *ie* in s*ie*ben	seat, green, believe, receive
[i]	wie *i* in b*i*n	finish, physic
[ɔ:]	wie *o* in P*o*st aber lang	shawl, tortoise
[ɔ]	wie *o* in P*o*st	not, want
[o]	wie *o* in M*o*ral	domain
[u:]	wie *u* in g*u*t	moon, tooth, truth
[u]	wie *u* in M*u*tter	good, July

Diphthonge

Ein Diphthong besteht aus zwei Vokalen, von denen der eine stärker (betont) und der andere schwächer (unbetont) ist und die zusammen als gleitender Laut ausgesprochen werden, wie z.B. *ai* in M*ai*. Im Englischen ist der zweite Vokal immer der schwächere. Manchmal folgt auf einen Diphthong noch ein [ə], wodurch der zweite Vokal etwas weiter abgeschwächt wird. Folgende Diphthonge sind zu beachten:

Deutsch		**Englisch**
[ai]	wie *ei* in m*ei*n	my, wife, high
[au]	wie *au* in H*au*s	house, how, bough
[ɛə]	wie *ä* in B*ä*r	bare, hair, their, dare, pear, scarce
[ei]	nicht wie in *ei*ns! Der erste Laut ist *e* wie in fest	same, day, they
[iə]	wie *ie* in B*ie*r	here, hear, pierce, interior
[ɔi]	wie *eu* in B*eu*tel	boy, noise, royal
[ou]	ungerundetes *ö* mit folgendem flüchtigem [u]-Laut	go, slow, owe, boat
[uə]	wie *uhe* in R*uhe*	sure, poor, doer
[ju:]	—	hue, acute, stew, beauty
[ju]	—	regulate, credulous

Konsonanten

Zeichen, die nicht erklärt sind, werden ungefähr wie die entsprechenden Buchstaben im Deutschen ausgesprochen.

Deutsch		**Englisch**
[j]	wie *j* in *j*ede	yellow, yawn
[kw]	—	queen, quantity, require
[l]	am Wortende oder vor Konsonant ist dunkel	—
[ŋ]	wie *ng* in Ri*ng*	hanging, thing, wringer, anxiety
[ŋg]	wie *ng* in La*ng*uste	linger, stronger, mangle
[ŋk]	wie *nk* in Ba*nk*	ink, sunken, anxious
[r]	schwer zu beschreiben! Die Zunge ist ungefähr in der gleichen Stellung wie bei [ʒ] (sie unten), aber viel tiefer, und die Lippen sind eher in einer neutralen Stellung	—

Erläuterung der englischen Aussprache

[s]	wie *s* in e*s*	*s*ee, *sc*ent, re*c*eive, *ps*ychology
[z]	wie *s* in Ro*s*e	hi*s*, *z*one, face*s*
[ʃ]	wie *sch* in ra*sch*	*sh*oe, bu*sh*, se*ss*ion, spe*c*ial
[ts]	wie *z* in *z*ehn	flo*ts*am, goa*ts*kin, boo*ts*
[tʃ]	wie *tsch* in deu*tsch*	ca*tch*, *ch*urn
[ʒ]	wie *g* in Eta*g*e	mea*s*ure, gara*g*e
[dʒ]	wie *dsch* in *Dsch*ungel	*j*ewel, *g*eology, dun*ge*on, dru*dge*
[ð]	wie *s* in Ro*s*e, aber gelispelt	*th*at, fa*th*er, pa*th*s
[θ]	wie *s* in e*s*, aber gelispelt	*th*ick, pa*th*
[v]	wie *w* in *w*o	*v*an, *v*ine, o*f*, gra*v*y
[w]	ein flüchtiger [u]-Laut, ungefähr wie in Rit*u*al	*w*ell, dou*gh*y, pers*u*ade
[x]	wie *ch* in Ba*ch*	lo*ch*

Amerikanische Aussprache

Unsere Umschrift gibt die übliche britische Aussprache an. Die amerikanische weicht davon in einigen Punkten ab (wobei es noch bedeutende regionale Unterschiede gibt). Hier einige der auffallendsten Abweichungen:

1 Im Gegensatz zum britischen Englisch wird *r* auch vor einem Konsonanten und am Wortende ausgesprochen.
2 In vielen Wörtern (z.B. *ask*, *castle*, *laugh* usw.) wird [ɑ:] zu [æ:].
3 Den [ɔ]-Laut spricht der Amerikaner [ɑ], vielfach auch [ɔ:].
4 In Wörtern wie *duty*, *tune*, *new* usw. entfällt oft der [j]-Laut vor [u:].
5 Schließlich werden eine Anzahl von Wörtern anders betont.

persönlich	*pers.*	personal
Pharmazie	*Pharm.*	pharmacy
Philosophie	*Phil.*	philosophy
Philologie	*Philol.*	philology
Phonetik	*Phonet.*	phonetics
Photographie	*Phot.*	photography
Physik	*Phys.*	physics
Physiologie	*Physiol.*	physiology
Plural	*pl.*	plural
Dichtkunst	*Poet.*	poetry
Politik	*Pol.*	politics
besitzanzeigend	*poss.*	possessive
Mittelwort der Vergangenheit	*p.p.*	past participle
prädikativ	*pred.*	predicative
Präfix	*pref.*	prefix
Präposition	*prep.*	preposition
Präsens	*pres.*	present
Druckerkunst	*Print.*	printing
Pronomen	*pron.*	pronoun
Prosodie	*Pros.*	prosody
Protestant	*Prot.*	Protestant
Sprichwort	*Prov.*	proverb
Mittelwort der Gegenwart	*pr. p.*	present participle
Psychologie	*Psych.*	psychology
quod vide	*q.v.*	*quod vide* (which see)
Rundfunk	*Rad.*	radio
römisch-katholisch	*R.C.*	Roman Catholic
Eisenbahn	*Railw.*	railways
Hinweis	*ref.*	reference
reflexiv	*refl.*	reflexive
regelmässig	*reg.*	regular
Religion	*Rel.*	religion
relativ	*rel.*	relative
Rhetorik	*Rhet.*	rhetoric
Sache	*S.*	*Sache* (= thing)
Substantiv, Hauptwort	*s.*	substantive
sein	s.	*sein* (= to be)
Skulptur	*Sculp.*	sculpture
trennbar	*sep.*	separable
Nähmaschine	*Sew.-mach.*	sewing machine
Schiffbau	*Shipb.*	shipbuilding
singular	*sing.*	singular
Slang	*sl.*	slang
Schmiedekunst	*Smith.*	smithery
jemand	*s.o.*	someone
Soziologie	*Soc.*	sociology
Sport	*Spt.*	sport
Statistik	*Stat.*	statistics
Börse	*St. Exch.*	Stock Exchange
etwas	*s.th.*	something
studenten Slang	*Studs. sl.*	students' slang
Konjunktiv	*subj.*	subjunctive
Suffix	*suff.*	suffix
Superlativ	*sup.*	superlative
Chirurgie	*Surg.*	surgery
Landvermessung	*Surv.*	surveying
Gerberei	*Tan.*	tanning
Technik	*Tech.*	technology
Telegraphie	*Tele.*	telegraphy
Tennis	*Tenn.*	tennis
Textilien	*Text.*	textiles
Ding, Sache	*th.*	thing
Theater	*Theat.*	theatre
Theologie	*Theol.*	theology
Topographie	*Top.*	topography
Fernsehen	*T.V.*	television
Universität	*Univ.*	university
gewöhnlich	*usu.*	usual(ly)
Verb	*v.*	verb
Hilfszeitwort	*v.aux.*	auxiliary verb
Tiermedizin	*Vet.*	veterinary medicine
intransitives Verb	*v.i.*	intransitive verb
reflexives Verb	*v.r.*	reflexive verb
transitives Verb	*v.t.*	transitive verb
vulgär	*vulg.*	vulgar
Weberei	*Weav.*	weaving
Zoologie	*Zool.*	zoology

A, a [ei], *s.* 1. das A, a; ***A 1,*** (*Comm.*) erstklassig, bester Qualität, von erster Güte, (*St. Exch.*) mündelsicher; (*coll.*) prima, famos; (*Mil.*) kriegsverwendungsfähig; 2. (*Mus.*) A; ***A flat,*** As; ***A major,*** A-Dur; ***A minor,*** a-Moll; ***A sharp,*** Ais. (*See Index of Abbreviations.*)

a [ei, ə], (*before vowel or silent h*) **an** [æn, ən], *indef.art.* ein, eine, ein; ***– few,*** (= *some*) ein paar, einige; (= ***not many***) wenige; ***– great deal,*** sehr viel; ***– great many,*** sehr viele; ***half – day,*** ein halber Tag; ***– little,*** etwas; ***many – man,*** mancher Mann; ***such – one,*** ein solcher; ***at – time,*** auf einmal, hintereinander; ***once – day,*** einmal am Tag; ***once – week,*** einmal wöchentlich, einmal die *or* in der Woche; ***2 marks – pound,*** 2 Mark das Pfund; ***3 marks – day,*** täglich 3 Mark, 3 Mark pro Tag; ***he is – poet,*** er ist Dichter; ***she died – widow,*** sie starb als Witwe; ***all of – size,*** alle von *or* in derselben Größe; ***two of – kind,*** zwei von derselben Art.

a- [ə], *prep. pref.* 1. (= *on, in, at etc.*); ***abed,*** im Bett(e); ***afoot,*** zu Fuß; 2. (*with forms in -ing*) ***go a-begging,*** betteln gehen; ***a-hunting we will go,*** wir gehen auf die Jagd; ***fall a-weeping,*** zu weinen anfangen.

a- [ei], *pref.* ohne, unempfindlich für, -los (*e.g.* ***amoral***).

aardvark [ˈɑːdvɑːk], *s.* (*Zool.*) das Erdferkel (*Orycteropus*).

Aaron [ˈɛərən], *s.* (*B.*) Aaron (*m.*); ***–'s rod,*** (*Archit.*) der Aaronsstab; (*Bot.*) die Königskerze (*Verbascum thapsus*).

aback [əˈbæk], *adv.* (*Naut.*) back; ***taken –,*** bestürzt, verblüfft; (*of sails*) ***be taken –,*** backbekommen.

abacus [ˈæbəkəs], *s.* das Rechenbrett, die Rechenmaschine; (*Archit.*) Säulendeckplatte, Kapitälsdeckplatte.

abaft [əˈbɑːft], *adv.* (*Naut.*) achtern (zu); ***– the beam,*** achterlicher als dwars.

abandon [əˈbændən], **1.** *v.t.* aufgeben, preisgeben, fallenlassen, überlassen (*to, Dat.*); im Stich lassen, verlassen; (*Law*) abandonnieren, abtreten; (*a child*) aussetzen; ***– o.s. to,*** sich ergeben *or* hingeben (*Dat.*); ***– him to his fate,*** ihn seinem Schicksal überlassen; ***– all hope,*** alle Hoffnung aufgeben *or* fahren lassen. **2.** *s.* die Ungezwungenheit, Ausgelassenheit, Unbeherrschtheit, Hemmungslosigkeit, das Sichgehenlassen; ***with –,*** rückhaltlos, mit Hingabe.

abandoned [əˈbændənd], *adj.* 1. verlassen; aufgegeben; ***– property,*** herrenloses Gut; 2. lasterhaft, liederlich, verworfen; hemmungslos, rückhaltlos, ungezwungen. **abandonment,** *s.* 1. (böswilliges) Verlassen; das Aufgeben, die Preisgabe; Verzichtleistung, Aufgabe, Abtretung, Überlassung, (*of a legal action*) Rücknahme, der Abandon; die Verlassenheit; 2. Selbstvergessenheit, Hingabe, Unbeherrschtheit, das Sichgehenlassen.

abase [əˈbeis], *v.t.* 1. senken; (*also* ***– o.s.***) (sich) demütigen, erniedrigen, entwürdigen, degradieren; 2. (*obs.*) niederlassen, senken. **abasement,** *s.* die Demütigung, Erniedrigung.

abash [əˈbæʃ], *v.t.* aus der Fassung *or* in Verlegenheit bringen, beschämen; ***be*** or ***stand –ed,*** in Verlegenheit sein, verlegen *or* betreten sein, sich schämen, beschämt sein (*at,* über (*Acc.*)). **abashment,** *s.* die Beschämung; Bestürzung, Betroffenheit, Verlegenheit.

abatable [əˈbeitəbl], *adj.* (*Law*) umstoßbar, aufhebbar, einstellbar. **abate, 1.** *v.t.* herabsetzen, ermäßigen, ablassen von (*price*); lindern, mildern, mäßigen, stillen (*pain etc.*); vermindern, verringern, heruntersetzen; (*Law*) abschaffen, umstoßen, aufheben. **2.** *v.i.* nachlassen, (an Stärke) abnehmen; (im Preise) fallen; (*Law*) ungültig werden; ***the wind –s,*** der Wind legt sich *or* flaut ab. **abatement,** *s.* die Verminderung, Abnahme; Linderung, Milderung; (*in price etc.*) der Nachlaß, Abzug, Rabatt, Preisabbau, die Herabsetzung; (*Law*) Abstellung, Beseitigung, Umstoßung, Abschaffung, Aufhebung; (*Law*) ***plea in –,*** die Einsprucherhebung.

abatis [ˈæbətis], *s.* (*Mil.*) der Verhau, die Baumsperre.

abattoir [ˈæbətwɑː], *s.* (öffentliches) Schlachthaus.

abbacy [ˈæbəsi], *s.* das Amt *or* die Würde *or* Gerichtsbarkeit eines Abtes. **abbatial** [əˈbeiʃəl], *adj.* Abts-, äbtlich; Äbtissinnen-; Abtei-, abteilich.

abbess [ˈæbes], *s.* die Äbtissin.

abbey [ˈæbi], *s.* die Abtei, das Kloster.

abbot [ˈæbət], *s.* der Abt. **abbotcy, abbotship,** *s. See* **abbacy.**

abbreviate [əˈbriːvieit], *v.t.* (ab)kürzen, zusammenziehen; (*Math.*) heben. **abbreviation** [–ˈeiʃən], *s.* die Abkürzung, Verkürzung; (*Math.*) das Heben (von Brüchen); (*Mus.*) die Kürzung, Abbreviatur.

A.B.C. [ˈeibiːˈsiː], *s.* das Alphabet, Abc, Abece; (*fig.*) die Anfangsgründe; (*Railw.*) der Eisenbahnfahrplan, das Abc-Kursbuch.

Abderite [ˈæbdərait], *s.* der Abderit, (*fig.*) Schildbürger, Krähwinkler.

abdicate [ˈæbdikeit], **1.** *v.t.* niederlegen, aufgeben, abtreten; (*Law*) enterben, verstoßen. **2.** *v.i.* abdanken, dem Throne entsagen. **abdication** [–ˈkeiʃən], *s.* die Niederlegung, Entsagung; Abdankung; der Verzicht (*of,* auf (*Acc.*)); (*Law*) die Enterbung, Verstoßung.

abdomen [æbˈdoumən, ˈæbdəmən], *s.* das Abdomen, der Unterleib, Bauch; (*Ent.*) Hinterleib. **abdominal** [–ˈdəminl], *adj.* Abdominal–, Unterleibs–, Bauch–, (*Ent.*) Hinterleibs–; ***– cavity,*** die Bauchhöhle; ***– segment,*** der Hinterleibsring; ***– wall,*** die Bauchdecke.

abducent [æbˈdjuːsənt], *adj.* (*Anat.*) abziehend; ***– muscle,*** der Abziehmuskel.

abduct [æbˈdʌkt], *v.t.* 1. (*Anat.*) abziehen; 2. entführen. **abduction,** *s.* 1. (*Anat.*) das Abziehen; 2. (*Law*) die Entführung. **abductor,** *s.* (*Anat.*) der Abziehmuskel; Entführer.

abeam [əˈbiːm], *pred.adj., adv.* (*Naut.*) dwars, querab.

abed [əˈbed], *adv.* zu Bett, im Bette.

Aberdonian [æbəˈdouniən], *s.* der Bewohner von Aberdeen.

aberrance, aberrancy [æbˈerəns(i)], *s.* die Abirrung (*from what is right*), Verirrung, der Irrtum, Fehler, (*Biol.*) die Abweichung (*from the norm*). **aberrant,** *adj.* irrig, irrtümlich, abirrend, (*Biol.*) abweichend, anomal. **aberration** [æbəˈreiʃən], *s.* die Abweichung, Abirrung; (*fig.*) der Irrgang, Irrweg; (*Opt.*) die (Brechungs)abweichung, (*Biol.*) Abweichung vom Typus, (*Astr.*) Aberration; ***mental –,*** Geistesverwirrung.

abet [əˈbet], *v.t.* anstiften, antreiben, aufhetzen, ermutigen, aufmuntern; helfen (*Dat.*), unterstützen, begünstigen (*Acc.*), Vorschub leisten (*Dat.*). **abetment,** *s.* die Anstiftung, Aufhetzung; der Vorschub, Beistand, die Beihilfe, Unterstützung. **abetter, abettor,** *s.* der Anstifter; (Helfers)-helfer.

abeyance [əˈbeiəns], *s.* die Unentschiedenheit, (der Zustand der) Ungewißheit; ***in –,*** noch nicht gerichtlich zugewiesen, herrenlos (*of lands*); unentschieden, in der Schwebe; ***fall into* –,** zeitweise ruhen, zeitweilig außer Kraft treten.

abhor [əb'hɔ:], *v.t.* verabscheuen, zurückschrecken vor (*Dat.*). **abhorrence** [-'hɔrəns], *s.* der Abscheu (*of*, vor (*Dat.*) *or* gegen), die Abneigung (gegen); ***hold in* –,** verabscheuen. **abhorrent,** *adj.* widerlich, verhaßt (***to,*** *Dat.*) (*a p.*); zuwider(laufend) (***to,*** *Dat.*), unverträglich, unvereinbar (mit) (*a th.*).

abide [ə'baid], **1.** *irr.v.t.* 1. bleiben, verweilen; fortdauern; (*obs.*) wohnen; 2. – ***by,*** verharren *or* ausharren bei, festhalten an (*Dat.*), sich halten an (*Acc.*), Folge leisten (*Dat.*); erdulden, sich ergeben in (*Acc.*), sich abfinden *or* begnügen mit; – ***by the consequences,*** die Folgen auf sich (*Acc.*) nehmen. **2.** *irr.v.t.* 1. warten auf (*Acc.*), erwarten; 2. (*only neg.*) aushalten, leiden, ertragen, vertragen, ausstehen. **abiding,** *adj.* dauernd, bleibend, anhaltend, beständig. **abiding-place,** *s.* (*obs.*) der Wohnort, Aufenthaltsort, die Wohnstätte.

abigail ['æbigeil], *s.* die Zofe, Kammerjungfer.

ability [ə'biliti], *s.* die Fähigkeit (***for,*** für *or* zu), Befähigung, Geschicklichkeit; das Geschick, Vermögen, Können, Talent; *pl.* geistige Anlagen, Gaben (*pl.*), die Veranlagung; ***to the best of my* –,** nach besten Kräften.

abiogenesis [æbio'dʒenisis], *s.* die Urzeugung, Selbstentstehung, Abiogenesis.

abject ['æbdʒekt], *adj.* verworfen, erniedrigt; kriechend, kriecherisch, unterwürfig; verächtlich, verachtenswert, zu verachten(d), gemein, niederträchtig; (*fig.*) äußerst, tiefst; ***in* – *misery,*** in tiefstem Elend, niedergeschlagen. **abjectness,** *s.* das Elend, die Niedergeschlagenheit; Verworfenheit, Niederträchtigkeit, Verächtlichkeit.

abjuration [æbdʒu'reiʃən], *s.* die Abschwörung, Entsagung. **abjure** [əb'dʒuə], *v.t.* abschwören, entsagen (*Dat.*), zurücknehmen, widerrufen; – ***the realm,*** eidlich versprechen das Land auf immer zu verlassen.

ablactation [æblæk'teiʃən], *s.* die Entwöhnung, Ablaktation, das Abstillen (*of a child*).

ablation [æb'leiʃən], *s.* (*Geol.*) das Abschmelzen (*of snow*), die Abtragung (*of rock*), (*Surg.*) Amputation, operative Entfernung.

ablative ['æblətiv], *s.* der Ablativ; – ***absolute,*** unabhängiger Ablativ.

ablaze [ə'bleiz], *pred.adj.* in Flammen, flammend, lodernd; (*fig.*) glänzend, beleuchtet (***with,*** von *or* vor (*Dat.*)); erregt (vor).

able [eibl], *adj.* 1. fähig, imstande, in der Lage (*to do*); – ***to do,*** tun können; – ***to pay,*** zahlungsfähig; ***as one is* –,** nach seinen Mitteln *or* Kräften; 2. geschickt, begabt, befähigt, tauglich, tüchtig. **able|-bodied,** *adj.* stark, kräftig, rüstig, gesund; (*Mil.*) diensttauglich, wehrfähig; – ***seaman,*** der Vollmatrose (*merchant navy*). **–-seaman,** *s.* der Matrosenobergefreite.

abloom [ə'blu:m], *adv.* in Blüte, blühend.

ablution [ə'blu:ʃən], *s.* die Abwaschung, Abwässerung, das Auswaschen, Auswässern, Ausspülen; (*R.C.*) die Ablution; *pl.* (*coll.*) Waschgelegenheit; der Waschraum; ***perform one's* –*s,*** sich waschen.

ably ['eibli], *adv.* geschickt, mit Geschick; *see* **able.**

abnegate ['æbnigeit], *v.t.* (ab)leugnen, verleugnen; aufgeben, sich (*Dat.*) versagen. **abnegation** [–'geiʃən], *s.* der Verzicht (*of,* auf (*Acc.*)), die Ableugnung; ***self–*–,** die Selbstverleugnung.

abnormal [æb'nɔ:məl], *adj.* ungewöhnlich, abnorm, anomal, regelwidrig, normwidrig; mißgestaltet; –***psychology,*** die Psychopathologie. **abnormality** [–'mæliti], *s.* die Unregelmäßigkeit, Regelwidrigkeit, Abweichung, (*Med.*) Deformität, Anomalie. **abnormity,** *s.* die Abnormität, Mißbildung, Mißgestalt, Ungeheuerlichkeit.

aboard [ə'bɔ:d], *adv.* an Bord; ***go* –,** sich einschiffen, an Bord gehen; (*coll.*) ***all* –*!*** alles einsteigen!

[1]**abode** [ə'boud], *s.* der Aufenthalt, Aufenthaltsort, Wohnort, Wohnsitz; die Wohnung; ***take up*** or ***make one's* –,** sich niederlassen; ***of no fixed* –,** ohne festen Wohnsitz.

[2]**abode,** *imperf., p.p. of* **abide.**

aboil [ə'bɔil], *pred.adj.* in Wallung, im Sieden; (*fig.*) in Wallung *or* großer Aufregung.

abolish [ə'bɔliʃ], *v.t.* aufheben, abschaffen; tilgen, ungültig machen; (*Poet.*) zerstören, vertilgen, vernichten. **abolition** [æbə'liʃən], *s.* die Abschaffung, Beseitigung, Tilgung, Aufhebung; (*Hist.*) Abschaffung der Sklaverei. **abolitionist,** *s.* (*Hist.*) der Abolitionist, Gegner der Sklaverei.

abomasum [æbə'meisəm], *s.* (*Zool.*) der Labmagen.

abominable [ə'bɔminəbl], *adj.* abscheulich, scheußlich, widerwärtig. **abominate,** *v.t.* verabscheuen. **abomination** [–'neiʃən], *s.* die Verabscheuung; der Abscheu (*of,* vor (*Dat.*)); die Schändlichkeit, Gemeinheit; der Gegenstand des Abscheus, etwas Widerliches, der Greuel; ***hold in* –,** verabscheuen; (*coll.*) ***it is his pet* –,** es ist ihm ein wahrer Greuel.

aboriginal [æbə'ridʒinl], **1.** *adj.* eingeboren, ureingesessen, einheimisch, ursprünglich, Ur–. **2.** *s.* der Ureinwohner. **aborigines** [–ni:z], *pl.* die Urbevölkerung, Ureinwohner (*pl.*).

abort [ə'bɔ:t], **1.** *v.t.* (*Med.*) nicht zur Entwicklung kommen lassen, zu einer Fehlgeburt bringen; (*fig., esp. Am.*) vorzeitig abschließen (*a project etc.*). **2.** *v.i.* fehlgebären, zu früh gebären; abortieren, (*Biol.*) verkümmern. **abortifacient** [–i'feiʃənt], *s.* das Abtreibungsmittel. **abortion** [–'bɔ:ʃən], *s.* die Frühgeburt, Fehlgeburt; (*Biol.*) Verkümmerung, Fehlbildung; Abtreibung; (*fig.*) (*coll.*) Mißgeburt, der Fehlschlag, das Mißlingen. **abortionist,** *s.* der Abtreiber. **abortive,** *adj.* unzeitig, zu früh geboren; (*Biol.*) verkümmert; (*fig.*) verfrüht, vorzeitig, mißlungen, fehlgeschlagen, verfehlt, fruchtlos; ***prove* –,** fehlschlagen, mißlingen, mißglücken.

abound [ə'baund], *v.i.* Überfluß haben, reich sein (*in,* an (*Dat.*)), gefüllt sein (***with,*** mit), voll sein, strotzen, wimmeln (von); reichlich *or* im Überfluß vorhanden sein. **abounding,** *adj.* reichlich vorhanden; reich (*in,* an (*Dat.*)), voll (***with,*** von).

about [ə'baut], **1.** *prep.* 1. um (. . . herum); ***beat* – *the bush,*** wie die Katze um den heißen Brei herumgehen; ***go the wrong way* – *s.th.,*** bei einer S. falsch zu Werke gehen; ***he is* – *the house,*** er ist irgendwo im Hause; ***the fields* – *the town,*** die Felder um die Stadt; ***he looked round* – *him,*** er sah umher *or* um sich her; 2. bei, an (*Dat.*); ***nothing strange* – *it,*** nichts Fremdes daran; ***I have no money* – *me,*** ich habe kein Geld bei mir; ***have one's wits* – *one,*** seine Gedanken beisammen haben; 3. um, gegen (*time*); ***it is* – *time,*** es wäre nun wohl (an der) Zeit; – ***3 o'clock,*** gegen 3 Uhr; 4. um, wegen, über, in, betreffs, in betreff, bezüglich (*Gen.*), in bezug auf (*Acc.*); ***go* – *your own business!*** kümmern Sie sich um Ihre Sachen! ***be quick* – *it!*** mach' schnell damit! ***what* – *it?*** wie steht's *or* wie wäre es damit? 5. im Begriff; ***be* – *to do,*** im Begriff sein *or* dabei sein zu tun, gerade tun wollen; 6. *many idiomatic usages after nouns and verbs, e.g.* ***doubt* –,** Zweifel an; ***fuss* –,** viel Wesens von; ***opinion* –,** Meinung über; ***bother* –,** sich kümmern um; ***care* –,** fragen nach; ***feel uneasy* –,** nicht wohl (zumute) sein bei; ***quarrel* –,** streiten über; *etc. See the nouns or verbs concerned.* **2.** *adv.* 1. (rund) herum *or* umher, ringsherum; im Kreise, in der Runde; überall, hier und da, irgendwo hier; ***I must be* – *early,*** ich muß früh auf den Beinen sein; ***bring* –,** zustande bringen; ***come* –,** geschehen, zugehen, zustande kommen; (*Naut.*) ***go* –,** wenden, lavieren, den Kurs ändern; ***be lying* –,** herumliegen, hier und da zerstreut liegen; ***look* – *one,*** sich umsehen; ***put a ship* –,** ein Schiff wenden; – ***turn!*** (*Am.* – ***face!***) (rechtsum) (*or in Germany* linksum) kehrt! (*coll.*) ***know what one is* –,** wissen was man tut; (*coll.*) ***what are you* –*?*** was machst du da? (*coll.*) ***mind what you are* –*!*** nimm dich in acht! 2. fast, beinahe, ungefähr, nahezu, etwa, zirka; – ***300 souls,*** an die *or* gegen 300 Seelen; – ***a year later,*** etwa ein Jahr später; (*coll.*) ***that's* – *right,*** das kommt so ungefähr hin, das stimmt ungefähr.

above [ə'bʌv], **1.** *prep.* über, oberhalb; (*fig.*) über;

mehr *or* stärker als; – ***all (things)***, vor allen Dingen, vor allem; – ***20 minutes***, über 20 Minuten; ***it is – my head***, es ist mir zu hoch, es geht über meinen Verstand; (*Comm.*) – ***par***, über pari; – ***party***, überparteilich; – ***praise***, über alles Lob erhaben; ***be – him***, ihm überlegen sein, ihn übertreffen *or* überflügeln; ***he is – it***, er ist darüber erhaben; ***he is – (doing*** *etc.*), er ist zu stolz (zu tun *etc.*); ***those – me***, meine Vorgesetzten; – ***300***, mehr als 300. **2.** *adv* (da) oben, droben; über, darüber (hinaus); ***over and –***, obendrein, überdies, noch dazu; ***the powers –***, die himmlischen Mächte; ***as noted –***, wie oben *or* vorher bemerkt. **3.** *s.* Obenerwähntes, Obiges.

above|-board, *pred.adj.* (*coll.*) offen, ehrlich, redlich. **--ground,** *pred.adj.* oberirdisch, (*Min.*) über Tag. **--mentioned,** *adj.* obenerwähnt. **--stairs,** *adv.* bei der Herrschaft.

abracadabra [æbrəkə'dæbrə], *s.* das Kauderwelsch, die Geheimnistuerei.

abrade [ə'breid], *v.t.* abreiben, abschaben, abschleifen; (*Geol.*) abscheuern, (*Tech.*) verschleißen, (*Med.*) abkratzen, abschürfen, abschälen; (*fig.*) schädigen, untergraben. **abraded,** *adj.* (*Med.*) abgeschürft, aufgeschürft, aufgescheuert, wund(gerieben).

abrasion [ə'breiʒən], *s.* das Abreiben, Abschaben, Abschleifen, (*Tech.*) der Abrieb, Verschleiß, die Reibung, Abnutzung, Abnützung, (*Med.*) Abschrammung, Scheuerstelle, Schürfwunde; Hautabschürfung, Schramme. **abrasive** [–siv], **1.** *adj.* abschleifend, abreibend, Scheuer–, Schleif–; Schmirgel–; – ***action***, die Scheuerwirkung; – ***hardness***, die Ritzhärte. **2.** *s.* das Schleifmittel, Abreibungsmittel, Putzmittel, Poliermittel, der Schmirgel.

abreact [æbri'ækt], *v.t.* (*Psych.*) abreagieren. **abreaction,** *s.* die Abreagierung.

abreast [ə'brest], **1.** *adv.* nebeneinander, Seite an Seite; (*Naut.*) dwars, querab; ***they walked three –***, sie gingen drei nebeneinander; – ***of***, gegenüber von, auf der (gleichen) Höhe von; ***the ship was – of the cape***, das Schiff lag auf der Höhe des Kaps; ***keep – of*** or ***with the progress of science***, mit der Wissenschaft Schritt halten. **2.** *adj.* (*Naut.*) ***line –***, die Dwarslinie.

abridge [ə'bridʒ], *v.t.* (ab)kürzen, verkürzen; zusammenfassen, zusammenziehen; (*fig.*) beschränken, einschränken, schmälern, vermindern, verringern; berauben (*of*, *Gen.*). **abridged,** *adj.* (ab)gekürzt, verkürzt, Kurz–. **abridg(e)ment,** *s.* die Abkürzung, (Ver)kürzung; der Abriß, Auszug; die Beschränkung, Einschränkung, Verminderung, Verringerung, Schmälerung.

abroad [ə'brɔ:d], *adv.* 1. im *or* ins Ausland, auswärts; ***go –***, ins Ausland reisen, in die Fremde ziehen; ***live –***, im Ausland leben; 2. draußen, außer dem Hause, im Freien; weit umher *or* auseinander, überallhin, weithin; ***scatter*** or ***spread –***, aussprengen, verbreiten; ***get –***, ruchbar werden; ***there is a rumour –***, es geht ein Gerücht (um).

abrogate ['æbrogeit], *v.t.* aufheben, widerrufen, außer Kraft setzen, beiseite setzen, beseitigen, abschaffen. **abrogation** [–'geiʃən], *s.* die Aufhebung, Abschaffung.

abrupt [ə'brʌpt], *adj.* abgebrochen, abgerissen; jäh, steil, schroff, abschüssig; plötzlich, unerwartet, hastig, übereilt; grob, kurz angebunden, ungeschliffen; zusammenhanglos, unzusammenhängend; – ***departure***, plötzliche *or* unvermittelte Abreise; – ***style***, schroffe *or* kurze Schreibweise. **abruptness,** *s.* die Zusammenhanglosigkeit, Abgerissenheit, Abgebrochenheit; Steilheit; Schroffheit, Rauheit, das Ungeschliffene (*of manner*); die Eile, Plötzlichkeit, Übereilung.

abscess ['æbses], *s.* das Geschwür, der Abszeß, die Eiterbeule.

abscissa [æb'sisə], *s.* (*pl.* **-ae** [–si:]) die Abszisse.

abscond [əb'skɔnd], *v.i.* (*Law*) flüchtig werden, flüchten (***from***, vor (*Dat.*)), (*coll.*) sich heimlich davonmachen, durchbrennen, sich drücken; sich verbergen *or* verstecken.

absence ['æbsəns], *s.* (*of a p.*) die Abwesenheit; das Nichterscheinen (***from***, in (*Dat.*) *or* zu), Ausbleiben, Fernbleiben (von); (*of a th.*) Nichtvorhandensein, Fehlen, der Mangel, die Ermangelung (***of***, an (*Acc.*)); – ***from duty***, die Dienstabwesenheit; – ***of mind***, die Zerstreutheit, Geistesabwesenheit, Gedankenlosenkeit, Unachtsamkeit; ***on leave of –***, auf Urlaub; (*Mil.*) – ***without leave***, unerlaubte Entfernung; ***in the – of***, in Ermangelung (*Gen.*).

absent, **1.** ['æbsənt], *adj.* (*of a p.*) nicht erschienen, abwesend, (*of a th.*) nicht vorhanden, fehlend; (*Prov.*) ***long –, soon forgotten***, aus den Augen, aus dem Sinn. **2.** [æb'sent], *v.t.* – ***o.s.***, sich entfernen (***from***, von, aus), sich fernhalten (von), fernbleiben (*Dat.* *or* von). **absentee** [–sən'ti:], *s.* Abwesende(r); – ***landlord***, nicht auf seinem Gut lebender Gutsherr. **absenteeism,** *s.* wiederholtes Fernbleiben (von der Arbeitsstelle), das Arbeitsversäumnis, der Arbeitsausfall; das Wohnen im Auslande, der Absentismus. **absent|-minded,** *adj.* zerstreut, geistesabwesend. **--mindedness,** *s.* die Geistesabwesenheit, Zerstreutheit.

absinth(e) ['æbsinθ], *s.* (*Bot.*) der Wermut (*Artemisia absinthium*); (*liqueur*) Absinth.

absolute ['æbsəlu:t], **1.** *adj.* unumschränkt, unbedingt, unbeschränkt, unabhängig, eigenmächtig, absolut; völlig, vollkommen, vollständig, vollendet; (*Chem.*) wasserfrei, unvermischt, rein; wirklich, tatsächlich; (*Phil.*) kategorisch, positiv, an und für sich bestehend; – ***alcohol***, wasserfreier *or* absoluter Alkohol; – ***fool***, völliger Narr; – ***monarchy***, absolute Monarchie; – ***music***, absolute Musik; (*Phys.*) – ***pressure***, der Absolutdruck; – ***vacuum***, absolute (Luft)leere. **2.** *s.* das Absolute. **absolutely,** *adv.* unumschränkt; vollends, völlig, vollkommen, gänzlich, an und für sich; tatsächlich, unbedingt, durchaus, überhaupt. **absoluteness,** *s.* das Absolute, die Absolutheit, Unbedingtheit, Unumschränktheit.

absolution [æbsə'lu:ʃən], *s.* (*Theol.*) der Sündenerlaß, die Absolution; (*Law*) Freisprechung, Lossprechung, Entbindung (***from***, von).

absolutism ['æbsəlu:tizm], *s.* der Absolutismus, unbeschränkte Herrschaft.

absolvable [əb'zɔlvəbl], *adj.* freizusprechen(d). **absolve,** *v.t.* lossprechen, freisprechen, entbinden (***of, from***, von), entheben (*Gen.*); (*Theol.*) Absolution erteilen (*Dat.*).

absorb [əb'sɔ:b], *v.t.* 1. ansaugen, einsaugen, aufsaugen, in sich (ein)ziehen; verschlingen, aufzehren, (ver)schlucken, in sich aufnehmen, einverleiben; (*Phys.*) absorbieren, resorbieren; 2. (*fig*) beschäftigen, in Anspruch nehmen, fesseln; ***–ed in thought***, in Gedanken vertieft; 3. auffangen, dämpfen, federn (*shocks*). **absorbency,** *s.* die Saugfähigkeit, Absorbierfähigkeit, das Absorptionsvermögen. **absorbent,** **1.** *adj.* aufsaugend, einsaugend, Absorptions–; – ***cotton wool***, die Verbandwatte. **2.** *s.* (*Chem.*) das Absorptionsmittel, (*Med.*) Absorbens. **absorbing,** *adj.* (*fig.*) packend, fesselnd.

absorption [əb'sɔ:pʃən], *s.* 1. die Einsaugung, Aufsaugung, Aufnahme, das Einfangen, Verschlucken; (*Chem.*) die Resorption, Absorption; 2. (*fig.*) das Vertieftsein, die Versunkenheit.

abstain [əb'stein], *v.i.* sich enthalten (***from***, *Gen.*), enthaltsam *or* abstinent leben. **abstainer,** *s.* der Abstinenzler, Temperenzler.

abstemious [əb'sti:miəs], *adj.* enthaltsam, mäßig, genügsam. **abstemiousness,** *s.* die Enthaltsamkeit, Mäßigkeit, Genügsamkeit.

abstention [əb'stenʃən], *s.* die Enthaltung (***from***, von).

abstergent [əb'stə:dʒənt], **abstersive** [əb'stə:siv], **1.** *adj.* reinigend; (*Med.*) abführend. **2.** *s.* das Reinigungsmittel, Abführmittel.

abstinence ['æbstinəns], *s.* die Enthaltsamkeit, Enthaltung, Abstinenz. **abstinent,** *adj.* enthaltsam, mäßig.

abstract, **1.** [æb'strækt], *v.t.* 1. abziehen, ablenken;

2. (ab)sondern, trennen, abstrahieren; für sich *or* abgesondert betrachten; (*Chem.*) destillieren; (*coll.*) entwenden, heimlich zu sich nehmen. **2.** ['æbstrækt], *adj.* abstrakt, theoretisch, rein begrifflich, absolut, gegenstandslos; abstrus, dunkel, tiefsinnig, schwer verständlich; – ***noun,*** das Begriffswort, Abstraktum; – ***number,*** unbenannte Zahl. **3.** ['æbstrækt], *s.* **1.** das Abstrakte, bloß Gedachtes; (*Gram.*) Abstraktum, Begriffswort; ***in the –,*** an und für sich, rein begrifflich, theoretisch betrachtet; 2. der Abriß, Auszug.

abstracted [æb'stræktid], *adj.* (ab)gesondert, abgezogen; getrennt, abstrahiert; (*fig.*) geistesabwesend, unaufmerksam, zerstreut.

abstraction [æb'strækʃən], *s.* 1. die Begriffsbildung, Verallgemeinerung; Abstraktion; das Abstrahieren; abstrakter Begriff, das bloß Gedachte, die Theorie; 2. Entwendung, Entfremdung, Wegnahme, der Unterschleif; 3. (*fig.*) die Geistesabwesenheit, Zerstreutheit; 4. (*Chem.*) Absonderung. **abstractness,** *s.* das Abstrakte, die Abstraktheit, Begrifflichkeit, Unwirklichkeit.

abstruse [æb'stru:s], *adj.* abstrus, dunkel, schwerverständlich, unklar, verworren, verborgen. **abstruseness,** *s.* die Dunkelheit, Unklarheit, Unverständlichkeit, Verworrenheit.

absurd [əb'sə:d], *adj.* absurd, sinnwidrig, widersinnig, unsinnig, sinnlos; albern, lächerlich, abgeschmackt; ***that's –!*** das ist Unsinn! **absurdity,** *s.* die Sinnwidrigkeit, Sinnlosigkeit, Unsinnigkeit, Absurdität, der Widersinn; Unsinn, die Albernheit, Ungereimtheit, Abgeschmacktheit.

abundance [ə'bʌndəns], *s.* große Anzahl, die Fülle, (*of,* von), Menge, der Überfluß (von, an (*Dat.*)); ***in –,*** in Hülle und Fülle, vollauf. **abundant,** *adj.* reich (*in,* an (*Dat.*)); reichlich (versehen mit), überschüssig, überflüssig, reichlich vorhanden. **abundantly,** *adv.* übergenug, vollauf; ***this will – show,*** dies wird völlig *or* zur Genüge beweisen.

abuse, 1. [ə'bju:z], *v.t.* mißbrauchen (*one's position etc.*); schlechten Gebrauch machen von, falsch gebrauchen (*one's resources etc.*); beschimpfen, schmähen, heruntermachen (*a p.*); mißhandeln, schänden, sich vergehen an (*Dat.*) (*a woman, child etc.*); täuschen (*a p.'s hopes, confidence etc.*); verraten (*a confidence*). **2.** [ə'bju:s], *s.* der Mißbrauch, Übergriff, Fehlgriff, falscher Gebrauch; Mißstand; die Mißhandlung, Schädigung, Schmähung, Beschimpfung; Schimpfworte (*pl.*), Beleidigungen (*pl.*); Entehrung, Schändung, Notzucht; – ***of authority,*** der Amtsmißbrauch; ***crying –,*** grober Mißbrauch. **abusive** [–siv], *adj.* schimpfend, beleidigend, schmähend; – ***language,*** Schimpfworte (*pl.*). **abusiveness,** *s.* das Beleidigende, grobe Beleidigung, beleidigendes Benehmen.

abut [ə'bʌt], *v.i.* angrenzen, anstoßen, anliegen (***against,*** (***up***)***on,*** an (*Acc.*)); vorspringen, auslaufen. **abutment,** *s.* das Angrenzen (***against,*** (***up***)***on,*** an (*Acc.*)), Aneinanderstoßen; (*Archit.*) der Strebepfeiler, Stützpfeiler, die Strebe, der Kämpfer; das Widerlager (*of a bridge*); – ***arch,*** der Endbogen; – ***beam,*** der Stoßbalken. **abuttal,** *s.* die Angrenzung, Berührung; ***come in –,*** angrenzen, sich berühren. **abutter,** *s.* der Anrainer, Anlieger; angrenzender Besitzer.

abysm [ə'bizm], *s.* (*Poet.*) *see* **abyss. abysmal,** *adj.* abgrundtief, bodenlos, unergründlich; – ***ignorance,*** grenzenlose Unwissenheit. **abyss** [ə'bis], *s.* der Abgrund, Schlund, unendliche *or* bodenlose Tiefe, (*fig.*) die Unendlichkeit, Unergründlichkeit.

Abyssinia [æbi'siniə], *s.* Abessinien (*n.*). **Abyssinian, 1.** *adj.* abessinisch. **2.** *s.* der Abessinier.

acacia [ə'keiʃə], *s.* (*Bot.*) die (falsche) Akazie, gemeine Robinie (*Robinia pseudacacia*).

academic [ækə'demik], **1.** *adj.* akademisch; gelehrt, wissenschaftlich; theoretisch, pedantisch, unpraktisch; – ***dress*** or ***robe(s),*** akademische Tracht; ***a purely – discussion,*** eine Auseinandersetzung ohne praktischen Nutzen, eine rein theoretische Erörterung. **2.** *s.* der Akademiker. **academical,** *adj.*, **academically,** *adv. see* **academic, 1. academician** [əkædə'miʃən], *s.* das Mitglied einer Akademie. **academy** [ə'kædəmi], *s.* die Akademie; literarische *or* gelehrte Gesellschaft, der Gelehrtenverein; höhere Bildungsanstalt, die Hochschule; (*Scots*) höhere Schule, das Gymnasium.

Acadian [ə'keidiən], **Acadic** [ə'kædik], *adj.* akadisch. **Acadis,** *s.* die Akadia.

acanthaceous [ækən'θeiʃəs], **acanthoid** [ə'kænθɔid], **acanthous,** *adj.* (*Bot.*) dornig, stach(e)lig.

acanthus [ə'kænθəs], *s.* (*Bot.*) die Bärenklau; (*Archit.*) Laubverzierung, das Laubwerk, der Akanthus.

acatalectic [əkætə'lektik], *adj.* (*Metr.*) vollzählig, akatalektisch.

acatalepsy [ə'kætəlepsi], *s.* (*Phil.*) die Akataleptik. **acataleptic** [–'leptik], *adj.* unfaßbar, unbegreiflich.

acaudal [ə'kɔ:dəl], *adj.* schwanzlos.

acauline [ə'kɔ:lain], **acaulose, acaulous,** *adj.* stengellos.

accede [ək'si:d], *v.i.* einwilligen (*to,* in (*Acc.*)), beipflichten, beitreten, beistimmen, zustimmen (*Dat.*), eingehen (auf (*Acc.*)); – ***to the throne,*** den Thron besteigen; – ***to an office,*** ein Amt antreten. **accedence,** *s.* die Einwilligung, Zustimmung; der Beitritt, das Antreten.

accelerate [ək'seləreit], **1.** *v.t.* beschleunigen. **2.** *v.i.* schneller gehen, die Geschwindigkeit erhöhen. **acceleration** [–'reiʃən], *s.* die Beschleunigung; – ***due to gravity,*** die Erdbeschleunigung. **accelerator,** *s.* (*Motor.*) das Gaspedal, der Gashebel, (*Chem., Phot.*) Beschleuniger; (*Anat.*) Treibmuskel.

accent, 1. [æk'sent], *v.t. See* **accentuate. 2.** ['æksənt], *s.* der Ton, die Betonung; der Akzent; (*Gram.*) das Tonzeichen; (*of speech*) der Tonfall, die Klangfärbung, (fremde) Aussprache; ***acute –,*** der Akut; ***grave –,*** der Gravis.

accentor [æk'sentə], *s.* (*Orn.*) die Braunelle (*Prunella*); ***hedge –,*** *see* **hedge-sparrow.**

accentuate [æk'sentjueit], *v.t.* betonen, akzentuieren; (*fig.*) hervorheben. **accentuation** [–'eiʃən], *s.* die Betonung, Akzentuation; Tonbezeichnung, (*Mus.*) Akzentuierung.

accept [ək'sept], *v.t.* annehmen, entgegennehmen; sich (*Dat.*) gefallen lassen, gelten lassen; hinnehmen, auf sich nehmen; (*Comm.*) akzeptieren; dafür halten, auffassen; zusagen, (damit) einverstanden sein; (*B.*) gnädiglich ansehen; – ***defeat,*** (eine) Niederlage hinnehmen; – ***the terms,*** die Bedingungen annehmen, auf die Bedingungen eingehen.

acceptability [əkseptə'biliti], *s.* die Annehmlichkeit, Erwünschtheit; Annehmbarkeit, Eignung. **acceptable,** *adj.*, **acceptably,** *adv.* annehmbar (*to,* für); (*Comm.*) akzeptabel; angenehm, willkommen.

acceptance [ək'septəns], *s.* die Annahme; Entgegennahme; günstige Aufnahme, der Empfang (***with,*** bei); die Billigung, Anerkennung, der Beifall; die Einwilligung, Zustimmung, Genehmigung; Annehmbarkeit, das Akzept (*of a bill*); die Geltung (*of a p.*); *see also* **acceptation**; (*Comm.*) ***qualified –,*** bedingtes Akzept; – ***under protest,*** das Interventionsakzept; (*at auctions*) – ***of a bid,*** der Zuschlag; ***find –,*** angenommen werden, Annahme *or* Geltung finden; ***my proposals did not meet with his –,*** er ging nicht auf meine Vorschläge ein.

acceptation [æksep'teiʃən], *s.* anerkannte Bedeutung, allgemein beigelegter *or* angenommener Sinn (*of a word etc.*).

accepted [ək'septid], *adj.* angenommen, gebilligt; allgemein anerkannt; (*Comm.*) anerkannt, akzeptiert; – ***bill,*** das Akzept; – ***before God,*** Gott angenehm. **accepter,** *s.* der Annehmer, Abnehmer, (*Comm.*) Akzeptant. **acceptor,** *s. see* **accepter**; (*Rad.*) – ***circuit,*** der Serienkreis, Saugkreis.

access ['ækses], *s.* der Zugang (*to,* zu), Zutritt (zu, bei); das Gehör, die Audienz (bei); Zugänglichkeit, Umgänglichkeit; (*Med.*) der Anfall, Eintritt (*of disease*); (*fig.*) Ausbruch, die Anwandlung; der Zugangsweg; ***easy of –,*** zugänglich; ***difficult of –,*** schwer zugänglich; – ***hatch*** (*of a tank etc.*), die Einsteigluke; – ***road,*** die Zufahrtsstraße; (*libraries*) ***open*** –, die Freihand.

accessary, *adj., s. See* **accessory.**

accessibility [əksesi'biliti], *s.* die Erreichbarkeit, Zugänglichkeit (***to,*** für). **accessible** [–'sesibl], *adj.* zugänglich (***to,*** für); erreichbar, ersteigbar; verfügbar.

accession [æk'seʃən], *s.* 1. der Zuwachs, die Zunahme, Vermehrung, Ausdehnung, Erweiterung, Vergrößerung, das Hinzukommen (*of property etc.*); – ***to knowledge,*** die Bereicherung *or* Erweiterung des Wissens; 2. (*libraries etc.*) die Akzession, (Neu)anschaffung; 3. Annäherung; der Beitritt, Eintritt, Hinzutritt; – ***to the throne,*** die Thronbesteigung; *see* **accede.**

accessory [æk'sesəri], **1.** *adj.* hinzugefügt, hinzukommend, zusätzlich, akzessorisch; Extra–, Ersatz–; beiläufig, nebensächlich, untergeordnet; Neben–, Bei–, Begleit–, Zusatz–; – ***phenomenon,*** die Begleiterscheinung; ***be*** – ***to,*** beitragen zu. **2.** *s.* 1. der Nebenumstand, die Begleiterscheinung; 2. (*Law*) der Helfershelfer, Mitschuldige(r); – ***after the fact,*** der Hehler; – ***before the fact,*** der Anstifter; 3. *pl.* die Staffage, das Beiwerk; (*Mech.*) Zubehör, Zubehörteile (*pl.*), Zubehörstücke (*pl.*).

accidence ['æksidəns], *s.* die Formenlehre, (*Gram.*) Flexionslehre.

accident ['æksidənt], *s.* 1. der Unfall; Unglücksfall; ***he met with an*** –, ihm stieß ein Unfall zu; 2. der Zufall, die Zufallserscheinung, zufällige Eigenschaft, Nebensache, das Unwesentliche, Zufällige; (*Log. etc.*) die Akzidenz; ***by*** –, zufällig(erweise), von ungefähr; ***it was by mere – that . . .,*** es war der reine Zufall daß . . .

accidental [æksi'dentl], **1.** *adj.* zufällig; unwesentlich, nebensächlich; (*Mus.*) tonartfremd, alteriert; – ***death,*** der Tod durch Unfall; – ***error,*** der Zufälligkeitsfehler; (*Mus.*) – ***sharp,*** das Erhöhungszeichen. **2.** *s.* das Zufällige; Unwesentliche, die Nebensache; (*Mus.*) das Versetzungszeichen. **accidentally,** *adv.* zufällig, durch Zufall, unbeabsichtigt.

accident-prone, *adj.* ***be*** –, ein Unglücksrabe sein.

acclaim [ə'kleim], **1.** *s.* (*Poet.*) *see* **acclamation. 2.** *v.t.* Beifall spenden *or* zurufen (*Dat.*), zujubeln (*Dat.*), zujauchzen (*Dat.*); – ***him king,*** ihn als König begrüßen.

acclamation [æklə'meiʃən], *s.* jauchzender Beifall; das Jubelgeschrei, der Zuruf; ***elected by*** –, durch Zuruf gewählt; ***with*** –, unter Beifall. **acclamatory** [ə'klæmətəri], *adj.* beifällig, Beifalls–, zurufend, zujauchzend.

acclimatization [ə'klaimətai'zeiʃən], *s.* die Akklimatisierung, Eingewöhnung, Einbürgerung. **acclimatize,** *v.t., v.i.* akklimatisieren, eingewöhnen, einbürgern; ***become*** –***d,*** sich akklimatisieren *or* gewöhnen (***to,*** an (*Acc.*)), sich eingewöhnen (in (*Dat.*)).

acclivity [ə'kliviti], *s.* (steile) Anhöhe, die Böschung.

accolade ['ækoleid], *s.* der Ritterschlag; (*fig.*) die Ehrung, Anerkennung; (*Mus.*) Systemklammer, Akkolade.

accommodate [ə'kɔmədeit], *v.t.* 1. in Übereinstimmung bringen (***to,*** mit), angleichen, anpassen (*Dat.*); – ***o.s. to circumstances,*** sich in die Umstände fügen *or* schicken, sich den Verhältnissen anpassen; 2. schlichten, beilegen (*a quarrel*); 3. beherbergen, unterbringen, einquartieren; ***be well*** –***d,*** bequem wohnen, gut untergebracht sein; 4. – ***him with s.th.,*** ihm mit etwas versehen *or* versorgen; ihm mit etwas aushelfen, ihm mit etwas eine Gefälligkeit erweisen. **accommodating,** *adj.* gefällig, zuvorkommend, entgegenkommend.

accommodation [əkɔmə'deiʃən], *s.* 1. die Anpassung (***to,*** an (*Acc.*)); 2. Beilegung, Schlichtung (*of a dispute*); Verständigung, gütlicher Vergleich; 3. der Komfort, die Annehmlichkeit, Bequemlichkeit; 4. der Vorschuß, die Anleihe, das Darleh(e)n, die Aushilfe (*with money*); 5. Unterkunft, das Unterkommen, die Unterbringung, Versorgung; ***have good*** –, gut untergebracht sein, behaglich wohnen; bequem eingerichtet sein (*as a hotel*); – ***for cyclists,*** Unterkunft für Radfahrer; ***find*** –, unterkommen; ***seating*** –, die Sitzgelegenheit; 6. die Gefälligkeit.

accommodation|-address, *s.* die Gefälligkeitsadresse. **--bill,** *s.* der Proformawechsel, das Gefälligkeitsakzept. **--ladder,** *s.* (*Naut.*) die Fallreeptreppe.

accompaniment [ə'kʌmpənimənt], *s.* (*Mus. etc.*) die Begleitung; Begleiterscheinung. **accompanist,** *s.* (*Mus.*) der (die) Begleiter(in).

accompany [ə'kʌmpəni], *v.t., v.i.* begleiten (*also Mus.*); (*of a p.*) geleiten (*Acc.*), Gesellschaft leisten (*Dat.*); (*of a th.*) ***be accompanied by*** or ***with,*** begleitet sein von, verbunden sein mit. **accompanying,** *adj.* begleitend, Begleit–.

accomplice [ə'kʌmplis, ə'kɔmplis], *s.* Mitschuldige(r), der Mittäter, Komplize (***in,*** bei, an (*Dat.*)).

accomplish [ə'kʌmpliʃ], *v.t.* vollenden, vollbringen, durchführen, ausführen, vollführen, zustandebringen; erlangen, erreichen, erfüllen. **accomplished,** *adj.* vorzüglich, vollendet, vollkommen, vollständig ausgeführt; (*of a p.*) gut beschlagen, wohl bewandert, (fein) gebildet; – ***fact,*** vollendete Tatsache. **accomplishment,** *s.* die Ausführung, Durchführung, Vollbringung, Erfüllung, Vollendung; das Eintreffen (*of prophecy etc.*); die Ausbildung, Vervollkommnung, Vollkommenheit; *pl.* vielseitige Ausbildung, Talente (*pl.*), Fertigkeiten (*pl.*), Kenntnisse (*pl.*); ***she has many*** –***s,*** sie ist vielseitig gebildet.

accord [ə'kɔ:d], **1.** *s.* (*of a p.*) die Zustimmung, Beistimmung; (*of a th.*) Übereinstimmung; Eintracht, Einigkeit, der Einklang; (*Mus.*) Akkord; (*Law*) Vergleich, das Abkommen, Übereinkommen; ***with one*** –, einstimmig, einmütig; ***of one's own*** –, aus eigenem Antrieb, freiwillig; ***of its own*** –, von selbst; ***in – with,*** in Einklang mit. **2.** *v.t.* (***him s.th.,*** ihm etwas) gewähren, einräumen, bewilligen, zuteil werden lassen. **3.** *v.i.* harmonieren, im Einklang sein, übereinstimmen (***with,*** mit). **accordance,** *s.* die Übereinstimmung, das Einverständnis; ***be in – with,*** übereinstimmen mit; ***in – with,*** gemäß, zufolge (*Dat.*), laut (*Gen.*). **accordant,** *adj.* im Einklang, übereinstimmend (***with,*** mit); gemäß, entsprechend (*Dat.*); (*Geol.*) gleich–; (*Biol.*) gleichsinnig.

according [ə'kɔ:diŋ], **1.** *conj.* – ***as,*** je nachdem (wie), insofern, in Verhältnis zu, so wie. **2.** *prep.* – ***to,*** gemäß, zufolge, entsprechend, nach (*Dat.*), laut (*Gen.*), mit Rücksicht auf (*Acc.*); – ***to circumstances,*** nach Lage der Dinge, den Umständen gemäß; ***cut one's coat – to one's cloth,*** sich nach der Decke strecken; – ***to Cocker,*** nach Adam Riese; – ***to taste,*** (je) nach Geschmack; – ***to that,*** demnach; – ***to report,*** laut Meldung; – ***to the latest intelligence,*** den letzten Nachrichten zufolge. **accordingly,** *adv.* danach, demnach, demgemäß, folglich, also, somit.

accordion [ə'kɔ:diən], *s.* die Ziehharmonika, das Akkordeon.

accost [ə'kɔst], **1.** *v.t.* anreden, ansprechen, herantreten an (*Acc.*). **2.** *s.* die Begrüßung, Anrede.

accouchement [ə'ku:ʃmã], *s.* die Entbindung, Niederkunft.

accoucheur [æku:'ʃə:], *s.* der Geburtshelfer. **accoucheuse,** *s.* die Hebamme, Geburtshelferin.

account [ə'kaunt], **1.** *s.* 1. die Berechnung, Rechnungslage, der Rechnungsauszug; das Soll und Haben, Einnahmen und Ausgaben (*pl.*), das Konto, die Rechnung, Note; ***bank*** –, das Bankkonto; ***cash*** –, das Kassenkonto; ***current*** –, – ***current,*** laufende Rechnung, das Kontokorrent; ***open*** –, offenes Konto, laufende Rechnung; – ***sales,*** Verkauf auf Rechnung; 2. der Bericht, die Erzählung, Darstellung; Beschreibung; 3. der Rechenschaftsbericht, die Rechenschaft, Verantwortung, der Grund, die Ursache; 4. der Vorteil, Gewinn, Nutzen; die Schätzung, Wertschätzung, Achtung, Wichtigkeit, Bedeutung, Geltung, das Ansehen, der Wert; 5. die Hinsicht, Erwägung, Berücksichtigung; 6. (*St. Exch.*) der Liquidationstermin.

(a) (*after preps.*) ***by all –s,*** wie man hört; (*Comm.*) ***for – and risk,*** auf Rechnung und Gefahr; ***from the latest –s,*** nach den neuesten Berichten; ***of no –,*** wertlos, unbedeutend, ohne Bedeutung; (*Comm.*) ***on –,*** a conto *or* Konto, als Akontozahlung, auf Abschlag; ***payment on –,*** die Abschlagszahlung, Teilzahlung, Anzahlung; ***on his –,*** um seinetwillen *or* seinetwegen; ***on – of,*** wegen, um . . . willen; ***on all –s,*** auf jeden Fall, in jeder Hinsicht; ***on another –,*** zudem; ***on one's own –,*** auf eigne Rechnung, auf eignes Risiko, für *or* aus sich; ***each on his own –,*** jeder für sich; ***on no –,*** keineswegs, unter keinen Umständen, auf keinen Fall; ***on that –,*** darum, deswegen.
(b) (*after verbs*) ***balance an –,*** ein Konto *or* eine Rechnung saldieren *or* ausgleichen; ***call to –,*** zur Rechenschaft ziehen; ***carry to a new –,*** auf neue Rechnung übertragen; ***debit s.th. to his –,*** ihm mit etwas belasten; ***give – of,*** Rechenschaft ablegen über (*Acc.*); ***give an – of,*** Bericht erstatten über (*Acc.*); ***he gave a good – of himself,*** er bewährte sich, er tat sich hervor; (*Poet.*) ***go to one's –,*** vor Gottes Richterstuhl treten; ***have an – with him,*** mit ihm in Rechnung stehen; ***keep –s,*** Buch führen; ***keep an – of,*** Rechnung führen über (*Acc.*); ***leave out of –,*** außer Betracht lassen; ***make out his –,*** ihm die Rechnung ausstellen; ***open an –,*** ein Konto eröffnen; ***overdraw one's –,*** sein Konto überziehen; ***place s.th. to his –,*** ihm etwas in Rechnung stellen, ihm etwas gutschreiben; ***put to –,*** verrechnen; ***render an –,*** eine Rechnung vorlegen; ***– rendered,*** laut eingeschickter Rechnung; ***settle an –,*** eine Rechnung bezahlen *or* begleichen; (*fig.*) ***settle –s with,*** abrechnen mit; ***take a th. into –*** or ***take – of a th.,*** eine S. berücksichtigen *or* beachten, eine S. in Betracht *or* Rechnung ziehen *or* in Anschlag bringen, einer S. Rechnung tragen; ***take no – of,*** nicht beachten; ***turn to –,*** sich (*Dat.*) zunutze machen, (gut) ausnützen.
2. *v.i.* Rechnung *or* Rechenschaft ablegen (***for,*** über (*Acc.*)), sich verantworten (für); die Verantwortung tragen, verantwortlich sein, einstehen (für); genügenden Grund angeben (für), begründen, erklären (*Acc.*); (*coll.*) ***– for,*** erledigen; ***there is no –ing for taste,*** über den Geschmack läßt sich nicht streiten.
3. *v.t.* betrachten *or* ansehen als, halten für; ***– o.s. lucky,*** sich glücklich schätzen.

accountability [əkauntə'biliti], *s.* die Verantwortlichkeit (***to him,*** ihm gegenüber; ***for a th.,*** für etwas). **accountable,** *adj.* 1. verantwortlich, rechenschaftspflichtig (***to him,*** ihm; ***for,*** für); ***be –,*** Rechenschaft schuldig sein; 2. erklärlich.

accountancy [ə'kauntənsi], *s.* die Buchhaltung, Buchführung, das Rechnungswesen. **accountant,** *s.* der Rechnungsführer, Wirtschaftsprüfer. Bücherrevisor, Buchhalter; ***chartered –,*** geprüfter Bücherrevisor; ***–-general,*** der Hauptrechnungsführer, Prokurist. **accounting,** *s.* das Rechnungswesen, die Buchführung.

accouter (*Am.*), **accoutre,** [ə'ku:tə], *v.t.* ausrüsten, ausstatten, ausstaffieren. **accoutrement,** *s.* (*Mil.*) die Ausstaffierung (*usu. pl.*), Ausrüstung.

accredit [ə'kredit], *v.t.* beglaubigen, akkreditieren; bevollmächtigen (***to,*** bei); ***– him with a th.,*** ihm etwas zuschreiben.

accretion [ə'kri:ʃən], *s.* das Wachstum; der Zuwachs, die Zunahme; der Zusatz, die Anfügung, Hinzufügung; (*Med.*) Verwachsung, Adhäsion, das Zusammenwachsen; (*Law*) der Erbzuwachs, Zuwachs durch Akkreszenz.

accrue [ə'kru:], *v.i.* zukommen, zufallen, zufließen, zulaufen, entstehen, erwachsen (***to,*** *Dat.*; ***from,*** aus); ***–d dividend,*** laufende Dividende; ***–d interest,*** aufgelaufene Zinsen.

accumulate [ə'kju:mjuleit], **1.** *v.t.* aufhäufen, anhäufen, anlagern, aufspeichern, ansammeln. **2.** *v.i.* sich anhäufen, sich ansammeln, sich vermehren, sich summieren, zunehmen, auflaufen, mehr werden. **accumulation** [–'leiʃən], *s.* die (An)häufung, Aufhäufung, Anlagerung, Ansammlung; (*Tech.*) Aufspeicherung, Stauung; angehäufte Masse, der Haufe(n). **accumulative** [-lətiv], *adj.* (sich) anhäufend, wachsend. **accumulator,** *s.* der Ansammler, Anhäufer; (*Elec.*) Akkumulator, (*coll.*) Akku; (*Tech.*) Sammler.

accuracy ['ækjurəsi], *s.* die Genauigkeit, Sorgfalt; Richtigkeit, Pünktlichkeit (*in time*); (*of aim*) Zielsicherheit, Treffsicherheit. **accurate,** *adj.* genau, sorgfältig, pünktlich, akkurat; fehlerfrei, exakt, richtig, getreu.

accursed [ə'kə:sid], (*Poet., Am.*) **accurst** [ə'kə:st], *adj.* verflucht, verdammt, verwünscht, (*coll.*) verflixt; verworfen, abscheulich.

accusation [ækju'zeiʃən], *s.* die Anklage, Anschuldigung, Beschuldigung; ***bring an – against him,*** eine Anklage gegen ihn erheben.

accusative [ə'kju:zətiv], *s.* der Akkusativ, Wenfall.

accusatory [ə'kju:zətəri], *adj.* anklagend, Klage–.

accuse [ə'kju:z], **1.** *v.t.* anklagen, anschuldigen (***of,*** wegen); beschuldigen (***of a th.,*** *Gen.*; ***of doing,*** getan zu haben); (*Poet.*) bezichtigen, zeihen (***of,*** *Gen.*). **2.** *v.i.* Anklage erheben. **accused,** *s.* Angeklagte(r), Angeschuldigte(r). **accuser,** *s.* der Ankläger. **accusing,** *adj.* anklagend, vorwurfsvoll.

accustom [ə'kʌstəm], *v.t.* gewöhnen (***to,*** an (*Acc.*)). **accustomed, 1.** *pred.adj.* ***be –,*** pflegen, gewohnt sein (***to doing,*** zu tun); ***get – to,*** sich gewöhnen an (*Acc.*), vertraut werden mit. **2.** *attrib.adj.* gewohnt, gewöhnlich; gebräuchlich, üblich.

ace [eis], *s.* (*Cards*) das As; (*dice*) die Eins; (*Av.*) der Spitzenflieger; (*Sp.*) (*sl.*) die Kanone; ***be within an – of (falling, being killed*** *etc.*), nahe daran sein (zu fallen, getötet zu werden *etc.*), um ein Haar *or* um eine Haaresbreite *or* beinahe (fallen, getötet werden *etc.*).

acephalous [ə'sefələs], *adj.* kopflos, ohne Kopf.

acerbate ['æsəbeit], *v.t.* bitter machen; (*fig.*) verbittern. **acerbity** [ə'sə:biti], *s.* die Herbheit; (*fig.*) Schärfe, Härte, Strenge, Barschheit.

acetate ['æsiteit], *s.* das Azetat, die Essigsäureverbindung, essigsaures Salz; ***aluminium –,*** essigsaure Tonerde. **acetic** [ə'si:tik] *adj.* essigsauer; ***–-acid,*** die Essigsäure. **acetify** [ə'setifai], **1.** *v.t.* sauer machen, (an)säuern, in Essig verwandeln. **2.** *v.i.* sauer werden, Essig bilden. **acetone** ['æsitoun], *s.* das Azeton, der Essiggeist. **acetose, acetous,** *adj.* essigsauer; ***– fermentation,*** die Essiggärung. **acetylene** [ə'setili:n], *s.* das Azetylen; ***– lamp,*** die Karbidlampe.

ache [eik], **1.** *s.* der Schmerz, das Weh. **2.** *v.i.* schmerzen, weh(e) tun; ***my head –s,*** ich habe Kopfweh *or* Kopfschmerzen; ***my heart –s for her,*** ich sehne mich schmerzlich *or* ich verlange schmerzlich nach ihr.

achievable [ə'tʃi:vəbl], *adj.* erreichbar, ausführbar. **achieve,** *v.t.* ausführen, zustandebringen, vollenden, vollbringen, erledigen, leisten; gewinnen, erlangen, erreichen, erzielen, erringen (*a goal etc.*). **achievement,** *s.* 1. die Ausführung, Durchführung, Vollendung; das vollendete Werk, die Leistung, Errungenschaft; Heldentat; 2. (*Her.*) das Wappenschild.

Achilles [ə'kili:z], *s.* Achill (*m.*); ***– heel,*** die Achillesferse; ***– tendon,*** die Achillessehne.

aching ['eikiŋ], **1.** *adj.* schmerzhaft, schmerzlich. **2.** *s.* der Schmerz, das Weh.

achromatic [ækro'mætik], *adj.* achromatisch, farblos.

achy ['eiki], *adj.* (*coll.*) *see* **aching, 1.**

acicular [ə'sikjulə], *adj.* (*Bot.*) nadelförmig, (*Zool.*) stachelborstig.

acid ['æsid], **1.** *adj.* sauer, herb, scharf; (*fig.*) bitter; bissig, beißend; (*Chem.*) Säure–, säurehaltig; ***– drops,*** saure Bonbons. **2.** *s.* die Säure; ***the – test,*** (*Chem.*) die Scheideprobe; (*fig.*) der Prüfstein, die Feuerprobe, Prüfung auf Herz und Nieren. **acidify** [ə'sidifai], **1.** *v.t.* sauer machen, (an)säuern, in Säure verwandeln. **2.** *v.i.* sauer werden. **acidimeter** [-'dimətə], *s.* der Säuremesser. **acidity** [ə'siditi], *s.* die Schärfe, Herbheit; der Säuregrad, Säuregehalt; (*Med.*) die Überazidität, Übersäuerung, Magensäure. **acidness,** *s.* die Schärfe, Herbheit. **acidosis** [-'dousis], *s.* (*Med.*) die Überazidität, Übersäuerung. **acidulate** [ə'sidjuleit], *v.t.* (an)säuern. **acidulous,** *adj.* säuerlich; – ***water*** der Sauerbrunnen.

ack-ack [æk'æk], *s., attrib.adj.* (*coll.*) die Flak; Flak–.

acknowledge [ək'nɔlidʒ], *v.t.* anerkennen; zugeben, einräumen, zugestehen, eingestehen, bestätigen; dankbar anerkennen, erkenntlich sein für; – ***the receipt of a letter,*** den (richtigen) Empfang eines Briefes bestätigen; – ***the receipt of money,*** den Empfang des Geldes bescheinigen *or* quittieren. **acknowledged,** *adj.* anerkannt, wohlbekannt, bewährt. **acknowledg(e)ment,** *s.* die Anerkennung; das Bekenntnis, Zugeständnis, Eingeständnis; die Bestätigung, Empfangsbescheinigung, Quittung, der Empfangsschein; (lobende) Anerkennung, die Erkenntlichkeit.

acme ['ækmi], *s.* der Gipfel, Höhepunkt, die Spitze, höchste Vollkommenheit.

acne ['ækni], *s.* (*Med*). der Finnenausschlag, die Akne.

acolyte ['ækolait], *s.* (*Eccl.*) der Altardiener, Meßgehilfe; (*Astr.*) Begleitstern; (*fig.*) Gefährte, Gehilfe.

aconite ['ækonait], *s.* (*Bot.*) der Eisenhut; (*Chem.*) das Akonit; (*Poet.*) tödliches Gift.

acorn ['eikɔ:n], *s.* die Eichel, Ecker.

acotyledon [əkɔti'li:dən], *s.* (*Bot.*) der Nacktkeimer, die Kryptogame, Akotyledone.

acoustic(al) [ə'ku:stik(əl)], *adj.* akustisch; – ***effect,*** die Schallwirkung, Klangwirkung; – ***mine,*** die Geräuschmine; – ***nerve,*** der Gehörnerv; – ***sounder,*** das Echolot. **acoustically,** *adv.* akustisch. **acoustics,** *pl.* (*sing.constr.*) die Akustik, Lehre vom Schall; (*pl.constr.*) die Akustik (*of a building*).

acquaint [ə'kweint], *v.t.* bekannt *or* vertraut machen (***with,*** mit), in Kenntnis setzen (von); mitteilen (***him,*** ihm; ***with,*** *Acc.*), berichten (von); ***be –ed with s.th.,*** etwas kennen; ***become –ed with,*** kennenlernen; – ***o.s. with*** . . ., sich mit . . . bekannt machen; ***we are –ed,*** wir sind Bekannte, wir kennen uns. **acquaintance,** *s.* die Bekanntschaft; Kenntnis (***with,*** von), das Vertrautsein (mit); (*of a p.*) Bekannte(r), die Bekanntschaft, *pl.* der Bekanntenkreis; ***on closer –,*** bei näherer Bekanntschaft; ***make his –,*** Bekanntschaft mit ihm machen; ***have – with a th.,*** Kenntnis von einer S. haben; ***an – of mine,*** eine(r) meiner Bekannten; ***keep up*** (***an***) – ***with,*** Umgang haben mit. **acquaintanceship,** *s.* die Bekanntschaft.

acquiesce [ækwi'es], *v.i.* ruhig hinnehmen; sich (*Dat.*) gefallen lassen (*in, Acc.*), sich beruhigen (bei), einwilligen, sich fügen *or* schicken (in (*Acc.*)). **acquiescence,** *s.* die Ergebung, Einwilligung (*in,* in (*Acc.*)), Beruhigung (bei). **acquiescent,** *adj.* nachgiebig, geduldig, ergeben, fügsam.

acquirable [ə'kwaiərəbl], *adj.* erlangbar, erreichbar, erwerbbar. **acquire** *v.t.* erlangen, gewinnen, bekommen, erreichen, an sich bringen, erwerben; (er)lernen; – ***a taste for,*** Geschmack finden an (*Dat.*); ***–d characteristics,*** erworbene Eigenschaften; ***–d taste,*** anerzogener Geschmack. **acquirement,** *s.* die Erwerbung, Erlangung; das Erworbene, Angeeignete; erworbene Fertigkeit *or* Fähigkeit.

acquisition [ækwi'ziʃən], *s.* die Erwerbung; Erlernung; der Erwerb, das Erworbene, die Errungenschaft, Anschaffung, Bereicherung, Eroberung. **acquisitive** [ə'kwizitiv], *adj.* gewinnsüchtig, erwerbslustig; habsüchtig, raubgierig. **acquisitiveness,** *s.* der Erwerbstrieb, Erwerbssinn, die Gewinnsucht.

acquit [ə'kwit], *v.t.* freisprechen, lossprechen, entlasten (*a p.*) (*of,* von); abzahlen, abtragen, quittieren (*a debt*); – ***o.s.,*** erfüllen (*of, Acc.*), sich entledigen (*Gen.*); – ***o.s. well,*** sich gut halten, seine S. gut machen. **acquittal,** *s.* 1. die Lossprechung, Freisprechung, der Freispruch, die Entlassung; 2. Abtragung, Erfüllung, Erledigung (*of duty etc.*). **acquittance,** *s.* die Bezahlung, Begleichung, Abtragung; Tilgung, Erfüllung; Empfangsbescheinigung, Empfangsbestätigung, Quittung.

Acre ['eikə], *s.* (*Geog.*) Akka (*n.*); (*Hist.*) Akko(n) (*n.*).

acre, *s.* der Morgen Landes (= *4840 Quadrat-Yards* or *0·40467 Hektar*); ***God's –,*** der Gottesacker. **acreage** [–ridʒ], *s.* der Flächeninhalt; die Anbaufläche.

acrid ['ækrid], *adj.* scharf, beißend, ätzend, herb, bissig.

acrimonious [ækri'mouniəs], *adj.* (*fig.*) scharf, beißend, bitter, verletzend. **acrimony** ['ækriməni], *s.* die Bitterkeit, Schärfe, Bissigkeit.

acrobat ['ækrəbæt], *s.* der Akrobat, Seiltänzer. **acrobatic** [–'bætik], *adj.* akrobatisch. **acrobatics,** *pl.* die Akrobatik, Kunststücke (*pl.*).

acronym ['ækrənim], *s.* das Akronym.

across [ə'krɔs], **1.** *adv.* kreuzweise, (quer) hinüber, (quer) herüber. **2.** *prep.* (quer) durch, (quer) über (*Acc.*), mitten durch; jenseits (*Gen.*), über (*Dat.*); – ***country,*** querfeldein; ***a short cut – the fields,*** ein Richtweg durch die Felder; ***I have come – this old book,*** ich bin auf dieses alte Buch gestoßen; ***it flashed – my mind,*** es fiel mir plötzlich ein; (*coll.*) ***put –,*** durchsetzen (*a plan etc.*); (*coll.*) ***put s.th. – to him,*** ihm etwas begreiflich *or* verständlich machen, ihm etwas klarmachen; (*sl.*) ***put it – him,*** ihn hereinlegen *or* beschummeln; (*coll.*) ***get –,*** verstanden werden (*of ideas*).

acrostic [ə'krɔstik], *s.* das Akrostichon.

act [ækt], **1.** *s.* 1. die Handlung, Tat; Leistung, Ausführung; das Vorgehen, Eingreifen, Handeln, der Schritt; ***the Acts*** (***of the Apostles***), die Apostelgeschichte; – ***of God,*** höhere Gewalt, das Naturereignis; ***in the – of doing,*** im Begriff zu tun; ***in the*** (***very***) ***–,*** auf frischer Tat; (*coll.*) ***he puts on his poverty –,*** er spielt sich als Bettler auf, er macht sein Theater als Verarmter; 2. (*Theat.*) der Aufzug, Akt; ***one-– play,*** der Einakter; 3. (*Law*) das Statut, Gesetz, der Beschluß, Erlaß, die Verordnung, Verfügung, Resolution; Akte, Urkunde; das Aktenstück; – ***of Parliament,*** die Parliamentsakte, der Parlamentsbeschluß. **2.** *v.t.* (*Theat.*) – ***a part,*** eine Rolle spielen *or* darstellen; (*fig.*) sich verstellen; – ***the part of,*** fungieren als; – ***a play,*** ein Stück aufführen. **3.** *v.i.* (*of a th.*) wirken, wirksam *or* tätig sein, dienen, fungieren, funktionieren; (*of a p.*) sich betragen *or* verhalten *or* benehmen; handeln, wirken, agieren, (*Theat.*) auftreten; (ein)wirken, Einfluß haben (***on,*** auf (*Acc.*)); spielen; – ***cautiously,*** vorsichtig zu Werke gehen; ***the play –s well,*** das Stück läßt sich gut spielen *or* aufführen; – ***well by him,*** an ihm gut handeln; – ***upon,*** sich richten nach; – ***up to,*** handeln gemäß *or* nach, entsprechen (*Dat.*).

acting ['æktiŋ], **1.** *s.* das Handeln, Tun; (*Theat.*) Spiel, die Darstellung, Schauspielkunst; (*fig.*) Verstellung. **2.** *adj.* handelnd, wirkend, tätig; stellvertretend, diensttuend, amtierend, geschäftsführend; interimistisch; ***self-–,*** selbstwirkend, selbsttätig; – ***copy,*** das Bühnenmanuskript; – ***manager,*** stellvertretender Direktor.

actinic [æk'tinik], *adj.* aktinisch, chemisch wirksam; – ***power of light,*** chemische Wirksamkeit des Lichts; – ***screen,*** der Leuchtschirm; – ***strength,*** der Helligkeitswert. **actinism** ['æktinizm], *s.* die (Licht)strahlenwirkung, Aktinität. **actinometer** [–'nɔmitə], *s.* der Strahlenmesser.

action ['ækʃən], *s.* die Tätigkeit, Bewegung; das Unternehmen, die Handlung, Tat; der Vorgang, Prozeß; die Wirkung, Wirksamkeit, wirkende Kraft, der Einfluß; das Funktionieren; (*Chem. etc.*) die Einwirkung; der Gang, die Haltung, Gangart (*of a horse*); Handlung (*of a play etc.*); (*Law*) der Rechtshandel, das Rechtsverfahren, der Prozeß, die Klage; (*Mil.*) das Treffen, Gefecht, die Kampfhandlung, Aktion, der Einsatz; (*Av.*) Feindflug; (*Mech.*) das Werk, der Mechanismus, die Mechanik, (*of an organ*) Traktur; ***double –,*** doppelte Wirkung; ***bring an – against,*** eine Klage anstrengen gegen; ***an – for debt,*** eine Schuldklage; ***be in –,*** in Bewegung *or* tätig sein, wirken; (*Mech.*) in *or* im Betrieb sein; (*Mech.*) ***put*** or ***set in –,*** in Betrieb *or* Gang setzen; ***put*** (*project etc.*) ***into –,***

in die Tat setzen; ***put*** *(troops etc.)* ***into*** **–**, einsetzen; ***ready for*** **–**, kampfbereit, einsatzbereit; *(Naut.)* klar zum Gefecht; ***readiness for*** **–**, die Einsatzbereitschaft; ***fight an*** **–**, eine Schlacht liefern; ***go into*** **–**, eingreifen, ins Gefecht kommen; ***killed in*** **–**, gefallen; ***man of*** **–**, Mann der Tat; *(Mech.)* ***out of*** **–**, außer Betrieb; *(Mil.)* ***put out of*** **–**, außer Gefecht setzen, kampfunfähig machen; **–** ***station,*** die Gefechtsstation; *(Naut.)* **–** ***stations!*** klar zum Gefecht! ***take*** **–** ***against,*** vorgehen gegen.

actionable ['ækʃənəbl], *adj.* *(of a p.)* verklagbar, *(of a deed)* gerichtlich verfolgbar.

activate ['æktiveit], *v.t.* aktivieren; *(Mech.)* in Betrieb setzen, *(Chem.)* radioaktiv machen, *(Mil.)* scharf machen *(a fuse).* **activation** [–'veiʃən], *s.* die Aktivierung, Erregung, Anregung.

active ['æktiv], *adj.* tätig; emsig, rührig, geschäftig; wirkend, wirksam, aktiv; behend, flink, mobil, energisch, lebhaft; *(Comm.)* produktiv, Aktiv–; belebt, rege, gesucht; zinstragend; *(Mil.)* aktiv; *(Gram.)* aktiv, transitiv; **–** ***bonds,*** festverzinsliche Obligationen; **–** ***debts,*** die Außenstände; ***an*** **–** ***life,*** ein tätiges Leben; **–** ***oxygen,*** das Ozon; ***an*** **–** ***part in,*** aktive Teilnahme an *(Dat.)*; **–** ***partner,*** tätiger Teilhaber; ***on*** **–** ***service,*** im aktiven Dienst; **–** ***service allowance,*** die Frontzulage; **–** ***service pay,*** der Wehrsold; *(Gram.)* **–** ***voice,*** das Aktiv(um).

activity [æk'tiviti], *s.* die Tätigkeit, Aktivität, Wirksamkeit; Behendigkeit, Lebhaftigkeit, Beweglichkeit; ***in full*** **–**, in vollem Gange *or* Betrieb; ***sphere of*** **–**, der Wirkungskreis, Tätigkeitsbereich.

actor ['æktə], *s.* der Täter, handelnde Person; *(Theat.)* der Schauspieler. **actor-manager,** *s.* Schauspieler und Theaterdirektor. **actress,** *s.* die Schauspielerin.

actual ['æktjuəl], **1.** *adj.* wirklich (vorhanden), tatsächlich, eigentlich, real; jetzig, gegenwärtig, vorliegend, aktuell, zeitgemäß, zeitnah; *(Comm.)* Effektiv–; **–** ***price,*** der Tagespreis; **–** ***receipts,*** Effektiveinnahmen; **–** ***state of affairs,*** die wirkliche Sachlage; *(Mil.)* **–** ***strength,*** die Iststärke, der Iststand; **–** ***value,*** der Realwert. **2.** *s.* das Wirkliche, die Wirklichkeit; *pl.* *(Comm.)* Effektiveinnahmen. **actuality** [–'æliti], *s.* die Wirklichkeit, Tatsächlichkeit; Wirklichkeitstreue, der Realismus; *pl.* Tatsachen, tatsächliche Umstände, Gegebenheiten. **actualization** [-lai'zeiʃən], *s.* die Verwirklichung. **actualize,** *v.t.* verwirklichen; realistisch darstellen. **actually,** *adv.* wirklich, tatsächlich, in der Tat, eigentlich, sogar.

actuarial [æktju'ɛəriəl], *adj.* versicherungsstatistisch; **–** ***rate,*** die Tafelziffer. **actuary** ['æktjuəri], *s.* der Versicherungsstatistiker; *(obs.)* Gerichtsschreiber, Aktuar, Urkundsbeamte(r).

actuate ['æktjueit], *v.t.* in Bewegung setzen, in Gang bringen, antreiben; **–*****d by the purest motives,*** von den reinsten Absichten getragen *or* geleitet. **actuation** [–'eiʃən], *s.* der Antrieb, Anstoß, die Betätigung, das Ingangsetzen.

acuity [ə'kju:iti], *s.* *(fig.)* die Schärfe.

acumen [ə'kju:mən, 'ækjumən], *s.* der Scharfsinn.

acupuncture ['ækjupʌŋktʃə], *s.* *(Med.)* die Nadelpunktierung, Akupunktur.

acute [ə'kju:t], *adj.* spitz(ig) zugespitzt, *(Math.)* spitz(wink(e)lig); scharf, stechend, heftig *(of pain)*; scharf, fein, klar *(of the senses)*; scharfsinnig, klug; kritisch, brennend, bedenklich, akut; **–** ***accent,*** der Akut; **–** ***angle,*** spitzer Winkel; **–** ***disease,*** heftige *or* akute Krankheit; **–** ***shortage,*** kritischer Mangel. **acuteness,** *s.* die Spitze, Schärfe; Klugheit, der Scharfsinn, die Schlauheit, Verschmitztheit, Schlagfertigkeit; Feinheit *(of senses),* Heftigkeit *(of a disease).*

ad [æd], *s.* *(sl.)* die Reklame, Annonce, Anzeige.

adage ['ædidʒ], *s.* das Sprichwort.

Adam ['ædəm], *s.* Adam *(m.)*; *(coll.)* ***I don't know him from*** **–**, ich kenne ihn überhaupt nicht; **–*****'s apple,*** der Adamsapfel.

adamant ['ædəmənt], **1.** *s.* sehr harter Stein; *(Poet.)* außerordentliche Härte. **2.** *adj.* unerbittlich, resolut, unnachgiebig, unerschütterlich, unverrückbar, felsenfest. **adamantine** [-'mæntain], *adj.* diamantenhart, demanten; *(fig.)* *see* **adamant, 2.**

adapt [ə'dæpt], *v.t.* anpassen *(to, Dat.)*, richten (nach), umstellen (auf *(Acc.)*), zurechtmachen; *(Theat.)* bearbeiten *(**from,** nach)*; **–** ***o.s. to circumstances,*** sich den Verhältnissen anpassen *or* nach den Verhältnissen richten. **adaptability** [–ə'biliti], *s.* die Anwendbarkeit (***to,*** auf *(Acc.)*), Anpassungsfähigkeit (an *(Acc.)*), Geeignetheit (zu, für). **adaptable,** *adj.* anwendbar (***to,*** auf *(Acc)*), anpassungsfähig (an *(Acc.)*), geeignet (zu, für); geschmeidig, biegsam. **adaptation** [ædæp'teiʃən], *s.* die Anwendung (***to,*** auf *(Acc.)*), Anpassung (an *(Acc.)*), Herrichtung, Umarbeitung, Bearbeitung. **adapter,** *s.* *(Mech.)* das Paßstück, Anschlußstück, Zusatzgerät, der Stutzen, die Verbindungsröhre; *(Phot.)* (Filmpack)kassette; *(Theat.)* der Bearbeiter; *(Elec.)* der Zwischenstecker, die Steckhülse. **adaption,** *s.* die Anpassung, Angleichung. **adaptive,** *adj.* anpassungsfähig. **adaptiveness,** *s.* die Anpassungsfähigkeit.

add [æd], **1.** *v.t.* hinzufügen, hinzurechnen, hinzuzählen, hinzusetzen (***to,*** zu), zusetzen, aufrechnen, aufschlagen (auf *(Acc.)*), einschließen, zuschließen, nachsetzen *(Dat.)*; *(Math.)* **–** (***up*** or ***together***), addieren, zusammenzählen; **–** ***in,*** einschließen, hinzurechnen; *(fig.)* **–** ***fuel to the fire,*** Öl ins Feuer gießen; **–** ***insult to injury,*** die schlimme Lage noch verschlimmern; **–** ***the interest to the capital,*** die Zinsen zum Kapital schlagen; **–*****ed to this,*** hinzu *or* dazu kommt noch, zuzüglich; **–*****ed to which,*** wozu kommt noch. **2.** *v.i.* **–** ***to,*** hinzukommen zu, vermehren; **–** ***up to,*** zusammenzählen auf *(Acc.)*; aufgehen *or* ausgehen *or* summieren *or* kommen auf *(Acc.)*; *(coll.)* ***that*** **–*****s up,*** das stimmt.

addendum [ə'dendəm], *s.* *(pl.* **-da**) der Zusatz, Anhang, Nachhang, Nachtrag, die Hinzufügung; *(Tech.)* **–** ***circle,*** der Kopfkreis *(of gear-wheel).*

adder ['ædə], *s.* die Natter, gemeine Kreuzotter *(Vipera berus).*

addict, 1. [ə'dikt], *v.t.* **–** ***o.s.,*** sich ergeben *or* hingeben *or* überlassen *(to, Dat.)*. **2.** ['ædikt], *s.* Süchtige(r). **addicted** [ə'diktid], *adj.* geneigt, zugetan, ergeben *(to, Dat.)*, –süchtig. **addiction** [–'dikʃən], *s.* die Hingabe (***to,*** an *(Acc.)*), Ergebung, Sucht; Neigung, der Hang (zu).

adding-machine ['ædiŋ–], *s.* die Rechenmaschine, Addiermaschine, Additionsmaschine.

addition [ə'diʃən], *s.* die Beifügung, Hinzusetzung, Hinzufügung, Beimengung; der Zusatz, Anhang, die Zugabe, Zutat; Vermehrung, der Zuwachs; *(Math.)* die Zusammenzählung, Addition, Addierung; **–** ***sign,*** das Pluszeichen; ***in*** **–** (***to this***), noch dazu, außerdem.

additional [ə'diʃənəl], *adj.* hinzugekommen, hinzukommend, beigefügt; nachträglich, Nach–, zusätzlich, Zusatz–, ergänzend; weiter; Mehr–, Auf–; **–** ***charge,*** der Zuschlag, Aufschlag; **–** ***charges,*** Mehrkosten; **–** ***clause,*** die Zusatzklausel; **–** ***duty,*** der Steuerzuschlag; **–** ***payment,*** die Nachzahlung. **additionally,** *adv.* als Zusatz, in verstärktem Maße, außerdem, noch dazu.

additive ['æditiv], **1.** *adj.* vermehrend, steigernd, hinzufügend. **2.** *s.* der Zusatz, die Zutat.

addle [ædl], **1.** *v.t.* unfruchtbar machen; *(fig.)* verwirren *(the brains).* **2.** *v.i.* faul werden; **–*****d egg,*** faules Ei, das Windei. **addle|-brained, –-pated,** *adj.* dumm, hohlköpfig.

address [ə'dres], **1.** *s.* 1. die Anrede, Ansprache, Rede, der Vortrag; die Denkschrift, Dankschrift, Eingabe; 2. Anschrift, Aufschrift, Adresse *(on a letter)*; ***in case of change of*** **–**, falls verzogen; 3. Gewandtheit, das Geschick; 4. Benehmen, die Haltung, Manieren *(pl.)*; ***pay one's*** **–*****es to a lady,*** einer Dame den Hof machen, um eine Dame anhalten. **2.** *v.t.* anreden, ansprechen *(a p.)*, adressieren, überschreiben *(a letter)*; richten *(words)* (***to,*** an *(Acc.)*); **–** ***a meeting,*** in *or* zu einer Versammlung sprechen, an eine Versammlung eine Ansprache halten, vor einer Versammlung eine Rede halten; *(coll.)* **–** ***the ball,*** den Ball anspielen *or* ansprechen *(golf).* **3.** *v.r.* sich wenden (*to*, an (*Acc.*)); – *o.s. to* (*a task etc.*), sich zu (einer Aufgabe *etc.*) anschicken *or* vorbereiten.

addressee [ædre'si:], *s.* der (die) Empfänger(in), Adressat(in).

adduce [ə'dju:s], *v.t.* anführen, beibringen, erbringen, sich berufen auf (*Acc.*), zitieren (*proofs, witnesses etc.*). **adducible,** *adj.* anführbar.

adductor [ə'dʌktə], *s.* der Anziehmuskel.

Adelaide ['ædəleid], *s.* Adelheid (*f.*).

ademption [ə'dempʃən], *s.* (*Law*) die Entziehung, Wegnahme.

adenoid ['ædənɔid], *s.* (*usu. pl.*) (*Med.*) Wucherungen (*pl.*), Polypen (in der Nase).

adept, 1. [ə'dept], *adj.* erfahren; geschickt; eingeweiht (*in*, in (*Dat.*)). **2.** ['ædept], *s.* Eingeweihte(r), der Kenner, Könner, Meister; (*obs.*) Goldmacher, Alchimist.

adequacy ['ædikwəsi], *s.* die Zulänglichkeit, Angemessenheit, Zweckdienlichkeit, Gemäßheit.

adequate ['ædikwit], *adj.* angemessen, genügend, hinlänglich, adäquat, ausreichend, hinreichend, zureichend (*to*, für), entsprechend (*Dat.*). **adequateness,** *s. See* **adequacy.**

adhere [əd'hiə], *v.i.* (an)kleben, (an)haften (*to*, an (*Dat.*)); (*Med.*) anhaften (*Dat.*), anwachsen (an (*Acc.*)), verwachsen sein (mit); (*fig.*) sich (an)klammern *or* (an)hängen (an (*Acc.*)), bleiben (bei), treu bleiben (*Dat.*); sich halten (zu), sich anschließen (*Dat. or* an (*Acc.*)), zugetan sein (*Dat.*); – ***to an opinion,*** bei einer Meinung bleiben, an einer Ansicht festhalten; – ***to the terms,*** die Vorschriften einhalten. **adherence,** *s.* das Festhalten; Anhaften, Hängenbleiben (*to*, an (*Dat.*)), Beharren (bei), die Anhänglichkeit (*to*, an (*Dat.*)). **adherent, 1.** *adj.* anhaftend, anklebend, sich anklammernd, festhaltend; (*fig.*) (fest) verbunden (mit), anhänglich; (*Med.*) angewachsen. **2.** *s.* der (die) Anhänger(in).

adhesion [əd'hi:ʒən], *s.* das Anhaften, Anhängen, Ankleben; die Adhäsion, Adhäsionskraft, das Haftvermögen, die Haftfestigkeit, Bindefestigkeit; (*Med.*) das Zusammenwachsen, die Verwachsung; (*fig.*) Anhänglichkeit, das Festhalten (*to*, an (*Dat.*)), der Beitritt; ***the – to an opinion,*** das Festhalten an einer Meinung; ***give one's – to a th.,*** sich für etwas erklären.

adhesive [əd'hi:siv], **1.** *adj.* anhaftend, klebend, klebrig, Kleb(e)–, Heft–, Haft–; – ***envelope,*** gummierter Briefumschlag; – ***force,*** die Klebkraft, Adhäsionskraft; – ***plaster,*** das Heftpflaster. **2.** *s.* das Bindemittel, der Klebstoff. **adhesiveness,** *s.* die Klebrigkeit, Adhäsion, das Haftvermögen; Anhaften.

ad hoc ['æd'hɔk], **1.** *adj.* Sonder–, besonder, speziell. **2.** *adv.* nur für diesen (besonderen) Zweck.

adieu [ə'dju:], **1.** *int.* lebewohl! **2.** *s.* (*pl.* **-s** *or* **-x** [–z]) das Lebewohl; ***bid*** or ***say –, make one's –x,*** Abschied nehmen, sich verabschieden.

Adige ['ɑ:didʒi], *s.* die Etsch.

adipose ['ædipous], *adj.* fett, fettig, fetthaltig, talgig, feist; – ***tissue,*** das Fettgewebe.

adit ['ædit], *s.* der Zugang, (*Min.*) Stollen.

adjacency [ə'dʒeisənsi], *s.* das Angrenzen, Naheliegen; Anliegende, Angrenzende, Anstoßende, unmittelbare Umgebung. **adjacent,** *adj.* anliegend, angrenzend, anschließend, anstoßend (*to*, an (*Acc.*)), naheliegend, benachbart; – ***angles,*** Nebenwinkel.

adjectival [ædʒək'taivəl], *adj.* adjektivisch. **adjective** ['ædʒiktiv], **1.** *s.* das Eigenschaftswort, Adjektiv. **2.** *adj.* adjektivisch.

adjoin [ə'dʒɔin], **1.** *v.i.* an(einander)grenzen, anliegen. **2.** *v.t.* (an)grenzen *or* (an)stoßen an (*Acc.*); beifügen (*to*, *Dat.*), anfügen (an (*Acc.*)), hinzufügen (zu). **adjoining,** *adj.* Neben–, anstoßend, angrenzend, benachbart; (*Math.*) ***be –,*** anliegen.

adjourn [ə'dʒə:n], **1.** *v.t.* vertagen, aufschieben. **2.** *v.i.* sich vertagen, die Sitzung vertagen; den Sitzungsort verlegen (*to*, nach). **adjournment,** *s.* die Vertagung, Verschiebung, der Aufschub.

adjudge [ə'dʒʌdʒ], *v.t.* entscheiden; (gerichtlich) zuerkennen, zusprechen; erklären; – ***him (to be) guilty,*** ihn für schuldig erklären; ***the prize was –d to the victor,*** der Preis wurde dem Sieger zuerkannt *or* zugesprochen.

adjudicate [ə'dʒu:dikeit], **1.** *v.t.* gerichtlich erklären (*to be*, für), (zu Recht) erkennen, zuerkennen (als). **2.** *v.i.* entscheiden, urteilen (*on*, über (*Acc.*)); als Schiedsrichter fungieren (*at*, bei). **adjudication** [–'keiʃən], *s.* die Zuerkennung, Zusprechung; (richterliche) Entscheidung, der Entscheid, Rechtsspruch, das Urteil. **adjudicator,** *s.* der Schiedsrichter.

adjunct ['ædʒʌŋkt], *s.* der Zusatz, Anhang, die Beigabe; das Anhängsel; zufällige Eigenschaft, der Nebenumstand; (*Gram.*) das Attribut; der (Amts)gehilfe, Beigeordnete(r), Adjunkt.

adjuration [ædʒu'reiʃən], *s.* die Beschwörung, inständige Bitte; Beschwörungsformel. **adjure** [ə'dʒuə], *v.t.* beschwören, inständig bitten.

adjust [ə'dʒʌst], *v.t.* zurechtmachen, ordnen; (*Tech.*) (richtig) einstellen, regulieren, regeln; anpassen, angleichen (*to*, *Dat. or* an (*Acc.*)); justieren; berichtigen, begleichen (*accounts*); ausgleichen, beseitigen, beilegen, schlichten (*disputes*); (*Naut.*) – ***the average,*** die Havarie berechnen. **adjustable,** *adj.* verschiebbar, regulierbar, einstellbar, verstellbar; *–**pitch airscrew,*** die Einstelluftschraube. **adjuster,** *s.* (*Insur.*) Feststellungsbeamte(r). **adjusting,** *adj.* (Ein)stell–, Justier–, Richt–. **adjustment,** *s.* (richtige) Anordnung, die Einrichtung, Einstellung; Ordnung, Anpassung, Angleichung, Abrichtung, Eichung, Justierung, Berichtigung; der Ausgleich, die Schlichtung, Beilegung (*of a quarrel*), (*Insur.*) Schadensfestsetzung, Regelung des Anspruchs; (*Naut.*) – ***of average,*** die Havarieberechnung; (*Artil.*) ***bracket –,*** das Gabelschießen; (*Artil.*) – ***of fire,*** das Einschießen.

adjutancy ['ædʒutənsi], *s.* die Adjutantur, Adjutantenstelle. **adjutant,** *s.* der Adjutant.

adjuvant ['ædʒuvənt], *adj.* hilfreich, förderlich, behilflich.

ad lib [æd'lib], *adv.* (*coll.*) nach Belieben. **ad-lib,** *v.t., v.i.* (*coll.*) extemporieren, improvisieren.

ad-man ['ædmæn], *s.* (*sl.*) der Werbefachmann.

admass ['ædmæs], *s.* (*coll.*) das Massenpublikum.

admeasurement [æd'meʒəmənt], *s.* (*Law*) die Zumessung; das Maß, der Umfang; das Messen, die Abmessung; (*Naut.*) ***bill of –,*** der Meßbrief.

administer [əd'ministə], **1.** *v.t.* verwalten (*city etc.*), ausüben, wahrnehmen (*affairs*), verabreichen (*medicine, blows*), leisten (*help*), abnehmen (*an oath*), spenden (*the sacraments*); – ***an oath to him,*** ihn vereidigen; – ***the law,*** Recht sprechen. **2.** *v.i.* behilflich sein; dienen; als Administrator walten. **administration** [–'treiʃən], *s.* die Verwaltung, Verwaltungsbehörde; Regierung, das Ministerium; die Austeilung, Darreichung, Spendung; Verabreichung (*of medicine*), Abnahme (*of an oath*); ***local –,*** der Ortsvorstand. **administrative** [–trativ], *adj.* verwaltend; administrativ; – ***body,*** die Behörde; – ***district,*** der Regierungsbezirk; – ***difficulties,*** Verwaltungsschwierigkeiten. **administrator** [–treitə], *s.* der Verwalter, Verweser; Spender; Verwaltungsbeamte(r), Administrator; Nachlaßverwalter, Testamentsvollstrecker. **administratrix,** *s.* die Verwalterin; Testamentsvollstreckerin.

admirable ['ædmərəbl], *adj.* bewunderungswürdig, bewundernswert, vortrefflich, herrlich. **admirableness,** *s.* die Trefflichkeit.

admiral ['ædmərəl], *s.* 1. der Admiral; – ***of the fleet,*** der Großadmiral; 2. (*Ent.*) Fleckenfalter (*Nymphalidae*). **admiralty,** *s.* das Marineamt, die Admiralität; das Oberkommando der Marine; ***High Court of Admiralty,*** das Admiralitätsgericht; ***First Lord of the Admiralty,*** der Marineminister.

admiration [ædmi'reiʃən], *s.* die Bewunderung (*of, for*, für); ***to –,*** in bewundernswerter Weise; ***be*** or ***become the – of everyone,*** bewundert werden von allen, der Gegenstand allgemeiner Bewunderung sein *or* werden.

admire [əd'maiə], *v.t.* bewundern, verehren, hochschätzen. **admirer,** *s.* der Bewunderer; Verehrer.

admissibility [ədmisi'biliti], *s.* die Zulässigkeit. **admissible,** *adj.* zulässig, erlaubt, annehmbar.

admission [əd'miʃən], *s.* die Zulassung, der Zugang, Eintritt, Zutritt, Einlaß, die Aufnahme; das Bekennen, Zugeben, Eingeständnis, Zugeständnis, die Einräumung; (*Tech.*) Zufuhr, der Einlaß (*of steam to cylinder etc.*); – *free!* Eintritt *or* Zutritt frei! **admission|-stroke,** *s.* (*Tech.*) der Einlaßhub. **--ticket,** *s.* die Eintrittskarte.

admit [əd'mit], **1.** *v.t.* 1. (her)einlassen ((*in*)*to,* in (*Acc.*)), zulassen (zu); aufnehmen (in); – ***into one's confidence,*** ins Vertrauen ziehen; ***this ticket –s two,*** diese Karte ist gültig für zwei Personen; 2. (ein)gestehen, zugeben (***to him,*** ihm gegenüber); einräumen, anerkennen, gelten lassen; ***I will – that,*** das gebe ich zu, das lasse ich gelten; 3. Platz *or* Raum haben für, Raum geben (*Dat.*). **2.** *v.i.* zulassen, erlauben, gestatten; ***it –s of no excuse,*** es läßt sich nicht entschuldigen; ***the words do not – of this construction,*** die Worte lassen diese Auslegung nicht zu; ***this ticket –s to the evening performance,*** diese Karte ist gültig für die Abendvorstellung. **admittance,** *s.* der Einlaß, Eintritt, Eingang, Zutritt, die Zulassung; (*Elec.*) der Scheinleitwert; ***no –!*** verbotener Eingang! Zutritt verboten! **admittedly,** *adv.* zugegeben, anerkanntermaßen, zugestandenermaßen.

admix [əd'miks], *v.t.* beimischen. **admixture** [–tʃə], *s.* die Beimischung, Beimengung; der Zusatz.

admonish [əd'mɔniʃ], *v.t.* ermahnen (*of,* an (*Acc.*)), warnen (vor (*Dat.*)). **admonition** [ædmo'niʃən], *s.* die Ermahnung; Warnung; der Verweis; (*Law*) die Verwarnung. **admonitory,** *adj.* ermahnend, warnend.

ado [ə'du:], *s.* das Tun, Treiben, Getue, Aufheben, Aufsehen, der Lärm; ***much – about nothing,*** viel Lärm um nichts; ***without more –,*** ohne weitere Umstände.

adobe [ə'doub(i)], *s.* luftgetrockneter Ziegelstein.

adolescence [ædo'lesəns], *s.* die Jugend(zeit), das Jünglingsalter. **adolescent, 1.** *adj.* jugendlich, Jugend–, Jünglings–, heranreifend, heranwachsend. **2.** *s.* der Jüngling; junges Mädchen; Jugendliche(r).

Adonijah [ædə'naidʒə], *s.* (*B.*) Adonai (*m.*).

adopt [ə'dɔpt], *v.t.* an Kindes Statt annehmen, adoptieren; (*fig.*) sich (*Dat.*) zu eigen machen, sich (*Dat.*) aneignen, annehmen; – ***an attitude,*** eine Haltung annehmen; – (***him as***) ***a candidate,*** einen (*or* ihn als) Kandidaten aufstellen; – ***a course,*** einen Weg einschlagen; ***–ed child,*** angenommenes Kind; ***his –ed country,*** seine Wahlheimat. **adopter,** *s.* der Adoptivvater. **adoption** [–pʃən], *s.* die Annahme an Kindes Statt, Adoption; (*fig.*) Annahme; Aneignung, Übernahme, Aufnahme; ***country of –,*** die Wahlheimat; ***brother by –,*** der Adoptivbruder. **adoptive,** *adj.* angenommen, Adoptiv–; übernommen.

adorable [ə'dɔ:rəbl], *adj.* anbetungswürdig, verehrungswürdig; (*coll.*) entzückend, allerliebst. **adoration** [ædɔ:'reiʃən], *s.* die Anbetung, Verehrung.

adore [ə'dɔ:], *v.t.* anbeten, verehren; (*coll.*) sehr gern haben, schwärmen für. **adorer,** *s.* der Anbeter, Verehrer.

adorn [ə'dɔ:n], *v.t.* schmücken, zieren; (mit Worten) ausschmücken, verschönern. **adornment,** *s.* der Schmuck, Zierat; die Verschönerung, Verzierung.

adrenal [ə'dri:nəl], *adj.* Nebennieren–; – ***glands,*** Nebennieren(drüsen).

Adriatic [eidri'ætik], *s.* die Adria.

adrift [ə'drift], *adv.* treibend, schwimmend, Wind und Wellen preisgegeben; (*fig.*) hilflos, dem Schicksal preisgegeben; ***set*** or ***cut –,*** treiben lassen; ***I was turned –,*** ich wurde hinausgesetzt *or* hinausgeworfen *or* fortgejagt; ***cut o.s. – from,*** sich absondern *or* losreißen von.

adroit [ə'drɔit], *adj.* geschickt, gewandt. **adroitness,** *s.* die Geschicklichkeit, Gewandtheit.

adsorb [əd'zɔ:b], *v.t.* adsorbieren, ansaugen. **adsorbent, 1.** *adj.* adsorbierend. **2.** *s.* der Adsorbent. **adsorption,** *s.* die Adsorption, Ansaugung.

adulation [ædju'leiʃən], *s.* die Lobhudelei, Speichelleckerei, Schmeichelei. **adulator** ['ædjuleitə], *s.* der Speichellecker, Schmeichler. **adulatory** ['ædjuleitəri], *adj.* schmeichlerisch, servil.

adult ['ædʌlt, ə'dʌlt], **1.** *adj.* erwachsen, reif. **2.** *s.* Erwachsene(r); – ***education,*** die Erwachsenenbildung.

adulterant [ə'dʌltərənt], *s.* das Verfälschungsmittel; Streckmittel, Verschnittmittel. **adulterate,** *v.t.* verfälschen, strecken; verschneiden, panschen (*wine*), verdünnen; (*fig.*) verderben. **adulteration** [–'reiʃən], *s.* die Verfälschung, Streckung; Verschneidung, das Panschen; der Verschnitt; – ***of food,*** die Nahrungsmittelverfälschung.

adulterer [ə'dʌltərə], *s.* der Ehebrecher. **adulteress,** *s.* die Ehebrecherin. **adulterous,** *adj.* ehebrecherisch. **adultery,** *s.* der Ehebruch.

adumbrate [ə'dʌmbreit, 'ædʌmbreit], *v.t.* andeuten, hindeuten auf (*Acc.*); flüchtig entwerfen, skizzieren. **adumbration** [–'breiʃən], *s.* die Andeutung; Skizze, flüchtiger Entwurf; die Vorahnung; (*Her.*) der Schattenriß.

advance [əd'vɑ:ns], **1.** *v.i.* vorrücken, vorgehen, vordringen, anrücken, vorwärtsgehen; Fortschritte machen, fortschreiten; vorwärtskommen, vorankommen, zunehmen (*in,* an (*Dat.*)); (*in price*) anziehen, in die Höhe gehen, (an)steigen; (*in rank*) befördert werden, aufrücken, avancieren. **2.** *v.t.* vorauszahlen, vorschießen, vorstrecken (*money*); befördern (*in rank*), beschleunigen (*growth*), erhöhen (*price*), vorwärtsbringen, voranbringen, fördern (*plans*), aufstellen, vorbringen, vortragen, äußern (*an opinion*), vorschieben, nach vorn verlegen (*troops*), ausstrecken (*a hand*), vorsetzen (*a foot*); – ***a claim,*** Ansprüche geltend machen; – ***his interests,*** seinen Interessen Vorschub leisten; – ***one's own interests,*** die Eigeninteressen fördern. **3.** *s.* der Vormarsch, Vorstoß, das Vorrücken, Anrücken, Vorschreiten; der Fortschritt, die Verbesserung, Vervollkommnung; Beförderung, das Aufrücken, Avancement (*in office*); der Vorschuß, Kredit, das Darlehen, die Auslage (*of money*); die Erhöhung, Steigerung, der Zuschlag, Aufschlag (*in price*); das Mehrgebot (*on an offer*); der Vorsprung (*in progress*); (*usu. pl.*) Antrag, das Anerbieten, Annäherungsversuche (*pl.*); (*Elec.*) die Voreilung; ***in –,*** vorn, voraus (*in position*), im voraus (*in time*); ***pay in –,*** im voraus zahlen; ***order in –,*** vorbestellen; ***be in – of him,*** Vorsprung haben vor ihm, ihm voraus sein. **4.** *adj.* Vor–, Voraus–, Vorher–, vorausgehend, (*Mil.*) vorgeschoben; – ***copy,*** das Vorausexemplar; – ***guard,*** die Vorhut, Avantgarde; – ***party,*** die Spitzenkompanie, der Vortrupp; – ***sale,*** der Vorverkauf.

advanced [əd'vɑ:nst], *adj.* vorgesetzt, vorgeschoben; vorgerückt; fortgeschritten, für Fortgeschrittene; fortschrittlich, modern, emanzipiert, extrem; – ***thinker,*** fortschrittlicher Denker; – ***age,*** vorgerücktes Alter. **advancement,** *s.* die Verbreitung, Förderung; der Fortschritt, das Anrücken, Vorrücken, Emporkommen; die Beförderung.

advantage [əd'vɑ:ntidʒ], **1.** *s.* der Vorteil (*also Tenn.*), Vorzug, Nutzen; Gewinn; die Überlegenheit, das Übergewicht; ***have the – of*** or ***over him,*** ihm überlegen sein, ihm etwas voraushaben, besser dran sein als er, ihm gegenüber im Vorteil sein; ***take – of a th.,*** etwas ausnutzen, einen Vorteil aus einer S. ziehen, sich (*Dat.*) etwas zunutze machen; ***take – of him,*** ihn übervorteilen *or* ausnutzen; ***turn s.th. to –,*** aus einer S. Nutzen ziehen, sich (*Dat.*) etwas zunutze machen; ***to the best –,*** auf das Vorteilhafteste; ***to –,*** vorteilhaft, mit Gewinn;

(*Tenn.*) – ***game,*** Spiel vor; – ***set,*** Satz mit Spielvorteil; ***personal –s,*** körperliche Vorzüge. **2.** *v.t.* (*a p.*) Vorteil gewähren; nützen (*Dat.*), (*a th.*) fördern. **advantageous** [ædvən'teidʒəs], *adj.* vorteilhaft, günstig, nützlich.

advent ['ædvənt], *s.* (*fig.*) die Ankunft, das Aufkommen; – ***to power,*** das Emporkommen zur Macht, (*Eccl.*) ***Advent,*** der Advent, die Adventzeit.

adventitious [ædvən'tiʃəs], *adj.* zufällig, fremd, nebensächlich, Neben –, hinzukommend, hinzugekommen.

adventure [əd'ventʃə], **1.** *s.* das Abenteuer; Erlebnis; Wagnis, Wagstück, gewagtes Unternehmen; die Spekulation. **2.** *v.t.* wagen, riskieren, aufs Spiel setzen. **3.** *v.i.* sich wagen (***upon,*** in *or* auf (*Acc.*)), Gefahr laufen, es darauf ankommen lassen. **adventurer,** *s.* der Abenteurer, Glücksritter; Spekulant. **adventuresome,** *adj.* verwegen, waghalsig. **adventurous,** *adj.* abenteuerlich; kühn, waghalsig, unternehmungslustig; riskant.

adverb ['ædvə:b], *s.* das Adverb(ium), Umstandswort. **adverbial** [–'və:biəl], *adj.* adverbial.

adversary ['ædvəsəri], *s.* der Gegner, Feind, Widersacher.

adversative [əd'və:sətiv], *adj.* (*Gram.*) gegensätzlich, adversativ.

adverse ['ædvə:s], *adj.* ungünstig, nachteilig (***to,*** für); gegenüberstehend, gegenüberliegend, gegnerisch, feindlich (gesinnt) (*to, Dat.*); entgegenwirkend, widrig (*as fate etc.*); (*pred.*) zuwider; – ***balance,*** die Unterbilanz; – ***fate,*** das Mißgeschick; – ***majority,*** Mehrheit gegen einen Antrag; – ***party,*** die Gegenpartei; – ***winds,*** widrige Winde. **adversity** [əd'və:siti], *s.* das Elend, die Not, das Unglück, Mißgeschick.

advert, 1. [əd'və:t] *v.i.* hinweisen, anspielen (***to,*** auf (*Acc.*)); aufmerken. **2.** ['ædvə:t], *s.* (*coll.*) *see* **advertisement.**

advertence, advertency [əd'və:təns(i)], *s.* die Beachtung, Aufmerksamkeit.

advertise ['ædvətaiz], **1.** *v.t.* (öffentlich) anzeigen *or* bekanntmachen, bekanntgeben, ankündigen, Reklame machen für; (*obs.*) in Kenntnis setzen, benachrichtigen. **2.** *v.i.* inserieren, annoncieren, Reklame machen; – ***for,*** durch Reklame *or* Inserat suchen. **advertisement** [əd'və:tismənt], *s.* die Anzeige, Bekanntmachung, Ankündigung, das Inserat, die Annonce, Reklame, Werbung; ***put*** or ***insert an – in a paper,*** ein Inserat in einer Zeitung aufgeben. **advertising, 1.** *s.* das Inserieren, Ankündigen; die Reklame, Werbung; das Reklamewesen; ***pictorial –,*** die Bildwerbung. **2.** *attrib. adj.* Reklame–, Inseraten–, Annoncen–, Werbe—; – ***agency,*** das Inseratenbüro, die Annoncenexpedition; – ***campaign,*** der Werbefeldzug.

advice [əd'vais], *s.* (*sing. only*) der Rat, Ratschlag; (*with pl.*) die Nachricht, Meldung, Mitteilung, Kunde, Anzeige, (*Comm.*) der Bericht, Avis; ***on my –,*** auf meinen Rat; ***on*** or ***by the – of,*** auf Rat von; ***ask*** or ***take*** or ***seek –,*** Rat holen *or* suchen, sich raten lassen; ***take my –!*** folge meinem Rate! ***take medical –,*** ärztlichen Rat einholen; ***he will not take any –,*** er läßt sich nicht raten; ***as per –,*** laut Bericht; ***a piece of –,*** ein (guter) Rat; ***according to –s from Rome,*** laut Berichten aus Rom; ***until further –,*** bis auf weitere Nachricht; ***letter of –,*** der Avisbrief. **advice-bureau,** *s.* die Beratungsstelle.

advisability [ədvaizə'biliti], *s.* die Ratsamkeit, Rätlichkeit, Zweckmäßigkeit. **advisable** [–'vaizəbl], *adj.* ratsam, rätlich; nützlich, zweckmäßig; ***it is –,*** es empfiehlt sich.

advise [əd'vaiz], **1.** *v.t.* (an)raten (*Dat.*); beraten (*a p.*); (an)empfehlen (*Dat.*); in Kenntnis setzen (*Dat.*), benachrichtigen, (*Comm.*) avisieren; – ***against,*** warnen vor (*Dat.*); ***I – you against it,*** ich rate es dir ab; ***be –d by me,*** laß dir von mir raten; – ***him to the contrary,*** ihm (von etwas) abraten; ***as –d,*** laut Bericht. **2.** *v.i.* (sich) beraten, zu Rate gehen, beratschlagen (***with,*** mit); – ***with one's pillow,*** etwas beschlafen.

advised [əd'vaizd], *adj.* überlegt, bedachtsam, absichtlich; ***ill-–,*** unbedachtsam, schlecht beraten; ***well-–,*** wohlbedacht, wohlüberlegt, wohlerwogen, vorsätzlich. **advisedly** [–zidli], *adv.* mit Bedacht *or* Vorbedacht *or* Überlegung. **adviser,** *s.* der Ratgeber, Berater. **advisory,** *adj.* beratend, ratgebend; – ***body,*** der Beratungsausschuß, die Gutachterkommission; – ***council,*** technischer Beirat.

advocacy ['ædvəkəsi], *s.* die Verteidigung, Befürwortung, Empfehlung (***of,*** *Gen.*), das Eintreten (für); (*Law*) die Anwaltschaft.

advocate, 1. ['ædvəkət], *s.* (*Scots*) der Anwalt, Rechtsanwalt, Rechtsbeistand, Advokat; (*fig.*) Verteidiger, Verfechter, Fürsprecher, Befürworter; ***I am a great – of,*** ich halte viel von *or* große Stücke auf (*Acc.*). **2.** [-keit], *v.t.* verteidigen, verfechten, empfehlen, befürworten; eintreten (für).

advowson [əd'vauzən], *s.* das Pfründenbesetzungsrecht, kirchliches Patronat.

adze [ædz], **1.** *s.* das Breitbeil, die Krummaxt. **2.** *v.t.* mit dem Breitbeil bearbeiten.

Aegean Sea, [i'dʒi:ən] *s.* Ägäisches Meer.

aegis ['i:dʒis], *s.* (*Hist.*) die Ägis; (*fig.*) Ägide, der Schutz.

Aeneid ['i:niid], *s.* die Äneide.

Aeolian [i'ouliən], *adj.* – ***harp,*** die Äolsharfe, Windharfe; (*Mus.*) – ***mode,*** Äolische Tonart.

aeon ['i:ən], *s.* der Äon, die Ewigkeit.

aerated ['ɛəreitid], *adj.* mit Kohlensäure *or* Luft durchsetzt, lufthaltig; – ***water,*** kohlensaures Wasser.

aerial ['ɛəriəl], **1.** *s.* (*Rad.*) die Antenne; ***directional –,*** die Richtantenne. **2.** *adj.* luftig; atmosphärisch; in der Luft, Luft–; (*fig.*) ätherisch, wesenslos; – ***camera,*** die Fliegerkamera; – ***combat,*** der Luftkampf; – ***defence,*** der Luftschutz; – ***escort,*** Begleitflugzeuge (*pl.*); – ***navigation,*** die Luft(schif)fahrt; – ***photograph,*** die Luftaufnahme; – ***survey,*** die Luftvermessung; – ***transport,*** der Lufttransport; – ***warfare,*** der Luftkrieg.

aerie ['ɛəri], *s.* der (Adler)horst, das Nest eines Raubvogels; erhöhter Standpunkt *or* Wohnort; junge Brut.

aero– ['ɛərou], *pref.* Aero–, Flug–, Luft–. **aerobatics** [–'bætiks], *s.* (*sing. constr.*) das Kunstfliegen. **aerodrome** [–droum], *s.* der Flughafen, Flugplatz; (*Mil.*) Fliegerhorst.

aero|dynamic, *adj.* aerodynamisch; (*Av.*) – ***centre,*** der Druckpunkt. **–dynamics,** *pl.* (*sing.constr.*) die Aerodynamik. **–-engine,** *s.* der Flugzeugmotor. **–foil,** *s.* die Tragfläche; – ***section,*** die Profildicke.

aerolite ['ɛəroulait], **aerolith** [–liθ], *s.* der Meteorstein, Aerolith.

aerometer [ɛə'rɔmitə], *s.* der Luftmesser, Dichtemesser.

aeronaut ['ɛərounɔ:t], *s.* der Luftfahrer, Flieger. **aeronautic(al),** *adj.* aeronautisch, Luftfahrt–. **aeronautics,** *s.pl.* (*sing.constr.*) die Luftfahrt, das Flugwesen.

aero|plane, *s.* das Flugzeug. **–static,** *adj.* aerostatisch. **–statics,** *pl.* (*sing. constr.*) die Aerostatik, Luftgleichgewichtslehre.

aeruginous [i'ru:dʒinəs], *adj.* grünspanartig, Grünspan–, patiniert.

aery ['ɛəri], *adj.* (*Poet.*) luftig, ätherisch.

Aesculapius [i:sku'leipiəs], *s.* (*Hist.*) Äskulap (*m.*).

aesthete ['i:sθi:t], *s.* der Ästhetiker; ästhetisch Gebildete(r); Ästhet, Schöngeist. **aesthetic** [i:s'θetik], *adj.* ästhetisch; Kunst–; geschmackvoll. **aestheticism** [–'θetisizm], *s.* die Schöngeistelei. **aesthetics,** *s.* (*sing. constr.*) der Schönheitssinn, Ästhetizismus; die Schönheitslehre, Ästhetik.

aestivate ['estiveit, 'i:stiveit], *v.i.* übersommern, Sommerschlaf halten. **aestivation** [–'veiʃən], *s.* (*Zool.*) der Sommerschlaf; (*Bot.*) die Knospenlage.

aether, aetherial, *see* **ether, etherial.**

aetiological [i:tio'lɔdʒikəl], *adj.* ursächlich, begrundend, ätiologisch. **aetiology** [–'ɔlədʒi], *s.* die Lehre von Ursachen; logische Begründung; (*Med.*) die Ätiologie.

afar [ə'fɑ:], *adv.* (*Poet.*) fern, weit (weg), entfernt; ***from* –**, aus weiter Ferne, von weit her.

affability [æfə'biliti], *s.* die Leutseligkeit, Freundlichkeit, Güte. **affable** ['æfəbl], *adj.*, **affably,** *adv.* leutselig, freundlich (***to,*** zu *or* gegen).

affair [ə'fɛə], *s.* die Angelegenheit; Sache; das Geschäft, die Affäre, das Ereignis, (*coll.*) die Liebschaft, das Liebesverhältnis; (*Mil.*) Treffen, Gefecht; (*coll.*) die Veranstaltung; ***family –s,*** Familienverhältnisse, Familienangelegenheiten; ***Secretary of State for foreign –s,*** der Minister des Auswärtigen, Außenminister; ***at the head of –s,*** an der Spitze des Unternehmens; ***– of honour,*** der Ehrenhandel, das Duell; ***love –,*** der Liebeshandel; (*coll.*) ***that's your –,*** das ist Ihre S.; (*coll.*) ***that's not my –,*** das geht mich nichts an; ***attend to your own –s,*** seinen eignen Geschäften nachgehen; ***as –s stand,*** wie die Dinge liegen *or* stehen; ***– of state,*** die Staatsangelegenheit; ***state of –s,*** die Lage der Dinge, Sachlage; ***a proper state of –s,*** geordnete Verhältnisse *or* Zustände.

¹**affect** [ə'fekt], *v.t.* 1. gern haben *or* mögen, Gefallen finden an (*Dat.*), mit Vorliebe tun, neigen zu, bevorzugen; 2. vorgeben, vortäuschen, affektieren, (er)heucheln; tun als ob (***to do,*** man tut); ***– a limp,*** sich hinkend stellen; ***– modesty,*** Bescheidenheit heucheln *or* zur Schau tragen.

²**affect,** **1.** *v.t.* (ein)wirken *or* Einfluß haben auf (*Acc.*), beeinflussen; betreffen, (be)rühren, bewegen, ergreifen; beeinträchtigen, schädlich wirken auf (*Acc.*), (*Med.*) angreifen, befallen, affizieren. **2.** *s.* (*Psych.*) der Affekt, die Gemütsbewegung, Erregung.

affectation [æfek'teiʃən], *s.* übertriebene Vorliebe (***of,*** für); die Zimperlichkeit, Geziertheit, Affektiertheit, Ziererei; Heuchelei, Verstellung.

¹**affected** [ə'fektid], *adj.* geziert, gekünstelt, affektiert; vorgetäuscht, angenommen, erheuchelt; gesinnt, geneigt.

²**affected,** *adj.* angegriffen, befallen, affiziert (***with,*** von); beeindruckt, betroffen, ergriffen, berührt, beeinträchtigt; bewegt, gerührt. **affecting,** *adj.* rührend, ergreifend.

affection [ə'fekʃən], *s.* die Gemütsbewegung, Rührung, Stimmung, der Affekt; die Neigung, Zuneigung, Liebe (***for, towards,*** zu); (*Med.*) Erkrankung, das Leiden, die Affektion; ***have an – for him,*** ihn lieb haben; ***set one's –s upon him,*** sein Herz an ihn hängen. **affectionate,** *adj.* liebevoll, zärtlich, herzlich; ***your – cousin,*** Dein Dich liebender Vetter. **affectionately,** *adv.* ***yours –,*** innigst *or* herzlichst *or* in Liebe dein. **affectionateness,** *s.* die Zärtlichkeit.

affective [ə'fektiv], *adj.* Gefühls–, Gemüts–, Affekt–, affektiv, emotional.

afferent ['æfərənt], *adj.* (*Med.*) zuführend; sensorisch.

affiance [ə'faiəns], **1.** *v.t.* verloben; ***–d bride,*** die Verlobte. **2.** *s.* die Verlobung; das Vertrauen (***in,*** in (*Acc.*)).

affidavit [æfi'deivit], *s.* eidesstattliche Erklärung, schriftliche Zeugenaussage; ***make an – of,*** eidlich erhärten, eidesstattlich erklären.

affiliate [ə'filieit], **1.** *v.t.* als Mitglied aufnehmen, anschließen, angliedern (***to,*** an (*Acc.*)); ***–d church,*** die Schwesterkirche; (*Law*) ***– a child on him,*** ihm die Vaterschaft eines Kindes zuschreiben *or* zuschieben; ***–d company,*** die Tochtergesellschaft; ***–d institution,*** die Zweiganstalt. **2.** *v.i.* sich anschließen (***with,*** *Dat. or* an (*Acc.*)), sich gesellen (zu), sich verbünden (mit). **affiliation** [–i'eiʃən], *s.* die Verbindung, Vereinigung, Angliederung, Anschließung; Aufnahme als Mitglied; (*Law*) Feststellung der Vaterschaft.

affinity [ə'finiti], *s.* die Verwandtschaft, Verschwägerung; (*Chem.*) Affinität; Ähnlichkeit, Übereinstimmung; Zuneigung, Hinneigung, gegenseitige Anziehung, Wahlverwandtschaft.

affirm [ə'fə:m], *v.t.* bestätigen, versichern, feierlich erklären; behaupten, bekräftigen; bejahen, bezeugen, (*Law*) eidesstattlich erklären. **affirmation** [æfə'meiʃən], *s.* die Behauptung, Bestätigung, Versicherung, Bejahung, Bekräftigung; eidesstattliche Erklärung. **affirmative** [–'fə:mətiv], **1.** *adj.* bejahend; zustimmend, (*Math.*) positiv. **2.** *s.* das Jawort, die Bejahung; ***answer in the –,*** bejahen; ***in the –,*** bejahend.

affix, 1. [ə'fiks], *v.t.* anheften, anhängen, aufkleben, anschlagen (***to,*** an (Acc.)), befestigen (an (*Dat.*)); (*fig.*) (hin)zufügen, beifügen; beilegen; ***– one's signature,*** unterschreiben; ***– one's seal,*** sein Siegel aufdrücken. **2.** ['æfiks], *s.* (*Gram.*) das Affix, der Anhang, die Beifügung.

afflatus [ə'fleitəs], *s.* die Eingebung; Begeisterung, Inspiration.

afflict [ə'flikt], *v.t.* betrüben; quälen, plagen, peinigen, kränken, heimsuchen. **afflicted,** *adj.* betrübt, bedrückt, niedergeschlagen; geplagt, befallen (***with,*** von); leidend, krank (an (*Dat.*)). **affliction** [–kʃən], *s.* die Betrübnis, Niedergeschlagenheit, Trauer; das Leid(en), Gebrechen; der Schmerz, Kummer, die Not.

affluence ['æfluəns], *s.* der Zufluß, das Zuströmen; (*fig.*) der Überfluß, Reichtum, die Fülle. **affluent,** **1.** *adj.* reichlich (fließend); wohlhabend, reich (***in,*** an (*Dat.*)). **2.** *s.* der Nebenfluß.

afflux ['æflʌks], *s.* der Zufluß, Zustrom, Zuwachs, (*Med.*) Andrang.

afford [ə'fɔ:d], *v.t.* 1. liefern, bieten, gewähren; ***– a good view,*** einen weiten Ausblick bieten; ***– satisfaction,*** Befriedigung gewähren; 2. (*with can etc.*) sich (*Dat.*) erlauben *or* leisten, die Mittel haben für, erübrigen, erschwingen, aufbringen; ***– a new suit,*** sich einen neuen Anzug leisten.

afforest [ə'fɔrəst], *v.t.* aufforsten. **afforestation** [–'teiʃən], *s.* die Aufforstung.

affranchise [ə'fræntʃaiz], *v.t.* befreien; freigeben.

affray [ə'frei], *s.* die Schlägerei, Rauferei, das Handgemenge, Geplänkel; der Aufruhr, (*coll.*) Krawall.

affricative [ə'frikətiv], *s.* (*Phonet.*) die Affrikata.

affright [ə'frait], **1.** *v.t.* (*Poet.*) erschrecken. **2.** *s.* (*Poet.*) der Schreck, das Erschrecken.

affront [ə'frʌnt], **1.** *s.* die Beleidigung, Beschimpfung, der Schimpf, Schmach; ***swallow an –,*** eine Beleidigung einstecken. **2.** *v.t.* beleidigen, beschimpfen; (*fig.*) trotzen, die Stirn bieten (*Dat.*).

affusion [ə'fju:ʒen], *s.* das Begießen, Übergießen, (*Med.*) der Guß, die Übergießung.

Afghan ['æfgæn], **1.** *s.* 1. der Afghane (die Afghanin); 2. (*language*) das Afghanisch(e). **2.** *adj.* afghanisch.

afield [ə'fi:ld], *adv.* im Felde; ins *or* aufs Feld; ***go far –,*** weit hinaus gehen, in die Ferne schweifen; ***look far –,*** sich weit umtun *or* umschauen.

afire [ə'faiə], *pred.adj.* in Brand *or* Flammen, brennend; (*fig.*) ***be all –,*** Feuer and Flamme sein.

aflame [ə'fleim], *pred.adj. See* **afire**; (*fig.*) flammend, glühend.

afloat [ə'flout], *pred.adj.* schwimmend, flott; auf See, auf dem Meere, zu Wasser, an Bord; (*fig.*) im Umlauf, in Kurs, zirkulierend; in (vollem) Gang; ***the rumour is –,*** das Gerücht geht um; ***keep –,*** sich über Wasser halten (*also fig.*); (*fig.*) ***set –,*** in Gang setzen *or* bringen; in Umlauf bringen.

aflutter [ə'flʌtə], *pred.adj.* flatternd; (*fig.*) aufgeregt, in Unruhe.

afoot [ə'fut], *pred.adj.* zu Fuße, auf den Beinen; (*fig.*) in Bewegung, im Gange.

afore [ə'fɔ:], **1.** *adv.* (*obs.*) zuvor, vorher; (*Naut.*) vorwärts. **2.** *prep.* (*Naut.*) vor. **afore|-mentioned, -named, -said,** *adj.* obengenannt, obenerwähnt, obig, besagt. **-thought,** *adj.* vorbedacht, vorsätzlich; ***with malice –,*** in böser Absicht. **-time,** *adv.* ehemals, ehedem, früher, vormals.

afraid [ə'freid], *pred.adj.* ängstlich, besorgt (***for,*** um; ***of,*** vor (*Dat.*)); ***be – of a th.,*** sich vor einer S. fürchten, Angst haben vor einer S.; ***be – that*** or ***lest,*** fürchten daß; ***be – to do*** or ***of doing,*** sich scheuen zu tun; (*coll.*) ***I am – I am late,*** es tut mir leid, daß ich zu spät komme.

afresh [ə'freʃ], *adv.* von neuem, aufs neue, wieder, abermals.

Africa ['æfrikə], *s.* Afrika (*n.*). **African, 1.** *s.* der (die) Afrikaner(in). **2.** *adj.* afrikanisch.

Afrikaans [æfri'kɑ:nz], *s.* das Afrikaans, Kapholländisch. **Afrikander,** *s.* der Afrikander, Südafrikanischer Weißer.

aft [ɑ:ft], *adv.* (*Naut.*) achtern (*on board ship*), achteraus (*behind the ship*); ***fore and –,*** vorn und achtern; in der Längsrichtung; ***right –,*** recht achteraus.

after ['ɑ:ftə], **1.** *prep.* 1. nach (*of time*); hinter (. . . her) (*in sequence*); – ***all,*** am Ende, letzten Endes, übrigens, bei alledem, also doch, schließlich; ***one – another,*** nacheinander; ***one – the other,*** einer nach dem andern; ***day – day,*** Tag für Tag; ***the day – tomorrow,*** übermorgen; ***the week – next,*** die übernächste Woche; – ***that,*** darauf, hierauf; – ***hours,*** nach der Polizeistunde, nach Büroschluß *or* Ladenschluß; (*coll.*) ***what are you –?*** was machst *or* willst du da? (*coll.*) ***I'll go – him,*** ich will ihm nach; (*coll.*) ***be – a th.,*** hinter etwas her sein; 2. nach, zufolge, entsprechend, gemäß; (*coll.*) – ***a fashion,*** recht und schlecht; – ***this fashion,*** auf diese Weise. **2.** *adv.* hinterher, nachher, danach, darauf(folgend), später; ***shortly –,*** kurz darauf; ***the day –,*** den Tag darauf. **3.** *adj.* (*Naut.*) achter, hinter; folgend, später; – ***ages,*** die Nachwelt; ***in – years,*** in späteren *or* zukünftigen Jahren. **4.** *conj.* nachdem; – ***having said so, he went away,*** nachdem er dies gesagt hatte, ging er fort.

after|birth, *s.* die Nachgeburt. **--care,** *s.* (*Med.*) die Nachbehandlung, (*Law*) Entlassungsfürsorge. **--compartment,** *s.* (*Naut.*) der Heckraum. **-damp,** *s.* die Nachschwaden (*pl.*). **-deck,** *s.* (*Naut.*) das Achterdeck. **--dinner,** *attrib.adj.* – ***nap,*** der Nachmittagsschlaf; – ***speech,*** die Tischrede. **--effect,** *s.* die Nachwirkung. **-glow,** *s.* das Nachglühen, Abendrot; (*fig.*) der Nachglanz. **--grass,** *s.* zweite Grasernte, das Grum(me)t. **--hold,** *s.* (*Naut.*) der Achter(lade)raum. **--life,** *s.* späteres *or* zukünftiges Leben; das Leben nach dem Tode. **-math,** *s.* 1. *See* **-grass**; 2. (*fig.*) Folgen, Nachwirkungen (*pl.*). **-most,** *adj.* hinterst.

afternoon [ɑ:ftə'nu:n], *s.* der Nachmittag; ***good –,*** guten Tag; ***in the –,*** am Nachmittag, nachmittags; – ***tea,*** der Fünfuhrtee.

after|-pains, *pl.* Nachwehen (*pl.*). **--piece,** *s.* (*Theat.*) das Nachstück. – **season,** *s.* (*Comm.*) stille Zeit. **--sight bill,** *s.* der Zeitsichtwechsel, Vistawechsel. **--taste,** *s.* der Nachgeschmack. **-thought,** *s.* nachträglicher Einfall. **--times,** *pl.* die Folgezeit. **--treatment,** *s.* die Nachbehandlung, Nachkur.

afterwards ['ɑ:ftəwədz], *adv.* später, nachher, hernach, hinterher, nachträglich, darauf, in der Folge.

again [ə'gein, ə'gen], *adv.* wieder, wiederum, abermals, nochmals, schon wieder, noch einmal, von neuem; noch dazu, ferner, außerdem, gleichfalls, ebenfalls; – ***and –, time and –,*** immer wieder; ***as much –,*** noch einmal soviel; ***now and –,*** ab und zu, dann und wann.

against [ə'geinst], *prep.* gegen, wider, entgegen; an, bei, auf (*Acc.*) . . . zu, nach . . . hin; im Vergleich zu, verglichen mit; – ***the grain,*** gegen den Strich, wider Willen, ungern; ***it hangs – the wall,*** es hängt an der Wand; – ***my arrival,*** auf mein Kommen; (*coll.*) – ***a rainy day,*** auf schlechte Zeiten hin, (in Vorsorge) für schlechte Zeiten; ***over –,*** nahe an, gegenüber; (*coll.*) ***be up – it,*** in der Klemme sein; (*coll.*) ***run up – him,*** auf ihn stoßen, ihn zufällig treffen.

agamic [ə'gæmik], **agamous** ['ægəməs], *adj.* (*Biol.*) geschlechtslos, ungeschlechtlich.

agape [ə'geip], *pred.adj.* gaffend, mit offenem Munde.

agaric ['ægərik, ə'gærik], *s.* der Blätterpilz, Blätterschwamm (*Agaricaceae*).

agasp [ə'gɑ:sp], *pred.adj.* keuchend, (*fig.*) schmachtend; verblüfft.

agate ['ægeit], **1.** *s.* der Achat. **2.** *adj.* achaten, Achat–.

Agatha ['ægəθə], *s.* Agathe (*f.*).

age [eidʒ], **1.** *s.* 1. das Alter, Lebensalter; die Reife, Volljährigkeit, Mündigkeit; ***old –,*** das hohe Alter, Greisenalter; – ***group,*** die Altersklasse, der Jahrgang; – ***limit,*** die Altersgrenze; ***be of –,*** volljährig *or* mündig sein; ***come of –,*** mündig werden; ***under –,*** minderjährig, unmündig; ***at an early –,*** frühzeitig; ***at the – of 16,*** im Alter von 16 Jahren; ***6 years of –,*** 6 Jahre alt; ***he is my –,*** er ist so alt wie ich, er ist in meinem Alter; 2. das Zeitalter, (*Geol.*) die Periode; das Menschenalter, die Generation; (*coll. oft. pl.*) lange Zeit, eine Ewigkeit; ***down the –s,*** durch die Jahrhunderte hindurch; ***former –s,*** frühere Zeiten; ***the Age of Goethe,*** das Zeitalter Goethes; ***the Ice Age,*** die Eiszeit; ***the Middle Ages,*** das Mittelalter; ***–s yet unborn,*** noch ungeborene Geschlechter. **2.** *v.i.* altern, alt werden. **3.** *v.t.* alt machen, ausreifen, zur Reife bringen.

aged, 1. [eidʒd], *p.p.* alt, im Alter von. **2.** ['eidʒid], *adj.* alt, bejahrt, betagt; ***the –,*** alte *or* die alten Leute.

ageing ['eidʒiŋ], **1.** *adj.* alternd. **2.** *s.* das Altern; (*Tech.*) Tempern, die Veredelung.

ageless ['eidʒlis], *adj.* zeitlos.

agency ['eidʒənsi], *s.* 1. die Wirkung, Wirksamkeit, Tätigkeit; ***by the – of,*** mit Hilfe von, vermittels (*Gen.*); 2. (*Comm.*) die Vertretung, Vermittlung, Agentur; – (***business***), das Kommissionsgeschäft.

agenda [ə'dʒendə], *s.* die Tagesordnung; (*obs.*) das Notizbuch.

agent ['eidʒənt], *s.* 1. Handelnde(r), Wirkende(r), der Urheber; 2. die Ursache, das Werkzeug; (*Chem.*) Agens, Mittel, wirkende Kraft; ***physical –s,*** Naturkräfte; 2. (*Comm.*) der Agent, Vertreter, Vermittler, Makler, Kommissionär, Handelsbeauftragte(r), Bevollmächtigte(r); Geschäftsträger, Gutsverwalter, Gutsinspektor; ***secret –,*** der Geheimagent.

age-old, *adj.* uralt.

agglomerate, 1. [ə'glɔməreit], *v.t.* zusammenballen, anhäufen, aufhäufen. **2.** [-reit], *v.i.* sich zusammenballen, sich (an)häufen. **3.** [-rət], *adj.* zusammengeballt, gehäuft. **4.** [-rət], *s.* (*Geol.*) das Agglomerat. **agglomeration** [–'reiʃən], *s.* die Ansammlung, Anhäufung, Zusammenballung; der Haufen, die Masse, das Durcheinander.

agglutinate [ə'glu:tineit], **1.** *v.t.* zusammenkleben, verbinden; (*Med., Gram.*) agglutinieren. **2.** *v.i.* sich verbinden. **3.** *adj.* zusammengeklebt, verbunden; (*Gram.*) agglutinierend. **agglutination** [–'neiʃən], *s.* das Zusammenkleben, Festkleben, (*Gram.*) die Agglutination. **agglutinative** [–nətiv], *adj.* zusammenklebend; (*Gram.*) agglutinierend.

aggrandize ['ægrəndaiz], *v.t.* vergrößern, ausdehnen, erweitern (*power etc.*); (*fig.*) erhöhen, erheben, verherrlichen. **aggrandizement** [ə'grændizmənt], *s.* die Vergrößerung, Erweiterung, Vermehrung, Zunahme, Erhöhung, Beförderung.

aggravate ['ægrəveit], *v.t.* erschweren, verschärfen, verschlimmern; (*coll.*) ärgern, reizen, aufbringen, erbittern. **aggravating,** *adj.* erschwerend; (*coll.*) ärgerlich, verdrießlich. **aggravation** [–'veiʃən], *s.* die Erschwerung, Verschlimmerung; (*coll.*) der Ärger, die Erbitterung.

aggregate, 1. ['ægrigeit], *v.t.* aufhäufen, zusammenhäufen, anhäufen, ansammeln, verbinden, vereinigen. **2.** [-geit], *v.i.* sich anhäufen, sich belaufen (*to,* auf (*Acc.*)). **3.** [–gət], *adj.* angehäuft, angesammelt, vereint, gesamt; (*Bot. etc.*) aggregiert; (*Geol.*) zusammengesetzt; (*Gram.*) Sammel–, kollektiv; – ***amount,*** der Gesamtbetrag. **4.** [-gət], *s.* das Aggregat, die Anhäufung, Ansammlung, Masse, Menge, Summe; ***in the –,*** im ganzen (genommen), alles zusammengerechnet, insgesamt. **aggregation** [–'geiʃən], *s.* die Ansammlung, Anhäufung, (*Biol.*) Aggregation, (*Phys.*) das Aggregat, (*Math.*) die Einklammerung.

aggression [ə'greʃən], *s.* der Angriff, Überfall; die Aggression; ***war of –,*** der Angriffskrieg. **aggressive** [–siv], *adj.* angreifend, kampflustig, aggressiv; ***take the –,*** aggresiv werden. **aggressiveness,** *s.* die Angriffslust. **aggressor,** *s.* der Angreifer.

aggrieve [ə'gri:v], *v.t.* kränken, betrüben; ***feel –d,*** sich gekränkt fühlen.

aghast [ə'gɑ:st], *pred.adj.* entsetzt, erschrocken, bestürzt (***at,*** über (*Acc.*)).

agile ['ædʒail], *adj.* beweglich, behend(e), flink, hurtig, gelenkig. **agility** [ə'dʒiliti], *s.* die Behendigkeit, Beweglichkeit, Flinkheit.

aging, (*Am.*) *see* **ageing.**

agio ['ædʒiou], *s.* (*Comm.*) das Aufgeld, Agio. **agiotage,** *s.* das Wechselgeschäft, die Agiotage, Börsenspekulation.

agitate ['ædʒiteit], **1.** *v.t.* bewegen, in Bewegung versetzen *or* bringen, schütteln, rühren, erschüttern, (*fig.*) erregen, aufregen, beunruhigen, stören; erörtern, verhandeln, zur Diskussion stellen, debattieren (*a question*). **2.** *v.i.* Propaganda machen, wühlen, agitieren (***for,*** für). **agitation** [–'teiʃən], *s.* 1. heftige Bewegung, das Schütteln; die Erschütterung, Erregung, Aufregung; Gemütsbewegung; Unruhe, der Aufruhr, die Agitation; 2. Erörterung. **agitator,** *s.* 1. der Aufwiegler, Agitator, Hetzredner; 2. (*Tech.*) Rührarm, das Rührwerk.

agley [ə'glei], *adj.* (*Scots*) krumm, schief.

aglow [ə'glou], *pred.adj.* glühend, gerötet; (*fig.*) erregt, errötend (***with,*** von *or* vor (*Dat.*)).

agnail ['ægneil], *s.* der Niednagel, Neidnagel.

agnate ['ægneit], *adj.* väterlicherseits verwandt, stammverwandt, agnatisch. **agnates,** *pl.* Agnaten (*pl.*), Verwandte väterlicherseits (*pl.*).

agnathic [æg'næθik], **agnathous,** *adj.* kieferlos.

agnostic [æg'nɔstik], **1.** *adj.* agnostisch. **2.** *s.* der Agnostiker. **agnosticism** [–sizm], *s.* der Agnostizismus.

ago [ə'gou], *adv.* ***a year –,*** vor einem Jahre; ***a little while –,*** vor kurzem; ***some time –,*** vor einiger Zeit; ***long –,*** lange her, vor langer Zeit; ***not long –,*** vor kurzem, vor kurzer Zeit; ***how long – is that?*** wie lange ist das her? ***no longer – than yesterday,*** erst gestern noch *or* erst noch gestern; ***it is but a few days – since . . .,*** es ist erst ein paar Tage her, daß . . ..

agog [ə'gɔg], *pred.adj.* (*coll.*) neugierig, gespannt, erpicht (***about, for,*** auf (*Acc.*)); ***set him –,*** seine Neugierde erregen.

agonistic(al) [ægə'nistik(l)], *adj.* streitsüchtig, polemisch; auf Effekt berechnet, angestrengt.

agonize ['ægənaiz], **1.** *v.t.* quälen, martern. **2.** *v.i.* mit dem Tode ringen *or* kämpfen, in den letzten Zügen liegen; (*fig.*) verzweifelt ringen, sich (ab)quälen, Qual erleiden. **agonizing,** *adj.* qualvoll.

agony ['ægəni], *s.* der Todeskampf; die Pein; ***– of mind,*** die Seelenangst, Seelenqual; (*coll.*) ***– column,*** die Seufzerspalte.

agoraphobia [ægərə'foubiə], *s.* (*Med.*) die Platzangst, Agoraphobie.

agrarian [ə'grɛəriən], *adj.* agrarisch, Agrar– landwirtschaftlich, Land–, Acker–; ***– law,*** das Agrargesetz, Ackergesetz; ***– party,*** die Bauernpartei.

agree [ə'gri:], *v.i.* übereinstimmen (***with,*** mit), entsprechen (*Dat.*); einwilligen (***to,*** in (*Acc.*)), zustimmen, beipflichten (*Dat.*), sich einverstanden erklären (mit); übereinkommen ((***up***)***on,*** in (*Dat.*)), einig werden, sich verständigen *or* einigen (über (*Acc.*)); sich vertragen, auskommen, einig sein, zusammenpassen; sich versöhnen *or* vergleichen; (*of food*) zuträglich sein, zusagen, bekommen (***with,*** *Dat.*); (miteinander) in Eintracht leben; stimmen, passen (***with,*** zu); ***as –d upon,*** wie vereinbart *or* verabredet; ***I have –d to act,*** ich habe mich bereit erklärt zu handeln; ***let us – to differ,*** streiten wir nicht mehr darüber; ***wine does not – with me,*** Wein bekommt mir nicht, ich kann keinen Wein vertragen; ***they all –d that . . .,*** sie vereinbarten, daß . . . *or* kamen alle überein, daß . . .; ***they are –d,*** sie sind sich einig; ***it is –d that . . .,*** man ist sich einig daß . . . ; ***–d!*** einverstanden! abgemacht!

agreeable [ə'gri:əbl], *adj.* liebenswürdig; angenehm (***to,*** *Dat. or* für), gefällig (*Dat.*); ***I am – to it,*** ich gehe darauf ein, ich bin damit einverstanden; (*coll.*) ***I am –,*** es ist mir recht. **agreeableness,** *s.* die Freundlichkeit, Annehmlichkeit.

agreement [ə'gri:mənt], *s.* die Übereinstimmung (***to, with,*** mit), Zustimmung (***to,*** zu), Vereinbarung, Verabredung ,Verständigung, Übereinkunft, das Abkommen, der Vertrag, Vergleich; Einklang, die Einigkeit, Eintracht; (*Gram.*) Übereinstimmung, Kongruenz; (*Law*) der Konsens; ***come to an –,*** ein Übereinkommen treffen, sich verständigen; ***by mutual –,*** in gegenseitigem Einvernehmen; ***be in –,*** übereinstimmen; ***reach*** (***an***) ***–,*** übereinkommen.

agricultural [ægri'kʌltʃərəl], *adj.* landwirtschaftlich, Landwirtschafts–, Land–, Ackerbau–; ***– labourer,*** der Landarbeiter; ***– produce,*** landwirtschaftliche Erzeugnisse; ***– wages,*** Landarbeiterlöhne. **agricultur(al)ist,** *s.* der Landwirt. **agriculture** ['ægrikʌltʃə], *s.* die Landwirtschaft, der Ackerbau; ***Ministry of Agriculture,*** das Landwirtschaftsministerium.

agrimony ['ægriməni], *s.* (*Bot.*) der Odermennig (*Agrimonia*).

agronomy [ə'grɔnəmi], *s.* die Ackerbaukunde.

aground [ə'graund], *pred.adj.* (*Naut.*) gestrandet; ***run –,*** auflaufen, stranden, auf (den) Grund laufen; ***run a ship –,*** ein Schiff auf (den) Grund setzen; ***be –,*** aufgelaufen sein.

ague ['eigju:], *s.* das Wechselfieber, der Fieberfrost, Schüttelfrost; das Zittern, Beben. **aguish** ['eigju:iʃ], *adj.* fieberhaft; zitternd.

ah! [ɑ:], *int.* ah! ha! ei! ach! **aha!** [ɑ:'hɑ:], *int.* aha! (*Scots coll.*) ja.

Ahasuerus [əhæzju'iərəs], *s.* (*B.*) Ahasver (*m.*).

ahead [ə'hed], *pred.adj.* vorwärts, voraus, voran, weiter vor, an der Spitze, vorn, nach vorn zu; ***straight –,*** geradeaus; (*coll.*) ***get –,*** vorwärts kommen, Karriere machen; ***get – of,*** überholen, (*fig.*) überflügeln; (*coll.*) ***go –!*** geh zu! mach weiter! ***go on –,*** vorgehen; ***full steam –,*** Volldampf voraus; (*Naut.*) ***right –,*** recht voraus; (*Naut.*) ***wind –,*** vorlicher Wind.

ahoy! [ə'hɔi], *int.* (*Naut.*) ahoi! ho!

aid [eid], **1.** *s.* die Hilfe (***to,*** für), der Beistand, die Unterstützung, Hilfeleistung (***in,*** bei); das Hilfsmittel; der Helfer, Gehilfe; ***by*** or ***with the – of,*** mit Hilfe (*Gen.*); ***come to his –,*** ihm zu Hilfe kommen; ***give*** or ***lend – to,*** Hilfe leisten (*Dat.*), unterstützen (*Acc.*); ***in – of,*** zum Besten (*Gen.*), zugunsten (*Gen. or* von). **2.** *v.t.* helfen (*Dat.*), beistehen (*Dat.*), behilflich sein (*Dat.*), Beistand leisten (*Dat.*), unterstützen, fördern (*digestion etc.*); (*Law*) ***– and abet,*** Vorschub *or* Beistand leisten (*Dat.*).

aide-de-camp ['eiddə'kã], *s.* der Adjutant (eines Generals), Flügeladjutant.

aide-mémoire [eidme'mwɑ:], *s.* die Denkschrift; Notiz, Gedächtnisstütze.

aigrette [ei'gret], *s.* der Federbusch, Kopfschmuck; die Reiherfeder; (*Bot.*) Haarkrone.

aiguille [ei'gwi:l], *s.* die Felsnadel.

aiguillette [eigwi'let], *s.* (*Mil.*) die Achselschnur.

ail [eil], **1.** *v.i.* unwohl *or* unpäßlich sein. **2.** *v.t.*(*imp.*) anfechten, weh tun (*Dat.*), schmerzen (*Dat.*); ***what –s him?*** was fehlt ihm?

aileron ['eilərɔn], *s.* (*Av.*) das Querruder, Quersteuer.

ailing ['eiliŋ], *adj.* unwohl, leidend, kränklich, unpäßlich. **ailment,** *s.* das Leiden, die Unpäßlichkeit.

aim [eim], **1.** *s.* die Richtung; das Ziel; (*fig.*) der Zweck, die Absicht, das Vorhaben; ***take – at a th.,*** zielen auf eine S. *or* nach einer S.; ***miss one's –,*** das Ziel verfehlen, fehlschießen; (*fig.*) seinen Zweck verfehlen. **2.** *v.i.* zielen (***at,*** nach *or* (*fig.*) auf (*Acc.*)); (*fig.*) streben (***at, for,*** nach); beabsichtigen, hinzielen auf (*Acc.*), bezwecken (*Acc.*), im Sinne haben (*Acc.*); ***– to do s.th.,*** etwas erstreben; (*fig.*) ***that was –ed at me,*** das galt mir *or* war auf mich abgesehen; (*fig.*) ***he –s too high***, er spannt die Saiten zu hoch, er steckt sich (*Dat.*) ein zu hohes Ziel. **3.** *v.t.* (*a weapon, blow etc.*) richten, anlegen (*at*, auf (*Acc.*)), (*fig.*) richten (*at*, gegen). **aimless,** *adj.* ohne Ziel, ziellos (*also fig.*), (*fig.*) planlos, zwecklos.

air [ɛə], **1.** *s.* 1. die Luft, Atmosphäre; Luftströmung, der Luftzug; ***by –***, per Flugzeug; (*fig.*) ***beat the –***, sich erfolglos bemühen; (*Min.*) ***foul –***, schlagende Wetter; (*fig.*) ***in the –***, ungewiß, in der Schwebe; ***there's s.th. in the –***, es liegt etwas in der Luft; ***castles in the –***, Luftschlösser (*pl.*); ***war in the –***, der Luftkrieg; ***in the open –***, im Freien, unter freiem Himmel, an der frischen Luft; ***open-–school***, die Freiluftschule, Waldschule; ***open-–theatre***, die Freilichtbühne; ***take the –***, (frische) Luft schöpfen; (*Av.*) abfliegen, aufsteigen; ***without a breath of –***, ohne ein Lüftchen, ohne daß sich ein Lüftchen regt; ***Secretary of State for Air***, der Luftfahrtminister; 2. (*Mus.*) die Melodie, Weise, Arie, das Lied; 3. Aussehen, die Miene, Gebärde, das Auftreten, Gebaren, Äußere(s); der Anschein, Stil, die Art; ***– of assurance***, dreistes Betragen; ***– of sadness***, Anflug der Traurigkeit; ***give o.s. –s***, vornehm tun, sich zieren *or* in die Brust werfen; ***–s (and graces)***, vornehmes Getue; 4. (*Rad., coll.*) der Äther; ***go off the –***, die Sendung beenden; ***on the –***, im *or* durch Rundfunk; ***be on the –***, senden; ***put on the –***, im Radio übertragen. **2.** *v.t.* lüften, ventilieren; der Luft aussetzen, an die Luft bringen, trocknen; (*fig.*) bekanntmachen, bekanntgeben, an die Öffentlichkeit bringen; sich groß tun mit, zur Schau tragen.

air|-arm, *s.* Luftstreitkräfte (*pl.*). **–-attack,** *s.* der Luftangriff, Fliegerangriff. **–-base,** *s.* der Fliegerstützpunkt. **–-bladder,** *s.* die Luftblase; (*Ichth*). Schwimmblase. **–borne, 1.** *pred.adj.* ***be –***, schon fliegen *or* in der Luft sein (*as aircraft*), per Luft befördert werden (*as supplies, reinforcments*). **2.** *attrib.adj.* ***– troops***, Luftlandetruppen (*pl.*). **– bubble,** *s.* die Luftblase. **Air Chief Marshal,** *s.* der General der Luftwaffe. **air| compressor,** der Preßlufterzeuger, Luftverdichter. **–-conditioning,** *s.* die Klimaanlage. **–-cooled,** *adj.* luftgekühlt. **–-cooling,** *s.* die Luftkühlung. **– corridor,** *s.* die Einflugschneise. **– cover,** *s.* die Luftsicherung. **–craft,** *s.* das Flugzeug; ***–-carrier***, der Flugzeugträger, das Flugzeugmutterschiff. **–crew,** *s.* fliegendes Personal, die Flugzeugbesatzung. **– current,** *s.* der Luftzug, die Zugluft; Luftströmung. **–field,** *s.* der Flugplatz, Flughafen, (*Mil.*) Fliegerhorst. **–flow,** *s.* der Luftstrom. **–foil,** *s.* die Tragfläche; ***– section***, das Tragflächenprofil. **– force,** *s.* die Luftwaffe, Luftstreitkräfte (*pl.*). **–frame,** *s.* die Zelle, das Gerippe (*of aircraft*). **–-gate,** *s.* (*Min.*) die Wettertür, das Schütz. **–graph letter,** *s.* der Photobrief. **–gun,** *s.* der Luftgewehr. **–-gunner,** *s.* der Bordschütze. **–-hole,** *s.* (*Av.*) die Fallbö, das Luftloch; (*Min.*) die Wetterleitung; (*Archit.*) das Zugloch; (*Metall.*) die Gußblase; (*on ice*) offene Stelle.

airily ['ɛərili], *adj.* (*fig.*) leichtfertig, leichten Sinnes. **airiness,** *s.* die Luftigkeit; Leichtigkeit; (*fig.*) Leichtfertigkeit, Munterkeit, Lebhaftigkeit. **airing,** *s.* das Lüften, die Lüftung, Belüftung, das Trocknen; der Spaziergang, Spazierritt, die Spazierfahrt; ***go for an –***, frische Luft schöpfen.

air|-inlet, –-intake, *s.* (*Tech.*) der Lufteinlaß, Lufteintritt. **– lane,** *s.* die Flugroute.

airless ['ɛəlis], *adj.* luftlos, stickig, dumpf.

air|-letter, *s.* der Luftpostbrief. **–-lift, 1.** *s.* (*Av.*) die Luftbrücke. **2.** *v.t.* auf dem Luftwege befördern. **–-line,** *s.* die Luftverkehrsgesellschaft; Luftverkehrslinie, Flugstrecke. **–-liner,** *s.* das Verkehrsflugzeug. **– lock,** *s.* die Druckstauung; Gasschleuse. **–mail,** *s.* die Luftpost, Flugpost. **–man,** *s.* der Flieger. **Air Marshal,** *s.* der Generalleutnant der Luftwaffe. **air|-mechanic,** *s.* der Bordmonteur. **–-mindedness,** *s.* die Flugbegeisterung. **Air Ministry,** *s.* das Luftfahrtministerium. **air| passenger,** *s.* der Fluggast. **–plane,** *s.* (*Am.*) das Flugzeug. **–-pocket,** *s.* (*Av.*) das Luftloch, die Fallbö. **– pollution,** *s.* die Luftverunreinigung. **–port,** *s.* der Flughafen. **– pressure,** *s.* der Luftdruck, Atmosphärendruck. **–proof,** *adj.* luftdicht. **–-raid,** *s.* der Fliegerangriff, Luftangriff; ***– precautions***, der Luftschutz; ***– shelter***, der Luftschutz|bunker, –raum, –keller; ***– warden***, der Luftschutzwart; ***– warning***, der Fliegeralarm. **– route,** *s.* die Flugstrecke. **–screw,** *s.* die Luftschraube, der Propeller. **–-shaft,** *s.* (*Min.*) der Wetterschacht. **–ship,** *s.* das Luftschiff. **–-sick,** *adj.* luftkrank. **– speed,** *s.* die Eigengeschwindigkeit; ***– indicator***, der Fahrtmesser. **–-strip,** *s.* der Landestreifen, Behelfsflugplatz. **– supply,** *s.* die Zuluft, Luftzufuhr. **– terminal,** *s.* der Großflughafen. **–tight,** *adj.* luftdicht, hermetisch; (*fig., coll.*) unangreifbar, todsicher. **– vesicle,** *s.* (*Zool.*) das Luftgefäß. **–way,** *s.* (*Min.*) der Wetterschacht; die Wetterstrecke; (*Av.*) Luftverkehrslinie, Flugstrecke. **–woman,** *s.* die Fliegerin. **–worthy,** *adj.* lufttüchtig, flugfähig.

airy ['ɛəri], *adj.* luftig; leicht, zierlich, zart, ätherisch; nichtig, eitel; leichtfertig, lebhaft, munter.

aisle [ail], *s.* das Seitenschiff, der Seitenchor (*in a church*); Gang (*in a hall*); die Schneise (*in a forest*).

aitch [eitʃ], *s.* der Buchstabe h; ***drop one's –es***, das h (im Anlaut) nicht aussprechen. **aitch-bone,** *s.* das Lendenstück.

Aix-la-Chapelle ['eikslaʃæ'pel], *s.* Aachen (*n.*).

ajar [ə'dʒɑ:], *pred.adj.* halb offen, angelehnt.

akimbo [ə'kimbou], *pred.adj.* ***with arms –***, die Arme in die Seiten gestemmt.

akin [ə'kin], *pred.adj.* (bluts)verwandt (*to*, mit); (*fig.*) (eng)verwandt (mit), ähnlich, entsprechend (*Dat.*).

alabaster [ælə'bɑ:stə], **1.** *s.* der Alabaster. **2.** *adj.* alabastern; (*fig.*) schimmernd weiß.

alack! [ə'læk], *int.* (*obs.*) o weh! ach! (*obs.*) ***–-a-day*** ach Gott!

alacrity [ə'lækriti], *s.* die Munterkeit, Lebhaftigkeit; Bereitwilligkeit, Dienstfertigkeit.

Aladdin [ə'lædin], *s.* Aladin (*m.*).

Alaric ['ælərik], *s.* Alarich (*m.*).

alarm [ə'lɑ:m], **1.** *s.* 1. der Alarm; Alarmruf, Warnruf, die Warnung; ***false –***, blinder Alarm; ***give or raise the –***, Larm schlagen, das Alarmzeichen geben; 2. der Schreck, die Furcht, Angst, Unruhe, Bestürzung; ***cause –***, Unruhe erregen; ***take –***, in Angst geraten, erschrecken, unruhig werden (*at*, über (*Acc.*)); 3. der Wecker (*in a clock*); 4. (*Fenc.*) Appell; 5. (*obs.*) Angriff, Überfall. **2.** *v.t.* 1. erschrecken, in Furcht setzen, beunruhigen, in Aufregung versetzen; 2. aufschrecken, warnen, alarmieren.

alarm|-bell, *s.* die Sturmglocke. **–-clock,** *s.* der Wecker, die Weckuhr. **alarming,** *adj.* beunruhigend, beängstigend. **alarmist, 1.** *s.* der Bangemacher, Schwarzseher. **2.** *adj.* beunruhigend. **alarm-post,** *s.* (*Mil.*) der Sammelplatz.

alarum [ə'lɑ:rəm], *s.* 1. (*obs.*) *see* **alarm, 1**; 2. die Alarmglocke, das Läutwerk.

alas! [ə'lɑ:s], *int.* leider! ach! o weh! ***– the day!*** o Unglückstag!

alate(d) ['eileit(id)], *adj.* (*Bot.*) geflügelt. **alation** [–'leiʃən], *s.* die Beflügelung.

alb [ælb], *s.* das Chorhemd, Meßhemd, die Albe.

albacore ['ælbəkɔ:], *s.* der Thunfisch.

Albanian [æl'beiniən], **1.** *s.* 1. der Albaner, Albanese; 2. (*language*) das Albanisch(e). **2.** *adj.* alban(es)isch.

albatross ['ælbətrɔs], *s.* (*Orn.*) der Albatros; ***black-browed –***, der Mollymauk (*Diomedea melanophris*); ***grey-headed –***, der Graukopfalbatros (*D. chrysostoma*); ***light-mantled sooty –***, der Rußalbatros (*Phoebetria palpebrata*); ***wandering –***, das Kapschaf (*D. exulans*); ***yellow-nosed –***, der Gelbnasenalbatros (*D. chlororhynchos*).

albeit [ɔ:l'bi:it], *conj.* (*also* ***– that***) obgleich, obwohl, ungeachtet, wiewohl.

albinism ['ælbinizm], *s.* der Albinismus, (*Bot.*) die Weißblättrigkeit. **albino** [æl'bi:nou], *s.* der Albino, Kakerlak.

album ['ælbəm], *s.* das Stammbuch, Album; (*Am.*) Fremdenbuch, Gästebuch.

albumen ['ælbjumin], *s.* (*Chem.*) das Albumin, der

Eiweißstoff, (*Zool., Bot.*) das Albumen, Eiweiß. **albuminate** [–'bju:minit], *s.* die Eiweißverbindung. **albuminous,** *adj.* eiweißhaltig.

alburnum [æl'bə:nəm], *s.* (*Bot.*) der Splint, das Splintholz.

Alcaic [æl'keiik], *adj.* (*Metr.*) alkäisch.

alchemical [æl'kemikəl], *adj.* alchimistisch. **alchemist** ['ælkimist], *s.* der Alchimist. **alchemy** ['ælkimi], *s.* die Alchimie.

alcohol ['ælkəhɔl], *s.* der Alkohol, Spiritus, Sprit, Weingeist. **alcoholic** [–'hɔlik], **1.** *adj.* alkoholisch; ***non–***, alkoholfrei; **– *liquor,*** geistige Getränke (*pl.*). **2.** *s.* der Säufer, Gewohnheitstrinker, Alkoholiker. **alcoholism,** *s.* der Alkoholismus, die Trunksucht; Alkoholvergiftung. **alcoholization** [–ai'zeiʃən], *s.* die Spiritusrektifikation; Sättigung mit Alkohol.

alcove ['ælkouv], *s.* (*Archit.*) der Alkoven; die Nische; Laube, Grotte.

aldehyde ['ældəhaid], *s.* (*Chem.*) der Aldehyd.

alder ['ɔ:ldə], **1.** *s.* (*Bot.*) die Erle. **2.** *adj.* erlen.

alderman ['ɔ:ldəmən], *s.* der Stadtrat, Ratsherr. **aldermanic** [–'mænik], *adj.* ratsherrlich; (*fig.*) würdevoll, gravitätisch.

ale [eil], *s.* englisches Bier, das Ale; ***pale –,*** helles Bier.

alee [ə'li:], *pred.adj.* (*Naut.*) leewärts, in Lee, unter dem Winde.

alembic [ə'lembik], *s.* der Destillierkolben.

alert [ə'lə:t], **1.** *adj.* wachsam, vorsichtig, umsichtig; (*pred.*) auf der Hut, (*coll.*) auf dem Posten; lebhaft, rege, munter, flink. **2.** *s.* die Alarmbereitschaft; Warnung, der Alarmruf; ***air-raid –,*** der Fliegeralarm; ***on the –,*** auf der Hut. **alertness,** *s.* die Wachsamkeit, Vorsicht; Munterkeit, Flinkheit.

alevin ['æləvin], *s.* (*Ichth.*) der Setzling, junge Fischbrut.

alexandrine [ælig'zɑ:ndrin], *s.* (*Metr.*) der Alexandriner.

alfresco [æl'freskou], *adj.* im Freien.

algae ['ældʒi:], *pl.* die Algen (*pl.*), das Seegras. **algal** ['ælgəl], *adj.* Algen–.

algebra ['ældʒibrə], *s.* die Algebra, Buchstabenrechnung. **algebraic(al)** [–'breiik(əl)], *adj.* algebraisch.

Algerian [æl'dʒiəriən], **1.** *s.* der (die) Algerier(in). **2.** *adj.* algerisch.

algid ['ældʒid], *adj.* (*Med.*) kalt, kühl. **algidity** [–'dʒiditi], *s.* die Kühle, Kälte.

algoid ['ælgɔid], *adj.* algenartig. **algological** [–gə'lɔdʒikəl], *adj.* algenkundlich. **algology** [–'gɔlədʒi], *s.* die Algenkunde.

algorithm ['ælgəriðm], *s.* das Rechenverfahren, die Rechnungsart, der Algorithmus.

alias ['eiliəs], **1.** *adv.* anders, sonst (. . . genannt). **2.** *s.* angenommener Name; ***under an –,*** unter falschem Namen.

alibi ['ælibai], *s.* (*Law*) das Alibi; (*coll.*) die Ausrede; ***establish*** or ***prove an –,*** sein Alibi beibringen.

alien ['eiliən], **1.** *adj.* fremd, ausländisch; (*fig.*) fernliegend, unsympathisch (*to, Dat.*), unangemessen (für *or Dat.*); ***it is – to my purpose,*** es entspricht nicht meiner Absicht *or* ist meiner Absicht zuwider. **2.** *s.* der (die) Ausländer(in), Fremde(r); (*fig.*) der Fremdling; ***–s' act,*** das Einwanderungsgesetz; ***undesirable –,*** lästiger Ausländer.

alienable ['eiliənəbl], *adj.* (*Law*) übertragbar, veräußerlich. **alienate,** *v.t.* 1. (*Law*) übertragen, veräußern (*property*); 2. entfremden, abspenstig machen (*a p.*) (*from, Dat. or* von). **alienation** [–'neiʃən], *s.* (*Law*) die Übertragung, Veräußerung; Entfremdung (***from,*** von); Abwendung, Abneigung, Abgeneigtheit; ***mental –, – of mind,*** die Geistesgestörtheit. **alienist,** *s.* der Psychiater, Irrenarzt, Nervenartzt.

[1]**alight** [ə'lait], *v.i.* (*of a bird*) sich niederlassen, sich setzen (***on,*** auf (*Acc.*)); (*Av.*) niedergehen, landen, wassern; absitzen (***from,*** von) (*a horse*), absteigen (von), aussteigen (aus) (*a vehicle*); (fig.) **– (*up*) *on,*** stoßen auf (*Acc.*).

[2]**alight,** *pred.adj.* in Flammen, brennend; (*fig.*) erleuchtet, erhellt (***with,*** von).

align [ə'lain], **1.** *v.t.* in eine (gerade) Linie bringen, in gerader Linie aufstellen; abmessen, abstecken; (*Artil.*) (aus)richten; (*fig.*) **– *o.s. with,*** sich anschließen an (*Acc.*). **2.** *v.i.* sich ausrichten (***with,*** nach), eine Linie bilden (mit). **alignment,** *s.* das Anordnen, die Anordnung, das Ausrichten, Abmessen, Abstecken, (*of a wheel*) Ausfluchten, die Fluchtung; der Gleichlauf, die Flucht; Richtung, aufgestellte Linie, Verlängerungslinie; (*Surv.*) Absteckline, Trasse; ***out of –,*** nicht gerade, schlecht ausgerichtet; ***in – with,*** in einer Linie mit.

alike [ə'laik], **1.** *pred.adj.* gleich, ähnlich. **2.** *adv.* gleich, gleicherweise, gleichermaßen, in gleicher Weise, ebenso; ***for you and me –,*** sowohl für dich wie mich.

aliment ['ælimənt], *s.* die Nahrung, Speise, das Futter, Nahrungsmittel, der Unterhalt. **alimental** [–'məntl], *adj.* nährend, nahrhaft. **alimentary,** *adj. See* **alimental**; Nahrungs–, Ernährungs–; Speise–; **– *canal,*** der Magendarmkanal, Verdauungskanal. **alimentation,** *s.* die Ernährung, Beköstigung, Verpflegung, Speisung; der Unterhalt; die Ernährungsweise, Ernährungsart.

alimony ['æliməni], *s.* (*Law*) der Unterhalt(sbeitrag), Alimente (*pl.*).

aliquant ['ælikwənt], *adj.* (*Math.*) nicht aufgehend, ungleichteilend. **aliquot,** *adj.* (ohne Rest) aufgehend, gleichteilend.

alive [ə'laiv], *adj.* (*usu. pred.*) lebend, lebendig, am Leben; lebendig, lebhaft, munter, belebt, rege, aufgeweckt; (*Elec.*) unter Spannung; **– *to,*** empfänglich für, achtsam *or* aufmerksam auf (*Acc.*); (*coll.*) ***look –!*** beeile dich! mach nur zu! ***there's not a man – who can . . .,*** niemand auf der Welt *or* kein Sterblicher kann . . .; ***be – with,*** wimmeln von (*fleas etc.*); (*coll.*) **– *and kicking,*** wohl und munter.

alizarin [ə'lizərin], *s.* das Krapprot.

alkali ['ælkəlai], *s.* das Alkali, Laugensalz. **alkalify** [–'kælifai], *v.t., v.i.* (sich) in Alkali verwandeln. **alkaline,** *adj.* alkalihaltig, alkalisch, basisch, laugensalzig; **– *salts,*** Abraumsalze (*pl.*). **alkaloid,** **1.** *adj.* alkaliartig, laugenhaft. **2.** *s.* das Alkaloid.

all [ɔ:l], **1.** *adj.* ganz, gesamt, vollständig, völlig, vollkommen; alle (*pl.*), sämtliche (*pl.*); all, jede(r), jedes; ***in – conscience,*** auf Ehre und Gewissen; ***lose – contact,*** jede Art von Kontakt verlieren; **– *day,*** den ganzen Tag; **– *Europe,*** ganz Europa; ***at – events,*** auf alle Fälle, unter allen Umständen; ***on – fours,*** auf allen vieren; ***with – my heart,*** von ganzem Herzen; ***till – hours of the night,*** bis spät in die Nacht; ***to – intents and purposes,*** mehr oder weniger, eigentlich, praktisch; **– *kinds*** or ***sorts of,*** allerlei; **– *good men,*** alle guten Menschen; **– *the men who,*** alle (die) Männer, die; ***with – speed,*** in aller Eile; ***he is – things to – men,*** er ist allen alles; **– *wool,*** reine Wolle; **– *the world,*** die ganze Welt, alle Welt; ***for – the world like,*** gerade *or* durchaus wie; ***not for – the world,*** nicht um alles in der Welt; **– *the world over,*** in der ganzen Welt. **2.** *adv.* (*when compounded with adjs. see compounds below*) ganz und gar, gänzlich, völlig; **– *along,*** die ganze Zeit über; **– *the better,*** um so besser, desto besser; ***be – ears,*** ganz Ohr sein; ***once and for –,*** ein für allemal; ***for good and –,*** für immer; (*coll.*) **– *in,*** total fertig *or* erledigt; (*coll.*) **– *out,*** mit aller Kraft *or* Macht; **– *over the town,*** durch die ganze Stadt, in der ganzen Stadt; ***that's Richard – over,*** das ist ganz *or* typisch Richard; Richard, wie er leibt und lebt; ***have pains – over,*** überall Schmerzen haben; ***tremble – over,*** am ganzen Leibe zittern; **– *right!*** ganz richtig! recht! gut! schön! schon gut! sehr wohl! einverstanden! alles in Ordnung! ***I am – right,*** es geht mir gut, ich bin ganz gesund; **– *round,*** rings umher, rund (her)um; (*coll.*) durchweg, in jeder Richtung, durch die Bank; ***taking it – round,*** im großen und ganzen; **– *the same,*** nichtsdestoweniger, ganz gleich; **– *the same, whether . . .,*** gleichgültig ob . . .; (*coll.*) **– *set,*** fertig, bereit; (*coll.*) **– *there,*** bei Sinnen, auf Draht, gewitzt, gescheit; **– *too dear,*** nur zu teuer; (*coll.*) **– *up,***

hoffnungslos (vorbei *or* verloren); (*coll.*) ***it's – up with him,*** es ist aus mit ihm; – ***in vain,*** völlig vergebens.
3. *pron.* alles; – ***but,*** beinahe, fast; – ***of us,*** wir alle; – ***of £10,*** volle zehn Pfund; – ***over,*** alles vorbei, alles zu Ende; – ***at once,*** auf einmal; ***one and –,*** alle zusammen *or* miteinander; ***it's – one to me,*** es ist mir einerlei *or* ganz gleich *or* alles eins; ***when – is said and done,*** im Grunde (genommen), letzten Endes; – ***and sundry,*** jedermann, alle, all und jeder; ***if that is –,*** wenn's weiter nichts ist; ***and – that,*** und dergleichen; ***that's – very well,*** das ist alles sehr schön; (*with preps.*) ***above –,*** vor allem, vor allen Dingen; ***after –,*** bei *or* trotz alledem, trotz *or* nach allem, schließlich, am Ende (doch), also doch, übrigens, im Grunde (genommen), nach reiflicher Überlegung; ***at –,*** überhaupt, durchaus; ***not at –,*** ganz und gar nicht, keineswegs; ***nothing at –,*** gar nichts; ***nowhere at –,*** nirgends; ***for – that,*** trotzdem, dessenungeachtet; ***for – I care,*** was mich betrifft, meinetwegen; ***for – I know,*** es ist ganz gut möglich, daß . . .; ***in –,*** in allem, im ganzen, alles zusammen (genommen).
4. *s.* das Ganze; Alles; der Gesamtbesitz; ***my –,*** mein alles; ***I lost my –,*** ich habe all mein Hab und Gut verloren.

all-absorbing, *adj.* völlig in Anspruch nehmend.

allay [ə'lei], *v.t.* lindern, mildern, dämpfen, mäßigen, stillen, beruhigen, beschwichtigen.

all-clear, *s.* (*coll.*) das Entwarnungssignal.

allegation [ælə'geiʃən], *s.* (unerwiesene) Behauptung, die Angabe, Anführung, (*Law*) Aussage, Aufzählung.

allege [ə'ledʒ], *v.t.* anführen, angeben, vorgeben, vorbringen, (Unerwiesenes) behaupten *or* versichern, (*Law*) aussagen, erklären. **alleged,** *adj.* angeblich. **allegedly** [–idli], *adv.* angeblich, vorgeblich.

allegiance [ə'li:dʒəns], *s.* die Untertanenpflicht, Untertanentreue, Lehnspflicht; Ergebenheit, Treue; ***oath of –,*** der Huldigungseid, Untertaneneid; ***conflict of –s,*** der Widerstreit der Bindungen.

allegoric(al) [ælə'gɔrik(əl)], *adj.* (sinn)bildlich, allegorisch. **allegorize** ['æləgəraiz], **1.** *v.t.* (sinn)bildlich darstellen. **2.** *v.i.* Allegorien gebrauchen. **allegory** ['æləgəri], *s.* die Allegorie, sinnbildliche Darstellung, das Sinnbild, Gleichnis.

allele ['æli:l], **allelomorph** ['æleləmɔ:f, ə'li:ləmɔ:f], *s.* (*Biol.*) das Allel, der Erbfaktor.

alleluia, allelujah [æli'lu:jə], *s.* das Hallelujah, Loblied.

allergic [ə'lə:dʒik], *adj.* überempfindlich, allergisch (*to,* gegen). **allergy** ['ælədʒi], *s.* die Überempfindlichkeit, Allergie; (*coll.*) Abneigung.

alleviate [ə'li:vieit], *v.t.* erleichtern, (ver)mindern, linden, mildern. **alleviation** [–'eiʃən], *s.* die Erleichterung, Linderung, Milderung, Abschwächung; – ***of tension,*** die Entspannung.

[1]**alley** ['æli], *s.* die Gasse, Seitenstraße, der Durchgang; die Allee, der (Baum)gang; ***blind –,*** die Sackgasse; ***skittle –,*** die Kegelbahn; (*coll.*) ***that's up*** or ***down my –,*** das ist gerade was für mich.

[2]**alley,** *s.* die (Glas)murmel.

All Fool's Day, *s.* der erste April.

All-Hallows, *s.* (*Eccl.*) Allerheiligen (*pl.*).

alliance [ə'laiəns], *s.* das Bündnis, der Bund, die Allianz; Verbindung, Verwandtschaft, Verschwägerung, Gemeinschaft; ***Dual Alliance,*** der Zweibund; ***Triple Alliance,*** der Dreibund; ***offensive and defensive –,*** das Schutz- und Trutzbündnis; ***enter into*** or ***form*** or ***make an –,*** sich verbinden, ein Bündnis schließen.

allied [ə'laid, 'ælaid], *adj.* verbündet; verwandt; ***Allied Control Commission,*** Alliierter Kontrollrat. *See* **ally.**

alligation [æli'geiʃən], *s.* (*Math.*) die Mischung; ***the rule of –,*** die Misch(ungs)rechnung, Alligationsrechnung.

alligator ['æligeitə], *s.* der Alligator, Kaiman.

all-in, *adj.* alles inbegriffen; ***–insurance,*** die Generalversicherung; – ***wrestling,*** das Freistilringen.

alliterate [ə'litəreit], *v.i.* (*Metr.*) alliterieren, mit demselben Buchstaben anfangen. **alliteration** [–'reiʃən], *s.* der Stabreim, die Alliteration. **alliterative** [–rətiv], *adj.* stabreimend, alliterierend; – ***poetry,*** die Stabreimdichtung.

all-metal, *adj.* Ganzmetall–.

allness ['ɔ:lnis], *s.* die Ganzheit, Totalität.

allocate ['ælokeit], *v.t.* zuteilen, zuweisen, anweisen (*to, Dat.*); beiseite legen. **allocation** [–'keiʃən], *s.* die Verteilung, Zuteilung, Anweisung, Zuweisung; das Kontingent; – ***of contracts,*** die Auftragslenkung.

allocution [ælə'kju:ʃən], *s.* die Anrede, Ansprache.

allodial [ə'loudiəl], *adj.* allodial, erbeigen, lehnzinsfrei; – ***lands,*** Allodialgüter (*pl.*). **allodium,** *s.* das Allod(ium), Freigut, freies Erbgut.

allopath ['ælopæθ], **allopathist** [ə'lɔpəθist], *s.* der Allopath. **allopathy** [ə'lɔpəθi], *s.* die Allopathie.

allot [ə'lɔt], *v.t.* anweisen, zuteilen, zumessen (***s.th. to him,*** ihm etwas); austeilen, verteilen. **allotment,** *s.* **1.** der Anteil, das Los; die Zuteilung, Zuweisung, Verteilung; (*Comm.*) ***on –,*** bei Zuteilung der Aktien; **2.** die Parzelle; kleines Pachtgrundstück; – (***garden***), der Schrebergarten; – ***holder,*** der Kleingärtner.

allotropy [ə'lɔtrəpi], *s.* (*Chem.*) die Allotropie, Vielgestaltigkeit.

all-out, *adj.* (*coll.*) unbedingt, uneingeschränkt; ***be*** or ***go – for,*** mit aller Macht hinterher sein (*Dat.*); – ***war,*** totaler Krieg.

allow [ə'lau], **1.** *v.t.* **1.** erlauben, gestatten, zugestehen, bewilligen, zubilligen, gewähren, gönnen (*Dat. of p.*); (*a th.*) zugeben, einräumen; dulden *or* gelten lassen, stattgeben (*Dat.*); ***I – her to go,*** ich erlaube ihr zu gehen, ich erlaube *or* gestatte, daß sie geht; ***they were not –ed out,*** sie durften nicht ausgehen; – ***me,*** gestatten Sie mir bitte; – ***o.s. a cigar after dinner,*** sich (*Dat.*) eine Zigarre nach dem Essen gönnen; – ***the paint to dry,*** die Farbe trocknen lassen; ***they would not – that he . . .,*** sie wollten nicht zugeben *or* einräumen, daß er . . .; **2.** abziehen, absetzen, abrechnen; anrechnen, vergüten, rabattieren, nachlassen, in Anrechnung *or* Anschlag bringen; bestimmen, ansetzen; ***I – him £30 a year,*** ich lasse ihm jährlich 30 Pfund zukommen; ***he –ed 3 hours for the work,*** er setzte 3 Stunden für die Arbeit an; **3.** versichern, behaupten. **2.** *v.i.* – ***for,*** in Anschlag bringen, in Betracht ziehen, berücksichtigen, Rücksicht nehmen auf (*Acc.*); – ***for waste,*** den Verlust in Anschlag bringen; – ***of,*** gestatten, zulassen, sich einverstanden erklären mit; ***his conduct –s of no excuse,*** sein Betragen läßt sich nicht entschuldigen *or* läßt keine Entschuldigung zu.

allowable [ə'lauəbl], *adj.* zulässig, erlaubt, rechtmäßig; (*as discount*) abziehbar.

allowance [ə'lauəns], **1.** *s.* die Einräumung, Genehmigung, Anerkennung, Billigung; Einwilligung, Bewilligung, Zulassung, Erlaubnis; angesetzte *or* ausgesetzte Summe (*e.g.* das Taschengeld, die Rente, jährliches Gehalt); zugeteilte Ration; die Nachsicht, Schonung, Rücksicht(nahme) (*for,* auf (*Acc.*)); Entschädigung, Vergütung, (*Comm.*) der Abzug, Nachlaß, Rabatt, die Ermäßigung; (*Tech.*) Toleranz; der Spielraum, zulässige Abweichung, das Remedium; (*Spt.*) die Vorgabe; ***education –,*** die Erziehungsbeihilfe; (*Mil.*) ***field –,*** die Feldzulage; ***mileage –,*** Kilometergelder (*pl.*); ***monthly –,*** das Monatsgeld, der Wechsel (*of a student*); ***short –,*** knappe Ration; ***make –*** (***for***), Nachsicht üben (bei), in Anschlag bringen, in Betracht ziehen, Rücksicht nehmen (auf (*Acc.*)), zugute halten; ***make him an –,*** ihm eine Summe *or* ein Taschengeld *or* Monatsgeld *etc.* zukommen lassen *or* aussetzen; (*Comm.*) ihm Rabatt gewähren, ihm vom Preis nachlassen. **2.** *v.t.* portionsweise austeilen, rationieren (*goods*); auf Rationen setzen (*a p.*).

alloy [ə'lɔi, 'ælɔi], **1.** *s.* die Legierung; (*fig.*) (Bei)mischung; – ***of gold,*** die Goldlegierung. **2.** *v.t.* legieren, mischen; (*fig.*) verschlechtern. **3.** *v.i.* sich vermischen.

all|-purpose, *adj.* Allzweck–, Mehrzweck. **--round,** *adj.* (*coll.*) vielseitig. **All| Saints' Day,** *s.* *See* **--Hallows. – Souls' Day,** *s.* (*Eccl.*) Allerseelen(tag).

allspice ['ɔ:lspais], *s.* (*Bot.*) der Nelkenpfeffer (*Pimenta officinalis*).

all-time, *adj.* (*coll.*) beispiellos, noch nie dagewesen, bisher unerreicht.

allude [ə'l(j)u:d], *v.i.* anspielen, hindeuten (*to,* auf (*Acc.*)); sprechen (von).

allure [ə'ljuə], **1.** *v.t.* anlocken, verlocken, ködern; (*fig.*) anziehen, reizen, bezaubern. **2.** *s.* der Reiz, Zauber, die Anziehungskraft. **allurement,** *s.* die Lockung, Verlockung, Reizung; das Lockmittel, der Köder; *see also* **allure, 2. alluring,** *adj.* reizend, bezaubernd, verlockend, verführerisch.

allusion [ə'l(j)u:ʒən], *s.* die Anspielung, Andeutung, Hinweisung, Bezugnahme (*to,* auf (*Acc.*)); (gelegentliche) Erwähnung (von); *make an – to,* anspielen auf (*Acc.*). **allusive** [–siv], *adj.* anspielend, verblümt.

alluvial [ə'lu:viəl], *adj.* (*Geol.*) angeschwemmt, angespült; Alluvial–; – *deposit,* die Anschwemmung, Aufschwemmung; – *plain,* die Schwemmlandebene. **alluvion,** *s.* die Überschwemmung, (*Law*) angeschwemmtes Land, die Landzunahme durch Anschwemmung. **alluvium,** *s.* (*Geol.*) angeschwemmtes Land, das Alluvium.

ally, 1. [ə'lai], *v.t.* verbinden, vereinigen, alliieren. **2.** [–'lai], *v.i., v.r.* sich verbünden *or* verbinden *or* vereinigen (*to, with,* mit). **3.** ['ælai], *s.* Verbündete(r), Alliierte(r), der Bundesgenosse; *the Allies,* die Alliierten.

almanac ['ɔ:lmənæk], *s.* der Almanach, Kalender, das Jahrbuch.

almightiness [ɔ:l'maitinis], *s.* die Allmacht. **almighty, 1.** *adj.* allmächtig; (*sl.*) kolossal, riesig. **2.** *s.* *the Almighty,* der Allmächtige.

almond ['ɑ:mənd], *s.* die Mandel; der Mandelbaum.

almoner ['ɑ:mənə, 'ælmənə], *s.* der Almosenpfleger; Krankenhausbeamte(r) für Sozialfürsorge.

almost ['ɔ:lmoust], *adv.* fast, beinahe, nahezu.

alms [ɑ:mz], *s.* (*also used as pl.*) das Almosen, die Armenhilfe, Liebesgabe, milde Gabe. **alms|-box,** *s.* die Almosenbüchse, Opferbüchse. **--giver,** *s.* der Almosenspender. **--giving,** *s.* das Almosenspenden. **–house,** *s.* das Armenhaus, Spital.

alodial, alodium, *see* **allodial, allodium.**

aloe ['ælou], *s.* (*Bot.*) die Aloe. **aloes,** *pl.* 1. (*B.*) das Aloeholz; 2. (*Pharm.*) der Aloesaft. **aloetic** [–'etik], *adj.* aloehaltig.

aloft [ə'lɔft], *adv.* (*Poet.*) hoch oben, droben, empor; in die *or* der Höhe, im *or* gen Himmel; (*Naut.*) in die *or* der Takelung.

alone [ə'loun], **1.** *pred.adj.* allein; *he –,* nur *or* bloß er; *leave* or *let him –,* ihn in Frieden *or* Ruhe lassen; *leave* or *let a th. –,* eine S. bleiben *or* sein lassen, die Finger von einer S. lassen; *he is not – in it,* er ist hierin nicht der Einzige. **2.** *adv.* nur, bloß, allein; *let – . . .,* geschweige (denn) . . ., abgesehen von.

along [ə'lɔŋ], **1.** *adv.* entlang, der Länge nach; weiter, fort, geradeaus; einher–, dahin–; *all –,* der ganzen Länge nach, überall; die ganze Zeit (hindurch), durchweg, fortwährend; *move –!* weiter! vorwärts! (*coll.*) *come – with me!* komm mit mir! *he drove –,* er fuhr dahin; (*coll.*) *get* or *go – with you!* packe dich! fort mit dir! *as we go –,* unterwegs; *take that – with you,* nimm das mit; – *with,* zusammen mit, nebst, samt. **2.** *prep.* entlang (*Dat. or Acc.*); längs (*Gen.*); an (*Dat.*) . . . vorbei; – *the road,* die Straße entlang; *we strolled – the river,* wir gingen den *or* am Fluß entlang. **alongside, 1.** *adv.* nebenan, Seite an Seite; (*Naut.*) Bord an Bord, längsseits. **2.** *prep.* längsseit(s) (*Gen.*), neben (*Dat.*), an der Seite von.

aloof [ə'lu:f], **1.** *pred.adj.* zurückhaltend, reserviert. **2.** *adv.* fern, weitab, abseits; *hold* or *keep* or *stand – from,* sich fernhalten von, neutral bleiben in (*Dat.*). **aloofness,** *s.* die Zurückhaltung, Reserviertheit.

alopecia [ælo'pi:ʃə], *s.* (*Med.*) der Haarausfall, die Alopezie.

aloud [ə'laud], *adv.* laut, vernehmlich, mit lauter Stimme.

alp [ælp], *s.* die Alm, Alpe.

alpaca [æl'pækə], *s.* (*Zool.*) das Alpaka, der Pako; die Alpakawolle; der Alpakastoff.

alpenglow ['ælpənglou], *s.* das Alpenglühen. **alpenstock,** *s.* der Bergstock.

alphabet ['ælfəbet], *s.* das Alphabet, Abc, Abece. **alphabetical** [–'betikl], *adj.* alphabetisch.

alpine ['ælpain], *adj.* alpin(isch); Alpen–, Hochgebirgs–; – *boots,* Bergschuhe, Nagelschuhe (*pl.*); – *club,* der Alpenklub *or* –verein; – *dweller,* der Älpler, Alpenbewohner; – *plant,* die Alpenpflanze; – *troops,* Gebirgsjäger (*pl.*). **alpinist** ['ælpinist], *s.* der Bergsteiger.

Alps [ælps], *pl.* Alpen (*pl.*).

already [ɔ:l'redi], *adv.* bereits, schon.

Alsace [æl'sæs], *s.* Elsaß (*n.*). **Alsatian** [–'seiʃən], **1.** *s.* 1. der (die) Elsässer(in); 2. deutscher Schäferhund, Wolfshund. **2.** *adj.* elsässisch.

also ['ɔ:lsou], *adv.* auch, ebenfalls, gleichfalls; ferner, außerdem, ebenso, dazu; (*Spt.*) . . . – *ran,* ferner liefen . . .; (*sl.*) *--ran,* der Versager, Nieter.

altar ['ɔ:ltə], *s.* der Altar. **altar|-cloth,** *s.* die Altarbekleidung, Altardecke. **--piece,** *s.* das Altarbild, Altargemälde. **--screen,** *s.* der Altarschrein.

alter ['ɔ:ltə], **1.** *v.t.* ändern, verändern, umändern, abändern, verwandeln, anders machen; *it does not – the fact,* es ändert nichts an der Tatsache. **2.** *v.i.* anders werden, sich (ver)ändern. **alterable,** *adj.* änderungsfähig, veränderlich, wandelbar. **alteration** [–'reiʃən], *s.* die Änderung (*to,* an (*Dat.*)), Veränderung; Umänderung, Abänderung, Abwechslung, Umbildung, Neuerung. **alterative** [–rətiv], *adj.* verändernd; (*Med.*) alterierend.

altercation [ɔ:ltə'keiʃən], *s.* der Streit, Zank, Wortwechsel.

alternate, 1. ['ɔ:ltəneit], *v.t.* wechselweise verrichten *or* verändern, abwechseln lassen, (aufeinander) folgen lassen. **2.** ['ɔ:ltəneit], *v.i.* (miteinander) abwechseln; wechselweise *or* aufeinander folgen. **3.** [ɔ:l'tə:nit], *adj.* abwechselnd; wechselseitig; (*Bot.*) wechselständig; – *angles,* Wechselwinkel; *on – days, on each – day,* einen Tag um den andern.

alternately [ɔ:l'tə:nitli], *adv.* abwechselnd, nacheinander, bald . . ., bald . . .; wechselweise. **alternating** ['ɔ:ltəneitiŋ], *adj.* abwechselnd, Wechsel–; – *current,* der Wechselstrom. **alternation** [–'neiʃən], *s.* die Abwechs(e)lung, der Wechsel, (*Math.*) die Permutation, Versetzung; das Responsorium. **alternative, 1.** *s.* die Wahl (zwischen zwei Dingen); das Entweder-Oder, die Alternative; *have no –,* keine Wahl haben, es bleibt (*Dat.*) nichts anderes übrig als. **2.** *adj.* alternativ, einander ausschließend; (*Mil.*) – *target,* das Ausweichziel. **alternator** ['ɔ:ltəneitə], *s.* der Wechselstromerzeuger, Wechselstromgenerator.

although [ɔ:l'ðou], *conj.* obgleich, obwohl, obschon, obzwar, wenn . . . schon, wenn . . . gleich, wenn . . . auch.

altimeter ['æltimi:tə], *s.* der Höhenmesser.

altitude ['æltitju:d], *s.* die Höhe; (*Av.*) Flughöhe; (*fig.*) Hoheit; *take the sun's –,* die Sonnenhöhe messen.

alto ['æltou], *s.* der Alt; – *clef,* der Altschlüssel; – *voice,* die Altstimme.

altogether [ɔ:ltə'geðə], **1.** *adv.* zusammen, insgesamt; gänzlich, ganz und gar, völlig, durchaus. **2.** *s.* (*coll.*) *in the –,* splitternackt.

alto-relievo ['æltorə'li:vou], *s.* das Hochrelief.

altruism ['æltruizm], *s.* die Selbstlosigkeit, Uneigennützigkeit, Nächstenliebe. **altruist,** *s.* uneigennütziger Mensch, der Altruist. **altruistic** [–'istik], *adj.* selbstlos, uneigennützig.

alum ['æləm], *s.* (*Chem.*) der Alaun.

alumina [ə'lju:minə], *s.* (*Chem.*) die Tonerde,

aluminate, *s.* das Aluminat, die Tonerdeverbindung.

aluminium [ælju'minjəm], *s.* das Aluminium; – *acetate,* essigsaure Tonerde.

aluminous [ə'lju:minəs], *adj.* alaunhaltig.

aluminum [ə'lu:minəm], *s.* (*Am.*) *see* **aluminium.**

alumnus [ə'lʌmnəs], *s.* (*pl.* **-ni** [–nai]) (*Am.*) Alter Herr (*University etc.*), ehemaliges Mitglied.

alveolar [æl'viələ], *adj.* (*Anat.*) alveolar; – *sound,* der Alveolarlaut. **alveolus,** *s.* die Bienenzelle; (*Anat.*) das Zahnfach.

always ['ɔ:lweiz], *adv.* immer, stets, ständig, jederzeit, allezeit.

am [æm, əm, *according to emphasis*], *first pers. sing. pres. indic. of* be; *I – to go, – I not?* ich soll gehen, nicht wahr? *I – going to see him tomorrow,* ich werde ihn morgen sehen; *I – told,* es wird mir gesagt, man sagt mir.

amain [ə'mein], *adv.* (*obs.*) mit voller Kraft, mit aller Macht, heftig, ungestüm.

amalgam [ə'mælgəm], *s.* das Amalgam; (*fig.*) die Mischung, innige Vermischung. **amalgamate, 1.** *v.t.* amalgamieren, vermischen, verschmelzen. **2.** *v.i.* sich vereinigen, sich zusammenschließen; (*fig.*) sich vermischen. **amalgamation** [–'meiʃən], *s.* die Amalgamierung, Vermischung, Verschmelzung; (*fig.*) Vereingung, der Zusammenschluß, die Fusion.

amanuensis [əmænju'ensis], *s.* der Sekretär, (Schreib)gehilfe, Amanuensis.

amaranth ['æmərænθ], *s.* (*Bot.*) der Amarant, das Tausendschön; (*fig.*) unverwelkliche Blume. **amaranthine** [–'rænθain], *adj.* amaranten, amarantfarben; (*fig.*) unverwelklich.

amaryllis [æmə'rilis], *s.* (*Bot.*) die Belladonnalilie.

amass [ə'mæs], *v.t.* (an)sammeln, anhäufen, (auf)häufen, zusammenscharren; (*troops*) zusammenziehen. **amassment,** *s.* die Anhäufung, Ansammlung.

amateur ['æmətə:, 'æmətjuə], *s.* der Liebhaber (der Kunst), Amateur, Dilettant; – *rider,* der Herrenreiter; – *theatricals,* das Liebhabertheater. **amateurish,** *adj.* laienhaft, dilettantisch; stümperhaft, unfachmännisch. **amateurishness,** *s.* die Liebhaberei, der Dilettantismus; die Stümperhaftigkeit. **amateurism,** *s.* der Amateursport.

amative ['æmətiv], *adj.* sinnlich, Liebes–. **amativeness,** *s.* die Sinnlichkeit, der Liebesdrang. **amatory,** *adj.* erotisch, verliebt, sinnlich, Liebes–.

amaze [ə'meiz], *v.t.* erstaunen, überraschen, in (Er)staunen setzen. **amazed,** *adj.* erstaunt (*at,* über (*Acc.*)). **amazement,** *s.* das (Er)staunen, die Überraschung, Verwunderung. **amazing,** *adj.* erstaunlich, wundervoll, verblüffend.

[1]**Amazon** ['æməzən], *s.* (*Geog.*) der Amazonas, Amazonenstrom.

[2]**Amazon,** *s.* (*Hist.*) die Amazone; (*fig.*) das Mannweib.

Amazonian [æmə'zouniən], **1.** *adj.* 1. (*Geog.*) Amazonas–; 2. (*Hist.*) amazonenhaft. **2.** *s.* Indianer aus dem Amazonasgebiet.

ambassador [æm'bæsədə], *s.* der Botschafter, Gesandte(r). **ambassadorial** [–'dɔ:riəl], *adj.* gesandtschaftlich, Botschafts–. **ambassadress,** *s.* die Gemahlin des Gesandten; Botschafterin.

amber ['æmbə], **1.** *s.* der Bernstein. **2.** *adj.* Bernstein–, bernsteinfarbig.

ambergris ['æmbəgri:s], *s.* graue Ambra.

ambiance ['æmbiəns], *s.* die Umwelt, Umgebung; (*Art.*) das Ambiente.

ambidexterity [æmbideks'teriti], *s.* die Beidhändigkeit, Ambidextrie; (*fig.*) Doppelzüngigkeit, Unaufrichtigkeit, Achselträgerei. **ambidextrous** [–'dekstrəs], *adj.* beidhändig, mit beiden Händen gleich geschickt; (*fig.*) doppelzüngig, achselträgerisch.

ambient ['æmbiənt], **1.** *adj.* umgebend, umlaufend, umkreisend. **2.** *s. See* **ambiance.**

ambiguity [æmbi'gju:iti], *s.* die Zweideutigkeit; Mehrdeutigkeit, Vieldeutigkeit, der Doppelsinn; die Ungewißheit, Dunkelheit. **ambiguous** [–'bigjuəs], *adj.* zweideutig, mehrdeutig, vieldeutig, doppelsinnig; (*fig.*) ungewiß, unklar, unbestimmt, dunkel.

ambit ['æmbit], *s.* der Umkreis, Umfang, Bereich, das Gebiet.

ambition [æm'biʃən], *s.* die Ehrsucht, der Ehrgeiz (*for,* nach); Gegenstand des Ehrgeizes. **ambitious,** *adj.* ehrgeizig, ehrsüchtig, hochstrebend; begierig (*of,* nach).

ambivalence, ambivalency [æm'bivələns(i)], *s.* die Doppelwertigkeit, Ambivalenz. **ambivalent,** *adj.* doppelwertig, ambivalent.

amble [æmbl], **1.** *s.* der Paßgang (*of horse*); gemächlicher Gang, das Schlendern (*of a p.*). **2.** *v.i.* den Paßgang gehen, im Paßgang reiten; (*fig.*) gemächlich gehen.

ambo ['æmbou], *s.* (*Eccl.*) die Kanzel, das Lesepult.

ambrosia [æm'brouziə], *s.* die Götterspeise, Ambrosia. **ambrosial,** *adj.* ambrosisch; (*fig.*) köstlich.

Ambrosian [æm'brouziən], *adj.* Ambrosianisch.

ambulance ['æmbjuləns], *s.* 1. (*Mil.*) das Feldlazarett; 2. der Krankenwagen, Santitätswagen; *motor* –, das Krankenauto. **ambulance|-man,** *s.* der Krankenträger, Sanitäter. **–-station,** *s.* die Unfallstation. **–-train,** *s.* der Lazarettzug.

ambulant ['æmbjulənt], *adj.* (*Med.*) ambulant; umherwandernd. **ambulatory, 1.** *adj.* veränderlich, vorübergehend; Wander–, Geh–, beweglich; (*Law*) nicht gesetzlich fest, widerruflich. **2.** *s.* (*Eccl.*) der Wandelgang, gedeckter Bogengang.

ambuscade [æmbəs'keid], *s.* (*obs.*) *see* **ambush.**

ambush ['æmbuʃ], **1.** *s.* der Hinterhalt, Versteck; Überfall aus dem Hinterhalt; *lie in –,* im Hinterhalt liegen, auf der Lauer liegen. **2.** *v.t.* aus dem Hinterhalt überfallen. **3.** *v.i.* im Hinterhalt *or* auf der Lauer liegen.

ameer [ə'miə], *s.* der Emir.

ameliorate [ə'mi:liəreit], **1.** *v.t.* verbessern. **2.** *v.i.* sich bessern, besser werden. **amelioration** [–'reiʃən], *s.* die Verbesserung; Läuterung, Veredelung. **ameliorative** [–rətiv], *adj.* (ver)bessernd.

amen [ɑ:'men], **1.** *int.* amen! **2.** *s.* das Amen.

amenability [əmi:nə'biliti], *s.* die Zugänglichkeit (*to,* für). **amenable** [ə'mi:nəbl], *adj.* (*of a p.*) willfährig; zugänglich (*to,* für); abhängig (von), unterworfen (*Dat.*); – *to law,* verantwortlich. **amenableness,** *s. See* **amenability.**

amend [ə'mend], **1.** *v.t.* verbessern; berichtigen, ausmerzen (*errors*); (*Parl.*) (ab)ändern, ergänzen (*a bill*); – *one's conduct,* sein Betragen bessern. **2.** *v.i.* sich bessern, besser werden. **amendable,** *adj.* verbesserungsfähig. **amendment,** *s.* die Verbesserung; Besserung (*conduct*), Berichtigung (*errors*); (*Parl.*) Ergänzung, der Zusatzantrag, Verbesserungsantrag, (Ab)änderungsantrag.

amends [ə'mendz], *pl.* der (Schaden)ersatz, die Entschädigung, Vergütung; Genugtuung; Schadloshaltung; *make –,*Schadenersatz leisten (*to, Dat.*; *for,* für), (*coll.*) sich entschädigen (*by,* durch); *make – for,* wiedergutmachen; *make – to him,* ihn entschädigen.

amenity [ə'mi:niti], *s.* die Annehmlichkeit, Artigkeit, Lieblichkeit, Anmut; *pl.* Vorzüge, Reize (*of a place*), Bequemlichkeiten (*of a building*).

amenorrhea [əmeno'riə], *s.* (*Med.*) das Ausbleiben der Regel, die Amenorrhö(e).

amerce [ə'mə:s], *v.t.* mit einer Geldstrafe belegen, eine Geldstrafe auferlegen (*Dat.*), bestrafen. **amercement,** *s.* die Geldstrafe; Bestrafung (durch Geldbuße). **amerciable,** *adj.* straffällig, strafbar.

America [ə'merikə], *s.* Amerika (*n.*). **American, 1.** *s.* der (die) Amerikaner(in). **2.** *adj.* amerikanisch; (*Orn.*) – *bittern,* Amerikanische Rohrdommel (*Botaurus lentiginosus*); (*Orn.*) – *golden plover,* Amerikanischer Goldregenpfeifer (*Charadrius dominicus dominicus*); (*Orn.*) – *kestrel,* see – *spar-*

row-hawk; (*Orn.*) – ***nightjar,*** see **night-hawk**; (*Orn.*) – ***robin,*** die Wanderdrossel (*Turdus migratorius*); (*Orn.*) – ***sparrow-hawk,*** der Buntfalke (*Falco sparverius*); (*Orn.*) – ***stint,*** Amerikanischer Zwergstrandläufer (*Calidris minutilla*); (*Orn.*) – ***wigeon,*** Nordamerikanische Pfeifente (*Anas americana*). **American-Indian,** *s.* der(die) Indianer(in).

amethyst [ˈæmiθist], **1.** *s.* der Amethyst. **2.** *adj.* amethystartig, amethystfarben.

amiability [eimiəˈbiliti], *s.* die Liebenswürdigkeit, Freundlichkeit, Leutseligkeit. **amiable** [ˈeimiəbl], *adj.* liebenswürdig, leutselig, freundlich; liebreich, reizend.

amianthus [æmiˈænθəs], *s.* der Amiant.

amicable [ˈæmikəbl], *adj.* freund(schaft)lich, friedlich; – ***settlement,*** gütlicher Vergleich, gütliche Einigung. **amicableness,** *s.* die Freund(schaft)lichkeit.

amice [ˈæmis], *s.* das Achseltuch (des Meßpriesters).

amidship(s) [əˈmidʃips], *adv.* (*Naut.*) mittschiffs.

amid(st) [əˈmid(st)], *prep.* mitten in *or* unter (*Dat.*), inmitten (*Gen.*), umgeben von; – ***tears,*** unter Tränen.

amir, *s. See* **ameer.**

amiss [əˈmis], *pred.adj.* verkehrt, falsch, verfehlt, fehlerhaft, schlecht; unrecht, unstatthaft, unpassend; ***if anything should happen –,*** wenn etwas schief gehen sollte; ***it would not be –,*** es wäre ganz in Ordnung; ***not –,*** nicht schlecht *or* übel; ***nothing comes – to him,*** ihm ist alles recht; ***not come –,*** nicht ungelegen kommen; ***nothing –,*** nichts für ungut; ***take –,*** übelnehmen.

amity [ˈæmiti], *s.* die Freundschaft, gutes Einvernehmen.

ammeter [ˈæmi:tə], *s.* (*Elec.*) das Amperemeter, der Strommesser.

ammo [ˈæmou], *s.* (*sl.*) die Muni(tion). **ammo-boots,** *pl.* (*sl.*) die Kommißstiefel.

ammonia [əˈmouniə], *s.* das Ammoniak; ***liquid –,*** der Salmiakgeist. **ammoniac** [–iˈæk], **ammoniacal** [æmouˈnaiəkl], *adj.* Ammoniak–, ammoniakalisch. **ammonium,** *s.* das Ammonium.

ammunition [æmjuˈniʃən], *s.* die Munition. **ammunition| belt,** *s.* der Patronengurt. **–-bread,** *s.* das Kommißbrot. **– clip,** *s.* der Ladestreifen. **–-wagon,** *s.* der Munitionswagen.

amnesia [æmˈni:ziə], *s.* die Amnesie, der Gedächtnisverlust.

amnesty [ˈæmnisti], **1.** *s.* (allgemeiner) Straferlaß, die Amnestie. **2.** *v.t.* begnadigen, amnestieren.

amnion [ˈæmniən], *s.* (*Anat.*) die Fruchthülle, Fruchthaut, Schafhaut, das Schafhäutchen. **amnionic** [–ˈɔnik], **amniotic,** *adj.* Schafhäutchen–; – ***fluid,*** das Fruchtwasser.

amoeba [əˈmi:bə], *s.* die Amöbe.

amok, *adj. See* **amuck.**

among(st) [əˈmʌŋ(st)], *prep.* (mitten) unter, zwischen, bei; ***from –,*** aus, aus . . . hervor, mitten aus . . .; ***be –,*** gehören *or* zählen zu; ***he is – the best,*** er ist mit der Beste.

amoral [æˈmɔrəl, eiˈmɔrəl], *adj.* amoralisch.

amorist [ˈæmərist], *s.* der Buhler, Liebhaber. **amorous,** *adj.* verliebt (*of,* in (*Acc.*)); Liebes–; – ***ditty,*** das Liebesliedchen. **amorousness,** *s.* die Verliebtheit.

amorphic [əˈmɔ:fik], *adj. See* **amorphous. amorphism,** *s.* die Formlosigkeit. **amorphous,** *adj.* (*Chem. etc.*) unkristallinisch, amorph, (*Anat.*) mißgestaltet, anomal; (*fig.*) formlos, gestaltlos, unregelmäßig.

amortizable [əˈmɔ:tizəbl], *adj.* tilgbar, amortisierbar. **amortization** [–ˈzeiʃən], *s.* die (Schulden)-tilgung, Amortisierung, Amortisation, Veräußerung an die tote Hand; ***bill of –,*** der Tilgungsschein. **amortize,** *v.t.* abzahlen, tilgen, amortisieren (*debts*), an die tote Hand veräußern (*land*).

amount [əˈmaunt], **1.** *s.* der Betrag; die (Gesamt)-summe, Menge, das Ausmaß, der Bestand; ***what is the –?*** wieviel macht *or* beträgt es? ***to the – of,*** im Betrage von, bis zur Höhe von; (*Comm.*) – ***carried forward,*** der Saldoübertrag; (*coll.*) ***any –,*** jede beliebige Menge; (*coll.*) ***any – of nonsense,*** nichts als Unsinn. **2.** *v.i.* sich belaufen *or* erstrecken (*to,* auf (*Acc.*)), ausmachen, betragen; (*fig.*) hinauslaufen (auf (*Acc.*)); (*coll.*) ***not – to much,*** belanglos sein; (*coll.*) ***it all –s to the same thing,*** es kommt *or* läuft auf dasselbe *or* eins hinaus.

amour [əˈmuə], *s.* die Liebschaft. **amour-propre** [æmuəˈprɔpr], *s.* das Selbstgefühl, die Selbstachtung, Eigenliebe, Eitelkeit.

amperage [ˈæmpəridʒ], *s.* die Amperezahl, Stromstärke. **ampere** [ˈæmpεə], *s.* das Ampere.

ampersand [ˈæmpəsænd], *s.* (*Typ.*) das Etzeichen.

amphetamine [æmˈfetəmin], *s.* (*Chem.*) das Benzedrin.

amphibian [æmˈfibiən], **1.** *s.* (*Zool.*) die Amphibie; der Lurch; (*Mil.*) Schwimmkampfwagen, (*Av.*) das Wasserlandflugzeug. **2.** *or* **amphibious,** *adj.* amphibisch, beidlebig; – ***tank,*** der Schwimmkampfwagen.

amphitheatre [ˈæmfiθiətə], *s.* das Amphitheater.

amphoric [æmˈfɔrik], *adj.* (*Med.*) hohlklingend (*breathing etc.*).

ample [æmpl], *adj.* weit, breit, geräumig, ausgedehnt, groß; weitläufig, ausführlich, umfassend; reich, reichlich, genügend; – ***means,*** reichliche Mittel; – ***satisfaction,*** völlige Genugtuung; ***it's –,*** es genügt vollständig.

amplification [æmplifiˈkeiʃən], *s.* die Erweiterung, Vergrößerung, (*Gram.*) Ausdehnung, weitere Ausführung; (*Rad.*) Verstärkung. **amplifier** [ˈæmplifaiə], *s.* (*Rad.*) der Verstärker. **amplify,** *v.t.* vergrößern, erweitern, ausdehnen; weiter ausführen, ausmalen, ausschmücken, ausführlich darstellen; (*Rad.*) verstärken.

amplitude [ˈæmplitju:d], *s.* der Umfang, die Größe, Weite; (*Phys.*) Schwingungsweite, Ausschlagsweite, Amplitude; (*Astr.*) Gestirnweite, der Polarwinkel; (*fig.*) Reichtum, die Fülle, Reichlichkeit.

amply [ˈæmpli], *adv.* reichlich; *see* **ample.**

ampoule [ˈæmpu:l], *s.* (*Med.*) die Ampulle.

ampulla [æmˈpulə], *s.* das Gefäß, die Phiole.

amputate [ˈæmpjuteit], *v.t.* (*Med.*) abnehmen, amputieren; abschneiden, stutzen. **amputation** [–ˈteiʃən], *s.* (*Med.*) die Abnahme, Amputation; Absetzung.

amuck [əˈmʌk], *adv.* ***run –,*** amoklaufen, wütend *or* tobend herumlaufen, blind losgehen.

amulet [ˈæmjulit], *s.* das Amulett, Zauber(schutz)-mittel.

amuse [əˈmju:z], *v.t.* unterhalten, vergnügen, amüsieren, belustigen, ergötzen; ***be –d by,*** Spaß haben an (*Dat.*), sich ergötzen an (*Dat.*); ***it –s me,*** es macht mir Spaß. **amusement,** *s.* die Unterhaltung, der Zeitvertreib, das Vergnügen, die Belustigung, Kurzweil; ***for –,*** zum Vergnügen; ***place of –,*** der Vergnügungsort. **amusing,** *adj.* unterhaltend, belustigend, ergötzlich, amüsant.

amylaceous [æmiˈleiʃəs], *adj. See* **amylous. amylate** [ˈæmilit], *s.* die Stärkeverbindung. **amyloid, amylous,** *adj.* stärkehaltig, mehlartig.

[1]**an** [æn, ən *according to emphasis*], *indef. art. used before a vowel or silent h,* ein *etc. See* **a.**

[2]**an,** *conj.* (*obs.*) wenn, falls.

Anabaptist [ænəˈbæptist], **1.** *s.* der Wiedertäufer. **2.** *adj.* wiedertäuferisch.

anabatic [ænəˈbætik], *adj.* (*Meteor.*) nach oben ziehend; – ***wind,*** der Aufwind; (*Med.*) zunehmend (*fever etc.*).

anachronism [əˈnækrənizm], *s.* der Anachronismus, Zeitverstoß.

anaconda [ænəˈkɔndə], *s.* (*Zool.*) die Riesenschlange (*Eunectes murinus*).

Anacreontic [ænəkriˈɔntik], *adj.* anakreontisch.

anacrusis [ænəˈkru:sis], *s.* (*Metr.*) der Vorschlag, Auftakt.

anaemia [əˈni:miə], *s.* die Blutarmut, Bleichsucht,

Anämie. **anaemic,** *adj.* blutarm, bleichsüchtig, anämisch.

anaesthesia [ænəs'θi:ziə], *s.* die Gefühllosigkeit, Empfindungslosigkeit; (*Med.*) Betäubung, Narkose. **anaesthetic** [–'θetik], **1.** *adj.* gefühllos, unempfindlich; (*Med.*) narkotisch, betäubend. **2.** *s.* das Betäubungsmittel, Narkotikum; ***general* –,** die Total- *or* Allgemein- narkose; ***local* –,** die Lokalanästhesie, örtliche Betäubung. **anaesthetist** [ə'ni:sθətist], *s.* der Narkosearzt, Narkositeur. **anaesthetize** [ə'ni:sθətaiz], *v.t.* anästhetisieren, narkotisieren, betäuben.

anaglyph ['ænəglif], *s.* flacherhabene Arbeit, das Bas relief.

anagoge [ænə'gɔdʒ], *s. See* **anagogy. anagogic(al),** *adj.* mystisch, allegorisch, sinnbildlich. **anagogy** ['ænəgɔdʒi], *s.* mystische *or* sinnbildliche Auslegung.

anagram ['ænəgræm], *s.* das Anagramm. **anagrammatical** [–'mætikl], *adj.* anagrammatisch.

anal ['einəl], *adj.* (*Anat.*) Steiß–, After–.

analecta [ænə'lektə], **analects** ['ænəlekts], *pl.* Auszüge, ausgewählte Stücke, Lesefrüchte, die Blumenlese.

analeptic [ænə'leptik], **1.** *adj.* stärkend, kräftigend, belebend. **2.** *s.* (*Med.*) das Anregungsmittel, Belebungsmittel, Kräftigungsmittel.

analgesia [ænəl'dʒi:ziə], *s.* die Schmerzlosigkeit. **analgesic, 1.** *adj.* schmerzlindernd, schmerzbetäubend. **2.** *s.* schmerzlinderndes Mittel, das Analgetikum.

analogical [ænə'lɔdʒikəl], **analogous** [ə'næləgəs], *adj.* ähnlich, entsprechend, analog (*to, Dat.*). **analogue** ['ænəlɔg], *s.* Ähnliches, Entsprechendes, die Entsprechung, das Seitenstück. **analogy** [ə'nælədʒi], *s.* die Analogie, Übereinstimmung, Verwandtschaft, Ähnlichkeit; ***by* – *with, on the* – *of*,** analogisch nach.

analyse ['ænəlaiz], *v.t.* analysieren, zerlegen, zergliedern, auflösen; (*fig.*) genau *or* kritisch untersuchen, durchforschen; auswerten.

analysis [ə'næləsis], *s.* (*pl.* **-ses** [–si:z]) (*Chem., fig.*) die Analyse, Zerlegung, (*Math.*) Analysis, Auflösung, (*Gram.*) Zergliederung, (*fig.*) Durchforschung, kritische Untersuchung, Darlegung, der Abriß; ***in the last* –,** letzten Endes, im Grunde; ***volumetric* –,** die Maßanalyse. **analyst** ['ænəlist], *s.* der Analytiker; ***public* –,** der Gerichtschemiker. **analytic(al)** [ænə'litik(l)], *adj.* analytisch.

analyze, (*Am.*) *see* **analyse.**

anapaest ['ænəpi:st], *s.* (*Metr.*) der Anapäst. **anapaestic** [–'pi:stik], *adj.* anapästisch.

anarchic(al) [ə'nɑ:kik(l)], *adj.* anarchisch, anarchistisch, zügellos. **anarchism** ['ænəkism], *s. See* **anarchy**; der Anarchismus. **anarchist,** *s.* der Anarchist. **anarchy,** *s.* die Anarchie, Regierungslosigkeit; Zügellosigkeit, Gesetzlosigkeit.

anathema [ə'næθəmə], *s.* der Kirchenbann, Bannfluch; (*fig.*) Fluch, die Verwünschung; (*coll.*) etwas Verhaßtes. **anathematize,** *v.t.* verfluchen, mit dem Bann belegen, in den Bann tun.

anatomic(al) [ænə'tɔmik(l)], *adj.* anatomisch. **anatomist** [ə'nætəmist], *s.* der Anatom. **anatomize,** *v.t.* zergliedern, (anatomisch) zerlegen, sezieren. **anatomy,** *s.* die Anatomie, (anatomische) Zerlegung; anatomischer Aufbau; (Textbuch über) Anatomie; (*fig.*) die Analyse, Zergliederung; das Skelett, Gerippe.

ancestor ['ænsestə], *s.* der Vorfahr, Stammvater (*also fig.*), (*Poet.*) Ahn(herr); *pl.* Vorfahren, Ahnen, Väter; – ***worship*,** der Ahnenkult. **ancestral** [–'sestrəl], *adj.* angestammt, Stamm–, Ahnen–, Ur–, (alt)ererbt; – ***castle*,** die Stammburg, das Ahnenschloß; – ***estate*,** das Erbgut, der Erbhof, ererbter Grundbesitz; – ***right*,** das Erbrecht. **ancestress,** *s.* die Stammutter; Ahnfrau, (*Poet.*) Ahne. **ancestry,** *s.* die Ahnen, Vorfahren (*pl.*); Abstammung, das Geschlecht.

anchor ['æŋkə], **1.** *s.* der Anker; (*Tech.*) Schlüsselanker, Querbolzen, das Zugeisen, die Schließe; (*fig.*) Zuflucht, der Rettungsanker, fester Grund; (*fig.*) ***sheet*-–,** der Notanker; ***cast*** or ***drop* –,** ankern, vor Anker gehen; ***drag the* –,** vor Anker treiben; ***weigh* –,** den Anker lichten; ***lie*** or ***ride at* –,** vor Anker liegen. **2.** *v.i.* ankern, vor Anker gehen. **3.** *v.t.* verankern, vor Anker legen; (*fig.*) befestigen; ***be* –*ed to*,** verankert sein in (*Dat.*). **anchorage** [–ridʒ], *s.* der Ankergrund, Ankerplatz; das Ankergeld; (*fig.*) fester Grund *or* Halt, verläßliche Stütze, sicherer Hafen; die Verankerung, Befestigung.

anchoret ['æŋkəret], **anchorite,** *s.* der Einsiedler Klausner.

anchovy ['æntʃəvi, æn'tʃouvi], *s.* die Anschovis, Sardelle; – ***paste*,** die Sardellenpaste.

[1]**ancient** ['einʃənt], **1.** *adj.* alt, uralt, ehemalig, vormalig, aus alter Zeit *or* alten Zeiten; (*fig.*) hochbetagt, (alt)ehrwürdig; ***that is* – *history*,** das ist eine altbekannte Geschichte. **2.** *s.* Alte(r), der (die) Greis(in); (*B.*) ***Ancient of Days*,** Gott der Vater; ***the* –*s*,** die Alten (Griechen und Römer).

[2]**ancient,** *s.* (*obs.*) 1. der Fähnrich; 2. die Fahne, Standarte.

anciently ['einʃəntli], *adv.* ehemals, von alters her, vor alter Zeit.

ancillary [æn'siləri], *adj.* untergeordnet, dienend (*to, Dat.*), ergänzend, Hilfs–.

and [ænd, ənd *according to emphasis*], *conj.* und; ***bread* – *butter*,** das Butterbrot; ***both* . . . – . . .,** sowohl . . . als auch . . .; ***a coach* – *four*,** eine Kutsche mit vier Pferden; ***there are dogs* – *dogs*,** es gibt solche Hunde und solche; ***good* – *loud*,** schön laut; ***a little more* – *he would* . . .,** es fehlte nicht viel, so wäre er . . .; ***how can you go out* – *not take him with you?*** wie können Sie ausgehen ohne ihn mitzunehmen? ***later* – *later*,** immer später; ***for miles* – *miles*,** viele Meilen weit; ***soap* – *water*,** das Seifenwasser; ***a hundred* – *one*,** hunderteins; ***she wept* – *wept*,** sie weinte in einem fort; ***both you* – *I*,** Sie sowohl wie ich; ***try* – *come*,** versuchen Sie zu kommen; ***walk two* – *two*,** zu zweien *or* zu zweit *or* paarweise gehen; ***go*** or ***look* – *see*,** sehen Sie nach; ***nice* – *warm*,** hübsch warm; ***years* – *years*,** viele Jahre; ***write* – *ask*,** fragen Sie mal an.

Andalusian [ændə'lu:ziən], **1.** *s.* der (die) Andalusier(in). **2.** *adj.* andalusisch.

Andes ['ændi:z], *s.* die Anden (*pl.*).

andiron ['ændaiən], *s.* der Feuerbock, Kaminbock.

Andrew ['ændru:], *s.* Andreas (*m.*).

androgynism [æn'drɔdʒinizm], *s.* der Hermaphroditismus, (*Bot.*) die Zwitterblütigkeit. **androgynous,** *adj.* androgyn(isch), zwitterartig, zweigeschlechtig, hermaphroditisch, (*Bot.*) zwitt(e)rig.

anecdotal [ænik'doutl], *adj.* anekdotisch; anekdotenhaft. **anecdote** ['ænikdout], *s.* das Geschichtchen, die Anekdote.

anemia, (*Am.*) *see* **anaemia.**

anemometer [æni'mɔmitə], *s.* der Wind(stärke- *or* geschwindigkeits)messer.

anemone [ə'neməni], *s.* (*Bot.*) das Windröschen, die Anemone; (*Zool.*) ***sea* –,** die Seeanemone.

anemoscope ['ænimoskoup], *s.* die Windfahne.

anent [ə'nent], *prep.* (*obs.*) betreffs, bezüglich (*Gen.*).

aneroid ['ænərɔid], *adj.* – ***barometer*,** das Aneroidbarometer, Druckdosenbarometer.

anesthesia, anesthetic, (*Am.*) *see* **anaesthesia, anaesthetic.**

aneurism, aneurysm ['ænjuərizm], *s.* die Pulsadergeschwulst, Arterienerweiterung.

anew [ə'nju:], *adv.* von neuem, aufs neue; wieder(um), noch einmal.

angel ['eindʒəl], *s.* der Engel; Gottesbote; (*coll.*) ***rush in where* –*s fear to tread*,** sich unbesonnen in eine heikle Angelegenheit einmischen; etwas auf sich nehmen, woran sich kein vernünftiger Mensch heranwagt; (*coll.*) ***be an* – *and* . . .!** sei doch so gut und . . .! (*coll.*) ***join the* –*s*,** in den Himmel kommen. **angel-fish,** *s.* (*Ichth.*) der Engelhai, gemeiner Meerengel. **angelic** [æn'dʒelik], *adj.* engelgleich, engelhaft, Engels–, (*obs., Eccl.*) englisch.

angelica [æn'dʒelikə], *s.* (*Bot.*) die Brustwurz, Engelwurz, Angelika.

angelical, *adj. See* **angelic.**

angel-noble, *s.* (*Hist.*) der Engelstaler.

angelus ['ændʒələs], *s.* der Angelus, das Angelusgeläut; die Angelusglocke; das Angelusgebet.

anger ['æŋgə], **1.** *s.* der Zorn, die Wut; der Unwille, Ärger (*at,* über (*Acc.*)); *fit of* –, der Zornausbruch, Wutanfall. **2.** *v.t.* erzürnen, aufbringen; böse machen, ärgern; ***become –ed,*** böse *or* ärgerlich werden, in Zorn *or* Wut geraten.

angina [æn'dʒainə, 'ændʒinə], *s.* die Hals–, Rachen– *or* Mandelentzündung; – ***pectoris,*** die Herzbräune, Stenokardie.

[1]**angle** [æŋgl], *s.* (*Geom. etc.*) der Winkel; (*Mech.*) das Knie(stück); (*Astr.*) Haus; (*fig.*) der Gesichtswinkel, Standpunkt, Aspekt, die Seite; (*coll.*) Methode, Taktik, der Winkelzug, Dreh, Kniff; ***right*** (***acute, obtuse***) –, rechter (spitzer, stumpfer) Winkel; ***adjacent*** (***alternate, exterior*** or ***external, vertical***) –, der Neben– (Wechsel–, Außen–, Scheitel)winkel; – ***of elevation,*** der Steigungswinkel; – ***of incidence,*** der Einfallswinkel; – ***of reflection,*** der Reflexionswinkel; – ***of refraction,*** der Brechungswinkel; – ***of sight, visual*** –, der Gesichtswinkel; (*Artil.*) – ***of traverse,*** der Schwenkwinkel, das Seitenrichtfeld; ***at right –s to,*** im rechten Winkel zu; ***at an – to,*** in einem Winkel stehend mit; (*fig.*) ***from a new*** –, von einem neuen Standpunkt *or* Gesichtspunkt, von einer neuen Seite.

[2]**angle, 1.** *s.* (*obs.*) die Angel, der Angelhaken. **2.** *v.i.* angeln (***for,*** nach).

angled [æŋgəld], *adj.* winklig, eckig.

angler ['æŋglə], *s.* der Angler.

Angles [æŋgəlz], *pl.* (*Hist.*) Angeln.

Anglican ['æŋglikən], **1.** *adj.* anglikanisch; staatskirchlich. **2.** *s.* der (die) Anglikaner(in), Hochkirchler(in).

anglice ['æŋglisi:], *adv.* auf englisch. **anglicism,** *s.* der Anglizimus. **anglicize,** *v.t.* anglisieren, englisch machen; ***become –d,*** englisch werden.

angling ['æŋgliŋ], *s.* das Angeln, der Angelsport.

Anglo– ['æŋglou], *pref.* **––French,** *s.* (*language*) das Anglonormannisch. **anglomania,** *s.* die Anglomanie. **anglophile,** *adj.* englandfreundlich. **anglophobic,** *adj.* englandfeindlich. **Anglo-Saxon, 1.** *s.* der Angelsachse; (*language*) das Angelsächsisch, Altenglisch. **2.** *adj.* angelsächsisch.

angrily ['æŋgrili], *adv.* voll Ärger, aufgebracht, verärgert.

angry ['æŋgri], *adj.* zornig, böse (***at, about*** (*a th.*), über (*Acc.*); ***with*** (*a p.*), auf (*Acc.*)), aufgebracht (über (*a th.*), gegen (*a p.*)), verärgert (über (*a p. or th.*)), ärgerlich (auf *or* über (*a p. or th.*)); (*Med.*) entzündet (*of a wound*); (*fig.*) heftig, erregt, stürmisch, aufgeregt; ***get*** –, in Zorn geraten; ***have an – look,*** böse aussehen.

anguish ['æŋgwiʃ], *s.* der Schmerz, die Pein, Qual; – ***of mind,*** die Seelenangst, Seelenqual.

angular ['æŋgjulə], *adj.* wink(e)lig, eckig, spitzkantig; (*fig.*) steif, ungelenk, eckig, linkisch; – ***distance,*** der Winkelabstand; – ***point,*** der Scheitelpunkt; – ***velocity,*** die Winkel–, *or* Dreh– *or* Umlaufgeschwindigkeit. **angularity** [–'læriti], *s.* die Winkligkeit, Eckigkeit; (*fig.*) Ungelenkheit, Steifheit.

anhydride [æn'haidraid], *s.* (*Chem.*) das Anhydrid. **anhydrite,** *s.* (*Min.*) der Anhydrit. **anhydrous,** *adj.* wasserfrei.

anigh [ə'nai], *adv.* (*obs.*) nahe.

anile ['ænail], *adj.* altweiberlich.

aniline ['ænilain], *s.* das Anilin; – ***dyes,*** Anilinfarbstoffe.

animadversion [ænimæd'və:ʃən], *s.* der Tadel, Verweis, die Rüge, Kritik (***on,*** an (*Dat.*)). **animadvert,** *v.i.* sich kritisch äußern, kritische Bemerkungen machen (***on, upon,*** über (*Acc.*)), kritisieren, rügen, tadeln.

animal ['æniməl], **1.** *s.* das Tier, Lebewesen, (*fig. of a p.*) Vieh, die Bestie. **2.** *adj.* Tier-, tierisch; (*fig.*) animalisch, sinnlich, fleischlich; – ***charcoal,*** die Knochenkohle; – ***food,*** die Fleischnahrung; – ***functions,*** tierische Verrichtungen; – ***husbandry,*** die Viehzucht; – ***kingdom,*** das Tierreich; – ***magnetism,*** tierischer Magnetismus; – ***spirits,*** Lebensgeister (*pl.*), die Vitalität, Lebenskraft.

animalcule [æni'mælkju:l], *s.* mikroskopisches Tierchen.

animalism ['æniməlizm], *s.* der Animalismus, Lebenstrieb, die Lebenskraft. **animality** [–'mæliti], *s.* die Vertiertheit, Tierheit; das Tierische.

animate ['ænimeit], **1.** *v.t.* beleben, beseelen; (*fig.*) anregen, anfeuern, aufmuntern. **2.** *or* **animated,** *adj.* belebt; beseelt (***with, by,*** von); lebndige, lebhaft, rege, angeregt, ermutigt, ***–d cartoon,*** der Zeichentrickfilm. **animation** [–'meiʃən], *s.* die Belebung, Beseelung; (*fig.*) das Leben, die Lebhaftigkeit, das Feuer.

animism ['ænimizm], *s.* die Naturbeseelung, der Animismus.

animosity [æni'mɔsiti], *s.* der Unwille, die Erbitterung, Abneigung, Feindseligkeit, der Haß, Groll. **animus** ['æniməs], *s. See* **animosity;** (*Law*) die Absicht.

anise ['ænis], *s.* (*Bot.*) der Anis. **aniseed** ['ænisi:d], *s.* der Anissamen.

ankle [æŋkl], *s.* der (Fuß)knöchel; ***sprain one's*** –, sich (*Dat.*) den Fuß verstauchen. **ankle|-bone,** *s.* der Fußknöchel, das Sprungbein. **--deep,** *adv., adj.* fußtief, bis über die Knöchel.

anklet ['æŋklit], *s.* die Fußspange; Halbsocke, das Knöchelsöckchen.

ankylosis [æŋki'lousis], *s.* (*Med.*) die Ankylose, Gelenkversteifung, Knochenverwachsung.

ankylostomiasis [ænkilɔstə'maiəsis], *s.* (*Med.*) die Hakenwurmkrankheit.

annalist ['ænəlist], *s.* der Chronist, Annalenschreiber. **annals,** *pl.* Annalen, Jahrbücher (*pl.*); die Chronik, chronologischer Bericht.

Annamese [ænə'mi:z], **1.** *s.* der Annamit(e) (die Annamitin). **2.** *adj.* annamitisch.

anneal [ə'ni:l], *v.t.* ausglühen, anlassen, tempern, vergüten (*metals*), kühlen (*glass*); (*fig.*) stählen, härten.

annelid ['ænəlid], *s.* (*Zool.*) der Ringelwurm.

annex, 1. [ə'neks], *v.t.* anhängen, beifügen (***to,*** an (*Acc.*)); (*Pol. etc.*) sich (*Dat.*) aneignen, einverleiben, annektieren; (*fig.*) verknüpfen, verbinden (***to,*** mit); (*Comm.*) ***as –ed,*** laut Anlage, anbei. **2.** ['æneks], *s. See* **annexe.**

annexation [ænek'seiʃən], *s.* die Hinzufügung, Anfügung (***to,*** zu); Vereinigung, Verknüpfung, Verbindung (***to,*** mit); (*Pol.*) Annektierung, Annexion, Einverleibung (***to,*** in (*Acc.*)).

annexe ['æneks], *s.* die Anlage, Beilage; der Anhang, Zusatz, Nachtrag; das Nebengebäude, der Anbau.

annihilate [ə'naiəleit], *v.t.* vernichten, zerstören, ausrotten, (*Mil.*) aufreiben, (*fig.*) aufheben, zunichte machen. **annihilation** [–'leiʃən], *s.* die Vernichtung, Zerstörung, Aufhebung.

anniversary [æni'və:səri], **1.** *s.* der Jahrestag, die Jahresfeier; das Jubiläum; ***15th*** –, fünfzehnjährige Wiederkehr; ***50th – of his death,*** sein fünfzigster Todestag. **2.** *adj.* Jahrestags–, Jubiläums–.

annotate ['ænoteit], *v.t.* mit Anmerkungen versehen, kommentieren; ***–d edition,*** Ausgabe mit Anmerkungen. **annotation** [–'teiʃən], *s.* das Kommentieren, Glossieren; die Anmerkung, Glosse. **annotator,** *s.* der Kommentator.

announce [ə'nauns], *v.t.* ankünd(ig)en, anzeigen, verkünd(ig)en, in Aussicht stellen, (an)melden, bekanntmachen; (*Rad.*) ansagen; – ***o.s.,*** sich anmelden. **announcement,** *s.* die Anzeige, Ankündigung, Verkündigung, Veröffentlichung, Bekanntmachung, (An)meldung. **announcer,** *s.* (*Rad.*) der (die) Ansager(in).

annoy [ə'nɔi], *v.t.* beunruhigen; stören; belästigen, plagen, ärgern, behelligen; ***be –ed,*** sich ärgern (***at*** (*a th.*), ***with*** (*a p.*), über (*Acc.*)). **annoyance,** *s.* der Ärger, Verdruß; die Störung, Beunruhigung,

Belästigung, Plage. **annoying,** *adj.* ärgerlich, lästig, verdrießlich, störend.

annual ['ænjuəl], **1.** *adj.* jährlich; (*Bot.*) einjährig; Jahres–; – ***balance,*** die Schlußbilanz, Jahresbilanz; – ***rainfall,*** jährliche Regenmenge; – ***report,*** der Jahresbericht; (*Bot.*) – ***ring,*** der Jahresring. **2.** *s.* 1. (*Bot.*) einjährige Pflanze; 2. die Jahresschrift, das Jahrbuch.

annuitant [ə'nju:itənt], *s.* der Leibrentner. **annuity,** *s.* die Jahresrente, Lebensrente; das Jahresgehalt, Jahreseinkommen, Jahrgeld; die Jahresrate, Jahreszahlung, jährliche Zinsen (*pl.*); ***government –,*** die Sozialrente; – ***bond,*** der Rentenbrief.

annul [ə'nʌl], *v.t.* für nichtig *or* ungültig erklären, widerrufen, kündigen, abschaffen, aufheben; vernichten, (aus)tilgen.

annular ['ænjulə], *adj.* ringförmig; (*Archit.*) – ***vault,*** das Ringgewölbe. **annulated,** *adj.* voller Ringe, geringelt. **annulet,** *s.* das Ringelchen, kleiner Ring, (*Her.*) das Ringlein; (*Archit.*) die Ringverzierung.

annullability [ənʌlə'biliti], *s.* die Tilgbarkeit. **annullable** [ə'nʌləbl], *adj.* tilgbar, aufhebbar. **annulment,** *s.* die Tilgung, Vernichtung, Aufhebung, Ungültigkeitserklärung, Nichtigkeitserklärung.

annulus ['ænjuləs], *s.* (*Bot.*) der Ring, (*Math.*) Kreisring, (*Astr.*) Lichtkreis.

Annunciation [ənʌnsi'eiʃən], *s.* (*Eccl.*) die Verkündigung.

anode ['ænoud], *s.* (*Elec.*) die Anode; – ***circuit,*** der Anodenkreis; – ***current,*** der Anodenstrom; – ***potential,*** die Anodenspannung.

anodyne ['ænodain], **1.** *adj.* schmerzstillend. **2.** *s.* schmerzstillendes Mittel.

anoint [ə'nɔint], *v.t.* einölen, einreiben, einfetten, einschmieren; (*Eccl.*) salben; (*B.*) ***Lord's Anointed,*** Gesalbte(r) des Herrn.

anomalous [ə'nɔmələs], *adj.* unregelmäßig, ungewöhnlich; abweichend, anomal, abnorm, normwidrig, regelwidrig. **anomaly,** *s.* die Unregelmäßigkeit; Abweichung von der Norm, Anomalie (*also Astr.*), (*Biol.*) Mißbildung.

anon [ə'nɔn], *adv.* bald, in kurzer Zeit; (*obs.*) sogleich, sofort, auf der Stelle; ***ever and –,*** immer wieder, wiederum, dann und wann; ***of this more –,*** hiervon bald mehr.

anonymity [æno'nimiti], *s.* die Anonymität. **anonymous** [ə'nɔniməs], *adj.* ohne Namen, namenlos, ungenannt, anonym.

anopheles [ə'nɔfəli:z], *s.* die Fiebermücke.

anorak ['ænəræk], *s.* der Anorak, die Windjacke.

another [ə'nʌðə], *adj., pron.* 1. ein anderer *etc.*, ein verschiedener *etc.*; 2. noch ein(er) *etc.*, ein zweiter *etc.*, ein weiterer *etc.*; – ***and –,*** immer noch mehr; ***give me –*** (= *different*) ***cup,*** geben Sie mir eine andere Tasse; ***give me –*** (= *one more*) ***cup,*** geben Sie mir noch eine Tasse; – ***day or two,*** noch einige Tage; ***just such –,*** gerade so einer; ***many –,*** manch andere(r); ***not – word,*** kein Wort mehr; ***one –,*** einander; gegenseitig; ***one after –,*** einer nach dem anderen; ***we are often taken for one –,*** wir werden oft miteinander verwechselt; ***one from –, from one –,*** von einander; ***one with –,*** miteinander, zusammengerechnet; ***it is one thing to promise, – to perform,*** Versprechen und Halten sind zweierlei; (*Parl.*) – ***place,*** das Oberhaus; – ***time,*** ein anderes Mal; ***that's – thing entirely,*** das ist etwas völlig anderes; ***one upon –,*** eins aufs andere; ***I am of – way of thinking,*** ich denke anders; ***yet –?*** noch einer? ***one thing with –,*** eins ins andere gerechnet; – ***Hitler,*** ein zweiter Hitler; (*Spt.*) ***A. N. Other,*** ungenannter Ersatzmann.

anserine ['ænsərain], *adj.* gänseartig, Gänse–; (*fig.*) albern.

answer ['ɑ:nsə], **1.** *s.* die Antwort, Erwiderung, Entgegnung (*to,* auf (*Acc.*)); (*Math.*) Lösung, das Resultat, Ergebnis; (*Law*) die Gegenschrift, Verteidigung, Replik; (*Naut.*) der Gegengruß; (*Fenc.*) Gegenhieb, Gegenstoß; (*fig.*) die Gegenmaßnahme, Reaktion; – ***in the affirmative*** (***negative***), eine bejahende (verneinende) Antwort; ***in – to,*** als Antwort auf (*Acc.*), in Beantwortung (*Gen.*). **2.** *v.t.* beantworten, antworten auf (*Acc.*) (*letter, question*), antworten, entgegnen, erwidern (*Dat.*) (*a p.*); erfüllen, befriedigen(*demands*); dienen, entsprechen, nachkommen, Folge leisten (*Dat.*), sich richten nach (*requirements*); (*Tech. etc.*) reagieren auf (*Acc.*), gehorchen (*Dat.*); – ***the door*** or (***door***) ***bell,*** die Tür öffnen; (*Comm.*) – ***a bill of exchange,*** einen Wechsel decken *or* honorieren; – ***a debt,*** eine Schuld abtragen; – ***his expectations,*** seine Wünsche erfüllen, seinen Erwartungen entsprechen; – ***the helm,*** dem Ruder gehorchen; – ***a prayer,*** ein Gebet erhören; – ***the purpose,*** dem Zwecke dienen *or* entsprechen; ***it –s no purpose,*** es hilft zu nichts; – ***a riddle,*** ein Rätsel lösen *or* herausbekommen; (*Law*) – ***a summons,*** einer Vorladung Folge leisten. **3.** *v.i.* antworten, eine Antwort geben, erwidern, entgegnen; (*coll.*) ***it will –,*** es stellt mich zufrieden, es genügt (mir); (*coll.*) – ***back,*** freche Antworten geben, widersprechen; – ***for,*** (*of a p.*) Rede (und Antwort) stehen für, Rechenschaft ablegen für; haften für, (sich ver)bürgen für, die Verantwortung tragen *or* verantwortlich sein für; (*of a th.*) taugen *or* ausreichen für, entsprechen (*Dat.*), dienen (*Dat.*); – ***to,*** reagieren auf (*Acc.*), gehorchen (*Dat.*); entsprechen (*Dat.*), gemäß sein (*Dat.*), übereinstimmen mit; ***he –s*** (***to***) ***the description,*** die Beschreibung paßt auf ihn; ***he –s to the name of Charles,*** er hört auf den Namen Karl.

answerable ['ɑ:nsərəbl], *adj.* verantwortlich, haftbar (***for,*** für); ***be – to him for s.th.,*** ihm dafür haften *or* bürgen, sich vor ihm *or* sich ihm gegenüber dafür verantworten müssen; ***be – for the work,*** für die Arbeit einstehen *or* verantwortlich sein.

answering-service, *s.* (*Tele.*) automatischer Anrufbeantworter.

ant [ænt], *s.* die Ameise.

antacid [ænt'æsid], **1.** *adj.* (Magen)säure neutralisierend *or* entgegenwirkend. **2.** *s.* gegen Magensäure wirkendes Mittel.

antagonism [æn'tægənizm], *s.* der Zwiespalt, Zwist; Widerstreit, Widerstand, die Feindschaft, das Widerstreben; der Antagonismus (*to,* gegen). **antagonist,** *s.* der Gegner, Widersacher. **antagonistic** [–'nistik], *adj.* gegnerisch, widerstreitend, entgegengesetzt, entgegenwirkend. **antagonize,** *v.t.* sich (*Dat.*) zum Gegner machen, sich verfeinden mit.

Antarctic [ænt'ɑ:ktik], **1.** *adj.* antarktisch, Südpol–; – ***Circle,*** südlicher Polarkreis; – ***expedition,*** die Südpolexpedition; – ***Ocean,*** Südliches Eismeer. **2.** *s.* ***the –,*** Südpolarländer (*pl.*).

ant-eater, *s.* (*Zool.*) der Ameisenbär.

antecedence [ænti'si:dəns], *s.* der Vortritt, Vorrang; (*Astr.*) die Rückläufigkeit. **antecedent, 1.** *adj.* vorhergehend, vorangehend, vorgängig, vorig; früher (*to,* als). **2.** *s.* das Vorhergehende; vorhergehender Umstand; (*Gram.*) das Beziehungswort; (*Phil.*) Antezedens, die Prämisse, der Vordersatz; (*Math.*) das Vorderglied, erstes Glied; *pl.* frühere Ereignisse, das Vorleben.

antechamber ['æntitʃeimbə], *s.* das Vorzimmer.

antechapel ['æntitʃæpəl], *s.* die Vorhalle einer Kapelle.

antedate ['æntideit], *v.t.* zurückdatieren, vordatieren (*a letter*); vorwegnehmen; vorangehen (*Dat.*).

antediluvian [æntidi'lu:viən], **1.** *adj.* vorsintflutlich, antediluvianisch; (*fig.*) altmodisch, veraltet, rückständig. **2.** *s.* vorsintflutliches Tier; altmodischer Mensch.

ant-egg, *s.* die Ameisenpuppe.

antelope ['æntiloup], *s.* die Antilope.

antemeridian [æntimə'ridiən], *adj.* Vormittags–, vormittägig.

antenatal [ænti'neitl], *adj.* vor der Geburt liegend, vorgeburtlich.
antenna [æn'tenə], *s.* (*Zool.*) das Fühlhorn, der Fühler; (*Am. Rad.*) die Antenne.
antenuptial [ænti'nʌpʃəl], *adj.* vorehelich, – ***contract,*** der Ehevertrag, die Gütertrennung.
antepenultimate [æntipə'nʌltimit], **1.** *adj.* drittletzt. **2.** *s.* drittletzte Silbe.
anterior [æn'tiəriə], *adj.* (*in time*) vorhergehend, vorangehend; früher, älter (***to,*** als); (*in space*) Vorder–, Vor–, vorder; voranstehend (***to,*** vor (*Dat.*)).
anteroom ['æntiru:m], *s.* das Vorzimmer, der Vorraum; das Wartezimmer.
anthelion [æn'θi:liən], *s.* die Gegensonne.
anthelmintic [ænθəl'mintik], **1.** *adj.* wurmvertreibend. **2.** *s.* das Wurmmittel.
anthem ['ænθəm], *s.* der Festgesang, Jubelgesang, die Hymne; (*Eccl.*) das Kirchenlied, der Choral; (*obs.*) Wechselgesang; ***national –,*** die Nationalhymne.
anther ['ænθə], *s.* der Staubbeutel.
ant-hill, *s.* der Ameisenhaufen.
anthology [æn'θɔlədʒi], *s.* die Anthologie, Gedichtsammlung, Blumenlese.
Anthony ['æntəni], *s.* Anton, Antonius (*m.*).
anthracite ['ænθrəsait], *s.* der Anthrazit, die Glanzkohle.
anthrax ['ænθræks], *s.* 1. (*Min.*) der Karfunkel; 2. (*Vet.*) Milzbrand.
anthropo– ['ænθrəpo], *pref.* Menschen–.
anthropoid ['ænθropɔid], **1.** *s.* menschenähnliches Tier. **2.** *adj.* menschenähnlich; – (***ape***), der Menschenaffe.
anthropological [ænθrəpo'lɔdʒikl], *adj.* anthropologisch. **anthropologist** [–'pɔlədʒist], *s.* der Anthropologe. **anthropology,** *s.* die Anthropologie.
anthropomorphic [ænθrəpo'mɔ:fik], *adj.* anthropomorph(isch). **anthropomorphism,** *s.* (*Eccl.*) die Vermenschlichung (Gottes); Übertragung menschlicher Eigenschaften. **anthropomorphous,** *adj.* menschenähnlich, von menschenähnlicher Gestalt.
anthropophagous [ænθrəpɔfəgəs], *adj.* menschenfressend. **anthropophagy** [–'pɔfədʒi], *s.* die Menschenfresserei, der Kannibalismus.
anti– ['ænti], *pref.* entgegen(gesetzt), gegen, Gegen–, Wider–, Anti–. **--aircraft,** *adj.* Flugabwehr–, Flak–, Luftschutz–.
antibiotic [æntibai'ɔtik], *s.* das Antibiotikum.
antibody ['æntibɔdi], *s.* der Immunkörper, Abwehrstoff.
antic ['æntik], **1.** *adj.* (*obs.*) grotesk, phantastisch, fratzenhaft, possierlich. **2.** *s.* (*usu. pl.*) die Posse, Fratze.
anti|christ, *s.* der Antichrist. **–christian,** *adj.* christenfeindlich.
anticipate [æn'tisipeit], **1.** *v.t.* 1. vorwegnehmen, im voraus tun (*s.th.*); zuvorkommen (*Dat.*) (*a p.*); ***she always –s my wishes,*** sie kommt meinen Wünschen immer zuvor; 2. im voraus erkennen, vorausempfinden, voraussehen, vorhersagen, ahnen; 3. erhoffen, erwarten; 4. (*Comm.*) im voraus *or* vor dem Termin bezahlen *or* einlösen (*a bill*); ***–d bill of exchange,*** vor der Verfallzeit eingelöster Wechsel. **2.** *v.i.* (*in narration*) vorgreifen. **anticipation** [–'peiʃən], *s.* die Vorwegnahme, Vorausnahme; das Zuvorkommen, Vorgreifen; Vorgefühl, der Vorgeschmack, die Vor(aus)empfindung, (Vor)-ahnung, der Vorgenuß; die Voraussicht, Erwartung; Hoffnung, Verfrühtheit; (*Comm.*) Vorauszahlung, Abschlagszahlung; ***by –,*** vorweg, im voraus; (*Comm.*) auf Abschlag; ***contrary to –,*** wider Erwarten; ***in – of,*** in Erwartung (*Gen.*), in der Voraussicht auf (*Acc.*); ***thanking you in –,*** Ihnen im voraus dankend. **anticipatory,** *adj.* vorgreifend, vorwegnehmend; erwartend; zuvorkommend.

anti|climax, *s.* die Antiklimax; (*fig.*) (enttäuschendes) Abfallen, der Niedergang, Abstieg. **--clockwise,** *adv.* (ent)gegen dem Uhrzeiger-(sinn), links herum; – ***rotation,*** die Linksdrehung. **–cyclone,** *s.* (*Meteor.*) das Hoch(druckgebiet). **–dazzle,** *adj.* (*Motor.*) Blendschutz–. **--distortion,** *adj.* (*Rad. etc.*) Entzerrungs–.
antidote ['æntidout], *s.* das Gegenmittel, Gegengift (***against, to,*** gegen).
anti|febrile, *adj. See* **–pyretic. –fouling paint,** *s.* (*Naut.*) die Unterwassergleitfarbe. **--freeze,** *s.* (*Motor.*) das Frostschutzmittel. **--gas,** *adj.* (*Mil.*) Gasabwehr–, Gasschutz–. **--interference,** *adj.* (*Rad.*) Entstörungs–. **--knock,** *adj.* (*Motor.*) klopffest. **–logarithm,** *s.* der Antilogarithmus, Numerus. **–macassar** [–mə'kæsə], *s.* der Sofaschoner. **--matter,** *s.* die Antimaterie. **--missile,** *attrib.adj.* – ***missile,*** die Gegenrakete, Antiraketen-Rakete. **--monarchist,** *s.* der Gegner der Monarchie.
antimonial [ænti'mouniəl], *adj.* (*Chem.*) Antimon–, antimonhaltig. **antimony** ['æntiməni], *s.* das Antimon, der Spießglanz.
antinode ['æntinoud], *s.* (*Phys.*) der Schwingungsbauch, Gegenknoten.
anti-noise, *adj.* geräuschdämpfend.
antinomian [ænti'noumiən], *adj.* gesetzwidrig; antinomistisch, Antinomisten–.
antinomy [æn'tinəmi], *s.* (*Law*) der Widerspruch, (*Phil.*) das Paradoxon.
antipathetic(al) [æntipə'θetik(l)], *adj.* abgeneigt (***to,*** *Dat.*); (*pred.*) zuwider (***to,*** *Dat.*). **antipathy** [æn'tipəθi], *s.* das Widerstreben, der Widerwille, die Abneigung, Antipathie (***to, against,*** gegen).
anti-personnel, *adj.* (*Mil.*) gegen Personen gerichtet; – ***bomb,*** die Splitterbombe.
antiphon ['æntifɔn], *s.* das Antiphon, der Wechselgesang. **antiphony** [–'tifəni], *s.* liturgischer Wechselgesang, der Wechselchor; (*fig.*) das Echo, die Antwort.
antipodal [æn'tipədəl], *adj.* antipodisch, gegenfüßlerisch; (*fig.*) völlig entgegengesetzt. **antipode** ['æntipoud], *s.* der Gegensatz, genaues Gegenteil. **antipodes** [–'tipədi:z], *pl.* gegenüberliegendes Erdteil.
anti|-pope, *s.* der Gegenpapst. **–pyretic** [–pai'retik], **1.** *adj.* fiebermildernd. **2.** *s.* das Fiebermittel.
antiquarian [ænti'kwεəriən], **1.** *adj.* altertümlich; – ***society,*** der Verein der Altertumsfreunde. **2.** *s. See* **antiquary. antiquarianism,** *s.* die Altertümerlei. **antiquary** ['æntikwəri], *s.* der Altertumsforscher, Altertumskenner; Altkunstsammler. **antiquated** ['æntikweitid], *adj.* veraltet, überlebt, überholt, altmodisch.
antique [æn'ti:k], **1.** *adj.* alt, antik; altmodisch; (*Bookb.*) blindgeprägt. **2.** *s.* die Antike, altes Kunstwerk, altes Möbelstück; *pl.* Antiquitäten (*pl.*). **antique|-dealer,** *s.* der Antiquitätenhändler. **--shop,** *s.* der Antiquitätenladen. **antiquity** [–'tikwiti], *s.* das Altertum, die Vorwelt, Vorzeit; klassisches Altertum; *pl.* Altertümer, Antiquitäten, alte Kunstgegenstände; ***of great –,*** von hohem Alter.
anti|-religious, *adj.* religionsfeindlich. **--resonant,** *adj.* (*Rad.*) – ***circuit,*** der Sperrkreis; – ***frequency,*** die Eigenfrequenz. **--roll,** *adj.* (*Naut.*) – ***device,*** der Schlingertank.
antirrhinum [ænti'rainəm], *s.* (*Bot.*) das Löwenmaul.
anti|-rust, *adj.* Rostschutz–. **–scorbutic, 1.** *adj.* skorbutheilend. **2.** *s.* das Skorbutmittel. **--Semite,** *s.* der Judenfeind, Judenhasser, Antisemit. **--semitic,** *adj.* judenfeindlich, antisemitisch. **–septic, 1.** *adj.* fäulnisverhindernd, keimtötend, antiseptisch. **2.** *s.* keimtötendes Mittel. **--skid,** *adj.* (*Motor.*) Gleitschutz–, rutschfest, rutschsicher, schleudersicher. **–social,** *adj.* asozial, gesellschaftsfeindlich. **--submarine,** *adj.* U-Boot-Abwehr–. **--tank,** *adj.* Panzerabwehr–.

antithesis [æn'tiθisis], *s.* (*pl.* **-ses** [-si:z]) die Antithese, der Gegensatz. **antithetic(al)** [-'θetik(l)], *adj.* gegensätzlich.

antitoxin [ænti'tɔksin], *s.* das Gegengift.

antitype ['æntitaip], *s.* das Gegenbild.

antler ['æntlə], *s.* die Geweihsprosse, Geweihzacke; *pl.* das Geweih; ***stag with ten -s,*** der Zehnender.

Antony, *see* **Anthony.**

antonym ['æntənim], *s.* das Wort von entgegengesetzter Bedeutung, entgegengesetzter Begriff. **antonymous** [-'tɔniməs], *adj.* entgegengesetzt.

antrum ['æntrəm], *s.* (*pl.* **-ra**) (*Anat.*) die Höhlung, Höhle.

Antwerp ['æntwə:p], *s.* Antwerpen (*n.*).

anuresis [ænju'ri:sis], **anuria** [æ'njuəriə], *s.* (*Med.*) die Anurie, Urinverhaltung.

anus ['einəs], *s.* (*Anat.*) der After; (*Bot.*) Ausgang, die Mündung.

anvil ['ænvil], *s.* der Amboß; (*fig.*) ***on the* –,** in Arbeit *or* Vorbereitung, im Werke.

anxiety [æŋ'zaiəti], *s.* die Angst, Sorge, Ängstlichkeit, Besorgnis, das Bangen (***for, about,*** wegen *or* um); eifriges Verlangen *or* Bestreben (***for,*** nach); die Unruhe, (*Med.*) Beängstigung, Beklemmung; ***causing* –,** besorgniserregend; ***in great* –,** sehr ängstlich *or* besorgt.

anxious ['æŋkʃəs], *adj.* **1.** angstvoll, ängstlich, bange, bekümmert, besorgt (***about,*** um *or* wegen); ***– times,*** unruhige *or* beunruhigende Zeiten; **2.** eifrig bemüht (***for,*** um), bedacht (auf (*Acc.*)), begierig (nach); ***be – to please,*** sich bemühen, alles recht zu machen; (*coll.*) ***I am – to see him,*** mir liegt viel daran, ihn zu sehen.

any ['eni], **1.** *adj.* **(a)** *affirmative*: jede(r, -s) *etc.*; jegliche(r, -s) *etc.*; jede(r, -s) *etc.* beliebige; beliebige(r, -s) *etc.*: (*coll.*) ***– amount,*** ein ganzer Haufen; ***– book you like,*** jedes beliebige Buch, ein beliebiges Buch; ***under – circumstances,*** unter allen Umständen; ***in – case, at – rate,*** auf jeden Fall; ***– number of,*** jede Menge *or* Anzahl von; ***at – time,*** jederzeit; **(b)** *neg. or inter.*: (irgend)ein(e) *etc.*, *pl.* einige; (irgend)welche; etwas; ***not* –,** (gar *or* überhaupt) kein(e) *etc.*; ***have you – sugar?*** hast du (etwas) Zucker? ***I haven't – (more) sugar,*** ich habe keinen Zucker (mehr); ***is there – hope?*** besteht noch irgendwelche Hoffnung? **2.** *pron.* irgendeine(r, -s) *etc.*, (irgend)welche(r, -s) *etc.*; ***he has no money and no prospects of* –,** er hat kein Geld und keine Aussicht auf welches; ***– of them, – at all,*** der *or* das *or* die erste beste; ***if (there are) – of*** or ***among you (who) are already tired,*** wenn irgendwelche von ihnen schon müde sind. **3.** *adv.* **1.** (*before comp.*) irgend(wie); ***not – better for it,*** keineswegs besser daran; ***– longer,*** (noch) länger; ***not – longer,*** nicht länger, nicht mehr; ***will you have – more?*** wollen Sie noch etwas *or* noch mehr *or* noch ein wenig haben? ***not – more,*** (*amount*) nichts mehr, (*time*) nicht mehr, nicht wieder; ***not – more than,*** ebensowenig wie; **2.** (*sl.*) (*neg.*) gar, überhaupt; ***that didn't help* –,** damit wurde gar nicht geholfen.

anybody ['enibɔdi], *pron.* irgendeine(r), irgend jemand, jeder(mann); ***– can do that,*** jeder kann das tun; ***not* –,** niemand, keine(r); ***scarcely* –,** fast niemand, kaum jemand; ***everybody who is* –,** alle, die überhaupt etwas sind; ***ask* –,** fragen Sie den ersten besten.

anyhow ['enihau], *adv.* irgendwie, auf irgendeine (Art und) Weise; jedenfalls, auf jeden Fall, wie dem auch sei, gleichwohl, gleichviel, sowieso, immerhin; (*coll.*) recht und schlecht, so gut wie's geht; ***not . . . –,*** auf keinen Fall; (*coll.*) ***muddle along* –,** fortwursteln.

anyone ['eniwʌn], *pron. See* **anybody.**

anything ['eniθiŋ], *pron.* (irgend) etwas; alles; (*coll.*) ***as cheeky as* –,** frech wie sonst was; ***– but,*** nichts weniger *or* weiter als, alles andere als; ***never – but trouble,*** immer nur Sorge; ***capable of* –,** zu allem fähig; ***for – I know,*** soviel ich weiß; ***if* –,** in gewissem Maße, womöglich; ***that is if – a little better,*** das ist eher etwas besser; ***not* –,** (gar) nichts; ***not for* –,** um keinen Preis; (*coll.*) ***not – so good,*** nicht im entferntesten so gut; ***– rather than,*** alles eher als; ***scarcely* –,** fast nichts, kaum etwas; ***– will do for him,*** er ist mit allem zufrieden.

anyway ['eniwei], *adv.* jedenfalls, sowieso, immerhin, wie dem auch sei.

anywhere ['eniwɛə], *adv.* irgendwo(hin), irgendwoher; ***not* –,** nirgendwo, nirgends; (*coll.*) ***not – near finished,*** nicht annähernd fertig, längst nicht fertig.

anywise ['eniwaiz], *adv.* (*rare*) irgendwie, auf irgendeine (Art und) Weise.

aorta [ei'ɔ:tə], *s.* (*Anat.*) die Aorta, Hauptschlagader.

apace [ə'peis], *adv.* (*obs.*) schnell, eilig, geschwind; eilends, flink. zusehends.

apanage ['æpənidʒ], *s.* das Jahrgeld, Leibgedinge; (*Pol.*) abhängiges Gebiet; (*fig.*) der Anteil; angeborene Eigenschaft, das Merkmal.

apart [ə'pɑ:t], *adv.* getrennt, (ab)gesondert (***from,*** von); abseits, beiseite; für sich, einzeln; ***fall* –,** auseinander fallen; ***keep* –,** getrennt halten; ***live* –,** getrennt leben; ***set* –,** beiseite setzen, aufbewahren, bestimmen, reservieren; ***take* –,** auseinandernehmen, zerlegen; ***joking* –,** Scherz beiseite; (*fig.*) ***– from,*** abgesehen von; ***a race* –,** eine Gattung für sich.

apartheid [ə'pɑ:thait], *s.* die Apartheid, (Politik der) Rassentrennung.

apartment [ə'pɑ:tmənt], *s.* das (Einzel)zimmer; (*Am.*) die (Etagen)wohnung; ***suite of -s,*** die Zimmerflucht; ***-s to let,*** Zimmer zu vermieten; ***furnished* –,** möbliertes Zimmer; (*Am.*) ***– house,*** der Luxuswohnblock.

apathetic(al) [æpə'θetik(l)], *adj.* gleichgültig, teilnahmslos, unempfänglich, apathisch (***towards,*** gegen); uninteressiert, lustlos, abgestumpft. **apathy** ['æpəθi], *s.* die Gleichgültigkeit, Teilnahmslosigkeit, Apathie (***towards,*** gegen), Unempfänglichkeit, Gefühllosigkeit (für), Interesselosigkeit, Stumpfheit; (*Med.*) Unempfindlichkeit (für).

ape [eip], **1.** *s.* der Affe. **2.** *v.t.* (*coll.*) nachäffen.

apeak [ə'pi:k], *adv.*, *pred. adj.* (*Naut.*) auf und nieder, senkrecht.

aperçu [əpɛə'su:], *s.* geistreiche Bemerkung, der Geistesblitz.

aperient [ə'piəriənt], **1.** *s.* das Abführmittel. **2.** *adj.* abführend.

aperiodic [eipiəri'ɔdik], *adj.* nichtperiodisch, aperiodisch, unregelmäßig; (*Phys.*) schwingungsfrei, gedämpft; (*Elec.*) frequenzunabhängig.

aperture ['æpətʃə], *s.* die Öffnung, der Schlitz, Spalt, die Spalte; (*Zool.*) Mündung; (*Opt.*) Blende; (*Med.*) das Ostium.

apetalous [ə'petələs], *adj.* (*Bot.*) blumenblattlos, kronenlos, apetal.

apex ['eipeks], *s.* (*pl.* **-es** *or* **apices** [-isi:z]) die Spitze, der Scheitel, Gipfel, (*Geom.*) Scheitelpunkt; (*fig.*) Gipfel, Höhepunkt.

aphasia [ə'feiʒə], *s.* (*Med.*) die Aphasie.

aphelion [ə'fi:liən], *s.* (*Astr.*) die Sonnenferne, das Aphel(ium).

aphesis ['æfəsis], *s.* (*Phonet.*) der Vokalschwund im Anlaut.

aphid ['eifid], **aphis,** *s.* (-, *pl.* **-ides** [-idi:z]) (*Ent.*) die Blattlaus.

aphorism ['æfərizm], *s.* der Aphorismus, Lehrspruch, die Maxime. **aphoristic** [-'ristik], *adj.* aphoristisch.

aphrodisiac [æfro'diziæk], **1.** *s.* den Geschlechtstrieb anregendes Mittel. **2.** *adj.* den Geschlechtstrieb anregend *or* erhöhend.

aphtha ['æfθə], *s.* (*Med.*) der Mundschwamm, die Schleimhautentzündung.

aphyllous [ə'filəs], *adj.* (*Bot.*) blattlos.

apiarist ['eipjərist], *s.* der Bienenzüchter, Imker. **apiary,** *s.* der Bienenstand, das Bienenhaus.

apical ['eipikəl], *adj.* an der Spitze befindlich, apikal, Spitzen–, Gipfel–, (*Bot.*) gipfelständig; – ***cone,*** die Wachstumsspitze; – ***angle,*** der Spitzenwinkel. **apices** [–si:z], *pl. of* **apex. apiculate(d)** [ə'pikjuleit(id)], *adj.* (*Bot.*) feinspitzig.

apiculture ['eipikʌltʃə], *s.* die Bienenzucht.

apiece [ə'pi:s], *adv.* für jedes Stück, pro Stück; pro Person *or* Kopf; ***he gave us an apple –,*** er gab jedem von uns einen Apfel.

apish ['eipiʃ], *adj.* affenartig, (*fig.*) affig, äffisch, närrisch, läppisch.

aplomb [ə'plɔm], *s.* (selbst)sicheres *or* selbstbewußtes Auftreten, die (Selbst)sicherheit, das Selbstbewußtsein.

Apocalypse [ə'pɔkəlips], *s.* (*B.*) die Offenbarung (Johannis), Apokalypse; ***the four horsemen of the –,*** die vier apokalyptischen Reiter.

apocope [ə'pɔkəpi], *s.* (*Phonet.*) die Endverkürzung (eines Wortes), Apokope.

Apocrypha [ə'pɔkrifə], *s.* die Apokryphen (*pl.*). **apocryphal,** *adj.* apokryph, unecht, verdächtig, zweifelhaft.

apodal ['æpədəl], *adj.* (*Zool.*) fußlos.

apodictic [æpə'diktik], *adj.* unwiderleglich, apodiktisch.

apodosis [ə'pɔdəsis], *s.* (*Gram.*) der Nachsatz.

apogee ['æpədʒi:], *s.* das Apogäum, die Erdferne des Mondes; (*fig.*) der Höhepunkt, Gipfel.

apologetic(al) [əpɔlə'dʒetik(l)], *adj.* entschuldigend, Entschuldigungs–, verteidigend, rechtfertigend, reumütig, apologetisch. **apologetics,** *pl.* die Apologetik.

apologia [æpə'loudʒə], *s.* die Verteidigung, Ehrenrettung; Entschuldigung, Abbitte, Selbstrechtfertigung. **apologist** [ə'pɔlədʒist], *s.* der Verteidiger, (*Eccl.*) Apologet; (*fig.*) Ehrenretter.

apologize [ə'pɔlədʒaiz], *v.i.* sich entschuldigen; um Entschuldigung *or* Vergebung bitten, Abbitte tun (***for,*** wegen; ***to,*** *Dat.*).

apologue ['æpəlɔg], *s.* der Apolog, die Lehrfabel.

apology, *s.* 1. die Entschuldigung, Abbitte; Rechtfertigung, Verteidigungsrede, Verteidigungsschrift; ***make an –,*** sich entschuldigen (***to,*** bei; ***for,*** für); ***in – for,*** als *or* zur Entschuldigung für; 2. (*coll.*) der Notbehelf, erbärmlicher *or* kümmerlicher *or* dürftiger Ersatz; ***an – for a hat,*** ein armseliger Hut.

apophthegm ['æpəθem], *s.* der Kernspruch, Denkspruch, Sinnspruch.

apoplectic [æpo'plektik], *adj.* apoplektisch, Schlagfluß–; – ***fit*** *or* **apoplexy** ['æpopleksi], *s.* der Schlagfluß, Schlaganfall, (*coll.*) Schlag.

apostasy [ə'pɔstəsi], *s.* der (Glaubens)abfall, die Abtrünnigkeit. **apostate** [–tit], **1.** *s.* der Apostat, Renegat, Abtrünnige(r). **2.** *adj.* abtrünnig. **apostatize,** *v.i.* abtrünnig *or* untreu werden (***from,*** *Dat.*), abfallen (von).

a posteriori ['eipɔsteri'ɔ:ri], *adv.* von Wirkung auf Ursache schließend; induktiv, empirisch, aus der Erfahrung *or* Beobachtung gewonnen.

apostle [ə'pɔsl], *s.* der Apostel, Jünger (*of Christ*); (*fig.*) Glaubensbote, Verfechter; ***Apostles' Creed,*** Apostolisches Glaubensbekenntnis. **apostolic(al)** [æpo'stɔlik(əl)], *adj.* apostolisch.

apostrophe [ə'pɔstrəfi], *s.* die Anrede; (*Typ., Gram.*) der Apostroph, das Auslassungszeichen; (*Bot.*) die Apostrophe. **apostrophize, 1.** *v.t.* (energisch *or* nachdrücklich) anreden; (*Typ.*) apostrophieren. **2.** *v.i.* (*Typ.*) einen Apostroph setzen.

apothecary [ə'pɔθəkəri], *s.* (*obs.*) der Apotheker; ***–'s shop,*** die Apotheke.

apothegm, *see* **apophthegm.**

apotheosis [əpɔθi'ousis], *s.* die Vergöttlichung, Apotheose; (*fig.*) Verherrlichung, Vergötterung.

appal [ə'pɔ:l], *v.t.* erschrecken, entsetzen. **appalling,** *adj.* entsetzlich, erschreckend, schrecklich.

appanage, *see* **apanage.**

apparatus [æpə'reitəs], *s.* der Apparat, das Gerät, die Vorrichtung, Einrichtung, Ausrüstung, Hilfsmittel (*pl.*); (*Gymn.*) das Turngerät, Übungsgerät; (*Naut. obs.*) Schiffsgerät, die Schiffsausrüstung; ***critical –,*** kritischer Apparat, Lesarten (*pl.*), Varianten (*pl.*); ***muscular –,*** das Muskelsystem, die Muskulatur; ***radio*** or ***wireless –,*** der Radioapparat.

apparel [ə'pærəl], **1.** *s.* die Kleidung, Tracht, das Gewand, Kleider (*pl.*). **2.** *v.t.* (*Poet.*) (be)kleiden, (aus)schmücken; (*Naut. obs.*) ausrüsten, ausstatten.

apparent [ə'pærənt], *adj.* sichtbar (***to,*** für), offenbar, offensichtlich, einleuchtend (*Dat.*); scheinbar, anscheinend, augenscheinlich, ersichtlich, Schein–; ***heir –,*** rechtmäßiger Erbe, der Erbprinz.

apparition [æpə'riʃən], *s.* die Erscheinung; das Gespenst, der Geist; (*Astr.*) das Sichtbarwerden.

appeal [ə'pi:l], **1.** *v.i.* 1. appellieren, sich wenden (***to,*** an (*Acc.*)), sich berufen (auf (*Acc.*)); (*Law*) Berufung einlegen (***against,*** gegen); 2. sich beschweren, Beschwerde führen (***to,*** bei); dringend ersuchen (***to,*** bei; ***for,*** *Acc.*); werben, sich einsetzen (***to,*** bei; ***for,*** um), bitten (***to,*** *Acc.*; ***for,*** um); ***– to arms,*** zu den Waffen greifen; (*Parl.*) ***– to the country,*** zur Neuwahl aufrufen; 3. gefallen, zusagen (***to,*** *Dat.*), Gefallen *or* Anklang finden (bei). **2.** *s.* 1. die Berufung, Verweisung (***to,*** auf (*Acc.*)), (*Law*) Appellation, das Appellationsrecht, Berufungsrecht; ***action upon –,*** die Appellationsklage; ***give notice of –,*** Berufung einlegen; ***the – was allowed,*** die Berufung wurde stattgegeben; ***the court of –,*** das Berufungsgericht; ***High Court of Appeal,*** das Oberberufungsgericht; 2. dringende Bitte (***for,*** um), der Aufruf, Appell (***to,*** an (*Acc.*)); ***an – to the people,*** ein Aufruf an das Volk; ***make an – to,*** appellieren *or* sich wenden an (*Acc.*); 3. der Anklang (***to,*** bei), die Anziehung(skraft) (auf (*Acc.*)); ***it makes no – to me,*** es findet bei mir keinen Anklang. **appealing,** *adj.* flehend, bittend, appellierend. **appealingly,** *adv.* flehentlich.

appear [ə'piə], *v.i.* 1. erscheinen, sichtbar werden, zum Vorschein kommen, sich zeigen; (*of actor*) (öffentlich) auftreten; (*of book*) erscheinen, herauskommen; (*Law*) (vor Gericht) erscheinen, sich stellen; ***– in print,*** im Druck erscheinen; ***– against him (in court),*** gegen ihn (vor Gericht) auftreten; (*Law*) ***failure to –,*** das Nichterscheinen vor Gericht; 2. scheinen, den Anschein haben, den Eindruck erwecken, aussehen, vorkommen; ***it –s to me,*** mir scheint; ***it would – as if,*** es scheint als ob; 3. sich ergeben *or* herausstellen, hervorgehen; ***it now –s that . . .,*** es stellt sich jetzt heraus, daß . . .; ***it –s from this,*** hieraus geht hervor.

appearance [ə'piərəns], *s.* 1. das Erscheinen, Sichtbarwerden, Auftreten, Vorkommen, (*of actor*) (öffentliches) Auftreten, (*of book*) Erscheinen, die Veröffentlichung, (*Law*) das Erscheinen (vor Gericht); ***make*** or (*coll.*) ***put in an*** or ***one's –,*** (*of a p.*) erscheinen, sich zeigen, (*of a th.*) auftreten, zum Vorschein kommen; ***non-–,*** das Nichterscheinen, Ausbleiben; 2. (äußere) Erscheinung, Äußere(s), das Aussehen, der Anblick; *pl.* Anschein, (äußerer) Schein; ***–s are against you,*** der Schein spricht gegen dich; ***to all –(s),*** allem Anschein nach; ***–s are deceptive,*** der Schein trügt; ***there is every – of an improvement,*** es hat ganz den Anschein, als ob eine Besserung eintritt; ***in –,*** anscheinend, dem Anschein nach; ***judge by –s,*** nach dem Schein *or* Äußeren urteilen; ***keep up –s,*** den Schein wahren; ***she thinks a great deal of her –,*** sie hat eine hohe Meinung von ihrer äußeren Erscheinung; ***for the sake of –s,*** des Scheines wegen, um den Schein zu wahren.

appease [ə'pi:z], *v.t.* (*anger etc.*) beruhigen, besänftigen, beschwichtigen; (*quarrel*) aussöhnen, versöhnen, beilegen, schlichten; (*hunger etc.*) befriedigen, lindern, löschen, stillen. **appeasement,** *s.* die Beruhigung, Besänftigung, Beschwichtigung; Stillung, Befriedigung; Versöhnung, Aussöhnung; ***policy of –,*** die Beschwichtigungspolitik.

appellant [ə'pelənt], **1.** *adj.* appellierend, Berufungs–. **2.** *s.* der Berufungskläger, Appellant, (*fig.*) Bittsteller.

appellation [æpə'leiʃən], *s.* die Benennung, Bezeichnung, der Name. **appellative** [ə'pelətiv], **1.**

adj. benennend, bezeichnend. **2.** *s.* (*Gram.*) das Appellativ(um), der Gattungsname; *see also* **appellation.**

appellee [æpe'li:], *s.* (*Law*) der Appellat, Berufungsbeklagte(r).

append [ə'pend], *v.t.* befestigen, festmachen, anbringen (*to*, an (*Dat.*)), anhängen (an (*Acc.*)), beifugen, hinzufügen (*Dat. or* zu), anfügen (*Dat. or* an (*Acc.*)). **appendage** [–idʒ], *s.* der Anhang, das Anhängsel, Zubehör, (*Anat. etc.*) der Ansatz, Fortsatz; (*fig.*) die Zugabe, Beigabe, das Beiwerk, die Begleiterscheinung; (*coll.*) der Anhänger, (ständiger) Begleiter, das Anhängsel.

appendectomy [æpen'dektəmi], *s.* (*Med.*) die Blinddarmoperation.

appendices [ə'pendisi:z], *pl. of* **appendix.**

appendicitis [əpendi'saitis], *s.* (*Med.*) die Blinddarmentzündung.

appendix [ə'pendiks], *s.* (*pl.* **-dices** [–isi:z]) der Anhang, Appendix; das Anhängsel, Zubehör; (*Anat.*) (Wurm)fortsatz, Blinddarm.

apperception [æpə'sepʃən], *s.* (*Phil.*) die Wahrnehmung, Erkenntnis, Auffassung, (*Psych.*) bewußtes Auffassen *or* Wahrnehmen, die Apperzeption. **apperceptive,** *adj.* apperzeptiv, apperzeptierend, wahrnehmend.

appertain [æpə'tein], *v.i.* – *to*, (zu)gehören, zustehen, zukommen, gebühren (*Dat.*), betreffen (*Acc.*), gehören zu; ***things –ing to this life,*** zeitliche Güter.

appetence, appetency ['æpitəns(i)], *s.* die Begierde, das Verlangen, Gelüst(e) (*for, after,* nach); der (Natur)trieb, Hang, (instinktive) Neigung.

appetite ['æpitait], *s.* der Appetit, Hunger (*for*, auf (*Acc.*)), die Eßlust; Begierde, das Verlangen (*for*, nach), der Trieb, die Neigung (zu), das Gefallen (an (*Dat.*)); ***have an* –,** Appetit haben; ***it will spoil your* –,** das nimmt dir den Appetit; (*Prov.*) ***a good – needs no sauce*** or ***is the best sauce,*** Hunger ist der beste Koch.

appetizer ['æpitaizə], *s.* pikante Vorspeise; der Aperitif. **appetizing,** *adj.* appetitanregend, appetitreizend, appetitlich; (*coll.*) verlockend, gewinnend, anziehend; lecker, schmuck.

Appian Way ['æpiən], *s.* (*Hist.*) die Appische Straße.

applaud [ə'plɔ:d], **1.** *v.i.* Beifall spenden *or* klatschen, applaudieren. **2.** *v.t.* Beifall spenden (*Dat.*), beklatschen; (*fig.*) billigen, zustimmen; loben, preisen. **applause** [–ɔ:z], *s.* der Beifall, Applaus, das Beifallklatschen; (*fig.*) die Billigung, Anerkennung, Zustimmung, der Beifall; ***round of* –,** lauter *or* begeisterter Beifall.

apple [æpl], *s.* der Apfel; – ***of discord,*** der Zankapfel; (*fig.*) – ***of the eye,*** der Augapfel, Liebling. **apple|cart,** *s.* der Apfelkarren; (*coll.*) ***upset the* –,** die Pläne über den Haufen werfen. **--dumpling,** *s.* der Apfelkloß. **--fritters,** *pl.* Apfelschnitten (*pl.*). **--pie,** *s.* (gedeckte) Apfeltorte; (*coll.*) ***in – order,*** in bester Ordnung, (*sl.*) in Butter. **--sauce,** *s.* das Apfelmus; (*Am. sl.*) der Quatsch; Schmus. **--tart,** *s.* die Apfeltorte. **--tree,** *s.* der Apfelbaum.

appliance [ə'plaiəns], *s.* **1.** der Apparat, das Gerät, die Vorrichtung; **2.** Anwendung.

applicability [æplikə'biliti], *s.* die Anwendbarkeit (*to*, auf (*Acc.*)), Eignung (für). **applicable,** *adj.* anwendbar (*to*, auf (*Acc.*)), geeignet, passend, angängig, verwendbar, zu gebrauchen(d) (für).

applicant ['æplikənt], *s.* der Bewerber (*for*, um), Stellungssuchende(r); Bittsteller, Antragsteller.

application [æpli'keiʃən], *s.* **1.** die Anwendung (*to*, auf (*Acc.*)), Verwendung, der Gebrauch (für); **2.** die Anwendbarkeit, Verwendbarkeit, Nutzanwendung; **3.** (*fig.*) Bedeutung (*to*, für), Beziehung (zu), der Zusammenhang (mit); **4.** die Bitte, Bewerbung, das Gesuch (*for*, um), der Antrag (auf (*Acc.*)); die Eingabe (*to*, an (*Acc.*)), das Stellengesuch; ***make (an) – for,*** sich bewerben um; ***on* –,** auf Wunsch *or* Ersuchen; ***on the – of,*** auf Ansuchen *or* auf das Gesuch von; **5.** (*fig.*) der Fleiß, Eifer, die Hingabe, (*coll.*) das Sitzfleische; ***close – is necessary,*** große Aufmerksamkeit ist erforderlich; **6.** (*Med.*) die Anlegung, Applikation, das Auflegen (*of bandage etc.*); der Verband, Umschlag; **7.** (*Phys.*) ***point of* –,** der Angriffspunkt.

application form, *s.* das Antragsformular, Anmeldungsformular.

applied [ə'plaid], *adj.* angewandt, praktisch. *See* **apply.**

appliqué [æ'pli:kei], *adj.* appliziert, Applikations–, (*Dressm.*) aufgesetzt, aufgenäht, Aufnäh–, (*Tech.*) aufgelegt, Auflege–.

apply [ə'plai], **1.** *v.t.* **1.** anwenden (*to*, auf (*Acc.*)), verwenden (auf (*Acc.*) *or* für), gebrauchen (zu); anlegen, auflegen, auftragen (*to*, auf (*Acc.*)), anbringen (an *or* auf (*Dat.*)); – ***the brake(s),*** bremsen; – ***one's knowledge,*** seine Kenntnisse verwerten *or* auswerten (*to*, für *or* zu); – ***one's mind to a th.,*** den Sinn auf eine S. lenken *or* richten, sich mit einer S. (eingehend) beschäftigen; (*Phys.*) ***be applied,*** (*force*) angreifen (*to*, an (*Dat.*)); **2.** – ***o.s.,*** sich widmen *or* hingeben (*to*, Dat.), sich legen (auf (*Acc.*)), sich Mühe geben (mit), sich befleißigen (*Gen.*). **2.** *v.i.* **1.** sich anwenden lassen, zur Anwendung kommen, anwendbar sein, sich beziehen (*to*, auf (*Acc.*)), passen (auf (*Acc.*) *or* zu), gelten (für); **2.** (*of a p.*) sich wenden (*to*, an (*Acc.*)), sich melden (bei) (*for*, wegen); – ***for,*** ersuchen *or* nachsuchen um, beantragen; – ***for a patent,*** ein Patent anmelden; – ***for a post,*** sich um eine Stelle bewerben; – ***for permission,*** Genehmigung einholen; – ***to him for help,*** ihn um Hilfe bitten *or* ersuchen, sich an ihn um Hilfe wenden.

appoggiatura [əpɔdʒə'tuərə], *s.* (*Mus.*) die Appoggiatur, der Vorschlag, freier Vorhalt.

appoint [ə'pɔint], *v.t.* **1.** (*a time*) bestimmen, festlegen, festsetzen, ansetzen, anberaumen, verabreden; **2.** (*a p.*) ernennen, anstellen, bestellen, berufen, einsetzen, machen zu; **3.** (*rules etc.*) anordnen, vorschreiben; **4.** (*premises etc.*) (*usu. p.p.*) ausrüsten, ausstatten, einrichten. **appointee** [–'ti:], *s.* Angestellte(r), Ernannte(r), Berufene(r), (*Law*) Bestallte(r), der Nutznießer.

appointment [ə'pɔintmənt], *s.* **1.** (*of a p.*) die Ernennung, Anstellung, Berufung, Bestellung, Bestallung; Stelle, Stellung, das Amt; ***purveyor by special – to the king,*** Königlicher Hoflieferant; ***hold an* –,** eine Stelle innehaben; **2.** (*in time*) die Bestimmung, Festlegung, Festsetzung, Anberaumung; Verabredung, Zusammenkunft, das Treffen; ***break an* –,** eine Verabredung nicht einhalten; ***keep an* –,** eine Verabredung einhalten; ***make an* –,** eine Verabredung treffen; ***by* –,** laut Verabredung, nach Vereinbarung; **3.** (*of rules*) die Anordnung, Vorschrift, der Beschluß, Befehl, Auftrag; **4.** *pl.* (*of premises*) die Ausstattung, Einrichtung.

apportion [ə'pɔ:ʃən], *v.t.* richtig *or* gerecht verteilen *or* zuteilen, zumessen, anweisen; – ***the costs,*** die Kosten umlegen. **apportionment,** *s.* richtige Verteilung *or* Zuteilung; – ***of costs,*** die Kostenumlage.

apposite ['æpəz(a)it], *adj.* passend, angemessen, geeignet (*to*, für); treffend, angebracht. **appositeness,** *s.* die Schicklichkeit, Angemessenheit.

apposition [æpə'ziʃən], *s.* das Nebeneinanderliegen; Nebeneinanderlegen, Nebeneinanderstellen; (*Gram.*) die Beifügung, Apposition; (*Bot. etc.*) Auflagerung, Anlagerung, Aneinanderlagerung.

appraisal [ə'preizəl], *s.* die Bewertung, (Ab)schätzung, Taxierung; (*fig.*) Würdigung, Wertschätzung. **appraise,** *v.t.* (ab)schätzen, bewerten, taxieren, (*fig.*) würdigen; ***–d value,*** der Schätzungswert. **appraisement,** *s. See* **appraisal**; der Schätz(ungs)wert. **appraiser,** *s.* der Schätzer, Taxator.

appreciable [ə'pri:ʃəbl], *adj.* **1.** nennenswert, beträchtlich, bemerkenswert; merklich; **2.** (ab)schätzbar, taxierbar.

appreciate [ə'pri:ʃieit], **1.** *v.t.* **1.** (hoch)schätzen, richtig einschätzen, würdigen, zu würdigen wissen; **2.** Gefallen finden an (*Dat.*), aufgeschlossen *or* empfänglich sein für, den Wert erkennen *or* einsehen (*Gen.*); **3.** schätzen, (dankbar) anerkennen; 4. erkennen, einsehen, erfassen, merken, wahrnehmen, gewahr werden (*Gen.*), sich (*Dat.*) bewußt sein *or* werden (*Gen.*). **2.** *v.i.* im Preis steigen, an Wert zunehmen.

appreciation [əpri:ʃi'eiʃən], *s.* 1. die Würdigung, das (Ab)schätzen; 2. die Anerkennung, (Wert)-schätzung; 3. das Verständnis, die Empfänglichkeit, Aufgeschlossenheit (*of, for,* für); 4. (dankbare) Anerkennung, der Ausdruck der Dankbarkeit; 5. die Wahrnehmung, (klares) Erkennen *or* Einsehen; 6. die Preiserhöhung, Aufwertung, Wertsteigerung, der Wertzuwachs.

appreciative [ə'pri:ʃiətiv], *adj.* achtungsvoll, anerkennend, würdigend; *see also* **appreciatory. appreciativeness,** *s.* die Empfänglichkeit, Aufgeschlossenheit (*of,* für). **appreciatory,** *adj.* verständnisvoll, empfänglich, aufgeschlossen (*of,* für).

apprehend [æpri'hend], *v.t.* fassen, ergreifen, festnehmen, gefangennehmen, verhaften; (*fig.*) (*a th.*) vernehmen, wahrnehmen, gewahren; gewahr werden (*Gen.*); (*fig.*) (*an idea*) erfassen, begreifen, verstehen, einsehen; (*fig.*) (be)fürchten, sich sorgen um, voraussehen.

apprehensible [æpri'hensibl], *adj.* wahrnehmbar, wahrzunehmen(d), erkennbar, zu erkennen(d); begreiflich, faßlich, verständlich.

apprehension [æpri'henʃən], *s.* 1. das Festnehmen, die Festnahme, Ergreifung, Verhaftung; 2. (*fig.*) das Erfassen, Begreifen, Verständnis, die Auffassung, Wahrnehmung; 3. Fassungskraft, Auffassungsgabe, das Auffassungsvermögen, Vorstellungsvermögen, der Verstand; ***dull of* –,** schwer von Begriff(en); ***be quick of* –,** schnell begreifen, leicht fassen; 4. der Begriff, die Vorstellung, Meinung, Ansicht; 5. Befürchtung, Besorgnis, Ahnung.

apprehensive [æpri'hensiv], *adj.* besorgt (*for,* um), furchtsam, ängstlich; ***be – of,*** befürchten, sich fürchten vor (*Dat.*). **apprehensiveness,** *s.* die Besorgnis, Ängstlichkeit, Furcht.

apprentice [ə'prentis], **1.** *s.* der Lehrling, Lehrjunge, Lehrbursche; (*fig.*) Neuling, Anfänger. **2.** *v.t.* in die Lehre geben (*to,* bei); ***be –d to,*** in der Lehre sein bei, in die Lehre kommen bei *or* zu. **apprenticeship,** *s.* die Lehre, Lehrzeit, Lehrjahre (*pl.*); das Lehrverhältnis, der Lehrlingsstand; ***serve one's* –,** in der Lehre sein, seine Lehrzeit durchmachen.

apprise [ə'praiz], *v.t.* benachrichtigen, in Kenntnis setzen (*of,* von).

appro ['æprou], (*abbr. of* **approval**) (*Comm.*) ***on* –,** zur Ansicht *or* Probe.

approach [ə'proutʃ], **1.** *v.i.* nahe *or* näher kommen, (heran)nahen, heranrücken, sich nähern; (*fig.*) grenzen (*to,* an (*Acc.*)), ähnlich sein, nahekommen (*Dat.*). **2.** *v.t.* sich nähern (*Dat.*), herantreten *or* herangehen an (*Acc.*); (*fig.*) nahekommen (*Dat.*), (*a p.*) sich wenden *or* heranmachen an (*Acc.*), angehen (*for,* um), (*a subject*) anschneiden, zu sprechen *or* reden kommen auf (*Acc.*). **3.** *s.* 1. das Herannahen, (Näher)kommen, (Her)anrücken, (*Mil.*) der Anmarsch, (*Av.*) Anflug; (*fig.*) das Nahekommen, (*to a p.*) Herantreten, die Annäherung; (*Av.*) ***– flight,*** der Anflug; (*Av.*) ***– path,*** der Anflugweg; (*Golf*) ***– shot,*** der Annäherungsschlag; 2. die Auffahrt, Zufahrt(sstraße), Zugangsstraße, der Zugang, Zutritt (*to,* zu), (*fig.*) Zugang, Weg (*to,* zu); *pl.* (*Mil.*) die Vormarschstraße; ***easy of* –,** leicht zugänglich; 3. erster Versuch *or* Schritt, Annäherungsversuch; die Betrachtungsweise (*to, Gen.*), Einstellung (zu), Stellungnahme, das Verhalten (gegenüber); ***method of* –,** die Betrachtungsweise, das Verhalten, (*Math.*) die Annäherungsmethode; ***make the first* –,** die ersten Schritte tun. **approachable,** *adj.* zugänglich, erreichbar.

approbate ['æprəbeit], *v.t.* (*Am.*) die Genehmigung erteilen zu, genehmigen, gutheißen, anerkennen, billigen. **approbation,** *s.* die Genehmigung, Billigung, Bestätigung; Zustimmung, der Beifall; (*Comm.*) ***on* –,** zur Ansicht *or* Einsichtnahme.

appropriate, 1. [ə'prouprieit], *v.t.* 1. sich aneignen, in Besitz nehmen, Besitz ergreifen von; 2. (*funds*) bestimmen, bewilligen, verwenden, anweisen. **2.** [–riət], *adj.* zuständig, zugehörig, eigen; zweckmäßig, angemessen, passend, geeignet (*to, for,* zu *or* für), dienlich (*Dat.*). **appropriateness,** *s.* die Angemessenheit, Zweckmäßigkeit. **appropriation** [–'eiʃən], *s.* 1. die Zueignung, Aneignung, Besitznahme, Besitzergreifung; 2. Anweisung, Verwendung, Zuwendung, Bestimmung, Bewilligung.

approvable [ə'pru:vəbl], *adj.* anerkennenswert, beifallswürdig, löblich. **approval,** *s.* 1. die Billigung, Bewilligung, Genehmigung, Gutheißung; ***give – to,*** billigen, gutheißen; 2. die Zustimmung, Anerkennung, der Beifall; ***meet with* –,** Anerkennung *or* Beifall finden; 3. (*Comm.*) die Prüfung, Probe; ***on* –,** zur Ansicht *or* Einsichtnahme. **approve, 1.** *v.t.* 1. genehmigen, billigen, gutheißen; anerkennen, gelten lassen; 2. (*rare*) ***– o.s.,*** sich erweisen (*to be,* als). **2.** *v.i.* ***– of,*** *see* **1.**; ***be –d of,*** Anklang finden (*by,* bei). **approved,** *adj.* anerkannt, bewährt, erprobt; (*Comm.*) ***– bill,*** anerkannter Wechsel; ***– school,*** die Besserungsanstalt. **approver,** *s.* Gutheißende(r), der Billiger, Gutheißer; (*Law*) Kronzeuge. **approvingly,** *adv.* beifällig, zustimmend.

approximate, 1. [ə'prɔksimit], *adj.* annähernd, Näherungs–; beiläufig, ungefähr; nahe, dicht (*to,* bei *or* an (*Dat.*)). **2.** [–meit], *v.i.* sich nähern, nahekommen (*to, Dat.*). **3.** [–meit], *v.t.* *See* **2.**; nahebringen, ähnlich machen, angleichen, anpassen. **approximation** [–'meiʃən], *s.* die (An)näherung (*to,* an (*Acc.*)); (*Math.*) der Annäherungswert; (*coll.*) annähernde Gleichheit; ***rough (close)* –,** grobe (genaue) Näherung. **approximative** [–mətiv], *adj.* annähernd.

appurtenance [ə'pə:tənəns], *s.* (*usu. pl.*) das *or* der Zubehör; *pl.* die Ausstattung, Gerätschaften (*pl.*); (*Law*) das Realrecht; Pertinenzstück, *pl.* Pertinenzien (*pl.*). **appurtenant,** *adj.* zugehörig (*to, Dat.*), gehörig (zu).

apricot ['eiprikɔt], *s.* die Aprikose, (*Austr.*) Marille.

April ['eiprəl], *s.* der April. **April-fool,** *s.* der Aprilnarr; ***make an – of him,*** ihn in den April schicken; ***–(s') day,*** der erste April.

a priori [eipri'ɔ:ri], *adj., adv.* deduktiv; von Ursache auf Wirkung schließend, unabhängig von aller Erfahrung, (*coll.*) mutmaßlich.

apron ['eiprən], *s.* die Schürze, (*Eccl.*) der Schurz, (*of a smith etc.*) Schurz, das Schurzfell; (*Tech.*) Schutzblech, die Schutzhaube (*on machines*), Schutzvorrichtung, das Schutzbrett, Schutzleder (*on carts etc.*); (*Naut.*) die Schutzleiste, der Binnenvorsteven; (*Av.*) das Rollfeld, die Landebahn; (*Geol.*) der Schuttfächer; (*Orn.*) die Bauchhaut (*ducks, geese*); (*Theat.*) Vorbühne; (*obs.*) Zündlochkappe (*on guns*). **apron-string,** *s.* das Schürzenband; ***be tied to one's mother's –s,*** ein Muttersöhnchen sein, an Mutters Schürzenzipfel hängen.

apropos [æprə'pou], **1.** *adv.* 1. gelegen, angemessen, zur rechten Zeit, (*coll.*) wie gerufen; 2. nebenbei (bemerkt), übrigens, beiläufig. **2.** *prep.* – (*of*), anläßlich, hinsichtlich (*Gen.*), in bezug auf, im Hinblick auf (*Acc.*), was . . . anbelangt.

apse [æps], *s.* (*Archit.*) die Apsis; *see also* **apsis.**

apsis ['æpsis], *s.* (*pl.* **apsides** [–di:z]) (*Astr.*) die Apside; ***higher* –,** das Aphel(ium); ***lower* –,** das Perihel(ium); *see also* **apse.**

apt [æpt], *adj.* 1. passend, tauglich, angemessen, geeignet; ***– remark,*** (zu)treffende *or* passende Bemerkung; 2. (*of a p.*) geeignet, willig, bereit; ***he is – to forget,*** er vergißt leicht; ***– to quarrel,*** streitsüchtig; 3. (*of a p.*) befähigt; fähig (*at,* für), gewandt, geschickt (in (*Dat.*)); ***– pupil,*** fähiger Schüler; 4. (*pred.*) (*Am.*) wahrscheinlich, voraussichtlich.

aptera ['æptərə], *pl.* (*Ent.*) flügellose Insekten. **apterous,** *adj.* (*Ent.*) flügellos, (*Bot.*) ungeflügelt. **apteryx** [–riks], *s.* (*Orn.*) der Kiwi, Schnepfenstrauß.

aptitude ['æptitju:d], *s.* 1. die Eigenschaft, (Sonder)begabung; Neigung, der Hang, (*Psych.*) die Fähigkeit, Eignung, Befähigung, Anlage (*for*, zu); 2. *See* **aptness. aptitude-test,** *s.* die Eignungsprüfung, der Test für Spezialbegabungen.

aptness ['æptnis], *s.* 1. die Angemessenheit, Geeignetheit, Tauglichkeit; 2. *See also* **aptitude.**

aqua fortis ['ækwəfɔ:tis], *s.* das Scheidewasser, Ätzwasser, die Salpetersäure.

aqualung ['ækwəlʌŋ], *s.* die Taucherlunge, das (Unterwasser-)Atmungsgerät.

aquamarine [ækwəmə'ri:n], *s.* 1. der Beryll, Aquamarin; 2. das Meergrün, Bläulichgrün.

aqua regia [ækwə'ri:dʒə], *s.* das Königswasser, (Gold)scheidewasser.

aquarelle [ækwə'rel], *s.* 1. die Aquarellmalerei; 2. das Aquarell.

aquarium [ə'kwɛəriəm], *s.* das Aquarium.

Aquarius [ə'kwɛəriəs], *s.* (*Astr.*) der Wassermann.

aquatic [ə'kwætik, ə'kwɔtik], *adj.* Wasser–. **aquatics,** *pl.* der Wassersport.

aquatint ['ækwətint], *s.* die Aquatintamanier, Tuschmanier; der Aquatintadruck.

aquavit, aqua vitae [ækwə'vi:t(ai)], *s.* der Aquavit, Branntwein.

aqueduct ['ækwədʌkt], *s.* (offene) Wasserleitung; (*Anat.*) der Kanal.

aqueous ['eikwiəs], *adj.* wässerig, wäßrig, wasserartig, wasserhaltig, Wasser–; (*Med.*) – ***humour,*** das Kammerwasser; – ***rocks,*** das Sediment– *or* Schichtgestein; – ***vapour,*** der Wasserdampf, Wasserdunst.

aquiline ['ækwilain], *adj.* Adler–, adlerartig; (*fig.*) gebogen, hakenförmig; – ***nose,*** die Adlernase.

Arab ['ærəb], **1.** *s.* der (die) Araber(in); (*pej.*) ***street arab,*** der Gassenjunge, das Straßenkind. **2.** *adj.* arabisch.

arabesque [ærə'besk], **1.** *s.* die Arabeske, Arabeskenarbeit. **2.** *adj.* arabesk(enartig).

Arabia [ə'reibiə], *s.* Arabien (*n.*). **Arabian, 1.** *s.* **1.** arabisches Pferd, der Araber; 2. *See* **Arab, 1. 2.** *adj. See* **Arab, 2.**; – ***Nights' (Entertainment),*** Tausendundeine Nacht. **Arabic** ['ærəbik], **1.** *s.* (*language*) das Arabisch(e); ***in* –,** auf arabisch. **2.** *adj.* arabisch; ***gum* –,** das Gummiarabikum.

arable ['ærəbl], **1.** *adj.* pflügbar, urbar, bestellbar, anbaufähig, kulturfähig. **2.** *s.* das Ackerland, (*Hist.*) die Feldmark.

Araby ['ærəbi], *s.* (*Poet.*) *see* **Arabia.**

arachnid [æ'ræknid], *s.* das Spinnentier. **arachnidium** [–'nidiəm], *s.* das Spinnwerkzeug (*of spiders*). **arachnoid** [–nɔid], *adj.* spinnenartig; spinnwebartig; (*Anat.*) – (*tunic*), die Spinnwebenhaut.

arbiter ['ɑ:bitə], *s.* der Schiedsrichter, Unparteiische(r); (*fig.*) der Gebieter, Herr, Richter. **arbitral,** *adj.* schiedsrichterlich. **arbitrament** [ɑ:'bitrəmənt], *s.* der Schiedsspruch, schiedsrichterliches Gutachten.

arbitrarily ['ɑ:bitrərili], *adv. See* **arbitrary. arbitrariness,** *s.* die Willkür. **arbitrary,** *adj.* willkürlich, beliebig; launenhaft; eigenmächtig, unumschränkt, despotisch; (*Math.*) – ***number,*** beliebige Zahl.

arbitrate ['ɑ:bitreit], **1.** *v.i.* als Schiedsrichter entscheiden *or* fungieren, Schiedsrichter sein; vermitteln. **2.** *v.t.* durch Schiedsspruch entscheiden *or* festsetzen *or* festlegen *or* bestimmen *or* schlichten *or* beilegen. **arbitration** [–'treiʃən], *s.* schiedsrichterliches Verfahren, das Schiedsspruchverfahren; (schiedsrichterliche) Entscheidung *or* Schlichtung, der Schiedsspruch, das Schiedsurteil; ***submit to* –,** einem Schiedsgericht unterwerfen; ***court of* –,** das Gewerbegericht; ***settle by* –,** durch Schiedsspruch schlichten; (*Comm.*) – ***of exchange,*** die Wechselarbitrage, Arbitragenrechnung, der Wechselkursvergleich. **arbitration|-committee,** *s.* der Schlichtungsausschuß. **–-court,** *s.* das Gewerbegericht. **arbitrator,** *s.* der Schiedsrichter, Unparteiische(r), (*Law*) Schlichter.

[1]**arbor** ['ɑ:bə], *s.* (*Mech.*) die Spindel, Welle Achse, der Drehstift, Drehbaum, Dorn, Bolzen.

[2]**arbor,** (*Am.*) *see* **arbour.**

arboraceous [ɑ:bə'reiʃəs], *adj. See* **arboreal, 1. arboreal** [ɑ:'bɔ:riəl], *adj.* 1. Baum–, baumartig; 2. auf Bäumen lebend. **arborescent** [ɑ:bə'resənt], *adj.* baumförmig, verzweigt. **arboriculture** ['ɑ:bərikʌltʃə], *s.* die Baumzucht. **arborization** [–'rai'zeiʃən], *s.* baumförmige *or* dendritenartige Bildung, die Verzweigung; der Dendrit.

arbor vitae ['ɑ:bə'vi:tai], *s.* (*Bot.*) der Lebensbaum.

arbour ['ɑ:bə], *s.* die Laube, der Laubengang.

arbutus [ɑ:'bju:təs], *s.* (*Bot.*) der Erdbeerbaum.

arc [ɑ:k], **1.** *s.* (*Geom.*) der Bogen, Arkus; (*Elec.*) (Licht)bogen; (*Astr.*) das Winkelgeschwindigkeitsmaß. **2.** *v.i.* Lichtbogen bilden, funken.

arcade [ɑ:'keid], *s.* der Bogengang, Säulengang, die Arkade; Passage, der Durchgang.

Arcadia [ɑ:'keidiə], *s.* Arkadien (*n.*). **Arcadian,** *adj.* arkadisch, (*fig.*) idyllisch. **Arcady** ['ɑ:kədi], *s.* (*Poet.*) *see* **Arcadia.**

arcane [ɑ:'kein], *adj.* geheim(nisvoll), verborgen. **arcanum,** *s.* 1. (*usu. pl.* **-na**) das Geheimnis, Mysterium, Hintergründige(s); 2. (*obs. Chem., Med.*) das Geheimmittel, Elixier, Arkanum.

[1]**arch** [ɑ:tʃ], **1.** *s.* (*Archit.*) der Bogen, die Wölbung, Rundung; das Gewölbe; – ***of the foot,*** der Rist, Spann; ***triumphal* –,** der Triumphbogen. **2.** *v.t.* wölben, runden, bogenförmig machen; – ***one's back,*** den Rücken krümmen, (*coll.*) einen Buckel machen; – ***over,*** überwölben, mit Bogen überspannen. **3.** *v.i.* sich wölben.

[2]**arch,** *adj.* schlau, listig, durchtrieben; schalkhaft, schelmisch, kokett.

[3]**arch,** *adj.*, **arch–,** *pref.* Haupt–, Erz–, erst, oberst, größt, führend.

Archaean [ɑ:'ki:ən], *adj.* (*Geol.*) azoisch.

archaeological [ɑ:kiə'lɔdʒikəl], *adj.* archäologisch, Altertums–. **archaeologist** [ɑ:ki'ɔlədʒist], *s.* der Archäologe, Altertumsforscher. **archaeology** [–'ɔlədʒi], *s.* die Archäologie, Altertumskunde, Altertumswissenschaft.

archaic [ɑ:'keiik], *adj.* altertümlich, archaisch; veraltet, altmodisch. **archaism** ['ɑ:keiizm], *s.* veralteter Ausdruck, der Archaismus; Veraltete(s), Altertümliche(s).

archangel ['ɑ:keindʒəl], *s.* 1. der Erzengel; 2. (*Bot.*) die Engelwurz, Angelika (*Archangelica officinalis*).

arch|bishop, *s.* der Erzbischof. **–bishopric,** *s.* das Erzbistum. **–-buttress,** *s.* der Strebebogen, Schwibbogen. **–deacon,** *s.* der Archidiakon. **–ducal,** *adj.* erzherzoglich. **–duchess,** *s.* die Erzherzogin. **–duchy,** *s.* das Erzherzogtum. **–duke,** *s.* der Erzherzog.

Archean, (*Am.*) *see* **Archaean.**

arched [ɑ:tʃt], *adj.* gewölbt, überwölbt; Bogen–, bogenförmig, gebogen, geschweift, gekrümmt; – ***roof,*** das Tonnendach.

arch-enemy, *s.* der Erzfeind; Satan, Teufel.

archeological, *etc.* (*Am.*) *see* **archaeological,** *etc.*

archer ['ɑ:tʃə], *s.* der Bogenschütze; (*Astr.*) Schütze. **archery,** *s.* das Bogenschießen.

archetypal ['ɑ:kitaipl], *adj.* urbildlich, vorbildlich, Muster–, original–. **archetype,** *s.* das Urbild, Vorbild, die Urform, das Muster, Original, (*Psych., Bot.*) der Archetyp(us).

arch|-fiend, *s. See* **–-enemy.**

archi– ['ɑ:ki], *pref.* 1. *See* **arch–**; 2. (*Bot., Zool. etc.*) primitiv, ursprünglich. **–diaconal,** *adj.* archidiakonisch. **–episcopal,** *adj.* erzbischöflich.

Archimedean [ɑ:ki'mi:diən], *adj.* archimedisch.

arching ['ɑ:tʃiŋ], **1.** *adj.* bogenförmig, gewölbt. **2.** *s.* das Gewölbe, der Bogen.

archipelago [ɑ:ki'peləgou], *s.* der Archipel, die Inselgruppe, das Inselmeer.

architect ['ɑ:kitekt], *s.* der Baumeister, Architekt; (*fig.*) Begründer, Urheber, Schöpfer; ***the* – *of his own fortune,*** seines eignen Glückes Schmied. **architectonic** [–'tɔnik], *adj.* architektonisch.

architectural [–'tektʃərəl], *adj.* baulich, baukünstlerisch, Bau–, Architektur–. **architecture,** *s.* die Baukunst, Architektur; der Baustil, die Bauart; der Bau, Aufbau, Bauplan, die Anlage, Struktur; *school of –,* die Bauschule; *naval –,* der Schiffsbau, die Schiffsbaukunst.

architrave ['ɑ:kitreiv], *s.* der Architrav, Säulenbalken.

archival [ɑ:'kaivəl], *adj.* Archiv–, archivalisch, urkundlich. **archives** ['ɑ:kaivz], *pl.* das Archiv, die Urkundensammlung; *keeper of the – or* **archivist** ['ɑ:kivist], *s.* der (die) Archivar(in).

archivolt ['ɑ:kivoult], *s.* die Archivolte, Bogeneinfassung, Bogenverzierung.

archness ['ɑ:tʃnis], *s.* die Schelmerei, Schalkhaftigkeit; der Mutwille; die Koketterie.

arch|-stone ['ɑ:tʃstoun], *s.* der Schlußstein. **--support,** *s.* die Plattfußeinlage. **–way,** *s.* der Bogengang, überwölbter Torweg.

arcing ['ɑ:kiŋ], *s.* (*Elec.*) die Lichtbogenbildung, das Funkenüberschlagen. **arc| lamp, – light,** *s.* die Bogen(licht)lampe, das Bogenlicht.

Arctic ['ɑ:ktik], **1.** *adj.* arktisch, nördlich, Polar–; *– Circle,* nördlicher Polarkreis; *– expedition,* die Nordpolexpedition; *– fox,* der Polarfuchs; *– Ocean,* Nördliches Eismeer; (*Orn*). *– tern,* die Küstenseeschwalbe (*Sterna macrura*). **2.** *s. the –,* die Arktis, nördliche Polargegend, Nordpolarländer (*pl.*).

arc welding, *s.* elektrische Schweißung, die Lichtbogenschweißung.

ardency ['ɑ:dənsi], *s.* die Hitze, Glut; (*fig.*) Inbrunst, Leidenschaft(lichkeit), Heftigkeit, das Feuer. **ardent,** *adj.* heiß, glühend, feurig, hitzig, brennend, (*fig.*) heiß, feurig, heftig, leidenschaftlich, innig, inbrünstig; eifrig.

ardor, (*Am.*) *see* **ardour.**

ardour ['ɑ:də], *s. See* **ardency**; die Begeisterung, der Eifer.

arduous ['ɑ:djuəs], *adj.* schwierig, mühsam; anstrengend, schwer; (*of a p.*) ausdauernd, eifrig, tätig, emsig, arbeitsam, energisch; (*obs.*) steil, jäh; *– efforts,* große Anstrengungen; *– winter,* strenger Winter. **arduousness,** *s.* die Schwierigkeit, Mühseligkeit, Mühsal.

[1]**are** [ɑ:, ə *according to emphasis*], *see* **be.**

[2]**are** [ɑ:], *s.* das Ar (= *100 sq. m.* or *approx. 120 sq. yards*).

area ['ɛəriə], *s.* die (Grund)fläche; der Raum, freier Platz; das Gebiet, die Zone, der Bezirk; (*fig.*) Bereich, Spielraum; (*Math.*) Flächeninhalt, Flächenraum; Vorplatz, Souterrainvorhof; *– of a circle,* die Kreisfläche; *– of a rectangle,* der Flächeninhalt eines Rechtecks; *prohibited –,* das Sperrgebiet. **area|-bell,** *s.* die Dienstbotenglocke. **– steps,** *pl.* die Außentreppe zum Souterrain.

[1]**arena** [ə'ri:nə], *s.* die Arena, der Kampfplatz, die Kampfbahn; (*fig.*) der Schauplatz.

[2]**arena,** *s.* (*Med.*) der Harngrieß. **arenaceous** [æri'neiʃəs], *adj.* sandig, sandhaltig; (*Bot.*) *– plants,* im sandigen Boden wachsende Pflanzen.

areola [ə'riələ], *s.* die Areole, Spiegelzelle; der Ring, Hof, (*esp.*) Brustwarzenhof. **areolar,** *adj.* netzförmig, zellig; (*Anat.*) *– tissue,* das Zellengewebe.

areometer [æri'ɔmitə], *s.* die Senkwaage, der Aräometer.

arête [æ'ret], *s.* der Bergkamm, (Fels)grat.

argent ['ɑ:dʒənt], *adj.* silberfarbig, glänzend, silbern; (*Her.*) silberweiß. **argentiferous** [–'tifərəs], *adj.* silberhaltig, silberführend.

Argentina [ɑ:dʒən'ti:nə], *s.* Argentinien (*n.*).

argentine ['ɑ:dʒəntain], *adj.* silbern, silberfarben, silberartig.

Argentine, 1. *adj.* argentinisch. **2.** *s. the –,* Argentinien (*n.*). **Argentinian** [–'tiniən], *s.* der (die) Argentinier(in).

argillaceous [ɑ:dʒi'leiʃəs], *adj.* lehmig, tonartig, tonhaltig, Ton–. **argilliferous** [–'lifərəs], *adj.* tonhaltig, tonreich.

argon ['ɑ:gən], *s.* (*Chem.*) das Argon.

argosy ['ɑ:gəsi], *s.* das Handelsschiff, (*coll.*) die Flotte.

argot ['ɑ:gou], *s.* die Geheimsprache, Gaunersprache.

arguable ['ɑ:gjuəbl], *adj.* diskutierbar, diskutabel; bestreitbar. **argue, 1.** *v.t.* **1.** erörtern, besprechen, diskutieren; *– the point,* die S. bestreiten; (*coll.*) *– the toss,* sich nicht überreden lassen; *– him into s.th.,* ihn zu etwas überreden; *– him out of s.th.,* ihn von etwas abbringen; **2.** bekunden, verraten, deuten auf (*Acc.*), zeugen von; *– sagacity,* Scharfsinn verraten. **2.** *v.i.* **1.** Gründe anführen, Schlüsse ziehen, argumentieren, schließen, folgern (*from,* von *or* aus); *– against,* Einwände machen gegen; *– for,* eintreten für, verteidigen; **2.** streiten, disputieren, hadern (*about,* über (*Acc.*)).

argument ['ɑ:gjumənt], *s.* **1.** der Beweis(grund), das Beweismittel; die Beweisführung, Erhärtung, Schlußfolgerung; *lame* or *weak –,* schwacher Beweis; *strong –,* stichhaltiger Beweis, wichtiges Argument; **2.** das Argument, die Verhandlung, Besprechung, Debatte, Erörterung; (*coll.*) Auseinandersetzung; der Streit; (*obs.*) Streitpunkt, die Streitfrage; *clinch an –,* triftige Beweisgründe anführen; *hold an –,* diskutieren; **3.** der (Haupt)-inhalt, Stoff, Gegenstand, das Thema.

argumentation [ɑ:gjumen'teiʃən], *s.* die Beweisführung, Schlußfolgerung; Erörterung. **argumentative** [–'mentətiv], *adj.* streitsüchtig, streitlustig. **argumentativeness,** *s.* die Streitlust.

aria ['ɑ:riə], *s.* die Arie.

Arian ['ɛəriən], **1.** *s.* der (die) Arianer(in). **2.** *adj.* arianisch.

arid ['ærid], *adj.* dürr, trocken; wasserlos, unfruchtbar; (*fig.*) reizlos, schal, trocken, leer, nüchtern. **aridity** [ə'riditi], *s.* die Dürre, Trockenheit.

Aries ['ɛərii:z], *s.* (*Astr.*) der Widder.

aright [ə'rait], *adv.* recht, richtig; zurecht, zu Recht.

arise [ə'raiz], *irr.v.i.* **1.** die Folge sein, herrühren (*from,* von), entstehen, hervorgehen, entspringen (aus); **2.** erscheinen, auftreten, aufkommen, auftauchen; *the question doesn't –,* es kommt gar nicht in Frage; **3.** (*Poet.*) sich erheben, aufstehen; *see also* **rise**; auferstehen (*from the dead*).

aristocracy [æris'tɔkrəsi], *s.* die Aristokratie, Adelsherrschaft; der Adel; (*fig.*) die Elite. **aristocrat** ['æristəkræt], *s.* der Aristokrat, Adlige(r). **aristocratic** [–'krætik], *adj.* aristokratisch, ad(e)lig, Adels–; (*fig.*) exklusiv, edel, vornehm.

Aristotelian [æristə'ti:liən], *adj.* aristotelisch. **Aristotle** ['æristɔtl], *s.* Aristoteles (*m.*).

arithmetic [ə'riθmətik], *s.* die Rechenkunst, Arithmetik; *mental –,* das Kopfrechnen. **arithmetic(al)** [æriθ'metik(l)], *adj.* arithmetisch; *– mean,* arithmetisches Mittel; *–al progression,* arithmetische Reihe. **arithmetician** [–mə'tiʃən], *s.* der Arithmetiker, Rechner.

ark [ɑ:k], *s.* die Arche, (*obs. or dial.*) Truhe, Kiste, Lade, der Kasten, Koffer; *– of the covenant,* die Bundeslade; *Noah's Ark,* die Arche Noah.

[1]**arm** [ɑ:m], *s.* der Arm (*also Mech.*); (*of a tree*) Ast, Zweig; (*of a chair*) die Seitenlehne; der Flügel (*of a windmill*); (*fig.*) die Macht, Stärke, Kraft, Gewalt; *at –'s length,* auf Armlänge; *hold at –'s length,* vor sich ausgestreckt halten; *keep him at –'s length,* sich (*Dat.*) ihn vom Leibe halten; (*Mech.*) *distributor –,* der Verteilerfinger; *fold one's –s,* die Arme kreuzen; *with folded –s,* mit verschränkten Armen; *go – in –,* Arm in Arm gehen; *child in –s,* das Tragkind, kleines Kind; *take him in one's –s,* ihn in die Arme schließen; *with a girl on his –,* mit einem Mädel am Arm; *with open –s,* mit offenen Armen; *– of the sea,* der Meeresarm; *the secular –,* die weltliche Macht, die Obrigkeit; *within –'s reach,* in Reichweite, in unmittelbarer Nähe.

[2]**arm, 1.** *s.* die Waffe, (*usu. pl.*) Waffen (*pl.*); die Waffengattung. *See* **arms. 2.** *v.t.* (be)waffnen, mit Waffen (aus)rüsten; armieren (*a magnet*); *– a*

grenade, eine Granate scharf machen. **3.** *v.i.* aufrüsten, sich rüsten *or* bewaffnen; ***–ed to the teeth,*** bis an die Zähne bewaffnet.

armada [ɑ:'mɑ:də], *s.* die Kriegsflotte, Armada.

armadillo [ɑ:mə'dilou], *s.* das Armadill, Gürteltier.

Armageddon [ɑ:mə'gedən], *s.* (*B.*) (der Berg) Harmagedon, (*fig.*) der Entscheidungskampf.

armament ['ɑ:məmənt], *s.* die Kriegsrüstung; Militärmacht, Kriegsstärke; Aufrüstung, Bewaffnung; Feuerstärke, Feuerkraft; Schiffsgeschütze (*pl.*); die Bestückung (*of a ship or tank*); –(*s*) ***race,*** das Wettrüsten.

armature ['ɑ:mətʃə], *s.* (*Elec.*) die Armatur, der Anker, Läufer; – ***winding,*** die Ankerwicklung.

arm|-band, *s.* die Armbinde. **–chair,** *s.* der Lehnstuhl, Sessel; – ***politician,*** der Bierbank– *or* Stammtischpolitiker.

armed [ɑ:md], *adj.* (*Mil.*) bewaffnet, (*of gun*) geladen, entsichert, (*of munitions*) scharf, zündfertig; (*Bot.*) dornig, stachelig; (*Zool.*) bewehrt, gepanzert; – ***assistance,*** der Waffenbeistand; – ***forces*** or ***services,*** Streitkräfte (*pl.*); – ***magnet,*** der Magnet mit Armatur; – ***neutrality,*** bewaffnete Neutralität; – ***service,*** der Dienst mit der Waffe.

–armed, *adj. suff.* –armig, mit . . . Armen.

armful ['ɑ:mful], *s.* der Armvoll; ***an – of books,*** ein Armvoll Bücher. **arm-hole,** *s.* (*Anat.*) die Achselhöhle; (*of clothes*) das Armloch.

armillary [ɑ:'miləri], *adj.* ringförmig, Ring–, Reifen–.

armistice ['ɑ:mistis], *s.* der Waffenstillstand, die Waffenruhe; ***Armistice Day,*** der Heldengedenktag.

armlet ['ɑ:mlit], *s.* die Armbinde; der Armreif; kurzer Ärmel; (*of the sea*) kleiner (Meeres)arm.

armor, (*Am.*) *see* **armour.**

armorial [ɑ:'mɔ:riəl], *adj.* heraldisch, Wappen–; – ***bearings,*** das Wappen(schild).

armour ['ɑ:mə], **1.** *s.* die Rüstung, der Harnisch, Panzer; die Panzerung, (*Zool.*) Schutzdecke; Bewehrung (*of a cable*); der Taucheranzug; (*collect.*) (*Mil.*) Panzertruppen, Panzerfahrzeuge (*pl.*); ***suit of –,*** die Rüstung. **2.** *v.t.* panzern, bewaffnen. **armour|-bearer,** *s.* der Waffenträger, Schildknappe. **--clad,** *adj. See* **--plated.**

armoured ['ɑ:məd], *adj.* gepanzert, Panzer–; – ***cable,*** das Panzerkabel, armiertes *or* bewehrtes Kabel; – ***car,*** der Panzer(kampf)wagen; – ***train,*** der Panzerzug. **armourer** [–rə], *s.* (*Hist.*) der Rüstmeister, Waffenschmied, Büchsenmacher; (*Mil.*) Waffenmeister.

armour|-piercing, *adj.* panzerbrechend; – ***bullet,*** das Panzer(spreng)geschoß, Stahlkerngeschoß; – ***gun,*** die Panzerabwehrkanone. **--plate,** *s.* die Panzerplatte, das Panzerblech. **--plated,** *adj.* gepanzert, Panzer–.

armoury ['ɑ:məri], *s.* die Waffenkammer, Rüstkammer, Rüsthalle, das Rüsthaus, Zeughaus (*also fig.*); die Waffenwerkstatt, Waffenmeisterei.

arms [ɑ:mz], *pl.* die Waffen, Bewaffnung; ***coat of –,*** das Wappen; ***companion in –,*** der Waffenbruder; ***passage of –,*** der Waffengang; ***profession of –,*** der Soldatenstand; – ***race,*** das Wettrüsten; ***bear*** or ***carry –,*** Waffen tragen *or* führen; ***capable of bearing –,*** waffenfähig; ***call to –,*** zu den Waffen rufen; ***ground*** or ***order –!*** Gewehr ab! ***lay down one's –,*** die Waffen strecken, sich ergeben; ***pile –!*** setzt die Gewehre zusammen! ***present –!*** präsentiert das Gewehr! ***rise in –,*** die Waffen ergreifen, sich erheben; ***shoulder*** or ***slope –!*** das Gewehr über! ***stand to your –!*** an die Gewehre! ***the men stood to their –,*** die Mannschaft trat unters Gewehr; ***take up –,*** die Waffen ergreifen, zu den Waffen greifen; ***by force of –,*** mit Waffengewalt; ***in*** or ***under –,*** unter Waffen, bewaffnet, gewaffnet, gerüstet, kampfbereit; ***up in –,*** in vollem Aufruhr, (*fig.*) in Harnisch, in hellem Zorn.

army ['ɑ:mi], *s.* das Heer, die Armee; Landstreitkräfte (*pl.*); (*fig.*) der Schwarm, die Schar; ***enter*** or ***go into the –,*** ins Heer eintreten (*as an officer*); ***join the –,*** Soldat werden (*in the ranks*). **army| bill,** *s.* (*Parl.*) die Wehrvorlage. **--chaplain,** *s.* Feldgeistliche(r). **--contractor,** *s.* der Heereslieferant. **--corps,** *s.* das Armeekorps. – **list,** *s.* die Rangordnung. – **nurse corps** (*Am.*), – **nursing service,** *s.* das Heereskrankenschwesternkorps. – **post office,** *s.* das Feldpostamt. – **register,** *s.* (*Am.*) *see* – **list.** – **regulations,** *pl.* die Heeresdienstvorschrift. – **service corps,** *s.* Nachschubtruppen, Versorgungstruppen, Fahrtruppen (*pl.*), der Train. – **welfare,** *s.* die Heeresbetreuung.

arnica ['ɑ:nikə], *s.* (*Bot.*) die Arnika, der (Berg)wohlverleih (*Arnica montana*).

aroma [ə'roumə], *s.* der Duft, Geruch, Wohlgeruch, das Aroma; Bukett, die Blume (*of wine*). **aromatic** [æro'mætik], *adj.* duftig, würzig, wohlriechend, aromatisch.

arose [ə'rouz], *imperf. of* **arise.**

around [ə'raund], **1.** *adv.* rundherum, ringsherum, ringsumher, rundum; (*sl.*) ***stick –!*** bleib in der Nähe! **2.** *prep.* 1. um . . . her(um), (rund) um; 2. (*coll.*) um (. . . herum), etwa, ungefähr.

arouse [ə'rauz], *v.t.* (auf)wecken; (*fig.*) erwecken, wachrufen, erregen, aufrütteln.

arquebus ['ɑ:kwibəs], *s. See* **harquebus.**

arrack ['ærək], *s.* der Arrak.

arraign [ə'rein], *v.t.* anklagen, beschuldigen; (*Law*) zur Anklage vernehmen, vor Gericht stellen; (*fig.*) zur Rechenschaft ziehen, anklagen, anfechten. **arraignment,** *s.* die Anklage, Beschuldigung, (*Law*) Vorführung zum Untersuchungsverhör, gerichtliche Belangung.

arrange [ə'reindʒ], **1.** *v.t.* ordnen, arrangieren; in Ordnung bringen; (ein)richten, Anstalten treffen, vorbereiten, planen, organisieren, veranstalten, anordnen; festsetzen, bestimmen, ausmachen, abmachen, vereinbaren, verabreden; (*Math.*) gruppieren, ansetzen, gliedern; bearbeiten (*music*); – ***a quarrel,*** einen Streit schlichten *or* beilegen; ***the matter has been –d,*** die S. ist abgemacht. **2.** *v.i.* sich verständigen *or* einigen (***about,*** über (*Acc.*)); Anordnungen *or* Vorkehrungen treffen, sorgen (***for,*** für); ***I will – for it*** (***to be done***), ich will dafür sorgen (daß . . . *etc.*).

arrangement [ə'reindʒmənt], *s.* das (An)ordnen, Aufstellen, Verteilen; die (An)ordnung, Einrichtung; Disposition, Gruppierung, Einteilung, Gliederung, Aufstellung, (*Math.*) Komplexion; der Vergleich, die Erledigung, Beilegung; Übereinkunft, Vereinbarung, Verabredung, Abmachung, das Abkommen; die Bearbeitung (*of music*); *pl.* Vorkehrungen, Vorbereitungen; ***come to an –,*** sich vergleichen, zu einem Vergleich kommen; ***enter into*** or ***make an – with,*** ein Übereinkommen treffen mit; ***make –s,*** Vorkehrungen treffen. **arranger,** *s.* der Anordner, (*Mus.*) Arrangeur, Bearbeiter.

arrant ['ærənt], *adj.* durchtrieben, abgefeimt, Erz–; – ***knave,*** der Erzgauner; – ***nonsense,*** ausgesprochener *or* offenkundiger Unsinn.

arras ['ærəs], *s.* gewirkter Teppich, gewirkte Tapete, der Wandteppich, Wandbehang.

array [ə'rei], **1.** *v.t.* 1. kleiden, putzen, schmücken; – ***o.s.,*** sich putzen *or* kleiden; 2. ordnen, in Ordnung bringen, aufstellen; – ***troops,*** Truppen aufstellen; (*Law*) – ***a panel,*** die Geschworenen aufrufen. **2.** *s.* 1. die Ordnung *or* Aufstellung (in Reih und Glied); Truppe; ***battle –,*** die Schlachtordnung, Gefechtsaufstellung; 2. das Aufgebot, die Schar, Menge, stattliche Reihe; 3. Anordnung, Verteilung, das Schema; (*Rad.*) ***aerial –,*** das Richtantennennetz; 4. die Kleidung, Tracht, Aufmachung, der Staat; ***in rich –,*** in prächtigen Gewändern; 5. (*Law*) die Geschworenenliste; Einsetzung der Geschworenen.

arrear [ə'riə], *s.* (*usu. pl.*) der Rückstand; rückständige Summe, Rückstände (*pl.*), Schulden (*pl.*), ausstehende Forderungen (*pl.*); ***in –s,*** im Rückstand; ***–s of*** or ***in rent,*** rückständige Miete.

arrest [ə'rest], **1.** *s.* 1. die Verhaftung, Festnahme, Inhaftnahme; der Arrest, die Haft; (*of goods*) Beschlagnahme, der Sequester; (*Mil.*) ***open –,*** der

Garnisonarrest; ***preventive*** **–**, die Schutzhaft; ***under*** **–**, in Haft *or* Gewahrsam, (*of goods*) in Beschlag; ***place under*** **–**, *see* **2,** 1; 2. die Hemmung, Stockung, der Stillstand, das Anhalten, Aufhalten, der Einhalt, die Unterbrechung; ***– of growth,*** der Wachstumsstillstand; (*Law*) ***– of judgement,*** die Urteilssistierung; (*Mil.*) ***close –,*** der Stubenarrest; ***lay – on the goods,*** die Waren mit Beschlag belegen. **2.** *v.t.* 1. verhaften, in Haft nehmen, festnehmen; (*goods*) in Beschlag nehmen, mit Beschlag belegen; 2. aufhalten, anhalten, zurückhalten, hemmen, hindern, zum Stillstand bringen; ***– his attention,*** seine Aufmerksamkeit festhalten *or* fesseln; (*Law*) ***– judgement,*** das Verfahren aussetzen.

arrester|-gear, *s.* (*Av.*) das Fangkabel. **--hook,** *s.* (*Av.*) der Fanghaken. **arresting,** *adj.* eindrucksvoll, fesselnd. **arresting-gear,** *s.* (*Tech.*) die Sperrvorrichtung, Abbremsvorrichtung, das Arretiergetriebe. **arrestment,** *s.* die Hemmung, das Hemmen; Hemmnis, Hindernis; (*Law*) die Beschlagnahme, (*Scots.*) Verhaftung, Festnahme.

arrhythmic(al) [ei'riðmik(l)], *adj.* unrhythmisch, rhythmuslos. **arrhythmous,** *adj.* (*Med.*) unregelmäßig (*pulse etc.*).

arrière|-ban ['æriɛə'bæn], *s.* (*Hist.*) der Landsturm, Heerbann. **--pensée** [–'pãsei], *s.* der Hintergedanke.

arrival [ə'raivəl], *s.* 1. die Ankunft, das Ankommen, Eintreffen, Erscheinen; ***on my –,*** bei meiner *or* gleich nach meiner Ankunft; ***– platform,*** der Ankunftsbahnsteig; 2. der Ankömmling, Angekommene(r); ***new –,*** Neuangekommene(r); (*coll.*) neugeborenes Kind; ***–s,*** angekommene Personen *or* Züge *etc.*; ***list of –s,*** die Fremdenliste; 3. (*Comm.*) (*usu. pl.*) Eingänge (*pl.*), die Zufuhr; 4. (*fig.*) Erreichung, das Gelangen.

arrive [ə'raiv], *v.i.* ankommen, eintreffen (***at,*** in *or* an (*Dat.*)); (*coll.*) Anerkennung finden, Erfolg haben, es zu etwas bringen, (*sl.*) es schaffen; (*fig.*) ***– at,*** kommen *or* gelangen zu, erreichen (*conclusion etc.*); ***the time has –d,*** die Zeit ist gekommen; ***it has just –d,*** es ist soeben eingelaufen; (*coll.*) ***– on the scene,*** auftauchen.

arrogance ['ærəgəns], *s.* die Arroganz, Vermessenheit, Anmaßung, Einbildung, der Hochmut, Dünkel. **arrogant,** *adj.* arrogant, vermessen, anmaßend, eingebildet, hochmütig.

arrogate ['ærəgeit], *v.t.* ***– to o.s.,*** sich (*Dat.*) anmaßen, für sich verlangen *or* beanspruchen; sich (*Dat.*) unrechtmäßig aneignen; ***– to him,*** ihm zuschreiben *or* zusprechen *or* zuschieben. **arrogation** [–'geiʃən], *s.* die Anmaßung; unrechtmäßige Aneignung.

arrow ['ærou], *s.* der Pfeil; (das) Pfeil(zeichen); (*Surv.*) der Zählstab, Markierstab; ***straight as an –,*** pfeilgerade; ***swift as an –,*** pfeilgeschwind; ***shower of –s,*** der Pfeilhagel. **arrow|-grass,** *s.* (*Bot.*) der Dreizack. **-head,** *s.* die Pfeilspitze; (*in diagrams*) der Pfeil; (*Bot.*) das Pfeilkraut. **-root,** *s.* (*Bot.*) die Pfeilwurz, (*Cul.*) das Pfeilwurzmehl. **--shaped, arrowy,** *adj.* pfeilförmig.

arse [ɑ:s], *s.* (*vulg.*) der Arsch, Steiß, Hintern.

arsenal ['ɑ:sənəl], *s.* das Zeughaus, Waffenlager; die Munitionsfabrik.

arsenate ['ɑ:səneit], **arseniate** [ɑ:'si:nieit], *s.* (*Chem.*) arsensäures Salz. **arsenic** ['ɑ:sənik], *s.* das Arsen; weißes Arsenik, arsenige Säure. **arsenical** [ɑ:'senikl], *adj.* arsen(ik)haltig, Arsen(ik)–. **arsenious** [ɑ:'siniəs], *adj.* arsenig, Arsen–; ***– acid,*** die Arsensäure. **arsenite** ['ɑ:sənait], *s.* arsenigsaures Salz. **arsenous** ['ɑ:sənəs], *adj. See* **arsenious.**

arsis ['ɑ:sis], *s.* (*Metr.*) die Hebung, (*Mus.*) der Aufschlag.

arson ['ɑ:sən], *s.* die Brandstiftung. **arsonist,** *s.* der Brandstifter.

[1]**art** [ɑ:t], *s.* 1. die Kunst; bildende Kunst; (*collect.*) Kunstwerke (*pl.*); ***applied –,*** angewandte Kunst, das Kunstgewerbe; ***–s and crafts,*** Kunst und Gewerbe; ***commercial –,*** die Gebrauchsgraphik; ***the fine –s,*** die schönen Künste; ***work of –,*** das Kunstwerk, der Kunstgegenstand; 2. die Kunstfertigkeit, Geschicklichkeit; 3. Findigkeit, Verschlagenheit, Schlauheit, List; (*coll.*) ***be – and part in*** or ***of it,*** die Hand im Spiele haben; 4. (*usu. pl.*) der Kunstgriff, Kniff; ***–s and wiles,*** Kniffe und Schliche; 5. *pl.* Geisteswissenschaften, (*Hist.*) die freien Künste; (*Univ.*) ***–s degree,*** der Grad in der philosophischen Fakultät; (*Univ.*) ***Faculty of Arts,*** philosophische Fakultät; (*Univ.*) ***Master of Arts,*** der Magister der philosophischen Fakultät *or* (*Hist.*) der freien Künste.

[2]**art** (*obs., Poet.*) *see* **be.**

artefact, *see* **artifact.**

arterial [ɑ:'tiəriəl], *adj.* Schlagader–, Arterien–, arteriell, arteriös; ***– road,*** die (Haupt)verkehrsader, Durchgangsstraße.

arteriosclerosis [ɑ:tiəriosklə'rousis], *s.* die Arterienverkalkung. **arteriotomy** [–ri'ɔtəmi], *s.* die Pulsaderöffnung, der Aderlaß.

artery ['ɑ:təri], *s.* die Pulsader, Schlagader, Arterie; (*fig.*) ***main arteries of trade,*** Hauptverkehrsadern, Haupthandelswege (*pl.*).

artesian well [ɑ:'ti:ʒən, –ziən], *s.* artesischer Brunnen.

artful ['ɑ:tful], *adj.* listig, schlau, verschlagen, gerissen, gerieben, verschmitzt; geschickt, gewandt, kunstvoll. **artfulness,** *s.* die List, Schlauheit, Schläue, Verschlagenheit, Gerissenheit, Verschmitztheit; Gewandtheit, das Geschick.

arthritic [ɑ:'θritik], *adj.* arthritisch, gichtisch. **arthritis** [ɑ:'θraitis], *s.* die Arthritis, Gicht, Gelenkentzündung.

arthropoda [ɑ:'θrɔpədə], *pl.* (*Zool.*) Gliederfüßler.

Arthurian [ɑ:'θjuəriən], *adj.* (König-)Artus–.

artichoke ['ɑ:titʃouk], *s.* die Artischocke; ***Jerusalem –,*** die Erdartischocke.

article ['ɑ:tikl], **1.** *s.* 1. der Abschnitt, Paragraph; Artikel, Punkt (*of faith etc.*); (*usu. pl.*) die Bedingung, Klausel (*of a treaty etc.*); der Aufsatz, Artikel (*in a newspaper*); ***–s of agreement,*** Vertragsbedingungen; ***–s of apprenticeship,*** der Lehrvertrag; ***–s of association,*** Satzungen, Vereinsstatuten; ***leading –,*** der Leitartikel; ***serve one's –s,*** als Lehrling dienen; ***ship's –s,*** der Heuervertrag; ***the Thirty-nine Articles,*** die Glaubensartikel (der Anglikanischen Kirche); ***–s of war,*** Kriegsartikel; 2. das Ding, die Sache, der Gegenstand; (*Comm.*) Artikel, das Stück, Gut, die Ware, der (Waren)posten, (Handels)artikel; ***– of clothing,*** das Kleidungsstuck; ***– of commerce,*** der Handelsposten; 3. (*Gram.*) der Artikel, das Geschlechtswort. **2.** *v.t.* schriftlich verklagen *or* anklagen (***for,*** wegen); kontraktlich binden, in die Lehre geben (***to,*** bei); ***–d clerk,*** der Buchhalter– *or* Kontorlehrling.

articulate, **1.** [ɑ:'tikjuleit], *v.t.* 1. zusammenfügen, aneinanderfügen, (gliedartig) verbinden; 2. deutlich aussprechen, artikulieren. **2.** [–leit], *v.i.* 1. ein Glied bilden, sich gliedartig verbinden; 2. deutlich *or* artikuliert sprechen. **3.** [–lit], *adj.* 1. gegliedert, gliedartig verbunden, Glieder–, Gelenk–; 2. artikuliert, deutlich ausgesprochen, verständlich, vernehmlich, klar erkenntlich, scharf ausgesprägt; (*of a p.*) imstande, sich verständlich zu machen. **articulated** [–leitid], *adj.* gegliedert, (*Phonet.*) artikuliert; (*Tech.*) Gelenk–; ***– lorry,*** der Gelenkwagen. **articulateness** [–litnis], *s.* die Deutlichkeit, Verständlichkeit. **articulation** [–'leiʃən], *s.* 1. die Zusammenfügung, Aneinanderfügung, Verbindung, Gliederung; Gelenkfügung, das Gelenk; 2. deutliche Aussprache, die Artikulation.

artifact ['ɑ:tifækt], *s.* das Kunsterzeugnis; (*Archaeol.*) Werkzeug, Gerät.

artifice ['ɑ:tifis], *s.* der Kunstgriff, Kniff; die Kunstfertigkeit; List, Schlauheit.

artificer [ɑ:'tifisə], *s.* der Mechaniker, Handwerker; (*Mil.*) Artillerietechniker, (*Naut.*) Maschinistenmaat; (*fig.*) Schöpfer, Stifter, Urheber.

artificial [ɑ:ti'fiʃəl], *adj.* künstlich, gekünstelt,

erkünstelt, erheuchelt, erdichtet, vorgetäuscht; künstlich, nachgemacht, unecht, falsch, Kunst–, Ersatz–; (*of a p.*) affektiert, geziert, unnatürlich; – ***flower,*** die Kunstblume; – ***insemination,*** künstliche Befruchtung; – ***limb,*** die Prothese; (*Law*) – ***person,*** juristische Person, die Körperschaft; – ***silk,*** die Kunstseide; – ***smile,*** gekünsteltes Lächeln; – ***stone,*** synthetischer Edelstein; – ***tears,*** erheuchelte Tränen; – ***teeth,*** falsche *or* künstliche Zähne, künstliches Gebiß. **artificiality** [–i'æliti], *s.* die Künstlichkeit, Gekünsteltheit.

artillery [ɑ:'tiləri], *s.* die Artillerie; Geschütze, Kanonen (*pl.*); ***under – fire,*** unter Beschuß. **artilleryman,** *s.* der Artillerist.

artisan ['ɑ:tizən, –'zæn], *s.* der Handwerker, Mechaniker.

artist ['ɑ:tist], *s.* (bildende(r)) Künstler(in); (*fig.*) der Könner. **artiste** [–'ti:st], *s.* der (die) Artist(in). **artistic(al)** [–'tistik(l)], *adj.* künstlerisch, kunstgemäß, kunstgerecht, Kunst–, Künstler–; kunstvoll, geschmackvoll, artistisch. **artistry,** *s.* der Kunstsinn, die Kunstfertigkeit, das Künstlertum, künstlerisches Können; künstlerische Vollendung *or* Leistung *or* Wirkung.

artless ['ɑ:tlis], *adj.* 1. kunstlos, unkünstlerisch, plump; 2. ungekünstelt, natürlich, einfach, schlicht, naiv; 3. offen, aufrichtig, arglos. **artlessness,** *s.* die Kunstlosigkeit, Plumpheit; Einfachheit, Natürlichkeit, Naivität, Schlichtheit; Arglosigkeit, Offenheit.

arty ['ɑ:ti], *adj.* künstlerartig, bohemienhaft (*of a p.*), künstlerisch aufgemacht (*of a th.*); (*coll.*) ***he's the – type,*** er macht auf Künstler. **arty-crafty,** *adj.* (*coll.*) kunstgewerblich, 'handgewebt'.

arum ['ɛərəm], *s.* (*Bot.*) der Aronstab (*Arum maculatum*); (*coll.*) das Schlangenkraut, die Drachenwurz (*Calla palustris*).

Aryan ['ɛəriən], **1.** *s.* der Arier, Indogermane; (*language*) die indo-iranische Sprachengruppe; (*Nat. Soc.*) der Arier, Nichtjude. **2.** *adj.* arisch, indogermanisch; indo-iranisch; arisch, nichtjüdisch.

as [æz], **1.** *adv.* (*in main clause*) (gerade) so, ebenso, genau so; – ***big as,*** (gerade) so *or* ebenso groß wie; ***I can see just – well without my glasses,*** ich kann ohne Brille genau so gut sehen; ***I would*** (***just***) ***– soon stay at home,*** ich würde ebenso *or* genau so gern zu Hause bleiben.
2. *conj.* (*in subord. clause*) **(a)** (*comparison of unlike things*) wie; ***as big –,*** so groß wie; ***no one suffered so much – he,*** niemand hat so viel gelitten wie er; *see also* **(k)** (ii); **(b)** (*similarity*) (eben)so wie, genau so wie, auf dieselbe Weise wie; – ***it is*** or ***stands,*** so wie die Dinge liegen; – ***usual,*** wie üblich *or* gewöhnlich, *see also* **(i)**; ***great men*** (***such***) ***– Caesar,*** große Männer wie Cäsar; ***he loves her – a father,*** er liebt sie (genau so) wie ein Vater; ***she is – a mother to me,*** sie ist (ebenso) wie eine Mutter zu mir; – ***like – two peas,*** wie ein Ei dem anderen; – ***yesterday so today,*** (auf dieselbe Weise) wie gestern so heute; – ***is the case,*** wie es der Fall ist; **(c)** (*in the capacity of*) als; ***he appears – Hamlet,*** er tritt als H. auf; ***he is employed – a teacher,*** er ist als Lehrer angestellt; ***let me tell you – a friend,*** laß mich dir als Freund sagen; ***it will serve – an example,*** es dient als Beispiel; – ***if*** or ***though,*** als ob; als *or* wie wenn; **(d)** (*time*) als, während, indem, sowie, (gerade) wie; ***he trembled – she spoke,*** er zitterte, während sie sprach; – ***he came in the music stopped,*** als *or* sowie *or* (gerade) wie er eintrat, hörte die Musik auf; ***it occurred to me – I was speaking,*** es fiel mir beim Reden ein *or* fiel mir ein, indem ich sprach; ***he waved to me – he passed,*** er winkte mir im Vorbeigehen; **(e)** (*consequence*) da, weil, insofern als; – ***you will not come, we must go alone,*** da du nicht kommen willst, müssen wir allein gehen; **(f)** (*concession*) obwohl, obgleich, wenn . . . auch; ***old – I am,*** wenn ich auch alt bin; ***try – he would,*** obwohl er alles versuchte; **(g)** (*with inf.*) so daß; ***do it so – not to offend him,*** tun Sie es so, daß er sich nicht verletzt fühlt; ***be so good – to send it to me,*** sei so gut und schicke es mir; sei so gut, es mir zu schicken; ***without so much – to move,*** ohne sich auch nur zu bewegen; – ***much – to say,*** mit anderen Worten; **(h)** (*with preps.*) (*coll.*) – ***for,*** *see* – ***regards***; (*Comm.*) – ***per bill of lading,*** laut Verladungsschein; – ***regards,*** was . . . (an)betrifft *or* angeht, betreffend (*Acc.*), im Hinblick auf, (*Acc.*), bezüglich (*Gen.*), hinsichtlich (*Gen.*); (*coll.*) – ***to,*** nach; ***he was questioned – to his income,*** er wurde nach seinem Einkommen befragt; *see also* – ***regards***; ***I was mistaken – to the day,*** ich habe mich in dem *or* in bezug auf den Tag geirrt; **(i)** (*with advs.*) – ***good – lost,*** so gut wie verloren, praktisch verloren; (*coll.*) – ***long – you stay, I'll stay too,*** wenn *or* insofern du bleibst, bleibe ich auch; (*coll.*) ***I thought – much,*** gerade *or* eben das habe ich mir gedacht, das dachte ich mir schon; – ***much – to say,*** mit anderen Worten, daß heißt; – ***such,*** als solche(r, –s), an sich; – ***usual,*** in gewohnter Weise; – ***well,*** auch, ferner, außerdem, ebenfalls, noch dazu; ***you might – well tell the truth,*** du könntest ebensogut die Wahrheit sagen; ***you might – well tell me,*** du würdest (wirklich) besser tun, es mir zu sagen; – ***yet,*** bisher, bis jetzt; ***not – yet,*** noch nicht; **(j)** (*other idioms*) ***according – the situation develops,*** je nachdem die Lage sich entwickelt; – ***it is*** or – ***things are,*** so wie die Dinge liegen; ***he is angry with me – it is,*** er ist sowieso böse auf mich; – ***it were,*** sozusagen gewissermaßen, gleichsam; (*Mil.*) – ***you were!*** Kommando zurück! (*coll.*) ***it's – broad – it's long,*** es läuft auf eins hinaus; – ***follows,*** wie folgt, folgendermaßen; – ***luck would have it,*** (un)glücklicherweise; ***I did not so much – see him,*** ich habe ihn nicht einmal gesehen; – ***requested,*** wunschgemäß; – ***a rule,*** in der Regel; **(k)** (*special constructions*) (i) (*compounds*) (–) ***clear – crystal,*** kristallhell; (–) ***clear – day,*** sonnenklar; (–) ***cold – ice,*** eiskalt; (–) ***large – life,*** lebensgroß, in Lebensgröße; (–) ***quiet – a mouse,*** mäuschenstill; (–) ***soft – butter,*** butterweich; (ii) (*contractions: with and without omission of conj.*) – ***far – I know,*** soviel ich weiß, soweit mir bekannt ist; – ***far – possible,*** soweit wie *or* als möglich; – ***far – I am concerned,*** was mich betrifft, meinetwegen; *see also* – ***regards*** *under* **(h)**; (*coll.*) – ***good –,*** see ***much the same –***; – ***little – possible,*** sowenig wie *or* als möglich; ***I have just – little money – you*** (***have***), ich habe sowenig Geld wie du; – ***long – I was ill,*** solang(e) ich krank war; *see also* **(i)**; – ***much – one can eat,*** soviel wie *or* als man essen kann; ***much the same – an oath,*** soviel wie ein Eid; ***much – I approve of it,*** sosehr ich es billige; – ***much again,*** noch einmal soviel; ***twice – much again,*** doppelt soviel; ***in – much – you do your duty,*** sofern du deine Pflicht tust; *see also* **(g) (i) (j)**; – ***soon – he came,*** sobald er kam; ***he – well – she,*** sowohl er *or* er sowohl wie *or* als auch sie; *see also* **(i).**
3. *rel. pron.* (*after same* or *such*) der *or* die *or* das, welche(r, –s); was, wie; ***such*** (***people***) ***– are homeless,*** diejenigen, die heimatlos sind; ***such things – I like,*** die, welche mir gefallen; das, was mir gefällt; ***the same beggar – was here last week,*** derselbe Bettler, der letzte Woche hier war; ***he was a Russian, – we noticed from his accent,*** er war Russe, was *or* wie wir an seinem Akzent merkten.

asafoetida [æsə'fetidə], *s.* der (Stink)asant, Teufelsdreck.

asbestos [æs'bestɔs], *s.* der Asbest, Steinflachs, Bergflachs.

ascend [ə'send], **1.** *v.i.* (hin)aufsteigen, (empor)steigen; (*Av.*) auffliegen, in die Höhe fliegen; (*as stairs*) ansteigen, in die Höhe gehen; (*fig.*) (*in rank*) aufsteigen, sich erheben, (*in time*) zürückgehen, hinaufreichen (***to*** or ***into,*** bis in *or* auf (*Acc.*)); (*Astr.*) aufgehen; (*Math.*) steigen, zunehmen; (*Mus.*) ansteigen, aufsteigen, aufwärtsgehen. **2.** *v.t.* besteigen, ersteigen, (hinauf)steigen auf (*Acc.*), erklettern, (*a river*) hinauffahren; – (***to***) ***the throne,*** den Thron besteigen.

ascendancy [ə'sendənsi], *s.* das Übergewicht, die Überlegenheit, Vorherrschaft (***over,*** über (*Acc.*)), bestimmender Einfluß (auf (*Acc.*)); ***gain*** (***the***) – ***over,*** bestimmenden Einfluß gewinnen über (*Acc.*); ***rise to –,*** die Oberhand gewinnen, zur

Macht *or* ans Ruder kommen. **ascendant, 1.** *adj.* (*Astr.*) aufsteigend, aufgehend; sich erhebend, (auf)steigend, emporkommend; (*fig.*) übertreffend, (vor)herrschend, überwiegend, vorwiegend; – ***over,*** überlegen (*Dat.*). **2.** *s.* 1. (*Astr.*) der Aufgangspunkt; das Horoskop, der Geburtsstern, Aszendent; (*fig.*) ***his star is in the –,*** sein Glück ist im Steigen; 2. (*Law*) der Vorfahr, Verwandte(r) in aufsteigender Linie, *pl.* Voreltern, Vorfahren; 3. (*Build.*) der Türpfosten, Fensterpfosten; 4. (*fig.*) *see* **ascendancy.**

ascendency, ascendent, *see* **ascendancy, ascendant.**

ascender [ə'sendə], *s.* 1. (*Typ.*) die Oberlänge; der Buchstabe mit Oberlänge; 2. (*a p.*) Ersteiger, Aufsteigende(r).

ascending [ə'sendiŋ], *adj.* (auf)steigend; ansteigend; nach oben strebend; (*Bot.*) razemos; (*Meteor.*) – ***air-current,*** der Aufwind; (*Av.*) – ***gust,*** die Steigbö.

ascension [ə'senʃən], *s.* das (Hin)aufsteigen, die Besteigung; der Aufstieg; das Steigen, die Auffahrt; (*Astr.*) das Aufsteigen; (*Astr.*) ***right –,*** die Rechtaszension; (*Eccl.*) ***the Ascension,*** Christi Himmelfahrt, die Himmelfahrt Christi; ***Ascension Day,*** der Himmelfahrtstag, (*Swiss*) Auffahrtstag

ascent [ə'sent], *s.* das (Auf)steigen, Ansteigen, (*Av.*) der Aufflug; die Besteigung, Ersteigung; der Aufstieg (***to,*** auf (*Acc.*)); Anstieg; die Auffahrt, Rampe; Anhöhe; (*Surv.*) Steigung, das Gefälle; (*Mus.*) Aufwärtsgehen, der Anstieg.

ascertain [æsə'tein], *v.t.* ermitteln, feststellen, erfahren, in Erfahrung bringen; genau angeben, nachweisen, bestimmen, festsetzen; ***–ed fact,*** festgestellte Tatsache. **ascertainable,** *adj.* ermittelbar, feststellbar, nachweisbar. **ascertainment,** *s.* die Feststellung, Ermittlung.

ascetic [ə'setik], **1.** *adj.* asketisch, enthaltsam. **2.** *s.* der Asket. **asceticism** [–sizm], *s.* die Askese, Enthaltsamkeit, Entsagung, harte Selbstzucht.

ascribable [ə'skraibəbl], *adj.* zuzuschreiben(d), beizulegen(d), zuschreibbar; ***it is – to him,*** es ist ihm zuzuschreiben. **ascribe,** *v.t.* zuschreiben, zuweisen, beimessen, beilegen (***to,*** *Dat.*), zurückführen (auf (*Acc.*)).

asepsis [æ'sepsis], *s.* keimfreie Behandlung, die Keimfreiheit. **aseptic,** *adj.* keimfrei, steril.

asexual [ei'seksjuəl], *adj.* ungeschlechtlich; geschlechtslos; – ***organism,*** die Amme; – ***reproduction,*** die Ammenzeugung.

[1]**ash** [æʃ], **1.** *s.* die Esche; das Eschenholz; ***mountain –,*** die Eberesche. **2.** *adj.* Eschen–, eschen, aus Eschenholz.

[2]**ash,** *s.* die Asche, der Verbrennungsrückstand; (*always pl.*) sterbliche Überreste, der Staub; ***the Ashes,*** das Symbol des Sieges im australisch-englischen Kricket-Wettkampf; ***in sackcloth and –es,*** in Sack und Asche; ***burn to –es,*** einäschern; ***lay in –es,*** niederbrennen; ***reduce to –es,*** in einen Aschenhaufen verwandeln.

ashamed [ə'ʃeimd], *pred. adj.* beschämt, verschämt; ***make him –,*** ihn beschämen; ***be*** or ***feel –,*** (*of o.s.*) sich schämen; ***be*** or ***feel –,*** (*of a th.*) sich schämen (*Gen.*); ***you ought to be – of yourself,*** schäme dich!

ash|-bin, --can (*Am.*), *s.* der Asch(en)kasten, Müllkasten, Kehrichtkasten, Mülleimer, Abfalleimer, Müllkübel, die Mülltonne.

ashen ['æʃən], *adj.* aschig; aschgrau, aschfarben.

ashes ['æʃiz], *pl. of* [2]**ash.**

ashlar ['æʃlə], *s.* (behauener) Bruchstein, der Quaderstein; die Quadermauer.

ashore [ə'ʃɔ:], *adv.* ans Ufer *or* Land; am Ufer, zu Lande, an(s) Land; gestrandet (*of a ship*); ***bring –,*** ans Land bringen; ***get –,*** landen, ans Land schaffen; ***go –,*** an Land gehen; ***run*** or ***be driven –,*** auf Strand laufen, stranden, auflaufen; ***run*** or ***cast a ship –,*** ein Schiff auf Strand setzen *or* ans Land werfen.

ash|-pan, *s.* die Aschenlade, der Aschenfall. **--tray,** *s.* der Aschenbecher, (*coll.*) Ascher. **Ash-Wednesday,** *s.* (*Eccl.*) der Aschermittwoch. **ashy,** *adj.* aschig, Aschen–; (*fig.*) totenblaß, totenbleich.

Asia ['eiʃə], *s.* Asien (*n.*); – ***Minor,*** Kleinasien (*n.*). **Asian, Asiatic** [eiʃi'ætik], **1.** *adj.* asiatisch. **2.** *s.* der (die) Asiat(in).

aside [ə'said], **1.** *adv.* seitwärts, abseits, auf der *or* die Seite, beiseite; (*Theat.*) leise, für sich; (*Am.*) außerdem; ***put –,*** auf die hohe Kante legen; ***she has laid – her mourning,*** sie hat die Trauer abgelegt; ***set – a judgement,*** ein Urteil aufheben; ***step –,*** zur Seite treten; ***he took him –,*** er nahm ihn beiseite; ***turn – from the path of virtue,*** vom Pfade der Tugend abweichen. **2.** *s.* (*Theat.*) beiseite gesprochenes Wort, die Aparte.

asinine ['æsinain], *adj.* eselartig, Esels–; (*fig.*) eselhaft, dumm.

ask [ɑ:sk], **1.** *v.t.* (*a p.*) fragen nach, erfragen; fragen *or* ersuchen *or* bitten (***for,*** um); (be)fragen, eine Frage stellen (*Dat.*); einladen, auffordern; (*a th.*) erbitten, verlangen, fordern, begehren; ***– him about a th.,*** sich bei ihm nach einer S. erkundigen; – (***him for***) ***his advice,*** ihn um seinen Rat fragen; – ***him a favour,*** ihn um einen Gefallen bitten; ***what price are you –ing?*** welchen Preis berechnen Sie? wieviel verlangen Sie? wieviel fordern Sie dafür? – ***her hand in marriage,*** um ihre Hand anhalten; – ***him home,*** ihn zu sich einladen; – ***him in,*** ihn hereinbitten; – ***his name,*** ihn nach seinem Namen fragen; ***may I – you to pass me the bread?*** darf ich Sie um das Brot bitten? ***be –ed out,*** eingeladen sein; – ***his permission,*** ihn um Erlaubnis bitten; – ***him a question,*** eine Frage an ihn *or* ihm eine Frage stellen; – ***a th. of him,*** etwas von ihm verlangen; – ***the gentlemen*** (***to come***) ***upstairs,*** bitten Sie den Herrn, sich heraufzubemühen; – (***him***) ***the way,*** (ihn) nach dem Wege fragen, sich (bei ihm) nach dem Wege erkundigen. **2.** *v.i.* fragen, sich erkundigen (***for, about*** or (*coll.*) ***after,*** nach), bitten (***for,*** um); (*coll.*) – ***after him,*** sich nach seinem Befinden erkundigen; – ***for him,*** nach ihm fragen, ihn zu sprechen wünschen; – ***for help,*** um Hilfe bitten *or* ersuchen; ***there's no harm in –ing,*** eine Frage schadet nichts; (*coll.*) – ***for trouble*** or (*sl.*) ***for it,*** es so haben wollen, herausfordernd wirken; – ***of him that . . .,*** von ihm verlangen, daß . . .

askance [ə'skɑ:ns], *adv.* seitwärts; ***look – at,*** von der Seite ansehen, (*fig.*) mißtrauisch betrachten, scheel *or* schief ansehen.

asker ['ɑ:skə], *s.* der (die) Frager(in), Bittsteller(in), Fragende(r), Bittende(r).

askew [ə'skju:], *adv.* schief, quer, schräg, (*Math.*) schiefwinklig, (*Tech.*) schiefliegend.

asking ['ɑ:skiŋ], *s.* die Bitte, Forderung, das Bitten, Fragen, Verlangen; (Ehe)aufgebot; (*coll.*) ***to be had for the –,*** mühelos *or* umsonst zu haben sein, nur eine Frage kosten; (*Eccl.*) ***for the second time of –,*** zweites Aufgebot.

aslant [ə'slɑ:nt], **1.** *adv.* schräg, schief(liegend), quer. **2.** *prep.* quer über (*Acc.*), durch.

asleep [ə'sli:p], *adv.*, *pred. adj.* schlafend, im Schlafe, in den Schlaf; ***be –,*** schlafen, eingeschlafen sein; ***be fast*** or ***sound –,*** in tiefem Schlafe liegen, fest eingeschlafen sein, fest schlafen; ***fall –,*** einschlafen; ***my foot has fallen –,*** der Fuß ist mir eingeschlafen; – ***in the Lord,*** im Herrn entschlafen.

aslope [ə'sloup], *adv.*, *pred. adj.* schief, schräg, abschüssig.

asocial [ei'souʃəl], *adj.* ungesellig, selbstisch.

asp [æsp], *s.* 1. (*Poet.*) *see* **aspen;** 2. (*Poet.*) die Natter, Giftschlange.

asparagus [əs'pærəgəs], *s.* der Spargel.

asparkle [ə'spɑ:kl], *pred. adj.* funkelnd, schimmernd.

aspect ['æspekt], *s.* der Anblick; die Erscheinung, Form, Gestalt, das Aussehen; der Gesichtsausdruck, die Miene; Aussicht, Lage, der Ausblick; (*fig.*) Blickpunkt, Gesichtspunkt, die Perspektive; Hinsicht, Beziehung, Seite; (*Gram.*) Aktionsart; (*Astr.*) der Aspekt; ***in all its –s,*** in jeder Hinsicht; ***southern –,*** die Lage nach Süden; ***in its true –,*** vom richtigen Gesichtspunkt aus, im richtigen Lichte; (*Av.*) – ***ratio,*** das Streckungsverhältnis.

aspen ['æspən], **1.** *s.* die Espe. **2.** *adj.* espen; ***tremble like an --leaf,*** wie Espenlaub zittern.

aspergill(um) ['æspədʒil (æspə'dʒiləm)], *s.* (*Eccl.*) der Weihwedel, Sprengwedel.

asperity [æs'periti], *s.* die Rauheit, Unebenheit (*of surface*); Unannehmlichkeit, Härte (*of sound*); Rauheit, Strenge (*of climate etc.*); Widerwärtigkeit, Borstigkeit, Schroffheit (*of character etc.*); Schärfe, Herbheit (*of taste*).

asperse [əs'pə:s], *v.t.* (*rare*) bespritzen, besprengen; (*fig.*) verleumden, schmähen, verdächtigen, anschwärzen, beschmutzen, in üblen Ruf bringen. **aspersion** [–'pə:ʃən], *s.* die Besprengung, Bespritzung, Benetzung; (*fig.*) Verleumdung, Anschwärzung, falsche Anschuldigung; Beschimpfung, Schmähung; ***cast –s on him,*** ihn verdächtigen *or* anschwärzen, seine Ehre beflecken.

aspersorium [æspə:'sɔ:riəm], *s.* (*Eccl.*) das Weihwasserbecken.

asphalt ['æsfælt], **1.** *s.* der Asphalt, das Erdharz, Erdpech. **2.** *adj.* Asphalt–. **3.** *v.t.* asphaltieren.

asphodel ['æsfədel], *s.* der Affodill; (*Poet.*) die Narzisse; ***bog –,*** der Beinbrech.

asphyxia [æs'fiksiə], *s.* die Erstickung, Asphyxie. **asphyxiate** [–ieit], *v.t., v.i.* ersticken. **asphyxiation** [–i'eiʃən], *s.* die Erstickung.

aspic ['æspik], *s.* die Sülze, der Aspik.

aspidistra [æspi'distrə], *s.* (*Bot.*) das Sternschild, die Schildblume.

aspirant [əs'paiərənt], *s.* der Bewerber (***for,*** um), Anwärter (*Gen.*), Kandidat (für); Emporstrebende(r) (nach); – ***to an office,*** der Amtsanwärter.

aspirate, 1. ['æspəreit], *v.t.* (*Phonet.*) aspirieren; (*Chem.*) ansaugen, absaugen, aufsaugen. **2.** [–rit], *adj.* behaucht, aspiriert. **3.** [–rit], *s.* die Aspirata, der Hauchlaut; Spiritus asper (*in Greek*). **aspirated** [–reitid], *adj. See* **aspirate, 2.**

aspiration [æspi'reiʃən], *s.* 1. (*Phonet.*) die Behauchung, Aspiration; der Hauchlaut; 2. (*Med.*) das Einatmen, der Atemzug, Hauch; 3. (*Chem.*) das Ansaugen, die Aufsaugung, Einsaugung; 4. (*fig.*) Bestrebung, das Streben, Trachten, heftiges Verlangen, die Sehnsucht (***for, after,*** nach).

aspire [əs'paiə], *v.i.* streben, trachten, sich sehnen, verlangen (***to, after,*** nach), (*Poet.*) sich erheben, emporsteigen, emporstreben.

aspirin ['æspərin], *s.* das Aspirin.

aspiring [əs'paiəriŋ], *adj.* (auf)strebend, trachtend (***to, after,*** nach); hochstrebend, strebsam, ehrgeizig; (*Poet.*) emporsteigend.

ass [æs], *s.* der Esel; (*fig.*) Dummkopf, Narr; ***she--,*** die Eselin; ***silly –!*** dummer Esel! ***make an – of o.s.,*** sich blamieren, sich lächerlich machen; ***make an – of him,*** ihn zum Narren halten.

assail [ə'seil], *v.t.* angreifen, anfallen, überfallen, bestürmen, berennen. **assailable,** *adj.* angreifbar; (*fig.*) anfechtbar. **assailant,** *s.* der Angreifer, Gegner.

assassin [ə'sæsin], *s.* der Meuchelmörder; ***hired –,*** gedungener Mörder. **assassinate,** *v.t.* meuchlerisch *or* meuchlings umbringen, ermorden. **assassination** [–'neiʃən], *s.* der Meuchelmord, die Ermordung.

assault [ə'sɔ:lt], **1.** *v.t.* angreifen, anfallen; (*Mil.*) (be)stürmen (*a position*); (*Law*) tätlich beleidigen; vergewaltigen (*a woman*). **2.** *s.* der Angriff, Anfall (***on, upon,*** auf (*Acc.*)); (*Mil.*) Sturm, die Bestürmung; (*Law*) gewalttätiger Angriff, die Gewalttätigkeit, körperliche *or* tätliche Beleidigung; (*Law*) – ***and battery,*** tätliche Beleidigung; – ***of*** or ***at arms,*** das Kontrafechten; die Fechtübung; (*Mil.*) ***carry*** or ***take by –,*** im Sturm nehmen, erstürmen; (*Mil.*) – ***detachment,*** der Stoßtrupp; ***indecent –,*** der Notzuchtversuch.

assay [ə'sei], **1.** *s.* die Erzprobe, Metallprobe; Untersuchung, Analyse, Probe, Prüfung, Erprobung (*of metals, drugs etc.*); (*fig., obs.*) das Prufungsergebnis, der Feingehalt; ***mark of –,*** das Probezeichen. **2.** *v.t.* (*Metall., Chem.*) prüfen, (er)proben, eichen, untersuchen, (*fig.*) (über)prüfen, untersuchen, bewerten; versuchen, probieren. **3.** *v.i.* (*Poet.*) versuchen, sich bemühen. **assay|-balance,** *s.* die Goldwaage, Probierwaage. **--office,** *s.* das Prüfungsamt.

assemblage [ə'semblidʒ], *s.* (*of people*) die Versammlung, Vereinigung, Zusammenkunft; das Versammeln, Zusammenrufen, Zusammenkommen; (*of things*) Zusammenbringen, Zusammentragen, Sammeln; (*Tech.*) Zusammenstellen, Zusammensetzen, Zusammenfügen, die Verbindung, Montierung, Montage, der Zusammenbau; (*of persons or things*) Haufen, die Menge, Schar, Ansammlung; (*Math.*) Menge.

assemble [ə'sembl], **1.** *v.t.* (ver)sammeln, zusammenbringen; (*Parl. etc.*) zusammenberufen; zusammenziehen, bereitstellen (*troops*); (*Tech.*) zusammensetzen, zusammenstellen, zusammenbauen, aufstellen, montieren. **2.** *v.i.* sich (ver)sammeln, zusammenkommen, (*Parl. etc.*) zusammentreten. **assembler,** *s.* (*Tech.*) der Monteur.

assembly [ə'sembli], *s. See* **assemblage**; (*Pol.*) gesetzgebende *or* beratende Körperschaft, das Plenum; (*Am.*) Repräsentantenhaus; (*Eccl.*) die Synode; (*Mil.*) Bereitsstellung; das Sammelsignal; ***General Assembly*** (*of the Church of Scotland*), die Generalsynode (der schottischen Staatskirche); ***place of –,*** der Treffpunkt, Versammlungsplatz.

assembly| area, *s.* (*Mil.*) der Bereitstellungsraum. **– belt, – line,** *s.* die Montagebahn, Montagerampe, das Montageband, Fließband, laufendes Band. **– room,** *s.* der Festsaal, Versammlungssaal. **– shop,** *s.* die Montagehalle.

assent [ə'sent], **1.** *s.* die Zustimmung, Beipflichtung; Einwilligung, Genehmigung, Billigung; ***royal –,*** königliche Genehmigung; ***with one –,*** einmütig, einstimmig. **2.** *v.i.* zustimmen, beistimmen, beipflichten (***to,*** *Dat.*), einwilligen (in (*Acc.*)), genehmigen, billigen, zugeben (*Acc.*).

assert [ə'sə:t], *v.t.* behaupten, erklären, versichern; einstehen für, bestehen auf (*Dat.*), verfechten, verteidigen, geltend machen; (*Math.*) behaupten, aussagen; ***– o.s.,*** sich geltend machen, sich zur Geltung bringen, sich durchsetzen, fest auftreten; ***– one's right(s),*** sein(e) Recht(e) verteidigen *or* geltend machen.

assertion [ə'sə:ʃən], *s.* die Behauptung, Erklärung, Versicherung; Verteidigung, Verfechtung, Geltendmachung (***of,*** *Gen.*), das Einstehen (für); (*Math.*) die Behauptung, Aussage; ***make an –,*** eine Behauptung aufstellen.

assertive [ə'sə:tiv], *adj.* bestimmt, ausdrücklich, zuversichtlich, bejahend, positiv; (*of a p.*) dogmatisch, aggressiv. **assertiveness,** *s.* zuversichtliche *or* selbstbewußte Art, die Anmaßung.

assess [ə'ses], *v.t.* festsetzen, festlegen, bestimmen (*damages etc.*); abschätzen, veranschlagen, bewerten, taxieren (***at,*** auf (*Acc.*)) (*for taxation*); (*fig.*) abschätzen, einschätzen, (be)werten. **assessable,** *adj.* steuerpflichtig, abgabepflichtig; (*fig.*) (ab)schätzbar. **assessment,** *s.* die (Ab)schätzung, Bewertung, Taxierung; Vermögensaufnahme, (Steuer)veranlagung, der Steueranschlag; die Besteuerung, das Steuersystem, der Steuertarif; die Festsetzung, Festlegung, Bestimmung (*of damages etc.*); (*fig.*) (Ab)schätzung, Einschätzung, (Be)wertung.

assessor [ə'sesə], *s.* der Assessor, Syndikus, Beisitzer; Taxator, Steuereinschätzer.

asset ['æset], *s.* (*Comm.*) der Posten auf der Aktivseite, das Haben; (*fig.*) Besitzstück; (*coll.*) der Wert, Vorzug, (wichtiger) Faktor, die Stütze, Hilfe. **assets,** *pl.* Aktivposten, Aktiva (*pl.*); das Vermögen, Gut(haben), der Vermögensstand; Nachlaß, die Hinterlassenschaft, Erbmasse; Konkursmasse, Fallitmasse; ***– and liabilities,*** Aktiva und Passiva, Soll und Haben; ***foreign –,*** Devisenwerte (*pl.*); ***frozen –,*** eingefrorene Guthaben (*pl.*); ***no –,*** kein Guthaben (*on cheques*).

asseverate [ə'sevəreit], *v.i.* beteuern, versichern,

feierlich erklären. **asseveration** [–'reiʃən], *s.* die Beteuerung, Versicherung.

assiduity [æsi'dju:iti], *s.* die Emsigkeit, Beharrlichkeit, anhaltender *or* ausdauernder Fleiß; die Aufmerksamkeit, Dienstfertigkeit, Dienstbeflissenheit. **assiduous** [ə'sidjuəs], *adj.* emsig, fleißig; unverdrossen, beharrlich, ausdauernd; aufmerksam, dienstfertig, dienstbeflissen.

assign [ə'sain], **1.** *v.t.* anweisen, zuweisen, zuteilen (*a share to a p., a p. to a place*); anvertrauen, übertragen, übergeben, aufgeben (*a task, duties to a p.*); zuschreiben (*responsibility etc.*); (*Law*) übermachen, überweisen, übertragen, übereignen, abtreten, zedieren (*to, Dat.*); ernennen, bestellen ((*a p.*) *to* (*a post*), zu); festlegen, festsetzen, bestimmen, vorschreiben (*a time*); angeben, anführen, vorbringen (*a reason*); (*Math.*) beilegen, zuordnen. **2.** *s.* (*usu. pl.*) (*Law*) der Rechtsnachfolger, Zessionar.

assignable [ə'sainəbl], *adj.* bestimmbar, zuweisbar, anweisbar, zuzuschreiben(d); (*of reasons*) angebbar, anführbar; (*Law*) übertragbar.

assignation [æsig'neiʃən], *s.* 1. *See* **assignment,** 1; 2. die Verabredung, das Stelldichein. **assignee** [æsi'ni:], *s. See* **assign, 2**; Bevollmächtigte(r); – ***in bankruptcy,*** der Konkursverwalter. **assigner,** *s. See* **assignor.**

assignment [ə'sainmənt], *s.* 1. die Zuweisung, Zuteilung, Anweisung; (*Law*) Übertragung, Abtretung, Übereignung, Zession; – ***of policy,*** die Abtretung der Versicherungsforderung; 2. Bestimmung, Festsetzung, Festlegung; Zuschreibung, Anführung, Angabe; (*Math.*) Zuordnung, Beilegung; – ***of dower,*** die Festsetzung des Witwenteils; 3. Schularbeit, (Schul)aufgabe; (*Journalism*) das Aufgabengebiet (*alloted to reporter*), die Zuweisung für einen Sonderbericht; 4. (*Comm.*) trassierter Wechsel, die Anweisung; (*Law*) Zessionsurkunde, Abtretungsurkunde; – ***in blank,*** das Blankoindossament.

assignor [ə'sainə], *s.* Anweisende(r), Zuteilende(r), (*Law*) Abtretende(r), der Zedent.

assimilate [ə'simileit], **1.** *v.t.* 1. angleichen, anpassen (*to, Dat. or* an (*Acc.*)); 2. gleich *or* ähnlich machen, als gleich *or* ähnlich hinstellen (*to, with, Dat.*), vergleichen (mit); 3. assimilieren, einverleiben, (in sich) aufnehmen, umsetzen (*nourishment*); sich aneignen, aufnehmen, aufsaugen, absorbieren, assimilieren (*influences etc.*). **2.** *v.i.* gleich *or* ähnlich werden, sich anpassen, sich angleichen (*to, with, Dat.*); (*of food*) umgesetzt *or* assimiliert werden, sich einverleiben *or* assimilieren lassen. **assimilation** [–'leiʃən], *s.* die Assimilation, Angleichung, Anpassung (*to,* an (*Acc.*)); Assimilierung, Einverleibung, Verwandlung in Körpersubstanz.

assist [ə'sist], **1.** *v.t.* beistehen, (aus)helfen, zu Hilfe kommen (*Dat.*), unterstützen, fördern. **2.** *v.i.* 1. (aus)helfen, mithelfen, Hilfe leisten; 2. (*obs.*) beiwohnen (*in, at, Dat.*), teilnehmen (an (*Dat.*)), dabei *or* zugegen sein (bei).

assistance [ə'sistəns], *s.* der Beistand, die Hilfe, Unterstützung; Mithilfe, Mitwirkung; ***afford –,*** Hilfe gewähren; ***lend*** or ***render –,*** Hilfe leisten. **assistant, 1.** *s.* der Gehilfe (die Gehilfin), der (die) Helfer(in), Mitarbeiter(in), Assistent(in), die Hilfskraft, der Beistand; ***shop –,*** der (die) Verkäufer(in). **2.** *adj.* Hilfs–; – ***editor,*** der Hilfsredakteur; – ***librarian,*** der Unterbibliothekar; – ***manager,*** stellvertretender Direktor; – ***master,*** der Lehrer, Studienrat; – ***secretary,*** zweiter Sekretär, (*civil service*) der Abteilungsleiter, Ministerialdirektor.

assize [ə'saiz], *s.* die Gerichtssitzung, gerichtliche Untersuchung *or* Verhandlung; richterlicher Beschluß, der (Urteils)spruch; *pl.* das Geschworenengericht, die Assisen (*pl.*); ***hold the –s,*** die Assisen abhalten.

associate, 1. [ə'souʃieit], *v.t.* zugesellen, anschließen (*with, Dat.*), verbünden, vereinigen, verbinden (mit); (*Math.*) zuordnen (*Dat.*). **2.** [–ieit], *v.i.* sich gesellen (*with,* zu), sich anschließen (an (*Acc.*)), sich verbinden, Umgang haben *or* pflegen, verkehren (mit); (*Comm.*) sich verbünden, assoziieren, zusammenarbeiten (mit). **3.** [–iit], *s.* der Amtsgenosse, Kollege, Mitarbeiter; (Bundes)genosse, Verbündete(r), Komplice, (Helfers)helfer, Spießgeselle; Beigeordnete(r), außerordentliches Mitglied; (*Comm.*) der Gesellschafter, Teilhaber, Teilnehmer. **4.** [–iit], *adj.* verbunden, verbündet, Mit–; Begleit–, beigeordnet, zugesellt; (*Math.*) zugeordnet, assoziiert; – ***editor,*** der Mitherausgeber; – ***member,*** außerordentliches Mitglied; (*Am.*) – ***professor,*** außerordentlicher Professor.

association [əsousi'eiʃən], *s.* die Verbindung, Vereinigung, der Anschluß; Verein, Bund, die Vereinigung, Gesellschaft, (*Comm.*) Genossenschaft, der Verband; das Bündnis; (*Psych.*) die Assoziation; (*coll.*) Kameradschaft, der Umgang, Verkehr; (*Biol.*) das Zusammenleben, die Vergesellschaftung; (*Chem.*) das Zusammentreten (*of molecules*) zu einem losen Verband; (*Stat.*) die Abhängigkeit; ***articles of –,*** Statuten der Handelsgesellschaft; – ***of ideas,*** die Ideenassoziation, Gedankenverbindung; ***Modern Language Association,*** der Neuphilologenverband; (*coll.*) ***pleasant –s,*** angenehme Erinnerungen.

assonance ['æsənəns], *s.* vokalischer Gleichklang, die Assonanz; (*fig.*) Ähnlichkeit, ungefähre Übereinstimmung. **assonant, 1.** *adj.* vokalisch gleichlautend, anklingend, assonierend. **2.** *s.* assonierendes Wort.

assort [ə'sɔ:t], **1.** *v.t.* passend zusammenstellen, ordnen, sortieren; (*Comm.*) assortieren. **2.** *v.i.* zusammenpassen, übereinstimmen (*with,* mit), passen (zu). **assorted,** *adj.* 1. geordnet, sortiert; zusammengestellt, assortiert, gemischt; 2. übereinstimmend, passend; ***ill-– couple,*** schlecht zueinander passendes Ehepaar. **assortment,** *s.* das Sortieren, Ordnen; die Sammlung, Zusammenstellung; (*Comm.*) das Sortimentlager, die Auswahl.

assuage [ə'sweidʒ], *v.t.* mildern, erleichtern, lindern (*pain*), stillen (*thirst*); besänftigen, beruhigen, mäßigen. **assuagement,** *s.* die Milderung, Linderung, Erleichterung, Stillung.

assume [ə'sju:m], *v.t.* 1. annehmen, auf sich (*Acc.*) nehmen, übernehmen (*responsibility etc.*), annehmen (*appearance etc.*), einnehmen, anlegen, sich (*Dat.*) geben, (er)heucheln, vorgeben (*false appearance*), sich (*Dat.*) aneignen *or* anmaßen; – ***a haughty air,*** eine hochmütige Miene anlegen; – ***the reins of government,*** die Regierung übernehmen; ***–d address,*** unechte *or* angenommene Adresse, Schein– *or* Deckadresse; 2. (als wahr) annehmen, voraussetzen, gelten lassen; ***assuming that . . .,*** angenommen *or* vorausgesetzt daß . . .. **assuming,** *adj.* vermessen, anmaßend; überheblich.

assumption [ə'sʌmpʃən], *s.* 1. das Übernehmen, Annehmen, Aufsichnehmen; die Übernahme, Annahme, Aneignung; ***the Assumption of the Blessed Virgin,*** Mariä Himmelfahrt; ***Christ's – of our flesh,*** Christi Menschwerdung; – ***of power,*** die Machtübernahme; 2. die Anmaßung, Überheblichkeit, Vermessenheit; 3. Annahme, Vermutung, Voraussetzung, das Postulat, (*Phil.*) logischer Untersatz; ***on the – that . . .,*** unter der Voraussetzung *or* in der Annahme, daß, ***by –,*** nach *or* gemäß der Annahme.

assurance [ə'ʃuərəns], *s.* 1. die Versicherung, Beteuerung; Zusicherung, Zusage; Sicherstellung, Bürgschaft, Garantie, Sicherheit; 2. Zuversicht(lichkeit), Selbstsicherheit, das Sicherheitsgefühl, (Selbst)vertrauen; die Anmaßung, Dreistigkeit, Unverschämtheit; – ***of manner,*** (selbst)sicheres Benehmen; ***air of –,*** dreiste *or* unerschrockene Miene; ***with –,*** mit zuversichtlichem Nachdruck; 3. (*Comm.*) (Lebens)versicherung, Assekuranz; – ***company,*** die Versicherungsgesellschaft.

assure [ə'ʃuə], *v.t.* 1. sichern, sicher machen, sicherstellen, garantieren (*against,* gegen); 2. Sicherheit geben (*Dat.*), Zuversicht einflößen (*Dat.*), zusichern (*Dat.*), überzeugen, versichern (*Acc.*), ermutigen; ***he –d me of his sympathy,*** er versicherte mich seiner Teilnahme; ***he is –d of a pension,*** ihm ist eine Rente zugesichert; ***his sympathy –d me,*** seine Teilnahme hat mich ermutigt; 3. mit Sicherheit sagen, versichern (*Dat.*); ***he –d me that . . .,*** er versicherte mir, daß . . .; 4. (*Comm.*) assekurieren, versichern (*Acc.*) (*one's life*).

assured [ə'ʃuəd], *adj.* 1. versichert, überzeugt; ***be – of s.th.,*** von einer S. überzeugt sein, einer S. (*Gen.*) versichert sein; 2. sicher, gewiß, unzweifelhaft, gesichert, gefestigt; ***be*** or ***rest – that . . .,*** sicher sein, daß . . ., sich darauf verlassen, daß . . .; ***his position is –,*** seine Stellung ist gesichert; 3. zuversichtlich, ermutigt, gestärkt, bestärkt; 4. selbstsicher, selbstbewußt; anmaßend, dreist, keck, unerschrocken. **assuredly** [–ridli], *adv.* sicherlich, zuversichtlich, unzweifelhaft, gewiß. **assuredness** [–ridnis], *s.* die Sicherheit, Gewißheit; Zuversicht(lichkeit), das Selbstvertrauen.

assurer [ə'ʃuərə], *s.* 1. der Ermutiger; 2. Versicherte(r); 3. *See* **assuror.**

assurgent [ə'sə:dʒənt], *adj.* (auf)steigend, emporstrebend; (*Bot.*) aufsteigend.

assuror [ə'ʃuərə], *s.* der Assekurant, Versicherer, Versicherungsträger.

Assyrian [ə'siriən], **1.** *s.* der (die) Assyrer(in). **2.** *adj.* assyrisch.

astatic [æ'stætik], *adj.* astatisch, unstet, unstabil.

aster ['æstə], *s.* (*Bot.*) die Aster, Sternblume.

asterisk ['æstərisk], *s.* (*Typ.*) das Sternchen.

astern [ə'stə:n], *adv.* achtern, achteraus (*of*, von); (nach) hinten, rückwärts; ***drop*** or ***fall –,*** achteraus sacken; ***wind –,*** achterlicher Wind.

asteroid ['æstərɔid], **1.** *s.* (*Astr.*) der Planetoid, Asteroid. **2.** *adj.* sternartig, sternförmig.

asthenia [æs'θi:niə], *s.* (*Med.*) die Körperschwäche, Kraftlosigkeit, Asthenie. **asthenic** [–'θenik], *adj.* schwach, kraftlos, asthenisch.

asthma ['æs(θ)mə], *s.* die Atemnot, Kurzatmigkeit, das Asthma. **asthmatic** [æs(θ)'mætik], **1.** *adj.* engbrüstig, kurzatmig, asthmatisch, (*fig.*) keuchend, schnaufend. **2.** *s.* der Asthmatiker.

astigmatic [æstig'mætik], *adj.* astigmatisch. **astigmatism** [əs'tigmətizm], *s.* der Astigmatismus.

astir [ə'stə:], *pred. adj.* in Bewegung, auf den Beinen; auf(gestanden), aus dem Bett; aufgeregt, in Aufruhr (***with***, von).

astonish [əs'tɔniʃ], *v.t.* in Erstaunen setzen; befremden, verblüffen, überraschen; ***be –ed,*** erstaunen, überrascht sein, sich wundern (***at***, über (*Acc.*)). **astonishing,** *adj.* überraschend, verblüffend, erstaunlich, wunderbar. **astonishment,** *s.* das (Er)staunen, die Überraschung, Bestürzung, Verwunderung (***at***, über (*Acc.*)); ***cause –,*** Staunen erregen; ***fill with –,*** in Staunen versetzen.

astound [əs'taund], *v.t.* in Staunen *or* Schrecken versetzen, verblüffen. **astounding,** *adj.* verblüffend, überraschend.

astraddle [ə'strædl], *pred. adj.* rittlings; ***– on,*** reitend auf (*Dat.*).

astragal ['æstrəgəl], *s.* (*Archit.*) der Rundstab; (*Anat.*) das Sprungbein; Band (*on fire-arms*).

astral ['æstrəl], *adj.* gestirnt, Stern(en)–, sternig, sternartig. **astral|-body,** *s.* der Astralleib. **--lamp,** *s.* die Astrallampe.

astray [ə'strei], *pred. adj., adv.* vom rechten Wege ab, irre, verirrt; ***go –,*** irregehen, sich verirren, sich verlieren, verlorengehen; (*fig.*) abschweifen; ***lead –,*** verleiten, verführen, irreführen.

astride [ə'straid], **1.** *pred. adj., adv.* rittlings, mit gespreizten Beinen; ***– of,*** rittlings auf (*Dat.*); ***ride –,*** im Herrensattel reiten. **2.** *prep.* ***– a horse,*** zu Pferd.

astringency [əs'trindʒənsi], *s.* zusammenziehende Kraft, (*fig.*) die Härte, Strenge, der Ernst. **astringent, 1.** *adj.* zusammenziehend, adstringierend; (*fig.*) streng, ernst. **2.** *s.* zusammenziehendes Mittel, das Adstringens.

astrolabe ['æstrəleib], *s.* das Astrolabium, der Sternhöhenmesser.

astrologer [əs'trɔlədʒə], *s.* der Sterndeuter, Astrologe. **astrological** [æstrə'lɔdʒikəl], *adj.* astrologisch. **astrology,** *s.* die Sterndeutekunst, Sterndeuterei, Astrologie.

astronaut ['æstrənɔ:t], *s.* der Weltraumfahrer.

astronomer [əs'trɔnəmə], *s.* der Astronom, Sternforscher. **astronomic** [æstrə'nɔmik], *adj.* (*fig.*) unermeßlich, übermäßig, astronomisch. **astronomical,** *adj.* astronomisch, Stern–; ***– tables,*** astronomische Tafeln; ***– year,*** siderisches Jahr, das Sternjahr. **astronomy,** *s.* die Sternkunde, Astronomie.

astute [əs'tju:t], *adj.* listig, schlau, gerieben, verschmitzt; klug, scharfsinnig. **astuteness,** *s.* der Scharfsinn, die Klugheit; Schlauheit, (Arg)list.

asunder [ə'sʌndə], **1.** *pred. adj.* abgesondert, auseinanderliegend, (voneinander) getrennt. **2.** *adv.* entzwei, in Stücke, auseinander; ***tear –,*** zerreißen.

asylum [ə'sailəm], *s.* das Asyl, die Freistätte, Zufluchtsstätte, der Zufluchtsort; die Anstalt, das Heim; (*coll.*) (*lunatic*) –, die Irrenanstalt; ***political –,*** (politisches) Asyl.

asymmetric(al) [æsi'metrik(əl)], *adj.* unsymmetrisch, unebenmäßig, ungleichförmig. **assymetry** [æ'simitri], *s.* die Asymmetrie, Ungleichförmigkeit, Unebenmäßigkeit.

asymptote ['æsimtout], *s.* die Asymptote.

asyndetic [æsin'detik], *adj.* (*Gram.*) verbindungslos.

at [æt, ət *according to emphasis*], *prep.* **(a)** (*place*) in (*Dat.*), an (*Dat.*), zu, bei; ***it happened – Oxford,*** es geschah in Oxford; ***he spent 3 years – Oxford*** (*i.e. at the university*), er verbrachte 3 Jahre in Oxford; ***– the battle of Hastings,*** in der Schlacht bei Hastings; ***– the corner,*** an der Ecke; ***– court,*** bei Hofe; ***– a distance,*** in einiger Entfernung; ***– hand,*** zur *or* bei der Hand; ***– home,*** zu Hause; ***– school,*** in der Schule; ***– sea,*** zur *or* auf der See; ***– table,*** bei Tisch; ***– the top,*** an der Spitze; ***– the baker's,*** beim Bäcker; ***– my uncle's,*** bei meinem Onkel; **(b)** (*time*) um, zu; ***– 2 o'clock,*** um 2 Uhr; ***– midnight,*** um Mitternacht; ***– Christmas,*** zu Weihnachten; ***– daybreak,*** bei Tagesanbruch; ***– his death,*** bei seinem Tod; ***– this moment,*** in diesem Augenblick; ***– the same time,*** zur selben Zeit; ***– the same hour,*** um dieselbe Stunde, zur selben Stunde; **(c)** (*condition*) in (*Dat.*), bei; ***– the age of 16,*** im Alter von 16 Jahren; ***– fault,*** im Irrtum; ***– large,*** im Freien; in Freiheit, auf freiem Fuß; (*fig.*) als Ganzes, in der Gesamtheit; ***– liberty,*** in Freiheit; ***– his mercy,*** in seiner Gewalt; ***– peace,*** im Frieden; ***– the point of death,*** im Sterben; ***– my time of life,*** in meinem Alter; ***– the sight of,*** beim Anblick (*Gen.*); ***– war,*** im Kriegszustand; ***– one's wits' end,*** in der größten Verlegenheit; ***take him – his word,*** ihn beim Wort nehmen; ***– work,*** bei der Arbeit; **(d)** (*number, price etc.*) zu, auf (*Acc.*)); ***– all events,*** auf alle Fälle; ***– my expense,*** auf meine Kosten; ***I estimate them – 20,*** ich schätze sie auf 20; ***– a low price,*** zu einem niedrigen Preis; ***– half-price,*** zum *or* um den halben Preis; ***– reduced prices,*** zu herabgesetzten Preisen; **(e)** (*origin, cause, reason*) aus, von, über (*Acc.*); ***laugh –,*** lachen über; ***receive – his hands,*** von ihm *or* aus seinen Händen empfangen; ***– second-hand,*** aus zweiter Hand; **(f)** (*various idioms*) ***– the beginning,*** am *or* zu Anfang, anfangs; ***– the door,*** an *or* vor der Tür; ***drink – one draught,*** auf einen Zug trinken; ***– an end,*** zu Ende, aus; ***– his feet,*** ihm zu Füßen; ***be laughed –,*** ausgelacht werden; ***– any moment,*** jeden Augenblick; ***– night,*** nachts, bei Nacht; ***– about 2 o'clock,*** gegen 2 Uhr; ***they were – one,*** sie waren einig *or* im Einverständnis *or* einer Meinung; ***– your*** (***his*** *etc.*) ***pleasure,*** nach Belieben; ***– any price,*** um jeden Preis; ***– your service,*** zu Ihren Diensten; ***– stake,*** auf dem Spiel; ***be – a standstill,*** stocken; ***two – a time,*** zwei auf einmal; ***– no time,*** niemals; ***– times,*** zuweilen, manchmal, bisweilen, mitunter; ***– the university,*** auf der Universität; (*coll.*) ***be – s.th.,*** bei einer S. sein, mit etwas beschäftigt sein; (*coll.*) ***you're always – him,*** du schikanierst ihn unbarmherzig *or* unablässig; **(g)** (*other common idioms*) ***– all,***

überhaupt; ***not – all,*** durchaus nicht, keineswegs; ***– best,*** bestenfalls, im besten Falle, höchstens; ***– one blow,*** mit einem Schlag; ***out – elbows,*** schäbig, zerlumpt; ***– first,*** zuerst; ***– last,*** zuletzt, endlich; ***– least,*** wenigstens, zum wenigsten; das heißt, jedoch, freilich; ***– length,*** endlich; ***– great length,*** ausführlich, weitläufig; ***– arm's length,*** vom Leibe; (*fig.*) ***you are – liberty to . . .,*** es steht Ihnen frei, zu . . .; – (***the***) ***most,*** höchstens; ***– once,*** sofort, auf der Stelle; ***all – once,*** auf einmal, plötzlich; (*Comm.*) ***– sight,*** auf Sicht; (*coll.*) ***we'll let it go*** or ***we'll leave it – that,*** wir wollen's damit bewenden lassen; (*coll.*) ***and stupid – that,*** und obendrein dumm, und dumm noch dazu; **(h)** (*after verbs expressing direction or aim*) auf (*Acc.*), nach; ***aim –,*** zielen auf, (*fig.*) streben nach; (*coll.*) ***what are you driving –?*** worauf zielst du hin? was willst du überhaupt? ***enter – the side door,*** durch die Seitentür eintreten; ***grab*** or ***snatch – the apple,*** nach dem Apfel greifen; ***point –,*** zielen nach, zeigen; ***throw a stone – the window,*** einen Stein gegen das Fenster werfen; **(i)** (*after adjectives*) ***angry –,*** zornig auf (*Acc.*), erzürnt über (*Acc.*); ***better – swimming than – running,*** besser im Schwimmen als im Laufen; ***good –,*** gut *or* geschickt in (*Dat.*); (*coll.*) ***hard – it,*** tüchtig hinterher, vollauf beschäftigt.

atavism ['ætəvizm], *s.* der Atavismus, Entwicklungsrückschlag, die Rückartung.

ataxia [ə'tæksiə], *s.* (*Med.*) die Bewegungsstörung, Koordinationsstörung, Ataxie.

ate [et], *imperf. of* **eat.**

Athanasian [æθə'neiʃən], *adj.* athanasianisch.

atheism ['eiθiizm], *s.* die Gottesleugnung, der Atheismus. **atheist,** *s.* der Gottesleugner, Atheist. **atheistic(al)** [–'istik(l)], *adj.* atheistisch.

Athenian [ə'θi:niən], **1.** *adj.* athenisch. **2.** *s.* der (die) Athener(in). **Athens** ['æθənz], *s.* Athen (*n.*).

athirst [ə'θə:st], *pred. adj.* (*Poet.*) durstig; (*fig.*) begierig (***for,*** nach).

athlete ['æθli:t], *s.* der Athlet, Wettkämpfer; Sportler, Sportsmensch; (*Med.*) ***–'s foot,*** die Dermatophytose, Epidermophytosis. **athletic** [–'letik], *adj.* athletisch; kräftig, stark, muskulös; ***– sports,*** **athletics,** *pl.* (*sing. constr.*) die Leichtathletik, der Sport; leichtathletische Wettspiele (*pl.*).

at-home, *s.* (*coll.*) zwangloser Empfang.

athwart [ə'θwɔ:t], **1.** *prep.* (quer) über (*Acc.*) *or* durch, (*Naut.*) dwars (über); (*Naut.*) ***lie – the waves,*** dwars See liegen. **2.** *adv.* schräg, schief, quer; (*Naut.*) dwars(über); (*Naut.*) ***– the beam,*** vorlicher als dwars. **athwart|-hawse,** *adv.* quer vor dem Bug (eines vor Anker liegenden Schiffes). **--ships,** *adv.* querschiffs, dwarsschiffs.

atilt [ə'tilt], *adv.* vorwärts *or* vorn gebeugt, vorgebeugt, vornüberkippend; (*Hist.*) mit gefällter Lanze; ***set a cask –,*** ein Faß kippen; (*fig.*) ***run – at,*** zu Felde ziehen gegen, losgehen auf (*Acc.*).

Atlantic [ət'læntik], *s.* der Atlantik, Atlantischer Ozean.

atlas ['ætləs], *s.* (*Myth., Geog.*) der Atlas; (*Archit.*) Atlas, Simsträger, Telamon; (*Anat.*) oberster Halswirbel; (*Bookb.*) das Atlastformat, Großfolio.

atmosphere ['ætməsfiə], *s.* die Atmosphäre, Lufthülle; (*Meteor.*) Luft; (*Tech.*) Atmosphäre (*unit of pressure*); (*fig.*) Stimmung, Umwelt; Umgebung, der Einfluß; ***moist –,*** feuchte Luft. **atmospheric** [–'ferik], *adj.* atmosphärisch, Luft–; Witterungs–; Wetter–; ***– conditions,*** die Wetterlage, Wetterverhältnisse (*pl.*), Witterung; ***– pressure,*** der Luftdruck. **atmospherical,** *adj. See* **atmospheric. atmospherics,** *pl.* (*Rad.*) atmosphärische Störungen, Nebengeräusche.

atoll ['ætəl, ə'tɔl], *s.* ringförmige Koralleninsel, das Atoll.

atom ['ætəm], *s.* das Atom; (*fig.*) winziges Teilchen, das bißchen, der Deut, die Spur, Kleinigkeit; ***smash*** (***in***)***to –s,*** in tausend Stücke *or* kurz und klein schlagen. **atom-bomb,** *s.* die Atombombe.

atomic [ə'tɔmik], *adj.* atomisch, atomartig, Atom–; ***– bomb,*** *see* **atom-bomb**; ***– energy,*** see ***– power***; ***– fission,*** die Atomspaltung; ***– index,*** see ***– number***; ***– nucleus,*** der Atomkern; ***– number,*** die Ordnungszahl, Kernladungszahl; ***– pile,*** die Atomsäule, der Atommeiler; ***– power,*** die Atomenergie; ***– scientist,*** der Atomforscher; ***– weight,*** das Atomgewicht.

atomize ['ætəmaiz], *v.t.* zerkleinern, zerstäuben. **atomizer,** *s.* der Zerstäuber, Zerstäubungsapparat.

atom-smasher, *s.* (*coll.*) das Zyklotron, der Teilchenbeschleuniger.

atone [ə'toun], *v.i.* ***– for,*** büßen, sühnen; wiedergutmachen, aufwiegen, Ersatz leisten für. **atonement,** *s.* die Buße, Sühne; (*B.*) das Sühnopfer (Christi); (*fig.*) ***make – for,*** abbüßen, wiedergutmachen, Genugtuung leisten für.

atonic [æ'tɔnik], *adj.* (*Gram.*) unbetont, tonlos, stimmlos; (*Med.*) schlaff, abgespannt, kraftlos. **atony** ['ætəni], *s.* die Schlaffheit, Schwäche, Kraftlosigkeit.

atop [ə'tɔp], **1.** *adv.* oben(auf), zuoberst. **2.** *prep.* (oben) auf (*Dat.*).

atrabilious [ætrə'biliəs], *adj.* schwarzgallig, schwermütig, melancholisch.

atremble [ə'trembl], *adv., pred. adj.* zitternd.

atrip [ə'trip], *adv.* (*Naut.*) gelichtet (*anchor*).

atrium ['eitriəm], *s.* (*Hist.*) die Vorhalle; (*Anat.*) Vorkammer, der Herzvorhof.

atrocious [ə'trouʃəs], *adj.* gräßlich, entsetzlich, schrecklich, scheußlich, schauderhaft, abscheulich, grausam; (*coll.*) furchtbar, miserabel. **atrociousness,** *s.* die Abscheulichkeit, Scheußlichkeit, Gräßlichkeit. **atrocity** [ə'trɔsiti], *s.* der Greuel, die Greueltat; *see also* **atrociousness**; (*coll.*) Ungeheuerlichkeit, grober Verstoß, der Schnitzer.

atrophied ['ætrəfid], *adj.* abgezehrt, ausgemergelt; verkümmert, geschrumpft. **atrophy, 1.** *s.* die Abzehrung, Verkümmerung, Abmagerung, Schrumpfung; der (Muskel)schwund, die Atrophie. **2.** *v.i.* absterben, verkümmern, einschrumpfen. **3.** *v.t.* absterben *or* einschrumpfen lassen.

attach [ə'tætʃ], **1.** *v.t.* 1. anheften, anknüpfen, anbinden, anfügen, festmachen, befestigen (***to,*** an (*Acc.*)), verbinden (mit); ***– o.s.,*** sich anschließen (***to,*** *Dat. or* an (*Acc.*)); 2. beifügen, beilegen, beimessen, zumessen, zurechnen (***to,*** *Dat.*); ***– blame to him,*** ihm Schuld geben (***for,*** wegen); ***I – no value to his remarks,*** ich lege seinen Äußerungen keinen Wert bei; 3. (*Mil.*) angliedern, zuweisen, zuteilen; ***he was –ed to the regiment,*** er wurde dem Regiment zugeteilt; 4. an sich ziehen, gewinnen, fesseln, für sich einnehmen; 5. (*Law*) (*a p.*) festnehmen, verhaften, (*goods*) beschlagnahmen, mit Beschlag belegen. **2.** *v.i.* haften (***to,*** an (*Dat.*)), sich knüpfen (an (*Acc.*)), zukommen (*Dat.*); verbunden *or* verknüpft sein (mit); ***no blame –es to him,*** ihn trifft keine Schuld.

attachable [ə'tætʃəbl], *adj.* (*Law*) mit Beschlag belegbar, verhaftbar; aufsteckbar, anfügbar; (*fig.*) verknüpfbar, zuzuschreiben(d), beizulegen(d).

attaché-case [ə'tæʃikeis], *s.* die Aktentasche, Aktenmappe, der Stadtkoffer.

attached [ə'tætʃt], *adj.,* 1. fest; unbeweglich; (*Archit.*) eingebaut; 2. (*fig.*) anhänglich; ***be*** (***very***) ***–,*** zugetan sein (***to,*** *Dat.*), hängen (an (*Dat.*)); ***become – to,*** liebgewinnen. **attachment,** *s.* 1. die Verbindung (***to,*** mit), Befestigung, Anbringung, Verknüpfung, Anknüpfung, Anfügung (an (*Acc.*)); 2. das Anhängsel, Beiwerk, (*Tech.*) Zusatzgerät; 3. (*of a p.*) die Anhänglichkeit, Ergebenheit (an (*Acc.*)), Zuneigung, Neigung (zu); 4. (*Mil.*) Angleiderung, Zuteilung; 5. (*Law*) Verhaftung, Beschlagnahme.

attack [ə'tæk], **1.** *v.t.* angreifen, anfallen, überfallen; in Angriff nehmen, anpacken, herfallen über (*Acc.*), sich machen an *or* über (*Acc.*) (*work*); (*Mus.*) ansetzen, anschlagen, antönen, einsetzen mit; (*as acid*) anfressen, (*as disease*) befallen. **2.** *v.i.* einen Angriff machen, (*Mus.*) ansetzen, einsetzen. **3.** *s.* der Angriff, Überfall; die Offensive; (*Med.*)

der Anfall, (*Mus.*) Einsatz, Ansatz, Anschlag; ***feigned*** or ***feint*** –, der Scheinangriff; ***surprise*** –, der Überfall. **attackable,** *adj.* angreifbar. **attacker,** *s.* der Angreifer; angreifender Teil.

attain [ə'tein], **1.** *v.t.* erreichen, gewinnen, erlangen, gelangen zu *or* an (*Acc.*); – ***one's end,*** seinen Zweck erreichen, zum Ziele gelangen. **2.** *v.i.* – ***to,*** gelangen *or* kommen zu, erreichen. **attainability** [–ə'biliti], *s.* die Erreichbarkeit. **attainable,** *adj.* erreichbar.

attainder [ə'teində], *s.* der Verlust der bürgerlichen Ehrenrechte, Ehr- und Eigentumsverlust; (*Hist.*) ***bill of*** –, der Parlamentsbeschluß zur Bestrafung des Hochverrats.

attainment [ə'teinmənt], *s.* die Erzielung, Erringung, Erlangung, Erwerbung, Erreichung; das Erreichte, Erworbene, die Errungenschaft; *pl.* Kenntnisse, Fertigkeiten, Errungenschaften.

attaint [ə'teint], **1.** *v.t.* eines Kapitalverbrechens überführen, zum Tode verurteilen, dem Verlust der bürgerlichen Ehrenrechte aussetzen; anstecken, befallen (*of disease*); (*fig.*) entehren, entweihen, schänden, beflecken, besudeln. **2.** *s. See* **attainder.**

attar ['ætə], *s.* die Blumenessenz; – ***of roses,*** das Rosenöl.

attemper [ə'tempə], *v.t.* durch Mischung verändern, tempern (*metals*), temperieren, regulieren (*temperature*); (*fig.*) mildern, lindern, mäßigen, dämpfen; in Anklang bringen (***to,*** mit), anpassen (*Dat. or* an (*Acc.*)).

attempt [ə'tempt], **1.** *v.t.* versuchen, probieren, wagen; unternehmen, sich machen an (*Acc.*), anpacken, angreifen; – ***his life,*** einen Mordanschlag auf ihn machen. **2.** *s.* der Versuch; die Bemühung, Unternehmung; der Anschlag, Angriff, das Attentat (***on,*** auf (*Acc.*)).

attend [ə'tend], **1.** *v.t.* 1. beiwohnen (*Dat.*), zugegen sein bei, besuchen (*school*), hören (*lectures*); – ***divine service,*** dem Gottesdienste beiwohnen; ***the theatre was poorly –ed,*** das Theater war schlecht besetzt *or* besucht; 2. aufwarten (*Dat.*), seine Aufwartung machen (*Dat.*), im Gefolge (*Gen.*) sein, (dienstlich) begleiten; 3. bedienen (*customers*), beaufsichtigen, warten, pflegen (*machines etc.*), behandeln, warten, pflegen (*invalids*); ***have you been –ed*** (***to***)***?*** werden Sie schon bedient? 4. (*fig.*) folgen (*Dat.*), begleiten; ***be –ed with difficulties,*** mit Schwierigkeiten verknüpft sein, Schwierigkeiten zur Folge haben *or* nach sich ziehen; ***success –ed his undertaking,*** Erfolg krönte sein Unternehmen. **2.** *v.i.* 1. merken, achtgeben, achten, aufpassen, hören (***to,*** auf (*Acc.*)); – ***on,*** *see* **1,** 2; dienen (*Dat.*), bedienen; – ***to,*** besorgen, erledigen, durchführen (*business*), sich kümmern um, sich befassen mit, sich widmen (*Dat.*), sehen nach; – ***to one's business,*** seiner Arbeit nachgehen; – ***to one's devotions,*** seine Andacht verrichten; ***I will – to it myself,*** ich will es selbst besorgen; 2. zugegen *or* anwesend sein (***at,*** bei), erscheinen, sich einfinden (***at, in,*** in *or* vor (*Dat.*)); – ***in person,*** persönlich erscheinen.

attendance [ə'tendəns], *s.* 1. die Bedienung, (Auf-)wartung, Pflege (***on,*** Gen.), Aufsicht (über (*Acc.*)); Dienstleistung, der Dienst; ***be in – on,*** aufwarten (*Dat.*); (*coll.*) ***dance –*** (***up***)***on him,*** ihm den Hof machen, um ihn herumscharwenzeln; ***hours of –,*** die Dienststunden; 2. die Bedienung, Dienerschaft, das Gefolge; 3. die Gegenwart, Anwesenheit, der Besuch (***at,*** bei), (*Med.*) Beistand, die Behandlung; ***be in – at,*** anwesend sein bei, teilnehmen an (*Dat.*); ***the doctor is in daily –,*** der Arzt kommt täglich; – ***at church,*** der Kirchenbesuch; – ***at lectures,*** der Besuch der Vorlesungen; 4. der Besuch, Besucher (*pl.*), die Besucherzahl, Frequenz; – ***list,*** die Präsenzliste, das Verzeichnis der Anwesenden.

attendant [ə'tendənt], **1.** *adj.* begleitend, folgend; aufwartend; (*Law*) abhängig (***to,*** von), verpflichtet (*Dat.*); gegenwärtig, anwesend; (*fig.*) verbunden ((***up***)***on,*** mit), anschließend (an (*Acc.*)), folgend (auf (*Acc.*)); – ***circumstances,*** Begleitumstände; – ***phenomenon,*** die Nebenerscheinung. **2.** *s.* der Gefährte (die Gefährtin), der (die) Begleiter(in), Gesellschafter(in); Aufwartende(r), der Diener; (*Hist.*) Knecht, Gefolgsmann; Aufseher, Wärter (*in hospitals etc.*); *pl.* die Dienerschaft, das Gefolge; die Begleitung.

attention [ə'tenʃən], *s.* die Aufmerksamkeit; Berücksichtigung, Beachtung; (*pl.*) Höflichkeitsbezeugungen; (*Mil.*) Grundstellung; (*Mil.*) –*!* gestanden! (*coll.*) Achtung! ***be all –,*** ganz Ohr sein; ***attract –,*** Aufmerksamkeit erregen; ***arrest his –,*** seine Aufmerksamkeit fesseln; ***call*** or ***draw – to,*** die Aufmerksamkeit lenken auf (*Acc.*); (*Mil.*) ***come to –,*** Front machen; (*Comm.*) ***for the – of,*** zu Händen von; ***focus one's – on,*** seine Aufmerksamkeit richten auf (*Acc.*); ***pay close –,*** gespannt aufmerken; ***pay close – to,*** genau achtgeben auf (*Acc.*); ***pay one's –s to him,*** ihm den Hof machen; ***stand at –,*** stramm stehen.

attentive [ə'tentiv], *adj.* aufmerksam, achtsam (***to,*** auf (*Acc.*)); aufmerksam, gefällig.

attenuate [ə'tenjueit], *v.t.* (ab)schwächen, verringern, vermindern, verkleinern, verjüngen, (*Chem. etc.*) verdünnen, verflüchtigen. **attenuated,** *adj.* verdünnt, abgeschwächt, vermindert; abgemagert, verschmälert, verjüngt, zugespitzt. **attenuation** [–ju'eiʃən], *s.* die Verdünnung; Verminderung, Abnahme, Schwächung, Abmagerung, Abzehrung; Verkleinerung, Verjüngung; Zerbröckelung, Verwitterung (*of stone*); Dämpfung (*of waves, sound etc.*); (*Brew.*) Vergärung; (*fig.*) Abschwächung, Verringerung.

attest [ə'test], **1.** *v.t.* beglaubigen, bezeugen, bekunden, bescheinigen; attestieren, amtlich bestätigen; zeigen, erweisen, zeugen von, bestätigen, beweisen; vereidigen (*soldiers etc.*). **2.** *v.i.* Zeugnis ablegen, zeugen (***to,*** für). **3.** *s. See* **attestation, 1.** **attestation** [ætes'teiʃən], *s.* 1. das Zeugnis, die Aussage; 2. der Schein, die Bescheinigung, Bestätigung, das Attest; die Bezeugung *or* Bekräftigung (durch Eid), Eidesleistung, Vereidigung. **attestor,** *s.* der Zeuge, Beglaubiger.

Attic ['ætik], *adj.* attisch, (*fig.*) klassisch; – ***order,*** attische Säulenordnung; – ***salt*** or ***wit,*** beißender Witz.

attic, *s.* die Dachstube; das Dachgeschoß; (*fig. coll.*) Oberstübchen (= *head*).

attire [ə'taiə], **1.** *s.* die Kleidung, Tracht, das Gewand; der Schmuck, Putz; das Geweih (*of stags*). **2.** *v.t.* (be)kleiden; putzen, schmücken, zieren.

attitude ['ætitju:d], *s.* die Stellung, (Körper)haltung, Lage, Positur; (*fig.*) Haltung, das Verhalten; die Stellung(nahme), Einstellung, der Standpunkt; – ***of mind,*** die Geisteshaltung; ***strike an –,*** sich in Positur setzen. **attitudinize** [–'tju:dinaiz], *v.i.* posieren, sich in Positur setzen, sich (selbst) ins Licht rücken. **attitudinizer,** *s.* der Poseur.

attorney [ə'tə:ni], *s.* der (Rechts)anwalt; Rechtsbeistand; (gesetzlicher) Vertreter, Bevollmächtigte(r), Sachwalter; – ***in fact,*** der Rechtswahrer, Bevollmächtigte(r); ***letter of –,*** schriftliche Vollmacht; ***power of –,*** die Bevollmächtigung, (gerichtliche) Vollmacht; ***prosecuting –,*** der Staatsanwalt. **attorney|-at-law,** *s.* der Rechtsanwalt, Rechtsbeistand. **–-general,** *s.* der Kronanwalt.

attract [ə'trækt], **1.** *v.t.* anziehen; an sich (*Acc.*) ziehen, auf sich (*Acc.*) ziehen, für sich einnehmen, (an)locken, fesseln, reizen; ***be –ed to,*** hingezogen werden zu; ***the magnet –s iron,*** der Magnet zieht das Eisen an; – ***attention,*** Aufmerksamkeit erregen. **2.** *v.i.* Anziehung(skraft) ausüben; anziehend wirken *or* sein, fesselnd *or* gewinnend sein. **attraction,** *s.* die Anziehung(skraft), der Reiz; das Reizende, Lockende; – ***of gravity,*** die Schwereanziehung, Gravitationskraft; ***the great – of the evening,*** die Hauptzugnummer des Abends; ***exert –,*** Anziehung ausüben. **attractive,** *adj.* anziehend; reizend, reizvoll, gewinnend, fesselnd; – ***force,*** die Zugkraft; – ***power,*** die Anziehungskraft. **attractiveness,** *s.* der Reiz, das Anziehende *or* Reizende, gewinnende Art.

attributable [ə'tribjutəbl], *adj.* zuzuschreiben(d), beizumessen(d). **attribute, 1.** [ə'tribju:t], *v.t.* zuschreiben, beimessen, beilegen, unterschieben (*to, Dat.*); zurückführen (auf (*Acc.*)). **2.** ['ætribju:t], *s.* charakteristische Eigenschaft, das Kennzeichen, (wesentliches) Merkmal; (*Gram.*) Attribut. **attribution** [ætri'bju:ʃən], *s.* die Zuschreibung, Beimessung, Beilegung, Zuerkennung, beigelegte Eigenschaft. **attributive, 1.** *adj.* (*Gram.*) attributiv. **2.** *s.* (*Gram.*) das Attribut.

attrition [ə'triʃən], *s.* die (Auf)reibung, Abreibung, Abnutzung; (*fig.*) Zermürbung, das Mürbemachen; (*Eccl.*) (unvollkommene) Reue; ***war of –,*** der Zermürbungskrieg.

attune [ə'tju:n], *v.t.* (ab)stimmen, einstimmen (*to*, auf (*Acc.*)), (*fig.*) einstellen (auf (*Acc.*)), in Einklang bringen (mit), anpassen (an (*Acc.*)).

atypical [ei'tipikəl], *adj.* von der Regel abweichend.

aubade [o'ba:d], *s.* das Morgenlied.

aubergine ['oubəʒi:n], *s.* (*Bot.*) die Eierfrucht (*Solanum melongena*).

auburn ['ɔ:bən], *adj.* rotbraun, kastanienbraun, nußbraun.

auction ['ɔ:kʃən], **1.** *s.* die Versteigerung, Auktion; ***sell by*** (or *Am.* ***at***) ***–, put up for*** (or *Am.* ***at***) ***–,*** *see* **2. 2.** *v.t.* versteigern, verauktionieren. **auctioneer** [–'niə], **1.** *s.* der Versteigerer, Auktionator. **2.** *v.t. See* **auction, 2.**

audacious [ɔ:'deiʃəs], *adj.* kühn, verwegen; keck, dreist, vermessen, unverschämt, frech. **audacity** [–'dæsiti], *s.* die Kühnheit, Verwegenheit; Keckheit, Dreistigkeit, Frechheit, Unverschämtheit.

audibility [ɔ:di'biliti], *s.* die Hörbarkeit, Vernehmbarkeit. **audible** ['ɔ:dibl], *adj.* hörbar, vernehmbar, vernehmlich (*to*, für).

audience ['ɔ:diəns], *s.* 1. die Audienz (***with***, bei); ***receive in –,*** (in Audienz) empfangen; ***grant*** or ***give an – to,*** eine Audienz erteilen (*Dat.*); 2. das Gehör, die Anhörung; ***give – to,*** Gehör schenken (*Dat.*); 3. das Publikum, die Zuhörerschaft, Zuhörer (*pl.*), der Leserkreis (*of a book*), (*Rad.*) die Hörerschaft. **audience-chamber,** *s.* der Audienzsaal.

audio-frequency ['ɔ:dio–], *s.* (*Rad.*) die Niederfrequenz, Tonfrequenz, Hörfrequenz.

audion ['ɔ:diɔn], *s.* (*Rad.*) die Kathodenröhre, das Audion.

audit ['ɔ:dit], **1.** *s.* 1. die Rechnungsabnahme, Rechnungsprüfung, Bücherrevision; 2. Bilanz, Schlußrechnung. **2.** *v.t.* prüfen, revidieren, abnehmen (*accounts*). **3.** *v.i.* die Bücher revidieren. **auditing,** *s. See* **audit, 1,** 1; ***– department,*** die Revisionsabteilung.

audition [ɔ:'diʃən], **1.** *s.* das Gehör, Hörvermogen; (*Theat., Mus. etc.*) Anhören, die Hörprobe. **2.** *v t.* einer Hörprobe unterziehen, anhören.

audit-office, *s.* das Rechnungsamt, die Rechnungskammer.

auditor ['ɔ:ditə], *s.* der (Bücher)revisor, Rechnungsprüfer; ***official –,*** Revisionsbeamte(r).

auditorium [ɔ:di'tɔ:riəm], *s.* (*Univ.*) der Hörsaal; Zuhörerraum, Zuschauerraum, Vortragsraum, das Auditorium.

auditory ['ɔ:ditəri], **1.** *adj.* Gehör–; ***– nerves,*** Gehörnerven. **2.** *s.* die Zuhörerschaft.

Augean [ɔ:'dʒi:ən], *adj.* Augias–; ***the – stables,*** der Augiasstall.

auger ['ɔ:gə], *s.* großer Bohrer, der Hohlbohrer.

aught [ɔ:t], *pron.* (*obs. or Poet.*) (irgend)etwas; ***for – I care,*** meinetwegen; ***for – I know,*** soviel ich weiß.

augment, 1. [ɔ:g'ment], *v.t.* vermehren; vergrößern (*also Mus.*), steigern; (*Gram.*) ein Augment vorsetzen (*Dat.*). **2.** [–'ment], *v.i.* zunehmen, sich vergrößern, sich vermehren. **3.** ['ɔ:gment], *s.* (*Gram.*) das Augment. **augmentation** [–'teiʃən], *s.* die Vermehrung, Vergrößerung, Zunahme, Erhöhung, das Wachstum; der Zusatz, Zuwachs; (*Mus.*) die Augmentation, (Themen)vergrößerung. **augmentative** [–'mentətiv], **1.** *adj.* vermehrend, vergrößernd, verstärkend, Verstärkungs–. **2.** *s.* (*Gram.*) die Verstärkungsform, das Augmentative. **augmented,** *adj.* vermehrt, verstärkt, (*Mus.*) übermäßig.

augur ['ɔ:gə], **1.** *s.* der Augur, Wahrsager. **2.** *v.t.* voraussagen, weissagen, prophezeien, verheißen, ankündigen. **3.** *v.i.* ***– ill*** (or ***well***), ein schlechtes (*or* gutes) Zeichen sein, böses (*or* gutes) versprechen. **augury** ['ɔ:gjuri], *s.* die Wahrsagung, Weissagung; das Anzeichen, Vorzeichen, die Vorbedeutung, Vorahnung.

august [ɔ:'gʌst], *adj.* erhaben, erlaucht, hehr, majestätisch, herrlich.

August ['ɔ:gəst], *s.* der August; ***in –,*** im August.

Augustan [ɔ:'gʌstən], *adj.* (*Hist.*) augusteisch; (*Eccl.*) augustanisch, augsburgisch; ***– Age*** (***of English literature***), das klassische Zeitalter (der englischen Literatur).

Augustinian [ɔ:gʌs'tiniən], **1.** *s.* der Augustiner(mönch). **2.** *adj.* augustinisch.

augustness [ɔ:'gʌstnis], *s.* die Erhabenheit, Hoheit, Herrlichkeit.

auk [ɔ:k], *s.* (*Orn*) der Alk; ***little –,*** der Krabbentaucher (*Plantus alle*).

auld lang syne [ɔ:ldlæŋ'sain], *s.* (*Scots*) die gute alte Zeit.

aulic ['ɔ:lik], *adj.* Hof–, fürstlich.

aunt [a:nt], *s.* die Tante, (*Poet.*) Muhme; ***great-–,*** die Großtante; ***Aunt Sally,*** das Knüttelwerfen. **auntie, aunty,** *s.* das Tantchen.

aura ['ɔ:rə], *s.* der Hauch, Duft, das Aroma; (*fig.*) die Atmosphäre, das Fluidum.

aural ['ɔ:rəl], *adj.* Ohr(en)–.

aureole ['ɔ:rioul], *s.* die Strahlenkrone, der Heiligenschein, Glorienschein; (*fig.*) Nimbus, Ruhmeskranz; (*Astr.*) Hof.

auric ['ɔ:rik], *adj.* Gold–.

auricle ['ɔ:rikl], *s.* äußeres Ohr, die Ohrmuschel; ***– of the heart,*** der Herzvorhof.

auricula [ɔ:'rikjulə], *s.* (*Bot.*) die Aurikel (*Primula auricula*).

auricular [ɔ:'rikjulə], *adj.* Ohr(en)–, ohrförmig; Hör–; (*fig.*) geflüstert, heimlich; ***– confession,*** die Ohrenbeichte; ***– tradition,*** mündliche Überlieferung.

auriferous [ɔ:'rifərəs], *adj.* goldhaltig; ***– quartz,*** der Goldquarz.

aurochs ['ɔ:rɔks], *s.* der Auerochs, Ur.

aurora [ɔ:'rɔ:rə], *s.* (*Poet.*) die Morgenröte, der Morgen. **aurora borealis,** *s.* das Nordlicht.

auscultate ['ɔ:skəlteit], *v.t.* (*Med.*) auskultieren, behorchen. **auscultation** [–'teiʃən], *s.* die Auskultation, Behorchung.

auspice ['ɔ:spis], *s.* das Auspizium; *pl.* (*fig.*) die Vorbedeutung; Anzeichen, Vorzeichen, Auspizien (*pl.*); *pl.* (*fig.*) die Schirmherrschaft, Leitung, der Schutz, Beistand; ***under favourable –s,*** unter günstigen Anzeichen; ***under the –s of,*** unter dem Schutz *or* der Leitung von. **auspicious,** [ɔ:s'piʃəs], *adj.* günstig, glücklich, glückverheißend.

Aussie ['ɔzi], *s.* (*sl.*) der Australier.

austere [ɔ:s'tiə], *adj.* nüchtern, ernst, einfach, schmucklos, ungeziert (*taste, style*); streng, hart, herb, rauh, unfreundlich, abweisend (*manner*). **austerity** [–'teriti], *s.* die Strenge, Härte, Unfreundlichkeit; Mäßigung, Enthaltsamkeit, Nüchternheit, Einfachheit, Schmucklosigkeit; der Ernst; (*coll.*) Sparmaßnahmen (*pl.*), wirtschaftliche Einschränkung.

austral ['ɔ:strəl], *adj.* südlich.

Australia [ɔs'treiliə], *s.* Australien. **Australian, 1.** *s.* der (die) Australier(in). **2.** *adj.* australisch.

Austria ['ɔstriə], *s.* Österreich (*n.*). **Austrian, 1.** *s.* der (die) Österreicher(in). **2.** *adj.* österreichisch. **Austro-Hungarian,** *adj.* österreichisch-ungarisch.

autarchy ['ɔ:ta:ki], *s.* die Autarchie, Selbstherrschaft.

autarky ['ɔ:tɑ:ki], *s.* die Autarkie, (wirtschaftliche) Unabhängigkeit.

authentic [ɔ:'θentik], *adj.* echt, wirklich, verbürgt, zuverlässig, glaubwürdig, authentisch; urschriftlich, eigenhändig, original; (*Law*) gültig, urkundlich belegt, rechtskräftig. **authenticate,** *v.t.* als echt erweisen, verbürgen; (*Law*) beglaubigen, gültig *or* rechtskräftig machen. **authentication** [–'keiʃən], *s.* die Beglaubigung. **authenticity** [–'tisiti], *s.* die Echtheit, Glaubwürdigkeit; Rechtsgültigkeit.

author ['ɔ:θə], *s.* 1. der Stifter, Urheber, Schöpfer, Begründer; (*fig.*) die Veranlassung, Ursache; ***the – of my being,*** mein Schöpfer; 2. der Verfasser, Autor, Schriftsteller; ***his profession as an –,*** sein Schriftstellerberuf; ***–'s copy,*** das Handexemplar. **authoress,** *s.* die Verfasserin, Schriftstellerin, Autorin.

authoritarian [ɔ:θɔri'tɛəriən], *adj.* autoritär; – ***principle,*** das Führerprinzip; – ***state,*** der Obrigkeitsstaat. **authoritative** [ɔ:'θɔritətiv], *adj.* autoritativ, Autorität habend, maßgebend, maßgeblich; bevollmächtigt; gebieterisch, herrisch. **authoritativeness,** *s.* gebieterisches Wesen; das Bevollmächtigtsein.

authority [ɔ:'θɔriti], *s.* 1. die Autorität, gesetzmäßige *or* rechtmäßige Macht, (Amts)gewalt; Vollmacht; (*Mil.*) Kommandogewalt, Befehlsgewalt; ***delegation of –,*** die Übertragung von Amtsgewalt; ***enforcement of –,*** die Gehorsamserzwingung; ***be in –,*** Vollmacht haben, die Gewalt in Händen haben; ***misuse of –,*** der Mißbrauch der Amtsgewalt; ***he has no – over them,*** er hat keine Macht über sie; ***have full – to act,*** volle Handlungsvollmacht besitzen; ***written –,*** schriftliche Vollmacht; 2. (*Law*) der Präzendenzfall, Vorgang; Beleg, die Quelle, (*fig.*) der Einfluß, das Gewicht, Ansehen, die Glaubwürdigkeit (***with,*** bei); ***on good –,*** aus guter Quelle; ***on the – of St. Paul,*** Paulus ist ein Gewährsmann dafür daß . . .; ***of unquestioned –,*** unbedingt glaubwurdig, unangefochten; 3. das Befugnis, der Befehl, Auftrag, die Ermächtigung; (*fig.*) (*of a p.*) Autorität, das Zeugnis; ***by –,*** mit amtlicher Erlaubnis; ***on the – of,*** im Auftrag von; ***on one's own –,*** aus eigener Machtbefugnis; 4. der Gewährsmann, Fachmann, Sachverständige(r), die Autorität, Fachgröße; ***he is an – on philology,*** er ist ein Fachmnan auf dem Gebiet der Philologie; 5. (*oft. pl.*) (Verwaltungs)behörde, Regierung; ***civil –,*** die Zivilbehörde; ***competent –,*** zuständige Behörde; (*Law*) ***confirming –,*** die Bestätigungsinstanz; (*Law*) ***reviewing –,*** die Revisionsinstanz; ***the authorities,*** die Behörde(n), Obrigkeit; ***local authorities,*** die Ortsbehörde.

authorization [ɔ:θərai'zeiʃən], *s.* die Ermächtigung, Bevollmächtigung; ***subject to –,*** genehmigungspflichtig. **authorize** ['ɔ:θəraiz], *v.t.* (*a p.*) bevollmächtigen, ermächtigen, autorisieren, den Auftrag geben (*Dat.*); (*an action*) rechtfertigen, genehmigen, billigen, gutheißen; ***–d agent,*** Bevollmächtigte(r), Beauftragte(r), (rechtsverbindlicher) Vertreter; ***–d capital,*** bewilligtes Kapital; ***Authorized Version,*** die englische Bibel von 1611.

authorship ['ɔ:θəʃip], *s.* die Verfasserschaft, Autorschaft (*of a work*); Schriftstellerei, Schriftstellerlaufbahn, der Schriftstellerberuf; (*fig.*) die Urheberschaft.

autobiographical [ɔ:təbaio'græfikəl], *adj.* autobiographisch. **autobiography** [–'ɔgrəfi], *s.* die Selbstbiographie.

autocade ['ɔ:tokeid], *s.* die Autokolonne.

autochthon [ɔ:'tɔkθən], *s.* (*usu. pl.* **-s** [–z] *or* **-es** [–i:z]) der Urbewohner. **autochthonal, autochthonic** [–'θɔnik], **autochthonous,** *adj.* ureingesessen, alteingeboren, bodenständig.

autoclave ['ɔ:təkleiv], *s.* der Autoklav, Dampfkochtopf.

autocracy [ɔ:'tɔkrəsi], *s.* die Selbstherrschaft, Autokratie. **autocrat** ['ɔ:tərkræt], *s.* der Selbstherrscher, Autokrat. **autocratic(al)** [–'krætik(l)], *adj.* selbstherrlich, alleinherrschend, unumschränkt, autokratisch.

auto-da-fé [ɔ:todɑ:'fei], *s.* das Ketzergericht.

autogiro [ɔ:to'dʒairou], *s.* der Tragschrauber.

autograph ['ɔ:təgrɑ:f], **1.** *s.* das Autograph, Original, die Originalhandschrift, Urschrift; das Autogramm, eigenhändige Unterschrift; ***– letter,*** eigenhändig geschriebener *or* unterzeichneter Brief. **2.** *v.t.* eigenhändig (unter)schreiben; mit einem Autogramm versehen. **autographic** [–'græfik], *adj.* eigenhändig geschrieben, autographisch.

autogyro, ***see*** **autogiro.**

auto|-hypnosis ['ɔ:tou–], *s.* die Selbsthypnose. **--ignition,** *s.* die Selbstzündung. **--intoxication,** *s.* die Selbstvergiftung, Autotoxikose.

automate ['ɔ:təmeit], *v.t.* automatisieren. **automated,** *adj.* vollautomatisiert.

automatic [ɔ:tə'mætik], **1.** *adj.* selbsttätig, selbstbeweglich, automatisch, Selbst–; (*Mil.*) Selbstlade–, Repetier–; (*Tech.*) maschinenmäßig, mechanisch; (*fig.*) unbewußt, mechanisch, unwillkürlich; – ***gun,*** das Selbstladegewehr; – ***machine,*** der Automat; (*Av.*) ***– pilot,*** automatische Steuerung; – ***telephone,*** das Selbstwähltelephon; – ***(telephone-)exchange,*** das Selbstwählamt, Selbstanschlußamt; (*Rad.*) – ***volume control,*** der Schwundausgleich. **2.** *s.* der Revolver, die Selbstladepistole. **automatically,** *adv.* automatisch, von sich selbst; (*fig.*) mechanisch, unwillkürlich, unbewußt; ohne weiteres.

automation [ɔ:tə'meiʃən], *s.* die Automatisierung, Automation.

automaton [ɔ:'tɔmətən], *s.* (*pl.* **-ta** *or* **-s**) der Automat (*also fig.*); die Gliederpuppe.

automobile ['ɔ:təmobi:l], *s.* das Auto, der Kraftwagen.

autonomous [ɔ:'tɔnəməs], *adj.* selbstregierend; unabhängig, selbständig. **autonomy,** *s.* die Selbstregierung, Selbständigkeit; Eigengesetzlichkeit; (*Phil.*) Willensfreiheit, Selbstbestimmung, Autonomie.

autopsy ['ɔ:tɔpsi], *s.* 1. eigene Anschauung, der Augenschein; 2. (*Med.*) die Leichenöffnung, Leichenschau, Autopsie, Obduktion; (*fig.*) Sezierung, Zergliederung.

auto-suggestion, *s.* die Autosuggestion, Selbstbeeinflussung.

autotype ['ɔ:totaip], **1.** *s.* (*Typ.*) die Autotypie, der Faksimileabdruck; (*Phot.*) das Rasterbild, die Rasterätzung. **2.** *v.t.* durch Autotypie vervielfältigen, autotypieren.

autumn ['ɔ:təm], *s.* der Herbst. **autumnal** [ɔ:'tʌmnəl], *adj.* herbstlich, Herbst–.

auxiliary [ɔ:g'ziliəri], **1.** *adj.* helfend, zusätzlich, Zusatz–, Hilfs–; mitwirkend; ***– engine,*** der Hilfsmotor; ***– forces*** or ***troops,*** die Hilfstruppen; ***– verb,*** das Hilfszeitwort. **2.** *s.* Verbündete(r), der Beistand, Helfer; (*Gram.*) das Hilfszeitwort; ***pl.*** (*Mil.*) Hilfstruppen.

avail [ə'veil], **1.** *v.t.* helfen (*Dat.*), nützen (*Dat.*), fördern; ***– o.s. of,*** sich (*Dat.*) zunutze machen, sich bedienen (*Gen.*); – ***o.s. of the opportunity,*** die Gelegenheit ausnützen. **2.** *v.i.* nutzen, nützen, helfen; nützlich sein, von Nutzen sein; ***what –s it?*** was nützt es? **3.** *s.* der Nutzen, Vorteil; ***all was of no –,*** es half alles nichts; ***without –,*** vergeblich, ohne Erfolg.

availability [əveilə'biliti], *s.* die Verwendbarkeit, Verfügbarkeit, das Vorhandensein; (*Law*) die Gültigkeit. **available,** *adj.* vorhanden, verfügbar, erhältlich, zu Gebote stehend; benutzbar, verwendbar, brauchbar, zugänglich; (*Law*) zulässig, statthaft, gültig; (*Comm.*) vorrätig, lieferbar; ***return ticket – for 3 days,*** Rückfahrkarte mit dreitägiger Gültigkeit; ***be –,*** zur Verfügung stehen.

avalanche ['ævəlɑ:nʃ], *s* die Lawine; ***– of words,*** der Wortschwall.

avant-garde ['ævɑ̃'gɑ:d], **1.** *s.* (*usu. fig.*) die Avantgarde. **2.** *adj.* avantgardistisch.

avarice ['ævəris], *s.* die Habsucht, der Geiz. **avaricious** [–'riʃəs], *adj.* habsüchtig, geizig.

avast! [ə'vɑ:st], *int.* (*Naut.*) fest(hieven)! stopp!

avaunt! [ə'vɔ:nt], *int.* (*obs.*) hinweg! fort!

avenge [ə'vendʒ], *v.t.* rächen; – ***o.s.*** or ***be -d,*** sich rächen (***on,*** an (*Dat.*)); – ***a murder,*** einen Mord rächen (*or Poet.* ahnden). **avenger,** *s.* der Rächer.

avenue ['ævinju:], *s.* die Allee; große breite Straße; (*fig.*) der Zugang, Weg.

aver [ə'və:], *v.t.* behaupten, als Tatsache hinstellen, versichern; beweisen, bekräftigen.

average ['ævəridʒ], **1.** *adj.* durchschnittlich, Durchschnitts–; ***the – man,*** der Durchschnittsmensch; – ***price,*** der Mittelpreis. **2.** *v.t.* den Durchschnitt ermitteln *or* nehmen (von *or* (*Gen.*)); (*Comm.*) anteilsmäßig aufgliedern (*losses etc.*). **3.** *v.i.* durchschnittlich betragen, einen Durchschnitt erzielen; – ***40 m.p.h.,*** eine Durchschnittsgeschwindigkeit von 40 Meilen pro Stunde fahren. **4.** *s.* 1. der Durchschnitt, Mittelwert; ***at an –,*** im Durchschnitt, durchschnittlich; ***general –,*** allgemeiner Durchschnittswert; ***rough –,*** mittleres Verhältnis, annähernder Durchschnitt; 2. (*Naut.*) die Havarie; ***general –,*** große Havarie; ***particular –,*** partikuläre Havarie; ***petty –,*** kleine *or* ordinäre Havarie.

averment [ə'və:mənt], *s.* die Behauptung, Bestätigung, Bekräftigung, (*Law*) der Beweisantrag.

averse [ə'və:s], *adj.* abgeneigt, abhold (*to, Dat.*); ***I am – to it,*** es ist mir zuwider; ***my father was – to my going,*** mein Vater war nicht geneigt, mich gehen zu lassen. **averseness,** *s.* die Abgeneigtheit (*to,* gegen). **aversion,** *s.* die Abneigung, Abscheu, der Widerwille (*to, for,* gegen; ***from,*** vor (*Dat.*)); Gegenstand des Abscheus, Greuel; (*coll.*) ***it is my pet –,*** es ist mir ein ausgesprochener Greuel.

avert [ə'və:t], *v.t.* abwenden, wegkehren (*one's face etc.*); ablenken, verhüten; vorbeugen (*Dat.*).

aviary ['eiviəri], *s.* das Vogelhaus.

aviation [eivi'eiʃən], *s.* das Flugwesen, Fliegen, die Luftfahrt; Fliegerei, der Flugsport. **aviator** ['eivieitə], *s.* der Flieger.

avid ['ævid], *adj.* (be)gierig (***of, for,*** nach). **avidity** [ə'viditi], *s.* die Gier(igkeit), Begierde (***of, for,*** nach).

avocation [ævo'keiʃən], *s.* 1. die Nebenbeschäftigung, der Nebenberuf; (*oft. improperly used* = **vocation**) das Berufsgeschäft; 2. (*obs.*) die Abhaltung, Zerstreuung (***from,*** von).

avocet ['ævəset], *s.* (*Orn.*) der Säbelschnäbler (*Recurvirostra avosetta*).

avoid [ə'vɔid], *v.t.* (*a p.*) meiden; (*a p. or th.*) vermeiden; ausweichen (*Dat.*), umgehen (*difficulties*); entgehen (*Dat.*), entrinnen (*danger*); (*Law*) aufheben, ungültig machen, umstoßen; ***he -s me,*** er geht mir aus dem Wege; ***in order to – delay,*** um Verzögerungen zu vermeiden. **avoidable,** *adj.* vermeidlich, vermeidbar, (*Law*) annulierbar. **avoidance,** *s.* das Meiden (*of a p.*), die Vermeidung (*of a th.*); das Freiwerden, die Vakanz (*of an office*), (*Law*) der Widerruf, die Aufhebung, Nichtigkeitserklärung.

avoirdupois [ævədə'pɔiz], *s.* gesetzliches (englisches) Handelsgewicht; (*hum.*) das Gewicht (*of a p.*).

avouch [ə'vautʃ], **1.** *v.t.* behaupten, bekennen, eingestehen, anerkennen, versichern, bekräftigen, verbürgen. **2.** *v.i.* einstehen, garantieren (***for,*** für).

avow [ə'vau], *v.t.* offen bekennen, anerkennen, (zu)gestehen, eingestehen. **avowal,** *s.* die Erklärung, das Bekenntnis, Geständnis. **avowed** [–d], *adj.* anerkannt; offen erklärt, ausgesprochen. **avowedly** [–idli], *adv.* offen, unverhohlen, eingestandenermaßen.

avuncular [ə'vʌŋkjulə], *adj.* Onkel–, onkelhaft.

await [ə'weit], *v.t.* erwarten, warten auf (*Acc.*), entgegensehen (*Dat.*); ***–ing your answer,*** in Erwartung Ihrer Antwort; – ***instructions,*** Anweisung abwarten.

awake [ə'weik], **1.** *irr.v.t.* erwecken, (auf)wecken; (*fig.*) aufrütteln (***from,*** aus), erregen (*suspicion*). **2.** *irr.v.i.* erwachen, aufwachen; (*fig.*) – ***to s.th.,*** sich (*Dat.*) einer S. bewußt werden, über eine S. Klarheit gewinnen. **3.** *pred. adj.* wach, wachend, munter; ***be wide –,*** ganz wach sein; (*fig.*) (*coll.*) wachsam *or* auf der Hut sein; ***be – to a th.,*** sich (*Dat.*) einer S. bewußt sein, etwas wohl wissen *or* kennen. **awaken,** *v.t., v.i. See* **awake. awakening,** *s.* das Erwachen; Erwecken; (*fig.*) (religiöse) Erweckung.

award [ə'wɔ:d], **1.** *v.t.* zuerkennen, zusprechen; gewähren, verleihen. **2.** *s.* das Urteil, die Entscheidung, der Schiedsspruch; Preis, die Auszeichnung, Prämie; zuerkannte Belohnung *or* Strafe; (Ehren)verleihung.

aware [ə'wɛə], *pred. adj.* gewahr (*of, Gen.*), unterrichtet (von), in Kenntnis (*Gen. or* von); ***be – of,*** wissen *or* Kenntnis haben von; ***become – of,*** merken, zur Kenntnis nehmen, gewahr werden (*Gen.*); ***he is – of it,*** er weiß es, es ist ihm bekannt, er hat Kenntnis davon; ***before I was –,*** ehe ich mich's versah. **awareness,** *s.* das Bewußtsein, die Bewußtheit, Erkenntnis.

awash [ə'wɔʃ], *pred. adj.* überspült, überflutet; (*Naut.*) zwischen Wind und Wasser.

away [ə'wei], *adv.* weg, hinweg, fort; fern von, entfernt, abwesend, auswärts, außer Hause, fort, verreist, nicht da; (*coll.*) immerzu, drauflos; (*coll.*) ohnmächtig, bewußtlos; ***come –!*** komm nur her! ***do – with,*** abschaffen, beseitigen, (*coll.*) verschwinden lassen; ***explain –,*** mit einer Erklärung rechtfertigen *or* beseitigen; ***fall –,*** abfallen; ***far and –,*** bei weitem; (*coll.*) ***fire –!*** schieß los! mach zu! ***give –,*** weggeben, verschenken; (*coll.*) ***give him*** (or ***o.s.*** or ***a secret***) ***–,*** ihn (*or* sich *or* ein Geheimnis) verraten; ***give one's daughter –,*** die Tochter dem Bräutigam übergeben; ***go –,*** weggehen, fortgehen; ***laugh –!*** lacht nur zu! ***make – with,*** umbringen (*a p.*), beiseitebringen, (*sl.*) verduften mit (*a th.*); (*coll.*) ***right –,*** sofort, (so)gleich; ***run – with the idea,*** es sich (*Dat.*) in den Kopf setzen; ***send –,*** wegsenden, fortschicken; ***throw –,*** wegwerfen, vergeuden; ***trifle –,*** vertrödeln, vertändeln; ***waste –,*** verfallen, abnehmen, vergehen, (dahin)schwinden; (*of invalids*) schwächer werden, herunterkommen, dahinsiechen; ***while – the time,*** die Zeit verbringen, sich (*Dat.*) die Zeit vertreiben; (*coll.*) ***work –,*** drauflos arbeiten.

away game, *s.* (*Footb.*) das Auswärtsspiel.

awe [ɔ:], **1.** *s.* die Furcht, Scheu, Ehrfurcht; ***in – of,*** aus Ehrfurcht vor (*Dat.*); ***inspire*** or ***fill him with –,*** ihm Ehrfurcht einflößen; ***stand in – of,*** sich fürchten *or* (*coll.*) einen gewaltigen Respekt haben vor (*Dat.*); ***strike with –,*** mit Ehrfurcht erfüllen. **2.** *v.t.* Ehrfurcht einflößen (*Dat.*) *or* gebieten (*Dat.*), mit (Ehr)furcht erfüllen; einschüchtern; ***be -d into silence,*** zum Stillschweigen eingeschüchtert werden. **awe-inspiring, awesome** [–səm], *adj.* erschreckend, ehrfurchtgebietend. **awe-struck,** *adj.* von Ehrfurcht *or* Scheu ergriffen.

awful ['ɔ:ful], **1.** *adj.* furchtbar, schrecklich, entsetzlich; (*coll.*) riesig, ungeheuer, kolossal; (*Poet.*) *see* **awesome. 2.** *adv.* (*sl.*), *or* **awfully,** *adv.* (*coll*). äußerst, höchst, sehr, ungemein, furchtbar, schrecklich; entsetzlich; – ***cold,*** furchtbar, entsetzlich *or* schrecklich kalt; – ***nice,*** riesig *or* furchtbar nett. **awfulness,** *s.* die Furchtbarkeit, Schrecklichkeit.

awhile [ə'wail], *adv.* eine Weile, eine Zeitlang; ***wait –,*** ein bißchen warten.

awkward ['ɔ:kwəd], *adj.* (*a p.*) ungeschickt, linkisch, plump, unbeholfen, verlegen, (*a th.*) unhandlich; (*a situation*) ungünstig, ungelegen, peinlich, unangenehm, mißlich; (*coll.*) – ***customer,*** unangenehmer Bursche. **awkwardness,** *s.* plumpes Wesen; die Ungeschicklichkeit; Unbeholfenheit; Unhandlichkeit; Verlegenheit; das Lästige, Unangenehme, Peinliche, Heikle (*of,* an (*Dat.*)).

awl [ɔ:l], *s.* die Ahle, der Pfriem.

awn [ɔ:n], **1.** *s.* die Granne, Achel. **2.** *v.t.* entgrannen.

awning ['ɔ:niŋ], *s.* die Plane, Zeltbahn; Markise; (*Naut.*) das Sonnensegel, Sonnenzelt.

awoke [ə'wouk], *imperf., p.p. See* **awake.**

awry [ə'rai], *adv.*, *pred. adj.* schief, krumm; (*fig.*) irre (*with* **sein** *and* **werden**, *otherwise as prefix*), verkehrt; *go* –, schiefgehen (*of things*), irren (*of persons*).

ax (*Am.*), *see* **axe.**

axe [æks], **1.** *s.* die Axt, Hacke, Haue, das Beil; (*coll.*) drastische Streichung der Staatsausgaben, drastische Sparmaßnahmen; *headman's* –, das Henkersbeil; *have an – to grind,* eigennützige Zwecke verfolgen. **2.** *v.t.* (*coll.*) rücksichtslos beseitigen; radikal herabsetzen, beschneiden (*expenses*), abbauen (*officials*). **axe-head,** *s.* das Eisen der Axt.

1**axes** ['æksiz], *pl. of* **axe.**

2**axes** ['æksi:z], *pl. of* **axis.**

axial ['æksiəl], *adj.* achsenförmig, Achsen–, achsrecht, (*Math.*) axial.

axil ['æksil], *s.* (*Bot.*) die (Blatt)achsel. **axile** ['æksail], *adj.* (*Bot.*) achselständig.

axilla [æk'silə], *s.* (*pl.* **-ae**) die Achselhöhle. **axillary,** *adj.* Achsel–; (*Bot.*) achselständig.

axiom ['æksiəm], *s.* das Axiom, der Grundsatz. **axiomatic(al)** [–'mætik(l)], *adj.* axiomatisch, grundsätzlich, unumstößlich, von vornherein erwiesen; allgemein anerkannt, einleuchtend.

axis ['æksis], *s.* (*pl.* **axes** [–i:z]) die Achse (*also Pol.*), Mittellinie, Hauptlinie; (*Anat.*) der Dreher, zweiter Halswirbel; *longitudinal* –, die Längsachse; *– of the earth,* die Erdachse; *– of oscillation,* die Mittellinie der Schwingung; *transverse* –, die Querachse; (*Geom.*) *vertical* –, die Höhe.

axle [æksl], *s.* die (Rad)achse, Welle; *driving* –, die Antriebachse; *independent* –, die Schwingachse; *wheel and* –, das Rad an der Welle. **axle|-base,** *s.* der Achsabstand. **--bearing,** *s.* das Achslager. **--bed,** *s.* das Achs(en)futter. **--box,** *s.* die Lagerschale, Achsbüchse, das Achsgehäuse. **– load,** *s.* die Achsbelastung. **--pin,** *s.* der Achsnagel, Splint, die Lünse. **--tree,** *s.* die Welle, Radachse.

ayah ['aiə], *s.* (*Anglo-Indian*) das Kindermädchen.

1**aye** [ai], **1.** *adv.* ja(wohl), freilich; (*Naut.*) –, –*!* zu Befehl! **2.** *s. the –s and the noes,* die Stimmen für und wider; *the –s have it,* die Mehrheit ist für den Antrag, der Antrag ist angenommen.

2**ay(e)** [ei], *adv.* (*Scots*) ewig, immer; *for ever and –,* auf immer und ewig.

azalea [ə'zeiliə], *s.* die Azalie.

azimuth ['æziməθ], *s.* (*Astr.*) der Azimut, Scheitelkreis; (*Artil.*) Seitenteilkreis, die Seitenrichtskala.

azoic [ə'zouik], *adj.* (*Geol.*) azoisch; *– period,* das Azoikum.

Azores [ə'zɔ:z], *pl.* die Azoren (*pl.*).

azote [ə'zout], *s.* der Stickstoff. **azotic** [ə'zɔtik], *adj.* Stickstoff–, stickstoffhaltig.

Azov ['ɑ:zɔv], *s. Sea of* –, das Asowsche Meer.

Aztec ['æztek], **1.** *s.* der Azteke (die Aztekin). **2.** *adj.* aztekisch.

azure ['eiʒ(ju)ə], **1.** *adj.* himmelblau, (*Poet.*) azurn; (*Her.*) blau. **2.** *s.* das Himmelblau, der Azur; (*Her.*) blaues Feld; (*Poet.*) das Himmelszelt, Blau des Himmels.

azyme ['æzaim], *s.* ungesäuertes Brot. **azymous** ['æziməs], *adj.* ungesäuert.

B

B, b [bi:], *s.* 1. das B, b; 2. (*Mus.*) das H; *B flat,* das B; *B major,* H-Dur; *B minor,* h-Moll; *B sharp,* His. *See Index of Abbreviations.*

baa [bɑ:], **1.** *s.* das Blöken, Geblök. **2.** *v.i.* blöken.

babble [bæbl], **1.** *v.i.* schwatzen, plappern, schnattern; plätschern, murmeln (*of brooks*); stammeln, lallen. **2.** *v.t.* ausschwatzen, ausplappern. **3.** *s.* das Geschwätz, Geplapper, Gestammel; Geplätscher, Gemurmel. **babbler,** *s.* der Schwätzer. **babbling,** *s. See* **babble, 3.**

babe [beib], *s.* (*B., Poet.*) kleines Kind, das Baby, der Säugling.

babel [beibl], *s.* der Lärm, die Verwirrung, das Durcheinander.

baboon [bə'bu:n], *s.* der Pavian; (*coll. of a p.*) Tölpel, Trottel.

baby ['beibi], **1.** *s.* das Kleinkind, Baby; der Säugling; (*fig.*) Kindskopf; (*sl. Am.*) Schatz, Mädchen; (*coll.*) *the – of the family,* der *or* die *or* das Jüngste in der Familie; (*coll.*) *carry* or *hold the* –, den Kopf hinhalten; (*sl.*) *his* –, das, worauf er sich etwas zugute hält; sein ganzer Stolz (*of his car, boat etc.*). **2.** *v.t.* (*coll.*) verzärteln. **3.** *attrib. adj.* (Klein)kinder–, Baby–, Säuglings–; kindisch; Klein–, klein.

baby|-carriage, *s.* der Kinderwagen. **--clothes,** *pl. See* **--linen. --farm,** *s.* das Säuglingsheim. **–grand,** *s.* (*Mus.*) der Stutzflügel.

babyhood ['beibihud], *s.* erste Kindheit, das Säuglingsalter. **babyish** [–iiʃ], *adj.* kindisch, kindhaft, kindlich.

baby|-linen, *s.* das Kinderzeug, die Kinderwäsche. **--sitter,** *s.* der Kinderhüter. **--snatcher,** *s.* der Kinderräuber. **– talk,** *s.* die Babysprache.

baccalaureate [bækə'lɔ:riət], *s.* das Bakkalaureat.

bacchanal ['bækənəl], **1.** *s.* der Bacchant; Bacchuspriester; *see also* **bacchanalia. 2.** *adj.* bacchantisch, schwelgerisch, ausschweifend, trunken. **bacchanalia** [–'neiliə], *pl.* Bacchanalien (*pl.*); die Orgie. **bacchanalian,** *adj. See* **bacchanal, 2.**

baccy ['bæki], *s.* (*coll.*) der Tabak.

bachelor ['bætʃələ], *s.* der Junggeselle, lediger Mann; (*Univ.*) Bakkalaureus; *knight* –, der Ritter (*as title*); *old* –, alter Hagestolz; *–'s button,* der Patentknopf; (*Bot.*) Scharfer Hahnenfuß. **bachelor-girl,** *s.* alleinstehendes Mädchen, die Junggesellin. **bachelorhood,** *s.* der Junggesellenstand; (*Univ.*) das Bakkalaureat.

bacillus [bæ'siləs], *s.* (*pl.* **-li** [–lai]) der Bazillus.

back [bæk], **1.** *s.* der Rücken; das Kreuz (*of a horse*); die Rückseite, Hinterseite; der Hintergrund; (*Footb.*) Verteidiger; die Kehrseite (*of a coin*); Rück(en)lehne (*of a chair*); linke Seite (*of cloth*); der Boden, die Platte (*of a violin*); der Rückenteil (*of a dress*).

(a) (*with nouns*) *in the – of the car,* auf dem Rücksitz des Wagens; *– of the chimney,* die Kaminplatte; *the Backs* (*of the Colleges*), die Parkseite der Cambridger Colleges; *– of the hand,* der Handrücken, die Rückseite der Hand; *– of the head,* der Hinterkopf; *at the – of the house,* hinter dem Haus; *– of the neck,* der Nacken, das Genick; *– of a sword,* der Rücken eines Schwertes.

(b) (*with verbs*) *break his* –, ihm das Rückgrat brechen, (*fig.*) ihn zugrunde richten; (*fig.*) *break the – of a th.,* das Schwerste *or* Schlimmste erledigen *or* hinter sich bringen; *break one's* –, sich (*Dat.*) das Kreuz brechen; *give* or *make a* –, sich bücken; *put one's – into a th.,* sich hinter eine S. (*or* sich dahinter) setzen; *put* or *get his – up,* ihn aufbringen *or* hochbringen *or* reizen *or* ärgern; *turn one's* –, sich umwenden; *turn one's – on him,* sich von ihm abwenden, ihm den Rücken kehren, (*fig.*) ihn im Stich lassen.

(c) (*with preps.*) *at the – of,* hinter (*Dat.*); *at the – of one's mind,* in seinen verborgensten Gedanken; *behind his* –, hinter seinem Rücken, im geheimen, insgeheim; (*coll.*) *like water off a duck's* –, ohne jede Wirkung; *be on one's* –, bettlägerig sein, auf dem Krankenlager liegen; (*coll.*) *have him always on one's* –, ihn dauernd auf dem Hals haben; *he hasn't a shirt to his* –, er hat kein Hemd auf dem Leibe; *– to* –, Rücken an Rücken; (*fig.*) *with one's – to the wall,* in die Enge getrieben, in großer Bedrängnis, hart bedrängt.

2. *adj.* Hinter–, Rück–, hinter, rückwärtig; fern, abgelegen; zurückliegend, rückständig; – ***alley,*** das Seitengäßchen; (*Tenn.*) – ***court,*** hinteres Spielfeld; – ***pay,*** rückständiges Gehalt; (*fig.*) ***take a – seat,*** in den Hintergrund treten, zurückgedrängt werden.

3. *adv.* zurück (*frequently as sep. pref.* zurück–), rückwärts; früher, vorher; hinten; – (***again***), wieder (*frequently as sep. pref.* wieder–), wieder zurück, wiederum; ***I shall be – (again) directly,*** ich bin gleich wieder da; – ***and forth,*** hin und her; ***a few years –,*** vor einigen Jahren; (*coll.*) ***get – at,*** den Spieß umkehren gegen, sich rächen an (*Dat.*), sich schadlos halten an (*Dat.*); ***get one's own –,*** sich rächen an (*Dat.*); ***go – on one's word,*** sein Versprechen nicht einhalten; ***keep – the truth,*** mit der Wahrheit zurückhalten, die Wahrheit für sich behalten; ***lie –,*** sich rückwarts legen; ***pay –,*** zurückbezahlen, (*fig.*) zurückzahlen, heimzahlen, vergelten; ***stand –!*** zurück! ***there and –,*** hin und zurück.

4. *v.t.* 1. (*also* – ***up***) den Rücken decken *or* stärken (*Dat.*), unterstützen, begünstigen, bekräftigen, beistehen (*Dat.*), (*Comm.*) gegenzeichnen, indossieren; 2. setzen *or* wetten auf (*Acc.*); – ***a horse,*** auf ein Pferd setzen *or* wetten; 3. an der Rückseite (ver)stärken (*a picture etc.*), mit einem Rücken *or* einer Lehne versehen (*a chair etc.*); 4. rückwärts fahren lassen (*a vehicle*); – ***the oars,*** see – ***water***; – ***the sails,*** die Segel backholen; – ***water,*** rückwärts rudern.

5. *v.i.* sich zurückbewegen, zurückgehen, zurücktreten, rückwärts gehen *or* fahren; (*Meteor.*) (*of wind*) zurückspringen, rückdrehen; (*coll.*) – ***down,*** abstehen, zurücktreten (***from,*** von), klein beigeben; – ***on to,*** (nach) hinten anstoßen an (*Acc.*); nach hinten blicken auf (*Acc.*) (*of rooms etc.*); – ***out,*** sich zurückziehen (***of, from,*** von *or* aus), zurücktreten (von), (*coll.*) sich drücken (von), kneifen (vor (*Dat.*)).

back|ache, *s.* Rückenschmerzen (*pl.*). **--band.** *s.* der Rückengurt, Kreuzriemen (*of harness*). **--basket,** *s.* die Kiepe, der Tragkorb. **--bencher,** *s.* Abgeordnete(r), der nicht Kabinettsmitglied ist. **-bite, 1.** *irr.v.t.* verleumden, herziehen über (*Acc.*). **2.** *irr.v.i.* nachreden. **-biter,** *s.* der Verleumder. **-biting, 1.** *adj.* verleumderisch. **2.** *s.* die Verleumdung. **--board,** *s.* das Rückenbrett, Lehnbrett, (*Med.*) der Geradehalter (*for improving posture*). **-bone,** *s.* das Rückgrat, die Wirbelsäule, (*fig.*) Willenskraft, Charakterstärke, Festigkeit; (*fig.*) ***to the –,*** bis auf die Knochen, eingefleischt, durch und durch, ganz und gar; (*fig.*) ***he has no –,*** er ist ein Waschlappen. **--breaking,** *adj.* zermürbend, erschöpfend. **--chat,** *s.* gegenseitige Unverschämtheiten, freche Antwort(en). **--cloth,** *s.* (*Theat.*) der Prospekt, die Kulisse. **--country,** *s.* das Hinterland. **--door, 1.** *s.* die Hintertür. **2.** *adj.* hinterlistig, heimlich. **-drop,** *s. See* **--cloth.**

backer ['bækə], *s.* der Helfer, Unterstützer, Beistand; (*Betting*) Wetter; (*Comm.*) Hintermann; Indossierer, Indossant.

back|fire, 1. *v.t.* (*Motor.*) frühzünden; (*guns*) fehlzünden, (*fig.*) fehlschlagen. **2.** *s.* (*Motor.*) die Frühzündung; der Auspuffknall; (*guns*) die Fehlzündung. **--formation,** *s.* (*Philol.*) die Rückbildung. **-gammon,** *s.* das Puffspiel. **-ground,** *s.* der Hintergrund; ***keep in the –,*** im Hintergrund bleiben; (*Rad.*) – ***noise,*** das Störgeräusch, die Geräuschkulisse. **-hand,** *s.* (*Spt.*) die Rückhand; – ***drive,*** der Rückhandschlag. **-hand(ed),** *adj.* mit dem Handrücken (*as a blow*), (*Spt.*) Rückhand–; (*fig.*) zweifelhaft, doppelsinnig; unerwartet, indirekt. **-hander,** *s.* (*coll.*) der Rückhandschlag, (*fig.*) unerwarteter *or* unfairer Angriff.

backing ['bækiŋ], *s.* 1. die Stütze, Hilfe, Unterstützung, (*Comm.*) Deckung, Indossierung; 2. Verstärkung, Ausfütterung; Rückenschicht, Unterlage, das Futter. **backing-plate,** *s.* die Stützplatte.

back|lash, *s.* (*Motor.*) toter Gang; heftiger Rückprall. **-log,** *s.* der Rückstand. **--number,** *s.* alte Nummer *or* Ausgabe (*of a periodical*); (*fig. coll.*) rückständiger Mensch; altmodische Angelegenheit. **--pedal,** *v.i.* (*Cycling*) rückwärtstreten; (*fig.*) einen Rückzieher machen; ***-ling brake,*** die Rücktrittbremse. **--room boy,** *s.* (*coll.*) technischer Experte (der Wehrmacht). **--seat driver,** *s.* der Besserwisser. **-side,** *s.* (*coll.*) das Gesäß, Hintere, der Popo. **-sight,** *s.* das Visier, die Kimme. **-slide,** *irr.v.i.* abfallen, abtrünnig werden; zurückfallen (***into,*** in (*Acc.*)). **-slider,** *s.* Abtrünnige(r), Rückfällige(r). **--somersault,** *s.* der Rückwärtssalto. **--spacer,** *s.* die Rücktaste (*of a typewriter*). **--spin,** *s.* das Rückeffet (*on a ball*). **-stage, 1.** *s.* die Hinterbühne. **2.** *adv.* hinten auf der Bühne. **-stair(s), 1.** *s.* die Hintertreppe, Dienstbotentreppe. **2.** *adj.* Hintertreppen–; hinterlistig. **-stay,** *s.* (*Naut.*) die Pardune. **-stitch,** *s.* der Steppstich. **-stroke,** *s.* der Rückschlag (*in ball games*); das Rückenschwimmen; (*Tech.*) der Rückschlag, Rücklauf. **-talk,** *s.* (*Am.*) *see* **--chat. --up,** *attrib. adj.* Hilfs–, Stütz–.

backward ['bækwəd], **1.** *adj.* spät eintretend *or* reifend, spätreif, zurückgeblieben, rückständig; zögernd, zurückhaltend, schüchtern, scheu; abgeneigt, widerwillig; träge, schwerfällig; rückwärtswirkend, rückwärts gerichtet, Rück–; – ***area,*** rückständige Gegend; – ***children,*** zurückgebliebene Kinder; – ***course,*** der Rücklauf; ***be – in doing one's duty,*** seine Pflicht vernachlässigen; ***he is – in learning,*** das Lernen fällt ihm schwer; ***he is – at school,*** er bleibt in der Schule zurück. **2.** *adv. See* **backwards.**

backwardation [bækwə'deiʃən], *s.* (*Comm.*) der Deport, Kursabschlag.

backwardness ['bækwədnis], *s.* das Zurücksein, Zurückbleiben; die Abgeneigtheit, der Widerwille, das Widerstreben; die Langsamkeit, Trägheit, langsames Wachstum, die Spätreife, Rückständigkeit. **backwards,** *adv.* rückwärts, zurück; rücklings, verkehrt; – ***and forwards,*** hin und her.

back|wash, *s.* (*Naut.*) die Kielwasserströmung, (*fig.*) (unangenehme) Nachwirkung. **-water,** *s.* das Stauwasser, totes Wasser, (*fig.*) rückständiger Ort, die Leere, Öde. **--wheel,** *s.* das Hinterrad. **-woods,** *pl.* Hinterwälder (*pl.*). **-woodsman,** *s.* der Hinterwäldler. **-yard,** *s.* der Hinterhof.

bacon ['beikən], *s.* der Speck; ***flitch of –,*** die Speckseite; ***gammon of –,*** der Schinken; ***rasher of –,*** die Speckschnitte; (*coll.*) ***save one's –,*** sich in Sicherheit bringen, mit heiler Haut davonkommen; (*sl.*) ***bring home the –,*** sich nicht umsonst bemühen. **bacon-rind,** *s.* die Speckschwarte.

bacteria [bæk'tiəriə], *pl. of* **bacterium. bacterial,** *adj.* Bakterien–. **bacteriologist** [-ri'ɔlədʒist], *s.* der Bakteriologe, Bakterienforscher. **bacteriology** [-i'ɔlədʒi], *s.* die Bakterienkunde, Bakteriologie. **bacterium,** *s.* (*usu. pl.* **-ia**) die Bakterie, der Spaltpilz.

bad [bæd], **1.** *adj.* schlecht, schlimm, arg, böse; (*as children*) böse, ungezogen; (*as influences*) übel, schädlich, ungesund; (*as foodstuff*) schlecht, verdorben, faul; (*ill-health*) krank, unwohl; – ***arm,*** kranker Arm; – ***bargain,*** schlechtes Geschäft; (*fig.*) – ***blood,*** der Groll, böses Blut; ***in his – books,*** schlecht bei ihm angeschrieben; – ***coin,*** falsche Münze; – ***cold,*** starke Erkältung, heftiger Schnupfen; – ***debts,*** nicht einziehbare Außenstände; – ***egg,*** faules Ei, (*fig., coll.*) übler Bursche *or* Kunde; – ***form,*** schlechte Manieren; ***it's – form,*** das schickt sich nicht; ***with a – grace,*** widerwillig, unfreundlich; – ***headache,*** übles Kopfweh; (*sl.*) – ***hat,*** see – ***egg*** (*fig.*); – ***heart,*** angegriffenes Herz; (*coll.*) – ***job,*** schlimmer Handel; – ***language,*** Flüche, Fluchworte; Zoten (*pl.*); – ***luck,*** das Unglück, (*coll.*) Pech; – ***news,*** schlechte Nachricht(en); (*coll.*) – ***shot,*** falsche Vermutung; (*coll.*) ***in a – way,*** in schlechten Verhältnissen; sehr krank; – ***ways,*** schlechte Angewohnheiten; ***he is too –,*** er treibt es zu bunt; ***that is too –,*** das ist zu dumm; (*coll.*) ***that is not –,*** das ist nicht übel; ***it was too – of you,*** es war nicht schön von dir; ***feel – about,*** sich ärgern über (*Acc.*); ***go –,*** verderben, verfallen. **2.** *s.* ***be £100 to the –,*** hundert Pfund

Verlust haben; ***from – to worse,*** schlimmer und schlimmer, immer schlimmer; (*coll.*) ***go to the –,*** auf die schiefe Bahn *or* auf Abwege geraten; ***take the – with the good,*** das Unangenehme hinnehmen.

bade [bæd], *imperf. of* **bid.**

badge [bædʒ], *s.* das Abzeichen, Rangabzeichen, Dienstabzeichen; die Marke, das Merkmal, Kennzeichen; (*Mil.*) die Auszeichnung, (Verdienst)-medaille.

badger ['bædʒə], **1.** *s.* (*Zool.*) der Dachs. **2.** *v.t.* (*coll.*) hetzen, plagen, belästigen.

badinage ['bædina:ʒ], *s.* der Scherz, die Neckerei, Schäkerei.

badly ['bædli], *adv.* schlecht, schlimm, (*coll.*) ernstlich, dringend, sehr; ***– needed*** or ***wanted,*** dringend erforderlich; ***be – in need*** or ***want of,*** dringend *or* nötig brauchen, sehr benötigen; ***he is – off, things go – with him,*** es geht ihm sehr schlecht, er ist übel daran.

badminton ['bædmintən], *s.* das Federballspiel.

badness ['bædnis], *s.* die Schlechtigkeit, Bösartigkeit; Schädlichkeit, Verderbtheit, schlechter Zustand.

baffle [bæfl], **1.** *v.t.* vereiteln; verwirren; (*obs.*) täuschen; ***it –s description,*** das spottet jeder Beschreibung; ***– his designs,*** seine Pläne durchkreuzen *or* vereiteln *or* zuschanden machen; ***– pursuit,*** die Verfolgung hindern; ***he was –d,*** es war ihm ein Rätsel. **2.** *s.* der (Schall)dämpfer, die Schallwand (*of loudspeaker*). **baffle|-paint,** *s.* der Tarnanstrich. **– plate,** *s.* die Ablenkplatte. **baffling,** *adj.* unverständlich, täuschend, verwirrend; vereitelnd, hinderlich; ***– winds,*** unstete Winde.

bag [bæg], **1.** *s.* der Beutel, Sack; die (Hand–, Reise– *or* Schul)tasche; (*Hunt.*) (Jagd)beute; (*sl.*) Schlampe; *pl.* (*coll.*) Hose(n); (*coll.*) ***with – and baggage,*** mit Sack und Pack, mit allem Drum und Dran; (*coll.*) ***– of bones,*** das Knochengerippe; ***let the cat out of the –,*** die Katze aus dem Sack lassen; ***Gladstone –,*** die Herrenreisetasche; ***make a good –,*** viel Jagdglück haben, viel Wild erlegen; ***lucky –,*** die Glückstüte; ***paper –,*** die Tüte; (*coll.*) ***the whole – of tricks,*** der ganze Kram; (*coll.*) ***it's in the –,*** es ist so gut wie sicher; das haben wir in der Tasche; ***– of wool,*** der Ballen Wolle (= *240 Pfd.*). **2.** *v.t.* einsacken, in einen Sack stecken; (*Hunt.*) erlegen, (*also fig.*) fangen, zur Strecke bringen; (*sl.*) beanspruchen, für sich in Anspruch nehmen. **3.** *v.i.* sich bauschen, aufschwellen, (*of clothes*) wie ein Sack sitzen, lose hängen.

bagasse [bə'gæs], *s.* Zuckerrohrrückstände (*pl.*).

bagatelle [bægə'tel], *s.* die Kleinigkeit, Lappalie, (*also Mus.*) Bagatelle; das Tivolispiel.

bagful ['bægful], *s.* der Sackvoll; ***in –s,*** sackweise.

baggage ['bægidʒ], *s.* das Gepäck, (*Am.*) Reisegepäck; (*Mil.*) der Troß, die Bagage; (*sl.*) (liederliches) Frauenzimmer, das Weibsbild; (*coll.*) der Fratz; ***bag and –,*** *see under* **bag. baggage| car,** *s.* (*Am.*) der Gepäckwagen. **– train,** *s.* (*Mil.*) der Troß.

bagginess ['bæginis], *s.* die Bauschigkeit, Aufgebauschtheit. **bagging, 1.** *s.* 1. das Einsacken, Einpacken in Säcke; 2. Aufbauschen, sackartiges Herabhängen; 3. die Packleinwand. **2.** *adj.* sich bauschend, ausbauschend, sackartig herabhängend. **baggy,** *adj.* bauschig, sackartig, aufgebauscht; *see also* **bagging, 2. bagman,** *s.* (*obs.*) Handlungsreisende(r).

bagnio ['bænjou], *s.* das Bad(ehaus); (*obs.*) Bordell; (Sklaven)gefängnis.

bagpipe ['bægpaip], *s.* der Dudelsack, die Sackpfeife. **bagpiper,** *s.* der Dudelsackpfeifer.

[1]**bail** [beil], **1.** *s.* die Bürgschaft, Kaution, Sicherheitsleistung; ***allow –,*** Bürgschaft zulassen; ***be (let) out on –,*** gegen Kaution auf freiem Fuß sein; ***find –,*** sich (*Dat.*) Bürgen verschaffen; ***forfeit one's –,*** die Kaution verfallen lassen; ***give –,*** eine Kaution hinterlegen; einen Bürgen stellen; ***go*** or ***stand – for him,*** für ihn Bürge sein *or* Bürgschaft leisten; ***let him out on –,*** ihn gegen Bürgschaft freilassen; ***refuse –,*** Bürgschaft ablehnen. **2.** *v.t.* 1. (*Comm.*) kontraktlich übergeben, hinterlegen, deponieren (*goods*); 2. (*obs.*) *see* ***let him out on –***; 3. (*obs.*) (*also – out*) durch Bürgschaft (aus der Haft) befreien.

[2]**bail,** *s.* der Henkel, (Hand)griff; Bügel, Reif(en); (*Crick.*) das Querholz.

[3]**bail, 1.** *v.t.* (*also – out*) ausschöpfen (*a boat, water from a boat*). **2.** *v.i.* (*coll.*) (*Av.*) ***– out,*** (mit dem Fallschirm) abspringen, aussteigen. *Also* **bale.**

bailable ['beiləbl], *adj.* 1. (*a p.*) gegen Bürgschaft freizulassen(d); 2. (*offence*) eine Entlassung gegen Bürgschaft zulassend. **bailee** [bei'li:], *s.* (*Law*) der Rechtsinhaber; Bewahrer, Depositar.

bailer ['beilə], *s.* der Schöpfeimer.

bailey ['beili], *s.* (*Hist.*) der Außenhof, Zwinger.

Bailey bridge, *s.* die Bailey-Behelfsbrücke.

bailie ['beili], *s.* (*Scots*) Stadtverordnete(r), das Magistratsmitglied.

bailiff ['beilif], *s.* 1. der Gerichtsdiener, Gerichtsvollstrecker, Büttel; 2. (Guts)verwalter, Inspektor; 3. Amtmann, Landvogt. **bailiwick** ['beiliwik], *s.* der Amtsbezirk; die Vogtei.

bailment ['beilmənt], *s.* 1. *See* [1]**bail, 1**; 2. die Freilassung gegen Bürgschaft. **bailor,** *s.* (*Law*) der Deponent, Hinterleger.

bairn [bɛən], *s.* (*Scots*) das Kind.

bait [beit], **1.** *s.* 1. der Köder, die Lockspeise; (*fig.*) der Köder, Reiz, die Lockung; ***take the –,*** sich ködern lassen, (*fig.*) in die Falle *or* auf den Leim gehen; 2. die Rast, Erfrischung(spause), der Imbiß. **2.** *v.t.* 1. (*a trap*) mit einem Köder versehen, (*fig.*) ködern, (an)locken; 2. (*Hunt.*) mit Hunden hetzen, (*fig.*) hetzen, plagen, quälen; 3. füttern und tränken (*horses*). **3.** *v.i.* Rast machen, einen Imbiß einnehmen; (*of horses*) futtern, fressen. **baiting,** *s.* 1. das Ködern; 2. Rastmachen, Einkehren, (*of horses*) Füttern; 3. (*fig.*) die Quälerei, Hetze. **baiting-place,** *s.* die Einkehr, der Ausspann.

baize [beiz], *s.* der Boi, Fries.

bake [beik], **1.** *v.t.* (*Cul.*) backen, im Ofen braten; (*bricks*) brennen; (*coll.*) ***half-–d,*** unreif, blöde. **2.** *v.i.* backen, gebacken werden; dörren, hart werden.

bakelite ['beikəlait], *s.* (*reg. trade name*) das Bakelit.

baker ['beikə], *s.* der Bäcker; ***–'s dozen,*** dreizehn (Stück); ***–'s (shop),*** die Bäckerei, der Bäckerladen. **bakery,** *s.* die Bäckerei. **baking, 1.** *s.* das Backen, (*of bricks*) Brennen; der Schub; ***at one –,*** auf einen Schub. **2.** *adj.,adv.* ***– (hot),*** glühend heiß. **baking|-powder,** *s.* das Backpulver. **–-soda,** *s.* das Natriumbikarbonat.

Balaam ['beilæm], *s.* (*B.*) Bileam (*m.*).

balance ['bæləns], **1.** *s.* 1. die Waage (*also Astr.*); (*Tech.*) ***hydrostatic –,*** die Senkwaage; 2. das Gleichgewicht (*also fig.*); (*fig.*) der Gleichmut, die (Gemüts)ruhe, Fassung; (*Art etc.*) Ausgewogenheit; ***– of mind,*** seelisches Gleichgewicht; ***– of power,*** politisches *or* internationales Gleichgewicht, das Gleichgewicht der Kräfte; ***adjust the –,*** das Gleichgewicht herstellen; ***hold the –,*** das Gleichgewicht bewahren, (*fig.*) das Zünglein an der Waage bilden; ***lose one's –,*** das Gleichgewicht verlieren, (*fig.*) die Fassung verlieren; ***throw him off his –,*** ihn aus dem Gleichgewicht bringen; ***tip*** or ***turn the –,*** den Ausschlag geben; (*fig.*) ***in the –,*** in der Schwebe; (*fig.*) ***on –,*** alles in allem genommen, wenn man alles berücksichtigt, nach gründlicher Überlegung; 3. das Gegengewicht, (*of clocks*) die Unruhe; 4. (*Comm.*) Bilanze, der Rechnungsabschluß; (Rechnungs)saldo, Kontostand, Bestand, Überschuß; (*coll.*) (Über)rest; ***– of accounts,*** der Rechnungsabschluß, die Bilanz; ***– at the bank,*** das Bankguthaben; ***– in cash,*** der Barbestand; ***– in favour,*** das Saldoguthaben; ***– in hand,*** der Kassenbestand, Überschuß; ***– of payments,*** die Zahlungsbilanz; ***– of trade,*** die Handelsbilanz; ***adverse –,*** die Unterbilanz; ***– carried forward,*** der Saldovortrag; ***– due,*** der Debitsaldo; ***show a –,*** einen Saldo aufweisen; ***strike a –,*** den Saldo *or* die Bilanz ziehen.

2. *v.t.* 1. im Gleichgewicht halten, ins Gleichgewicht bringen, ausgleichen, aufwiegen, (*a wheel*)

auswuchten, (*Elec.*) ausbalancieren, abgleichen; ***more than -d by,*** überwogen durch; 2. (*fig.*) (*in one's mind*) wägen, erwägen, abwägen; ***- one th. against another,*** eine S. gegen die andere aufrechnen *or* abwägen; 3. (*Comm.*) begleichen, saldieren, bilanzieren; ***to - your account,*** zum Ausgleich ihrer Rechnung; ***- the ledger,*** das Hauptbuch abschließen; ***the expenses - the receipts,*** die Ausgaben stehen mit den Einnahmen gleich.
3. *v.i.* im Gleichgewicht sein, sich im Gleichgewicht halten; sich ausgleichen, balancieren; (*Comm.*) Bilanz machen.

balanced ['bælənst], *adj.* ausgewogen, ausgeglichen, im Gleichgewicht; ***- diet,*** ausgeglichene Kost. **balancer,** *s.* (*Tech.*) der Schwinghebel, Stabilisator, (*Elec.*) Ausgleichsregler; (*Ent.*) Schwingkölbchen.

balance|-sheet, *s.* der Rechnungsabschluß, Bilanzbogen, die Bilanzaufstellung, Kassenübersicht. **--spring,** *s.* die Unruhefeder. **--weight,** *s.* das Gegengewicht. **--wheel,** *s.* die Unruhe, das Hemmungsrad.

balancing ['bælənsiŋ], *s.* die Ausbalancierung, Ausgleichung, Kompensation; Aufrechnung, Anrechnung; (*Comm.*) das Saldieren, Bilanzieren; (*Elec.*) Abgleichen, der Abgleich; (*of a wheel*) das Auswuchten.

balcony ['bælkəni], *s.* der Balkon; Altan, Söller, (*Naut.*) die Achtergalerie, (*Theat.*) zweiter Rang.

bald [bɔ:ld], *adj.* kahl(köpfig), unbehaart; (*fig.*) kahl, nackt, schmucklos, nüchtern, dürftig, armselig; ***- lie,*** glatte Lüge; ***- translation,*** dürftige Übersetzung; ***- truth,*** nackte Wahrheit.

baldachin ['bældəkin], *s.* der Baldachin, Thronhimmel, Traghimmel.

balderdash ['bɔ:ldədæʃ], *s.* (*coll.*) der Quatsch, das Geschwätz.

bald|head, *s.* der Kahlkopf, Glatzkopf. **-headed,** *adj.* kahlköpfig; (*coll.*) ***go - for*** or ***at it,*** sich Hals über Kopf hineinstürzen *or* darauf stürzen. **baldly,** *adv.* (*fig.*) knapp, kahl, schmucklos; geradezu, schlechtweg, unverblümt, ungeschminkt. **baldness,** *s.* die Kahlheit, (*fig.*) Dürftigkeit, Nüchternheit, Schmucklosigkeit. **bald|-pate,** *s.* 1. *See* **-head**; 2. (*Orn.*) *see* ***American wigeon.***

baldric ['bɔ:ldrik], *s,* der Gürtel, das Wehrgehänge, Wehrgehenk.

[1]**bale** [beil], **1.** *s.* der Ballen. **2.** *v.t.* in Ballen verpacken, emballieren.

[2]**bale,** *s.* (*obs.*) das Elend, Leid, Weh, die Qual; Not, das Unglück, Unheil.

[3]**bale,** *v.t., v.i. See* [3]**bail.**

Balearic Islands [bæli'ærik], *pl.* die Balearen (*pl.*).

balefire ['beilfaiə], *s.* das Signalfeuer; Freudenfeuer; (*obs.*) der Scheiterhaufen.

baleful ['beilful], *adj.* unheilvoll, verderblich; (*obs.*) elend, kläglich.

balk [bɔ:k], **1.** *s.* der (Furchen)rain; (*Archit.*) (Haupt)balken, Spannbalken; (*Bill.*) Kessel, das Quartier; (*fig.*) Hindernis; (*Bill.*) ***miss-in--,*** absichtlicher Fehlstoß. **2.** *v.t.* aufhalten, hemmen, hindern; vereiteln, durchkreuzen; ausweichen, umgehen, meiden. **3.** *v.i.* (plötzlich) anhalten, stocken, stutzen, (*of horse*) störrisch werden, scheuen (*at,* vor (*Dat.*)).

Balkan ['bɔ:lkən], **1.** *adj.* Balkan-. **2.** ***the -s,*** der Balkan, die Balkanstaaten.

balk-line, *s.* (*Bill.*) die Feldlinie.

[1]**ball** [bɔ:l], **1.** *s.* der Ball; die Kugel (*also of guns*); der Ballen (*also Anat.*); (*of wool etc.*) Knäuel; *pl.* (*vulg.*) Eier, (*as exclamation*) Quatsch! ***- and chain,*** die Kugel- und Kettenfessel; (*sl.*) der Klotz am Bein; ***- of the eye,*** der Augapfel; ***- of the foot,*** der Fußballen; ***- and socket joint,*** das Kugelgelenk; ***- of the thumb,*** der Handballen; (*coll.*) ***have the - at one's feet,*** Herr der Situation sein, das Spiel in der Hand haben; (*fig.*) ***keep the - rolling,*** das Gespräch in Gang halten; (*Bill.*) ***miss the -,*** einen Kicks machen; (*Crick.*) ***no -,*** spielwidriger Wurf; (*sl.*) ***play -,*** mitwirken, mitspielen, zueinander halten; (*sl.*) ***play - with him,*** es ehrlich mit ihm meinen; (*Bill.*) ***pocket a -,*** einen Ball machen, ins Loch spielen; (*fig.*) ***set the - rolling,*** es in Gang bringen; ***have a game of -,*** Ball spielen; (*fig.*) ***keep one's eye on the -,*** auf dem Damm sein; (*sl.*) ***be on the -,*** auf Draht sein; (*Mil.*) ***load with -,*** scharf laden. **2.** *v.t.* zusammenballen; (*sl.*) ***- up,*** durcheinanderbringen, hoffnungslos verwirren.

[2]**ball,** *s.* der Ball, die Tanzgesellschaft; ***fancy-dress -,*** der Kostümball; ***masked -,*** der Maskenball.

ballad ['bæləd], *s.* die Ballade. **ballad| concert,** *s.* der Liederabend. **--monger,** *s.* der Bänkelsänger.

ballast ['bæləst], **1.** *s.* (*Naut.*) der Ballast, (*Railw. etc.*) die Bettung, das Bettungsmaterial, der (Stein)-schotter; (*Naut.*) ***in -,*** ohne Ladung; (*fig.*) ***mental -,*** innere Festigkeit, sittlicher Halt; ***- tank,*** die Tauchzelle (*submarine*). **2.** *v.t.* ballasten, mit Ballast beladen; (*Railw. etc.*) beschottern; (*fig.*) im Gleichgewicht halten.

ball|-bearing, *s.* das Kugellager. **--boy,** *s.* (*Tenn.*) der Balljunge. **--cartridge,** *s.* die Kugelpatrone, Vollpatrone. **--cock,** *s.* der Schwimmerhahn, das Schwimmerventil. **- control,** *s.* (*Footb.*) die Ballbeherrschung.

ballet ['bælei], *s.* das Ballett.

ball game, *s.* das Ballspiel, (*usu.*) Baseballspiel.

ballista [bə'listə], *s.* (*Hist.*) das Wurfgeschütz, die Balliste.

ballistic [bə'listik], *adj.* ballistisch. **ballistics,** *pl.* (*sing. constr.*) die Ballistik, Schießlehre.

ball|-joint, *s.* das Kugelgelenk. **--journal,** *s.* der Kugelzapfen.

balloon [bə'lu:n], **1.** *s.* der Ballon, Luftballon; (*Chem.*) Rezipient; (*Archit.*) die Kugel; ***barrage -,*** der Sperrballon; ***captive -,*** der Fesselballon; ***pilot -,*** der Registrierballon; ***- barrage,*** die Ballonsperre; ***- tyre,*** der Ballonreifen. **2.** *v.i.* aufschwellen, sich blähen. **3.** *v.t.* (*Spt.*) (*sl.*) hoch in die Luft schlagen.

ballot ['bælət], **1.** *s.* die Wahlkugel, der Wahl- *or* Stimmzettel; geheime Abstimmung; die Gesamtzahl der abgegebenen Stimmen; ***by -,*** durch (geheime) Abstimmung; ***second*** (or ***final***) ***-,*** die Stichwahl. **2.** *v.i.* abstimmen, wählen; ***- for,*** abstimmen über (*Acc.*), losen um. **ballot|-box,** *s.* die Wahlurne. **--paper,** *s.* der Stimmzettel, Wahlzettel, Wahlschein, Wählerschein.

ball|-point pen, *s.* der Kugelschreiber. **--race,** *s.* der Kugellagerring.

ballroom ['bɔ:lru:m], *s.* der Tanzsaal. **ballroom dancing,** *s.* der Gesellschaftstanz.

bally ['bæli], *adj.* (*sl.*) verdammt, verflixt. **ballyhoo** [-'hu:], *s.* (*sl.*) das Tamtam, Reklamegeschrei, der Reklamerummel.

balm [bɑ:m], *s.* der Balsam; (*Bot.*) die Melisse; (*fig.*) der Trost, die Linderung. **balmy,** *adj.* balsamisch; heilend, lindernd; (*of weather*) mild, lind.

balsam ['bɔ:lsəm], *s.* der Balsam; (*Bot.*) das Springkraut, die Balsamine. **balsamic** [-'sæmik], *adj.* lindernd, erquickend, balsamisch.

balsa(wood) ['bɔ:lsəwud], *s.* das Balsa(holz).

Baltic ['bɔ:ltik], **1.** *s.* - (***Sea***), die Ostsee. **2.** *adj.* Ostsee-, baltisch; ***- provinces,*** das Baltikum.

baluster ['bæləstə], *s.* die Geländersäule, Geländerdocke. **balustrade** [-'treid], *s.* die Brüstung, das (Treppen)geländer.

bamboo [bæm'bu:], *s.* der Bambus, das Bambusrohr; ***- cane,*** der Bambusstock.

bamboozle [bæm'bu:zl], *v.t.* (*coll.*) beschwindeln, beschummeln, beschuppen; verwirren, verblüffen.

ban [bæn], **1.** *s.* (amtliches) Verbot; der Bann, die Acht, Verbannung, Landesverweisung; (*Eccl.*) der (Kirchen)bann, das Anathem; (*fig.*) der Fluch; Verwünschung, Ächtung; ***under a -,*** verboten; geächtet; (*Hist.*) ***laid*** or ***placed under the - of the empire,*** in die Reichsacht erklärt *or* getan. **2.** *v.t.* verbieten (*a p., Dat.*); ***- him from speaking,*** ihm verbieten zu sprechen; – ***a play,*** ein Schauspiel verbieten; – ***him from the place,*** ihm den Ort verbieten.

banal [bə'nɑ:l], *adj.* abgedroschen, alltäglich, banal. **banality** [bə'næliti], *s.* die Alltäglichkeit, Banalität; der Gemeinplatz.

banana [bə'nɑ:nə], *s.* die Banane.

[1]**band** [bænd], *s.* das Band, die Bande, der Bund; die Schnur; (*Bookb.*) Heftschnur; Borte, Leiste, der Reifen, Streifen; (*Mech.*) Lauf- *or* Treibriemen; ***endless –,*** das Band ohne Ende; (*Rad.*) ***frequency*** or ***wave*** –, das Frequenzband; ***rubber –,*** das Gummiband.

[2]**band, 1.** *s.* 1. die Bande, Gruppe, Schar, Kompagnie, Truppe; – ***of robbers,*** die Räuberbande; 2. die (Musik)kapelle, das (Unterhaltungs)-orchester, (*Mil.*) Musikkorps, die Regimentsmusik; ***German –,*** umherziehende Musikanten. **2.** *v.i.* (*v.t.*) – (***themselves***) ***together,*** sich zusammentun *or* vereinigen *or* verbinden.

bandage ['bændidʒ], **1.** *s.* der Verband, die Binde, Bandage. **2.** *v.t.* verbinden.

bandanna [bæn'dænə], *s.* buntes Kopftuch.

band|box, *s.* die Hutschachtel; (*fig.*) ***as if come out of the –,*** wie aus dem Ei gepellt. **--conveyor,** *s.* das Fließband, Transportband.

bandeau ['bændou], *s.* (*pl.* **-x** [–z]) das Stirnband, die Kopfbinde.

banderol(e) ['bændəroul], *s.* (*Hist.*) das (Lanzen)-fähnlein; (*Her.*) der Wimpel; (*Archit.*) das Inschriftenband, Spruchband.

bandit ['bændit], *s.* der Bandit, Räuber; (*Av.*) (*sl.*) feindlicher Flieger. **banditry,** *s.* (*collect.*) Räuber, Banditen (*pl.*); das Banditenwesen. **banditti** [–'diti], *pl.* die Räuberbande.

bandmaster ['bændmɑ:stə], *s.* der Kapellmeister, Musikmeister.

bandog ['bændɔg], *s.* der Kettenhund, Bullenbeißer.

bandoleer [bændə'liə], *s.* der Patronengurt, die Patronentasche, das Bandelier.

band|-pass filter, *s.* (*Rad.*) das Bandfilter, die Siebkette. **--saw,** *s.* die Bandsäge.

bandsman ['bændzmən], *s.* der (Militär)musiker, Spielmann.

band|-spread, *s.* (*Rad.*) die Bandspreizung. **–stand,** *s.* der Musikpavillon. **--wagon,** *s.* (*fig., coll.*) die Woge der Volksgunst; ***jump on the –,*** sich dem Sieger anschließen, zur Siegerpartei umschwenken.

[1]**bandy** ['bændi], *v.t.* wechseln, (aus)tauschen, sich (*Dat.*) zuwerfen (*words, glances etc.*), hin- und herschleudern (*a ball etc.*); – ***words,*** hin- und herstreiten; ***her name was freely bandied about,*** ihr Name war in aller Leute Munde.

[2]**bandy(-legged),** *adj.* krummbeinig, O-beinig.

bane [bein], *s.* das Gift (*only in compounds, e.g.* rats–, Rattengift); (*fig.*) Verderben; ***he was the – of her existence,*** er war der Fluch ihres Lebens. **baneful,** *adj.* verderblich, tödlich; giftig.

[1]**bang** [bæŋ], **1.** *s.* schallender Schlag, der Schall, Knall, Krach, (*coll.*) Bums; (*coll., fig.*) Schwung; – ***on the head,*** der Schlag auf dem Kopf; ***it went off with a –,*** es knallte los. **2.** *int.* bums! (*coll.*) – ***went all my money,*** bums war mein Geld weg; – ***went the door,*** bums flog die Tür zu. **3.** *v.t.* schlagen; – ***the table with one's fist,*** – ***one's fist on the table,*** mit der Faust auf den Tisch schlagen; – ***the door*** (***to***), die Tür (heftig) zuschlagen; – ***about,*** unsanft behandeln, mißhandeln; – ***sense into him,*** ihm Vernunft einhämmern *or* einbleuen; – ***off fireworks,*** das Feuerwerk losknallen. **4.** *v.i.* schallen, knallen; (*as a door*) zuknallen, zuschlagen; – ***away,*** drauflosknallen.

[2]**bang, 1.** *s.* die Ponyfrisur. **2.** *v.t.* stutzen, kurz abschneiden (*hair*).

banger ['bæŋə], *s.* 1. der Knallkörper; 2. (*sl.*) die Mordslüge; 3. (*sl.*) Wurst.

bangle [bæŋgl], *s.* der Arm- *or* Fußring, Armreif, das Armband; die Spange.

banian ['bænjən], *s.* indischer Kaufmann, der Händler. **banian-days,** *s.* (*Naut.*) fleischloser Tag, der Fasttag.

banish ['bæniʃ], *v.t.* verbannen, ausweisen (***from,*** aus), (*fig.*) vertreiben, verscheuchen, bannen; – ***him*** (***from the country***), ihn des Landes verweisen; – ***the thought of s.th.,*** sich (*Dat.*) etwas aus dem Sinne schlagen. **banishment,** *s.* die Verbannung, Ausweisung, (*fig.*) Vertreibung.

banister ['bænistə], *s.* der Geländerstab, die Geländersäule; *pl.* das Treppengeländer.

banjo ['bændʒou], *s.* das Banjo.

[1]**bank** ['bænk], **1.** *s.* der Damm, Deich, die Böschung, der Erdwall; (*of rivers, lakes*) das Ufer, Gestade; (*of a corner*) die Überhöhung; (*dial.*) Anhöhe, der Abhang; (*Av.*) die Querneigung, Querlage; (*Bill.*) Bande; – ***of sand,*** die Sandbank; – ***of clouds,*** die Wolkenbank, Wolkenwand. **2.** *v.t.* eindämmen, aufhäufen; überhöhen (*a corner*); (*Av.*) in Schräglage bringen, in die Kurve legen; – ***up the fire,*** das Feuer belegen. **3.** *v.i.* (*Av.*) in die Kurve *or* Schräglage gehen; – ***up,*** eine Bank bilden, sich aufhäufen (*as clouds*).

[2]**bank, 1.** *s.* (*Comm., Cards*) die Bank; ***branch –,*** die Filialbank; ***he is at the –,*** er ist auf der Bank; ***break the –,*** die Bank sprengen; – ***of circulation,*** die Girobank; – ***of deposit,*** die Depositenbank; ***deposit money in the –,*** Geld in *or* bei der Bank deponieren; (*Cards*) ***go –,*** Bank setzen; – ***of issue,*** die Notenbank; ***joint-stock –,*** die Aktienbank; ***savings –,*** die Sparkasse. **2.** *v.t.* in *or* bei der Bank deponieren, auf die Bank bringen. **3.** *v.i.* Bankgeschäfte machen; ein Bankkonto haben (***with,*** bei); (*coll.*) – ***on,*** zählen *or* bauen *or* sich verlassen auf (*Acc.*).

bankable ['bæŋkəbl], *adj.* diskontierbar, bankfähig. **bank|-account,** *s.* das Bankkonto, Bankguthaben; ***open a –,*** ein Konto einrichten. **--bill,** *s.* der Bankwechsel. **--book,** *s.* das Kontobuch. **--clerk,** *s.* Bankbeamte(r), Bankangestellte(r). **banker,** *s.* der Bankier; (*Cards*) Bankhalter; ***–'s order,*** der Zahlungsauftrag an die Bank. **bank holiday,** *s.* der Bankfeiertag.

[1]**banking** ['bæŋkiŋ], *s.* (*Av.*) die Querneigung, Schräglage.

[2]**banking,** *s.* das Bankwesen, Bankgeschäft, der Geldhandel; ***--house,*** die Bank.

bank|-note, *s.* die Banknote, der Geldschein. **--paper,** *s.* das Bankpostpapier. **--rate,** *s.* der Bankdiskont. Diskontsatz, amtlicher Zinsfuß. **--roll,** *s.* (*Am.*) der Stoß Banknoten.

bankrupt ['bæŋkrʌpt], **1.** *s.* der Bankrotteur, Zahlungsunfähige(r); ***–'s creditor,*** der Konkursgläubiger; ***–'s assets*** or ***estate,*** die Konkursmasse. **2.** *adj.* bank(e)rott, zahlungsunfähig, (*coll.*) pleite; (*fig.*) arm (***in,*** an (*Dat.*)); ***go –,*** Konkurs machen, (*coll.*) Pleite gehen *or* machen; ***declare o.s. –,*** den Konkurs anmelden; – ***in health,*** am Ende mit seiner Gesundheit. **3.** *v.t.* bankrott machen, zugrunde richten (*a p.*). **bankruptcy** [–rəpsi], *s.* die Zahlungseinstellung, der Bank(e)rott, Konkurs; (*fig.*) Ruin, Schiffbruch; ***court of –,*** das Konkursgericht; ***file a petition in –,*** den Konkurs anmelden.

bank swallow, *s.* (*Am.*) *see* **sandmartin.**

banner ['bænə], **1.** *s.* die Fahne; das Banner, Panier (*also fig.*); (*Bot.*) Fähnchen. **2.** *attrib. adj.* (*Am.*) führend, hervorragend. **banneret,** *s.* (*Hist.*) der Bannerherr. **banner|-line,** *s.* (*Am.*) die Schlagzeile. **– screen,** *s.* der Ofenschirm, Kaminschirm.

bannister, *s. See* **banister.**

bannock ['bænək], *s.* (*Scots.*) der Haferkuchen.

banns [bænz], *pl.* das Heiratsaufgebot; ***their – have been published,*** sie sind aufgeboten worden; ***forbid the –,*** gegen die Heirat Einspruch erheben.

banquet ['bæŋkwit], **1.** *s.* das Gastmahl, Festessen, Bankett. **2.** *v.i.* schmausen, bankettieren.

banquette [bæŋ'ket], *s.* 1. (*Mil.*) der Auftritt, die Grabenstufe, der Schützenstand; 2. (*Railw. etc.*) die Bankette, Bahnböschung; (*Am.*) der Gehweg, Bürgersteig.

banquetter, *s.* der Schmauser, Festteilnehmer.

banshee ['bænʃiː], *s.* (*Scots, Irish*) die (Todes)fee, todverkündender Geist.

bantam ['bæntəm], **1.** *s.* das Bantamhuhn, Zwerghuhn; (*fig.*) der Knirps. **2.** *pred. adj.* Zwerg–, (*fig.*) winzig. **bantam-weight,** *s.* (*Spt.*) das Bantamgewicht; der Bantamgewichtler.

banter ['bæntə], **1.** *s.* die Neckerei, der Scherz. **2.** *v.t., v.i.* necken, hänseln, aufziehen; (*Am.*) auffordern, herausfordern (*for*, zu).

bantling ['bæntliŋ], *s.* kleines Kind, der Balg.

banyan(-tree) ['bænjən], *s.* indischer Feigenbaum (*Ficus bengalensis*).

baptism ['bæptizm], *s.* die Taufe; ***certificate of –***, der Taufschein; ***– of fire,*** die Feuertaufe; ***private –***, die Haustaufe. **baptismal** [–'tizməl], *adj.* Tauf–; ***– font,*** der Taufstein, das Taufbecken. **Baptist,** *s.* der (die) Täufer(in); Baptist; ***John the –,*** Johannes der Täufer. **baptistery** [–tistri], *s.* die Taufkapelle; der Taufstein. **baptize** [–'taiz], *v.t.* taufen, (*fig.*) einen Namen geben (*Dat.*).

bar [bɑː], **1.** *s.* 1. die Stange, Barre, der Stab; Riegel, Querbalken; die Barriere, Schranke; (*Naut.*) Barre, Sandbank (am Hafeneingang); ***–s,*** das Gitter; ***– of chocolate,*** die Stange *or* der Riegel Schokolade; ***– of gold,*** die Goldbarre; ***– of a grate,*** der Roststab; ***harbour –,*** die Hafenbarre; ***– of iron,*** die Eisenstange; (*Motor.*) ***torsion –,*** der Drillstab; ***– of wood,*** der Holzstab; (*Naut.*) ***cross the –,*** in einen Hafen einlaufen; (*Gymn.*) ***horizontal –(s),*** das Reck; (*Gymn.*) ***parallel –s,*** der Barren; ***window –s,*** Fensterstäbe (*pl.*), das Fenstergitter; 2. (*fig.*) das Hindernis (*to*, für), die Schranke (gegen), der Querstrich; ***colour –,*** der Ausschluß von Farbigen; 3. (*Law*) der Anwaltsstand, die Gerichtsschranke, das Gericht; die (Rechts)anwaltschaft, Advokatur; ***the bench and the –,*** Richter und Advokaten; ***the – of God,*** Jüngstes Gericht; ***the prisoner at the –,*** der *or* die Gefangene vor den Schranken; ***he is at the –,*** er ist Anwalt; ***bring before the – of public opinion,*** vor die Schranke der Öffentlichkeit bringen; ***he was called to the –,*** er wurde als Anwalt zugelassen; ***he was educated for the –,*** er hat Jura studiert; 4. der Streifen, (dicker) Strich; (*Mus.*) Takt(strich); (*Her.*) Querbalken, Querstreifen; die Ordensspange (*to a medal*); (*Mus.*) ***– rest,*** die (Ganz)taktpause; (*Her.*) ***– sinister,*** das Zeichen der Illegitimität; 5. der Schenktisch, das Büfett, die Schenke, der Ausschank; die Bar; (*coll.*) ***prop up the –,*** in der Kneipe hocken.
2. *v.t.* verriegeln, zuriegeln; vergittern; (*fig.*) sperren, versperren, verhindern; hemmen, hindern (***from,*** an (*Dat.*)), aufhalten, Einhalt tun (*Dat.*); verbieten, untersagen; ausschließen, abhalten (***from,*** von); ausnehmen, absehen von; (*coll.*) beanstanden.
3. *prep.* ***– one,*** außer einem, abgesehen von einem; ***– none,*** alle ohne Ausnahme, niemand ausgenommen.

[1]**barb** [bɑːb], **1.** *s.* (*Bot.*) der Bart; Widerhaken (*of a hook, arrow etc.*); die Fahne (*of a feather*), (*fig.*) der Stachel. **2.** *v.t.* mit Widerhaken versehen; ***–ed wire,*** der Stacheldraht; ***–ed-wire entanglement,*** der *or* das Drahtverhau.

[2]**barb,** *s.* (*Poet.*) das Berberroß.

barbarian [bɑː'bɛəriən], **1.** *adj.* barbarisch, unzivilisiert; roh, ungebildet, ungesittet. **2.** *s.* der Barbar, roher *or* ungebildeter *or* ungesitteter Mensch; Unmensch, grausamer Mensch. **barbaric** [–'bærik], *adj. See* **barbarian, 1**; ausländisch, fremd. **barbarism** ['bɑːbərizm], *s.* die Roheit, Wildheit, Unkultur; Sprachwidrigkeit, der Barbarismus. **barbarity** [–'bæriti], *s.* die Grausamkeit, Unmenschlichkeit, Roheit. **barbarous** ['bɑːbərəs], *adj.* barbarisch, unmenschlich, roh, grausam, unkultiviert, ungesittet, ungebildet.

Barbary ['bɑːbəri], *s.* die Berberei. **Barbary-horse,** *s.* das Berberpferd.

barbate ['bɑːbeit], *adj.* bärtig, gebärtet.

barbecue ['bɑːbikjuː], **1.** *s.* der Bratrost; am Spieß gebratenes Tier; das Festessen im Freien; (*Am.*) der Röstboden (*for coffee beans*). **2.** *v.t.* unzerlegt (am Spieß *or* auf dem Rost) braten (*animals*); rösten, dörren (*coffee*).

barbed [bɑːbd], *adj. See* [1]**barb.**

barbel ['bɑːbəl], *s.* (*Ichth.*) die Barbe.

bar-bell, *s.* (*Gymn.*) die (Kugel)hantel.

barbellate ['bɑːbəleit], *adj. See* **barbate.**

barber ['bɑːbə], **1.** *s.* der Friseur, Frisör, Barbier; (*obs.*) ***surgeon –***, der Bader, Wundarzt; ***–'s rash,*** die Bartflechte. **2.** *v.t.* (*Am.*) barbieren.

barberry ['bɑːbəri], *s.* die Berberitze, Berbesbeere.

barbershop ['bɑːbəʃɔp], *s.* (*Am.*) der Friseurladen.

barbette [bɑː'bet], *s.* die Geschützlafette, der Geschützstand, die Kasematte.

barbican ['bɑːbikən], *s.* das Außenwerk, Vorwerk; der Wachtturm.

barbiturate [bɑː'bitjurit], *s.* das Barbitursäurepräparat.

bard [bɑːd], *s.* der Barde, Sänger; (*Poet.*) Dichter. **bardic,** *adj.* bardisch, Barden–.

bare [bɛə], **1.** *adj.* nackt, unbekleidet, bloß, entblößt; unverhüllt, offen(bar); kahl, unbehaart; entlaubt; (*fig.*) bar, blank, schmucklos, leer; arm (***of,*** an (*Dat.*)), entblößt (von); ***the – facts,*** die nackten Tatsachen; ***the – idea,*** die bloße Idee; ***lay –,*** bloßlegen, (*fig.*) offen darlegen, aufdecken; ***at the – mention of it,*** bei der bloßen Erwähnung davon; ***the – necessities of life,*** die allernotwendigsten ***or*** kaum hinreichenden Lebensbedürfnisse, das Nötigste zum Leben; (*Naut.*) ***under – poles,*** vor Topp und Takel. **2.** *v.t.* entblößen, entkleiden, (*fig.*) enthüllen, bloßlegen, offenbaren; ***– one's heart to him,*** ihm sein Herz erschließen.

bare|back(ed), *adj., adv.* ungesattelt (*of horses*); ***ride –,*** ohne Sattel reiten. **–faced,** *adj.* (*fig.*) frech, unverschämt, schamlos; ***– lie,*** schamlose Lüge. **–foot(ed),** *adj., adv.* barfuß. **–-headed,** *adj., adv.* barhaupt, barhäuptig, mit bloßem Kopfe, unbedeckt(en Hauptes). **–-legged,** *adj., adv.* nacktbeinig. **barely,** *adv.* bloß, gerade, kaum; ***– 3 feet,*** knapp *or* kaum 3 Fuß. **bare-necked,** *adj., adv.* mit bloßem Halse. **bareness,** *s.* die Nacktheit, Blöße; Kahlheit, Unbehaartheit; Knappheit, Dürftigkeit; Leere, Armut.

baresark ['bɛəsɑːk], **1.** *s.* der Berserker. **2.** *adv.* ohne Rüstung, unbewaffnet.

bargain ['bɑːgin], **1.** *s.* der Handel, Kauf(vertrag), das Geschäft; der Vertrag, die Abmachung, Übereinkunft; vorteilhaftes Geschäft, vorteilhafter (Ver)kauf, billiger Einkauf, der Gelegenheitskauf, das Sonderangebot; günstig gekaufter Artikel; ***it's a –,*** es ist spottbillig; (*fig.*) es bleibt dabei! abgemacht! ***bad –,*** böser (*or* unvorteilhafter) Handel; ***strike a –,*** einen Handel abschließen, handelseinig werden; ***make the best of a bad –,*** sich mit Humor aus der Affäre ziehen; ***drive a hard –,*** um den Pfennig feilschen, rücksichtslos seinen Vorteil wahren; ***into the –,*** obendrein, noch dazu, in den Kauf. **2.** *v.i.* handeln; feilschen, schachern (***for,*** um); ***by –ing I got it cheaper,*** ich habe vom Preise etwas abgehandelt; ***as –ed for,*** wie abgeredet; ***– for,*** (*usu. neg.*) rechnen mit; gefaßt sein auf (*Acc.*); ***this was more than I –ed for,*** dies habe ich nicht erwartet, da bin ich schön reingefallen. **3.** *v.t.* (ein)tauschen (***for,*** gegen); ***– away,*** verschachern. **--counter,** *s.* der Ramschverkaufsstand. **--sale.** *s.* der Ausverkauf von Sonderangeboten.

barge [bɑːdʒ], **1.** *s.* der Lastkahn, Schleppkahn, Leichter, das Kanalschiff, die Zille, Schute; das Vergnügungsboot, Galaruderboot. **2.** *v.i.* stürzen, rennen, torkeln; (*coll.*) ***– in,*** sich (uneingeladen) einmischen, hereinplatzen. **bargee** [–'dʒiː], *s.* der Kahnführer, Leichterführer, Schutenschiffer. **barge-pole,** *s.* die Bootstange; (*coll.*) ***I wouldn't touch it with a –,*** ich möchte es nicht mit der Feuerzange berühren.

baritone ['bæritoun], *s.* der Bariton(sänger); die Baritonstimme.

[1]**bark** [bɑːk], **1.** *s.* die (Baum)rinde, Borke; ***tanner's –,*** die (Gerber)lohe. **2.** *v.t.* abrinden, entrinden (*trees etc.*); ***– one's shin,*** sich (*Dat.*) das Schienbein abschürfen.

²**bark,** *s. See* **barque**; (*Poet.*) das Schiff, die Barke.

³**bark,** **1.** *v.i.* bellen, kläffen; (*fig.*) belfern; – ***when one cannot bite,*** den Mond anbellen; – ***up the wrong tree,*** auf falscher Fährte *or* auf dem Holzweg sein. **2.** *s.* das Bellen, Kläffen; Gebell; (*fig.*) Gebelfer; ***his – is worse than his bite,*** Hunde, die viel bellen *or* bellende Hunde beißen nicht. **barker,** *s.* (*coll.*) der Kundenwerber, Anpreiser, Ausrufer.

barley ['bɑ:li], *s.* die Gerste; ***French*** or ***pot –,*** Graupen (*pl.*); ***pearl –,*** Perlgraupen (*pl.*). **barley|-corn,** *s.* das Gerstenkorn; (*coll.*) ***John Barleycorn,*** der Gerstensaft, Whisky. **--sugar,** *s.* der Gerstenzucker. **--water,** *s.* der Gerstenschleim.

barm [bɑ:m], *s* die Hefe, Bärme.

bar-magnet, *s.* der Stabmagnet.

barmaid ['bɑ:meid], *s.* das Schankfräulein, die Bardame. **barman** [–mən], *s.* der Schankkellner, Barkellner.

barmy ['bɑ:mi], *adj.* hefig, schaumig, gärend; (*coll.*) verdreht, verrückt, blöd.

barn [bɑ:n], *s.* die Scheune, Scheuer, (*Am.*) der (Vieh)stall.

¹**barnacle** ['bɑ:nəkl], *s.* 1. (*Orn.*) (*also* – ***goose***) die Weißwangengans (*Branta leucopsis*); 2. (*Zool.*) Entenmuschel; (*fig.*) Klette.

²**barnacle,** *s.* die Bremse, der Nasenknebel (*for unruly horses*); *pl.* (*coll.*) Kneifer, Klemmer, Zwicker.

barn|-dance, *s.* der Ländler. **--door,** *s.* das Scheunentor; – ***fowl,*** das Haushuhn. **--owl,** *s.* (*Orn.*) die Schleiereule (*Tyto alba*). **-stormer,** *s.* der Schmiererschauspieler. **--swallow,** *s.* (*Am.*) *see* **swallow. -yard,** *s.* der Scheunenhof.

barometer [bə'rɔmitə], *s.* das Barometer, Wetterglas, (*fig.*) der Stimmungsmesser. **barometric-(al)** [bærə'metrik(l)], *adj.* barometrisch; – ***level*** or ***reading,*** der Barometerstand; – ***pressure,*** der Luftdruck.

baron ['bærən], *s.* der Baron, Freiherr; (*fig.*) Magnat; – ***of beef,*** das Lendenstück des Rinds. **baronage** [–idʒ], *s.* die Freiherrschaft; Barone (*pl.*). **baroness,** *s.* die Baronin, Freifrau, Freiin. **baronet,** *s.* der Baronet. **baronetcy** [–etsi], *s.* die Baronetswürde. **baronial** [bə'rouniəl], *adj.* freiherrlich, Barons–; (*fig.*) prunkvoll. **barony,** *s.* die Baronie, der Freiherrnstand.

baroque [bə'rɔk, bə'rouk], **1.** *adj.* barock; überladen, verschnörkelt, wunderlich, verschroben; schiefrund (*of pearls*). **2.** *s.* der Barock(stil).

barouche [bə'ru:ʃ], *s.* viersitziger Landauer.

bar-parlour, *s.* die Schenkstube, Schankstube.

barque [bɑ:k], *s.* die Bark, das Barkschiff.

barrack ['bærək], **1.** *s.* die Baracke, Hütte; *pl.* (*Mil.*) (*sing. constr.*) Kaserne; (*Mil.*) ***confined to –s,*** unter Kasernenarrest; – ***yard,*** – ***square,*** der Kasernenhof. **2.** *v.t.* (*coll.*) verhöhnen, verspotten. **3.** *v.i.* (*coll.*) Partei ergreifen, Zwischenrufe machen.

barracuda [bærə'kju:də], *s.* (*Ichth.*) der Pfeilhecht.

barrage ['bærɑ:ʒ], *s.* der Damm, die Sperre, Buhne, das Wehr, Stauwerk; (*Mil.*) Sperrfeuer; (*fig.*) der Ansturm, Schwall (*of questions etc.*); – ***balloon,*** der Sperrballon; (*Mil.*) ***box –,*** das Abriegelungsfeuer; (*Mil.*) ***creeping –,*** die Feuerwalze.

barred [bɑ:d], *adj.* verriegelt, verschlossen, (ab)-gesperrt; *see* **bar.**

barrel ['bærəl], **1.** *s.* 1. das Faß, die Tonne; ***by the –,*** faßweise; 2. der (Gewehr)lauf, das (Geschütz)-rohr, (*Horol.*) Federgehäuse; die Walze, Trommel, der Zylinder; ***built-up –,*** das Ringrohr; ***one-piece –,*** das Vollrohr; ***smooth –,*** der Schrotlauf, das Glattrohr; ***sub-calibre –,*** der Einstecklauf, das Einlegerohr; 3. der Rumpf, Leib (*of cattle*). **2.** *v.t.* – ***off,*** – ***up,*** eintonnen, auf Fässer füllen.

barrel-burst, *s.* (*Mil.*) der Rohrzerspringer, Rohrkrepierer. **barrelled,** *adj.* in ein Faß abgefüllt; ***double-– gun,*** zweiläufiges Gewehr. **barrel|-maker,** *s.* der Faßbinder. **--organ,** *s.* die Drehorgel, der Leierkasten; ***--grinder,*** der Orgeldreher, Leier(kasten)mann. – **roll,** *s.* (*Av.*) der Überschlag über den Flügel. **--vault,** *s.* (*Archit.*) das Tonnengewölbe.

barren ['bærən], *adj.* unfruchtbar, steril, öde, trocken, dürr; leer, arm (*of,* an (*Dat.*)); unproduktiv, wertlos, seicht; (*Min.*) taub; gelt (*cow*); tot (*capital*). **barrenness,** *s.* die Unfruchtbarkeit, Dürre; Leere, Armut, Dürftigkeit, der Mangel (*of,* an (*Dat.*)).

barretter [bæ'retə], *s.* (*Rad.*) die Überlagerungsröhre.

barricade [bæri'keid], **1.** *s.* die Barrikade, Verschanzung, Sperre, das Hindernis. **2.** *v.t.* verrammeln, sperren, verschanzen.

barrier ['bæriə], *s.* die Schranke, Sperre, Barriere, das Schutzgatter, der Schlagbaum; (*Geog.*) – ***reef,*** das Wallriff.

barring ['bɑ:riŋ], *prep.* ausgenommen, abgesehen von, wenn . . . nicht eintritt. *See* **bar.**

barrister(-at-law) ['bæristə], *s.* der Rechtsanwalt, Advokat.

¹**barrow** ['bærou], *s.* der Schubkarren, Schiebkarren; die Trage, Bahre.

²**barrow,** *s.* der Grabhügel, das Hünengrab.

barter ['bɑ:tə], **1.** *s.* der Tausch, Tauschhandel. **2.** *v.t.* vertauschen, austauschen, umtauschen, eintauschen (*for,* gegen). **3.** *v.i.* Tauschhandel treiben. **bartering,** *s.* der Tauschhandel, das Tauschgeschäft.

baryta [bə'raitə], *s.* die Baryterde, das Bariumoxyd. **barytes** [–i:z], *pl.* der Schwerspat, das Bariumsulfat.

barytone, *see* **baritone.**

basal ['beisəl], *adj.* fundamental, Grund–, (*fig.*) grundlegend.

basalt ['bæsɔ:lt], *s.* der Basalt. **basaltic** [–'sɔ:ltik], *adj.* basaltisch, Basalt–.

basan ['bæzən], *s.* gegerbtes Schaffell.

bascule-bridge ['bæskju:l–], *s.* die Fallbrücke, Zugbrücke.

¹**base** [beis], *adj.* niederträchtig, gemein, verächtlich; minderwertig, gering, unedel (*as metals*), unecht, falsch (*as coins*); (*obs.*) niedrigen Standes.

²**base,** **1.** *s.* 1. der Grund, die Grundlage, Basis; (*Chem.*) Base, der Grundstoff, Hauptbestandteil; (*Geom.*) die Grundfläche, Grundlinie, (*Surv.*) Standlinie; (*Math.*) Grundzahl, Basis; (*fig.*) Basis, Grundlage, der Ausgangspunkt; 2. (*Archit.*) Fuß, Sockel, Träger, das Fußgestell, Postament, Fundament; (*Anat. etc.*) der Unterteil, unterster Teil, die Basis; (*Tech.*) Grundplatte, Unterlage, Standfläche, Bettung, das Gestell; Fundament, der Sockel; (*Mil.*) Stützpunkt, die Operationsbasis, Etappe, (*Naut.*) der Einsatzhafen, (*Av.*) (Flieger)-horst; (*Spt.*) das Mal; ***naval –,*** der Flottenstützpunkt; (*game*) ***prisoner's –,*** das Barlaufspiel. **2.** *v.t.* gründen, stützen (*on,* auf (*Acc.*)); (*Mil.*) ***be –d at . . ., . . .*** als Basis haben; ***be –d on,*** beruhen *or* basieren auf (*Dat.*).

base| angle, *s.* (*Geom.*) der Basiswinkel. **-ball,** *s.* der Baseball. **--born,** *adj.* von niedriger Geburt. **--burner,** *s.* der Füllofen, Regulierofen. **-- camp,** *s.* (*Mil.*) das Hauptlager, Ausgangslager. **--court,** *s.* (*Hist.*) äußerer Hof (*of a castle*). – **depot,** *s.* (*Mil.*) das Hauptdepot. **--hearted,** *adj.* gemein, niederträchtig, verräterisch, treulos. **baseless,** *adj.* (*fig.*) grundlos, unbegründet. **baseline,** *s.* (*Surv.*) die Standlinie, (*Tenn.*) Grundlinie, (*Baseball*) Lauflinie.

basement ['beismənt], *s.* das Untergeschoß, Kellergeschoß, Parterre(geschoß), Souterrain; (*Archit.*) die Grundmauer, der Grundbau; Sockel, das Fundament.

base-minded, *adj.* von unedler Gesinnung. **baseness,** *s.* die Niedrigkeit, Gemeinheit, Niederträchtigkeit; Minderwertigkeit, Unechtheit, Falschheit. **base|plate,** *s.* die Bodenplatte, Lagerplatte, Abstützplatte, Unterlage, das Fundament, der Sockel. **--wallah,** *s.* (*Mil. sl.*) das Etappenschwein.

bash [bæʃ], **1.** *v.t.* (*coll.*) heftig schlagen, schmeißen; (*usu. fig.*) – ***one's head against a brick wall,*** mit dem Kopf gegen die Wand rennen; – ***his head in,*** ihm den Schädel einschlagen. **2.** *s.* (*sl.*) ***have a –*** (***at a th.***), es versuchen, an die S. herangehen.

bashful [ˈbæʃful], *adj.* schüchtern, verschämt. **bashfulness,** *s.* die Schüchternheit, Verschämtheit.

basic [ˈbeisik], *adj.* grundlegend, fundamental, Grund–, (*Chem.*) basisch; – ***English,*** vereinfachte Grundlagen des Englischen; – ***industry,*** die Grundstoffindustrie, Schlüsselindustrie; (*Metall.*) – ***iron,*** das Thomaseisen; – ***load,*** ständige Grundlast; – ***material,*** der (Ausgangs)werkstoff; (*Mil.*) – ***pay,*** der Wehrsold; – ***research,*** die Grundlagenforschung; – ***size,*** das Sollmaß; (*Metall.*) – ***steel,*** der Seimens-Martin-Stahl; – ***training,*** die Grundausbildung; – ***wage,*** der Grundlohn. **basically,** *adv.* im Grunde, im wesentlichen, grundsätzlich.

basil [ˈbæzil], *s.* (*Bot.*) das Basilienkraut.

basilica [bəˈsilikə], *s.* die Basilika.

basilisk [ˈbæzilisk], *s.* (*Myth.*) der Basilisk; (*Zool.*) die Kroneidechse.

basin [beisn], *s.* das Becken; die Schüssel, Schale; der Wasserbehälter, das Bassin; Stromgebiet (*of a river*); (*Geol.*) die Mulde, der Kessel, das (Tal)becken; (*Naut.*) Hafenbecken, der Innenhafen; ***wash –,*** das Waschbecken.

basinet [ˈbæsinet], *s.* (*Hist.*) die Kesselhaube.

basis [ˈbeisis], *s.* die Grundlage, Basis, der Grund.

bask [bɑːsk], *v.i.* sich sonnen, sich wärmen.

basket [ˈbɑːskit], *s.* der Korb; (*Av.*) die Ballongondel; ***the pick of the –,*** das beste vom Ganzen; ***put all one's eggs in one –,*** alles auf eine Karte setzen. **basket|-ball,** *s.* das Korbballspiel. **--carriage,** *s.* der Korbwagen. **--chair,** *s.* der Korbsessel. **basketful,** *s.* der Korbvoll; ***by –s,*** korbweise, in Körben. **basket|-handle,** *s.* der Korbhenkel. **--hilt,** *s.* der Säbelkorb. **basketry,** *s.* *See* **basketwork. basket|-stitch,** *s.* der Korbstich. **-work,** *s.* das Flechtwerk; Korbwaren (*pl.*).

Basle [bɑːl], *s.* (*Geog.*) Basel.

Basque [bɑːsk], **1.** *s.* 1. der Baske (die Baskin); 2. (*language*) das Baskisch(e). **2.** *adj.* baskisch.

bas-relief [ˈbæsrəˈliːf], *s.* das Basrelief, Flachbildwerk.

[1]**bass** [beis], **1.** *s.* der Baß, die Baßstimme; der Bassist, Baßsänger, Baßspieler; Baßschlüssel, das Baßregister. **2.** *adj.* – ***clef,*** der Baßschlüssel; – ***drum,*** die Pauke, große Trommel; – ***singer,*** der Bassist; – ***string,*** die Baßsaite; – ***voice,*** die Baßstimme; – ***viol,*** die Gambe.

[2]**bass** [bæs], *s.* der (Linden)bast; die Bastmatte.

[3]**bass** [bæs], *s.* (*Ichth.*) der Seebarsch, Flußbarsch.

bass-bar [ˈbeis–], *s.* der Balken (*of violin*).

basset| horn [ˈbæsit], *s.* das Bassetthorn. **– hound,** *s.* der Dachshund.

bassinet [bæsiˈnet], *s.* der Kinderwagen; die Korbwiege.

bassoon [bəˈsuːn], *s.* das Fagott; ***double –,*** das Kontrafagott. **bassoonist,** *s.* der Fagottist.

bast [bæst], *s.* der Bast; das Bastseil; *see* [2]**bass.**

bastard [ˈbɑːstəd], **1.** *s.* der Bastard, Bankert; (*sl.*) Schweinehund. **2.** *adj.* unehelich; unecht, falsch; (*Bot.*) – ***branch,*** der Seitentrieb; – ***file,*** die Bastardfeile; (*Typ.*) – ***title,*** der Schmutztitel. **bastardize,** *v.t.* für unehelich *or* zum Bastard erklären. **bastardy,** *s.* uneheliche Geburt, die Bastardschaft.

[1]**baste** [beist], *v.t.* 1. mit Fett begießen; 2. (*coll.*) verprügeln, verhauen.

[2]**baste,** *v.t.* lose (zusammen)nähen, (an)heften.

bastinado [bæstiˈneidou], **1.** *s.* die Bastonade, Prügelstrafe. **2.** *v.t.* die Bastonade geben (*Dat.*).

[1]**basting** [ˈbeistiŋ], *s.* 1. das Begießen mit Fett; Fett zum Begießen; 2. (*coll.*) Prügel (*pl.*), Schläge (*pl.*); *see* [1]**baste.**

[2]**basting,** *s.* das Anheften, loses Zusammennähen; Vorderstiche, weite Stiche (*pl.*); *see* [2]**baste.**

bastion [ˈbæstiən], *s.* die Bastion, Bastei, das Bollwerk (*also fig.*).

[1]**bat** [bæt], *s.* die Fledermaus; ***as blind as a –,*** stockblind; (*coll.*) ***he has –s in the belfry,*** er hat einen Vogel, er hat Raupen im Kopf, er ist nicht recht gescheit.

[2]**bat, 1.** *s.* das Schlagholz, der Schläger; (*sl.*) das Tempo; (*sl.*) ***at a good –,*** mit raschem Schritt; (*coll.*) ***off one's own –,*** auf eigne Faust. **2.** *v.i.* schlagen; am Schlagen sein.

[3]**bat,** *v.t.* (*only in*) (*coll.*) ***without batting an eyelid,*** ohne mit der Wimper zu zucken.

batch [bætʃ], *s.* der Schub (*bread*), Satz (*pottery etc.*); die Schicht, Partie, der Stoß (*of things*), die Menge, Gruppe, der Trupp (*of persons*).

bate [beit], **1.** *v.t.* herabsetzen, vermindern, verringern, schwächen, mäßigen; ***with –d breath,*** mit verhaltenem Atem. **2.** *v.i.* nachlassen, abnehmen, sich vermindern.

bath [bɑːθ], **1.** *s.* (*pl.* **-s** [–ðz]) das (Wannen)bad; die Badewanne; (*Chem.*) Waschung; ***have*** or ***take a –,*** ein Bad nehmen; ***Order of the Bath,*** der Bathorden; ***Commander of the Bath,*** der Komtur des Bathordens; (*Phot.*) ***fixing –,*** das Fixierbad; (*Dye.*) ***initial –,*** das Ansatzbad; ***standing –,*** laufendes Bad; ***charge*** or ***prepare a –,*** ein Bad ansetzen; ***reinforce the –,*** die Flotte ergänzen. **2.** *v.t.* baden. **3.** *v.i.* (sich) baden, ein Bad nehmen. **bath| brick,** *s.* der Putzstein. **– chair,** *s.* der Rollstuhl.

bathe [beið], **1.** *v.i.* (im Freien) baden, baden *or* schwimmen gehen; *see also* **bath, 3. 2.** *v.t.* waschen, befeuchten, benetzen; (*Poet.*) bespülen, umspülen; (*fig.*) baden, umhüllen (*as light*); *see also* **bath, 2**; ***be –d in tears,*** in Tränen schwimmen. **3.** *s.* das Bad (im Freien).

bathing [ˈbeiðiŋ], *s.* das Baden; ***mixed –,*** das Familienbad. **bathing|-beauty,** *s.* die Badeschönheit. **--costume,** *s.* der Badeanzug, das Badekostüm. **--drawers,** *pl. See* **--trunks. --machine,** *s.* der Badekarren, die Badekabine. **--place,** *s.* die Badestelle, der Badeplatz; Badeort. **--season,** *s.* die Badezeit, Badesaison. **--trunks,** *pl.* die Badehose. **--wrap,** *s.* der Bademantel.

bathos [ˈbeiθɔs], *s.* der Übergang vom Erhabenen zum Lächerlichen; die Trivialität, der Gemeinplatz.

bath| robe, *s.* (*Am.*) der Bademantel. **-room,** *s.* das Badezimmer; (*coll.*) die Toilette.

baths [bɑːðz], *pl.* die Badeanstalt; das Badehaus; – ***attendant,*** der Badewärter.

bath| salts, *pl.* das Badesalz. **--sheet,** *s.* das Badelaken. **--towel,** *s.* das Badetuch. **--tub,** *s.* die Badewanne.

bathymetry [bæˈθimitri], *s.* die Tiefseemessung. **bathysphere** [ˈbæθisfiə], *s.* die Tiefsee-Taucherkugel.

batiste [bæˈtiːst], *s.* der Batist.

batman [ˈbætmən], *s.* (*Mil.*) der Offiziersbursche.

baton [ˈbætən], *s.* der Stock, Stab; Knüppel, Knüttel; (*Mus.*) Taktstock; (*Spt.*) Staffelstab; (*Her.*) Querstab; ***marshal's –,*** der Feldherrnstab, Marschallstab.

batrachian [bəˈtreikiən], **1.** *adj.* Frosch–. **2.** *s.* der Froschlurch.

batsman [ˈbætsmən], *s.* (*Crick., Baseball*) der Schläger, Schlagmann.

battalion [bəˈtæljən], *s.* das Bataillon, die Abteilung.

[1]**batten** [bætn], **1.** *s.* die Latte, Leiste; (*Naut.*) Schalkleiste (*for hatches*); Lade (*of looms*); – ***door,*** die Leistentür; – ***fence,*** der Lattenzaun. **2.** *v.t.* mit Latten verkleiden *or* verschalen (*a wall*); (*Naut.*) – ***down,*** schalken (*hatches*).

[2]**batten, 1.** *v.i.* sich mästen, fett werden (***on,*** an (*Dat.*)); (*fig.*) gedeihen; sich gütlich tun, sich weiden (***on,*** an (*Dat.*)), schwelgen (in (*Dat.*)). **2.** *v.t.* mästen (***on,*** mit).

[1]**batter** [ˈbætə], *s.* geschlagener Teig, der Eierteig.

[2]**batter,** *s. See* **batsman.**

[3]**batter,** *v.t.* (heftig) schlagen *or* stoßen gegen; zerschlagen, zerschmettern; (*Mil.*) beschießen;

abnutzen, beschädigen, arg mitnehmen, böse zurichten; – *down,* zusammenschießen; niederreißen; – *in,* einschlagen. **battered,** *adj.* zerschlagen, schäbig, abgenutzt, arg mitgenommen. **battering|-ram,** *s.* der Sturmbock, Mauerbrecher. **--train,** *s.* der Belagerungstrain.

battery ['bætəri], *s.* 1. (*Law*) tätliche Beleidigung, die Mißhandlung, Körperverletzung; ***action for assault and*** –, Klage wegen Tätlichkeiten; 2. (*Mil.*) die Batterie, Artillerieabteilung; Geschützstellung; – ***of field-artillery,*** fahrende Batterie; – ***of horse-artillery,*** reitende Batterie; ***floating*** –, schwimmende Batterie; 3. (*Elec.*) die Batterie, der Sammler; ***dry*** –, das Trockenelement; (*Rad.*) – ***eliminator,*** die Netzanode; 4. (*Opt.*) das Linsen- *or* Prismensystem; 5. (*fig.*) der Satz, die Reihe (*of questions, tests etc.*).

battery|-charger, *s.* (*Elec.*) die Lademaschine. **--charging station,** *s.* die Ladestation. **--operated,** *adj.* mit Batterieanschluß, batteriegespeist.

batting ['bætiŋ], *s.* (*Crick., Baseball*) das Schlagen; – ***average,*** die Durchschnittsleistung des Schlägers (für die Saison).

battle [bætl], **1.** *s.* die Schlacht, das Gefecht, Treffen, die Kampfhandlung; (*fig.*) der Kampf, das Ringen (*for,* um); ***drawn*** –, unentschiedene Schlacht; ***do – for,*** kämpfen *or* sich schlagen um; ***a good start is half the*** –, frisch gewagt ist halb gewonnen; ***that is half the*** –, das ist schon ein großer Vorteil; ***fight a*** –, einen Kampf führen; ***fight one's own –(s),*** sich allein durchschlagen; ***give*** or ***join*** –, eine Schlacht liefern, sich zum Kampfe stellen; ***pitched*** –, regelrechte Schlacht; – ***royal,*** allgemeine Schlägerei, das Handgemenge; ***the – is to the strong,*** der Sieg gehört den Starken; ***Battle of Waterloo,*** die Schlacht bei Belle-Alliance; – ***of words,*** das Wortgefecht. **2.** *v.i.* – ***against,*** bekämpfen; –***for,*** kämpfen *or* fechten *or* streiten um; (*coll.*) – ***it out,*** es auskämpfen.

battle|-area, *s.* der Kampfraum. **--array,** *s.* die Schlachtordnung. **--axe,** *s.* 1. die Streitaxt; 2. (*coll.*) der Drache. **--cruiser,** *s.* der Schlachtkreuzer. **--cry.** *s.* der Schlachtruf, das Kriegsgeschrei.

battledore ['bætldɔ:], *s.* das Rakett, der Federballschläger; – ***and shuttlecock,*** das Federballspiel.

battle|-dress, *s.* der Dienstanzug, Feldanzug. **-field,** *s.* das Schlachtfeld. **--fleet,** *s.* die Hochseeflotte. – **formation,** *s.* die Gefechtsgliederung, Schlachtordnung. **-ground,** *s. See* **-field**; (*usu. fig.*) der Kampfplatz, die Streitursache.

battlement ['bætlmənt], *s.* (*usu. pl.*) die Brustwehr, Festungsmauer, Zinnen (*pl.*).

battle| order, 1. *See* – **formation**; 2. der Gefechtsbefehl. **--piece,** *s.* das Schlachtgemälde, Schlachtszene. **-ship,** *s.* das Schlachtschiff, Kriegsschiff, Linienschiff. **--stations,** *pl.* (*Naut.*) die Gefechtsstation.

battue [bæ'tu:], *s.* die Treibjagd, (*fig.*) das Gemetzel, die Metzelei, Niedermetzelung.

batty ['bæti], *adj.* (*sl.*) plemplem.

bauble [bɔ:bl], *s.* das Spielzeug; der Tand; (*fig.*) die Kleinigkeit, Spielerei; (*obs.*) der Narrenstab.

baulk, *see* **balk.**

bauxite ['bɔ:ksait, 'bouzait], *s.* das Bauxit.

Bavaria [bə'vɛəriə], *s.* Bayern (*n.*). **Bavarian, 1.** *s.* der (die) Bayer(in). **2.** *adj.* bay(e)risch, bajuvarisch.

bawd [bɔ:d], *s.* die Kupplerin. **bawdiness,** *s.* die Unflätigkeit, Unzüchtigkeit. **bawdry,** *s.* die Unflätigkeit, Zoten (*pl.*); Unzucht, Hurerei. **bawdy,** *adj.* unzüchtig, unflätig; ***talk*** –, Zoten reißen. **bawdy-house,** *s.* (*coll.*) das Bordell.

bawl [bɔ:l], **1.** *v.t.* (*also* – ***out***) laut ausrufen, brüllen; (*sl.*) (*Am.*) anschnauzen, anbrüllen (*a p.*). **2.** *v.i.* schreien, brüllen, (*of children*) heulen, plärren; – ***at,*** anbrüllen.

[1]**bay** [bei], **1.** *adj.* rötlichbraun, kastanienbraun. **2.** *s.* der Braune, Fuchs (*horse*).

[2]**bay,** *s.* (*also* – ***tree***) der Lorbeer(baum).

[3]**bay,** *s.* 1. die Bai, Bucht; der Meerbusen; 2. (*Build.*) das Fach, die Abteilung; Banse (*of a barn*); der Zwischenraum, die Lücke, Nische, der Erker; (*Av.*) ***bomb*** –, die Bombenschacht.

[4]**bay,** *s.* (*Hunt.*) das Gestelltsein (*of game*); ***be at*** –, gestellt sein, (*fig.*) sich zur Wehr setzen, in Bedrängnis sein; ***hold*** or ***keep at*** –, hinhalten, in Schach halten.

[5]**bay,** *v.i.* bellen; anschlagen, Laut geben. **baying,** *s.* das Gebell.

bay leaf, *s.* das Lorbeerblatt.

bayonet ['beiənet], **1.** *s.* das Seitengewehr, Bajonett; ***at the point of the*** –, mit dem Bajonett; ***with fixed*** –***s,*** mit aufgepflanztem Seitengewehr. **2.** *v.t.* mit dem Bajonett erstechen.

bayou ['baiju:], *s.* (*Am.*) die Sumpfstelle an See *or* Fluß.

bay| rum, *s.* der Bayrum. – **salt,** *s.* das Seesalz. – **tree,** *s. See* [2]**bay. -window,** *s.* das Erkerfenster.

bazaar [bə'zɑ:], *s.* (orientalischer) Basar, die Ladenstraße; der Wohltätigkeitsbasar; billiges Warenhaus.

bazooka [bə'zu:kə], *s.* das Panzergeschütz, die Panzerbüchse, (*coll.*) Panzerfaust.

be [bi:], **1.** *irr.v.i.* (vorhanden) sein, existieren, bestehen; sich befinden, (der Fall) sein; ***there is, there are,*** es gibt (*Acc.*); es ist, es sind (*Nom.*); ***there is plenty to eat,*** es gibt eine Menge zu essen; ***there is no bread on the table,*** es ist kein Brot auf dem Tisch; ***as it is,*** so wie die Dinge liegen; (*Mil., Gymn.*) ***as you were!*** in die Stellung zurück! herstellt euch! ***so – it,*** so sei es, gut so; ***let it*** –! laß es bleiben! ***how is it that . . . ?*** wie kommt es daß . . .? ***what is it now?*** was willst du nun? ***how are you?*** wie geht es dir? ***how have you been?*** wie ist es dir ergangen? – ***that as it may,*** das mag sein wie es will; ***twice two is four,*** zweimal zwei macht vier; ***are you coming? of course I am,*** kommst du? Jawohl, natürlich; ***are you coming? I am not,*** kommst du? Keineswegs *or* auf keinen Fall; ***he lived to – 70,*** er wurde 70 Jahre alt.

(a) (*with adjs., advs.*) – ***about to do,*** im Begriffe sein zu tun; ***I will – along soon,*** ich komme bald; ***there you are!*** da hast du es! (*coll.*) ***how much is it?*** wieviel kostet das? wieviel macht das? – ***ill*** (or ***well***), sich übel (*or* wohl) befinden; – ***in,*** zu Hause sein; angekommen sein; (*Pol.*) an der Macht *or* Spitze *or* am Ruder sein; (*Spt.*) daran sein; ***do not – long!*** bleiben Sie nicht lange; – ***a long time doing,*** lange gebrauchen, um zu tun; – ***off,*** fortgehen, abreisen; (*coll.*) ausfallen; – ***off!*** fort mit dir! packe dich! ***I must – off,*** ich muß fort; – ***well placed,*** gut situiert sein; (*coll.*) – ***on,*** auf dem Programm stehen; – ***out,*** nicht zu Hause sein; im Irrtum sein; streiken, im Ausstand sein; – ***over,*** vorbei sein; (*coll.*) – (***all***) ***up,*** zu Ende sein, um *or* aus sein; (*coll.*) – ***up to s.th.,*** etwas vorhaben *or* im Schilde führen.

(b) (*with preps.*) – ***about,*** handeln von; ***I will – after you,*** ich will hinter dir her sein; – ***at,*** zugegen sein bei; ***what is she at?*** was hat sie vor? (*coll.*) ***they are at it again,*** sie sind wieder dabei; ***I am for the former suggestion,*** ich erkläre mich für den ersten Vorschlag; ***is this the train for London?*** fährt dieser Zug nach London? ***it is for him to apologize,*** es kommt ihm zu, sich zu entschuldigen; (*coll.*) – ***for it,*** schön in der Patsche sitzen; ***she was not of the party,*** sie gehörte nicht zur Gesellschaft; ***what is that to you?*** was macht Ihnen das aus? was kümmert Sie das? was bedeutet das für Sie? ***it is just the same with me,*** es geht mir genau so; ***I am with you,*** ich bin eins mit dir.

(c) (*in questions*) ***he is not dead, is he?*** er lebt doch noch, nicht wahr? ***the weather is fine today, is it not?*** nicht wahr, das Wetter ist heute schön?

2. *irr.v.aux.* 1. (*with pres. participle expressing continuous action*) ***I am reading,*** ich bin am *or* beim Lesen, ich lese gerade; ***the house is being built,*** das Haus ist im Bau, das Haus wird gerade gebaut; ***I have just been drinking tea,*** ich habe eben Tee getrunken; ***I shall – writing soon,*** ich werde bald schreiben; 2. (*with inf. expressing necessity or* *obligation*) sollen, müssen; ***he is to come today,*** er soll heute kommen; ***he is to die,*** er muß sterben; ***if I were to die,*** wenn ich sterben sollte; ***it was not to –,*** es sollte nicht sein; ***what am I to do?*** was soll ich tun? ***it is to – hoped,*** es ist zu hoffen, man darf *or* kann hoffen; ***the house is to – sold,*** das Haus ist zu verkaufen; ***that is to say,*** das heißt; 3. (*aux. of the passive*) werden; ***I am told,*** mir wurde gesagt; ***I shall – loved,*** ich werde geliebt werden.

beach [bi:tʃ], **1.** *s.* der Strand, das Gestade, flaches Ufer. **2.** *v.t.* auf den Strand setzen *or* ziehen, stranden lassen. **beach|comber,** *s.* der Strandguträuber; (*Am.*) die Strandwelle. **–head,** *s.* der Brückenkopf, Landekopf. **--wear,** *s.* die Strandkleidung.

beacon ['bi:kən], *s.* die Bake; der Leuchtturm, das Leuchtfeuer, Signalfeuer; (*fig.*) der Leitstern, die Leuchte, das Fanal; (*Av.*) ***landing –,*** das Ansteuerungsfeuer; ***radio –,*** die Funkbake; ***traffic –,*** das Verkehrs(warn)zeichen. **beaconage** [–idʒ], *s.* das Bakengeld. **beacon-buoy,** *s.* die Bakenboje.

bead [bi:d], *s.* die Perle (*of glass etc.*), das Kügelchen, Körnchen, Knöpfchen; (*fig.*) der Tropfen (*of liquid*); das Korn (*of a gun*); *pl.* die Perlschnur, das Halsband, der Rosenkranz; (*sl.*) ***draw a – on,*** zielen auf (*Acc.*); ***string –s,*** Perlen (auf eine Schnur) aufziehen; ***tell one's –s,*** den Rosenkranz beten. **beading,** *s.* die Perlstickerei; (*Archit.*) Rundstabverzierung, Perlstabverzierung.

beadle [bi:dl], *s.* der Kirchendiener; (*Law, obs.*) Gerichtsdiener, Büttel; (*Univ.*) Pedell.

bead|-moulding, *s.* (*Archit.*) der Perlstab, Rundstab. **–work,** *s.* die Perlarbeit, Perlstickerei.

beady ['bi:di], *adj.* perlartig. **beady-eyed,** *adj.* rundäugig, kleinäugig.

beagle [bi:gl], *s.* der Spürhund, Stöber.

beak [bi:k], *s.* der Schnabel (*of birds*); (*sl. of a p.*) die Schnauze; der Ausguß, die Schneppe, Tülle (*of vessels etc.*); (*Naut., obs.*) der Rammschnabel, Sporn; (*sl.*) der Polizeirichter; (*sl.*) Pauker. **beaked,** *adj.* mit einem Schnabel, geschnäbelt; Schnabel–, schnabelförmig, spitz.

beaker ['bi:kə], *s.* der Becher, Humpen; (*Chem.*) das Becherglas.

be-all ['bi:ɔ:l], *s.* das Ganze, Alleinseiende; ***the – and end-all,*** der Hauptzweck, das ein und alles.

beam [bi:m], **1.** *s.* 1. der Balken, Träger, Trag(e)-balken, (Trag)baum, Holm, die Schwelle; der Ketten– *or* Weberbaum (*of a loom*); Pflugbaum (*of a plough*); die Deichsel (*of a cart*); der Arm, Waagebalken (*of a balance*); Balancier, Schwinghebel, Ausgleichshebel (*of steam-engines*); ***cantilever –,*** der Ausleger(balken); ***cross –,*** der Querbalken, Scherstock, die Ducht; (*coll.*) ***kick the –,*** zu leicht sein; ***supporting –,*** der Tragbalken; ***– of a windlass,*** der Haspelbaum; (*Av.*) ***wing –,*** der Flügelholm; 2. (*Naut.*) die Breite (*of a ship*); ***abaft the –,*** achterlicher als querab; ***off the –,*** (*Naut.*) dwars, querab; (*fig.*) weit vom Ziel, fehlgeschossen; ***right on the –,*** dwars ein; ***– wind,*** der Dwarswind, Seitenwind, halber Wind; ***wind on the starboard –,*** der Steuerbordwind; 3. der Strahl, Lichtstrahl, Lichtkegel, das Bündel (*of light etc.*); ***–s of the moon,*** die Mondstrahlen; ***radio –,*** die Funkbake, der (Funk)leitstrahl, Richtstrahl, Peilstrahl; ***searchlight –,*** der Lichtkegel. **2.** *v.i.* strahlen, Strahlen werfen, anstrahlen; ***–ing countenance,*** strahlendes Gesicht. **3.** *v.t.* (aus)strahlen; (*Radio, T.V.*) senden.

beam|-aerial, – antenna, *s.* die Richt(strahl)-antenne, der Richtstrahler. **--callipers,** *pl.* der Stangentastzirkel. **--compasses,** *pl.* der Stangenzirkel. **--ends,** *pl.* (*Naut.*) Querbalkenköpfe (*pl.*); ***the ship is on her –,*** das Schiff liegt auf der Seite; (*sl.*) ***he is on his –,*** er ist pleite, er pfeift auf dem letzten Loch, er sitzt in der Klemme. **--engine,** *s.* die Balanciermaschine. **– sea,** *s.* die Dwarssee. **--transmitter,** *s.* (*Rad.*) der Richtstrahler.

beamy ['bi:mi], *adj.* (*Naut.*) (übermäßig) breit; (*coll.*) wuchtig, massiv.

bean [bi:n], *s.* die Bohne; (*sl.*) Birne (= *head*); ***broad –,*** die Saubohne, Puffbohne; ***French dwarf –,*** die Zwerg– *or* Busch– *or* Zuckerbohne; ***kidney –, haricot –,*** die Schmink– *or* Veits– *or* Steigbohne; ***scarlet runner –,*** die Stangen– *or* Feuerbohne; (*coll.*) ***not have a –,*** keinen roten Heller haben; (*coll.*) ***old –,*** Alte(r), altes Haus, mein Lieber; (*coll.*) ***be full of –s,*** springlebendig *or* lebensprudelnd sein; (*coll.*) ***give him –s,*** ihn tüchtig prügeln; (*coll.*) ***spill the –s,*** aus der Schule plaudern, alles ausquatschen. **bean-feast, beano,** *s.* (*coll.*) das Fest, Gelage, die Lustbarkeit, Zecherei. **beanstalk,** *s.* die Bohnenranke.

1**bear** [bɛə], **1.** *s.* der Bär; (*coll., fig.*) Tolpatsch, ungeschliffener Mensch; (*Comm.*) Baissier, Baissespekulant; ***she-–,*** die Bärin; (*Astr.*) ***the Great and Little Bear,*** der große und der kleine Bär. **2.** *v.i.* (*Comm.*) auf Baisse spekulieren. **3.** *v.t.* (*Comm.*) drücken (*the market*).

2**bear, 1.** *irr.v.t.* 1. (*p.p.* **borne**) tragen; (über)-bringen (*message etc.*); hegen, nähren (*ill will etc.*); führen (*a name, weapons etc.*); vertragen, aushalten, (er)tragen, (er)dulden, (er)leiden (*pain etc.*), ausstehen, leiden (*a p.*); 2. (*p.p.* **born**) zur Welt bringen, gebären (*children*).

(a) (*with nouns*) ***fit to – arms,*** waffenfähig; ***– arms against,*** Krieg führen gegen; ***– the blame,*** es auf sich nehmen, die Schuld tragen; ***– the brunt,*** der Wucht ausgesetzt sein; ***– him company,*** ihm Gesellschaft leisten; ***– comparison with,*** Vergleich aushalten mit; ***– fruit,*** Frucht tragen (*also fig.*); ***– him good will,*** ihm gewogen sein; ***– him a grudge, – a grudge against him,*** einen Groll gegen ihn hegen; ***– inspection,*** sich sehen lassen können; ***the text will not – such an interpretation,*** die Stelle kann nicht so ausgelegt werden; ***– a likeness to him,*** ihm ähneln; ***– a loss,*** einen Verlust tragen *or* leiden; ***not – repeating,*** sich nicht wiederholen lassen; ***– no relation to,*** in keinem Verhältnis stehen zu; ***– a resemblance to,*** Ähnlichkeit haben mit; ***– witness to,*** zeugen *or* Zeugnis ablegen für.

(b) (*with preps. or advs.*) ***– away,*** fort– *or* davontragen; hinreißen; ***– down,*** überwinden, überwältigen, niederdrücken; niederschlagen, niederwerfen, unterdrücken; ***it was borne in upon me that . . .,*** es drängte sich mir auf *or* es wurde mir klar, daß . . .; ***– in mind,*** sich (*Dat.*) merken; denken *or* sich erinnern an (*Acc.*), gedenken (*Gen.*), erwägen, berücksichtigen, (*coll.*) sich (*Dat.*) hinters Ohr schreiben; ***–ing in mind the conditions,*** wenn man die Bedingungen bedenkt; ***– off,*** wegtragen, fortführen, entführen, (*a prize*) davontragen; (*fig.*) ***– out,*** unterstützen, verteidigen; (*an assertion*) bestätigen, bekräftigen, erhärten; ***she bore him out,*** sie gab ihm recht; ***– up,*** (unter)stützen, aufrechterhalten; ***– o.s. well,*** sich gut betragen *or* benehmen *or* halten.

2. *irr.v.i.* (*p.p.* **borne**) 1. tragen; 2. trächtig sein (*as animals*); fruchtbar werden, Früchte tragen (*as plants*); ***this tree will – next year,*** dieser Baum wird nächstes Jahr tragen; 3. tragfähig sein (*as ice etc.*); 4. sich halten, gerichtet sein (*direction*); (*Naut.*) ***the buoy –s due east,*** die Boje liegt bei *or* auf Ost; 5. leiden, dulden; ***– and forbear,*** leide und meide. (*with preps. or advs.*) ***– against,*** drücken *or* sich lehnen gegen, (*obs.*) angreifen, losgehen auf (*Acc.*); (*Naut.*) ***– away,*** abfallen, ablaufen, abfahren; ***– down upon,*** schwer liegen *or* lasten auf (*Dat.*), drücken *or* einen Druck ausüben auf (*Acc.*); zuhalten *or* zusteuern auf (*Acc.*); (*fig.*) ***– on,*** Bezug haben *or* sich beziehen auf (*Acc.*); einwirken *or* einen Einfluß haben auf (*Acc.*); im Zusammenhang stehen mit; ***bring to –,*** geltend machen, zur Geltung bringen; ausüben (*pressure*); einwirken *or* eindrucksvoll wirken (*on,* auf (*Acc.*)); ***– out to sea,*** auslaufen, in See stechen; ***– to the right*** (***left***), sich rechts (links) halten; ***– up,*** ausharren, standhaft sein, festbleiben, nicht verzagen; ***– up against,*** widerstehen (*Dat.*); standhalten *or* sich behaupten gegen; ***– up towards,*** zusegeln auf (*Acc.*); ***– with,*** geduldig ertragen, auskommen mit, Nachsicht haben mit.

bearable ['bɛərəbl], *adj.* erträglich, zu ertragen(d).

bear-baiting, *s.* die Bärenhetze.

beard [biəd], **1.** *s.* der Bart, Vollbart; (*Bot.*) die Granne (*oft. pl.*), Fasern (*pl.*), (*Zool.*) die Barte (*of whales*) (*oft. pl.*). **2.** *v.t.* (*fig.*) Trotz bieten (*Dat.*), kühn entgegentreten (*Dat.*). **bearded,** *adj.* bärtig; mit Grannen; Barten–.

bearer [ˈbɛərə], *s.* der Träger; Leichenträger (*at funerals*); Überbringer (*of a letter etc.*); (*Comm.*) Inhaber; (*Her.*) Schildhalter; (*Tech.*) Träger, die Stütze.

bear garden, *s.* der Bärenzwinger; (*fig.*) lärmende Versammlung.

bearing [ˈbɛəriŋ], *s.* 1. das Tragen; (*fig.*) Ertragen, Dulden; ***his arrogance is past* –,** sein Hochmut ist unerträglich; ***the tree is past* –,** der Baum trägt keine Früchte mehr; 2. das Betragen, Verhalten; die (Körper)haltung; (*fig.*) Beziehung, der Bezug (*on*, auf (*Acc.*)), Zusammenhang (mit), das Verhältnis (zu), der Einfluß (auf (*Acc.*)); (*fig.*) ***have no – on,*** keinen Einfluß haben auf (*Acc.*), keine Beziehung haben zu, in keinem Zusammenhang stehen mit; 3. die Richtung, Lage, (*Surv.*) Visierlinie, (*Naut., Av.*) Peilung, *pl.* (*fig.*) Orientierung; (*fig.*) ***find one's –s,*** sich orientieren; (*fig.*) ***lose one's –s,*** sich verirren *or* verlaufen; ***take*** or ***obtain a – on,*** anpeilen; peilen *or* orten an (*Acc.*); ***magnetic*** or ***compass* –,** mißweisende Peilung; ***true* –,** rechtweisende Peilung; ***radio* –,** die Funkpeilung; ***reciprocal* –,** die Gegenpeilung; 4. (*Archit.*) die Tragweite, Tracht, Spannweite, freitragende Länge; 5. (*Tech.*) das Lager, Auflager, die Lagerung; ***ball –s,*** das Kugellager; ***friction* –,** das Gleitlager; ***journal* –,** das Zapfen– *or* Achsen– *or* Wellenlager; ***roller* –,** das Rollenlager; ***trunnion* –,** das Zapfen– *or* Schildlager; 6. *pl.* (*Her.*) das Wappenbild; ***armorial –s,*** das Wappen.

bearing| angle, *s.* der Peilwinkel. **--rein,** *s.* der Ausbindezügel. **--seat,** *s.* die Lagerschale. **—spring,** *s.* die Tragfeder. **– surface,** *s.* die Auflage– *or* Lauf– *or* Führungsfläche.

bearish [ˈbɛəriʃ], *adj.* bärenhaft, (*fig.*) plump, täppisch, tolpatschig; (*Comm.*) Baisse–, baissetendenziös, flau; (*coll.*) brummig, unfreundlich.

bear's|-ear, *s.* (*Bot.*) die Aurikel. **--foot,** *s.* (*Bot.*) stinkende Nieswurz.

bearskin [ˈbɛəskin], *s.* das Bärenfell; (*Mil.*) die Bären(fell)mütze.

beast [bi:st], *s.* das Tier; (Mast)vieh; (*coll.*) der Rohling, roher *or* brutaler Mensch, die Bestie, das Biest; ***– of burden,*** das Lasttier; ***– of prey,*** das Raubtier; ***– epic,*** das Tierepos; (*coll.*) ***a – of a day,*** ein scheußlicher Tag. **beastliness,** *s.* die Bestialität, Schweinerei; Gemeinheit, Roheit, (*coll.*) Scheußlichkeit. **beastly,** *adj.* tierisch; viehisch, bestialisch; roh, gemein, brutal; (*coll.*) scheußlich, abscheulich, ekelhaft, garstig; (*sl.*) ***– shame,*** die Gemeinheit, Affenschande; (*coll.*) ***– weather,*** das Hundewetter, Sauwetter.

beat [bi:t], **1.** *s.* 1. das Schlagen, Pochen, Klopfen; der Schlag, Hieb; (*Med.*) Pulsschlag; (*Mus.*) Takt(schlag); (*Metr.*) Ton, die Hebung; (*Phys.*) Schwebung (*between two frequencies*); ***– of the drum,*** der Trommelschlag; 2. die Runde, das Revier, der (Amts)bereich, Bezirk; 3. (*Am. sl.*) Nichtsnutz, Schmarotzer.

2. *irr.v.t.* schlagen, (ver)prügeln (*a p.*), schlagen, besiegen, überwältigen (*the enemy*), übertreffen, überbieten (*a rival*), schlagen, drücken (*a record*); klopfen, (zer)stoßen, (zer)stampfen, zerschlagen, zertrümmern; hämmern, schmieden (*metal*), dreschen (*corn*), schwingen (*flax*), schlagen, rühren (*eggs, a drum*), (aus)klopfen (*clothes, carpets*); treten, stampfen, (sich (*Dat.*)) bahnen (*a path*), (*Hunt.*) abklopfen, durchstreifen, durchstöbern (*the ground*), aufjagen (*game*).

(a) (*with nouns*) ***– the air,*** in den Wind reden, gegen Windmühlen kämpfen; (*coll.*) ***– the band,*** alles übertreffen, dem Faß den Boden ausschlagen; ***– the bounds,*** um die (Kreis)grenzen *or* die Gemarkung umgehen; ***– one's breast,*** sich an die Brust schlagen; (*Mil.*) ***– the retreat,*** zum Rückzug trommeln; (*fig.*) ***– a retreat,*** sich zurückziehen, sich aus dem Staub machen; klein beigeben, das Feld räumen; (*Mil.*) ***– a tattoo,*** (den) Zapfenstreich schlagen; (*Mus.*) ***– time,*** den Takt schlagen; ***– the wings,*** mit den Flügeln schlagen.

(b) (*with prons.*) ***that –s everything!*** das übertrifft alles! da hört alles auf! (*sl.*) ***– it,*** abhauen, verduften; (*coll.*) ***can you – it?*** das ist ja unerhört; (*coll.*) ***there's nothing to – it,*** darüber geht nichts; ***that –s me,*** da kann ich nicht mehr mit; ***I'll – you to it,*** ich komme dir zuvor.

(c) (*with advs. or preps.*) ***– back,*** zurücktreiben, zurückschlagen, abschlagen; ***– down,*** niederschlagen, bedrücken; herunterhandeln, drücken (*price*), (*coll.*) übertrumpfen (*a p.*); (*coll.*) ***– hollow,*** glatt besiegen; ***– into his head,*** ihm einhämmern *or* einbleuen; (*coll.*) ***– into a cocked hat,*** vernichtend schlagen, total fertigmachen; ***– off,*** see ***– back***; ***– out,*** aushauen, aushämmern, (*fig.*) herausarbeiten, ausknobeln; ***– up,*** (*Mil.*) zusammentrommeln, (*recruits*) werben; (*eggs, dough etc.*) schlagen, rühren, quirlen; (*coll.*) auftreiben, aufstöbern; (*sl.*) verdreschen, verhauen.

3. *irr.v.i.* schlagen, pochen, klopfen; (*as wind, waves etc.*) peitschen, tosen, wüten; (*Naut.*) lavieren, kreuzen; (*Phys.*) Schwebungen ergeben; ***the drums are –ing,*** es wird getrommelt, die Trommeln ertönen; ***the sun –s (down) fiercely,*** die Sonne strahlt heftig herab (*on*, auf (*Acc.*)); (*coll.*) ***– about the bush,*** wie die Katze um den heißen Brei herumgehen; (*Naut.*) ***– to quarters,*** Klarschiff zum Gefecht blasen; (*Naut.*) ***– to windward,*** aufkreuzen, anluven, gegen den Wind segeln.

4. *adj.* (*coll.*) zerschlagen, (wie) erschlagen, erschöpft, kaputt.

beaten [bi:tn], *adj.* geschlagen, besiegt; (*Tech.*) gehämmert; (*coll.*) verblüfft, am Ende seiner Weisheit; (*fig.*) breitgetreten, abgedroschen; ***– gold,*** das Blattgold, die Goldfolie; ***– path,*** gebahnter *or* ausgetretener *or* vielbegangener Weg; (*fig.*) ***– track,*** herkömmliche Art und Weise, üblicher Weg, ausgetretener Pfad; (*fig.*) ***off the – track,*** ungewöhnlich; (*Mil.*) ***– zone,*** bestrichener Raum.

beater [ˈbi:tə], *s.* der Schläger (*a p.*), (*Hunt.*) Treiber; (*a tool*) Schlegel, Klöpfel, die Ramme, das Rammeisen, Schlageisen; die Stampfe, Stoffmühle.

beat-frequency, *s.* (*Rad.*) die Schwebungs– *or* Überlagerungsfrequenz; ***– oscillator,*** der Schwebungssummer, Überlagerungsoszillator.

beatific [biəˈtifik], *adj.* beseligend, seligmachend; (glück)selig, glückstrahlend. **beatification** [biætifiˈkeiʃən], *s.* die Seligsprechung. **beatify** [biˈætifai], *v.t.* (*R.C.*) seligmachen, seligsprechen.

beating [ˈbi:tiŋ], *s.* das Schlagen, Klopfen; Schläge (*pl.*), Prügel (*pl.*), die Züchtigung; Niederlage; (*Naut.*) das Lavieren, Kreuzen; (*Hunt.*) Treiben; ***give him a sound –,*** ihn tüchtig durchprügeln; ***get a sound –,*** eine Tracht Prügel bekommen; ***– of the heart,*** der Herzschlag; ***– of the drum(s),*** der Trommelschlag.

beatitude [biˈætitju:d], *s.* die (Glück)seligkeit; (*B.*) ***the Beatitudes,*** die Seligpreisungen.

beat-music, *s.* Schlager (*pl.*).

beatnik [ˈbi:tnik], *s.* (*coll.*) der Gammler.

beat-note, *s.* (*Phys.*) der Schwebungs– *or* Interferenzton.

beau [bou], *s.* (*pl.* **-x** [–z]) der Stutzer, Geck; Verehrer, Courmacher. **beau-ideal,** *s.* das Ideal, Vorbild, Muster.

beauteous [ˈbju:tiəs], *adj.* (*Poet.*) schön. **beauteousness,** *s.* die Schönheit. **beautician** [–ˈtiʃən], *s.* (*Am.*) der (die) Schönheitspfleger(in). **beautification** [–tifiˈkeiʃən], *s.* die Verschönerung. **beautiful** [ˈbju:tiful], *adj.* schön; (*coll.*) wunderschön, bewundernswert. **beautify** [–fai], *v.t.* verschöne(r)n, schön(er) machen, ausschmücken.

beauty [ˈbju:ti], *s.* die Schönheit, das Schöne; (*a p.*) die Schöne, Schönheit; (*a th., coll.*) das Prachtexemplar; die Anmut, der Reiz; ***the – of it,*** das Schönste daran; ***a thing of –,*** etwas Schönes; (*coll.*) ***it is really a –,*** es ist eine wahre Pracht; ***– is but***

skin-deep, man kann nach dem Äußeren nicht urteilen; ***Beauty and the Beast,*** die Schöne und das Tier; ***Sleeping Beauty,*** Dornröschen; (*Ent.*) ***Camberwell –,*** der Trauermantel. **beauty| contest,** *s.* der Schönheitswettbewerb. **--culture,** *s.* die Schönheitspflege. **--parlour,** *s.* der Schönheitssalon. **--sleep,** *s.* (*coll.*) der Schlaf vor Mitternacht. **--spot,** *s.* das Schönheitspflästerchen; schöne Gegend.

[1]beaver ['bi:və], *s.* (*Zool.*) der Biber; Biberpelz; (*sl.*) Bart; bärtiger Mann; – ***hat,*** der Kastorhut.

[2]beaver, *s.* (*Hist.*) das Visier, der Helmsturz.

beaver|-dam, --lodge, *s.* der Biberbau.

becalm [bi'kɑ:m], *v.t.* beruhigen, besänftigen, stillen; (*Naut.*) bekalmen; ***be –ed,*** in Windstille geraten, eine Flaute haben, blind liegen.

became [bi'keim], *imperf. of* **become.**

because [bi'kɔz], *conj.* weil; – ***of,*** wegen, auf Grund (*Gen.*), aufgrund (*Gen.*), infolge (*Gen.*), infolge von, auf Grund von; – ***of you,*** Ihretwegen; um Ihretwillen.

bechamel ['beʃəmel], *s.* weiße Rahmsoße.

[1]beck [bek], *s.* (*dial., Poet.*) das Bächlein.

[2]beck, *s.* der Wink, das Kopfnicken; ***be at his – and call,*** auf seinen Wink und Ruf bereit sein.

becket ['bekit], *s.* (*Naut.*) der Stropp.

beckon ['bekən], **1.** *v.t.* (zu)winken, (zu)nicken (*Dat.*), herbeiwinken. **2.** *v.i.* winken; – ***to him,*** ihm zunicken *or* zuwinken.

becloud [bi'klaud], *v.t.* umwölken (*also fig.*), (*fig.*) trüben.

become [bi'kʌm], **1.** *irr.v.i.* werden (zu); ***they became acquainted,*** sie wurden miteinander bekannt; ***he became a doctor,*** er wurde Arzt; ***it became a fashion,*** es wurde zur Mode; ***they became friends,*** sie wurden Freunde; ***what is to – of her?*** was soll aus ihr werden? **2.** *irr.v.t.* sich (ge)ziemen *or* schicken für; (*clothes*) stehen (*Dat.*), passen zu, kleiden; ***it ill –s you,*** es steht Ihnen übel an, es geziemt sich nicht für Sie, es paßt sich schlecht für Sie; ***the hat –s you,*** der Hut steht Ihnen *or* kleidet Sie.

becoming [bi'kʌmiŋ], **1.** *s.* das Entstehen, Werden. **2.** *adj.* geziemend, passend, schicklich; (*clothes*) passend, kleidend, kleidsam; ***with – respect,*** mit gehöriger *or* geziemender Hochachtung; ***as is –,*** wie es sich gebührt.

bed [bed], **1.** *s.* das Bett (*also of a river*); Lager (*of animals*); (*fig.*) Logis, die Übernachtung, Schlafstätte; (*Archit.*) Unterlage, Bettung, Lagerung, Lage, Schicht; (*Geol.*) Schicht, Lage, Lagerung, das Lager, Geleg, Flöz; (*Railw.*) Schotterbett, der Unterbau; das Beet (*of flowers*); – ***of clay,*** die Tonschicht; – ***of ease,*** das Faulbett; – ***of the ocean,*** der Meeresgrund; – ***of a river,*** das Flußbett; – ***of roses,*** rosige Lage; – ***of sickness,*** das Krankenlager; – ***of state,*** das Paradebett; – ***of straw,*** das Strohlager; (*fig.*) – ***of thorns,*** das Schmerzenslager; ***double –,*** das Doppelbett, Ehebett, zweischläfriges Bett; ***flower –,*** das Blumenbeet; – ***and board,*** Tisch und Bett; – ***and breakfast,*** das Zimmer mit Frühstück; ***be brought to –,*** niederkommen, entbunden werden; ***be confined to one's –,*** bettlägerig sein; ***get into –,*** ins Bett gehen, sich zu Bett legen; ***get out of –,*** aufstehen; (*coll.*) ***get out of – on the wrong side,*** mit dem linken *or* verkehrten Fuß aus dem Bett steigen; ***go to –,*** schlafen *or* zu Bett gehen; (*Prov.*) ***early to – and early to rise, makes a man healthy, wealthy and wise,*** Morgenstunde hat Gold im Munde; ***keep one's –,*** daniederliegen, das Bett hüten; (*Prov.*) ***as one makes one's –, so one must lie,*** wie man sich bettet, so liegt man; ***put to –,*** schlafen legen, zu Bett bringen; ***take to one's –,*** sich hinlegen, sich (krank) ins Bett legen; ***turn down the –,*** das Bett aufdecken. **2.** *v.t.* betten (*beasts*), pflanzen, einbetten (*plants*); – ***down,*** mit Streu versorgen (*beasts*); – ***out,*** verpflanzen, ins Freie setzen. **3.** *v.i.* (*coll.*) – ***down,*** sich schlafen legen, sich ein Lager bereiten.

bedaub [bi'dɔ:b], *v.t.* beschmieren, beschmutzen.

bed|-bug, *s.* die Wanze. **--chamber,** *s.* das Schlafgemach; ***Gentleman of the King's –,*** königlicher Kammerherr; ***Lady of the Queen's –,*** königliche Hofdame. **--clothes,** *pl.* das Bettzeug, die Bettwäsche. **--curtains,** *pl.* die Bettvorhänge.

bedded ['bedid], *adj.* (ein)gebettet, gelagert, geschichtet; (*Hort.*) in Beeten wachsend, ins Freie verpflanzt. **-bedded,** *adj. suff.* -bettig. **bedder,** *s.* **1.** *See* **bedmaker**; 2. (*Hort.*) der Freilandsetzling. **bedding,** *s.* das Bettzeug; (*for cattle*) die (Lager)streu; (*Geol.*) Schichtung, Schichtenbildung; (*Tech.*) Bettung, das Lager; (*Archit.*) Fundament, die Unterlage, Untermauerung.

bedeck [bi'dek], *v.t.* schmücken, zieren.

bedevil [bi'devl], *v.t.* behexen, verhexen; quälen, plagen; (*fig.*) verpfuschen, vermasseln. **bedevilled,** *adj.* verhext, besessen. **bedevilment,** *s.* die Verhexung, Besessenheit; (*fig.*) heillose Verwirrung.

bedew [bi'dju:], *v.t.* betauen, benetzen, besprengen.

bed|fellow, *s.* der Schlafkamerad; (*fig.*) Genosse. **--head,** *s.* das Kopfende (des Bettes).

bedizen [bi'd(a)izn], *v.t.* herausputzen, ausstaffieren, (*coll.*) aufdonnern.

bedlam ['bedləm], *s.* (*Hist.*) das Tollhaus, Irrenhaus; (*fig.*) Tollhaus, toller Lärm. **bedlamite,** *s.* (*Hist.*) der Tollhäusler, Wahnsinnige(r).

bed|-linen, *s.* die Bettwäsche. **-maker,** *s.* (*Univ.*) die Aufwartefrau.

Bedouin ['beduin], **1.** *s.* der Beduine. **2.** *adj.* Beduinen–, beduinisch.

bed|pan, *s.* die Leibesschüssel, das Stechbecken. **--plate,** *s.* die Bodenplatte, Grundplatte, Unterlagsplatte, Bettung. **--post,** *s.* der Bettpfosten.

bedraggle [bi'drægl], *v.t.* beschmutzen, ramponieren.

bed|ridden, *adj.* bettlägerig. **-rock,** *s.* (*Geol.*) die Grundschicht, das Grundgestein, Muttergestein; (*fig.*) Fundament, die Grundlage; – ***truth,*** die Grundwahrheit; – ***price,*** niedrigster *or* äußerster Preis. **-room,** *s.* das Schlafzimmer. **-side,** *s.* die Bettseite; ***by her –,*** an ihrem Bette; – ***carpet,*** der Bettvorleger; ***have a good – manner,*** mit den Kranken gut umzugehen wissen, sich taktvoll verhalten beim Krankenbesuch. **--sitter, --sitting room,** *s.* das Wohnschlafzimmer. **-sore,** *s.* (*Med.*) der Dekubitus; ***get –s,*** sich wundliegen. **-spread,** *s.* die Tagesdecke, (Zier)bettdecke. **-stead,** *s.* das Bettgestell, die Bettstelle. **--tick,** *s.* der Matratzenüberzug, das (Oberbett)inlett. **-time,** *s.* die Schlafenszeit; (***long***) ***past –,*** höchste Zeit zum Schlafengehen.

bee [bi:], *s.* **1.** die Biene; (*fig.*) arbeitsamer Mensch; (*coll.*) ***have a – in one's bonnet,*** einen Vogel haben, Grillen im Kopf haben; (***as***) ***busy as a –,*** emsig wie eine Biene; ***queen –,*** der Weisel, die Bienenkönigin; ***swarm of –s,*** der Bienenschwarm; 2. (*coll.*) das Arbeitskränzchen; ***spelling –,*** das Buchstabierspiel.

bee-bread, *s.* das Bienenbrot.

beech [bi:tʃ], *s.* die Buche; ***common –,*** die Rotbuche; ***copper –,*** die Blutbuche. **beechen,** *adj.* buchen, aus Buchenholz. **beech|-mast,** *s.* die Buchmast. **--nut,** *s.* die Buchecker, Buchel. **--oil,** *s.* das Bucheckeröl. **--tree,** *s.* die Buche.

bee-eater, *s.* der Bienenfresser.

beef [bi:f], **1.** *s.* **1.** (*pl.* **beeves**) das Rind; 2. (*no pl.*) Rindfleisch, Ochsenfleisch; ***corned –,*** das Büchsenfleisch; ***roast –,*** der Rindsbraten, Rostbraten; ***sirloin of –,*** der Lendenbraten; 3. (*fig., coll.*) die Muskelkraft. **2.** *v.i.* (*sl.*) meckern, nörgeln. **beef|-cake,** *s.* (*sl.*) das Bild eines Muskelprotzen. **--cube,** *s.* der Bouillonwürfel. **-eater,** *s.* königlicher Leibgardist. **-steak,** *s.* die Lendenschnitte, das Beefsteak. **--tea,** *s.* die Kraftbrühe, Fleischbrühe. **beefy,** *adj.* (*coll.*) kräftig, muskulös.

bee|-glue, *s.* das Bienenharz, Klebwachs. **-hive,** *s.* der Bienenstock, Bienenkorb. **-keeper,** *s.* der Bienenzüchter, Imker. **-keeping,** *s.* die Bienenzucht. **--line,** *s.* (*fig.*) kürzester *or* gerader Weg, die Luftlinie; ***make a – for,*** schnurgerade *or* schnurstracks losgehen auf (*Acc.*)

been [bi:n], *p.p. of* **be.**

beer [biə], *s.* das Bier; ***life is not all – and skittles,*** das Leben ist nicht eitel Freude; ***small –,*** das Dünnbier; (*coll.*) ***think no small – of,*** sehr viel halten von. **beer|-barrel,** *s.* das Bierfaß. **--engine,** *s.* der Bierdruckapparat. **--garden,** *s.* das Gartenlokal. **--house,** *s.* die Bierhalle, Bierstube, Schenke, Kneipe. **--mat,** *s.* der Bierdeckel. **--mug,** *s.* der Bierkrug, das Seidel. **--pull,** *s.* die Bierpumpe. **beery,** *adj.* Bier–, bierartig; (*coll.*) (*of a p.*) bierselig, bierduselig.

bee-sting, *s.* der Bienenstich.

beestings ['bi:stiŋz], *pl.* die Biestmilch, der Biest.

beeswax ['bi:zwæks], **1.** *s.* das Bienenwachs. **2.** *v.t.* bohnern, wachsern. **bee's-wine,** *s.* der Blütennektar.

beet [bi:t], *s.* die Rünkelrube, Bete; ***red –,*** rote Bete *or* Rübe; ***sugar –,*** die Zuckerrübe.

[1]**beetle** [bi:tl], **1.** *s.* (*Tech.*) der Schlegel, Bleuel, die Ramme, Stampfe. **2.** *v.t.* rammen, (ein)stampfen; (*textiles*) kalandern, ***beetling machine*** or ***mill,*** der Stampfkalander.

[2]**beetle,** *s.* (*Ent.*) der Käfer; ***Colorado –,*** der Kartoffelkäfer.

[3]**beetle,** *v.i.* überhängen, vorstehen, hervorragen.

beetle|browed, *adj.* mit überhängenden Augenbrauen. **--crushers,** *pl.* (*sl.*) Quadratlatschen (*pl.*).

beet|root, *s.* rote Rübe *or* Bete. **--sugar,** *s.* der Rübenzucker.

beeves [bi:vz], *pl. of* **beef, 1.**

befall [bi'fɔ:l], **1.** *irr.v.t.* begegnen, zustoßen, widerfahren (*Dat.*). **2.** *irr.v.i.* sich ereignen, sich zutragen.

befit [bi'fit], *v.t.* sich schicken *or* ziemen für; anstehen (*Dat.*). **befitting,** *adj.* geziemend, passend, schicklich, angemessen.

befog [bi'fɔg], *v.t.* in Nebel hüllen; (*fig.*) umnebeln, verwirren.

befool [bi'fu:l], *v.t.* betören, anführen, zum Narren halten *or* haben.

before [bi'fɔ:], **1.** *adv.* (*place*) vorn, voran, voraus; (*time*) vorher, zuvor, vormals, ehemals, ehedem, eher, früher, bereits, schon; ***an hour –,*** eine Stunde früher *or* vorher; ***go on –,*** vorausgehen, vorangehen; ***that was never known –,*** ehemals wußte man das nicht; ***I have told him –,*** ich habe es ihm schon gesagt. **2.** *prep.* vor; ***– all,*** vor allem; ***– his arrival,*** vor seiner Ankunft; ***– the door,*** vor der Tür; ***– my very eyes,*** gerade vor meinen Augen; ***swear – God,*** vor *or* bei Gott schwören; ***the week – last,*** vorletzte Woche; ***– long,*** in Kürze, bald; (*Naut.*) ***– the mast,*** als gewöhnlicher Matrose; ***– now,*** schon früher; ***he carries everything – him,*** er siegt auf der ganzen Linie; ***the question – us,*** die (uns) vorliegende Frage; ***sail – the wind,*** vor dem Wind segeln; ***the day – yesterday,*** vorgestern. **3.** *conj.* bevor, ehe; ***not –,*** erst als *or* wenn; ***– you know where you are,*** im Handumdrehen; ***I would die – I would . . .,*** eher *or* lieber würde *or* will ich sterben, als daß ich *or* zu (*inf.*) . . .; ***it will not be long – you repent of it,*** es dauert nicht lange, bis Sie es bereuen.

before|hand, *adv.* vorher, zuvor, im voraus; ***I think it necessary to observe –,*** ich halte es für notwendig, von vornherein zu bemerken; ***be – with s.th.,*** es vorwegnehmen, einer S. (*Dat.*) zuvorkommen. **--mentioned,** *adj.* vorhererwähnt, obenerwähnt.

befoul [bi'faul], *v.t.* besudeln, beschmutzen.

befriend [bi'frend], *v.t.* als Freund behandeln, Freundschaft erzeigen (*Dat.*); unterstützen, begünstigen; ***she –ed him,*** sie nahm sich seiner an.

beg [beg], **1.** *v.t.* 1. betteln um, erbetteln; 2. bitten *or* ersuchen (*a p.*) um (*a th.*), erbitten (*a th.*) von (*a p.*); ***– him to come,*** ihn bitten zu kommen; ***– leave,*** um Erlaubnis bitten; ***I – your pardon,*** verzeihen Sie! wie bitte? ***– the question,*** den (Frage)punkt als bewiesen annehmen, (*coll.*) dem wahren Sachverhalt ausweichen. **2.** *v.i.* 1. betteln (***for,*** um); (*of dogs*) Männchen machen; 2. flehen (***for,*** um); ***– for mercy,*** um Gnade flehen; ***– of him not to go,*** ihn dringend bitten, nicht zu gehen; ***I – to differ,*** ich erlaube mir anderer Ansicht zu sein; ***I – to remain yours respectfully,*** ich verbleibe mit vorzüglicher Hochachtung Ihr sehr ergebener; ***I – to inform you,*** ich gestatte mir Ihnen mitzuteilen.

began [bi'gæn], *imperf. of* **begin.**

begat [bi'gæt], (*obs.*) *imperf. of* **beget.**

beget [bi'get], *irr.v.t.* zeugen; (*fig.*) hervorbringen, in die Welt setzen, erzeugen. **begetter,** *s.* der Erzeuger, Vater; (*fig.*) Veranlasser, Urheber.

beggar ['begə], **1.** *s.* der (die) Bettler(in); (*coll.*) Bursche, Kerl; (*Prov.*) ***–s must not be choosers,*** einem geschenkten Gaul sieht man nicht ins Maul; (*coll.*) ***lucky –,*** der Glückspilz. **2.** *v.t.* 1. zum Bettler machen, an den Bettelstab bringen; 2. berauben, entblößen; (*fig.*) übertreffen, übersteigen; ***it –s description,*** es spottet jeder Beschreibung, es geht über alle Beschreibung.

beggar-boy, *s.* der Betteljunge. **beggarliness,** *s.* die Bettelarmut; Armseligkeit; Erbärmlichkeit, Dürftigkeit. **beggarly,** *adj.* bettelhaft; armselig, erbärmlich, (*coll.*) lumpig; ***– price,*** der Bettelpreis. **beggar-my-neighbour,** *s.* (*Cards*) Tod und Leben, der Bettelmann. **Beggar's Opera,** *s.* die Dreigroschenoper. **beggary,** *s.* die Bettelarmut; ***reduce to –,*** an den Bettelstab bringen.

begging ['begiŋ], **1.** *s.* das Betteln, die Bettelei; das Bitten, Ersuchen; ***– the question,*** die Petitio principii, Annahme einer erst zu beweisender S. **2.** *adj.* bettelnd; ***– letter,*** der Bittbrief, das Bittschreiben.

begin [bi'gin], *irr.v.t., irr.v.i.* anfangen, beginnen; ***– a journey,*** eine Reise antreten; ***– again,*** von neuem anfangen; ***– by doing s.th.,*** damit anfangen, etwas zu tun; ***– on a th.,*** etwas in Angriff nehmen; ***to – with,*** erstens, anfangs, am Anfang, vorerst, zunächst; ***I – to see,*** es geht mir ein Licht auf; (*Prov.*) ***well begun is half done,*** wohl begonnen ist halb gewonnen. **beginner,** *s.* der (die) Anfänger(in).

beginning [bi'giniŋ], *s.* der Anfang, Beginn; Ursprung; ***in*** or ***at the –,*** bei Beginn, im *or* am *or* zu Anfang; ***the – of the end,*** der Anfang vom Ende; ***from the –,*** von Anfang an; ***from – to end,*** von Anfang bis (zu) Ende. **beginnings,** *pl.* die ersten Anfänge, das Anfangsstadium; ***small –,*** ein kleiner Anfang.

begird [bi'gə:d], *irr.v.t.* umgürten; (*fig.*) umgeben, umringen, einschließen.

begirt [bi'gə:t], *p.p. of* **begird.**

begone! [bi'gɔn], *int.* hinweg! fort! weg (mit dir)! packe dich!

begonia [bi'gouniə], *s.* (*Bot.*) die Begonie, das Schiefblatt.

begot [bi'gɔt], *imperf. of* **beget.**

begotten [bi'gɔtn], *adj.* ***the only – Son of God,*** Gottes eingeborener Sohn. *See* **beget.**

begrime [bi'graim], *v.t.* beschmieren, besudeln, beschmutzen.

begrudge [bi'grʌdʒ], *v.t.* mißgönnen, neiden, ungern geben (***him a th.,*** ihm etwas), beneiden (ihn um etwas).

beguile [bi'gail], *v.t.* betrügen (***of,*** um), verleiten, verführen (***into doing,*** zu tun); bestricken, bezaubern, betören (*a p.*), vertreiben, hinbringen, verkürzen (*time*). **beguilement,** *s.* der Betrug, die Täuschung, Hintergehung; der Zeitvertreib. **beguiling,** *adj.* verführerisch, betrügerisch, täuschend; verlockend, bezaubernd, bestrickend, berückend.

begum ['bi:gəm], *s.* die Begum, Begam.

begun [bi'gʌn], *p.p. of* **begin.**

behalf [bi'hɑ:f], *s.* (*obs.*) der Behuf, Vorteil, Nutzen; (*only in*) ***on my –, on – of myself,*** für mich; in meinem Namen, in meinem Interesse, um meinetwillen, meinetwegen; ***on – of the poor,*** zugunsten *or* zum Besten der Armen.

behave [bi'heiv], **1.** *v.i.* handeln, sich benehmen, sich betragen; sich anständig benehmen; sich verhalten, fungieren (*of things*); funktionieren (*of machines*); ***– badly,*** sich schlecht betragen. **2.** *v.r.*

sich (anständig) benehmen. **-behaved,** *adj. suff. well--*, wohlerzogen, artig; *ill--* or *badly* -, ungezogen, unartig.

behavior (*Am.*), **behaviour** [bi'heivjə], *s.* das Betragen, Verhalten, Benehmen; Auftreten, die Führung, der Anstand; ***he is on his good*** or ***best*** -, er achtet sehr auf sein Benehmen; (*Psych.*) - ***pattern,*** das Verhaltensmuster. **behaviourism,** *s.* (*Psych.*) der Behaviorismus.

behead [bi'hed], *v.t.* enthaupten, köpfen. **beheading,** *s.* die Enthauptung.

beheld [bi'held], *imperf., p.p. of* **behold.**

behest [bi'hest], *s.* (*Poet.*) das Geheiß, der Befehl.

behind [bi'haind], **1.** *adv.* hinten(nach), dahinter, hinterher; ***fall*** -, zurückbleiben; ***get up*** -, hinten aufsteigen; ***leave*** -, zurücklassen, hinter sich lassen. **2.** *pred. adj.* zurück, im Rückstand. **3.** *prep.* hinter; - ***his back,*** hinter seinem Rücken; ohne sein Wissen, heimlich; ***she is not - him in zeal,*** sie steht ihm an Eifer nicht nach; ***she looked - (her),*** sie blickte zurück *or* sah sich um; ***the groom rode - him,*** der Diener ritt hinter ihm her; - ***the scenes,*** hinter den Kulissen, im geheimen; ***be - time,*** zu spät (daran) sein, Verspätung *or* sich verspätet haben; - ***the times,*** rückständig; ***there is something - all that,*** es steckt etwas dahinter. **4.** *s.* (*coll.*) der Hintern.

behindhand [bi'haindhænd], *adv., pred. adj.* im Rückstand, zurück (***with,*** mit); verspätet; (*fig.*) rückständig.

behold [bi'hould], **1.** *irr.v.t.* (*Poet.*) anschauen, ansehen, betrachten; sehen, erblicken. **2.** *int.* sieh (da)!

beholden [bi'houldn], *pred. adj.* verpflichtet, verbunden (*to, Dat.*).

beholder [bi'houldə], *s.* der Beschauer, Zuschauer, Beobachter.

behoove [bi'hu:v] (*Am.*), **behoof** [bi'hu:f], *s.* (*obs.*) *see* **behalf.**

behove [bi'houv], *v.imp.* gebühren (*Dat.*), erforderlich sein *or* sich ziemen *or* sich schicken für; ***it -s me,*** es geziemt mir, es gehört sich für mich, es liegt mir ob.

beige [beiʒ], **1.** *s.* die Beige (*textile*); das Beige (*colour*). **2.** *adj.* gelbgrau, sandfarben, beige.

being ['bi:iŋ], **1.** *pres. p. of* **be. 2.** *s.* das Sein, Dasein, die Existenz; das Wesen, die Kreatur; ***in*** -, (tatsächlich) vorhanden, existierend; ***call into*** -, ins Leben rufen; ***come into*** -, entstehen; ***human*** -, der Mensch; ***living*** -, lebendes Wesen, das Lebewesen; ***the Supreme Being,*** das höchste Wesen.

bejewel [bi'dʒu:əl], *v.t.* (*usu. p.p.*) mit Edelsteinen schmücken.

belabour [bi'leibə], *v.t.* tüchtig prügeln, durchprügeln.

belated [bi'leitid], *adj.* verspätet; (*obs.*) von der Nacht überrascht.

belay [bi'lei], **1.** *v.t.* (*Naut.*) belegen; (*Mount.*) sichern. **2.** *s.* (*Mount.*) die Sicherung. **belaying-pin,** *s.* (*Naut.*) der Belegnagel.

belch [beltʃ], **1.** *v.i.* rülpsen, aufstoßen. **2.** *v.t.* (*fig.*) - (***forth***), ausstoßen, ausspeien. **3.** *s.* das Rülpsen, Aufstoßen; (*fig.*) der Ausbruch.

beldam(e) ['beldəm], *s.* (*obs.*) altes Weib, alte Vettel, das Mütterchen.

beleaguer [bi'li:gə], *v.t.* belagern, (*fig.*) umgeben, blockieren.

belemnite ['beləmnait], *s.* der Donnerkeil, Belemnit.

bel esprit [beles'pri:], *s.* (*pl.* **beaux esprits** [bouzes'pri:]) geistreicher Mensch, das Genie.

belfry ['belfri], *s.* der Glockenturm, Glockenstuhl; (*coll.*) ***he has bats in the*** -, er hat einen Vogel.

Belgian ['beldʒən], **1.** *s.* der (die) Belgier(in). **2.** *adj.* belgisch. **Belgium** [-əm], *s.* Belgien (*n.*).

belie [bi'lai], *v.t.* widersprechen, nicht entsprechen (*Dat.*); als falsch erweisen, Lügen strafen; täuschen (*hopes*).

belief [bi'li:f], *s.* der Glaube (***in,*** an (*Acc.*)), das Vertrauen (auf (*Acc.*) (*a th.*), zu (*a p.*)); die Meinung; Überzeugung; (*Eccl.*) das Glaubensbekenntnis; *pl.* Glaubensanschauungen (*pl.*); ***to the best of my*** -, nach bestem Wissen (und Gewissen); ***past*** (***all***) -, unglaublich.

believable [bi'li:vəbl], *adj.* glaublich, glaubhaft.

believe, 1. *v.t.* glauben, meinen; ***he is not to be -d,*** man darf ihm keinen Glauben schenken; ***I - him to be a fool,*** ich halte ihn für einen Narren; ***make him - it,*** ihn es glauben machen, ihm es weismachen. **2.** *v.i.* glauben (***in,*** an (*Acc.*)); vertrauen (auf (*Acc.*)), Vertrauen haben (zu), Hoffnung setzen (auf (*Acc.*)), viel halten (von); ***I - so,*** das glaube ich, ich denke *or* glaube ja; ***I - not,*** das glaube ich nicht, ich glaube nein; ***make*** -, vorgeben, vorschützen. **believer,** *s.* Gläubige(r); ***be a great - in,*** fest glauben an (*Acc.*), viel halten von; ***true*** -, Rechtgläubige(r). **believing, 1.** *adj.* glaubend, gläubig. **2.** *s.* das Glauben; ***seeing is*** -, Sehen ist Glauben.

belike [bi'laik], *adv.* (*obs.*) wahrscheinlich, vermutlich.

belittle [bi'litl], *v.t.* verkleinern, schmälern, herabsetzen.

bell [bel], **1.** *s.* die Glocke, Schelle, Klingel; der Glockenklang, das Glockenzeichen; (*Bot., Archit.*) der Kelch; Schalltrichter, die Stürze (*of a trumpet*); *pl.* das Läutewerk; (Glocken)geläut(e); (*on harness*) Schellengeläut; (*Naut.*) Glasen (*pl.*); (*Naut.*) ***eight -s,*** acht Glasen; ***answer the (door)*** -, auf die Klingel hören; ***carry off the*** -, den Preis davontragen, der Erste sein; ***cap and -s,*** die Schellenkappe; ***chime*** or ***peal of -s,*** das (Glocken)geläut(e); ***as clear as a*** -, glockenrein, glockenhell; ***curse by -, book and candle,*** in Grund und Boden verfluchen; ***ring the*** -, klingeln; (*coll.*) ***that rings a*** -, das kommt mir vertraut *or* bekannt vor; ***as sound as a*** -, kerngesund; ***toll the*** - läuten. **2.** *v.t.* - ***the cat,*** der Katze die Schelle umhängen. **3.** *v.i.* (*of stags*) rö(h)ren.

belladonna [belə'dɔnə], *s.* (*Bot.*) die Tollkirsche, (*Med.*) Belladonna, das Atropin.

bell|-bottomed, *adj.* unten weit (*of trousers*). **--boy,** *s.* (*Am.*) der Hotelpage. **--buoy,** *s.* die Glockenboje, Glockentonne. **--clapper,** *s.* der Glockenklöppel.

belle [bel], *s.* die Schöne, Schönheit; - ***of the ball,*** die Ballkönigin.

belles-lettres [bel'letr], *pl.* schöne Literatur, die Belletristik. **belletristic** [-lə'tristik], *adj.* Unterhaltungs-, schöngeistig, belletristisch.

bell|flower, *s.* die Glockenblume. **--founder,** *s.* der Glockengießer. **--founding,** *s.* der Glockenguß. **--foundry,** *s.* die Glockengießerei. **--glass,** *s.* die Glasglocke. **--hop,** *s.* (*coll.*) *see* **--boy.**

bellicose ['belikous], *adj.* kriegslustig, kriegerisch, kampflustig. **bellicosity** [-'kɔsiti], *s.* die Kriegslust, Kampf(es)lust.

bellied ['belid], *adj.* geschwollen, bauchig; (*as suff.*) -bäuchig.

belligerence [bə'lidʒərəns], *s.* die Streitsucht, Angriffslust; Kriegführung. **belligerency,** *s.* der Kriegszustand. **belligerent, 1.** *adj.* kriegführend; streitsüchtig, angriffslustig, herausfordernd. **2.** *s.* Kriegführende(r).

bell|-jar, *s. See* **--glass. --metal,** *s.* die Glockenspeise. **--mouth,** *s.* der Schalltrichter. **--mouthed,** *adj.* trichterförmig.

bellow ['belou], **1.** *v.i.* brüllen, heulen, laut schreien. **2.** *s.* das Gebrüll.

bellows ['belouz], *pl.* der Blasebalg, (*Tech.*) das Gebläse, (*Phot. etc.*) der Balgen. **bellows-blower,** *s.* der Balg(en)treter.

bell|-pull, *s.* der Glockenzug, Klingelzug. **--push,** *s.* der Klingelknopf, die Klingeltaste. **--ringer,** *s.* der Glöckner. **--rope,** *s.* die Klingelschnur, der Glockenstrang, das Glockenseil. **--shaped,** *adj.* glockenförmig. **--tent,** *s.* das Rundzelt. **--tower,** *s.* der Glockenturm, Bergfried. **--wether,** *s.* der Leithammel; (*fig.*) Anführer. **--wire,** *s.* der Klingeldraht.

belly ['beli], **1.** *s.* der Bauch, Unterleib; (*sl.*) Magen; Wanst, Schmerbauch; (*of a violin*) die Decke, (*of a vase, sail etc.*) Ausbauchung, (*of a ship*) das Innere. **2.** *v.i.* sich ausbauchen, (an)schwellen; ***the –ing canvas,*** die schwellenden Segel.

belly|-ache, 1. *s.* (*sl.*) die Leibschmerzen (*pl.*), das Bauchweh. **2.** *v.i.* (*sl.*) jammern, quengeln. **--band,** *s.* (*Med.*) die Bauchbinde, der Bauchgurt; (*harness*) Bauchriemen. **--button,** *s.* (*coll.*) der (Bauch)nabel. **--flop,** *s.* (*sl.*) der Bauchklatscher. **bellyful,** *s.* der Bauchvoll; (*sl.*) ***have had a –,*** die Nase voll haben. **belly-worship,** *s.* die Schlemmerei.

belong [bi'lɔŋ], *v.i.* gehören (*as possessions*) (*to, Dat.*), (*as integral part*) (*to,* zu), zugehören, angehören (*as one of a group*) (*to, Dat.*); (*fig.*) zukommen, gebühren (*to, Dat.*), sich gehören (für); ***it –s to me,*** es gehört mir; ***essays of Schiller which – to this period,*** Aufsätze Schillers, welche dieser Zeit angehören; ***this town –s to Hesse,*** diese Stadt gehört zu Hessen; ***it –s here,*** es gehört hierher; ***I – here,*** ich bin von hier *or* bin hier ansässig. **belongings,** *pl.* die Habe, der Besitz, das Eigentum, Habseligkeiten (*pl.*), das Zubehör; ***with all his –,*** mit seinem ganzen Gepäck.

beloved, 1. [bi'lʌvd], *pred. adj.* geliebt (*of, by,* von). **2.** [–vid], *attrib. adj.* geliebt. **3.** [–vid], *s.* Geliebte(r); (*Eccl.*) ***dearly –!*** liebe Gemeinde!

below [bi'lou], **1.** *adv.* unten; auf Erden; ***down –,*** in der Hölle; ***here –,*** hienieden; ***as stated –,*** wie unten bemerkt. **2.** *prep.* unter, unterhalb; (*fig.*) ***– the belt,*** unehrlich, unfair; (*Min.*) ***– ground,*** unter Tage; ***– par,*** unter Pari; (*fig.*) mittelmäßig; ***– stairs,*** bei den Dienstboten.

belt [belt], **1.** *s.* der Gürtel; (*Archit.*) das Kranzgesims; (*Mech.*) der (Treib)riemen; das Fließband, Förderband, laufendes Band; (*Mil.*) Gehenk, Gehänge, Koppel; (*Naut.*) der Panzergürtel; (*Geog.*) Belt, die Meerenge; Zone, das Gebiet, der Bereich; (*Boxing*) die Gürtellinie; ***ammunition –,*** der Patronengurt; Gurt (*of machine gun*); ***blow below the –,*** (*Boxing*) unerlaubter Schlag, der Tiefschlag; (*fig.*) unfaire Handlung; ***– of fire,*** der Feuergürtel; ***green –,*** der Grünstreifen (*round towns*); ***–s of Jupiter,*** die Streifen Jupiters. **2.** *v.t.* (um)gürten; (*coll.*) schlagen, prügeln.

belt|-drive, *s.* der Riemenantrieb. **--feed,** *s.* die Gurtenzuführung; der Zuführer (*machine-gun*). **--pulley,** *s.* die Gurtscheibe, Riemenscheibe.

bemoan [bi'moun], **1.** *v.t.* betrauern, beweinen, beklagen. **2.** *v.i.* trauern, klagen.

bemuse [bi'mju:z], *v.t.* benebeln, verwirren.

bench [bentʃ], *s.* 1. die Bank; Werkbank, der Arbeitstisch; ***carpenter's –,*** die Hobelbank; (*Parl.*) ***the opposition –es,*** die Reihen der Opposition; 2. (*Law*) die Richterbank, Richter (*pl.*), das Richterkollegium; der Gerichtshof, das Gericht; ***the – and the bar,*** Richter und Advokaten, alle Rechtsgelehrten; ***be on the –,*** Richter sein; ***the Queen's Bench,*** das Oberhofgericht; ***Queen's Bench division,*** höchster Gerichtshof in Strafsachen.

bencher ['bentʃə], *s.* das Vorstandsmitglied eines Gerichtshofs (*Inn of Court*). **bench|-mark,** *s.* der Abrißpunkt, (*Surv.*) das Nivellier(ungs)zeichen. **--plane,** *s.* der Bankhobel. **--warrant,** *s.* der Verhaftungsbefehl, Haftbefehl. **-work,** *s.* die Werkbankarbeit.

bend [bend], **1.** *irr.v.t.* biegen, krümmen; beugen, neigen; spannen (*a bow*); (*Naut.*) befestigen, festmachen, anstecken (*a rope*); (*Naut.*) anschlagen, anreihen, anmarlen (*sails*); (*fig.*) unterwerfen, zwingen (*a p.*) (*to,* unter (*Acc.*)); richten, lenken, wenden (*thoughts, steps, glances etc.*) (*to, on,* auf (*Acc.*)); ***– one's head,*** den Kopf neigen; ***– the knee,*** das Knie beugen; ***– one's energies to*** or ***on,*** seine ganze Kraft verwenden auf (*Acc.*); ***– him to one's will,*** sich (*Dat.*) ihn gefügig machen; ***– one's steps towards home,*** die Schritte heimwärts lenken. **2.** *irr.v.i.* (*of a th.*) sich biegen, sich krümmen; (*of a p.*) sich (ver)beugen, sich neigen; (*fig.*) sich fügen, sich unterwerfen, sich beugen, nachgeben (*to, Dat.*); ***– back,*** sich zurückbeugen; ***– down,*** sich niederbeugen; ***– forward,*** sich bücken, sich neigen; ***he is bent on mischief,*** er führt Böses im Schilde; ***he is bent on his work,*** er geht seiner Arbeit eifrig nach; ***he is bent upon (doing) it,*** es ist ihm sehr daran gelegen *or* er ist darauf versessen *or* erpicht (es zu tun); ***he bent to her will,*** er beugte sich ihrem Willen. **3.** *s.* 1. die Biegung, Krümmung, Kurve; (*sl.*) ***he is round the –,*** er spinnt; 2. (*Her.*) der Schrägbalken; ***– sinister,*** der Schräglinksbalken; 3. (*Naut.*) der Knoten; ***fisherman's –,*** der Fischerknoten; ***sheet –,*** der Schotstek; 4. (*Gymn.*) die Beuge; 5. (*Tech.*) der Bogen, Krümmer, das Knierohr; 6. *pl.* (*coll.*) die Luftdruckkrankheit.

bendable ['bendəbl], *adj.* biegsam. **bended,** *adj.* (*obs. except in*) ***on – knee,*** kniefällig. **bender,** *s.* (*Am. sl.*) die Bierreise, Sauferei.

bending ['bendiŋ], *attrib. adj.* (*Tech.*) Biegungs–, Biege–. **bending|-strength,** *s.* die Knickfestigkeit, Biegesteifigkeit. **--stress,** *s.* die Biegespannung, Biegebeanspruchung. **--test,** *s.* die Biegeprobe.

bend| leather, *s.* das Sohlenleder, Kernleder. **-test,** *s.* *See* **bending-test. -wise,** *adv.* (*Her.*) diagonal. **bendy,** *adj.* (*coll.*) *see* **bendable.**

beneath [bi'ni:θ], **1.** *adv.* unten. **2.** *prep.* unter, unterhalb; ***– contempt,*** unter aller Würde; ***– me,*** unter meiner Würde; ***– notice,*** nicht der Beachtung wert.

benedick ['benidik], *s.* (*coll.*) neuverheirateter Ehemann.

Benedictine [beni'dikti:n], **1.** *s.* 1. (*Eccl.*) der (die) Benediktiner(in); 2. (*liqueur*) der Benediktiner. **2.** *adj.* benediktinisch, Benediktiner–.

benediction [beni'dikʃən], *s.* der Segen, Segensspruch, Danksagungsgottesdienst, das Dankgebet; (*R.C.*) die Weihe, Segnung.

benefaction [beni'fækʃən], *s.* die Wohltat; Spende, wohltätige Gabe. **benefactor** ['benifæktə], *s.* der Wohltäter. **benefactress,** *s.* die Wohltäterin.

benefice ['benifis], *s.* die Pfründe; (*Hist.*) das Lehen. **beneficed,** *adj.* mit einer Pfründe bedacht.

beneficence [bi'nefisəns], *s.* die Wohltätigkeit. **beneficent,** *adj.* wohltätig, mildtätig.

beneficial [beni'fiʃəl], *adj.* heilsam, zuträglich (*to, Dat.*), vorteilhaft, nützlich (für), (*Law*) nutznießend. **beneficiary,** *s.* der Pfründner; Almosenempfänger, Unterstützungsempfänger, Bezugsberechtigte(r); (*Law*) Nießbraucher, Nutznießer, Versicherungsnehmer, Erbberechtigte(r).

benefit ['benifit], **1.** *s.* der Vorteil, Nutzen, Gewinn; (*Law*) das Vorrecht, Privileg(ium); (*Insur.*) die Versicherungsleistung; Unterstützung, Beihilfe; (*Spt., Theat.*) das Benefiz; ***– of clergy,*** das Vorrecht des Klerus; ***for the – of,*** zum Nutzen von; ***derive – from,*** Nutzen ziehen aus; ***give him the – of the doubt,*** ihm im Zweifelsfalle recht geben, zu seinem Gunsten entscheiden; (*Law*) *in dubio pro reo* genießen lassen; (*Insur.*) ***be in –,*** unterstützungsberechtigt sein. **2.** *v.t.* begünstigen, fördern (*Acc.*), Nutzen bringen, nützen, zugutekommen, zuträglich *or* vorteilhaft sein (*Dat.*). **3.** *v.i.* Vorteil haben (*by* or *from,* von *or* durch), Nutzen ziehen (aus); ***he –ed by this,*** dies kam ihm zugute.

benefit|-match, *s.* das Benefizspiel. **--performance,** *s.* die Benefizvorstellung. **--society,** *s.* der Wohltätigkeitsverein; Versicherungsverein auf Gegenseitigkeit.

benevolence [bi'nevələns], *s.* die Güte, Nächstenliebe, Mildtätigkeit, Wohltätigkeit; das Wohlwollen; ***act of –,*** die Wohltat. **benevolent,** *adj.* wohltätig, mildtätig, menschenfreundlich, gütig; wohlwollend; ***– fund,*** der Unterstützungsfonds.

Bengal [beŋ'gɔ:l], **1.** *s.* Bengalen (*n.*). **2.** *adj.* bengalisch. **Bengali,** *s.* 1. der Bengale (die Bengalin); 2. (*language*) das Bengali, Bengalische.

benighted [bi'naitid], *adj.* von der Nacht überfallen; (*fig.*) unwissend, unaufgeklärt.

benign [bi'nain], *adj.* gütig, liebevoll, huldvoll; (*fig.*) wohltuend, heilsam, (*Med.*) gutartig; (*climate*) günstig, mild, zuträglich. **benignant** [bi'nignənt], *adj. See* **benign. benignity** [-'nigniti], *s.* die Güte, Freundlichkeit, Gunst, das Wohlwollen, (*Med.*) die Gutartigkeit.

[1]**bent** [bent], **1.** *adj.* gebeugt, gebogen; krumm, gekrümmt; *see* **bend. 2.** *s.* die Neigung, der Hang (*for*, zu); ***to the top of one's –,*** bis zum äußersten, nach Herzenslust.

[2]**bent,** *s.* (*also –* ***grass***) das Straußgras.

benumb [bi'nʌm], *v.t.* erstarren lassen, gefühllos machen, betäuben, (*fig.*) lähmen. **benumbed,** *adj.* erstarrt, gefühllos, betäubt, benommen.

benzene ['benzi:n], *s.* das Benzol, Kohlenbenzin. **benzine** [-i:n], *s.* das Benzin. **benzoic** [-'zouik], *adj.* **– *acid,*** die Benzoesäure. **benzol(e)** ['benzɔl], *s. See* **benzene. benzolize,** *v.t.* mit Benzol sättigen *or* behandeln.

bequeath [bi'kwi:ð], *v.t.* (*Law*) testamentarisch vermachen (*to*, *Dat.*); hinterlassen; (*fig.*) überliefern. **bequest** [-'kwest], *s.* das Vermächtnis, Erbteil; (*fig.*) Erbe, die Hinterlassenschaft.

berate [bi'reit], *v.t.* ausschelten, ausschimpfen.

bereave [bi'ri:v], *irr.v.t.* berauben (*of*, *Gen.*). **bereaved,** *adj.* durch Tod beraubt, verwaist; ***the –,*** die Hinterbliebenen. **bereavement,** *s.* die Beraubung; schmerzlicher Verlust; ***in their –,*** in ihrer Verlassenheit; ***a – in the family,*** ein Trauerfall in der Familie.

bereft [bi'reft], **1.** *pred. adj.* leer (*of*, an (*Dat.*)), beraubt. **2.** *imperf., p.p. of* **bereave.**

beret ['berei], *s.* die Baskenmütze.

bergamot ['bə:gəmɔt], *s.* die Bergmottenbirne; ***essence of –,*** das Bergamottöl.

beribboned [bi'ribənd], *adj.* mit (Ordens)bändern geschmückt.

beri-beri ['beriberi], *s.* die Reisesserkrankheit.

berm [bə:m], *s.* (*Mil.*) die Grabenstufe, Bankette, der Böschungsabsatz; (*roads*) das Bankett, die Berme.

Bermud(i)an [bə'mju:d(i)ən], *s.* der Bermuda-Insulaner. **Bermud(i)an-rigged,** *adj.* (*Naut.*) hochgetakelt.

Berne [bə:n], *s.* Bern (*n.*). **Bernese, 1.** *s.* der (die) Berner(in). **2.** *adj.* Berner; ***– Alps,*** Berner Alpen.

berry ['beri], *s.* die Beere; (*coffee*) Bohne. **berry-bearing,** *adj.* beerentragend.

berserk ['bə:sə:k], **1.** *s.* der Berserker, Wüterich. **2.** *adj.* rasend, wütend, Berserker–.

berth [bə:θ], **1.** *s.* (*Naut.*) die Koje, das Kajütenbett; (*Railw.*) Bett; (*Naut.*) der Liegeplatz, Ankerplatz; (*Naut.*) Seeraum, (*fig.*) Abstand; (*coll.*) die Anstellung, Unterkunft; ***loading –,*** die Ladestelle; ***give a wide –,*** guten Abstand halten, weit abhalten, gut frei halten (*to*, von), (*fig.*) einen Bogen machen (um), weit aus dem Wege gehen (*Dat.*). **2.** *v.t.* vor Anker gehen, ankern lassen; am Kai festmachen; (*coll.*) einen (Schlaf)platz anweisen (*Dat.*), unterbringen. **3.** *v.i.* (*Naut.*) anlegen.

beryl ['beril], *s.* der Beryll. **berylline** [-ain], *adj.* beryllartig; hellgrün.

beseech [bi'si:tʃ], *irr.v.t.* ersuchen, anflehen, dringend bitten (*for*, um). **beseeching,** *adj.* flehend. **beseechingly,** *adv.* flehentlich, eindringlich.

beseem [bi'si:m], **1.** *v.t.* (*obs.*) sich ziemen *or* schicken für. **2.** *v.i.* (*obs.*) sich ziemen *or* schicken, angemessen *or* schicklich sein.

beset [bi'set], *irr.v.t.* umringen, einschließen, umgeben, umlagern; besetzen, schmücken (*with jewels*); (*fig.*) bedrängen, bestürmen, verfolgen; ***hard –,*** hart bedrängt; ***– with difficulties,*** von Schwierigkeiten überhäuft; ***he was – with entreaties,*** man bestürmte ihn mit Bitten. **besetting,** *adj.* beständig drohend, hartnäckig; ***– sin,*** die Gewohnheitssünde.

beshrew [bi'ʃru:], **1.** *v.t.* (*obs.*) verwünschen, verfluchen. **2.** *int.* (*obs.*) zum Kuckuck damit! der Teufel soll mich holen!

beside [bi'said], *prep.* neben, nahe *or* dicht bei; (*coll.*) ***– o.s.,*** aus dem Häuschen; ***he is – himself with rage,*** er ist außer sich vor Wut; ***he sat – me,*** er saß neben mir; ***come and sit – me,*** setzen Sie sich neben mich; ***– the point,*** nebensächlich, belanglos, unwichtig, unerheblich, abwegig, nicht zur Sache gehörig; ***– the purpose,*** unzweckmäßig. **besides, 1.** *adv.* überdies, außerdem, zudem, abgesehen davon, noch dazu; ***nobody –,*** sonst niemand. **2.** *prep.* außer, abgesehen von, über (*Acc.*) . . . hinaus.

besiege [bi'si:dʒ], *v.t.* belagern; (*fig.*) bedrängen, bestürmen.

beslaver [bi'slævə], *v.t.* begeifern.

beslobber [bi'slɔbə], *v.t.* begeifern; (*coll.*) abküssen.

besmear [bi'smiə], *v.t.* beschmieren, besudeln, beschmutzen.

besmirch [bi'smə:tʃ], *v.t.* (*usu. fig.*) besudeln.

besom ['bi:zəm], *s.* der (Reisig)besen; (*Scots*) die Schlampe, das Weibsbild.

besot [bi'sɔt], *v.t.* betören; berauschen; verdummen. **besotted,** *adj.* betört, töricht; betrunken, berauscht; vernarrt (*on*, in (*Acc.*)).

besought [bi'sɔ:t], *imperf., p.p. of* **beseech.**

bespatter [bi'spætə], *v.t.* bespritzen.

bespeak [bi'spi:k], *irr.v.t.* 1. (voraus)bestellen; ***– a book*** (*at a library*), ein Buch vormerken lassen; 2. kundgeben, zeigen; zeugen von, verraten; ***his manners – the gentleman,*** sein Benehmen verrät den Mann von Bildung.

bespectacled [bi'spektəkld], *adj.* brillentragend, bebrillt.

bespoke [bi'spouk], **1.** *adj.* nach Maß, besonders *or* auf Bestellung angefertigt; ***– tailor,*** der Maßschneider; ***– work,*** die Maßarbeit. **2.** *imperf. of* **bespeak.**

besprinkle [bi'spriŋkl], *v.t.* besprengen, bestreuen.

best [best], **1.** *adj.* (*sup. of* ***good***) best, feinst, vornehmst; ***he was on his – behaviour,*** er achtete sehr auf sein Benehmen; ***put the – construction on it,*** es im günstigsten Sinne auslegen; (*coll.*) ***put one's – foot forward,*** tüchtig ausschreiten, (*fig.*) sein Bestes tun; ***his – girl,*** sein Schatz; ***the – man,*** der Beistand des Bräutigams; ***the – part,*** der größere *or* größte Teil, das meiste. **2.** *adv.* (*sup. of* ***well***) am besten, aufs beste; ***as – he could,*** so gut er konnte; ***what had I – do?*** was sollte ich wohl tun, was täte ich am besten? ***I think it – not to go,*** ich halte es für das beste, nicht zu gehen. **3.** *s.* das Beste; die Besten (*pl.*); (*coll.*) ***the – of it is that . . .,*** der Witz der Sache ist daß . . .; ***do one's*** (***level***) ***–,*** sein Möglichstes tun; ***get*** or ***have the – of it,*** am besten dabei abschneiden *or* wegkommen; ***make the – of,*** sich abfinden *or* zufriedengeben mit; ***make the – of a bad job,*** gute Miene zum bösen Spiel machen; ***his Sunday –,*** sein Sonntagsanzug; ***the very –,*** der *or* das *or* die Allerbeste; ***at*** (***the***) ***–,*** höchstens, bestenfalls, im besten *or* günstigsten Falle; ***be at one's –,*** in bester Form *or* Verfassung sein; ***for the –,*** in bester Absicht; ***to the – of my knowledge*** or ***belief,*** nach bestem Wissen (und Gewissen); ***to the – of my power,*** nach besten Kräften; ***to the – of my recollection,*** soviel ich mich erinnere; ***with the –,*** so gut wie nur einer. **4.** *v.t.* (*coll.*) übertreffen; übervorteilen, übers Ohr hauen.

beste(a)d [bi'sted], *adj.* (*obs., only in*) ***well-*** (***ill-***) ***–,*** gut (schlecht) situiert.

bestial ['bestiəl], *adj.* (*fig.*) tierisch, viehisch, bestialisch, entmenscht. **bestiality** [-'æliti], *s.* viehisches Wesen, die Bestialität. **bestialize,** *v.t.* vertieren, verrohen, entmenschlichen.

bestiary ['bestjəri], *s.* das Bestiarium.

bestir [bi'stə:], *v.r.* sich rühren, sich regen; ***– yourself!*** streng dich doch an!

bestorm [bi'stɔ:m], *v.t.* bestürmen, umstürmen.

bestow [bi'stou], *v.t.* 1. geben, schenken, erteilen, spenden, verleihen ((*up*)*on*, *Dat.*); 2. (*obs*) unterbringen, aufbewahren. **bestowal,** *s.* die Schenkung, Verleihung (*on*, an (*Acc.*)).

bestrew [bi'stru:], *irr.v.t.* bestreuen.

bestride [bi'straid], *irr.v.t.* besteigen, rittlings sitzen auf (*Dat.*) (*a horse*); mit gespreizten Beinen stehen über *or* auf (*Dat.*); durchschreiten, hinwegschreiten über (*Acc.*); (*fig.*) sich spannen *or* wölben über (*Dat.*).

bestrode [bi'stroud], *imperf. of* **bestride.**

bestseller ['best'selə], *s.* der Bucherfolg, Bestseller, Verkaufsschlager. **bestselling,** *adj.* meistverkauft.

bet [bet], *s.* die Wette; ***even –,*** Wette mit gleichen Chancen; ***heavy –,*** hohe Wette; ***lay*** or ***make a –,*** wetten (***on,*** auf (*Acc.*)); ***safe –,*** sicherer Tip; ***take a –,*** eine Wette annehmen. **2.** *reg. or irr.v.t., v.i.* wetten; setzen; ***what do you –?*** was gilt die Wette? (*sl.*) ***– one's bottom dollar,*** den letzten Heller wetten; ***I will – (you) five to one,*** ich wette (mit Ihnen) fünf gegen eins; ***I will – you £100,*** ich wette mit Ihnen um 100 Pfund; (*sl.*) ***(you can) – your life (on it),*** darauf können Sie Gift nehmen; (*sl.*) ***you –!*** aber sicher! und ob!

betake [bi'teik], *irr.v.r.* (*Poet.*) sich begeben *or* verfügen (***to,*** nach), sich wenden (an (*Acc.*)), (*fig.*) seine Zuflucht nehmen (zu), seine Rettung suchen (in (*Dat.*)); ***– o.s. to flight,*** die Flucht ergreifen.

bethink [bi'θiŋk], *irr.v.r.* (*rare*) sich besinnen (*of,* auf (*Acc.*)); sich erinnern (an (*Acc.*)); sich bedenken (*Gen.*), überlegen, nachdenken.

betide [bi'taid], **1.** *v.t.* (*only in*) ***woe – him!*** wehe ihm! **2.** *v.i.* geschehen, sich ereignen.

betimes [bi'taimz], *adv.* beizeiten, (recht)zeitig, bald.

betoken [bi'toukən], *v.t.* bezeichnen, andeuten; anzeigen, verkünden.

betony ['betəni], *s.* (*Bot.*) das Zehrkraut, rote Betonie.

betook [bi'tuk], *imperf. of* **betake.**

betray [bi'trei], *v.t.* verraten (*to, Dat. or* an (*Acc.*)); die Treue brechen (*Dat.*), im Stich lassen, hintergehen; verleiten, verführen (***into,*** zu); (*fig.*) zur Schau stellen, an den Tag legen. **betrayal,** *s.* der Verrat, Treubruch (*of,* an (*Dat.*)); ***– of confidence,*** der Vertrauensbruch.

betroth [bi'trouð], *v.t.* (*usu. pass.*) verloben (***to,*** mit). **betrothal,** *s.* die Verlobung. **betrothed,** *s.* ***your –,*** Ihre Braut *or* Verlobte; Ihr Bräutigam *or* Verlobter.

[1]**better** ['betə], *s.* Wettende(r), der Wetter. *See* **bet.**

[2]**better, 1.** *adj.* (*comp. of* ***good***) besser, geeigneter, passender, günstiger, vorteilhafter; gesünder; ***upon – acquaintance,*** bei näherer Bekanntschaft; ***the – the day, the – the deed,*** je heiliger der Tag, desto besser *or* heiliger die Tat; (*coll.*) ***his – half,*** seine Frau; ***the – part of an hour,*** fast eine ganze Stunde; ***his – self,*** seine bessere Seite; ***he is no – than he should be,*** man kann nichts besseres von ihm erwarten; ***she is no – than she should be,*** sie ist ein lockeres Mädchen, sie führt einen unsittlichen Lebenswandel; ***I am none the – for it,*** es hat mir nichts genützt; ***be – than one's word,*** mehr tun als man versprochen hat. **2.** *adv.* (*comp. of* ***well***) besser, wohler, mehr; ***– and –,*** immer besser; ***I am*** or ***feel –,*** es geht mir besser, ich befinde *or* fühle mich wohler; ***be – off,*** besser daran sein, (*financially*) in besseren Umständen sein; ***get –,*** sich erholen; (*coll.*) ***go one –,*** übertrumpfen; ***all the –,*** see ***so much the –; you had – (sl. you –) go at once,*** am besten gehen Sie sofort; (*coll.*) ***you had – (sl. you –) not!*** das will ich dir nicht raten; ***he knows –,*** er weiß es besser; ***he always knows –,*** er läßt sich nichts vormachen; ***I like her – than him,*** ich habe sie lieber als ihn; ***I like this –,*** dies ziehe ich vor; ***so much the –,*** desto besser, um so besser; ***I thought – of it,*** ich habe mich eines Besseren besonnen, ich habe es mir genauer überlegt. **3.** *s.* das Bessere; ***his –,*** der ihm Überlegene; ***my –s,*** (*in rank*) meine Vorgesetzten, die Höherstehenden, (*financially*) Bessergestellten; ***for – for worse,*** auf Glück und Unglück, in Freud und Leid; auf Gedeih und Verderb; ***change for the –,*** sich bessern; ***a change for the –,*** eine Wendung zum Besseren; ***get the – of him,*** ihn ausstechen *or* besiegen, die Oberhand über ihn gewinnen; ***get the – of it,*** es überwinden. **4.** *v.i.* sich (ver)bessern, besser werden. **5.** *v.t.* bessern, verbessern, vervollkommen; ***– o.s.,*** sich *or* seine Lage verbessern, vorwärtskommen.

bettering ['betəriŋ], **betterment,** *s.* die Verbesserung, Veredelung, Melioration (*of land*), Besserung, das Besserwerden (*of health*).

betting ['betiŋ], **1.** *s.* das Wetten. **2.** *adj.* Wett–; ***– man,*** gewohnheitsmäßiger *or* versessener Wetter. **bettor,** *s. See* [1]**better.**

between [bi'twi:n], **1.** *adv.* dazwischen; ***few and far –,*** vereinzelt, selten; ***in –,*** mitten darin; ***space –,*** der Zwischenraum. **2.** *prep.* zwischen; ***in –,*** mitten in; ***– the devil and the deep sea,*** unrettbar verloren, in einer hoffnungslosen Klemme; ***– ourselves*** or ***you and me,*** unter uns, unter vier Augen, im Vertrauen; (*Railw.*) ***– stations,*** auf freier Strecke; ***there is nothing – them,*** sie stehen in keinem besonderen Verhältnis zueinander; ***– two and three years ago,*** vor etwa zwei bis drei Jahren; ***we bought it – us,*** wir kauften es zusammen *or* gemeinschaftlich.

between|-decks, *s.* (*adv.*) (im) Zwischendeck. **--maid,** *s.* (*obs.*) das Aushilfsmädchen. **– times, – whiles,** *adv.* dann und wann, zuweilen, von Zeit zu Zeit.

betwixt [bi'twikst], **1.** *adv.* (*obs., Poet.*) *see* **between;** ***– and between,*** weder das eine noch das andere, in der Mitte, halb und halb. **2.** *prep.* (*obs.*) zwischen.

bevel [bevl], **1.** *adj.* schräg(kantig), schief(winkelig), abgekantet. **2.** *s.* die (Ab)schrägung, Abgratung, Schräge, Gehrung; Fase, schräger Ausschnitt, schräge Richtung; (*instrument*) der Stellwinkel, Winkelpasser, die Schmiege; ***on a –,*** schräg, schiefwinklig. **3.** *v.t.* schräg abschneiden, abschrägen, abkanten, gehren, facettieren. **4.** *v.i.* ***– off,*** schräg verlaufen, eine schräge Richtung haben.

bevel|-edge, *s.* schräge Kante, die Facette. **--gear(ing),** *s.* die Schrägverzahnung; das Stirnrad, Kegelrad(getriebe). **bevelled,** *adj.* schräg (geschnitten), abgeschrägt, schiefwinkelig, facettiert. **bevelling, 1.** *s.* das Abschrägen, Abflächen, Abkanten, Abfasen. **2.** *adj.* Schräg(schnitt)–. **bevel-wheel,** *s.* das Kegelrad, konisches Zahnrad.

beverage ['bevəridʒ], *s.* das Getränk, der Trank.

bevy ['bevi], *s.* der Flug, Truppe (*of birds*); das Rudel, die Herde (*of animals*), (*fig.*) Schar, der Schwarm, Flor (*of girls*).

bewail [bi'weil], **1.** *v.t.* beklagen, beweinen. **2.** *v.i.* (weh)klagen, trauern.

beware [bi'wɛə], *v.i.* (*only inf. & imper.*) sich hüten, sich in Acht nehmen (*of,* vor (*Dat.*)); ***– lest you fall,*** nimm dich in Acht, daß du nicht fällst! ***– how you step out,*** hüte dich beim Aussteigen! ***– of pickpockets!*** vor Taschendieben wird gewarnt!

bewilder [bi'wildə], *v.t.* verwirren, verblüffen, bestürzen, irreführen, irremachen. **bewildered,** *adj.* verwirrt, bestürzt, verblüfft, konfus. **bewildering,** *adj.* verwirrend, verblüffend, irreführend. **bewilderment,** *s.* die Verwirrung, Bestürzung.

bewitch [bi'witʃ], *v.t.* behexen; (*fig.*) bezaubern, bestricken, in seinen Bann ziehen. **bewitching,** *adj.* bezaubernd, berückend, anziehend, reizend. **bewitchment,** *s.* die Bestrickung, Bezauberung.

bey [bei], *s.* (*Hist.*) der Bei.

beyond [bi'jɔnd], **1.** *adv.* darüber hinaus; jenseits. **2.** *prep.* jenseits, über (*Acc.*) (. . . hinaus), weiter als, außer; ***– belief,*** unglaublich; ***– all blame,*** über jeden Tadel erhaben; ***– all bounds,*** über alle Maßen; ***she is – my control,*** sie ist mir über den Kopf gewachsen; ***go – one's depth,*** den Boden verlieren (*in water*), (*fig.*) den Grund unter den Füßen verlieren; ***– dispute,*** außer allem Zweifel, unzweifelhaft, zweifellos, fraglos, unstreitig; ***– doubt,*** einwandfrei; ***– endurance,*** nicht auszuhalten, unerträglich; ***– human aid,*** nicht mehr zu retten; (*coll.*) ***that is – me,*** das geht über meine Begriffe *or* meinen Horizont, da komme ich nicht mehr mit; ***live – one's means,*** über sein Vermögen *or* seine Mittel leben; ***– measure,*** see ***– all bounds; – possibility,*** unmöglich; ***it is – my power,*** es übersteigt meine Kraft; – *all praise,* über alles Lob erhaben; – *all price,* unbezahlbar; – *recognition,* bis zur Unkenntlichkeit; – *recovery,* (*of a th.*) unrettbar, nicht mehr wiederherzustellen; (*of a p.*) unheilbar krank; – *reproach,* tadellos, einwandfrei. **3.** *s.* das Jenseits; (*coll.*) *the back of –,* das Ende der Welt.

bezel [bezl], *s.* der Kasten (*of a ring*), die Rille (*of a watch*); Kante, Schneide (*of a chisel*); Schrägfläche, Rautenfläche (*of a jewel*).

bezique [bə'zi:k], *s.* (*Cards*) das Besik.

bhang [bæŋ], *s.* das Haschisch.

bi- [bai], *pref.* zwei(mal), doppelt, zweifach. **-angular,** *adj.* zweiwinklig. **-annual,** *adj.* halbjährlich. *For other examples see below.*

bias ['baiəs], **1.** *adj., adv.* schräg *or* quer (geschnitten), schief. **2.** *s.* 1. schiefe *or* schwere Seite; 2. (*Dressm.*) schräger Schnitt, der Keil, Schrägstreifen; *cut on the –,* schräg schneiden; 3. (*Bowls*) schiefer Lauf, Überhang; 4. (*Rad.*) die Gittervorspannung; – *battery,* die (Gitter)vorspannungs- *or* Speisespannungsbatterie; – *resistor,* der Gitter(ableit)widerstand, Kathodenwiderstand; 5. (*fig.*) Hang; die (Zu)neigung, Vorliebe; das Vorurteil; *free from* or *without –,* vorurteilsfrei, unvoreingenommen, unbefangen. **3.** *v.t.* eine Richtung geben (*Dat.*), auf eine Seite lenken, (*fig.*) beeinflussen, bestimmen. **biased,** *adj.* voreingenommen, tendenziös; – *in his favour,* für ihn eingenommen.

[1]**bib** [bib], *s.* das (Kinder- *or* Geifer)lätzchen; der Schürzenlatz; (*coll.*) *in best – and tucker,* im Sonntagsstaat.

[2]**bib,** *v.t., v.i.* gern und oft trinken. **bibacious** [bi'beiʃəs], *adj.* dem Trunk ergeben. **bibber,** *s.* der (Gewohnheits)trinker.

bible [baibl], *s.* die Bibel, Heilige Schrift; – *oath,* der Eid auf die Bibel, heiliger Schwur. **biblical** ['biblikl], *adj.* biblisch, Bibel-.

bibliographer [bibli'ɔgrəfə], *s.* der Bücherkenner, Bibliograph. **bibliographic(al)** [-'græfik(əl)], *adj.* bibliographisch. **bibliography,** *s.* die Bücherkunde, Bibliographie; gesamte *or* einschlägige Literatur, das Literaturverzeichnis (*on a subject*).

bibliolatry [bibli'ɔlətri], *s.* die Bibelverehrung, der Buchstabenglaube.

bibliophile ['bibliofail], *s.* der Bücherfreund, Bücherliebhaber.

bibulous ['bibjuləs], *adj.* trunksüchtig, dem Trunk ergeben; saugfähig, schwammig.

bicarbonate [bai'kɑ:bənit], *s.* das Bikarbonat, doppel(t)kohlensaures Salz; – *of soda,* doppel(t)kohlensaures Natron.

bicentenary [baisen'ti:nəri], **1.** *adj.* zweihundertjährig. **2.** *s.* die Zweihundertjahrfeier, zweihundertjähriges Jubiläum. **bicentennial** [-'teniəl], **1.** *adj.* zweihundertjahrelang. **2.** *s.* der Zeitraum von zweihundert Jahren.

biceps ['baiseps], *s.* der Bizeps, zweiköpfiger Armmuskel.

bichloride [bai'klɔ:raid], *s.* das Bi- *or* Dichlorid.

bichromate [bai'kroumit], *s.* das Bi- *or* Dichromat; doppeltchromsaures Salz; – *of potash,* doppeltchromsaures Kali.

bicker ['bikə], *v.i.* zanken, streiten, hadern; (*Poet.*) rauschen, prasseln, plätschern. **bickering,** *s.* der Hader, Zwist, Streit, Zank.

bicuspid [bai'kʌspid], **1.** *adj.* doppelspitzig. **2.** *s.* kleiner Backenzahn.

bicycle ['baisikl], **1.** *s.* das Fahrrad, (*coll.*) Rad; *ride a –,* radfahren. **2.** *v.i.* radfahren, (*coll.*) radeln. **bicyclist,** *s.* der Radfahrer.

bid [bid], **1.** *irr.v.t.* 1. (*imperf. bade, p.p. bid or bidden*) heißen, befehlen (*Dat.*), gebieten (*Dat.*); wünschen, entbieten (*greeting*); – *him go,* ihn gehen heißen; – *him good morning,* ihm einen guten Morgen sagen *or* wünschen; – *him welcome,* ihn willkommen heißen; *do as you are –,* tue was man dir sagt; 2. (*imperf. bid, p.p. bid*) (*auctions*) (an)bieten; (*Cards*) reizen, bieten; (*obs.*) bitten, einladen; – *up,* (den Preis) in die Höhe treiben; – *defiance,* Trotz bieten. **2.** *irr.v.i.* bieten, ein Angebot machen; werben (*for,* um), (*Cards*) reizen; – *for an article,* auf einen Artikel bieten; – *for safety,* vorsichtig zu Werke gehen; (*Cards*) – *against him,* ihn reizen; – *fair,* zu Hoffnungen berechtigen, viel versprechen, auf dem besten Wege sein. **3.** *s.* das (An)gebot; (*Cards*) Reizen, die Meldung; (*fig.*) Bewerbung (*for,* um); *make a – for,* sich bewerben um; (*fig.*) sich bemühen um, sich (*Dat.*) zu sichern suchen.

biddable ['bidəbl], *adj.* (*coll.*) folgsam, fügsam; gehorsam, willig. **bidder,** *s.* der Bieter, Bewerber, Offertsteller; *highest –,* Meistbietende(r). **bidding,** *s.* der Befehl, die Anordnung; Aufforderung, Einladung; (*Cards*) das Reizen, Bieten; (*at auctions*) Gebot; *start the –,* das Erstangebot machen; *do his –,* ihm gehorchen.

bide [baid], **1.** *irr.v.i.* (*Scots*) bleiben, verharren; – *by,* beharren bei. **2.** *irr.v.t.* (*only in*) – *one's time,* seine Zeit *or* den rechten Augenblick abwarten.

bidet ['bi:dei], *s.* das Sitzbad, Bidet.

biennial [bai'eniəl], **1.** *adj.* zweijährig. **2.** *s.* zweijährige Pflanze.

bier [biə], *s.* die (Toten)bahre.

biestings, *see* **beestings.**

biff [bif], **1.** *s.* (*sl.*) der Schlag. **2.** *v.t.* schlagen, hauen.

bifid ['baifid], *adj.* zweispaltig.

bifocal [bai'foukəl], **1.** *adj.* Zweistärken-. **bifocals,** *pl.* die Zweistärkenbrille.

bifoliate [bai'fouliit], *adj.* (*Bot.*) einpaarig gefiedert.

bifurcate ['baifə:keit], **1.** *adj.* zweizackig, zweizinkig, zweiästig, gabelförmig, gegabelt. **2.** *v.i.* sich gabeln, sich abzweigen (*of a way*). **bifurcation** [-'keiʃən], *s.* die Spaltung, Gabelung; der Gabelungspunkt.

big [big], *adj.* groß; dick, stark; weit, breit; (hoch)schwanger (*of woman*), trächtig (*of animal*); erwachsen; (*sl.*) – *bug,* see – *pot*; – *business,* das Großunternehmen; die Finanzwelt; – *drum,* große Trommel; (*coll.*) *get too – for one's boots,* eingebildet werden; – *game,* das Hochwild; (*sl.*) *the – idea,* die Absicht, der Zweck; (*fig.*) – *man,* wichtige Persönlichkeit; (*coll.*) – *money,* ein Haufen Geld; (*sl.*) – *noise,* große Kanone; (*sl.*) – *pot* or *shot,* hohes *or* großes Tier; (*coll.*) – *talk,* die Prahlerei, Aufschneiderei; – *toe,* große Zehe; – *wheel,* das Riesenrad; – *with child,* (hoch)schwanger; – *with pride,* aufgeblasen, hochmütig; – *with significance,* voll von Bedeutung.

bigamist ['bigəmist], *s.* der Bigamist. **bigamous,** *adj.* der Bigamie schuldig, in Bigamie lebend. **bigamy,** *s.* die Doppelehe, Bigamie.

big|-bellied, *adj.* dickbäuchig. **--boned,** *adj.* starkknöchig, vierschrötig. **--end,** *s.* (*Mech.*) das Kurbelwellenende; (*Tech.*) – *bearing,* das Pleuellager. **bigger,** *comp.,* **biggest,** *sup. adj. See* **big. biggish,** *adj.* (*coll.*) ziemlich groß. **big-hearted,** *adj.* großherzig, großmütig, großzügig, edelmütig.

bight [bait], *s.* (*Geog.*) die Bucht, Einbuchtung; Krümmung; (*Naut.*) Bucht, das Los (*of rope*).

big-mouthed, *adj.* (*sl.*) großmäulig, prahlerisch. **bigness,** *s.* die Größe, Dicke, der Umfang.

bigot ['bigət], *s.* der Frömmler, Bigotte(r); Eiferer, Fanatiker, blinder Anhänger. **bigoted,** *adj.* fanatisch fromm, bigott; blind ergeben, voreingenommen. **bigotry,** *s.* die Frömmelei, Bigotterie; der Fanatismus, blinder Eifer.

big|-time, *adj.* (*sl.*) erstklassig. **--top,** *s.* das Zirkuszelt, der Zirkus. **-wig,** *s.* (*coll.*) der Bonze.

bike [baik], *s. coll. for* **bicycle.**

bikini [bi'ki:ni], *s.* (*coll.*) der Bikini, zweiteiliger Badeanzug.

bilabial [bai'leibiəl], *adj.* (*Phonet.*) mit beiden Lippen gesprochen. **bilabiate,** *adj.* (*Bot.*) zweilippig.

bilateral [bai'lætərəl], *adj.* zweiseitig; (*Comm., Law*) gegenseitig, beiderseitig; (*Tech.*) doppelseitig.

bilberry ['bilbəri], *s.* die Heidelbeere, Blaubeere.
bilbo ['bilbou], *s.* (*Poet.*) das Schwert, die Klinge. **bilboes,** *pl.* Fußfesseln (*pl.*).
bile [bail], *s.* die Galle; (*fig.*) der Ärger, die Verdrießlichkeit, Bitterkeit. **bile-duct,** *s.* der Gallengang.
bilge [bildʒ], *s.* 1. der Bauch (*of a cask etc.*); 2. (*Naut*) die Bilge, Kimm, der Kielraum; 3. *See* **bilge-water**; (*sl.*) Quatsch, Unsinn. **bilge|-keel,** *s.* der Kimmkiel, Schlingerkiel. **--pump,** *s.* die Lenzpumpe, Sodpumpe. **--water,** *s.* das Schlagwasser, Sodwasser. **-ways,** *s.* Schlittenbalken (*pl.*).
biliary ['biliəri], *adj.* Gallen–, biliar.
bilingual [bai'liŋgwəl], *adj.* zweisprachig. **bilingualism,** *s.* die Zweisprachigkeit.
bilious ['biljəs], *adj.* Gallen–; gallenartig, gallig; – *attack,* der Gallenfieberanfall. **biliousness,** *s.* die Gallenkrankheit; (*fig.*) schlechte Laune.
bilk [bilk], *v.t.* betrügen, prellen; (*coll.*) durchbrennen mit; (*coll.*) – *one's fare,* schwarzfahren.
[1]**bill** [bil], *s.* (*obs.*) die Pike.
[2]**bill, 1.** *s.* der Schnabel (*of a bird*), die Spitze (*of a ship*). **2.** *v.i.* sich schnäbeln (*of birds*); (*fig.*) – *and coo,* liebkosen.
[3]**bill, 1.** *s.* 1. das Plakat, der Anschlag(zettel); Schein, die Bescheinigung; Aufstellung, Liste, das Verzeichnis, Inventar; 2. (*Parl.*) der Gesetzentwurf, Gesetzesantrag, die Gesetzvorlage, Bill; (*Law*) Anklageakte, Klageschrift; 3. (*Comm.*) der Wechsel, die Schuldverschreibung, Rechnung; (*Am.*) Banknote, (Geld)schein.
(a) (*with adjs., nouns*) *accommodation* –, das Gefälligkeitsakzept; – *of costs,* die Spesenrechnung; – *of credit,* der Kreditbrief; – *of entry,* die Zolldeklaration; – *of exchange,* der Wechsel, die Tratte; – *of fare,* die Speisekarte; – *of health,* der Gesundheitspaß, das Gesundheitsattest; *clean – of health,* gesund, ohne Krankheit; – *of indictment,* die Anklageschrift; – *of lading,* der Frachtbrief; Verladungsschein, das Konnossement; *–s and money,* Brief und Geld; – *of mortality,* die Sterbeliste; *private* –, der Gesetzesantrag in privatem Interesse; *–s receivable,* Wechselforderungen (*pl.*); *Bill of Rights,* die Freiheitsurkunde (*1689*); – *of sale,* der Kaufvertrag; (*Law*) die Übertragungsurkunde, Mobiliarschuldverschreibung; – *of sight,* der Zollgutbesichtigungsschein; – *of specie,* der Sortenzettel.
(b) (*with verbs*) *accept a* –, einen Wechsel akzeptieren; *bring in a* –, eine Gesetzvorlage einbringen; *bring in a true* –, see *find a true* –; *the – was carried,* die Vorlage ging durch, der Entwurf wurde angenommen; *draw a – on,* einen Wechsel ziehen *or* trassieren auf; (*coll.*) *fill the* –, allen Anforderungen genügen; *find a true* –, die Anklage annehmen, die Anklage für begründet erklären; (*coll.*) *foot a* –, eine Rechnung bezahlen; *ignore a* –, die Anklage für unbegründet erklären, die Anklage verwerfen; *make out a* –, eine Rechnung ausstellen; *pass a* –, ein Gesetz verabschieden; *post* or *stick –s,* Zettel ankleben; *protest a* –, einen Wechsel protestieren; *stick no –s!* Zettelankleben verboten! *table the* –, die Vorlage vertagen; *take up a* –, einen Wechsel honorieren; *throw out a* –, einen Gesetzentwurf ablehnen. **2.** *v.t.* anzeigen, (durch Anschlag) bekanntmachen; (*Comm.*) (*goods*) auf die Rechnung setzen, (*coll.*) (*purchaser*) eine Rechnung schicken (*Dat.*); (*Theat.*) *–ed to appear,* im Programm aufgenommen.
bill|board, *s.* (*Am.*) das Anschlagbrett. **--book,** *s.* das Wechselbuch. **--broker,** *s.* der Wechselmakler. **--brokerage,** *s.* die Wechselcourtage. **--business,** *s.* das Wechselgeschäft.
[1]**billet** ['bilit], **1.** *s.* (*Mil.*) der Quartierzettel; das Quartier, die Unterkunft; (*coll.*) *good* –, gute Stellung; (*Prov.*) *every bullet has its* –, jede Kugel hat ihre Bestimmung. **2.** *v.t.* einquartieren, unterbringen (*on, with,* bei).
[2]**billet,** *s.* das (Holz)scheit, (*Her.*) die Schindel.
billet-doux ['bilei'du:], *s.* (*pl.* **billets-doux**) (*coll.*) der Liebesbrief.
billetee [bili'ti:], *s.* Einquartierte(r). **billeting** ['bilitiŋ], *s.* die Einquartierung; – *officer,* der Quartiermacher.
bill|fold, *s.* (*Am.*) die Brieftasche. **--holder,** *s.* der Wechselinhaber.
billhook ['bilhuk], *s.* die Hippe, das Gartenmesser, Heckenmesser, Baummesser.
billiard|ball ['biljəd–], *s.* die Billardkugel. **--cue,** *s.* der Billardstock, das Queue. **--marker,** *s.* der (Billard)markör. **billiards,** *pl.* (*sing. constr.*) das Billard(spiel). **billiard-table,** *s.* der Billardtisch.
Billingsgate ['biliŋzgeit], *s.* (*sl.*) die Pöbelsprache.
billion ['biljən], *s.* (*U.K.*) die Billion (= *1,000,000 millions*); (*Am.*) Milliarde (= *1,000 millions*).
billow ['bilou], **1.** *s.* die Woge, Welle. **2.** *v.t.* wogen, sich türmen. **billowy,** *adj.* schwellend, wogend.
bill|-poster, --sticker, *s.* der Zettelankleber, Plakatkleber.
billy ['bili], *s.* der Kochkessel; (*Am.*) die Keule, der Knüppel, Knüttel. **billy|can,** *s.* der Kochkessel. **-cock,** *s.* (*coll.*) die Melone (*hat*). **--goat,** *s.* der Ziegenbock. **--ho,** *s.* (*sl.*) *like* –, wie verrückt, wie die Wilden.
bimetallism [bai'mətəlizm], *s.* der Bimetallismus, die Doppelwährung.
bi-monthly [bai'mʌnθli], *adj.* vierzehntägig, halbmonatlich; zweimonatlich.
bin [bin], **1.** *s.* der Kasten, Behälter. **2.** *v.t.* lagern (*wine*); aufbewahren.
binary ['bainəri], *adj.* binär, zweizählig; – *arithmetic,* dyadisches Zahlensystem, die Dyadik; – *compound,* binäre Verbindung; – *fission,* die Zweiteilung; (*Mus.*) – *measure,* gerader Takt; – *star,* der Doppelstern.
binate ['bainit], *adj.* (*Bot.*) zweiteilig, gepaart.
bind [baind], **1.** *irr.v.t.* 1. binden, befestigen, festmachen; (ein)binden (*books*), einfassen (*a dress etc.*), beschlagen (*a wheel*); – *up,* verbinden (*a wound*); zusammenbinden (*pamphlets etc.*); *his interests are bound up with mine,* seine Interessen hängen mit meinen aufs engste zusammen, seine Interessen sind mit meinen aufs engste verknüpft; 2. (*fig.*) verbinden, verpflichten; *be bound to do,* verpflichtet sein zu tun; (*coll.*) *I'll be bound,* ohne Zweifel, ich bürge dafür, ich stehe dafür ein; *bound by a promise,* durch ein Versprechen gebunden; – *over,* durch Bürgschaft verpflichten; *be bound over for a year in the sum of £100,* eine Bewährungsfrist von einem Jahr unter Kaution von £100 erhalten; 3. verstopfen (*the bowels*). *See also* [1]**bound. 2.** *irr.v.i.* 1. steif *or* hart werden, binden; (*Med.*) stopfen; (*Mech.*) feststecken, stocken, hängenbleiben, gehemmt werden; 2. (*fig.*) bindend sein, verpflichten. **3.** *s.* (*coll.*) die Bürde, lästige Pflicht.
binder ['baində], *s.* der Binder; Buchbinder; Garbenbinder (*a p. or machine*); das Bindemittel, Band, die Binde; (*for papers*) der Einband, Umschlag, Hefter; (*Med.*) die Leibbinde; (*Build.*) der Bindestein, Bindebalken, Zugbalken; *–'s board,* die Buchbinderpappe; *–'s press,* die Heftlade. **bindery,** *s.* die Buchbinderei.
binding ['baindiŋ], **1.** *adj.* 1. bindend, verbindlich (*on,* für); *not* –, unverbindlich, freibleibend; 2. (*Med.*) verstopfend. **2.** *s.* die Bindung; Binde, der Verband; Einband (*of a book*); Besatz, die Einfassung, Borte, das Einfaßband (*of a dress*). **binding|-agent,** *s.* das Bindemittel. **--course,** *s.* (*Build.*) die Binderschicht. **--screw,** *s.* die Klemmschraube.
bindweed ['baindwi:d], *s.* (*Bot.*) die Winde.
binge [bindʒ], *s.* (*sl.*) die Bierreise, der Saufabend.
bingo ['biŋgou], *s.* (*coll.*) (eine Art) Lottospiel.
binnacle ['binəkl], *s.* (*Naut.*) die Kompaßhaube, das Kompaßhäuschen, Nachthaus.
binocular [bi'nɔkjulə], **1.** *s.* (*usu. pl.*) der Feldstecher, das Feldglas, Opernglas. **2.** *adj.* zweiäugig, beidäugig.
binomial [bai'noumiəl], **1.** *s.* (*Math.*) zweigliedrige

Größe, das Binom. **2.** *adj.* (*Math.*) binomisch, zweigliedrig.

binominal [bai'nɔminəl], *adj.* zweinamig; – ***system,*** das System der Doppelbenennung.

biochemist [baio'kemist], *s.* der Biochemiker. **biochemistry,** *s.* die Biochemie.

biographer [bai'ɔgrəfə], *s.* der Biograph. **biographic(al)** [–o'græfik(əl)], *adj.* biographisch. **biography,** *s.* die Biographie, Lebensbeschreibung.

biologic(al) [baio'lɔdʒik(əl)], *adj.* biologisch; – (***pest***) ***control,*** biologische Schädlingsbekämpfung; – ***warfare,*** der Bakterien– *or* Bazillenkrieg. **biologist** [–'ɔlədʒist], *s.* der Biologe. **biology** [–'ɔlədʒi], *s.* die Biologie.

bipartite [bai'pɑ:tait], *adj.* (*Bot.*) zweiteilig; in doppelter Ausfertigung (*of documents etc.*); (*Law*) zweiseitig (*contract etc.*).

biped ['baiped], *s.* der Zweifüß(l)er.

biplane ['baiplein], *s.* der Doppeldecker, Zweidecker.

bipod ['baipɔd], *s.* der Zweifuß, das Zweibein, zweibeiniges Gestell.

birch [bə:tʃ], **1.** *s.* die Birke; – (***rod***), die Rute. **2.** *v.t.* mit der Rute züchtigen. **3.** *adj.* birken. **birching,** *s.* die Züchtigung. **birch| tree,** *s.* die Birke. **–wood,** *s.* der Birkenwald. **–wood,** *s.* das Birkenholz.

bird [bə:d], *s.* der Vogel; (*coll.*) Bursche; (*sl.*) das Mädchen; ***cock* –,** das Männchen; (*Prov.*) ***the early – catches the worm,*** Morgenstunde hat Gold im Munde; (*fig.*) ***–s of a feather,*** gleiche Brüder; ***–s of a feather flock together,*** gleich und gleich gesellt sich gern; ***fine feathers make fine –s,*** Kleider machen Leute; (*sl.*) ***give him the –,*** ihn auszischen *or* auspfeifen; (*Prov.*) ***a – in the hand is worth two in the bush,*** ein Sperling in der Hand ist besser als eine Taube auf dem Dach; ***hen –,*** das Weibchen; – ***of paradise,*** der Paradiesvogel; – ***of passage,*** der Durchzügler; – ***of prey,*** der Raubvogel; (*coll.*) ***queer –,*** komischer Kauz; ***a little – told me,*** ich habe ein Vögelchen singen hören; ***kill two –s with one stone,*** zwei Fliegen mit einer Klappe schlagen; (*coll.*) ***wise old –,*** schlauer Bursche.

bird|-bath, *s.* die Vogeltränke. **--cage,** *s.* der *or* das Vogelbauer. **--call,** *s.* der Vogelruf; die Lockpfeife. **--catcher,** *s.* der Vogelfänger, Vogelsteller. **--cherry,** *s.* (*Bot.*) die Vogelkirsche, Traubenkirsche. **--fancier,** *s.* der Vogelliebhaber, Vogelzüchter.

birdie ['bə:rdi], *s.* (*coll.*) das Vöglein; (*Phot. coll.*) ***watch the –!*** schau' den Piepmatz!

bird|-lime, *s.* der Vogelleim. **--lover,** *s.* der Vogelfreund. **--sanctuary,** *s.* das Vogelschutzgebiet. **--seed,** *s.* das Vogelfutter.

bird's| egg, *s.* das Vogelei. **--eye,** *s.* (*Bot.*) das Adonisröschen; – ***tobacco,*** der Feinschnitt(abak); ***--eye view,*** die Vogelperspektive, (der Blick aus der) Vogelschau, (*fig.*) allgemeiner Überblick. **--nest, 1.** *s.* das Vogelnest (*also Cul.*); (*Naut.*) der Ausguck, Mastkorb. **2.** *v.i.* Vogelnester ausnehmen; ***they went bird('s)-nesting,*** sie gingen auf die Suche nach Vogelnestern.

bird|-table, *s.* der Futtertisch. **--watcher,** *s.* der Vogelbeobachter.

biretta [bi'retə], *s.* (*R.C.*) das Birett, Barett.

birth [bə:θ], *s.* die Geburt; Herkunft, Abstammung; (*fig.*) Abkunft, Entstehung, der Ursprung; ***at his –,*** bei seiner Geburt; ***by –,*** von Geburt; ***give – to,*** gebären, zur Welt bringen; (*fig.*) Veranlassung geben zu, hervorbringen; ***of noble –,*** von adliger Abkunft.

birth|-certificate, *s.* der Geburtsschein. **--control,** *s.* die Geburtenregelung, Geburtenbeschränkung, Empfängnisverhütung. **–day,** *s.* der Geburtstag; – ***present,*** das Geburtstagsgeschenk; (*coll.*) ***in one's – suit,*** im Adamskostüm, splitternackt. **--mark,** *s.* das Muttermal. **–place,** *s.* der Geburtsort. **--rate,** *s.* die Geburtenziffer; ***falling –,*** der Geburtenrückgang. **–right,** *s.* das Geburtsrecht, angestammtes Recht.

biscuit ['biskit], *s.* der Zwieback, der *or* das Biskuit *or* Keks; (*Naut.*) ***ship's –,*** der Schiffszwieback; – (***china***), das Biskuitporzellan; (*coll.*) ***that takes the –,*** das ist ja *or* doch die Höhe! das setzt allem die Krone auf!

bisect [bai'sekt], **1.** *v.t.* (*Math.*) halbieren; in zwei Teile schneiden, in zwei teilen; ***–ing line,*** die Mittellinie, Halbierungslinie, Halbierende. **2.** *v.i.* sich teilen, sich gabeln. **bisection,** *s.* die Halbierung. **bisector,** *s.* *See* ***bisecting line.***

bisexual [bai'seksjuəl], *adj.* zweigeschlechtig, gemischtgeschlechtig, zwitterhaft, zwitterig.

bishop ['biʃəp], *s.* der Bischof; (*Chess*) Läufer. **bishopric,** *s.* das Bistum.

bismuth ['bizməθ], *s.* der *or* das Wismut.

bison [baisn], *s.* amerikanischer Büffel, der Bison.

bissextile [bi'sekstail], **1.** *adj.* Schalt–; – ***day,*** der Schalttag; – ***year,*** das Schaltjahr. **2.** *s.* das Schaltjahr.

bister, (*Am.*) *see* **bistre.**

bistoury ['bisturi], *s.* das *or* der Bistouri, das Klappmesser.

bistre ['bistə], **1.** *s.* der *or* das Bister, das Nußbraun. **2.** *adj.* nußbraun, bisterfarben.

bisulphate [bai'sʌlfeit], *s.* das Bisulfat, doppeltschwefelsaures Salz; – ***of potash,*** doppeltschwefelsaures Kalium. **bisulphite** [–ait], *s.* das Bisulfit, doppeltschwefligsaures Salz.

[1]**bit** [bit], *s.* (*of a bridle*) das Gebiß; (*Tech.*) der Bohrer, das Bohreisen, die Schneide, (*of a plane*) das (Hobel)eisen; (*of a key*) der Bart; ***centre –,*** der Herzbohrer; ***curb –,*** das Stangengebiß; ***snaffle –,*** das Trensengebiß; ***take the – in*** or ***between one's teeth,*** (*of a horse*) durchgehen, (*fig.*) auf die Stange beißen, störrisch *or* widerspenstig werden.

[2]**bit,** *s.* der Bissen, Happen, das Stück; (*coll.*) ***a –,*** ein wenig *or* bißchen, ein Stückchen, eine Kleinigkeit; (*Am. coll.*) das 25-Cent-Stück; (*coll.*) ***he's a – of a fool,*** er hat etwas von einem Narr; – ***by –,*** Stück für Stück, stückweise, allmählich, nach und nach; ***not care a –,*** sich gar nichts daraus machen; (*coll.*) ***do one's –,*** das Seine tun, seine Pflicht und Schuldigkeit tun, seinen Teil dazu *or* sein Scherflein beitragen; ***every –,*** ganz und gar, gänzlich, in jeder Beziehung; ***give him a – of one's mind,*** ihm gehörig die Meinung sagen; ***a good –,*** ein tüchtiges *or* ordentliches Stück; ***a little*** or ***tiny –,*** ein ganz klein wenig; ***not a –,*** ganz und gar nicht, nicht im geringsten, keine Spur; (*coll.*) ***wait a –,*** warte einen Augenblick *or* ein Weilchen.

[3]**bit,** *imperf. of* **bite.**

bitch [bitʃ], **1.** *s.* die Hündin, Petze; (*vulg.*) das Weib(sbild); die Hure, Metze; (*vulg.*) ***you son of a –!*** du Arsch mit Ohren! **2.** *v.t.* (*sl.*) versauen.

bite [bait], **1.** *irr.v.t.* 1. beißen; stechen (*of insects*); – ***the dust,*** ins Gras beißen; – ***one's lip,*** sich (*Dat.*) auf die Lippe beißen; – ***one's nails,*** an den Nägeln kauen; – ***off,*** abbeißen; (*coll.*) – ***off more than one can chew,*** zu viel unternehmen, sich (*Dat.*) zuviel zumuten; 2. (*Tech.*) fassen, eingreifen, einschneiden; (*Chem.*) angreifen, zerfressen, ätzen, beizen (*metals*); – ***into,*** tief einschneiden in (*Acc.*); 3. (*coll.*) ***be bitten,*** betrogen werden, hereinfallen; ***once bitten twice shy,*** gebranntes Kind scheut das Feuer; (*coll.*) ***be bitten by,*** angesteckt sein von, sich begeistern für. **2.** *irr.v.i.* 1. beißen, schnappen (***at,*** nach), (*of fish*) anbeißen; (*fig.*) beißen, schneiden (*as wind, cold*), stechen, brennen (*as mustard etc.*); 2. eingreifen (*of wheels*); fassen, halten (*of the anchor*). **3.** *s.* 1. das Beißen, der Biß, die Bißwunde; der Stich (*of insects*); 2. das Anbeißen (*of fish*); 3. (*Tech.*) Fassen, Eingreifen; (*Chem.*) Beizen, Ätzen; (*fig.*) die Schärfe, Bissigkeit; 4. (*coll.*) der Bissen, Happen; ***will you have a – to eat?*** wollen Sie eine Kleinigkeit essen? ***I haven't had a –*** (***to eat***) ***since yesterday,*** ich habe seit gestern keinen Bissen gegessen; ***give me a –,*** laß mich mal abbeißen. **biter,** *s.* ***the – bit,*** der betrogene Betrüger; wer anderen eine Grube gräbt, fällt selbst hinein.

biting ['baitiŋ], *adj.* beißend, scharf, schneidend;

(*fig.*) bissig, sarkastisch; *– jest,* beißender Scherz; *– wind,* scharfer *or* schneidend kalter Wind.

bitt [bit], *s.* (*usu. pl.*) (*Naut.*) der Poller; *mooring –s,* der Vertäupoller; *towing –s,* der Schleppoller.

bitten [bitn], *p.p. of* **bite.**

bitter ['bitə], **1.** *adj.* bitter, herb; hart, heftig, schmerzhaft; (*fig. of a p.*) erbittert, verbittert; (*of weather etc.*) rauh, streng, unfreundlich; *– beer,* helles Bier; *– blast,* schneidender Wind; *to the – end,* bis aufs letzte, bis zum äußersten, bis zum Tode; *– enemy,* der Todfeind; *as – as gall,* gallenbitter; (*Chem.*) *– principle,* der Bitterstoff; *– quarrel,* heftiger Streit; *– sorrow,* herber Schmerz; *– words,* verbitterte Worte. **2.** *adv.* bitter–; *– cold,* bitterkalt. **3.** *s.* 1. das Bittere, die Bitterkeit; 2. helles Bier; 3. *pl.* der Magenbitter, das Bittermittel, Bittertropfen (*pl.*).

bitter-gourd, *s.* (*Bot.*) die Koloquinte.

bittern ['bitən], *s.* (*Orn.*) Große Rohrdommel (*Botaurus stellaris*); *little –,* die Zwergrohrdommel (*Ixobrychus minutus*).

bitterness ['bitənis], *s.* die Bitterkeit, Herbheit; Strenge, Härte, Schmerzlichkeit; Verbitterung, Grausamkeit.

bittersweet ['bitəswi:t], **1.** *adj.* bittersüß. **2.** *s.* (*Bot.*) das Bittersüß.

bitumen ['bitjumən, bi'tju:mən], *s.* das Erdpech, der Bergteer, Asphalt. **bituminous** [–'tju:minəs], *adj.* bituminös; pechhaltig, asphalthaltig; *– cement,* der Asphaltkitt; *– coal,* die Fettkohle.

bivalence [bai'veiləns], *s.* (*Chem.*) die Zweiwertigkeit, (*Biol.*) doppelte Chromosomenzahl. **bivalent,** *adj.* (*Chem.*) zweiwertig, (*Biol.*) doppelchromosomig.

bivalve ['baivælv], *s.* zweischalige Muschel; zweiklappige Frucht. **bivalvular** [–'vælvjulə], *adj.* zweischalig; (*Bot.*) zweiklappig.

bivouac ['bivuæk], **1.** *s.* das Biwak, Feldlager, Nachtlager. **2.** *v.i.* biwakieren, im Freien übernachten.

bizarre [bi'zɑ:], *adj.* wunderlich, seltsam, phantastisch, grotesk, bizarr.

blab [blæb], **1.** *s.* (*coll.*) das Geschwätz, die Plapperei; der (die) Schwätzer(in), die Klatschbase. **2.** *v.t.* – (*out*), ausschwatzen, ausplaudern, verraten. **3.** *v.i.* schwatzen, ein Geheimnis verraten.

black [blæk], **1.** *adj.* schwarz; (*fig.*) dunkel, finster, düster; schändlich, abscheulich (*as a crime*). **(a)** (*with nouns*) *the – art,* schwarze Magie *or* Kunst; *I am in his – books,* ich bin bei ihm schlecht angeschrieben; *– cap,* schwarze Kappe (*of a judge*); *Black Death,* die Pest, der Schwarze Tod; *– and white drawing,* die Schwarzweißzeichnung; *– eye,* blaues Auge; *Black Forest,* der Schwarzwald; *Black Friar,* der Dominikaner; *– frost,* trockener Frost; *– heart,* böses Herz; *– letter,* die Fraktur; *– list,* schwarze Liste; *– look,* drohender *or* mißmutiger Blick; *– magic,* see *– art*; *– man,* Schwarze(r), Eingeborene(r); *Black Maria,* der Gefangenenwagen, grüne Minna; *– mark,* der Tadel, schlechtes Zeugnis; *get a – mark,* in üblen Ruf kommen; *– market,* schwarzer Markt, der Schwarzmarkt, Schwarzhandel; *– marketeer,* der Schwarzhändler, Schieber; *Black Monday,* der Unglückstag; erster Schultag; (*Bot.*) *– poplar,* die Schwarzpappel; *– pudding,* die Blutwurst; *Black Sea,* das Schwarze Meer; *– sheep,* räudiges Schaf; (*usu. fig.*) der Taugenichts. **(b)** (*with verbs, preps.*) *beat – and blue,* grün und blau schlagen; *things look –,* die Aussicht ist finster *or* düster; *go – in the face,* blau werden (*through choking*); *not so – as he is painted,* besser als sein Ruf. **2.** *s.* **1.** das Schwarz, die Schwärze; das Trauerkleid; *bone –,* die Knochenkohle, das Beinschwarz; *speck of –,* der Rußfleck, Schmutzfleck; *wear –,* Trauer(kleidung) tragen; (*Comm.*) *in the –,* ohne Schulden, zahlungsfähig; *have a th. in – and white,* etwas schriftlich *or* etwas schwarz auf weiß haben; 2. **Schwarze**(r), der (die) Neger(in). **3.** *v.t.* 1. schwärzen, wichsen; *– out,* verdunkeln; 2. (*coll.*) auf die schwarze Liste setzen. **4.** *v.i. – out,* eine Bewußtseinsstörung haben.

blackamoor ['blækəmuə], *s.* Schwarze(r), der Neger, Mohr.

black|ball, **1.** *s.* schwarze Wahlkugel, (*fig.*) die Gegenstimme. **2.** *v.t.* stimmen gegen, ausschließen. **--beetle,** *s.* die Küchenschabe. **–berry,** *s.* die Brombeere. **–bird,** *s.* (*Orn.*) die Amsel (*Turdus merula*). **–board,** *s.* die Wandtafel. **–cap,** *s.* (*Orn.*) die Mönchsgrasmücke, das Schwarzplättchen (*Silvia atricapilla*). **--coated,** *adj.* *– worker,* Büroangestellte(r). **--cock,** *s.* (*Orn.*) der Birkhahn (*Lyrurus tetrix*). **--currant,** *s.* die Johannisbeere.

blacken [blækn], **1.** *v.t.* schwarz machen, schwärzen; (*fig.*) anschwärzen, verleumden. **2.** *v.i.* schwarz werden. **blackening,** *s. See* **blacking.**

black-eyed, *adj.* schwarzäugig.

blackguard ['blægɑ:d], **1.** *s.* der Schuft, Lump, *pl.* das Lumpenpack, schmutziges Gesindel. **2.** *v.t.* beschimpfen. **blackguardly,** *adv.* roh, gemein, pöbelhaft, schuftig.

black|head, *s.* der Mitesser. **--hearted,** *adj.* bösartig, boshaft.

blacking ['blækiŋ], *s.* das Schwärzen, Wichsen; die Schwärze, Wichse; *– brush,* die Wichsbürste. **blackish,** *adj.* schwärzlich.

black|jack, *s.* die Piratenflagge; (*Am.*) der Totschläger. **–lead, 1.** *s.* der Graphit, das Reißblei; die Ofenwichse, Ofenschwärze; *– pencil,* der Bleistift. **2.** *v.t.* schwärzen (*a stove etc.*). **–leg,** *s.* der Streikbrecher. **--leg,** *s.* (*Vet.*) die Klauenseuche. **--legged,** *adj.* (*Orn.*) (*Am.*) *– kittiwake, see* **kittiwake.** **–list,** *v.t.* auf die schwarze Liste setzen. **–mail,** **1.** *s.* die Erpressung; das Erpressergeld. **2.** *v.t.* Geld erpressen von, erpressen. **–mailer,** *s.* der (die) Erpresser(in).

blackness ['blæknis], *s.* die Schwärze; Dunkelheit; (*fig.*) Abscheulichkeit, Verderbtheit.

black|-out, *s.* die Verdunkelung; (*fig.*) die Bewußtseinsstörung, der Bewußtseinsschwund; (*of news*) die Blockierung, Sperre. **--rimmed,** *adj.* schwarzumrandet. **–shirt,** *s.* das Schwarzhemd, der Faschist. **–smith,** *s.* der Grobschmied, Hufschmied. **–thorn,** *s.* (*Bot.*) der Schwarzdorn, Schlehdorn.

bladder ['blædər], *s.* die Blase; Schwimmblase; (*Anat.*) (Harn)blase. **bladder|-fern,** *s.* (*Bot.*) der Blasenfarn. **--wort,** *s.* (*Bot.*) der Wasserschlauch, Wasserfenchel. **--wrack,** *s.* (*Bot.*) der Blasentang.

blade [bleid], *s.* 1. das Blatt, der Halm (*of grass etc.*); die Klinge (*of a knife etc.*); (*Poet.*) der Degen, das Schwert; der Flügel (*of fan, propellor*); das Blatt (*of saw, axe, spade, oar*); *razor –,* die Rasierklinge; *shoulder –,* das Schulterblatt; *in the –,* auf dem Halm; 2. (*coll.*) der Raufbold, Haudegen; frecher Bursche.

blain [blein], *s.* die Beule, das Geschwür.

blamable ['bleiməbl], *adj.* tadelnswert, strafbar. **blame,** **1.** *s.* der Tadel, Vorwurf, die Rüge; Schuld, Verantwortung; *bear* or *take the –,* die Schuld auf sich nehmen; *lay* or *put* or *throw the – on him,* ihm die Verantwortung *or* Schuld zuschieben *or* geben. **2.** *v.t.* tadeln, rügen (*for,* wegen); verantwortlich machen (*for,* für), die Schuld geben (*Dat.*) (*for,* an (*Dat.*)); *be to – for,* schuld sein an (*Dat.*), die Schuld tragen an (*Dat.*); *I have only myself to –,* die Schuld habe ich allein, es ist meine eigne Schuld; *no one can – you for it,* das kann Ihnen niemand verargen. **blameless,** *adj.* untadelig, schuldlos (*of,* an (*Dat.*)). **blamelessness,** *s.* die Tadellosigkeit, Schuldlosigkeit. **blameworthy,** *adj.* tadelnswert, schuldig.

blanch [blɑ:ntʃ], **1.** *v.t.* weiß machen, bleichen; beizen, weiß sieden (*metals*); abhülsen, schälen (*almonds*); (*fig.*) *– over,* beschönigen. **2.** *v.i.* erbleichen, erblassen, bleich werden.

blancmange [blə'mɔnʒ], *s.* der Pudding, Flammeri.

bland [blænd], *adj.* (ein)schmeichelnd; mild, sanft.

blandish ['blændiʃ], *v.t.* schmeicheln (*Dat.*), liebkosen. **blandishment,** *s.* die Schmeichelei; *pl.* schmeichelhafte Worte.

blandness ['blændnis], *s.* die Milde, Sanftheit.

blank [blæŋk], **1.** *adj.* 1. unbeschrieben, leer (*of* *paper etc.*), unausgefüllt, Blanko– (*of a form*); – ***acceptance***, das Blankoakzept; – ***cheque***, der Blankoscheck, unausgefüllter Wechsel; (*fig.*) unbeschränkte Vollmacht; – ***endorsement***, das Blankoindossement; offenes Giro; – ***line***, blinde Zeile; – ***space***, leerer Raum; – ***window***, blindes Fenster; ***leave*** –, leer *or* unbeschrieben lassen; ***leave a line*** –, eine Zeile frei lassen; 2. reimlos (*of verse*); – ***verse***, der Blankvers, reimloser Vers; 3. (*fig.*) verblüfft, bestürzt, verwirrt, fassungslos; ***in – astonishment***, in sprachlosem Erstaunen; ***look*** –, verblüfft aussehen; ***his mind went*** –, seine Erinnerung ließ ihn in Stich; 4. (*Mil.*) blind (*ammunition*); – ***ammunition***, die Exerziermunition; – ***cartridge***, die Platzpatrone; 5. (*obs.*) blank, weiß. **2.** *s.* 1. (*Mil.*) die Platzpatrone; 2. der Vordruck, unausgefülltes Formular, unbeschriebenes Blatt; ***his mind became a*** –, seine Erinnerung ließ ihn in Stich; ***leave a*** –, einen freien Raum lassen; (*coll.*) ***what the*** (*–ety*) – . . .? Verflixt nochmal! was zum Teufel . . .? 3. (*Typ.*) der Durchschuß, das Blindmaterial, (*Tech.*) ungeprägte Münzplatte, der Rohling, rohes Formstück, das Werkstück; 4. (*lottery*) die Niete; ***draw a*** –, eine Niete ziehen; 5. (*fig.*) die Öde, das Nichts.

blanket ['blæŋkit], **1.** *s.* die Wolldecke, Bettdecke, Schlafdecke; (*Tech.*) (Filz)unterlage; (*fig.*) Decke, Hülle (*of snow etc.*); (*fig.*) ***wet*** –, der Dämpfer, kalte Dusche; der Miesmacher, Spaß– *or* Spielverderber; ***saddle*** –, die Satteldecke, der Woilach; (*coll.*) ***on the wrong side of the*** –, unehelich. **2.** *v.t.* zudecken; (*Rad.*) überlagern; (*Naut.*) den Wind fangen (*Dat.*); (*fig.*) totschweigen (*news etc.*). **3.** *attrib. adj.* Gesamt–, generell, umfassend; – ***insurance***, die Kollektivversicherung. **blanketing,** *s.* das Wollzeug zu Bettdecken; (*fig.*) (*Rad.*) die Überlagerung (von Signalen). **blanket-stitch,** *s.* der Knopflochstich.

blanquette [blæŋ'ket], *s.* das (Kalb)frikassee.

blare [blɛə], **1.** *v.i.* schmettern; – ***forth***, ausschmettern. **2.** *s.* das Geschmetter.

blarney ['blɑːni], *s.* (*coll.*) (*Irish*) grobe Schmeichelei, die Flunkerei.

blasé [blɑː'zei], *adj.* blasiert.

blaspheme [blæs'fiːm], *v.t.*, *v.i.* lästern; – ***against***, fluchen gegen *or* über (*Acc.*). **blasphemer,** *s.* der Gotteslästerer. **blasphemous** ['blæsfiməs], *adj.* lästernd, lästerlich. **blasphemy** ['blæsfimi], *s.* die (Gottes)lästerung.

blast [blɑːst], **1.** *s.* 1. der Windstoß, Sturm; 2. Schall, Stoß, das Geschmetter (*of trumpets*); 3. die Sprengladung; Detonation, Explosion, Druckwelle; (*Artil.*) ***muzzle*** –, der Mündungsknall; 4. (*Bot.*) der Meltau, Brand; Pesthauch; 5. (*Tech.*) die Zugluft, das Gebläse; (*coll.*) ***at*** or ***in full*** –, auf (Hoch)touren, mit Volldampf, im Gange, in Tätigkeit. **2.** *v.t.* sprengen; versengen, verdorren; (*fig.*) vernichten, verderben, vereiteln; verdammen, verfluchen; – ***his reputation***, ihn um seinen guten Namen bringen; ***–ed hopes***, vereitelte Hoffnungen; ***–ed corn***, verbranntes Getreide. **blasted,** *adj.* (*vulg.*) verdammt.

blast|-furnace, *s.* der Hochofen. **–-hole,** *s.* das Bohrloch, Sprengloch. **blasting,** *s.* das Sprengen; die Sprengung; (*fig.*) Vernichtung; ***–-cartridge*** or ***-charge***, die Bohrpatrone, Bohrladung, Sprengladung, der Sprengkörper.

blastoderm ['blɑːstədəːm], *s.* die Keimhaut.

blatancy ['bleitənsi], *s.* anmaßendes Benehmen, die Angeberei. **blatant,** *adj.* blökend, plärrend; lärmend, laut, dreist; – ***nonsense***, himmelschreiender Unsinn.

blather ['blæðə], *see* **blether.**

[1]**blaze** [bleiz], **1.** *s.* (lodernde) Flamme, (loderndes) Feuer, der Brand, die Glut; (*Poet.*) Lohe; (*of light*) das Strahlen, Leuchten, der Glanz; (*fig.*) das Auflodern, (plötzlicher) Ausbruch (*of enthusiasm etc.*); – ***of colour***, die Farbenpracht; ***it went up in a*** –, es ging in Flammen auf; (*sl.*) ***go to –s***, zum Teufel gehen; (*sl.*) ***what the –s . . .?*** was zum Teufel . . .? (*coll.*) ***like –s***, wie verrückt; (*sl.*) ***run like –s***, laufen was das Zeug hält. **2.** *v.i.* aufflammen, lodern; leuchten, glühen, glänzen; ***the fire was blazing*** (***away***), das Feuer brannte lichterloh; (*coll.*) – ***away at***, drauflosschießen an (*Acc.*), (*fig.*) herangehen an (*Acc.*); ***in a blazing temper***, in heller Wut; – ***up***, aufflammen, auflodern, (*fig.*) (in Zorn) entbrennen.

[2]**blaze, 1.** *s.* die Blesse (*on a horse's forehead*); Wegmarkierung, Anschalmung, der Einschnitt (*on a tree*). **2.** *v.t.* markieren, anschalmen (*a tree*); – ***the trail***, den Weg bahnen, (*fig.*) Pionierarbeit leisten, Bahn brechen.

blazer ['bleizə], *s.* bunte *or* leichte Sportjacke.

blazon ['bleizən], **1.** *s.* die Wappenkunde; das Wappen(schild), Panier; (*fig.*) die Verkündigung. **2.** *v.t.* (*Her.*) (heraldisch) erklären *or* beschreiben; verzieren, schmücken; (*fig.*) verkünden, (*usu.*) – ***abroad*** or ***forth***, verherrlichen, rühmen, ausposaunen; ***–ed windows***, wappengeschmückte Fenster. **blazonment,** *s.* die Wappenmalerei, (*fig.*) Ausschmückung; das Ausposaunen. **blazonry,** *s.* die Wappenkunde; heraldische Kunst; (*fig.*) pomphafte Hervorhebung, der Farbenschmuck.

bleach [bliːtʃ], **1.** *v.t.* bleichen. **2.** *v.i.* weiß werden, erbleichen. **3.** *s.* das Bleichmittel, der Chlorkalk. **bleacher,** *s.* der Bleicher; *pl.* (*Am. coll.*) unbedeckte Zuschauersitze. **bleaching,** *s.* das Bleichen, die Bleiche. **bleaching|-agent,** *s.* das Bleichmittel. **–-powder,** *s.* das Bleichpulver; der Chlorkalk.

[1]**bleak** [bliːk], *s.* (*Ichth.*) der Ukelei.

[2]**bleak,** *adj.* öde, kahl; rauh (*as climate*), windig; ungeschützt; (*fig.*) trübe, freudlos. **bleakness,** *s.* die Öde, Kahlheit, Rauheit, Kälte; Freudlosigkeit, Trübheit.

blear [bliə], *adj.* trüb(e), umnebelt, verschwommen. **blear-eyed,** *adj.* triefäugig. **bleariness,** *s.* die Trübheit, Verschwommenheit. **bleary,** *adj. See* **blear.**

bleat [bliːt], **1.** *v.i.* blöken (*sheep*), meckern (*goats*). **2.** *or* **bleating,** *s.* das Blöken, Gemecker.

bleb [bleb], *s.* kleine Blase, das Bläschen; die Pustel.

bled [bled], *imperf.*, *p.p. of* **bleed.**

bleed [bliːd], **1.** *irr.v.i.* bluten; (*Tech.*) lecken, leck sein; – ***to death***, verbluten; ***my heart –s for you***, mir blutet das Herz um dich. **2.** *irr.v.t.* bluten lassen, zur Ader lassen; abzapfen (*trees*); auslaufen *or* ausströmen *or* abfließen lassen (*liquid*); (*fig.*, *coll.*) schröpfen, rupfen; – ***him white***, ihn aussaugen, ihn um sein Letztes bringen. **bleeder,** *s.* 1. (*Med.*) der Bluter, Hämophile; 2. (*sl.*) Schmarotzer, gemeiner Schuft; 3. (*Tech.*) das Ablaß– *or* Auslaßbentil; (*Elec.*) – (***resistor***), der Nebenschlußwiderstand. **bleeding, 1.** *adj.* 1. blutend; 2. (*vulg.*) verflucht. **2.** *s.* die Blutung; das Bluten; (*Surg.*) der Aderlaß; (*Tech.*) das Auslaufen; Abzapfen (*of trees*); – ***from the nose***, das Nasenbluten.

blemish ['blemiʃ], **1.** *s.* der Makel, Flecken; Fehler, Mangel, das Gebrechen; (*fig.*) der Schandfleck. **2.** *v.t.* verunstalten, entstellen; schänden, brandmarken; (*Law*) verleumden.

blench [blentʃ], *v.i.* zurückschrecken, zurückfahren, zurückbeben, zurückweichen, stutzen.

blend [blend], **1.** *v.t.* (ver)mischen, (ver)mengen, verschmelzen; melieren, verschneiden (*wine*). **2.** *v.i.* ineinander übergehen, verschmelzen; sich (harmonisch) verbinden, sich vermischen (***with***, mit), gut passen (zu). **3.** *s.* die Mischung; der Verschnitt (*of wine*); (harmonische) Zusammenstellung.

blende [blend], *s.* (*Min.*) die (Zink)blende.

blennorrhoea [blenə'riə], *s.* (*Med.*) der Schleimfluß.

bless [bles], *v.t.* segnen, weihen; beglücken, glücklich machen; preisen, loben, verherrlichen; – ***one's lucky stars***, sich glücklich schätzen; (*coll.*) – ***me! – my soul!*** verflixt! du meine Güte! ***I haven't a penny to – myself with***, ich habe nicht einen roten Heller; (*coll.*) ***be –ed with***, beglückt *or* gesegnet sein mit; (*coll.*) ***well I'm -ed!*** see - ***me!*** **blessed** ['blesid], *attrib. adj.* glücklich, (glück)selig; gesegnet; (*coll.*) verwünscht, verflixt; ***Blessed Virgin,*** Jungfrau Maria; ***of - memory,*** seligen Angedenkens; (*coll.*) ***the whole - day,*** den lieben langen Tag. **blessedness** [-idnis], *s.* die Glückseligkeit, das Glück, der Segen; die Seligkeit, das Heil; (*coll.*) ***single--,*** die Unvermähltheit, lediger Stand.

blessing ['blesiŋ], *s.* der Segen, Segensspruch, die Segnung; Wohltat, Gnade; das Glück; ***by the - of God,*** durch Gottes Segen *or* Huld; ***ask a -,*** das Tischgebet sprechen; (*coll.*) ***that's a -!*** das ist ein Glück! - ***in disguise,*** das Glück im Unglück.

blest [blest], *adj.* (*Poet.*) glücklich, selig.

blether ['bleðə], **1.** *s.* das Geschwätz, Gequassel; (*coll.*) der Schwätzer, Quatschkopf. **2.** *v.i.* Unsinn schwatzen.

blew [blu:], *imperf. of* **blow.**

blight [blait], **1.** *s.* der Meltau, Brand, die Trockenfäule; (*fig.*) der Pesthauch, Gifthauch; die Vereitelung, Zerstörung; (*coll.*) schädlicher Einfluß. **2.** *v.t.* durch Brand verderben; (*fig.*) am Gedeihen hindern, im Keim ersticken, zunichte machen, vernichten, vereiteln. **blighter,** *s.* (*sl.*) der Nichtsnutz, Schuft, Lump.

Blighty ['blaiti], *s.* (*sl.*) die Heimat (*England*); ***a - one,*** der Heimatschuß.

blimey! ['blaimi], *int.* (*sl.*) potztausend! zum Kuckuck!

blimp [blimp], *s.* (*coll.*) kleines unstarres Luftschiff.

blind [blaind], **1.** *adj.* blind (*also fig. to,* gegen; *with,* vor (*Dat.*)); (*fig.*) unbesonnen, verständnislos, urteilslos, wahllos; ziellos, zwecklos; verdeckt, verborgen, unsichtbar; ***strike -,*** blenden; - ***from birth,*** blind geboren; - ***alley,*** die Sackgasse; (*fig.*) totes Gleis; ***--alley occupation,*** der Beruf ohne Aussichten; - ***coal,*** der Anthrazit; - ***corner,*** unübersichtliche Straßenecke; (*fig.*) ***turn a - eye,*** ein Auge zudrücken (*to,* bei), absichtlich übersehen (*Acc.*); - ***flying,*** der Blindflug, das Blindfliegen; ***--flying instrument,*** das Blindfluggerät; ***in a - fury,*** in blinder Wut; - ***letter,*** unbestellbarer Brief; - ***man,*** Blinde(r); ***--man's-buff,*** die Blindekuh; ***--man's holiday,*** das Zwielicht, die Dämmerung; (*Artil.*) - ***shell,*** der Blindgänger; (*fig.*) ***his - side,*** seine schwache Seite; - ***spot,*** (*Tech.*) tote Zone, der Totpunkt; (*fig.*) schwacher *or* wunder Punkt; (*Bookb.*) - ***tooling,*** die Blindprägung, Blindpressung; - ***wall,*** blinde Mauer; - ***in*** or ***of one eye,*** auf einem Auge blind; - ***to one's own failings,*** gegen die eigenen Fehler blind; - ***with rage,*** blind vor Wut. **2.** *adv.* (*coll.*) - ***drunk,*** sinnlos betrunken, besoffen. **3.** *s.* die Blende, der Schirm; Vorhang, die Jalousie, das Rouleau (*at a window*); die Scheuklappe (*of harness*); (*fig.*) der Vorwand, die Bemäntelung; ***Venetian -,*** die Jalousie. **4.** *v.t.* blind machen, blenden; verblenden (*to,* gegen); - ***o.s. to the facts,*** sich den Tatsachen verschließen. **5.** *v.i.* (*sl.*) 1. blind drauflossausen; 2. fluchen.

blindfold ['blaindfould], **1.** *adj., adv.* mit verbundenen Augen; (*fig.*) blind(lings). **2.** *v.t.* die Augen verbinden (*Dat.*); (*fig.*) (ver)blenden. **3.** *s.* die Augenbinde. **blindly,** *adv.* (*fig.*) blind, blindlings, unbesonnen, ins Blaue hinein. **blindness,** *s.* die Blindheit (*also fig.*) (*to,* gegen), (*fig.*) Verblendung. **blindworm,** *s.* die Blindschleiche.

blink [bliŋk], **1.** *s.* das Blinzeln; der Schimmer, das Blinken. **2.** *v.t.* absichtlich übersehen, nicht sehen wollen; - ***the facts,*** die Wahrheit ignorieren. **3.** *v.i.* blinken, blinzeln, zwinkern, mit den Wimpern zucken; schimmern (*of light*). **blinker, 1.** *s.* die Klappe, Scheuklappe; das Blinklicht; Blinkgerät. **2.** *v.t.* mit Scheuklappen versehen. **blinking, 1.** *s.* das Blinzeln. **2.** *adj.* blinzelnd; (*sl.*) verflixt.

blip [blip], *s.* der Leuchtfleck, das Echosignal (*radar*).

bliss [blis], *s.* die Seligkeit, Wonne, das Entzücken. **blissful,** *adj.* (glück)selig, wonnig, wonnevoll. **blissfulness,** *s. See* **bliss.**

blister ['blistə], **1.** *s.* die Blase, Hautblase; Pustel; (*Med.*) das Zugmittel, Blasenpflaster; Schwalbennest (*on aircraft*). **2.** *v.t.* Blasen ziehen auf (*Dat.*); Zugpflaster auflegen (*Dat.*). **3.** *v.i.* Blasen ziehen, sich mit Blasen bedecken. **blistered,** *adj.* voller Blasen, blasig. **blistering, 1.** *adj.* blasenziehend; (*fig.*) brennend (*heat*); (*fig.*) - ***attack,*** der Verriß (*of a critic etc.*). **2.** *s.* die Blasenbildung. **blister-steel,** *s.* der Blasenstahl, Zementstahl.

blithe [blaið], *adj.* (*Poet.*) munter, froh, fröhlich, lustig, heiter, vergnügt, wohlgemut.

blithering ['bliðəriŋ], *adj.* (*sl.*) - ***idiot,*** der Vollidiot.

blithesome ['blaiðsəm], *adj. See* **blithe.**

blizzard ['blizəd], *s.* heftiger Schneesturm, das Schneegestöber.

bloat [blout], **1.** *v.i.* aufblasen, aufblähen, aufschwellen. **2.** *v.t.* - ***herrings,*** Heringe räuchern. **bloated,** *adj.* aufgedunsen, (an)geschwollen, aufgeblasen, gebläht. **bloater,** *s.* der Räucherhering, Bück(l)ing.

blob [blɔb], *s.* (*coll.*) der Klacks.

bloc [blɔk], *s.* (*Pol.*) der Block.

block [blɔk], **1.** *s.* 1. der Block, Klotz; (*Naut., Tech.*) die Flasche, Rolle; der Häuserblock; die Hutform, der Hutstock; (*Typ.*) Farbstein, Bildstock; das Klischee; Lochholz, der Leisten (*of cobblers*); Richtblock (*of the executioner*); Perückenstock (*of wigmakers*); - ***and tackle,*** der Flaschenzug; ***a chip of(f) the old -,*** ganz der Vater; - ***of houses,*** Reihenhäuser (*pl.*), der Häuserkomplex, Häuserblock; - ***of marble,*** der Marmorblock; ***pulley -,*** der Flaschenzug; ***put on the -,*** (auf dem Stock) formen; 2. (*Railw.*) die Blockstrecke; 3. (*fig.*) das Hindernis, die Sperre; Absperrung, Blockierung, Stockung, Lahmlegung; ***road -,*** die Straßensperre; ***traffic -,*** die Verkehrsstockung; 4. (*fig.*) der Tölpel, Klotz, Dummkopf. **2.** *v.t.* (ver)sperren, absperren; (*also* - ***up***) einschließen, blockieren, verstopfen; (*Parl.*) aufhalten, verhindern, hinausschieben (*a bill*); (*Comm.*) sperren (*an account*), einfrieren (*payments*); (*Crick.*) stoppen (*a ball*); ***be no longer -ed,*** entblockt sein (*of a railway line*); - ***in*** or ***out,*** entwerfen, skizzieren; - ***a hat,*** einen Hut (auf dem Block) formen.

blockade [blɔ'keid], **1.** *s.* die Blockade, Sperre; Barrikade; ***run the -,*** die Blockade brechen. **2.** *v.t.* blockieren, (ver)sperren, absperren; ***-d area,*** das Sperrgebiet. **blockade-runner,** *s.* der Blockadebrecher.

blockage ['blɔkidʒ], die Stockung, Blockierung, Hemmung, Sperre.

block| booking, *s.* das Blockbuchung. **--buster,** *s.* (*Av., coll.*) die Bezirksbombe. - **calendar,** *s.* der Abreißkalender. **-head,** *s.* der Dummkopf. **-headed,** *adj.* dumm. **-house,** *s.* das Blockhaus. - **letters,** *pl.* (*Typ.*) die Blockschrift. **--making,** *s.* (*Typ.*) das Klischieren. **--printing,** *s.* der Holzdruck; Handdruck. - **vote,** *s.* die Sammelstimme.

bloke [blouk], *s.* (*sl.*) der Bursche, Kerl.

blond(e) [blɔnd], *adj.* blond(haarig), hell(farbig). **blonde,** *s.* die Blondine. **blonde-lace,** *s.* die Blonde, geklöppelte Spitz.

blood [blʌd], **1.** *s.* 1. das Blut; ***loss of -,*** der Blutverlust; - ***and thunder,*** Mord und Totschlag; ***blue -,*** adliges Blut; ***in cold -,*** kaltblütig, kalten Blutes; ***in hot -,*** im Zorn; (*coll.*) ***young -,*** junges Blut, der Hitzkopf, Draufgänger; ***his - is up,*** sein Blut ist in Wallung; (*Prov.*) - ***is thicker than water,*** Blut ist dicker als Wasser; ***get - from a stone,*** Geld vom Geizigen bekommen; ***let -,*** zur Ader lassen; ***make his - run cold,*** sein Blut gerinnen machen; ***spill -,*** Blut vergießen; 2. die Abstammung, Herkunft, Rasse, das Geblüt; die Blutsverwandtschaft; ***princes of the -,*** Prinzen von königlichem Geblüt; ***fresh -,*** neues Blut (*in a family*); ***full -,*** das Vollblut(pferd); ***half--,*** das Halbblut(pferd); halbbürtige Geschwister (*of persons*); ***next of -,*** am nächsten verwandt; ***breed bad -,*** böses Blut machen; ***it runs in the -,*** es steckt im Blute; 3. das Leben; der Saft. **2.** *v.t.* an Blut gewöhnen (*a dog*).

blood|-and-thunder, *attrib. adj.* Mord-, Schauer-, sensationell. - **bank,** *s.* die Blutbank. **-bath,** *s.*

(*fig.*) das Blutbad, Gemetzel. – **brother,** *s.* leiblicher Bruder; (*fig.*) der Blutsbruder. – **clot,** *s.* der Blutklumpen, Thrombus. – **corpuscle,** *s.* das Blutkörperchen. – **count,** *s.* die Blutkörperchenzählung, das Blutbild. –**-curdling,** *adj.* haarsträubend, grausig. – **donor,** *s.* der Blutspender. – **feud,** *s.* die Blutfehde. – **group,** *s.* die Blutgruppe. –**-guilt(iness),** *s.* die Blutschuld. –**-guilty,** *adj.* mit Blutschuld beladen. – **heat,** *s.* die Blutwärme, Körpertemperatur. –**hound,** *s.* der Blut– *or* Schweißhund; (*fig.*) Verfolger, Häscher, Spürhund.

bloodless ['blʌdlis], *adj.* blutlos, blutleer; unblutig; ohne Blutvergießen (*victory etc.*); (*fig.*) farblos, leblos.

blood|letting, *s.* der Aderlaß. – **money,** *s.* das Blutgeld, Sühnegeld. – **orange,** *s.* die Blutapfelsine. – **plasma,** *s.* die Blutflüssigkeit. – **poisoning,** *s.* die Blutvergiftung. – **pressure,** *s.* der Blutdruck. –**-red,** *adj.* blutrot. – **relation,** *s.* Blutsverwandte(r). – **relationship,** *s.* die Blutsverwandtschaft. –**shed,** *s.* das Blutvergießen. –**shot,** *adj.* blutunterlaufen. –**stain,** *s.* die Blutspur, der Blutfleck. –**stained,** *adj.* blutbefleckt. –**stock,** *s.* das Vollblut(pferd). –**stone,** *s.* der Blutstein, Roteisenstein. –**sucker,** *s.* der Blutigel; (*fig.*) Blutsauger. – **test,** *s.* die Blutprobe. –**thirstiness,** *s.* der Blutdurst, die Blutgier. –**thirsty,** *adj.* blutdürstig, blutrünstig. – **transfusion,** *s.* die Blutübertragung. – **vessel,** *s.* das Blutgefäß. –**wort,** *s.* (*Bot.*) der Hainampfer.

bloody ['blʌdi], *adj.* blutig; blutrot, blutbefleckt; grausam, blutdürstig; (*vulg.*) saumäßig, verdammt, verflucht; (*Bot.*) – ***dock,*** *see* **bloodwort**; – ***flux,*** der Blutfluß; – ***sweat,*** blutiger Schweiß; – ***tyrant,*** blutrünstiger Tyrann. **bloody minded,** *adj.* blutgierig, mordsüchtig; (*fig., vulg.*) widerborstig, trotzig.

[1]**bloom** [blu:m], **1.** *s.* die Blüte, Blume; der Flor, die Jugendfrische, Jugendblüte; Blütenpracht, Fülle; der Flaum, Hauch (*on peaches etc.*), Schmelz (*on porcelain etc.*); Gärungsschaum (*on beer*); ***in (full)*** –, in Blüte, blühend; – ***of youth,*** die Jugendblüte; ***take the – off s.th.,*** etwas der Frische *or* des Glanzes *or* des Zaubers berauben. **2.** *v.i.* blühen, in Blüte stehen, (*fig.*) (er)blühen, (er)strahlen.

[2]**bloom,** *s.* (*Metall.*) die Luppe; – ***iron,*** das Luppeneisen.

bloomer ['blu:mə], *s.* (*sl.*) der Schnitzer, Bock.

bloomers ['blu:məz], *pl.* (*obs. or hum.*) die Schlupfhose.

bloomery ['blu:məri], *s.* (*Metall.*) die Luppenfrischarbeit; Luppenfrischhütte.

[1]**blooming** ['blu:miŋ], **1.** *adj.* aufblühend, (*pred.*) in voller Blüte; (*fig.*) blühend, strahlend; (*sl.*) verflixt. **2.** *s.* das Blühen, die Blüte(zeit).

[2]**blooming,** *s.* (*Metall.*) das Luppenwalzen.

blossom ['blɔsəm], **1.** *s.* die Blüte; der Blütenstand. **2.** *v.i.* blühen, Blüten treiben; (*fig.*) gedeihen; (*fig.*) – ***out into,*** sich entwickeln zu.

blot [blɔt], **1.** *v.t.* beflecken, beklecksen; (*with blotting paper*) auftrocknen, (ab)löschen; (*fig.*) – ***out,*** tilgen, (aus)löschen, aus der Welt schaffen; (*coll.*) – ***one's copybook,*** sich blamieren, einen Bock schießen. **2.** *v.i.* (*as a pen*) Kleckse machen; (*of ink*) zerfließen, verlaufen. **3.** *s.* der Klecks, (Tinten)fleck; (*sl.*) die Sau; (*fig.*) der Makel, Schandfleck; ***a – on the escutcheon,*** ein Fleck auf der (Familien)ehre; ***a – on his character,*** ein Makel seines Charakters; – ***on the landscape,*** Verunstaltung der Landschaft.

blotch [blɔtʃ], *s.* die Pustel, der Ausschlag; Fleck, Klecks. **blotchy,** *adj.* fleckig, gefleckt.

blotter ['blɔtə], *s.* der (Tinten)löscher; *see also* **blotting paper. blotting| pad,** *s.* die Schreibunterlage. – **paper,** *s.* das Löschpapier.

blotto ['blɔtou], *adj.* (*sl.*) besoffen.

blouse [blauz], *s.* die Bluse.

[1]**blow** [blou], *s.* der Schlag, Streich, Hieb, Stoß; (*coll.*) (Schicksals)schlag, das Unglück; ***be at –s,*** sich schlagen; ***come to*** or ***exchange –s,*** handgemein werden; ***without striking a –,*** ohne Mühe, ohne einen Streich *or* Schlag zu tun; ***strike a – for,*** sich einsetzen für; ***strike a – against,*** sich entgegenstellen (*Dat.*); ***at one*** or ***a (single)*** –, mit einem Schlag *or* Streich, auf einmal.

[2]**blow, 1.** *irr.v.i.* (*Poet.*) (auf)blühen, zur Blüte kommen; (*fig.*) erblühen, sich entfalten. **2.** *s.* (*Poet.*) die Blüte(zeit).

[3]**blow, 1.** *irr.v.i.* blasen, wehen (*as wind*); keuchen, schnaufen (*of a p.*); (er)schallen, ertönen (*of trumpets*); (*Elec.*) durchbrennen (*of a fuse*); (*sl.*) abhauen, verduften, türmen; ***it is –ing,*** es ist windig; ***he knows which way the wind –s,*** er weiß wie der Hase läuft; – ***hot and cold,*** wetterwendisch sein, bald so bald anders sein, sich in einem Atem widersprechen; (*sl.*) ***I'm –ed if I will!*** zum Teufel wenn ich's täte! (*sl.*) – ***in,*** auftauchen, hereingeschneit kommen; – ***out,*** ausgehen, (v)erlöschen (*of light etc.*); (*coll.*) – ***over,*** vorüberziehen, vorübergehen; (*fig.*) nachlassen, sich legen; – ***up,*** auffliegen, in die Luft fliegen, explodieren; sich erheben (*of wind*); (*coll. of a p.*) auffahren. **2.** *irr.v.t.* blasen; wehen, treiben; anblasen, entfachen, anfachen (*the fire etc.*); aufblasen, aufblähen (*also fig.*); (*sl.*) vergeuden (*money*); – ***the bellows,*** den Blasebalg treten; – ***bubbles,*** Seifenblasen machen; – ***an egg,*** ein Ei ausblasen; (*sl.*) – ***the gaff,*** das Spiel verraten, petzen, pfeifen; – ***him a kiss,*** ihm eine Kußhand zuwerfen; – ***one's nose,*** sich (*Dat.*) die Nase putzen, sich schneuzen; – ***the tanks,*** anblasen (*submarine*); – ***one's own trumpet,*** sein eigenes Lob(lied) singen; – ***away,*** wegblasen; – ***down,*** umwehen, umblasen; – ***in,*** eindrücken (*a window*); – ***off steam,*** Dampf abblasen *or* ablassen; (*fig.*) den Zorn verrauchen lassen, die Wut abreagieren; – ***out,*** ausblasen, (aus)löschen (*light*); – ***one's brains out,*** – ***out one's brains,*** sich (*Dat.*) eine Kugel durch den Kopf jagen; – ***one's cheeks out,*** – ***out one's cheeks,*** seine Wangen aufblasen; – ***up,*** aufblasen, aufblähen; (in die Luft) sprengen, springen lassen; aufwirbeln, aufwehen (*dust*); (*coll.*) vergrößern (*a photo*); (*coll.*) – ***him up,*** ihn anranzen, anschnauzen *or* tüchtig ausschelten. **3.** *s.* (*Naut.*) starker Wind, steife Brise; (*coll.*) die Verschnaufpause; das Blasen, der Stoß (*on a horn*); ***have a –,*** blasen (***on,*** auf (*Dat.*)); ***the – on the whistle,*** der Pfiff.

blow|-back, *s.* (*Tech., fig.*) der Rückstoß, Rückschlag. –**cock,** *s.* (*Tech.*) der Ablaßhahn. **blower,** *s.* der Bläser; das Schiebeblech (*of a furnace*); Gebläse; (*sl.*) die Strippe (= *telephone*); ***organ–-,*** der Balgtreter. **blow|fly,** *s.* die Schmeißfliege. –**-hole,** *s.* das Luftloch, Zugloch; (*Mus.*) Blasloch, Mundloch; Atemloch (*in ice*); Nasenloch (*of a whale*); (*Tech.*) der Lunker. –**lamp,** *s.* die Gebläselampe.

blown [bloun], **1.** *p.p. of* **blow. 2.** *adj.* (*coll.*) außer Atem; – ***up,*** aufgeblasen, (auf)gebläht, aufgedunsen, geschwollen.

blow|-off, *attrib. adj.* Ablaß–, Abblase–. –**-out,** *s.* das Durchbrennen (*of a fuse*); Platzen (*of a tyre*); (*sl.*) die Futterei. –**pipe,** *s.* das Blasrohr; Lötrohr; die Pfeife (*of glass-blowers*). –**torch,** *s.* (*Am.*) *see* –**lamp.**

blowy ['bloui], *adj.* (*coll.*) windig, luftig.

blowzy ['blauzi], *adj.* pausbäckig, hochrot; zerzaust, nachlässig, unordentlich, schlampig.

[1]**blubber** ['blʌbə], *s.* der (Braun)tran, Walfischspeck; (*coll.*) Speck, das Fett (*on a p.*).

[2]**blubber,** *v.i.* (*coll.*) flennen, plärren, heulen, weinen.

bludgeon ['blʌdʒən], **1.** *s.* der Knüttel, Knüppel, die Keule. **2.** *v.t.* niederknüppeln, (*fig.*) zwingen (*into,* zu).

blue [blu:], **1.** *adj.* blau; (*coll.*) ängstlich, mutlos; (*coll.*) niedergeschlagen, schwermütig; (*coll.*) schlüpfrig, unanständig, obszön; – ***baby,*** blau(süchtig)es Baby; – ***blood,*** adliges Blut; (*coll.*) – ***devils,*** Spukgestalten (*of the drunkard*); (*Naut.*) – ***ensign,*** die Flagge der Reserveflotte; ***feel –,*** in gedrückter Stimmung sein; (*coll.*) ***be in a – funk,*** einen Bammel *or* Dampf *or* (*vulg.*) Schiß haben;

– ***jaundice,*** die Blausucht, Zyanose; (*Am.*) – ***laws,*** streng puritanische Sittengesetze; ***once in a – moon,*** höchst selten; – ***pill,*** die Quecksilberpille; – ***ribbon,*** der Hosenbandorden, (*fig.*) höchste Auszeichnung, Blaues Band; ***true –,*** treu, unwandelbar. **2.** *s.* 1. das Blau, blaue Farbe; (*laundry*) das Waschblau, die Bläue; blauer Himmel; (weite) Ferne; offenes Meer; ***bolt from the –,*** der Blitz aus heiterm Himmel; ***fire into the –,*** drauflosknallen; ***navy –,*** das Marineblau; ***Prussian –,*** das Berlinerblau; ***true –,*** der Konservative; ***the Blues,*** die englischen königlichen Gardereiter; 2. (*Spt.*) die Mitgliedschaft der ersten Mannschaft (*school* or *univ.*); das Mitglied der ersten Mannschaft; ***dark –,*** die Oxforder Farbe; ***light –,*** die Cambridger Farbe; ***rowing –,*** das Mitglied der ersten Rudermannschaft (*of school* or *univ.*); ***get one's –,*** als Mitglied der ersten Mannschaft erwählt werden; 3 *pl.* (*coll.*) der Trübsinn, die Schwermut, Melancholie; *pl.* (*Mus.*) der Blues; ***have a fit of the –s,*** Trübsal blasen. **3.** *v.t.* 1. blau färben, (*laundry*) (an)bläuen; 2. (*sl.*) vergeuden, verschleudern.

Bluebeard ['blu:biəd], *s.* Ritter Blaubart.

blue|bell, *s.* (*England*) Nickende Sternhyazinthe (*Scilla nonscripta*), (*Scots, Am.*) Rundblättrige Glockenblume (*Campanula rotundifolia*). **–berry,** *s.* (*Am.*) die Blaubeere, Heidelbeere. **–-black,** *adj.* dunkelblau. – **book,** *s.* das Blaubuch, staatliche Veröffentlichung (*in Germany usu.* das Weißbuch, *in France* das Gelbbuch). **–bottle,** *s.* (*Ent.*) die Schmeißfliege; (*Bot.*) Kornblume. **–-eyed,** *adj.* blauäugig; (*coll.*) ***he is his grannie's – boy,*** die Oma hat an ihm einen Narren gefressen; ***he is the boss's – boy,*** er macht sich lieb Kind bei dem Chef. **–grass,** *s.* (*Am.*) das Riedgras, Rispengras. **–jacket,** *s.* (*coll.*) die Blaujacke, der Matrose.

blueness ['blu:nis], *s.* blaue Farbe, die Bläue.

blue-pencil, *v.t.* (*coll.*) durchstreichen, zensieren. **Blue Peter,** *s.* (*Naut.*) die Abfahrtssignalflagge. **blue|print,** *s.* die Blaupause, der Blaudruck; (*fig.*) Entwurf, Plan, Vorschlag. **–stocking,** *s.* der Blaustrumpf. **–stone,** *s.* das Kupfervitriol. **–-tit-(mouse),** *s.* (*Orn.*) die Blaumeise (*Parus caerulis*).

¹**bluff** [blʌf], **1.** *adj.* plump, derb, barsch; gutmütig, freimütig (*of manner*); steil, schroff (*coast*); (*Naut.*) voll, breit. **2.** *s.* steiles Felsenufer.

²**bluff, 1.** *s.* der Bluff, die Spiegelfechterei, Irreführung, Täuschung; ***call his –,*** ihn zwingen Farbe zu bekennen. **2.** *v.t.* (*Cards*) bluffen, (*fig.*) verblüffen, einschüchtern, täuschen, irreführen, ins Bockshorn jagen. **3.** *v.i.* (*Cards*) bluffen, (*fig.*) großtun, sich aufspielen.

bluffness ['blʌfnis], *s.* plumpe Gutmütigkeit.

bluish ['blu:iʃ], *adj.* bläulich.

blunder ['blʌndə], **1.** *s.* der Schnitzer, (grober) Fehler, Mißgriff; ***commit a –,*** einen Bock schießen. **2.** *v.i.* einen Schnitzer machen, einen Bock schießen; – ***about,*** umhertappen; – ***along*** or ***on,*** blindlings weitergehen; immer weiter Fehler machen; – ***out,*** herausplatzen (***with,*** mit); – ***upon,*** durch Zufall stoßen auf (*Acc.*). **3.** *v.t.* verderben, verpfuschen, verhunzen, (*coll.*) verkorksen, vermasseln.

blunderbuss ['blʌndəbʌs], *s.* die Donnerbüchse.

blunderer ['blʌndərə], *s.* der Pfuscher, Stümper. **blunderheaded,** *adj.* tölpelhaft. **blundering,** *adj.* ungeschickt, taktlos.

blunt [blʌnt], **1.** *adj.* stumpf; abgestumpft, unempfindlich; plump, grob, barsch, derb, unbeholfen, ungeschliffen; ungezwungen, ungeziert, unverblümt; ***grow –,*** sich abstumpfen; ***be – with him,*** es ihm offen heraus sagen. **2.** *v.t.* stumpf machen, abstumpfen (*also fig.*). **3.** *s.* (*sl.*) (*obs.*) Moneten (*pl.*). **bluntness,** *s.* die Stumpfheit; (*fig.*) Plumpheit, Derbheit, (taktlose) Offenheit.

blur [blə:], **1.** *s.* der Fleck, verwischte Stelle, (*fig.*) verwischter Eindruck, die Unklarheit, Verschwommenheit; (*fig.*) der Makel. **2.** *v.t.* verschmieren, verwischen; (*fig.*) trüben, verdunkeln.

blurb [blə:b], *s.* (*sl.*) der Reklamestreifen, Waschzettel (*of a book*); (*fig.*) (maßlose) Anpreisung.

blurred [blə:d], *adj.* verwischt, verschwommen, unscharf, unklar.

blurt [blə:t], *v.t.* – ***out,*** ausschwatzen, (unbesonnen) herausplatzen mit.

blush [blʌʃ], **1.** *s.* das Erröten; die (Scham)röte; (*fig.*) rosiger Glanz; ***put him to the –,*** ihn beschämen; ***spare her –es,*** sie nicht in Velegenheit bringen; ***at the first –,*** auf den ersten Blick. **2.** *v.i.* erröten (***at,*** über (*Acc.*)), (scham)rot werden; (*fig.*) sich schämen. **blushing, 1.** *adj.* errötend; (*fig.*) rosig, rötlich. **2.** *s.* das Erröten. **blush-rose,** *s.* blaßrote Rose.

bluster ['blʌstə], **1.** *s.* 1. das Brausen, Toben; Getöse, der Tumult, Lärm; 2. das Prahlen, die Prahlerei, Großtuerei. **2.** *v.i.* 1. brausen, tosen; lärmen, toben; 2. prahlen, aufbegehren, den Mund voll nehmen. **blustering,** *adj.* tobend, stürmisch; lärmend, prahlend; – ***fellow,*** das Großmaul, der Prahlhans. **blustery,** *adj.* böig (*of wind*).

¹**bo!** [bou], *int.* buh! huh! ***he cannot say – to a goose,*** er kann den Mund nicht auftun.

²**bo,** *s.* (*Am. sl.*) der Mensch, Bursche.

boa ['bouə], *s.* 1. die Riesenschlange; 2. Boa (*lady's fur*). **boa-constrictor,** *s.* die Königsschlange, Abgottschlange.

boar [bɔ:], *s.* der Eber, Keiler; ***wild –,*** das Wildschwein; ***young wild –,*** der Frischling; ***–'s head,*** der Schweinskopf.

board [bɔ:d], **1.** *s.* 1. das Brett, die Diele, Planke, Bohle; der Tisch, die Tafel; (*Naut.*) der Bord; (*Bookb.*) die Pappe, der Pappdeckel, Karton; (*Bookb.*) ***–s,*** der Pappband; (*Theat.*) ***the –s,*** die Bühne, die Bretter (*pl.*); ***above –,*** offen, ehrlich, einwandfrei; ***bound in –s,*** kartoniert; ***chess –,*** das Spielbrett, Schachbrett; ***diving-–,*** das Sprungbrett; ***drawing-–,*** das Reißbrett; ***duck-–,*** das Laufbrett; ***floor –,*** die Diele; ***go by the –,*** über Bord gehen; (*fig.*) verlorengehen, zugrunde gehen, fehlschlagen, scheitern; ***on –,*** an Bord; (*Comm.*) ***free on –,*** frei an Bord; (*Naut.*) ***go on –,*** an Bord gehen; ***on the –s,*** am Theater; ***plotting-–,*** der Meßtisch; (*fig.*) ***sweep the –,*** den Sieg davontragen; 2. (*fig.*) die Kost, Beköstigung, Pension, der Unterhalt; das Kostgeld; ***accommodation and –, – and lodging,*** freie Station, Kost und Logis, volle Pension; ***bed and –,*** Tisch und Bett; ***free –,*** freie Kost; ***put out to –,*** in Kost geben; 3. der Ausschuß, das Komitee, Kollegium, die Kommission; Körperschaft, Behörde; der Rat, das Amt; (*Am.*) ***Board of Assessment,*** see ***Inland Revenue Board;*** – ***of control,*** die Aufsichtsbehörde; – ***of directors,*** der Aufsichtsrat, Verwaltungsrat, die Direktion, das Direktorium; – ***of examiners,*** die Prüfungskommission; ***Inland Revenue Board,*** die Steuerbehörde, Finanzkammer; (*Mil.*) ***medical –,*** die Sanitätskommission; ***statutory –,*** gesetzlich genehmigte Körperschaft; (*Univ.*) ***–s of study,*** die Fakultätsausschüsse; ***Board of Trade,*** das Handelsministerium, (*Am.*) die Handelskammer; (*Elec.*) ***Board of Trade unit,*** die Kilowattstunde; – ***of trustees,*** der Treuhänderausschuß, das Kuratorium. **2.** *v.t.* 1. täfeln, dielen, verschalen; – ***up,*** mit Brettern verschlagen; 2. (*Naut.*) entern; an Bord gehen, (*train etc.*) (ein)steigen in (*Acc.*), besteigen; 3. in Kost nehmen, beköstigen; – ***out,*** in Kost geben; 4. (*coll.*) vor einem Ausschuß prüfen (*a p.*). **3.** *v.i.* 1. in Kost *or* Pension sein; – ***out,*** auswärts essen; 2. einschiffen, einsteigen.

boarder ['bɔ:də], *s.* 1. der Kostgänger, Pensionär; 2. Internatsschüler; 3. (*Naut.*) Enterer. **boarding,** *s.* 1. die Verschalung, Bretterverkleidung, Täfelung, der Dielenbelag; Verschlag, Latten (*pl.*), Schalbretter (*pl.*); 2. die Beköstigung, Verpflegung; 3. (*Naut.*) das Entern. **boarding|-house,** *s.* die Pension. **–-party,** *s.* (*Naut.*) die Entermannschaft. **–-school,** *s.* das Internat, Pensionat, die Heimschule.

board|-meeting, *s.* die Vorstandssitzung. **–-room,** *s.* das Sitzungszimmer. **–-school,** *s.* (*obs.*) die Volksschule. **–-wages,** *pl.* das Kostgeld.

boast [boust], **1.** *v.i.* sich rühmen (***of, about,*** *Gen.*), prahlen, großsprechen, großtun (mit); (*coll.*) ***that's nothing to – about,*** das ist nicht weit her. **2.** *v.t.* (*usu. iron.*) sich rühmen (*Gen.*), aufzuweisen haben; ***she can – two fur coats,*** sie ist stolz darauf, zwei Pelzmäntel zu besitzen. **3.** *s.* die Prahlerei, das Großtun; der Stolz; (*Prov.*) ***great –, small roast,*** viel Geschrei und wenig Wolle; ***make great – of,*** sich etwas einbilden auf (*Acc.*). **boaster,** *s.* der Prahler, Prahlhans, Wichtigtuer, Großsprecher. **boastful,** *adj.* prahlerisch, großsprecherisch, ruhmredig. **boastfulness,** *s.* die Prahlsucht, Ruhmredigkeit.

boat [bout], **1.** *s.* das Boot, der Kahn, Nachen; das Schiff, der Dampfer; (*fig.*) ***be in the same –,*** in der gleichen (schlechten) Lage sein, dasselbe Schicksal teilen; (*fig.*) ***burn one's –s,*** alle Brücken hinter sich abbrechen; – ***drill,*** das Bootsmanöver; – ***song,*** das Schifferlied; ***sauce-–,*** die Sauciere. **2.** *v.i.* in einem Boote fahren, rudern, segeln.

boater [ˈboutə], *s.* (*coll.*) steifer Strohhut.

boat-hook, *s.* der Bootshaken. **boating,** *s.* das Bootfahren, der Segelsport, Rudersport; die Wasserfahrt, Bootfahrt; ***go –,*** rudern, segeln; – ***pond,*** der Bootsteich. **boat|load,** *s.* die Bootsladung. **–man** [–mən], *s.* der Jollenführer. **–-race,** *s.* das Wettrudern, die Ruderregatta. **–-shaped,** *adj.* kahnförmig, nachenförmig. **–swain** [bousn], *s.* der (Ober)bootsmann;**–*'s chair,*** der Bootsmannsstuhl; ***–'s mate,*** der Bootsmannsmaat. **–-train,** *s.* der Zug mit Dampferanschluß.

bob [bɔb], **1.** *s.* 1. die Quaste, das Gehänge; der Haarknoten; (*pendulum*) das Gewicht, die Linse; (*plumb-line*) das Senkblei; 2. der Bubikopf; 3. Ruck, Stoß, ruckartige Bewegung; der Knicks; 4. (*sl.*) das 5-Pence-Stück, (*obs.*) der Schilling. **2.** *v.i.* 1. baumeln, springen; – ***about,*** umherspringen; – ***up,*** emporschnellen, (*fig.*) plötzlich auftauchen; – ***up like a cork,*** sich nicht unterkriegen lassen; – ***up and down,*** sich auf und ab bewegen; 2. einen Knicks machen. **3.** *v.t.* 1. ruckweise bewegen; – ***a curts(e)y,*** einen Knicks machen; – ***one's head up,*** plötzlich aufblicken; 2. stutzen (*tail*), kurz schneiden (*hair*). **bobbed,** *adj.* kurz geschnitten, gestutzt; – ***hair,*** der Bubikopf.

bobbin [ˈbɔbin], *s.* die Spule, Haspel, Garnrolle, der Klöppel; die Strähne (*of flax*); (*Elec.*) Induktionsrolle. **bobbinet,** *s.* Englischer Tüll. **bobbin|-frame,** *s.* die Spindelbank, Spulmaschine. **–-lace,** *s.* geklöppelte Spitzen (*pl.*).

bobbish [ˈbɔbiʃ], *adj.* (*coll.*) lebhaft, munter, wohlauf.

bobby [ˈbɔbi], *s.* (*sl.*) der Schupo.

bobby-soxer [ˈbɔbisɔksə], *s.* (*Am. sl.*) der Backfisch.

bob|-run, *s.* die Bobbahn. **–sleigh,** *s.* der Bob(sleigh), Rennschlitten.

bobtail [ˈbɔbteil], *s.* der Stutzschwanz; ***rag-tag and –,*** Krethi und Plethi, das Lumpenpack, Gesindel.

[1]**bode** [boud], *v.t., v.i.* vorhersagen, voraussehen, ahnen (lassen); – ***ill,*** von schlechter Vorbedeutung sein, Unheil verkünden.

[2]**bode,** *imperf. of* **bide.**

bodice [ˈbɔdis], *s.* das (Schnür)leibchen; Mieder, (*Dressm.*) die Taille.

-bodied [ˈbɔdid], *adj. suff.* –leibig, –gestaltet; ***able-–,*** gesund, stark, handfest; dienstfähig (*of sailors*); ***full-–,*** voll, stark (*of wine*).

bodiless [ˈbɔdilis], *adj.* unkörperlich, körperlos. **bodily, 1.** *adj.* Körper–, körperlich, physisch; – ***exercise,*** die Leibesübung; – ***injury,*** die Körperverletzung. **2.** *adv.* persönlich, leibhaftig; als Ganzes, ganz und gar, gänzlich, völlig.

boding [ˈbouding], *s.* die Vorahnung, Vorbedeutung.

bodkin [ˈbɔdkin], *s.* die Schnürnadel, Durchziehnadel; Haarnadel; (*Typ.*) Ahle, (*Bookb.*) der Pfriem, Stecher.

body [ˈbɔdi], *s.* der Körper, Leib; die Leiche, der Leichnam; (*of a th.*) Hauptteil, Rumpf, Stamm, Tragkörper; Rahmen, das Gestell, Gehäuse; (*of a cart*) der Kasten, (*of a car*) die Karosserie, (*of a cannon*) Lafette; (*coll.*) Person, der Mensch; (*Dressm.*) die Taille; (*Archit.*) das Schiff (*of a church*), der Schaft (*of a pillar*); (*Chem.*) die Substanz, der Stoff; die Masse, Menge, Gesamtheit, Mehrheit; das Gros, Wesentliche, Innere, der Kern; (*of wine*) Gehalt, (*of fabric*) die Dichtigkeit, (*of paper*) Stärke, (*of paint*) Deckfähigkeit, (*of sound*) Tonstärke, Tonfülle; (*fig. of people*) Körperschaft, Gesellschaft, das Gremium; ***keep – and soul together,*** Leib und Seele zusammenhalten; (*Scots*) ***what's a – to do?*** was soll man tun? **(a)** (*with adjs.*) ***advisory –,*** der Beirat; (*Chem.*) ***compound –,*** die Verbindung, zusammengesetzter Stoff; – ***corporate,*** die Körperschaft, juristische Person; ***heavenly –,*** der Himmelskörper; ***legislative –,*** gesetzgebende Körperschaft; – ***politic,*** der Staat(skörper); ***solid –,*** fester Körper; **(b)** (*with nouns*) – ***of cold air,*** kalte Luftmasse; ***main – of the army,*** das Gros *or* der Hauptteil des Heeres; ***main – of a building,*** das Hauptgebäude; ***the – of the clergy,*** die gesamte Geistlichkeit, der Klerus; – ***of civil law,*** das Corpus Juris; – ***of a letter,*** der Text eines Briefes; – ***of a ship,*** der Schiffsrumpf; – ***of troops,*** die Mannschaft, Truppe, der Truppenkörper; **(c)** (*with preps.*) ***in a –,*** zusammen, auf einmal, in Masse.

body| belt, *s.* die Leibbinde, der Leibgurt. – **blow,** *s.* (*Boxing*) der Körperschlag; (*fig.*) vernichtender Schlag (*to,* für). **–-building,** *s.* die Körperbildung. – **cloth,** *s.* die Pferdedecke, Schabracke. – **colour,** *s.* die Deckfarbe. **–guard,** *s.* die Leibwache. **–snatcher,** *s.* der Leichenräuber. **–work,** *s.* (*Motor.*) die Karosserie.

Boer [ˈbuə, ˈbouə], *s.* der Bur(e); – ***War,*** der Burenkrieg.

boffin [ˈbɔfin], *s.* (*sl.*) (vom Kriegsministerium beauftragter) Technokrat.

bog [bɔg], **1.** *s.* der Sumpf, Morast, das Moor; (*vulg.*) der Lokus. **2.** *v.t.* in Schlamm versenken; ***be*** or ***get bogged down,*** in Schlamm versinken, (*fig.*) sich festfahren, steckenbleiben. **bog| asphodel,** *s.* (*Bot.*) der Beinbrech. **–berry,** *s.* die Moosbeere. – **bilberry,** *s.* die Moorbeere, Rauschbeere.

bogey [ˈbougi], *s.* (*Golf*) die Norm für gute Spieler, (*fig.*) guter Durchschnitt; *see also* **bogy.**

boggle [bɔgl], *v.i.* stutzen, stutzig werden (*at,* vor (*Dat.*)); unschlüssig sein, zögern, schwanken (bei); (*of horses etc.*) scheuen, zusammenfahren (vor (*Dat.*)); ***the mind –s at,*** gar kein Verständnis haben für; nicht die blasseste Ahnung haben von; nicht klug werden aus; nicht wissen, woran man ist, bei.

boggy [ˈbɔgi], *adj.* sumpfig, morastig.

bogie [ˈbougi], *s.* das Drehgestell; (*Railw.*) der Blockwagen (mit Drehgestell); (*Min.*) der Förderkarren. **bogie| engine,** *s. See* **bogie** (*Railw.*). – **wheel,** *s.* das Laufrad.

bog|land, *s.* das Moorland, Marschland. **–trotter,** *s.* (*pej.*) der Ire, Irländer.

bogus [ˈbougəs], *adj.* (*coll.*) falsch, unecht; schwindelhaft, Schwindel–; – ***bill,*** fingierter Wechsel, der Kellerwechsel.

bogy [ˈbougi], *s.* der Teufel, Kobold, das (Schreck)gespenst; – ***man,*** der schwarze Mann, Butzemann.

Bohemia [bouˈhiːmiə], *s.* Böhmen (*n.*). **Bohemian, 1.** *s.* 1. der Böhme (die Böhmin); (*language*) das Böhmische; 2. der Bohemien, leichtlebiger Literat *or* Künstler, verbummeltes Genie. **2.** *adj.* 1. böhmisch; 2. bohemehaft, unkonventionell, leichtlebig.

[1]**boil** [bɔil], *s.* der Furunkel, das Blutgeschwür.

[2]**boil, 1.** *v.i.* kochen, sieden, (*fig.*) wallen, brausen; – ***away,*** einkochen, verdampfen; (*coll.*) ***it –s down to this,*** es kommt (letzten Endes) auf folgendes heraus; – ***gently,*** schwach kochen; (*coll.*) ***keep the pot –ing,*** die S. in Gang halten; – ***over,*** überkochen, überlaufen, überschäumen; (*fig.*) – ***with rage,*** rasend werden, vor Wut schäumen; – ***up,*** (auf)wallen, aufsieden. **2.** *v.t.* zum Kochen bringen, kochen (lassen); blau kochen (*fish*); – ***away*** or ***down,*** verdampfen *or* einkochen (lassen); (*fig. coll.*) – ***down,*** kürzen; – ***off,*** abkochen; – ***up,*** auf-

kochen (lassen). **3.** *s.* das Kochen, Sieden; ***on the –,*** im *or* am Kochen; ***bring to the –,*** zum Kochen bringen; ***go off the –,*** zu kochen aufhören.

boiled [bɔild], *adj.* gekocht, gesotten; ***– oil,*** trocknendes Öl; (*coll.*) ***– shirt,*** das Frackhemd.

boiler ['bɔilə], *s.* der Sieder; Kochtopf, Kochkessel; (*Tech.*) (Dampf)kessel; (*coll.*) Heißwasserspeicher. **boiler|maker,** *s.* der Kesselschmied. **– scale,** *s.* der Kesselstein. **– suit,** *s.* der Overall.

boiling ['bɔiliŋ], **1.** *adj.* kochend, siedend, Siede–; ***– point,*** der Siedepunkt. **2.** *adv.* ***– hot,*** siedeheiß. **3.** *s.* das Kochen, Sieden; (auf einmal) Gekochte(s); ***fast to –,*** kochfest; (*sl.*) ***the whole –,*** (*of persons*) die ganze Sippschaft, (*of things*) der ganze Schub.

boisterous ['bɔistərəs], *adj.* stürmisch, heftig, unbändig, ungestüm; lärmend, tobend, geräuschvoll. **boisterousness,** *s.* das Ungestüm, die Heftigkeit, Unbändigkeit.

boko ['boukou], *s.* (*sl.*) die Schnauze, der Zinken.

bold [bould], *adj.* kühn, mutig, unerschrocken, beherzt; keck, frech, dreist, verwegen, unverschämt; (*coll.*) ***as – as brass,*** frech wie Oskar; (*Typ.*) ***– face,*** fette Schrift; (*fig.*) ***put a – face on a th.,*** sich kühn über eine S. hinwegsetzen; ***make –,*** sich (*Dat.*) Freiheiten herausnehmen (***with,*** gegen); ***make*** or ***be so – as to do,*** es wagen zu tun; sich erdreisten *or* erkühnen *or* erfrechen zu tun; so frei sein *or* sich (*Dat.*) die Freiheit nehmen zu tun; ***– outline(s),*** deutliche Umrisse; ***– plan,*** kühner *or* gewagter Plan; ***in – relief,*** sich deutlich abhebend, scharf hervortretend; ***speak –ly,*** ohne Rückhalt *or* frei sprechen. **bold-faced,** *adj.* 1. (*Typ.*) fett; 2. (*fig.*) unverschämt. **boldness,** *s.* der Mut, die Kühnheit, Unerschrockenheit; Keckheit, Frechheit, Dreistigkeit, Verwegenheit, Unverschämtheit; (*fig.*) deutliches Hervortreten.

[1]**bole** [boul], *s.* der (Baum)stamm.

[2]**bole,** *s.* der Bolus, die Siegelerde.

boletus [bo'li:təs], *s.* (*Bot.*) der Röhrenpilz, Röhrling.

boll [boul], *s.* die Samenkapsel, Schote; runder Knopf.

bollard ['bɔləd], *s.* (*Naut.*) der (Beleg)poller.

boloney [bə'louni], *s.* (*sl.*) der Quatsch.

Bolshevik ['bɔlʃəvik], **1.** *s.* der Bolschewik. **2.** *adj.* bolschewistisch. **Bolshevism,** *s.* der Bolschewismus. **Bolshevist,** *s., adj. See* **Bolshevik.**

bolster ['boulstə], **1.** *s.* das Polster, (Keil)kissen; die Unterlage. **2.** *v.t.* (aus)polstern; (*coll.*) ***– up,*** (künstlich) aufrechterhalten, unterstützen.

[1]**bolt** [boult], **1.** *s.* 1. der Bolzen, Pfeil; (*coll.*) ***shoot one's –,*** sein Pulver verschießen; ***– upright,*** kerzengerade; 2. der Donnerkeil; ***a – from the blue,*** der Blitz aus heiterm Himmel; (*coll.*) ***make a –,*** stürzen (***for,*** nach); (*coll.*) ***make a – for it,*** (*sl.*) ***do a –,*** sich aus dem Staub machen, Reißaus nehmen; 3. (*Tech.*) der (Schrauben)bolzen, die Schraube; 4. (*on doors*) der Riegel, Schieber, Verschluß; Schließhaken; ***shoot the –,*** den Riegel vorschieben; 5. (*on guns*) der (Nadel)bolzen, das Schloß, die Sperrklaue; 6. (*of cloth etc.*) Rolle, das Bündel, Bund. **2.** *v.t.* (*Tech.*) verbolzen, mit Bolzen befestigen; (*door etc.*) verriegeln, zuriegeln, abriegeln; (*coll.*) (hastig) hinunterschlingen, hinunterwürgen (*food*). **3.** *v.i.* durchbrennen, ausreißen, davonstürzen, sich davonmachen, sich aus dem Staub machen; (*of horses*) durchgehen; (*coll.*) ***– into the next room,*** ins Nebenzimmer stürzen *or* springen.

[2]**bolt,** *v.t.* beuteln, sieben, sichten, prüfen.

[1]**bolter** ['boultə], *s.* (*horse*) der Durchgänger, Ausreißer.

[2]**bolter,** *s.* der (Mehl)beutel, das Beutelwerk.

bolt|-head, *s.* (*Tech.*) der Bolzenkopf, (*Chem.*) die Blase, der (Destillier)kolben. **–-hole,** *s.* (*Tech.*) das Bolzenloch; (*coll.*) Schlupfloch, der Schlupfwinkel.

bolting cloth, *s.* das Siebtuch, Beutelsieb.

bolt| mechanism, *s.* (*Artil.*) das Gewehrschloß. **– rope,** *s.* (*Naut.*) das Liek, der Segelsaum.

bolus ['bouləs], *s.* (*Med.*) große Pille; der Klumpen, Kloß; (*Geol.*) Bolus, Pfeifenton.

bomb [bɔm], **1.** *s.* die Bombe (*also fig.*); Handgranate. **2.** *v.t.* mit Bomben belegen, Bombenabwerfen auf (*Acc.*); (*coll.*) ***– up,*** mit Bomben beladen. **3.** *v.i.* ***– up,*** Bomben aufladen. **bomb aimer,** *s.* (*Av.*) der Bombenschütze.

bombard [bɔm'bɑ:d], *v.t.* bombardieren, beschießen, (*fig.*) bestürmen. **bombardier** [–bə'diə], *s.* der Artillerieunteroffizier, (*Am. Av.*) Bombenschütze. **bombardment,** *s.* die Beschießung, Bombardierung, Belegung mit Bomben.

bombast ['bɔmbəst], *s.* der Wortschwall, Schwulst. **bombastic** [–'bæstik], *adj.* schwülstig, hochtrabend.

bomb| bay, *s.* (*Av.*) die Bombenschacht, das Bombenmagazin. **– disposal,** *s.* die Bombenräumung, Blindgängerbeseitigung; ***– squad,*** die Sprengtruppe. **– door,** *s.* die Bombenklappe.

bomber ['bɔmə], *s.* (*Av.*) der Bomber, das Bombenflugzeug. **bombing,** *s.* der Bombenabwurf; ***– run,*** der Zielanflug.

bomb|proof, *adj.* bombensicher, bombenfest. **– rack,** *s.* der Bombenträger. **–shell,** *s.* (*fig.*) die Bombe. **–-sight,** *s.* das Bombenzielgerät, Bombenvisier.

bona fide [bounə'faidi], *adj., adv.* auf Treu und Glauben, in gutem Glauben, gutgläubig; echt, zuverlässig, (*Comm., coll.*) solid; redlich, ehrlich, aufrichtig. **bona fides,** *pl.* ehrliche Absichten (*pl.*), die Ehrlichkeit, Aufrichtigkeit, Treuherzigkeit, Geradheit, der Geradsinn.

bonanza [bə'nænzə], *s.* (*Min.*) (*Am.*) reiche Erzader; (*coll.*) die Glücksquelle, Goldgrube; günstige Gelegenheit, glücklicher Griff.

[1]**bond** [bɔnd], **1.** *s.* 1. die Bindung; Verbindung, der Bund, das Bündnis; 2. (*Comm.*) die Schuldverschreibung, Obligation, der Rückschein, Gutschein, Schuldschein, Anleihschein, (Hypotheken)pfandbrief; 3. die Verpflichtung, Bürgschaft; der Bürge; 4. (*Archit.*) Verband; 5. (*customs*) Zollverschluß; ***goods in –,*** Waren unter Zollverschluß; 6. *pl.* Fesseln (*pl.*), Bande (*pl.*); ***– of friendship,*** die Bande der Freundschaft. **2.** *v.t.* 1. unter Zollverschluß legen; 2. verpfänden; 3. (*Build.*) verbinden.

[2]**bond,** *adj.* (*obs.*) leibeigen. **bondage** ['bɔndidʒ], *s.* die Leibeigenschaft, Knechtschaft, Sklaverei; Gefangenschaft, Haft; (*fig.*) der Zwang.

bond debts, *pl.* Obligationsschulden (*pl.*). **bonded,** *adj.* (durch Verpflichtung) gebunden; (mit Schulden) belastet, verpfändet; unter Zollverschluß; ***– debt,*** die Obligationsschuld; ***– goods,*** Waren unter Zollverschluß; ***– warehouse,*** das Freilager, der Zollspeicher. **bonder,** *s.* (*Build.*) der Binder, Bindestein. **bond holder,** *s.* der Obligationsinhaber.

bond servant, bond(s)man, *s.* Leibeigene(r), Fronpflichtige(r), unfreier Bauer.

bone [boun], **1.** *s.* der Knochen, das Bein, (*of fish*) die Gräte; *pl.* (*corsets etc.*) (Fischbein)stäbchen (*pl.*); *pl.* (*coll.*) Würfel (*pl.*); *pl.* (*coll.*) Kastagnetten, Handklappern (*pl.*); ***– of contention,*** der Zankapfel; (*coll.*) ***make no –s about,*** keine (großen) Umstände machen wegen; nicht viel Federlesens machen mit; (*coll.*) ***feel it in one's –s,*** es instinktiv spüren; (*coll.*) ***have a – in one's leg,*** zu faul zum Gehen sein; ***I have a – to pick with him,*** ich habe mit ihm ein Hühnchen zu rupfen *or* pflücken; (*Prov.*) ***what is bred in the – will come out in the flesh,*** Art läßt nicht von Art; ***cut to the –,*** bis auf den Knochen schneiden, (*fig.*) (*of prices*) auf das alleräußerste herabsetzen. **2.** *adj.* beinern, knöchern. **3.** *v.t.* 1. die Knochen *or* Gräten herausnehmen aus, (*meat*) ausbeinen, (*fish*) entgräten, ausgräten; 2. (*dress etc.*) (Fischbein)stäbchen einsetzen in (*Acc.*); 3. (*sl.*) klauen, stiebitzen. **4.** *v.i.* (*sl.*) ***– up (on),*** einpauken.

bone black, *s.* das Beinschwarz, die Knochenkohle.

boned [bound], *adj.* ausgebeint, ausgegrätet, entgrätet. **–boned,** *adj. suff.* –knochig.

bone|-dry, *adj.* knochentrocken. – **dust,** *s.* das Knochenmehl. – **earth,** *s.* die Knochenerde, Knochenasche. – **glue,** *s.* der Knochenleim. –**head,** *s.* (*sl.*) der Dummkopf, Holzkopf. --**idle,** *adj.* (*coll.*) stinkfaul. --**lace,** *s.* die Klöppelspitze. **boneless,** *adj.* knochenlos, (*fig.*) haltlos, ohne Rückgrat. **bone manure,** *s.* das Knochenmehl, der Knochendünger. **boner,** *s.* (*Am. sl.*) der Schnitzer. **bone|setter,** *s.* der Knocheneinrichter. --**shaker,** *s.* (*Motor. coll.*) die Klapperkiste. – **spavin,** *s.* (*Vet.*) der Hufspat. –**yard,** *s.* (*Am.*) die Abdeckerei, der Schindanger.

bonfire ['bɔnfaiə], *s.* das Freudenfeuer; Feuer (*for garden refuse etc.*).

bonhomie [bɔnə'mi:], *s.* die Gutmütigkeit.

bonito [bə'ni:tou], *s.* (*Ichth.*) der Blaufisch.

bonnet ['bɔnit], *s.* die Damenmütze, Haube; Kappe, (*Scots*) (*for men*) Mütze; (*Motor.*) Haube; Kappe (*of a chimney*); ***have a bee in one's* –,** einen Vogel haben.

bonny [bɔni], *adj.* gesund, strahlend, drall; (*Scots*) hübsch, schön, fein, nett.

bonus ['bounəs], *s.* die Prämie, Extradividende, der Gewinnanteil, die Tantieme; (Gehalts)zulage; der (Teuerungs)zuschlag; die Gratifikation; ***cash* –,** bar ausgezahlte Dividende; – ***share,*** die Gratisaktie.

bony ['bouni], *adj.* knöchern, beinern, Knochen–; (*meat*) (stark)knockig, voll Knochen; (*fish*) grätig, voll Gräten; (*fig.*) knochenhart; (*coll. of a p.*) mager, hager, klapperdürr.

boo [bu:], **1.** *int.* buh! huh! pfui! **2.** *v.t., v.i.* muhen; auszischen, auspfeifen.

boob [bu:b], *s.* 1. (*coll.*) der Bock, Schnitze; 2. (*sl.*) *see* **booby, 1. booby,** *s.* 1. der Tölpel, Einfaltspinsel, Dussel; 2. (*Orn.*) Tölpel. **booby|-hatch,** *s.* (*Naut.*) die Schiebeluke, Achterlukenkappe; (*sl.*) Klapsmühle; (*sl.*) das Kittchen. --**prize,** *s.* der Trostpreis. --**trap, 1.** *s.* derber Streich; (*Mil.*) die Schreckladung, Sprengfalle. **2.** *v.t.* Sprengfallen legen *or* setzen in (*Dat.*).

book [buk], **1.** *s.* das Buch; – ***of commission,*** das Auftragsbuch; – ***for complaints,*** das Beschwerdebuch; ***copy*** or ***exercise* –,** das Schreibheft; – ***of reference,*** das Nachschlagewerk; – ***of sales,*** das (Waren)-verkaufsbuch; ***be at his –s,*** über seinen Büchern sitzen; ***he is deep in our –s,*** er steckt bei uns tief in Schulden; ***be in his good*** (***bad***) ***–s,*** bei ihm gut (schlecht) angeschrieben sein; ***be on the –s,*** eingetragenes Mitglied sein, auf der Liste stehen; (*coll., fig.*) auf dem Programm stehen; ***bring to* –,** zur Rechenschaft *or* Verantwortung ziehen, zur Rede stellen; ***do s.th. by the* –,** etwas vorschriftsmäßig verrichten; ***keep the –s,*** die Bücher führen; ***kiss the* –,** auf die Bibel schwören; ***make a* –,** Wetten eintragen; ***repeat*** or ***say without the* –,** auswendig hersagen; ***speak without the* –,** ohne Autorität reden; (*coll.*) ***suit his* –,** ihm passen; ***swear on the* –,** see ***kiss the* –**; ***take a leaf out of his* –,** sich (*Dat.*) ihn zum Muster nehmen; ***talk like a* –,** wie ein Buch *or* wie gedruckt reden. **2.** *v.t.* aufschreiben, notieren; eintragen, (ver)buchen (*entry in a book*); im voraus bestellen, (vor)bestellen, belegen (*seat, room etc.*); lösen (*ticket*); im Vorverkauf besorgen (*theatre ticket*); engagieren (*performer*); vormerken (*a library book*); anmelden (*phone call*); ***all rooms are –ed,*** alle Zimmer sind besetzt *or* reserviert; ***all the seats have been –ed,*** das Haus ist ausverkauft; ***be –ed,*** eine gebührenpflichtige Verwarnung bekommen; ***be –ed up,*** besetzt *or* ausverkauft sein; (*coll.*) vorläufig beschäftigt sein; (*coll.*) ***be –ed to do,*** verpflichtet sein zu tun; (*coll.*) ***I am –ed to see him tomorrow,*** ich habe mich auf morgen mit ihm verabredet. **3.** *v.i.* sich vormerken lassen; eine Karte lösen (*to,* nach); – ***through to Basle,*** bis Basel durchlösen.

bookable ['bukəbl], *adj.* im Vorverkauf erhältlich. **book|binder,** *s.* der Buchbinder. –**binding,** *s.* das Buchbinden, die Buchbinderei. –**case,** *s.* der Bücherschrank. --**club,** *s.* der Lesezirkel. --**ends,** *pl.* Bücherstützen.

bookie ['buki], *s.* (*coll.*) *see* **bookmaker.**

booking ['bukiŋ], *s.* das Buchen, Bestellen, die Bestellung; (Karten)ausgabe, der Vorverkauf; (*Comm.*) die Buchung, Eintragung, Notierung; (*Spt. etc.*) bestellter Platz, gelöste Karte; ***advance* –,** der Vorverkauf; ***cancel a* –,** Karten abbestellen. **booking|-clerk,** *s.* Schalterbeamte(r), der Fahrkartenverkäufer. --**form,** *s.* der Bestellzettel. --**office,** *s.* (*Railw.*) der (Fahrkarten)schalter; die (Theater)kasse, Vorverkaufsstelle.

bookish ['bukiʃ], *adj.* (*coll.*) den Büchern ergeben, auf Bücher versessen; belesen; geschraubt, pedantisch; – ***person,*** der Büchernarr, die Leseratte. **bookishness,** *s.* trockene Gelehrsamkeit, die Stubengelehrsamkeit, das Buchwissen.

book|keeper, *s.* der Buchhalter, Rechnungsführer. –**keeping,** *s.* die Buchhaltung, Buchführung. – **knowledge,** – **learning,** *s.* die Buchgelehrsamkeit, Schulweisheit.

booklet ['buklit], *s.* die Broschure, das Büchlein.

book| lover, *s.* der Bücherfreund. –**maker,** *s.* (*Spt.*) der Buchmacher. –**man,** *s.* (Buch)gelehrte(r). –**mark(er),** *s.* das Lesezeichen. –**plate,** *s.* das Exlibris. --**post,** *s.* die Drucksachenpost; ***by* –,** unter Kreuzband. – **rack,** *s.* das Büchergestell. – **rest,** *s.* das Lesepult. – **review,** *s.* die Buchbesprechung. –**seller,** *s.* der Buchhändler, Sortimenter. –**selling,** *s.* der Buchhandel. –**shelf,** *s.* das Bücherbord, Bücherbrett, Bücherregal. –**shop,** *s.* die Buchhandlung. –**stall,** *s.* der Bücherverkaufsstand; ***railway* –,** die Bahnhofsbuchhandlung, der Zeitungsstand. –**stand,** *s.* das Büchergestell. –**store,** *s.* (*Am.*) *see* –**shop.** --**trade,** *s.* der Buchhandel. –**worm,** *s.* der Bücherwurm (*also fig.*). --**wrapper,** *s.* die Buchhülle, der Schutzumschlag.

[1]**boom** [bu:m], *s.* (*Naut.*) der Baum, die Spiere; (*of crane*) der Ausleger, Schnabel; (*for camera or microphone*) Galgen; (*of harbour*) Ausleger, Hafenbaum, die (Hafen)sperre; (*Naut.*) ***main* –,** der Großbaum.

[2]**boom, 1.** *v.i.* dröhnen, brummen, brüllen, schallen, brausen, summen, (*of bitterns*) schreien. **2.** *s.* das Dröhnen, Brüllen, Gebrumme.

[3]**boom, 1.** *s.* (*Comm.*) der Aufschwung, die (Hoch)-konjunktur, Hausse; (*fig.*) Blüte(zeit), Glanzzeit; (*Am.*) Stimmungsmache, (Wahl)propaganda, der Reklamerummel. **2.** *v.i.* in die Höhe schnellen, einen (plötzlichen) Aufschwung nehmen, blühen, sich schnell entwickeln. **3.** *v.t.* in die Höhe treiben; Reklame machen für.

boomerang ['bu:mərӕŋ], **1.** *s.* der Bumerang. **2.** *v.i.* (*coll.*) – (***on him***), (ihm) zum eigenen Schaden gereichen.

[1]**boon** [bu:n], *s.* die Wohltat, Gnade, Gabe; (*Hist.*) unentgeltliche Dienstleistung.

[2]**boon,** *adj.* (*Poet.*) fröhlich, munter; – ***companion,*** (lustiger) Zechbruder.

boor [buə], *s.* der Lümmel, Grobian. **boorish,** *adj.* bäurisch, grob, lümmelhaft, ungeschliffen. **boorishness,** *s.* die Grobheit, Ungeschliffenheit.

boost [bu:st], **1.** *v.t.* nachhelfen (*Dat.*), voranhelfen (*Dat.*), fördern, unterstützen; (*coll.*) anpreisen, Reklame machen für; (*Elec. etc.*) verstärken; (*Comm.*) ankurbeln (*business*), in die Höhe treiben (*prices*). **2.** *s.* der Aufschwung; (*Mech.*) Auftrieb, (*Elec.*) Ladedruck; (*coll.*) die Förderung, Unterstützung; (*coll.*) Reklame, Propaganda. **booster,** *s.* (*coll.*) der Reklamemacher; (*Elec.*) Zusatzdynamo; – ***battery,*** die Zusatzbatterie; – ***rocket,*** die Hilfs(antrieb)rakete; (*Med. coll.*) – ***shot,*** die Wiederholungsimpfung.

[1]**boot** [bu:t], **1.** *s.* (*obs.*) (*only in*) ***to* –,** obendrein, überdies, außerdem, noch dazu. **2.** *v.t.* (*obs.*) nützen, frommen; (*only in*) ***what –s it?*** was hilft es?

[2]**boot, 1.** *s.* 1. der Stiefel, hoher Schuh; (*coll.*) ***you can bet your –s on it,*** darauf kannst du Gift nehmen; ***elastic* –,** der Zugstiefel; ***fishing –s,*** Wasserstiefel (*pl.*); ***in –s,*** gestiefelt; ***die in one's –s, die with one's –s on,*** in den Sielen sterben; ***he had his heart in his –s,*** ihm saß das Herz in der Hose; ***the***

– is on the other foot, der Fall *or* die S. *or* Wahrheit liegt genau umgekehrt; 2. der Wagenkasten, Kutschkasten, (*Motor.*) Kofferraum, (*obs.*) Dienersitz; 3. (*torture*) Spanischer Stiefel; 4. (*sl.*) der Fußtritt; (sofortige) Entlassung, der Laufpaß; (*sl.*) ***get the –,*** fliegen; (*sl.*) ***give him the –,*** ihn herausschmeißen; (*sl.*) ***give him a good –,*** ihm einen heftigen *or* kräftigen *or* tüchtigen Fußtritt geben. **2.** *v.t.* (*coll.*) (mit dem Fuß) wuchtig stoßen, (*Footb.*) kräftig kicken; (*sl.*) ***– him out,*** ihn herausschmeißen.

bootblack ['bu:tblæk], *s.* der Schuhputzer. **booted,** *adj.* gestiefelt. **bootee** [–'ti:], *s.* der Damenhalbstiefel; (wollener) Kinderschuh.

Boötes [bo'outi:z], *s.* (*Astr.*) der Bärenhüter.

booth [bu:θ, bu:ð], *s.* die Bude, der Marktstand; (*telephone or voting*) die Zelle.

boot|-jack, *s.* der Stiefelknecht. **–lace,** *s.* der Schuhriemen, Schnürsenkel. **--last,** *s.* der Schuhleisten, das Stiefelholz. **–leg,** *v.t., v.i.* schmuggeln. **–legger,** *s.* (*coll.*) der (Alkohol)schmuggler.

bootless ['bu:tlis], *adj.* (*Poet.*) nutzlos, zwecklos, erfolglos, vergeblich, unnütz.

boot|-licking, *s.* die Kriecherei, Speichelleckerei. **–maker,** *s.* der Schuhmacher, Schuster. **– polish,** *s.* die Schuhkrem. **boots,** *s.* (*coll.*) der Stiefelputzer, Hausdiener (*in hotels*). **boot|-top(ping),** *s.* (*Naut.*) der Wassergang. **--tree,** *s.* der Stiefelspanner.

booty ['bu:ti], *s.* die (Kriegs)beute, der Raub; die (Aus)beute.

booze [bu:z], **1.** *v.i.* (*sl.*) saufen, zechen, süffeln. **2.** *s.* (*sl.*) der Schnaps, Fusel; Suff, die Sauferei; ***go on the –,*** saufen, zechen, süffeln, fuseln. **boozed,** *adj.* (*sl.*) besoffen, schief geladen, blau. **boozer,** *s.* (*sl.*) 1. der Säufer, Trunkenbold, Saufbruder; 2. die Kneipe. **boozy,** *adj.* (*sl.*) versoffen, trunksüchtig.

boracic [bə'ræsik], *adj. See* **boric. borate** ['bɔ:reit], *s.* das Borat, borsaures Salz. **borax** ['bɔ:ræks], *s.* der Borax, das Natriumborat, borsaures Natrium.

border ['bɔ:də], **1.** *s.* der Rand, Saum, die Borte, Leiste, Bordüre, der Besatz; die Umrandung, Einfassung; (*gardens*) das Randbeet, die Rabatte, (*of a wood etc.*) der Rain; (*of a country*) (*oft. pl.*) die (Landes)grenze; (*Typ.*) Randleiste, Zierleiste; (*Archit.*) Einfassung, Randverzierung. **2.** *v.t.* einfassen, (ein)säumen, besetzen, bordieren (*a dress etc.*), (*Tech.*) umranden, (um)bordeln, rändern. **3.** *v.i.* (an)stoßen, (an)grenzen ((***up***)*on*, on (*Acc.*)), (*fig.*) grenzen (an (*Acc.*)), nahekommen (*Dat.*). **borderer,** *s.* der Grenzbewohner. **border|land,** *s.* das Grenzland, (*fig.*) Grenzgebiet. **–line, 1.** *s.* die Grenzlinie. **2.** *adj.* Grenz–; ***– case,*** der Grenzfall.

bordure ['bɔ:djuə], *s.* (*Her.*) der Wappen– *or* Schildrand, die Wappen– *or* Schildumrandung *or* –einfassung.

[1]**bore** [bɔ:], **1.** *v.t.* (an)bohren, ausbohren, durchbohren; (*Min.*) teufen; (*fig.*) durchdringen; (*Spt.*) (ab)drängen, verdrängen. **2.** *v.i.* (*Min.*) Bohrungen machen, bohren, schürfen (***for,*** nach); ***the wood –s easily,*** das Holz läßt sich leicht bohren. **3.** *s.* das Bohrloch, die Bohrung; (*of a cylinder*) innerer Zylinderdurchmesser, (*of a pipe*) die Höhlung, (*of a gun*) Seele, das Kaliber, Rohr; ***smooth*** (***rifled***) ***–,*** glatte (gezogene) Bohrung.

[2]**bore, 1.** *v.t.* langweilen, belästigen; (*coll.*) ***be –d stiff,*** sich zu Tode langweilen. **2.** *s.* langweilige *or* lästige S.; langweiliger Mensch; ***what a –!*** wie ärgerlich!

[3]**bore,** *imperf. of* [1]**bear.**

[4]**bore,** *s.* brandende Flutwelle.

boreal ['bɔ:riəl], *adj.* (*Poet.*) nördlich. **Boreas,** *s.* (*Poet.*) der Nordwind.

boredom ['bɔ:dəm], *s.* die Langeweile; Lästigkeit.

borer ['bɔ:rə], *s.* der Bohrer, das Bohreisen; der Bohrarbeiter; (*Ent.*) Bohrwurm.

boric ['bɔ:rik], *adj.* Bor–, boraxhaltig; ***– acid,*** die Borsäure.

[1]**boring** ['bɔ:riŋ], **1.** *adj.* Bohr–. **2.** *s.* das Bohren, die Bohrung; das Bohrloch; *pl.* Bohrspäne (*pl.*).

[2]**boring,** *adj.* langweilig.

born [bɔ:n], **1.** *p.p. of* [2]**bear,** 2. **2.** *adj.* geboren; ***be a – actor,*** zum Schauspieler geboren sein; ***– blind,*** blind geboren; (*coll.*) ***in all my – days,*** mein Lebtag, in meinem ganzen Leben; ***Dante was – and bred a Guelph,*** Dante war seiner Geburt und Erziehung nach ein Welfe; ***a nobleman –,*** ein geborener Edelmann; ***– fool,*** vollkommener Narr; ***– to renown,*** zum Ruhme bestimmt; ***be – with a silver spoon in one's mouth, be – under a lucky star,*** ein Glückskind *or* Sonntagskind sein.

borne [bɔ:n], *p.p. of* [1]**bear, 1.**

boron ['bɔ:rən], *s.* (*Chem.*) das Bor(on).

borough ['bʌrə], *s.* der Stadtbezirk, die Stadt(gemeinde), städtischer Wahlbezirk; ***– council(lor),*** der Stadtrat; ***parliamentary –,*** wahlberechtigter Ort; (*Pol. Hist.*) ***rotten –s,*** Wahlkreise ohne Wähler.

borrow ['bɔrou], *v.t.* borgen, (ent)leihen, sich (*Dat.*) leihen; (*fig.*) entlehnen, entnehmen (***from,*** von); ***he has –ed from me,*** er hat mich angepumpt; ***–ed plumes,*** fremde Federn; ***–ed word,*** das Lehnwort. **borrower,** *s.* der Borger, Entleiher; (*Comm.*) Kreditnehmer; (*fig.*) Entlehner. **borrowing, 1.** *s.* das (Aus)borgen, Entleihen, (*Comm.*) die Kreditaufnahme; *pl.* aufgenommene Schulden. **2.** *adj.* (*Comm.*) Kredit–.

Borstal (Institution) ['bɔ:stl], *s.* die Besserungsanstalt für jugendliche Verbrecher.

boscage ['bɔskidʒ], *s.* (*Poet.*) das Gebüsch, Gehölz, Unterholz, Dickicht.

bosh [bɔʃ], *s.* (*sl.*) der Unsinn, Quatsch.

bosky ['bɔski], *adj* (*Poet.*) buschig, waldig.

bosom ['buzəm], *s.* die Brust, der Busen; (*of a dress*) Brustteil; (*fig.*) das Herz, Innere, die Tiefe, der Schoß; ***in Abraham's –,*** in Abrahams Schoß, hingeschieden; ***– of the earth,*** das Erdinnere; ***in the – of the family,*** im Schoß der Familie; ***– of the sea,*** die Tiefe des Meeres; ***come to my –,*** komm an mein Herz; ***– friend*** or (*coll.*) ***pal,*** der Busenfreund, Herzensfreund, Spezi.

Bosphorus ['bɔsfərəs], *s.* der Bosporus.

[1]**boss** [bɔs], *s.* der Buckel (*of a shield*), Knopf, Knauf, die Beule; Nabe (*of a wheel*); (*Archit.*) der Bossen, die Bosse(l).

[2]**boss, 1.** *s.* (*coll.*) der Meister, Chef, Boß, Arbeitgeber, Vorgesetzte(r); (*fig.*) Tonangebende(r), Macher; (*Pol.*) Bonze. **2.** *v.t.* (*sl.*) arrangieren, dirigieren, leiten; ***– the show,*** der Hauptmacher sein, den Laden schmeißen; ***– him around*** or ***about,*** ihn herumkommandieren.

boss-eyed, *adj.* (*sl.*) schielend, (*fig.*) schief, einseitig.

bossiness ['bɔsinis], *s.* (*coll.*) die Rechthaberei, Großspurigkeit.

[1]**bossy** ['bɔsi], *adj.* rechthaberisch, großspurig, herrschsüchtig; *see* [2]**boss.**

[2]**bossy,** *adj.* mit Buckeln *or* Bossen verziert; *see* [1]**boss.**

bosun [bousn], *s.* (*coll.*) *see* **boatswain.**

bot [bɔt], *s.* die Dassellarve.

botanic(al) [bo'tænik(l)], *adj.* botanisch, Pflanzen–. **botanist** ['bɔtənist], *s.* der Botaniker. **botanize** ['bɔtənaiz], *v.i.* Pflanzen sammeln, botanisieren. **botany** ['bɔtəni], *s.* die Botanik, Pflanzenkunde.

botch [bɔtʃ], **1.** *s.* (*obs.*) die Beule, das Geschwür; (*coll.*) Flickwerk; die Pfuscharbeit; ***make a – of a job,*** eine Arbeit verhunzen *or* verpfuschen. **2.** *v.t.* (zusammen)flicken; verhunzen, verpfuschen; ***–ed work,*** das Flickwerk, die Pfuscherei. **botcher,** *s.* der Flickschneider, Flickschuster; (*fig.*) Pfuscher, Stümper.

bot-fly, *s.* die Dasselfliege.

both [bouθ], **1.** *adj., pron.* beide, beides; ***I will take them –*** or ***– of them,*** ich will sie alle beide mitnehmen; ***make – ends meet,*** sich nach der Decke strecken; ***– her sisters,*** ihre beiden Schwestern; ***– are true,*** beides ist wahr. **2.** *conj.* ***– . . . and,*** sowohl

. . . als (auch), ebenso . . . wie; – ***by day and by night,*** bei Tag wie bei *or* sowohl als bei Nacht; – ***in word and deed,*** in *or* mit Wort und Tat.

bother ['bɔðə], **1.** *v.t.* plagen, belästigen, beunruhigen, stören, ärgern; (*coll.*) – ***the boys!*** die verflixten Jungen! (*coll.*) – ***it!*** zum Henker *or* Kuckuck! ***don't – me!*** laß mich in Ruhe! ***I can't be –ed with it,*** ich kann mich nicht damit abgeben; – ***one's head about,*** sich (*Dat.*) den Kopf zerbrechen über (*Acc.*); ***I am –ed about him,*** ich bin über ihn beunruhigt. **2.** *v.i.* sich bemühen *or* befassen *or* abgeben (***with, about,*** mit); sich (*Dat.*) Sorgen *or* Gedanken machen, sich aufregen (über (*Acc.*)); ***I shan't –,*** ich mache mir keine Gedanken darüber; ***please don't –!*** bemühen Sie sich bitte nicht! **3.** *s.* der Verdruß, Ärger, die Sorge; Störung, Belästigung, Plage, Mühe, Schikane, Schererei, viel Aufhebens. **botheration!** [–'reiʃən], *int.* (*coll.*) verflixt! wie ärgerlich! **bothersome** [–səm], *adj.* lästig, ärgerlich.

Bothnia ['bɔθniə], *s.* Botten (*n.*); ***Gulf of –,*** der Bottnische Meerbusen.

bothy ['bɔθi], *s.* (*Scots*) die Hütte, Baracke.

[1]**bottle** [bɔtl], **1.** *s.* die Flasche; ***bring up on the –,*** mit der Flasche aufziehen; ***by the –,*** flaschenweise; ***crack a – together,*** eine Flasche zusammen trinken; ***be fond of the –,*** gern trinken; ***chat over a – of beer,*** beim Glase Bier plaudern; ***stone –,*** der Steinkrug, Tonkrug. **2.** *v.t.* auf Flaschen ziehen *or* füllen; – ***up one's wrath,*** seinen Zorn zurückhalten *or* unterdrücken; ***–d beer,*** das Flaschenbier.

[2]**bottle,** *s.* das Bund, Bündel (*of hay*).

bottle|-fed, *adj.* – ***child,*** das Flaschenkind. **--feeding,** *s.* die Ernährung mit der Flasche. **--glass,** *s.* grünes Flaschenglas. **--gourd,** *s.* der Flaschenkürbis. **--green,** *adj.* dunkelgrün. **--holder,** *s.* (*Spt. sl.*) der Sekundant. **–neck,** *s.* 1. der Flaschenhals; 2. (*fig.*) Engpaß, die Enge, Stauung; Straßenverengung, enge Straßenmündung. **--nose,** *s.* die Schnapsnase. **--nosed,** *adj.* mit aufgedunsener Nase; (*Zool.*) – ***whale,*** der Butzkopf. **--party,** *s.* zwanglose Party. **--washer,** *s.* (*coll.*) das Faktotum.

bottling ['bɔtliŋ], *s.* die Flaschenfüllung.

bottom ['bɔtəm], **1.** *s.* 1. der Boden (*of cask, cup etc.*), Fuß (*of mountain, page*), die Sohle (*of ditch, pit etc.*), der Grund (*of water*); (*Naut.*) ***go to the –,*** versinken, untergehen; ***from the – of my heart,*** aus Herzensgrund *or* tiefstem Herzen; (*coll.*) ***knock the – out of,*** den Boden entziehen (*Dat.*); – ***of the sea,*** der Meeresgrund; (*Naut.*) ***send to the –,*** versenken, auf den Grund schicken; ***from top to –,*** von oben bis unten; ***touch –,*** auf Grund geraten; (*fig.*) den Tiefpunkt *or* tiefsten Stand erreichen; (*sl.*) ***–s up!*** Prosit! Trink zu! ***valley –,*** die Talsohle; 2. (*fig.*) die Grundlage, Basis, das Fundament, Wesen; die Ursache, der Grund, Ursprung; ***at –,*** im Grunde, in Wirklichkeit; ***be at the – of,*** zugrunde liegen (*Dat.*), der (wahre) Grund sein (für); ***get to the – of,*** auf den Grund gehen *or* kommen (*Dat.*); 3. (*Naut.*) der Schiffsboden, (*fig.*) das Schiff; – ***up(wards),*** (*Naut.*) kieloben; das Unterste zu oberst; verkehrt liegend; 4. (*usu. pl.*) der Bodensatz, die Hefe (*of beer etc.*); 5. (*coll.*) der Hintern, das Gesäß; 6. (*coll.*) die Ausdauer, Stärke (*of a horse etc.*); 7. das Ende; – ***of the bed,*** unteres Ende des Bettes; ***he is at the – of his class,*** ist der Letzte *or* Unterste (in) seiner Klasse; ***at the – of the street,*** am Ende der Straße. **2.** *adj.* unterst, tiefst, niedrigst; – ***coat,*** erster Auftrag (*of paint*); (*Motor.*) – ***gear,*** erster Gang; (*sl.*) ***bet one's – dollar,*** den letzten Pfennig darauf setzen, darauf Gift nehmen; (*coll.*) – ***drawer,*** der Hamsterkasten für die Aussteuer; – ***price,*** niedrigster Preis, äußerster Kurs; – ***view,*** die Ansicht von unten. **3.** *v.t.* einen Boden einsetzen; (*fig. usu. pass.*) gründen, stützen, bauen (***on,*** auf (*Acc.*)); grundieren, vorfärben (*painting*). **–bottomed,** *adj. suff.* ***double-–,*** mit doppeltem Boden; ***flat-– boat,*** der Prahm; ***full-– wig,*** die Allongeperücke; ***leather-– chair,*** der Lederstuhl.

bottom| fermentation, *s.* die Untergärung. **– fishing,** *s.* das Grundangeln. **bottomless,** *adj.* bodenlos, grundlos; (*fig.*) unergründlich; ***the – pit,*** die tiefste Tiefe, die Hölle. **bottommost, 1.** *adj.* tiefst, unterst. **2.** *adv.* ganz zu unterst. **bottomry,** *s.* (*Naut.*) die Bodmerei.

botulism ['bɔtjulizm], *s.* die Fleisch– *or* Wurstvergiftung.

boudoir ['bu:dwɑ:], *s.* das Boudoir, Damenzimmer.

bough [bau], *s.* der Zweig, Ast.

bought [bɔ:t], *imperf., p.p. of* **buy.**

bougie ['bu:ʒi:], *s.* 1. die Wachskerze, das Wachslicht; 2. (*Med.*) die Dehnsonde, der Dilatator.

bouillon ['bu:jɔ̃], *s.* die Fleischbrühe, Kraftbrühe.

boulder ['bouldə], *s.* der Uferkiesel, Flußstein; Felsblock; (*Geol.*) ***erratic –,*** der Findling, erratischer Block. **boulder|-clay,** *s.* (*Geol.*) (eiszeitlicher) Geschiebelehm. **--period,** *s.* die Eiszeit.

bounce [bauns], **1.** *v.i.* springen, aufschlagen, anprallen, aufprallen; (*fig.*) stürzen, platzen; (*coll.*) großsprechen, aufschneiden, prahlen; (*Comm. sl.*) (*as a cheque*) retourniert werden; – ***about,*** herumspringen; – ***into a room,*** ins Zimmer hineinplatzen *or* hineinstürzen. **2.** *v.t.* aufspringen *or* aufprallen lassen (*a ball*); (*coll.*) – ***him into doing s.th.,*** ihn einschüchtern, etwas zu tun. **3.** *s.* der Sprung, Rückprall, Aufprall; die Sprungkraft; (*fig.*) der Schwung, (*sl.*) die Prahlerei. **bouncer,** *s.* (*sl.*) unverschämte Lüge; (*sl.*) der Aufschneider, Angeber; (*Comm., sl.*) ungedeckter Scheck; (*sl.*) der Rausschmeißer (*in a club*); ***the ball is a good –,*** der Ball springt gut. **bouncing,** *adj.* (*fig.*) lebenslustig, stramm, drall.

[1]**bound** [baund], **1.** *imperf., p.p. of* **bind. 2.** *adj.* 1. gebunden, verpflichtet; (*of a th.*) bestimmt, verurteilt; (*coll.*) ***I'll be –,*** ich stehe dafür ein, auf mein Wort; ***he is – to go,*** er wird auf jeden Fall *or* unbedingt gehen; ***it is – to fail,*** es ist zum Mißlingen bestimmt *or* verurteilt; 2. (*Med.*) hartleibig; ***fog-–,*** vom Nebel gehindert; ***ice-–,*** von Eis umgeben *or* im Eis eingeschlossen; 3. (*fig.*) – ***up,*** (untrennbar) verknüpft (***with,*** mit), (völlig) in Anspruch genommen (***in,*** von).

[2]**bound,** *adj.* bestimmt, unterwegs (***for,*** nach); ***London-– train,*** der nach London fahrende Zug; ***where are you – for?*** wo geht die Reise hin? wohin geht's? wo wollen Sie hin? ***homeward-–,*** auf der Heim– *or* Rückreise; ***outward-–,*** auf der Ausreise.

[3]**bound, 1.** *s.* der Sprung, Satz; Prall, Anprall, Aufprall, Rückprall; ***at a –,*** mit einem Satze; ***by leaps and –s,*** in gewaltigen Sätzen, in raschem Tempo. **2.** *v.i.* springen, hüpfen, (auf)prallen.

[4]**bound, 1.** *s.* (*usu. pl.*) die Grenze; Schranke, das Maß; ***beyond all –s,*** über alle Grenzen, übermäßig, außer Rand und Band; ***out of –s,*** verboten; ***overstep the –s,*** die Grenze überschreiten; ***put out of –s,*** verbieten; ***set –s to one's desires,*** seine Wünsche in Schranken halten; ***within –s,*** mit Maß, in Schranken, mäßig; ***within the –s of possibility,*** im Bereich des Möglichen; ***keep within the –s of propriety,*** sich in den Grenzen des Anstands halten. **2.** *v.t.* abgrenzen, eingrenzen, begrenzen, die Grenze bilden von, (*fig.*) beschränken, einschränken, in Schranken halten.

boundary ['baundri], *s.* 1. die Grenze, Grenzlinie, der Rand; die Begrenzung, Abgrenzung; 2. (*Crick.*) Schlag bis zur Spielfeldgrenze. **boundary line,** *s.* die Grenzlinie.

bounden [baundən], *adj.* (*obs.*) (*only in*) – ***duty,*** die Pflicht und Schuldigkeit; ***I am – to you,*** ich bin Ihnen verbunden *or* verpflichtet.

bounder ['baundə], *s.* der Prolet, Schuft, Rabauke; (*coll.*) unartiges Kind.

boundless ['baundlis], *adj.* grenzenlos, unbegrenzt, unbeschränkt.

bounteous ['bauntiəs], **bountiful,** *adj.* freigebig, großzügig, mildtätig, gütig (*of persons*); reichlich (*of things*). **bounty,** *s.* 1. die Freigebigkeit, Großmut, Mildtätigkeit, Wohltätigkeit; Wohltat, Gabe; 2. (*Comm.*) Subvention, Prämie; (*Mil.*) das Handgeld.

bouquet [bu'kei], *s.* 1. der (Blumen)strauß, das Bukett; 2. (*of wine*) der Duft, die Blume.
bourdon ['buədən], *s.* der Brummbaß (*organ*).
[1]**bourgeois** [bəː'dʒɔis], *s.* (*Typ.*) die Borgis(schrift).
[2]**bourgeois** ['buəʒwɑː], **1.** *s.* der Bürger; Philister, Spießbürger. **2.** *adj.* (spieß)bürgerlich, philisterhaft. **bourgeoisie** [–'ziː], *s.* der Bürgerstand.
bourn(e) [buən], *s.* (*Poet.*) 1. der Bach; 2. Bereich, das Ziel.
bout [baut], *s.* die Reihe, Wechselfolge, der Gang, die Tour; (*Boxing etc.*) der (Wett)kampf; ***drinking* –**, das Zechgelage, der Schmaus; ***– of illness,*** der (Krankheits)anfall.
bovine ['bouvain], *adj.* Ochsen–, Rinder–; (*fig.*) träge.
[1]**bow** [bau], *s.* 1. (*Naut.*) (*oft. pl.*) der Bug; ***on the port –***, an Backbord voraus; 2. (*Rowing*) Bugmann, Bugriemen.
[2]**bow** [bau], **1.** *s.* die Verbeugung, Verneigung; ***make one's –***, abtreten, sich zurückziehen; ***make one's (first) –***, zum ersten Male auftreten. **2.** *v.t.* biegen, beugen, neigen; ***–ed (down)***, niedergedrückt *or* gebeugt (***by***, with, von); ***– one's assent,*** seine Genehmigung durch eine Verbeugung ausdrücken; ***– one's head,*** den Kopf neigen; ***– one's knee,*** das Knie beugen; ***– the knee to,*** sich in Ehrfurcht beugen vor (*Dat.*); ***– him out,*** ihn hinauskomplimentieren; ***– one's thanks,*** sich dankend verneigen. **3.** *v.i.* sich (ver)beugen, sich bücken, sich (ver)neigen; eine Verbeugung machen (***to***, vor (*Dat.*)); (*fig.*) sich fügen, sich unterwerfen, sich beugen; ***– and scrape,*** Kratzfüße machen; ***– down,*** sich niederbeugen, sich unterwerfen (***to, before,*** *Dat.*); ***have a –ing acquaintance with,*** auf dem Grußfuße stehen mit, nur flüchtig kennen; ***– to the inevitable,*** sich ins Unvermeidliche fügen.
[3]**bow** [bou], **1.** *s.* der (Schieß)bogen; (*Mus.*) (Streich)bogen; Bogen, die Kurve; Schleife (*of ribbons*); ***draw a –***, einen Bogen spannen; ***draw the long –***, aufschneiden; ***draw a – at a venture,*** auf den Busch klopfen; ***have more than one string to one's –***, mehrere Eisen im Feuer haben; ***tie a –***, eine Schleife knüpfen; ***violin –***, der (Geigen)bogen. **2.** *v.i.* den Bogen führen (*violin etc.*).
bow| arm ['bou], *s.* rechter Arm (*of violinist etc.*). **– compasses,** *pl.* der Null(en)zirkel, Bogenzirkel.
bowdlerization ['baudlerai'zeiʃən], *s.* die Verballhornung, Verschlimmbesserung. **bowdlerize,** *v.t.* von anstößigen Stellen reinigen, verballhornen, verschlimmbessern.
[1]**bowed** [baud], *adj.* gebeugt, gebückt; *see* [2]**bow.**
[2]**bowed** [boud], *adj.* bogenförmig, geschweift; *see* [3]**bow.**
bowel ['bauəl], *s.* (*Med.*) der Darm; *pl.* das Eingeweide, Gedärme; *pl.* (*fig.*) Innere; (*obs.*) ***–s of compassion,*** das Mitleid; ***action*** *or* ***motion of the –s,*** der Stuhlgang; ***–s of the earth,*** das Erdinnere.
[1]**bower** ['bauə], *s.* die Laube; (*obs.*) das Frauengemach.
[2]**bower,** *s.* (*Naut.*) der Buganker.
bow hair ['bou], *s.* (*Mus.*) der (Haar)bezug des Bogens.
bow-heavy ['bau], *adj.* (*Naut.*) buglastig; *see* [1]**bow.**
bowie-knife ['boui], *s.* das Jagdmesser.
bowing ['bouiŋ], *s.* (*Mus.*) die Bogenführung, der Strich.
[1]**bowl** [boul], *s.* der Becher, Napf, das Becken, die Schale, Schüssel, (*Chem.*) Kuvette; (*drink*) Bowle; Höhlung (*of spoon*); der (Pfeifen)kopf.
[2]**bowl, 1.** *s.* die Holzkugel; (*at bowls etc.*) der Wurf. **2.** *v.t.* rollen (lassen), kugeln; (*skittles*) schieben, (*Crick.*) werfen; treiben, schlagen (*a hoop*); ***– down,*** umwerfen, niederwerfen; ***– out,*** (*Crick.*) absetzen; (*fig.*) schlagen, besiegen; ***– over,*** umwerfen, über den Haufen werfen; (*fig.*) überraschen, niederschmettern, erledigen. **3.** *v.i.* rollen, kegeln; (*Crick.*) den Ball werfen; ***– along,*** dahinrollen.
bow|-legged ['bou], *adj.* krummbeinig, O-beinig. **–-legs,** *pl.* krumme Beine, O-Beine (*pl.*).
bowler ['boulə], *s.* 1. der Bowlingspieler, (*Crick.*) Ballmann, Werfer; 2. (*coll.*) (*also* ***– hat***) die Melone.
bowline ['boulin], *s.* (*Naut.*) die Bulin(e), Buleine; (*knot*) der Paalsteek.
bowling ['bouliŋ], *s.* das Bowlingspiel; (*Am.*) Kegeln, Kegelschieben; (*Crick.*) Werfen; ***– alley,*** die Kegelbahn; ***– green,*** der Rasen zum Bowlingspiel. **bowls,** *pl.* (*sing. constr.*) das Bowlingspiel.
bowman ['boumən], *s.* der Bogenschütze.
bow oar ['bauɔː], *s. See* [1]**bow,** 2.
bow saw ['bousɔː], *s.* die Bügelsäge, Schweifsäge.
bowse [bauz], *v.t.* (*Naut.*) anholen, auftaljen.
bow|-shaped ['bou], *adj.* bogenförmig, geschweift. **–shot,** *s.* ***within –***, in Bogenschußweite.
bowsprit ['bousprit], *s.* (*Naut.*) das Bugspriet.
bow|string ['bou], *s.* die Bogensehne. **– tie,** *s.* die (Frack)schleife, Fliege, der Schmetterlingsbinder. **– window,** *s.* rundes Erkerfenster.
bow-wow ['bau'wau], **1.** *int.* wauwau! **2.** *s.* (*nursery talk*) der Wauwau.
bowzer ['bauzə], *s.* (*sl.*) der Tankwagen.
[1]**box** [bɔks], **1.** *s.* (*Bot.*) der Buchsbaum. **2.** *adj.* Buchsbaum–.
[2]**box, 1.** *s.* die Schachtel, Büchse, Dose; Kiste, der Kasten; (Kutsch)bock; (*Theat.*) die Loge; (*Tech.*) Hülse, Kapsel, Muffe, Kassette, das Gehäuse; (*Typ.*) Fach des Schriftkastens; Häuschen; der Stand, die Abteilung (*stables etc.*); (*in newspaper*) Einrahmung, der Kasten; ***axle –***, die Radbüchse, Achsenbüchse; ***ballot –***, die Wahlurne; ***– of bricks,*** der Baukasten; ***cardboard –***, die Pappschachtel, der Karton; ***– of chocolates,*** die Schachtel Schokolade; ***Christmas –***, das Weihnachtsgeschenk; ***cigar –***, die Zigarrenkiste; (*Elec.*) ***junction –***, die Abzweigdose; ***letter –***, der Briefkasten; ***– of matches,*** die Schachtel Streichhölzer; ***money –***, die Sparbüchse; ***musical –***, die Spieldose; ***– of paints,*** der Tuschkasten; ***sentry –***, das Schilderhaus; ***shooting –***, das Jagdhäuschen; (*Railw.*) ***signal –***, die Blockstelle; ***strong –***, die Kassette; (*coll.*) ***the whole – of tricks,*** der ganze Kram; ***witness –***, der Zeugenstand; ***be in the wrong –***, auf dem Holzweg sein. **2.** *v.t.* in Büchsen *or* Schachteln (ein)packen *or* verschließen, einschachteln; (*a wheel*) mit Büchsen versehen; (*a tree*) anzapfen; ***– the compass,*** (*Naut.*) die Kompaßpunkte in der Ordnung hersagen; (*fig.*) sich gänzlich umstellen; ***– in, see – up***; ***– off,*** in Fächer abteilen; (*Artil.*) abriegeln; (*fig.*) ***– up,*** einschließen.
[3]**box, 1.** *s.* ***– on the ear,*** die Ohrfeige, (*B.*) der Backenstreich. **2.** *v.t.* 1. (mit der Hand) schlagen; ***– his ears,*** ihn ohrfeigen; 2. boxen (mit *or* gegen). **3.** *v.i.* (sich) boxen.
box| barrage, *s.* (*Artil.*) das Abriegelungsfeuer. **–-bed,** *s.* der Bettschrank. **– camera,** *s.* die Box(kamera). **–car,** *s.* (*Am.*) der Güterwagen.
[1]**boxer** ['bɔksə], *s.* der Boxer, Faustkämpfer; *see* [3]**box.**
[2]**boxer,** *s.* der Boxer (*dog*).
boxful ['bɔksful], *s.* der Kastenvoll, die Büchsevoll.
[1]**boxing** ['bɔksiŋ], *s.* das Einpacken *or* Verpacken (in Kästen *etc.*); ***Boxing Day,*** der zweite Weihnachtstag.
[2]**boxing,** *s.* das Boxen, der Boxsport; ***– glove,*** der Boxhandschuh; ***– match,*** der Boxkampf; ***– ring,*** der Boxring.
box|-iron, *s.* das Bügeleisen mit Einsteckheizer. **–-keeper,** *s.* (*Theat.*) der Logenschließer. **–-kite,** *s.* der Kastendrachen, Rahmendrachen. **– number,** *s.* die Chiffre(nummer). **–-office,** *s.* die (Theater)kasse, Kinokasse; ***– attraction,*** die Anziehungskraft (*of play, film*); ***– success,*** der Kassenerfolg. **–-pleat,** *s.* (*Dressm.*) die Kellerfalte. **–room,** *s.* die Rumpelkammer. **–-spanner,** *s.* der (Auf)steckschlüssel.
boy [bɔi], *s.* der Knabe, Junge, (*dial.*) Bub(e); ***old –***, früherer Schüler, alter Herr; (*coll.*) lieber Freund, alter Knabe; (*Prov.*) ***–s will be –s,*** Jugend kennt keine Tugend.
boycott ['bɔikɔt], **1.** *v.t.* boykottieren, in Verruf tun

or erklären, verfemen, kaltstellen. **2.** *s.* der Boykott, die Boykottierung, Verrufserklärung.
boyfriend, *s.* der Freund.
boyhood ['bɔihud], *s.* das Knabenalter, die Jugend. **boyish,** *adj.* knabenhaft, jungenhaft. **boyishness,** *s.* knabenhaftes Wesen, die Jungenhaftigkeit, Knabenart. **Boy Scout,** *s.* der Pfadfinder.
bra [brɑ:], *s.* (*coll.*) *abbr. for* **brassière.**
brace [breis], **1.** *s.* 1. das Band, die Binde, der Gurt, Bügel, Halter, Gürtel, Riemen; (*Archit.*) die Strebe, Stütze, Verstrebung, Versteifung, Klammer, der Anker, Stützbalken, das Tragband; (*Dentistry*) die Zahnklammer; (*Carp.*) (*– and bit*), Brustleier, Bohrwinde; Spannschnur (*of a drum*); (*Mus., Typ.*) Systemklammer, geschweifte Klammer, die Akkolade; (*Naut.*) Brasse; ***splice the main –,*** (*Naut.*) Besanschot an! (*coll.*) Grog trinken; 2. (*pl.* -) das Paar (*game etc.*); 3. *pl.* (***pair of –s***) Hosenträger (*pl.*). **2.** *v.t.* straff ziehen, spannen, verspannen, verstreben, versteifen, klammern, gurten, stützen, festigen, abspreizen, absteifen; (*Naut.*) brassen; (*Av.*) abstreben; (*fig.*) stärken, kräftigen; ***– o.s. for,*** die Kräfte zusammennehmen für; ***– o.s.*** (***up***), sich aufraffen *or* zusammenziehen *or* anspannen (***to***, zu).
bracelet ['breislit], *s.* das Armband, der Armreif, die Armspange; *pl.* (*sl.*) Handschellen (*pl.*).
bracer ['breisə], *s.* (*Hist.*) die Armschiene; (*coll.*) der Nervenstärker, Schluck Schnaps.
braces ['bresiz], *pl. See* **brace,** 3.
brach [brætʃ], *s.* (*obs.*) die Bracke; (Spür)hündin.
brachial ['breikiəl], *adj.* Arm–. **brachiate,** *pred. adj.* (*Bot.*) gegenständig. **brachiopoda** [bræki'ɔpədə], *pl.* (*Zool.*) Armfüßer (*pl.*).
brachycephalic [brækisə'fælik], *adj.* kurzköpfig, brachyzephal.
bracing ['breisiŋ], **1.** *s.* die Verspannung, Versteifung, Verankerung, das Absteifen, Abspreizen; (*Naut.*) Brassen. **2.** *adj.* stärkend, kräftigend, erfrischend.
bracken ['brækən], *s.* das Farnkraut, der Adlerfarn.
bracket ['brækit], **1.** *s.* 1. (*Archit.*) der Kragstein, Tragstein, Träger; das Wandbrett, die Konsole, Krage, der (Wand)arm; (*Artil.*) die Gabel, (Ein)gabelung; ***– mounting,*** der Drehkranz (*of guns*); ***corner –,*** das Eckbrett; ***lamp –,*** der Lampenarm; ***spring –,*** der Federbock (*of a vehicle*); ***wall –,*** der Mauerbügel; Wandarm; 2. (*Typ.*) die Klammer; ***in –s,*** in Klammern *or* Parenthese; 3. (*fig.*) die Rubrik, Gruppe, (Steuer)klasse. **2.** *v.t.* 1. (*Typ.*) einklammern, in Klammern setzen; 2. (*Artil.*) eingabeln; 3. (*fig.*) gleichstellen, in dieselbe Rubrik *or* Klasse bringen; ***they were –ed together,*** sie wurden in eine Gruppe zusammengefaßt; sie wurden auf eine Stufe gestellt *or* gleich gut erklärt. **bracketing,** *s.* die Gabelbilding; (*Artil.*) das Gabelschießen.
brackish ['brækiʃ], *adj.* (etwas) salzig; brackig; ***– water,*** das Brackwasser.
bract ['brækt], *s.* (*Bot.*) das Deckblatt, Hochblatt, die Braktee. **bracteate** [–iit], **1.** *adj.* mit Brakteen. **2.** *s.* (*Hist.*) der Brakteat (*coin*).
brad [bræd], *s.* kopfloser Nagel, der Drahtstift; Bodennagel; die Schuhzwecke. **bradawl** [–ɔ:l], *s.* der Vorstechbohrer.
brae [brei], *s.* (*Scots*) der Abhang, Hügel.
brag [bræg], **1.** *s.* die Prahlerei. **2.** *v.i.* aufschneiden, prahlen (***about***, mit); sich rühmen (*Gen.*). **braggadocio** [–ə'douʃiou], *s.* die Prahlerei; der Prahlhans, Aufschneider. **braggart** [–ət], *s.* der Prahler, Aufschneider.
Brahman ['brɑ:mən], *s.* der Brahmane. **Brahmanee,** *s.* die Brahmanin.
braid [breid], **1.** *s.* die Borte, Schnur, Litze, Tresse, der Paspel, das Zierband; die (Haar)flechte. **2.** *v.t.* flechten (*the hair*); mit Borten *or* Litzen besetzen; (*wire etc.*) umspinnen. **braided,** *adj.* geflochten; umsponnen; ***– wire,*** die Litze. **braiding,** *s.* Litzen (*pl.*), der Besatz.
brail [breil], (*Naut.*) **1.** *s.* das Geitau. **2.** *v.t.* ***– up,*** aufgeien.

Braille [breil], *s.* die Blindenschrift.
brain [brein], **1.** *s.* (*Anat.*) das Gehirn; (*fig. usu. pl.*) Hirn, der Verstand, Intellekt, Kopf, die Intelligenz; ***blow his –s out,*** ihm eine Kugel durch den Kopf jagen; ***dash his –s out,*** ihm den Schädel einschlagen; ***he hasn't much –,*** er ist keiner von den Klügsten; ***have s.th. on the –,*** von einer S. besessen sein; ***cudgel*** or ***puzzle*** or ***rack one's –s,*** sich (*Dat.*) den Kopf zerbrechen; (*sl.*) ***pick his –s,*** ihn ausquetschen; ***softening of the –,*** die Gehirnerweichung; ***turn his –,*** ihm den Kopf verdrehen. **2.** *v.t.* den Schädel einschlagen (*Dat.*).
brain|-box, *s. See* **--pan.** **– cell,** *s.* die Gehirngewebezelle. **--child,** *s.* (*coll.*) das Geistesprodukt. **--fag,** *s.* geistige Übermüdung *or* Überanstrengung. **– fever,** *s.* die Gehirnentzündung, Hirnhautentzündung.
brainless ['breinlis], *adj.* (*fig.*) ohne Verstand, geistlos, gedankenlos, unvernünftig, dumm.
brain|-pan, *s.* die Hirnschale. **–storm,** *s.* geistige Umnachtung, die Geistesstörung, (*coll.*) hirnverbrannte Idee. **--teaser, --twister,** *s.* kopfzerbrechendes Rätsel. **–wash,** *v.t.* Gehirnwäsche vornehmen bei. **–washing,** *s.* die Gehirnwäsche. **–wave,** *s.* der Geistesblitz, geistreicher Einfall. **–work,** *s.* die Geistesarbeit, Kopfarbeit. **–worker,** *s.* der Geistesarbeiter, Kopfarbeiter.
brainy ['braini], *adj.* (*coll.*) intelligent, geistreich, klug.
braise [breiz], *v.t.* schmoren.
[1]**brake** [breik], *s.* (*Bot.*) das Farnkraut; (*Poet.*) Dickicht, Gebüsch, (Dorn)gestrüpp.
[2]**brake,** **1.** *s.* 1. die (Flachs– *or* Hanf)breche, Bracke; 2. (*Agr.*) schwere Egge; (*obs.*) vierrädriger Wagen. **2.** *v.t.* brechen (*flax*), aufbrechen (*ground*).
[3]**brake,** (*obs. Poet.*) *imperf. of* **break.**
[4]**brake,** **1.** *s.* die Bremse, Hemmvorrichtung; (*fig.*) der Einhalt, Zügel; ***external contraction –,*** die Außenbackenbremse; ***internal expanding –,*** die Innenbackenbremse; ***four-wheel –s,*** Vierradbremsen; ***put on*** or ***apply the –(s),*** bremsen; (*fig.*) ***put a – on a th.,*** einer S. Einhalt gebieten. **2.** *v.i.* (ab)bremsen.
brake|-block, *s. See* **–shoe.** **--cable,** *s.* die Bremstrosse. **– (horse)power,** *s.* die Bremsleistung (in PS). **–shoe,** *s.* die Bremsbacke. **brake(s)man,** *s.* der Bremser. **brake-van,** *s.* (*Railw.*) der Bremswagen.
bramble [bræmbl], *s.* der Brombeerstrauch; (*Poet.*) das Dorngestrüpp.
brambling ['bræmbliŋ], *s.* (*Orn.*) der Bergfink (*Fringilla montifringilla*).
bran [bræn], *s.* die Kleie.
branch [brɑ:ntʃ], **1.** *s.* der Ast, Zweig (*of a tree*), Arm (*of river, candlestick*), Ausläufer (*of mountains*), Zinken, Zacken, die Sprosse (*of antlers*); (*Comm.*) Zweigstelle, Nebenstelle, Filiale, Niederlassung, das Zweiggeschäft; der Zweig, die Linie (*of a family*); (*fig.*) Branche, das Fach, Gebiet (*of knowledge*), der Abschnitt, Teil, die Unterabteilung (*of a whole*); ***– of industry,*** der Erwerbszweig; (*Mil.*) ***– of service,*** die Waffengattung, Truppengattung; ***– establishment,*** die Zweigstelle, Filiale, das Zweiggeschäft; ***– line,*** (*Railw.*) die Zweigbahn, Nebenlinie, Seitenlinie, (*Elec.*) Anschlußleitung, Abzweigleitung; Seitenlinie (*of a family*); ***local –,*** die Ortsgruppe (*of a society*); (*fig.*) ***root and –,*** völlig, gründlich, mit Stumpf und Stiel. **2.** *v.i.* Zweige *or* Äste treiben; (*fig.*) (*usu.* ***– off***) abzweigen; ***– out,*** sich verzweigen, (*also fig.*) sich ausbreiten (***into***, in (*Acc.*)), (*fig.*) abschweifen, sich ergehen (***into***, in (*Dat.*)).
branchia ['bræŋkiə], *s.* (*pl.* **-e** [–kii:]) (*Zool.*) die Kieme. **branchial,** *adj.* Kiemen–. **branchiate,** *adj.* kiementragend.
brand [brænd], **1.** *s.* 1. der (Feuer)brand; Kien, die Fackel; 2. das Brandmal, (*fig.*) der Schandfleck, Makel; 3. (*Comm.*) das Warenzeichen, die (Fabrik– *or* Handels)marke, Warengattung, Sorte; 4. (*Bot.*) der Brand (*on corn*); 5. (*Poet.*) das Schwert, die Klinge. **2.** *v.t.* Zeichen einbrennen

(*Dat.*), (*fig.*) brandmarken; (*Comm.*) mit einem Warenzeichen versehen; (*fig.*) ***-ed on his memory,*** seinem Gedächtnis unauslöschlich eingeprägt. **branded,** *adj.* mit einem eingebrannten Zeichen *or* (*Comm.*) einem Warenzeichen *or* einer Fabrikmarke versehen. **branding,** *s.* das Einbrennen, (*fig.*) Brandmarken. **branding-iron,** *s.* das Brenneisen.

brandish ['brændiʃ], *v.t.* schwingen, schwenken.

brand-new, *adj.* (*coll.*) funkelnagelneu.

brandy ['brændi], *s.* der Kognak, Weinbrand, Branntwein. **brandy-snap,** *s.* der Pfefferkuchen.

brant [brænt], *s.* (*Am.*) *see* **brent goose.**

brash [bræʃ], **1.** *s.* 1. (*Med.*) das Sodbrennen; 2. (*Geol.*) Trümmergestein; (*Naut.*) Eistrümmer (*pl.*). **2.** *adj.* brüchig, bröckelig, morsch, spröde; (*coll.*) unverschämt, draufgängerisch, dreist, keck.

brass [brɑ:s], **1.** *s.* das Messing; (*Mus.*) Blech, Blechinstrumente (*pl.*), (*players*) Blechbläser (*pl.*); (*sl.*) die Frechheit, Unverschämtheit, Stirn; (*sl.* = *money*) Pinke, der Draht; die Grabplatte, Gedenktafel; ***bold as* –,** frech wie Oskar; (*sl.*) ***top* –,** hohe Tiere (*pl.*). **2.** *adj.* Messing–, messingen; – ***band,*** die Blaskapelle, Blechmusik; – ***farthing,*** roter Heller, der Deut, Pfifferling; (*sl.*) – ***hat,*** hohes Tier, der Stabsoffizier; – ***plate,*** das Namenschild; (*sl.*) – ***tacks,*** die Hauptsache; ***get down to – tacks,*** zur S. kommen.

brassard ['bræsɑ:d], *s.* die Armbinde, das Armband.

brasserie ['bræsəri], *s.* die Bierstube.

brassie ['brɑ:si], *s.* (eine Art) Golfschläger (mit Messingbeschlag).

brassière ['bræsiɛə], *s.* der Büstenhalter.

brassy ['brɑ:si], *adj.* messingartig; (*fig.*) frech, unverschämt, (*of sound*) blechern.

brat [bræt], *s.* (*sl.*) der Balg, Fratz, die Range, Blage, das Gör.

bravado [brə'vɑ:dou], *s.* die Prahlerei, herausforderndes Benehmen, die Bravade.

brave [breiv], **1.** *adj.* 1. tapfer, mutig, unerschrocken; brav, rechtschaffen; 2. (*obs.*) ansehnlich, prächtig, stattlich. **2.** *v.t.* mutig begegnen *or* entgegentreten (*Dat.*); trotzen (*Dat.*), die Stirn bieten (*Dat.*), herausfordern, standhalten; – ***it out,*** es trotzig durchsetzen. **3.** *s.* (indianischer) Krieger, (*Poet.*) (tapferer) Held. **bravery,** *s.* 1. der Mut, die Tapferkeit, Unerschrockenheit; 2. Pracht, Stattlichkeit, der Glanz; Staat, Putz, das Gepränge.

[1]**bravo** ['brɑ:vou], *s.* der Bravo, Bandit, Räuber, Meuchelmörder.

[2]**bravo** [brɑ:'vou], **1.** *s.* das Bravo, der Bravoruf. **2.** *int.* bravo!

bravura [brə'vuərə], *s.* die Bravour, (*Mus. etc.*) das Bravourstück.

brawl [brɔ:l], **1.** *v.i.* laut zanken, lärmen, krakeelen; (*Poet.*) murmeln, rauschen (*as a stream*). **2.** *s.* der Aufruhr, Krakeel, die Keilerei. **brawling,** *s.* die Keilerei, Stänkerei, das Gezänk, (*Law*) die Ruhestörung.

brawn [brɔ:n], *s.* 1. die Schweinesülze; 2. (*coll.*) das Muskelfleisch; (*fig.*) die Muskelkraft, Muskelfülle. **brawny,** *adj.* sehnig, muskulös, stämmig.

[1]**bray** [brei], **1.** *v.i.* schreien (*of donkeys*); (*fig.*) gellen, kreischen, schmettern (*as trumpets*). **2.** *v.t.* – ***out,*** gellend ausposaunen, kreischend verkünden. **3.** *s.* das Eselgeschrei; (*fig.*) Kreischen, Schmettern.

[2]**bray,** *v.t.* zerstoßen, zerreiben, zerstampfen, zermalmen.

braze [breiz], *v.t.* hartlöten, schweißen.

brazen [breizn], **1.** *adj.* ehern, messingen; (*fig.*) (*also* ***--faced***) frech, schamlos, unverschämt; mit eherner Stirn. **2.** *v.t.* – ***it out,*** sich unverschämt durchsetzen.

brazier ['breiziə], *s.* 1. der Kupferschmied, Gelbgießer; 2. die Kohlenpfanne, Feuerschale.

Brazil [brə'zil], *s.* Brasilien (*n.*). **Brazilian, 1.** *s.* der (die) Brasilianer(in). **2.** *adj.* brazilianisch. **Brazil nut,** *s.* die Paranuß.

breach [bri:tʃ], **1.** *s.* der Bruch, Riß, Sprung, die Lücke; (*Mil.*) Bresche, Einbruchstelle; (*fig.*) Übertretung, Verletzung, der Verstoß; die Uneinigkeit, der Zwiespalt, Zwist; ***stand in the* –,** den Angriff aushalten; ***step into the* –,** in die Bresche springen; (*Law*) – ***of close,*** unbefugtes Betreten; – ***of contract*** or ***covenant,*** der Vertragsbruch; – ***of discipline,*** das Disziplinarvergehen; – ***of etiquette,*** der Verstoß gegen den guten Ton; – ***of honour,*** die Verletzung der Ehre; – ***of the law,*** die Übertretung des Gesetzes; – ***of an oath,*** der Eidbruch; (*Law*) – ***of the peace,*** öffentliche Ruhestörung; – ***of privilege,*** die Übertretung der Machtbefugnis, Zuständigkeitsübertretung; – ***of promise*** (***of marriage***), der Bruch des Eheversprechens; – ***of trust,*** die Veruntreuung, Wortbrüchigkeit, der Vertrauensbruch, Vertrauensmißbrauch. **2.** *v.t.* (*Mil.*) eine Bresche schlagen in (*Acc.*), durchbrechen (*also fig.*).

bread [bred], *s.* das Brot; (*fig.*) der Lebensunterhalt, tägliches Brot; (*Eccl.*) die Hostie; ***black* –,** das Roggenbrot; ***brown* –,** das Weizenschrotbrot; (***piece*** or ***slice of***) – ***and butter,*** das Butterbrot; ***quarrel with one's – and butter,*** seinen eignen Interessen schaden, sich (*Dat.*) selbst im Lichte stehen; ***he knows on which side his – is buttered,*** er versteht sich auf seinen Vorteil; er weiß, wo Barthel den Most holt; – ***and cheese,*** das Käsebrot; ***consecrated* –,** die Hostie; ***eat the – of idleness,*** ein faules Leben führen; ***loaf of* –,** das (*or* der Laib) Brot; ***piece*** or ***slice of* –,** die Scheibe Brot; (*coll.*) – ***and scrape,*** dünn geschmiertes Brot; (*fig.*) knappe Nahrung; ***take the – out of his mouth,*** ihn brotlos machen, ihm den Lebensunterhalt rauben; ***be*** (***put***) ***on – and water,*** nur Wasser und Brot bekommen.

bread|-and-butter, *attrib. adj.* – ***business,*** das Geschäft, das seinen Mann ernährt; – ***education,*** die Erziehung, die nur auf den Broterwerb hinzielt. **--basket,** *s.* der Brotkorb; (*sl.*) Magen. **--bin,** *s.* der Brotkasten. **--board,** *s.* das Brotschneidebrett. **--crumb,** *s.* die Brotkrume. **--cutter,** *s.* die Brotschneidemaschine. – **fruit,** *s.* die Frucht des Brot(frucht)baumes. **-knife,** *s.* das Brotmesser. **--line,** *s.* (*Am.*) die Schlange der Bedürftigen bei Verteilungen von Speisen; (*coll.*) ***be on the* –,** keine sichere Existenz haben.

breadth [bredθ], *s.* die Breite, Weite; (*of cloth*) Bahn; (*fig.*) das Ausmaß, die Ausdehnung, Fülle, Größe; (*of concept*) der Umfang, (*of mind*) die Weitherzigkeit, Großzügigkeit; ***to a hair's* –,** aufs Haar genau. **breadth|ways, -wise,** *adv.* der Breite nach, in der Breite.

breadwinner ['bredwinə], *s.* 1. der Ernährer, (Geld– *or* Brot)verdiener; 2. Erwerb, die Verdienstquelle.

break [breik], **1.** *s.* 1. der Bruch, die Bruchstelle; Öffnung, Lücke, Bresche, der Durchbruch, Riß; Zwischenraum, Einschnitt (*in, Gen.*); (*Elec.*) – ***in the circuit,*** die Stromabbrechung; – ***of day,*** der Tagesanbruch; ***a – in the weather,*** ein Witterungsumschwung; 2. die Unterbrechung, (Ruhe)pause; ***at* –,** in der Pause (*at schools*); ***without a* –,** ohne Unterbrechung; 3. der Übergang, Wechsel, die Abwechs(e)lung; 4. (*Typ.*) der (Gedanken)strich; (*Typ.*) Absatz; 5. (*Archit.*) blinde Nische, die Vertiefung; Lichtung, der Durchhau (*in woods*); 6. (*Bill.*) die Serie, Tour; 7. (*Crick.*) das Effet; 8. (*coll.*) Ausbrechen, der Fluchtversuch (*from prison*); 9. (*sl.*) die Chance, günstige Gelegenheit; (*sl.*) ***bad* –,** tückischer Zufall.

2. *irr.v.t.* brechen, durchbrechen; zerbrechen, zerschlagen, zertrümmern, zersprengen; aufreißen (*the surface*); umbrechen (*the ground*); aufbrechen, erbrechen (*locks, doors, letters etc.*); (*fig., coll.*) bankrott machen, zugrunde richten (*a p. financially*); degradieren (*an officer*); (*Elec.*) unterbrechen (*a curcuit*), ausschalten (*the current*).

(a) (*with nouns*) – ***his neck*** or ***back,*** ihm den Hals *or* das Rückgrat brechen, (*fig.*) ihn zugrunde richten; (*coll.*) – ***the back of s.th.,*** das Schwerste einer S. hinter sich bringen; – ***the bank,*** die Bank sprengen; – ***bounds,*** die erlaubte Grenze überschreiten; (*Naut.*) – ***bulk,*** zu löschen anfangen; – ***camp,*** das

Lager abbrechen; – ***cover,*** aus dem Lager hervorbrechen, ins Freie gehen (*of game*); – ***the engagement,*** die Verlobung auflösen; –***faith with him,*** ihm die Treue brechen; – (***the force of***) ***a fall,*** den Fall abfangen *or* aufhalten *or* dämpfen *or* abschwächen; – ***one's fast,*** das Fasten unterbrechen; (*obs.*) frühstücken, (*coll.*) etwas zu sich nehmen; – ***a flag,*** eine Flagge ausbreiten; (*coll.*) – ***gaol,*** aus dem Gefängnis ausbrechen; – (***new***) ***ground,*** (ein Brachfeld) (um)pflügen *or* umgraben, (*fig.*) ein neues Gebiet erschließen; – ***his heart,*** ihm das Herz brechen; – ***a horse to harness,*** ein Pferd einfahren; (*fig.*) – ***the ice,*** das Eis brechen; – ***one's journey,*** die Reise unterbrechen; – ***the law,*** das Gesetz übertreten; – ***the news*** (***gently***), die Nachricht (schonend) beibringen; – ***o.s. of a habit,*** sich (*Acc.*) von einer Gewohnheit abbringen *or* einer S. (*Gen.*) entwöhnen; sich (*Dat.*) etwas abgewöhnen; – ***his pride,*** seinen Stolz demütigen; – ***a promise,*** ein Versprechen nicht halten; (*Mil.*) – ***ranks,*** wegtreten; (*Spt.*) – ***a record,*** den Rekord schlagen; – ***the rules,*** die Regeln verletzen; – ***the silence,*** das Schweigen brechen; – ***the spell,*** den Zauber brechen; – ***step,*** ohne Tritt (marschieren); – ***stones,*** Steine klopfen; – ***water,*** an die Oberfläche kommen; – ***wind,*** einen Wind abgehen lassen; ***they broke his windows,*** sie warfen ihm die Fenster ein; – ***one's word,*** see – ***a promise.***
(b) (*with adverbs*) – ***down,*** abbrechen, niederreißen; – ***down opposition,*** Widerstand *or* Widerspruch beseitigen; – ***in,*** aufbrechen (*a door*); eintreten (*shoes*); bändigen, abrichten, zureiten (*a horse*); – ***off,*** abbrechen, losbrechen, lösen; unterbrechen (*conversation etc.*); – ***off an engagement,*** eine Verlobung auflösen; – ***open,*** aufbrechen, erbrechen; – ***to pieces,*** zerschlagen, zertrümmern; – ***up,*** zerkleinern, zerteilen, zerfasern, aufspalten, auflösen, zersprengen, zerschmettern; abwracken (*a ship*); auseinandertreiben (*a gathering*).
3. *irr.v.i.* brechen, zerbrechen, zerspringen, reißen (*of ropes etc.*), zerreißen, bersten, platzen, in Stücke gehen, entzweigehen; (*as a crowd*) weichen, zersprengt werden, auseinandergehen, sich auflösen; branden, sich brechen, schlagen, stürzen (***over,*** über (*Acc.*)) (*as waves*); ausbrechen, losbrechen, hereinbrechen (*as a storm*); anbrechen, grauen (*of day*); wechseln, umschlagen (*of the voice*); umschlagen (*of weather*); abspringen (*of a ball*); (*sl.*) – ***even,*** ungeschoren davonkommen; ***my heart is ready to*** –, mir will das Herz zerspringen; – ***away,*** sich losmachen, sich lossagen, losbrechen, abbrechen, abfallen, sich losreißen (***from,*** von); sich davonmachen; – ***down,*** zusammenbrechen, in die Brüche gehen, zerbrechen, zerfallen; versagen, steckenbleiben; (*Motor.*) eine Panne haben; ausgehen, zu Ende gehen, abnehmen, aussetzen; – ***forth,*** ausbrechen, hervorbrechen; – ***in,*** einbrechen, eindringen; unterbrechen; – ***into,*** einbrechen in (*Acc.*); ausbrechen in (*Acc.*) (*laughter etc.*); plötzlich anfangen (***a run,*** zu laufen); ***the house was broken into,*** in das Haus wurde eingebrochen; – ***in upon,*** (*a p.*) hereinplatzen bei, (*a th.*) unterbrechen, einfallen in (*Acc.*); – ***loose,*** sich losreißen *or* befreien; ausreißen, ausbrechen; – ***off,*** aufhören, abbrechen; – ***out,*** ausbrechen; hervorbrechen, auftreten, sich zeigen; – ***out in a rash,*** einen Ausschlag bekommen; ***I broke out in sweat,*** mir brach der Schweiß aus; – ***through,*** durchbrechen, hervorkommen, durchdringen (durch); – ***to pieces,*** in Trümmer gehen; – ***up,*** sich auflösen, auseinanderfallen, auseinandergehen, in Stücke gehen; (für die Ferien) schließen (*of school*); verfallen, zusammenbrechen (*as health*); ***he is –ing up,*** es geht mit ihm zu Ende; (*coll.*) – ***with him,*** sich mit ihm überwerfen, mit ihm brechen *or* zerfallen.

breakable ['breikəbl], *adj.* zerbrechlich. **breakables,** *pl.* zerbrechliche Waren. **breakage** [–idʒ], *s.* das Brechen; der Bruch; Bruchschaden; (*Comm.*) ***payment for*** –, die Refaktie.

breakdown ['breikdaun], *s.* der Zusammenbruch, das Versagen, die Zerrüttung (*of health*); (*Tech.*) (Betriebs)störung, technische Störung, das Scheitern; (*Motor.*) die Panne; (*Chem.*) Zersetzung, Aufspaltung; (*fig.*) Aufgleiderung, Zerlegung, Analyse, Verteilung; ***nervous*** –, der Nervenzusammenbruch, (*coll.*) Nervenklaps; – ***crane,*** der Bergungskran; – ***gang,*** die Hilfsmannschaft, Unfallkolonne; – ***lorry,*** der Abschleppwagen; – ***of negotiations,*** das Scheitern der Verhandlungen.

breaker ['breikə], *s.* **1.** der Brecher, Zerstörer, Zertrümmerer; **2.** die Sturzwelle, Sturzsee; *pl.* Brandung; (*fig.*) –***s ahead!*** Gefahr in Sicht!

breakfast ['brekfəst], **1.** *s.* das Frühstück. **2.** *v.i.* frühstücken; – ***on an egg,*** ein Ei zum Frühstück essen.

break-in, *s.* (*coll.*) der Einbruch.

breaking ['breikiŋ], *s.* die Brechung; das Brechen, Abreißen; (*Law*) – ***and entering,*** der Einbruch; – ***of the voice,*** der Stimmbruch, Stimmwechsel. **breaking|-in,** *s.* der Einbruch; das Zureiten, Abrichten (*of animals*). **--load,** *s.* die Bruchbelastung, Reißbelastung. **--off,** *s.* der Abbruch. **--point,** *s.* die Bruchstelle; (*Tech.*) Festigkeitsgrenze; (*fig.*) das Ende der Kräfte. **--strain,** *s. See* **--stress. --strength,** *s.* die Reißfestigkeit, Bruchfestigkeit. **--stress,** *s.* die Bruchbeanspruchung. **--up,** *s.* der (Schul)schluß.

break|neck, *adj.* halsbrecherisch. **--through,** *s.* (*Mil., fig.*) der Durchbruch. **--up,** *s.* das Aufbrechen, der Aufbruch, die Auflösung. **–water,** *s.* der Wellenbrecher, die Buhne.

[1]**bream** [bri:m], *s.* (*Ichth.*) der Brassen.

[2]**bream,** *v.t.* (*Naut.*) reinbrennen, abflammen.

breast [brest], **1.** *s.* (*Anat.*) die Brust; (*fig.*) der Busen, das Herz; (*Archit.*) die Brüstung (*of window*); ***a child at her*** –, ein Kind an der Brust; ***make a clean – of it,*** es offen bekennen *or* eingestehen *or* heraussagen, reinen Wein einschenken. **2.** *v.t.* sich stemmen gegen, trotzen (*Dat.*), Trotz *or* die Stirn bieten (*Dat.*); gerade losgehen auf (*Acc.*); – ***a hill,*** einen Hügel ansteigen; – ***the waves,*** gegen die Wellen ankämpfen.

breastbone ['brestboun], *s.* das Brustbein.

–breasted ['brestid], *adj. suff.* (*Anat.*) –brüstig; (*of garment*) –reihig.

breast|-fed, *adj.* mit Muttermilch genährt; – ***child,*** das Brustkind. **--feeding,** *s.* das Stillen. **--glass,** *s.* (*Med.*) die Milchpumpe. **--harness,** *s.* das Sielengeschirr. **--high,** *adj.* brusthoch. **--pin,** *s.* die Vorstecknadel, Schlipsnadel. **–plate,** *s.* der Brustharnisch, Brustpanzer (*of armour*); das Vorderzeug (*of harness*); der Bauchschild (*of tortoises*). **--rope,** *s.* (*Naut.*) das Dwarstau. **–strap,** *s.* das Blatt (*of harness*). **–stroke,** *s.* das Brustschwimmen. **–work,** *s.* (*Fort.*) die Brustwehr, Schulterwehr; (*Naut.*) das Schanzkleid, die Reeling.

breath [breθ], *s.* der Atem; Hauch; Atemzug; (*Phonet.*) stimmloser Hauch; **(a)** (*with nouns*) – ***of air,*** das Lüftchen; – ***of scandal, suspicion etc.,*** eine Spur *or* leiseste Andeutung von Verleumdung *or* Verdacht *etc.*; ***shortness of*** –, die Kurzatmigkeit; **(b)** (*with verbs*) ***draw*** –, Atem schöpfen *or* holen; ***draw a deep*** –, tief aufatmen; ***give me time to draw*** –, laß mich ein wenig zu Atem kommen! ***gasp for*** –, nach Luft schnappen; ***get one's*** – (***back***), Atem holen, verschnaufen; ***hold one's*** –, den Atem anhalten; (*coll.*) ***keep your – to cool your porridge,*** spare deine Worte! behalte deinen Rat für dich! ***that knocks the – out of me*** or ***takes my – away,*** das benimmt *or* raubt *or* verschlägt *or* versetzt mir den Atem; ***waste one's*** –, in den Wind reden; **(c)** (*with preps.*) ***at every*** –, bei jedem Atemzuge; ***in one*** –, in einem Atem; ***in the same – with,*** in demselben Augenblick wie, zugleich mit; ***out of*** –, außer Atem; ***to one's dying*** –, bis zum letzten Atemzug; ***under one's*** –, im Flüsterton, leise flüsternd; ***with bated*** –, mit verhaltenem Atem.

breathalyser ['breθəlaizə], *s.* (*Motor.*) das Alkoholteströhrchen; (*coll.*) ***be given the – test,*** in die Tüte blasen (müssen).

breathe [bri:ð], **1.** *v.i.* atmen, Atem holen, Luft einholen; – ***in,*** einatmen; – ***out,*** ausatmen; – ***again*** or ***freely,*** erleichtert aufatmen; – (***up***)***on,*** anhauchen;

(*coll.*) ***give me a chance to –!*** laß mich verschnaufen! **2.** *v.t.* atmen, einatmen, ausatmen (*the air*); hauchen, flüstern (*words*), (*fig.*) verlauten lassen, verraten; verschnaufen lassen (*horses*); – ***one's last,*** den letzten Atemzug tun, in den letzten Zügen liegen; – ***vengeance,*** Rache schnauben; – ***a wish,*** einen Wunsch leise äußern *or* schüchtern an den Tag legen; ***not – a word of*** or ***about it,*** kein Wort davon erwähnen.

breathed [bri:ðd], *adj.* (*Phonet.*) stimmlos. **breather,** *s.* (*coll.*) die Atempause; ***go for a –,*** Luft schöpfen gehen; ***take a –,*** Ruhepause machen.

breathing ['bri:ðiŋ], **1.** *adj.* leibhaftig, lebenswahr, sprechend (*as a portrait*). **2.** *s.* das Atmen, die Atmung; Atemübung; (*Phonet.*) der Hauchlaut; ***deep –*** (***exercises***), die Atemgymnastik. **breathing| apparatus,** *s.* der Sauerstoffapparat, das Atemgerät. **--hole,** *s.* das Luftloch. **--pipe,** *s.* der Schnorchel (*submarines*). **--space,** *s.* die (Atem)-pause, Zeit zum Atemschöpfen.

breathless ['breθlis], *adj.* atemlos, außer Atem; (*fig.*) außer sich (***with,*** vor (*Dat.*)); atemlos, atemberaubend (*attention, excitement etc.*); schwül, windstill (*weather*). **breathlessness,** *s.* die Atemnot, Atemlosigkeit. **breathtaking,** *adj.* atemberaubend.

bred [bred], *imperf., p.p. of* **breed.**

breech [bri:tʃ], **1.** *s.* 1. der Hintere, das Gesäß, Hinterteil; der Boden (*of trousers*); – ***leather,*** das Hinterleder, Fahrleder (*of miners*); 2. das Verschlußstück, der Laderaum (*of a gun*). **2.** *v.t.* die ersten Hosen anziehen (*Dat.*). **breech|-action,** *s.* die Hinterladevorrichtung. **--block,** *s.* der Verschluß, Verschlußblock, Blockverschluß; Verschlußkeil. **– delivery,** *s.* (*Med.*) die Steißgeburt. **breeched** [–t], *adj.* hosentragend.

breeches ['britʃəz], *pl.* die Reithose(n), Kniehose(n); (*coll.*) ***wear the –,*** die Hosen anhaben, das Regiment führen (*of a wife*). **breeches-buoy,** *s.* (*Naut.*) die Hosenboje. **breeching,** *s.* das Hinterzeug, der Umgang (*of harness*).

breech|-loader, *s.* der Hinterlader. **--loading,** *s.* die Hinterladung. **--pin, --plug,** *s.* der Verschlußkeil. **– presentation,** *s.* (*Med.*) die Steißlage.

breed [bri:d], **1.** *irr.v.i.* sich vermehren, sich fortpflanzen, Nachkommenschaft zeugen; brüten, erzeugt werden; – ***in-and-in,*** Inzucht treiben; (*Biol.*) – ***true,*** sich rein vererben **2.** *irr. v.t.* erzeugen, gebären, hervorbringen; ziehen, züchten (*plants*), züchten (*animals*); (*fig.*) hervorrufen, herbeiführen, entstehen lassen; aufziehen, ausbilden; ausbrüten, aushecken; – ***ill blood,*** böses Blut machen; ***bred in the bone,*** angeboren. **3.** *s.* die Brut, Zucht, Rasse, Art; (*fig.*) Herkunft, der Stamm, Schlag.

breeder ['bri:də], *s.* der Erzeuger; Züchter (*of cattle*); das Zuchttier. **breeding,** *s.* 1. das Züchten, (Auf)ziehen, die Züchtung, (Auf)zucht (*of plants, animals*), das Gebären, (Er)zeugen, die Fortpflanzung; das Brüten; 2. die Erziehung, Bildung; ***bad –,*** schlechte Manieren; ***good –,*** feine Lebensart. **breeding| ground,** *s.* die Brutstätte, der Brutplatz, (*fig.*) Nährboden. **– mare,** *s.* die Zuchtstute. **– place,** *s. See* **– ground. --pond,** *s.* der Laichteich. **– season,** *s.* die Fortpflanzungsperiode, Brutzeit.

breeks [bri:ks], *pl.* (*Scots*) *see* **breeches.**

[1]**breeze** [bri:z], *s.* die Brise, leichter Wind; (*coll.*) der Zank, Streit; (*coll.*) ***kick up a –,*** Krach machen; ***light –,*** leichte Brise; ***gentle –,*** schwacher Wind; ***moderate –,*** mäßiger Wind; ***fresh –,*** frischer Wind; ***strong –,*** steifer Wind (*the above are Beaufort Scale 2 to 6*).

[2]**breeze,** *s.* (*Ent.*) die Bremse, Biesfliege.

[3]**breeze,** *s.* das Kohlenklein, die Lösche.

breezy [bri:zi], *adj.* luftig, windig; (*coll.*) lebhaft, munter, flott, forsch.

brehon ['bri:hən], *s.* (*Hist.*) irischer Landrichter.

brent goose ['brentgu:s], *s.* die Wildgans, Ringelgans (*Branta bernicla*).

brethren ['breðrən], *pl.* (*obs.*) die Brüder; (*Eccl.*) ***my –,*** liebe Brüder.

Breton ['bretən], **1.** *s.* 1. der Bretone (die Bretonin); 2. (*language*) das Bretonische. **2.** *adj.* bretonisch.

breve [bri:v], *s.* (*Mus.*) die Brevis, doppelte Taktnote; (*Phonet.*) das Kürzezeichen.

brevet ['brevit], *s.* – (***rank***), der Titularrang (***of,*** als); – ***major,*** der Hauptmann mit Rang eines Majors.

breviary ['bri:vjəri], *s.* (*R.C.*) das Brevier, Stundenbuch.

brevier [brə'viə], *s.* (*Typ.*) die Petit(schrift).

brevity ['breviti], *s.* die Kürze; (*Prov.*) – ***is the soul of wit,*** Kürze ist des Witzes Würze.

brew [bru:], **1.** *v.t.* brauen (*beer*); kochen, (zu)bereiten (*tea etc.*); (*fig.*) schmieden, (aus)brüten, anzetteln (*mischief*). **2.** *v.i.* (*usu.* ***be –ing***) im Anzug sein, sich vorbereiten *or* zusammenziehen, aufziehen, heranziehen (*as a storm etc.*). **3.** *s.* das Gebräu, Bräu. **brewer,** *s.* der (Bier)brauer. **brewery,** *s.* die Brauerei, das Brauhaus.

briar, *s. see* **brier.**

bribable ['braibəbl], *adj.* bestechlich, käuflich. **bribe, 1.** *s.* das Bestechungsgeschenk, Bestechungsgeld, die Bestechung; ***offer him a –,*** ihn bestechen wollen; ***take a –,*** sich bestechen lassen. **2.** *v.t.* bestechen, durch Bestechung verleiten. **bribery,** *s.* die Bestechung; ***open to –,*** bestechlich.

bric-à-brac ['brikəbræk], *s.* Antiquitäten (*pl.*), Raritäten (*pl.*), Nippsachen (*pl.*).

brick [brik], **1.** *s.* der Ziegel(stein), Backstein; Würfel, (Bau)klotz; (*coll.*) famoser *or* prima Kerl; (*coll.*) ***drop a –,*** eine Taktlosigkeit begehen, ins Fettnäpfchen treten; ***box of*** (***wooden***) ***–s,*** der Holzbaukasten; ***swim like a –,*** wie eine bleierne Ente schwimmen; ***like a ton of –s,*** mit Riesenkrach. **2.** *adj.* Backstein–; – ***colour,*** ziegelrot; – ***facing,*** die Backsteinverkleidung; – ***wall,*** die Backsteinmauer; ***he can see through a – wall,*** er hört das Gras wachsen, er kann alles. **3.** *v.t.* mit Ziegeln *or* Backsteinen bauen *or* pflastern; – ***up,*** zumauern.

brick|bat, *s.* der Ziegelbrocken; (*fig.*) Anwurf, die Verunglimpfung, schmähliche *or* schnöde Kritik. **--built,** *adj.* gemauert. **--clay,** *s.* die Ziegelerde. **--dust,** *s.* das Ziegelmehl. **--kiln,** *s.* der Ziegelofen, die Ziegelei. **–layer,** *s.* der Maurer. **–laying,** *s.* die Maurerei. **--making,** *s.* das Ziegelbrennen. **--red,** *adj.* ziegelrot. **–work,** *s.* der Backsteinbau; die Maurerarbeit. **–works,** *pl. See* **–yard. bricky,** *s.* (*coll.*) *see* **bricklayer. brickyard,** *s.* die Ziegelei.

bridal [braidl], **1.** *adj.* bräutlich, Braut–, hochzeitlich, Hochzeits–; – ***chamber,*** das Brautgemach; – ***suite,*** das (Hotel)zimmer für Hochzeitsreisende; – ***wreath,*** der Brautkranz, Jungfernkranz. **2.** *s.* (*obs.*) die Hochzeit, das Hochzeitsfest.

bride [braid], *s.* neuvermählte Frau; die Braut am Tag der Trauung; – ***and bridegroom,*** das junge Paar, die Neuvermählten; ***give the – away,*** Brautvater sein. **bridegroom,** *s.* der Bräutigam am Hochzeitstag, junger Ehemann, Neuvermählte(r). **bridesmaid** [–zmeid], *s.* die Brautjungfer.

[1]**bridge** [bridʒ], **1.** *s.* die Brücke; der Steg (*of stringinstruments*); (Nasen)rücken (*of the nose*); Nasensteg (*of spectacles*); (*Naut.*) die (Kommando)-brücke; (*fig.*) Überleitung, der Übergang; – ***of boats,*** die Schiffsbrücke; ***cable-suspension –,*** die Drahtseilbrücke; ***cantilever –,*** die Auslegerbrücke; ***girder –,*** die Fachwerk– *or* Trägerbrücke; ***suspension –,*** die Hängebrücke; ***swing –,*** die Drehbrücke. **2.** *v.t.* eine Brücke schlagen über (*Acc.*); überbrücken; (*fig.*) – ***over,*** überbrücken.

[2]**bridge,** *s.* (*Cards*) das Bridge; ***auction –,*** das Auktionsbridge, Lizitationsbridge; ***contract –,*** das Kontraktbridge, Plafondbridge.

bridgeable ['bridʒəbl], *adj.* überbrückbar. **bridge|-building,** *s.* der Brückenbau. **–head,** *s.* (*Mil.*) der Brückenkopf.

bridle [braidl], **1.** *s.* der Zaum, Zügel; ***give a horse the –,*** einem Pferd die Zügel schießen lassen. **2.** *v.t.* den Zaum anlegen (*Dat.*), (auf)zäumen (*a* *horse*), (*also fig.*) im Zaume halten, zügeln, (*fig.*) einschränken, (be)zähmen, bändigen; – ***one's tongue,*** seine Zunge zügeln *or* im Zaum halten. **3.** *v.i.* (*of horse*) den Kopf aufwerken, (*fig.*) Anstand nehmen, sich brüsten; beleidigt tun (***at,*** über (*Acc.*)). **bridle|-bit,** *s.* das Stangengebiß, die Kandare. **--hand,** *s.* die Zügelhand, linke Hand. **--path,** *s.* der Reitweg. **--rein,** *s.* der Zügel.

bridoon [bri'du:n], *s.* die Trense. **bridoon-bit,** *s.* das Trensengebiß.

brief [bri:f], **1.** *adj.* kurz, knapp, bündig, kurz gefaßt; flüchtig; ***in* –,** mit wenigen *or* kurzen Worten, kurz gesagt, in kurzem; ***be* –,** sich kurz fassen; ***be – with him,*** ihn kurz abfertigen. **2.** *s.* das Breve (*of the Pope*); (*Law*) der Schriftsatz (*of solicitor for barrister*); das Memorandum, schriftliche Zusammenfassung; ***hold a – for,*** (*Law*) als Anwalt *or* vor Gericht vertreten; (*coll.*) sprechen für, eingenommen sein für; (*coll.*) ***hold no – for,*** nicht viel übrig haben für. **3.** *v.t.* einweisen, unterweisen, in Kenntnis setzen, Anweisungen geben (*Dat.*); (*Law*) – ***a lawyer,*** den Fall einem Rechtsanwalt übergeben.

brief-case, *s.* die Aktentasche, Aktenmappe. **briefing,** *s.* (*Av.*) die Flugberatung, Flugbesprechung; (*Mil.*) der Einsatzbefehl; (*Law*) die Anweisung, Instruktion. **briefless,** *adj.* (*Law.*) ohne Praxis.

briefly ['bri:fli], *adv. See in brief.* **briefness,** *s.* die Kürze, Knappheit, Bündigkeit. **briefs,** *pl.* (*coll.*) der Slip (*for men and women*).

brier ['braiə], *s.* 1. der Dornstrauch; wilde Rose; (*Poet.*) das Dorngestrüpp; 2. Bruyèreholz; 3. (*also* – ***pipe***) die Bruyèrepfeife.

brig [brig], *s.* (*Naut.*) die Brigg.

brigade [bri'geid], *s.* die Brigade; (*Artil.*) Abteilung. **brigade major,** *s.* der Brigadeadjutant. **brigadier** [brigə'diə], *s.* (*Am.* – ***general***) der Brigadegeneral.

brigand ['brigənd], *s.* der (Straßen)räuber, Bandit, Brigant. **brigandage** [–idʒ], *s.* der Straßenraub, die Räuberei, Plünderung.

brigantine ['brigənti:n], *s.* (*Naut.*) die Brigantine, der Briggschoner.

bright [brait], *adj.* hell, glänzend, leuchtend, strahlend, licht, klar; (*fig.*) heiter, lebhaft; (*coll.*) aufgeweckt, gescheit; – ***colour,*** lebhafte *or* leuchtende Farbe; – ***day,*** heiterer Tag; (*coll.*) – ***and early,*** recht früh; – ***prospects,*** günstige Aussichten; ***–ly shining,*** hell glänzend.

brighten [braitn], **1.** *v.t.* heller *or* glänzend machen, erhellen, erleuchten; (*fig.*) (*also* – ***up***) aufhellen; aufheitern; (*Dye.*) abklären, auffrischen, beleben; polieren, glänzen, glätten. **2.** *v.i.* – ***up,*** hell(er) werden, sich aufklären, sich aufhellen.

bright|-eyed, *adj.* helläugig. **--hued,** *adj.* hellfarbig, bunt. **brightness,** *s.* der Glanz, die Klarheit, Helligkeit; (*Phys.*) Leuchtstärke; (*fig.*) Heiterkeit, Lebhaftigkeit; (*coll.*) Aufgewecktheit; Helle, Glätte (*as a polish etc.*); (*T.V.*) – ***control,*** die Helligkeitsregelung.

Bright's disease, *s.* (*Med.*) die Nierenschrumpfung, Brightsche Krankheit.

brill [bril], *s.* (*Ichth.*) der Meerbutt.

brilliance, brilliancy ['briljəns(i)], *s.* das Leuchten, der Glanz, die Klarheit, Pracht; (*of colour*) Helligkeit, Buntheit; (*of gems*) das Feuer; (*fig.*) der Scharfsinn, geistige Überlegenheit. **brilliant, 1.** *adj.* hell, glänzend, leuchtend, strahlend; (*coll.*) glänzend, hervorragend, ausgezeichnet, blendend, prächtig; (*a p.*) hochbegabt, hochintelligent, geistreich, (*an idea*) genial; – ***gloss,*** der Hochglanz. **2.** *s.* der Brillant; (*Typ.*) die Brillant(schrift). **brilliantine** [–ti:n], *s.* die Brillantine.

brim [brim], **1.** *s.* der Rand; die Krempe (*of a hat*); ***full to the* –,** bis zum Rande voll. **2.** *v.i.* – ***over,*** übervoll seine, überlaufen; (*fig.*) übersprudeln (*with,* von). **brimful,** *pred. adj.* bis zum Rande voll, übervoll (***of,*** an (*Dat.*)). **-brimmed,** *adj. suff.* -krempig. **brimmer,** *s.* volles Glas; (*coll.*) steifer Strohhut. **brimming,** *adj.* voll bis zum Rande, übervoll; – ***eyes,*** tränende Augen.

brimstone ['brimstən], *s.* (*obs.*) der Schwefel; – ***butterfly,*** der Zitronenfalter.

brindle(d) [brindl(d)], *adj.* gestreift, getigert; scheckig.

brine [brain], *s.* das Salzwasser, die Salzlösung, Salzbrühe, Salzlauge, Sole, Lake; (*Poet.*) das Meer. **brine-bath,** *s.* das Solbad. **--gauge,** *s.* die Salzwaage. **--pit,** *s.* die Salzquelle, Salzgrube.

bring [briŋ], *irr.v.t.* bringen; herbringen, mitbringen, überbringen, herbeischaffen, (her)führen; – ***about,*** zuwege *or* zustande bringen, veranlassen, verursachen, hervorrufen, bewerkstelligen; (*Naut.*) umdrehen; (*Law*) – ***an action against him,*** ihn verklagen, ihn gerichtlich belangen, ihn unter Anklage stellen; – ***away,*** wegbringen, wegschaffen; – ***back,*** zurückbringen; – ***back to life,*** ins Leben zurückrufen; – ***it back to mind,*** sich dessen entsinnen; – ***down,*** herunterbringen *or* –holen; erlegen (*game*), abschießen, niederholen (*an aircraft*); (*fig.*) – ***down the house,*** stürmischen Beifall hervorrufen; – ***down prices,*** die Preise herabsetzen; ***his illness has brought him down greatly,*** seine Krankheit hat ihn sehr geschwächt *or* entkräftet *or* heruntergebracht; – ***down*** (*punishment etc.*) ***upon him,*** auf ihn laden; – ***forth,*** hervorbringen, ans Licht bringen, mit sich bringen; gebären (*children*), werfen (*animals*); – ***forward,*** vorwärtsbringen, fördern; vorbringen, beibringen (*excuses etc.*), anführen, zitieren (*reasons, suggestions etc.*); (*Comm.*) vortragen, übertragen; – ***home to him,*** ihm klarmachen *or* nahebringen *or* eindringlich erklären *or* vorstellen, ihm zu Gemüte führen; ihn überzeugen von; (*sl.*) – ***home the bacon,*** Erfolg haben; – ***in,*** hereinbringen, hineinbringen, einführen; einbringen (*money, a bill*), abwerfen (*profit*); – ***him in guilty,*** ihn für schuldig erklären *or* erkennen; – ***him in not guilty,*** ihn freisprechen; – ***into accord,*** in Übereinstimmung bringen; – ***into notice,*** bekanntmachen; – ***into play,*** in Gang bringen; – ***into the world,*** erzeugen, zur Welt bringen; – ***off,*** fortbringen, wegschaffen; (*coll.*) zustande bringen, fertigbringen, schaffen; – ***on,*** heranbringen, herbeiführen, verursachen, veranlassen; – ***out,*** herausbringen, in die Gesellschaft einführen (*a young lady*); aufdecken, enthüllen, zutage treten lassen, an den Tag bringen; zu Gehör bringen, erweisen; hervorheben, hervortreten lassen (*contrast, colour etc.*); herausgeben, veröffentlichen, verlegen (*a book*); auf den Markt bringen (*wares*); – ***over,*** herüberbringen, herüberziehen; – ***him over to one's own way of thinking,*** ihn umstimmen *or* zu seiner eigenen Meinung bekehren, ihn für die eigene Meinung gewinnen; – ***round,*** wiederherstellen, wieder zu sich *or* zu Bewußtsein bringen; bekehren, umstimmen, überreden, (*coll.*) herumkriegen (*s.o. with differing views*); vorfahren (*a car*); ***I will – it round tomorrow,*** ich bringe es morgen herüber; – ***through,*** durchbringen; wiederherstellen; (*Naut.*) – ***to,*** beidrehen; – ***to account,*** in Rechnung stellen, (*fig.*) *see* – ***to book***; – ***to bear,*** anwenden, anbringen, zur Geltung bringen, wirken lassen; ***be brought to bed*** (***of a son***), (von einem Sohne) entbunden werden; – ***to book,*** zur Rechenschaft ziehen; – ***to a close,*** zum Abschluß bringen; ***I cannot – myself to do it,*** ich kann es nicht über mich *or* übers Herz bringen *or* ich bringe mich nicht dazu *or* dahin, es zu tun; – ***to a head,*** zur Entscheidung bringen; – ***to heel,*** zur Strecke bringen; – ***him to*** (***himself***), ihn wieder zu sich bringen; – ***to an issue,*** zum Austrag bringen; – ***him to justice,*** ihn gerichtlich belangen; – ***to life,*** Leben verleihen (*Dat.*) (*a th.*); – ***to light,*** ans Licht bringen, aufdecken; – ***to*** (***one's***) ***mind,*** (sich) erinnern an (*Acc.*); – ***s.th. to his notice,*** ihm etwas bekanntmachen, ihn mit etwas bekannt machen; – ***to pass,*** zustande bringen, in die Tat umsetzen, geschehen lassen; – ***him to his senses,*** ihn zur Vernunft bringen; – ***to subjection,*** unterwerfen; – ***together,*** zusammenbringen, (*fig.*) versöhnen; – ***things under one heading,*** Sachen in einer Gruppe einschließen; – ***up,*** hinaufbringen, heraufbringen, heranschaffen (*a th.*), vorbringen, anführen, zur Sprache bringen (*a subject*), erziehen, aufziehen (*a* *child*), einsetzen, heraufführen (*troops*); ausbrechen, herausbrechen (*food*); aufhalten, zum Stehen *or* Halten *or* Stillstand bringen (*s.th. moving*); (*Naut.*) vor Anker legen; – ***up the rear,*** (*Mil.*) den Nachtrab bilden, den Rückzug decken; (*fig.*) der letzte sein; – ***up to date,*** auf den gegenwärtigen Stand bringen; – ***upon o.s.,*** sich (*Dat.*) zuziehen, auf sich (*Acc.*) laden, heraufbeschwören.

brink [briŋk], *s.* der Rand, die Kante; der Bord, das Ufer; ***on the – of,*** kurz *or* dicht vor, nahe (*Dat.*); ***on the – of doing,*** im Begriff sein zu tun; ***hover on the –,*** unschlüssig sein. **brinkmanship,** *s.* (*coll.*) politische Seiltanzerei.

briny ['braini], **1.** *adj.* salzig. **2.** *s.* (*coll.*) die See.

briquet(te) [bri'ket], *s.* das Brikett, die Preßkohle.

brisk [brisk], **1.** *adj.* lebhaft, frisch, munter, rege, flink, flott; schäumend, perlend, moussierend (*as beer*); – ***sale*** or ***trade,*** flotter Absatz. **2.** *v.i.* (*coll.*) – ***up,*** munter werden. **3.** *v.t.* beleben, anfeuern, anregen, aufheitern, aufmuntern.

brisket ['briskit], *s.* das Bruststück (*of meat*).

briskness ['brisknis], *s.* die Lebhaftigkeit, Flottheit, Munterkeit.

brisling ['brisliŋ], *s.* (*Ichth.*) die Sprotte.

bristle [brisl], **1.** *s.* die Borste (*also Bot.*). **2.** *v.i.* sich sträuben; – (***up***), auffahren; – ***with,*** strotzen *or* starren vor (*Dat.*) *or* von. **bristled,** *adj.* borstig, stachelig. **bristly,** *adj. See* **bristled**; (*coll., fig.*) kratzbürstig.

Britain ['britən], *s.* Britannien (*n.*). **British,** *adj.* britisch. **Britisher,** *s.* (*Am.*) der (die) Engländer(in). **Briton** ['britən], *s.* der Brite (die Britin); (*Hist.*) Britannier.

Brittany ['britəni], *s.* Bretagne (*f.*).

brittle [britl], *adj.* spröde, brüchig, bröckelig, zerbrechlich. **brittleness,** *s.* die Sprödigkeit, Spröde, Brüchigkeit, Zerbrechlichkeit.

broach [broutʃ], **1.** *s.* (*Cul.*) der Bratspieß; (*Archit.*) (achteckige) Turmspitze; (*Mech.*) die (Räum)ahle, der Pfriem; (Zieh)dorn (*of a lock*). **2.** *v.t.* 1. anzapfen, anbohren (*a cask etc.*); (aus)bohren (*a hole*); 2. (*fig.*) das Gespräch bringen auf (*Acc.*), aufs Tapet *or* (als erste(r)) zur Sprache bringen (*a subject*). **3.** *v.i.* (*Naut.*) – ***to,*** querschlagen.

broad [brɔ:d], **1.** *adj.* breit, weit, ausgedehnt; (*fig.*) frei, derb, grob, plump; umfassend, umfangreich; ***in – daylight,*** am hellen *or* hellichten Tag; – ***hint,*** der Wink mit dem Zaunpfahl; – ***joke,*** derber Spaß; ***it's as – as it's long,*** es läuft auf eins hinaus, es kommt auf eins heraus, es ist eins wie das andere; ***in – outlines,*** in großen Zügen, in groben Umrissen; ***in – Scots,*** im (ausgeprägt) schottischen Dialekt; ***in the –est possible sense,*** im allerweitesten Sinn; – ***stare,*** dreistes Angaffen, frecher Blick; – ***sympathies,*** weitreichende Sympathien; – ***views,*** aufgeklärte *or* weitherzige *or* großzügige *or* liberale *or* tolerante Ansichten. **2.** *s.* 1. breiter *or* Teil; (*Geog.*) ***the Broads,*** Binnenseen Ostenglands; 2. (*obs., Am.*) das Frauenzimmer, Weib; 3. *pl.* (*sl.*) Spielkarten.

broad| arrow, *s.* breitköpfiger Pfeil. **––axe,** *s.* die Streitaxt, das Breitbeil. **––bean,** *s.* die Saubohne. **––brimmed,** *adj.* breitkrempig, breitrandig (*as a hat*). **––built,** *adj.* breitgebaut; breitschult(e)rig, untersetzt.

broadcast ['brɔ:dkɑ:st], **1.** *v.t.* 1. breitwürfig säen, (*fig.*) verbreiten, ausstreuen; 2. durch Rundfunk verbreiten, im Radio übertragen, senden, ausstrahlen. **2.** *v.i.* im Rundfunk sprechen *or* singen *etc.* **3.** *s.* 1. die Breitsaat; 2. das Rundfunkprogramm, die (Rundfunk)sendung *or* –übertragung; ***schools –,*** der Schulfunk. **4.** *adj., adv.* 1. mit der Hand gesät; ausgestreut, weit verbreitet; ***sow –,*** breitwürfig säen; 2. Rundfunk –; ***advertising,*** der Werbefunk; – ***programme,*** das Rundfunkprogramm; – ***receiver,*** der Radioempfänger. **broadcaster,** *s.* der Sänger *or* Vortragende *etc.* am Rundfunk. **broadcasting,** *s.* der Rundfunk, das Radio; die Rundfunkübertragung; – ***station,*** der Sender; – ***studio,*** der Senderaum.

broadcloth ['brɔ:dklɔθ], *s.* feiner Wollstoff.

broaden [brɔ:dn], **1.** *v.t.* breiter machen, verbreitern, erweitern, ausdehnen. **2.** *v.i.* breiter werden, sich weiten *or* erweitern. **broadening,** *s.* die Verbreiterung.

broad|-gauge(d), *adj.* (*Railw.*) breitspurig (*more than 1,435 mm.*). **–jump,** *s.* (*Spt.*) der Weitsprung. **broadly,** *adv.* allgemein; – ***speaking,*** allgemein gesprochen. **broad|-minded,** *adj.* weitherzig, tolerant, liberal (gesinnt), großzügig, duldsam. **––mindedness,** *s.* die Weitherzigkeit, Großzügigkeit, liberale Gesinnung. **broadness,** *s.* die Derbheit, Grobheit, Anstößigkeit, Schlüpfrigkeit. **broad|sheet,** *s.* das Flugblatt, Plakat. **––shouldered,** *adj.* breitschult(e)rig. **–side,** *s.* (*Naut.*) die Breitseite, Abfeuerung aller Geschütze der Breitseite; (*coll.*) schimpfliche Anwürfe (*pl.*), die Schimpfkanonade; – ***on,*** mit der Breitseite zugekehrt (*to, Dat.*). **–sword,** *s.* der Säbel, breites Schwert. **–ways, –wise,** *adv.* der Breite nach.

brocade [bro'keid], *s.* der Brokat. **brocaded,** *adj.* mit Brokat geschmückt.

broccoli ['brɔkəli], *s.* der Spargelkohl, Brokkoli (*pl.*).

brochure [brɔ'ʃuə, 'brouʃə], *s.* die Broschüre, Flugschrift.

brock [brɔk], *s.* der Dachs.

brocket ['brɔkit], *s.* der Spießer, zweijähriger Hirsch.

brogue [broug], *s.* 1. derber Schuh (mit Lochmuster); 2. irischer Akzent; ausgeprägt dialektische Aussprache.

[1]**broil** [brɔil], *s.* der Lärm, Streit, Zank, Tumult, die Zwistigkeit.

[2]**broil,** **1.** *v.t.* auf dem Roste braten, rösten. **2.** *v.i.* (*coll.*) (in der Sonne) schmoren. **broiler,** *s.* das Brathuhn, Brathühnchen. **broiling,** *adj.* (*coll.*) glühend *or* brennend heiß; (*Cul.*) – ***hot,*** kochend heiß.

broke [brouk], **1.** *imperf. of* **break.** **2.** *pred. adj.* (*sl.*) (***stony***) –, abgebrannt, pleite.

broken [broukn], **1.** *p.p. of* **break.** **2.** *adj.* gebrochen, zerbrochen, (*coll.*) kaputt; angebrochen, unterbrochen, fehlerhaft, unvollständig, fragmentarisch; zerrüttet; bankrott, ruiniert; (*Phonet.*) diphthongiert; – ***English,*** gebrochenes Englisch; – ***glass,*** zerbrochenes Glas; – ***ground,*** unebenes Gelände; – ***health,*** geschwächte *or* zerrüttete Gesundheit; – ***heart,*** gebrochenes Herz; – ***home,*** zerrüttete Familie; – ***horse,*** zugerittenes Pferd; – ***man,*** ein gebrochener Mann; – ***meat,*** übriggebliebene Speisen, Speisereste, Brocken (*pl.*); (*fig.*) – ***reed,*** schwankendes Rohr; – ***sleep,*** unterbrochener Schlaf, gestörte Ruhe; – ***spirit,*** niedergeschlagener Geist; – ***stones,*** der Steinschlag; – ***time,*** der Verdienstausfall; die Kurzarbeit; – ***week,*** unvollständige *or* angebrochene Arbeitswoche.

broken|-backed, *adj.* (*Naut.*) kielbrüchig, (*pred. only*) mit einem Katzenrücken. **––down,** *adj.* zusammengebrochen, niedergebrochen; heruntergekommen, verfallen, unbrauchbar, ruiniert, (*Chem. etc.*) zersetzt. **––hearted,** *adj.* verzweifelt, niedergeschlagen, mit gebrochenem Herzen. **––spirited,** *adj.* entmutigt, seelisch gebrochen. **––winded,** *adj.* (*Vet.*) dämpfig, kurzatmig. **––winged,** *adj.* fügellahm.

broker ['broukə], *s.* der Makler, Agent, Vermittler, Unterhändler, Zwischenhändler, Mittelsmann, Kommissionär; Trödler, Pfandleiher. **brokerage** [–ridʒ], *s.* die Maklergebühr, Provision, Courtage; das Maklergeschäft.

brolly ['brɔli], *s.* (*sl.*) *see* **umbrella.**

bromate ['broumeit], *s.* bromsaures Salz, das Bromat. **bromic,** *adj.* bromhaltig; – ***acid,*** die Bromsäure. **bromide** [–aid], *s.* 1. das Bromid; (*Phot.*) – ***paper,*** das Bromsilberpapier; – ***of potassium,*** das Bromkali; 2. (*Am. sl.*) Phrasen (*pl.*), der Gemeinplatz, die Binsenwahrheit; der Phrasendrescher. **bromine** [–in], *s.* das Brom.

bronchia ['brɔŋkjə], *pl.* (*Anat.*) Bronchien (*pl.*). **bronchial,** *adj.* Luftröhren–, bronchial; – ***tube,*** die Luftröhre. **bronchitis** [–'kaitis], *s.* der Luftröhrenkatarrh. **bronchocele** [–kəsi:l], *s.* der Kropf.

bronco ['brɔŋkou], *s.* (*coll.*) wildes Pferd. **broncobuster,** *s.* (*coll.*) der Zureiter.

bronze [brɔnz], **1.** *s.* die Bronze; Bronzefigur; Bronzefarbe; – ***age,*** das Bronzezeitalter. **2.** *v.t.* bronzieren; ***his –d countenance,*** sein gebräuntes Gesicht.

brooch [broutʃ], *s.* die Brosche, Spange; Vorstecknadel.

brood [bru:d], **1.** *s.* die Brut; Hecke; (*fig.*) Sippe, das Geschlecht. **2.** *v.i.* brüten; (*fig.*) – ***on*** or ***over,*** brüten über (*Acc.*); – ***over,*** schwer lasten auf (*Dat.*). **brood|-hen,** *s.* die Bruthenne. **--mare,** *s.* die Zuchtstute. **broody,** *adj.* brütig (*of hens*).

[1]**brook** [bruk], *v.t.* (*always neg.*) (er)dulden, ertragen, sich (*Dat.*) gefallen lassen; – ***no delay,*** keinen Aufschub dulden.

[2]**brook,** *s.* der Bach. **brooklet,** *s.* das Bächlein.

[1]**broom** [bru:m], *s.* (*Bot.*) der Geißklee.

[2]**broom,** *s.* der Besen; (*fig.*) ***new*** –, der Auskehrer; (*Prov.*) ***a new – sweeps clean,*** neue Besen kehren gut. **broom|-handle, –stick,** *s.* der Besenstiel.

brose [brouz], *s.* (*Scots*) die Hafergrütze.

broth [brɔθ], *s.* die Fleischbrühe, Kraftbrühe, Bouillon; (*Irish*) – ***of a boy,*** famoser Kerl.

brothel [brɔθl], *s.* das Bordell, (*sl.*) der Puff.

brother ['brʌðə], *s.* der Bruder; (*fig.*) Mitmensch, Mitbruder, Amtsbruder, Kollege; – ***in arms,*** der Waffenbruder, Kriegskamerad, Kampfgenosse; – ***german,*** der Vollbruder; – ***officer,*** der Kamerad; ***–s and sisters,*** Geschwister (*pl.*); – ***in affliction,*** Leidensgefährte(r). **brotherhood,** *s.* (*Eccl.*) die Bruderschaft; (*relationship*) Brüderschaft. **–in-law,** *s.* der Schwager. **brotherliness,** *s.* die Brüderlichkeit. **brotherly,** *adj.* brüderlich.

brougham [bru:(ə)m], *s.* der Brougham, geschlossener (vierrädriger) Einspänner.

brought [brɔ:t], *imperf., p.p. of* **bring.**

brow [brau], *s.* die (Augen)braue; Stirn; Miene, das Aussehen; der Rand, Vorsprung (*of a cliff etc.*); ***knit*** or ***wrinkle one's*** –, die Stirn runzeln; ***by the sweat of one's*** –, im Schweiße seines Angesichts. **brow|-antlers,** *pl.* die Augensprosse. **–beat,** *irr. v.t.* einschüchtern, drohend anfahren.

brown [braun], **1.** *adj.* braun; (*of complexion*) gebräunt, bräunlich, brünett; ***as – as a berry,*** wie eine Kastanie gebräunt; – ***bread,*** das (Weizen)-schrotbrot; – ***coal,*** die Braunkohle; (*sl.*) ***do him*** –, ihn anschmieren *or* hereinlegen; (*Orn.*) – ***owl,*** der Waldkauz (*Strix aluco*); – ***paper,*** das Packpapier; ***in a – study,*** in tiefes Nachsinnen versunken, in Gedanken verloren; – ***sugar,*** der Sandzucker; – ***ware,*** das Steingut. **2.** *v.t.* (an)bräunen; (*Tech.*) braun beizen, brünieren; (*sl.*) ***be –ed off,*** die Nase voll haben, restlos bedient sein. **3.** *s.* das Braun.

brownie ['brauni], *s.* das Heinzelmännchen; junge Pfadfinderin, das Jungmädel.

browning ['brauniŋ], *s.* das Bräunen, die Bräunung, (*Tech.*) Brünierung. **brownish,** *adj.* bräunlich. **brownness,** *s.* die Bräune, braune Farbe. **brownshirt,** *s.* (*coll.*) der Nazi.

browse [brauz], **1.** *s.* junges Laub, junge Triebe (*pl.*); das Viehfutter. **2.** *v.t.* abäsen, abweiden, abgrasen, abfressen. **3.** *v.i.* grasen, weiden, äsen; (*fig.*) – ***in*** or ***through,*** durchblättern, schmökern in (*Dat.*) (*a book*).

Bruges [bru:ʒ], *s.* Brügge (*n.*).

Bruin ['bru:in], *s.* der Bär, (Meister) Braun.

bruise [bru:z], **1.** *v.t.* (zer)quetschen, zermalmen, zerreiben, zerstoßen; wund *or* braun und blau schlagen, (*fig.*) verletzen (*feelings etc.*); – ***malt,*** Malz schroten; ***–d malt,*** das Malzschrot. **2.** *s.* die Quetschung, Prellung, Kontusion, (*coll.*) blauer Fleck. **bruiser,** *s.* 1. (*Opt.*) die Schleifschale; 2. Presse, Quetsche; 3. (*sl.*) der Boxer, Preiskämpfer; Kraftmeier, Raufbold.

bruit [bru:t], **1.** *s.* (*obs.*) das Gerücht. **2.** *v.t.* verkünden, verbreiten, aussprengen.

brume [bru:m], *s.* (*Poet.*) der Nebel, Dunst.

brunch [brʌntʃ], *s.* (*coll.*) das Gabelfrühstück.

brunette [bru:'net], **1.** *s.* die Brünette. **2.** *adj.* brünett.

Brunswick ['brʌnzwik], *s.* Braunschweig (*n.*).

brunt [brʌnt], *s.* der Angriff, Anfall, Anprall; ***bear the*** –, der (ganzen) Wucht ausgesetzt sein.

brush [brʌʃ], **1.** *s.* 1. die Bürste, der Pinsel; Pinsel- *or* Bürstenstrich; das Abbürsten; 2. (*Hunt.*) die Rute, Lunte, buschiger Schweif, der Schwanz, Bruch; 3. das Unterholz, Gebüsch, Gestrüpp, Dickicht, Strauchwerk; 4. (*Mil.*) Scharmützel; (*Artil.*) die Lunte; (*coll.*) ***have a – with him,*** mit ihm aneinandergeraten; 5. (*Tech.*) (Kontakt- *or* Draht)bürste; der Stromabnehmer; (*Elec.*) elektrische Entladung, das Strahlenbüschel. **2.** *v.t.* (ab)bürsten, abwischen, kehren, fegen; (*fig.*) leicht berühren, streifen; – ***off,*** abbürsten, wegbürsten, wegfegen, wegwischen; (*sl. fig.*) rausschmeißen, abfertigen (*a p.*); – ***on one side,*** beiseite schieben; (*fig.*) – ***up,*** auffrischen (*one's memory etc.*). **3.** *v.i.* – ***by*** or ***past,*** vorbeieilen.

brush|-discharge, *s.* (*Elec.*) die Glimmentladung. **--down,** *s.* (*coll.*) ***give me a*** –, bürsten Sie mich ab! – **off,** *s.* (*sl.*) ***get the*** –, eine Abfuhr erleiden, die Entlassung *or* eine Absage *or* Weigerung bekommen. **--proof,** *s.* (*Typ.*) der Bürstenabzug. **--up,** *s.* (*coll.*) das Reinigen, Abbürsten. **–wood,** *s.* das Dickicht, Gestrüpp, Unterholz; Reisig. **–work,** *s.* (*Paint.*) die Pinselführung.

brusque [brusk], *adj.* barsch, schroff, kurz angebunden, brüsk. **brusqueness,** *s.* die Barschheit, Schroffheit.

Brussels [brʌslz], *s.* Brüssel (*n.*); – ***lace,*** Brüsseler Spitzen (*pl.*); ***Brussels or Brussel sprouts,*** der Rosenkohl.

brutal [bru:tl], *adj.* unmenschlich, brutal, roh, tierisch, viehisch. **brutality** [–'tæliti], *s.* die Unmenschlichkeit, Roheit, Brutalität. **brutalization** [–lai'zeiʃən], *s.* die Verrohung, Verwilderung. **brutalize** [–laiz], **1.** *v.t.* brutal *or* unmenschlich *or* roh behandeln, zum Tier machen. **2.** *v.i.* unmenschlich *or* tierisch werden, vertieren.

brute [bru:t], **1.** *s.* unvernünftiges Wesen, das Tier, Vieh; (*fig.*) der Unmensch, brutaler *or* roher Mensch, Rohling, das Untier, Scheusal. **2.** *adj.* tierisch; gefühllos, roh; unvernünftig, sinnlos, seelenlos; – ***force,*** rohe Gewalt. **brutish,** *adj.* tierisch, viehisch; (*fig.*) roh, vertiert; – ***pleasures,*** fleischliche Lüste. **brutishness,** *s.* die Roheit, Sinnlichkeit.

bryony ['braiəni], *s.* (*Bot.*) die Zaunrübe.

bubble [bʌbl], **1.** *s.* die Blase, Luftblase, Seifenblase (*also fig.*); (*fig.*) leerer Schein, der Schaum; Schwindel, das Schwindelgeschäft, betrügerisches *or* unsolides Unternehmen; ***rise in –s,*** wallen, sprudeln; (*Hist.*) ***South Sea*** –, der Südseeschwindel; (*sl.*) – ***and squeak,*** zusammen gebratene Kartoffeln- und Kohlreste; – ***bath,*** das Schaumbad; (*coll.*) – ***car,*** der Kleinstwagen, Kabinenroller; – ***company,*** die Schwindelgesellschaft; (*coll.*) – ***gum,*** der Knallkaugummi. **2.** *v.i.* (auf)-wallen, Blasen aufwerfen, schäumen, perlen, sprudeln, brodeln; (*fig.*) – ***over with,*** übersprudeln vor (*Dat.*). **bubbly, 1.** *adj.* sprudelnd, perlend, voller Blasen. **2.** *s.* (*sl.*) der Champagner.

bubo ['bju:bou], *s.* (*Med.*) die Lymphdrüsenschwellung, Leistenbeule. **bubonic** [–'bɔnik], *adj.* – ***plague,*** die Beulenpest. **bubonocele** [–'bounosi:l], *s.* der Leistenbruch.

buccaneer [bʌkə'niə], **1.** *s.* der Seeräuber, Freibeuter. **2.** *v.i.* Seeräuberei betreiben. **buccaneering,** *s.* die Seeräuberei.

Bucharest [bju:kə'rest], *s.* Bukarest (*n.*).

[1]**buck** [bʌk], **1.** *s.* 1. (*Zool.*) der Bock (*also Gymn.*); Rehbock; Ziegenbock; das Männchen (*of rabbits etc.*); 2. (*obs.*) der Stutzer, Geck, Lebemann, Modeheld; 3. (*sl.*) ***pass the*** –, sich (von der Verantwortung) drücken. **2.** *v.t.* – ***off,*** abwerfen (*horseman*); – ***up,*** aufmuntern, aufmöbeln. **3.** *v.i.* bocken (*as a horse*); (*sl.*) bockig sein; (*coll.*) – ***up,*** **1.** *v.i.* 1. sich beeilen; 2. sich zusammenraffen,

zusammenreißen *or* aufrappeln; (*coll.*) – ***up!*** 1. mach schnell! 2. Kopf hoch!

[2]**buck, 1.** *s.* (*obs.*) die Lauge, Beuche. **2.** *v.t.* (*obs.*) beuchen.

[3]**buck,** *s.* (*Am. sl.*) der Dollar.

buck|bean, *s.* (*Bot.*) der Sumpfklee. **–board,** *s.* (*Am.*) einfacher (vierrädriger) Wagen.

bucket ['bʌkit], **1.** *s.* 1. der Eimer, Kübel; (*sl.*) ***kick the –***, ins Gras beißen; 2. (*Naut.*) die Pütz(e); 3. (*Mil.*) der Lanzenschuh; 4. Pumpenkolben. **2.** *v.i.* schlecht reiten *or* rudern. **bucket| conveyor,** *s.* das Becherwerk. – **dredger,** *s.* der Löffelbagger. **bucketful,** *s.* der Eimervoll; ***in –s,*** eimerweise. **bucket| seat,** *s.* (*Motor.*) der Schalensitz. **--shop,** *s.* die Winkelbörse. **--wheel,** *s.* das Zellenrad, Schöpfrad.

buckle [bʌkl], **1.** *s.* 1. die Schnalle, Spange, (*Mil.*) das Koppelschloß; 2. der Knick, die Stauchung. **2.** *v.t.* 1. (zu)schnallen; – ***on,*** anschnallen, umschnallen; – ***up,*** zuschnallen; 2. biegen, krümmen (*a wheel etc.*). **3.** *v.i.* einknicken, sich krümmen, sich verziehen *or* (ver)biegen; (*coll.*) – (***down***) ***to a th.***, sich eifrig *or* ernstlich an eine S. machen, tüchtig daran gehen.

buckler ['bʌklə], *s.* kleiner runder Schild.

[1]**buckling** ['bʌkliŋ], *s.* (*Tech.*) die Knickung, Stauchung, das Krümmen, Verziehen; – ***load,*** die Knicklast; – ***strength,*** die Knickfestigkeit.

[2]**buckling,** *s.* (*Ichth.*) der Bückling.

buckram ['bʌkrəm], *s.* das Steifleinen, der Buckram; (*fig.*) die Steifheit, Geziertheit, Förmlichkeit.

buckshee ['bʌkʃi:], *adj.* (*sl.*) gratis, kostenfrei, (*pred. only*) umsonst.

buck|shot, *s.* der Rehposten, grober Schrot. **–skin,** *s.* das Rehfell, Wildleder. **–thorn,** *s.* (*Bot.*) der Wegedorn, Kreuzdorn. – **tooth,** *s.* (*coll.*) vorstehender Zahn. **–wheat,** *s.* der Buchweizen.

bucolic [bju:'kɔlik], **1.** *adj.* ländlich, idyllisch, bukolisch, Hirten–; – ***poetry,*** die Hirtendichtung, Schäferdichtung. **2.** *s.* (*usu. pl.*) das Hirtengedicht, die Idylle.

bud [bʌd], **1.** *s.* (*Bot.*) die Knospe, das Auge, (*Zool.*) der Keim; ***in –***, in der Knospe; (*fig.*) ***in the –***, im Keim, im Entstehen; ***nipped in the –***, im Keime erstickt. **2.** *v.i.* Knospen treiben, knospen, keimen, sprossen, (*fig.*) sich entwickeln (***into***, zu (*Dat.*)); aufblühen, heranreifen; – ***off,*** entstehen (***from***, aus); ***budding love,*** aufkeimende Liebe; ***budding scholar,*** angehender Gelehrter. **3.** *v.t.* (*Hort.*) pfropfen, äugeln, okulieren.

buddle [bʌdl], **1.** *s.* der Schlämmgraben, Schlämmtrog. **2.** *v.t.* waschen, schlämmen (*ore*).

buddy ['bʌdi], *s.* (*sl.*) (*Am.*) der Kamerad, Genosse, Kumpan, Kumpel.

budge [bʌdʒ], **1.** *v.i.* (*coll.*) sich rühren *or* regen, sich (von der Stelle) bewegen. **2.** *v.t.* (*coll.*) (*usu. neg.*) vom Fleck bewegen.

budgerigar ['bʌdʒəriga:], *s.* der Wellensittich.

budget ['bʌdʒit], **1.** *s.* (*Parl.*) der Haushaltsplan, Etat, Staatshaushalt, das Budget; (*fig.*) der Vorrat, Inhalt; – ***of news,*** der Stoß Neuigkeiten; ***open the –***, den Haushaltsplan vorlegen. **2.** *v.i.* – ***for,*** im Budget vorsehen, (*coll.*) rechnen mit.

budgie ['bʌdʒi], *s.* (*coll.*) *see* **budgerigar.**

buff [bʌf], **1.** *s.* das Büffelleder, Sämischleder; (*colour*) Braungelb, die Lederfarbe; (*coll.*) bloße Haut; ***in –***, nackt. **2.** *adj.* ledergelb, lederfarben, isabellfarbig; – ***coat,*** – ***jerkin,*** der Lederkoller. **3.** *v.t.* mit Leder polieren.

buffalo ['bʌfəlou], *s.* der Büffel. **buffalo|-grass,** *s.* das Ellengras. **--hide,** *s.* das Büffelfell.

buffer ['bʌfə], *s.* der Puffer, Prellbock; Stoßdämpfer, die Stoßscheibe, das Stoßpolster; (*sl.*) ***old –***, alter Tropf. **buffer| amplifier,** *s.* (*Rad.*) der Trennverstärker. – **state,** *s.* der Pufferstaat. **--stop,** *s.* der Anschlagblock, Prellbock.

[1]**buffet** ['bʌfit], **1.** *s.* der Puff, Stoß, (Faust)schlag; ***–s of fate,*** Schicksalsschläge (*pl.*). **2.** *v.t.* puffen, stoßen, (mit der Faust) schlagen; (*fig.*) ankämpfen gegen, bekämpfen.

[2]**buffet** ['bufei], *s.* das Büfett, der Schenktisch; Kredenztisch, die Anrichte; das Selbstbedienungsrestaurant; (*Railw.*) – ***car,*** der Büfettwagen.

buffeting ['bʌfitiŋ], *s.* der Anprall, Stöße (*pl.*), Schläge (*pl.*).

buffing ['bʌfiŋ], *s.* der Nachschliff, das Polieren. **buffing wheel,** *s.* die Schwabbelscheibe.

buffoon [bə'fu:n], *s.* der Possenreißer, Spaßmacher, Narr, Hanswurst. **buffoonery,** *s.* Possen (*pl.*), das Possenreißen.

bug [bʌg], **1.** *s.* 1. (*Ent.*) die Wanze; (*Am.*) das Insekt, der Käfer; (*coll.*) Bazillus, die Bakterie; 2. (*sl.*) Panne, technische Störung; 3. (*sl.*) ***big –***, großes *or* hohes Tier, der Bonze; 4. (*Am. sl.*) ***be a – on,*** verrückt sein nach, Fanatiker sein über (*Acc.*). **2.** *v.t.* (*sl.*) eine Abhöranlage einbauen in (*Acc.*) (*a room*).

bugbear ['bʌgbɛə], *s.* der Popanz, das Schreckgespenst.

bugger ['bʌgə], **1.** *s.* (*Law*) der Sodomit; (*vulg.*) Lump, Schuft. **2.** *v.t.* Unzucht treiben mit. **buggery,** *s.* die Unzucht, Sodomie.

[1]**buggy** ['bʌgi], *adj.* verwanzt.

[2]**buggy,** *s.* zwei– (*Am.* vier)rädriger Einspänner.

bug|house, *s.* (*sl.*) die Klapsmühle. – **hunter,** *s.* (*coll.*) der Käfersammler.

[1]**bugle** [bju:gl], *s.* das Jagdhorn.

[2]**bugle,** *s.* die Schmelzperle, (schwarze) Glasperle.

[3]**bugle,** *s.* (*Bot.*) der Günsel.

bugle|-call, *s.* das Hornsignal. – **horn,** *s.* *See* **bugle. bugler,** *s.* der Hornist.

bugloss ['bju:glɔs], *s.* (*Bot.*) der Natternkopf (*Echium vulgare*); ***dyer's*** or ***Spanish –***, die Ochsenzunge (*Anchusa tinctoria*).

buhl(-work) ['bu:l–], *s.* eingelegte Arbeit.

build [bild], **1.** *irr.v.t.* 1. bauen; erbauen, errichten, aufbauen, konstruieren; – ***a fire,*** ein Feuer anrichten; – ***castles in the air,*** Luftschlösser bauen; – ***one's hopes on,*** seine Hoffnungen gründen auf (*Acc.*); 2. (*fig.*) – ***up,*** aufbauen, gründen; – ***up a case,*** Argumente zusammenstellen; – ***up a reputation,*** sich einen Namen machen; (*Elec.*) – ***up the current,*** den Strom einschwingen *or* aufschaukeln. **2.** *irr.v.i.* – ***up to,*** entwickeln zu; – ***upon,*** bauen *or* sich stützen *or* sich verlassen auf (*Acc.*). **3.** *s.* der Bau, Schnitt, Stil, die Form, Gestalt, Bauart; (*of a p.*) der Körperbau, die Figur. **builder,** *s.* der Baumeister, Bauunternehmer; Erbauer.

building ['bildiŋ], *s.* das (Er)bauen, Errichten; Bauwesen; Gebäude, Bauwerk, der Bau; ***public –***, öffentliches Gebäude; öffentliches Bauprogramm. **building|-contract,** *s.* der Baukontrakt. **--contractor,** *s.* der Bauunternehmer. **--line,** *s.* die Bauflucht, Fluchtlinie. **--lot,** *s.* *See* **--plot. --material,** *s.* das Baumaterial, der Baustoff. **--plot,** *s.* das Baugrundstück, die Bauparzelle. **--site,** *s.* der Bauplatz, die Baustelle. – **society,** *s.* die Bausparkasse, Baugenossenschaft. – **trade,** *s.* das Baugewerbe.

build-up, *s.* 1. der Aufbau; 2. (*fig.*) die Propaganda.

built [bilt], **1.** *imperf., p.p. of* **build. 2.** *adj.* gebaut, geformt, konstruiert; (*coll.*) ***I'm – that way,*** ich bin eben so. **built|-in,** *adj.* Einbau–, eingebaut (*furniture etc.*). **--up,** *adj.* zusammengesetzt; – ***area,*** bebautes Gelände, geschlossene Ortschaft; – ***gun,*** die Ringkanone.

bulb [bʌlb], *s.* (*Bot.*) die Zwiebel, Knolle, der Knollen; die Wurzel (*of hair etc.*); Kugel (*of thermometer*); der Apfel (*of the eye*); (Glas)kolben; (***electric light***) –, die (Glüh)birne. **bulbous** [–əs], *adj.* zwiebelförmig, zwiebelartig, knollig; – ***root,*** die Knollenwurzel.

bulge [bʌldʒ], **1.** *v.i.* (*also – out*) hervortreten, hervorragen, hervorstehen, vorspringen, sich ausbauchen, sich bauschen, sich aufblähen, anschwellen. **2.** *s.* die Anschwellung, Ausbuchtung, Ausbauchung; Rundung, der Bauch (*of a cask*); (*Mil.*) Frontvorsprung; (*fig. coll.*) das (An)steigen,

Anwachsen, Anschwellen (*of birth-rate, students etc.*). **bulginess,** *s.* die Bauchigkeit. **bulgy,** *adj.* bauchig, (an)geschwollen.

bulk [bʌlk], **1.** *s.* der Umfang, die Größe, Masse, Menge, das Volumen; der Hauptteil, Großteil, größerer Teil, die Hauptmenge, Hauptmasse, Mehrzahl; (*Naut.*) lose *or* unverpackte (Schiffs)-ladung; (*Naut.*) ***break –,*** zu löschen anfangen; ***in –,*** lose, unverpackt; (*coll.*) ***in*** or ***by –,*** in großen Mengen; ***in the –,*** in Bausch und Bogen; ***– purchase,*** der Masseneinkauf. **2.** *v.i.* Umfang *or* Bedeutung haben, umfangreich *or* wichtig sein; ***– large,*** großen Umfang haben, (*fig.*) eine wichtige Rolle spielen. **3.** *v.t.* aufhäufen, aufstapeln; (*coll.*) ***– everything together,*** alles zusammennehmen.

bulk|-cargo, *s.* (*Naut.*) das Schüttgut. **--goods,** *pl.* Massengüter (*pl.*).

bulkhead ['bʌlkhed], *s.* (*Naut.*) das Schott.

bulkiness ['bʌlkinis], *s.* die Größe, (großer) Umfang. **bulky,** *adj.* groß, massig, umfangreich, voluminös; unhandlich, sperrig; ***– goods,*** das Sperrgut.

[1]**bull** [bul], **1.** *s.* 1. der Stier, Bulle; ***like a – in a china-shop,*** wie ein Elephant im Porzellanladen; ***take the – by the horns,*** den Stier bei *or* an den Hörnern fassen; 2. (*Comm.*) der Haussier, Haussespekulant. **2.** *v.i.* (*Comm.*) auf Hausse spekulieren. **3.** *v.t.* (*Comm.*) (die Preise (*Gen. or* für)) in die Höhe treiben.

[2]**bull,** *s.* (*R.C.*) päpstliche Bulle.

[3]**bull,** *s.* (***Irish –***) der Unsinn, die Ungereimtheit, der Kalauer.

bullace ['buləs], *s.* (*Bot.*) die Krieche, Haferschlehe.

bull|-baiting, *s.* die Stierhetze. **–dog,** *s.* 1. die Bulldogge, der Bullenbeißer; 2. (*fig.*) Starrkopf; 3. (*sl.*) Universitätsdiener. **–doze,** *v.t.* (*sl.*) einschüchtern. **–dozer,** *s.* der Erdbagger, die Planierraupe, Schuttramme; Panzerschaufel.

bullet ['bulit], *s.* das Geschoß, die Kugel; ***armour-piercing –,*** das Panzergeschoß, Stahlkerngeschoß; ***explosive –,*** das Sprenggeschoß; ***incendiary –,*** das Brandkerngeschoß; ***spent –,*** matte Kugel; ***tracer –,*** das Leuchtspurgeschoß; (*Prov.*) ***every – has its billet,*** jede Kugel hat ihre Bestimmung. **bullet|-headed,** *adj.* rundköpfig. **--hole,** *s.* das Schußloch.

bulletin ['bulitin], *s.* das Bulletin, der Tagesbericht, (kurze) Bekanntmachung.

bullet-proof, *adj.* kugelsicher, kugelfest, schußsicher; ***– glass,*** das Panzerglas.

bull|fight, *s.* der Stierkampf. **–fighter,** *s.* der Stierkämpfer. **–finch,** *s.* 1. (*Orn.*) der Dompfaff, Gimpel (*Pyrrhula pyrrhula*); 2. die (Grenz)hecke. **–frog,** *s.* der Ochsenfrosch, Brüllfrosch. **–head,** *s.* (*Ichth.*) der Kaulkopf. **--headed,** *adj.* dickköpfig, hartnäckig, dumm.

bullion ['buljən], *s.* der Münzbarren, ungemünztes Edelmetall; die Franse, Gold- *or* Silberschnur.

bull-necked, *adj.* stiernackig.

bullock ['bulək], *s.* der Ochse.

bullring ['bulriŋ], *s.* die Stierkampfarena.

bull's-eye, *s.* (*Naut.*) die Blendlaterne; das Ochsenauge, Bullauge; (*of target*) Zentrum, Schwarze; der Kernschuß, Schuß ins Schwarze; (*Opt.*) die Konvexlinse; Pfefferminzkugel; ***– pane,*** die Butzenscheibe; ***hit the –,*** ins Schwarze treffen (*also fig.*).

bullshit ['bulʃit], *s.* (*sl.*) krasser Unsinn.

bully ['buli], **1.** *s.* 1. der Raufbold, Renommist; Schinder, Tyrann (*among schoolboys*); 2. (*Hockey*) Abschlag; 3. (*coll.*) *see* **bully beef. 2.** *v.t.* tyrannisieren, unterdrücken, einschüchtern, drangsalieren, schurigeln, kujonieren. **3.** *v.i.* (*Hockey*) (***– off***) abschlagen. **4.** *adj.* (*sl.*) famos, erstklassig, prima. **bully beef,** *s.* (*coll.*) das Büchsenfleisch.

bulrush ['bulrʌʃ], *s.* (*Bot.*) die Teich- *or* Sumpfbinse.

bulwark ['bulwək], *s.* das Bollwerk (*also fig.*), der Wall, die Bastei, Verschanzung; (*Naut.*) das Schanzkleid, die Reling; (*fig.*) der Schutz, Halt, die Stütze.

bum [bʌm], **1.** *s.* 1. (*vulg.*) der Hintere, Hintern, Steiß, das Gesäß; 2. (*Am. sl.*) der Landstreicher, Stromer, Schnorrer; (*Am. sl.*) ***on the –,*** auf der Walze. **2.** *v.i.* (*Am. sl.*) vagabundieren, herumlungern, faulenzen, schmarotzen, schnorren. **3.** *adj.* (*Am. sl.*) mies. **bum-bailiff,** *s.* der Büttel, Scherge, Gerichtsdiener.

bumble-bee ['bʌmblbi:], *s.* die Hummel.

bumbledom ['bʌmbldəm], *s.* (*coll.*) die Wichtigtuerei, der Beamtendünkel.

bum-boat, *s.* das Proviantboot.

bumf [bʌmf], *s.* (*vulg.*) das Klosettpapier; (*sl.*) der Wisch, Papierkram.

bump [bʌmp], **1.** *s.* 1. der Schlag, Stoß, Puff, (*coll.*) Bums; die Beule; ***nasty – on the head,*** böse Beule am Kopf; 2. (*Phrenology*) der Höcker (am Schädel), (*coll.*) Sinn, das Organ (***of,*** für); ***– of locality,*** der Ortssinn, Orientierungssinn. **2.** *v.t.* stoßen, schlagen (***against,*** gegen; ***on,*** an (*Dat.*)); ***– one's head on*** or ***against the door,*** mit dem Kopf gegen die Tür rennen, sich (*Dat.*) den Kopf an der Tür stoßen; (*sl.*) ***– off,*** umbringen, um die Ecke bringen, kaltmachen. **3.** *v.i.* ***– into, – against,*** zusammenstoßen mit, schlagen *or* stoßen gegen *or* an (*Acc.*).

bumper ['bʌmpə], **1.** *s.* 1. volles Glas; der Humpen; 2. (*Motor.*) die Stoßstange. **2.** *attrib. adj.* (*coll.*) zufriedenstellend; (*Theat.*) ***– audience,*** volles Haus; ***– crop,*** die Rekordernte; ***– edition,*** ungewöhnlich große Auflage.

bumpiness ['bʌmpinis], *s.* die Holprigkeit (*as a road*), (*Av.*) Böigkeit.

[1]**bumpkin** ['bʌmpkin], *s.* der Bauernlümmel, Tölpel.

[2]**bumpkin,** *s.* (*Naut.*) der Butenluv.

bumptious ['bʌmpʃəs], *adj.* aufgeblasen, anmaßend.

bumpy ['bʌmpi], *adj.* holperig (*as a road*), (*Av.*) böig, (*coll.*) bockig.

bun [bʌn], *s.* 1. das Korinthenbrötchen; ***hot-cross –,*** die Karfreitagssemmel; 2. (*of hair*) der Dutt.

bunch [bʌntʃ], **1.** *s.* das Bund, Bündel, der Strauß (*of flowers*), das Büschel (*of hair etc.*); (*Min.*) das Erznest, der Butzen; (*coll.*) die Gruppe, Gesellschaft; ***– of feathers,*** der Federbusch; ***– of grapes,*** die Weintraube; ***– of keys,*** der *or* das Schlüsselbund; ***– of radishes,*** das Bund Radieschen; ***the best of the –,*** der (die, das) Beste von allen. **2.** *v.i.* (***– together***), sich zusammenschließen; (***– out***) aufschwellen, hervortreten. **3.** *v.t.* bündeln, zusammenbinden, (*fig.*) zusammenfassen. **bunching,** *s.* die Häufung, Bündelung. **bunchy,** *adj.* in Büscheln wachsend, büschelig; buschig; traubenförmig.

buncombe ['bʌŋkəm], *s.* (*coll.*) leeres Geschwätz, der Quatsch.

bundle [bʌndl], **1.** *s.* das Bund, Bündel, der Pack, das Paket; die Rolle, der Ballen; (*fig.*) (*a p.*) ***– of nerves,*** das Nervenbündel. **2.** *v.t.* ***– away*** or ***off*** or ***out,*** eilig fortjagen *or* wegschaffen; ***– (up),*** zusammenrollen, zusammenpacken. **3.** *v.i.* ***– off*** or ***out,*** sich packen *or* eilig davonmachen.

bung [bʌŋ], **1.** *s.* der Spund, Zapfen, Stöpsel. **2.** *v.t.* 1. (zu)spunden, verspunden; (*sl.*) ***– up,*** verstopfen; (*sl.*) ***–ed up,*** verstopft, (*as eyes*) geschwollen; 2. (*sl.*) werfen, schleudern.

bungalow ['bʌŋgəlou], *s.* einstöckiges (Sommer)-haus.

bung|-full, *adj.* (*coll.*) gestopft voll. **--hole,** *s.* das Spund- *or* Zapfloch.

bungle [bʌŋgl], **1.** *s.* die Pfuscherei, Stümperei. **2.** *v.t.* verpfuschen, verpatzen, verhunzen; ***–d work,*** die Pfuscharbeit. **3.** *v.i.* stümpern, pfuschen, patzen. **bungler,** *s.* der Stümper, Pfuscher. **bungling, 1.** *adj.* ungeschickt, stümperhaft. **2.** *s.* das Ungeschick, die Ungeschicklichkeit; *see also* **bungle, 1.**

bunion ['bʌnjən], *s.* die Fußballenentzündung.

[1]**bunk** [bʌnk], *s.* (*Naut.*) die Koje, (*coll.*) das Bett,

die Schlafstelle; (*Mil.*) – *inspection,* der Stubenappell.

²**bunk,** *v.i.* (*sl.*) (*also* ***do a*** *–*) ausreißen, verduften, abhauen.

³**bunk,** *s.* (*sl.*) *see* **buncombe.**

bunker ['bʌŋkə], *s.* (*Naut., Mil., Golf*) der Bunker, (*Naut.*) *esp.* Kohlenbunker, (*Mil.*) Unterstand, (*Golf*) das Hindernis, die Sandgrube.

bunkum, *s.* (*sl.*) *see* **buncombe.**

bunny ['bʌni], *s.* (*coll.*) das Kaninchen.

¹**bunt** [bʌnt], *s.* der Bauch (*of a sail*).

²**bunt,** *s.* (*Bot.*) der Weizenbrand.

³**bunt,** *v.t., v.i.* mit dem Kopf *or* den Hörnern stoßen.

¹**bunting** ['bʌntiŋ], *s.* das Flaggentuch; der Flaggenschmuck, Flaggen (*pl.*).

²**bunting,** *s.* (*Orn.*) die Ammer (*Emberiza*).

buoy [bɔi], **1.** *s.* die Boje, Bake, das Seezeichen; ***whistling*** *–,* die Heulboje. **2.** *v.t.* durch Bojen bezeichnen, ausbojen (*a channel etc.*); – ***up,*** aufbojen; flott *or* schwimmend erhalten, über Wasser halten; (*fig.*) Auftrieb geben (*Dat.*), aufrechterhalten (*hope etc.*). **buoyage** ['bɔiidʒ], *s.* die Markierung (durch Bojen); (*collect.*) Bojen (*pl.*).

buoyancy ['bɔiənsi], *s.* die Schwimmkraft, das Tragvermögen; (statischer) Auftrieb; (*fig.*) die Schwungkraft, Spannkraft, Lebenskraft; – ***aid,*** die Schwimmweste; – ***tank,*** der Auftriebstank. **buoyant,** *adj.* 1. schwimmend, schimmkräftig, tragfähig, leicht; 2. (*fig.*) lebensfroh, lebhaft, heiter; unbekümmert, in gehobener Stimmung; 3. (*Comm.*) steigend (*of prices*).

bur [bə:], *s.* (*Bot.*) die Klette; ***cling like a –,*** wie eine Klette haften.

burble [bə:bl], *v.i.* gurgeln, murmeln; unverständlich reden.

burbot ['bə:bət], *s.* (*Ichth.*) die Aalraupe, Quappe.

burden [bə:dn], **1.** *s.* 1. die Bürde, Last; Belastung, Verantwortung, der Druck; (*Naut.*) Tonnengehalt, die Tragkraft (*of a ship*); ***be a – to him,*** ihm zur Last fallen; ***beast of –,*** das Lasttier; ***the – of proof,*** die Beweislast; ***ship of 2,000 tons –,*** ein Schiff von 2000 Tonnen; 2. (*fig.*) der Hauptgedanke, Hauptpunkt, die Hauptidee, das Hauptthema, der Schwerpunkt, Kern; das Leitmotiv, der Refrain. **2.** *v.t.* belasten, beladen; – ***him with a th.,*** ihm etwas aufbürden. **burdensome** [–səm], *adj.* drückend, lästig, beschwerlich.

burdock ['bə:dɔk], *s.* (*Bot.*) die Klette.

bureau [bju'rou, 'bjuərou], *s.* (*pl.* **-s** *or* **-x** [–z]) 1. das Geschäftszimmer, Amt, Kontor, Büro, Bureau; 2. (*Am.*) (*Pol.*) die Abteilung eines Ministeriums *or* einer Behörde; 3. (verschließbares) Schreibpult; 4. (*Am.*) die Kommode.

bureaucracy [bju'rɔkrəsi], *s.* die Bürokratie, Beamtenherrschaft; (*collect.*) Beamtenschaft. **bureaucrat** ['bjuərəkræt], *s.* der Bürokrat; (*coll.*) Aktenkrämer. **bureaucratic** [–'krætik], *adj.* bürokratisch; (*pred.*) (*iron.*) nach Schema F, den Amtsschimmel reitend.

burette [bju'ret], *s.* (*Chem.*) die Bürette, Meßröhre.

burgee [bə:'dʒi:], *s.* (*Naut.*) dreieckiger Wimpel.

burgeon ['bə:dʒən], **1.** *s.* (*Bot.*) die Knospe, das Auge, der Sproß, (*Zool.*) Keim. **2.** *v.i.* Knospen treiben, keimen, ausschlagen, (*fig.*) (*also* – ***out*** or ***forth***) hervorsprießen.

burgess ['bə:dʒis], *s.* (*Hist.*) der (Wahl)bürger, Wähler; Abgeordnete(r).

burgh ['bʌrə], *s.* (*Scots*) die Stadt(gemeinde). **burgher** ['bə:gə], *s.* (*not only Scots*) der Bürger.

burglar ['bə:glə], *s.* der Einbrecher; ***cat-–,*** der Fassadenkletterer. **burglar alarm,** *s.* die Alarmglocke. **burglarize,** *v.t.* (*Am.*) *see* **burgle. burglar-proof,** *adj.* einbruchsicher, diebessicher. **burglary,** *s.* der Einbruch, Einbruchsdiebstahl; ***insurance against –,*** die Einbruchsversicherung. **burgle,** *v.t.* einbrechen in (*Acc.*).

burgomaster ['bə:gomɑ:stə], *s.* der Bürgermeister.

Burgundian [bə'gʌndiən], **1.** *s.* der (die) Burgunder(in). **2.** *adj.* burgundisch. **Burgundy** ['bə:gəndi], *s.* 1. Burgund (*n.*) (*district*); 2. der Burgunder (*wine*).

burial ['beriəl], *s.* das Begräbnis, die Beerdigung, Beisetzung, Bestattung. **burial|-ground,** *s.* der Begräbnisplatz, Kirchhof, Friedhof, (*Poet.*) Gottesacker. **--mound,** *s.* der Grabhügel. **--place,** *s.* das Grab, die Grabstätte. – **service,** *s.* die Trauerfeier, Totenfeier, Totenmesse.

burke [bə:k], *v.t.* (heimlich) ermorden, ersticken, erwürgen; (*fig.*) vertuschen, (in aller Stille) unterdrücken, beiseiteschaffen.

burl [bə:l], **1.** *s.* der Knoten (*in yarn*) (*Am. also in wood*). **2.** *v.t.* noppen (*cloth*). **burlap,** *s.* das Sackleinen, die Packleinwand, grobe Leinwand.

burlesque [bə:'lesk], **1.** *adj.* burlesk, possenhaft, possierlich, lächerlich. **2.** *s.* (*Theat.*) die Burleske, Posse, Parodie, Satire. **3.** *v.t.* lächerlich machen, possenhaft behandeln, travestieren, parodieren.

burly ['bə:li], *adj.* stämmig, kräftig; stark, beleibt.

Burma ['bə:mə], *s.* Birma (*n.*). **Burman, Burmese** [–'mi:z], **1.** *s.* 1. der Birmane (die Birmanin); 2. das Birmanisch(e) (*language*). **2.** *adj.* birmanisch.

¹**burn** [bə:n], *s.* (*Scots*) der Bach.

²**burn, 1.** *irr.v.t.* in Brand stecken, (ver)brennen; anbrennen (*meat etc.*); einbrennen (*a mark etc.*); bräunen (*of the sun*); – ***alive,*** lebendig verbrennen; (*fig.*) – ***one's boats,*** alle Brücken hinter sich abbrechen; (*fig.*) – ***the candle at both ends,*** seine Gesundheit untergraben, seine Kräfte vergeuden, sich allzusehr ausgeben; – ***to death,*** verbrennen; – ***one's fingers,*** sich (*Dat.*) die Finger verbrennen (*also fig.*); (*coll.*) ***he has money to –,*** er hat Geld wie Heu; ***the money –s a hole in his pocket,*** das Geld juckt *or* brennt ihm in der Tasche; – ***the midnight oil,*** bis spät in die Nacht arbeiten; – ***down,*** abbrennen, niederbrennen; – ***out,*** ausbrennen, ausräuchern; – ***to the ground,*** bis auf den Grund niederbrennen; – ***up,*** gänzlich verbrennen. **2.** *irr.v.i.* brennen, in Flammen stehen, entbrennen, aufflammen; (*as of food*) anbrennen, verbrennen; (*fig.*) glühen, brennen (***with,*** vor); (*fig.*) ***my ears are –ing,*** mir klingen die Ohren; – ***away,*** abbrennen; – ***into,*** sich tief einfressen in (*Acc.*); ***it –ed itself into my mind,*** es machte auf mich einen unauslöschlichen Eindruck; – ***out,*** ausbrennen; (*Elec.*) durchbrennen; – ***up,*** aufflammen; gänzlich verbrennen. **3.** *s.* das Brandmal, die Brandstelle, Brandwunde; Verbrennung.

burnable ['bə:nəbl], *adj.* (ver)brennbar. **burner,** *s.* der Brenner; ***Bunsen –,*** der Bunsenbrenner; ***charcoal –,*** der Köhler, Kohlenbrenner.

burnet ['bə:nit], *s.* (*Bot.*) der Wiesenknopf.

burning ['bə:niŋ], **1.** *adj.* brennend (*also fig.*); (*fig.*) glühend (***with,*** vor (*Dat.*)), leidenschaftlich, feurig, heiß; (*B.*) ***the – bush,*** die feurige Flamme aus dem *or* die Feuerflamme im Busch; – ***question,*** brennende Frage; – ***shame,*** schreiende Ungerechtigkeit, wahre Schmach. **2.** *s.* das Brennen, Verbrennen; der Brand; ***smell of –,*** der Brandgeruch; ***it smells of –,*** es riecht nach Brand. **burning|-bush,** *s.* (*Bot.*) der Diptam. **--glass,** *s.* das Brennglas. **--test,** *s.* die Verbrennungsprobe.

burnish ['bə:niʃ], **1.** *v.t.* glätten, (hoch)polieren, glanzschleifen, brünieren. **2.** *s.* die Politur, der Hochglanz (*of metals*). **burnisher,** *s.* der Polierer; Polierstahl, Brünierstahl.

burnous [bə:'nu:s], *s.* der Burnus.

burnt [bə:nt], **1.** *imperf., p.p. of* ²**burn. 2.** *adj.* gebrannt, verbrannt; – ***almonds,*** gebrannte Mandeln; (*Prov.*) ***a – child dreads the fire,*** gebranntes Kind scheut das Feuer; – ***gas,*** das Abgas, Auspuffgas; – ***lime,*** der Ätzkalk; – ***offering,*** das Brandopfer; – ***sienna,*** die Siennaerde; ***taste –,*** angebrannt schmecken.

burp [bə:p], (*coll.*) **1.** *v.i.* rülpsen, aufstoßen. **2.** *s.* der Rülpser.

¹**burr** [bə:], *s. See* **bur.**

²**burr, 1.** *s.* gutturale *or* schnarrende Aussprache

(des Zäpfchen-R) (*as in northern England*); undeutliche *or* unartikulierte Aussprache (*as in western England*). **2.** *v.t.* guttural aussprechen (*one's r's*).

[3]**burr,** *s.* der Mühlstein, Schleifstein, Wetzstein.

[4]**burr,** *s.* (*Tech.*) der Grat, die Naht, rauhe Kante (*on metal*).

burrow ['bʌrou], **1.** *s.* der Bau (*rabbits etc.*). **2.** *v.i.* wühlen, einen Bau *or* ein (Erd)loch graben; sich eingraben, sich in eine Erdhöhle verkriechen; (*fig.*) sich verkriechen *or* verbergen (*into,* in (*Acc.*)). **3.** *v.t.* aufwühlen, graben.

bursar ['bəːsə], *s.* der Schatzmeister, Zahlmeister, Kassenwart; (*Univ.*) Quästor; Stipendiat (*in Scottish universities*). **bursary,** *s.* das Schatzamt, die Kasse, Quästur; (*Scots*) das Stipendium.

burst [bəːst], **1.** *irr.v.i.* bersten, platzen (*with,* vor (*Dat.*)); aufplatzen, zerspringen (*as a bubble*); (*Artil.*) explodieren, zerknallen, krepieren; – *asunder,* auseinanderspringen, aufplatzen; – *forth,* ausbrechen, hervorsprudeln; – *in,* hineinplatzen, hereinplatzen; – *in upon him,* über ihn hereinbrechen; – *into blossom,* knospen, aufblühen; – *into flame,* aufflammen; – *into a room,* in ein Zimmer herein- *or* hineinstürzen; – *into tears,* in Tränen ausbrechen; – *into view,* plötzlich sichtbar werden; – *on,* herfallen über (*Acc.*); – *open,* aufspringen, aufplatzen; – *out,* hervorbrechen, ausbrechen; ausrufen; – *out laughing,* in Gelächter ausbrechen; – *out with,* herausplatzen mit; – *upon,* stoßen auf (*Acc.*); – *with* (*usu. be -ing with*), überfließen von, platzen vor (*Dat.*). **2.** *irr.v.t.* (auf)-sprengen, zersprengen, zum Platzen bringen; *the river -s its banks,* der Fluß durchbricht seine Dämme; *I have – a blood-vessel,* mir ist eine Ader geplatzt; – *one's sides with laughing,* vor Lachen platzen; – *open the door,* die Tür aufbrechen. **3.** *s.* das Bersten, Platzen; die Explosion, Detonation, Sprengung; der Stoß (*of gunfire*); (*Cycl., Motor.*) Reifenschaden; (*fig.*) plötzlicher Ausbruch; der Riß, Bruch; – *of applause,* der Beifallssturm; – *of laughter,* die Lachsalve; (*Artil.*) *premature –,* der Frühzerspringer; (*coll.*) – *of speed,* plötzliche Anstrengung, der Spurt.

bursting|-charge, *s.* die Sprengladung. – **stress,** *s.* die Bruchfestigkeit.

burthen [bəːðn], *s. See* **burden** (*Naut.*).

bury ['beri], *v.t.* begraben, beerdigen, bestatten (*a corpse*); verbergen, eingraben, vergraben; – *alive,* verschütten; – *the hatchet,* die Streitaxt begraben; – *o.s. in one's work,* sich in die Arbeit vergraben, sich in die Arbeit vertiefen. **burying|-beetle,** *s.* der Totengräberkäfer. **--ground.** *s.* der Friedhof, Kirchhof, die Grabstätte.

bus [bʌs], **1.** *s.* der (Auto)bus, Omnibus, Verkehrskraftwagen; (*sl.*) (*Motor., Av.*) die Kiste; (*sl.*) *miss the –,* die Gelegenheit verpassen. **2.** *v.i.* (*coll.*) – *it,* mit dem Bus fahren. **3.** *v.t.* mit dem Bus befördern. **bus-bar,** *s.* (*Elec.*) die Sammelschiene.

busby ['bʌzbi], *s.* der (Husaren)kalpak, die Bärenmütze.

bus| conductor, *s.* der Autobusschaffner. – **driver,** *s.* der Autobusfahrer.

[1]**bush** [buʃ], **1.** *s.* der Busch, Strauch; *pl.* das Gebüsch, Gestrüpp, Dickicht; der (Laub)kranz (*of a tavern*); das Büschel (*of hair*); (*Geog.*) der Urwald (*esp. Australia*); *beat about the –,* wie die Katze um den heißen Brei herumgehen; *good wine needs no –,* gute Ware braucht keine Empfehlung; *take to the –,* Buschklepper werden. **2.** *v.i.* buschig wachsen *or* werden.

[2]**bush,** *s.* (*Tech.*) die Lagerschale, Buchse, Büchse, Pfanne, Hülse; das Lagerfutter, Zapfen- *or* Pfannenlager.

bushel [buʃl], *s.* (englischer) Scheffel (= 36½ (*Am.* 35¼) *litres*); *hide one's light under a –,* sein Licht unter den Scheffel stellen.

bush-fighting, *s.* der Buschkrieg.

bushing ['buʃiŋ], *s. See* [2]**bush**; (*Elec.*) – (*insulator*), die Durchführungshülse, das Isolationsfutter.

bush|man, *s.* der Buschmann (*S. Africa, Austral.*). **-ranger,** *s.* der Buschklepper, Strauchdieb. **--whacker,** *s.* (*Austral.*) der Holzfäller, (*coll.*) Hinterwäldler; (*Am.*) Guerillakämpfer. **bushy,** *adj.* buschig.

busily ['bizili], *adv. See* **busy.**

business ['biznis], *s.* das Geschäft, die Beschäftigung, Arbeit; Aufgabe, Pflicht, Obliegenheit; Angelegenheit, Sache, das Anliegen; (*Comm.*) kaufmännischer Beruf, das Geschäftsleben, der Handel, das Gewerbe; der Geschäftsgang, die Markttätigkeit; das Geschäft, Unternehmen, die Firma; – *before pleasure,* erst die Arbeit, dann das Vergnügen; *that's my –,* das ist meine S.; *that's none of my –,* das geht mich nichts an; *on –,* geschäftlich, in geschäftlichen Angelegenheiten; *no – done,* ohne Umsatz; *bad –,* schlimme S.; *hours of –,* Geschäftsstunden (*pl.*); *line* or *branch of –,* die Geschäftsbranche, der Geschäftszweig; (*coll.*) *that is not my line of –,* das liegt außer meinem Bereich; *good* (*stroke of*) –, gutes Geschäft. (*with verbs*) *attend to one's own –,* see *mind one's own –*; *be away on –,* auf Geschäftsreise sein; *be in –,* geschäftlich tätig sein; (*coll.*) *come* (*down*) *to –,* zur S. kommen; *do –,* Geschäfte machen; *do – with,* geschäftliche Verbindungen haben mit; *go about one's –,* seiner Arbeit nachgehen; *go into –,* Kaufmann werden; *have no – there,* dort nichts zu suchen haben; *have no – to be here,* kein Recht haben, hier zu sein; *what – have you to say that?* wie kommst du dazu, das zu sagen? *make a – of* (*doing*) *a th.,* viel Aufhebens machen über eine S.; *make it one's – to do,* es sich (*Dat.*) zur Aufgabe machen zu tun; *mean –,* Ernst machen, es ernst meinen; *mind one's own –,* sich um seine eigenen Angelegenheiten kümmern; *open a –,* ein Geschäft eröffnen; *retire from –,* sich geschäftlich zur Ruhe setzen; *send him about his –,* ihn kurz abfertigen, ihm die Tür weisen; *set up in –,* sich geschäftlich niederlassen, ein Geschäft gründen; (*coll.*) *settle his – for him,* ihm den Garaus machen, ihn gehörig zurechtsetzen; *settle down to –,* sich an die Arbeit machen; *be sick of* or *fed up with the whole –,* den ganzen Kram satt haben; *talk –,* über Geschäfte sprechen, (*coll.*) kein Blatt vor den Mund nehmen; *transact –,* geschäftliche Verbindungen haben.

business| affair, *s.* geschäftliche Angelegenheit. **--capital,** *s.* das Betriebskapital. – **career,** *s.* kaufmännische Laufbahn. – **connections,** *pl.* Geschäftsverbindungen (*pl.*). – **hours,** *pl.* die Geschäftszeit, Geschäftsstunden (*pl.*). **-like,** *adj.* geschäftsmäßig, geschäftstüchtig; nüchtern, sachlich, praktisch. **-man,** *s.* der Geschäftsmann, Kaufmann. – **manager,** *s.* der Geschäftsführer. – **outlook,** *s.* die Geschäftslage, Konjunktur. – **transactions,** *pl.* Geschäfte (*pl.*). **-woman,** *s.* die Geschäftsfrau.

busk [bʌsk], *s.* die Planchette, Korsettstange, das Miederstäbchen.

busker ['bʌskə], *s.* der Bettelmusikant, Straßensänger.

buskin ['bʌskin], *s.* der Halbstiefel; Kothurn; (*fig.*) – *style,* tragischer Stil.

busman ['bʌsmən], *s.* das Omnibusfahrer; *-'s holiday,* die Berufsarbeit während des Urlaubs.

buss [bʌs], **1.** *s.* (*obs.*) der Kuß, (*dial.*) das Busserl. **2.** *v.t.* (*obs.*) küssen.

[1]**bust** [bʌst], *s.* 1. die Büste, weiblicher Busen; 2. das Brustbild.

[2]**bust,** **1.** *v.t., v.i.* (*sl.*) *see* **burst. 2.** *adv. go –,* kaputtgehen, bankrott machen. **3.** *s. go on the –,* eine Bierreise machen, auf den Bummel gehen.

bustard ['bʌstəd], *s.* (*Orn.*) die Trappe (*Otididae*).

[1]**bustle** [bʌsl], *s.* die Turnüre, der Bausch (*of dress*).

[2]**bustle,** **1.** *v.i.* sich rühren, geschäftig sein, hasten, hetzen; – *about,* geschäftig tun, umherlaufen, herumhantieren. **2.** *s.* der Lärm, Tumult, das Getöse, Geräusch, Gewühl, Aufsehen; die Geschäftigkeit, Aufregung, der Übereifer. **bustling,** *adj.* geschäftig, rührig, (über)eifrig.

bust-up, *s.* (*sl.*) der Krach, Krakeel.

busy ['bizi], **1.** *adj.* beschäftigt; geschäftig, emsig, arbeitsam, rührig, fleißig, eifrig; – ***at work,*** fleißig an *or* bei der Arbeit; ***be* – *with,*** beschäftigt sein mit; – ***bee,*** emsige Biene; – ***day,*** arbeitsvoller Tag; – ***life,*** arbeitsreiches Leben; (*Tele.*) – ***line,*** besetzte Leitung; – ***street,*** belebte Straße; ***he is* – *reading,*** er liest eifrig. **2.** *v.t.* beschäftigen; – ***o.s.,*** beschäftigt sein *or* sich beschäftigen (***with,*** mit). **3.** *s.* (*sl.*) der Detektiv. **busybody,** *s.* der Geschaftlhuber, Wichtigtuer. **busyness,** *s.* die Geschäftigkeit, das Beschäftigtsein.

but [bʌt, bət], **1.** *conj.* **(a)** aber, allein, dessenungeachtet, indessen, nichtsdestoweniger, dennoch, jedoch; (*contradicting a neg.*) sondern; ***not only*** ... – ***also*** . . ., nicht nur . . ., sondern auch . . .; **(b)** (*after neg. or inter. and before inf.*) außer, als; ***nothing remains* – *to thank him,*** nichts bleibt als *or* außer ihm zu danken; ***one cannot* – *hope,*** man kann nicht umhin zu hoffen, man kann nur hoffen; **(c)** (*introd. subord. clause after neg. or inter.*) ohne daß, daß nicht, ob nicht; ***she is not so old* – (*that*) *she may learn,*** sie ist nicht zu alt, um nicht zu lernen *or* daß sie nicht lernen kann; ***who knows* – (*that*) *he may be ill?*** wer weiß ob er nicht vielleicht krank ist? ***not* – *that I have warned him,*** nicht als ob ich ihn nicht gewarnt hätte; ***there is no doubt* – (*that*) *she will come,*** es besteht kein Zweifel, daß sie kommen wird; ***I do not deny* – *that he*** . . ., ich bezweifle nicht, daß er . . .; ***I could do it* – *that I am afraid,*** ich könnte es tun, wenn ich nicht Angst hätte; – ***then,*** aber schließlich *or* andererseits; – ***yet,*** aber doch, dennoch. **2.** *prep.* außer, mit Ausnahme von; ***the last* – *one,*** der vorletzte; ***the last line* – *one,*** die vorletzte Zeile; ***the last* – *two,*** der drittletzte; ***all* – *he*** or ***him,*** alle außer ihm, alle bis auf ihn, nur er nicht; – ***for him,*** wenn er nicht gewesen wäre, ohne ihn; ***nothing* –,** nichts als. **3.** *adv.* nur, bloß, lediglich; gerade, (gerade) erst; ***all* –,** fast, beinahe, nahezu, um ein Haar; ***all* – *impossible,*** nahezu unmöglich; ***she all* – *told him,*** fast sagte sie es ihm; – ***a child,*** bloß ein Kind; ***anything* – *clever,*** alles andere als klug, nichts weniger als klug; – ***last week,*** erst vorige Woche; ***nothing* – *trouble,*** nichts als Verdruß. **4.** (*as neg. rel. pron.* = ***that . . . not,*** *after neg. main clause*) ***there is nothing here* – *is*** (*or literary* – ***that is*** or *coll.* – ***what is***) ***needed,*** hier ist nichts, das nicht notwendig ist. **5.** *s.* das Aber; ***but me so* –*s!*** keine Widerrede! komme mir nicht mit deinen Einwendungen! hier gibt es kein Aber! **6.** *v.t. See under* **5.**

butcher [ˈbutʃə], **1.** *s.* der Fleischer, Metzger, Schlächter; (*fig.*) blutgieriger *or* grausamer Mörder; (*coll.*) Pfuscher, Stümper; –***'s meat,*** das Schlächterfleisch; –***'s shop,*** der Fleischerladen, die Metzgerei. **2.** *v.t.* schlachten, (*fig.*) abschlachten, hinschlachten, niedermetzeln; (*coll.*) verpfuschen (*a job*). **butcher-bird,** *s.* (*Orn.*) der Würger (*Lanius*). **butchery,** *s.* das Schlachthaus, die Schlächterei; das Fleischerhandwerk; (*fig.*) die Metzelei, das Gemetzel, die Niedermetzelung, Bluttat, das Blutbad.

butler [ˈbʌtlə], *s.* der Kellermeister, Mundschenk; oberster Diener; –***'s pantry,*** die Anrichtekammer.

[1]**butt** [bʌt], *s.* das Faß, Stückfaß, die Butte.

[2]**butt, 1.** *s.* 1. der Kopfstoß; 2. Kolben (*of rifle*), dickes Ende, der Griff, Stiel (*of tools*), unterer Stamm (*of a tree*), Stummel (*of a cigar*); (*Build.*) Stoß (*of beams etc.*); (*Carp. etc.*) – ***and* –,** der Anstoß; 3. *pl.* Scheiben- *or* Schießstand; (*fig.*) das Ziel, die Zielscheibe; ***he is the* – *of the company,*** er dient der ganzen Gesellschaft als Zielscheibe *or* Gegenstand des Spottes. **2.** *v.t.* 1. mit dem Kopfe stoßen; 2. (*Tech.*) (in einer Linie) aneinanderfügen, zusammenstoßen (lassen). **3.** *v.i.* sich anfügen, stoßen (***against, on,*** an (*Acc.*)); aneinanderstoßen, zusammenstoßen; (*coll.*) – ***into,*** stoßen auf (*Acc.*), zusammenstoßen mit; (*coll.*) – ***in,*** sich (unbefugt) einmischen, sich aufdrängen.

[3]**butt,** *s.* (*Ichth.*) der Plattfisch (*generic name of numerous varieties*).

butt-end, *s.* (*coll.*) (dickes) Ende, das Endstück.

butter [ˈbʌtə], **1.** *s.* die Butter; ***bread and* –,** das Butterbrot; ***she looks as if* – *would not melt in her mouth,*** sie sieht aus, als ob sie kein Wässerchen trüben könnte. **2.** *v.t.* mit Butter bestreichen; (*coll.*) – ***him up,*** ihm Honig um den Mund *or* Bart *or* ums Maul schmieren; ***know on which side one's bread is* –*ed,*** seinen Vorteil kennen, wissen wo Barthel den Most holt. **butter|-bean,** *s.* die Wachsbohne. **–cup,** *s.* (*Bot.*) die Butterblume, der Hahnenfuß. **--dish,** *s.* die Butterdose. **--fingered,** *adj.* (*coll.*) ungeschickt beim Fangen, tolpatschig. **--fingers,** *s.* (*coll.*) der Tolpatsch; einer, der nicht fangen kann.

butterfly [ˈbʌtəflai], *s.* der Schmetterling (*also fig.*), Tagfalter. **butterfly|-nut,** *s.* die Flügelmutter. **--screw,** *s.* die Flügelschraube. **--valve,** *s.* die Drosselklappe.

butter|milk, *s.* die Buttermilch. **--pat,** *s.* die Butterscheibe. **--print,** *s.* die Butterform. **–scotch,** *s.* die Butterkaramelle. **–wort,** *s.* (*Bot.*) das Fettkraut.

buttery [ˈbʌtəri], **1.** *adj.* butterig, butterartig. **2.** *s.* die Speisekammer; (*esp. Univ.*) Kantine. **buttery|-bar,** *s.* die Speiseausgabe. **--hatch,** *s.* die Durchreiche, Servierluke.

butt|-hinge, *s.* das Fischband. **--joint,** *s.* (*Tech.*) stumpfer Stoß, der Stumpfstoß, die Stoßfuge, Stoßverbindung.

buttock [ˈbʌtək], *s.* die Hinterbacke; das Hinterteil; (*usu. pl.*) Gesäß, der Steiß, Hintern.

button [bʌtn], **1.** *s.* der Knopf; Knauf (*of a sword etc.*); (*Metall.*) das Korn; (*Bot.*) die Knospe, das Auge, der Knoten; (*Zool.*) Hoden; Saitenhalterstift (*of violin etc.*); ***boy in* –*s,*** der Page in Livree; ***not care a* – *for,*** sich nicht das geringste machen aus, sich den Teufel scheren um; ***covered* –,** überzogener Knopf; ***press the* –,** auf den Knopf drücken; ***it's not worth a* –,** es ist keinen Deut *or* Pfifferling wert. **2.** *v.t.* (– ***up***) zuknöpfen; (*coll.*) –***ed up,*** zugeknöpft, zurückhaltend. **3.** *v.i.* sich knöpfen lassen; – ***at the back,*** hinten geknöpft werden. **button|hole, 1.** *s.* 1. das Knopfloch; 2. die Knopflochblume. **2.** *v.t.* (*coll.*) anhalten, aufhalten, festhalten, abhalten, sich (*Dat.*) vorknöpfen; – ***stitch,*** der Langettenstich. **--hook,** *s.* der Stiefelknöpfer. **buttons,** *s.* (*coll.*) der Page, Hoteldiener.

butt-plate, *s.* die Kolbenkappe (*of rifle*); (*Tech.*) Stoßplatte.

buttress [ˈbʌtris], **1.** *s.* der Strebepfeiler, das Widerlager; (*fig.*) die Stütze. **2.** *v.t.* stützen, (*fig.*) (*also* – ***up***) unterstützen, untermauern.

butt|-swivel, *s.* der Klammerfuß (*of rifle*). **– weld,** *s.* die Stoß- *or* Stumpf(schweiß)naht. **– welding,** *s.* die Stoß- *or* Stumpfschweißung.

butyric [bju:ˈtirik], *adj.* butterig; – ***acid,*** die Buttersäure. **butyrin(e)** [ˈbju:tirin], *s.* das Butterfett.

buxom [ˈbʌksəm], *adj.* gesundheitstrotzend, drall, stramm; mollig (*of women only*).

buy [bai], **1.** *irr.v.t.* kaufen, einkaufen; teuer zahlen für, erkaufen (*experience etc.*); – ***a pig in a poke,*** die Katze im Sack kaufen; ***everything that money can* –,** alles was für Geld zu haben ist; – ***and sell,*** Handel treiben; – ***s.th. for him,*** ihm etwas kaufen; – ***s.th. from*** or ***of him,*** etwas von ihm kaufen *or* beziehen, ihm etwas abkaufen; – ***a ticket,*** eine Karte lösen; (*Comm.*) – ***forward,*** auf Spekulation kaufen; – ***in,*** einkaufen, sich eindecken mit; zurückkaufen (*at auctions*); – ***off,*** loskaufen (*a p. from an obligation*), abfinden (*a p.'s interest in a th.*); (*coll.*) durch Versprechungen abbringen *or* abhalten; erkaufen (*a th.*); – ***out,*** auskaufen, loskaufen (*a p.*), ablösen (*a p. from an obligation*); durch Ankauf um das Eigentum bringen; – ***over,*** durch Bestechung (für sich) gewinnen, bestechen (*a p.*); – ***up,*** aufkaufen. **2.** *s.* (*coll.*) der Kauf.

buyer [ˈbaiə], *s.* der Käufer, Einkäufer, Abnehmer; (*Comm.*) – ***of a bill,*** der Wechselnehmer; (*St. Exch.*) –***'s option,*** die Kaufoption; (*St. Exch.*) –***s over,*** mehr Geld als Brief. **buying,** *s.* das Kaufen, der Ankauf, Abkauf; – ***power,*** die Kaufkraft.

buzz [bʌz], **1.** *v.i.* brummen, summen; dröhnen, surren, schwirren; ***the place* –*ed with visitors,*** Besucher schwirrten im Ort herum; ***the place* –*ed***

with rumours, Gerüchte summten durch den Ort; (*coll.*) – *about,* herumschwirren; (*sl.*) – *off,* abhauen, verduften. **2.** *v.t.* (*Av.*) (*coll.*) sehr nahe heranfliegen an (*Acc.*). **3.** *s.* das Summen, Surren, Schwirren, Brummen, (*fig.*) Gesumme, Geflüster, Gerede.

buzzard ['bʌzəd], *s.* (*Orn.*) der Mäusebussard (*Buteo buteo*).

buzzer ['bʌzə], *s.* (*Elec.*) der Summer; – *key,* der Summerknopf; – *set,* der Summerzusatz.

by [bai], **1.** *prep.* **(a)** (*place*) neben (*Dat.*), (nahe *or* dicht) an (*Dat.*) *or* bei, nahebei; *the house – the river,* das Haus beim *or* am Fluß; *side – side,* Seite an Seite; – *his bedside,* an seinem Bett; *I have no money – me,* ich habe kein Geld bei mir.
(b) (*direction*) durch, über (*Acc.*), auf (*Dat.*), entlang (*Acc.*); an (*Dat.*) . . . vorbei *or* vorüber; *travel – Paris,* über Paris fahren; *come – the other road,* die andere Straße entlang kommen.
(c) (*relation*) nach, gemäß, –weise; – *appearances,* nach dem Anschein; – *birth,* von Geburt; – *blood,* von Geblüt, der Abstammung nach; – *degrees,* allmählich, nach und nach, stufenweise; – *the dozen,* dutzendweise; – *experience,* aus Erfahrung; – *the hour,* stundenweise; – *hundreds,* zu Hunderten; – *the hundredweight,* zentnerweise; – *the laws of nature,* nach dem Naturgesetz; – *his looks,* an seinen Blicken; – *name,* mit Namen, dem Namen nach; *he goes – the name of . . .,* er führt den Namen . . .; – *nature,* von Natur; – *profession* or *trade,* von Beruf; – *turns,* der Reihe nach, wechselweise, abwechselnd; – *my watch,* nach meiner Uhr; – *way of example,* beispielsweise.
(d) (*means*) von, durch, mit (Hilfe von), vermöge, (ver)mittels, (*Comm.*) per; – *air,* mit dem Flugzeug; *represented – attorney,* durch einen Anwalt vertreten; – *boat,* mit dem (*or Comm.* per) Schiff; – *chance,* durch Zufall, zufällig; – *force,* mit Gewalt; – *land,* zu Lande; – *leaps and bounds,* in raschem Tempo, sprungweise; – *letter,* brieflich; – *mistake,* aus Versehen, versehentlich; – *order of,* auf Verordnung (*Gen.*); – *permission of,* mit Erlaubnis (*Gen.*); – *post,* mit der (*or Comm.* per) Post; – *rail,* mit der (Eisen)bahn; – *the nearest road,* auf dem kürzesten Wege; – *sea,* zu Wasser; – *stealth,* verstohlen, heimlich; *die – the sword,* durch das Schwert umkommen; – *which train?* mit welchem Zuge? – *word of mouth,* mündlich.
(e) (*time*) bei, während; bis zu, bis um, bis (spätestens); – *day,* bei Tage; – *next week,* bis (spätestens) nächste Woche; – *now,* – *this time,* (jetzt) schon, inzwischen, mittlerweile, unterdessen; – *this time tomorrow,* bis morgen um diese Zeit; *be back – Tuesday,* bis Dienstag zurück sein.
(f) (*other idioms*) *day – day,* Tag für Tag, jeden Tag, (tag)täglich; – *dint of,* kraft, vermöge; – *the* –(*e*), see – *the way*; – *far,* bei weitem; *5 feet – 4 feet,* 5 Fuß zu 4 Fuß, 5 Fuß lang und 4 Fuß breit; – *heart,* auswendig; – *itself,* (an und) für sich, allein; selbsttätig; – *o.s.,* für sich, allein; selbst, selbständig, aus eigener Kraft; *little – little,* nach und nach, allmählich; *man – man,* Mann für Mann; – *all means,* auf alle Fälle, auf jeden Fall; durchaus, unbedingt; gewiß, freilich; – *means of,* (ver)mittels; – *no means,* keinesfalls, auf keinen Fall, keineswegs; – *so much more,* um so mehr; *one – one,* einzeln, eins nach dem andern; *point – point,* Punkt für Punkt; – *reason of,* wegen; – *right*(*s*), von Rechts wegen; *seize – the hand,* bei der Hand fassen; *seize – the waist,* um die Taille fassen; *two – two,* – *twos,* zwei und zwei, zu zweien; – *the way,* nebenbei (bemerkt), beiläufig; *word – word,* Wort für Wort.
2. *adv.* 1. nahe (dabei); *close* or *hard* –, dicht dabei; (*Mil.*) *stand* –, bereit stehen; – *and* –, in der (nicht zu weiten) Zukunft, nächstens, bald; – *and large,* im großen und ganzen; 2. vorbei, vorüber; *go* –, vorbei– *or* vorübergehen *or* –kommen; *times gone* –, vergangene Zeiten; *pass* –, see *go* –; *pass s.th.* –, an einer S. vorübergehen; (*fig.*) *pass him* –, ihn übergehen; 3. beiseite; *lay* or *put* –, beiseite legen *or* stellen.

by(e)– [bai], *pref.* Neben–, Seiten–.

bye, *s.* etwas Untergeordnetes (*esp. Spt.*); (*Golf*) am Ende des Spiels nicht gespielte Löcher; (*Crick.*) dem Schläger zugeteilter Punkt wenn der Ball von den Verteidigern nicht abgefangen wird; (*Tenn.*) das Aufsteigen in die nächste Runde.

bye-bye, 1. *s.* (*nursery talk*) die Heia; *go to –s,* in die Heia gehen. **2.** *int.* (*coll.*) auf Wiedersehen!

by-election, *s.* die Nachwahl, Ersatzwahl.

bygone ['baigɔn], **1.** *adj.* vergangen. **2.** *s. let –s be –s,* laß das Vergangene ruhen, (*sl.*) Schwamm darüber!

by|-law, *s.* das Ortsstatut, örtliche *or* städtische Bestimmung *or* Verordnung; (*esp. Am.*) die Satzung. **--pass, 1.** *s.* die Entlastungs– *or* Umgehungsstraße; (*Tech.*) Nebenleitung; – (*burner*), der Kleinsteller; – *condenser,* der Nebenschluß– *or* Ableitkondensator. **2.** *v.t.* umgehen (*obstruction, enemy*), (*Tech.*) umleiten, ableiten, vorbeileiten. **--play,** *s.* stummes Spiel, das Gebärdenspiel. **--product,** *s.* das Nebenerzeugnis, Abfallprodukt, (*fig.*) die Nebenerscheinung.

byre ['baiə], *s.* der Kuhstall.

byrnie ['bə:ni], *s.* (*Hist.*) die Brünne.

by|-road, *s.* die Seitenstraße, der Nebenweg. **–stander,** *s.* der Zuschauer; *pl.* Umstehende (*pl.*). **--way,** *s. See* **--road** (*also fig.*). **–word,** *s.* das Sprichwort; Schlagwort, stehende Redensart; die Zielscheibe des Spottes, das Gespött; der Gegenstand der Verachtung, warnendes Beispiel.

Byzantian [bai'zæntiən], **Byzantine** [–tain], **1.** *s.* der (die) Byzantiner(in). **2.** *adj.* byzantinisch. **Byzantium,** *s.* (*Hist.*) Byzanz (*n.*).

C

C, c [si:], *s.* das C, c (*also Mus.*); *C flat,* Ces; *C major,* C-Dur; *C Minor,* c-Moll; *C sharp,* Cis. (*See Index of Abbreviations.*)

cab [kæb], *s.* 1. die Droschke, der Fiaker; 2. (*Railw.*) Führerstand.

cabal [kə'bæl], **1.** *s.* die Kabale, Intrige, Ränke (*pl.*), Machenschaften (*pl.*); die Clique, der Geheimbund, Klüngel. **2.** *v.i.* Ränke schmieden, intrigieren, sich verschwören.

cabaret ['kæbərei], *s.* das Kabarett, die Kleinkunstbühne, das Überbrettl.

cabbage ['kæbidʒ], *s.* der Kohl; Kohlkopf. **cabbage|-butterfly,** *s.* der Kohlweißling. **--lettuce,** *s.* der Kopfsalat. **--rose,** *s.* die Zentifolie. **--tree,** *s.* die Kohlpalme. **--white,** *s. See* **--butterfly.**

cabbala [kə'bɑ:lə], *s.* die Kabbala. **cabbalism** ['kæbəlizm], *s.* die Kabbalistik, Geheimlehre (der Kabbalisten). **cabbalist,** *s.* der Kabbalist. **cabbalistic(al)** [–'listik(l)], *adj.* kabbalistisch, esoterisch.

cabby ['kæbi], *s.* (*coll.*) *see* **cabman.**

cabin ['kæbin], *s.* 1. die Hütte; 2. (*Naut.*) Kajüte, (*Av.*) Kabine. **cabin|-boy,** *s.* der Schiffsjunge. **– class,** *s.* zweite Klasse, die Kajütsklasse (*on liners*). **– cruiser,** *s.* der Kabinenkreuzer. **cabined,** *adj.* (*Poet.*) eingepfercht.

cabinet ['kæbinit], *s.* 1. das Zimmerchen, Kabinett; die Vitrine, der Schrank; (*Rad. etc.*) das Gehäuse, die Truhe; (*obs.*) (wertvolle) Sammlung; *medicine* –, der Medizinschrank; 2. (*Pol.*) der Ministerrat, das Kabinett. **cabinet| edition.** *s.* bibliophile Ausgabe. **--maker,** *s.* der Kunsttischler. **--mak-**

ing, *s.* die Kunsttischlerei. – **meeting,** *s.* die Kabinettssitzung. – **minister,** *s.* der Staatsminister, das Kabinettsmitglied. **--size,** *s.* (*Phot.*) das Kabinettformat (*10 × 14 cm.*).

cable [keibl], **1.** *s.* das Kabel, (Kabel)tau, die (Stahl)trosse, das (Draht)seil; (*coll.*) die Depesche; (*Naut.*) ***a –'s length,*** eine Kabellänge (= *200 yds.*); ***anchor –,*** das Ankertau; ***armoured –,*** das Panzerkabel, Armierungskabel; ***buried –,*** das Erdkabel; ***conducting –,*** das Zuleitungskabel; ***ground –,*** see ***buried –***; ***lead-covered –,*** das Blei(mantel)kabel; ***marine –,*** das Seekabel; ***overhead –,*** das Luftkabel; ***rubber-insulated –,*** das Gummikabel; ***underground –,*** see ***buried –***. **2.** *v.t.* (*coll.*) telegraphieren, drahten, kabeln. **cable|gram,** *s.* die Kabeldepesche. **--laid,** *adj.* kabelartig gedreht (*rope*). **--moulding,** *s.* (*Archit.*) die Schiffstauverzierung. **--railway,** *s.* die (Draht)seilbahn, Schwebebahn. – **transfer,** *s.* telegraphische Geldüberweisung.

cabman ['kæbmən], *s.* der Droschkenkutscher; Taxifahrer.

caboodle [kə'bu:dl], *s.* (*sl.*) (*of things*) der Kram, Plunder, Schmarren; (*of persons*) das Pack, die Bande, Sippschaft.

caboose [kə'bu:s], *s.* (*Naut.*) die Kombüse, Schiffsküche; (*Am. Railw.*) der Bremswagen.

cab-rank, *s.* der Droschkenstand.

cabriole ['kæbrioul], *s.* das Stuhlbein in Pfotenform.

cabriolet [kæbrio'lei], *s.* das Kabriolett, zweirädriger Einspänner.

ca'canny [kɑ:'kæni], *s.* die Produktionseinschränkung, passiver Widerstand.

cacao [kə'keiou], *s.* die Kakaobohne. **cacao-tree,** *s.* der Kakaobaum.

cachalot ['kæʃəlɔt], *s.* der Pottwal.

cache [kæʃ], **1.** *s.* der Aufbewahrungsort, das Versteck, geheimes Lager. **2.** *v.t.* versteckt aufbewahren, verbergen.

cachectic [kə'kektik], *adj.* kränklich.

cachet ['kæʃei], *s.* 1. (*Med.*) die Arzneikapsel, das Kachet; 2. Siegel, der Stempel; (*usu. fig.*) Stempel, das Gepräge.

cachexy [kæ'keksi], *s.* (*Med.*) ungesunder Zustand, der Körperverfall, die Kachexie.

cachinnation [kæki'neiʃən], *s.* lautes Gelächter.

cackle [kækl], **1.** *v.i.* gackern (*hens*), schnattern (*geese*), (*fig.*) schnattern, schwatzen, plappern; gackernd lachen. **2.** *s.* das Gegacker, Geschnatter; (*fig.*) Geschwätz, Geschnatter, Geplapper; (*sl.*) ***cut the –!*** Schluß mit dem Geschwätz!

cacophonous [kə'kɔfənəs], *adj.* mißlautend, mißtönend, übelklingend. **cacophony,** *s.* der Mißklang.

cactus ['kæktəs], *s.* der Kaktus.

cad [kæd], *s.* gemeiner *or* ordinärer Kerl.

cadaver [kə'dɑ:və], *s.* (*Med.*) der Leichnam. **cadaverous** [kə'dævərəs], *adj.* leichenhaft, leichenblaß, totenblaß.

caddie ['kædi], *s.* der Golfjunge, Träger.

caddish ['kædiʃ], *adj.* gemein, niederträchtig, schuftig. **caddishness,** *s.* die Gemeinheit, Niedertracht.

caddy ['kædi], *s.* die Teebüchse.

cadence ['keidəns], *s.* der Takt(schlag), (Sprech– *or* Vers)rhythmus; Tonfall, die Modulation (*of speech*), (*Mus.*) Kadenz, Schlußphrase, der Schluß(fall); ***perfect –,*** der Ganzschluß; ***imperfect –,*** der Halbschluß; ***interrupted –,*** gestörter Schluß.

cadenza [kə'denzə], *s.* (*Mus.*) die Kadenz, Solopassage.

cadet [kə'det], *s.* jüngster Sohn *or* Bruder; (*Mil.*) der Kadett, Offiziersanwärter, Fahnenjunker; ***– ship,*** das Schulschiff. **cadetship,** *s.* die Kadettenstelle.

cadge [kædʒ], **1.** *v.i.* (*coll.*) schnorren, nassauern; betteln (***for,*** um). **2.** *v.t.* (*coll.*) erbetteln. **cadger,** *s.* der Schmarotzer, Schnorrer, Nassauer.

cadmium ['kædmiəm], *s.* das Kadmium.

cadre ['kɑ:də], *s.* (*Mil.*) der Kader, die Stammeinheit.

caducity [kə'dju:siti], *s.* die Hinfälligkeit, Vergänglichkeit; (*Bot., Zool.*) das Abfallen, Absterben; (*Law*) Verfallensein. **caducous** [–kəs], *adj.* hinfällig, vergänglich; (*Bot., Zool.*) frühzeitig absterbend *or* abfallend *or* ausfallend *or* eingehend *or* verwelkend.

caecum ['si:kəm], *s.* (*Anat.*) der Blinddarm.

Caesar ['si:zə], *s.* Cäsar (*m.*). **Caesarian** [si'zɛəriən], *s.* (*Med.*) (*also* ***– operation, – section***) der Kaiserschnitt.

caesura [si'zjuərə], *s.* der (Vers)einschnitt, die Zäsur.

café ['kæfei], *s.* 1. das Café, Kaffee(haus), alkoholfreies Restaurant (*in England*); 2. der Kaffee; ***– au lait,*** der Milchkaffee, Kaffee verkehrt.

cafeteria [kæfə'tiəriə], *s.* das Selbstbedienungsrestaurant, Automatenbüfett.

caffeine ['kæfi:n], *s.* das Koffein.

cage [keidʒ], **1.** *s.* der Käfig, das (Vogel)bauer (*for birds*); Gehege (*for animals*); der Förderkorb, Fahrkorb (*mines*); (*fig.*) das Gefängnis, (Kriegs)gefangenenlager. **2.** *v.t.* in einen Käfig sperren, einsperren. **cage-bird, cageling,** *s.* der Vogel im Käfig, Stubenvogel. **cagey** ['keidʒi], *adj.* (*sl.*) schlau, argwöhnisch, vorsichtig, berechnend, gewieft.

cahoots [kə'hu:ts], *pl.* (*sl.*) ***in – with,*** unter einer Decke stecken mit, gemeinsame S. machen mit.

Cain [kein], *s.* Kain (*m.*); (*coll.*) ***raise –,*** Krach machen.

caïque [kɑ:'i:k], *s.* der Kaik, türkische Barke.

cairn [kɛən], *s.* der Steinhügel, Grabhügel, Steinhaufen.

cairngorm ['kɛəngɔ:m], *s.* der Rauchtopas.

caisson ['keisən], *s.* der Senkkasten, Schwimmkasten; (*Mil.*) Munitionswagen.

caitiff ['keitif], **1.** *s.* (*Poet.*) Elende(r), der Schurke, Lump. **2.** *adj.* elend, schuftig, schurkisch.

cajole [kə'dʒoul], *v.t.* schmeicheln (*Dat.*), gut zureden (*Dat.*), beschwatzen; verführen, herumkriegen (***into,*** zu); ***– s.th. out of him,*** ihm etwas abbetteln. **cajolery,** *s.* die Schmeichelei, Lobhudelei, Liebedienerei, gutes Zureden.

cake [keik], **1.** *s.* der Kuchen; ***–s and ale,*** das Wohlleben, vergnügliches Leben; ***not all –s and ale,*** nicht eitel Freude; ***go like hot –s,*** wie warme Semmeln (weg)gehen; ***you can't have your – and eat it,*** du kannst nicht alles haben; entweder oder! (*sl.*) ***a piece of –,*** eine Leichtigkeit *or* Spielerei; ***– of soap,*** das Stück Seife; (*coll.*) ***take the –,*** den Vogel abschießen, alles überbieten *or* übertreffen; (*coll.*) ***that takes the –!*** das ist (ja *or* doch) die Höhe! **2.** *v.i.* zusammenbacken; ***–d with,*** dick beschmiert mit. **cake-walk,** *s.* (eine Art) Tanz, der Cakewalk; (*coll.*) die Spielerei, das Kinderspiel.

calabash ['kæləbæʃ], *s.* die Kalabasse, der Flaschenkürbis.

calaboose [kælə'bu:s], *s.* (*Am. sl.*) der Kerker, das Loch, Kittchen.

calamanco [kælə'mæŋkou], *s.* der Kalmank.

calamine ['kæləm(a)in], *s.* der Galmei, Zinkspat.

calamint ['kæləmint], *s.* die Bergminze, Kölle.

calamitous [kə'læmitəs], *adj.* unheilvoll, verhängnisvoll, unselig, unglücklich. **calamity,** *s.* das Unglück, Unheil; Elend, die Trübsal.

calamus ['kæləməs], *s.* (*Hist.*) die Schreibfeder (aus Schilfrohr); (*Bot.*) Gemeiner Kalmus.

calash [kə'læʃ], *s.* die Kalesche.

calcareous [kæl'kɛəriəs], *adj.* kalkig, kalkreich, kalkhaltig; kalkartig, Kalk–.

calceolaria [kælsiə'lɛəriə], *s.* die Pantoffelblume, Kalzeolarie.

calcification [kælsifi'keiʃən], *s.* die Kalkbildung. **calcify** ['kælsifai], *v.t., v.i.* verkalken. **calcination** [–'neiʃən], *s.* die Verkalkung; (*of lime etc.*) das Brennen, Kalzinieren. **calcine** ['kæls(a)in],

1. *v.t.* verkalken; brennen, kalzinieren, (aus)glühen (*lime etc.*). **2.** *v.i.* kalziniert *or* (aus)geglüht werden.

calcium ['kælsiəm], *s.* das Kalzium; – ***carbide,*** das (Kalzium)karbid; – ***carbonate,*** die Schlämmkreide; – ***chloride,*** das Chlorkalzium; – (***hydr***)***oxide,*** gelöschter *or* gebrannter Kalk, der Ätzkalk.

calculable ['kælkjuləbl], *adj.* berechenbar, (*of a p.*) verläßlich. **calculate** [–leit], **1.** *v.t.* berechnen, errechnen, ausrechnen; kalkulieren, abschätzen; bestimmen, beabsichtigen; (*Am. coll.*) glauben, vermuten, rechnen. **2.** *v.i.* rechnen, zählen, sich verlassen (***on,*** auf (*Acc.*)). **calculated,** *adj.* (wohl)überlegt, beabsichtigt, gewollt; – ***for,*** dafür *or* dazu geeignet *or* darauf berechnet; – ***risk*** berechnetes Risiko. **calculating,** *adj.* 1. (*Tech.*) Rechen–; – ***machine,*** die Rechenmaschine; 2. (*of a p.*) berechnend, abwägend, (kühl) überlegend. **calculation** [–'leiʃən], *s.* die Berechnung; Veranschlagung, Schätzung; der Überschlag, Kostenanschlag; ***be out in one's –***(***s***), sich verrechnet haben; ***at the lowest –,*** bei niedrigster Berechnung.

calculous ['kælkjuləs], *adj.* (*Med.*) 1. Stein–; 2. steinkrank.

[1]**calculus** ['kælkjuləs], *s.* der (Blasen– *or* Nieren)stein.

[2]**calculus,** *s.* die Rechnung, das Kalkül; ***differential –,*** die Differentialrechnung; ***integral –,*** die Integralrechnung.

caldron, *see* **cauldron.**

Caledonia [kæli'dounjə], *s.* (*Poet.*) Schottland, Kaledonien (*n.*). **Caledonian,** *adj.* schottisch, kaledonisch.

calefaction [kæli'fækʃən], *s.* die Erhitzung, Erwärmung.

calendar ['kælində], **1.** *s.* der Kalender; (*Law*) die Liste, Rolle; – ***month,*** der Kalendermonat; ***university –,*** das Vorlesungsverzeichnis, Hochschulbestimmungen (*pl.*). **2.** *v.t.* (*Law*) registrieren, eintragen, einschreiben.

calender ['kælində], **1.** *s.* der Kalander, die Glättmaschine, Satiniermaschine. **2.** *v.t.* kalandern, glätten, satinieren.

calends ['kæləndz], *pl.* (*Hist.*) Kalenden (*pl.*); (*coll.*) ***at the Greek –,*** niemals.

[1]**calf** [kɑ:f], *s.* (*pl.* **calves** [kɑ:vz]) 1. das Kalb; ***with*** or ***in –,*** trächtig; ***–'s–*** or ***calves-foot jelly,*** die Kalbspfotensülze; (*coll.*) – ***love,*** erste Liebe, (unreife) Jugendliebe; 2. Kalbleder; ***bound in –,*** in Leder gebunden; – ***binding,*** der Franzband, (Kalb)lederband.

[2]**calf,** *s.* (*pl.* **calves**) (*Anat.*) die Wade.

calfskin ['kɑ:fskin], *s.* das Kalbsfell, Kalbleder.

caliber, (*Am.*) *see* **calibre.**

calibrate ['kælibreit], *v.t., v.i.* eichen, kalibrieren. **calibrated,** *adj.* graduiert (*as a dial*). **calibration** [–'breiʃən], *s.* die Eichung, Kalibrierung; Gradeinteilung (*of a dial*).

calibre ['kælibə], *s.* 1. das Kaliber, die Rohrweite, Seelenweite, innerer Durchmesser; 2. (*fig.*) die Qualität, Eigenschaft, Befähigung, der Wert, das Format.

calices ['keilisi:z], *pl. of* **calix.**

calico ['kælikou], *s.* der Kattun, Zitz.

California [kæli'fɔ:njə], *s.* Kalifornien (*n.*). **Californian, 1.** *s.* der (die) Kalifornier(in). **2.** *adj.* kalifornisch.

caliper, *see* **calliper.**

caliph ['keilif, 'kælif], *s.* der Kalif. **caliphate** ['kælifeit], *s.* das Kalifat.

calisthenic [kælis'θenik], *adj.* gymnastisch. **calisthenics,** *pl.* (*sing. constr.*) die (Lehre von der) Gymnastik; (*pl. constr.*) (Frauen)gymnastik, Freiübungen (*pl.*).

calix ['keiliks], *s.* (*pl.* **calices** [–lisi:z]) der Kelch.

[1]**calk** [kɔ:k], *v.t.* durchzeichnen, durchpausen.

[2]**calk, 1.** *v.t.* 1. scharf beschlagen (*a horse*); mit Stollen versehen (*a horseshoe*); 2. *See* **caulk. 2.** *s.* (*Am.*) *or* **calkin** ['kɔ:kin, 'kælkin], *s.* der (Huf)stollen.

call [kɔ:l], **1.** *v.t.* rufen, kommen lassen, herbeirufen (*a p.*), wecken (*from sleep*); einberufen, zusammenrufen (*a meeting*); heißen, nennen (*a p. by a name*), (be)nennen, bezeichnen (*a th. by a name*); zitieren, aufrufen (*a p. to judgement*); ernennen, berufen (*a p. to a post*); anrufen, antelephonieren (*by phone*); (*coll.*) schätzen auf (*Acc.*); – ***his attention to,*** ihn aufmerksam machen auf (*Acc.*); (*sl.*) – ***it a day!*** mach' Schluß damit! – ***a halt,*** Halt machen, Einhalt gebieten (*Dat.*); – ***him names,*** ihn beschimpfen; ***not a moment to – one's own,*** keinen Augenblick für sich; (*Mil.*) – ***the roll,*** Appell abhalten; (*coll.*) – ***a spade a spade,*** das Kind beim rechten Namen nennen; (*Cards*) – (***one's trump*** or ***hand***), (Trumpf) ansagen.

(a) (*with advs.*) – ***aside,*** beiseite rufen, auf die Seite nehmen; – ***away,*** abrufen, wegrufen; – ***back,*** zurückrufen; – ***down,*** herunterrufen; herabrufen (*blessings, curses etc.*); – ***forth,*** hervorrufen, auslösen (*consequences*), aufbieten (*efforts etc.*), aufrufen (*a p.*); – ***in,*** hereinrufen, herbeirufen (*a p.*), zu Rate ziehen, (hin)zuziehen (*for advice*); einziehen, einfordern, kündigen (*debts*), außer Umlauf setzen, einziehen (*money*); (*coll.*) – ***off,*** abrufen (*a dog etc.*); (*coll.*) absagen, rückgängig machen, (*sl.*) abblasen; – ***out,*** ausrufen, laut rufen; (heraus)fordern (*to a duel etc.*); (*Mil.*) einberufen, aufrufen, aufbieten, ausheben (*troops*); einsetzen (*in an emergency*); – ***over,*** verlesen (*names*); – ***together,*** zusammenrufen, einberufen; – ***up,*** (her)aufrufen, erwecken; (*Tele.*) anrufen; (*coll.*) einberufen, einziehen, ausheben (*troops*); (*fig.*) hervorrufen, wachrufen, vergegenwärtigen, heraufbeschwören (*ideas, memories etc.*), beschwören, zitieren (*spirits*).

(b) (*with preps.*) – ***in***(***to***) ***question,*** bezweifeln, anzweifeln, in Frage stellen; – ***into being,*** ins Leben rufen; – ***into play,*** in Tätigkeit setzen; – ***over the coals,*** gehörig den Kopf waschen (*Dat.*); – ***to account,*** zur Rechenschaft ziehen; – ***to the bar,*** als Advokat zulassen; – ***to mind,*** sich (*Dat.*) ins Gedächtnis zurückrufen, sich erinnern an (*Acc.*); – ***to order,*** zur Ordnung rufen.

2. *v.i.* rufen, schreien (***for,*** nach), ausrufen; einen Besuch machen, vorsprechen (***on,*** bei), anlegen (*of a ship*) (***at,*** in (*Dat.*)); – ***at a port,*** einen Hafen anlaufen; (*fig.*) – ***for,*** (er)fordern, (dringend) verlangen; abholen (*a p. or th.*); ***an article much –ed for,*** vielbegehrter Artikel; ***to be –ed for,*** postlagernd (*on letters*); – ***in,*** einen kurzen Besuch machen, kurz vorsprechen (***on,*** bei); – ***on,*** besuchen (*a p.*), *see also* – ***upon;*** (*B.*) – ***on the name of the Lord,*** den Namen des Herrn anrufen; – ***out,*** aufschreien; – ***to,*** zurufen (*Dat.*); – ***upon,*** sich wenden an (*Acc.*), ersuchen, auffordern (***for,*** um *or* wegen); ***be*** or ***feel –ed upon,*** sich berufen *or* gedrungen *or* genötigt fühlen.

3. *s.* 1. der Ruf, Schrei (***for,*** nach); ***at –,*** bereit, des Rufs gewärtig; (*Comm.*) auf tägliche Kündigung, auf Abruf; – ***to arms*** or ***the colours,*** die Einberufung; – ***of duty,*** das Gebot der Pflicht; – ***for help,*** der Hilferuf; (*coll.*) ***obey the – of nature,*** seine Notdurft verrichten; ***within –,*** in Rufweite, innerhalb Hörweite, gleich zu erreichen; 2. (*Tele.*) der Anruf, das (Telephon)gespräch; (*coll.*) ***give me a –,*** ruf' mich an! 3. (*Theat.*) das Herausrufen (*before the curtain*), der Aufruf (*to the stage*); 4. (*fig.*) (innere) Berufung, der Beruf; 5. (*fig.*) die Aufforderung ((***up***)***on,*** an (*Acc.*)), Inanspruchnahme (*Gen.*); ***have the first – on,*** das Vorrecht haben auf (*Acc.*); 6. kurzer Besuch, (*Naut.*) das Anlaufen; ***port of –,*** der Anlaufhafen; 7. das Signal, Kommando; ***bugle –,*** das Trompetensignal; 8. (*of animals, birds*) der (Lock)ruf; (*Hunt.*) die Lockpfeife; (*fig.*) Lockung, Anziehung(skraft); 9. (*Cards*) Ansage; – ***for trumps,*** den Trumpf bedienen; 10. (*Comm.*) die Nachfrage (***for,*** nach); 11. (*St. Exch.*) Kaufoption, das Prämiengeschäft; ***first –,*** erste Notierung; 12. (*fig.*) (*neg. only*) das Recht, der Grund, die Veranlassung, Befugnis; ***no – to blush,*** kein Grund *or* keine Veranlassung zu erröten.

call|-bird, *s.* der Lockvogel. **--box,** *s.* 1. die Fernsprechzelle, öffentlicher Fernsprecher; 2.

(*Am.*) das Postschließfach. **--boy,** *s.* der Hotelpage; Theaterbursche.

caller ['kɔ:lə], *s.* der (die) Rufer(in), Rufende(r); Besucher(in); (*Tele.*) Sprecher(in); ***many -s,*** viel Besuch.

call-girl, *s.* (*coll.*) (telephonisch erreichbare) Prostituierte.

calligrapher [kə'ligrəfə], *s.* der Schreibkünstler, Schönschreiber, Kalligraph. **calligraphy,** *s.* die Schönschreibkunst, Kalligraphie; Schönschrift, schöne Handschrift.

calling ['kɔ:liŋ], *s.* 1. der Ruf, das Rufen; – ***of the plaintiff,*** das Vorrufen des abwesenden Klägers; 2. der Beruf. das Geschäft; (*Eccl.*) die Berufung. **calling-card,** *s.* (*Am.*) die Visitenkarte.

calliper ['kælipə], *s.* (*usu. pl.*) der Taster, Greifzirkel; ***internal -s,*** der Innen- *or* Lochtaster; ***external -s,*** der Außentaster, Greifzirkel.

callisthenic, *see* **calisthenic.**

call|-loan, *s.* das Darlehen auf tägliche Kündigung. **--money,** *s.* tägliches Geld, das Tagesgeld. **--note,** *s.* der Lockruf (*of birds*). – **number,** *s.* (*Am.*) die Standortnummer (*libraries*).

callosity [kæ'lɔsiti], *s.* die Schwiele, Hautverhärtung, Hornhautbildung.

callous ['kæləs], *adj.* (*Med.*) schwielig, verhärtet, harthäutig; (*fig.*) gefühllos, unempfindlich, abgestumpft, gleichgültig. **callousness,** *s.* (*fig.*) die Härte, Gefühllosigkeit; Unempfindlichkeit, Gleichgültigkeit.

callow ['kælou], *adj.* ungefiedert, kahl; (*fig.*) unerfahren, unreif.

callus ['kæləs], *s.* (*Med.*) die Schwiele, Hornhaut; Knochennarbe; (*Bot.*) verhärtete Stelle, der Kallus.

calm [kɑ:m], **1.** *adj.* ruhig, still; gelassen; – ***day,*** windstiller Tag. **2.** *s.* die Stille, Ruhe; (*Naut. etc.*) Windstille, Flaute; ***dead -,*** völlige Flaute; ***after a storm comes a -,*** auf Regen folgt Sonnenschein. **3.** *v.t.* beruhigen, besänftigen. **4.** *v.i.* – ***down,*** sich beruhigen, ruhig werden, sich legen. **calmness,** *s.* die Stille, Ruhe; Gemütsruhe, Gelassenheit.

calomel ['kælomel], *s.* das Kalomel, Quecksilberchlorür.

calorescence [kælə'resəns], *s.* der Wechsel von Wärmestrahlen in Lichtstrahlen, die Kaloreszenz. **caloric** [kə'lɔrik], **1.** *s.* die Wärme. **2.** *adj.* – ***engine,*** die Heißluftmaschine; – ***unit,*** die Wärmeeinheit. **calorie** ['kæləri], *s.* die Kalorie, Wärmeeinheit. **calorific** [–'rifik], *adj.* Wärme erzeugend, erhitzend; – ***power,*** die Heizkraft; – ***rays,*** die Wärmestrahlen; – ***value,*** der Heizwert. **calorimeter** [–'rimitə], *s.* der Wärmemesser.

calotte [kæ'lɔt], *s.* (*Eccl.*) das Scheitelkäppchen; (*Geom.*) der Kugelabschnitt; (*Med.*) die Schädeldecke; (*Orn.*) Haube; (*Archit.*) Kuppel; (*Mech.*) Kappe, Haube.

caltrop ['kæltrɔp], *s.* die Fußangel; (*Bot.*) Sterndistel.

calumniate [kə'lʌmnieit], *v.t.* verleumden. **calumniation** [–'eiʃən], *s.* die Verleumdung. **calumniator,** *s.* der Verleumder, Ehrabschneider. **calumniatory** [–niətəri], *adj.* verleumderisch, falsch (*of statement*). **calumnious,** *adj.* verleumderisch, lästerlich (*of a p.*). **calumny** ['kæləmni], *s.* die Verleumdung.

Calvary ['kælvəri], *s.* (*B.*) Golgotha (*n.*), die Schädelstätte; (*fig.*) der Leidensweg.

calve [kɑ:v], *v.i.* 1. kalben, ein Kalb werfen; 2. Stücke abstoßen (*of icebergs*).

calves, *pl. See* **calf.**

Calvinism ['kælvinizm], *s.* der Kalvinismus. **Calvinist,** *s.* der (die) Kalvinist(in). **Calvinistic(al)** [–'nistik(l)], *adj.* kalvinistisch.

calx [kælks], *s.* (*obs.*) der Metallkalk, das Oxyd.

calypso [kə'lipsou], *s.* der Kalypso.

calyx ['keiliks], *s.* (*Bot.*) der Kelch.

cam [kæm], *s.* der Daumen, Nocken, die Nocke; Knagge.

camaraderie [kæmə'rɑ:dəri], *s.* die Kameradschaft.

camarilla [kæmə'rilə], *s.* die Hofclique, Hofkabale.

camber ['kæmbə], **1.** *v.t.* wölben, biegen, krümmen. **2.** *s.* die Wölbung, Biegung, Krümmung (*of road etc.*); der Radsturz (*of wheel*). **cambered,** *adj.* gewölbt, gekrümmt, geschweift.

cambist ['kæmbist], *s.* der Wechsler, Wechselmakler.

Cambrian ['kæmbriən], *adj.* walisisch, (*Geol.*) kambrisch.

Cambodia [kæm'boudiə], *s.* die Kambodscha. **Cambodian, 1.** *s.* der (die) Kambodschaner(in). **2.** *adj.* kambodschanisch.

cambric ['keimbrik], *s.* der Battist, Kambrik.

came [keim], *imperf. of* **come.**

camel ['kæməl], *s.* das Kamel (*also Naut.*). **camel|-backed,** *adj.* buckelig. **--driver, cameleer** [–'liə], *s.* der Kameltreiber. **camel-hair,** *s.* das Kamelhaar.

camellia [kə'mi:ljə], *s.* (*Bot.*) die Kamelie.

camelopard ['kæmilopɑ:d], *s.* (*obs.*) die Giraffe.

cameo ['kæmiou], *s.* die Kamee.

camera ['kæmərə], *s.* 1. die Kamera, der Photoapparat, (photographischer) Apparat; 2. (*Law*) das Richterzimmer; ***in -,*** unter Ausschluß der Öffentlichkeit; 3. (*Archit.*) Gewölbe.

cameralist ['kæmərəlist], *s.* (*Hist.*) Staatswissenschaftskundige(r), der Kameralist. **cameralistics** [–'listiks], *pl.* (*sing. constr.*) die Staatswissenschaftskunde, Kameralistik.

camera|man, *s.* der Kameramann, (*coll.*) Kurbler. **--obscura,** *s.* die Lochkamera.

Cameroons ['kæməru:nz], *s.* Kamerun (*n.*).

cam-gear, *s.* (*Mech.*) die Nockensteuerung.

camiknickers ['kæminikəz], *pl.* die Hemdhose.

camisole ['kæmisoul], *s.* das Damenhemd; (*obs.*) Wams, Kamisol.

camlet ['kæmlit], *s.* der Kamelott.

camomile ['kæməmail], *s.* die Kamille. **camomile-tea,** *s.* der Kamillentee.

camouflage ['kæmuflɑ:ʒ], **1.** *s.* die Tarnung, Schutzfärbung, Verschleierung, der Blendanstrich; (*fig.*) die Täuschung, Irreführung. **2.** *v.t.* tarnen; (*fig.*) verschleiern, vertuschen.

[1]**camp** [kæmp], **1.** *s.* das Lager, Feldlager; Zeltlager, Ferienlager; (*fig.*) die Partei, Anhänger (*pl.*); ***pitch -,*** das Lager aufschlagen; ***strike*** or ***break -,*** das Lager abbrechen. **2.** *v.i.* (sich) lagern, das Lager aufschlagen; – ***out,*** im Freien lagern, zelten, kampieren.

[2]**camp,** *adj.* (*sl.*) affektiert, geziert; kitschig.

campaign [kæm'pein], **1.** *s.* der Feldzug; (*fig.*) Kampf, die Schlacht, Kampagne; – ***medal,*** die Erinnerungsmedaille; ***electoral -,*** der Wahlkampf; ***publicity -,*** der Werbefeldzug. **2.** *v.i.* einen Feldzug mitmachen, zu Felde ziehen; (*fig.*) Propaganda machen, werben. **campaigner,** *s.* der Veteran, alter Soldat, (*sl.*) der Zwölfender; (*fig.*) (Mit)kämpfer.

campanile [kæmpə'ni:li], *s.* (freistehender) Glockenturm.

campanologist [kæmpə'nɔlədʒist], *s.* der Glockenläuter. **campanology,** *s.* die Glockenkunde.

campanula [kæm'pænjulə], *s.* (*Bot.*) die Glockenblume.

camp|-bed, *s.* das Feldbett. **--chair,** *s. See* **--stool,**

campeachy-wood [kæm'pi:tʃi], *s.* das Kampescheholz, Blauholz.

camper ['kæmpə], *s.* der Zeltbewohner, Lagerbewohner. **camp|-fever,** *s.* die Lagerseuche, das Fleckfieber. – **fire,** *s.* das Lagerfeuer. **--follower,** *s.* der Schlachtenbummler.

camphor ['kæmfə], *s.* der Kampfer; – ***ball*** die Mottenkugel. **camphorated** [–reitid], *adj.* mit Kampfer gesättigt; – ***spirit(s),*** der Kampferspiritus. **camphoric** [–'fɔrik], *adj.* kampferhaltig; – ***acid,*** die Kampfersäure.

camping [ˈkæmpiŋ], *s.* das Lagern, Zelten, Kampieren; – ***ground*** or ***place*** or ***site,*** der Lagerplatz, Zeltplatz.
campion [ˈkæmpiən], *s.* (*Bot.*) die Lichtnelke, Feuernelke.
camp|-meeting, *s.* (*Am.*) der Feldgottesdienst. – **site,** *s. See* ***camping site.*** **--stool,** *s.* der Klappstuhl.
campus [ˈkæmpəs], *s.* (*Am.*) die (Hoch)schulanlage, das (Hoch)schulgelände; (*fig.*) akademische Welt.
camshaft [ˈkæmʃɑːft], *s.* (*Motor.*) die Nockenwelle, Steuerwelle.
camwood [ˈkæmwud], *s.* das Kam(bal)holz, Rotholz.
¹can [kæn], *irr.v.aux.* 1. kann(st) (*sing.*), können (*pl.*) (***do,*** tun); vermag(st) (*sing.*), vermögen (*pl.*) (zu tun); bin (*etc.*) fähig (zu tun); 2. (*coll.*) *see* **may**; ***as good as – be,*** so gut wie (nur) möglich, (*coll. of a child*) ganz artig; (*coll.*) – ***I go now?*** darf ich jetzt gehen?
²can, 1. *s.* die Dose, Büchse, (Blech)kanne; (*sl.*) ***carry the –,*** den Sündenbock spielen; zahlen *or* blechen müssen. **2.** *v.t.* in Büchsen *or* Dosen einmachen *or* konservieren, eindosen; (*sl.*) – ***it!*** Schluß damit! halt's Maul!
Canaan [ˈkeinən], *s.* (*B.*) Kanaan (*n.*). **Canaanite** [–ait], **1.** *s.* der (die) Kanaaniter(in). **2.** *adj.* kanaanitisch, kanaanäisch.
Canada [ˈkænədə], *s.* Kanada (*n.*). **Canadian** [kəˈneidjən], **1.** *s.* der (die) Kanadier(in). **2.** *adj.* kanadisch.
canaille [kæˈnai], *s.* der Pöbel, das Pack, Gesindel.
canal [kəˈnæl], *s.* der Kanal, (*obs.*) die Wasserstraße; (*Anat.*) Röhre, der Gang; – ***barge*** or ***boat,*** das Kanalboot, der Schleppkahn; – ***lock,*** die Kanalschleuse; – ***navigation,*** die Kanalschiffahrt. **canalization** [kænəlaiˈzeiʃən], *s.* der Kanalbau, die Kanalisation, Kanalisierung. **canalize** [ˈkænəlaiz], *v.t.* kanalisieren, durch Kanalbauten schiffbar machen; (*fig.*) in eine vorbedachte Richtung zielen, in eine vorgeschriebene *or* vorgesehene *or* vorgezeichnete Bahn *or* auf ein vorgestecktes Ziel leiten.
canard [keˈnɑː(d)], *s.* die Zeitungsente, Falschmeldung, falsches Gerücht.
canary [kəˈnɛəri], *s.* (*obs.* – ***bird***) der Kanarienvogel; – ***yellow,*** kanariengelb.
canasta [kəˈnæstə], *s.* das Kanasta.
canaster [kəˈnæstə], *s.* (– ***tobacco***) der Knaster.
can-buoy, *s.* (*Naut.*) die Tonnenboje.
cancel [kænsl], **1.** *v.t.* (aus)streichen, durchstreichen; (*Comm.*) abbestellen, stornieren, rückgängig machen; aufheben, annullieren, widerrufen (*instructions*), absagen (*plans etc.*), tilgen, ausgleichen (*debt*), entwerten, ungültig machen (*postage stamp*); (*Math.*) heben; (*Mus.*) aufheben, auflösen; – ***a booking,*** eine Karte abbestellen; – ***a performance,*** eine Vorstellung absagen; ***until cancelled,*** bis auf Widerruf; – ***a will,*** ein Testament für nichtig erklären. **2.** *v.i.* (*Math.*) – ***out,*** sich aufheben; (*fig.*) sich gegenseitig widerlegen.
cancellate(d) [ˈkænsəleit(id)], *adj.* (*Anat.*) netzförmig, gegittert.
cancellation [kænsəˈleiʃən], *s.* die (Durch)streichung, (*Comm.*) Abbestellung, Rückgängigmachung, Stornierung; Abschaffung, Aufhebung, Annullierung, der Widerruf; (*postage stamps*) die Entwertung.
cancer [ˈkænsə], *s.* 1. (*Med.*) der Krebs, das Karzinom; (*fig.*) der Krebsschaden; 2. (*Astr.*) ***Cancer,*** der Krebs. **cancerous,** *adj.* krebsartig, karzinomatös.
candelabrum [kændəˈlɑːbrəm], *s.* (*pl.* **-bra**) (*usu. pl. with sing. constr.*) der Kandelaber, Armleuchter.
candescent [kænˈdesənt], *adj.* (weiß)glühend.
candid [ˈkændid], *adj.* aufrichtig, ehrlich, redlich, offen; – ***camera,*** unparteiische *or* unvoreingenommene Bildberichterstattung.
candidate [ˈkændidit], *s.* der Bewerber (***for,*** um), Kandidat (für). **candidature** [–tʃə], *s.* die Kandidatur, Bewerbung, Anwartschaft.
candied [ˈkændid], *adj.* überzuckert, kandiert; (*fig.*) honigsüß; – ***peel,*** das Zitronat.
candle [kændl], *s.* die Kerze, das Licht; Kerzenlicht; (*coll.*) ***the game isn't worth the –,*** die S. ist der Mühe nicht wert; (*fig.*) ***burn the – at both ends,*** sich übernehmen, sich allzusehr ausgeben, seine Kräfte vergeuden, seine Gesundheit untergraben; (*fig.*) ***he couldn't hold a – to him,*** er konnte ihm das Wasser nicht reichen, er konnte mit ihm keinen Vergleich aushalten.
candle|berry tree, *s.* der Kerzennußbaum. **--end,** *s.* der Lichtstumpf. – **extinguisher,** *s.* das Lichthütchen. **--holder,** *s. See* **–stick. –light,** *s.* das Kerzenlicht, die Kerzenbeleuchtung; ***by –,*** bei Kerzenlicht.
Candlemas [ˈkændlməs], *s.* (*Eccl.*) die Lichtmeß.
candle|-power, *s.* die Lichtstärke, (*norm*) Normalkerze. **–stick,** *s.* der Leuchter, Kerzenhalter, Kerzenständer. **--wick,** *s.* der Kerzendocht; das Frotté, Frottee (*material*).
candour [ˈkændə], *s.* die Offenheit, Redlichkeit, Aufrichtigkeit.
candy [ˈkændi], **1.** *s.* (*Am.*) das Zuckerwerk, Konfekt; Süßwaren (*pl.*), Süßigkeiten (*pl.*), Bonbons (*pl.*); ***sugar –,*** der Kandiszucker. **2.** *v.t.* in Zucker einmachen; kristallisieren lassen (*of sugar*). **3.** *v.i.* kandieren, kristallisieren. **candy|-floss,** *s.* die Zuckerwatte. **--store,** *s.* (*Am.*) das Bonbongeschäft. **--striped,** *adj.* buntgestreift.
candytuft [ˈkænditʌft], *s.* (*Bot.*) die Schleifenblume.
cane [kein], **1.** *s.* das (Schilf)rohr; der Rohrstock; (Spazier)stock; (***sugar--***) das Zuckerrohr. **2.** *v.t.* züchtigen. **cane|-brake,** *s.* das Röhricht. **--chair,** *s.* der Rohrstuhl, Korbstuhl. **--plaiting,** *s.* das Rohrgeflecht. **--sugar,** *s.* der Rohrzucker. **--trash,** *s.* die Bagasse, Zuckerrohrrückstände (*pl.*). **--worker,** *s.* der Rohrflechter.
canicular [kəˈnikjulə], *adj.* – ***days,*** die Hundstage.
canine [ˈkeinain, ˈkænain], *adj.* Hunde–, Hunds–; – ***madness,*** die Tollwut, Hundswut; – ***teeth,*** Eckzähne, Augenzähne; – ***varieties,*** Hundespielarten.
caning [ˈkeiniŋ], *s.* die Tracht Prügel, Züchtigung, Prügelstrafe.
canister [ˈkænistə], *s.* die Blechbüchse. **canister-shot,** *s.* die Kartätsche.
canker [ˈkæŋkə], **1.** *s.* (*Med.*) das Krebsgeschwür; (*Bot.*) der Rost, Brand, Fraß, Baumkrebs; (*fig.*) Krebsschaden, das Grundübel, nagender Wurm. **2.** *v.t.* anfressen, zerfressen, vergiften, anstecken. **3.** *v.i.* angenagt *or* angefressen *or* angesteckt *or* vergiftet werden, (langsam) verderben. **cankered,** *adj.* angefressen, zerfressen, vergiftet, verdorben; (*fig.*) mürrisch, verdrießlich, bösartig, mißgünstig. **cankerous,** *adj.* krebsig, krebsartig; verderblich, (an)fressend. **canker-worm,** *s.* schädliche Raupe; (*fig.*) nagender Wurm, fressendes Übel.
cannabis [ˈkænəbis], *s.* indischer Hanf, der Haschisch.
canned [kænd], *adj.* 1. Dosen–, Büchsen–, konserviert, eingedost; (*coll.*) – ***music,*** die Konservenmusik; 2. (*sl.*) besoffen; *see* **²can.**
cannel-coal [ˈkænlkoul], *s.* die Kännelkohle.
canner [ˈkænə], *s.* der Konservenfabrikant. **cannery,** *s.* die Konservenfabrik. *See* **²can.**
cannibal [ˈkænibl], *s.* der Menschenfresser, Kannibale. **cannibalism,** *s.* der Kannibalismus, die Menschenfresserei. **cannibalize,** *v.t.* (*coll.*) ausschlachten.
canniness [ˈkæninis], *s.* (*Scots*) die Klugheit, Schlauheit, Erfahrenheit; Umsicht, Vorsicht, Sparsamkeit.
canning [ˈkæniŋ], *s.* die Konservenfabrikation; *see* **²can.**
cannon [ˈkænən], **1.** *s.* 1. die Kanone, das Geschütz; (*collect.*) Geschütze (*pl.*), Kanonen (*pl.*), die Artillerie; 2. (*Bill.*) Karambolage. **2.** *v.i.* (*Bill.*) karambolieren; (*fig.*) – ***into,*** rennen *or* stoßen an

(*Acc.*) *or* gegen. **cannonade, 1.** *s.* die Kanonade, Beschießung, Bombardierung, (*fig.*) das Donnern. **2.** *v.t.* beschießen, bombardieren.

cannon|ball, *s.* die Kanonenkugel. **--bit,** *s.* das Mundstück des Stangengebisses. **--bone,** *s.* der Mittelfußknochen, das Sprungbein (*of horse*). **– fodder,** *s.* (*fig.*) das Kanonenfutter. **--foundry,** *s.* die Stückgießerei. **--pinion,** *s.* (*Horol.*) der Zapfen des Minutenzeigers. **--shot,** *s.* der Kanonenschuß, Kanonenkugeln (*pl.*); die Schußweite.

cannot ['kænɔt], *neg. indic. of* [1]**can.**

canny ['kæni], *adj.* (*Scots*) klug, schlau, erfahren; vorsichtig, umsichtig, sparsam.

canoe [kə'nu:], **1.** *s.* das Kanu, Paddelboot. **2.** *v.i.* paddeln, in einem Kanu fahren. **canoeing,** *s.* der Kanusport, das Paddeln.

[1]**canon** ['kænən], *s.* (*Eccl.*) kirchliche Vorschrift, der Kanon; (*fig.*) die Vorschrift, Regel, Richtschnur, der Maßstab, Wertmesser Grundsatz, das Prinzip; (*B.*) kanonische Bücher (*pl.*), (*fig.*) (*of any author*) authentische Schriften (*pl.*); (*Mus.*) der Kanon; (*Typ.*) die Kanonschrift; *– **law,*** das Kirchenrecht; ***the sacred –,*** der Meßkanon.

[2]**canon,** *s.* der Domherr, Stiftsherr, Kanonikus; ***regular –,*** regulierter Domherr; ***secular –,*** weltlicher Domherr. **canoness,** *s.* die Stiftsdame, Kanonissin.

canonic [kæ'nɔnik], *adj.* (*Mus.*) kanonartig, kanonisch, Kanon–. **canonical,** *adj.* (*Eccl.*) kanonisch, vorschriftsmäßig; anerkannt; ***– books,*** kanonische Bücher; ***– hours,*** vorgeschriebene Gebetsstunden; ***– punishment,*** die Kirchenstrafe. **canonicals,** *pl.* das Ornat, der Talar, kirchliche Amtstracht, Meßgewände (*pl.*). **canonicity** [–'nisiti], *s.* die Kirchengemäßheit, das Kanonische, die Echtheit. **canonist** ['kænənist], *s.* der Kirchenrechtslehrer. **canonization** [–nai'zeiʃən], *s.* die Heiligsprechung. **canonize,** *v.t.* heiligsprechen, (*fig.*) sanktionieren, gutheißen.

canonry ['kænənri], *s.* die Stiftspfründe, das Kanonikat; *see* [2]**canon.**

canoodle [kə'nu:dl], *v.i.* (*sl.*) liebkosen, flirten.

can-opener, *s.* der Dosenöffner.

canopy ['kænəpi], **1.** *s.* der Baldachin, Betthimmel, Thronhimmel, Traghimmel; das Schutzdach, die Decke, Hülle; (*Poet.*) der Himmel, das Firmament; ***– of a pulpit,*** der Schalldeckel; ***– of heaven,*** das Himmelszelt. **2.** *v.t.* (mit einem Baldachin) bedecken *or* überdachen.

can't [kɑ:nt], (*coll.*) (*abbr. of* **cannot**) *see* [1]**can.**

[1]**cant** [kænt], **1.** *s.* die Schrägung, geneigte Lage *or* Fläche; die Neigung, schiefer Stand. **2.** *v.t.* (*also **– over***) schräg *or* auf die Seite legen, kanten, (um)kippen; (*Tech.*) (schräg) abkanten, abschrägen. **3.** *v.i.* (*also **– over***) sich auf die Seite legen; schräg liegen *or* stehen.

[2]**cant, 1.** *s.* 1. die Scheinheiligkeit, Frömmelei, Heuchelei; 2. Zunftsprache, Fachsprache, der Jargon; die Gaunersprache, das Rotwelsch; (*fig.*) Kauderwelsch; ***– phrase,*** stehende Redensart, nichtssagendes Schlagwort. **2.** *v.i.* (*rare*) scheinheilig reden, sich scheinheilig benehmen; kauderwelschen.

cantaloup ['kæntəlu:p], *s.* die Beutelmelone.

cantankerous [kæn'tæŋkərəs], *adj.* mürrisch, streitsüchtig, rechthaberisch.

cantata [kæn'tɑ:tə], *s.* (*Mus.*) die Kantate.

canted ['kæntid], *adj.* gekantet, (auf die Seite) geneigt, umgekippt; *see* [1]**cant.**

canteen [kæn'ti:n], *s.* 1. die Feldflasche; das Kochgeschirr; 2. die Kantine, der Speiseraum, Erfrischungsraum; ***– of cutlery,*** der Besteckkasten.

canter ['kæntə], **1.** *s.* leichter *or* kurzer Galopp, der Kanter; (*coll.*) ***win in a –,*** mühelos gewinnen. **2.** *v.i.* im leichten Galopp reiten, kantern.

cantharides [kæn'θæridi:z], *pl.* Spanische Fliegen (*pl.*).

cant-hook, *s.* (*Naut.*) der Kanthaken; *see* [1]**cant.**

canticle ['kæntikl], *s.* (*Eccl.*) der (Lob)gesang. **Canticles,** *pl.* (*B.*) das Hohelied Salomo(ni)s.

cantilever ['kæntili:və], **1.** *s.* der Ausleger, vorspringender Träger. **2.** *adj.* freitragend; ***– bridge,*** die Auslegerbrücke; ***– monoplane,*** freitragender Eindecker.

canting ['kæntiŋ], *adj.* scheinheilig, heuchlerisch; *see* [2]**cant.**

cantle [kæntl], *s.* die Hinterzwiesel (*of saddle*).

canto ['kæntou], *s.* (*pl.* **-s**) der Gesang (*of a long poem*).

canton, 1. ['kæntən, kæn'tɔn], *s.* 1. der Kanton, Bezirk (*esp. Switzerland*); 2. (*Her.*) das Quartier, Eckschildchen. **2.** [kæn'tɔn, –'tu:n], *v.t.* (*Mil.*) (*also **– out***) unterbringen, einquartieren; Quartiere zuweisen (*Dat.*). **cantonal** ['kæntənl], *adj.* kantonal, Bezirks–. **cantonment** [kæn'tɔnmənt, –'tu:nmənt], *s.* die Kantonierung, Einquartierung; (Orts)unterkunft, das Quartier.

cantor ['kæntɔ], *s.* der Kantor, Vorsänger.

cant-timbers, *pl.* (*Naut.*) Kantspanten (*pl.*); *see* [1]**cant.**

canvas ['kænvəs], *s.* das Segeltuch, der Drillich; (*for embroidery*) Kanevas, das Gitterleinen; (*for painting*) die (Maler)leinwand, (*fig.*) das (Öl)gemälde (auf Leinwand); (*Naut.*) Segel (*pl.*); (*fig.*) das Zelt; ***under –,*** in Zelten; (*Naut.*) ***under full –,*** mit allen Segeln; ***– bucket,*** der Wassersack, die Pütze.

canvass ['kænvəs], **1.** *s.* sorgfältige Prüfung; (*Pol.*) die Stimmenwerbung, Wahlpropaganda. **2.** *v.t.* sorgfältig prüfen, genau untersuchen, eingehend erörtern; (*Pol.*) ausfragen (*voters*); werben um (*votes*); bearbeiten, (*coll.*) abklappern (*constituency*). **3.** *v.i.* (Stimmen) werben (*for*, um). **canvasser,** *s.* (*Pol.*) der Stimmenwerber, (*Comm.*) Kundenwerber, Abonnentensammler. **canvassing,** *s.* die Erörterung, Untersuchung; (*Pol.*) Stimmenwerbung, Wahlpropaganda, (*Comm.*) (Kunden)werbung, Reklame.

canyon ['kænjən], *s.* (tiefe) Bergschlucht.

caoutchouc ['kautʃu:k], *s.* der Kautschuk, Gummi.

cap [kæp], **1.** *s.* 1. die Kappe, Mütze, Haube; ***– and bells,*** die Schellenkappe; (*Spt.*) ***get one's –,*** die Klubmütze *or* Mannschaftsmütze bekommen, ausgezeichnet werden, in die Mannschaft aufgenommen werden; (*Univ.*) ***– and gown,*** akademische Tracht; Barett und Talar; (*fig.*) ***that's a feather in his –,*** darauf kann er stolz sein; (*fig.*) ***the – fits him,*** er fühlt sich betroffen; (*Prov.*) ***if the – fits wear it,*** wen's juckt, der kratze sich; wem die Jacke paßt, der ziehe sie sich an; (*fig.*) ***– in hand,*** demütig, unterwürfig; (*Hist.*) ***– of maintenance,*** die Schirmhaube; (*coll.*) ***put on one's thinking –,*** die Gedanken zusammennehmen; (*coll.*) ***she sets her – at him,*** sie ist hinter ihm her, sie angelt nach ihm; 2. Zündkapsel, Sprengkapsel, das Zündhütchen, (*for toy guns*) Zündplättchen; 3. die Kapsel, der Verschluß, Deckel; Aufsatz, Knauf; (*Naut.*) das Eselshaupt. **2.** *v.t.* bedecken, mit einem Deckel versehen; krönen, oben liegen auf (*Dat.*); (*Univ.*) einen akademischen Grad verleihen (*Dat.*); (*Spt.*) auszeichnen, in die Mannschaft aufnehmen; (*fig.*) übertreffen, ausstechen; ***– a joke,*** einen Witz überbieten; (*Motor.*) ***– a tyre,*** einen Reifen runderneuern; ***– verses,*** Verse um die Wette hersagen.

capability [keipə'biliti], *s.* die Fähigkeit, Tauglichkeit (*of*, zu); Befähigung, Begabung, das Talent, Vermögen. **capable** ['keipəbl], *adj.* fähig (*of*, zu *or Gen.*), tauglich (zu), imstande (***of doing***, zu tun); (*of a p.*) befähigt, begabt, (leistungs)fähig, tüchtig; (*Law*) befähigt, berechtigt, ermächtigt.

capacious [kə'peiʃəs], *adj.* weit, umfassend, geräumig, aufnahmefähig. **capaciousness,** *s.* die Geräumigkeit, Weite.

capacitance [kə'pæsitəns], *s.* (*Elec.*) kapazitive Reaktanz, kapazitiver (Blind)widerstand, die Kapazitanz, Kondensanz.

capacitate [kə'pæsiteit], *v.t.* befähigen, (*Law*) ermächtigen, berechtigen.

capacity [kə'pæsiti], **1.** *s.* 1. der Inhalt, Gehalt, Umfang, das Volumen; die Geräumigkeit, Aufnahmefähigkeit, der Raum, das Fassungsvermögen, (*of* (*vehicles*) die Ladefähigkeit; ***measure of* –**, das Hohlmaß; ***filled*** or ***full to* –**, gedrängt *or* gesteckt voll; 2. (*of an engine*) der (Gesamt)hubraum; 3. (*Elec.*) die Kapazität; 4. (*fig.*) Aufnahmefähigkeit, (geistige) Fassungskraft; die (Leistungs)fähigkeit, Kraft, das Vermögen; der Charakter, die Eigenschaft; (*Law*) Zuständigkeit, Kompetenz; ***in his* – *as,*** in seiner Eigenschaft als; ***official* –**, dienstliche Eigenschaft; (*Comm.*) **– *to pay,*** die Zahlungsfähigkeit; ***productive* –**, die Leistungsfähigkeit; ***working to* –**, mit voller Leistungsfähigkeit arbeiten. **2.** *adj.* (*coll.*) (*Theat.*) **– *house,*** ausverkauftes Haus.

cap-à-pie [kæpə'pi:], *adv.* von Kopf (bis) zu Fuß.

caparison [kə'pærizn], *s.* die Schabracke; Pferdedecke; (*fig.*) Ausstaffierung, Ausstattung, Ausrüstung.

1**cape** [keip], *s.* der Umhang, das Cape.

2**cape,** *s.* das Vorgebirge, Kap, die Landzunge; ***Cape Colony,*** die Kapkolonie; ***Cape Dutch,*** Kapholländer, Buren (*pl.*); (*language*) das Kapholländisch, Afrikaans; ***Cape gooseberry,*** die Erdkirsche; ***Cape of Good Hope,*** das Kap der Guten Hoffnung; ***Cape Town,*** Kapstadt (*f.*); ***Cape Verde Islands,*** die Kapverdischen Inseln.

1**caper** ['keipə], **1.** *s.* der Bocksprung, Luftsprung, Freudensprung, die Kapriole; der Schabernack, dummer Streich; ***cut* –*s,*** Kapriolen *or* Dummheiten machen. **2.** *v.i.* Freudensprünge machen, (vor Freude) hüpfen.

2**caper,** *s.* der Kapernstrauch; (*usu. pl.*) die Kaper; **– *sauce,*** die Kapernsoße.

capercaillie, capercailzie [kæpə'keilji], *s.* (*Orn.*) das Auerhuhn (*Tetrao urogallus*).

Capetian [kə'pi:ʃən], **1.** *s.* der Kapetinger. **2.** *adj.* kapetingisch.

capful ['kæpful], *s.* (*Naut.*) ***a* – *of wind,*** vorübergehender *or* eine Mütze Wind; *see* **cap.**

capillarity [kæpi'læriti], *s.* die Kapillarwirkung, Kapillarität. **capillary** [kə'piləri], **1.** *adj.* haarförmig, haarfaserig, haarfein, kapillar; **– *attraction,*** die Kapillaranziehung; **– *pyrites,*** der Haarkies. **2.** *s.* (*Anat.*) das Kapillargefäß, die Kapillare.

1**capital** ['kæpitl], **1.** *adj.* 1. (*of crimes*) Todes–, todeswürdig, kapital; **– *crime,*** das Kapitalverbrechen; **– *punishment,*** die Todesstrafe; 2. (*fig.*) größt, höchst, äußerst, wichtigst, Haupt–; (*coll.*) vortrefflich, vorzüglich, herrlich, glänzend, ausgezeichnet, großartig, erstklassig, famos, Mords–; **– *city,*** die Hauptstadt; ***of* – *importance,*** von äußerster Wichtigkeit; **– *joke,*** der Mordsspaß; **– *letter,*** großer Anfangsbuchstabe; **– *ship,*** (großes) Kriegsschiff. **2.** *s.* 1. die Hauptstadt; 2. großer Anfangsbuchstabe.

2**capital,** *s.* (*Archit.*) das Kapitäl, Kapitell, der Säulenknauf.

3**capital,** *s.* (*Comm.*) das Kapital, (Rein)vermögen; (*collect.*) Unternehmertum; (*fig.*) der Vorteil, Nutzen; **– *gains tax,*** die Kapitalertragssteuer; ***floating* –**, das Betriebskapital; ***invested* –**, das Anlagekapital; ***invest*** or ***sink* – *in,*** Geld anlegen in (*Acc.*); ***make* – *out of,*** Kapital schlagen aus, Nutzen *or* Vorteil ziehen aus; ***unproductive* –**, totes Kapital. **capitalism,** *s.* der Kapitalismus. **capitalist,** *s.* der Kapitalist. **capitalistic** [–'listik], *adj.* kapitalistisch.

capitalization [kæpitəlai'zeiʃən], *s.* 1. (*Comm.*) die Kapitalisierung, Kapitalausstattung; 2. (*Typ.*) Großschreibung. **capitalize, 1.** *v.t.* 1. (*Comm.*) kapitalisieren, in Kapital umsetzen, zum Kapital schlagen; mit Kapital ausstatten (*an undertaking*); 2. (*Typ.*) mit großen Buchstaben schreiben. **2.** *v.i.* (*fig.*) Nutzen ziehen (*on*, aus).

capitation [kæpi'teiʃən], *s.* die Kopfzählung; Kopfsteuer; **– *fee,*** das Kopfgeld.

Capitol ['kæpitəl], *s.* (*Rome*) das Kapitol; (*Am.*) Kongreßgebäude.

capitular [kə'pitjulə], **1.** *adj,* 1. (*Eccl.*) Kapitel–, kapitular, Stifts–; 2. (*Anat., Bot.*) Köpfchen–, köpfchenförmig. **2.** *s.* der Stiftsherr, Kapitular, das Mitglied eines Domkapitels; (*Hist.*) Kapitulare (*pl.*).

capitulary [kə'pitjuləri], **1.** *adj.* *See* **capitular, 1,** 1. **2.** *s.* *See* **capitular, 2.**

capitulate [kə'pitjuleit], *v.i.* kapitulieren (*to*, vor (*Acc.*)), sich unterwerfen *or* ergeben (*Dat.*); (*fig.*) die Waffen strecken. **capitulation** [–'leiʃən], *s.* die Übergabe, Kapitulation, Waffenstreckung.

capon ['keipɔn], *s.* der Kapaun. **caponize** [–aiz], *v.t.* kapaunen, kastrieren (*fowl*).

capot [kə'pɔt], *s.* der Matsch (im Pikett).

capote [kə'pout], *s.* die Kapotte, der Kapuzenmantel.

caprice [kə'pri:s], *s.* die Laune, Grille; Launenhaftigkeit; (*Mus.*) das Capriccio. **capricious** [kə'priʃəs], *adj.* launisch, launenhaft, unberechenbar, mutwillig, unbeständig. **capriciousness,** *s.* die Launenhaftigkeit.

Capricorn ['kæprikɔ:n], *s.* (*Astr.*) der Steinbock; ***capricorn beetle,*** der Bockkäfer.

capriole ['kæprioul], *s.* die Kapriole, der Bocksprung.

capsicum ['kæpsikəm], *s.* spanischer Pfeffer.

capsize [kæp'saiz], **1.** *v.t.* zum Kentern bringen, umwerfen. **2.** *v.i.* kentern, umschlagen, umkippen.

capstan ['kæpstən], *s.* (*Naut.*) die Ankerwinde, das (Gang)spill; (*Tech.*) die (Erd)winde, (*of tape recorder*) Bandantriebsachse. **capstan-bar,** *s.* die (Gang)spillspake, Handspake.

capsular ['kæpsjulə], *adj.* kapselförmig; (*Anat.*) **– *ligament,*** das Kapselband. **capsulate(d)** [–leit(id)], *adj.* verkapselt, eingekapselt. **capsule,** *s.* die Kapsel, Schale, Hülle; (*Chem.*) Abdampfschale, der Schmelztiegel, die Kupelle, Kapelle; (*Artil.*) ***primer* –**, die Zündpille.

captain ['kæptin], *s.* (*Naut.*) der Kapitän, (*Mil.*) Hauptmann, (*cavalry*) Rittmeister, (*Spt.*) Mannschaftsführer, (*of a school*) Primus; **– *of industry,*** Großindustrielle(r), der Industrieführer. **captaincy** [–si], *s.* der Rang eines Hauptmanns *etc.* **captainship,** *s.* die Führerrolle, Führung.

caption ['kæpʃən], *s.* die Überschrift, Rubrik, der Titel, (Titel)kopf, (*Films*) Zwischentitel; (*illustrations*) Bildtext, die (Bild)unterschrift, Legende; (*Law*) Einleitungsformel, Präambel; (*rare*) (*Law*) Verhaftung, Wegnahme.

captious ['kæpʃəs], *adj.* verfänglich, heikel; spitzfindig, krittelig; **– *critic,*** der Besserwisser, Nörgler, Meckerer, Kritikaster. **captiousness,** *s.* die Verfänglichkeit (*of a question*), Spitzfindigkeit, Tadelsucht, der Widerspruchsgeist (*of a p.*).

captivate ['kæptiveit], *v.t.* (*fig.*) fesseln, gefangennehmen, (für sich) einnehmen; gewinnen, bestricken, bezaubern. **captivating,** *adj.* fesselnd, bezaubernd, einnehmend.

captive ['kæptiv], **1.** *adj.* gefangen, festgehalten; **– *balloon,*** der Fesselballon; ***take* –**, gefangennehmen. **2.** *s.* Gefangene(r), (*fig.*) der Sklave, das Opfer. **captivity** [–'tiviti], *s.* die Gefangenschaft, (*fig.*) Knechtschaft.

captor ['kæptə], *s.* der Fänger, Erbeuter; (*Naut.*) Kaper.

capture ['kæptʃə], **1.** *s.* das Fangen; die Gefangennahme (*of prisoners*), Einnahme, Eroberung (*of a place*), das Erbeuten (*of stores*); (*Naut.*) die Prise, Aufbringung, das Kapern; der Fang, Raub, die Beute; ***right of* –**, das Prisenrecht. **2.** *v.t.* fangen, abfangen; (*Mil.*) erobern, einnehmen (*a place*), gefangennehmen (*prisoners*), erbeuten (*stores*); (*Naut.*) kapern, aufbringen (*a ship*); (*fig.*) ergreifen, erlangen, gewinnen; ***it* –*d my fancy,*** es fesselte mich; (*Mil.*) ***be* –*d,*** in Gefangenschaft kommen.

capuchin ['kæputʃin], *s.* 1. die Kapuze; 2. der Kapuziner(mönch). **capuchin|-monkey,** *s.* der Rollschwanzaffe, Kapuzineraffe. **–-pigeon,** *s.* die Haubentaube.

car [kɑ:], *s.* der (Kraft)wagen, das Auto(mobil); der Wagen, Karren; die Gondel (*of a balloon*); (*Railw.*)

(*esp. Am.*) der Eisenbahnwagen, Waggon; ***dining-–,*** der Speisewagen; ***sleeping-–,*** der Schlafwagen; (***tram*** (*Am.* ***street***)) –, der Straßenbahnwagen; ***triumphal –,*** der Triumphwagen; – ***driver,*** der Kraftfahrer, Autofahrer; – ***park,*** der Parkplatz.

carabineer [kærəbi'niə], *s.* der Karabinier.

caracol(e) ['kærəkoul], **1.** *s.* 1. halbe Wendung, die Karakole (*of a horse*); 2. Wendeltreppe. **2.** *v.i.* halbe Wendungen machen, karakolieren.

carafe [kə'ræf], *s.* die Wasserflasche, Karaffe.

caramel ['kærəməl], *s.* der Karamel; gebrannter Zucker; (*sweetmeat*) die Karamelle, der *or* das Sahnebonbon.

carapace ['kærəpeis], *s.* der Rückenschild.

carat ['kærət], **1.** *s.* das Karat; der Goldfeingehalt. **2.** *adj.* karätig.

caravan ['kærəvæn], **1.** *s.* 1. die Karawane; 2. der Wohnwagen, Reisewagen; Menageriewagen; – ***site,*** der Campingplatz. **2.** *v.i.* im Wohnwagen reisen. **caravansary, caravanserai** [–'vænsərai], *s.* die Karawanserei.

caraway ['kærəwei], *s.* der Kümmel. **caraway-seed,** *s.* der Kümmelsamen, *pl.* der Kümmel.

carbide ['kɑ:baid], *s.* das Karbid.

carbine ['kɑ:bain], *s.* der Karabiner.

carbohydrate [kɑ:bo'haidreit], *s.* das Kohlehydrat.

carbolic [kɑ:'bɔlik], *adj.* karbolsauer; – ***acid,*** die Karbolsäure, das Phenol; – ***soap*** die Karbolseife.

carbon ['kɑ:bən], *s.* 1. (*Chem.*) der Kohlenstoff; – ***dioxide,*** das Kohlendioxyd, die Kohlensäure; – ***monoxide,*** das Kohlenoxyd; – ***tetrachloride,*** der Tetrachlorkohlenstoff; 2. (*Elec.*) die Kohlestift, die Kohle(elektrode); – (***filament***) ***lamp,*** die Kohle(n)fadenlampe; – ***pile,*** graphitmoderierter Reaktor; 3. die Ölkohle (*in cylinder*); 4. (*coll.*) das Kohlepapier; (*coll.*) der Durchschlag; – ***copy,*** der Durchschlag; – ***paper,*** das Kohlepapier, Durchschlagpapier. **carbonaceous** [–'neiʃəs], *adj.* (*Geol.*) kohlenhaltig, kohlenreich, (*Chem.*) kohlenstoffhaltig, Kohlen–, kohleartig. **carbonate, 1.** [–neit], *v.t.* (*Chem.*) mit Kohlensäure sättigen; karbonisieren. **2.** [–nit], *s.* das Karbonat, kohlensaures Salz; – ***of soda,*** kohlensaures Natron. **carbonic** [–'bɔnik], *adj.* kohlensauer, Kohlen–; – ***acid,*** die Kohlensäure; – ***acid gas,*** das Kohlensäuregas. **carboniferous** [–'nifərəs], *adj.* kohlen(stoff)haltig, kohlig, (*Geol.*) kohleführend; – ***limestone,*** der Kohlenkalkstein; – ***period,*** die Steinkohlenzeit, das Karbon. **carbonization** [–nai'zeiʃən], *s.* (*Chem.*) die Verbindung mit Kohlenstoff, Karbonisation; (*Tech.*) Verkohlung, Verkokung, Verschwelung; (*Geol.*) Inkohlung; – ***plant,*** die Kokerei. **carbonize,** *v.t.* (*Chem.*) mit Kohlenstoff verbinden, karbonisieren, (*Tech.*) verkohlen, verkoken; (*Geol.*) inkohlen; ***partially –,*** ankohlen.

carborundum [kɑ:bə'rʌndəm], *s.* das Siliziumkarbid, Karborundum.

carboy ['kɑ:bɔi], *s.* (*Chem.*) die Korbflasche, der Ballon.

carbuncle ['kɑ:bʌŋkl], *s.* (*Med.*) der Karbunkel, Furunkel; (*Min.*) (*obs.*) Karfunkel(stein).

carburation [kɑ:bju'reiʃən], *s. See* **carburetion. carburet** [–'ret], *v.t.* karburieren, vergasen. **carburetion** [–'reʃən], *s.* die Vergasung, Karburierung. **carburetted,** *adj.* mit Kohlenstoff verbunden, karburiert; – ***hydrogen,*** das Kohlenwasserstoffgas. **carburettor,** *s.* (*Motor.*) der Vergaser.

carcass ['kɑ:kəs], *s.* der Kadaver, die Tierleiche; (*hum.*) Leiche, der Leichnam, Körper; (*fig.*) das Gerippe, Skelett, der Rumpf.

carcinogenic [kɑ:sino'dʒi:nik], *adj.* (*Med.*) krebserzeugend, karzinogen. **carcinoid** ['kɑ:sinɔid], *adj.* krebsähnlich. **carcinoma** [–'noumə], *s.* (*Med.*) das Krebsgeschwür, Karzinom.

[1]**card** [kɑ:d], *s.* die Karte; Postkarte; Spielkarte; Visitenkarte; Mitgliedskarte; (*fig.*) Mitteilung, Anzeige; (*horse-racing*) das Programm; *pl.* (*usu. sing. constr.*) Kartenspiel(en); (*coll.*) (*of a p.*) Original, der Kauz; (*coll.*) *see* **cardboard**; ***compass –,*** die Windrose; ***identification –,*** die Ausweiskarte; (*coll.*) ***get one's –s,*** den Laufpaß bekommen; ***have a – up one's sleeve,*** einen Trumpf in der Hand *or* etwas in petto haben; ***lay one's –s on the table,*** mit offenen Karten spielen; (*coll.*) ***on the –s,*** durchaus möglich, gut denkbar; ***pack of –s,*** das Spiel Karten; (*coll.*) ***queer –,*** komische Nummer; ***ration –,*** die Lebensmittelkarte, der Bezugsschein; ***show one's –s,*** die Karten aufdecken; ***throw up one's –s,*** das Spiel aufgeben; ***trump –,*** der Trumpf, das Trumpfblatt; – ***to view,*** die Erlaubniskarte zur Besichtigung; ***visiting –,*** die Visitenkarte.

[2]**card, 1.** *s.* die Karde, Kardätsche, (Woll)kratze, Krempel(maschine). **2.** *v.t.* kardätschen, krempeln, karden (*wool etc.*); ***–ed yarn,*** das Kammgarn, Halbgarn.

cardan| joint ['kɑ:dən], *s.* das Kreuzgelenk, Kardangelenk. – **shaft,** *s.* die Gelenkwelle, Kardanwelle.

cardboard ['kɑ:dbɔ:d], *s.* der Karton, die Pappe; – ***box,*** die Pappschachtel.

card|-catalogue, *s. See* **–-index.**

carder ['kɑ:də], *s.* der Wollkämmer, Krempler; *see* [2]**card.**

card-game, *s.* das Kartenspiel.

cardiac ['kɑ:diæk], **1.** *adj.* Herz–; – ***murmur,*** das Herzgeräusch. **2.** *s.* herzstärkendes Mittel.

cardialgia [kɑ:di'ældʒiə], *s.* (*Med.*) das Sodbrennen.

cardigan ['kɑ:digən], *s.* die Wolljacke, Strickweste, Strickjacke.

[1]**cardinal** ['kɑ:dinəl], *adj.* 1. vornehmlich, vornehmst, hauptsächlich, Grund–, Haupt–, Kardinal–; ***of – importance,*** von grundsätzlicher Bedeutung; – (***number***), die Kardinal– *or* Grundzahl; (*fig.*) – ***point,*** der Haupt– *or* Angelpunkt; – ***points,***Kardinalpunkte (*of the compass*); – ***principle,*** das Grundprinzip; – ***virtues,*** Kardinaltugenden; 2. hochrot, scharlachfarben.

[2]**cardinal,** *s.* 1. (*Eccl.*) der Kardinal; 2. (*Orn.*) Kardinal(vogel). **cardinalate** [–it], *s.* die Kardinalswürde; (*collect.*) das Kardinalskollegium.

card-index, *s.* die Kartei, Kartothek, der Zettelkatalog.

carding ['kɑ:diŋ], *s.* das Krempeln, Karden, Kratzen, Rauhen, Kardätschen; – ***machine,*** die Krempel– *or* Kratz– *or* Rauhmaschine; *see* [2]**card.**

cardio– ['kɑ:diou], *pref.* Herz–. **cardiogram,** *s.* das Kardiogramm. **cardiograph,** *s.* der Kardiograph. **cardiography** [–'ɔgrəfi], *s.* die Kardiographie. **cardiologist** [–'ɔlədʒist], *s.* der Herzspezialist. **cardiology** [–'ɔlədʒi], *s.* die Herzheilkunde.

cardoon [kɑ:'du:n], *s.* (*Bot.*) die Kardone(artischocke).

card|-playing, *s.* das Kartenspiel(en). **–-room,** *s.* das Spielzimmer. **–sharper,** *s.* der Falschspieler. **–-trick,** *s.* das Kartenkunststück, *pl.* die Kartenkunst. **–-vote,** *s.* die Abstimmung durch Wahlmänner.

care [kɛə], **1.** *s.* 1. die Sorge, Besorgnis, der Kummer (*for,* um); ***cast aside all –,*** alle Sorgen von sich werfen; ***free from –,*** sorgenfrei; – ***will kill a cat,*** Kummer macht vor der Zeit alt; 2. die Aufmerksamkeit, Vorsicht, Sorgfalt, Acht(samkeit); ***take – to do,*** nicht vergessen zu tun, trachten *or* sich bemühen zu tun; ***take – not to do,*** sich hüten zu tun; 3. die Pflege, Betreuung, Wartung, Aufsicht, Obhut, der Schutz; – ***of,*** per Adresse, bei; ***entrust to his –,*** seiner Obhut anvertrauen; ***have a –! take –!*** Vorsicht! Achtung! sei vorsichtig! nimm dich in acht! (*coll.*) paß auf! ***in*** or ***under his –,*** in seiner Obhut; ***under the – of Dr. F.,*** unter der Aufsicht *or* in der Behandlung des Herrn Doktor F.; ***take – of,*** aufpassen auf (*Acc.*), behüten; (*coll.*) besorgen, erledigen (*a task*); (*sl.*) kaltmachen (*a p.*); ***he is well taken – of,*** er ist in guter Obhut *or* ist gut aufgehoben *or* ist gut versorgt; ***take – of o.s.,*** sich schonen; (*fig.*) ***he can take – of himself,*** er hat sein eigenes Interesse im Auge; er kann in Notwehr handeln.

2. *v.i.* 1. sorgen (*for*, für), sich kümmern (um); 2. sich sorgen, besorgt sein (*about*, um), sich ängstigen (um *or* wegen), sich Sorgen machen (um *or* über (*Acc.*)); 3. – *for*, zugetan sein (*Dat.*), gern haben; *he* –*s for her*, er hat sie gern, er ist ihr zugetan; – *for nobody*, sich um niemanden kümmern; – *for nothing*, nach nichts fragen, sich um nichts kümmern; 4. (*neg. and inter.*) sich etwas daraus machen; Interesse *or* Lust haben, es gern sehen; *what do I* –? was frage ich danach! was kümmert's mich? was geht's mich an? (*coll.*) *I don't* –, es macht mir nichts aus; es ist mir egal *or* Wurst *or* ganz gleich; (*sl.*) *I don't* or *couldn't – a damn, I couldn't – less*, ich mache mir nicht das geringste daraus, das kümmert mich nicht im geringsten, das ist mir total schnuppe; *nobody* –*s about it*, danach kräht kein Hahn; *for all I* –, meinetwegen, wenn es nach mir ginge; *I don't – if I do*, ich habe nichts dagegen, es ist mir ganz gleich, es macht mir nichts aus, meinetwegen; *I don't – for strawberries*, ich mache mir nichts aus Erdbeeren; *would you – for a cup of tea?* hättest du Lust auf eine Tasse Tee?

careen [kə'ri:n], **1.** *v.t.* kielholen, umlegen (*a ship*). **2.** *v.i.* sich auf die Seite legen, krängen. **careenage** [–idʒ], *s.* die Kielholungskosten; der Kielholplatz.

career [kə'riə], **1.** *s.* 1. die Laufbahn, Karriere; der Werdegang, Lebensweg; *enter upon a* –, eine Laufbahn einschlagen; *make a – for o.s.*, Karriere machen; –*s guidance*, die Berufsberatung; 2. schneller Lauf, gestreckter Galopp, (*of hawk etc.*) der Flug; *in full* –, in vollem Lauf. **2.** *v.i.* (*coll.*) rennen, eilen, jagen, rasen. **careerist,** *s.* der Karrieremacher, Postenjäger.

carefree ['kɛəfri:], *adj.* sorglos, sorgenfrei. **careful,** *adj.* 1. bedacht, behutsam, sorgsam, achtsam (*of, about*, auf (*Acc.*)); 2. gründlich, genau, sorgfältig (*inquiry etc.*); 3. vorsichtig, achtsam; *be –!* nimm dich in acht! gib acht! Vorsicht! *be – to do*, nicht vergessen zu tun; *be – not to do*, sich hüten zu tun; 4. (*coll.*) sparsam. **carefulness,** *s.* die Sorgsamkeit, Sorgfalt; Aufmerksamkeit, Vorsicht; Gründlichkeit, Genauigkeit. **care|-laden,** *adj. See* **–worn.**

careless ['kɛəlis], *adj.* 1. sorglos, unbekümmert (*of, about*, um), gleichgültig (gegen); unachtsam (auf (*Acc.*)); *be – about one's appearance*, um sein Aussehen unbekümmert sein; 2. unüberlegt, unbedacht (*remark etc.*), unvorsichtig, fahrlässig, nachlässig. **carelessness,** *s.* die Sorglosigkeit; Unachtsamkeit; Fahrlässigkeit; Nachlässigkeit.

caress [kə'res], **1.** *s.* die Liebkosung. **2.** *v.t.* liebkosen, herzen, umarmen; streichen, tätscheln; (*fig.*) schmeicheln (*as music etc.*).

caret ['kærət], *s.* das Einschaltungszeichen; Auslassungszeichen.

care|taker, *s.* der (die) Hausmeister(in), (Haus)-verwalter(in), Hausbesorger(in); der Wärter, Wächter; – *government*, die Übergangsregierung. **–worn,** *adj.* sorgenvoll, abgehärmt.

cargo ['kɑ:gou], *s.* die (Schiffs)ladung, Fracht; das Frachtgut. **cargo|-carrying,** *adj.* Lasten–. **– ship, – vessel,** *s.* das Frachtschiff.

Carib ['kærib], *s.* der Kar(a)ibe. **Caribbean** [kæri'bi:ən], *adj.* kar(a)ibisch; – *sea*, Kar(a)ibisches Meer.

caribou [kæri'bu:], *s.* das Karibu.

caricature [kærikə'tjuə], **1.** *s.* die Karikatur, (*fig.*) das Zerrbild. **2.** *v.t.* karikieren, (*fig.*) lächerlich machen *or* darstellen. **caricaturist,** *s.* der Karikaturenzeichner.

caries ['kɛərii:z], *s.* der Knochenfraß; die Zahnfäule.

carillon [kə'riljən], *s.* das Glockenspiel.

carinal [kə'ri:nl], **carinate** ['kærineit], *adj.* (*Bot., Zool.*) kielförmig, kammähnlich, Kiel–, Kamm–.

Carinthia [kə'rinθiə], *s.* Kärnten (*n.*). **Carinthian, 1.** *s.* der (die) Kärntner(in). **2.** *adj.* kärntnerisch.

carious ['kɛəriəs], *adj.* angefressen, verfault, kariös.

carking ['kɑ:kiŋ], *adj.* kummervoll; – *care*, nagende Sorge.

carl(e) [kɑ:l], *s.* (*Scots*) der Kerl, kräftiger Bursche.

carline ['kɑ:lin], *s.* – *thistle*, die Eberwurz.

Carlovingian [kɑ:lə'vindʒən], *adj. See* **Carolingian.**

Carmelite ['kɑ:məlait], **1.** *s.* (*Eccl.*) der (die) Karmeliter(in). **2.** *adj.* Karmeliter–.

carminative ['kɑ:minətiv], **1.** *adj.* Blähungen beseitigend. **2.** *s.* das Mittel gegen Blähungen.

carmine ['kɑ:m(a)in], **1.** *s.* der *or* das Karmin, das Karminrot. **2.** *adj.* karminrot.

carnage ['kɑ:nidʒ], *s.* das Blutbad, Gemetzel.

carnal [kɑ:nl], *adj.* fleischlich, sinnlich, körperlich; geschlechtlich, sexuell; weltlich, irdisch, diesseitig; – *desire*, sinnliche Begierde; – *intercourse* (*with*), (*Law*) – *knowledge* (*of*), geschlechtlicher Umgang (mit). **carnality** [–'næliti], *s.* die Sinneslust, Fleischeslust, Sinnlichkeit, sinnliche Begierde; weltlicher Sinn, die Diesseitigkeit.

carnation [kɑ:'neiʃən], *s.* 1. (*Bot.*) die Nelke; 2. (*painting*) Fleischfarbe.

carnelian [kɑ:'ni:liən], *s.* der Karneol.

Carniola [kɑ:ni'oulə], *s.* Krain (*n.*). **Carniolan, 1.** *s.* der (die) Krainer(in). **2.** *adj.* krainisch.

carnival ['kɑ:nivl], *s.* der Karneval, Fasching; Vergnügungspark; das Kostümfest; (*fig.*) Schwelgen (*of*, in (*Dat.*)).

carnivore ['kɑ:nivɔ:], *s.* das Raubtier, der Fleischfresser. **carnivorous** [–'nivərəs], *adj.* fleischfressend.

carob ['kærəb], *s.* – *bean*, das Johannisbrot; –*-tree*, der Johannisbrotbaum.

carol ['kærəl], **1.** *s.* der Lobgesang, das Jubellied; *Christmas* –, das Weihnachtslied; – *singers*, Weihnachtssänger (*pl.*). **2.** *v.i.* (fröhlich) singen, (*of birds*) singen, jubilieren.

Carolingian [kærə'lindʒən], *adj.* (*Hist.*) karolingisch.

carom ['kærəm], **1.** *s.* (*Am.*) (*Bill.*) die Karombol(ag)e. **2.** *v.i.* karombolieren.

carotid [kə'rɔtid], *s.* (*Anat.*) die Halsschlagader, Karotis.

carousal [kə'rauzl], *s.* das Trinkgelage, die Zecherei. **carouse,** *v.i.* zechen, trinken.

carousel [kæru'sel], *s.* (*Am.*) das Karussell.

[1]**carp** [kɑ:p], *s.* (*Ichth.*) der Karpfen.

[2]**carp,** *v.i.* kritteln (*at*, über (*Acc.*) *or* an (*Dat.*)), nörgeln (an (*Dat.*)); – *at*, bekritteln.

carpal [kɑ:pl], *adj.* (*Anat.*) Handwurzel–.

Carpathian Mountains [kɑ:'peiθiən], *pl.* Karpathen (*pl.*).

carpel [kɑ:pl], *s.* (*Bot.*) das Fruchtblatt.

carpenter ['kɑ:pintə], **1.** *s.* der Zimmermann, Zimmerer, Tischler; – *bee*, die Holzbiene; –*'s bench*, die Hobelbank; –*'s rule*, der Zollstock. **2.** *v.i.* zimmern. **carpentering,** *s.* die Zimmermannsarbeit, Tischlerarbeit. **carpentry,** *s.* die Tischlerei, das Zimmerhandwerk; *see also* **carpentering.**

carper ['kɑ:pə], *s.* der Nörgler, Krittler, Kritikaster; *see* [2]**carp.**

carpet ['kɑ:pit], **1.** *s.* der Teppich; *bedside* –, der Bettvorleger; *stair* –, der Treppenläufer; (*fig.*) *be on the* –, aufs Tapet kommen, zur Debatte stehen; (*coll.*) (*of a p.*) gemaßregelt *or* abgekanzelt *or* zur Verantwortung gezogen werden. **2.** *v.t.* 1. mit Teppichen belegen; 2. (*coll.*) maßregeln, zur Verantwortung ziehen, zur Rede stellen.

carpet|-bag, *s.* der Reisesack. **–bagger,** *s.* (*Am.*) (politischer) Abenteurer, der Schwindler. **–beater,** *s.* der Teppichklopfer. **–-bombing,** *s.* der Bombenteppichwurf. **carpeting,** *s.* der Teppichstoff. **carpet|-knight,** *s.* der Salonheld. **–-rod,** *s.* die Läuferstange. **–-slippers,** *pl.* Hausschuhe (*pl.*). **– sweeper,** *s.* die Teppichkehrmaschine.

carping ['kɑ:piŋ], **1.** *s.* die Nörgelei, Krittelei. **2.** *adj.* krittelig, tadelsüchtig; – *criticism*, kleinliche Kritik; *see* [2]**carp.**

carpolite ['kɑːpəlait], *s.* (*Geol.*) die Fruchtversteinerung.

carpus ['kɑːpəs], *s.* die Handwurzel.

carrag(h)een ['kærəgiːn], *s.* (*Bot.*) irländisches Moos, das Perlmoos, der Perltang, Knorpeltang (*Chondrus crispus*).

carrel ['kærəl], *s.* (*library*) die Lesenische.

carriage ['kæridʒ], *s.* 1. die Kutsche, Equipage, der Wagen; (*Railw.*) Waggon, Personenwagen; ***one-horse* –**, der Einspänner; ***– and pair,*** der Zweispänner; 2. das Tragen, Fahren, der Transport, die Beförderung, Verfrachtung; (*Comm.*) das Fuhrgeld, Frachtgeld, Rollgeld, die Fracht(gebühr); Transportkosten (*pl.*), Transportspesen (*pl.*); ***– by sea,*** der Seetransport; ***by –,*** per Achse; 3. die (Körper)haltung; (*obs.*) das Auftreten, Betragen, Benehmen; 4. (*fig.*) die Ausführung, Durchführung; (*Pol.*) Annahme (*of a bill*); 5. (*Tech.*) das (Fahr)gestell, der Wagen, Schlitten (*of typewriter*), Karren (*of printing press*), das Fahrwerk, Fahrgestell (*of aircraft*), die Lafette (*of a gun*).

carriage| body, *s.* die Karosserie. **– builder,** *s.* der Wagenbauer, Wagner. **– building,** *s.* der Wagenbau. **– door,** *s.* der Wagenschlag. **– drive,** *s.* die Durchfahrt, Auffahrt. **– entrance,** *s.* die Einfahrt. **– forward,** *adv.* unter Nachnahme, unfrankiert. **– frame,** *s.* das Wagengestell. **--free,** *adj.* portofrei, frachtfrei, franko. **– horse,** *s.* das Kutschpferd. **--paid,** *adv. See* **--free.** **– road, –way,** *s.* der Fahrweg, Fahrdamm, die Fahrbahn; ***dual carriageway,*** doppelte Fahrbahn.

carried ['kærid], *imperf., p.p. of* **carry.**

carrier ['kæriə], *s.* 1. der Spediteur, Fuhrmann, (*Naut.*) Verfrachter; ***common –,*** der Lohnfuhrmann; 2. Überbringer, Bote, Träger, Beförderer; (*Med.*) Übertrager, (*Chem. etc.*) Katalysator, Träger, die Trägersubstanz; 3. (*Tech.*) Führungsrolle, das Zwischenrad, (*Lathe*) Drehherz, der Mitnehmer; (*Phot.*) Halterahmen, (*Elec.*) Trägerstrom, (*Rad.*) die Trägerwelle; 4. (*bicycle*) der Gepäckträger; 5. ***aircraft –,*** das Flugzeugmutterschiff; ***troop –,*** das Truppentransportflugzeug, (*ship*) der Truppentransporter. **carrier|-bag,** *s.* die Einkaufstasche. **--based,** *adj.* Träger–, Bord–, Decklande– (*aircraft*). **--broadcasting,** *s.* der Drahtfunk. **--pigeon,** *s.* die Brieftaube. **--wave,** *s.* (*Rad.*) die Trägerwelle.

carrion ['kæriən], *s.* das Aas, der Kadaver, (*fig.*) Unrat, Unflat. **carrion crow,** *s.* (*Orn.*) die Rabenkrähe (*Corvus corone corone*).

carronade [kærə'neid], *s.* (*obs.*) die (Schiffs)haubitze.

carrot ['kærət], *s.* die Karotte, Möhre, Mohrrübe, gelbe Rübe; (*coll.*) *–s,* der Rotkopf. **carroty,** *adj.* (*of hair*) rötlich, gelbrot.

carrousel, *see* **carousel.**

carry ['kæri], 1. *v.t.* tragen, führen, bringen, befördern. schaffen; (*on one's person*) mit sich tragen, mitnehmen, mitführen; verbreiten, übertragen (*disease*); (*Math.*) vortragen, übertragen (*figures*); (*Mil.*) erobern, einnehmen (*a position*); (*Comm.*) führen (*stock, goods*); (*Pol.*) annehmen, zur Annahme bringen, durchsetzen (*a motion*); ***– all before one,*** auf der ganzen Linie siegen; ***– arms,*** Waffen tragen; ***– the audience with one,*** die Zuhörer mitreißen; ***– coals to Newcastle,*** Eulen nach Athen tragen; ***– conviction,*** überzeugen, überzeugend wirken; ***– the day,*** siegen, den Sieg davontragen; ***– interest,*** Zinsen tragen *or* einbringen; ***– it with a high hand,*** gebieterisch auftreten; (*coll.*) ***he carries his liquor well,*** er kann eine Menge Alkohol vertragen; ***the motion was carried,*** der Antrag ging durch; ***– o.s. with courage,*** sich tapfer halten *or* betragen; ***– one's point,*** seinen Zweck *or* sein Ziel erreichen, seinen Willen *or* Standpunkt durchsetzen; ***– a th. too far,*** es übertreiben *or* zu weit treiben; ***– too much sail,*** zu viele Segel führen; ***carried unanimously,*** einstimmig angenommen; (*fig.*) ***– weight,*** von Bedeutung sein, ins Gewicht fallen, Einfluß haben.

(*with advs.*) ***– away,*** wegtragen, fortschaffen; (*fig.*) verleiten, hinreißen, (mit sich) fortreißen; ***a mast was carried away,*** ein Mast wurde abgebrochen *or* weggerissen; (*fig.*) ***– back,*** zurückversetzen (***to,*** in (*Acc.*)); (*Comm.*) ***– forward,*** vortragen, übertragen; (erfolgreich) fortführen, fortsetzen; ***amount carried forward,*** der Übertrag; ***– into effect,*** ausführen, durchsetzen; ***– off,*** wegführen, abführen, wegtragen, wegnehmen, (*of disease*) fortraffen, hinwegraffen, (*a prize*) gewinnen, erringen, davontragen; ***– it off well,*** mit Erfolg auftreten, sich darüber hinwegsetzen; ***– on,*** führen, betreiben, (*a business*) (weiter)führen; fortsetzen, fortführen; ***– on a conversation,*** ein Gespräch führen; ***– out,*** ausführen, durchführen, durchsetzen, verwirklichen, zum Abschluß bringen, vollenden, vollstrecken; ***– over,*** hinüberführen, hinüberschaffen; (*fig.*) verschieben, aufschieben; (*Comm.*) *see* ***– forward;*** ***– through,*** durchführen, durchsetzen, ausführen, zum Abschluß bringen (*a task*), durchbringen, durchhelfen (*Dat.*) (*a p.*); ***– to a new account,*** auf neue Rechnung vortragen; (*fig.*) ***– with it,*** mit sich bringen, an sich haben, in sich schließen, nach sich ziehen.

2\. *v.i.* tragen, vernehmbar sein (*of sound*), reichen (*of shots*), apportieren (*of dog*); (*coll.*) ***fetch and –,*** geschäftig hin– und herlaufen, Handlanger sein; (*coll.*) ***– on,*** weitermachen; sich aufregen, stark ins Zeug gehen, ein Theater machen; (*sl.*) sich abgeben, anbändeln, ein Verhältnis haben, verkehren (***with,*** mit); ***he gave me money to – on with,*** er half mir mit Geld aus.

3\. *s.* die Flugstrecke; Reichweite.

carrying ['kæriiŋ], *s.* das Fuhrwesen, die Beförderung, der Transport; ***– agent,*** der Spediteur; ***– capacity,*** die Ladefähigkeit (*of vehicle*), Tragfähigkeit (*of structure*), das Fassungsvermögen (*of container*), (*Elec.*) die Belastbarkeit; ***– roller,*** die Laufrolle, Führungsrolle; ***– trade,*** das Transportgeschäft, Speditionsgeschäft; (*Railw.*) ***– traffic,*** der Güterverkehr. **carryings-on,** *pl.* (*coll.*) das Gehabe, tolle Sachen (*pl.*), dumme Streiche (*pl.*). **carry-on,** *s.* (*sl.*) unliebsame Szene.

cart [kɑːt], 1. *s.* der (Last)karren, Frachtwagen, die Karre; das Fuhrwerk, die Fuhre; (*sl.*) ***be in the –,*** in der Tinte *or* Patsche sitzen, in der Klemme sein; ***put the – before the horse,*** das Pferd beim Schwanze aufzäumen, die S. verkehrt anpacken. 2. *v.t.* karren, befördern; (*sl.*) ***– about,*** (mit sich) herumschleppen; ***– away,*** wegschaffen, fortschaffen, abkarren. **cartage** [–idʒ], *s.* das Fahren, Karren; der Fuhrlohn, das Rollgeld, Transportkosten (*pl.*).

carte [kɑːt], *s.* (*Fenc.*) die Quart.

carte-blanche [kɑːt'blɑ̃ʃ], *s.* das Blankett, (*usu. fig.*) unbeschränkte Vollmacht.

cartel ['kɑːtəl], *s.* (*Comm.*) das Kartell, (*Pol.*) die Konvention, der Auslieferungsvertrag; (*obs.*) schriftliche Herausforderung. **cartellization** [–lai'zeiʃən], *s.* die Kartellisierung.

carter ['kɑːtə], *s.* der Fuhrmann, Kärrner.

Cartesian [kɑː'tiːʒən], 1. *s.* der Kartesianer. 2. *adj.* kartes(ian)isch.

Carthage ['kɑːθidʒ], *s.* Karthago (*n.*). **Carthaginian** [kɑːθə'dʒiniən], 1. *s.* (die) Karthager(in). 2. *adj.* karthagisch.

cart-horse, *s.* das Zugpferd.

Carthusian [kɑː'θjuːziən], *s.* der Kartäuser(mönch).

cartilage ['kɑːtilidʒ], *s.* der Knorpel. **cartilaginous** [–'lædʒinəs], *adj.* knorpelig, knorpelartig, Knorpel–.

cartload ['kɑːtloud], *s.* die Wagenladung, Fuhre, das Fuder; (*coll.*) ***come down on him like a – of bricks,*** ihn restlos niederschmettern.

cartography [kɑː'tɔgrəfi], *s.* das Kartenzeichnen.

carton ['kɑːtən], *s.* die Pappschachtel, der Karton.

cartoon [kɑː'tuːn], 1. *s.* die Karikatur, Witzzeichnung, (*Films*) der Zeichentrickfilm; (*Paint.*) Karton, Entwurf, die Vorlage. 2. *v.t.* karikieren. **cartoonist,** *s.* der Karikaturenzeichner.

cartouche [kɑː'tuːʃ], *s.* (*Archit.*) die Kartusche, Randverzierung, der Zierrahmen.

cartridge ['kɑːtridʒ], *s.* die Patrone; (*Phot.*) Spule;

blank –, die Platzpatrone; *dummy* –, die Exerzierpatrone. **cartridge| base,** *s.* der Hülsenboden. – **belt,** *s.* der Patronengurt. – **case,** *s.* die Patronenhülle, Kartuschhülse. – **clip,** *s.* der Ladestreifen. – **paper,** *s.* das Zeichenpapier, Kartonpapier.

cart|wheel, *s.* das Wagenrad, (*Gymn.*) Rad; *do* or *turn a* –, radschlagen. **–wright,** *s.* der Wagenbauer, Wagner, Stellmacher.

caruncle [kæ'rʌŋkl], *s.* (*Zool.*) der Fleischauswuchs, Fleischlappen; (*Bot.*) Fruchthüllenauswuchs; (*Med.*) die Fleischgeschwulst.

carve [kɑ:v], **1.** *v.t.* vorschneiden, tranchieren, zerlegen (*meat*); schnitzen (*wood*); meißeln (*stone*), einschneiden, einmeißeln (*designs*); (*fig.*) (*also* – *out*) gestalten, sich (*Dat.*) bahnen (*career etc.*); (*coll.*) (*fig.*) – *up*, aufteilen. **2.** *v.i.* vorschneiden (*at table*); schnitzen, meißeln.

carvel-built ['kɑ:vəl], *adj.* (*Naut.*) kraweelgebaut; – *boat*, das Kraweelboot.

carver ['kɑ:və], *s.* 1. der Vorschneider; (Holz)-schnitzer, Bildhauer; 2. das Vorlegemesser; *pl.* Tranchierbesteck. **carve-up,** *s.* (*sl.*) der Schwindel. **carving,** *s.* das Vorschneiden, Tranchieren; Schnitzen, Meißeln; Schnitzwerk, die Schnitzerei; Bildhauerarbeit; – *knife*, das Vorlegemesser.

cascade [kæs'keid], **1.** *s.* der Wasserfall; – *of sparks*, der Feuerregen. **2.** *v.i.* in Strömen *or* Wellen herunterstürzen, (*fig.*) regnen.

[1]**case** [keis], **1.** *s.* der Kasten, die Kiste; das Futteral, Gehäuse, Etui, der Behälter, das Behältnis, Fach; die Tasche, Hülle, Scheide, Hülse; der Bezug, Überzug (*of pillow etc.*); (*Tech.*) die Bekleidung, Verkleidung, Umkleidung, Einfassung, das Futter, der Mantel; (*Min.*) (Schacht- *or* Stollen)rahmen; (*Bookb.*) die Einbanddecke; – *of bottles*, der Flaschenkeller; (*Med.*) – *of instruments*, das Besteck; – *of mathematical instruments*, das Reißzeug; – *of whisky*, die Kiste Whisky; *cigarette* –, das Zigarettenetui; *dispatch* –, die Aktenmappe; *dressing* –, das Reisenecessaire; (*Typ.*) *letter* –, der Setzkasten; (*Typ.*) *lower* –, der Unterkasten; Kleinbuchstaben (*pl.*); *map* –, die Kartenschutzhülle; *music* –, die Notentasche; *packing* –, die Packkiste; (*Typ.*) *upper* –, der Oberkasten; Großbuchstaben (*pl.*); *violin* –, der Geigenkasten; *watch* –, das Uhrgehäuse; *writing* –, das Schreibetui, die Schreibmappe. **2.** *v.t.* mit einem Überzug *or* Futteral versehen; (*Tech.*) verkleiden, ummanteln, verschalen, umhüllen, umgeben (*in*, mit), einhüllen (in (*Acc.*)).

[2]**case,** *s.* der Fall, Umstand, Vorfall, Zustand, die Lage; (Tat)sache, Angelegenheit, Frage; (*Law*) (Streit)sache, der (Rechts)fall; (*Med.*) (Krankheits)fall; (*Gram.*) Kasus, Fall; (*coll.*) Argumente (*pl.*), (triftige) Gründe (*pl.*); *good – for complaint*, guter Anlaß zum Klagen; – *in point*, der vorliegende Fall; *leading* –, der Präzedenzfall; *it is a – of*, es handelt sich um; – *of conscience*, die Gewissensfrage; *that is not the* – (*with me*), das trifft (bei mir *or* auf mich) nicht zu; *I have a strong* or *good* –, ich habe das Recht auf meiner Seite, die Tatsachen sprechen für mich; *a* (*good*) – *can be made for it*, es läßt sich viel dafür sagen; *the – is this*, es hat (damit) folgende Bewandtnis; *as the – may be*, je nach den Umständen, je nachdem; *as the – stands*, wie die S. (nun einmal) liegt, wie die Sachen stehen; *state one's* –, seinen Standpunkt darlegen; *in* – (*that*), im Falle daß, falls; *in – of*, im Falle von (*or Gen.*); *in – of need*, im Notfall; *in any* –, sowieso, jedenfalls, auf jeden Fall; *in no* –, keinesfalls, auf keinen Fall; *in that* –, in dem Falle, wenn das so ist.

case|-book, *s.* (*Med.*) das Patientenbuch. – **ending,** *s.* (*Gram.*) die Kasusendung.

case|-harden, *v.t.* (*Metall.*) hartgießen, einsatzhärten, verstählen, (*fig.*) abhärten. **--hardened,** *adj.* (*Metall.*) hartgegossen, im Einsatz gehärtet, schalenhart; (*fig.*) abgehärtet, abgebrüht, unempfindlich. **--hardening,** *s.* (*Metall.*) das Einsetzen, Einsatzhärten, die Einsatzhärtung.

case history, *s.* (*Med.*) die Krankengeschichte; Personalakte; (*Law etc.*) Vorgeschichte.

casein(e) ['keisiin], *s.* das Kasein, der Käsestoff.

case law, *s.* das Fallrecht.

casemate ['keismeit], *s.* die Kasematte.

casement ['keismənt], *s.* der Fensterflügel, Flügelrahmen; – *window*, das Flügelfenster.

caseous ['keisiəs], *adj.* käsig, käseartig.

case-shot, *s.* (*Hist.*) die Kartätsche.

case study, *s.* die Einzelfallstudie.

[1]**casework** ['keiswə:k], *s.* soziale Einzelarbeit, das Milieustudium.

[2]**casework,** *s.* (*Typ.*) der Handsatz.

cash [kæʃ], **1.** *s.* bares Geld, das (Bar)geld; (*Comm.*) die Barzahlung, Kasse; – *and carry*, nur gegen Barzahlung und bei eigenem Transport; – *down*, bar, gegen Barzahlung; *for* –, gegen Barzahlung, gegen Kasse; *in* –, bar, per Kassa; (*coll.*) *be in* –, bei Kasse sein; *£15 in* –, 15 Pfund bar *or* in barer Münze *or* in barem Geld; *net – in advance*, netto Kasse im voraus; – *in bank*, das Bankguthaben; – *in hand*, der Kassenbestand, Barbestand; *loose* –, das Kleingeld, Münzgeld; – *on delivery*, unter Nachnahme; (*coll.*) *be out of* –, nicht bei Kasse sein; *ready* –, sofortige Kasse; (*coll.*) *short of* –, knapp (bei Kasse); *turn into* –, einlösen, zu Geld machen. **2.** *v.t.* zu Geld machen; einwechseln, einkassieren, einlösen (*cheque etc.*); (*sl.*) – *in one's checks* or *chips*, krepieren, abtreten. **3.** *v.i.* (*coll.*) – *in*, kassieren; (*sl.*) – *in on*, sich (*Dat.*) zunutze machen, ausnützen, profitieren von, Kapital schlagen *or* einen Vorteil ziehen aus.

cash| account, *s.* das Kassenkonto. – **advance,** *s.* der Barvorschuß. **--and-carry (store),** *s.* der C-und-C-Laden. – **balance,** *s.* der Kassensaldo, Kassenbestand, das Barguthaben. **–book,** *s.* das Kassenbuch. **–box,** *s.* der Geldkasten, die Geldkassette, Schatulle. – **discount,** *s.* der *or* das Kassenskonto.

cashew ['kæʃu:, kə'ʃu:], *s.* der Nierenbaum. **cashew-nuts,** *pl* Elefantenläuse (*pl.*).

[1]**cashier** [kæ'ʃiə], *s.* der (die) Kassierer(in), (*Austr.* Kassier(in)).

[2]**cashier,** *v.t.* (*Mil.*) entlassen, kassieren. **cashiering, cashierment,** *s.* die Entlassung, Kassierung, Kassation.

cashmere ['kæʃmiə], **1.** *s.* der Kaschmir. **2.** *adj.* Kaschmir-.

cash| payment, *s.* die Barzahlung. – **price,** *s.* der Bar(zahlungs)preis, Kassapreis. – **purchase,** *s.* der Bareinkauf. **--register,** *s.* die Kontrollkasse, Registrierkasse. – **sale,** *s.* der Verkauf gegen Barzahlung, Barverkauf, das Kassageschäft.

casing ['keisiŋ], *s.* der Überzug, die (Schutz)hülle; Umhüllung, Ummantelung, (Ver)schalung, Verkleidung, Bekleidung; das Verschalungs- *or* Bekleidungsmaterial; Futter, Gehäuse, (*of a tyre*) der Mantel.

casino [kə'si:nou], *s.* das Gesellschaftshaus; Tanzlokal, Spiellokal.

cask [kɑ:sk], **1.** *s.* das Faß, die Tonne. **2.** *v.t.* auf Fässer ziehen.

casket [kɑ:skit], *s.* das Kästchen, die Schatulle; (*Am.*) der Sarg.

casque [kɑ:sk], *s.* (*obs.*) der Helm.

cassation [kæ'seiʃən], *s.* (*Law*) die Kassation, Aufhebung.

casserole ['kæsəroul], *s.* die Schmorpfanne; (*coll.*) Geschmorene(s).

cassia ['kæsiə], *s.* die Kassie.

cassock ['kæsək], *s.* der Meßrock, Chorrock; (*R.C.*) die Soutane.

cassowary ['kæsəwəri], *s.* (*Orn.*) der Kasuar.

cast [kɑ:st], **1.** *irr.v.t.* 1. werfen, hinwerfen, auswerfen (*anchor, nets etc.*); abwerfen, verlieren (*horns, teeth etc.*); – *the blame on him*, ihm die Schuld zuschieben *or* geben (*for*, an (*Dat.*)); *the die is* –, der Würfel ist gefallen; – *one's eyes upon*, sein Auge werfen *or* seine Blicke richten auf (*Acc.*); – *the lead*, loten; – *a look behind*, zurückblicken; – *lots for*, losen um; – *the skin*, sich

abhäuten; – *a spell on him,* ihn behexen; – *s.th. in his teeth,* ihm etwas vorwerfen; – *one's vote,* seine Stimme abgeben; 2. (*Tech.*) gießen, foremen; 3. (*of animals*) werfen, gebären (*young*); 4. (*fig.*) berechnen, ausrechnen, aufrechnen, errechnen (*accounts*); – *a balance,* den Saldo ziehen; – *a horoscope,* ein Horoskop stellen; 5. (*Theat.*) verteilen (*parts*), besetzen (*a play*); *the play is well* –, das Stück ist gut besetzt.
(b) (*with advs.*) – *about,* umherwerfen; – *aside,* beiseite schieben *or* legen, wegwerfen, verwerfen; – *away,* verwerfen, wegwerfen; (*Naut.*) *be – away,* verschlagen *or* schiffbrüchig werden; – *away care,* die Sorgen verbannen; – *down,* niederwerfen; (*fig.*) entmutigen, deprimieren, niederschlagen; senken, niederschlagen (*the eyes*); *be – down,* niedergeschlagen *or* betrübt *or* bedrückt sein (*about,* über (*Acc.*)); – *in one's lot with,* das Los teilen mit, gemeinsame S. machen mit; – *off,* abwerfen, ablegen, von sich werfen, abschütteln; verstoßen (*son etc.*); (*Naut.*) fieren; – *off stitches,* Maschen abnehmen; – *on stitches,* (die ersten) Maschen aufnehmen; – *out,* (hin)auswerfen, ausstoßen, austreiben, verstoßen, vertreiben; – *up,* in die Höhe werfen; aufschlagen (*the eyes*); berechnen, errechnen, zusammenrechnen, ausrechnen (*accounts*); erbrechen, auswerfen (*food*).
2. *v.i.* die Angel auswerfen; (*Tech.*) sich gießen *or* formen lassen; – *about,* suchen, sich umsehen (*for,* nach); (*Naut.*) umherlavieren; (*fig.*) sinnen (*for,* nach); (*Naut.*) – *off,* abfieren.
3. *s.* 1. der Wurf; das Werfen. Auswerfen (*of nets*); die Wurfweite; 2. (*Tech.*) Gußform; der Guß, Abguß, Abdruck; *plaster* –, der Gipsabdruck; (*Med.*) Gipsverband; *take a* –, prägen, abdrucken; 3. (*Theat.*) die Rollenverteilung, (Rollen)besetzung; 4. (*fig.*) Nuance, Färbung, Schattierung, der Anflug, Stich; Anschein, die Anlage, Form, Gattung, Art, Manier, der Schlag, Typ; *it has a green* –, es spielt ins Grüne; *have a – in one's eye,* schielen, einen Augenfehler haben; 5. die Berechnung, Aufrechnung; 6. der Angelhaken mit Köder; 7. (*of worms*) das Erdhäufchen.

castanet [kæstə'net], *s.* die Kastagnette.

castaway ['kɑ:stəwei], **1.** *adj.* weggeworfen, unnütz, wertlos; (*Naut.*) schiffbrüchig, gestrandet. **2.** *s.* Schiffbrüchige(r); (*fig.*) Verstoßene(r), Verworfene(r).

cast concrete, *s.* der Betonguß.

caste [kɑ:st], *s.* die Kaste, gesellschaftliche Stellung; *lose* –, auf gesellschaftlich niedere Stufe herabsinken; – *feeling,* der Kastengeist.

castellan ['kæstələn], *s.* der Kastellan, Burgvogt. **castellated** [–leitid], *adj.* mit Zinnen *or* Türmen versehen, burgartig.

caster ['kɑ:stə], *s.* der Werfer; Berechner (*of accounts*); (*Metall.*) Gießer; *see also* **²castor, ³castor.**

castigate ['kæstigeit], *v.t.* züchtigen. **castigation** [–'geiʃən], *s.* die Züchtigung.

Castile [kæs'ti:l], *s.* Kastilien (*n.*). **Castilian** [–'tiljən], **1.** *s.* 1. der (die) Kastilier(in); 2. (*language*) das Kastilisch(e) **2.** *adj.* kastilisch.

casting ['kɑ:stiŋ], **1.** *adj.* den Ausschlag gebend, entscheidend; – *vote,* ausschlaggebende *or* entscheidende Stimme. **2.** *s.* das Gießen; der Guß, Abguß, das Gußstück, der Gußteil, *pl.* das Gußwerk, Gußwaren (*pl.*); – *in chills,* der Schalenguß, Kokillenguß; – *on a core,* der Hohlguß, Kernguß; *open sand* –, der Herdguß. **casting|-box,** *s.* der Gießkasten, Formkasten. **--mould,** *s.* die Gießform.

cast| iron, *s.* das Roheisen, Gußeisen, der Grauguß. **--iron,** *adj.* gußeisern, (*fig.*) unumstößlich, unbeugsam, starr.

castle [kɑ:sl], **1.** *s.* die Burg, das Schloß; (*Chess*) der Turm; –*s in the air,* Luftschlösser (*pl.*). **2.** *v.i.* (*Chess*) rochieren. **castle-builder,** *s.* (*fig.*) der Projektemacher.

cast-off, **1.** *adj.* abgelegt, (*coll.*) ausrangiert. **2.** *s.* (*usu. pl.*) abgelegtes Kleidungsstück, *pl.* abgelegte Kleider.

¹castor ['kɑ:stə], *s.* (*obs.*) der Biber; Biberhut; (*Med.*) das Bibergeil.

²castor, *s.* die Streubüchse.

³castor, *s.* die Laufrolle, Möbelrolle.

castor|-oil, *s.* das Rizinusöl. – **sugar,** *s.* der Streuzucker, Puderzucker.

castrate [kæs'treit], *v.t.* kastrieren, verschneiden, entmannen; (*fig.*) verstümmeln. **castration** [–'treiʃən], *s.* die Kastrierung, Entmannung, (*fig.*) Verstümmelung; Ausmerzung (*of passages in a book*).

casual ['kæʒuəl], **1.** *adj.* zufällig, gelegentlich, beiläufig; unbestimmt, gleichgültig, nachlässig, zwanglos, inkonsequent; (*of clothing*) salopp, sportlich; – *acquaintance,* flüchtige Bekanntschaft; – *labourer,* der Gelegenheitsarbeiter. **2.** *s.* 1. Obdachlose(r); der Gelegenheitsarbeiter; gelegentlicher Kunde; 2. *pl.* die Sportshose; leichte Schuhe.

casualty ['kæʒuəlti], *s.* der Unglücksfall; Verwundete(r), Verunglückte(r); *pl.* Verluste (*pl.*) (*in battle*), Opfer (*pl.*) (*of an accident*); – *list,* – *returns,* die Verlustliste; – *ward,* die Unfallstation.

casuist ['kæʒuist], *s.* der Kasuist. **casuistic(al)** [–'istik(l)], *adj.* kasuistisch, spitzfindig. **casuistry,** *s.* die Kasuistik; Spitzfindigkeit.

cat [kæt], **1.** *s.* 1. die Katze, der Kater; *domestic* –, die Hauskatze; *Manx* –, schwanzlose Katze; *neuter* –, verschnittener Kater; *tom*–, der Kater; *when the* –*'s away the mice will play,* wenn die Katze nicht zu Hause ist, spielen *or* tanzen die Mäuse (auf dem Tisch); (*sl.*) *not a – in hell's chance,* nicht die geringste Aussicht; *by night all* –*s are grey,* alle Kühe (*or* Katzen) sind in der Nacht schwarz (*or* grau); *see how* (or *which way*) *the – jumps,* sehen wie der Hase läuft; *wait for the – to jump,* die Ereignisse abwarten; *lead a* –*-and-dog life,* wie Hund und Katze leben; *let the – out of the bag,* die Katze aus dem Sack lassen; *a – may look at a king,* sieht doch die Katz' den Kaiser an; *it was raining* –*s and dogs,* es regnete Bindfaden; *not room to swing a* – (*in*), beschränkter *or* knapper *or* (zu) enger Raum; 2. (*Naut.*) die Katt, der Kattanker; 3. *See* **cat-o'nine-tails.** **2.** *v.t.* – *the anchor,* den Anker katten.

catabolism [kə'tæbəlizm], *s.* (*Med. etc.*) der Abbau, Stoffwechsel, Zersetzungsvorgang.

cataclysm ['kætəklizm], *s.* die Überschwemmung, Sintflut; (*fig.*) verheerende Umwälzung, völliger Umsturz. **cataclysmal** [–'klizml], **cataclysmic** [–'klizmik], *adj.* umwälzend, umstürzend.

catacomb ['kætəku:m], *s.* die Katakombe.

catafalque ['kætəfælk], *s.* der Katafalk, das Leichengerüst.

catalectic [kætə'lektik], *adj.* (*Metr.*) katalektisch, unvollständig.

catalepsy ['kætəlepsi], *s.* (*Med.*) der Starrkrampf. **cataleptic** [–'leptik], *adj.* starrsüchtig, kataleptisch.

catalogue ['kætəlɔg], **1.** *s.* das Verzeichnis, der Katalog, (*Comm.*) die Preisliste. **2.** *v.t.* in ein Verzeichnis aufnehmen, einen Katalog aufstellen von. **cataloguer** [–ə], *s.* (*library*) Katalogbeamte(r), der (die) Katalogbearbeiter(in).

catalyse ['kætəlaiz], *v.t.* katalysieren, katalytisch beeinflussen, durch Katalyse beschleunigen. **catalysis** [kə'tælisis], *s.* die Katalyse. **catalyst** ['kætəlist], *s.* der Katalysator.

catamaran [kætəmə'ræn], *s.* 1. das Floß; 2. Katamaran; 3. zänkisches Weib.

catamenia [kætə'mi:niə], *s.* (*Med.*) der Monatsfluß.

cataplasm ['kætəplæzm], *s.* der Breiumschlag.

cataplexy ['kætəpleksi], *s.* die Schrecklähmung.

catapult ['kætəpʌlt], **1.** *s.* (*Hist.*) die Wurfmaschine, der *or* das Katapult; die Schleuder (*also Av.*), Zwille. **2.** *v.t.* (ab)schleudern, mit der Zwille schießen; (*Av.*) katapultieren.

cataract ['kætərækt], *s.* 1. der Katarakt, Wasserfall; 2. (*Med.*) die Katarakte, grauer Star; *couch the* –, den Star stechen.

catarrh [kə'tɑ:], *s.* der Katarrh, Schnupfen. **catarrhal** [–rəl], *adj.* katarrhalisch, Schnupfen–.

catastrophe [kə'tæstrəfi], *s.* die Katastrophe (*drama*); der Schicksalsschlag, das Verhängnis, Unheil, großes Unglück. **catastrophic** [kætə'strɔfik], *adj.* verhängnisvoll, katastrophal.

cat| block, *s.* (*Naut.*) der Kattblock. **–boat,** *s.* kleines Segelboot. **--burglar,** *s.* der Fassadenkletterer. **–call, 1.** *s.* schrilles Pfeifen, das Auspfeifen. **2.** *v.t.* auspfeifen.

catch [kætʃ], **1.** *irr.v.t.* fangen, einfangen, auffangen; erfassen, ergreifen, packen, (er)haschen; einholen (*a p.*), (rechtzeitig) erreichen (*a train etc.*), ertappen, erwischen, abfassen (*a p. doing s.th.*); klemmen, hängenbleiben mit (*one's fingers, foot etc.*); sich (*Dat.*) zuziehen *or* holen, befallen *or* ergriffen *or* angesteckt werden von (*a disease*); (*fig.*) erfassen, begreifen, vernehmen, verstehen; – ***his attention,*** seine Aufmerksamkeit auf sich lenken; – ***the ball,*** den Ball auffangen; (*coll.*) – ***him a blow,*** ihm eins versetzen; – ***one's breath,*** den Atem (plötzlich) anhalten; – (***a***) ***cold,*** sich erkälten; (*coll.*) – ***a crab,*** einen Krebs fangen; (*coll.*) einen Luftschlag machen; (*coll.*) – ***one's death*** (***of cold***), sich schrecklich erkälten; – ***his eye,*** ihm ins Auge fallen (*of a th.*), seine Aufmerksamkeit auf sich ziehen (*of a p.*); (*Parl.*) – ***the Speaker's eye,*** das Wort erhalten; – ***fire,*** Feuer fangen, in Brand geraten; – ***a glimpse of,*** erblicken; – ***hold of,*** fassen, ergreifen, anpacken, habhaft werden (*Gen.*); – ***him napping,*** ihn überrumpeln; – ***the scent,*** die Spur finden; – ***sight of,*** erblicken; – ***a Tartar,*** übel ankommen, an den Unrechten kommen; ***without –ing a word,*** ohne ein Wort zu verstehen *or* begreifen; (*coll.*) – ***it,*** was abkriegen, sein Fett kriegen; (*coll.*) – ***me*** (***doing that***)***!*** das fällt mir nicht ein! ich werde mich davor hüten! da kannst du lange warten! – ***him at it,*** – ***him in the act,*** ihn dabei ertappen; – ***him on one foot,*** ihn überrumpeln; – ***out,*** (*Crick.*) durch Auffangen (des Balles) erledigen (*the batsman*); ertappen, überraschen (***in,*** bei); – ***up,*** aufraffen; einholen.
2. *irr.v.i.* halten, fassen, greifen, ineinandergreifen; einschnappen (*as a lock*); Feuer fangen; – ***at,*** schnappen *or* haschen *or* greifen nach; ***caught in the rain,*** vom Regen überrascht; – ***on,*** hängenbleiben (*as a dress on a nail*); (*coll.*) einschlagen, Erfolg haben, Anklang finden, in Mode kommen; (*sl.*) – ***on to,*** erfassen, begreifen; – ***up with,*** einholen.
3. *s.* 1. das Fangen; Gefangene(s), der Fang, die (Aus)beute, (*fig.*) der Vorteil, Gewinn; ***good –,*** (*Crick. etc.*) guter Fang, (*Fishing*) guter Fang *or* Zug, (*coll.*) glänzende Partie (*marriage*); 2. (*Mus.*) der Rundgesang; 3. (*Tech.*) Schließhaken (*of lock*), (Sperr)haken, Schnäpper, die Klinke; Arretiervorrichtung, Knagge; 4. (*fig. coll.*) Falle, Täuschung, der Kniff, Haken; das Stocken, Anhalten (*in speaking*); ***there is a – in it,*** die S. hat einen Haken.

catch-as-catch-can, *s.* das Freistilringen. **catching,** *adj.* (*Med.*) ansteckend, übertragbar; gefällig, einschmeichelnd (*tune*), anziehend, einnehmend, fesselnd; verfänglich. **catchment,** *s.* die Wasserstauung; Sammelanlage; – ***area,*** das Sammelbecken, Abflußgebiet (*of rivers*), (*fig.*) Sammelgebiet; – ***basin,*** das Nährgebiet (*of glacier*). **catch|penny, 1.** *s.* der Schund, die Schundware, der Schleuderartikel, Lockartikel. **2.** *adj.* marktschreierisch; wertlos, Schund–. **--phrase,** *s.* das Schlagwort. **–pole, –poll,** *s.* der Büttel, Häscher. **–word,** *s.* das Stichwort, (*Typ.*) der Kustos; das Schlagwort. **catchy,** *adj.* (*coll.*) schwierig, verfänglich, heikel (*question*), einschmeichelnd, gefällig, fasselnd, zugkräftig (*tune etc.*).

catechesis [kætə'ki:sis], *s.* die Katechese. **catechetic(al)** [–'ketik(l)], *adj.* katechetisch. **catechism** ['kætəkizm], *s.* der Katechismus, (*fig.*) die Reihe von Fragen. **catechist,** *s.* der Katechet. **catechize** ['kætəkaiz], *v.t.* katechisieren; (*fig.*) ausfragen, befragen. **catechumen** [–'kju:mən], *s.* der (die) Konfirmand(in), (*fig.*) Anfänger(in), der Neuling.

categorical [kæti'gɔrikl], *adj.* kategorisch; (*fig.*) bestimmt, unbedingt. **category** ['kætigəri], *s.* die Kategorie; (*fig.*) Ordnung, Art, Klasse.

catenarian [kæti'nɛəriən], *adj.* kettenartig, Ketten–. **catenary** [kə'ti:nəri], **1.** *adj.* *See* **catenarian. 2.** *s.* die Kettenlinie.

cater ['keitə], *v.i.* Lebensmittel anschaffen *or* einkaufen (***for,*** für); (*fig.*) sorgen (***for,*** für); (*fig.*) – ***to,*** schmeicheln, etwas bieten (*Dat.*), befriedigen. **caterer,** *s.* der Lebensmittellieferant, Proviantmeister. **catering,** *s.* die Lebensmittelversorgung; das Verpflegungswesen; – ***college*** or ***school,*** die Hotelschule; --***trade,*** das Lebensmittelgewerbe.

caterpillar ['kætəpilə], *s.* 1. die Raupe; 2. (*Tech.*) Gleiskette. **caterpillar-tractor,** *s.* (*regd. trade name*) der Raupenschlepper.

caterwaul ['kætəwɔ:l], *v.i.* miauen, schreien, (*fig.*) jaulen, johlen, zetern. **caterwauling,** *s.* das Katzengeschrei, die Katzenmusik, (*fig.*) das Gejohle, Gezeter.

cat|fall, *s.* (*Naut.*) der Kattläufer. **–fish,** *s.* (*Ichth.*) der Seewolf (*Annarrhichas*); Katzenwels (*Amiurus*). **--footed,** *adj.* (*fig.*) auf leisen Sohlen. **–gut,** *s.* die Darmsaite.

catharsis [kə'θɑ:sis], *s.* 1. (*Med.*) die Abführung, Reinigung; 2. (*fig.*) (*Theat.*) Katharsis, Läuterung, Entspannung. **cathartic, 1.** *adj.* abführend, reinigend; (*fig.*) erlösend. **2.** *s.* (*Med.*) das Abführmittel, (*also fig.*) Reinigungsmittel.

cathead ['kæthed], *s.* (*Naut.*) der Kranbalken, Ankerkran.

cathedra [kə'θi:drə], *s.* der Bischofsstuhl; (*fig.*) ***ex*** –, maßgebend, authoritativ.

cathedral [kə'θi:drəl], *s.* der Dom, die Kathedrale.

Catherine-wheel ['kæθərin], *s.* (*fireworks*) das Feuerrad; (*Gymn.*) Rad; (*Archit.*) Radfenster, die Fensterrose.

catheter ['kæθitə], *s.* der Katheter.

cathode ['kæθoud], *s.* die Kathode; – ***rays,*** Kathodenstrahlen; --***ray tube,*** die Kathodenstrahlröhre, Braunsche Röhre.

catholic ['kæθəlik], **1.** *adj.* (all)umfassend, universal, allgemein(gültig); vorurteilslos; (*Eccl.*) ***Catholic,*** katholisch. **2.** *s.* (***Roman***) ***Catholic,*** der (die) Katholik(in). **Catholicism** [kə'θɔlisizm], *s.* der Katholizismus. **catholicity** [–'lisiti], *s.* die Allgemeinheit, Allgemeingültigkeit, Universalität; Vorurteilslosigkeit. **catholicize** [kə'θɔlisaiz], *v.t.* katholisch machen.

cat-ice, *s.* unsichere Eisschicht.

catkin ['kætkin], *s.* (*Bot.*) das Kätzchen.

cat|-lick, *s.* (*coll.*) flüchtiges Waschen. **–like,** *adj.* katzenartig.

catling ['kætliŋ], *s.* 1. (*Surg.*) das Zergliederungsmesser; 2. (*obs.*) *see* **catgut.**

cat|-nap, *s,* (*coll.*) das Nickerchen. **--o'nine-tails,** *s.* neunschwänzige Katze.

catoptric [kə'tɔptrik], *adj.* katoptrisch, Reflexions–, Spiegel–. **catoptrics,** *pl.* (*sing. constr.*) die Katoptrik.

cat's| cradle, *s.* das Abnehmespiel, Schnurspiel. **--eye,** *s.* (*Geol.*) das Katzenauge; (*Bot.*) der Ehrenpreis; (*Motor.*) Rückstrahler. **--paw,** *s.* (*fig.*) (willenloses) Werkzeug, der Handlanger, Gefoppte(r); (*Naut.*) leichte Brise, die Kühlte; ***make a – of him,*** ihn die Kastanien *or* sich (*Dat.*) von ihm die Kastanien aus dem Feuer holen lassen. **--whisker,** *s.* *See* **cat-whisker.**

cattiness ['kætinis], *s.* (*coll.*) die Gehässigkeit, Bosheit; *see* **catty.**

cattle [kætl], *s.* (*usu. pl. constr.*) das (Rind)vieh, Hornvieh; (*derogatory*) Viehzeug; ***6 head of –,*** 6 (Stück) Vieh. **cattle| breeder,** *s.* der Viehzüchter. **– breeding,** *s.* die Viehzucht. **– feeder,** *s.* die Futtermaschine, der Futterschütter. **– lifter,** *s.* *See* **– rustler. –man,** *s.* der Viehknecht, (*Am.*) *see* **– breeder. – plague,** *s.* die Rinderpest. **– ranch,** *s.* (*Am.*) die Viehfarm. **– range, – run,** *s.* die Viehtrift, Viehweide. **– rustler,** *s.* (*Am.*) der Viehdieb. **– shed,** *s.* der Viehstall. **– show,** *s.* die

Tierschau, viehausstellung. – **trucks,** *s.* der Viehwagen.

catty [kæti], *adj.* (*coll.*) gehässig, boshaft, heimtückisch.

cat|walk, *s.* der Steg, Laufgang, die Laufplanke. **--whisker,** *s.* (*Rad. obs.*) der Kontaktdraht, die Detektornadel.

caucus ['kɔ:kəs], **1.** *s.* die Parteiclique; politische Intriguen (*pl.*); (*Am.*) der Parteiausschuß bei Wahlvorbereitungen; – *funds,* Gelder für Parteizwecke. **2.** *v.t.* durch den Parteiausschuß beeinflussen.

caudal [kɔ:dl], *adj.* Schwanz–. **caudate** [–deit], *adj.* geschwänzt.

caudle [kɔ:dl], *s.* die Krankensuppe, der Stärkungstrank.

caught [kɔ:t], *imperf., p.p. of* **catch.**

caul [kɔ:l], *s.* (*Anat.*) die Eihaut, (*coll.*) Glückshaube; das Haarnetz.

cauldron ['kɔ:ldrən], *s.* großer Kessel; *witches'* –, der Hexenkessel.

cauliflower ['kɔliflauə], *s.* der Blumenkohl.

cauline ['kɔ:lain], *adj.* Stengel–, stengelständig.

caulk [kɔ:k], *v.t.* (ab)dichten, verstemmen; (*Naut.*) kalfatern.

causal ['kɔ:zəl], *adj.* ursächlich, kausal; (*Gram.*) kausal, begründend. **causality** [–'zæliti], *s.* die Kausalität; der Kausalzusammenhang, Kausalnexus; *law of* –, das Kausalgesetz. **causation** [–'zeiʃən], *s.* die Verursachung, Ursächlichkeit; Ursache. **causative** [–zətiv], **1.** *adj.* verursachend, bewirkend, begründend; (*Gram.*) *see* **causal. 2.** *s.* (*Gram.*) das Kausalitivum.

cause [kɔ:z], **1.** *s.* die Ursache, der Grund; Anlaß, die Veranlassung (*for,* zu); gute *or* gerechte S.; (*Law*) der Rechtsfall, Rechtsstreit, Rechtshandel, Prozeß; (*Phil.*) *final* –, der Endzweck; *first* –, der Urgrund, Gott; (*Law*) – *list,* die Terminliste; *die for* or *in a good* –, für eine gute S. sterben; *gain one's* –, obsiegen; *give – for,* Anlaß geben zu; *– for complaint,* Grund zum Klagen; *make common – with,* gemeinsame S. machen mit; *plead a* –, eine Rechtssache führen; *show* –, seine Gründe angeben; *for the* –, für die gute S. *or* unsre S.; *not without* (*some*) –, nicht ohne Grund. **2.** *v.t.* verursachen, veranlassen, bewirken; Anlaß geben (*Dat.*) zu; – *him grief,* ihm Kummer machen *or* verursachen; *he –d me to be invited,* er ließ mich einladen; *he –d me to be late,* er verursachte, daß ich spät ankam; *– trouble,* Schwierigkeiten *or* (*coll.*) Krach machen. **causeless,** *adj.* grundlos, unbegründet, ohne Ursache *or* Grund. **causelessness,** *s.* die Grundlosigkeit. **causer,** *s.* der Urheber.

causerie [kouzə'ri:], *s.* die Plauderei, zwanglose Ansprache.

causeway ['kɔ:zwei], *s.* der Fußweg, Damm.

caustic ['kɔ:stik], **1.** *adj.* ätzend, beizend, brennend, (*fig.*) scharf, beißend, satirisch, sarkastisch, kaustisch; *– bath,* das Laugenbad; *– curve,* die Brennlinie; *– potash,* das Ätzkali; *– soda,* das Natriumhydroxyd, (Ätz)natron; – *wit,* beißender Witz. **2.** *s.* das Ätzmittel, Beizmittel, die Alkalilauge, Beize. **causticity** [–'tisiti], *s.* die Ätzwirkung, Beizkraft, (*fig.*) Schärfe, der Sarkasmus.

cauterization [kɔ:tərai'zeiʃən], *s.* das (Aus)brennen, Ätzen, die Ätzung. **cauterize** ['kɔ:təraiz], *v.t.* (aus)brennen, (ver)ätzen, wegätzen. **cautery** [–ri], *s.* das Brenneisen; Ätzmittel, der Ätzstift; das (Aus)brennen, Ätzen.

caution ['kɔ:ʃən], **1.** *s.* **1.** die Vorsicht, Umsicht, Behutsamkeit; *ride with –!* vorsichtig fahren! 2. (Ver)-warnung; *by way of* –, als Warnung; *be let off with a* –, mit einer Verwarnung davonkommen; 3. (*sl.*) etwas Bemerkenswertes; (*sl.*) *he is a* –, er ist eine Nummer für sich. **2.** *v.t.* warnen (*against,* vor (*Dat.*)); verwarnen; *I –ed him against leaving,* ich warnte ihn fortzugehen. **cautionary,** *adj.* warnend, Warnungs–, Warn–. **caution-money,** *s.* die Kaution.

cautious ['kɔ:ʃəs], *adj.* vorsichtig, umsichtig, behutsam; achtsam (*of,* auf (*Acc.*)). **cautiousness,** *s.* die Vorsicht, Behutsamkeit.

cavalcade [kævl'keid], *s.* der Reiter(auf)zug.

cavalier [kævə'liə], **1.** *s.* der Reiter; Ritter; Kavalier, Verehrer; (*Hist.*) Kavalier, Royalist; *Cavaliers and Roundheads,* Royalisten und Puritaner. **2.** *adj.* arrogant, anmaßend, hochmütig, rücksichtslos, verächtlich.

cavalry ['kævlri], *s.* die Reiterei, Kavallerie; – *sergeant,* der Wachtmeister; *troop of* –, die Reiterschwadron. **cavalry|man,** *s.* der Reiter, Kavallerist. **--sword,** *s.* der Schleppsäbel, Reitersäbel.

[1]**cave** [keiv], **1.** *s.* 1. die Höhle, Grube; 2. (*Pol.*) Parteispaltung Absonderung, Sezession; Sezessionsgruppe, Sezessionisten (*pl.*); 3. (*Am.*) der Erdrutsch. **2.** *v.t.* (*usu.* – *in*) eindrücken, aushöhlen. **3.** *v.i.* 1. (*Pol.*) sich abspalten; 2. (*usu.* – *in*) einstürzen, (*sl.*) klein beigeben, zusammenklappen.

[2]**cave!** ['keivi], *int.* (*school sl.*) aufpassen! *keep* –, aufpassen.

caveat ['keiviæt], *s.* (*Law*) der Einspruch, die Verwahrung; (*Am.*) Patentanmeldung; Warnung; der Vorbehalt; *enter a* –, Einspruch erheben, Verwahrung einlegen.

cave|-dweller, *s.* der Höhlenbewohner. **-man,** *s.* (*Archaeol.*) der Höhlenbewohner; (*coll.*) Naturmensch, Gewaltmensch.

cavern ['kævən], *s.* die Höhle. **cavernous,** *adj.* voller Höhlen, höhlenreich; (*fig.*) hohl, eingefallen (*cheeks*), tief (*darkness*).

caviar(e) ['kævia:], *s.* der Kaviar; – *to the general,* Kaviar für das Volk.

cavil ['kævil], **1.** *v.i.* kritteln, nörgeln (*at, about,* an (*Dat.*) *or* über (*Acc.*)). **2.** *s.* die Spitzfindigkeit, Krittelei, Nörgelei, spitzfindiger Einwand. **caviller,** *s.* der Nörgler, Krittler. **cavilling, 1.** *adj.* spitzfindig, krittelig, nörglerisch. **2.** *s. See* **cavil, 2.**

cavitation [kævi'teiʃən], *s.* (*Metall.*) die Hohlraumbildung, (*Med.*) Höhlenbildung. **cavity** ['kæviti], *s.* die (Aus)höhlung, der Hohlraum; die Vertiefung, Mulde; (*Anat.*) (Körper)höhle, (*in teeth*) das Loch.

cavort [kə'vɔ:t], *v.i.* sich bäumen, umherspringen.

cavy ['keivi], *s.* (*Zool.*) das Meerschweinchen.

caw [kɔ:], **1.** *v.i.* krächzen. **2.** *int.* krah!

cay [kei], *s.* die Sandbank.

cayenne-pepper ['keijən], *s.* spanischer Pfeffer.

cayman ['keimən], *s.* (*Zool.*) der Kaiman.

cease [si:s], **1.** *v.i.* aufhören, enden, zu Ende gehen; – *from,* anhalten mit, ablassen *or* abstehen von. **2.** *v.t.* einstellen, aufhören mit; – *fire,* das Feuer einstellen; – *work,* die Arbeit einstellen, Feierabend machen. **3.** *s.* (*only in*) *without* –, *see* **ceaseless. cease-fire,** *s.* die Feuereinstellung, Waffenruhe. **ceaseless,** *adj.* unaufhörlich, unablässig.

cecity ['si:siti], *s.* (*fig.*) die Blindheit.

cedar ['si:də], *s.* (*Bot.*) die Zeder. **cedar(wood),** *s.* das Zedernholz.

cede [si:d], **1.** *v.t.* abtreten, abgeben (*to, Dat. or* an (*Acc.*)), überlassen (*Dat.*). **2.** *v.i.* zugeben, (*obs.*) weichen, nachgeben.

cedilla [sə'dilə], *s.* die Cedille.

ceil [si:l], *v.t.* verschalen, täfeln, verputzen (*a room*); (*Naut.*) bewegern. **ceiling,** *s.* die (Zimmer)decke; (*Naut.*) Wegerung, Innenbeplankung; (*Av.*) Gipfelhöhe, Steighöhe; (*Meteor.*) untere Wolkengrenze; (*Comm. etc.*) Höchstgrenze, das Höchstmaß; *credit* –, der Kreditrahmen.

celandine ['seləndain], *s.* (*greater* –) das Schöllkraut, Schellkraut; (*lesser* –) die Feigwurz.

celebrant ['selibrənt], *s.* (*Eccl.*) der Zelebrant.

celebrate ['selibreit], **1.** *v.t.* feiern, festlich begehen (*a feast*); feiern, verherrlichen, preisen (*a p.*); (*Eccl.*) abhalten, zelebrieren. **2.** *v.i.* feiern. **celebrated,** *adj.* berühmt, gefeiert. **celebration** [–'breiʃən], *s.* die Feier, das Fest, Begängnis; Feiern, Begehen (*of a feast*); die Verherrlichung, der Preis (*of a p.*); – *of the Lord's supper,* die

Abendmahlsfeier. **celebrity,** *s.* die Berühmtheit, der Ruhm: berühmte Persönlichkeit.

celeriac [sə'leriæk], *s.* der *or* die Knollensellerie.

celerity [sə'leriti], *s.* die Geschwindigkeit, Schnelligkeit.

celery ['seləri], *s.* der *or* die Sellerie; ***stick of –,*** der Selleriestengel.

celestial [si'lestjəl], **1.** *adj.* himmlisch, (*also Astr.*) Himmels–; – ***body,*** der Himmelskörper; ***the – empire,*** das Reich des Himmels (*China*); – ***harmony,*** die Sphärenharmonie. **2.** *s.* Selige(r).

celibacy ['selibəsi], *s.* die Ehelosigkeit; lediger Stand; der *or* das Zölibat (*of clergy*). **celibate, 1.** *s.* der Junggeselle, Unverheiratete(r). **2.** *adj.* unverheiratet, ledig.

cell [sel], *s.* die Zelle (*of prisoner, monk etc.*) (*also Bot., Biol., Zool.*); (*Poet.*) Klause, Hütte (*of recluse*); (*Pol.*) Arbeitsgruppe; (*Elec.*) das Element; – ***formation,*** die Zell(en)bildung; – ***wall,*** die Zellwand.

cellar ['selə], **1.** *s.* der Keller; ***keep a good –,*** einen guten Weinkeller halten. **2.** *v.t.* einkellern. **cellarage** [–ridʒ], *s.* 1. das Kellergeschoß, Kellerräume (*pl.*); 2. die Kellermiete. **cellarer,** *s.* der Kellermeister. **cellaret** [–'ret], *s.* der Flaschenschrank, Flaschenständer. **cellarman,** *s. See* **cellarer.**

cellist ['tʃelist], *etc. See* **violoncellist** *etc.*

cellophane ['seləfein], *s.* das Zellophan(papier), die Glashaut.

cellular ['seljulə], *adj.* zellig, zellenartig, Zell(en)–; – ***fibre,*** die Zellfaser; – ***tissue,*** das Zellgewebe; – ***vest,*** die Netzjacke. **cellule** [–ju:l], *s.* kleine Zelle.

celluloid ['seljulɔid], *s.* das Zelluloid, Zellhorn. **cellulose** [–lous], **1.** *adj.* Zellulose–. **2.** *s.* der Zellstoff, die Zellulose. **cellulous,** *adj. See* **cellular.**

Celt [kelt, selt], *s.* der Kelte (die Keltin). **Celtic, 1.** *adj.* keltisch. **2.** *s.* (*language*) das Keltisch(e).

cement [si'ment], **1.** *s.* der Zement, Mörtel; Kitt; (*fig.*) Band, die Bindung; ***mastic –,*** der Steinkitt. **2.** *v.t.* zementieren, (an)kitten, zusammenkitten, verkitten; (*fig.*) verbinden, (be)festigen, schmieden, vereinigen. **cementation** [–'teiʃən], *s.* (*Metall.*) die Einsatzhärtung; Zementstahlbereitung; ***steel of –,*** der Zementstahl; – ***furnace,*** der Zementierofen.

cemetery ['semitri], *s.* der Friedhof.

cenobite ['si:nəbait], *s.* der Klostermönch.

cenotaph ['senətɑ:f], *s.* das Ehrengrabmal, Ehren(denk)mal.

censer ['sensə], *s.* das Weihrauchfaß.

censor ['sensə], **1.** *s.* der Zensor; Sittenrichter (*of,* über); (*Psych.*) die Zensur. **2.** *v.t.* zensieren. **censorial** [–'sɔ:riəl], *adj.* zensorisch, Zensor–, Zensur–. **censorious** [–'sɔ:riəs], *adj.* streng kritisch (***towards, of,*** gegen), tadelnd, tadelsüchtig, krittelig. **censoriousness,** *s.* die Tadelsucht, Krittelei. **censorship,** *s.* das Zensoramt; die Zensur.

censurable ['senʃərəbl], *adj.* tadelhaft, tadelnswert. **censure, 1.** *s.* der Tadel, die Kritik (*of,* an (*Dat.*)); Mißbilligung; Rüge, der Verweis; ***vote of –,*** das Mißtrauensvotum. **2.** *v.t.* tadeln, rügen, mißbilligen, verurteilen.

census ['sensəs], *s.* die (Volks)zählung, der Zensus; ***take a –,*** eine Volkszählung vornehmen.

cent [sent], *s.* 1. ***per –,*** Prozent, aufs Hundert; ***at 5 per –,*** zu 5 Prozent; ***a loan at 5 per –,*** eine fünfprozentige Anleihe; 2. (*Am.*) der Cent; (*coll.*) Heller, Pfennig.

centaur ['sentɔ:], *s.* der Zentaur, Kentaur, Pferdemensch.

centaury ['sentəri], *s.* (*Bot.*) das Tausendgüldenkraut, die Flockenblume.

centenarian [senti'nɛəriən], **1.** *s.* Hundertjährige(r). **2.** *adj.* hundertjährig. **centenary** [–'ti:nəri], **1.** *adj.* hundertjährig. **2.** *s.* der Zeitraum von hundert Jahren; die Hundertjahrfeier, hundertjähriges Jubiläum. **centennial** [–'teniəl], **1.** *adj.* hundertjährig. **2.** *s.* die Hundertjahrfeier.

center (*Am.*), *see* **centre.**

centesimal [sen'tesiməl], *adj.* hundertteilig; Zentesimal–.

centigrade ['sentigreid], *adj.* hundertgradig, hundertteilig; – ***scale,*** die Zentesimaleinteilung; – ***thermometer,*** das Celsiusthermometer; ***20 degrees –,*** 20 Grad Celsius. **centigramme,** *s.* das Zentigramm. **centimetre,** *s.* das Zentimeter. **centipede** [–pi:d], *s.* (*Zool.*) der Tausendfuß, Tausendfüß(l)er.

centner ['sentnə], *s.* der Zentner (*50 kg.*).

cento ['sentou], *s.* die Kompilation, das Flickwerk.

central ['sentrəl], *adj.* zentral (gelegen), zentrisch, den Mittelpunkt bildend, (*fig.*) Zentral–, Mittel–, Haupt–; ***be –,*** im Mittelpunkt sein; – ***heating,*** die Zentralheizung; – ***office,*** die Zentralstelle, Zentrale; – ***point,*** der Mittelpunkt; (*Elec.*) Nullpunkt; (*Hist.*) – ***powers,*** die Mittelmächte; – (***railway-***) ***station,*** der Hauptbahnhof. **centrality** [–'træliti], *s.* die Zentralität, zentrale Lage.

centralization [sentrəlai'zeiʃən], *s.* die Zentralisierung, Zentralisation. **centralize** ['sentrəlaiz], *v.t.* zentralisieren.

centre ['sentə], **1.** *s.* der Mittelpunkt (*also fig.*), die Mitte, das Zentrum; (*Pol.*) die Zentrumspartei, Mittelpartei; – ***of an arch,*** der Lehrbogen; – ***of attraction,*** der Anziehungs(mittel)punkt; ***communication –,*** die Nachrichtenstelle; (*Tech.*) ***dead –,*** der Totpunkt; – ***of gravity,*** der Schwerpunkt; (*Artil.*) – ***of impact,*** mittlerer Auftreff– *or* Aufschlagpunkt; – ***of interest,*** das Hauptinteresse; – ***of motion,*** der Drehpunkt; (*Mil.*) – ***of resistance,*** der Anklammerungspunkt; – ***of rotation,*** der Drehpunkt; ***training –,*** das Ausbildungslager. **2.** *v.t.* 1. konzentrieren (***on,*** auf (*Acc.*)); 2. (*Tech.*) zentrieren, einmitten, ankörnen; in den Mittelpunkt stellen; 3. (*Footb.*) auf die Mitte zuspielen. **3.** *v.i.* sich konzentrieren (*on,* auf (*Acc.*)), (*fig.*) sich gründen, beruhen (auf (*Dat.*)).

centre|-bit, *s.* der Zentrier– *or* Zentrumsbohrer. **–board,** *s.* (*Naut.*) das (Kiel)schwert; – ***vessel,*** das Schwertboot. **–-forward,** *s.* (*Footb.*) der Mittelstürmer. **–-half,** *s.* (*Footb.*) der Mittelläufer, – **line,** *s.* die Mittellinie, Mitte; (*Naut.*) Mitschiffslinie. **–piece,** *s.* der Tafelaufsatz. – **punch,** *s.* das Locheisen, der (An)körner. **–-second hand,** *s.* der Zentralsekundenzeiger. – **section,** *s.* das Mittelstück, der Mittelteil.

centrifugal [sen'trifjugl, –'fju:gl], *adj.* zentrifugal; – ***force,*** die Fliehkraft, Zentrifugalkraft; – ***machine,*** die Zentrifuge, Schleudermaschine; – ***pump,*** die Kreiselpumpe. **centrifuge** ['sentrifju:dʒ], **1.** *s.* der (Trenn)schleuder. **2.** *v.t.* (aus)schleudern.

centripetal [sen'tripitl], *adj.* zentripetal; – ***force,*** die Zentripetalkraft.

centuple ['sentjupl], **1.** *adj.* hundertfach, hundertfältig. **2.** *v.t.* verhundertfachen. **centuplicate** [–'tju:plikeit], *v.t.* hundertfach anfertigen.

centurion [sen'tjuəriən], *s.* (*Hist.*) der Zenturio.

century ['sentʃəri], *s.* 1. das Jahrhundert; ***centuries old,*** jahrhundertealt; ***for centuries,*** jahrhundertelang; 2. der Satz von hundert; (*Crick.*) volles Hundert.

cephalic [se'fælik], *adj.* Kopf–, Schädel–. **cephalopod** ['sefələpɔd], *s.* (*Zool.*) der Kopffüß(l)er.

ceramic [sə'ræmik], *adj.* keramisch; – ***art*** or **ceramics,** *pl.* (*sing. constr.*) die Keramik, Töpferkunst.

cerate ['siərət], *s.* die Wachssalbe. **cerated** [–reitid], *adj.* mit Wachs überzogen.

cere [siə], *s.* (*Orn.*) die Wachshaut.

cereal ['siəriəl], **1.** *adj.* Getreide–. **2.** *s.* die Frühstücksmehlspeise; *pl.* das Getreide, Getreidearten (*pl.*).

cerebellum [seri'beləm], *s.* das Kleinhirn. **cerebral** ['seribrəl], *adj.* Gehirn–. **cerebration** [–'breiʃən], *s.* die Gehirntätigkeit, der Denkprozeß.

cerebro-spinal meningitis ['seribrou–], *s.* (*Med.*) die Genickstarre. **cerebrum,** *s.* das Großhirn.

cere-cloth, *s.* das Wachstuch; Leichentuch. **cerements,** *pl.* das Totenhemd, Leichengewand.

ceremonial [seri'mouniəl], **1.** *adj.* zeremoniell, feierlich; förmlich, rituell. **2.** *s.* das Zeremoniell. **ceremonious,** *adj.* zeremoniös, steif, förmlich, umständlich. **ceremoniousness,** *s.* die Feierlichkeit, Förmlichkeit, Umständlichkeit.

ceremony ['seriməni], *s.* 1. die Zeremonie; Feier(lichkeit), feierliche Handlung; ***master of ceremonies,*** der Zeremonienmeister, Conférencier; 2. die Förmlichkeit; ***no – please!*** bitte, keine Umstände! ***stand on –,*** förmlich sein; ***without –,*** ohne Umstände, kurzweg.

cereous ['siərəs], *adj.* wachsartig, wächsern.

ceriph, *see* **serif.**

cerise [sə'ri:z], *adj.* kirschrot.

cerium ['siəriəm], *s.* (*Chem.*) das Cer, Zer.

cerous ['siərəs], *adj.* (*Orn.*) wachshautartig.

certain [sə:tn], *adj.* 1. (*pred.*) sicher, gewiß (*of p. or th.*), (*of th.*) unbestreitbar, (*of p.*) überzeugt; ***be – of,*** sicher *or* gewiß sein (*Gen.*), überzeugt sein von; ***feel –,*** überzeugt sein; ***make – of,*** sich (*Dat.*) sichern, sich vergewissern (*Gen.*); ***come for –,*** mit Sicherheit kommen; 2. (*attrib.*) gewiß, bestimmt, festgesetzt; unfehlbar, zuverlässig, verläßlich, sicher; ***to my – knowledge,*** wie ich gewiß weiß; ***a – cure,*** zuverlässiges *or* sicheres (Heil)mittel; 3. gewiß; ***– of your friends,*** einige Ihrer Freunde *or* unter Ihren Freunden; ***a – George Miller,*** ein gewisser G. M.; ***a – reluctance,*** eine gewisse Abneigung; ***under – circumstances,*** unter gewissen *or* bestimmten Umständen; ***have a – doubt,*** einigen Zweifel haben. **certainly,** *adv.* gewiß, bestimmt, sicher(lich), zweifellos, allerdings. **certainty,** *s.* die Bestimmtheit, Sicherheit, Zuverlässigkeit; Gewißheit, Überzeugung; ***for a –,*** mit Bestimmtheit, ganz bestimmt *or* gewiß; (*coll.*) ***a dead –*** or (*sl.*) ***cert.,*** eine unumstößliche Gewißheit; ein todsicherer Tip.

certes ['sə:tiz], *adv.* (*obs.*) fürwahr.

certifiable ['sə:tifaiəbl], *adj.* 1. zu bestätigen(d); 2. (*of the mentally ill*) meldepflichtig, anmeldungspflichtig; (*coll.*) wahnsinnig.

certificate, 1. [sə'tifikit], *s.* das Zeugnis, Attest, die Bescheinigung, Urkunde, der Schein; (*Naut.*) Befähigungsschein; ***– of baptism,*** der Taufschein; ***– of birth,*** die Geburtsurkunde; ***– of character,*** das Leumundszeugnis; ***General Certificate of Education,*** das Schul(abgangs)zeugnis (mit 16 Jahren), (*approx.* =) (*coll.*) Einjährige(zeugnis); ***General Certificate of Education (advanced level),*** das Schulabgangszeugnis (mit 18 Jahren), (*approx.* =) Abitur, Reifezeugnis, die Reifeprüfung; ***– of health, health –,*** das Gesundheitsattest, der Gesundheitspaß; ***– of merit,*** schriftliche Belobigung; (*Comm.*) ***– of origin,*** das Ursprungszeugnis; ***– of posting,*** die Postquittung, der Postempfangsschein; ***school (leaving) –,*** *see* ***General Certificate of Education***; ***higher school –,*** see ***General Certificate of Education (advanced level).*** **2.** [–keit], *v.t.* ein Zeugnis ausstellen (*Dat.*) (***for,*** über (*Acc.*)), bescheinigen. **certificated,** *adj.* staatlich anerkannt *or* beglaubigt; ***– engineer,*** der Diplomingenieur; ***– teacher,*** geprüfter Lehrer. **certification** [–'keiʃən], *s.* die Bescheinigung, (amtliche) Beglaubigung; das Zeugnis.

certify ['sə:tifai], *v.t.* 1. bescheinigen, beglaubigen, bezeugen, beurkunden, attestieren, bestätigen; ***this is to – . . .,*** hiermit wird bestätigt . . . *or* bezeugt . . .; 2. versichern, vergewissern (*a p.*) (***of,*** *Gen.*); 3. für geisteskrank erklären.

certitude ['sə:titju:d], *s.* die Überzeugung, (innere) Gewißheit.

cerulean [sə'ru:liən], *adj.* himmelblau.

cerumen [sə'ru:min], *s.* das Ohrenschmalz.

ceruse ['siəru:s], *s.* das Bleiweiß; Weißbleierz.

cervical ['sə:vikl, sə'vaikl], *adj.* Nacken–, Hals–.

cervine ['sə:vain], *adj.* Hirsch–.

cervix ['sə:viks], *s.* das Genick, (*of an organ*) der Hals.

cess [ses], *s.* (*Irish*) die Steuer, Gebühr; (*coll. obs.*) ***bad – to you!*** hol' dich der Teufel! die Pest über dich!

cessation [sə'seiʃən], *s.* das Aufhören, Einstellen, die Beendigung; Ruhe, der Einstand; ***– of hostilities,*** die Einstellung der Feindseligkeiten; ***without –,*** unaufhörlich.

cession ['seʃən], *s.* die Abtretung, Zession, Überlassung, Übertretung (***to,*** an (*Acc.*)); der Verzicht (***of,*** auf (*Acc.*)). **cessionary,** *s.* der Zessionär, Rechtsnachfolger.

cess|pit, –pool, *s.* die Senkgrube, Abtritt(s)grube, Jauchengrube; (*fig.*) der Pfuhl.

cestoid ['sestɔid], **1.** *s.* der Bandwurm. **2.** *adj.* bandwurmartig.

cetacean [si'teiʃən], **1.** *s.* der Wal(fisch). **2.** *adj.* Wal–, walartig.

chafe [tʃeif], **1.** *v.t.* scheuern, wundreiben; durchreiben, aufreiben; frottieren, warmreiben. **2.** *v.i.* scheuern, schaben (***on, against,*** an (*Dat.*)), sich reiben (auf (*Dat.*)); (*Naut.*) schamfilen; (*fig.*) sich ärgern (***at,*** über (*Acc.*)), sich abhärmen (um); wüten, toben.

chafer ['tʃeifə], *s.* (*Ent.*) der (Mai)käfer.

chaff [tʃɑ:f, tʃæf], **1.** *s.* 1. die Spreu, das Kaff; der *or* das Häcksel; 2. (*coll.*) die Neckerei. **2.** *v.t., v.i.* (*coll.*) necken, aufziehen. **chaff-cutter,** *s.* die Häckselbank, der Häckselschneider.

chaffer ['tʃæfə], *v.i.* handeln, schachern, feilschen.

chaffinch ['tʃæfintʃ], *s.* (*Orn.*) der Buchfink (*Fringilla coelebs*).

chafing ['tʃeifiŋ], *s.* das Wundreiben, Scheuern; Aufreiben, Durchreiben; (*Naut.*) Schamfilen; (*Med.*) wunde *or* wundgeriebene Stelle, der Wolf.

chafing|-dish, *s.* die Wärmepfanne. **––gear,** *s.* (*Naut.*) das Umkleidungsmaterial (*for ropes etc.*).

chagrin [ʃægrin, ʃæ'gri:n], **1.** *s.* der Ärger, Verdruß; Kummer, die Enttäuschung. **2.** *v.t.* (ver)ärgern, verdrießen; Kummer bereiten (*Dat.*), enttäuschen.

chain [tʃein], **1.** *s.* die Kette; (*Surv.*) Meßkette (= *66 feet, approx. 20 m.*); (*fig.*) Kette, Verkettung, Reihe, Folge; (*Comm.*) das Kettenunternehmen; *pl.* Fesseln (*pl.*), Bande (*pl.*); ***drag––,*** die Hemmkette; ***link in the –,*** das Kettenglied; (*fig.*) ***a link in the – of reasoning,*** ein Glied in der (Kette der) Argumentation *or* Beweisführung; ***– of mountains,*** die Bergkette, Gebirgskette, der Höhenzug. **2.** *v.t.* (***also – up***) mit einer Kette befestigen, anketten, an die Kette legen; ketten, fesseln, in Ketten legen (*a prisoner*).

chain| adjuster, *s.* (*Cycl.*) der Kettenspanner. **– armour,** *s.* der Kettenpanzer. **– bridge,** *s.* die Kettenbrücke, Hängebrücke. **– cable,** *s.* (*Naut.*) die Ankerkette. **– drive,** *s.* der Kettenantrieb. **– gang,** *s.* aneinandergekettete Sträflinge (*pl.*). **– locker,** *s.* (*Naut.*) der Kettenkasten. **– mail,** *s.* *See* **– armour. – plate,** *s.* (*Naut.*) die Pütting. **– pump,** *s.* das Paternosterwerk, die Kettenpumpe. **– reaction,** *s.* die Kettenreaktion. **– smoker,** *s.* (*coll.*) der Kettenraucher. **– stitch,** *s.* der Kettenstich. **– store,** *s.* das Zweiggeschäft, der Filialbetrieb.

chainwale [tʃænl], *s.* (*usu. pl.*) (*Naut.*) Rüsten (*pl.*).

chair [tʃɛə], *s.* 1. der Stuhl, Sessel; ***easy –,*** der Lehnstuhl; ***folding –,*** der Klappstuhl; ***sedan –,*** der Tragsessel, die Sänfte; ***upholstered –,*** der Polsterstuhl; ***take a –,*** sich setzen, Platz nehmen; 2. (*Univ.*) der Lehrstuhl, die Professur; ***hold the – for German,*** den Lehrstuhl für Deutsch innehaben; 3. (*Railw.*) der Schienenstuhl; 4. (*fig.*) Vorsitz, Vorsitzende(r); ***–! –!*** zur Ordnung! ***address the –,*** sich an den Vorsitzenden wenden; ***be in the –,*** den Vorsitz führen; ***take the –,*** den Vorsitz übernehmen. **2.** *v.t.* auf die Schultern nehmen (*a p.*); ***– a meeting,*** den Vorsitz einer Versammlung übernehmen.

chair| attendant, *s.* der Stuhlvermieter. **––back,** *s.* die Stuhllehne. **––bottom,** *s.* der Stuhlsitz. **––lift,** *s.* der Sessellift.

chairman ['tʃɛəmən], *s.* Vorsitzende(r), der Präsident. **chairmanship,** *s.* der Vorsitz.

chaise [ʃeiz], *s.* die Chaise, Kalesche. **chaise longue** [–lɔŋ], *s.* das Liegesofa.

chalcedony [kæl'sedəni], *s.* der Chalzedon.

chalcographer [kæl'kɔgrəfə], *s.* der Kupferstecher.

chaldron ['tʃɔ:ldrən], *s.* (*obs.*) ein Kohlenmaß (= *36 bushels, approx. 1200 litres*).

chalet ['ʃælei], *s.* die Sennhütte; das Sommerhäuschen.

chalice ['tʃælis], *s.* der Meßkelch, Abendmahlsbecher; (*Bot.*) Kelch.

chalk [tʃɔ:k], **1.** *s.* die Kreide; Zeichenkreide, der Kreidestift; ***coloured –***, der Buntstift, Farbstift; ***– formation***, das Kreidegebirge; (*coll.*) ***not by a long –***, lange *or* bei weitem nicht; ***red –***, der Rotstift, Rötel; ***they are as unlike as – and cheese***, sie gleichen einander wie Tag und Nacht. **2.** *v.t.* mit Kreide zeichnen *or* schreiben; (*coll.*) ***– up***, rot im Kalender anstreichen (*s.th. memorable*); ankreiden, auf die Rechnung schreiben, auf Rechnung setzen (*an account*). **chalk|-cutter,** *s.* der Kreidegräber. **--mark,** *s.* der Kreidestrich. **--pit,** *s.* die Kreidegrube. **--stone,** *s.* (*Med.*) der Gichtknoten. **chalky,** *adj.* kreidig, kreideartig; kreidehaltig, Kreide–; kreideweiß; ***– clay***, der Mergel.

challenge ['tʃæləndʒ], **1.** *s.* die Herausforderung (***to***, zu) (*a duel etc.*), Aufforderung (an (*Acc.*)) (*a p.*); das Anrufen (*of a sentry*); die Ablehnung (*of jurymen etc.*); (*Hunt.*) das Anschlagen. **2.** *v.t.* **1.** herausfordern, auffordern (***to***, zu); **2.** (*Mil.*) anrufen; (*Law*) ablehnen; sich aussprechen gegen, Einwendungen machen gegen, in Frage stellen, bestreiten, anzweifeln. **challenge trophy,** *s.* (*Spt.*) der Wanderpreis.

chalybeate [kə'libiit], *adj.* stahlhaltig; ***– spring***, die Stahlquelle.

chamade [ʃə'mɑ:d], *s.* (*Mil.*) die Schamade, der Rückzug.

chamber ['tʃeimbə], *s.* **1.** (*Poet.*) die Kammer, das Zimmer, Gemach; (*Parl.*) die Kammer, der Sitzungssaal; (*Comm.*) die Kammer; (*Law*) das Kammergericht, Gerichtszimmer; ***bridal –***, das Brautgemach; ***– of commerce***, die Handelskammer; (*Parl.*) ***second*** or ***upper –***, das Oberhaus; 2. der Laderaum (*of a gun*); ***ammunition –***, die Munitionskammer; ***combustion –***, der Verbrennungsraum; ***compression –***, der Verdichtungsraum; 3. (*Anat.*) die Kammer; 4. (*coll.*) *see* **chamber-pot**; 5. *pl.* Junggesellenwohnung; Geschäftsräume (*pl.*) (*of a barrister*).

chamber|-concert, *s.* das Kammerkonzert. **--counsel,** *s.* der Rechtskonsulent. **chambered,** *adj.* mit Kammern versehen; ***six-- revolver***, sechsschüssiger Revolver.

chamberlain ['tʃeimbəlin], *s.* der Kämmerer, Kammerherr; Haushofmeister; ***the Lord Chamberlain of the Household***, der Oberhofmeister; ***the Lord Great Chamberlain***, der Großkämmerer.

chamber|maid, *s.* das Zimmermädchen, Stubenmädchen. **--music,** *s.* die Kammermusik. **--organ,** *s.* die Zimmerorgel. **--pot,** *s.* das Nachtgeschirr, der Nachttopf. **--practice,** *s.* die Privatpraxis eines Anwalts.

chameleon [kə'mi:ljən], *s.* (*Zool.*) das Chamäleon (*also fig.*), (*fig.*) die Wetterfahne. **chameleon-like,** *adj.* (*fig.*) wankelmütig, wetterwendisch, unbeständig.

chamfer ['tʃæmfə], **1.** *v.i.* (*Archit.*) kannelieren, auskehlen; (*Tech.*) abschrägen, abkanten. **2.** *s.* die Kannelierung, Auskehlung, Hohlrinne; (*Tech.*) Schrägkante, Abschrägung, Fase.

chamois, *s.* **1.** ['ʃæmwɑ:] (*Zool.*) die Gemse; 2. ['ʃæmi] (*– leather*) das Sämischleder.

[1]**champ** [tʃæmp], *v.t., v.i.* geräuschvoll kauen; (*fig.*) mit den Zähnen knirschen; ***– the bit***, auf die Stange beißen, am Gebiß kauen; (*coll.*) ***– at the bit***, ungeduldig sein *or* werden.

[2]**champ,** *s.* (*sl.*) *see* **champion.**

champagne [ʃæm'pein], *s.* der Champagner, Sekt, Schaumwein.

champaign [tʃæm'pein], *s.* (*Poet.*) die Ebene, offenes *or* freies Feld.

champion ['tʃæmpjən], **1.** *s.* **1.** der Kämpfer, Held, Kämpe; (*Spt.*) Meister, Sieger; ***– boxer***, der Meisterschaftskämpfer, Boxmeister; ***– turnip***, preisgekrönte Rübe; 2. (*fig.*) der Verfechter, Fürsprecher; ***– of the truth***, der Wahrheitsverfechter. **2.** *v.t.* eintreten für, verfechten, verteidigen. **3.** *adj.* (*coll.*) erstklassig. **championship,** *s.* **1.** die Verteidigung, Verfechtung; das Eintreten (***of***, für); 2. (*Spt.*) die Meisterschaft.

chance [tʃɑ:ns], **1.** *s.* **1.** der Zufall; das Schicksal, Geschick, Los; ***game of –***, ein Glücksspiel; ***happy*** or ***lucky –***, glücklicher Zufall; ***mere –***, reiner Zufall; ***leave it to –***, es darauf ankommen lassen, es dem Zufall überlassen; ***take a –***, ein Risiko auf sich nehmen, es darauf ankommen lassen, sein Glück versuchen; ***not take any –s***, auf Nummer Sicher gehen; ***take –s***, ein Risiko eingehen, die Gefahr auf sich nehmen; ***by –***, zufällig, durch Zufall, von ungefähr; 2. die Gelegenheit, Chance, Aussicht (***of***, auf), Möglichkeit, Wahrscheinlichkeit; (*coll.*) ***not a dog's*** or ***an earthly –***, nicht die geringste Aussicht; ***the –s are that***, es ist mit Wahrscheinlichkeit anzunehmen, daß; ***an even –***, eine ebensogute Chance wie gar keine; (*coll.*) ***look to the main –***, auf den eigenen Vorteil sehen; ***give him a –!*** versuche es mit ihm doch noch einmal! ***stand a good –***, gute Aussicht(en) haben; ***on the –***, für den Fall. **2.** *v.t.* (*coll.*) wagen, riskieren, (auf gut Glück) versuchen, es ankommen lassen auf (*Acc.*); (*coll.*) ***– it***, es darauf ankommen lassen. **3.** *v.i.* sich zufällig ereignen, unerwartet eintreten, sich fügen, sich treffen; ***I –d to see him***, ich sah ihn zufällig; es traf sich gerade, daß ich ihn sah; ***if my letter should – to get lost***, falls mein Brief verloren gehen sollte; ***– upon s.th.***, auf eine S. zufällig stoßen. **4.** *adj.* zufällig; ***– comer***, unerwartet Kommende(r); ***– customer***, zufälliger Kunde.

chancel ['tʃɑ:nsəl], *s.* der Altarplatz, Chor.

chancellery ['tʃɑ:nsələri], *s.* die Kanzlei, das Kanzleramt. **chancellor,** *s.* der Kanzler (*also Univ.*); Kanzleivorstand; ***Chancellor of the Exchequer***, der Schatzkanzler, Finanzminister; ***Lord High Chancellor***, der Großkanzler (*highest legal authority in England*). **chancellorship,** *s.* die Kanzlerwürde.

chancery ['tʃɑ:nsəri], *s.* (*Law*) das Kanzleigericht; (*Am.*) Billigkeitsgericht; ***be in –***, (*Law*) unter gerichtlicher Verwaltung sein; (*wrestling*) im Schwitzkasten sein; (*fig.*) in der Klemme sitzen *or* sein; ***bill in –***, die Rechtsklage bei dem Kanzleigericht; ***ward in –***, das Mündel unter Amtsvormundschaft.

chancre ['ʃæŋkə], *s.* der Schanker. **chancrous** [-krəs], *adj.* schankerartig.

chancy ['tʃɑ:nsi], *adj.* (*coll.*) gewagt, ungewiß, riskant, unsicher.

chandelier [ʃændi'liə], *s.* der Armleuchter, Kronleuchter.

chandler ['tʃɑ:ndlə], *s.* **1.** der Kerzenzieher; 2. Händler, Krämer; ***corn –***, der Kornhändler; ***ship –***, der Schiffslieferant. **chandlery,** *s.* der Krämerladen, (*coll.*) Krämerwaren (*pl.*).

change [tʃeindʒ], **1.** *v.t.* wechseln, auswechseln, (ver)tauschen; ändern, abändern, verändern, umändern, umgestalten, verwandeln (***from***, von; ***to***, zu; ***into***, in (*Acc.*)); umwechseln, umtauschen (*money*), einwechseln (*a cheque*) (***for***, gegen); trockenlegen (*a baby*); ***– the bed***, das Bett frisch beziehen; ***– one's clothes***, sich umziehen, die Kleider wechseln; ***– colour***, blaß werden; ***– one's condition***, heiraten; sich verändern; ***– gear***, den Gang wechseln, schalten; ***– the guard***, die Wache *or* Posten (*pl.*) ablösen; ***– hands***, in andere Hände übergehen, den Besitzer wechseln; ***– one's lodgings***, umziehen; ***– one's mind***, sich anders besinnen; (*coll.*) ***– one's spots***, sein Verhalten ändern; ***– step***, den Tritt wechseln; ***– the subject***, das Thema wechseln; ***– trains etc.***, umsteigen; (*coll.*) ***– one's tune***, einen anderen Ton anschlagen. **2.** *v.i.* sich (ver)ändern, anders werden, umschlagen; umsteigen (***for***, nach) (*trains etc.*); (*coll.*) sich umkleiden; ***all –!*** alle umsteigen! ***the moon –s***, es ist Mondwechsel; ***– for the better***, sich (ver)-

bessern, sich zum Besseren wenden; – ***for the worse,*** sich verschlimmern, sich zum Schlechteren wenden; – ***into,*** übergehen *or* sich verwandeln in (*Acc.*); – ***into evening dress,*** einen Frack anziehen. **3.** *s.* 1. die Änderung, Veränderung; der Wechsel, Übergang, Umschwung; Wandel, die Wandlung, Abänderung, Abwechslung; der (Aus)tausch; die Ablösung (*of sentries*); – ***of air,*** die Luftveränderung; – ***of clothes,*** frische Wäsche; die Kleidung zum Wechseln; – ***of life,*** das Klimakterium, Wechseljahre (*pl.*); – ***of the moon,*** der Mondwechsel; – ***of name,*** die Namensänderung; – ***of position,*** der Stellungswechsel; – ***of the tide,*** der Gezeitenwechsel, Wechsel von Ebbe und Flut; – ***of voice,*** der Stimmwechsel; – ***in the*** or ***of weather,*** der Witterungsumschlag; ***ring the –s,*** wechselläuten; (*fig.*) ***ring the –s with a th.,*** dasselbe in stets verschiedener Weise behandeln, alle Möglichkeiten ausprobieren; ***for a –,*** zur Abwechslung; – ***for the better,*** die (Ver)besserung; – ***for the worse,*** die Verschlimmerung; 2. (*also* ***small*** –) das Kleingeld, Wechselgeld; ***have you got – for a pound?*** können Sie mir ein Pfund wechseln? ***give me – for a pound,*** geben Sie mir auf ein Pfund heraus; (*coll.*) ***get no – out of him,*** aus ihm nichts herausbekommen; ***I have no – on*** or ***about me,*** ich habe kein Kleingeld bei mir; 3. (*coll.*) die Börse.

changeability [tʃeindʒə'biliti], *s.* die Veränderlichkeit, Unbeständigkeit, der Wankelmut. **changeable,** *adj.* veränderlich, unbeständig, wandelbar, ungleich, wankelmütig. **changeableness,** *s. See* **changeability. changeful,** *adj.* (*rare*) wechselvoll, veränderlich. **changeless,** *adj.* unveränderlich, beständig. **changelessness,** *s.* die Unveränderlichkeit, Beständigkeit. **changeling,** *s.* der Wechselbalg, untergeschobenes Kind. **changeover,** *s.* (*Mech.*) die Umschaltung; (*fig.*) Umstellung; Wandlung, Umwälzung, (völliger) Wechsel (***from,*** von; ***to,*** auf (*Acc.*)); (*Elec.*) – ***switch,*** der Umschalter, Polwender.

[1]**channel** [tʃænl], **1.** *s.* 1. das Flußbett, die Stromrinne; der Wasserweg, Kanal, das Fahrwasser, Gatt; die (Hafen)einfahrt; Kille, Rinne, Gosse; ***the (English) Channel,*** der Ärmelkanal; 2. (*Archit.*) die Auskehlung, Kannelierung, Kehlleiste, Hohlkehle; 3. (*Rad.*) das Frequenzband; 4. (*Tech.*) die Rille, Furche, Riefe, Nut, der Falz; 5. (*fig.*) Weg, die Bahn; – ***of communication,*** der Nachrichtenweg; ***through diplomatic –s,*** auf diplomatischem Wege; ***official –,*** der Dienstweg, Instanzenweg; (*Parl.*) ***'the usual –s',*** Vereinbarung zwischen Regierung und Opposition. **2.** *v.t.* furchen, auskehlen; (*fig.*) in eine (gewisse) Richtung lenken; – ***out,*** rinnenförmig aushöhlen.

[2]**channel,** *s. See* **chainwale.**

chant [tʃɑ:nt], **1.** *s.* der Gesang, die Weise; Kirchenmelodie; liturgischer Gesang; (*fig.*) der Sing-Sang, eintöniges Lied. **2.** *v.t.* besingen, preisen; intonieren; (*also v.i.*) singen. **chanter,** *s.* der Sänger; (*in a choir*) Vorsänger, Kantor; (*of bagpipes*) die Diskantpfeife.

chanterelle [tʃæntə'rel], *s.* der Pfifferling.

chanticleer ['tʃɑ:ntikliə], *s.* (*Poet.*) der Hahn, Kikeriki.

chantry ['tʃɑ:ntri], *s.* die Votivkapelle, der Votivaltar; die Messenstiftung.

chaos ['keiɔs], *s.* das Chaos; (*fig.*) Durcheinander, Gewirr, die Verwirrung, der Wirrwarr. **chaotic** [–'ɔtik], *adj.* chaotisch, wüst, verworren, wirr.

[1]**chap** [tʃæp], **1.** *s.* (*usu. pl.*) der Spalt, Sprung, Riß; die (Haut)schrunde. **2.** *v.t., v.i.* aufspringen (lassen), spalten; Risse verursachen *or* bekommen, rissig machen *or* werden; ***chapped hands,*** aufgesprungene Hände.

[2]**chap,** *s.* die Kinnbacke, Kinnlade (*of animals*); (*usu. pl.*) das Maul, der Kinnbacken.

[3]**chap,** *s.* (*coll.*) der Bursche, Kerl; ***old –,*** alter Knabe.

chapbook ['tʃæpbuk], *s.* das Volksbuch, die Flugschrift.

chapel [tʃæpl], *s.* die Kapelle, Betkapelle; das Gotteshaus (*of dissenters*); (*Typ.*) die Druckerei, Offizin; ***church versus –,*** Staatskirche gegen Sekten; – ***of ease,*** die Filialkirche.

chaperon ['ʃæpəroun], **1.** *s.* die Anstandsdame, Begleiterin. **2.** *v.t.* (als Anstandsdame) begleiten *or* beschützen, chaperonieren, bemuttern.

chap-fallen, *adj.* (*fig.*) entmutigt, niedergeschlagen.

chapiter ['tʃæpitə], *s.* (*Archit.*) das Kapitäl.

chaplain ['tʃæplin], *s.* der Kaplan; Geistliche(r); Hausprediger; ***army –,*** Feldgeistliche(r). **chaplaincy** [–si], *s.* die Kaplanstelle.

chaplet ['tʃæplit], *s.* der Kranz; (*Eccl.*) Rosenkranz.

chapman ['tʃæpmən], *s.* (*obs.*) der Hausierer, Höker.

chapped [tʃæpt], *adj. See* [1]**chap.**

chapter ['tʃæptə], *s.* das Kapitel (*also fig., Eccl.*), der Abschnitt; (*coll.*) – ***of accidents,*** eine Reihe von Unglücksfällen; (*fig.*) ***to the end of the –,*** bis ans Ende; (*fig.*) ***give – and verse,*** eingehend begründen, genaue Angaben *or* Beweise geben. **chapter-house,** *s.* das Domkapitel.

chaptrel ['tʃæptrəl], *s.* (*Archit.*) der Knauf, Kämpfer.

[1]**char** [tʃɑ:], **1.** *v.i.* scheuern; ***go out charring,*** als Reinmachefrau arbeiten. **2.** *s.* (*coll.*) *see* **charwoman.**

[2]**char, 1.** *v.t.* verkohlen; verbrennen, versengen, anbrennen. **2.** *v.i.* verkohlen, zu Kohle werden.

[3]**char,** *s.* (*Ichth.*) die Rotforelle, der Seibling.

[4]**char,** *s.* (*sl.*) der Tee.

char-à-banc, charabanc ['ʃærəbəŋ], *s.* der Ausflugsautobus.

character ['kærəktə], *s.* 1. das (Schrift)zeichen, der Buchstabe, die Schrift; Ziffer, das Zahlzeichen; 2. der Charakter, die Persönlichkeit; ***public –,*** bekannte Persönlichkeit; 3. die Charakterstärke; 4. das (Führungs- *or* Leumunds)zeugnis, der Leumund, Ruf; ***she has not a good –,*** sie steht in keinem guten Rufe; ***give a servant a good –,*** einem Dienstboten ein gutes Zeugnis ausstellen; ***take away his –,*** ihm den guten Ruf nehmen; 5. die Eigenschaft, Eigenart, Wesensart, Anlage, Beschaffenheit, Natur; das Kennzeichen, (Wesens)merkmal, Gepräge, der Stempel; Rang, Stand, die Stellung; (*Biol.*) ***generic –,*** das Gattungsmerkmal; ***set the – of a th.,*** einer S. das Gepräge geben; (*Biol.*) ***specific –,*** das Artmerkmal; 6. (*Theat.*) die Rolle, Figur, Gestalt, handelnde Person (*of a novel*); ***in –,*** der Rolle gemäß; ***out of all –,*** völlig unpassend; ***act out of –,*** aus der Rolle fallen; 7. (*coll.*) das Original, der Sonderling, Kauz; ***he is a bad –,*** er ist ein ehrloser Mensch; (*coll.*) ***he is quite a –,*** er ist eine wahres Original.

characteristic [kærəktə'ristik], **1.** *adj.* charakteristisch, bezeichnend, typisch (***of,*** für); ***this is – of the man,*** es charakterisiert *or* kennzeichnet den Mann. **2.** *s.* das Merkmal, Kennzeichen, charakteristische Eigenschaft, bezeichnender Zug; die Eigentümlichkeit, Besonderheit; Kennziffer, der Index (*of a logarithm*).

characterization [kærəktərai'zeiʃən], *s.* die Kennzeichnung, Charakterisierung, Kenntlichmachung. **characterize** ['kærəktəraiz], *v.t.* characterisieren, kennzeichnen, charakteristisch sein für; eingehend schildern.

characterless ['kærəktəlis], *adj.* (*of a p. or th.*) charakterlos, (*of a th.*) ohne besonderes Merkmal.

charade [ʃə'rɑ:d], *s.* das Silbenrätsel, die Scharade.

charcoal ['tʃɑ:koul], *s.* die Holzkohle, Knochenkohle; Zeichenkohle, Reißkohle. **charcoal|-burner,** *s.* der Köhler, Kohlenbrenner. **–-burning,** *s.* die Köhlerei, Holzverkohlung. **– drawing,** *s.* die Kohlezeichnung. **– pencil,** *s.* (*Elec.*) die Kohlenspitze. **–-pile,** *s.* der Kohlenmeiler.

charge [tʃɑ:dʒ], **1.** *s.* 1. (*Elec., guns, bombs etc.*) die Ladung; ***blasting –,*** die Sprengladung, Bohrladung; ***booster –,*** die Zündladung, Eingangszündung; ***multiple –,*** gestreckte Ladung; ***priming –,*** die Zündladung; ***weak –,*** der Ausblaser; 2. (*Tech.*) die Füllung, Beschickung; Gicht, das

Beschickungsgut; 3. (*Law*) die Verwahrung, Obhut, Aufsicht, Verantwortung; das Mündel, der Schützling, Pflegling, Pflegebefohlene(r); Anvertraute(s); ***be in – of,*** in Obhut haben (*a p.*), leiten, mit der Führung beauftragt werden (*an undertaking*); ***give in –,*** in Gewahrsam übergeben, der Polizei ausliefern (*a p.*), zur Verantwortung geben (*a th.*); ***the pastor's –,*** Pfarrkinder (*pl.*), der Pfarrbezirk; ***put him in –,*** ihn mit der Führung beauftragen; ***take – of,*** übernehmen, sorgen für; ***take him in –,*** ihn in Haft nehmen; 4. (*Comm.*) (Un)kosten (*pl.*), Spesen (*pl.*), die Forderung, Gebühr, Taxe, der Betrag, Preis; ***after deduction of all –s,*** nach Abzug aller Lasten; ***free of –,*** kostenlos, unentgeltlich; ***no – for admission!*** Eintritt frei! 5. (*fig.*) der Auftrag, Befehl, feierliche Anrede, die Ermahnung, (*of a judge to a jury*) Rechtsbelehrung; 6. (*Mil.*) das Signal zum Angriff; der Angriff, Ansturm; ***sound the –,*** das Signal zum Angriff geben; 7. (*Law*) die Beschuldigung, Anklage, der Anklagepunkt; ***bring a – against him,*** eine Anklage gegen ihn vorbringen; ***–s pending,*** schwebende Anklagen; 8. (*Her.*) das Wappenbild.

2. *v.t.* 1. beladen, belasten, beschweren, anfüllen, beschicken (*a stove etc.*), (auf)laden (*a gun, battery etc.*), bestellen, (*Chem.*) ansetzen, sättigen (*a solution*); 2. (*Law*) beschuldigen, anklagen, bezichtigen (***with***, *Gen.*); (*with Dat. of p.*) vorwerfen, aufbürden, zur Last legen (***with***, *Acc.*); 3. (*Comm.*) (*a p., an account*) belasten (***with***, mit), (*a sum*) anrechnen, in Rechnung stellen, anschreiben, debitieren; ***–d at £5,*** zu 5 Pfund berechnet; ***how much do you – for it?*** wieviel verlangen *or* berechnen Sie dafür? ***– it to his account,*** es ihm in Rechnung stellen, sein Konto damit belasten; 4. (*fig.*) beauftragen (***with***, mit), (*with Dat. of p.*) (an)befehlen, einschärfen, zur Pflicht machen, ans Herz legen (***with***, *Acc.*); ***– the jury,*** die Geschworenen belehren *or* ermahnen; 5. (*Mil.*) anfallen, stürmen, in Sturm angreifen, (*Spt.*) anrennen, rammen, sich stürzen gegen, anrempeln.

3. *v.i.* 1. (*Comm.*) Zahlung verlangen; 2. (*Mil.*) einen Angriff machen, anstürmen, angreifen.

chargeable ['tʃɑːdʒəbl], *adj.* (*Law*) zu beschuldigen(d), anklagefähig; (*Comm.*) zur Last fallend, anzurechnen(d), anrechenbar; ***a duty is – on wine,*** Wein ist mit einer Abgabe zu versteuern; ***be – to him,*** ihm zur Last fallen; ***– offence,*** gerichtlich zu belangendes Vergehen.

chargé d'affaires ['ʃɑːʒeidæ'fɛə], *s.* (diplomatischer) Geschäftsträger.

charger ['tʃɑːdʒə], *s.* 1. das Offizierspferd, Chargenpferd, Schlachtroß; 2. (*Elec.*) die Ladevorrichtung; 3. (*obs.*) Platte, Schüssel.

charging ['tʃɑːdʒiŋ], *s.* (*Elec.*) die (Auf)ladung, (*Tech.*) Beschickung, Begichtung, Möllerung; ***– voltage,*** die Ladespannung.

charily ['tʃɛərili], *adv.* behutsam, vorsichtig; sparsam. **chariness,** *s.* die Behutsamkeit, Vorsicht, Bedenklichkeit; Sparsamkeit.

charion ['tʃɑːriən], *s.* die Haut, Schalenhaut.

chariot ['tʃæriət], *s.* der Streitwagen; Triumphwagen. **charioteer** [–'tiə], *s.* der Wagenlenker; (*Astr.*) Fuhrmann.

charitable ['tʃæritəbl], *adj.* wohltätig, mild(tätig); barmherzig, gütig, nachsichtig; ***– interpretation,*** nachsichtige *or* günstige Auslegung; ***– institution,*** milde Stiftung; ***– organization,*** der Wohltätigkeitsverein; ***for – purposes,*** für mildtätige Zwecke. **charitableness,** *s.* die Mildtätigkeit, Wohltätigkeit; Milde, Nachsicht.

charity ['tʃæriti], *s.* (christliche) Nächstenliebe; die Mildtätigkeit, Güte, Nachsicht; Wohltat, das Almosen, milde Gabe; (*also pl.*) wohltätige Stiftung, die Wohlfahrtseinrichtung; (*Prov.*) ***– begins at home,*** jeder ist sich selbst der Nächste; ***as cold as –,*** bitter wie das Brot der Barmherzigkeit; ***for –'s sake,*** um Gotteslohn; ***sister of –,*** barmherzige Schwester. **charity-school,** *s.* die Armenschule, Freischule.

charivari [ʃɑːri'vɑːri], *s.* die Katzenmusik.

charlatan ['ʃɑːlətən], *s.* der Quacksalber, Kurpfuscher, Charlatan. **charlatanism,** *s.* das Quacksalbertum, die Kurpfuscherei. **charlatanry,** *s.* die Marktschreierei, Prahlerei.

Charles [tʃɑːlz], *s.* Karl (*m.*); (*Astr.*) ***–'s Wain,*** der Große Bär.

charlock ['tʃɑːlɔk], *s.* (*Bot.*) der Ackersenf.

charm [tʃɑːm], **1.** *s.* das Zauberwort, die Zauberformel; (*fig.*) der Zauber, (Lieb)reiz, Charme, die Anmut; der Talisman, das Amulett; ***break the –,*** den Zauber *or* Bann brechen. **2.** *v.t.* bezaubern, (*fig.*) entzücken, erfreuen, reizen, fesseln; ***– away,*** wegzaubern; (*coll.*) ***I shall be –ed,*** ich werde mich außerordentlich freuen; ***–ed with,*** bezaubert *or* entzückt von; ***have*** or ***bear a –ed life,*** fest *or* gefeit sein. **charmer,** *s.* der Zauberer, die Zauberin (*also fig.*). **charming,** *adj.* entzückend, bezaubernd, reizend, charmant.

charnel-house ['tʃɑːnl], *s.* das Leichenhaus, Beinhaus, der Karner.

charred [tʃɑːd], *adj.* verkohlt, angebrannt; *see* [2]**char.**

chart [tʃɑːt], **1.** *s.* die Tabelle, Tafel, das Diagramm, Schaubild; (*Naut.*) die Seekarte, (*Astr.*) Himmelskarte. **2.** *v.t.* auf einem Diagramm verzeichnen; (*usu. fig.*) skizzieren, entwerfen.

charter ['tʃɑːtə], **1.** *s.* die Stiftungsurkunde, Verleihungsurkunde, Verfassungsurkunde; der Gnadenbrief, Freibrief, das Privileg, Patent; (*Naut.*) die Befrachtung, Charterung, das Mieten, Heuern; ***– of incorporation,*** der Schutzbrief, das Patent; ***royal –,*** königliches Privilegium. **2.** *v.t.* privilegieren; chartern (*a ship, plane*), befrachten, heuern (*a ship*); mieten (*a vehicle*). **chartered,** *adj.* privilegiert, verbrieft, konzessioniert; ***– accountant,*** der Wirtschaftsprüfer, beeidigter Bücherrevisor; ***– company,*** privilegierte *or* gesetzlich geschützte Gesellschaft; ***– rights,*** Privilegien, verbriefte Rechte. **charter|-flight,** *s.* der Charterflug. **--party,** *s.* die Charterpartie; der Befrachtungsvertrag.

charwoman ['tʃɑːwumən], *s.* die Rein(e)machefrau.

chary ['tʃɛəri], *adj.* sparsam (***of***, mit); behutsam, vorsichtig, sorgfältig (***in, of***, bei *or* in (*Dat.*)).

[1]**chase** ['tʃeis], **1.** *s.* 1. die (Hetz)jagd; (*fig.*) Verfolgung; gehetztes Wild; das Gehege, Jagdrevier; ***wild-goose –,*** vergebliche Bemühung, fruchtloses Unternehmen; ***I sent him on a wild-goose –,*** ich schickte ihn von Pontius zu Pilatus; ***give –,*** Jagd machen (***to***, auf (*Acc.*)), nachjagen, nachstellen (***to***, *Dat.*), verfolgen (*Acc.*). **2.** *v.t.* jagen, Jagd machen auf (*Acc.*), nachjagen (*Dat.*), nachsetzen (*Dat.*), verfolgen, hetzen; ***– away,*** verjagen, vertreiben, verscheuchen. **3.** *v.i.* (*aux.* s.) (*coll.*) eilen, hasten; ***– after him,*** ihm nachjagen.

[2]**chase,** **1.** *s.* (*Typ.*) der Formrahmen. **2.** *v.t.* treiben, ziselieren, ausmeißeln; ***–d work,*** getriebene Arbeit.

[3]**chase,** *s.* das Längsfeld (*of gun*); die Rinne, Furche.

chase-gun, *s.* (*Naut.*) das Jagdstück, Buggeschütz.

[1]**chaser** ['tʃeisə], *s.* der Jäger, Verfolger; das Geleitschiff; Jagdflugzeug; (*sl.*) der Nachschluck (Schnaps auf Kaffee, Bier auf Schnaps *etc.*).

[2]**chaser,** *s.* 1. der Ziseleur; 2. Treibmeißel. **chasing,** *s.* die Ziselierung.

chasm [kæzm], *s.* der Abgrund, die Schlucht, Klamm, (*fig.*) Spalte, Kluft, (*Tech.*) der Riß, Spalt.

chassis ['ʃæsi], *s.* (*Motor.*) das Fahrgestell, der Rahmen, (*Av.*) das Untergestell, (*Artil.*) der Lafettenrahmen, (*Rad.*) die Grundplatte, das Montagegestell.

chaste [tʃeist], *adj.* keusch, züchtig, rein, unbefleckt, (*fig.*) stilrein, einfach, ungeziert (*as language*).

chasten [tʃeisn], *v.t.* züchtigen, strafen; mäßigen, dämpfen; läutern, reinigen.

chastise [tʃæs'taiz], *v.t.* züchtigen, strafen. **chastisement** ['tʃæstizmənt], *s.* die Züchtigung, Strafe.

chastity ['tʃæstiti], *s.* die Keuschheit, Reinheit, Unbeflecktheit.

chasuble ['tʃæzjubl], *s.* das Meßgewand, die Kasel.

[1]**chat** [tʃæt], **1.** *v.i.* plaudern, schwatzen. **2.** *v.t.* (*sl.*) – *up,* anbändeln mit (*a girl*). **3.** *s.* die Plauderei, der Plausch, das Geplauder, zwangloses Gespräch.

[2]**chat,** *s.* (*Orn.*) der Schmätzer.

chattel [tʃætl], *s.* (*usu. pl.*) bewegliche Habe, bewegliches Eigentum *or* Vermögen, Mobilien (*pl.*); ***goods and –s,*** das Hab und Gut.

chatter ['tʃætə], **1.** *v.i.* schwatzen, plappern; schnattern (*of birds*); plätschern (*of brooks*); rattern (*as machinery*); ***his teeth are –ing,*** er klappert mit den Zähnen. **2.** *s.* das Geplauder, Geplapper, Geschwätz; Geschnatter, Gezwitscher (*of birds*). **chatterbox,** *s.* (*coll.*) der Schwätzer, die Plaudertasche, das Plappermaul.

chatty ['tʃæti], *adj.* geschwätzig, gesprächig, redselig, plaudernd, unterhaltsam.

chauffeur [ʃou'fə:, 'ʃoufə], *s.* der (Kraft)fahrer, Kraftwagenführer, Chauffeur.

chauvinism ['ʃouvinizm], *s.* der Chauvinismus, Hurrapatriotismus.

cheap [tʃi:p], *adj.* billig, preiswert, wohlfeil; wertlos, minderwertig, kitschig; (*fig. coll.*) schäbig; (*coll.*) ***dirt –,*** spottbillig; (*coll.*) ***on the –,*** auf billigste Art; – ***ticket,*** ermäßigte (Eintritts)karte; – ***trip,*** der Ausflug mit Fahrpreisermäßigung; (*coll.*) ***feel –,*** verdattert sein; ***get off –ly,*** leichten Kaufs *or* mit einem blauen Auge davonkommen; ***hold –,*** geringschätzen, verachten (*a th.*); ***make o.s. –,*** sich wegwerfen. **cheapen,** *v.t.* im Preis herabsetzen, billiger machen, verbilligen, (*fig.*) schlechtmachen; – ***o.s.,*** see ***make o.s. cheap.*** **cheap-jack, 1.** *s.* der Marktschreier, wahrer Jakob. **2.** *adj.* marktschreierisch, minderwertig, Schund–. **cheapness,** *s.* die Billigkeit, Wohlfeilheit.

cheat [tʃi:t], **1.** *s.* der Betrug, Schwindel; Betrüger, Schwindler. **2.** *v.t.* betrügen, beschwindeln, (*coll.*) bemogeln (*of,* (*coll.*) ***out of,*** um); irreführen, hinters Licht führen; – ***death,*** dem Tod ein Schnippchen schlagen. **3.** *v.i.* betrügen, schwindeln, (*coll.*) mogeln. **cheating,** *s.* die Betrügerei, Schwindelei, Mogelei.

check [tʃek], **1.** *s.* 1. das Hindernis, Hemmnis; der Einhalt, die Hemmung, Unterbrechung, Pause; 2. (Über)prüfung, Kontrolle; Probe, Nachprüfung; ***keep him in –,*** ihn in Schach *or* im Zaume halten; ***keep a – on a th.,*** etwas unter Kontrolle halten; 3. Kontrollmarke, der Kontrollabschnitt, Kontrollschein; Gutschein, Bon; Kassenschein, Rechnungszettel; (*Am.*) Gepäckschein; (*Am.*) die Garderobenmarke; (*sl.*) ***hand in one's –s,*** krepieren, ins Gras beißen; 4. (*Am.*) *see* **cheque**; 5. (*Chess*) die Schachstellung, das Schach; 6. Karomuster, Schachbrettmuster; Karo, Viereck; karierter Stoff; 7. (*Hunt.*) der Verlust der Fährte; (*Chess*) ***–!*** Schach dem König! **2.** *v.t.* 1. Einhalt tun (*Dat.*), zurückhalten, aufhalten, hemmen, hindern; 2. kontrollieren, überprüfen, nachprüfen, revidieren; nachrechnen; (*Am.*) – ***one's baggage,*** das Gepäck aufgeben; – ***an invoice,*** eine Faktura auf ihre Richtigkeit nachprüfen; (*coll.*) – ***up,*** kontrollieren, nachprüfen, nachsehen, nachrechnen. **3.** *v.i.* (überein)stimmen, genau entsprechen; (*coll.*) – ***in,*** sich (in einem Hotel *or* zur Arbeit) anmelden; (*coll.*) – ***out,*** das Hotel verlassen; sich (von der Arbeit) abmelden; (*coll.*) – ***up on a th.,*** einer S. nachgehen.

check|-account, *s.* die Gegenrechnung, das Kontrollkonto. **--book,** *s.* (*Am.*) *see* **cheque-book. checked,** *adj.* kariert. **checker,** *s.* 1. der Kontrolleur, Überprüfer; 2. (*Am.*) *see* **chequer. checkered,** *adj. See* **chequered. checkers,** *s. See* **chequers. check|-list,** *s.* die Kontrolliste, Vergleichsliste **–mate, 1.** *s.* (*Chess*) das Schachmatt, die Mattstellung. **2.** *v.t.* (schach)matt setzen. **--nut,** *s.* die Gegenmutter. – **point,** *s.* der Eichpunkt, Orientierungspunkt, Bezugspunkt, (*Pol.*) Kontrollpunkt, Grenzübergang. **--rail,** *s.* die Gegenschiene. **–rein,** *s.* der Ausbindezügel. **--ring,** *s.* der Trensenring (*of harness*), (*Tech.*) Stoßring, Anschlagring. **--up,** *s.* (*coll.*) die Kontrolle, Überprüfung; (*Med. coll.*) ärztliche Untersuchung. **--valve,** *s.* das Absperrventil, Rückschlagventil.

cheek [tʃi:k], **1.** *s.* 1. die Backe, Wange (*also Tech.*); ***with one's tongue in one's –,*** schalkhaft; – ***by jowl,*** dicht aneinander, in vertraulichem Zusammensein; 2. (*coll.*) die Unverschämtheit, Frechheit, Stirn; (*coll.*) ***none of your –!*** sei nicht so frech! **2.** *v.t.* (*coll.*) frech sein gegen, Frechheiten sagen (*Dat.*). **--bone,** *s.* der Backenknochen. **cheekiness,** *s.* (*coll.*) die Frechheit, Unverschämtheit. **cheek-piece,** *s.* das Kopfstück (*harness*). **cheeky,** *adj.* (*coll.*) frech, dreist, unverschämt; – ***fellow,*** der Frechdachs.

cheep [tʃi:p], *v.i.* piep(s)en.

cheer [tʃiə], **1.** *s.* 1. das Hurra, der Hurraruf, Hochruf, Beifallsruf; ***three –s for,*** ein dreifaches Hoch auf (*Acc.*); 2. die Kost, Bewirtung, Speisen und Getränke (*pl.*); 3. Laune, Stimmung, Ermunterung, Erheiterung, Ermutigung, der Trost; Frohsinn, die Heiterkeit, Lustigkeit, Fröhlichkeit; ***be of good –,*** guter Dinge *or* guten Mutes sein; ***what –?*** was gibt's? wie geht's? **2.** *v.t.* 1. mit Beifall begrüßen; zujubeln (*Dat.*), Beifall spenden (*Dat.*); 2. aufmuntern, aufheitern, ermuntern, ermutigen; – ***on,*** anspornen, anfeuern; – ***up, see* 2,** 2. **3.** *v.i.* applaudieren, Beifall spenden, Hurra rufen; (*coll.*) – ***to the echo,*** applaudieren, daß die Wände wackeln; – ***up,*** Mut fassen; – ***up!*** sei guten Mutes!

cheerful ['tʃiəful], *adj.* (*of a p.*) heiter, munter, froh, fröhlich; (*of a th.*) freudebringend, erfreuend, erfreulich, freundlich; ***do –ly,*** willig tun. **cheerfulness, cheeriness,** *s.* der Frohsinn, die Fröhlichkeit, Heiterkeit.

cheerio ['tʃiəriou], *int.* (*coll.*) alles Gute! viel Glück! Prost! auf Wiedersehen! **cheer-leader,** *s.* (*coll.*) der Anführer (beim Beifallrufen). **cheerless,** *adj.* freudlos, trostlos. **cheery,** *adj.* heiter, munter, froh.

[1]**cheese** [tʃi:z], **1.** *s.* der Käse; ***as different as chalk from –,*** grundverschieden. **2.** *v.t.* (*sl.*) – ***it!*** sei still! halt's Maul! (*sl.*) ***I'm –d off with it,*** es hängt mir zum Halse heraus.

[2]**cheese,** *s.* (*sl.*) das einzig Wahre, eigentlich Richtige.

cheese|-cake, *s.* der Quarkkuchen. **--cloth,** *s.* das Nesseltuch. **--headed,** *adj.* Rundkopf– (*screw*). **--maggot,** *s.* die Käsemade. **--mite,** *s.* die Käsemilbe. **--parer,** *s.* (*coll.*) der Knauser, Knicker. **--paring, 1.** *s.* 1. die Käserinde; 2. (*fig.*) Knauserei, Knickerigkeit. **2.** *adj.* knauserig, knickerig. **--straw,** *s.* die Käsestange. **cheesy,** *adj.* käsig, (*sl.*) schlecht, schäbig, kläglich.

cheetah ['tʃi:tə], *s.* der Jagdleopard, Gepard.

chef [ʃef], *s.* der Küchenmeister, Küchenchef.

cheiroptera [kai'rɔptərə], *pl.* die Fledermäuse, Handflügler. **cheiropterous,** *adj.* fledermausartig.

chemical ['kemikl], **1.** *adj.* chemisch; – ***action,*** chemischer Eingriff; – ***affinity,*** chemische Verwandtschaft; – ***conversion,*** chemische Umsetzung; – ***decomposition,*** chemischer Abbau; – ***engineering,*** die Industriechemie; ***–ly pure,*** chemisch rein; – ***structure,*** chemischer Bau; – ***warfare,*** der Gaskrieg; – ***works,*** chemische Fabrik. **2.** *s.* chemisches Präparat; *pl.* Chemikalien.

chemise [ʃə'mi:z], *s.* das (Frauen)hemd, Leibchen.

chemist ['kemist], *s.* der Chemiker; Apotheker, Drogist; ***analytical –,*** der Chemiker; ***dispensing –,*** der Apotheker; ***–'s*** (***shop***), die Drogerie, Apotheke; ***works –,*** der Betriebschemiker. **chemistry,** *s.* die Chemie; ***analytical –,*** die Scheidekunst; ***applied –,*** angewandte *or* technische Chemie; – ***of food,*** die Nahrungsmittelchemie; – ***of plants,*** die Pflanzenchemie.

chenille [ʃə'ni:l], *s.* die Chenille.

cheque [tʃek], *s.* der Scheck, die Zahlungsanweisung; (*fig.*) ***give him a blank –,*** ihm freie Hand lassen; ***crossed –,*** der Verrechnungsscheck; – ***for £10,*** der Scheck über 10 Pfund; – ***on London,*** der Scheck auf London. **cheque-book,** *s.* das Scheckbuch.

chequer ['tʃekə], **1.** *s.* kariertes Zeug; das Karomuster. **2.** *v.t.* scheckig verzieren, karieren, (*fig.*) variieren. **chequered,** *adj.* kariert; (*fig.*) bunt, bewegt, wechselvoll. **chequers,** *pl.* (*sing. constr.*) das Damespiel.

cherish [ˈtʃeriʃ], *v.t.* pflegen, sorgen für; unterhalten, hegen; zugetan sein (*Dat.*), (wert)schätzen; – ***hope,*** Hoffnung nähren; – ***an idea,*** an einer Idee festhalten.

cheroot [ʃəˈru:t], *s.* der Stumpen.

cherry [ˈtʃeri], **1.** *s.* die Kirsche. **2.** *adj.* kirschrot. **cherry|-brandy,** *s.* das Kirschwasser, der Kirschlikör. **--stone,** *s.* der Kirschkern. **--tree,** *s.* der Kirschbaum. **-wood,** *s.* das Kirschbaumholz.

chersonese [ˈkə:səni:z], *s.* die Halbinsel. **Chersonese,** *s.* (*Geog.*) der Chersones.

chert [tʃə:t], *s.* der Feuerstein, Hornstein.

cherub [ˈtʃerəb], *s.* (*pl.* **-im** *or* **-s**) der Cherub, Engelskopf; (*fig.*) Engel, das Herzchen. **cherubic** [–ˈru:bik], *adj.* engelhaft, cherubinisch. **cherubim,** *pl.* Cherubim (*pl.*).

chervil [ˈtʃə:vil], *s.* (*Bot.*) der Kerbel.

chess [tʃes], *s.* das Schach(spiel); ***a game of –,*** eine Schachpartie. **chess|board,** *s.* das Schachbrett. **-man,** *s.* die Schachfigur, der Stein.

chest [tʃest], *s.* 1. die Kiste, Truhe, der Kasten; (*obs.*) Fonds, die Kasse; – ***of drawers,*** die Kommode; 2. (*Anat.*) die Brust, der Brustkasten; ***get*** (***s.th.***) ***off one's –,*** seinem Herzen Luft machen, sich (*Dat.*) (etwas) von der Seele schaffen; ***have – trouble,*** brustkrank sein. **-chested,** *adj. suff.* -brüstig.

chesterfield [ˈtʃestəfi:ld], *s.* 1. der Überzieher zum Knöpfen; 2. das Schlafsofa.

chestnut [ˈtʃesnʌt], **1.** *s.* 1. die (Edel)kastanie; ***pull the -s out of the fire,*** die Kastanien aus dem Feuer holen; 2. (*coll.*) alte Geschichte, abgedroschener Witz, olle Kamelle. **2.** *adj.* kastanienbraun; – ***horse,*** Braune(r), der Fuchs. **chestnut|-brown,** *s.* das Kastanienbraun. **--tree,** *s.* der Kastanienbaum.

chesty [ˈtʃesti], *adj.* 1. (*coll.*) ***be –,*** es auf der Brust haben; 2. (*esp. Am. sl.*) anmaßend, aufgeblasen.

cheval|-de-frise [ʃəˈvældəˈfri:z], *s.* spanischer Reiter. **--glass,** *s.* der Drehspiegel.

chevalier [ʃevəˈliə], *s.* der Ritter.

cheviot [ˈtʃeviət], *s.* 1. der Wollstoff; 2. das Bergschaf.

chevron [ˈʃevrən], *s.* (*Her.*) der Sparren; (*Mil.*) das Dienstabzeichen, der (Uniform)winkel, die Unteroffiziertresse; (*Archit.*) Zickzackleiste.

chevrotain [ˈʃevrotein], *s.* das Zwergmoschustier.

chew [tʃu:], *v.t.* kauen; priemen (*tobacco*); (*sl.*) sinnen (***on,*** auf (*Acc.*)); – ***the cud,*** wiederkäuen; (*sl.*) – ***the rag,*** schwätzen, quasseln, tratschen. **chewing-gum,** *s.* der Kaugummi.

chiaroscuro [kiɑ:rəsˈkuərou], *s.* das Helldunkel; die Licht- und Schattenwirkung.

chibouque [tʃiˈbu:k], *s.* der Tschibuk.

chic [ʃi:k], **1.** *adj.* schick, elegant. **2.** *s.* der Schick, die Eleganz.

chicane [ʃiˈkein], *v.t.* übervorteilen, schikanieren. **chicanery** [–əri], *s.* die Spitzfindigkeit, Schikane, der Rechtskniff.

chick [tʃik], *s.* (*coll.*) *see* **chicken**; (*coll.*) liebes Kind, das Herzchen; (*sl.*) junges Mädchen, das Küken. **chickadee** [–əˈdi:], *s.* (*Orn., Am.*) ***black-capped –,*** *see* **willow-tit.**

chicken [ˈtʃikin], **1.** *s.* das Hühnchen, Küken, Kücken; (*Cul.*) Huhn, Geflügel; (*sl.*) ***no –,*** nicht mehr jung, kein Kind mehr; ***count one's -s before they are hatched,*** die Rechnung ohne den Wirt machen, zu früh triumphieren. **2.** *pred. adj.* feige, kleinmütig, zaghaft. **chicken|-broth,** *s.* die Hühnersuppe. **--feed,** *s.* das Hühnerfutter; (*sl.*) die Lappalie, geringer Lohn, Pfennige (*pl.*). **--hearted, --livered,** *adj.* feige, kleinmütig, zaghaft. **-pox,** *s.* (*Med.*) Windpocken (*pl.*), Varizellen (*pl.*). **--run,** *s.* der Hühnerhof.

chick|-pea, *s.* (*Bot.*) die Kichererbse. **-weed,** *s.* (*Bot.*) die Vogelmiere, Sternmiere (*Stellaria media*); Getreidemiere (*Alsine media*); ***mouse-eared –,*** das Hornkraut (*Cerastium hirsutum*).

chicory [ˈtʃikəri], *s.* (*Bot.*) die Zichorie, Wegwarte.

chide [tʃaid], *irr.v.t., v.i.* (aus)schelten, tadeln.

chief [tʃi:f], **1.** *adj.* höchst, oberst, erst, wichtigst, hauptsächlich(st), vornehmlichst, Ober–, Höchst–, Haupt–; – ***clerk,*** erster Kommis; – ***justice,*** der Oberrichter; – ***mourner,*** Hauptleidtragende(r); (*Naut.*) – ***petty officer,*** der Oberbootsmann, (*Am.*) Stabsbootsmann. **2.** *s.* 1. das Haupt, Oberhaupt; Vorgesetzte(r), der (An)führer, Leiter, Prinzipal, Chef, (*of tribes*) Häuptling; ***in –,*** hauptsächlich, im besondern, besonders; (*Mil.*) – ***of staff,*** der Generalstabschef; 2. (*Her.*) das Schildhaupt.

chiefly [ˈtʃi:fli], *adv.* größtenteils, hauptsächlich, meistens.

chieftain [ˈtʃi:ftən], *s.* (*of tribe*) der Häuptling, (*of robber band etc.*) Anführer.

chiffchaff [ˈtʃiftʃæf], *s.* (*Orn.*) der Weidenlaubsänger, Zilpzalp (*Phylloscopus collybita*).

chiffonier [ʃifəˈniə], *s.* (kleiner) Schrank (mit Schubfächern).

chignon [ˈʃi:njɔ̃], *s.* der (Haar)wulst, Kauz, Dutt.

chilblain [ˈtʃilblein], *s.* die Frostbeule.

child [tʃaild], *s.* (*pl.* **children** [ˈtʃildrən]) das Kind; ***from a –,*** von Kindheit an; ***with –,*** schwanger; – ***labour,*** die Kinderarbeit; – ***murder,*** der Kindermord.

child|-bearing, *s.* das Gebären, die Niederkunft; ***be past –,*** keine Kinder mehr haben können. **-bed,** *s.* das Wochenbett; ***be in –,*** in den Wochen sein; ***die in –,*** im Wochenbett sterben; ***woman in –,*** die Wöchnerin. **-birth,** *s.* die Niederkunft, Entbindung. **--care,** *s.* die Kinderfürsorge.

childe [tʃaild], *s.* (*obs.*) der Junker.

child-guidance, *s.* heilpädagogische Beratung. **childhood,** *s.* die Kindheit. **childish,** *adj.* 1. (*of* (*children*) kindlich; 2. (*of adults etc.*) kindisch, infantil. **childishness,** *s.* die Kindlichkeit; kindisches Wesen, die Kinderei. **childless,** *adj.* kinderlos. **childlike,** *adj. See* **childish,** 1.

children [ˈtʃildrən], *pl. of* **child**; ***-'s allowance,*** die Kinderbeihilfe; ***-'s books,*** Jugendschriften (*pl.*); (*Rad.*) ***-'s hour,*** der Kinderfunk.

child's-play, s. (*fig.*) das Kinderspiel, die Kleinigkeit. **child-welfare,** *s.* die Jugendfürsorge; – ***worker,*** der Jugendpfleger.

Chile [ˈtʃili], *s.* Chile (*n.*); – ***saltpeter,*** salpetersaures Natron, das Natriumnitrat. **Chilean, 1.** *s.* der Chilene (die Chilenin). **2.** *adj.* chilenisch.

chili [ˈtʃili], *s.* (*Bot.*) der Cayennepfeffer (*Capsicum frutescens*).

chiliad [ˈkiliæd], *s.* das (Jahr)tausend.

chill [tʃil], **1.** *s.* 1. der Schauer, (Fieber)frost, das Frösteln; (*coll.*) die Erkältung; ***catch a –,*** sich erkälten; 2. die Kälte, Kühle; ***take the – off,*** leicht erwärmen; ***water with the – off,*** verschlagenes Wasser; 3. (*Tech.*) die Gußform, Schale, Kokille. **2.** *adj.* kühl, kalt, frostig. **3.** *v.t.* kalt machen, abkühlen (lassen); (*Tech.*) abschrecken, härten; (*fig.*) entmutigen, niederschlagen; (*fig.*) ***it -s my blood,*** mein Blut erstarrt; ***it -s my hopes,*** es zerschlägt meine Hoffnung; ***-ed meat,*** das Kühlfleisch; ***-ed shot,*** das Hartblei. **chill-casting,** *s.* (*Tech.*) der Hartguß, Schalenguß, Kokillenguß.

chilli, *see* **chili.**

chilliness [ˈtʃilinis], *s.* die Kälte, Kühle. **chilling, 1.** *s.* die Abkühlung, (*Tech.*) das Abschrecken. **2.** *adj.* (*usu. fig.*) frostig. **chilly,** *adj.* kalt, kühl, (*fig.*) kühl, frostig; ***feel –,*** frösteln.

[1]**chime** [tʃaim], **1.** *s.* (*oft. pl.*) das Glockenspiel, Läuten; (*fig.*) der Einklang, Zusammenklang. **2.** *v.t.* läuten, ertönen lassen, anschlagen; – ***the hours,*** die Stunden schlagen. **3.** *v.i.* tönen, läuten, klingen, (*of clocks*) schlagen; (*fig.*) übereinstimmen; (*coll.*) – ***in,*** sich (ins Gespräch) einmischen, gelegentlich bemerken; (*coll.*) – ***in with,*** übereinstimmen mit, beistimmen (*Dat.*).

[2]**chime,** *s.* die Kimme, Zarge.

chimera [kiˈmiərə], *s.* (*Myth.*) die Chimäre, (*fig.*)

das Schreckbild, Schreckgespenst; Hirngespinst, die Schimäre. **chimerical** [–'merikl], *adj.* (s)chimärisch, schimärenhaft, visionär, trügerisch, phantastisch.

chimney ['tʃimni], *s.* (*outside*) der Schornstein, Schlot, (*inside*) Rauchfang, Kamin; (*of volcano*) Schlot, Ausbruchskanal; (*of lamps*) Zylinder; (*Mount.*) Kamin, (enge) Kluft. **chimney|-breast,** *s.* der Oberteil des Kamins. **--cap,** *s. See* **--pot. --corner,** *s.* die Kaminecke, Sitzecke am Kamin. **--head,** *s.* der Schornsteinkranz. **--piece,** *s.* der Kaminsims. **--pot,** *s.* die Schornsteinkappe, der Schornsteinaufsatz. **--stack,** *s.* der Schornsteinkasten. **--sweep,** *s.* der Schornsteinfeger, Essenkehrer, Rauchfangkehrer. **--top,** *s. See* **--pot**; ***over the –s,*** über die Giebel.

chimpanzee [tʃimpæn'zi:], *s.* der Schimpanse.

chin [tʃin], *s.* das Kinn; ***up to the –,*** bis ans *or* zum Kinn, (*fig.*) bis über die Ohren; (*fig.*) ***take it on the –,*** die Ohren steif halten; (*coll.*) ***keep your – up!*** Kopf hoch! laß dich nicht 'runterkriegen! **2.** *v.i.* (*sl.*) quasseln, schwatzen.

china 'tʃainə], *s.* das Porzellan; (Porzellan)geschirr; ***– clay,*** die Porzellanerde, das Kaolin.

China, *s.* China (*n.*); ***– bark,*** die Chinarinde, Fieberrinde.

china tea ['tʃainə 'ti:], *s.* chinesischer Tee.

china-shop, *s.* der Porzellanladen; (*coll.*) ***like a bull in a –,*** wie ein Elefant im Porzellanladen.

Chinatown ['tʃainətaun], *s.* das Chinesenviertel.

chinaware ['tʃainəwɛə], *s. See* **china.**

chinchilla [tʃin'tʃilə], *s.* (*Zool.*) die Chinchilla; der Chinchillapelz.

chine [tʃain], *s.* 1. der Rückgrat, Kreuz; (*of meat*) das Rückenstück, Lendenstück; 2. der Bergrücken, (Berg)kamm, (Fels)grat; (*Naut.*) die Kimme; ***– boat,*** das Knickspantboot.

Chinese [tʃai'ni:z], **1.** *s.* 1. der Chinese (die Chinesin); 2. (*language*) das Chinesisch(e). **2.** *adj.* chinesisch; ***– lantern,*** der Lampion; ***– puzzle,*** das Mosaikspiel, Vexierspiel, (*fig.*) komplizierte Angelegenheit.

¹**chink,** *s.* die Ritze, Spalte, der Riß, Spalt.

²**chink,** **1.** *s.* 1. das Klingen, Klirren, Geklimper; 2. (*sl.*) Moos, die Pinkepinke. **2.** *v.i.* klirren, klingen, klimpern. **3.** *v.t.* klingen lassen, klimpern mit.

chin|-rest, *s.* der Kinnhalter (*of violin etc.*). **--strap,** *s.* (*harness*) der Kinnriemen, (*of helmet*) Sturmriemen.

chintz [tʃints], *s.* der (Möbel)kattun, Zitz.

chinwag ['tʃinwæg], *s.* (*sl.*) der Plauscher.

chip [tʃip], **1.** *s.* das Stückchen, Schnittchen, Schnitzel, der Splitter, Span; ***a – of(f) the old block,*** aus gleichem Holz geschnitzt, ein Ast vom alten Stamm, der leibhafte Vater; (*Prov.*) ***from chipping come –s,*** wo gehobelt wird, da fallen Späne; (*coll.*) ***– on the shoulder,*** leicht gekränkter Eigensinn. **2.** *v.t.* 1. behauen (*stone*), abhacken, abschaben, abschnitzeln (*wood*), abschlagen, anschlagen (*crockery etc.*); 2. (*Golf*) aus dem Handgelenk anschlagen. **3.** *v.i.* abbrechen, abbröckeln; (*sl.*) ***– in,*** sich einmischen, dazwischenfahren (*in conversation*), mitmachen, einspringen (*with help*); ***– off,*** abbrechen, abbröckeln, abspringen, abblättern.

chipboard, *s.* die Kunstholzplatte, Spanplatte.

chip-hat, *s.* der Basthut.

chipmunk ['tʃipmʌŋk], *s.* (*Am.*) (*Zool.*) das Backenhörnchen.

chipped [tʃipt], *adj.* angeschlagen, angestoßen; ***– potatoes,*** *see* **chips** (*Cul.*). **chipper,** *adj.* (*sl.*) lebhaft, munter. **chippy,** *s.* 1. (*sl.*) der Zimmermann; 2. (*Am. sl.*) das Flittchen. **chips,** *pl.* 1. Späne, Splitter (*pl.*); 2. (*sl.*) *see* **chippy,** 1.; 3. (*sl.*) Spielmarken (*pl.*); ***have plenty of –,*** Zaster haben; (*sl.*) ***hand in one's–,*** abkratzen, krepieren; (*sl.*) ***you've had your –,*** du hast ausgespielt; 4. (*Cul.*) pommes frites (*pl.*).

chirographer [kai'rɔgrəfə], *s.* (*Hist.*) der Gerichtsschreiber, Amtsschreiber. **chirographic** [–'græfik], *adj.* (hand)schriftlich. **chirography,** *s.* die Schreibkunst.

chiromancer ['kairomænsə], *s.* der Handliniendeuter, Chiromant. **chiromancy,** *s.* die Handlesekunst, Chiromantie.

chiropodist [ki'rɔpədist], *s.* der (die) Fußpfleger(in), die Pediküre. **chiropody,** *s.* die Fußpflege, Pediküre.

chirp [tʃə:p], *v.i.* zirpen, zwitschern, piep(s)en. **chirping,** *s.* das Gezirp, Gezwitscher. **chirpy,** *adj.* (*coll.*) quietschvergnügt.

chirrup ['tʃirəp], *v.i.* 1. *See* **chirp**; 2. (mit der Zunge) schnalzen.

chisel [tʃizl], **1.** *s.* der Meißel, Beitel, das Stemmeisen; ***cold –,*** der Schrotmeißel; ***engraver's –,*** der Grabstichel. **2.** *v.t.* (aus)meißeln; (*sl.*) beschwindeln, 'reinlegen. **3.** *v.i.* meißeln; (*sl.*) schwindeln. **chiselled,** *adj.* ausgemeißelt; (*fig.*) ***finely – features,*** wohlgeformte Gesichtszüge. **chiseller,** *s.* (*sl.*) der Schwindler, Gauner, Nassauer.

¹**chit** [tʃit], *s.* kleines Geschöpf; ***– of a girl,*** junges Ding.

²**chit,** *s.* 1. der Gutschein, Bon, die Marke; 2. das Zettelchen, kurze Notiz.

chit-chat, *s.* (*coll.*) das Geplauder, der Tratsch, Schnickschnack.

chit(ter)ling ['tʃit(ə)liŋ], *s.* (*usu. pl.*) das (Schweins)gekröse.

chitty ['tʃiti], *s.* (*coll.*) *see* ²**chit,** 2.

chivalrous ['ʃivəlrəs], *adj.* ritterlich, galant. **chivalry,** *s.* 1. das Ritterwesen, Rittertum; 2. die Ritterlichkeit; 3. Ritterschaft.

chive [tʃaiv], *s.* (*Bot.*) der Schnittlauch, Schnittling.

chloral ['klɔ:rəl], *s.* (*Chem.*) das Chloral. **chlorate** [–reit], *s.* das Chlorat, chlorsaures Salz; ***– of lime,*** chlorsaurer Kalk. **chloric** ['klɔ(:)rik], *adj.* Chlor–, chlorsauer; ***– acid,*** die Chlorsäure. **chloride** [–raid], *s.* das Chlorid, die Chlorverbindung; ***– of lime,*** der Chlorkalk. **chlorinate** [–rineit], *v.t.* chlorieren, (*water etc.*) chloren. **chlorine** [–ri(:)n], *s.* das Chlor(gas). **chlorite** [–rait], *s.* chlorigsaures Salz.

chloroform ['klɔrəfɔ:m], **1.** *s.* das Chloroform. **2.** *v.t.* chloroformieren, betäuben.

chlorophyll ['klɔ(:)rəfil], *s.* das Blattgrün, Chlorophyll.

chlorosis [klə'rousis], *s.* (*Med., Bot.*) die Bleichsucht, Chlorose. **chlorotic** [–'rɔtik], *adj.* bleichsüchtig, chlorotisch.

chlorous ['klɔ:rəs], *adj.* (*Chem.*) chlorhaltig, chlorig.

chock [tʃɔk], **1.** *s.* der Bremskeil, Hemmkeil; (*Naut.*) die (Boots)klampe. **2.** *v.t.* festkeilen, (*Naut.*) abkeilen. **3.** *adv.* dicht *or* eng (anliegend). **chock|-a-block,** *adv.* (*coll.*) dicht zusammengedrängt. **--full,** *adv., pred. adj.* (*coll.*) gedrängt voll, zum Überlaufen voll.

chocolate ['tʃɔk(ə)lit], **1.** *s.* die Schokolade; ***bar of –,*** die Tafel Schokolade; ***– cream,*** die Praline. **2.** *adj.* schokolade(n)farben.

choice [tʃɔis], **1.** *s.* die (Aus)wahl; Auslese, Elite, das Beste; (*Comm*) Sortiment, der Vorrat; ***by*** or ***for –,*** am liebsten, vorzugsweise; ***Hobson's –,*** das Nehmenmüssen ohne Wahl; ***make*** or ***take one's –,*** wählen, seine Wahl treffen, nach Belieben auswählen; ***give him his –,*** ihm die Wahl lassen; ***this is his –,*** seine Wahl ist auf dieses gefallen; ***have no (other) –,*** keine andere Möglichkeit *or* Wahl haben; ***the – lies*** or ***is with you,*** die Wahl liegt bei dir; ***wide*** or ***good –,*** reiche Auswahl. **2.** *adj.* auserlesen, ausgesucht; ausgezeichnet, vorzüglich, vortrefflich; ***– fruit,*** erlesenes Obst; ***a few – words,*** einige wohlerwogene *or* sorgfältig gewählte Worte. **choiceness,** *s.* die Erlesenheit, Gewähltheit, Feinheit, Vorzüglichkeit. **choicy,** *adj.* (*Am.*) *see* **choosy.**

choir ['kwaiə], **1.** *s.* 1. (*Eccl.*) der (Kirchen)chor, Sängerchor; 2. Gesangverein; 3. (*Archit.*) der *or* das Chor, der Chorraum, Altarraum. **2.** *v.i.* im Chor singen. **choir|boy,** *s.* der Chorknabe, Chorsänger, Sängerknabe. **--loft,** *s.* die Empore.

--master, *s.* der Chorleiter. **--stalls,** *pl.* das Chorgestühl.
choke [tʃouk], **1.** *v.t.* ersticken, (er)würgen, erdrosseln; (*also* – *up*) verstopfen, versperren; (*fig.*) unterdrücken, hemmen, hindern, dämpfen; (*Motor., Elec.*) (ab)drosseln; – ***down,*** verschlucken, hinunterwürgen (*food*), ersticken, unterdrücken (*feelings, laughter etc.*); ***–d (up) with mud,*** verschlammt; (*sl.*) – ***him off,*** ihm den Mund stopfen; ihn loswerden. **2.** *v.i.* ersticken; sich verstopfen. **3.** *s.* (*Tech.*) die Würgebohrung, Verengung, (*Elec.*) Drosselspule, (*Motor.*) Starterklappe, Drosselklappe.
choke|-coil, *s. See* **choke, 3.** (*Elec.*). **--damp,** *s.* der (Nach)schwaden, Ferch, das Grubengas, Stickwetter, schlagende Wetter (*pl.*). **choker,** *s.* (*sl.*) der Vatermörder. **chok(e)y,** *s.* (*sl.*) das Kittchen, Loch. **choking,** *adj.* ***with a – voice,*** mit erstickter Stimme.
choler [ˈkɔlə], *s.* (*obs.*) die Galle; (*fig.*) der Zorn.
cholera [ˈkɔlərə], *s.* die Cholera, der Brechdurchfall.
choleric [ˈkɔlərik], *adj.* (*obs.*) gallsüchtig; (*fig.*) jähzornig, cholerisch.
cholesterol [kəˈlestərəl], *s.* das Gallenfett, Cholesterin.
choose [tʃu:z], **1.** *irr.v.t.* (aus)wählen, aussuchen; (*with inf.*) vorziehen, wünschen, wollen, mögen, belieben; ***take whichever you –,*** nehmen Sie wie es Ihnen beliebt; ***I do as I –,*** ich tue was ich will; ***I – to stay,*** ich ziehe es vor zu bleiben. **2.** *irr.v.i.* die Wahl haben, wählen (können); ***he cannot – but come,*** er kann nicht umhin, zu kommen; ***there's nothing to – between them,*** es ist kaum ein Unterschied zwischen ihnen; ***pick and –,*** lange aussuchen, wählerisch sein. **chooser,** *s.* der (die) (Aus)wähler(in), (Aus)wählende(r); ***beggars can't be –s,*** friß Vogel oder stirb! in der Not frißt der Teufel Fliegen. **choosing,** *s.* die Wahl; ***this is not of my –,*** diese Wahl hätte ich nicht getroffen. **choosy,** *adj.* (*coll.*) heikel, wählerisch.
chop [tʃɔp], **1.** *s.* **1.** der Schlag, (Axt)hieb; 2. (*of meat*) das Kotelett; 3. (*Naut.*) die Kabbelung; 4. *pl.* (*sl.*) (Kinn)backen (*pl.*), das Maul. **2.** *v.t.* hauen, (zer)hacken; – ***down,*** niederhauen, fällen (*trees*); – ***off,*** abhauen, abhacken (*branches*); – ***up,*** zerhacken, kleinhacken (*wood*); – ***logic,*** hin und her argumentieren. **3.** *v.i.* 1. ***the wood –s easily,*** das Holz läßt sich leicht spalten; 2. wenden, plötzlich umschlagen; – ***and change,*** unschlüssig *or* unentschlossen sein, hin und her schwanken.
chop-house, *s.* das Speiselokal, die Wirtschaft.
chopper [ˈtʃɔpə], *s.* das Hackmesser, Hackbeil. **chopping,** *s.* das (Zer)hacken; – ***and changing,*** ewiges Hin und Her. **chopping|-block,** *s.* der Hackblock, Hackklotz. **--board,** *s.* das Hackbrett. **--knife,** *s.* das Hackmesser, Wiegemesser.
choppy [ˈtʃɔpi], *adj.* (*Naut.*) kabbelig.
chop|stick, *s.* das Eßstäbchen. **–suey** [–ˈsu:i], *s.* (eine Art) chinesisches Gericht.
choral [ˈkɔ:rəl], *adj.* Chor–; – ***service,*** der Chorgottesdienst; – ***society,*** der Gesangverein. **choral(e)** [kɔˈrɑ:l], *s.* der Choral.
chord [kɔ:d], *s.* 1. (*Math.*) die Sehne, (*Tech.*) Spannweite, (*Av.*) Profilsehne; 2. (*Mus.*) der Akkord, Zusammenklang; ***common –,*** der Dreiklang; ***major –,*** der Durakkord; ***minor –,*** der Mollakkord; 3. (*Poet., fig.*) die Saite, der Ton; (*fig.*) ***touch*** or ***strike the right –,*** den richtigen Ton anschlagen; 4. (*obs.*) (*Anat.*) das Band, der Strang; *see* **cord.**
chore [tʃɔ:], *s.* 1. (*usu. pl.*) (*coll.*) die Hausarbeit, Alltagsarbeit; 2. unangenehme Aufgabe.
chorea [kɔˈriə], *s.* (*Med.*) der Veitstanz.
choreographer [kɔriˈɔgrəfə], *s.* der Ballettmeister, Tanzgestalter, Choreograph. **choreography,** *s.* die Tanzgestaltung; Tanzschrift.
choriamb(us) [ˈkɔriæmb (kɔriˈæmbus)], *s.* (*Metr.*) der Choriambus.
chorioid [ˈkɔriɔid], *s. See* **choroid.**
chorion [ˈkɔ:riən], *s.* (*Med.*) die Fruchthaut, Eihaut, Zottenhaut.
chorister [ˈkɔristə], *s.* der (Kirchen)chorsänger, Chorist; (*Am.*) (Kirchen)chorleiter.
choroid [ˈkɔ:rɔid], *s.* (*Anat.*) die Aderhaut des Auges, Augapfelgefäßhaut.
chortle [tʃɔ:tl], **1.** *v.i.* vergnügt kichern. **2.** *s.* vergnügtes Kichern.
chorus [ˈkɔ:rəs], **1.** *s.* 1. der Chor, Sängerchor, Chorsänger (*pl.*); ***sing in –,*** gemeinsam singen; 2. der Chorgesang, das Chorwerk; 3. der (Chor)-refrain, Kehrreim. **2.** *v.t.* gemeinsam *or* im Chor ausrufen. **chorus-girl,** *s.* die Revuetänzerin.
chose [tʃouz], *imperf. of* **choose. chosen,** *adj.* (*B.*) ***the – people,*** das auserwählte Volk.
chough [tʃʌf], *s.* (*Orn.*) die Alpenkrähe, Steinkrähe (*Pyrrhocorax pyrrhocorax*).
chow [tʃau], *s.* 1. (*sl.*) das Futter; 2. (*Zool.*) der Chow-Chow, chinesischer Spitz.
chowder [ˈtʃaudə], *s.* (*Am.*) (eine Art) Fischgericht.
chrism [krizm], *s.* 1. das Salböl, Chrisam; die Salbung; 2. griechisch-orthodoxe Firmung. **chrismatory** [ˈkrizmətəri], *s.* das Salbölgefäß, der Chrisambehälter.
chrisom [ˈkrisəm], *s.* (*Hist.*) das Taufkleid.
Christ [kraist], *s.* Christus (*m.*).
christen [krisn], *v.t.* taufen; (*ship etc.*) benennen; (*coll.*) zum ersten Mal benützen, einweihen; – ***him John,*** ihn auf den Namen Johann taufen. **Christendom** [–dəm], *s.* die Christenheit, christliche Welt. **christening, 1.** *s.* die Taufe. **2.** *attrib. adj.* Tauf–.
Christian [ˈkristjən], **1.** *adj.* christlich; – ***name,*** der Vorname, Taufname; – ***science,*** der Szientismus. **2.** *s.* der (die) Christ(in); (*coll.*) der Christenmensch, anständiger Kerl. **Christianity** [–iˈæniti], *s.* 1. christlicher Glaube, das Christentum; 2. die Christenheit. **christianize** [–aiz], *v.t.* zum Christentum bekehren.
Christmas [ˈkrisməs], *s.* (*usu. without art.*) (die) Weihnacht, (das) *or* (die (*f.pl.*)) Weihnachten; das Christfest, Weihnachtsfest; ***Father –,*** der Weihnachtsmann. **Christmas|-box,** *s.* das Weihnachtsgeschenk. **– card,** *s.* die Weihnachtskarte. **– carol,** *s.* das Weihnachtslied. **– Day,** *s.* der Christtag, erster Weihnachtstag. **– Eve,** *s.* Heiliger Abend, Heiligabend, Weihnachtsabend, Heilige *or* Stille Nacht. **– present,** *s. See* **--box. – pudding,** *s.* der Plumpudding. **– rose,** *s.* die Christrose, schwarze Nieswurz. **– tree,** *s.* der Weihnachtsbaum, Christbaum. **Christmasy,** *adj.* (*coll.*) weihnachtlich.
chromate [ˈkroumeit], *s.* chromsaures Salz, das Chromsalz; – ***of potash,*** chromsaures Kali.
chromatic [kroˈmætik], *adj.* chromatisch, Farben–; (*Mus.*) chromatisch, alteriert; – ***printing,*** der Farbendruck; – ***scale,*** chromatische Tonleiter. **chromatics,** *pl.* (*sing. constr.*) die Farbenlehre; (*Mus.*) Chromatik. **chromatism** [ˈkroumətizm], *s.* (*Bot.*) (unnatürliche) Färbung. **chromatophore** [–ˈmætəfɔ:], *s.* (*Bot.*) der Farbstoffträger, (*Zool.*) die Farbzelle.
chrome [kroum], *s.* (*Chem.*) *see* **chromium**; (*Dye.*) das Chromgelb, Kaliumdichromat; – ***steel,*** der Chromstahl; ***--yellow,*** das Chromgelb, Bleichromat. **chromic,** *adj.* chromhaltig, Chrom–; – ***acid,*** die Chromsäure. **chromium,** *s.* das Chrom; ***--plated,*** verchromt.
chromogen [ˈkroumədʒən], *s.* der Farbenerzeuger. **chromogenesis** [–ˈdʒenəsis], *s.* die Farbstoffbildung. **chromogenic,** *adj.* farbgebend, chromogen.
chromo|lithograph, *s.* (*product*), **–lithography,** *s.* (*process*) die Chromolithographie, lithographischer Farb(en)druck, der Mehrfarbensteindruck.
chromosome [ˈkrouməsoum], *s.* das Chromosom, Kernstäbchen.
chromotype [ˈkroumətaip], *s.* (*product*), **chromotypy,** *s.* (*process*) der Farbdruck, die Chromotypie.
chronic [ˈkrɔnik], *adj.* chronisch, (an)dauernd, stetig, (be)ständig; (*sl.*) schlecht.
chronicle [ˈkrɔnikl], **1.** *s.* die Chronik; das Jahrbuch; (*coll.*) der Bericht, die Erzählung. **2.** *v.t.* (in zeit-

licher Folge) berichten *or* aufzeichnen. **chronicler,** *s.* der Chronikenschreiber, Chronist. **Chronicles,** *pl.* (*B.*) Bücher (*pl.*) der Chronika.

chronogram ['krɔnəgræm], *s.* das Chronogramm. **chronograph,** *s.* der Chronograph.

chronological [krɔnə'lɔdʒikl], *adj.* chronologisch, zeitlich geordnet; ***in – order,*** in der Zeitfolge, der Zeitfolge nach. **chronologist** [–'nɔlədʒist], *s.* der Chronolog(e), Zeit(rechnungs)forscher. **chronology** [–'nɔlədʒi], *s.* die Chronologie, Zeitbestimmung, Zeitrechnung; Zeittafel, Zeitfolge; chronologische Anordnung *or* Aufstellung.

chronometer [krɔ'nɔmitə], *s.* das Chronometer, der Zeitmesser, die Präzisionsuhr. **chronometry,** *s.* die Zeitmessung.

chrysalis ['krisəlis], *s.* (*Ent.*) die (Schmetterlings)-puppe.

chrysanthemum [kri'sænθəməm], *s.* die Goldblume, das Chrysanthemum.

chrysolite ['krisolait], *s.* der Chrysolith, Olivin. **chrysoprase** [–preiz], *s.* der Chrysopras.

chub [tʃʌb], *s.* (*Ichth.*) der Döbel, Aitel.

chubbiness ['tʃʌbinis], *s.* die Pausbäckigkeit. **chubby,** *adj.* pausbackig, pausbäckig, mollig, rundlich.

[1]**chuck** [tʃʌk], **1.** *v.i.* glucken, schnalzen. **2.** *s.* das Glucken.

[2]**chuck,** *s.* (*coll.*) der Schnuck.

[3]**chuck, 1.** *v.t.* sanft schlagen (*under the chin*); (*coll.*) werfen, schmeißen; (*sl.*) ***– it,*** es aufgeben, es sausen lassen, es hinschmeißen; (*coll.*) ***– away,*** wegschmeißen, verplempern; (*coll.*) ***– out,*** an die Luft setzen, hinauswerfen; (*coll.*) ***– (up) a job,*** eine Stellung an den Nagel hängen. **2.** *s.* sanfter Schlag *or* Stoß; (*coll.*) der Wurf; (*sl.*) ***give him the –,*** ihn an die Luft setzen; ihm den Laufpaß geben.

[4]**chuck,** *s.* (*Tech.*) das Bohrfutter, (Auf)spannfutter, Klemmfutter, die Klemme, der Spannkopf.

chucker-out, *s.* (*sl.*) der Rausschmeißer.

chuckle [tʃʌkl], *v.i.* (vergnügt) in sich hineinlachen. **chucklehead,** *s.* (*Am.*) der Dummkopf.

chug [tʃʌg], *v.i.* (*coll.*) schuckeln, puckern, knattern.

chum [tʃʌm], **1.** *s.* (*coll.*) der Kamerad, Gefährte, Busenfreund, (*coll.*) Kumpel; Stubengenosse. **2.** *v.i.* (*coll.*) ***– up with,*** sich eng befreunden mit, dicke Freundschaft schließen mit. **chummy,** *adj.* (*coll.*) gesellig, freundlich; engbefreundet.

chump [tʃʌmp], *s.* 1. dickes Ende, der Klotz; (*of meat*) die Fleischkeule; 2. (*coll.*) der Dickkopf, Dummkopf, Tolpatsch; 3. (*sl.*) die Birne (= *head*); (*sl.*) ***be off one's –,*** verdreht *or* verrückt sein.

chunk [tʃʌŋk], *s.* (*coll.*) dickes Stück, der Klumpen.

church [tʃə:tʃ], **1.** *s.* die Kirche; Geistlichkeit; christliche Gemeinschaft; (*without art.*) der Gottesdienst; ***at –,*** in der Kirche; ***Church of England,*** anglikanische Kirche; ***enter the –,*** see ***go into the –; established –,*** die Staatskirche; ***go to –,*** zur Kirche gehen; ***go into the –,*** Geistlicher werden; ***– is over,*** die Kirche ist aus. **2.** *v.t.* Dankgottesdienst halten für; ***be –ed,*** ausgesegnet werden (*after childbirth*).

church|-burial, *s.* kirchliches Begräbnis. **–goer,** *s.* der (die) Kirchgänger(in). **churching,** *s.* die Aussegnung. **church|-lands,** *pl.* das Kirchengut. **–man,** *s.* der Theologe, Geistliche(r). **– militant,** *s.* die streitende Kirche. **--mouse,** *s.* ***poor as a –,*** arm wie eine Kirchenmaus. **--parade,** *s.* (*Mil.*) der Kirchgang. **– preferment,** *s.* die Pfründe. **– school,** *s.* von der Staatskirche geleitete Volksschule. **--service,** *s.* der Gottesdienst. **–warden,** *s.* 1. der Kirchenvorsteher; 2. (*coll.*) lange Tonpfeife. **–yard,** *s.* der Kirchhof; (*coll.*) ***– cough,*** böser Husten.

churl [tʃə:l], *s.* der Flegel, Grobian, Raubein; (*Hist.*) Bauer; (*coll.*) Knicker, Knauser. **churlish,** *adj.* grob, rauhbeinig, ungehobelt; (*coll.*) geizig, filzig, knauserig.

churn [tʃə:n], **1.** *s.* das Butterfaß, die Buttermaschine; (große) Milchkanne. **2.** *v.t.* aufwühlen, kneten; (*coll.*) ***– out,*** serienmäßig herstellen. **3.** *v.i.* buttern; aufwallen, schäumen. **churning,** *s.* das Buttern; Aufwallen, heftige Bewegung. **churn-staff,** *s.* der Butterstößel, Butterstempel.

chute [ʃu:t], *s.* 1. die Rutsche, Schüttelrinne; starkes Gefälle, die Stromschnelle; (*Am.*) Wasserrutschbahn, Gleitbahn; 2. (*coll.*) *abbr. of* **parachute.**

chutney ['tʃʌtni], *s.* die Würztunke.

chyle [kail], *s.* der Milchsaft, Speisesaft, Chylus.

chyme [kaim], *s.* der Speisebrei, Magenbrei, Chymus.

ciborium [si'bɔ:riəm], *s.* (*Eccl.*) das Hostiengefäß, die Monstranz; (*Archit.*) der Altarüberhang.

cicada [si'keidə, –'kɑ:də], *s.* die Zikade, Grille, Zirpe.

cicatrice ['sikətris], *s.* die Narbe, das Wundmal. **cicatrization** [–trai'zeiʃən], *s.* die Vernarbung, Narbenbildung. **cicatrize,** *v.t., v.i.* vernarben.

cicely ['sisəli], *s.* (*Bot.*) die Myrrhe.

cicerone [tʃitʃə'rouni, sisə–], *s.* (*pl.* **-ni** [–ni:]) der Cicerone, Fremdenführer.

cider ['saidə], *s.* der Apfelmost, Apfelwein. **cider-press,** *s.* die Apfelpresse.

cigar [si'gɑ:], *s.* die Zigarre; ***--box,*** die Zigarrenkiste; ***– case,*** das Zigarrenetui; ***– cutter,*** der Zigarrenabschneider; ***– end,*** der Zigarrenstummel.

cigarette [sigə'ret], *s.* die Zigarette; ***--end,*** die Kippe; ***– holder,*** die (Zigaretten)spitze; ***– lighter,*** das Feuerzeug.

cilia ['siliə], *pl.* die (Augen)wimpern (*pl.*); (*Bot., Zool.*) Flimmerhärchen (*pl.*). **ciliary,** *adj.* Wimper–; ***– process,*** der Ziliarfortsatz. **ciliate** [–iit], *adj.* bewimpert.

cinch [sintʃ], *s.* der Sattelgurt; (*sl.*) ***a (dead) –,*** todsichere S., die Spielerei, das Kinderspiel.

cinchona [siŋ'kounə], *s.* die Chinarinde.

cincture ['siŋktʃə], **1.** *s.* der Gürtel, Gurt; die Umzäunung; (*Archit.*) der (Säulen)kranz. **2.** *v.t.* umgürten, umzäunen, einschließen.

cinder ['sində], *s.* ausgeglühte Kohle, die Asche; (*Metall.*) Schlacke; ***live –,*** glühende Kohle; ***burnt to a –,*** zu Kohle verbrannt, verkohlt.

Cinderella [sində'relə], *s.* Aschenbrödel, Aschenputtel (*n.*).

cinder|-path, --track, *s.* (*Spt.*) die Aschenbahn.

cine– ['sini], *pref.* Film–, Kino–; ***--camera,*** die Filmkamera; ***--film,*** der Kinofilm, Schmalfilm; ***--projector,*** der Schmalfilm-Vorführapparat, Kinoprojektor.

cinema ['sinimə], *s.* das Kino, Lichtspieltheater; der Film, die Filmkunst. **cinematograph** [–'mætəgrɑ:f], *s.* der Filmvorführapparat. **cinematographer** [–'tɔgrəfə], *s.* der Kameramann. **cinematographic** [–'græfik], *adj.* Film–, kinematographisch.

cineraria [sinə'rɛəriə], *s.* (*Bot.*) das Aschenkraut.

cinerary ['sinərəri], *adj.* ***– urn,*** die Totenurne, Aschenurne.

cinnabar ['sinəbɑ:], *s.* der Zinnober.

cinnamon ['sinəmən], *s.* der Zimt, Kaneel.

cinque [siŋk], *s.* (*Cards etc.*) die Fünf. **cinquecento** [tʃiŋkwi'tʃentou], *s.* italienische Kunst des 16. Jahrhunderts. **cinquefoil** ['siŋkfɔil], *s.* (*Bot.*) das Fünffingerkraut; (*Archit.*) Fünfblatt.

cipher ['saifə], **1.** *s.* 1. die Ziffer, Nummer; (*Math.*) (*also fig. of a p.*) Null, (*fig.*) (*of a th.*) das Nichts, wertlose S., (*of a p.*) unbedeutende Person; 2. die Chiffre, Geheimschrift; der Schlüssel (zu einer Geheimschrift); das Monogramm. **2.** *v.i.* rechnen. **3.** *v.t.* berechnen, ausrechnen; chiffrieren, verschlüsseln; ***– out,*** dechiffrieren, entziffern, (*coll.*) austüfteln, ausknobeln.

circa ['sə:kə], *adv.* zirka, ungefähr, etwa.

Circassian [sə'kæsiən], **1.** *s.* der Tscherkesse (die Tscherkessin). **2.** *adj.* tscherkessisch.

circle [sə:kl], **1.** *s.* der Kreis, (*Geom.*) die Kreislinie; der Umkreis, Umfang; Zirkel, (Bekannten)kreis; (*Log.*) Zyklus; die Serie, Periode, der Zirkelschluß; (*Theat.*) Rang; Ring, Reif, Kranz; ***Antarctic Circle,*** südlicher Polarkreis; ***Arctic Circle,*** nördlicher

Polarkreis; (*Theat.*) ***dress –,*** erster Rang; ***full –,*** (*used as adv.*) rund *or* die Reihe herum; ***inner –,*** die Ringbahn; (*Theat.*) ***upper –,*** zweiter Rang; ***vicious –,*** der Zirkelschluß, die Schraube ohne Ende; ***argue in a –,*** einen Zirkelschluß machen; ***square the –,*** den Kreis quadrieren, (*fig.*) Unmögliches leisten. **2.** *v.t.* umgehen, herumgehen um; umgeben, umzingeln, einkreisen, einschließen. **3.** *v.i.* sich im Kreise bewegen, kreisen. **circlet** [–klit], *s.* kleiner Ring, das Ringlein, der Reif.

circlip [ˈsəːklip], *s.* (*Mech.*) der Sprengring.

circuit [ˈsəːkit], **1.** *s.* die Kreisbewegung, Umdrehung; der Kreislauf, Umlauf; Umkreis, Umfang; Umweg, die Runde, der Bogen; (*Law*) Gerichtsbezirk, die Rundreise (*of judges etc.*); (*Elec.*) der Stromkreis, die Leitung, Schaltung, das Schaltsystem; (*Av.*) der Rundflug; (*Elec.*) ***in –,*** angeschlossen; ***make a –,*** einen Umgang machen; ***make a – of,*** herumgehen um; ***go on –,*** die Assisen abhalten; ***within a – of 10 miles,*** im Umkreise von 10 Meilen; ***cinema –,*** der Kinoring; (*Rad.*) ***grid –,*** der Gitterkreis; (*Rad.*) ***rejector –,*** der Sperrkreis; (*Elec.*) ***short –,*** der Kurzschluß. **2.** *v.t.* bereisen, umkreisen.

circuit|-breaker, *s.* der Stromunterbrecher, Trennschalter, Ausschalter. **– diagram,** *s.* (*Elec.*) das Schaltbild, Schaltschema.

circuitous [səːˈkjuitəs], *adj.* weitläufig, weitschweifig; ***– route,*** der Umweg.

circuitry [ˈsəːkitri], *s.* (*Elec.*) die Schaltungstechnik; Schaltung.

circular [ˈsəːkjulə], **1.** *adj.* kreisförmig, (kreis)rund, Kreis–; (*Geom.*) ***– area,*** die Kreisfläche; ***– letter,*** das Rundschreiben, der Laufzettel; (*Geom.*) ***– measure,*** das (Kreis)bogenmaß; ***– motion,*** die Kreisbewegung; ***– numbers,*** Zirkularzahlen; ***– railway,*** die Ringbahn; ***– saw,*** die Kreissäge; (*Geom.*) ***– section,*** kreisrunder Querschnitt; (*Archit.*) ***– style,*** der Rundbogenstil; ***– ticket,*** das Rundreisebillet; ***– tour,*** die Rundfahrt, Rundreise; (*Tech.*) ***– track,*** der (Dreh)kranz; (*Geom.*) ***– triangle,*** das Kreisbogendreieck, Kugeldreieck, sphärisches Dreieck; ***– velocity,*** die Umdrehungsgeschwindigkeit. **2.** *s.* das Rundschreiben, Zirkular; ***Court –,*** die Hofnachrichten. **circularize** [–raiz], *v.t.* durch Rundschreiben benachrichtigen, Werbeschriften versenden an (*Acc.*).

circulate [ˈsəːkjuleit], **1.** *v.i.* umlaufen, zirkulieren, (*of money*) kursieren, im Umlauf sein; sich im Kreise bewegen; (*sl.*) verkehren. **2.** *v.t.* in Umlauf setzen, verbreiten (*rumour etc.*); (*Comm.*) girieren (*bills*). **circulating,** *adj.* umlaufend; kursierend; ***– decimal,*** periodischer Dezimalbruch; ***– library,*** die Leihbibliothek; ***– medium,*** das Zahlungsmittel, Tauschmittel, Umlaufsmittel; ***– pump,*** die Zirkulationspumpe. **circulation** [–ˈleiʃən], *s.* der Kreislauf (*of blood etc.*), Umlauf (*of money etc.*); Absatz (*of goods*); die Verbreitung (*of a report*); Auflage (*of a paper*); das im Umlauf befindliche Geld; ***be in –,*** in Umlauf sein, zirkulieren; ***– of air,*** die Ventilation, der Durchzug; die Bewetterung (*in mines*); ***bank of –,*** die Girobank; (*Comm.*) ***– of bills,*** der Wechselverkehr; ***withdraw*** (*bills*) ***from –,*** aus dem Verkehr ziehen; ***out of –,*** außer Kurs (gesetzt).

circum|ambient [səːkəmˈæmbiənt], *adj.* umgebend, umschließend, ringsum einschließend. **–ambulate, 1.** *v.i.* herumgehen, umhergehen; (*fig.*) Umschweife machen, um die S. herumreden, (*coll.*) auf den Busch klopfen. **2.** *v.t.* umgehen, herumgehen um. **–ambulation** [–bjuˈleiʃən], *s.* der Umweg, (*fig.*) Umschweif.

circumcise [ˈsəːkəmsaiz], *v.t.* beschneiden. **circumcision** [–ˈsiʒən], *s.* die Beschneidung.

circumference [səˈkʌmfərəns], *s.* der Umkreis, Kreisumfang, die Kreislinie, Peripherie. **circumferential** [–ˈrenʃəl], *adj.* Umkreis–, Umfangs–.

circumflex [ˈsəːkəmfleks], **1.** *s.* der Zirkumflex. **2.** *adj.* (*Med.*) gebogen, gekrümmt. **circumflexion** [–ˈflekʃən], *s.* die Biegung, Krümmung.

circum|gyrate, *v.i.* sich (um die Achse) drehen, rotieren, kreisen. **–-jacent** [–ˈdʒeisənt], *adj.* umliegend, umgebend. **circum|locution,** *s.* die Umschreibung; der Umschweif, die Weitschweifigkeit. **–locutory** [–ˈlɔkjutəri], *adj.* umschreibend, weitschweifig. **–navigate,** *v.t.* umschiffen, umfahren, umsegeln. **–navigation,** *s.* die Umschiffung, Umseg(e)lung.

circumscribe [ˈsəːkəmskraib], *v.t.* (*Geom.*) umschreiben; umgeben, umgrenzen; (*fig.*) umschreiben, einschränken, definieren. **circumscription** [–ˈskripʃən], *s.* die Umschreibung, Begrenzung, Beschränkung; Umgrenzung, Peripherie; Umschrift (*on coins etc.*).

circumspect [ˈsəːkəmspekt], *adj.* behutsam, umsichtig, vorsichtig, wohlüberlegt, wohlerwogen. **circumspection** [–ˈspekʃən], *s.* die Umsicht, Vorsicht, Behutsamkeit.

circumstance [ˈsəːkəmstəns], *s.* der Umstand; Fall, die Einzelheit, Tatsache, das Ereignis; *pl.* nähere Umstände (*pl.*), Verhältnisse (*pl.*), die (Sach)lage, der Sachverhalt, das Nähere; ***extenuating –s,*** mildernde Umstände, (*Law*) der Strafmilderungsgrund; ***easy –s,*** gute Verhältnisse; ***reduced*** or ***straitened –s,*** beschränkte Verhältnisse; ***–s demand it,*** die Lage bringt es so mit sich; ***–s alter cases,*** neue Umstände ergeben neue Verhältnisse; ***pomp and –,*** Pomp und Staat; ***in*** or ***under the –s,*** unter den gegenwärtigen *or* obwaltenden Umständen; ***under no –s,*** unter keinen Umständen, auf keinen Fall. **circumstanced,** *adj.* in einer Lage befindlich, in eine Lage versetzt; ***– as I was,*** in meiner Lage.

circumstantial [səːkəmˈstænʃl], *adj.* 1. umständlich, eingehend, ausführlich; ***– report,*** der Tatbestand; 2. nebensächlich, untergeordnet, zufällig; ***– evidence,*** der Indizienbeweis, Indizien (*pl.*). **circumstantiality** [–ʃiˈæliti], *s.* die Umständlichkeit, Ausführlichkeit. **circumstantiate** [–ʃieit], *v.t.* mit allen Einzelheiten darstellen; (*Law*) auf Grund der Indizien beweisen. **circumstantiation** [–ʃiˈeiʃən], *s.* die Ausstattung mit Einzelheiten; (*Law*) Beweisführung auf Grund der Indizien.

circumvallation [səːkəmvəˈleiʃən], *s.* die Umwallung, Umschanzung.

circumvent [səːkəmˈvent], *v.t.* überlisten, übervorteilen, hintergehen (*a p.*), verhindern, vereiteln, hintertreiben (*a th.*). **circumvention** [–ˈvenʃən], *s.* die Überlistung, Vereitelung.

circumvolution [səːkəmvəˈljuːʃən], *s.* die Umdrehung, Umwälzung; Windung, Krümmung.

circus [ˈsəːkəs], *s.* 1. der Zirkus, die Zirkustruppe; Zirkusarena; Zirkusvorstellung; 2. große Wegkreuzung, runder Platz.

cirrhosis [siˈrousis], *s.* (*Med.*) die Zirrhose, Leberschrumpfung.

cirro-cumulus [ˈsiroukjuːmjuləs], *s.* die Lämmerwolke, Schäfchenwolke.

cirrose [ˈsirous], *adj. See* **cirrous.**

cirro-stratus [ˈsiroustrɑːtəs], *s.* die Schleierwolke.

cirrous [ˈsirəs], *adj.* rankig, rankenartig; federartig, büschelartig.

cirrus [ˈsirəs], *s.* (*Bot.*) die Ranke, (*Zool.*) der Rankenfuß, (*Meteor.*) die Federwolke.

cisalpine [sisˈælpain], *adj.* zisalpin(isch), diesseits der Alpen (gelegen).

cissy [ˈsisi], **1.** *s.* (*coll.*) der Weichling; (*sl.*) Homo. **2.** *adj.* (*coll.*) verweichlicht, weibisch.

cist [sist], *s.* 1. die Kiste, Ziste, Truhe, das Kästchen; 2. keltisches Steingrab.

Cistercian [sisˈtəːʃən], **1.** *s.* der Zisterzienser(mönch). **2.** *adj.* zisterziensisch.

cistern [ˈsistən], *s.* die Zisterne, der Wasserbehälter, Bottich; Wasserspeicher, das Reservoir, Bassin.

cistus [ˈsistəs], *s.* (*Bot.*) die Zistrose.

citable, *see* **citeable.**

citadel [ˈsitədəl], *s.* die Burg, Zitadelle.

citation [saiˈteiʃən], *s.* 1. die Anführung, das Zitieren, (*Law*) die Vorladung, (*Mil.*) ehrenvolle Erwähnung; 2. das Zitat. **citatory** [ˈsitətəry], *adj.* (*Law*) ***letters –,*** schriftliche Vorladung. **cite**

[sait], *v.t.* zitieren; (als Beispiel) anführen *or* erwähnen; (*Law*) vorladen. **citeable** ['saitəbl], *adj.* zitierbar, anführbar.

cither(n) ['siðə(n)], *s.* (*Poet.*) die Zither, Laute.

citizen ['sitizən], *s.* 1. der Staatsbürger, Staatsangehörige(r); – ***of the world,*** der Weltbürger, Kosmopolit; 2. Bürger, Städter, Stadtbewohner; 3. Einwohner (*of a country*), Zivilist (*opp. of military*). **citizenry,** *s.* die Bürgerschaft. **citizenship,** *s.* die Staatsbürgerschaft, Staatsangehörigkeit; das Bürgerrecht; die Bürgerkunde.

citrate ['sitreit], *s.* (*Chem.*) das Zitrat, zitronensaures Salz; – ***of iron,*** zitronensaures Eisenoxyd. **citreous** [–iəs], *adj.* zitronengelb. **citric,** *adj.* – ***acid,*** die Zitronensäure. **citron,** *s.* (*Bot.*) gemeiner Zitronenbaum; (*obs.*) die Zitrone.

city ['siti], *s.* 1. die (Groß)stadt; – ***authorities*** or ***council,*** die Stadtbehörde, der Stadtrat; – ***father,*** der Stadtrat, das Mitglied des Stadtrats; – ***hall,*** das Rathaus, Magistratsgebäude; (*sl.*) – ***slicker,*** plausibler Gauner; – ***state,*** autonomer Stadtstaat; ***the – of Berlin,*** die Stadt B.; ***freedom of the –,*** das (Ehren)bürgerrecht der Stadt; 2. (*Comm.*) die City, das Geschäftszentrum; – ***editor,*** der Redakteur des Handelsteils, (*Am.*) Lokalredakteur; – ***page,*** der Handelsteil (*of newspaper*).

civet ['sivit], *s.* 1. der Zibet; 2. (*also* –***-cat***) die Zibetkatze.

civic ['sivik], *adj.* bürgerlich, Bürger–; städtisch, Stadt–; – ***centre,*** das (Stadt)verwaltungsviertel; – ***duties,*** die Bürgerpflicht; – ***reception,*** der Empfang durch die Stadtverwaltung. **civics,** *pl.* (*sing. constr.*) die (Staats)bürgerkunde.

civies (*Am.*), *see* **civvies.**

civil ['sivil], *adj.* 1. (*Law*) zivilrechtlich, privatrechtlich; zivil, Zivil–; bürgerlich, Bürger–; Staats–; – ***affairs,*** Verwaltungsangelegenheiten (*pl.*); – ***authorities,*** Zivilbehörden (*pl.*); – ***aviation,*** die Zivilluftfahrt; ***Civil Court,*** das Zivilgericht; – ***defence,*** zivile Verteidigung; – ***disobedience,*** bürgerlicher Ungehorsam; – ***engineer,*** der (Tief)bauingenieur; – ***engineering,*** der Tiefbau, Ingenieurbau; – ***government,*** die Zivilverwaltung; – ***law,*** das Privatrecht, Zivilrecht; – ***liberty,*** bürgerliche Freiheit; – ***list,*** die Zivilliste; – ***marriage,*** standesamtliche Trauung, die Zivilehe; – ***rights,*** Bürgerrechte (*pl.*), bürgerliche Ehrenrechte (*pl.*); – ***servant,*** Staatsbeamte(r), Verwaltungsbeamte(r); – ***service,*** der Staatsdienst, die Zivilverwaltung; – ***suit,*** der Zivilrechtsfall; – ***war,*** der Bürgerkrieg; (***American***) ***Civil War,*** (amerikanischer) Sezessionskrieg; 2. höflich, zuvorkommend, gesittet, anständig; – ***attitude,*** anständige Haltung; ***keep a – tongue in one's head,*** hübsch höflich bleiben.

civilian [si'viljən], **1.** *s.* der Zivilist, die Zivilperson; Staatsbeamte(r) (in Indien). **2.** *adj.* bürgerlich, zivil, Zivil–; – ***life,*** das Zivilleben; – ***population,*** die Zivilbevölkerung, Zivilisten (*pl.*).

civility [si'viliti], *s.* die Artigkeit, Höflichkeit, Gefälligkeit.

civilization [sivilai'zeiʃən], *s.* die Zivilisation, Kultur; Kulturwelt, zivilisierte Welt. **civilize** ['sivilaiz], *v.t.* zivilisieren, verfeinern; ***–d nations,*** Kulturvölker (*pl.*).

civvies ['siviz], *pl.* (*coll.*) Zivilklamotten (*pl.*). **civvy street,** *s.* (*sl.*) das Zivilleben.

clachan ['klæxən], *s.* (*Scots*) (kleines) Dorf.

clack [klæk], **1.** *v.i.* klappern, rasseln; (*coll.*) plappern. **2.** *s.* 1. das Klappern, Geklapper, Rasseln, Gerassel; 2. die Klapper; Ventilklappe; 3. (*coll.*) das Plappern, Geplapper. **clack-valve,** *s.* das Klappenventil.

clad [klæd], **1.** (*Poet.*) *imperf., p.p. of* **clothe. 2.** *adj.* (an)gekleidet. **3.** *v.t.* (*Metall.*) plattieren; (*Build.*) verkleiden.

claim [kleim], **1.** *v.t.* fordern, beanspruchen, Anspruch erheben auf (*Acc.*); für sich in Anspruch nehmen, geltend machen; behaupten; reklamieren; – ***attention,*** Aufmerksamkeit erfordern; – ***payment,*** Zahlung fordern. **2.** *s.* der Anspruch, die Forderung, das Recht; der Rechtsanspruch, Rechtstitel, das Anrecht (***to, on,*** auf (*Acc.*)); (*Insur.*) die Reklamation, der Schadenersatzanspruch; (*Min.*) die Mutung, der Grubenanteil; – ***for compensation,*** der Ersatzanspruch; ***enter*** or ***lodge a – for,*** Anspruch erheben *or* Forderung anmelden auf (*Acc.*); ***give up*** or ***waive all – to,*** Verzicht leisten auf (*Acc.*); ***have a – on him,*** eine Forderung gegen ihn haben; ***lay – to s.th.,*** etwas in Anspruch nehmen, Anspruch *or* eine Forderung erheben auf eine S.; ***put in*** or ***submit a – for damages,*** Schadenersatz beanspruchen; ***substantiate a –,*** den Rechtsanspruch nachweisen; ***waive a –,*** auf einen Anspruch verzichten; (*Insur.*) ***no –s bonus,*** der Schadenfreiheitrabatt.

claimable ['kleiməbl], *adj.* zu beanspruchen(d). **claimant,** *s.* Beanspruchende(r), Anspruchererhebende(r), Anspruchsberechtigte(r), der (die) Anwärter(in), Bewerber(in), (*to the throne etc.*) Prätendent(in). **claim jumper,** *s.* (*Am. coll.*) widerrechtlicher Besitzergreifer eines fremden Grubenanteils.

clairvoyance [klɛə'vɔiəns], *s.* das Hellsehen. **clairvoyant, 1.** *s.* der (die) Hellseher(in). **2.** *adj.* hellsehend, hellseherisch.

clam [klæm], *s.* eßbare Muschel.

clamant ['kleimənt], *adj.* (*elevated style*) lärmend, (*fig.*) schreiend (*injustice etc.*), (*Scots*) dringend.

clamber ['klæmbə], *v.i.* klettern, klimmen; – ***up,*** erklettern, erklimmen.

clamminess ['klæminis], *s.* (feuchtkalte) Klebrigkeit. **clammy,** *adj.* feuchtkalt und klebrig.

clamor ['klæmə], (*Am.*) *see* **clamour. clamorous,** *adj.* laut, lärmend; ungestüm. **clamour, 1.** *s.* das Geschrei, Getöse, der Lärm, Tumult; laute Klage. **2.** *v.i.* schreien (*for,* nach); – ***against,*** Klage erheben gegen.

[1]**clamp** [klæmp], **1.** *s.* die Klampe, Klammer, Kluppe, Krampe, Klemmschraube, Zwinge; Schelle, Einschubleiste (*of a door etc.*). **2.** *v.t.* festklemmen, einklemmen, einspannen, verklammern.

[2]**clamp, 1.** *s.* der Haufen, Meiler, die Miete (*of potatoes etc.*). **2.** *v.t.* aufhäufen, aufschichten, aufstapeln, einmieten (*potatoes etc.*).

clamping ['klæmpiŋ], *adj.* Klemm–, Spann–.

clan [klæn], *s.* (*Scots*) der Stamm, Clan; (*coll.*) die Sippe, Familie; Sippschaft, Clique; – ***spirit,*** das Stammesbewußtsein.

clandestine [klæn'destin], *adj.* heimlich, verstohlen; – ***trade,*** der Schleichhandel.

clang [klæŋ], **1.** *s.* der Klang, Schall, das Geklirr. **2.** *v.t.* schallen *or* klirren lassen. **3.** *v.i.* schallen, klirren. **clanger,** *s.* (*sl.*) der Verstoß, Fehltritt; (*sl.*) ***drop a –,*** ins Fettnäpfchen treten. **clangor,** (*Am.*) *see* **clangour. clangorous** [–ərəs], *adj.* schmetternd, klirrend, schallend; schrill, gellend. **clangour** [–ə], *s.* der Schall, Klang, das Schmettern, Geschmetter, Gellen.

clank [klæŋk], **1.** *s.* das Gerassel, Geklirr, Klirren. **2.** *v.t.* rasseln mit, klirren lassen. **3.** *v.i.* rasseln, klirren.

clannish ['klæniʃ], *adj.* Stammes–, stammverbunden; (*fig. coll.*) fest zusammenhaltend. **clannishness,** *s.* das Stammesgefühl; (*fig.*) Zusammenhalten. **clanship,** *s.* das Stammesbewußtsein, die Stammesverbundenheit. **clansman,** *s.* der Stammesgenosse, Stammverwandte(r), das Stammesmitglied, Angehörige(r) eines Clans.

[1]**clap** [klæp], **1.** *v.i.* in die Hände klatschen, Beifall klatschen; – ***to,*** zuschlagen (*as a door*); – ***together,*** zusammenklappen. **2.** *v.t.* beklatschen, applaudieren; Beifall klatschen (*Dat.*); klopfen, schlagen; – ***him on the back,*** ihm auf den Rücken klopfen; (*coll.*) – ***one's eyes on,*** zu sehen bekommen; – ***one's hands,*** in die Hände klatschen, Beifall klatschen; – ***the handcuffs on him,*** ihm Handschellen anlegen; – ***one's hat on one's head,*** sich (*Dat.*) den Hut aufstülpen; (*coll.*) – ***hold of,*** (plötzlich) ergreifen; – ***import duties on,*** mit Einfuhrzoll belegen; – ***a pistol to his breast,*** ihm eine Pistole auf die Brust setzen; (*coll.*) – ***into prison,*** (ohne weiteres) einstecken; – ***spurs to a horse,*** einem Pferde die

Sporen geben. **3.** *s.* der Knall, Schlag, Klaps; Applaus, das Händeklatschen; – ***of thunder,*** der Donnerschlag.

[2]**clap,** *s.* (*Med.*) (*vulg.*) der Tripper.

clap|-board, *s.* die Schindel; Faßdaube. **--net,** *s.* das Schlagnetz. **clapper,** *s.* 1. die Klapper; der Schwengel, (*of a bell*) Klöppel; 2. Beifallsspender, Händeklatscher; 3. (*sl.*) die Zunge. **clapper|-board(s),** *s.* (*pl.*) (*Films*) die Klappe. **--boy,** *s.* (*Films*) der Klappenmann. **clap-trap, 1.** *s.* (*coll.*) die Effekthascherei, der Theaterkniff; Klimbim, das Blech, die Phrasendrescherei. **2.** *adj.* effekthaschend, trügerisch, täuschend.

claque [klæk], *s.* die Claque, Claqueure (*pl.*).

clarendon ['klærəndən], *s.* (*Typ.*) der Fettdruck.

claret ['klærət], *s.* der Rotwein; das Weinrot; (*sl.*) Blut; – ***cup,*** die Rotweinbowle; ***mulled*** –, der Glühwein.

clarification [klærifi'keiʃən], *s.* (*Tech.*) die (Ab)-klärung, (Ab)läuterung; (*fig.*) (Er)klärung, Aufhellung; – ***plant,*** die Kläranlage. **clarifier** ['klærifaiə], *s.* das Klärmittel, die Kläre; Klärpfanne. **clarify** [–fai], *v.t.* (*Tech.*) (ab)klären, abschlämmen, läutern (*fluids*); abschleifen, ausseimen (*sugar*); reinigen (*air*); (*fig.*) (er)klären, erhellen, aufklären, klarmachen.

clarinet [klæri'net], *s.* die Klarinette.

clarion ['klæriən], **1.** *s.* (*Poet.*) die Zinke, Trompete; heller Trompetenton. **2.** *adj.* (*Poet.*) laut, schmetternd. **3.** *v.t.* (*Poet.*) – ***forth,*** ausposaunen. **clarionet,** *s. See* **clarinet.**

clarity ['klæriti], *s.* die Klarheit, Reinheit.

clary ['klɛəri], *s.* (*Bot.*) das Schlarlachkraut; ***meadow*** –, der Wiesensalbei.

clash [klæʃ], **1.** *v.i.* 1. klirren, rasseln, prasseln; aneinanderstoßen, zusammenprallen; 2. (*fig.*) (*of events*) (zeitlich) zusammenfallen, kollidieren; (*of persons*) im Widerspruch stehen, nicht zusammenpassen, unvereinbar sein, aneinandergeraten, (*of colours etc.*) nicht harmonieren, sich nicht vertragen, nicht zusammenpassen. **2.** *v.t.* klirren lassen, (klirrend) aneinanderstoßen *or* zusammenschlagen. **3.** *s.* der Zusammenstoß, Zusammenprall; das Geklirr; Gerassel, Geschmetter; (*fig.*) (*of persons*) der Widerstreit, Widerspruch, Konflikt; (*of events*) die Kollision, (zeitliches) Zusammentreffen; – (***of arms***), bewaffneter Zusammenstoß, feindliches Zusammentreffen; – ***of opinions,*** die Meinungsverschiedenheit.

clasp [klɑ:sp], **1.** *v.t.* zuhaken, einhaken, festschnallen; ergreifen, umklammern, festhalten; umfangen, umranken (*as tendrils*); umfassen (*the knees etc.*); – ***hands,*** sich die Hände reichen; – ***one's hands*** (***together***), die Hände falten; – ***in one's arms,*** umarmen; – ***to one's bosom,*** ans Herz drücken. **2.** *s.* der Haken, die Klammer; Schnalle (*of a belt*); (*Mil.*) Ordensspange; Umklammerung, Umarmung, der Händedruck; die Schließe (*of a book*); das Schließeisen, der Riegelhaken (*of a lock*). **clasp|-knife,** *s.* das Klappmesser. **--lock,** *s.* das Schnappschloß. **--nail,** *s.* der Schindelnagel.

class [klɑ:s], **1.** *s.* die Klasse, Gruppe, Kategorie, Gattung, Art, Sorte; Rangstufe, Wertklasse, Qualität, der Grad; die Schulklasse; (*Mil.*) der Rekrutenjahrgang; Stand, gesellschaftlicher Rang, soziale Stellung, die Gesellschaftsschicht, Gesellschaftsklasse; ***attend –es,*** am Unterricht teilnehmen; (*at school*) ***be*** (***at the***) ***top of one's*** –, der Klassenerste sein; ***be in the same – with,*** gleichwertig sein mit; ***first--*** or ***high--,*** erstklassig, hervorragend; ***first-- compartment,*** das Abteil erster Klasse; ***first-- performance,*** hervorragende Leistung; ***the lower –(es),*** die unteren Bevölkerungsschichten; ***the middle –(es),*** der Mittelstand; ***the upper –(es),*** die obere Gesellschaftsschicht. **2.** *v.t.* in Klassen einteilen *or* einordnen, einstufen; – ***with,*** gleichstellen mit; ***be –ed as*** or ***with,*** zählen zu, angesehen werden als, angehören (*Dat.*).

class|-book, *s.* das Schulbuch, Lehrbuch. **--conflict,** *s.* der Klassenkampf. **--conscious,** *adj.* klassenbewußt. **– hatred,** *s.* der Klassenhaß.

classic ['klæsik], **1.** *adj.* klassisch, vollendet, mustergültig; erstklassig, ausgezeichnet; – ***example,*** klassisches *or* mustergültiges Beispiel; – ***races,*** die berühmten Pferderennen. **2.** *s.* 1. klassischer Schriftsteller, der Klassiker; 2. klassisches (Kunst)werk; 3. griechisch-römischer Schriftsteller; 4. ***the –s,*** klassische Philologie; klassische (griechisch-römische) Literatur; die klassischen Schriftsteller, die Klassiker; klassische Werke der Literatur.

classical ['klæsikl], *adj.* 1. klassisch, griechisch-römisch; klassizistisch; – ***architecture,*** (*of antiquity*) klassischer *or* antiker Baustil, (*of modern times*) klassizistischer Baustil; – ***education,*** klassische *or* humanistische Bildung; 2. *See* **classic, 1.**

classicism ['klæsisizm], *s.* der Klassizismus; die Klassik (*in German lit.*); klassische Bildung. **classicist,** *s.* klassischer Philologe. **classics,** *pl. See* **classic, 2.**

classifiable ['klæsifaiəbl], *adj.* klassifizierbar. **classification** [–fi'keiʃən], *s.* die Klassifizierung, (Klassen)einteilung, (*Bot., Zool.*) Gruppeneinteilung; Eingruppierung, Einstufung, Anordnung, Sortierung. **classificatory,** *adj.* klassenbildend. **classify** ['klæsifai], *v.t.* (in *or* nach Klassen *or* Gruppen) einteilen, einordnen, einstufen, (ein)-gruppieren, klassifizieren, sortieren; (*Mil., Pol.*) ***classified matter,*** die Verschlußsache.

class|-list, *s.* die Prüfungsliste, Benotungsliste. **--mate,** *s.* der (die) Klassenkamerad(in), Mitschüler(in). **-room,** *s.* das Klassenzimmer. **– war,** *s. See* **– conflict.**

classy ['klɑ:si], *adj.* (*sl.*) erstklassig, pfundig, Klasse–.

clatter ['klætə], **1.** *v.i.* klappern, klirren, rasseln; – ***about,*** umhertrappeln, umhertrampeln. **2.** *v.t.* klirren *or* klappern lassen. **3.** *s.* das Gerassel, Geklirr, Geklapper, Getrappel; Geplapper.

clause [klɔ:z], *s.* 1. der Satzteil, das Satzglied; ***principal*** –, der Hauptsatz; ***subordinate*** –, der Nebensatz; 2. (*Law*) der Vorbehalt, die Klausel.

claustral ['klɔ:strəl], *adj.* klösterlich, Kloster–.

claustrophobia [klɔ:strə'foubiə], *s.* die Angst vor geschlossenen Räumen, Klaustrophobie.

clavecin ['klævisin], *s.* (*Mus.*) das Cembalo. **clavichord** [–kɔ:d], *s.* (*Mus.*) das Klavichord.

clavicle ['klævikl], *s.* (*Anat.*) das Schlüsselbein.

claw [klɔ:], **1.** *s.* die Klaue, Kralle, der Fang; (*of crabs etc.*) die Schere; (*Tech.*) Klaue, der Haken; – ***of a hammer,*** die Hammerklaue, gespaltene Finne; (*coll.*) ***get one's –s into him,*** ihn zu fassen kriegen. **2.** *v.t.* (zer)kratzen; (*Naut.*) – ***off,*** vom Ufer abhalten. **3.** *v.t.* (*coll.*) – ***at,*** krabbeln an (*Dat.*). **claw|-hammer,** *s.* der Splitthammer. **– setting,** *s.* die Ajourfassung (*of a ring*).

clay [klei], *s.* der Ton, Lehm, Mergel, die Tonerde, (*fig.*) Erde, Staub und Asche; (*Eccl.*) irdische Hülle, sterblicher Teil; (*fig.*) ***feet of*** –, tönerne Füße. **clayey** [–i:], *adj.* tonig, lehmig, lehmhaltig, Ton–, Lehm–. **clay| hut,** *s.* die Lehmhütte. **--marl,** *s.* der Tonmergel.

claymore ['kleimɔ:], *s.* (*Hist.*) altschottisches Breitschwert.

clay| pigeon, *s.* die Tontaube. **– pipe,** *s.* die Tonpfeife. **--pit,** *s.* die Lehmgrube. **– soil,** *s.* der Lehmboden.

clean [kli:n], **1.** *adj.* rein; reinlich, sauber, stubenrein (*as animals*); sauber, einwandfrei (*as food*); lauter, fehlerfrei, schuldlos (*morals*); leer, unbeschrieben (*paper*); sauber, fehlerlos (*printer's copy*); geschickt, gewandt, sauber, glatt, tadellos, gut ausgeführt (*as actions*); (*Comm.*) – ***acceptance,*** bedingungsloses Akzept; (*Comm.*) – ***bill,*** einwandfreier Wechsel; – ***bill of health,*** reiner Gesundheitspaß; (*Comm.*) – ***bill of lading,*** echtes Konnossement; ***make a – breast of it,*** es sich (*Dat.*) vom Herzen reden, es offen eingestehen; – ***cut,*** glatter Schnitt; ***make a – sweep of,*** aufräumen mit, reinen Tisch machen mit. **2.** *adv.* rein, sauber, reinlich, sorgfältig; (*coll.*) glatt, gänzlich, völlig, ganz und gar, absolut, direkt; (*sl.*) ***come*** –, mit der Sprache herausrücken, alles eingestehen; ***cut it – off,*** es glatt abschneiden; (*coll.*) ***– forget about it,*** es total vergessen; (*coll.*) ***go – off one's head,*** den Kopf völlig verlieren; (*coll.*) ***– gone,*** spurlos verschwunden; ***leap – over,*** direkt 'rüber springen. **3.** *v.t.* reinigen, säubern, reinmachen, putzen; (*Tech.*) klären, waschen, abschwemmen; ***– a gun,*** ein Gewehr putzen; ***– out,*** reinigen, reinmachen; aufräumen, leeren; (*sl.*) ausnehmen, schröpfen (*a p.*); ***– up,*** gründlich reinigen, aufräumen, in Ordnung bringen, (*sl.*) beiseiteschaffen, einheimsen.

clean-cut, *adj.* scharf abgeschnitten, klar umrissen, (*as features*) wohlgeformt. **cleaner,** *s.* der Reiniger; die Reinigungsmaschine; *pl.* die Reinigungs(anstalt); Scheuerfrauen (*pl.*); (*sl.*) ***take to the –s,*** schröpfen, ausrauben. **clean-handed,** *adj.* mit reinen Händen; unbestochen, sauber. **cleaning,** *s.* die Reinigung, das Putzen; Reinemachen. **clean-limbed,** *adj.* ebenmäßig gebaut, wohlproportioniert.

cleanliness ['klenlinis], *s.* die Reinheit, Reinlichkeit, Sauberkeit.

clean-living, *adj.* mit sauberem Charakter *or* einwandfreiem Lebenswandel.

cleanly ['klenli], *adj.* reinlich, säuberlich; nett; geschickt, gewandt.

cleanness ['kli:nnis], *s.* die Sauberkeit, Reinheit. **clean-out,** *s.* (*coll.*) das Reinemachen, Ausräumen.

cleanse [klenz], *v.t.* reinigen, säubern, reinwaschen; abscheuern, ausputzen (*vessels etc.*); (*Metall.*) (ab)beizen; (*fig.*) heilen, befreien, freisprechen, lossprechen. **cleanser,** *s.* das Reinigungsmittel.

clean-shaven, *adj.* glattrasiert.

cleansing ['klenziŋ], *s.* die Reinigung, (*fig.*) der Freispruch, die Befreiung, Lossprechung; ***– cream,*** die Abschminkcreme.

clean-up, *s.* (*coll.*) gründliche Reinigung; (*fig. sl.*) die Beseitigung, (*Mil. sl.*) Auswäsche.

clear [kliə], **1.** *adj.* 1. klar, hell, durchsichtig, rein; heiter (*of the sky*); ***as – as a bell,*** glockenrein; ***– day,*** heiterer Tag; ***– sky,*** heiterer Himmel; ***– soup,*** (klare) Kraftbrühe; ***– water,*** reines Wasser; (*Naut.*) offenes Fahrwasser; ***– weather,*** heiteres Wetter; 2. deutlich, kenntlich, (leicht)verständlich, übersichtlich; scharfsichtig; ***be – about,*** im klaren sein über (*Acc.*); ***make it – to him,*** es ihm klarmachen; ***make o.s. –,*** sich verständlich machen; (*fig.*) ***as – as day,*** sonnenklar; ***– head,*** klarer Kopf; ***– judgement,*** scharfsichtiges Urteil; (*fig.*) ***as – as mud,*** klar wie Kloßbrühe; ***– style,*** klare *or* leichtverständliche Schreibart; ***– voice,*** deutliche *or* durchdringende Stimme; 3. unbefangen, offen, frei, unbehindert; unschuldig, schuldlos, frei (*of,* von), unbelastet (mit); ***all –!*** alles klar! fertig! Gefahr vorbei! (*coll.*) ***be – of,*** überwunden haben, hinter sich (*Dat.*) gelassen haben, los sein; ***be – of debt,*** frei von Schulden *or* unbelastet sein; ***be – of guilt,*** schuldlos sein; (*fig. coll.*) ***the coast is –,*** nichts steht im Wege, die Luft ist rein; ***– conscience,*** reines *or* unbelastetes Gewissen; 4. (*Comm.*) ohne Abzug, netto, Rein–; ***– profit,*** der Reingewinn; 5. zuversichtlich, außer Zweifel, sicher; zweifellos, unleugbar, unbestreitbar, unanfechtbar; ***– case,*** unbestreitbare *or* zweifellose S.; ***the – contrary,*** genau *or* gerade das *or* das genaue *or* gerade Gegenteil; ***– title,*** unbestrittenes Recht; 6. voll; ***four – days,*** vier volle Tage. **2.** *adv.* gänzlich, völlig, ganz (und gar); ***two weeks –,*** zwei volle Wochen; ***get – of,*** loskommen von; ***jump –,*** abspringen; ***keep – of,*** abseits stehen von, (*fig.*) sich fernhalten von, meiden; ***leap – over,*** frei springen über (*Acc.*); ***stand –,*** abseits stehen.

3. *s.* die Helle; (*Tech.*) lichte Weite; (*of message, signal etc.*) ***in (the) –,*** der Klartext; (*fig.*) ***in the –,*** nicht unter Verdacht (stehend), über jeden Verdacht erhaben.

4. *v.t.* säubern, reinigen; lichten, abholzen, roden (*a wood*); löschen (*cargo*), leeren, entladen (*a ship*); befreien, frei machen, entlasten, reinwaschen (*from guilt*); (*Comm.*) einlösen (*a cheque*); aus dem Wege räumen, abräumen, abdecken, aufräumen, wegräumen, wegschaffen, entfernen; bezahlen, abtragen (*a debt*), begleichen, ins Reine bringen (*an account*); verzollen, klarieren (*goods at the customs*), ausklarieren (*ship at the customs*); (*Naut.*) klarmachen (*ship for action*); hinwegspringen *or* –setzen über (*Acc.*) (*an obstacle*); ***– the coast,*** von der Küste freikommen; ***– o.s. of a debt,*** sich einer Schuld entledigen; ***– a place of the enemy,*** einen Ort vom Feinde säubern; ***– an estate,*** ein Gut entlasten; ***– the ground,*** das Land urbar machen; ***– the letter-box,*** den Briefkasten leeren; (*Railw.*) ***– the line,*** freie Fahrt geben (***for,*** *Dat.*); ***– an obstacle,*** an einem Hindernis vorbeikommen; ***– a port,*** aus einem Hafen auslaufen; ***– a profit of £10,*** 10 Pf. als Reingewinn erzielen, 10 Pf. netto einnehmen; ***– a room,*** ein Zimmer (aus– *or* auf)räumen; ***– a ship for action,*** ein Schiff klar zum Gefecht *or* gefechtsklar machen; ***– the table,*** abdecken; ***– one's throat,*** sich räuspern; ***– the way!*** Platz da! aus dem Wege! ***– away,*** wegräumen, abräumen; ***– (off) a debt,*** eine Schuld tilgen *or* abbezahlen; ***– out,*** ausräumen, ausleeren; ***his stock was –ed out,*** sein Lager wurde ausverkauft; ***– up,*** aufklären, erklären, erhellen; aufräumen, in Ordnung bringen.

5. *v.i.* (*also* ***– up***) sich aufhellen, sich aufklären, sich aufheitern (*as weather*), sich klären, hell *or* klar werden (*as liquids*), (*Naut.*) klarkommen; ***– away,*** abräumen; (*sl.*) ***– off,*** verduften; (*coll.*) ***– out,*** sich packen, sich davonmachen, sich aus dem Staube machen.

clearage ['kliəridʒ], *s.* die Bodenfreiheit, der Bodenabstand (*of vehicles etc. from the ground*).

clearance ['kliərəns], *s.* 1. das (Auf)räumen, Wegräumen; 2. (*Comm.*) die Verrechnung (*of cheques etc.*), Tilgung, volle Bezahlung (*of debts*); 3. Lichtweite, der Spiel(raum), (*of a bridge*) lichte Höhe; *see also* **clearage**; 4. (*of a wood*) die (Aus)lichtung, Rodung, Abholzung; 5. (*at the customs*) Verzollung, Ausklarierung; der Zollschein; 6. (*Av.*) die Abfertigung, Freigabe (*of aircraft by flight control*). **clearance|-sale,** *s.* der (Räumungs)ausverkauf. **--space,** *s.* (*Tech.*) das Toleranzfeld.

clear|-cut, *adj.* scharfgeschnitten, klar umrissen, (*fig.*) deutlich, klar. **--eyed,** *adj.* helläugig. **--headed,** *adj.* verständig, scharfsinnig, einsichtig, (*pred.*) klar im Kopf.

clearing ['kliəriŋ], *s.* 1. das Aufräumen, Ausräumen; 2. die Lichtung, Rodung, Reute, der (Kahl)schlag, die Abholzung (*in a wood*); 3. (*Comm.*) Clearing, der Verrechnungsverkehr. **clearing|-bank,** *s.* die Girobank. **--certificate,** *s.* der Zollabfertigungsschein. **--house,** *s.* die Verrechnungskasse, Abrechnungsbörse, Girozentrale, das Clearinginstitut. **--office,** *s.* die Ausgleichstelle, Verrechnungsstelle. **--station,** *s.* (*Mil.*) die Verwundetensammelstelle, das Durchgangslager. **--system,** *s.* der Clearingverkehr.

clearly ['kliəli], *adv.* klar, deutlich; offenbar. **clearness,** *s.* die Klarheit, Deutlichkeit. **clear|-sighted,** *adj.* scharfsichtig; (*fig.*) scharfsinnig, einsichtig. **--starch,** *v.t.* stärken. **–way,** *s.* die Halteverbotstraße.

cleat [kli:t], *s.* (*Naut.*) die Klampe; (*Tech.*) Querleiste, das Kreuzholz; (*Elec.*) die Isolierschelle; der Schuhnagel.

cleavable ['kli:vəbl], *adj.* spaltbar. **cleavage** [–vidʒ], *s.* das Spalten; die Spaltung (*also Chem.*), Zerspaltung, Aufspaltung; (*Biol.*) (Zell)teilung; Spaltbarkeit (*of crystals*); (*Geol.*) der Spalt; (*coll.*) der Brustansatz.

[1]**cleave, 1.** *irr.v.t.* spalten, aufspalten, zerspalten; sich (*Dat.*) bahnen (*a way*); durchdringen (*the air*). **2.** *irr.v.i.* sich spalten, aufspringen, bersten.

[2]**cleave,** *v.i.* kleben, haften, hängenbleiben (***to,*** an (*Acc.*)); (*fig.*) halten (zu).

cleaver ['kli:və], *s.* die Baumhacke, das Hackmesser.

cleavers ['kli:vəz], *pl.* (*Bot.*) das Klebkraut.

clef [klef], *s.* (*Mus.*) der (Noten)schlüssel.

cleft [kleft], **1.** *imperf., p.p. of* **cleave. 2.** *s.* die Spalte, Ritze, Kluft, der Spalt, Schlitz, Riß, Sprung. **3.** *adj.* (ein)gespalten; ***– palate,*** die

Gaumenspalte, der Wolfsrachen; (*fig.*) ***in a – stick,*** in der Klemme *or* Patsche. **cleft-footed,** *adj.* mit Spalthuf; – ***animal,*** der Spalthufer.

cleg [kleg], *s.* (*dial.*) die Pferdefliege, Bremse.

clem [klem], **1.** *v.i.* (*dial.*) verschmachten. **2.** *v.t.* (*dial.*) verschmachten lassen.

clematis ['klemətis], *s.* (*Bot.*) die Waldrebe.

clemency ['klemənsi], *s.* die Gnade, Nachsicht, Schonung, Milde (*also of weather*). **clement,** *adj.* gnädig, gütig, nachsichtig; sanft, mild.

clench [klentʃ], *v.t.* vernieten (*rivet*); festmachen (*rope*); zusammenpressen; – ***one's fist,*** die Faust ballen; – ***one's teeth,*** die Zähne zusammenbeißen.

clerestory ['kliəstɔ:ri], *s.* (*Archit.*) der Lichtgaden.

clergy ['klə:dʒi], *s.* die Geistlichkeit, Geistliche (*pl.*), der Klerus; ***benefit of –,*** das Vorrecht der Geistlichen vor dem Gericht. **clergyman** [–mən], *s.* Geistliche(r), der Pfarrer, Pastor.

cleric ['klerik], *s.* Geistliche(r), der Pfaffe, Kleriker. **clerical,** *adj.* 1. geistlich, klerikal; 2. Büro–, Schreib–; – ***error,*** der Schreibfehler; – ***staff,*** Büroangestellten (*pl.*); – ***work,*** die Büroarbeit. **clericalism,** *s.* der Klerikalismus, die Pfaffenherrschaft; klerikaler Einfluß.

clerk [klɑ:k, (*Am.*) klə:k], *s.* der Schreiber, Schriftführer, Buchhalter; Kontorist, Handlungsgehilfe, kaufmännische(r) Angestellte(r), Sekretär, (*Am.*) Verkäufer; (*obs.*) Geistliche(r); Gelehrte(r); Schreibkundige(r); ***articled –,*** der Rechtspraktikant; ***bank-–,*** Bankbeamte(r), Bankangestellte(r); ***chief –,*** see ***head –***; ***confidential –,*** der Geheimsekretär; ***correspondence –,*** der Korrespondent; ***head –,*** erster Buchhalter, der Bürovorsteher, (*Am.*) erster Verkäufer; ***signing –,*** der Prokurist; ***town –,*** der Stadtsyndikus; – ***of the assizes,*** der Gerichtsschreiber; ***Clerk of the House of Commons,*** der Sekretär des Unterhauses; – ***of the weather,*** Petrus, der Wettergott; – ***of works,*** der Bauleiter. **clerkess,** *s.* (*Scots*) kaufmännische Angestellte, die Kontoristin, Sekretärin. **clerkly,** *adj.* (*obs.*) gelehrt, Schreiber–. **clerkship,** *s.* der Buchhalterposten, die Stellung als Schreiber *or* (*Am.*) als Verkäufer(in), das Amt eines Sekretärs.

clever ['klevə], *adj.* klug, gescheit, begabt, intelligent, talentiert; geschickt, gewandt; geistreich (*as an answer*). **cleverness,** *s.* die Klugheit, Begabung, Intelligenz, das Talent; die Geschicklichkeit, Gewandtheit.

Cleves [kli:vz], *s.* (*Geog.*) Kleve (*n.*).

clew [klu:], **1.** *s.* der Knäuel; (*Naut.*) das Schothorn. **2.** *v.t.* (*Naut.*) aufgeien. **clew-line,** *s.* das Geitau.

cliché ['kli:ʃei], *s.* 1. (*Typ.*) das Klischee, die Druckplatte, der Druckstock; 2. (*fig.*) abgedroschene Redensart, der Gemeinplatz.

click [klik], **1.** *s.* das Ticken, Klicken, Knacken, Knipsen; (*as of a door*) Einschnappen; (*Tech.*) die Sperrklinke, der Sperrhaken; – ***of the tongue,*** das Schnalzen. **2.** *v.i.* ticken, klicken, knacken, knipsen; (*sl.*) (*of a th.*) klappen, gerade in den Kram passen, wie gerufen kommen; (*sl.*) (*of persons*) Gefallen aneinander finden; (*as a lock*) – ***to*** or ***shut,*** zuklinken, zuschnappen. **3.** *v.t.* – ***one's heels,*** die Hacken zusammenschlagen; – ***one's tongue,*** schnalzen.

client ['klaiənt], *s.* (*Law*) der (die) Klient(in), Mandant(in); Kunde (Kundin). **clientage** [–tidʒ], **clientele** [–'tel, kli:ätel], *s.* (*Law*) die Klientel, (*Comm.*) der Kundenkreis, die Kundschaft, Kunden (*pl.*).

cliff [klif], *s.* die Klippe, Felswand, steiler Abhang. **cliff|-dweller,** *s.* der Felsenbewohner. **–-hanger,** *s.* (*sl.*) atemlos packende(r) Fortsetzung(sroman).

climacteric [klaimæk'terik], **1.** *adj.* entscheidend, kritisch. **2.** *s.* Wechseljahre (*pl.*), kritisches Alter, das Klimakterium.

climate ['klaimit], *s.* das Klima, der Himmelsstrich; (*fig.*) die Stimmung, Atmosphäre. **climatic** [–'mætik], *adj.* klimatisch, Klima–. **climatology** [–ə'tɔlədʒi], *s.* die Witterungskunde.

climax ['klaimæks], **1.** *s.* die Steigerung; der Gipfel, Höhepunkt. **2.** *v.i.* gipfeln, sich steigern. **3.** *v.t.* auf einen Höhepunkt bringen.

climb [klaim], **1.** *v.t.* ersteigen, erklettern, erklimmen, besteigen, klettern auf (*Acc.*), (*of plants*) sich hinaufranken auf (*Acc.*), umranken. **2.** *v.i.* klettern, emporsteigen, (*as a road*) ansteigen, (*Av.*) steigen; – ***down,*** hinunter- *or* heruntersteigen, (*fig. coll.*) klein beigeben, einen Rückzieher machen, nachgeben; – ***up,*** hinaufsteigen, hinaufklettern. **3.** *s.* der Aufstieg; die Besteigung; (*Av.*) der Steilflug; (*Av.*) ***rate of –,*** die Steigleistung.

climbable ['klaiməbl], *adj.* ersteigbar. **climb-down,** *s.* (*coll.*) das Nachgeben, Aufgeben, der Rückzieher, Rückzug. **climber,** *s.* der Kletterer, Bergsteiger; die Kletterpflanze, Schlingpflanze; (*fig.*) der Streber.

climbing ['klaimiŋ], *s.* das Bergsteigen, Klettern. **climbing|-irons,** *pl.* Steigeisen (*pl.*). **–-rope,** *s.* das Kletterseil. – **turn,** *s.* (*Av.*) gezogene Kurve.

clime [klaim], *s.* (*Poet.*) der Landstrich, Himmelsstrich, die Gegend.

clinch [klintʃ], **1.** *v.t.* (ver)nieten, festmachen; (*fig.*) endgültig regeln, entscheiden, erledigen; ***this –es matters,*** das bringt die S. zum Abschluß; das gibt den Ausschlag; damit ist der Fall erledigt. **2.** *v.i.* (*Boxing*) clinchen, in den Clinch gehen; sich umklammern. **3.** *s.* die Vernietung; (*Boxing*) Umklammerung, der Clinch. **clincher,** *s.* (*coll.*) entscheidendes Argument, treffender Beweis, das Ausschlaggebende. **clinch-nail,** *s.* der Niet(nagel).

cling [kliŋ], *irr.v.i.* (sich) festhalten, hängen(bleiben) (*to,* an (*Dat.*)), anhaften (*Dat.*), haften (an (*Dat.*)), sich heften, sich klammern, festsitzen (an (*Acc.*)); (*fig.*) sich hängen, anhänglich sein (an (*Acc.*)), treu bleiben (*Dat.*). **clinging,** *adj.* anhängend; eng anliegend (*as a dress*), (*fig. of a p.*) anhänglich.

clinic ['klinik], *s.* die (Poli)klinik, das (Universitäts)-krankenhaus; Klinikum, klinisches Praktikum. **clinical,** *adj.* klinisch; (*fig.*) streng objectiv, vorurteilsfrei; – ***conversion,*** die Bekehrung am Sterbebett; – ***thermometer,*** das Fieberthermometer. **clinician** [–'niʃən], *s.* der Kliniker.

clink [kliŋk], **1.** *s.* 1. das Geklirr, Klirren, Klimpern; 2. (*sl.*) Gefängnis, Loch, Kittchen. **2.** *v.i.* klirren, klimpern. **3.** *v.t.* klirren lassen, klimpern mit; – ***glasses,*** anstoßen.

clinker ['kliŋkə], *s.* 1. der Klinker, Hartziegel; 2. die Schlacke; 3. Nietnagel. **clinker|-built,** *adj.* (*Naut.*) klinkergebaut, in Klinkerbauart, mit Klinkerbeplankung. – **screen,** *s.* der Schlackensieb.

clinometer [klai'nɔmitə], *s.* der Winkelmesser, Neigungsmesser, das Klinometer.

[1]**clip** [klip], *v.t.* beschneiden, stutzen, (*sheep*) scheren, (*coin*) kippen, (*tickets*) (durch)lochen; (*fig.*) – ***his wings,*** ihm die Flügel stutzen; – ***one's words,*** die Silben verschlucken. **2.** *s.* 1. die (Schaf)-schur; der (Haar)schnitt; 2. (*coll.*) Klaps; (*sl.*) – ***on the ear,*** der Nasenstüber.

[2]**clip, 1.** *v.t.* festhalten, befestigen. **2.** *s.* die Klammer, Klemme, (*Tech.*) Kluppe, Schelle, Lasche, der Bügel, (*Elec.*) die Halterung; ***cartridge –,*** der Patronenrahmen, Ladestreifen, das Einsteckmagazin; ***paper –,*** die Büroklammer; ***pipe –,*** die Rohrschelle; (*Cycl.*) ***trouser –,*** die Hosenklammer.

clip-joint, *s.* (*sl.*) der Neppladen.

clipper ['klipə], *s.* 1. der Beschneider; 2. (*Naut.*) Klipper, Schnellsegler; 3. (*sl.*) Prachtkerl; 4. *pl.* die Schere, Haarschneidemaschine, Schneidzange. **clippie,** *s.* (*sl.*) die Schaffnerin. **clipping,** *s.* 1. das Beschneiden, Stutzen, Scheren; 2. der (Zeitungs)-ausschnitt; *pl.* Abfälle (*pl.*), Schnitzel (*pl.*). **clipping shears,** *pl.* die Pferdeschere, Schafschere.

clique [kli:k], *s.* der Klüngel, die Clique. **cliquish,** *adj.* (*coll.*) cliquenhaft. **cliquishness,** *s.* die Klüngelei, Cliquenwirtschaft. **cliquy,** *adj. See* **cliquish.**

clitoris ['klitəris], *s.* (*Anat.*) der Kitzler.

cloaca [klou'eikə], *s.* 1. die Senkgrube, der Abzugskanal, (*fig.*) Pfuhl, Sumpf; 2. (*Anat., Zool.*) die Kloake.

cloak [klouk], **1.** *s.* (loser) Mantel; (*fig.*) der Deckmantel, Vorwand, die Bemäntelung, Decke. **2.** *v.t.* einhüllen; (*fig.*) bemänteln, verbergen, vertuschen. **cloak|-and-dagger,** *attrib. adj.* Spionage-. **-room,** *s.* die Garderode, Kleiderablage; (*euphemism.*) Toilette.

[1]**clobber** ['klɔbə], *v.t.* (*sl.*) zusammenhauen.

[2]**clobber,** *s.* (*sl.*) Dinger, (*clothes*) Klamotten (*pl.*).

cloche [klɔʃ], *s.* 1. die Glasglocke (*for plants*); 2. (glockenförmige) Damenhut.

[1]**clock** [klɔk], **1.** *s.* die (Wand- *or* Stand)uhr; (*in taxis etc.*) Kontrolluhr; (*coll.*) Federkrone, Pusteblume (*of dandelions*); (*coll.*) ***like one o'–,*** wie verrückt; ***musical –,*** die Spieluhr; (*obs.*) ***what o'– is it?*** wieviel Uhr ist es? ***four o'–,*** vier Uhr. **2.** *v.t.* (*Spt. coll.*) erzielen (*a certain time*), abstoppen (*a runner*). **3.** *v.i.* ***– in*** (***out***), den Arbeitsanfang (Arbeitsschluß) (an der Kontrolluhr) stempeln *or* stechen *or* registrieren.

[2]**clock,** *s.* der Zwickel (*in stockings*). **clocked,** *adj.* mit Zwickel.

clock|-face, *s.* das Zifferblatt. **--golf,** *s.* das Minigolf. **--hand,** *s.* der (Uhr)zeiger. **-maker,** *s.* der Uhrmacher. **-wise,** *adj., adv.* rechtsdrehend, rechtslaufend, rechtsläufig, im Uhrzeigersinn; ***– rotation,*** der Rechtslauf. **-work,** *s.* das Uhrwerk, Räderwerk; ***like –,*** pünktlich, mechanisch, automatisch; regelmäßig, (*coll.*) wie geölt; ***– toy,*** das Spielzeug zum Aufziehen.

clod [klɔd], *s.* 1. der (Erd)klumpen; die Scholle; 2. (*fig.*) der Tölpel, Tolpatsch. **clodhopper,** *s.* 1. (*coll.*) der Bauernlümmel, Tölpel, Tolpatsch, der *or* die *or* das Trampel; 2. *pl.* (*coll.*) klobige Schuhe (*pl.*).

clog [klɔg], **1.** *v.t.* (be)hindern, hemmen; verstopfen. **2.** *v.i.* sich verstopfen. **3.** *s.* das Fesselholz, der Holzklotz; Holzschuh, die Pantine; (*fig.*) der Hemmschuh, das Hemmnis, Hindernis; die Verstopfung; (*Tech.*) der Knebel. **clog dance,** *s.* der Schuhplattler.

cloister ['klɔistə], **1.** *s.* das Kloster; (*Archit.*) (*usu. pl.*) der Kreuzgang, gedeckter Gang. **2.** *v.t.* ins Kloster stecken. **cloistered,** *adj.* (*Archit.*) mit Kreuzgängen umgeben; (*fig.*) einsam, abgeschieden, zurückgezogen. **cloistral,** *adj.* Kloster-, klösterlich, klosterartig.

[1]**close** [klous], **1.** *adj.* 1. geschlossen (*also Phonet.*), verschlossen, zugeschlossen, (*pred. only*) zu(gemacht); eingeschlossen, umgeben; abgeschlossen, abgeschieden, zurückgezogen; (*of air*) dumpf, schwül, drückend; (*fig.*) verschlossen, verschwiegen, zurückhaltend, schweigsam, in sich gekehrt; (*Naut.*) ***– box,*** der Verschlag; ***– cell,*** enge Zelle; ***– confinement,*** strenge Haft; (*coll.*) ***– customer,*** verschlossener Mensch; ***– formation*** or ***order,*** geschlossene (Marsch- *or* Flug)ordnung; ***– prisoner,*** streng bewachter Gefangener; ***– scholarship,*** bedingtes Stipendium; ***– season,*** die Schonzeit; 2. nah, dicht (*in space*), dicht, fest (*fabric*), (*Typ.*) gedrängt, kompreß; ***– attack,*** der Nahangriff; (*Mil.*) ***– column,*** geschlossene Marschkolonne; ***– combat,*** der Nahkampf; (*Mil.*) ***– fire,*** die Feuerkonzentration; ***– fit,*** enge Paßform, (*Tech.*) die Edelpassung; ***– harmony,*** enger Satz; ***– proximity,*** unmittelbare Nähe; ***come to – quarters,*** handgemein werden; ***– range,*** nächste Entfernung, die Kernschußweite; (*coll.*) ***– shave,*** die Rettung mit knapper Not, knappes Entkommen *or* Entrinnen; ***– style,*** gedrängter *or* bündiger *or* knapper Stil; (*Mil., fig.*) ***– touch,*** die Tuchfühlung; 3. (*of a p.*) sparsam, geizig, knickerig, filzig karg; ***– fist,*** karge Hand; 4. genau (*resemblance*), (wort)getreu (*translation*); scharf; gründlich; ***– attention,*** gespannte Aufmerksamkeit; ***– observer,*** sorgfältiger *or* scharfer Beobachter; ***– reasoning,*** lückenlose Beweisführung; ***– study,*** gründliches *or* eingehendes Studium; 5. eng, vertraut, innig, intim (*friend*); ***in – conversation,*** in eifrigem Gespräche; 6. fast gleich(wertig), unentschieden (*contest*); ***– fight,*** lange unentschiedener Kampf; (*coll.*) ***a – thing,*** knappes Erreichen, knapper Sieg.

2. *adv.* nahe, eng, dicht; ***– by,*** dicht dabei *or* daneben; ***come –,*** nahe herankommen; ***cut a th. –,*** etwas kurz abschneiden; ***– to the ground,*** dicht am Boden; ***be – at hand,*** dicht bevorstehen; ***– on a hundred,*** annähernd *or* fast 100, nahe an 100; ***follow – upon him,*** ihm auf den Fersen folgen, dicht hinter ihm kommen; ***keep – (to),*** sich dicht anschließen (an (*Acc.*)); ***lie –,*** dicht an (*Dat.*) *or* bei etwas sein; ***sail – to the wind,*** (dicht *or* hoch *or* hart) am Winde segeln; (*fig.*) Gefahr laufen, beinahe Anstoß geben; ***sit – (together),*** eng zusammensitzen; ***sit – round the fire,*** dicht ums Feuer sitzen; ***stick – to him,*** sich dicht an ihn halten.

[2]**close** [klous], *s.* eingeschlossener Raum; die Sackgasse; das Gehege; die Umzäunung, Einfried(ig)ung; das Klostergebiet, bischöflicher Machtbezirk; die Domfreiheit, der Domplatz, Hofraum; (*Scots*) das Treppenhaus.

[3]**close** [klouz], **1.** *v.t.* 1. schließen, zuschließen, einschließen, abschließen, verschließen, zumachen, zutun; (*Comm.*) ***– the books,*** die Bücher schließen; ***– the current,*** den Stromkreis schließen; ***– the door on him,*** die Tür hinter ihm zumachen, (*fig.*) ihn verstoßen; (*fig.*) ***– the door on a th.,*** den Weg zu etwas abschneiden; ***– one's eyes to a th.,*** die Augen vor etwas verschließen, etwas absichtlich übersehen; ***– one's mind to a th.,*** sich einer S. verschließen; (*Mil.*) ***– the ranks,*** die Glieder schließen; ***– down,*** schließen, zumachen, einstellen, stillegen; ***– in,*** einschließen; ***– off,*** abschließen; ***– up,*** (ver)schließen, zumachen; zusammenrücken, (*Typ.*) verbinden; 2. beschließen, abschließen, beenden, endigen, zu Ende führen; ***– an account,*** ein Konto abschließen; (*fig.*) ***– accounts with,*** abrechnen mit; ***– an affair,*** einer S. ein Ende machen, eine S. beendigen; ***– a bargain,*** ein Geschäft abmachen, einen Kauf abschließen; ***– a sentence,*** einen Satz beenden *or* schließen; 3. (*Naut.*) ***– the wind,*** an den Wind kommen.

2. *v.i.* 1. (sich) schließen, geschlossen werden; zuheilen (*of wounds*); ***– up,*** aufschließen, aufrücken, zusammenrücken; sich füllen, sich schließen; 2. heranrücken, näher kommen, sich nähern, eng zusammenrücken, sich zusammenschließen (um); aneinandergeraten, handgemein werden (***with,*** mit); ***– about*** or ***around him,*** von allen Seiten auf ihn eindringen; ***– in,*** herankommen, hereinbrechen; auf den Leib rücken (***upon,*** *Dat.*); (*Naut.*) ***– with the land,*** sich dem Lande nähern; 3. aufhören, end(ig)en, zu Ende gehen, abschließen; ***– down,*** schließen, stillgelegt werden; 4. sich einigen (***with,*** mit) (*a p.*); ***– with an offer,*** ein Angebot annehmen.

3. *s.* der (Ab)schluß, das Ende; ***bring to a –,*** schließen, beendigen; ***draw to a –,*** sich dem Ende nähern; ***at the – of the year,*** am Jahresende. *See* **closing, closure.**

close-cropped ['klous-], *adj.* kurzgeschoren.

closed [klouzd], *adj. See* [3]**close, 1, 2. closed| circuit,** *s.* der Ruhestromkreis; ***– current,*** der Ruhestrom; ***– television,*** das Betriebsfernsehen. **– shop,** *s.* das Geschäft mit Gewerkschaftszwang.

close|-fisted ['klous-], *adj.* geizig, knauserig, filzig. **--fitting,** *adj.* eng anliegend *or* anschließend. **--grained,** *adj.* dichtfaserig; feinkörnig. **--hauled,** *adj.* (*Naut.*) dicht *or* hoch *or* hart am Wind.

closely ['klousli], *adv.* eng, dicht, fest; streng, genau, scharf; ***– allied,*** eng verbunden; ***attend –,*** genau *or* scharf aufpassen; ***– contested,*** hart umstritten.

closeness ['klousnis], *s.* 1. die Nähe; (*of translation*) Treue, Genauigkeit; ***– to life,*** die Lebensnähe; 2. (*of confinement*) Schärfe, Strenge; 3. (*of air*) Schwüle, Dumpfheit, Stickigkeit; 4. (*of fabric*) Dichtheit, Dichtigkeit, Festigkeit; 5. (*of a p.*) Verschwiegenheit, Verschlossenheit; 6. (*coll.*) (*of a p.*) Knickerigkeit, der Geiz.

[1]**closer** [ˈklouzə], *s.* der (Be)schließer; (*Archit.*) Kopfziegel, Schlußstein.
[2]**closer** [ˈklousə], *comp. adj. See* [1]**close.**
close-range [ˈklous-], *adj.* Nah-, aus nächster Nähe.
closet [ˈklɔzit], **1.** *s.* das Kabinett, kleines Zimmer; (*Am.*) der Wandschrank; (*water*) -, der Abort, Abtritt, das Klosett. **2.** *v.t.* ***be -ed with him,*** mit ihm eine vertrauliche Unterredung haben.
close|-tongued [ˈklous-], *adj.* verschwiegen, vorsichtig im Gespräch. **--up, 1.** *s.* die Nahaufnahme, Großaufnahme. **2.** *adj.* Nah-.
closing [ˈklouziŋ], *adj.* - ***date,*** letzter Termin; (*Theat.*) - ***scene,*** die Schlußszene; - ***time,*** die Polizeistunde (*for public houses etc.*); der Geschäftsschluß, Feierabend; - ***word,*** das Schlußwort.
closure [ˈklouʒə], *s.* das (Zu)schließen, Verschließen; der Verschluß; (*Pol.*) Schluß (der Debatte); ***apply the -,*** den Antrag auf Schluß der Debatte stellen.
clot [klɔt], **1.** *s.* 1. der Klumpen, das Klümpchen; Gerinnsel; 2. (*sl.*) der Trottel. **2.** *v.i.* gerinnen, koagulieren, Klümpchen bilden.
cloth [klɔθ], *s.* das Tuch, Gewebe, Zeug, der Stoff; (*Bookb.*) die Leinwand, das Leinen; (*fig.*) ***the -,*** der geistliche Stand, die Geistlichkeit; ***American -,*** das Wachstuch; ***cut one's coat according to one's -,*** sich nach der Decke strecken; ***lay the -,*** den Tisch decken; ***remove the -,*** abdecken; ***twilled -,*** das Köperzeug; - ***binding,*** der Leinenband; - ***board,*** der Leinwanddeckel; - ***cap,*** die Tuchmütze.
clothe [klouð], *reg. & irr.v.t.* (an)kleiden, bekleiden; anziehen (*a child etc.*), (*fig.*) (ein)kleiden, einhüllen (*thoughts etc.*).
clothes [klouðz], *pl.* Kleider (*pl.*), die Kleidung; Wäsche; ***baby -,*** die Säuglingswäsche, Windeln; ***cast-off -,*** alte *or* abgetragene Kleider; ***in plain -,*** in Zivil; (*obs.*) ***small -,*** Beinkleider (*pl.*); ***soiled -,*** schmutzige Wäsche; ***change one's -,*** sich umziehen; ***put on one's -,*** sich ankleiden *or* anziehen; ***take off one's -,*** sich ausziehen *or* entkleiden.
clothes|-bag, *s.* der Wäschebeutel. **--basket,** *s.* der Wäschekorb. **--brush,** *s.* die Kleiderbürste. **--hanger,** *s.* der Kleiderbügel. **--horse,** *s.* das Wäschegestell, der Trockenständer. **--line,** *s.* die Wäscheleine. **--peg,** (*Am.*) **--pin,** *s.* die Wäscheklammer. **--pole,** (*Am.*) **--post, --prop,** *s.* die Wäschestange.
clothier [ˈklouðiə], *s.* der Kleiderhändler, Tuchhändler.
clothing [ˈklouðiŋ], *s.* die (Be)kleidung; ***article of -,*** das Kleidungsstück; (*Mil.*) - ***allowance,*** der Bekleidungszuschuß; - ***industry,*** die Bekleidungsindustrie.
clotted [ˈklɔtid], *adj.* klumpig, geronnen; - ***cream,*** verdickter Rahm. **clotting,** *s.* die Gerinnung, Koagulation, Klumpenbildung.
cloud [klaud], **1.** *s.* die Wolke; (*fig.*) Schar, der Schwarm, Haufe(n); trüber Fleck, Schatten, die Trübung, Verdüsterung, Düsterheit, Dunkelheit; - ***of dust,*** die Staubwolke; - ***of tobacco smoke,*** der Tabaksqualm; (*fig.*) ***be in the -s,*** träumen, in Gedanken vertieft sein; ***under a -,*** in Ungnade *or* Verruf; ***cast a - upon*** or ***over,*** einen Schatten werfen auf (*Acc.*), trüben; ***live in a -,*** in höheren Regionen leben *or* schweben. **2.** *v.t.* 1. bewölken, trüben, verdunkeln, überschatten; 2. (*Tech.*) schattieren, ädern, flammen; moirieren, wässern (*fabrics*). **3.** *v.i.* (- ***over***) sich bewölken, sich trüben, trübe werden.
cloud| bank, *s.* die Wolkenbank. **-burst,** *s.* der Wolkenbruch. **--capped,** *adj.* von Wolken umgeben, wolkenbedeckt. **--covered,** *adj.* wolkenumhüllt (*as mountains*), bewölkt, wolkenbedeckt (*as sky*). **--cuckoo-land,** *s.* das Wolkenkuckucksheim. **--drift,** *s.* der Wolkenzug.
clouded [ˈklaudid], *adj.* umwölkt, getrübt; moiriert. **cloudiness,** *s.* die Bewölkung, Trübheit; der Schleier, die Trübung, Unklarheit, Dunkelheit. **clouding,** *s.* die Trübung (*of stones*); Äderung, das Moirémuster (*of fabrics*); (*fig.*) die Umwölkung, Trübung (*of the mind*). **cloudless,** *adj.* wolkenlos, unbewölkt, klar, hell. **cloudlet** [-lit], *s.* das Wölkchen. **cloudy,** *adj.* wolkig, bewölkt, (von Wolken) bedeckt; (*fig.*) (*of a liquid*) wolkig, trübe, (*of fabrics*) gewässert, geädert, moiriert; (*fig.*) finster, traurig, düster; dunkel, zweifelhaft, verschwommen, unklar.
clout [klaut], **1.** *s.* 1. (*obs., dial.*) der Lappen, Wisch; (*obs.*) Fleck, das Flicken (*on shoes etc.*); 2. die Achsscheibe (*of wheels*); das Zentrum (*of target*), der Treffer; (*coll.*) Schlag, Hieb; - ***on the ear,*** die Ohrfeige; - ***on the head,*** die Kopfnuß. **2.** *v.t.* 1. (*obs., dial.*) flicken; beschlagen; 2. (*coll.*) schlagen, ohrfeigen. **clout-nail,** *s.* der Schuhnagel, Blattnagel.
[1]**clove** [klouv], *s.* (*Bot.*) die Brutzwiebel, Nebenzweibel.
[2]**clove,** *s.* die Gewürznelke; (*Poet.*) das Nägelein; ***oil of -s,*** das Nelkenöl.
[3]**clove,** *s.* (*obs.*) *imperf. of* [1]**cleave,** [2]**cleave.**
clove-hitch, *s.* (*Naut.*) der Mastwurf.
cloven [ˈklouvən], *adj.* gespalten; - ***hoof,*** der Spaltfuß, (*fig.*) Teufel; ***show the - hoof,*** sein wahres Gesicht zeigen. **cloven-hoofed,** *adj.* spaltfüßig, paarzehig; (*fig.*) teuflisch.
clove-pink, *s.* (*Bot.*) die Gartennelke (*Dianthus caryophyllus*).
clover [ˈklouvə], *s.* der Klee; ***be in -,*** es gut haben, üppig leben. **clover-leaf,** *s.* 1. das Kleeblatt; 2. die Kleeblattkreuzung (*on motorways*).
clown [klaun], *s.* der Grobian, Tölpel; (*Theat.*) Hanswurst, Possenreißer (*also fig.*), Clown. **clownish,** *adj.* bäuerisch, grob, plump, tölpelhaft, ungeschliffen.
cloy [klɔi], *v.t.* übersättigen, überladen; (*fig.*) anwidern, anekeln.
club [klʌb], **1.** *s.* 1. die Keule, der Knüppel, Knüttel; (*Spt.*) Schläger, das Schlagholz; ***Indian -s,*** Keulen (*pl.*); 2. (*Cards*) das Treff, Kreuz, die Eichel; ***queen of -s,*** die Treffdame; 3. (geschlossene) Gesellschaft, der Klub, Verein; das Kasino. **2.** *v.t.* 1. mit einer Keule schlagen; - ***a musket,*** mit dem Kolben dreinschlagen; 2. zusammenschließen, vereinigen; ***we must - out efforts,*** wir müssen uns gemeinsam bemühen. **3.** *v.i.* (*coll.*) (- ***together***) sich zusammentun, gemeinschaftlich beisteuern; für die Auslagen gemeinsam aufkommen, sich in die Ausgaben teilen; (*coll.*) - ***up,*** zusammenlegen (*money*).
club|foot, *s.* der Klumpfuß. **-footed,** *adj.* klumpfüßig. **--haul,** *v.i.* (*Naut.*) mit dem Leeanker wenden. **-house,** *s.* das Klublokal, Klubhaus, Kasino, Vereinshaus. **-land,** *s.* das Klubviertel (in London). **--law,** *s.* das Faustrecht. **-man,** *s.* das Klubmitglied, (*coll.*) der Vereinsmeier. **--moss,** *s.* (*Bot.*) das Kolbenmoos, der Bärlapp. **-room,** *s.* das Vereinszimmer. **--rush,** *s.* (*Bot.*) die Simse; breitblättriger Rohrkolben. **--shaped,** *adj.* keulenförmig.
cluck [klʌk], *v.i.* gluck(s)en.
clue [klu:], *s.* 1. der Faden (*of a tale*); (*fig.*) Fingerzeig, Anhaltspunkt, Schlüssel, das Losungswort (*to,* zu, für); (*coll.*) ***I haven't a -,*** ich habe keinen Schimmer; 2. *See* **clew. clueless,** *adj.* (*sl.*) unklug, täppisch, läppisch, töricht.
clump [klʌmp], **1.** *s.* der Klotz, Klumpen, Kloß; Haufen, die Masse, Gruppe; Doppelsohle; das Trampeln; - ***of trees,*** die Baumgruppe, das Gehölz. **2.** *v.t.* mit Doppelsohlen versehen. **3.** *v.i.* (*coll.*) schwer auftreten, schwerfällig gehen, trampen, trapsen.
clumsiness [ˈklʌmzinis], *s.* das Ungeschick, die Ungeschicklichkeit, Schwerfälligkeit, Unbeholfenheit, Plumpheit. **clumsy,** *adj.* schwerfällig, unbeholfen, ungeschickt; plump.
clung [klʌŋ], *imperf., p.p. of* **cling.**
cluster [ˈklʌstə], **1.** *s.* die Traube, das Büschel; der Haufen, die Gruppe; der Schwarm; (*Stat.*) die Häufungsstelle; - ***of stars,*** der Sternhaufen; - ***of trees,*** die Baumgruppe. **2.** *v.i.* in Büscheln *or* Trauben wachsen; sich (ver)sammeln *or* zusammenscharen; schwärmen (*of bees*); - ***around,*** in

Gruppen herumstehen; (*Archit.*) *-ed column,* der Bündelpfeiler.

[1]**clutch** [klʌtʃ], **1.** *s.* 1. (krampfhafter) Griff, die Umklammerung; Klaue, Kralle, Pranke; (*fig.*) Macht, Gewalt; ***fall into his -es,*** ihm in die Klauen geraten; ***keep out of his -es,*** sich vor seiner Macht hüten; 2. (*Tech.*) die Kupplung; (*Motor.*) ***let in*** or ***engage the -,*** einkuppeln. **2.** *v.t.* 1. (er)greifen, (er)fassen, packen; 2. (*Tech.*) kuppeln. **3.** *v.i.* (krampfhaft) greifen (***at,*** nach).

[2]**clutch,** *s.* die Brut.

clutch|-lining, *s.* der Kupplungsbelag. **--pedal,** *s.* das Kupplungspedal. **--plate,** *s.* die Kupplungsscheibe.

clutter [ˈklʌtə], **1.** *s.* das Durcheinander, Gewirr, der Wirrwarr, die Unordnung. **2.** *v.t.* durcheinanderwerfen, umherstreuen; ***-ed up with,*** überhäuft *or* unordentlich vollgestopft mit.

clypeate [ˈklipieit], **clypeiform,** *adj.* (*Bot.*) schildförmig.

clyster [ˈklistə], *s.* (*Med.*) das Klistier, der Einlauf.

coach [koutʃ], **1.** *s.* 1. (vierrädrige) Kutsche; (*Railw.*) der Personenwagen; - ***and four,*** vierspännige Kutsche, der Vierspänner; (***motor***) -, der (Fern)autobus; ***stage -,*** die Eilkutsche; 2. Privatlehrer, Hauslehrer, Einpauker, Repetitor, (*Spt.*) Trainer. **2.** *v.t.* einpauken, (*Spt.*) trainieren (***for,*** zu). **coach|-box,** *s.* der Kutschersitz, Kutscherbock. **--builder,** *s.* der Wagenbauer. **--horse,** *s.* das Kutschpferd. **--house,** *s.* die Wagenremise. **coaching, 1.** *adj.* ***the old - days,*** als man noch Kutsche fuhr. **2.** *s.* der Nachhilfeunterricht, Privatunterricht; (*Spt.*) das Training. **coach|man,** *s.* der Kutscher. **-work,** *s.* die Karosserie. **--wrench,** *s.* der Engländer.

coaction [kouˈækʃən], *s.* das Zusammenwirken, die Zusammenarbeit. **coactive,** *adj.* zusammenwirkend, mitwirkend.

coadjutor [kouˈædʒutə], *s.* der Gehilfe, Mitarbeiter, (*Eccl.*) Koadjutor.

coagulant [kouˈægulənt], *s.* der Gerinnstoff, das Gerinnungsmittel. **coagulate** [-ˈleit], **1.** *v.i.* gerinnen, koagulieren. **2.** *v.t.* gerinnen lassen. **coagulation** [-ˈleiʃən], *s.* das Gerinnen; die Koagulierung. **coagulum,** *s.* das Gerinnsel, die Koagulatmasse.

coal [koul], **1.** *s.* die (Stein)kohle; ***bituminous -,*** die Fettkohle, bituminöse Kohle; (*coll.*) ***call*** or ***haul him over the -s,*** ihm den Text *or* die Leviten lesen, ihn zur Rechenschaft ziehen; ***carry -s to Newcastle,*** Eulen nach Athen tragen; ***hard -,*** der Anthrazit, die Glanzkohle; ***heap -s of fire on his head,*** feurige Kohlen auf sein Haupt sammeln; ***live -,*** glühende *or* glimmende Kohle; ***rich -,*** die Fettkohle; (*Pol.*) ***Coal and Steel Community,*** die Montanunion; ***vegetable -,*** die Braunkohle. **2.** *v.i.* (*Naut.*) Kohlen einnehmen, bunkern. **3.** *v.t.* bekohlen (*a ship etc.*).

coal|-bin, *s.* der Kohlenverschlag. **--black,** *adj.* kohlschwarz. **--box,** *s.* (*Railw.*) der Kohlenkasten. **--bunker,** *s.* (*Naut.*) der Kohlenraum. **--cellar,** *s.* der Kohlenkeller. **--dust,** *s.* der Kohlengrus.

coalesce [kouəˈles], *v.i.* sich verbinden *or* vereinigen, verschmelzen, zusammenwachsen. **coalescence,** *s.* das Zusammenfließen; die Vereinigung, Verschmelzung.

coal|face, *s.* das Ort, der Stoß. **-field,** *s.* das Kohlengebiet *or* -revier. **--formation,** *s.* (*Geol.*) die Steinkohlenformation. **--gas,** *s.* das Kohlengas, Leuchtgas, Steinkohlenleuchtgas. **--heaver,** *s.* der Kohlenträger. **--hole,** *s.* der Kohlenraum, Kohlenkeller, (*Am.*) die Kohlenschacht, (*Naut.*) das Kohlengatt. **coaling,** *s.* das Kohleneinnehmen; - ***station,*** die Kohlenstation, Bunkerstation.

coalition [kouəˈliʃən], *s.* das Bündnis, die Koalition; Vereinigung, der Zusammenschluß; ***- government,*** die Koalitionsregierung.

coal|-measures, *pl.* (*Geol.*) das Kohlengebirge. **--merchant,** *s.* der Kohlenhändler. **--mine,** *s.* das Kohlenbergwerk, die Kohlengrube, Zeche. **--miner,** *s.* der Bergarbeiter, Grubenarbeiter, Bergmann. **--mining,** *s.* der Kohlenbergbau. **--oil,** *s.* (*Am.*) das Kerosin. **--owner,** *s.* der Bergwerkbesitzer. **--pit,** *s.* die Kohlengrube, (*Am.*) der (Holz)kohlenmeiler. **--scuttle,** *s.* der Kohlenkasten, Kohleneimer. **--seam,** *s.* das Kohlenflöz. **--tar,** *s.* der (Stein)kohlenteer; - ***dye,*** der Teerfarbstoff; - ***soap,*** die Kohlenseife. **--tit(mouse),** *s.* (*Orn.*) die Tannenmeise (*Parus ater*). **--wharf,** *s.* der Kohlenabladeplatz.

coamings [ˈkoumiŋz], *pl.* (*Naut.*) der *or* das Süll, die Lukenkimming.

coarse [kɔːs], *adj.* grob, rauh; grobkörnig; (*fig.*) roh, grob, derb, plump, ungebildet, ungeschliffen; gemein, unanständig; (*Tech.*) (*of screw-thread*) steilgängig, grobgängig; - ***bread,*** das Schrotbrot; - ***language,*** derbe Sprache, rohe *or* anstößige Ausdrucksweise; - ***manners,*** rauhe Manieren; - ***meal,*** das Schrotmehl. **coarse-grained,** *adj.* grobkörnig; (*fig.*) ungehobelt, ungeschliffen. **coarsen, 1.** *v.t.* vergröben, grob machen. **2.** *v.i.* grob werden, (*fig.*) verrohen. **coarseness,** *s.* die Grobheit, Rauheit; (*fig.*) Roheit, Ungeschliffenheit, Ruppigkeit, Gemeinheit.

coast [koust], **1.** *s.* 1. die Küste; der Strand, das Meeresufer, Gestade; (*fig.*) ***the - is clear,*** die Bahn ist frei; die Luft ist rein; 2. (*Am.*) die Rodelbahn. **2.** *v.i.* 1. Küstenschiffahrt treiben; die Küste entlangfahren; 2. (*Am.*) rodeln; 3. (*Tech.*) leerlaufen; - ***along,*** (*Cycl.*) mit Freilauf bergab fahren; (*fig.*) ohne Anstrengung weiterkommen. **coastal,** *adj.* Küsten-. **coast|-battery,** *s.* die Küstenbatterie. **--defence,** *s.* die Küstenverteidigung.

coaster [ˈkoustə], *s.* 1. der Küstenfahrer; 2. das Tablett, Servierbrett (*for wine*); 3. (*Am.*) der Rodelschlitten. **coaster|-brake,** *s.* (*Cycl.*) die Rücktrittbremse. **--hub,** *s.* (*Cycl.*) die Freilaufnabe.

coastguard [ˈkoustgɑːd], *s.* die Küstenwache, Strandwache. **coasting,** *s.* 1. die Küstenschiffahrt, der Küstenhandel; 2. (*Am.*) das Rodeln; - ***trade,*** der Küstenhandel; - ***vessel,*** das Küstenschiff. **coast|line,** *s.* die Küstenlinie. **-wise, 1.** *adj.* Küsten-. **2.** *adv.* an der Küste entlang, längs der Küste.

coat [kout], **1.** *s.* der Rock, die Jacke, das Jackett; der Mantel; (*of animals*) Pelz, das Fell, (*of birds*) Gefieder; (*of paint etc.*) der Anstrich, Aufstrich, (*of plaster*) Belag, Bewurf; Überzug, die Schicht, Lage, Haut; - ***of arms,*** das Wappen(schild); - ***of dust,*** die Staubschicht; - ***of mail,*** der Panzer, Harnisch, das Panzerhemd; - ***of paint,*** der Anstrich; - ***of plaster,*** der Gipsbewurf; ***fur -,*** der Pelzmantel; ***apply the first -,*** den Grundanstrich auftragen; ***cut one's - according to one's cloth,*** sich nach der Decke strecken; (*coll.*) ***dust his -,*** ihn verprügeln; (*fig.*) ***turn one's -,*** den Mantel nach dem Winde hängen, abtrünnig werden; - ***and skirt,*** Jacke und Rock, das (Schneider)kostüm; ***wear the king's -,*** Soldat sein. **2.** *v.t.* überziehen; auftragen, anstreichen, überstreichen; belegen, bestreichen.

coated [ˈkoutid], **1.** *adj.* bedeckt, überzogen, bekleidet; (*Med.*) belegt (*as the tongue*). **2.** (*as suff.*) -röckig; (*of animals*) -haarig; ***black-- worker,*** der Kopfarbeiter. **coatee** [-ˈtiː], *s.* kurzes Damenjackett, die Jacke, Weste. **coat|-hanger,** *s.* der Kleiderbügel. **--hook,** *s.* der Kleiderhaken. **coating,** *s.* 1. der Überzug, Anstrich; Belag, Beschlag, die Schicht; - ***of plaster,*** der Bewurf, Verputz; 2. der Mantelstoff. **coat|-stand,** *s.* der Kleiderständer. **--tail,** *s.* der Rockschoß; ***hang on to his -s,*** sich an seinen Rockschoß klammern.

co-author [kouˈɔːθə], *s.* der Mitverfasser.

coax [kouks], **1.** *v.t.* beschwatzen, überreden; - ***him into (doing) a th.,*** ihm gut zureden, daß er etwas tut; ***he -ed money out of her,*** er schwatzte ihr Geld ab. **2.** *v.i.* schmeicheln.

[1]**cob** [kɔb], *s.* 1. (starkes) Reitpferd, das Halbblut; 2. männlicher Schwan; 3. der Maiskolben; 4. Klumpen.

[2]**cob,** *s.* (*Build.*) die Fachwerkfüllung, das Wellerbaumaterial.

cobalt [kəˈbɔ:lt, ˈkoubɔ:lt], *s.* der Kobalt. **cobalt|-blue,** *s.* das Kobaltblau, die Schmalte. **--glance,** *s. See* **cobaltine. cobaltic** [koˈbɔ:ltik], *adj.* Kobalt–, kobalthaltig. **cobaltine, cobaltite,** *s.* der Kobaltglanz.

cobble [kɔbl], *v.t.* flicken (*shoes*); (*fig.*) (zusammen)-pfuschen, zusammenschustern; *–d job,* das Flickwerk, gepfuschte Arbeit. **cobbler,** *s.* der (Flick)schuster, (*fig.*) Pfuscher, Stümper; *–'s wax,* das Schusterpech, Schuhmacherpech, Schnittwachs.

cobbles [kɔblz], *pl.* 1. das Kopfsteinpflaster; 2. die Stückkohle, Nußkohle. **cobblestone,** *s.* der Feldstein, Pflasterstein, Kopfstein.

co-belligerent [koubiˈlidʒərənt], **1.** *s.* Mitkriegführende(r). **2.** *adj.* mitkriegführend.

coble [kɔbl], *s.* flaches Fischerboot.

cob| loaf, *s.* runder Laib Brot. – **nut,** *s.* die Haselnuß.

cobra [ˈkoubrə], *s.* die Brillenschlange.

cobweb [ˈkɔbweb], *s.* das Spinn(en)gewebe, die Spinnwebe, der Spinnenfaden; feiner Faden, feines Gewebe; ***blow away the –s,*** sich (*Dat.*) einen klaren Kopf schaffen.

coca [ˈkoukə], *s.* (*Bot.*) die Koka. **coca-cola** [–ˈkoulə], *s.* das (Coca-)Cola.

cocain(e) [kəˈkein], *s.* das Kokain. **cocainism,** *s.* die Kokainvergiftung.

coccyx [ˈkɔksiks], *s.* (*Anat.*) das Steißbein.

cochineal [ˈkɔtʃini:l], *s.* die Koschenille(farbe).

cochlea [ˈkɔkliə], *s.* (*Anat.*) die Schnecke (*of the ear*).

[1]**cock** [kɔk], **1.** *s.* 1. (*of poultry*) der Hahn, (*of any bird*) das Männchen; – ***bird,*** das Vogelmännchen; ***--and-bull story,*** das Ammenmärchen, die Lügengeschichte; ***fighting –,*** der Kampfhahn; ***live like fighting –s,*** wie die Made im Speck leben; (*coll.*) ***that – won't fight,*** damit geht's nicht; – ***of the roost*** or ***walk,*** der Hahn im Korb; 2. (*of gun*) der Hahn, (*for water, gas etc.*) (Absperr)hahn; ***blow-off –,*** der Ablaßhahn; ***at full –,*** Hahn gespannt; ***at half –,*** Hahn in Ruh'; ***go off at half –,*** (*of gun*) vorzeitig losgehen, (*fig.*) voreilig *or* überstürzt handeln; 3. (*of hay etc.*) der (Heu)haufen, Schober; 4. (*coll.*) Kerl, Bursche; (*sl.*) (An)führer; (*coll.*) ***old –,*** alter Junge; 5. (*vulg.*) der Schwanz (= *penis*). **2.** *v.t.* in die Höhe richten, aufrichten (*also – up*); aufschichten, zusammenhäufen, schobern (*hay etc.*); (den Hahn) spannen (*of a gun*); – ***one's ears,*** die Ohren spitzen; – ***one's eye at him,*** ihm zublinzeln *or* zublinken; – ***one's hat,*** den Hut schief *or* keck aufsetzen; (*sl.*) – ***a snook,*** eine lange Nase machen.

cockade [kɔˈkeid], *s.* die Kokarde.

cock|-a-doodle-doo [kɔkədu:dlˈdu:], *a.* 1. (*call*) das Kikeriki; 2. (*nursery talk for* **cock,** 1.) der Kikeriki. **--a-hoop,** *adj.* frohlockend, triumphierend; anmaßend.

Cockaigne [kɔˈkein], *s.* das Schlaraffenland.

cockatoo [kɔkəˈtu:], *s.* der Kakadu.

cockatrice [ˈkɔkətri:s], *s.* der Basilisk.

cock-boat, *s.* das Beiboot.

cockchafer [ˈkɔktʃeifə], *s.* der Maikäfer.

cock-crow, *s.* der Hahnenschrei; (*fig.*) Tagesanbruch, die Morgendämmerung.

cocked [kɔkt], *adj.* aufgestülpt (*hat*), gespannt (*gun*); ***half-–,*** see ***at half cock;*** – ***hat,*** der Dreispitz, Dreimaster; (*coll.*) ***knock into a – hat,*** überrumpeln, total fertigmachen.

cocker [ˈkɔkə], *v.t.* verhätscheln, verzärteln.

Cocker, *s.* (*only in*) ***according to –,*** nach Adam Riese.

cockerel [ˈkɔkərəl], *s.* junger Hahn, das Hähnchen.

cocker spaniel, *s.* der Schnepfenhund.

cocket [ˈkɔkit], *s.* (*obs.*) das Zollsiegel.

cock|-eyed, *adj.* (*sl.*) schielend; (*fig.*) schief; schiefgeladen. **--fight,** *s.* der Hahnenkampf.

cockiness [ˈkɔkinis], *s.* (*sl*) die Keckheit, Frechheit; Hochnäsigkeit, Anmaßung.

cockle [kɔkl], **1.** *s.* (*Bot.*) die Kornrade; (*Mollusc.*) Herzmuschel; (*coll.*) ***warm the –s of my heart,*** mich im innersten Herzen erfreuen. **2.** *v.i.* sich runzeln, sich kräuseln. **3.** *v.t.* falten, runzeln, kräuseln. **cockle| boat,** *s. See* **cock-boat. -shell,** *s.* die Muschelschale, (*coll.*) kleines Boot, die Nußschale.

cock-loft, *s.* die Dachkammer.

cockney [ˈkɔkni], **1.** *s.* das Londoner Stadtkind; der Londoner Dialekt. **2.** *attrib. adj.* Londoner. **cockneyism,** *s.* Londoner Ausdruck.

cockpit [ˈkɔkpit], *s.* 1. (*Hist.*) der Hahnenkampfplatz; (*fig.*) Kampfplatz; 2. (*obs. Naut.*) Lazarettraum auf dem Orlogdeck; (*Naut.*) die Plicht; 3. (*Av.*) der Pilotensitz, die Pilotenkabine, Führerkabine, Kanzel.

cockroach [ˈkɔkroutʃ], *s.* die Küchenschabe, der Kakerlak.

cockscomb [ˈkɔkskoum], *s.* 1. der Hahnenkamm; 2. (*Bot.*) gemeiner Hahnenkamm, der Klappertopf; 3. *See* **coxcomb.**

cockshy [ˈkɔkʃai], *s.* (*sl.*) die Zielscheibe (*usu. fig.*).

cockspur [ˈkɔkspə:], *s.* (*Bot.*) gemeiner Hahnendorn.

cocksure [ˈkɔkʃuə], *adj.* (*coll.*) selbstsicher, vollkommen überzeugt. **cocksureness,** *s.* (übertriebene) Selbstsicherheit.

cocktail [ˈkɔkteil], *s.* 1. der Cocktail; 2. das Halbblut (mit gestutztem Schweif); 3. (*Ent.*) der Kurzflügler.

cock-tread, *s.* der Hahnentritt (*in egg*).

cocky [ˈkɔki], *adj.* (*sl.*) keck, frech; hochnäsig, unverschämt arrogant.

coco [ˈkoukou], *s.* die Kokospalme; Kokosnuß.

cocoa [ˈkoukou], *s.* der Kakao. **cocoa-butter,** *s.* die Kakaobutter.

coconut [ˈkoukənʌt], **1.** *s.* die Kokosnuß. **2.** *attrib. adj.* Kokos–.

cocoon [kəˈku:n], **1.** *s.* der Kokon, das Gespinst, (*of silkworms*) die Puppe. **2.** *v.i.* einen Kokon bilden, sich einspinnen.

cocotte [kɔˈkɔt], *s.* die Kokotte, Halbweltdame.

[1]**cod** [kɔd], *s.* der Kabeljau, Dorsch; ***dried –,*** der Stockfisch, Klippfisch.

[2]**cod,** *v.t., v.i.* (*sl.*) foppen, narren.

coda [ˈkoudə], *s.* (*Mus.*) der Schlußsatz.

coddle [kɔdl], *v.t.* verhätscheln, verzärteln, verwöhnen, verweichlichen; (*Cul.*) dünsten, dämpfen.

code [koud], **1.** *s.* 1. das Gesetzbuch; der Kodex, die Vorschriftensammlung; ***civil –,*** die Zivilprozeßordnung; ***commercial –,*** das Handelsgesetzbuch; ***criminal*** or ***penal –,*** das Strafgesetzbuch; – ***of honour,*** der Ehrenkodex; – ***of laws,*** das Gesetzbuch; 2. der Schlüssel, Kode, die Chiffre; Geheimschrift, Schlüsselschrift; – ***of signals,*** das Flaggensignalsystem. **2.** *v.t.* chiffrieren, kodieren, schlüsseln.

codeine [ˈkoudi:n], *s.* (*Chem.*) das Kodein.

code|-name, *s.* der Deckname. **--telegram,** *s.* das Schlüsseltelegramm.

codex [ˈkoudeks], *s.* (*pl.* **codices** [–disi:z]) alte Handschrift, der Kodex.

codfish [ˈkɔdfiʃ], *s.* (*esp. Am.*) see [1]**cod.**

codger [ˈkɔdʒə], *s.* (*coll.*) der Kauz, Sonderling.

codices [ˈkoudisi:z], *pl. See* **codex.**

codicil [ˈkɔdisil], *s.* das Kodizill, der Testamentsnachtrag; Anhang, Zusatz.

codification [koudifiˈkeiʃən], *s.* die Kodifizierung. **codify** [koudifai], *v.t.* kodifizieren, systematisch aufzeichnen.

codling [ˈkɔdliŋ], *s.* 1. junger Kabeljau; 2. (eine Art) Kochapfel.

cod|-liver oil, *s.* der Lebertran. **--piece,** *s.* (*Hist.*) der Hosenlatz.

co-driver [ˈkouˈdraivə], *s.* der Beifahrer.

co-ed [kouˈed], *s.* (*Am.*) (*coll.*) die Schülerin einer Gemeinschaftsschule.

co-editor [ˈkouˈeditə], *s.* der Mitherausgeber.

co-education [kouedju'keiʃən], *s.* gemeinsame Erziehung beider Geschlechter, die Koedukation.

coefficient [koui'fiʃənt], **1.** *adj.* mitwirkend. **2.** *s.* der Koeffizient; – ***of linear expansion,*** linearer Ausdehnungskoeffizient.

coeliac ['si:liæk], *adj.* Unterleibs–, Bauch–, abdominal.

coenobite ['senobait], *s.* der Klostermönch.

coequal [kou'i:kwəl], *adj.* gleichrangig, gleichgestellt; (*Theol.*) gleich.

coerce [kou'ə:s], *v.t.* zwingen, nötigen (***into,*** zu); erzwingen. **coercible,** *adj.* (er)zwingbar. **coercion** [–'ə:ʃən], *s.* der Zwang, die Nötigung; Zwangsgewalt; ***by*** –, durch Zwang, unter Druck, zwangsweise. **coercive,** *adj.* zwingend, Zwangs–; (*Phys.*) – ***force,*** die Koerzitivkraft; – ***measures,*** Zwangsmaßnahmen, Zwangsmaßregeln (*pl.*).

coessential [koui'senʃəl], *adj.* (*Theol.*) wesensgleich, gleichen Wesens.

coeternal [koui'tə:nl], *adj.* gleich ewig.

Coeur de Lion [kə:də'li:ɔ̃], *s.* Löwenherz (*n.*).

coeval [kou'i:vəl], *adj.* gleichzeitig, zeitgenössisch; gleichaltrig, gleichen Alters.

coexecutor [kouig'zekjutə], *s.* der Mitvollstrecker. **coexecutrix,** *s.* die Mitvollstreckerin.

coexist [kouig'zist], *v.i.* gleichzeitig vorhanden sein, nebeneinander bestehen, zusammenexistieren. **coexistence,** *s.* gleichzeitiges Bestehen *or* Dasein, die Koexistenz. **coexistent,** *adj.* gleichzeitig (vorhanden).

coextend [kouiks'tend], *v.i.* gleichen Umfang *or* gleiche Dauer haben, (sich) gleich weit ausdehnen (***with,*** wie). **coextension** [–'tenʃən], *s.* gleiche Ausdehnung *or* Dauer. **coextensive,** *adj.* von gleicher Dauer *or* Ausdehnung.

coffee ['kɔfi], *s.* der Kaffee. **coffee|-bar,** *s.* das Café. **--bean,** *s.* die Kaffeebohne. **--cup,** *s.* die Kaffeetasse. **--grinder,** *s.* die Kaffeemühle. **--grounds,** *s.* der Kaffeesatz. **--house,** *s.* das Kaffeehaus, Café. **--pot,** *s.* die Kaffeekanne. **--room,** *s.* das Frühstückszimmer (*in a hotel etc.*), die Kaffeestube. **--service,** *s.* das Kaffeegeschirr, Kaffeeservice. – **substitute,** *s.* der Kaffee-Ersatz.

coffer ['kɔfə], *s.* 1. der Kasten, die Kiste, Truhe; Kammer (*of locks*); 2. *See* **coffer-dam**; 3. (*Archit.*) Kassette, das Deckenfeld; 4. *pl.* die Schatzkammer, Schätze (*pl.*). **coffer-dam,** *s.* der Fangdamm, Kastendamm; Caisson.

coffin ['kɔfin], **1.** *s.* 1. der Sarg; 2. (*Typ.*) Karren. **2.** *v.t.* einsargen. **coffin|-bone,** *s.* das Hufbein. **--nail,** *s.* (*sl.*) schlechte Zigarette, der Sargnagel.

[1]**cog** [kɔg], **1.** *s.* der Kamm, Zahn; Mitnehmer, Hebedaumen; (*fig.*) (*of a p. in an organization*) das Rädchen. **2.** *v.t.* zahnen.

[2]**cog,** *v.t.* mit Blei beschweren (*dice*); – ***the dice,*** (beim Würfeln) falsch spielen.

cogency ['koudʒənsi], *s.* überzeugende *or* zwingende Kraft; die Überzeugungskraft, Beweiskraft, Triftigkeit. **cogent,** *adj.* zwingend, überzeugend, triftig, schlagend.

cogged [kɔgd], *adj.* gezahnt; *see* [1]**cog.**

cogitate ['kɔdʒiteit], **1.** *v.i.* (nach)sinnen; (nach)denken (***upon,*** über (*Acc.*)). **2.** *v.t.* (aus)denken, erdenken, ersinnen; überlegen, nachdenken über (*Acc.*). **cogitation** [–'teiʃən], *s.* das (Nach)denken, (Nach)sinnen, die Überlegung. **cogitative** [–tətiv], *adj.* (nach)sinnend, (nach)denkend; nachdenklich.

cognac ['kɔnjæk], *s.* der Kognak, (französischer) Weinbrand.

cognate ['kɔgneit], **1.** *adj.* verwandt; (*Gram.*) – ***accusative,*** inneres Objekt, das Object des Inhalts; – ***words,*** verwandte Wörter, Wörter gleichen Ursprungs. **2.** *s.* verwandtes Wort; (*Law*) Verwandte(r). **cognation** [–'neiʃən], *s.* (sprachliche) Verwandtschaft, (*Law*) die (Bluts)verwandtschaft.

cognition [kɔg'niʃən], *s.* die Erkenntnis, Wahrnehmung; das Erkennen, Erkennungsvermögen; (*obs.*) Wissen; (*Scots Law*) gerichtliches Erkenntnis. **cognitive** ['kɔgnitiv], *adj.* Erkenntnis–.

cognizable ['kɔ(g)nizəbl], *adj.* erkennbar, wahrnehmbar; (*Law*) der Gerichtsbarkeit unterworfen, gerichtlich verfolgbar. **cognizance,** *s.* die Kenntnis(nahme), Erkenntnis, Anerkennung; Erkenntnissphäre, der Wissensbereich; (*Law*) gerichtliches Erkenntnis, die Gerichtsbarkeit, Zuständigkeit; Anerkennung der Klage, das Eingeständnis des Tatbestands; (*Her.*) Abzeichen, Kennzeichen; ***take*** – ***of a th.,*** von einer S. Kenntnis nehmen, etwas zur Kenntnis nehmen. **cognizant,** *adj.* (*Law*) wissend; (*Phil.*) erkennend; zuständig; ***be*** – ***of a th.,*** über etwas unterrichtet sein, um etwas wissen.

cognomen [kɔg'noumen], *s.* der Zuname, Familienname; Beiname, Spitzname.

cognoscente [kɔnɔ'ʃenti], *s.* (*usu. pl.* **-ti**) der (Kunst)kenner.

cog|-rail, *s.* die Zahnschiene. **--railway,** *s.* die Zahnradbahn. **–wheel,** *s.* das Zahnrad, Kammrad.

cohabit [kou'hæbit], *v.i.* (als Eheleute) zusammenleben, in wilder Ehe leben. **cohabitation** [–'teiʃən], *s.* wilde Ehe, das Beisammenwohnen; der Beischlaf, Geschlechtsverkehr.

coheir [kou'ɛə], *s.* der Miterbe. **coheiress** [–ris], *s.* die Miterbin.

cohere [kou'hiə], *v.i.* 1. zusammenhängen (*also fig.*), zusammenhalten; (*fig.*) in logischem Zusammenhang stehen; 2. (*Rad.*) fritten. **coherence, coherency** [–rəns(i)], *s.* 1. der Zusammenhang, Zusammenhalt, die Kohärenz; logischer Zusammenhang, die Klarheit (*of ideas*); 2. (*Rad.*) Frittung. **coherent,** *adj.* zusammenhängend, kohärent; klar, verständlich, logisch (zusammenhängend). **coherer,** *s.* (*Rad.*) der Fritter, Kohärer.

cohesion [kou'hi:ʒən], *s.* die Kohäsion, Bindekraft; der Zusammenhalt; (*fig.*) Zusammenhang. **cohesive** [–ziv], *adj.* fest zusammenhängend *or* zusammenhaltend; Kohäsions–, Binde–. **cohesiveness,** *s.* die Bindekraft, Kohäsion(skraft).

cohort ['kouhɔ:t], *s.* (*Hist.*) die Kohorte; (*Poet.*) (Kriegs)schar.

coif [kɔif], *s.* die Kappe, Haube.

coiffeur [kwɑ'fə:], *s.* der Friseur. **coiffure** [–'fjuə], *s.* die Frisur, Haartracht; der Kopfputz.

coign [kɔin], *s.* (*obs.*) die Ecke; der Eckstein; – ***of vantage,*** vorteilhafte *or* günstige Stellung.

coil [kɔil], **1.** *s.* die Rolle; Locke, der Wickel (*of hair etc.*); die Spirale, Schlange (*of pipes*); (einzelne) Windung (*of rope*); (*Elec.*) Wicklung, Spule; ***induction*** –, die Induktionsspule; ***moving*** –, die Schwingspule; – ***of rope,*** die Rolle Tauwerk, der Taukranz; (*Rad.*) ***tuning*** –, die Abstimmspule. **2.** *v.t.* (*also* ***–up***) (auf)wickeln, aufrollen; aufschießen (*rope*), (auf)spulen (*on a reel*); spiralförmig winden (*springs etc.*); – ***o.s. up,*** sich zusammenrollen. **3.** *v.i.* sich winden; – (***a***)***round,*** sich winden *or* wickeln *or* schlingen um; – ***up,*** sich zusammenrollen (*as snakes*).

coil| antenna, *s.* die Spiralantenne. – **ignition,** *s.* die Abreißzündung. – **spring,** *s.* die Spiralfeder.

coin [kɔin], **1.** *s.* das Geldstück, die Münze; (*collect.*) das Metallgeld, gemünztes Geld; ***base*** or ***counterfeit*** –, falsche Münze; ***current*** –, gangbare Münze; ***small*** –, die Scheidemünze; ***pay him*** (***back***) ***in his own*** –, ihm mit gleicher Münze heimzahlen. **2.** *v.t.* Münzen schlagen; prägen, münzen; (*fig.*) ***be –ing money,*** schwer verdienen, Geld wie Heu verdienen; – ***a phrase,*** eine Redewendung erfinden. **coinage** [–idʒ], *s.* das Münzen, Prägen; (*collect.*) gemünztes Geld; Münzsystem; (*fig.*) die Prägung, Erfindung (*of expressions etc.*); Neuprägung, geprägtes Wort; ***decimal*** –, das Dezimalmünzsystem; (*fig.*) ***the*** – ***of his*** (***overheated***) ***brain,*** das Hirngespinst. **coin box,** *s.* (*coll.*) der Münzfernsprecher.

coincide [kouin'said], *v.i.* zusammentreffen, zusammenfallen; (*fig.*) übereinstimmen, sich decken, in Einklang stehen (***with,*** mit), (genau) entsprechen (*Dat.*). **coincidence** [–'insidəns], *s.* das Zusammentreffen; (*fig.*) Zusammenfallen, die Übereinstimmung; ***mere*** –, bloßer Zufall. **coincident**

[–'insidənt], *adj.* zusammentreffend, zusammenfallend; in Einklang stehend, sich deckend, (genau) übereinstimmend *or* entsprechend. **coincidental** [–'dentl], *adj.* zufällig.

coiner ['kɔinə], *s.* der Münzschläger, (Falsch)münzer; (*fig.*) Präger (*of words etc.*).

coir ['kɔiə], *s.* der Kokosbast, die Kokosfaser.

coition [kou'iʃən], **coitus** ['kouitəs], *s.* der Beischlaf, Geschlechtsverkehr, Koitus.

[1]**coke** [kouk], **1.** *s.* der (Gas)koks. **2.** *v.t.* verkoken (lassen).

[2]**coke,** *s.* (*sl.*) das Kokain, der Koks.

[3]**coke,** *s.* (*coll.*) *see* **coca-cola.**

col [kɔl], *s.* der Gebirgspaß, das Joch; (*Meteor.*) schmales Tief.

colander ['kʌlində], *s.* der Durchschlag, Seiher, die Seihe, das Sieb.

colchicum ['kɔlkikəm], *s.* (*Bot.*) die Herbstzeitlose.

colcothar ['kɔlkoθɑː], *s.* das Eisenrot, die Eisenmennige, englisches Rot, der Kolkothar, rotes Eisenoxyd.

cold [kould], **1.** *adj.* kalt, frostig; (*fig.*) kalt, gefühllos, teilnahmslos, gleichgültig, kühl, zurückhaltend (***towards***, gegen), nüchtern, ruhig, gelassen; (*Med.*) leidenschaftslos, gefühlskalt, frigid; ***in – blood,*** kaltblütig, kalten Blutes; ***as – as charity,*** hart wie Stein; ***– chisel,*** der Hartmeißel, Kaltschrottmeißel; ***– comfort,*** magerer *or* schwacher *or* schlechter Trost; ***– cream,*** die Hautcreme; (*Metall.*) ***– drawing,*** das Kaltstrecken; ***the – facts,*** die nackten Tatsachen; (*coll.*) ***have – feet,*** Angst haben; (*Meteor.*) ***– front,*** die Kaltluftfront, Einbruchsfront; ***as – as ice,*** eiskalt; ***– look,*** kalter *or* unfreundlicher Blick; ***– meat,*** kalte Küche, kalte Platte; ***– reason,*** nüchterner Verstand; ***– reception,*** frostiger Empfang; (*Hunt.*) ***– scent,*** kalte Fährte; ***give him the – shoulder,*** ihm die kalte Schulter zeigen, ihn kühl *or* geringschätzig behandeln; ***– snap,*** plötzlich eintretendes kaltes Wetter; ***– steel,*** blanke Waffe; ***– storage,*** die Kühlraumlagerung, Kaltlagerung; (*fig.*) ***put into – storage,*** auf die lange Bank schieben; ***– store,*** die Kühlhalle, das Kühlhaus, der Kühlraum; ***– war,*** kalter Krieg; (*fig., coll.*) ***throw – water on,*** dämpfen, abkühlen; ***– working,*** die Kaltverarbeitung; ***I am –,*** mich friert, mir ist kalt; (*coll.*) ***that leaves me –,*** das läßt mich kalt; ***my blood runs –,*** mich gruselt's; ***it makes my blood run –,*** es läßt mein Blut erstarren. **2.** *s.* 1. die Kälte, der Frost; ***keep out the –,*** die Kälte abhalten *or* vertreiben; (*fig.*) ***leave him out in the –,*** ihn kaltstellen *or* ignorieren; 2. (*Med.*) die Erkältung, der Schnupfen; ***catch (a) –,*** sich erkälten, sich (*Dat.*) einen Schnupfen holen; ***have a (bad*** or ***severe) – (in the head),*** sich (stark) erkältet haben, einen (heftigen) Schnupfen haben.

cold|-blooded, *adj.* (*Zool.*) wechselwarm, kaltblütig, (*coll. of a p.*) kälteempfindlich; (*fig.*) kaltblütig, gefühllos. **--drawn,** *adj.* (*Tech.*) kaltgezogen, kaltgestreckt. **--hearted,** *adj.* kaltherzig, hartherzig. **coldish,** *adj.* ziemlich kalt, kühl. **coldness,** *s.* die Kälte (*also fig.*). **cold|-short,** *adj.* (*Tech.*) kaltbrüchig, spröde. **--shoulder,** *v.t.* die kalte Schulter zeigen (*Dat.*), kaltstellen, ignorieren.

cole [koul], *s.* (eine Art) Kohl; *see* **cole|-seed, --wort.**

coleoptera [kɔli'ɔptərə], *pl.* Käfer (*pl.*). **coleopterous,** *adj.* Käfer–, käferartig.

cole|-seed, *s.* der Raps, Rübsen; Rübsamen. **--wort,** *s.* der Grünkohl.

colic ['kɔlik], *s.* der Darmkatarrh, die Kolik.

coliseum, *see* **colosseum.**

colitis [ko'laitis], *s.* der Dickdarmkatarrh, die Kolitis.

collaborate [kə'læbəreit], *v.i.* mitwirken, mitarbeiten, zusammenarbeiten; (*Pol.*) mit dem Feind zusammenarbeiten. **collaboration** [–'reiʃən], *s.* die Mitwirkung, Mitarbeit, Zusammenarbeit; (*Pol.*) Kollaboration; ***in – with,*** gemeinsam mit. **collaborator,** *s.* der Mitarbeiter, Mitwirkende(r); (*Pol.*) Kollaborator, Kollaborateur.

collage [kɔ'lɑːʒ], *s.* die Collage.

collapse [kə'læps], **1.** *s.* das Zusammenfallen, der Einsturz (*of buildings etc.*), (*fig.*) Zusammenbruch, das Scheitern, die Vernichtung (*of hopes*), (*Med.*) der Kraftverfall, Kollaps; (*Comm.*) Sturz, Krach; ***nervous –,*** der Nervenzusammenbruch; ***– of a bank,*** der Bankkrach; ***– of a lung,*** die Atelektase; ***– of prices,*** der Preissturz. **2.** *v.i.* zusammenfallen, einfallen, einstürzen; (*as a table, seat etc.*) sich zusammenklappen lassen, zusammenlegbar sein; (*Med.*) zusammenbrechen, einen Kollaps erleiden; (*fig.*) zusammenbrechen, scheitern, zu Fall kommen, vereitelt werden, ins Wasser fallen. **3.** *v.t.* zusammenklappen (lassen), zusammenlegen. **collapsible,** *adj.* zusammenlegbar, zusammenklappbar, Klapp–, Falt–; ***– boat,*** das Faltboot.

collar ['kɔlə], **1.** *s.* der Kragen, (*for dog*) das Halsband, (*of harness*) Kum(me)t; (*of pearls etc.*) Kollier; (*Her.*) die Halskette, Ordenskette; (*of animals*) der Halskragen, Halsstreifen; (*Tech.*) Ring, Bund, Reif(en), Flansch, die Manschette, Hülse, Zwinge, Schelle; ***stand-up –,*** der Stehkragen; ***turn-down –,*** der Umlegekragen; (*coll.*) ***get hot under the –,*** aufgeregt *or* verärgert werden, sich aufregen *or* ärgern. **2.** *v.t.* 1. beim Kragen fassen *or* packen, (*coll.*) fassen, packen, festnehmen (*a p.*), (*sl.*) erwischen, sich aneignen (*a th.*); 2. (*Cul.*) zusammenrollen (*meat*).

collar|-beam, *s.* (*Archit.*) der Querbalken. **--bone,** *s.* (*Anat.*) das Schlüsselbein. **--button,** *s.* (*Am.*) *see* **--stud. collaret,** *s.* (*Hist.*) die Halsrüstung, Halsberge; (kleiner) Spitzenkragen. **collar-stud,** *s.* der Kragenknopf.

collate [kə'leit], *v.t.* kollationieren (*also Typ.*), kritisch vergleichen (*texts*); (*Eccl.*) einsetzen (*to*, in (*Acc.*)).

collateral [kə'lætərəl], **1.** *adj.* seitlich, Seiten–, kollateral; begleitend, Neben–, untergeordnet, zusätzlich, indirekt; in der Seitenlinie verwandt; gleichzeitig (auftretend); (*Bot.*) nebenständig; ***– circumstances,*** Nebenumstände, Begleitumstände (*pl.*); ***– descent,*** die Abstammung von einer Seitenlinie; ***– loan,*** der Lombardkredit, das Lombarddarlehen; ***– security,*** die Nebensicherheit, Nebenbürgschaft; Sicherstellung. **2.** *s.* 1. Verwandte(r) einer Nebenlinie; 2. (*Comm.*) *see* ***– security.***

collation [kə'leiʃən], *s.* 1. die Textvergleichung; bibliographische Beschreibung; 2. (*Eccl.*) die Einsetzung (*to a living*), Verleihung einer Pfründe; 3. der Imbiß, die Kollation. **collator,** *s.* der Textvergleicher; (*Eccl.*) (Pfründen)verleiher, Patron.

colleague ['kɔliːg], *s.* der Kollege (die Kollegin), Amtsgenosse (–genossin), Mitarbeiter(in).

[1]**collect** [kə'lekt], **1.** *v.t.* versammeln; (ein)sammeln; (*money*) (ein)kassieren, eintreiben, (*taxes*) einziehen, erheben; (*coll.*) abholen; ***– one's thoughts,*** seine Gedanken zusammennehmen; ***– o.s.,*** sich zusammennehmen *or* sammeln *or* fassen. **2.** *v.i.* sich (ver)sammeln; sich ansammeln *or* (an)häufen.

[2]**collect** ['kɔlekt], *s.* kurzes (Kirchen)gebet, die Kollekte.

collected [kə'lektid], *adj.* gesammelt, (*fig.*) gefaßt. **collectedness,** *s.* die Gefaßtheit, Fassung, Sammlung. **collecting, 1.** *s.* das Sammeln, (*Comm.*) die (Ein)kassierung, Eintreibung, Einziehung, das Inkasso. **2.** *adj.* Sammel–.

collection [kə'lekʃən], *s.* 1. das (Ein)sammeln; 2. die Sammlung; (*Comm.*) (*of goods*) Auswahl, Kollektion, das Sortiment; die Ansammlung, Anhäufung; ***stamp –,*** die Briefmarkensammlung; ***the Paris spring –s,*** die Pariser Frühjahrskollektionen; ***a disgusting – of all sorts of junk,*** eine ekelhafte Ansammlung allerhand Krimskrams; 2. (*fig.*) *see* **collectedness**; 3. die Leerung (des Briefkastens); ***ready for –,*** zum Abholen bereit.

collective [kə'lektiv], **1.** *adj.* gesammelt, zusammengefaßt, vereint; gesamt, gemeinsam; kollektiv, Gesamt–, Kollektiv–, Sammel–, Gemeinschafts–; ***– agreement*** der Kollektivvertrag (über Lohnsätze und Arbeitsbedingungen); ***– bargaining,*** Tarifverhandlungen (zwischen Arbeitgebern und

Gewerkschaften) (*pl.*); – ***farm,*** die Kolchose (*of U.S.S.R.*); – ***noun,*** der Sammelname, das Sammelwort, Kollektivum; – ***ownership,*** gemeinsamer Besitz. **2.** *s.* **1.** *See* – ***noun***; 2. *See* – ***farm***; die Produktionsgemeinschaft, das Kollektiv (*in U.S.S.R.*).

collector [kəˈlektə], *s.* **1.** der Sammler; –***'s item*** or ***piece,*** das Sammlerstück; 2. (*Comm.*) der Einsammler, Kassierer, Inkassobeamte(r); ***tax*** –, der Steuereinnehmer; ***ticket*** –, der Schaffner; 3. (*Elec.*) der (Strom)abnehmer, Schleifbügel, Kollektor, die Sammelscheibe.

colleen [ˈkɔli:n], *s.* (*Irish*) das Mädchen.

college [ˈkɔlidʒ], *s.* höhere Schule, die Akademie, Hochschule, Universität; das College (*Oxford and Cambridge*); (*Eccl.*) Kollegium; – ***of cardinals,*** das Kardinalkollegium; ***commercial*** –, die Handelshochschule; – ***dues,*** Studiengebühren; ***go to*** –, die Universität beziehen; ***military*** –, die Kadettenanstalt; ***naval*** –, die Marineakademie; ***training*** –, die Lehrerbildungsanstalt. **collegian** [kəˈli:dʒiən], *s.* der Student. **collegiate** [–iit], *adj.* studentisch, akademisch, Universitäts–, Studenten–; – ***church,*** die Stiftskirche; – ***school,*** die Stiftsschule, Stiftung.

collide [kəˈlaid], *v.i.* zusammenstoßen (*also fig.*), stoßen, rennen (***with,*** gegen); (*fig.*) im Widerspruch stehen (zu), kollidieren (mit), sich überschneiden (*as interests*).

collie [ˈkɔli], *s.* schottischer Schäferhund.

collier [ˈkɔliə], *s.* **1.** der Kohlenarbeiter, Grubenarbeiter, Bergmann; 2. das Kohlenschiff. **colliery,** *s.* das Kohlenbergwerk, die Kohlengrube, Zeche.

colligate [ˈkɔligeit], *v.t.* vereinigen, (logisch) verbinden.

collimation [kɔliˈmeiʃən], *s.* (*Astr., Opt.*) die Kollimation; das Einstellen, Visieren; ***line of*** –, die Sehlinie, optische Achse. **collimator** [ˈkɔlimeitə], *s.* der Kollimator, das Richtglas, die Visiervorrichtung.

collision [keˈliʒən], *s.* der Zusammenstoß, die Karambolage; (*fig.*) der Widerspruch, Widerstreit, Konflikt; die Überschneidung (*of interests*); (*fig.*) ***come into – with,*** in Konflikt geraten mit.

collocate [ˈkɔlokeit], *v.t.* (zusammen)stellen, (an)ordnen. **collocation** [–ˈkeiʃən], *s.* die (Zusammen)stellung, (An)ordnung; (*fig.*) (Rede)wendung.

collocutor [ˈkɔləkju:tə], *s.* der Gesprächsteilnehmer.

collodion [kəˈloudiən], *s.* (*Chem.*) das Kollodium.

collogue [kəˈloug], *v.i.* (*coll.*) eine vertrauliche Besprechung halten, sich heimlich besprechen.

colloid [ˈkɔlɔid], *s.* (*Chem.*) das Kolloid.

collop [ˈkɔləp], *s.* die Fleischschnitte.

colloquial [kəˈloukwiəl], *adj.* Umgangs–, Alltags–, umgangssprachlich, familiär. **colloquialism,** *s.* der Ausdruck der Umgangssprache, familiärer Ausdruck. **colloquium,** *s.* das Kolloquium, wissenschaftliche Erörterung; mündliche Hochschulprüfung. **colloquy** [ˈkɔləkwi], *s.* formelle Besprechung, das Gespräch.

collotype [ˈkɔlətaip], *s.* der Lichtdruck, das Lichtdruckverfahren.

collusion [kəˈlu:ʒən], *s.* betrügerisches Einverständnis, vorherige Abmachung. **collusive** [–siv], *adj.* heimlich verabredet, abgekartet.

collywobbles [ˈkɔliwɔblz], *s.* (*coll.*) das Bauchweh.

colocynth [ˈkɔlosinθ], *s.* (*Bot.*) der Koloquinte.

Cologne [kəˈloun], *s.* Köln (*n.*); – ***cathedral,*** der Kölner Dom; ***eau de*** –, das Kölnischwasser.

[1]**colon** [ˈkoulən], *s.* (*Typ.*) der Doppelpunkt, das Kolon.

[2]**colon,** *s.* (*Anat.*) der Grimmdarm, Dickdarm.

colonel [kə:nl], *s.* der Oberst. **colonelcy** [–si], *s.* die Oberstenstelle; der Oberstenrang.

colonial [kəˈlounjəl], **1.** *adj.* Kolonial–, kolonial. **2.** *s.* der Bewohner einer Kolonie. **colonialism,** *s.* die Kolonialpolitik. **colonist** [ˈkɔlənist], *s.* der Ansiedler, Kolonist. **colonization** [kɔlənaiˈzeiʃən], *s.* die Kolonisierung, Kolonisation, Besiedlung. **colonize** [ˈkɔlənaiz], **1.** *v.t.* kolonisieren, besiedeln (*territory*), ansiedeln (*people*). **2.** *v.i.* eine Kolonie gründen; sich ansiedeln. **colonizer,** *s.* der (An)siedler, Besiedler.

colonnade [kɔləˈneid], *s.* (*Archit.*) der Säulengang, die Säulenhalle; Baumreihe, Allee (*of trees*).

colony [ˈkɔləni], *s.* die Kolonie (*also Zool.*), das Kolonialgebiet; die Siedlung; ***penal*** –, die Strafkolonie; – ***of artists,*** die Künstlerkolonie.

colophon [ˈkɔləfən], *s.* (*Typ.*) der Kolophon.

colophony [koˈlɔfəni], *s.* das Kolophonium, Geigenharz.

color, (*Am.*) *see* **colour.**

coloration [kʌləˈreiʃən], *s.* das Färben; die Färbung (*of animals, plants etc.*); (*Paint.*) Farbengebung, Farbenverteilung, das , Kolorit. **coloratura** [–rəˈtjuərə], *s.* (*Mus.*) die Koloratur. **colorific** [–ˈrifik], *adj.* färbend, farbgebend; farbenfreudig; Farb–, Farben–. **colorimeter** [–ˈrimitə], *s.* der Farbenmesser.

colossal [kəˈlɔsəl], *adj.* riesenhaft, riesig, Riesen–, (*coll.*) riesig, enorm, ungeheuer, kolossal.

colosseum [kɔləˈsiəm], *s.* (*Rome*) das Kolosseum; Amphitheater, Stadion, die Sporthalle.

Colossians [kəˈlɔʃəns], *pl.* (*B.*) Kolosser (*pl.*); ***Epistle to the*** –, der Kolosserbrief.

colossus [kəˈlɔsəs], *s.* der Riese, Koloß; die Riesengestalt.

colour [ˈkʌlə], **1.** *s.* die Farbe; Anstrichfarbe; der Farbstoff; die Färbung, das Kolorit; (gesunde) Gesichtsfarbe, die (Gesichts)röte; (dunkle) Hautfarbe; (*Mus.*) Tonfärbung, Klangfarbe; der Anstrich, Anschein; Charakter, Ton, die Stimmung, Färbung, Schattierung; der Deckmantel, Vorwand; *pl.* (*Mil.*) die Fahne, Standarte; (*Naut.*) Flagge; (*Spt.*) Auszeichnung als Mannschaftsmitglied; ***complementary*** –, die Gegenfarbe, Ergänzungsfarbe; ***composite –s,*** Mischfarben (*pl.*); ***fast*** –, echte *or* beständige Farbe; ***fugitive*** –, unechte *or* unbeständige Farbe; ***local*** –, das Lokalkolorit; ***national –s,*** Nationalfarben (*pl.*); ***primary –s,*** Grundfarben (*pl.*); ***priming*** –, die Grundierfarbe; ***prismatic –s,*** Prismenfarben (*pl.*); ***secondary –s,*** Mischfarben (*pl.*); ***coat of*** –, der Farbenauftrag; ***play of*** –, das Farbenspiel; ***theory of –s,*** die Farbenlehre; ***trooping (of) the*** –, die Fahnenparade; ***change*** –, (*of a th.*) verfärben, die Farbe wechseln; (*of a p.*) erröten; erblassen; (*Spt.*) ***get one's –s,*** Mitglied der ersten Mannschaft werden; ***give*** or ***lend – to a th.,*** einer S. den Anschein der Wahrscheinlichkeit geben; ***have a*** –, blühend aussehen; ***join the –s,*** Soldat werden; (*fig.*) ***nail one's –s to the mast, stick to one's –s,*** hartnäckig bei seinem Standpunkt bleiben; (*fig.*) ***come out in one's true –s*** or ***show one's –s,*** sich im wahren Lichte zeigen, sein wahres Gesicht zeigen, Farbe bekennen; ***serve with the –s,*** im Heere dienen; (*coll.*) ***be*** or ***feel off*** –, unpäßlich sein, nicht auf der Höhe sein, sich nicht wohl fühlen; ***paint him in his true –s,*** ihn zeigen wie er ist; ***under false –s,*** unter falscher Flagge (*also fig.*); (*fig.*) ***come off with flying –s,*** den Sieg davontragen. **2.** *v.t.* färben, kolorieren, anstreichen, bemalen; (*fig.*) einen Anstrich geben (*Dat.*), beschönigen, bemänteln, übertreiben, entstellen; (*fig.*) beeinflussen, sich abfärben auf (*Acc.*). **3.** *v.i.* erröten, Farbe annehmen; ***she –ed up to the eyes,*** sie wurde über und über rot.

colourable [ˈkʌlərəbl], *adj.* plausibel, annehmbar; fingiert, vorgeblich, mutmaßlich. **colour| bar,** *s.* die Rassenschranke, Rassendiskriminierung. **--bearer,** *s.* der Fahnenträger. **--blind,** *adj.* farbenblind. **--box,** *s.* der Malkasten, Farbenkasten.

coloured [ˈkʌləd], **1.** *adj.* gefärbt, koloriert; bunt, farbig; (*fig.*) beschönigt; – ***crayon,*** die Farbkreide; – ***paper,*** das Buntpapier; – ***pencil,*** der Farbstift, Buntstift; – ***print,*** der Farben(kunst)druck. **2.** *s.* Farbige(r).

colour|-fast, *adj.* farbecht. – **filter,** *s.* (*Phot.*) das Farbfilter. **colourful,** *adj.* farbenreich, farbenprächtig, farbenfreudig, (*fig.*) farbig, lebhaft.

colouring, *s.* das Färben; der Farbton, die Färbung; Gesichtsfarbe; (*Paint.*) Farb(en)gebung, das Kolorit; – ***agent,*** das Farbmittel; – ***matter,*** der Farbstoff. **colourist,** *s.* der Meister der Farbgebung. **colourless,** *adj.* farblos; (*fig.*) matt, nichtssagend, neutral. **colour| photography,** *s.* die Farbphotographie. – **printing,** *s.* der Buntdruck, Farbendruck. – **scheme,** *s.* die Farbgebung. – **sergeant,** *s.* (*Mil.*) der Oberfeldwebel. – **television,** *s.* das Farbfernsehen.

colportage [ˈkɔlpɔːtidʒ], *s.* der Hausierhandel (mit Büchern), die Kolportage. **colporteur** [–əː], *s.* der (Bibel)hausierer.

colt [koult], *s.* das Füllen, Fohlen; (*fig.*) der Neuling, Grünschnabel.

colter, *see* **coulter.**

coltish [ˈkoultiʃ], *adj.* übermütig, wild, ausgelassen. **coltsfoot,** *s.* (*Bot.*) der Huflattich.

columbine [ˈkɔləmbain], *s.* (*Bot.*) die Akelei.

column [ˈkɔləm], *s.* die Säule (*also smoke etc.*), der Pfeiler, Träger, Pfosten; (*Mil.*) die Kolonne (*also of figures*); (*Typ.*) Spalte, Kolumne; Rubrik (*of a ledger*); ***advertisement*** –, die Anschlagsäule, Litfaßsäule; – ***of figures,*** die Zahlenkolonne; ***spinal*** or ***vertebral*** –, die Wirbelsäule, der Rückgrat. **columnar** [kɔˈlʌmnə], *adj.* säulenförmig, Säulen–. **columnist** [–nist], *s.* der Feuilletonist, Kolumnist, (*Am.*) Leitartikelschreiber.

colure [kəˈljuə], *s.* (*Astr.*) der Deklinationskreis, Kolur.

colza [ˈkɔlzə], *s.* der Raps.

[1]**coma** [ˈkoumə], *s.* (*Bot.*) das Haarbüschel, der Schopf, die Federkrone; (*Astr.*) Koma, der Schweif.

[2]**coma,** *s.* (*Med.*) das Koma; der Dämmerzustand, die Bewußtlosigkeit. **comatose,** *adj.* (*Med.*) komatös.

comb [koum], **1.** *s.* 1. der Kamm, Striegel, (*Weav.*) die Hechel; 2. Honigwabe; 3. der Kamm (*of a cock*). **2.** *v.t.* kämmen; striegeln (*horse*); krempeln (*wool*), hecheln (*flax*); (*fig.*) absuchen (*the ground*); – ***one's hair,*** sich kämmen; – ***out,*** durchkämmen; sieben, sichten, aussondern. **3.** *v.i.* sich brechen, sich überstürzen (*of waves*).

combat [ˈkɔmbæt], **1.** *s.* der Kampf, das Gefecht; ***close*** –, der Nahkampf; ***hand-to-hand*** –, das Handgemenge, der Nahkampf; ***single*** –, der Zweikampf. **2.** *v.t.* kämpfen gegen, bekämpfen. **combatant** [–bətənt], *s.* der Kämpfer, Kämpfende(r). **combative,** *adj.* kampfbereit, kampflustig, rauflustig.

combe, *see* **coomb.**

comber [ˈkoumə], *s.* 1. der Wollkämmer, Krempler; Flachshechler; 2. (*of sea*) Brecher, die Sturzwelle.

combination [kɔmbiˈneiʃən], *s.* 1. die Vereinigung, Verknüpfung, Verbindung, Zusammenstellung; das Bündnis, Abkommen, der Zusammenschluß; (*Math.*) die Kombination, (*Spt.*) das Zusammenspiel; ***chemical*** –, chemische Verbindung; 2. das Schlüsselwort, die Buchstabenkombination (*of a lock*); – ***lock,*** das Vexierschloß; 3. das Motorrad mit Beiwagen; *pl.* die Hemdhose.

combine, 1. [kəmˈbain], *v.t.* verbinden, (in sich) vereinigen, zusammensetzen, kombinieren. **2.** [–bain], *v.i.* (*Chem.*) sich verbinden; sich vereinigen, eine Einheit bilden; sich zusammenschließen, sich verbünden, einen Bund schließen. **3.** [ˈkɔmbain], *s.* 1. (*Comm.*) der Verband, Ring, Trust, das Kartell; 2. – ***harvester,*** der Mähdrescher. **combined** [kəmˈbaind], *adj.* vereinigt; gemeinsam, gemeinschaftlich; verbündet; (*Chem., Mil.*) verbunden; – ***arms,*** verbundene Waffen; (*Mil.*) – ***operation,*** die Operation verbundener Waffen; – ***transmitter and receiver,*** der Senderempfänger.

combings [ˈkoumiŋs], *pl.* ausgekämmte Haare *or* Fasern.

combustibility [kəmbʌstiˈbiliti], *s.* die (Ver)brennbarkeit, Entzündlichkeit. **combustible** [kəmˈbʌstibl], *adj.* (ver)brennbar, entzündlich, feuergefährlich; (*fig.*) leicht erregbar; – ***matter,*** der Zündstoff. **combustibles,** *pl.* der Brennstoff. **combustion** [–ˈbʌstʃən], *s.* die Verbrennung, Entzündung; (***internal-***)– ***engine,*** der Verbrennungsmotor; ***spontaneous*** –, die Selbstentzündung; – ***chamber,*** der Verbrennungsraum, die Brennkammer.

come [kʌm], **1.** *irr.v.i.* kommen; gelangen, geraten, sich erstrecken, reichen; herankommen, herbeikommen; erscheinen, auftreten, sich ereignen, sich zutragen, geschehen; entstehen, zum Vorschein kommen, sich herausstellen, sich erweisen; (*before inf.*) sich bilden *or* entwickeln, werden; herkommen, herrühren, abstammen; (*coll.*) ***it –s expensive,*** es wird teuer; ***I have*** –, ich bin gekommen; ***how –s it to be yours?*** wie sind Sie dazu gekommen? (*coll.*) ***how –s it that . . .?*** wie ist es möglich, daß . . .? (*sl.*) ***how –?*** wieso? (*coll.*) – ***a cropper,*** zu Fall kommen (*also fig.*); ***the malt –s,*** das Malz keimt; ***there is cheese to*** –, es kommt noch Käse; ***for a year to*** –, noch ein Jahr, ein weiteres Jahr; ***the life to*** –, künftiges Leben; ***Christmas –s but once a year,*** es ist nicht alle Tage Weihnachten; (*coll.*) ***a year – Christmas,*** Weihnachten in einem Jahr; (*coll.*) ***he is as stupid as they*** –, er ist so dumm wie nur möglich; ***someone is coming,*** es kommt jemand; ***it –s as a shock,*** es ist ein schwerer Schlag (*to,* für); – ***what may,*** komme, was da wolle; es mag kommen, was da will; ***the dress –s*** (***to***) ***below her knees,*** das Kleid reicht ihr bis über die Knie; (*coll.*) ***take it as it –s,*** wie's kommt, wird's genommen; ***nothing has – my way,*** ich habe nichts gefunden, mir ist nichts begegnet.

(a) (*as int.*) bitte! nun! – –! (*encouragement*) na komm schon! versuch's doch mal! (*warning*) sachte! nanu! – ***now!*** ach gar! geh' doch!

(b) (*with advs.*) – ***about,*** sich ereignen, zustandekommen, passieren; (*of wind*) sich drehen, umspringen; – ***after,*** nachkommen, (nach)folgen (*Dat.*); – ***along,*** mitkommen; (*coll.*) – ***along nicely,*** Fortschritte machen, gut vorwärtskommen; (*coll.*) – ***along!*** beeile dich! (*Naut.*) – ***alongside,*** längsseit anlegen; – ***apart,*** auseinanderfallen; – ***away,*** (*of a p.*) weggehen; (*of a th.*) abgehen, sich loslösen; – ***away empty-handed,*** mit leeren Händen ausgehen; – ***back,*** zurückkommen, wiederkehren; (*coll.*) wieder einfallen (*to, Dat.*); – ***by,*** vorbeikommen, vorübergehen; (*sl.*) – ***clean,*** mit der Wahrheit herausrücken; – ***down,*** herunterkommen, herabkommen, (*of prices*) fallen, sich senken, heruntergehen; – ***down a peg,*** mildere Saiten aufziehen, kleinlaut werden; ***he has – down in the world,*** er hat bessere Tage gesehen; (*coll.*) – ***down on him,*** ihm Vorwürfe machen, über ihn herfallen; (*coll.*) – ***down on him like a ton of bricks,*** ihn gehörig 'runterputzen; (*sl.*) – ***down handsomely,*** sich nicht lumpen lassen; – ***forth,*** hervorkommen, herauskommen; – ***forward,*** vorwärtskommen, hervorkommen, hervortreten, auftreten, sich melden; – ***home,*** nach Hause kommen; (*fig.*) ***it came home to him at last,*** es leuchtete ihm endlich ein, es wurde ihm endlich nahegebracht; (*coll.*) – ***home to roost,*** sich endlich rächen; – ***in,*** hereinkommen, eintreten, (*of trains etc.*) eintreffen, einlaufen, (*of orders*) eingehen, (*Spt.*) durchs Ziel gehen, (*of fashions*) aufkommen; ***that will – in handy*** or ***useful,*** das kann man noch gut gebrauchen; (*coll.*) ***where do I – in?*** wo bleibe ich? was ist mit mir? ***where does the joke – in?*** wo steckt der Witz? – ***in for,*** sich (*Dat.*) zuziehen, erhalten, bekommen; – ***in for a good thrashing,*** eine Tracht Prügel abkriegen, sich (*Dat.*) eine Tracht Prügel aufhalsen; – ***loose,*** sich lösen, locker werden; – ***near,*** (*of a p.*) nahe *or* näher kommen, sich nähern (*to, Dat.*), (*of a th.*) Ähnlichkeit haben (mit), ähnlich sein (*Dat.*), nahekommen (*Dat.*), beinahe erreichen; ***I came near*** (***to***) ***breaking my neck,*** ich hätte mir beinahe das Genick gebrochen; – ***next,*** darauf folgen (*Dat.*); – ***off,*** sich (los)lösen, abgehen, abfallen; (*coll.*) stattfinden, erfolgen, vor sich gehen; (*of plays*) abgesetzt werden; – ***off creditably,*** mit Ehren hervorgehen; ***the lid won't – off,*** der Deckel will nicht ab; (*coll.*) – ***off*** (***well***), gut abschneiden; (*coll.*) – ***off a loser,*** den kürzeren ziehen;

(*coll.*) *it didn't – off*, es glückte nicht; (*sl.*) – *off it!* hör damit auf! – *on*, herankommen, heranrücken, vorrücken; (*fig.*) vorwärtskommen, Fortschritte machen, (*of plants etc.*) wachsen, gedeihen, (*as night, winter etc.*) beginnen, anbrechen, hereinbrechen, eintreten, heraufziehen; – *on!* komm nur her! komm schon! (*fig.*) nur weiter! vorwärts! los! – *out*, herauskommen, hervorkommen, (*of publications*) herauskommen, erscheinen, veröffentlicht werden, (*of news, truth etc.*) bekanntwerden, an den Tag kommen, ruchbar werden, (*as puzzles*) aufgehen, (*as hair*) ausgehen, ausfallen, (*as stains*) herausgehen, (*as a débutante*) in die Gesellschaft eingeführt werden, debütieren; (*coll.*) – *out against*, sich offen erklären gegen; – *out in spots*, einen Ausschlag bekommen, an einem Ausschlag leiden; – *out on strike*, streiken, in Streik treten; – *out into the open*, ins Freie treten, (*fig.*) seine Karten aufdecken, vor die Öffentlichkeit treten (*with*, mit); – *out of*, herauskommen aus, (*fig.*) hervorgehen aus; *he came out with his good news*, er platzte mit seiner guten Nachricht heraus; – *over*, herüberkommen; (*fig.*) übertreten, umschwenken; (*coll.*) – *over faint*, einen Schwächeanfall bekommen; – *round*, vorbeikommen, her(über)kommen; (*Med.*) wieder zum Bewußtsein kommen, wieder zu sich kommen; (*Naut.*) sich wenden *or* drehen, (*of wind*) umspringen; (*as anniversaries etc.*) wiederkehren; (*in one's opinions*) sich anders *or* sich eines Besseren besinnen, einlenken, (*to a point of view*) sich bekehren; – *short of*, zurückbleiben hinter, nachstehen (*Dat.*), nicht gleichkommen (*Dat.*), nicht erreichen; – *through*, durchkommen; (*coll.*) Erfolg haben, das Ziel erreichen; – *to*, see – *round* (*Med.*); – *true*, in Erfüllung gehen, zur Wirklichkeit werden, sich verwirklichen; – *undone*, aufgehen (*of button, knot*); (*sl.*) – *unstuck*, Mißerfolg haben; – *up*, heraufkommen, (*of plants*) aufgehen, keimen, (*fig.*) (*of a question*) zur Sprache kommen, aufgeworfen *or* aufgerollt werden; (*as lottery number*) herauskommen; (*coll.*) die Universität beziehen; – *up against*, stoßen auf (*Acc.*); – *up for discussion*, zur Diskussion *or* auf die Tagesordnung kommen; – *up to*, herantreten an (*Acc.*), zutreten auf (*Acc.*), (*fig.*) erreichen, reichen bis an (*Acc.*) *or* zu, gleichkommen (*Dat.*); – *up to expectations*, den Erwartungen entsprechen; (*coll.*) – *up to the mark*, den Ansprüchen genügen; (*coll.*) – *up smiling*, lächelnd überstehen.

(c) (*with preps.*) – *across*, zufällig finden (*a th.*) *or* treffen (*a p.*), stoßen auf (*Acc.*); – *after*, (*a p.*) (nach)folgen (*Dat.*), hergehen hinter (*Dat.*), nachkommen (*Dat.*), (*a th.*) kommen um abzuholen; – *at*, losgehen auf (*Acc.*); gewinnen, erreichen, gelangen zu; – *by*, bekommen, erlangen, gelangen zu; *how did you – by that?* wie kommen Sie dazu? wo haben Sie das her? – *by one's death*, ums Leben kommen; – *for*, kommen um abzuholen; – *from*, (*of a th.*) kommen *or* herrühren von, zurückzuführen sein auf (*Acc.*), (*of a p.*) kommen *or* stammen aus; – *into*, eintreten in (*Acc.*); – *into action*, in Tätigkeit treten, eingreifen; – *into being*, ins Dasein treten, entstehen; – *into danger*, in Gefahr geraten; – *into effect* or *force*, wirksam werden, in Kraft treten; – *into money*, zu Geld kommen, Geld erben; – *into one's own*, auf seine Rechnung kommen, zur Geltung kommen; – *into play*, in Tätigkeit treten, sich bemerkbar machen; – *into possession*, den Besitz antreten, in den Besitz gelangen (*of*, *Gen.*); – *into property*, (unbewegliches) Vermögen erben; – *into sight*, in Sicht kommen; – *into use*, in Gebrauch kommen, eingeführt werden; – *into vogue*, modern werden, sich durchsetzen; – *into the world*, auf die Welt kommen; – *of*, see – *from* (*of a th.*); – *of age*, mündig *or* großjährig werden; – *off duty*, mit dem Dienst fertig sein; – *over*, überkommen, befallen; *what has – over him?* was ist mit ihm los? – *to*, (*of amounts*) sich belaufen auf (*Acc.*); (*usu. of inheritance*) zufallen (*Dat.*); kommen zu; – *to blows*, handgemein werden; – *to an end*, aufhören, zu Ende gehen, ein Ende nehmen *or* haben; – *to grief*, versagen, fehlschlagen; ein schlimmes Ende nehmen, zu Fall kommen; (*coll.*) kaputt gehen; – *to hand*, zum Vorschein kommen; (*Comm.*) *your letter has – to hand*, ich habe Ihr Schreiben erhalten; – *to harm*, verunglücken, zu Schaden kommen; – *to a head*, kritisch werden, zur Entscheidung kommen, sich spitzen, (*Med.*) zum Durchbruch kommen, (*as a boil*) am Aufbrechen sein; – *to my knowledge*, mir zu Ohren kommen; – *to life*, sich wiederbeleben, (*coll.*) Interesse zeigen, aufwachen; – *to light*, zum Vorschein kommen, ans Licht *or* an den Tag kommen; – *to nothing*, zu nichts führen, sich zerschlagen, ins Wasser fallen, zu Wasser werden; – *to a point*, spitz zulaufen; (*fig.*) – *to the point*, zur S. kommen; – *to rest*, zur Ruhe kommen, (*of machinery*) nicht mehr laufen; – *to the same* (*th.*), auf eins *or* dasselbe hinauskommen *or* hinauslaufen; – *to one's senses* or *to o.s.*, (wieder) zur Besinnung *or* zu sich kommen; – *to terms*, sich einigen *or* vergleichen, handelseinig werden; (*with inf.*) – *to be*, schließlich werden; – *to believe*, zu der Überzeugung kommen; – *to know*, kennenlernen; – *to pass*, zustandekommen, sich ereignen, passieren; – *to regret it*, es noch bereuen; – *to see*, einsehen, Verständnis aufbringen für; *in time you will – to see that I am right*, mit der Zeit wirst du einsehen, daß ich recht habe; – *under*, unterstehen, unterliegen (*Dat.*); – *under a separate heading*, in eine besondere Rubrik gehören; – *under consideration*, in Betracht kommen, berücksichtigt werden; – *upon*, (*of a p.*) zufällig finden *or* treffen, stoßen auf (*Acc.*), (*of a th.*) überfallen, hereinbrechen über (*Acc.*), zustoßen (*Dat.*), befallen.

2. *irr.v.t.* (*coll.*) spielen, sich aufspielen als; – *the fine gentleman*, den vornehmen Herrn spielen; *don't – that trick on me!* damit kommst du bei mir nicht an! du kannst mir doch keinen (blauen) Dunst vormachen! (*sl.*) – *it strong*, weit übers Ziel hinausgehen, es bis zum äußersten treiben; das Maul voll nehmen, es dick auftragen, dicke Töne reden.

come-back, *s.* **1.** (*coll.*) die Wiederkehr, Rückkehr, Rehabilitierung; 2. (*sl.*) schlagfertige Antwort; 3. (*sl.*) der Beschwerdegrund.

comedian [kə'mi:diən], *s.* (*Theat.*) der Komiker; Komödiant; Lustspieldichter; (*coll.*) Spaßvogel. **comedienne** [kəmi:di'en], *s.* die Komödiantin, Komikerin.

come-down, *s.* (*coll.*) der Reinfall.

comedy ['kɔmidi], *s.* das Lustspiel, die Komödie; *light –*, der Schwank, die Posse; – *of manners*, die Sittenkomödie; *musical –*, das Singspiel, die Operette.

come-hither, *adj.* (*sl.*) – *look*, das Bett im Netzhaut.

comeliness ['kʌmlinis], *s.* die Anmut, Grazie, Schönheit. **comely**, *adj.* anmutig; hübsch.

comer ['kʌmə], *s.* Kommende(r); *all –s*, all und jeder; *first-–*, Zuerstkommende(r), erste(r) Beste(r).

comestible [kɔ'mestibl], *adj.* eßbar, genießbar. **comestibles**, *pl.* Eßwaren, Nahrungsmittel (*pl.*).

comet ['kɔmit], *s.* der Komet, Schweifstern.

comfit ['kʌmfit], *s.* das Konfekt, Zuckerwerk.

comfort ['kʌmfət], **1.** *s.* die Behaglichkeit, Bequemlichkeit, der Komfort; Trost, die Tröstung, Erleichterung; Stärkung, Erquickung, Wohltat, das Labsal (*to*, für); der Tröster; *cold –*, schlechter Trost; *creature –(s)*, leiblicher Genuß; *take* or *derive – from*, Trost finden in (*Dat.*); *take –*, sich trösten, Mut fassen; *–s for the troops*, Liebesgaben (*pl.*). **2.** *v.t.* trösten; erquicken, erfreuen; ermutigen, Mut zusprechen (*Dat.*).

comfortable ['kʌmfətəbl], *adj.* bequem, behaglich, gemütlich, komfortabel; behäbig, wohlhabend (*of a p.*); genügend, ausreichend (*income*); – *circumstances*, der Wohlstand; *make o.s. –*, es sich (*Dat.*) bequem machen; *feel more –*, Erleichterung spüren (*as an invalid*). **comforter**, *s.* der Tröster; (*for infants*) Schnuller; *Job's –*, der Hiobströster, schlechter Tröster. **comforting**, *adj.* tröstlich, ermutigend. **comfortless,** *adj.* trostlos; unbequem, unbehaglich; unerquicklich, unerfreulich.

comfrey ['kʌmfri], *s.* (*Bot.*) die Schwarzwurz.

comfy ['kʌmfi], *adj.* (*coll.*) bequem, behaglich, gemütlich.

comic ['kɔmik], **1.** *adj,* komisch, Lustspiel–, Komödien–; komisch, humoristisch, heiter; – ***opera,*** komische Oper, die Operette; – ***strip,*** der Karikaturstreifen. **2.** *s.* (*coll.*) der Komiker; das Witzblatt. **comical,** *adj.* lustig, drollig, spaßig, ulkig, possierlich, (*pred.*) zum Lachen. **comicality** [–'kæliti], *s.* das Komische, die Komik.

coming ['kʌmiŋ], **1.** *pres.p. of* **come**; – ***Sir!*** gleich *or* sofort mein Herr! **2.** *adj.* künftig, kommend; – ***man,*** kommender Mann; – ***week,*** nächste *or* künftige Woche. **3.** *s.* das Kommen, die Ankunft; – ***of age,*** das Mündigwerden. **coming-in,** *s.* der Anfang, Beginn, Eintritt. **comings-in,** *pl.* (*Comm.*) Einnahmen (*pl.*).

comity ['kɔmiti], *s.* die Höflichkeit, gutes Einvernehmen; – ***of nations,*** das Konzert der Mächte.

comma ['kɔmə], *s.* der Beistrich, das Komma; ***inverted –s,*** Anführungszeichen, (*coll.*) Gänsefüßchen (*pl.*).

command [kə'mɑ:nd], **1.** *v.t.* befehlen, gebieten (*Dat.*); fordern, verlangen, verfügen, anordnen, beanspruchen; (*Mil.*) befehligen, kommandieren, führen; beherrschen, in der Gewalt haben, verfügen über (*Acc.*), zu Verfügung haben; abnötigen, hervorrufen, einflößen (*respect admiration etc.*); – ***him to come,*** ihm befehlen zu kommen, ihn kommen heißen; – ***a good price,*** einen guten Preis einbringen *or* erzielen; – ***a ready sale,*** guten Absatz finden; – ***silence,*** Stillschweigen gebieten; – ***a fine view,*** eine schöne Aussicht gewähren *or* bieten. **2.** *v.i.* befehlen, gebieten, herrschen, (*Mil.*) den Befehl haben, das Kommando führen, kommandieren; ***as far as the eye –s,*** soweit das Auge reicht. **3.** *s.* die Herrschaft, Führung, Verfügung, Gewalt (***of,*** über (*Acc.*)); der Auftrag, das Gebot, der Befehl; (*Mil.*) das Kommando, der (Ober)-befehl; die Beherrschung (*of a language*); ***be in –,*** das Kommando führen; ***be at my –,*** mir zur Verfügung stehen; ***by –,*** laut Befehl; (*Mil.*) ***chain of –,*** die Befehlerteilungsfolge; – ***of language,*** die Sprachbeherrschung, Redegewandtheit; – ***over o.s.,*** die Selbstbeherrschung; ***supreme –,*** oberste Heeresleitung; ***take – of,*** das Kommando übernehmen über (*Acc.*); ***under the – of,*** befehligt von; (*Mil.*) ***word of –,*** das Kommandowort.

commandant [kɔmən'dænt], *s.* der Kommandant (*of a camp*), Kommandeur (*of a training school*).

commandeer [kɔmən'diə], *v.t.* zum Dienst pressen, beitreiben, requirieren (*stores*); (*coll.*) sich aneignen, (*sl.*) kapern, organisieren.

commander [kə'mɑ:ndə], *s.* der Befehlshaber (*of an army*), Chef (*of a company*), Kommandant (*of airplane or tank*), Kommandeur (*of regiment, battalion, corps*), (Truppen)führer (*of platoon*); (*Naut.*) Fregattenkapitän; (*Av.*) ***wing –,*** der Fliegeroberstleutnant; Komtur (*of Order of Knighthood*); ***—in-chief,*** der Oberbefehlshaber, Höchstkommandierende(r). **commandery,** *s.* die Komturei, Kommende.

commanding [kə'mɑ:ndiŋ], *adj.* herrschend, gebietend, (*Mil.*) befehlshabend, kommandierend; beherrschend, hervorragend, überragend (*of situation*); (*fig.*) eindrucksvoll, dominierend, imponierend; – ***officer,*** der Einheitsführer, Kommandeur.

commandment [kə'mɑ:ndmənt], *s.* der Befehl, die Vorschrift; das Gesetz, Gebot; ***the ten –s,*** die zehn Gebote.

commando [kə'mɑ:ndou], *s.* das Kommando, die Truppeneinheit; der Sabotagetrupp.

command|-paper, *s.* (*Pol.*) königlicher Erlaß. **—performance,** *s.* die Aufführung auf Allerhöchsten Befehl. **—post,** *s.* der Gefechtsstand, Feuerleitungsstand.

commemorate [kə'meməreit], *v.t.* gedenken (*Gen.*), (das Andenken (*Gen.*)) feiern, eine Gedenkfeier abhalten für; gedenkend erwähnen, erinnern an (*Acc.*). **commemoration** [–'reiʃən], *s.* die Gedächtnisfeier, Gedenkfeier, das Gedenkfest; ***in – of,*** zum Gedächtnis (*Gen.*), zur Erinnerung *or* zum Andenken an (*Acc.*). **commemorative** [–rətiv], *adj.* Gedächtnis–, Gedenk–, Erinnerungs–.

commence [kə'mens], **1.** *v.i.* anfangen, beginnen. **2.** *v.t.* anfangen, beginnen; (*Univ.*) promovieren zu. **commencement,** *s.* der Anfang, Beginn; (*Univ.*) die Promotion.

commend [kə'mend], *v.t.* loben, lobend erwähnen; empfehlen; anvertrauen; – ***o.s.,*** sich empfehlen. **commendable,** *adj.* lobenswert, empfehlenswert, löblich. **commendation** [kɔmen'deiʃən], *s.* die Empfehlung, das Lob, der Preis. **commendatory** [–dətəri], *adj.* empfehlend, lobend, anerkennend; – ***letter,*** das Empfehlungsschreiben.

commensal [kə'mensəl], **1.** *adj.* am gleichen Tisch essend; (*Biol.*) parasitisch, Schmarotzer–. **2.** *s.* der Tischgenosse; (*Biol*). Schmarotzer.

commensurability [kəmenʃərə'biliti], *s.* die Vergleichbarkeit, Kommensurabilität; Angemessenheit. **commensurable,** *adj.* mit gleichem Maße meßbar *or* zu messen(d) (***with,*** wie), kommensurabel (mit); angemessen, im richtigen Verhältnis. **commensurate** [kə'menʃərit], *adj.* von gleichem Ausmaß *or* Umfang *or* gleicher Dauer, gleich groß (***with,*** wie); entsprechend, angemessen (***to, with,*** *Dat.*).

comment ['kɔment], **1.** *v.i.* 1. Bemerkungen machend (***upon,*** über (*Acc.*)); 2. kritische Anmerkungen *or* Erläuterungen machen (***on,*** zu). **2.** *s.* der Kommentar, die Erklärung, (kritische) Anmerkung *or* Erläuterung (***on,*** zu); Stellungnahme (zu), Kritik, kritische Bemerkungen (*pl.*) (über (*Acc.*)). **commentary** ['kɔməntəri], *s.* der Kommentar (***on,*** zu) (*also Rad.*); ***running –,*** erläutender Bericht *or* Kommentar. **commentate** [–teit], *v.t.* *See* **comment, 1,** 2. **commentator,** *s.* der Ausleger, Erläuterer, Kommentator; (*Rad.*) Funkberichter(statter).

commerce ['kɔmə:s], *s.* der Handel, Handelsverkehr; (*fig.*) Umgang, Verkehr; ***Chamber of Commerce,*** die Handelskammer.

commercial [kə'mə:ʃəl], **1.** *adj.* kaufmännisch, kommerziell, Geschäfts–, Handels–; handelsüblich, technisch rein (*of chemicals*); – ***advertising,*** die Wirtschaftswerbung; – ***art,*** die Gebrauchsgraphik; – ***aviation,*** die Handelsluftfahrt, Verkehrsluftfahrt; – ***college,*** die Handelshochschule; – ***directory,*** das Handelsadreßbuch; – ***education,*** kaufmännische Bildung; – ***hotel,*** der Gasthof für Geschäftsreisende; – ***law,*** das Handelsrecht; – ***plane,*** das Zivilflugzeug, Verkehrsflugzeug; – ***school,*** die Handelsschule; – ***television,*** das Werbefernsehen; – ***traveller,*** Handlungsreisende(r), Geschäftsreisende(r), der Vertreter; – ***vehicle,*** das Nutzfahrzeug. **2.** *s.* 1. (*Rad., T.V.*) die Werbesendung, Reklamesendung; 2. (*coll.*) *see* – ***traveller.*** **commercialism,** *s.* der Handelsgeist. **commercialization** [–lai'zeiʃən], *s.* kaufmännische Ausnutzung *or* Verwertung. **commercialize,** *v.t.* in den Handel bringen, marktfähig machen, kaufmännisch ausnutzen *or* verwerten.

commination [kɔmi'neiʃən], *s.* (*Eccl.*) die (Straf)-androhung. **comminatory** ['kɔminətəri], *adj.* (an)drohend, racheverkündend.

commingle [kə'miŋgl], *v.t.* (*v.i.*) (sich) vermischen, (sich) vermengen.

comminute ['kɔminju:t], *v.t.* zerkleinern, zersplittern, zerstückeln; (*Med.*) ***–d fracture,*** der Splitterbruch, die (Knochen)splitterung. **comminution** [–'nju:ʃən], *s.* die Zerkleinerung, Zerstückelung.

commiserate [kə'mizəreit], *v.t.* (*v.i.* – ***with***) bemitleiden, bedauern. **commiseration** [–'reiʃən], *s.* das Mitleid, Erbarmen.

commissar [kɔmi'sɑ:], *s.* (*esp. U.S.S.R.*) der Kommissar. **commissariat** [–'sɛəriət], *s.* das Kommissariat; (*Mil.*) Verpflegungsamt, die Intendantur, Lebensmittelversorgung. **commissary**

['kɔmisəri], *s.* Bevollmächtigte(r), Beauftragte(r), der Kommissar, (*esp. France*) Kommissär; (*Mil.*) Intendanturbeamte(r); (*Eccl.*) bischöflicher Vertreter.

commission [kə'miʃən], **1.** *s.* 1. der Auftrag, die Anweisung, Bestellung, Instruktion; ***discharge a –***, einen Auftrag ausführen; 2. die Vollmacht, Bevollmächtigung, Beauftragung, Anvertrauung, Übertragung; 3. (*of a crime*) Verübung, Begehung; ***sin of –***, die Begehungssünde; 4. (*Comm.*) die Kommissions- *or* Vermittlungs- *or* Maklergebühr, Provision, Courtage; ***sell on –***, gegen Provision verkaufen; ***– agent***, der Kommissionär, Provisionsvertreter; ***– business***, das Kommissionsgeschäft; 5. amtliche Stellung, das Amt; (*Mil.*) die Offiziersstelle, das Offizierspatent; ***hold a –***, eine Offiziersstelle innehaben; ***resign one's –***, seinen Abschied nehmen; 6. der Ausschuß, die Kommission; ***– of inquiry***, der Untersuchungsausschuß; 7. (*Naut.*) die Diensttauglichkeit, Einsatzbereitschaft, (*coll.*) gebrauchsfähiger Zustand; ***in –***, in Dienst gestellt (*of ships*); (*coll.*) ***be out of –***, außer Betrieb sein, nicht funktionieren. **2.** *v.t.* beauftragen, bevollmächtigen, autorisieren (*a p.*), ein Amt übertragen (*Dat.*), (*Mil.*) das Offizierspatent verleihen (*Dat.*); einen Auftrag geben (*Dat.*), abordnen; bestellen (*a th.*), (*Naut.*) in Dienst stellen (*a ship*); ***–ed officer***, (durch Patent bestallter) Offizier.

commissionaire [kəmiʃə'nɛə], *s.* der Dienstmann, Portier.

commissioner [kə'miʃənə], *s.* Beauftragte(r), Bevollmächtigte(r); das Mitglied eines Regierungsausschusses; ***High Commissioner***, der Oberkommissar (*of Dominions in London*); ***income-tax –s***, der Steuerappelationsausschuß; ***– for oaths***, beeidigter Notar; ***Commissioner of Works***, der Minister für Staatsbauten.

commissure ['kɔmiʃə], *s.* die Verbindungsstelle, Naht, Fuge, der Saum; (*Anat.*) Nervenstrang.

commit [kə'mit], *v.t.* 1. begehen, verüben (*a crime*); ***– adultery***, Ehebruch begehen; ***– suicide***, Selbstmord begehen; 2. übergeben, überliefern (*a p.*); anvertrauen, überlassen, überantworten (***s.th. to him***, ihm etwas); ***– one's soul to God***, seine Seele Gott befehlen; ***– to the grave***, der Erde übergeben; ***– to memory***, dem Gedächtnis einprägen; ***– to paper*** or ***to writing***, zu Papier bringen; ***– to prison***, einsperren, einliefern; ***committed for trial***, dem Gerichte zur Aburteilung überliefert; 3. (*also* ***– o.s.***, sich) binden, festlegen, verpflichten; ***stand*** or ***be committed***, sich festgelegt haben (*to*, auf (*Acc.*)).

commitment [kə'mitmənt], *s.* 1. die Verhaftung, Einlieferung; Übergabe, Überweisung, Übertragung, Überantwortung (*to*, an (*Acc.*)); 2. Festlegung (*to*, auf (*Acc.*)), Verpflichtung (zu), Bindung (an (*Acc.*)); Verbindlichkeit, das Engagement; ***undertake a –***, eine Verpflichtung eingehen; ***without any –s***, ganz unverbindlich.

committal [kə'mitl], *s.* 1. das Übergeben, Überweisen; 2. die Begehung, Verübung; 3. Verpflichtung; (*Mil.*) der Einsatz (*of forces*).

committee [kə'miti], *s.* der Ausschuß, das Komitee, die Kommission; (*Parl.*) ***go into –***, in Sonderausschüssen beraten; ***joint –***, zusammengesetzter Ausschuß; ***– of management***, der Verwaltungsausschuß; ***select –***, der Sonderausschuß; ***standing –***, ständiger Ausschuß; (*Parl.*) ***Committee of Ways and Means***, der Steuerbewilligungsausschuß.

commix [kə'miks], (*obs.*) *v.t.* (*v.i.* sich) (ver)mischen. **commixture** [–tʃə], *s.* die Mischung, das Gemisch.

commode [kə'moud], *s.* der Nachtstuhl; die (Wasch)kommode.

commodious [kə'moudiəs], *adj.* geräumig.

commodity [kə'mɔditi], *s.* die Ware, der (Handels)-artikel, *pl.* Gebrauchsgegenstände, Waren (*pl.*).

commodore ['kɔmədɔ:], *s.* der Kommodore, Kapitän zur See, Kommandeur (eines Geschwaders); Präsident (eines Segelklubs).

common ['kɔmən], **1.** *adj.* gewöhnlich, üblich, gebräuchlich, alltäglich, normal, Gewohnheits–; allgemein, öffentlich; gemeinschaftlich, gemeinsam; (*coll.*) gemein, gewöhnlich, ordinär, vulgär; ***– carrier***, der Fuhrunternehmer, Spediteur; ***make – cause with***, gemeinsame S. machen mit; (*Her.*) ***– charges***, gemeine Figuren; ***– chord***, der Dreiklang; ***by – consent***, mit allgemeiner Zustimmung; ***– criminal***, der Gewohnheitsverbrecher; ***– decency***, natürlicher Anstand; (*Math.*) ***– denominator***, der Hauptnenner, gemeinsamer Nenner; (*Math.*) ***– divisor***, gemeinsamer Teiler; (*Math.*) ***– fraction***, gemeiner Bruch; (*coll.*) ***– or garden***, landläufig, gewöhnlich; (*Gram.*) ***– gender***, doppeltes Geschlecht; ***be on – ground with***, von den gleichen Voraussetzungen ausgehen wie, auf den gleichen Grundlagen fußen wie; (*Orn.*) ***– gull***, die Sturmmöwe (*Larus canus*); ***the – herd***, gemeines *or* niedriges Volk; ***– law***, das Gewohnheitsrecht; ***–-law marriage***, das Zusammenleben, wilde Ehe; ***Common Market***, Gemeinsamer Markt; ***– measure***, gerader Takt; ***– noun***, das Appellativ(um), Guttangswort; ***– phrase***, abgedroschene Redensart; ***the – people***, das gewöhnliche Volk; ***Court of Common Pleas***, der Zivilgerichtshof; ***it is – practice***, es ist allgemein üblich; ***Book of Common Prayer***, anglikanische Liturgie, anglikanisches Gebetbuch; ***– rights***, Menschenrechte (*pl.*); ***– salt***, das Kochsalz, Natriumchlorid; ***a – sight***, ein alltäglicher *or* vertrauter Anblick; ***– soldier***, gemeiner Soldat; ***– talk***, das Stadtgespräch; ***– time***, see ***– measure***; ***– usage***, weit verbreiteter Gebrauch; ***the – weal***, das Gemeinwesen, Gemeinwohl; ***– woman***, ordinäres Weib, die Hure.

2. *s.* 1. der Gemeindeplatz, die Gemeindewiese, Allmende; 2. das Gemeinsame, Allgemeine; ***act in –***, gemeinsam vorgehen; ***have in –***, gemeinschaftlich besitzen; ***in – with***, gemeinsam mit, in Übereinstimmung mit, ebenso wie; ***out of the –***, außergewöhnlich, über das Gewöhnliche hinaus; ***right of –***, das Mitbenutzungsrecht; ***– of pasturage*** das Weiderecht.

commonalty ['kɔmənəlti], *s.* gemeines Volk, die Allgemeinheit, Gesamtheit. **commoner,** *s.* Nichtadelige(r), Bürgerliche(r); (*Univ.*) der Student, der seinen Unterhalt bezahlt.

commonly ['kɔmənli], *adv.* meistens, gewöhnlich, normalerweise, (im) allgemein(en). **commonness,** *s.* häufiges Vorkommen, die Gewöhnlichkeit; Gemeinheit; Gemeinschaftlichkeit, Gemeinsamkeit.

common|place, 1. *adj.* alltäglich, gewöhnlich, banal, abgedroschen; ***– book***, das Kollektaneenbuch, Sammelheft. **2.** *s.* der Gemeinplatz, die Binsenwahrheit; das Alltägliche, Platte, Gewöhnliche. **--room,** *s.* das Lehrerzimmer (*in schools*); der Gemeinschaftsraum, das Klubzimmer.

commons ['kɔmənz], *pl.* 1. die Gemeinen, Bürgerlichen, Nichtadligen; ***the (House of) Commons***, das Unterhaus; 2. die Ration, gemeinschaftliche Kost; ***be kept on short –***, nicht satt zu essen bekommen, von schmaler Kost leben.

common|-sense, *s.* gesunder Menschenverstand, schlichte Vernunft. **–wealth,** *s.* das Gemeinwesen; der Staat; (*Hist.*) ***the Commonwealth***, die englische Republik (1649–60); ***Australian Commonwealth***, Australischer Staatenbund; ***the – of learning***, die Gelehrtenwelt, Gelehrtenrepublik; ***British Commonwealth of Nations***, Britische Nationengemeinschaft, das Commonwealth.

commotion [kə'mouʃən], *s.* heftige Bewegung, die Verwirrung, Erregung; der Tumult, Aufruhr; ***make a –***, Aufsehen erregen.

communal ['kɔmjunl], *adj.* Gemeinde–, Kommunal–; Gemeinschafts–; ***– kitchen***, die Volksküche. **communalize,** *v.t.* eingemeinden.

[1]**commune** ['kɔmju:n], *s.* die Gemeinde, Kommune.

[2]**commune** [kə'mju:n], *v.i.* sich unterhalten, sich beraten, Gedanken austauschen; (*Eccl.*) das Abendmahl empfangen, kommunizieren; ***– with o.s.***, mit sich zu Rate gehen.

communicable [kə'mju:nikəbl], *adj.* mitteilbar,

erzählbar; übertragbar (*of disease*); mitteilsam (*of a p.*). **communicant,** *s.* der Kommunikant, (regelmäßiger) Abendmahlsgast.

communicate [kəˈmjuːnikeit], **1.** *v.t.* mitteilen (*to, Dat.*); übertragen (auf (*Acc.*)) (*disease*). **2.** *v.i.* 1 (*Eccl.*) kommunizieren, das Abendmahl empfangen; 2. in Verbindung treten, sich in Verbindung setzen; (*as rooms etc.*) miteinander in Verbindung stehen, zusammenhängen. **communication** [–ˈkeiʃən], *s.* die Mitteilung (*to*, an (*Acc.*)); Bekanntmachung, Nachricht; der Verkehr, die Verbindung; der Durchgang, Verkehrsweg, Verbindungsweg; die Übertragung, Fortpflanzung (*of power, motion etc.*); *pl.* das Fernmeldewesen, (*Mil.*) Nachschublinien (*pl.*); – ***centre,*** die Fernmeldezentrale, Nachrichtensammelstelle; ***channel of*** –, der Nachrichtenweg; (*Railw.*) – ***cord,*** die Notleine, Notbremse; (*Prov.*) ***evil –s corrupt good manners,*** schlechter Umgang verdirbt gute Sitten; (*Av.*) ***ground*** –, die Boden-zu-Bord-Verbindung *or* Verständigung; (*Mil.*) ***line of –s,*** die Etappe; ***means of*** –, Verkehrsmittel (*pl.*); – ***by rail,*** die Eisenbahnverbindung; – ***satellite,*** der Nachrichtensatellit; (*Mil.*) ***–s trench,*** der Verbindungsgraben, Stichgraben; ***two-way*** –, der Wechselverkehr.

communicative [kəˈmjuːnikətiv], *adj.* mitteilsam, offenherzig; redselig, gesprächig. **communicativeness,** *s.* die Mitteilsamkeit. **communicator** [–keitə], *s.* 1. Mitteilende(r); 2. (*Railw.*) die Notleine.

communion [kəˈmjuːnjən], *s.* 1. die Gemeinschaft (*of persons*); Verbindung, der Umgang, Verkehr; ***hold – with him,*** mit ihm Umgang pflegen; – ***with o.s.,*** die Einkehr bei sich; 2. (*Eccl.*) Heiliges Abendmahl, (*R.C.*) die Kommunion. **communion|-bread,** *s.* das Abendmahlsbrot, die Oblate, Hostie. **--cup,** *s.* der Abendmahlskelch. **--rail,** *s.* das Altargitter. **--service,** *s.* die Abendmahlsfeier. **--table.** *s.* der Altar, Tisch des Herrn.

communiqué [kɔˈmjuːnikei], *s.* die Meldung, Verlautbarung, amtliche Mitteilung, amtlicher Bericht.

communism [ˈkɔmjunizm], *s.* der Kommunismus. **communist, 1.** *s.* der (die) Kommunist(in). **2.** *adj.* kommunistisch.

community [kəˈmjuːniti], *s.* die Gemeinschaft, Gemeinsamkeit; Gemeinde; der Staat, das Gemeinwesen; die Allgemeinheit, Öffentlichkeit, das Volk; – ***centre,*** das Gemeinschaftszentrum; – ***of goods,*** die Gütergemeinschaft; – ***of interests,*** die Interessengemeinschaft; – ***singing,*** das Gemeinschaftssingen.

commutability [kəmjuːtəˈbiliti], *s.* die Vertauschbarkeit, Austauschbarkeit; (*into money*) Ablösbarkeit. **commutable** [–ˈmjuːtəbl], *adj.* vertauschbar; austauschbar, (*into money*) ablösbar. **commutation** [kɔmjuˈteiʃən], *s.* 1. die Umänderung; Umwandlung; der (Um)tausch, Austausch; 2. (*Law*) die (Straf)milderung; – ***of sentence,*** die Strafmilderung, der Strafnachlaß; 3. die Ablösung (*of obligations*); 4. (*Elec.*) Stromwendung, Stromumkehrung; 5. (*Am.*) – ***ticket,*** die Abonnementskarte, Zeitkarte. **commutator** [ˈkɔmjuteitə], *s.* (*Elec.*) der Umschalter, Umsetzer, Polwender, Stromwender, Kommutator.

commute [kəˈmjuːt], **1.** *v.t.* 1. austauschen, umtauschen, vertauschen, eintauschen; umwandeln, auswechseln, verändern; 2. (*Law*) herabsetzen (*to*, auf (*Acc.*)), mildern (zu); 3. (*Comm.*) ablösen (***for,*** durch). **2.** *v.i.* mit Zeitkarte fahren, pendeln. **commuter,** *s.* der Zeitkarteninhaber, (*coll.*) Pendler.

Como [ˈkoumou], *s.* ***Lake*** –, der Comer See.

compact, 1. [kəmˈpækt], *adj.* dicht, fest, kompakt, (zusammen)gedrängt; gedrängt, knapp, (kurz und) bündig (*style*). **2.** [–pækt], *v.t.* zusammendrängen, fest miteinander verbinden, verdichten, festigen, konsolidieren. **3.** [ˈkɔmpækt], *s.* 1. der Vertrag, Pakt, die Übereinkunft; 2. (*coll.*) Puderdose. **compactness** [kəmˈpæktnis], *s.* die Dichte, Dichtigkeit, Festigkeit; Gedrängtheit, Knappheit, Bündigkeit (*of style*).

1**companion** [kəmˈpænjən], **1.** *s.* 1. der (die) Gesellschafter(in), Begleiter(in); Kamerad(in), Genosse (Genossin), Gefährte (Gefährtin); ***--in-arms,*** der Waffenbruder; ***boon*** –, der Zechkumpan; ***travelling*** –, Mitreisende(r); 2. (*of a th.*) das Seitenstück, Gegenstück; 3. (*of a book*) der Ratgeber, Leitfaden; 4. der Ritter; ***Companion of the Bath,*** der Ritter des Bath-Ordens. **2.** *attrib. adj.* dazu passend, dazugehörig, Gegen–, Seiten–, Begleit–.

2**companion,** *s.* 1. (*also* ***--hatch***) (*Naut.*) die Kajütsluke, Kajütskappe; 2. (*also* ***--ladder, --way***) die Kajütstreppe, der Niedergang.

companionable [kəmˈpænjənəbl], *adj.* gesellig, umgänglich. **companionableness,** *s.* die Geselligkeit, Umgänglichkeit. **companionate** [–nit], *adj.* – ***marriage,*** die Kameradschaftsehe. **companionship,** *s.* die Kameradschaft, Gesellschaft.

company [ˈkʌmpəni], *s.* die Begleitung, Gesellschaft, der Umgang; (*coll.*) Besuch, Gäste (*pl.*) *or* der Gast; ***be fond of*** –, gerne Gesellschaft haben, Geselligkeit lieben; ***they have*** –, sie haben Gäste; ***be good*** –, ein guter Gesellschafter sein; ***in – with,*** zusammen mit, in Gesellschaft *or* Begleitung von; (*coll.*) ***I sin in good*** –, das haben Bessere auch getan; ***keep him*** –, ihm Gesellschaft leisten; ***keep – with,*** verkehren *or* Umgang haben mit; ***part*** – (***with him***), sich (von ihm) trennen, (*fig.*) anderer Meinung sein (als er); ***receive*** –, Gesellschaft bei sich empfangen; (*Am.*) ***see no*** –, keinen Umgang haben; 2. (*Mil.*) die Kompanie; (*Naut.*) Besatzung, Mannschaft; 3. (*Comm.*) (Handels)gesellschaft, Genossenschaft; (*Hist.*) Zunft, Innung; ***chartered*** –, gesetzlich genehmigte Gesellschaft; ***joint-stock*** –, die Aktiengesellschaft; ***limited*** (***liability***) –, die Gesellschaft mit beschränkter Haftung; ***publishing*** –, der Verlag; ***trading*** –, die Handelsgesellschaft; 4. (*Theat.*) – ***of actors,*** die Schauspielertruppe; ***touring*** (***Am. road***) –, die Wandertruppe.

comparability [kɔmpərəˈbiliti], *s.* die Vergleichbarkeit. **comparable** [ˈkɔmpərəbl], *adj.* vergleichbar. **comparative** [kəmˈpærətiv], **1.** *adj.* 1. vergleichend; – ***anatomy,*** vergleichende Anatomie; – ***value,*** der Vergleichswert; 2. (*coll.*) nicht unbedingt, relativ; – ***beauty,*** relative Schönheit; 3. (*Gram.*) steigernd; 4. (*coll.*) ziemlich. **2.** *s.* (*Gram.*) der Komparativ. **comparatively,** *adv.* (*coll.*) ziemlich, verhältnismäßig.

compare [kəmˈpɛə], **1.** *v.t.* 1. (*one th. with another*) vergleichen (***with, to,*** mit); (*two things*) miteinander vergleichen, nebeneinanderstellen; gleichstellen, gleichsetzen, auf eine Stufe stellen (*to*, mit); ***as –d with*** or ***to,*** im Vergleich zu, gegenüber (*Dat.*); ***not to be –d with,*** nicht zu vergleichen mit; (*coll.*) – ***notes,*** Meinungen austauschen, sich berat(schlag)en; 2. (*Gram.*) steigern. **2.** *v.i.* sich vergleichen (lassen), den Vergleich aushalten, wetteifern (***with,*** mit). **3.** *s.* (*only in*) ***beyond*** or ***past*** or ***without*** –, unvergleichlich.

comparison [kəmˈpærisən], *s.* 1. der Vergleich, die Nebeneinanderstellung; (*Rhet.*) das Gleichnis; ***bear – with,*** den Vergleich aushalten mit, sich sehr wohl vergleichen lassen mit; ***beyond*** –, unvergleichlich; ***by*** –, vergleichsweise, zum Vergleich; ***in – with,*** verglichen mit, im Vergleich zu; ***make*** or ***draw a*** –, einen Vergleich anstellen *or* ziehen; (*coll.*) ***there's no*** – (***between them***), sie lassen sich nicht vergleichen; 2. (*Gram.*) die Steigerung.

compartment [kəmˈpɑːtmənt], *s.* die Abteilung; der Abschnitt, Sektor; (abgeteiltes) Fach; die Kassette, Zelle; (*Railw.*) das Abteil; ***luggage*** –, der Gepäckraum; ***smoking*** –, das Raucherabteil; ***water-tight*** –, wasserdichte Abteilung. **compartmentalize** [–ˈmentəlaiz], *v.t.* in Fächer einteilen.

compass [ˈkʌmpəs], **1.** *s.* 1. der Umfang, Umkreis, die Ausdehnung; der Zeitraum; Bezirk, Bereich, das Gebiet, die Sphäre; Grenzen (*pl.*), Schranken (*pl.*); (*obs.*) der Umweg, die Abschweifung; ***keep within*** –, in Schranken halten; ***within the – of,*** innerhalb (*Gen.*); ***reduce in*** –, in engere Rahmen fassen; – *of the eye,* der Gesichtskreis; – *of the voice,* der Stimmumfang; 2. (*usu. pl.*) *see* **compasses**; 3. (*magnetic*) –, die Bussole, der Kompaß; *prismatic* –, die Patentbussole; *repeater* –, der Tochterkompaß; *point of the* –, der Kompaßstrich; – *bearing,* die Peilung; – *card,* die Windrose; – *deviation,* die Fehlweisung, der Kompaßfehler; – *error,* die Abweichung (von der rechtweisenden Peilung); – *needle,* die Magnetnadel; – *variation,* die Mißweisung, magnetische Deklination. **2.** *v.t.* 1. (*obs.*) *see* **encompass**; 2. bewerkstelligen, zustandebringen, zeitigen; erzielen, erreichen, vollenden, durchsetzen (*one's purpose*); anstiften, planen, anzetteln.

compasses ['kʌmpəsəz], *pl.* (*also pair of* –) der (Einsatz)zirkel; *beam*––, der Stabzirkel; *bow*––, der Nullenzirkel; *measure with* –, abzirkeln.

compassion [kəm'pæʃən], *s.* das Mitleid, Mitgefühl, Erbarmen (*for, with,* mit); *have* or *take* – *on,* Mitleid empfinden mit. **compassionate, 1.** [-nit], *adj.* mitleidig, mitleidsvoll, mitfühlend; – *allowance,* die Gnadenzulage; (*Mil.*) – *leave,* der Sonderurlaub aus Familiengründen. **2.** [-neit], *v.t.* bemitleiden. **compassionateness,** *s. See* **compassion.**

compass-saw, *s.* die Stichsäge, Schweifsäge, Lochsäge.

compatibility [kəmpæti'biliti], *s.* die Verträglichkeit, Vereinbarkeit; – *of temper,* verträgliches Gemüt. **compatible** [-'pætibl], *adj.* verträglich, vereinbar (*with,* mit); angemessen (*with, Dat.*), widerspruchsfrei.

compatriot [kəm'pætriət], *s.* der Landsmann (die Landsmännin).

compeer ['kɔmpiə], *s.* Gleichstehende(r), Gleichgestellte(r), der Genosse (die Genossin); *have no* –, nicht seinesgleichen haben.

compel [kəm'pel], *v.t.* zwingen, nötigen (*a p.*); erzwingen, abnötigen (*a th.*); *be compelled to do or* (*coll.*) *into doing,* gezwungen sein zu tun, tun müssen. **compelling,** *adj.* zwingend, unwiderstehlich.

compendious [kəm'pendiəs], *adj.* kurz (gefaßt), gedrängt. **compendiousness,** *s.* die Kürze, Gedrängtheit. **compendium,** *s.* das Handbuch, der Grundriß, Leitfaden; Auszug, Abriß, die Zusammenfassung.

compensate ['kɔmpənseit], **1.** *v.t.* ersetzen, Ersatz leisten für, vergüten (*to, Dat.*); ausgleichen, aufwiegen, wiedergutmachen (*a th.*); entschädigen (*a p.*) (*for,* für). **2.** *v.i.* aufwiegen, kompensieren, Ersatz geben für. **compensating,** *adj.* ausgleichend, Ausgleichs–. **compensation** [–'seiʃən], *s.* der Ersatz, die Ersetzung, (Rück)erstattung, Vergütung; Entschädigung; der Schadenersatz; die Abfindung(ssumme), das Abstandsgeld; (*Tech.*) die Ausgleichung, Kompensation, der Ausgleich; (*Am.*) die Bezahlung, der Lohn, das Entgelt; (*fig.*) *find* –, sich entschädigen lassen (*in,* durch); *make* – *for,* Ersatz bieten *or* leisten für (*to him,* ihm); (*fig.*) ausgleichen, aufwiegen; *pay* –, Schadenersatz leisten; *as* –, *by way of* –, als Ersatz; *disability* –, die Invaliditätsentschädigung; *workmen's* –, die Arbeitsunfallversicherung. **compensatory** [kəm'pensətəri], *adj.* ausgleichend, Ausgleichs–, Entschädigungs–; (*Gram.*) – (*vowel-*) *lengthening,* die Ersatzdehnung.

compère ['kɔmpɛə], **1.** *s.* der (die) Ansager(in), der Conférencier. **2.** *v.t.* ansagen bei.

compete [kəm'pi:t], *v.i.* sich mitbewerben, sich als Mitbewerber bemühen, in Mitbewerb *or* Konkurrenz treten, konkurrieren (*for,* um) (*a th.*); wetteifern, sich messen (*with,* mit) (*a p.*); (*Spt.*) am Wettkampf teilnehmen.

competence ['kɔmpitəns], *s.* die Fähigkeit, Befähigung (*for,* zu), Tauglichkeit (für); (*Law*) Kompetenz, Qualifikation, Zuständigkeit, (Rechts)befugnis. **competency,** *s.* (ausreichendes) Auskommen. **competent,** *adj.* zulänglich, hinlänglich, hinreichend, ausreichend (*for,* für), entsprechend, angemessen (*Dat.*); (*Law*) zuständig, kompetent, befugt, maßgeblich; (*coll.*) tüchtig, (leistungs)fähig; – *authority,* zuständige Behörde; (*fig.*) – *judge,* sachkundiger Beurteiler; (*coll.*) – *p.,* fähiger Kopf.

competition [kɔmpi'tiʃən], *s.* der Wettbewerb, Wettkampf, Wettstreit, (*Comm.*) die Konkurrenz (*for,* um); das Preisausschreiben; *enter into* – *with him,* mit ihm in Wettstreit treten (*for,* um); *enter a* –, an einem Preisausschreiben teilnehmen; – *in armaments,* das Wettrüsten; *unfair* –, unlauterer Wettbewerb. **competitive** [kəm'petitiv], *adj.* auf Wettbewerb eingestellt, wetteifernd; Konkurrenz–; konkurrenzfähig (*price*); – *examination,* die Ausleseprüfung. **competitor** [–'petitə], *s.* der (die) Mitbewerber(in), (*Comm.*) Konkurrent(in); (*Spt.*) (Wettbewerbs)teilnehmer(in) (*for,* um; *in,* an (*Dat.*)).

compilation [kɔmpi'leiʃən], *s.* die Zusammenstellung, Sammlung, Kompilation; das Sammelwerk. **compile** [kəm'pail], *v.t.* zusammentragen, zusammenstellen, sammeln, kompilieren (*from,* aus). **compiler,** *s.* der Kompilator.

complacence, complacency [kəm'pleisəns(i)], *s.* die Selbstzufriedenheit, Selbstgefälligkeit, das Wohlgefallen, Behagen. **complacent,** *adj.* selbstzufrieden, selbstgefällig, behaglich.

complain [kəm'plein], *v.i.* klagen, jammern (*of,* über (*Acc.*)), sich beklagen *or* beschweren, Klage *or* Beschwerde führen (*about,* über (*Acc.*); *to,* bei). **complainant,** *s.* (*Law*) der (die) Kläger(in). **complainer,** *s.* (*coll.*) der Jammerlappen. **complaint,** *s.* die Klage (*also Law*), Beschwerde (*about,* über (*Acc.*)); (*Med.*) das Leiden, Übel, die Beschwerde; (*Comm.*) Beanstandung, Reklamation; *make a* –, *see* **complain**; (*Comm.*) reklamieren; – *book,* das Beschwerdebuch.

complaisance [kəm'pleisəns], *s.* die Willfährigkeit, Zuvorkommenheit, Gefälligkeit, Höflichkeit, das Entgegenkommen. **complaisant,** *adj.* willfährig, zuvorkommend, entgegenkommend, nachgiebig (*to,* gegen).

complement, 1. ['kɔmplimənt], *s.* die Ergänzung, Vervollständigung; Vollständigkeit, Vollzähligkeit, volle Anzahl, die Gesamtzahl, (*Naut.*) vollzählige Besatzung; (*Gram.*) Ergänzung; (*Math.*) das Komplement; (*Mus.*) komplementäres *or* umgekehrtes Intervall. **2.** [–ment], *v.t.* ergänzen, vervollständigen. **complementary** [–'mentəri], *adj.* ergänzend, Ergänzungs–, komplementär; – *angles,* Ergänzungswinkel (*pl.*); – *colours,* Komplementärfarben (*pl.*).

complete [kəm'pli:t], **1.** *adj.* vollständig, vollzählig; ganz, völlig, total, komplett; vollkommen, vollendet; *Ovid's* – *works,* Ovids sämtliche Werke. **2.** *v.t.* vervollständigen, ergänzen; beend(ig)en, vollenden, abschließen; – *the enclosed form,* das beigelegte Formular ausfüllen. **completeness,** *s.* die Vollständigkeit, Vollkommenheit. **completion** [–'pli:ʃən], *s.* die Vervollständigung, Vervollkommnung, Vollendung; Erfüllung, der Abschluß; (*Gram.*) – *of the predicate,* die Ergänzung des Prädikats; *bring to* –, zum Abschluß bringen.

complex ['kɔmpleks], **1.** *adj.* zusammengesetzt, (*Math.*) komplex; (*fig.*) verwickelt, kompliziert; (*Gram.*) – *sentence,* das Satzgefüge. **2.** *s.* 1. die Gesamtheit, das Ganze, der Inbegriff; *building* –, der Gebäudekomplex; 2. (*Psych.*) der Komplex; *inferiority* –, das Minderwertigkeitsgefühl.

complexion [kəm'plekʃən], *s.* die Hautfarbe, Gesichtsfarbe, der Teint; (*fig.*) Charakter, das Aussehen; *put a fresh* – *on a th.,* einer S. einen neuen Zug *or* Anstrich verleihen.

complexity [kəm'pleksiti], *s.* die Zusammengesetztheit, Verschlungenheit; (*fig.*) Verzweigtheit, Verflechtung, Verwicklung, Kompliziertheit.

compliable [kəm'plaiəbl], *adj.* willfährig, fügsam, nachgiebig. **compliance,** *s.* die Willfährigkeit, Unterwürfigkeit; Einwilligung, Erfüllung, Gewährung; *in* – *with your wishes,* Ihren Wünschen gemäß *or* entsprechend. **compliant,** *adj. See* **compliable.**

complicacy ['kɔmplikəsi], *s.* die Verwicklung,

Kompliziertheit. **complicate** [–keit], *v.t.* verwickeln, verflechten; komplizieren, erschweren. **complicated,** *adj.* verwickelt, kompliziert, (*Math.*) verschlungen. **complication** [–'keiʃən], *s.* die Verflechtung, Verwick(e)lung, (*fig.*) Erschwerung; (*Math.*) Verschlingung; (*Med.*) Komplikation.

complicity [kəm'plisiti], *s.* die Mitschuld (*in*, an (*Dat.*)).

compliment, 1. ['kɔmplimənt], *s.* das Kompliment; (*pl.*) Empfehlungen, Grüße (*pl.*); ***give her my –s,*** grüßen Sie sie von mir, empfehlen Sie mich ihr; ***pay him a –,*** ihm ein Kompliment machen; ***pay him the –,*** ihm die Ehre erweisen (***of doing,*** zu tun); ***send one's –s to him,*** sich ihm empfehlen; ***the – of the season!*** frohe Weihnachten! **2.** [–ment], *v.t.* beglückwünschen (*Acc.*), gratulieren (*Dat.*) (***on,*** zu); beehren, auszeichnen. **complimentary** [–'mentəri], *adj.* schmeichelhaft; Höflichkeits–, Ehren–; – ***copy,*** das Freiexemplar; – ***ticket,*** die Freikarte.

comply [kəm'plai], *v.i.* willfahren (***with,*** *Dat.*), sich fügen (*Dat.*), nachkommen (*Dat.*), einwilligen (in (*Acc.*)); sich halten (an (*Acc.*)), sich unterwerfen (*Dat.*), erfüllen.

component [kəm'pounənt], **1.** *adj.* einen Teil ausmachen; – ***force,*** die Teilkraft; – ***part,*** der Bestandteil. **2.** *s.* der (Bestand)teil, das Einzelteil, Glied, (*Math.*) die Komponente.

comport [kəm'pɔ:t], *v.t.* – ***o.s.,*** sich betragen *or* (auf)führen *or* verhalten *or* benehmen, auftreten. **comportment,** *s.* das Benehmen, Verhalten, Betragen.

compose [kəm'pouz], *v.t.* 1. zusammensetzen, zusammenstellen, bilden, ausmachen; verfassen, abfassen, ausarbeiten (*text etc.*), dichten (*a poem*); (*Mus.*) komponieren; (*Typ.*) (ab)setzen; 2. besänftigen, beruhigen (*the mind etc.*); beilegen, schlichten (*a quarrel*); – ***o.s.,*** sich beruhigen; sich fassen; – ***o.s. to sleep,*** sich zum Schlafe anschicken. **composed,** *adj.* 1. gefaßt, gesetzt, gelassen, ruhig; 2. zusammengesetzt; ***be – of,*** bestehen aus. **composedness,** *s.* die Gelassenheit, Ruhe. **composer,** *s.* der (die) Verfasser(in) (*of a poem*); (*usu. Mus.*) Komponist(in).

composing [kəm'pouziŋ], **1.** *adj.* Beruhigungs–; – ***draught,*** das Beruhigungsmittel, der Schlaftrunk. **2.** *s.* 1. das Komponieren; Dichten; 2. (*Typ.*) Schriftsetzen. **composing|-machine,** *s.* die Setzmaschine. **–-room,** *s.* der Setzersaal, die Setzerei. **–-stick,** *s.* der Winkelhaken.

composite ['kɔmpəzit], **1.** *adj.* 1. zusammengesetzt, gemischt; 2. (*Bot.*) Kornblüter–, Kompositen–. **2.** *s.* die Mischung, Zusammensetzung.

composition [kɔmpə'ziʃən], *s.* 1. die Zusammensetzung, der Aufbau, die Synthese; Zusammenstellung, Gestaltung, Anordnung, Einrichtung, Ausarbeitung; Komposition, Verbindung; Beschaffenheit, Art, Anlage, Natur; ***chemical –,*** chemisches Präparat; 2. der Aufsatz, schriftliche Arbeit; (*Mus.*) die Komposition; ***German –,*** die Übersetzung ins Deutsche; 3. (*Typ.*) das Setzen, der Satz; 4. (*Comm., Law*) die Übereinkunft, das Abkommen, der Vergleich, Akkord, der *or* das Kompromiß; die Abfindungssumme. **compositor** [kəm'pɔzitə], *s.* der (Schrift)setzer.

compost ['kɔmpɔst], *s.* der Kompost, Mischdünger.

composure [kəm'pouʒə], *s.* die (Gemüts)ruhe, Fassung, Gelassenheit.

compote ['kɔmpɔt], *s.* Eingemachte(s), das Kompott.

compound, 1. ['kɔmpaund], *adj.* zusammengesetzt; – ***engine,*** die Verbundmaschine; – ***eye,*** das Netzauge; (*Med.*) – ***fracture,*** komplizierter Bruch; (*Math.*) – ***fraction,*** zusammengesetzter Bruch, der Doppelbruch; – ***interest,*** der Zinseszins; – ***number,*** zusammengesetzte Zahl; – ***pillar,*** der Bündelpfeiler; – ***word,*** *see* **2,** 1. **2.** ['kɔmpaund], *s.* 1. (*Gram.*) zusammengesetztes Wort, das Kompositum; 2. die Zusammensetzung, Mischung; Masse, das Präparat; (*Chem.*) die Verbindung; 3. umzäuntes Gelände. **3.** [kəm'paund], *v.t.* 1. zusammensetzen, (ver)mischen; 2. beilegen, schlichten (*a quarrel*); (*Law*) gegen Entschädigung beilegen; ablösen, entrichten (*an obligation*), tilgen (*a debt*); (*Law*) – ***a felony,*** ein Verbrechen (infolge erhaltener Entschädigung) nicht verfolgen. **4.** [kəm'paund], *v.i.* sich abfinden *or* einigen *or* vergleichen, akkordieren (***for,*** über (*Acc.*); ***with,*** mit); – ***with one's creditors,*** ein Abkommen mit seinen Gläubigern treffen.

comprehend [kɔmpri'hend], *v.t.* 1. enthalten, einschließen, in sich schließen *or* fassen; 2. begreifen, verstehen, erfassen. **comprehensible,** *adj.* faßlich, begreiflich, verständlich. **comprehension** [–'henʃən], *s.* 1. der Umfang; die Einbeziehung, Einschließung; 2. das Verständnis, der Verstand, die Einsicht; das Fassungsvermögen, Erkenntnisvermögen; ***that is beyond my –,*** das geht über meinen Horizont. **comprehensive,** *adj.* umfassend, weit; – ***insurance,*** die Kaskoversicherung; – ***school,*** die Einheitsschule. **comprehensiveness,** *s.* die Weite, Ausdehnung, der Umfang; die Reichhaltigkeit.

compress, 1. [kəm'pres], *v.t.* zusammenpressen, zusammendrängen, zusammendrücken, komprimieren; verdichten, kondensieren; ***–ed air,*** die Preßluft, Druckluft; ***–ed brick,*** der Preßziegel; ***–ed style,*** gedrängter Stil. **2.** ['kɔmpres], *s.* (*Med.*) die Kompresse, der Umschlag. **compressibility** [–i'biliti], *s.* die Kompressionsfähigkeit, Verdichtbarkeit, Zusammendrückbarkeit. **compressible** [–'presibl], *adj.* zusammendrückbar, verdichtbar.

compression [kəm'preʃən], *s.* das Zusammenpressen, Zusammendrücken; der Druck, die Druckbeanspruchung, Druckspannung; (*Motor. etc.*) Kompression, Verdichtung; (*fig.*) Zusammendrängung; – ***chamber,*** der Kompressionsraum; – ***spring,*** die Druckfeder; – ***ratio,*** der Verdichtungsgrad. **compressive,** *adj.* Druck–. **compressor,** *s.* der Kompressor, Verdichter, Druckluftkessel, die Preßluftmaschine.

comprise [kəm'praiz], *v.t.* in sich fassen, enthalten, einschließen, einbegreifen, umfassen (***within,*** in (*Acc.*)); bestehen aus.

compromise ['kɔmprəmaiz], **1.** *s.* gütlicher Vergleich; der *or* das Kompromiß. **2.** *v.i.* einen Vergleich schließen, sich vergleichen, übereinkommen (***on,*** über (*Acc.*)), Entgegenkommen zeigen (***on,*** in (*Dat.*)). **3.** *v.t.* (*also* – ***o.s.,*** sich) kompromittieren *or* bloßstellen; aufs Spiel setzen, gefährden; beeinträchtigen.

comptometer [kɔm'tɔmitə], *s.* die Rechenmaschine.

compulsion [kəm'pʌlʃən], *s.* der Zwang; (*Psych.*) Trieb, unwiderstehlicher Drang; ***under*** or ***upon –,*** gezwungen, zwangsweise, unter Zwang. **compulsive** [–siv], *adj.* zwingend, Zwangs–; unumgänglich, unabwendbar. **compulsively,** *adv.* zwangsweise, unter Zwang *or* Nötigung. **compulsorily** [–sərili], *adv.* zwangsweise. **compulsory,** *adj.* Zwangs–, zwangsmäßig, obligatorisch; – ***education,*** allgemeine Schulpflicht; – ***lecture,*** die Pflichtvorlesung; – ***military service,*** allgemeine Wehrpflicht.

compunction [kəm'pʌŋkʃən], *s.* Gewissenbisse (*pl.*), Bedenken (*pl.*), die Reue.

computable [kəm'pju:təbl], *adj.* berechenbar, zu berechnen(d). **computation** [kɔmpju'teiʃən], *s.* die Berechnung, Schätzung, der Kostenanschlag, Überschlag. **compute, 1.** *v.t.* berechnen, schätzen (***at,*** auf (*Acc.*)); ***–d tare,*** die Durchschnittstara. **2.** *v.i.* rechnen. **computer,** *s.* 1. (*the p.*) der (Be)rechner, Kalkulator; 2. (*machine*) die Rechenmaschine, der Rechenautomat, der Computer, (*coll.*) das Elektronengehirn. **computing centre,** *s.* die Auswertstelle, Rechenstelle.

comrade ['kɔmr(e)id], *s.* der (die) Kamerad(in), Genosse (Genossin), Gefährte (Gefährtin); (*Pol.*) (Partei)genosse. **comradeship,** *s.* die Kameradschaft, Kameradschaftlichkeit.

[1]**con** [kɔn], *s.* (*abbr. of* **contra**) ***pro and –,*** das Für und Wider; ***pros and –s,*** Gründe für und wider.

[2]**con,** *v.t.* fleißig studieren, wiederholt lesen, prüfen.

^{3}**con,** *v.t.* (*Naut.*) steuern.

^{4}**con,** *v.t.* (*sl.*) betrügen, beschwindeln, überlisten; (*sl.*) – ***man,*** der Betrüger, Schwindler, Hochstapler.

conation [kɔ'neiʃən], *s.* der Willenstrieb, das Wollen, Begehren. **conative** ['kɔnətiv], *adj.* Willens–, triebhaft, strebend, begehrlich.

concatenate [kən'kætineit], *v.t.* verketten, zusammenknüpfen. **concatenation** [–'neiʃən], *s.* die Verkettung, (*fig.*) Kette, Reihe.

concave [kɔn'keiv], **1.** *adj.* konkav, hohl(geschliffen), ausgehöhlt, Hohl–; ***double*** –, bikonkav; – ***glasses,*** Hohlgläser (*pl.*); – ***lens,*** die Zerstreuungs– *or* Konkavlinse; – ***mirror,*** der Hohlspiegel. **2.** *s.* die (Aus)höhlung, konkave Fläche. **concavity** [–'kæviti], *s.* die Höhlung, Wölbung, Hohlrundung. **concavo|-concave,** *adj.* bikonkav. **--convex,** *adj.* konkavkonvex, hohlerhaben.

conceal [kən'si:l], *v.t.* verhehlen, verheimlichen, verborgen halten, geheimhalten, verschweigen, verbergen, verstecken, (*Mil.*) gegen Sicht decken (***from,*** vor (*Dat.*)). **concealed,** *adj.* verborgen; unübersichtlich (*as a turning*); – ***lighting,*** indirekte Beleuchtung. **concealment,** *s.* die Verheimlichung, Verschleierung, Verhehlung, Verschweigung, Geheimhaltung, Verbergung; Verborgenheit, (*Mil.*) Deckung; – ***of birth,*** die Geburtsverschweigung; ***in*** –, verborgen; – ***of material facts and circumstances,*** die Verhehlung wesentlicher Tatsachen; ***place of*** –, das Versteck.

concede [kən'si:d], *v.t.* einräumen, zugeben, anerkennen, zugestehen, bewilligen, gewähren; (*coll.*) – ***a point,*** in einem Punkt nachgeben.

conceit [kən'si:t], *s.* die Eitelkeit, Eingebildetheit; der (Eigen)dünkel; phantastischer Einfall; weithergeholte Idee, gesuchter Gedankengang, (*Liter.*) das Concetto, Sinnspiel, gedankliche Spielerei; ***idle –s,*** törichte Einfälle; ***out of – with,*** unzufrieden mit *or* über (*Acc.*); ***put him out of*** –, ihm die Lust nehmen (***with,*** an (*Dat.*)). **conceited,** *adj.* eingebildet, eitel (***about,*** auf (*Acc.*)).

conceivable [kən'si:vəbl], *adj.* (er)denkbar; vorstellbar, begreiflich, faßlich; ***the best relation*** –, das denkbar beste Verhältnis. **conceive, 1.** *v.t.* **1.** fassen, begreifen, verstehen (*an idea*); sich (*Dat.*) denken *or* vorstellen, sich (*Dat.*) eine Vorstellung *or* einen Begriff machen von; 2. erdenken, ersinnen, ausdenken (*a plan*), fassen, hegen (*an inclination etc.*); 3. (*Med.*) empfangen (*a child*). **2.** *v.i.* **1.** – ***of,*** sich (*Dat.*) eine Vorstellung *or* einen Begriff machen von, sich (*Dat.*) denken *or* vorstellen; 2. (*Med.*) empfangen, schwanger werden (*of women*), trächtig werden (*of beasts*).

concentrate ['kɔnsəntreit], **1.** *v.t.* **1.** konzentrieren, zusammenfassen, zusammendrängen, zusammenziehen, vereinigen; 2. richten, hinlenken (*attention*) (***upon,*** auf (*Acc.*)); 3. (*Chem.*) verdichten, verstärken, eindicken, sättigen. **2.** *s.* das Konzentrat. **concentrated,** *adj.* konzentriert, verdichtet, gesättigt; – ***charge,*** geballte Ladung; – ***fire,*** das Massenfeuer, die Feuerzusammenfassung, zusammengefaßtes *or* geballtes Feuer. **concentration** [–'treiʃən], *s.* **1.** die Konzentrierung, Konzentration; Zusammenfassung, Zusammenziehung; (*Chem.*) Verdichtung, Verstärkung, Sättigung; Dichte, Grädigkeit; – ***of fire,*** die Feuerzusammenfassung; – ***camp,*** das Konzentrationslager; 2. die Hinlenkung, Richtung (*of attention*) (***on,*** auf (*Acc.*)); (gespannte) Aufmerksamkeit; (*Mil.*) die Massierung, Ansammlung, Bereitstellung, Schwerpunktbildung, der Aufmarsch. **concentrative,** *adj.* konzentrierend.

concentre [kən'sentə], **1.** *v.i.* sich vereinigen, (in einem Punkt) zusammentreffen. **2.** *v.t.* vereinigen, auf einen Punkt bringen. **concentric,** *adj.* konzentrisch, gleichachsig, (*Elec.*) koaxial (*cable*). **concentricity** [kɔnsen'trisiti], *s.* die Konzentrizität.

concept ['kɔnsept], *s.* (*Phil.*) der Begriff; (*coll.*) Gedanke; die Planung.

conception [kən'sepʃən], *s.* **1.** (*Med.*) die Empfängnis (*of women*); (*Eccl.*) ***Immaculate Conception,*** unbefleckte Empfängnis; 2. das Erfassen, Begreifen; Auffassungsvermögen, die Fassungskraft; Auffassung, Vorstellung, der Begriff; Entwurf, Plan, die Anlage, Idee; ***form a – of,*** sich (*Dat.*) einen Begriff machen von; ***this passes all*** –, das übersteigt alle Begriffe. **conceptional, conceptive, conceptual,** *adj.* begrifflich, Begriffs–, abstrakt.

concern [kən'sə:n], **1.** *v.t.* **1.** (*of a th.*) betreffen, angehen, sich beziehen auf (*Acc.*), anbelangen; interessieren, von Interesse *or* Belang *or* Wichtigkeit sein für; ***to (all) whom it may*** –, an alle, die es angeht; ***that does not – you,*** das geht Sie nichts an; 2. (*of a p.*) ***be –ed,*** sich (*Dat.*) Sorgen machen (***about,*** wegen; ***for,*** um); besorgt sein (***about, for,*** um); sich bemühen, es sich (*Dat.*) zur Aufgabe machen (***in doing,*** zu tun); verwickelt sein (***in,*** in (*Acc.*)), beteiligt sein (an (*Dat.*) *or* bei), ein Interesse haben (an (*Dat.*)); sich beschäftigen *or* befassen (***with,*** mit); 3. – ***o.s.,*** sich beschäftigen *or* befassen (***with,*** mit); sich kümmern (***about,*** um), sich (*Dat.*) Sorgen machen (wegen).
2. *s.* **1.** das Interesse (***with, for, about,*** für), der Anteil, die Teilnahme (an (*Dat.*)); ***with deep*** –, mit großer Teilnahme; ***feel – for,*** besorgt sein um, Teilnahme *or* Anteil haben an (*Dat.*); ***he has no – for*** or ***shows no – about it,*** er kümmert sich nicht darum; 2. die Unruhe, Beunruhigung, Sorge, Besorgnis (***at, for, about,*** wegen); ***it causes me considerable*** –, es macht mir große Sorge; 3. die Angelegenheit, Sache, (*coll.*) das Ding, der Krempel; ***that's your own*** –, das ist Ihre S.; ***that is no – of yours,*** das geht dich nichts an; ***petty –s,*** Lappalien (*pl.*); 4. die Bedeutung, Wichtigkeit, der Belang; ***a matter of the utmost*** –, eine S. von äußerster Wichtigkeit *or* von höchstem Belang; 5. die Beziehung, das Verhältnis (***with,*** zu); ***exclusive – with,*** ausschließliche Beschäftigung mit; ***have no – with,*** nichts zu tun haben mit; 6. das Geschäft, Unternehmen, die Firma; ***big*** –, großes Unternehmen, der Großbetrieb; ***flourishing*** –, blühendes Geschäft; ***paying*** –, rentables Geschäft.

concerned [kən'sə:nd], *adj.* **1.** verwickelt (***in,*** in (*Acc.*)), beteiligt (bei *or* an (*Dat.*)), interessiert (an (*Dat.*)); ***the parties*** or ***people*** –, die Beteiligten; 2. besorgt (***about, for, at,*** um), beunruhigt (wegen), betrübt, bekümmert (über (*Acc.*)).

concerning [kən'sə:niŋ], *prep.* hinsichtlich, bezüglich, wegen, betreffs (*Gen.*), betreffend (*Acc.*), in Hinsicht *or* in bezug auf (*Acc.*); – ***him,*** was ihn (an)betrifft *or* anbelangt; – ***it,*** mit bezug darauf, diesbezüglich.

concernment [kən'sə:nmənt], *s. See* **concern, 3.,** 2, 3, 4, 5; (*obs.*) 1.

concert, 1. ['kɔnsət], *s.* **1.** das Einvernehmen, Einverständnis, die Übereinstimmung, Harmonie; (*Hist.*) – ***of Europe,*** Europäisches Konzert; ***in – with,*** in Übereinstimmung *or* im Einverständnis mit; 2. (*Mus.*) das Konzert. **2.** [kən'sə:t], *v.t.* verabreden, vereinbaren, abmachen, gemeinsam besprechen, anordnen, planen; vereinigen (*forces*). **3.** [kən'sə:t], *v.i.* zusammenarbeiten (***with,*** mit). **concerted** [kən'sə:tid], *adj.* gemeinsam (ausgeführt *or* geplant), gemeinschaftlich; (*Mus.*) mehrstimmig; – ***effort,*** gemeinsame Bemühungen (*pl.*); – ***move,*** verabredete Maßnahme.

concert|-goer, *s.* der Konzertbesucher. **--grand,** *s.* der (Konzert)flügel. **--hall,** *s.* der Konzertsaal.

concertina [kɔnsə'ti:nə], **1.** *s.* die Ziehharmonika. **2.** *v.t.* (*coll.*) zusammendrücken. **3.** *v.i.* (*coll.*) zusammenklappen.

concerto [kən'tʃɛətou], *s.* das Konzert, Concerto.

concert|-party, *s.* **1.** die (Künstler)truppe; 2. buntes Programm. **--pitch,** *s.* der Kammerton; (*fig.*) ***up to*** –, auf der Höhe. **--room,** *s. See* **--hall.**

concession [kən'seʃən], *s.* **1.** zugeteilter Grund und Boden, die Konzession; 2. das Zugeständnis, Gewähren, die Einräumung, Anerkennung, Bewilligung, Genehmigung; das Entgegenkommen. **concessionaire** [–'nɛə], *s.* der Konzessionsinhaber, Monopolinhaber, Konzessionär. **con-**

cessive [–'sesiv], *adj.* (*Gram.*) – *clause,* der Konzessivsatz, einräumender Satz.

conch [kɔŋk], *s.* die Muschel(schale), (*Archit.*) Koncha, Halbkuppel. **conchoid,** *s.* (*Math.*) die Schneckenlinie, Konchoide. **conchoidal** [–'kɔidl], *adj.* (*Math.*) schnecken(linien)förmig. **conchological** [–kə'lɔdʒikl], *adj.* Muschel–. **conchology** [–'kɔlədʒi], *s.* die Muschelkunde.

conchy ['kɔntʃi], *s.* (*sl.*) der (Kriegs)dienstverweigerer.

concierge [kɔnsi'ɛəʒ], *s.* der (die) Hausmeister(in), der Portier, Pförtner.

conciliate [kən'silieit], *v.t.* aussöhnen, versöhnen, beschwichtigen; gewinnen. **conciliation** [–'eiʃən], *s.* die Versöhnung, Aussöhnung; Schlichtung, der Ausgleich; – *board,* der Schlichtungsausschuß. **conciliator,** *s.* der Vermittler, Versöhner. **conciliatory** [–ətəri], *adj.* versöhnlich, vermittelnd, Versöhnungs–, Vermittlungs–, gewinnend.

concise [kən'sais], *adj.* kurz, gedrängt, knapp, bündig, prägnant, präzis(e); – *edition,* die Handausgabe. **conciseness,** *s.* die Kürze, Knappheit, Gedrängtheit, Bündigkeit, Prägnanz.

conclave ['kɔnkleiv], *s.* das Konklave, geheime Versammlung; *sit in* –, geheime Sitzung halten.

conclude [kən'klu:d], **1.** *v.t.* **1.** schließen, (be)-endigen, beenden, zu Ende führen, abschließen, beschließen; *to be –d,* Schluß folgt; 2. entscheiden, sich entschließen; 3. (ab)schließen (*contract etc.*). **2.** *v.i.* **1.** aufhören, endigen, enden, zu Ende gehen, ein Ende nehmen; *to* –, zum Schluß, schließlich; 2. beschließen, zu einer Entscheidung kommen; 3. schließen, folgern (*from,* aus). **concluding,** *adj.* (ab)schließend, Schluß–, End–.

conclusion [kən'clu:ʒən], *s.* **1.** der (Ab)schluß, Ausgang, das Ende, Ergebnis; *bring to a* –, zum Abschluß bringen; *in* –, zum Schluß, schließlich, endlich; 2. die (Schluß)folgerung, (logischer) Schluß; die Entscheidung; der Entschluß, Beschluß; *come to the* –, zu der Überzeugung *or* dem Schluß kommen; *draw one's own –s,* seine eigenen Schlüsse ziehen; *jump at –s,* voreilig(e) Schlüsse ziehen; – *of peace,* der Friedensschluß; *try –s with,* es versuchen mit, sich messen mit.

conclusive [kən'klu:siv], *adj.* entscheidend, endgültig; überzeugend, beweiskräftig; – *evidence,* schlagender Beweis. **conclusiveness,** *s.* das Entscheidende, Überzeugende, die Endgültigkeit.

concoct [kən'kɔkt], *v.t.* (zusammen)brauen, auskochen, aussieden, ausziehen; (*fig.*) erfinden, aussinnen, aushecken (*a plot*). **concoction** [–'kɔkʃən], *s* das Brauen, Auskochen, die Zubereitung, der Absud, das Dekokt, Gebräu, Präparat, die Mischung; (*fig.*) Erfindung, das Ausbrüten (*of a scheme*); (*coll.*) *a – from beginning to end,* von A bis Z rein erfunden.

concomitance, concomitancy [kən'kɔmitəns(i)], *s.* das Zusammenbestehen, gleichzeitiges Vorhandensein; (*Eccl.*) die Koexistenz. **concomitant, 1.** *adj.* begleitend, gleichzeitig; (*Eccl.*) mitwirkend; – *circumstances,* Begleitumstände (*pl.*). **2.** *s.* die Begleiterscheinung, der Begleitumstand.

concord ['kɔŋkɔ:d], *s.* die Eintracht, Einmütigkeit, Harmonie, der Einklang; die Übereinstimmung (*also Gram.*); (*Mus.*) der Einklang, Zusammenklang; (*Law*) Vertrag, das Übereinkommen. **concordance** [kən'kɔ:dəns], *s.* die Übereinstimmung; Konkordanz (*to the Bible etc.*); *in – with,* in Übereinstimmung mit. **concordant,** *adj.* übereinstimmend; harmonisch. **concordat** [–'kɔ:dæt], *s.* das Konkordat, Übereinkommen.

concourse ['kɔŋkɔ:s], *s.* der (Menschen)auflauf, die Ansammlung, (Menschen)menge, das Gedränge, Gewühl, der Haufen; das Zusammenlaufen, Zusammenkommen, Zusammentreffen.

concresence [kɔn'kresəns], *s.* (*Med., Bot. etc.*) die (Zellen)verwachsung.

concrete ['kɔnkri:t], **1.** *adj.* **1.** wirklich, dinglich, greifbar, wesenhaft, gegenständlich, körperlich, konkret; (*Math.*) benannt (*as a number*); – *noun,* das Konkretum, Dingwort; 2. dicht, fest, kompakt; 3. (*Tech.*) Beton–, betoniert. **2.** *s.* **1.** der Beton, Zement, Steinmörtel; – *mixer,* die Betonmischmaschine; *reinforced* –, der Eisenbeton; 2. (*Phil.*) das Konkrete; konkreter Begriff; *in the* –, in Wirklichkeit, im konkreten Falle. **3.** *v.t.* zu einer festen Masse verdinden, betonieren. **4.** *v.i.* eine feste Masse bilden, fest werden; anschießen (*of crystals*). **concreteness,** *s.* die Festigkeit, Körperlichkeit; das Konkrete.

concretion [kən'kri:ʃən], *s.* das Zusammenwachsen, die Verwachsung; das Gerinnen, Festwerden; (*Geol.*) die Zusammenhäufung, Ablagerung, Konkretion; (*Med.*) steinige Absonderung, das Konkrement; der Knoten, das Klümpchen, feste Masse.

concubinage [kən'kju:binidʒ], *s.* wilde Ehe, das Konkubinat. **concubine** ['kɔŋkjubain], *s.* die Konkubine, (*of primitive tribes*) Nebenfrau.

concupiscence [kən'kju:pisəns], *s.* sinnliche Begierde, die Sinnlichkeit, Fleischeslust, Sinnenlust. **concupiscent,** *adj.* lüstern, sinnlich, wollüstig.

concur [kən'kə:], *v.i.* (*of events*) zusammentreffen, zusammenfallen; mitwirken, beitragen; (*of persons*) übereinstimmen, einverstanden sein (*with,* mit; *in,* in (*Dat.*)); *I – with your view,* ich stimme Ihrer Meinung bei.

concurrence [kən'kʌrəns], *s.* das Zusammentreffen; (*Law*) der Konflikt, die Kollision; Übereinstimmung, Zustimmung, das Einverständnis; (*Geom.*) der Schnittpunkt. **concurrent,** *adj.* zusammenwirkend, mitwirkend; übereinstimmend, gleichzeitig, gleichlaufend; (*Geom.*) in einem Punkte treffend, sich schneidend; (*Law*) gleich kompetent, gleichberechtigt; *–ly with,* zusammen *or* gleichzeitig mit.

concuss [kən'kʌs], *v.t.* **1.** erschüttern (*with,* durch); 2. durch Drohung zwingen, einschüchtern. **concussion** [–'kʌʃən], *s.* die Erschütterung; – *of the brain,* die Gehirnerschütterung; *–-fuse,* der Aufschlagzünder. **concussive** [–siv], *adj.* erschütternd.

condemn [kən'dem], *v.t.* **1.** verdammen; verurteilen schuldig sprechen (*of, Gen.*); mißbilligen, tadeln, abfällig urteilen über (*Acc.*); 2. verwerfen, als unbewohnbar *or* unbrauchbar *or* untauglich erklären; *the ship was –ed,* das Schiff wurde für seeuntüchtig erklärt *or* wurde ausrangiert. **condemnable,** *adj.* verwerflich, verdammenswert; strafbar. **condemnation** [kɔndem'neiʃən], *s.* die Verurteilung, Schuldigsprechung; Verdammung, Mißbilligung, Verwerfung, der Tadel; die Untauglichkeitserklärung. **condemnatory** [–nətəri], *adj.* verurteilend, verdammend.

condensability [kəndensə'biliti], *s.* die Verdichtbarkeit, Kondensierbarkeit. **condensate** [–'denseit], *s.* das Kondensationsprodukt. **condensation** [kɔnden'seiʃən], *s.* **1.** die Verdichtung, Kondensation; Zusammendrängung, Anhäufung; (*Av.*) – *trail,* der Kondensstreifen; 2. (*Meteor.*) der Niederschlag, das Niederschlagwasser; 3. (*fig.*) die Abkürzung, Zusammenfassung.

condense [kən'dens], **1.** *v.t.* verdichten, eindicken, kondensieren (*liquids*), niederschlagen, verflüssigen (*gases*); zusammendrängen, zusammenfassen, abkürzen; *–d milk,* die Kondensmilch. **2.** *v.i.* sich verdichten (*of liquids*), sich verflüssigen (*of gases*). **condenser,** *s.* **1.** (*Elec.*) der Kondensator; *fixed* –, der Blockkondensator; *variable* –, der Drehkondensator; 2. (*Opt.*) der Kondensor; die Kondensorlinse; 3. das Kühlrohr, der Kühler, Verdichter, Verflüssiger.

condescend [kɔndi'send], *v.i.* sich herablassen (*to,* zu), leutselig sein (gegen), geruhen, belieben (*to do,* zu tun). **condescending,** *adj.* herablassend, leutselig. **condescension** [–'senʃən], *s.* die Herablassung, Leutseligkeit.

condign [kən'dain], *adj.* verdient; gehörig, gebührend, angemessen (*of punishment*).

condiment ['kɔndimənt], *s.* die Würze, Zutat.

condition [kən'diʃən], **1.** *s.* **1.** die Beschaffenheit,

Lage, der Zustand; Familienstand; die Vermögenslage; der Rang, Stand, (gesellschaftliche) Stellung; (*Spt.*) die Form, Kondition; *pl.* Umstände (*pl.*), Verhältnisse (*pl.*); (*Mil.*) ***–s on the ground,*** Geländeverhältnisse (*pl.*); ***all sorts and –s of men,*** alle Arten von Menschen; ***change one's –,*** sich verändern, heiraten; ***in –,*** in Form *or* Kondition; ***in an interesting –,*** in anderen Umständen, schwanger; ***every – of life,*** jede Lebenslage; ***under existing –s,*** unter diesen Umständen. 2. die (Vor)bedingung, Voraussetzung, das Erfordernis; (*Law*) der Vorbehalt, die Klausel; (*Gram.*) Protasis, der Bedingungssatz; ***essential –,*** wesentliche Voraussetzung; ***fundamental –,*** die Grundbedingung; ***implied –s,*** stillschweigende Bedingungen; ***make it a – that,*** es zur Bedingung machen daß; ***on – that,*** unter der Bedingung, daß; ***favourable peace –s,*** günstige Friedensbedingungen; ***working –s,*** Arbeitsbedingungen. **2.** *v.t.* 1. bedingen, die Bedingung *or* Voraussetzung sein für; zur Bedingung machen, die Bedingung stellen daß, bestimmen, ausmachen; 2. abhängig machen (*on*, von), in den gewünschten Zustand bringen; ***be –ed by,*** abhängen von.

conditional [kən'diʃənl], **1.** *adj.* bedingt ((*up*)*on*, durch), abhängig (von); freibleibend; (*Gram.*) konditional; ***– acceptance,*** freibleibende Annahme; ***– clause,*** der Bedingungssatz. **2.** *s.* (*Gram.*) die Bedingungsform, das Konditional. **conditionality** [–'næliti], *s.* die Bedingtheit. **conditionally,** *adv.* unter der Bedingung. **conditioned,** *adj.* 1. bedingt, eingeschränkt, relativ, abhängig; ***– reflex,*** bedingter Reflex; 2. (*as suff.*) geartet, beschaffen.

condolatory [kən'doulətəri], *adj.* Beileid bezeigend, Beileids–. **condole,** *v.i.* sein Beileid bezeigen *or* bezeugen (***with***, *Dat.*). **condolence,** *s.* (*oft. pl.*) die Beileidsbezeigung, das Beileid; ***letter of –,*** der Beileidsbrief.

condonation [kɔndo'neiʃən], *s.* die Vergebung, Verzeihung, stillschweigende Einwilligung. **condone** [kən'doun], *v.t.* verzeihen, vergeben, entschuldigen, nachsehen (***his mistake***, ihm seinen Fehltritt).

condor ['kɔndɔ:], *s.* (*Orn.*) der Kondor.

conduce [kən'dju:s], *v.i.* beitragen, dienen, führen (*to*(***wards***), zu), förderlich sein (*Dat.*). **conducive,** *adj.* förderlich, dienlich (*to*, *Dat.*), nützlich (für); ***be – to,*** herbeiführen.

conduct, 1. ['kɔndʌkt], *s.* 1. die Führung, Leitung, Verwaltung (*of affairs*); ***safe –,*** der Geleitsbrief, sicheres Geleit; 2. das Betragen, Benehmen, Verhalten, Gebaren, die Führung; (*Law*) ***disorderly –,*** grober Unfug; (*Mil.*) ***good –,*** gute Führung; (*Mil.*) ***– prejudicial to good order and discipline,*** Ordnung und Disziplin gefährdendes Verhalten; ***– unbecoming a gentleman,*** ungebührliches Betragen; ***– of war,*** die Kriegführung. **2.** [kən'dʌkt], *v.t.* 1. (ge)leiten, (zu)führen; verwalten, anordnen, leiten, führen (*a business*), dirigieren (*an orchestra*), leiten (*heat, electricity etc.*); ***– away,*** ableiten; ***–ed tour,*** die Gesellschaftsreise (*holidays*), Führung (*round the sights*); 2. ***– o.s.,*** sich benehmen *or* betragen *or* (auf)führen.

conductance [kən'dʌktəns], *s.* die Leitfähigkeit, das Leitvermögen, der Wirkleitwert. **conductibility** [–i'biliti], *s.* die Leitfähigkeit. **conducting, 1.** *adj.* Leit(ungs)–; ***– wire,*** der Leitungsdraht, die Drahtleitung. **2.** *s.* das Leiten; ***capable of –,*** leitungsfähig. **conduction** [–'dʌkʃən], *s.* die Leitung, Übertragung; (Zu)führung. **conductive,** *adj.* leitend, leitfähig, Leitungs–. **conductivity** [kɔndʌk'tiviti], *s.* das Leitvermögen, der Leitwert.

conductor [kən'dʌktə], *s.* der Führer, Begleiter; Verwalter, Leiter (*also Phys., Elec.*), (*Elec.*) Leitungsdraht, die Zuleitung, (*Build.*) das Fallrohr; (*Mus.*) der Dirigent; (*on trams etc.*) Schaffner, (*Am.*) Zugführer; ***–'s baton,*** der Taktstock; ***lightning –,*** der Blitzableiter; ***– rail,*** die Stromschiene, Leit(ungs)schiene. **conductress,** *s.* die Schaffnerin.

conduit ['kʌnd(ju)it], *s.* die (Rohr)leitung, Wasserleitung, Röhre; der Kanal, Abzug; (*Elec.*) ***– box,*** die Abzweigsdose; ***– pipe,*** das Leitungsrohr, (*Elec.*) Isolierrohr.

condyle ['kɔndil], *s.* (*Anat.*) der Gelenkhöcker.

cone [koun], *s.* (*Geom.*) der Kegel, (*of firs*) Zapfen; (*ice-cream*) die (Waffel)tüte; (*of loudspeaker*) der Konus; (*firearms*) ***– of dispersion,*** die Streugarbe; ***– of rays,*** das Strahlenbündel; ***– of shade,*** der Schattenkegel. **cone|-bearing,** *adj.* zapfentragend. **– bearing,** *s.* (*Tech.*) das Kegellager, Zapfenlager. **– clutch,** *s.* (*Motor.*) die Konuskupplung.

coney, *see* **cony.**

confab ['kɔnfæb], *coll. for* **confabulate** *and* **confabulation. confabulate** [kən'fæbjuleit], *v.i.* vertraulich plaudern. **confabulation** [–'leiʃən], *s.* vertrauliches Gespräch, gemütliche Plauderei.

confection [kən'fekʃən], *s.* 1. die Zubereitung, Zusammensetzung, Mischung; 2. das Konfekt, (mit Zucker) Eingemachte(s); 3. (*ladies' wear*) der Konfektionsartikel; 4. (*Med.*) die Latwerge. **confectioner,** *s.* der Konditor, Zuckerbäcker; ***–'s shop,*** die Konditorei. **confectionery,** *s.* das Konfekt, Zuckerwerk, Süßwaren (*pl.*); die Konditorei; das Kompott.

confederacy [kən'fedərəsi], *s.* das Bündnis, der (Staaten)bund; das Komplott, die Verschwörung. **confederate, 1.** [–rit], *s.* Verbündete(r), der Bundesgenosse; Mitschuldige(r), Helfershelfer; (*Hist.*) Südstaatler (*Am. Civil War*). **2.** [–rit], *adj.* verbündet, verbunden, Bundes–; (*Hist.*) ***Confederate States of America,*** die Südstaaten von Amerika. **3.** [–reit], *v.t.* (*v.i.* sich) verbünden. **confederation** [–'reiʃən], *s.* das Bündnis, der (Staaten)bund; (*Switzerland*) die Eidgenossenschaft.

confer [kən'fə:], **1.** *v.t.* erteilen, verleihen, zuteil werden lassen ((*up*)*on*, *Dat.*); ***– a degree,*** einen (akademischen) Grad verleihen; ***– a favour on him,*** ihm eine Gefälligkeit erweisen; (*Eccl.*) ***– a living,*** eine Pfründe zuteilen. **2.** *v.i.* unterhandeln, sich besprechen *or* beraten, beratschlagen (***with him about a th.***, mit ihm über (*Acc.*)). **conference** ['kɔnfərəns], *s.* die Unterredung, Verhandlung, Beratung, Besprechung; Konferenz, Sitzung, Tagung; ***hold a –,*** eine Sitzung (ab)halten; ***sit in –,*** tagen. **conferment** [kən'fə:mənt], *s.* die Verleihung, Erteilung, Zuteilung ((*up*)*on*, an (*Acc.*)).

confess [kən'fes], **1.** *v.t.* zugestehen, zugeben, anerkennen, bekennen, (ein)gestehen; (*Eccl.*) beichten (*sins*), (*of the priest*) die Beichte abnehmen (*Dat.*); ***– o.s.,*** sich bekennen (***to be***, als). **2.** *v.i.* sich bekennen (*to*, zu), ein Bekenntnis ablegen; (*esp. Eccl.*) sich schuldig bekennen (*to*, *Gen. or* an (*Dat.*)), beichten; ***– to doing,*** eingestehen, getan zu haben. **confessed,** *adj.* zugestanden, offenbar; ***stand – as a liar,*** als Lügner dastehen. **confessedly** [–idli], *adv.* offenbar, zugestandenermaßen.

confession [ken'feʃən], *s.* das Geständnis (*also Law*), Zugeständnis, Bekenntnis; (*Eccl.*) Sündenbekenntnis, die Beichte; (*Eccl.*) Glaubensgemeinschaft; ***auricular –,*** die Ohrenbeichte; ***dying –,*** das Bekenntnis auf dem Sterbebett; ***– of faith,*** das Glaubensbekenntnis. **confessional, 1.** *s.* der Beichtstuhl. **2.** *adj.* Beicht–, Bekenntnis–; konfessionell, Konfessions–. **confessor,** *s.* der (Glaubens)bekenner, Glaubenszeuge; ***father –,*** der Beichtvater; ***Edward the Confessor,*** Eduard der Bekenner.

confidant [kɔnfi'dænt], *s.* Vertraute(r), der Mitwisser. **confidante,** *s.* die Vertraute, Mitwisserin.

confide [kən'faid], **1.** *v.t.* anvertrauen, vertraulich mitteilen (*secret etc.*), zu treuen Händen übergeben (*a task etc.*) (*to*, *Dat.*). **2.** *v.i.* vertrauen (*in*, *Dat. or* auf (*Acc.*)), Vertrauen schenken (*Dat.*); sich anvertrauen (*Dat.*), sein Vertrauen setzen, sich verlassen (auf (*Acc.*)).

confidence ['kɔnfidəns], *s.* 1. das Vertrauen (*in*, zu *or* auf (*Acc.*)), Zutrauen (zu); Selbstvertrauen, die Zuversicht; ***be in his –,*** sein Vertrauen genießen; ***have every –,*** unbedingte Zuversicht haben;

in –, vertraulich, im Vertrauen; ***have – in him,*** Vertrauen in ihm setzen, Vertrauen zu ihm haben; ***– man,*** see ***– trickster; take him into one's –,*** ihn ins Vertrauen ziehen; ***– trick,*** die Bauernfängerei; ***– trickster,*** der Bauernfänger, Schwindler; ***vote of –,*** das Vertrauensvotum; ***vote of no –,*** das Mißvertrauensvotum; 2. vertrauliche Mitteilung.

confident ['kɔnfidənt], *adj.* voll Vertrauen (*of*, auf (*Acc.*)), gewiß, sicher, überzeugt; selbstsicher, kühn; ***– of victory,*** siegesgewiß; ***– of success,*** des Erfolges sicher *or* gewiß. **confidential** [–'denʃəl], *adj.* vertraulich, geheim; Vertrauens–; ***– clerk,*** der Prokurist; ***– secretary,*** der Privatsekretär. **confidently,** *adv.* zuversichtlich, des Erfolges gewiß; selbstsicher, kühn; ***speaking –,*** unter uns gesagt. **confiding** [kən'faidiŋ], *adj.* zutraulich, vertrauensvoll.

configuration [kɔnfigə'reiʃən], *s.* die Gestaltung, Bildung, Gestalt, Struktur, der Bau; (*Chem., Phys.*) die Anordnung; (*Math.*) Figur, Zusammenstellung; (*Astr.*) Konfiguration, der Aspekt, Aspekte (*pl.*), das Sternbild, der Planetenstand.

confine, 1. [kən'fain], *v.t.* 1. begrenzen, beschränken, einschränken (*to*, auf (*Acc.*); ***within***, in (*Acc.*)); einsperren, einkerkern; (*fig.*) ***– o.s. to,*** sich beschränken auf (*Acc.*); ***be –d to bed,*** bettlägerig sein; ***be –d to one's room,*** ans Zimmer gefesselt sein; 2. (*Med.*) ***be –d,*** in den Wochen kommen; ***be –d of a son,*** einen Sohn gebären, mit einem Sohn niederkommen, von einem Sohn entbunden werden. **2.** ['kɔnfain], *s.* (*usu. pl.*) die Grenze; (*fig.*) Schwelle, der Rand; (*Poet.*) die Gefangenschaft.

confinement [kən'fainmənt], *s.* 1. die Beengtheit; Beschränkung, Einschränkung (***to***, auf (*Acc.*)); Haft, Gefangenschaft, (*Mil.*) der Arrest; ***– to (one's) bed,*** die Bettlägerigkeit; (*Mil.*) ***– to quarters,*** der Stubenarrest; ***close –,*** strenge Haft; ***solitary –,*** die Einzelhaft; ***place under –,*** in Haft nehmen, (*Mil.*) in Arrest schicken; 2. (*Med.*) das Wochenbett, die Niederkunft, Entbindung.

confirm [kən'fə:m], *v.t.* bekräftigen, bestärken, bestätigen, (*position, power etc.*) festigen; (*Eccl.*) konfirmieren (*Prot.*), firmeln (*R.C.*); ***– my resolution,*** mich in meinem Entschluß bestärken; ***– my suspicion,*** meinen Verdacht bestätigen; ***this –s my words,*** dies bestätigt die Richtigkeit meiner Worte; ***– by oath,*** eidlich erhärten.

confirmation [kɔnfə'meiʃən], *s.* die Bestätigung; Bekräftigung, Stärkung; Festigung; (*Eccl.*) Konfirmation (*Prot.*), Firmelung (*R.C.*); ***– of signature,*** die Unterschriftsbeglaubigung.

confirmative [kən'fə:mətiv], **confirmatory** [–təri], *adj.* bestätigend, bekräftigend, beglaubigend, Bestätigungs–. **confirmed,** *adj.* 1. bestätigt, bestärkt; 2. (*fig.*) fest, gefestigt, eingefleischt, eingewurzelt, unverbesserlich, Erz–; ***– bachelor,*** eingefleischter Junggeselle; ***– drunkard,*** der Trunkenbold, Gewohnheitssäufer; ***– invalid,*** chronisch Leidende(r); ***– sceptic,*** der Erzzweifler.

confiscate ['kɔnfiskeit], **1.** *v.t.* beschlagnahmen, einziehen, konfiszieren. **2.** *adj.* beschlagnahmt, konfisziert, verfallen. **confiscation** [–'keiʃən], *s.* die Beschlagnahme, Einziehung, Konfiszierung, Konfiskation, Verfallserklärung. **confiscatory** [kən'fiskətəri], *adj.* Einziehungs– (*powers*).

conflagration [kɔnflə'greiʃən], *s.* (großer) Brand, die Feuersbrunst.

conflate [kən'fleit], *v.t.* vereinigen, verschmelzen (*texts*). **conflation** [–'fleiʃən], *s.* die Verschmelzung.

conflict, 1. ['kɔnflikt], *s.* der Kampf, Streit, Konflikt, Zusammenstoß; (*fig.*) Widerstreit, Widerspruch; ***– of allegiances,*** der Widerstreit der Pflichten; ***– of ideas,*** der Ideenkonflikt; ***mental –,*** der Seelenkampf; ***come into – with,*** in Streit *or* (*fig.*) Widerstreit geraten mit. **2.** [kən'flikt], *v.i.* in Konflikt *or* im Widerspruch stehen, sich widersprechen (*with*, mit), im Gegensatz stehen (zu); ***–ing ideas,*** (einander) widersprechende Ideen.

confluence ['kɔnfluəns], *s.* der Zusammenfluß (*of rivers*), Zustrom, Zulauf, Auflauf (*of people*).

confluent, 1. *adj.* zusammenfließend, zusammenlaufend; (*Med.*) zusammenwachsend, verwachsen. **2.** *s.* der Nebenfluß. **conflux** [–flʌks], *s. See* **confluence** (*esp. of people*).

conform [kən'fɔ:m], **1.** *v.t.* anpassen (*to*, *Dat. or* an (*Acc.*)). **2.** *v.i.* sich anpassen *or* angleichen (*to*, *Dat.*), sich fügen *or* schicken (in (*Acc.*)), sich richten (nach); entsprechen (*Dat.*); (*Eccl.*) anglikanisch sein, sich der Staatskirche unterwerfen. **conformable,** *adj.* gleichförmig, übereinstimmend, vereinbar, konform (***to***, ***with***, mit), angemessen (*Dat.*); (*of a p.*) fügsam, nachgiebig, unterwürfig; ***be – to,*** entsprechen (*Dat.*). **conformance,** *s.* die Anpassung, Angleichung (***to***, ***with***, an (*Acc.*)), Übereinstimmung (mit); ***in – with,*** gemäß (*Dat.*).

conformation [kɔnfɔ:'meiʃən], *s.* 1. *See* **conformance**; 2. die Fügsamkeit, Unterwürfigkeit (***to***, gegenüber); 3. Gestaltung, Formgebung; Gestalt, Form, Struktur; (gegenseitige) Anordnung, (übereinstimmendes) Verhalten, die Gleichförmigkeit. **conformity** [kən'fɔ:miti], *s.* die Gleichförmigkeit, Übereinstimmung (***with***, mit), Anpassung, Fügsamkeit (***to***, gegenüber); (*Eccl.*) Konformität; ***in – with,*** in Übereinstimmung mit, übereinstimmend mit, gemäß (*Dat.*); ***be in – with,*** übereinstimmen mit.

confound [kən'faund], *v.t.* vermengen, durcheinanderbringen; verwechseln; verwirren; verwirrt *or* bestürzt machen; vereiteln, vernichten, zugrunde richten; (*B.*) beschämen; (*coll.*) ***– him!*** zum Teufel mit ihm! (*coll.*) ***– it!*** zum Teufel *or* Henker! verdammt! (*coll.*) ***– his cheek!*** so eine Frechheit! **confounded,** *adj.* verlegen, verwirrt, bestürzt; (*coll.*) verflucht, verdammt, verflixt, verteufelt.

confraternity [kɔnfrə'tə:niti], *s.* die Bruderschaft, (brüderliche) Gemeinschaft.

confrère ['kɔnfrɛə], *s.* der Kollege, Genosse.

confront [kən'frʌnt], *v.t.* entgegenhalten (***him with a th.***, ihm etwas); gegenüberstehen *or* –liegen *or* –treten (*Dat.*); die Stirn bieten, trotzig entgegentreten (*Dat.*); ***be –ed with,*** stehen vor (*Dat.*), gegenüberstehen (*Dat.*). **confrontation** [kɔnfrʌn'teiʃən], *s.* die Gegenüberstellung.

Confucian [kən'fju:ʃən], **1.** *adj.* konfuzianisch. **2.** *s.* der (die) Konfuzianer(in). **Confucius,** *s.* Konfuzius (*m.*).

confuse [kən'fju:z], *v.t.* vermengen (***with***, mit), durcheinanderbringen, (miteinander) verwechseln; in Unordnung bringen, verwirren; (*a p.*) verwirren, außer Fassung bringen, verlegen machen. **confused,** *adj.* verwirrt, bestürzt, verlegen (*of persons*); wirr, verworren (*of things*). **confusing,** *adj.* irreführend, verwirrend. **confusion** [–'fju:ʒən], *s.* die Verwirrung, Unordnung, das Durcheinander, die Verworrenheit; Verwechs(e)lung; (*of a p.*) Verlegenheit, Bestürzung, Verwirrung.

confutable [kən'fju:təbl], *adj.* widerlegbar. **confutation** [kɔnfju'teiʃən], *s.* die Widerlegung. **confute,** *v.t.* widerlegen; zum Schweigen bringen.

congé ['kɔ̃ʒei], *s.* der Abschied; die Verabschiedung, Entlassung, Beurlaubung.

congeal [kən'dʒi:l], **1.** *v.i.* (ge)frieren, zusammenfrieren, zu Eis werden; dick *or* fest werden, gerinnen; ***be –ed,*** erstarren. **2.** *v.t.* gefrieren *or* gerinnen lassen; erstarren. **congealable** [–əbl], *adj.* gefrierbar. **congealing, congealment,** *s.* das Gefrieren, die Zusammenfrierung; das Gerinnen, Erstarren, Festwerden.

congelation [kɔndʒi'leiʃən], *s. See* **congealing.**

congener ['kɔndʒinə], *s.* Stammverwandte(r), Artverwandte(r), verwandtes *or* gleichartiges Wesen *or* Ding. **congenial** [kən'dʒi:niəl], *adj.* gleichartig, geistesverwandt (***with***, *Dat. or* mit); zusagend, sympathisch; zuträglich, passend, angemessen, entsprechend (*to*, *Dat.*); ***be – to him,*** ihm passen *or* zusagen. **congeniality** [–ni'æliti], *s.* die Gleichartigkeit, Geistesverwandtschaft; Angemessenheit.

congenital [kən'dʒenitəl], *adj.* angeboren. **congenitally,** *adv.* von Geburt (an).

conger(-eel) ['kɔŋgə–], *s.* der Seeaal, Meeraal.

congeries [kɔn'dʒeriiːz], *s.* der Haufen, die Anhäufung, Masse (*of stars*).

congest [kən'dʒest], **1.** *v.i.* sich ansammeln *or* stauen *or* verstopfen. **2.** *v.t.* überfüllen, verstopfen; (*Phys.*) ineinanderdrängen. **congested,** *adj.* überfüllt (*with*, von), übervölkert; (*Med.*) mit Blut überfüllt. **congestion** [–ʃən], *s.* die Anhäufung, Ansammlung, der Andrang, (*Med.*) Blutandrang; – ***of the brain,*** der Blutandrang zum Gehirn; ***traffic*** –, die Verkehrsstockung.

conglobate, 1. ['kɔnglobeit], *v.t.* (*v.i.* sich) zusammenballen (***into***, zu). **2.** [–bit], *adj.* (zusammen)geballt. **conglobation** [–'beiʃən], *s.* die Kugelbildung, Zusammenballung; Anhäufung.

conglomerate, 1. [kən'glɔmərit], *adj.* zusammengeballt, (zusammen)geknäuelt, (*fig.*) zusammengewürfelt, gemischt; – ***rocks,*** *see* **2. 2.** [–rit], *s.* (*Geol.*) das Konglomerat; (*fig.*) Gemisch, die Anhäufung. **3.** [–reit], *v.t.* (*v.i.* sich) zusammenballen *or* –knäueln, verbinden (***into***, zu); (*usu. v.i.* sich) ansammeln, anhäufen, aufhäufen, zusammenhäufen. **conglomeration** [–'reiʃən], *s.* die Anhäufung, Zusammenhäufung; (*Geol.*) Ballung, (*Math.*) Häufung; (*fig.*) Masse, das Knäuel, Gemisch.

conglutinate [kən'gluːtineit], **1.** *v.t.* zusammenleimen, zusammenkitten. **2.** *v.i.* zusammenkleben. **conglutination** [–'neiʃən], *s.* das Zusammenkleben; (*fig.*) die Vereinigung.

congratulate [kən'grætjuleit], *v.t.* beglückwünschen (*Acc.*), Glück wünschen, gratulieren (*Dat.*) (***on***, zu). **congratulation** [–'leiʃən], *s.* (*oft. pl.*) der Glückwunsch (***on***, zu); –***s!*** meinen Glückwunsch! ich gratuliere! **congratulator,** *s.* der (die) Gratulant(in). **congratulatory** [–lətəri], *adj.* (be)glückwünschend, Glückwunsch–, Gratulations–.

congregate ['kɔŋgrigeit], **1.** *v.t.* (ver)sammeln, zusammenbringen. **2.** *v.i.* sich (ver)sammeln, zusammenkommen, sich zusammenscharen. **congregation** [–'geiʃən], *s.* das (An)sammeln; die Versammlung, Ansammlung, Zusammenkunft; (*of things*) Sammlung, Menge; (*Eccl.*) (Kirchen)gemeinde. **congregational,** *adj.* (*Eccl.*) Gemeinde–; (*Eccl.*) independent. **Congregationalism,** *s.* die Selbstverwaltung der Kirchengemeinde. **Congregationalist,** *s.* (*Eccl.*) der Independent.

congress ['kɔŋgres], *s.* die Tagung, Versammlung, (*also Am. Pol.*) der Kongreß. **congressional** [kən'greʃənl], *adj.* Kongreß–. **congress-man,** *s.* (*Am.*) Kongreßabgeordnete(r).

congruence, congruency ['kɔŋgruəns(i)], *s.* die Übereinstimmung; (*Math.*) Kongruenz. **congruent,** *adj.* gemäß, entsprechend (***with***, *Dat.*), übereinstimmend (mit); (*Math.*) kongruent, deckungsgleich; (*Log.*) sich deckend.

congruity [kɔŋ'gruːiti], *s.* die Übereinstimmung (***with***, mit), Folgerichtigkeit, Angemessenheit; (*Math.*) Kongruenz. **congruous** ['kɔŋgruəs], *adj.* übereinstimmend (***to***, ***with***, mit), folgerichtig, angemessen, gemäß, entsprechend (*Dat.*).

conic(al) ['kɔnik(l)], *adj.* kegelförmig, konisch; ***conic section,*** der Kegelschnitt; ***conical buoy,*** die Spitzboje; ***conical frustrum,*** der Kegelstumpf. **conicity** [kɔ'nisiti], *s.* die Kegelform. **conics,** *pl.* (*sing. constr.*) die Lehre von den Kegelschnitten.

conifer ['kounifə, 'kɔ–], *s.* der Nadelbaum, Zapfenträger, die Konifere; *pl.* Nadelhölzer (*pl.*). **coniferous** [–'nifərəs], *adj.* zapfentragend, Nadel(holz)–.

conjecturable [kən'dʒektʃərəbl], *adj.* zu vermuten(d), erratbar. **conjectural,** *adj.* mutmaßlich. **conjecture, 1.** *s.* die Mutmaßung, Vermutung, Annahme; ***make a*** –, eine Mutmaßung anstellen. **2.** *v.t.* mutmaßen, vermuten, erraten. **3.** *v.i.* Vermutungen anstellen, raten (***about***, über (*Acc.*)).

conjoin [kən'dʒɔin], *v.t.* (*v.i.* sich) verbinden, vereinigen. **conjoint,** *adj.* verein(ig)t, verbunden, gemeinsam.

conjugal ['kɔndʒugl], *adj.* ehelich, Ehe–; – ***love,*** die Gattenliebe; – ***rights,*** eheliche Rechte. **conjugality** [–'gæliti], *s.* der Ehestand.

conjugate, 1. ['kɔndʒugit], *adj.* gepaart; (*Bot.*) paarig; (*Math.*) konjugiert, zugeordnet; (*Chem.*) assoziiert, konjugiert; (*Gram.*) wurzelverwandt. **2.** [–geit], *v.t.* (*Gram.*) beugen, konjugieren (*a verb*). **3.** [–geit], *v.i.* (*Biol.*) sich paaren. **conjugation** [–'geiʃən], *s.* (*Gram.*) die Beugung, Abwandlung, Konjugation, (*Biol.*) Vereinigung.

conjunct [kən'dʒʌŋkt], *adj.* verbunden, verein(ig)t. **conjunction** [–'dʒʌŋkʃən], *s.* 1. die Vereinigung, Verbindung; das Zusammentreffen (*of events*); (*Astr.*) die Konjunktion; ***in – with,*** zusammengenommen mit; 2. (*Gram.*) das Bindewort, die Konjunktion.

conjunctiva [kɔndʒʌŋk'taivə], *s.* (*Anat.*) die Bindehaut (*of the eye*).

conjunctive [kən'dʒʌŋktiv], *adj.* 1. verbindend, Verbindungs–; (*Anat.*) Binde–; 2. (*Gram.*) konjunktional, konjunktivisch; – ***adverb,*** verbindendes Umstandswort; – ***mood,*** die Möglichkeitsform, der Konjunktiv.

conjunctivitis [kəndʒʌŋkti'vaitis], *s.* (*Med.*) die Bindehautentzündung.

conjuncture [kən'dʒʌŋktʃə], *s.* das Zusammentreffen (*of events*); die Krise.

conjuration [kɔndʒu'reiʃən], *s.* feierliche Anrufung, die Beschwörung; Zauberformel; Zauberei. **conjure, 1.** [kən'dʒuə], *v.t.* inständig bitten, feierlich anflehen. **2.** ['kʌndʒə], *v.t.* beschwören; behexen, verhexen, bezaubern; – ***away,*** weghexen, bannen; – ***up,*** heraufbeschwören, zitieren (*spirits*). **3.** ['kʌndʒə], *v.i.* hexen, zaubern, Zauberei treiben; ***a name to – with,*** ein Name von mächtigem Einfluß. **conjurer** ['kʌndʒərə], *s.* der Zauberer, Hexenmeister; Zauberkünstler, Taschenspieler. **conjuring** ['kʌndʒəriŋ], **1.** *adj.* Zauber–. **2.** *s.* die Zauberei, Hexerei; Taschenspielerei; – ***trick,*** das Zauberkunststück.

¹conk [kɔŋk], *s.* (*sl.*) die Schnauze, der Riecher.

²conk, *v.i.* (*sl.*) (*usu.* – ***out***) aussetzen, versagen, streiken, kaputtgehen.

conker ['kɔŋkə], *s.* (*coll.*) die Roßkastanie; *pl.* (*coll.*) ein Kinderspiel mit Kastanien.

connate ['kɔneit], *adj.* angeboren (***with***, *Dat.*); (*Bot.*) verwachsen; – ***notions,*** angeborene Begriffe. **connatural** [kə'nætʃərəl], *adj.* gleicher Natur (***to***, wie), verwandt (*Dat.*).

connect [kə'nekt], **1.** *v.t.* verbinden, verknüpfen (***with***, mit); (*Tech.*) zusammenfügen, kuppeln, koppeln; (*Elec.*) anschließen; einschalten, anschalten. **2.** *v.i.* in Verbindung treten, in Zusammenhang stehen (***with***, mit), sich anschließen (an (*Acc.*)), (*of trains*) Anschluß haben.

connected [kə'nektid], *adj.* verbunden, verknüpft; verwandt; zusammenhängend; (*Elec.*) geschaltet; – ***by marriage,*** verschwägert; (*Tele.*) ***be*** –, angeschlossen sein (*to the system*), verbunden sein (*with a caller*); ***be – with the affair,*** in die Angelegenheit verwickelt sein; ***be well-–,*** gute Beziehungen *or* einflußreiche Verwandte haben. **connectedly,** *adv.* logisch, in logischem Zusammenhang. **connectedness,** *s.* die Folgerichtigkeit, logischer Zusammenhang (*of thought*).

connecting [kə'nektiŋ], *adj.* Binde–; Verbindungs–; – ***line,*** (*Railw.*) das Anschlußgleis, (*Geom.*) die Verbindungsgerade; – ***link,*** das Bindeglied, Zwischenglied; – ***passage,*** der Durchgang; – ***piece,*** das Ansatzstück; (*Tech.*) – ***rod,*** die Schubstange, Pleuelstange.

connection [kə'nekʃən], *s.* 1. die Verbindung, Verknüpfung; (*Tele., Railw. etc.*) Verbindung, der Anschluß; (*Elec.*) Anschluß, die Schaltung; (*Tech.*) das Bindeglied, verbindender Teil; ***miss one's*** –, seinen Anschluß versäumen; 2. (*fig.*) der Zusammenhang; ***no – between them,*** kein Zusammenhang zwischen ihnen; ***in this*** –, in diesem Zusammenhang, in dieser Beziehung *or* Hinsicht; ***in – with,*** anläßlich, betreffs (*Gen.*), in bezug auf (*Acc.*); 3. die Beziehung, (persönliche) Verbindung;

Bekannte(r), Verwandte(r), *pl.* die Verwandtschaft, der Bekanntenkreis; Kundenkreis, die Kundschaft, Klientel, Konnexionen (*pl.*); ***business -s,*** geschäftliche Beziehungen (*pl.*); ***establish a -,*** Verbindungen anknüpfen.

connective, *adj.* verbindend; – ***tissue,*** das Bindegewebe, Zellgewebe. **connector,** *s.* der Ansatz, das Ansatzstück, Verbindungsstück; die Verbindungsschraube, Verbindungsröhre, Klemme, Klemmschraube; (*Railw.*) Kupplung.

connexion, *s. See* **connection.**

conning tower ['kɔniŋ], *s.* (*Naut.*) der Kommandoturm.

connivance [kə'naivəns], *s.* die Nachsicht, wissentliches Gewährenlassen (***at, in,*** bei), stillschweigende Einwilligung (in (*Acc.*)), (*Law*) strafbares Einverständnis (mit), die Duldung des Ehebruchs. **connive,** *v.i.* stillschweigend dulden, gewähren lassen (***at,*** *Acc.*), ein Auge zudrücken (bei); (*Law*) stillschweigend Vorschub leisten (*Dat.*). **connivent,** *adj.* (*Bot.*) zusammenlaufend, konvergierend; (*Anat.*) – ***valves,*** Darmfalten (*pl.*).

connoisseur [kɔnə'sə:], *s.* der (Kunst)kenner.

connotation [kɔno'teiʃən], *s.* die Mitbezeichnung, (Neben)bedeutung; (*Log.*) der Begriffsinhalt. **connotative** ['kɔnəteitiv], *adj.* mitbedeutend; (*Log.*) umfassend. **connote** [kə'nout], *v.t.* mitbezeichnen, zugleich bedeuten, in sich schließen, mit einbegreifen.

connubial [kə'nju:biəl], *adj.* ehelich, Ehe–. **connubiality** [–'æliti], *s.* der Ehestand; *pl.* eheliche Zärtlichkeiten (*pl.*).

conoid ['kounɔid], *s.* (*Geom.*) das Konoid; (*Anat.*) (*also* – ***body***) die Zirbeldrüse. **conoid(al)** [–'nɔid(l)], *adj.* kegelförmig.

conquer ['kɔŋkə], **1.** *v.t.* besiegen, überwinden, überwältigen, bezwingen, unterwerfen (*a p.*), erobern, einnehmen, unterwerfen (*territory*); (*fig.*) Herr werden über (*Acc.*), beherrschen, bewältigen (*one's feelings etc.*). **2.** *v.i.* siegen; Eroberungen machen. **conquerable,** *adj.* besiegbar, überwindlich. **conquering,** *adj.* siegend, siegreich. **conqueror,** *s.* der Eroberer, Sieger.

conquest ['kɔŋkwest], *s.* die Eroberung, Unterwerfung, Unterjochung; der Sieg, die Überwindung; erobertes Land, die Beute; (*coll.*) ***make a -,*** (ihn, sie *etc.*) erobern, (seine, ihre *etc.*) Zuneigung gewinnen; ***the (Norman) Conquest,*** die normannische Eroberung.

consanguineous [kɔnsæŋ'gwiniəs], *adj.* blutsverwandt. **consanguinity,** *s.* die Blutsverwandtschaft.

conscience ['kɔnʃəns], *s.* das Gewissen; ***clear -,*** reines Gewissen; ***have on one's -,*** auf dem Gewissen haben; (*coll.*) ***have the - to do a th.,*** die Stirn *or* Frechheit haben, etwas zu tun; ***matter of -,*** die Gewissenssache, Gewissensfrage; ***make it a matter of -,*** sich (*Dat.*) ein Gewissen daraus machen; ***in all -,*** mit gutem Gewissen, wahrhaftig, sicherlich; ***out of all -,*** unverschämt, über alle Maßen; ***pangs of -,*** Gewissensbisse (*pl.*).

conscience-clause, *s.* die Gewissensklausel. **conscienceless,** *adj.* gewissenlos. **conscience|-money,** *s.* das Reugeld, in die öffentliche Kasse gezahltes Geld (um Steuerhinterziehung gutzumachen). **--proof,** *adj.* gegen Gewissensbisse unempfindlich. **--smitten, --stricken,** *adj.* reuig, reuevoll.

conscientious [kɔnʃi'enʃəs], *adj.* gewissenhaft; Gewissens–; – ***objector,*** der Kriegsdienstverweigerer; – ***scruples,*** Gewissensskrupel (*pl.*). **conscientiousness,** *s.* die Gewissenhaftigkeit.

conscious ['kɔnʃəs], *adj.* **1.** (*pred.*) bei *or* mit (vollem) Bewußtstein; 2. bewußt; – ***of a th.,*** sich (*Dat.*) einer S. (*Gen.*) bewußt; ***be - that,*** wohl wissen daß, davon überzeugt sein daß. **consciously,** *adv.* bewußt, wissentlich. **consciousness,** *s.* **1.** das Bewußtsein, der Bewußtseinszustand; ***lose -,*** das Bewußtsein verlieren; 2. die Kenntnis (***of,*** von), das Wissen (um).

conscript, 1. ['kɔnskript], *adj.* zwangsweise ausgehoben. **2.** ['kɔnskript], *s.* (Wehr)dienstpflichtige(r), (eingezogener *or* ausgehobener) Rekrut. **3.** [kən'skript], *v.t.* zwangsweise ausheben *or* einziehen. **conscription** [kən'skripʃən], *s.* die (Zwangs)aushebung; Einberufung; ***universal -,*** allgemeine Wehrpflicht.

consecrate ['kɔnsikreit], **1.** *v.t.* (ein)weihen, einsegnen; (*fig.*) widmen (***to,*** *Dat.*); (*Eccl.*) heiligsprechen. **2.** *or* **consecrated,** *adj.* geweiht (***to,*** *Dat.*), geheiligt; (*fig.*) – ***by tradition,*** durch Sitte und Brauch geheiligt. **consecration** [–'kreiʃən], *s.* die Weihe, (Ein)weihung, Einsegnung; (*fig.*) Widmung, Hingabe (***to,*** an (*Acc.*)).

consecution [kɔnsi'kju:ʃən], *s.* die Serie, (Aufeinander)folge; (*Gram.*) Zeitfolge, Wortfolge; logische Folge, die Folgerung. **consecutive** [kən'sekjutiv], *adj.* aufeinanderfolgend, zusammenhängend; Folge–; – ***clause,*** der Folgesatz; (*Mus.*) – ***fifths,*** Quintparallelen (*pl.*); – ***narrative,*** zusammenhängende Erzählung; ***three - weeks,*** drei Wochen hintereinander. **consecutively,** *adv.* hintereinander, nacheinander, fortlaufend. **consecutiveness,** *s.* das Aufeinanderfolgen; logische Aufeinanderfolge, die Folgerichtigkeit.

consensus [kən'sensəs], *s.* **1.** (allgemeine) Übereinstimmung; – ***of opinion,*** allseitige Zustimmung, übereinstimmende Meinung; 2. (*Med.*) die Wechselwirkung.

consent [kən'sent], **1.** *s.* die Einwilligung (***to,*** in (*Acc.*)), Zustimmung (zu), Genehmigung (für); ***age of -,*** das Mündigkeitsalter; ***by common -,*** mit allgemeiner Zustimmung; ***mutual -,*** gegenseitige Übereinkunft; ***silence gives -,*** Stillschweigen bedeutet Zustimmung; ***with one -,*** einmütig, einstimmig; ***the parents gave their -,*** die Eltern gaben den Ehekonsens. **2.** *v.i.* einwilligen (***to,*** in (*Acc.*)), zustimmen, beistimmen (*Dat.*). **consentaneous** [kɔnsen'teiniəs], *adj.* (*rare*) übereinstimmend (***to, with,*** mit); einmütig.

consequence ['kɔnsikwəns], *s.* **1.** die Folge, das Resultat, Ergebnis, die Wirkung; (*Log.*) Folgerung, der Schluß(satz); *pl.* der Steckbrief (*parlour game*); ***in -,*** in der Folge, folglich, infolgedessen, deshalb, daher; ***in - of,*** infolge von *or* (*Gen.*), wegen (*Gen.*), zufolge (*follows Dat.*); ***in - of which,*** weswegen; ***take the -s,*** die Folgen tragen; ***with the - that,*** mit dem Ergebnis daß; 2. die Wichtigkeit, Bedeutung, der Einfluß, das Ansehen; ***of -,*** bedeutend, wichtig (***to,*** für); ***man of -,*** einflußreicher *or* angesehener *or* bedeutender Mann, Mann von Bedeutung; ***be of little -,*** nichts auf sich haben, von geringer Bedeutung sein (***to,*** für); ***of no -,*** ohne Bedeutung, unbedeutend, unwichtig (***to,*** für).

consequent ['kɔnsikwənt], **1.** *adj.* (nach)folgend ((***up***)***on,*** auf (*Acc.*)); (*Log.*) folgerichtig, konsequent; – ***on,*** die Folge von, infolge (*Gen.*) *or* von. **2.** *s.* die Folge(erscheinung); logische Folge, Folgerung, der Schluß; (*Math.*) das Hinterglied (*of a ratio*). **consequential** [–'kwenʃəl], *adj.* **1.** folgernd, konsequent (***on,*** aus), folgend auf (*Acc.*); ***be - on,*** folgen auf (*Acc.*), sich ergeben aus; 2. logisch richtig, folgerecht, folgerichtig, konsequent; 3. wichtigtuend, hochtrabend, überheblich. **consequently,** *conj.* in der Folge, folglich, infolgedessen, deshalb, daher.

conservable [kən'sə:vəbl], *adj.* erhaltbar. **conservancy,** *s.* die Kontrollbehörde (*for waters, forests etc.*), Fischereikontrolle, Forsterhaltung; ***Thames Conservancy Board,*** die Kontrollbehörde für die Themse. **conservation** [kɔnsə'veiʃən], *s.* **1.** die (Aufrecht)erhaltung, Bewahrung; (*Phys.*) – ***of energy,*** die Energieerhaltung; 2. der (Natur)schutz; – ***area,*** das Naturschutzgebiet; 3. das Haltbarmachen, Konservieren (*of fruit*).

conservatism [kən'sə:vətizm], *s.* der Konservatismus. **conservative, 1.** *adj.* **1.** erhaltend; mäßig, vorsichtig; ***be - of,*** erhalten, vorsichtig umgehen mit; – ***estimate,*** vorsichtige Einschätzung; **2.** (*Pol.*) konservativ. **2.** *s.* Konservative(r).

conservatoire [kən'sə:vətwa:], *s.* (*Mus.*) die Hochschule für Musik, Musikakademie, das Konservatorium.

conservator ['kɔnsəveitə], *s.* der Erhalter, Beschützer; Konservator, Aufseher, Aufsichtsbeamte(r).

conservatory [kən'sə:vətəri], *s.* 1. das Treibhaus, Gewächshaus, der Wintergarten (*for plants*); 2. (*esp. Am.*) *see* **conservatoire.**

conserve [kən'sə:v], **1.** *v.t.* erhalten, (auf)bewahren; konservieren, einmachen (*fruit*); (*fig.*) aufrechterhalten, beibehalten; – ***one's energy,*** seine Energie aufspeichern. **2.** *s.* Eingemachte(s), die Konserve.

consider [kən'sidə], **1.** *v.t.* 1. sorgfältig ansehen, eingehend betrachten, ins Auge fassen; 2. sich (*Dat.*) überlegen, erwägen, in Erwägung ziehen, nachdenken über (*Acc.*); – ***the matter!*** denken Sie darüber nach! ***I will – it,*** ich werde es mir überlegen; ***–ed action,*** wohlüberlegte *or* wohlerwogene *or* wohldurchdachte Handlung; 3. berücksichtigen, in Betracht ziehen, in Anschlag bringen; – ***a th. on its merits,*** etwas auf seinen Wert hin betrachten; ***all things –ed,*** wenn man alles erwägt *or* in Betracht zieht; 4. Rücksicht nehmen auf (*Acc.*), denken an (*Acc.*); ***he never –s me,*** er denkt nie an mich, er nimmt keine Rücksicht auf mich; 5. denken, glauben, meinen, der Meinung sein, finden, halten für, ansehen als; ***I – him clever,*** ich halte ihn für klug; ***I – he acted wisely,*** ich finde daß er klug gehandelt hat; ***he may – himself lucky,*** er kann sich glücklich nennen; – ***yourself at home,*** tun Sie, als wären Sie zuhause; ***they wish to be –ed cultured,*** sie möchten für kultiviert gelten. **2.** *v.i.* nachdenken, überlegen.

considerable [kən'sidərəbl], *adj.* beträchtlich, beachtlich, ansehnlich, bedeutend; (*coll.*) nicht wenig, viel, eine ganze Menge. **considerate** [–rit], *adj.* rücksichtsvoll, aufmerksam (*to(****wards****)*, gegen); bedächtig, umsichtig, wohlbedacht, überlegt. **considerateness,** *s.* die Rücksichtnahme, Aufmerksamkeit.

consideration [kənsidə'reiʃən], *s.* 1. die Betrachtung, Überlegung, Erwägung; ***on further –,*** bei weiterer Überlegung; ***take into –,*** in Betracht ziehen; ***the matter is under –,*** die S. schwebt noch *or* wird erwogen; 2. die Bedeutung, Wichtigkeit, der Belang, das Ansehen; ***it is of no –,*** es spielt keine Rolle *or* kommt darauf nicht an; ***a p. of some –,*** eine P. von einiger Bedeutung; 3. die Rücksicht(nahme), Berücksichtigung (***for, of,*** auf (*Acc.*)); ***lack*** or ***want of –,*** die Rücksichtslosigkeit; ***a matter for –,*** eine S., die Berücksichtigung verdient; ***in – of,*** in Anbetracht, hinsichtlich (*Gen.*); ***out of – for,*** aus Rücksicht auf (*Acc.*); ***on*** or ***under no –,*** unter keinen Umständen; 4. (*Comm.*) das Entgelt, die Entschädigung, Gegenleistung, Vergütung, das Äquivalent; ***for a –,*** gegen Entgelt *or* Vergütung; 5. der (Beweg)grund; ***that is a –,*** das ist ein triftiger Grund.

considering [kən'sidəriŋ], **1.** *prep.* betreffend (*Acc.*), in Anbetracht (*Gen.*). **2.** *adv.* (*coll.*) wenn man alles in Betracht zieht; ***that is very well done –,*** das ist unter den Umständen recht hübsch gemacht.

consign [kən'sain], *v.t.* übergeben, überliefern, (*Comm.*) übersenden, zusenden, verschicken, adressieren (***to,*** an (*Acc.*)); überweisen, deponieren, hinterlegen (*money*); anvertrauen (*Dat.*); – ***to oblivion,*** der Vergessenheit überliefern. **consignation** [kɔnsig'neiʃən], *s.* (*money*) die Überweisung, (*goods*) Übersendung, Verschickung; Hinterlegung; ***to the – of,*** unter der *or* an die Adresse von. **consignee** [kɔnsai'ni:], *s.* der (Waren)empfänger, Bezieher, Adressat. **consignment,** *s.* 1. die Verschickung, Zustellung, Übersendung, Zusendung, Versendung, Konsignation; Hinterlegung; – ***of specie,*** die Barsendung; ***in –,*** in Konsignation, mit Rücksenderecht; 2. die Sendung, Lieferung; – ***note,*** der Frachtbrief. **consignor** [–nə], *s.* der Hinterleger, Deponent; (*Comm.*) Verfrachter, Versender; Absender, Übersender, Überweiser, Konsignant.

consist [kən'sist], *v.t.* bestehen, sich zusammensetzen (***of,*** aus); – ***in,*** bestehen in (*Dat.*), enthalten, ausmachen; (*obs.*) – ***with,*** zusammen bestehen mit, vereinbar sein mit, sich vertragen.

consistence [kən'sistəns], *s.* die Festigkeit, Dichtigkeit, Dicke, Konsistenz. **consistency,** *s.* 1. *See* **consistence**; 2. (*fig.*) die Vereinbarkeit, Übereinstimmung, Folgerichtigkeit, Konsequenz. **consistent,** *adj.* 1. fest, dicht; 2. (*fig.*) übereinstimmend, vereinbar, verträglich (***with,*** mit), gemäß (*Dat.*); folgerichtig, konsequent; ***make – with,*** in Einklang bringen mit; ***he is at least –,*** er ist wenigstens konsequent. **consistently,** *adv.* durchweg, regelmäßig.

consistorial [kɔnsis'tɔ:riəl], *adj.* Konsistorial–. **consistory** [kən'sistəri], *s.* das Konsistorium, (*R.C.*) die Kardinalsversammlung, (*Prot.*) kirchliche Behörde, der Kirchenrat.

consol ['kɔnsɔl], *s.* (*usu. pl.*) (*Comm.*) konsolidierte Staatsanleihe, der Konsol.

consolation [kɔnsə'leiʃən], *s.* der Trost, die Tröstung, das Trösten; – ***prize,*** der Trostpreis; ***poor –,*** schlechter Trost. **consolatory** [–'sɔlətəri], *adj.* tröstend, tröstlich.

[1]**console** [kən'soul], *v.t.* trösten.

[2]**console** ['kɔnsoul], *s.* 1. (*Archit.*) der Tragstein, Kragstein, die Konsole; 2. (*Rad.*) ***mixing –,*** der Mischtisch (*of sound engineer*). **console| model,** *s.* (*Rad. T.V.*) das Stehmodell. **–-table,** *s.* das Wandtischchen.

consolidate [kən'sɔlideit], **1.** *v.t.* verdichten; (be)festigen, (ver)stärken; vereinigen, zusammenlegen, zusammenziehen; (*Comm.*) konsolidieren, fundieren. **2.** *v.i.* sich verdichten, fest werden; sich festigen, stark *or* stärker werden. **consolidated,** *adj.* dicht, fest, kompakt; verstärkt, gefestigt; (*Comm.*) vereinigt, konsolidiert; *see* **consol.** **consolidation** [–'deiʃən], *s.* die Verdichtung, (Ver)festigung, Vereinigung, Konsolidierung, Kombinierung; (*Geol.*) das Festwerden.

consols, *pl. of* **consol.**

consommé [kɔ̃'sɔmei], *s.* die Kraftbrühe.

consonance ['kɔnsənəns], *s.* (*Mus.*) der Einklang, Zusammenklang, Gleichklang, die Konsonanz; (*fig.*) Übereinstimmung, Harmonie. **consonant, 1.** *adj.* (*Mus.*) zusammenklingend, konsonant; (*fig.*) übereinstimmend, vereinbar (***with,*** mit); gemäß, entsprechend (*Dat.*), passend (zu). **2.** *s.* (*Gram.*) der Mitlaut(er), Konsonant; ***back –,*** der Gaumenlaut; ***dental –,*** der Zahnlaut; ***front –,*** der Palatallaut; ***labial*** or ***lip –,*** der Lippenlaut; ***lingual –,*** der Zungenlaut; ***stopped –,*** der Verschlußlaut. **consonantal** [–'næntl], *adj.* konsonantisch. **consonant-shift,** *s.* die Lautverschiebung.

consort, 1. ['kɔnsɔ:t], *s.* 1. der Gemahl, Gatte; die Gemahlin, Gattin; ***Prince Consort,*** der Prinzgemahl; 2. (*Naut.*) das Geleitschiff. **2.** [kən'sɔ:t], *v.i.* sich gesellen (***with,*** zu), verkehren, umgehen (mit); (*fig.*) passen (zu); übereinstimmen (mit). **consortium** [–'sɔ:tiəm], *s.* das Konsortium, die Vereinigung, Genossenschaft.

conspectus [kən'spektəs], *s.* die Übersicht (***of,*** über (*Acc.*)), Zusammenfassung, das Resümee.

conspicuous [kən'spikjuəs], *adj.* deutlich, ersichtlich, auffallend, auffällig, (*fig.*) bemerkenswert, hervorragend (***by,*** durch; ***for,*** wegen); ***be –,*** in die Augen fallen; ***be – by one's absence,*** durch Abwesenheit glänzen; ***make o.s. –,*** sich auffällig benehmen, auffallen.

conspiracy [kən'spirəsi], *s.* die Verschwörung, das Komplott, geheime Abrede; – ***of silence,*** verabredetes Stillschweigen. **conspirator** [–rətə], *s.* der Verschwörer. **conspire** [kən'spaiə], **1.** *v.i.* sich verschwören, ein Komplott schmieden; ***all things – to make him happy,*** alles trifft zu seinem Glück zusammen. **2.** *v.t.* planen, anstiften, anzetteln.

constable ['kʌnstəbl], *s.* der Schutzmann, Polizist; (*Hist.*) Konnetabel; ***Chief Constable,*** der Polizeipräsident; ***Lord High Constable of England,*** der Großkonnetabel von England; ***special –,*** der Hilfspolizist. **constabulary** [kən'stæbjuləri], **1.** *s.* die Schutzmannschaft, Polizei. **2.** *adj.* Polizei–.

Constance ['kɔnstəns], *s.* (*Geog.*) Konstanz (*n.*); ***Lake –,*** der Bodensee.

constancy ['kɔnstənsi], *s.* 1. die Standhaftigkeit,

Treue; 2. Beständigkeit, Beharrlichkeit, Unveränderlichkeit, Unwandelbarkeit; Dauer, der Bestand. **constant, 1.** *adj.* beständig, stet(ig), unveränderlich, gleichbleibend; gleichmäßig, unaufhörlich, fortwährend, anhaltend; (*fig.*) standhaft, beharrlich, unwandelbar, unerschütterlich, unverrückbar; verläßlich, treu; (*Math., Phys.*) konstant; – ***change,*** stetiger Wechsel; – ***current,*** konstanter Strom; – ***noise,*** unaufhörliches Geräusch; – ***rain,*** anhaltender Regen. **2.** *s.* das Beständige, Unveränderliche; (*Math., Phys.*) konstante Größe, die Konstante, der Exponent.

constellation [kɔnstə'leiʃən], *s.* (*Astr.*) das Sternbild, die Konstellation; (*fig.*) glänzende Gruppe.

consternation [kɔnstə'neiʃən], *s.* die Bestürzung.

constipate ['kɔnstipeit], *v.t.* (*Med.*) verstopfen. **constipation** [–'peiʃən], *s.* die Verstopfung, Hartleibigkeit.

constituency [kən'stitjuənsi], *s.* die Wählerschaft; der Wahlkreis, Wahlbezirk. **constituent, 1.** *adj.* 1. (*Pol.*) wählend, Wähler–, Wahl–; verfassunggebend; (*Pol.*) – ***assembly,*** konstituierende Nationalversammlung; – ***body,*** der Wahlkörper, die Wählerschaft; 2. einen Teil ausmachend, Teil–; – ***part,*** der Bestandteil, wesentliches Element. **2.** *s.* 1. (*Pol.*) der Wähler; 2. Bestandteil, (*Chem.*) die Komponente; 3. (*Law*) der Auftraggeber, Vollmachtgeber.

constitute ['kɔnstitju:t], *v.t.* 1. festsetzen, einrichten, errichten, gründen; 2. bilden, darstellen, ausmachen, in sich enthalten; ***this –s a precedent,*** dies gibt einen Präzedenzfall ab; 3. (*a p.*) ernennen, bestellen, einsetzen; beauftragen, bevollmächtigen; (*Parl.*) konstituieren; – ***o.s. as a judge,*** sich zum Richter aufwerfen; ***the –d authorities,*** die verfassungsmäßigen Behörden.

constitution [kɔnsti'tju:ʃən], *s.* 1. das Festsetzen, die Anordnung, Einrichtung, Errichtung, Bildung; 2. Natur, Gemütsart, Veranlagung, das Temperament; die Konstitution, (Körper)beschaffenheit; ***strong –,*** kräftige Konstitution; ***by –,*** von Natur; 3. der Bau, die Struktur, Zusammensetzung; 4. (*Pol.*) Konstitution, Verfassung; Satzungen (*pl.*). **constitutional, 1.** *adj.* 1. körperlich bedingt *or* begründet, von Natur angeboren, temperamentsmäßig; – ***disease,*** angeborenes Übel; 2. (*Pol.*) gesetzmäßig, verfassungsmäßig, konstitutionell; – ***charter,*** die Verfassungsurkunde; – ***liberty,*** verfassungsmäßige Freiheit. **2.** *s.* (*coll.*) der Verdauungsspaziergang. **constitutionalism,** *s.* verfassungsmäßige Regierungsform. **constitutionalist,** *s.* der Anhänger verfassungsmäßiger Regierungsformen.

constitutive [kən'stitjutiv], *adj.* richtunggebend, grundlegend, wesentlich.

constrain [kən'strein], *v.t.* zwingen, drängen, nötigen; fesseln. **constrained,** *adj.* gezwungen, unfrei, verkrampft, befangen, verlegen, unnatürlich. **constraint,** *s.* der Zwang, die Nötigung; Einschränkung, Beschränkung, (*fig.*) Gezwungenheit, Verlegenheit, Befangenheit, Zurückhaltung; Haft; ***under –,*** zwangsweise.

constrict [kən'strikt], *v.t.* zusammenziehen, zusammenschnüren, zusammenpressen, verengen, einengen. **constriction** [–'strikʃən], *s.* die Zusammenziehung, Zusammenpressung, Verengung, Einengung, Einschnürung; Beengtheit. **constrictive,** *adj.* zusammenziehend, verengend, einschnürend. **constrictor,** *s.* 1. (*Anat.*) der Schließmuskel; 2. (*Zool.*) *see* **boa-constrictor.**

constringent [kən'strindʒənt], *adj. See* **constrictive.**

construct [kən'strʌkt], *v.t.* errichten, aufführen, aufbauen, (er)bauen; (*Math.*) konstruieren; (*fig.*) bilden, erdenken, ausarbeiten, ersinnen.

construction [kən'strʌkʃən], *s.* 1. das (Er)bauen. die Aufführung, Errichtung, der (Aus)bau; ***cost of –,*** Baukosten (*pl.*); ***type of –,*** die Bauart; ***under –,*** im Bau; 2. der Bau, das Gebäude, Bauwerk, die Baulichkeit; ***brick –,*** der Ziegelbau; 3. (*Gram.*) der Satzbau, das Satzgefüge, die Wortfügung; (*Math*) Konstruktion; Gestaltung; 4. Bauweise; Bauart, der Aufbau, die Struktur, Anlage, Form; (*fig.*) Auslegung, Deutung; ***put the worst – on a th.,*** eine S. im schlechtesten Sinne auffassen *or* auslegen. **constructional,** *adj.* Bau–, bautechnisch. **constructive** [–tiv], *adj.* 1. aufbauend, konstruktiv, schöpferisch; Bau–, Konstruktions–, baulich; 2. (*Law*) gefolgert, abgeleitet, de facto; 3. – ***criticism,*** positive *or* fördernde Kritik. **constructor,** *s.* der Erbauer, Konstrukteur.

construe [kən'stru:], **1.** *v.t.* (*Gram.*) konstruieren, analysieren; wörtlich übersetzen; (*fig.*) auslegen, deuten. **2.** *v.i.* sich konstruieren *or* grammatisch erklären lassen.

consubstantial [kɔnsəb'stænʃəl], *adj.* wesensgleich. **consubstantiality** [–i'æliti], *s.* (*Eccl.*) die Wesenseinheit. **consubstantiate** [–ʃieit], *v.t.* zu einem (einzigen) Wesen vereinigen. **consubstantiation** [–'eiʃən], *s.* die Konsubstantiation.

consuetude ['kɔnswitju:d], *s.* der Brauch, die Gewohnheit. **consuetudinary** [–'tju:dinəri], *adj.* gewohnheitsmäßig, Gewohnheits–.

consul ['kɔnsəl], *s.* der Konsul. **consular** [–sjulə], *adj.* konsularisch, Konsulats–, Konsular–. **consulate** [–sjulit], *s.* das Konsulat (*office and premises*). **consul-general,** *s.* der Generalkonsul. **consulship,** *s.* das Amt des Konsuls.

consult [kən'sʌlt], **1.** *v.i.* (sich) beraten, beratschlagen (***with him about a th.,*** mit ihm über eine S.). **2.** *v.t.* zu Rate ziehen, um Rat fragen, konsultieren (*a doctor*); nachschlagen in (*Dat.*) (*a book*); (*fig.*) Rücksicht nehmen auf (*Acc.*), berücksichtigen, beachten, im Auge haben, ins Auge fassen; – ***one's pillow,*** es beschlafen; – ***one's watch,*** nach der Uhr sehen. **consultant,** *s.* fachmännischer Berater, der Gutachter, (*Med.*) Spezialarzt, fachärztlicher Berater.

consultation [kɔnsəl'teiʃən], *s.* die Berat(schlag)ung, Aussprache, Konsultation, Konferenz; ***after – with,*** nach Rücksprache mit. **consultative** [kən'sʌltətiv], *adj.* beratend. **consulting| engineer,** *s.* technischer Berater. **–-room,** *s.* das Sprechzimmer (*of a doctor*).

consumable [kən'sju:məbl], *adj.* verzehrbar, verbrauchbar, zerstörbar. **consume,** *v.t.* verzehren, aufbrauchen, verbrauchen; vergeuden, verschwenden; benötigen, in Anspruch nehmen (*time*); vernichten, zerstören; ***be –d with,*** erfüllt sein von, sich verzehren vor (*Dat.*) *or* in (*Dat.*). **consumer,** *s.* (*Comm.*) der Verbraucher, Abnehmer, Konsument; – ***goods,*** Konsumgüter (*pl.*); – ***resistance,*** die Kaufunlust.

consummate, 1. ['kɔnsəmeit], *v.t.* vollziehen, durchführen, vollbringen, vollenden; – ***the marriage,*** den Eheakt vollziehen. **2.** [ken'sʌmit), *adj.* vollendet, vollkommen; – ***art,*** künstlerische Vollendung; – ***fool,*** ausgemachter Narr; – ***scoundrel,*** abgefeimter Gauner. **consummation** [kɔnsə'meiʃən], *s.* die Vollziehung, Vollendung; das Ende, Ziel; – ***of the marriage,*** die Vollziehung des Eheaktes.

consumption [kən'sʌmpʃən], *s.* 1. der Verbrauch, Aufwand (*of,* an (*Dat.*)); (*Comm.*) Absatz, Konsum, Bedarf; ***fit for human –,*** für die menschliche Ernährung geeignet; 2. (*Med.*) die Auszehrung, Schwindsucht. **consumptive** [–tiv], **1.** *adj.* 1. (ver)zehrend; 2. (*Med.*) schwindsüchtig. **2.** *s.* Schwindsüchtige(r).

contact ['kɔntækt], **1.** *s.* 1. die Berührung; ***come in(to) – with,*** in Berührung kommen mit; ***point of –,*** der Berührungspunkt; 2. (*Elec.*) der Kontakt, Anschluß; das Kontaktstück; ***make –,*** den Kontakt herstellen; 3. (*Mil.*) die Feindberührung, Fühlung; 4. (*Med., coll.*) ansteckungsverdächtige Person; 5. (*fig.*) Fühlung, Beziehung, Verbindung; ***establish –,*** Fühlung aufnehmen; (*fig.*) – ***with the soil,*** die Erdverbundenheit. **2.** *v.t.* sich in Verbindung setzen mit, in Verbindung treten mit, in Berührung kommen mit, Beziehungen aufnehmen mit.

contact|-box, *s.* die Anschlußdose. **–-breaker,** *s.* der Stromunterbrecher, Ausschalter. **–-lens,** *s.* die

Haftschale. --**mine,** *s.* (*Mil.*) die Flattermine, Tretmine. **contactor,** *s.* (*Elec.*) (automatischer) Kontaktgeber; – ***switch,*** der Kontaktschalter. **contact|print,** *s.* (*Phot.*) der Abzug, die Kopie. --**rail,** *s.* die Kontaktschiene.

contagion [kən'teidʒən], *s.* die Ansteckung; der Ansteckungsstoff; ansteckende Krankheit, die Seuche; (*fig.*) Verseuchung. **contagious,** *adj.* ansteckend, direkt übertragbar; (*fig.*) ***his good humour is –,*** seine Fröhlichkeit steckt an.

contain [kən'tein], *v.t.* 1. enthalten; umfassen, einschließen; fassen, messen (*measures and weights*); 2. (*fig.*) im Zaume halten, zurückhalten, zügeln (*feelings etc.*), (*Mil.*) festhalten, hinhalten, abriegeln, fesseln; – ***o.s.,*** (an) sich halten, sich beherrschen *or* fassen *or* zügeln; ***I could not – myself for laughing,*** ich konnte mich vorm Lachen kaum fassen, ich konnte das Lachen nicht unterdrücken. **container,** *s.* der Behälter (*also Comm., Railw.*), das Gefäß.

contaminate [kən'tæmineit], *v.t.* beflecken, beschmutzen, verunreinigen, besudeln; anstecken, infizieren, vergiften, verseuchen. **contamination** [-'neiʃən], *s.* die Verunreinigung, Befleckung, Beschmutzung, Besudelung; Verseuchung.

contango [kən'tæŋgou], **1.** *s.* (*Comm.*) das Aufgeld, der Report; die Reportprämie; – ***rate,*** der Reportsatz, die Prolongationsgebühr. **2.** *v.i.* Reportgeschäfte abschließen.

contemn [kən'tem], *v.t.* (*Poet.*) verachten, verschmähen, geringschätzen.

contemplate ['kɔntəmpleit], **1.** *v.t.* 1. betrachten, beschauen; 2. vorhaben, beabsichtigen, erwägen, im Sinne haben, ins Auge fassen; 3. rechnen mit, voraussehen; 4. (nach)sinnen *or* nachdenken über (*Acc.*), überlegen, bedenken. **2.** *v.i.* (nach)sinnen, nachdenken. **contemplation** [-'pleiʃən], *s.* die Beobachtung, Betrachtung; das Sinnen, Nachdenken; die Beschaulichkeit, Meditation; Erwägung, Beabsichtigung, das Vorhaben; ***be in –,*** beabsichtigt *or* geplant werden; ***have in –,*** in Erwägung ziehen, vorhaben, beabsichtigen. **contemplative** [kən'templətiv], *adj.* nachdenklich, gedankenvoll, sinnend, tiefsinnig; beschaulich.

contemporaneity [kəntempərə'neiiti], *s.* die Gleichzeitigkeit. **contemporaneous** [-'reiniəs], *adj.* gleichzeitig (***with,*** mit). **contemporaneousness,** *s. See* **contemporaneity.**

contemporary [kən'tempərəri], **1.** *adj.* zeitgenössisch, gleichzeitig; ***be – with,*** zeitlich zusammenfallen mit. **2.** *s.* der Zeitgenosse (die Zeitgenossin); Altersgenosse (Altersgenossin); ***our –,*** unsere Kollegin (*referring to a newspaper etc.*).

contempt [kən'tempt], *s.* 1. die Verachtung (*for, Gen.*), Geringschätzung (gegen); Schmähung, Schmach, Schande; ***beneath –,*** nicht einmal der Verachtung wert; ***bring into –,*** verächtlich machen; ***hold in –,*** mit Verachtung strafen, verachten; ***hold him up to –,*** ihn verächtlich machen, ihn der Verachtung preisgeben; 2. (*Law*) die Mißachtung; das Nichterscheinen vor Gericht, die Kontumaz; – ***of court,*** vorsätzliches Nichterscheinen; die Mißachtung des Gerichts.

contemptible [kən'temptibl], *adj.* verächtlich, verachtenswert; nichtswürdig, niederträchtig, gemein; (*coll.*) ***Old Contemptibles,*** britisches Heer in Frankreich, 1914. **contemptibleness,** *s.* die Verächtlichkeit, Nichtswürdigkeit, Gemeinheit, Niedertracht. **contemptuous** [-juəs], *adj.* verachtend, verachtungsvoll, geringschätzig; – ***air,*** verächtliche Miene; ***be – of,*** verachten; ***speak -ly of him,*** von ihm mit Verachtung reden. **contemptuousness,** *s.* verächtliches Wesen; die Verachtung, Geringschätzigkeit.

contend [kən'tend], **1.** *v.t.* kämpfen, ringen; wetteifern, sich bewerben (***for,*** um); beharren auf (*Dat.*); – ***for mastery,*** um den Vorzug streiten. **2.** *v.t.* verfechten. **contender,** *s.* der (die) Kämpfer(in), Streiter(in); Verfechter(in), Disputant(in). **contending,** *adj.* streitend; widerstreitend (*claims etc.*), gegenüberstehend (*claimants*).

[1]**content** [kən'tent], **1.** *pred. adj.* (leidlich) zufrieden; (*Parl.*) einverstanden; bereit, willens; (*Parl.*) ***not –,*** dagegen. **2.** *v.t.* befriedigen, zufriedenstellen; – ***o.s. with,*** sich begnügen mit. **3.** *s.* die Zufriedenheit; ***to one's heart's –,*** nach Herzenslust.

[2]**content** ['kɔntent], *s.* der Gehalt, (Raum)inhalt, das Fassungsvermögen, der Umfang; (*fig. of a book etc.*) Inhalt, Gehalt; *pl.* Inhalt; ***cubic –,*** der Kubikinhalt; ***solid –,*** das Volumen; ***table of -s,*** das Inhaltsverzeichnis.

contented [kən'tentid], *adj.* zufrieden; genügsam; ***be – with it,*** sich damit begnügen, sich damit zufrieden geben. **contentedness,** *s.* die Zufriedenheit, Genügsamkeit.

contention [kən'tenʃən], *s.* der Streit, Zank, Hader, die Streitigkeit, das Wortgefecht, der Wortstreit; Streitpunkt; das Argument, die Behauptung, Beweisführung; ***bone of –,*** der Zankapfel. **contentious,** *adj.* streitsüchtig, zänkisch; umstritten, strittig (*point*); (*Law*) streitig; (*Law*) ***non--,*** freiwillig. **contentiousness,** *s.* die Streitsucht.

contentment [kən'tentmənt], *s. See* **contentedness.**

contents, *pl. See* [2]**content.**

conterminal [kɔn'tə:minl], *adj.* anstoßend, (an)grenzend (***to, with,*** an (*Acc.*)). **conterminous,** *adj.* 1. *See* **conterminal**; ***be –,*** eine gemeinsame Grenze haben (***with,*** mit); 2. (*fig.*) sich deckend, gleichbedeutend, zusammenfallend (***with,*** mit).

contest, 1. ['kɔntest], *s.* der Streit, Kampf; Wettkampf (***for,*** um). **2.** [kən'test], *v.i.* (sich) streiten, wetteifern (***with him,*** mit ihm; ***for, about,*** um). **3.** [kən'test], *v.t.* streiten *or* kämpfen um, wetteifern um; sich bewerben um; bestreiten, anfechten, anzweifeln (*an opinion*); (*Parl.*) – ***a seat*** or ***an election,*** kandidieren (für eine Wahl). **contestable** [kən'testəbl], *adj.* bestreitbar, anfechtbar, strittig. **contestant,** *s.* der (die) Streiter(in), streitende Partei; der (die) Kandidat(in), Bewerber(in).

context ['kɔntekst], *s.* der Zusammenhang; (*fig.*) die Umgebung. **contextual** [-'tekstjuəl], *adj.* vom Zusammenhang abhängig. **contexture** [kən'tekstʃe], *s.* das Gewebe, Gefüge, Netz, der Bau, die Zusammensetzung, Struktur.

contiguity [kɔnti'gju:iti], *s.* die Berührung (***to,*** mit), das Angrenzen (an (*Acc.*)); Aneinandergrenzen, Aneinanderstoßen, die Nähe, Nachbarschaft, (*Psych.*) Kontiguität. **contiguous** [kən'tigjuəs], *adj.* anstoßend, angrenzend (***to,*** an (*Acc.*)), nahe, benachbart (*Dat.*); aneinandergrenzend, aneinanderstoßend; (*Math.*) anliegend.

continence ['kɔntinəns], *s.* (geschlechtliche) Enthaltsamkeit, die Keuschheit; Mäßigung.

[1]**continent,** *adj.* keusch; enthaltsam, mäßig.

[2]**continent,** *s.* (europäisches) Festland; der Erdteil, Kontinent; ***the Dark Continent,*** der dunkle Erdteil. **continental** [-'nentl], **1.** *adj.* Kontinental-; (*Geog.*) – ***basin,*** binnenländische Beckengegend; – ***plateau,*** die Kontinentaltafel; – ***shelf,*** der Kontinentalsockel, Schelf; – ***travel,*** das Auslandsreisen. **2.** *s.* der Bewohner des (europäischen) Festlandes, Europäer.

contingency [kən'tindʒənsi], *s.* 1. die Zufälligkeit, Ungewißheit, Möglichkeit; der Zufall, möglicher Fall, zufälliges Ereignis; *pl.* Zufälle (*pl.*); 2. *pl.* unvorhergesehene Ausgaben (*pl.*). **contingent, 1.** *adj.* zufällig, zufallsbedingt, ungewiß; möglich, eventuell; (*Phil.*) nebensächlich, unwesentlich, nicht notwendig wahr; – (***up***)***on,*** abhängig von, bedingt durch. **2.** *s.* 1. der Beitrag, Anteil, die Beteiligungsquote; 2. das Kontingent (*of soldiers*).

continual [kən'tinjuəl], *adj.* ununterbrochen, anhaltend, fortgesetzt, fortwährend, immerwährend, fortdauernd, beständig, unablässig, unaufhörlich; (*coll.*) ständig, oft wiederholt, immer wiederkehrend. **continuance,** *s.* die (Fort)dauer, der Fortgang, das Fortbestehen, Anhalten; die Stetigkeit, Beständigkeit; das (Ver)bleiben, Verweilen; (*Law*) der Aufschub, die Aussetzung, Vertagung. **continuant,** *s.* (*Phonet.*) der Dauerlaut. **continuation** [-'eiʃən], *s.* die Fortsetzung,

Weiterführung; Fortdauer, der Fortbestand; die Erweiterung, Verlängerung, das Verlängerungsstück; (*Comm.*) die Prolongation; – *school,* die Fortbildungsschule. **continuative** [–ətiv], *adj.* weiterführend, fortführend, fortsetzend.

continue [kən'tinju:], **1.** *v.t.* fortsetzen, fortführen, fortfahren mit; erhalten, beibehalten, belassen; verlängern (*a line etc.*), weiterführen, ausdehnen; (*Law*) aufschieben, vertagen; *to be –d,* Fortsetzung folgt; *he –d his story,* er setzte seine Erzählung fort. **2.** *v.i.* (ver)bleiben, verweilen, verharren, beharren (*in,* in (*Dat.*)); fortfahren, weitermachen, weitergehen, sich fortsetzen; anhalten, andauern, fortdauern; *please –!* bitte fahren Sie fort! – *in office,* im Amt bleiben; – *in sin,* in der Sünde beharren; *he –d to smoke,* er rauchte weiter. **continued,** *adj.* anhaltend, fortlaufend, fortgesetzt, unaufhörlich, stetig; (*Math.*) – *fraction,* kontinuierlicher Bruch, der Kettenbruch; (*Math.*) – *proportion,* stetiges Verhältnis.

continuity [kɔnti'nju:iti], *s.* 1. die Stetigkeit, gleichmäßige Fortdauer, ununterbrochenes Bestehen; die Kontinuität; 2. zusammenhängendes Ganzes, ununterbrochene Folge *or* Reihe, innerer Zusammenhang; 3. (*Films*) das Drehbuch, (*T.V. etc.*) Manuskript; – *girl,* das Skriptgirl; 4. (*fig.*) roter Faden. **continuous** [kən'tinjuəs], *adj.* ununterbrochen, fortdauernd, (fort)laufend, stetig, kontinuierlich; unaufhörlich, andauernd, anhaltend; (*Archit.*) durchlaufend (*support*); (*Elec.*) – *current,* der Gleichstrom; – *operation* or *working,* der Dauerbetrieb; – *performance,* die Nonstopvorstellung; (*Rad.*) – *wave,* ungedämpfte Welle. **continuum,** *s.* ununterbrochene Folge *or* Reihe, zusammenhängendes Ganzes; (*Math.*) das Kontinuum.

contort [kən'tɔ:t], *v.t.* verdrehen, verzerren, verziehen (*one's features*); zusammenziehen, krümmen. **contortion** [–'tɔ:ʃən], *s.* die Krümmung (*also Geol.*); Verzerrung, Verdrehung. **contortionist,** *s.* der Schlangenmensch, Kautschukmensch.

contour ['kɔntuə], *s.* der Umriß, die Umrißlinie, Kontur, (*Mil.*) Außenlinie. **contour|-line,** *s.* (*Surv.*) die Höhenlinie, Isohypse. **--map,** *s.* die Höhenlinienkarte.

contra ['kɔntrə], **1.** *prep.* (*usu. as pref.*) wider, gegen. **2.** *s.* (*Comm.*) die Kreditseite, Gegenseite; (*Comm.*) *per –,* als Gegenrechnung *or* Gegenleistung.

contraband ['kɔntrəbænd], **1.** *adj.* verboten, gesetzwidrig, Schmuggel–. **2.** *s.* die Konterbande; Bannware, Schmuggelware; der Schleichhandel, Schmuggel.

contra|-bass [–beis], *s.* die Baßgeige; der Kontrabaß. **--bassoon,** *s.* das Kontrafagott.

contraception [kɔntrə'sepʃən], *s.* die Schwangerschafts– *or* Empfängnisverhütung. **contraceptive** [–tiv], **1.** *adj.* schwangerschaftsverhütend, empfängnisverhütend. **2.** *s.* schwangerschaftsverhütendes *or* empfängnisverhütendes Mittel.

[1]**contract, 1.** ['kɔntrækt], *s.* der Vertrag, Kontrakt; die Vertragsurkunde; Verdingung; der Akkord; *by –,* vertraglich; *give by –,* in Submission vergeben; *by private –,* unter der Hand; *under – to,* vertraglich verpflichtet (*Dat.*); *draw up a –,* einen Vertrag aufsetzen; *fulfil or discharge a –,* einen Vertrag erfüllen; *marriage –,* der Ehevertrag. **2.** [kən'trækt], 1. *v.t.* eingehen, (ab)schließen (*agreement*), geraten in (*Acc.*), machen (*debts*), sich (*Dat.*) zuziehen (*illness*), annehmen, sich (*Dat.*) aneignen (*habits*), schließen, machen (*friendship etc.*); 2. [–'trækt], *v.i.* einen Vertrag eingehen *or* schließen, kontrahieren; sich vertraglich verpflichten (*for,* zu); – *out,* sich (vertraglich) freimachen *or* befreien (*of,* von).

[2]**contract** [kən'trækt], **1.** *v.t.* zusammenziehen; verengen, einschränken; (*Gram.*) kontrahieren, verkürzen, zusammenziehen; runzeln (*eyebrows, forehead*). **2.** *v.i.* sich zusammenziehen, (ein)schrumpfen; sich verkleinern, kleiner *or* kürzer *or* enger werden. **contracted,** *adj.* zusammengezogen, zusammengeschrumpft; verkürzt; gerunzelt. **contracti(bi)lity** [–i'biliti], *s.* die Zusammenziehbarkeit. **contracti(b)le,** *adj.* zusammenziehbar.

contracting [kən'træktiŋ], *adj.* – *party,* vertragschließende Partei, der Kontrahent.

contraction [kən'trækʃən], *s.* 1. die Abschließung (*of an agreement*), Zuziehung (*of an illness*), Aneignung (*of habits*); – *of debts,* die Verschuldung; 2. die Zusammenziehung; Verkürzung, (*Med.*) Kontraktur; (*Gram.*) Verkürzung; Abkürzung, das Kurzwort.

contractor [kən'træktə], *s.* 1. der (die) Kontrahent(in), Vertragschließende(r); 2. der Lieferer, Lieferant, Unternehmer; *building –,* der Bauunternehmer; 3. (*Anat.*) Schließmuskel.

contractual [kən'træktjuəl], *adj.* vertraglich, vertragsmäßig, kontraktlich, Vertrags–.

contradict [kɔntrə'dikt], *v.t.* widersprechen (*Dat.*) (*a p. or th.*), widerrufen, bestreiten, in Abrede stellen (*a th.*), unvereinbar sein mit, im Widerspruch stehen zu (*of a th.*); – *each other,* sich (*Dat.*) widersprechen. **contradiction** [–'dikʃən], *s.* der Widerspruch, die Widerrede; Bestreitung (*of a statement*); Unvereinbarkeit (*of things*); *in – to,* im Widerspruch zu; – *in terms,* der Widerspruch in sich, innerer Widerspruch; *spirit of –,* der Widerspruchsgeist; *without –,* ohne Widerrede. **contradictious** [–ʃəs], *adj.* streitsüchtig, zum Widerspruch geneigt. **contradictoriness,** *s.* (*of things*) der Widerspruch (*to,* zu), die Unvereinbarkeit (mit), (*of a p.*) Unverträglichkeit, der Widerspruchsgeist. **contradictory, 1.** *adj.* (*of things*) widersprechend (*to, Dat.*), unvereinbar (mit), im Widerspruch stehend (zu); sich (*Dat.*) *or* einander widersprechend *or* widerstreitend, unvereinbar; (*of a p.*) *see* **contradictious. 2.** *s.* (*with def. art. only*) der Widerspruch, Gegensatz.

contradistinction [kɔntrədis'tiŋkʃən], *s.* die Unterscheidung; *in – to,* im Gegensatz zu.

contralto [kən'træltou], **1.** *s.* der Alt, die Altistin; Altstimme, Altlage. **2.** *adj.* Alt–.

contraption [kən'træpʃən], *s.* (*coll.*) die Vorrichtung, der Apparat, Mechanismus, technischer Kniff, (*sl.*) der Kasten, das Ungetüm, Dingsda.

contrapuntal [kɔntrə'pʌntl], *adj.* kontrapunktisch.

contrariety [kɔntrə'raiəti], *s.* 1. die Gegensätzlichkeit, Unvereinbarkeit; der Gegensatz, Widerspruch; 2. (*of wind etc.*) *see* **contrariness. contrariness,** *s.* 1. [kən'trɛərinis], (*of a p.*) der Eigensinn, die Widerspenstigkeit, Widerborstigkeit, (*of wind etc.*) Widrigkeit, Ungunst; 2. ['kɔntrərinis], *see* **contrariety. contrariwise** [kən'trɛəriwaiz], *adv.* (*coll.*) im Gegenteil, andererseits, umgekehrt.

contrary ['kɔntrəri], **1.** *adj.* 1. entgegengesetzt, widersprechend (*to, Dat.*), im Widerspruch (zu), verstoßend (gegen); sich (*Dat.*) widersprechend *or* widerstreitend, einander entgegengesetzt, gegensätzlich; (*Log.*) konträr, Gegen–, (*as winds etc.*) widrig, ungünstig; *that is – to the rules,* das verstößt gegen die Regeln; *in the – case,* widrigenfalls; 2. (*coll.*) [kən'trɛəri] (*of a p.*) aufsässig, widersetzlich, widerspenstig, widerborstig, eigensinnig. **2.** *adv.* im Gegensatz *or* Widerspruch (*to,* zu); – *to,* zuwider (*follows Dat.*), entgegen (*sometimes follows Dat.*), gegen. **3.** *s.* (*with def. art. only*) das Gegenteil (*to,* zu *or* von); *on the –,* im Gegenteil, hingegen; *quite the –,* ganz im Gegenteil; *to the –,* dagegen, gegenteilig.

contrast, 1. [kən'trɑ:st], *v.t.* entgegensetzen, gegenüberstellen (*with, Dat.*), kontrastieren, vergleichen (mit). **2.** [–'trɑ:st], *v.i.* sich abheben, abstechen (*with,* von *or* gegen), kontrastieren (mit), im Gegensatz stehen, einen Gegensatz bilden (zu). **3.** ['kɔntrɑ:st], *s.* der Gegensatz, Kontrast (*to,* zu); *by – with,* im Vergleich mit; *in – to,* im Gegensatz zu.

contravene [kɔntrə'vi:n], *v.t.* im Widerspruch stehen zu, widersprechen, zuwiderhandeln (*Dat.*); verletzen, übertreten, verstoßen gegen (*laws*). **contravention** [–'venʃən], *s.* das Zuwiderhandeln (*of*, gegen), die Übertretung (*Gen.*); ***in – of***, zuwider (*follows Dat.*), entgegen (*sometimes follows Dat.*).

contretemps ['kɔntrətã], *s.* unglücklicher *or* widriger Zufall.

contribute [kən'tribju:t], **1.** *v.t.* beitragen, beisteuern (***to***, zu *or* für), (*to a newspaper*) beitragen (zu). **2.** *v.i.* einen Beitrag leisten; beitragen (***to***, zu), mitwirken (an (*Dat.*)); – ***to a newspaper***, für eine Zeitung schreiben. **contribution** [kɔntri'bju:ʃən], *s.* die Beitragung, Beisteuerung; der Beitrag, die Beisteuer, (Geld)spende, Zuwendung, Abgabe; (*Hist.*) Kriegssteuer, Zwangsauflage, Brandschatzung; (*fig.*) Mitwirkung (***to***, an (*Dat.*)). **contributive,** *adj.* beisteuernd (***to***, zu); mitwirkend (an (*Dat.*)). **contributor,** *s.* Beitragende(r), Beisteuernde(r), Beitragleistende(r); Mitwirkende(r), der (die) Mitarbeiter(in) (***to***, bei *or* an (*Dat.*)). **contributory, 1.** *adj.* 1. *See* **contributive**; – ***cause***, mitwirkende Ursache; 2. beitragspflichtig; 3. förderlich (***to***, *Dat.*), unterstützend, fördernd. **2.** *s.* 1. *See* **contributor**; 2. Beitragspflichtige(r); 3. fördernder *or* mitwirkender Umstand.

contrite ['kɔntrait], *adj.* zerknirscht, reuevoll, reuig, reumütig; (*Eccl.*) bußfertig; – ***tears***, Tränen der Reue. **contriteness, contrition** [kən'triʃən], *s.* die Zerknirschung, Reue; (*Eccl.*) Bußfertigkeit.

contrivable [kən'traivəbl], *adj.* erfindbar, erdenkbar; herstellbar, durchführbar. **contrivance,** *s.* 1. die Erfindung, Bewerkstelligung, Planung; Findigkeit, Erfindungsgabe; der Plan, Kniff, Kunstgriff; ***full of –s***, erfinderisch, findig; 2. die Einrichtung, Vorrichtung, der Apparat. **contrive, 1.** *v.t.* erfinden, ersinnen, erdenken, ausdenken, entwerfen, sinnen auf (*Acc.*); bewerkstelligen, zustande *or* zuwege bringen, Mittel und Wege finden; es verstehen *or* einrichten *or* fertigbringen (***to do***, zu tun). **2.** *v.i.* Pläne machen, Ränke schmieden, intrigieren.

control [kən'troul], **1.** *s.* die Überwachung, Prüfung; Einschränkung, der Einhalt, Zwang, (*Comm.*) die Bewirtschaftung, Zwangswirtschaft; Leitung, (Ober)aufsicht, Kontrolle, Macht, Gewalt, Herrschaft (***of, over***, über (*Acc.*)); Bekämpfung, Verhütung (*of disease etc.*); (*Tech.*) Regelung, Führung, Steuerung, Regulierung; der Regler, die Kontrollvorrichtung, Reguliervorrichtung; *pl.* (*Tech.*) das Bedienungsgestänge; (*Comm.*) Steuerorgane (*pl.*); (*Av.*) das Leitwerk; ***board of –***, der Aufsichtsrat; ***dual –***, die Doppelsteuerung; ***he gets beyond my –***, er wächst mir über den Kopf; ***be in – of***, unter sich haben; ***lose – (of o.s.)***, die (Selbst)beherrschung verlieren; ***press-button –***, die Druckknopfsteuerung; ***radio –***, die Funklenkung, Fernlenkung; ***remote –***, die Fernsteuerung; ***be under –***, unter Kontrolle stehen; ***bring under –***, bewältigen, meistern (*a fire etc.*); ***have the situation under –***, Herr der Lage sein; ***keep under –***, im Zaume halten; (*Rad.*) ***volume –***, der Lautstärkenregler; ***without –***, frei, uneingeschränkt, ohne Aufsicht. **2.** *v.t.* (nach)prüfen, revidieren, überwachen, beaufsichtigen; (*Tech.*) regulieren, kontrollieren, steuern, lenken, leiten; beherrschen, die Herrschaft *or* Kontrolle haben über (*Acc.*), einschränken, zurückhalten, in Grenzen *or* im Zaume halten; bekämpfen, verhüten (*disease etc.*); (*Comm.*) unter Zwangswirtschaft stellen (*industry etc.*); – ***o.s.***, sich beherrschen.

control| board, *s.* 1. (*Comm.*) die Bewirtschaftungsstelle; 2. (*Elec. etc.*) *see* – **panel.** – **centre,** *s.* das Kontrollzentrum. – **column,** *s.* (*Av.*) der Steuerknüppel. – **experiment,** *s.* der Gegenversuch. – **grid,** *s.* (*Rad.*) der Steuergitter. – **knob,** *s.* der Bedienungsknopf.

controllable [kən'trouləbl], *adj.* kontrollierbar, regulierbar, lenkbar, steuerbar. **controller,** *s.* der Kontrolleur, Aufseher; Revisor, (Rechnungs)prüfer; (*fig.*) Leiter; (*Elec.*) (Strom)regler, (*elec. Railw.*) Fahrschalter.

control| lever, *s.* der Schalthebel. – **panel,** *s.* (*Elec.*) die Schalttafel, Bedienanlage. – **room,** *s.* (*Mil.*) die (Befehls)zentrale, (*Rad., T.V.*) der Regieraum. – **surface,** *s.* (*Av.*) die Steuerfläche. – **tower,** *s.* (*Av.*) der Kontrollturm, (*Naut.*) Kommandoturm. – **valve,** *s.* (*Rad.*) die Steuerröhre.

controversial [kɔntrə'və:ʃəl], *adj.* streitig, strittig, umstritten, Streit–; streitend, polemisch; streitlustig. **controversialist,** *s.* der Polemiker. **controversy** ['kɔntrəvə:si, kən'trɔvəsi], *s.* die Kontroverse, Debatte, Diskussion, Disputation; der Meinungsstreit, Disput; Streitpunkt, die Streitfrage, Streitsache; ***without*** or ***beyond –***, ohne Frage, fraglos, unstreitig, unzweifelhaft.

controvert ['kɔntrəvə:t], *v.t.* bestreiten, anfechten, bekämpfen (*opinions*), widersprechen (*Dat.*) (*a p.*). **controvertible,** *adj.* bestreitbar, anfechtbar; streitig, strittig.

contumacious [kɔntju'meiʃəs], *adj.* halsstarrig, aufsässig, widerspenstig, (*Law*) ungehorsam. **contumaciousness, contumacy** ['kɔntjuməsi], *s.* 1. die Halsstarrigkeit, Aufsässigkeit, Widerspenstigkeit; 2. (*Law*) Kontumaz, das Nichterscheinen (vor Gericht).

contumelious [kɔntju'mi:liəs], *adj.* verächtlich, verachtenswert, schmählich, schändlich, schimpflich; unverschämt, schnöde, frech. **contumely** ['kɔntjuməli], *s.* die Beschimpfung, Schmähung, Verachtung; Schmach, der Schimpf, Hohn.

contuse [kən'tju:z], *v.t.* quetschen. **contusion** [–'tju:ʒən], *s.* die Quetschung; Quetschwunde.

conundrum [kə'nʌndrəm], *s.* das (Scherz)rätsel, die Vexierfrage.

conurbation [kɔnə:'beiʃən], *s.* ineinandergreifende Stadtgebiete (*pl.*).

convalesce [kɔnvə'les], *v.i.* genesen, gesund werden. **convalescence,** *s.* die Genesung, Gesundung, Rekonvaleszenz. **convalescent, 1.** *adj.* genesend, rekonvaleszent; ***he is –***, er ist gut auf dem Wege der Besserung. **2.** *s.* Genesende(r), der (die) Rekonvaleszent(in); – ***home***, das Genesungsheim, die Heilanstalt.

convection [kən'vekʃən], *s.* (*Phys.*) die Konvektion. **convectional,** *adj.* Konvektions–. **convector** [–ktə], *s.* (*also – heater*) der Konvektor.

convene [kən'vi:n], **1.** *v.t.* zusammenrufen, (ein)berufen, versammeln; (*Law*) vorladen, zitieren (***before***, vor (*Acc.*)). **2.** *v.i.* zusammenkommen, zusammentreffen, sich versammeln. **convener,** *s.* der Einberufer; (*Scots*) Vorsitzende(r).

convenience [kən'vi:niəns], *s.* 1. die Schicklichkeit, Angemessenheit; Bequemlichkeit, Annehmlichkeit; der Vorteil; ***at your earliest –***, so bald wie möglich, baldmöglichst, bei erster Gelegenheit; ***every –***, aller Komfort, jede Bequemlichkeit; ***make a – of***, ausnutzen; ***marriage of –***, die Verstandesheirat; ***at one's –***, wenn es gerade paßt, gelegentlich, nach Belieben; ***to suit your own –***, ganz nach Ihrem Belieben; 2. (*coll.*) (*also* ***public –***) die Bedürfnisanstalt.

convenient [kən'vi:niənt], *adj.* passend, (zweck)dienlich, angebracht; günstig, geeignet; bequem gelegen; ***it will not be – for me to see him today***, es paßt mir schlecht, ihn heute zu sehen; – ***for the purpose***, zu dem Zwecke geeignet, zweckdienlich; (*coll.*) – ***for*** or ***to the station***, nahe an *or* bei dem Bahnhof, in der Nähe von dem Bahnhof; ***with – speed***, mit möglichster Eile.

convent ['kɔnvənt], *s.* das (Nonnen)kloster.

conventical [kən'ventikl], *s.* die Versammlung; das Konventikel (*of Nonconformists*).

convention [kən'venʃən], *s.* 1. die Versammlung, Zusammenkunft, Tagung; (*Law*) der Vertrag, das Abkommen, Übereinkommen, die Übereinkunft, Abmachung; (*Pol.*) Konvention; (*Hist.*) ***National Convention***, der Nationalkonvent; 2. (*oft. pl.*) das Herkommen, der Brauch.

conventional [kən'venʃənl], *adj.* üblich, herkömmlich, konventionell, traditionsgemäß; (*Law*) vertragsgemäß, vereinbart, willkürlich festgesetzt; – ***signs***, Kartenzeichen (*pl.*) (*of a map*); – ***treatment***, die Behandlung nach der Schablone. **conven-**

tionalism, *s.* das Haften am Hergebrachten. **conventionality** [-'næliti], *s.* die Herkömmlichkeit, Schablonenhaftigkeit.

conventual [kən'ventjuəl], *adj.* klösterlich, Kloster-.

converge [kən'və:dʒ], *v.i.* zusammenlaufen, (*Math. etc.*) konvergieren; sich nähern (*to(wards)*, *Dat.*). **convergence, convergency,** *s.* die Annäherung (*to(wards)*, an (*Acc.*)), das Zusammenlaufen, die Konvergenz. **convergent,** *adj.* (*esp. Math.*) *see* **converging. converging,** *adj.* zusammenlaufend, verjüngend, konvergent, konvergierend; – ***lens,*** die Sammellinse; – ***point,*** der Knotenpunkt.

conversable [kən'və:səbl], *adj.* unterhaltend, gesprächig; gesellig, umgänglich, mitteilsam. **conversance,** *s.* die Vertrautheit. **conversant,** *adj.* bekannt, vertraut (***with,*** mit); erfahren, geübt, bewandert (in (*Dat.*)), kundig (*Gen.*).

conversation [kɔnvə'seiʃən], *s.* 1. das Gespräch, die Unterredung, Unterhaltung, Konversation; ***enter into – with,*** ein Gespräch anknüpfen mit; (*Art*) – ***piece,*** das Genrebild; ***subject of –,*** das Gesprächsthema; 2. (*obs.*) der Umgang, Verkehr; (*Law*) ***criminal –,*** der Geschlechtsverkehr. **conversational,** *adj.* gesprächig, Unterhaltungs–; – ***powers,*** die Unterhaltungsgabe; – ***style,*** der Gesprächsstil, Umgangsstil. **conversationalist,** *s.* guter Gesellschafter, gewandter Gesprächspartner. **conversazione** [–sætsi'ouni], *s.* die Abendgesellschaft; (literarischer) Unterhaltungsabend.

[1]**converse,** 1. [kən'və:s], *v.i.* sich unterhalten, sprechen, reden (***with,*** mit); (*obs.*) verkehren (***with,*** mit). 2. ['kɔnvə:s], *s.* das Gespräch, die Unterhaltung, Unterredung; der Umgang, Verkehr.

[2]**converse** ['kɔnvə:s], 1. *adj.* umgekehrt, gegenteilig. 2. *s.* die Umkehrung, das Gegenteil.

conversion [kən'və:ʃən], *s.* 1. die Umänderung, Verwandlung, Umwandlung (***into,*** in (*Acc.*)), (*Math.*) (*inches to cm. etc.*) Umrechnung, (*of equations*) Reduktion, Umstellung; (*Comm.*) Konvertierung, Einlösung, (*currency*) Umwechslung; (*Chem.*) Umsetzung; (*Elec.*) Umformung; (*Log.*) Umkehrung; (*Eccl.*) Bekehrung, (*fig.*) Wandlung, Besserung, Meinungsänderung; – ***table,*** die Umrechnungstabelle; 2. (*Law*) widerrechtliche Aneignung *or* Verwendung; ***fraudulent –,*** die Veruntreuung, Unterschlagung.

convert, 1. [kən'və:t], *v.t.* 1. umwandeln, verwandeln (***into,*** in (*Acc.*)), umformen, umändern (zu); (*Comm.*) konvertieren, einlösen (*bonds*), einwechseln, umwechseln (*money*), umsetzen, umrechnen; (*Log.*) umkehren; (*Theol. etc.*) bekehren (zu); – ***a house,*** ein Haus in kleine Wohnungen einteilen; – ***everything into money,*** alles zu Geld machen *or* flüssig machen; 2. (*Law*) (widerrechtlich) verwenden (zu), sich (*Dat.*) unbefugt aneignen, unterschlagen; – ***a th. to one's own use,*** etwas für sich verwenden, sich (*Dat.*) etwas aneignen; 3. (*Rugby*) erhöhen; 4. (*Tech.*) bessemern, frischen, (*steel*) zementieren; ***–ed steel,*** der Zementstahl. 2. ['kɔnvə:t], *s.* Bekehrte(r), Übergetretene(r), der (die) Konvertit(in), Proselyt(in); ***become a – to,*** sich bekehren zu; ***make a –,*** einen Proselyten machen.

converter [kən'və:tə], *s.* 1. der Bekehrer; 2. (*Elec.*) Umformer; ***rotary –,*** der Drehumformer, Einankerumformer; 3. (*Metall.*) die Bessemerbirne. **convertibility** [–'biliti], *s.* die Umwandelbarkeit, Verwandelbarkeit; (*Comm.*) Umsetzbarkeit, Konvertierbarkeit. **convertible,** 1. *adj.* (um)wandelbar; bekehrbar; umkehrbar, auswechselbar; (*Math.*) umrechenbar; (*Comm.*) umsetzbar, konvertierbar, einlösbar; – ***bond,*** die Wandelschuldverschreibung; – ***terms,*** gleichwertige *or* gleichbedeutende Ausdrücke. 2. *s.* (*coll.*) (*Motor.*) das Kabriolett.

convex ['kɔnveks], *adj.* konvex, nach außen gewölbt, erhaben. **convexity** [kən'veksiti], *s.* konvexe Form.

convey [kən'vei], *v.t.* zuführen, überbringen, übergeben, übersenden, übertragen, übermitteln; (*Comm.*) spedieren, befördern, transportieren, versenden; (*fig.*) mitteilen, vermitteln, ausdrücken, zu verstehen geben; (*Law*) übertragen, abtreten, auflassen, zedieren (***to,*** an (*Acc.*)); (*Phys.*) (über)tragen, leiten, fortpflanzen; – ***greetings,*** Grüße übermitteln *or* überbringen *or* bestellen; – ***an idea,*** einen Begriff geben; – ***one's meaning clearly,*** sich klar ausdrücken; – ***by water,*** verschiffen.

conveyance [kən'veiəns], *s.* das Wegführen, Forttragen, Fortschaffen; (*Law*) die Übergabe, Abtretung; Auflassung, Zession, Übertragung(surkunde); (*Comm.*) Beförderung, Übersendung, Überbringung, Spedition, der Transport; (*fig.*) die Vermittlung, Übermittlung, Mitteilung; (*coll.*) das Transportmittel, Beförderungsmittel, Fuhrwerk, Fahrzeug; ***bill of –,*** die Speditionsrechnung; ***charges for –,*** Transportkosten; ***deed of –,*** die Übertragungsurkunde; ***means of –,*** das Beförderungsmittel, Transportmittel; ***mode of –,*** die Versendungsart.

conveyancer [kən'veiənsə], *s.* der Notar für Übertragungsgeschäfte. **conveyancing,** *s.* die Grundeigentumsübertragung.

conveyer, conveyor [kən'veiə], *s.* 1. der Beförderer; 2. (*also – chain*) die Förderkette, Becherkette; (*also – belt*) laufendes Band, das Förderband, Transportband.

convict, 1. [kən'vikt], *v.t.* überführen, für schuldig erklären; – ***him of an error,*** ihm einen Irrtum nachweisen *or* zum Bewußtsein bringen; ***be –ed of murder,*** des Mordes überführt werden. 2. ['kɔnvikt], *s.* der Sträfling, Zuchthäusler; (*obs.*) überführter Missetäter; – ***settlement,*** die Sträflingskolonie.

conviction [kən'vikʃən], *s.* 1. (*Law*) die Überführung, Verurteilung; Schuldigerklärung, Schuldigsprechung; ***previous*** or ***prior –,*** die Vorstrafe; 2. Gewißheit, Überzeugung; ***the – grows on me,*** ich komme immer mehr zu der Überzeugung; ***be open to –,*** sich gern überzeugen lassen; – ***of sin,*** das Sündenbewußtsein; ***strong –,*** feste Überzeugung; ***carry –,*** überzeugend klingen; ***live up to one's –s,*** seiner Überzeugung gemäß handeln.

convince [kən'vins], *v.t.* überzeugen; – ***him of a th.,*** ihn von etwas überzeugen, ihm etwas zum Bewußtsein bringen. **convincible,** *adj.* überzeugbar. **convincing,** *adj.* überzeugend; ***be –,*** überzeugend wirken, überzeugen; – ***proof,*** schlagender Beweis.

convivial [kən'viviəl], *adj.* gesellig; lustig, heiter; festlich; – ***evening,*** der Festabend. **conviviality** [–'æliti], *s.* die Geselligkeit; Fröhlichkeit (bei Tafel).

convocation [kɔnvo'keiʃən], *s.* die Zusammenberufung, Einberufung; Versammlung; Provinzialsynode (*of Church of England*); (*Univ.*) gesetzgebende Versammlung.

convoke [kən'vouk], *v.t.* (amtlich) zusammenberufen *or* einberufen.

convolute ['kɔnvəlju:t], 1. *s.* (*Math.*) die Rollkurve, Zykloide. 2. *v.t.* (*v.i.* sich) (zusammen)rollen. 3. *adj.* (*Bot.*) zusammengerollt, zusammengewickelt, ringelförmig. **convoluted,** *adj.* (*Med.*) geschlängelt, knäuelförmig, (*Biol., Zool.*) zusammengerollt, gewunden. **convolution** [–'lju:ʃən], *s.* die Zusammenrollung, Zusammenwick(e)lung, Einrollung (*also Bot.*); (*Tech.*) der Umlauf, Umgang, die Windung (*also Anat.*).

convolve [kən'vɔlv], *v.t., v.i. See* **convolute, 2.**

convolvulus [kən'vɔlvjuləs], *s.* (*Bot.*) die Winde.

convoy, 1. [kən'vɔi], *v.t.* (*Mil. etc.*) geleiten, decken. 2. ['kɔnvɔi], *s.* das Geleit, die (Schutz)begleitung, Deckung, der Schutz; (*Naut.*) Geleitzug, Konvoi; ***lorry –,*** die Lastkraftwagenkolonne; ***travel in –,*** im Geleitzug fahren.

convulse [kən'vʌls], *v.t.* erschüttern; ***be –d with laughter,*** sich vor Lachen biegen *or* krümmen; ***be –d with pain,*** sich vor Schmerzen winden. **convulsion** [–'vʌlʃən], *s.* (*Med.*) (*oft. pl.*) die Zuckung, der Krampf; (*fig.*) die Erschütterung; ***–s of laughter,*** Lachkrämpfe. **convulsive,** *adj.* krampfhaft, krampfartig, zuckend; (*fig.*) erschütternd.

cony ['kouni], *s.* das Kaninchen; Kaninchenfell.

coo [ku:], *v.i.* girren, gurren; ***bill and* –,** (sich) schnäbeln; (*coll.*) zärtlich tun, liebkosen. **cooing,** *s.* das Girren; (*coll.*) ***billing and* –,** Zärtlichkeiten (*pl.*).

cook [kuk], **1.** *s.* der Koch (die Köchin); (*Prov.*) ***too many –s spoil the broth,*** viele Köche verderben den Brei. **2.** *v.t.* kochen, abkochen, backen, braten, zubereiten; (*coll.*) – ***the accounts*** or (*sl.*) ***books,*** die Abrechnung fälschen *or* schminken *or* frisieren; (*sl.*) – ***his goose,*** ihm den Garaus machen; – ***up,*** aufwärmen; (*sl.*) zusammenlügen, erdichten, vorschwindeln. **3.** *v.i.* kochen, Speisen zubereiten; (*sl.*) ***what's –ing?*** was tut sich?

cook-book, *s.* (*Am.*) das Kochbuch. **cooker,** *s.* 1. der Kocher; das Kochgerät, Kochgefäß; 2. *pl.* Kochobst; ***the apples are good –s,*** die Äpfel lassen sich gut kochen.

cookery ['kukəri], *s.* das Kochen; die Kochkunst; – ***book,*** das Kochbuch. **cook-house,** *s.* (*Mil.*) die Feldküche, (*Naut.*) Schiffsküche, Kombüse. **cookie,** *s.* 1. (*Am.*) der Keks; 2. *See* **cooky. cooking, 1.** *s. See* **cookery**; die Kochweise, Küche. **2.** *adj.* Koch–; – ***apple,*** der Kochapfel; – ***range,*** der Kochherd. **cook-shop,** *s.* die Garküche. **cooky,** *s.* 1. (*Scots*) das Brötchen; 2. (*coll.*) die Köchin.

cool [ku:l], **1.** *adj.* kühl, frisch; (*fig.*) gleichgültig, abweisend, lau, teilnahmslos; ruhig, bedächtig, besonnen, gelassen; (*sl.*) unverfroren, frech; – ***cheek,*** die Frechheit, Stirn; (*coll.*) – ***as a cucumber,*** frech wie Oskar; (*coll.*) – ***customer,*** geriebener Kunde; – ***dress,*** leichtes Kleid; ***get* –,** sich abkühlen; (*coll.*) ***keep* –,** einen kühlen Kopf behalten; (*sl.*) ***a – thousand,*** glatte tausend (*pounds, dollars etc.*). **2.** *s.* die Kühle, Frische. **3.** *v.t.* (ab)kühlen (lassen); (*coll.*) – ***one's heels,*** lange *or* vergeblich warten. **4.** *v.i.* (*also* – ***down***) sich (ab)kühlen, kühl werden, erkalten; (*fig.*) – ***down,*** sich legen, sich beruhigen.

coolant ['ku:lənt], *s.* das Kühlmittel. **cooler,** *s.* 1. der Kühler; 2. (*sl.*) das Kittchen.

cool-headed ['ku:l'hedid], *adj.* 1. besonnen, kaltblütig; 2. schwer erregbar.

coolie ['ku:li], *s.* der Kuli, chinesischer Lastträger.

cooling ['ku:liŋ], **1.** *s.* die (Ab)kühlung; ***gravity system water* –,** die Thermosyphonkühlung. **2.** *adj.* kühlend, erfrischend; (*Tech.*) Kühl–; – ***agent,*** das Kühlmittel; – ***chamber,*** der Kühlraum; – ***fin,*** die Kühlrippe (*of an engine*); – ***tower,*** der Kondensationsturm; – ***water,*** das Kühlwasser. **coolly** ['ku:lli], *adv. See* **cool, 1.** (*fig.*). **coolness,** *s.* die Kühle; (*fig.*) Gelassenheit, Ruhe; Lauheit, Gleichgültigkeit, Unfreundlichkeit; Kälte, Kaltblütigkeit; (*sl.*) Frechheit.

coomb [ku:m], *s.* (*dial.*) die Talmulde, Senkung.

coon [ku:n], *s.* (*Zool.*) Schupp, gemeiner Waschbär.

coop [ku:p], **1.** *v.t.* (– ***up***) einsperren, einpferchen. **2.** *s.* der Hühnerkorb.

co-op ['kouɔp], *s.* (*coll.*) *see* ***co-operative society*** or ***store.***

cooper ['ku:pə], **1.** *s.* der Küfer, Böttcher, Faßbinder. **2.** *v.i.* Fässer machen *or* binden. **cooperage** [–ridʒ], *s.* die Küferei, Böttcherei; der Küferlohn.

co-operate [kou'ɔpəreit], *v.i.* mitwirken (***in,*** an (*Dat.*)), beitragen (zu), zusammenwirken, zusammenarbeiten. **co-operation** [–'reiʃən], *s.* die Mitwirkung, Mitarbeit, Zusammenarbeit, das Zusammenarbeiten, Zusammenwirken. **co-operative,** *adj.* mitwirkend, zusammenarbeitend; gegenseitig förderlich; (*Comm.*) Genossenschafts–, genossenschaftlich; – ***movement,*** die Genossenschaftsbewegung; – ***society,*** der Konsumverein, die Genossenschaft; – ***store,*** der Konsumladen. **co-operator,** *s.* Mitwirkende(r), der Mitarbeiter; (*Comm.*) das Konsumvereinsmitglied.

co-opt [kou'ɔpt], *v.t.* hinzuwählen, kooptieren. **co-op(ta)tion** [–'ɔpʃən (–ɔp'teiʃən)], *s.* die Zuwahl, Kooptierung.

co-ordinate, 1. [kou'ɔ:dinit], *adj.* beigeordnet, gleichgeordnet, koordiniert; gleichrangig, gleichgestellt, gleichartig. **2.** [–neit], *v.t.* beiordnen, gleichordnen, gleichstellen, koordinieren, gleichschalten; richtig anordnen, aufeinander abstimmen, in Einklang bringen. **3.** [–neit], *v.i.* sich einordnen, zusammenwirken, sich aufeinander abstimmen. **4.** [–nit], *s.* (*Math.*) die Koordinate. **co-ordination** [–'neiʃən], *s.* die Beiordnung, Gleichordnung, Gleichstellung, Nebenordnung, Gleichschaltung, Koordinierung, Koordination; Übereinstimmung, Zusammenfassung, richtige Anordnung, harmonische Vereinigung, das Zusammenwirken, Zusammenspiel. **co-ordinator,** *s.* der Koordinator.

coot [ku:t], *s.* (*Am.* ***European*** –) (*Orn.*) das Bläßhuhn, schwarzes Wasserhuhn (*Fulica atra*); (*coll.*) der Tolpatsch, Tölpel; ***as bald as a* –,** völlig kahl.

[1]**cop** [kɔp], *s.* der Garnwickel, der *or* das Knäuel, der Kötzer, die (Garn)winde, Spule.

[2]**cop, 1.** *v.t.* (*sl.*) fangen, erwischen; (*sl.*) – ***it,*** Prügel bekommen. **2.** *s.* (*sl.*) der Polyp (= *policeman*).

copaiba [kə'paibə], *s.* der Kopaivabalsam.

copal [koupl], *s.* der Kopal.

coparcenary [kou'pɑ:sənəri], *adj.* gemeinsamer Besitz, die Miterbschaft. **coparcener,** *s.* der Miterbe (die Miterbin).

co-partner [kou'pɑ:tnə], *s.* der Teilhaber, Mitinhaber, Kompagnon, Associé. **co-partnership,** *s.* die Teilhaberschaft, Mitbeteiligung; das Mitbeteiligungssystem; – ***of labour,*** die Gewinnbeteiligung (der Arbeitnehmer).

[1]**cope** [koup], **1.** *s.* 1. (*Eccl.*) der Priesterrock, Chorrock; 2. (*Archit.*) die Mauerkappe, Mauerabdeckung; (*Found.*) der Außenmantel, die Oberform; (*fig.*) Decke, das Dach, Zelt, Gewölbe. **2.** *v.t.* (be)decken, einhüllen.

[2]**cope,** *v.i.* sich messen, es aufnehmen (***with,*** mit); fertig werden (mit), gewachsen sein (*Dat.*); – ***with the situation,*** die Lage meistern *or* bewältigen.

copeck ['koupek], *s.* die Kopeke.

Copenhagen [koupən'heigən], *s.* Kopenhagen (*n.*).

coper ['koupə], *s.* der Pferdehändler.

Copernican [kə'pə:nikn], *adj.* kopernikanisch.

cope-stone, *s. See* ***coping stone***; (*fig.*) der Schlußstein, die Krönung, Krone.

copied ['kɔpid], *see* **copy. copier** ['kɔpiə], *s.* 1. der (die) Abschreiber(in), Kopist(in); 2. Plagiator(in), Nachahmer(in).

co-pilot ['koupailət], *s.* zweiter Pilot, der Mitpilot.

coping ['koupiŋ], *s.* die Mauerkappe, Mauerkrönung; – ***saw,*** die Laubsäge; – ***stone,*** der Deckstein, Kappenstein.

copious ['koupiəs], *adj.* reich(lich), ausgiebig; weitläufig; weitschweifig, wortreich. **copiousness,** *s.* die Fülle, Reichlichkeit, der Überfluß, Reichtum; die Weitläufigkeit, Weitschweifigkeit.

copper ['kɔpə], **1.** *s.* 1. das Kupfer; ***sheet* –,** das Kupferblech; – ***pyrites,*** der Kupferkies, Chalcopyrit; – ***sulphate,*** schwefelsaures Kupfer; – ***sulphide,*** das Schwefelkupfer; 2. die Kupfermünze; *pl.* das Kupfergeld, (*coll.*) Kleingeld; 3. der (Kupfer)kessel, Kochkessel, das (Kupfer)gefäß; 4. (*sl.*) *see* [2]**cop, 2. 2.** *adj.* kupfern, Kupfer–; –(-***wing***) ***butterfly,*** der Bläuling; – ***sheathing,*** der Kupferbeschlag; – ***wire,*** der Kupferdraht.

copperas ['kɔpərəs], *s.* das Vitriol; ***blue* –,** das Kupfervitriol; ***green* –,** das Eisenvitriol, Ferrosulfat; ***white* –,** das Zinkvitriol.

copper|-beech, *s.* (*Bot.*) die Blutbuche (*Fagus silvatica*). **--bottomed,** *adj.* (*Shipb.*) mit Kupferverkleidung, (*fig.*) seetüchtig; kerngesund. **--coloured,** *adj.* kupferrot. **--engraving,** *s.* 1. die Kupferstechkunst; 2. der Kupferstich. **–glance,** *s.* der Kupferglanz, das Chalcosin. **–head,** *s.* (*Zool.*) die Mokassinschlange. **–plate, 1.** *s.* die Kupferstichplatte; der Kupferstich. **2.** *adj.* Kupferstech–, Kupferstich–; (*fig.*) (*of handwriting*) wie gestochen; – ***engraving,*** *see* **--engraving. --plate,** *s.* der Kupferüberzug, die Verkupferung. **--plated,** *adj.* verkupfert. **–smith,** *s.* der Kupferschmied. **coppery,** *adj.* kupferig, kupferartig, kupferähnlich; kupferhaltig, Kupfer–.

coppice ['kɔpis], *s.* das Unterholz, Dickicht, Gehölz, Gebüsch, Gestrüpp.

copra ['kɔprə], *s.* die Kopra.

copse [kɔps], *s. See* **coppice.**

Copt [kɔpt], *s.* der Kopte (die Koptin). **Coptic, 1.** *adj.* koptisch. **2.** *s.* das Koptisch (*language*).

copula ['kɔpjulə], *s.* 1. (*Gram.*) das Bindewort, die Kopula; 2. (*Anat.*) das Bindeglied.

copulate ['kɔpjuleit], *v.i.* sich paaren, sich begatten. **copulation** [–'leiʃən], *s.* die Paarung, Begattung, der Beischlaf, Koitus; die Verbindung, Zusammenfügung. **copulative** [–lətiv], **1.** *adj.* Binde–, verbindend. **2.** *s.* (*Gram.*) *see* **copula. copulatory** [–lətəri], *adj.* Paarungs–, Begattungs–.

copy ['kɔpi], **1.** *s.* die Abschrift, Kopie; Nachahmung, Nachbildung, Reproduktion; der Abzug, die Pause, (*typewriter*) der Durchschlag; ***carbon –,*** der Durchschlag; ***make*** or ***take a –,*** eine Abschrift nehmen; 2. die Vorlage, das Muster, Modell; (*Typ.*) druckfertiges Manuskript, die (Satz)vorlage; (*journalism*) literarisches Material, der (Zeitungs)stoff; ***clean*** or ***fair –,*** die Reinschrift; ***foul*** or ***rough –,*** die Kladde, das Konzept, erster Entwurf; 3. (*of a document*) die Ausfertigung, (*of a newspaper*) Nummer, (*of a book*) der Abdruck, das Exemplar. **2.** *v.t.* abschreiben; durchpausen, kopieren; (*Phot.*) einen Abzug *or* eine Kopie machen von, abziehen; reproduzieren, abzeichnen, nachbilden, nachahmen; ***– out,*** abschreiben, ins reine schreiben. **3.** *v.i.* kopieren, nachahmen; (*at school*) (vom Nachbar) abschreiben.

copy|-book, *s.* das Schreibheft; (*coll., fig.*) ***blot one's –,*** sich blamieren. **--cat,** *s.* 1. (*coll.*) der Nachäffer; 2. (*coll.*) Vervielfältigungsapparat. **–hold,** *s.* das Zinslehen. **–holder,** *s.* 1. der Erbpächter, Zinslehensbesitzer; 2. (*Typ.*) Korrekturgehilfe.

copying ['kɔpiiŋ], **1.** *s.* das Abschreiben. **2.** *adj.* Kopier–. **copying|-clerk,** *s.* der Kopist. **--ink,** *s.* die Kopiertinte; ***– pencil,*** der Tintenstift. **--machine,** *s. See* **--press. --paper,** *s.* das Durchschlagpapier. **--pencil,** *s.* der Tintenstift. **--press,** *s.* die Kopiermaschine, Kopierpresse.

copyist ['kɔpiist], *s.* der Abschreiber, Kopist. **copyright, 1.** *s.* das Verlagsrecht, Urheberrecht (*in*, von *or* für). **2.** *adj.* verlagsrechtlich geschützt; ***– edition,*** urheberrechtliche Ausgabe. **3.** *v.t.* verlagsrechtlich schützen. **copy-writer,** *s.* (*advertising*) der Texter.

coquet [kɔ'ket], **1.** *v.i.* kokettieren, flirten; (*fig.*) liebäugeln, es nicht ernst meinen (***with,*** mit). **2.** *adj.* kokett. **coquetry** ['koukitri], *s.* die Gefallsucht, Koketterie. **coquette,** *s.* die Kokette, Gefallsüchtige. **coquettish,** *adj.* gefallsüchtig, kokett.

coracle ['kɔrəkl], *s.* primitives Boot (aus überzogenem Flechtwerk).

coracoid ['kɔrəkɔid], *adj.* (*Anat., Zool.*) Rabenschnabel–; ***– bone,*** das Rabenschnabelbein; ***– process,*** der Rabenschnabelfortsatz.

coral ['kɔrəl], **1.** *s.* die Koralle; der Korallenpolyp. **2.** *adj.* Korallen–; ***– beads,*** Korallen (*pl.*), das Korallenhalsband; ***– island,*** die Koralleninsel; ***– reef,*** das Korallenriff. **corallin,** *s.* (*Chem.*) das Korallin. **coralline** [–lain], **1.** *adj.* korallenartig; korallenrot; Korallen–. **2.** *s.* die Korallenalge. **corallite** [–lait], *s.* fossile Koralle, das Korallenskelett. **coralloid,** *adj.* korallenähnlich, korallenartig.

corbel [kɔ:bl], **1.** *s.* (*Archit.*) der Kragstein, die Konsole, der Balkenträger. **2.** *v.t.* durch Kragsteine stützen. **corbel-table,** *s.* auf Kragsteinen ruhender Mauervorsprung, der Bogenfries.

corbie ['kɔ:bi], *s.* (*Scots*) der Rabe. **corbie-steps,** *pl.* (*Archit.*) die Giebelstufen.

cord [kɔ:d], **1.** *s.* 1. der Strick, das Seil, die Leine; Schnur (*also Anat.*); der Strang (*also Anat.*); (*Anat.*) das Band; ***spinal –,*** das Rückenmark; ***vocal –s,*** Stimmbänder (*pl.*); 2. die Klafter (*of wood = 128 cu. ft.*); ***– of wood,*** eine Klafter Holz; 3. *See* **corduroy**; *pl.* (*coll.*) Kordhose. **2.** *v.t.* zuschnüren, verschnüren; festbinden; ***– wood,*** Holz (auf)klaftern. **cordage** [–idʒ], *s.* das Tauwerk, Seilwerk.

cordate ['kɔ:deit], *adj.* herzförmig.

corded ['kɔ:did], *adj.* verschnürt, zugeschnürt; gerippt (*of cloth*).

Cordelier [kɔ:də'liə], *s.* der Franziskanermönch.

cordial ['kɔ:diəl], **1.** *adj.* herzlich, aufrichtig; (*Med.*) belebend, herzstärkend, magenstärkend; (*coll.*) ***– dislike,*** gründliche Abneigung. **2.** *s.* der Magenlikör, herzstärkendes *or* magenstärkendes Mittel; (*fig.*) das Labsal. **cordiality** [–'æliti], *s.* die Herzlichkeit, Wärme.

cordite ['kɔ:dait], *s.* das Kordit.

1**cordon** ['kɔ:dən], **1.** *s.* 1. (*Mil.*) die Postenkette, (Ab)sperrkette, der Kordon; ***form a –,*** Spalier bilden; 2. (*Archit.*) der Mauerkranz, das Kranzgesims; (*Hort.*) der Spalierbaum. **2.** *v.t.* ***– off,*** abriegeln, absperren, umzingeln, einschließen.

2**cordon** [kɔ:'dɔ̃], *s.* die Schnur, Litze, Kordel, das Ordensband; (*Her.*) der Strick, Knoten; (*fig.*) ***– bleu,*** höchste Auszeichnung, (*coll.*) erstklassiger Koch.

cordovan ['kɔ:dəvən], *s.* das Korduan(leder).

corduroy ['kɔ:djurɔi], *s.* der Kord(samt), Kordstoff, Rippssamt, *pl.* die Kordhose; ***– road,*** der Knüppeldamm.

cordwain ['kɔ:dwein], *s.* (*obs.*) *see* **cordovan. cordwainer,** *s.* ***Cordwainers' Company,*** die Londoner Schuhmacherinnung.

core [kɔ:], **1.** *s.* das Kerngehäuse, der Griebs, Kern; (*fig.*) Kern, das Innerste, Herz, Mark, die Ader; (*of wire, cable etc.*) Seele, der Kabelkern, (*of magnet etc.*) (Anker)kern; ***the heart's –,*** der Herzensgrund; ***rotten at*** or ***to the –,*** im Innersten faul; ***to the –,*** bis ins Innerste, bis auf den Grund. **2.** *v.t.* entkernen.

co-regent ['kouri:dʒənt], *s.* der Mitregent.

co-religionist ['kourilidʒənist], *s.* der Glaubensgenosse.

co-respondent ['kourispɔndənt], *s.* Mitgeklagte(r) (*in divorce suit*).

corf [kɔ:f], *s.* (*Min.*) der Förderkorb.

coriacious [kɔri'eiʃəs], *adj.* ledern, Leder–; lederartig, zäh, (*Bot.*) lederig.

Corinth ['kɔrinθ], *s.* Korinth (*n.*). **Corinthian** [kə'rinθiən], **1.** *s.* der (die) Korinther(in); (*B.*) ***Epistle to the –s,*** der Korintherbrief. **2.** *adj.* korinthisch; (*Archit.*) ***– order,*** korinthische Säulenordnung.

Coriolanus [kɔriə'leinəs], *s.* Koriolan (*m.*).

cork [kɔ:k], **1.** *s.* (*Bot.*) die Korkrinde, der Kork; Kork(en), Stöpsel, Pfropfen; (*fishing etc.*) Schwimmer, Angelkork; ***draw the –,*** den Kork ziehen; ***rubber –,*** der Gummistöpsel. **2.** *v.t.* verkorken, zukorken, verstöpseln, zustöpseln (*a bottle*); (mit verbranntem Kork) schwärzen; (*sl.*) ***– it!*** halt's Maul! **corkage** [–idʒ], *s.* das Korkengeld. **corkboard,** *s.* die Korkplatte. **corked,** *adj.* (*of bottles*) verkorkt, zugekorkt, verstöpselt; (*of wine*) korkig; ***be –,*** nach dem Kork schmecken. **corker,** *s.* (*sl.*) prima S.; famoser Kerl. **corking,** *adj.* (*sl.*) prima, famos, fabelhaft, großartig.

cork| jacket, *s.* die Schwimmweste. **– leg,** *s.* die Beinprothese. **--oak,** *s.* die Korkeiche. **–screw, 1.** *s.* der Korkenzieher. **2.** *v.t.* (*v.i.* sich) (durch)winden, (durch)schlängeln. **3.** *adj.* spiralig gewunden; ***– curls,*** Ringellocken (*pl.*). **– sole,** *s.* die Korkeinlegesohle.

corm [kɔ:m], *s.* (*Bot.*) der Kormus.

cormorant ['kɔ:mərənt], *s.* (*Am.* ***Great –***) (*Orn.*) der Kormoran (*Phalacrocorax carbo*); (*fig.*) Vielfraß.

1**corn** [kɔ:n], *s.* (*Med.*) das Hühnerauge; (*fig.*) ***tread on his –s,*** ihm auf die Hühneraugen treten.

2**corn, 1.** *s.* das Korn, Getreide; der Weizen (*in England*), Hafer (*in Scotland and Ireland*), (*Am.*)

(*also* ***Indian*** *–*) Mais, (*coll.*) Maisschnaps; **– *on the cob,*** Maiskörner am Kolben. **2.** *v.t.* (ein)pökeln, einsalzen; ***–ed beef,*** das Pökelfleisch, Büchsen(rind)fleisch.
corn|-belt, *s.* der Getreidegürtel (*U.S.A.*). **--bin,** *s.* die Kornlade. **--bind,** *s.* (*Bot.*) die Ackerwinde. **--bunting,** *s.* (*Orn.*) die Grauammer (*Emberiza callandra*). **--chandler,** *s.* der Getreidehändler. **--cob,** *s.* der Maiskolben. **--cockle,** *s.* (*Bot.*) die Kornrade. **–crake,** (*Am.*) **– crake,** *s.* der Wiesenknarrer, Wachtelkönig (*Crex crex*).
cornea ['kɔ:niə], *s.* die Hornhaut (*of eye*).
corned [kɔ:nd], *adj.* *See* **²corn, 2.**
cornel [kɔ:nl], *s.* (*Bot.*) die Kornel(ius)kirsche, der Hornstrauch, Hartriegel.
cornelian [kɔ:'ni:liən], *s.* der Karneol.
corneous ['kɔ:niəs], *adj.* hornig, Horn–.
corner ['kɔ:nə], **1.** *s.* 1. die Ecke, der Winkel; (*fig.*) die Verlegenheit, Klemme; ***at the – of the street,*** an der Straßenecke; ***blind –,*** unübersichtliche Biegung *or* Ecke; ***cut (off) a –,*** ein Stück (vom Wege) abschneiden; ***all the –s of the earth,*** alle Ecken und Enden *or* alle Gegenden der Erde; (*fig.*) ***be in a –,*** in der Klemme *or* Patsche sitzen, in Verlegenheit sein; (*fig.*) ***drive him into a –,*** ihn in die Enge treiben *or* in Verlegenheit bringen; (*fig.*) ***we are not round the – yet,*** wir sind noch nicht über den Berg; ***tight –,*** schwierige Lage; (*Motor.*) ***take a –,*** eine Kurve nehmen; ***turn the –,*** um die Ecke biegen, (*fig.*) über das Schlimmste hinweg sein, über den Berg hinwegkommen; 2. (*Comm.*) die Schwänze, Aufkäufergruppe, der Spekulantenring; Aufkauf, Corner, das Aufkaufen, die Monopolbildung; 3. (*Footb.*) *see* **corner-kick. 2.** *v.t.* 1. (*fig.*) in die Enge treiben, in Verlegenheit bringen; 2. (*Comm.*) aufkaufen, cornern, aufschwänzen; (durch Aufkauf *or* Vereinbarung) hohe Preise aufzwingen (*Dat.*); ***– the market,*** den Markt aufkaufen. **3.** *v.i.* (*Motor.*) in die Kurve fahren.
corner-cupboard, *s.* der Eckschrank. **cornered,** *adj.* 1. (*as suff.*) –eckig; 2. (*fig.*) in Verlegenheit, in die Enge getrieben; in der Klemme *or* Patsche; 3. (*Comm.*) aufgekauft, aufgeschwänzt. **corner| house,** *s.* das Eckhaus. **--kick,** *s.* (*Footb.*) der Eckball, (freier) Eckstoß, die Ecke. **–piece,** *s.* der Dreikantbeschlag, die Eckverzierung. **–stone,** *s.* (*Archit.*) der Eckstein, (*fig.*) Eckpfeiler, Grundstein. **–ways, –wise,** *adv.* mit der Ecke nach vorn, diagonal.
cornet ['kɔ:nit], *s.* 1. (*Mus.*) das (Ventil)kornett; 2. (spitze) Tüte; ***ice-cream –,*** die Eistüte; 3. (*Hist.*) der Fahnenjunker, Fähnrich, Kornett. **cornetcy** [–si], *s.* (*Hist.*) die Kornettstelle. **cornet player,** *s.* der Kornettbläser, Kornettist.
cornett ['kɔ:nit], *s.* (*Mus., obs.*) die Zinke.
corn| exchange, *s.* die Getreidebörse. **– factor,** *s.* der Getreide(groß)händler. **–field,** *s.* das Kornfeld, Getreidefeld. **– flakes,** *pl.* Maisflocken (*pl.*). **–flour,** *s.* das Maismehl. **–flower,** *s.* (*Bot.*) die Kornblume.
cornice ['kɔ:nis], *s.* (*Archit.*) das Karnies, Gesims, der Sims; die Mauerbrüstung; Bilderleiste; (*on furniture*) Kranzleiste, Randleiste; (*of snow*) Wächte.
Cornish ['kɔ:niʃ], **1.** *adj.* aus Cornwall, kornisch. **2.** *s.* das Kornisch (*language*).
corn| laws, *pl.* (*Hist.*) das Korn(zoll)gesetz. **–loft,** *s.* der Kornboden, Getreidespeicher. **--plaster,** *s.* das Hühneraugenpflaster. **--poppy,** *s.* (*Bot.*) die Klatschrose, der Klatschmohn.
cornucopia [kɔ:nju'koupiə], *s.* das Füllhorn, (*fig.*) die Fülle, der Überfluß.
¹corny ['kɔ:ni], *adj.* 1. kornreich; 2. Korn–, Getreide–, (*Am.*) Mais–; 3. körnig, körnerreich; 4. (*sl.*) abgedroschen, kitschig, schmalzig.
²corny, *adj.* voller Hühneraugen.
corolla [kə'rɔlə], *s.* (*Bot.*) die Blumenkrone.
corollary [kə'rɔləri], *s.* (*Log., Math.*) der Folgesatz, Zusatz, (*fig.*) (logische) Folge(erscheinung), das Ergebnis; selbstverständliche Folgerung.
corona [kə'rounə], *s.* (*Astr.*) der Hof, Lichtkranz, (*of sun*) die Korona, Leuchtatmosphäre; (*Elec.*) Korona, Glimmentladung; (*Archit.*) Kranzleiste, das Kranzgesims; (*dentistry*) die (Zahn)krone; (*Bot.*) Federkrone, Nebenkrone, der Pappus, Randblütenkranz; (*Eccl.*) runder Kronleuchter. **coronal, 1.** *adj.* Kranz–, Kron(en)–; ***– bone,*** das Stirnbein; – (***suture***), die Kranznaht. **2.** *s.* der Stirnreif, das Diadem; der (Blumen)kranz.
coronary ['kɔrənəri], *adj.* Kronen–, Kranz–, kronenartig, kranzartig; (*Anat.*) ***– artery,*** die Kranzarterie; (*Med.*) – (***thrombosis***), die Koronarthrombose.
coronation [kɔrə'neiʃən], *s.* die Krönung(sfeier); ***– oath,*** der Krönungseid.
coroner ['kɔrənə], *s.* amtlicher Leichenbeschauer; ***–'s inquest,*** gerichtliche Leichenschau; ***–'s jury,*** die Leichenkommission.
coronet ['kɔrənet], *s.* 1. kleine Krone, die Adelskrone; 2. (*of horse*) Hufkrone.
¹corporal ['kɔ:pərəl], *s.* (*Mil.*) Obergefreite(r).
²corporal, *adj.* körperlich, leiblich; ***– punishment,*** körperliche Züchtigung, die Prügelstrafe, (*Law*) Körperstrafe. **corporality** [kɔ:pə'ræliti], *s.* die Körperlichkeit, körperliche Existenz; *pl.* körperliche Bedürfnisse (*pl.*).
corporate ['kɔrpərit], *adj.* korporativ, körperschaftlich, Körperschafts–, inkorporiert, vereinigt, verbunden; ***– body,*** die Körperschaft, juristische P.; ***– effort,*** vereinte Bemühungen (*pl.*); ***– property,*** das Körperschaftseigentum.
corporation [kɔ:pə'reiʃən], *s.* 1. die Korporation, Körperschaft, juristische P.; die Gilde, Zunft, Innung, (Handels)gesellschaft; Stadtbehörde; ***mayor and –,*** Bürgermeister und (Stadt)rat; ***– tax,*** die Körperschaftssteuer; 2. (*sl.*) der Schmerbauch.
corporeal [kɔ:'pɔ:riəl], *adj.* körperlich; physisch, materiell, greifbar. **corporeality** [–'æliti], *s.* die Körperlichkeit, körperliche Existenz *or* Form.
corposant ['kɔ:pəzənt], *s.* das (Sankt) Elmsfeuer.
corps [kɔ:], *s.* (*Mil.*) (*also* ***army*** *–*) das (Armee)korps; Korps, die Truppe; (*Univ.*) Korporation, das Corps.
corpse ['kɔ:ps], *s.* die Leiche, der Leichnam.
corpulence, corpulency ['kɔ:pjuləns(i)], *s.* die Beleibtheit, Korpulenz, Körperfülle. **corpulent,** *adj.* beleibt, korpulent.
corpus ['kɔ:pəs], *s.* 1. das Korpus, der Hauptkörper, Stamm, die Hauptmasse; (*Comm.*) das Stammkapital; 2. (*Law*) ***– delici,*** der Tatbestand; ***– juris,*** die Gesetzessammlung; 3. (*Eccl.*) ***Corpus Christi,*** der Fronleichnam; das Fronleichnamsfest.
corpuscle ['kɔ:pəsl], *s.* das (Blut)körperchen; (*Chem. etc.*) Elementarteilchen, Korpuskel. **corpuscular** [–'pʌskjulə], *adj.* Korpuskular–, korpuskular. **corpuscule** [–'pʌskju:l], *s.* *See* **corpuscle.**
corral [kə'rɑ:l], *s.* die Hürde, der Pferch, das Gehege; die Wagenburg.
correct [kə'rekt], **1.** *adj.* richtig, fehlerfrei; genau, wahr; vorschriftsmäßig, einwandfrei, tadellos, korrekt; ***be –,*** (*of a th.*) stimmen, (*of a p.*) recht haben; (*Comm.*) ***if found –,*** nach Rechtbefinden; ***that is the – thing to do,*** das gehört sich nun einmal, das ist nun das Gegebene. **2.** *v.t.* berichtigen, richtigstellen, verbessern, korrigieren (*mistakes*); tadeln, zurechtweisen (*wrongdoings*), (*obs.*) strafen, züchtigen; beheben, beseitigen, abstellen (*defects*); ***– o.s.,*** sich verbessern; ***stand –ed,*** einen Fehler eingestehen; (*Typ.*) ***– proofs,*** Korrekturen lesen, durchkorrigieren.
correction [kə'rekʃən], *s.* die Berichtigung, Richtigstellung, Verbesserung (*of mistakes*); Zurechtweisung, der Tadel, Verweis (*of wrongdoings*), (*obs.*) die Bestrafung, Züchtigung, Strafe; Behebung, Beseitigung, Abstellung (*of defects*); (*Typ.*) Korrektur; (*Math.*) der Korrektionsfaktor; (*obs.*) ***house of –,*** die Besserungsanstalt; ***subject to –,*** ohne Gewähr; ***I speak under –,*** ich kann mich irren, wenn ich mich nicht irre, dies ist meine

unmaßgebliche Meinung. **correctional,** *adj.* Berichtigungs–, Korrektions–; verbessernd, Besserungs–.

correctitude [kə'rektitju:d], *s.* die Korrektheit (*of behaviour*). **corrective, 1.** *adj.* berichtigend, richtigstellend, verbessernd, korrigierend, Verbesserungs–; lindernd, mildernd, neutralisierend. **2.** *s.* das Besserungsmittel, Gegenmittel, Korrektiv, die Abhilfe. **correctness,** *s.* die Richtigkeit, Genauigkeit; *see also* **correctitude. corrector,** *s.* der Berichtiger, Verbesserer; Zurechtweiser, Tadler; (*Typ.*) Korrektor.

correlate ['kɔrəleit], **1.** *s.* das Korrelat, die Ergänzung. **2.** *v.i.* sich aufeinander beziehen, in Wechselbeziehung *or* Wechselwirkung stehen (***with,*** mit). **3.** *v.t.* in Wechselbeziehung *or* Wechselwirkung bringen (***with,*** mit), aufeinander beziehen. **correlation** [–'leiʃən], *s.* die Wechselbeziehung, Wechselwirkung; gegenseitige Abhängigkeit, wechselseitiges Verhältnis, (*Math.*) die Korrelation. **correlative** [kə'relətiv], *adj.* wechselseitig bedingt, sich gegenseitig ergänzend, voneinander abhängig, einander entsprechend.

correspond [kɔri'spɔnd], *v.i.* 1. übereinstimmen (***to, with,*** mit), entsprechen, gemäß sein (*Dat.*), passen (zu); 2. in Briefwechsel *or* (*Comm.*) in Geschäftsbeziehungen stehen (***with,*** mit). **correspondence,** *s.* 1. die Übereinstimmung; Angemessenheit, Entsprechung, Gemäßheit; 2. Korrespondenz, brieflicher Verkehr, der Briefwechsel, (*Comm.*) die (Geschäfts)verbindung; ***break off – with,*** die Verbindung abbrechen mit; ***keep up a –,*** einen Briefwechsel unterhalten. **correspondent, 1.** *adj.* übereinstimmend (***with,*** mit), entsprechend (*Dat.*). **2.** *s.* der (die) Briefpartner(in), Korrespondent(in); (*press*) Berichterstatter(in), (*Comm.*) der Geschäftsfreund. **corresponding,** *adj.* entsprechend, gemäß (***to,*** *Dat.*), (*Math.*) (einander) zugeordnet; ***– member,*** korrespondicrendes Mitglied.

corridor ['kɔridɔ:], *s.* der Korridor (*also Pol.*), Gang, Flur; ***–-train,*** der Durchgangszug, D-Zug.

corrie ['kɔri], *s.* (*Scots*) das (Gelände)becken, der (Tal)kessel.

corrigible ['kɔridʒibl], *adj.* verbesserlich, besserungsfähig; fügsam, lenksam.

corroborate [kə'rɔbəreit], *v.t.* bestätigen, bekräftigen, erhärten. **corroboration** [–'reiʃən], *s.* die Bestätigung, Bekräftigung, Erhärtung; ***in – of,*** zur Bestätigung von. **corroborative** [–rətiv], **corroboratory** [–rətəri], *adj.* bestätigend, bekräftigend, erhärtend.

corrode [kə'roud], **1.** *v.t.* anfressen, angreifen, zerfressen, (weg)ätzen, (weg)beizen; (*fig.*) angreifen, zerstören. **2.** *v.i.* zerfressen werden, rosten; fressen (***into,*** an (*Dat.*)), sich einfressen (in (*Acc.*)). **corrosion** [–'rouʒən], *s.* die Anfressung, Zerfressung; Verrostung, Rostbildung; (*fig.*) Zerstörung. **corrosive, 1.** *adj.* zerfressend, ätzend, Ätz–, Beiz–; (*fig.*) nagend, quälend; ***– sublimate,*** das Ätzsublimat. **2.** *s.* das Ätzmittel, Beizmittel, die Beize. **corrosiveness,** *s.* ätzende Schärfe, die Beizkraft.

corrugate ['kɔrəgeit], *v.t.* wellen, riefe(l)n, rippen; runzeln, (zer)furchen. **corrugated,** *adj.* gewellt, geriffelt, gerunzelt; ***– iron,*** das Wellblech; ***– paper,*** die Wellpappe. **corrugation** [–'geiʃən], *s.* das Furchen, Runzeln; die Runzel, Falte, Welle, Rippe.

corrupt [kə'rʌpt], **1.** *v.t.* verderben, korrumpieren, bestechen, (er)kaufen; verleiten, verführen; verfälschen, entstellen (*text*). **2.** *v.i.* verfaulen, verderben, verkommen. **3.** *adj.* faul, verfault, verdorben, schlecht; verfälscht, unecht (*text etc.*); (*of a p.*) verworfen, ruchlos, ehrlos, unehrlich, unredlich, korrupt, bestechlich, käuflich; (*Pol.*) ***– practices,*** der Stimmenkauf, die Wahlfälschung, Bestechung (*at elections*); ***the text is –,*** der Text ist verderbt.

corruptibility [kərʌpti'biliti], *s.* die Bestechlichkeit, Käuflichkeit; Verführbarkeit, Neigung zum Schlechten. **corruptible,** *adj.* bestechlich, käuflich, verführbar; (*B.*) vergänglich. **corruption** [kə'rʌpʃən], *s.* die Fäulnis, Verwesung, der Verfall; (*fig.*) die Verderbtheit, Verderbnis, Verdorbenheit, Entartung; (*of text*) Verfälschung, Entstellung; Bestechung(spolitik), Korruption; (*of a p.*) Bestechlichkeit, Korruptheit. **corruptive,** *adj.* zersetzend, verderblich, ansteckend. **corruptness,** *s. See* **corruption** (*fig.*).

corsage ['kɔ:sɑ:ʒ], *s.* das Mieder, Leibchen, die Taille.

corsair ['kɔ:sɛə], *s.* der Seeräuber, (*Hist.*) Korsar; das Seeräuberschiff.

corse [kɔ:s], *s.* (*Poet.*) *see* **corpse.**

corselet ['kɔ:slit], *s.* (*Hist.*) der Brustharnisch; (*Ent.*) Brustschild; das Mieder, Korselett.

corset ['kɔ:sit], *s.* das Korsett.

Corsica ['kɔ:sikə], *s.* Korsika (*n.*). **Corsican, 1.** *s.* der Korse (die Korsin). **2.** *adj.* korsisch.

corslet, *see* **corselet.**

cortège [kɔ:'teiʒ], *s.* das Gefolge, der Zug; ***funeral –,*** der Leichenzug.

cortex ['kɔ:teks], *s.* (*pl.* **-tices** [–tis:z]) die Rinde; ***cerebral –,*** die Großhirnrinde. **cortical** [–tikl], *adj.* Rinden–. **corticate** [–tikit], *adj.* rindig, rindenartig; berindet. **cortication** [–'keiʃən], *s.* die Rindenbildung.

corundum [kə'rʌndəm], *s.* (*Min.*) der Korund.

coruscate ['kɔrəskeit], *v.i.* (auf)blitzen, funkeln, (*also fig.*) glänzen. **coruscation** [–'keiʃən], *s.* das (Auf)blitzen, Funkeln, Schimmern; der Glanz, Blitz.

corvette [kɔ:'vet], *s.* (*Naut.*) die Korvette.

corvine ['kɔ:vain], *adj.* rabenartig, krähenartig.

corymb ['kɔrim(b)], *s.* (*Bot.*) der Ebenstrauß, die Doldentraube. **corymbiferous** [–'bifərəs], *adj.* Doldentrauben tragend.

coryphaeus [kɔri'feiəs], *s.* der Chorführer; (*fig.*) Vornehmste(r), Hauptvertreter, die Koryphäe.

coryza [kə'raizə], *s.* (*Med.*) der Schnupfen.

cosecant [kou'si:kənt], *s.* die Kosekante.

[1]**cosh** [kɔʃ], **1.** *s.* (*sl.*) der Knüppel, Totschläger. **2.** *v.t.* niederknüppeln, (*sl.*) prügeln, vermöbeln.

[2]**cosh,** *s.* (*Math.*) hyperbolischer Kosinus.

cosher ['kɔʃə], *v.t.* verhätscheln, verpäppeln.

co-signatory [kou'signətəri], *s.* der (die) Mitunterzeichner(in).

cosily ['kouzili], *adv. See* **cosy, 1.**

cosine ['kousain], *s.* der Kosinus.

cosiness ['kouzinis], *s.* die Behaglichkeit, Gemütlichkeit, Traulichkeit.

cosmetic [kɔz'metik], **1.** *adj.* kosmetisch, Schönheits–. **2.** *s.* das Schönheitsmittel. **cosmetics,** *pl.* (*sing. constr.*) die Schönheitspflege, Kosmetik.

cosmic(al) ['kɔzmik(l)], *adj.* kosmisch, Weltall–; (*fig.*) weltumfassend, unermeßlich, gewaltig.

cosmogony [kɔz'mɔgəni], *s.* die Weltentstehungslehre. **cosmographic** [–'græfik], *adj.* kosmographisch. **cosmography** [–'mɔgrəfi], *s.* die Weltbeschreibung. **cosmological** [–mə'lɔdʒikl], *adj.* kosmologisch. **cosmology** [–'mɔlədʒi], *s.* die Lehre vom Weltall, Kosmologie. **cosmonaut** ['kɔzmənɔ:t], *s.* der (Welt)raumfahrer. **cosmopolitan** [–mə'pɔlitən], **1.** *adj.* weltbürgerlich, kosmopolitisch. **2.** *s.* der (die) Kosmopolit(in), Weltbürger(in). **cosmopolitanism,** *s.* der Kosmopolitismus, das Weltbürgertum.

cosmos ['kɔzmɔs], *s.* das Weltall, der Kosmos; die Weltordnung, (*fig.*) Welt für sich.

Cossack ['kɔsæk], *s.* der Kosak.

cosset ['kɔsit], *v.t.* verhätscheln, verpäppeln.

cost [kɔst], **1.** *s.* 1. (*only sing.*) der Preis; Kosten (*pl.*), Auslagen (*pl.*); (*Comm.*) Unkosten (*pl.*), (Geschäfts)kosten (*pl.*); (*Law*) (*only pl.*) (Gerichts)kosten (*pl.*), Gebühren (*pl.*); ***– of living,*** Lebenshaltungskosten (*pl.*); ***– of living bonus,*** die Teuerungszulage; (*Comm.*) ***at –,*** zum Selbstkostenpreis; ***excess –,*** Mehrkosten (*pl.*); (*Comm.*) ***prime –,*** der Gestehungspreis, Selbstkostenpreis;

(*Law*) *with* **–***s*, nebst (Tragung der) (Gerichts)-kosten; *it will not repay the* –, es macht sich nicht bezahlt, es lohnt nicht die Kosten nicht; 2. (*fig.*) das Opfer, der Verlust, Schaden, Nachteil; *at all* –*s*, *at any* –, auf jeden Fall, unter allen Umständen, um jeden Preis; *at a heavy* –, unter schweren Opfern; *at the* – *of his life*, auf Kosten seines Lebens; *to my* –, zu meinem Schaden; (*fig.*) *without counting the* –, ohne Rücksicht auf die Folgen, ohne sich (*Dat.*) die Folgen zu überlegen. **2.** *v.t.*, *v.i.* kosten; – *dear*, teuer zu stehen kommen; *it* – *me £2*, es kostete mich *or* mir zwei Pfund; *it* – *him his life*, es kostete ihn *or* ihm das Leben; *it* – *him much time and trouble*, es verursachte ihm *or* kostete ihn viel Zeit und Mühe. **3.** *v.t.* (*Comm.*) den Preis berechnen *or* festsetzen.

costal [kɔstl], *adj.* Rippen–; (*Bot.*) (Blatt)rippen–.

co-star [ˈkoustɑː], **1.** *v.i.* als Hauptdarsteller mitspielen (*films etc.*). **2.** *s.* eine(r) der Hauptdarsteller.

costate [ˈkɔsteit], *adj.* (*Bot.*) gerippt.

coster(-monger) [ˈkɔstə], *s.* der (Straßen)händler, Höker.

costing [ˈkɔstiŋ], *s.* die Kostenberechnung.

costive [ˈkɔstiv], *adj.* (*Med.*) verstopft, hartleibig; (*fig.*) zugeknöpft, knauserig, geizig. **costiveness,** *s.* die Verstopfung; (*fig.*) Knauserigkeit, der Geiz.

costliness [ˈkɔstlinis], *s.* die Kostbarkeit, Kostspieligkeit. **costly,** *adj.* teuer, kostspielig, kostbar, wertvoll. **cost| plus,** *s.* (*Comm.*) Gestehungskosten einschließlich Gewinnspanne. **–-price,** *s.* der Selbstkostenpreis, Einkaufspreis.

costume [ˈkɔstjuːm], *s.* das Kostüm, die Tracht; *tailor-made* –, das (Schneider)kostüm, Kostümkleid; (*Theat.*) Bühnenkostüm; *fancy-dress* –, das Maskenkostüm; – *jewellery*, der Modeschmuck. **costumier** [–ˈtjuːmiə], *s.* der Kostümschneider, Theaterschneider; Kostümverleiher.

cosy [ˈkouzi], **1.** *adj.* behaglich, bequem, traulich, gemütlich. **2.** *s.* der Kaffeewärmer, Teewärmer, die Teehaube.

[1]**cot** [kɔt], *s.* das Kinderbett; (*Naut.*) die Hängematte, Koje.

[2]**cot,** *s.* das Häuschen, der Schuppen, Stall; (*Poet.*) die Hütte, Kate.

cotangent [kouˈtænʒənt], *s.* der Kotangens, die Kotangente.

cote [kout], *s.* der Stall, Verschlag; *dove*–, der Taubenschlag; *sheep*–, der Schafstall.

coterie [ˈkoutəri], *s.* die Koterie, exklusiver Kreis; geschlossene Gesellschaft, die Clique, der Klüngel.

cothurn(us) [kouˈθəːn(əs)], *s.* 1. der Kothurn, Stelzenschuh; 2. (*fig.*) tragischer *or* erhabener Stil.

cotillion [koˈtiljən], *s.* der Kotillon.

cottage [ˈkɔtidʒ], *s.* das Häuschen, Landarbeiterhaus, die Hütte, Kate, der Kotten; kleines Landhaus, die Sommerwohnung; – *cheese*, der Landkäse, Quark; – *industry*, die Heimarbeit; – *piano*, das Pianino. **cottager,** *s.* der Hüttenbewohner, kleiner Bauer, Häusler, Kätner, Kossäte.

cottar [ˈkɔtə], *s.* (*Scots*) *see* **cottager.**

[1]**cotter** [ˈkɔtə], *s.* *See* **cottager.**

[2]**cotter,** *s.* der Schließkeil, Splint, Bolzen, Pflock, Vorstecker, Sicherungsstift. **cotter-pin,** *s.* der Schließbolzen, Splint, Vorstecker, Vorsteckkeil.

cotton [kɔtn], **1.** *s.* die Baumwolle; das (Baumwoll)-garn, der (Baumwoll)zwirn; das Baumwollzeug, der Kattun, Baumwollstoff, *pl.* Baumwollwaren (*pl.*); *reel of* –, die Zwirnrolle; *sewing* –, das Nähgarn. **2.** *adj.* baumwollen, Baumwoll–. **3.** *v.i.* (*coll.*) – *on to him*, sich mit ihm anfreunden or befreunden; (*coll.*) – *on to a th.*, sich zu einer S. bequemen, sich mit einer S. zurechtfinden.

cotton|-belt, *s.* (*Am.*) die Baumwollgegend. **–-cake,** *s.* der Baumwollkuchen (*for cattle*). **–-gin,** *s.* die Egreniermaschine. **–-grass,** *s.* (*Bot.*) das Wollgras. **–-grower,** *s.* der Baumwollpflanzer. **–-mill,** *s.* die Baumwollspinnerei. **–-plant,** *s.* die Baumwollstaude. **–-print,** *s.* bedruckter Kattun. **–-reel,** *s.* die Zwirnrolle. **–-waste,** *s.* der Baumwollabfall. **–wood,** *s.* (*Bot.*) Dreieckblättrige Pappel. **–wool,** *s.* die (Roh)baumwolle; Watte. **cottony,** *adj.* baumwollartig, (*fig.*) weich.

cotyledon [kɔtiˈliːdən], *s.* (*Bot.*) das Keimblatt, der Samenlappen; (*Bot.*) das Nabelkraut. **cotyledonous** [–əs], *adj.* Keimblatt–.

couch [kautʃ], **1.** *s.* 1. das Ruhebett, Liegesofa, die Liege, Chaiselongue; (*Poet.*) das Bett, Lager, die Lagerstätte; 2. (*of paint etc.*) Grundierung, Unterlage, (Grund)schicht, der Grund; 3. (*Tech.*) die Gautschpresse. **2.** *v.t.* 1. senken, einlegen (*lance etc.*); 2. ausdrücken, formulieren, in Worte fassen *or* kleiden (*thoughts etc.*); 3. (*Med.*) stechen (*a cataract*); 4. gautschen (*paper*); 5. (*pass. only*) *be* –*ed*, liegen. **3.** *v.i.* sich niederlegen, sich lagern (*of animals*), (*fig.*) kauern, versteckt liegen, sich ducken. **couched,** *adj.* 1. (*Hunt.*) im Lager; 2. (*Her.*) mit erhobenem Kopf liegend.

couch-grass, *s.* (*Bot.*) Gemeine Quecke.

couching [ˈkautʃiŋ], *s.* 1. die Plattstickerei; 2. (*Med.*) das Starstechen; – *needle*, die Starnadel; 3. (*Tech.*) Gautschen.

cougar [ˈkuːgə], *s.* (*Zool.*) der Puma, Kuguar.

cough [kɔf], **1.** *s.* der Husten; (*coll.*) *churchyard* –, böser Husten; *give a* (*slight*) –, sich räuspern, hüsteln. **2.** *v.i.* husten. **3.** *v.t.* – *up*, aushusten (*phlegm*); (*sl.*) herausrücken mit, blechen (*money*). **cough-drop,** *s.* der Hustenbonbon. **coughing,** *s.* das Husten. **cough|-lozenge,** *s.* *See* **–-drop.** **–-mixture,** *s.* Hustentropfen (*pl.*).

could [kud, kəd], *imperf. of* [1]**can. couldn't** = *could not.*

coulisse [kuːˈliːs], *s.* die Kulisse.

couloir [ˈkuːlwɑː], *s.* die Bergschlucht.

coulomb [ˈkuːləm], *s.* (*Elec.*) das Coulomb, die Amperesekunde.

coulter [ˈkoultə], *s.* die Pflugschar, das Pflugeisen.

council [ˈkaunsil], *s.* die Ratssitzung, Ratsversammlung; beratende Versammlung, der Rat; (*Eccl.*) das Konzil; die Synode; *cabinet* –, der Kabinettsrat; *county* –, der Grafschaftsrat; *order in* –, der Kabinettsbefehl; *privy* –, geheimer Staatsrat; *Council of Europe*, der Europarat; – *of state*, der Staatsrat; *Council of States*, der Ständerat (*Switzerland*); (*Hist.*) *Council of Trent*, Tridentinisches Konzil; – *of war*, der Kriegsrat (*also fig.*).

council|-chamber, *s.* die Ratsstube. **–-house,** *s.* das Gemeindewohnhaus. **councillor,** (*Am.*) **councilor,** *s.* das Ratsmitglied, der Rat(sherr).

counsel [kaunsl], **1.** *s.* 1. die Beratung, Beratschlagung; der Rat(schlag); (*Theol.*) *God's* –, Gottes Rat, der Ratschluß Gottes; – *of perfection*, idealer Rat; eine Unmöglichkeit; *keep one's* (*own*) –, seine Absicht *or* Meinung für sich behalten; *take* –, sich beraten; *take* – *of one's pillow*, es beschlafen; *take* – *with*, sich (*Dat.*) Rat holen bei; 2. (*Law*) (*oft. without art.*) der (Rechts)anwalt, Rechtsbeistand, Rechtsvertreter, Rechtsberater; – *for the defence*, der Plädeur, (Straf)verteidiger, Anwalt der Verteidigung; – *for the prosecution*, der Staatsanwalt, Anklagevertreter; *King's* (*Queen's*) *Counsel*, der Kronanwalt. **2.** *v.t.* raten, (einen) Rat geben *or* erteilen (*Dat.*); beraten; empfehlen (*Dat.*); ermahnen. **counsellor** [–ə], *s.* 1. der Ratgeber; 2. (*Am.*) Anwalt, Rechtsbeistand.

[1]**count** [kaunt], *s.* der Graf.

[2]**count, 1.** *v.t.* 1. zählen; ausrechnen, berechnen; in Rechnung stellen, mitzählen, mitrechnen, mit einrechnen, anrechnen; – *one's chickens before they are hatched*, die Rechnung ohne den Wirt machen; (*fig.*) – *the cost*, sich (*Dat.*) die Folgen überlegen; *without* –*ing the others*, ohne die anderen mitzurechnen, abgesehen von den anderen, die anderen abgesehen; – *in*, mitzählen, mitrechnen, mit einberechnen; – *out*, auszählen (*also Boxing*); (*Parl.*) die Sitzung aufheben, vertagen; (*sl.*) außer acht *or* unberücksichtigt lassen, nicht berücksichtigen, ausnehmen; – *over*, durchzählen, nachzählen; – *up*, zusammenzählen; 2. be-

trachten als, halten für; – ***o.s. lucky,*** sich glücklich schätzen. **2.** *v.i.* rechnen, zählen, ins Gewicht fallen, von Wert sein; ***he does not –,*** auf ihn kommt es nicht an; ***that does not –,*** das zählt nicht, das fällt nicht ins Gewicht, das ist ohne Belang; ***every little –s,*** jede Kleinigkeit zählt; ***every minute –s,*** auf jede Minute kommt es an; – ***for nothing,*** nichts gelten, keinen Wert haben, von keinem Belang sein; – ***on,*** zählen *or* sich verlassen auf (*Acc.*), rechnen mit. **3.** *s.* 1. die (Be)rechnung, (Ab)zählung; (*Boxing*) das Auszählen; die (End)zahl, Endsumme, das Ergebnis; ***keep – (of),*** genau zählen; ***lose –,*** sich verzählen; (*Boxing*) ***take the –,*** ausgezählt werden; ***take no – of,*** nicht berücksichtigen, unberücksichtigt *or* außer acht lassen; 2. (*Law*) der (An)klagepunkt; (*fig.*) ***on all –s,*** in jedem Punkt, in jeder Hinsicht.

count-down, *s.* das Abzählen, die Startzählung.

countenance ['kauntinəns], **1.** *s.* das Gesicht, Antlitz; der (Gesichts)ausdruck, die Miene; Fassung, Gemütsruhe; (moralische) Unterstützung, die Gunst(bezeigung); ***change (one's) –,*** die Farbe wechseln; ***his – fell,*** er machte ein langes *or* bestürztes Gesicht; ***give*** or ***lend – to the rumour,*** dem Gerücht Glaubwürdigkeit verleihen; ***keep one's –,*** die Fassung *or* ernste Miene bewahren; ***keep him in –,*** ihn ermutigen *or* ermuntern *or* unterstützen; ***put a good – on the matter,*** gute Miene zum bösen Spiel machen; ***put him out of –,*** ihn verblüffen *or* verwirren *or* aus der Fassung bringen. **2.** *v.t.* begünstigen, unterstützen, Vorschub leisten (*Dat.*), ermutigen, ermuntern; zulassen, dulden, hingehen lassen, gutheißen.

[1]**counter** ['kauntə], *s.* 1. der Zähler; 2. (*Tech.*) Zähler, Zählapparat, das Zählwerk; 3. (*Cards*) die Spielmarke, der Zahlpfennig.

[2]**counter,** *s.* (*Naut.*) die Gillung, Gilling; (*of horse*) Brustgrube.

[3]**counter,** *s.* der Ladentisch; Zahltisch, (Kassen)schalter; die Theke; ***sell over*** or ***across the –,*** im Laden verkaufen.

[4]**counter, 1.** *adv.* in entgegengesetzter Richtung; (*fig.*) im Gegensatz *or* Widerspruch (*to*, zu); – ***to,*** entgegen, zuwider; ***run –,*** zuwiderlaufen (*to, Dat.*). **2.** *adj.* entgegengesetzt, Gegen–; gegenseitig. **3.** *v.i.* einen Gegenschlag führen, einen Gegenzug machen; (*Boxing etc.*) gegenschlagen, kontern, mit einem Gegenhieb parieren; entgegengesetzt handeln, opponieren. **4.** *v.t.* bekämpfen, entgegen; entgegenwirken (*Dat.*), entgegentreten (*Dat.*), widerstreben (*Dat.*), widersprechen (*Dat.*), zuwiderhandeln (*Dat.*), durchkreuzen; (*attack, blow*) mit einem Gegenschlag *or* Gegenzug beantworten. **5.** *s.* 1. das Gegenteil; 2. (*Boxing etc.*) der Gegenhieb, Gegenschlag, (*Fenc.*) die Parade.

counter|act, *v.t.* bekämpfen, Widerstand leisten (*Dat.*), entgegenarbeiten (*Dat.*), entgegenwirken (*Dat.*); aufwiegen, neutralisieren; hintertreiben, vereiteln, durchkreuzen. **–action,** *s.* die Gegenwirkung, der Widerstand; die Hintertreibung, Durchkreuzung. **––attack, 1.** *s.* der Gegenangriff. **2.** *v.t.* einen Gegenangriff richten gegen. **3.** *v.i.* einen Gegenangriff durchführen. **––attraction,** *s.* entgegengesetzte Anziehung(skraft); (*fig.*) die Gegenattraktion.

counter|-balance, 1. *s.* das Gegengewicht, Ausgleichsgewicht. **2.** *v.t.* ausgleichen, aufwiegen, das Gegengewicht bilden zu, die Waage halten (*Dat.*). **–blast, 1.** *s.* der Gegenstoß; (*fig.*) kräftige Gegenerklärung *or* Entgegnung. **–bore,** *v.t.* ausfräsen, ansenken (*a hole*), versenken (*a screw-head*).

counter|-charge, 1. *s.* (*Law*) die Gegenklage; (*Mil.*) der Gegenstoß. **2.** *v.i.* (*Mil.*) einen Gegenstoß richten gegen. **––check,** *s.* 1. die Gegenwirkung, (*fig.*) der Einhalt, das Hindernis; 2. nochmalige Überprüfung. **2.** *v.t.* 1. entgegenwirken, aufhalten, verhindern; 2. nochmals überprüfen. **––claim, 1.** *s.* der Gegenanspruch, die Gegenforderung. **2.** *v.i.* Gegenforderungen stellen; – ***for,*** als Gegenforderung verlangen. **––clockwise,** *adj., adv.* gegen den *or* entgegen dem Uhrzeigersinn, linksläufig; – ***rotation,*** die Linksdrehung, der Linkslauf. **–current,** *s.* (*Elec.*) der Gegenstrom.

counter|-espionage, *s.* die Spionageabwehr, der Abwehrdienst. **––evidence,** *s.* der Gegenbeweis.

counterfeit ['kauntəfit], **1.** *s.* die Nachahmung, Fälschung; das Falschgeld; unerlaubter *or* unrechtmäßiger Nachdruck. **2.** *adj.* nachgemacht, gefälscht, falsch, unecht; (*fig.*) geheuchelt, erheuchelt, verstellt, vorgetäuscht. **3.** *v.t.* nachmachen, nachahmen, fälschen; heucheln, vortäuschen, vorgeben, simulieren; – ***illness,*** sich krank stellen. **counterfeiter,** *s.* der (die) Nachahmer(in), Nachmacher(in); der Falschmünzer; der (die) Heuchler(in).

counter|foil, *s.* der Kontrollabschnitt, Abreißzettel, Kupon, Talon; Empfangsschein, die Empfangsquittung. **–fort,** *s.* (*Archit.*) der Strebepfeiler.

counter|-irritant, *s.* das Gegen(reiz)mittel. **––jumper,** *s.* (*coll.*) der Ladenschwengel.

countermand [kauntə'mɑ:nd], **1.** *s.* 1. der Gegenbefehl; 2. die Widerrufung, Annullierung, Abbestellung, der Storno. **2.** *v.t.* widerrufen, umstoßen; abbestellen, absagen, rückgängig machen, stornieren.

counter|march, 1. *s.* der Rückmarsch. **2.** *v.i.* zurückmarschieren. **––measure,** *s.* die Gegenmaßnahme. **––motion,** *s.* 1. die Gegenbewegung; 2. (*Parl.*) der Gegenantrag. **––movement,** *s.* die Gegenbewegung; (*Mil.*) der Gegenzug.

counter|-offensive, *s.* (*Mil.*) die Gegenoffensive. **––order,** *s.* der Gegenbefehl; (*Comm.*) Gegenauftrag.

counter|pane, *s.* die Steppdecke, Bettdecke. **–part,** *s.* das Gegenstück, Seitenstück (*to*, zu); Ergänzungsstück, Komplement, (genaue) Ergänzung; das Ebenbild, Duplikat, die Kopie. **––plea,** *s.* (*Law*) der Gegeneinspruch. **––plead,** *v.i.* Gegeneinspruch erheben. **––plot, 1.** *s.* der Gegenanschlag. **2.** *v.i.* einen Gegenanschlag ausführen. **–point,** *s.* (*Mus.*) der Kontrapunkt. **–poise,** *s.* das Gegengewicht (*to*, zu *or* gegen).

Counter-Reformation, *s.* (*Hist.*) die Gegenreformation. **counter|-revolution,** *s.* die Konterrevolution. **––revolutionary, 1.** *s.* der (die) Konterrevolutionär(in). **2.** *adj.* konterrevolutionär. **––rotation,** *s.* die Gegendrehung.

counter|-sabotage, *s.* die Sabotageabwehr. **–scarp,** *s.* (*Mil.*) die Gegenböschung, Kontereskarpe, äußere Grabenböschung. **––shaft,** *s.* (*Tech.*) die Vorgelegewelle. **–sign, 1.** *v.t.* gegenzeichnen, mitunterschreiben; (*fig.*) bestätigen. **2.** *s.* (*Mil.*) die Parole, Losung, das Losungswort. **––signature,** *s.* die Gegenzeichnung. **–sink, 1.** *irr.v.t.* ausfräsen, ansenken (*a hole*), versenken, einlassen (*a screw*). **2.** *s.* der Versenkbohrer, (Spitz)senker, Versenker, Krauskopf. **–stroke,** *s.* der Gegenstoß, Gegenhieb. **––tenor,** *s.* männliche Altstimme, hoher Tenor.

countervail [kauntə'veil], **1.** *v.t.* aufwiegen, ausgleichen. **2.** *v.i.* gleich stark sein (***against,*** wie), stark genug sein, ausreichen (gegen); ***–ing duty,*** der Ausgleichszoll.

counterweight ['kauntəweit], *s.* das Gegengewicht (*to*, gegen).

countess ['kauntis], *s.* die Gräfin (*wife of count*), Komtesse, Komteß (*daughter of count*).

counting ['kauntiŋ], **1.** *s.* das Rechnen, Zählen. **2.** *adj.* Rechen–. **counting-house,** *s.* das Kontor, Büro, die Buchhaltungsabteilung.

countless ['kauntlis], *adj.* zahllos, unzählig.

countrified ['kʌntrifaid], *adj.* ländlich; bäurisch.

country ['kʌntri], **1.** *s.* 1. das Land, der Staat; ***foreign –,*** das Ausland; ***fly the –,*** landesflüchtig werden; ***from all over the –,*** aus allen Teilen des Landes; (*Am.*) (*coll.*) ***God's own –,*** Vereinigte Staaten; ***leave the –,*** auswandern; 2. die Gegend, Landschaft, der Landstrich, das Gebiet; ***go into the –,*** aufs Land gehen; ***go down into the –,*** in die Provinz gehen; ***go up –,*** sich ins Innere des Landes begeben; ***in the –,*** auf dem Lande; 3. der Vaterland, Heimatland, die Heimat; ***die for one's –,*** für das Vaterland sterben; ***mother –, native –,*** das Vaterland, Heimatland, Geburtsland; 4. die

Bevölkerung, Einwohner (*pl.*), das Volk, die Nation; (*Pol.*) Wähler (*pl.*); (*Parl.*) ***appeal to the –,*** an das Volk appellieren. **2.** *adj.* Land-, ländlich; – ***air,*** die Landluft; (*of a p.*) baurisches Aussehen; – ***bumpkin,*** der Bauernlümmel; – ***club*** (*esp. Am.*), der Sport- und Freizeitsklub (auf dem Lande); – ***cousin,*** Verwandte(r) aus der Provinz, (*coll.*) die Unschuld vom Lande; – ***doctor,*** der Landarzt; – ***gentleman,*** der (Land)gutsbesitzer, Landedelmann; – ***house,*** der Landsitz, das Landhaus, die Villa; – ***life,*** das Landleben; – ***squire,*** der Landedelmann, Landjunker; – ***town,*** die Landstadt.

country|-bred, *adj.* auf dem Lande aufgewachsen. **--dance,** *s.* der Bauerntanz, Volkstanz. **-folk,** *s.* das Landvolk. **-man** [-mən], *s.* 1. der Landsmann, Mitbürger; 2. Landmann, Bauer. **--party,** *s.* (*Pol.*) der Landbund, die Bauernpartei. **-people,** *pl. See* **-folk.** **--seat,** *s.* der Landsitz. **-side,** *s.* das Land, die Landschaft, der Landstrich. **--wide,** *adj.* über das ganze Land verbreitet, im ganzen Land. **-woman,** *s.* 1. die Bäuerin, Bauersfrau; 2. Landsmännin, Mitbürgerin.

county [ˈkaunti], *s.* die Grafschaft, (*Am.*) der Kreis. **county| borough, --corporate,** *s.* die Stadt als Grafschaftsbezirk. – **council,** *s.* der Grafschaftsrat. – **councillor,** *s.* das Mitglied des Grafschaftsrates. – **court,** *s.* das Provinzialgericht für Zivilsachen. – **family,** *s.* die (Land)adelsfamilie. **--palatine,** *s.* die Pfalzgrafschaft. **--town,** *s.* die Kreisstadt, Hauptstadt einer Grafschaft.

coup [ku:], *s.* der Streich, Putsch; – ***d'état,*** der Staatsstreich; – ***de grâce,*** der Gnadenstoß; – ***de main,*** der Handstreich; – ***de théâtre,*** der Theatercoup.

coupé [ˈku:pei], *s.* 1. (*Motor.*) das Coupé, geschlossener Zweisitzer; 2. (*Railw.*) das Halbabteil.

couple [kʌpl], **1.** *s.* 1. das Paar; Ehepaar, Liebespaar, (*coll.*) Pärchen; Tanzpaar; ***a – of words,*** etliche *or* ein paar Worte; ***married –,*** das Ehepaar; 2. (*Hunt.*) die Koppel; 3. (*Tech.*) Verbindung, das Verbindungsglied; 4. (*Archit.*) Gebinde, Bundgespärre, der Dachbund. **2.** *v.t.* (*Elec., Mus., dogs*) koppeln; (*Tech.*) (ver)kuppeln, ankuppeln, einkuppeln, zusammenkuppeln; verbinden, vereinigen, ehelich verbinden, paaren. **3.** *v.i.* sich paaren. **coupled,** *adj.* gepaart, (*Tech.*) gekuppelt, gekoppelt, verkoppelt; – ***axle,*** die Kuppelachse; (*Railw.*) – ***engine,*** die Zwillingsmaschine. **coupler,** *s.* (*Mus.*) die Koppel, Kopplung; (*Elec.*) der Koppler; (*Tech.*) die Kupp(e)lung. **couplet** [-lit], *s.* das Reimpaar.

coupling [ˈkʌpliŋ], *s.* (*Tech.*) das Verbindungsstück, die Kupplung, (*Elec., Rad.*) Kopplung; Verbindung, Paarung (*of animals*); (*Rad.*) ***feed-back –, reaction –,*** die Rückkopplung. **coupling|-box,** *s.* die Muffe, Kupplungshülse. **--coil,** *s.* (*Rad.*) die Kopplungsspule. **--rod,** *s.* die Kuppelstange.

coupon [ˈku:pɔn], *s.* der Gutschein, Kupon, Kassenzettel, Bon; (Kontroll)abschnitt.

courage [ˈkʌridʒ], *s.* der Mut, die Tapferkeit; ***Dutch –,*** angetrunkener Mut; ***have the – of one's convictions,*** Zivilcourage haben; ***pluck up*** or ***take –,*** Mut fassen; ***screw up one's –, take one's – in both hands,*** seinen ganzen Mut zusammennehmen. **courageous** [kəˈreidʒəs], *adj.* mutig, tapfer, beherzt.

courier [ˈkuriə], *s.* der Eilbote, Kurier; Reiseführer.

course [kɔ:s], **1.** *s.* der Lauf, Gang; Verlauf (*of time*); – ***of a disease,*** der Verlauf einer Krankheit; ***the – of law,*** der Rechtsgang; ***by due – of law,*** dem Rechte gemäß; – ***of nature,*** natürlicher Lauf der Dinge; ***in due –,*** zu seiner *or* zur rechten Zeit; ***in the ordinary –,*** normalerweise; ***let it take its –,*** es seinen Weg gehen lassen; ***in – of construction,*** im Bau (begriffen); ***in (the) – of time,*** im Laufe der Zeit; ***in the – of a year,*** binnen Jahresfrist; ***a matter of –,*** eine Selbstverständlichkeit; ***of –,*** natürlich, selbstverständlich; 2. die Richtung, (*Naut.*) der Kurs; ***alter –,*** den Kurs ändern; ***direct –,*** gerader Kurs; ***magnetic –,*** mißweisender Kurs; ***true –,*** rechtweisender Kurs; 3. (*fig.*) der Weg, die Methode, Handlungsweise, das Verfahren; – ***of action,*** die Handlungsweise; ***adopt a –,*** einen Weg einschlagen; 4. der Lehrgang, Kurs(us), Zyklus (*of lectures etc.*); Reihe(nfolge); – ***of instruction,*** der Lehrgang, Lehrkursus; – ***of lectures,*** die Vortragsreihe; – ***of training,*** der Übungskurs; (*Med.*) – ***of treatment,*** die Kur; 5. die Laufbahn, Karriere, der Lebenslauf; 6. der Gang, das Gericht (*of food*); 7. (*Spt.*) die (Renn)strecke, Rennbahn, der Rennplatz; (Golf)platz; (*Motor.*) die Fahrbahn; ***clear the –!*** (macht die) Bahn frei! (*coll.*) ***stay the –,*** bis zum Ende aushalten; 8. die Schicht, Lage (*of bricks*); 9. (*Comm.*) der Kurs, die Notierung; – ***of exchange,*** der Wechselkurs, die Notierung; 10. (*Hunt.*) Hasenhetze; 11. *pl.* (*Med.*) der Monatsfluß, die Regel. **2.** *v.t.* mit Hunden jagen *or* hetzen *or* verfolgen (*usu. hares*). **3.** *v.i.* (*coll.*) rennen, eilen, jagen; (*of liquids*) rinnen, fließen.

courser [ˈkɔ:sə], *s.* (*Poet.*) das Rennpferd; der Jagdhund. **coursing,** *s.* die Hetzjagd, Hetze.

court [kɔ:t], **1.** *s.* 1. (*space*) der (Vor)hof, Platz; schmale *or* enge Gasse; (*Spt.*) der Spielplatz, das Feld; 2. (fürstlicher *or* königlicher) Hof, die Residenz; der Herrensitz, das Palais; (*Law*) der Gerichtshof, Gerichtssaal, das Gericht; ***at –,*** bei Hofe; (*fig.*) ***have a friend at –,*** einen einflußreichen Fürsprechen haben; ***have the – cleared,*** den Gerichtssaal räumen lassen; ***hold a –,*** eine Cour abhalten; (*Law*) ***appear in –,*** vor Gericht erscheinen; (*Law*) ***bring into –,*** vor (das) Gericht bringen, verklagen; ***in open –,*** in öffentlicher Sitzung *or* Verhandlung; (*fig.*) ***out of –,*** nicht zur S. gehörig, indiskutabel; ***put s.th. out of –,*** etwas von der Verhandlung ausschließen; ***the case was settled out of –,*** der Fall wurde außergerichtlich *or* auf gütlichem Wege beigelegt; ***go to –,*** den Gerichtsweg beschreiten, zu Gericht gehen; – ***of arbitration,*** die Schlichtungskammer; – ***of inquiry,*** der Untersuchungsausschuß; – ***of honour,*** das Ehrengericht, der Disziplinarausschuß; 3. (*people*) fürstlicher *or* königlicher Hof *or* Haushalt, fürstliche Familie, der Hofstaat, die Hofgesellschaft, Hofleute (*pl.*); (*Law*) das Gericht, die (Gerichts)sitzung; ***hold*** or ***keep –,*** Hofstaat halten; 4. (*fig.*) der Hof, die Cour; Aufwartung; ***pay (one's) – to her,*** ihr den Hof machen; ***pay (one's) – to him,*** ihm seine Aufwartung machen. **2.** *v.t.* den Hof machen (*Dat.*), huldigen (*Dat.*); (*a lady*) werben *or* freien um; (*fig.*) sich bemühen um; – ***disaster,*** mit dem Feuer spielen, ein Unheil heraufbeschwören; – ***his favour,*** sich um seine Gunst bemühen, um seine Gunst buhlen; – ***sleep,*** (den) Schlaf suchen. **3.** *v.i.* freien; (*usu.*) ***go -ing,*** auf Freiersfüßen gehen; ***-ing couple,*** das Liebespaar.

court| calendar, *s.* der Hofalmanach. – **card,** *s.* die Bilderkarte, Figurenkarte. – **chaplain,** *s.* der Hofprediger. – **circular,** *s.* Hofnachrichten (*pl.*). – **day,** *s.* (*Law*) der Gerichtstag, Termin. – **dress,** *s.* die Hoftracht.

courteous [ˈkə:tiəs], *adj.* höflich, verbindlich, liebenswürdig.

courtesan [ˈkɔ:tizæn], *s.* die Kurtisane.

courtesy [ˈkə:təsi], *s.* die Höflichkeit, Verbindlichkeit, Gefälligkeit (*to(wards)*, gegen); ***by – of,*** durch freundliches Entgegenkommen (*Gen.*), mit freundlicher Genehmigung von; ***be in – bound,*** anstandshalber verpflichtet sein; – ***title,*** der Ehrentitel, Höflichkeitstitel.

courtezan, *s. See* **courtesan.**

court| fool, *s.* der Hofnarr. **--house,** *s.* (*Law*) das Gerichtsgebäude.

courtier [ˈkɔ:tiə], *s.* der Höfling, Hofmann.

courtliness [ˈkɔ:tlinis], *s.* die Würde, Vornehmheit. **courtly,** *adj.* vornehm, elegant.

court|-martial, 1. *s.* (*pl.* **-s-martial**) das Kriegsgericht. **2.** *v.t.* vor ein Kriegsgericht stellen. – **plaster,** *s.* das Heftpflaster, Englischpflaster. **-room,** *s.* der Gerichtssaal.

courtship [ˈkɔ:rtʃip], *s.* das Werben, Freien, die Werbung; Gunstbewerbung, Huldigung.

courtyard [ˈkɔ:tjɑ:d], *s.* der Hof(raum), Innenhof.

cousin [kʌzn], *s.* (*male*) der Vetter, Cousin, (*female*) die Cousine, Kusine, Base; ***first –s, –s german,*** leibliche Vettern *or* Basen (*pl.*), (*of opp. sexes*) Geschwisterkinder (*pl.*); (***first***) ***– once removed,*** der Vetter *or* die Base eines Elternteils; das Kind eines Vetters *or* einer Base; ***second –s,*** Vettern *or* Basen zweiten Grades, (*of opp. sexes*) Kinder der Geschwisterkinder; (*fig.*) ***our American –s,*** unsere amerikanischen Vettern. **cousinly,** *adj.* vetterlich. **cousinship,** *s.* die Vetter(n)schaft, (*fig.*) Verwandtschaft.

couvade [ku'vɑ:d], *s.* das Männerkindbett.

[1]**cove** [kouv], **1.** *s.* (kleine) Bucht; (*Archit.*) die Wölbung; (*fig.*) der Schlupfwinkel. **2.** *v.t.* (*Archit.*) (über)wölben. **3.** *v.i.* (*Archit.*) sich wölben.

[2]**cove,** *s.* (*sl.*) der Kerl, Bursche.

coved [kouvd], *adj.* (*Archit.*) überwölbt, gewölbt; *see* [1]**cove.**

coven [kʌvn], *s.* die Hexenversammlung.

covenant ['kʌvənənt], *s.* der Vertrag; die Vertragsurkunde; Vertragsklausel; (*Eccl.*) der Bund, das Bündnis; (*Eccl.*) ***Ark of the Covenant,*** die Bundeslade; (*Eccl.*) ***land of the –,*** Gelobtes Land. **2.** *v.i.* übereinkommen (***with,*** mit; ***for,*** um), sich (schriftlich) verpflichten. **3.** *v.t.* (vertraglich) gewähren *or* festlegen *or* vereinbaren. **covenanter,** *s.* der Kontrahent, Vertragschließende(r); (*Hist.*) das Mitglied des Bundes der schottischen Protestanten.

cover ['kʌvə], **1.** *v.t.* 1. bedecken, zudecken; überziehen, umhüllen, umwickeln, umspinnen (***with,*** mit), einhüllen, einwickeln, einschlagen (***in, with,*** in (*Acc.*)); ***– in,*** decken, bedachen; ***– over,*** überdecken, überziehen; ***– up,*** verdecken, zudecken; (*fig.*) verbergen, verhehlen, verheimlichen, verhüllen; ***– one's head,*** seinen Kopf *or* sich bedecken; ***– o.s. with glory,*** sich mit Ruhm bedecken; 2. (*area*) sich ausdehnen *or* erstrecken über (*Acc.*), umfassen, einnehmen; (*distance*) zurücklegen; 3. (*fig.*) verdecken, verbergen, verhehlen; ***– one's tracks,*** die Spuren verdecken *or* (*fig.*) verhüllen; 4. (*Mil.*) decken, sichern, schützen, abschirmen (***from,*** vor (*Dat.*)); 5. (*Comm.*) decken, bestreiten, ausgleichen; (*Insur.*) versichern; (*coll.*) ausreichen *or* genügen für; ***be –ed,*** (*Comm.*) Deckung in Händen haben, (*Insur.*) versichert sein, (*fig.*) gedeckt *or* geschützt sein; (*Comm.*) ***receipts do not – the outlay,*** die Einnahme deckt die Kosten nicht; 6. (*as a book etc.*) umfassen, einschließen, enthalten, behandeln, beinhalten; 7. (*as a salesman*) bereisen, bearbeiten; 8. (*with firearms*) zielen auf (*Acc.*); (*Mil.*) als Vordermann nehmen; 9. (*of male animals*) decken, bespringen (*the female*), (*of stallions*) beschälen (*the mare*).
2. *s.* 1. die Decke, der Deckel, (*of book*) Einband; (Schutz)umschlag, Bezug, Überzug, (*of tyre*) Mantel, das Futteral, die Hülle, Kappe, Haube; ***from – to –,*** vom Anfang bis zum Ende (*of a book*); ***under the same –,*** beiliegend (*of post*); ***under separate –,*** als gesondertes Paket (*of post*); 2. (*Comm.*) die Deckung, Sicherheit, Bürgschaft; 3. (*Mil.*) Deckung (***from,*** vor (*Dat.*)), der Schutz (gegen); das Obdach, (*Hunt.*) Lager; Dickicht, schützendes Gebüsch; (*fig.*) der Vorwand, Deckmantel; (*Mil.*) ***air –,*** die Luftsicherung; (*Hunt.*) ***break –,*** aus dem Lager hervorbrechen; ***take –,*** Deckung suchen, in Deckung gehen; ***under –,*** unter Obdach, (*Mil.*) unter Deckung; ***get under –,*** sich unterstellen; ***under*** (***the***) ***– of darkness,*** unter dem *or* im Schutz der Finsternis; 4. (*at table*) das Gedeck, Kuvert; 5. (*philately*) die Ganzsache.

cover address, *s.* die Deckadresse.

coverage ['kʌvəridʒ], *s.* der Geltungsbereich, (*of newspaper*) die Verbreitung, (*radio etc.*) Reichweite, (*reporting*) Berichterstattung (***of,*** über (*Acc.*)).

cover charge, *s.* das Gedeck (*in restaurants*).

covered ['kʌvəd], *adj.* bedeckt, (zu)gedeckt; (*buttons*) überzogen, (*wire*) umsponnen, (*violin strings*) übersponnen; ***– wagon,*** der Planwagen; ***– way,*** überdachter Gang; *see also under* **cover, 1.**

covering ['kʌvəriŋ], **1.** *adj.* deckend, Deck–, Schutz–, (*Mil.*) Deckungs–, Sicherungs–. **2.** *s.* die Decke, Bedeckung, Umhüllung; der Mantel, das Futteral, die Hülle; Bekleidung, Bespannung, Verkleidung, Beplankung, Beschalung; der Bezug, Überzug; die Dachdeckung.

covering| force, *s.* (*Mil.*) Deckungstruppen (*pl.*). **– letter,** *s.* das Begleitschreiben. **– note,** *s.* *See* **cover note. – party,** *s.* (*Mil.*) der Deckungstrupp.

coverlet ['kʌvəlit], *s.* der Überwurf, die Bettdecke.

cover| note, *s.* (*Insur.*) der Vorvertrag. **– plate,** *s.* die (Ab)deckplatte.

covert ['kʌvət], **1.** *adj.* (*obs.*) gedeckt, verborgen, geschützt; (*Law*) ***feme –,*** verheiratete Frau. **2.** *s.* (*Hunt.*) das Lager, Dickicht; Versteck, der Schlupfwinkel, **covertly,** *adv.* verborgen, (ins)geheim. **coverture** [–tʃə], *s.* 1. das Versteck, Obdach, die Deckung, der Schutz; 2. (*Law*) Stand der Ehefrau.

covet ['kʌvət], *v.t.* verlangen *or* trachten nach, begehren, sich gelüsten lassen nach. **covetous,** *adj.* verlangend, (be)gierig, lüstern (***of,*** nach); habsüchtig. **covetousness,** *s.* das Verlangen, die Begierde, Gier; Habsucht, der Geiz.

covey ['kʌvi], *s.* die Brut, Hecke; (*of partridge*) das Volk; (*fig.*) der Schwarm, die Schar.

coving ['kouviŋ], **1.** *adj.* (*Archit.*) überhängend, vorgekragt. **2.** *s.* (*Archit.*) überhängendes Obergeschoß; *see* [1]**cove.**

[1]**cow** [kau], *s.* die Kuh; (*of whale, elephant etc.*) das Weibchen; (*vulg.*) der *or* die *or* das Trampel.

[2]**cow,** *v.t.* einschüchtern.

coward ['kauəd], *s.* der Feigling, die Memme. **cowardice** [–dis], **cowardliness,** *s.* die Feigheit. **cowardly,** *adj., adv.* feig(e).

cow|bane, *s.* (*Bot.*) der Wasserschierling. **–boy,** *s.* der Rinderhirt, Cowboy. **--catcher,** *s.* (*Railw.*) der Schienenräumer. **--dung,** *s.* der Kuhmist.

cower ['kauə], *v.i.* (zusammen)kauern, (nieder)hocken; sich verkriechen *or* ducken.

cow|-hand, *s.* *See* **–boy. --heel,** *s.* die Kalbsfußsülze. **--herd,** *s.* der Kuhhirt. **–hide,** *s.* die Kuhhaut, das Rindleder; – (***whip***), der Ochsenziemer. **--house,** *s.* der Kuhstall.

cowl [kaul], *s.* die Kapuze, Mönchskutte; (*Build.*) Schornsteinkappe; (*Tech.*) Verschalung, der Mantel. **cowling,** *s.* (*esp. Av.*) die Verschalung, Verkleidung, Haube.

cow|-man, *s.* der Kuhknecht; (*Am.*) Rinderzüchter. **--parsley,** *s.* (*Bot.*) Gemeiner Kerbel. **--parsnip,** *s.* (*Bot.*) der Bärenklau, das Herkuleskraut. **--pen,** *s.* die Kuhhürde. **–pox,** *s.* Kuhpocken (*pl.*). **–puncher,** *s.* (*sl.*) *see* **–boy.**

cowrie, cowry ['kauri], *s.* die Kaurischnecke; Kaurischale; das Muschelgeld.

cow|-shed, *s.* der Kuhstall. **–slip,** *s.* (*Bot.*) die Schlüsselblume, Primel; (*Am.*) Kuhblume, Sumpfdotterblume; ***American –,*** die Götterblume.

cox [kɔks], **1.** *s.* (*coll.*) *abbr.* *See* **coxswain. 2.** *v.t.* (*coll.*) steuern; ***–ed four,*** der Vierer mit (Steuermann).

coxcomb ['kɔkskoum], *s.* der Geck, Stutzer, Laffe. **coxcombry** [–ri], *s.* die Geckenhaftigkeit, Affektiertheit.

coxless ['kɔkslis], *adj.* (*coll.*) ohne Steuermann; ***– pair,*** der Zweier ohne (Steuermann).

coxswain [kɔksn], *s.* der Steuermann, Boot(s)führer.

coy [kɔi], *adj.* spröde, blöde, scheu, schüchtern, zurückhaltend, zimperlich. **coyness,** *s.* die Sprödigkeit, Zurückhaltung, Scheu, Zimperlichkeit.

coyote [kɔ'jouti], *s.* der Präriewolf, Steppenwolf.

coyp(o)u ['kɔipu:], *s.* die Biberratte; (*fur*) Nutria, der Nutriapelz.

coz [kʌz], *s.* (*obs. usu. fig.*) *abbr. of* **cousin.**

cozen [kʌzn], *v.t.* (*obs.*) betrügen, prellen (***out of,*** um); (ver)locken (***into doing,*** zu tun), ködern.

coziness, *s.*, **cozy,** *adj.* *See* **cosiness, cosy.**

[1]**crab** [kræb], *s.* 1. die Krabbe; der Krebs (*also Astr.*), Taschenkrebs; (*coll.*) ***catch a –,*** einen

Krebs fangen; einen Luftschlag machen; 2. (*Tech.*) die Winde, das Gangspill, Hebezeug, die Laufkatze.

²**crab,** *s. See* **crab-apple.**

³**crab, 1.** *s.* (*coll.*) der Sauertopf, Miesmacher, Griesgram, Nörgler, Querulant, Querkopf. **2.** *v.t.* (*coll.*) meckern *or* (herum)nörgeln an (*Dat.*), bekritteln, heruntermachen.

crab-apple, *s.* der Holzapfel(baum).

crabbed [kræbd], *adj.* (*of a p.*) mürrisch, grämlich, griesgrämig, kratzbürstig; (*as handwriting*) kritz(e)lig, unleserlich, verzwickt. **crabby,** *adj.* (*coll.*) *see* **crabbed** (*usu. of a p.*).

crab-louse, *s.* (*Ent.*) die Filzlaus.

crack [kræk], **1.** *v.t.* (zer)spalten, (zer)sprengen, zerbrechen; (auf)knacken (*nuts*), knallen lassen (*a whip*); zerstören, vernichten (*reputation etc.*); (*Chem.*) kracken (*oils*); (*coll.*) – ***a bottle together,*** eine Flasche zusammen trinken; (*sl.*) – ***a crib,*** in ein Haus *etc.* einbrechen; – ***an egg,*** ein Ei aufschlagen; – ***one's fingers,*** mit den Fingern knacken; – ***a joke,*** einen Witz reißen; – ***a safe,*** einen Geldschrank knacken; (*sl.*) – ***up,*** in den Himmel heben, herausstreichen. **2.** *v.i.* (*physical*) rissig werden, Sprünge *or* Risse bekommen, (zer)springen, aufspringen; (zer)brechen, (zer)bersten, (zer)platzen, aufreißen, sich spalten; (*audible*) knacken, krachen, knallen; (*of the voice*) brechen, umschlagen; (*coll.*) (*also* – ***up***) zusammenbrechen, in die Brüche gehen, kaputt gehen; (*coll.*) – ***down on,*** unter die Fuchtel nehmen; (*coll.*) – ***on,*** alles hergeben. **3.** *s.* 1. (*physical*) der Riß, Ritz, Sprung, Bruch, Schrund, Schlitz, Spalt, die Spalte, Schrunde; (*audible*) der Krach, Knacks, Knall, Klaps, Schlag; ***the – of doom,*** der Jüngste Tag, das Jüngste Gericht; – ***of the whip,*** der Peitschenknall, (*sl.*) die Chance; 2. (*sl.*) der Versuch; 3. (*sl.*) Witz. **4.** *adj.* (*coll.*) großartig, Elite–; – ***regiment,*** feudales Regiment; – ***shot,*** der Meisterschütze; – ***team,*** erstklassige Mannschaft. **5.** *int.* klatsch! patsch!

crack-brained, *adj.* (*coll.*) *see* **cracked** (*coll.*). **cracked,** *adj.* rissig, gesprungen; zerbrochen, zersprungen; (*Tech.*) gekrackt, Krack–, Spalt– (*oil*); ***be –,*** zersprungen sein, einen Sprung haben; (*coll.*) (*of a p.*) verdreht *or* übergeschnappt sein, einen Vogel haben; – ***voice,*** rauhe *or* gebrochene Stimme. **cracker,** *s.* 1. (*fireworks*) der Schwärmer, Frosch; 2. (*Cul.*) Keks, Biskuit; 3. (*also* ***Christmas*** –) der *or* das Knallbonbon; 4. ***nut –s,*** der Nußknacker. **crackerjack,** *adj.* (*coll.*) famos, Pracht–, Pfunds–.

cracking [ˈkrækiŋ], **1.** *adj.* (*coll.*) ***at a – pace,*** mit Volldampf voraus. **2.** *s.* die Sprungbildung; (*Tech.*) Kracking, das Kracken. **cracking|-plant,** *s.* die Krack(ings)anlage, (Spalt)destillieranlage, Fraktionierungsanlage. **–-process,** *s.* das Kracken, Krackverfahren, die Spaltdestillation.

crackle [krækl], **1.** *v.i.* knistern, knattern, prasseln. **2.** *v.t.* 1. knistern *or* krachen lassen; 2. (*glass etc.*) krakelieren; –***(d) glass,*** das Krakeeleglas. **crackling,** *s.* **1.** das Knistern, Prasseln, Geknister, Geknatter; 2. knusprige Kruste (*of roast pork*). **crackly,** *adj.* (*coll.*) knusprig.

cracknel [ˈkræknəl], *s.* die Brezel.

crack-pot, *s.* **1.** *adj.* (*sl.*) verrückt, bekloppt. **2.** *s.* (*sl.*) Verrückte(r), der Spinner. **cracksman,** *s.* (*coll.*) der Einbrecher, Geldschrankknacker. **crack-up,** *s.* (*sl.*) der Zusammenbruch, (*Motor.*) Zusammenstoß, (*Av.*) Bruch, die Bruchlandung. **crack-willow,** *s.* (*Bot.*) die Knackweide.

cradle [kreidl], **1.** *s.* die Wiege, (*fig.*) Kindheit, der Anfang, das Anfangsstadium; (*Tech.*) Gerüst, Gestell, der Schlitten, die Stütze, (*Med.*) Beinschiene, das Schutzgestell, (*Shipb.*) der Stapelschlitten, (*gold mining*) Schwingtrog, (*Tele.*) die Gabel, (*Engr.*) das Gründungseisen, Wiegemesser, (*of a scythe*) Reff, der Korb, (*Railw.*) Schienenstuhl; ***from the –,*** von (der) Kindheit an, von Jugend auf; ***rock the –,*** wiegen. **2.** *v.t.* in die Wiege legen, (ein)wiegen, (*fig.*) bergen, umfangen, (*Tech.*) stützen. **cradled,** *adj.* (*fig.*) geborgen, eingeschlossen (***in,*** in (*Dat.*)), (*Tech.*) gestützt. **cradle|-snatching,** *s.* (*coll.*) der Kinderraub. **–-song,** *s.* das Wiegenlied.

craft [krɑːft], *s.* 1. das Handwerk, Gewerbe; (*Prov.*) ***every man to his –,*** Schuster, bleib bei deinem Leisten! 2. die Zunft, Innung, Gilde; – ***guild,*** die Handwerkerinnung; 3. die Fertigkeit, Geschicklichkeit, Kunst; 4. List, Schlauheit, Geriebenheit, Verschlagenheit, Verschmitztheit; 5. das Schiff; (*pl. constr.*) Fahrzeuge (*pl.*), Flugzeuge (*pl.*), (*usu.*) Schiffe (*pl.*). **craftiness,** *s. See* **craft,** 4. **craftsman,** *s.* (gelernter) Handwerker, (*fig.*) der Künstler. **craftsmanship,** *s.* die Kunstfertigkeit, handwerkliches Geschick; (*fig.*) das Künstlertum. **crafty,** *adj.* schlau, listig, gerieben, verschlagen, verschmitzt.

crag [kræg], *s.* die Felsspitze, Klippe. **cragginess,** *s.* die Felsigkeit, Schroffheit. **craggy,** *adj.* felsig, schroff. **cragsman,** *s.* erfahrener Kletterer.

crake [kreik], *s. See* **corncrake.**

cram [kræm], *v.t.* vollstopfen, überfüllen, anfüllen; mästen, nudeln (*poultry*); überfüttern, überladen (*with food*); hineinstopfen, hineinzwängen (***into,*** in (*Acc.*)); (*sl.*) einpauken; (*fig., coll.*) – ***s.th. down his throat,*** ihm etwas mit aller Gewalt aufdrängen, ihm etwas recht deutlich machen. **2.** *v.i.* (*sl.*) ochsen, büffeln, pauken (*for an examination*).

crambo [ˈkræmbou], *s.* das Reimspiel.

cram-full, *adj.* vollgepfropft. **crammer,** *s.* (*coll.*) der Einpauker. **cramming,** *s.* das Einpauken; (*coll.*) – ***establishment,*** die Presse.

¹**cramp** [kræmp], *s.* (*Med.*) der (Muskel)krampf; ***be seized with –,*** einen Krampf bekommen; ***writer's –,*** der Schreibkrampf.

²**cramp, 1.** *s.* (*Tech.*) die Krampe, Klammer, Schraubzwinge. **2.** *v.t.* (*Tech.*) ankrampen, anklammern; (*fig.*) einengen, einzwängen, einschränken; hemmen; ***be –ed for space,*** zusammengepfercht sein, zu wenig Platz haben; (*fig., coll.*) – ***his style,*** ihm die Flügel stutzen, ihm die Bäume nicht in den Himmel wachsen lassen. **cramped,** *adj.* steif, verkrampft; beengt, eng; – ***hand,*** steife Hand(schrift). **cramp|-fish,** *s.* der Zitterrochen. **–-iron,** *s.* eiserne Klammer, das Kropfeisen; (*Archit.*) der Anker; (*Naut.*) Enterhaken. **crampons,** *pl.* das Steigeisen.

cranage [ˈkreinidʒ], *s.* die Krangebühr, das Krangeld.

cranberry [ˈkrænbəri], *s.* die Moosbeere, Kronsbeere, Preiselbeere.

crane [krein], **1.** *s.* 1. (*Orn.*) der Kranich (*Grus grus*); 2. (*Tech.*) Kran; (*Railw.*) ***feeding –,*** der Speisewasserkran; ***hoisting –,*** der Hebekran; ***travelling –,*** der Laufkran. **2.** *v.t.* – ***one's neck,*** sich (*Dat.*) den Hals ausrecken (***for,*** nach). **3.** *v.i.* sich (*Dat.*) den Hals ausrecken; (*fig.*) zaudern, zögern (***at,*** bei, vor (*Dat.*)). **crane-jib,** *s.* der Kranausleger. **cranesbill,** *s.* (*Bot.*) der Storchschnabel.

cranial [ˈkreiniəl], *adj.* Hirn–, Schädel–. **craniology** [–ˈɔlədʒi], *s.* die Schädellehre. **cranium,** *s.* (*Anat.*) die Hirnschale; (*coll.*) der Schädel.

crank [kræŋk], **1.** *s.* 1. die Kurbel, der Schwengel, Hebel; die Kröpfung (*of a shaft*); 2. (*coll.*) wunderlicher Kauz, komische Kruke; (*coll.*) ***he is a –,*** er hat einen Sparren; 3. verschrobener Einfall, die Verdrehung, Schnurre. **2.** *adj.* leicht kenterbar, rank (*of a ship*); unsicher, baufällig (*of buildings*). **3.** *v.t.* (– ***up***) ankurbeln, andrehen, (*Motor.*) anwerfen. **crank|-case,** *s.* das Kurbelgehäuse. **–-handle,** *s.* die Andrehkurbel, der Kurbelgriff. **crankiness,** *s.* die Verschrobenheit, Grillenhaftigkeit, Wunderlichkeit. **crankshaft,** *s.* die Kurbelwelle, gekröpfte Welle. **cranky,** *adj.* (*of a p.*) exzentrisch, verdreht, grillenhaft, launisch, verschroben; voreingenommen; (*of a th.*) wackelig, baufällig, unsicher; *see also* **crank, 2.**

cranny [ˈkræni], *s.* der Riß, die Ritze, Spalte; das Versteck, der (Schlupf)winkel.

crap [kræp], *s.* 1. (*Am.*)(eine Art) Würfelspiel; 2. (*sl.*) der Schund.

crape [kreip], *s.* der Krepp, (Trauer)flor.

craps, *pl.* (*sing. constr.*)(*Am.*) *see* **crap, 1.**

crapulence ['kræpjuləns], *s.* der Kater; die Sauferei, Völlerei. **crapulent,** *adj.* unmäßig; verkatert.

[1]**crash** [kræʃ], **1.** *s.* der Krach, das Krachen; (*Av.*) der Absturz, die Bruchlandung, (*Motor.*) der Zusammenstoß; (*Comm.*) Zusammenbruch, Krach. **2.** *v.i.* einstürzen, zusammenstürzen, zusammenkrachen; krachen, stürzen, (*Av.*) abstürzen, Bruch machen; (*Motor.*) zusammenstoßen. **3.** *v.t.* 1. zerbrechen, zerschmettern; zum Absturz bringen (*a plane*); 2. (*sl.*) uneingeladen eindringen (*a party*). **4.** *adj.* (*coll.*) – ***programme,*** (eilig vorgenommenes) Aushilfsprogramm.

[2]**crash,** *s.* (*fabric*) der Leinendrell, grober Drillich.

crash| barrier, *s.* die Leitplanke (*on motorway*). **--dive, 1.** *v.i.* schnelltauchen, (*sl.*) eine Ente machen (*submarines*). **2.** *s.* das Schnelltauchen. **--helmet,** *s.* der Sturzhelm, die Sturzhaube. **--land,** *v.i.* (*Av.*) bruchlanden, (eine) Bruch(landung) machen. **--landing,** *s.* die Bruchlandung.

crasis ['kreisis], *s.* (*Gram.*) die Zusammenziehung, Krasis.

crass [kræs], *adj.* grob, kraß. **crassness,** *s.* krasse Dummheit.

crate [kreit], *s.* großer Korb; die Lattenkiste; der Verschlag; (*sl.*) die Kiste. **crate-car,** *s.* (*Railw.*) der Verschlagwagen.

crater ['kreitə], *s.* (*Geol.*) der Krater, (*fig.*) Trichter; (*Astr.*) Becher. **crateriform** [–rifɔ:m], *adj.* kraterförmig. **crater-lake,** *s.* (*Geol.*) das Maar.

cravat [krə'væt], *s.* die Krawatte, Halsbinde, das Halstuch.

crave [kreiv], **1.** *v.t.* flehen *or* bitten um, erflehen, (dringend) erbitten; (dringend) benötigen. **2.** *v.i.* sich sehnen (***for***, ***after***, nach), inständig bitten (***for***, um).

craven [kreivn], **1.** *adj.* feig(herzig), zaghaft. **2.** *s.* die Memme, der Feigling.

craving ['kreiviŋ], *s.* heftiges Verlangen, die Sehnsucht, Begierde (***for***, nach).

craw [krɔ:], *s.* der Kropf (*of fowls*).

crawfish ['krɔ:fiʃ], *s.* (*esp. Am.*) *see* **crayfish.**

crawl [krɔ:l], **1.** *v.i.* kriechen, krabbeln; (*fig.*) sich hinschleppen, schleichen; wimmeln (***with***, von), kribbeln; kraulen (*swimming*). **2.** *s.* das Kriechen, Schleichen; Kraul(schwimmen); ***go at a –,*** sehr langsam gehen *or* fahren. **crawler,** *s.* kriechendes Ungeziefer, der Kriecher; (*fig.*, *coll.*) Kriecher, Speichellecker; (*coll.*) langsam fahrendes Fahrzeug. **crawlers,** *pl.* der Strampelanzug. **crawling, 1.** *adj.* kriechend; schleichend; (*fig.*) kriecherisch, servil; ***be – with vermin,*** von Ungeziefer wimmeln. **2.** *s.* das Kriechen, Krabbeln *etc.*

crayfish ['kreifiʃ], *s.* der Flußkrebs, Bachkrebs; ***sea-–,*** die Languste.

crayon ['kreiən], *s.* der Farbstift, Buntstift, Zeichenstift, Pastellstift; ***red –,*** der Rotstift; – ***drawing,*** die Kreidezeichnung, Pastellzeichnung, das Pastell.

craze [kreiz], **1.** *s.* die Verrücktheit; fixe Idee, die Manie; (*coll.*) Schrulle, der Fimmel; die Modetorheit; ***the latest –,*** der letzte (Mode)schrei; ***be all the –,*** überall Mode sein. **2.** *v.t.* 1. zum Wahnsinn treiben, verrückt *or* toll machen; 2. (*Tech.*) krakelieren (*porcelain etc.*). **crazed,** *adj.* verrückt (***about***, nach), versessen (auf (*Acc.*)); – ***with fear,*** wahnsinnig vor Angst. **craziness,** *s.* die Verrücktheit. **crazy,** *adj.* 1. wahnsinnig, toll, verrückt (***with***, vor (*Dat.*)); (*fig.*) unsinnig begeistert (***about***, für), erpicht, versessen (auf (*Acc.*)), besessen (von); ***go –,*** aus dem Häuschen geraten; 2. gebrechlich, wack(e)lig, baufällig; – ***pavement,*** das Mosaikpflaster.

creak [kri:k], **1.** *v.i.* knarren, knirschen, quietschen. **2.** *v.t.* knarren mit, knirschen lassen. **3.** *s.* das Knarren, Knirschen, Geknarre, Geknirsche. **creaky,** *adj.* knarrend, knirschend, quietschend.

cream [kri:m], **1.** *s.* 1. die Sahne, der Rahm; ***clotted –,*** verdickter Rahm; ***whipped –,*** die Schlagsahne; 2. die Creme, Krem, Salbe; ***cold –,*** die Kühlsalbe; 3. (*fig.*) das Beste, die Auslese, Blüte, der Kern; – ***of society,*** die Elite der Gesellschaft; 4. (*Chem.*) – ***of tartar,*** gereinigter Weinstein. **2.** *v.t.* 1. abrahmen (*milk*); 2. (*Cul.*) zu Schaum schlagen. **3.** *v.i.* 1. Rahm ansetzen; 2. schäumen.

cream|-cake, *s.* die Kremtorte. **--cheese,** *s.* der Rahmkäse, Weichkäse, Quarkkäse. **--coloured,** *adj.* gelblichweiß, cremefarben, kremfarben. **creamery,** *s.* die Butterei; das Milchgeschäft, die Molkerei. **cream-laid,** *adj.* Velin– (*of paper*). **creamy,** *adj.* voller Sahne, sahnig; (*fig.*) sämig, ölig.

crease [kri:s], **1.** *s.* 1. die Falte; Bügelfalte, der Bruch, Kniff (*in trousers etc.*); Einschlag, Umschlag, Knick, Falz, das Eselsohr (*in a book*); 2. (*Crick.*) der Torstrich. **2.** *v.t.* falten, knicken, kniffen, umbiegen. **3.** *v.i.* Falten werfen, knittern. **crease|proof, – resistant,** *adj.* knitterfest, knitterfrei.

create [kri'eit], **1.** *v.t.* (er)schaffen, erzeugen, ins Leben rufen, hervorbringen; hervorrufen, machen (*an impression etc.*); (*Theat.*) darstellen, kreieren (*a role*); (*a p.*) ernennen *or* erheben *or* machen zu. **2.** *v.i.* (*sl.*) Aufhebens machen (***about***, von). **creation** [–eiʃən], *s.* die Schöpfung (*also artistic product*); das Geschöpf, Erzeugnis; die Modeschöpfung (*clothes*); Erschaffung, Hervorbringung, Erzeugung; (*Theat.*) Gestaltung (*of a role*); Schaffung, Ernennung (*of peers etc.*).

creative [kri'eitiv], *adj.* (er)schaffend, Schöpfungs–; schöpferisch (*as genius*); ***be – of,*** hervorbringen, hervorrufen, erzeugen, erregen. **creativeness, creativity** [–'tiviti], *s.* schöpferische Kraft, die Schaffenskraft, Schöpferkraft, Produktivität. **creator** [–tə], *s.* der Schöpfer, Erzeuger, Erschaffer, (*fig.*) Urheber.

creature ['kri:tʃə], *s.* das Geschöpf, Wesen; die Kreatur; (*fig.*) das Werkzeug, der Sklave, Handlanger; ***dumb –,*** stumme Kreatur; ***fellow –,*** der Mitmensch; ***living –,*** lebendes Wesen, das Lebewesen; (*coll.*) ***silly –,*** dummes Ding; – ***comforts,*** das Wohlleben, materielle Annehmlichkeiten des Daseins (*pl.*).

crèche [kreiʃ], *s.* die Kleinkinderbewahranstalt, der Kinderhort.

credence ['kri:dəns], *s.* 1. der Glaube(n); ***give – to a story,*** einer Geschichte Glauben schenken; 2. (*also* – ***table***) (*Eccl.*) der Kredenztisch.

credentials [kri'denʃəlz], *pl.* das Beglaubigungsschreiben, Empfehlungsschreiben, der Ausweis; (*diplomat*) das Kreditiv.

credibility [kredi'biliti], *s.* die Glaubwürdigkeit. **credible** ['kredibl], *adj.* glaublich, glaubwürdig; ***be credibly informed,*** von zuverlässiger Seite erfahren.

credit ['kredit], **1.** *s.* 1. der Glaube(n); die Glaubwürdigkeit, Zuverlässigkeit; (guter) Ruf, das Ansehen, die Ehre, Achtung, Anerkennung, das Verdienst; ***be a – to,*** see ***reflect – on***; ***it does him –,*** es gereicht ihm zur Ehre; ***he does me –,*** mit ihm lege ich Ehre ein; ***deserve –,*** Anerkennung verdienen; ***give – to a story,*** einer Geschichte Glauben schenken; ***give him*** (***the***) – ***for s.th.,*** ihm etwas hoch *or* als Verdienst anrechnen, ihm etwas zutrauen; ***reflect – on him,*** ihm Ehre machen *or* einbringen; ***take*** (***the***) – ***for a th.,*** sich (*Dat.*) etwas zum Verdienst anrechnen; ***worthy of –,*** glaubwürdig; ***it is to his –,*** see ***it does him –***; ***with –,*** ehrenvoll; 2. (*Comm.*) der Kredit, die Kreditfähigkeit, Kreditwürdigkeit; das Kredit, (Gut)haben, der Kreditposten, die Kreditseite; – ***balance,*** das Guthaben; ***letter of –,*** der Kreditbrief, das Akkreditiv; – ***note,*** der Gutschein, die Gutschriftsanzeige; – ***slip,*** der Einzahlungsbeleg; – ***standing,*** die Bonität; Kreditwürdigkeit; ***at*** or ***on a year's –,*** auf ein Jahr Zeit; ***give –,*** Kredit geben (***for***, in Höhe von); ***open a –,*** einen Kredit eröffnen; ***on –,*** auf Zeit *or* Kredit; ***transactions on –,*** Zeitgeschäfte; ***to his –,*** zu seinen Gunsten; ***place*** or ***put*** or ***enter it to my –,*** schreiben Sie es mir gut; 3. (*Am. Univ.*) der Anrechnungspunkt. **2.** *v.t.* 1.

Glauben schenken (*Dat.*), glauben (*Dat.*), (ver)-trauen (*Dat.*); – ***him with s.th.,*** ihm etwas zutrauen *or* beilegen *or* beimessen *or* zuschreiben; 2. (*Comm.*) kreditieren, gutschreiben (*to, Dat.*); erkennen (***him with a sum,*** ihn für eine Summe).

creditable ['kreditəbl], *adj.* ehrenwert, lobenswert, löblich, achtbar, rühmlich; ***it is very – to him,*** es macht ihm alle Ehre. **creditor,** *s.* der Gläubiger; ***–'s side,*** die Kreditseite, der Kreditposten, das Kredit, Haben.

credulity [krə'dju:liti], *s.* die Leichtgläubigkeit. **credulous** ['kredjuləs], *adj.* leichtgläubig. **credulousness,** *s. See* **credulity.**

creed [kri:d], *s.* das Glaubensbekenntnis, Kredo; der Glaube(n), die Konfession; ***Apostles' –,*** Apostolisches Glaubensbekenntnis.

creek [kri:k], *s.* (kleine) Bucht; (*esp. Am.*) der Nebenfluß, kleiner Fluß.

creel [kri:l], *s.* 1. der Weidenkorb, Fischkorb; die Reuse; 2. (*Weav.*) das Spulrahmengestell, Lieferwerk, (Aufsteck)gatter.

creep [kri:p], **1.** *irr.v.i.* kriechen; schleichen, sich ranken (*of plants*); kribbeln, schaudern (*as flesh*); – ***into his favour,*** sich bei ihm einschmeicheln; ***I felt my flesh –,*** es überlief mich eiskalt, mich überlief eine Gänsehaut; ***it makes my flesh –,*** es macht mich schaudern; – ***forward,*** heranschleichen; – ***in,*** hineinkriechen; ***an error has crept in,*** ein Fehler hat sich eingeschlichen; – ***up,*** langsam steigen (*of prices*); – ***up*** (*to*), heranschleichen. **2.** *s.* 1. (*Geol.*) der Rutsch; (*Tech.*) die Kriechdehnung, das Wandern, Verschieben; 2. (*sl.*) (*of a p.*) der Kriecher, Schmarotzer, Speichellecker, die Kreatur, das Geschmeiß; 3. (*coll.*) ***the –s,*** die Gänsehaut, das Gruseln, Kribbeln, der Schauder; ***it gives me the –s,*** es macht mich schaudern.

creepage ['kri:pidʒ], *s.* (*Elec.*) das Kriechen. **creeper,** *s.* der Kriecher; das Kriechtier; (*Bot.*) Rankengewächs, die Schlingpflanze; (*Orn.*) der Baumläufer (*Certhiidae*); ***Virginia –,*** wilder Wein. **creepiness,** *s.* (*coll.*) die Gruseligkeit. **creeping,** *adj.* kriechend, schleichend; (*fig.*) – ***sensation,*** gruseliges Gefühl, die Gänsehaut; (*Artil.*) – ***barrage,*** die Feuerwalze, das Rollsperrfeuer; (*Elec.*) – ***current,*** der Kriechstrom. **creepy,** *adj.* (*coll.*) *adj.* kriechend; unheimlich, schauerlich, gruselig, schaurig. **creepy-crawly,** *s.* (*coll.*) der Wurm, das Gewürm; der Floh, die Wanze, Laus.

cremate [kri'meit], *v.t.* einäschern; verbrennen. **cremation** [–'meiʃən], *s.* die Einäscherung, Feuerbestattung; Leichenverbrennung. **crematorium** [kremə'tɔ:riəm], (*Am.*) **crematory** ['kremətəri], *s.* die Einäscherungshalle, Feuerbestattungsanstalt, das Krematorium.

cremona [kri'mounə], *s.* (*Mus.*) das Krummhorn (*organ stop*).

crenate(d) ['kri:neit(id)], *adj.* (*Bot.*) zackig, gekerbt. **crenation** [–'neiʃən], **crenature** [–nətʃə], *s.* (*Bot.*) die (Ein)kerbung, Auszackung.

crenel [krenl], *s.* die Schießscharte. **crenellate** [–nileit], *v.t.* mit Zinnen versehen, zinnenförmig ornamentieren. **crenelation** [–'leiʃən], *s.* die Zinne; Zinnenbildung, Zackenbildung. **crenelle** [krə'nel], *s. See* **crenel.**

Creole ['kri:oul], **1.** *s.* der Kreole (die Kreolin). **2.** *adj.* kreolisch, Kreolen–.

creosote ['kriəsout], **1.** *s.* das Kreosot. **2.** *v.t.* mit Kreosot durchtränken *or* beschmieren.

crêpe [kreip], *s.* der Krepp; – ***de Chine,*** der Chinakrepp; – ***paper,*** das Kreppapier; – ***rubber,*** das or der Krausgummi, Kreppgummi.

crepitate ['krepiteit], *v.i.* knistern, knirschen, knacken, knarren, rasseln, prasseln. **crepitation** [–'teiʃən], *s.* das Knistern *etc.*; (*Med.*) die Krepitation.

crept [krept], *imperf., p.p. of* **creep.**

crepuscular [kri'pʌskjulə], *adj.* dämmend, dämmerig, Dämmer(ungs)–; (*Zool.*) im Zwielicht erscheinend.

crescendo [kri'ʃendou], **1.** *adv.* (*Mus.*) an Stärke zunehmend. **2.** *s.* das Crescendo, zunehmende Stärke.

crescent [kresnt], **1.** *s.* 1. zunehmender *or* abnehmender Mond, der Halbmond; 2. (*Mus.*) Schellenbaum; 3. halbmondförmige Straße; 3. (*Cul.*) das Hörnchen. **2.** *adj.* (*also* ***–-shaped***) halbmondförmig.

cress [kres], *s.* (*Bot.*) die Kresse.

cresset ['kresit], *s.* die Pechpfanne, Kohlenpfanne; Stocklaterne; (*fig.*) Fackel.

crest [krest], **1.** *s.* der Kamm (*of a cock*); Schopf, die Haube (*on birds etc.*); Mähne (*of horse etc.*), der Federbusch, Helmbusch (*of a helmet*); (*Her.*) Helmschmuck; (*fig., Poet.*) Helm; (Höhen)-rücken, Grat, Kamm, Gipfel; Firstkamm, die Bekrönung; (*fig.*) ***on the – of the wave,*** auf dem Gipfel des Glücks. **2.** *v.t.* den Gipfel erreichen *or* ersteigen von. **crested,** *adj.* Schopf–, Hauben–; mit Kamm *or* Schopf *or* Helmschmuck; (*Orn.*) – ***lark,*** die Haubenlerche. **crestfallen,** *adj.* niedergeschlagen, beschämt.

cretaceous [kri'teiʃəs], *adj.* kreidig, kreideartig, Kreide–; kreidehaltig; – ***period,*** die Kreide(zeit).

Cretan ['kri:tən], **1.** *s.* der (die) Kreter(in). **2.** *adj.* kretisch. **Crete** [kri:t], *s.* Kreta (*n.*).

cretin ['kretin], *s.* der Kretin. **cretinism,** *s.* der Kretinismus. **cretinous,** *adj.* kretinhaft.

cretonne [kre'tɔn], *s.* die Kretonne, der Zitz.

crevasse [kri'væs], *s.* die Gletscherspalte; (*Geol.*) der Durchbruch.

crevice ['krevis], *s.* der Riß, Spalt, die Spalte.

[1]**crew** [kru:], *imperf. of* [2]**crow.**

[2]**crew,** *s.* die Schar; der Haufen, die Rotte, Bande; Bemannung, Bedienung (*of a gun*), Mannschaft, Besatzung (*of a ship*), das (Dienst)personal (*of a train etc.*). **crew cut,** *s.* (*coll.*) der Bürstenschnitt.

crewel ['kru:əl], *s.* feine Wolle. **crewel-work,** *s.* die Plattstichstickerei.

crew| list, *s.* die Mannschaftsrolle. – **space,** *s.* (*Av.*) die Kabine, (*Naut.*) das Logis.

crib [krib], **1.** *s.* 1. die (Futter)krippe, Raufe; der Stall, Pferch, Stand; die Hütte, Kate; das Kinderbett; 2. (*coll.*) kleiner Diebstahl, kleines Plagiat, die Eselsbrücke, Klatsche; 3. (*Am. sl.*) Spelunke, der Puff; (*sl.*) ***crack a –,*** in ein Haus einbrechen. **2.** *v.t.* 1. einpferchen; 2. (*coll.*) mausen, stibitzen; (*at school*) abschreiben.

cribbage ['kribidʒ], *s.* (*Cards*) das Cribbage.

crib-biter, *s.* (*Vet.*) der Krippensetzer.

cribriform ['kribrifɔ:m], *adj.* (*Anat.*) siebförmig.

crick [krik], **1.** *s.* der Krampf; – ***in the back,*** der Hexenschuß; – ***in the neck,*** steifer Hals. **2.** *v.t.* – ***one's neck,*** sich (*Dat.*) den Hals verrenken.

[1]**cricket** ['krikit], *s.* (*Ent.*) die Grille, das Heimchen; ***merry as a –,*** vergnügt wie ein Lämmerschwänzchen, kreuzfidel.

[2]**cricket,** *s.* (*Spt.*) das Kricket; (*coll., fig.*) die Fairneß; (*coll.*) ***not –,*** nicht ehrlich *or* fair; (*coll.*) ***play –,*** ehrlich spielen. **cricket-bat,** *s.* das Schlagholz. **cricketer,** *s.* der Kricketspieler. **cricket|-field,** *s.* der Kricketspielplatz. **–-match,** *s.* die Kricketpartie. **–-pitch,** *s.* der Rasen zum Kricketspielen.

cricoid ['kraikɔid], *adj.* ringförmig; – ***cartilage,*** der Ringknorpel.

cried [kraid], *imperf., p.p. of* **cry. crier** ['kraiə], *s.* der Schreier, Ausrufer; ***town –,*** öffentlicher Ausrufer.

crime [kraim], **1.** *s.* das Verbrechen, (*Law*) strafbare Handlung; (*fig.*) der Frevel, die Übeltat; ***capital –,*** das Kapitalverbrechen; ***commit a –,*** ein Verbrechen begehen. **2.** *v.t.* (*coll.*) anklagen, beschuldigen.

Crimea [krai'miə], *s.* die Krim. **Crimean,** *adj.* Krim–; – ***War,*** der Krimkrieg.

criminal ['kriminl], **1.** *adj.* 1. verbrecherisch, strafbar, kriminell; – ***conversation,*** der Ehebruch; 2. (*Law*) Kriminal–, Straf–; – ***code,*** das Strafgesetzbuch; – ***law,*** das Strafrecht. **2.** *s.* der (die) Verbrecher(in). **criminality** [–'næliti], *s.* die Strafbarkeit; Schuld; Kriminalität. **criminate** [–neit], *v.t.* beschuldigen, anklagen. **crimination** [–'neiʃən], *s.* die Beschuldigung, Anklage. **criminology** [–'nɔlədʒi], *s.* die Kriminalistik.

¹**crimp** [krimp], **1.** *v.t.* fälteln, kräuseln, krausen, kreppen, knittern; (*Tech.*) bördeln, rändeln, randkehlen; (*Cul.*) – ***fish,*** Fische schlitzen. **2.** *s.* die Falte, Krause; Welligkeit, Kräuselung; (*Tech.*) der Falz.

²**crimp, 1.** *v.t.* gewaltsam anwerben, pressen (*sailors etc.*). **2.** *s.* der Werber, Matrosenmakler. **crimper** ['krimpə], *s.* (*Tech.*) die Kräusel- *or* Bördel- *or* Rändelmaschine.

crimping-house, *s.* die Preßspelunke.

crimpy ['krimpi], *adj.* (*coll.*) gekräuselt, wellig.

crimson [krimzn], **1.** *s.* das Karm(es)in, Hochrot. **2.** *adj.* karm(es)in, hochrot. **3.** *v.i.* erröten, rot werden.

cringe [krindʒ], **1.** *v.i.* sich ducken, sich krümmen, zusammenfahren, zusammenzucken; (*fig.*) kriechen (***to,*** vor (*Dat.*)). **2.** *s.* kriechende Höflichkeit. **cringing, 1.** *adj.* kriechend, kriecherisch. **2.** *s.* die Speichelleckerei, das Kriechen.

cringle [kriŋgl], *s.* (*Naut.*) der Legel.

crinkle [kriŋkl], **1.** *s.* die Falte, Runzel; Windung, Krümmung. **2.** *v.t.* faltig machen; kräuseln. **3.** *v.i.* Falten werfen, sich kräuseln, sich falten; sich krümmen *or* schlängeln *or* winden. **crinkly,** *adj.* wellig, faltig, gekräuselt.

crinoline ['krinəlin], *s.* 1. der Reifrock, die Krinoline; der Roßhaarstoff; 2. (*Naut.*) das Torpedoabwehrnetz.

cripple [kripl], **1.** *s.* der Krüppel. **2.** *adj.* lahm, gelähmt, verkrüppelt. **3.** *v.t.* verkrüppeln, zum Krüppel machen; (*fig.*) entkräften, lähmen; (*Mil., Av. etc.*) kampfunfähig machen. **crippled,** *adj.* verkrüppelt, lahm, krüppelhaft; (*fig.*) lahmgelegt.

crisis ['kraisis], *s.* (*pl.* **crises** [–si:z]) die Krise; der Entscheidungspunkt, Wendepunkt.

crisp [krisp], **1.** *adj.* kraus, gekräuselt (*of hair*); bröckelig, knusperig, mürbe (*of cakes*); frisch, scharf (*of air*); klar, entschieden, kurz (*of manner*). **2.** *v.t.* kräuseln; mürbe *or* knusperig machen; braun rösten (*meat etc.*). **3.** *v.i.* sich kräuseln, knusperig werden. **crispate** [–eit], *adj.* gekräuselt, kraus. **crispation** [–'peiʃən], *s.* das Kräuseln, die Kräuselung; Gänsehaut. **crispness,** *s.* die Krausheit; Knusperigkeit; Schärfe, Lebendigkeit, Frische. **crisps,** *pl.* geröstete Kartoffelscheiben. **crispy,** *adj.* (*coll.*) *see* **crisp.**

criss-cross ['kriskrɔs], **1.** *s.* das Kreuz, Netz (*of lines*), Gewirr. **2.** *adj.* gekreuzt, Kreuz–, sich überschneidend. **3.** *adv.* in die Quere, kreuz und quer. **4.** *v.t.* durchkreuzen.

criterion [krai'tiəriən], *s.* (*pl.* **-ria**) das Unterscheidungszeichen, Kennzeichen, Merkmal, Kriterium, der Prüfstein, die Norm; ***that is no – for,*** das ist nicht maßgebend für.

critic ['kritik], *s.* der Kunstrichter; Rezensent, Kritiker; Tadler, Kritikaster, Krittler. **critical,** *adj.* 1. kunstverständig; 2. kritisch (***of him,*** ihm gegenüber); tadelsüchtig, krittelig; ***be – of a th.,*** an einer S. etwas auszusetzen haben; 3. kritisch, ausschlaggebend, entscheidend; – ***moment,*** entscheidender Augenblick; 4. kritisch, ernst, bedenklich, gefährlich, bedrohlich, brenzlig; – ***position,*** brenzlige Lage; – ***times,*** bedenkliche Zeiten. **criticism** [–sizm], *s.* 1. die Kritik; Kunstbeurteilung; Rezension, Besprechung; ***make a –,*** Kritik üben; 2. der Tadel; ***above –,*** über jeden Tadel erhaben; ***open to –,*** anfechtbar. **criticize** [–saiz], **1.** *v.t.* 1. (abfällig) kritisieren, tadeln, bemäkeln; 2. kritisch beurteilen; besprechen, rezensieren. **2.** *v.i.* (abfällig) kritisieren, kritisch urteilen, mäkeln, kritteln.

critique [kri'ti:k], *s.* die Besprechung, Kritik, Rezension.

croak [krouk], *v.i.* 1. krächzen (*as a raven*); quaken, quäken (*of frogs*); heiser *or* krächzend sprechen, 2. (*fig.*) Unglück prophezeien, unken, jammern; 3. (*sl.*) abkratzen. **croaker,** *s.* (*sl.*) der Unglücksprophet, Miesmacher. **croaking,** *s.* das Gequake, Gekrächze. **croaky,** *adj.* krächzend (*as voice*).

Croat ['krouæt], *s.* 1. der Kroate (die Kroatin); 2. das Kroatisch (*language*). **Croatian** [–'eiʃən], *adj.* kroatisch.

crochet ['krouʃi], **1.** *s.* die Häkelarbeit, Häkelei. **2.** *v.t., v.i.* häkeln. **crocheted** ['krouʃid], *adj.* gehäkelt. **crochet-hook,** *s.* die Häkelnadel. **crocheting** [–ʃiiŋ], *s.* das Häkeln. **crochet-work,** *s.* die Häkelarbeit.

crock [krɔk], **1.** *s.* der Topf; (*sl.*) (*of a p.*) das Wrack, der Krüppel; (*of a horse*) alter Gaul, der Klepper, die Kracke; (*of a vehicle*) der Karren, Klapperkasten. **2.** *v.i.* (*also –* ***up***) (*coll.*) versagen, zusammenbrechen. **3.** *v.t.* (*coll.*) – ***o.s.,*** sich verletzen. **crocked,** *adj.* (*coll.*) verletzt, ausgemergelt. **crockery,** *s.* das Steingut, irdenes Geschirr, die Tonware, Töpferware.

crocket ['krɔkit], *s.* (*Archit.*) die Kriechblume, Krabbe.

crocodile ['krɔkədail], *s.* das Krokodil; (*coll.*) die Schlange (*of schoolchildren*); – ***tears,*** Krokodilstränen.

crocus ['kroukəs], *s.* (*Bot.*) der Krokus, Safran.

Croesus ['kri:səs], *s.* Krösus (*m.*).

croft [krɔft], *s.* kleines Feldstück *or* Pachtgut. **crofter,** *s.* (*Scots*) der Kleinbauer, Kätner.

cromlech ['krɔmlek], *s.* vorgeschichtlicher Steinbau.

cromorne [krə'mɔ:n], *s.* *See* **cremona.**

crone [kroun], *s.* altes Weib.

crony ['krouni], *s.* alte(r) Bekannte(r), der (die) vertraute Freund(in), Busenfreund(in).

crook [kruk], **1.** *s.* 1. der Haken; Krummstab, Bischofsstab, Hirtenstab; (*Tech.*) das Kniestück; (*coll.*) ***by hook or by –,*** auf Biegen oder Brechen; 2. (*coll.*) der Schwindler, Schieber, Hochstapler. **2.** *v.t.* krümmen, krumm biegen; beugen (*knee or elbow*). **crooked,** *adj.* 1. ['krukid], krumm, gekrümmt, gebogen, (*with age*) gebeugt, (*with disease etc.*) bucklig, verwachsen; (*coll.*) unehrlich, unehrenhaft, falsch, betrügerisch, verbrecherisch; – ***ways,*** krumme Wege; 2. [krukt], Krück–, Krumm–; – ***stick,*** der Krückstock, Stock mit einer Krücke. **crookedness** ['krukidnis], *s.* die Gekrümmtheit, Krummheit, Krümmung; Verkrümmung; (*coll.*) Falschheit, Unehrlichkeit, Verderbtheit.

croon [kru:n], *v.i.* leise und schmachtend singen, vor sich hin summen. **crooner,** *s.* der Schnulzensänger.

crop [krɔp], **1.** *s.* 1. der Vormagen, Kropf (*of a fowl*); 2. Peitschenstock, die Reitgerte; 3. der Stutzkopf; ***she has an Eton –,*** sie trägt Herrenschnitt; 4. (*oft. pl.*) die Ernte, (Feld)frucht, der (Ernte)ertrag, das Getreide auf dem Halm, eingebrachtes Getreide; (*fig. sing. only*) der Haufen, die Menge, Ausbeute (***of,*** an (*Dat.*)); ***in*** or ***under –,*** bebaut, in Bebauung; (*coll.*) ***a – of mistakes,*** ein Haufen *or* eine Menge Fehler. **2.** *v.t.* 1. kurz schneiden (*hair*), beschneiden, stutzen (*a tail*); 2. (*of animals*) abfressen, abweiden; (*of a p.*) (ab)mähen, abschneiden (*grass etc.*), pflücken, ernten (*fruit etc.*); 3. bepflanzen, bebauen, besäen (*land*). **3.** *v.i.* 1. (*of animals*) grasen, weiden; 2. (*of land*) (Ernte) tragen; – ***well*** or ***heavily,*** gut tragen, reichen Ertrag bringen; 3. (*Geol.*) – ***out,*** anstehen, ausbeißen, zutage ausgehen; (*coll.*) – ***up,*** zum Vorschein kommen, zutage treten, auftauchen.

crop-eared, *adj.* mit gestutzten Ohren. **cropped** [krɔpt], *adj.* (ab)geschnitten, gestutzt, (*of a p.*) kahlgeschoren, (*of a book*) beschnitten. **cropper,** *s.* der Abschneider; Abmäher, Schnitter; Bebauer, Pächter; (*Orn.*) Kröpfer, die Kropftaube; (*coll.*) schwerer Sturz, (*fig.*) der Fehlschlag; ***good –,*** guter Träger (*plant etc.*); (*coll.*) ***come a –,*** der Länge nach hinfallen, (*fig.*) reinfallen.

croquet ['krouki], *s.* das Krocket(spiel).

croquette [kro'ket], *s.* (*Cul.*) das Bratklößchen.

crosier ['krouziə], *s.* der Bischofsstab, Krummstab.

cross [krɔs], **1.** *s.* 1. das Kreuz; Kruzifix, (*fig.*) Lei-

den, die Trübsal, Not, Widerwärtigkeit; das Kreuz(zeichen) (*as signature*), der Querstrich (*on letter 't'*); ***fiery –***, das Feuerkreuz; ***make the sign of the –***, sich bekreuzigen; ***mark with a –***, ankreuzen; (*coll.*) ***on the –***, schräg; (*fig.*) ***take up one's –***, sein Kreuz auf sich nehmen; ***Red Cross Society***, die Rotkreuzgesellschaft; (*Astr.*) ***Southern Cross***, das Kreuz des Südens; 2. (*Biol.*) die Kreuzung, Kreuzungsprodukt, Hybride, (*fig.*) das Zwischending, Mittelding.
2. *adj.* 1. quer, Quer–, kreuzweise liegend; (*Naut.*) – ***bearing***, die Kreuzpeilung; – ***current***, die Gegenströmung; (*Comm.*) – ***entry***, die Umbuchung, Gegenbuchung; (*Spt.*) – ***kick***, die Flanke; – ***multiplication***, kreuzweise Multiplikation; – ***wind***, der Seitenwind; 2. (*coll.*) verstimmt, verärgert, ärgerlich, verdrießlich, mürrisch, ungehalten, übelgelaunt; ***exchange*** or ***have – words with***, ärgerlich anfahren, zornige Worte wechseln mit.
3. *adv.* quer, schief.
4. *v.t.* 1. (*Eccl.*) das Kreuzzeichen machen über (*Dat.*) *or* auf (*Acc.*), bekreuz(ig)en; – ***o.s.***, sich bekreuzigen; 2. mit einem Kreuz bezeichnen, ankreuzen; – ***a cheque***, einen Scheck kreuzen; (*coll.*) – ***his hand*** (or ***palm***) ***with money***, ihn bestechen *or* schmieren; – ***off*** or ***out***, ausstreichen, durchstreichen; ***you must – your 't's'***, du mußt den Querstrich im 't' ziehen; 3. kreuzen, kreuzweise legen; 4. überschreiten, durchqueren, überqueren, (hinüber)gehen über (*Acc.*); – ***the Channel***, den Kanal überqueren; ***your route*** (***letter etc.***) ***must have –ed mine***, dein Weg (Brief *etc.*) muß sich mit meinem gekreuzt haben; (*Pol.*) – ***the floor*** (***of the House***), zur anderen Seite übergehen; (*obs.*) – ***a horse***, ein Pferd besteigen; ***it –ed my mind***, es kam mir in den Sinn; (*fig.*) – ***his path***, ihm in die Quere kommen; – ***the threshold***, die Schwelle überschreiten; 5. (*Biol.*) kreuzen; 6. (*fig.*) durchkreuzen, vereiteln (*plans etc.*), in die Quere kommen, entgegentreten, Widerstand leisten (*a p., Dat.*); ***be –ed***, Widerstand finden, auf Schwierigkeiten stoßen; ***be –ed in love***, Unglück in der Liebe haben.
5. *v.i.* sich kreuzen, sich (über)schneiden, sich treffen; aneinander vorbeigehen *or* vorbeifahren; – ***over***, hinübergehen *or* hinüberfahren (***to***, zu), übersetzen (nach), (*as a bridge*) hinüberreichen (bis); (*coll.*) über die Straße gehen.

cross|-action, *s.* (*Law*) die Gegenklage, Widerklage. **–bar,** *s.* der Querbalken, Querträger, Querriegel, Querstock, Spannbalken, das Querholz, Querstück, die Querstange, Querstrebe, (*Footb.*) Torlatte, (*high jump*) Latte, (*bicycle*) oberes Rahmenrohr. **–beam,** *s.* der Querbalken, das Querholz, (*Naut.*) der Dwarsbalken. **––bench,** **1.** *s.* (*Pol.*) die Querbank. **2.** *adj.* (*Pol.*) parteilos, unabhängig. **–bill,** *s.* (*Orn.*) (*Am.* ***Red*** –) der Fichten-Kreuzschnabel (*Loxia curvirostra*). **–bones,** *pl.* gekreuzte Knochen (*pl.*). **–bow,** *s.* die Armbrust. **––bowman,** *s.* der Armbrustschütze. **–bred,** *adj.* durch Kreuzung erzeugt, hybrid. **–breed,** *s.* der Bastard, Hybride; Mischling, die Mischrasse. **––channel,** *adj.* – ***steamer***, der Kanaldampfer. **––check,** **1.** *v.t., v.i.* (gegen)-kontrollieren. **2.** *s.* die (Gegen)kontrolle.

cross-country, *adj.* – ***flight***, der Überlandflug; – ***performance***, die Geländegängigkeit (*of a vehicle*); – ***race***, der Geländelauf, Waldlauf, das Querfeldeinrennen; – ***vehicle***, geländegängiges Fahrzeug.

cross-cut, **1.** *s.* (*Carp.*) der Hirnschnitt; (*Min.*) Querschlag, Querstollen; – ***file***, die Kreuzhiebfeile; – ***saw***, die Schrotsäge. **2.** *v.t., v.i.* (*Carp.*) über Hirn sägen.

crossed [krɔst], *adj.* 1. gekreuzt, geschränkt; 2. mit einem Kreuzzeichen vermerkt, angekreuzt; – ***cheque***, gekreuzter Scheck, der Verrechnungsscheck; – ***through*** or ***off*** or ***out***, ausgestrichen, durchgestrichen.

cross|-examination, *s.* das Kreuzverhör. **––examine,** **1.** *v.t.* ins Kreuzverhör nehmen. **2.** *v.i.* ein Kreuzverhör vornehmen. **––eyed,** *adj.* (nach innen) schielend. **––fertilization,** *s.* die Kreuzbefruchtung, Fremdbefruchtung. **––fertilize,** *v.i.* sich kreuzweise befruchten. **–fire,** *s.* (*Mil.*) das Kreuzfeuer (*also fig.*). **––grain,** *s.* (*Carp.*) die Hirnseite, Stirnseite. **––grained,** *adj.* quer zur Faser geschnitten; (*fig.*) eigensinnig, widerspenstig, widerborstig, widerhaarig, störrisch; – ***timber***, das Hirnholz. **––hairs,** *pl. See* **––wires.** **––hatching,** *s.* die (Kreuz)schraffierung. **––head,** *s.* (*Tech.*) der Kreuzkopf. **––heading,** *s.* (spaltenlange) Überschrift, die Auszeichnungszeile.

crossing ['krɔsiŋ], *s.* 1. das Kreuzen, die Kreuzung; 2. Überquerung, Durchquerung; Überfahrt, Reise zur See; Überschreitung (*of a frontier*); – ***the line***, die Überquerung des Äquators; ***rough –***, stürmische Überfahrt; 3. (***pedestrian –***) (Straßen)-kreuzung, der Fußgängerüberweg, Straßenübergang; die Übergangsstelle, Überfahrtsstelle (*ferry etc.*); ***level –***, der Bahnübergang; – ***sweeper***, der Straßenkehrer; 4. (*Biol.*) die Kreuzung; 5. (*Archit.*) Vierung.

cross-legged, *adj.* mit gekreuzten *or* übereinandergeschlagenen Beinen.

crossly ['krɔsli], *adv.* ungehalten, mürrisch, verdrießlich, ärgerlich. **crossness,** *s.* die Verdrießlichkeit, Ärgerlichkeit, schlechte Laune.

cross|patch, *s.* (*coll.*) der Brummbär, Murrkopf. **–piece,** *s.* der Querbalken, Querverband, das Querstück, Querhaupt, Querholz. **––pollination,** *s.* die Fremdbestäubung. **––purposes,** *pl.* das Rätselspiel; (*coll.*) ***be at –***, sich (gegenseitig) mißverstehen, einander (unabsichtlich) entgegenhandeln. **––question,** *v.t. See* **––examine.** **––reference,** *s.* der Kreuzverweis. **–road,** *s.* die Querstraße, Seitenstraße; *pl.* (*oft. sing. constr.*) der Kreuzweg, die (Weg)kreuzung, Straßenkreuzung; (*fig.*) ***at the –s***, am Scheideweg. **––section,** *s.* der Querschnitt (***of***, durch). **––stitch,** *s.* der Kreuzstich. **––talk,** *s.* (*Rad.*) das Nebensprechen. **––trees,** *pl.* (*Naut.*) die Saling. **–wires,** *pl.* das Fadenkreuz. **–wise,** *adv.* quer, kreuzweise. **–word (puzzle),** *s.* das Kreuzworträtsel.

crotch [krɔtʃ], *s.* die Gabel(ung). **crotched** [–t], *adj.* gegabelt.

crotchet ['krɔtʃit], *s.* 1. (*Mus.*) die Viertelnote; 2. (*fig.*) Grille, Schrulle. **crotchety,** *adj.* schrullenhaft; (*coll.*) ärgerlich, verstimmt.

croton ['krоutən], *s.* (*Bot.*) der Kroton; – ***oil***, das Krotonöl.

crouch [krautʃ], **1.** *v.i.* 1. hocken, sich bücken, sich ducken, sich zusammenkauern (***before***, vor (*Dat.*)); ***be –ed***, kauern; 2. (*fig.*) sich demütigen, kriechen (vor (*Dat.*)). **2.** *s.* die Hockstellung.

[1]**croup** [kru:p], *s.* (*Med.*) der Krupp.

[2]**croup,** *s.* das Kreuz, die Kruppe (*of horses*); der Steiß, Bürzel (*of birds*).

croupier ['kru:piə], *s.* der Bankhalter.

[1]**crow** [krou], *s.* die Krähe; (*Orn.*) ***carrion –***, die Rabenkrähe (*Corvus corone*); ***hooded –***, die Nebelkrähe (*Corvus cornix*); ***have a – to pluck with him***, mit ihm ein Hühnchen zu rupfen haben; ***as hoarse as a –***, heiser wie ein Rabe; ***as the – flies***, schnurgerade, in der Luftlinie; (*fig.*) ***a white –***, ein weißer Rabe, eine Seltenheit.

[2]**crow,** *irr.v.i.* krähen; (*coll.*) frohlocken, triumphieren (***over***, über (*Acc.*)).

crowbar ['kroubɑ:], *s.* das Brecheisen, Stemmeisen.

crowd [kraud], **1.** *s.* das Gedränge; der Haufen, die Masse, dichte Menge (*of people*); der Pöbel, gemeines Volk; ***–s of people***, Menschenmassen (*pl.*). **2.** *v.t.* stoßen, vorwärtsschieben; hineinpressen, hineinpferchen (***into***, in (*Acc.*)); vollstopfen (*a space*) (***with***, mit); zusammendrängen; (*Am., fig.*) (be)drängen; – (***all***) ***sail***, alle Segel beisetzen; – ***out***, verdrängen. **3.** *v.i.* sich drängen; – ***in(to)***, sich hineindrängen (in (*Acc.*)); hineindringen; – ***in upon***, bedrängen, bestürmen. **crowded,** *adj.* (über)voll, wimmelnd (***with***, von), überfüllt, vollgestopft (mit); gedrängt, zusammengepfercht; übervölkert; – ***to suffocation***, zum Ersticken voll.

crowfoot ['kroufut], *s.* (*pl.* **-s**) (*Bot.*) der Hahnenfuß.

crown [kraun], **1.** *s.* 1. die Krone, (*fig.*) Herrschermacht, Herrscherwürde, der Souverän; (Sieger)-kranz; 2. (*fig.*) Gipfel(punkt), Schlußstein, die Spitze, Krönung, Vollendung; 3. der Scheitel, Wirbel (*of the head*); (*fig.*) Schädel, Kopf; ***from the – of the head to the sole of the foot,*** von Kopf zu Fuß, vom Scheitel bis zur Sohle; 4. das (Anker)-kreuz; 5. die (Zahn)krone; 6. (Baum)krone; 7. ein Papierformat (*15 in.* × *20 in.*); 7. (*obs.*) englische Silbermünze (*5 shillings* = *25p*); (*obs.*) ***half a –,*** eine halbe Krone (= *12½p*). **2.** *v.t.* krönen; (*fig.*) bekränzen; schmücken, auszeichnen, Ehre bringen (*Dat.*); die Krone aufsetzen (*Dat.*), den Höhepunkt bilden von, glorreich abschließen, vollenden, vervollkommnen; (*sl.*) eins aufs Dach geben (*Dat.*); ***to – all,*** als Letztes *or* Höchstes; (*Draughts*) ***– a man,*** einen Stein zur Dame machen; ***– a tooth,*** einen Zahn eine (neue) Krone aufsetzen; ***–ed heads,*** gekrönte Häupter.

crown|-bit, *s.* der Kronenbohrer. **– colony,** *s.* die Kronkolonie. **–-escapement,** *s.* (*Horol.*) die Spindelhemmung. **–-glass,** *s.* das Kronglas. **crowning,** *adj.* höchst, letzt, oberst. **crown|-jewels,** *pl.* die Reichskleinodien. **–-lands,** *pl.* Krongüter, Staatsdomänen (*pl.*). **– octavo,** *s.* das Kleinoktav. **– prince,** *s.* der Kronprinz. **–-setting,** *s.* die Kastenfassung (*jewels*). **–-wheel,** *s.* (*Horol.*) das Kronrad.

crow's|-feet, *pl.* Krähenfüße, Fältchen unter den Augen (*pl.*). **–-nest,** *s.* (*Naut.*) das Krähennest, der Ausguck.

crozier, *see* **crosier.**

crucial ['kru:ʃəl], *adj.* entscheidend, kritisch; kreuzförmig; ***– point,*** springender Punkt; ***– test,*** die Feuerprobe.

crucian ['kru:ʃiən], *s.* (*Ichth.*) die Karausche.

crucible ['kru:sibl], *s.* der (Schmelz)tiegel; (*fig.*) die Feuerprobe. **crucible-steel,** *s.* der Tiegelgußstahl.

cruciferous [kru'sifərəs], *adj.* ***– plant,*** der Kreuzblüter. **crucifix** ['kru:sifiks], *s.* das Kruzifix. **crucifixion** [–'fikʃən], *s.* die Kreuzigung. **cruciform** ['kru:sifɔ:m], *adj.* kreuzförmig. **crucify** ['kru:sifai], *v.t.* kreuzigen, ans Kreuz schlagen.

crude [kru:d], *adj.* roh, unreif, ungekocht; grell (*as colour*); (*Tech.*) Roh–, unfertig, unverarbeitet, unbearbeitet; (*fig.*) unreif, unverdaut; (*as manners*) grob, unfein, ungeschliffen, ungehobelt, plump; ***the – facts,*** die ungeschminkten *or* nackten Tatsachen; ***– iron,*** das Roheisen; ***– oil,*** das Rohöl; ***– sugar,*** der Rohzucker. **crudeness, crudity,** *s.* die Roheit, Unfertigkeit, Unreife; Grobheit, Ungeschliffenheit, Plumpheit, Geschmacklosigkeit.

cruel ['kruəl], **1.** *adj.* grausam (*to*, gegen), hart, gefühllos, unbarmherzig, unmenschlich; entsetzlich, schrecklich. **2.** *adv.* (*also coll.*) sehr, äußerst, höchst. **cruelty,** *s.* die Grausamkeit, Unmenschlichkeit, Härte (*to*, gegen(über)); ***– to animals,*** die Tierquälerei; ***Society for the Prevention of Cruelty to Animals,*** der Tierschutzverein.

cruet ['kru:it], *s.* das Ölfläschchen, Essigfläschchen. **cruet-stand,** *s.* die Menage.

cruise [kru:z], **1.** *s.* die Seereise; Erholungsreise, Vergnügungsfahrt (zur See). **2.** *v.i.* kreuzen, (ziellos) herumfahren; (*Av. etc.*) mit Reisegeschwindigkeit fahren. **cruiser,** *s.* 1. der Kreuzer; Segler, die Jacht; ***armoured –,*** der Panzerkreuzer; ***cabin –,*** das Kajütboot; ***motor –,*** der Motorkreuzer; ***sailing –,*** der Segelkreuzer; 2. (*Boxing*) ***– weight,*** das Halbschwergewicht. **cruising| altitude,** *s.* die Normalflughöhe. **– radius, – range,** *s.* der Aktionsradius. **– speed,** *s.* (*Naut.*) die Marschfahrt, (*Av., Motor.*) Reisegeschwindigkeit.

crumb [krʌm], **1.** *s.* die Krume, Brosame, der Krümel, Brosel; (*fig.*) das Bißchen, Bröckchen, der Splitter. **2.** *v.t.* zerkrümeln, (*Cul.*) panieren. **crumb brush,** *s.* der Tischbesen.

crumble [krʌmbl], **1.** *v.t.* zerkrümeln, zerbröckeln, zerstückeln. **2.** *v.i.* zerfallen, zerbröckeln; ***– to pieces,*** in Stücke zerfallen, (*fig.*) zunichte werden, zugrunde gehen; ***– into dust,*** in Staub zerfallen. **crumbly,** *adj.* krümelig, bröckelig.

crumby ['krʌmi], *adj.* (*coll.*) *see* **crumbly**; (*sl.*) schäbig, lausig.

crumhorn ['krʌmhɔ:n], *s.* (*Mus., obs.*) das Krummhorn.

crumpet ['krʌmpit], *s.* 1. flacher Sauerteigkuchen; 2. (*vulg.*) das Weibsbild; 3. (*sl.*) ***be off one's –,*** eine weiche Birne haben.

crumple [krʌmpl], **1.** *v.t.* zerknüllen, zerknittern, ramponieren; ***– up,*** zusammenknüllen. **2.** *v.i.* zerknittert *or* faltig werden; ***– up,*** zusammenschrumpfen, (*fig.*) zusammenbrechen, versagen.

crunch [krʌntʃ], **1.** *v.t.* zerknirschen, zermalmen. **2.** *v.i.* knirschen. **3.** *s.* das Knirschen; (*sl.*) ***when it comes to the –,*** wenn es auf (des) Messers Schneide steht.

crupper ['krʌpə], *s.* (*of horse*) die Kruppe, das Kreuz; (*of harness*) der Schwanzriemen.

crural ['kru:rəl], *adj.* Bein–, Schenkel–.

crusade [kru:'seid], **1.** *s.* der Kreuzzug (*also fig.*). **2.** *v.i.* einen Kreuzzug unternehmen, (*fig.*) zu Felde ziehen. **crusader,** *s.* der Kreuzfahrer, Kreuzritter.

cruse [kru:z], *s.* (*obs.*) der Topf, Krug, die Schale, das Gefäß.

crush [krʌʃ], **1.** *v.t.* (zer)quetschen, zerdrücken, zermalmen; (*Tech.*) zerstoßen, zerreiben, zerstampfen, zerkleinern, (*ore*) brechen, pochen, (*grain*) mahlen, schroten; (*as clothes*) zerdrücken, zerknittern; (*fig.*) (*population*) bedrücken, unterdrücken, (*resistance*) überwältigen, niederwerfen, niederschmettern, vernichten; ***– out,*** ausdrücken, auspressen (*cigarette etc.*). **2.** *v.i.* sich falten, zerknittern, zerdrückt werden; (*of a p.*) sich vorwärts dränge(l)n. **3.** *s.* 1. das Gedränge, Gewühl, die Menschenmenge; 2. (*sl.*) der Schwarm; (*sl.*) ***have a – on him,*** in ihn vernarrt sein.

crusher ['krʌʃə], *s.* der Zerdrücker; (*Tech.*) Brecher, das Brechwerk, die Brechwalze, Zerkleinerungsmaschine, Presse, Quetsche. **crush-hat,** *s.* der Klapphut. **crushing,** *adj.* zermalmend, (*Tech.*) Brech–, Mahl–; (*fig.*) vernichtend, überwältigend, niederschmetternd. **crushing-mill,** *s.* das Brechwerk, der Stampfgang, die Erzquetsche. **crush-room,** *s.* (*Theat.*) das Foyer, die Wandelhalle.

crust [krʌst], **1.** *s.* die Kruste, Rinde, Schale, (*of bread*) der Knust, Anschnitt, (*of pastry*) Teig, die Kruste; (*Med.*) der Schorf, Grind; (*coll.*) trockenes Stück Brot; (*in wine bottles*) der Niederschlag, (*in boilers*) Kesselstein; ***the earth's –,*** die Erdrinde. **2.** *v.t.* (*usu.* ***– over***) mit einer Kruste überziehen, überkrusten; (*Tech.*) mit Belag überziehen, inkrustieren. **3.** *v.i.* eine Kruste bilden, verkrusten.

crustacean [krʌs'teiʃən], **1.** *adj.* (*Zool.*) Krebs–. **2.** *s.* das Krebstier, Krustentier. **crustaceous,** *adj.* Krusten–, krustenartig.

crusted ['krʌstid], *adj.* bekrustet, verkrustet; (*of wine*) abgelagert; ***– snow,*** der Harsch; ***– over with ice,*** mit einer Eiskruste bedeckt.

crustiness ['krʌstinis], *s.* die Krustigkeit, (*fig., coll.*) Reizbarkeit, Bärbeißigkeit. **crusty,** *adj.* krustig, (*fig., coll.*) reizbar, bärbeißig, mürrisch.

crutch [krʌtʃ], *s.* die Krücke, Stütze; (*Tech.*) Gabel; (*Naut.*) (*for the boom*) Baumschere, (*for the gaff*) Gaffelklaue, (*for a sweep*) Rudergabel.

crux [krʌks], *s.* (*Her.*) das Kreuz; (*fig.*) die Schwierigkeit, harte Nuß; springender *or* entscheidender Punkt.

cry [krai], **1.** *v.i.* 1. schreien, (laut) rufen; ***– after him,*** ihm nachrufen; ***– for the moon,*** nach Unmöglichem verlangen; ***– out,*** aufschreien; ***– out against,*** mißbilligen, sich beschweren über (*Acc.*); ***– out for,*** dringend verlangen nach; ***– to him to stop,*** ihm zurufen, daß er stehenbleiben soll; 2. weinen, heulen (***for***, um; ***over***, über (*Acc.*) *or* wegen); ***the child is –ing for its mother,*** das Kind verlangt seine Mutter unter Tränen; (*Prov.*) ***it's no good –ing over spilt milk,*** hin ist hin; geschehene Dinge sind nicht zu ändern; 3. (*Hunt.*) bellen, anschlagen, Laut geben (*of hounds*); 4. (*coll.*) ***– off,*** sich lossagen, absagen, zurücktreten. **2.** *v.t.* schreien, rufen, verkünden; ausrufen, ausbieten (*wares*); –

down, herabsetzen, heruntersetzen, verschreien; niederschreien; (*coll.*) – *off,* absagen; – *one's eyes* or *heart out,* sich (*Dat.*) die Augen ausweinen; (*Prov.*) – *stinking fish,* sein Licht unter den Scheffel stellen; – *halt,* Einhalt gebieten; – *o.s. to sleep,* sich in den Schlaf weinen; – *bitter tears,* bittere Tränen weinen; – *up,* rühmen, preisen, in den Himmel heben, Reklame machen für; – *wolf,* blinden Alarm schlagen. **3.** *s.* der Schrei, Ruf (*for,* nach); das Schreien, Geschrei; der Ausruf, Zuruf, die Bitte; das Losungswort, Schlagwort; Weinen, (Weh)klagen; (*of hounds*) Gebell, Anschlagen; (*fig.*) *a far* –, weit entfernt; *in full* –, mit lautem Gebell, (*fig.*) mit großer Begeisterung; *have a good* –, sich ordentlich ausweinen; *the cries of London,* die Ausrufe der Londoner Straßenverkäufer; *the popular* –, die Volksstimme, das Gerücht; *within* –, in Rufweite.

cry-baby, *s.* (*coll.*) der Heulpeter, die Heulsuse. **crying,** *adj.* schreiend; rufend; weinend; (*fig.*) (himmel)schreiend, dringend; – *shame,* schreiendes Unrecht.

crypt [kript], *s.* die Gruft, Krypta; (*Anat.*) Absonderungsdrüse. **cryptic,** *adj.* geheim, verborgen, rätselhaft.

cryptogam [ˈkriptəgæm], *s.* (*pl.* **-ia**) (*Bot.*) die Kryptogame. **cryptogamous** [–ˈtɔgəməs], *adj.* (*Bot.*) kryptogamisch.

cryptograph [ˈkriptəgrɑːf], *s.* die Geheimschrift. **cryptography** [–ˈtɔgrəfi], *s.* die (Kunst der Verschlüsselung und Entschlüsselung von) Geheimschrift(en).

crystal [kristl], **1.** *s.* der Kristall; das Kristall(glas); Uhrglas; (*Elec.*) – *control,* die Quarzsteuerung; (*Rad.*) – *detector,* der (Kristall)detektor, Kristallgleichrichter; (*Rad.*) – *set,* der (Kristall)detektorempfänger. **2.** *adj.* Kristall–, kristallen, kristallartig.

crystal|-clear, *adj.* kristallhell, kristallklar. **--gazer,** *s.* der Hellseher. **--gazing,** *s.* das Kristallsehen. **crystalline** [–lain], *adj.* Kristall–, kristallen; kristallinisch, kristallisiert; kristallhell; – *rock,* der Bergkristall.

crystallization [ˈkristəlaiˈzeiʃən], *s.* die Kristallisation, Kristallisierung, Kristallbildung; *water of* –, das Konstitutionswasser. **crystallize, 1.** *v.t.* kristallisieren; (*fruits*) kandieren; (*fig.*) feste *or* konkrete Form geben (*Dat.*), konkretisieren, verfestigen. **2.** *v.i.* kristallisieren; (*fig.*) feste *or* konkrete Form annehmen.

crystallographer [kristəˈlɔgrəfə], *s.* der Kristallograph. **crystallography,** *s.* die Kristallographie, Kristallehre. **crystalloid** [ˈkristəlɔid], *adj.* kristallähnlich.

csardas, *see* **czardas.**

ctenoid [ˈtiːnɔid], *adj.* Kamm–, kammartig; (*Ichth.*) kammschuppig; – *fish,* der Kammschupper.

cub [kʌb], **1.** *s.* 1. das Junge (*of many wild animals*); (*fig.*) ungeschlachter Bengel; (*fig.*) *unlicked* –, der Flegel, Tolpatsch; 2. (*wolf-*)–, der Pimpf, Wölfling, das Mitglied der Jungabteilung der Pfadfinder. **2.** *v.i.* Junge werfen.

Cuba [ˈkjuːbə], *s.* Kuba (*n.*). **Cuban, 1.** *s.* der (die) Kubaner(in). **2.** *adj.* kubanisch.

cubature [ˈkjuːbətʃə], *s.* die Raum(inhalts)berechnung.

cubby-hole [ˈkʌbi-], *s.* (*coll.*) gemütliche Ecke, kleiner gemütlicher Raum.

cube [kjuːb], **1.** *s.* 1. der Würfel, Kubus, das Hexaeder; – *sugar,* der Würfelzucker; 2. (*Math.*) (*also* – *number*) der Kubus, die Kubikzahl, dritte Potenz; – *root,* die Kubikwurzel, dritte Wurzel. **2.** *v.t.* kubieren, zur dritten Potenz erheben; den Rauminhalt berechnen von; *seven* –*d,* sieben zur dritten Potenz, sieben hoch drei; *see also* **cubic.**

cubeb [ˈkjuːbeb], *s.* (*Bot.*) die Kubebe.

cubic [ˈkjuːbik], *adj.* Kubik–, Raum–; (*of crystals*) isometrisch; *see also* **cubical;** – *content,* das Volumen, der Rauminhalt; – *equation,* kubische Gleichung, die Gleichung dritten Grades; – *metre,* das Kubikmeter; – *number, see* **cube** (*Math.*). **cubical,** *adj.* würfelförmig, Würfel–.

cubicle [ˈkjuːbikl], *s.* abgeschlossener (Schlaf)raum; die Einzelzelle, Nische; Badezelle.

cubiform [ˈkjuːbifɔːm], *adj.* *See* **cubical.**

Cubism [ˈkjuːbizm], *s.* der Kubismus. **Cubist, 1.** *s.* der Kubist. **2.** *adj.* kubistisch.

cubit [ˈkjuːbit], *s.* (*obs.*) die Elle.

cuboid [ˈkjuːbɔid], *adj.* würfelähnlich; (*Anat.*) Würfel–; – (*bone*), das Würfelbein.

cuckold [ˈkʌkəld], **1.** *s.* der Hahnrei. **2.** *v.t.* Hörner aufsetzen (*Dat.*), zum Hahnrei machen. **cuckoldry,** *s.* die Hahnreischaft, das Hörneraufsetzen.

cuckoo [ˈkukuː], **1.** *s.* (*Orn.*) der Kuckuck (*Cuculus canorus*); (*coll.*) Dummkopf, Einfaltspinsel. **2.** *adj.* (*coll.*) plemplem, bekloppt. **3.** *v.i.* kuckuck rufen. **cuckoo|-clock,** *s.* die Kuckucksuhr. **--flower,** *s.* (*Bot.*) das Wiesenschaumkraut. **--pint** [pint], *s.* (*Bot.*) Gefleckter Aron. **--spit,** *s.* (*Ent.*) der Kuckucksspeichel, die Schaumzikade.

cucumber [ˈkjuːkʌmbə], *s.* die Gurke; (*coll.*) *cool as a* –, gelassen, ohne Aufregung.

cucurbit [kjuˈkəːbit], *s.* der Kürbis. **cucurbitaceous** [–ˈteiʃəs], *adj.* Kürbis–.

cud [kʌd], *s.* zurückgebrachtes Futter zum Wiederkäuen; *chew the* –, wiederkäuen, (*fig., coll.*) nachsinnen (*over,* über (*Acc.*)).

cuddle [kʌdl], **1.** *v.t.* hätscheln, herzen, liebkosen, an sich drücken, (*sl.*) knutschen. **2.** *v.i.* sich herzen; – *up,* sich schmiegen *or* kuscheln (*to,* an (*Acc.*)); – *up in bed,* sich im Bett warm einmummeln *or* zusammenkuscheln. **3.** *s.* die Umarmung, Liebkosung. **cuddly,** *adj.* kuschelig; – *toy,* das Stofftier, (*coll.*) Kuscheltier(chen).

cuddy [ˈkʌdi], *s.* (*Naut.*) die Kajüte.

cudgel [kʌdʒl], **1.** *s.* der Knüttel, Knüppel, die Keule; (*fig.*) *take up the* –*s,* in den Kampf eingreifen; *take up the* –*s for him,* für ihn eintreten, für ihn Partei nehmen *or* ergreifen. **2.** *v.t.* prügeln; – *one's brains about a th.,* sich (*Dat.*) den Kopf über eine S. zerbrechen. **cudgel-play,** *s.* das Stockfechten.

1**cue** [kjuː], *s.* 1. der Haarzopf; 2. Billardstock, das Queue.

2**cue,** *s.* (*Theat.*) das Stichwort; (*Mus.*) der Kustos; (*fig.*) Wink, Fingerzeig; *give him his* –, ihm die Worte in den Mund legen; *take one's* – *from him,* sich nach ihm richten.

1**cuff** [kʌf], **1.** *s.* der Puff, Knuff. **2.** *v.t.* puffen, knuffen, ohrfeigen.

2**cuff,** *s.* die Manschette, Stulpe, der (Ärmel)aufschlag. **cuff-link,** *s.* der Manschettenknopf.

cuirass [kwiˈræs], *s.* der (Brust)harnisch, Panzer (*also Zool.*), Küraß. **cuirassier** [kwirəˈsiə], *s.* der Kürassier.

cuisine [kwiˈziːn], *s.* die Küche, Kochkunst.

cul-de-sac [ˈkuldəsæk], *s.* die Sackgasse.

culinary [ˈkʌlinəri], *adj.* Küchen–, Koch–; – *art,* die Kochkunst; – *herbs,* Küchenkräuter.

cull [kʌl], *v.t.* pflücken; aussuchen, auslesen.

cullender [ˈkʌlində], *s.* *See* **colander.**

cullet [ˈkʌlit], *s.* das Bruchglas.

1**culm** [kʌlm], *s.* der Halm, Stengel.

2**culm,** *s.* der Kohlenstaub, (Kohlen)grus, das Kohlenklein, die Staubkohle.

culminate [ˈkʌlmineit], *v.i.* den Höhepunkt erreichen (*in,* mit *or* bei), gipfeln (in (*Dat.*)), (*Astr.*) kulminieren. **culmination** [–ˈneiʃən], *s.* (*Astr.*) die Kulmination; (*fig.*) der Gipfel, Höhepunkt, die Gipfelhöhe, höchster Stand.

culpability [kʌlpəˈbiliti], *s.* die Sträflichkeit, Schuld(haftigkeit). **culpable** [ˈkʌlpəbl], *adj.* sträflich, schuldhaft, tadelnswert.

culprit [ˈkʌlprit], *s.* der Verbrecher, Schuldige(r); (*Law*) Angeklagte(r), Beschuldigte(r).

cult [kʌlt], *s.* der Kult, Kultus; die Huldigung, (kultische) Verehrung; Kultgemeinschaft.

cultivable [ˈkʌltivəbl], **cultivatable** [–veitəbl],

adj. (*of land*) bestellbar, bebaubar, kultivierbar, anbaufähig; (*of plants*) züchtbar, kultivierbar. **cultivate,** *v.t.* bearbeiten, bestellen, bebauen, kultivieren (*land*); (an)bauen, ziehen, züchten (*crops etc.*); (*fig.*) (aus)bilden, entwickeln, veredeln, verfeinern, gesittet machen; ausüben, betreiben, pflegen, sich befleißigen (*Gen.*), Wert legen auf (*Acc.*), (*friendship etc.*) pflegen, hegen. **cultivated,** *adj.* bebaut, bestellt, kultiviert (*land*); angebaut, Kultur– (*plants*); gebildet, zivilisiert, kultiviert, verfeinert (*a p.*); – ***area,*** die Kulturfläche, das Anbaugebiet; – ***plant,*** die Kulturpflanze. **cultivation** [–'veiʃən], *s.* der Anbau, Ackerbau; die Bebauung, Bestellung, Bearbeitung, Anpflanzung, Urbarmachung, Kultivierung; Ausbildung, Verfeinerung, Veredelung; Kultur, Bildung; Pflege, Übung. **cultivator,** *s.* der Bebauer, Landwirt.

cultural ['kʌltʃərəl], *adj.* kulturell, Kultur–. **culture, 1.** *s.* 1. die Kultur (*also fig.*); (Geistes)-bildung, Kultiviertheit, Zivilisation; 2. Pflege, Zucht; ***physical –,*** die Körperpflege; 3. (*Biol.*) Kultur; – ***medium,*** künstlicher Nährboden, das Kultursubstrat; *see also* **cultivation. 2.** *v.t.* züchten (*bacteria*). **cultured,** *adj.* zivilisiert, gebildet, kultiviert.

culver ['kʌlvə], *s.* die Waldtaube.

culverin ['kʌlvərin], *s.* (*Hist.*) die Feldschlange.

culvert ['kʌlvət], *s.* der Abzugskanal, Abflußgraben, Durchlaß; (*Naut.*) die Dole.

cumber ['kʌmbə], *v.t.* beschweren, belasten, überladen; lästig sein (*Dat.*), zur Last fallen (*Dat.*), (be)hindern, hemmen. **cumbersome** [–səm], *adj.* beschwerlich, lästig, hinderlich; schwerfällig. **cumbersomeness,** *s.* die Beschwerlichkeit, Lästigkeit, Schwerfälligkeit. **cumbrous** [–brəs], *adj. See* **cumbersome.**

cumin ['kʌmin], *s.* (*Bot.*) der Kruzkümmel.

cummberbund ['kʌməbʌnd], *s.* der Leibgurt, die Schärpe.

cumulative ['kju:mjulətiv], *adj.* sich (an)häufend, sich steigernd; (*Law, Comm.*) zusätzlich, kumulativ, Zusatz–, (noch) hinzukommend, verstärkend.

cumulus ['kju:mjuləs], *s.* die Haufenwolke, der Kumulus.

cuneate ['kju:niit], *adj.* keilförmig, Keil–. **cuneiform** [–niifɔ:m, –'neiifɔ:m], **1.** *adj. See* **cuneate. 2.** *s.* die Keilschrift.

cunning ['kʌniŋ], **1.** *adj.* (*of a p.*) listig, schlau, verschlagen, verschmitzt; (*of a th.*) geschickt. **2.** *s.* die (Arg)list, Schlauheit, Verschlagenheit, Verschmitztheit; Geschicklichkeit.

cup [kʌp], **1.** *s.* die Tasse, Schale; (*Bot., Eccl.*) der Becher, Kelch; Pokal (*trophy*); Trunk; die (kalte) Bowle; ***challenge –,*** der Wanderpreis, Preispokal; ***claret –,*** die Rotweinbowle; ***drinking –,*** der Trinkbecher; ***an early morning – of tea,*** eine Tasse Tee vor dem Aufstehen; (*coll.*) ***that's not my – of tea,*** das ist nichts für mich; ***be fond of the –,*** dem Trunk ergeben sein; (*fig.*) ***his – was full,*** der Kelch *or* das Maß seiner Leiden war voll; ***in one's –s,*** betrunken, im Rausch; ***parting –,*** der Abschiedstrunk; (*Prov.*) ***there's many a slip 'twixt (the) – and (the) lip,*** es ist noch nicht aller Tage Abend. **2.** *v.t.* 1. (*Surg.*) schröpfen; 2. – ***your hand!*** mach eine hohle Hand!

cup-bearer, *s.* der Mundschenk.

cupboard ['kʌbəd], *s.* der Schrank; (*coll.*) ***–-love,*** eigennützige Liebe, berechnende Liebenswürdigkeit(en).

cupel [kju:pl], **1.** *s.* (*Tech., Chem.*) die Kapelle, Kupelle, der Schmelztiegel. **2.** *v.t.* kupellieren, abtreiben. **cupellation** [–'leiʃən], *s.* das Kupellieren, Abtreiben, der Treibprozeß.

cup final, *s.* (*Footb.*) das Pokalendspiel. **cupful,** *s.* die Tassevoll, der Bechervoll.

Cupid ['kju:pid], *s.* Kupido, Amor (*m.*); ***–'s bow,*** der Amorsbogen.

cupidity [kju:'piditi], *s.* die Habgier, Habsucht; Gier, Begierde.

cup-moss, *s.* (*Bot.*) die Becherflechte.

cupola ['kju:pələ], *s.* die Kuppel; das Kuppeldach, Kuppelgewölbe; (*Metall.*) der Kuppelofen; (*Mil.*) Panzerturm.

cupping ['kʌpiŋ], *s.* (*Surg.*) das Schröpfen; – ***glass,*** das Schröpfglas.

cupreous ['kju:priəs], *adj.* kupfern, kupferartig, kupferfarbig; kupferhaltig. **cupric,** *adj.* (*Chem.*) Kupfer–; – ***oxide,*** das Kupferoxyd. **cuprous,** *adj.* (*Chem.*) Kupfer–; – ***oxide,*** das Kupferoxydul.

cup-shaped, *adj.* becherförmig, kelchförmig.

cur [kə:], *s.* der Köter, (*fig.*) Schuft, Schurke, Halunke, Hund.

curability [kjuərə'biliti], *s.* die Heilbarkeit. **curable** ['kjuərəbl], *adj.* heilbar.

curacy ['kjuərəsi], *s.* die Unterpfarre, das Hilfspfarramt. **curate** [–rit], *s.* der Hilfspfarrer, Unterpfarrer.

curative ['kjuərətiv], **1.** *adj.* heilend, Heil–. **2.** *s.* das Heilmittel.

curator [kju'reitə], *s.* 1. der Museumsdirektor, Konservator, Kustos; 2. (*Scots Law*) Vormund, Verwalter.

curb [kə:b], **1.** *s.* 1. (*harness*) die Kandare, Kinnkette, (*fig.*) der Einhalt, Zaum, Zügel; 2. (*Vet.*) Spat, Hasenfuß; 3. (*Am.*) *see* **kerb. 2.** *v.t.* an die Kandare legen (*a horse*), (*fig.*) zügeln, im Zaum halten, bändigen. **curb|-bit,** *s.* die Kinnkettenstange, Kandarenstange. **--roof,** *s.* das Mansard(en)dach.

curd [kə:d], *s.* (*oft. pl.*) geronnene Milch, der Quark; ***turn to –s,*** gerinnen; – ***soap,*** die Kernseife; ***–s and whey,*** dicke Milch. **curdle, 1.** *v.t.* gerinnen lassen, (*fig.*) erstarren lassen. **2.** *v.i.* gerinnen, dick werden, (*fig.*) erstarren; ***it makes my blood –,*** es geht mir durch Mark und Bein.

cure [kjuə], **1.** *s.* 1. die Kur, Behandlung, das Heilverfahren; ***undergo a –,*** eine Kur machen; 2. die Heilung, Genesung; ***past –,*** (*disease*) unheilbar, (*a p.*) unheilbar krank; 3. das Heilmittel; ***a – for rheumatism,*** ein Mittel gegen Rheuma; 4. (*Eccl.*) die Seelsorge; Pfarre. **2.** *v.t.* 1. (*Med.*) heilen, kurieren (*of,* von); (*fig.*) – ***him of it,*** es ihm abgewöhnen, ihm davon abbringen; 2. trocknen, räuchern (*meat*), einsalzen, einpökeln (*fish*), beizen (*tobacco*), vulkanisieren, schwefeln (*rubber*).

cure-all, *s.* (*coll.*) das Universalmittel, Allheilmittel.

curetage [kju'retidʒ], *s.* (*Med.*) die Küretage, Ausschabung, Auskratzung, Ausräumung. **curette** [–'ret], **1.** *s.* die Kürette, der Auskratzer, Ausräumer. **2.** *v.t.* ausschaben, auskratzen, ausräumen.

curfew ['kə:fju:], *s.* das Abendläuten; (*Mil. etc.*) Ausgangsverbot, die Sperrstunde, Polizeistunde; –(***-bell***), die Abendglocke.

curia ['kjuəriə], *s.* die Kurie. **curial,** *adj.* Kurial–.

curing ['kjuəriŋ], *s.* das Heilen *etc. See* **cure, 2.**

curio ['kjuəriou], *s.* die Rarität, Kuriosität.

curiosity [kjuəri'ɔsiti], *s.* 1. die Neugier, Wißbegierde; ***out of –,*** aus Neugier; 2. *See* **curio;** (*old*) – ***shop,*** der Antiquitätenladen; 3. die Merkwürdigkeit, Wunderlichkeit; 4. (*coll.*) komischer Kauz; das Kuriosum.

curious ['kjuəriəs], *adj.* 1. neugierig, wißbegierig; (*coll.*) ***I'm – about what*** or ***– to know what will happen,*** ich bin gespannt, was noch wird; 2. seltsam, merkwürdig, wunderlich; ***–ly enough,*** merkwürdigerweise.

curl [kə:l], *s.* die Locke, der Ringel; – ***of smoke,*** die Rauchwindung, der Rauchwirbel; – ***of the lip(s),*** das Kräuseln *or* Krausziehen *or* Aufwerfen der Lippen; ***put (hair) in –s,*** locken. **2.** *v.t.* locken, ringeln, kräuseln, frisieren (*hair*); drehen, winden, (zusammen)rollen; – ***one's lip,*** die Lippen kräuseln. **3.** *v.i.* sich locken *or* ringeln *or* kräuseln (*as hair*); – ***up,*** sich zusammenrollen, (*as a serpent*) sich schlängeln *or* winden, (*as smoke*) sich hochringeln *or* hochwirbeln, in Ringeln *or* Wirbeln hochsteigen; – ***up at the edges,*** sich am Rande aufbiegen; ***her hair -ed down over her shoulders,*** ihre Haare fielen in Locken über die Schulter nieder.

curler [ˈkəːlə], *s.* 1. der Lockenwickel; 2. Curlingspieler; *see* **curling, 2,** 2.

curlew [ˈkəːljuː], *s.* (*Am. Eurasian* –) (*Orn.*) Großer Brachvogel (*Numenius arquata*).

curliness [ˈkəːlinis], *s.* die Lockigkeit, Krausheit. **curling, 1.** *adj.* kräuselnd, sich windend *or* wirbelnd. **2.** *s.* 1. das Kräuseln, Ringeln; Winden, Krümmen, Wirbeln; 2. (*Spt.*) Eisschießen, Curlingspiel. **curling|-iron(s),** *s. See* **--tongs. --stone,** *s.* das Curlingstein. **--tongs,** *s.* das Brenneisen, Onduliereisen, die Brennschere.

curl-paper, *s. See* **curler,** 1. **curly,** *adj.* lockig, gekräuselt, gelockt. **curly|-haired, --headed,** *adj.* krausköpfig, lockenköpfig.

curmudgeon [kəˈmʌdʒən], *s.* der Griesgram, Brummbär; Geizhals, Knicker, Filz.

currant [ˈkʌrənt], *s.* (*soft fruit*) die Johannisbeere, (*dried*) Korinthe.

currency [ˈkʌrənsi], *s.* 1. der Umlauf, die Zirkulation, Währung, Valuta, das Umlaufsmittel, Zahlungsmittel, Kurant(geld); (amtlicher) Kurs; (*of a bill*) die Laufzeit; – *note,* die Schatzanweisung; 2. (*fig.*) Gültigkeit, Geltung, allgemeine Anerkanntheit, die Gebräuchlichkeit, Geläufigkeit, Verbreitung, Bekanntheit; ***give* – *to,*** in Umlauf bringen.

current [ˈkʌrənt], **1.** *adj.* 1. (*of time*) laufend, jetzig, gegenwärtig, augenblicklich, aktuell, Tages–; ***at the* – *exchange,*** zum Tageskurs; – ***expenses,*** laufende Ausgaben; – ***opinion,*** die gegenwärtige *or* augenblickliche Meinung; ***for* – *payment,*** gegen bar; – ***price,*** der Tageskurs; – ***year,*** laufendes Jahr; 2. (*Comm. esp. of money*) umlaufend, kursierend, zirkulierend, kurant, gangbar, gültig; 3. (*fig.*) anerkannt, allgemein angenommen *or* gültig; allgemein üblich *or* gebraucht, geläufig, bekannt, verbreitet, gang und gäbe; ***pass* –,** für gültig *or* voll angenommen werden, gang und gäbe sein; ***in* – *use,*** allgemein üblich; 4. (*obs.*) fließend; – ***account,*** das Verrechnungskonto, Girokonto, Kontokorrent; – ***hand***(*writing*), die Kurrentschrift. **2.** *s.* der Strom (*esp. Elec.*); (*of water*) die Strömung, (*of air*) der Zug; (*fig.*) Gang, (Ver)lauf (*of events*), die Tendenz, Richtung (*of ideas*); (*Elec.*) ***alternating* –,** der Wechselstrom; (*Elec.*) ***continuous*** or ***direct* –,** der Gleichstrom; (*Meteor.*) ***down* –,** der Abwind; (*fig.*) ***the* – *of modern opinion,*** die moderne Geistesrichtung; (*Meteor.*) ***up* –,** der Aufwind.

current| density, – intensity, – strength, *s.* (*Elec.*) die Stromstärke. – **supply,** *s.* die Stromversorgung. – **transformer,** *s.* der Stromwandler.

curricle [ˈkʌrikl], *s.* zweirädriger Zweispänner, das Karriol, die Karriole.

curricular [kəˈrikjulə], *adj.* Lehrplan–. **curriculum,** *s.* der Lehrplan, Studienplan; – ***vitae,*** der Lebenslauf.

curried [ˈkʌrid], *imperf., p.p. of* **curry.**

currier [ˈkʌriə], *s.* der Lederzurichter, Gerber.

currish [ˈkəːriʃ], *adj.* bissig, knurrig; mürrisch, bösartig; *see* **cur.**

[1]**curry** [ˈkʌri], *v.t.* striegeln, abreiben (*a horse*); zurichten, gerben (*leather*); – ***favour with him,*** sich bei ihm einschmeicheln, um seine Gunst buhlen; (*sl.*) – ***his hide,*** ihm das Fell gerben, ihn vermöbeln.

[2]**curry, 1.** *s.* indisches Ragoutpulver, der *or* das Curry; gewürztes Reisragout, das Currygericht. **2.** *v.t.* mit Currysoße zubereiten.

curry-comb, *s.* der Striegel; *see* [1]**curry.**

curry-powder, *s. See* [2]**curry.**

curse [kəːs], **1.** *v.t.* verfluchen, verwünschen, verdammen; – ***him,*** ihm fluchen, auf ihn fluchen; – ***him!*** zum Teufel mit ihm! – ***it!*** verdammt noch mal! zum Kuckuck damit! **2.** *v.i.* fluchen, lästern. **3.** *s.* der Fluch; die Verwünschung, das Fluchwort; (*Eccl.*) die Verdammung, Verdammnis, der Bann(fluch); (*fig.*) das Elend, Unglück.

cursed, 1. [ˈkəːsid], *attrib. adj.* verflucht, verdammt, verwünscht, (*coll.*) verflixt. **2.** [kəːst], *pred. adj.* ***be* – *with,*** bestraft *or* gequält sein *or* werden mit. **cursing,** *s.* das Fluchen.

cursive [ˈkəːsiv], *adj.* kursiv, Kursiv–, Kurrent–(*handwriting*); (*Typ.*) – ***characters,*** die Schreibschrift.

cursor [ˈkəːsə], *s.* der Schieber, Läufer.

cursorial [kəːˈsɔːriəl], *adj.* (*Orn.*) Lauf–.

cursoriness [ˈkəːsərinis], *s.* die Flüchtigkeit, Oberflächlichkeit. **cursory,** *adj.* flüchtig, oberflächlich, eilfertig.

curt [kəːt], *adj.* kurz(gefaßt), knapp, gedrängt (*of style*); ***be* – *with him,*** mit ihm kurz angebunden *or* gegen ihn schroff sein.

curtail [kəːˈteil], *v.t.* (ver)kürzen, abkürzen; beschneiden, stutzen; (*fig.*) beschränken, einschränken, herabsetzen,, vermindern, schmälern, beeinträchtigen; – ***expenses,*** Ausgaben einschränken; – (***him of***) ***his rights,*** ihn in seinen Rechten schmälern; – ***wages,*** Löhne herabsetzen. **curtailment,** *s.* die (Ver)kürzung, Abkürzung; Beschneidung, Beschränkung, Einschränkung, Herabsetzung, Verminderung, Schmälerung, Beeinträchtigung.

curtain [kəːtn], **1.** *s.* der Vorhang, die Gardine; (*Fort.*) Kurtine, der Zwischenwall; (*fig.*) Schleier, die Hülle; (*Theat.*) *see* **curtain(-fall)**; (*fig.*) ***behind the* –,** hinter den Kulissen; ***draw the* –,** die Gardine zuziehen *or* vorziehen; (*fig.*) ***draw the* – *over a th.,*** etwas begraben; (*Mil.*) – ***of fire,*** der Feuervorhang; (*fig.*) ***lift the* –,** den Schleier lüften; (*Theat.*) ***the* – *rises,*** der Vorhang geht hoch; (*fig.*) ***under the* – *of night,*** unter dem Schleier der Nacht. **2.** *v.t.* mit Vorhängen versehen; – ***off,*** mit Vorhängen abschließen.

curtain|-call, *s.* (*Theat.*) der Hervorruf. **–(-fall),** *s.* (*Theat.*) das Fallen des Vorhangs. **--fire,** *s.* (*Mil.*) das Sperrfeuer. **--lecture,** *s.* (*coll.*) die Gardinenpredigt. **--pole,** *s. See* **--rod. --raiser,** *s.* (*Theat.*) kurzes Vorspiel, der Eröffnungseinakter. **--rod,** *s.* die Gardinenstange.

curtilage [ˈkəːtilidʒ], *s.* die Umfriedung, (umfriedeter) Innenhof.

curtly [ˈkəːtli], *adv.* schroff, rundweg. **curtness,** *s.* die Kürze, Knappheit, Gedrängtheit; Barschheit.

curts(e)y [ˈkəːtsi], **1.** *s.* der Knicks; ***drop*** or ***make a* –,** *see* **2. 2.** *v.i.* knicksen, einen Knicks machen (*to,* vor (*Dat.*)).

curvaceous [kəːˈveiʃəs], *adj.* (*coll.*) kurvenreich (*of woman*).

curvature [ˈkəːvətʃə], *s.* die Krümmung, Biegung; (Ab)rundung, Wölbung; – ***of the spine,*** die Rückgratsverkrümmung.

curve [kəːv], **1.** *s.* die Kurve, Krümmung, Biegung, Rundung, Windung; (*Math., Stat.*) Kurve, Schaulinie; ***sharp* –,** die Steilkurve, Kniebiegung. **2.** *v.t.* (*v.i.* sich) krümmen, biegen. **curved,** *adj.* gebogen, gekrümmt; gerundet, geschweift; (*Archit.*) gewölbt, Bogen–; (*Math.*) – ***line,*** die Bogenlinie; (*Math.*) – ***surface,*** krumme *or* gekrümmte Fläche.

curvet [kəːˈvet, ˈkəːvit], **1.** *s.* die Kurbette (*of horse*), (*fig.*) der Luftsprung, Bocksprung. **2.** *v.i.* kurbettieren; (*fig.*) Bocksprünge machen. **3.** *v.t.* kurbettieren lassen.

curvilinear [kəːviˈliniə], *adj.* krummlinig.

cushat [ˈkuʃət], *s.* die Ringeltaube.

cushion [ˈkuʃən], **1.** *s.* das Kissen, Polster; (*Bill.*) die Bande; (*Archit.*) das Polsterkapitell; (*Tech.*) die Polsterschicht, Zwischenlage, das Prellkissen, der Dämpfer, Puffer; (*Bill.*) – ***cannon*** or (*Am.*) ***carom,*** der Bandenball; – ***cover,*** der Kissenbezug; – ***tyre,*** der Halbluftreifen. **2.** *v.t.* mit Kissen versehen, polstern; (*Tech.*) abfedern; (*fig.*) dämpfen (*vibration etc.*); (*fig.*) ***he* –*ed himself on her lap,*** er machte sich bequem auf ihrem Schoß; (*Bill.*) – ***the ball,*** den Ball dublieren; –***ed seat,*** die Polsterbank.

cushy [ˈkuʃi], *adj.* (*sl.*) (kinder)leicht, bequem, angenehm; (*coll.*) – ***job,*** ruhige Nummer.

cusp [kʌsp], *s.* die Spitze; (*Math.*) der Scheitelpunkt (*of curve*); (*Anat.*) Zipfel (*of heart-valve*); (*Archit.*) die Nase (*of Gothic arch*); das Horn (*of crescent moon*); (*Zool.*) der Höcker (*of teeth*).

cuspate(d) [-eit(id)], *adj.* spitz (zulaufend), zugespitzt, Spitz-. **cuspidal** [-pidl], *adj.* (*esp. Math.*) Spitzen-. **cuspidate(d),** *adj.* (*Bot.*) spitzig. **cuspidation** [-'deiʃən], *s.* (*Archit.*) die Nasenverzierung.

cuspidor ['kʌspidɔ:], *s.* der Spucknapf.

cuss [kʌs], **1.** *s.* 1. (*sl.*) *see* **curse**; (*coll.*) ***he doesn't care a tinker's* –**, es ist ihm völlig schnuppe; 2. (*coll.*) der Bursche, Kerl; (*sl.*) ***a queer* –**, eine dufte Nummer. **2.** *v.t., v.i.* (*sl.*) *see* **curse. cussed** ['kʌsid], *adj.* (*sl.*) *see* **cursed, 1. cussedness,** *s.* (*coll.*) die Sturheit, Widerborstigkeit, Widerhaarigkeit.

custard [kʌstəd], *s.* die Vanillesoße, der Pudding. **custard|-pie,** *attrib. adj.* (*Theat.*) – ***farce,*** das Klamaukstück. **--powder,** *s.* das Puddingpulver.

custodial [kʌs'toudiəl], **1.** *adj.* vormundschaftlich, Vormundschafts-; Bewahrungs-, Aufsichts-. **2.** *s.* (*Eccl.*) das Reliquienkästchen. **custodian,** *s.* der Vormund, Aufseher, Wächter, Hüter, (*of museum*) Kustos. **custody** ['kʌstədi], *s.* die Aufsicht (*of,* über (*Acc.*)), (Ob)hut, Verwahrung, Bewachung, der Schutz, (*Law*) Gewahrsam, die Haft; – ***of a child,*** die Obhut *or* Aufsicht über ein Kind; ***in his* –**, in seiner Obhut, unter seinem Schutz; ***hand over to his* –**, ihm in Verwahrung geben; (*Law*) ***protective* –**, die Schutzhaft; (*Law*) ***remand in* –**, in Untersuchungshaft zurücksenden; (*Law*) ***take into* –**, verhaften, in Haft nehmen.

custom ['kʌstəm], **1.** *s.* 1. die Gewohnheit, Sitte, der Brauch; (*collect.*) Sitten (*pl.*), Bräuche (*pl.*), das Herkommen; (*Law*) Gewohnheitsrecht, fester Brauch; 2. (*Comm.*) Kunden (*pl.*), die Kundschaft, der Kundenkreis. **2.** *attrib. adj. See* **custom-built.**

customable ['kʌstəməbl], *adj.* zollpflichtig, abgabepflichtig, gebührenpflichtig.

customary ['kʌstəməri], *adj.* gebräuchlich, üblich, gewöhnlich, gewohnt, herkömmlich, Gewohnheits-.

custom-built, *adj.* einzeln *or* speziell angefertigt *or* gebaut.

customer ['kʌstəmə], *s.* der Kunde (die Kundin), der (die) Abnehmer(in), Käufer(in); *pl. See* **custom,** 2; (*coll.*) der Kerl, Bursche; (*coll.*) ***queer* –**, seltsamer Kerl; ***regular* –**, der Stammkunde, (*of restaurant etc.*) Stammgast; (*coll.*) ***rough* –**, roher Kunde.

customs ['kʌstəmz], *s.* der Zoll; das Zollamt; die Zollbehörde; – ***clearance,*** die Zollabfertigung; – ***declaration*** or ***entry,*** die Zollangabe, Zollerklärung; – ***examination,*** die Zollrevision; – ***house,*** das Zollamt; – ***officer,*** Zollbeamte(r); – ***union,*** der Zollverein, die Zollunion.

custos ['kʌstɔs], *s.* der Aufseher; – ***rotulorum,*** der Archivar.

cut [kʌt], **1.** *irr.v.t.* schneiden, durchschneiden, abschneiden, beschneiden, zerschneiden, zu(recht)schneiden; mähen (*grass, corn*), bohren (*tunnel*), stechen (*ditch*), schleifen (*gems*), hauen (*coal, stone*), (*Math.*) durchschneiden, durchstoßen, kreuzen (*a line*); (*fig., coll.*) kürzen, beschneiden.

(a) (*with nouns*) – ***a book,*** ein Buch aufschneiden; (*sl.*) – ***the cackle,*** das Schwatzen sein lassen, mit dem Gequatsche Schluß machen; – ***capers,*** Luftsprünge machen; – ***the cards,*** die Karten abheben; (*Prov.*) – ***one's coat according to one's cloth,*** sich nach der Decke strecken; – ***the umbilical cord,*** abnabeln; (*coll.*) – ***a dash,*** großtun; (*coll.*) – ***a figure,*** eine (bedeutende) Rolle spielen; – ***a film,*** einen Film edieren; – ***one's finger,*** sich in den Finger schneiden; – ***the ground from under his feet,*** ihm dem Boden unter den Füßen wegziehen; ***have one's hair* –**, sich (*Dat.*) die Haare schneiden lassen; – ***a hedge,*** eine Hecke stutzen *or* beschneiden; (*sl.*) ***it –s no ice with me,*** es läßt mich kalt, es macht auf mich gar keinen Eindruck; (*fig.*) – ***the (Gordian) knot,*** den (gordischen) Knoten durchhauen; (*coll.*) – ***a lecture,*** ein Kolleg schwänzen; (*Math.*) ***the lines* – *each other,*** die Linien schneiden sich; (*coll.*) – ***one's losses,*** die Verluste abschreiben *or* abbuchen; (*coll.*) – ***him (dead),*** ihn ignorieren *or* schneiden; (*fig.*) – ***the painter,*** sich loslösen, sich selbständig machen; (*coll.*) – ***the price,*** den Preis herabsetzen *or* drücken; (*Mount.*) – ***steps,*** Stufen schlagen; – ***one's teeth,*** zahnen, Zähne durchbrechen lassen; (*fig.*) – ***one's own throat,*** sich ins eigne Fleisch schneiden; – ***turf,*** Rasen stechen; (*fig.*) – ***one's way,*** sich (*Dat.*) einen Weg bahnen.

(b) (*with advs.*) – ***across,*** quer abschneiden; – ***away,*** abschneiden, abhauen, wegschneiden; – ***back,*** (*plants*) beschneiden, stutzen, (*fig.*) (*speed*) drosseln; – ***down,*** niederhauen; (*trees*) fällen, (*forests*) abholzen, (*crops*) mähen, (*troops*) niedermetzeln, zusammenhauen; (*fig.*) (*prices*) herabsetzen, senken, (*costs*) beschneiden, (ver)kürzen, verringen, einschränken, (*manuscript*) zusammenstreichen; (*coll.*) – ***it fine,*** in Zeitnot kommen, es auf den letzten Moment ankommen lassen; – ***in pieces,*** zerhauen; – ***in two,*** entzweischneiden, durchschneiden; – ***loose,*** lösen, trennen; (*fig.*) – ***o.s. loose from,*** sich lossagen von; – ***off,*** abschneiden, abhauen; (*supply*) absperren, abdrehen, abstellen; (*fig.*) trennen, ausschließen; – ***off an entail,*** die Beschränkung der Erbfolge aufheben; – ***off with a shilling,*** bis auf den letzten Pfennig enterben; – ***off his head,*** ihn köpfen; (*coll.*) – ***off one's nose to spite one's face,*** sich (*Dat.*) die Rache allzuviel kosten lassen; – ***off the enemy's retreat,*** dem Feinde den Rückzug abschneiden; ***be – off in one's prime,*** in den besten Jahren dahingerafft werden; – ***out,*** (her)ausschneiden, (*dresses etc.*) zuschneiden; (*fig.*) (*an opponent*) verdrängen, ausstechen, ausschalten; (*a th.*) entfernen, fernhalten, abstellen; (*Rad.*) – ***out interference,*** Störungen entfernen; (*coll.*) – ***it out!*** (unter)lassen Sie es! ***he is – out for it,*** er ist wie dafür *or* dafür wie geschaffen; ***he has his work – out,*** er hat (mehr als) genügend zu tun; (*fig.*) – ***short,*** plötzlich beenden; ***he – me short,*** er fiel mir ins Wort; ***to – a long story short,*** um es kurz zu machen; – ***to bits*** or ***pieces,*** in Stücke (zer)hauen, zerstückeln; (*fig.*) – ***him to the heart,*** ihm ins Herz schneiden, ihm in der Seele wehtun; – ***to the quick,*** (bis) ins Mark treffen, (*fig.*) aufs tiefste kränken *or* verwunden; – ***up,*** zerschneiden, zerlegen; (*coll.*) einer vernichtenden Kritik unterziehen, heruntermachen; (*coll.*) ***he was – up about it,*** er wurde darüber sehr betrübt *or* mitgenommen.

2. *irr.v.i.* schneiden, hauen; sich schneiden lassen; ***it –s both ways,*** es ist ein zweischneidiges Schwert; – ***and come again!*** greif tüchtig zu! (*coll.*) – ***and run,*** sich aus dem Staube machen; ***badly – about,*** übel hergerichtet; – ***across,*** einen kürzeren Weg einschlagen (durch); ***it –s across my plans,*** es steht in Widerspruch zu meinen Plänen, es läßt sich mit meinen Plänen nicht vereinbaren; – ***back,*** (*Films*) (zu)rückblenden; (*Cards*) – ***for deal,*** zum Geben abheben; – ***in,*** plötzlich eingreifen, unterbrechen, sich einmischen; (*Motor.*) sich (nach Überholen) wieder einreihen; (*Danc.*) abklatschen; – ***loose,*** alle Verbindungen abbrechen; (*Motor.*) – ***out,*** scharf ausbiegen zum Überholen; (*of engine*) aussetzen; (*sl.*) – ***up rough,*** rauhbeinig *or* grob werden.

3. *s.* 1. der Schnitt, Hieb, Stich; ***—and-thrust,*** das Hieb- und Stoßfechten; ***—and-thrust weapon,*** die Hieb- and Stoßwaffe; (*coll.*) ***that was an unfriendly* –**, das war ein unfreundlicher Seitenhieb; 2. der Schmiß, die Schnittwunde, Schmarre; (*coll.*) ***he's a – above me,*** er steht eine Stufe *or* ein gutes Stück über mir; (*coll.*) ***that's a – above me,*** das ist mir zu hoch; 3. der Kupferstich; Holzschnitt; 4. (*of clothes*) (Zu)schnitt, die Form, Fasson; ***I don't like the – of his jib,*** seine Nase paßt mir nicht; 5. der Einschnitt, Durchstich, kleiner Graben, die Rinne; der Kanal; 6. (*Tech.*) der Einschnitt, Anschnitt, Ritz, die Kerbe; 7. (*of meat etc.*) der Abschnitt, Aufschnitt, die Schnitte, das Stück(chen); 8. (*fig.*) (*of prices, wages etc.*) die Beschneidung, Kürzung, Senkung, der Abstrich, Abzug; (*in a play etc.*) die Streichung, Kürzung, Auslassung; ***short* –**, der Abkürzungsweg, Durchgang, die Weg(ab)kürzung; 9. (*coll.*) das Schneiden,

Nichtsehenwollen; 10. (*sl.*) der Anteil; (*sl.*) ***his – is at least 10%,*** sein Anteil ist *or* er bekommt wenigstens 10%; 11. (*Cards*) das Abheben; ***whose – is it?*** wer hebt ab?
4. *adj.* geschnitten, beschnitten; (*glass*) geschnitzt, geschliffen; ***– flowers,*** Schnittblumen (*pl.*); (*coll.*) ***– and dry*** or ***dried,*** fix und fertig, abgemacht; schablonenhaft; ***– horse,*** der Wallach.

cutaneous [kju:'teiniəs], *adj.* Haut–, kutan.

cut|-away, *adj.* Schnitt–; ***– view of the engine,*** der Motor im Schnitt. **–away,** *s.* der Cut(away), Herrenrock mit abgerundeten Vorderschößen. **--back,** *s.* 1. (*Films*) die Rückblende; 2. (*coll.*) Kürzung, Senkung, Einschränkung, der Abstrich, Abzug.

cute [kju:t], *adj.* (*coll.*) klug, schlau, scharfsinnig, aufgeweckt; (*esp. Am.*) nett, niedlich, hübsch, süß. **cutey** [–i], *s.* (*sl. esp. Am.*) fesches Mädel.

cuticle ['kju:tikl], *s.* die Oberhaut, Epidermis, (*also Bot.*) Kutikula.

cutlas(s) ['kʌtləs], *s.* das Entermesser.

cutler ['kʌtlə], *s.* der Messerschmied. **cutlery,** *s.* 1. das Messerschmiedhandwerk; 2. (*collect.*) Schneidewaren (*pl.*); das Eßbesteck, Tischbesteck.

cutlet ['kʌtlit], *s.* das Rippenstück, Rippchen, Kotelett, die Karbonade.

cut|-off, *s.* (*Elec.*) die (Ab)sperrung, Abschaltung, Ausschaltung; (*rockets*) der Brennschluß; (*Rad.*) ***– bias,*** die Sperrspannung; (*Elec.*) ***– point,*** der Sperrpunkt, die Sperrstelle; (*Elec.*) ***– time,*** die Abschaltperiode. **--out,** *s.* 1. der Ausschnitt; die Ausschnittstelle; Ausschneidefigur (*for children*); 2. (*Elec.*) der Ausschalter, Unterbrecher, automatische Sicherung. **--price, 1.** *s.* der Schleuderpreis. **2.** *adj.* ermäßigt, reduziert, Schleuder–. **–purse,** *s.* der Taschendieb, Beutelschneider.

cutter ['kʌtə], *s.* 1. (*Tail.*) der (die) Zuschneider(in); (*Films*) Schnittmeister(in); 2. (*Tech.*) die Schneidemaschine, das Schneidewerkzeug, der Schneidezahn, (*Cul.*) die Ausstechform; 3. (*Naut.*) der Kutter, das Beiboot; ***coastguard –,*** das Küstenwachfahrzeug. **cutter-head,** *s.* die Bohrkrone, der Messerkopf, (*of plane*) das Hobelmesser, (*of electric razor*) der Scherkopf.

cut-throat, 1. *s.* der Meuchelmörder, (*also fig.*) Halsabschneider. **2.** *adj.* (*usu. fig.*) mörderisch, halsabschneiderisch; ***– competition,*** mörderische Konkurrenz; ***– price,*** der Wucherpreis; (*coll.*) ***– razor,*** das Rasiermesser.

cutting ['kʌtiŋ], **1.** *s.* 1. das (Be)schneiden; (*of trees*) Fällen; (*Films*) der Schnitt; (*fig.*) das (Ver)kürzen, die Kürzung; 2. der Einschnitt, Ritz, Schlitz; (*Railw. etc.*) Durchstich; 3. Abschnitt, Ausschnitt; (*Hort.*) Ableger, Steckling, Setzling; *pl.* Späne (*pl.*), Abfälle (*pl.*), Schnitzel (*pl.*); ***newspaper –,*** der Zeitungsausschnitt; 4. ***– of the teeth,*** der Durchbruch der Zähne. **2.** *adj.* Schneid(e)–, Schnitt–, schneidend; (*fig.*) schneidend, beißend, scharf; (*fig.*) ***– glance,*** durchdringender Blick; (*fig.*) ***– remark,*** beißende Bemerkung; (*fig.*) ***– wind,*** schneidender Wind.

cutting|-angle, *s.* der Schneidewinkel, Schnittwinkel. **--board,** *s.* der Zuschneidetisch (*tailoring*). **--die,** *s.* die Schnittmatrize, Stanzschablone. **--edge,** *s.* die Schneide. **--line,** *s.* (*Typ.*) die Schnittlinie. **--out,** *s.* das Zuschneiden (*tailoring*); ***– board,*** *see* **--board. --tool,** *s.* das Schneidewerkzeug. **--torch,** *s.* der Schneidbrenner.

cuttle|-bone ['kʌtl], *s.* der (Kalk)schulp, das Blackfischbein. **–fish,** *s.* der Tintenfisch, Blackfisch, Kuttelfisch, gemeine Sepie.

cutwater ['kʌtwɔ:tə], *s.* 1. (*Naut.*) der Schegg, das Galion; 2. (*of bridge*) der Pfeilerkopf.

cwm [ku:m], *s. See* **coomb.**

cyanate ['saiəneit], *s.* zyansaures Salz. **cyanic** [–'ænik], *adj.* Zyan–, zyansauer. **cyanide** [–naid], *s.* das Zyanid; ***– of potash,*** das Zyankali. **cyanogen** [–'ænədʒin], *s* das Zyan.

cybernetic [saibə'netik], *adj.* kybernetisch. **cybernetics,** *pl.* (*sing. constr.*) die Kybernetik.

Cyclads ['saiklædz], *pl.* Zykladen (*pl.*).

cyclamen ['sikləmən], *s.* (*Bot.*) das Alpenveilchen.

cycle [saikl], **1.** *s.* 1. der Kreis(lauf), Zyklus, (*Phys., Elec.*) die Periode; (*Biol.*) der Entwicklungsgang; (*Chem.*) Ring, Kreisprozeß; (*Tech.*) Arbeitsgang, (Motor)takt; (*of publications etc.*) die Reihe, Folge, Serie; (*Motor.*) ***combustion –,*** der Verbrennungsvorgang; ***compression –,*** der Verdichtungstakt; ***exhaust –,*** der Auspufftakt; ***legendary –,*** der Sagenkreis; ***recurring in –s,*** periodisch wiederkehrend; (*Phys.*) ***–s per second,*** Perioden pro Sekunde; ***song –,*** der Liederzyklus; 2. (*coll.*) *see* **bicycle, tricycle. 2.** *v.i.* (*coll.*) radfahren, radeln.

cycle| car, *s.* der Kleinstwagen. **– track,** *s.* der Radfahrweg.

cyclic ['saiklik], *adj.* zyklisch, periodisch (*or* regelmäßig) wiederkehrend; (*Chem.*) Ring–, Zyklo–; (*Bot.*) zyklisch (angeordnet).

cycling ['saikliŋ], *s.* das Radfahren; der Radrennsport; ***– club,*** der Radfahrverein; ***– race,*** das Radrennen; ***– track,*** die Radrennstrecke. **cyclist,** *s.* der (die) Radfahrer(in).

cycloid ['saiklɔid], **1.** *s.* (*Geom.*) die Zykloide, Radlinie. **2.** *adj.* ringförmig, kreisförmig. **cycloidal** [–'klɔidl], *adj.* Zykloiden–, radlinig.

cyclometer [sai'klɔmitə], *s.* der Wegmesser.

cyclone ['saikloun], *s.* der Wirbelsturm; (*Meteor.*) das Tief(druckgebiet). **cyclonic** [–'klɔnik], *adj.* zyklonisch.

cyclop(a)edia [saiklo'pi:diə], *s.* die Enzyklopädie, das Konversationslexikon. **cyclop(a)edic,** *adj.* enzyklopädisch, umfassend, universal.

Cyclopean [saiklo'piən], *adj.* Zyklopen–; (*fig.*) zyklopisch, gigantisch, (*Archit.*) megalithisch. **cyclopia** [–'kloupiə], *s.* die Einäugigkeit. **Cyclops** ['saiklɔps], *s.* (*Myth.*) Zyklop (*m.*).

cyclostyle ['saiklostail], **1.** *s.* der Vervielfältigungsapparat. **2.** *v.t.* vervielfältigen.

cyclotron ['saiklətrɔn], *s.* das Zyklotron, der (Teilchen)beschleuniger.

cyder, (*obs.*) *see* **cider.**

cygnet ['signit], *s.* junger Schwan.

cylinder ['silində], *s.* (*Geom., Tech.*) der Zylinder, die Walze; (*Tech.*) der Trommel, die Rolle; (*Motor.*) der Zylinder; (*of a pump*) Stiefel; ***gas –,*** die Gasflasche. **cylindric(al)** [–'lindrik(l)], *adj.* (*Geom.*) zylindrisch, Zylinder–; (*Tech.*) zylinderförmig, walzenförmig.

cymbal [simbl], *s.* (*Mus.*) das Becken; (*organ*) die Zimbel.

cyme [saim], *s.* (*Bot.*) zymöser Blütenstand, die Trugdolde. **cymoid, cymose,** *adj.* zymös, trugdoldig.

Cymric ['kimrik, 'simrik], **1.** *adj.* walisisch, kymrisch. **2.** *s.* das Kymrisch(e) (*language*).

cynic ['sinik], *s.* der Zyniker, Spötter. **cynical,** *adj.* zynisch, spöttisch; verbittert. **cynicism** [–isizm], *s.* der Zynismus.

cynosure ['sainəʃuə], *s.* (*Astr.*) Kleiner Bär; (*fig.*) der Leitstern, die Richtlinie; der Anziehungspunkt.

cypher, (*obs.*) *see* **cipher.**

cypress ['saiprəs], *s.* (*Bot.*) die Zypresse.

Cyprian ['siprian], **1.** *s. See* **Cypriot(e). 2.** *adj.* zyprisch; ***– wine,*** der Zyperwein. **Cypriot(e)** [–iət], **1.** *s.* 1. der (die) Zyprer(in), Zypriot(in); 2. (*language*) das Zyprisch. **2.** *adj. See* **Cyprian. Cyprus** ['saiprəs], *s.* Zypern (*n.*).

Cyrillic [si'rilik], *adj.* kyrillisch.

cyrtosis [sə:'tousis], *s.* (*Med.*) die Rückgrat(s)-verkrümmung.

cyst [sist], *s.* (*Med.*) die Zyste; (*Anat., Zool., Bot.*) Blase, Kapsel, Hülle, Zelle. **cystic,** *adj.* (*Anat.*) (Gallen– *or* Harn)blasen–; ***– duct,*** der Gallenblasengang. **cystitis** [–'taitis], *s.* (*Med.*) die Blasenentzündung. **cystocele** ['sistəsi:l], *s.* (*Med.*) der (Harn)blasenbruch. **cystoid,** *adj.* blasenähnlich. **cystolith** [–əliθ], *s.* (*Med.*) der Blasenstein. **cystoma** [–'toumə], *s.* (*Med.*) zystische Geschwulst, die Sackgeschwulst. **cysto-**

scope [–əskoup], *s.* (*Med.*) der Blasenspiegel. **cystotomy** [–'tɔtəmi], *s.* (*Med.*) die Blaseneröffnung, der Blasen(stein)schnitt.

cyto– ['saito], *pref.* Zell(en)–. **cytoblast,** *s.* der Zellkern. **cytogenous** [–'tɔdʒinəs], *adj.* zellbildend. **cytoid,** *adj.* zellähnlich. **cytology** [–'tɔlədʒi], *s.* die Zellenlehre. **cytolysis** [–'tɔlisis], *s.* der Zellzerfall, die Zellauflösung.

czar [zɑ:], *s.* der Zar.

czardas ['tʃɑ:dæʃ], *s.* der Tschardasch.

czardom ['zɑ:dəm], *s.* das Zarenreich. **czarevitch** ['zɑ:rəvitʃ], *s.* der Zarewitsch. **czarina** [–'ri:nə], *s.* die Zarin.

Czech [tʃek], **1.** *s.* 1. der Tscheche (die Tschechin); 2. (*language*) das Tschechisch(e). **2. Czechish,** *adj.* tschechisch. **Czechoslovak** [–o'slouvæk], **1.** *s.* der (die) Tschechoslowak(in). **2.** *adj.* tschechoslowakisch. **Czechoslovakia** [–'vækiə], *s.* die Tschechoslowakei. **Czechoslovakian,** *s., adj. See* **Czechoslovak.**

D

D, d, *s.* das D, d (*also Mus.*); ***D flat,*** das Des, des; ***D major,*** D-Dur; ***D minor,*** d-Moll; ***D sharp,*** das Dis, dis. (*See Index of Abbreviations.*)

[1]**dab** [dæb], **1.** *v.t.* leicht schlagen, (*coll.*) antippen; betupfen, abtupfen; (*Tech.*) abklatschen, klischieren. **2.** *s.* der Klaps, Tupper, sanfter Schlag; das Klümpchen, der Klumpen, Klecks; (*coll.*) ***be a* – (*hand*) *at a th.,*** sich auf eine S. verstehen.

[2]**dab,** *s.* (*Ichth.*) die Kliesche.

dabber ['dæbə], *s.* der Tupfbeutel, Tupfer, (Watte)bausch, (*Typ.*) Farbballen, die Klopfbürste.

dabble [dæbl], **1.** *v.t.* benetzen, bespritzen. **2.** *v.i.* plätschern, planschen; sich aus Liebhaberei abgeben *or* befassen (*in,* mit); pfuschen (in (*Acc.*)), sich als Dilettant *or* sich dilettantisch beschäftigen (mit). **dabbler,** *s.* der Stümper, Pfuscher, Dilettant.

dabchick ['dæbtʃik], *s.* (*coll.*) der Zwergtaucher, (*Orn.*) Zwergsteißfuß (*Podiceps ruficollis*).

dace [deis], *s.* (*Ichth.*) der Hasel, Häsling.

dacoit [də'kɔit], *s.* der Bandit, Räuber.

dactyl ['dæktil], *s.* der Daktylus. **dactylic** [–'tilik], *adj.* daktylisch.

dactylogram [dæk'tiləgræm], *s.* der Fingerabdruck. **dactylology** [–'lɔlədʒi], *s.* die Fingersprache.

dad [dæd], **dada, daddy,** *s.* (*coll.*) der Vati, Papi. **daddy-long-legs,** *s.* (*Ent.*) langbeinige Spinne; die Bachmücke, der Kanker, Weberknecht.

dado ['deidou], *s.* untere Wandbekleidung *or* Wandbemalung *or* Wandtäfelung; (*Archit.*) der Postamentwürfel.

daemon, *see* **demon.**

daffodil ['dæfədil], *s.* gelbe Narzisse, (*coll.*) die Osterblume, der Märzbecher.

daft [dɑ:ft], *adj.* (*sl.*) albern, dämlich, einfältig; verdreht, verrückt, doof.

dagger ['dægə], *s.* der Dolch; (*Typ.*) das Kreuz(zeichen); ***look –s at,*** mit Blicken durchbohren; ***be at –s drawn,*** auf Kriegsfuß stehen.

dahlia ['deiljə], *s.* (*Bot.*) die Georgine, Dahlie.

daily ['deili], **1.** *adj.* täglich; ständig, tagtäglich, alltäglich, üblich; ***our – bread,*** unser täglich Brot; – (***help***), das Tagmädchen; – (***paper***), die Tageszeitung; ***the dailies,*** die Tagespresse. **2.** *adv.* täglich, Tag für Tag.

daintiness ['deintinis], *s.* die Niedlichkeit, Zierlichkeit; wählerisches Wesen, die Verwöhntheit; Geziertheit, Zimperlichkeit; (*of food*) Leckerhaftigkeit, Schmackhaftigkeit. **dainty, 1.** *adj.* niedlich, zierlich; wählerisch, verwöhnt, geziert, zimperlich; (*of food*) schmackhaft, delikat. **2.** *s.* der Leckerbissen; *pl.* das Naschwerk, Näschereien (*pl.*).

dairy ['dɛəri], *s.* der Milchraum (*of a farm*); die Milchwirtschaft, Molkerei, Meierei; Milchhandlung, das Milchgeschäft. **dairy| cattle,** *s.* das Milchvieh. **–-farm,** *s.* die Meierei, Milchwirtschaft. **–maid,** *s.* das Milchmädchen. **–-man,** *s.* der Milchhändler, Milchmann. **– produce,** *s.* Molkereiprodukte (*pl.*).

dais ['deiis], *s.* das Podium, die Estrade.

daisy ['deizi], **1.** *s.* (*Bot.*) das Gänseblümchen, Maßliebchen; ***as fresh as a* –,** quicklebendig; (*sl.*) ***push up the daisies,*** die Radieschen von unten wachsen sehen. **2.** *adj.* (*sl.*) großartig, prima. **daisy|-chain,** *s.* die Blumenkette. **–-cutter,** *s.* (*sl.*) das Pferd mit schleppendem Gang; (*sl.*) (*esp. Crick.*) der Bodenflitzer.

dale [deil], *s.* das Tal. **dalesman,** *s.* der Talbewohner.

dalliance ['dæliəns], *s.* die Tändelei, Spielerei; Bummelei, Trödelei, Zeitvergeudung; Verzögerung, der Aufschub; die Liebelei, das Geschäker. **dally,** *v.i.* tändeln, spielen, liebängeln; liebeln, schäkern; bummeln, Zeit vergeuden.

Dalmatian [dæl'meiʃən], **1.** *s.* der (die) Dalmatiner(in); der Dalmatiner (*dog*). **2.** *adj.* dalmat(in)isch.

Daltonism ['dɔ:ltənizm], *s.* die Farbenblindheit.

[1]**dam** [dæm], **1.** *s.* der Deich, (Stau)damm, das Wehr; die Talsperre; ***beaver* –,** das Biberwehr; ***coffer* –,** der Fangdamm, Kastendamm. **2.** *v.t.* (*also – up*) eindeichen, (ab)dämmen, eindämmen, stauen; (*fig.*) hemmen, (ab)sperren, blockieren.

[2]**dam,** *s.* die Mutter (*of animals*), das Muttertier; ***the devil's* –,** des Teufels Großmutter.

damage ['dæmidʒ], **1.** *s.* der Schaden (*oft. pl.* Schäden), die Beschädigung (*to,* an (*Dat.*)); *pl. See* **damages**; ***– by sea,*** die Havarie; ***do him* –,** ihm schaden, ihm Schaden zufügen; ***do – to a th.,*** eine S. beschädigen, einer S. Schaden anrichten, (*fig.*) einer S. schaden (*as reputation*); (*sl.*) ***what's the –?*** was macht die Zeche? **2.** *v.t.* (*a th.*) Schaden anrichten (*Dat.*), beschädigen; (*a p.*) schaden (*Dat.*), Schaden zufügen (*Dat.*), schädigen. **3.** *v.i.* ***it –s easily,*** es wird leicht beschädigt.

damageable ['dæmidʒəbl], *adj.* leicht zu beschädigen(d), zerbrechlich. **damaged,** *adj.* beschädigt, schadhaft. **damages,** *pl.* (*Law*) der Schadenersatz; ***assess* –,** Schadenersatzansprüche festsetzen; ***claim* –,** Schadenersatzansprüche stellen; ***pay* –,** Schadenersatz leisten; ***recover* –,** entschädigt werden, Schadenersatz erhalten. **damaging,** *adj.* schädlich, beeinträchtigend, nachteilig (*to,* für).

damascene [dæmə'si:n], **1.** *v.t.* damaszieren. **2.** *adj.* damasziert.

damask ['dæməsk], **1.** *s.* der Damast; ***linen* –,** das Damastleinen; ***silk* –,** die Damastseide. **2.** *adj.* damasten, rosarot; ***– carpet,*** der Damastteppich; ***– rose,*** die Damaszenerrose; ***– steel,*** der Damaszenerstahl. **3.** *v.t.* damaszieren (*steel*); damastieren, damastartig weben; (*fig.*) verzieren.

dame [deim], *s.* (*Poet.*) die Dame; (*as title*) Freifrau; (*sl.*) das Frauenzimmer, Weibsbild. **dame(s')-school,** *s.* (*obs.*) private Elementarschule.

damn [dæm], **1.** *v.t.* verdammen, verurteilen, verschreien, verwerfen, tadeln, in Verruf bringen; ***– me! – it!*** verdammt! verflucht! verwünscht! ***– you!*** hol' dich der Teufel! (*sl.*) ***know – all,*** gar nichts wissen; (*sl.*) ***a –(ed) sight too much,*** verflixt viel; ***the –ed,*** die Verdammten; (***I'll be***) ***–ed if,*** ich will verflucht sein wenn; ***– with faint praise,*** trotz freundlicher Aufnahme seine Ablehnung durchblicken lassen. **2.** *s.* (*coll.*) ***I don't care a*** (***twopenny***) **–,** ich schere mich den Teufel darum, es ist mir völlig schnuppe.

damnable ['dæmnəbl], *adj.* verdammenswürdig,

verwerflich, verdammlich; verdammt, verflucht, abscheulich. **damnation** [–ˈneiʃən], **1.** *s.* (*Eccl.*) die Verdammnis; Verdammung, Verurteilung, Verwerfung. **2.** *int.* verdammt! verwünscht! verflucht! **damnatory** [–nətəri], *adj.* verdammend, Verdammungs–. **damning** [ˈdæmiŋ], *adj.* verdammend, vernichtend, belastend.

damp [dæmp], **1.** *adj.* feucht; *– rot,* nasse Fäulnis. **2.** *s.* 1. die Feuchtigkeit; 2. *pl.* das Grubengas, der Schwaden. **3.** *v.t.* 1. anfeuchten, befeuchten, benetzen; 2. (*Elec., Mus., fig.*) dämpfen; – (***down***), (ab)dämpfen, (ab)schwächen, hemmen; ***– his spirits,*** ihn entmutigen, ihm die Stimmung trüben; ***–ed wave,*** gedämpfte Welle. **4.** *v.i.* feucht werden; ***– off,*** abfaulen (*of plants*).

damp-course, *s.* (*Build.*) die Schutzschicht, Sperrbahn. **dampen** [ˈdæmpən], **1.** *v.t.* anfeuchten, befeuchten, benetzen; (*fig.*) niederdrücken, niederschlagen, entmutigen. **2.** *v.i. See* **damp, 4. damper,** *s.* der Schieber, die Ofenklappe; der Zugregler (*of stoves etc.*); (*Elec. etc.*) die Dämpfung(svorrichtung); (*fig.*) Dämpfer; ***be a – to, cast a – on,*** dämpfen, entmutigen, lähmend wirken auf (*Acc.*). **damping,** *s.* (*Phys., Elec.*) die Dämpfung. **dampish,** *adj.* etwas feucht, dumpfig. **dampness,** *s.* die Feuchtigkeit. **damp-proof,** *adj.* feuchtigkeitsbeständig; gegen Feuchtigkeit geschützt.

damsel [ˈdæmzəl], *s.* (*Poet.*) junges Mädchen, das Fräulein, die Jungfrau.

damson [ˈdæmzən], *s.* die Damaszenerpflaume.

dance [dɑ:ns], **1.** *v.i.* tanzen; hüpfen (***with, for,*** vor (*Dat.*)); (*fig.*) ***– to his tune,*** nach seiner Pfeife tanzen. **2.** *v.t.* ***– a waltz,*** einen Walzer tanzen; (*fig.*) ***– attendance on him,*** bei ihm antichambrieren; ***– the baby up and down,*** das Kind schaukeln *or* wiegen. **3.** *s.* der Tanz; die Tanzgesellschaft, der Ball; ***– of death,*** der Totentanz; ***lead the –,*** den Reigen eröffnen; (*coll.*) ***lead him a –,*** ihn an der Nase herumführen, ihn zum Narren halten, ihn von Pontius zu Pilatus schicken; ***St. Vitus's –,*** der Veitstanz.

dance|-floor, *s.* der Tanzboden, die Tanzfläche. **--hall,** *s.* der Tanzsaal, das Tanzlokal. **--music,** *s.* die Tanzmusik. **dancer,** *s.* der (die) Tänzer(in).

dancing [ˈdɑ:nsiŋ], *s.* das Tanzen; die Tanzkunst. **dancing|-girl,** *s.* (berufsmäßige) Tänzerin. **--lesson,** *s.* die Tanzstunde. **--master,** *s.* der Tanzlehrer. **--school,** *s.* die Tanzschule.

dandelion [ˈdændilaiən], *s.* (*Bot.*) der Löwenzahn.

dander [ˈdændə], *s.* (*coll.*) der Zorn, Ärger; ***get his – up,*** ihn in Wut *or* Harnisch bringen.

dandified [ˈdændifaid], *adj.* 1. stutzerhaft, geckenhaft; 2. *See* **dandy, 2.**

dandle [dændl], *v.t.* auf dem Schoße *or* auf den Knien *or* in den Armen schaukeln (*a child*).

dandruff [ˈdændrʌf], *s.* der (Kopf)schorf, Kopfschuppen (*pl.*).

dandy [ˈdændi], **1.** *s.* 1. der Stutzer, Geck, Modenarr; 2. (*Naut.*) die Schaluppe mit Treibmast. **2.** *adj.* (*Am. sl.*) großartig, erstklassig. **dandyish,** *adj. See* **dandified. dandyism,** *s.* die Geckenhaftigkeit, Stutzerhaftigkeit. **dandy-roll,** *s.* (*Typ.*) die Draht(sieb)walze.

Dane [dein], *s.* 1. der Däne (die Dänin); 2. ***Great –,*** dänische Dogge.

danger [ˈdeindʒə], *s.* die Gefahr (*to,* für); Gefährdung, Bedrohung (*to, Gen.*); ***in – of death,*** in Todesgefahr; ***be in – of falling,*** Gefahr laufen, zu fallen; ***in case of –,*** im Falle der Not; ***go in – of one's life,*** in Lebensgefahr schweben; (*Naut.*) ***– angle,*** der Gefahrenwinkel; ***– area,*** das Alarmgebiet, Warngebiet; die Gefahrenzone, das Sperrgebiet; ***– point,*** der Gefahrenpunkt; ***– signal,*** das Notsignal; (*Mil.*) ***– zone,*** bestrichener Raum. **dangerous** [–rəs], *adj.* gefährlich, gefahrvoll (***to,*** *Dat. or* für).

dangle [dæŋgl], **1.** *v.i.* (herab)hängen, baumeln; ***– after girls,*** den Mädchen nachlaufen. **2.** *v.t.* baumeln lassen, schlenkern.

Danish [ˈdeiniʃ], **1.** *adj.* dänisch. **2.** *s.* (*language*) das Dänisch(e).

dank [dæŋk], *adj.* dunstig, dumpfig, feucht, naßkalt.

danseuse [dɑ:nˈsə:z], *s.* die Ballettänzerin.

Danube [ˈdænju:b], *s.* die Donau. **Danubian** [–ˈnju:biən], *adj.* Donau–.

dapper [ˈdæpə], *adj.* nett, adrett, schmuck, flink.

dapple [dæpl], *v.t.* sprenkeln, tupfeln, scheckig machen. **dappled,** *adj.* gesprenkelt, gefleckt, scheckig.

dapple-grey, **1.** *adj.* apfelgrau. **2.** *s.* (*horse*) der Apfelschimmel.

darbies [ˈdɑ:biz], *pl.* (*sl.*) Handschellen (*pl.*).

dare [dɛə], **1.** *v.i.* es wagen, sich erkühnen, sich erdreisten, sich getrauen, sich unterstehen; ***he – not do it, he does not – to do it,*** er wagt es nicht zu tun; ***if I may – to say so,*** wenn ich so sagen darf; ***I – say,*** ich darf wohl behaupten, ich glaube wohl; ***I – not tell him,*** ich getraue mich *or* mir nicht, es ihm zu sagen; ***how – you?*** wie können Sie sich unterstehen? **2.** *v.t.* (*a p.*) herausfordern, trotzen (*Dat.*), Trotz bieten (*Dat.*); (*a th.*) wagen, sich heranwagen an (*Acc.*), unternehmen, riskieren.

dare|-devil, **1.** *s.* der Teufelskerl, Wagehals. **2.** *adj.* wag(e)halsig, tollkühn. **–devilry,** *s.* die Tollkühnheit, Wagehalsigkeit, Verwegenheit.

daren't [dɛənt] = ***dare not.***

daring [ˈdɛəriŋ], **1.** *adj.* kühn, tapfer, wagemutig, verwegen; dreist, unverschämt, anmaßend. **2.** *s.* die Kühnheit, der (Wage)mut.

dark [dɑ:k], **1.** *adj.* dunkel, finster; brünett (*hair*); (*fig.*) unerforschlich, geheimnisvoll, verborgen, unklar, unaufgeklärt; trostlos, düster, finster, trübe; böse, verbrecherisch (*deed*); ***the Dark Ages,*** frühes Mittelalter; ***the – continent,*** der dunkle Erdteil; ***– glasses,*** die Schutzbrille; (*coll.*) ***he is a – horse,*** er hat es dick hinter den Ohren; ***keep s.th –,*** etwas geheimhalten; ***– lantern,*** die Blendlaterne; ***look on the – side,*** schwarzsehen, nur die Schattenseite sehen; (*Phot.*) ***– slide,*** die Kassette. **2.** *s.* das Dunkel, die Dunkelheit, Finsternis; *pl.* (*Paint.*) Schatten (*pl.*); ***after –,*** nach Eintritt der Dunkelheit; (*fig.*) ***keep*** or ***leave him in the –,*** ihn im ungewissen lassen; ***a leap in the –,*** ein Sprung ins Ungewisse; ***I'm still in the –,*** ich tappe noch im dunkeln.

darken [dɑ:kn], **1.** *v.t.* verdunkeln, verfinstern; dunkler machen, nachdunkeln, abdunkeln (*colours*); (*fig.*) verdüstern, trüben, schwärzen; ***I shall never – his doors again,*** ich werde seine Schwelle nie wieder betreten. **2.** *v.i.* sich verdunkeln *or* verfinstern, dunkler *or* dunkel werden; (*fig.*) sich verdüstern *or* trüben. **darkish,** *adj.* schwärzlich (*of colour*); etwas dunkel, trübe; dämmerig.

darkling [ˈdɑ:kliŋ], (*Poet.*) **1.** *adv.* im Dunkeln. **2.** *adj.* dunkel; (*fig.*) düster. **darkly,** *adv.* (*usu. fig.*) geheimnisvoll, insgeheim, heimlich. **darkness,** *s.* die Finsternis, Dunkelheit; (*fig.*) Unwissenheit, Unklarheit, Undeutlichkeit; Heimlichkeit, Verborgenheit; ***powers of –,*** die Mächte der Finsternis. **darkroom,** *s.* (*Phot.*) die Dunkelkammer. **darksome** [–səm], *adj.* (*Poet.*) finster, dunkel, trübe.

darling [ˈdɑ:liŋ], **1.** *adj.* teuer, lieb, (aller)liebst, Herzens–, Lieblings–. **2.** *s.* der Liebling, Schatz, Liebste(r), Geliebte(r); (*coll.*) ***be a –!*** sei ein Engel! ***– of fortune,*** das Glückskind.

[1]**darn** [dɑ:n], (*coll.*) *see* **damn.**

[2]**darn,** **1.** *v.t.* stopfen, ausbessern. **2.** *s.* das Gestopfte, gestopftes Loch.

darnel [dɑ:nl], *s.* (*Bot.*) der Lolch.

darner [ˈdɑ:nə], *s.* 1. die Stopfnadel; 2. das Stopfei, die Stopfkugel, der Stopfpilz. **darning,** *s.* das Stopfen, die Stopfarbeit; ***– needle,*** *see* **darner,** 1; ***– wool,*** die Stopfwolle, das Stopfgarn.

dart [dɑ:t], **1.** *s.* 1. der Wurfspieß, Speer; Pfeil; *pl.* das Pfeilwurfspiel; 2. (*Dressm.*) abgenähte Falte, der Abnäher; 3. plötzliche Bewegung, der Sturz, Sprung, Satz; ***make a – for,*** losstürzen auf (*Acc.*). **2.** *v.t.* schleudern, werfen; schießen; ***– a glance at him,*** ihm einen Blick zuwerfen. **3.** *v.i.* fliegen, schießen, stürzen, losstürmen (***at, on,*** auf

(*Acc.*)), herfallen (über (*Acc.*)); – ***forth,*** hervorschießen, hervorbrechen (***from,*** aus); – ***off,*** davonschießen. **dartboard,** *s.* das Zielbrett fürs Pfeilwurfspiel. **darter,** *s.* (*Orn.*) der Schlangenhalsvogel; (*Ichth.*) Spritzfisch.

dash [dæʃ], **1.** *v.t.* schlagen, stoßen; schmeißen, schleudern, werfen; übergießen, bespritzen, besprengen; (*fig.*) zerschlagen, zerschmettern, zerstören, vernichten, vereiteln; vermischen, vermengen; – ***his brains out,*** – ***out his brains,*** ihm den Schädel einschlagen; – ***his hopes,*** seine Hoffnungen zunichte machen; – ***a pen through the line,*** die Zeile durchstreichen; – ***his spirits,*** ihn niederschlagen *or* entmutigen; (*coll.*) – ***s.th. off,*** etwas flüchtig entwerfen *or* aufs Papier werfen *or* in aller Eile schreiben; – ***water in his face,*** sein Gesicht mit Wasser bespritzen, ihm Wasser ins Gesicht spritzen; (*coll.*) – ***it!*** verwünscht! **2.** *v.i.* (sich) stürzen, stürmen, jagen; – ***about,*** umherjagen; – ***against,*** (*of a th.*) aufschlagen, prallen, stoßen; (*of a p.*) sich stürzen *or* rennen gegen *or* an (*Acc.*), (*fig.*) scheitern (an (*Dat.*)); – ***away,*** davonstürzen, wegeilen; – ***into,*** hineinstürzen *or* einbrechen in (*Acc.*); – ***off,*** hinwegeilen, dahinsprengen; – ***out,*** hinausstürzen; (*coll.*) – ***out for a minute,*** auf einen Augenblick hinausgehen; – ***over,*** überlaufen; ***the water –ed over the ship's side,*** das Wasser stürzte über die Seiten des Schiffes. **3.** *s.* **1.** der (Auf)-schlag, Prall, das Prallen, Fallen; der Sturm, Anlauf, Vorstoß; ***make a – for,*** losstürzen auf (*Acc.*); ***at one –,*** mit einem Schlage *or* Zuge, auf einmal; 2. (*fig.*) die Kühnheit, der Schneid, Elan, Glanz, die Eleganz; ***cut a –,*** eine Rolle spielen, von sich reden machen; 3. der Federstrich, Gedankenstrich; (*Mus., Tele.*) Strich; 4. (*fig.*) Zusatz, Schuß; Anflug; ***coffee (with) –,*** Kaffee verkehrt; (*coll.*) ***a – of eccentricity,*** ein Anflug von Überspanntheit; ***a – of red,*** ein Stich ins Rote.

dashboard ['dæʃbɔ:d], *s.* das Armaturenbrett, Schaltbrett, Instrumentenbrett. **dasher,** *s.* 1. der Butterstößel; 2. (*Am.*) *see* **dashboard. dashing,** *adj.* 1. schneidig, forsch, ungestüm, feurig, stürmisch (*attack*); klatschend, platschend, rauschend; 2. (*coll.*) elegant, glänzend, fesch, patent.

dastard ['dæstəd], *s.* der Feigling, die Memme. **dastardliness,** *s.* die Feigheit. **dastardly,** *adj.* feig(e), memmenhaft; heimtückisch.

data ['deitə], *pl. of* **datum**; Werte, Daten (*pl.*); Angaben, Unterlagen, Grundlagen, Einzelheiten (*pl.*); ***personal –,*** Personalien (*pl.*); – ***processing,*** die Datenverarbeitung.

[1]**date** [deit], **1.** *s.* das Datum, die Zeitangabe; der Monatstag, die Jahreszahl; Zeit, Periode, Epoche, der Zeitraum, Zeitpunkt; (*Comm.*) Termin, die Frist, Verfall(s)zeit; (*coll.*) Verabredung, das Rendezvous; (*sl.*) der (die) Verabredungspartner(in); (*Comm.*) ***two months after –,*** zwei Monate nach dato von heute; ***at an early –,*** in nicht zu langer Zeit; (*Comm.*) ***at a long –,*** auf lange Sicht; ***fix a –,*** einen Termin festsetzen, eine Frist bestimmen; (*sl.*) ***make a –,*** sich verabreden; ***of this –,*** vom heutigen Datum; ***of recent –,*** modern, neu(eren Datums); ***out of –,*** überholt, veraltet; ***(down) to –,*** bis auf den heutigen Tag; ***up to –,*** zeitgemäß, modern, auf der Höhe der Zeit; ***what is today's –?*** der wievielte ist heute? **2.** *v.t.* datieren; herleiten (***from,*** von *or* aus); eine Zeit bestimmen *or* angeben *or* ansetzen *or* festsetzen für; (*coll.*) sich verabreden mit; (*coll.*) ***we've got him –d,*** wir kennen unsere Pappenheimer. **3.** *v.i.* das Datum tragen, datiert sein; (*coll.*) veraltert *or* überholt wirken, sich überlebt haben; – ***back,*** zurückreichen (***to,*** bis in (*Acc.*)), zurückgehen (auf (*Acc.*)); – ***from,*** sich herleiten aus, stammen aus, entstanden sein *or* seinen Ursprung haben in (*Dat.*).

[2]**date,** *s.* die Dattel.

dateless ['deitlis], *adj.* ohne Datum, undatiert; zeitlos.

date-line, *s.* die Datumsgrenze.

date-palm, *s.* die Dattelpalme.

date-stamp, *s.* der Poststempel, Datumstempel.

dative ['deitiv], **1.** *s.* (– *case*) der Wemfall, Dativ. **2.** *adj.* 1. dativisch, Dativ–; 2. (*Law*) verfügbar, vergebbar, absetzbar; gerichtlich ernannt, übertragen.

datum ['deitəm], *s.* (*pl.* **data**) (*Math.*) gegebene Tatsache *or* Größe; die Grundlage, Voraussetzung, Prämisse; – ***line,*** die Grundlinie, Standlinie; – ***point,*** der Bezugspunkt.

daub [dɔ:b], **1.** *v.t.* verputzen, bewerfen; beschmieren, verschmieren, überstreichen (*a wall etc.*), streichen, schmieren (***on,*** auf (*Acc.*)), verschmieren (auf (*Dat.*)) (*mud etc.*); (*fig.*) beschmutzen, besudeln. **2.** *v.i.* (*Paint.*) schmieren, klecksen. **3.** *s.* 1. der Klecks; (*Paint.*) die Kleckserei, Schmiererei, das Geschmiere; 2. (*Build.*) der (Rauh)putz. **dauber,** *s.* der Schmierer, Farbenkleckser.

daughter ['dɔ:tə], *s.* die Tochter. **daughter-in-law,** *s.* die Schwiegertochter.

daunt [dɔ:nt], *v.t.* entmutigen, einschüchtern, schrecken. **dauntless,** *adj.* furchtlos, unerschrocken.

davenport ['dævnpɔ:t], *s.* der Schreibtisch, Sekretär.

davit ['dævit], *s.* (*usu. pl.*) (*Naut.*) der Davit, Bootskran.

davy ['deivi], *s.* (*coll.*) der Eid; (*coll.*) ***on my –!*** auf mein Wort.

Davy Jones's locker, *s.* (*coll.*) das Grab in Meerestiefe.

daw [dɔ:], *s.* (*Orn.*) (*coll.*) die Dohle.

dawdle [dɔ:dl], **1.** *v.i.* bummeln, herumtrödeln. **2.** *v.t.* – ***one's time away,*** die Zeit vertrödeln *or* totschlagen. **3.** *s.* die Bummelei, Zeitvergeudung; (*coll.*) *see* **dawdler. dawdler,** *s.* der Müßiggänger, Bummler, Trödler, Tagedieb, die Schlafmütze.

dawn [dɔ:n], **1.** *s.* die (Morgen)dämmerung, das Morgengrauen, der Tagesanbruch; (*fig.*) Beginn, Anfang, Anbruch, das Anbrechen, Dämmern, Erwachen; ***at the crack of –,*** bei Tagesanbruch; – ***of hope,*** erster Hoffnungsschimmer; – ***chorus,*** der Frühgesang. **2.** *v.i.* dämmern, tagen; (*fig.*) heraufdämmern, erwachen; ***when day –ed,*** als der Tag anbrach; ***it –ed upon me,*** es kam mir zum Bewußtsein, es ging mir ein Licht auf, es wurde mir klar (daß . . .). **dawning, 1.** *s.* (*Poet.*) *see* **dawn, 1. 2.** *adj.* dämmernd, beginnend, anbrechend, erwachend.

day [dei], *s.* der Tag; das Tageslicht; (*oft. pl.*) die (Lebens)zeit; der Termin, festgesetzter Tag; ***all (the) – (long),*** den ganzen Tag; (*coll.*) ***she has seen her best –s,*** sie ist nicht mehr die jüngste; ***every –,*** alle Tage; ***every second*** or ***other –,*** alle zwei Tage, einen Tag um den andern; ***end one's –s,*** sterben; ***fall on evil –s,*** ins Unglück geraten; ***the good old –s,*** die gute alte Zeit; ***–s of grace,*** (*Law*) Verzugstage, (*Comm.*) Respekttage; ***have had one's –,*** überlebt sein; ***every dog has his –,*** jedem lacht einmal das Glück; ***intercalary –,*** der Schalttag; ***one –,*** eines Tages, einst; ***one of these –s,*** eines schönen Tages, demnächst, nächstens; ***the other –,*** neulich; ***order of the –,*** die Tagesordnung; ***some –,*** eines Tages, der(mal)einst (*future time*); ***some – or other,*** irgendeinmal; ***student –s,*** die Studentenzeit; ***what's the time of –?*** wie spät ist es? (*coll.*) ***know the time of –,*** wissen was es geschlagen hat, (genau) Bescheid wissen; ***win the –,*** den Sieg davontragen.

(a) (*other idioms*) – ***and – about,*** jeden zweiten Tag; (*coll.*) ***call it a –!*** mach Schluß! laß es jetzt genug sein! (*coll.*) ***that will be the –,*** ich halte das nicht für wahrscheinlich; ***thirty if a –,*** mindestens 30 Jahre alt; ***this many a –,*** jetzt schon lange Zeit; ***this – week,*** heute über acht Tage; ***this – last week,*** heute vor acht Tagen; ***these –s,*** heutzutage; ***twice a –,*** zweimal am Tage.

(b) (*with preps. or advs.*) ***the – after,*** am nächsten Tag, tags darauf; ***the – after tomorrow,*** übermorgen; – ***after –,*** see – ***by –***; (*fig.*) ***at the end of the –,*** letzten Endes; – ***by –,*** Tag für Tag, (tag)-täglich; ***the – before,*** der vorhergehende Tag, tags zuvor, am Tag vorher; ***the – before yesterday,*** vorgestern; ***by –,*** bei Tage; ***by the –,*** tageweise;

for ever and a –, für immer und ewig; *from this – forth* or *forward,* von heute an; *from – to –,* von Tag zu Tag, zusehends; *from one – to another,* von einem Tag zum andern; *in all my born –s,* mein Lebtag; *in his –,* (zu) seiner Zeit, in seinen Tagen; *in this – and age,* zu der heutigen Zeit; *in those –s,* damals; *– in – out,* tagaus tagein; *in these –s,* heutzutage; *in (the) –s of old,* vormals, einst, in alten Zeiten; *in –s to come,* in zukünftigen Zeiten; *late in the –,* reichlich spät; (*coll.*) *all in a –'s work,* das muß man mit in Kauf nehmen, es gehört alles mit dazu; (*Comm.*) *– to – money,* tägliches Geld; *to a –,* (genau) auf den Tag; *to this –,* bis auf den heutigen Tag.

day|-bed, *s.* das Ruhebett, die Chaiselongue. **--boarder,** *s.* der Halbpensionär, Tagesschüler. **-book,** *s.* (*Comm.*) das Tagebuch, Journal. **--boy,** *s.* Externe(r). **-break,** *s.* der Tagesanbruch, die Morgendämmerung, das Morgengrauen. **-dream,** **1.** *s.* wacher Traum, der Wachtraum, die Träumerei; *pl.* Phantasiegebilde, Luftschlösser. **2.** *v.i.* Luftschlösser bauen. **--fly,** *s.* die Eintagsfliege. **--labourer,** *s.* der Tag(e)löhner. **-light,** *s.* das Tageslicht, Sonnenlicht; (*fig.*) der Abstand, Zwischenraum; *before –,* vor dem Morgengrauen; (*Phot.*) *– printing paper,* das Lichtpauspapier; *– saving,* die Sommerzeit, vorverlegte Stundenzählung; *in broad –,* am hellichten Tage; *as clear as –,* sonnenklar; (*fig.*) *he begins to see –,* ihm geht ein Licht auf. **--nursery,** *s.* die Kinderkrippe, der Kleinkindergarten. **--off,** *s.* freier Tag. **--out,** *s.* der Ausgang. **--scholar,** *s.* *See* **--boy.** **--school,** *s.* die Tagesschule; das Externat. **--shift,** *s.* die Tagschicht.

day's|-journey, *s.* die Tagereise. **– run,** *s.* (*Naut.*) das Etmal.

day-star, *s.* der Morgenstern.

day's-work, *s.* das Tagewerk.

day|-ticket, *s.* die Tagesrückfahrkarte. **-time,** *s.* der Tag, die Tageszeit; *in the –,* bei Tage. **--work,** *s.* die Tagarbeit.

daze [deiz], **1.** *v.t.* blenden; betäuben, verwirren. **2.** *s.* die Betäubung, Verwirrung, Bestürzung, Benommenheit; *be in a –,* verwirrt *or* benommen sein. **dazed,** *adj.* betäubt, benommen.

dazzle [dæzl], *v.t.* blenden (*also fig.*), (*fig.*) verblüffen. **dazzle-painting,** *s.* (*Mil.*) die Tarnung. **dazzling,** *adj.* blendend, (*fig.*) verblüffend.

deacon ['di:kən], *s.* der Diakon(us). **deaconess,** *s.* die Diakonisse. **deaconry.** *s.* das Diakonat.

dead [ded], **1.** *adj.* tot, gestorben (*of persons*); leblos, geistlos, kraftlos, wirkungslos (*of things*); unempfänglich, unzugänglich (*to,* für), gleichgültig, abgestumpt, unempfindlich (*to,* gegen); leer, öde (*of a district*); verwelkt, abgestorben, dürr (*as plants*); (*Comm.*) unbelebt, still, flau; glanzlos, matt, trüb, stumpf, unbelebt (*of colours*); klanglos, dumpf (*of sound*); ausgestorben, erloschen (*as volcano, feelings etc.*); verloschen (*as a fire*); tief (*of sleep*); (*Mil.*) *– angle,* toter Winkel; *– ball,* der Ball außer Spiel; (*coll.*) *– bargain,* der Spottpreis; spottbillige Ware; *– body,* die Leiche, der Leichnam; *– calm,* völlige Windstille, die Flaute; (*Tech.*) *– centre,* die Totlage, toter Punkt; (*coll.*) *– certainty,* völlige Gewißheit; *– colouring,* die Grundierung; (*as*) *– as a doornail,* mausetot; *in – earnest,* in vollem Ernst; *– faint,* tiefe Ohnmacht; *– gold,* mattes Gold; (*Mil.*) *– ground,* toter Winkel(bereich); *– heat,* totes *or* unentschiedenes Rennen; (*coll.*) *flog a – horse,* sich aussichtslos bemühen; sich vergeblich anstrengen; *– language,* tote Sprache; *– level,* einförmige Ebene; (*fig.*) die Eintönigkeit; *in a – (straight) line,* schnurgerade; *– load,* die Eigenbelastung, das Eigengewicht; (*coll.*) *– loss,* der Totalverlust; *be a – man,* ein Kind des Todes sein; *– matter,* tote Materie, (*Typ.*) der Ablegesatz; (*sl.*) *– men,* leere Flaschen; *wait for – men's shoes,* lange auf Beförderung warten; *– men tell no tales,* die Toten verraten nichts; *as – as mutton,* mausetot; *– point,* see *– centre*; *– reckoning,* (*Naut.*) die Gissung, gegißtes Besteck, der Koppelkurs; (*fig.*) ungefähre Berechnung; (*Naut.*) *position by – reckoning,* gegißter *or* gekoppelter Standort; *Dead Sea,* Totes Meer; (*fig.*) *Dead Sea apples* or *fruit,* Sodomsäpfel (*pl.*), die Täuschung, täuschender Reiz; *– season,* geschäftslose Zeit; (*coll.*) *– secret,* tiefes Geheimnis; (*Hunt.*) *– set,* das Stehen; (*fig.*) *make a – set at,* energisch angreifen; beharrlich werben um; (*coll.*) *– shot,* unfehlbarer Schütze; *– silence,* die Totenstille; *– sleep,* tiefer *or* todähnlicher Schlaf; *– steam,* der Ab(gangs)dampf; *– stock,* totes Inventar; (*Comm.*) unverkaufbare Waren (*pl.*); *come to a – stop,* plötzlich anhalten; *strike –,* erschlagen; *– water,* der Sog, das Kielwasser; *– weight,* das Eigengewicht; (*fig.*) drückende Last; *– wood,* das Reisig; (*fig.*) Veraltete(s), Überholte(s); wertloser Plunder.
2. *adv.* völlig, ganzlich, restlos, absolut; *be – against,* restlos voreingenommen gegen; (*coll.*) *– beat,* gänzlich erschöpft, kaputt; (*coll.*) *cut him –,* ihn schneiden, ihn wie Luft behandeln; *– drunk,* völlig betrunken; *– opposite,* genau gegenüber (*to, Dat. or* von); (*sl.*) *– right,* absolut richtig; *– slow,* (*Naut.*) langsame Fahrt; (*fig.*) ganz langsam; *stop –,* plötzlich stehenbleiben; *– straight,* schnurgerade; *– sure,* todsicher; *– tired,* todmüde.
3. *s.* 1. die Totenstille; *in the – of (the) night,* mitten in der Nacht; *in the – of winter,* im tiefsten Winter; 2. *the –,* Tote (*pl.*); *risen from the –,* von den Toten *or* vom Tode auferstanden.

dead|(-and)-alive, *adj.* halbtot, langweilig. **-beat,** *adj.* (*Phys.*) aperiodisch (gedämpft). **--beat,** *s.* (*sl.*) (*Am.*) der Schorrer, Nassauer.

deaden [dedn], *v.t.* (ab)schwächen, dämpfen, (*of sounds, feelings etc.*) abtöten, abstumpfen (*to,* gegen); (*gold etc.*) mattieren, abmatten.

dead|-end, **1.** *s.* die Sackgasse. **2.** *adj.* (*coll.*) ausweglos; (*of job*) aussichtslos; (*Am.*) *– kid,* verwahrlostes (Stadt)kind. **--eye,** *s.* (*Naut.*) die Jungfer. **-head,** *s.* (*sl.*) der (die) Frei(fahr)karteninhaber(in); blinder Passagier. **--letter,** *s.* 1. ungültig gewordenes Gesetz; 2. unzustellbarer Brief; *– office,* das Amt für unzustellbare Briefe. **-light,** *s.* (*Naut.*) der Lukendeckel, die Fensterblende. **-line,** *s.* der Drucktermin, Redaktionsschluß; Stichtag; (*fig.*) äußerster Termin.

deadliness ['dedlinis], *s.* die Tödlichkeit, das Tödliche.

deadlock ['dedlɔk], *s.* 1. das Einriegelschloß; 2. (*fig.*) der Stillstand, vollige Stockung; *break the –,* den toten Punkt überwinden; *come to a –,* steckenbleiben, sich festfahren, auf ein totes Gleis kommen, auf einem toten Punkt gelangen.

deadly ['dedli], *adj.* tödlich, todbringend; giftig, äußerst schädlich; Todes–, totenähnlich; (*fig.*) Tod–, unversöhnlich; (*coll.*) äußerst, außerordentlich; *– enemy,* der Todfeind; *– pale,* totenblaß, leichenblaß; *– pallor,* die Todesblässe; *– sin,* die Todsünde; *– tired,* todmüde. **deadly-nightshade,** *s.* (*Bot.*) die Tollkirsche.

dead-march, *s.* der Trauermarsch.

deadness ['dednis], *s.* die Erstarrung, Leblosigkeit; (*fig.*) Leere, Öde, Eintönigkeit, (*of sound*) Klanglosigkeit, Dumpfheit, (*of colour*) Glanzlosigkeit, Mattheit, (*of trade*) Unbelebtheit, Flauheit, Mattheit; Empfindungslosigkeit, Kälte, Gleichgültigkeit, Abgestumpftheit.

dead|-nettle, *s.* (*Bot.*) die Taubnessel. **--pan,** **1.** *adj.* ausdruckslos, dämlich. **2.** *s.* (*sl.*) das Schafsgesicht, (*of comedian*) der Ölgötze.

deaf [def], *adj.* taub, schwerhörig; *– as a post,* stocktaub; *– and dumb,* taubstumm; (*fig.*) *turn a – ear to,* taub sein gegen; *– in one ear,* auf einem Ohr taub; (*fig.*) *fall on – ears,* kein Gehör finden; (*fig.*) *– to,* taub gegen, unzugänglich für. **deafen** [-n], *v.t.* taub machen, (*fig.*) betäuben (*with,* durch). **deaf-mute,** **1.** *adj.* taubstumm. **2.** *s.* Taubstumme(r). **deafness,** *s.* die Taubheit, Schwerhörigkeit; (*fig.*) Taubheit (*to,* gegen), Unzugänglichkeit (für).

[1]**deal** [di:l], **1.** *irr.v.t.* (*usu. – out*) austeilen, verteilen; zuteilen, zukommen lassen; (*Cards*) geben; *– him a blow,* ihm einen Schlag versetzen. **2.** *irr.v.i.*

handeln, Handel treiben (*in*, mit); (*Cards*) geben; – ***in foodstuffs,*** Lebensmittel führen; – ***in politics,*** sich mit Politik abgeben; – ***with*** (*a th.*), (*of a p.*) behandeln, sich befassen *or* beschäftigen mit, zu tun haben mit; (*of a subject*) handeln von, sich befassen mit, zum Thema haben; – ***with*** (*a p.*), verfahren *or* umgehen mit, sich verhalten gegen, handeln an (*Dat.*), behandeln; verkehren *or* zu tun haben mit, Beziehung haben zu; (*Comm.*) Geschäftsverbindung haben *or* in Geschäftsverkehr stehen *or* Handel treiben *or* Geschäfte machen mit, kaufen bei; (*coll.*) – ***with*** (*a p. or a th.*), fertig werden mit, erledigen; ***I will – with it at once,*** ich nehme es sofort in Angriff; – ***fairly with him,*** anständig an ihm handeln, sich anständig gegen ihn verhalten, ihn anständig behandeln; ***it was –t with out of hand,*** es wurde kurz abgefertigt, man machte kurzen Prozeß damit. **3.** *s.* 1. (*Cards*) das (Karten)geben; ***it's my –,*** ich muß geben; 2. (*Comm.*) (*coll.*) der Handel; das Geschäft; die Übereinkunft, Abmachung, das Abkommen; (*coll.*) ***do a – with,*** einen Abschluß machen mit; (*coll.*) ***a fair –,*** anständige Behandlung; (*sl.*) ***a raw –,*** unfaire Behandlung; ***the New Deal,*** (Roosevelts) wirtschaftliche Reformpolitik; (*coll.*) ***it's a –!*** abgemacht! es gilt!

[2]**deal,** *s.* die Menge; (*usu. with attrib. adj.*) ***a good –,*** eine ganze Menge, ziemlich viel; ***a*** (***good***) ***– better,*** entschieden *or* erheblich besser; ***a good – of sense,*** ein gut Stück Verstand; ***a great –,*** sehr viel; ***make a great – of him,*** viel Wesens von ihm machen; ***think a great – of him,*** ihn hochschätzen, große Stücke auf ihn halten.

[3]**deal, 1.** *s.* die Diele, Bohle, das Brett (*of pine wood*); das Tannenholz, Kiefernholz. **2.** *adj.* Kiefern–, Tannen–.

dealer [ˈdiːlə], *s.* 1. der Händler, Krämer, Kaufmann, Handeltreibende(r); 2. (*Cards*) (Karten)geber. **dealing,** *s.* 1. (*Cards*) das Geben, Austeilen; 2. (*usu. pl.*) Verfahren, Verhalten, die Handlungsweise; der Umgang, Verkehr, Verbindungen (*pl.*); (*Comm.*) das Geschäft, der Handel(sverkehr); ***have –s with him,*** mit ihm zu tun haben; ***there's no – with him,*** mit ihm ist nicht auszukommen.

dealt [delt], *imperf., p.p. of* [1]**deal.**

dean [diːn], *s.* der Dechant, Dekan (*also Univ.*). **deanery,** *s.* die Dekanei, Dechantenwürde, Dekanswürde; das Amtshaus eines Dechanten.

dear [diə], **1.** *adj.* 1. teuer, kostbar, kostspielig; 2. lieb(st), teuer, wert; – ***Doctor,*** sehr geehrter Herr Doktor! ***for – life,*** als wenn es ums Leben ginge; – ***Madam,*** gnädige Frau! ***near and –,*** nahestehend (*to, Dat.*); – ***Sir,*** sehr geehrter Herr! ***his –est wish,*** sein Herzenswunsch. **2.** *adv.* teuer; ***that will cost him –,*** das wird ihm teuer zu stehen kommen; ***pay – for,*** teuer bezahlen. **3.** *s.* der Liebling, Schatz; ***my –,*** meine Liebe *or* Teure; ***Lizzie is a –,*** Lieschen ist ein gutes Kind *or* ein Engel; ***the poor –,*** der *or* die Ärmste; ***there's a –!*** sei doch so nett! **4.** *int.* ***oh –! – me! – –!*** du liebe Zeit! ach du lieber Himmel! **dearie** [–ri], *s.* (*coll.*) das Liebchen, die Liebste. **dearly,** *adv. See* **dear, 1**; ***love her –,*** sie von ganzem Herzen lieben; – ***beloved,*** innig geliebt, heißgeliebt; – ***bought,*** teuer erkauft. **dearness,** *s.* die Kostspieligkeit; teurer Preis, hoher Wert; ***her – to me,*** ihr Wert für mich, meine Liebe für sie.

dearth [dəːθ], *s.* 1. der Mangel (*of*, an (*Dat.*)), das Fehlen (von); 2. die Teu(e)rung.

death [deθ], *s.* der Tod, das Sterben; der Todesfall, *pl.* Todesfälle (*pl.*); (*fig.*) ***in at the –,*** den Schluß mitmachen *or* miterleben; ***bleed to –,*** sich verbluten; (*coll.*) ***catch one's –,*** sich (*Dat.*) den Tod holen; ***come by one's –,*** ums Leben kommen; ***die the – of a hero,*** den Heldentod sterben; ***do him to –,*** ihn töten; ***be at –'s door,*** an der Schwelle des Todes sein, in den letzten Zügen liegen; (*fig.*) ***like grim –,*** verbissen; ***hour of –,*** die Todesstunde; (*coll.*) ***it will be the – of me,*** es bringt mich noch ins Grab; ***at the point of –,*** see ***at –'s door***; (*fig.*) ***to the –,*** bis zum äußersten; ***the fight to the –,*** der Kampf bis aufs Messer; ***laugh o.s. to –,*** sich totlachen; ***put to –,*** hinrichten; ***send him to his –,*** ihn dem Tod entgegenschicken; ***sick to – of a th.,*** einer S. überdrüssig; ***as sure as –,*** todsicher, bombensicher; ***tired to –,*** todmüde.

death|-agony, *s.* der Todeskampf. **–-bed,** *s.* das Sterbebett, Totenbett. **–-blow,** *s.* der Todesstreich; (*fig.*) Todesstoß. **–-cell,** *s.* die Todeszelle. **–-certificate,** *s.* der Totenschein. **–-duty,** *s.* die Nachlaßsteuer, Erbschaftssteuer. **–-knell,** *s.* die Sterbeglocke, das Totengeläut; (*fig.*) ***sound the –,*** das letzte Stündlein läuten, den Rest geben. **deathless,** *adj.* unsterblich. **deathlessness,** *s.* die Unsterblichkeit. **death-like, deathly,** *adj.* totenähnlich, Toten–, Todes–; ***deathly pale,*** totenblaß, leichenblaß; ***deathly silence,*** die Totenstille.

death|-mask, *s.* die Totenmaske. **–-penalty,** *s.* die Todesstrafe. **–-rate,** *s.* die Sterblichkeitsziffer. **–-rattle,** *s.* das Todesröcheln. **–-ray,** *s.* der Todesstrahl. **–-roll,** *s.* (*Mil.*) die Verlustliste, Gefallenenliste; (*of an accident*) Zahl der Todesopfer. **–-sentence,** *s.* das Todesurteil.

death's-head, *s.* der Totenkopf; (*Ent.*) – ***moth,*** der Totenkopfschwärmer.

death|-throes, *pl.* der Todeskampf. **–-trap,** *s.* lebensgefährlicher Platz *or* Raum *or* Bau. **–-warrant,** *s.* der Hinrichtungsbefehl; (*fig.*) das Todesurteil. **–-watch,** *s.* (*Ent.*) (*also* – ***beetle***) der Klopfkäfer, die Totenuhr.

débâcle [diˈbɑːkl], *s.* 1. der Zusammenbruch, die Katastrophe, das Debakel; 2. (*Geol.*) die Mure, der Eisgang, Murgang.

debar [diˈbɑː], *v.t.* ausschließen (***from***, von), hindern (***from doing,*** zu tun); ***he is debarred the liberty . . .,*** ihm wird die Freiheit . . . entzogen; – ***o.s. of a pleasure,*** sich (*Dat.*) ein Vergnügen versagen.

debase [diˈbeis], *v.t.* verschlechtern, verderben; (herab)mindern (*value*); (*Chem.*) denaturieren. **debasement,** *s.* die Verschlechterung, Verringerung, Herabminderung; Verfälschung; Erniedrigung, Entwürdigung.

debatable [diˈbeitəbl], *adj.* strittig, umstritten; fraglich; diskutierbar, (*Law*) streitig, anfechtbar; – ***ground,*** umstrittenes Gebiet; (*fig.*) ***that is – ground,*** darüber läßt sich streiten. **debate, 1.** *s.* (*Parl.*) die Debatte, Verhandlung; Diskussion, Erörterung, der Disput, Wortstreit. **2.** *v.t.* debattieren, disputieren, erörtern. **3.** *v.i.* debattieren; – ***with o.s.,*** sich (*Dat.*) überlegen, mit sich zu Rate gehen. **debater,** *s.* der Disputant, Debattierende(r). **debating-society,** *s.* der Debattierklub.

debauch [diˈbɔːtʃ], **1.** *v.t.* verführen, verleiten; korrumpieren, (moralisch) verderben. **2.** *s.* die Schwelgerei, Ausschweifung. **debauched,** *adj.* verderbt, ausschweifend, verkommen, liederlich. **debauchee** [debɔːˈtʃiː], *s.* der Wüstling, Schwelger. **debaucher,** *s.* der Verführer. **debauchery,** *s.* die Schwelgerei, Ausschweifung, Liederlichkeit.

debenture [diˈbentʃə], *s.* der Schuldschein, die Schuldverschreibung, Obligation; der Rückzollschein (*customs*); – ***bonds,*** – ***stock,*** Obligationen (*pl.*), festverzinsliche Schuldverschreibungen (*pl.*). **debentured,** *adj.* Rückzoll–.

debilitate [diˈbiliteit], *v.t.* schwächen, entkräften. **debilitation** [–ˈteiʃən], *s.* die Schwächung, Entkräftigung. **debility,** *s.* die Schwäche, Hinfälligkeit.

debit [ˈdebit], **1.** *s.* das Soll, Debet; der Schuldposten; die Kontobelastung; Debetseite (*of a ledger*); ***to the – of his account,*** zu seinen Lasten; ***place a sum to his –,*** ihn mit einer Summe belasten; – ***and credit,*** Soll und Haben; – ***side,*** die Debetseite, das Debetkonto; – ***slip,*** der Belastungszettel. **2.** *v.t.* belasten, debitieren (***with***, mit), zur Last schreiben (*Dat.*).

debonair [deboˈnɛə], *adj.* anmutig, höflich, gefällig, liebenswürdig, heiter.

debouch [diˈbuːʃ], *v.i.* (*Mil.*) hervorbrechen, herauskommen, debouchieren; sich ergießen, (ein)münden (*of a river*). **debouchment,** *s.* (*Mil.*) *s.* der Ausfall, das Hervorbrechen; die Mündung, der Ausgang.

débris ['debri:], *s.* Bruchstücke (*pl.*); Trümmer (*pl.*), der Schutt.

debt [det], *s.* die Schuld (*also fig.*); Verpflichtung, Obligation; – ***of gratitude,*** die Dankesschuld; – ***of honour,*** die Ehrenschuld; ***pay the – of*** or ***one's – to nature,*** sterben; ***active –s,*** Außenstände (*pl.*); ***–s active and passive,*** Aktiva und Passiva; ***bad –s,*** zweifelhafte Außenstände (*pl.*); ***floating –,*** schwebende Schuld *or* Forderung; ***national –,*** die Staatsschuld; ***outstanding –s,*** see ***active –s***; ***be in –,*** verschuldet sein, Schulden haben; ***be in his –,*** ihm schuldig *or* verpflichtet sein; ***contract*** or ***incur –s,*** see ***run up –s***; ***honour a –,*** eine Schuld begleichen; ***run into –, run up –s,*** Schulden machen. **debtor,** *s.* der Schuldner, Debitor; – ***side,*** die Debetseite.

debunk [di'bʌŋk], *v.t.* (*sl.*) entlarven, ins rechte Licht setzen; den Nimbus nehmen (*Dat.*). **debunking** [di'bʌŋkiŋ], *s.* die Entlarvung.

début ['deib(j)u:], *s.* (*esp. Theat.*) erstes Auftreten, das Debüt; (*of a girl*) Debüt, die Einführung in die Gesellschaft. **débutant** [debju'tã], *s.* der Debütant. **débutante** [–ta:nt], *s.* die Debütantin.

decade ['dekeid], *s.* 1. das Jahrzehnt, Dezennium; 2. die Zehnergruppe.

decadence ['dekədəns], *s.* der Verfall, Zerfall, Niedergang, die Entartung, Dekadenz. **decadent,** *adj.* verfallend, im Verfall *or* Niedergang begriffen; entartet, dekadent.

decagon ['dekəgən], *s.* das Zehneck. **decagram(me),** *s.* das Dekagramm. **decahedron** [–'hi:drən], *s.* der Zehnflächner, das Dekaeder.

decalcification [–fi'keiʃən], *s.* die Entkalkung.

decalcify [di'kælsifai], *v.t.* entkalken.

decalitre ['dekəli:tə], *s.* das *or* (*coll.*) der Dekaliter. **decalogue** [–lɔg], *s.* die zehn Gebote (*pl.*), der Dekalog. **decametre,** *s.* das *or* (*coll.*) der Dekameter.

decamp [di'kæmp], *v.i.* das Lager abbrechen; (*coll.*) sich aus dem Staube machen, sich davonmachen, ausreißen, türmen. **decampment,** *s.* der Abzug, Aufbruch, das Abmarschieren (aus dem Lager).

decant [di'kænt], *v.t.* umfüllen, abfüllen, abgießen; abschlämmen, abklären, dekantieren. **decantation** [di:kæn'teiʃən], *s.* das Abgießen, Umfüllen. **decanter,** *s.* die Karaffe (*for wine*).

decapitate [di'kæpiteit], *v.t.* enthaupten, köpfen. **decapitation** [–'teiʃən], *s.* die Enthauptung.

decapod ['dekəpɔd], *s.* (*Zool.*) der Zehnfüßer, Zehnfußkrebs.

decarbonization [di:ka:bənai'zeiʃən], *s.* die Entkohlung, Entrußung. **decarbonize,** *v.t.* entkohlen, entrußen. **decarburation** [–bju'reiʃən], **decarburize,** *see* **decarbonization, decarbonize.**

decasyllabic [dekəsi'læbik], *adj.* zehnsilbig.

decathlon [di'kæθlən], *s.* (*Spt.*) der Zehnkampf.

decay [di'kei], 1. *v.i.* verfallen, zerfallen, in Verfall geraten, vermodern, verwesen, verfaulen, (*of teeth*) faulen, schlecht werden, (*Geol.*) verwittern; (*fig.*) verblühen, verwelken, absterben, abnehmen, sinken. 2. *s.* der Verfall, Zerfall, die Verwesung, Vermoderung, das Verfaulen, (*of teeth*) Faulen, Schlechtwerden, (*Geol.*) die Verwitterung; (*fig.*) das Verblühen, Verwelken, die (Kraft)abnahme, der Rückgang, (*of sound etc.*) das Abklingen; ***fall into –,*** in Verfall geraten, zugrunde gehen, (*of buildings*) baufällig werden. **decayed,** *adj.* verfallen, vermodert, verfault, morsch, (*of teeth*) faul, schlecht, kariös, (*Geol.*) verwittert; (*fig.*) verblüht, verwelkt, heruntergekommen, zerrüttet.

decease [di'si:s], 1. *v.i.* sterben, verscheiden, hinscheiden. 2. *s.* der Tod, das Verscheiden, Hinscheiden. **deceased,** 1. *adj.* gestorben, verstorben. 2. *s.* Verstorbene(r).

deceit [di'si:t], *s.* die Falschheit, (Hinter)list, Täuschung, Betrügerei, der Betrug; Trug, Ränke (*pl.*), Tücken (*pl.*). **deceitful,** *adj.* (be)trügerisch, (hinter)listig, falsch. **deceitfulness,** *s.* die Falschheit, Hinterlist, Arglist.

deceivable [di'si:vəbl], *adj.* täuschbar, betrügbar, leicht zu täuschen(d). **deceive,** *v.t.* täuschen, irreführen; betrügen, hintergehen, hinters Licht führen; ***be –d,*** sich täuschen (lassen), sich irren (***in,*** in (*Dat.*)); – ***o.s.,*** sich täuschen, sich einer Täuschung hingeben. **deceiver,** *s.* der (die) Betrüger(in), Schwindler(in), (*of the opp. sex*) Verführer(in).

decelerate [di:'seləreit], 1. *v.i.* sich verlangsamen, die Geschwindigkeit verringern, (*Motor.*) langsamer fahren. 2. *v.t.* verlangsamen, die Geschwindigkeit vermindern von. **deceleration** [–'reiʃən], *s.* die Verlangsamung; Geschwindigkeitsabnahme.

December [di'sembə], *s.* der Dezember; ***in –,*** im Dezember.

decemvir [di'semviə], *s.* der Dezemvir. **decemvirate** [–vireit], *s.* das Dezemvirat.

decency ['di:sənsi], *s.* die Schicklichkeit, (Wohl)anständigkeit, der Anstand; die Sittsamkeit; (*pl.*) Anstandsformen (*pl.*), der Anstand; ***for –'s sake,*** anstandshalber.

decennary [di'senəri], *s. See* **decennium. decennial,** *adj.* zehnjährig. **decennially,** *adv.* alle zehn Jahre. **decennium,** *s.* das Jahrzehnt.

decent ['di:sənt], *adj.* schicklich, anständig, (sich) ziemend; sittsam, züchtig, dezent, bescheiden; (*coll.*) (ganz) anständig, passabel, ordentlich; (*coll.*) nett, freundlich.

decentralization [di:sentrəlai'zeiʃən], *s.* die Dezentralisierung. **decentralize** [di:'sentrəlaiz], *v.t.* dezentralisieren.

deception [di'sepʃən], *s.* die Täuschung, Irreführung; Betrügerei, der Betrug. **deceptive** [–tiv], *adj.* täuschend, irreführend; (be)trügerisch, Trug–.

decibel ['desibel], *s.* (*Phys.*) das Dezibel.

decide [di'said], 1. *v.t.* entscheiden (*also a battle*), einer Lösung zuführen, schlichten (*an issue*), bestimmen, zum Entschluß bringen (*a p.*); ***that –d it,*** das gab den Ausschlag. 2. *v.i.* beschließen, (sich) entschließen *or* entscheiden, zu der Meinung *or* Überzeugung *or* zum Schluß kommen; die Entscheidung treffen; den Ausschlag geben; – ***(up)on a th.*** or ***in favour of a th.,*** sich für etwas entschließen; – ***to do*** or ***on doing,*** beschließen zu tun; – ***against doing,*** beschließen nicht zu tun.

decided [di'saidid], *adj.* entschieden, eindeutig, bestimmt (*as attitudes*); (*of a p.*) (fest) entschlossen. **decidedly,** *adv.* sicher, bestimmt, unzweifelhaft; entschieden, ausgesprochen. **decidedness,** *s.* die Entschiedenheit, Bestimmtheit, Eindeutigkeit, (*of a p.*) Entschlossenheit, Festigkeit. **decider,** *s.* 1. der (die) Entscheider(in), Entscheidende(r), Schiedsrichter(in); 2. (*Spt.*) der Entscheidungskampf, das Entscheidungsrennen.

deciduous [di'sidjuəs], *adj.* (jedes Jahr) abfallend, laubwechselnd; – ***tree,*** der Laubbaum.

decigram(me) ['desigræm], *s.* das Dezigramm, Zehntelgramm. **decilitre** [–li:tə], *s.* das Deziliter.

decimal ['desiməl], 1. *adj.* dezimal; – ***currency,*** *see* **decimalism**; – ***fraction,*** der Dezimalbruch; – ***place,*** die Dezimalstelle; – ***point,*** der Dezimalstrich, das Komma; – ***system,*** das Dezimalsystem. 2. *s.* der Dezimalbruch; ***recurring –,*** unendliche Dezimalzahl. **decimalism,** *s.* das Dezimalsystem. **decimalize** [–aiz], 1. *v.t.* auf das Dezimalsystem zurückführen. 2. *v.i.* das Dezimalsystem einführen. **decimally,** *adv.* nach dem Dezimalsystem.

decimate ['desimeit], *v.t.* 1. (*Hist.*) den Zehnten hinrichten von; 2. (*fig.*) dezimieren, Verheerung anrichten unter (*Dat.*). **decimation** [–'meiʃən], *s.* die Dezimierung.

decimetre ['desimi:tə], *s.* das Dezimeter.

decipher [di'saifə], *v.t.* entziffern, dechiffrieren; (*fig.*) enträtseln. **decipherable,** *adj.* entzifferbar.

decision [di'siʒən], *s.* 1. die Entscheidung (*also Law*), der Entschluß, (*Law*) Beschluß, Entscheid, Bescheid, Schiedsspruch, das Urteil; ***arrive at*** or ***come to a –,*** zu einem Entschluß kommen (***about,*** über (*Acc.*)); ***make a –,*** eine Entscheidung treffen;

2. die Entschlossenheit, Entschlußkraft, Festigkeit (*of character*); **man of –**, entschlossener Mann.

decisive [di'saisiv], *adj.* 1. entscheidend, maßgebend, bestimmend, ausschlaggebend; **– battle**, der Entscheidungskampf; 2. entschieden, eindeutig, bestimmt, klar; 3. (*of a p.*) fest, entschlossen. **decisively,** *adv.* in entscheidender Weise. **decisiveness,** *s.* die Entschiedenheit, Eindeutigkeit, Endgültigkeit, (*of a p.*) Entschlossenheit.

deck [dek], **1.** *v.t.* 1. (*also* **– out**) bekleiden; (aus)-schmücken, zieren; 2. (*Naut.*) mit einem Deck versehen. **2.** *s.* 1. (*Naut.*) das (Ver)deck; **below –**, unter Deck; **clear the –s,** das Schiff klar zum Gefecht machen (*also fig.*); **lower –**, das Unterdeck; **main –**, das Hauptdeck; **on –**, auf Deck; **go on –**, an Deck gehen; **all hands on –**, alle Mann an Deck; **'tween –s**, das Zwischendeck; 2. (*Cards*) (*esp. Am.*) das Spiel, Pack.

deck|-chair, *s.* der Liegestuhl. **--games,** *pl.* Bordspiele (*pl.*). **--hand,** *s.* der Matrose (*on fishing boats etc.*).

deckle [dekl], *adj.* **– edge,** der Büttenrand (*of paper*).

deck-tennis, *s.* das Ringtennis.

declaim [di'kleim], **1.** *v.t.* hersagen, vortragen, deklamieren. **2.** *v.i.* eine Rede halten (**about, on,** über (*Acc.*)); **– against,** eifern *or* losziehen gegen.

declamation [deklə'meiʃən], *s.* die Deklamation, das Deklamieren; schwungvolle Rede, der (Rede)-erguß. **declamatory** [di'klæmətəri], *adj.* deklamatorisch; schwülstig, pathetisch.

declarable [di'klɛərəbl], *adj.* zollpflichtig, steuerpflichtig. **declaration** [deklə'reiʃən], *s.* die Erklärung, Verkündung, Aussage; Proklamation, das Manifest; (*customs*) die Deklaration, Zollerklärung; (*Cards*) Ansage; (*Law*) Klageschrift. **declarative** [–'klærətiv], *adj.* Erklärungs–; (*Gram.*) Aussage–; **be – of,** ausdrücken, aussagen. **declaratory** [–'klærətəri], *adj.* erklärend, verkündend, feststellend; **be – of,** erklären, verkünden, feststellen, darlegen.

declare [di'klɛə], **1.** *v.t.* erklären, verkünd(ig)en, bekanntgeben, kundtun, aussagen, behaupten, versichern; (*customs*) deklarieren, anmelden, verzollen; (*dividend*) festsetzen; (*Cards*) ansagen; **nothing to –**, nichts zu verzollen; **– o.s.,** sich erklären, seine Meinung kundtun. **2.** *v.i.* 1. sich erklären, sich entscheiden, sich aussprechen; (*coll.*) **I –!** wahrhaftig! so etwas! ich muß (schon) sagen! 2. (*Crick.*) (vor dem Abschluß) vom Spiele zurücktreten. **declared,** *adj.* offen (erklärt), zugegeben.

declension [di'klenʃən], *s.* 1. die Abweichung, Neigung; der Verfall; 2. (*Gram.*) die Beugung, Abwandlung, Deklination.

declinable [di'klainəbl], *adj.* (*Gram.*) deklinierbar. **declination** [dekli'neiʃən], *s.* die Neigung, Schräglage, Abschüssigkeit; (*Phys., Astr.*) Abweichung, Deklination; **compass –**, die Mißweisung; **local –**, die Ortsmißweisung; **magnetic –**, die Nadelabweichung. **declinator** ['deklineitə], *s.* der Abweichungsmesser. **declinatory** [di-'klainətəri], *adj.* abweichend.

decline [di'klain], **1.** *v.t.* 1. neigen, senken; 2. (*Gram.*) beugen, deklinieren; 3. ablehnen, ausschlagen, nicht annehmen; **he –d the honour,** er verbat sich die Ehre. **2.** *v.i.* 1. sich neigen *or* senken, abfallen; (*of prices*) fallen, sinken; (*fig.*) sich verschlechtern, in Verfall geraten, verfallen, abnehmen, zurückgehen, sinken, (*coll.*) bergab gehen; sich neigen, zur Neige gehen, dem Ende zugehen; **his strength –s,** er kommt von Kräften; 2. ablehnen, absagen, sich weigern. **3.** *s.* die Neigung, Senkung; der Abhang; (*as of sun etc.*) Untergang, das Sinken, (*of prices*) Fallen, der Rückgang, Sturz; (*fig.*) Niedergang, Verfall, die Abnahme, Verminderung, Verschlechterung, (*Med.*) das Siechtum, die Auszehrung; **be on the –**, im Niedergang begriffen sein, zu Ende *or* auf die Neige gehen; (*of prices*) zurückgehen, sinken, fallen; **go into a –**, (dahin)-siechen; **– of life,** der Lebensabend, vorgerücktes Alter.

declivitous [di'klivitəs], *adj.* abschüssig, steil.

declivity, *s.* der (Ab)hang; die Abschüssigkeit. **declivous** [–'klaivəs], *adj.* abfallend, geneigt.

declutch [di:'klʌtʃ], *v.t.* (*Motor.*) auskuppeln; **double-—**, Zwischengas geben.

decoct [di'kɔkt], *v.t.* abkochen; absieden, ausziehen. **decoction** [–'kɔkʃən], *s.* das Abkochen, Absieden; der Absud, die Abkochung, der Auszug.

decode [di:'koud], *v.t.* entziffern, dechiffrieren.

décolleté [dei'kɔltei], *adj.* dekolletiert (*a lady*), (tief) ausgeschnitten (*a dress*).

decolorant [di:'kʌlərənt], **1.** *adj.* bleichend, entfärbend. **2.** *s.* das Bleichmittel, Entfärbungsmittel. **decolorize** [–raiz], *v.t.* entfärben, bleichen.

decomposable [di:kəm'pouzəbl], *adj.* scheidbar, zersetzbar, zerlegbar. **decompose, 1.** *v.t.* zersetzen; zerlegen, scheiden, spalten. **2.** *v.i.* verwesen, sich zersetzen, sich auflösen, zerfallen (*into*, in (*Acc.*)). **decomposed,** *adj.* faul, verfault, verwest, morsch. **decomposition** [di:kɔmpə-'ziʃən], *s.* die Zersetzung, der Zerfall; die Auflösung, Verwesung, Fäulnis; Zerlegung, Aufspaltung.

decompress [di:kəm'pres], *v.t.* dekomprimieren. **decompression** [–'preʃən], *s.* die Entkompression, Druckverminderung, Druckentlastung; **– chamber,** die Höhenkammer.

decontaminate [di:kən'tæmineit], *v.t.* entgiften, entseuchen, (*radioactivity*) entstrahlen, (*Mil.*) entgasen. **decontamination** [–'neiʃən], *s.* die Entgiftung, Entseuchung, Entstrahlung, Entgasung; **– squad,** der Entgasungstrupp.

decontrol [di:kən'troul], **1.** *v.t.* von der Kontrolle befreien, freigeben (*goods*). **2.** *s.* der Abbau der Zwangswirtschaft; die Freigabe.

décor ['deikɔ:], *s.* die Ausschmückung, Dekorierung, (*Theat.*) Ausstattung, der Dekor.

decorate ['dekəreit], *v.t.* 1. schmücken, (ver)zieren; (*Archit.*) **–d style,** englische Gotik; 2. auszeichnen (*a p.*). **decoration** [–'reiʃən], *s.* 1. die Verzierung, Ausschmückung; der Schmuck, Zierat; *pl.* die Dekoration(en) (*in a theatre etc.*); 2. die Auszeichnung, das Ehrenzeichen, der Orden. **decorative** [–rətiv], *adj.* verzierend, schmückend, dekorativ, Dekorations–, Schmuck–, Zier–. **decorator** [–reitə], *s.* der Dekorateur, Dekorationsmaler; Anstreicher und Tapezierer.

decorous ['dekərəs], *adj.* geziemend, schicklich; sittsam, (wohl)anständig, gebührlich.

decorticate [di'kɔ:tikeit], *v.t.* abrinden, entrinden, (ab)schälen. **decortication** [–'keiʃən], *s.* die Entrindung, Abschälung.

decorum [di'kɔ:rəm], *s.* der Anstand, die Schicklichkeit, (Wohl)anständigkeit; Etikette, Anstandsregeln (*pl.*).

decoy, 1. [di'kɔi], *v.t.* locken, ködern; (*fig.*) verleiten, (ver)locken. **2.** ['di:kɔi], *s.* die Entenfalle; Lockspeise, der Köder; Lockvogel (*also fig. of a p.*); **– duck,** die Lockente.

decrease, 1. [di'kri:s], *v.i.* abnehmen, sich verringern *or* vermindern; **– in length,** kürzer werden; **– in strength,** schwächer werden. **2.** [–'kri:s], *v.t.* verringern, vermindern, verkürzen, verkleinern, reduzieren; **– speed,** die Geschwindigkeit herabsetzen. **3.** ['di:kri:s], *s.* der Rückgang, die Abnahme, Verminderung, Verringerung, Verkürzung, Verkleinerung.

decree [di'kri:], **1.** *s.* die Verordnung, Verfügung, Vorschrift, der Erlaß, Bescheid, das Edikt, Dekret; (*Law*) der Entscheid, das Urteil; der Ratschluß, die Bestimmung (*of God*); **– of fate,** die Schicksalsfügung; **– nisi,** provisorisches Scheidungsurteil. **2.** *v.t., v.i.* anordnen, verordnen, verfügen, bestimmen.

decrement ['dekrəmənt], *s.* die Verminderung, Abnahme, (*Math. etc.*) das Dekrement.

decrepit [di'krepit], *adj.* altersschwach, hinfällig, (*fig.*) verfallen, klapprig.

decrepitate [di'krepiteit], **1.** *v.i.* zerknistern, verprasseln. **2.** *v.t.* (*Chem.*) dekrepitieren lassen.

decrepitation [–'teiʃən], *s.* die Verknisterung, Dekrepitation; das Knistern, Prasseln.
decrepitude [di'krepitju:d], *s.* die Hinfälligkeit, Altersschwäche, Gebrechlichkeit.
decrescent [di'kresənt], *adj.* abnehmend (*moon etc.*).
decretal [di'kri:tl], **1.** *adj.* Dekretal–. **2.** *s.* das Dekretale, *pl.* Dekretal(i)en (*pl.*). **decretive, decretory,** *adj.* dekretorisch, entscheidend.
decrial [di'kraiəl], *s.* das Verschreien, Heruntermachen, die Herabsetzung. **decrier** [di'kraiə], *s.* der Schlechtmacher. **decry** [di'krai], *v.t.* verschreien, verdammen, in Verruf bringen; heruntermachen, schlechtmachen, herabsetzen.
decubitus [di'kju:bitəs], *s.* (*Med.*) das Wundliegen.
decumbence, decumbency [di'kʌmbəns(i)], *s.* das Liegen, liegende Stellung. **decumbent,** *adj.* (*Bot.*) liegend; (*Zool.*) anliegend.
decuple ['dekjupl], **1.** *adj.* zehnfach. **2.** *s.* das Zehnfache. **3.** *v.t.* verzehnfachen.
decussate, 1. [di'kʌsit], *adj.* sich kreuzend *or* schneidend, gekreuzt, (*Bot.*) gegenständig. **2.** [–seit], *v.t.* (*v.i.* sich) kreuzen. **decussation** [–'seiʃən], *s.* die (Durch)kreuzung.
dedicate ['dedikeit], *v.t.* weihen (*to God*), widmen (*time or a book*), zueignen (*a book*) (*to*, *Dat.*). **dedication** [–'keiʃən], *s.* die Weihung; Widmung, Zueignung (*to*, an (*Acc.*)) (*of a book etc.*); Zueignungsschrift; (*fig.*) Hingabe (*to*, an (*Acc.*)). **dedicator,** *s.* der Widmer, Zueigner. **dedicatory** [–kətəri], *adj.* Widmungs–, Zueignungs–.
deduce [di'dju:s], *v.t.* schließen, folgern (***from***, aus); verfolgen, ableiten, herleiten (von). **deducible,** *adj.* herzuleiten(d), zu schließen(d), schließbar.
deduct [di'dʌkt], *v.t.* abziehen, abrechnen, absetzen; ***after –ing*** . . ., nach Abzug (von) . . .; ***–ing expenses,*** abzüglich der Kosten. **deductible,** *adj.* abziehbar, abrechenbar. **deduction** [–'dʌkʃən], *s.* 1. das Abziehen, der Abzug, die Abrechnung, Absetzung (***from***, von); (*Comm.*) der Rabatt, Nachlaß; ***tax –***, die Rückstellung für Steuern; 2. (*Log.*) das Schließen, Folgern (***from***, aus), die (Schluß)folgerung, der (Erkenntnis)schluß; ***make –s,*** Schlüsse ziehen. **deductive,** *adj.* folgernd, deduktiv, erschließbar, ableitbar.
deed [di:d], **1.** *s.* 1. die Tat, Handlung; Ausführung; Heldentat, Großtat; ***in*** (***very***) ***–***, in Wahrheit, in der Tat; ***take the will for the –***, den guten Willen für die Tat nehmen; 2. (*Law*) die Urkunde, das Instrument, Dokument; ***– of gift,*** die Schenkungsurkunde. **2.** *v.t.* urkundlich übertragen (*to*, *Dat. or* auf (*Acc.*)). **deed|-box,** *s.* die Kassette. **–-poll,** *s.* einseitige Rechtsgeschäftsurkunde.
deem [di:m], **1.** *v.t.* halten *or* erachten für, betrachten als. **2.** *v.i.* eine Meinung haben, meinen, glauben, denken; ***– highly of,*** hochschätzen. **deemster,** *s.* der Richter (*Isle of Man*).
deep [di:p], **1.** *adj.* tief, tiefliegend, niedrig gelegen; (*fig.*) unergründlich, dunkel (*also of colours*), tiefsinnig, schwer verständlich; geheim, verborgen; listig, verschlagen; tiefgehend, eingehend, gründlich, durchdringend, mächtig, stark; innig empfunden, inbrünstig (*of feelings*); tieftönend (*of sounds*); versunken, vertieft (***in***, in (*Acc.*)); ***drawn up two –***, in zwei Gliedern aufgestellt; ***– border,*** breiter Rand; ***take a – breath,*** tief atmen; ***– designs,*** versteckte Absichten, geheime Pläne; ***– disappointment,*** schwere Enttäuschung; (*coll.*) ***go off the – end,*** die Fassung verlieren; ***– fellow,*** durchtriebener Bursche, schlauer Kopf *or* Fuchs; ***– grief,*** schwerer Kummer; ***– impression,*** starker *or* mächtiger *or* tief(gehend)er Eindruck; ***– influence,*** mächtiger Einfluß; ***– mourning,*** tiefe Trauer; ***– problem,*** schwerwiegendes Problem; ***– sense of gratitude,*** aufrichtiges Dankgefühl; ***– silence,*** vollkommenes Schweigen; ***in – thought,*** in Gedanken vertieft; ***be in – water,*** den Boden unter den Füßen verlieren; ***– wrongs,*** schweres Unrecht. **2.** *adv.* ***drink –***, reichlich trinken; ***– into the night,*** bis tief in die Nacht; ***– in debt,*** tief verschuldet; ***– in thought,*** see ***in – thought***; ***still waters run –***, stille Wasser sind tief. **3.** *s.* (*Poet.*) die Tiefe; See, das Meer, der Ozean; (*Naut.*) tiefe Stelle.
deep-breathing, *s.* die Atemübung.
deepen ['di:pən], **1.** *v.t.* tiefer machen, vertiefen, (*Min.*) abteufen; (*Naut.*) austiefen, ausbaggern; (*fig.*) verdunkeln (*colours*); steigern, verstärken, vergrößern; tiefer stimmen (*tones*). **2.** *v.i.* tiefer werden, sich vertiefen; (*fig.*) sich steigern *or* verstärken; nachdunkeln, dunkler *or* stärker werden.
deep|-felt, *adj.* tiefempfunden. **–-freeze, 1.** *s.* der Tiefkühlschrank. **2.** *irr.v.t.* tiefkühlen. **–-fry,** *v.t.* in schwimmendem Fett backen. **–-laid,** *adj.* ***– schemes,*** schlau angelegte Pläne.
deeply ['di:pli], *adv.* tief, sorgfältig, gründlich, heftig, unmäßig; ***– affected,*** tief ergriffen; ***– hurt,*** schwer gekränkt; ***– indebted,*** zu großem Dank verpflichtet; ***– in love,*** schwer verliebt; ***– offend,*** großen Anstoß geben; ***– read*** or ***versed,*** gründlich bewandert.
deep-mouthed, *adj.* mit tiefer Stimme (*of dogs*); tieftönend. **deepness,** *s.* die Tiefe; Schwerverständlichkeit, Verborgenheit. **deep|-rooted,** *adj.* tiefwurzelnd, (*fig.*) tiefverwurzelt. **–-sea,** *attrib. adj.* Hochsee–; ***– fishing,*** die Hochseefischerei. **–-seated,** *adj.* tiefsitzend, festsitzend, fest verwurzelt. **–-set,** *adj.* tiefliegend (*as eyes*). **–-throated, –-toned,** *adj.* tieftönend.
deer [diə], *s.* (*pl.* -) der Hirsch, das Reh; (*collect.*) Wild, Rotwild, Hochwild; ***fallow –***, der Damhirsch, das Damwild; ***red –***, der Edelhirsch, Rothirsch. **deer|-forest,** *s.* das Hochwildgehege. **–hound,** *s.* der Jagdhund. **–-hunt,** *s.* die Hochwildjagd. **–-lick,** *s.* die Salzlecke. **–-park,** *s.* der Wildpark. **–skin,** *s.* das Hirschleder, Rehleder. **–-stalker,** *s.* 1. der Pirscher; 2. die Jagdmütze. **–-stalking,** *s.* die Pirsch.
deface [di'feis], *v.t.* entstellen, verunstalten; unleserlich machen; (*postage stamp*) entwerten. **defacement,** *s.* die Entstellung, Verunstaltung; Entwertung.
de facto [di:'fæktou], *adv.* (*Law*) tatsächlich.
defalcate ['di:fəlkeit], *v.i.* Veruntreuungen *or* Unterschlagungen begehen. **defalcation** [–'keiʃən], *s.* die Veruntreuung, Unterschlagung; die Unterschlagungssumme.
defamation [defə'meiʃən], *s.* die Verleumdung, Schmähung; ***– of character,*** die Ehrabschneidung. **defamatory** [di'fæmətəri], *adj.* verleumderisch, ehrenrührig, schmähend, Schmäh–; ***be – of,*** verleumden; ***– libel,*** die Schmähschrift. **defame** [di'feim], *v.t.* verleumden, verunglimpfen. **defamer,** *s.* der Verleumder.
default [di'fɔ:lt], **1.** *s.* die Unterlassung, Vernachlässigung, das Versäumnis; (*Comm.*) die Nichterfüllung, Zahlungseinstellung, der Verzug; (*obs.*) Fehler, Mangel; das Vergehen; (*Law*) Nichterscheinen; ***be in –***, im Verzug sein; ***in – of,*** in Ermang(e)lung von, mangels; ***in – whereof,*** widrigenfalls; ***let go by –***, unausgenützt vorübergehen lassen, unterlassen; ***make –***, nicht (vor Gericht) erscheinen; ***judgement by –***, das Säumnisurteil. **2.** *v.i.* (vor Gericht) nicht erscheinen; im Verzug sein, einer Verpflichtung nicht nachkommen; ***– on a debt,*** einer Schuld nicht nachkommen. **3.** *v.t.* wegen Nichterscheinens verurteilen. **defaulter,** *s.* säumiger Zahler *or* Schuldner, der Insolvent, Zahlungsunfähige(r), (*Law*) Nichterscheinende(r); (*Mil.*) Delinquent.
defeasance [di'fi:zəns], *s.* (*Law*) die Ungültigkeitserklärung, Aufhebung, Annullierung; Nichtigkeitsklausel. **defeasible,** *adj.* anfechtbar, aufhebbar, umstoßbar, annullierbar.
defeat [di'fi:t], **1.** *s.* die Niederlage; das Zurückschlagen, die Niederschlagung (*of an attack*); Besiegung, Niederwerfung (*of the enemy*); (*Law*) Aufhebung, Annullierung, Ungültigkeitserklärung; (*Parl.*) Ablehnung (*of a motion*); (*of hopes etc.*) Durchkreuzung, Vereitelung; ***inflict a –***, eine Niederlage beibringen (***on***, *Dat.*); ***suffer a –***, eine Niederlage erleiden, geschlagen werden. **2.** *v.t.* besiegen, schlagen, überwinden (*an army*), niederschlagen, zurückschlagen, abschlagen, abweisen (*an onslaught*); zu Fall bringen (*a motion*); vereiteln, zunichte machen, durchkreuzen (*hopes*

etc.); (*Law*) annullieren, umstoßen, aufheben. **defeatism,** *s.* der Defätismus, die Miesmacherei, Flaumacherei. **defeatist,** *s.* der Miesmacher.

defecate ['di:fəkeit], **1.** *v.t.* (ab)klären, reinigen, scheiden, läutern (*of*, von). **2.** *v.i.* den Darm entleeren, Stuhlgang haben. **defecation** [–'keiʃən], *s.* der Stuhlgang, die Darmentleerung; Reinigung, Klärung.

defect [di'fekt], **1.** *s.* der Fehler, Defekt, (*Med.*) das Gebrechen; die Unvollkommenheit; der Mangel (*of*, an (*Dat.*)); – ***of memory,*** die Gedächtnisschwäche. **2.** *v.i.* abfallen, abtrünnig *or* treulos werden; übertreten (*to*, zu). **defection** [–'fekʃən], *s.* der Abfall, die Lossagung (***from,*** von), der Übertritt (*to*, zu); die Abtrünnigkeit, Pflichtvergessenheit, der Treubruch.

defective [di'fektiv], *adj.* mangelhaft, unvollkommen, lückenhaft, unzulänglich, unvollständig (*also Gram.*); (*Comm.*) defekt, schadhaft; (*Gram.*) defektiv; ***be – in,*** mangeln an (*Dat.*); ***mentally –,*** schwachsinnig. **defectiveness,** *s.* die Mangelhaftigkeit, Unzulänglichkeit; Schadhaftigkeit.

defence [di'fens], *s.* die Verteidigung (*also Law*); Gegenwehr; (*Law*) Rechtfertigung; Abwehr, der Schutz; (*Spt.*) die Verteidigung; Hintermannschaft; *pl.* Befestigungsanlagen, Verteidigungswerke, Abwehrstellungen (*pl.*); ***anti-aircraft –,*** die Fliegerabwehr, der Luftschutz; ***coast –,*** die Küstenverteidigung; ***counsel for the –,*** der Verteidiger; ***conduct one's own –,*** sich selbst verteidigen; ***come to his –,*** ihn verteidigen; ***home –,*** die Landesverteidigung, der Heimatschutz; ***in one's own –,*** zu seiner Rechtfertigung; ***in self-–,*** in Selbstverteidigung, in Notwehr; ***Minister of Defence,*** der Verteidigungsminister; ***witness for the –,*** der Entlastungszeuge. **defenceless,** *adj.* schutzlos, wehrlos; unbefestigt; hilflos, schwach. **defencelessness,** *s.* Schutzlosigkeit.

defend [di'fend], *v.t.* verteidigen, schützen, sichern (***against,*** gegen); schützen, bewahren (***from,*** vor (*Dat.*)); rechtfertigen, wahren, aufrechterhalten (*rights etc.*). **defendant,** *s.* (*Law*) Angeklagte(r) (*criminal case*), Beklagte(r) (*civil case*). **defender,** *s.* der Verteidiger, (Be)schützer; – ***of the faith,*** der Schutzherr des Glaubens.

defense [di'fens], *s.* (*Am.*) *see* **defence. defensible,** *adj.* verteidigungsfähig, zu verteidigen(d); zu rechtfertigen(d), haltbar, vertretbar, verfechtbar. **defensive, 1.** *adj.* verteidigend, schützend, Abwehr–, Schutz–, Verteidigungs–; – ***arms,*** Schutzwaffen (*pl.*); – ***measures,*** Schutzmaßnahmen (*pl.*); – ***position,*** die Abwehrstellung; – ***war,*** der Defensivkrieg. **2.** *s.* die Defensive, Abwehr, Verteidigung; ***act*** or ***be*** or ***stand on the –,*** sich defensiv verhalten.

defer [di'fə:], **1.** *v.t.* aufschieben, verschieben, vertagen (*to*, auf (*Acc.*)); (ver)zögern, hinausschieben, (*Mil.*) zurückstellen (*as military service*); ***deferred annuity,*** die Anwartschaftsrente; ***deferred payment,*** die Ratenzahlung, Abzahlung; ***deferred stock,*** Nachzugsaktien (*pl.*). **2.** *v.i.* zögern, (ab)warten; nachgeben (*to*, *Dat.*), sich beugen (vor (*Dat.*)).

deference ['defərəns], *s.* die Achtung, Ehrerbietung (***to,*** vor (*Dat.*) *or* gegenüber), Nachgiebigkeit (***to,*** gegenüber), Unterwerfung (unter (*Acc.*)), Rücksicht(nahme) (auf (*Acc.*)); ***in –*** or ***out of – to,*** mit *or* aus Rücksicht auf (*Acc.*), aus Achtung vor (*Dat.*); ***show – to him,*** ihm Achtung zollen; ***with all (due) – to,*** bei aller Hochachtung vor (*Dat.*). **deferential** [–'renʃəl], *adj.* achtungsvoll, ehrerbietig.

deferment [di'fə:mənt], *s.* die Verzögerung, der Aufschub; die Zurückstellung (*of military service*).

defiance [di'faiəns], *s.* die Herausforderung; der Trotz, Hohn; ***bid – to,*** Trotz bieten (*Dat.*), Hohn sprechen (*Dat.*); ***in – of,*** trotz, ungeachtet (*Gen.*), zuwider (*with preceding Dat.*); ***in – of him,*** ihm zum Trotze; ***set at –,*** see ***bid – to.*** **defiant,** *adj.* trotzig, keck, herausfordernd.

deficiency [di'fiʃənsi], *s.* die Mangelhaftigkeit, Unzulänglichkeit, Unvollkommenheit; der Mangel (***of,*** an (*Dat.*)), das Fehlen (von); die Schwäche, der Defekt; (*Comm.*) das Defizit, Manko, der Ausfall, Fehlbetrag; ***mental –,*** der Schwachsinn; ***make good a –,*** das Fehlende ergänzen; – ***disease,*** die Mangelkrankheit, Avitaminose. **deficient,** *adj.* mangelhaft, unzulänglich; unzureichend, ungenügend (***in,*** an (*Dat.*)); ***be – in,*** Mangel leiden an (*Dat.*), es mangeln *or* fehlen lassen an (*Dat.*); (*Poet.*) (er)mangeln (*Gen.*); ***she is – in the social graces,*** es mangelt ihr an Charme; ***mentally –,*** schwachsinnig.

deficit ['defisit], *s.* der Fehlbetrag, Ausfall, das Defizit.

defilade [defi'leid], **1.** *v.t.* (*Mil.*) gegen Feuer decken, defilieren. **2.** *s.* die Deckung, gedeckte Stellung.

[1]**defile** [di'fail], **1.** *v.i.* (*Mil.*) vorbeimarschieren, defilieren. **2.** [*also* 'di:fail], *s.* der Engpaß, Hohlweg, die Talschlucht, Enge; (*Mil.*) der Vorbeimarsch.

[2]**defile,** *v.t.* verunreinigen, besudeln, beschmutzen; (*fig.*) entehren, schänden (*a woman*), beflecken, verunglimpfen (*good name*), entweihen (*holy place*). **defilement,** *s.* die Verunreinigung, Befleckung, Beschmutzung, Besudelung; Schändung; Unreinheit, der Schmutz.

definable [di'fainəbl], *adj.* bestimmbar, erklärbar, genau umgrenzbar, definierbar. **define,** *v.t.* begrenzen, abgrenzen, umgrenzen; genau bezeichnen *or* umreißen, kennzeichnen, bestimmen, festlegen, definieren, genau erklären.

definite ['definit], *adj.* genau umgrenzt *or* umrissen, festgesetzt, festgelegt, bestimmt (*also Gram.*); definitiv, ausdrücklich, eindeutig, unzweideutig, präzis, klar, deutlich; – ***answer,*** endgültige Antwort. **definiteness,** *s.* die Bestimmtheit. **definition** [–'niʃən], *s.* 1. die (Begriffs)bestimmung, Erklärung, Definition; 2. Deutlichkeit, Bestimmtheit, (*Rad.*) Trennschärfe, (*T.V.*) Bildschärfe, (*Opt.*) Präzision. **definitive** [di'finitiv], *adj.* bestimmt, genau festgelegt, klar umrissen, (*opinion*) fest, entschlossen, entschieden; endgültig, definitiv.

deflagrate ['di:fləgreit], **1.** *v.i.* aufflackern, abbrennen, verpuffen. **2.** *v.t.* abbrennen *or* verbrennen (lassen); ***deflagrating spoon,*** der Abbrennlöffel.

deflate [di'fleit], **1.** *v.t.* 1. die Luft *etc.* ablassen aus, von Luft *etc.* entleeren; 2. (*fig.*) herabsetzen, herunterbringen (*prices*); (*fig.*) klein und häßlich machen (*a p.*). **2.** *v.i.* den Zahlungsmittelumlauf einschränken. **deflation** [–'fleiʃən], *s.* 1. die Ablassung *or* Entleerung der Luft *etc.*; 2. (*Pol. etc.*) Deflation. **deflationary,** *adj.* (*Pol.*) Deflations–.

deflect [di'flekt], **1.** *v.t.* ablenken, abwenden, abbiegen. **2.** *v.i.* abweichen. **deflection,** *s. See* **deflexion.**

deflexion [di'flekʃən], *s.* die Abweichung (*also fig.*), Ablenkung, Abbiegung; (*Phys.*) der Ausschlag (*of a needle etc.*), die Beugung (*of rays*); (*Artil.*) der Seitenvorhalt, Seitenwinkel; ***lateral –,*** die Seitenverschiebung; – ***correction,*** die Seitenvorhaltverbesserung.

deflorate ['di:flɔ:reit], *v.t. See* **deflower. defloration** [–'reiʃən], *s.* die Entjungferung; (*fig.*) Plünderung, Schändung.

deflower [di:'flauə], *v.t.* entjungfern; (*fig.*) plündern, schänden.

defoliate [di:'foulieit], *v.t.* entblättern. **defoliation** [–'eiʃən], *s.* die Entblätterung, der Laubfall.

deforest [di:'fɔrist], *v.t.* abholzen, abforsten, entwalden. **deforestation** [–'teiʃən], *s.* die Abforstung, Abholzung, Entwaldung, der Abtrieb.

deform [di'fɔ:m], *v.t.* entstellen, verunstalten, verzerren, deformieren. **deformation** [–'meiʃən], *s.* die Entstellung, Verunstaltung; Verzerrung, Mißbildung, (*Tech.*) Formveränderung, Verformung. **deformed,** *adj.* entstellt, verunstaltet, mißgestalt(et). **deformity,** *s.* die Mißgestaltung, Mißbildung; Mißgestalt, Unförmigkeit, Häßlichkeit.

defraud [di'frɔ:d], *v.t.* betrügen (***of,*** um); ***with***

intent to –, in betrügerischer Absicht; ***– the revenue,*** Steuern hinterziehen. **defraudation** [–'deiʃən], *s.* die Unterschlagung, Hinterziehung.

defray [di'frei], *v.t.* bezahlen, bestreiten, tragen, decken (*expenses*). **defrayment,** *s.* die Bezahlung, Deckung, Bestreitung.

defrock [di:'frɔk], *v.t. See* **unfrock.**

defrost [di:'frɔst], *v.t.* enteisen.

deft [deft], *adj.* geschickt, gewandt, flink. **deftness,** *s.* die Gewandtheit, Geschicklichkeit, Flinkheit.

defunct [di'fʌŋkt], *adj.* verstorben, (*fig.*) (*as a newspaper*) eingegangen.

defuse [di:'fju:z], *v.t.* entschärfen (*bombs*).

defy [di'fai], *v.t.* herausfordern; Trotz bieten (*Dat.*), trotzen (*Dat.*); ***– all description,*** jeder Beschreibung spotten.

degauss [di:'gaus], *v.t.* (*Mil.*) entmagnetisieren (*mines etc.*).

degeneracy [di'dʒenərəsi], *s.* die Degeneration, Entartung, Verderbtheit, Verkommenheit. **degenerate, 1.** [–reit], *v.i.* degenerieren, entarten, ausarten (***into***, in (*Acc.*) *or* zu). **2.** [–rit], *adj.* entartet, verderbt, verkommen, degeneriert. **3.** [–rit], *s.* verkommener Mensch. **degeneration** [–'reiʃən], *s.* die Ausartung, Degeneration, (*Chem.*) der Abbau.

deglutition [di:glu:'tiʃən], *s.* das Schlucken, der Schluckakt.

degradation [degrə'deiʃən], *s.* die Absetzung, Entsetzung; (*Mil.*) Degradation, Degradierung; Verschlechterung, Schwächung, Verkleinerung, Verringerung, Verminderung; (*fig.*) Erniedrigung, Entwürdigung, Schande; (*Biol.*) Degeneration, Entartung; (*Geol.*) Verwitterung, Abtragung. **degrade** [di'greid], **1.** *v.t.* herabsetzen, degradieren (*in rank*); heruntersetzen, verkleinern, vermindern, verringern, verschlechtern, abschwächen; (*fig.*) entwürdigen, entehren, erniedrigen; (*Geol.*) abnutzen, abtragen; (*Univ.*) auf ein Jahr zurückstellen. **2.** *v.i.* entarten, degenerieren, herunterkommen. **degrading,** *adj.* (*fig.*) entehrend, entwürdigend, erniedrigend; ***speak –ly,*** geringschätzig sprechen.

degree [di'gri:], *s.* 1. die Stufe, der Grad, das (Aus)-maß; ***– of relationship,*** der Verwandtschaftsgrad; (*sl.*) ***third –***, Polizeizwangsmaßnahmen (*pl.*), das Folterverhör; ***by –s,*** allmählich, Schritt für Schritt, nach und nach, stufenweise; ***by slow –s,*** ganz allmählich; ***in no small –***, in nicht geringem Grade; ***in no –***, keineswegs; ***in some –***, einigermaßen; ***not in the slightest –***, nicht im geringsten; ***to a certain –***, bis zu einem gewissen Grade, gewissermaßen, einigermaßen, ziemlich; ***to a high –***, (*coll.*) ***to a –***, in hohem Grade *or* Maße, äußerst; ***to an unusual –***, in ungewöhnlichem Maße; 2. der Rang, Stand; ***men of high –***, Männer von hohem Stande; 3. (*Univ.*) akademische Würde, akademischer Grad; ***honours –***, akademischer Grad höherer Ordnung; ***ordinary*** or ***pass –***, akademischer Grad ohne Spezialisierung; ***confer an honorary – on him,*** ihm die Würde eines Ehrendoktors verleihen; ***he obtained the doctor's –***, er errang die Doktorwürde; ***take one's –***, promovieren, einen akademischen Grad erlangen; 4. (*Mus.*) das Intervall, die Tonstufe; 5. (*Math.*) der Grad; ***three –s of frost,*** 3 Grad unter Null; ***– of latitude,*** der Breitengrad; ***– of longitude,*** der Längengrad; 6. (*Gram.*) ***– of comparison,*** die Steigerungsstufe.

dehiscence [di:'hisəns], *s.* (*Bot.*) das Aufspringen (*of seed pods*).

dehortatory [di:'hɔ:tətəri], *adj.* abratend, abmahnend.

dehumanize [di:'hju:mənaiz], *v.t.* entseelen, entmenschlichen.

dehydrate [di:'haidreit], *v.t.* entwässern; ***–d egg,*** das Trockenei. **dehydration** [–'dreiʃən], *s.* die Entwässerung, Wasserentziehung.

de-ice [di:'ais], *v.t.* (*Av.*) enteisen.

deification [di:ifi'keiʃən], *s.* die Vergötterung; Vergöttlichung, Apotheose. **deiform** ['di:ifɔ:m], *adj.* gottähnlich, göttlich, von göttlicher Gestalt. **deify** [–fai], *v.t.* vergöttlichen; (*fig.*) vergöttern.

deign [dein], **1.** *v.i.* geruhen, belieben; sich herablassen. **2.** *v.t.* gewähren, würdigen, sich herablassen zu; ***he did not – me a glance,*** er gewährte mir keinen Blick, er würdigte mich keines Blickes.

deism ['di:izm], *s.* der Deismus. **deist,** *s.* der (die) Deist(in). **deistic(al)** [–'istik(l)], *adj.* deistisch.

deity ['di:iti], *s.* die Gottheit; der Gott.

dejected [di'dʒektid], *adj.* niedergeschlagen, verzagt, betrübt. **dejectedness,** *s.* die Niedergeschlagenheit, Betrübtheit, Schwermut, Verzagtheit, der Kleinmut, Trübsinn. **dejection** [–'dʒekʃən], *s.* 1. *See* **dejectedness**; 2. (*Med.*) der Stuhlgang, die Defäkation. **dejecture** [–tʃə], *s.* (*Med.*) der Stuhl, Fäzes (*pl.*).

dekko ['dekou], *s.* (*sl.*) der Blick.

delactation [di:læk'teiʃən], *s.* die Entwöhnung (von der Mutterbrust).

delaine [də'lein], *s.* bunter Damenkleidstoff.

delate [di'leit], *v.t.* (*Scots Law*) anzeigen, denunzieren. **delation** [–'leiʃən], *s.* die Anzeige, Denunziation.

delay [di'lei], **1.** *v.t.* verzögern, aufschieben, hinausschieben, verschieben; hindern, hemmen, aufhalten; ***– going,*** säumen zu gehen; ***– payment,*** mit der Zahlung säumen; ***–ed action,*** die Verzögerung; Zeitzündung (*bombs etc.*); ***–ed ignition,*** die Spätzündung; (*Mil.*) ***–ing action,*** hinhaltendes Gefecht. **2.** *v.i.* säumen, zögern, zaudern; sich aufhalten. **3.** *s.* die Verzögerung, Verschiebung, der Aufschub, Verzug; ***the train has an hour's –***, der Zug hat eine Stunde Verspätung; ***without –***, ohne Aufschub, unverzüglich; ***– of payment,*** der Zahlungsaufschub, die Stundung.

dele ['di:li:], **1.** *imper.* zu tilgen! tilge! **2.** *s.* das Deleatur, Tilgungszeichen.

delectable [di'lektəbl], *adj.* erfreulich, ergötzlich, köstlich. **delectation** [di:lek'teiʃən], *s.* der Genuß, das Vergnügen, Ergötzen.

delegacy ['deligəsi], *s.* die Abordnung, Delegation, der Ausschuß. **delegate, 1.** [–geit], *v.t.* übertragen, überweisen, anvertrauen (*a th.*) (***to***, *Dat.*); bevollmächtigen, abordnen (*a p.*); ***– authority to him,*** ihm Vollmacht erteilen. **2.** [–git], *s.* Abgeordnete(r), Bevollmächtigte(r), Delegierte(r); *pl. See* **delegacy. delegation** [–'geiʃən], *s.* 1. die Überweisung (*of a debt etc.*), Übertragung (*of authority*), Bevollmächtigung; Abordnung, Delegierung (*of a p.*) (***to***, zu); ***– of powers,*** die Vollmachtsübertragung; 2. Abordnung, Deputation, Delegation, Abgeordnete (*pl.*).

delete [di'li:t], *v.t.* (aus)streichen, ausmerzen, tilgen, ausradieren.

deleterious [deli'tiəriəs], *adj.* schädlich, verderblich.

deletion [di'li:ʃən], *s.* die Tilgung, (Aus)streichung, Ausmerzung.

delf(t) [delf(t)], **1.** *s.* Delfter Porzellan. **2.** *adj.* (*Scots*) Steingut–, irden.

deliberate, 1. [di'libəreit], *v.t.* überlegen, erwägen. **2.** [–reit], *v.i.* sich beraten, sich bedenken, beratschlagen, nachdenken ((***up)on***, über (*Acc.*)). **3.** [–rit], *adj.* 1. vorsätzlich, absichtlich, bewußt; 2. bedächtig, vorsichtig, bedachtsam, besonnen, überlegt, wohlerwogen. **deliberateness** [–'ritnis], *s.* die Bedachtsamkeit, Bedächtigkeit, Besonnenheit, Vorsätzlichkeit, Vorsichtigkeit. **deliberation** [–'reiʃən], *s.* 1. die Überlegung, Beratung; 2. *See* **deliberateness. deliberative** [–rətiv], *adj.* überlegend; beratend.

delicacy ['delikəsi], *s.* 1. der Leckerbissen, die Delikatesse (*foodstuffs*); 2. Feinheit, Zartheit (*of texture, character etc.*); Zierlichkeit, Niedlichkeit (*of appearance*); Empfindlichkeit, Genauigkeit (*of instruments*), Zärtlichkeit, Schwächlichkeit, Anfälligkeit, Weichlichkeit (*of health*); Nachsicht, Feinfühligkeit, der Takt, das Zartgefühl (*of feelings*); ***negotiations of the utmost –***, Verhandlungen heikelster *or* kitzligster Natur.

delicate [ˈdelikit], *adj.* köstlich, schmackhaft, wohlschmeckend (*of food*); zart leicht, dünn, fein (*of materials*); feinfühlig, taktvoll, zartfühlend (*of a p.'s feelings*); zierlich, niedlich, elegant (*in appearance*), kränklich, schwächlich, anfällig (*in health*); heikel, kitzlig, bedenklich (*of problems*); zart (*of colour*).

delicatessen [delikəˈtesn], *s.* die Feinkost; das Feinkostgeschäft.

delicious [diˈliʃəs], *adj.* köstlich, wohlschmeckend; (*coll.*) lieblich, herrlich.

delict [diˈlikt], *s.* das Vergehen, Delikt.

delight [diˈlait], **1.** *s.* das Vergnügen, Ergötzen; die Freude, Lust, Wonne; ***take – in,*** seine Freude haben an (*Dat.*), Vergnügen finden an (*Dat.*); ***take a – in,*** sich (*Dat.*) ein Vergnügen machen aus; ***to the – of the onlookers,*** zum Ergötzen der Zuschauer. **2.** *v.t.* ergötzen, erfreuen, entzücken. **3.** *v.i.* sich (er)freuen, ein Vergnügen finden (***in,*** an (*Dat.*)); ***– in flowers,*** große Freude an Blumen haben; ***– in mischief,*** schadenfroh sein. **delighted,** *adj.* erfreut, entzückt; ***be –,*** entzückt sein, sich freuen (***with, at,*** über (*Acc.*)); ***I am – to accept,*** ich nehme mit (dem größten) Vergnügen an. **delightful,** *adj.* entzückend, reizend, köstlich; ***– news,*** der Ohrenschmauß. **delightfulness,** *s.* die Ergötzlichkeit, Köstlichkeit, Herrlichkeit.

delimit [di:ˈlimit], *v.t.* abgrenzen. **delimitation** [–ˈteiʃən], *s.* die Abgrenzung.

delineate [diˈlinieit], *v.t.* 1. entwerfen, skizzieren, zeichnen; 2. abgrenzen; 3. schildern, beschreiben, darstellen. **delineation** [–ˈeiʃən], *s.* 1. der Entwurf, die Skizze; 2. Schilderung.

delinquency [diˈliŋkwənsi], *s.* 1. die Pflichtvergessenheit, Pflichtverletzung; 2. das Vergehen, Verbrechen; ***juvenile –,*** die Jugendkriminalität. **delinquent, 1.** *adj.* 1. pflichtvergessen; 2. verbrecherisch, straffällig. **2.** *s.* der Verbrecher, Missetäter, Straffällige(r), Gestrauchelte(r).

deliquesce [deliˈkwes], *v.i.* (*Chem.*) zergehen, zerschmelzen, zerfließen. **deliquescence,** *s.* die Zerfließbarkeit; das Zerschmelzen. **deliquescent,** *adj.* zerfließend, zerfließlich, zerschmelzend.

delirious [diˈliriəs], *adj.* irre redend, phantasierend, im Fieberwahn; (*fig.*) rasend, wahnsinnig; ***be –,*** Fieberphantasien haben, phantasieren; ***– with joy,*** vor Freude rasend. **delirium,** *s.* das Phantasieren, Irrereden, der Fieberwahn; (*fig.*) Wahnsinn, Taumel, die Raserei; ***– tremens,*** der Säuferwahnsinn.

deliver [diˈlivə], *v.t.* 1. (*persons*) befreien (***from, out of,*** von *or* aus), (er)retten, erlösen; (*B.*) ***– us from evil,*** erlöse uns von dem Übel; 2. entbinden (*a woman of a child*); ***she was –ed of a boy,*** sie wurde von einem Knaben entbunden; 3. (*things*) übergeben, überreichen, überlassen, einhändigen (***to,*** *Dat.*); liefern (an (*Acc.*)), abliefern, ausliefern, überliefern, übertragen, überbringen, aufgeben, aushändigen, ausrichten (*Dat.*); zustellen, austragen (*letters*); ***to be –ed at B.,*** Erfüllungsort B.; ***– a blow,*** einen Schlag verabreichen *or* versetzen; ***to be –ed in eight days,*** mit achttägiger Lieferungsfrist, in acht Tagen lieferbar; ***– judgement,*** ein Urteil verkünden *or* aussprechen; ***– a lecture,*** einen Vortrag halten; ***– a message,*** eine Nachricht überbringen; ***– one's opinion,*** sein Urteil abgeben; ***– o.s. of a secret,*** ein Geheimnis von sich geben; ***– up,*** aufgeben, abtreten (*a th.*), überantworten (*a p. to justice*); ***– o.s. up,*** sich ergeben, sich stellen (***to,*** *Dat.*); ***– a warning,*** eine Warnung aussprechen *or* loslassen.

deliverable [diˈlivərəbl], *adj.* lieferbar, zu liefern(d). **deliverance,** *s.* die Befreiung, Erlösung, (Er)rettung. **deliverer,** *s.* der Befreier; (Er)retter, Erlöser. **delivery** [diˈlivəri], *s.* 1. (*Med.*) die Entbindung, Niederkunft; 2. Übergabe, (Aus)lieferung, Überbringung, Zusendung, Ablieferung, Abgabe (***to,*** an (*Acc.*)); Zustellung, Austragung (*of letters*); (*Comm.*) *see* **delivery-service**; ***bill of –,*** der Lieferungsschein; ***cash*** or (*Am.*) ***collect on –,*** Zahlung gegen Nachnahme; ***special –,*** die Zustellung durch Eilbote; ***take – of,*** abnehmen; 3. die Vortragsart, Vortragsweise, der Vortrag (*of a speech*); 4. das (Ab)werfen (*of a ball*). **delivery|-date,** *s.* der Liefertermin. **--pipe,** *s.* das Ablaufrohr, Ausflußrohr. **--service,** *s.* der Zustelldienst. **--van,** *s.* der Lieferwagen.

dell [del], *s.* enges Tal.

delouse [di:ˈlaus], *v.t.* entlausen.

delphinium [delˈfiniəm], *s.* (*Bot.*) der Rittersporn.

delta [ˈdeltə], *s.* das Delta. **delta-connection,** *s.* (*Elec.*) die Dreieckschaltung. **deltoid, 1.** *adj.* (*Anat.*) deltaförmig. **2.** *s.* der Deltamuskel.

delude [diˈl(j)u:d], *v.t.* betrügen, täuschen, irreführen; ***– into,*** verleiten zu; ***– o.s.,*** sich Illusionen hingeben.

deluge [ˈdelju:dʒ], **1.** *s.* die Überschwemmung; (*fig.*) Flut, (Un)menge; (*B.*) ***the Deluge,*** die Sintflut. **2.** *v.t.* überfluten, überschwemmen; (*fig.*) überschütten.

delusion [diˈl(j)u:ʒən], *s.* die Irreführung, (Selbst)-täuschung, Verblendung; der Irrtum, Wahn, Irrglauben; ***–s of grandeur,*** der Größenwahn; ***be*** or ***labour under the –,*** in dem Wahn leben. **delusive** [–siv], *adj.* irreführend, trügerisch, täuschend. **delusiveness,** *s.* das Trügerische, die Trüglichkeit. **delusory,** *adj. See* **delusive.**

de luxe [diˈluks, –lʌks], *adj.* luxuriös, Luxus–.

delve [delv], **1.** *v.t.* (*obs.*) graben. **2.** *v.i.* (*fig.*) sich eingraben (***into,*** in (*Acc.*)), graben (***for,*** nach), stöbern (***among,*** in (*Dat.*)).

demagnetize [di:ˈmægnitaiz], *v.t.* entmagnetisieren.

demagogic(al) [deməˈgɔdʒik(l)], *adj.* demagogisch. **demagogue** [ˈdeməgɔg], *s.* der Demagog. **demagogy** [ˈdeməgɔgi], *s.* die Demagogie.

demand [diˈmɑ:nd], **1.** *v.t.* 1. verlangen, fordern, fragen nach, ersuchen, begehren (***of, from,*** von); 2. erfordern, erheischen, beanspruchen, Anspruch erheben auf (*Acc.*), Forderungen stellen an (*Acc.*). **2.** *s.* 1. das Verlangen, die Forderung (***for,*** nach; ***on,*** an (*Acc.*)); ***on –,*** auf Verlangen *or* Aufforderung, (*Comm.*) auf Sicht; ***bill payable on –,*** der Sichtwechsel; 2. (*fig.*) die Anforderung (***on,*** an (*Acc.*)), Inanspruchnahme (*Gen.*); ***make great –s on,*** große Anforderungen stellen an (*Acc.*), stark in Anspruch nehmen; 4. (*Comm.*) der Bedarf (***for,*** an (*Dat.*)), die Nachfrage (nach); ***supply and –,*** Angebot und Nachfrage; ***in –,*** begehrt, gesucht; 4. (*Law*) der (Rechts)anspruch (***on,*** an (*Acc.*) (*a p.*), auf (*Acc.*) (*a th.*)). **demanding,** *adj.* (*fig.*) anspruchsvoll. **demand-note,** *s.* die Zahlungsaufforderung.

demarcate [ˈdi:mɑ:keit], *v.t.* abgrenzen (***from,*** von *or* gegen). **demarcation** [–ˈkeiʃən], *s.* die Abgrenzung; ***line of –,*** die Grenzlinie, Scheidelinie.

démarche [deiˈmɑ:ʃ], *s.* diplomatischer Schritt, die Demarche.

demean [diˈmi:n], *v.t.* 1. ***– o.s.,*** sich benehmen *or* verhalten *or* betragen; 2. ***– o.s.,*** sich erniedrigen *or* herabwürdigen. **demeaning,** *adj.* erniedrigend. **demeanour,** *s.* das Benehmen, Betragen, Verhalten, Auftreten.

demented [diˈmentid], *adj.* wahnsinnig.

démenti [deiˈmenti], *s.* die Richtigstellung, Ableugnung, das Dementi.

demerit [di:ˈmerit], *s.* das Verschulden, Versehen, Vergehen; der Mangel, Fehler; die Unwürdigkeit, Verwerflichkeit.

demesne [diˈmi:n], *s.* das Erbgut, freies Grundeigentum, die Domäne; der Eigenbesitz; (*fig.*) das Gebiet; ***royal –,*** das Kronland.

demi– [ˈdemi], *pref.* halb, Halb–. **–god,** *s.* der Halbgott. **–john,** *s.* die Korbflasche, der Glasballon.

demilitarization [di:militəraiˈzeiʃən], *s.* die Entmilitarisierung. **demilitarize** [–ˈmilitəraiz], *v.t.* entmilitarisieren.

demi|-mondaine [demimɔnˈdein], *s.* die Halbweltdame. **--monde** [ˈdemimɔnd], *s.* die Halbwelt. **--rep,** *s.* (*sl.*) die Frau von zweifelhaftem Ruf.

demisable [di'maizəbl], *adj.* (*Law*) verpachtbar, übertragbar. **demise, 1.** *s.* das Ableben, Hinscheiden; (*Law*) die (Grundstücks)übertragung, Verpachtung. **2.** *v.t.* (*Law*) übertragen (*landed property*), verpachten; vermachen.

demisemiquaver ['demisemikweivə], *s.* (*Mus.*) die Zweiunddreißigstelnote.

demission [di'miʃən], *s.* das Niederlegen, die Zurückziehung, Abdankung, der Rücktritt.

demobilization [di:moubilai'zeiʃən], *s.* die Demobilisierung, Demobilmachung, Abrüstung. **demobilize** [-'moubilaiz], *v.t.* auflösen (*an army*), entlassen (*troops*), außer Dienst stellen (*a ship*).

democracy [di'mɔkrəsi], *s.* die Demokratie. **democrat** ['deməkræt], *s.* der (die) Demokrat(in). **democratic** [demə'krætik], *adj.* demokratisch.

demographic(al) [demə'græfik(l)], *adj.* bevölkerungsstatistisch. **demography** [de'mɔgrəfi], *s.* die Bevölkerungsstatistik.

demolish [di'mɔliʃ], *v.t.* demolieren, niederreißen, abreißen, schleifen; (*fig.*) vernichten, zerstören. **demolition** [demə'liʃən], *s.* die Demolierung, das Niederreißen, Schleifen; (*fig.*) die Zerstörung, Vernichtung; – ***charge,*** die Sprengladung, geballte Ladung; – ***party,*** das Sprengkommando.

demon ['di:mən], *s.* böser Geist, der Teufel, Dämon; (*coll.*) Teufelskerl; ***a – for work,*** unermüdlicher *or* unersättlicher Arbeiter.

demonetize [di:'mʌnitaiz], *v.t.* außer Kurs setzen, entwerten.

demoniac [di'mouniæk], **1.** *adj.* dämonisch, teuflisch, besessen. **2.** *s.* Besessene(r). **demoniacal** [di:mə'naiəkl], *adj. See* **demoniac, 1. demonic** [di'mɔnik], *adj.* dämonisch, übermenschlich. **demonism** ['di:mənizm], *s.* der Dämonenglaube. **demonology** [di:mɔ'nɔlədʒi], *s.* die Dämonenlehre.

demonstrable [di'mɔnstrəbl], *adj.* sichtbar (*to*, für), beweisbar, erweislich, nachweislich. **demonstrate** ['demənstreit], **1.** *v.t.* anschaulich machen, dartun, darlegen, an den Tag legen, zeigen, erweisen; beweisen, demonstrieren; (*goods, instruments etc.*) vorführen. **2.** *v.i.* (*Pol.*) eine Kundgebung veranstalten, demonstrieren. **demonstration** [-'treiʃən], *s.* 1. anschauliche Darstellung, die Veranschaulichung; Demonstrierung, Vorführung; 2. Kundgebung, Äußerung, (*also Pol.*) Demonstration; 3. (*Log.*) der Beweis (*of*, für), die Beweisführung, Darlegung; 4. (*Mil.*) das Ablenkungsmanöver, der Scheinangriff. **demonstrative** [di'mɔnstrətiv], *adj.* 1. beweiskräftig; überzeugend, schlagend; ***be – of,*** deutlich zeigen, beweisen; 2. ausdrucksvoll, auffällig, überschwenglich; 3. (*Gram.*) – ***pronoun,*** hinweisendes Fürwort. **demonstrativeness,** *s.* die Überschwenglichkeit. **demonstrator** ['demənstreitə], *s.* 1. der Beweisführer, Erklärer; (*Comm.*) Demonstrator, Vorführer; 2. (*Anat.*) Prosektor; 3. Demonstrant, Teilnehmer an einer Demonstration.

demoralization [dimɔrəlai'zeiʃən], *s.* die Demoralisierung, Entmutigung; Zuchtlosigkeit. **demoralize** [-'mɔrəlaiz], *v.t.* entsittlichen, moralisch verderben; (*fig.*) demoralisieren, entmutigen, entkräften, zermürben. **demoralizing,** *adj.* verderblich (*to*, für), demoralisierend, zersetzend, zermürbend.

demote [di:'mout], *v.t.* (*Mil.*) (*coll.*) degradieren. **demotion** [-'mouʃən], *s.* (*Mil.*) die Degradierung, Absetzung.

demur [di'mə:], **1.** *v.i.* Einwendungen machen, Anstand nehmen, Bedenken äußern (*to*, gegen); (*Law*) (Rechts)einwände erheben; – ***to,*** beanstanden. **2.** *s.* der Zweifel, Skrupel; Einwand, die Einwendung; Bedenklichkeit, Unentschlossenheit; ***without –,*** ohne Einwendung; ***make – to,*** bezweifeln.

demure [di'mjuə], *adj.* ernst(haft), gesetzt, zurückhaltend; zimperlich, spröde. **demureness,** *s.* die Gesetztheit; Sprödigkeit.

demurrage [di'mʌridʒ], *s.* (*Naut.*) das Überliegegeld; die Überliegezeit; (*coll.*) das Lagergeld; ***be on –,*** die Liegezeit überschreiten.

demurrer [di'mə:rə], *s.* (*Law*) der (Rechts)einwand, Einspruch, die Einrede.

demy [di'mai], *s.* englisches Papierformat ($17\frac{1}{2}$ *in.* × $22\frac{1}{2}$ *in.*). **demyship** [-ʃip], *s.* ein Universitätsstipendium (*in Oxford*).

den [den], *s.* das Lager, der Bau (*of animals*); (*fig.*) die Höhle, Grube; (*coll.*) Bude; (*fig.*) ***the lion's –,*** die Höhle des Löwen; ***robber's –,*** die Räuberhöhle, das Räubernest; (*B.*) – ***of thieves,*** die Mördergrube.

denationalize [di:'næʃənəlaiz], *v.t.* entnationalisieren, des Nationalcharakters berauben; (*industry etc.*) entstaatlichen, reprivatisieren.

denaturalize [di:'nætʃərəlaiz], *v.t.* (*a th.*) seiner Natur berauben; (*a p.*) ausbürgern, der Staatsbürgerschaft *or* des Heimatrechts berauben.

denature [di:'neitʃə], *v.t.* (*Chem.*) denaturieren; (*alcohol*) vergällen.

denazification [di:nɑ:tsifi'keiʃən], *s.* die Entnazifizierung.

dendriform ['dendrifɔ:m], *adj.* baumförmig, baumartig. **dendrite** [-rait], *s.* der Dendrit. **dendroid,** *adj.* verästelt, baumähnlich. **dendrolite** [-əlait], *s.* der Dendrolith, die Pflanzenversteinerung. **dendrology** [-'drɔlədʒi], *s.* die Baumkunde.

deniable [di'naiəbl], *adj.* verneinbar, zu verneinen(d), ableugbar, abzuleugnen(d). **denial,** *s.* die Verneinung, (Ab)leugnung; Verweigerung, Ablehnung, Abweisung, abschlägige Antwort, Absage; ***official –,*** das Dementi; ***self-–,*** die Selbstverleugnung.

denigrate ['denigreit], *v.t.* anschwärzen, verunglimpfen. **denigration** [-'greiʃən], *s.* die Anschwärzung, Verunglimpfung.

denim ['denim], *s.* grober Drillich; *pl.* der Drillichanzug; Drillichhosen (*pl.*).

denizen ['denizn], **1.** *s.* der Bewohner; eingebürgerter Ausländer. **2.** *v.t.* bevölkern.

Denmark ['denmɑ:k], *s.* Dänemark (*n.*).

denominate [di'nɔmineit], *v.t.* (be)nennen, bezeichnen. **denomination** [-'neiʃən], *s.* die Benennung, Bezeichnung; Kategorie, Klasse, (*Math.*) (benannte) Einheit; der Nennwert (*currency*); (*Eccl.*) das Bekenntnis, die Sekte, Konfession. **denominational,** *adj.* konfessionell, Sekten–; – ***school,*** konfessionelle Schule. **denominationalism,** *s.* das Sektierertum, der Sektengeist; konfessioneller Unterricht. **denominative** [-nətiv], *adj.* benennend. **denominator,** *s.* (*Math.*) der Nenner; ***common –,*** der Generalnenner.

denotation [di:no'teiʃən], *s.* die Bezeichnung; Bedeutung, (*Log.*) der Begriffsumfang. **denotative** [di'noutətiv], *adj.* bezeichnend, andeutend. **denote** [di'nout], *v.t.* bezeichnen, kennzeichnen; (an)zeigen, angeben, andeuten, bedeuten.

denouement [dei'nu:mã], *s.* (*Theat.*) die Lösung (des Knotens); (*fig.*) der Ausgang, die Entscheidung.

denounce [di'nauns], *v.t.* anzeigen (*to, Dat. or* bei), denunzieren (bei); bloßstellen, brandmarken, öffentlich anklagen *or* rügen; – ***a treaty,*** einen Vertrag kündigen. **denouncement,** *s.* die Bloßstellung, Brandmarkung, Denunziation, Anzeige, öffentliche Anklage.

dense [dens], *adj.* 1. dicht (*as a crowd*); dick (*as a fog*); – ***smoke,*** der Qualm; 2. (*coll.*) beschränkt, dumm, schwerfällig; 3. (*Phot.*) gut belichtet. **denseness,** *s.* 1. die Dichte, Dichtheit, Dichtigkeit; 2. Schwerfälligkeit, Beschränktheit. **density,** *s.* die Dichte (*also Phot., Phys.*), Dichtigkeit, Dichtheit; (*Chem.*) Grädigkeit; (*Elec.*) ***field –,*** die Feldstärke.

dent [dent], **1.** *s.* der Einschnitt, die Kerbe; Beule, Delle, Einbeulung. **2.** *v.t.* auszacken, kerben; einbeulen. **3.** *v.i.* sich einbeulen.

dental [dentl], **1.** *adj.* Zahn–; zahnärztlich; (*Phonet.*) Dental–; – ***hospital,*** die Zahnklinik; – ***surgeon,*** der Zahnarzt; – ***surgery,*** die Zahnheilkunde. **2.** *s.* (*Phonet.*) der Zahnlaut, Dental(laut).

dentate(d) ['denteit (–'teitid)], *adj.* (*Bot.*) gezähnt. **dentation** [–'teiʃən], *s.* (*Bot.*) die Bezahnung, Zähnung. **denticle** [–tikl], *s.* das Zähnchen. **denticulate(d)** [–'tikjuleit(id)], *adj.* gezahnt, gezähnelt, ausgezackt. **denticulation** [–'leiʃən], *s.* die Zähnelung, Auszackung. **dentiform,** *adj.* zahnförmig. **dentifrice** [–fri:s], *s.* das Zahnputzmittel.

dentil ['dentil], *s.* (*Archit.*) der Zahnschnitt, die Zahnverzierung. **dentine** [–ti:n], *s.* das Zahnbein, Dentin. **dentist,** *s.* der Zahnarzt. **dentistry,** *s.* die Zahnheilkunde. **dentition** [–'tiʃən], *s.* das Zahnen (*of children*); Zahnsystem, die Zahnordnung. **denture** ['dentʃə], *s.* künstliches Gebiß, die Zahnprothese.

denudation [di:nju:'deiʃən], *s.* (*Geol.*) die Entblößung; Abtragung. **denude** [di'nju:d], *v.t.* entblößen (*of*, von), (*fig.*) berauben (*Gen.*); (*Geol.*) durch Abtragung freilegen.

denunciate [di'nʌnsieit], *v.t. See* **denounce. denunciation** [–'eiʃən], *s.* (drohende) Anzeige, die Brandmarkung, Denunziation, (*of a treaty*) Kündigung. **denunciator,** *s.* der Angeber, Denunziant. **denunciatory** [–siətəri], *adj.* anklagend, denunzierend, brandmarkend, drohend.

deny [di'nai], *v.t.* verneinen, negieren; in Abrede stellen, abstreiten, (ab)leugnen, dementieren; verweigern, versagen, abschlagen; verleugnen, nicht anerkennen; – ***on oath,*** abschwören; ***I – having*** or ***that I have said it,*** ich leugne, es gesagt zu haben; – ***o.s. a pleasure,*** sich (*Dat.*) ein Vergnügen versagen, sich (*Dat.*) ein Vergnügen nicht gönnen; ***there's no –ing it, it cannot be denied,*** es läßt sich nicht bestreiten, es ist nicht zu leugnen; – ***o.s.,*** sich verleugnen lassen (***to***, vor (*Dat.*)); ***he will not be denied,*** er läßt sich nicht zurückweisen *or* abweisen.

deodand ['di:oudænd], *s.* dem Staat verfallenes Gut.

deodorant [di:'oudərənt], *s.* das Desodorierungsmittel. **deodorize,** *v.t.* desodorieren, von Gerüchen befreien. **deodorizer,** *s. See* **deodorant.**

deoxid(iz)ation [di:ɔksi'deiʃən (–dai'zeiʃən)], *s.* die Desoxydation, Reduktion. **deoxidize** [–'ɔksidaiz], *v.t.* desoxydieren, reduzieren.

deoxygenate [di:'ɔksidʒəneit], *v.t.* den Sauerstoff entziehen (*Dat.*). **deoxygen(iz)ation** [–'neiʃən (–nai'zeiʃən)], *s.* die Sauerstoffentziehung.

depart [di'pɑ:t], **1.** *v.i.* **1.** abreisen; weggehen, fortgehen (*as a p.*), abfahren, abgehen (*as trains etc.*) (***for***, nach); **2.** abweichen, ablassen (***from***, von); – ***from a plan,*** einen Plan ändern *or* aufgeben; – ***from one's word,*** sein Wort nicht halten. **2.** *v.t.* – ***this life,*** dahinscheiden. **departed, 1.** *adj.* vergangen; verstorben; (*as adv.*) dahin. **2.** *s.* Verstorbene(r) (*usu. pl.*).

department [di'pɑ:tmənt], *s.* **1.** die Abteilung; **2.** (*Comm.*) Branche, der Geschäftszweig *or* –kreis, die Dienststelle; der Zweig; **3.** (*in France*) (Verwaltungs)bezirk, das Departement; **4.** (*usu. Am.*) Ministerium; (*Am.*) ***Department of State,*** Auswärtiges Amt; (*Am.*) – ***of war,*** das Kriegsministerium. **departmental** [di:pɑ:t'mentl], *adj.* Abteilungs–; Bezirks–; – ***chief,*** der Abteilungsvorsteher. **departmentalization** [–mentəlai'zeiʃən], *s.* die Aufteilung in Abteilungen. **departmentalize,** *v.t.* in Abteilungen einteilen. **department store,** *s.* das Warenhaus, Kaufhaus.

departure [di'pɑ:tʃə], *s.* **1.** das Weggehen, der Weggang; die Abreise, Abfahrt, (*Av.*) der Abflug; ***take one's –,*** fortgehen, sich verabschieden; **2.** (*fig.*) der Abgang, die Abweichung, Abwendung, das Ablassen (***from***, von), Aufgeben (*Gen.*); der Anfang, Beginn; ***a new –,*** neuer Anfang, etwas ganz Neues; ***a – from the usual practice,*** eine Abweichung von dem gewöhnlichen Vorgang; ***point of –,*** der Ausgang. **departure-platform,** *s.* der Abfahrtsbahnsteig.

depend [di'pend], *v.i.* **1.** abhängen, abhängig sein ((***up***)***on***, von), angewiesen sein auf (*Acc.*)), bedingt sein (durch), darauf ankommen; ***that –s,*** das kommt darauf an, je nachdem; ***that –s upon circumstances,*** das hängt von den Umständen ab; **2.** (*of a p.*) sich verlassen, zählen, rechnen (auf (*Acc.*)); – ***on it,*** verlassen Sie sich darauf! **3.** (*Law*) (*usu.* ***be –ing***) in der Schwebe sein, anhängig sein, schweben.

dependability [dipendə'biliti], *s.* die Zuverlässigkeit, Verläßlichkeit. **dependable** [–'pendəbl], *adj.* zuverlässig, verläßlich. **dependant,** *s.* **1.** Unterstützungsberechtigte(r), Angehörige(r), Abhängige(r); **2.** der Diener, Vasall, Anhänger.

dependence [di'pendəns], *s.* **1.** die Abhängigkeit ((***up***)***on***, von); das Bedingtsein (durch); **2.** Vertrauen, der Verlaß (auf (*Acc.*)); **3.** (*Law*) die Schwebe, Anhängigkeit. **dependency,** *s.* die Abhängigkeit, das Bedingtsein; (*Pol.*) abhängiges Gebiet, die Kolonie. **dependent, 1.** *adj.* abhängig, abhängend (***on***, von), angewiesen (auf (*Acc.*)); bedingt (durch); unterworfen, untergeordnet (*Dat.*). **2.** *s. See* **dependant.**

depict [di'pikt], *v.t.* (ab)malen; schildern, beschreiben, darstellen, zeichnen. **depiction** [–'pikʃən], *s.* das Zeichnen; die Zeichnung, Schilderung, Darstellung.

depilate ['depileit], *v.t.* enthaaren. **depilatory** [di'pilətəri], **1.** *adj.* enthaarend. **2.** *s.* das Enthaarungsmittel.

deplane [di:'plein], *v.i.* aus dem Flugzeug (aus)-steigen.

deplenish [di:'pleniʃ], *v.t.* entleeren.

deplete [di'pli:t], *v.t.* (ent)leeren; (*fig.*) erschöpfen. **depletion** [–'pli:ʃən], *s.* die Entleerung; (*Med.*) der Flüssigkeitsentzug; (*fig.*) die Erschöpfung; – ***of capital,*** die Kapitalentblößung. **depletive, depletory,** *adj.* entleerend.

deplorable [di'plɔ:rəbl], *adj.* bedauerlich, bedauernswert, beklagenswert; kläglich, jämmerlich, erbärmlich. **deplore,** *v.t.* bedauern, beweinen, beklagen, betrauern; mißbilligen.

deploy [di'plɔi], **1.** *v.t.* (*Mil.*) aufmarschieren lassen, Gefechtsformation annehmen lassen; (*fig.*) entfalten, entwickeln. **2.** *v.i.* (*Mil.*) die Gefechtsformation annehmen, ausschwärmen. **deployment,** *s.* (*Mil.*) der Aufmarsch; (*fig.*) die Entfaltung, Entwicklung; – ***area,*** das Aufmarschgebiet; – ***in depth,*** die Tiefengliederung.

depolarization [di:poulərai'zeiʃən], *s.* die Depolarisierung. **depolarize** [–'pouləraiz], *v.t.* depolarisieren.

depone [di'poun], *v.t.* (*Scots*) eidlich aussagen.

deponent [di'pounənt], **1.** *adj.* – ***verb,*** das Deponens. **2.** *s.* (*Scots*) vereidigter Zeuge.

depopulate [di:'pɔpjuleit], *v.t.* (*v.i.* sich) entvölkern. **depopulation** [–'leiʃən], *s.* die Entvölkerung.

deport [di'pɔ:t], *v.t.* **1.** verbannen, deportieren, des Landes verweisen, fortschaffen; ausweisen, abschieben (*aliens*); **2.** – ***o.s.,*** sich benehmen *or* betragen *or* verhalten. **deportation** [di:pɔ:'teiʃən], *s.* die Verbannung, Landesverweisung; Zwangsverschickung, Deportation, Ausweisung, Abschiebung (*of aliens*). **deportee** [–'ti:], *s.* Deportierte(r). **deportment,** *s.* das Benehmen, Betragen, Verhalten; die (Körper)haltung.

deposable [di'pouzəbl], *adj.* absetzbar. **deposal,** *s.* die Absetzung. **depose, 1.** *v.t.* absetzen; entsetzen (***from***, *Gen.*); entthronen (*a king etc.*). **2.** *v.i.* (*Law*) eidlich bezeugen *or* aussagen.

deposit [di'pɔzit], **1.** *s.* **1.** (*Geol.*) die Lagerstätte, das Lager, (*Chem., Geol.*) die Ablagerung, (*Chem.*) der Niederschlag, (Boden)satz; (*Tech.*) (galvanischer) Überzug, Belag; – ***in a boiler,*** der Kesselstein; **2.** (*Comm.*) die Deponierung, Hinterlegung, Einzahlung (*of money*), Anzahlung (*as part-payment*); (*money deposited*) (Geld)einlage; Kaution, das Reugeld, Depositum, (Unter)pfand; *pl.* Einlagen (*pl.*), Depositengelder (*pl.*); – ***account,*** das Einlagekonto, Depositenkonto; – ***in a bank,*** das Bankdepositum; ***make a –,*** eine Anzahlung leisten; ***place on –,*** in Depot geben, deponieren. **2.** *v.t.* **1.** abstellen, absetzen, ablegen, niederstellen, niedersetzen, niederlegen; (*Chem., Geol.*)

absetzen, ablagern; anschwemmen, aufschütten (*land*); (ab)legen (*eggs*); 2. (*Comm.*) anzahlen (*as part-payment*), einzahlen, hinterlegen, deponieren (*in a bank etc.*). **3.** *v.i.* (*Chem.*) absitzen, sich ablagern *or* abscheiden, sich absetzen *or* niederschlagen.

depositary [di'pɔzitəri], *s.* der Verwahrer, Depositar. **deposition** [di:pə'ziʃən], *s.* 1. (eidliche) Zeugenaussage; die Erklärung, Behauptung; 2. (*Comm.*) Deponierung, Hinterlegung, Einzahlung; 3. Amtsenthebung, Absetzung, Entsetzung (*from an office etc.*), Entthronung; 4. (*Chem., Geol.*) Ablagerung, Anlagerung, der Niederschlag; 5. (*Art*) die Kreuzabnahme (*of Christ*). **depositor,** *s.* der Depositeninhaber, Deponent, Einzahler, Hinterleger; *–'s book,* das Einlagebuch. **depository,** *s.* der Stapelplatz, Verwahrungsort, das Magazin, Depositorium, die Niederlage; (*fig.*) Fundgrube.

depot ['depou], *s.* die Niederlage, Sammelstelle, der Sammelplatz; das Magazin, Lagerhaus; (*Mil.*) (Sammel)lager, Depot, der Park; (*Am.*) Bahnhof; *– ship,* das Mutterschiff.

depravation [deprə'veiʃən], *s.* 1. *See* **depravity**; 2. die Entsittlichung, Verführung zum Schlechten. **deprave** [di'preiv], *v.t.* (moralisch) verderben. **depraved,** *adj.* verderbt, verdorben, verworfen, (sittlich) entartet, lasterhaft. **depravity** [di'præviti], *s.* die Verderbtheit, Verdorbenheit, Verworfenheit, Lasterhaftigkeit, Sittenlosigkeit, (sittliche) Entartung, die Schlechtigkeit.

deprecate ['deprikeit], *v.t.* mißbilligen, tadeln, verwerfen; ablehnen, von sich weisen, abzuwenden suchen. **deprecating,** *adj.* mißbilligend, abweisend, ablehnend. **deprecation** [–'keiʃən], *s.* die Mißbilligung, der Tadel, die Abweisung, Ablehnung. **deprecatory** [–kətəri], *adj.* 1. *See* **deprecating**; 2. Entschuldigungs–, abbittend.

depreciate [di'pri:ʃieit], **1.** *v.t.* herabsetzen (*prices*), entwerten, abwerten (*currency*); (*fig.*) heruntersetzen, heruntermachen, herabwürdigen; gering denken von, geringschätzen, unterschätzen. **2.** *v.i.* (im Preis) fallen; an Wert verlieren, im Wert sinken, abgeschrieben werden. **depreciation** [–'eiʃən], *s.* der Wertverlust, die Wertminderung; (*currency*) Abwertung, Entwertung; Herabsetzung, Herabwürdigung; Geringschätzung, Mißachtung, Unterschätzung; (*Tech.*) Abschreibung (*for wear and tear*); *– account,* das Abschreibungskonto; *– allowance,* der Abschreibungsbetrag. **depreciatory** [–iətəri], *adj.* herabsetzend; geringschätzig, verächtlich.

depredation [deprə'deiʃən], *s.* die Verwüstung, Verheerung, Plünderung; Räuberei, der Raub. **depredator** ['deprədeitə], *s.* der Plünderer, Verwüster, Räuber. **depredatory** [di'predətəri], *adj.* verheerend.

depress [di'pres], *v.t.* niederdrücken, herunterdrücken, (*trade etc.*) einschränken, abflauen lassen, (*prices*) herabsetzen, senken, (herab)drücken; (*Mus.*) senken (*pitch*), erniedrigen (*a note*); senken, mäßigen (*one's voice*), senken, niederschlagen (*one's eyes*); (*fig.*) (*a p.*) deprimieren, (nieder)drücken, bedrücken, entmutigen. **depressant, 1.** *adj.* (*Med.*) dämpfend, beruhigend; (*fig.*) bedrückend, (nieder)drückend. **2.** *s.* (*Med.*) das Beruhigungsmittel.

depressed [di'prest], *adj.* eingedrückt, zusammengedrückt, abgeflacht, abgeplattet; (*Comm.*) flau, matt (*business*), gesenkt, herabgesetzt (*prices*), verringert, vermindert (*value*); (*fig.*) deprimiert, bedrückt, niedergedrückt, niedergeschlagen (*a p.*), gedrückt (*spirits*); *– area,* das Notstandsgebiet; *– classes,* (*in India*) Parias (*pl.*); (*Pol.*) die wirtschaftlich Schlechtgestellten. **depressing,** *adj.* niederdrückend, bedrückend, deprimierend; (*coll.*) (*of sights etc.*) kläglich, erbärmlich.

depression [di'preʃən], *s.* 1. (*on a surface*) die Vertiefung, (Ein)senkung, (*Geol.*) Mulde, Landsenke; 2. (*Comm.*) Geschäftsstille, Flaute, Depression (*of trade*), Baisse, der Tiefstand (*of the market*), das Sinken, Fallen, die Senkung (*of prices*); 3. (*Meteor.*) das Tief(druckgebiet); 4. (*Astr.*) der Tiefstand, die Depression; 5. (*Med.*) Depression, Bedrücktheit, Gedrücktheit, Niedergeschlagenheit, gedrückte Stimmung, die Melancholie. **depressor** [–sə], *s.* (*Anat.*) der Niederzieher, Herabdrücker, Senker (*muscle*).

deprivation [depri'veiʃən], *s.* die Beraubung, Entziehung, der Entzug; schmerzlicher Verlust, die Entbehrung; Absetzung, Entsetzung (*of office*). **deprive** [di'praiv], *v.t.* berauben (*a p., Acc.*; *of, Gen.*), nehmen *or* entziehen (*a p., Dat.*; *of, Acc.*); ausschließen, fernhalten (*of,* von), vorenthalten (*Dat.*) (*of, Acc.*); (*esp. Eccl.*) entsetzen (*of, Gen.*), absetzen; ***I must – myself of this pleasure,*** ich muß mir das Vergnügen versagen.

depth [depθ], *s.* die Tiefe (*also fig.*); (*fig.*) (*of feeling*) Intensität, (*of knowledge*) der Umfang, das Ausmaß, (*of thought*) die Tiefgründigkeit, (*of meaning*) Unergründlichkeit, Dunkelheit, Unverständlichkeit, Unklarheit, (*of colour*) Kraft, Stärke, Fülle; (*oft. pl.*) der Abgrund, das Innerste; ***three feet in –,*** 3 Fuß tief; ***get out of one's –,*** den (sicheren) Grund unter den Füßen verlieren; (*fig.*) ***be*** or ***get out of one's –,*** den Boden unter den Füßen verlieren, ratlos davor stehen; (*Mil.*) ***– of column,*** die Marschtiefe; (*Opt.*) ***– of field*** or ***focus,*** die Schärfentiefe, (*esp. Phot.*) Tiefenschärfe; ***–(s) of misery,*** der Abgrund des Elends; ***in the – of the night,*** mitten in der Nacht, in tiefer Nacht; ***in the – of winter,*** mitten im Winter.

depth|-charge, *s.* die (Unter)wasserbombe. **--gauge,** *s.* die Tiefenlehre, der Tiefenmesser. **--sounder,** *s.* das Echolot.

depurate ['depjureit], *v.t.* (*Chem.*) reinigen, läutern. **depuration** [–'reiʃən], *s.* die Reinigung, Läuterung. **depurative** [di'pjuərətiv], **1.** *adj.* reinigend. **2.** *s.* das Reinigungsmittel.

deputation [depju'teiʃən], *s.* die Abordnung, Delegation, Deputation; Abgesandte (*pl.*). **depute, 1.** [di'pju:t], *v.t.* (*a p.*) abordnen, delegieren, bevollmächtigen, (*a task etc.*) übertragen (*to, Dat.*). **2.** ['depju:t], *adj.* (*Scots*) stellvertretend (*follows noun*). **deputize** ['depjutaiz], *v.i.* als Vertreter fungieren; *– for,* vertreten, (*coll.*) einspringen für. **deputy** ['depjuti], *s.* (*Pol.*) Abgeordnete(r), Abgesandte(r), (*Law*) Bevollmächtigte(r), der Stellvertreter, (*Comm.*) Geschäftsträger; ***by –,*** durch Stellvertretung; ***chamber of deputies,*** das Abgeordnetenhaus; ***– chairman,*** stellvertretende(r) Vorsitzende(r), der Vizepräsident.

deracinate [di'ræsineit], *v.t.* entwurzeln, (mit der Wurzel) ausrotten.

derail [di'reil], **1.** *v.t.* zum Entgleisen bringen. **2.** *v.i.* entgleisen. **derailment,** *s.* die Entgleisung.

derange [di'reindʒ], *v.t.* in Unordnung bringen, durcheinanderbringen, verwirren; aus der Ordnung bringen, unterbrechen, stören; (*the mind*) zerrütten. **deranged,** *adj.* in Unordnung, durcheinander, verwirrt, gestört, (*of the mind*) wahnsinnig, verrückt, geistesgestört. **derangement,** *s.* die Unordnung, Verwirrung, das Durcheinander; die Störung, Unterbrechung; Geistesgestörtheit, Geistesstörung, Geisteszerrüttung.

derate [di:'reit], *v.t.* von städtischer Steuer befreien.

de-register ['di:–], *v.t.* (*v.i.*) (sich) abkündigen.

derelict ['derəlikt], **1.** *adj.* verlassen, herrenlos. **2.** *s.* herrenloses Gut, (*Naut.*) (treibendes) Wrack; (*a p.*) Hilflose(r). **dereliction** [–'likʃən], *s.* 1. das Aufgeben, Verlassen, die Preisgabe; schuldhafte Vernachlässigung, schuldhaftes Versäumnis; ***– of duty,*** das Pflichtversäumnis, die Pflichtverletzung, Pflichtvergessenheit; 2. das Zurücktreten (*of the sea*); trockengelegtes Land.

de-requisition ['di:–], *v.t.* freigeben. **de-requisitioning,** *s.* die Aufhebung der Beschlagnahme, Freigabe.

de-restrict ['di:–], *v.t.* die Bewirtschaftung (*Gen.*) lockern. **de-restriction,** *s.* die Lockerung der Bewirtschaftung.

deride [di'raid], *v.t.* verlachen, verhöhnen, verspotten, verächtlich behandeln. **derisible**

[–'rizibl], *adj.* lächerlich. **derision** [–'riʒən], *s.* der Hohn, Spott; das Gespött, die Zielscheibe des Spottes; ***hold in –***, *see* **deride. derisive** [–'raisiv], *adj.* spöttisch, verächtlich, höhnisch. **derisory** [–'raizəri], *adj. See* **derisive**; lächerlich.

derivable [di'raivəbl], *adj.* ableitbar, herleitbar (***from***, von); erreichbar (aus); ***be – from,*** sich herleiten lassen von. **derivate** ['deriveit], *s.* (*Math.*) die Abgeleitete. **derivation** [–'veiʃən], *s.* die Ableitung (*also Math., Gram.*), Herleitung; Herkunft, Abstammung, der Ursprung. **derivative** [di'rivətiv], **1.** *adj.* abgeleitet, hergeleitet. **2.** *s.* Abgeleitete(s); (*Gram.*) abgeleitetes Wort, das Derivat(um), (*Math.*) der Differenzialkoeffizient, (*Chem.*) Abkömmling, das Derivat.

derive [di'raiv], **1.** *v.t.* ableiten (*also Math., Chem.*), herleiten, übernehmen (***from***, von); gewinnen, erlangen, erhalten, bekommen; ***be –d from,*** sich ableiten von, herstammen *or* herrühren von, übernommen sein von; ***– benefit from,*** Nutzen ziehen aus; ***– pleasure from,*** Freude haben *or* finden an (*Dat.*); ***– profit from,*** Gewinn schöpfen aus. **2.** *v.i.* abstammen, herstammen, herkommen, herrühren (***from***, von *or* aus), ausgehen (von), seinen Ursprung haben (in (*Dat.*)), sich ableiten *or* herleiten (von).

derma ['də:mə], *s.* (*Anat.*) die (Leder)haut. **dermal,** *adj.* (Leder)haut–. **dermatitis** [–'taitis], *s.* die Hautentzündung. **dermatoid,** *adj.* hautähnlich. **dermatologist** [–'tɔlədʒist], *s.* der Facharzt für Hautkrankheiten. **dermatosis** [–'tousis], *s.* die Hautkrankheit. **dermic,** *adj.* Haut–. **dermoid,** *adj. See* **dermatoid.**

derogate ['derəgeit], *v.i.* ***– from,*** beeinträchtigen, schmälern, abträglich sein (*Dat.*), Abbruch tun (*Dat.*), zum Nachteil gereichen (*Dat.*), schaden (*Dat.*); ***– from o.s.,*** sich erniedrigen, sich (*Dat.*) etwas vergeben; ***– from rules,*** von den Regeln abgehen. **derogation** [–'geiʃən], *s.* die Herabsetzung, Erniedrigung, Entwürdigung; Beeinträchtigung, Schmälerung, der Abbruch (***from***, *Gen.*).

derogative [di'rɔgətiv], *adj.* nachteilig (***to, of***, für), von Nachteil (*Dat.*), abträglich (*Dat.*), schädlich (*Dat. or* für), beeinträchtigend, schmälernd. **derogatory,** *adj.* **1.** *See* **derogative**; ***be – to,*** schaden (*Dat.*), beeinträchtigen; **2.** unwürdig, herabwürdigend, herabsetzend (*as behaviour*), abschätzig, abfällig (*as remarks*); ***– to o.s.,*** seiner unwürdig.

derrick ['derik], *s.* (*Naut.*) der Ladebaum; beweglicher Ausleger, der Dreh– und Wippkran; (*oil-well*) Bohrturm.

dervish ['də:viʃ], *s.* der Derwisch.

descant, 1. [dis'kænt], *v.i.* **1.** Diskant *or* Sopran singen; **2.** (*fig.*) sich verbreiten ((***up***)***on***, über (*Acc.*)). **2.** ['deskænt], *s.* der Diskant, Sopran, die Oberstimme, Gegenstimme; Variierung, variierte Melodie.

descend [di'send], **1.** *v.i.* hinab–, hinunter–, herab– *or* herunterfahren, –fließen, –gehen, –kommen, –sinken *or* –steigen, niederfallen (*as rain*), niederfahren (*into hell*), niedergehen (*as a shaft*); sinken, fallen (*as the sun etc.*); absteigen, absitzen (*from a horse etc.*), aussteigen (*from a vehicle*), (*Av.*) niedergehen, landen; (*Mus.*) absteigen, tiefer werden, fallen; ***– from*** (*usu.* ***be –ed from***), abstammen von; ***–*** (***up***)***on,*** herfallen über (*Acc.*), (sich) stürzen auf (*Acc.*), überfallen (*a p.*), einbrechen *or* einfallen in (*Acc.*) (*a place*), (*fig.*) hereinbrechen über (*Acc.*); (*of legacy*) ***– to him,*** ihm anheimfallen, auf ihn übergehen, sich auf ihn vererben; (*of a p.*) ***– to s.th.,*** sich zu etwas herablassen *or* herabwürdigen *or* hergeben *or* erniedrigen, sich auf etwas einlassen. **2.** *v.t.* herab–, herunter–, hinab– *or* hinuntergehen, –kommen *or* –steigen (*stairs*), abwärts– *or* hinunterfahren (*river*).

descendant [di'sendənt], *s.* der Abkömmling, Nachkomme; *pl.* Nachkommen (*pl.*), die Nachkommenschaft. **descender,** *s.* (*Typ.*) die Unterlänge; der Buchstabe mit Unterlänge.**descending,** *adj.* absteigend, fallend; ***– line***, absteigende Linie (*of family*); ***– rhythm***, fallender Rhythmus; (*Math.*) ***– series***, fallende Reihe.

descent [di'sent], *s.* **1.** der Abstieg, das Hinab–, Herab–, Hinunter– *or* Heruntersteigen; der Abhang, Abfall, die Neigung, Senkung, das Gefälle; (*fig.*) Sinken, der Verfall, Niedergang, Abstieg; ***Descent from the Cross,*** die Kreuzabnahme; ***Descent into Hell,*** die Höllenfahrt; **2.** die Abstammung, Abkunft, Herkunft, Geburt; ***of German –***, deutscher Herkunft; **3.** (*Law*) (*of property*) Vererbung; Übertragung, der Heimfall; **4.** (*Av.*) das Niedergehen, die Landung; ***make a –***, eine Landung machen, landen; ***parachute –***, der (Fallschirm)absprung; ***rate of –***, die Sinkgeschwindigkeit; **5.** (*into a mine*) die Einfahrt; **6.** (*Mil. etc.*) der Überfall (***on***, auf (*Acc.*)), Einfall (in (*Acc.*)), das Herfallen (über (*Acc.*)).

describable [dis'kraibəbl], *adj.* beschreibbar. **describe,** *v.t.* beschreiben, schildern, darstellen, bezeichnen (***as***, als); ***– a circle,*** einen Kreis beschreiben; ***– o.s. as an actor,*** sich als Schauspieler ausgeben.

description [dis'kripʃən], *s.* **1.** die Beschreibung, Schilderung, Darstellung; ***beggar*** or ***defy –***, jeder Beschreibung spotten; ***beyond*** or ***past all –***, unbeschreiblich; **2.** die Gattung, Sorte, Art; ***all books of this –***, alle Bücher dieser Art. **descriptive** [–tiv], *adj.* beschreibend, schildernd, darstellend; ***be – of,*** beschreiben, bezeichnen; ***– power,*** die Darstellungsgabe; ***– geometry,*** darstellende Geometrie; ***– language,*** anschauliche Sprache.

descry [dis'krai], *v.t.* gewahren, wahrnehmen, erspähen.

desecrate ['desikreit], *v.t.* entweihen, entheiligen, profanieren, schänden. **desecration** [–'kreiʃən], *s.* die Entweihung, Entheiligung, Profanierung.

desensitize [di:'sensitaiz], *v.t.* (*Phot.*) lichtunempfindlich machen, desensibilisieren. **desensitizer,** *s.* der Desensibilisator.

[1]**desert** ['dezət], **1.** *s.* die Wüste, Einöde; (*fig.*) Öde, das Ödland. **2.** *adj.* Wüsten–; öde, wüst, verlassen.

[2]**desert** [di'zə:t], *s.* (*oft. pl.*) das Verdienst, die Verdienstlichkeit; verdienter Lohn; verdiente Strafe; ***get one's –s,*** die verdiente Strafe bekommen.

[3]**desert** [di'zə:t], **1.** *v.t.* verlassen, im Stich lassen (*a p.*); abfallen von, untreu *or* abtrünnig werden (*Dat.*) (*a cause*); (*Mil.*) ***– the colours,*** *see* **2. 2.** *v.i.* (*Mil.*) fahnenflüchtig werden; ausreißen, desertieren (***from***, aus).

deserted [di'zə:tid], *adj.* unbewohnt, unbelebt (*district*), verlassen (*wife etc.*). **deserter,** *s.* (*Mil.*) Fahnenflüchtige(r), der Ausreißer, Deserteur, Überläufer. **desertion** [–'zə:ʃən], *s.* das Verlassen, Imstichlassen (*of a p.*), der Abfall, die Abtrünnigkeit (*of a cause*), (*Law*) böswilliges Verlassen (*of one's wife*); (*Mil.*) die Fahnenflucht, Desertion.

deserts [di'zə:ts], *pl. See* [2]**desert.**

deserve [di'zə:v], **1.** *v.t.* verdienen, verdient haben; würdig sein (*Gen.*), Anspruch haben auf (*Acc.*). **2.** *v.i.* sich (wohl)verdient machen (***of***, um). **deservedly** [–idli], *adv.* verdientermaßen, nach Verdienst, mit Recht. **deserving,** *adj.* verdienstvoll; verdienstlich; wert, würdig (***of***, *Gen.*); ***be – of***, wert *or* würdig sein (*Gen.*), verdienen; ***the – poor***, die verschämten Armen.

desiccant ['desikənt], *s.* das (Aus)trocknungsmittel. **desiccate** [–keit], **1.** *v.t.* (aus)trocknen. **2.** *v.i.* (aus)trocknen, (aus)dörren, trocken werden. **desiccation** [–'keiʃən], *s.* die (Aus)trocknung. **desiccative** [di'sikətiv], *adj.* (aus)trocknend. **desiccator** [–keitə], *s.* der Trockenapparat, Exsikkator.

desiderate [di'sidəreit], *v.t.* brauchen, nötig haben, benötigen, bedürfen (*Gen.*), vermissen; ersehnen. **desiderative** [–rətiv], **1.** *adj.* bedürfend (*Gen.*), benötigend; (*Gram.*) desiderativ. **2.** *s.* (*Gram.*) das Desiderativum. **desideratum** [–'reitəm], *s.* (*pl.* **-ta**) das Bedürfnis, Erfordernis, Erwünschte(s), Benötigte(s); der Mangel, die Lücke.

design [di'zain], **1.** *v.t.* **1.** aufzeichnen, entwerfen, skizzieren; – ***a dress,*** ein Kleid entwerfen; 2. (*fig.*) ersinnen, ausdenken; planen, vorhaben, sich (*Dat.*) vornehmen, beabsichtigen, im Sinne haben; 3. vorsehen, ausersehen (***for,*** für), bestimmen (zu) (*a p.*), vorsehen, bestimmen (für) (*a th.*); ***his father –ed him for the bar,*** sein Vater bestimmte ihn zum Rechtsanwalt *or* ihn für die Rechtsanwaltslaufbahn. **2.** *s.* 1. der Entwurf, Plan, die Zeichnung, Skizze; das Muster, Dessin, die Musterung; Ausführung, Konstruktion, Bauform, der Bau; die Formgebung, (künstlerische) Gestaltung; die Anordnung, Anlage; ***registered –,*** das Gebrauchsmuster; 2. (*fig.*) die Absicht, das Vorhaben, Projekt, der Plan, Anschlag; (End)zweck, das Ziel; ***by accident or (by) –,*** durch Zufall oder mit Absicht; ***have –s on*** or ***against,*** etwas (Böses) im Schilde führen gegen.

designate ['dezigneit], **1.** *v.t.* bezeichnen. kennzeichnen; betiteln, benennen; (*a th.*) bestimmen, vorsehen (***for,*** für); (*a p.*) ernennen, ausersehen, bestimmen (***for,*** für (*a post*); ***as,*** zu (*incumbent*)); (*Mil.*) ansprechen (*target*). **2.** *adj.* (*follows noun*) ausersehen, designiert. **designation** [–'neiʃən], *s.* die Bezeichnung, Benennung; Bestimmung, Ernennung (***to, for,*** für (*a post*); ***as,*** zu (*incumbent*)).

desingedly [di'zainidli], *adv.* absichtlich, vorsätzlich. **designer,** *s.* der Entwerfer, (Muster)-zeichner; Erfinder, Konstrukteur; (*fig.*) Projektenmacher; Ränkeschmied, Intrigant. **designing,** *adj.* (*fig.*) hinterhältig, ränkevoll.

desilver(ize) [di:'silvə(raiz)], *v.t.* entsilbern.

desirability [dizaiərə'biliti], *s.* die Erwünschtheit. **desirable** [–'zaiərəbl], *adj.* wünschenswert, erwünscht; angenehm; ***it is – that,*** es wird erwünscht, daß; – ***residence,*** angenehme Wohnung.

desire [di'zaiə], **1.** *v.t.* wünschen, verlangen, begehren; bitten, ersuchen; ***as –d,*** wie gewünscht; ***if –d,*** auf Wunsch; ***leave much (nothing) to be –d,*** viel (nichts) zu wünschen übriglassen. **2.** *s.* das Verlangen, Begehren (***for,*** nach); der Wunsch, die Bitte; Begierde, Lust, Sehnsucht; ***in accordance with one's –,*** wie gewünscht, wunschgemäß. **desirous** [–rəs], *pred. adj.* begierig, verlangend (***of,*** nach); ***be – of doing,*** danach verlangen *or* trachten zu tun; ***be – to do,*** gern tun wollen.

desist [di'sist], *v.i.* abstehen, ablassen, Abstand nehmen (***from,*** von), aufhören (mit *or* zu (*with inf.*)). **desistance,** *s.* das Abstehen, Ablassen.

desk [desk], *s.* das Pult; der Schreibtisch; ***cash-*** or ***pay-–,*** die Kasse; ***reading-–,*** das Lesepult; ***writing-–,*** der Schreibtisch

desolate, 1. ['desolit], *adj.* einsam, verlassen (*a p. or place*), leer, wüst, verwüstet (*place*), vereinsamt, allein (*a p.*), (*fig.*) öde, trostlos (*place*), betrübt, trostlos, niedergeschlagen, traurig (*a p.*). **2.** [–leit], *v.t.* verwüsten, verheeren; betrüben, betrübt *or* traurig machen. **desolateness** ['desolitnis], *s.* die Verlassenheit, Einsamkeit, Vereinsamung; Öde, Trostlosigkeit, Traurigkeit, Niedergeschlagenheit, der Gram. **desolation** [–'leiʃən], *s.* die Verödung, Verwüstung, Verheerung; Einöde; das Elend, der Gram, die Trostlosigkeit.

despair [dis'pɛə], **1.** *s.* die Hoffnungslosigkeit, Verzweiflung (***at,*** über (*Acc.*)); ***drive to –,*** zur Verzweiflung bringen; ***he is the – of his teachers,*** er gibt seinen Lehrern Grund zur Verzweiflung. **2.** *v.i.* verzweifeln, ohne Hoffnung sein, die Hoffnung aufgeben; – ***of,*** verzweifeln an (*Dat.*). **despairing,** *adj.* verzweifelnd, verzweifelt, verzweiflungsvoll, hoffnungslos.

despatch, *see* **dispatch.**

desperado [despə'ra:dou], *s.* der Wagehals, Tollkopf, Heißsporn; Schwerverbrecher, Bandit.

desperate ['despərit], *adj.* hoffnungslos, ausweglos, verzweifelt; verwegen, tollkühn; (*coll.*) arg, schlecht; ungeheuer, toll; ***rendered –,*** zur Verzweiflung gebracht; – ***deed,*** der Verzweiflungsakt; – ***effort,*** verzweifelte Anstrengung; – ***remedy,*** äußerstes Mittel. **desperation** [–'reiʃən], *s.* die Verzweiflung, Hoffnungslosigkeit; Raserei, Wut; ***drive to –,*** rasend machen, zur Verzweiflung bringen.

despicable ['despikəbl], *adj.* verächtlich, verachtenswert, verachtenswürdig.

despise [dis'paiz], *v.t.* verachten, geringschätzen; verschmähen.

despite [dis'pait], **1.** *s.* die Verachtung, Beschimpfung; der Trotz; Haß, die Tücke, Bosheit; (*rare*) ***in – of,*** *see* **2**; ***in – of you,*** dir zum Trotz; ***in – of himself,*** ohne es zu wollen, wider seinen Willen. **2.** *prep.* trotz (*Dat. or Gen.*), ungeachtet (*Gen.*). **despiteful,** *adj.* (*obs.*) boshaft, tückisch, gehässig.

despoil [dis'pɔil], *v.t.* plündern, berauben. **despoliation** [dispouli'eiʃən], *s.* die Plünderung, Beraubung.

despond [dis'pɔnd], *v.i.* verzagen, verzweifeln (***of,*** an (*Dat.*)). **despondence, despondency,** *s.* die Verzweiflung, Verzagtheit, Mutlosigkeit. **despondent, desponding,** *adj.* verzweifelt, verzagt, mutlos, kleinmütig.

despot ['despɔt], *s.* der Gewaltherrscher, Selbstherrscher, Autokrat, Despot; Tyrann. **despotic** [–'pɔtik], *adj.* despotisch, herrisch, gebieterisch, unumschränkt. **despotism,** *s.* die Gewaltherrschaft, Autokratie, der Despotismus, Absolutismus.

desquamate ['deskwəmeit], *v.i.* sich abschuppen. **desquamation** [–'meiʃən], *s.* (*Med.*) das Abschuppen, (*Geol.*) Abblättern.

dessert [di'zə:t], *s.* der Nachtisch, das Dessert, die Süßspeise. **dessert-spoon,** *s.* der Desertlöffel.

destination [desti'neiʃən], *s.* die Bestimmung, das Ziel; der Bestimmungsort, das Reiseziel; die Adresse (*of a letter*).

destine ['destin], *v.t.* bestimmen, vorsehen (*a th.*), (voraus)bestimmen, ausersehen (*a p.*) (***for,*** für); ***–d to do,*** tun sollen; (*of a ship etc.*) ***–d for Oslo,*** unterwegs nach Oslo.

destiny ['destini], *s.* das Schicksal, Geschick, Los, Verhängnis; die Notwendigkeit, Schicksalsgewalt.

destitute ['destitju:t], *adj.* bar, ermangelnd (***of,*** *Gen.*), entblößt, beraubt (*Gen.*); hilflos, mittellos, verarmt, notleidend. **destitution** [–'tju:ʃən], *s.* das Fehlen (***of,*** *Gen. or* von), der Mangel (an (*Dat.*)); bittere Not, das Elend, äußerste Armut.

destroy [dis'trɔi], *v.t.* zerstören, vernichten, verheeren; niederreißen, demolieren (*buildings etc.*), töten, umbringen (*a p.*), aufreiben (*enemy forces*), ausrotten, vertilgen (*vermin etc.*); (*Chem.*) zersetzen, auflösen; – ***his health,*** seine Gesundheit zerrütten; – ***his hopes,*** seine Hoffnungen zunichte machen. **destroyable,** *adj.* zerstörbar. **destroyer,** *s.* der Zerstörer (*also Naut.*). **destroying,** *adj. See* **destructive**; – ***angel,*** der Würgengel.

destructibility [distrʌkti'biliti], *s.* die Zerstörbarkeit. **destructible,** *adj.* zerstörbar. **destruction** [–'trʌkʃən], *s.* die Zerstörung, Vernichtung, Demolierung, Zertrümmerung, Verwüstung, Verheerung, das Zugrunderichten; die Ausrottung, Vertilgung; Tötung, (*fig.*) das Verderben, der Zerfall, Untergang; ***work one's own –,*** seinen eignen Untergang herbeiführen. **destructive** [–tiv], *adj.* zerstörend, vernichtend, verheerend; verderblich, schädlich; zersetzend, zerrüttend; ***be – of,*** untergraben, zerstören; – ***criticism,*** negative *or* verneinende Kritik. **destructiveness,** *s.* zerstörende Gewalt, vernichtende Wirkung, die Verderblichkeit, Zerstörungswut. **destructor,** *s.* die Verbrennungsanlage.

desuetude [di'sju:itju:d], *s.* das Aufhören eines Gebrauchs; die Ungebräuchlichkeit; ***fall into –,*** außer Gebrauch kommen; ***lost by –,*** infolge Nichtgeltendmachung verloren.

desulphurate [di:'sʌlfəreit], **desulphurize** [–raiz], *v.t.* entschwefeln.

desultoriness ['desəltərinis], *s.* die Flüchtigkeit, Flatterhaftigkeit, Unbeständigkeit; Zusammenhanglosigkeit, Ziellosigkeit, Planlosigkeit, Oberflächlichkeit. **desultory,** *adj.* unzusammenhängend, planlos, ziellos, abschweifend, flatterhaft, unbeständig; – ***remark,*** beiläufige Bemerkung.

detach [di'tætʃ], *v.t.* 1. losmachen, loslösen, ablösen, (los)trennen, abtrennen, abnehmen; absondern, freimachen, herauslösen; 2. (*Mil.*) detachieren, abkommandieren. **detachable,** *adj.* abnehmbar, (ab)trennbar, lösbar; – ***magazine,*** das Ansteckmagazin. **detached,** *adj.* 1. (ab)getrennt, (ab)gesondert, losgelöst; einzeln (*as events*); freistehend, alleinstehend (*as houses*); 2. (*Mil.*) abkommandiert, (*pred.*) zur besonderen Verwendung; 3. (*fig.*) objektiv, unparteiisch, unvoreingenommen; gleichgültig (***about,*** gegen), uninteressiert (an (*Dat.*)). **detachment,** *s.* 1. die Absonderung, (Ab)trennung, (Los)lösung, das Losmachen; 2. (*Mil.*) die Abteilung, der Trupp, das (Sonder)kommando; 3. (*fig.*) die Unparteilichkeit, Objektivität; Gleichgültigkeit (***from,*** gegen).

detail, 1. [di'teil], *v.t.* 1. ausführlich beschreiben *or* behandeln *or* berichten; einzeln eingehen auf (*Acc.*) *or* aufzählen; 2. (*Mil.*) einteilen, abkommandieren. **2.** ['di:teil], *s.* 1. die Einzelheit, das Detail, (*collect.*) Einzelheiten (*pl.*), Nähere(s); die Detailarbeit; Detailbehandlung; (*of a large picture*) der Einzelteil, Ausschnitt; (*coll.*) Nebenumstand, die Nebensache; *pl.* (*coll.*) nähere Angaben, das Nähere; ***in –,*** ausführlich, im einzelnen; ***go into*** or ***come down to –(s),*** auf Einzelheiten eingehen, ins Detail gehen; ***down to the smallest –,*** bis ins einzelne; 2. (*Mil.*) *see* **detachment** (*Mil.*); (*Mil.*) die Abkommandierung; (*Mil.*) der Tagesbefehl. **detailed** ['di:teild], *adj.* eingehend, ausführlich, umständlich.

detain [di'tein], *v.t.* aufhalten, abhalten, zurückhalten, hindern, (*a p.*) warten lassen; nachsitzen lassen (*at school*); (*Law*) in Haft (be)halten, festhalten (*in prison*). **detainer,** *s.* (*Law*) die Haft, (widerrechtliche) Vorenthaltung; ***writ of –,*** der Haftverlängerungsbefehl.

detect [di'tekt], *v.t.* entdecken, ausfindig machen, (heraus)finden, ermitteln, feststellen, nachweisen; aufdecken (*crime etc.*), ertappen (*a p. in wrongdoing*), (*Mil.*) spüren (*mines, gas etc.*). **detectable,** *adj.* entdeckbar, feststellbar, nachweisbar. **detection** [–'tekʃən], *s.* die Entdeckung, Ermittlung, Feststellung, der Nachweis; die Aufdeckung, Ertappung, Entlarvung; (*Rad.*) Gleichrichtung. **detective,** *s.* der Geheimpolizist, Kriminalbeamte(r), Detektiv; ***– force,*** die Geheimpolizei; ***– story,*** der Kriminalroman, die Detektivgeschichte. **detector,** *s.* (*Rad.*) der Detektor, Gleichrichter; (*Tech.*) Anzeiger; (*Mil.*) das Spürgerät; ***submarine –,*** das Ortungsgerät.

detent [di'tent], *s.* der Sperrkegel, Sperrhaken; (*Horol.*) Einfall, Vorfall, Einfallshaken.

détente [dei'tɑ̃t], *s.* (*Pol.*) die Entspannung.

detention [di'tenʃən], *s.* die Zurückhaltung, Vorenthaltung; Abhaltung, Beschlagnahme; (*Law*) Haft, Gefangenhaltung; (*Mil.*) der Arrest; das Nachsitzen (*at school*); ***– camp,*** das Internierungslager; ***– centre,*** die Besserungsanstalt; ***– colony,*** die Strafkolonie; ***preventive –,*** die Schutzhaft, Sicherungsverwahrung; ***unlawful –,*** die Freiheitsberaubung.

deter [di'tə:], *v.t.* abschrecken, zurückschrecken, abhalten (***from,*** von), verhindern (an (*Dat.*)).

detergent [di'tə:dʒənt], **1.** *adj.* reinigend. **2.** *s.* das Reinigungsmittel.

deteriorate [di'tiəriəreit], **1.** *v.t.* verschlechtern, verschlimmern, beeinträchtigen, verderben, herabsetzen. **2.** *v.i.* sich verschlimmern *or* verschlechtern, verderben; entarten, verfallen. **deterioration** [–'reiʃən], *s.* die Verschlimmerung, Verschlechterung, Entartung, der Zerfall, Verderb.

determent [di'tə:mənt], *s.* die Abschreckung; das Abschreckungsmittel.

determinable [di'tə:minəbl], *adj.* bestimmbar, festsetzbar, entscheidbar. **determinant, 1.** *adj.* bestimmend. **2.** *s.* das Bestimmende; (*Math.*) die Determinante. **determinate** [–nit], *adj.* bestimmt, entschieden, entschlossen, fest(gesetzt), festgelegt, endgültig. **determination** [–'neiʃən], *s.* 1. die Entschlossenheit, Entschiedenheit, Bestimmtheit, Entschlußkraft; 2. Festsetzung, Festlegung, Bestimmung; Feststellung, Ermittlung; der Beschluß, Entschluß, die Entscheidung, Resolution; 3. feste Absicht, der Zweck, Vorsatz, das Ziel, Streben; 4. die Richtung, Neigung, Tendenz; 5. (*Law*) der Ablauf (*of agreement etc.*). **determinative** [–nətiv], **1.** *adj.* bestimmend, Bestimmungs–, einschränkend (*of words etc.*); entscheidend. **2.** *s.* das Charakteristische, Bestimmende; (*Gram.*) Determinativ(um).

determine [di'tə:min], **1.** *v.t.* 1. entscheiden, bestimmen, festlegen, ansetzen, festsetzen; 2. feststellen, ermitteln, herausfinden, ausfindig machen; 3. veranlassen (*a p.*); 4. (*Law*) ablaufen lassen. **2.** *v.i.* beschließen, sich entschließen (***on,*** zu), sich entscheiden (für); ***– on doing,*** sich dazu entschließen zu tun, beschließen zu tun. **determined,** *adj.* entschlossen, entschieden; bestimmt, festgelegt.

deterrent [di'terənt], **1.** *s.* das Abschreckungsmittel (***to,*** gegen). **2.** *adj.* abschreckend.

detersive [di'tə:siv], *s., adj. See* **detergent.**

detest [di'test], *v.t.* verabscheuen. **detestable,** *adj.* verabscheuungswürdig, abscheulich. **detestableness,** *s.* die Abscheulichkeit. **detestation** [di:tes'teiʃən], *s.* die Verabscheuung, der Abscheu (***of, for,*** gegen *or* vor (*Dat.*)); ***hold in –,*** verabscheuen.

dethrone [di'θroun], *v.t.* entthronen (*also fig.*). **dethronement,** *s.* die Entthronung.

detonate ['detəneit], **1.** *v.i.* (ab)knallen, detonieren, explodieren. **2.** *v.t.* detonieren lassen. **detonating,** *adj.* Knall–, Spreng–, Zünd–; ***– composition,*** der Knallsatz, Zündsatz. **detonation** [–'neiʃən], *s.* der Knall, die Detonation, Explosion, Zündung. **detonator,** *s.* (*Railw.*) der Knallkörper, das Knallsignal; der Zünder, die Zündkapsel, Sprengkapsel, Zündpatrone.

detour [dei'tuə, 'di:tuə], *s.* der Umweg, Abstecher, die Umgehung, Umleitung.

detract [di'trækt], *v.t., v.i.* abziehen, wegnehmen, entziehen (***from,*** *Dat.*); ***– from,*** Eintrag *or* Abbruch tun (*Dat.*), beeinträchtigen, heruntersetzen, herabsetzen, vermindern, schmälern; ***– from his reputation,*** ihn herabsetzen *or* verunglimpfen. **detraction** [–'trækʃən], *s.* die Herabsetzung, Beeinträchtigung; Verleumdung. **detractive,** *adj.* verleumderisch; ***be – from,*** herabsetzen. **detractor,** *s.* 1. der Verleumder; 2. (*Anat.*) Abziehmuskel.

detrain [di:'trein], **1.** *v.t.* (*Mil.*) ausladen, absetzen (*persons*). **2.** *v.i.* aussteigen. **detrainment,** *s.* (*Mil.*) die Ausladung (*of troops*).

detriment ['detrimənt], *s.* der Nachteil, Schaden, Verlust (***to,*** für), Abbruch; ***to the – of,*** zum Schaden (*Gen.*); ***without – to,*** ohne Schaden für. **detrimental** [–'mentl], *adj.* schädlich, nachteilig, ungünstig (***to,*** für); ***be – to,*** schaden (*Dat.*).

detrital [di'traitl], *adj.* (*Geol.*) (Stein)schutt–, Geröll–. **detrited,** *adj.* abgenützt, verwittert. **detrition** [–'triʃən], *s.* die Abnützung, Abreibung, Abtragung. **detritus,** *s.* das Geröll, der (Gestein)schutt.

[1]**deuce** [dju:s], *s.* (*Cards, dice*) die Zwei, das Daus; (*Tenn.*) der Einstand; ***– ace,*** der Wurf (mit) Zwei und Eins.

[2]**deuce,** *s.* der Teufel; (*sl.*) ***what the – do you mean?*** was zum Teufel wollen Sie damit sagen? (*sl.*) ***the – of a noise,*** der Höllenlärm; ***play the – with,*** Schindluder treiben mit. **deuced,** *adj.* (*sl.*) verflucht, verteufelt.

Deuteronomy [dju:tə'rɔnəmi], *s.* (*B.*) das fünfte Buch Mosis.

devaluate [di'væljueit], *v.t.* abwerten, entwerten. **devaluation** [–'eiʃən], *s.* die Abwertung, Entwertung. **devalue,** *v.t. See* **devaluate.**

devastate ['devəsteit], *v.t.* verwüsten, verheeren. **devastating,** *adj.* verheerend, (*coll.*) phantastisch, enorm. **devastation** [–'teiʃən], *s.* die Verwüstung, Verheerung.

develop [di'veləp], **1.** *v.t.* entwickeln (*also Phot.*), entfalten; zeigen, an den Tag legen, enthüllen; erschließen, nutzbar machen (*resources*), hervorbringen, sich zuziehen (*ailment*); (*fig.*) (her)-ausarbeiten, ausbauen. **2.** *v.i.* sich entfalten *or* entwickeln (***from***, aus; ***into***, zu), entstehen; ***slow to –***, entwicklungsträge. **developer,** *s.* **1.** (*Phot.*) der Entwickler; 2. (*coll.*) *late* or *slow –*, der Spätentwickler, (*coll.*) Spätblütler. **development,** *s.* die Entwick(e)lung; Entfaltung, (Aus)bildung, das Werden, Entstehen, Wachstum, der Verlauf; Ausbau, die Erschließung; (*fig.*) Ausarbeitung, (*Mus.*) Durchführung; *– **area,*** das Entwicklungsgebiet. **developmental** [–'mentl], *adj.* Entwicklungs–, Wachstums–.

deviate ['di:vieit], *v.i.* abweichen, abgehen, abkommen (***from***, von). **deviation** [–'eiʃən], *s.* die Abweichung (*also Stat.*), (*Opt.*) Ablenkung, (*Magnet.*) Fehlweisung; (*Stat.*) ***standard –***, mittlere quadratische Abweichung; *– **of a balance,*** der Ausschlag einer Waage. **deviationism,** *s.* (*Pol.*) das Abweichen. **deviationist,** *s.* (*Pol.*) der Abweichler.

device [di'vais], *s.* **1.** die Einrichtung, Vorrichtung, das Gerät, der Apparat; 2. Plan, Einfall, die Erfindung; List, der Anschlag, Kunstgriff, Schlich, das Manöver; ***be left to one's own –s,*** sich (*Dat.*) selbst überlassen werden; 3. (*Her.*) das Sinnbild, Motto, der Wappenspruch, Wahlspruch, die Devise.

devil [devl], **1.** *s.* **1.** der Teufel; Höllengeist, Dämon, böser Geist; (*coll.*) toller Bursche, der Teufelskerl; (*sl.*) ***the –!*** alle Teufel! zum Henker! (*sl.*) ***the – a bit,*** nicht die Spur; (*sl.*) ***the – a one,*** nicht ein einziger; (*sl.*) ***how the –?*** wie zum Teufel? ***the –'s in it,*** das geht mit dem Teufel zu; (*sl.*) ***like the –,*** wie wild *or* verrückt; (*sl.*) ***that's the – of it,*** da liegt der Hund begraben; ***poor –,*** armer Schlucker *or* Teufel; (*sl.*) ***it's the very –,*** es ist eine verflixte S.; ***–'s advocate,*** (*Eccl.*) der Teufelsadvokat, (*fig.*) Widerspruchsgeist; *– **of a fellow,*** der Teufelskerl; (*sl.*) *– **of a job,*** eine Heidenarbeit; (*sl.*) *– **of a mess,*** ein Mordsdurcheinander; (*sl.*) *– **of a time,*** eine verdammt aufregende Zeit; ***cast out the –,*** den Teufel austreiben; ***needs must when the – drives,*** in der Not frißt der Teufel Fliegen; ***give the – his due,*** jedem das Seine lassen; ***go to the –,*** vor die Hunde *or* zugrunde gehen; ***go to the –!*** scher' dich zum Teufel! ***there's the – to pay,*** der Teufel ist los; das dicke Ende kommt noch; ***play the – with,*** arg mitspielen (*Dat.*); *– **take him!*** hol' ihn der Teufel! *– **take the hindmost,*** den letzten beißen die Hunde; ***talk of the – (and he's sure to appear),*** wenn man den Teufel an die Wand malt, ist er schon da; ***between the – and the deep blue sea,*** zwischen Scylla und Charybdis; 2. (*Typ.*) der Laufbursche; (*Law*) Hilfsanwalt; Handlanger; 3. (*Cul.*) scharf gewürztes Gericht; 4. (*Tech.*) der (Reiß)wolf. **2.** *v.t.* **1.** (*Tech.*) zerfasern, zerkleinern; 2. (*Cul.*) scharf gewürzt braten.

devil-fish, *s.* der Hornfisch. **devilish, 1.** *adj.* teuflisch, (*coll.*) verdammt. **2.** *adv.* (*coll.*) schrecklich, fürchterlich, verdammt. **devilishness,** *s.* Teuflische(s), die Teufelei. **devilled,** *adj.* (*Cul.*) zerhackt und gewürzt. **devil-may-care,** *adj.* sorglos, unbekümmert, verantwortungslos, leichtsinnig, rücksichtslos, verwegen. **devilment,** *s.* die Schelmerei, der Ulk, Unfug, Possen (*pl.*); die Ausgelassenheit, Tollkühnheit, der Mutwillen. **devilry,** *s.* die Teufelei, teuflische Kunst; die Grausamkeit, Schurkerei, Schlechtigkeit. **devil-worship,** *s.* der Teufelsdienst.

devious ['di:viəs], *adj.* abgelegen, ausgefallen, abschweifend; geschlängelt, gewunden, umherirrend; abwegig, irrig; (*coll.*) (*of a p.*) unaufrichtig, verschlagen; *– **paths,*** Abwege; *– **step,*** der Fehltritt. **deviousness,** *s.* die Abweichung, Verirrung; (*of a p.*) Verschlagenheit.

devisable [di'vaizəbl], *adj.* erdenkbar, erdenklich, (*Law*) vererbbar. **devise, 1.** *v.t.* **1.** ersinnen, erdenken, ausdenken, erfinden; (*coll.*) *– **ways and means,*** Mittel und Wege ausfindig machen; 2. (*Law*) hinterlassen, letztwillig vermachen. **2.** *s.* (*Law*) die Hinterlassung, das Vermachen; Vermächtnis, Legat, vermachter Besitz; das Testament. **devisee** [devai'zi:], *s.* der Legatar, Testamentserbe. **deviser,** *s.* der Erfinder. **devisor,** *s.* (*Law*) der Erblasser.

devitalize [di:'vaitəlaiz], *v.t.* entkräften, entnerven.

devitrification [di:vitrifi'keiʃən], *s.* die Entglasung. **devitrify** [di:'vitrifai], *v.t.* entglasen.

devoid [di'vɔid], *adj.* *– **of,*** ohne (*Acc.*), bar (*Gen.*), frei von, leer an (*Dat.*), –los; *– **of fear,*** furchtlos; *– **of all feelings,*** aller Gefühle bar, ohne jedes Gefühl; *– **of understanding,*** ohne Verständnis, verständnislos.

devoir ['devwɑ:], *s.* (*obs.*) die Höflichkeitsbezeigung; ***pay one's –s,*** seine Aufwartung machen (***to,*** *Dat.*).

devolution [di:və'lu:ʃən], *s.* **1.** der Verlauf, Ablauf, das Abrollen (*of time*); 2. (*Law*) der Übergang, die Übertragung, Weitergabe, der Heimfall (an (*Acc.*)); 3. (*Biol.*) die Entartung.

devolve [di'vɔlv], **1.** *v.t.* weitergeben (***upon,*** *Dat. or* an (*Acc.*)), übertragen (*Dat. or* auf (*Acc.*)). **2.** *v.i.* übertragen werden ((***up***)***on,*** ***to,*** *Dat. or* auf (*Acc.*)), weitergegeben werden (*Dat. or* an (*Acc.*)), anheimfallen, zufallen (*Dat.*), übergehen (auf (*Acc.*)); ***the crown –s on his eldest son,*** die Krone fällt an seinen ältesten Sohn; ***it –s upon me to tell him,*** es liegt mir ob, es ihm zu sagen.

devote [di'vout], *v.t.* widmen, weihen (***to,*** *Dat.*); hingeben, zuwenden (*time etc.*) (***to,*** *Dat.*). **devoted,** *adj.* (*pred.*) ergeben, gewidmet (*Dat.*); (*attrib.*) treu, hingebungsvoll, anhänglich; dem Untergang geweiht. **devotedness,** *s.* die Ergebenheit, Anhänglichkeit, Hingebung. **devotee** [devo'ti:], *s.* der Anhänger, Anbeter, Verehrer, Verfechter; (*Eccl.*) Eiferer, Zelot, Frömmler.

devotion [di'vouʃən], *s.* die Widmung, Weihung; Hingabe (***to,*** an (*Acc.*)), Hingebung, Aufopferung (für); Frömmigkeit, Andacht; Zuneigung, innige Liebe (***to,*** zu), Anhänglichkeit (an (*Acc.*)), Ergebenheit (in (*Acc.*)), Treue (gegen); der Eifer (für); *pl.* die Andacht(sübung), das Gebet; *– **to duty,*** der Eifer in der Erfüllung der Pflicht; ***be at one's –s,*** seine Andacht verrichten. **devotional,** *adj.* andächtig, fromm; *– **book,*** das Erbauungsbuch; *– **frame of mind,*** fromme Gemütsart.

devour [di'vauə], *v.t.* verschlingen, verzehren, fressen; (*fig.*) vernichten, zerstören, wegraffen; ***–ed by jealousy,*** von Eifersucht verzehrt; *– **a book,*** ein Buch (förmlich) verschlingen. **devouring,** *adj.* verschlingend, brennend.

devout [di'vaut], *adj.* andächtig, fromm, gläubig, gottesfürchtig; innig, inbrüstig. **devoutness,** *s.* die Frömmigkeit, Gottesfurcht, Andächtigkeit; Hingabe, Hingegebenheit, Inbrunst, Innigkeit.

dew [dju:], *s.* der Tau; ***the – is falling,*** es taut. **dew|berry,** *s.* die Ackerbeere. **–drop,** *s.* der Tautropfen. **dewiness** [–inis], *s.* die (Tau)feuchtigkeit.

dewlap ['dju:læp], *s.* die Wamme, der Triel.

dew-point, *s.* der Taupunkt. **dewy,** *adj.* betaut, tauig, taufeucht.

dexter ['dekstə], *adj.* (*Her.*) recht, recht(s)seitig (*left of the observer*). **dexterity** [–'teriti], *s.* **1.** die Gewandtheit, Geschicklichkeit, (Hand)fertigkeit; Behendigkeit, Flinkheit; 2. Rechtshändigkeit. **dexterous** [–tərəs], *adj.* **1.** flink, behend; gewandt, geschickt; 2. rechtshändig. **dextral,** *adj.* rechtshändig. **dextrality** [–'træliti], *s.* die Rechtshändigkeit.

dextrin ['dekstrin], *s.* das Dextrin; Stärkegummi, Röstgummi.

dextro– ['dekstrou], *pref.* rechts–; ***––acid,*** die Rechtssäure; ***––rotatory,*** rechtsdrehend.

dextrose ['dekstrous], *s.* der Traubenzucker, die Dextrose.

dextrous ['dekstrəs], *adj. See* **dexterous.**

dhow [dau], *s.* die D(h)au.

di– [dai], *pref.* (*Chem.*) zwei, doppelt.

diabetes [daiə'bi:ti:z], *s.* die Zuckerkrankheit, Harnruhr, der Diabetes. **diabetic** [–'betik], **1.** *adj.* zuckerkrank. **2.** *s.* der (die) Diabetiker(in), Zuckerkranke(r).

diablerie [di'ɑ:bləri], *s.* die Teufelskunst, Zauberei, Hexerei. **diabolic(al)** [daiə'bɔlik(l)], *adj.* teuflisch, böse, boshaft.

di-acid [dai'æsid], *adj.* zweisäurig.

diaconal [dai'ækənl], *adj.* Diakons–, Diakonats–.

diacritic [daiə'kritik], **1.** *adj.* diakritisch, unterscheidend. **2.** *s.* diakritisches Zeichen. **diacritical,** *adj. See* **diacritic, 1**; – ***mark,*** *see* **diacritic, 2.**

diadem ['daiədem], *s.* das Stirnband, Diadem; (*fig.*) der Kranz, die Krone; Königswürde, Hoheit, Herrschaft.

diaeresis [dai'erəsis], *s.* die Diärese, Diäresis; das Trema.

diagnose [daiəg'nouz], **1.** *v.i.* eine Diagnose stellen. **2.** *v.t.* diagnostizieren, (*also fig.*) bestimmen. **diagnosis** [–'nousis], *s.* die Diagnose; (*fig.*) Bestimmung, Beurteilung; ***make a –,*** *see* **diagnose, 1. diagnostic** [–'nɔstik], **1.** *adj.* diagnostisch; (*fig.*) bezeichnend, charakteristisch. **2.** *s.* das Merkmal, Kennzeichen. **diagnostician** [–nɔs'tiʃən], *s.* der Diagnostiker. **diagnostics,** *pl.* (*sing. constr.*) die Diagnostik.

diagonal [dai'ægənl], **1.** *adj.* diagonal, schräg(laufend), querlaufend. **2.** *s.* die Diagonale, der Schrägschnitt.

diagram ['daiəgræm], *s.* (erläuternde) Figur, schematische *or* graphische Darstellung, das Diagramm, Schema, Schaubild; (*Rad.*) ***circuit –,*** das Schaltschema, Schaltbild; (*Bot.*) ***floral –,*** der Blütengrundriß. **diagrammatic** [–grə'mætik], *adj.* schematisch, graphisch.

dial ['daiəl], **1.** *s.* das Zifferblatt (*clock etc.*); (*Tele.*) der Wähler, die Wählscheibe, (*Tech.*) Skala, Skalenscheibe, das Skalenblatt; (*sl.*) die Visage; – ***telephone,*** das Selbstanschlußtelephon, Selbstwähltelephon. **2.** *v.t.* (*Tele.*) wählen; ***dial(l)ing tone,*** das Amtszeichen.

dialect ['daiəlekt], *s.* die Mundart, der Dialekt. **dialectal** [–'lektl], *adj.* mundartlich; dialektisch.

dialectic [daiə'lektik], *s.* die Dialektik. **dialectic(al),** *adj.* dialektisch, logisch; spitzfindig. **dialectician** [–'tiʃən], *s.* der Dialektiker, Logiker. **dialectics,** *pl.* (*usu. sing. constr.*) die Dialektik.

dial(l)ing ['daiəliŋ], *see* **dial, 2.**

dialogue ['daiəlɔg], *s.* das (Zwie)gespräch, die Unterredung, der Dialog.

diameter [dai'æmitə], *s.* der Durchmesser; ***inner*** – (***of a cylinder***), lichte Weite, die Zylinderbohrung; ***in –,*** im Durchmesser. **diametrical** [daiə'metrikl], *adj.* diametrisch; – ***opposites,*** diametrale Gegensätze; ***–ly opposed,*** diametral *or* genau entgegengesetzt.

diamond ['dɑiəmənd], *s.* 1. der Diamant, (*Poet.*) Demant; ***black –,*** dunkler Diamant; (*coll.*) die Steinkohle; ***faceted –,*** der Rautenbrillant; ***glazier's –,*** der Glaserdiamant; ***rough –,*** ungeschliffener Diamant; (*fig.*) Mensch mit rauhem Äußeren aber gutem Kern; – ***cut –,*** List gegen List; (*coll.*) Wurst wider Wurst; 2. (*Geom.*) der Rhombus, die Raute; 3. (*Cards*) das Karo, Schellen (*pl.*); ***nine of –s,*** die Karoneun; ***queen of –s,*** die Karodame; 4. (*Typ.*) die Diamant(schrift).

diamond|-cutter, *s.* der Diamantschleifer. **--mine,** *s.* die Diamantgrube. **--setter,** *s.* der Diamantenfasser. **--shaped,** *adj.* rautenförmig, rhombisch. **- wedding,** *s.* diamantene Hochzeit.

diandrian [dai'ændriən], *adj.* (*Bot.*) zweimännig, diandrisch.

diapason [daiə'peizn], *s.* die Oktave; Mensur (*of organs*); (*Poet.*) der Tonumfang, Einklang, harmonisches Ganze; ***open –,*** das Prinzipal (*organ*).

diaper ['daiəpə], **1.** *s.* 1. rautenförmig gemusterte Leinwand; 2. (*Archit.*) rautenförmiges Muster; 3. (*Am.*) die Windel (*of a baby*). **2.** *v.t.* rautenförmig mustern.

diaphanous [dai'æfənəs], *adj.* durchsichtig, transparent; diaphan.

diaphoretic [daiəfə'retik], **1.** *adj.* schweißtreibend. **2.** *s.* schweißtreibendes Mittel.

diaphragm ['daiəfræm], *s.* (*Anat.*) das Zwerchfell; die Scheidewand; (*Opt.*) Blende; (*Tele.*) Membran, das Schallblech.

diapositive [daiə'pɔzitiv], *s.* das Diapositiv; durchsichtiges Bild.

diarist ['daiərist], *s.* der Tagebuchschreiber.

diarrhoea [daiə'riə], *s.* der Durchfall, die Diarrhö(e), (*vulg.*) der Dünnpfiff, Dünnschiß.

diary ['daiəri], *s.* das Tagebuch; der (Taschen)kalender; ***keep a –,*** ein Tagebuch führen.

diastole [dai'æstəli], *s.* (*Med.*) die Diastole; (*Metr.*) Dehnung; (*fig.*) ***systole and –,*** das Auf und Ab.

diathermacy [daiə'θə:məsi], *s.* die Wärmedurchlässigkeit. **diathermic,** *adj.* wärmedurchlässig, diatherm(an).

diathesis [dai'æθisis], *s.* (*Med.*) die Anlage, Neigung (*to,* zu), Empfänglichkeit (für).

diatom ['daiətɔm], *s.* (*Bot.*) die Kieselalge, Diatomee. **diatomaceous** [–'meiʃəs], *adj.* Diatomeen–; – ***earth,*** die Infusorienerde, Kieselgur.

diatomic [daiə'tɔmik], *adj.* (*Chem.*) zweiatomig, zweiwertig.

diatonic [daiə'tɔnik], *adj.* (*Mus.*) diatonisch.

diatribe ['daiətraib], *s.* die Schmährede, Schmähschrift; kritischer Ausfall, der Protest.

dibble [dibl], **1.** *s.* der Pflanzstock, Dibbelstock, das Setzholz, Steckholz. **2.** *v.t., v.i.* mit dem Setzholz pflanzen.

dice [dais], **1.** *pl.* (*see* [2]**die**) Würfel (*pl.*). **2.** *v.t.* in Würfel schneiden. **3.** *v.i.* würfeln, knobeln; (*sl.*) – ***with death,*** mit dem Leben spielen, das Leben aufs Spiel setzen. **dice-box,** *s.* der Würfelbecher, Knobelbecher.

dicephalous [dai'sefələs], *adj.* zweiköpfig.

dichotomy [dai'kɔtəmi], *s.* die (Zwei)teilung, (Auf)spaltung; (*Bot.*) Gabelspaltung, Gabelung; (*Astr.*) Halbsicht.

dick [dik], *s.* (*sl.*) der Schnüffler, Spitzel.

dickens ['dikinz], *s.* (*coll.*) der Teufel, Kuckuck; (*coll.*) ***what the –?*** was zum Teufel? – ***of a noise,*** der Mordslärm.

[1]**dicker** ['dikə], *s.* zehn Stück (*esp. hides*), das Dutzend.

[2]**dicker, 1.** *v.i.* (*sl.*) schachern, feilschen; Tauschhandel treiben, Tauschgeschäfte machen. **2.** *v.t.* schachern *or* feilschen mit; tauschen, Tauschhandel treiben mit.

dick(e)y ['diki], *s.* 1. der Bedientensitz (*of a coach*); (*Motor.*) Rücksitz; 2. die Hemd(en)brust, das Vorhemd, der (Blusen)einsatz; Schurz, das Lätzchen; 3. (*coll.*) der Esel.

dicky, *adj.* (*sl.*) kränklich, unwohl, unpäßlich; (*fig.*) klapp(e)rig, wackelig, brüchig, kümmerlich.

dicky(-bird), *s.* (*coll.*) der Piepmatz.

dicotyledon [daikɔti'li:dən], *s.* der Blattkeimer, die Dikotyle, zweikeimblättrige Pflanze. **dicotyledonous** [–əs], *adj.* zweikeimblättrig, dikotyl.

dictaphone ['diktəfoun], *s.* das Diktaphon, der Diktierapparat.

dictate, 1. [dik'teit], *v.t.* 1. vorschreiben, befehlen, gebieten, aufzwingen, auferlegen; – ***terms,*** Bedingungen auferlegen; 2. diktieren, ansagen (*letter etc.*) (*to, Dat.*); 3. (*fig.*) einflößen, eingeben. **2.** [–'teit], *v.i.* befehlen, Befehle geben; ***he will not be –d to,*** er läßt sich (*Dat.*) nichts vorschreiben *or* keine Vorschriften machen. **3.** ['dikteit], *s.* die Vorschrift, der Befehl, das Gebot; ***–s of conscience*** (or ***reason***), das Gebot des Gewissens (*or* der Vernunft). **dictation** [–'teiʃən], *s.* 1. das Diktieren; Diktat(schreiben); ***write from –,*** nach Diktat schreiben; 2. das Geheiß, Gebot, der Befehl, die Vorschrift.

dictator [dik'teitə], *s.* der Diktator, unumschränkter Machthaber, Gewalthaber. **dictatorial** [–tə'tɔ:riəl], *adj.* diktatorisch, absolut, unumschränkt; gebieterisch, befehlshaberisch. **dictatorship,** *s.* die Diktatur; unumschränkte Macht, die Gewaltherrschaft.

diction ['dikʃən], *s.* die Ausdrucksweise, Redeweise,

Diktion, Sprache, der Stil; die Aussprache, der Vortrag.

dictionary ['dikʃənəri], *s.* das Wörterbuch, Lexikon; (*fig.*) ***walking –,*** wandelndes Lexikon.

dictum ['diktəm], *s.* (*pl.* **-ta**) der Spruch. geflügeltes Wort, die Maxime; der Ausspruch, Entscheid.

did [did], *imperf. of* **do.**

didactic [di'dæktik], *adj.* lehrhaft, didaktisch; (*of a p.*) schulmeisternd, belehrend; – ***poem,*** das Lehrgedicht.

diddle [didl], *v.t.* (*sl.*) beschwindeln, betrügen, hereinlegen; prellen (***out of,*** um). **diddler,** *s.* (*sl.*) der (die) Schwindler(in).

didn't [didnt] = ***did not.***

[1]**die** [dai], *v.i.* sterben (***of,*** an (*Dat.*); ***from,*** vor (*Dat.*)); krepieren (*of animals; also sl.*); absterben, eingehen (*as a plant*); (*fig.*) vergehen, dahinschwinden, erlöschen, aufhören; ***never say –!*** Kopf hoch! nur nicht nachgeben! – ***an early death,*** eines frühen Todes sterben; – ***a natural death,*** eines natürlichen Todes sterben; – ***a rich man,*** als reicher Mann sterben.

(*with advs.*) – ***away,*** sich legen (*as the wind*), sich verlieren, verklingen, verhallen, ersterben (*as sounds*); schwinden, schwächer werden, vergehen; – ***down,*** schwinden, allmählich vergehen; verhallen (*of sound*); erlöschen (*of fire*); – ***game,*** kämpfend sterben; (*coll.*) – ***hard,*** nicht nachgeben wollen, stur weiterkämpfen; (*fig.*) (*as habits etc.*) sich lange halten, ein zähes Leben haben; – ***off,*** absterben, hinsterben, eingehen; – ***out,*** aussterben (*as races*); *see also* – ***away,*** – ***down.***

(*with preps.*) – ***by one's own hand,*** Selbstmord begehen; – ***by the sword,*** durch das Schwert umkommen; – ***for one's country,*** für sein Vaterland sterben; ***though I were to – for it,*** sollte es mir den Kopf kosten; (*coll.*) ***I am dying for a letter,*** ich sehne mich *or* schmachte *or* verlange nach einem Brief; – ***for love,*** vor Liebe sterben; – ***from one's wounds,*** an den Verwundungen sterben, den Verwundungen erliegen; – ***in one's bed,*** eines natürlichen Todes sterben; – ***in harness,*** in den Sielen sterben; – ***of hunger,*** verhungern, Hungers *or* vor Hunger sterben; – ***of an illness,*** an einer Krankheit sterben; – ***of shame,*** vor Scham vergehen; (*coll.*) ***I am dying to see him,*** ich möchte ihn schrecklich gern sehen; (*coll.*) – ***with one's boots on,*** eines gewaltsamen *or* plötzlichen Todes sterben; – (***with***) ***laughing,*** sich totlachen, vor Lachen sterben (wollen).

[2]**die,** *s.* 1. (*usu. pl.* **dice**) der Würfel; ***the – is cast,*** die Würfel sind gefallen; ***the dice are loaded against him,*** er hat geringe Chancen; ***straight as a –,*** kerzengerade, (*fig.*) grundehrlich; ***risk all on the throw of a –*** or ***dice,*** alles auf einen Wurf setzen, alles dem Zufall überlassen; 2. (*pl.* **-s**) der (Münz)-stempel, Prägestock, Stanzer, die Preßform, Matrize; (*for screw thread*) das Schneideisen, die Schneidbacke, Kluppe; (*Archit.*) der Postamentwürfel.

die|-block, *s.* das Gesenk, die Gußform, Kokille. **--casting,** *s.* der Schalenguß. **--hard,** *s.* Unentwegte(r), hartnäckiger Kämpfer; (*Pol.*) der Reaktionär, *pl.* die Alte Garde. **--head,** *s.* der Schneidkopf.

dielectric [daiə'lektrik], *s.* das Dielektrikum; – ***constant,*** die Dielektrizitätskonstante.

diesel|-engine [di:zl], *s.* der Dieselmotor. **--oil,** *s.* das Dieselöl.

die|-sinker, *s.* der Stempelschneider. **--stock,** *s.* der Schneideisenhalter, die Kluppe.

[1]**diet** ['daiət], **1.** *s.* (*Med.*) die Diät, Krankenkost, Schonkost; Ernährung, Nahrung, Kost, Speise; ***be on a –,*** Diät halten, diät leben, auf Diät sein; ***low –,*** magere Kost; ***put on a –,*** auf Diät setzen; ***strict –,*** strenge Diät. **2.** *v.t.* Diät vorschreiben (*Dat.*), auf Diät setzen. **3.** *v.i.* nach Diät leben, Diät halten, diät leben.

[2]**diet,** *s.* (*esp. Hist.*) der Landtag, Bundestag, Reichstag; (*Scots*) die Sitzung, Tagung, Versammlung.

dietary ['daiətəri], **1.** *s.* die Diätvorschrift; Ration. **2.** *adj.* diätetisch, Diät–. **dieter,** *s.* der (die) Diätpatient(in). **dietetic** [–'tetik], *adj. See* **dietary, 2. dietetics,** *pl.* (*sing. constr.*) die Diätetik, Diätkunde.

differ ['difə], *v.i.* sich unterscheiden, verschieden sein, abweichen (***from,*** von); (*of a p.*) anderer Meinung sein (als), nicht übereinstimmen (mit), (*of opponents*) sich (*Dat.*) nicht einig sein (***on,*** über (*Acc.*)), (*of opinions*) auseinandergehen; ***agree to –,*** sich auf verschiedene Standpunkte einigen; ***I beg to –,*** ich bin leider anderer Meinung.

difference ['difərəns], *s.* 1. der Unterschied, die Verschiedenheit, Abweichung; Unterscheidung, das Unterscheidungsmerkmal, Kennzeichen; – ***in price,*** der Preisunterschied; ***that makes a –,*** das ändert die S., das gibt der S. ein anderes Gesicht; ***that makes all the*** or ***a great –,*** das ist ein himmelweiter Unterschied, das macht viel aus, das ist von wesentlicher Bedeutung (***to,*** für); ***that makes no –,*** das macht nichts aus; – ***of opinion,*** die Meinungsverschiedenheit; 2. (*Math., Comm.*) die Differenz, (*Math.*) der Rest; ***make up the –,*** das Fehlende ersetzen; ***split the –,*** sich in die Differenz teilen, (*fig.*) zu einem Kompromiß kommen; 3. (*coll.*) der Streitpunkt; Streit, Zwiespalt, die Uneinigkeit; ***settle a –,*** einen Streit beilegen *or* schlichten.

different ['difərənt], *adj.* (*non-identity*) verschieden, abweichend (***from,*** von), ander(er, –es, –e) (als), (*pred.*) anders (als); (*non-similarity*) verschieden-(artig), anders(artig), ungleich, unähnlich; ***as – as chalk from cheese,*** so verschieden wie Tag und Nacht; ***that is quite a – matter,*** das ist eine ganz andere S., das ist etwas ganz anderes; ***in a – way,*** anders.

differentiable [difə'renʃ(i)əbl], *adj.* unterscheidbar; (*Math.*) differenzierbar.

differential [difə'renʃəl], **1.** *adj.* unterscheidend, Unterscheidungs–; Differenzial–; – ***calculus,*** die Differenzialrechnung; – ***gear,*** *see* **2.** (*Motor.*); – ***tariff,*** der Staffeltarif. **2.** *s.* (*Math.*) die Differenziale; (*Motor.*) das Differenzial(getriebe), Ausgleichsgetriebe.

differentiate [difə'renʃieit], **1.** *v.t.* einen Unterschied erkennen *or* machen, unterscheiden (***between,*** zwischen (*Dat.*)); (unter)scheiden, (aus)-sondern, trennen (***from,*** von); (*Math.*) differenzieren; ***be –d,*** *see* **2. 2.** *v.i.* sich unterscheiden *or* differenzieren, sich verschieden(artig) entwickeln; sich sondern *or* entfernen (***from,*** von); (*of a p.*) Unterschiede machen, diskriminieren. **differentiation** [–'eiʃən], *s.* die Unterscheidung; (*Math., Biol.*) Differenzierung; (Aus)sonderung, Scheidung.

differently ['difərəntli], *adv.* anders, unterschiedlich.

difficult ['difikəlt], *adj.* schwer, schwierig; beschwerlich, mühsam; (*of a p.*) schwierig, schwer zu behandeln, eigensinnig, diffizil; (*as ground*) unwegsam; – ***of access,*** schwer zugänglich. **difficulty,** *s.* die Schwierigkeit; Mühe; Unverständlichkeit; schwierige S., das Problem; (*usu. pl.*) schwierige Lage, die Verlegenheit; ***come up against*** or ***experience a –,*** auf Widerstand stoßen; ***find – in a th.,*** es schwierig finden; ***have – in doing it,*** Mühe haben, es zu tun; ***make difficulties,*** Schwierigkeiten bereiten (***for,*** *Dat.*); ***in –*** or ***difficulties,*** in Verlegenheit; ***with –,*** mit Mühe.

diffidence ['difidəns], *s.* der Mangel an *or* mangelndes Selbstvertrauen (***in,*** zu), die Schüchternheit. **diffident,** *adj.* scheu, schüchtern; ***be –,*** sich scheuen (***about doing,*** zu tun).

diffract [di'frækt], *v.t.* beugen. **diffraction** [–'frækʃən], *s.* die Beugung, Diffraktion.

diffuse, 1. [di'fju:s], *adj.* weitverbreitet, diffus, ausgebreitet, (weit) zerstreut; (*fig.*) weitschweifig, langatmig, wortreich. **2.** [di'fju:z], *v.t.* ausschütten, ausgießen; (*fig.*) ausbreiten, verbreiten, zerstreuen. **3.** [di'fju:z], *v.i.* sich verbreiten *or* zerstreuen; (*esp. Chem.*) zerfließen, sich vermischen, diffundieren. **diffuseness** [di'fju:snis], *s.* die Zerstreuung, (*esp. fig.*) Weitschweifigkeit, Langatmigkeit.

diffusibility [difju:zi'biliti], *s.* das Diffusionsvermögen, die Diffusionsfähigkeit. **diffusible** [–'fju:zibl], *adj.* verbreitbar; diffusionsfähig. **diffusion** [–'fju:ʒən], *s.* die Ausbreitung, Ausstreuung, Zerstreuung; (*Chem. etc.*) Diffusion; (*fig.*) Verbreitung. **diffusive** [–'fju:siv], *adj.* verbreitungsfähig, ausbreitungsfähig; (*fig.*) weitschweifig, weitläufig. **diffusiveness,** *s. See* **diffuseness.**

dig [dig], **1.** *irr.v.t.* 1. (*also* – *up*) graben in (*Dat.*), umgraben (*ground*), ausgraben (*potatoes etc.*); – ***a hole,*** eine Grube ausheben; (*fig.*) – ***a pit for him,*** ihm eine Grube graben *or* eine Falle stellen; – ***o.s. in,*** sich verschanzen; (*coll.*) – ***one's teeth into,*** seine Zähne graben in (*Acc.*); (*coll.*) – ***him in the ribs,*** ihn in die Rippen stoßen; (*fig.*) – ***up,*** entdecken, aufdecken, ans Tageslicht bringen (*facts*); (*coll.*) – ***one's heels in,*** sich steifen, auf seinem Sinn *or* Kopf bestehen *or* beharren; 2. (*sl.*) schwärmen für; kapieren. **2.** *irr.v.i.* 1. graben, schürfen (***for,*** nach); – ***in,*** sich eingraben *or* verschanzen; (*sl.*) sich an die Arbeit machen; 2. (*sl.*) hausen, wohnen, Quartier nehmen. **3.** *s.* 1. die Grabung; (*coll.*) der Stoß, Puff; die Stichelei, böswillige Bemerkung; – ***in the ribs,*** der Rippenstoß; 2. *pl.* (*sl.*) die Bude, das Quartier.

digest, 1. [d(a)i'dʒest], *v.t.* 1. verdauen (*food*); (*Chem.*) versetzen, einweichen, digerieren; 2. (*fig.*) ordnen, einteilen, in ein System bringen; überlegen, durchdenken, in sich aufnehmen, verarbeiten (*of the mind*); 3. erdulden, ertragen, hinunterschlucken, verwinden; – ***one's anger,*** seinen Ärger verbeißen. **2.** [–'dʒest], *v.i.* verdauen; sich verdauen lassen, verdaut werden; (*Chem.*) sich auflösen, digerieren. **3.** ['daidʒest], *s.* (*Law*) die Gesetzessammlung; Digesten (*pl.*), Pandekten (*pl.*); die Auswahl, Auslese, der Überblick, Auszug, Abriß.

digester [d(a)i'dʒestə], *s.* 1. *See* **digestive, 2**; 2. (*Tech.*) der Digestor, Autoklav, Papinscher Topf; 3. (*Cul.*) Kochkessel, Dampfkochtopf. **digestibility** [–ə'biliti], *s.* die Verdaulichkeit. **digestible,** *adj.* verdaulich, bekömmlich. **digestion** [–tʃən], *s.* die Verdauung; (*Chem.*) Digestion. **digestive, 1.** *adj.* verdauungsfördernd, bekömmlich; – ***biscuits,*** leichtverdauliche Keks; – ***organs,*** Verdauungsorgane. **2.** *s.* verdauungsförderndes Mittel.

digger ['digə], *s.* 1. der Gräber, Schipper; Löffelbagger, die Grabmaschine; 2. (*sl.*) der Australier. **digging,** *s.* das Graben, die Erdarbeit, Tiefbauarbeit; (*Min.*) (*oft. pl.*) Schürfung, der Schurf; *pl.* (*coll.*) *see* **digs.**

digit ['didʒit], *s.* 1. die Fingerbreite, (*Astr.*) astronomischer Zoll; 2. (*Zool.*) der Finger, die Zehe; 3.(*Math.*) einstellige Zahl. **digital, 1.** *adj.* Finger–; – ***computer,*** der Digitalrechner; (*Med.*) – ***pressure,*** der Fingerdruck. **2.** *s.* (*Mus.*) die Taste. **digitalis** [–'teilis], *s.* (*Bot.*) der Fingerhut. **digitate,** *adj.* (*Zool.*) gefingert, (*Bot.*) fingerförmig. **digitigrade** [–igreid], **1.** *adj.* auf Zehen gehend. **2.** *s.* (*Zool.*) der Zehengänger.

dignified ['dignifaid], *adj.* würdevoll, würdig, erhaben. **dignify** [–fai], *v.t.* verherrlichen, ehren, zieren; – ***with the name of*** . . ., hochtrabend bezeichnen als . . .. **dignitary** [–təri], *s.* der Würdenträger; (*Eccl.*) Prälat. **dignity** [–ti], *s.* die Erhabenheit, Hoheit, Würde, das Ansehen; hohe Stellung, die Ehrenstelle, der Rang, hoher Stand; ***beneath my*** –, unter meiner Würde; ***stand on one's*** –, auf Würde halten, sich nichts vergeben.

digraph ['daigra:f], *s.* (*Phonet.*) der Digraph.

digress [dai'gres], *v.i.* abschweifen. **digression** [–'greʃən], *s.* die Abschweifung. **digressive,** *adj.* abschweifend, abwegig.

digs [digz], *pl. See* **dig, 3,** 2.

dihedral [dai'hi:drəl], *s.* (*Av.*) der Neigungswinkel der Tragflächen, die V-Stellung, V-Form; (*Math.*) der Zweiflächner, Dieder, das Zweiflach.

dike [daik], **1.** *s.* der Deich, Damm, Erdwall; (*Scots*) die Grenzmauer; der Graben, Kanal; (*Geol.*) Gangstock, Eruptivgang. **2.** *v.t.* eindeichen, eindämmen. **dike|-reeve,** *s.* der Deichaufseher. **–-rocks,** *pl.* (*Geol.*) Ganggesteine (*pl.*).

dilapidate [di'læpideit], **1.** *v.t.* verfallen lassen, in Verfall geraten lassen. **2.** *v.i.* in Verfall geraten, verfallen. **dilapidated,** *adj.* verfallen, baufällig; schäbig, verwahrlost. **dilapidation** [–'deiʃən], *s.* die Baufälligkeit, der Verfall; das Verfallenlassen.

dilatability [d(a)ileitə'biliti], *s.* die Dehnbarkeit. **dilatable** [–'leitəbl], *adj.* dehnbar. **dilatation** [–'teiʃən], *s.* die Ausdehnung, Erweiterung. **dilate** [–'leit], **1.** *v.t.* (aus)dehnen, erweitern. **2.** *v.i.* sich (aus)dehnen, sich erweitern; (*fig.*) sich verbreiten, sich auslassen ((***up***)***on,*** über (*Acc.*)). **dilation** [–'leiʃən], *s. See* **dilatation. dilator,** *s.* (*Med.*) der Dilatator; (*Anat.*) Dehner (*muscle*).

dilatoriness ['dilətərinis], *s.* die Saumseligkeit, das Zögern, Zaudern. **dilatory,** *adj.* aufschiebend, hinauszögernd, hinhaltend, Verzögerungs–; zögernd, zaudernd, saumselig; langsam, schleppend; (*Law*) – ***plea,*** das Fristgesuch.

dilemma [di'lemə], *s.* (*Log.*) das Dilemma; (*fig.*) die Verlegenheit, (*coll.*) Klemme; ***in a*** – or ***on the horns of a*** –, in einer Zwickmühle, in Verlegenheit, in der Klemme.

dilettante [dili'tænti], **1.** *s.* (*pl.* **-ti**) der Dilettant, Nichtfachmann, Kunstliebhaber. **2.** *adj.* dilettantisch, nichtfachmännisch. **dilettantism,** *s.* der Dilettantismus.

diligence ['dilidʒəns], *s.* 1. der Fleiß, Eifer, die Emsigkeit; Sorgfalt; 2. Postkutsche. **diligent,** *adj.* fleißig, emsig; sorgfältig.

dill [dil], *s.* (*Bot.*) der Dill.

dilly-dally ['dilidæli], *v.i.* (*coll.*) die Zeit vertrödeln.

diluent ['diljuənt], **1.** *adj.* verdünnend. **2.** *s.* das Streckmittel, Verdünnungsmittel, Verschnittmittel. **dilute, 1.** [d(a)i'l(j)u:t], *v.t.* verdünnen, strecken, verschneiden, verwässern; (*fig.*) abschwächen; – ***labour,*** ungelernte Arbeiter einstellen. **2.** ['dailju:t], **diluted** [d(a)i'l(j)u:tid], *adj.* verdünnt, verwässert, geschwächt. **dilution** [–'lju:ʃən], *s.* die Verdünnung, Verwässerung.

diluvial [di'l(j)u:viəl], *adj.* sintflutlich; (*Geol.*) diluvial. **diluvian,** *adj.* Sintflut–. **diluvium,** *s.* (*Geol.*) das Diluvium.

dim [dim], **1.** *adj.* düster, (halb)dunkel, blaß, trübe, matt (*of colours*); undeutlich, unklar, verschwommen, schwach (*of sound*); (*coll.*) dumm, einfältig; (*coll.*) ***take a – view of,*** über die Achsel ansehen. **2.** *v.t.* verdüstern, verdunkeln, abmatten, trüben; abblenden (*dazzling light*).

dime [daim], *s.* (*Am.*) das Zehncentstück.

dimension [di'menʃən], **1.** *s.* die Ausdehnung, Ausmessung, Abmessung, das Maß; (*fig.*) der Umfang, das Ausmaß; (*Math.*) die Dimension; ***of enormous -s,*** riesengroß; (*fig.*) von riesenhaftem Ausmaß. **2.** *v.t.* bemessen; (*Tech.*) bemaßen. **dimensional,** *adj.* (*Math.*) dimensional; – ***stability,*** die Maßhaltigkeit.

dimeter ['dimitə], *s.* (*Metr.*) der Dimeter.

diminish [di'miniʃ], **1.** *v.t.* vermindern, verringern; verkleinern; (*Archit.*) verjüngen; (*fig.*) (ab)schwächen, herabsetzen, beeinträchtigen; (*Mus.*) ***-ed interval,*** vermindertes Intervall; (*Law*) ***-ed responsibility,*** verminderte Zurechnungsfähigkeit. **2.** *v.i.* abnehmen, sich verringern *or* vermindern (***in,*** an (*Dat.*)).

diminution [dimi'nju:ʃən], *s.* die Verkleinerung, Verminderung, Verringerung, Abnahme; (*Archit.*) Verjüngung; (*Mus.*) Verkürzung, Verkleinerung (*value of note*). **diminutive** [di'minjutiv], **1.** *adj.* klein, winzig, (*Gram.*) verkleinernd, Verkleinerungs–. **2.** *s.* (*Gram.*) das Diminutiv. **diminutiveness,** *s.* die Kleinheit, Winzigkeit.

dimissory [di'misəri], *adj.* entlassend; ***letter*** –, das Entlassungsschreiben.

dimity ['dimiti], *s.* geköperter Barchent, der Dimitz.

dimness ['dimnis], *s.* die Düsterheit, Dunkelheit; Mattheit, Trübheit, Unklarheit, Undeutlichkeit; (*coll.*) Dummheit.

dimorphic [dai'mɔ:fik], **dimorphous** [–fəs], *adj.* dimorph, zweigestaltig.

dimple [dimpl], **1.** *s.* das Grübchen. **2.** *v.i.* Grübchen bekommen. **3.** *v.t.* Grübchen machen in (*Acc.*); kräuseln (*as the surface of water*). **dimpled,** *adj.* mit Grübchen.

dimwit ['dimwit], *s.* (*coll.*) der Dussel. **dimwitted,** *adj.* (*coll.*) dusselig, dämlich.

din [din], **1.** *s.* das Getöse, der Lärm; das Geklirr (*clashing*); Gerassel (*rattling*). **2.** *v.t.* durch Lärm betäuben; – ***it into his ears,*** es ihm einhämmern, es ihm dauernd vorpredigen.

dine [dain], **1.** *v.i.* essen, speisen; – ***off*** or ***on roast pork,*** Schweinebraten (zu Mittag) essen; – ***out,*** außer dem Hause essen, zum Essen geladen sein; – ***with him,*** mit ihm zu Tisch sein; (*fig.*) – ***with Duke Humphrey,*** nichts zu essen bekommen, das (Mittag)essen überschlagen. **2.** *v.t.* zu essen geben (*Dat.*), speisen, bewirten, bei sich zu Gast haben; ***a room capable of dining 300 people,*** ein Saal, in dem für 300 Personen gedeckt werden kann. **diner,** *s.*1. der Tischgast; 2. (*Railw.*) Speisewagen. **dinette** [dai'net], *s.* (*Am.*) die Speisenische.

ding [diŋ], *v.t.* – ***s.th. into him,*** *see* **din, 2. dingdong, 1.** *int.* bim bam bum! **2.** *s.* der Kling-klang, das Bimbam; (*coll.*) – ***battle,*** hin und her wogender Kampf.

dinghy ['diŋgi], *s.* das Beiboot, die Jolle, der Kutter (*in the navy*); ***rubber*** –, das Schlauchboot, der Floßsack.

dinginess ['dindʒinis], *s.* dunkle Farbe, die Trübheit, Schmutzfarbe; Schäbigkeit, schmutziges Äußere.

dingle [diŋgl], *s.* die Waldschlucht, waldiges Tal.

dingo ['diŋgou], *s.* wilder Hund (*of Australia*).

dingy ['dindʒi], *adj.* trüb, dunkelfarbig, schmutzigbraun; schmutzig; schäbig.

dining|-car ['dainiŋ], *s.* (*Railw.*) der Speisewagen. **--hall,** *s.* der Speisesaal. **--room,** *s.* das Eßzimmer, Speisezimmer. **--saloon,** *s.* (*Naut.*) der Speiseraum.

dinky ['diŋki], *adj.* (*coll.*) nett, niedlich, zierlich.

dinner ['dinə], *s.* die Hauptmahlzeit, das Essen; Mittagessen, Mittagsmahl; Abendessen; Festessen, Diner; ***after*** –, nach dem Essen, nach Tisch; ***early*** –, das Mittagessen; ***late*** –, das Abendessen; ***public*** –, das Zweckessen; – ***is ready*** or ***served,*** das Essen steht auf dem Tisch; ***ask him to*** –, ihn zum Essen einladen; ***what did you have for*** –? was haben Sie zum Essen bekommen? ***stay for*** –, zum Essen bleiben.

dinner|-bell, *s.* die Tischglocke, Essensglocke. **--hour,** *s.* die Mittagspause. **--jacket,** *s.* der Smoking. **--party,** *s.* die Tischgesellschaft, Abendgesellschaft. **--service,** *s.* das Tafelgeschirr, Tafelservice. **--table,** *s.* der Eßtisch. **--time,** *s.* die Essenszeit, Tischzeit. **--wagon,** *s.* der Servierwagen.

dinosaur ['dainəsɔ:], *s.* der Dinosaurier.

dint [dint], **1.** *s.* 1. (*only in*) ***by*** – ***of,*** kraft, vermöge, mittels, vermittelst (*Gen.*); 2. der Eindruck, die Druckspur, Vertiefung, Delle, Strieme, Beule; *see* **dent. 2.** *v.t.* eindrücken, eindellen, einbeulen.

diocesan [dai'ɔsisən], **1.** *adj.* Diözesan–. **2.** *s.* der Diözesanbischof. **diocese** ['daiəsis], *s.* der Sprengel, die Diözese.

diode ['daioud], *s.* (*Rad.*) die Zweielektrodenröhre, Zweipolröhre, Diode.

diopter [dai'ɔptə], *s.* die Dioptrie. **dioptric, 1.** *adj.* dioptrisch. **2.** *s. See* **diopter. dioptrics,** *pl.* (*sing. constr.*) die Dioptrik, (Licht)brechungslehre.

dioxide [dai'ɔksaid], *s.* das Dioxyd.

dip [dip], **1.** *v.t.* (ein)tauchen, (ein)tunken (*in(to)*, in (*Acc.*)); anfeuchten (*a hide*); waschen (*sheep*); färben, blauen; (*Naut.*) dippen (*flag*); abblenden (*headlights*); ziehen (*candles*); – ***one's head,*** den Kopf senken. **2.** *v.i.* untertauchen (und wieder auftauchen), eintauchen; sinken (***below,*** unter (*Acc.*)); sich neigen *or* senken, (*Geol.*) abfallen, einfallen; – ***into a book,*** ein Buch (flüchtig) durchblättern, einen Blick in ein Buch werfen; – ***into one's purse,*** in die Tasche greifen. **3.** *s.* 1. das Tauchen, Eintauchen; (*coll.*) – ***in the sea,*** das (kurze) Bad (im Meer); 2. die Neigung, Senkung, der Fallwinkel; (*Dye.*) kurzes Bad, die Lösung; (*Geol.*) das Einfallen; die Höhlung, Vertiefung, Einsenkung, Bodensenke; Inklination (der Magnetnadel); gezogene Kerze; – ***of the horizon,*** die Kimmtiefe, Depression, der Depressionswinkel.

diphtheria [dif'θiəriə], *s.* die Diphtherie, Diphtheritis. **diphtherial, diphtheric** [–'θerik], **diphtheritic** [–'ritik], *adj.* diphtheritisch.

diphthong ['difθɔŋ], *s.* der Doppelvokal, Diphthong. **diphthongal** [–'θɔŋgl], *adj.* diphthongisch. **diphthongization** [–ai'zeiʃən], *s.* die Diphthongierung.

diploma [di'ploumə], *s.* das Diplom, die Urkunde.

diplomacy [di'ploumәsi], *s.* die Diplomatie; (*fig.*) diplomatisches Vorgehen, politischer Takt, kluge Berechnung; (*fig.*) ***use a bit of*** –, diplomatisch vorgehen. **diplomat** ['diplomæt], *s. See* **diplomatist. diplomatic** [–'mætik], *adj.* 1. diplomatisch; (*fig.*) taktvoll; 2. urkundlich. **diplomatics,** *pl.* (*sing. constr.*) die Diplomatik, Urkundenlehre. **diplomatist** [di'ploumətist], *s.* der Diplomat.

dipole ['daipoul], *s.* (*Rad.*) der Dipol

dipper ['dipə], *s.* 1. (*Orn.*) die Wasseramsel (*Cinclus* *cinclus*), (*Am.*) (*Orn.*) die Büffelkopfente (*Clangula albeola*); 2. Schöpfkelle; 3. (*Eccl.*) (*coll.*) der Wiedertäufer; 4. (*Am.*) (*Astr.*) Wagen; 5. ***the big*** –, die Achterbahn (*at fairs*).

dippy ['dipi], *adj.* (*sl.*) verdreht, verrückt.

dipsomania [dipso'meiniə], *s.* die Trunksucht, Dipsomanie. **dipsomaniac** [–iæk], *s.* Trunksüchtige(r), der Dipsomane (die Dipsomanin).

dip|stick, *s.* der (Öl)meßstab. **--switch,** *s.* (*Motor.*) der Abblendschalter.

diptera ['diptərə], *pl.* Zweiflügler (*pl.*). **dipteral, dipterous,** *adj.* zweiflügelig.

diptych ['diptik], *s.* das Diptychon.

dire [daiə], *adj.* schrecklich, entsetzlich, schauderhaft, gräßlich, grauenhaft, fürchterlich; unheilbringend, unheilverkündend; (*coll.*) äußerst, höchst.

direct [d(a)i'rekt], **1.** *adj.* gerade, direkt; unmittelbar; (*Astr.*) rechtläufig; offen, klar, deutlich, unzweideutig; (*Pol.*) – ***action,*** direkte Aktion; (*Elec.*) – ***current,*** der Gleichstrom; (*Artil.*) – ***hit,*** der Volltreffer; ***in the*** – ***line,*** in gerader Linie; (*Gram.*) – ***object,*** das Akkusativobjekt; – ***method,*** direkte Methode; ***in*** – ***opposition to,*** genau das Gegenteil von; – ***route,*** gerader Weg; – ***sale,*** der Direktverkauf; (*Gram.*) – ***speech,*** direkte Rede; – ***taxes,*** direkte Steuern; – ***train,*** durchgehender Zug. **2.** *v.t.* 1. richten, lenken, zielen (***to***(***wards***), auf (*Acc.*) *or* nach); hinweisen, (ver)weisen (***to,*** an (*Acc.*)), den Weg zeigen (*Dat.*) (***to,*** nach); 2. anordnen, verfügen, anweisen, bestimmen, befehlen, beauftragen; ***as*** –***ed,*** nach Vorschrift *or* Angabe; laut Verfügung; 3. disponieren, führen, leiten, beaufsichtigen; (*Theat. etc.*) in Regie nehmen *or* haben; 4. richten (*remarks*) (***to,*** an (*Acc.*)), adressieren (*a letter*) (***to,*** an (*Acc.*)). **3.** *v.i.* anordnen, befehlen, Befehle erteilen.

direction [d(a)i'rekʃən], *s.* 1. die Richtung; ***from all*** –***s,*** von allen Seiten; ***from that*** –, aus jener Richtung; ***in the*** – ***of,*** in (der) Richtung nach *or* auf (*Acc.*); ***in all*** –***s,*** nach allen Seiten *or* Richtungen; (*fig.*) ***in many*** –***s,*** in vieler *or* mancherlei Hinsicht; – ***of motion,*** die Bewegungsrichtung, Bahnrichtung; – ***of rotation,*** der Drehsinn; ***sense of*** –, der Orientierungssinn, das Ortsgedächtnis; 2. die Lenkung, das Lenken, Richten, (*of letters*) Adressieren; 3. die Leitung, Führung, Direktion; (*Theat. etc.*) Regie, Spielleitung; ***under the*** – ***of,*** unter der Leitung von; 4. (*usu. pl.*) die (An)weisung, Anordnung, Vorschrift, Richtlinie, Bestimmung, Verfügung, der Hinweis; ***according to*** –***s,*** den Anweisungen gemäß, vorschriftsmäßig; ***by*** – ***of,*** auf Anweisung *or* Anordnung von; –***s for use,*** die Gebrauchsanweisung, Anwendungsvorschrift.

directional [d(a)i'rekʃənl], *adj.* Richt–, Richtungs–; (*Rad.*) – ***aerial,*** die Richtantenne. **direction|-finder,** *s.* das Peilgerät, Ortungsgerät; die Peilfunkeinrichtung; (*Phot.*) der Sucher. **--finding,** *s.* die (Funk)peilung, Ortung. **--line,** *s.* (*Typ.*) die Normzeile.

directive [d(a)i'rektiv], **1.** *s.* die (An)weisung, Verhaltungsregel, Direktive. **2.** *adj.* anweisend, richtunggebend, maßgebend, maßgeblich. **directly, 1.** *adv.* 1. in gerader Richtung, geradlinig, gerade; direkt, unmittelbar; – ***opposed,*** gerade *or* genau entgegengesetzt; – ***proportional,*** direkt proportional; 2. sofort, (so)gleich, augenblicklich, unverzüglich, bald. **2.** *conj.* (*coll.*) sobald (als), unmittelbar nachdem, sowie. **directness,** *s.* gerade Richtung; die Geradheit, Geradlinigkeit; Unmittelbarkeit; Offenheit, Deutlichkeit, Eindeutigkeit, Unumwundenheit.

director [d(a)i'rektə], *s.* 1. der Direktor, Leiter, Vorsteher, Chef, (*Theat. etc.*) Spielleiter, Regisseur; 2. (*Tech.*) das Richtgerät; ***board of –s,*** der Aufsichtsrat, das Direktorium. **directorate** [–rit], *s.* das Direktorat; Direktorium, der Aufsichtsrat. **directorial** [–'tɔ:riəl], *adj.* leitend, Aufsichts–; Direktorial–. **directorship,** *s.* das Direktorat, die Direktor(en)stelle. **directory,** *s.* 1. das Adreßbuch, Telephonbuch; 2. (*Hist.*) Direktorium (*in France*); 3. (*Eccl.*) die Anweisung, der Leitfaden. **directress,** *s.* die Direktorin, Direktrice, Vorsteherin, Leiterin. **directrix,** *s.* 1. (*rare*) *see* **directress**; 2. (*Geom.*) die Leitlinie.

direful ['daiəful], *adj. See* **dire.**

dirge [də:dʒ], *s.* der Trauergesang, Grabgesang, das Klagelied, Trauerlied, die Klage.

dirigible ['diridʒibl], **1.** *adj.* lenkbar. **2.** *s.* der Lenkballon, das Luftschiff.

dirk [də:k], *s.* der Dolch.

dirt [də:t], *s.* der Schmutz, Dreck, Kot; ***as cheap as*** –, spottbillig; ***have to eat*** –, sich demütigen müssen; ***spot of*** –, der Schmutzfleck; ***throw*** or ***fling – at him,*** ihn mit Schmutz bewerfen, ihn in den Schmutz ziehen; ***treat him like*** –, ihn wie Dreck *or* wie einen Schuhputzer behandeln.

dirt-cheap, *adj.* (*coll.*) spottbillig. **dirtiness,** *s.* der Schmutz; die Schmutzigkeit; (*fig.*) Gemeinheit, Niederträchtigkeit. **dirt-track,** *s.* die Aschenbahn.

dirty ['də:ti], **1.** *adj.* schmutzig, kotig, dreckig, beschmutzt; (*fig.*) gemein, niederträchtig; (*sl.*) ***do the – on him,*** ihn gemein behandeln; – ***brown,*** schmutzigbraun; – ***linen,*** schmutzige Wäsche (*also fig.*); (*coll.*) – ***look,*** scheeler Blick; – ***trick,*** die Gemeinheit; – ***weather,*** schlechtes Wetter; – ***work,*** niedere Arbeit; (*fig.*) unsauberes Geschäft, verdecktes *or* doppeltes Spiel, die Schurkerei; – ***wound,*** septische Wunde. **2.** *v.t.* beschmutzen, besudeln. **3.** *v.i.* schmutzig werden, schmutzen.

disability [disə'biliti], *s.* 1. das Unvermögen, die Unfähigkeit, (*oft. pl.*) Unzulänglichkeit; 2. (*Law*) Rechtsunfähigkeit; ***lie under a*** –, rechtsunfähig sein; 3. die Körperbehinderung; (*Mil.*) ***partial*** –, beschränkte Dienstunfähigkeit; (*Mil.*) ***permanent*** –, dauernde Dienstunfähigkeit; – ***pension,*** die Invalidenrente.

disable [dis'eibl], *v.t.* 1. untauglich *or* unbrauchbar machen, außer Stand setzen; 2. (*Mil.*) kampfunfähig *or* dienstuntauglich *or* außer Gefecht setzen; 3. körperlich behindern, lähmen, verkrüppeln, entkräften; 4. (*Law*) rechtsunfähig machen. **disabled,** *adj.* 1. körperlich behindert, schwerverletzt; arbeitsunfähig, invalid(e), (*Mil.*) kampfunfähig, dienstunfähig, kriegsversehrt, kriegsbeschädigt; (*Naut.*) seeuntüchtig, manövrierunfähig; ***permanently*** –, dauernd untauglich; – ***soldier,*** Kriegsbeschädigte(r). **disablement,** *s.* die Invalidität, (Dienst– *or* Arbeits)unfähigkeit, (*Mil.*) Dienstuntauglichkeit, Kampfunfähigkeit.

disabuse [disə'bju:z], *v.t.* von einem Irrtum befreien, eines Besseren belehren (***of,*** über (*Acc.*)); – ***o.s.*** or ***one's mind of s.th.,*** sich (*Dat.*) etwas aus dem Kopfe schlagen.

disaccord [disə'kɔ:d], **1.** *v.i.* nicht übereinstimmen. **2.** *s.* der Widerspruch, das Mißverhältnis, Mißverständnis, die Uneinigkeit, Nichtübereinstimmung.

disaccustom [disə'kʌstəm], *v.t.* abgewöhnen (***him to a th.,*** ihm etwas), entwöhnen (ihn einer S. (*Gen.*)). **disaccustomed,** *adj.* nicht gewöhnt (***to,*** an (*Acc.*)).

disadvantage [disəd'vɑ:ntidʒ], *s.* der Nachteil; Schaden, Verlust (***to,*** für); ungünstige Lage; ***be at*** or ***labour under a*** –, im Nachteil sein; ***labour under the – of being . . .,*** den Nachteil haben . . . zu sein; ***put o.s. at a – with him,*** sich ihm gegenüber in den Nachteil setzen; ***sell to*** –, mit Verlust verkaufen; ***take him at a*** –, seine ungünstige Lage ausnutzen. **disadvantageous** [–ædvən'teidʒəs], *adj.* unvorteilhaft, nachteilig, schädlich, abträglich, ungünstig (***to,*** für).

disaffected [disə'fektid], *adj.* 1. (*usu. Pol.*) unzufrieden (***towards,*** mit), abgeneigt (*Dat.*); 2. unzuverlässig (*as troops*). **disaffection** [–'fekʃən], *s.* 1. die Unzufriedenheit (***towards,*** mit), Abgeneigtheit (gegen); 2. Unzuverlässigkeit.

disaffirm [disə'fə:m], *v.t.* (*Law*) aufheben.

disafforest [disə'fɔrist], *v.t.* 1. abholzen, abforsten, entwalden; 2. des Forstrechts berauben.

disagree [disə'gri:], *v.i.* 1. nicht übereinstimmen (***with,*** mit), in Widerspruch stehen (zu *or* mit), nicht zustimmen (*Dat.*), widersprechen (*Dat.*); uneins *or* uneinig sein, verschiedener Meinung sein (***on*** or ***about,*** über (*Acc.*)); 2. (*as food*) nicht zuträglich sein, schlecht *or* nicht bekommen (***with,*** *Dat.*).

disagreeable [disə'griəbl], *adj.* unangenehm, lästig, widerlich, widerwärtig; übelgelaunt, unliebenswürdig, verdrießlich. **disagreeableness,** *s.* die Unannehmlichkeit, Lästigkeit, Widerlichkeit, Widerwärtigkeit. **disagreement,** *s.* die Verschiedenheit, Nichtübereinstimmung, der Widerspruch; die Meinungsverschiedenheit, Streitigkeit, Mißhelligkeit; ***in – from,*** zum Unterschied von, abweichend von.

disallow [disə'lau], *v.t.* nicht zugeben *or* erlauben *or* gestatten; nicht gelten lassen, nicht billigen *or* anerkennen, verwerfen, zurückweisen. **disallowable,** *adj.* nicht zu billigen(d), ungültig.

disappear [disə'piə], *v.i.* verschwinden; (*coll.*) verlorengehen; – ***from circulation,*** außer Umlauf kommen. **disappearance** [–rəns], *s.* das Verschwinden.

disappoint [disə'pɔint], *v.t.* enttäuschen; vereiteln, täuschen (*hopes*); ***be –ed,*** enttäuscht sein *or* werden (***at, with*** (*a th.*), über (*Acc.*); ***in*** (*a p. or th.*), in (*Dat.*)); ***be –ed of,*** gebracht *or* betrogen werden um; ***it is –ing,*** es entspricht nicht den Erwartungen. **disappointment,** *s.* die Enttäuschung (***at*** (*a th.*), ***in*** (*a p.*), über (*Acc.*)); Vereitelung, der Fehlschlag, Mißerfolg; ***meet with a*** –, enttäuscht werden, eine Enttäuschung erleben.

disapprobation [disæpro'beiʃən], *s.* die Mißbilligung. **disapprobative** [–'æprobeitiv], **disapprobatory,** *adj.* mißbilligend.

disappropriate [disə'prouprieit], *v.t.* enteignen. **disappropriation** [–'eiʃən], *s.* die Enteignung.

disapproval [disə'pru:vl], *s.* die Mißbilligung (***of,*** *Gen.*), das Mißfallen (über (*Acc.*)). **disapprove, 1.** *v.t.* mißbilligen, tadeln, verwerfen, zurückweisen. **2.** *v.i.* Mißfallen äußern (***of,*** über (*Acc.*)); – ***of,*** *see also* **1.**; ***be –d of,*** Mißfallen erregen.

disarm [dis'ɑ:m], **1.** *v.t.* entwaffnen; (*fig.*) unschädlich machen, besänftigen; (*Mil.*) abrüsten. **2.** *v.i.* abrüsten. **disarmament,** *s.* die Abrüstung. **disarming, 1.** *s.* die Entwaffnung. **2.** *adj.* (*fig.*) besänftigend, einschmeichelnd, einnehmend, gewinnend.

disarrange [disə'reindʒ], *v.t.* durcheinanderbringen, in Unordnung bringen, verwirren. **disarrangement,** *s.* die Unordnung, Verwirrung, das Durcheinander.

disarray [disə'rei], **1.** *s.* die Unordnung, Verwirrung. **2.** *v.t.* verwirren, in Verwirrung *or*

Unordnung bringen; (*Poet.*) entkleiden; entwaffnen (*a knight*).

disassemble [disə'sembl], *v.t.* demontieren, auseinandernehmen.

disaster [di'zɑ:stə], *s.* das Unglück (*to*, für), Mißgeschick; der Unfall, die Katastrophe; ***bring to* –,** ins Unglück bringen; ***bring* –,** Unheil bringen. **disastrous** [–trəs], *adj.* unglücklich, verhängnisvoll, unheilvoll; unselig, schrecklich, verheerend (*to*, für).

disavow [disə'vau], *v.t.* (ab)leugnen, nicht wahrhaben wollen, nicht eingestehen *or* anerkennen, in Abrede stellen, abrücken von. **disavowal,** *s.* die Nichtanerkennung, Verwerfung; das Ableugnen, Dementi.

disband [dis'bænd], **1.** *v.t.* auflösen, entlassen (*troops etc.*); verabschieden (*an individual*). **2.** *v.i.* sich auflösen, auseinandergehen. **disbandment,** *s.* die Auflösung.

disbelief [disbi'li:f], *s.* der Unglaube, Zweifel (***in***, an (*Dat.*)). **disbelieve,** *v.t.* keinen Glauben schenken, nicht glauben (*a p., Dat.*); nicht glauben, bezweifeln (*a th.*). **disbeliever,** *s.* der (die) Zweifler(in), Ungläubige(r).

disburden [dis'bə:dn], *v.t.* befreien, entlasten; – ***one's heart*** or ***mind*** or ***feelings,*** sein Herz ausschütten.

disburse [dis'bə:s], *v.t.* auszahlen, ausgeben, auslegen. **disbursement,** *s.* die Ausgabe, Auslage, Auszahlung.

disc, *see* **disk.**

discard [dis'kɑ:d], **1.** *v.t.* ablegen (*also fig.*), beiseite legen, (*coll.*) ausrangieren; (*fig.*) aufgeben; (*Cards*) abwerfen; (*workers etc.*) entlassen, verabschieden. **2.** *v.i.* Karten abwerfen. **3.** [*also* 'diskɑ:d], *s.* das Abwerfen; abgeworfene Karte.

discern [di'sə:n], **1.** *v.t.* wahrnehmen, erkennen, feststellen, bemerken; (heraus)finden, dahinterkommen; unterscheiden (können). **2.** *v.i.* (*obs.*) unterscheiden. **discernible,** *adj.* wahrnehmbar, feststellbar, unterscheidbar, erkennbar, sichtbar, merklich. **discerning,** *adj.* einsichtsvoll, scharfsichtig, scharfsinnig, urteilsfähig. **discernment,** *s.* die Einsicht, Urteilskraft, das Urteil, der Scharfsinn, Scharfblick; das Erkennen, Wahrnehmen, Unterscheiden.

discharge [dis'tʃɑ:dʒ], **1.** *v.t.* 1. abladen, ausladen, löschen (*cargo*), absetzen, ausschiffen (*passengers*), entladen (*a ship*); (*Elec.*) entladen; abschießen, abfeuern (*a gun*); 2. bezahlen, begleichen, entrichten (*debts etc.*); quittieren, einlösen (*a bill*); befriedigen (*one's creditors*); – ***the debt of nature,*** der Natur ihren Tribut bezahlen; 3. entlassen; verabschieden, abdanken, ausmustern (*soldiers*); ablohnen (*sailors*); entlassen, freilassen, in Freiheit setzen (*a prisoner*); freisprechen, entlasten (*the accused*); 4. nachkommen (*Dat.*), erfüllen (*duty*); – ***one's office,*** das Amt versehen *or* verrichten; 5. auslassen (*anger*) (***on***, an (*Dat.*)); ausfließen *or* ablaufen *or* auslaufen lassen, abführen, ablassen (*liquids*); ***the ulcer –s matter,*** das Geschwür eitert; – ***smoke,*** Rauch aussenden *or* auswerfen, Rauch von sich geben; 6. (*Law*) tilgen, aufheben; 7. – ***itself,*** sich ergießen, münden (***into***, in (*Acc.*)).
2. *v.i.* (*Med.*) eitern; (*of liquid*) hervorströmen, (*of container*) ausströmen lassen, (*of gun*) sich entladen, (*coll.*) losgehen; *see also* **1.,** 7.
3. [*also* 'distʃɑ:dʒ], *s.* 1. das Abfeuern, der Abschuß (*of fire-arms*); (*Elec.*) die Entladung; 2. der Abfluß, Ausfluß, das Ausfließen, Auswerfen, Ausströmen (*of water etc.*); (*Med.*) die Absonderung, Eiterung, der Eiterausfluß, Auswurf; 3. (*Comm.*) die Bezahlung, Entrichtung, Quittung, Begleichung; – ***in full,*** vollständige Quittung; 4. (*Mil. etc.*) die (Dienst)entlassung, Verabschiedung; (*Law*) Entlassung, Freisprechung, Freilassung; – ***of a bankrupt,*** die Aufhebung des Konkursverfahrens; ***get one's* –,** seinen Abschied bekommen; (*Mil.*) – ***with ignominy,*** schimpflicher Abschied; 5. die Verrichtung, Erfüllung (*of a duty*); 6. (*Naut.*) Ausladung, Löschung (*of cargo*); ***port of* –,** der Löschplatz.

discharge-pipe, *s.* das Abflußrohr. **discharger,** *s.* (*Tech.*) die Entladevorrichtung, (*Elec.*) der Entlader. **discharging|-arch,** *s.* (*Archit.*) der Entlastungsbogen. **--rod,** *s. See* **discharger** (*Elec.*).

disciple [di'saipl], *s.* (*B.*) der Jünger; (*fig.*) Schüler, Gefolgsmann, Anhänger. **discipleship,** *s.* die Jüngerschaft, Anhängerschaft.

disciplinable ['disiplinəbl], *adj.* gelehrig, fügsam, folgsam. **disciplinarian** [–'nɛəriən], *s.* der Zuchtmeister. **disciplinary,** *adj.* disziplinarisch, Disziplinar–, erzieherisch, Zucht–; – ***action,*** die Disziplinarmaßnahme; – ***punishment,*** die Disziplinarstrafe.

discipline ['disiplin], **1.** *s.* 1. die Zucht, Manneszucht, Schulzucht, Kirchenzucht, Disziplin; ***maintain* –,** Disziplin halten; ***military* –,** soldatische Zucht, die Manneszucht; 2. der Wissenszweig, das Wissensgebiet, (Unterrichts)fach; 3. die Züchtigung, Bestrafung. **2.** *v.t.* 1. erziehen, schulen, (aus)bilden; 2. zur Zucht anhalten, an Disziplin gewöhnen; 3. züchtigen, (be)strafen.

disclaim [dis'kleim], *v.t.* nicht anerkennen, ablehnen; abstreiten, dementieren, in Abrede stellen, (ver)leugnen; (*Law*) entsagen (*Dat.*), Verzicht leisten auf (*Acc.*), nicht beanspruchen. **disclaimer,** *s.* (*Law*) der Verzicht, die Verzichtleistung; Ableugnung; der Widerruf, das Dementi.

disclose [dis'klouz], *v.t.* aufdecken, ans Licht bringen; offenbaren, enthüllen. **disclosure** [–ʒə], *s.* die Enthüllung, Erschließung, Aufdeckung, Offenbarung; Mitteilung, das Enthüllte.

discolor, (*Am.*) *see* **discolour. discoloration** [diskʌlə'reiʃən], *s.* die Entfärbung, Verfärbung, der Farbverlust; Fleck. **discolour** [dis'kʌlə], **1.** *v.t.* verfärben, anders färben, (*fig.*) entstellen. **2.** *v.i.* sich verfärben, die Farbe verlieren; verschießen, verblassen. **discoloured,** *adj.* verschossen, entfärbt; verfärbt.

discomfit [dis'kʌmfit], *v.t.* (zer)schlagen, besiegen; entmutigen, verwirren, aus der Fassung bringen. **discomfiture** [–ʃə], *s.* die Niederlage, Besiegung; Verwirrung, Enttäuschung, Vereitelung, Durchkreuzung.

discomfort [dis'kʌmfət], **1.** *s.* das Unbehagen, die Unannehmlichkeit; körperliche Beschwerde. **2.** *v.t.* (*rare*) unbehaglich sein (*Dat.*), beunruhigen.

discompose [diskəm'pouz], *v.t.* durcheinanderbringen, in Unordnung bringen; verwirren, beunruhigen, bestürzen, aus der Fassung bringen. **discomposure** [–'pouʒə], *s.* die Beunruhigung, Unruhe, Aufregung, Verwirrung, Fassungslosigkeit.

disconcert [diskən'sə:t], *v.t.* vereiteln, zunichte machen, durcheinanderbringen; beunruhigen, verwirren, bestürzen, aus der Fassung bringen.

disconnect [diskə'nekt], *v.t.* trennen, loslösen; (*Elec.*) trennen, unterbrechen, abschalten, ausschalten; (*Tech.*) abstellen, entkuppeln, auskuppeln. **disconnected,** *adj.* losgelöst, (ab)getrennt; unzusammenhängend, zusammenhang(s)los. **disconnection, disconnexion,** *s.* die Entkuppelung, Abschaltung, Unterbrechung, Abstellung.

disconsolate [dis'kɔnsəlit], *adj.* trostlos, freudlos; verzweifelt, untröstlich. **disconsolateness,** *s.* die Trostlosigkeit.

discontent [diskən'tent], **1.** *s.* die Unzufriedenheit, das Mißvergnügen. **2.** *pred. adj. See* **discontented. 3.** *v.t.* unzufrieden machen. **discontented,** *adj.* unzufrieden (***with***, mit), mißvergnügt (über (*Acc.*)); mißmutig. **discontentedness, discontentment,** *s. See* **discontent, 1.**

discontinuance [diskən'tinjuəns], *s. See* **discontinuation**; (*Law*) – ***of a suit,*** die Absetzung einer Klage. **discontinuation** [–'eiʃən], *s.* die Unterbrechung; Einstellung, das Aufhören, der Abbruch, die Beendigung. **discontinue, 1.** *v.t.*

unterbrechen, aussetzen; einstellen, nicht weiterführen, aufgeben, abbrechen, unterlassen; – ***a newspaper,*** die Zeitung abbestellen. **2.** *v.i.* aufhören, eingestellt *or* unterbrochen werden. **discontinuity** [diskɔnti'nju:iti], *s.* die Zusammenhang(s)losigkeit; Lücke, Unterbrechung; (*Math.*) Diskontinuität. **discontinuous,** *adj.* unterbrochen, zusammenhang(s)los, unzusammenhängend, (*Math.*) diskontinuierlich.

discord ['diskɔ:d], *s.* die Zwietracht, Uneinigkeit, der Zank, Streit, Zwist; (*Mus.*) die Dissonanz, der Mißklang, (*fig.*) Mißklang, Mißton; ***be at – with,*** im Widerspruch stehen zu. **discordance, discordancy** [–'kɔ:dəns(i)], *s.* der Mißklang, die Dissonanz; Nichtübereinstimmung, Uneinigkeit, Zwistigkeit, Mißhelligkeit. **discordant,** *adj.* uneinig, nicht übereinstimmend (***with,*** mit), widersprechend (*Dat.*); entgegengesetzt, sich widersprechend; (*Mus.*) dissonant, unharmonisch, mißtönend.

discount, 1. ['diskaunt], *s.* der Rabatt, Preisnachlaß, Abschlag, der *or* das Skonto, der Diskont, das Disagio, der Zinsabzug; (*fig.*) Vorbehalt; ***allow a –,*** Rabatt gewähren; ***be at a –,*** unter Pari stehen; (*fig.*) in Mißkredit stehen, unbeliebt *or* nicht geschätzt sein; ***sell at a –,*** mit *or* unter Verlust verkaufen; – ***broker,*** der Wechselmakler, Diskontmakler; – ***rate,*** der Diskontsatz, Bankdiskont. **2.** [–'kaunt], *v.t.* 1. diskontieren (*a bill*); 2. (*fig.*) nur halbwegs glauben, mit Vorsicht hinnehmen; 3. beeinträchtigen, verringern; 4. nicht mitzählen *or* mitrechnen. **discountable** [–'kauntəbl], *adj.* diskontierbar, diskontfähig.

discountenance [dis'kauntinəns], *v.t.* verwirren, aus der Fassung bringen (*a p.*); (offen) mißbilligen, ablehnen, nicht unterstützen. **discountenanced,** *adj.* entmutigt, verwirrt.

discourage [dis'kʌridʒ], *v.t.* 1. entmutigen; 2. abhalten, abschrecken (***from doing,*** zu tun); abraten (*Dat.*) (***from,*** von); mißbilligen; verhindern. **discouragement,** *s.* 1. die Entmutigung; Enttäuschung; 2. Verhinderung, das Hindernis; Abschreckungsmittel.

discourse, 1. ['diskɔ:s], *s.* das Gespräch; die Rede, der Vortrag; die Predigt; (*obs.*) Abhandlung. **2.** [–'kɔ:s], *v.i.* einen Vortrag halten, reden, sprechen, sich unterhalten (***on,*** über (*Acc.*)).

discourteous [dis'kə:tjəs], *adj.* unhöflich, unartig. **discourtesy** [–tisi], *s.* die Unhöflichkeit.

discover [dis'kʌvə], *v.t.* 1. entdecken, ausfindig machen, auskundschaften; ermitteln, feststellen (*truth etc.*); (*fig.*) erkennen, einsehen; 2. (*obs.*) aufdecken, enthüllen; (*Chess*) – ***check,*** maskiertes Schach bieten. **discoverable,** *adj.* entdeckbar; wahrnehmbar, sichtbar. **discoverer,** *s.* der Entdecker. **discovery,** *s.* 1. die Entdeckung; Auffindung; Enthüllung; der Fund, die Entdeckung; ***voyage of –,*** die Forschungsreise, Entdeckungsfahrt; 2. (*Law*) zwangsweise Aufdeckung.

discredit [dis'kredit], **1.** *s.* 1. schlechter Ruf; der Mißkredit, die Unehre, Schande; ***bring him into –, bring – on him,*** ihn in Mißkredit bringen; ***to the – of their family,*** zur Schande ihrer Familie; 2. der Zweifel, das Mißtrauen; ***cast*** or ***throw – on a th.,*** etwas zweifelhaft erscheinen lassen. **2.** *v.t.* 1. (*a th.*) keinen Glauben schenken (*Dat.*), nicht glauben, anzweifeln, bezweifeln; 2. (*a p.*) in Verruf *or* Mißkredit bringen (***with,*** bei). **discreditable,** *adj.* schändlich, entehrend, schimpflich. **discredited,** *adj.* unglaubwürdig.

discreet [dis'kri:t], *adj.* umsichtig, vorsichtig, besonnen, verständig; taktvoll, verschwiegen, diskret. **discreetness,** *s.* die Verschwiegenheit, der Takt.

discrepancy [dis'krepənsi], *s.* die Verschiedenheit, Nichtübereinstimmung; der Widerspruch, Zwiespalt. **discrepant,** *adj.* abweichend, verschieden (***from,*** von); nicht übereinstimmend, sich widersprechend, widerstreitend.

discrete [dis'kri:t], *adj.* getrennt, einzeln; (*Math.*) unstetig, diskontinuierlich, diskret; (*Log.*) disjunktiv, abstrahiert.

discretion [dis'kreʃən], *s.* die Klugheit, Umsicht, Vorsicht, Besonnenheit; das Ermessen, Belieben, Gutdünken; die Verfügungsfreiheit, Machtbefugnis; *see also* **discreetness**; ***age*** or ***years of –,*** mündiges Alter; ***at –,*** nach Belieben *or* Gutdünken; ***it is at*** or ***within my –,*** es steht mir frei; – ***is the better part of valour,*** das bessere Teil der Tapferkeit ist Vorsicht; ***surrender at –,*** sich bedingungslos *or* auf Gnade und Ungnade ergeben; ***use one's –,*** nach eigenem Gutdünken handeln; ***act with –,*** mit Einsicht *or* taktvoll handeln. **discretional, discretionary,** *adj.* willkürlich, beliebig; – ***powers,*** unumschränkte Vollmacht.

discretive [dis'kri:tiv], *adj.* (*Log., Chem.*) trennend, disjunktiv.

discriminate [dis'krimineit], **1.** *v.t.* auseinanderhalten, (voneinander) unterscheiden, abheben, absondern. **2.** *v.i.* einen Unterschied machen, unterscheiden; – ***against,*** nachteilig behandeln, benachteiligen, diskriminieren, herabsetzen; – ***between,*** unterschiedlich behandeln; – ***in favour of,*** begünstigen. **discriminating,** *adj.* unterscheidend, charakteristisch; scharf(sinnig); urteilsfähig, umsichtig; – ***duties,*** Differenzialzölle; – ***taste,*** feingebildeter Geschmack. **discrimination** [–'neiʃən], *s.* 1. die Unterscheidung, unterschiedliche Behandlung; die Diskriminierung; (*in favour*) Begünstigung, (*against*) Benachteiligung, Zurücksetzung; 2. der Scharfsinn, das Unterscheidungsvermögen, die Einsicht, Urteilskraft. **discriminative** [–nətiv], *adj.* unterscheidend, Unterscheidungs–, charakteristisch; einen Unterschied beobachtend *or* machend, diskriminierend. **discriminatory,** *adj. See* **discriminative**; – ***law,*** das Ausnahmegesetz.

discursive [dis'kə:siv], *adj.* 1. abschweifend, unzusammenhängend; 2. (*Phil.*) logisch fortschreitend, diskursiv; – ***faculty,*** logische Denkkraft.

discus ['diskəs], *s.* die Wurfscheibe, der Diskus.

discuss [dis'kʌs], *v.t.* 1. reden *or* sprechen *or* sich unterhalten über (*Acc.*), diskutieren, debattieren, erörtern, besprechen, verhandeln; 2. untersuchen, behandeln. **discussion** [–'kʌʃən], *s.* die Diskussion, Debatte, Erörterung, Besprechung, Aussprache, der Meinungsaustausch; ***enter into*** or ***upon a –,*** in eine Diskussion eintreten; ***matter for –,*** der Diskussionsgegenstand; ***under –,*** zur Erörterung stehend.

discus|-throw, *s.* der Diskuswurf. **–-throwing,** *s.* (***throwing the discus***) das Diskuswerfen.

disdain [dis'dein], **1.** *s.* die Verachtung, Geringschätzung, Verschmähung; ***hold in –,*** geringschätzen; ***smile in –,*** geringschätzig lächeln. **2.** *v.t.* verachten, verschmähen; – ***to do,*** es für unter seiner Würde halten, zu tun. **disdainful,** *adj.* 1. verächtlich, geringschätzig; ***be – of,*** *see* **disdain, 2.**; 2. hochmütig; höhnisch.

disease [di'zi:z], *s.* die Krankheit, das Leiden. **diseased,** *adj.* krank, erkrankt; (*fig.*) krankhaft.

disembark [disim'bɑ:k], **1.** *v.t.* an Land setzen, ausschiffen, landen. **2.** *v.i.* an Land gehen, landen, aussteigen. **disembarkation** [–embɑ:'keiʃən], *s.* die Landung, Ausschiffung.

disembarrass [disim'bærəs], *v.t.* aus der Verlegenkeit ziehen *or* befreien; (*fig.*) befreien, loslösen (***of,*** von), herausziehen, herauslösen (***from,*** aus); – ***o.s. of,*** sich befreien *or* freimachen von. **disembarrassment,** *s.* die Befreiung aus einer Verlegenheit; (*fig.*) Befreiung.

disembodied [disim'bɔdid], *adj.* entkörpert, körperlos. **disembodiment,** *s.* 1. die Entkörperlichung; 2. Auflösung (*of troops*). **disembody,** *v.t.* 1. entkörperlichen; 2. (*Mil.*) entlassen, auflösen.

disembogue [disim'boug], **1.** *v.t.* fließen *or* ausströmen lassen, entladen. **2.** *v.i.* sich ergießen *or* entladen, fließen, münden (***into,*** in (*Acc.*)).

disembowel [disim'bauəl], *v.t.* ausweiden; den Bauch aufschlitzen (*Dat.*).

disembroil [disim'brɔil], *v.t.* aus der Zwicklage helfen (*Dat.*).

disenchant [disin'tʃɑ:nt], *v.t.* ernüchtern, desillusionieren, enttäuschen. **disenchantment,** *s.* die Enttäuschung, Desillusionierung, Ernüchterung.

disencumber [disin'kʌmbə], *v.t.* entlasten, befreien (*of, from*, von).

disendow [disin'dau], *v.t.* die Pfründe *or* Stiftung entziehen (*Dat.*).

disenfranchise [disin'fræntʃaiz], *v.t.* das Wahlrecht entziehen (*Dat.*), entrechten. **disenfranchisement** [–tʃizmənt], *s.* die Entziehung *or* der Entzug des Wahlrechts, die Entrechtung.

disengage [disin'geidʒ], **1.** *v.t.* befreien, freimachen, loslösen, losmachen (*from*, von); (*Chem., Phys.*) entwickeln, auslösen, abscheiden; (*Tech.*) ausrücken, ausklinken, loskuppeln, entkuppeln; (*fig.*) entlasten, entbinden, befreien; (*Motor.*) – ***the clutch,*** auskuppeln. **2.** *v.i.* sich losmachen *or* freimachen; sich absetzen (*also Mil.*), loskommen. **disengaged,** *adj.* frei, unbeschäftigt, zu sprechen; (*Tele.*) frei, nicht besetzt. **disengagement,** *s.* die Loslösung, Freimachung, Befreiung; (*Tech.*) das Ausrücken; (*Chem.*) die Ausscheidung, Entbindung; (*Pol. etc.*) das Auseinanderrücken.

disentangle [disin'tæŋgl], *v.t.* entwirren, auseinanderwickeln (*knots etc.*); (*fig.*) befreien (*from*, von *or* aus), herauslösen (aus). **disentanglement,** *s.* die Entwirrung, Entflechtung, (*fig.*) Herauslösung, Befreiung.

disenthral(l) [disin'θrɔ:l], *v.t.* (von Knechtschaft) befreien.

disestablish [disis'tæbliʃ], *v.t.* aufheben, abschaffen; – ***the church,*** die Kirche entstaatlichen. **disestablishment,** *s.* die Entstaatlichung.

disfavour [dis'feivə], **1.** *s.* die Ungnade, Ungunst, Mißgunst, Mißbilligung, der Unwillen, das Mißfallen; ***fall into*** –, in Ungnade fallen; ***in – with,*** in Ungnade bei; ***in his*** –, zu seinen Ungunsten; ***look upon with*** –, mit Mißfallen betrachten. **2.** *v.t.* mißbilligen, ungnädig behandeln.

disfiguration [disfigju'reiʃən], *s.* die Entstellung, Verunstaltung. **disfigure** [–'figə], *v.t.* entstellen, verunstalten (*with*, durch). **disfigurement,** *s. See* **disfiguration.**

disfranchise [dis'fræntʃaiz], *v.t.* 1. *See* **disenfranchise**; 2. die Vorrechte *or* Freiheiten entziehen (*Dat.*). **disfranchisement** [–tʃizmənt], *s.* 1. *See* **disenfranchisement**; 2. die Entziehung *or* der Entzug der Vorrechte.

disgorge [dis'gɔ:dʒ], **1.** *v.t.* auswerfen, ausstoßen, ausspeien; (*fig.*) (widerwillig) herausgeben (*booty etc.*). **2.** *v.i.* sich entladen.

disgrace [dis'greis], **1.** *s.* die Ungnade; Schande, Unehre (*to*, für); *in* –, in Ungnade; ***bring – on him,*** ihm Schande bereiten; ***he is a – to his family,*** er ist eine Schande *or* ein Schandfleck für seine Familie. **2.** *v.t.* in Ungnade stürzen; entehren, schänden; – ***o.s.,*** sich blamieren; ***be –d,*** in Ungnade fallen. **disgraceful,** *adj.* schimpflich, schmählich, schmachvoll, entehrend, schändlich.

disgruntled [dis'grʌntld], *adj.* verstimmt, verärgert, übelgelaunt, mürrisch, unzufrieden (*at*, über (*Acc.*)).

disguise [dis'gaiz], **1.** *v.t.* verkleiden, vermummen, maskieren; (*fig.*) verstellen, verhüllen, verschleiern, verbergen, verhehlen, bemänteln. **2.** *s.* die Verkleidung, Vermummung; Maske; (*fig.*) Verstellung, Verschleierung, der Schein; Vorwand; ***in*** –, verkleidet, maskiert; ***a blessing in*** –, das Glück im Unglück; ***under the – of,*** unter dem Vorwand (*Gen.*).

disgust [dis'gʌst], **1.** *s.* der Ekel, Widerwille, Abscheu (*at*, über (*Acc.*) *or* vor (*Dat.*)). **2.** *v.t.* anwidern, (an)ekeln; ***it –s me,*** es ekelt mich (an); ***be –ed with*** or ***at*** or ***by,*** Ekel empfinden über (*Acc.*) (*a th.*); (*coll.*) ***be –ed with him,*** über ihn verärgert *or* empört sein; ***he has become –ed with life,*** er ist des Lebens überdrüssig geworden, das Leben ist ihm zum Ekel geworden. **disgusting,** *adj.* ekelhaft, widerlich, abscheulich. **disgustingly,** *adv.* (*also coll.*) entsetzlich, schrecklich (*rich, fat etc.*).

dish [diʃ], **1.** *s.* 1. die Schüssel, Platte, Schale; 2. das Gericht, die Speise. **2.** *v.t.* 1. (*Cul.*) (*usu.* – ***up***) anrichten, auftragen, servieren; (*fig., coll.*) – ***out,*** austeilen, verteilen; (*fig., coll.*) – ***up,*** auftischen, herrichten, mundgerecht darbieten; 2. (*sl.*) vereiteln (*a th.*), erledigen, abtun, kaltstellen (*a p. or th.*); (*sl.*) anschmieren, hereinlegen, hereinfallen lassen (*a p.*); 3. (*Tech.*) wölben, buckeln, tiefziehen, (*wheel*) stürzen.

dishabille [disə'bi:l], *s.* das Morgenkleid, Hauskleid; Negligé, (*coll.*) nachlässige Kleidung; (*coll.*) ***in*** –, nachlässig gekleidet.

disharmony [dis'hɑ:məni], *s.* der Mißklang, die Dissonanz, (*fig.*) Mißhelligkeit.

dish-cloth, *s.* das Geschirrtuch, Spültuch, der Abwaschlappen.

dishearten [dis'hɑ:tn], *v.t.* entmutigen; niedergeschlagen *or* verzagt machen. **disheartening,** *adj.* entmutigend.

dished [diʃt], *adj.* 1. (*Tech.*) konkav gewölbt, (*wheel*) gestürzt; 2. (*sl.*) fertig, kaputt.

dishevel [di'ʃevl], *v.t.* zerzausen, in Unordnung bringen. **dishevelled,** *adj.* aufgelöst, zerzaust, wirr (*as hair*); unordentlich, ungepflegt, schlampig.

dishonest [dis'ɔnist], *adj.* unehrlich, unredlich. **dishonesty,** *s.* die Unredlichkeit, Unehrlichkeit.

dishonour [dis'ɔnə], **1.** *s.* die Schmach, Schande, der Schimpf. **2.** *v.t.* 1. entehren, schänden (*a woman*), verächtlich behandeln, in Unehre bringen; 2. (*Comm.*) nicht akzeptieren *or* honorieren (*a cheque*); – ***one's word,*** sein Wort nicht einlösen; ***return a bill –ed,*** einen Wechsel mit Protest zurückschicken. **dishonourable,** *adj.* ehrlos, unehrenhaft (*a p.*); entehrend, schimpflich, schändlich, gemein (*action*); (*Mil.*) – ***discharge,*** die Entlassung wegen Wehrunwürdigkeit. **dishonourableness,** *s.* die Ehrlosigkeit, Unehrenhaftigkeit; Schändlichkeit.

dish|-washer, *s.* der Geschirrspüler, Geschirrspülautomat. **–-water,** *s.* das Spülwasser, Abwaschwasser.

disillusion [disi'l(j)u:ʒən], **1.** *s.* die Enttäuschung, Ernüchterung (*with*, über (*Acc.*)). **2.** *v.t.* ernüchtern, von Illusionen befreien, desillusionieren. **disillusionment,** *s. See* **disillusion, 1. disillusionize,** *v.t. See* **disillusion, 2.**

disinclination [disinkli'neiʃən], *s.* die Abneigung, Abgeneigtheit (*for, to*, gegen). **disincline** [–'klain], *v.t.* abgeneigt machen (*from*, gegen). **disinclined,** *adj.* abgeneigt.

disinfect [disin'fekt], *v.t.* desinfizieren. **disinfectant, 1.** *s.* das Desinfektionsmittel. **2.** *adj.* desinfizierend, keimtötend. **disinfection** [–'fekʃən], *s.* die Desinfektion, Desinfizierung.

disingenuous [disin'dʒenjuəs], *adj.* unaufrichtig, unredlich, hinterlistig. **disingenuousness,** *s.* die Unredlichkeit, Unaufrichtigkeit.

disinherit [disin'herit], *v.t.* enterben. **disinheritance,** *s.* die Enterbung.

disintegrate [dis'intigreit], **1.** *v.t.* auflösen, aufschließen, aufspalten, zersetzen, zerstückeln, zertrümmern, zerteilen, zerfasern, zerkleinern. **2.** *v.i.* zerfallen, sich auflösen, (*fig.*) verfallen, (*Geol.*) verwittern. **disintegration** [–'greiʃən], *s.* die Auflösung, der Zerfall, die Zersetzung, Zertrümmerung, Zerstörung, Zerstückelung, (*Geol.*) Verwitterung. **disintegrator,** *s.* die Stampfmaschine, Schlagmühle, der Desintegrator, Zerkleinerer.

disinter [disin'tə:], *v.t.* (wieder) ausgraben, exhumieren, (*fig.*) ans Licht bringen.

disinterest [dis'intərist], *v.t.* – ***o.s.,*** uninteressiert sein (*from*, an (*Dat.*)); gleichgültig gegenüber stehen (*Dat.*). **disinterested,** *adj.* uneigennützig, selbstlos; unparteiisch, unbefangen. **disinterestedness,** *s.* die Uneigennützigkeit, Selbstlosigkeit; Unparteilichkeit.

disinterment [disin'tə:mənt], *s.* die Ausgrabung, Exhumierung.

disjoin [dis'dʒɔin], *v.t.* trennen.

disjoint [dis'dʒɔint], *v.t.* verrenken, ausrenken; auseinandernehmen, zergliedern, zerlegen, zerstückeln; (ab)trennen (*from*, von); (*fig.*) den Zusammenhang zerstören, aus den Fugen bringen. **disjointed,** *adj.* abgerissen, zusammenhang(s)los, unzusammenhängend. **disjointedness,** *s.* die Zusammenhang(s)losigkeit.

disjunction [dis'dʒʌŋkʃən], *s.* die Trennung, Absonderung. **disjunctive** [–tiv], *adj.* (ab)trennend; (*Gram.*) disjunktiv.

disk [disk], *s.* 1. die Scheibe, Platte, der Teller; 2. (*coll.*) die (Schall)platte. **disk|-brake,** *s.* die Scheibenbremse. **--clutch,** *s.* die Lamellenkupplung. **--jockey,** *s.* (*Rad. coll.*) der Schallplattenjockey. **--valve,** *s.* das Tellerventil.

dislike [dis'laik], **1.** *s.* die Abneigung, der Widerwille (*of, for*, gegen), das Mißfallen; *take a – to a th.*, eine Abneigung gegen eine S. fassen. **2.** *v.t.* nicht gern haben, nicht mögen, nicht lieben, nicht leiden mögen *or* können, mißbilligen; ***I – doing it,*** ich tue es ungern, ich mag es nicht tun; ***you will make yourself –d,*** du machst dich unbeliebt.

dislocate ['dislokeit], *v.t.* 1. (*Med.*) verrenken, ausrenken; – ***one's shoulder,*** sich (*Dat.*) die Schulter verrenken; 2. (*Tech.*) verschieben, verrücken; 3. (*Geol.*) verwerfen, versetzen; 4. (*fig.*) in Verwirrung bringen. **dislocation** [–'keiʃən], *s.* (*Med.*) die Verrenkung; (*Tech.*) Verrückung, Verschiebung; (*Geol.*) Verwerfung; (*fig.*) Verwirrung.

dislodge [dis'lɔdʒ], *v.t.* verjagen, vertreiben, verdrängen, entfernen.

disloyal [dis'lɔiəl], *adj.* treulos, ungetreu (*to* (*a p.*), *Dat.*), treulos, illoyal, verräterisch (gegen). **disloyalty,** *s.* die Untreue, Treulosigkeit.

dismal ['dizməl], *adj.* trüb(e), düster; traurig, trostlos, bedrückend, elend; gräßlich, schrecklich. **dismalness,** *s.* die Trübheit, Düsterheit; Traurigkeit, Trostlosigkeit; Schrecklichkeit.

dismantle [dis'mæntl], *v.t.* 1. abmontieren, abbauen, auseinandernehmen; niederreißen, abbrechen, schleifen; abtakeln (*a ship*); 2. (*obs.*) entblößen, entkleiden.

dismast [dis'mɑ:st], *v.t.* entmasten.

dismay [dis'mei], **1.** *s.* der Schreck(en), die Bestürzung, das Entsetzen; ***filled with –,*** verzweifelt, schreckerfüllt. **2.** *v.t.* in Schrecken versetzen, erschrecken, entsetzen; ***be –ed,*** entsetzt *or* verzagt sein.

dismember [dis'membə], *v.t.* zergliedern; zerreißen, zerstückeln. **dismemberment,** *s.* die Zergliederung, Zerreißung, Zerstückelung.

dismiss [dis'mis], **1.** *v.t.* fortschicken, wegschicken, verabschieden; entlassen (*from*, aus) (*from office*); (*Mil.*) wegtreten lassen (*a parade*); (*fig.*) aufgeben, ablehnen, ablegen; abtun, hinweggehen über (*Acc.*), fallenlassen; (*Law*) abweisen; (*Spt.*) ausschalten; ***I –ed him without ceremony,*** ich fertigte ihn ohne Umstände ab; – ***a th. from one's mind,*** sich (*Dat.*) eine S. aus dem Sinn *or* Kopf schlagen. **2.** *v.i.* (*Mil.*) wegtreten, abtreten. **dismissal,** *s.* die Entlassung (*from*, aus), der Abschied, die Verabschiedung; (*Law*) Abweisung; – ***with costs*** kostenpflichtige Abweisung.

dismount [dis'maunt], **1.** *v.i.* absteigen; (*Mil.*) absitzen; (*Mil.*) *–!* abgesessen! **2.** *v.t.* 1. absteigen von (*a horse*); 2. vom Pferde werfen, aus dem Sattel heben (*a rider*); 3. demontieren, aus der Lafette heben (*a gun*); (*Tech.*) auseinandernehmen.

disobedience [diso'bi:djəns], *s.* der Ungehorsam, die Widerspenstigkeit, Gehorsamsverweigerung (*as a p.*); – ***of a law,*** die Nichtbefolgung eines Gesetzes. **disobedient,** *adj.* ungehorsam (*to*, gegen). **disobey** [–'bei], *v.t.* nicht gehorchen (*Dat.*), ungehorsam sein gegen (*as a p.*); verletzen, übertreten, nicht befolgen, mißachten (*commands*); ***I will not be –ed,*** ich dulde keinen Ungehorsam.

disoblige [diso'blaidʒ], *v.t.* ungefällig sein gegen; vor den Kopf stoßen, kränken, verletzen. **disobliging,** *adj.* ungefällig, unhöflich, unartig, unfreundlich. **disobligingness,** *s.* die Ungefälligkeit.

disorder [dis'ɔ:də], **1.** *s.* die Unordnung, Verwirrung, das Durcheinander; (*Pol.*) die Ruhestörung, der Aufruhr, (*coll.*) Krawall; (*Med.*) die Erkrankung, Krankheit; ***mental –,*** die Geistesstörung. **2.** *v.t.* durcheinanderbringen, in Unordnung bringen, stören, verwirren; zerrütten (*body or mind*); ***my stomach is –ed,*** ich habe mir den Magen verdorben. **disorderliness,** *s.* die Unordnung, Verwirrung; (*of a p.*) Unordentlichkeit, Schlampigkeit; *see also* ***disorderly conduct.*** **disorderly,** *adj.* unordentlich, verwirrt; (*of a p.*) unsystematisch; liederlich, schlampig; (*Law etc.*) gesetzwidrig, unbotmäßig, aufrührerisch; – ***conduct,*** ordnungswidriges *or* ungebührliches Benehmen; (*obs.*) – ***house,*** das Bordell.

disorganization [disɔ:gənai'zeiʃən], *s.* die Auflösung, Zerrüttung; Unordnung, Verwirrung, das Durcheinander. **disorganize** [–'ɔ:gənaiz], *v.t.* auflösen, zerrütten; in Unordnung bringen, durcheinanderbringen.

disorient(ate) [dis'ɔ:riənt(eit)], *v.t.* verwirren, desorientieren (*also Psych.*). **disorientated,** *adj.* verwirrt, desorientiert. **disorientation** [–'teiʃən], *s.* die Verwirrtheit, Desorientiertheit.

disown [dis'oun], *v.t.* nicht (als sein eigen) anerkennen; verstoßen; verleugnen, ableugnen.

disparage [dis'pæridʒ], *v.t.* herabsetzen, in Verruf bringen, geringschätzen, verunglimpfen. **disparagement,** *s.* die Herabsetzung, Geringschätzung, Verunglimpfung, der Verruf; ***no –! without – to you!*** ohne Ihnen nahetreten zu wollen! **disparaging,** *adj.* herabsetzend, verächtlich, geringschätzig.

disparate ['dispərit], *adj.* ungleichartig, unvereinbar, grundverschieden; disparat. **disparates,** *pl.* unvereinbare *or* unvergleichbare Dinge. **disparity** [–'pæriti], *s.* die Ungleichheit, Verschiedenheit, Unvereinbarkeit, der Unterschied.

[1]**dispart** [dis'pɑ:t], **1.** *v.t.* trennen, (auf)teilen, (zer)spalten. **2.** *v.i.* sich teilen *or* spalten *or* trennen.

[2]**dispart,** **1.** *v.t.* (*Artil.*) kalibrieren. **2.** *s.* der Visierwinkel. **dispart-sight,** *s.* das Richtkorn.

dispassionate [dis'pæʃənit], *adj.* leidenschaftslos; nüchtern, sachlich, ruhig, gelassen; unbefangen, unparteiisch, objektiv.

dispatch [dis'pætʃ], **1.** *v.t.* 1. befördern, (ab)senden, (ab)schicken, spedieren, versenden, abgehen lassen; 2. schnell erledigen, ausführen, abfertigen; 3. beseitigen, abtun, ins Jenseits befördern; 4. (*coll.*) rasch aufessen, verputzen. **2.** *s.* 1. schnelle Abfertigung, die Ausführung, Erledigung; 2. Absendung, Beförderung, der Versand; 3. die Eile, Promptheit; ***with –,*** eiligst; 4. die Beseitigung; 5. Depesche, Eilbotschaft; ***bearer of –es,*** der Eilbote, Depeschenträger, Kurier; (*Mil.*) ***mentioned in –es,*** in Depeschen erwähnt.

dispatch|-boat, *s.* das Depeschenboot, der Aviso. **--box,** *s.* (*Pol.*) die Depeschentasche. **--case,** *s.* die Aktenmappe, Aktentasche. **--goods,** *pl.* das Eilgut. **--note,** *s.* die Versandanzeige. **--rider,** *s.* (*Mil.*) der Meldereiter, Meldefahrer.

dispel [dis'pel], *v.t.* zerstreuen; (*fig.*) verbannen, verjagen, vertreiben (*doubt, care etc.*).

dispensability [dispensə'biliti], *s.* 1. die Verteilbarkeit; 2. Entbehrlichkeit, Erläßlichkeit; (*Eccl.*) Dispensierbarkeit. **dispensable,** *adj.* 1. verteilbar; 2. erläßlich, entbehrlich, unwesentlich.

dispensary [dis'pensəri], *s.* die (Armen)apotheke; Poliklinik.

dispensation [dispen'seiʃən], *s.* 1. die Zuteilung, Austeilung, Verteilung; 2. (*Eccl.*) der Dispens, die Dispensation; (*Law*) Ausnahmebewilligung, Erlassung; Fügung, Ordnung, Lenkung; Vorkehrung, Einrichtung; ***divine –,*** göttliche Fügung; – ***of Providence,*** das Walten der Vorsehung.

dispense [dis'pens], **1.** *v.t.* austeilen, verteilen, spenden, verschenken; verabreichen, nach Rezept anfertigen; – ***drugs,*** Arzneien verabreichen; – ***justice,*** Recht sprechen. **2.** *v.i.* 1. Dispens(ation) erteilen, eine Ausnahme bewilligen; 2. Arzneien verabreichen; 3. – ***with,*** erlassen, nicht anwenden; entbehren, verzichten auf (*Acc.*), fertig werden ohne; ***it cannot be –d with,*** es darf nicht unterbleiben; ***we can – with your company,*** wir können Ihre Gesellschaft entbehren; ***– with formalities,*** von Förmlichkeiten Abstand nehmen. **dispenser,** *s.* 1. der Austeiler, Verteiler, Spender; 2. (*also* ***dispensing chemist***) Arzneihersteller, Apotheker.

dispersal [dis'pə:sl], *s.* 1. *See* **dispersion**; 2. (*Mil.*) die Auflockerung. **disperse,** 1. *v.t.* zerstreuen, zersprengen, auseinandertreiben; verteilen, verbreiten, ausbreiten (***over,*** über (*Acc.*)); (*Mil.*) auflockern (*ranks*), auseinandersprengen (*enemy*). 2. *v.i.* zerstreut werden, sich zerstreuen *or* auflösen; auseinandergehen. **dispersion** [–'pə:ʃən], *s.* die Verstreuung, Zerstreuung, (*also Stat.*) Streuung; Auflösung, Auflockerung; Verbreitung, Verteilung, Ausbreitung (***over,*** über (*Acc.*)); (*Stat.*) – ***error,*** der Streu(ungs)fehler; (*marksmanship*) – ***pattern,*** das Trefferbild.

dispirit [di'spirit], *v.t.* entmutigen, niederdrücken, deprimieren. **dispirited,** *adj.* mutlos, entmutigt, niedergeschlagen, niedergedrückt, deprimiert.

displace [dis'pleis], *v.t.* 1. versetzen, verschieben, verlagern, verrücken, (*also Naut.*) verdrängen; 2. (*a p.*) absetzen, entheben, entlassen; (*Pol.*) ***–d p.,*** Verschleppte(r); 3. (*also Chem.*) ersetzen. **displacement,** *s.* 1. die Versetzung, Verschiebung, Verlagerung, Verrückung, (*Naut.*) (Wasser)verdrängung; ***– tonnage,*** die Verdrängungstonnage; 2. (*Motor.*) der Hubraum; 3. die Absetzung, (*also Chem.*) Ersetzung; 4. (*of population*) Verschleppung.

display [dis'plei], 1. *v.t.* entfalten, ausbreiten, enthüllen, zeigen, offenbaren; (*goods*) ausstellen, auslegen; zur Schau stellen; ***– one's courage*** seinen Mut zeigen; ***– one's common sense,*** seinen Mutterwitz erkennen lassen. 2. *s.* die Entfaltung, Schaustellung, (*of goods*) Ausstellung, Auslage; (*Typ.*) Aufmachung, Auszeichnung, Hervorhebung; der Aufwand, Prunk, Pomp; (*Orn.*) das Balzen; ***make a great –,*** großen Aufwand machen; ***make a great – of,*** auffällig zur Schau tragen, prunken mit; ***grand – of fireworks,*** großes Feuerwerk; ***– of power,*** die Machtentfaltung.

displease [dis'pli:z], *v.t.* mißfallen (*Dat.*), zuwider sein (*Dat.*), ärgern, kränken; ***– the eye*** das Auge beleidigen. **displeased,** *adj.* mißvergnügt; ungehalten (***at, with,*** über (*Acc.*)), unzufrieden (mit). **displeasing,** *adj.* unangenehm, anstößig, mißfällig. **displeasure** [–'pleʒə], *s.* das Mißfallen, Mißvergnügen; der Ärger, Verdruß, Unwille (***at, over,*** über (*Acc.*)); ***incur his –,*** sich (*Dat.*) sein Mißfallen zuziehen.

disport [di'spɔ:t], *v.i.* (*also* ***– o.s.***) sich belustigen *or* ergötzen *or* vergnügen; herumtollen.

disposable [dis'pouzəbl], *adj.* 1. verfügbar, disponibel; 2. Wegwerf–, wegzuwerfen(d) (*container etc.*). **disposal,** *s.* 1. die Anordnung, Aufstellung; Verwendung; 2. Beseitigung, Erledigung; 3. Übertragung, Übergabe, der Verkauf; 4. die Verfügung, Disposition, Willkür, das Verfügungsrecht (***of,*** über (*Acc.*)); ***have the – of,*** verfügen über (*Acc.*); ***be at his –,*** ihm zur Verfügung stehen; ***put*** or ***place at his –,*** ihm zur Verfügung stellen.

dispose [dis'pouz], 1. *v.t.* 1. (an)ordnen, verteilen, einteilen, einrichten, einreihen, aufstellen, zurechtlegen (*things*); 2. geneigt machen, veranlassen, bewegen, stimmen, verleiten (*a p.*). 2. *v.i.* ordnen, lenken, verfügen; ***man proposes, God –s,*** der Mensch denkt, Gott lenkt; ***– of,*** verfügen *or* entscheiden über (*Acc.*), verwenden, anwenden; (*goods*) verkaufen, veräußern, verschenken, aushändigen, übertragen, übergeben; (*a p.*) erledigen, abfertigen, beseitigen, abschaffen, wegschaffen, wegschicken; abtun, loswerden, (*coll.*) um die Ecke bringen; ***– of a matter,*** eine S. erledigen; ***– of by will,*** testamentarisch vermachen; ***– of in marriage,*** durch Heirat versorgen, verheiraten (***to,*** an (*Acc.*)); ***– of once and for all,*** ein für allemal aus dem Weg räumen; ***–d of,*** verkauft, veräußert, abgegeben.

disposed [dis'pouzd], *adj.* geneigt, gewillt, gesonnen, bereit; aufgelegt, eingestellt, gesinnt, gestimmt; ***– to mirth,*** zur Fröhlichkeit aufgelegt; ***ill-–,*** übelgesinnt (***towards,*** *Dat.*); ***well-–,*** wohlgesinnt (***towards,*** *Dat.*).

disposition [dispə'ziʃən], *s.* 1. die Anordnung, Aufstellung, Gliederung, Verteilung, Einteilung, Einrichtung; Anlage, der Plan; 2. die Verfügung, Bestimmung, Disposition, *pl.* Dispositionen, Vorkehrungen, Vorbereitungen (*pl.*); 3. die Verleihung, Verschenkung, Übertragung, Übergabe; 4. (*of a p.*) der Hang, die Neigung (***to,*** zu), Gesinnung, Stimmung, Anlage, Veranlagung, Charakteranlage, Gemütsart.

dispossess [dispo'zes], *v.t.* enteignen; vertreiben; (*fig.*) berauben (***of,*** *Gen.*), befreien (von). **dispossession** [–'zeʃən], *s.* die Enteignung; Beraubung.

dispraise [dis'preiz], 1. *v.t.* tadeln, herabsetzen, schmähen. 2. *s.* der Tadel, die Geringschätzung, Herabsetzung, Schmähung.

disproof [dis'pru:f], *s.* die Widerlegung.

disproportion [disprə'pɔ:ʃən], *s.* das Mißverhältnis. **disproportionate** [–nit], *adj.* in einem Mißverhältnis *or* in keinem Verhältnis stehend (***to,*** zu); unangemessen, unverhältnismäßig, übertrieben.

disprove [dis'pru:v], *v.t.* widerlegen.

disputable [dis'pju:təbl], *adj.* bestreitbar, strittig, fraglich, unerwiesen. **disputant,** *s.* der Streiter; Gegner, Disputant. **disputation** [–'teiʃən], *s.* der Wortstreit, Disput; (gelehrter) Redestreit, die Disputation. **disputatious** [–'teiʃəs], *adj.* streitsüchtig, zänkisch. **disputatiousness,** *s.* die Streitsucht. **disputative** [–tətiv], *adj.* *See* **disputatious.**

dispute [dis'pju:t], 1. *s.* 1. der Streit, Zank, die Auseinandersetzung; ***in –,*** streitig, strittig, umstritten; 2. die Diskussion, Debatte, Kontroverse; ***beyond –,*** unstreitig, fraglos, zweifellos, unzweifelhaft. 2. *v.t.* 1. bestreiten, in Zweifel ziehen, bezweifeln; 2. streiten *or* kämpfen um, abstreiten, widerstreben (*Dat.*), widerstehen (*Dat.*); ***– every inch of ground,*** jeden Zollbreit Landes streitig machen; 3. erörtern, diskutieren. 3. *v.i.* (sich) streiten, zanken (***about,*** um); disputieren, debattieren; ***– about nothing,*** sich um des Kaisers Bart streiten.

disqualification [diskwɔlifi'keiʃən], *s.* die Untauglichkeit, Ungeeignetheit; Untauglichkeitserklärung, Ausschließung, das Unfähigmachen; (*Spt.*) der Ausschluß. **disqualify** [dis'kwɔlifai], *v.t.* ungeeignet *or* untauglich machen (***for,*** für), (für) untauglich *or* unfähig erklären (***for,*** zu), (*Spt.*) ausschließen.

disquiet [dis'kwaiət], 1. *v.t.* beunruhigen. 2. *s.* die Unruhe, Besorgnis, Angst. **disquieting,** *adj.* beunruhigend. **disquietude** [–tju:d], *s.* *See* **disquiet, 2.**

disquisition [diskwi'ziʃən], *s.* (ausführliche) Rede, die Abhandlung (***on,*** über (*Acc.*)).

disrate [dis'reit], *v.t.* (her)absetzen, degradieren.

disregard [disri'gɑ:d], 1. *s.* die Mißachtung, Nichtachtung, Geringschätzung (***of, for,*** für *or Gen.*); Vernachlässigung, Ignorierung, Nichtbeachtung, das Außerachtlassen (*Gen.*), die Gleichgültigkeit (gegenüber). 2. *v.t.* mißachten, geringschätzen; nicht achten auf (*Acc.*), nicht beachten, übersehen, ignorieren, vernachlässigen, außer Acht lassen. **disregardful,** *adj.* unachtsam (***of,*** auf (*Acc.*)); ***be – of,*** mißachten, vernachlässigen.

disrepair [disri'pɛə], *s.* die Baufälligkeit, der Verfall; ***be in a state of –,*** baufällig sein; ***fall into –,*** verfallen, in Verfall geraten.

disreputable [dis'repjutəbl], *adj.* verrufen, von schlechtem Ruf; gemein, schimpflich. **disrepute** [–ri'pju:t], *s.* übler Ruf, der Verruf, die Verrufenheit, Schande, der Mißkredit; ***bring (fall) into –,*** in Verruf bringen (kommen).

disrespect [disri'spekt], 1. *s.* die Nichtachtung, Mißachtung (***to,*** für), Geringschätzung (*Gen.*); Respektlosigkeit, Unhöflichkeit, Unehrerbietigkeit (gegen). 2. *v.t.* nicht achten, geringschätzen.

disrespectful, *adj.* respektlos, unehrerbietig; unhöflich (*to*, gegen). **disrespectfulness,** *s.* die Respektlosigkeit, Unehrerbietigkeit, Unhöflichkeit.

disrobe [dis'roub], **1.** *v.t.* entkleiden, (*also fig.*) entblößen. **2.** *v.r.* sich entkleiden.

disroot [dis'ru:t], *v.t.* entwurzeln.

disrupt [dis'rʌpt], *v.t.* (zer)spalten, zersprengen, (auseinander)sprengen; (*fig.*) (zer)trennen, zerreißen, auseinanderreißen. **disruption** [–'rʌpʃən], *s.* das Auseinanderreißen, die Zerschlagung, Zerspaltung, Zerreißung; Zerrissenheit, Spaltung, der Bruch, Riß. **disruptive,** *adj.* (zer)spaltend, zertrümmernd; Zertrümmerungs–, Bruch–.

dissatisfaction [disætis'fækʃən], *s.* die Unzufriedenheit (***at***, ***over***, ***with***, über (*Acc.*) *or* mit). **dissatisfactory,** *adj.* unbefriedigend.

dissatisfied [di'sætisfaid], *adj.* unzufrieden (***with***, ***at***, über (*Acc.*) *or* mit), mißvergnügt, verdrießlich (über (*Acc.*)), unbefriedigt (von). **dissatisfy,** *v.t.* nicht befriedigen; unzufrieden machen; mißfallen (*Dat.*).

dissect [di'sekt], *v.t.* zerlegen; zergliedern (*also fig.*); (*Anat.*) sezieren; (*fig.*) analysieren. **dissecting,** *adj.* (*Anat.*) Sezier–, Sektions–. **dissection** [–'sekʃən], *s.* die Zerlegung, Zergliederung; (*Anat.*) Sektion, das Sezieren; (*fig.*) die Zergliederung, (genaue) Analyse.

disseise [dis'si:z], *v.t.* (*Law*) widerrechtlich enteignen. **disseisin,** *s.* widerrechtliche Enteignung *or* Besitzergreifung. **disseize,** *etc. See* **disseise.**

dissemble [di'sembl], **1.** *v.t.* verbergen, verhehlen, verhüllen, sich (*Dat.*) nicht anmerken lassen. **2.** *v.i.* heucheln, sich verstellen. **dissembler,** *s.* der Heuchler.

disseminate [di'semineit], *v.t.* ausstreuen (*seed*); (*fig.*) verbreiten. **dissemination** [–'neiʃən], *s.* die Ausstreuung; Verbreitung, Ausbreitung.

dissension [di'senʃən], *s.* die Zwietracht, Uneinigkeit; der Streit, Zwist; ***sow*** –, Zwietracht stiften.

dissent [di'sent], **1.** *s.* die Nichtübereinstimmung; abweichende Meinung, die Meinungsverschiedenheit; (*Eccl.*) Abweichung von der Staatskirche, der Dissent. **2.** *v.i.* nicht zustimmen (***from***, *Dat.*), nicht übereinstimmen (mit), anderer Meinung sein (als); (*Eccl.*) (von der Staatskirche) abweichen. **dissenter,** *s.* Andersdenkende(r), (*Eccl.*) der Dissident, Dissenter, Sektierer, Nonkonformist. **dissentient** [–'senʃənt], **1.** *adj.* andersdenkend, abweichend, nicht übereinstimmend; – ***vote,*** die Gegenstimme; ***without a – vote,*** einstimmig. **2.** *s.* Andersdenkende(r); die Gegenstimme.

dissertation [disə'teiʃən], *s.* (gelehrte) Abhandlung; die Dissertation (***on***, über (*Acc.*)); ***doctoral*** –, die Doktorarbeit.

disservice [dis'sə:vis], *s.* der Nachteil, Schaden, schlechter Dienst; ***be of – to him,*** ihm schaden, ihm zum Nachteil gereichen; ***do him a*** –, ihm einen schlechten Dienst erweisen.

dissever [di'sevə], *v.t.* trennen, absondern; (zer)teilen, zerlegen. **disseverance, disseverment,** *s.* die Trennung, Absonderung; Zerteilung.

dissidence ['disidəns], *s.* die Uneinigkeit, Nichtübereinstimmung, Meinungsverschiedenheit. **dissident,** **1.** *adj.* nicht übereinstimmend, andersdenkend, abweichend. **2.** *s.* der Sezessionist, Dissident, Andersdenkende(r).

dissimilar [di'similə], *adj.* unähnlich, ungleich(artig); verschieden (***to***, ***from***, von). **dissimilarity** [–'læriti], **dissimilitude** [–'militju:d], *s.* die Ungleichheit, Unähnlichkeit, Verschiedenartigkeit, Verschiedenheit.

dissimulate [di'simjuleit], **1.** *v.t.* verhehlen, verheimlichen, verbergen, verstecken. **2.** *v.i.* sich verstellen, heucheln. **dissimulation** [–'leiʃən], *s.* die Verstellung, Heuchelei.

dissipate ['disipeit], **1.** *v.t.* zerstreuen, zerteilen; ableiten (*heat*); (*fig.*) vertreiben, verscheuchen (*care*); vergeuden, verschwenden (*resources*). **2.** *v.i.* sich zerstreuen, sich auflösen, verschwinden. **dissipated,** *adj.* ausschweifend, liederlich. **dissipation** [–'peiʃən], *s.* die Zerstreuung (*also fig.*); Auflösung (*of smoke etc.*), (*fig.*) Vertreibung, Verscheuchung (*of cares etc.*), Vergeudung, Verschwendung (*of resources*); der Zeitvertreib, die Ausschweifung, Liederlichkeit, ausschweifendes Leben.

dissociable [di'souʃjəbl], *adj.* (ab)trennbar. **dissociate** [–ʃieit], **1.** *v.t.* trennen, loslösen, absondern (***from***, von); – ***o.s. from,*** abrücken von, sich lossagen von, nichts zu tun haben mit. **2.** *v.i.* sich spalten, aufspalten, zerfallen. **dissociation** [–'eiʃən], *s.* die Trennung, Absonderung; (*Chem.*) Auflösung, Zersetzung, Spaltung, der Zerfall; (*Psych.*) die Dissoziation, Assoziationsstörung, Bewußtseinsspaltung.

dissolubility [disɔlju'biliti], *s.* die (Auf)lösbarkeit, Trennbarkeit. **dissoluble,** *adj.* (auf)lösbar, trennbar.

dissolute ['disəlju:t], *adj.* ausschweifend, liederlich. **dissoluteness,** *s.* die Liederlichkeit, Ausschweifung.

dissolution [disə'lju:ʃən], *s.* die Auflösung (*also fig.*), Zersetzung; (*fig.*) Zerstörung, Vernichtung, der Tod; Zusammenbruch, Verfall; die Aufhebung, Trennung; – ***of the body,*** die Zersetzung *or* der Zerfall des Körpers; – ***of marriage,*** die Auflösung *or* Trennung einer Ehe; ***Dissolution of Parliament,*** die Auflösung des Parlaments.

dissolvable [di'zɔlvəbl], *adj.* auflösbar, löslich. **dissolve,** **1.** *v.t.* (auf)lösen (*also fig.*), (*fig.*) umstoßen, aufheben, annulieren; – ***a marriage,*** eine Ehe lösen; – ***a partnership,*** ein Gesellschaftsverhältnis auflösen; – ***one picture in another,*** ein Bild in das andere übergehen lassen *or* überblenden. **2.** *v.i.* sich auflösen, zergehen; (*fig.*) vergehen, verschwinden, hinschwinden; auseinandergehen (*as Parliament*), ineinander übergehen *or* überblenden (*as pictures*); – ***in(to) tears,*** sich in Tränen auflösen. **dissolvent,** **1.** *adj.* (auf)lösend, zersetzend. **2.** *s.* (*Tech.*) das Lösungsmittel, (*fig.*) Auflösungsmittel.

dissonance ['disonəns], *s.* der Mißklang, die Dissonanz; (*fig.*) Unstimmigkeit, Uneinigkeit, Mißhelligkeit. **dissonant,** *adj.* mißtönend, unharmonisch; (*fig.*) unvereinbar, abweichend.

dissuade [di'sweid], *v.t.* abraten (*Dat.*), abbringen (***from***, von). **dissuasion** [–'sweiʒən], *s.* das Abraten, Abbringen; die Abmahnung. **dissuasive** [–siv], *adj.* abratend, abmahnend.

dissyllabic, *see* **disyllabic.**

distaff ['distɑ:f], *s.* der Spinnrocken, die Kunkel; (*fig.*) – ***side,*** weibliche Linie, weibliches Geschlecht, (*obs.*) Kunkelmagen (*pl.*).

distal [distl], *adj.* (*Anat.*) der Körpermitte entfernt.

distance ['distəns], **1.** *s.* die Entfernung; Ferne, Weite; der Abstand (*also fig.*); (*Spt.*) die Strecke; (*Paint.*) der Hintergrund; (*fig.*) die Distanz, Reserve, Zurückhaltung; ***at a*** –, von weitem *or* fern(e); ***at an equal*** –, gleich weit (entfernt); ***action at a*** –, die Fernwirkung; ***keep at a*** –, fernhalten, vom Leibe halten; ***at this – of time,*** bei diesem Zeitabstand; ***from a*** –, aus einiger Entfernung; ***in the*** –, in der Ferne; (*Paint.*) ***in the middle*** –, in der Mitte; ***cover a*** –, eine Strecke zurücklegen; – ***covered,*** zurückgelegte Strecke; (*fig.*) ***keep one's*** –, Distanz halten, zurückhaltend sein; ***within driving*** –, mit dem Wagen (ohne weiteres) zu erreichen; ***within easy*** –, bequem zu erreichen; (*fig.*) ***within striking*** –, in Wirkungsabstand; (*Opt.*) ***focal*** –, die Brennweite; ***a good – off,*** ziemlich weit entfernt; (*Motor.*) ***stopping*** –, die Bremsstrecke; ***visual*** –, die Sehweite. **2.** *v.t.* distanzieren, hinter sich lassen (*also fig.*), (*fig.*) überholen, übertreffen, überflügeln.

distance|-post, *s.* (*Spt.*) der Distanzpfahl. **–-shot,** *s.* (*Phot.*) die Fernaufnahme.

distant ['distənt], *adj.* fern, weit, entfernt (***from***, von); (*fig.*) kühl, zurückhaltend, abweisend; – ***allusion,*** leichte Anspielung; (*fig.*) – ***prospect,*** schwache *or* geringe Hoffnung; – ***relation,*** weitläufige(r) Verwandte(r); – ***resemblance,***

entfernte Ähnlichkeit; – ***times,*** ferne Zeiten. **distant-signal,** *s.* (*Railw.*) das Vorsignal.

distaste [dis'teist], *s.* die Abneigung, der Widerwille (*for*, gegen), Abscheu (vor (*Dat.*)). **distasteful,** *adj.* ekelhaft, widerlich, unangenehm, zuwider (*to*, *Dat.*). **distastefulness,** *s.* die Widerwärtigkeit, Ekelhaftigkeit, Unannehmlichkeit.

[1]**distemper** [dis'tempə], **1.** *s.* die Temperafarbe, Leimfarbe. **2.** *v.t.* mit Leimfarbe streichen (*walls*); in Temperamanier malen.

[2]**distemper,** *s.* (*Vet.*) die Staupe (*dogs*), Druse (*horses*); Krankheit, Unpäßlichkeit; Verstimmung, üble Laune. **distempered,** *adj.* unwohl, unpäßlich; übelgelaunt, mißgestimmt, verärgert; zerrüttet, (geistes)gestört.

distend [dis'tend], **1.** *v.t.* (aus)dehnen; aufblasen, aufblähen; – ***the lungs,*** die Lunge füllen. **2.** *v.i.* sich (aus)dehnen, (*fig.*) anschwellen. **distensible** [–sibl], **distensile** [–sail], *adj.* (aus)dehnbar. **distension, distention** [–'tenʃən], *s.* die (Aus)-dehnung; Aufblasung; das Dehnen, Strecken, (*fig.*) die Anschwellung.

distich ['distik], *s.* (*Metr.*) das Distichon, (gereimtes) Verspaar. **distichous,** *adj.* (*Bot.*) zweireihig.

distil [dis'til], **1.** *v.t.* destillieren, (*spirits*) brennen; (*fig.*) (das Beste) entnehmen *or* abziehen (***from,*** aus). **2.** *v.i.* destillieren, kondensieren; herabtröpfeln, triefen, rinnen, rieseln. **distillate** ['distilit], *s.* das Destillat. **distillation** [–'leiʃən], *s.* die Destillation, das Destillieren, (*spirits*) Brennen; Destillat, Konzentrat, der Extrakt, Auszug; (*fig.*) Kern, das Wesen, die Quintessenz. **distiller,** *s.* der Destillateur, Branntweinbrenner. **distillery,** *s.* die (Branntwein)brennerei.

distinct [dis'tiŋkt], *adj.* **1.** abgesondert, getrennt, einzeln; verschieden, unterschieden (***from,*** von); 2. klar, deutlich, bestimmt, eindeutig, entschieden, ausgeprägt; 3. verschiedenartig. **distinction** [–'tiŋkʃən], *s.* **1.** die Unterscheidung; der Unterschied; die Verschiedenheit; das Kennzeichen, Unterscheidungsmerkmal; 2. die Auszeichnung, das Ehrenzeichen; die Würde, Vornehmheit.

distinctive [dis'tiŋktiv], *adj.* unterscheidend, Unterscheidungs–; bezeichnend, kennzeichnend, charakteristisch (*of*, für); ausgeprägt, spezifisch; ***be – of,*** kennzeichnen; – ***feature,*** das Unterscheidungsmerkmal. **distinctiveness,** *s.* **1.** das Unterscheidende, die Eigentümlichkeit, Besonderheit, charakteristische Eigenart; 2. die Deutlichkeit, Ausgeprägtheit. **distinctly,** *adj.* klar, deutlich, unzweideutig, unmißverständlich. **distinctness,** *s.* 1. die Klarheit, Deutlichkeit, Bestimmtheit; 2. Verschiedenheit, Verschiedenartigkeit.

distinguish [dis'tiŋgwiʃ], **1.** *v.t.* **1.** unterscheiden (***from,*** von); kennzeichnen, charakterisieren; bemerken, erkennen, wahrnehmen, auseinanderhalten (können); ***be –ed by,*** sich unterscheiden *or* auszeichen durch; 2. ehrend hervorheben, auszeichnen; – ***o.s.,*** sich auszeichnen. **2.** *v.i.* unterscheiden, einen Unterschied machen. **distinguishable,** *adj.* unterscheidbar; kenntlich, erkennbar, wahrnehmbar. **distinguished,** *adj.* 1. kenntlich (***by,*** an (*Dat.*)), bemerkenswert (***by,*** durch; ***for,*** wegen); 2. hervorragend, ausgezeichnet; berühmt (***for,*** wegen); vornehm; ***Distinguished Conduct Medal,*** die Verdienstmedaille (*Army, R.A.F.*: *other ranks*); ***Distinguished Flying Cross,*** das Verdienstkreuz (*R.A.F.*: *officers*); ***Distinguished Flying Medal,*** die Verdienstmedaille (*R.A.F.*: *other ranks*); ***Distinguished Service Cross,*** das Verdienstkreuz (*Navy*: *officers*); ***Distinguished Service Medal,*** die Verdienstmedaille (*Navy*: *other ranks*); ***Distinguished Service Order,*** (höherer) Verdienstorden (*Army, Navy, R.A.F.*: *officers*). **distinguishing,** *adj.* unterscheidend, Unterscheidungs–, bezeichnend, kennzeichnend, charakteristisch; – ***mark,*** das Kennzeichen.

distort [dis'tɔ:t], *v.t.* verdrehen, verbiegen, verrenken, verformen; (*Opt., Rad. etc.*) verzerren; (*fig.*) entstellen, verdrehen; ***be –ed,*** sich verziehen.

distortion [–'tɔ:ʃən], *s.* die Verdrehung, Verbiegung, Verformung, (*Acoust., Rad., Opt.*) Verzerrung, (*fig.*) Entstellung.

distract [dis'trækt], *v.t.* **1.** ablenken (*the attention*); 2. verwirren, aufwühlen, beunruhigen; rasend machen, zur Raserei treiben, von Sinnen bringen. **distracted,** *adj.* verwirrt, zerstreut; von Sinnen, wahnsinnig, verrückt; – ***with pain,*** verrückt *or* außer sich vor Schmerz. **distraction** [–'trækʃən], *s.* 1. die Ablenkung; 2. Verwirrung, (heftige) Erregung, die Erregtheit; der Wahnsinn, die Raserei; ***to –,*** bis zur Raserei; ***drive to –,*** zum Wahnsinn treiben; 3. die Zerstreuung, Unterhaltung, Erholung.

distrain [dis'trein], *v.i.* – (***up***)***on,*** mit Beschlag belegen, beschlagnahmen (*a th.*), pfänden (*a p.*) (*for*, wegen). **distrainable,** *adj.* mit Beschlag belegbar, pfändbar. **distrainee** [–'ni:], *s.* Gepfändete(r). **distrainer, distrainor,** *s.* der Pfänder. **distraint,** *s.* die Pfändung, Beschlagnahme, Zwangsvollstreckung.

distraught [dis'trɔ:t], *adj.* bestürzt, verwirrt, (heftig) erregt, aufgewühlt (***with,*** von *or* durch); rasend, toll, wahnsinnig (vor (*Dat.*)).

distress [dis'tres], **1.** *s.* **1.** die Not, das Elend, Leiden; die Notlage, der Notstand; Kummer, die Trübsal, Sorge, Bedrängnis; Qual, Pein; Erschöpfung; ***brothers in –,*** Leidengenossen (*pl.*); – ***call,*** das Notzeichen; – ***at sea,*** die Seenot; ***signal of –, – signal,*** das Notsignal; 2. (*Law*) die Beschlagnahme, Pfändung, Zwangsvollstreckung; ***levy a – on,*** pfänden, mit Beschlag belegen; ***warrant of –,*** der Vollstreckungsbefehl. **2.** *v.t.* **1.** plagen, peinigen, bedrücken; beunruhigen, betrüben, unglücklich machen; 2. (*Law*) *see* **distrain. distressed,** *adj.* in Not, notleidend, bedrängt; unglücklich, bekümmert, betrübt, besorgt (***about,*** um); – ***area,*** das Notstandsgebiet. **distressful,** *adj.* unglücklich, elend, notleidend, gequält, quälend, qualvoll, unselig, jämmerlich. **distressing,** *adj.* schmerzlich, peinlich, beunruhigend.

distributable [dis'tribjutəbl], *adj.* verteilbar. **distribute** [–bju:t], *v.t.* verteilen, austeilen, verbreiten, ausbreiten (***among,*** unter (*Acc. or Dat.*); ***to,*** an (*Acc.*)); einteilen, anorden; zuteilen, spenden (*alms etc.*); (*Typ.*) ablegen. **distribution** [–'bju:ʃən], *s.* die Verteilung, Austeilung; der Absatz, Vertrieb (*of goods*), Verleih (*of films etc.*); die Einteilung (*into classes*); Ausschüttung, Zuteilung (*of profits etc.*); (*Log.*) Anwendung auf alle in einer Klasse; (*Typ.*) das Ablegen; ***cost of –,*** Vertriebskosten, Absatzkosten (*pl.*); – ***of alms,*** die Almosenspende, Verteilung milder Gaben. **distributive, 1.** *adj.* austeilend, verteilend, zuteilend; ausgleichend (*justice*); (*Math., Gram.*) distributiv; – ***trades,*** das Vertriebsgewerbe. **2.** *s.* (*Gram.*) das Distributivum. **distributor,** *s.* **1.** (*Comm.*) der Vertreiber (*of goods*); 2. das Verteilgerät, die Streumaschine; (*Tech., Motor.*) der (Zünd)verteiler; – ***arm,*** der Verteilerfinger; – ***head,*** der Zündverteiler.

district ['distrikt], *s.* der (Verwaltungs)bezirk, Kreis, (*Hist.*) Gau; das Gebiet, die Gegend, der Landstrich.

district|-attorney, *s.* (*Am.*) der Staatsanwalt. **--court,** *s.* das Bezirksgericht, Kreisgericht. **--heating,** *s.* die Fernheizung. **--nurse,** *s.* die Armenkrankenschwester, Diakonisse, Diakonieschwester. **--railway,** *s.* die Vorortbahn. **--rate,** *s.* die Kreissteuer, Kommunalsteuer. **--visitor,** *s.* der Pfarrkreisgehilfe.

distrust [dis'trʌst], **1.** *v.t.* mißtrauen (*Dat.*). **2.** *s.* das Mißtrauen, der Argwohn (*of*, gegen); ***hold him in –,*** mißtrauisch gegen ihn sein. **distrustful,** *adj.* mißtrauisch, argwöhnisch (***of,*** gegen); – ***of o.s.,*** gehemmt, voll Hemmungen, ohne Selbstvertrauen. **distrustfulness,** *s.* das Mißtrauen, der Argwohn.

disturb [dis'tə:b], *v.t.* stören; beunruhigen, erregen, aufregen; aufrühren, aufschrecken, aufscheuchen; verwirren, durcheinanderbringen; – ***a train of thought,*** einen Gedankengang unterbrechen; ***don't – yourself!*** lassen Sie sich nicht stören! **disturb-**

ance, *s.* die Störung, Beunruhigung; (seelische) Erregung, die Aufregung, Aufgeregtheit, Verwirrung; (*Pol.*) Unruhe, der Aufruhr, Tumult; (*Law*) die Behinderung, Belästigung, Beeinträchtigung; – ***of the peace,*** die Ruhestörung. **disturbing,** *adj.* störend; beunruhigend (*to*, für).

disunion [dis'ju:njən], *s.* die Trennung, Spaltung; (*fig.*) Uneinigkeit, Zwietracht, Entzweiung. **disunite** [–'nait], **1.** *v.t.* (*usu. fig.*) entzweien, trennen; ***become –d,*** uneinig werden. **2.** *v.i.* sich trennen, auseinandergehen. **disunity,** *s.* die Uneinigkeit.

disuse, 1. [dis'ju:s], *s.* der Nichtgebrauch, die Nichtverwendung, Nichtbenutzung; das Aufhören eines Brauches; ***fall into –,*** ungebräuchlich werden, außer Gebrauch kommen. **2.** [–'ju:z], *v.t.* nicht mehr gebrauchen. **disused** [–'ju:zd], *adj.* außer Gebrauch, veraltet, ungebräuchlich.

disyllabic [disi'læbik], *adj.* zweisilbig. **disyllable** [di'siləbl], *s.* zweisilbiges Wort.

ditch [ditʃ], **1.** *s.* der Graben, die Gosse; ***drainage –,*** der Entwässerungsgraben, Dräniergraben, Abzugsgraben; ***foundation –,*** die Schachtgrube; ***dig a –,*** einen Graben ziehen; (*fig.*) ***to the last –,*** bis zum Äußersten. **2.** *v.i.* einen Graben ziehen *or* ausbessern. **3.** *v.t.* 1. mit einem Graben umgeben; 2. (*sl.*) notwassern (*an aircraft*); (*sl.*) den Laufpaß geben (*Dat.*), loswerden (*a p.*), wegschmeißen (*a th.*). **ditcher,** *s.* der Grabenbauer. **ditch-water,** *s.* abgestandenes Wasser; (*fig.*) ***as dull as –,*** langweilig, fade.

dither ['diðə], **1.** *v.i.* zittern, zappeln; – ***about,*** unschlüssig *or* verdattert sein. **2.** *s.* das Zittern, Gezitter, der Tatterich; (*coll.*) ***in a –*** or ***all of a –,*** tatterig, verdattert.

dithyramb ['diθiræm(b)], *s.* der Dithyrambus, die Dithyrambe. **dithyrambic** [–'ræmbik], **1.** *adj.* dithyrambisch, schwungvoll. **2.** *s. See* **dithyramb.**

dittany ['ditəni], *s.* (*Bot.*) der Diptam.

ditto ['ditou], *adv.* desgleichen, dito; ebenfalls, ebenso.

ditty ['diti], *s.* das Liedchen; ***popular –,*** der Gassenhauer.

ditty|-bag, *s.* (*Naut.*) der Nähbeutel. **--box,** *s.* (*Naut.*) der Utensilienkasten.

diuretic [daiju'retik], **1.** *adj.* harntreibend. **2.** *s.* harntreibendes Mittel.

diurnal [dai'ə:nl], *adj.* Tag–, Tages–, täglich.

divagate ['daivəgeit], *v.i.* abschweifen, herumschweifen. **divagation** [–'geiʃən], *s.* die Abweichung, Abwendung, Abkehr; Abschweifung.

divalent [dai'veilənt], *adj.* (*Chem.*) zweiwertig.

divan [di'væn], *s.* 1. das (Liege)sofa, die Chaiselongue, der Diwan; 2. (*rare*) das Rauchzimmer.

divaricate [dai'værikeit], *v.i.* abzweigen, sich trennen, sich gabeln, sich spalten. **divarication** [–'keiʃən], *s.* 1. die Gabelung; 2. (*fig.*) Mißhelligkeit, Meinungsverschiedenheit.

dive [daiv], **1.** *v.i.* tauchen (***into,*** in (*Acc.*); ***for,*** nach); untertauchen, (*Naut.*) tauchen; (*Spt.*) einen Kopfsprung machen; (*Av.*) stürzen, einen Sturzflug machen, sturzfliegen; (*Spt.*) – ***for,*** sich werfen *or* stürzen nach; – ***into,*** plötzlich verschwinden in (*Acc.*), (*fig.*) tief eindringen in (*Acc.*), sich stürzen *or* vertiefen *or* versenken in (*Acc.*); – ***into one's pocket,*** in die Tasche greifen. **2.** *s.* 1. das Tauchen; der Kopfsprung; (*Av.*) Sturzflug; (*Naut.*) die Tauchfahrt; ***make a – at,*** einen Griff tun nach, haschen *or* langen nach; ***make a – for,*** stürzen auf (*Acc.*); 2. (*sl.*) die Spelunke. **dive-bomber,** *s.* (*Av.*) der Sturz(kampf)bomber. **diver,** *s.* der Taucher (*also Orn.* (*Gaviidae*)).

diverge [dai'və:dʒ], *v.i.* auseinandergehen, auseinanderlaufen, sich (voneinander) trennen, divergieren; abweichen, abzweigen (***from,*** von). **divergence, divergency,** *s.* das Auseinandergehen, Auseinanderlaufen, die Abweichung; Streuung, Divergenz. **divergent, diverging,** *adj.* divergierend, divergent, auseinandergehend, auseinanderlaufend, abweichend; (*Opt.*) Streu–, Zerstreuungs–.

divers ['daivəz], *adj.* etliche, verschiedene, mehrere, mancherlei.

diverse [dai'və:s], *adj.* verschieden, andersartig, ungleich; mannigfaltig. **diversification** [–sifi'keiʃən], *s.* die Abänderung, Veränderung; Mannigfaltigkeit. **diversified** [–faid], *adj.* abwechslungsreich, mannigfaltig, verschiedenartig. **diversify** [–fai], *v.t.* verschiedenartig gestalten, variieren, Mannigfaltigkeit *or* Abwechslung bringen in (*Acc.*).

diversion [dai'və:ʃən], *s.* 1. die Abwendung, Ableitung, Ablenkung (***from,*** von); Umleitung (*of traffic*); (*Mil.*) das Ablenkungsmanöver; 2. die Zerstreuung, der Zeitvertreib.

diversity [dai'və:siti], *s.* die Verschiedenheit, Ungleichheit; Vielförmigkeit, Mannigfaltigkeit, Abwechslung.

divert [dai'və:t], *v.t.* 1. abwenden, ablenken, ableiten (***from,*** von); lenken (***to,*** auf (*Acc.*)), (*resources*) abzweigen (***to,*** für); – ***him from his purpose,*** ihn von seinem Vorhaben abbringen; – ***traffic,*** Verkehr umleiten; 2. (*fig.*) unterhalten, belustigen, ergötzen, zerstreuen. **diverting,** *adj.* unterhaltend, unterhaltsam, belustigend, amüsant.

divest [d(a)i'vest], *v.t.* entkleiden (***of,*** *Gen.*); (*fig.*) berauben, entblößen (***of,*** *Gen.*); – ***o.s. of,*** ablegen; (*fig.*) aufgeben, entsagen (*Dat.*), verzichten auf (*Acc.*) (*a th.*); – ***o.s. of a right,*** sich eines Rechts begeben. **divestiture** [–itʃə], **divestment,** *s.* die Entkleidung, Entblößung, (*fig.*) Beraubung.

divide [di'vaid], **1.** *v.t.* teilen, einteilen (***in(to),*** in (*Acc.*)); verteilen, austeilen (***among, between,*** unter (*Dat. or Acc.*)); absondern, trennen, scheiden (***from,*** von); spalten, zerteilen; (*fig.*) entzweien, uneinig machen; (*Math.*) dividieren (***by,*** durch); aufgehen in (*Acc.*); – ***12 by 3,*** dividiere 12 durch 3; ***3 –s into 12,*** 3 geht in 12 auf; ***he –d the loaf with his comrade,*** er teilte sich in das Brot mit dem Kamerad; ***the book is –d into two parts,*** das Buch zerfällt in zwei Teile. **2.** *v.i.* sich teilen; sich trennen *or* abspalten *or* absondern (***from,*** von); sich aufteilen *or* auflösen (***into,*** in (*Acc.*)); (*Parl.*) abstimmen, **3.** *s.* die Wasserscheide, (*fig.*) Scheidelinie.

dividend ['dividend], *s.* (*Comm.*) der Gewinnanteil, die Dividende; (*Math.*) Teilungszahl, der Dividend; – ***warrant,*** der Dividendenschein.

dividers [di'vaidəz], *pl.* der Teilzirkel, Stechzirkel. **dividing,** *adj.* teilend; – ***line,*** die Trennungslinie, Scheidelinie.

divination [divi'neiʃən], *s.* die Wahrsagung, Weissagung; Ahnung.

[1]**divine** [di'vain], **1.** *v.i.* wahrsagen, weissagen. **2.** *v.t.* (voraus)ahnen; erraten.

[2]**divine, 1.** *adj.* göttlich; (*fig., coll.*) himmlisch, herrlich, köstlich; – ***grace,*** göttliche Gnade; – ***right of kings,*** das Königtum von Gottes Gnaden; ***king by – right,*** König von Gottes Gnaden; – ***service*** or ***worship,*** der Gottesdienst; ***–ly inspired,*** gottbegeistert. **2.** *s.* Geistliche(r), der Theologe.

diviner [di'vainə], *s.* der Wahrsager, Weissager; (***water-***)–, der (Wünschel)rutengänger; *see* [1]**divine.**

diving ['daiviŋ], *s.* das Tauchen; (*Spt.*) Kunstspringen. **diving|-bell,** *s.* die Taucherglocke. **--board,** *s.* das Sprungbrett. **--helmet,** *s.* der Taucherhelm. **--suit,** *s.* der Taucheranzug.

divining rod, *s.* die Wünschelrute; *see* [1]**divine.**

divinity [di'viniti], *s.* 1. die Gottheit; Göttlichkeit; 2. Gottesgelehrsamkeit, Theologie; ***professor of –,*** der Professor der Theologie; 3. der Religionsunterricht; – ***lesson,*** die Religionsstunde.

divisibility [divizi'biliti], *s.* die Teilbarkeit, Spaltbarkeit. **divisible** [–'vizibl], *adj.* teilbar, spaltbar.

division [di'viʒən], *s.* 1. die Teilung, Trennung, Zerteilung, Spaltung; 2. Verteilung, Austeilung, Aufteilung, Einteilung (***into,*** in (*Acc.*)); – ***of labour,*** die Arbeitsteilung; 3. die Trennlinie, Scheidelinie, Grenzlinie, Grenze; 4. Abteilung, der Abschnitt, die Klasse, Kategorie, (Unter)stufe, (*Spt.*) Spielklasse, Liga, (*Mil.*) Division; 5. (*Math.*)

Division; *long –,* ungekürzte Division; (*Math.*) – *sign,* das Divisionszeichen, Teilungszeichen; – *sum,* die Divisionsaufgabe; 6. (*Parl.*) (namentliche) Abstimmung, die Stimmenzählung; *go into –,* zur Abstimmung schreiten; 7. (*fig.*) der Zwist, die Zwietracht, Uneinigkeit; *cause a – between friends,* Freunde entzweien.

divisional [di'viʒənl], *adj.* Teilungs–; (*Mil.*) Divisions–; – *commander,* der Divisionskommandeur.

divisive [di'vaiziv], *adj.* teilend, unterscheidend; verteilend; entzweiend. **divisor,** *s.* (*Math.*) der Teiler, Divisor, (*of a fraction*) Nenner.

divorce [di'vɔ:s], **1.** *s.* die (Ehe)scheidung, (*fig.*) Scheidung, Trennung; *get* or *obtain a –,* geschieden werden; *seek a –,* sich scheiden lassen; – *court,* das Scheidungsgericht. **2.** *v.t.* sich scheiden lassen von; (*fig.*) scheiden, trennen; (*fig.*) *–d from its context,* aus dem Zusammenhang gerissen. **divorcee** [–'si:], *s.* Geschiedene(r).

divot ['divət], *s.* das Rasenstück, die Sode.

divulge [d(a)i'vʌldʒ], *v.t.* enthüllen, bekanntmachen, bekanntgeben, verbreiten, ausplaudern. **divulgement, divulgence,** *s.* die Enthüllung, Verbreitung, Bekanntmachung.

dixie ['diksi], *s.* (*coll.*) der Feldkessel, das Kochgeschirr.

dizygotic [daizai'gɔtik], *adj.* (*Biol.*) zweieiig.

dizziness ['dizinis], *s.* der Schwindel, die Schwind(e)ligkeit, Benommenheit; der Schwindelanfall; (*fig.*) die Verwirrtheit. **dizzy,** *adj.* schwind(e)lig, benommen, (*fig.*) verwirrt, unbesonnen; (*heights*) schwindelerregend, schwindelnd.

Dnieper ['dni:pə], *s.* (*Geog.*) der Dnjepr. **Dniester,** *s.* (*Geog.*) der Dnjestr.

[1]**do** [du:], **1.** *irr.v.t.* tun, machen; verrichten, ausführen, vollbringen, leisten; (*p.p. only*) zustandebringen, vollenden, zu Ende bringen, erledigen; tätigen, bewirken, erziehen, erreichen; (*to a p., Dat.*) zufügen, erweisen, erzeigen, gewähren, widerfahren lassen; (*coll.*) zubereiten, kochen (*food*), frisieren, (her)richten (*hair*), putzen (*teeth*), aufräumen (*room*), abwaschen (*crockery*), zurücklegen, schaffen (*a distance*), besichtigen (*sights*); (*sl.*) übers Ohr hauen, anführen, reinlegen; (*sl.*) absitzen (*time in prison*).

(a) (*with nouns*) – *battle,* kämpfen, fechten (*for,* um); – *one's best,* sein möglichstes tun, sich (*Dat.*) alle Mühe geben; – *better,* Besseres leisten; – *his bidding,* seinen Befehl ausführen; (*coll.*) – *one's bit,* seinen Teil dazu beitragen, seine Pflicht tun; (*coll.*) – *business,* Geschäfte tätigen; (*coll.*) – *one's business,* sein Geschäft verrichten; – *homage to,* huldigen (*Dat.*); (*Scots*) – *the messages,* Einkäufe machen; – *penance,* Buße tun; (*coll.*) – *the talking,* allein das Wort führen; (*coll.*) – *o.s. well,* sich gütlich tun, sich (*Dat.*) etwas zukommen lassen.

(b) (*with Dat.*) – *him credit,* ihm Ehre einbringen, ihm zur Ehre gereichen; – *him a favour,* ihm den Gefallen tun; – *him good,* ihm bekommen; – *him harm,* ihm schaden; – *him the honour,* ihm die Ehre erweisen; – *him an injustice,* ihm unrecht tun *or* ein Unrecht zufügen; – *him justice,* ihm Gerechtigkeit widerfahren lassen; (*coll.*) – *it justice,* einer S. gerecht werden; (*coll.*) – *justice to the meal,* dem Essen tüchtig zusprechen; – *justice to o.s.,* sein wahres Können zeigen; – *him a good turn,* ihm einen guten Dienst erweisen, ihm einen Gefallen tun.

(c) (*with advs.*) – *away with,* loswerden, wegschaffen, beseitigen; – *away with o.s.,* sich umbringen, sich (*Dat.*) das Leben nehmen; (*sl.*) – *him down,* ihn übers Ohr hauen; (*sl.*) – *in,* umbringen, um die Ecke bringen; (*coll.*) *done in,* ermüdet, abgespannt, ausgepumpt, erledigt; – *him out of his money,* ihn um sein Geld bringen; – *out a room,* ein Zimmer ausräumen *or* ausfegen; – *up,* zusammenbinden, zusammenschnüren, verschnüren, zurechtmachen (*parcel*), zuknöpfen (*coat*), (*coll.*) herrichten, reparieren; (*coll.*) *done up,* see *done in.*

2. *irr.v.i.* tun, handeln, vorgehen, sich verhalten; weiterkommen, fortkommen, vorankommen; sich befinden, ergehen; dem Zwecke dienen *or* entsprechen, genügen, ausreichen, auskommen, angehen, sich schicken, recht sein, passen; *that will –,* das genügt, so ist es recht; *that won't –,* das geht nicht (an), das reicht nicht (aus); *it will – tomorrow,* es hat Zeit bis morgen; *it will – for the present,* es ist für den Augenblick gut genug; *it did perfectly,* es paßte vortrefflich, es ging vorzüglich; *will ordinary paper –?* ist gewöhnliches Papier gut genug? *how do you –?* guten Tag! wie gehts? – *as I –,* mach's (so) wie ich; (*Prov.*) *when in Rome – as the Romans –,* mit den Wölfen muß man heulen; – *badly,* schlechte Geschäfte machen, schlecht daran sein; – *right,* recht tun; – *well,* seine S. gut machen, gut vorwärtskommen, Erfolg haben, gut abschneiden; *he is –ing well,* es geht ihm gut; *he does well to come,* er tut gut daran, zu kommen; – *wrong,* unrecht tun.

(*with preps.*) – *by,* behandeln, sich verhalten gegen, handeln an (*Dat.*); – *as you would be done by,* was du nicht willst das man dir tu', das füg' auch keinem andern zu; – *for,* passen für, sich eignen für, bestimmt sein für, zusagen (*Dat.*), richtig *or* ausreichend sein für, ausreichen; (*coll.*) verderben, erledigen, abtun; (*coll.*) umbringen, zugrunde richten; (*sl.*) betrügen um; (*coll.*) den Haushalt führen für *or* (*Dat.*); *he is done for!* mit ihm ist's aus! er ist geliefert! – *to death,* totschlagen, umbringen; (*fig. coll.*) herumreiten auf (*Dat.*); – *with,* sich begnügen mit, auskommen mit, fertig werden mit, (*coll.*) (sehr gut) brauchen können; *I could – with a drink,* ich könnte einen Schluck vertragen; *have to – with,* zu tun *or* schaffen haben mit; *what has that to – with me?* was geht das mich an? *what am I to – with it?* was soll ich damit anfangen? *I did not know what to – with myself,* ich wußte nicht was ich anfangen *or* wie ich die Zeit hinbringen *or* (*coll.*) totschlagen sollte; *be done with a th.,* mit etwas fertig sein; *I have done with him,* ich will mit ihm nichts mehr zu schaffen haben, ich bin mit ihm fertig; – *without,* entbehren, verzichten auf (*Acc.*), auskommen ohne, fertig werden ohne.

3. *irr.v.aux. and absolute* **(a)** (*inter.*) – *you learn English?* lernen Sie Englisch? *you learn English, don't you?* Sie lernen Englisch, nicht wahr? **(b)** (*neg.*) *I – not know him,* ich kenne ihn nicht; *did you not see him?* sahen Sie ihn nicht? **(c)** (*concessive*) *only once did he come,* nur einmal kam er; **(d)** (*emph.*) – *make haste!* beeile dich doch! *I did see him,* ich sah ihn tatsächlich *or* auch wirklich; *send it, –!* schicke es doch! **(e)** (*absolute*) *he sings better than he did,* er singt besser als vorher; *he sings better than I –,* er singt besser als ich; – *you like the German language? I –!* gefällt Ihnen die deutsche Sprache? ja! *you could surely see him? I did!* Sie konnten ihn doch sicherlich sehen? Gewiß! Jawohl!

4. *special idiomatic forms*: – *or die,* kämpfen oder untergehen; *it was – or die with him,* es ging bei ihm um Leben oder Tod; (*sl.*) *nothing doing!* es kommt gar nicht in Frage! *have done!* genug! mach Schluß! hör' auf! *have you done talking?* sind Sie mit Reden fertig? *it can't be done,* es kann nicht geschehen, es geht nicht; *what's to –?* was ist los? *what is to be done?* was ist zu tun? *it isn't done,* es schickt sich nicht; *this done . . .,* nachdem dies geschehen war, . . .; *well done!* bravo! *no sooner said than done,* gesagt, getan.

5. *s.* 1. (*sl.*) der Schwindel; 2. die Feier, Festlichkeit, das Fest, der Schmaus, große S.; 3. (*coll.*) *–s and don'ts,* Regeln (*pl.*).

[2]**do** [dou], *s.* (*Mus.*) das C.

doable ['du:əbl], *adj.* (*coll.*) ausführbar, tunlich.

docile ['dousail], *adj.* gelehrig, gefügig, fügsam, lenksam, willig. **docility** [–'siliti], *s.* die Gelehrigkeit, Fügsamkeit, Lenksamkeit.

[1]**dock** [dɔk], *s.* (*Bot.*) der Ampfer.

[2]**dock, 1.** *s.* (*Naut.*) das Dock, der Anlegeplatz; (*Railw. esp. Am.*) die Ladebühne, Verladerampe; *pl.* Hafenanlagen (*pl.*). **2.** *v.t.* (ein)docken, ins Dock bringen. **3.** *v.i.* docken, ins Dock gehen.

[3]**dock, 1.** *v.t.* stutzen; (*fig.*) kürzen, beschneiden

(*wages etc.*); abschneiden (*supply*). **2.** *s.* der Stummel, Stumpf, Stutzschwanz; (*Vet.*) die Schwanzrübe.

⁴**dock,** *s.* **1.** (*Law*) die Anklagebank; ***be in the –***, auf der Anklagebank sitzen; 2. (*Mil. sl.*) das Lazarett; ***be in –***, im Lazarett liegen.

dockage [ˈdɔkidʒ], *s.*, **dock dues,** *pl.* Dockgebühren (*pl.*). **docker,** *s.* der Hafenarbeiter, Dockarbeiter, Schauermann.

docket [ˈdɔkit], **1.** *s.* kurze Inhaltsangabe, das Inhaltsverzeichnis, der Inhaltsvermerk; amtliche Beglaubigung, die Kaufbewilligung, Einkaufsgenehmigung; der Adreßzettel, Lieferschein, das Etikett; (*Law*) der Terminkalender, die Prozeßliste. **2.** *v.t.* (*documents etc.*) mit Inhaltsvermerk versehen; (*goods etc.*) mit Adreßzettel *or* Etikett versehen, etikettieren, beschriften.

dock|-gate, *s.* das Schleusentor. **–land,** *s.* das Hafenviertel. **--worker,** *s.* *See* **docker. –yard,** *s.* die Marinestation.

doctor [ˈdɔktə], **1.** *s.* 1. (*Univ.*) der Doktor; ***– of laws*** (***of medicine***), Doktor der Rechte (der Medizin); ***take one's –('s degree)***, promovieren; ***– and Mrs. S.***, Herr und Frau Dr. S.; ***dear –***, Sehr geehrter Herr Doktor! 2. der Arzt, Doktor; ***lady –***, die Ärztin; 3. (*Weav.*) der Schaber, das Abstreichmesser. **2.** *v.t.* (ärztlich) behandeln, kurieren; (*fig.*) ausbessern (*a th.*); verfälschen, verpanschen (*wine etc.*); (*fig.*) fälschen, zurechtmachen, zustutzen. **3.** *v.i.* als Arzt praktizieren. **doctoral,** *adj.* (*Univ.*) Doktor–. **doctorand,** *s.* (*Univ.*) der Doktorand. **doctorate** [–rit], *s.* (*Univ.*) die Doktorwürde, das Doktorat.

doctrinaire [dɔktriˈnɛə], **1.** *s.* der Prinzipienreiter. **2.** *adj.* doktrinär, schulmeisterlich; ***– socialism,*** der Kathedersozialismus. **doctrinal** [–ˈtrainl], *adj.* Lehr–, dogmatisch, lehrmäßig; ***– theology,*** die Dogmatik. **doctrine** [ˈdɔktrin], *s.* die Lehre; Doktrin, Lehrmeinung, der Grundsatz.

document [ˈdɔkjumənt], **1.** *s.* die Urkunde, das Dokument, Aktenstück, Schriftstück; *pl.* (*coll.*) Papiere (*pl.*). **2.** *v.t.* dokumentieren, dokumentarisch belegen. **documentary** [–ˈmentəri], *adj.* urkundlich, dokumentarisch; ***– evidence,*** das Beweisstück; ***– (film)***, der Bildbericht, Lehrfilm, Kulturfilm. **documentation** [–ˈteiʃən], *s.* die Urkundenbenutzung, Quellenbenutzung, Heranziehung von Dokumenten.

¹**dodder** [ˈdɔdə], *s.* (*Bot.*) die Klebe, Seide, der Teufelszwirn.

²**dodder,** *v.i.* (*coll.*) (sch)wanken, wackeln. **doddering, doddery,** *adj.* (sch)wankend, zittrig; senil, blöd.

dodecagon [douˈdekəgən], *s.* das Zwölfeck. **dodecahedral** [–ˈhi:drəl], *adj.* zwölfflächig. **dodecahedron** [–ˈhi:drən], *s.* das Zwölfflach, der Zwölfflächner, Dodekaeder.

Dodecanese [doudekəˈni:z], **1.** *s.* (*Geog.*) der Dodekanes. **2.** *adj.* dodekanesisch.

dodge [dɔdʒ], **1.** *v.t.* 1. ausweichen, umgehen, aus dem Wege gehen (*Dat.*), sich entziehen (*Dat.*), vermeiden; (*coll.*) ***– the issue,*** den Folgen aus dem Wege gehen; 2. zum besten haben, aufziehen. **2.** *v.i.* plötzlich zur Seite springen, ausweichen; sich drücken, Ausflüchte *or* Winkelzüge machen. **3.** *s.* 1. der Seitensprung; 2. (*coll.*) Schlich, Kniff, Kunstgriff; die Ausflucht; (*coll.*) geeignetes Hilfsmittel, das Patent; (*coll.*) ***be up to a – or two,*** es faustdick hinter den Ohren haben. **dodger,** *s.* 1. der Schwindler, geriebener Kerl; der Drückeberger; ***artful –***, der Schlaufuchs; 2. (*Naut.*) der Wetterunterstand. **dodgy,** *adj.* (*coll. of a p.*) gerieben, verschlagen; (*sl. of a th.*) kniffelig, heikel.

dodo [ˈdoudou], *s.* (*Orn.*) die Dronte.

doe [dou], *s.* 1. die Damhirschkuh, Hindin; 2. das Weibchen (*of rabbits etc.*).

doer [ˈdu:ə], *s.* der Täter, Ausführer, Handelnde(r). **does** [dʌz], *see* ¹**do.**

doeskin [ˈdouskin], *s.* das Rehfell, Rehleder.

doesn't [dʌznt] = ***does not***; *see* ¹**do.**

doff [dɔf], *v.t.* abnehmen (*hat*), ablegen, ausziehen (*clothes*).

dog [dɔg], **1.** *s.* 1. der Hund; (*coll.*) ***the –s,*** *see* **dog racing**; (*coll.*) ***hot –***, das Brötchen mit heißem Würstchen; ***hunting –***, der Jagdhund; (*coll.*) ***spotted –***, der Korinthenkloß; (*coll.*) ***go to the –s,*** zugrunde gehen, vor die Hunde gehen; (*fig.*) ***throw to the –s,*** wegwerfen, opfern, an den Haken hängen; (*coll.*) ***not a –'s chance,*** nicht die geringste Aussicht; ***every – has his day,*** jedem lacht einmal das Glück; ***die a –'s death,*** in Elend umkommen; ***give a – a bad name,*** ihn verleumden; ***help a lame – over a stile,*** ihm in der Not beistehen; ***lead a –'s life,*** ein Hundeleben führen; ***lead him a –'s life,*** ihm das Leben zur Hölle machen; ***– in the manger,*** der Neidhammel; ***let sleeping –s lie,*** laß den Hund begraben sein; ***let slip the –s of war,*** die Kriegsfurie entfesseln; (*coll.*) ***take a hair of the – that bit you,*** den Kater in Alkohol ersäufen; (*coll.*) ***it's raining cats and –s,*** es gießt in Strömen; ***it's hard to teach an old – new tricks,*** was Hänschen nicht lernt, lernt Hans nimmermehr; 2. (*of fox, wolf etc.*) der Rüde, das Männchen; 3. (*coll.*) der Bursche, Kerl; (*sl.*) Schurke, Hund; (*fig.*) ***gay –***, lustiger Bursche; (*fig.*) ***lazy –***, fauler Kerl; (*coll.*) ***lucky –***, der Glückspilz; (*coll.*) ***old –***, schlauer alter Fuchs; (*fig.*) ***sly –***, geriebener Bursche; 4. (*Tech.*) die Klaue, Klammer, der Klammerhaken, Greifhaken; Dorn, Mitnehmer(stift), Sperrklinkenzahn; Sperrhaken, Nocken, die Klemmschraube; 5. (*Min.*) Lore, der Förderwagen; Bock, das Gestell. **2.** *v.t.* 1. (*usu.* ***– his steps***) (ihm) auf den Fersen bleiben, (ihm) auf Schritt und Tritt folgen; 2. (*fig.*) verfolgen; schädigen; 3. (*Tech.*) mit einer Klaue *or* Klammer befestigen.

dog|bane, *s.* (*Bot.*) der Hundstod. **–berry,** *s.* (*Bot.*) die Hundsbeere. **--biscuit,** *s.* der Hundekuchen. **--box,** *s.* (*Railw.*) das Hundeabteil. **–cart,** *s.* zweirädriger Einspänner. **--clutch,** *s.* (*Tech.*) die Klauenkupplung. **--collar,** *s.* das Hundehalsband; (*coll.*) steifer Kragen (*esp.* eines Geistlichen). **–days,** *pl.* Hundstage (*pl.*).

doge [douʒ], *s.* der Doge (*of Venice*).

dog|-ear, **1.** *s.* (*fig.*) das Eselsohr. **2.** *v.t.* Eselsohren machen in (*Dat.*) (*a book*). **--eared,** *adj.* mit Eselsohren. **--end,** *s.* (*sl.*) die Kippe. **– fancier,** *s.* der Hundezüchter; Hundeliebhaber. **--fight,** *s.* (*Av.*) der Einzelkampf, (*Mil.*) Nahkampf (*tanks etc.*), (*coll.*) die Balgerei, das Handgemenge. **–fish,** *s.* ***spiny –***, gemeiner Dornhai; ***smooth –***, der Hundshai, Sternhai; ***spotted –***, kleinfleckiger Katzenhai.

dogged [ˈdɔgid], *adj.* verbissen, hartnäckig, zäh; (*coll.*) ***– does it!*** Zähigkeit siegt! **doggedness,** *s.* die Verbissenheit, Hartnäckigkeit, Zähigkeit.

doggerel [ˈdɔgərəl], **1.** *s.* der Knittelvers, Knittelverse (*pl.*); holprige Verse (*pl.*). **2.** *adj.* holprig, plump, burlesk (*of verse*).

doggo [ˈdɔgou], *adv.* ***lie –***, sich versteckt *or* regungslos halten, sich nicht rühren.

doggone [ˈdɔgɔn], *adj., int.* (*esp. Am.*) verflucht, verdammt.

dog-grass, *s.* (*Bot.*) die Hundsquecke. **doggy, 1.** *adj.* hundeartig, Hunde–; (*coll.*) ***– p.***, der Hundenarr. **2.** *s.* (*coll.*) das Hündchen. **dog|-house,** *s.* (*Am.*) *see* **--kennel**; (*sl.*) ***in the –***, in Ungnade. **--kennel,** *s.* die Hundehütte. **--Latin,** *s.* das Küchenlatein. **--licence,** *s.* die Hundesteuer.

dogma [ˈdɔgmə], *s.* der Lehrsatz, Glaubenssatz, das Dogma. **dogmatic** [–ˈmætik], *adj.* dogmatisch, doktrinär, autoritär, gebieterisch, anmaßend. **dogmatics,** *pl.* (*sing. constr.*) (*Eccl.*) die Dogmatik. **dogmatism** [–mətizm], *s.* der Dogmatismus, (anmaßende) Selbstsicherheit, (doktrinäre) Entschiedenheit. **dogmatist,** *s.* (*Eccl.*) der Dogmatiker. **dogmatize, 1.** *v.i.* dogmatisieren, sich dogmatisch äußern, anmaßende Behauptungen aufstellen (*on*, über (*Acc.*)). **2.** *v.t.* mit (dogmatischer) Bestimmtheit behaupten.

do-gooder [du:ˈgudə], *s.* (*coll.*) der Weltverbesserer, Humanitätsapostel.

dog| racing, *s.* das Hundewettrennen. **–rose,** *s.* (*Bot.*) wilde Rose, die Heckenrose.
dog's-ear, *s. See* **dog-ear.**
dog show, *s.* die Hundeausstellung.
dog's lead, *s.* die Hundeleine.
dog|-sledge, *s.* der Hundeschlitten. **--sleep,** *s.* (*coll.*) leichter Schlaf.
dog's|-meat, *s.* das (Pferde)fleisch für Hunde. **--mercury,** *s.* (*Bot.*) das Bingelkraut.
Dog-star, *s.* (*Astr.*) der Hundsstern. **dog|-tired,** *adj.* (*coll.*) hundsmüde, hundemüde, todmüde. **--tooth,** *s.* (*Archit.*) das (Hund)zahnornament. **--track,** *s.* die Hunderennbahn. **--violet,** *s.* (*Bot.*) das Hundsveilchen. **--watch,** *s.* (*Naut.*) der Plattfuß, die Spaltwache. **--whip,** *s.* die Hundepeitsche. **–wood,** *s.* (*Bot.*) der Hartriegel, Hornstrauch.
doily ['dɔili], *s.* das Deckchen, die Tassenunterlage, Tellerunterlage.
doing ['du:iŋ], *s.* das Tun, Handeln; die Tat; *pl.* Taten, Handlungen (*pl.*), die Tätigkeit, (*coll.*) Vorfälle (*pl.*), Begebenheiten (*pl.*); (*sl.*) Notwendige(s), das Drum und Dran; ***that's none of my –,*** ich bin nicht schuld daran, es hat mit mir nichts zu tun; (*coll.*) ***up and –,*** tätig, an der Arbeit; (*sl.*) ***nothing –!*** kommt gar nicht in Frage! nichts zu machen!
doit [dɔit], *s.* (*Hist.*) der Deut, Heller, (*fig.*) Pfifferling.
do-it-yourself, 1. *adj.* Selbstanfertigungs–, Maches-selbst–. **2.** *s.* das Selbstanfertigen.
doldrums ['dɔldrəmz], *pl.* 1. äquatoriale Windstillen (*pl.*); die Kalmenzone; 2. (*fig.*) Niedergeschlagenheit, der Trübsinn; (*fig.*) ***in the –,*** verdrießlich, übelgelaunt; niedergeschlagen.
[1]**dole** [doul], **1.** *s.* milde Gabe, das Almosen; (*coll.*) die Arbeitslosenunterstützung; (*coll.*) ***be on the –,*** stempeln gehen. **2.** *v.t.* (*coll.*) ***– out,*** verteilen, austeilen.
[2]**dole,** *s.* (*Poet.*) der Kummer, das Leid; die Klage. **doleful,** *adj.* traurig. **dolefulness,** *s.* die Traurigkeit, der Kummer.
dolichocephalic [dɔlikousi'fælik], *adj.* langköpfig.
doll [dɔl], **1.** *s.* die Puppe; ***–'s-house,*** die Puppenstube, das Puppenhaus. **2.** *v.t.* (*coll.*) ***– up,*** aufputzen, aufdonnern. **3.** *v.i.* (*coll.*) ***– up,*** sich aufdonnern.
dollar ['dɔlə], *s.* (*Am.*) der Dollar; (*Engl. sl.*) 25 Pence; (*Hist.*) der Taler.
dollop ['dɔləp], *s.* (*sl.*) der Klumpen, Happen.
dolly ['dɔli], *s.* 1. das Püppchen; 2. (*for washing*) der Stampfer, Stößel, (*Tech.*) Rührer; 3. (*Films*) Kamerawagen, Montagewagen. **dolly|-dye,** *s.* die Haushaltfarbe. **--shot,** *s.* (*Films*) die Fahraufnahme. **--tub,** *s.* das Waschfaß, Schlämmfaß.
dolman ['dɔlmən], *s.* der Dolman, die Husarenjacke.
dolmen ['dɔlmən], *s.* das Hünengrab, Steingrabmal.
dolomite ['dɔləmait], *s.* der Dolomit, Bitterspat. **Dolomites,** *pl.* (*Geog.*) Dolomiten (*pl.*).
dolor ['dɔlə], *s.* (*Am.*) *see* **dolour. dolorous,** *adj.* (*Poet.*) traurig, schmerzlich. **dolour,** *s.* (*Poet.*) die Pein, Qual, der Gram, Schmerz, das Leid.
dolphin ['dɔlfin], *s.* 1. (*Ichth.*) der Delphin; 2. (*Naut.*) die Dalbe, Ankerboje.
dolt [doult], *s.* der Tölpel, Einfaltspinsel. **doltish,** *adj.* tölpelhaft. **doltishness,** *s.* die Tölpelhaftigkeit.
domain [do'mein], *s.* Ländereien (*pl.*), der Landbesitz, das Erbgut, Grundeigentum; Staatsgut, die Domäne; (*fig.*) das Gebiet, der Bereich, die Sphäre; (*Law*) das Verfügungsrecht, die Herrschaft.
dome [doum], *s.* die Kuppel, das (Kuppel)gewölbe, die Wölbung. **domed,** *adj.* gewölbt.
Domesday-Book ['du:mzdei], *s.* (*Hist.*) das Reichsgrundbuch.
dome-shaped, *adj.* kuppelförmig.
domestic [də'mestik], **1.** *adj.* 1. Haushalt(s)–, Haus–, Familien–, häuslich; ***– affairs,*** häusliche Angelegenheiten; *see also* 2; ***– animal,*** das Haustier; ***– appliances,*** Haushaltungsgeräte; ***– cattle,*** das Nutzvieh; ***– drama,*** bürgerliches Drama; ***– duties,*** häusliche Pflichten; ***– quarrels*** or ***strife,*** Familienstreitigkeiten; ***– remedy,*** die Hausarznei; ***– science,*** die Hauswirtschaftslehre; ***– servant,*** Hausangestellte(r), der Dienstbote; ***– service,*** die Dienstbotentätigkeit; ***– washing,*** die Hauswäsche; 2. inländisch, Innen–, Binnen–, einheimisch, Landes–; ***– affairs*** *see* ***– policy; – consumption,*** inländischer Verbrauch; ***– policy,*** die Innenpolitik; ***– trade,*** der Binnenhandel.
domesticate [də'mestikeit], *v.t.* ans häusliche Leben gewöhnen; zähmen (*beasts*), domestizieren, zu Kulturpflanzen züchten (*plants*); ***become –d,*** häuslich *or* heimisch *or* zahm werden. **domestication** [–'keiʃən], *s.* die Eingewöhnung, Zähmung (*also Zool.*); (*Bot.*) Kultivierung; häusliches Leben, die Häuslichkeit. **domesticity** [dɔmes'tisiti], *s.* die Häuslichkeit, häusliches Leben, das Familienleben.
domicile ['dɔmis(a)il], **1.** *s.* 1. die Wohnung; der Aufenthalt(sort), Wohnort, (ständiger) Wohnsitz, das Domizil; 2. (*Comm.*) der Zahlungsort, die Zahlstelle, (*Law*) der Gerichtsstand. **2.** *v.t.* 1. wohnhaft *or* ansässig machen, ansiedeln; 2. (*Comm.*) domizilieren, auf bestimmten Ort ausstellen. **domiciled,** *adj.* wohnhaft, ansässig, beheimatet; (*Comm.*) domiziliert. **domiciliary** [–'siljəri], *adj.* Haus–, Wohnungs–; ***– visit,*** die Haussuchung.
dominance ['dɔminəns], *s.* das Vorherrschen, die (Vor)herrschaft. **dominant, 1.** *adj.* (vor)herrschend; (*fig.*) beherrschend, weithin sichtbar, überragend, emporragend; (*Mus.*) ***– chord,*** der Dominantakkord; ***– factor,*** entscheidender Faktor; ***– sex,*** herrschendes Geschlecht. **2.** *s.* (*Mus.*) die Dominante. **dominate** [–neit], **1.** *v.t.* beherrschen, emporragen über (*Acc.*). **2.** *v.i.* vorherrschen, herrschen (***over,*** über (*Acc.*)). **domination** [–'neiʃən], *s.* die (Vor)herrschaft.
domineer [dɔmi'niə], *v.i.* den Herrn spielen; despotisch herrschen; ***– over,*** tyrannisieren. **domineering,** *adj.* herrisch, gebieterisch, tyrannisch; anmaßend.
dominical [də'minikl], *adj.* des Herrn, Christi; sonntäglich; ***– day,*** der Sonntag; ***– letter,*** der Sonntagsbuchstabe; ***– prayer,*** das Vaterunser; ***– year,*** das Jahr des Herrn.
Dominican [də'minikən], *s.* (***– friar***) der Dominikaner. **Dominican Republic,** *s.* Dominikanische Republik.
dominie ['dɔmini], *s.* (*Scots*) der Schulmeister.
dominion [də'minjən], *s.* 1. die (Ober)herrschaft; (Regierungs)gewalt, das Besitzrecht (***over,*** über (*Acc.*)); (*fig.*) der Einfluß, die Herrschaft; 2. das (Herrschafts)gebiet; der Staat im Britischen Staatenbund; selbständige Kolonie; ***Dominion of Canada,*** das Dominion Kanada; ***– status,*** das Selbstverwaltungsrecht einer Kolonie.
domino ['dɔminou], *s.* (*pl.* **–es**) 1. der Domino, die Halbmaske; 2. der Dominostein; *pl.* das Dominospiel; ***play –es,*** Domino spielen.
[1]**don** [dɔn], *s.* der Don (*Spanish title*); (*Univ.*) Universitätslehrer, akademische Respektsperson; ***Don Quixote,*** Don Quichotte *or* Quijote.
[2]**don,** *v.t.* anziehen (*clothes*), aufsetzen (*hat*).
donate [do'neit], *v.t.* schenken, verleihen. **donation** [–'neiʃən], *s.* die Schenkung, Gabe. **donative** ['dounətiv], **1.** *adj.* durch Schenkung übertragen, Schenkungs–. **2.** *s.* offizielle Gabe *or* Schenkung; (*Eccl.*) ohne Präsentation übertragene Pfründe.
done [dʌn], **1.** *p.p. of* [1]**do. 2.** *adj.* fertig, ausgeführt; vorbei, erledigt; (*Cul.*) gekocht, gebraten, gar; (*coll.*) (*also* ***– in*** or ***up***) erschöpft, kaputt; (*sl.*) (*also* ***– brown***) betrogen, beschwindelt; ***– to a turn,*** gerade richtig gekocht *or* gebraten; ***that's not –,*** das schickt sich nicht; (*coll.*) ***– for,*** verloren, aus, geliefert.
donee [dou'ni:], *s.* (*Law*) Beschenkte(r), der (die) Schenkungsempfänger(in).

donjon ['dʌndʒən], *s.* der Schloßturm, das Burgverlies, der Bergfried.

donkey ['dɔŋki], *s.* der Esel; (*fig.*) Dummkopf; (*sl.*) *for –'s years,* seit anno Tobak. **donkey|-engine,** *s.* die Hilfsmaschine. **--work,** *s.* die Kuliarbeit, Plackerei.

donnish ['dɔniʃ], *adj.* gravitätisch, steif; *see* [1]**don.**

donor ['dounə], *s.* der Geber, Stifter, Schenker, Spender; *blood-–,* der Blutspender.

don't [dount] = *do not, see* [1]**do. I.** *int.* laß das! nicht doch! bitte nicht! **2.** *s.* das Verbot; (*coll.*) *dos and –s,* Regeln (*pl.*), Weisungen und Verbote (*pl.*).

doodah ['du:dɑ:], *s.* (*sl.*) das Dingsda; (*sl.*) *all of a –,* aus dem Häuschen.

doodle [du:dl], *v.i.* (*coll.*) gedankenlos hinkritzeln.

doom [du:m], **I.** *v.t.* verurteilen, verdammen (*to,* zu). **2.** *s.* das Schicksal, Verhängnis, Los, böses Geschick; der Untergang, das Verderben; (*obs.*) (Verdammungs)urteil, der Urteilsspruch; *crack* or *day of –,* Jüngstes Gericht. **doomed,** *adj.* gerichtet, verurteilt, verloren, dem Untergang geweiht. **doomsday,** *s.* Jüngstes Gericht, das Weltgericht; (*coll.*) *till –,* ewig, immerfort. **Doomsday-Book,** *s. See* **Domesday-Book.**

door [dɔ:], *s.* die Tür; (*fig.*) der Eingang; *back –,* die Hintertür; *communicating –,* die Verbindungstür; *double –s,* die Doppeltür; *folding –,* die Flügeltür; *front –, street-–,* die Haustür; *sliding –,* die Schiebetür; *the first – from the corner,* das erste Haus von der Ecke; *next –,* nebenan, im Nebenhaus *or* nächsten Hause; (*fig.*) *be next – to,* beinahe *or* nahezu sein, grenzen an (*Acc.*), nicht weit sein von; *next – but one,* zwei Häuser weiter, übernächstes Haus; *close* or *shut the – against him,* ihm die Tür verschließen; *close the – on him,* die Tür hinter ihm zumachen; *close the – on one's fingers,* sich (*Dat.*) den Finger in der Tür klemmen; (*fig.*) *bang* or *close* or *slam the – on a th.,* etwas unmöglich machen; *he shall never darken my –(s) again,* er soll meine Schwelle nie wieder betreten; (*fig.*) *lay a th. at his –,* ihm etwas zur Last legen; *open the – to him,* ihm (die Tür) öffnen, ihn hereinlassen; (*fig.*) *open the – to* or *for a th.,* etwas möglich machen; *see him to the –,* ihn zur Tür begleiten; *show him the –,* ihm die Tür weisen; (*fig.*) *throw the – open to s.th.,* die Tür öffnen für etwas; *at the –,* vor der Tür; *at death's –,* am Rande des Grabes; *from – to –,* von Haus zu Haus; *out of –s,* außer *or* aus dem Hause; im Freien, draußen; *packed to the –s,* voll besetzt, gedrängt voll; *within –s,* im Hause.

door|-bell, *s.* die Türklingel. **--case, --frame,** *s.* die Türeinfassung, Türzarge, das Türfutter, der Türrahmen. **--handle,** *s. See* **--knob. --jamb,** *s.* das Türgewände. **--keeper,** *s.* der Pförtner, Portier. **-key,** *s.* der Schlüssel. **--knob,** *s.* der Türknopf, Türgriff. **-man,** *s. See* **--keeper. -mat,** *s.* der Fußabtreter, die Fußmatte. **--money,** *s.* das Eintrittsgeld. **-nail,** *s. dead as a –,* mausetot. **--plate,** *s.* das Türschild, Namenschild. **-post,** *s.* der Türpfosten. **--scraper,** *s.* der Fußabstreicher. **-step,** *s.* die Stufe vor der Haustür. **--stop,** *s.* der Anschlag. **-way,** *s.* der Torweg; Türeingang; (*fig.*) Zugang; *in the –,* in der Tür.

dope [doup], **I.** *s.* I. (*Av. etc.*) der (Imprägnier)lack, Spannlack; 2. (*Motor. etc.*) das Benzinzusatzmittel; 3. (*sl.*) (Rausch)gift, Opium, Narkotikum; *– fiend,* (Rauschgift)süchtige(r); *– pedlar,* der Dealer; 4. (*sl.*) (*oft. inside –*) Informationen (*pl.*), das Neueste. **2.** *v.t.* lackieren; (*Spt. sl.*) dopen; *–d petrol,* das Bleibenzin. **dopey** [–i], *adj.* (*coll.*) benebelt, benommen, dämlich, dusselig; dus(e)lig.

dor [dɔ:], *s.* (*Ent.*) der Roßkäfer; Maikäfer.

Dorian ['dɔriən], *adj.* (*Mus.*) dorisch. **Doric, I.** *adj.* (*Archit.*) dorisch. **2.** *s.* dorischer Dialekt; rauhe *or* grobe Mundart.

dormancy ['dɔ:mənsi], *s.* der Schlafzustand, die Ruhe. **dormant,** *adj.* schlafend, ruhend, (*as volcano*) untätig; (*Zool.*) Winterschlaf haltend; (*fig.*) unbeansprucht, unbenutzt, ungebraucht; (*Comm.*) brach(liegend), tot, (*Law*) nicht ausgenützt, ruhend; (*Her.*) *lion –,* schlafender Löwe; (*Comm.*) *– partner,* stiller Teilhaber; *– passions,* schlummernde Leidenschaften.

dormer ['dɔ:mə], *s.* (*also –window*) das Dachfenster, Bodenfenster.

dormitory ['dɔ:mitəri], *s.* der Schlafsaal; *– suburb,* großstädtisches Wohnviertel.

dormouse ['dɔ:maus], *s.* die Haselmaus.

Dorothy ['dɔrəθi], *s.* Dorothea (*f.*).

dorsal [dɔ:sl], *adj.* Rücken–, dorsal.

[1]**dory** ['dɔ:ri], *s.* (*also John –*) der Heringskönig.

[2]**dory,** *s.* kleines Fischerboot.

dosage ['dousidʒ], *s.* die Dosierung. **dose, I.** *s.* die Dosis; Portion, das Quantum. **2.** *v.t.* dosieren; eine Dosis verschreiben, Arznei eingeben (*Dat.*); (*wine*) Zucker zusetzen (*Dat.*).

doss [dɔs], **I.** *s.* (*sl.*) das Bett; der Schlaf. **2.** *v.i.* (*sl.*) pennen. **doss-house,** *s.* die Penne.

dossier ['dɔsiei], *s.* das Aktenbündel, Aktenheft, Akten (*pl.*).

[1]**dot** [dɔt], **I.** *s.* der Punkt; Tupfen, das Tüpfelchen; (*fig.*) der Knirps; (*coll.*) *on the –,* auf die Minute pünktlich. **2.** *v.t.* I. punktieren; tupfen, tüpfeln, sprenkeln; das I-Punkt machen auf (*Acc.*) (*letter i*); (*fig.*) *– the i's and cross the t's,* peinlich genau sein; (*coll.*) *– down,* rasch notieren; (*coll.*) *– and carry one,* hinken, hinkend gehen; (*sl.*) *– him one,* ihm eins versetzen; 2. (*fig.*) hinstreuen, verstreuen.

[2]**dot,** *s. See* **dowry.**

dotage ['doutidʒ], *s.* die Senilität, Altersschwäche; *he is in his –,* er ist kindisch geworden. **dotard** [–təd], *s.* kindischer Greis. **dote,** *v.i.* kindisch sein, faseln; *– on,* schwärmen für, vernarrt sein in (*Acc.*).

doth [dʌθ], (*Poet.*) = *does*; *see* [1]**do.**

doting ['doutiŋ], *adj.* kindisch, faselnd; verliebt, vernarrt (*on,* in (*Acc.*)).

dotted ['dɔtid], *adj.* I. punktiert (*also Mus.*); gesprenkelt, übersät; *– line,* punktierte Linie; (*fig.*) *sign on the – line,* sich unwiderruflich verpflichten; 2. *– about,* verstreut, hingestreut.

dotterel ['dɔtərəl], *s.* (*Orn.*) der Mornellregenpfeifer (*Charadrius morinellus*).

dottle [dɔtl], *s.* der Tabaksrest (*in a pipe*).

dotty ['dɔti], *adj.* (*sl.*) verdreht, beklapst, übergeschnappt; *– on,* vernarrt in (*Acc.*).

double [dʌbl], **I.** *adj.* Doppel–, doppelt, zweifach, gepaart; (*fig.*) zwiespältig, zweideutig, heuchlerisch, unaufrichtig, scheinheilig; verdoppelt, verstärkt, vermehrt, vergrößert, (*Bot.*) gefüllt, (*Mus.*) Kontra–; *– ale,* das Starkbier; *– the amount,* doppelter *or* zweifacher Betrag; *– chin,* das Doppelkinn; (*coll.*) *– Dutch,* das Kauderwelsch; *– eagle,* (*Her.*) der Doppeladler; (*Am.*) das Zwanzigdollarstück; (*Comm.*) *– entry,* doppelte Buchführung; (*Univ.*) *– first,* akademischer Grad mit Auszeichnung in zwei Fächern; *– game,* falsches Spiel; *– line,* (*Railw.*) das Doppelg(e)leis(e), (*Tele.*) die Doppelleitung; *– meaning,* der Doppelsinn; *– room,* das Schlafzimmer mit Doppelbett; *– track,* see *– line* (*Railw.*); (*Comm.*) *– usance,* doppelte Wechselfrist.

2. *adv.* doppelt, paarweise, zu zweit *or* zweien.

3. *s.* I. das Doppelte, Zweifache; 2. Seitwärtsspringen, der Seitensprung, Quersprung, (*Hunt.*) Hakenschlag; 3. (*of a p.*) Doppelgänger, das Ebenbild, (*of a th.*) Seitenstück, Gegenstück, Duplikat; 4. (*Mil.*) der Laufschritt; *at the –,* im Laufschritt; 5. (*Theat. etc.*) zweite Besetzung, das Double; 6. (*Spt.*) der Doppellauf, Doppeltreffer, Doppelsieg, die Doublette; 7. *pl.* (*Tenn.*) das Doppel(spiel).

4. *v.t.* I.verdoppeln; 2.(*oft. – up*) umfalten, zusammenfalten, zusammenlegen, kniffen, (*the fist*) ballen; *– down,* umfalten, einschlagen (*a page*); *– in,* nach innen falten, einbiegen; *– up,* zusammenfalten, zusammenlegen; (*fig.*) *be –d up with,* sich krümmen vor (*Dat.*) (*pain, laughter etc.*); 3. (*Naut.*) umschiffen, umsegeln, umfahren (*a headland*); 4. (*Cards*) doppeln; 5. (*Theat.*) mit übernehmen (*a*

role); – ***the parts,*** beide Rollen spielen; 6. (*Weav.*) doublieren, duplieren.
5. *v.i.* 1. sich verdoppeln; 2. (*Theat.*) als Double spielen; 2. (*Hunt.*) einen Haken(sprung) machen; 4. (*Mil.*) im Laufschritt marschieren, (*coll.*) Tempo an den Tag legen; 5. (*gambling*) den Einsatz verdoppeln; 6. – ***back,*** kehrtmachen (***on,*** auf (*Dat.*)); 7. – ***up,*** sich biegen *or* falten; (*fig.*) sich (zusammen)krümmen (***with,*** vor (*Dat.*)); das Quartier teilen (müssen).

double|-acting, *adj.* doppeltwirkend. **--barrelled,** *adj.* doppelläufig, (*fig.*) zweischneidig; – ***gun,*** die Doppelflinte; (*coll.*) – ***name,*** der Doppelname. **--bass,** *s.* (*Mus.*) der Kontrabaß. **--bed,** *s.* das Doppelbett, Ehebett. **--bedded,** *adj.* – ***room,*** see ***double room.*** **--breasted,** *adj.* zweireihig (*coat*). **--chinned,** *adj.* mit Doppelkinn. **--cross,** **1.** *v.t.* (*coll.*) verraten, 'reinlegen. **2.** *s.* (*coll.*) der Betrug, Verrat. **--dealing,** *s.* die Achselträgerei, Doppelzüngigkeit, Falschheit, der Betrug. **--decker,** *s.* der Doppeldecker. **--dyed,** *adj.* (*fig.*) eingefleischt, Erz–. **--edged,** *adj.* zweischneidig (*also fig.*). **--faced,** *adj.* doppelzüngig, heuchlerisch. **--lock,** *v.t.* doppelt verschließen. **--quick,** *adv.* (*coll.*) schnellstens, sehr rasch. **--stop,** **1.** *s.* (*Mus.*) der Doppelgriff. **2.** *v.i.* in Doppelgriffen spielen.

doublet ['dʌblit], *s.* (*Hist.*) das *or* der Wams; (*Philol.*) die Doppelform; (*of things*) D(o)ublette, das Doppelstück; (*dice*) der Pasch.

doubling ['dʌbliŋ], *s.* die Verdoppelung; (*Bot.*) Blütenfüllung; (*Weav.*) das Doublieren, Duplieren; (Zusammen)falten (*of pages etc.*). **doubly,** *adv.* doppelt, zweifach.

doubt [daut], **1.** *v.i.* zweifeln (***about,*** an (*Dat.*)); ***whether, if,*** ob; (*with neg.*) ***but*** (***that***), daß); zweifelhaft *or* im Zweifel sein (über (*Acc.*)); Bedenken haben *or* tragen (über (*Acc.*) *or* wegen), unentschlossen sein, schwanken, zögern. **2.** *v.t.* zweifeln an (*Dat.*), bezweifeln; anzweifeln, in Zweifel ziehen; (*a p.*) mißtrauen (*Dat.*); – ***his ability,*** seine Fähigkeit anzweifeln; – ***his words,*** seinen Worten keinen Glauben schenken; – ***it,*** es bezweifeln; – ***his coming,*** (be)zweifeln, daß er kommt. **3.** *s.* der Zweifel (***about, of,*** an (*Dat.*)), die Ungewißheit, das Bedenken (über (*Acc.*)), die Besorgnis (um); ***beyond*** or ***without*** –, ohne Zweifel, zweifellos, fraglos, unzweifelhaft; ***no*** –, vermutlich, wahrscheinlich; ***have no – of,*** nicht zweifeln an (*Dat.*), keinen Zweifel haben an (*Dat.*); ***have no – that,*** nicht bezweifeln daß; ***there is no – but*** (***that***), es besteht kein Zweifel darüber (daß); ***make no*** –, sicher sein, keinen Zweifel hegen; ***raise –s,*** Bedenken erregen; ***have one's –s about,*** seine Bedenken haben über (*Acc.*); ***it is not in any*** –, darüber besteht kein Zweifel; ***give him the benefit of the*** –, ihn mangels Beweises freisprechen, im Zweifelsfalle zu seinen Gunsten entscheiden.

doubtful ['dautful], *adj.* (*of a p.*) zweifelnd, unschlüssig, unsicher, schwankend; (*of a th.*) bedenklich, zweifelhaft, fraglich, ungewiß, fragwürdig; unsicher, unklar; ***be – of*** or ***about,*** zweifeln an (*Dat.*); – ***character,*** verdächtiges Element. **doubtfulness,** *s.* die Zweifelhaftigkeit, Bedenklichkeit, Fragwürdigkeit, Ungewißheit. **doubtless,** *adv.* ohne Zweifel, zweifellos, zweifelsohne, unzweifelhaft, fraglos, gewiß; wahrscheinlich, sicher(lich), wohl, ich gebe zu.

douce [du:s], *adj.* (*Scots*) gesetzt, gelassen, besonnen, nüchtern.

douche [du:ʃ], **1.** *s.* die Dusche, Brause; (*Med.*) der Irrigator; (*fig.*) ***throw a cold – on a th.,*** etwas dämpfen. **2.** *v.t.* (ab)duschen. **3.** *v.i.* sich (ab)-duschen.

dough [dou], *s.* 1. der Teig; 2. (*sl.*) die Pinke, der Zaster, Moneten (*pl.*). **dough|boy,** *s.* (*Am. sl.*) der Landser. **-nut,** *s.* der Krapfen, (Berliner) Pfannkuchen.

doughtiness ['dautinis], *s.* (*Poet.*) die Tapferkeit. **doughty,** *adj.* tapfer, mannhaft, beherzt, wacker.

doughy ['doui], *adj.* teigig, klitschig, weich.

dour [duə], *adj.* (*Scots*) ernst, streng; stur, störrisch, starrköpfig.

douse [daus], *v.t.* 1. begießen, durchtränken; löschen (*fire*), auslöschen (*light*); 2. (*Naut.*) laufen lassen (*sails*).

[1]**dove** [douv], (*Am.*) *imperf. of* **dive. 1.**

[2]**dove** [dʌv], *s.* die Taube (*Columbidae*); (*coll.*) das Täubchen, der Liebling; (*Bot.*) ***–'s foot,*** der Storchschnabel; – ***of peace,*** die Friedenstaube. **dove|-colour,** *s.* das Taubengrau. **-cot(e),** *s.* der Taubenschlag; (*fig.*) ***flutter the –s,*** die Spießbürger erschrecken.

dovekie ['dʌvki], *s.* (*Am.*) *see* **little auk.**

dovetail ['dʌvteil], **1.** *s.* (*Carp.*) der Schwalbenschwanz. **2.** *v.t.* durch Schwalbenschwanz verbinden; (*fig.*) fest verbinden, zusammenfügen; einfügen, eingliedern (***into,*** in (*Acc.*)). **3.** *v.i.* (*usu. fig.*) genau passen (***into,*** in (*Acc.*)), ineinandergreifen.

dowager ['dauidʒə], *s.* die Witwe von Stande; (*coll.*) Matrone; ***queen*** –, die Königinwitwe, Königinmutter; – ***Lady C.,*** die verwitwete Lady C.

dowdiness ['daudinis], *s.* die Schlampigkeit.

dowdy ['daudi], **1.** *adj.* unelegant; nachlässig angezogen, schlampig. **2.** *s.* schlampige Frau, die Schlampe.

dowel ['dauəl], **1.** *s.* der Dübel, Döbel, Diebel, Holzpflock, Zapfen. **2.** *v.t.* mit Dübeln befestigen.

dower ['dauə], **1.** *s.* die Mitgift, das Wittum, (*fig.*) die Begabung. **2.** *v.t.* mit einer Mitgift ausstatten. **dowerless,** *adj.* ohne Mitgift.

dowlas ['dauləs], *s.* grobe Leinwand, die Sackleinwand.

[1]**down** [daun], *s.* die Daune, Flaumfeder, (*usu. pl.*) Daunen (*pl.*), Flaumfedern (*pl.*); (*Bot., beard etc.*) der Flaum; – ***quilt,*** die Daunendecke.

[2]**down,** *s.* (*usu. pl.*) das Hügelland, grasbewachsener Höhenzug, die Heide, Geest.

[3]**down,** **1.** *adv.* (*direction*) herunter, hinunter, herab, hinab, abwärts, nieder(wärts), nach unten, zum Boden; (*position*) unten, nieder, herunter; am Boden (liegend), hingestreckt; (*prices*) gefallen, heruntergekommen, (*stars etc.*) untergegangen; (*fig.*) (*spirits*) niedergeschlagen, niedergedrückt, entmutigt, deprimiert, (*health*) erschöpft, ermattet, geschwächt; (*coll.*) – ***and out,*** völlig heruntergekommen *or* mittellos, ruiniert, erledigt, auf den Hund gekommen; (*coll.*) – ***at heel,*** schäbig, verwahrlost, verkommen, zerlumpt; (*Spt.*) ***2 points*** –, 2 Punkte zurück; ***£1*** –, ein Pfund bar auf den Tisch (*in payment*),(*coll.*) ein Pfund ärmer (*of a p.*); ***sugar is*** –, Zucker ist billiger geworden; ***the temperature is 6 degrees*** – or – ***by 6 degrees,*** die Temperatur ist um 6 Grad gefallen; – ***from London,*** von London (weg); – ***for tomorrow,*** für morgen angesetzt, an der Tagesordnung für morgen; ***he is not – yet,*** er ist noch nicht auf(gestanden), er ist noch oben; (*coll.*) – ***in the mouth,*** bedrückt, niedergeschlagen; – ***on one's luck,*** vom Pech verfolgt; (*coll.*) – ***on him,*** streng gegen ihn; – ***there,*** dort unten; (*fig.*) – ***to the ground,*** in jeder Hinsicht, ganz und gar, durchaus, von Grund aus; – ***to the last man,*** bis auf den letzten Mann; (*coll.*) – ***under,*** in Australien; ***upside*** –, das Oberste zuunterst; ***turn upside*** –, auf den Kopf stellen (*also fig.*), umdrehen; ***be – with 'flu,*** an der Grippe daniederliegen;
(*with verbs*) ***boil*** –, einkochen; ***bring*** –, drücken (*prices*); ***burn*** –, niederbrennen; ***come – in the world,*** sehr herunterkommen; ***he has come – in the world,*** er hat bessere Tage gesehen; ***get*** –, (*v.i.*) herunterkommen, (*v.t.*) herunterbekommen (*food*); auf die Nerven fallen (*Dat.*) (*a p.*); ***go*** –, (*wind*) sich legen, (*sun etc.. ship*) sinken, untergehen, (*food*) hinunterrutschen; (*Univ.*) in die Ferien gehen, die Universität verlassen; (*coll.*) ***go*** – (***well***), Anklang finden; ***hunt*** –, stellen; ***knock*** –, zu Boden schlagen, (*Motor.*) überfahren; (*coll.*) ***let him*** –, ihn enttäuschen; (*fig.*) ***look – on,*** herabsehen auf (*Acc.*); ***look – one's nose at,*** die Nase rümpfen über (*Acc.*); ***note*** –, notieren, zu Papier bringen;

pay –, (in) bar bezahlen; *run* –, endlich finden; (*Motor.*) überfahren; (*Univ.*) *send* –, relegieren, von der Universität verweisen; *settle* –, sich niederlassen, (*fig.*) sich einleben; *settle – to,* sich machen *or* setzen an (*Acc.*); *take* –, see *note* –; *thin* –, verdünnen; *track* –, endlich finden; *write* –, niederschreiben.
2. *prep.* (*direction*) hinunter, herunter, hinab *or* herab (in (*Acc.*)), (*position*) unten an (*Dat.*) *or* in (*Dat.*), (*time*) durch . . . (hindurch); *all – the ages,* durch die ganzen Zeitalter hindurch; (*fig., coll.*) *all – the line,* vom Anfang bis zum Ende; *fall – a hole,* in eine Grube fallen; – *the hill,* den Berg hinab *or* hinunter; – *the river,* den Fluß abwärts *or* hinunter, stromabwärts; *further – the river,* weiter unten am Fluß; *cut – the middle,* durch die Mitte durchschneiden; *pace up and – the room,* im Zimmer auf und ab schreiten; (*esp. Am.*) – *town,* in die Stadt(mitte); (*Naut.*) – (*the*) *wind,* mit dem Wind.
3. *adj. See* **downward**; (*Mus.*) – *beat,* der Niederschlag; – *gradient,* das Gefälle, die Gefallstrecke; – *payment,* die Anzahlung; – *pipe,* das Fallrohr; – *platform,* der Bahnsteig für Züge aus (*London or other large town*); – *stage,* im Vordergrund der Bühne; – *stroke,* der Abstrich, Grundstrich (*writing*), (*Tech.*) Abwärtshub, Leerhub (*of piston*); – *train,* der Zug aus (*London or other large town*).
4. *int.* hinab! nieder! (*to dog*) kusch (dich)! – *on your knees!* auf die Knie mit dir! (*Naut.*) – *helm!* Ruder in Lee!
5. *s.* 1. die Abwärtsbewegung; *ups and –s,* das Steigen und Fallen, Auf und Ab; (*fig.*) *ups and –s of life,* die Höhen und Tiefen *or* die Wechselfälle des Lebens; 2. (*coll.*) der Groll; (*coll.*) *have a – on him,* ihn nicht leiden können.
6. *v.t.* niederwerfen, bezwingen, demütigen; (*sl.*) hinuntergießen, hinunterkippen (*a drink*); (*coll.*) – *tools,* in den Streik treten, die Arbeit einstellen.

down|-and-out, *s.* (*coll.*) heruntergekommener Mensch. **--bow,** *s.* (*Mus.*) der Abstrich (*violin etc.*), Herstrich (*cello etc.*). **-cast, 1.** *adj.* niedergeschlagen, gesenkt (*eyes*), (*fig.*) niedergeschlagen, entmutigt, deprimiert. **2.** *s.* (*Min.*) einziehende Schacht, die Wetterschacht. **--draught,** *s.* (*Tech.*) der Fallstrom. **-fall,** *s.* der Fall, Sturz; starker Regenfall; (*fig.*) der Untergang, Niedergang, Verfall. **-grade, 1.** *s. See down gradient*; (*fig.*) der Niedergang, das Fallen, Sinken; *on the* –, im Niedergang, auf dem absteigenden Ast. **2.** *v.t.* degradieren, herabsetzen (*in rank*), auf eine niedrigere Stufe heruntersetzen (*in importance, secrecy etc.*). **-haul,** *s.* (*Naut.*) der Niederholer. **--hearted,** *adj.* niedergeschlagen, gedrückt, entmutigt, verzagt; *are we –?* bange machen gilt nicht! **-hill, 1.** *adv.* bergab, ins *or* zum Tal, abwärts; (*fig.*) *he is going* –, es geht bergab mit ihm. **2.** *adj.* bergabgehend, abschüssig; (*skiing*) Abfahrts–. **--lead,** *s.* (*Rad.*) die Niederführung. **-pour,** *s.* der Regenguß, Platzregen.

down|right, 1. *adj.* 1. völlig, vollkommen, total, ausgesprochen; – *fool,* ausgesprochener Narr; – *lie,* glatte Lüge; – *madness,* heller Wahnsinn; – *nonsense,* barer *or* völliger Unsinn; – *rejection,* kategorische Absage; 2. offen(herzig), ehrlich, redlich, bieder, gerade, unverstellt. **2.** *adv.* 1. geradezu, ganz und gar, durch und durch, gänzlich, durchaus; 2. gerade heraus, ohne Umstände, unzweideutig. **-rightness,** *s.* die Offenheit, Gradheit, Biederkeit.

downsman ['daunzmən], *s.* der Hügelbewohner, Geestbewohner; *see* [2]**down.**

down|stairs, 1. *adv.* die Treppe hinunter *or* hinab, treppab; unten (im Hause); *he is* –, er ist unten. **2.** *adj.* – *room,* unteres Zimmer. **-stream,** *adv.* stromabwärts. **-throw,** *s.* der Sturz, das Niederwerfen. **--to-earth,** *attrib. adj.* praktisch. **-trodden,** *adj.* (*fig.*) unterdrückt, mit Füßen getreten.

downward ['daunwəd], *adj.* absteigend, nach unten führend, sich neigend, sich senkend, Abwärts–; (*fig.*) *on the – grade,* auf dem absteigenden Ast, im Niedergang (begriffen). **downward(s),** *adv.* abwärts, hinab, hinunter, nach unten.

down-wind, *s.* (*Meteor.*) der Abwind.

downy ['dauni], *adj.* daunenartig, flaumig, weich; – *beard,* der Milchbart. (*See* [1]**down**).

dowry ['dauri], *s.* die Mitgift, Aussteuer, Ausstattung.

[1]**dowse** [daus], *v.t. See* **douse.**

[2]**dowse** [dauz], *v.i.* mit der Wünschelrute (Wasser) suchen. **dowser,** *s.* der Rutengänger. **dowsing,** *s.* das Rutengehen; – *rod,* die Wünschelrute.

doxology [dɔk'sɔlədʒi], *s.* (liturgischer) Lobgesang, die Lobpreisung Gottes.

doxy ['dɔksi], *s.* (*obs.*) die Dirne.

doyen ['dɔijən], *s.* der Wortführer, Sprecher; Rangälteste(r).

doyl(e)y, *s. See* **doily.**

doze [douz], **1.** *v.i.* schlummern, dösen; – *off,* einnicken, einschlummern. **2.** *s.* das Schläfchen, Nickerchen, der Schlummer.

dozen [dʌzn], *s.* das Dutzend; *10p a* –, 10 Pence das Dutzend; *baker's* –, 13 Stück; *–s of,* Dutzende von; *some –s of,* einige Dutzend; *–s of times,* dutzendmal; *by the* –, *in –s,* zu Dutzenden; *cheaper by the* –, im Dutzend billiger; *round* –, volles Dutzend; *talk nineteen to the* –, das Blaue vom Himmel herunterschwatzen; (*coll.*) *do one's daily* –, tägliche Körperübungen machen.

doziness ['douzinis], *s.* die Schläfrigkeit, Verschlafenheit. **dozy,** *adj.* schläfrig, verschlafen; (*fig.*) träge, faul.

[1]**drab** [dræb], *adj.* graubraun, gelblich grau, mausgrau, schmutzfarben; (*fig.*) düster, eintönig, langweilig, fad(e).

[2]**drab,** *s.* die Schlampe; Dirne.

drabble [dræbl], *v.t. See* **draggle.**

drabness ['dræbnis], *s.* (*usu. fig.*) die Eintönigkeit, Langweiligkeit, Fadheit.

drachm [dræm], *s.* die Drachme, das Quentchen. **drachma** ['drækmə], *s.* die Drachme.

draconian [dræ'kouniən], **draconic** [–'kɔnik], *adj.* drakonisch, streng.

draff [dræf], *s.* der Bodensatz, Treber, Trester; Viehtrank; (*fig.*) Auswurf, Abfall.

draft [drɑ:ft], **1.** *s.* 1. (*Comm.*) die Tratte, der Wechsel; *make a – on,* abheben von (*an account*), einen Wechsel ziehen auf (*Acc.*) (*a p.*); *make the – payable to him,* die Tratte auf ihn ausstellen; – *at sight on London,* die Sichttratte auf London; 2. die Auswahl, Abordnung; (*Mil.*) das (Kriegs)aufgebot; die Aushebung, Musterung; Abteilung, (Ersatz)truppe, das Kommando; 3. der Plan, Entwurf, (Auf)riß, Abriß, die Skizze, das Konzept; – *agreement,* der Vertragsentwurf; 4. *See* **draught. 2.** *v.t.* 1. entwerfen, skizzieren; abfassen, aufsetzen (*a lease etc.*); 2. auswählen, abordnen; (*Mil.*) ausheben, einberufen; abkommandieren, detachieren.

draft board, *s.* (*Mil.*) die Musterungskommission. **draftee** [–'ti:], *s.* Wehrdienstpflichtige(r). **draft exemption,** *s.* die Wehrdienstbefreiung. **draft horse, draftiness, draftsman, drafty,** *see under* **draught.**

drag [dræg], **1.** *v.t.* schleppen, schleifen, zerren; (*Agr.*) eggen; dreggen, absuchen (*river etc.*); – *the anchor,* vor Anker treiben; – *one's feet,* mit den Füßen schlurren; (*fig.*) sich Zeit lassen; (*fig.*) – *in,* an den Haaren herbeiziehen; – *into,* hineinziehen in (*Acc.*) (*a p.*); – *out* (or *on*), (da)hinschleppen, ausdehnen; (*coll.*) – *up,* unsanft aufziehen (*a child*). **2.** *v.i.* geschleift *or* geschleppt werden, schleifen, schleppen, schlurren; sich (da)hinschleppen, langweilig werden; mit einem Grundnetz suchen (*for,* nach); – *on* or *out,* sich hinziehen *or* dahinschleppen, in die Länge ziehen. **3.** *s.* 1. die Schleife, der Holzschlitten; (*Agr.*) schwere Egge; schwerer Vierspänner; 2. das Schleppnetz, Baggernetz; 3. der Suchanker, Dregghaken, die Dregge; der Hemmschuh; 4. Strömungswiderstand; 5. (*fig.*) das Hindernis, die Hemmung, Belastung (*on,* für).

drag-chain, *s.* die Hemmkette, Sperrkette.

draggle [drægl], **1.** *v.t.* durch den Schmutz ziehen, beschmutzen. **2.** *v.i.* schleppen, (nach)schleifen. **draggled,** *adj.* schmutzig, schlampig. **draggle-tail,** *s.* (*coll.*) die Schlampe, Schmutzliese.

drag-net, *s.* das Schleppnetz.

dragoman ['drægomən], *s.* der Dolmetscher.

dragon ['drægən], *s.* der Drache; (*Poet.*) Lindwurm, die (Riesen)schlange; (*B.*) der Teufel, das Untier; (*fig.*) böses Weib. **dragonet** [-'net], *s.* (*Ichth.*) der Spinnenfisch. **dragonfly,** *s.* (*Ent.*) die Wasserjungfrau, Libelle. **dragon's|-blood,** *s.* (*Bot.*) das Drachenblut. **– teeth,** *pl.* (*Mil.*) das Panzerhindernis, (*fig.*) die Drachensaat. **dragon-tree,** *s.* der Drachenbaum.

dragoon [drə'gu:n], **1.** *s.* 1. (*Mil.*) der Dragoner; 2. (*fig.*) Rohling, Grobian. **2.** *v.t.* schinden, unterdrücken; zwingen (*into*, zu).

drag-shoe, *s.* der Hemmschuh.

drain [drein], **1.** *v.t.* abtropfen lassen, abfließen lassen, austropfen lassen (*liquids*); entwässern, trockenlegen, dränieren (*ground*); abziehen, ableiten (*pus etc.*); (aus)leeren, austrinken (*a jug etc.*); (*fig.*) verzehren, aufzehren, aufbrauchen; berauben (*of*, *Gen.*), entblößen (von); *– off,* ablassen, abführen, abziehen, ableiten. **2.** *v.i.* ablaufen, abfließen, sickern (*of liquids*); entwässern (*into*, in (*Acc.*)) (*of land*); austrocknen; leerlaufen (*of vessel*); *– away,* abfließen, wegfließen, sich verlaufen. **3.** *s.* 1. das Ableiten, die Ableitung; 2. der Drän, Entwässerungsgraben, Abzugskanal, Ablaufkanal, die (Abzugs)rinne; Gosse, Straßenrinne; das Kanalisationsrohr; die Senkgrube; (*Med.*) Kanüle; *pl.* Abflußrohranlage, Kanalisation; (*sl.*) *down the –,* zum Fenster hinaus; 3. (*fig.*) der Abfluß (*of money*), die Inanspruchnahme, Belastung, Verminderung, Schwächung (*on*, *Gen.*); *that is a – on my purse,* das nimmt meinen Geldbeutel (zu) stark in Anspruch.

drainable ['dreinəbl], *adj.* dränierbar, entwässerbar. **drainage** [-idʒ], *s.* das Ablaufen, Abfließen (*of liquids*); die Entleerung (*of vessels*); Entwässerung, Trockenlegung, Dränage (*of land*); Entwässerungsanlage, (*in the house*) Kanalisation; das Abwasser; *– area* or *basin,* das Stromgebiet; *– system,* die Entwässerungsanlage; (*Med.*) *– tube,* die (Abfluß)kanüle.

drain-cock, *s.* der Ablaßhahn, Ablaufhahn. **drainer,** *s.* der Ableiter, das Tropfbrett. **draining|-board,** *s.* das Abtropfbrett. **–-rack,** *s.* (*Phot.*) der Trockenständer. **drain|-pipe,** *s.* das Abzugsrohr, Abflußrohr. **–-trap,** *s.* der Wasserabschluß, Geruchverschluß.

drake [dreik], *s.* der Enterich.

dram [dræm], *s.* 1. *See* **drachm**; 2. der Schluck, das Schlückchen (*of spirits*); (*fig.*) die Kleinigkeit, das bißchen; (*coll.*) *– shop,* die Branntweinschenke.

drama ['drɑ:mə], *s.* das Schauspiel, (*also fig.*) Drama; die Schauspielkunst; dramatische Dichtkunst, die Dramatik. **dramatic** [drə'mætik], *adj.* dramatisch, Schauspiel(er)–, Theater–; (*fig.*) erregend, handlungsreich, spannend; *– art,* die Theaterwissenschaft; *– critic,* der Theaterkritiker; *– rights,* Aufführungsrechte, Bühnenrechte (*pl.*); *– school,* die Schauspielerschule.

dramatis personae ['dræmətispə'so:ni:], *pl.* das Rollenverzeichnis, Personen (der Handlung) (*pl.*).

dramatist ['dræmətist], *s.* der Dramatiker, Schauspieldichter. **dramatization** [-tai'zeiʃən], *s.* die Dramatisierung, Bühnenbearbeitung. **dramatize,** *v.t.* dramatisieren (*also fig.*), für die Bühne bearbeiten. **dramaturgy** [-tə:dʒi], *s.* die Dramaturgie, Theaterwissenschaft.

drank [dræŋk], *imperf. of* **drink.**

drape [dreip], *v.t.* (malerisch) behängen, drapieren, in Falten legen. **draper,** *s.* der Tuchhändler, Stoffhändler, Textilhändler, Schnittwarenhändler; *–s' company,* die Tuchhändlerinnung. **drapery,** *s.* 1. der Textilhandel, Stoffhandel, Tuchhandel; 2. das Tuch, der Stoff, Tuche (*pl.*), Stoffe (*pl.*), Textilien (*pl.*); 3. die Drapierung, der Faltenwurf. **drapes,** *pl.* (*Am.*) der Vorhang, die Gardine.

drastic ['drɑ:stik], *adj.* kräftig, energisch, drastisch; gründlich, durchgreifend.

drat [dræt], *int.* (*coll.*) zum Henker mit . . .! der Teufel soll . . . holen! *– it!* zum Teufel damit! **dratted,** *adj.* (*coll.*) verflucht, verflixt.

draught [drɑ:ft], *s.* das Ziehen; der Zug (*also drink, of air, of fish*); Tiefgang (*of a ship*); Schluck; Luftzug; die Arznei, Dosis; *see also* **draft**; *drink off at one –,* auf einen Zug austrinken; *there is a –,* es zieht; (*sl.*) *feel the –,* den kürzeren ziehen; *beer on –,* Bier vom Faß, das Abzugbier.

draught|-animal, *s.* das Zugtier. **–board,** *s.* das Dam(espiel)brett. **–-hole,** *s.* das Zugloch. **–-horse,** *s.* das Zugpferd. **draughtiness,** *s.* die Zugigkeit. **draught-marks,** *pl.* (*Naut.*) die Ahmung, Ahming. **draughts,** *pl.* (*sing. constr.*) das Damespiel; (*pl. constr.*) Damebrettsteine (*pl.*); *play at –,* Dame spielen. **draughtsman,** *s.* 1. der Damstein; 2. (*also* **draftsman**) (Muster)-zeichner, Konstruktionszeichner; (*usu.* **draftsman**) Entwerfer, Konzipist. **draughty,** *adj. it is –,* es zieht.

Drave [dreiv], *s.* (*Geog.*) die Drau.

Dravidian [drə'vidiən], **1.** *adj.* drawidisch. **2.** *s.* das Drawida (*language*).

draw [drɔ:], **1.** *irr.v.t.*

1. ziehen, zerren, schleppen, schleifen; (*fig.*) anziehen, an *or* zu sich ziehen, fesseln; (*Tech.*) (aus)-walzen, recken, strecken, dehnen; *I felt –n to him,* ich fühlte mich zu ihm hingezogen; *– applause,* Beifall hervorrufen; *– applause from,* Beifall entlocken *or* abringen (*Dat.*); *– attention to,* Aufmerksamkeit lenken auf (*Acc.*); *– a bead,* zielen (*on*, nach); *– beer,* Bier abziehen *or* abzapfen; *– a bird,* Geflügel ausnehmen; *– a blank,* eine Niete ziehen, (*fig.*) einen Fehlschlag erleiden; *– blood,* verwunden; *– the bow,* den Bogen spannen; (*fig.*) *– the long bow,* aufschneiden, prahlen, angeben; *– breath,* Atem holen, Luft schöpfen; *– a cheque on the account,* sich (*Dat.*) einen Scheck von dem Konto auszahlen lassen; *– comparisons,* Vergleiche aufstellen *or* anstellen; *– a conclusion from,* einen Schluß ziehen aus; *– consolation from,* Trost schöpfen aus; *– fresh courage from,* neuen Mut schöpfen aus; *– the curtain,* die Gardine aufziehen *or* zuziehen; *at daggers –n,* auf gespanntem Fuße; *– one's finger over,* mit dem Finger fahren über; (*Theat.*) *– a full house,* das Haus füllen; (*Hunt.*) *– the game,* das Wild aufstöbern; *– interest,* Zinsen abwerfen; *– a loser,* eine Niete auslosen; *– lots,* losen (*for*, um); *– money from an account,* Geld von einem Konto abheben; *– a parallel,* eine Parallele ziehen; *– one's pen through,* ausstreichen, durchstreichen; *– a good price,* einen guten Preis einbringen; *– rein,* die Zügel anziehen; *– a salary,* ein Gehalt beziehen; *– a sigh,* aufseufzen, einen Seufzer ausstoßen; (*Crick.*) *– stumps,* dem Spiel ein Ende machen; *– the sword,* das Schwert ziehen *or* zücken; *– tea,* Tee ziehen lassen; *– a tooth* einen Zahn ziehen; *– one's wages,* seinen Lohn beziehen *or* in Empfang nehmen; *– water,* Wasser holen *or* schöpfen; (*Hunt.*) *– a wood,* einen Wald durchsuchen *or* durchstöbern;

2. (ab)zeichnen, schildern, darstellen; (*coll.*) *– the line at,* nicht mehr mitmachen *or* Schluß machen bei, ablehnen, nicht dulden;

3. (*Spt.*) unentschieden beenden; *– a game,* ein Spiel unentschieden beenden;

4. (*Naut.*) einen Tiefgang haben von;

5. (*coll.*) aus der Reserve herauslocken (*a p.*); (*coll.*) *– him,* ihn aushorchen *or* auspumpen.

(*with advs. and preps.*) *– aside,* beiseitenehmen, zur Seite ziehen; *– away,* wegziehen, zurückziehen; ablenken (*attention*); *– back,* zurückziehen; *– down,* herablassen; auf sich ziehen, herabbeschwören (*curse*); *– forth,* herausziehen, hervorziehen, (*fig.*) herauslocken, entlocken; *– in,* einziehen; zusammenziehen; (*fig.*) beschränken, einschränken; (*fig.*) *– in one's horns,* die Hörner einziehen, sich mäßigen; *– into,* hineinziehen in

(*Acc.*); verlocken *or* verleiten zu; – *off,* abziehen, abzapfen (*fluids*); abziehen, zurückziehen (*troops*); ablenken (*the attention etc.*); – *on,* anziehen (*boots etc.*); (*fig.*) anlocken; – *out,* herausziehen, herausholen (*from,* aus); hinausziehen, verlängern, ausdehnen; (*fig.*) in die Länge ziehen; – *out troops,* Truppen detachieren *or* aufstellen; (*coll.*) – *him out, see* – **1.** 5; – *together,* zusammenziehen; – *up,* aufstellen, aufrichten; (her)aufziehen, in die Höhe ziehen; – *up boats,* Boote ans Land ziehen; – *up a petition,* eine Bittschrift abfassen *or* aufsetzen; – *up in order of battle,* in Schlachtordnung aufstellen; – *o.s. up,* sich recken *or* emporrichten *or* aufrichten *or* erheben.
2. *irr.v.i.* 1. ziehen; eine Karte ziehen; das Schwert ziehen (*on,* gegen); *we must let the tea* –, der Tee muß ziehen; – *at long date,* auf lange Zeit ziehen *or* ausstellen (*bills*); – *for the move,* um den Zug losen; 2. zeichnen; 3. (*Spt.*) unentschieden spielen; 4. (*with advs. or preps.*) sich begeben, sich bewegen; herankommen (*to,* an (*Acc.*)), sich nähern (*to, Dat.*); – *aside,* zur Seite treten *or* gehen, ausweichen; – *away,* sich entfernen; (*Spt.*) sich weiter nach vorn schieben; – *back,* sich zurückziehen, zurückweichen; – *in,* sich neigen (*as the day*), kürzer werden (*as the days*); – *level,* auf gleiche Höhe kommen; – *level with,* aufholen, einholen, herankommen an (*Acc.*); – *near* or (*Poet.*) *nigh,* sich nähern (*to, Dat.*), näherrücken, näher herankommen (an (*Acc.*)); *harvest is –ing near,* es geht auf die Ernte zu, die Ernte steht vor der Tür; *the time is –ing near,* die Zeit rückt heran; – *off,* sich zurückziehen, zurücktreten, (*Mil.*) abziehen; – *on,* nahen, anrücken, herankommen, sich nähern; (*fig.*) – (*up*)*on,* beanspruchen, Anspruch erheben auf (*Acc.*), in Anspruch nehmen; – *on one's savings,* die Ersparnisse angreifen *or* heranziehen; (*coll.*) – *on him,* ihn angehen (*for,* um); – *out,* länger werden (*as the days*); – *round,* sich versammeln; – *round the table,* sich um den Tisch versammeln, einen Kreis um den Tisch bilden; – *to,* herankommen an (*Acc.*), sich nähern (*Dat.*); – *to an end* or *a close,* zu Ende gehen, sich dem Ende nähern; – *to a head,* reifen (*also Med.*), reif werden, den Höhepunkt erreichen; *I felt –n to him,* ich fühlte mich zu ihm hingezogen; – *together,* sich sammeln, zusammenziehen; – *up,* vorfahren (*before,* vor (*Dat.*)); stehenbleiben, (an)halten; (*of troops*) sich aufstellen; – *up to* or *with,* herankommen an (*Acc.*), aufholen, einholen.
3. *s.* 1. das Ziehen, der Zug; das Los, Schicksal; die Ziehung, Verlosung; (*fig.*) Anziehungskraft; (*Theat.*) das Zugstück, der Schlager; (*sl.*) *quick on the* –, schnell mit dem Revolver bei der Hand; 2. (*Spt.*) unentschiedenes Spiel; *end in a* –, unentschieden enden *or* bleiben *or* ausgehen.

draw|back, *s.* 1. der Nachteil, das Hindernis (*to,* für), die Behinderung, Beeinträchtigung (*Gen.*); 2. Kehrseite, Schattenseite; 3. (*Comm.*) (Zoll)rückvergütung. **–bridge,** *s.* die Zugbrücke. **drawee** [drɔːˈiː], *s.* (*Comm.*) der Akzeptant, Bezogene(r), Trassat. **drawer,** *s.* 1. [ˈdrɔːə], (*Comm.*) der Zieher, Aussteller, Trassant; Zeichner; 2. [drɔː], die Schublade, das Schubfach; (*a chest of*) *–s,* die Kommode. **drawers** [drɔːz], *pl.* (*pair of*) –, die Unterhose (*for men*), der Schlüpfer (*for women*); *bathing* –, die Badehose.

drawing [ˈdrɔːiŋ], *s.* 1. das Ziehen; (*lottery*) die Ziehung, Verlosung, Auslosung; (*of money*) Abhebung; *pl.* (*Comm.*) Bezüge (*pl.*); (*Comm.*) – *account,* das Girokonto; 2. das Zeichnen; die Zeichnung, Skizze; Zeichenkunst; *out of* –, verzeichnet; – *board,* das Zeichenbrett, Reißbrett; – *compasses,* der Reißzirkel; – *ink,* die (Auszieh)tusche; – *master,* der Zeichenlehrer; – *office,* das Zeichenbüro; – *paper,* das Zeichenpapier; – *pen,* die Reißfeder; – *pin,* die Reißzwecke, Heftzwecke.

drawing-room, 1. *s.* das Gesellschaftszimmer, der Salon. **2.** *adj.* (*coll.*) gesellschaftsfähig, anständig.

drawl [drɔːl], **1.** *v.t., v.i.* affektiert sprechen. **2.** *s.* affektierte Sprechweise.

drawn [drɔːn], **1.** *p.p. of* **draw. 2.** *adj.* – *battle,* unentschiedene Schlacht; – *bird,* ausgeweidetes Geflügel; – *butter,* zerlassene Butter; – *expression,* verzerrtes Gesicht; – *sword,* blankes Schwert; –(*thread*)*work,* die Hohlsaumarbeit; – *wire,* gezogener Draht.

draw|plate, *s.* die (Draht)lochplatte. **–string,** *s.* die Zugschnur, das Zugband. **–-well,** *s.* der Ziehbrunnen.

dray [drei], *s.* der Rollwagen. **drayage** [–idʒ], *s.* das Rollgeld. **dray|-cart,** *s. See* **dray. –-horse,** *s.* der Karrengaul. **–man,** *s.* der Rollkutscher, Rollfuhrmann, Bierkutscher.

dread [dred], **1.** *s.* große Furcht *or* Angst, der Schrecken; die Scheu, Ehrfurcht; das Grauen (*of,* vor (*Dat.*)). **2.** *adj.* (*Poet.*) schrecklich, furchtbar; gefürchtet; erhaben, hehr. **3.** *v.t.* fürchten, sich fürchten vor (*Dat.*). **dreadful, 1.** *adj.* schrecklich, furchtbar, fürchterlich, (*coll.*) sehr, entsetzlich. **2.** *s. penny-–,* billiger Schauerroman, die Gruselgeschichte. **dreadnought,** *s.* 1. das Großkampfschiff; 2. wetterfester Stoff *or* Mantel.

dream [driːm], **1.** *s.* der Traum; die Träumerei, der Traumzustand; – *world,* die Traumwelt; 2. das Ideal; (*coll.*) *a – of a dress,* ein Wunder *or* Gedicht von einem Kleid. **2.** *reg. & irr.v.t.* träumen. **3.** *reg. & irr.v.i.* träumen; träumerisch sein; – *away,* verträumen, vor sich (*Dat.*) hinträumen (*time etc.*); *I –ed that,* mir träumte daß; *I never –t of such a thing,* so etwas ist mir nie im Traume eingefallen, so etwas habe ich mir nie träumen lassen; *without –ing that he might come,* ohne zu ahnen daß er kommen könnte. **dreamer,** *s.* der Träumer, Phantast. **dreaminess,** *s.* die Verträumtheit. **dreaming,** *adj.* verträumt. **dreamland,** *s.* das Märchenland. **dreamless,** *adj.* traumlos. **dreamlike,** *adj.* traumartig, traumähnlich, traumhaft.

dreamt [dremt], *imperf., p.p. of* **dream.**

dreamy [ˈdriːmi], *adj.* träumerisch, verträumt.

drear [driə], *adj.* (*Poet.*) *see* **dreary. dreariness** [–rinis], *s.* die Öde, Trostlosigkeit, Düsterkeit, Düsterheit. **dreary,** *adj.* trostlos, öde, düster; langweilig.

[1]**dredge** [dredʒ], *v.t.* bestreuen, panieren (*with flour etc.*), streuen (*flour etc.*).

[2]**dredge, 1.** *s.* das Schleppnetz, Grundnetz, die Kurre; der Bagger. **2.** *v.t.* ausbaggern; (*Naut.*) dreggen; mit Schleppnetzen fangen.

[1]**dredger** [ˈdredʒə], *s.* der (Schwimm)bagger, die Baggermaschine.

[2]**dredger,** *s.* die Streubüchse.

dreg [dreg], *s.* letzter Rest, (*usu. pl.*) die Hefe, der (Boden)satz; (*fig.*) Abschaum, Auswurf; *to the –s,* bis zur Neige.

drench [drentʃ], **1.** *s.* (*Vet.*) der Trank, die Arznei. **2.** *v.t.* 1. durchnässen, durchtränken; *–ed in tears,* in Tränen gebadet; *–ed with rain,* bis auf die Haut durchnäßt; 2. Arznei eingeben (*Dat.*) (*animals*). **drencher,** *s.* (*coll.*) der Regenguß.

Dresden china [ˈdrezdən], *s.* Meißner Porzellan.

dress [dres], **1.** *v.t.* 1. anziehen, ankleiden; bekleiden, mit Kleidung (*or Theat.* Kostümen) versorgen; schmücken, verzieren, dekorieren (*as a window*); bearbeiten, zurechtmachen; verbinden, behandeln (*wound*), düngen (*soil*), anrichten, zubereiten (*food*), anmachen (*salad*), frisieren (*hair*), behauen (*stones*), aufbereiten (*ore*), abputzen, hobeln (*timber*), stärken, appretieren, glätten (*cloth*), zurichten, bereiten (*leather*), hecheln (*flax*), beizen (*corn*), brechen (*hemp*); (*Typ.*) bestoßen, abhobeln; – *a ship,* die Flaggengala setzen; – *the vine,* den Weinstock beschneiden; – *o.s.,* sich (an)kleiden *or* anziehen; (*coll.*) – *him down,* ihn abkanzeln *or* anschnauzen; ihm eine Strafpredigt halten; – *him out with,* ihn herausputzen *or* ausschmücken mit; – *him up,* ihm Galakleidung anziehen, ihn verkleiden; 2. (*Mil.*) (aus)richten; – *the ranks,* sich ausrichten. **2.** *v.i.* 1. sich (an)kleiden, sich anziehen; – *for dinner,* sich zum Abendessen umkleiden; – *well,* sich geschmackvoll kleiden; – *up,* sich in Gala werfen, sich verkleiden; sich fein machen, sich aufdonnern; 2. (*Mil.*) sich richten; –*!* richt euch! – *by the right,* sich nach rechts ausrichten.

3. *s.* die (Be)kleidung; das (Damen)kleid; (*Mil.*) der Anzug, die Uniform; (*fig.*) Gestalt, das Gewand; ***battle –,*** der Kampfanzug; ***evening –,*** der Gesellschaftsanzug; Frack(*for men*), die (Ball)-toilette (*for women*); ***fancy –,*** das Maskenkostüm; ***full –,*** der Paradeanzug, Galaanzug, die Gala; ***morning –,*** der Straßenanzug, schwarzer Rock mit gestreifter Hose; ***summer –,*** das Sommerkleid.

dressage ['dresɑːʒ], *s.* (*Equest.*) das Schulreiten.

dress| allowance, *s.* das Nadelgeld. **– circle,** *s.* (*Theat.*) erster Rang. **–-clothes,** *pl.* die Gesellschaftskleidung. **–-coat,** *s.* der Frack. **– designer,** *s.* der (die) Moderzeichner(in).

dresser ['dresə], *s.* **1.** (*Theat.*) die Ankleidefrau, Ankleiderin; (*Tech.*) der Aufbereiter, Zurichter, Appretierer, Steinhauer; (*Med.*) Assistenzarzt, Operationsgehilfe; 2. die Anrichte, das Büffet, der Geschirrschrank, Küchenschrank. **dressiness,** *s.* (*coll.*) auffällige Eleganz (*of clothes*), die Putzsucht (*of a p.*).

dressing ['dresiŋ], *s.* 1. das Ankleiden; die Bekleidung; 2. das Verbinden, Behandeln (*of a wound*), (*Surg.*) der Verband, Verbandstoff; (*Mil.*) ***field –,*** der Notverband; 3. (*Tech.*) die Aufbereitung, Zurichtung, Appretur, Nachbearbeitung; (*of food*) Zubereitung; (*Cul.*) Zutat, Füllung, Soße, Tunke; (*Agr.*) Düngung; der Dünger.

dressing|-case, *s.* das Toilettenkästchen, Reisenecessaire. **–-down,** *s.* (*coll.*) die Standpauke, Gardinenpredigt. **–-gown,** *s.* der Schlafrock. **–-jacket,** *s.* der Frisiermantel. **–-room,** *s.* das Ankleidezimmer, (*Spt.*) Umkleidezimmer. **–-station,** *s.* (*Mil.*) der Verbandplatz. **–-table,** *s.* der Toilettentisch, die Frisierkommode.

dress|maker, *s.* die Damenschneiderin. **–making,** *s.* die Damenschneiderei. **– parade,** *s.* die Modeschau. **– pattern,** *s.* das Schnittmuster. **– preserver,** *s. See* **– shield. –-rehearsal,** *s.* (*Theat.*) die Generalprobe, Hauptprobe. **– shield,** *s.* das Schweißblatt. **–-shirt,** *s.* das Frackhemd. **–-suit,** *s.* der Gesellschaftsanzug, Frackanzug. **–-sword,** *s.* der Galadegen.

dressy ['dresi], *adj.* (*coll.*) schick, modisch, (auffällig) elegant (*of clothes*), herausgeputzt, aufgedonnert, stutzerhaft, modesüchtig, putzsüchtig (*of a p.*).

drew [druː], *imperf. of* **draw.**

drib [drib], *s.* (*only in*) ***in –s and drabs,*** in kleinen Mengen, tropfenweise.

dribble [dribl], **1.** *v.i.* 1. rieseln, tröpfeln; (*as a child*) sabbern, geifern; 2. (*Footb.*) dribbeln. **2.** *v.t.* 1. tröpfeln lassen; 2. (*Footb.*) vor sich (*Dat.*) hertreiben, dribbeln (*the ball*).

driblet ['driblit], *s.* (*coll.*) (das) bißchen, der Tropfen, die Kleinigkeit; ***in –s,*** in kleinen Mengen, tropfenweise.

dried [draid], **1.** *imperf., p.p. of* **dry. 2.** *adj.* getrocknet, Trocken–, Dörr–; ***– fruit,*** das Dörrobst; ***– milk,*** die Trockenmilch. **drier, 1.** *s.* 1. der Trockner, Trockenapparat; 2. das Trockenmittel, Sikkativ. **2.** *comp. adj. See* **dry. driest** ['draiist], *sup. adj. See* **dry.**

drift [drft], **1.** *s.* 1. das (An)treiben; ***– from the land,*** die Landflucht; 2. (*Geog.*) die Driftgeschwindigkeit, (Drift)strömung; (*Naut.*) Abtrift, der Abtrieb, (*Av.*) die (Kurs)versetzung, (*Artil.*) Seitenabweichung; 3. (*fig.*) das (Sich)gehenlassen, (Sich)treibenlassen, die Untätigkeit; 4. der (An)trieb, die Neigung, Richtung, Tendenz, der Lauf; (*coll.*) Zweck, die Absicht; der Gedankengang, Sinn, die Bedeutung; 5. (*of snow*) Wehe, Verwehung, (*of sand etc.*) der Haufen, (*of rain etc.*) Guß, das Gestöbe; (*Geol.*) Geschiebe; (*Min.*) der Stollen, die Strecke; 6. (*Tech.*) der Lochhammer, Austreiber, Dorn. **2.** *v.i.* treiben, getrieben werden, (*of snow*) verweht werden, sich häufen; (*Naut.*) triftig sein; (*fig.*) (*of a p.*) geraten, gezogen werden (***into,*** in (*Acc.*)), sich (willenlos) treiben lassen; ***– apart,*** auseinanderkommen (*also fig.*); ***– away,*** abwandern, wegziehen; (*fig.*) ***let things –,*** den Dingen ihren Lauf lassen.

drift|-anchor, *s.* der Treibanker. **–-angle,** *s.* der Abtriftwinkel. **drifter,** *s.* 1. der Treibnetzfischdampfer; 2. (*coll.*) unschlüssiger *or* zielloser Mensch. **drift|-ice,** *s.* das Treibeis. **–-net,** *s.* das Treibnetz. **–-sand,** *s.* der Triebsand, Flugsand. **–-way,** *s.* die Trift (*for cattle*), (*Min.*) Strecke, (*Naut.*) Abtrift. **–wood,** *s.* das Treibholz.

[1]**drill** [dril], *s.* der Drell, Drill(ich), Zwil(li)ch (*cloth*).

[2]**drill, 1.** *s.* (*Tech.*) der (Drill)bohrer, die Bohrmaschine. **2.** *v.t.* bohren (*hole*), durchbohren (*wood etc.*), ausbohren (*a tooth*).

[3]**drill, 1.** *s.* (*Mil.*) das Exerzieren, der Drill, (*fig.*) die Schulung, Übung, Ausbildung, das Drillen, (Ein)pauken; ***Swedish –,*** Freiübungen (*pl.*). **2.** *v.t.* (*Mil.*) drillen, einexerzieren, (*fig.*) (gründlich) ausbilden (*a p.*), eindrillen, einpauken (*a subject*) (***into,*** *Dat.*).

[4]**drill, 1.** *s.* (*Agr.*) 1. die Furche, (Saat)rille; 2. Drillmaschine, Reihensämaschine. **2.** *v.t.* in Reihen pflanzen *or* säen (*seed*), in Reihen bepflanzen *or* besäen (*field*).

drill| book, *s.* das Exerzierreglement. **– chuck,** *s.* das Bohrfutter, der Bohrkopf. **– ground,** *s.* der Exerzierplatz. **– hall,** *s.* die Exerzierhalle. **–-harrow,** *s.* die Bohregge.

drilling ['driliŋ], *s.* 1. das Bohren; 2. *See* [3]**drill, 1.**; 3. Drillen, Reihensäen; 4. *pl.* Bohrspäne (*pl.*). **drilling|-machine,** *s.* der Bohrer, die Bohrmaschine. **–-rig,** *s.* die Bohranlage, der Bohrturm.

drill|-plough, *s. See* [4]**drill, 1,** 2. **–-sergeant,** *s.* der Ausbildungsunteroffizier.

drily, *adv. See* **dryly.**

drink [driŋk], **1.** *irr.v.t.* trinken, (*of beasts*) saufen; (*fig.*) absorbieren, aufsaugen; ***– a glass,*** ein Glas austrinken *or* leeren; ***– one's fill,*** sich satt *or* voll trinken; ***– his health,*** auf seine Gesundheit *or* sein Wohl trinken; (*coll.*) ***– him under the table,*** ihn unter den Tisch trinken; ***– the waters,*** Brunnen trinken; ***– o.s. to death,*** sich zu Tode trinken; (*with advs.*) ***– away,*** vertrinken (*sorrow etc.*); ***– down,*** see ***– up***; (*fig.*) ***– in,*** aufsaugen; (*air*) (ein)-schlürfen, (*ideas etc.*) (gierig) aufnehmen, verschlingen; ***– off*** or ***up,*** (auf einen Zug) austrinken *or* leeren. **2.** *irr.v.i.* trinken; übermäßig trinken, dem Alkohol zusprechen, saufen; ***– deep,*** einen tiefen Zug tun; ***– like a fish,*** wie ein Loch saufen; ***– to him,*** auf ihn anstoßen *or* trinken. **3.** *s.* 1. das Getränk; der Trunk, Zug, Schluck (*of water etc.*); geistiges Getränk; das Trinken, der Trunk; ***food and –,*** Speisen und Getränke, Speise und Trank; ***have a –,*** einen Schluck zu sich nehmen; ***have a – with him,*** mit ihm ein Glas *or* eins trinken; ***in –,*** betrunken, berauscht; (*coll.*) ***be on the –,*** dem Trunk frönen; ***take a –,*** see ***have a –***; ***take to –,*** sich dem Trunk ergeben; ***the worse for –,*** see ***in –***; 2. (*sl.*) der Teich, Bach.

drinkable ['driŋkəbl], *adj.* trinkbar. **drinker,** *s.* der Trinker, Zecher; Säufer, Trunkenbold. **drinking,** *s.* das Trinken. **drinking|-bout,** *s.* das Trinkgelage, Zechgelage. **– companion,** *s.* der Zechkumpan, Trinkkumpan. **–-cup,** *s.* der Becher. **–-fountain,** *s.* der Trinkbrunnen. **–-horn,** *s.* das Trinkhorn. **–-song,** *s.* das Trinklied. **–-water,** *s.* das Trinkwasser.

drip [drip], **1.** *v.i.* (herab)tropfen, (herab)tröpfeln (***from,*** von), triefen (***with,*** von). **2.** *s.* 1. das Tröpfeln, (*oft. pl.*) der Nachlauf; 2. (*sl.*) Waschlappen (*a p.*); 3. *See* **dripstone, 1. drip|-dry,** *adj.* tropfnaß aufzuhängen, schnelltrocknend, bügelfrei (*as shirts*). **–-feed,** *s.* die Tropfschmierung.

dripping ['dripiŋ], **1.** *adj.* tröpfelnd; triefend, durchnäßt; ***– wet,*** triefend naß, durchnäßt. **2.** *s.* 1. das Herabtropfen, Tröpfeln, Triefen; 2. (*Cul.*) Bratenfett, Schmalz. **dripping-pan,** *s.* die Bratpfanne.

dripstone ['dripstoun], *s.* 1. (*Archit.*) das Traufdach, die Traufleiste; 2. (*Min.*) der Tropfstein.

drive [draiv], **1.** *irr.v.t.* treiben, antreiben, vorwärtstreiben; forttreiben, vertreiben (***from,*** von); (*fig.*) nötigen, zwingen, (dazu) bringen; jagen, hetzen

(*game*); lenken, fahren (*a car etc.*); führen (*an engine*); bohren (*a tunnel*); (ein)schlagen (*nail*), (ein)treiben, (ein)rammen (*piles*); (*Spt.*) kräftig schlagen, (*Golf*) vom Abschlagrasen abspielen; (*fig.*) – ***all before one,*** jeden Widerstand überwinden; – ***an argument home,*** einen Beweis erbringen; ***he –s a hard bargain,*** es ist nicht gut mit ihm Kirschen essen, er ist eine harte Nuß; – ***a car,*** ein Auto fahren; – ***a coach,*** kutschieren; – ***him hard,*** ihn zur Arbeit antreiben, ihn schinden *or* überanstrengen; – ***home,*** nach Hause fahren; – ***a nail home,*** einen Nagel ganz einschlagen; – ***it home to him,*** es ihm klarmachen *or* zu Bewußtsein bringen *or* zu Gemüte führen; – ***it into his head,*** es ihm einbleuen; – ***him mad,*** ihn verrückt machen; ***it was enough to – one mad,*** es war zum Rasendwerden; – ***him from pillar to post,*** ihn von Pontius zu Pilatus schicken; – ***him out of his mind*** or ***senses,*** ihn um den Verstand bringen; – ***him to despair*** or ***distraction,*** ihn zur Verzweiflung treiben *or* bringen.
(*with advs.*) – ***away,*** verjagen, vertreiben, zerstreuen; – ***back,*** zurücktreiben; – ***in,*** eintreiben (*cattle*), einschlagen (*nails*); – ***on,*** vorwärtstreiben; – ***out,*** (hin)austreiben, forttreiben, vertreiben, verjagen; – ***up,*** in die Höhe treiben, hinauftreiben (*prices*).
2. *irr.v.i.* (dahin)treiben, getrieben *or* getragen werden; fahren (*in a vehicle*); (*coll.*) – ***at,*** hinzielen *or* abzielen *or* hinauswollen auf (*Acc.*); (*coll.*) ***what are you driving at?*** was meinst du überhaupt damit? worauf willst du hinaus? ***let – at,*** losschlagen auf (*Acc.*); – ***off,*** wegfahren; – ***on,*** weiterfahren, zufahren; – ***out,*** ausfahren, spazierenfahren; – ***up,*** vorfahren (***to,*** vor (*Dat.*)).
3. *s.* 1. die (Spazier)fahrt, Ausfahrt; ***go for*** or ***take a –,*** ausfahren; 2. der Fahrweg, die Auffahrt; 3. das Hetzen, die Treibjagd (*of game*); 4. Stoßkraft, Triebkraft, Energie, der Schwung; 5. (*Mil.*) Vorstoß; 6. (*Comm. etc.*) (Werbe)feldzug, die Kampagne, (Werbe)aktion; 7. (*Tech.*) der Antrieb; (*Motor.*) ***rear –,*** der Hinterradantrieb; ***remote –,*** der Fernantrieb; 8. (*Psych.*) die Tendenz, Neigung, der Antrieb; 9. (*Spt.*) Weitschlag, (*Golf*) erster Schlag, (*Tenn.*) der Treibschlag.

drive-in, *attrib. adj.* Einfahr–, Auto–.

drivel [drivl], **1.** *v.i.* geifern, sabbern (*as infants*); (*fig.*) schwatzen, faseln. **2.** *s.* der Geifer, Sabber; das Gefasel, Geplapper, die Faselei, leeres Geschwätz. **driveller,** *s.* der Faselhans, Schwätzer.

driven [drivn], *p.p. of* **drive.**

driver ['draivə], *s.* 1. der Treiber (*of oxen etc.*); Fuhrmann, Kutscher (*of cart*), Führer (*of train, tramcar*), (*Motor.*) Chauffeur, Schofför, Fahrer, Lenker; ***–'s cab,*** der Führerstand; ***–'s mate,*** der Beifahrer; ***–'s seat,*** der Kutschersitz, Führersitz; 2. (*Tech.*) das Triebrad, der Mitnehmer (*on lathes etc.*); 3. (*Build.*) Rammblock, die Ramme; 4. (*Golf*) erster Schläger; 5. (*fig.*) der Antreiber, Schinder.

drive-shaft, *s. See* **driving-shaft.**

driving ['draiviŋ], **1.** *adj.* treibend; Treib–, Trieb–, Antriebs–; – ***force,*** treibende Kraft; – ***rain,*** strömender Regen. **2.** *s.* das Autofahren; ***be good at –,*** gut (auto)fahren können; ***within – distance*** im Wagen leicht zu erreichen.

driving|-axle, *s.* die Triebwelle, Antriebswelle, Triebachse. **--band,** *s.* (*Artil.*) das Führungsband. **--belt,** *s.* der Treibriemen. **--box,** *s.* der Kutsch(er)bock, Kutschersitz. **--gear,** *s.* das Getriebe; Triebwerk. **--instructor,** *s.* der Fahrlehrer. – **lessons,** *pl.* der Fahrunterricht. **--licence,** *s.* der Führerschein. **--mirror,** *s.* (*Motor.*) der Rück(blick)spiegel. **--power,** *s.* die Antriebskraft, Antriebsleistung. **--reins,** *pl.* Leitriemen (*pl.*). **--seat,** *s.* (*Motor.*) der Führersitz. **--shaft,** *s.* die Antriebswelle, Getriebewelle, Triebachse; (*Motor.*) Kardanwelle. **--test,** *s.* die Fahrprüfung. **--wheel,** *s.* das Antriebsrad, Triebrad.

drizzle [drizl], **1.** *s.* der Sprühregen. **2.** *v.i.* rieseln, nieseln. **drizzly,** *adj.* rieselnd, regnerisch.

drogue [droug], *s.* der Windsack.

droit [drɔit, drwa:], *s.* (*Law*) das Recht, der Rechtsanspruch.

droll [droul], **1.** *adj.* drollig, possierlich, spaßig, komisch. **2.** *s.* (*rare*) der Possenreißer. **drollery,** *s.* die Posse, Schnurre, der Spaß; die Spaßhaftigkeit, Komik.

dromedary ['drɔmədəri], *s.* das Dromedar.

[1]**drone** [droun], **1.** *s.* das Summen, Brummen, Gebrumm, der Brummton; (*fig.*) eintöniges Sprechen; der Brummer (*of bagpipes*). **2.** *v.i.* brummen, summen, dröhnen; (*fig.*) eintönig reden, leiern. **3.** *v.t.* eintönig herunterleiern.

[2]**drone,** **1.** *s.* die Drohne, (*fig.*) der Faulenzer, Schmarotzer. **2.** *v.i.* faulenzen. **3.** *v.t.* – ***away,*** müßig verbringen.

drool [dru:l], *v.i.* (*sl.*) 1. *See* **drivel**; 2. – ***about*** or ***over,*** verknallt sein in (*Acc.*) (*a p.*).

droop [dru:p], **1.** *v.t.* sinken lassen, (herab)hängen lassen. **2.** *v.i.* sich senken, (dahin)sinken; ermatten, erschlaffen, zusammensinken, schmachten (***with,*** vor (*Dat.*)), (ver)welken (*as flowers*); (*Comm.*) sinken (*as prices*); (*fig.*) den Kopf hängenlassen. **droopy,** *adj.* (*coll.*) schlaff, matt, erschlafft, ermattet.

drop [drɔp], **1.** *s.* 1. der Tropfen, (*coll.*) das Schlückchen, Tröpfchen; *pl.* (Arznei)tropfen (*pl.*), Fruchtbonbons (*pl.*), Zuckerplätzchen (*pl.*); – ***by –, in –s,*** tropfenweise; ***add by –s,*** einträufeln; (*coll.*) ***a – too much,*** ein Trunk über den Durst; (*fig.*) ***a – in the ocean,*** ein Tropfen auf den heißen Stein; 2. der Fall, Sturz, das Niedergehen, (Herab)fallen, Sinken (*of prices, temperature etc.*); die Fallweite, Falltiefe; Senkung, das Gefälle, der Abfall, steiler Abhang; (*of gallows*) die Falltür, (*Theat.*) *see* **drop-curtain**; (*coll.*) ***at the – of a hat,*** bei erster bester Gelegenheit; ***a – of 40 feet,*** ein Fall aus 12 Meter Höhe *or* aus einer Höhe von 12 Metern.
2. *v.t.* 1. (herab)tröpfeln *or* (herab)tropfen lassen; – ***a tear,*** eine Träne vergießen; 2. fallen lassen; senken, herablassen; werfen, gebären (*the young of beasts*); fällen, zu Fall bringen, zu Boden schlagen, niederschlagen; (*coll.*) einstellen, aufgeben; (*coll.*) – ***an acquaintance,*** eine Bekanntschaft fallenlassen; – ***anchor,*** den Anker auswerfen *or* ausbringen; ***the bill was dropped,*** der Antrag fiel durch; – ***a bird on the wing,*** einen Vogel im Flug herunterschießen; – ***bombs,*** Bomben abwerfen; (*coll.*) – ***a brick,*** einen groben Schnitzer machen; – ***a curts(e)y,*** einen Knicks machen; – ***one's eyes,*** die Augen senken *or* niederschlagen; (*Footb.*) – ***a goal,*** ein Tor durch Sprungtritt schießen *or* erzielen; – ***one's h's,*** das h nicht aussprechen; – ***a hint,*** einen Wink fallen lassen *or* von sich geben; (*coll.*) – ***it!*** laß das! hör' auf damit! – ***a letter in the box,*** einen Brief in den Briefkasten werfen; – ***me a line,*** lassen Sie mir ein paar Zeilen zukommen; – ***the matter,*** die S. fallenlassen; – ***money on s.th.,*** Geld bei etwas verlieren; – ***passengers,*** Passagiere absetzen; – ***the pilot,*** den Lotsen entlassen; – ***a stitch,*** eine Masche fallen lassen; – ***one's voice,*** die Stimme senken.
3. *v.i.* 1. tröpfeln, triefen; 2. herunterfallen, (herab)fallen; sinken, zurückgehen; sich senken (*as voice*), sich legen (*as wind*); niederfallen, umfallen, hinsinken; (*fig.*) aufhören, eingehen; ***so quiet that you could hear a pin –,*** mäuschenstill; ***be ready to –,*** zum Umfallen *or* Hinsinken müde sein; (*coll.*) – ***across,*** zufällig stoßen auf (*Acc.*); – ***asleep,*** in Schlaf sinken, einschlafen; (*Naut.*) – ***astern,*** achteraussacken, zurückbleiben; – ***away,*** allmählich abfallen; – ***back*** or ***behind,*** zurückfallen, zurückbleiben; – ***down,*** niederfallen; (*coll.*) – ***in,*** vorsprechen (***at,*** bei), einen unerwarteten Besuch machen (***on,*** *Dat.*); – ***in at his brother's*** or ***on his brother,*** bei seinem Bruder hereinschneien; – ***off,*** abtropfen; abfallen; (*coll.*) zurückgehen, sich zurückziehen, abnehmen; (*coll.*) einschlafen; (*coll.*) – ***on,*** anfahren, herfallen über (*Acc.*); – ***out,*** ausscheiden, sich zurückziehen (***of,*** von), nicht mehr mitmachen *or* daran teilnehmen; verschwinden, ausfallen, fortfallen.

drop|-annunciator, *s.* (*Tele.*) das Fallklappenbrett. **--curtain,** *s.* (*Theat.*) der Vorhang. **--forge,** *s.*

die Gesenkschmiede. **--forging,** *s.* das Gesenkschmieden; Gesenkschmiedestück. **--hammer,** *s.* das Hammerfallwerk, der Gesenkhammer. **--head,** *adj.* abklappbar, versenkbar. **--kick,** *s.* (*Footb.*) der Sprungtritt. **droplet** [–lit], *s.* das Tröpfchen. **drop-out,** *s.* (*Footb.*) der Sprungtritt aus dem Gedränge; (*coll. esp. Univ.*) Versager, Durchgefallene(r). **dropper,** *s. See* **dropping-bottle.**

dropping ['drɔpiŋ], *s.* das (Herab)tropfen, (Herab)tröpfeln; (Herab)fallen, Sinken; (*of bombs etc.*) Abwerfen; *pl.* der Mist, Dung, Tierexkremente (*pl.*); ***constant – wears the stone,*** stetes Tropfen höhlt den Stein. **dropping|-bottle,** *s.* (*Med.*) die Tropfflasche, das Tropfglas, der Tropfenzähler. **--fire,** *s.* (*Mil.*) unregelmäßiges Gewehrfeuer. **--zone,** *s.* (*Av.*) die Landezone.

drop|-scene, *s.* (*Theat.*) der Vorhang. **--shot,** *s.* (*Tenn.*) der Stoppball, kurzer Flugball. **--shutter,** *s.* (*Phot.*) die Fallscheibe.

dropsical ['drɔpsikl], *adj.* wassersüchtig. **dropsy,** *s.* die Wassersucht.

dros(h)ky ['drɔski ('drɔʃki)], *s.* die Droschke.

dross [drɔs], *s.* (*Metall.*) die Schlacke; (*fig.*) der Unrat, Abfall, Auswurf, die Spreu, wertloses Zeug.

drought [draut], *s.* die Dürre, Trockenheit, der Wassermangel; (*obs.*) Durst. **droughty,** *adj.* dürr, trocken; (*fig.*) durstig.

drove [drouv], **1.** *imperf. of* **drive. 2.** *s.* die Viehherde; (*fig.*) Herde, Menge. **drover,** *s.* der Viehtreiber.

drown [draun], **1.** *v.t.* ertränken, ersäufen; überströmen, überfluten, überschwemmen; (*fig.*) übertäuben, betäuben; überschlagen, übertönen (*sounds*); ersticken; ***be –ed,*** ertrinken, ersaufen; ***–ed by the noise,*** vom Lärm übertönt; ***like a –ed rat,*** pudelnaß; ***–ed in tears,*** in Tränen gebadet. **2.** *v.i.* ertrinken, ersaufen; ***she is –ing,*** sie ertrinkt. **drowning, 1.** *adj.* – *p.*, Ertrinkende(r). **2.** *s.* das Ertrinken.

drowse [drauz], **1.** *v.i.* schlummern, (dahin)dösen, schläfrig sein. **2.** *v.t.* schläfrig machen. **drowsiness,** *s.* die Schläfrigkeit. **drowsy,** *adj.* schläfrig, schlaftrunken; einschläfernd.

drub [drʌb], *v.t.* schlagen, prügeln; (*fig.*) ***– s.th. into him,*** ihm etwas einbleuen. **drubbing,** *s.* die Tracht Prügel; (*fig.*) Niederlage.

drudge [drʌdʒ], **1.** *s.* der Knecht, Sklave, Handlanger, Packesel, Kuli. **2.** *v.i.* (*fig.*) schuften, rackern, sich abplacken *or* schinden. **drudgery,** *s.* die Schufterei, Schinderei, Plackerei.

drug [drʌg], **1.** *s.* 1. die Apothekerware, Droge, das Arzneimittel; *pl.* pharmazeutische Präparate (*pl.*), Apothekerwaren (*pl.*); 2. das Narkotikum, Rauschgift; ***– addict,*** Rauschgiftsüchtige(r); ***– habit,*** die Rauschgiftsucht; 3. ***a – on*** or ***in the market,*** der Ladenhüter. **2.** *v.t.* betäuben; ***– wine,*** Wein verfälschen. **3.** *v.i.* Rauschgift nehmen.

drugget ['drʌgit], *s.* grober Wollstoff, grobes Gewebe; der Teppich, Läufer.

druggist ['drʌgist], *s.* der Drogist, Drogenhändler, Apotheker. **drugstore,** *s.* (*Am.*) der Drugstore.

Druid ['dru:id], *s.* der Druide. **Druidess,** *s.* die Druidin. **druidic(al)** [–'idik(l)], *adj.* druidisch; Druiden–. **Druidism,** *s.* das Druidentum.

drum [drʌm], **1.** *s.* 1. die Trommel; ***beat the –,*** die Trommel rühren, trommeln; ***with –s beating,*** unter Trommelschlag, mit klingendem Spiel; ***roll of –s,*** Trommelwirbel (*pl.*); 2. (*Anat.*) die Mittelohrhöhle; 2. (*Tech.*) Trommel, Spule, Walze, der Zylinder; das Trommelmagazin (*of machine-gun*); die Büchse, (zylindrischer) Behälter; 4. (*obs.*) die Abendgesellschaft; 5. (*Archit. obs.*) Säulentrommel, der Tambour. **2.** *v.i.* trommeln; (*fig.*) klopfen, pochen; klimpern (*on piano*); burren (*of partridges*), meckern (*of snipe*). **3.** *v.t.* trommeln auf (*Acc.*); ***– s.th. into his head*** or ***into him,*** ihm etwas einpauken; ***– out of,*** hinauswerfen *or* schimpflich ausstoßen aus; ***– up,*** zusammentrommeln; (*coll.*) (an)werben.

drum|-beat, *s.* der Trommelschlag. **–fire,** *s.* (*Mil.*) das Trommelfeuer. **–head,** *s.* das Trommelfell (*also Anat.*); ***– court-martial,*** das Standgericht; ***– service,*** der Feldgottesdienst. **--major,** *s.* der Tambourmajor. **drummer,** *s.* (*Mus.*) der Trommler, Schlagzeuger; (*Mil.*) Trommelschläger, Tambour. **drumstick,** *s.* der Trommelstock, Trommelschlegel.

drunk [drʌŋk], **1.** *p.p. of* **drink. 2.** *adj.* (*rarely attrib.*) betrunken; (*fig.*) trunken, berauscht (***with,*** von *or* vor (*Dat.*)); ***blind*** or ***dead –, – as a lord,*** sinnlos betrunken; ***get –,*** sich betrinken; ***– with joy,*** trunken vor Freude, freudetrunken. **3.** *s.* (*coll.*) Betrunkene(r), der Trunkenbold; (*Law*) Trunkenheitsfall. **drunkard** [–əd], *s.* der (Gewohnheits)trinker, Säufer, Trunkenbold, versoffener Kerl. **drunken,** *attrib. adj.* betrunken; trunksüchtig; ***– man,*** Betrunkene(r); ***– sleep,*** der Schlaf der Trunkenheit, Rausch; ***– song,*** das Zechlied. **drunkenness,** *s.* die Trunkenheit, der Rausch; die Trunksucht.

drupe [dru:p], *s.* die Steinfrucht.

dry [drai], **1.** *adj.* trocken, getrocknet; vertrocknet, ausgetrocknet, versiegt; dürr, ausgedörrt; (*Meteor.*) niederschlagsfrei, regenarm, regenlos; (*of wine*) herb; (*coll.*) durstig; (*fig.*) (*of a th.*) nackt, nüchtern, ledern, langweilig, schmucklos, (*of a p.*) derb, humorlos, stur, gleichgültig, teilnahm(s)los; (*coll.*) unter Alkoholverbot, trocken(gelegt); (*as a cow*) trockenstehend, milchlos, gelt; ***– as a bone,*** knochentrocken; ***– bread,*** Brot ohne Aufstrich; ***– battery*** or ***cell,*** das Trockenelement; ***– cough*** trockener Husten; ***the cow is –,*** die Kuh steht trocken; ***– crust,*** das Stück trockenes Brot; ***– dock,*** das Trockendock; (*fig.*) ***as – as dust,*** höchst langweilig; ***with – eyes,*** ohne Rührung, ungerührt; ***– facts,*** nüchterne *or* nackte *or* ungeschminkte Tatsachen; (*coll.*) ***go –,*** das Alkoholverbot einführen; ***– goods,*** Schnittwaren, Kurzwaren (*pl.*); ***high and –,*** (*Naut.*) auf dem Trockenen, gestrandet; (*fig.*) auf dem toten Gleis; ***– humour,*** trockener *or* sarkastischer Humor; ***– measure,*** das Trocken(hohl)maß; ***– nurse,*** die Kinderfrau, Säuglingsschwester; (*Phot.*) ***– plate,*** die Trockenplatte; ***– point,*** die Kaltnadel; Kaltnadelradierung; das Kaltnadelverfahren; ***– rot,*** die Trockenfäule, (*fig.*) der Verfall; ***run –,*** (*v.i.*) leer werden; (*v.t.*) leerlaufen lassen; ***– shampoo,*** das Trockenschampun *or* –shampoo; ***– spell,*** die Trockenperiode. **2.** *v.t.* (ab)trocknen; (*fruit etc.*) dörren; ***– one's hands,*** sich (*Dat.*) die Hände abtrocknen; ***– one's eyes*** or ***tears,*** die Tränen trocknen; ***– o.s.,*** sich abtrocknen; ***– up,*** auftrocknen (*s.th. spilt*). **3.** *v.i.* trocken werden, trocknen; ***– out,*** vertrocknen, austrocknen; ***– up,*** eintrocknen, vertrocknen; (*coll.*) versiegen, steckenbleiben; (*sl.*) (endlich) still sein, das Maul halten.

dryad ['draiæd], *s.* die Dryade, Waldnymphe.

dry|-as-dust, 1. *attrib. adj.* (*fig.*) pedantisch, langweilig. **2.** *s.* trockene(r) Stubengelehrte(r). **--casting,** *s.* (*Metall.*) der Sandguß, Masselguß. **--clean,** *v.t.* chemisch reinigen. **--cleaning,** *s.* chemische Reinigung, die Trockenreinigung. **--cure,** *v.t.* dörren (*fruit*), einsalzen (*meat*).

dryer ['draiə], *s. See* **drier, 1.**

dry|-eyed, *adj.* trockenen Auges. **--fly,** *s.* künstliche Fliege (*fishing*).

drying ['draiiŋ], **1.** *adj.* trocknend, Trocken–. **2.** *s.* das Trocknen, (*of fruit*) Dörren. **drying|-agent,** *s.* das Trockenmittel. **– ground,** *s.* der Trockenplatz. **– kiln,** *s.* der Trockenofen. **– loft,** *s.* der Trockenboden. **– oil,** *s.* der Ölfirnis. **– room,** *s.* der Trockenraum.

dryly ['draili], *adv.* (*fig.*) kühl, gleichgültig; sarkastisch. **dryness,** *s.* 1. die Trockenheit; Dürre; 2. (*fig.*) Trockenheit, Kühlheit, Teilnahm(s)losigkeit; Langweiligkeit. **dry|-salter,** *s.* der Drogenhändler, Drogist. **--shod,** *adj.* trockenen Fußes. **--wall,** *s.* die Trockenmauer.

dual ['djuəl], **1.** *s.* (*Gram.*) der Dual(is), die Zweizahl. **2.** *adj.* doppelt, zweifach, Zwei–; ***– alliance,*** der Zweibund; ***– carriage-way,*** doppelte Fahrbahn; (*Motor., Av.*) ***– control,*** die Doppelsteuerung; ***– monarchy,*** die Doppelmonarchie;

(*Gram.*) – ***number***, *see* **1. dualism,** *s.* (*Phil., Pol.*) der Dualismus; die Zwei(geteilt)heit, Doppelheit. **duality** [-'æliti], *s.* die Zweiheit. **dual-purpose,** *adj.* Mehrzweck-.

dub [dʌb], *v.t.* 1. (zum Ritter) schlagen *or* ernennen; (*coll.*) (be)nennen, betiteln, titulieren; 2. (*Tech.*) schmieren, schlichten (*leather*), zurichten, glätten (*wood*); 3. (*Films*) nachsynchronisieren. **dubbin(g),** *s.* das Lederfett, die Lederschmiere. **dubbing,** *s.* 1. der Ritterschlag; die Benennung, Titulierung; 2. (*Films*) Nachsynchronisierung, das Überspielen.

dubiety [dju'baiiti], *s.* die Ungewißheit, Unbestimmtheit, Unklarheit, Unsicherheit, Zweifelhaftigkeit. **dubious** ['dju:biəs], *adj.* ungewiß, unbestimmt, unklar, unsicher, zweifelhaft, zweideutig; – ***character,*** verdächtiger Charakter; ***be – about,*** im Zweifel sein über (*Acc.*). **dubiousness,** *s. See* **dubiety. dubitation** [-'teiʃən], *s.* das Zögern, Schwanken; der Zweifel, die Unentschlossenheit. **dubitative** ['dju:bitətiv], *adj.* zögernd, zweifelnd, unschlüssig.

ducal [dju:kl], *adj.* herzoglich, Herzogs-.

ducat ['dʌkit], *s.* der Dukaten.

duchess ['dʌtʃis], *s.* die Herzogin. **duchy,** *s.* das Herzogtum.

[1]**duck** [dʌk], *s.* 1. die Ente; ***play at –s and drakes,*** Hüpfsteine *or* (Wasser)jungern werfen; (*fig.*) ***play –s and drakes with, make –s and drakes of,*** verschleudern, zum Fenster hinauswerfen; (*coll.*) ***like water off a –'s back,*** ohne die geringste Wirkung (zu haben); (*coll.*) ***like a – in a thunderstorm,*** verblüfft, bestürzt, platt; (*fig.*) ***lame –,*** (*Comm.*) Zahlungsunfähige(r), (*coll.*) der Versager, die Niete; krankes Huhn, der Pechvogel; (*coll.*) ***in two shakes of a –'s tail,*** im Handumdrehen; ***he's taken to it like a – (takes) to water,*** er ist dabei in seinem Element; 2. (*coll.*) der Liebling, das Schätzchen; 3. (*sl. Crick.*) die Null.

[2]**duck,** *s.* das Segeltuch, Schiertuch; *pl.* die Segeltuchhose.

[3]**duck, 1.** *v.i.* sich ducken *or* bücken; (unter)tauchen; (*Am. coll.*) – ***out,*** auskneifen, türmen, verduften. **2.** *v.t.* ducken (*one's head etc.*); (ein)tauchen; (*coll.*) sich ducken vor (*Dat.*) (*a blow*), sich drücken von (*a problem*).

duck|bill, -billed platypus, *s.* (*Zool.*) das Schnabeltier. **-board,** *s.* (*oft. pl.*) das Laufbrett, der Holzrost, Bretterrost. **– egg,** *s.* das Entenei.

ducking ['dʌkiŋ], *s.* das (Unter)tauchen, Eintauchen, (*Naut.*) die Taufe; ***get a –,*** tüchtig naß werden; ***give him a –,*** ihn untertauchen; (*Hist.*) ***– stool,*** der Tauchstuhl.

duckling ['dʌkliŋ], *s.* das Entchen, Entlein. **duck-pond,** *s.* der Ententeich.

duck's egg, *s. See* [1]**duck.**

duck|-shooting, *s.* die Entenjagd. **--shot,** *s.* der Entenschrot. **-weed,** *s.* (*Bot.*) die Wasserlinse, Entengrütze.

ducky ['dʌki], **1.** *adj.* (*sl.*) lieb(lich), niedlich. **2.** *s. See* [1]**duck** (*coll.*).

duct [dʌkt], *s.* (*Bot., Zool., Anat.*) der Gang, Kanal; die (Leitungs)röhre, Leitung.

ductile ['dʌktail], *adj.* dehnbar, streckbar; (*fig.*) fügsam, geschmeidig, lenksam, biegsam. **ductility** [-'tiliti], *s.* die Dehnbarkeit, Streckbarkeit; Biegsamkeit, Fügsamkeit.

ductless ['dʌktlis], *adj.* ohne Kanal; (*Anat.*) – ***glands,*** Hormondrüsen (*pl.*).

dud [dʌd], **1.** *s.* (*Artil.*) der Blindgänger; (*sl.*) Versager, Fehlschlag, die Niete; *pl.* (*sl.*) Klamotten (*pl.*), Siebensachen (*pl.*). **2.** *adj.* (*sl.*) unbrauchbar, wertlos; – ***stock,*** Ladenhüter (*pl.*).

dude [dju:d], *s.* (*Am. sl.*) der Geck, Gigerl.

dudgeon ['dʌdʒən], *s.* der Groll, Unwille, Ärger; ***be in high – about,*** es sehr übelnehmen.

due [dju:], **1.** *adj.* 1. gebührend, geziemend, gehörig, angemessen, hinreichend; vorschriftsmäßig, passend, recht, richtig, genau; ***after – consideration,*** nach reiflicher Überlegung; ***in – course,*** zur rechten Zeit, zu seiner *or* gehöriger Zeit; ***in – form,*** vorschriftsmäßig; ***take – note,*** gehörige Notiz nehmen; – ***respect,*** gebührende Hochachtung; ***his – reward,*** der ihm gebührende Lohn; ***in – time,*** zur rechten Zeit; ***it is – to him,*** es gebührt ihm, es kommt ihm zu; (*coll.*) es ist ihm zuzuschreiben, ihm verdanken wir (es); ***honour to whom honour is –,*** Ehre wem Ehre gebührt; 2. (*Comm.*) sofort zahlbar, fällig; – ***bill,*** die Promesse, Schuldverschreibung; – ***date,*** der Fälligkeitstermin, Verfallstag; ***when –,*** zur Verfallszeit, bei Verfall; ***become*** or ***fall –,*** fällig werden; 3. (*of time*) fällig; ***the train is – (in) at 8 o'clock,*** der Zug soll um 8 Uhr ankommen; ***it is already –,*** es müßte schon da sein; (*coll.*) – ***for retirement,*** reif zur Pensionierung; 4. (*coll.*) – ***to,*** infolge von (*or Gen.*), wegen (*Gen.*), veranlaßt durch, zurückführbar auf (*Acc.*), zuzuschreiben(d) (*Dat.*); (*coll.*) – ***to carelessness,*** auf Nachlässigkeit zurückzuführen, eine Folge *or* infolge der Nachlässigkeit. **2.** *adv.* gerade, genau, direkt; – ***east,*** gerade östlich, genau nach Osten. **3.** *s.* das Recht, (rechtmäßiger) Anspruch *or* Anteil, zustehender *or* gebührender Lohn, das Zustehende, Gebührende; *pl.* Gebühren, Abgaben (*pl.*); (*coll.*) der Vereinsbeitrag; ***give the devil his –,*** selbst dem Teufel Gerechtigkeit widerfahren lassen; ***give everyone his –,*** jedem das Seine geben *or* lassen; (*coll.*) ***pay one's –s,*** seinen Verpflichtungen nachkommen; (*Naut.*) ***for a full –,*** vollständig, vollkommen.

duel ['djuəl], **1.** *s.* der Zweikampf, das Duell; ***student's –,*** die Mensur; ***fight a –,*** sich duellieren, (*Studs. sl.*) auf die Mensur gehen. **2.** *v.i.* sich duellieren; (*Studs. sl.*) pauken. **duelling,** *s.* das Duellieren, (*sl.*) Pauken. **duellist,** *s.* der Duellant, (*sl.*) Paukant.

duenna [dju'enə], *s.* die Anstandsdame.

duet [dju'et], *s.* das Duett, Duo; ***play a –,*** ein Duo spielen, (*piano*) vierhändig spielen.

duffel [dʌfl], *s.* der Düffel, dickes Wolltuch. **duffel|-bag,** *s.* der Seesack. **--coat,** *s.* der Düffelmantel.

duffer ['dʌfə], *s.* (*coll.*) der Dummkopf, Stümper.

duffle, *s. See* **duffel.**

[1]**dug** [dʌg], *s.* die Zitze.

[2]**dug,** *imperf., p.p. of* **dig.**

dugong ['du:gɔŋ], *s.* (*Zool.*) die Seekuh.

dug-out, *s.* (*Mil.*) der Unterstand, Bunker, (*sl.*) Heldenkeller; – (***canoe***), der Einbaum.

duke [dju:k], *s.* der Herzog. **dukedom,** *s.* das Herzogtum; die Herzogswürde.

dulcet ['dʌlsit], *adj.* wohlklingend, lieblich; beruhigend, lind. **dulcify** [-fai], *v.t.* versüßen; (*fig.*) besänftigen, beschwichtigen.

dulcimer ['dʌlsimə], *s.* (*Mus.*) das Hackbrett.

dull [dʌl], **1.** *adj.* (*of a p.*) dumm, schwer von Begriff(en), stumpfsinnig, beschränkt; schwerfällig, träge; (*of a th.*) dumpf (*as pain or sound*), stumpf (*as a knife*), trübe (*as weather*), fad(e), langweilig (*as a book*), getrübt (*as spirits*), schwach (*as light or fire*), matt, düster (*as colour*), leblos, glanzlos (*as eyes*); flau, still, stockend, lustlos (*as trade*); ***as – as ditchwater,*** höchst langweilig. **2.** *v.t.* stumpf machen (*a knife*), abstumpfen, mattieren (*a colour*), trüben (*eyes etc.*), betäuben, mildern (*pain*).

dullard ['dʌləd], *s.* der Einfaltspinsel, Dummkopf. **dullish,** *adj.* etwas *or* ziemlich dumm *or* langweilig. **dullness,** *s.* die Stumpfheit; Stumpfsinnigkeit, Dummheit, der Stumpfsinn; die Schwerfälligkeit, Trägheit, Mattigkeit, (*of colour*) Mattheit, Düsterheit, Glanzlosigkeit, (*of weather*) Trübheit; (*of sound*) Dumpfheit; (*of trade*) Flauheit, Flaute, Stagnation.

duly ['dju:li], *adv. See* **due**; pünktlich, rechtzeitig; gehörig, ordnungsgemäß, vorschriftsmäßig.

dumb [dʌm], *adj.* 1. stumm; ***deaf and –,*** taubstumm; – ***animals*** or ***brutes*** or ***creatures*** or ***friends,*** stumme Geschöpfe; ***strike –,*** sprachlos machen, zum Schweigen bringen; 2. (*sl.*) dumm, blöd, doof. **dumb|-bell,** *s.* 1. (*Spt.*) die Hantel; 2. (*sl.*) der

Dummkopf. **-found** [-faund], *v.t.* sprachlos machen, verblüffen. **-founded,** *adj.* verblüfft, sprachlos. **dumbness,** *s.* die Stummheit. **dumb|-show,** *s.* stummes Spiel, das Gebärdenspiel, die Pantomime. **--waiter,** *s.* der Drehtisch, stummer Diener; (*Am.*) der Speiseaufzug.

dummy ['dʌmi], **1.** *s.* 1. (*Theat.*) stumme Person, der (die) Statist(in); (*fig.*) der Strohmann (*also Cards*); die Kleiderpuppe, Schaufensterpuppe; Attrappe, leere Packung; 2. das Lutschgummi, der (Gummi)lutscher, Schnuller (*for babies*); 3. (*Cards*) das Whistspiel mit Strohmann. **2.** *adj.* unecht, (*Mil.*) Schein-; – ***cartridge,*** die Exerzierpatrone; – ***run,*** die Probefahrt, Testfahrt; Testreihe, Testfolge.

dump [dʌmp], **1.** *s.* 1. dumpfer Schlag, der Plumps, Bums; 2. Abfallhaufen, Schutthaufen, (Müll)abladeplatz, die Schutthalde; Sammelstelle, Abladestelle; (*Min.*) (Abraum)halde; (*Mil.*) das Lager, Depot, der Lagerplatz, Park; (*sl.*) verwahrloster Ort. **2.** *v.t.* abladen, auskippen; (*coll.*) hinfallen lassen, hinplumpsen, hinwerfen, absetzen, abstellen; (*Mil.*) stapeln, lagern; (*Comm.*) verschleudern, zu Schleuderpreisen absetzen (*surplus goods etc.*). **dump-cart,** *s.* (*Am.*) der Kippwagen. **dumper,** *s.* 1. der Schmutzkonkurrent; 2. *See* **dump-cart. dumping,** *s.* das (Schutt)abladen; (*Comm.*) der Schleuderverkauf (ans Ausland), das Dumping. **dumping-ground,** *s.* der Abladeplatz, die Schutthalde.

dumpling ['dʌmpliŋ], *s.* der Kloß, Knödel.

dumps [dʌmps], *pl.* (*coll.*) trübe Stimmung, die Niedergeschlagenheit; schlechte Laune; (*coll.*) (***down***) ***in the*** –, niedergeschlagen, trübsinnig; schlechtgelaunt, verdrießlich.

dump| truck, *s. See* **--cart.**

dumpy ['dʌmpi], *adj.* (*coll.*) untersetzt, rundlich.

[1]**dun** [dʌn], *adj.* schwarzbraun, graubraun; (*Poet.*) dunkel.

[2]**dun, 1.** *s.* drängender Gläubiger; der Mahnbrief, die Zahlungsaufforderung. **2.** *v.t.* ungestüm mahnen, drängen, (*sl.*) treten; belästigen, bedrängen, plagen (***with,*** mit); ***dunning letter,*** der Mahnbrief.

dunce [dʌns], *s.* der Dummkopf; ***–'s cap,*** die Narrenkappe.

dunderhead ['dʌndəhed], *s.* (*coll.*) der Dummkopf. **dunderheaded,** *adj.* (*coll.*) dumm.

dune [dju:n], *s.* die Düne.

dung [dʌŋ], **1.** *s.* der Dünger, Dung, Mist. **2.** *v.t., v.i.* düngen.

dungaree [dʌŋgə'ri:], *s.* grobes Kattunzeug; *pl.* der Arbeitsanzug, das Überkleid.

dung-beetle, *s.* der Mistkäfer.

dungeon ['dʌndʒən], *s.* das (Burg)verlies, der Kerker.

dung|-heap, --hill, *s.* der Misthaufen.

dunk [dʌŋk], *v.t.* (*coll.*) eintauchen (*in,* in (*Acc.*)).

Dunkirk [dʌn'kə:k], *s.* (*Geog.*) Dünkirchen (*n.*).

duo ['dju:ou], *s.* (*pl.* **-s**) das Duett. **duo|decimal,** *adj.* duodekadisch, duodezimal. **-decimo,** *s.* das Duodez(format); *pl.* das Buch im Duodezformat.

duodenal [djuə'di:nl], *adj.* (*Anat.*) Duodenal-, Zwölffingerdarm-. **duodenary,** *adj.* zwölffach, deodekadisch. **duodenitis** [-'naitis], *s.* (*Med.*) die Zwölffingerdarmentzündung. **duodenum,** *s.* (*Anat.*) der Zwölffingerdarm.

dupability [dju:pə'biliti], *s.* die Leichtgläubigkeit, Vertrauensseligkeit. **dupable,** *adj.* leicht anzuführen(d), vertrauensselig, leichtgläubig. **dupe, 1.** *s.* Betrogene(r), Angeführte(r), Gefoppte(r); Leichtgläubige(r), der Gimpel; ***be the – of,*** sich anführen *or* sich täuschen lassen von, hereinfallen auf (*Acc.*). **2.** *v.t.* betrügen, überlisten, übertölpeln, hinters Licht führen, anführen; ***be –d by,*** see ***be the – of.*** **dupery,** *s.* die Täuschung, Überlistung, Übertölpelung.

duple [dju:pl], *adj.* (*Mus.*) – ***time,*** der Zweiertakt. **duplex** [-eks], *adj.* doppelt, zweifach; – ***burner,*** der Doppelbrenner; – ***telegraphy,*** die Duplex-Telegraphie; – ***turret,*** der Zwillingsturm.

duplicate, 1. ['dju:plikit], *adj.* doppelt, zweifach, Doppel-; genau gleich, Duplikat-, Nach- (*as key etc.*). **2.** [-kit], *s.* das Duplikat, die Kopie, Abschrift; das Seitenstück; ***in*** –, in doppelter Ausführung, in zwei Exemplaren. **3.** [-keit], *v.t.* verdoppeln; kopieren, vervielfältigen, im Duplikat herstellen. **duplication** [-'keiʃən], *s.* die Verdopp(e)lung; Vervielfältigung. **duplicator** [-keitə], *s.* der Vervielfältigungsapparat.

duplicity [dju:'plisiti], *s.* die Zweiheit, Zweifältigkeit, Doppelheit; (*fig.*) Falschheit, Doppelzüngigkeit.

durability [djuərə'biliti], *s.* die Dauer(haftigkeit), Beständigkeit. **durable** ['djuərəbl], *adj.* dauerhaft, beständig, haltbar. **durableness,** *s. See* **durability.**

duralumin [dju'ræljəmin], *s.* das Dural.

durance ['djuərəns], *s.* (*Poet.*) der Gewahrsam, die Haft; (*Poet.*) ***in – vile,*** hinter Schloß und Riegel; ***keep in*** –, gefangen halten.

duration [djuə'reiʃən], *s.* die (Fort)dauer, Zeitdauer; – ***of life,*** die Lebensdauer; ***of short*** –, von kurzer Dauer; (*coll.*) ***for the*** –, bis Kriegsende. **durative** ['djuərətiv], **1.** *adj.* dauernd; (*Gram.*) Dauer-. **2.** *s.* (*Gram.*) die Dauerform.

duress [dju'res], *s.* 1. der Zwang, Druck, die Nötigung; ***act under*** –, unter Zwang handeln; 2. (*Law*) die Haft, Freiheitsberaubung.

during ['djuəriŋ], *prep.* während (*Gen.*), im Laufe von *or* (*Gen.*); (*Law*) – ***Her Majesty's pleasure,*** auf Lebenszeit.

durst [də:st], (*Poet.*) *see* **dare.**

dusk [dʌsk], **1.** *adj.* (*Poet.*) düster, dämmerig, dunkel, finster. **2.** *s.* die (Abend)dämmerung, das Halbdunkel, Zwielicht; ***after*** –, nach Einbruch der Dunkelheit. **duskiness,** *s.* dunkle Färbung. **dusky,** *adj.* schwärzlich; düster, trüb.

dust [dʌst], **1.** *s.* der Staub; Kehricht, Müll, Schutt; (*coll.*) ***bite*** or ***kiss the*** –, ins Gras beißen; ***fall to*** –, zerfallen; ***fine as*** –, staubfein; ***gather*** –, staubig werden; (*fig.*) ***in the*** –, gedemütigt; ***make*** or ***raise*** or (*sl.*) ***kick up a*** –, Staub aufwirbeln, Lärm machen; ***lay the*** –, den Staub dämpfen; ***reduce to*** –, zerstäuben; ***shake the – off one's feet,*** voll Entrüstung fortgehen; ***throw – in his eyes,*** ihm Sand in die Augen streuen. **2.** *v.t.* 1. abstauben, abwischen; ausklopfen, ausbürsten (*clothes*); 2. bestäuben, bestreuen (*a th. with powder*).

dust|-bin, *s.* der Aschenkasten, Müllkasten, Mülleimer. **--cart,** *s.* der Müllwagen. **--cloth,** *s.* die Staubdecke, der Überzug (*for furniture*). **--coat,** *s.* der Staubmantel. **--cover,** *s.* der Schutzumschlag (*on books*). **duster,** *s.* das Staubtuch, der Wischlappen. **dustiness,** *s.* die Staubigkeit, Bestaubtheit. **dusting,** *s.* 1. das Staubwischen, Abstauben; 2. (*coll.*) (*also* ***--down***) die Tracht Prügel. **dust|-jacket,** *s. See* **--cover.** **-man** [-mən], *s.* der Müllfuhrmann. **-pan,** *s.* die Kehrichtschaufel. **--proof,** *adj.* staubdicht. **--storm,** *s.* der Staubsturm. **dusty,** *adj.* staubig, bestaubt, voll(er) Staub; staubfarben, schmutzig; (*sl.*) ***not so*** –, nicht so schlimm, nicht zu verachten.

Dutch [dʌtʃ], **1.** *adj.* holländisch, niederländisch. **2.** *adv.* (*only in*) ***go*** –, getrennte Kasse machen. **3.** *s.* 1. das Holländisch, Niederländisch (*language*); (*coll.*) ***double*** –, das Kauderwelsch; 2. ***the*** –, die Holländer (*pl.*). **Dutch| auction,** *s.* die Auktion mit Abschlag. **– courage,** *s.* (*coll.*) angetrunkener Mut. **-man** [-mən], *s.* der Holländer, Niederländer; (*coll.*) ***or I'm a*** –, oder ich will Hans heißen. **– oven,** *s.* das Röstblech. **– uncle,** *s.* (*only in*) ***talk like a – uncle,*** deutlich seine Meinung sagen. **– ware,** *s.* das Delfter Geschirr. **-woman,** *s.* die Holländerin, Niederländerin.

duteous ['dju:tiəs], *adj.* pflichtbewußt, gewissenhaft; *see also* **dutiful. dutiable** [-iəbl], *adj.* zollpflichtig, steuerpflichtig. **dutiful,** *adj.* pflichtgetreu, gehorsam; ehrerbietig.

duty ['dju:ti], *s.* 1. die Pflicht, Schuldigkeit, Verpflichtung (*to(wards)*, gegen(über)); Ehrerbietung; *do one's – by him,* seine Pflicht an ihm tun; *in – bound,* pflichtschuldig, von Rechts wegen, pflichtgemäß; *– call,* der Pflichtbesuch; *neglect of –,* die Pflichtverletzung, das Pflichtversäumnis; 2. der Dienst; *do – for,* vertreten (*a p.*), (*fig.*) dienen als (*a th.*); *tour of –,* die Dienstzeit; *be off –,* dienstfrei haben, nicht im Dienst sein; *officer on –,* Diensttuender *or* diensthabender Offizier; *be on –,* Dienst haben; *go on –,* in den Dienst gehen; 3. (*Comm.*) die Gebühr, Abgabe, Auflage, Steuer, der Zoll; *pay – on goods,* Waren versteuern *or* verzollen; *ad valorem –,* der Wertzoll; *customs –,* der Einfuhrzoll; *stamp –,* die Stempelgebühr; *transit –,* der Durchgangszoll; *– off,* unverzollt; *– paid,* verzollt, versteuert; *liable to –,* zollpflichtig; 4. (*Tech.*) der Nutzeffekt, die Nutzleistung.

duty|-free, *adj.* zollfrei, steuerfrei, abgabefrei; *– goods,* das Freigut. **– station,** *s.* der Dienstort.

duumvir [dju'ʌmvə], *s.* der Duumvir. **duumvirate** [–rit], *s.* das Duumvirat.

dwarf [dwɔ:f], **1.** *s.* der (die) Zwerg(in). **2.** *adj.* (*Bot.*) Zwerg–. **3.** *v.t.* im Wachstum hindern; (*fig.*) klein(er) erscheinen lassen, in den Schatten stellen. **dwarfed,** *adj.* verkümmert, verkrüppelt, zusammengeschrumpft. **dwarfish,** *adj.* zwerg(en)haft, zwergig.

dwell [dwel], *irr.v.i.* wohnen; bleiben, verweilen, sich aufhalten; (*fig.*) *– (up)on,* verweilen bei, näher eingehen auf (*Acc.*); bestehen *or* Nachdruck legen auf (*Acc.*); brüten *or* nachdenken über (*Acc.*); *– upon a syllable,* eine Silbe anhalten *or* dehnen. **dweller,** *s.* der (die) Bewohner(in). **dwelling,** *s.* die Wohnung, Behausung; der Wohnsitz, Aufenthalt. **dwelling|-house,** *s.* das Wohnhaus. **–-place,** *s.* der Wohnort, Aufenthaltsort.

dwelt [dwelt], *imperf., p.p. of* **dwell.**

Dwina ['dwi:nə], *s.* (*Geog.*) *Northern –* die Dwina; *Southern –,* die Düna.

dwindle [dwɪndl], *v.i.* abnehmen, schwinden, sinken, heruntergehen, zusammenschrumpfen, einschrumpfen; entarten, ausarten, verfallen (*into,* zu); *– away,* dahinschwinden.

dyad ['daiæd], *s.* das Paar, die Zweiheit; (*Mus.*) der Zweiklang; (*Chem.*) die Dyade.

dye [dai], **1.** *v.t.* färben; *– (s.th.) another colour,* umfärben; *– in the grain* or *wool,* im Rohzustand *or* in der Wolle färben; (*fig.*) *–d-in-the-wool,* von echtem Schrot und Korn, unverfälscht. **2.** *v.i.* sich färben (lassen). **3.** *s.* der Farbstoff, die Farbe; (*fig.*) Tönung, Färbung; *fast –,* haltbare *or* echte Farbe; *a rogue of the deepest –,* ein Schurke von der übelsten Sorte. **dye-house,** *s.* die Färberei. **dyeing,** *s.* das Färben; Färbereigewerbe. **dyer,** *s.* der Färber. **dyer's|-broom,** *s.* (*Bot.*) der Färberginster. **–-weed,** *s.* (*Bot.*) der Wau. **dyestuffs,** *pl.* Farbestoffe (*pl.*).

dying ['daiiŋ], **1.** *pres.p. of* **die. 2.** *adj.* sterbend; (*fig.*) ersterbend, verhallend; *be –,* im Sterben liegen; *the –,* die Sterbenden; *– bed,* das Sterbebett, Totenbett; *till his – day,* bis zu seinem Todestag; *his – wish,* sein letzter Wunsch; *– words,* letzte Worte, Worte auf dem Sterbebett. **3.** *s.* das Sterben.

dyke, *s. See* **dike.**

dynamic(al) [dai'næmik(l)], *adj.* dynamisch; (*fig.*) wirksam, kräftig. **dynamics,** *pl.* (*sing. constr.*) die Dynamik; (*fig.*) das Kräftespiel. **dynamism** ['dainəmizm], *s.* (*Phil.*) der Dynamismus; (*fig.*) die Dynamik, das Dynamische.

dynamite ['dainəmait], **1.** *s.* das Dynamit. **2.** *v.t.* mit Dynamit sprengen.

dynamo ['dainəmou], *s.* der Dynamo, die Dynamomaschine; (*Cycl.*) Lichtmaschine. **dynamometer** [–'mɔmitə], *s.* der Kraftmesser.

dynast ['dinæst], *s.* der Herrscher. **dynastic** [–'næstik], *adj.* dynastisch. **dynasty** ['dinəsti], *s.* das Herrschergeschlecht, Herrscherhaus, die Dynastie.

dyne [dain], *s.* (*Phys.*) das Zentimetergramm, die Krafteinheit, das Dyn.

dysenteric [disən'terik], *adj.* ruhrartig, Ruhr–; ruhrkrank. **dysentery** ['disəntri], *s.* (*Med.*) die Ruhr.

dyspepsia [dis'pepsiə], *s.* die Verdauungsstörung. **dyspeptic, 1.** *adj.* magenschwach, magenkrank; (*fig.*) mißgestimmt, mürrisch. **2.** *s.* der Dyspeptiker.

dyspnoea [dis'pniə], *s.* die Atembeschwerde, Atemnot, Kurzatmigkeit.

E

E, e [i:], *s.* das E, e; (*Mus.*) *E flat,* das Es, es; *E major,* E-Dur; *E minor,* e-Moll; *E sharp,* das Eis, eis. (*See Index of Abbreviations.*)

each [i:tʃ], **1.** *adj.* jede(r, –s) einzelne; *– one, see* **2**; *– way,* auf Gewinn beziehungsweise Placierung (*betting*). **2.** *pron.* (ein) jeder *or* jedes, (eine) jede; *– and all,* jeder einzelne; *– and every,* all und jeder; *they deceive – other,* jeder täuscht den anderen; *they love – other,* sie lieben sich; *they help – other,* sie helfen einander. **3.** *adv. a shilling –,* je ein Schilling, ein Schilling pro Person, ein Schilling das Stück; *he gave us – 2 marks,* er gab uns je 2 Mark.

eager ['i:gə], *adj.* eifrig; begierig (*for,* nach), erpicht (auf (*Acc.*)); *– for knowledge,* wißbegierig; *be – for news,* ungeduldig auf Nachricht warten. **eagerly,** *adv.* begierig, gespannt, ungeduldig. **eagerness,** *s.* der Eifer, heftiges Verlangen, die Begierde; Spannung, Ungeduld.

eagle [i:gl], *s.* der Adler. **eagle|-eyed,** *adj.* adleräugig, scharfsichtig. **–-owl,** *s.* (*Orn.*) der Uhu (*Bubo bubo*). **eaglet** [–lit], *s.* junger Adler.

eagre ['i:gə], *s.* die Flutwelle, Springflut.

[1]**ear** [iə], *s.* die Ähre.

[2]**ear,** *s.* (*Anat.*) das Ohr, (*Mus.*) Gehör; der Henkel; das Öhr, die Öse; *be all –(s),* ganz Ohr sein; *an – for music,* ein musikalisches Gehör; *not believe one's –s,* es nicht für möglich halten, seinen Ohren nicht trauen; *bring s.th. about his –s,* ihm etwas auf den Hals laden; *my –s are burning,* mir klingen die Ohren; *by –,* nach dem Gehör; *come* or *get to his –s,* ihm zu Ohren kommen; *fall on deaf –s,* taube Ohren finden; *give –,* aufmerksam zuhören (*to, Dat.*); *give one's –s for,* kein Opfer scheuen um; *have a good –,* feines Gehör haben; *have a quick –,* scharfes Gehör haben; *have his –,* seine Aufmerksamkeit besitzen, sein Vertrauen genießen; (*coll.*) *have one's – to the ground,* auf dem laufenden sein; *in (at) one – and out (at) the other,* zu einem Ohr hinein und zum anderen wieder hinaus; *lend an – to him,* ihn anhören, auf ihn hören, ihm Gehör schenken; *over head and –s,* ganz und gar, vollkommen, restlos; befangen (*in,* in (*Dat.*)); *prick up one's –s,* die Ohren spitzen; *send him away with a flea in his –,* ihm gehörig den Kopf waschen; *set (them) by the –s,* (sie) gegen einander hetzen; *turn a deaf – to,* taub sein gegen, taube Ohren haben für; *up to the –s,* bis über die Ohren; *just a word in your –,* ein schnelles Wort im Vertrauen.

ear|-ache, *s.* der Ohrenschmerz, das Ohrenreißen. **–-drops,** *pl.* das Ohrgehänge. **–drum,** *s.* das Trommelfell. **eared** [iəd], *adj.* mit Ohren *or* Henkel (versehen); *lop-–,* mit Hängeohren; *quick-–,* von scharfem Gehör.

earing ['iəriŋ], *s.* (*Naut.*) der Nockbändsel, das Nockhorn.

earl [ə:l], *s.* der Graf. **earldom** [–dəm], *s.* die Grafschaft; Grafenwürde.

earlier [ˈə:liə], **1.** *adj.* früher. **2.** *adv.* früher, zuvor, vorher. **earliest** [–iist], **1.** *adj.* frühest; (*Comm.*) ***at your – convenience,*** so bald wie möglich, umgehend. **2.** *adv.* frühestens, am frühesten; ***at the –,*** frühestens. **earliness,** *s.* die Frühzeitigkeit, Frühe.

Earl Marshal, *s.* königlicher Zeremonienmeister.

early [ˈə:li], **1.** *adj.* früh, (früh)zeitig; ***– bird*** or ***riser,*** der Frühaufsteher; (*Prov.*) ***the – bird catches the worm,*** wer zuerst kommt, mahlt zuerst; ***– closing,*** früher Ladenschluß; (*coll.*) ***it is still – days,*** der Erfolg bleibt abzuwarten, (*sl.*) abwarten und Tee trinken! ***in his – days,*** in seiner Jugend; ***– death,*** vorzeitiger Tod; ***keep – hours,*** früh schlafen gehen; ***– history,*** die Frühgeschichte; ***in – life,*** in der Jugendzeit; ***– vegetable,*** das Frühgemüse; ***– warning,*** die Vorwarnung; ***– warning system,*** das Vorwarnsystem. **2.** *adv.* früh, (früh)zeitig; beizeiten, zu früh; ***– in the day,*** früh am Tag; ***– in the morning,*** früh morgen; ***as – as Chaucer,*** schon bei C.; (*Prov.*) ***– to bed and – to rise makes a man healthy, wealthy, and wise,*** Morgenstunde hat Gold im Munde.

earmark [ˈiəmɑ:k], **1.** *s.* (*fig.*) das Kennzeichen, Merkmal. **2.** *v.t.* kennzeichnen, bezeichnen; (*fig.*) zurückstellen, zurücklegen (*money*), bestimmen, vorsehen, sich (*Dat.*) vorbehalten.

earn [ə:n], *v.t.* (*as a p.*) erwerben, verdienen, (*as a th.*) einbringen.

[1]**earnest** [ˈə:nist], *s.* das Angeld, Aufgeld, Draufgeld, Handgeld; (*fig.*) die Probe, der Vorbote, Vorgeschmack; ***as an – of his determination,*** als Beweis dafür, daß er entschlossen ist.

[2]**earnest, 1.** *adj.* ernst(haft), gewissenhaft, emsig, eifrig; ernstlich, dringend; im Ernst, aufrichtig. **2.** *s.* der Ernst; ***in –,*** ernst, im Ernst; ***in dead*** or ***good –,*** in vollem Ernst; ***are you in –?*** ist das Ihr Ernst? ist es Ihnen ernst damit? **earnestly,** *adv.* ernstlich, ernsthaft, inständig, eifrig. **earnestness,** *s.* der Ernst, die Ernsthaftigkeit; der Eifer.

earning [ˈə:niŋ], *s.* 1. der Erwerb, das (Geld)verdienen; ***– power,*** (*of a p.*) die Erwerbskraft, (*of a th.*) Rentabilität, der Ertragswert; 2. *pl.* der Lohn, Verdienst, das Einkommen; der Gewinn, Erlös, Ertrag, Einnahmen (*pl.*).

ear|phone, *s.* (*oft. pl.*) der Kopfhörer. **–piece,** *s.* (*Tele.*) der Hörer, die Hörmuschel. **–-piercing,** *adj.* ohrenzerreißend, ohrenbetäubend. **–-ring,** *s.* der Ohrring. **–shot,** *s.* die Hörweite. **–-splitting,** *adj. See* **–-piercing.**

earth [ə:θ], **1.** *s.* 1. die Erde; der (Erd)boden, (trockenes) Land; ***the –,*** die Erde, Welt, der Erdball; (*coll.*) ***of the –,*** erdgebunden, erdnahe; ***on –,*** auf Erden; (*coll.*) ***what*** or ***why on –?*** was *or* warum in aller Welt? (*coll.*) ***come (down) to –,*** wieder nüchtern denken; ***fall to the –,*** zu Boden *or* zur Erde *or* auf den Boden fallen; ***run to –,*** (*v.t.*) stellen (*a p.*), (*coll.*) aufstöbern, ausfindig machen (*a th.*); (*v.i.*) sich verkriechen; 2. der Bau (*of a fox etc.*); 3. (*Elec.*) die Erdung, Erdleitung, der Erdschluß; 4. (*Chem.*) die Erde. **2.** *v.t.* 1. in den Bau treiben (*a fox*); 2. (*Elec.*) erden; 3. ***– up,*** häufeln, mit Erde bedecken. **3.** *v.i.* in den Bau flüchten (*of a fox*).

earth|-born, *adj.* erdgeboren, staubgeboren, irdisch, sterblich. **–-bound,** *adj.* erdgebunden. **–-connection,** *s. See* **earth, 1,** 3.

earthen [ə:θn], *adj.* Erd–, irden; ***– pot,*** irdener Topf. **earthenware,** *s.* die Töpferware, das Steingut.

earthiness [ˈə:θinis], *s.* die Erdigkeit, das Erdige. **earth-light,** *s.* der Erdschein. **earthliness,** *s.* das Irdische, Körperliche, die Weltlichkeit. **earthly,** *adj.* irdisch, weltlich; (*coll.*) denkbar; ***– bliss,*** das Erdenglück; (*coll.*) ***no – reason,*** kein denkbarer Grund, nicht der geringste Grund; (*sl.*) ***not an –,*** gar keine *or* nicht die geringste Aussicht *or* Chance. **earthly-minded,** *adj.* weltlich gesinnt.

earth|-nut, *s.* die Erdnuß. **–quake,** *s.* das Erdbeben, der Erdstoß. **–-shaking,** *adj.* welterschütternd. **earthward(s)** [–wəd(z)], *adj.* erdwärts. **earth|-work,** *s.* der Erdwall; (*pl.*) (*Mil.*) die Feldschanze. **–worm,** *s.* der Regenwurm. **earthy,** *adj.* erdig, Erd–; (*fig.*) irdisch; (*coll.*) erdgebunden, erdnahe; ***– smell,*** der Erdgeruch.

ear|-trumpet, *s.* das Hörrohr. **–-wax,** *s.* das Ohrenschmalz. **–wig,** *s.* (*Ent.*) der Ohrwurm.

ease [i:z], **1.** *s.* die Bequemlichkeit, Behaglichkeit, Gemächlichkeit, das Wohlgefühl, Behagen; die Ruhe; Erleichterung, Linderung; Ungezwungenheit, Unbefangenheit, Sorglosigkeit; Leichtigkeit, Mühelosigkeit; ***at –,*** bequem, ruhig, zwanglos; ***ill at –,*** unbehaglich, unruhig; ***at one's –,*** ungezwungen, ungeniert, wie zu Hause; ***put*** or ***set him at his –,*** ihm die Schüchternheit *or* Befangenheit nehmen; (*Mil.*) ***(stand) at –!*** rührt euch! ***take one's –,*** es sich bequem machen; ***with –,*** mit Leichtigkeit, mühelos, leicht. **2.** *v.t.* erleichtern, lindern, bequem(er) machen, beruhigen; abhelfen (*Dat.*), befreien, entlasten (*of,* von); auslassen (*a seam*), ausschneiden (*an arm-hole*), (*Tech.*) locker machen, lockern, den Spielraum vergrößern; ***– away, – off,*** abfieren (*rope*); ***– the helm,*** mit dem Ruder aufkommen; ***– the ship,*** die Fahrt vermindern. **3.** *v.i.* (*usu.*) ***– off,*** nachlassen; (*Comm.*) fallen.

easel [i:zl], *s.* die Staffelei, das Gestell.

easement [ˈi:zmənt], *s.* 1. (*obs.*) die Linderung, Erleichterung; Erlösung, Befreiung; 2. (*Law*) Grundstückslast, das Servitut.

easier [ˈi:ziə], *comp. adj.,* **easiest,** *sup. adj. See* **easy. easily,** *adv.* leicht, mühelos, mit Leichtigkeit, ohne Schwierigkeit; (*coll.*) bei weitem. **easiness,** *s.* die Bequemlichkeit, Behaglichkeit; Leichtigkeit, Mühelosigkeit; Natürlichkeit, Ungezwungenheit.

east [i:st], **1.** *s.* der Osten, (*Naut.*) Ost; ***the East,*** Orient, das Morgenland; ***– by south,*** Ost zu Süd; ***the three kings from the East,*** die Weisen aus dem Morgenlande; ***the Far East,*** der Ferne Osten; ***in the –,*** im Osten; ***the wind is in the –,*** der Wind kommt von Osten; ***the Near East,*** der Nahe Osten; ***(to the) – of,*** östlich von, im Osten von. **2.** *adj.* Ost–; ***the East End of London,*** der Ostteil Londons; ***the East Indies,*** Ostindien (*n.*); ***East India Company,*** die Ostindische Kompanie; ***East Side,*** New York östlich von Broadway; ***– wind,*** der Ostwind. **3.** *adv.* östlich, ostwärts.

Easter [ˈi:stə], **1.** *s.* das Ostern, Osterfest; ***at –,*** zu Ostern. **2.** *attrib. adj.* Oster–; ***– egg,*** das Osterei; ***– greetings,*** Ostergrüße; ***– Monday,*** der Ostermontag.

easterly [ˈi:stəli], **1.** *adj.* Ost–, östlich (gelegen), Ost–; ***– wind,*** der Ostwind, Wind aus *or* von Osten. **2.** *adv.* ostwärts, nach Osten. **eastern,** *attrib. adj.* östlich, morgenländisch, orientalisch; nach Osten, Ost–, östlich gelegen. **easterner,** *s.* der Ostländer. **easternmost,** *adj.* am weitesten östlich, östlichst. **easting,** *s.* (*Naut.*) zurückgelegter östlicher Kurs; östliche Entfernung; die Ostrichtung; Umschlagung nach Ost (*of wind*). **eastwardly** [–wəd(li)], **1.** *adj.* östlich, ostwärts gerichtet; ***– wind,*** see ***easterly wind.*** **2.** *or* **eastwards,** *adv.* ostwärts, nach Osten.

easy [ˈi:zi], **1.** *adj.* 1. leicht, mühelos; leicht, einfach; ***– to understand,*** leicht verständlich; ***the work is –,*** die Arbeit ist leicht (zu bewältigen); ***the language is –,*** die Sprache ist leicht (zu erlernen); ***it is – for you to talk,*** da haben Sie gut reden; ***– of access,*** leicht zugänglich; (*sl.*) ***– meat,*** kein ernst zu nehmender Gegner; ***– money,*** billiges Geld; ***– victory,*** müheloser Sieg; 2. bequem, behaglich; ***make o.s. –,*** es sich (*Dat.*) bequem machen; ***– chair,*** der Lehnstuhl, Sessel; ***in – circumstances,*** in guten Verhältnissen; ***an – fit,*** bequemer *or* loser Sitz; ***– pace,*** bequemes *or* gemächliches *or* lässiges Tempo; (*sl.*) ***on – street,*** see ***in – circumstances;*** ***on – terms,*** unter günstigen Bedingungen, auf Abzahlung; 3. sorglos, unbekümmert, unbeschwert, unbesorgt, ruhig (***about,*** um); ungezwungen, frei, natürlich, unbefangen; ***free and –,*** ohne (alle) Formalitäten; ***I am quite – about the future,*** um die Zukunft bin ich ganz unbesorgt; ***make your mind –!*** beruhige dich! sei unbesorgt! ***– manners,*** ungezwungenes

Benehmen; – *morals,* freie *or* lockere Sitten; – *style* (*of writing*), flüssige *or* glatte Schreibweise; *woman of – virtue,* die Hure, Dirne, feiles Weib; 4. willig, bereitwillig, nachgiebig, gefügig; 5. (*Comm.*) wenig gesucht *or* gefragt (*goods*), lustlos, flau (*trade*). **2.** *adv.* leicht; (*Naut.*) –*!* langsam! *go –,* sich schonen, es nicht so schwer nehmen; (*coll.*) *go – with* or (*sl.*) *on,* nicht zuviel nehmen, sparsam umgehen mit; (*Mil.*) *stand –!* rührt euch! *take things –,* es sich (*Dat.*) bequem machen, sich nicht überanstrengen; (*coll.*) *take it –!* nur ruhig! sachte! *easier said than done,* leichter gesagt als getan; – *come – go,* wie gekommen, so zerronnen.

easy|-going, *adj.* bequem, gemächlich, lässig, unbekümmert, gutmütig, behäbig. **--tempered,** *adj.* gutmütig.

eat [i:t], **1.** *irr.v.t.* essen; fressen (*of beasts*); zerfressen, ätzen; verzehren; verschlingen; (*sl.*) *what's –ing you,* was ist dir über die Leber gelaufen; (*coll.*) *you can't have your cake and – it,* für eines von beiden mußt du entscheiden; *have to – dirt,* sich demütigen müssen; *dog does not – dog,* eine Krähe hackt der anderen kein Auge aus; (*coll.*) *I'll – my hat,* ich lasse mich hängen; – *away,* abfressen, zerfressen, abätzen; – *one's fill,* sich anessen, sich satt essen; *the horse –s its head off,* das Pferd frißt mehr als es wert ist; (*coll.*) *he –s his head off* er frißt unmäßig; – *one's heart out,* sich vor Gram verzehren; – *him out of house and home,* ihn arm essen, ihn zugrunde richten; – *humble pie,* zu Kreuze kriechen; – *salt with him,* sein Gast sein; – *up,* aufessen, verzehren; (*fig.*) *be –en up with,* vergehen *or* sich verzehren vor (*Dat.*); – *one's words,* seine Worte zurücknehmen *or* widerrufen. **2.** *irr. v.i.* essen; *good to –,* gut zum Essen; –*in*(*to*), anfressen; sich einfressen *or* eindringen (in (*Acc.*)); (*fig.*) – *out of his hand,* ihm aus der Hand fressen; – *well,* einen guten Appetit haben.

eatable ['i:təbl], *adj.* eßbar, genießbar. **eatables,** *pl.* Eßwaren (*pl.*), Lebensmittel (*pl.*). **eaten,** *p.p. of* **eat. eater,** *s.* der Esser. **eating, 1.** *s.* das Essen. **2.** *attrib. adj.* Eß–; – *apple,* der Eßapfel; – *house,* das Speisehaus.

eau-de|-cologne [oudəkə'loun], *s.* Kölnisch Wasser, Kölnischwasser. **--vie** [–'vi:], *s.* der Branntwein.

eaves [i:vz], *pl.* die Traufe, Dachrinne. **eaves|drop,** *v.i.* lauschen, (heimlich) horchen (*on,* auf (*Acc.*)). **-dropper,** *s.* der Lauscher, (heimlicher) Horcher. **-dropping,** *s.* das (Be)lauschen, (heimliches) Horchen.

ebb [eb], **1.** *s.* die Ebbe; (*fig.*) Ebbe, das Zurückfluten; (*fig.*) die Abnahme, Neige, der Verfall; – *and flow,* Ebbe und Flut; (*fig.*) *be at a low –,* sehr schlecht *or* heruntergekommen sein, (*as prices*) gedrückt *or* im Tiefstand sein, (*as a p.*) traurig dastehen. **2.** *v.i.* (ver)ebben; (*fig.*) zurückgehen, abnehmen, versiegen, sinken, (dahin)schwinden; – *and flow,* ebben und fluten, (*fig.*) steigen und fallen. **ebb tide,** *s.* die Ebbe.

ebonite ['ebənait], *s.* das Ebonit, Hartgummi. **ebonize,** *v.t.* schwarz beizen, schwärzen. **ebony** [–ni], *s.* das Ebenholz.

ebriate ['i:briit], *adj.* (*obs.*) berauscht. **ebriety** [i'braiəti], *s.* die Trunkenheit.

ebullience, ebulliency [i'bʌljəns(i)], *s.* das Überwallen, Überschäumen, Sprudeln; die Überschwenglichkeit; *see also* **ebullition. ebullient,** *adj.* aufwallend, kochend; (*usu. fig.*) sprudelnd, überschäumend (*with,* von); überschwenglich. **ebullition** [ebə'liʃən], *s.* das Aufwallen, Aufbrausen, Sieden, die Aufwallung; (*fig.*) der Ausbruch (*of passion etc.*).

eccentric [ik'sentrik], **1.** *adj.* nicht zentral, nicht rund, exzentrisch (*also fig.*); (*fig.*) (*as a p.*) wunderlich, verschroben, überspannt, (*as behaviour etc.*) ungewöhnlich, ausgefallen; – *rod,* die Exzenterstange. **2.** *s.* 1. (*Tech.*) der Exzenter; 2. (*fig.*) exzentrischer Mensch, der Sonderling. **eccentricity** [eksen'trisiti], *s.* die Exzentrizität; (*fig.*) Wunderlichkeit, Überspanntheit, Verschrobenheit, Absonderlichkeit (*of a p.*); verschrobener *or* wunderlicher Einfall.

Ecclesiastes [ikli:zi'æsti:z], *s.* (*B.*) Prediger Salomonis. **ecclesiastic,** *s.* Geistliche(r). **ecclesiastic(al),** *adj.* kirchlich, geistlich, Kirchen–; – *history,* die Kirchengeschichte. **ecclesiasticism** [–tisizm], *s.* die Kirchlichkeit, das Kirchentum.

ecdysis [ek'daisis], *s.* die Häutung (*of snakes*).

echelon ['eʃələn], **1.** *s.* (*Mil.*) die Staffelstellung, Staffelung; Staffel; (*fig.*) Ebene, Stufe, der Rang; *in –,* staffelförmig. **2.** *v.t.* staffeln, gliedern, staffelweise aufstellen.

echidna [e'kidnə], *s.* (*Zool.*) der Ameisenigel. **echinite** ['ekinait], *s.* fossiler Seeigel. **echinoderm** [i'kainədə:m], *s.* (*Zool.*) der Stachelhäuter. **echinus** [i'kainəs], *s.* (*pl.* **-ni** [–nai]) 1. (*Zool.*) der Seeigel; 2. (*Archit.*) Echinus.

echo ['ekou], **1.** *s.* 1. der Widerhall, das Echo; *cheer him to the –,* ihm begeistert zujubeln; 2. (*fig., coll.*) der Nachahmer, Nachbeter; (*fig.*) genaue Wiedergabe; der Anklang, annähernde Wiederholung; 3. (*T.V. etc.*) das Geisterbild, Schattenbild. **2.** *v.t.* widerhallen lassen, zurückwerfen; (*fig.*) – *his words,* seine Worte nachsagen *or* nachplappern. **3.** *v.i.* widerhallen (*with,* von); (nach)hallen. **echo|-sounder,** *s.* (*Naut.*) das Echolot. **--sounding,** *s.* die Echolotmessung.

éclair [ei'klɛə], *s.* der Liebesknochen.

éclat [ei'klɑ:], *s.* allgemeiner Beifall, offenbarer Erfolg, öffentliches Aufsehen; (*fig.*) die Auszeichnung.

eclectic [e'klektik], **1.** *adj.* eklektisch, auswählend, zusammengestellt. **2.** *s.* der Eklektiker. **eclecticism** [–tisizm], *s.* der Eklektizismus.

eclipse [i'klips], **1.** *s.* 1. die Verfinsterung, Finsternis; – *of the moon,* die Mondfinsternis; 2. (*fig.*) die Überschattung, Verdüsterung, Verdunkelung; der Schwund, Wegfall, das (Ver)schwinden; (*fig.*) *in –,* in Verfall, im Sinken *or* Schwinden *or* Abnehmen. **2.** *v.t.* verfinstern; (*fig.*) verdunkeln, trüben, verdüstern; überragen, übertreffen, in den Schatten stellen. **ecliptic,** *s.* die Ekliptik, Sonnenbahn.

eclogue ['eklɔg], *s.* das Hirtengedicht, die Ekloge.

ecology [i'kɔlədʒi], *s.* die Ökologie.

economic [i:kə'nɔmik], *adj.* ökonomisch, wirtschaftlich, rationell, rentabel; volkswirtschaftlich, staatswirtschaftlich, nationalökonomisch, Wirtschafts–; – *conditions,* die Wirtschaftslage; – *development,* wirtschaftliche Entwicklung. **economical,** *adj.* sparsam, haushälterisch (*of,* mit); billig, preiswert; Spar–; – *cruising speed,* die Sparfluggeschwindigkeit. **economics,** *pl.* (*sing. constr.*) die Volkswirtschaft(slehre), Nationalökonomie.

economist [i'kɔnəmist], *s.* (*also political –*) der Volkswirtschaftler, Nationalökonom. **economize** [–aiz], **1.** *v.i.* sparen, sparsam wirtschaften, Einsparungen machen; sich einschränken (*in,* an (*Dat.*)), sparsam umgehen (mit). **2.** *v.t.* sparsam wirtschaften *or* umgehen mit, besser ausnützen, haushälterisch *or* sparsam anwenden *or* gebrauchen. **economizer,** *s.* (*Tech.*) der Vorwärmer, die Sparanlage. **economy,** *s.* 1. die Wirtschaftlichkeit, Sparsamkeit; Ersparnis, Einsparung, *pl.* Sparmaßnahmen (*pl.*); (*Pol. etc.*) die Wirtschaft, Ökonomie; *planned –,* die Planwirtschaft; *political –,* die Volkswirtschaft(slehre), Nationalökonomie; 2. die Organisation, Anordnung, innere Verfassung, der Aufbau, organisches System.

ecstasy ['ekstəsi], *s.* (*Med.*) krankhafte Erregung, die Ekstase; der Freudentaumel, das Entzücken, die Entzückung, Begeisterung, Überschwenglichkeit; (*Eccl.*) Verzückung; *be in –,* außer sich sein; *be in ecstasies over,* entzückt sein über (*Acc.*), begeistert sein von. **ecstatic** [eks'tætik], *adj.* (*Med.*) ekstatisch, verzückt; schwärmerisch, überschwenglich; entzückt, begeistert, hingerissen.

ectoblast ['ektoblɑ:st], **ectoderm,** *s.* äußeres Keimblatt. **ectoplasm** [–plæzm], *s.* äußere

Protoplasmaschicht. **ectozoon** [–zouɔn], *s.* der Außenparasit.

ecumenic(al), *see* **oecumenic(al).**

eczema [ˈekzmə], *s.* das Ekzem.

edacious [eˈdeiʃəs], *adj.* gefräßig, gierig.

eddy [ˈedi], **1.** *s.* der Wirbel, Strudel; (*Elec.*) – ***current,*** der Wirbelstrom. **2.** *v.i.* wirbeln.

edentate [iːˈdenteit], *adj.* (*Zool.*) zahnlos.

edge [edʒ], **1.** *s.* 1. die Schärfe, Schneide (*of a knife etc.*); ***blunt the – of,*** abstumpfen; ***cutting––,*** die Schneide, Schneidkante; ***the knife has no –,*** das Messer schneidet nicht; ***on –,*** nervös, gereizt, aufs äußerste gespannt; ***put an – on,*** schärfen, schleifen; (*B.*) ***put to the – of the sword,*** über die Klinge springen lassen; ***set his teeth on –,*** ihn kribbelig *or* nervös machen; ***take the – off,*** abstumpfen, (*fig.*) die Spitze *or* Wirkung nehmen (*Dat.*); 2. (scharfe) Kante, die Schmalseite, Ecke; der Saum, (äußerster) Rand; der Schnitt (*of a book*); ***with gilt –,*** mit Goldschnitt; (*Av.*) ***leading –,*** die Profilvorderkante, Leitkante; ***set a th.*** (*up*) ***on –,*** etwas hochkant(ig) stellen; ***– to –,*** Kante auf Kante; (*Av.*) ***trailing –,*** die Profilhinterkante, Schleppkante; ***the – of the water,*** der Rand des Wassers; 3. (*fig.*) die Schärfe, Spitze, der Schliff (*of wit etc.*); ***give an – to,*** verschärfen, verstärken; ***not put too fine an – on it,*** kein Blatt vor den Mund nehmen; 4. (*Spt., fig.*) der Vorteil; (*coll.*) ***have the – on him,*** ihm gegenüber einen Vorteil haben. **2.** *v.t.* 1. schärfen, (ab)schleifen; 2. umranden, (um)säumen, einfassen, einschließen; 3. abkanten, abranden, beschneiden; 4. (*coll.*) (unbemerkt) schieben *or* schlängeln *or* rücken *or* drängen; ***– o.s. into,*** sich (hin)eindrängen in (*Acc.*); ***– one's way through,*** sich (durch)schlängeln durch. **3.** *v.i.* sich seitwärts (heran)bewegen; ***– away,*** wegschleichen, wegrücken, sich langsam absetzen; ***– forward,*** langsam vorrücken; (*Naut.*) ***– off,*** abhalten von.

edged [edʒd], *adj.* 1. schneidend, scharf; (*as suff.*) –schneidig; ***– tool,*** schneidendes Werkzeug; ***play with – tools,*** mit dem Feuer spielen, mit gefährlichen Dingen umgehen. 2. eingefaßt, gesäumt; (*as suff.*) –randig. **edgeless,** *adj.* stumpf. **edge|-plane,** *s.* der Bestoßhobel. **––rail,** *s.* die Kantenschiene. **––tool,** *s.* das Schneid(e)werkzeug. **–ways, –wise,** *adv.* seitwärts, seitlich, von der Seite; hochkant(ig); Kante an Kante; ***not get a word in –,*** kein einziges Wort einwerfen *or* anbringen können, gar nicht zu Worte kommen.

edging [ˈedʒiŋ], *s.* die Einfassung; Litze, Borte, der Besatz. **edgy,** *adj.* 1. kantig; 2. (*usu. fig. coll.*) reizbar, gereizt, kratzbürstig.

edibility [ediˈbiliti], *s.* die Eßbarkeit, Genießbarkeit. **edible** [ˈedibl], *adj.* eßbar, genießbar.

edict [ˈiːdikt], *s.* die Verordnung, der Erlaß, das Edikt.

edification [edifiˈkeiʃən], *s.* (*fig.*) die Erbauung.

edifice [ˈedifis], *s.* das Gebäude; (*fig.*) Gefüge.

edify [ˈedifai], *v.t.* (*fig.*) erbauen; (*fig.*) belehren. **edifying,** *adj.* erbaulich; belehrend, lehrreich.

Edinburgh [ˈedinbərə], *s.* Edinburg (*n.*).

edit [ˈedit], *v.t.* herausgeben, edieren, redigieren, druckfertig machen; (*film, tape*) schneiden. **edition** [iˈdiʃən], *s.* die Auflage, Ausgabe; ***evening –,*** die Abendausgabe (*of a paper*); ***popular –,*** die Volksausgabe; ***third –,*** dritte Auflage (*of a book*); ***– de luxe,*** die Prachtausgabe. **editor,** *s.* der Herausgeber (*of a book*); Schriftleiter, Redakteur (*of a journal etc.*). **editorial** [–ˈtɔːriəl], **1.** *adj.* Redaktions–, redaktionell; ***– notes,*** Herausgeberanmerkungen (*pl.*); ***– staff,*** die Redaktion. **2.** *s.* der Leitartikel. **editorship,** *s.* die Schriftleitung, Redaktion; das Amt eines Herausgebers.

educable [ˈedjukəbl], *adj.* erziehbar. **educate** [–keit], *v.t.* erziehen, (aus)bilden, unterrichten; aufziehen, trainieren, dressieren (*animals*); ***be –d at . . .,*** die Schule in . . . besuchen. **educated,** *adj.* erzogen, gebildet; ***– man,*** gebildeter Mensch; ***– speech,*** kultivierte Sprache; ***be well –,*** gebildet sein. **education** [–ˈkeiʃən], *s.* die Erziehung, Bildung, Ausbildung; das Erziehungswesen, Schulwesen; die Pädagogik, Erziehungswissenschaft; (*Univ.*) ***department of –, – department,*** pädagogisches Seminar *or* Institut; ***liberal –,*** gelehrte Bildung; ***ministry of –,*** das Unterrichtsministerium; ***primary*** (or ***elementary***) –, das Volksschulwesen; ***secondary –,*** höheres Schulwesen. **educational,** *adj.* erzieherisch, pädagogisch, Unterrichts–, Erziehungs–, Bildungs–; ***– establishment,*** die Erziehungsanstalt; ***– film,*** der Lehrfilm; ***– journey,*** die Studienreise; ***– value,*** der Erziehungswert. **educationalist,** *s.* der Schulmann, Pädagog. **educative** [–kətiv], *adj.* Bildungs–, Erziehungs–, erzieherisch. **educator** [–keitə], *s.* der Erzieher.

educe [iˈdjuːs], *v.t.* hervorziehen, hervorholen, herausholen; (*Chem.*) ausziehen, extrahieren; (*Log.*) ableiten, ziehen (***from,*** aus). **educible,** *adj.* ableitbar. **educt** [ˈiːdʌkt], *s.* (*Chem.*) der Auszug, das Edukt; (*Log.*) Ergebnis, der Schluß, die (Schluß)folge, Ableitung, Folgerung. **eduction** [iˈdʌkʃən], *s.* der Herausholen, Hervorholen, die Entwicklung, Ableitung; ***– pipe,*** das Abzugsrohr.

edulcorate [iˈdʌlkəreit], *v.t.* auswässern, reinigen. **edulcoration** [–ˈreiʃən], *s.* die Reinigung.

eel [iːl], *s.* der Aal; ***as slippery as an –,*** aalglatt. **eel|-fishing,** *s.* der Aalfang. **––pot,** *s.* die Aalreuse. **––pout,** *s.* die Aalraupe. **––spear,** *s.* die Aalgabel.

e'en [iːn], *Poet. abbr. of* **even.**

e'er [εə], *Poet. abbr. of* **ever.**

eerie [ˈiəri], *adj.* unheimlich, grausig; (*rare*) furchtsam.

efface [iˈfeis], *v.t.* auswischen, (aus)löschen, (aus)tilgen, (aus)streichen, verwischen; (*fig.*) in den Schatten stellen; ***– o.s.,*** sich zurückhalten *or* zurückziehen, sich im Hintergrund halten, in den Hintergrund treten. **effaceable,** *adj.* tilgbar, auslöschbar. **effacement,** *s.* die Auslöschung, Tilgung, Streichung.

effect [iˈfekt], **1.** *s.* 1. die (Ein)wirkung, der Effekt, Eindruck, Einfluß ((*up*)*on,* auf (*Acc.*)); die Folge, Auswirkung, Konsequenz, das Resultat, Ergebnis; ***bring*** or ***carry into –,*** verwirklichen, ausführen, bewerkstelligen; zur Ausführung bringen; ***cause and –,*** Ursache und Wirkung; ***for –,*** auf Effekt berechnet, um Eindruck zu machen; ***have an – on,*** wirken auf (*Acc.*); ***in –,*** in der Tat, in Wirklichkeit, tatsächlich; ***of no –,*** erfolglos, ergebnislos, wirkungslos, ohne Erfolg; ***to good –,*** erfolgreich, mit guter Wirkung; ***to no –,*** see ***without –***; ***with telling –,*** mit eindeutigem Erfolg; ***without –,*** vergeblich, umsonst, unwirksam; 2. die Kraft, Gültigkeit; ***give – to a th.,*** einer S. Nachdruck verleihen, etwas in Kraft treten lassen, etwas verwirklichen; ***take –,*** in Kraft treten, wirksam werden, Wirkung haben; 3. der Inhalt, Sinn, Nutzen, Zweck, die Absicht; ***to that –,*** dementsprechend, diesbezüglich; ***to this –,*** in der Absicht, zu dem Ende; ***to the – that,*** dem Sinne nach; ***to the following –,*** folgenden Inhalts; ***to the same –,*** in demselben Sinne, desselben Inhalts; 4. (*Tech.*) die (Nutz)leistung; 5. *pl. See* **effects. 2.** *v.t.* bewirken, erwirken, veranlassen, verursachen; bewerkstelligen, vornehmen, ausführen, durchführen, vollbringen, vollziehen, erledigen, besorgen, zuwegebringen, zustandebringen; ***– a compromise,*** zu einem Vergleich kommen; ***– an insurance policy,*** eine Versicherung abschließen; ***– payment,*** Zahlung leisten.

effective [iˈfektiv], **1.** *adj.* wirkend; erfolgreich, wirksam, wirkungsvoll; effektvoll, eindrucksvoll; wirklich, tatsächlich, effektiv; (*Tech.*) Effektiv–, Nutz–, nutzbar; (*Mil.*) einsatzbereit, (dienst)tauglich, kampffähig; ***be –,*** wirken, Wirkung *or* Erfolg haben; ***become –,*** in Kraft treten; ***– range,*** der Wirkungsbereich, (*Artil.*) Schußbereich; (*Elec.*) ***– resistance,*** der Wirkwiderstand; (*Mil.*) ***– strength,*** die Iststärke; (*Tech.*) ***– work,*** die Nutzleistung. **2.** *s.* 1. diensttauglicher Soldat, (*usu. pl.*) der Effektivbestand, Istbestand; 2. (*Comm.*) das Bargeld. **effectiveness,** *s.* die Wirksamkeit.

effects [iˈfekts], *pl.* (*Comm.*) Effekten, Aktiva, Vermögenswerte (*pl.*); das Guthaben, der Barbestand;

die Habe, bewegliches Eigentum; (*coll.*) Habseligkeiten (*pl.*).

effectual [iˈfektjuəl], *adj.* wirksam, erfolgreich; ausreichend, hinreichend, genügend; (rechts)-kräftig, gültig; ***be* –,** wirken, Wirkung haben. **effectuate** [–eit], *v.t.* verwirklichen, durchführen, ausführen, bewerkstelligen, bewirken, erwirken.

effeminacy [iˈfeminəsi], *s.* die Verweichlichung, Weichlichkeit, Unmännlichkeit. **effeminate** [–nit], *adj.* weibisch, unmännlich, weichlich, verweichlicht, verzärtelt.

efferent [ˈefərənt], *adj.* nach außen führend.

effervesce [efəˈves], *v.i.* (auf)brausen, sprudeln, (auf)schäumen, moussieren, aufwallen. **effervescence,** *s.* das Aufbrausen, Schäumen. **effervescent, effervescing,** *adj.* (auf)brausend, sprudelnd, moussierend, schäumend, Brause–; (*fig.*) (über)-sprudelnd, überschäumend.

effete [iˈfiːt], *adj.* erschöpft, kraftlos, entkräftet; abgenutzt, ausgemergelt.

efficacious [efiˈkeiʃəs], *adj.* wirksam, wirkungsvoll, kräftig. **efficaciousness, efficacy** [ˈefikəsi], *s.* die Wirksamkeit, Wirkung(skraft).

efficiency [iˈfiʃənsi], *s.* (*Tech.*) die (Nutz)leistung, Leistungsfähigkeit, der Nutzeffekt, Wirkungsgrad; (*of a p.*) die Tüchtigkeit, (Leistungs)-fähigkeit, (*of a th.*) Tauglichkeit, Brauchbarkeit, Wirksamkeit; – ***expert,*** (*Comm. etc.*) der Betriebswirtschaftler, Wirtschaftsberater, (*Tech. etc.*) Rationalisierungsfachmann. **efficient,** *adj.* (leistungs)fähig, tüchtig, brauchbar, wirksam, tauglich; (be)wirkend.

effigy [ˈefidʒi], *s.* das Bild(nis), Abbild; ***burn in* –,** im Bilde verbrennen.

effloresce [efləˈres], *v.i.* (*Bot., fig.*) aufblühen, zur Entfaltung kommen; (*Chem.*) ausblühen, auskristallisieren, auswittern; Kristalle ansetzen. **efflorescence,** *s.* (*Bot.*) die Blüte, das (Auf)blühen; (*Chem.*) Ausblühen, Auskristallisieren, die Ausblühung, Auswitterung, der Beschlag. **efflorescent,** *adj.* (*Bot.*) (auf)blühend; (*Chem.*) ausblühend, auskristallisierend, auswitternd.

effluence [ˈefluəns], *s.* der Ausfluß, Abfluß, das Ausfließen, Ausströmen. **effluent, 1.** *adj.* ausströmend. **2.** *s.* der Ausfluß, Abfluß, das Abwasser, Sielwasser.

effluvium [iˈfluːviəm], *s.* (*pl.* **-via**) die Ausdünstung.

efflux [ˈeflʌks], *s.* das Ausfließen, Ausströmen, der Abfluß, Ausfluß, Auslauf, Austritt, Erguß; (*fig.*) das Verfließen, Vergehen.

effort [ˈefət], *s.* die Anstrengung, Mühe, Bemühung, angestrengter Versuch, das Bestreben; (*coll.*) ***a fine* –,** eine gute Leistung; ***make an* –,** sich anstrengen *or* bemühen, sich Mühe geben; ***make every* –,** alles aufbieten, alle Kräfte anspannen, sich (*Dat.*) alle Mühe geben; ***spare no* –,** keine Mühe scheuen; ***with an* –,** mühsam. **effortless,** *adj.* ohne Anstrengung, mühelos.

effrontery [əˈfrʌntəri], *s.* die Frechheit, Unverschämtheit, Unverfrorenheit.

effulge [iˈfʌldʒ], *v.i.* strahlen. **effulgence,** *s.* der Glanz, Schimmer. **effulgent,** *adj.* strahlend, glänzend.

effuse, 1. [iˈfjuːs], *adj.* (*Bot.*) ausgebreitet, sich ausbreitend. **2.** [iˈfjuːz], *v.t.* ausstrahlen, ausgießen, hervorquellen lassen, verbreiten. **effusion** [iˈfjuːʒən], *s.* das Ausgießen, Vergießen, Ausströmen; (*Med.*) der Erguß, Verlust; (*coll.*) Herzenserguß, Wortschwall; – ***of blood,*** der Blutverlust; – ***of the Holy Spirit,*** die Ausgießung des heiligen Geistes. **effusive** [–siv], *adj.* (*fig.*) überschwenglich; (*Geol.*) – ***rock,*** das Effusivgestein. **effusiveness,** *s.* die Überschwenglichkeit.

eft [eft], *s.* (*Zool.*) der Wassermolch.

egad! [iˈgæd], *int.* (*obs.*) wahrhaftig! meiner Treu!

egalitarian [igæliˈtɛəriən], **1.** *s.* der Gleichmacher. **2.** *adj.* gleichmacherisch.

[1]**egg** [eg], *v.t.* (*usu.* – *on*) anreizen, anstacheln, antreiben, anfeuern, aufreizen, aufhetzen.

[2]**egg,** *s.* das Ei; (*Av. sl.*) die Bombe; ***addled* –,** das Windei; ***have all one's –s in one basket,*** alles auf eine Karte setzen; ***bad* –,** faules Ei; (*fig.*) der Tunichtgut, Nichtsnutz; ***hard (soft) boiled* –,** hart (weich) gekochtes Ei; ***like the curate's* –,** teilweise gut; ***fried* –,** das Spiegelei, Setzei; (*sl.*) ***good* –!** prima! glänzend; (*sl.*) ***be on a good* –,** glänzende Aussichten haben; ***poached* –,** verlorenes Ei; ***rotten* –,** see ***bad* –**; ***scrambled* –,** das Rührei; ***as sure as –s are*** or ***is –s,*** so sicher wie nur was; (*coll.*) ***teach one's grandmother to suck –s,*** Unnötiges erörtern; ***white of* –,** das Eiweiß; ***yolk of* –,** der Eidotter, das Eigelb.

egg|-and-spoon race, *s.* das Eierlaufen. **--beater,** *s. See* **--whisk. –cup,** *s.* der Eierbecher. **--flip,** *s.* der Eierpunsch. **–head,** *s.* (*sl.*) Intellektuelle(r). **--nog,** *s. See* **--flip. –plant,** *s.* die Eierpflanze, Aubergine. **--shaped,** *adj.* eiförmig. **–shell,** *s.* die Eierschale. **--timer,** *s.* die Eieruhr. **--whisk,** *s.* der Eierschläger, Schaumschläger, Eierschlegel, Schlagbesen, Schneebesen.

eglantine [ˈegləntain], *s.* die Heckenrose, wilde Rose.

ego [ˈegou, ˈiːgou], *s.* das Ich, Selbst. **egocentric** [–ˈsentrik], *adj.* egozentrisch, ichbezogen, ichbewußt. **egocentricity** [–ˈtrisiti], *s.* die Ichbezogenheit, Egozentrik. **egoism,** *s.* die Selbstsucht, Eigennützigkeit, der Eigennutz, Egoismus. **egoist,** *s.* der (die) Egoist(in). **egoistic(al)** [–ˈistik(l)], *adj.* selbstsüchtig, egoistisch. **egomania,** *s.* krankhafte Selbstsucht, die Selbstgefälligkeit. **egotism,** *s.* die Selbstgefälligkeit, Selbstüberhebung, Selbstbespieglung, das Geltungsbedürfnis, Eigenlob, der Eigendünkel, Egotismus. **egotist,** *s.* der (die) Egotist(in). **egotistic(al)** [–ˈtistik(l)], *adj.* selbstgefällig, egotistisch.

egregious [iˈgriːdʒəs], *adj.* ungeheuer(lich), entsetzlich, unerhört. **egregiousness,** *s.* die Ungeheuerlichkeit, Unerhörtheit.

egress [ˈiːgres], *s.* der Ausgang, (*of water*) Ausfluß; (*Astr.*) Austritt, (*fig.*) Ausweg. **egression** [iˈgreʃən], *s.* das Heraustreten, der Austritt.

egret [ˈiːgret], *s.* **1.** (*Orn.*) (*Am.* ***Large* –**) der Silberreiher (*Egretta alba*); **2.** (*Bot.*) Pappus, die Samenkrone.

Egypt [ˈiːdʒipt], *s.* Ägypten (*n.*). **Egyptian** [iˈdʒipʃən], **1.** *s.* der (die) Ägypter(in). **2.** *adj.* ägyptisch; (*Orn.*) – ***vulture,*** der Schmutzgeier, Aasgeier (*Nephron percnopterus*).

eh? [ei], *int.* nicht wahr? wie? was? nun?

eider [ˈaidə], *s.* (*Am.*) *see* **eider-duck. eider|-down,** *s.* Eiderdaunen (*pl.*); (*coll.*) – (***quilt***), die Daunendecke. **--duck,** *s.* (*Orn.*) die Eiderente (*Somateria mollissima*).

eidetic [aiˈdetik], *adj.* anschaulich, wesensmäßig, eidetisch; (*Psych.*) – ***imagery,*** Anschauungsbilder (*pl.*).

eight [eit], **1.** *num. adj.* acht; ***--hour day,*** der Achtstundentag; – ***times,*** achtmal; ***at --twenty,*** um acht Uhr zwanzig; ***half-past* –,** halb neun. **2.** *s.* die Acht; der Achter (*boat*); die Achtermannschaft; ***figure of* –,** die Acht; (*sl.*) ***have one over the* –,** ein Glas *or* einen *or* eins über den Durst getrunken haben. **eighteen** [–ˈtiːn], **1.** *num. adj.* achtzehn. **2.** *s.* die Achtzehn. **eighteenth, 1.** *num. adj.* achtzehnt. **2.** *s.* das Achtzehntel. **eightfold,** *adj.* achtfach. **eighth** [–tθ], **1.** *num. adj.* acht. **2.** *s.* das Achtel. **eighthly,** *adv.* achtens. **eightieth** [–tiiθ], **1.** *adj.* achtzigst. **2.** *s.* das Achtzigstel. **eighties** [–tiz], *pl.* die achtziger Jahre. **eighty, 1.** *num. adj.* achtzig. **2.** *s.* die Achtzig.

Eire [ˈɛərə], *s.* Irische Republik.

eisteddfodd [aiˈsteðvɔd], *s.* walisisches Sängerfest.

either [ˈaiðə], **1.** *adj.* (irgend)ein; jede(r, -s), beide; – ***answer is correct,*** beide Antworten sind richtig; ***in – case,*** in beiden Fällen; – ***side,*** eine der beiden Parteien (***persons***); ***on – side,*** auf beiden Seiten; ***it can be done – way,*** es kann auf die eine oder die andere Art gemacht werden. **2.** *pron.* irgendein, beides; – ***of them,*** eins von beiden; ***not – of them,*** keiner *etc.* von beiden; – ***is possible,*** beides ist möglich. **3.** *conj.* – . . . *or* . . ., entweder . . . oder; (*after neg.*) weder . . . noch; ***I did not see – him or his son,*** ich sah weder ihn noch seinen Sohn. **4.** *adv.* (*with neg.*) auch nicht; ***I did not see him nor his son –,*** ich sah ihn nicht, und seinen Sohn auch nicht; ***I shall not go –,*** ich gehe auch nicht; ***without gifts – of mind or of character,*** weder mit geistiger noch charakterlicher Begabung.

ejaculate [i'dʒækjuleit], *v.t.* ausstoßen, von sich geben. **ejaculation** [–'leiʃən], *s.* **1.** das Ausstoßen; (*Med.*) (*semen*) der Samenerguß, die Samenabgabe; 2. der Ausruf; das Stoßgebet, der Stoßseufzer. **ejaculatory** [–lətəri], *adj.* ausstoßend, Ausstoß–; Stoß–, hastig; (*Anat.*) – ***duct,*** der Samenausführungsgang.

eject [i'dʒekt], *v.t.* (hin)auswerfen, verstoßen (***from,*** aus), ausstoßen (von), vertreiben (von *or* aus); (*Law*) zwangsweise entfernen (aus), exmittieren; – ***from office,*** aus dem Amt entfernen, eines Amtes entsetzen. **ejection** [i'dʒekʃən], *s.* die Ausweisung, Ausstoßung, Auswerfung (***from,*** aus), (*from office*) Entsetzung, Entfernung (aus), (*from possession*) Vertreibung (von *or* aus). **ejectment,** *s.* (*Law*) die Vertreibung, Exmittierung. **ejector,** *s.* **1.** der Vertreiber; 2. (*Tech.*) die Ausstoßvorrichtung, der Ejektor, Ausblaseapparat, Auswerfer (*of rifle etc.*); (*Av.*) – ***seat,*** der Schleudersitz.

[1]**eke** [i:k], *v.t.* (*usu.* – ***out***) (mühsam) ergänzen, zusammenstückeln, verlängern; – ***out a miserable existence,*** sich kümmerlich durchschlagen.

[2]**eke,** *adv., conj.* (*obs.*) auch.

elaborate [i'læbəreit], **1.** *v.t.* (sorgsam) ausarbeiten, erarbeiten, herausarbeiten. **2.** [–reit], *v.i.* – ***on,*** ausführlich behandeln, sich verbreiten über (*Acc.*). **3.** [–rit], *adj.* sorgfältig ausgearbeitet; ausführlich, umständlich; kompliziert, kunstvoll, vollendet. **elaborateness,** *s.* sorgfältige Ausführung *or* Ausarbeitung, die Sorgfalt, Ausgefeiltheit. **elaboration** [–'reiʃən], *s.* die Ausarbeitung; sorgfältige Ausführung, ausführliche Behandlung; die Entwicklung, Vervollkommnung.

élan [ei'lã], *s.* das Feuer, der Schwung, die Begeisterung.

eland ['i:lænd], *s.* die Elenantilope.

elapse [i'læps], *v.i.* verfließen, verstreichen, vergehen (*of time*).

elastic [i'læstik], **1.** *adj.* elastisch, bruchfest, dehnbar, federnd, spannkräftig; biegsam, geschmeidig (*also fig.*); – ***band,*** das Gummi(band); – ***conscience,*** weites Gewissen; –-***sided boots,*** Zugstiefel (*pl.*). **2.** *s.* das Gummiband, der Gummizug. **elasticity** [–'tisiti], *s.* die Elastizität, Bruchfestigkeit, Dehnbarkeit, Federkraft, Spannkraft, Springkraft, Schnellkraft; (*fig.*) Biegsamkeit, Geschmeidigkeit, Fügsamkeit; Spannkraft.

elate [i'leit], *v.t.* erheben, ermutigen, stolz machen. **elated,** *adj.* erhoben, stolz (***at,*** über (*Acc.*); ***with,*** von); freudig (erregt), übermütig, in gehobener Stimmung (über (*Acc.*)). **elater,** *s.* **1.** (*Ent.*) der Schnellkäfer; 2. (*Bot.*) die Schleuderzelle, der Springfaden. **elation** [i'leiʃən], *s.* der Stolz; die Begeisterung, freudige Erregung, gehobene Stimmung.

elbow ['elbou], **1.** *s.* der Ell(en)bogen; (*Tech.*) die Krümmung, Biegung, Ecke, das Knie(stück), Winkelstück, der Krümmer, Winkel; ***at one's –,*** bei der Hand; ***out at –s,*** zerlumpt, schäbig; ***be up to the –s,*** alle Hände voll zu tun haben; (*sl.*) ***lift the –,*** einen heben. **2.** *v.t.* (mit dem Ellbogen) stoßen *or* drängen *or* schieben; – ***him out,*** ihn beiseite drängen, ihn verdrängen; – ***one's way through,*** sich drängen *or* sich (*Dat.*) einen Weg bahnen durch.

elbow|-chair, *s.* der Armstuhl, Lehnstuhl. **–-grease,** *s.* (*coll.*) die Kraft, Energie. – **joint,** *s.* (*Anat.*) das Ell(en)bogengelenk; (*Tech.*) das Winkelverbindungsstück. **–-rest,** *s.* die Armstütze. **–-room,** *s.* (*fig.*) die Bewegungsfreiheit, der Spielraum.

eld [eld], *s.* (*Poet.*) das Alter, (*obs.*) alte Zeiten (*pl.*).

[1]**elder** ['eldə], **1.** *attrib. adj.* älter; – ***statesman,*** erfahrener Staatsmann. **2.** *s.* (*Eccl.*) (Kirchen)älteste(r), der Presbyter; (*of tribes*) (Stammes)älteste(r); (*usu. pl.*) ältere Person; ***my –s,*** ältere Leute als ich; ***–s and betters,*** Respektspersonen (*pl.*).

[2]**elder,** *s.* (schwarzer) Holunder. **elderberry,** *s.* die Holunderbeere.

elderly ['eldəli], *adj.* ältlich; – ***lady,*** ältere Dame. **eldership,** *s.* (*Eccl.*) das Ältestenamt. **eldest** [–ist], *attrib. adj.* ältest, erstgeboren.

elect [i'lekt], **1.** *v.t.* (er)wählen (*a p.*) (***to,*** zu); (aus)wählen, sich entschließen zu, sich entscheiden für (*a th.*); (*Eccl.*) ausersehen, auserwählen. **2.** *v.i.* sich entschließen, für richtig halten (***to do,*** zu tun). **3.** *adj.* designiert; (*Eccl.*) auserwählt, ausersehen; ***the –,*** die Auserwählten (*pl.*); ***bishop –,*** designierter Bischof; ***bride –,*** die Verlobte, Braut.

election [i'lekʃən], *s.* die Wahl; das Wählen; (*Eccl.*) die (Aus)erwählung, Gnadenwahl; – ***campaign,*** der Wahlkampf; – ***meeting,*** die Wahlversammlung; – ***returns,*** Wahlergebnisse (*pl.*). **electioneer** [–'niə], *v.i.* Wahlpropaganda machen, Wahlagitation treiben. **electioneering,** *s.* die Wahlagitation; Wahlumtriebe (*pl.*).

elective [i'lektiv], *adj.* wählend, Wahl–; durch Wahl, gewählt; wahlberechtigt; – ***affinity,*** die Wahlverwandtschaft. **elector,** *s.* **1.** (stimmberechtigter) Wähler, Wahlberechtigte(r); 2. (*Hist.*) der Kurfürst. **electoral,** *adj.* **1.** Wahl–, Wähler–; – ***college,*** der Wahlausschuß; – ***reform,*** die Wahlreform; – ***roll,*** die Wählerliste; 2. (*Hist.*) kurfürstlich. **electorate** [–rit], *s.* **1.** (*Hist.*) die Kurwürde; das Kurfürstentum; 2. (*Parl.*) die Wählerschaft. **electress,** *s.* die Kurfürstin.

electric [i'lektrik], *adj.* elektrisch; (*fig.*) wie elektrisiert; – ***battery,*** elektrische Batterie; – ***blanket,*** die Heizdecke; – ***blue,*** stahlblau; – ***chair,*** elektrischer Stuhl; – ***charge,*** elektrische Ladung; – ***current,*** elektrischer Strom; (*Ichth.*) – ***eel,*** der Zitteraal; – ***field,*** elektrostatisches Feld; – ***light,*** elektrisches Licht; – ***motor,*** der Elektromotor; – ***railway,*** elektrische Eisenbahn; (*Ichth.*) – ***ray,*** der Zitterrochen; – ***shock,*** elektrischer Schlag. **electrical,** *adj.* Elektrizitäts–, Elektro–; (*fig.*) elektrisierend, faszinierend; – ***appliances,*** Elektrogeräte (*pl.*); – ***engineer,*** der Elektrotechniker; – ***engineering,*** die Elektrotechnik. **electrician** [–'triʃən], *s.* der Elektriker, Elektrotechniker, Elektromechaniker. **electricity** [–'trisiti], *s.* die Elektrizität. **electrification** [–fi'keiʃən], *s.* die Elektrisierung. **electrify** [–fai], *v.t.* elektrifizieren, elektrisieren, elektrisch laden; (*fig.*) elektrisieren, hinreißen, entflammen, begeistern.

electro-chemistry [i'lektro–], *s.* die Elektrochemie.

electrocute [i'lektrəkju:t], *v.t.* durch elektrischen Strom töten *or* hinrichten. **electrocution** [–'kju:ʃən], *s.* die Hinrichtung *or* tödlicher Unfall durch elektrischen Strom.

electrode [i'lektroud], *s.* die Elektrode.

electrodynamics [ilektrodai'næmiks], *pl.* (*usu. sing. constr.*) die Elektrodynamik.

electrolier [ilektrə'liə], *s.* elektrischer Kronleuchter.

electrolysis [ilek'trɔlisis], *s.* die Elektrolyse. **electrolyte** [i'lektrəlait], *s.* der Elektrolyt, (*in batteries*) die Füllsäure. **electrolytic** [–'litik], *adj.* elektrolytisch; – ***condenser,*** der Elektrolytkondensator.

electro|-magnet, *s.* der Elektromagnet. **–magnetic,** *adj.* elektromagnetisch. **–magnetism,** *s.* der Elektromagnetismus. **–motive,** *adj.* elektromotorisch. **–motor,** *s.* der Elektromotor.

electron [i'lektrɔn], *s.* das Elektron. **electronic** [–'trɔnik], *adj.* Elektronen–; – ***brain,*** das Elektronengehirn. **electronics,** *pl.* (*sing. constr.*) die Elektronik, Elektronenlehre, Elektronenphysik.

electro|plate, **1.** *v.t.* galvanisch versilbern. **2.** *s.* (galvanisch) versilberte Ware. **–scope,** *s.* das Elektroskop. **–statics,** *s.* (*sing. constr.*) die Elektrostatik. **–therapy,** *s.* die Elektrotherapie. **–type,** **1.** *s.* die Elektrotype, das Galvano. **2.** *v.t.* galvanographisch abbilden.

electrum [i'lektrəm], *s.* die Goldsilberlegierung.

electuary [i'lektjuəri], *s.* die Latwerge.

eleemosynary [el(i)i:'mɔzinəri], *adj.* Almosen–, Wohltätigkeits–.

elegance ['eligəns], *s.* geschmackvolle Erscheinung, die Zierlichkeit, Anmut, Feinheit, Eleganz; (*also* **elegancy**) Vornehmheit, Gewähltheit, Gepflegtheit (*style etc.*). **elegant,** *adj.* zierlich, anmutig, niedlich, gepflegt, gefällig, gewählt, elegant, geschmackvoll.

elegiac [eli'dʒaiik], **1.** *adj.* elegisch; (*fig.*) klagend, schwermütig; – ***poet,*** der Elegiendichter; – ***couplet*** *or* **2.** *s.* das Distichon. **elegiacs,** *pl.* elegische Verse, Distichen (*pl.*). **elegize** ['elidʒaiz], *v.t.* in Elegien besingen, eine Elegie schreiben auf (*Acc.*). **elegy** ['elidʒi], *s.* die Elegie, das Klagelied, Trauergedicht.

element ['elimənt], *s.* (*Chem.*) der Urstoff, Grundstoff, das Element; wesentlicher Bestandteil, der Grundbestandteil; (*coll.*) das (Lebens)element, die Sphäre, gewohnte Umgebung; (*fig.*) das Körnchen, Fünkchen; *pl. See* **elements**; ***be in one's –,*** in seinem Element sein, sich wohl fühlen; ***be out of one's –,*** sich unglücklich *or* unbehaglich fühlen; ***an – of truth,*** ein Körnchen Wahrheit; – ***of uncertainty,*** der Unsicherheitsfaktor. **elemental** [–'mentl], *adj.* elementar, Elementar–, primär, grundlegend; urkräftig, Ur–; – ***power,*** die Naturgewalt; – ***spirits,*** Elementargeister (*pl.*).

elementary [eli'mentəri], *adj.* Elementar–, Anfangs–, Einführungs–, Grund–; einfach, rudimentär; – ***education,*** die Volksschulbildung; – ***school,*** die Grundschule, Volksschule.

elements ['elimənts], *pl.* 1. Grundlagen, Grundzüge, Anfangsgründe, Elemente (*pl.*); 2. Naturgewalten, Wetterverhältnisse (*pl.*), das Wetter; 3. (*Eccl.*) Brot und Wein.

elenchus [i'leŋkəs], *s.* der Gegenbeweis, die Widerlegung.

elephant ['elifənt], *s.* der Elefant; ein Papierformat (*28 in.* × *23 in.*); (*fig.*) ***white –,*** kostspieliger *or* lästiger Besitz. **elephantiasis** [–'taiəsis], *s.* die Elefantiasis. **elephantine** [–'fæntain], *adj.* Elefanten–; (*fig.*) elefantenhaft, ungeheuer, plump, schwerfällig, unbeholfen.

elevate ['eliveit], **1.** *v.t.* 1. aufheben, hochheben, emporheben; aufrichten, aufstellen (*a pole etc.*); – ***the voice,*** lauter sprechen, die Stimme heben; 2. (*Artil.*) die Höhenrichtung geben (*Dat.*); 3. erheben, erhöhen, befördern (*a p.*) (*to,* zu); 4. (*fig.*) heben, veredeln (*the mind etc.*); aufmuntern, beleben, erheitern, aufheitern (*the spirits etc.*). **2.** *v.i.* 1. (*Artil.*) Erhöhung nehmen; 2. (*fig.*) erhebend sein. **elevated,** *adj.* hoch; (*fig.*) gehoben, erhaben, edel; – ***with,*** erhoben von; – ***railway,*** die Hochbahn; – ***with wine,*** angeheitert, weinselig. **elevating,** *adj.* (*Tech.*) Hebe–, Aufzieh–; (*Artil.*) Höhenricht–; (*fig.*) erhebend.

elevation [eli'veiʃən], *s.* 1. das Emporheben, Hochheben, (Auf)heben; Aufstellen, die Aufrichtung; 2. (*fig.*) Erhebung, Erhöhung, Beförderung; (Boden)erhebung, (An)höhe; 3. (*fig.*) Erhabenheit, Vornehmheit, Hoheit, Würde; 4. (*Archit.*) Vorderansicht, der Aufriß; (*Astr.*) die Höhe; (*Artil.*) der Erhöhungswinkel, Aufsatzwinkel, Visierwinkel, die Höhenrichtung, Richthöhe; ***high – fire,*** das Steilfeuer; (*Astr.*) – ***of the pole,*** die Polhöhe; ***sectional –,*** der Längsschnitt, Querschnitt; ***side –,*** die Seitenansicht.

elevator ['eliveitə], *s.* 1. (*Anat.*) der Hebemuskel, Levator; 2. (*Dentistry*) Wurzelheber; 3. (*Tech.*) das Förderwerk, Hebewerk; (*Am.*) der Aufzug, Fahrstuhl, Lift; (*Min.*) – ***cage,*** der Förderkorb; ***grain –,*** der Getreidespeicher; 4. (*Av.*) das Höhensteuer, Höhenruder. **elevatory** [–vətəri], *adj.* emporhebend, Hebe–.

eleven [i'levn], **1.** *num. adj.* elf. **2.** *s.* die Elf; (*Spt.*) Elf(ermannschaft). *For clock-times see* **eight. eleven-plus,** *s.* (*also* – ***examination***) die Ausleseprüfung für die höhere Schule. **elevenses** [–ziz], *pl.* (*sing. constr.*) (*coll.*) zweites Frühstück. **eleventh, 1.** *num. adj.* elft; ***at the – hour,*** in zwölfter Stunde. **2.** *s.* das Elftel.

elf [elf], *s.* (*pl.* **elves** [elvz]) der Elf, die Elfe, der Kobold; Zwerg. **elfin, 1.** *adj.* Zwerg–, Elfen–. **2.** *s. See* **elf. elfish,** *adj.* elfisch, schalkhaft, neckisch, schelmisch. **elf|-locks,** *pl.* der Weichselzopf, verfilztes Haar. **--struck,** *adj.* verhext.

elicit [i'lisit], *v.t.* herausholen, hervorlocken (***from,*** aus), entlocken (*Dat.*); herausbekommen, ans Licht bringen, (*a response*) auslösen. **elicitation** [–'teiʃən], *s.* das Herauslocken, die Auslösung.

elide [i'laid], *v.t.* (*Gram.*) elidieren, ausstoßen.

eligibility [elidʒi'biliti], *s.* die Wählbarkeit; Annehmbarkeit, Eignung, Qualifiziertheit, Qualifikation. **eligible** ['elidʒibl], *adj.* wählbar; annehmbar, geeignet, passend, akzeptabel, erwünscht; wünschenswert; – ***bachelor,*** in Frage kommender Junggeselle.

Elijah [i'laidʒə], *s.* (*B.*) Elias (*m.*).

eliminate [i'limineit], *v.t.* ausstoßen, ausschließen, aussondern, ausscheiden; ausmerzen, ausschalten, beseitigen, entfernen; (*Math.*) eliminieren. **elimination** [–'neiʃən], *s.* die Ausstoßung, Ausschließung, Aussonderung, Ausscheidung (*also Med., Spt.*), Ausmerzung, Ausschaltung, Beseitigung, Eliminierung, Wegschaffung, das Entfernen; (*Math.*) die Elimination. **eliminator,** *s.* (*Rad.*) der Sperrkreis, Siebkreis.

elision [i'liʒən], *s.* (*Gram.*) die Ausstoßung (eines Vokals), Elision.

élite [ei'li:t], *s.* die Elite, Auslese; (*Mil.*) Elite(truppe); Führerschicht (*of society*).

elixir [i'liksə], *s.* der Zaubertrank, das Elixier; der Heiltrank; (*fig.*) die Quintessenz, der Kern.

Elizabeth [i'lizəbəθ], *s.* Elisabeth (*f.*). **Elizabethan** [–'bi:θn], *adj.* elisabethanisch.

elk [elk], *s.* der Elch, das Elentier.

ell [el], *s.* die Elle; (*Prov.*) ***give him an inch and he'll take an –,*** gib ihm den kleinen Finger, so nimmt er die ganze Hand.

ellipse [i'lips], *s.* (*Math.*) die Ellipse. **ellipsis,** *s.* (*pl.* **-ses** [–si:z]) (*Gram.*) die Ellipse, Auslassung (eines Worts). **ellipsoid,** *s.* (*Math.*) das Ellipsoid. **elliptic(al),** *adj.* (*Math.*) elliptisch, Ellipsen–. **elliptical,** *adj.* (*Gram.*) elliptisch, unvollständig.

elm [elm], *s.* die Ulme, Rüster.

elocution [elo'kju:ʃən], *s.* der Vortrag, die Vortragsweise; Redekunst, Vortragskunst; – ***classes*** Vortragsübungen. **elocutionary,** *adj.* Vortrags–, rednerisch. **elocutionist,** *s.* der Vortragskünstler, Redekünstler.

elongate ['i:lɔŋgeit], **1.** *v.t.* verlängern, ausdehnen. **2.** *adj.* (*Bot.*) zugespitzt, länglich. **elongated,** *adj.* verlängert. **elongation** [–'geiʃən], *s.* die Verlängerung, Ausdehnung; (*Tech.*) Dehnung, Streckung; das Verlängerungsstück; (*Astr.*) der Winkelabstand.

elope [i'loup], *v.i.* (*of man or woman*) durchgehen, entlaufen (***with,*** mit); – ***with,*** (*of man*) entführen, (*of woman*) sich entführen lassen von. **elopement,** *s.* das Entlaufen.

eloquence ['elokwəns], *s.* die Beredtheit, Beredsamkeit, Redegabe, der Redefluß. **eloquent,** *adj.* beredt, beredsam, redegewandt; (*fig.*) ausdrucksvoll, sprechend (*as eyes etc.*); ***be – of,*** deutlich zum Ausdruck bringen.

else [els], *adv.* andere(r, -s); (*after neg. or inter.*) sonst, außerdem, weiter; (*after or, expressed or implied*) oder, sonst, wenn . . . nicht; ***anyone –,*** irgend ein anderer; ***anyone –?*** sonst noch jemand? ***anything –,*** irgend etwas anderes; ***anything –?*** sonst noch etwas? ***everybody –,*** alle anderen; ***no one –,*** sonst *or* weiter niemand; ***nothing –,*** sonst nichts; ***nowhere –,*** sonst nirgends; ***somebody*** or ***someone –,*** ein anderer (eine andere); ***something –,*** etwas anderes; ***somewhere –,*** *see* **elsewhere**; ***what –?*** was sonst (noch)? ***where –?*** wo anders? wo sonst? ***who –?*** wer sonst? wer anders? wer weiter? **elsewhere,** *adv.* sonstwo, sonst irgendwo, anderswo, irgendwo anders, anderwärts; anderswohin, woanders hin.

elucidate [i'lu:sideit], *v.t.* aufhellen, aufklären;

erklären, erläutern. **elucidation** [–'deiʃən], *s.* die Erläuterung, Erklärung, Klarstellung, Aufklärung; der Aufschluß (*of*, über (*Acc.*)). **elucidatory** [–deitəri], *adj.* aufklärend, erläuternd, aufhellend.

elude [i'l(j)u:d], *v.t.* ausweichen, entgehen, aus dem Wege gehen, sich entziehen (*Dat.*); (*fig.*) entgehen, sich entziehen (*Dat.*) (*the understanding etc.*). **elusion** [i'l(j)u:ʒən], *s.* die Umgehung, das Entkommen, Entweichen, Ausweichen. **elusive** [–siv], *adj.* ausweichend; (*fig.*) schwer feststellbar *or* faßbar. **elusory,** *adj.* trügerisch, täuschend.

elutriate [i'lju:trieit], *v.t.* auswaschen, abklären, (ab)schlämmen, abschwemmen. **elutriation** [–'eiʃən], *s.* die Auswaschung, Abklärung, Schlämmung.

elver ['elvə], *s.* junger Aal.

elves [elvz], *pl. of* **elf. elvish,** *adj. See* **elfish.**

Elysian [e'liziən], *adj.* elysisch, elysäisch; (*fig.*) wonnig, beseligend, paradiesisch, himmlisch. **Elysium,** *s.* das Paradies, Elysium.

elzevir ['elzivə], *s.* (*Typ.*) die Elzevir(schrift).

em [em], *s.* (*Typ.*) das Quadrätchen, Geviert.

'em [əm], (*coll.*) = ***them.***

emaciate [i'meiʃieit], *v.t.* abzehren, ausmergeln; abmagern, erschöpfen (*soil*). **emaciation** [–'eiʃən], *s.* die Abmagerung, Abzehrung, Auszehrung, Ausmergelung.

emanate ['eməneit], *v.i.* ausfließen (***from***, aus), ausgehen, ausströmen, ausstrahlen (von); (*fig.*) herrühren, herstammen, ausgehen (von). **emanation** [–'neiʃən], *s.* die Ausströmung, Ausstrahlung, Ausdünstung, der Ausfluß, (*Phil., Phys.*) die Emanation; (*fig.*) Austrahlung, Auswirkung.

emancipate [i'mænsipeit], *v.t.* freigeben, freilassen, befreien (*as slaves*), freimachen, losmachen, unabhängig machen (***from***, von), gleichstellen, gleiche Rechte zugestehen (*Dat.*) (*as women*). **emancipated,** *adj.* frei; (*Pol.*) gleichberechtigt, (*slaves*) emanzipiert; (*coll.*) vorurteilslos. **emancipation** [–'peiʃən], *s.* die Freimachung, Losmachung; Freilassung, Befreiung (*of slaves*), Emanzipation, Gleichberechtigung, Gleichstellung (*of women*).

emasculate, 1. [i'mæskjulit], *adj.* entmannt, kastriert; (*fig.*) unmännlich, weichlich, weibisch. **2.** [–leit], *v.t.* entmannen, kastrieren; (*fig.*) schwächen, entkräften, verweichlichen. **emasculation** [–'leiʃən], *s.* die Kastrierung, Entmannung; (*fig.*) Verweichlichung, Schwächung, Entkräftung; Verwässerung (*as style*), Verstümmelung (*as a book*); Unmännlichkeit, Schwächlichkeit.

embalm [im'bɑ:m], *v.t.* salben, (ein)balsamieren; (*fig.*) sorgsam bewahren, erhalten; (*fig.*) ***be –ed in,*** fortleben in (*Dat.*). **embalmment,** *s.* die Einbalsamierung.

embank [im'bæŋk], *v.t.* eindeichen, eindämmen. **embankment,** *s.* die Eindeichung, Eindämmung; der Damm, Deich, (*Railw.*) Bahndamm; die Uferanlage; ***the Thames Embankment,*** der Themsekai.

embargo [em'bɑ:gou], **1.** *s.* die Beschlagnahme, der Arrest, das Embargo (*on, Gen.*), die (Handels)-sperre, das (Handels)verbot (***on***, auf (*Dat.*)); ***lay an – on,*** mit Beschlag belegen (*ship*), sperren (*port*); ***lift the –,*** die Beschlagnahme *or* Sperre aufheben; ***be under –,*** unter Beschlagnahme stehen. **2.** *v.t.* sperren; mit Beschlag belegen, beschlagnahmen.

embark [im'bɑ:k], **1.** *v.t.* einschiffen (*persons*), verladen (*goods*) (***for***, nach). **2.** *v.i.* sich einschiffen, an Bord gehen (***for***, nach); (*fig.*) ***– in*** or (***up***)***on,*** sich einlassen in *or* auf (*Acc.*), beginnen, (*coll.*) einsteigen in (*Acc.*). **embarkation** [embɑ:'keiʃən], *s.* die Einschiffung; Verladung.

embarrass [im'bærəs], *v.t.* verwirren, aus der Fassung bringen, in Verlegenheit bringen *or* setzen (*a p.*); erschweren, (be)hindern (*movement*); erschweren, verwickeln. **embarrassed,** *adj.* verlegen, in Verlegenheit, peinlich berührt (***by***, über (*Acc.*)); verwirrt, bestürzt; in Geldverlegenheit; behindert. **embarrassing,** *adj.* peinlich, ungelegen, unbequem, befremdlich (***to***, *Dat.*). **embarrassment,** *s.* die Verlegenheit, Verwirrung; das Hindernis, die Schwierigkeit; Störung, Behinderung, Beeinträchtigung, Erschwerung; Geldverlegenheit.

embassy ['embəsi], *s.* die Botschaft, Gesandtschaft.

embattle [im'bætl], *v.t.* 1. in Schlachtordnung aufstellen; 2. mit Zinnen *or* Schießscharten versehen, befestigen; (*Her.*) ***–d,*** mit Zinnen gespalten.

embed [im'bed], *v.t.* (ein)betten, (ein)lagern, eingraben; umschließen, einschließen, einmauern, verankern, fest vergraben.

embellish [im'beliʃ], *v.t.* verschöne(r)n, schmücken, verzieren; (*fig.*) ausschmücken. **embellishment,** *s.* die Verschönerung, Verzierung, Ausschmückung, (*Mus.*) Verzierung, das Ornament.

ember ['embə], *s.* (*usu. pl.*) glimmende Kohle, glühende Asche; (*fig.*) (letzte) Funken (*pl.*).

ember|-days, *pl.* der Quatember. **--goose,** *s.* (*Orn.*) die Imbergans, der Eistaucher. **--week,** *s.* die Quatemberwoche.

embezzle [im'bezl], *v.t.* veruntreuen, unterschlagen. **embezzlement,** *s.* die Veruntreuung, Unterschlagung. **embezzler,** *s.* der (die) Veruntreuer(in).

embitter [im'bitə], *v.t.* verbittern; erbittern (*a p.*). **embitterment,** *s.* die Verbitterung.

emblazon [im'bleizn], *v.t.* 1. heraldisch bemalen, blasonieren; (*fig.*) schmücken, (ver)zieren; 2. feiern, verherrlichen, ausposaunen. **emblazonment,** *s.* die Wappenmalerei, Blasonierung; der Wappenschmuck.

emblem ['embləm], *s.* das Sinnbild, Symbol; Wahrzeichen, Kennzeichen, Abzeichen, Erkennungszeichen, Emblem. **emblematic(al)** [–'mætik(l)], *adj.* sinnbildlich; ***be – of,*** versinnbildlichen. **emblematize** [em'blemətaiz], *v.t.* sinnbildlich darstellen, versinnbildlichen.

emblement ['emblmənt], *s.* (*usu. pl.*) die Ernte, der Ernteertrag.

embodiment [im'bɔdimənt], *s.* die Verkörperung; Darstellung, das Verkörpern; die Einfügung, Aufnahme, Einverleibung. **embody,** *v.t.* konkrete Form geben (*Dat.*), verkörpern, in konkreter Form zum Ausdruck bringen, darstellen, (*of a th.*) einfügen, einverleiben, aufnehmen (***in***, in (*Acc.*)), in sich schließen *or* vereinigen, umfassen, einschließen.

embolden [im'bouldn], *v.t.* ermutigen.

embolism ['embəlizm], *s.* die Embolie.

embonpoint ['ɑ̃bɔ̃pwɛ̃], *s.* die (Wohl)beleibtheit, Körperfülle.

embosom [im'buzm], *v.t.* ins Herz schließen, ans Herz drücken; (*fig.*) einhüllen, einschließen (***in***, in (*Acc.*)), umschließen (von).

emboss [im'bɔs], *v.t.* in erhabener Arbeit anfertigen, erhaben ausarbeiten, mit erhabener Arbeit schmücken; hämmern, treiben, bossieren, bosseln (*metal*), prägen, gaufrieren (*fabric*). **embossed,** *adj.* getrieben, erhaben gearbeitet, gebosselt, bossiert (*metal*), gaufriert (*fabric*); ***– leather,*** genarbtes Leder; ***– printing,*** der Blindendruck; ***– wallpaper,*** die Relieftapete. **embossing,** *s.* erhabene Arbeit, die Bossierarbeit. **embossing-press,** *s.* die Prägepresse.

embouchure [ɔmbu'ʃuə], *s.* 1. die Mündung (*of river*); 2. (*Mus.*) das Mundstück (*of instrument*), der Zungenschlag (*of performer*).

embowel [im'bauəl], *v.t.* ausweiden.

embower [im'bauə], *v.t.* (wie) in einer Laube einschließen.

[1]**embrace** [im'breis], **1.** *v.t.* umarmen, in die Arme schließen; (*of a th.*) einschließen, in sich schließen, umfassen, umschließen; (*fig.*) annehmen (*religion*), einschlagen (*career*), ergreifen (*career, opportunity*), annehmen (*offer*); (*with the mind*) sich (*Dat.*) zu eigen machen, in sich aufnehmen. **2.** *v.i.* sich umarmen. **3.** *s.* die Umarmung.

[2]**embrace,** *v.t.* (*Law*) bestechen, zu bestechen versuchen. **embracer,** *s.* der Bestecher. **embracery,** *s.* die Bestechung, der Bestechungsversuch.

embranchment [im'brɑ:ntʃmənt], *s.* die Verzweigung, Gabelung.

embrasure [im'breiʒə], *s.* die Leibung; (*Fort.*) (Schieß)scharte.

embrocate ['embrokeit], *v.t.* einreiben. **embrocation** [–'keiʃən], *s.* das Einreibemittel.

embroider [im'brɔidə], *v.t.* sticken (*a design*); mit Stickerei schmücken, besticken (*material etc.*); (*fig.*) ausschmücken. **embroidery,** *s.* das Sticken, die Stickerei(arbeit); ***do –,*** sticken; ***openwork –,*** durchbrochene Stickerei. **embroidery|-cotton,** *s.* das Stickgarn. **--frame,** *s.* der Stickrahmen.

embroil [im'brɔil], *v.t.* verwickeln; in einen Streit hineinziehen. **embroilment,** *s.* die Verwick(e)lung; Streitigkeit.

embryo ['embriou], *s.* der (Frucht)keim, Embryo; (*fig.*) Keim; ***in –,*** im Keim, im Werden, im Entstehen. **embryonic** [–'ɔnik], *adj.* Embryo–; (*fig.*) unentwickelt, rudimentär.

embus [em'bʌs], **1.** *v.t.* (*Mil., coll.*) auf Kraftfahrzeuge verladen. **2.** *v.i.* auf Kraftfahrzeuge verladen werden.

emend [i'mend], *v.t.* verbessern, berichtigen, emendieren, korrigieren. **emendation** [i:men'deiʃən], *s.* die Textverbesserung, Berichtigung. **emendator** ['i:mendeitə], *s.* der Textverbesserer, Berichtiger. **emendatory** [–dətəri], *adj.* textverbessernd, Verbesserungs–.

emerald ['emərəld], **1.** *s.* 1. der Smaragd; die Smaragdfarbe; 2. (*Typ.*) Insertie. **2.** *adj.* smaragdgrün; ***Emerald Isle,*** Grüne Insel (***Ireland***).

emerge [i'mə:dʒ], *v.i.* herauskommen, hervortreten, zutage treten, auftauchen, zum Vorschein kommen (***from,*** aus); (*fig.*) eintreten, in Erscheinung treten, auftreten, entstehen, hervorgehen, davonkommen, sich entwickeln, sich herausstellen; sich erheben (***from,*** aus). **emergence,** *s.* das Auftauchen, Sichtbarwerden, Hervortreten, Emporkommen, Auftreten, Zutagetreten.

emergency [i'mə:dʒənsi], *s.* unerwartetes Ereignis, die Not(lage), der Notfall, Notstand, Ernstfall; ***in case of*** or ***in an –,*** im Notfall *or* Ernstfall, notfalls; ***– aid*** (***programme***), die Soforthilfe; ***– brake,*** die Notbremse; ***– decree,*** die Notverordnung; ***– exit,*** der Notausgang; (*Av.*) ***– landing,*** die Notlandung; ***– measure,*** die Notstandsmaßnahme; ***– ration,*** eiserne Ration; ***state of –,*** der Ausnahmezustand, Notstand.

emergent [i'mə:dʒənt], *adj.* auftauchend, aufsteigend, hervorgehend, emporkommend; (*fig.*) entspringend, entstehend, neu auftretend; ***– nations,*** Entwicklungsländer (*pl.*).

emeritus [i'meritəs], *adj.* emeritiert.

emersion [i'mə:ʃən], *s.* das Auftauchen, Hervorkommen, Heraustreten (***from,*** aus); (*Astr.*) der Austritt.

emery ['eməri], *s.* der Schmirgel, Korund. **emery|-cloth,** *s.* das Schmirgelleinen. **--paper,** *s.* das Schmirgelpapier. **--wheel,** *s.* die Schmirgelscheibe.

emetic [i'metik], **1.** *adj.* erbrechenerregend. **2.** *s.* das Brechmittel.

emigrant ['emigrənt], **1.** *adj.* auswandernd, Auswanderer–, Auswanderungs–. **2.** *s.* der Auswanderer. **emigrate** [–eit], *v.i.* auswandern. **emigration** [–'greiʃən], *s.* die Auswanderung.

eminence ['eminəns], *s.* 1. die Erhöhung, (An)höhe; 2. (*fig.*) hohe Stellung, hoher Rang, die Auszeichnung, Berühmtheit, der Ruhm; Vorrang, Vorzug; (*Eccl. as title*) die Eminenz; ***rise to –,*** zu Rang und Würde gelangen. **eminent,** *adj.* hervorragend, herausstehend, erhaben; (*fig.*) hervorragend, bedeutend, berühmt, ausgezeichnet; (*coll.*) bemerkenswert, außergewöhnlich, beispielhaft. **eminently,** *adv.* in hohem Maße, (ganz) besonders, ausnehmend, überaus.

emissary ['emisəri], *s.* Abgesandte(r), der (Geheim)bote, Sendbote, Sendling, Emissär.

emission [i'miʃən], *s.* 1. das Aussenden, die Ausströmung, (Aus)strahlung; der Ausfluß, Erguß; 2. (*Comm.*) die Ausgabe, Emission. **emissive** [–siv], *adj.* (*Phys.*) Strahlungs–, ausstrahlend.

emit, *v.t.* ausstrahlen, ausströmen (lassen), aussenden, entsenden; ausstoßen, auswerfen, von sich geben; (*Comm.*) ausgeben, in Umlauf setzen, emittieren; (*Phys.*) ausstrahlen, emittieren; ***– an opinion,*** eine Meinung äußern *or* von sich geben.

emmet ['emit], *s.* (*Poet.*) die Ameise.

emollient [i'mɔliənt], **1.** *adj.* erweichend. **2.** *s.* erweichendes Mittel.

emolument [i'mɔljumənt], *s.* die Vergütung, *pl.* (Neben)einkünfte (*pl.*), (Neben)bezüge (*pl.*).

emotion [i'mouʃən], *s.* die Gemütsbewegung, (Gefühls)regung, Erregung, Rührung, das Gefühl. **emotional,** *adj.* gefühlsbedingt, gefühlsmäßig, Gefühls–, Affekt–; gefühlsbetont, empfindsam, leicht erregbar *or* gerührt; rührend, herzbewegend. **emotionalism,** *s.* die Empfindsamkeit, Gefühlsbetontheit; Gefühlsseligkeit, Gefühlsduselei; Gefühlsäußerung, der Gefühlsausbruch. **emotionalist,** *s.* der Gefühlsmensch. **emotionality** [–'næliti], *s.* die Gefühlsbedingtheit, Gefühlsmäßigkeit, Erregbarkeit. **emotionalize** [–aiz], *v.t.* mit Gefühl behandeln, zur Gefühlssache machen. **emotionless,** *adj.* gefühllos, unempfindsam; ungerührt, unbewegt.

emotive [i'moutiv], *adj.* gefühlsmäßig, Gefühls–, affektiv; gefühlsbetont, gefühlvoll.

empanel [im'pænl], *v.t.* ernennen, eintragen; zusammenrufen (*a jury*).

empathy ['empəθi], *s.* (*Psych.*) die Einfühlung, das Einfühlungsvermögen.

empennage [em'penidʒ], *s.* (*Av.*) das Leitwerk.

emperor ['empərə], *s.* der Kaiser; ***– moth,*** Kleines Nachtpfauenauge; (*Ent.*) ***Purple Emperor,*** Großer Schillerfalter.

emphasis ['emfəsis], *s.* (*Phonet.*) die Betonung, der Akzent (***on,*** auf (*Dat.*)); (*fig.*) die Betonung, das Gewicht, der Nachdruck, die Emphase; der Schwerpunkt. **emphasize** [–saiz], *v.t.* (nachdrücklich) betonen, Nachdruck legen auf (*Acc.*), (*fig.*) hervorheben, unterstreichen. **emphatic** [im'fætik], *adj.* nachdrücklich, betont, unterstrichen; deutlich, eindringlich, ausdrücklich.

emphysema [emfi'si:mə], *s.* das Emphysem, die Wundgeschwulst.

empire ['empaiə], **1.** *s.* das Reich, Kaiserreich; die (Ober)herrschaft, Gewalt (***over,*** über (*Acc.*)); ***British Empire,*** britisches Weltreich; ***Empire Day,*** britischer Staatsfeiertag; ***Holy Roman Empire,*** das Heilige Römische Reich (Deutscher Nation). **2.** *attrib. adj.* (*style*) Empire–; ***– furniture,*** das Empiremöbel.

empiric [em'pirik], *s.* *See* **empiricist. empiric(al),** *adj.* auf Erfahrung gegründet, erfahrungsmäßig, empirisch. **empiricism** [–risizm], *s.* 1. der Empirismus, die Empirie, Erfahrungsmethode; 2. Kurpfuscherei, Quacksalberei. **empiricist** [–risist], *s.* 1. der Empiriker; 2. Kurpfuscher, Quacksalber.

emplacement [im'pleismənt], *s.* der Geschützstand; die Bettung.

employ [im'plɔi], **1.** *v.t.* gebrauchen, benutzen, anwenden, verwenden (*a th.*); beschäftigen; einsetzen, einstellen, anstellen (*a p.*); ***– o.s.*** or ***one's energies,*** sich beschäftigen (***with,*** mit *or* in (*Dat.*)), sich widmen (*Dat.*); ***– one's time,*** seine Zeit verbringen (***in, with,*** mit); ***be –ed,*** angestellt sein (***with,*** bei); beschäftigt sein (***on,*** an *or* mit; ***in doing,*** zu tun). **2.** *s.* die Beschäftigung; ***in his –,*** bei ihm angestellt. **employable,** *adj.* anwendbar, brauchbar, verwendbar, verwendungsfähig (*of a th.*), arbeitsfähig (*of a p.*). **employee,** *s.* Angestellte(r), der Lohnempfänger, Arbeitnehmer. **employer,** *s.* der Arbeitgeber, Unternehmer, Dienstherr; ***–'s liability,*** die Unfallhaftpflicht des Arbeitgebers. **employment,** *s.* 1. die Beschäftigung, Arbeit; das Geschäft, der Dienst, Beruf, die Tätigkeit, (An)stellung; ***be in –,*** beschäftigt sein; ***be thrown out of –,*** arbeitslos *or* stellenlos werden; ***– agency, – bureau, – exchange,*** der Arbeitsnach-

weis, die Arbeitsvermittlung; 2. die Anwendung, Verwendung, Benützung, der Einsatz, Gebrauch.
emporium [em'pɔ:riəm], *s.* der Stapelplatz, (Haupt)handelsplatz; das Warenhaus, Magazin.
empower [im'pauə], *v.t.* ermächtigen, bevollmächtigen, befähigen; ***be -ed,*** befugt *or* berechtigt sein.
empress ['empris], *s.* die Kaiserin.
emprise [em'praiz], *s.* (*obs.*) ritterliches *or* abenteuerliches Unternehmen, das Wagnis.
emptiness ['emptinis], *s.* die Leere, Leerheit; (*fig.*) Nichtigkeit, Hohlheit, Wertlosigkeit. **empty, 1.** *adj.* leer (*of*, an (*Dat.*)), ausgeleert; (*of building*) leerstehend, unbesetzt, unbewohnt; (*fig.*) eitel, nichtig, nichtssagend, inhaltslos, hohl; (*coll.*) hungrig, nüchtern; – ***room,*** leerstehendes Zimmer; ***on an – stomach,*** auf nüchternem Magen; – ***talk,*** hohles Gerede; – ***weight,*** das Eigengewicht. **2.** *v.t.* entleeren, (aus)leeren; abfüllen, ablassen (*boiler*); – ***itself,*** sich ergießen, münden (*as a river*). **3.** *v.i.* sich leeren, leer werden. **4.** *s.* (*usu. pl.*) leere Flasche, leeres Faß; (*Comm.*) das Leergut, Emballagen (*pl.*); (*Artil.*) abgeschossene Hülse; (*Railw.*) das Leermaterial. **empty|-handed,** *adj.* mit leeren Händen. **--headed,** *adj.* hohlköpfig.
empyema [emp(a)i'i:mə], *s.* (*Med.*) das Empyem, die Eiteransammlung.
empyreal [empi'riəl], *adj.* empyreisch, himmlisch. **empyrean, 1.** *s.* der Feuerhimmel, Lichthimmel, (höchster) Himmel, (*coll.*) das Weltall, Firmament. **2.** *adj. See* **empyreal.**
empyreumatic [empiru'mætik], *adj.* brenzlich.
emu ['i:mju:], *s.* (*Orn.*) der Emu, australischer Kasuar.
emulate ['emjuleit], *v.t.* wetteifern mit, es gleichtun (*Dat.*), nacheifern (*Dat.*). **emulation** [–'leiʃən], *s.* der Wetteifer, die Nacheiferung; ***in – of him,*** ihm nacheifernd. **emulative** [–lətiv], **emulous,** *adj.* wetteifernd (*of*, mit), nacheifernd (*Dat.*); eifersüchtig (auf (*Acc.*)), begierig (nach).
emulsifiable [i'mʌlsifaiəbl], *adj.* emulgierbar. **emulsification** [–fi'keiʃən], *s.* die Emulsionsbildung. **emulsifier** [–faiə], *s.* der Emulgator, das Emulgiermittel. **emulsify,** *v.t.* emulgieren. **emulsion** [i'mʌlʃən], *s.* die Emulsion; – ***paint,*** die Emulsionsfarbe. **emulsive,** *adj.* emulsionsbildend, Emulsions–.
emunctory [i'mʌŋktəri], **1.** *s.* (*Anat.*) das Absonderungsorgan, Ausscheidungsorgan. **2.** *adj.* Ausscheidungs–.
en [en], *s.* (*Typ.*) das Halbgeviert.
enable [i'neibl], *v.t.* befähigen, in den Stand setzen, es möglich machen (*Dat.*), ermächtigen, die Möglichkeit geben (*Dat.*) (*a p.*), ermöglichen, möglich machen (*a th.*); ***be -d,*** imstande sein; (*Pol.*) ***enabling act,*** das Ermächtigungsgesetz.
enact [i'nækt], *v.t.* 1. verordnen, verfügen; erlassen (*a law*); Gesetzeskraft verleihen (*Dat.*); 2. (*Theat.*) spielen, darstellen (*a rôle*), inszenieren, aufführen (*a play*); ***be -ed,*** sich abspielen, stattfinden, vor sich gehen (*of events*). **enaction** [i'nækʃən], *s.* gesetzliche Bestimmung, das Erlassen, die Verfügung, Verordnung. **enactive,** *adj.* Verfügungs–. **enactment,** *s.* 1. gesetzliche Verfügung, das Gesetz, der Erlaß; (*Parl.*) die Erhebung zum Gesetz; 2. (*Theat.*) Darstellung.
enamel [i'næml], **1.** *s.* das Email, die Emaille, Emailfarbe, der Lack, Schmelz, die Glasur; (*of teeth*) der (Zahn)schmelz; – ***ware,*** das Emaillegeschirr. **2.** *v.t.* emaillieren, mit Email *or* Schmelz überziehen; glasieren, firnissen, lackieren; überschmelzen, in Email arbeiten *or* malen; (*fig.*) bunt machen, schmücken. **enamel(l)er,** *s.* der Emailleur, Schmelzarbeiter. **enamel(l)ing,** *s.* das Emaillieren, die Lackierung.
enamour [i'næmə], *v.t.* verliebt machen; (*usu. pass.*) ***be -ed,*** verliebt sein (*of*, in (*Acc.*)); (*coll.*) hingezogen sein (zu), versessen sein (auf (*Acc.*)), gefesselt sein (von), sehr gern haben.
en bloc [ã'blɔk], *adv.* en bloc, im ganzen.
encaenia [en'si:niə], *s.* die Gründungsfeier (*Oxford Univ.*).
encage [in'keidʒ], *v.t.* einschließen, einsperren.
encamp [in'kæmp], **1.** *v.t.* lagern lassen. **2.** *v.i.* (sich) lagern, ein Lager aufschlagen; ***be -ed,*** lagern. **encampment,** *s.* das Lagern; (Zelt)lager.
encase [in'keis], *v.t.* in einen Behälter einschließen; umhüllen.
encash [in'kæʃ], *v.t.* in Geld umsetzen, in bar einlösen, einkassieren. **encashment,** *s.* die Einkassierung, das Inkasso.
encaustic [en'kɔ:stik], **1.** *adj.* enkaustisch, eingebrannt; – ***tiles,*** glasierte Ziegel. **2.** *s.* eingebrannte Wachsmalerei.
enceinte [ɔn'sænt], **1.** *adj.* schwanger. **2.** *s.* (*Fort.*) die Umwallung.
encephalitis [ensefə'laitis], *s.* die Gehirnentzündung.
enchain [in'tʃein], *v.t.* anketten, verketten; (*fig.*) fesseln, ketten, festhalten.
enchant [in'tʃɑ:nt], *v.t.* verzaubern, verhexen, behexen; (*fig.*) bezaubern, entzücken; ***-ed castle,*** das Zauberschloß. **enchanter,** *s.* der Hexenmeister, Zauberer. **enchanting,** *adj.* (*fig.*) bezaubernd, hinreißend, reizend, entzückend. **enchantment,** *s.* die Verzauberung; der Zauber(bann), die Hexerei, Zauberei; (*fig.*) der Zauber. **enchantress,** *s.* die Zauberin, Hexe.
enchase [in'tʃeis], *v.t.* ziselieren, erhaben verzieren (*metal*), fassen (*gems etc.*); (*fig.*) schmücken; ***-d work,*** getriebene *or* ziselierte Arbeit.
encipher [in'saifə], *v.t.* verschlüsseln, chiffrieren.
encircle [in'sə:kl], *v.t.* umringen, umzingeln, umgeben, einkreisen, einkesseln; (*fig.*) umschließen, umschlingen, umfassen. **encirclement,** *s.* die Einkreisung, Einkesselung.
enclave ['enkleiv], *s.* die Enklave.
enclitic [in'klitik], **1.** *adj.* enklitisch. **2.** *s.* das Enklitikon.
enclose [in'klouz], *v.t.* 1. umzäunen, einfriedigen, einhegen (*land*); einschließen (*in*, in (*Dat. or Acc.*)), umgeben, umringen (mit); 2. (*in a letter*) beilegen, beischließen, beifügen (*in*, ***with***, *Dat.*), in sich schließen, enthalten. **enclosed,** *adj.* (*Comm. etc.*) beiliegend, anbei, in der Anlage; ***the –,*** die Einlage, Anlage. **enclosure** [–'klouʒə], *s.* 1. (*wall etc.*) der Zaun, die Mauer, Einfassung; 2. (*land*) Umzäunung, Einhegung, Einfriedigung; Koppel, das Gehöft, Gehege (*in a wood*); 3. die Anlage, Beilage, Einlage (*in a letter*).
encode [in'koud], *v.t. See* **encipher.**
encomiast [en'koumiæst], *s.* der Lobredner, Schmeichler. **encomiastic(al)** [–'æstik(l)], *adj.* lobend, (lob)preisend. **encomium,** *s.* die Lobrede, Lobpreisung, das Loblied, Enkomion.
encompass [in'kʌmpəs], *v.t.* umgeben, umringen, umfassen, einschließen (***with***, mit); (*fig.*) fassen, enthalten.
encore ['ɔŋkɔ:], **1.** *int.* (*Theat. etc.*) noch einmal! da capo! **2.** *v.t.* um Wiederholung *or* um eine Zugabe bitten. **3.** *s.* die Zugabe; Wiederholung, das Dakapo.
encounter [in'kauntə], **1.** *s.* die Begegnung, zufälliges Zusammentreffen (***with***, mit); (*Mil.*) das Zusammentreffen, der Zusammenstoß, das Gefecht, Treffen. **2.** *v.t.* begegnen (*Dat.*), treffen (*Acc.*); zusammentreffen *or* zusammenstoßen mit, entgegentreten (*Dat.*); stoßen auf (*Acc.*); – ***opposition,*** Widerstand finden.
encourage [in'kʌridʒ], *v.t.* 1. ermutigen, ermuntern, aufmuntern; begeistern, anregen, antreiben, anreizen (***to***, zu); 2. fördern, unterstützen, Vorschub leisten (*Dat.*), bestärken (***in***, in (*Dat.*)). **encouragement,** *s.* die Aufmunterung, Ermunterung, Ermutigung, der Antrieb (***to***, für); die Förderung, Unterstützung, Begünstigung, Gunst. **encouraging,** *adj.* ermutigend; vielversprechend, hoffnungsvoll.
encroach [in'kroutʃ], *v.i.* unberechtigt eindringen, eingreifen ((***up***)***on***, in (*Acc.*)), übergreifen (auf

(*Acc.*)); (*fig.*) – (*up*)*on*, mißbrauchen, über Gebühr in Anspruch nehmen; schmälern, beeinträchtigen. **encroachment,** *s.* der Eingriff, Übergriff ((*up*)*on*, in (*Acc.*)), die Verletzung, Schmälerung, Beeinträchtigung (*Gen.*); das Vordringen, Übergreifen (*as the sea*).

encrust [in'krʌst], *v.t.* mit Rinde *etc.* überziehen, inkrustieren.

encumber [in'kʌmbə], *v.t.* belasten, beschweren, überladen; (be)hindern; versperren; – ***an estate,*** ein Gut mit Schulden belasten. **encumberment,** *s.* die Belastung, Behinderung, Versperrung. **encumbrance,** *s.* die Belastung, Last; Behinderung, Beschwerde, Belästigung, das Hindernis; (*Law*) die Schuldenlast, Hypothekenlast; ***without*** –(*s*), ohne Kinder *or* Verpflichtungen. **encumbrancer,** *s.* der Pfandgläubiger.

encyclical [en's(a)iklikl], **1.** *adj.* enzyklisch. **2.** *s.* (päpstliche) Enzyklika.

encyclop(a)edia [ensaiklo'pi:diə], *s.* die Enzyklopädie, das Konversationslexikon. **encyclop(a)edic,** *adj.* enzyklopädisch; (*fig.*) umfassend.

encyst [en'sist], *v.t.* (*only pass.*) ***–ed,*** verkapselt, abgekapselt, eingekapselt. **encystation** [–'teiʃən], **encystment,** *s.* die Einkapselung, Verkapselung.

end [end], **1.** *s.* 1. (*temporal*) das Ende, der Schluß; das Aufhören, Zuendegehen; 2. (*spatial*) Ende; (*of a town*) der Teil, die Gegend; 3. (*fig.*) das Ergebnis, Resultat, die Konsequenz, Folge; (*oft. pl.*) Absicht; der (End)zweck, das Ziel; 4. (*coll.*) Endchen, Stück(chen), der Rest.

(a) (*with nouns*) ***candle –,*** der Kerzenstummel; ***the –s of the earth,*** das äußerste Ende der Welt; ***odds and –s,***(Über)reste, allerhand Kleinigkeiten; ***rope's –,*** der Tamp, das Tauende; ***shoemaker's –,*** der Pechdraht; ***no – of trouble,*** nichts als Unannehmlichkeiten, unendliche Mühe; (*fig.*) ***the thin – of the wedge,*** ein schwacher Anfang, einmal ein Anfang; ***the West End of London,*** der Westen Londons, westlicher Teil von London.

(b) (*with verbs*) ***there's an – of it,*** und damit gut *or* basta; ***there must be an – of,*** es muß ein Ende haben mit; ***there's an – to everything,*** alles hat mal ein Ende; ***you will be the – of me,*** du bringst mich noch ins Grab; ***bring to an –,*** zu Ende führen *or* bringen; ***come to an –,*** zu Ende gehen *or* kommen, ein Ende nehmen *or* finden; ***come to a bad –,*** ein böses Ende nehmen; ***gain one's –,*** sein Ziel erreichen; (*coll.*) ***go off the deep –,*** die Fassung verlieren, aus der Haut fahren, in Harnisch geraten; ***the – justifies the means,*** der Zweck heiligt die Mittel; (*coll.*) ***keep one's – up,*** seinen Mann stehen, durchhalten, nicht nachgeben; ***make an – of,*** Schluß machen mit, ein Ende machen (*Dat.*); ***make both –s meet,*** gerade auskommen, sein Auskommen finden, sich nach der Decke strecken; ***put an – to,*** see ***make an – of***; ***serve one's –,*** seine Privatinteressen *or* seinen eignen Vorteil wahren.

(c) (*with preps.*) ***at the – of June,*** Ende Juni; (*coll.*) ***at our –,*** hier bei uns; ***be at an –,*** zu Ende sein, vorbei *or* aus sein; (*coll.*) ***be at a loose –,*** nichts zu tun haben, untätig *or* müßig sein; ohne feste Bindung; ***have at one's fingers' –s,*** am Schnürchen haben; (*fig.*) ***be at the – of one's tether,*** ratlos dastehen, nicht mehr weiter wissen; ***be at one's wits' –,*** sich (*Dat.*) nicht mehr zu helfen wissen, am Ende seiner Weisheit sein; ***for one's own*** (***private***) ***–s,*** zum eigenen Nutzen; ***in the –,*** am Ende, schließlich; auf die Dauer; ***it comes to very much the same thing in the –,*** es kommt schließlich auf eins hinaus; ***be near one's –,*** dem Tode nahe sein; ***on –,*** aufrecht, hochkant; (*fig.*) ununterbrochen, hintereinander; ***his hair stood on –,*** die Haare standen ihm zu Berge; ***for hours on –,*** stundenlang; ***– on,*** mit dem Ende zugewandt (*to, Dat.*); ***– to –,*** mit den Enden aneinander; ***from – to –,*** der Länge nach, von einem Ende zum anderen; ***to no –,*** vergebens; ***to this –,*** zu diesem Zwecke; ***to the – that,*** damit; ***to what –?*** wozu? zu welchem Zweck? ***to the bitter –,*** bis aufs äußerste *or* zum äußersten; ***without –,*** unaufhörlich, fortwährend, immer und ewig; ***world without –,*** von Ewigkeit zu Ewigkeit, für immer und immer.

2. *v.t.* (be)enden, beendigen, vollenden, abschließen, zu Ende bringen *or* führen, ein Ende machen (*Dat.*); – ***one's days,*** den Lebensabend zubringen *or* verbringen.

3. *v.i.* enden, endigen, zu Ende kommen, schließen, aufhören; – ***by saying,*** schließlich sagen; (*Prov.*) ***all's well that –s well,*** Ende gut, alles gut; – ***in,*** damit endigen *or* auslaufen *or* ausgehen daß, dazu führen daß; – ***in nothing*** or ***smoke,*** zu Wasser werden, im Sand verlaufen, verpuffen, zu nichts führen; – ***with,*** ein Ende finden mit; (*coll.*) ***– up in,*** see – ***in.***

endanger [in'deindʒə], *v.t.* gefährden, in Gefahr bringen.

endear [in'diə], *v.t.* lieb *or* wert *or* teuer machen; – ***o.s. to*** or ***with,*** sich lieb Kind machen bei. **endearing,** *adj.* zärtlich, lockend (*as words*), reizend, lieblich, gefällig (*of persons*). **endearment,** *s.* die Liebkosung, Zärtlichkeit; Beliebtheit; ***term of –,*** das Kosewort, der Kosename.

endeavour [in'devə], **1.** *s.* die Bemühung, Anstrengung, das Bestreben; ***make every –,*** alles Mögliche versuchen. **2.** *v.i.* sich bemühen, streben, trachten, (ver)suchen (***to do,*** zu tun).

endemic [en'demik], *s.* endemische Krankheit. **endemic(al),** *adj.* endemisch, örtlich beschränkt.

endermic [en'də:mik], *adj.* auf die Haut wirkend.

ending ['endiŋ], *s.* das Ende, die Beendigung, Vollendung, der (Ab)schluß; (*Gram.*) die Endung.

endive ['endiv], *s.* die Endivie.

endless ['endlis], *adj.* endlos, unendlich, ohne Ende; fortdauernd, unaufhörlich, ununterbrochen, ständig; – ***band,*** das Transportband, Raupenband, endloses Band; – ***chain,*** das Paternosterwerk, die Eimerkette; (*fig.*) endlose Kette (*of events etc.*); – ***screw,*** die Schnecke, Schraube ohne Ende. **endlessness,** *s.* die Endlosigkeit, Unendlichkeit.

endoblast ['endoblɑ:st], *s.* inneres Keimblatt.

endocarditis [endoukɑ:'daitis], *s.* die Herzklappenentzündung. **endocardium** [–'kɑ:diəm], *s.* die Herzinnenhaut.

endocarp ['endokɑ:p], *s.* (*Bot.*) das Endokarp, innere Fruchthaut.

endocrine ['endokrin], *adj.* endokrin, inkretorisch, mit innerer Sekretion (*of glands*).

endogen ['endodʒən], *s.* (*Bot.*) die Monokotyle(done). **endogenous** [–'dɔdʒinəs], *adj.* (*Bot., Geol.*) endogen.

endoplasm ['endoplæzm], *s.* innere Plasmaschicht.

endorse [in'dɔ:s], *v.t.* 1. auf der Rückseite überschreiben, vermerken; indossieren, girieren (*a cheque*); 2. überweisen, übertragen ((*over*) *to, Dat.*); 3. beipflichten, gutheißen, bekräftigen, bestätigen (*opinions etc.*). **endorsee** [–'si:], *s.* der Indossat, Girat. **endorsement,** *s.* 1. (*Comm.*) die Aufschrift, der Akzeptvermerk, das Indossement, Indossament, Giro; (*on documents*) der Nachtrag, Vermerk, Zusatz; 2. die Übertragung, Zession; 3. (*fig.*) Genehmigung, Bestätigung, Bekräftigung. **endorser,** *s.* der Indossant, Girant.

endosperm ['endouspə:m], *s.* das Endosperm, Nährgewebe.

endow [in'dau], *v.t.* 1. gründen, stifen; ***–ed school,*** die Stiftungsschule; 2. subventionieren, dotieren; (*fig.*) ausstatten; (*fig.*) ***–ed with,*** begabt mit. **endowment,** *s.* 1. die Ausstattung; – ***insurance,*** die Lebensversicherung auf den Erlebensfall; 2. die Stiftung, Dotation; 3. (*usu. pl.*) Gabe, Begabung.

end|-paper, *s.* (*Bookb.*) der Vorsatz, das Vorsatzpapier. **–piece,** *s.* das Endstück, der Zipfel. **– play,** *s.* (*Tech.*) das Endspiel. **–-product,** *s.* das Schlußergebnis; (*fig.*) der Endeffekt.

endue [in'dju:], *v.t.* anziehen, anlegen (*clothes etc.*), (be)kleiden (*a p.*); (*usu. fig.*) ausstatten, ausrüsten, versehen, begaben (***with,*** mit).

endurable [in'djuərəbl], *adj.* erträglich, leidlich.

endurance, *s.* die Dauer(haftigkeit), Fortdauer; das Ertragen, Aushalten, Erdulden, Erleiden; die Ausdauer, Geduld, Beharrlichkeit; ***beyond*** or ***past*** –, unausstehlich, unerträglich; – ***flight,*** der Dauerflug; – ***test,*** die Belastungsprobe (*of material*); (*fig.*) Geduldsprobe; (*Motor.*) – ***trial,*** die Dauerfahrt. **endure, I.** *v.t.* aushalten, ertragen, erdulden; erfahren, durchmachen; (*fig. only neg.*) ausstehen, leiden; ***not to be*** **–*d*,** nicht auszuhalten, unerträglich. **2.** *v.i.* Dauer haben, ausdauern, fortdauern; (*fig.*) aushalten, ausharren. **enduring,** *adj.* dauernd, bleibend, fortdauernd, andauernd.

end|ways, -wise, *adv.* aufrecht, gerade; mit dem Ende zugewandt (***to***, *Dat.*).

enema ['enimə], *s.* das Klistier; die Klistierspritze.

enemy ['enimi], **I.** *s.* der Feind, Gegner, Widersacher; (*B.*) Teufel, der böse Feind; ***sworn*** –, der Todfeind; ***be one's own*** (***worst***) –, sich selbst im Wege stehen; (*sl.*) ***how's*** or ***how goes the*** –? wie spät ist es? **2.** *adj.* feindlich, Feind(es)–; – ***action,*** die Kriegseinwirkung; – ***alien,*** feindlicher Ausländer; – ***position,*** die Feindstellung.

energetic [enə'dʒetik], *adj.* tatkräftig, energisch; tätig, wirksam; kraftvoll, nachdrücklich. **energize** ['enədʒaiz], *v.t.* (*Tech.*) erregen, mit Energie speisen; (*fig.*) anspornen, mit Tatkraft erfüllen (*a p.*), kräftig machen, kräftigen. **energy** ['enədʒi], *s.* die Tatkraft, Energie, Arbeitsfähigkeit, Kraft; der Nachdruck, Kraftaufwand, die Wirksamkeit; ***conservation of*** –, die Erhaltung der Kraft; ***nuclear*** –, die (Atom)kernenergie; ***potential*** –, potentielle Energie.

enervate, I. [i'nə:vit], *adj.* kraftlos, entnervt, abgespannt, schlaff. **2.** ['enəveit], *v.t.* entkräften, entnerven, abspannen, schwächen. **enervating** ['enəveitiŋ], *adj.* entkräftend, abspannend, schwächend. **enervation** [–'veiʃən], *s.* die Entkräftung, Entnervung, Schwächung; Schwäche, Abgespanntheit.

enfeeble [in'fi:bl], *v.t.* schwächen, entkräften. **enfeeblement,** *s.* die Schwächung, Entkräftung; Schwäche.

enfeoff [in'fef, –'fi:f], *v.t.* belehnen; (*fig.*) ausliefern, übergeben. **enfeoffment,** *s.* die Belehnung; der Lehnsbrief.

enfilade [enfi'leid], **I.** *s.* (*Mil.*) das Flankenfeuer, Längsfeuer. **2.** *v.t.* der Länge nach beschießen, mit Flankenfeuer bestreichen. **enfilading,** *adj.* Flanken–, Flankierungs–.

enfold [in'fould], *v.t.* einhüllen (***in***, in (*Acc.*)), umhüllen (***with***, mit); (*fig.*) umfassen, umschließen.

enforce [in'fɔ:s], *v.t.* erzwingen, durchsetzen; Geltung verschaffen (*Dat.*), durchführen; aufzwingen, auferlegen, mit Nachdruck einschärfen ((***up***)***on***, *Dat.*); zur Geltung bringen, geltend machen. **enforceable,** *adj.* erzwingbar, durchsetzbar. **enforced,** *adj.* erzwungen, aufgezwungen, notgedrungen; – ***sale,*** der Zwangsverkauf. **enforcement,** *s.* die Durchsetzung, Vollziehung, Vollstreckung, gewaltsame Durchführung; die Erzwingung, Geltendmachung; der Zwang.

enfranchise [in'fræntʃaiz], *v.t.* I. befreien, freilassen, für frei erklären; 2. das Bürgerrecht *or* Wahlrecht erteilen (*Dat.*); ***be*** **–*d*,** das Wahlrecht erhalten. **enfranchisement** [–tʃizmənt], *s.* I. die Freilassung, Befreiung; 2. Einbürgerung; 3. Erteilung des Bürgerrechts *or* Wahlrechts.

engage [in'geidʒ], **I.** *v.t.* I. verpflichten, binden; 2. auf sich (*Acc.*) ziehen; – ***his attention,*** seine Aufmerksamkeit für sich gewinnen *or* auf sich ziehen; 3. (*usu. pass.*) beschäftigen (***in***, mit), in Anspruch nehmen (von); 4. einstellen, anstellen, in Dienst nehmen, engagieren, dingen, heuern; 5. (vorher)bestellen, belegen, besetzen (*seats*); mieten (*room etc.*); 6. (*Tech.*) einrücken, kuppeln, einschalten; 7. (*fig.*) fesseln, verwickeln (***in***, in (*Acc.*)); 8. einsetzen (*troops*), angreifen, binden (*the enemy*); – ***him in conversation,*** ein Gespräch mit ihm anknüpfen. **2.** *v.i.* I. sich verpflichten, sich binden; Gewähr leisten, einstehen; 2. sich einlassen (***in***, auf (*Acc.*)), sich befassen *or* abgeben *or* beschäftigen (mit), sich beteiligen (an (*Dat.*)); 3. (*Mil.*) anbinden, angreifen; 4. (*Tech.*) einklinken, ineinandergreifen.

engaged [in'geidʒd], *adj.* I. verpflichtet, gebunden; 2. (*of a p.*) beschäftigt, vergeben, nicht abkömmlich; (*phone, seat etc.*) besetzt, (*room*) belegt, (*table*) reserviert; (*Tele.*) – ***signal,*** das Besetztzeichen; 3. – (***to be married***), verlobt, versprochen; ***become*** or (*coll.*) ***get*** –, sich verloben; – ***couple,*** das Brautpaar. **engagement,** *s.* I. die Verpflichtung, Verbindlichkeit (***to***, gegenüber); ***meet one's*** **–*s*,** seinen (Zahlungs)verpflichtungen nachkommen; ***be under an*** – ***to him,*** ihm vertraglich verpflichtet sein; 2. die Verlobung (***to***, mit); ***break off the*** –, die Verlobung auflösen; – ***ring,*** der Verlobungsring; 3. das Engagement (*of an actor etc.*); die Beschäftigung, Anstellung; 4. Einladung, Verabredung, Vereinbarung, das Übereinkommen; ***I have an*** – ***with him,*** ich habe eine Verabredung mit ihm; – ***book,*** das Merkbuch für Verabredungen; 5. (*Mil.*) das Gefecht, Treffen, die Kampfhandlung. **engaging,** *adj.* (*fig.*) einnehmend, gewinnend, anziehend, reizend.

engender [in'dʒendə], *v.t.* (*fig.*) erzeugen, hervorbringen, hervorrufen, verursachen.

engine ['endʒin], **I.** *s.* die Maschine; der Motor; (*Railw.*) die Lokomotive; (*fig.*) das Werkzeug, Mittel; ***internal combustion*** –, der Verbrennungsmotor; ***in-line*** –, der Reihenmotor; ***marine*** –, die Schiffsmaschine; ***radial*** –, der Sternmotor. **2.** *v.t.* (*Nav.*) mit Maschinen *or* Motoren versehen.

engine|-builder, *s.* der Maschinenbauer. **--capacity,** *s.* die Motorenleistung. **--cowling,** *s.* die Motorhaube. **--driver,** *s.* (*Railw.*) der Lokomotivführer.

engineer [endʒi'niə], **I.** *s.* der Ingenieur, Techniker; Maschinenbauer, Maschinist; (*Mil.*) Pionier; (*Am.*) Lokomotivführer; (*coll.*) Organisator; ***chief*** –, der Oberingenieur; ***civil*** –, der Bauingenieur, Zivilingenieur; ***electrical*** –, der Elektrotechniker; ***marine*** –, der Schiff(s)bauingenieur; ***mechanical*** –, der Maschinenbauer; ***mining*** –, der Bergwerksingenieur. **2.** *v.t.* (er)bauen, errichten, konstruieren; (*fig.*) einrichten, ausführen, durchführen, durchsetzen, (*coll.*) einfädeln, deichseln, herbeiführen, bewerkstelligen. **engineering,** *s.* das Ingenieurwesen, der Maschinenbau, die Maschinenbaukunst; (*coll.*) Mache, das Getue, Manipulationen (*pl.*), Umtriebe (*pl.*); ***civil*** –, die Ziviltechnik; ***electrical*** –, die Elektrotechnik; ***marine*** –, der Schiff(s)bau; ***mechanical*** –, der Maschinenbau; (*obs.*) ***military*** –, das Geniewesen; – ***drawing,*** die Konstruktionszeichnung.

engine|-failure, *s.* der Motordefekt, Motorausfall. **--fitter,** *s.* der Maschinenschlosser, Monteur. **--house,** *s.* (*Railw.*) der Lok(omotiv)schuppen; das Maschinenhaus. **--room,** *s.* der Maschinenraum. **--speed,** *s.* die Motordrehzahl. **--trouble,** *s.* der Maschinenschaden, die Motorpanne.

engird [in'gə:d], *irr.v.t.* (***p.p.*** **engirt**) umgürten, umschließen, umgeben.

English ['ingliʃ], **I.** *adj.* englisch; – ***Channel,*** der Ärmelkanal; ***Old*** – (***type***), die Fraktur(schrift). **2.** *s.* I. das Englisch(e) (*language*); ***Queen's*** (or ***King's***) –, reines English; (*fig.*) ***in plain*** –, auf gut deutsch; 2. ***the*** –, das englische Volk, die Engländer. **Englishman,** *s.* der Engländer. **Englishwoman,** *s.* die Engländerin.

engraft [in'grɑ:ft], *v.t.* pfropfen (***upon***, auf (*Acc.*)); (*fig.*) einpflanzen, einprägen (***in***, *Dat.*). **engraftation** [–'teiʃən], *s.* das Pfropfen; (*fig.*) Einprägen.

engrail [in'greil], *v.t.* (*usu. p.p.*) (*Her.*) auszacken; (*coins*) rändeln. **engrailment,** *s.* (*Her.*) gezahnter Rand; die Rändelung.

engrain [in'grein], *v.t.* in der Wolle färben, tief färben; (*fig.*) (*usu. pass.*) unauslöschlich einprägen, tief einwurzeln *or* einpflanzen. **engrained,** *adj.* in der Wolle gefärbt; (*fig.*) fest verwurzelt, in Fleisch und Blut übergegangen.

engrave [in'greiv], *v.t.* gravieren, stechen; einschneiden, eingraben ((*up*)*on*, auf (*Acc.*)); (*fig.*) einprägen (*Dat.*). **engraver,** *s.* der Graveur, Kunststecher; Kupferstecher; ***wood*--,** der Holzschneider. **engraving,** *s.* das Gravieren, die Gravierkunst; der Stich, Kupferstich, Holzschnitt; ***copperplate*--,** der Kupferstich; ***photographic* –,** die Photogravüre.

engross [in'grous], *v.t.* 1. an sich ziehen *or* reißen, ganz (für sich) in Anspruch nehmen, monopolisieren; 2. (*Comm.*) (im großen) (auf)kaufen; eine Reinschrift anfertigen von, ins reine *or* in großer Schrift (ab)schreiben; (*Law*) in rechtsgültiger *or* gesetzlicher Form ausdrücken, mundieren. **engrossed,** *adj.* (*fig.*) voll in Anspruch genommen, eingenommen (***by***, von), versunken, vertieft (***in***, ***with***, in (*Acc.*)). **engrosser,** *s.* der Urkundenabschreiber. **engrossing,** *adj.* 1. fesselnd, spannend; 2. – ***hand***, die Kanzleischrift. **engrossment,** *s.* 1. (*Comm.*) der Aufkauf; (*Law*) (mundierte) Urkunde; die Reinschrift, Abschrift; Anfertigung, Ausfertigung, Mundierung; 2. (*fig.*) völliges Aufgehen (***in***, ***with***, in (*Dat.*)), die Inanspruchnahme (durch).

engulf [in'gʌlf], *v.t.* verschlingen; in einen Abgrund stürzen, versenken; (*fig.*) überschütten, überwältigen, begraben.

enhance [in'hɑ:ns], *v.t.* erhöhen, vergrößern, steigern; (*fig.*) übertreiben. **enhancement,** *s.* die Erhöhung, Steigerung, Verstärkung, Vergrößerung.

enharmonic [enhɑ:'mɔnik], **1.** *adj.* enharmonisch. **2.** *s.* enharmonischer Akkord.

enigma [i'nigmə], *s.* das Rätsel; rätselhafte S. *or* P. **enigmatic(al)** [enig'mætik(l)], *adj.* rätselhaft; dunkel, geheimnisvoll, unverständlich.

enjambment [in'dʒæmmənt], *s.* das Enjambement, die Versbrechung, der Zeilensprung.

enjoin [in'dʒɔin], *v.t.* auferlegen, vorschreiben, einschärfen, zur Pflicht machen (***on***, *Dat.*), auftragen, befehlen (***him***, ihm; ***to do***, zu tun); (*Law*) – ***him from doing***, ihm verbieten zu tun, ihn davon zurückhalten daß er tut.

enjoy [in'dʒɔi], *v.t.* sich erfreuen (*Gen.*), genießen, besitzen (*as good health etc.*); sich erfreuen an (*Dat.*), Gefallen *or* Vergnügen finden an (*Dat.*), Freude *or* Vergnügen haben an (*Dat.*); ***I – the coffee***, der Kaffee schmeckt mir; – ***o.s.***, sich gut unterhalten, sich amüsieren. **enjoyable,** *adj.* genießbar (*of food*); genußreich, erfreulich. **enjoyment,** *s.* der Genuß (***of***, *Gen.*), die Freude, das Vergnügen, Gefallen (an (*Dat.*)).

enkindle [in'kindl], *v.t.* (*fig.*) entzünden, entflammen.

enlace [in'leis], *v.t.* umschlingen, fest umgeben, verschlingen, verflechten, verstricken.

enlarge [in'lɑ:dʒ], **1.** *v.t.* erweitern, ausweiten, verbreitern, ausdehnen, (*also Phot.*) vergrößern; (*Tech.*) – ***a hole***, ein Loch aufdornen; – ***one's mind***, seinen Gesichtskreis erweitern; ***–d and revised edition***, vermehrte und verbesserte Auflage. **2.** *v.i.* 1. (*Phot.*) sich vergrößern lassen; sich erweitern, sich ausdehnen, sich vergrößern, zunehmen; 2. (*fig.*) sich (weitläufig) auslassen, sich verbreiten ((***up***)***on***, über (*Acc.*)). **enlargement,** *s.* 1. die Vergrößerung (*also Phot.*), Ausdehnung, Zunahme, Erweiterung (*of the heart etc.*); 2. (*fig.*) Verbreitung ((***up***)***on***, über (*Acc.*)). **enlarger,** *s.* (*Phot.*) der Vergrößerungsapparat.

enlighten [in'laitn], *v.t.* erleuchten, aufklären, belehren, unterrichten (***on***, über (*Acc.*)). **enlightened,** *adj.* erleuchtet, aufgeklärt, vorurteilsfrei. **enlightenment,** *s.* die Aufklärung.

enlist [in'list], **1.** *v.t.* anwerben (*soldiers*), einstellen, werben, in Dienst stellen (*employees*); (*fig.*) gewinnen, engagieren, in Anspruch nehmen; – ***his services***, seine Dienste in Anspruch nehmen; – ***his sympathy***, Stimmung bei ihm machen; (*Am.*) ***–ed men***, Mannschaften (*pl.*). **2.** *v.i.* sich anwerben lassen, Soldat werden; sich freiwillig melden (***in***, zu). **enlistment,** *s.* die (An)werbung, Einstellung; Gewinnung (*of help*), Hinzuziehung (*of helpers*); ***age at*** –, das Eintrittsalter; ***date of*** –, der Einstellungstermin.

enliven [in'laivn], *v.t.* beleben, beseelen, anfeuern, ermuntern, erheitern.

en masse [ã'mæs], *adv.* als Ganzes, alle(s) zusammen; in Massen, in der Masse.

enmesh [in'meʃ], *v.t.* verstricken, umgarnen.

enmity ['enmiti], *s.* die Feindschaft; Feindseligkeit, Abneigung, das Übelwollen, der Haß; ***be at – with***, verfeindet sein mit, feindlich gegenüberstehen (*Dat.*); ***bear him no*** –, ihm nicht nachtragen, es ihm nicht übelnehmen.

ennoble [i'noubl], *v.t.* adeln, in den Adelsstand erheben; (*fig.*) veredeln. **ennoblement,** *s.* die Erhebung in den Adelsstand; (*fig.*) Veredelung.

ennui [ɔn'wi:], *s.* die Langeweile.

enormity [i'nɔ:miti], *s.* die Ungeheuerlichkeit, Unmäßigkeit, Enormität; Abscheulichkeit, der Greuel, Frevel. **enormous,** *adj.* ungeheuer, gewaltig, riesig; (*coll.*) kolossal, enorm. **enormousness,** *s.* ungeheure Größe.

enough [i'nʌf], **1.** *adv.* genug; genügend, hinlänglich; ***curiously*** –, eigentümlicherweise; ***please be kind – to shut the window***, bitte seien Sie so gut *or* freundlich und machen Sie das Fenster zu; ***like(ly)*** –, sehr wahrscheinlich; ***are you man – to do it?*** bist du Manns genug es zu tun? ***natural*** –, ganz natürlich; ***safe*** –, durchaus sicher; – ***and to spare***, übergenug; ***sure – there he was***, freilich *or* gewiß *or* und richtig *or* und tatsächlich, da war er; ***true*** –, nur zu wahr; ***are you warm –?*** ist es Ihnen warm genug? ***well*** –, recht gut, (zwar) ganz leidlich. **2.** *adj.* ausreichend, hinlänglich; (*indecl.*) genug; ***we have time*** – or – ***time***, wir haben Zeit genug *or* genug Zeit *or* ausreichende Zeit; ***it is – for me***, es genügt mir. **3.** *s.* die Genüge; ***I have had (more than) – (of it)***, ich habe *or* bin es (mehr als) satt; – ***of that!*** genug davon! laß das! Schluß damit! ***have – to do to get finished***, seine Mühe haben, fertig zu werden; (*Prov.*) – ***is as good as a feast***, allzuviel ist ungesund.

enounce [i'nauns], *v.t.* verkünden, ankündigen, bekanntgeben, bekanntmachen, erklären; aussprechen, äußern.

en passant [ã'pæsã], *adv.* nebenbei, beiläufig, im Vorbeigehen.

enquire, *etc. See* **inquire.**

enrage [in'reidʒ], *v.t.* wütend *or* rasend machen, aufbringen, erzürnen. **enraged,** *adj.* wütend, rasend (***at***, über (*Acc.*) (*a th.*); ***with***, auf (*Acc.*) (*a p.*)).

enrapture [in'ræptʃə], *v.t.* entzücken. **enraptured,** *adj.* hingerissen, entzückt.

enrich [in'ritʃ], *v.t.* bereichern (*a p., also fig.*), anreichern, fruchtbar machen (*land*); (*fig.*) (aus)schmücken, reich verzieren (*as a building*), befruchten (*as the mind*); (*Tech.*) anreichern. **enrichment,** *s.* die Bereicherung; Verzierung, Ausschmückung; Anreicherung.

enrol [in'roul], **1.** *v.t.* einschreiben, eintragen; (*Mil.*) (an)werben; anmustern (*sailors*), einstellen (*workers*), als Mitglied aufnehmen (*in a society*); (*Law*) amtlich aufzeichnen, protokollieren; – ***o.s.***, sich einschreiben lassen, sich als Mitglied eintragen lassen; – ***o.s. in***, eintreten bei, beitreten (*Dat.*). **2.** *v.i. See* – ***o.s.***; (*Univ.*) sich immatrikulieren (lassen); – ***for lectures***, Vorlesungen belegen. **enrolment,** *s.* die Eintragung, Einschreibung; Aufnahme, Beitrittserklärung (*in a society*); (*Mil.*) Anwerbung; (*Law*) das Verzeichnis, Register; (*Univ.*) (zugelassene) Studentenzahl.

en route [ã'ru:t], *adv.* unterwegs, auf dem Wege (***for***, nach).

ensconce [in'skɔns], *v.t.* verstecken, verbergen; (*usu.* – ***o.s.***) sich bequem niederlassen.

ensemble [ã'sɑ:mbl], *s.* das Ganze, die Gesamtheit; (*Theat., Mus.*) das Ensemble(spiel); die Gesamtwirkung; (*clothes*) das Komplet.

enshrine [in'ʃrain], *v.t.* in einen Schrein einschließen, (als Heiligtum) verwahren. **enshrinement,** *s.* die Einschließung, Verwahrung.

enshroud [in'ʃraud], *v.t.* (ver)hüllen, einhüllen.

ensign ['ens(ə)in], *s.* 1. (*Nav.*) die (Schiffs)flagge; Fahne, Standarte, Nationalflagge; das Abzeichen, Kennzeichen; 2. (*Hist., Mil.*) der Fahnenjunker, Fähnrich; (*Am.*) Leutnant zur See. **ensigncy** [-si], *s.* (*Hist., Mil.*) die Fähnrichsstelle.

ensilage ['ensilidʒ], *s.* das Gärfutter, Grünfutter, Süßpreßfutter.

enslave [in'sleiv], *v.t.* zum Sklaven machen, versklaven, unterjochen, knechten; (*fig.*) fesseln, binden (*to*, an (*Acc.*)). **enslavement,** *s.* die Versklavung, Unterjochung, Knechtung; Knechtschaft; (*fig.*) sklavische Bindung (*to*, an (*Acc.*)).

ensnare [in'snɛə], *v.t.* fangen; (*fig.*) verstricken, bestricken, verführen. **ensnarement,** *s.* (*fig.*) die Verstrickung, Verführung.

ensue [in'sju:], *v.i.* darauf folgen, erfolgen, sich ergeben (*from*, aus). **ensuing,** *adj.* (darauf)-folgend, bevorstehend; – ***ages,*** die Nachwelt.

ensure [in'ʃuə], *v.t.* sichern, sicherstellen (***against, from***, gegen), schützen (vor (*Dat.*)); versichern, garantieren, Gewähr leisten für.

enswathe [in'sweið], *v.t.* (*Poet.*) umhüllen, einhüllen.

entablature [in'tæblətʃə], *s.* (*Archit.*) das Säulengebälk, Hauptgesims.

entail [in'teil], **1.** *s.* (*Law*) unveräußerliches Erbgut, das Erblehen, Fideikommiß; ***cut off*** or ***break the*** –, das Fideikommiß aufheben; ***set up an*** –, ein Fideikommiß einsetzen; ***in strict*** –, als unveränderliches Erblehen. **2.** *v.t.* 1. als Fideikommiß vererben (*on*, auf (*Acc.*)); in ein unveräußerliches Erblehen verwandeln; übertragen (*on*, auf (*Acc.*)), als unveräußerlichen Besitz verleihen (*Dat.*); 2. (*fig.*) mit sich bringen, nach sich ziehen, zur Folge haben. **entailed,** *adj.* – ***estate,*** das Erbgut; – ***property,*** unveräußerlicher Grundbesitz. **entailment,** *s.* die Übertragung als Fideikommiß.

entangle [in'tæŋgl], *v.t.* verwickeln, verstricken, verwirren; ***be -d in,*** verstrickt sein in (*Dat.*), sich verwickeln in (*Acc.*); ***become -d with,*** sich kompromittieren mit. **entanglement,** *s.* 1. die Verwick(e)lung, Verwirrung; 2. (*coll.*) Liebschaft; 3. (*Mil.*) der Verhau.

entelechy [en'teləki], *s.* (*Phil.*) die Entelechie, Eigengesetzlichkeit.

entente [ã'tãt], *s.* das Bündnis.

enter ['entə], **1.** *v.t.* betreten, hineingehen *or* -kommen *or* -treten in (*Acc.*), eintreten *or* -steigen *or* -fahren *or* -laufen in (*Acc.*), sich begeben in (*Acc.*), (*as a river*) sich ergießen in (*Acc.*); (*fig.*) eintreten in (*Acc.*), antreten, beginnen (*an era*); beitreten (*Dat.*), Mitglied werden von (*a society*); einschreiben, eintragen, melden (*name etc.*); (*Comm.*) – (*up*), regelrecht buchen; (*Law*) – ***an action against him,*** ihn verklagen; – ***the army,*** Soldat werden; – ***a claim,*** eine Klage einreichen, eine Forderung erheben (*for*, auf (*Acc.*)); – ***a convent,*** Nonne werden; – ***it to his credit,*** es ihm gutschreiben; – ***it to his debit,*** ihn damit belasten, es ihm in Rechnung stellen; – ***goods at the custom-house,*** Waren deklarieren; – ***a harbour,*** in einen Hafen einlaufen; ***the thought -ed my head,*** der Gedanke kam mir in den Sinn, mir kam der Gedanke; – ***a horse*** (***for a race***), ein Pferd (für ein Rennen) anmelden; – ***a hospital,*** ein Krankenhaus aufsuchen; – ***judgement,*** ein Urteil fällen; – ***the lists,*** in die Schranken treten; – ***it in the minutes,*** es protokollieren (lassen); – ***one's name,*** sich eintragen *or* einschreiben; ***have one's name -ed,*** sich einschreiben lassen; – ***a profession,*** einen Beruf ergreifen; – ***a protest,*** Verwahrung einlegen, Einspruch erheben (***with***, bei; ***against***, gegen); – ***his service,*** in seine Dienste treten; – ***the university,*** die Hochschule beziehen; – ***the war,*** in den Krieg eintreten; – ***one's fiftieth year,*** das fünfzigste Jahr antreten.
2. *v.i.* eintreten, herein- *or* hineintreten, herein- *or* hineinkommen, herein- *or* hineingehen; (*Spt.*) sich anmelden; (*Theat.*) auftreten; (*fig.*) – ***into,*** sich hineindenken in (*Acc.*), zu würdigen wissen; eingehen *or* sich einlassen auf (*Acc.*); teilnehmen *or* sich beteiligen an (*Dat.*); einen Bestandteil bilden von; – ***into an agreement,*** auf einen Vergleich eingehen; – ***into correspondence,*** in Briefwechsel treten; – ***into details,*** ins einzelne gehen, sich auf Einzelheiten einlassen; – ***into his feelings,*** seine Gefühle würdigen *or* verstehen, mit ihm sympathisieren; – ***into the joke,*** auf den Scherz eingehen; – ***into partnership,*** sich assoziieren, sich geschäftlich verbinden; ***that does not – into my plan,*** das gehört nicht in meinen Plan, (*coll.*) das paßt mir nicht in den Kram; – ***into the spirit of an author,*** in den Geist eines Schriftstellers eindringen; – ***into the spirit of it,*** mit bei der S. sein; – ***into a treaty,*** einen Vertrag abschließen; (*fig.*) – (***up***)***on,*** eintreten *or* sich einlassen in (*Acc.*); vornehmen, beginnen, anschneiden; antreten (*an office*); (*Law*) in Besitz nehmen, Besitz ergreifen von; – ***on a new phase,*** in ein neues Stadium treten.

enteric [en'terik], *adj.* Darm-; – ***fever,*** der (Unterleibs)typhus.

entering ['entəriŋ], *s.* 1. das Eintreten, der Eintritt, Einzug; (*Law*) ***breaking and*** –, der Einbruch; 2. (*fig.*) das Antreten, der Antritt; 3. die Eintragung.

enteritis [entə'raitis], *s.* (*Med.*) der Darmkatarrh. **enterocele** ['entərosi:l], *s.* der Darmbruch.

enterprise ['entəpraiz], *s.* 1. die Unternehmung, das (Geschäfts)unternehmen, der Betrieb; die Spekulation, das Wagnis, Wag(e)stück; ***private*** –, freie Wirtschaft; 2. der Unternehmungsgeist, die Unternehmungslust, Initiative. **enterprising,** *adj.* unternehmend, unternehmungslustig; wagemutig, verwegen, kühn.

entertain [entə'tein], **1.** *v.t.* 1. gastlich bewirten, gastfreundlich aufnehmen; – ***them to dinner,*** sie als Gast zum Mittagessen sehen; 2. hegen (*opinions, resentment*), in Erwägung *or* Betrachtung ziehen (*suggestion*); – ***doubts,*** Zweifel hegen; – ***an idea,*** sich mit einem Gedanken tragen; – ***the proposal,*** auf den Vorschlag eingehen *or* sich einlassen, den Vorschlag in Erwägung ziehen; – ***thoughts of revenge,*** Rachegedanken Raum geben; 3. belustigen, (angenehm) unterhalten, ergötzen; – ***o.s.,*** sich amüsieren; 4. (*obs.*) aufrechterhalten, unterhalten. **2.** *v.i.* Gäste haben, Gäste bei sich sehen. **entertainer,** *s.* der Unterhaltungskünstler. **entertaining,** *adj.* unterhaltend, unterhaltsam, amüsant, ergötzlich. **entertainment,** *s.* 1. gastliche Aufnahme, die Bewirtung, Gastfreundschaft; – ***allowance,*** die Aufwandsentschädigung; 2. die Unterhaltung, Belustigung, Ablenkung, der Zeitvertreib; ***afford*** –, amüsieren, belustigen; ***for their*** –, zu ihrer Unterhaltung *or* Belustigung; ***place of*** –, die Vergnügungsstätte; – ***tax,*** die Lustbarkeitssteuer; 3. die Vorstellung, Aufführung; ***give an*** –, eine Aufführung veranstalten.

enthral(l) [in'θrɔ:l], *v.t.* 1. (*obs.*) unterjochen, versklaven; 2. (*fig.*) fesseln, einnehmen, bezaubern. **enthralling,** *adj.* entzückend, fesselnd, faszinierend, bezaubernd, einnehmend. **enthral(l)ment,** *s.* 1. die Unterjochung; 2. (*fig.*) Fesselung, Bezauberung.

enthrone [in'θroun], *v.t.* auf den Thron setzen; (*Eccl.*) einsetzen; ***be -d,*** thronen. **enthronement,** *s.* die Thronerhebung; (*Eccl.*) Einsetzung.

enthuse [in'θju:z], *v.i.* (*coll.*) schwärmen (***about, over***, für), sich begeistern (über (*Acc.*)), begeistert sein *or* werden (von). **enthusiasm** [-iæzm], *s.* der Enthusiasmus, die Begeisterung (***for***, für; ***about***, über (*Acc.*)), Schwärmerei (für), das Entzücken (über (*Acc.*)). **enthusiast,** *s.* der Schwärmer, Enthusiast. **enthusiastic** [-'æstik], *adj.* enthusiastisch, begeistert (***about***, über (*Acc.*)); schwärmerisch.

entice [in'tais], *v.t.* (an)locken, verlocken; weglocken (***from***, von); verführen, verleiten, reizen (***into***, zu). **enticement,** *s.* die (Ver)lockung, der (An)reiz; die Verleitung, Verführung. **enticing,** *adj.* verlockend, verführerisch, reizend.

entire [in'taiə], **1.** *adj.* 1. ganz, völlig, vollständig, vollkommen, komplett; 2. unversehrt, unbeschädigt, unbeschadet, ungeschmälert, unvermindert, vollzählig, Gesamt–; unvermischt, ungeteilt, uneingeschränkt, voll, aufrichtig, echt; nicht kastriert (*of horses*). **2.** *s.* (*rare*) *see* **entirety. entirely,** *adv.* völlig, gänzlich, ganz und gar, durchaus, lediglich. **entirety** [–riti], *s.* die Ganzheit, Ungeteiltheit, Gesamtheit, Vollständigkeit; das Ganze; ***in its –,*** als Ganzes, in seiner Gesamtheit, in seinem ganzen Umfang.

entitle [in'taitl], *v.t.* betiteln; ***– to,*** berechtigen zu, ein Recht geben auf (*Acc.*); ***be –d to,*** berechtigt sein zu, ein Recht *or* einen (Rechts)anspruch haben auf (*Acc.*). **entitlement,** *s.* das, worauf man berechtigten Anspruch hat, zustehende Quote.

entity ['entiti], *s.* die Wesenheit, das Wesen, Dasein.

entomb [in'tu:m], *v.t.* begraben, bestatten, beerdigen; (*fig.*) vergraben, einschließen. **entombment,** *s.* das Begräbnis, die Beerdigung.

entomological [entəmə'lɔdʒikl], *adj.* entomologisch, Insekten–. **entomologist** [–'mɔlədʒist], *s.* Insektenkundige(r), der Entomologe. **entomology** [–'mɔlədʒi], *s.* die Insektenkunde, Entomologie. **entomophagous** [–'mɔfəgəs], *adj.* insektenfressend. **entomophilous** [–'mɔfiləs], *adj.* insektenblütig.

entophyte ['entəfait], *s.* die Schmarotzerpflanze. **entophytic** [–'fitik], *adj.* (*Bot.*) Innenschmarotzer–.

entourage [ãtu'rɑ:ʒ], *s.* die Umgebung; Begleitung.

entozoon [entə'zouən], *s.* (*pl.* **-zoa**) der Eingeweidewurm.

entr'acte [ɔn'trækt], *s.* (*Theat.*) der Zwischenakt, das Zwischenspiel.

entrails ['entreilz], *pl.* Eingeweide (*pl.*); (*fig.*) das Innere.

entrain [in'trein], **1.** *v.t.* (*Mil.*) verladen (*troops*). **2.** *v.i.* in den Zug einsteigen, verladen werden. **entrainment,** *s.* die (Truppen)verladung.

entrammel [in'træml], *v.t.* (*fig.*) verwickeln; hemmen.

[1]**entrance** ['entrəns], *s.* der Eintritt, Einzug, die Einfahrt, das Eintreten; der Eingang, Zugang, Torweg; Einlaß, Zutritt; (*of an actor*) Auftritt; (*fig.*) Antritt; ***at the –,*** am Eingang; ***no –,*** Eintritt verboten; ***– upon an office,*** der Amtsantritt; ***– to the attic is by a ladder,*** der Zutritt zum Dachzimmer ist über eine Leiter; ***– examination,*** die Aufnahmeprüfung; ***– fee,*** das Eintrittsgeld, die Eintrittsgebühr, der Eintritt; die Einschreibegebühr; ***– hall,*** die Vorhalle, Eingangshalle, (*of house*) der (Haus)flur; ***– money,*** das Eintrittsgeld.

[2]**entrance** [in'trɑ:ns], *v.t.* entzücken, hinreißen, in Verzückung versetzen; außer sich bringen, überwältigen (***with,*** vor (*Dat.*)). **entrancement,** *s.* das Entzücken, die Bezauberung; Verzückung. **entrancing,** *adj.* entzückend, bezaubernd.

entrant ['entrənt], *s.* Eintretende(r); (*Spt.*) der (die) Teilnehmer(in) (***for,*** an (*Dat.*)), Bewerber(in).

entrap [in'træp], *v.t.* fangen; (*fig.*) bestricken, verstricken; verleiten, verführen (***into doing,*** zu tun); überlisten.

entreat [in'tri:t], *v.t.* ersuchen, anflehen, ernstlich bitten (***for,*** um) (*a p.*); erbitten (***of,*** von) (*a th.*). **entreating,** *adj.* flehentlich. **entreaty,** *s.* dringende Bitte, das Gesuch.

entre|chat [ãtr'ʃɑ:], *s.* (*ballet*) der Kreuzsprung. **–cote** ['ãtrəkɔt], *s.* (*Cul.*) das Rippenstück.

entrée ['ãtrei], *s.* **1.** der Eintritt, Zutritt (***of,*** zu); **2.** (*Cul.*) das Zwischengericht.

entremets ['ɔntrəmei], *s.* das Zwischengericht, Nebengericht.

entrench [in'trentʃ], *v.t.* (*Mil.*) mit Gräben versehen, befestigen, verschanzen; ***– o.s.,*** sich eingraben *or* verschanzen; (*fig.*) sich festsetzen. **entrenchment,** *s.* die Verschanzung; Feldschanze, der Schützengraben; Schanzarbeiten (*pl.*).

entre| nous [ãtrə'nu:], *adv.* unter uns, im Vertrauen. **–pôt** [–pou], *s.* die Niederlage, Warenlage, der Lagerplatz. **–preneur** [–prə'nə:], *s.* der Unternehmer. **–sol** [–soul], *s.* das Halbgeschoß, der Zwischenstock.

entropy ['entrəpi], *s.* das Wärmegewicht.

entrust [in'trʌst], *v.t.* anvertrauen (***to,*** *Dat.*), betrauen (*a p.*) (***with,*** mit).

entry ['entri], *s.* **1.** das Eintreten; der Einzug, Eintritt; (*of actor*) Auftritt; (*of immigrants*) Zuzug, die Einreise; (*of goods*) Einfuhr; (*Law*) der Besitzantritt, die Besitzergreifung (***into, upon,*** *Gen.*); ***make one's –,*** (*of a p.*) eintreten, (*of an actor*) auftreten, (*of troops*) seinen Einzug halten; ***no –!*** gesperrt! (*Law*) ***unlawful –,*** der Hausfriedensbruch; **2.** (*Comm.*) die Eintragung, Buchung; der Eintrag, Posten; die Einklarierung, Zollangabe, Zolldeklaration (*at the custom-house*); ***make an – of,*** buchen, eintragen; ***credit –,*** die Gutschrift; ***bookkeeping by double –,*** doppelte Buchführung; **3.** (*Spt.*) die Nennung, Meldung (*for events*), (*a p.*) der Bewerber, (*collect. also pl.*) die Nennungsliste, Teilnehmerliste, (*horse-racing*) Renn-Nennung; **4.** (*coll.*) der Garteneingang, Zugang(sweg); (*Geog.*) die Mündung.

entry| door, *s.* die Eingangstür. **– fee,** *s.* die Nenngebühr. **– form,** *s.* der Anmeldeschein. **– permit,** *s.* die Einreisegenehmigung.

entwine [in'twain], **1.** *v.t.* umwinden, umschlingen, umflechten. **2.** *v.r.* sich winden, verflochten werden.

enucleate [i'nju:klieit], *v.t.* klarlegen, aufklären, erläutern; (*Med.*) herausnehmen (*a tumour*). **enucleation** [–'eiʃən], *s.* die Klarlegung, Bloßlegung. **enucleator,** *s.* (*Surg.*) die Knopfsonde.

enumerate [i'nju:məreit], *v.t.* aufzählen, verzeichnen, spezifizieren. **enumeration** [–'reiʃən], *s.* die Aufzählung; Liste, das Verzeichnis.

enunciate [i'nʌnsieit], *v.t.* verkünden, aussagen; ausdrücken, behaupten; formulieren, aufstellen (*a proposition*); (deutlich) aussprechen. **enunciation** [–'eiʃən], *s.* die Aussprache, Ausdrucksweise, Vortragsart, der Ausdruck; die Kundgebung, (öffentliche) Erklärung, der Ausspruch; die Formulierung, Aufstellung (*of a proposition*). **enunciative** [–siətiv], *adj.* erklärend, ausdrückend, Ausdrucks–.

enuresis [enju'ri:sis], *s.* der Harnfluß, die Blasenschwäche; ***nocturnal –,*** das Bettnässen.

envelop [in'veləp], *v.t.* einwickeln, einschlagen; (*fig.*) verhüllen, einhüllen, umhüllen (***in,*** in (*Acc.*)); (*Mil.*) umfassen, umklammern, umzingeln, einkreisen, einkesseln.

envelope ['envəloup, 'ɔnvəloup], *s.* **1.** die Decke; der (Brief)umschlag, das Kuvert; **2.** (*Fort.*) der Vorwall; **3.** (*Av.*) die Hülle, Haut; **4.** (*Bot.*) der Kelch.

envelopment [in'veləpmənt], *s.* die Einwicklung, Einhüllung, Umhüllung, Hülle; (*Mil.*) Umfassung, Umklammerung, Umzingelung, Einschließung.

envenom [in'venəm], *v.t.* vergiften (*also fig.*); (*fig.*) verbittern, erbittert machen.

enviable ['enviəbl], *adj.* beneidenswert, zu beneiden(d). **envier,** *s.* der (die) Neider(in). **envious,** *adj.* neidisch (***of,*** auf (*Acc.*)); ***be – of him,*** ihn beneiden (***because of,*** um).

environ [in'vairən], *v.t.* umgeben, umringen; umschließen; umlagern, umzingeln. **environment,** *s.* die Umgebung; (*Soc.*) äußere Lebensbedingungen (*pl.*), die Umwelt, Außenwelt; (*Bot.*) der Standort. **environmental** [–'mentl], *adj.* Umgebungs–, (*Biol.*) Umwelt–. **environs,** *pl.* die Umgegend, Umgebung, (*of a town*) Vororte (*pl.*).

envisage [in'vizidʒ], *v.t.* ins Auge fassen, im Geiste betrachten, sich (*Dat.*) vorstellen; (*coll.*) beabsichtigen, in Betracht ziehen; (*Phil.*) intuitiv wahrnehmen.

envoy ['envɔi], *s.* Gesandte(r); der Bote, Bevollmächtigte(r).

envy ['envi], **1.** *s.* der Neid (***of,*** auf (*Acc.*) (*a p.*); ***of,***

at, über (*Acc.*) (*a th.*)); die Mißgunst (*of*, gegen); der Gegenstand des Neides; ***be eaten up with –***, vor Neid vergehen *or* platzen; ***green with –***, blaß vor Neid. **2.** *v.t.* beneiden; neiden, mißgönnen (***him***, ihm; ***it***, es); ***I – (him) his success,*** ich beneide ihn um seinen Erfolg; ***better envied than pitied,*** besser beneidet als bemitleidet.

enwrap [in'ræp], *v.t.* einwickeln, einhüllen, umhüllen.

enzyme ['enzaim], *s.* das Enzym, Ferment.

Eocene ['i:osi:n], *s.* (*Geol.*) das Eozän. **eolith** [–liθ], *s.* das Steinwerkzeug. **eolithic** [–'liθik], *adj.* frühsteinzeitlich.

eon, *see* **aeon.**

eophyte ['i:ofait], *s.* (*Geol.*) versteinerte Pflanze. **Eozoic** [–'zouik], *adj.* (*Geol.*) eozoisch.

epact ['i:pækt], *s.* (*Astr.*) die Epakte.

epaulement [i'pɔ:lmənt], *s.* (*Fort.*) die Schulterwehr, Brustwehr.

epaulet(te) ['epəlet], *s.* die Epaulette, das Epaulett, Schulterstück, Achselstück.

épée ['epei], *s.* der Fechtdegen.

epergne [i'pə:n], *s.* der Tafelaufsatz.

epexegesis [ipeksə'dʒi:sis], *s.* erklärender Zusatz, die Hinzufügung.

ephemera [i'femərə], *s.* (*pl.* **-rae**) **1.** (*Ent.*) die Eintagsfliege; 2. (*fig.*) das Strohfeuer, vorübergehende Erscheinung. **ephemeral,** *adj.* eintägig, Eintags–; kurzlebig, vergänglich, rasch vorübergehend, flüchtig. **ephemerid,** *s.* die Eintagsfliege. **ephemeris,** *s.* (*pl.* **-ides** [efi'meridi:z]) astronomischer Almanach. **ephemeron,** *s.* (*pl.* **-ra**) *see* **ephemera.**

epiblast ['epiblæst], *s.* das Ektoderm, (*Biol.*) äußeres Keimblatt. **epiblastic** [–'blæstik], *adj.* ektoderm.

epic ['epik], **1.** *adj.* episch, erzählend; (*fig.*) heldenhaft, heldisch, heroisch, Helden–. **2.** *s.* das Heldengedicht, Epos. **epical,** *adj.* episch, erzählend.

epicene ['episi:n], *adj.* (*Gram.*) beiderlei Geschlechts.

epicentre [epi'sentə], *s.* (*Geol.*) das Epizentrum; (*fig.*) der Mittelpunkt.

epicure ['epikjuə], *s.* der Feinschmecker, Genießer; Genußmensch. **Epicurean** [–'riən], (*Phil.*) **1.** *adj.* epikureisch. **2.** *s.* der Epikureer. **epicurean, 1.** *adj.* feinschmeckerisch, schwelgerisch, genußsüchtig. **2.** *s.* *See* **epicure. Epicureanism,** *s.* die Lehre Epikurs, der Epikureismus. **epicureanism, epicurism,** *s.* die Genußsucht.

epicycle ['episaikl], *s.* der Epizykel, Nebenkreis. **epicyclic** [–'siklik], *adj.* (*Tech.*) Umlauf–, Planeten– (*gear*). **epicycloid** [–'saiklɔid], *s.* (*Geom.*) die Epizykloide, Radlinie.

epidemic [epi'demik], **1.** *adj.* seuchenartig, epidemisch; (*fig.*) grassierend, weit verbreitet. **2.** *s.* epidemische Krankheit, die Seuche, Epidemie.

epidermis [epi'də:mis], *s.* die Oberhaut, Epidermis.

epidiascope [epi'daiəskoup], *s.* das Epidiaskop.

epigastrium [epi'gæstriəm], *s.* (*Anat.*) die Oberbauchgegend.

epiglottis [epi'glɔtis], *s.* der Kehldeckel.

epigram ['epigræm], *s.* das Sinngedicht, Epigramm, der Spruch. **epigrammatic** [–grə'mætik], *adj.* epigrammatisch; (*fig.*) schlagkräftig, kurz und treffend. **epigrammatist** [–'græmətist], *s.* der Epigrammdichter, Spruchdichter.

epigraph ['epigrɑ:f], *s.* die Inschrift, Aufschrift; der Sinnspruch, Denkspruch, das Motto.

epilepsy ['epilepsi], *s.* die Fallsucht, Epilepsie. **epileptic** [–'leptik], **1.** *adj.* fallsüchtig, epileptisch. **2.** *s.* der (die) Epileptiker(in).

epilogue ['epilɔg], *s.* das Nachwort, Schlußwort, der Epilog; (*Theat.*) die Schlußrede; der Epilogsprecher (*actor*).

Epiphany [i'pifəni], *s.* (*Eccl.*) der Dreikönigstag, das Epiphaniasfest, Epiphanienfest.

epiphyte ['epifait], *s.* (*Bot.*) der Scheinschmarotzer, die Afterpflanze.

episcopacy [i'piskəpəsi], *s.* bischöfliche Verfassung; die gesamten Bischöfe (*pl.*). **episcopal,** *adj.* bischöflich, Bischofs–; ***Episcopal Church,*** die Episkopalkirche, (*Scots*) anglikanische Kirche in Schottland. **episcopalian** [–'peiliən], **1.** *adj.* Episkopal–. **2.** *s.* das Mitglied der Episkopalkirche, (*Scots*) der Anglikaner. **episcopate** [–pit], *s.* das Episkopat, die Bischofswürde; das Bistum; die gesamten Bischöfe (*pl.*).

episode ['episoud], *s.* die Nebenhandlung, Zwischenhandlung; Episode. **episodic(al)** [–'sɔdik(l)], *adj.* eingeschaltet, nebensächlich, episodisch, gelegentlich auftretend.

epistemology [ipistə'mɔlədʒi], *s.* die Erkenntnistheorie.

epistle [i'pisl], *s.* das Sendschreiben, der Brief; die Epistel; (*coll.*) weitschweifiger Brief; (*B.*) ***the Epistle to the Romans,*** der Römerbrief. **epistolary** [–tələri], *adj.* brieflich; Brief–.

epistyle ['epistail], *s.* (*Archit.*) der Architrav, Hauptbalken.

epitaph ['epitɑ:f], *s.* die Grabschrift, das Totengedicht.

epithalamium [epiθə'leimiəm], *s.* das Hochzeitsgedicht, Hochzeitslied.

epithelium [epi'θi:liəm], *s.* das Epithel, Zell(en)-gewebe.

epithet ['epiθet], *s.* das Beiwort, Attribut, Epitheton; die Benennung, Bezeichnung, der Beiname.

epitome [i'pitəmi], *s.* der Auszug, Abriß, die Inhaltsangabe; der Inbegriff. **epitomize** [–maiz], *v.t.* einen Auszug machen aus *or* von; kurz darstellen, einen Abriß *or* eine kurze Darstellung geben von.

epizoon [epi'zouən], *s.* (*pl.* **-zoa**) der Außenschmarotzer. **epizootic** [–'ɔtik], *adj.* (*Vet.*) epidemisch, seuchenartig.

epoch ['i:pɔk], *s.* die Epoche, der Zeitabschnitt, Zeitraum; Wendepunkt, Markstein. **epochal** [–'pɔkl], *adj.* epochemachend, Epochen–. **epoch-making,** *adj.* bahnbrechend, epochemachend.

epode ['epoud], *s.* die Epode.

eponym ['eponim], *s.* der Stammvater. **eponymous** [i'pɔniməs], *adj.* namengebend.

epopee ['epopi:], *s.* episches Gedicht, das Heldengedicht, Epos, die Epopöe; epische Dichtung.

epos ['epəs], *s.* das Epos, episches Gedicht.

equability [ekwə'biliti], *s.* 1. die Gleichmäßigkeit, Gleichförmigkeit; 2. der Gleichmut. **equable,** *adj.*, **equably,** *adv.* 1. gleichförmig, gleichmäßig, gleich(bleibend); 2. gleichmütig, ausgeglichen, ausgewogen, ruhig, gelassen.

equal ['i:kwəl], **1.** *adj.* gleich (*to*, *Dat.*), gleichförmig, gleichwertig (*in*, an (*Dat.*)), gleichmäßig; ***be – to,*** gleichen (*Dat.*); ***be – to doing,*** imstande *or* fähig sein zu tun; ***be – to the task,*** der Aufgabe gewachsen sein; ***all*** or ***other things being –,*** unter sonst gleichen Umständen; ***– to the demand,*** der Nachfrage angemessen; ***– in size,*** gleich groß, von gleicher Größe, gleich an Größe; (*Geom.*) ***of – area,*** flächentreu; ***with – ease,*** mit derselben Leichtigkeit. **2.** *s.* 1. (*of a p.*) Gleichgestellte(r); ***be his –,*** ihm ebenbürtig sein; ***he has not his –*** or ***has no –*** or ***is without –,*** er hat nicht *or* sucht seinesgleichen; ***his –s in age,*** seine Altersgenossen; 2. *pl.* (*Math.*) das Gleiche; ***–s from –s leaves –s,*** Gleiches von Gleichem bleibt Gleiches. **3.** *v.t.* (*with Dat.*) gleichen, entsprechen, gleich sein, gleichkommen (***in***, an (*Dat.*)).

equality [i'kwɔliti], *s.* die Gleichheit; Gleichförmigkeit, Gleichmäßigkeit; ***be on – with,*** (*a p.*) auf gleicher Stufe stehen mit; (*a th.*) gleich(bedeutend) *or* identisch sein mit; ***on a footing of –,*** auf der Basis der Gleichberechtigung; ***– of status,*** die Gleichberechtigung; ***political –,*** politische Gleichberechtigung; (*Math.*) ***sign of –*** das Gleichheitszeichen.

equalization [i:kwəlai'zeiʃən], *s.* die Gleichmachung, Gleichstellung; Ausgleichung, der

Ausgleich, (*Tech.*) Abgleich. **equalize** [ˈiːkwəlaiz], **1.** *v.t.* gleichmachen, gleichsetzen, gleichstellen; ausgleichen. **2.** *v.i.* (*Spt.*) ausgleichen. **equalizer,** *s.* 1. (*Tech.*) der Stabilisator, Ausgleicher; 2. (*Spt.*) Ausgleichspunkt, das Ausgleichstor.

equally [ˈiːkwəli], *adv.* in gleicher Weise, in gleichem Maße, ebenso; – ***distant,*** gleich weit entfernt; – ***good,*** ebensogut; – ***with,*** ebenso wie.

equanimity [iːkwəˈnimiti], *s.* der Gleichmut.

equate [iˈkweit], *v.t.*gleichsetzen, gleichstellen (***with,*** *Dat.*) (*also Math.*); auf gleiche Stufe stellen. **equation** [iˈkweiʒən], *s.* 1. (*Math.*) die Gleichung; ***simple –,*** die Gleichung ersten Grades; 2. die Ausgleichung, der Ausgleich; 3. (*fig.*) die Gleichheit, das Gleichgewicht.

equator [iˈkweitə], *s.* der Äquator. **equatorial** [ekwəˈtɔːriəl], *adj.* äquatorial.

equerry [ˈekwəri], *s.* der Stallmeister; Bediente(r) des königlichen Haushalts.

equestrian [iˈkwestriən], **1.** *adj.* Reit–, Reiter–; – ***statue,*** das Reiterstandbild. **2.** *s.* der (die) (Kunst- *or* Turnier)reiter(in). **equestrianism,** *s.* die Reitkunst.

equi|angular [iːkwi–], *adj.* gleichwink(e)lig. **–distant,** *adj.* gleich weit entfernt. **–lateral,** *adj.* gleichseitig.

equilibrate [iːkwiˈlaibreit], **1.** *v.t.* im Gleichgewicht halten, ins Gleichgewicht bringen. **2.** *v.i.* im Gleichgewicht sein. **equilibrist** [–ˈlibrist], *s.* der Akrobat, Seiltänzer. **equilibrium** [–ˈlibriəm], *s.* das Gleichgewicht; ***be in (a state of) –,*** sich (*Dat.*) das Gleichgewicht halten.

equine [ˈekwain], *adj.* pferdeartig, Pferde–.

equinoctial [iːkwiˈnɔkʃəl], **1.** *adj.* äquinoktial; – ***gales,*** Äquinoktialstürme. **2.** *s.* die Äquinoktiallinie, der Himmelsäquator. **equinox** [ˈiːkwinɔks], *s.* die Tagundnachtgleiche, das Äquinoktium; ***vernal –,*** das Frühlingsäquinoktium.

equip [iˈkwip], *v.t.* ausrüsten (*also Mil., Naut.*), ausstatten, ausstaffieren; ***well equipped,*** mit allem Nötigen (*or fig.* geistigem Rüstzeug) reichlich versehen.

equipage [ˈekwipidʒ], *s.* die Equipage, der Wagen mit Pferden; (*Mil.*) die Ausrüstung; Begleitung, das Gefolge.

equipment [iˈkwipmənt], *s.* die Einrichtung, Ausstattung, (*Mil.*) Ausrüstung; Anlage, Apparatur, das Gerät, die Gerätschaft; (*fig.*) geistiges Rüstzeug.

equipoise [ˈekwipɔiz], *s.* (*fig.*) das Gleichgewicht; Gegengewicht.

equipollent [iːkwiˈpɔlənt], *adj.* gleichwertig, gleichstark, gleichbedeutend.

equitable [ˈekwitəbl], *adj.* (recht und) billig, gerecht; unparteiisch; (*Law*) billigkeitsgerichtlich. **equitableness,** *s.* die Billigkeit, Unparteilichkeit.

equitation [ekwiˈteiʃən], *s.* das Reiten; die Reitkunst, (Dressur)reiterei.

equity [ˈekwiti], *s.* die Billigkeit, Gerechtigkeit, Unparteilichkeit; (*Law*) das Billigkeitsrecht; ***Court of Equity,*** das Billigkeitsgericht.

equivalence [iˈkwivələns], *s.* die Gleichwertigkeit, gleicher Wert, gleiche Bedeutung. **equivalent, 1.** *adj.* gleichwertig, gleichbedeutend, äquivalent (***to,*** mit); ***be – to,*** gleichen Wert haben mit, gleichkommen (*Dat.*), ebensoviel gelten wie; so viel heißen wie; (*Chem.*) – ***number,*** die Valenzzahl. **2.** *s.* 1. der Gegenwert, gleicher Wert, gleicher Betrag; 2. volle Entsprechung, das Seitenstück, Gegenstück (***of,*** zu); 3. (*Phys.*) Äquivalent (***of,*** für).

equivocal [iˈkwivəkl], *adj.* doppelsinnig, zweideutig, unbestimmt, ungewiß, zweifelhaft, fraglich (*of a th.*), fragwürdig, verdächtig. **equivocalness,** *s.* der Doppelsinn, die Zweideutigkeit. **equivocate** [–keit], *v.i.* zweideutig *or* doppelzüngig reden; Ausflüchte gebrauchen. **equivocation** [–ˈkeiʃən], *s.* die Zweideutigkeit; Ausflucht. **equivocator,** *s.* der Wortverdreher.

era [ˈiərə], *s.* die Ära, Zeitrechnung; Epoche, (neuer) Zeitabschnitt; geschichtliche Periode, das Zeitalter.

eradicable [iˈrædikəbl], *adj.* ausrottbar; ***not –,*** nicht auszurotten(d). **eradicate** [–keit], *v.t.* entwurzeln, ausrotten (*usu. fig.*). **eradication** [–ˈkeiʃən], *s.* die Entwurzelung, Ausrottung.

erasable [iˈreizəbl], *adj.* vertilgbar, auslöschbar. **erase,** *v.t.* auskratzen, ausstreichen, ausradieren; (*fig.*) auslöschen, (ver)tilgen (***from,*** aus); – ***from one's memory,*** aus dem Gedächtnis tilgen. **eraser,** *s.* das Radiermesser; der Radiergummi. **erasion** [iˈreiʒən], **erasure** [iˈreiʒə], *s.* das Auskratzen, Ausradieren; die Rasur, ausradierte Stelle; (*fig.*) die (Ver)tilgung, Entfernung.

ere [ɛə], **1.** *conj.* (*Poet.*) ehe, bevor. **2.** *prep.* vor (*Dat.*); – ***long,*** binnen kurzem, demnächst, bald; – ***now,*** schon früher, bis jetzt, bereits; – ***this,*** schon vorher, vordem, zuvor.

erect [iˈrekt], **1.** *adj.* aufrecht, aufgerichtet, gerade; ***with head –,*** mit erhobenem Kopf; ***spring –,*** in die Höhe springen; (*Gymn.*) kerzenspringen; ***stand –,*** gerade stehen. **2.** *v.t.* 1. aufrichten, in die Höhe richten; 2. bauen, errichten (*a building*), montieren, zusammenbauen, aufstellen (*equipment*); 3. (*Geom.*) errichten, fällen (*perpendicular*); 4. (*fig.*) aufstellen, aufführen. **erectile** [–tail], *adj.* hochstehend; (*Anat.*) anschwellbar, erektil. **erection** [iˈrekʃən], *s.* 1. das Aufrichten, Errichten; die Errichtung, Aufführung; 2. der Bau, das Gebäude; 3. (*Anat.*) die Erektion. **erectness,** *s.* die Gradheit, aufrechte Haltung. **erector,** *s.* 1. der Erbauer, Errichter; 2. (*Anat.*) Aufrichtmuskel.

eremite [ˈerimait], *s.* der Einsiedler, Eremit.

erg [əːg], *s.* (*Phys.*) das Erg.

ergo [ˈəːgou], *adv.* also, folglich.

ergot [ˈəːgət], *s.* 1. (*Bot.*) das Mutterkorn; 2. (*Vet.*) die Flußgalle. **ergotism,** *s.* 1. (*Bot.*) der Mutterkornbefall; 2. (*Med.*) die Kornstaupe, Kriebelkrankheit, Mutterkornvergiftung.

Eric [ˈerik], *s.* Erich (*m.*).

Erica [ˈerikə], *s.* *See* **Heather.**

erica, *s.* *See* **heather.**

ermine [ˈəːmin], *s.* 1. der Hermelin; Hermelin(pelz); 2. (*fig.*) das Richteramt, die Richterwürde, Richtertracht.

erne [əːn], *s.* (*Orn.*) der Seeadler (*Haliaeetus albicilla*).

Ernest [ˈəːnist], *s.* Ernst (*m.*).

erode [iˈroud], *v.t.* zerfressen, anfressen; (*Geol.*) wegfressen, abtragen, auswaschen. **erosion** [iˈrouʒən], *s.* die Zerfressung (*by acids etc.*), Abtragung, Auswaschung (*by water*); (*Med.*) der Krebs; (*Tech.*) Verschleiß, die Abnützung; Ausbrennung (*of a gun-barrel*).

erotic [iˈrɔtik], **1.** *adj.* erotisch, Liebes–. **2.** *s.* erotisches Gedicht. **eroticism** [–tisizm], *s.* die Erotik.

err [əː], *v.i.* (sich) irren; unrichtig sein, fehlgehen (*of statements*); (*fig.*) abweichen, abirren (***from,*** von); (*obs.*) sündigen, auf Abwege geraten; – ***on the right*** or ***safe side,*** sichergehen.

errand [ˈerənd], *s.* der Auftrag, die Botschaft; die Besorgung, der (Boten)gang; ***go on an –,*** einen Gang tun; ***go*** or ***run –s,*** Wege besorgen; ***fool's –,*** unnützer Gang. **errand-boy,** *s.* der Laufbursche.

errant [ˈerənt], *adj.* fahrend, wandernd, (umher)ziehend; (*fig.*) abweichend (***from,*** von); ***knight –,*** fahrender Ritter. **errantry,** *s.* das Umherschweifen; die Irrfahrt (*of a knight*); fahrendes Rittertum.

errata [eˈrɑːtə], *pl.* das Druckfehlerverzeichnis.

erratic [iˈrætik], *adj.* (*Med.*) wandernd; (*Geol.*) erratisch; unregelmäßig, regellos, ziellos, ungleichmäßig (*as movement*), sprunghaft, wandelbar, launenhaft, unberechenbar (*as moods*).

erroneous [iˈrouniəs], *adj.* irrig, irrtümlich, falsch, unrichtig. **erroneously,** *adv.* irrtümlicherweise, zu Unrecht. **erroneousness,** *s.* der Irrtum, die Irrigkeit.

error [ˈerə], *s.* der Irrtum, Fehler, das Vergehen,

Versehen, der Verstoß, Fehltritt; die Abweichung (*of the compass*); (*Law*) der Formfehler; (*Comm.*) *–s excepted,* Irrtümer vorbehalten; ***be in –***, sich irren; ***in –***, im Irrtum, aus Versehen, irrtümlicherweise; ***clerical –***, der Schreibfehler; ***– of judgement,*** die Täuschung, irrige Ansicht; ***margin of –***, die Fehlergrenze; (*Law*) ***writ of –***, der Revisionsbefehl; ***see the – of one's ways,*** seine Fehler einsehen.

Erse [ə:s], *s.* das Gälisch, Ersisch.

erst [ə:st], *adv.* (*obs.*) ehedem, einst, vormals. **erstwhile, 1.** *adj.* ehemalig, früher. **2.** *adv.* *See* **erst.**

eructate [i'rʌkteit], *v.i.* aufstoßen, rülpsen. **eructation** [–'teiʃən], *s.* das Aufstoßen, Rülpsen.

erudite ['eru:dait], *adj.* gelehrt, belesen. **erudition** [–'diʃən], *s.* die Gelehrsamkeit, Belesenheit, gelehrte Bildung.

erupt [i'rʌpt], *v.i.* ausbrechen (*of volcano*); durchbrechen (*of teeth*); ausschlagen (*of pimples etc.*); hervorkommen, herauskommen (***from***, aus). **eruption** [i'rʌpʃən], *s.* der Ausbruch, Durchbruch; (*Med.*) Hautausschlag. **eruptive,** *adj.* ausbrechend, hervorbrechend; (*fig.*) losbrechend, gewaltsam; stürmisch; (*Geol.*) eruptiv; (*Med.*) ausschlagartig, von Ausschlag begleitet.

eryngo [e'riŋgou], *s.* (*Bot.*) die (Meerstrands)-männertreu.

erysipelas [eri'sipiləs], *s.* (*Med.*) die (Wund)rose, der Rotlauf.

escalade [eskə'leid], **1.** *s.* (*Mil., Hist.*) die Eskalade, (Mauer)ersteigung, Erstürmung; ***by –***, mit Sturmleitern. **2.** *v.t.* mit Sturmleitern ersteigen, erstürmen.

escalate ['eskəleit], **1.** *v.i.* hochschnellen. **2.** *v.t.* eskalieren, stufenweise steigern. **escalation** [–'leiʃən], *s.* die Eskalation. **escalator,** *s.* die Rolltreppe.

escal(l)op [əs'kɔləp], *s.* die Jakobsmuschel, Kammmuschel.

escapade [eskə'peid], *s.* toller Streich, der Jugendstreich.

escape [is'keip], **1.** *v.t.* (*with Dat.*) (*of a p.*) entkommen, entfliehen, entlaufen, entrinnen, entschlüpfen, entwischen, (*fig. and of a th.*) entgehen; ***the meaning –s me,*** der Sinn leuchtet mir nicht ein; ***not a word –d my lips,*** kein Wort kam über meine Lippen; ***it –d my notice,*** ich übersah es; ***it –s me*** or ***my memory,*** es fällt mir nicht ein, es ist mir entfallen; ***– being laughed at,*** der Gefahr entgehen, ausgelacht zu werden. **2.** *v.i.* entlaufen, entkommen, entrinnen, entwischen, entschlüpfen (***from***, aus *or* von); (mit dem Leben) davonkommen; ausfließen (*as liquid*), ausströmen, entweichen (*as gas*) (***from***, aus); ***– scot-free,*** ungestraft davonkommen; (*coll.*) ***– by the skin of one's teeth,*** mit knapper Not entkommen. **3.** *s.* das Entrinnen, Entkommen, die Flucht; der Ausfluß (*of liquid*), das Ausströmen, Entweichen, der Abgang (*of gas*); ***have a narrow –***, mit knapper Not entkommen; ***make (good) one's –***, entweichen, sich aus dem Staube machen.

escape-apparatus, *s.* der Tauchretter (*submarines*).

escapee [eskei'pi:], *s.* der Ausbrecher, Flüchtling.

escape|-hatch, *s.* die Notluke (*tanks*). **– literature,** *s.* die Entspannungs– *or* Zerstreuungslektüre. **–-mechanism,** *s.* (*Psych.*) der Ausfluchtmechanismus.

escapement [is'keipmənt], *s.* (*Horol.*) die Hemmung; (*typewriter*) der Vorschub.

escape|-pipe, *s.* das Abflußrohr, Abzugsrohr. **–-shaft,** *s.* der Rettungsschacht. **–-valve,** *s.* das Auslaßventil. **–-velocity,** *s.* (*rocketry*) kosmische Geschwindigkeit. **–-wheel,** *s.* (*Horol.*) das Hemmungsrad.

escapism [is'keipizm], *s.* die Abkehr von der Wirklichkeit, Wirklichkeitsflucht, Vergnügungssucht. **escapist,** *s.* Wirklichkeitsflüchtige(r), Vergnügungssüchtige(r). **escapologist** [eskə'pɔlədʒist], *s.* der Entfesselungskünstler.

escargot [es'kɑ:gou], *s.* eßbare Schnecke.

escarp [is'kɑ:p], **1.** *v.t.* abdachen, böschen, mit einer Böschung versehen. **2.** *s.* (*Fort.*) innere Grabenböschung, vordere Grabenwand. **escarpment,** *s.* die Böschung, steiler Abhang; (*Geol.*) der Steilabbruch; (*Fort.*) das Schanzwerk.

eschalot [eʃə'lɔt], *s.* *See* **shallot.**

eschatology [eskə'tɔlədʒi], *s.* (*Theol.*) die Lehre von den letzten Dingen.

escheat [is'tʃi:t], **1.** *s.* (*Law*) der Heimfall; heimgefallenes Gut. **2.** *v.i.* anheimfallen. **3.** *v.t.* beschlagnahmen.

eschew [is'tʃu:], *v.t.* (ver)meiden, unterlassen, scheuen. **eschewal,** *s.* die Scheu (***of***, vor (*Dat.*)), das Vermeiden (*Gen.*).

escort, 1. ['eskɔ:t], *s.* die Begleitung; Begleitperson; das Geleit, der Schutz; (*Mil.*) die Begleitmannschaft, Bedeckung, Eskorte, (*Naut.*) das Geleitschiff, (*Av.*) der Geleitschutz. **2.** [is'kɔ:t], *v.t.* begleiten; geleiten, decken, eskortieren.

escritoire [eskri'twɑ:], *s.* das Schreibpult.

esculent ['eskjulənt], **1.** *adj.* eßbar, genießbar. **2.** *s.* das Nahrungsmittel.

escutcheon [is'kʌtʃən], *s.* das (Wappen)schild; Wappen; Namenschild; Schloßblech; (*Hunt.*) der Spiegel (*of deer*), (*Ent.*) das Schildchen; (*fig.*) ***a blot on his –***, ein Fleck(en) *or* Makel auf seinem Ruf *or* seiner Ehre; (*Hort.*) ***– grafting,*** das Schildpfropfen.

esoteric [eso'terik], *adj.* esoterisch, nur für Eingeweihte bestimmt; vertraulich, geheim; dunkel, tief.

espalier [is'pæljə], *s.* das Spalier; der Spalierbaum.

esparto [es'pɑ:tou], *s.* das Espartogras, Spartgras.

especial [is'peʃəl], *adj.* besonder, speziell, hauptsächlich, Haupt–, hervorragend, vorzüglich. **especially,** *adv.* besonders, insbesondere, im besonderen, vorzüglich, vornehmlich, hauptsächlich, in hohem Maße.

espial [is'paiəl], *s.* das (Er)spähen, (Aus)kundschaften, Spionieren; die Entdeckung.

espionage ['espiənɑ:ʒ], *s.* das Spionieren, die Spionage.

esplanade [esplə'neid], *s.* die Promenade, freier Platz; (*Fort.*) das Glacis.

espousal [is'pauzl], *s.* 1. das Eintreten, die Parteinahme (***of***, für), der Anschluß (***of***, an (*Acc.*)), die Annahme (von), Verteidigung (*Gen.*); 2. (*usu. pl.*) Eheschließung, Vermählung. **espouse,** *v.t.* 1. heiraten (*of the man*); verheiraten (***to***, an (*Acc.*)) (*the girl*); 2. (*fig.*) sich annehmen (*Gen.*), sich anschließen an (*Acc.*), annehmen; eintreten für, Partei ergreifen für.

esprit [es'pri:], *s.* der Geist, Witz; ***– de corps,*** der Korpsgeist, das Zusammengehörigkeitsgefühl.

espy [is'pai], *v.t.* erspähen, gewahren, erblicken, entdecken.

esquire [is'kwaiə], *s.* (*Hist.*) der Landedelmann, Junker; (*as title following name*: *abbr.* Esq.) Wohlgeboren; (*on letters*) ***W. G. Carr, Esq.,*** Herrn W. G. Carr.

essay, 1. [ə'sei], *v.t.* versuchen, probieren, erproben. **2.** ['esei], *s.* 1. der Versuch (***at***, mit); 2. Aufsatz, die Abhandlung, schriftliche Arbeit, der Essay; ***prize –***, die Preisarbeit. **essayist** ['eseiist], *s.* der Verfasser von Essays, Essayist.

essence ['esəns], *s.* (*Phil.*) die Substanz, absolutes Sein; (*fig.*) (innerstes) Wesen, der Hauptinhalt, Kern, wesentliche Eigenschaft, das Wesentliche; der Auszug, Geist, Extrakt, die Essenz; (*Chem.*) das Extrakt; ***the very – of the matter,*** des Pudels Kern.

essential [i'senʃəl], **1.** *adj.* 1. wesentlich; 2. unentbehrlich, unbedingt notwendig, erforderlich; durchaus wichtig, bedeutend (***to***, für); ***– goods,*** lebenswichtige Güter; 3. (*Chem.*) ätherisch; ***– oils,*** ätherische Öle. **2.** *s.* (*usu. pl.*) das Wesentliche, die Hauptsache, wesentliche Eigenschaft(en), Wesensmerkmale (*pl.*). **essentiality** [–i'æliti], *s.* die Wirklichkeit, Wesentlichkeit, das Wesentliche. **essenti-**

ally, *adv.* im wesentlichen, in der Hauptsache, ganz besonders, in hohem Maße.

establish [is'tæbliʃ], *v.t.* festsetzen, einsetzen; aufstellen, einrichten, einführen, schaffen, herstellen, durchsetzen; bilden, stiften, etablieren, (be)gründen, errichten; (*fig.*) feststellen, festlegen, außer Frage stellen, bestätigen, begründen, beweisen, erweisen, nachweisen; unterbringen, versorgen, selbständig machen (*one's children etc.*); *– the church,* die Kirche verstaatlichen; *–ed church,* die Staatskirche; *– a connection,* eine Verbindung herstellen; *– contact,* Fühlung aufnehmen; *–ed facts,* feststehende Tatsachen; *–ed laws,* bestehende Gesetze; *– o.s.,* sich niederlassen, sich etablieren; *– order,* Ordnung schaffen; *– a record,* einen Rekord aufstellen; *– a reputation for o.s.,* sich (*Dat.*) einen Namen machen.

establishment [is'tæbliʃmənt], *s.* 1. die (Be)gründung, Errichtung, Einrichtung, Stiftung, Schaffung, Etablierung; Festsetzung, Einsetzung; (*fig.*) Feststellung, Bestätigung; (*Law*) *– of paternity,* der Vaterschaftsnachweis; 2. der Haushalt; die Anstalt, das Institut; (*Comm.*) Etablissement, Geschäft, Unternehmen, die Firma; *the Establishment,* das Establishment; *Church –,* staatskirchliche Verfassung; *educational –,* die Erziehungsanstalt; *keep up a large –,* ein großes Haus führen; *separate –,* getrennter Haushalt; 3. (*Mil.*) der (Mannschafts– *or* Personal)bestand, das Personal; die (Soll)stärke; *military –,* stehendes Heer, die Kriegsmacht; *naval –,* die Flotte; *peace –,* der Friedensstand; *war –,* die Kriegsstärke.

estate [is'teit], *s.* 1. (*Law*) der Besitz, das Besitztum, Besitzrecht; Vermögen, der Nachlaß, die Erbschaftsmasse, (*of a bankrupt*) Konkursmasse; (*Law*) *personal –,* bewegliche Habe, das Mobiliar(vermögen); (*Law*) *real –,* unbewegliche Habe, der Grundbesitz, das Immobiliarvermögen, Immobilien (*pl.*), Liegenschaften (*pl.*); *residuary –,* der Nachlaß eines Verstorbenen nach Abzug der Legate; *wind up an –,* die Vermögensangelegenheiten abwickeln *or* regeln; 2. der Landsitz, das Gut, Grundstück, Anwesen, die Besitzung; 3. (*Hist.*) der Rang, Stand, die Klasse; (*B.*) der Zustand; (*coll.*) *fourth –,* die Presse; *owner of large –s,* der Großgrundbesitzer; *man's –,* das Mannesalter; *come to man's –,* mannbar werden; *–s of the realm,* die Reichsstände; *the three –s of the realm,* die drei Stände des Reiches (= die hohe Geistlichkeit, der Adel, die Gemeinen).

estate|agent, *s.* der Grundstücksmakler. **– car,** *s.* der Kombiwagen. **– duty,** *s.* die Nachlaßsteuer, Erbschaftssteuer.

esteem [is'ti:m], **1.** *v.t.* (hoch)schätzen, (hoch)achten; ansehen *or* erachten als, halten für. **2.** *s.* die Wertschätzung (*for, Gen.*), Achtung (vor (*Dat.*)); *be in great – with,* in großem Ansehen stehen bei; *hold in –,* achten.

ester ['estə], *s.* (*Chem.*) der Ester.

esthete, *etc. See* **aesthete.**

Esthonia [es'touniə], *s.* (*Geog.*) Estland (*n.*). **Esthonian, 1.** *s.* 1. der Este (die Estin), der (die) Estländer(in); 2. das Estnisch(e) (*language*). **2.** *adj.* estnisch, estländisch.

estimable ['estiməbl], *adj.* schätzenswert, achtungswert. **estimate, 1.** [–meit], *v.t.* 1. würdigen, beurteilen, bewerten; 2. (ab)schätzen, berechnen, veranschlagen, taxieren (*at,* auf (*Acc.*)). **2.** [–mit], *s.* 1. die Beurteilung, Bewertung, Meinung; *form an – of,* beurteilen, abschätzen; 2. (*Comm.*) der Überschlag, (Kosten)anschlag, die (Ab)schätzung, Veranschlagung; *pl.* (*Parl.*) der Voranschlag, veranschlagter Etat; *rough –,* ungefährer Überschlag. **estimation** [–'meiʃən], *s.* 1. die (Ab)schätzung, Veranschlagung, der Überschlag; 2. die Ansicht, Meinung, das Urteil, Gutachten; *in my –,* nach meiner Ansicht; 3. die (Hoch)achtung, (Wert)schätzung; *hold in –,* hochschätzen.

estival, *etc. See* **aestival.**

Estonia, *etc. See* **Esthonia.**

estop [i'stɔp], *v.t.* abhalten (*from,* von), (*Law*) hemmen, hindern (an (*Dat.*)).

estrade [es'trɑ:d], *s.* erhöhter Platz, die Estrade.

estrange [i'streindʒ], *v.t.* entfremden, abwendig machen (*from, Dat.* (*a p.*)), abwenden, abhalten, fernhalten, entfernen (von). **estrangement,** *s.* die Entfremdung (*from,* von).

estreat [i'stri:t], **1.** *v.t.* (*Law*) vollstrecken, zahlen lassen (*a fine or bail*). **2.** *s.* (*Law*) die Protokollabschrift.

estuary ['estjuəri], *s.* der Meeresarm, die Meeresbucht; Seemündung, weite Flußmündung.

et cetera [et'setrə], (*abbr.* **etc.** or **&c.**) und so weiter (usw.).

etch [etʃ], *v.t.* ätzen; radieren, kupferstechen. **etching,** *s.* 1. das Ätzen, Radieren, Kupferstechen; die Radierkunst, Kupferstecherei; 2. Radierung, der Kupferstich. **etching-needle,** *s.* die Radiernadel.

eternal [i'tə:nl], **1.** *adj.* ewig, immerwährend, zeitlos; ständig, bleibend, unabänderlich, unveränderlich; (*coll.*) unaufhörlich, beständig, dauernd; (*coll.*) *– triangle,* dreieckiges Verhältnis. **2.** *s.* das Ewige; *pl.* ewige Dinge; *the Eternal,* Gott. **eternalize** [–aiz], *v.t.* verewigen; unsterblich *or* unvergeßlich machen. **eternity** [–niti], *s.* die Ewigkeit; (*coll.*) das Jenseits. **eternize,** *v.t. See* **eternalize.**

ether ['i:θə], *s.* (*Phys., Chem.; also fig.*) der Äther; *acetic –,* der Essigäther; *– waves,* Ätherwellen. **ethereal** [i'θiəriəl], *adj.* ätherisch (*also fig.*); (*Chem.*) ätherartig; (*fig.*) himmlisch, zart, vergeistigt. **etherealize** [–laiz], *v.t.* ätherisch machen, verflüchtigen; (*fig.*) vergeistigen, verklären. **etherize,** *v.t.* mit Äther betäuben.

ethic ['eθik], **1.** *s. See* **ethos** *and* **ethics. 2.** *adj.* (*rare*), **ethical,** *adj.* sittlich, moralisch, ethisch; (*Gram.*) *ethic dative,* ethischer Dativ. **ethics,** *pl.* (*sing. constr.*) die Sittenlehre, Moralphilosophie; (*pl. constr.*) Ethik, Moral.

Ethiopia [i:θi'oupiə], *s.* Äthiopien (*n.*). **Ethiopian, 1.** *s.* der (die) Äthiopier(in). **2.** *adj.* äthiopisch.

ethmoid ['eθmɔid], *adj.* zellig; *– bone,* das Siebbein.

ethnic(al) ['eθnik(l)], *adj.* ethnisch, volkisch, völkisch; heidnisch; *ethnic group,* die Volksgruppe. **ethnographer** [–'nɔgrəfə], *s.* der Ethnograph. **ethnographic(al)** [–nə'græfik(l)], *adj.* ethnographisch. **ethnography** [–'nɔgrəfi], *s.* die Völkerbeschreibung. **ethnological** [–nə'lɔdʒikl], *adj.* völkerkundlich, ethnologisch. **ethnologist** [–'nɔlədʒist], *s.* der Ethnologe. **ethnology** [–'nɔlədʒi], *s.* die Völkerkunde.

ethos ['i:θɔs], *s.* sittlicher Gehalt, das Ethos; ethische Grundsätze, der Lebensgrundsatz.

ethyl ['eθil], *s.* das Äthyl; *– alcohol,* der Äthylalkohol, Spiritus, (*coll.*) Sprit. **ethylene** [–i:n], *s.* das Äthylen, Kohlenwasserstoffgas.

etiolate ['i:tioleit], *v.t.* (durch Ausschluß des Lichts) bleichen. **etiolation** [–'leiʃən], *s.* das Entfärben, Bleichwerden; (*fig.*) Siechtum.

etiological, *see* **aetiological.**

etiquette ['etiket], *s.* gesellschaftliche Umgangsformen (*pl.*), die Etikette, das Hofzeremoniell.

Etna ['etnə], *s.* Ätna (*m.*).

Eton| collar ['i:tn], *s.* breiter Steifkragen. **– crop,** *s.* der Herrenschnitt. **– jacket,** *s.* kurze Schülerjacke.

etui [e'twi:], *s.* der Behälter, das Etui, Futteral.

etymological [etimə'lɔdʒikl], *adj.* etymologisch. **etymologist** [–'mɔlədʒist], *s.* der Etymologe. **etymology** [–'mɔlədʒi], *s.* die Wortableitung; Etymologie, Wortforschung.

etymon ['etimɔn], *s.* das Stammwort, Grundwort.

eucalyptus [ju:kə'liptəs], *s.* der Eukalyptus.

Eucharist ['ju:kərist], *s.* heiliges Abendmahl. **Eucharistic** [–'ristik], *adj.* Abendmahls–.

euchre ['ju:kə], **1.** *s.* (*Cards*) das Euchrespiel. **2.** *v.t.* (*sl.*) übertreffen, überlisten, schlagen.

eudiometer [ju:di'ɔmitə], *s.* der Eudiometer, Sauerstoffmesser.

eugenic [ju'dʒenik], *adj.* rassenhygienisch. **euge-**

nics, *pl.* (*sing. constr.*) die Rassenhygiene, Rassenpflege, Eugenik.

eulogist ['ju:lədʒist], *s.* der Lobpreiser, Lobredner. **eulogistic(al)** [–'dʒistik(l)], *adj.* (lob)preisend, rühmend, lobend. **eulogium** [–'loudʒiəm], *s. See* **eulogy. eulogize** [–dʒaiz], *v.t.* loben, preisen. **eulogy,** *s.* die Lobrede, Lobpreisung, das Lob (*on*, auf (*Acc.*)).

eunuch ['ju:nək], *s.* Verschnittene(r), Entmannte(r), der Eunuch; Haremaufseher.

euonymus [ju'ɔniməs], *s.* die Spindelbaumwurzel.

eupepsia [ju'pepsiə], *s.* gute Verdauung. **eupeptic,** *adj.* leicht verdaulich, verdauungsfördernd; gut verdauend.

euphemism ['ju:fəmizm], *s.* beschönigender Ausdruck, (sprachliche) Verhüllung, die Beschönigung, Milderung, der Euphemismus. **euphemistic(al)** [–'mistik(l)], *adj.* mildernd, beschönigend, euphemistisch.

euphonious [ju'founiəs], *adj.* wohlklingend. **euphonium,** *s.* (*Mus.*) das Baritonhorn. **euphony** ['ju:fəni], *s.* der Wohlklang.

euphorbia [ju'fɔ:biə], *s.* (*Bot.*) die Wolfsmilch.

euphoria [ju'fɔ:riə], *s.* das Wohlbefinden.

Euphrates [ju'freiti:z], *s.* der Euphrat.

euphuism ['ju:fjuizm], *s.* der Euphuismus, schwülstige *or* gespreizte *or* gezierte Ausdrucksweise, der Schwulst. **euphuistic** [–'istik], *adj.* geziert, gespreizt, schwülstig.

eurhythmics [ju'riðmiks], *pl.* (*sing. constr.*) rhythmische Gymnastik.

Europe ['juərəp], *s.* Europa (*n.*); ***Central –,*** Mitteleuropa. **European** [–'piən], **1.** *s.* der (die) Europäer(in). **2.** *adj.* europäisch; (*Spt.*) ***– championship,*** die Europameisterschaft; ***– Economic Community,*** Europäische Wirtschaftsgemeinschaft (EWG).

euthanasia [ju:θə'neiziə], *s.* leichter *or* sanfter Tod; die Euthanasie, Sterbehilfe.

evacuant [i'vækjuənt], **1.** *adj.* (*Med.*) abführend. **2.** *s.* das Abführmittel. **evacuate** [–eit], **1.** *v.i.* sich zurückziehen, aussiedeln. **2.** *v.t.* (ent)leeren, ausleeren, ausräumen; (*Med.*) entleeren, abführen; räumen, verlassen (*town etc.*), verlegen (*troops*), evakuieren, abschieben, abtransportieren (*people*); ***– the air,*** die Luft absaugen. **evacuation** [–'eiʃən], *s.* **1.** die Entleerung; das Auspumpen (*of air*); (*Med.*) die Ausleerung, der Stuhlgang; 2. die Aussiedlung, Umsiedlung, Verschickung, der Abtransport, Abschub (*of population*); die Evakuierung, Räumung (*of territory*). **evacuee** [–'i:], *s.* Evakuierte(r), Verschickte(r), der Umsiedler.

evade [i'veid], *v.t.* ausweichen, sich entziehen, aus dem Weg gehen, entgehen, entwischen, entrinnen (*Dat.*); umgehen, vermeiden; ***– definition,*** sich nicht definieren lassen; ***– detection,*** der Entdeckung entgehen; ***– the regulations,*** die Bestimmungen umgehen.

evaluate [i'væljueit], *v.t.* abschätzen, berechnen, bewerten; ausrechnen, zahlenmäßig bestimmen. **evaluation** [–'eiʃən], *s.* die Abschätzung, Bewertung; (*Math.*) Ausrechnung, Auswertung, Berechnung, (Wert)bestimmung.

evanesce [evə'nes], *v.i.* (ver)schwinden, vergehen. **evanescence,** *s.* das (Dahin)schwinden; die Vergänglichkeit. **evanescent,** *adj.* dahinschwindend, (ver)schwindend; (*Math.*) unendlich klein.

evangel [i'vændʒəl], *s.* (*rare*) das Evangelium. **evangelic(al)** [i:væn'dʒelik(l)], *adj.* evangelisch; Evangelien–. **evangelical,** *s.* evangelischer Protestant. **evangelicalism,** *s.* die Lehre der evangelischen Kirche, evangelischer Glaube. **evangelism,** *s.* die Verkündung des Evangeliums. **evangelist,** *s.* der Evangelist, Glaubensbote; Wanderprediger. **evangelize** [–laiz], **1.** *v.i.* das Evangelium predigen. **2.** *v.t.* (zum Christentum) bekehren.

evaporable [i'væpərəbl], *adj.* verdunstbar, verdampfbar. **evaporate** [–reit], **1.** *v.i.* verdunsten, verdampfen, verfliegen, verflüchtigen; (*fig.*) verschwinden. **2.** *v.t.* abdampfen, eindampfen, einkochen; verdampfen *or* verdunsten lassen; ***–d milk,*** die Kondensmilch. **evaporation** [–'reiʃən], *s.* die Verdampfung, Verdunstung; (*Tech.*) das Eindampfen, Abdampfen, Einkochen; die Ausdünstung. **evaporative,** *adj.* Ausdünstungs–, Verdampfungs–. **evaporator** [–reitə], *s.* die Abdampfschale, das Eindampfgefäß, der Verdampfer.

evasion [i'veiʒən], *s.* das Ausweichen, die Umgehung; Ausflucht, Ausrede; ***tax –,*** die Steuerhinterziehung. **evasive** [–siv], *adj.* ausweichend; schwer faßbar; ***– action,*** das Ausweichmanöver. **evasiveness,** *s.* ausweichendes Benehmen.

eve [i:v], *s.* (*Poet.*) der Abend; Vorabend; ***Christmas Eve,*** der Weihnachtsabend, Heiligabend, Heiliger Abend; ***New Year's Eve,*** der Silvester; ***on the – of,*** am Vorabend (*Gen.*); (*fig.*) nahe an (*Dat.*), unmittelbar vor (*Dat.*).

Eve, *s.* (*B.*) Eva (*f.*); (*coll.*) ***a daughter of –,*** typische Frau.

[1]**even** [i:vən], *s.* (*Poet.*) der Abend.

[2]**even, 1.** *adj.* **1.** eben, gerade, waagerecht, horizontal; flach, glatt; ***on an – keel,*** (*Naut.*) auf ebenem Kiel; (*fig.*) ausgeglichen, im Gleichgewicht; ***– number,*** gerade Zahl; ***make a th. – with the ground,*** etwas dem Boden gleichmachen; 2. gleichmäßig, regelmäßig, gleichförmig, gleich, identisch; (*Comm.*) ***of – date,*** gleichen Datums; ***on – terms,*** in gutem Einvernehmen; 3. (*fig.*) gelassen, gleichmütig, ausgeglichen, ruhig; ***of an – temper,*** ruhigen Gemüts; 4. unparteiisch; 5. (*coll.*) quitt; ***be – with him,*** ihm nichts mehr schuldig sein, mit ihm quitt sein; (*usu. fig.*) ***get – with him,*** mit ihm abrechnen *or* ins reine kommen. **2.** *adv.* selbst, sogar, auch; gerade, genau; (*before comp.*) noch; ***– as,*** gerade als; genau wie; ***– more,*** (sogar) noch mehr; ***– now,*** selbst jetzt; eben *or* gerade jetzt; ***not –,*** nicht einmal; ***or –,*** oder auch nur; ***– so,*** immerhin, allerdings, wenn schon; ***– if*** or ***though,*** wenn auch, selbst wenn. **3.** *v.t.* (ein)ebnen, gleichmachen, glätten; ***– up,*** ausgleichen; (*coll.*) ***– matters up,*** sich revanchieren (***with,*** an (*Dat.*)), es heimzahlen *or* vergelten (*Dat.*), ins reine kommen (mit).

even|-handed, *adj.* unparteilich, unparteiisch. **–-handedness,** *s.* die Unparteilichkeit.

evening ['i:vniŋ], **1.** *s.* der Abend; die Abendunterhaltung, geselliger Abend; ***in the –,*** am Abend, abends; ***late in the –,*** spätabends; ***in the –s,*** in den Abendstunden, abends; ***on the – of,*** am Abend des; ***on Sunday –s,*** an Sonntagabenden; ***one –,*** eines Abends; ***this –,*** heute abend; ***tomorrow –,*** morgen abend; ***yesterday –,*** gestern abend. **2.** *adj.* Abend–; abendlich; ***– dress,*** der Gesellschaftsanzug, Frack (*for men*); das Abendkleid, die Balltoilette (*for women*); ***– service,*** der Abendgottesdienst; ***–-star,*** der Abendstern.

evenness ['i:vənnis], *s.* die Ebenheit, Geradheit, Glätte; (*fig.*) Gleichmäßigkeit, Gleichförmigkeit, (*of temperament*) Gelassenheit, (Seelen)ruhe, der Gleichmut; *see* [2]**even.**

evensong ['i:vənsɔŋ], *s.* das Abendgebet, der Abendgottesdienst, die Vesper; *see* [1]**even.**

event [i'vent], *s.* das Ereignis, der Vorfall, die Begebenheit, das Vorkommnis; der Ausgang, das Ergebnis; der Fall; (*Spt.*) die (Programm)-nummer; ***at all –s,*** auf alle Fälle; ***athletic –s,*** sportliche Veranstaltung; (*Spt.*) ***field –s,*** Sprung- und Wurfwettkämpfe (*pl.*); (*coll.*) ***a happy –,*** ein freudiges Ereignis (*baby*); ***in any –,*** sowieso; (*coll.*) ***in the –,*** schließlich; ***in the – of his arrival,*** im Falle seiner Ankunft; ***in the – of his arriving,*** falls er ankommen sollte; (*coll.*) ***quite an –,*** ein besonderes Ereignis; (*Spt.*) ***track –s,*** Laufwettkämpfe (*pl.*).

even-tempered, *adj.* gleichmütig, gelassen.

eventful [i'ventful], *adj.* ereignisreich, ereignisvoll.

eventide ['i:vəntaid], *s.* (*usu. Poet.*) *see* **evening;** ***– home,*** das Altersheim.

eventual [i'ventjuəl], *adj.* schließlich, endlich; möglich, etwaig. **eventuality** [–'æliti], *s.* die Möglichkeit. **eventually,** *adv.* endlich, am Ende, schließlich. **eventuate** [–eit], *v.i.* ausgehen, ausfallen, endigen; stattfinden, sich ereignen.

ever ['evə], *adv.* immer, stets, unaufhörlich; (*esp. in inter., neg. and conditional*) je(mals); überhaupt, nur; – ***after(wards)***, seit der Zeit, von der Zeit an, seitdem; – ***and anon***, dann und wann, immer wieder; ***as good as*** –, so gut wie nur je; ***as soon as – I can***, sobald ich nur irgend kann; (*coll.*) ***did you –?*** hast du überhaupt so etwas gehört (*or* gesehen)? so etwas! ***for*** – (***and*** – or ***and a day***), auf ewig, für immer, in alle Ewigkeit; ***Scotland for –!*** es lebe Schottland! Schottland hoch! ***he is for – making mischief***, er stiftet stets Unheil an; – ***increasing***, immer (mehr) wachsend; ***more than*** –, mehr denn je; (*coll.*) ***be – so pleased***, sich wirklich sehr freuen; (*coll.*) – ***so many***, sehr viele, unzählige; (*coll.*) – ***so much***, wirklich sehr; – ***since***, see – ***after***; ***scarcely*** –, fast nie; ***were he – so rich***, wäre er noch so reich; (*coll.*) – ***so long***, sehr lange; (*coll.*) ***not . . . for – so much***, nicht um alles in der Welt; ***what*** (***where, who etc.***) – ***can it be?*** was (wo, wer *etc.*) kann es nur *or* bloß sein? ***yours*** –, immer der Ihrige (*in letters*).

ever|green, 1. *s.* das Immergrün. **2.** *adj.* immergrün. **–lasting, 1.** *adj.* ewig, immerwährend; (*fig.*) dauerhaft, unverwüstlich (*cloth*); (*coll.*) unaufhörlich, immer wiederholt; – ***flower***, die Strohblume, Immortelle. **2.** *s.* die Ewigkeit. **–lastingly,** *adv.* auf ewig. **–more,** *adv.* (*usu.* ***for*** –) immerfort, immerzu, stets, für immer; ***now and*** –, auf immer und ewig, jetzt und in alle Zukunft.

eversion [i'və:ʃən], *s.* das Auswärtskehren, die Umkehrung, Umstülpung. **evert,** *v.t.* nach außen kehren, umkehren, umstülpen.

every ['evri], *attrib. adj.* jede(r, –s); alle; ***all*** or ***each and*** –, all und jeder; – ***bit as good***, genau so gut; ***have – confidence in***, volles Vertrauen haben zu; – ***day***, jeden Tag, alle Tage, täglich (*see* **everyday**); – ***now and then***, – ***once in a while***, see – ***so often***; (*coll.*) – ***man Jack***, – ***mother's son***, Hinz und Kunz; – ***one***, jeder einzelne (*see* **everybody**); – ***one of them***, ein jeder von ihnen; – ***other*** or ***second day***, – ***two days***, jeden zweiten Tag, alle zwei Tage; – ***third day***, – ***three days***, jeden dritten Tag; – ***ten days***, alle zehn Tage; ***from – side***, von allen Seiten; – ***so often***, hin und wieder, dann und wann, von Zeit zu Zeit, ab und zu, gelegentlich, immer wieder; ***my – thought***, jeder meiner *or* alle meine Gedanken; – ***time***, jedesmal, stets, ohne Ausnahme; ***in – way***, in jeder Weise.

every|body, *s.* jeder(mann), ein jeder. **–day,** *adj.* (all)täglich, tagtäglich, Alltags–. **–one,** *s. See* **–body. –thing,** *s.* alles; (*coll.*) die Hauptsache, das (Aller)wichtigste; (*coll.*) ***think – of***, große Stücke halten auf (*Acc.*); – ***that***, alles was. **–where,** *adv.* überall, allenthalben.

evict [i'vikt], *v.t.* (*Law*) aus dem Besitze vertreiben, exmittieren. **eviction** [i'vikʃən], *s.* (*Hist.*) der Abtrieb; gerichtliche Vertreibung *or* Entsetzung, die Exmission; (*Law*) – ***order***, der Räumungsbefehl.

evidence ['evidəns], **1.** *s.* (*Law*) der (Zeugen)beweis, das Zeugnis (***of, for***, für), die Zeugenaussage; das Beweisstück, Beweismittel, Beweismaterial; (*fig.*) die Spur, das (An)zeichen; ***be – of***, beweisen, bezeugen; – ***of character***, das Leumundszeugnis; ***circumstantial*** –, der Indizienbeweis; (*Law*) – ***for the defence***, das Entlastungsmaterial; ***documentary*** –, urkundlicher Beweis; ***external*** –, äußere Beweise (*pl.*); ***furnish – of***, bezeugen, Zeugnis ablegen für, beweisen; (*coll.*) ***be in*** –, sichtbar sein, zutage treten, auffallen; ***be much in*** –, stark vertreten sein; ***admit in*** –, als Beweis zulassen; ***call him in*** –, ihn als Zeugen anrufen; ***give*** –, Beweise erbringen, Zeugenaussage machen, Zeugnis ablegen; ***piece of*** –, das Beweisstück, der Beleg; ***prima facie*** –, die Rechtsvermutung, vollgültiger Beweis; (*Law*) – ***for the prosecution***, das Belastungsmaterial; ***rules of*** –, Bestimmungen für die Beweiserhebung; ***turn king's*** or ***queen's*** –, Kronzeuge werden. **2.** *v.t.* augenscheinlich machen, zeigen, beweisen, erweisen, dartun.

evident ['evidənt], *adj.* augenscheinlich, einleuchtend; offenbar, klar (ersichtlich), offensichtlich, offenkundlich, handgreiflich. **evidently,** *adv.* augenscheinlich, offenbar, offensichtlich, zweifelsohne.

evil [i:vl], **1.** *adj.* übel, böse, schlimm; schlecht, bösartig, boshaft, gottlos; – ***communications***, schlechte Gesellschaft; ***fall on – days***, ins Unglück geraten; – ***eye***, böser Blick, der Augenzauber; ***look with an – eye upon***, mißfällig *or* scheel ansehen; ***the Evil One***, der böse Feind. **2.** *s.* das Übel, Böse; Unglück, Unheil; ***do*** –, Böses tun, freveln, sündigen; (*B.*) ***full of*** –, voll Arges; ***for good or*** (***for***) –, auf Gedeih und Verderb; ***King's*** –, Skrofeln (*pl.*), die Skrofulose; ***powers of*** –, die Mächte der Finsternis; ***shun*** –, die Sünde meiden; ***speak – of***, schlecht sprechen von; ***wish him*** –, ihm Unglück wünschen. **evil|-disposed,** *adj.* boshaft, übelgesinnt. **–-doer,** *s.* der (die) Übeltäter(in). **–-minded,** *adj.* bösartig, boshaft. **–-mindedness,** *s.* die Bösartigkeit, Boshaftigkeit.

evince [i'vins], *v.t.* beweisen, bekunden, erweisen, zeigen, dartun, an den Tag legen.

eviscerate [i'visəreit], *v.t.* ausweiden; (*fig.*) bedeutungslos machen. **evisceration** [–'reiʃən], *s.* die Ausweidung.

evocation [evo'keiʃən], *s.* die Hervorrufung, (*fig.*) Erzeugung; (Geister)beschwörung. **evocative** [i'vɔkətiv], *adj.* im Geiste hervorrufend; ***be – of***, erinnern an (*Acc.*). **evoke** [i'vouk], *v.t.* hervorrufen, wachrufen; bannen, (herauf)beschwören (*spirits*).

evolute ['i:vəlju:t], *s.* (*Math.*) die Evolute. **evolution** [–'lu:ʃən], *s.* 1. die Entwick(e)lung, Entfaltung, der Werdegang; 2. (*Math.*) das Wurzelausziehen; 3. (*Biol.*) die Evolution; 4. (*Chem.*) Entbindung; 5. (*Mil.*) taktische Bewegung, das Manövrieren; 6. (*fig.*) Ergebnis, die Folge, Reihe; 7. Bewegung, Umdrehung. **evolutionary,** *adj.* **1.** Entwicklungs–, Evolutions–; 2. (*Mil.*) Schwenkungs–, Manövrier–.

evolve [i'vɔlv], **1.** *v.t.* 1. entwickeln, entfalten, enthüllen; 2. (*Chem.*) ausscheiden, entbinden, von sich geben. **2.** *v.i.* entstehen (***from***, aus); sich entwickeln, sich entfalten (***into***, in (*Acc.*) *or* zu).

ewe [ju:], *s.* das Mutterschaf; – ***lamb***, das Schaflamm.

ewer ['ju:ə], *s.* die Wasserkanne, der Wasserkrug.

ex [eks], **1.** *prep.* 1. aus; – ***mine***, ab Bergwerk; – ***ship***, aus dem Schiffe; – ***works***, ab Werk; 2. ohne, abzüglich, exklusive; – ***dividend***, ohne Dividende. **2.** *pref.* ehemalig, früher; –***-queen***, ehemalige Königin.

exacerbate [eg'zæsəbeit], *v.t.* verschlimmern (*a th.*); erbittern (*a p.*). **exacerbation** [–'beiʃən], *s.* die Erbitterung, Verschärfung; (*Med.*) Verschlimmerung.

exact [ig'zækt], **1.** *adj.* genau, richtig, exakt; (*of a p.*) sorgfältig, pünktlich, gewissenhaft. **2.** *v.t.* eintreiben (*payment*); erpressen (*money*); (er)fordern, verlangen, erzwingen, erheischen. **exacting,** *adj.* anstrengend, anspruchsvoll; ***he was very*** –, er stellte hohe Anforderungen, er war sehr genau. **exaction** [–'zækʃən], *s.* die Beitreibung, Eintreibung (*of money, debts etc.*); unrechtmäßige Forderung; hohe Anforderung; der Tribut, erpreßte Abgabe. **exactitude** [–itju:d], *s.* die Genauigkeit, Exaktheit. **exactly,** *adv.* genau, richtig; –! ganz recht *or* richtig! – ***the man for the post***, gerade der Richtige für diesen Posten; ***not*** –, nicht eben *or* gerade. **exactness,** *s.* die Genauigkeit, Richtigkeit, Pünktlichkeit, Sorgfalt, Regelmäßigkeit. **exactor,** *s.* der Eintreiber; Erpresser; Forderer.

exaggerate [ig'zædʒəreit], **1.** *v.t.* übertreiben; (unangemessen) hervorheben, zu viel machen aus, (*coll.*) hochschrauben, verstärken, verschlimmern, zu stark betonen. **2.** *v.i.* übertreiben. **exaggerated,** *adj.* übertrieben. **exaggeration** [–'reiʃən], *s.* die Übertreibung.

exalt [ig'zɔ:lt], *v.t.* erheben; erhöhen, veredeln;

(lob)preisen; – *to the skies,* in den Himmel heben.
exaltation [egzɔ:l'teiʃən], *s.* 1. die Erhebung, Erhöhung; (*Eccl.*) – *of the cross,* die Kreuzeserhöhung; 2. (*fig.*) die Begeisterung, Verzückung, Erregung, gehobene Stimmung; 3. (*Astrol.*) höchster Stand. **exalted,** *adj.* erhaben, hoch; (*fig.*) begeistert, exaltiert; gehoben (*as style*).

exam [ig'zæm], (*coll. for*) **examination.**

examination [igzæmi'neiʃən], *s.* 1. die Prüfung, das Examen; ***competitive –,*** die Konkurrenzprüfung; ***entrance –,*** die Aufnahmeprüfung; ***fail (in) an –,*** bei einer Prüfung durchfallen; ***go in for an –,*** see ***sit an –; pass an –,*** eine Prüfung bestehen; (*sl.*) ***plough an –,*** see ***fail an –; get through an –,*** see ***pass an –; sit for*** or ***take an –,*** sich prüfen lassen, sich einer Prüfung unterziehen; 2. die Prüfung, Untersuchung, Besichtigung, Durchsicht (*of, into, Gen.*), (Zoll)revision, Kontrolle; (*Law*) Untersuchung, Vernehmung, das Verhör; ***make an – of,*** besichtigen; ***medical –,*** ärztliche Untersuchung; ***post-mortem –,*** die Leichenöffnung; ***be under –,*** erwogen *or* geprüft werden; (*Law*) unter Verhör stehen; (***up***)***on –,*** bei näherer Prüfung. **examination-paper,** *s.* 1. schriftliche Prüfung; 2. die Prüfungsarbeit.

examine [ig'zæmin], *v.t.* untersuchen, prüfen, revidieren, besichtigen; (*Law*) ausfragen, vernehmen, verhören; (*a th.*) einer Prüfung unterwerfen; – ***accounts,*** Rechnungen überprüfen; – ***one's conscience,*** sein Gewissen prüfen; ***be –d by a doctor,*** sich von einem Arzt untersuchen lassen. **examinee** [–'ni:], *s.* der Prüfling, Prüfungskandidat. **examiner,** *s.* der (die) Prüfer(in), Prüfende(r), der Untersucher, Untersuchende(r), Kontrollbeamte(r), der Revisor, Examinator; (*Law*) Vernehmer, Verhörer.

example [ig'zɑ:mpl], *s.* das Beispiel, Vorbild (*of,* für); Muster, Exemplar, die Probe; warnendes Beispiel, die Warnung (*to,* für); ***by way of –,*** (***as***) ***for –,*** zum Beispiel, um ein Beispiel zu geben; ***hold up as an –,*** als Beispiel hinstellen (*to, Dat.*); ***let this be an – to you,*** möge dir dies eine Warnung sein; ***make an – of him,*** ein Exempel an ihm statuieren, ihn exemplarisch bestrafen; ***set an –,*** ein Beispiel geben; ***set a bad –,*** ein schlechtes Beispiel geben; ***set a good –,*** mit gutem Beispiele vorangehen; ***take – by,*** sich (*Dat.*) ein Beispiel nehmen an (*Dat.*), sich (*Dat.*) zur Warnung dienen lassen.

exasperate [ig'zɑ:spəreit], *v.t.* 1. (auf)reizen, aufbringen, ärgern, entrüsten, erzürnen, erbittern; 2. (*Med.*) verschlimmern. **exasperation** [–'reiʃən], *s.* 1. die Erbitterung, Entrüstung, der Ärger; 2. (*Med.*) die Verschlimmerung.

ex cathedra [ekskə'θi:drə], *adv.* von maßgebender Seite.

excavate ['ekskəveit], *v.t.* ausgraben, aushöhlen. **excavation** [–'veiʃən], *s.* die Aushöhlung; (Aus)grabung, Ausschachtung, Baugrube, Höhle. **excavator,** *s.* der Löffelbagger, Trockenbagger.

exceed [ik'si:d], **1.** *v.t.* überschreiten, übertreffen, übersteigen, hinausgehen über (*Acc.*), in den Schatten stellen. **2.** *v.i.* 1. zu weit gehen, das Maß überschreiten (*in,* in (*Dat.*)); 2. sich auszeichnen. **exceeding,** *adj.* übermäßig, äußerst, außerordentlich; mehr als, übersteigend. **exceedingly,** *adv.* überaus, außerordentlich, äußerst, höchst.

excel [ik'sel], **1.** *v.i.* (*also – o.s.*) sich hervortun, sich auszeichnen, hervorragen (***in, at,*** in (*Dat.*)). **2.** *v.t.* übertreffen, überragen.

excellence ['eksələns], *s.* die Vortrefflichkeit, Vorzüglichkeit, Güte; ausgezeichnete Leistung, der Vorzug. **Excellency,** *s.* die Exzellenz (*in titles*). **excellent,** *adj.* ausgezeichnet, (vor)trefflich, vorzüglich.

excelsior [ek'selsiɔ], **1.** *adj.* (*Comm.*) Prima–. **2.** *s.* (*Typ.*) die Brillant.

except [ik'sept], **1.** *v.t.* ausnehmen, ausschließen (***from,*** von *or* aus), vorbehalten (von); ***present company –ed,*** Anwesende ausgenommen; (*Comm.*) ***errors –ed,*** Irrtümer vorbehalten. **2.** *conj.* außer daß, es sei denn daß, ausgenommen daß; – ***for,*** abgesehen von, bis auf (*Acc.*). **3.** *or* **excepting,** *prep.* außer, mit Ausnahme von, ausgenommen.

exception [ik'sepʃən], *s.* 1. die Ausnahme (***to, from,*** von); ***admit of no –,*** keine Ausnahme zulassen; ***by way of –,*** ausnahmsweise; ***make an – of,*** als Ausnahme betrachten; ***the – proves the rule,*** die Ausnahme bestätigt die Regel; ***no – to the rule,*** keine Ausnahme von der Regel; ***with the – of,*** mit Ausnahme von, ausgenommen, außer, bis auf (*Acc.*); ***with this –,*** ausgenommen davon; ***without –,*** ohne Ausnahme, ausnahmslos; 2. die Einwendung, der Einwand, Einwurf, (*Law*) Vorbehalt (*to,* gegen); die Einrede, Beanstandung, Ausschließung; ***beyond –,*** unanfechtbar; ***take – to,*** Vorstellungen erheben *or,* Einwendungen machen gegen, Anstoß nehmen an (*Dat.*), sich stoßen an (*Dat.*), übelnehmen.

exceptionable [ik'sepʃənəbl], *adj.* anfechtbar; tadelnswert, anstößig. **exceptional,** *adj.* außergewöhnlich; Sonder–, Vorzugs–, Ausnahme–. **exceptionally,** *adv.* ausnahmsweise, außerordentlich, außergewöhnlich.

excerpt, **1.** [ek'sə:pt], *v.t.* ausziehen, exzerpieren (***from,*** aus). **2.** ['eksə:pt], *s.* der Auszug, das Exzerpt; (*Typ.*) der Sonderdruck, Separatdruck.

excess [ik'ses], **1.** *s.* 1. das Übermaß, der Überfluß (*of,* an (*Dat.*)); (*Math.*) das Mehr, der Mehrbetrag, Überschuß; ***in – of,*** mehr als; ***be in – of,*** überschreiten, übersteigen, hinausgehen über (*Acc.*), überwiegen; ***in –,*** im Übermaß; 2. die Unmäßigkeit, Ausschweifung; *pl.* Exzesse (*pl.*), Ausschreitungen (*pl.*); ***carry to –,*** bis zum Übermaß treiben, übertreiben; ***drink to –,*** übermäßig trinken. **2.** *adj.* Über–, überzählig; ***– fare,*** der Zuschlag; ***– freight,*** die Überfracht; ***– luggage,*** das Übergewicht; ***– postage,*** das Strafporto, die Nachgebühr; ***– profits duty,*** die Mehrgewinnsteuer; ***– purchasing power,*** der Kaufkraftüberhang.

excessive [ik'sesiv], *adj.* übermäßig, übertrieben; – ***charge,*** die Überforderung; – ***demand,*** der Überbedarf; – ***interest,*** Wucherzinsen (*pl.*); – ***supply,*** das Überangebot. **excessiveness,** *s.* die Übermäßigkeit.

exchange [iks'tʃeindʒ], **1.** *v.t.* (aus–, um–, ver)tauschen; (*money*) eintauschen, (um)wechseln (***for,*** gegen); ersetzen (***for,*** durch); – ***books, compliments, greetings, ideas,*** Bücher, Komplimente, Grüße, Gedanken austauschen; – ***presents,*** sich gegenseitig beschenken; – ***prisoners,*** Gefangene austauschen; – ***shots,*** Schüsse wechseln. **2.** *s.* 1. der (Aus– *or* Um)tausch, die Auswechs(e)lung; ***give in –,*** in Tausch geben, einwechseln; ***in – for,*** als Entgelt für *or* gegen; – ***of letters,*** der Schriftwechsel; ***make an –,*** tauschen; ***take in part –,*** in Zahlung nehmen; – ***of prisoners,*** der Gefangenenaustausch; – ***is no robbery,*** Tausch ist kein Raub; – ***of shots,*** der Kugelwechsel; – ***of views,*** der Meinungsaustausch, Gedankenaustausch; 2. (*Comm.*) das (Um)wechseln, der Wechselverkehr; Tauschhandel; ***bill of –,*** die Tratte, der Wechsel; ***foreign –,*** die Valuta, Devisen (*pl.*); – ***of money,*** der Geldwechsel; ***par of –,*** das Wechselpari; ***under the quoted –,*** unter dem Kurse; ***rate of –,*** der Umrechnungskurs, Wechselkurs; 3. (*Boxing, etc.*) der Wechsel; 4. (*St. Exch.*) die Börse; ***on –,*** an *or* auf der Börse; 5. (*Tele.*) das (Fernsprech)amt, die Vermittlung, Zentrale.

exchangeability [ikstʃeindʒə'biliti], *s.* die (Aus)tauschbarkeit, Auswechselbarkeit. **exchangeable** [–'tʃeindʒəbl], *adj.* (aus)tauschbar, auswechselbar (***for,*** gegen); vertauschbar; – ***value,*** der Tauschwert.

exchange| advice, *s.* der Börsenbericht. – **broker,** *s.* der Wechselmakler, Börsenmakler, Kursmakler. – **control,** *s.* die Paritätskontrolle. – **rate,** *s.* der Wechselkurs, Umrechnungskurs. – **regulations,** *pl.* Devisenverordnungen. – **student,** *s.* der Austauschstudent

exchequer [iks'tʃekə], *s.* das Schatzamt, die Staatskasse; der Fiskus, das Finanzministerium; die Kasse, der Geldvorrat, Finanzen (*pl.*) (*of private firms*); ***Chancellor of the Exchequer,*** der Schatzkanzler, Finanzminister; ***Court of Exchequer,*** das Finanzgericht. **exchequer| bill,** *s.* (kurzfristige) verzinsliche Schatzanweisung. – **bond,** *s.* die Staatsobligation, langfristige Schatzanweisung.

excisable [ek'saizəbl], *adj.* (be)steuerbar.

[1]**excise** ['eksaiz, ek'saiz], **1.** *s.* die Verbrauchssteuer, Verbrauchsabgabe, Akzise; Finanzabteilung für indirekte Steuern; – ***duties,*** Steuerabgaben (*pl.*). **2.** *v.t.* besteuern.

[2]**excise** [ek'saiz], *v.t.* herausschneiden; (*fig.*) ausschneiden, ausmerzen (***from,*** aus).

exciseman ['eksaizmæn], *s.* der Akzisen– *or* Steuereinnehmer.

excision [ek'siʒən], *s.* die Ausschneidung, Abschneidung; (*fig.*) Ausrottung, Ausscheidung (***from,*** aus).

excitability [iksaitə'biliti], *s.* die Erregbarkeit, Reizbarkeit, Nervosität. **excitable,** *adj.* erregbar, reizbar, nervös. **excitableness,** *s. See* **excitability. excitant** ['eksitənt], *s.* das Reizmittel. **excitation** [eksi'teiʃən], *s.* die Reizung, Erregung; Aufregung, Anregung; der Reiz, Stimulus.

excite [ik'sait], *v.t.* erregen, aufregen; aufreizen, (an)reizen; (*fig.*) hervorrufen, erwecken, wachrufen; – ***o.s., get –d,*** sich aufregen. **excitement,** *s.* die Erregung, Aufregung (***over,*** über (*Acc.*)), Aufgeregtheit. **exciter,** *s.* 1. der Anreger, Erreger; 2. (*Med.*) das Reizmittel; 3. (*Elec.*) die Erregermaschine; – ***current,*** der Erregerstrom. **exciting,** *adj.* aufregend, anregend, erregend; spannend.

exclaim [iks'kleim], **1.** *v.i.* ausrufen, schreien; – ***against,*** eifern gegen. **2.** *v.t.* ausrufen.

exclamation [ekskla'meiʃən], *s.* der Ausruf; die Ausrufung; *pl.* das Geschrei; – ***mark,*** das Ausrufungszeichen. **exclamatory** [iks'klæmətəri], *adj.* ausrufend; – ***words,*** Ausrufeworte.

exclude [iks'klu:d], *v.t.* ausschließen, ausscheiden, ausstoßen. **exclusion** [–'klu:ʒən], *s.* die Ausschließung, Ausschaltung, der Ausschluß (***from,*** von); (*Law*) die Präklusion; ***to the – of,*** unter Ausschluß von. **exclusive,** *adj.* 1. ausschließend, ausschließlich, alleinig, Allein–; – ***of,*** abgesehen *or* mit Ausschluß von; ***be – of,*** ausschließen; – ***of other charges,*** andere Kosten ungerechnet; – ***report,*** der Sonderbericht; – ***sale,*** der Alleinverkauf; 2. vornehm, wählerisch, exklusiv. **exclusively,** *adv.* ausschließlich. **exclusiveness,** *s.* 1. die Ausschließlichkeit; 2. Abgeschlossenheit, Exklusivität.

excogitate [eks'kɔdʒiteit], *v.t.* ausdenken, erdenken, aussinnen, ersinnen. **excogitation** [–'teiʃən], *s.* das Ausdenken; Nachdenken (***of,*** über (*Acc.*)); die Erfindung.

excommunicate [ekskə'mju:nikeit], *v.t.* in den Bann tun, exkommunizieren. **excommunication** [–'keiʃən], *s.* der (Kirchen)bann, die Exkommunikation; Ausstoßung, Auschließung.

excoriate [eks'kɔ:rieit], *v.t.* die Haut abschälen (*Dat.*); wund reiben, abschürfen (*skin*). **excoriation** [–'eiʃən], *s.* das Abschälen, Abschürfen; die Wundreibung.

excorticate [eks'kɔ:tikeit], *v.t.* entrinden.

excrement ['ekskrimənt], *s.* das Exkrement, der Auswurf, Kot, Stuhl. **excremental** [–'mentl], *adj.* Kot–, kotartig.

excrescence [iks'kresns], *s.* der Auswuchs; Vorsprung; (*fig.*) krankhafte *or* abnorme Entwicklung. **excrescent,** *adj.* auswachsend; (*fig.*) überflüssig, überschüssig; (*Phonet.*) eingeschoben.

excreta [iks'kri:tə], *s.* Auswurfstoffe, Ausscheidungsstoffe (*pl.*). **excrete,** *v.t.* ausscheiden, absondern. **excretion** [–'kri:ʃən], *s.* die Ausscheidung, Absonderung; der Auswurf. **excretive, excretory,** *adj.* ausscheidend, absondernd, abführend, Ausscheidungs–.

excruciate [iks'kru:ʃieit], *v.t.* martern, quälen, foltern. **excruciating,** *adj.* peinigend, qualvoll; (*coll.*) peinlich, unausstehlich. **excruciation** [–'eiʃən], *s.* das Martern, Peinigen; die Marter, Qual.

exculpate ['ekskʌlpeit], *v.t.* entlasten, rechtfertigen, freisprechen, rein waschen (***from,*** von). **exculpation** [–'peiʃən], *s.* die Entschuldigung, Entlastung, Rechtfertigung. **exculpatory** [–'kʌlpətəri], *adj.* rechtfertigend, entlastend, Rechtfertigungs–.

excursion [iks'kə:ʃən], *s.* 1. der Ausflug, die Partie; der Abstecher, Streifzug; 2. (*Astr.*) die Ausweichung; 3. (*Phys.*) Schwingung, das Ausschlag (*of pendulum*); 4. (*fig.*) die Abschweifung. **excursionist,** *s.* der Ausflügler, Tourist. **excursion| ticket,** *s.* die Ausflugsfahrkarte. – **train,** *s.* der Sonderzug.

excursive [eks'kə:siv], *adj.* sprunghaft, unzusammenhängend; abschweifend, umherschweifend. **excursus,** *s.* die Abschweifung; der Exkurs, angehängte Erörterung.

excusable [iks'kju:zəbl], *adj.* entschuldbar, verzeihlich. **excusal,** *s.* die Befreiung (*from taxes*). **excuse, 1.** [–'kju:z], *v.t.* (*a p.*) entschuldigen, rechtfertigen; verzeihen (*Dat.*), Nachsicht haben mit; (*a th.*) verzeihen (*Acc.*), entschuldigen, übersehen, als Entschuldigung dienen für, eine Entschuldigung finden für, (*only neg.*) gutheißen, rechtfertigen; (*usu. pass.*) – ***him from,*** ihm erlassen (*Acc.*), ihn entheben (*Gen.*) *or* befreien von; – ***me!*** verzeihen Sie! Verzeihung! entschuldigen Sie! ***may I be –d?*** ich bitte, mich zu entschuldigen; ***I must be –d from speaking,*** ich muß leider ablehnen zu sprechen; – ***o.s.,*** sich entschuldigen, sich rechtfertigen; ***he was –d attendance,*** ihm wurde das Erscheinen erlassen; ***that does not – his rudeness,*** das dient nicht als Entschuldigung für seine Grobheit. **2.** [–'kju:s], *s.* die Entschuldigung, Rechtfertigung; der Milderungsgrund, Rechtfertigungsgrund; die Ausrede, Ausflucht, der Vorwand; die Bitte um Verzeihung *or* Entschuldigung *or* Nachsicht; ***make –s,*** Ausflüchte gebrauchen; ***make one's –s to him,*** sich bei ihm entschuldigen; ***in – of,*** zur *or* als Entschuldigung für; ***there is no – for it, it admits of no –,*** es läßt sich nicht entschuldigen *or* rechtfertigen.

exeat ['eksiæt], *s.* der Urlaub.

execrable ['eksikrəbl], *adj.* scheußlich, abscheulich. **execrate** [–kreit], **1.** *v.t.* verfluchen; verabscheuen. **2.** *v.i.* fluchen. **execration** [–'kreiʃən], *s.* die Verwünschung, der Fluch; Abscheu; ***hold in –,*** verabscheuen.

executant [ig'sekjutənt], *s.* (*Mus.*) Vortragende(r), Ausführende(r), Ausübende(r). **execute** ['eksikju:t], *v.t.* 1. durchführen, ausführen, vollführen, vollziehen, vollstrecken, verrichten; (*Theat., Mus.*) vortragen, spielen; (*Law*) ausfertigen, rechtsgültig machen; ausüben (*an office*); 2. hinrichten (*a p.*). **executer,** *s.* der Vollzieher, Vollstrecker.

execution [eksi'kju:ʃən], *s.* 1. die Durchführung, Ausführung, Vollstreckung, Vollziehung, Erfüllung; (*Law*) Ausfertigung (*of a deed*); (*Mus.*) der Vortrag, das Spiel, die Ausführung, Technik; ***carry*** or ***put into –,*** ausführen, vollziehen; 2. die Hinrichtung (*of a criminal*); ***place of –,*** die Richtstätte, der Richtplatz; 3. die Zwangsvollstreckung, Pfändung, Exekution (*for debt*); ***take out an – against him,*** ihn auspfänden lassen; ***take goods in –,*** Güter exekutieren; (*Law*) ***writ of –,*** der Vollstreckungsbefehl; 4. ***do –,*** Schaden anrichten, (*coll.*) Wirkung haben, wirken. **executioner,** *s.* der Henker, Scharfrichter.

executive [ig'zekjutiv], **1.** *adj.* vollziehend, ausübend, Exekutiv–; – ***ability,*** praktische Geschicklichkeit; – ***committee,*** der Verwaltungsrat, geschäftsführender Ausschuß; (*Am.*) – ***council,*** der Ministerrat; – ***power,*** die Exekutive, vollziehende Gewalt. **2.** *s.* (*Pol.*) ausübende Gewalt, die Vollziehungsgewalt, Exekutive; (*Comm.*) der Geschäftsführer, geschäftsführender Beamter.

executor [ig'zekjutə], *s.* der Testamentsvollstrecker; ***literary –,*** der Nachlaßverwalter. **executorial** [–'tɔ:riəl], *adj.* Vollstreckungs–. **executory,** *adj.* ausübend, vollstreckend, vollziehend, Ausführungs–, Ausübungs–, Vollziehungs–. **executrix,** *s.* die Testamentsvollstreckerin.

exegesis [eksi'dʒi:sis], *s.* die Bibelauslegung,

Bibelerklärung, Exegese. **exegete** ['eksidʒi:t], *s.* der Bibelerklärer, Exeget. **exegetic(al)** [-'dʒetik(l)], *adj.* exegetisch, auslegend, erklärend. **exegetics,** *pl.* die Exegetik.

exemplar [ig'zemplə], *s.* das Muster(beispiel), Vorbild, (typisches) Beispiel (*of,* für); das Urbild, der Archetyp. **exemplariness,** *s.* die Musterhaftigkeit. **exemplary,** *adj.* musterhaft, mustergültig, Muster–, vorbildlich, nachahmungswert; abschreckend, exemplarisch (*of punishment*).

exemplification [igzemplifi'keiʃən], *s.* die Belegung *or* Erläuterung durch Beispiele; der Beleg, das Beispiel, Muster; (*Law*) beglaubigte Abschrift; ***in* – *of,*** zur Erläuterung (*Gen.*). **exemplify** [ig'zemplifai], *v.t.* durch Beispiele belegen *or* erläutern; als Beispiel *or* Beleg dienen für, an Beispielen illustrieren; (*Law*) eine rechtsgültige Abschrift nehmen von.

exempt [ig'zempt], **1.** *v.t.* befreien, freimachen, freistellen, ausnehmen (***from,*** von), verschonen (mit); (*Mil.*) zurückstellen. **2.** *pred. adj.* befreit, verschont, frei (***from,*** von), (*Mil.*) zurückgestellt. **3.** *s.* Bevorrechtigte(r), Privilegierte(r), Befreite(r). **exemption** [-'zempʃən], *s.* die Befreiung, (*Mil.*) Zurückstellung; das Freisein; die Sonderstellung, Ausnahmestellung; ***– from taxation,*** die Steuerfreiheit.

exequies ['eksikwiz], *pl.* das Leichenbegängnis, die Totenfeier.

exercisable ['eksəsaizəbl], *adj.* ausführbar, anwendbar, anzuwenden(d). **exercise, 1.** *v.t.* 1. anwenden, gebrauchen; ausüben, geltend machen (*power, influence*); verwalten (*an office*); ***– authority,*** die Herrschaft besitzen; ***– patience,*** Geduld üben; 2. üben, drillen, einexerzieren (*a p.*), in Bewegung halten, bewegen, in Übung halten (*a horse*); ***– one's mind,*** sich geistig beschäftigen. **2.** *v.i.* (*Mil.*) exerzieren, (*Spt.*) trainieren; sich (*Dat.*) Bewegung machen. **3.** *s.* 1. der Gebrauch, die Anwendung, Ausübung; ***in the – of his duty,*** in Ausübung *or* Erfüllung seiner Pflicht; 2. die Übung, (*Mil.*) (*usu. pl.*) (Waffen)übung, das Manöver, Exerzieren; die (Schul)aufgabe; (*Mus.*) das Übungsstück; (*oft. pl.*) die Leibesübung, (Körper)bewegung; ***physical –(s),*** die Leibesübung; ***religious –(s),*** die Andachtsübung, der Gottesdienst; ***take –,*** sich (*Dat.*) Bewegung (im Freien) machen; ***written –,*** schriftliche Aufgabe *or* Arbeit.

exert [ig'zə:t], *v.t.* anwenden, (ge)brauchen, ausüben; ***– o.s.,*** sich anstrengen, sich bemühen; ***– one's influence,*** seinen Einfluß geltend machen. **exertion** [-'zə:ʃən], *s.* 1. die Anwendung, Ausübung; 2. Anstrengung, Anspannung, Bemühung, das Streben.

exeunt ['eksiunt], (*Theat.*) (sie gehen) ab.

exfoliate [eks'foulieit], *v.i.* sich abblättern, sich abschälen, (*Geol.*) sich abschiefern. **exfoliation** [-'eiʃən], *s.* die Abblätterung, Abschieferung, Häutung.

exhalation [eksə'leiʃən], *s.* die Ausdünstung, Ausdunstung; Ausatmung; der Brodem, Nebel, Dunst. **exhale** [eks'heil], *v.t.* ausdünsten; ausatmen, aushauchen, (*fig.*) von sich geben; ***be –d,*** ausdunsten.

exhaust [ig'zɔ:st], **1.** *v.t.* erschöpfen, ermüden; erschöpfend behandeln (*a subject*); aufbrauchen (*supplies*); erschöpfen, aussaugen (*soil*), aushauen (*a mine*); absaugen, herauspumpen, herausziehen (***from,*** aus) (*air etc. from a vessel*); ausschöpfen, auspumpen, entleeren (*vessel*); ***– the air in . . .,*** . . . luftleer pumpen; ***– the land,*** Raubbau treiben; ***– his patience,*** seine Geduld erschöpfen. **2.** *s.* (*Motor.*) der Auspuff, das Auspuffrohr; Auspuffgase (*pl.*). **exhausted,** *adj.* erschöpft, ermattet; verbraucht, abgebaut (*of a mine*); ***be –,*** versiegen; vergriffen sein (*of a book*). **exhaustible,** *adj.* erschöpflich. **exhausting,** *adj.* anstrengend, ermüdend, mühselig. **exhaustion** [-tʃən], *s.* die Erschöpfung; Ausziehung, Ausschöpfung, Ausleerung, Entleerung, das Ausströmen, Auspumpen; der Abbau (*of mine etc.*), (*Comm.*) Verbrauch, Konsum; (*Math.*) die Approximation, Exhaustion. **exhaustive,** *adj.* erschöpfend; vollständig. **exhaust| manifold,** *s.* das Auspuffsammelrohr. **– pipe,** *s.* das Auspuffrohr. **– steam,** *s.* der Abdampf. **– valve,** *s.* die Auspuffklappe, das Auslaßventil.

exhibit [ig'zibit], **1.** *v.t.* (*goods*) auslegen, ausstellen, zur Schau stellen; zeigen, sehen lassen, aufweisen, darlegen, an den Tag legen, entfalten; (*Law*) vorbringen, anbringen, einreichen (*evidence etc.*), zustellen, vorlegen (*a charge etc.*). **2.** *s.* (*Law*) das Beweisstück, der Beleg, die Eingabe; der Ausstellungsgegenstand.

exhibition [eksi'biʃən], *s.* 1. die Darlegung, Darstellung, Entfaltung, Bekundung, Äußerung; (*of goods*) Schaustellung, Ausstellung, Messe; (*Law*) Vorlage, Vorzeigung, Einreichung; (*Spt.*) ***– bout,*** der Schaukampf; ***international –,*** die Weltausstellung; ***make an – of o.s.,*** eine lächerliche Figur machen, sich lächerlich *or* zum Gespött machen; ***be on public –,*** öffentlich ausgestellt sein; 2. (*Univ.*) (kleines) Stipendium. **exhibitioner,** *s.* der Stipendiat. **exhibitionism,** *s.* (*Psych.*) der Exhibitionismus. **exhibitionist,** *s.* (*Psych.*) der Exhibitionist.

exhibitive [ek'zibitiv], *adj.* ***be – of,*** darstellen, vorstellen. **exhibitor,** *s.* der Aussteller (*of goods*); Darsteller (*of qualities*).

exhilarate [ig'ziləreit], *v.t.* erheitern, aufheitern. **exhilarated,** *adj.* heiter, lebhaft, angeregt. **exhilarating,** *adj.* erheiternd, anregend. **exhilaration** [-'reiʃən], *s.* die Erheiterung, Heiterkeit.

exhort [ig'zɔ:t], *v.t.* zureden (*Dat.*), ermahnen, ermuntern (***to,*** zu); dringend raten *or* empfehlen (*Dat.*). **exhortation** [eksɔ:'teiʃən], *s.* die Ermahnung, Ermunterung. **exhortatory** [-tətəri], *adj.* (er)mahnend, Ermahnungs–.

exhumation [ekshju'meiʃən], *s.* die (Wieder)-ausgrabung, Exhumierung. **exhume** [eks'hju:m], *v.t.* (wieder) ausgraben, exhumieren; (*fig.*) ans Tageslicht bringen.

exigence, exigency ['eksidʒəns(i)], *s.* die Dringlichkeit, (dringendes) Bedürfnis, das Erfordernis; dringender Fall, der Notfall, die Notlage, Zwangslage, kritische Lage. **exigent,** *adj.* dringend, dringlich, kritisch; anspruchsvoll (*of a p.*).

exiguity [eksi'gjuiti], *s.* die Kleinheit, Winzigkeit, Geringfügigkeit, Spärlichkeit, Unerheblichkeit. **exiguous** [ek'zigjuəs], *adj.* klein, winzig, geringfügig, spärlich, dürftig, unerheblich, unbedeutend.

exile ['eksail], **1.** *s.* 1. das Exil, die Verbannung; Abgeschiedenheit; 2. Verbannte(r), Vertriebene(r). **2.** *v.t.* verbannen, verweisen, vertreiben (***from,*** aus).

exist [ig'zist], *v.i.* existieren, vorhanden sein, (da)-sein, sich finden (***in,*** in (*Dat.*)); leben, bestehen, dauern, vegetieren; ***able to –,*** existenzfähig; ***the right to –,*** die Existenzberechtigung. **existence,** *s.* das (Da)sein, Vorhandensein, Leben, Bestehen, die Existenz; Dauer, das Fortbestehen; ***be in –,*** bestehen, existieren, vorhanden sein; ***call into –,*** ins Leben rufen; ***remain in –,*** weiterbestehen; ***struggle for –,*** der Daseinskampf. **existent,** *adj.* vorhanden, bestehend, existierend.

existential [ekzis'tenʃl], *adj.* Existenz–, Daseins–; (*Phil.*) existentiell, Existential–. **existentialism,** *s.* (*Phil.*) die Existenzphilosophie, der Existentialismus. **existentialist,** *s.* (*Phil.*) der (die) Existentialist(in).

existing [ig'zistiŋ], *adj.* *See* **existent.**

exit ['egzit, 'eksit], **1.** *v.i.* abtreten, abgehen; (*Theat.*) (geht) ab. **2.** *s.* das Abtreten, der Abgang (*also fig.*), (*fig.*) Tod; Ausgang; (*Tech.*) Austritt, Ausfluß; ***make one's –,*** abtreten, (*fig.*) verscheiden. **exit| angle,** *s.* der Austrittswinkel. **– permit,** *s.* (*Pol.*) die Ausreisegenehmigung. **– port,** *s.* die Ausflußöffnung.

ex libris [eks'li:bris], *s.* das Exlibris, Buch(eigner)-zeichen.

exodus ['eksədəs], *s.* der Auszug, die Abwanderung,

Auswanderung; (*B.*) ***Exodus,*** Zweites Buch Mosis; (*coll.*) ***general* –,** allgemeiner Aufbruch.

ex officio [eksə'fiʃiou], **1.** *adj.* Amts–, amtlich. **2.** *adv.* von Amts wegen.

exogamy [ek'sɔgəmi], *s.* (*Biol.*) die Kreuzungspaarung.

exogen ['eksədʒən], *s.* (*Bot.*) die Dikotyledone. **exogenous** [–'sɔdʒinəs], *adj.* (*Geol.*) exogen, von außen wirkend.

exonerate [ig'zɔnəreit], *v.t.* entlasten, befreien, freisprechen (***from***, von) (*a charge*), entbinden, entheben (*Gen.*) (*a duty*). **exoneration** [–'reiʃən], *s.* die Entlastung, Befreiung; Entbindung. **exonerative** [–rətiv], *adj.* entlastend.

exophthalmus [eksɔf'θælməs], *s.* (*Med.*) die Glotzäugigkeit, der Augapfelvorfall.

exorbitance, exorbitancy [ig'zɔ:bitəns(i)], *s.* die Unmäßigkeit, Maßlosigkeit, Überschreitung (der Grenze *or* des zulässigen Maßes), Grenzenlosigkeit, das Übermaß; die Habgier, Habsucht, der Wucher. **exorbitant,** *adj.* übermäßig, maßlos, grenzenlos; übertrieben, ungeheuer, unerschwinglich; – ***price,*** der Wucherpreis.

exorcism ['eksɔ:sizm], *s.* die Geisterbeschwörung, Teufelsbannung. **exorcist,** *s.* der Geisterbeschwörer, Teufelsaustreiber. **exorcize** [–saiz], *v.t.* bannen, austreiben (*evil spirits*), beschwören, herbeirufen (*spirits*), befreien (*a p. or place*).

exordium [eg'zɔ:diəm], *s.* die Einleitung, der Anfang, Eingang.

exoteric(al) [eksə'terik(l)], *adj.* gemeinverständlich, öffentlich, populär.

exotic [ig'zɔtik], **1.** *adj.* ausländisch, fremd(artig), exotisch. **2.** *s.* fremdartiges Gewächs; das Fremdwort.

expand [iks'pænd], **1.** *v.t.* ausspannen, ausbreiten; ausdehnen, entfalten, entwickeln, erweitern; (*Math.*) entwickeln. **2.** *v.i.* sich ausbreiten *or* ausdehnen *or* erweitern; (*fig.*) freundlich entgegenkommen (***towards,*** *Dat.*); ***his heart –s with joy,*** sein Herz schwillt vor Freude. **expander,** *s.* (*Spt.*) der Muskelstrecker. **expanding| brake,** *s.* die Spreizringbremse. – **bullet,** *s.* das Expansionsgeschoß.

expanse [iks'pæns], *s.* die Ausdehnung, Weite; weiter Raum, weite Fläche; (*of wings*) die Spanne, Spannweite: ***the – of heaven,*** die Himmelswölbung. **expansibility** [–i'biliti], *s.* die (Aus)dehnbarkeit. **expansible,** *adj.* (aus)dehnbar. **expansion** [–'pænʃən], *s.* die Ausdehnung, Ausbreitung; Erweiterung (*as of business*), Ausweitung (*as of capital*); (*Math.*) Entwicklung; (*Pol.*) Expansion; der Umfang, Raum. **expansionism,** *s.* die Expansionspolitik. **expansive,** *adj.* ausdehnend; ausdehnungsfähig; (*fig.*) gefühlvoll, überschwenglich, mitteilsam (*of feelings*), ausgedehnt, weit, breit, umfassend (*of views*); – ***force,*** die Ausdehnungskraft. **expansiveness,** *s.* die Ausdehnungsfähigkeit; (*fig.*) Freundlichkeit, Offenheit, Mitteilsamkeit, Überschwenglichkeit.

expatiate [eks'peiʃieit], *v.t.* weitläufig sprechen, sich auslassen *or* verbreiten (***on,*** über (*Acc.*)). **expatiation** [–'eiʃən], *s.* weitläufige Erörterung. **expatiatory** [–ʃiətəri], *adj.* weitläufig, langatmig.

expatriate [eks'pætrieit], *v.t.* (aus dem Vaterlande) verbannen, ausbürgern, die Staatsbürgerschaft entziehen (*Dat.*); – ***o.s.,*** sein Vaterland verlassen, auswandern. **expatriation** [–'eiʃən], *s.* die Verbannung, Vertreibung; Ausbürgerung, Aberkennung der Staatsangehörigkeit; Auswanderung.

expect [iks'pekt], *v.t.* erwarten; entgegensehen (*Dat.*); (*oft. neg.*) rechnen *or* zählen auf (*Acc.*), gefaßt sein auf (*Acc.*); (*coll.*) annehmen, vorhersehen, vermuten, denken, glauben; ***that is what is –ed of you,*** das erwartet man von dir; (*coll.*) ***I – so,*** ich glaube schon, ich nehme es an.

expectancy [iks'pektənsi], *s.* die Erwartung, Aussicht, Hoffnung, der Anspruch; (*Law*) die Anwartschaft (***of,*** auf (*Acc.*)). **expectant, 1.** *adj.* 1. erwartend; erwartungsvoll, zuversichtlich; (*Law*) ***fee –,*** die zu erwartende Gebühr; ***heir –,*** der Anwärter auf ein Erbe; Thronanwärter; (*Med.*) – ***method,*** abwartende Methode; 2. (*coll.*) in anderen Umständen; – ***mother,*** werdende Mutter. **2.** *s.* der (die) Anwärter(in) (***of,*** auf (*Acc.*)).

expectation [ekspek'teiʃən], *s.* die Erwartung, das Erwarten; die Hoffnung, Aussicht; (*usu. pl.*) der Gegenstand der Erwartung; abwartende Haltung, der Zustand der Erwartung; ***according to –s,*** erwartungsgemäß; ***beyond –,*** über Erwarten; ***against*** or ***contrary to (all) –(s),*** entgegen allen Erwartungen, wider Erwarten; (*coll.*) ***have –s,*** einmal etwas zu erwarten haben; ***in the – of,*** entgegensehend (*Dat.*); ***fall short of –s,*** die Erwartungen enttäuschen, hinter den Erwartungen zurückbleiben, den Erwartungen nicht entsprechen; – ***of life,*** mutmaßliche Lebensdauer.

expecting [iks'pektiŋ], *adj.* (*coll.*) ***be –,*** in anderen Umständen sein.

expectorant [eks'pektərənt], *s.* (*Med.*) schleimlösendes Mittel. **expectorate, 1.** *v.t.* auswerfen, aushusten, ausspeien. **2.** *v.i.* spucken; Blut husten. **expectoration** [–'reiʃən], *s.* das Auswerfen, (Aus)spucken; der (Schleim)auswurf.

expedience, expediency [iks'pi:diəns(i)], *s.* die Zweckdienlichkeit, Zweckmäßigkeit, Tunlichkeit, Ratsamkeit, Angemessenheit, Schicklichkeit; Vorteilhaftigkeit, Nützlichkeit. **expedient, 1.** *adj.* tunlich, angebracht, angemessen, ratsam, passend; nützlich, zweckmäßig, zweckdienlich, vorteilhaft. **2.** *s.* das Hilfsmittel, (Behelfs)mittel, der (Not)behelf; Ausweg, die Ausflucht; ***hit on an –,*** einen Ausweg finden. **expediently,** *adv.* zweckmäßigerweise.

expedite ['ekspidait], *v.t.* beschleunigen, fördern; (ab)senden, befördern, expedieren. **expedition** [–'diʃən], *s.* 1. die Eile, Schnelligkeit, Geschwindigkeit; 2. der Feldzug, das Unternehmen; die Forschungsreise, Expedition. **expeditionary,** *adj.* Expeditions–. **expeditious** [–'diʃəs], *adj.* schnell, geschwind, eilig, emsig.

expel [iks'pel], *v.t.* ausstoßen, austreiben, forttreiben, wegtreiben, vertreiben, verweisen, ausweisen, verbannen, (*from school*) ausschließen, (*Univ.*) relegieren; (*Chem.*) abtreiben (***from,*** von, aus).

expend [iks'pend], *v.t.* ausgeben, auslegen (*money*); verwenden, aufwenden (*labour, time etc.*) (***on,*** auf (*Acc.*)); verzehren, verbrauchen. **expendable,** *adj.* verbrauchbar, entbehrlich, Verbrauchs–. **expenditure** [–ditʃə], *s.* die Ausgabe, Auslage, Verausgabung (***on,*** für); (*Comm.*) Auslagen (*pl.*), Ausgänge (*pl.*); die Aufwendung, der Aufwand, Verbrauch (***of,*** an (*Dat.*)) (*of time etc.*).

expense [iks'pens], *s.* die (Geld)ausgabe, Auslage, der Aufwand, Verbrauch; *pl.* (Un)kosten (*pl.*), Spesen (*pl.*); ***at an – of,*** unter Verlust von, mit einem Aufwand von; ***at great –,*** teuer erkauft; ***at my –,*** auf meine Kosten; ***at the – of,*** auf Kosten von, (*fig.*) zum Nachteil *or* Schaden von; ***bear the –,*** die Kosten tragen; ***cover –s,*** die Auslagen decken; ***current –s,*** laufende Ausgaben (*pl.*); ***cut down –s,*** sich einschränken; ***go to great –,*** sich (*Dat.*) große Kosten machen, es sich (*Dat.*) viel kosten lassen; ***go to the – of,*** soweit gehen, . . . zu kaufen; ***incidental –s,*** Nebenausgaben (*pl.*); ***out-of-pocket –s,*** Barauslagen (*pl.*); ***put him to great –,*** ihn in große Kosten stürzen, ihm große Kosten verursachen; ***running –s,*** see ***current –s***; ***spare no*** or ***not spare any –,*** keine Kosten scheuen; ***travelling –s,*** Reisekosten (*pl.*); ***working –s,*** Betriebs(un)kosten (*pl.*).

expensive [iks'pensiv], *adj.* kostspielig, teuer; ***come –,*** teuer (zu stehen) kommen. **expensiveness,** *s.* die Kostspieligkeit.

experience [iks'piəriəns], **1.** *s.* 1. das Erlebnis; 2. die Erfahrung; Praxis, (in der Praxis erworbene) Kenntnisse (*pl.*); ***know by*** or ***from –,*** aus (eigener) Erfahrung wissen; ***man of –,*** erfahrener Mann. **2.** *v.t.* erfahren, erleben, stoßen auf (*Acc.*); aus Erfahrung wissen, erleiden, durchmachen; – ***difficulties,*** auf Schwierigkeiten stoßen; – ***losses,*** Verluste erleiden; – ***pleasure,*** Vergnügen empfinden. **experienced,** *adj.* erfahren, erprobt, bewandert; – ***in business,*** geschäftskundig.

experiment [iks'perimənt], **1.** *s.* der Versuch, das Experiment, die Probe (*on*, an (*Dat.*)). **2.** *v.i.* Versuche anstellen, experimentieren (*on*, an (*Dat.*); ***with,*** mit); – ***with s.th.,*** etwas versuchen *or* erproben. **experimental** [–'mentl], *adj.* 1. experimentell, Experimental–, Versuchs–; – ***chemistry,*** die Experimentalchemie; – ***error,*** der Versuchsfehler; ***in*** or ***at the – stage,*** im Versuchsstadium; – ***station,*** die Versuchsstation; 2. auf Erfahrung gegründet, Erfahrungs–, Erlebnis–. **experimentalist,** *s.* der Experimentierer. **experimentally,** *adv.* durch Experiment. **experimentation** [–'teiʃən], *s.* das Experimentieren. **experimenter,** *s.* der Experimentator.

expert ['ekspə:t], **1.** *adj.* 1. erfahren, kundig; geschickt, gewandt (*in, at*, in (*Dat.*)); – ***swimmer,*** ausgezeichneter Schwimmer; 2. fachmännisch (*work*). **2.** *s.* Sachverständige(r), die Autorität, der Spezialist, Gutachter; Fachmann, (Sach)kundige(r), der Kenner (*on*, für); – ***opinion,*** (fachmännisches) Gutachten. **expertise** [–'ti:z], *s.* die Sachkenntnis, fachmännisches Können. **expertness,** *s.* die Erfahrenheit, Geschicklichkeit, Gewandtheit.

expiable ['ekspiəbl], *adj.* sühnbar. **expiate** [–eit], *v.t.* (ab)büßen, sühnen, wiedergutmachen. **expiation** [–'eiʃən], *s.* die Sühne, Buße, (Ab)büßung; ***in – of,*** um zu sühnen; ***make – for,*** sühnen; (*Eccl.*) ***Feast of Expiation,*** das Versöhnungsfest. **expiatory** [–ətəri], *adj.* sühnend, Sühn–, Buß–.

expiration [ekspi'reiʃən], *s.* 1. die Ausatmung, (*fig.*) das Verscheiden, letzter Atemzug; 2. der Schluß, Ablauf, Verlauf, das Ende; (*Comm.*) ***at the time of –,*** zur Verfall(s)zeit; ***on the – of,*** nach Ablauf von. **expiratory** [iks'pairətəri], *adj.* ausatmend, Ausatmungs–, Atem–.

expire [iks'paiə], *v.i.* 1. aushauchen, ausatmen; 2. sterben, verscheiden; 3. enden, zu Ende gehen, ablaufen (*as time*), erlöschen (*as a title*); verfallen, fällig *or* ungültig werden (*as a contract*). **expiring,** *adj.* sterbend, Todes–. **expiry** [–ri, 'ekspiri], *s.* das Ende, der Ablauf.

explain [iks'plein], **1.** *v.t.* erklären, erläutern, verständlich *or* klar machen; auseinandersetzen; rechtfertigen, begründen; – ***o.s.,*** sich rechtfertigen *or* (deutlich) erklären; – ***away,*** wegerklären, beseitigen. **2.** *v.i.* eine Erklärung geben, sich erklären. **explainable,** *adj.* erklärlich, erklärbar.

explanation [eksplə'neiʃən], *s.* 1. die Erklärung (*of*, für), Erläuterung (zu), Auslegung, Aufklärung, Aufhellung (*Gen.*); ***in – of,*** als Erklärung für, zur Erklärung von, um zu erklären; ***make some –,*** sich erklären, eine Erklärung abgeben; 2. (*obs.*) die Auseinandersetzung, Verständigung. **explanatory** [iks'plænətəri], *adj.* erklärend, erläuternd; ***be self––,*** sich von selbst verstehen.

expletive [eks'pli:tiv], **1.** *adj.* ausfüllend, Ausfüll–. **2.** *s.* 1. das Füllwort, Flickwort; der Lückenbüßer, das Füllsel; 2. (*coll.*) der Fluch, die Verwünschung.

explicable ['eksplikəbl], *adj.* erklärlich, erklärbar. **explicate** [–keit], *v.t.* erläutern, erklären, auseinandersetzen. **explication** [–'keiʃən], *s.* die Erläuterung, Erklärung. **explicative** [–kətiv], **explicatory** [–kətri], *adj.* erklärend, erläuternd.

explicit [eks'plisit], *adj.* ausdrücklich, deutlich, klar, bestimmt (*of statements*); offen, rückhaltlos (*of a p.*); (*Math.*) explizit. **explicitness,** *s.* die Deutlichkeit, Bestimmtheit.

explode [iks'ploud], **1.** *v.t.* explodieren lassen, detonieren, (in die Luft) sprengen; (*fig.*) über den Haufen werfen, verwerfen, beseitigen; (*fig.*) ***be –d,*** überlebt *or* veraltet sein, keine Geltung mehr haben. **2.** *v.i.* abknallen, zersprengen, (zer)platzen, sich entladen, in die Luft fliegen, explodieren; (*fig.*) – ***with fury,*** vor Wut platzen; (*fig.*) – ***with laughter,*** in Gelächter ausbrechen. **exploded view,** *s.* (*Tech.*) auseinandergezogene Darstellung.

exploit, **1.** ['eksplɔit], *s.* die Großtat, Heldentat. **2.** [–'plɔit], *v.t.* ausnutzen, ausnützen, auswerten, ausbeuten. **exploitable** [–'plɔitəbl], *adj.* (aus)nutzbar. **exploitation** [eksplɔi'teiʃən], *s.* die Ausnützung, Ausnutzung, Ausbeutung; ***wasteful –,*** der Raubbau.

exploration [eksplɔ'reiʃən], *s.* die Erforschung, Untersuchung. **explorative** [iks'plɔ:rətiv], **exploratory** [–rətri], *adj.* (er)forschend, untersuchend, Erkundungs–, Forschungs–, Untersuchungs–; informatorisch, Informations–, Versuch–, Probe–. **explore** [iks'plɔ:], *v.t.* erforschen, auskundschaften, untersuchen, (*Surg.*) sondieren. **explorer,** *s.* der (Er)forscher, Forschungsreisende(r).

explosion [iks'plouʒən], *s.* der Knall, die Detonation, Explosion, Entladung; das Bersten, Platzen, Sprengen, die Sprengung; (*fig.*) der Ausbruch. **explosive** [–siv], **1.** *adj.* 1. explosiv, Knall–, Spreng–, Explosions–; – ***bullet,*** das Sprenggeschoß; – ***charge,*** die Sprengladung; – ***force*** or ***power,*** die Sprengkraft, Sprengwirkung, Brisanz; – ***gas,*** das Knallgas; 2. (*fig.*) aufbrausend; – ***situation,*** explosive *or* gefährliche *or* aufbrausende Situation. **2.** *s.* 1. der Sprengstoff, das Sprengmittel; ***high –,*** der Brisanzsprengstoff; 2. (*Phonet.*) der Verschlußlaut. **explosiveness,** *s.* die Explosionsfähigkeit.

exponent [eks'pounənt], *s.* der Repräsentant, Vertreter, Verfechter (*of opinion etc.*); (*Math.*) Exponent, die Hochzahl; der Erklärer, Ausleger. **exponential** [–'nenʃl], **1.** *adj.* (*Math.*) Exponential–. **2.** *s.* die Exponentialgröße.

export, **1.** [eks'pɔ:t], *v.t.* ausführen, versenden, exportieren. **2.** ['ekspɔ:t], *s.* die Ausfuhr, der Export; Ausfuhrartikel; *pl.* die Ausfuhrware, Gesamtausfuhr. **exportable** [–'pɔ:təbl], *adj.* ausführbar, Ausfuhr–, exportierbar. **exportation** [–'teiʃən], *s.* die Ausfuhr, das Exportieren, der Export. **exporter** [–'pɔ:tə], *s.* der Exporteur, Ausfuhrhändler. **export-trade,** *s.* der Ausfuhrhandel, Außenhandel, Aktivhandel.

exposal [iks'pouzl], *s. See* **exposure. expose,** *v.t.* 1. aussetzen (*a child etc.*); 2. aussetzen, unterwerfen, preisgeben (*to, Dat.*) (*danger etc.*); ***be –d to,*** ausgesetzt sein (*Dat.*); – ***o.s. to ridicule,*** sich lächerlich machen; 3. ausstellen, auslegen, feilhalten (*goods for sale*); 4. (*Phot.*) belichten; 5. aufdecken, entlarven (*an impostor etc.*), enthüllen, an den Tag legen, bloßstellen, bloßlegen, entblößen; – ***o.s.,*** sich entblößen, (*fig.*) sich bloßstellen, sich (*Dat.*) eine Blöße geben.

exposé [ekspou'zei], *s.* 1. die Denkschrift, Auseinandersetzung, Darlegung; 2. Entlarvung, Enthüllung.

exposed [iks'pouzd], *adj.* 1. offen, frei(stehend), freiliegend; ***be –,*** freistehen, freiliegen; 2. exponiert, gefährdet, ungeschützt; ausgesetzt, preisgegeben (***to,*** *Dat.*); (*Mil.*) – ***position,*** gefährdete *or* exponierte Lage; 3. (*Phot.*) belichtet.

exposition [ekspə'ziʃən], *s.* 1. die Erklärung, Auslegung (*of, Gen.*), Ausführung(en), Darlegung(en), (über (*Acc.*)); (*Theat., Mus.*) Exposition; 2. (öffentliche) Ausstellung; die Aussetzung, Preisgabe. **expositor** [–'pɔzitə], *s.* der Ausleger, Erklärer, Deuter. **expository,** *adj.* erklärend, erläuternd.

ex post facto [ekspoust'fæktou], **1.** *adj.* nach geschehener Tat, hintennach; – ***law,*** rückwirkendes Gesetz. **2.** *adv.* nach geschehener Tat.

expostulate [iks'pɔstjuleit], *v.i.* protestieren; – ***with him,*** ihm (ernste) Vorhaltungen machen, ihn zurechtweisen *or* zur Rede stellen. **expostulation** [–'leiʃən], *s.* ernste Vorstellung *or* Vorhaltung, der Protest. **expostulative** [–lətiv], **expostulatory** [–lətri], *adj.* Vorhaltungen machend, mahnend; – ***letter,*** die Beschwerdeschrift.

exposure [iks'pouʒə], *s.* 1. die Ausstellung, das Feilhalten (*of goods for sale*); 2. die Aussetzung (*of children*); 3. das Ausgesetztsein, die Preisgabe; ***death from –,*** der Tod durch Erfrieren; 4. die Enthüllung, Entlarvung, Aufdeckung, Bloßstellung; (*Law*) ***indecent –,*** die Erregung öffentlichen Ärgernisses; 5. (ungeschützte) Lage; ***southern –,***

die Südlage; 6. (*Phot.*) die Belichtung(szeit); ***time* –**, die Zeitaufnahme. **exposure meter,** *s.* der Belichtungsmesser.

expound [iks'paund], *v.t.* auslegen, erläutern, erklären.

express [iks'pres], **1.** *v.t.* 1. ausdrücken, auspressen (***from***, aus); 2. (*fig.*) äußern, ausdrücken, zum Ausdruck bringen, aussprechen (*opinions*); bezeigen, offenbaren, zu erkennen geben, an den Tag legen (*feelings etc.*); darstellen, vorstellen, bezeichnen, bedeuten, bekunden (*motives, intentions etc.*); – ***o.s.***, sich äußern, sich erklären; – ***itself,*** sich zeigen, sich ausdrücken, sich offenbaren. **2.** *adj.* 1. ausdrücklich, deutlich, bestimmt; ***for this – purpose,*** eigens zu diesem Zweck; ***his – words,*** seine ausdrücklichen Worte; 2. Eil–, Schnell–; – ***delivery,*** die Eilbeförderung, Eilzustellung; – ***letter,*** der Eilbrief; – ***messenger,*** der Eilbote; – ***train,*** der Schnellzug, D-Zug. **3.** *adv.* 1. eigens, expreß; 2. durch Eilboten; ***by –***, per Eilgut. **4.** *s.* der Eilbote; das Eilgut; der Schnellzug, Eilzug. **expressible,** *adj.* ausdrückbar.

expression [iks'preʃən], *s.* 1. der Ausdruck, die Redensart, Äußerung; Ausdrucksweise, Ausdruckskraft; (*Math.*) Formel, der Terminus; ***beyond –***, über alle Beschreibung, unaussprechlich; ***give – to,*** Ausdruck verleihen (*Dat.*); ***speak*** (***sing, play the piano etc.***) ***with –***, mit Gefühl sprechen *etc.*; 2. der (Gesichts)ausdruck; 3. das Auspressen, Ausdrücken (*of juice*). **expressionism,** *s.* der Expressionismus. **expressionistic** [–'nistik], *adj.* expressionistisch. **expressionless,** *adj.* ausdruckslos. **expressive** [–siv], *adj.* ausdrückend (***of,*** *Acc.*), bezeichnend (für); ausdrucksvoll, nachdrücklich, kräftig; ***be – of,*** ausdrücken. **expressiveness,** *s.* das Ausdrucksvolle, die Ausdruckskraft; Ausdrücklichkeit, der Nachdruck. **expressly,** *adv.* ausdrücklich; besonders, eigens. **expressway,** *s.* (*Am.*) die Schnellverkehrsstraße.

expropriate [eks'prouprieit], *v.t.* enteignen, des Eigentums berauben. **expropriation** [–'eiʃən], *s.* die Enteignung, Eigentumsberaubung.

expulsion [iks'pʌlʃən], *s.* die Austreibung, Vertreibung, Ausweisung, Ausstoßung (***from***, aus), Abschiebung, Entfernung (von); – ***order,*** der Ausweisungsbefehl. **expulsive** [–siv], *adj.* vertreibend, austreibend, Abtreib–.

expunge [iks'pʌndʒ], *v.t.* ausstreichen, durchstreichen; streichen (***from***, aus); (*fig.*) vernichten, (aus)tilgen.

expurgate ['ekspə:geit], *v.t.* reinigen, säubern (*a book*), ausmerzen, streichen (*obscenities etc.*) (***from***, von). **expurgation** [–'geiʃən], *s.* die Reinigung, Säuberung, Ausmerzung, Streichung. **expurgatory** [iks'pə:gətəri], *adj.* reinigend, säubernd; (*R.C.*) ***Expurgatory Index,*** der Reinigungskatalog.

exquisite ['ekskwizit], **1.** *adj.* vortrefflich, vorzüglich, ausgezeichnet, köstlich; gepflegt, verfeinert, vollkommen, höchst empfindlich, äußerst fein; hochgradig, heftig (*pain, joy etc.*). **2.** *s.* (*obs.*) der Stutzer, Geck. **exquisiteness,** *s.* die Vorzüglichkeit, Vortrefflichkeit; Schärfe, Feinheit (*of judgement etc.*); Heftigkeit, Stärke (*of pain*).

ex-serviceman, *s.* ehemaliger Frontsoldat, der Veteran.

extant [iks'tænt, 'ekstənt], *adj.* existierend, (noch) vorhanden *or* zu finden(d).

extemporaneous [ekstempə'reiniəs], *adj. See* **extemporary. extemporarily** [–'tempərərili], *adv. See* **extempore. extemporary,** *adj.*, **extempore** [–'tempəri], *adj.*, *adv.* aus dem Stegreif, improvisiert, unvorbereitet. **extemporize** [–raiz], *v.t.*, *v.i.* aus dem Stegreif reden *or* spielen *or* dichten, frei sprechen, extemporieren, improvisieren. **extemporizer,** *s.* der Stegreif|redner *or* –spieler *or* –dichter; Improvisator.

extend [iks'tend], **1.** *v.t.* (aus)dehnen, strecken, ausziehen, verlängern; (*fig.*) erweitern, vergrößern, ausbauen; fortsetzen, fortführen; (*as one's hand*) ausstrecken, (*as one's tongue*) vorstrecken, (*as one's arms*) ausbreiten; (*fig.*) gewähren, erweisen, erteilen, erzeigen (***to,*** *Dat.*) (*a welcome etc.*); voll ausschreiben (*abbreviations*), in gewöhnliche Schrift umsetzen (*shorthand*); (*Comm.*) verlängern, prolongieren (*a term*); (*Math.*) erweitern, vergrößern; (*coll.*) – ***o.s.***, sich ins Zeug legen, sich anstrengen; (*Geom.*) – ***a line,*** eine Linie ziehen; (*Mil.*) ***–ed order*** or ***formation,*** ausgeschwärmte Schützenlinie, geöffnete Ordnung. **2.** *v.i.* sich erstrecken, reichen, sich ausdehnen (***over,*** über (*Acc.*); ***from,*** von; ***to,*** bis); hinausgehen (***beyond,*** über (*Acc.*)). **extendible,** *adj. See* **extensible. extending,** *adj.* – ***ladder,*** die Ausziehleiter; – ***table,*** der Ausziehtisch.

extensibility [ikstensi'biliti], *s.* die Dehnbarkeit. **extensible** [–'tensibl], *adj.* (aus)dehnbar, streckbar; ausstreckbar, vorstreckbar. **extension** [–'tenʃən], *s.* die Ausdehnung (***to,*** auf (*Acc.*)); Verlängerung, Erweiterung, Vergrößerung, (*Surg.*) das Strecken, (*Comm.*) die Verlängerung, Prolongation, der Umfang; (*Tele.*) Nebenanschluß; Ansatz (*to a th.*), Anbau (*to a building*); (*Elec.*) – ***lead,*** die Verlängerungsschnur; (*Mil.*) – ***of leave,*** die Urlaubsverlängerung, der Nachurlaub; – ***rod,*** das Aufsteckrohr; – ***of the term of payment,*** die Verlängerung *or* Hinausschiebung des Zahlungstermins; ***university –***, die Volkshochschule. **extensive,** *adj.* sich weit erstreckend, ausgedehnt; umfassend, geräumig. **extensiveness,** *s.* die Ausdehnung, Weite, Größe, der Umfang. **extensor,** *s.* (*Anat.*) der Streckmuskel.

extent [iks'tent], *s.* 1. die Ausdehnung, Weite, Strecke, Größe, Länge, Höhe; der Raum, Umfang; ***in –***, an Umfang; 2. (*fig.*) der Grad, das (Aus)maß; ***to the – of,*** bis zum Betrage *or* zur Höhe von; ***to a certain –***, gewissermaßen, bis zu einem gewissen Grade; ***to the full –***, völlig, in vollem Umfang; ***to a great*** or ***large –***, in großem Umfang, in hohem Grade, großenteils; ***to some –***, in gewissem Grade, einigermaßen.

extenuate [iks'tenjueit], *v.t.* schwächen, entkräften, verringern, verkleinern; mildern, beschönigen, bemänteln; ***extenuating circumstances,*** mildernde Umstände. **extenuation** [–'eiʃən], *s.* die Milderung, Abschwächung, Beschönigung; ***in – of,*** zur Milderung (*Gen.*), um . . . zu mildern.

exterior [eks'tiəriə], **1.** *adj.* äußerlich, äußer; – ***angle,*** der Außenwinkel; – ***to,*** außerhalb (*Gen.*), abseits von. **2.** *s.* 1. das Äußere, die Außenseite (*of a th.*), äußeres Ansehen (*of a p.*); 2. (*Films*) die Außenaufnahme.

exterminate [eks'tə:mineit], *v.t.* ausrotten, vertilgen, wegschaffen. **extermination** [–'neiʃən], *s.* die Vertilgung, Ausrottung, Wegschaffung.

external [eks'tə:nl], **1.** *adj.* außen befindlich; äußer, äußerlich, (*Math.*) Außen–; sichtbar, wahrnehmbar, körperlich; (*Pol.*) Außen–, auswärtig; ***minister for – affairs,*** der Außenminister; – ***angle,*** see ***exterior angle***; – ***debt,*** auswärtige Schuld; – ***to,*** außerhalb (*Gen.*); ***the – world,*** die Außenwelt, Erscheinungswelt. **2.** *s.* (*usu. pl.*) das Äußere; Äußerlichkeiten (*pl.*), Nebensächlichkeiten (*pl.*). **externalize** [–laiz], *v.t.* veräußerlichen, verkörper(liche)n, objektivieren.

exterritorial [eksteri'tɔ:riəl], *adj. See* **extraterritorial.**

extinct [iks'tiŋkt], *adj.* ausgelöscht, erloschen, (*fig.*) ausgestorben, untergegangen (*race, animal*), erloschen (*title*), abgeschafft, aufgehoben; ***become –***, erlöschen, aussterben, untergehen; – ***volcano,*** ausgebrannter Vulkan. **extinction** [–'tiŋkʃən], *s.* das Erlöschen, Auslöschen, die (Aus)löschung; (*fig.*) Tilgung (*of debts*), Vernichtung, Vertilgung, Ausrottung, Abschaffung; der Untergang, das Aussterben.

extinguish [iks'tiŋgwiʃ], *v.t.* (aus)löschen, ersticken; (*fig.*) vernichten, töten, zerstören, abschaffen, aufheben (*a th.*), tilgen (*debt*); (*fig.*) in den Schatten stellen, zum Schweigen bringen, (*coll.*) kaltstellen (*a p.*). **extinguisher,** *s.* das Löschhütchen, Lichthütchen. **extinguishment,** *s.* (*Law*) die Aufhebung; *see also* **extinction.**

extirpate ['ekstəpeit], *v.t.* ausrotten, vertilgen, vernichten; (*Surg.*) entfernen, ausschneiden. **extirpation** [–'peiʃən], *s.* die Ausrottung, Ausschneidung.

extol [iks'toul], *v.t.* erheben, loben, preisen; – ***to the skies,*** in den Himmel heben.

extort [iks'tɔ:t], *v.t.* erpressen, abnötigen; erzwingen (***from,*** von), abzwingen, abringen (*Dat.*). **extortion** [–'tɔ:ʃən], *s.* die Erpressung; Geldschneiderei, der Wucher. **extortionate** [–nit], *adj.* erpresserisch, wucherisch; – ***price,*** der Wucherpreis. **extortioner,** *s.* der Erpresser, Wucherer.

extra ['ekstrə], **1.** *adj.* zusätzlich, nachträglich, Extra–, Neben–, Sonder–; außergewöhnlich, besonder; – ***charge,*** der (Sonder)aufschlag, Nebenspesen (*pl.*), Nebenkosten (*pl.*); – ***edition,*** die Spätausgabe; – ***pay,*** die Zulage; – ***profit,*** der Nebenverdienst, Übergewinn; – ***work,*** zusätzliche Arbeit, (*at school*) die Strafarbeit; ***I had to pay an – nine pence,*** ich mußte noch neun Pence zulegen. **2.** *adv.* besonders, ungewöhnlich, extra; (*Typ.*) – ***bold,*** der Fettdruck; ***charged (for) –,*** gesondert berechnet; ***an – high tide,*** eine besonders *or* ungewöhnlich hohe Flut. **3.** *s.* **1.** Außergewöhnliche(s); (besonderer) Zusatz; (*newspaper*) die Spätausgabe, Sonderausgabe; 2. (*usu. pl.*) Sonder– *or* Nebenausgaben *or* –einnahmen (*pl.*); 3. der Zuschlag, die Sonderberechnung; 4. (*Films*) der (die) Statist(in), der Komparse; 5. (*Crick.*) Zusatzpunkt; 6. *pl.* das Sonderzubehör.

extract, **1.** [iks'trækt], *v.t.* herausziehen; (*a tooth*) ziehen; (*from a book*) ausziehen, exzerpieren; (*Chem.*) ausziehen, extrahieren, ausscheiden, auslaugen (***from,*** aus), (*Tech.*) gewinnen (aus); (*fig.*) herausholen (aus), entlocken, abringen (*Dat.*); herleiten, ableiten (von); (*Math.*) – ***the root of a number,*** aus einer Zahl die Wurzel ziehen. **2.** ['ekstrækt], *s.* (*Chem.*) der Auszug, Absud, das Extrakt; (*from a book*) der Auszug, Ausschnitt, das Exzerpt, Zitat. **extraction** [–'trækʃən], *s.* das (Her)ausziehen; (*Chem.*) Ausziehen, Extrahieren, Auslaugen, die Absonderung, Ausscheidung; Extraktion (*of tooth*); (*Tech.*) Gewinnung, Extraktion (*of ore*) (***from,*** aus); (*flour*) Ausmahlung; (*Math.*) Radizierung, das (Aus)ziehen; die Abkunft, Abstammung, Herkunft. **extractor** [–'træktə], *s.* der Auszieher (*also Tech.*); (*Artil.*) Entlader, (*Surg.*) die Zange, (*Tech.*) der Schleuder; Ausziehhebel, die Ausziehkralle.

extra-curricular, *adj.* außerplanmäßig.

extraditable ['ekstrədaitəbl], *adj.* der Auslieferung unterliegend (*offence*), auszuliefern(d) (*offender*). **extradite,** *v.t.* ausliefern. **extradition** [–'diʃən], *s.* die Auslieferung.

extrados [eks'treidɔs], *s.* (*Archit.*) der Bogenrücken, Gewölberücken.

extra|-judicial, *adj.* außergerichtlich. **--marital,** *adj.* außerehelich. **--mural,** *adj.* – ***student,*** der Gasthörer; – ***class,*** der Volkshochschulekurs; *pl.* die Volkshochschule.

extraneous [eks'treiniəs], *adj.* nicht gehörig (***to,*** zu), fremd, unwesentlich (*Dat.*), von außen kommend; ***be – to,*** nicht gehören zu.

extraordinarily [iks'trɔ:dinərili], *adv. See* **extraordinary. extraordinariness,** *s.* die Ungewöhnlichkeit, Merkwürdigkeit. **extraordinary,** *adj.* ungewöhnlich, außergewöhnlich, außerordentlich, merkwürdig, seltsam; – ***charges,*** Extrakosten (*pl.*); ***ambassador –,*** der Sonderbotschafter.

extrapolate [iks'træpəleit], **1.** *v.t.* extrapolieren, schließen lassen auf (*Acc.*). **2.** *v.i.* zu mutmaßlichen Ergebnissen kommen, annähernde Berechnungen anstellen.

extra-territorial, *adj.* exterritorial; – ***waters,*** Außengewässer (*pl.*).

extravagance, extravagancy [iks'trævəgəns(i)], *s.* die (Geld)verschwendung; das Übermaß, die Übertriebenheit, Überspanntheit, Extravaganz, Abgeschmacktheit; Zügellosigkeit, Ausschweifung. **extravagant,** *adj.* verschwenderisch; übertrieben, übermäßig; zügellos, überspannt, ausschweifend. **extravaganza** [–və'gænzə], *s.* fantastisches Werk, die Burleske, (Zauber)posse, das Ausstattungsstück.

extravasate [iks'trævəseit], **1.** *v.t.* (*Med.*) austreten lassen; ***–d blood,*** ausgetretenes Blut. **2.** *v.i.* ausfließen, heraustreten. **extravasation** [–'seiʃən], *s.* der (Blut)erguß, Austritt.

extreme [iks'tri:m], **1.** *adj.* äußerst, letzt, weitest; (*fig.*) außergewöhnlich, höchst, übertrieben, extrem; – ***case,*** äußerster Notfall; – ***danger,*** höchste Gefahr; ***to an – degree,*** im höchsten Grade; – ***measure,*** äußerstes Mittel; – ***necessity,*** dringende Notwendigkeit; – ***old age,*** hohes Greisenalter; (*Eccl.*) – ***unction,*** Letzte Ölung; – ***views,*** radikale Ansichten. **2.** *s.* das Äußerste, äußerstes Ende, äußerste Grenze; höchster Grad, das Extrem; äußerste Maßnahme; das Übermaß, die Übertreibung; ***at the other –,*** am entgegengesetzten Ende; ***in the –,*** aufs äußerste, übermäßig; ***stupid in the –,*** äußerst dumm; (*Math.*) ***–s of a proportion,*** die äußeren Glieder einer Proportion; ***carry s.th. to –s*** or ***to the –,*** etwas zu weit treiben; ***fly*** or ***go to the other –,*** ins andere Extrem verfallen; ***go from one – to the other,*** von einem Extrem ins andere fallen; ***go to –s,*** zum Äußersten schreiten, vor nichts zurückschrecken.

extremism [iks'tri:mizm], *s.* die Neigung zur Maßlosigkeit; (*Pol.*) (ultra)radikale Einstellung. **extremist,** *s.* der Fanatiker; (*Pol.*) Radikale(r).

extremity [iks'tremiti], *s.* das Äußerste, äußerstes Ende, äußerste Grenze; die Spitze, der Rand; (*fig.*) das Übermaß, höchster Grad; (*oft. pl.*) äußerste Verlegenheit *or* Not; (*usu. pl.*) äußerste Maßnahme; *pl.* Gliedmaßen (*pl.*), Extremitäten (*pl.*), Hände und Füße; ***to the last –,*** bis zum Äußersten; ***carry to extremities,*** übertreiben, zu weit treiben, auf die Spitze treiben; ***go*** or ***proceed to extremities,*** zum Äußersten schreiten, die äußersten Maßnahmen ergreifen; ***be reduced to extremities,*** in äußerster Not sein.

extricable ['ekstrikəbl], *adj.* herausziehbar (***from,*** aus). **extricate,** *v.t.* befreien (***from,*** von), herausziehen, herauswickeln (aus); (*Chem.*) freimachen, entwickeln (*heat etc.*). **extrication** [–'keiʃən], *s.* die Befreiung, das Freimachen, Losmachen.

extrinsic [eks'trinsik], *adj.* äußer, äußerlich, von außen wirkend; ***be – to,*** außerhalb (*Gen.*) liegen, nicht gehören zu.

extroversion [ekstro'və:ʃən], *s.* 1. (*Med.*) die Umstülpung; 2. (*Psych.*) das Extravertiertsein. **extrovert** ['ekstrəvə:t], **1.** *adj.* 1. (*Med.*) umgestülpt, extravert; 2. (*Psych.*) extravertiert. **2.** *s.* Extravertierte(r).

extrude [eks'tru:d], *v.t.* herauspressen, austreiben, verdrängen; (*Tech.*) auspressen, strangpressen. **extrusion** [–'tru:ʒən], *s.* die Verdrängung, Vertreibung; (*Geol.*) Extrusion; (*Tech.*) das Strangpreßprofil.

exuberance, exuberancy [ig'zju:bərəns(i)], *s.* der Überfluß, das Übermaß, die Fülle, Üppigkeit; Überschwenglichkeit, der Redeschwall. **exuberant,** *adj.* (über)reichlich; üppig, wuchernd; überschwenglich; – ***spirits,*** sprudelnde Laune. **exuberate** [–reit], *v.i.* strotzen (***with,*** von).

exudation [egzju:'deiʃən], *s.* die Ausschwitzung, Auswitterung, Ausblühung, der Ausschlag. **exude** [ig'zju:d], **1.** *v.t.* ausschwitzen, auswittern, ausblühen, ausschlagen; (*fig.*) ausstrahlen. **2.** *v.i.* ausgeschieden werden, hervorkommen (***from,*** aus).

exult [ig'zʌlt], *v.i.* jauchzen, frohlocken, triumphieren (***at, over, in,*** über (*Acc.*)). **exultant,** *adj.* frohlockend, jauchzend, triumphierend. **exultation** [egzʌl'teiʃən], *s.* das Jauchzen, Frohlocken, der Jubel.

eye [ai], **1.** *s.* 1. das Auge (*also fig.*), (*fig.*) Augenmerk, der Blick; 2. Gesichtssinn; Sinn, Geschmack; 3. (*Tech.*) das Öhr, die Öse (*of needle etc.*), (*Naut.*) Kausch(e) (*on a sail*); 4. (*Bot.*) Knospe, das Auge.
(a) (*with adj.*) (*coll.*) (***all***) ***my –!*** Unsinn! Quatsch!

evil –, böser Blick, der Augenzauber; (*coll.*) ***give him the glad –,*** mit ihm kokettieren; ***if you had half an –,*** wenn du nicht ganz blind wärest; ***be born with one's –s open,*** Haare auf den Zähnen haben; ***be in the public –,*** in der Öffentlichkeit bekannt sein.
(b) (*with verbs*) ***be all –s,*** ganz Auge sein, seine Augen überall haben; (*sl.*) ***his –s are bigger than his belly,*** seine Augen sind größer als der Magen; ***believe one's –s,*** seinen Augen trauen; ***cast an – over,*** einen Blick werfen auf (*Acc.*); ***catch the –,*** ins Auge fallen, auffallen; ***catch his –,*** seine Aufmerksamkeit auf sich ziehen; (*Parl.*) ***catch the Speaker's –,*** das Wort erhalten; (*coll.*) ***clap –s on,*** see ***set –s on***; ***cry one's –s out,*** sich ausweinen; ***give an – to,*** ein Auge haben auf (*Acc.*); ***have an – for,*** Sinn *or* ein (offenes) Auge haben für; ***have one's –s about one,*** die Augen überall haben; ***have an – to,*** achten auf (*Acc.*), im Auge behalten; (*coll.*) ***keep one's –s skinned*** or ***peeled,*** wie ein Schießhund aufpassen; ***keep a strict*** or ***an – on,*** ein wachsames Auge haben auf (*Acc.*); ***lay –s on,*** see ***set –s on***; ***make (sheep's) –s at,*** Augen machen (*Dat.*); ***more in*** or ***to it than meets the –,*** mehr dahinterstecken als den Anschein hat; (*coll.*) ***mind your –!*** paß auf! ***offend the –,*** dem Auge weh tun; ***open his –s to the facts,*** ihm die Augen über die Tatsachen öffnen, ihm den tatsächlichen Sachverhalt klarmachen; ***set –s on,*** zu Gesicht bekommen; ***shut one's –s to,*** die Augen verschließen gegen *or* vor (*Dat.*); ***strike the –,*** in die Augen springen.
(c) (*with nouns*) ***apple of the –,*** der Augapfel; ***see it out of the corner of one's –,*** einen flüchtigen Blick von etwas erhaschen; ***–s front!*** Augen geradeaus! ***mind's –,*** geistiges Augen; ***–s like saucers,*** Glotzaugen (*pl.*); ***– of the storm,*** (windstilles) Zentrum des Sturms; ***in the twinkling of an –,*** im Nu.
(d) (*with preps.*) (*B.*) ***(an) – for (an) –,*** Auge um Auge; (*coll.*) ***a sight for sore –s,*** eine Augenweide, erfreulicher Anblick; ***have a cast in one's –,*** schielen; ***in the –(s) of the law,*** vom Standpunkt des Gesetzes aus; ***in my –s,*** in meinen Augen, nach meiner Ansicht *or* Meinung, nach meinem Urteil; (*sl.*) ***do him in the –,*** ihn übers Ohr hauen; ***find favour in his –s,*** vor ihm Gnade finden; ***be wise in one's own –s,*** sich klug dünken; ***in(to) the wind's –,*** gegen den Wind; ***keep him under one's –,*** ihn überwachen, ihn im Auge behalten *or* haben; ***up to the –s in work,*** bis über die Ohren in der Arbeit; ***see – to – with,*** völlig übereinstimmen mit; ***under the – of,*** beaufsichtigt von, unter den Augen von; ***with an – to,*** mit Rücksicht auf (*Acc.*); ***with the naked –,*** mit bloßem Auge; ***with one's –s shut,*** mit geschlossenen Augen (*also fig.*).
2. *v.t.* ansehen, anschauen, betrachten, mustern, beobachten, ins Auge fassen, begucken, beäugeln; ***– up and down*** or ***from head to foot*** or ***from top to toe,*** von oben bis unten mustern.

eye|ball, *s.* der Augapfel. **--bolt,** *s.* der Ringbolzen. **--bright,** *s.* (*Bot.*) der Augentrost. **–brow,** *s.* die (Augen)braue; (*fig.*) ***raise one's –s,*** hochnäsig dreinschauen; ***– pencil,*** der Augenbrauenstift. **--catcher,** *s.* (*coll.*) der Blickfang.

eyed [aid], *adj. suff.* –äugig.

eye|glass, *s.* das Augenglas, Monokel, Lorgnon; (*usu. pl.*) die Brille, Augengläser (*pl.*), der Kneifer, Zwicker, Klemmer; (*Opt.*) das Okular. **--hole,** *s.* das Guckloch. **–lash,** *s.* die Augenwimper.

eyelet ['ailit], *s.* die Öse, das Loch, Äuglein.

eye|lid, *s.* das Augenlid. **--lotion,** *s.* das Augenwasser. **--opener,** *s.* (*coll.*) die Überraschung, schlagender Beweis; ***it was an – to me,*** es belehrte mich eines Besseren, es öffnete mir die Augen. **--piece,** *s.* (*Opt.*) das Okular. **--shade,** *s.* der Augenschirm. **–sight,** *s.* die Sehkraft, das Sehvermögen, Augenlicht, Gesicht, der Gesichtssinn. **–sore,** *s.* unschöne Stelle, häßlicher Zug, störender Anblick, der Ekel, Dorn im Auge. **--splice,** *s.* (*Naut.*) der Augspleiß. **–strain,** *s.* die Überanstrengung der Augen. **–tooth,** *s.* der Augenzahn, Eckzahn. **–wash,** *s.* das Augenwasser, (*sl.*) der Schwindel, die Augenwischerei; Spiegelfechterei, der Bluff, das Täuschungsmanöver. **--witness,** **1.** *s.* der Augenzeuge; ***– account,*** der Augenzeugenbericht. **2.** *v.t.* als Augenzeuge beobachten.

eyot ['eiət], *s.* der Werder, das Inselchen.

eyre [ɛə], *s.* die Rundreise der Richter; ***Justices in Eyre,*** das Land bereisende Richter.

eyrie, *see* **aerie.**

F

F, f [ef], *s.* das F, f (*also Mus.*); ***F flat,*** das Fes, fes; ***F-hole,*** das Schalloch (*of violin etc.*); ***F major,*** F-Dur; ***F minor,*** f-Moll; ***F sharp,*** das Fis, fis. (*See Index of Abbreviations.*)

fa [fɑ:], *s.* (*Mus.*) das F.

Fabian ['feibiən], *adj.* zögernd, zaudernd; fabianisch; (*Hist.*) ***– Society,*** der Verein der Fabier.

fable [feibl], **1.** *s.* die Fabel; das Märchen, erfundene Geschichte, die Erdichtung, Lüge; Sage, Mythe, Legende; ***it is a mere –,*** es ist völlig aus der Luft gegriffen. **2.** *v.t.* erdichten, fabeln, zusammenlügen. **fabled,** *adj.* in Fabeln gepriesen, legendenhaft, sagenhaft, legendär, erdichtet.

fabric ['fæbrik], *s.* das Gebäude, der Bau; (*fig.*) das Gefüge, System, die Struktur; das Zeug, Gewebe, der Stoff; (*Av.*) die Bespannung. **fabricate** [–keit], *v.t.* (ver)fertigen, anfertigen, herstellen, fabrizieren; (*fig.*) erfinden, erdichten, ersinnen, schmieden. **fabrication** [–'keiʃən], *s.* die Herstellung, Anfertigung, Fabrikation; (*fig.*) Erdichtung, Erfindung, Fälschung, Lüge. **fabricator,** *s.* der Hersteller, Verfertiger; (*fig.*) Erfinder, Erdichter (*of falsehood*).

fabulist ['fæbjulist], *s.* der Fabeldichter; *see also* **fabricator** (*fig.*). **fabulous,** *adj.* legendenhaft, mythisch, sagenhaft, Fabel–; (*fig.*) fabelhaft, unglaublich, ungeheuer, sagenhaft.

façade [fæ'sɑ:d], *s.* die Vorderseite, Stirnseite, Fassade (*also fig.*).

face [feis], **1.** *s.* 1. das (An)gesicht, Antlitz; Aussehen, der (Gesichts)ausdruck, die Miene; (*coll.*) Fratze, Grimasse; 2. (*of a th.*) Fläche, Oberfläche, Schlagfläche; Vorderseite, Fassade, Außenseite, Front; Bildseite (*of cards*), der Avers (*of a coin*), (*Typ.*) das Bild (*of type*); Zifferblatt (*of a clock*), rechte Seite (*of cloth*); (*Min.*) die Wand, das Ort, der Stob; 3. (*coll., fig.*) die Stirn, Unverschämtheit, Dreistigkeit.
(a) (*with verbs*) ***have the – to . . .,*** so unverschämt sein *or* die Stirn haben zu . . .; ***lose –,*** den guten Ruf verlieren; ***make*** or ***pull a –,*** Fratzen *or* ein Gesicht schneiden; ***make*** or ***pull a long –,*** ein langes Gesicht machen; ***put a bold – on the matter,*** sich (*Dat.*) etwas nicht anmerken lassen; ***put a good*** or ***the best – on the matter,*** gute Miene zum bösen Spiel machen; (*coll.*) ***put on one's –,*** sich pudern und schminken; ***save one's –,*** das Gesicht wahren, sein Prestige retten, seinen Ruf schützen; ***set one's – against,*** entschieden mißbilligen; sich sträuben *or* widersetzen *or* wenden *or* stemmen gegen; ***show one's –,*** sich sehen lassen.
(b) (*with preps.*) ***before his –,*** vor seinen Augen; ***in – of,*** gegenüber, direkt vor (*Dat.*); ***in the – of,*** angesichts (*Gen.*), trotz (*Gen.*); ***fly in the – of danger,*** der Gefahr mutig entgegentreten; ***with the wind in one's –,*** gegen den Wind; ***laugh in his –,*** ihm ins Gesicht lachen; ***look him in the –,*** ihm ins Gesicht sehen; ***shut the door in his –,*** ihm die Tür vor der Nase zuschlagen; ***ruin stared him in the –,*** der Untergang starrte ihm entgegen;

on the – of it, auf den ersten Blick, augenscheinlich; ***put him out of –,*** ihn aus der Fassung bringen; ***to my –,*** mir ins Gesicht; ***– to –,*** Angesicht zu Angesicht; ***bring them – to –,*** sie (einander) gegenüberstellen; ***– to – with,*** gegenüber (*Dat.*), angesichts (*Gen.*).

(c) (*with adjs.*) ***be full in the –,*** ein volles Gesicht haben; ***full –,*** die Vorderansicht; ***half*** or ***side –,*** das Profil; ***wry –,*** schiefes Gesicht.

2. *v.t.* **1.** ins Gesicht *or* Auge sehen (*Dat.*), das Gesicht zuwenden (*Dat.*), entgegenblicken (*Dat.*), sich gegenübersehen (*Dat.*), gegenüber|sein *or* –treten *or* –liegen *or* –sitzen *or* –stehen (*Dat.*); (hinaus)gehen nach *or* auf (*Acc.*), zuliegen nach (*as a house* or *window*); (*fig.*) entgegentreten (*Dat.*), trotzen (*Dat.*), Trotz *or* die Stirn bieten (*Dat.*); ***– death,*** dem Tode ins Angesicht sehen; ***– the engine,*** vorwärts *or* mit dem Gesicht nach vorn fahren; ***– facts,*** sich mit den Tatsachen abfinden; ***this window –s the garden,*** dieses Fenster geht auf den Garten (hinaus); (*sl.*) ***– the music,*** die Folgen tragen, die Suppe auslöffeln, dafür geradestehen; ***– (the) south,*** nach Süden liegen; ***the problem that –s us,*** die Aufgabe *or* Frage, die uns hier entgegentritt; (*coll.*) ***let's – it,*** seien wir ehrlich; (*coll.*) ***– it out,*** fest durchhalten, es überwinden; **2.** (*Tech.*) plandrehen (*on a lathe*), glätten, ebnen (*stone*), belegen, verblenden, verkleiden (*a wall*), einfassen, verbrämen, besetzen (*a dress etc.*); (*Typ.*) auf der gegenüberliegende Seite stehen von; ***– a jacket,*** Aufschläge auf einen Rock setzen.

3. *v.i.* ***– about,*** sich umwenden, kehrtmachen; (*Am., Mil.*) ***right about –!*** rechtsum kehrt! (*Am. Mil.*) ***right –!*** rechts um! ***– up to,*** entgegentreten (*Dat.*), auf sich nehmen.

face|-ache, *s.* der Gesichtsschmerz, das Zahnweh. **--card,** *s.* die Bildkarte. **--cloth,** *s.* der Waschlappen. **faced,** *adj.* ***– with cement,*** mit Mörtel verkleidet *or* belegt; ***– card,*** aufgedeckte Karte; ***– jacket,*** die Jacke mit Aufschlägen; ***full-–,*** mit rundem, vollem Gesicht; ***two-–,*** doppelzüngig. **face-guard,** *s.* die Schutzmaske. **faceless,** *adj.* gesichtslos. **face|-lift,** *s.* die Gesichtsstraffung; (*fig.*) Verschönerung, Erneuerung, Renovierung. **--pack,** *s.* die Gesichtsmaske. **-plate,** *s.* die Frontplatte, (*lathe*) Planscheibe. **--presentation,** *s.* die Gesichtslage (*at birth*). **facer,** *s.* (*coll.*) der Schlag ins Gesicht; plötzliche Schwierigkeit. **face-saving,** *adj.* den (An)schein wahrend; ehrenrettend.

facet ['fæsit], *s.* die Facette, Rautenfläche, Schleiffläche, Schliffläche; (*fig.*) Seite, der Aspekt. **faceted,** *adj.* facettiert; (*Zool.*) ***– eye,*** das Netzauge, Facettenauge.

facetious [fə'si:ʃəs], *adj.* witzig, drollig, spaßhaft, spaßig, scherzhaft. **facetiousness,** *s.* die Drolligkeit, Witzigkeit, Scherzhaftigkeit.

face| value, *s.* der Nominalwert, Nennwert; (*fig.*) scheinbarer Wert; ***take his words at their –,*** seine Worte für bare Münze nehmen. **-work,** *s.* (*Archit.*) äußeres Mauerwerk.

facia ['feiʃə], *s.* **1.** das Firmenschild; **2.** Armaturenbrett.

facial ['feiʃəl], **1.** *adj.* Gesichts–; ***– angle,*** der Gesichtswinkel; ***– artery,*** die Gesichtsschlagader. **2.** *s.* (*also **– massage***) die Gesichtsmassage.

facile ['fæsail], *adj.* leicht (zu tun); gefällig, gefügig, umgänglich, nachgiebig, fügsam; leicht, gewandt. **facilitate** [fə'siliteit], *v.t.* erleichtern, fördern. **facilitation** [–'teiʃən], *s.* die Erleichterung, Förderung. **facility** [fə'siliti], *s.* **1.** die Leichtigkeit, Gewandtheit; Nachgiebigkeit; **2.** (*usu. pl.*) (günstige) Gelegenheit, die Möglichkeit; **3.** (*usu. pl.*) Erleichterung(en), der Vorteil, Vorteile (*pl.*).

facing ['feisiŋ], *s.* die Schutzbedeckung, Einfassung, (*of wall*) Verkleidung, Verblendung, (*Dressm.*) (*usu. pl.*) der Aufschlag, Besatz; (*Mil.*) die Wendung, Schwenkung; ***– board,*** das Blendholz; ***– brick,*** der (Ver)blendstein; ***– hammer,*** der Bahnschlegel; ***– lathe,*** die Plandrehbank; ***– tool,*** der Plandrehstahl.

facsimile [fæk'simili], *s.* das Faksimile, die Kopie, genaue Nachbildung.

fact [fækt], *s.* die Tatsache, das Faktum; (*without art. or pl.*) die Wirklichkeit, Wahrheit, Tatumstände (*pl.*); (*Law*) der Sachverhalt, Tatbestand; ***hard –s,*** nackte *or* unumstößliche Tatsachen; ***matter of –,*** feststehende Tatsache; ***as a matter of –,*** in Wirklichkeit, tatsächlich; ***the – (of the matter) is that . . .,*** um die Wahrheit zu sagen, offen gesagt; ***–s are –s,*** Tatsache bleibt Tatsache; ***in (point of) –,*** tatsächlich, in der Tat, faktisch; eigentlich, vielmehr. **fact-finding,** *attrib. adj.* Untersuchungs–, Informations–. *See* **factual.**

faction ['fækʃən], *s.* **1.** die Partei, Faktion, Clique; **2.** der Parteigeist, die Parteisucht; **3.** Zwietracht, Uneinigkeit. **factional,** *adj.* Partei–, Faktions–. **factionist,** *s.* der Parteigänger. **factious,** *adj.* parteieifrig, parteisüchtig, Partei–; aufrührerisch. **factiousness,** *s.* der Parteigeist, die Parteisucht.

factitious [fæk'tiʃəs], *adj.* (nach)gemacht, künstlich, unecht, gekünstelt.

factitive ['fæktitiv], *adj.* (*Gram.*) faktitiv, kausativ.

factor ['fæktə], *s.* **1.** (*Comm.*) der Agent, Faktor, Kommissionär, Vertreter, Disponent; (*Scots*) Verwalter (*of an estate*); **2.** (*fig.*) Faktor (*also Math.*), (mitwirkender) Umstand, das Moment; (*Biol.*) die Erbanlage; ***determining –,*** bestimmender Umstand; ***safety –,*** der Sicherheitskoeffizient. **factorage** [–ridʒ], *s.* die Provision, Kommissionsgebühr. **factorial** [–'tɔ:riəl], *s.* (*Math.*) die Fakultät. **factorization** [–rai'zeiʃən], *s.* (*Math.*) die Faktorenzerlegung. **factorize,** *v.t.* (*Math.*) in Faktoren zerlegen *or* auflösen.

factory ['fæktəri], *s.* die Fabrik(anlage), das Fabrikgebäude; (*obs.*) die Faktorei, Handelsniederlassung; ***– chimney,*** der Fabrikschornstein; ***– hand*** or ***worker,*** der Fabrikarbeiter; ***– inspector,*** Gewerbeaufsichtsbeamte(r); ***– system,*** das Fabrikwesen.

factotum [fæk'toutəm], *s.* das Faktotum, der Allerweltskünstler; (*fig.*) das Mädchen für alles, die Stütze, rechte Hand.

factual ['fæktjuəl], *adj.* Tatsachen–, tatsächlich.

facultative ['fækəltətiv], *adj.* wahlfrei, beliebig, freigestellt, fakultativ, Wahl–.

faculty ['fækulti], *s.* **1.** die Fähigkeit, (geistige *or* seelische) Kraft, das Vermögen, die Anlage, Gabe, das Talent; die Gewandtheit, Geschicklichkeit; **2.** (*R.C., Law*) Ermächtigung, Erlaubnis, Befugnis, Dispensation; **3.** (*Univ.*) Fakultät, Fakultätsmitglieder (*pl.*); (*Am.*) der Lehrkörper.

fad [fæd], *s.* (*coll.*) die Grille, Schrulle, Marotte, Liebhaberei, das Steckenpferd; fixe Idee, die Mode(torheit). **faddist,** *s.* der Grillenfänger, Fex. **faddy,** *adj.* grillenhaft, schrullenhaft, launenhaft, launisch, schrullig.

fade [feid], **1.** *v.i.* (ver)welken; verbleichen, verblassen, sich entfärben, abfärben, verschießen; ***– away,*** (dahin)schwinden, abklingen, vergehen (*of sound*), (ver)schwinden (*of sights*), (*Rad.*) (*also **– out***) schwinden, verklingen. **2.** *v.t.* verwelken lassen, zum Verblassen bringen; ***– in,*** aufblenden, einblenden; ***– out,*** abblenden, ausblenden. **faded,** *adj.* verschossen, verblichen; (*Bot.*) (*also fig. of a p.*) verblüht, fahl, verwelkt, welk. **fadeless,** *adj.* lichtecht; unverwelklich, unvergänglich. **fading,** **1.** *adj.* vergänglich, verblühend, (hin)schwindend. **2.** *s.* das Verblassen, Verschießen, die Verfärbung; (*Rad.*) der Schwund(affekt), die Schwunderscheinung, das Fading.

faecal [fi:kl], *adj.* Kot–, kotig, fäkal. **faeces** ['fi:si:z], *pl.* Exkremente, Fäkalien (*pl.*).

[1]**fag** [fæg], **1.** *v.i.* sich abmühen *or* (ab)schinden *or* abarbeiten *or* abplagen *or* (ab)placken, ochsen, büffeln; ***– for him,*** sein Fuchs sein (*in schools*). **2.** *v.t.* (*– o.s.*) (sich) erschöpfen *or* ermüden. **3.** *s.* die Plackerei, Schinderei; (*school sl.*) der Fuchs.

[2]**fag,** *s.* (*sl.*) der Glimmstengel. **fag-end,** *s.* die Kippe; (*of cloth*) Salleiste, das Salband; (*Naut.*) aufgedrehtes Tauende; (*fig. sl.*) letzter Rest, das Überbleibsel.

fagged [fægd], *adj.* (*coll.*) (*also* – *out*) erschöpft, ermüdet, völlig fertig *or* ausgepumpt.

faggot [ˈfægət], *s.* 1. das Reisigbündel, die Faschine; (*Tech.*) das Paket (*of steel rods*); 2. (*Cul.*) die Leberfrikandelle; 3. (*sl.*) Schlampe. **fagot,** *s.* (*Am.*) *see* **faggot.**

faience [faiˈɑ̃s], *s.* die Fayence.

fail [feil], **1.** *v.i.* fehlen, mangeln (*in*, an (*Dat.*)), ermangeln (*Gen.*); fehlschlagen, fehlgehen, scheitern, (den Zweck) verfehlen, mißlingen, Mißerfolg haben; (*with inf.*) verfehlen, versäumen, unterlassen; (*Comm.*) zahlungsunfähig werden, Bankrott machen, fallieren; durchfallen (*in an examination*); zu Ende gehen, ausgehen, vergehen, schwinden, aufhören, ausbleiben; (*as an engine*) versagen, stocken; abnehmen, schwach werden, nachlassen, ermatten; versiegen (*as a well*); nicht aufgehen (*as seed*), mißraten (*as harvest*); ***the attempt –ed***, der Versuch schlug fehl; ***it –ed in its effect***, es hatte nicht die beabsichtigte Wirkung; ***if everything else –s***, wenn alle Stricke reißen; ***his strength –s***, seine Kräfte lassen nach; ***it never –s***, es verfehlt nie; ***the plan –ed owing to the weather***, der Plan scheiterte an dem Wetter; ***he –ed to see***, es war ihm unmöglich einzusehen; ***he cannot – to see***, er muß (unfehlbar) einsehen, er kann nicht umhin einzusehen; ***his voice –ed***, seine Stimme versagte. **2.** *v.t.* 1. im Stich lassen, verlassen; enttäuschen; ***my courage –s me***, mir sinkt der Mut; ***he will never – you***, er enttäuscht dich nie, er läßt dich nie im Stich; ***words – me***, es fehlen mir Worte; 2. durchfallen lassen (*in an examination*); ***– an examination***, in einer Prüfung durchfallen. **3.** *s.* 1. (*only in*) ***without –***, unfehlbar, unbedingt, ganz bestimmt *or* gewiß; 2. (*in an examination*) Durchgefallene(r).

failing [ˈfeiliŋ], **1.** *adj.* fehlend, ausbleibend; schwindend, versagend; ***never –***, unfehlbar, nie versagend; nie versiegend. **2.** *prep.* in Ermangelung (*Gen.*), mangels (*Gen.*); ***– this***, andernfalls, wenn nicht; ***– which***, widrigenfalls. **3.** *s.* der Mangel, Fehler, die Schwäche.

failure [ˈfeiljə], *s.* 1. das Fehlen, Ausbleiben, Versagen; 2. Versäumnis, die Unterlassung; ***– to obey***, die Gehorsamsverweigerung; ***– to pay***, das Zahlungsversäumnis; 3. die Abnahme, der Verfall, Zusammenbruch; Fehlschlag, das Fehlschlagen, Mißlingen, der Mißerfolg; ***crop –***, die Mißernte; ***be doomed to –***, keine Aussicht auf Erfolg haben; 4. der Versager, fehlgeschlagene S.; untauglicher *or* mißglückter Mensch, der Taugenichts, verkrachte Existenz; 5. (*Comm.*) die Zahlungseinstellung, der Konkurs, Bankrott; 6. (*in examinations*) das Durchfallen; 7. (*Mech.*) der Defekt, die Störung.

fain [fein], **1.** *pred. adj.* (*obs.*) froh, erfreut; geneigt, bereit. **2.** *adv.* gern; (*only in*) ***I would – do it***, ich möchte es gern tun.

faint [feint], **1.** *adj.* 1. ohnmächtig; kraftlos, schwach (***with***, vor (*Dat.*)); 2. leise (*sounds, also fig.*); matt, blaß (*colour*); (*Prov.*) ***– heart never won fair lady***, wer nicht wagt, der gewinnt nicht; ***– hope***, leise *or* geringe Hoffnung; ***– idea***, leise Ahnung; ***– recollection***, undeutliche *or* schwache Erinnerung. **2.** *v.i.* 1. ohnmächtig werden, in Ohnmacht fallen (***with***, vor (*Dat.*)); 2. (*Poet.*) matt *or* schwach werden; verzagen. **3.** *s.* die Ohnmacht, der Ohnmachtsanfall.

faint|-hearted, *adj.* mutlos, kleinmütig, zaghaft. **--heartedness,** *s.* der Kleinmut, die Verzagtheit. **fainting (fit),** *s. See* **faint, 3. faintness,** *s.* die Schwäche, Mattigkeit; Erschöpfung, Schwachheit, Ohnmacht; das Ohnmachtsgefühl; ***– of heart***, die Verzagtheit, Mutlosigkeit.

[1]**fair** [fɛə], **1.** *adj.* 1. schön, hübsch; ***the – sex***, das schöne Geschlecht; 2. hell(farbig), blond; 3. beständig, heiter, klar (*weather*), deutlich, sauber, leserlich (*handwriting etc.*), unbehindert, klar, offen, frei (*view etc.*); ***– catch***, der Freifang; ***– copy***, die Reinschrift, druckfertiges Manuskript; ***– game***, das Freiwild (*also fig.*), jagdbares Wild; 4. (*fig.*) aussichtsreich, vielversprechend, günstig, gut, glücklich; ***– chance***, aussichtsreiche Chance; ***be in a – way***, auf dem besten Wege sein, gute Aussichten haben; 5. unbescholten, tadellos, aufrichtig, ehrlich, redlich, gerecht, anständig, (recht und) billig, unparteiisch, fair (***with***, gegen); ***– dealing***, die Redlichkeit; ***be a – judge***, ziemlich gutes Urteil haben; ***by – means***, auf ehrliche Weise; ***– play***, ehrliches Spiel *or* (*fig.*) Vorgehen; ***– trial***, unparteiische Untersuchung; ***– warning***, rechtzeitige Warnung; ***give him – warning***, ihn rechtzeitig warnen; 6. reichlich, beträchtlich, befriedigend, leidlich, erträglich, ziemlich *or* einigermaßen gut; (*coll.*) ***pretty –***, ganz leidlich; 7. freundlich, gefällig, angenehm, artig; ***– promises***, schöne Versprechungen; ***– words***, gefällige *or* schmeichelnde Worte. **2.** *adv.* gut, schön; unmittelbar, direkt; anständig, ehrlich, gerecht, billig; ***bid –***, sich gut anlassen, zu Hoffnungen berechtigen; ***play –***, ehrlich *or* fair spielen; (*fig.*) ehrliches Spiel treiben; ***promise –***, viel versprechen; ***the wind sits –***, der Wind ist günstig; ***speak him –***, ihm freundliche Worte sagen; ***– and square***, offen und ehrlich; ***– and square in the face***, direkt ins Gesicht. **3.** *s.* die Schöne; ***the –***, das schöne Geschlecht.

[2]**fair,** *s.* die Messe, Ausstellung; der Jahrmarkt, das Volksfest. **fair-ground,** *s.* das Messegelände; der Rummelplatz.

fair-haired, *adj.* blond, hellhaarig.

fairing [ˈfɛəriŋ], *s.* (*Av., Motor.*) die Verkleidung, Verschalung.

fairish [ˈfɛəriʃ], *adj.* (*coll.*) leidlich. **fairlead** [–liːd], *s.* (*Naut.*) der Führungsring, die Führung. **fairly,** *adv.* 1. leidlich, ziemlich, mäßig; 2. billig, unparteiisch, gerecht, rechtmäßig; 3. richtig, völlig, vollkommen, gänzlich, ganz und gar. **fair|-minded,** *adj.* ehrlich (gesinnt), aufrichtig. **--mindedness,** *s.* ehrliche Gesinnung, die Ehrlichkeit, Aufrichtigkeit. **fairness,** *s.* die Schönheit; Blondheit; Ehrlichkeit, Redlichkeit, Billigkeit, Unparteilichkeit, (*esp. Spt.*) Fairneß; ***in –***, von Rechts wegen; ***in – to him***, um ihm gerecht zu sein. **fair|-spoken,** *adj.* höflich, gefällig. **–way,** *s.* (*Naut.*) das Fahrwasser, die Fahrrinne; (*Golf*) gepflegte Bahn; (*Naut.*) ***– marker***, die Anseglungsboje. **--weather,** *adj.* Schönwetter–; ***– friend***, der Freund im Glück, unzuverlässiger Freund.

fairy [ˈfɛəri], **1.** *adj.* feenhaft, zauberisch, zauberhaft, Feen–, Zauber–. **2.** *s.* der Elf, die Fee. **fairy|-dance,** *s.* der Feenreigen. **–land,** *s.* das Elfenreich, Feenland; (*fig.*) Märchenland, Zauberland. **–like,** *adj.* feenhaft. **--ring,** *s.* (*Bot.*) der Feenring, Hexenring. **–tale,** *s.* das Märchen.

fait accompli [fetəkɔmˈpliː], *s.* vollendete Tatsache.

faith [feiθ], *s.* das Vertrauen (*in*, auf (*Acc.*) *or* zu); der Glaube(n) (an (*Acc.*)); (*Eccl.*) das Glaubensbekenntnis; die (Pflicht)treue, Redlichkeit; das Versprechen, die Zusage; (*obs.*) (*i'*) ***–!*** meiner Treu! auf Ehre! ***in (all) good –***, in gutem Glauben, in guter Absicht, auf Treu' und Glauben; ***break (one's) –***, sein Versprechen brechen; ***keep (one's) –***, Wort halten; ***pledge*** or ***plight one's –***, sein Wort *or* Versprechen geben; ***pin one's – on, put one's –*** or ***have – in***, Vertrauen haben zu *or* setzen in (*Acc.*). **faith|-cure,** *s. See* **--healing.**

faithful [ˈfeiθful], *adj.* 1. treu (***to***, *Dat.*); pflichttreu; aufrichtig, ehrlich, gewissenhaft; 2. wahr, (wahrheits)getreu, zuverlässig, glaubwürdig; 3. (recht)gläubig; (*Eccl.*) ***the –***, die Gläubigen. **faithfully,** *adv.* treu, ergeben; genau, getreu; ***carry out –***, genau *or* gewissenhaft ausführen; ***promise –***, hoch und heilig versprechen; ***yours –***, Ihr ergebener (*in letters*). **faithfulness,** *s.* die (Pflicht)treue; Genauigkeit, Zuverlässigkeit, Gewissenhaftigkeit.

faith|-healer, *s.* der Gesundbeter. **--healing,** *s.* das Gesundbeten. **faithless,** *adj.* treulos, untreu; ungläubig. **faithlessness,** *s.* die Untreue, Treulosigkeit (***towards***, gegen); der Unglaube.

fake [feik], **1.** *v.t.* (*sl.*) nachmachen; fälschen, zurechtmachen, frisieren (*report*), vortäuschen, heucheln (*surprise etc.*). **2.** *s.* (*sl.*) 1. der Betrug,

Schwindel; die Fälschung, Attrappe; 2. der Betrüger, Schwindler.

fakir [fɑ:'kiə], *s.* der Fakir.

falchion ['fɔ:l(t)ʃən], *s.* (*Hist.*) der Krummschwert, Pallasch.

falcon ['fɔ:lkən], *s.* der Falke; (*Hist.*) die Falkaune. **falconer,** *s.* der Falkner, Falkenier. **falconry,** *s.* die Falknerei, Falkenbeize.

falderal ['fældəræl], **falderol,** *s.* (*coll.*) der Firlefanz, das Larifari.

fall [fɔ:l], **1.** *irr.v.i.* fallen; (*of a p.*) hinfallen, niederfallen, umfallen, zu Boden fallen *or* stürzen, zu Fall kommen; (*fig.*) umkommen, erliegen; (*of a woman*) die Unschuld verlieren; (*of a th.*) zusammenfallen, zusammenbrechen, (nieder)stürzen; einfallen, einstürzen; abfallen, sich neigen *or* senken (*as terrain*), gestürzt werden (*as government*), genommen werden (*as a fortress*), (ab)fallen (*as leaves*), herabfallen (*as hair, drapery*), niedergehen (*as a curtain*); sich legen, nachlassen (*as wind*); heruntergehen, abnehmen, sinken (*as prices*); eintreffen, eintreten, hereinbrechen (*as time and events*); geworfen werden (*as lambs*); ***his courage fell,*** der Mut sank ihm; ***her eyes fell,*** sie senkte den Blick; ***his face fell,*** er machte ein langes Gesicht; ***night fell,*** die Nacht brach herein.
(a) (*with preps.*) – ***among,*** geraten unter (*Acc.*); – ***among thieves,*** unter die Räuber geraten, unter die Mörder fallen; – ***behind,*** zurückbleiben hinter (*Dat.*), überholt werden von; – ***between two stools,*** sich zwischen zwei Stühle setzen; – ***down the stairs,*** die Treppe hinunterfallen; (*sl.*) – ***for,*** sich einnehmen lassen von, gefesselt werden von, schwärmen für, vernarrt sein in (*Acc.*), reinfallen auf (*Acc.*); – ***from,*** abfallen von; ***an exclamation of displeasure fell from him,*** ihm entfuhr ein Ausruf des Mißfallens; – ***from favour,*** in Ungnade fallen; – ***from grace,*** sündigen, in Sünde fallen; (*coll.*) in Ungnade fallen; – ***in,*** fallen *or* schlagen in (*Acc.*), gehören zu; – ***in love,*** sich verlieben (***with,*** in (*Acc.*)); – ***in two,*** entzweigehen, auseinanderfallen; – ***in value,*** an Wert verlieren; – ***into,*** sich einfügen in (*Acc.*), kommen *or* geraten in (*Acc.*); – ***into a category,*** zu einer Gruppe gehören; – ***into conversation,*** ins Gespräch kommen; – ***into disrepair,*** verfallen; – ***into disrepute,*** in Verruf kommen; – ***into disuse,*** außer Gebrauch kommen; – ***into four divisions,*** in vier Teile zerfallen; – ***into error,*** einem Irrtum verfallen; – ***into a habit,*** eine Gewohnheit annehmen; – ***into line,*** (*Mil.*) (in Reih und Glied) antreten; (*fig.*) übereinstimmen (***with,*** mit), sich fügen *or* anschließen (*Dat.*); – ***into oblivion,*** in Vergessenheit geraten; (*fig.*) – ***into place,*** ohne Schwierigkeit zurechtkommen; – ***into a rage,*** in Wut geraten; – ***into ruin,*** zerfallen, in Trümmer sinken; ***the river –s into the sea,*** der Fluß ergießt sich *or* mündet ins Meer; (*Mil.*) – ***into step,*** Tritt fassen; – ***on,*** fallen auf (*Acc.*); (*fig.*) stoßen *or* verfallen auf (*Acc.*), treffen; anfallen, überfallen, angreifen, herfallen über (*Acc.*); – ***on evil days,*** ins Unglück *or* in Not geraten; (*fig.*) – ***on one's feet,*** auf die Füße fallen; – ***on his neck,*** ihm um den Hals fallen; – ***on a Sunday,*** auf einen Sonntag fallen; – ***on one's sword,*** sich ins Schwert stürzen; (*coll.*) – ***over,*** herfallen über (*Acc.*); (*coll.*) – ***over o.s.,*** sich anstrengen; ***her hair –s over her shoulders,*** ihre Haare hängen über die Schultern; – ***to,*** fallen an (*Acc.*), zufallen (*Dat.*), anheimfallen (*Dat.*), zuteil werden (*Dat.*) (*a p.*), beginnen, anfangen, sich machen an (*Acc.*), sich widmen (*Dat.*) (*a task etc.*); (*fig.*) – ***to the ground,*** scheitern, fehlschlagen, unter den Tisch *or* ins Wasser fallen; ***it –s to my lot,*** es fällt mir das Los zu, es ist mir beschieden; ***it –s to me to do it,*** es liegt mir ob, es zu tun; – ***to pieces,*** zerfallen, in Stücke fallen; – ***to work,*** sich an die Arbeit machen; (*fig.*) – ***under,*** gerechnet werden unter (*Acc.*), gehören zu; – ***under censure,*** dem Tadel unterliegen, sich dem Tadel aussetzen; – ***upon,*** see – ***on***; (*fig.*) – ***within,*** gerechnet werden zu.
(b) (*with advs.*) – ***asleep,*** einschlafen; – ***astern,*** achteraus sacken; – ***asunder,*** see – ***in two***; – ***away,*** (*of a p.*) abfallen (***from,*** von), abtrünnig werden (*Dat.*) (*from a cause*); abnehmen, abmagern, Gewicht verlieren; (*of strength etc.*) nachlassen; – ***back,*** sich zurückziehen, zurücktreten, zurückweichen; (*fig.*) zurückkommen, sich verlegen ((***up***)***on,*** auf (*Acc.*)); Hilfe suchen (bei), seine Zuflucht nehmen (zu), einen Rückhalt haben (an (*Dat.*)); – ***behind,*** zurückbleiben, ins Hintertreffen geraten; – ***behind in one's payments,*** in Zahlungsverzug geraten; – ***down,*** hinfallen, umfallen (*of a p.*), (*in respect*) niederfallen, auf die Knie sinken; einstürzen (*as buildings*); (*fig. coll.*) versagen (***on,*** bei); – ***in,*** einfallen, einstürzen (*as buildings, tunnels etc.*); (*Mil.*) antreten; (*Comm.*) fällig werden, ablaufen (*as a lease*); (*fig.*) – ***in with,*** stoßen auf (*Acc.*), zufällig treffen (*a p.*), eingehen auf (*Acc.*), einverstanden sein *or* überstimmen mit, beipflichten (*Dat.*), zustimmen (*Dat.*) (*a suggestion*), passen zu, entsprechen (*Dat.*) (*preconceived idea*); – ***off,*** herabfallen, (*as leaves*) abfallen; (*fig.*) fallen (*in value*), nachlassen, abflauen (*in strength*), sich vermindern *or* verschlechtern; (*Naut.*) (leewärts) absacken, vom Strich abfallen; – ***out,*** heraus- *or* hinausfallen (***of,*** aus); (*fig.*) ausgehen, ausfallen, sich herausstellen (*with adv.*); (*Mil.*) wegtreten, austreten; (*coll.*) sich entzweien *or* zanken *or* überwerfen (***with,*** mit); – ***out of cultivation,*** nicht mehr bebaut werden; – ***out of his hands,*** seinen Händen entfallen; – ***out of use,*** außer Gebrauch kommen; – ***over,*** umfallen, umkippen, überkippen; (*sl.*) – ***over backwards,*** sich beinahe umbringen (***to be,*** um zu sein); – ***through,*** durchfallen; (*coll.*) ins Wasser fallen, mißglücken, mißlingen; – ***to,*** ins Schloß fallen (*of a door*); (*fig.*) handgemein werden; (*coll.*) zugreifen, zupacken (*at meals*); – ***together,*** zusammenfallen.
(c) (*with adjs.*) – ***dead,*** tot hinfallen; – ***due,*** fällig werden; (*coll.*) – ***flat,*** fehlschlagen, keinen Eindruck machen; – ***foul of,*** zusammenstoßen *or* sich überwerfen mit, in Streit *or* Konflikt geraten mit; – ***foul of each other,*** sich in die Haare geraten; – ***ill,*** erkranken, krank werden; – ***short of,*** mangeln an (*Dat.*), knapp werden an (*Dat.*); zurückbleiben hinter (*Dat.*), nicht entsprechen (*Dat.*), nicht erreichen (*expectations etc.*); (*Artil.*) zu kurz gehen; (*fig. coll.*) – ***short of the mark,*** das Ziel nicht treffen; – ***vacant,*** frei werden.
(d) (*with nouns*) – ***heir to,*** erben; – ***a prey*** or ***victim to,*** zum Opfer fallen (*Dat.*), das Opfer werden von, überwältigt werden von.
(e) (*with verbs*) (*Poet.*) – ***a-weeping,*** zu weinen anfangen.
2. *s.* 1. der Fall, Sturz; ***break his –,*** ihn (im Fallen) auffangen; ***have*** or ***sustain a –,*** zu Falle kommen, fallen, stürzen; ***ride for a –,*** waghalsig reiten; (*fig.*) auf die schiefe Ebene geraten; 2. das Fallen, (Ab)fallen (*of leaves*), Herabfallen, der Faltenwurf (*of drapery*), das Niedergehen (*of a curtain*), Sinken, der Sturz (*of prices*), Niedergang (*of piston etc.*), Einsturz, das Zusammenfallen (*of a roof etc.*); (*Comm.*) ***on the –,*** im Fallen begriffen; – ***in prices,*** der Preissturz; – ***of rain,*** der Regenfall; (*Comm.*) ***speculate on the –,*** auf Baisse spekulieren; – ***of the tide,*** das Fallen der Flut; 3. (*fig.*) der Untergang, Niedergang, Abstieg, Verfall, Sturz, Zusammenbruch; die Einnahme (*of a fortress*); ***the Fall*** (***of man***), der Sündenfall; ***decline and –,*** Abstieg und Ende; ***rise and –,*** Aufstieg und Untergang; 4. die Absenkung, Neigung, der Abfall, das Gefälle (*of terrain*); 5. Werfen, der Wurf (*of lambs*); 6. (*Mus.*) die Kadenz; 7. (*Naut.*) das Fall (*pl.* Fallen) (*of hoisting tackle*); 8. der Niederwurf (*wrestling*); 9. die Fallhöhe, Fallstrecke; 10. (*usu. pl.*) der Wasserfall; 11. (*Am.*) Herbst.

fallacious [fə'leiʃəs], *adj.* falsch, irrig; trügerisch, täuschend, irreführend. **fallaciousness,** *s.* die Falschheit, Irrigkeit; Trüglichkeit. **fallacy** ['fæləsi], *s.* der Irrtum, Trugschluß; die Täuschung, Irreführung; (*Poet.*) ***pathetic –,*** die Vermenschlichung der Natur.

fallen [fɔ:lən], **1.** *p.p. of* **fall. 2.** *adj.* – ***angel,*** gestürzter Engel; – ***arch,*** der Senkfuß; – ***woman,*** gefallene Frau; ***the –,*** die Gefallenen, Kriegsopfer (*pl.*).

fall guy, *s.* (*Am.*) *see* **scapegoat.**

fallibility [fæli'biliti], *s.* die Fehlbarkeit. **fallible** ['fælibl], *adj.* fehlbar.

falling ['fɔ:liŋ], **1.** *s.* das Fallen, Sinken, (*Med.*) der Vorfall; – *sickness*, die Fallsucht. **2.** *adj.* fallend, sinkend, abnehmend; – *star*, die Sternschnuppe. **falling|-away,** *s.* der Abfall; das Abfallen, Wegfallen; Abmagern. **--off,** *s.* (*coll.*) der Rückgang, die Abnahme.

Fallopian [fə'loupiən], *adj.* (*Anat.*) fallopisch; – *tube*, der Eileiter, die Mutterröhre, Muttertrompete.

fall-out, *s.* (radioaktiver) Niederschlag.

fallow ['fælou], **1.** *adj.* 1. fahl, falb, fahlgelb; – *deer*, das Damwild; 2. (*of land*) brach (liegend), unbebaut; *lie* –, brachliegen. **2.** *s.* das Brachfeld, die Brache. **3.** *v.t.* aufbrechen (*land*).

false [fɔ:ls], **1.** *adj.* falsch, unrichtig, irrig, unwahr, fehlerhaft; (*of a p.*) trügerisch, verräterisch, treulos (*to*, gegen(über)), untreu (*Dat.*); (*of a th.*) unecht, gefälscht, nachgemacht, vorgetäuscht, Schein–; – *alarm*, blinder Alarm; – *bottom*, der Doppelboden; – *ceiling*, die Einschubdecke; *under – colours*, (*Naut.*) unter falscher Flagge; (*fig.*) mit betrügerischer Aufmachung; (*Scots*) – *face*, die Maske; – *horizon*, künstlicher Horizont; – *impression*, falsches Bild; – *imprisonment*, rechtswidrige Verhaftung; – *keel*, der Loskiel; – *key*, der Nachschlüssel, Dietrich; – *pregnancy*, eingebildete Schwangerschaft; (*Law*) – *pretences*, die Vorspiegelung falscher Tatsachen; – *start*, der Fehlstart; – *step*, der Fehltritt; – *verdict*, das Fehlurteil. **2.** *adv. play him* –, ein falsches Spiel mit ihm treiben.

false-hearted, *adj.* verräterisch, treulos, falsch. **falsehood,** *s.* die Lüge, Unwahrheit; Falschheit. **falseness,** *s.* die Falschheit, Unrichtigkeit, Unwahrheit; Unredlichkeit, Unaufrichtigkeit; Treulosigkeit, der Verrat.

falsetto [fɔ:l'setou], *s.* (*Mus.*) die Fistel(stimme), das Falsett; der (die) Falsettsänger(in).

falsification [fɔ:lsifi'keiʃən], *s.* die (Ver)fälschung. **falsifier** ['fɔ:lsifaiə], *s.* der Fälscher. **falsify** [–fai], *v.t.* fälschen (*coin*); verfälschen (*writings etc.*); als falsch erweisen, (ent)täuschen, vereiteln (*hopes etc.*). **falsity** [–ti], *s.* die Unrichtigkeit, Unwahrheit, Falschheit.

falter ['fɔ:ltə], **1.** *v.i.* stottern, stammeln (*in speaking*); stolpern, straucheln, wanken, schwanken, taumeln (*in walking*); (*fig.*) zögern, zaudern, stocken, (*as memory, courage etc.*) versagen. **2.** *v.t.* stammeln(d äußern). **faltering,** *adj.* stammelnd, stotternd; zögernd, schwankend, wankend, taumelnd.

fame [feim], *s.* 1. der Ruhm, die Berühmtheit, (guter) Ruf; 2. (*obs.*) das Gerücht; *of ill* –, berüchtigt; *house of ill* –, das Freudenhaus, Bordell. **famed,** *adj.* berühmt, bekannt (*for*, wegen).

familiar [fə'miljə], **1.** *adj.* (wohl)bekannt, vertraut; (allgemein) bekannt, (alt)gewohnt, gebräuchlich, alltäglich, gewöhnlich; geläufig (*to*, *Dat.*); vertraulich, intim, ungezwungen, familiär, (zu) frei, zudringlich, aufdringlich; *make o.s.* – *with*, sich bekannt machen mit; – *quotation*, geflügeltes Wort; – *sight*, gewohnter Anblick; – *spirit*, der Schutzgeist; – *style*, ungezwungene Schreibart; *be on – terms*, auf vertrautem Fuße stehen, freundschaftliche Beziehungen haben. **2.** *s.* 1. Vertraute(r); 2. der Hausgeist. **familiarity** [–i'æriti], *s.* die Bekanntschaft, Vertrautheit; Vertraulichkeit, Ungezwungenheit, Zwanglosigkeit, Leutseligkeit; *pl.* familiärer Umgangston; (*Prov.*) – *breeds contempt*, allzugroße Vertrautheit führt zur Geringschätzung. **familiarization** [–rai'zeiʃən], *s.* die Gewöhnung (*with*, an (*Acc.*)). **familiarize,** *v.t.* gewöhnen (*with*, an (*Acc.*)); bekannt *or* vertraut machen (mit).

family ['fæmili], **1.** *s.* die Familie; der Stamm, das Geschlecht, Vorfahren (*pl.*); (*Bot., Zool.*) die Gattung, (*Math.*) Schar, (*Chem. etc.*) Gruppe; *father of a* –, der Familienvater; *of good* –, aus guter *or* vornehmer Familie *or* gutem Haus; *have you a* –? haben Sie Familie? *have a large* –, viele Kinder haben; *old* –, altes Geschlecht; *raise a* –, Kinder aufziehen. **2.** *attrib. adj.* Familien–, zur Familie gehörig; – *allowance*, die Familienzulage, Kinderzulage; – *Bible*, die Familienbibel; – *circle*, der Familienkreis; – *doctor*, der Hausarzt; – *likeness*, die Familienähnlichkeit; – *man*, der Familienvater; häuslicher Mensch; – *name*, der Familienname, Zuname; – *prayers*, die Hausandacht; – *tree*, der Stammbaum; (*coll.*) *in the – way*, in anderen Umständen, guter Hoffnung.

famine ['fæmin], *s.* die Hungersnot; (*fig.*) Not, der Mangel; *die of* –, vor Hunger sterben; *water* –, der Wassermangel.

famish ['fæmiʃ], **1.** *v.t.* aushungern (lassen), (ver)hungern *or* verschmachten *or* darben lassen. **2.** *v.i.* hungern, fast verhungern, darben; (*coll.*) *be –ed*, großen Hunger haben.

famous ['feiməs], *adj.* berühmt (*for*, wegen); (*coll.*) prima, famos. **famously,** *adv.* (*coll.*) famos, glänzend.

[1]**fan** [fæn], **1.** *s.* der Fächer; (*Agr.*) die Wanne, Schwinge; (*Tech.*) der Lüfter, Ventilator, das Gebläse; der Flügel, die Windfahne (*of windmill*); (*Naut.*) das (Schrauben)blatt; Flügelrad (*of turbine*); *electric* –, der Lüfter. **2.** *v.t.* fächeln, wedeln; schwingen, worfeln (*corn*); (*fig.*) anfachen, entfachen (*into*, zu); (*fig.*) – *the flame*, Öl ins Feuer gießen. **3.** *v.i.* – *out*, ausschwärmen.

[2]**fan,** *s.* (*coll.*) (*Spt. etc.*) leidenschaftlicher Liebhaber, begeisterter Anhänger, der Fanatiker, Narr, Fex; – *mail*, Briefe aus dem Anhängerkreis.

fanatic [fə'nætik], **1.** *s.* der Fanatiker, Eiferer, Schwärmer. **2.** *or* **fanatical,** *adj.* fanatisch, schwärmerisch. **fanaticism** [–tisizm], *s.* der Fanatismus, blinder Eifer; (religiöse) Schwärmerei.

fan|-belt, *s.* (*Motor.*) der Keilriemen, (Treib)riemen. **--blade,** *s.* der Windflügel.

fancier ['fænsiə], *s.* der Liebhaber, Kenner, Züchter. **fanciful,** *adj.* phantasiereich, phantasievoll, phantastisch, unrealistisch, schwärmerisch; wunderlich, grillenhaft, schrullig, spielerisch. **fancifulness,** *s.* der Phantasiereichtum, die Grillenhaftigkeit, Phantasterei.

fancy ['fænsi], **1.** *s.* 1. die Phantasie, Einbildungskraft; Einbildung, Eingebung, Vorstellung, der Einfall; die Grille, Laune, Schrulle; 2. persönlicher Geschmack, die Neigung (*for*, zu), Vorliebe (für), das Gefallen (an (*Dat.*)), Interesse (an (*Dat.*) *or* für); *catch* or *take* or *tickle his* –, sein Interesse erwecken, ihm gefallen, bei ihm Anklang finden; *strike one's* –, sich (*Dat.*) in den Sinn kommen; *take a – to*, eingenommen sein für, eine Neigung fassen zu, Gefallen finden an (*Dat.*); 3. (*sl.*) *the* –, die Sportwelt. **2.** *v.t.* 1. sich (*Dat.*) einbilden *or* vorstellen *or* denken, annehmen, meinen, wähnen, halten für; (*coll.*) – *o.s.*, sich wichtig vorkommen; (*just* or *only*) – (*that*)! stellen Sie sich vor! denken Sie sich nur! 2. gern haben *or* mögen, eingenommen sein für. **3.** *attrib. adj.* Mode–, Luxus–, Galanterie–; Phantasie–, übertrieben; bunt, vielfarbig, gemustert; – *cakes*, feines Gebäck, Torten (*pl.*); – *dress*, das Maskenkostüm; – *dress ball*, der Maskenball, das Kostümfest; – *goods*, Galanteriewaren, Modewaren (*pl.*); – *handkerchief*, buntes *or* farbiges Taschentuch; – *man*, (*coll.*) Geliebte(r); (*sl.*) der Zuhälter; – *paper*, das Buntpapier, Phantasiepapier; – *price*, der Liebhaberpreis, (*coll.*) Wucherpreis; (*Comm.*) – *stocks*, Spekulationspapiere (*pl.*); (*coll.*) – *woman*, Geliebte, die Mätresse; – *work*, feine Handarbeit, das Zierwerk, Ornament.

fandango [fæn'dæŋgou], *s.* der Fandango.

fane [fein], *s.* (*Poet.*) der Tempel.

fanfare ['fænfɛə], *s.* der Tusch, die Fanfare. **fanfaronade** [fænfærə'neid], *s.* die Prahlerei, Aufschneiderei, Großtuerei.

[1]**fang** [fæŋ], *s.* der Fang, Hauer, Hauzahn; Giftzahn (*of snakes*); (*fig.*) die Klaue; Zahnwurzel; der Stift, Zapfen.

[2]**fang,** *v.t.* mit Wasser auffüllen, in Tätigkeit setzen (*pump*).

fan|-heater, *s.* der Heizlüfter. **–light,** *s.* die Lünette, das Fächerfenster. **--palm,** *s.* (*Bot.*) die Fächerpalme. **--shaped,** *adj.* fächerförmig. **–tail,** *s.* (*Orn.*) die Pfau(en)taube.

fantasia [fæn'teiziə, fæntə'ziə], *s.* (*esp. Mus.*) die Phantasie. **fantastic** [fæn'tæstik], *adj.* phantastisch, wunderlich, grotesk, seltsam, eingebildet. **fantasy** ['fæntəsi], *s.* das Phantasiegebilde, Traumgebilde, Hirngespinst, Trugbild, (*Psych.*) der Wachtraum, die Phantasiefolge; *see also* **phantasy.**

fan|-tracery, *s.* (*Archit.*) das Fächermaßwerk. **--vaulting,** *s.* (*Archit.*) das Fächergewölbe.

far [fɑ:], **1.** *adj.* fern, (weit) entfernt; ***Far East,*** Ferner Osten; ***in the – corner,*** in der gegenüberliegenden Ecke; ***on the – side,*** auf der anderen Seite. **2.** *adv.* fern, weit, weitaus, um vieles, bei weitem; ***as – as,*** soweit (wie), insofern als; nicht weiter als, bis (nach); ***as – as that goes,*** was das betrifft; ***so –,*** bisher, bis jetzt; bis hierher; ***in so*** or ***in as – as,*** insoweit *or* insofern als; ***not so – as I am aware,*** nicht daß ich wüßte; ***so – so good,*** soweit geht's noch; ***thus –,*** so weit, bis dahin; ***carry (a th.) too –,*** (eine S.) zu weit treiben; ***he will go –,*** er wird es weit bringen; ***this went – to convince us,*** dies trug wesentlich dazu bei, uns zu überzeugen; dies überzeugte uns geradezu; ***– and away,*** bei weitem, weitaus; ***– and near,*** nahe und fern; ***– and wide,*** weit und breit, allenthalben; (*with advs. or preps.*) ***– away,*** weit weg, weit entfernt; ***– the best,*** weitaus am besten, bei weitem das beste; ***– better,*** weitaus *or* viel besser; ***few and – between,*** vereinzelt, dünn gesät; ***by –,*** weitaus, bei weitem; ***– be it from me,*** es sei fern von mir, es liegt mir fern; ***– from being offended,*** weit (davon) entfernt, beleidigt zu sein; ***– from finished,*** weit entfernt, vollendet zu sein; (*coll.*) ***– from it,*** bei weitem nicht, keineswegs, ganz im Gegenteil; ***– from rich,*** keineswegs reich; ***– into the night,*** bis spät in die Nacht; ***– off,*** weit weg; ***– out,*** weit draußen; (*fig.*) weit gefehlt; ***– up,*** hoch oben.

farad ['færəd], *s.* (*Elec.*) das Farad.

far-away, *adj.* (weit) entfernt; (*fig.*) träumerisch, entrückt.

farce [fɑ:s], **1.** *v.t.* (*Cul.*) füllen, farcieren. **2.** *s.* (*Theat.*) der Schwank, die Posse; (*fig.*) das Possenspiel, Theater; (*fig.*) ***complete –,*** reiner Schwindel, ausgesprochene Komödie. **farcical,** *adj.* possenhaft; (*fig.*) lächerlich, absurd.

fardel [fɑ:dl], *s.* (*obs.*) das Bündel; (*fig.*) die Bürde, Last.

fare [fɛə], **1.** *v.i.* ergehen (*Dat.*), sich befinden, daran sein, (*impers.*) ergehen (*with Dat. of p.*); (*Poet.*) fahren, reisen; ***how did you – subsequently?*** wie ist es dir seither ergangen? (*Poet.*) ***– forth,*** sich aufmachen; ***go farther and – worse,*** aus dem Regen in die Traufe kommen; ***– well*** (or ***ill***), gut (*or* schlecht) abschneiden; (*Poet.*) ***– thee well!*** laß es dir gut gehen! **2.** *s.* 1. das Fahrgeld, der Fahrpreis; ***excess –,*** der Zuschlag; ***– stage,*** die Teilstrecke, Tarifgrenze; ***what is the –?*** was kostet die Fahrt *or* Fahrkarte? 2. der Fahrgast, Passagier; 3. die Beköstigung, Nahrung, Kost; ***bill of –,*** die Speisekarte; ***poor –,*** schmale Kost, schlechte Verpflegung.

farewell [fɛə'wel], **1.** *int.* lebe wohl! leben Sie wohl! **2.** *attrib. adj.* Abschieds–. **3.** *s.* das Lebewohl, der Abschied(sgruß); ***bid him –*** or ***– to him,*** ihm Lebewohl sagen, von ihm Abschied nehmen; ***make one's –s,*** sich verabschieden.

far|-famed, *adj.* weithin berühmt *or* bekannt. **--fetched,** *adj.* weit hergeholt, übertrieben, gezwungen, gesucht, an *or* bei den Haaren herbeigezogen. **--flung,** *adj.* weit ausgebreitet *or* ausgedehnt. **--gone,** *adj.* weit fortgeschritten *or* vorgerückt; (*coll.*) stark benebelt; restlos verliebt (*on,* in (*Acc.*)); in den letzten Zügen.

farina [fə'ri:nə], *s.* das Stärkemehl, Kartoffelmehl.

farinaceous [færi'neiʃəs], *adj.* mehlig; stärkehaltig, mehlhaltig; ***– food,*** Mehlspeisen (*pl.*).

farm [fɑ:m], **1.** *s.* das Bauerngut, der Bauernhof; das Gehöft, der Pachthof; die Farm (*in the colonies*); das Bauernhaus, Gutshaus; ***dairy –,*** die Meierei; ***home –,*** selbstbewirtschaftetes Gut; ***poultry –,*** die Hühnerfarm. **2.** *v.t.* bebauen, bewirtschaften; ***– out,*** verpachten, in Pacht geben (*land*); verdingen (*people*), vergeben, weitergeben (*contracts*), gegen Bezahlung ausgeben (*children*). **3.** *v.i.* Landwirtschaft betreiben.

farmer ['fɑ:mə], *s.* der Bauer, Landwirt, Pächter; ***cattle –,*** der Viehzüchter; ***dairy –,*** der Milchproduzent. **farm|hand,** *s.* der Landarbeiter. **–house,** *s.* das Bauernhaus, Gutshaus. **farming,** **1.** *attrib. adj.* landwirtschaftlich, Land–, Acker(bau)–; ***– implements,*** Ackergeräte (*pl.*). **2.** *s.* die Landwirtschaft, der Landbau, Ackerbau. **farm|-labourer,** *s. See* **–hand. –land,** *s.* das Ackerland, der Ackerboden, die Ackerfläche. **--servant,** *s.* der Bauernknecht, die Bauernmagd. **–stead,** *s.* der Bauernhof, das Gehöft. **--worker,** *s. See* **–hand. –yard,** *s.* der Wirtschaftshof.

faro ['fɛərou], *s.* das Pharo(spiel).

far-off, *adj.* abgelegen, entlegen.

farouche [fə'ru:ʃ], *adj.* (menschen)scheu.

farrago [fə'ra:gou], *s.* das Gemisch, der Mischmasch.

far-reaching, *adj.* weitreichend; (*fig.*) schwerwiegend, tiefgreifend, folgenschwer.

farrier ['færiə], *s.* der Hufschmied; (*Mil.*) Fahnenschmied; (*obs.*) Roßarzt. **farriery,** *s.* das Hufschmiedehandwerk.

farrow ['færou], **1.** *s.* der Wurf (*of pigs*); ***in*** or ***with –,*** trächtig (*of sows*). **2.** *v.i.* ferkeln, (Ferkel) werfen, frischen.

far|-seeing, *adj.* (*fig.*) weitsichtig, weitblickend. **--sighted,** *adj.* 1. (*Med.*) weitsichtig; 2. (*fig.*) *see* **--seeing. --sightedness,** *s.* 1. (*Med.*) die Weitsichtigkeit; 2. (*fig.*) Umsicht, der Weitblick.

fart [fɑ:t], (*vulg.*) **1.** *s.* der Furz. **2.** *v.i.* furzen.

farther ['fɑ:ðə], **1.** *comp. adj. See* **far**; entfernter. **2.** *adv.* weiter, ferner. **farthest, 1.** *sup. adj.* fernst, weitest, entferntest; ***at the –,*** höchstens. **2.** *adv.* weitestens, am weitesten; spätestens.

farthing ['fɑ:ðiŋ], *s.* (*obs.*) der Heller.

farthingale ['fɑ:ðiŋgeil], *s.* (*obs.*) der Reifrock.

fasces ['fæsi:z], *pl.* (*Hist.*) das Liktorenbündel, Faszes (*pl.*).

fascia ['feiʃə], *s.* das (Quer)band, Bandgesims, (*Archit.*) der Bund, Gurtsims; (*Astr.*) Ring, Gürtel; (*Zool.*) Farbstreifen; (*Anat.*) die Faszie, Muskelbinde; *see also* **facia. fasciated** [–ieitid], *adj.* (*Bot.*) verbändert; (*Zool.*) gestreift. **fasciation** [–'eiʃən], *s.* das Zusammenbündeln; (*Anat.*) Verbinden; (*Bot.*) die Verbänderung.

fascicle ['fæsikl], *s.* 1. das Bündel, (*Bot.*) Büschel; 2. die (Teil)lieferung, das (Einzel)heft (*of a book*); (*Law*) der Faszikel, das Aktenbündel. **fascicular** [fə'sikjulə], **fasciculate(d),** *adj.* büschelförmig.

fascinate ['fæsineit], *v.t.* bezaubern, bestricken, betören, fesseln, packen, hinreißen, faszinieren. **fascination** [–'neiʃən], *s.* die Bezauberung, Bestrickung; der Zauber, Reiz.

fascine [fæ'si:n], *s.* die Faschine, das Reisigbündel, Strauchbüschel.

fascism ['fæʃizm], *s.* der Faschismus. **fascist, 1.** *s.* der Faschist. **2.** *adj.* faschistisch.

fash [fæʃ], (*Scots*) **1.** *v.t.* quälen, plagen, ärgern; ***– o.s.,*** sich ärgern *or* aufregen, sich (*Dat.*) Sorgen machen (***about,*** über (*Acc.*)). **2.** *s.* der Ärger, die Plage.

fashion ['fæʃən], **1.** *s.* 1. die Mode; ***come into –,*** Mode werden; ***– conscious,*** modebewußt, modisch; ***the height of –,*** die neueste Mode; ***in (the) –,*** modisch (*of clothes etc.*), modern (*of persons*); ***– magazine,*** die Modezeitschrift; ***out of –,*** außer Mode, veraltet, unmodern; ***people*** or ***world of –,*** die Modewelt; ***set the –,*** den Ton angeben, die Mode einführen; 2. die Art und Weise, Manier, der Stil; (Zu)schnitt, die Machart, Fasson, Form, Art, Sorte; ***after the – of,*** nach (der) Art von, auf die Weise von, im Stil von; (*coll.*) ***after*** or ***in a –,*** einigermaßen, oberflächlich, nachlässig, halb und halb. **2.** *v.t.* bilden, gestalten, formen, machen; (*Tech.*) ausarbeiten, zuschneiden; zurechtmachen (***to,*** für), anpassen (*Dat. or* an (*Acc.*)).

fashionable [ˈfæʃənəbl], *adj.* modisch, Mode–, modern, fein, elegant; ***it is –,*** es ist Mode; ***– party,*** feine Gesellschaft; ***– resort,*** eleganter Kurort; ***– woman,*** modisch gekleidete Dame; ***dress fashionably,*** sich nach der Mode kleiden. **fashionableness,** *s.* das Modische, Moderne, die Modernität, Eleganz. **fashioner,** *s.* der Gestalter. **fashioning,** *s.* die Form(geb)ung. **fashion|-monger,** *s.* der Modeheld, Stutzer. **--parade,** *s.* die Mode(n)-schau. **--plate,** *s.* das Modebild, die Modezeichnung. **--show,** *s. See* **--parade.**

[1]**fast** [fɑːst], *adj., adv.* (*pred. only*) fest, befestigt, festgemacht, unbeweglich; (*attrib. and pred.*) haltbar, dauerhaft, beständig; ***– aground,*** festgefahren; ***be – asleep,*** fest schlafen; ***– colour,*** echte Farbe; ***– friends,*** feste *or* unzertrennliche Freunde; ***hold –,*** festhalten; ***make –,*** festmachen, befestigen; (*Naut.*) festzurren; ***hard and – rule,*** feste Regel; ***play – and loose,*** Schindluder treiben, Katz und Maus spielen; ***stick –,*** feststecken; ***take – hold of,*** fest anpacken.

[2]**fast,** *adj.* schnell, geschwind, rasch; vorgehend (*of a watch*); (*coll.*) flott, leichtlebig, locker, ausschweifend; (*Phot.*) ***– film,*** lichtempfindlicher Film; ***– girl,*** lockeres *or* leichtlebiges Mädchen; (*Phot.*) ***– lens,*** lichtstarkes Objektiv; ***– life,*** ausschweifendes Leben; ***– train,*** der Schnellzug, Eilzug; ***my watch is –,*** meine Uhr geht vor; ***it is raining –,*** es regnet stark *or* tüchtig.

[3]**fast, 1.** *v.i.* fasten. **2.** *s.* das Fasten; die Fastenzeit; ***break one's –,*** frühstücken. **fast-day,** *s.* der Fast(en)tag.

fasten [fɑːsn], **1.** *v.t.* festmachen, festbinden, befestigen, anbinden (***to,*** an (*Dat.*)); (ver)schließen, abschließen, fest zumachen; verriegeln, abriegeln, zuriegeln (*as a door*), verschnüren, zuschnüren (*as a parcel*), zuknöpfen (*as a coat*); (*fig.*) zuschieben, anhängen, beilegen (***upon,*** *Dat.*), heften, richten (*eyes, thoughts etc.*), setzen (*hopes*) (***on,*** auf (*Acc.*)); ***– down,*** befestigen; (*Sewing*) ***– off,*** mit Knoten abschließen; ***– a crime on him,*** ihn eines Verbrechens beschuldigen; ***– a nickname on him,*** ihm einen Spitznamen beilegen. **2.** *v.i.* schließen, sich schließen *or* zumachen lassen (*of door*); sich festhalten *or* heften (***on,*** an (*Dat.*)); (*fig.*) ***– upon,*** sich heften *or* halten *or* richten *or* klammern an (*Acc.*); ***– upon it as a pretext,*** es zum Vorwand nehmen.

fastener [ˈfɑːsnə], *s.* der Befestiger, Verschluß, Schließer, Halter, Hefter, Druckknopf. **fastening,** *s.* das Befestigungsmittel, die Verschlußvorrichtung, Verankerung, Sicherung, der Riegel, das Schloß, Band.

fastidious [fæsˈtidiəs], *adj.* verwöhnt, wählerisch, anspruchsvoll; mäk(e)lig, schwer zu befriedigen(d). **fastidiousness,** *s.* die Verwöhntheit, Überempfindlichkeit, Mäkelei.

fastness [ˈfɑːstnis], *s.* 1. die Haltbarkeit, Beständigkeit, Festigkeit, (*of colours*) Echtheit; *see* [1]**fast**; 2. Festung, Feste; 3. Schnelligkeit, Raschheit; (*coll.*) Leichtlebigkeit; *see* [2]**fast.**

fat [fæt], **1.** *adj.* 1. fett; fettig, ölig; fruchtbar (*as soil*); bituminös (*of coal*); 2. dick, korpulent, beleibt (*of a p.*); (*fig.*) lohnend, ergiebig, einträglich; ***grow –,*** fett werden; (*coll., iron.*) ***a – lot,*** herzlich wenig; ***– profit,*** reicher Gewinn; ***– purse,*** dicker Beutel. **2.** *s.* das Fett (*also Chem., fig.*), Schmalz; ***incline to –,*** Fett ansetzen; ***live on the – of the land,*** in Saus und Braus leben; aus dem vollen schöpfen; ***the – was in the fire,*** der Teufel war los.

fatal [feitl], *adj.* 1. verhängnisvoll, unheilvoll, schicksalhaft, schicksalsschwer(***to,*** für); ***the Fatal Sisters,*** die Parzen (*pl.*); 2. tödlich, mit tödlichem Ausgang; ***– accident,*** tödlicher Unfall; ***– stroke,*** der Todesstreich. **fatalism,** *s.* der Fatalismus, Schicksalsglaube. **fatalist,** *s.* der Fatalist. **fatalistic** [–ˈlistik], *adj.* fatalistisch. **fatality** [fəˈtæliti], *s.* der Todesfall, tödlicher Unfall; das Todesopfer; Verhängnis, Geschick; der Schicksalsschlag.

Fata Morgana [fɑːtəmɔːˈgɑːnə], *s.* die Luftspiegelung.

fate [feit], *s.* das Schicksal, die Schicksalsmacht; das Schicksal, Geschick, Los; Verhängnis, Verderben, der Untergang; ***go to one's –,*** seinem Schicksal entgegengehen; ***he met his –,*** das Schicksal ereilte ihn; ***seal*** or ***decide his –,*** sein Schicksal besiegeln *or* entscheiden; ***the (three) Fates,*** die Nornen, Parzen, Schicksalsgöttinnen (*pl.*). **fated,** *adj.* vom Schicksal verhängt *or* bestimmt; dem Verderben *or* Untergang geweiht, dem Schicksal verfallen. **fateful,** *adj.* verhängnisvoll, schicksalsschwer, schicksalhaft, Schicksals–; unheilverkündend, prophetisch.

fat|head, *s.* (*coll.*) der Dummkopf, Trottel. **–headed,** *adj.* (*coll.*) dumm, dickköpfig.

father [ˈfɑːðə], **1.** *s.* der Vater; (*R.C.*) Pater; ***adoptive –,*** der Adoptivvater; ***Father Christmas,*** der Weihnachtsmann; ***city –s,*** Stadtälteste (*pl.*); ***– confessor,*** der Beichtvater; ***the early –s,*** die Kirchenväter; ***from – to son,*** von Geschlecht zu Geschlecht; ***be gathered to one's –s,*** zu seinen Vätern versammelt werden; ***the Holy Father,*** der Papst; ***like – like son,*** der Apfel fällt nicht weit vom Stamm; ***Father Time,*** Chronos; (*Prov.*) ***the wish is – to the thought,*** der Wunsch ist der Vater des Gedankens; ***your –,*** Ihr (Herr) Vater. **2.** *v.t.* zeugen, Vater werden von; (*fig.*) erzeugen, ins Leben rufen, hervorbringen; väterlich betreuen, verantwortlich sein für; ***– a cause,*** sich (*Acc.*) einer S. annehmen; sich (*Acc.*) zu einer S. *or* als Urheber einer S. bekennen; ***– a child upon him,*** ihm ein Kind zuschreiben; ***– s.th. upon him,*** ihm etwas zuschieben *or* in die Schuhe schieben.

father-figure, *s.* geistiger Vater. **fatherhood,** *s.* die Vaterschaft. **father|-in-law,** *s.* der Schwiegervater. **–land,** *s.* das Vaterland. **fatherless,** *adj.* vaterlos. **fatherliness,** *s.* die Väterlichkeit. **fatherly,** *adj.* väterlich.

fathom [ˈfæðəm], **1.** *s.* die Klafter, der Faden. **2.** *v.t.* loten, sondieren, (*usu. fig.*) abmessen, ergründen, erforschen, erfassen, verstehen, eindringen in (*Acc.*). **fathomable,** *adj.* meßbar; ergründlich. **fathomless,** *adj.* unergründlich, bodenlos.

fatigue [fəˈtiːg], **1.** *s.* 1. die Ermüdung, Ermattung, Erschöpfung; schwere Arbeit, die Strapaze; (*Tech.*) Ermüdung (*of materials*); 2. (*Mil.*) der Arbeitsdienst. **2.** *v.t.* ermüden, erschöpfen. **3.** *v.i.* ermüden, erschöpft werden. **fatigue|-dress,** *s.* (*Mil.*) die Arbeitskleidung, der Drillichanzug. **--party,** *s.* (*Mil.*) das Arbeitskommando. **--test,** *s.* die Ermüdungsprobe. **fatiguing,** *adj.* ermüdend, mühsam.

fatling [ˈfætliŋ], *s.* junges Masttier. **fatness,** *s.* 1. die Fettigkeit, Öligkeit; 2. Dicke, Fettheit, Beleibtheit (*of a p.*), (*fig.*) Fruchtbarkeit, Ergiebigkeit. **fatstock,** *s.* das Mastvieh.

fatten [fætn], **1.** *v.t.* mästen. **2.** *v.i.* fett werden, sich mästen (***on,*** von), (*fig.*) sich bereichern. **fattening,** *s.* das Mästen. **fattiness,** *s. See* **fatness, 1. fattish,** *adj.* etwas *or* ziemlich dick *or* fett. **fatty, 1.** *adj.* fettig, fetthaltig, fettartig; ***– acid,*** die Fettsäure; ***– degeneration,*** die Verfettung; ***– heart,*** die Herzverfettung; ***– tissue,*** das Fettgewebe. **2.** *s.* (*coll.*) das Dickchen.

fatuity [fəˈtjuːiti], *s.* die Albernheit, Dummheit, Einfältigkeit. **fatuous** [ˈfætjuəs], *adj.* albern, einfältig, dumm.

faucal [fɔːkl], *adj.* Kehl–, Rachen–. **fauces** [ˈfɔːsiːz], *pl.* der Rachen, Schlund.

faucet [ˈfɔːsit], *s.* (*esp. Am.*) der (Wasser)hahn, (Faß)zapfen.

faugh! [fɔː], *int.* pfui!

fault [fɔːlt], **1.** *s.* 1. der Mangel, Fehler; ***find –,*** tadeln, mißbilligen, kritteln, nörgeln; ***find – with,*** etwas auszusetzen haben an (*Dat.*); ***to a –,*** bis zum Übermaß; ***generous to a –,*** allzu freigebig; 2. der Fehltritt, das Vergehen; der Irrtum, das Versehen,

Verschulden, die Schuld; ***it is my –,*** ich habe die Schuld, es ist meine Schuld; ***be at –,*** im Unrecht sein, zu tadeln sein; sich irren, auf falscher Fährte sein; ***commit a –,*** sich versehen, einen Fehler machen; 3. (*Hunt.*) verlorene Spur, (*Elec.*) die Störung, der (Leitungs)fehler, fehlerhafte Isolierung; (*Tech.*) die Störung, der Defekt; (*Geol.*) (Schichten)bruch, die Kluft, Spalte, Verwerfung; 4. (*Tenn.*) der Fehler. **2.** *v.t. See* ***find – with.***

fault|-finder, *s.* der Besserwisser, Tadler, Krittler, Nörgler. **--finding,** *s.* das Schulmeistern, die Besserwisserei, Krittelei, Nörgelei. **faultiness,** *s.* die Fehlerhaftigkeit. **faulting,** *s.* (*Geol.*) die Verwerfung, Verschiebung, Bruchbildung, **faultless,** *adj.* fehlerfrei, fehlerlos, untadelig, tadellos. **faultlessness,** *s.* die Fehlerlosigkeit, Tadellosigkeit. **fault-line,** *s.* (*Geol.*) die Verwerfungslinie. **faultsman,** *s.* (*Tele.*) der Störungssucher. **faulty,** *adj.* fehlerhaft, mangelhaft, unvollkommen, (*Tech.*) schadhaft, Fehl–.

faun [fɔ:n], *s.* der Faun.

fauna [ˈfɔ:nə], *s.* die Fauna; (Abhandlung über) die Tierwelt.

fauteuil [foˈtə:i], *s.* der Lehnsessel; (*Theat.*) Sperrsitz.

faux-pas [ˈfouˈpɑ:], *s.* der Fehltritt, Mißgriff, die Taktlosigkeit, der Schnitzer, Verstoß.

favor, *etc.* (*Am.*) *see* **favour.**

favour [ˈfeivə], **1.** *s.* 1. die Gunst, Gnade, Gewogenheit, das Wohlwollen; ***be in – of,*** einverstanden sein mit; ***be (high) in his –*** or ***in – with him,*** bei ihm (sehr) gut angeschreiben sein, bei ihm in (besonderer) Gunst stehen; ***in his –,*** zugunsten von ihm, zu seinen Gunsten; (*Comm.*) ***balance in your –,*** Saldo zu Ihren Gunsten; ***look with – on,*** mit Wohlwollen betrachten; ***out of –,*** in Ungnade gefallen; ***bestow one's –s,*** (*of a woman*) ihre Liebe *or* Neigung schenken (*on, Dat.*); ***curry –,*** sich einschmeicheln (***with,*** bei); ***find – in his eyes*** or ***with him,*** bei ihm Gnade *or* Gunst finden; ***grant him a –,*** ihm eine Gunst gewähren; 2. der Gefallen, die Gefälligkeit, Gunstbezeigung; Genehmigung, Erlaubnis; ***do me the – to . . .,*** tun Sie mir den Gefallen und . . .; (*Comm.*) ***your – of the 20th inst.,*** Ihr geehrtes Schreiben vom 20. d. Mts; ***by – of,*** mit gütiger Erlaubnis von, überreicht von; ***ask him a –*** or ***ask a – of him,*** ihn um einen Gefallen bitten, von ihm eine Gefälligkeit erbitten; ***ask for –s,*** besondere Ansprüche stellen; ***I request the – of your company,*** ich beehre mich, Sie einzuladen; (*Comm.*) ***the – of an early answer is requested,*** um gefällige baldige Antwort wird gebeten; 3. der Schutz, die Unterstützung, Hilfe, Begünstigung, Bevorzugung, der Vorteil; ***under – of night,*** unter dem Schutze *or* mit Hilfe der Nacht; ***without fear or –,*** unparteiisch; 4. die Bandschleife, Rosette, das Angebinde. **2.** *v.t.* begünstigen, bevorzugen, vorziehen; gewogen *or* geneigt sein, günstig gesinnt sein (*Dat.*); unterstützen, bestätigen, bekräftigen (*opinion etc.*); ***the child –s his father,*** das Kind ähnelt seinem Vater; ***– him with,*** ihm schenken *or* verehren (*Acc.*); ihm die Ehre geben (*Gen.*), ihn beehren mit; ***– me with an answer,*** antworten Sie mir gefälligst! ***– us with a song,*** geben Sie uns ein Lied zum besten!

favourable [ˈfeivərəbl], *adj.* vorteilhaft, günstig (***to, for,*** für); geneigt, gewogen, günstig gesinnt (***to,*** *Dat.*); vielversprechend, dienlich, förderlich (*to, Dat.*); ***– balance of trade,*** aktive Handelsbilanz; ***– reply,*** bejahende *or* zustimmende Antwort; ***– terms,*** günstige Preise. **favoured** [–vəd], *adj.* begünstigt; (*Comm.*) ***– by,*** überreicht von; ***the – few,*** die wenigen Begünstigten; ***ill––,*** häßlich; ***well––,*** wohlgestaltet, hübsch. **favourite** [–rit], **1.** *s.* 1. der Günstling; Liebling, der (*or* die) Liebste; 2. (*Spt.*) mutmaßlicher Sieger, der Favorit. **2.** *attrib. adj.* Lieblings–. **favouritism,** *s.* die Günstlingswirtschaft; Bevorzugung, Begünstigung.

[1]**fawn** [fɔ:n], **1.** *s.* das Rehkalb, (Dam)kitz; die Rehfarbe, das Bisterbraun. **2.** *v.t.* (*v.i.*) (Kitze) werfen *or* setzen. **3.** *adj.* rehfarbig, bisterbraun.

[2]**fawn,** *v.i.* schwänzeln, (schweif)wedeln (*of dogs*); (*fig.*) sich anschmeicheln (***(up)on,*** bei), kriechen, katzbuckeln (vor (*Dat.*)), scharwenzeln (um).

fawn-coloured, *adj. See* [1]**fawn, 3.**

fawner [ˈfɔ:nə], *s.* der Schmeichler, Kriecher. **fawning,** *adj.* sich anschmeichelnd, schmeichlerisch, kriechend, kriecherisch; *see* [2]**fawn.**

fay [fei], *s.* die Fee, Elfe.

fealty [ˈfiəlti], *s.* (*Hist.*) die Mannestreue, Leh(e)nstreue; (*fig.*) Treue (***to,*** zu), Anhänglichkeit (an (*Acc.*)).

fear [fiə], **1.** *s.* die Furcht, Angst (***of,*** vor (*Dat.*)), Sorge, Befürchtung, Besorgnis (***for,*** um); *pl.* Befürchtungen (*pl.*), die Besorgnis; Ängstlichkeit, Furchtsamkeit; ***– of death, – of one's life,*** die Todesangst; ***– of the Lord,*** die Gottesfurcht, Ehrfurcht vor dem Herrn; ***go*** or ***stand in – of,*** sich fürchten vor (*Dat.*); ***have (one's) –s,*** besorgt sein; ***for – of,*** in der Furcht vor (*Dat.*), um . . . zu verhüten; ***for – of offending him,*** um ihn nicht zu kränken, damit er nicht gekränkt wird; (*coll.*) ***no –!*** keine Bange! auf keinen Fall! beileibe nicht! ***there is no – of that,*** das ist nicht zu befürchten. **2.** *v.t.* (be)fürchten (*a th.*), Angst haben *or* sich fürchten vor (*Dat.*) (*a p.*); ***I – his revenge,*** ich fürchte mich vor seiner Rache; ***there is nothing to –,*** da ist nichts zu befürchten. **3.** *v.i.* sich fürchten, Furcht haben; bangen, besorgt sein (***for,*** um); ***never –!*** keine Angst! sei unbesorgt!

fearful [ˈfiəful], *adj.* (*of a p.*) furchtsam, ängstlich; sehr besorgt, bange (***of,*** um); (*of a th.*) furchtbar, fürchterlich; (*coll.*) schrecklich, gräßlich, furchtbar. **fearfulness,** *s.* (*of a th.*) die Furchtbarkeit, Fürchterlichkeit, Schrecklichkeit; (*of a p.*) Furchtsamkeit, Ängstlichkeit. **fearless,** *adj.* furchtlos, unerschrocken. **fearlessness,** *s.* die Furchtlosigkeit. **fearsome** [–səm], *adj.* schrecklich, furchtbar.

feasance [ˈfi:zəns], *s.* (*Law*) die Erfüllung.

feasibility [fi:zəˈbiliti], *s.* die Durchführbarkeit, Tunlichkeit, Eignung, Möglichkeit. **feasible** [ˈfi:zəbl], *adj.* ausführbar, durchführbar, möglich, angängig, angänglich, tunlich, geeignet; wahrscheinlich.

feast [fi:st], **1.** *s.* das Fest, der Festtag, die Festlichkeit; das Festessen, Gastmahl, der Schmaus; (*fig.*) (Hoch)genuß; (*coll.*) ***a – for the eyes,*** die Augenweide. **2.** *v.t.* festlich bewirten; (*fig.*) ergötzen, erquicken; ***– one's eyes on,*** seine Augen weiden an (*Dat.*). **3.** *v.i.* schmausen (***on,*** von), sich gütlich tun; (*fig.*) sich ergötzen *or* laben *or* weiden (an (*Dat.*)).

feat [fi:t], *s.* die Heldentat, Großtat; das Kunststück, Glanzstück, Bravourstück, die Kraftleistung; ***– of arms,*** die Waffentat.

feather [ˈfeðə], **1.** *s.* die Feder (*pl.* das Gefieder), (*on helmet etc.*) der Federbusch; ***birds of a – flock together,*** gleich und gleich gesellt sich gern; ***fine –s make fine birds,*** Kleider machen Leute; ***fur and –,*** Wild und Federwild; ***a – in his cap,*** ehrende Auszeichnung; etwas, worauf er stolz sein kann; ***light as a –,*** federleicht; ***show the white –,*** sich feige zeigen, sich drücken; ***in full*** or ***high –,*** in gehobener Stimmung. **2.** *v.t.* befiedern; mit Federn bedecken *or* schmücken; (*Hunt.*) ***– a bird,*** einen Vogel anschießen; ***– one's nest,*** sein Schäfchen ins trockene bringen; ***– the oars,*** die Riemen flach *or* platt werfen.

feather|-bed, *s.* das Federunterbett. **--brained,** *adj.* unbesonnen, leichtsinnig. **feathered** [–ðəd], *adj.* befiedert, gefiedert; ***– game,*** das Federwild. **feather|-edge,** *s.* zugespitzte Kante. **--grass,** *s.* das Federgras. **feathering,** *s.* 1. das Gefieder; der Federschmuck; 2. (*rowing*) das Federn, (*propeller*) die Leerlaufstellung; 3. *pl.* (*Archit.*) Spitzen der Maßwerkverzierung (*pl.*). **feather|-star,** *s.* (*Zool.*) der Haarstern. **--stitch,** *s.* der Grätenstich, Hexenstich. **–weight,** *s.* (*Spt.*) das Federgewicht; (*fig.*) belanglose Person. **feathery,** *adj.* federartig, federleicht, federweich; gefiedert, befiedert.

feature [ˈfi:tʃə], **1.** *s.* 1. der Gesichtszug (*pl. also* die

Gesichtsbildung); charakteristischer Zug, der Grundzug, die Eigenschaft, das Kennzeichen, Merkmal, Charakteristische, Gepräge; ***distinctive –,*** das Unterscheidungsmerkmal; ***make a – of doing it,*** sich dabei besonders hervortun, es sich (*Dat.*) angelegen sein lassen zu tun; ***redeeming –,*** der Lichtblick; ***topographical –s,*** die Bodengestaltung; 2. (*newspaper*) die Beigabe, der Sonderartikel; 3. (*Films*) Hauptfilm, Spielfilm; (*Rad.*) ***– programme,*** die Hörfolge. **2.** *v.t.* kennzeichnen, charakterisieren, in den Hauptzügen schildern *or* darstellen; den Vorrang einräumen (*Dat.*), großartig aufziehen; (*Films*) in der Hauptrolle darstellen; ***film featuring*** . . ., der Film mit . . . in der Hauptrolle. **3.** *v.i.* (*of actor*) in der Hauptrolle erscheinen, (*of th.*) bezeichnend sein (***in,*** für), den Vorrang einnehmen (in (*Dat.*) *or* bei), als Hauptschlager dargestellt *or* hingestellt werden, in den Grundzügen geschildert werden. **featured,** *adj.* gestaltet, gebildet, geformt; (*fig.*) betont, hervorgehoben. **feature film,** *s.* der Spielfilm. **featureless,** *adj.* (*fig.*) ohne bestimmte Züge, einförmig, eintönig, monoton, uninteressant.

febrifuge [ˈfebrifjuːdʒ], **1.** *s.* das Fiebermittel. **2.** *adj.* fiebervertreibend. **febrile** [ˈfiːbrail], *adj.* fieberhaft, fiebernd, Fieber–.

February [ˈfebruəri], *s.* der Februar.

fecal, *etc.* (*Am.*) *see* **faecal.**

feckless [ˈfeklis], *adj.* hilflos, unfähig, untauglich, wirkungslos, nutzlos, wertlos.

feculence [ˈfekjuləns], *s.* das Trübe, Schlammige; die Hefe, der Bodensatz. **feculent,** *adj.* hefig, trübe, schlammig, schmutzig; (*fig.*) widerwärtig, ekelhaft.

fecund [ˈfekənd], *adj.* fruchtbar, schöpferisch; (*Biol.*) befruchtungsfähig. **fecundate** [–deit], *v.t.* befruchten, schwängern. **fecundation** [–ˈdeiʃən], *s.* die Befruchtung, Schwängerung. **fecundity** [fiˈkʌnditi], *s.* die Fruchtbarkeit, (*fig.*) befruchtende Kraft, die Gestaltungskraft, Schöpferkraft.

fed [fed], *imperf., p.p. of* **feed.**

federacy [ˈfedərəsi], *s.* der (Staaten)bund. **federal, 1.** *adj.* föderativ, Bundes–; (*Swiss*) eidgenössisch; (*Am. Civil War*) unionistisch; ***Federal Republic,*** die Bundesrepublik (*W. Germany*); ***– states,*** Bundesstaaten (*pl.*). **2.** *s. See* **federalist. federalism,** *s.* der Föderalismus; Partikularismus; (*Am. Hist.*) Zentralismus. **federalist,** *s.* der Föderalist. **federalize** [–laiz], *v.t.* verbünden. **federate, 1.** [–rit], *adj.* verbündet, Bundes–. **2.** [–reit], *v.t.* zu einem Staatenbund vereinigen, verbünden. **3.** [–reit], *v.i.* sich verbünden. **federation** [–ˈreiʃən], *s.* (*Pol.*) der Staatenbund, Bundesstaat; (*Comm.*) Bund, (Zentral)verband, Dachverband; die Vereinigung, das Bündnis. **federative** [–rətiv], *adj.* föderativ, bundesmäßig.

fee [fiː], **1.** *s.* die Gebühr; das Honorar, die Bezahlung, Vergütung, Belohnung; (*Law*) das Lehen, Lehngut, Erbgut; *pl.* Schulgeld; ***admission*** or ***entrance –,*** das Eintrittsgeld; (*Law*) ***retaining –,*** der Honorarvorschuß; ***– simple,*** das Eigengut, Allodialgut; ***hold in – (simple),*** zu eigen besitzen; ***estate in – tail,*** begrenztes Lehen. **2.** *v.t.* bezahlen, belohnen, honorieren; (*coll.*) ein Trinkgeld geben (*Dat.*), schmieren.

feeble [fiːbl], *adj.* schwach, schwächlich, hinfällig; (*fig.*) kraftlos, wirkungslos, (*as sound*) undeutlich, leise, schwach; (*coll. of a p.*) wankelmütig, unentschlossen; ***– joke,*** billiger Witz. **feeble|-minded,** *adj.* geistesschwach, schwachsinnig. **--mindedness,** *s.* der Schwachsinn, die Geistesschwäche. **feebleness,** *s.* die Schwäche, Entkräftung; Kraftlosigkeit, Wirkungslosigkeit; (*coll.*) Schwachheit, Unentschlossenheit, der Wankelmut.

feed [fiːd], **1.** *irr.v.t.* füttern (*cattle*); nähren (***on, with,*** mit), Nahrung zuführen (*Dat.*), zu essen geben (*Dat.*); ernähren (***on,*** von); versorgen, unterhalten (*a fire*); beschicken (*a furnace*); zuführen (*fuel, material*); (*coll.*) ***– the fishes,*** seekrank werden; ertrinken; ***– hope,*** Hoffnung nähren *or* Nahrung geben; ***– o.s.,*** ohne Hilfe essen, sich selbst nähren; ***– the eyes on,*** das Auge weiden an (*Dat.*); ***– up,*** mästen; (*sl.*) ***be fed up with,*** gründlich satt haben. **2.** *irr.v.i.* essen; (*beasts*) fressen, weiden; (*sl.*) futtern; leben, sich nähren ((***up***)***on,*** von); (*fig.*) ***– out of his hand,*** ihm aus der Hand fressen, gefügig sein. **3.** *s.* 1. das Füttern; (Vieh)futter, die Nahrung; (*coll.*) Mahlzeit, das Essen; 2. (*Tech.*) die Speisung, Beschickung, Zuführung, Zufuhr, der Zufluß (*of material*); Vorschub, Zuführer (*of a lathe etc.*).

feed|back, *s.* (*Rad.*) die Rückkopplung; (*Psych.*) Reafferenz; (*fig.*) Rückbeeinflussung, Rückwirkung. **--bag,** *s.* der Futtersack. **--belt,** *s.* (*machine gun*) der Patronengurt. **--cock,** *s.* der Speisehahn, Einfüllhahn. **--current,** *s.* (*Elec.*) der Speisestrom.

feeder [ˈfiːdə], *s.* der Esser, Fresser; Fütterer; Nebenfluß, Zufuhrkanal, Zuflußgraben, Bewässerungsgraben; (*Tech.*) die Speisevorrichtung, der Zuführer; (*Elec.*) die Speiseleitung; der Kinderlatz (*for infants*). **feeder-line,** *s.* (*Railw. etc.*) die Zubringerlinie; (*Elec.*) Speiseleitung.

feeding [ˈfiːdiŋ], *s.* die Nahrung(saufnahme), (*of cattle*) Fütterung, das Füttern; (*Tech.*) die Beschickung, Speisung, Zuleitung; (*dial.*) Weide, das Futter; ***bottle –,*** die Flaschennahrung; ***forcible –,*** die Zwangsernährung. **feeding|-bottle,** *s.* die Saugflasche. **--crane,** *s.* (*Railw.*) der Speisekran. **--cup,** *s.* die Schnabeltasse. **--hair,** *s.* (*Bot.*) das Futterhaar. **--stuff,** *s.* das Futter.

feed|-mechanism, *s.* (*Tech.*) das Vorschubgetriebe. **--pipe,** *s.* die Speiseröhre, das Zuleitungsrohr, Zuführungsrohr. **--pump,** *s.* die Speisepumpe. **--tank,** *s.* der Speisewasserbehälter, Zuflußbehälter. **--water,** *s.* das Speisewasser.

feel [fiːl], **1.** *irr.v.t.* (be)fühlen, betasten; merken, wahrnehmen, (ver)spüren, zu spüren bekommen, empfinden, erfahren, halten für; ***– the draught,*** den Zug merken; (*fig.*) unannehmliche Folgen zu spüren bekommen, in arger Bedrängnis sein; (*fig.*) ***– one's feet,*** Vertrauen fassen; ***– the helm,*** dem Ruder gehorchen; ***– one's legs,*** festen Boden unter den Füßen gewinnen *or* haben; ***– his pulse,*** ihm den Puls betasten; ***– one's way,*** sich tastend zurechtfinden, (*fig.*) vorsichtig vorgehen, sich einfühlen (***into,*** in (*Acc.*)); ***I felt it deeply,*** es schmerzte mich tief, ich empfand es sehr schmerzlich; ***– it one's duty,*** es für seine Pflicht halten. **2.** *irr.v.i.* fühlen (***for,*** nach), durch Fühlen feststellen; sich fühlen, das Gefühl haben von, sich bewußt werden (*Gen.*); Teilnahme empfinden (***with, for,*** für), Mitgefühl *or* Mitleid haben (mit), sich (*Dat.*) zu Herzen nehmen; den Eindruck geben, sich anfühlen; **(a)** (*with adjs. etc.*) (*coll.*) ***– bad about it,*** es bedauern; ***I – better,*** es geht mir besser; ***– certain,*** ein sicheres Gefühl haben; (*coll.*) ***– cheap,*** sich gedemütigt fühlen; ***I – cold,*** mich friert; ***how do you –?*** wie befinden Sie sich? ***– hungry,*** Hunger haben; ***– hurt,*** sich beleidigt fühlen; ***– inclined,*** sich geneigt fühlen, geneigt *or* aufgelegt sein; ***I – queer,*** mir ist sonderbar zumute; (*coll.*) ***not – quite o.s.,*** nicht ganz beieinander sein; (*coll.*) ***– quite o.s. again,*** sich ganz wiederhergestellt fühlen; ***it –s soft,*** es fühlt sich weich an; ***– strongly,*** entschiedene Ansichten haben (***about,*** über (*Acc.*)); ***– sure of,*** überzeugt sein von; ***I – warm,*** mir ist warm; **(b)** (*with preps. etc.*) ***how do you – about it?*** was meinen Sie dazu? ***– for,*** fühlen *or* greifen *or* tasten nach (*a th.*); (*Mil.*) Fühlung nehmen mit; ***we – for them,*** wir fühlen mit ihnen, sie dauern uns sehr, sie tun uns leid; (*coll.*) ***I do not – up to much,*** ich bin nicht ganz auf der Höhe; ***I do not – up to work,*** ich fühle mich der Arbeit nicht gewachsen; ***I do not – like work,*** ich habe keine Lust zur Arbeit; ***I know what it –s like to be poor,*** ich weiß, was es heißt, arm zu sein; ***I – as if I shall stifle,*** es ist mir, als wenn ich ersticke; ***it made itself felt,*** es machte sich fühlbar. **3.** *s.* das Gefühl, die Empfindung; ***the – of the cloth,*** der Griff des Stoffes; ***a homely –,*** anheimelnde Stimmung *or* Atmosphäre; ***it is rough to the –,*** es fühlt sich rauh an, es ist dem Anfühlen nach rauh.

feeler [ˈfiːlə], *s.* (*Ent., fig.*) der Fühler, (*Ent.*) das Fühlhorn; (*fig.*) der Versuchsballon; (*fig.*) ***put*** or

throw out a –, auf den Busch klopfen, einen Fühler ausstrecken; (*Tech.*) ***– gauge***, die Fühl(er)-lehre. **feeling, 1.** *adj.* fühlend, mitfühlend, gefühlvoll. **2.** *s.* das Gefühl, der Gefühlssinn; die Rührung, Erregung; Empfindung, Stimmung, Haltung, der Gefühlseindruck, die Aufregung; ***good –***, das Wohlwollen, Entgegenkommen; ***hard –***, der Groll, das Ressentiment; ***ill –***, der Unwille, Verdruß, die Verstimmung; ***man of –***, Mann von Gefühl; ***hurt his –s***, ihn kränken *or* verletzen, ihm weh tun; *–(s)* ***ran high***, die Gemüter erregten *or* erhitzten sich; ***have strong –s about it***, aus innerer Überzeugung dazu Stellung nehmen.

feet, *pl. of* **foot.**

feign [fein], *v.t.* simulieren, (vor)heucheln, vortäuschen, vorgeben; ***– sickness***, sich krank stellen. **feigned,** *adj.* simuliert, verstellt, vorgeblich, fingiert, Schein–. **feigning,** *s.* die Verstellung, Heuchelei.

feint [feint], **1.** *s.* (*Fenc., fig.*) die Finte; das Täuschungs– *or* Ablenkungsmanöver, der Scheinangriff; (*fig.*) die Verstellung. **2.** *v.i.* fintieren.

feldspar ['feldspɑ:], *s. See* **felspar.**

felicitate [fi'lisiteit], *v.t.* gratulieren (*Dat.*), beglückwünschen (***upon***, zu); (*obs.*) beglücken. **felicitation** [–'teiʃən], *s.* der Glückwunsch. **felicitous,** *adj.* glücklich; gut gewählt, treffend (*expressions*). **felicity,** *s.* (*rare*) das Glück, die Glückseligkeit; (*usu.*) treffender Ausdruck, glücklicher Griff *or* Einfall; die Trefflichkeit, Gefälligkeit (*of expression etc.*), Sicherheit (*in doing*).

feline ['fi:lain], *adj.* katzenartig, Katzen–.

[1]**fell** [fel], *v.t.* 1. fällen (*trees*); niederstrecken (*men*); 2. (*Sewing*) kappen, (ein)säumen, umnähen.

[2]**fell,** *adj.* (*Poet.*) grausam, grimmig; ***at one – swoop***, auf einen Hieb *or* Streich.

[3]**fell,** *s.* (*dial.*) der Hügel, das Moorland, Hügelland.

[4]**fell,** *s.* das Fell, die (Tier)haut, der Balg.

[5]**fell,** *imperf. of* **fall.**

fellah ['felə], *s.* (*pl.* **-een** [–'hi:n]) der Fellache.

[1]**feller** ['felə], *s.* (*coll.*) der Bursche, Kerl.

[2]**feller,** *s.* der (Holz)fäller; *see* [1]**fell.**

felling ['feliŋ], *s.* der Einschlag, das Fällen (*of trees*).

felloe ['felou], *s.* die Felge, der Radkranz.

fellow ['felou], *s.* 1. der Gefährte (die Gefährtin), der Genosse (die Genossin), der (die) Kamerad(in); der Mitmensch, Zeitgenosse; (*Univ. etc.*) das Mitglied einer Körperschaft; (*coll.*) der Kerl, Bursch(e), Mensch; ***this – of a barber***, dieser Kerl von Barbier; ***cunning –***, schlauer Bursche; ***my dear –***, lieber Freund; ***my good –***, lieber Mann; ***fine*** or ***good –***, guter *or* netter Kerl, famoser Mensch; (*coll.*) ***he's hail – well met with everyone***, er steht mit allen *or* jedem auf du und du; (*coll.*) ***let a – alone!*** laß mich in Frieden! ***odd –***, komischer Kauz; ***old –***, alter Junge, altes Haus; ***poor –***, armer Kerl; 2. das Gegenstück, das *or* der *or* die Dazugehörige; ***two shoes that are not –s***, zwei unzusammengehörige Schuhe; ***where is the – of this glove?*** wo ist der andere Handschuh? ***this man has not his –***, dieser Mann hat nicht seinesgleichen.

fellow|-being, *s.* der Mitmensch. **--citizen,** *s.* der Mitbürger. **--countryman,** *s.* der Landsmann. **--creature,** *s.* der Mitmensch. **--feeling,** *s.* das Mitgefühl, Zusammengehörigkeitsgefühl. **--member,** *s.* der Parteigenosse. **--men,** *pl.* Mitmenschen (*pl.*). **--passenger,** *s.* der Reisegefährte, Mitreisende(r). **--prisoner,** *s.* Mitgefangene(r).

fellowship ['felouʃip], *s.* 1. die Gemeinschaft, Kameradschaft, Zusammengehörigkeit, gegenseitige Verbundenheit; ***good –***, die Geselligkeit, Gemütlichkeit; 2. die (Interessen)gemeinschaft, Gesellschaft, Brüderschaft, Körperschaft; 3. das Universitätsstipendium.

fellow|-soldier, *s.* der Mitkämpfer, Waffenbruder, (Kriegs)kamerad. **--student,** *s.* der Kommilitone. **--sufferer,** *s.* der Leidensgefährte. **--traveller,** *s.* 1. der Reisegefährte; 2. (*coll.*) (kommunistischer) Mitläufer.

felly ['feli], *s. See* **felloe.**

felo-de-se ['fi:loudisi:], *s.* der Selbstmörder; Selbstmord.

felon ['felən], **1.** *s.* der (Schwer)verbrecher. **2.** *adj.* (*Poet.*) grausam. **felonious** [fi'louniəs], *adj.* verbrecherisch, mit böser Absicht. **felony,** *s.* schweres Verbrechen, das Schwerverbrechen; (*Hist.*) der Bruch der Lehnstreue, die Felonie.

felspar ['felspɑ:], *s.* der Feldspat. **felspathic** [–'spæθik], *adj.* Feldspat–.

[1]**felt** [felt], **1.** *imperf., p.p. of* **feel. 2.** *adj.* ***– want***, dringendes Erfordernis, ausgesprochener Mangel.

[2]**felt, 1.** *s.* der Filz; ***carpet –***, die Teppichunterlage; ***– hat***, der Filzhut; ***roofing –***, die Dachpappe. **2.** *v.t.* (ver)filzen; ***– a roof***, ein Dach mit Dachpappe überziehen; ***–ed cloth***, das Filztuch.

felucca [fe'lʌkə], *s.* (*Naut.*) die Feluke.

female ['fi:meil], **1.** *adj.* weiblich; ***– child***, das Mädchen; ***– companion***, die Begleiterin; ***– dog***, die Hündin; ***– friend***, die Freundin; ***– labour***, die Frauenarbeit; (*Tech.*) ***– screw***, die Schraubenmutter; ***– servant***, die Magd, das Dienstmädchen; ***– slave***, die Sklavin; ***– student***, die Studentin; (*Tech.*) ***– thread***, das Muttergewinde. **2.** *s.* das Weib, die Frau, das Mädchen, (*pej.*) Weib(sbild), Frauenzimmer; Weibchen (*of beasts etc.*).

feme [fem], *s.* (*Law*) die (Ehe)frau; ***– covert***, verheiratete Frau; ***– sole***, unverheiratete Frau.

feminine ['feminin], **1.** *adj.* weiblich (*also Gram.*), Frauen–; fraulich, zart, sanft; weibisch, unmännlich (*of men*); (*Metr.*) ***– ending***, weiblicher Endreim. **2.** *s.* (*Gram.*) das Femininum, weibliches Geschlecht. **femininity** [–'niniti], *s.* die Fraulichkeit, Weiblichkeit. **feminism,** *s.* das Frauenrechtlertum. **feminist,** *s.* der (die) Frauenrechtler(in).

femoral ['femərəl], *adj.* Oberschenkel–. **femur** ['fi:mə], *s.* (*pl.* **-s, femora**) der Oberschenkel-(knochen), das (Ober)schenkelbein.

fen [fen], *s.* der Sumpf, das Moor, Marschland; *pl.* Niederungen (*pl.*). **fen-berry,** *s.* die Moosbeere.

[1]**fence** [fens], **1.** *s.* der Zaun, die Umzäunung, Einzäunung, Einfriedung, das Gehege; (*Spt.*) die Hürde; das Hindernis, (*Tech.*) Schutzgatter; ***sit on*** (*Am.* ***ride***) ***the –***, sich neutral verhalten, abwarten, unentschlossen sein. **2.** *v.t.* einhegen, einfrieden, einzäunen; (*fig.*) verteidigen, schützen, sichern; ***– about, – in, – off, – round***, einzäunen, umzäunen, umgeben.

[2]**fence, 1.** *v.i.* fechten; (*fig.*) abwehren, parieren, ausweichen; Spiegelfechterei treiben. **2.** *v.t.* ***– off***, abwehren, abhalten, absperren.

[3]**fence,** *s.* (*coll.*) der Hehler.

fenceless ['fenslis], *adj.* offen, uneingezäunt; (*Poet.*) wehrlos. **fence-month,** *s.* die Schonzeit.

fencer ['fensə], *s.* der Fechter, Fechtmeister.

fencible ['fensibl], **1.** *adj.* (*Scots*) verteidigungsfähig, wehrfähig. **2.** *s.* (*Hist.*) der Landwehrsoldat; *pl.* die Landwehr, Miliz.

[1]**fencing** ['fensiŋ], *s.* die Einzäunung, Einfriedigung; das Zaunmaterial; (*collect.*) Zäune (*pl.*).

[2]**fencing,** *s.* das Fechten, die Fechtkunst. **fencing| club,** *s.* der Fechtverein. **--foil,** *s.* das Florett. **--gloves,** *pl.* die Fechthandschuhe.

fend [fend], **1.** *v.t.* (***– off***) abwehren, abhalten (***from***, von); (*Naut.*) abscheren. **2.** *v.i.* ***– for***, sorgen für; ***– for o.s.***, sich allein durchschlagen. **fender,** *s.* der Kaminvorsetzer; die Schutzvorrichtung, das Schutzholz, Schutzbrett, Schutzblech; (*Railw.*) der Stoßfänger; (*Am. Motor.*) das Schutzblech, der Kotflügel; (*Naut.*) Fender.

fenestral [fi'nestrəl], *adj.* Fenster–. **fenestrate** [–it], *adj.* (*Bot., Zool.*) mit kleinen Löchern. **fenestration** [fenis'treiʃən], *s.* (*Archit.*) das Fensterwerk, die Fensteranlage; (*Med.*) der Fensterverband.

Fenian ['fi:niən], **1.** *s.* (*Hist.*) der Fenier. **2.** *adj.* fenisch.

fenman ['fenmən], *s.* der Marschlandbewohner.

fennel [fenl], *s.* (*Bot.*) der Fenchel. **fennel-flower,** *s.* der Schwarzkümmel, Gretchen im Busch (*n.*).

fenny ['feni], *adj.* sumpfig, Sumpf–, Moor–.

feoff [fef], *s. See* **fief. feoffee** [fe'fi:], *s.* (*Law*) Belehnte(r). **feoffer,** *s.* der Lehnsherr. **feoffment,** *s.* die Belehnung. **feoffor,** *s. See* **feoffer.**

feral ['fiərəl], *adj.* unkultiviert, wild(lebend), verwildert.

feretory ['ferətəri], *s.* (*R.C.*) der Reliquienschrein.

ferial ['fiəriəl], *adj.* Alltags–, (*Eccl.*) Wochentags–.

ferment, 1. ['fə:mənt], *s.* das Gärmittel, Enzym, der Gärungserreger, Gärstoff; (*fig.*) die Gärung, Wallung, der Aufruhr. **2.** [fə'ment], *v.t.* gären lassen, in Gärung bringen; (*fig.*) erregen. **3.** [fə'ment], *v.i.* gären, in Gärung sein (*also fig.*). **fermentable** [–'mentəbl], *adj.* gär(ungs)fähig. **fermentation** [–'teiʃən], *s.* die Gärung, der Gärungsprozeß; (*fig.*) die Wallung, das Aufbrausen. **fermenting** [–'mentiŋ], **1.** *adj.* gärend. **2.** *s.* das Gären; – *vat,* der Gärbottich.

fern [fə:n], *s.* der Farn, das Farnkraut. **fernery,** *s.* die Farnkrautpflanzung. **ferny,** *adj.* mit Farn(kraut) überwachsen; farnartig.

ferocious [fə'rouʃəs], *adj.* wild, grausam; bissig (*as a dog*); – ***animals,*** Raubtiere. **ferocity** [fə'rɔsiti], *s.* die Wildheit, Grausamkeit.

ferrate ['fereit], *s.* (*Chem.*) eisensaures Salz. **ferreous** ['feriəs], *adj.* eisenhaltig.

ferret ['ferit], **1.** *s.* das Frettchen. **2.** *v.t.* – ***out,*** herausjagen (*rabbits*); (*fig.*) ausforschen, aufspüren, aufstöbern, auskundschaften. **3.** *v.i.* frettieren, mit Frettchen jagen; (*fig.*) – ***about,*** (herum)suchen (***for***, nach).

ferric ['ferik], *adj.* (*Chem.*) Ferri–, Eisen–; – ***compound,*** die Eisenoxydverbindung; – ***oxide,*** das Eisenoxyd. **ferriferous** [fe'rifərəs], *adj.* eisenhaltig, eisenschüssig, eisenführend.

ferro– ['ferou], *pref.* Eisen–. **–-concrete,** *s.* der Eisenbeton. **–type,** *s.* (*Phot.*) die Ferrotype.

ferrous ['ferəs], *adj.* (*Chem.*) Eisen–, Ferro–; – ***oxide,*** (schwefelsaures) Eisenoxydul. **ferruginous** [fe'ru:dʒinəs], *adj. See* **ferriferous**; rostfarbig.

ferrule ['ferul], *s.* die Zwinge (*on a stick*); (*Tech.*) Buchse, der Metallring.

ferry ['feri], **1.** *s.* 1. die Fähre, das Fährboot, Fährschiff; ***train*** –, das Trajekt, die Eisenbahnfähre; 2. (*Law*) Fährrecht. **2.** *v.t., v.i.* (hin)übersetzen; (*Av.*) überführen. **ferry|-boat,** *s. See* **ferry, 1,** 1. – **command,** *s.* (*Av.*) das Überführungskommando, Abholkommando. **–man,** *s.* der Fährmann.

fertile ['fə:tail], *adj.* fruchtbar, reich, ergiebig (***in***, an (*Dat.*)), (*as an egg*) befruchtet; (*fig.*) schöpferisch. **fertility** [fə'tiliti], *s.* die Fruchtbarkeit, Ergiebigkeit, der Reichtum (*also fig.*). **fertilization** [fə:tilai'zeiʃən], *s.* die Befruchtung, Fruchtbarmachung; (*of soil*) Düngung, das Düngen; (*Bot.*) die Bestäubung. **fertilize** [–tilaiz], *v.t.* befruchten, fruchtbar machen; (*soil*) düngen; (*Bot.*) bestäuben. **fertilizer,** *s.* das Düngemittel, der (Kunst)dünger.

ferule ['feru:l], **1.** *s.* der Stock, die Rute; das Lineal. **2.** *v.t.* züchtigen, mit der Rute schlagen.

fervency ['fe:vənsi], *s.* die Glut, Inbrunst, das Feuer, der Eifer. **fervent,** *adj.* glühend, feurig, inbrünstig, heftig; – ***prayer,*** inniges Gebet; – ***in spirit,*** eifrigen Geistes; – ***zeal,*** glühender Eifer.

fervid ['fə:vid], *adj.* (*esp. Poet.*) glühend (heiß), brennend; feurig, hitzig, leidenschaftlich (erregt), eifrig. **fervour** [–və], *s.* die Hitze, der (Feuer)eifer; die Glut, Leidenschaft, Inbrunst; – ***of love,*** die Liebesglut.

fescue ['feskju:], *s.* (*Bot.*) (*also* – ***grass***) der Wiesenschwingel, das Schwingelgras.

fesse [fes], *s.* (*Her.*) der (Quer)balken.

festal [festl], *adj.* (*Poet.*) festlich, Fest–.

fester ['festə], **1.** *v.i.* schwären, eitern; verwesen, verfaulen, modern; (*fig.*) nagen, um sich fressen. **2.** *v.t.* zum Schwären *or* Eitern bringen. **3.** *s.* das Geschwür, eiternde Wunde, die Fistel, Pustel.

festival ['festivl], *s.* der Festtag, das Fest; Festspiele (*pl.*), Festspieltage (*pl.*), Festspielwochen (*pl.*); ***Salzburg*** –, Salzburger Festspiele; – ***performance,*** das Festspiel. **festive,** *adj.* festlich, fröhlich, heiter. **festivity** [–'tiviti], *s.* das Fest, die Festlichkeit, festlicher Anlaß; festliche Stimmung, die Feststimmung, Fröhlichkeit.

festoon [fes'tu:n], **1.** *s.* die Girlande; das Blumengewinde; (*Archit.*) Fruchtgehänge, Laubgehänge. **2.** *v.t.* mit Girlanden behängen *or* schmücken.

fetal, (*Am.*) *see* **foetal.**

fetch [fetʃ], **1.** *v.t.* holen, heranholen, herbeiholen, abholen; hervorholen (***from***, aus); einbringen, eintragen, erzielen; fließen lassen (*tears, blood*); (*coll.*) – ***him a blow,*** ihm einen Schlag versetzen; – ***a deep breath,*** tief Atem holen, tief einatmen; – ***a high price,*** einen hohen Preis einbringen *or* erzielen; – ***down,*** herunterholen, niederschießen (*bird, plane etc.*); – ***out,*** herausholen (***from***, aus), zum Vorschein bringen; – ***up,*** aufholen, einholen (*distance*); ausspeien (*food*). **2.** *v.i.* (*Naut.*) Kurs nehmen; (*Hunt.*) apportieren; – ***and carry,*** niedrige Dienste verrichten, Handlanger sein; – ***up,*** stillstehen, zum Stehen kommen; – ***up at,*** erreichen, gelangen nach. **3.** *s.* (*coll.*) der Kniff, Kunstgriff, die Finte. **fetching,** *adj.* (*coll.*) einnehmend, reizend, fesselnd, bezaubernd.

fête [feit], **1.** *s.* das Fest, die Festlichkeit, (*esp.*) das Gartenfest. **2.** *v.t.* feiern (*an occasion*), festlich bewirten (*a p.*).

fetid ['fetid], *adj.* stinkend, übelriechend.

fetish ['fetiʃ], *s.* der Fetisch, das Götzenbild. **fetishism,** *s.* der Götzendienst, die Fetischverehrung; (*Psych.*) der Fetischismus.

fetlock ['fetlɔk], *s.* die Köte, das Kötengelenk, Fesselgelenk; Hufhaar, Kötenhaar.

fetter ['fetə], **1.** *v.t.* fesseln; (*fig.*) zügeln, einschränken. **2.** *s.* (*usu. pl.*) die Fessel (*also fig.*); *pl.* (*fig.*) der Zwang, Hemmschuh.

fettle [fetl], *s.* (*coll.*) ***in good*** or ***fine*** –, in Form.

fetus, *s. See* **foetus.**

feu [fju:], (*Scots*) **1.** *s.* das Lehen, der Lehnbesitz. **2.** *v.t.* in Lehen geben (*land*).

[1]**feud** [fju:d], *s.* die Fehde.

[2]**feud,** *s.* (*Law*) das Lehen, Lehnsgut. **feudal,** *adj.* feudal, Lehns–; – ***system,*** das Feudalsystem. **feudalism,** *s.* der Feudalismus, das Feudalsystem. **feudality** [–'dæliti], *s.* die Lehnbarkeit; Lehnsverfassung, das Lehenswesen. **feudalize** [–laiz], *v.t.* lehnbar machen. **feudatory** [–təri], **1.** *s.* der Lehnsmann, Vasall. **2.** *adj.* lehnspflichtig, Lehns–.

feu-duty, *s.* (*Scots*) der Bodenzins.

feuilleton ['fə:itɔ̃], *s.* das Feuilleton, der Unterhaltungsteil (*of newspaper*).

fever ['fi:və], *s.* das Fieber; (*fig.*) die Erregung, Aufregung. **fevered,** *adj.* fiebrig, fiebernd; (*fig.*) fieberhaft, erregt, aufgeregt. **feverish,** *adj.* (*Med.*) fiebrig, fieberkrank; (*fig.*) fieberhaft, aufgeregt; ***be*** –, Fieber haben. **feverishness,** *s.* das Fieber; die Fieberhaftigkeit.

few [fju:], *pron., adj.* wenige; ***a*** –, ***some*** –, einige (wenige), ein paar; ***quite a*** –, (*coll.*) ***a good*** –, ziemlich viele, eine beträchtliche Anzahl; ***not a*** –, nicht wenige; – ***and far between,*** sehr selten; ***every*** – ***days,*** alle paar Tage; ***the chosen*** –, die wenigen Auserwählten; ***a select*** –, ein paar *or* einige Auserwählte; ***only a*** –, nur wenige. **fewer,** *pron., comp. adj.* weniger. **fewness,** *s.* geringe Anzahl.

fez [fez], *s.* der *or* das Fes.

fiancé [fi'ãsei], *s.* Verlobte(r), der Bräutigam. **fiancée,** *s.* die Braut, Verlobte.

fiasco [fi'æskou], *s.* der Mißerfolg, das Fiasko; die Blamage.

fiat ['faiæt], *s.* der Befehl, Machtspruch; (*Law*) die Ermächtigung.

fib [fib], **1.** *s.* (*coll.*) die Lüge, Flunkerei; ***tell a*** –, flunkern. **2.** *v.i.* lügen, flunkern. **fibber,** *s.* der Flunkerer.

fiber, (*Am.*) *see* **fibre.**

fibre ['faibə], *s.* die Faser, Fiber; (*collect.*) das Fasergefüge, die Textur; (*fig.*) der Charakter, die

Struktur; (*of a p.*) Charakterstärke, das Rückgrat. **fibre|board,** *s.* die Holzfaserplatte, Hartpappe. **--glass,** *s.* die Glasfiber, der Kunststoff. **fibreless,** *adj.* faserlos; (*fig.*) kraftlos.

fibril ['faibril], *s.* das Fäserchen; (*Bot.*) die Wurzelfaser. **fibrilation** [-'leiʃən], *s.* die Faserbildung; (*Med.*) das Flattern, Flimmern (*of heart*).

fibrin ['faibrin], *s.* der Faserstoff, das Fibrin. **fibroid, 1.** *adj.* faserartig, Faser–. **2.** *s.* (*Med.*) die Fasergeschwulst. **fibrositis** [-brə'saitis], *s.* der Muskelrheumatismus. **fibrous,** *adj.* faserig, faserartig, fibrinös; – ***membrane,*** die Faserhaut.

fibula ['fibjulə], *s.* (*pl.* **-e** [–li:], **-s**) das Wadenbein; (*Hist.*) die Fibel, Spange.

fichu ['fiʃu:], *s.* das Halstuch.

fickle [fikl], *adj.* wankelmütig, unbeständig, launisch, wandelbar. **fickleness,** *s.* der Wankelmut, die Unbeständigkeit.

fictile ['fiktail], *adj.* Ton–, tönern, irden; Töpfer(ei)–; – ***art,*** die Töpferkunst; – ***ware,*** das Steingut.

fiction ['fikʃən], *s.* die Erdichtung, (freie) Erfindung; die Prosadichtung, Erzählungsliteratur, Romane (*pl.*); (*Law, Phil.*) die Fiktion, (bloße) Annahme; ***work of*** –, der Roman. **fictional,** *adj.* erdichtet; Roman–, Erzählungs–. **fictitious** [–'tiʃəs], *adj.* (*Law*) fingiert, fiktiv, (bloß) angenommen, Schein–; unecht, nachgemacht; erdichtet, erfunden; (*Comm.*) – ***bill,*** der Reitwechsel, Kellerwechsel; – ***character,*** erfundene Person; – ***name,*** der Deckname; (*Law*) – ***person,*** juristische P.; – ***purchase,*** der Scheinkauf. **fictitiousness,** *s.* die Unechtheit, Falschheit.

fid [fid], *s.* (*Naut.*) das Schloßholz.

fiddle [fidl], **1.** *s.* **1.** (*coll.*) die Fiedel, Geige; ***play first*** (***second***) –, erste (zweite) Geige spielen; (*fig.*) die Hauptrolle (Nebenrolle) spielen; ***have a face as long as a*** –, ein langes *or* trauriges Gesicht machen; ***fit as a*** –, kerngesund; 2. (*sl.*) der Betrug, Schwindel. **2.** *v.i.* 1. geigen; 2. (*coll.*) tändeln, spielen; geschäftig sein, sich zu tun machen (***with,*** mit); (*sl.*) sich (*Dat.*) Übergriffe erlauben, nach Recht und Gerechtigkeit nicht fragen; – ***about,*** nichts vernünftiges tun, herumtändeln. **3.** *v.t.* auf der Geige spielen, fiedeln (*a tune*); (*sl.*) (auf)frisieren (*accounts*); – ***away,*** vertändeln (*time*).

fiddle|-bow, *s.* der Fiedelbogen. **--case,** *s.* der Geigenkasten. **--de-dee!** *int. See* ***fiddlesticks!*** **--faddle,** *s.* (*coll.*) die Lappalie, der Unsinn. **fiddler,** *s.* der Geiger, Fiedler. **fiddle|stick,** *s.* der Fiedel- *or* Geigenbogen; (*coll.*) ***–s!*** Unsinn! Quatsch! dummes Zeug! **--string,** *s.* die Geigensaite.

fiddling ['fidliŋ], *adj.* (*coll.*) unnütz, trivial, läppisch, fipsig.

fidelity [f(a)i'deliti], *s.* die Treue (*to,* zu *or* gegenüber); (*fig.*) Genauigkeit; das Festhalten (*to,* an (*Dat.*)), genaue Übereinstimmung (mit), getreue Wiedergabe (*Gen.*).

fidget ['fidʒit], **1.** *v.i.* unruhig sein, (herum)zappeln. **2.** *v.t.* beunruhigen, nervös machen. **3.** *s.* 1. der Zappelphilipp, unruhige P.; 2. (*usu. pl.*) nervöse Unruhe; (*coll.*) ***have the –s,*** kein Sitzfleisch haben. **fidgetiness,** *s.* die Unruhe, Nervosität, Zappelei. **fidgety,** *adj.* unruhig, nervös, zappelig.

fid-pin, *s.* (*Naut.*) der Marlspieker.

fiduciary [fi'dju:ʃiəri], **1.** *adj.* (*Law*) Treuhänder–; anvertraut, Vertrauens–; (*Comm.*) ungedeckt; – ***currency,*** das Kreditgeld; – ***issue,*** ungedeckte Notenausgabe. **2.** *s.* der Treuhänder, Vertrauensmann.

fie! [fai], *int.* pfui! – ***upon you!*** pfui über dich! schäme dich!

fief [fi:f], *s.* das Leh(e)n, Lehngut.

field [fi:ld], **1.** *s.* 1. das Feld (*also Her., Magnet.*), Ackerland, der Acker; (weite) Fläche, (*Mil.*) das (Schlacht)feld, (*Spt.*) (Spiel)feld, (*Min.*) Flöz; ***hold the*** –, das Feld behaupten; ***take the*** –, (*Mil.*) ins Feld rücken, den Kampf eröffnen; (*Spt.*) den Spielplatz betreten; ***in the*** –, (*Mil.*) im Felde, an der Front; (*Comm. etc.*) im Außendienst; (*Crick.*) als Angreifer; (*fig.*) im Wettbewerb; ***bring into the*** –, ins Gefecht bringen; 2. (*fig.*) das Gebiet, der Bereich; – ***of application,*** das Verwendungsgebiet; (*Artil.*) – ***of fire,*** das Schußfeld; (*Artil.*) – ***of traverse,*** der Schwenkungsbereich; – ***of vision*** or ***view,*** das Gesichtsfeld, Blickfeld; (*fig.*) der Gesichtskreis; 3. (*Spt.*) die Gesamtheit der Teilnehmer *or* Wettbewerber; ***back a horse against the*** –, auf ein Pferd gegen alle andern Renner setzen; 4. (*Comm. etc.*) Praxis, (praktischer) Einsatz, der Außendienst. **2.** *v.i.* (*Crick.*) als Angreifer *or* Fänger spielen. **3.** *v.t.* (*Crick.*) auffangen und zurückwerfen (*the ball*).

field|-allowance, *s.* die Kriegszulage. **--ambulance,** *s.* der Sanitätskrankenwagen. **--artillery,** *s.* die Feldartillerie. **--base,** *s.* (*baseball*) das Laufmal. **--battery,** *s.* (*Mil.*) die Feldbatterie. – **coil,** *s.* (*Elec.*) die Erregerspule. **--day,** *s.* (*Mil.*) die Felddienstübung; (*fig.*) ereignisvoller Tag. **--dressing,** *s.* der Notverband. – **dressing-station,** *s.* (*Mil.*) der Verbandplatz. **fielder,** *s.* (*Crick.*) der Angreifer, Fänger, Spieler der nichtschlagenden Mannschaft.

field| events, *pl.* (*Spt.*) Sprung– und Wurfwettspiele. **–fare,** *s.* (*Orn.*) die Wacholderdrossel, der Krammetsvogel (*Turdus pilaris*). **--glass(es),** *s.* (*pl.*) der Feldstecher, das Feldglas. **–gun,** *s. See* **–piece. --hospital,** *s.* das Feldlazarett. **--kitchen,** *s.* die Feldküche. **–marshal,** *s.* der Feldmarschall. **--mouse,** *s.* die Feldmaus. **--officer,** *s.* der Stabsoffizier. **–piece,** *s.* das Feldgeschütz. – **recording,** *s.* die Außenaufnahme (*tape*).

fieldsman ['fi:ldzmən], *s. See* **fielder.**

field|-sports, *pl.* der Sport im Freien. – **strength,** *s.* (*Elec.*) die Feldstärke. **--training,** *s.* (*Mil.*) die Geländeausbildung. – **trial(s),** *s.* (*pl.*) (*Hunt.*) die Hundeprobe. **--winding,** *s.* (*Elec.*) die Erregerwicklung. **–work,** *s.* (*oft. pl.*) (*Mil.*) die Feldschanze; Schanzarbeit. – **work,** *s.* (*fig.*) praktische Arbeit, der Außeneinsatz.

fiend [fi:nd], *s.* böser Feind, der Teufel; (*fig.*) Unhold, die Furie; (*coll.*) Besessene(r), Süchtige(r); (*coll.*) der Fex, Narr. **fiendish,** *adj.* teuflisch, unmenschlich; (*coll.*) verflucht, verflixt. **fiendishness,** *s.* teuflische Bosheit, die Grausamkeit, Unmenschlichkeit.

fierce [fiəs], *adj.* wild, grimmig, wütend, grausam; heftig, hitzig, ungestüm; grell (*of light*). **fierceness,** *s.* die Wildheit, Wut, Grimmigkeit; Heftigkeit, das Ungestüm.

fieriness ['faiərinis], *s.* die Hitze, das Feuer. **fiery,** *adj.* Feuer–, glühend, brennend; (*fig.*) feurig, hitzig, heftig, leidenschaftlich, unbändig (*as a horse*); – ***red,*** feuerrot; – ***temper,*** der Jähzorn.

fife [faif], **1.** *s.* die Querpfeife. **2.** *v.i.* auf der Querpfeife blasen, pfeifen.

fifteen [fif'ti:n], **1.** *num. adj.* fünfzehn. **2.** *s.* die Fünfzehn; (*Spt.*) Rugbymannschaft. **fifteenth, 1.** *num. adj.* fünfzehnt. **2.** *s.* das Fünfzehntel.

fifth [fifθ], **1.** *num. adj.* fünft. **2.** *s.* das Fünftel; (*Mus.*) die Quinte; (*Pol.*) – ***column,*** fünfte Kolonne; – ***columnist,*** das Mitglied der fünften Kolonne. **fifthly,** *adv.* fünftens.

fifties ['fiftiz], *pl.* die fünfziger Jahre; ***by*** –, zu Fünfzigen. **fiftieth** [–iiθ], **1.** *num. adj.* fünfzigst. **2.** *s.* das Fünfzigstel. **fifty, 1.** *num. adj.* fünfzig; ***–one,*** einundfünfzig. **2.** *s.* die Fünfzig. **fifty-fifty, 1.** *adj.* (*coll.*) fünfzigprozentig. **2.** *adv.* halbpart, (*coll.*) halb und halb, zu gleichen Teilen.

[1]**fig** [fig], **1.** *s.* (*coll.*) der Putz, die Ausrüstung; (*only in*) ***in full*** –, in vollem Wichs. **2.** *v.t.* – ***out,*** herausputzen.

[2]**fig,** *s.* die Feige; der Feigenbaum; (*fig.*) Pfifferling, Deut; ***a – for,*** zum Teufel mit . . ., was frage ich nach . . .? ***I don't care a – for it,*** ich mache mir nichts daraus.

fight [fait], **1.** *irr.v.i.* kämpfen, fechten; sich schlagen *or* raufen; (*fig.*) – ***against,*** sich widersetzen (*Dat.*); – ***back,*** sich zur Wehr setzen, widerstehen, abwehren; – ***for,*** kämpfen um, (*fig.*) verfechten; –

shy of, aus dem Wege gehen (*Dat.*), meiden; – *to the last ditch,* bis zum Letzten kämpfen. **2.** *irr.v.t.* kämpfen (mit *or* gegen); bekämpfen, sich schlagen mit; verfechten, verteidigen (*a question*); im Kampf führen (*troops, ships*); – *a battle,* eine Schlacht liefern, einen Kampf führen; – *one's own battles,* sich allein durchschlagen; – *a duel,* sich duellieren; – *a good fight,* sich wacker schlagen; – *a fire,* gegen ein Feuer kämpfen; – *him,* mit ihm kämpfen, sich mit ihm boxen *or* schlagen; (*fig.*) ihn bekämpfen, gegen ihn kämpfen; – *it out,* es ausfechten; – *a war,* einen Krieg führen; – *one's way,* sich durchschlagen. **3.** *s.* das Gefecht, der Kampf, das Treffen; der Streit, Konflikt; die Schlägerei; der Boxkampf; die Kampflust; *be full of* –, kampflustig sein; *hand-to-hand* –, das Handgemenge; *there is no – left in him,* er ist kampfmüde *or* abgekämpft; *there is – in him yet,* er ist noch kampffähig, er ist noch nicht geschlagen; *make a – for,* kämpfen um; *make a – of it,* sich kräftig zur Wehr setzen; *put up a good* –, sich wacker schlagen; *running* –, das Rückzugsgefecht; *show* –, sich zur Wehr setzen, nicht nachgeben; *stand-up* –, regelrechter Kampf.

fighter ['faitə], *s.* 1. der Kämpfer, Streiter, Krieger, Fechter; 2. (*Av.*) Jäger, Jagdflieger, das Jagdflugzeug; – *aircraft,* das Jagdflugzeug; – *escort,* der Jagdschutz; – *pilot,* der Jagdflieger; – *squadron,* die Jagdstaffel. **fighting, 1.** *attrib. adj.* Kampf–; – *chance,* die Aussicht auf Erfolg, Gewinnchance; – *cock,* der Kampfhahn; – *efficiency,* der Gefechtswert; – *equipment,* die Feldausrüstung; – *force,* die Kampftruppe; – *line,* die Front; (*Naut.*) – *top,* der Kommandoturm, Gefechtsmars. **2.** *s.* das Gefecht, der Kampf; *way of* –, die Kampfesart.

fig-leaf, *s.* das Feigenblatt.

figment ['figmənt], *s.* die Erdichtung; – *of one's imagination,* (reine) Erdichtung, das Produkt der Phantasie.

fig-tree, *s.* der Feigenbaum.

figurant ['figjurənt], *s.* der Chortänzer; Statist, stumme P. **figurante** [figu'rɑ:nt], *s.* die Chortänzerin, Statistin.

figurate [figjuərit], *adj.* (*esp. Mus.*) verziert. **figuration** [–'reiʃən], *s.* bildliche Darstellung, die Gestaltung, Formgebung; Gestalt, Form; (*Mus.*) Verzierung, Figuration. **figurative** [–rətiv], *adj.* figürlich, metaphorisch, (sinn)bildlich, übertragen; bilderreich. **figurativeness,** *s.* der Bilderreichtum; die (Sinn)bildlichkeit.

figure ['figə], **1.** *s.* 1. die Gestalt, Form, Figur (*also Geom., Math., Mus.*); der Charakter, die Person, Persönlichkeit (*in a play etc.*); – *of fun,* komische Figur, groteske P.; *lay* –, die Gliederpuppe; (*Geom.*) *solid* –, der Körper; *cut a poor* –, eine armselige Rolle spielen; *keep one's* –, nicht dick werden, eine gute Figur behalten; *make a – (in the world),* eine glänzende Rolle spielen; 2. die Abbildung, Tafel, Zeichnung, das Diagramm, Bild; (Stoff)muster; 3. Zahlzeichen, die Zahl, Ziffer, Nummer, Summe, der Betrag (*of money*); *be good at –s,* ein guter Rechner sein, tüchtig im Rechnen sein; *at a high* –, teuer; *at a low* –, billig; *Roman –s,* römische Zahlen; *run into three –s,* in die Hunderte gehen; 4. (*Danc., skating*) die (Tanz)figur, Tour; (*Rhet.*) Redewendung, Sprachfigur; – *of speech,* die Sprachfigur, Redewendung. **2.** *v.t.* 1. (ab)-bilden, gestalten, formen; (symbolisch) darstellen; – *to o.s.,* sich (*Dat.*) denken, sich *or* im Geist vorstellen; 2. mustern, blümen (*fabric*); (*Mus.*) figurieren; 3. (*Comm.*) mit Zahlen bezeichnen, mit Figuren versehen; 4. (*coll.*) – *out,* ausrechnen, berechnen; ausfindig machen, ausknobeln. **3.** *v.i.* 1. eine Rolle spielen, sich zeigen, auftreten, erscheinen (*as,* als); 2. (*coll. esp. Am.*) glauben, meinen; (*coll.*) – *on,* rechnen mit, zählen auf (*Acc.*), beabsichtigen, im Auge haben; – *out at,* veranschlagt werden auf.

figured ['figəd], *adj.* gemustert, geblümt (*fabric*); (*Mus.*) figuriert, verziert; (*Mus.*) – *bass,* bezifferter Baß, der Generalbaß. **figure|-head,** *s.* (*Naut.*) die Galionsfigur, der Bugschmuck; (*fig.*) das Aushängeschild, die Repräsentationsfigur, Puppe, der Strohmann. **--of-eight knot,** *s.* (*Naut.*) der Achterstich. **--skating,** *s.* der Eiskunstlauf.

figwort ['figwə:t], *s.* (*Bot.*) die Braunwurz.

filament ['filəmənt], *s.* die Faser, das Fäserchen, der Faden, das Fädchen; der Glühfaden (*of a lamp*); (*Rad.*) Heizfaden, die Kathode; (*Bot.*) der Staubfaden; (*Rad.*) – *battery,* die Heizbatterie; (*Rad.*) – *voltage,* die Heizspannung. **filamentous** [–'mentəs], *adj.* (haar)faserig, fadenartig; (*Bot.*) Faden–.

filbert ['filbət], *s.* die Haselnuß; der Hasel(nuß)-strauch.

filch [filtʃ], *v.t.* (*coll.*) mausen, klauen, stibitzen.

[1]**file** [fail], **1.** *s.* 1. das Aktenbündel, Aktenheft, die Sammelmappe, der Stoß (*of papers*); (Brief)-ordner, Registrator; *in the –, on (the)* –, geordnet, aufgereiht, unter den Akten; 2. (*Mil.*) die Reihe; *blank* –, halbe *or* blinde Rotte; *in* –, einer hinter dem anderen, im Gänsemarsch; *in double* –, zu zweien hintereinander; *rank and* –, Mannschaften (*pl.*); (*fig.*) die große Masse; *single* or *Indian* –, die Reihe zu einem Glied, der Gänsemarsch. **2.** *v.t.* aufreihen, gliedern, ordnen, heften, einregistrieren; – *away letters,* Briefe ablegen; – *a bill,* eine Klage vorlegen; – *a petition,* ein Gesuch einreichen, einen Antrag stellen. **3.** *v.i.* (*Mil.*) defilieren, in Reihe vorbeiziehen; – *in (out),* im Gänsemarsch *or* in Reih und Glied eintreten (austreten).

[2]**file, 1.** *s.* (*Tech.*) die Feile; *smooth* –, die Schlichtfeile. **2.** *v.t.* feilen; (*fig.*) zurechtfeilen, feilen an (*Dat.*), glätten (*style etc.*).

file| card, *s.* (*Tech.*) die Feilenbürste. – **clerk,** *s.* (*Am.*) der Registrator. – **copy,** *s.* die Aktenkopie. **--cutter,** *s.* der Feilenhauer. **--leader,** *s.* der Rottenführer, Vordermann.

filial ['filiəl], *adj.* kindlich, Kindes–, Sohnes–Tochter–.

filiation [fili'eiʃən], *s.* die Kindschaft, das Kindschaftsverhältnis; die Herkunft, Abstammung; (*Law*) Feststellung der Vaterschaft, (*fig.*) das Verwandtschaftsverhältnis, Abhängigkeitsverhältnis (*of languages etc.*).

filibeg ['filibeg], *s. See* **kilt.**

filibuster ['filibʌstə], **1.** *s.* 1. (*Hist.*) der Seeräuber, Abenteurer, Freibeuter, Filibustier; 2. (*Am.*) die Obstruktion, Verschleppungstaktik; der Verschleppungstaktiker. **2.** *v.i.* 1. (*Hist.*) freibeutern; 2. (*Am.*) Obstruktion treiben, die Debatte lahmlegen.

filigree ['filigri:], *s.* das Filigran, die Filigranarbeit.

[1]**filing** ['failiŋ], *s.* das Ordnen, Ablegen; – *cabinet,* der Aktenschrank; – *clerk,* der Registrator.

[2]**filing,** *s.* (*Tech.*) das Feilen; *pl.* Feilspäne (*pl.*), das Feilicht.

fill [fil], **1.** *v.t.* (an)füllen, einfüllen; (voll)stopfen; ausfüllen; innehaben, besetzen, bekleiden (*a post*); sättigen, befriedigen; (*Naut.*) vollbrassen; auffüllen, spachteln (*paintwork*); (*coll.*) – *the bill,* allen Anforderungen *or* Ansprüchen genügen, der geeignete Mann sein; – *his glass,* ihm einschenken; *courage –ed their hearts,* Mut erfüllte ihre Herzen; – *his place,* seine Stelle einnehmen, ihn ersetzen; – *a tooth,* einen Zahn füllen *or* plombieren; – *in,* eintragen, einsetzen, hineinschreiben (*one's name etc.*), ergänzen (*missing items*), ausfüllen (*a form*); (*coll.*) – *in the time,* die Zeit ausfüllen *or* totschlagen; – *him in on,* ihn informieren über (*Acc.*); – *out,* ausfüllen; ausdehnen; vollfüllen; (*esp. Am.*) ausfüllen (*a form*); – *up,* nachfüllen, vollfüllen, auffüllen, anfüllen; ausfüllen (*a form*). **2.** *v.i.* sich füllen, voll werden (*with,* von); – *out,* schwellen (*as sails*); sich ausdehnen, dicker werden; – *up,* sich anfüllen. **3.** *s.* die Fülle, Genüge; *have one's – of,* genug haben von, überdrüssig sein von; *drink (eat) (gaze) one's* –, sich satt trinken (essen) (sehen) (*of,* an (*Dat.*)). **filler,** *s.* 1. der Füller, Auffüller; 2. Trichter, Füllapparat; (*Motor.*) – *cap,* der (Ein)füllstutzen; 3. der

Spachtel; (*Build. etc.*) Füllkörper, das Streckmittel; 4. Füllsel.

fillet ['filit], **1.** *s.* 1. die Kopfbinde, das Haarband, Stirnband; (*Archit.*) die Leiste, der Streifen; Reif; (*on books*) Zierstreifen, das Filet; 2. (*of meat*) Filet, Lendenstück; (*Cul.*) Rollfleisch, die Roulade. **2.** *v.t.* 1. mit einer Kopfbinde schmücken, mit Reifen *or* Leisten zieren; mit Goldstreifen verzieren; 2. (*Cul.*) von Gräten befreien (*fish*), zu Roulade herrichten (*meat*).

filling ['filiŋ], **1.** *See* **fill. 2.** *adj.* sättigend. **3.** *s.* die Füllung, Füllmasse, Einlage, das Füllsel; (*Cul.*) die Farce; (*Dentistry*) Plombe; (*Weav.*) der Einschlag; (*fig.*) die Ergänzung, Zutat, das Füllsel, der Lückenbüßer. **filling-station,** *s.* (*Motor.*) die Tankstelle.

fillip ['filip], **1.** *s.* der Schneller, Schnalzer, Nasenstüber, das Schnippchen; (*coll.*) der Fips; (*fig.*) die Anregung, der Ansporn, Anreiz (*to*, für). **2.** *v.i.* (mit dem Finger) schnellen *or* schnalzen *or* schnippen. **3.** *v.t.* einen Nasenstüber geben (*Dat.*); (*fig.*) antreiben, anstrengen, einen Schubs geben (*Dat.*) (*one's memory*).

filly ['fili], *s.* das Stutenfüllen; (*coll.*) ausgelassenes Mädchen, wilde Hummel.

film [film], **1.** *s.* 1. das Häutchen, die Membran(e); Lage, Schicht, der Überzug, Anstrich, Belag (*on teeth*); die Trübung (*of eyes*); der Dunst, Schleier; 2. (*Phot.*) (Roll)film, (*Cinema*) (Ton)film; ***colour* –,** der Farbfilm; ***full-length* –,** der Hauptfilm; ***make a* –,** einen Film drehen; ***silent* –,** stummer Film; ***talking* –,** der Tonfilm; ***the –s,*** das Kino, Lichtspiele (*pl.*). **2.** *v.i.* sich mit einem Häutchen überziehen; (*Cinema*) sich zum (Ver)filmen eignen (*of a subject*), filmen, einen Film drehen (*of a p.*). **3.** *v.t.* (ver)filmen.

film| actor, *s.* der Filmschauspieler. – **fan,** *s.* der Kinofex, Kinonarr. **--pack,** *s.* (*Phot.*) die Filmpackung. – **speed,** *s.* (*Phot.*) die Lichtempfindlichkeit (*of the emulsion*), Laufgeschwindigkeit (*in the camera*). – **star,** *s.* der Filmstar, die Filmdiva. **--strip,** *s.* der Stehfilm, Bildstreifen. – **version,** *s.* die Verfilmung.

filmy ['filmi], *adj.* (hauch)dünn, häutig; trübe, verschleiert.

filose ['failous], *adj.* (*Zool.*) fadenförmig.

filoselle [filo'sel], *s.* das Filosellegarn.

filter ['filtə], **1.** *s.* 1. das *or* der Filter, das Seihtuch, Sieb, der Seiher, Sieber, Filtrierapparat; 2. (*Rad.*) die Siebkette, der Saugkreis; ***band-pass* –,** das Bandfilter; ***high-pass* –,** der Hochpaß, die Kondensatorkette; ***low-pass* –,** der Tiefpaß, die Spulenkette. **2.** *v.t.* (durch)seihen, aussieben, filtern, filtrieren, abklären. **3.** *v.i.* kolieren, passieren; durchsickern, durchlaufen; (*fig.*) – ***in,*** sich einfädeln; (*fig.*) – ***through,*** allmählich hervorkommen *or* bekanntwerden.

filter|-bed, *s.* die Kläranlage, das Rieselfeld. **--circuit,** *s.* (*Rad.*) der Sperrkreis. **--paper,** *s.* das Filtrierpapier. **--tip,** *s.* das Filtermundstück (*on cigarettes*).

filth [filθ], *s.* der Schmutz, Dreck, Kot. **filthiness,** *s.* die Unreinlichkeit, Unflätigkeit, der Schmutz. **filthy,** *adj.* schmutzig; unflätig, zotig (*as conversation*).

filtrate ['filtreit], **1.** *s.* das Filtrat, filtrierte Flüssigkeit. **2.** *v.t.* durchseihen, filtern, filtrieren, abläutern. **filtration** [–'treiʃən], *s.* das Filtrieren; die Filtrierung.

fimbriate ['fimbrieit], *adj.* mit behaartem Rand, befranst.

fin [fin], *s.* die Flosse, Finne; (*Av.*) Seitenflosse, Kielflosse; (*sl.*) Pfote.

final [fainl], **1.** *adj.* letzt, schließlich, endgültig, End–, Schluß–; (*Phonet.*) auslautend, End–; (*Gram.*) Absicht–; (*Law*) entscheidend, definitiv, rechtskräftig; – ***aim,*** das Endziel; – ***cause,*** der Endzweck; (*Gram.*) – ***clause,*** der Absichtsatz; – ***consonant,*** der Endkonsonant; – ***examination,*** die Abschlußprüfung; – ***result,*** das Endergebnis; (*Spt.*) – ***spurt,*** der Endspurt. **2.** *s.* 1. (*Spt.*) die Schlußrunde, das Endspiel; 2. (*oft. pl.*) (*Univ.*) *see* – ***examination***; 3. ***late night* –,** die Spätausgabe (*of newspaper*).

finale [fi'nɑ:li], *s.* das Finale, (*Mus.*) der Schlußsatz.

finalist ['fainəlist], *s.* der Endspielteilnehmer. **finality** [fai'næliti], *s.* die Unwiderruflichkeit, Endgültigkeit; der Endzustand; (*Phil.*) Zweckbestimmtheit. **finalize** [–laiz], *v.t.* beenden, vollenden. **finally,** *adv.* zuletzt, zum Schluß, endlich, schließlich, letztlich, endgültig; (*Phonet.*) im Auslaut.

finance [fi'næns, 'fainæns], **1.** *s.* das Finanzwesen, die Finanzwirtschaft, Geldwirtschaft; Finanzwissenschaft, *pl.* Finanzen (*pl.*), Einkünfte (*pl.*); (*coll.*) ***his –s are low,*** er ist nicht bei Kasse; (*Pol.*) – ***bill,*** das Steuergesetz; – ***company,*** die Finanzierungsgesellschaft. **2.** *v.t.* finanzieren, finanziell unterstützen. **financial** [–'nænʃl], *adj.* finanziell, Finanz–, Geld–; – ***column,*** der Handelsteil (*of newspaper*); – ***embarrassment,*** die Geldverlegenheit; – ***position,*** die Finanzlage, Vermögensverhältnisse (*pl.*); – ***standing,*** die Kreditfähigkeit; – ***year,*** (*Comm.*) das Betriebsjahr, (*Pol.*) Rechnungsjahr. **financier** [–'nænsiə], *s.* der Finanzmann, Geldgeber, Kapitalist.

finch [fintʃ], *s.* (*Orn.*) der Fink (*Fringilla*).

find [faind], **1.** *irr.v.t.* 1. finden, (an)treffen, (heraus)finden, entdecken, herausbekommen, feststellen, erfahren; (auf)finden, ermitteln, entdecken, gewahr werden (*Gen.*); – ***expression,*** sich ausdrücken (*of a th.*); – ***fault with,*** mißbilligen, tadeln, etwas auszusetzen haben mit; – ***favour with,*** Gunst gewinnen bei; – ***one's feet,*** Selbstvertrauen gewinnen; sich einarbeiten; sich hineinfinden *or* zurechtfinden; – ***it in one's heart,*** es über sich *or* übers Herz bringen; ***make him* – *his legs* (*his tongue*),** ihm Beine machen (die Zunge lösen); – ***pleasure in,*** Freude haben an (*Dat.*); ***take it as you* – *it,*** es nehmen wie es ist; – ***one's way,*** sich (zurecht)finden (*to*, nach; *in*, in (*Dat.*)); ***I found myself surrounded by,*** ich sah mich umgeben von; ***I found myself in a strange house,*** ich befand mich in einem fremden Haus; 2. (*Law*) befinden, erklären, erkennen; – ***a* (*true*) *bill,*** die Anklagepunkte für gültig erklären; ***be found guilty,*** für schuldig erklärt *or* erkannt *or* befunden werden; 3. verschaffen, auftreiben, aufbringen, stellen, liefern; versehen, versorgen, ausstatten (*in*, mit); ***all found,*** freie Station, volle Unterkunft und Verpflegung; ***he must* – *himself in boots,*** er muß selbst seine Stiefel stellen; – ***me a car!*** suchen *or* holen Sie mir ein Auto! ***I will make the dress but you must* – *the material,*** ich mache Ihnen das Kleid, Sie müssen aber den Stoff selbst liefern *or* anschaffen; – ***the money for,*** das Geld besorgen für; – ***him in pocket-money,*** ihn mit Taschengeld versorgen; – ***time,*** die Zeit aufbringen, sich (*Dat.*) die Zeit verschaffen; 4. – ***out,*** erfahren, auffinden, herausfinden, ermitteln, herausbekommen, entdecken; – ***out the secret,*** das Geheimnis enträtseln; (*coll.*) – ***him out,*** ihn erwischen *or* ertappen; ***be found out in a lie,*** auf einer Lüge *or* beim Lügen ertappt werden.
2. *irr.v.i.* (*Law*) – ***for him,*** zu seinen Gunsten entscheiden, für ihn erklären, ihn freisprechen.
3. *s.* der Fund.

finder ['faində], *s.* 1. der Finder, Entdecker; 2. (*Phot.*) Sucher; (*Opt.*) das Suchglas. **finding,** *s.* die Entdeckung, das Finden, der Fund; (*oft. pl.*) Befund, Ausspruch, das Urteil, Ermittlungsergebnis, die Entscheidung; ***the* – *of the jury,*** der Beschluß der Geschworenen.

[1]**fine** [fain], **1.** *adj.* 1. schön, fein, edel, gut; (*coll.*) ausgezeichnet, glänzend, vortrefflich, hervorragend, großartig; ***the* – *arts,*** die schönen Künste; (*coll.*) ***one* (*of these*) – *day*(*s*),** eines schönen Tages; ***you are a* – *fellow,*** du bist mir ein netter Kerl! – ***gentleman,*** vornehmer Herr; (*coll. iron.*) ***these are* – *goings-on,*** das sind mir schöne Geschichten; – ***scholar,*** großer Gelehrter; ***they had* – *sport,*** sie hatten großen Spaß; (*coll.*) ***a* – *time,*** eine herrliche *or* glänzende Zeit; – ***weather,*** schönes Wetter;

(*Prov.*) – ***words butter no parsnips,*** schöne Worte machen den Kohl nicht fett; (*coll.*) ***that's –!*** das ist herrlich! ***that is all very –, but . . .,*** das ist alles recht gut und schön, aber . . .; 2. dünn (*as hair etc.*); scharf, spitz (*as an edge or point*); – ***dust,*** feiner Staub; 3. rein (*of metals*), verfeinert, gebildet (*as taste*); zierlich, elegant, hübsch, schmuck (*in appearance*); subtil, diffizil (*as work*); (*Prov.*) – ***feathers make – birds,*** Kleider machen Leute. **2.** *v.t.* (*also* – ***down***) abklären (*wine*), abläutern (*beer*), abtreiben (*metal*). **3.** *adv.* (*coll.*) ***cut*** or ***run it –,*** mit der Zeit in die Enge kommen; ***that will suit me –,*** das paßt mir ausgezeichnet. **4.** *s.* (*only in*) ***in rain or –,*** bei Regen oder Sonnenschein.

[2]**fine, 1.** *s.* 1. die Geldstrafe, Geldbuße; Strafsumme, Abstandsumme; 2. (*obs.*) das Ende (*only in*) ***in –,*** endlich, schließlich, kurz(um); *see also* [3]**fine. 2.** *v.t.* zu einer Geldstrafe verurteilen.

[3]**fine** [ˈfi:nei], *s.* (*Mus.*) das Ende.

fine|-draw, *irr.v.t.* (*Semp.*) kunststopfen; (*Tech.*) fein ausziehen (*wire*). **--drawn,** *adj.* fein ausgezogen, (*fig.*) fein gesponnen, subtil. **fineness,** *s.* die Feinheit, (*of gold etc.*) Reinheit, der Feingehalt; (*fig.*) die Zartheit (*of feelings*), Schärfe, Genauigkeit (*of judgment etc.*); (*coll.*) Vortrefflichkeit. **finery,** *s.* 1. der Putz, Staat; 2. (*Metall.*) Frischherd, Frischofen. **fine-spun,** *adj.* feingesponnen, dünn; (*fig.*) subtil.

finesse [fiˈnes], **1.** *s.* 1. die Feinheit, Finesse; 2. Spitzfindigkeit, Schlauheit, List; 3. (*Whist*) das Schneiden, der Impasse. **2.** *v.i.* Kunstgriffe anwenden. **3.** *v.t.* (*Whist*) schneiden *or* impassieren mit.

finger [ˈfiŋgə], **1.** *s.* der Finger; Zeiger (*of clock etc.*); ***have a – in the pie*** (or ***many pies***), die Hand (überall) im Spiele haben; ***count on the –s of one hand,*** an den Fingern abzählen; (*fig.*) ***cross one's –s,*** den Daumen halten; ***his –s are all thumbs,*** er ist sehr ungeschickt; ***his –s are itching to do it,*** es juckt ihm in den Fingern, es zu tun; ***point the – of scorn at,*** mit Verachtung strafen, der (allgemeinen) Verachtung preisgeben; ***put one's – on a th.,*** auf eine S. genau hinweisen; ***slip through his –s,*** ihm entschlüpfen *or* entwischen; ***snap one's –s at,*** ein Schnippchen schlagen (*Dat.*), verhöhnen; ***not move*** or ***stir a –,*** keinen Finger rühren *or* krumm machen; ***twist him round one's little –,*** ihn um den Finger wickeln; ***work one's –s to the bone,*** sich (*Dat.*) die Hände wund arbeiten. **2.** *v.t.* 1. betasten, befühlen, befingern, (leicht) berühren, in die Finger nehmen; 2. (*Mus.*) mit dem Fingersatz versehen.

finger|-board, *s.* das Griffbrett (*of violin*); die Klaviatur (*of piano*). **--bowl,** *s.* die Spülschale. **fingered,** *adj.* –fing(e)rig; (*Bot.*) fingerförmig; ***light--,*** langfingerig, diebisch. **finger-grass,** *s.* (*Bot.*) die Fingerhirse, Bluthirse. **fingering,** *s.* 1. die Fingerspur; das Betasten; 2. (*Mus.*) der Fingersatz, die Fingertechnik. **finger|mark,** *s.* der Schmutzfleck, die Berührungsstelle. **–nail,** *s.* der Fingernagel. **--plate,** *s.* der Türschoner (*on doors*). **--post,** *s.* der Wegweiser. **-print,** *s.* der Fingerabdruck. **--stall,** *s.* der Fingerling, Däumling. **--tip,** *s.* die Fingerspitze; ***have at one's –s,*** am Schnürchen haben, im kleinen Finger haben, parat haben, auswendig können, ganz genau kennen, vollständig beherrschen; ***to one's –s,*** durch und durch.

finical [ˈfinikl], *adj.* geziert, zimperlich, affektiert; übertrieben genau, peinlich, knifflig. **finicalness,** *s.* die Geziertheit, Zimperlichkeit; Peinlichkeit. **finicking,** *adj.* (*coll.*) *see* **finical.**

fining [ˈfainiŋ], *s.* das Klären, Reinigen; (*usu. pl.*) Reinigungsmittel, Läuterungsmittel.

finis [ˈfainis], *s.* das Ende, der Abschluß.

finish [ˈfiniʃ], **1.** *v.t.* (be)enden, beendigen, aufhören mit; fertigmachen, vollenden, erledigen; verbrauchen, aufbrauchen; aufessen, austrinken; vervollkommnen, ausarbeiten; fertigmachen, fertigstellen (*goods*); zubereiten, zurichten, appretieren (*cloth*); – ***a letter,*** einen Brief fertig schreiben; (*coll.*) – ***him,*** ihn töten, ihm den Rest geben; (*coll.*) – ***off,*** fertigmachen, abtun, vervollständigen, erledigen; (*coll.*) den Rest geben (*Dat.*), zugrunde richten; (*coll.*) – ***up,*** aufessen, austrinken. **2.** *v.i.* aufhören, zum Ende kommen, Schluß machen, enden; (*Spt.*) ans Ziel kommen; – ***up by doing,*** zum Schluß dazu kommen *or* damit schließen, daß man tut; – ***with,*** abschließen mit; ***have -ed with,*** fertig sein mit. **3.** *s.* das Ende, der (Ab)schluß, die Entscheidung, der Endkampf (*race etc.*); die Vollendung, feine Qualität; letzte Hand, letzter Schliff, die Ausarbeitung, Ausführung; Appretur (*on cloth*); ***be in at the –,*** (mit) in den Endkampf kommen; ***fight to the –,*** bis zur Entscheidung kämpfen.

finished [ˈfiniʃt], *adj.* fertig, abgeschlossen, beendet, beendigt; vollendet, vollkommen; – ***goods,*** Fertigwaren (*pl.*). **finisher,** *s.* der Fertigsteller, Vollender; Appretierer; (*coll.*) vernichtender Schlag. **finishing, 1.** *adj.* abschließend, vollendend; – ***agent,*** das Appreturmittel (*for cloth*); – ***coat,*** der Deckanstrich, Überzugslack; (*Spt.*) – ***post,*** das Ziel; – ***process,*** das Veredelungsverfahren; – ***school,*** (vornehmes) Mädchenpensionat; ***put the – stroke*** or ***give the – touch to,*** die letzte Hand legen an (*Acc.*); (*Hunt.*) – ***stroke,*** der Gnadenstoß. **2.** *s.* das Fertigstellen, die Nachbearbeitung; Veredelung, (*of cloth*) Appretur, Zurichtung; (*Archit.*) Verzierung; Ausarbeitung, das Fertigmachen, Beenden, Vollenden.

finite [ˈfainait], *adj.* endlich (*also Math.*), begrenzt; – ***verb,*** das Verbum finitum. **finiteness,** *s.* die Endlichkeit, Begrenztheit.

Finland [ˈfinlənd], *s.* Finnland (*n.*). **Finn,** *s.* der Finne (die Finnin). **Finnish, 1.** *adj.* finnisch. **2.** *s.* (*language*) das Finnisch(e).

fiord [fjɔ:d], *s.* der Fjord, die Förde.

fir [fə:], *s.* die Tanne, der Tannenbaum; das Tannenholz; ***Scotch –,*** die Kiefer, Föhre; ***silver –,*** die Weißtanne, Edeltanne, Silbertanne; ***spruce--,*** die Rottanne, gemeine Fichte. **fir-cone,** *s.* der Kienapfel, Tannenzapfen.

fire [ˈfaiə], **1.** *s.* 1. das Feuer (*also Mil., of jewels and fig.*); der Brand, die Feuersbrunst; 2. (*fig.*) Flamme, Hitze, Glut, Begeisterung, Leidenschaft; 3. der Glanz.

(a) (*with adjs.*) (*Mil.*) ***blind –,*** Feuer ohne Zielbeobachtung; (*Mil.*) ***concentrated –,*** die Feuerzusammenfassung, das Massenfeuer, Punktschießen; (*Med.*) ***St. Anthony's –,*** der Rotlauf, die Rose; (*Naut.*) ***St. Elmo's –,*** das St. Elmsfeuer; ***wild –,*** das Lauffeuer; (*Mil.*) ***withering –,*** vernichtendes Feuer.

(b) (*with verbs*) ***catch –,*** Feuer fangen; (*Mil.*) ***cease –,*** das Feuer einstellen; ***hang –,*** (*Artil.*) zu spät losgehen; (*fig.*) sich verzögern, ohne Wirkung bleiben; ***lay the –,*** das Feuer anlegen; ***make up the –,*** das Feuer schüren; ***miss –,*** versagen; (*fig.*) fehlschlagen; (*Mil.*) ***open –,*** das Feuer eröffnen, Feuer geben; ***put on the –,*** aufs Feuer setzen; ***set – to,*** in Brand stecken, anstecken, anzünden; ***take –,*** see ***catch –***; (*fig.*) in Wut geraten (*at,* über (*Acc.*)).

(c) (*with preps.*) (*fig.*) ***between two –s,*** zwischen zwei Feuern; ***sit by the –,*** am Ofen sitzen; (*coll.*) ***the fat's in the –,*** der Teufel ist los; ***be on –,*** in Brand stehen, brennen; (*fig.*) in Feuer und Flamme stehen, erregt werden; ***like a house on –,*** wie der Wind, wie toll; ***set on –,*** see ***set – to***; (*fig.*) entflammen (*a p.*); (*Prov.*) ***set the Thames on –,*** Außergewöhnliches leisten; ***sit over the –,*** in den Ofen kriechen; ***over a slow –,*** bei langsamem Feuer; ***go through – and water,*** durchs Feuer gehen (***for,*** für); (*fig.*) ***add fuel to the –,*** Öl ins Feuer gießen; ***under –,*** (*Mil.*) im Feuer, unter Beschuß; (*fig.*) heftig angegriffen; ***no smoke without –,*** an jedem Gerücht ist etwas Wahres. **2.** *v.t.* in Brand stecken, anzünden, entzünden; abfeuern (*a gun*); zünden (*a charge*); brennen (*bricks*); (*fig.*) anfeuern, entflammen; (*Naut.*) – ***a broadside,*** eine Salve abgeben; (*sl.*) – ***him,*** ihn entlassen; – ***off,*** abfeuern, losschießen (*gun*).

3. *v.i.* Feuer fangen, sich entzünden, anbrennen; (*with gun*) Feuer geben, feuern, schießen (***at, on,*** auf (*Acc.*)); (*of an engine*) zünden; (*fig.*) rot werden (*as cheeks*); (*fig.*) – ***away,*** losschießen, anfangen; – ***up at,*** in Feuer und Flammen *or* Hitze *or* Wut geraten *or* auffahren über (*Acc.*).

fire|-alarm, *s.* der Feueralarm; (*instrument*) Feuermelder. **-arms,** *pl.* Schußwaffen (*pl.*). **-ball,** *s.* (*Mil.*) die Feuerkugel, Brandkugel. **--balloon,** *s.* der Feuerballon. **--bar,** *s.* der Roststab. **--bomb,** *s.* die Brandbombe. **--box,** *s.* (*locomotive etc.*) die Feuerbüchse, der Feuerraum. **-brand,** *s.* brennendes Stück Holz; (*fig.*) der Unruhestifter. **-brick,** *s.* feuerfester Ziegel, der Schamottestein. **--brigade,** *s.* die Feuerwehr. **-clay,** *s.* die Schamotte, feuerfester Ton. – **company,** *s.* (*Am.*) *see* **--brigade. --control,** *s.* (*Artil.*) die Feuerleitung; Feuerleitstelle. **--cracker,** *s.* der Schwärmer, Frosch. **--curtain,** *s.* (*Theat.*) der Sicherheitsvorhang, eiserner Vorhang. **-damp,** *s.* das Grubengas; schlagende Wetter (*pl.*). – **department,** *s.* (*Am.*) *see* **--brigade. --dog,** *s.* der Feuerbock. **--drill,** *s.* die Feuerlöschübung; der Probefeueralarm. **--eater,** *s.* der Feuerfresser; (*fig.*) Streithahn, Eisenfresser, Hitzkopf, Raufbold. **--engine,** *s.* das Feuerwehrfahrzeug, die Feuerspritze. **--escape,** *s.* die Rettungsleiter, Nottreppe. **--extinguisher,** *s.* der Feuerlöscher, chemischer Löschapparat. **--fighter,** *s.* der Feuerwehrmann. **-fly,** *s.* der Leuchtkäfer. **-grate,** *s.* der Feuerrost. **--guard,** *s.* das Kamingitter. **--hose,** *s.* die Schlauchleitung. **--hydrant,** *s.* der Wasseranschluß, Hydrant, Feuerhahn. **--insurance,** *s.* die Feuerversicherung, Brandversicherung. **--irons,** *pl.* das Kamingerät. **-light,** *s.* der Feuerschein. **--lighter,** *s.* der Feueranzünder. **-lit,** *adj.* durch Feuer beleuchtet (*as a room*). **-lock,** *s.* das Luntenschloß (*on the gun*); die Muskete. **fire|man,** *s.* 1. (*Railw.*) der Heizer; 2. Feuerwehrmann; *pl.* die Löschmannschaft, Feuerwehr. **--office,** *s.* die Feuerversicherungsanstalt. – **order,** *s.* (*Mil.*) die Zielansprache. **-place,** *s.* (offener) Kamin; der Herd. **--plug,** *s.* *See* **--hydrant.** – **power,** *s.* (*Mil.*) die Feuerkraft. **-proof,** 1. *adj.* feuerfest, feuerbeständig, flammsicher; – ***bulkhead,*** das Brandspant, Brandschott; – ***cement,*** feuerfester Kitt, der Schamottemörtel. 2. *v.t.* flammsicher machen. **-proofing,** *s.* Feuerschutzmittel (*pl.*). **--raising,** *s.* die Brandstiftung. **--screen,** *s.* der Ofenschirm. **--ship,** *s.* (*Naut.*) der Brander. **-side,** 1. *s.* der Herd, Kamin; (*fig.*) häusliches Leben, der Familienkreis. 2. *adj.* häuslich; – ***chat,*** trauliche Plauderei; – ***tale,*** eine Geschichte für die ganze Familie. **--station,** *s.* die Feuerwehrwache. **--step,** *s.* (*Mil.*) der Schützenauftritt. **-stone,** *s.* der Feuerstein. **--tongs,** *pl.* die Kohlenzange. **--watcher,** *s.* die Brandwache. **--water,** *s.* (*coll.*) das Feuerwasser, der Branntwein. **-wood,** *s.* das Brennholz. **-works,** *pl.* 1. das Feuerwerk; 2. (*fig. coll.*) begeisterter Wortschwall; –(*s*) ***display,*** die Feuerwerkveranstaltung. **--worship,** *s.* die Feueranbetung.

firing ['fairiŋ], *s.* (*Mil.*) das Feuer, Feuern, Schießen; die Heizung; Feuerung, der Brennstoff, das Brennmaterial; (*Tech.*) die Zündung; (*of bricks*) das Brennen; – ***data,*** Schußwerte, Schießgrundlagen (*pl.*); – ***hole,*** das Schürloch (*of furness*); – ***lever,*** der Abfeuerungshebel; – ***line,*** die Kampffront, Feuerstellung (*also fig.*); – ***order,*** (*Mil.*) der Schießbefehl; (*Motor.*) die Zündfolge; – ***party,*** – ***squad,*** das Exekutionskommando; die Ehrenabordnung.

firkin ['fə:kin], *s.* das Viertelfaß (= *41 litres*: (*Am.*) *34 litres*); (*of butter*) Fäßchen.

[1]**firm** [fə:m], 1. *adj.* fest, hart; stabil, beständig, haltbar; (*fig.*) treu, standhaft, entschlossen, (*as decree*) bestimmt; – ***friends,*** enge Freunde; (*fig.*) ***be on – ground,*** festen Boden unter den Füßen haben. 2. *adv.* fest, sicher; ***hold – to,*** aufrechterhalten; ***make –,*** befestigen; ***stand –,*** entschlossen dastehen.

[2]**firm,** *s.* die (Handels)firma, Unternehmung, der Betrieb, das Geschäft, Unternehmen.

firmament ['fə:məmənt], *s.* das Himmelsgewölbe, Sternenzelt, Firmament.

firman ['fə:mən], *s.* der Ferman, landesherrlicher Befehl.

firmness ['fə:mnis], *s.* die Festigkeit; Entschlossenheit, Standhaftigkeit, Beständigkeit; *see* [1]**firm.**

first [fə:st], 1. *adj.* erst; – ***claim,*** erster Anspruch, die Vorhand; – ***cost,*** der Selbstkostenpreis, Einkaufspreis; – ***cousin,*** das Geschwisterkind; – ***draft,*** erster Entwurf, das Konzept; – ***floor,*** erster Stock; erstes Stockwerk; (*Am.*) das Erdgeschoß; – ***form,*** die Sexta (*at school*); – ***fruit(s),*** Erstlinge (*pl.*), (*fig.*) das Erstlingswerk, der Erstlingserfolg; (*Am.*) – ***grade,*** see – ***form;*** (*Am.*) – ***lady,*** die Frau des Präsidenten; – ***lieutenant,*** der Oberleutnant; ***First Lord of the Admiralty,*** der Marineminister; – ***maid,*** die Großmagd (*on a farm*); (*Naut.*) – ***mate,*** der Obersteuermann; – ***member of a series,*** das Anfangsglied einer Reihe; – ***name,*** der Vorname; (*Theat. etc.*) – ***night,*** die Erstaufführung, Uraufführung, Premiere; – ***offender,*** noch nicht Vorbestrafte(r); (*Gram.*) – ***person,*** erste Person; – ***quality,*** prima Qualität; – ***refusal,*** das Vorkaufsrecht; ***First Sea Lord,*** der Chef des Flottenstabs; ***in the – place,*** zuerst, erstens, an erster Stelle; ***at – sight,*** beim ersten (An)blick; – ***stage,*** die Vorstufe; – ***thing,*** als erstes, an erster Stelle; (*coll.*) in aller Früh; ***you don't know the – thing about it,*** du hast keine Ahnung davon; ***put – things –,*** alles der Reihe nach tun, Dringendem den Vortritt *or* Vorrang geben; – ***violin(ist),*** der Konzertmeister; – ***water,*** reinstes Wasser (*of diamonds*); (*fig.*) erste Qualität, höchster Rang. 2. *adv.* zuerst, zuvörderst, an erster Stelle, vor anderen; zum ersten Mal, erstens, fürs erste; eher, lieber; ***at –,*** zuerst, anfangs, im *or* am Anfang; – ***of all,*** vor allen Dingen, in allererster Linie, zuallererst; – ***come – served,*** wer zuerst kommt, mahlt zuerst; – ***and foremost,*** see – ***of all;*** ***go –,*** vorangehen; ***head –,*** mit dem Kopf voran, kopfüber; – ***and last,*** alles in allem; im (großen) ganzen; –, ***last and all the time,*** ein für alle Mal. 3. *s.* der *or* die *or* das Erste; (*Railw. etc.*) erste Klasse; (*coll. Univ.*) höchste Note (bei der Abschlußprüfung); *pl.* (*Comm.*) Waren erster Qualität (*pl.*); ***from the –,*** von vornherein, von Anfang an; – ***of exchange,*** der Primawechsel; ***the – of May,*** der 1. Mai; ***travel –,*** erster Klasse fahren.

first|-aid, *s.* erste Hilfe, die Nothilfe; – ***kit,*** das Verbandpäckchen; – ***post,*** die Verbandstelle, Sanitätswache. **--born,** 1. *adj.* erstgeboren, ältest. 2. *s.* Erstgeborene(r). **--class,** 1. *adj.* erstklassig; ausgezeichnet; – ***mail,*** bevorzugte Post, (*esp. Am.*) die Briefpost. 2. *adv.* erster Klasse; (*coll.*) *see* **--rate, 2. 3.** erste Klasse, höchste Stufe. **--comer,** *s.* Erste(r), Erstbeste(r), x-beliebige(r). **--foot,** *v.t.* (*Scots*) ersten Besuch am Neujahrstag machen bei. **--hand,** 1. *adj.* direkt, unmittelbar; – ***account,*** der Tatsachenbericht; – ***bill,*** eigener Wechsel. 2. *adv.* (*also* ***at*** –) aus erster Hand. **firstling,** *s.* der Erstling. **firstly,** *adv.* erstlich, erstens, zum ersten, zuerst. **first|-nighter,** *s.* der Premierenbesucher. **--rate,** 1. *adj.* ersten Ranges, erstklassig, ausgezeichnet, vorzüglich. 2. *adv.* (*coll.*) glänzend, tadellos, großartig, famos, prima.

firth [fə:θ], *s.* (*Scots*) der Meeresarm, die Mündung, Förde.

fir|-tree, *s.* der Tannenbaum. **--wood,** *s.* der Tannenwald.

fiscal [fiskl], 1. *adj.* fiskalisch; – ***reform,*** die Steuerreform; – ***year,*** das Finanzjahr, Etatsjahr. 2. *s.* der Fiskal, Fiskusbeamte(r).

[1]**fish** [fiʃ], 1. *s.* der Fisch; (*collect.*) Fische (*pl.*); ***drink like a –,*** saufen wie ein Loch; (*coll.*) ***feed the –es,*** seekrank werden; ertrinken; ***there are as good – in the sea as ever came out of it,*** es gibt noch mehr davon in der Welt; es gibt keinen, der nicht zu ersetzen wäre; (*coll.*) ***have other – to fry,*** Wichtigeres zu tun haben; (*coll.*) ***a pretty kettle of –,*** eine schöne Bescherung; (*fig.*) ***loose –,*** lockerer Vogel; ***all is – that comes to his net,*** er steckt ein, was ihm in die Hände kommt; (*fig.*) ***queer –,*** wunderlicher Kauz; ***he takes to it like a – to the water,*** er ist in seinem Element; ***be like a – out of water,*** nicht in seinem

Element sein; (*fig.*) ***neither – nor flesh (nor good red herring)***, weder Fisch noch Fleisch; nichts Halbes und nichts Ganzes; vollkommen undefinierbar. **2.** *v.t.* fischen, holen, ziehen (*out of*, aus), fangen; abfischen, absuchen (*a river*) (*for*, nach); (*fig.*) – ***out***, herausholen (*facts etc.*); – ***up***, auffischen, retten. **3.** *v.i.* fischen, angeln; (*fig. coll.*) haschen (*for*, nach); – ***for compliments***, nach Komplimenten haschen; – ***for pike***, nach Hechten angeln *or* fischen; – ***in troubled waters***, im trüben fischen.

[2]**fish, 1.** *s.* (*Railw.*) die Lasche. **2.** *v.t.* verbinden, verlaschen; – ***the anchor***, den Anker festmachen.

fish| ball, *s. See* **– cake. – basket,** *s.* die Reuse. **– bolt,** *s.* der Laschenbolzen. **–bone,** *s.* die Gräte. **– cake,** *s.* der Fischklops. **--carver,** *s.* das Fischmesser. **fisher,** *s.* der Fischer; (*Zool.*) der Zobel, das Zobelwiesel. **fisherman,** *s.* der Fischer, Angler; ***–'s bend***, der Fischerknoten. **fishery,** *s.* der Fischfang; die Fischerei; das Fischereigebiet. **fish|-glue,** *s.* der Fischleim. **--hook,** *s.* der Angelhaken. **fishiness,** *s.* (*coll.*) die Zweifelhaftigkeit, Mißlichkeit.

fishing ['fiʃiŋ], *s.* das Fischen, Angeln, die Fischerei, der Fischfang; ***go –***, auf den Fischfang ausgehen. **fishing|-boat,** *s.* das Fischerboot. **--boots,** *pl.* Wasserstiefel. **--fly,** *s.* künstliche Fliege. **--gear,** *s. See* **--tackle. --ground,** *s.* der Fischereigrund. **--limits,** *pl.* die Fischereigrenze. **--line,** *s.* die Angelschnur. **--rights,** *pl.* das Fischereirecht. **--rod,** *s.* die Angelrute. **--smack,** *s.* der Fischkutter. **--tackle,** *s.* das Angelgerät, Fischereigerät. **--village,** *s.* das Fischerdorf.

fish|-knife, *s.* das Fischmesser. **--like,** *adj.* fischartig, fischähnlich. **–monger,** *s.* der Fischhändler. **--oil,** *s.* der Fischtran. **--plate,** *s. See* [2]**fish, 1. –pond,** *s.* der Fischteich. **--slice,** *s.* die Fischkelle. **--sound,** *s.* die Fischblase. **–wife,** *s.* die Fischverkäuferin, das Fischweib.

fishy ['fiʃi], *adj.* 1. fischartig, Fisch–; fischreich; 2. (*coll.*) verdächtig, zweifelhaft, mißlich, anrüchig, faul, nicht geheuer, nicht in Ordnung.

fissile ['fisail], *adj.* spaltbar. **fission** ['fiʃən], *s.* die Spaltung; ***nuclear –***, die Kernspaltung. **fissure** ['fiʃə], **1.** *s.* der Spalt, (Ein)riß, Sprung, die Ritze. **2.** *v.t.* (*v.i.*) (sich) spalten. **fissured,** *adj.* gespalten, zerkluftet, rissig.

fist [fist], **1.** *s.* die Faust; ***make money hand over –***, schweres Geld verdienen; ***shake one's – at him***, ihn mit der Faust bedrohen. **2.** *v.t.* (*Naut.*) handhaben (*a sail*); – ***off***, mit der Faust abwehren. **fisticuffs** [–ikʌfs], *pl.* Faustschläge (*pl.*), der Faustkampf.

fistula ['fistjulə], *s.* (*Med.*) die Fistel; Rohrflöte (*of an organ*). **fistular,** *adj.* röhrenförmig. **fistulous,** *adj. See* **fistular**; (*Med.*) fistelartig.

[1]**fit** [fit], **1.** *adj.* 1. passend, geeignet, angemessen, geziemend; (*only pred.*) schicklich; fähig, tauglich; ***more than is –***, über Gebühr, übermäßig; ***see*** or ***think –***, es für richtig halten; ***be – for***, taugen zu, reif sein für; geeignet *or* bereit sein zu; – ***for habitation***, bewohnbar; ***a meal – for a king***, ein königliches Mahl; – ***for service***, dienstfähig, diensttauglich; (*coll.*) ***he laughed – to burst***, er lachte daß er beinahe platzte; (*coll.*) – ***to drop***, zum Umsinken erschöpft; ***not – to eat***, ungenießbar; (*coll.*) ***dressed – to kill***, aufgedonnert; 2. (*coll.*) gesund, in (guter) Form; ***as – as a fiddle, fighting –***, in bester Verfassung, kerngesund; ***keep –***, sich gesund erhalten, in Form bleiben. **2.** *s.* genaues Passen, der Sitz (*of clothes*), (*Tech.*) die Passung; ***it is a bad –***, es paßt schlecht; ***be an excellent –***, wie angegossen sitzen; ***be a tight –***, eng *or* knapp passen. **3.** *v.t.* 1. aufstellen, anbringen, montieren, einfügen, einordnen; – ***in***, einfügen, einpassen (in (*Acc.*)); – ***out***, ausrüsten, ausstatten; – ***together***, montieren, zusammenfügen; – ***up***, einrichten, zurechtmachen; ausrüsten, ausstatten; montieren; – ***with***, versehen *or* versorgen mit; 2. (*as clothes*) anstehen (*Dat.*), sitzen (*Dat.*), passen (für *or* auf (*Acc.*)), angemessen sein für; passend *or* geeignet machen, befähigen (*for*, zu); anpassen, anprobieren (*clothes*); ***this coat doesn't – me***, dieser Rock paßt *or* sitzt mir nicht; – ***him to a T***, ihm wie angegossen passen; – ***him for***, ihn ausbilden *or* bereiten für *or* auf (*Acc.*); – ***on***, anpassen, anprobieren. **4.** *v.i.* angemessen *or* passend sein; (*as clothes*) sitzen, passen; – ***in with***, passen zu; ***it –s in with my plans***, es trifft sich gut, es paßt mir in den Kram; – ***into***, sich (hinein)passen in.

[2]**fit,** *s.* (*Med.*) der Anfall, Ausbruch; die Anwandlung, (*coll.*) Stimmung, Laune; ***apoplectic –***, der Schlaganfall; – ***of coughing***, der Hustenanfall; ***drunken –***, der Rausch; ***epileptic –***, epileptischer Anfall; ***fainting –***, der Ohnmachtsanfall; – ***of hysterics***, hysterischer Anfall; – ***of jealousy***, die Anwandlung von Eifersucht; – ***of laughter***, der Lachkrampf; (*coll.*) ***in –s (of laughter)***, hilflos vor Lachen; – ***of rage***, der Wutanfall; ***by –s and starts***, stoßweise, rückweise; dann und wann, von Zeit zu Zeit; ***if the – takes me***, wenn mich die Laune anwandelt.

[3]**fit,** *s.* der Abschnitt eines altgermanischen epischen Gedichtes.

fitful ['fitful], *adj.* abwechselnd, unterbrochen, ungleichmäßig, veränderlich; unbeständig, launenhaft, launisch. **fitfulness,** *s.* die Unbeständigkeit, Ungleichmäßigkeit, Launenhaftigkeit.

fitly ['fitli], *adv.* sachgemäß, auf passende Art, sinngemäß; zur rechten Zeit. **fitment,** *s.* die Einrichtung; der Einrichtungsgegenstand, Einbauteil. **fitness,** *s.* die Angemessenheit, Schicklichkeit; Brauchbarkeit, Eignung, Tauglichkeit; Gesundheit, (*Mil.*) Dienstfähigkeit; ***certificate of –***, das Gesundheitsattest; (*Scots*) (*Univ.*) die Zulassung zum Studium. **fitted,** *adj.* ausgestattet, ausgerüstet; montiert, eingebaut. **fitter,** *s.* der Zuschneider, Anpasser; Schlosser, Klempner, Monteur, Installateur. **fitting, 1.** *adj.* schicklich, passend, angemessen; geeignet, angebracht. **2.** *s.* 1. die Anprobe (*of clothes*); das Anpassen, Zurechtmachen; Einstellen, Einrichten, die Aufstellung, Montage, Installation; Paßarbeit; 2. (*Tech.*) das Verbindungsstück, Kupplungsstück; (*usu. pl.*) Zubehör, Beschläge (*pl.*), Armaturen (*pl.*), Zubehörteile (*pl.*), Ausrüstungsgegenstände (*pl.*). **fitting|-shop,** *s.* die Montagehalle. **--yard,** *s.* (*Shipb.*) die Bauwerft.

five [faiv], **1.** *num. adj.* fünf; ***--barred gate***, der Schlagbaum mit fünf Barren; ***--day week***, die Fünftagewoche; ***--figure tables***, fünfstellige Tafeln; (*Mus.*) ***--finger exercises***, Fingerübungen; – ***times***, fünfmal; ***--year plan***, der Fünfjahresplan. **2.** *s.* die Fünf; der Fünfer. *For clock-times see under* **eight. fivefold,** *adj.* fünffach. **fiver,** *s.* (*coll.*) die Fünf-pfundnote. **fives,** *pl.* (eine Art) Wandballspiel; ***--court***, die Wandballanlage.

fix [fiks], **1.** *v.t.* 1. befestigen, festmachen (*to*, an (*Acc.*)), anheften; (*fig.*) ansetzen, festlegen, festsetzen, bestimmen, anberaumen (*a meeting, time etc.*); (*Phot.*) fixieren (*also fig. with one's eyes*); – ***the attention***, die Aufmerksamkeit festhalten *or* fesseln; – ***the attention (eyes) upon***, die Aufmerksamkeit (Augen) richten *or* heften auf (*Acc.*); – ***bayonets!*** Seitengewehr pflanzt auf! – ***in one's memory***, sich (*Dat.*) einprägen; (*Naut. etc.*) – ***the position***, orten; – ***the price***, den Preis festlegen *or* festsetzen *or* bestimmen *or* verabreden; 2. verhärten, fest machen, feste Form geben (*Dat.*), (*Chem.*) zum Erstarren *or* Gestehen bringen, erstarren lassen; 3. (*coll.*) in Ordnung bringen, reparieren, herrichten; zubereiten (*a meal*); (*coll.*) – ***a quarrel***, einen Streit beilegen; 4. (*sl.*) zu seinem eigenen Vorteil beeinflussen; (*an antagonist*) beseitigen, ausschalten, kaltstellen; 5. (*coll.*) – ***on***, sich entschließen für, wählen, festsetzen (*a date etc.*); 6. (*coll.*) – ***up***, anordnen, festsetzen; in Ordnung bringen, herrichten, organisieren, arrangieren; (*sl.*) unterbringen, versorgen. **2.** *v.i.* (*coll.*) sich niederlassen; sich entscheiden (*on*, für). **3.** *s.* 1. (*Naut.*) das Besteck; 2. (*coll.*) die Verlegenheit, Klemme; 3. (*sl.*) abgekartetes Spiel; 4. (*sl. drugs*) der Fix.

fixate [fik'seit], *v.t.* fixieren, die Augen richten auf

(*Acc.*); festhalten. **fixation** [–'seiʃən], *s.* das Befestigen, Festmachen; (*fig.*) die Fixierung, Festlegung, Festsetzung, Bestimmung; (*Chem.*) Verdichtung; (*Psych.*) der Komplex.

fixative ['fiksətiv], *s.* das Fixativ, Fixiermittel.

fixed [fikst], *adj.* fest(gemacht), befestigt; (*fig.*) fest(gesetzt), festgelegt, bestimmt, feststehend, festliegend, ständig; fest eingebaut; (*Chem.*) nicht flüchtig, feuerbeständig; starr (*of eyes*); (*coll.*) erledigt, beigelegt; repariert, hergerichtet; – ***acid,*** gebundene Säure; ***with – bayonets,*** mit aufgepflanztem Seitengewehr; – ***idea,*** fixe Idee; ***with – ideas,*** mit bestimmten Ansichten; – ***income,*** ständiges Einkommen; – ***price,*** fester *or* stehender Preise, der Richtpreis; – ***sight,*** das Standvisier; – ***star,*** der Fixstern; – ***sum,*** bestimmte Summe; (*Av.*) – ***undercarriage,*** starres Fahrwerk; (*coll.*) ***be well –,*** gut gestellt sein. **fixedly** ['fiksidli], *adv.* starr, unverwandt. **fixedness,** *s.* die Festigkeit; (*fig.*) Standhaftigkeit, Beharrlichkeit. **fixer,** *s.* (*Phot.*) das Fixiermittel.

fixing ['fiksiŋ], *s.* das Aufstellen, Festmachen, Befestigen, die Einspannung, Montierung; (*Chem., Phot.*) Fixierung; (*coll.*) Instandsetzung; *pl.* das Zubehör, Einrichtungen (*pl.*), die Garnierung; – ***agent,*** das Bindemittel; – ***bath,*** das Fixierbad; – ***bolt,*** der Haltebolzen; – ***point,*** die Einspannstelle; – ***solution,*** die Fixierlösung.

fixity ['fiksiti], *s.* die Festigkeit, Beständigkeit, Stabilität; – ***of purpose,*** die Zielstrebigkeit; – ***of tenure,*** die Ständigkeit des Lehens, festes Lehen.

fixture ['fikstʃə], *s.* das Inventarstück, Pertinenzstück, (nagel)fester Gegenstand, feste Anlage; (*Law*) das Zubehör, festes Inventar; (*Spt.*) festgesetzte Veranstaltung; (*coll.*) ***be a –,*** (*of a p.*) unverrückbar sein, (*of a th.*) ein altes Inventarstück sein; (*Spt.*) – ***list,*** das Spielprogramm.

fizz [fiz], **1.** *v.i.* zischen, sprudeln, sprühen. **2.** *s.* das Zischen, Sprudeln, Sprühen, Gezische; (*coll.*) der Champagner, Sekt. **fizzle, 1.** *v.i.* zischen, brausen, sprühen; (*Am. sl.*) mißglücken, durchfallen; – ***out,*** verpuffen, abflauen, im Sand verlaufen. **2.** *s.* (*sl.*) der Mißerfolg, die Pleite. **fizzy,** *adj.* (*coll.*) sprudelnd, sprühend.

flabbergast ['flæbəgɑ:st], *v.t.* (*coll.*) verblüffen; (*coll.*) ***be –ed,*** platt sein.

flabbiness ['flæbinis], *s.* die Schlaffheit. **flabby,** *adj.* schlaff, weich; schlapp, matt, lappig; (*fig.*) kraftlos, gehaltlos.

flaccid ['flæksid], *adj.* weich, schlaff, schlapp, schlotterig, kraftlos. **flaccidity** [–'siditi], *s.* die Schlaffheit, Weichheit, Schwäche.

[1]**flag** [flæg], **1.** *s.* die Fahne, (*Naut.*) Flagge; ***black –,*** die Seeräuberflagge; ***break out*** or ***unfurl a –,*** die (aufgerollte) Fahne entfalten; ***dip the –,*** die Flagge niederholen und wieder hissen; ***hoist a –,*** eine Flagge setzen; ***hoist one's –,*** das Kommando übernehmen (*of an admiral*); ***keep the – flying,*** die Fahne hochhalten; ***run up a –,*** see ***hoist a –***; (*esp. fig.*) ***show the –,*** die Fahne wehen lassen; ***strike*** or ***lower the –,*** die Flagge streichen *or* niederholen; ***strike one's –,*** das Kommando aufgeben (*of an admiral*); – ***of convenience,*** fremde Flagge; – ***of truce,*** die Parlamentärfahne. **2.** *v.t.* (mit Flaggen) ein Signal geben (*Dat.*) (*a p.*), signalisieren (*a th.*); (*esp. Naut.*) mit Flaggen schmücken, beflaggen; – ***the course,*** die Rennbahn ausflaggen; – ***a train*** (***down***), einen Zug anhalten.

[2]**flag,** *v.i.* ermatten, erschlaffen, nachlassen, nachgeben, (*as atttenion, interest etc.*) erlahmen; (*sl.*) schlappmachen.

[3]**flag, 1.** *s.* die Fliese, Steinplatte. **2.** *v.t.* mit Fliesen belegen *or* pflastern; ***flagged pavement,*** das Fliesenpflaster.

[4]**flag,** *s.* (*Bot.*) die Schwertlilie, Ilge; (*Bot.*) ***sweet –,*** der Kalmus.

flag-day, *s.* die Wohltätigkeitssammlung, der Opfertag; (*Am.*) Nationalfeiertag (*14. Juni*).

flagellant ['flædʒilənt], **1.** *s.* der Geißler, (*Eccl.*) Geißelbruder, Flagellant. **2.** *adj.* geißelnd. **flagellate** [–leit], **1.** *v.t.* geißeln. **2.** *s.* (*Zool.*) der Flagellat, das Geißeltierchen. **3.** *adj.* (*Bot.*) Schößlings–. **flagellation** [–'leiʃən], *s.* die Geißelung.

flageolet [flædʒo'let], *s.* das Flageolett.

[1]**flagging** ['flægiŋ], *adj.* nachlassend, erschlaffend, erlahmend; *see* [2]**flag.**

[2]**flagging,** *s.* (*collect.*) Fliesen, Pflastersteine (*pl.*).

flagitious [flə'dʒiʃəs], *adj.* abscheulich, schändlich, verworfen. **flagitiousness,** *s.* die Abscheulichkeit, Schändlichkeit, Verworfenheit.

flag|man, *s.* (*Naut.*) der Winker. **--officer,** *s.* (*Naut.*) der Flaggoffizier.

flagon ['flægən], *s.* der Bocksbeutel, runde Tafelflasche.

flagpole ['flægpoul], *s.* der Fahnenmast.

flagrancy ['fleigrənsi], *s.* offenkundige Schamlosigkeit, die Schändlichkeit, Abscheulichkeit, Ungeheuerlichkeit. **flagrant,** *adj.* abscheulich, entsetzlich, schändlich; offenkundig, schreiend, schamlos, empörend.

flag|ship, *s.* das Flaggschiff. **–staff,** *s.* der Flaggenstock. **–stone,** *s.* *See* [3]**flag. --wagging,** *s.* (*coll.*) das Fahnenschwenken. **--waver,** *s.* (*coll.*) der Chauvinist. **--waving,** *s.* (*coll.*) der Chauvinismus.

flail [fleil], *s.* der Dreschflegel.

flair [flɛə], *s.* (*Hunt.*) der Spürsinn, die Witterung; (*fig.*) feine Nase (***for,*** für); natürliche Begabung.

flake [fleik], **1.** *s.* die Flocke (*of snow etc.*); dünne Schicht, die Lage; Schuppe, Platte, das Blatt; ***oat–s,*** Haferflocken (*pl.*). **2.** *v.t.* 1. zu Flocken ballen; 2. ausflocken, abschuppen, abblättern; 3. mit Flocken bedecken, sprenkeln. **3.** *v.i.* zu Flocken werden, sich flocken, sich schuppen; – ***off,*** abblättern, sich abschuppen, abschälen. **flake-white,** *s.* das Schieferweiß. **flakiness,** *s.* das Flockige; Schuppige. **flaky,** *adj.* flockenartig, flockig, blattförmig, schuppig; blätterig (*as pie-crust*); – ***pastry,*** der Blätterteig.

flambeau ['flæmbou], *s.* die Fackel, der Leuchter.

flamboyance [flæm'bɔiəns], *s.* überladener Schmuck. **flamboyant,** *adj.* (*Archit.*) flammenähnlich, wellenförmig; (*fig.*) grell, leuchtend, überladen, auffallend; (*Archit.*) – ***style,*** der Flammenstil.

flame [fleim], **1.** *s.* 1. die Flamme; das Feuer; (*fig.*) die Hitze, Glut, Heftigkeit, Leidenschaft; ***burst into –(s),*** in Flammen aufgehen; 2. (*sl.*) Geliebte(r), der Schatz; ***old –,*** alte Flamme. **2.** *v.i.* flammen, (auf)lodern; (*fig.*) glühen, leuchten (***with,*** von); – ***up,*** aufflammen; (*fig.*) erröten; auffahren, aufbrausen, in hellem Zorn ausbrechen.

flame|-coloured, *adj.* feuerfarben. **--proof,** *adj.* feuerfest, flammsicher. **--thrower,** *s.* (*Mil.*) der Flammenwerfer. **flaming,** *adj.* flammend, lodernd; feurig, brennend; (*fig.*) hitzig, glühend, heftig, hell.

flamingo [flə'miŋgou], *s.* der Flamingo.

flammable ['flæməbl], *adj.* *See* **inflammable.**

flan [flæn], *s.* die Obsttorte.

Flanders ['flɑ:ndəz], *s.* Flandern (*n.*).

flange [flændʒ], **1.** *s.* der Flan(t)sch; Gurt, Kragen; Radkranz, Spurkranz (*of a wheel*). **2.** *v.t.* flan(t)schen. **flange-rail,** *s.* die Randschiene.

flank [flæŋk], **1.** *s.* 1. die Flanke, Seiche (*of animals*); 2. (*Mil.*) Flanke, der Flügel; ***exposed –,*** offener Flügel; ***take the enemy in the –,*** dem Feinde in die Flanken fallen; ***turn the –,*** die Flanke aufrollen; – ***attack,*** der Flankenangriff; – ***guard,*** die Seitendeckung. **2.** *v.t.* 1. flankieren, umgehen; seitlich begrenzen *or* abschließen; 2. (*Mil.*) die Flanke decken; die Flanke bedrohen, in der Flanke angreifen, in die Flanke fallen (*Dat.*). **flanker,** *s.* 1. (*Fort.*) das Flankenwerk; 2. *pl.* Flankierer (*pl.*), Plänkler (*pl.*). **flanking,** *adj.* – ***fire,*** das Flankenfeuer; – ***march,*** seitlicher Abmarsch; – ***movement,*** das Flankierungsmanöver.

flannel [flænl], **1.** *s.* 1. der Flanell; (*coll.*) Waschlappen; 2. (*sl.*) blauer Dunst; 3. *pl.* (*Spt.*) die Flanellhose, der Flanellanzug, weiße Sportkleidung. **2.** *v.i* (*sl.*) schummeln. **flannelet(te)** [–'let], *s.* der Baumwollflanell, die Flanellimitation.

flap [flæp], **1.** *s.* 1. der Lappen; die Krempe (*of a hat*); Klappe (*of a table*); Lasche (*of a shoe*), Patte (*of a pocket*); (*Surg.*) – ***amputation,*** die Lappenamputation; (*Av.*) ***wing* –,** die Bremsklappe; 2. der (Flügel)schlag, das Flattern, flatternde Bewegung; (*sl.*) die Aufregung, Panik. **2.** *v.t.* schlagen mit (*wings etc.*); (*coll.*) einen Klaps versetzen (*Dat.*). **3.** *v.i.* lose herabhängen, sich hin- und herbewegen, baumeln, flattern; flappen, killen (*as sails*); (*sl.*) sich aufregen.

flap|doodle, *s.* (*coll.*) der Unsinn, Quatsch, Mumpitz. **--eared,** *adj.* schlappohrig. **-jack,** *s.* der Pfannkucken; (*coll.*) die Puderdose.

flapper ['flæpə], *s.* 1. die Klapper, der Klöppel, Schlegel; die Flosse; 2. (*sl.*) der Backfisch, Fratz. **flapper-bracket,** *s.* (*sl.*) der Soziussitz (*of motorcycle*).

flare [flɛə], **1.** *v.i.* flackern, flammen, lodern; sich bauschen (*as a dress*); überhängen (*as ship's bows*); – ***up,*** aufflackern, aufleuchten, aufflammen; (*fig.*) aufbrausen, losbrechen, in Hitze geraten. **2.** *s.* 1. flackerndes Licht, plötzliches Aufleuchten, das Aufflackern; 2. Aufbauschen (*of a dress*), die Ausbauchung; 3. (*esp. Naut.*) das Lichtsignal; (*Av.*) die Leuchtkugel, Leuchtbombe. **flare|-path,** *s.* (*Av.*) der Leuchtpfad. **--up,** *s.* (*coll.*) das Aufbrausen, der (Zorn)ausbruch; Skandal.

flash [flæʃ], **1.** *s.* 1. plötzliches Aufleuchten *or* Aufflammen, das Aufblitzen; lodernde Flamme, der Blitz; (*of gun*) das Mündungsfeuer; (*Phot.*) Blitzlicht; (*fig.*) Aufblitzen, Auflodern; – ***of hope,*** der Hoffnungsstrahl; – ***of lightning,*** der Blitz(strahl); – ***of wit,*** witziger Einfall; (*fig.*) – ***in the pan,*** das Strohfeuer, mißlungener Versuch; 2. (*coll.*) der Augenblick; ***in a* –,** im Nu; 3. die Kurzmeldung; ***news* –,** die Kurznachricht; 4. (*coll.*) die Pracht, der Glanz. **2.** *adj.* (*sl.*) grell, auffällig, aufgedonnert, protzig; falsch, unecht (*as jewels*); – ***language,*** die Gaunersprache. **3.** *v.i.* 1. auflodern, aufblitzen, aufflammen, aufblinken, blitzartig aufleuchten; glänzen, glitzern; ***the lightning -ed,*** der Blitz zuckte; 2. (*fig.*) ausbrechen, hervorbrechen; sich plötzlich bewegen, springen, flitzen; ***the thought -ed across my mind,*** der Gedanke fuhr mir blitzartig durch den Kopf. **4.** *v.t.* auflodern *or* aufleuchten lassen, durchzucken; blitzschnell verbreiten (*news*); – ***a light,*** ein Licht aufblitzen lassen; – ***a light in his face,*** ihn blenden; ***his eyes -ed fire,*** seine Augen sprühten Feuer.

flash|-back, *s.* 1. (*Tech.*) der Rückschlag der Flamme; 2. (*Films etc.*) die Rückblende, Rückschau. **--bulb,** *s.* (*Phot.*) das Blitzlichtlampe. **flasher,** *s.* (*Motor.*) der Blinker. **flashiness,** *s.* (*sl.*) äußerer Glanz, auffallender Prunk, die Auffälligkeit.

flashing| indicator, *s.* (*Motor.*) der Blinker. **- light,** *s.* (*Naut.*) das Blinkfeuer.

flash|lamp, *s.* die Taschenlampe. **-light,** *s.* 1. (*Phot.*) das Blitzlicht; 2. die Taschenlampe. **--over,** *s.* (*Elec.*) der Überschlag. **--point,** *s.* der Flammpunkt. **- spotter,** *s.* (*Artil.*) der Richtkreisdiopter. **- spotting,** *s.* (*Artil.*) das Lichtmeßverfahren.

flashy ['flæʃi], *adj.* (*coll.*) grell, auffällig, auffallend, aufdringlich.

flask [flɑːsk], *s.* die Flasche; (*Chem.*) der (Glas)kolben.

flat [flæt], **1.** *adj.* 1. platt, flach; eben, glatt; (*fig.*) schal, flau, geschmacklos, (*as drink*) abgestanden; plump, langweilig, uninteressant, fade; trüb, matt, glanzlos, kontrastlos, undeutlich, seicht, oberflächlich; – ***beer,*** schales Bier; (*Railw.*) – ***car,*** der Plattformwagen; – ***coat,*** der Grundanstrich (*paint*); – ***foot,*** der Plattfuß, Senkfuß; – ***seam,*** flache Naht; (*sl.*) ***be in a – spin,*** nicht aus noch ein wissen; (*Artil.*) – ***trajectory,*** die Rasenz; – ***tyre,*** die Reifenpanne; 2. ausdrücklich, unbedingt, entschieden, glatt, klar, rund herausgesprochen; (*coll.*) ***that's* –,** das ist mein letztes Wort; – ***denial,*** glatte Ableugnung; – ***refusal,*** glatte Absage, unbedingte Verweigerung; 3. (*Mus.*) vermindert, tief, erniedrigt; 4. (*Comm.*) flau, lustlos, leblos. **2.** *adv.* 1. platt, ausgestreckt; ***fall* –,** lang hinfallen; (*fig.*) mißglücken, fehlschlagen; keinen Anklang finden, durchfallen; ein glatter Versager sein, mit Pauken und Trompeten durchfallen; ***knock him* –,** ihn zu Boden strecken; (*fig.*) ihn platt machen; ***lay*** (***lie***) **–,** platt machen (liegen); 2. glatt, direkt, rundweg; ***tell him* –,** ihm rundweg heraussagen; 3. ***sing* –,** zu tief singen. **3.** *s.* 1. die Fläche, Ebene; ebene Oberfläche (*of a solid body*); flache Seite (*of a sword*); (*usu. pl.*) die Untiefe, das Watt, (*Naut.*) die Sandbank; das Flachland, die Niederung; ***on the* –,** auf ebenem Boden; 2. (*Mus.*) das B (♭); ***sharps and -s,*** Kreuze und B's; 3. die Mietwohnung, Etagenwohnung; (*Scots*) das Stockwerk, die Etage; 4. (*sl.*) der Einfaltspinsel; 5. (*sl.*) die Reifenpanne, der Platter, Plattfuß.

flat|-bottomed, *adj.* Steh-; – ***boat,*** der Prahm. **--fish,** *s.* der Plattfisch. **-foot,** *s.* (*sl.*) der Polyp (*see also* ***flat foot***). **--footed,** *adj.* plattfüßig; (*fig.*) schwerfällig. **--iron,** *s.* das Plätteisen, Bügeleisen. **flatlet,** *s.* die Kleinwohnung. **flatly,** *adv.* glatt; geradezu, rundweg. **flatness,** *s.* die Flachheit, Plattheit; Entschiedenheit; Eintönigkeit; (*Comm.*) Flauheit. **flat|-nosed,** *adj.* stumpfnasig. **--race, --racing,** *s.* das Flachrennen. **--rate,** *s.* die Pauschalgebühr, der Einheitssatz. **--roofed,** *adj.* mit flachem Dache.

flatten [flætn], **1.** *v.t.* glatt *or* platt *or* flach machen, ebnen, glätten, ausbeulen; (*Tech.*) abflachen, breitschlagen, strecken; abstumpfen, dämpfen (*colours*), (*Mus.*) erniedrigen, (*fig.*) niederringen, niederdrücken. **2.** *v.i.* platt *or* flach werden; (*Av.*) – ***out,*** abfangen, ausschweben. **flattening,** *s.* Abflachung, Abplattung; (*Metall.*) das Strecken; flache *or* ebene Stelle.

[1]**flatter** ['flætə], *v.t.* schmeicheln (*Dat.*), Komplimente machen (*Dat.*); günstig darstellen (*as portraits*); – ***his hopes,*** ihn mit unbegründeter Hoffnung erfüllen; – ***o.s.,*** sich einbilden, sich (*Dat.*) in dem Gedanken gefallen; – ***o.s. on,*** sich beglückwünschen zu; – ***his vanity,*** seine Eitelkeit befriedigen.

[2]**flatter,** *s.* (*Tech.*) der Streckhammer, Breithammer; die Streckwalze.

[3]**flatter,** *comp. adj. See* **flat.**

flattering ['flætəriŋ], *adj.* schmeichelhaft, schmeichlerisch, schmeichelnd; geschmeichelt (*as portraits*). **flattery,** *s.* die Schmeichelei.

flatting ['flætiŋ], *s.* das Platthämmern; – ***mill,*** das Streckwerk.

flatulence, flatulency ['flætjuləns(i)], *s.* die Blähung; (*Med.*) Blähsucht; (*fig.*) Aufgeblasenheit, Nichtigkeit, Eitelkeit, Anmaßung. **flatulent,** *adj.* blähend, blähsüchtig; (*fig.*) aufgeblasen, aufgebläht, schwülstig, nichtig.

flatus ['fleitəs], *s.* die Blähung.

flaunt [flɔːnt], **1.** *v.t.* paradieren *or* prunken mit, (stolz) zur Schau tragen. **2.** *v.i.* prangen, (herum)stolzieren, paradieren.

flautist ['flɔːtist], *s.* der Flötenspieler, Flötist.

flavor (*Am.*), *see* **flavour.**

flavour ['fleivə], **1.** *s.* der (Wohl)geschmack; Wohlgeruch, Duft, das Aroma; die Blume (*of wine*); (*fig.*) der Beigeschmack, die Würze. **2.** *v.t.* Geschmack *or* Duft geben (*Dat.*), schmackhaft machen, würzen. **flavoured,** *adj.* schmackhaft, würzig; wohlriechend; ***full*-–,** schwer, stark (*as cigars*), mit starker Blume (*as wine*), stark gewürzt (*as food*). **flavouring,** *s.* die Würze. **flavourless,** *adj.* geschmacklos, schal, fade.

flaw [flɔː], *s.* der Fehler, Makel; fehlerhafte Stelle; der Sprung, Riß, Bruch; (*Tech.*) die Blase, Wolke, der Flecken (*in cast metal, gems etc.*); (*Law*) Formfehler. **flawless,** *adj.* makellos, fehlerlos, fehlerfrei; (*fig.*) tadellos.

flax [flæks], *s.* der Flachs, Lein; die Leinpflanze. **flax|-comb,** *s.* die Flachshechel. **--dresser,** *s.* der Flachsbereiter. **flaxen,** *adj.* Flachs-, flachsen, flächse(r)n, flachsartig; flachsfarben, flachsgelb; – ***hair,*** flachsblondes Haar. **flaxen-haired,** *adj.*

flachshaarig; – *child*, kleiner Flachskopf. **flax-seed,** *s.* der Leinsamen. **flaxy,** *adj. See* **flaxen.**

flay [flei], *v.t.* schinden; die Haut abziehen (*Dat.*); (*fig.*) heruntermachen, scharf kritisieren.

flea [fli:], *s.* der Floh; ***send him away with a – in his ear,*** ihm gehörig den Kopf waschen. **flea|-bag,** *s.* (*sl.*) die Flohkiste, der Schlafsack. **–bane,** *s.* (*Bot.*) das Flohkraut. **–bite,** *s.* der Flohstich; (*coll.*) geringfügige Verletzung; die Kleinigkeit, Bagatelle. **–-bitten,** *adj.* von Flöhen gebissen *or* zerstochen.

fleam [fli:m], *s.* (*Vet.*) die Fliete, Lanzette.

flea-pit, *s.* der *or* das Kintopp.

fleck [flek], **1.** *v.t.* sprenkeln, tüpfeln. **2.** *s.* kleiner Fleck(en).

flection, *see* **flexion.**

fled [fled], *imperf., p.p. of* **flee.**

fledge [fledʒ], **1.** *v.t.* befiedern, mit Federn versehen (*as an arrow*). **2.** *v.i.* flügge werden, Federn bekommen (*as a bird*). **fledged,** *adj.* flügge, befiedert; (*fig.*) ***fully*** –, erwachsen, fertig. **fledg(e)ling,** *s.* junger Vogel; (*fig.*) unerfahrener Mensch, der Grünschnabel.

flee [fli:], **1.** *irr.v.t.* fliehen, plötzlich verlassen, meiden, ausweichen (*Dat.*), sich fernhalten von; – ***one's country,*** sein Vaterland verlassen. **2.** *irr.v.i.* fliehen, die Flucht ergreifen (***from,*** vor (*Dat.*)), entfliehen, schwinden.

fleece [fli:s], **1.** *s.* das Vlies, (Schaf)fell; geschorene Wolle, die Schur. **2.** *v.t.* scheren; (*fig.*) rupfen, ausrauben, plündern. **fleecy,** *adj.* wollig; flockig; weich; – ***clouds,*** Schäfchen(wolken) (*pl.*).

fleer [fliə], **1.** *v.i.* höhnisch lachen, spotten (***at,*** über (*Acc.*)). **2.** *s.* der Spott, das Hohngelächter.

[1]**fleet** [fli:t], **1.** *adj.* (*Poet.*) schnell, flink, flüchtig; – ***of foot,*** schnellfüßig. **2.** *v.i.* (*rare*) dahineilen, dahinfliehen, flüchtig sein.

[2]**fleet,** *s.* die (Kriegs)flotte; ***Admiral of the Fleet,*** der Großadmiral; ***Fleet Air Arm,*** die Marineluftwaffe; – ***of cars,*** der Wagenpark.

fleet-footed, *adj. See* ***fleet of foot.*** **fleeting,** *adj.* dahineilend, flüchtig, vergänglich; (*Mil.*) – ***target,*** das Augenblicksziel. **fleetness,** *s.* die Schnelligkeit, Flüchtigkeit.

Fleming ['flemiŋ], *s.* der Flame (die Flamin *or* Flämin). **Flemish, 1.** *adj.* flämisch, flandrisch. **2.** *s.* das Flämisch(e) (*language*).

flense [flens], *v.t.* flensen, abhäuten (*whales etc.*).

flesh [fleʃ], **1.** *s.* das Fleisch; ***become one –,*** ein Leib und eine Seele werden; ***my own – and blood,*** mein Fleisch und Blut, meine Blutsverwandten; ***it makes my – creep,*** mich überläuft eine Gänsehaut; ***in the –,*** leibhaftig, höchstpersönlich; ***in –,*** korpulent, wohlbeleibt; (*B.*) ***be made –,*** Mensch werden; ***proud –,*** wildes Fleisch; ***run to –,*** zur Beleibtheit neigen; ***pleasures of the –,*** die Fleischeslust, Sinnenlust; ***put on –,*** dick werden. **2.** *v.t.* **1.** Fleisch kosten lassen (*hounds*); (*fig.*) kampfmutig machen; abrichten, einweihen, gewöhnen an (*Acc.*); – ***one's sword,*** das Schwert (zum erstenmal) üben; 2. vom Fleisch befreien, abschaben, ausfleischen (*skins*).

flesh|-brush, *s.* die Frottierbürste. **–-colour,** *s.* die Fleischfarbe. **–-coloured,** *adj.* fleischfarben. **flesher,** *s.* (*Scots*) der Fleischer; (*Tan.*) Ausfleischer; das Ausfleischmesser. **flesh-hook,** *s.* der Fleischhaken. **fleshiness,** *s.* die Fleischigkeit, Beleibtheit. **fleshing,** *s.* 1. (*Tan.*) das Ausfleischen; *pl.* Fleischreste (*pl.*), Abschabsel (*pl.*); 2. *pl.* fleischfarbener Trikot. **fleshliness,** *s.* die Fleischlichkeit, Sinnlichkeit. **fleshly,** *adj.* fleischlich, körperlich, sinnlich; irdisch, weltlich, diesseitig, sterblich. **flesh|-pots,** *pl.* (*coll.*) Fleischtöpfe (*pl.*), üppiges Leben. **–-wound,** *s.* die Fleischwunde. **fleshy,** *adj.* fleischig, fleischartig.

fleur-de-lis [flə:də'li:], *s.* (*Her.*) die Lilie; (*Bot.*) Schwertlilie.

flew [flu:], *imperf. of* **fly.**

flews [flu:z], *pl.* Lefzen (*pl.*) (*of hounds*).

flex [fleks], **1.** *s.* die Litze, der Litzendraht, die Anschlußschnur, Kontaktschnur. **2.** *v.t., v.i.* biegen, beugen. **flexibility** [–i'biliti], *s.* die Biegsamkeit, Geschmeidigkeit (*also fig.*); (*fig.*) Fügsamkeit, Anpassungsfähigkeit. **flexible,** *adj.* biegsam, geschmeidig; (*Tech.*) unstarr, beweglich, bewegungsfrei; (*fig.*) lenksam, fügsam, anpassungsfähig, nachgiebig; – ***axle,*** die Lenkachse; – ***coupling,*** die Gelenkkupplung; – ***mind,*** fügsames Gemut; – ***rule,*** das Bandmaß.

flexile ['fleksail], *adj. See* **flexible** (*fig.*). **flexion** ['flekʃən], *s.* die Biegung, Beugung; (*Gram.*) Flexion. **flexional,** *adj.* (*Gram.*) Biegungs–, Beugungs–, Flexions–, flektierend. **flexor,** *s.* der Beugemuskel, (*Anat.*) Beuger. **flexural** ['flekʃərəl], *adj.* (*Tech.*) Biege–, Biegungs–. **flexure,** *s.* das (Um)biegen; die Biegung, Beugung, Krümmung; (*Geol.*) Flexur.

flibbertigibbet [flibəti'dʒibit], *s.* (*coll.*) leichtsinniger *or* unbeständiger Mensch.

flick [flik], **1.** *s.* 1. leichter Schlag *or* Hieb, der Ruck; das Schnippchen; 2. *pl.* (*sl.*) die Flimmerkiste, der *or* das Kintopp. **2.** *v.t.* leicht schlagen *or* berühren, schnellen, schnippen; – ***away*** or ***off,*** abklopfen, wegschnellen. **3.** *v.i.* sich ruckartig bewegen.

flicker ['flikə], **1.** *v.i.* flackern, flimmern; flattern. **2.** *s.* das (Auf)flackern, Flimmern; Flattern, Zucken; flackerndes Licht; (*fig.*) der Funke(n) (*of hope etc.*).

flick-knife, *s.* das Schnappmesser.

flier, *see* **flyer.**

flight [flait], *s.* 1. die Flucht, das Entrinnen; ***put to –,*** in die Flucht schlagen; ***take to –,*** die Flucht ergreifen, fliehen, flüchten; 2. das Fliegen, der Flug; die Luftfahrt, Fliegerei; Flugreise, Luftreise; Flugstrecke; (***cross-***)***Atlantic –,*** der Ozeanflug; – ***of fancy,*** der Flug *or* Schwung *or* Ausbruch der Phantasie; (*fig.*) ***in the first –,*** in der vordersten Reihe, in der Vorhut, an der Spitze; (*Av.*) ***make*** or ***take a –,*** fliegen; – ***of time,*** der Flug der Zeit; 3. die Schar, der Schwarm (*of birds*), Regen, Hagel (*of missiles*); (*Av.*) Verband, die Kette; – ***of pigeons,*** der Flug von Tauben; 4. – ***of stairs*** or ***steps,*** die Treppenflucht.

flight|-commander, *s.* (*Av.*) der Kettenführer. **–-deck,** *s.* (*Naut.*) das Flugdeck. **flightiness,** *s.* die Fahrigkeit, Flatterhaftigkeit. **flight|-lane,** *s.* die Flugschneise. **–-lieutenant,** *s.* (*Av.*) der Fliegerhauptmann. **–-mechanic,** *s.* (*Av.*) der Bordwart, Bordmechaniker. **–-personnel,** *s.* fliegendes Personal. **–-sergeant,** *s.* (*Av.*) der Oberfeldwebel der Luftwaffe. **flighty,** *adj.* launisch, fahrig, flatterhaft, leichtsinnig, zerstreut.

flim-flam ['flimflæm], *s.* (*sl.*) der Unsinn, Unfug, Mumpitz, Schwindel.

flimsiness ['flimzinis], *s.* die Dünnheit, Lockerheit; (*fig.*) Nichtigkeit, Fadenscheinigkeit. **flimsy, 1.** *adj.* locker, lose, dünn; (*fig.*) schwach, dürftig, nichtig, fadenscheinig. **2.** *s.* 1. dünnes Kopierpapier; (*sl.*) die Banknote; 2. *pl.* (*sl.*) das Damenunterzeug.

flinch [flintʃ], *v.i.* (zurück)weichen, zurückschrecken (***from,*** vor (*Dat.*)), abstehen (von), ausweichen (*Dat.*); zusammenfahren, wanken, zucken.

fling [fliŋ], **1.** *irr.v.t.* werfen, schleudern; – ***away,*** wegwerfen, verschleudern; fahren lassen (*a chance etc.*); (*fig.*) – ***back,*** hitzig erwidern; – ***down,*** zu Boden werfen, niederwerfen; – ***s.th. in his teeth,*** ihm etwas ins Gesicht schleudern; (*fig.*) – ***o.s. into,*** sich stürzen in (*Acc.*); – ***off,*** abwerfen; (*fig.*) – ***o.s. on him,*** sich ihm anvertrauen; – ***open,*** aufreißen (*a door*); – ***out,*** hinauswerfen; ungestüm ausstrecken (*one's arms*); – ***to,*** zuwerfen (*a door*); – ***up,*** in die Höhe werfen. **2.** *irr.v.i.* (*also* – ***up***) hinten ausschlagen (*as a horse*); unbändig werden (*of a p.*). **3.** *s.* der Wurf; das Ausschlagen (*of a horse*); (*fig.*) toller Ausbruch; der Hieb, die Stichelei; ***Highland –,*** schottischer Tanz; ***have a – at,*** werfen nach; (*coll.*) versuchen; ***let him have his –,*** laß ihn austoben! laß ihn sich (*Dat.*) die Hörner abstoßen!

flint [flint], *s.* der Kiesel, Feuerstein; ***heart of –,*** ein

Herz wie Stein; (*coll.*) ***skin a –***, geizig sein; – ***and steel***, das Feuerzeug. **flint|-glass,** *s.* das Kieselglas, Flintglas. **--hard,** *adj.* kieselhart. **-lock,** *s.* das Steinschloß. **flinty,** *adj.* kieselartig, kieselhaltig; (*fig.*) hart.

flip [flip], **1.** *v.t.* leicht schlagen, klapsen, schnellen. **2.** *v.i.* (*of a th.*) schnippen, schnipsen. **3.** *s.* der Klaps, Ruck; (*sl.*) kurze Fahrt, kurzer Flug.

flippancy ['flipənsi], *s.* die Leichtfertigkeit (im Reden), der Leichtsinn; die Frivolität, Keckheit, schnippisches *or* vorlautes Wesen. **flippant,** *adj.* vorlaut, schnippisch, leichtfertig, respektlos, frivol, keck. **flippantly,** *adv.* leichthin, obenhin.

flipper ['flipə], *s.* (*coll.*) der Ruderschwanz, die (Schwimm)flosse; (*sl.*) Hand.

flirt [flə:t], **1.** *v.i.* flirten, kokettieren; (*fig.*) liebäugeln, spielen. **2.** *v.t.* spielen mit, schnellen, schnipsen. **3.** *s.* die Kokette; der Courschneider, Schäker, Hofmacher. **flirtation** [-'teiʃən], *s.* der Flirt, die Liebelei. **flirtatious,** *adj.* kokett, gefallsüchtig, kokettierend, flirtend.

flit [flit], **1.** *v.i.* 1. huschen, flitzen, hin- und herflattern; – ***by*** or ***past***, verfliegen, vorbeihuschen; 2. (*Scots*) umziehen, ausziehen. **2.** *s.* (*sl.*) ***do a*** (***moonlight***) –, (heimlich *or* verstohlen) umziehen *or* ausziehen.

flitch [flitʃ], *s.* – ***of bacon***, geräucherte Speckseite.

flivver ['flivə], *s.* (*sl.*) billiges Auto, die Kiste, alte Karre.

float [flout], **1.** *s.* das Schwimmende; Floß; der Kork(schwimmer) (*angling*); die (Rad)schaufel (*of a paddle wheel*); das Flott (*of a fishing-net*); die Schwimmblase (*of fishes*); das Reibebrett (*of masons*); Schwimmgestell (*of seaplane*), der Schwimmer (*of carburettor etc.*); Förderkarren, Plattformwagen; (*Theat.*) (*usu. pl.*) das Rampenlicht. **2.** *v.i.* (obenauf) schwimmen, (*Naut.*) flott sein; schweben, (dahin)treiben; gleiten; (*Comm.*) in Umlauf sein. **3.** *v.t.* 1. unter Wasser setzen, überschwemmen, überfluten; 2. (*Naut.*) flottmachen; zum Schwimmen bringen, schwimmen *or* treiben lassen; (*fig.*) gründen, in Gang bringen (*an enterprise*), verbreiten, in Umlauf setzen (*rumour*); auflegen, ausgeben (*a loan*).

floatable ['floutəbl], *adj.* schwimmfähig, flößbar. **floatage** [-tidʒ], *s.* die Schwimmfähigkeit, Schwimmkraft; das Schwimmen, Treiben; Schwimmende(s). **floatation** [-'teiʃən], *s.* *See* **floatage**; die Gründung (*of a company*); Auflegung (*of a loan*). **float-chamber,** *s.* (*Motor.*) das Schwimmergehäuse. **floater,** *s.* 1. Schwimmende(r, -s); 2. der Gründer (*of a company*); 3. (*St. Exch.*) anerkanntes Papier; 4. (*coll.*) parteiloser Wähler; 5. der Gelegenheitsarbeiter. **float|-feed,** *s.* schwimmerregulierte Zuleitung. **--gauge,** *s.* der Schwimmer.

floating ['floutiŋ], *adj.* schwimmend, treibend, Schwimm-, Treib-; (*Comm.*) zirkulierend, im Umlauf befindlich; (*fig.*) schwebend, schwankend, unsicher; – ***anchor***, der Treibanker; – ***assets***, Aktiven, flüssige Anlagen (*pl.*); – ***battery***, schwimmende Batterie; – ***bridge***, die Floßbrücke; – ***capital***, flüssiges Kapital; das Umlaufskapital, Betriebskapital; – ***debt***, schwebende Schuld; – ***dock***, das Schwimmdock; – ***ice***, das Treibeis; – ***kidney***, die Wanderniere; – ***light***, die Leuchtboje, das Leuchtschiff; – ***mine***, die Treibmine; – ***population***, schwankende Bevölkerung; – ***vote***, nichtparteigebundene Wählerschaft.

floccose [flɔ'kous], *adj.* (*Bot.*) wollig, flockig. **flocculate** ['flɔkjuleit], *v.t.* ausflocken. **flocculent,** *adj.* flockig, flockenartig, wollig.

[1]**flock** [flɔk], *s.* die Flocke (*of wool*); *pl.* der Wollabfall (*for cushions etc.*).

[2]**flock, 1.** *s.* die Herde (*of sheep*); der Flug (*of birds*); (*Eccl.*) die Gemeinde; (*fig.*) der Haufen, die Menge, Schar. **2.** *v.i.* sich scharen, zusammenströmen; – ***out of the room***, aus dem Zimmer herausströmen; – ***to him***, ihm zuströmen; – ***to a meeting***, in (hellen) Scharen zu einer Versammlung kommen; – ***together***, sich zusammenscharen.

flock| bed, *s.* das Wollbett. – **mattress,** *s.* die Wollmatratze. **--paper,** *s.* die Samttapete, Flocktapete.

floe [flou], *s.* die Eisscholle, treibendes Eis(feld); *pl.* das Treibeis.

flog [flɔg], *v.t.* (aus)peitschen, prügeln, züchtigen; – ***a horse on***, ein Pferd antreiben; (*coll.*) – ***a dead horse***, sich vergeblich anstrengen. **flogging,** *s.* das Peitschen; die Prügelstrafe, körperliche Züchtigung; ***get a –***, (durch)geprügelt werden.

flood [flʌd], **1.** *s.* die Flut, Überschwemmung (*also fig.*), das Hochwasser; (*fig.*) der Erguß, Schwall, die Fülle, Flut; (*Poet.*) der Strom; (*B.*) die Sintflut; ***-s of tears***, die Tränenflut, der Tränenstrom; – ***of words***, der Wortschwall. **2.** *v.t.* überfluten, überschwemmen, unter Wasser setzen; (*submarine tanks*) fluten. **3.** *v.i.* fluten, strömen, sich ergießen; steigen (*as the tide*); – ***in upon***, überfluten, sich ergießen über (*Acc.*).

flood|-bound, *adj.* ringsum von Wasser eingeschlossen. – **disaster,** *s.* die Hochwasserkatastrophe. **-gate,** *s.* die Schleuse (*also fig.*), das Schleusentor. **flooding,** *s.* das Überfließen, die Überschwemmung, Überflutung; das Fluten (*submarine tanks etc.*); (*Med.*) die Gebärmutterblutung. **flood|light, 1.** *s.* (*usu. pl.*) das Bühnenlicht; der Scheinwerfer; (*fig.*) das Schlaglicht. **2.** *v.t.* (mit Scheinwerfern) anstrahlen *or* beleuchten. **-lighting,** *s.* die Scheinwerferbeleuchtung, das Flutlicht. **-lit,** *adj.* von Scheinwerfern beleuchtet; (*Spt.*) – ***game***, das Flutlichtspiel. **--mark,** *s.* das Hochwasserstandszeichen. **--tide,** *s.* die Flut.

floor [flɔ:], **1.** *s.* der (Fuß)boden, die Diele; (*of a building*) der Stock, das Geschoß, Stockwerk; (*of the sea*) der Grund, Boden, (*of a barn*) die Tenne; (*of a trench etc.*) Sohle; (*Parl.*) (*fig.*) der Sitzungssaal; ***ground--*** (*Am.* ***first –***), das Erdgeschoß, Parterre; ***on the first –*** (*Am.* ***second –***), im ersten Stock; (*Parl.*) – ***of the House***, der Sitzungssaal; ***inlaid –***, das Parkett; (*Parl.*) ***have*** (***take***) ***the –***, das Wort haben (ergreifen); ***take the –***, tanzen; (*sl.*) ***wipe the – with him***, ihn gehörig zurichten *or* vollkommen erledigen. **2.** *v.t.* 1. dielen, pflastern, mit Fußboden versehen (*a room*); 2. (*coll.*) zu Boden strecken (*a p.*); (*fig.*) verblüffen, zum Schweigen bringen, auf den Sand setzen.

floorage ['flɔ:ridʒ], *s.* die (Fuß)bodenfläche. **floorcloth,** *s.* der Wischlappen, Scheuerlappen. **flooring,** *s.* der Fußboden; die Dielung, das Bodenmaterial, der Fußbodenbelag. **floor|-lamp,** *s.* (*Am.*) die Stehlampe. – **manager,** *s.* der Abteilungsleiter (*in large stores*). – **plan,** *s.* der Grundriß. **--polish,** *s.* das Bohnerwachs. **--show,** *s.* die Kabarettvorstellung. **--space,** *s.* die Grundfläche. **--stain,** *s.* die Bodenbeize. **--timbers,** *pl.* (*Shipb.*) Kielplanken. **-walker,** *s.* (*Am.*) die Aufsicht (*in large stores*). **--wax,** *s.* *See* **--polish.**

flop [flɔp], **1.** *v.i.* 1. (*coll.*) schwerfällig niederfallen, hinplumpsen; lose herunterhängen; 2. (*sl.*) scheitern, versagen, durchfallen. **2.** *s.* 1. der Plumps, das Plumpsen; 2. (*sl.*) der Mißerfolg, Versager, Durchfall; (*of a p.*) die Niete. **3.** *int.* plumps! **floppiness,** *s.* (*coll.*) die Schlaffheit, Schlappheit. **floppy,** *adj.* schlaff, schlapp(ig), schlotterig.

flora ['flɔ:rə], *s.* die Pflanzenwelt, Flora. **floral,** *adj.* Blüten-, Blumen-; (*Her.*) – ***emblem***, die Wappenblume.

Florence ['flɔrəns], *s.* (*Geog.*) Florenz (*n.*). **Florentine** [-tain], **1.** *adj.* Florentiner-, florentinisch. **2.** *s.* der (die) Florentiner(in).

florescence [flɔ'resəns], *s.* die Blüte(zeit). **florescent,** *adj.* (auf)blühend. **floret** ['flɔ:ret], *s.* (*Bot.*) das Blümchen, Blütchen. **floriculture** ['flɔ:rikʌltʃə], *s.* die Blumenzucht.

florid ['flɔrid], *adj.* blühend, rot, gerötet; (*Archit.*) überladen; dekorativ, (*Mus.*) figural; blumenreich (*as language*); (*obs.*) blumig, blütenreich.

florin ['flɔrin], *s.* der Gulden (*Holland*), (*obs.*) das 10-Pence-Stück (*England*).

florist ['flɔrist], *s.* der Blumenhändler; Blumenzüchter.

floss [flɔs], *s.* die Rohseide, der Seidenflaum; ungezwirnte Seidenfäden (*pl.*), das Florettgarn. **floss-silk,** *s.* die Wattseide, Florettseide. **flossy,** *adj.* seidenweich, seidenähnlich.

flotage, flotation, *see* **floatage, floatation.**

flotilla [flo'tilə], *s.* die Flotille.

flotsam ['flɔtsəm], *s.* das Treibgut, treibendes Wrackgut, die Seetrift, seetriftiges Gut; (*fig.*) das Strandgut; – ***and jetsam,*** das Strandgut, Wrackgut; (*fig.*) wertlose Kleinigkeiten (*pl.*), Überbleibsel (*pl.*), Reste (*pl.*).

[1]**flounce** [flauns], *v.i.* – ***in,*** hereinstürmen; – ***out of the room,*** trotzig *or* ungehalten aus dem Zimmer stürzen.

[2]**flounce, 1.** *s.* die Falbel, Krause, loser Besatz, der Volant. **2.** *v.t.* mit Falbeln *or* Volants besetzen.

[1]**flounder** ['flaundə], *v.i.* sich wühlen *or* abquälen; umherstolpern, zappeln, taumeln; (*fig.*) nicht weiterwissen, stocken (*in speaking*).

[2]**flounder,** *s.* (*Ichth.*) die Flunder.

flour ['flauə], **1.** *s.* das Mehl; ***coarse –,*** das Schrot. **2.** *v.t.* mit Mehl bestreuen.

flourish ['flʌriʃ], **1.** *v.i.* 1. blühen, gedeihen, in Blüte sein, florieren; 2. leben, wirken, tätig sein; 3. Schnörkel machen (*in writing*), sich geziert ausdrücken; 4. einen Tusch blasen, schmettern (*of trumpets*); 5. (*fig.*) protzen, prahlen. **2.** *v.t.* schwingen (*a sword*); schwenken (*a flag*), protzen mit, zur Schau stellen. **3.** *s.* 1. der Schnörkel, die Floskel; ***write one's name with a –,*** seinen Namen zierlich verschnörkeln; 2. das Schwingen (*of a sword*), Schwenken (*of a flag*), (*Mus.*) Vorspiel; ***in full –,*** in voller Blüte; – ***of trumpets,*** die Trompetenfanfare, der Tusch; ***do with a –,*** prahlend tun. **flourishing,** *adj.* blühend, gedeihend, (*of trade*) schwunghaft.

flour| mill, *s.* die (Mahl)mühle. – **mite,** *s.* die Mehlmilbe. **floury,** *adj.* mehlartig, mehlig; mehlbestreut.

flout [flaut], **1.** *v.t.* verhöhnen, verspotten, verächtlich machen. **2.** *v.i.* spotten (***at,*** über (*Acc.*)); – ***at fortune,*** dem Glücke Hohn sprechen.

flow [flou], **1.** *v.i.* sich ergießen, fließen, strömen, fluten, rinnen, quellen; lose herabhängen, wallen (*as garments etc.*); – ***from,*** fließen aus, entfließen, entströmen (*Dat.*); (*fig.*) herrühren von, sich ergeben aus, entstehen aus, entspringen (*Dat.*); ***–ing with milk and honey,*** wo Milch und Honig fließt. **2.** *s.* 1. der Fluß, Lauf, die Strömung, Flut; der Zufluß, Zustrom; 2. (*fig.*) Strom, Schwall, Erguß (*of words*); das Wogen, Wallen (*of dress*); 3. Überschäumen, der Überfluß, die Ergießung.

flow-chart, *s.* das Flußschema, Verarbeitungsdiagramm.

flower ['flauə], **1.** *s.* 1. die Blume; (*Bot.*) Blüte (*also fig.*); ***artificial –s,*** künstliche Blumen; ***cut –s,*** Schnittblumen; ***in –,*** in Blüte; ***no –s by request,*** Blumenspenden dankend verbeten; ***say it with –s!*** laßt Blumen sprechen! 2. (*fig.*) das Beste, Feinste, die Auslese, Zierde, der Schmuck; ***the – of chivalry,*** die Zierde der Ritterschaft; ***–s of rhetoric,*** Redeblüten; ***the – of the troops,*** die Besten *or* Auslese der Truppen; 3. (*Typ.*) die Vignette, Leiste; 4. (*Chem.*) ***–s of sulphur,*** Schwefelblumen; sublimierter Schwefel. **2.** *v.i.* blühen (*also fig.*); (*fig.*) in höchster Blüte stehen. **3.** *v.t.* mit Blumenmuster schmücken, blümen.

flowerage ['flauəridʒ], *s.* der Blütenreichtum, Blumenflor. **flower|-bed,** *s.* das Blumenbeet. **–-de-luce,** *s.* (*Am.*) *see* **fleur-de-lis. flowered,** *adj.* geblümt, blumig. **flower-girl,** *s.* die Blumenverkäuferin. **floweriness,** *s.* der Blütenreichtum; (*fig.*) blumenreicher Schmuck, die Geblümtheit, Geziertheit (*of speech*). **flowering, 1.** *adj.* blühend, blütentragend; ***be –,*** in Blüte stehen. **2.** *s.* die Blüte, das (Auf)blühen; – ***time,*** die Blütezeit. **flower|-leaf,** *s.* das Blütenblatt. **–pot,** *s.* der Blumentopf. **–-show,** *s.* die Blumenausstellung. **–-stalk,** *s.* der Blütenstiel. **–-vase,** *s.* das Blumengefäß, die Blumenvase. **flowery,** *adj.* blütenreich, blumig; (*fig.*) blumenreich, geziert; geblümt (*pattern*).

flowing ['flouiŋ], *adj.* fließend, strömend; flatternd, wallend, lose hängend; (*fig.*) fließend, schwungvoll; ununterbrochen; (*Poet.*) – ***cup,*** überschäumender Becher.

flown [floun], *p.p. of* **fly.**

flow-pattern, *s.* das Strömungsbild.

flu [flu:], *s.* (*coll.*) *see* **influenza.**

fluctuate ['flʌktjueit], *v.i.* schwanken, sich ständig ändern, (*as prices*) steigen und fallen. **fluctuation** [–'eiʃən], *s.* (*Comm., Elec. etc.*) das Schwanken, Wogen, die Schwankung.

[1]**flue** [flu:], *s.* der Rauchfang, die Esse; das Flammrohr, Heizrohr, (*of organ*) die Kernspalte; ***–-gas,*** das Abgas; ***–-pipe,*** die Lippenpfeife (*of organ*); ***–-stop,*** das Lippenregister (*of organ*).

[2]**flue,** *s.* der Flaum, die Staubflocke.

[3]**flue,** *s.* das Schleppnetz.

fluency ['flu:ənsi], *s.* der Fluß (*of speech*); die Geläufigkeit, Sprachfertigkeit, (*fig.*) Flüssigkeit. **fluent,** *adj.* fließend; geläufig; (*fig.*) flüssig, leicht.

fluff [flʌf], **1.** *s.* leichte Staubflocke, die Federflocke, der Flaum; (*sl.*) ***bit of –,*** das Mädchen. **2.** *v.t.* zu Flaum machen; (*coll.*) verpfuschen; – ***up*** or ***out,*** aufplustern. **fluffiness,** *s.* die Flaumigkeit, Flockigkeit. **fluffy,** *adj.* flaumig, flockig; mit Flaum bedeckt.

fluid ['flu:id], **1.** *s.* die Flüssigkeit; (*Anat.*) der Saft, die Sekretion. **2.** *adj.* (dünn)flüssig; (*fig.*) fließend, in Bewegung, im Fluß; – ***mechanics,*** die Strömungslehre, Hydromechanik; – ***ounce*** (= *28.5* (*Am. 29.5*) *ccm.*) (ein Flüssigkeitsmaß). **fluidity** [–'iditi], *s.* die Flüssigkeit (*also fig.*), Leichtflüssigkeit; flüssiger Zustand.

[1]**fluke** [flu:k], *s.* (*Ichth.*) die Flunder.

[2]**fluke,** *s.* der Ankerarm, Ankerflügel, die Ankerhand, Ankerschaufel; *pl.* Schwanzflossen (*pl.*) (*of a whale*).

[3]**fluke,** *s.* (*coll.*) glücklicher Zufall, der Dusel; (*Bill.*) Fuchs; ***by a –,*** durch Zufall. **fluky,** *adj.* unsicher, Zufalls–.

flume [flu:m], *s.* künstlicher Wasserlauf; die Klamm.

flummery ['flʌməri], *s.* (*Cul.*) der Flammeri; (*fig., coll.*) leeres Geschwätz, das Gewäsch.

flummox ['flʌməks], *v.t.* (*sl.*) verblüffen.

flung [flʌŋ], *imperf., p.p. of* **fling.**

flunk [flʌŋk], (*Am.*) **1.** *v.i.* sich drücken, kneifen; durchfallen, durchrasseln. **2.** *v.t.* durchfallen lassen.

flunkey ['flʌŋki], *s.* Livreebediente(r), der Lakai; Speichellecker, Kriecher; Handlanger. **flunkeydom** [–dəm], *s.* Livreebedienten (*pl.*), die Dienerschaft. **flunkeyism,** *s.* der Knechtssinn, die Kriecherei, Speichelleckerei.

fluor ['flu:ɔ:], *s. See* **fluorite. fluoresce** [fluə'res], *v.i.* schillern, fluoreszieren. **fluorescence,** *s.* die Fluoreszenz. **fluorescent** *adj.* schillernd, fluoreszierend; – ***lamp,*** die Leuchtstofflampe. **fluoric** [–'ɔrik], *adj.* Fluor–; – ***acid,*** die Fluorwasserstoffsäure. **fluoride** ['fluəraid], *s.* das Fluorsalz, die Fluorverbindung; – ***of,*** Fluor–. **fluorine** [–ri:n], *s.* das Fluor. **fluorite** [–rait], *s.* der Flußspat, das Fluorkalzium. **fluorspar,** *s. See* **fluorite.**

flurry ['flʌri], **1.** *s.* die Verwirrung, ängstliche Eile; nervöse Aufregung; das (Schnee)gestöber; der Windstoß; ***in a –,*** aufgeregt, verwirrt. **2.** *v.t. See* **fluster, 2.**

[1]**flush** [flʌʃ], **1.** *v.i.* 1. erröten, rot werden; erglühen; 2. (*of blood*) strömen, sich ergießen, ins Gesicht steigen; 3. (*Bot.*) sprießen. **2.** *v.t.* 1. erröten machen, erhitzen; (*fig.*) beleben, erregen, entflammen; ***–ed with anger,*** mit Zornröte übergossen; ***–ed with joy,*** freudetrunken; ***–ed with victory,*** siegestrunken; ***–ed with wine,*** vom Wein erhitzt; 2. (*Bot.*) zum Sprießen bringen. **3.** *s.* 1. das Erröten, die Röte, Glut; 2. (*fig.*) Aufwallung (*of joy*); Flut, der Sturm (*of passion*); die Fülle, Blüte,

Kraft, der Glanz, Überfluß (*of youth etc.*); 3. (*Med.*) die Fieberhitze; 4. (*Bot.*) üppiges Wachstum.

[2]**flush,** *adj.* 1. (*Tech.*) (plan)eben, in gleicher Ebene; (*Typ.*) ohne Einzug, stumpf; ***fit – together,*** (*v.t.*) planeben zusammenfügen; (*v.i.*) planeben zusammengefügt sein; ***– with,*** bündig mit; (*Naut.*) ***– deck,*** das Glattdeck; ***– head,*** der Versenkkopf; ***– rivet,*** die Senkniete; 2. (*coll.*) ***be –,*** Geld haben, bei Kasse sein.

[3]**flush, 1.** *v.t.* 1. ausspülen, durchspülen; überschwemmen; 2. (*Hunt.*) aufscheuchen, aufjagen (*birds etc.*). **2.** *v.i.* 1. sich durchspülen lassen; 2. (*Hunt.*) auffliegen, aufgescheucht werden.

[4]**flush,** *s.* (*Cards*) (*also* ***– hand***) die Flöte, lange Farbe.

flushing ['flʌʃiŋ], *s.* (*Geog.*) Vlissingen (*n.*).

flush toilet, *s.* das Spülklosett.

fluster ['flʌstə], **1.** *s.* die Verwirrung, Aufregung; (*coll.*) ***all in a –,*** ganz verwirrt. **2.** *v.t.* verwirren, aufregen, nervös machen.

flute [flu:t], **1.** *s.* 1. (*Mus.*) die Flöte; ***– stop,*** das Flötenregister (*of organ*); 2. (*Archit.*) die Rinne, Rille, Hohlkehle, Riefe, Riffel, Kannelierung; (*Dressm.*) Rüsche. **2.** *v.t.* auskehlen, kannelieren, riffeln; rüschen, gaufrieren. **fluted,** *adj.* ausgekehlt, kanneliert, geriffelt; (*Dressm.*) gaufriert. **fluting,** *s.* die Rinne, Riefe, Kannelierung; (*Dressm.*) Falten (*pl.*), Rüschen (*pl.*).

flutter ['flʌtə], **1.** *v.i.* flattern, wehen; sich aufgeregt *or* unruhig bewegen; ***– about,*** ziellos hin und her eilen. **2.** *v.t.* flattern lassen, hin und her bewegen; (*coll.*) ***– the dovecot(e)s,*** Verwirrung verursachen, die Spießbürger erschrecken. **3.** *s.* das Flattern, Geflatter; (*fig.*) die Aufregung, Verwirrtheit; (*coll.*) ***all in a –,*** in großer Aufregung; (*coll.*) ***have a –,*** wetten, spekulieren.

fluvial ['flu:viəl], *adj.* Fluß–.

flux [flʌks], *s.* das Fließen, der Fluß; Strom, Ausfluß, die Flut; (*Tech.*) das Flußmittel, Schmelzmittel, der Zuschlag; (*fig.*) ständiger Wechsel, dauernde Veränderung; (*Med.*) ***bloody –,*** rote Ruhr; (*fig.*) ***in –,*** im Fluß; (*Elec.*) ***– density,*** die Flußdichte, Stromdichte; (*Elec.*) ***– linkage,*** die Induktivkupplung. **fluxion** ['flʌkʃən], *s.* das Fließen, der Fluß, die Fluxion (*also Med.*), (*Math.*) Fluxion; (*Math.*) ***method of –s,*** die Differentialrechnung. **fluxional,** *adj.* Fluxions–, Differential–.

[1]**fly** [flai], **1.** *irr.v.i.* fliegen (*also Av.*); (*as time*) entfliehen, enteilen, verfliegen, vergehen; (*as flags*) wehen, flattern; (*only inf., pres. part. and pres.*) fliehen, davonlaufen; (*fig.*) ***– at his throat,*** ihm an die Kehle gehen; (*Av.*) ***– blind,*** blindfliegen; ***as the crow flies,*** in *or* nach der Luftlinie; (*fig.*) ***the bird is flown,*** der Vogel ist ausgeflogen; (*fig.*) ***– high,*** hohe Ziele haben, hoch hinauswollen; ***let –,*** abschießen, losschießen; (*fig.*) losgehen, losschlagen; (*fig.*) ***let – at him,*** über ihn herfallen, auf ihn losgehen, ihn anfahren, gegen *or* auf ihn loswettern; ***– in the face of,*** mutig entgegentreten (*Dat.*) (*danger*), trotzen *or* (offen) widersprechen (*Dat.*) (*a p.*); ***– into a rage,*** in Wut geraten; (*sl.*) ***– off the handle,*** aus dem Häuschen geraten (***at,*** über (*Acc.*)); ***– to arms,*** zu den Waffen eilen; ***– to pieces,*** zerspringen, zerbrechen, zerplatzen.
(*with advs.*) ***– about,*** herumfliegen, (*as rumour*) sich verbreiten; ***– apart,*** see ***– to pieces***; ***– off,*** fortfliegen, wegfliegen; (*fig.*) ***– off at a tangent,*** plötzlich abspringen *or* abschwenken *or* vom Thema abschweifen; ***– open,*** auffliegen (*as a door*); ***– out of the room,*** aus dem Zimmer hinausstürzen.
2. *irr.v.t.* fliegen lassen (*as hawks*), steigen lassen (*a kite*), wehen lassen, hissen, führen (*a flag*); fliegen, führen, steuern (*a plane*); fliehen aus *or* vor (*Dat.*), meiden (*danger etc.*); ***he flew the Atlantic,*** er überflog den Atlantik; ***– food to Biafra,*** Lebensmittel nach B. im Flugzeug befördern; ***– a kite,*** (*Comm.*) auf Wechsel borgen, (*fig.*) einen Versuchsballon loslassen; (*Av.*) ***– a sortie,*** Einsatz fliegen.
3. *s.* (*coll.*) ***go for a –,*** einen Flug machen, fliegen.

[2]**fly,** *s.* 1. die Fliege, (*angling*) künstliche Fliege; ***break flies on a wheel,*** mit Kanonen nach Spatzen schießen; ***a – in the ointment,*** ein Haar in der Suppe; (*sl.*) ***there are no flies on him,*** auf ihn lasse ich nichts kommen; 2. frei flatternder Teil (*of flag etc.*); die Flaggenlänge; (*Typ.*) der (Bogen)ausleger; Latz, (Hosen)schlitz, die Klappe, Patte; 3. (*obs.*) Droschke, der Einspänner; 4. *pl.* (*Theat.*) Soffitten (*pl.*). (*See also* **flyer,** 3. *and* **flysheet,** 2.)

[3]**fly,** *adj.* (*coll.*) schlau, gerissen, pfiffig.

fly|-agaric, *s.* (*Bot.*) der Fliegenpilz. **–bane,** *s.* (*Bot.*) das Leimkraut. **–blow,** *s.* Fliegeneier (*pl.*), der Fliegenschmutz. **–blown,** *adj.* von Fliegen beschmutzt, (*fig.*) besudelt; unsauber. **–-by-night,** *s.* (*coll.*) der Nachtschwärmer. **–catcher,** *s.* (*Orn.*) der Schnäpper (*Muscicapidae*).

flyer ['flaiə], *s.* 1. (*Av.*) der Flieger; 2. (*coll.*) Expreßzug, Schnellautobus, gutes Rennpferd; 3. (*Tech.*) das Schwungrad, der Spindelflügel, (*of clocks*) die Unruhe; 4. (*rare*) der Flüchtling, Fliehende(r).

fly-fishing, *s.* das Angeln mit künstlichen Fliegen.

flying ['flaiiŋ], **1.** *adj.* fliegend; wehend, flatternd, wallend; eilend, eilig; flüchtig, vorübergehend; (*coll.*) ***– bedstead,*** fliegendes Bettgestell; ***– bomb,*** die Raketenbombe; ***– buttress,*** der Strebebogen; ***– circus,*** das Kunstfliegergeschwader; (*fig.*) ***with – colours,*** siegreich; (*Mil.*) ***– column,*** fliegende Kolonne; (*Ichth.*) ***– fish,*** fliegender Fisch; (*Zool.*) ***– fox,*** der Flughund; (*Naut.*) ***– jib,*** der Außenklüver, Flieger; ***– jump,*** der Sprung mit Anlauf; (*coll.*) ***– saucer,*** fliegende Untertasse; (*Zool.*) ***– squirrel,*** das Flughörnchen; ***– start,*** fliegender Start; ***– visit,*** die Stippvisite, flüchtiger Besuch; (*Av.*) ***– wing,*** das Nurflügelflugzeug. **2.** *s.* das Fliegen; die Fliegerei, das Flugwesen.

flying| accident, *s.* der Flugunfall. **– altitude,** *s.* die Flughöhe. **–-boat,** *s.* das Flugboot. **–-field,** *s.* der Flugplatz. **–-instructor,** *s.* der Fluglehrer. **–-machine,** *s.* (*obs.*) das Flugzeug. **–-officer,** *s.* der Oberleutnant der Luftwaffe. **–-school,** *s.* die Flugschule, Fliegerschule. **–-speed,** *s.* die Fluggeschwindigkeit. **–-squad,** *s.* das Überfallkommando.

fly|leaf, *s.* (*Typ.*) das Vorsatzblatt. **–-over,** *s.* kreuzungsfreier Übergang, die Überführung. **–-paper,** *s.* das Fliegenpapier. **–-past,** *s.* die Luftparade, der Vorbeiflug. **–-press,** *s.* das Stoßwerk. **–sheet,** *s.* 1. das Flugblatt; 2. (*of tent*) äußeres Zeltdach. **–-swat(ter),** *s.* der Fliegenwedel, die Fliegenklatsche. **–weight,** *s.* (*Spt.*) das Fliegengewicht; der Fliegengewichtler. **–wheel,** *s.* das Schwungrad.

foal [foul], **1.** *s.* das Fohlen, Füllen; ***with*** or ***in –,*** trächtig. **2.** *v.i.* fohlen, (ein Füllen) werfen. **foalfoot,** *s.* (*Bot.*) der Huflattich.

foam [foum], **1.** *s.* der Schaum; ***– extinguisher,*** das Schaumlöschgerät; ***– rubber,*** der Schaumgummi. **2.** *v.i.* schäumen; (*fig.*) wüten, (vor Wut) schäumen (***at,*** über (*Acc.*)); ***he –ed at the mouth,*** sein Mund schäumte. **foaming,** *adj.* schäumend, schaumbedeckt. **foamy,** *adj.* schaumig, schaumartig, Schaum–.

[1]**fob** [fɔb], *s.* (*obs.*) die Uhrtasche.

[2]**fob,** *v.t.* foppen, zum besten haben; ***– s.th. off on him, – him off with s.th.,*** ihn mit etwas abwimmeln *or* abspeisen, ihm etwas andrehen *or* anhängen.

focal [foukl], *adj.* im Brennpunkt stehend, Brenn(punkt)–; (*Med.*) fokal, Herd–; ***– distance*** or ***length,*** die Brennweite; ***–-plane shutter,*** der Schlitzverschluß; ***– point,*** der Brennpunkt (*also fig.*).

fo'c'sle, *s.* (*Naut.*) *see* **forecastle.**

focus ['foukəs], **1.** *s.* (*pl.* **foci** [–ki:], **-es**) der Brennpunkt (*also fig.*); scharfe Einstellung; ***in –,*** scharf eingestellt, (*fig.*) scharf dargestellt; ***bring into –,*** scharf einstellen, (*fig.*) in den Brennpunkt rücken; ***out of –,*** nicht scharf eingestellt. **2.** *v.t.* (richtig *or* scharf) einstellen; im Brennpunkt vereinigen. **focusing,** *s.* (*Opt.*) die (Scharf)einstellung; (*Phot.*) ***–-screen,*** die Mattscheibe.

fodder ['fɔdə], **1.** *s.* das Trockenfutter, Dürrfutter. **2.** *v.t.* füttern.

foe [fou], *s.* der Feind, Gegner, Widersacher (***to,*** *Gen.*). **foeman,** *s.* (*Poet.*) der Feind.

foetal [fi:tl], *adj.* fötal, Fötus–. **foetus,** *s.* die Leibesfrucht, der Fötus.

fog [fɔg], **1.** *s.* (dichter) Nebel; (*fig.*) die Umnebelung, Verwirrung, Unsicherheit; (*Phot.*) der Dunst, (Grau)schleier; (*fig.*) ***in a –,*** in Verwirrung *or* Unsicherheit. **2.** *v.t.* (*fig.*) umnebeln, verwirren. **fog|bank,** *s.* die Nebelbank. **–bound,** *adj.* in Nebel eingehüllt; durch Nebel zurückgehalten (*of ships*).

fogey ['fougi], *s.* (*coll.*) (*usu.*) ***old –,*** altmodischer Mensch, alter Knopf, der Philister.

fogginess ['fɔginis], *s.* die Nebligkeit; (*fig.*) Unklarheit, Verworrenheit. **foggy,** *adj.* neblig, dunstig, (*Naut.*) mistig; (*fig.*) umnebelt, wirr, verworren, nebelhaft, unklar, unsicher; (*Phot.*) verschleiert; (*coll.*) ***not the foggiest notion,*** keine blasse Ahnung. **fog|horn,** *s.* das Nebelhorn. **–-lamp,** *s.* (*Motor.*) der Nebelscheinwerfer. **–-signal,** *s.* (*Railw.*) das Nebelsignal.

fogy, *see* **fogey.**

foible [fɔibl], *s.* die Schwäche, schwache Seite.

[1]**foil** [fɔil], *s.* die Folie, das Blattmetall; Metallblättchen; Glanzblättchen (*for gems*); der Belag, die Folie (*for mirrors*); (*fig.*) Folie, Unterlage, der Hintergrund, Kontrast; (*Archit.*) die Blattverzierung, das Laubwerk; ***metal –,*** das Blattmetall; ***tin –,*** das Blattzinn.

[2]**foil, 1.** *v.t.* verhindern, vereiteln, zunichte *or* zuschanden machen (*efforts, plans etc.*), entgegentreten (*Dat.*) (*a p.*); (*Hunt.*) verwischen (*the scent*). **2.** *s.* (*Hunt.*) die Fährte, Spur.

[3]**foil,** *s.* (*Fenc.*) das Florett.

foist [fɔist], *v.t.* unterschieben, einschmuggeln; ***– s.th. on him,*** ihm etwas aufhalsen *or* andrehen *or* anhängen.

[1]**fold** [fould], **1.** *s.* die Falte (*in cloth etc.; also Geol.*); (*Bookb.*) der Falz; Kniff, Bruch (*in paper etc.*). **2.** *v.t.* falten; falzen, umbiegen, kniffen (*paper*); übereinanderlegen, kreuzen (*the arms etc.*); ***with –ed arms,*** mit untergeschlagenen *or* verschränkten Armen; ***– down a leaf,*** ein Blatt einschlagen *or* umkniffen; ***– in one's arms,*** umarmen, in die Arme schließen; ***– up,*** zusammenlegen. **3.** *v.i.* (*oft.* ***– up***) sich (zusammen)falten, sich zusammenlegen, sich zusammenfalten lassen, zusammenklappen.

[2]**fold, 1.** *s.* die (Schaf)hürde, der Pferch; (*Eccl.*) die Herde, Gemeinde. **2.** *v.t.* einpferchen.

-fold, *suff.* –fach, –fältig.

folder ['fouldə], *s.* 1. (*Bookb.*) (*a p.*) der Falzer, (*instrument*) das Falzbein, die Falzmaschine; 2. Mappe, der Hefter, Umschlag, Aktendeckel; 3. Prospekt, die Broschüre, das Heft; 4. *pl.* der Klappkneifer, Zwicker.

folding ['fouldiŋ], *adj.* zusammenlegbar, zusammenklappbar, Falt–, Klapp–; ***– bed,*** das Feldbett, Klappbett; ***– boat,*** das Faltboot; ***– camera,*** die Klappkamera; ***– chair,*** der Klappstuhl; ***– door,*** die Flügeltür; ***–hat,*** der Klapphut; ***– rule,*** der Gliedermaßstab; ***– screen,*** spanische Wand; ***– seat,*** der Klappsitz; ***– stick,*** das Falzbein; ***– table,*** der Klapptisch.

folderol ['fɔldərɔl], *s.* der Schnickschnack, Firlefanz, das Larifari.

foliaceous [fouli'eiʃəs], *adj.* blätterig, beblättert, Blätter–. **foliage** ['fouliidʒ], *s.* das Laub(werk), Blätter (*pl.*); (*Archit. etc.*) das Blattwerk, die Blattverzierung. **foliate, 1.** [–iit], *adj.* blätterig, blattähnlich, blattartig, blattförmig; blattreich, belaubt. **2.** [–ieit], *v.i.* 1. (*Bot.*) Blätter treiben; 2. (*Geol.*) sich in Blättchen spalten. **3.** [–ieit], *v.t.* 1. (mit Folie) belegen (*a mirror*); (*Archit.*) mit Blattverzierung schmücken; 2. paginieren (*a book*). **foliation** [–'eiʃən], *s.* 1. (*Bot.*) die Blattbildung, Blattentwicklung, der Blätterwuchs; Blattstand, die Blattstellung, Belaubung; 2. (*Archit.*) das Laubwerk, Blattwerk, der Laubschmuck, Blätterschmuck, die Blattverzierung; 3. (*Tech.*) Herstellung von Folien; 4. (*Geol.*) Lagerung in Schichten, Schieferung; 5. (*of a book*) Blattzählung, Paginierung; Blattzahl.

folio ['fouliou], *s.* das Folio(blatt); Folio(format); (*Comm.*) die Kontobuchseite, Seitenzahl; ***–*** (***volume***), der Foliant.

folk [fouk], *s.* (*pl. constr.*) Leute (*pl.*); (*obs.*) das Volk; (*coll.*) (*only pl.*) Verwandte (*pl.*), Angehörige (*pl.*). **folk|-dance,** *s.* der Volkstanz. **–lore,** *s.* die Volkskunde. **–lorist,** *s.* der Volkskundler. **–song,** *s.* das Volkslied. **folksy,** *adj.* (*Am.*) gesellig. **folk|-tale,** *s.* die Volkssage. **–weave,** *s.* handgewebte Stoffe (*pl.*).

follicle ['fɔlikl], *s.* das Drüsenbläschen, der Drüsenbalg, Follikel.

follow ['fɔlou], **1.** *v.t.* (nach)folgen, nachgehen, nachlaufen (*Dat.*); folgen (*Dat.*), folgen auf (*Acc.*); verfolgen (*also fig.*); (*fig.*) gehorchen, dienen (*a p.*) (*Dat.*); befolgen, sich halten an (*Acc.*) (*instructions*); folgen aus, sich ergeben aus, die Folge sein von (*an example*), ausüben, betreiben (*career*); (*coll.*) verstehen, begreifen, erfassen; ***– his advice,*** seinem Rat folgen; ***– his example,*** seinem Beispiel folgen; ***– the fashion,*** die Mode mitmachen; ***– the hounds,*** an der Fuchsjagd teilnehmen; (*coll.*) ***– one's nose,*** immer der Nase nach gehen; ***– one's pleasure,*** seinem Vergnügen nachgehen; ***– the plough,*** Landmann sein; ***– the sea,*** Seemann sein; ***– suit,*** (*Cards*) Farbe bekennen; (*fig.*) dem Beispiel folgen; sich anschließen; (*with advs.*) ***– out*** or ***through,*** (bis zum Ende) durchführen, weiterverfolgen, (beharrlich) ausführen; ***– up,*** energisch verfolgen, ausnutzen (*an advantage*); ***– up one th. with another,*** auf eine S. eine andere (sofort) folgen lassen. **2.** *v.i.* (nach)folgen, nachkommen; ***as –s,*** folgendermaßen, wie folgt; ***– from,*** sich ergeben aus; ***– in his footsteps,*** ihm auf dem Fuße folgen; ***–*** (***up***)***on,*** folgen auf (*Acc.*); ***– on,*** gleich weitergehen *or* (*fig.*) weitermachen; (*Crick.*) sofort (zum Schlagen) wieder antreten; (*Spt.*) ***– through,*** (ganz) durchziehen; (*Mil.*) ***– up,*** nachdrängen, nachstoßen.

follower ['fɔlouə], *s.* der (die) Nachfolger(in), Anhänger(in), Schüler(in), Jünger(in); Verfolger(in); Begleiter(in); (*Hist.*) der Gefolgsmann; (*pl.*) das Gefolge, die Gefolgschaft; (*coll.*) der Verehrer, Anhang; (*Tech.*) das Nebenrad, (*of gun*) der Zubringer. **following, 1.** *adj.* (nächst)folgend, anschließend, nächst; ***on the – day,*** am Tag darauf; ***– wind,*** der Rückenwind. **2.** *s.* 1. Folgende(s); 2. das Gefolge, der Anhang, die Gefolgschaft, Anhängerschaft, Anhänger (*pl.*).

follow|-on, *s.* (*Crick.*) sofortiges Wiederantreten. **–-through,** *s.* (*Spt.*) das Durchziehen, Durchschwingen. **–-up, 1.** *s.* die Nachuntersuchung, weitere Verfolgung, (*Mil.*) frontales Nachdrängen. **2.** *adj.* weiter, Nach–.

folly ['fɔli], *s.* die Torheit, Narrheit, der Unsinn; die Unsinnigkeit; ***piece of –,*** törichtes Unternehmen, dummer Streich.

foment [fo'ment], *v.t.* warm baden, bähen; (*fig.*) fördern, pflegen, erregen, schüren, anfachen, anstiften. **fomentation** [–'teiʃən], *s.* 1. die Bähung, das Bähen; Dampfbad, Bähmittel, heißer Umschlag; 2. (*fig.*) die Anstiftung, Aufreizung, Schürung.

fond [fɔnd], *adj.* 1. liebevoll, zärtlich; ***– father,*** übertrieben zärtlicher Vater; 2. kühn (*dreams, hope etc.*); 3. ***be – of,*** gern haben, (gern) mögen, lieben; ***– of swimming,*** gern schwimmen.

fondle [fɔndl], **1.** *v.t.* liebkosen, streicheln, herzen. **2.** *v.i.* kosen, tändeln.

fondly ['fɔndli], *adv.* 1. *See* **fond,** 1.; 2. in unkritischer Zuversicht; ***he – imagined,*** er bildete sich in seiner Unwissenheit ein. **fondness,** *s.* 1. die Liebe, Zärtlichkeit; 2. Vorliebe (***for,*** für), der Hang (zu).

font [fɔnt], *s.* der Taufstein, das Taufbecken.

fontanel(le) [fɔntə'nel], *s.* (*Anat.*) die Fontanelle.

food [fu:d], *s.* das Essen, die Speise, Kost, Nahrung; Nahrungsmittel (*pl.*), Lebensmittel (*pl.*), das Futter (*of beasts*); ***– and drink,*** Essen und Trinken, Speise und Trank; ***– for thought,*** der Stoff zum Nachdenken; ***– card,*** die Lebensmittelkarte; –

office, das Ernährungsamt; *– shortage,* die Lebensmittelknappheit; *– supply,* die Verpflegung, Lebensmittelzufuhr; der Lebensmittelvorrat; *– value,* der Nährwert. **foodstuff,** *s.* Nahrungsmittel, Lebensmittel (*pl.*); der Nährstoff.

[1]**fool** [fu:l], **1.** *s.* der Narr (die Närrin), der Tor; (*coll.*) Dummkopf; (*Theat. etc.*) Narr, Hanswurst; ***he's no –,*** er läßt sich nicht übervorteilen *or* hinters Licht führen; ***there's no – like an old –,*** Alter schützt vor Torheit nicht; ***he would be a – to do it,*** er wäre dumm *or* töricht, es zu tun; ***make a – of o.s.,*** sich blamieren, sich (*Dat.*) eine Blöße geben, sich lächerlich machen; ***make a – of him,*** ihn zum Narren halten; ***make an April – of him,*** ihn in den April schicken; ***play the –,*** Possen treiben; ***–'s cap,*** die Narrenkappe; ***All Fools' Day,*** der erste April; ***–'s errand,*** vergeblicher Gang; ***–'s paradise,*** das Schlaraffenland; ***live in a –'s paradise,*** sich goldene Berge versprechen, sich Illusionen hingeben, in einem verhängnisvollen Irrtum befangen sein; (*Bot.*) ***–'s parsley,*** der Gartenschierling. **2.** *v.t.* zum Narren halten, äffen, hänseln; täuschen, betören; verleiten (***into doing,*** zu tun); betrügen (***him out of s.th.,*** ihn um etwas); ***– away,*** unnütz vergeuden *or* vertrödeln *or* vertändeln. **3.** *v.i.* Possen treiben, Faxen machen; spielen, tändeln (***with,*** mit); ***– around*** or ***about,*** Unsinn machen; sich herumtreiben, herumlungern. **4.** *adj.* (*coll.*) töricht, närrisch.

[2]**fool,** *s.* (*Cul.*) das Mus, die Krem.

foolery ['fu:ləri], *s.* die Torheit, Narrheit. **fool|hardiness,** *s.* die Tollkühnheit. **–hardy,** *adj.* tollkühn. **fooling,** *s.* die Dummheit, Albernheit, Faxen (*pl.*); ***stop your –!*** mach keinen Unsinn! **foolish,** *adj.* närrisch, töricht, albern, dumm, unklug; lächerlich, läppisch. **foolishness,** *s.* die Torheit, Dummheit, Albernheit. **foolproof,** *adj.* absolut sicher, narrensicher, ungefährlich, einfach zu handhaben; (*Tech.*) betriebssicher. **foolscap,** *s.* das Kanzleipapier, Propatriapapier, Aktenpapier; Aktenformat (= $13\frac{1}{2}$ *in.* $\times$ $8\frac{1}{2}$ *in.*).

foot [fut], **1.** *s.* (*pl.* **feet** [fi:t]) 1. der Fuß (*also fig. and measure*); ***–-and-mouth disease,*** die Maul- und Klauenseuche; (*coll.*) ***I know the length of his –,*** ich kenne seine Schwächen genau; ***be on one's feet,*** (wieder) auf den Beinen sein; ***catch on the wrong –,*** überraschen, überrumpeln; (*coll.*) ***fall on one's feet,*** immer Glück haben; ***get off on the wrong –,*** den falschen Weg einschlagen; ***get on*** or ***to one's feet,*** sich erheben, aufstehen; (*coll.*) ***get one's – in,*** sich hineindrängen; ***have both feet on the ground,*** mit beiden Füßen auf der Erde stehen; ***have one – in the grave,*** mit einem Fuß *or* Bein im Grabe stehen; ***help him to his feet,*** ihm auf die Beine helfen; ***jump to one's feet,*** auf die Füße springen; ***put one's – down,*** Einspruch erheben, energisch werden *or* auftreten, ein Machtwort sprechen, auftrumpfen; (*Motor. coll.*) Gas geben; (*coll.*) ***put one's – in it,*** schön herein fallen, sich blamieren, ins Fettnäpfchen treten; ***put one's best – forward,*** tüchtig ausschreiten, sich nach Kräften anstrengen; (*fig.*) ***put one's – on s.th.,*** etwas abstellen, mit etwas ein Ende machen; ***run him off his feet,*** ihn zum Tode hetzen; ***set – in*** or ***on,*** betreten; ***set on –,*** in die Wege leiten, in Gang bringen, ins Werk setzen; ***not stir a – from*** or ***out of,*** sich nicht rühren von . . . weg; ***sweep him off his feet,*** ihn fortreißen *or* hinreißen; ***at his feet,*** ihm zu Füßen; ***light of –,*** leichtfüßig; ***on –,*** zu Fuß, (*fig.*) am Werk, im Gange, in Tätigkeit; ***from head to –,*** von Kopf bis Fuß; ***under –,*** unter dem Fuße, auf dem Boden; (*fig.*) unter die Füße; ***tread under –,*** mit Füßen treten; 2. unteres Ende, das Fußende (*of a bed, page etc.*); ***at the –,*** am Schluß, unten; 3. der Füßling (*of a stocking*); 4. (*Naut.*) das Unterliek (*of sail*); 5. (*Mil.*) Fußvolk, die Infanterie; ***horse and –,*** Kavallerie und Infanterie; ***the 125th (regiment of) –,*** das 125. Infanterieregiment; 6. der Versfuß. **2.** *v.t.* 1. anstricken (*socks*); 2. (*coll.*) bezahlen, begleichen, bestreiten (*a bill*); ***– up,*** zusammenrechnen, addieren, summieren. **3.** *v.i.* ***– it,*** tanzen, trippeln, (*rare*) zu Fuße gehen; ***– up to,*** sich belaufen auf (*Acc.*).

footage ['futidʒ], *s.* die Gesamtlänge (*film*). **foot|-ball,** *s.* der Fußball; das Fußballspiel; ***– match*** (***Am. game***), das Fußballspiel; ***– pools,*** der Toto. **–baller,** *s.* der Fußballspieler. **–board,** *s.* das Fußbrett (*of a bed*); (*Motor.*) Trittbrett; (*Railw.*) Laufbrett, der Tritt. **–boy,** *s.* der Laufbursche, Page. **–-brake,** *s.* die Fußbremse. **–bridge,** *s.* der (Lauf)steg. **footed,** *suff.* -füßig. **footer,** *s.* (*sl.*) der Fußball. **foot|fall,** *s.* der Tritt, Schritt. **–-fault,** *s.* (*Tenn.*) der Fußfehler. **–-gear,** *s. See* **–wear. –-guards,** *pl.* die Gardeinfanterie, das Garderegiment zu Fuß. **–-hills,** *pl.* das Vorgebirge. **–hold,** *s.* die Fußstütze, fester Stand; der Raum zum Stehen; (*fig.*) Halt, die Stütze; ***gain a –,*** Fuß fassen.

footing ['futiŋ], *s.* 1. der Halt, Stand, die Stellung, fester Fuß; (*Archit. etc.*) die Bankette; ***get*** or ***gain a –,*** festen Fuß fassen; ***lose*** or ***miss one's –,*** stolpern, einen Fehltritt machen, ausgleiten; 2. (*fig.*) die Lage, Basis, der Zustand; das Verhältnis; ***be on a friendly –,*** auf freundschaftlichem Fuße stehen; ***pay one's –,*** seinen Einstand geben; (*Scots*) ***first –,*** der Neujahrsbesuch; ***on a war –,*** auf Kriegsbasis; ***he is not on a – with us,*** er steht uns nicht gleich; ***place*** or ***put on a – with*** or ***the same – as*** or ***with,*** gleichstellen (*Dat.*), auf gleichem Fuße stellen mit; 3. das Anfußen (*of socks*).

footlights ['futlaits], *pl.* Rampenlichter (*pl.*); ***get across the –,*** auf das Publikum wirken.

footling ['fu:tliŋ], *adj.* albern, blöde, nichtig, fipsig.

foot|-loose, *adj.* frei, ungebunden, unbeschwert, unbehindert. **–man** [-mən], *s.* der Lakai, Bediente(r). **–mark,** *s. See* **–print. –-muff,** *s.* der Fußwärmer, Fußsack. **–note,** *s.* die Fußnote, Anmerkung. **–-pace,** *s.* langsamer Schritt, der Spazierschritt. **–pad,** *s.* (*Hist.*) der Wegelagerer, Straßenräuber. **–-passenger,** *s.* der Fußgänger. **–path,** *s.* der Fußweg, (Fuß)pfad, Steg. **–-pedal,** *s.* der Fußhebel. **–plate,** *s.* (*Railw.*) der Führerstand. **–plate-man,** *s.* der Lokomotivführer. **–-pound,** *s.* (*Phys.*) das Fußpfund. **–print,** *s.* die Fußstapfe, (Fuß)spur. **–-race,** *s.* der Wettlauf. **–-rail,** *s.* die Fußleiste. **–-rest,** *s.* das Fußbänkchen; (*of a chair etc.*) die Fußleiste; (*Cycl.*) Fußruhe. **–-rot,** *s.* (*Vet.*) die Fußfäule. **–-rule,** *s.* der Zollstock.

foots [futs], *pl.* der Bodensatz, die Hefe.

foot|-scraper, *s.* der Fußabtreter. **–-slogger,** *s.* (*sl.*) der Fußlatscher, Stoppelhopser. **–-soldier,** *s.* der Fußsoldat, Infanterist. **–sore,** *adj.* marschkrank, fußwund. **–stalk,** *s.* der Stengel, Stiel. **–-starter,** *s.* (*Motor. etc.*) der Tretanlasser. **–step,** *s.* der (Fuß)tritt, Schritt; *see also* **–print**; ***follow in his –s,*** in seine Fußstapfen treten, seinem Beispiel folgen. **–stool,** *s.* der Schemel, die Fußbank. **–wear,** *s.* das Schuhzeug, Schuhwerk, die Fußbekleidung. **–work,** *s.* (*Spt.*) die Beinarbeit.

foozle [fu:zl], *v.t.* (*sl.*) (*esp. Spt.*) verpfuschen, vermasseln.

fop [fɔp], *s.* der Geck, Stutzer. **foppery,** *s.* der Tand, Flitter; die Geckenhaftigkeit, Ziererei. **foppish,** *adj.* geckenhaft, stutzerhaft.

for [fɔ:, fə], **1.** *prep.* 1. (= *in place of, instead of*) für, (an)statt, an Stelle von; ***once and – all,*** ein für allemal; ***change it – s.th. better,*** es gegen etwas Besseres tauschen; ***in mistake –,*** irrtümlich *or* aus Versehen an Stelle von; ***take –,*** irrtümlich halten für; 2. (= *in support of*) ***fight – one's country,*** für sein Land kämpfen; ***take my word – it,*** verlassen Sie sich darauf! 3. (= *with the aim of*) um (. . . willen), (mit der Absicht) zu, zum Zwecke von, für, halber; ***it is – art to express,*** es ist S. *or* die Aufgabe der Kunst auszudrücken; ***give up law – the church,*** das Rechtsstudium aufgeben um Theologe zu werden; ***go – a walk,*** spazierengehen; ***good –,*** gut für *or* zu; ***try – a job,*** sich um eine Stellung bewerben; ***– God's sake,*** um Gottes willen; ***write – money,*** für Geld schreiben; ***all – nothing,*** alles umsonst; ***be good – nothing,*** nichts taugen; ***what –?*** warum? weshalb? weswegen? wofür? ***he gave orders – the charge to be made,*** er gab Befehl anzugreifen; ***– hire!*** zu vermieten! frei! (*of taxicabs*); ***– a holiday,*** auf Urlaub; ***– sale,*** zum

Verkauf; 4. (= *destination*) nach, (in Richtung) auf (*Acc.*); ***leave – the continent,*** nach dem Kontinent reisen; ***I am off – L.,*** ich reise nach L. ab; ***it is getting on – midnight,*** es geht auf Mitternacht; ***now – it!*** jetzt ans Werk! nun los! jetzt gilt's! jetzt geht's los! (*coll.*) ***be in – it,*** es ausbaden müssen; ***oh, – money!*** hätte ich nur Geld! 5. (= *fitness*) (passend *or* geeignet *or* bestimmt) für *or* zu; ***that's the man – me!*** das ist mein Mann! ***there's a man – you!*** das nenne ich einen Kerl! ***it is – you to say,*** es liegt bei *or* an dir zu sagen; ***there is nothing – it but to go,*** es läßt sich nichts anderes machen als wegzugehen, weggehen ist der einzige Weg; ***it is not – me to . . .,*** es ziemt mir nicht *or* geziemt sich nicht für mich zu . . .; 6. (= *relation*) im Verhältnis zu, im Hinblick auf (*Acc.*), angesichts, für; ***tall – his age,*** groß für sein Alter; ***line – line,*** Zeile für *or* um Zeile; ***word – word,*** Wort für Wort; 7. (= *as, as being*) ***– certain,*** sicherlich, gewiß; ***– example, – instance,*** zum *or* als Beispiel; ***– the first time,*** zum ersten Mal; ***count – little,*** wenig zählen; ***I – one,*** ich zum Beispiel, ich meinerseits; ***give up – lost,*** verloren geben; ***a curse upon thee – a traitor!*** fluch dir, Verräter! 8. (= *in spite of*) trotz, ungeachtet, bei; ***not – the life of me,*** beim besten Willen nicht; ***– all he is so rich,*** obgleich er so reich ist; ***– all that,*** bei *or* trotz alledem; ***nothing happened – all his efforts,*** es geschah nichts, trotz *or* ungeachtet aller seiner Anstrengungen; ***but – you,*** ohne dich; ***but – this,*** wenn dies nicht wäre, abgesehen von dem; 9. (= *as regards, on account of*) betreffs, in Anbetracht, soweit *or* soviel in Betracht *or* Frage kommt, was . . . an(be)langt; ***– all I know,*** soviel ich weiß; (***as***) ***– me,*** meinetwegen, was mich an(be)langt *or* betrifft; ***treat – cancer,*** auf Krebs behandeln; ***– fun,*** aus Spaß; ***– joy,*** vor *or* aus Freude; ***he could not speak – laughing,*** er konnte vor Lachen nicht sprechen; ***at a loss –,*** verlegen um; ***– that matter,*** was das betrifft; ***– my part,*** see (***as***) ***– me***; ***– this reason,*** aus diesem Grunde; ***– shame!*** pfui! schäme dich! 10. (= *duration*) während, seit, für die Dauer von; ***– ages,*** schon ewig; ***– some days,*** einige Tage lang, schon einige Tage; ***not – some days,*** nicht vor einigen Tagen; ***– ever,*** für immer, auf ewig *or* immer; ***Willi Brandt – ever!*** W.B. soll leben! ***– good,*** für *or* auf immer; ***– life,*** lebenslänglich; ***– long,*** auf lange Zeit; ***– the next 3 weeks,*** die *or* in den nächsten 3 Wochen; ***– the present,*** im Augenblick; ***– some time past,*** seit längerer Zeit; ***– a while,*** auf einige Zeit; 11. (= *for the benefit of*) im Interesse *or* Auftrag von; zu Ehren von, zugunsten *or* zum Besten von; ***buy – him,*** für ihn kaufen; ***earn s.th. – him,*** ihm etwas einbringen; ***hold it – me!*** halte es mir! **2.** *conj.* denn.

forage ['fɔridʒ], **1.** *s.* das (Vieh)futter, (*Mil.*) die Furage; das Furagieren; (*fig.*) ***on the – for,*** umherstöbern nach. **2.** *v.i.* Futter suchen, furagieren; (*fig.*) *see* ***on the –***. **3.** *v.t.* durch Furagieren ausplündern (*country*); (*fig.*) durchstöbern. **forage-cap,** *s.* (*Mil.*) die Feldmütze. **forager,** *s.* (*Mil. Hist.*) der Furier. **foraging-party,** *s.* der Furagierzug.

foramen [fo'reimin], *s.* (*pl.* **-mina** [-'ræminə]) (*Zool., Bot., Anat.*) das Loch, die Öffnung.

forasmuch [fərəz'mʌtʃ], *adv.* insofern.

foray ['fɔrei], **1.** *s.* räuberischer Einfall, der Raubzug, Beutezug. **2.** *v.t.* plündern.

forbade [fə'bæd], *imperf. of* **forbid.**

[1]**forbear** [fɔ:'bɛə], **1.** *irr.v.t.* sich enthalten (*Gen.*), unterlassen, abstehen von; ***I cannot – smiling,*** ich kann nicht umhin zu lächeln. **2.** *irr.v.i.* sich gedulden; Geduld haben, nachsichtig *or* geduldig sein (***with,*** mit); abstehen, ablassen (***from,*** von).

[2]**forbear** ['fɔ:bɛə], *s. See* **forebear.**

forbearance [fɔ:'bɛərəns], *s.* die Schonung, Geduld, Nachsicht; Unterlassung, Enthaltung.

forbearing, [fɔ:'bɛəriŋ], *adj.* geduldig, nachsichtig, langmütig.

forbid [fə'bid], *irr.v.t.* 1. ***– him s.th.,*** ihm etwas verbieten *or* untersagen; 2. (*a th.*) ausschließen, (ver)hindern; ***circumstances – it,*** die Lage macht es unmöglich; ***God –!*** Gott behüte *or* bewahre! **forbidden,** *adj.* verboten, untersagt; ***– fruit,*** unerlaubte Frucht. **forbidding,** *adj.* verbietend; abstoßend, abschreckend; ***– appearance,*** bedrohliches Aussehen; ***– rocks,*** gefährliche Klippen.

forbore [fɔ:'bɔ:], *imperf.*, **forborne,** *p.p. of* [1]**forbear.**

force [fɔ:s], **1.** *s.* 1. die Kraft, Macht, Stärke, Wucht, Gewalt; Kraftanwendung, der Zwang, Druck, Einfluß; ***brute –,*** rohe Gewalt; ***by –,*** gewaltsam; ***by main –,*** mit roher Gewalt, mit aller Kraft; ***centrifugal –,*** die Fliehkraft, Schwungkraft; ***centripetal –,*** die Anziehkraft; ***explosive –,*** die Brisanz; ***– of gravity,*** die Schwerkraft, Erdschwere; ***– of impact,*** die Aufschlagskraft; ***in –,*** in großer Menge *or* Zahl; (*Law etc.*) gültig, in Kraft; ***in full –,*** in voller Kraft, voll wirksam; 2. (*Law*) die Gewaltanwendung, Gewalttätigkeit; (*Law*) Gültigkeit, bindende Kraft; der Nachdruck, das Gewicht, die Wirkung; Bedeutung, der Gehalt (*of a word etc.*); ***by – of,*** vermittels, mit Hilfe von; ***– of circumstances,*** die Macht *or* der Zwang der Verhältnisse; ***come into –,*** in Kraft treten; ***– of law,*** die Gesetzeskraft; ***put into –,*** in Kraft setzen; 3. (*Mil.*) die Truppe, Formation, der Verband; *pl.* Truppen (*pl.*), Streitkräfte (*pl.*); ***armed –s,*** die Wehrmacht; (*Mil.*) ***field –,*** Feldtruppen (*pl.*); ***labour –,*** der Arbeitertrupp, die Belegschaft; ***land –s,*** Landstreitkräfte (*pl.*); ***police –,*** die Polizei. **2.** *v.t.* zwingen, nötigen, treiben; erstürmen, durch Sturm einnehmen (*a city etc.*); aufbrechen, erbrechen, sprengen (*a door, lock etc.*); aufdrängen, aufnötigen, aufzwingen (***upon,*** *Dat.*); erkünsteln, erzwingen (*a smile*); schänden, notzüchtigen (*a woman*); (*Hort.*) hochzüchten; künstlich in die Höhe treiben (*prices etc.*); Gewalt antun (*Dat.*) (*the meaning*), zu Tode hetzen (*a simile*); (*Cards*) zum Trumpfen zwingen; (*fig.*) ***– s.th. down his throat,*** ihm etwas aufzwingen; ***– his hand,*** ihn unter Druck setzen, ihn nötigen; ***– the pace,*** das Tempo beschleunigen; ***– along,*** vorwärtstreiben; ***– back,*** zurücktreiben; ***– down,*** hinunterdrücken; (*Av.*) zur Notlandung zwingen; (*Av.*) ***be –d down,*** notlanden; ***– on,*** antreiben; (*Hort.*) beschleunigen; ***– open,*** mit Gewalt aufbrechen *or* erbrechen, sprengen; ***– out of,*** vertreiben aus; ***– through,*** durchsetzen.

forced [fɔ:st], *adj.* gezwungen, gekünstelt, künstlich, forciert; erzwungen, Zwangs–; (*Tech.*) ***– feed,*** die Druckschmierung; ***– labour,*** die Zwangsarbeit; ***– landing,*** die Notlandung; ***– loan,*** die Zwangsanleihe; ***– march,*** der Gewaltmarsch; ***– smile,*** gezwungenes Lächeln; ***– style,*** gekünstelter *or* unnatürlicher Stil. **forceful,** *adj.* kräftig, wirkungsvoll, eindrucksvoll; eindringlich, ungestüm, gewaltsam. **forcefulness,** *s.* das Ungestüm, die Eindringlichkeit, der Schwung, Schmiß.

forcemeat ['fɔ:smi:t], *s.* gehacktes Füllfleisch, das Füllsel.

forceps ['fɔ:seps], *s.* die Pinzette, Zange.

force-pump, *s.* die Druckpumpe.

forcible ['fɔ:sibl], *adj. See* **forceful**; wirksam, zwingend; (*Law*) ***– detainer,*** gewaltsame Entziehung; ***– feeding,*** die Zwangsernährung. **forcing,** *s.* das Zwingen; (*of a lock etc.*) Aufbrechen, Sprengen, (*of defences*) Erstürmen, (*of plants*) Hochzüchten, Treiben; ***–-house,*** das Treibhaus; ***–-pump,*** see **force-pump.**

ford [fɔ:d], **1.** *s.* die Furt. **2.** *v.t.* durchwaten.

fore [fɔ:], **1.** *adv.* vorn; (*Golf*) ***–!*** Achtung! (*Naut.*) ***– and aft,*** längsschiffs, in Kielrichtung; ***–-and-aft sail,*** das Stagsegel. **2.** *s.* der Vorderteil, die Vorderseite; ***to the –,*** bei der *or* zur Hand, zur Stelle; (nach) vorn, voran; im Vordergrund; (*coll.*) am Ruder; ***be well to the –,*** sehr im Vordergrund stehen; ***come to the –,*** hervortreten, in den Vordergrund treten, (*of a p.*) ans Ruder kommen, (*of a th.*) zum Vorschein kommen. **3.** *adj.* Vor–, vorder.

fore|arm, **1.** ['fɔ:rɑ:m], *s.* der Unterarm. **2.** [fɔ:-'ɑ:m], *v.t.* im voraus bewaffnen. **–bear,** *s.* (*usu. pl.*) der Vorfahr, Ahne, Ahnherr.

fore|bode [fɔ:'boud], *v.t.* weissagen, voraussagen, vorhersagen, prophezeien; anzeigen, vorbedeuten, ankündigen; voraussehen, ahnen. **-boding,** *s.* das Anzeichen, Vorzeichen; die Vorhersage, Voraussage, Prophezeiung; (böse) (Vor)-ahnung. **--cabin,** *s.* vordere Kajüte. **-cast, 1.** *s.* die Vorhersage, Voraussage; ***weather –,*** der Wetterbericht, die Wettervorhersage. **2.** *v.t.* vorhersehen, voraussagen, im voraus feststellen. **-castle** ['fouksl], *s.* (*Naut.*) die Back, das Vorderdeck; ***– crew*** or ***men,*** die Backsdivision. **-close** [-'klouz], *v.t.* ausschließen, abweisen, (*Law*) präkludieren; ***– a mortgage,*** eine Hypothek für verfallen erklären. **-closure,** *s.* (*Law*) die Rechtsausschließung; Verfallserklärung, Präklusion. **-court,** *s.* der Vorhof; (*Tenn.*) das Aufschlagsfeld. **--deck,** *s.* das Vorderdeck. **-doom** [-'du:m], *v.t.* vorher bestimmen (*to*, zu, für); im voraus verurteilen (zu). **-fathers,** *pl.* Vorfahren, Ahnen (*pl.*). **-finger,** *s.* der Zeigefinger. **-foot,** *s.* (*Zool.*) der Vorderfuß; (*Naut.*) Stevenanlauf. **-front,** *s.* die Vorderseite; erste *or* vorderste Reihe; ***– of the battle,*** vorderste Schlachtlinie; (*usu. fig.*) ***be in the –,*** im Vordergrund stehen. **-gather,** *v.i. See* **forgather. -go** [-'gou], *irr.v.t., v.i.* 1. (*rare*) vorangehen, vorhergehen (*Dat.*); 2. *See* **forgo. -going,** *adj.* vorhergehend, vorangehend, vorig, früher erwähnt, obig. **-gone,** *adj.* von vornherein feststehend, vorherbestimmt, unvermeidlich; ***– conclusion,*** ausgemachte S., die Selbstverständlichkeit, unvermeidlicher Schluß; ***– opinion,*** vorgefaßte Meinung. **-ground,** *s.* der Vordergrund; ***in the left –,*** im Vordergrund links. **-hand,** *s.* die Vorderhand (*of horse*); (*Tenn.*) ***– (stroke),*** der Vorhandschlag. **-handed,** *adj.* (*Tenn.*) mit Vorhand. **-head** ['fɔrid], *s.* die Stirn. **--hold,** *s.* (*Naut.*) der Vorderraum.

foreign ['fɔrin], *adj.* ausländisch, auswärtig; Auslands–, Außen–; (*fig.*) fremd (*to, Dat.*), nicht gehörig *or* passend (zu); ***– affairs,*** die Außenpolitik; ***Secretary of State for Foreign Affairs,*** der Minister des Äußeren, Außenminister; ***– assets,*** Devisenwerte (*pl.*); (*Law*) ***– attachment,*** die Beschlagnahme fremden Eigentums; ***– bill,*** der Auslandswechsel; ***– body,*** der Fremdkörper (*in eye*), Fremdstoff; ***– country,*** das Ausland; ***– department,*** die Auslandsabteilung (*of a bank etc.*); ***– exchange,*** Devisen (*pl.*); ***– language,*** die Fremdsprache; ***Foreign Legion,*** die Fremdenlegion; ***– mission(s),*** äußere Mission, die Mission im Ausland; ***Foreign Office,*** das Ministerium des Äußeren, Außenministerium; Auswärtiges Amt; ***– parts,*** see ***– country***; (*Law*) ***– plea,*** der Einspruch gegen den Richter; ***– policy,*** die Außenpolitik; ***– to my purpose,*** meinem Zwecke fernliegend; ***Foreign Secretary,*** der Außenminister; ***– trade,*** (*Comm.*) der Außenhandel, (*Naut.*) große Fahrt. **foreigner,** *s.* der (die) Ausländer(in), Fremde(r). **foreignness,** *s.* die Fremdheit; Fremdartigkeit; (*Law*) Inkompetenz.

fore|judge [-'dʒʌdʒ], *v.t.* im voraus *or* voreilig entscheiden *or* (be)urteilen. **-know** [-'nou], *irr.v.t.* vorherwissen, im voraus wissen. **-knowledge,** *s.* das Vorherwissen. **-land,** *s.* das Vorland; Vorgebirge, die Landspitze. **-leg,** *s.* das Vorderbein. **-lock,** *s.* die Stirnlocke; ***take time by the –,*** die Gelegenheit beim Schopf fassen. **-man** [-mən], *s.* der Obmann, Sprecher (*of a jury*); Bauführer, Werkführer, Werkmeister, Vorarbeiter, Polier, Aufseher. **-mast,** *s.* der Fockmast. **-mentioned** [-'menʃənd], *adj.* vor(her)erwähnt, besagt. **-most, 1.** *adj.* vorderst, erst, vornehmst. **2.** *adv.* zuerst; voran, voraus, an erster Stelle; ***first and –,*** zu allererst, in erster Linie; ***feet –,*** mit den Füßen zuvorderst. **-noon,** *s.* der Vormittag.

forensic [fo'rensik], *adj.* gerichtlich, Gerichts–; ***– medicine,*** die Gerichtsmedizin.

fore|ordain [–ɔ:'dein], *v.t.* vorherbestimmen. **-quarters,** *pl.* die Vorhand (*of a horse*). **-reach** [-'ri:tʃ], *v.t., v.i.* (*Naut.*) überholen, übersegeln. **-runner,** *s.* der Vorgänger, Vorläufer; Vorfahr; (*fig.*) Vorbote, das Anzeichen. **-sail** [fɔ:sl], *s.* das Focksegel. **-see** [-'si:], *irr.v.t.* voraussehen, vorhersehen, vorherwissen. **-seeable,** *adj.* ***in the – future,*** in absehbarer Zeit. **-shadow** [-'ʃædou], *v.t.* ahnen lassen, vorher andeuten. **--sheet,** *s.* (*Naut.*) die Fockschot. **-shore,** *s.* das (Küsten)-vorland, Uferland, Gestade, der Strand. **-shorten** [-'ʃɔ:tn], *v.t.* in Verkürzung zeichnen, verkürzen. **-shortening,** *s.* die Verkürzung. **-show** [-'ʃou], *v.t.* vorher anzeigen, vorbedeuten. **-sight,** *s.* 1. der Blick in die Zukunft, die Voraussicht; 2. Vorsorge, Fürsorge; 3. das (Visier)korn (*of a gun*). **-skin,** *s.* (*Anat.*) die Vorhaut.

forest ['fɔrist], **1.** *s.* der Wald, Forst, die Waldung; ***– fire,*** der Waldbrand; (*Am.*) ***– ranger,*** *see* **forester,** 1. **2.** *v.t.* aufforsten.

forestall [fɔ:'stɔ:l], *v.t.* (*a p.*) zuvorkommen (*Dat.*), (*a th.*) vorbeugen (*Dat.*), vorwegnehmen, vereiteln; (*Comm.*) im voraus aufkaufen; ***– the market,*** durch Aufkauf den Markt beherrschen.

forestation [fɔris'teiʃən], *s.* die Aufforstung.

fore-stay, *s.* (*Naut.*) das Fockstag.

forester ['fɔristə], *s.* 1. der Förster; 2. Waldbewohner. **forestry,** *s.* die Forstkultur, Forstwirtschaft, das Forstwesen.

fore|taste, *s.* der Vorgeschmack. **-tell** [-'tel], *irr.v.t.* vorhersagen, voraussagen; im voraus anzeigen. **-thought,** *s.* der Vorbedacht, die Vorsorge. **-top,** *s.* (*Naut.*) der Fockmars, Vormars. **--topgallant,** *adj.* (*Naut.*) Vorbram–; ***– mast,*** die Vorbramstenge. **--topmast** [-'tɔpmɑ:st], *s.* die Vormarsstenge.

forever [fɔr'evə], *adv.* (*Am.*) (= ***for ever***) für *or* auf immer, für alle Zeit, ewig; dauernd, ständig.

fore|-warn [-'wɔ:n], *v.t.* vorher warnen, vorhersagen. **-woman,** *s.* die Vorsteherin, Vorarbeiterin, Aufseherin, Werkführerin. **-word,** *s.* das Vorwort. **-yard,** *s.* (*Naut.*) die Fockrahe.

forfeit ['fɔ:fit], **1.** *v.t.* verwirken, verlieren, einbüßen, verscherzen. **2.** *adj.* verwirkt, verfallen. **3.** *s.* die Verwirkung, der Verlust; die Buße, (verwirktes) Pfand; das Reugeld; *pl.* Pfänderspiel; ***pay a –,*** ein Pfand geben; ***pay the –,*** das Reugeld zahlen; ***play (at) –s,*** Pfänderspiele machen. **forfeitable,** *adj.* verlierbar, verwirkbar. **forfeiture** [-fitʃə], *s.* die Verwirkung, Einbuße, der Verlust, Verfall; ***– of civil rights,*** der Verlust der bürgerlichen Ehrenrechte; ***– of a deposit,*** der Depotverfall.

forfend [fɔ:'fend], *v.t.* verteidigen, sichern; verwehren, fernhalten; ***Heaven –!*** Gott behüte!

forgather [fɔ:'gæðə], *v.i.* zusammenkommen, sich (ver)sammeln; zusammentreffen, sich begegnen *or* treffen.

forgave [fə'geiv], *imperf. of* **forgive.**

[1]**forge** [fɔ:dʒ], **1.** *v.t.* 1. schmieden; (*fig.*) sich (*Dat.*) ausdenken, erfinden, ersinnen, erdichten; 2. fälschen, nachmachen (*a document*). **2.** *s.* die Schmiede; Esse, das Schmiedefeuer, der Schmiedeherd; ***drop-–,*** die Gesenkschmiede.

[2]**forge,** *v.i.* mit Wucht dahinfahren; ***– ahead,*** immer (mühsam) vorwärtskommen; die Führung übernehmen, sich an die Spitze drängen.

forgeable ['fɔ:dʒəbl], *adj.* schmiedbar. **forger,** *s.* 1. der Hammerschmied, Grobschmied; 2. Fälscher, Falschmünzer; (*fig.*) Erfinder, Erdichter. **forgery,** *s.* das Fälschen, die Fälschung.

forget [fə'get], **1.** *irr.v.t.* vergessen; unterlassen, vernachlässigen, außer Acht lassen; ***– o.s.,*** sich vergessen; (*coll.*) ***don't you – it!*** merk es dir! (*sl.*) ***– it!*** Schwamm darüber! **2.** *irr.v.i.* vergessen; ***I –,*** ich habe vergessen, ich weiß (es) nicht mehr; ***he will – about it,*** er wird sich nicht (mehr) daran erinnern. **forgetful,** *adj.* vergeßlich; ***be – of,*** vergessen. **forgetfulness,** *s.* die Vergeßlichkeit; Achtlosigkeit, Vernachlässigung; Vergessenheit. **forget-me-not,** *s.* (*Bot.*) das Vergißmeinnicht.

forging ['fɔ:dʒiŋ], *s.* 1. das Schmieden (*also fig.*), die Schmiedearbeit; das Schmiedestück; 2. Fälschen.

forgivable [fə'givəbl], *adj.* verzeihlich. **forgive,** *irr.v.t.* (*a p.*) vergeben, verzeihen (*Dat.*); erlassen (*a debt etc.*); ***his mistake was forgiven him, he was forgiven his mistake,*** sein Fehler wurde ihm verziehen; ***not to be forgiven,*** unverzeihlich. **forgiveness,** *s.* die Vergebung, Verzeihung. **forgiv-**

ing, *adj.* nachsichtig, versöhnlich, mild. **forgivingness,** *s.* die Versöhnlichkeit.

forgo [fɔː'gou], *irr.v.t.* verzichten auf (*Acc.*), abstehen von, entsagen (*Dat.*), aufgeben.

forgot [fə'gɔt], *imperf. of* **forget. forgotten,** *p.p. of* **forget**; ***never-to-be—,*** unvergeßlich; ***it is easily —,*** das vergißt sich leicht; ***that will soon be —,*** das vergißt sich rasch.

fork [fɔːk], **1.** *s.* 1. die Gabel, (*Agr.*) Forke; (*Mus.*) ***tuning —,*** die Stimmgabel; 2. die Gabelung, Abzweigung (*of a road etc.*). **2.** *v.t.* mit der Gabel aufladen; (*sl.*) ***— out*** or ***up money,*** Geld herausrücken, blechen. **3.** *v.i.* sich gabeln, abzweigen; sich teilen *or* spalten; (*sl.*) ***— out,*** blechen, bluten. **forked,** *adj.* gabelig, gegabelt, gabelförmig, gabelspaltig, gespalten; (*as lightning*) Zickzack–.

forlorn [fə'lɔːn], *adj.* verlassen, einsam; hilflos, hoffnungslos, unglücklich, elend; ***all —,*** mutterseelenallein; ***— hope,*** (*Mil.*) verlorener Posten, (*sl.*) das Himmelfahrtskommando; (*fig.*) verzweifeltes *or* aussichtsloses Unternehmen.

form [fɔːm], **1.** *s.* 1. die Gestalt, Form, Figur; das Muster, Modell, die Schablone; (*fig.*) Erscheinungsform, Art und Weise, Natur, Struktur, Methode, (An)ordnung, das System, Schema; ***— of prayer,*** die Gebetformel; ***— of worship,*** vorgeschriebene Gottesdienst; 2. der (Ge)brauch, die Sitte; Manier, der Anstand, gesellschaftliche Form; die Förmlichkeit, Zeremonie, Formalität; ***matter of —,*** die Formsache, Formalität, bloße Äußerlichkeit; ***that is bad —,*** das schickt sich nicht; ***good —,*** guter Ton, der Takt; ***mere —,*** see ***matter of —***; ***for —'s sake,*** der bloßen Form wegen; ***in due —,*** in gehöriger Form, vorschriftsmäßig; 3. die (Schul)bank, der Sitz; die (Schul)klasse; ***the second —,*** die Quinta; ***the sixth —,*** die Prima; 4. der Vordruck, das Formular; ***application —,*** das Antragsformular; ***requisition —,*** der Bestellzettel; 5. (*coll.*) (körperliche) Verfassung, die Leistungsfähigkeit; (*Spt.*) (*coll.*) ***in*** or ***on —,*** in Form *or* guter Verfassung; (*coll.*) ***in good*** or ***great —,*** in bester Verfassung; ***out of —,*** nicht in Form; 6. *See* **forme. 2.** *v.t.* formen, bilden, gestalten (***into,*** zu); (*Tech.*) verformen, fassonieren; ausbilden, heranbilden, schulen (*a p.*), hervorbringen, schaffen, entwickeln, annehmen; (an)ordnen, aufstellen, zusammenstellen; fassen; entwerfen, erdenken, ersinnen (*a plan etc.*); (*Mil.*) formieren (***into,*** in (*Acc.*)); bilden, darstellen, ausmachen, dienen als; ***— an alliance,*** eine Verbindung eingehen, ein Bündnis schließen; ***— an estimate,*** abschätzen, eine Schätzung machen; ***— a friendship,*** eine Freundschaft anknüpfen *or* schließen; ***— a habit,*** eine Gewohnheit annehmen; ***— an idea,*** eine Idee fassen; ***— an opinion,*** sich (*Dat.*) eine Meinung bilden; ***— a part,*** einen Teil ausmachen *or* darstellen; (*Gram.*) ***— the passive,*** das Passiv bilden; ***— a plan,*** einen Plan fassen *or* ausdenken *or* ersinnen; ***— a society,*** eine Gesellschaft gründen. **3.** *v.i.* sich bilden *or* gestalten *or* formen, Form *or* Gestalt annehmen; (*Mil.*) ***— up,*** antreten; ***— up into line,*** sich in eine Linie formieren.

formal [fɔːml], *adj.* 1. formal, gehörig, in gehöriger Form, bindend; formell, förmlich, feierlich, umständlich, steif; 2. gewohnheitsgemäß, äußerlich, scheinbar; 3. (*Phil.*) formal, wesentlich.

formaldehyde [fɔː'mældihaid], **formalin** ['fɔːməlin], *s.* (*Chem.*) das Formaldehyd.

formalism ['fɔːməlizm], *s.* der Formalismus, die Förmlichkeit. **formalist,** *s.* der Formenmensch. **formalistic** [–'listik], *adj.* formalistisch. **formality** [–'mæliti], *s.* die Förmlichkeit, Formsache, Formalität; Steifheit, Umständlichkeit; ***without —,*** ohne Umstände. **formalize** [–laiz], *v.t.* zur Formsache machen; feste Form geben (*Dat.*). **formally,** *adv.* formell, in aller Form; formal, förmlich.

format ['fɔːmæt], *s.* das Format.

formation [fɔː'meiʃən], *s.* 1. das Bilden, die Formung, Gestaltung; Bildung, Entstehung; 2. der Aufbau, die Struktur, Zusammensetzung, Anordnung, Gliederung; (*Geol., Mil.*) Formation; (*Mil.*) der (Truppen)verband; (*Av.*) die Flugordnung; ***— flying,*** das Verbandfliegen. **formative** ['fɔːmətiv], **1.** *adj.* bildend, formend; (*Gram., Geol.*) formbildend; (*Biol.*) Bildungs–, Gestaltungs–, morphogen. **2.** *s.* (*Gram.*) formbildendes Element.

forme [fɔːm], *s.* (*Typ.*) die (Druck)form.

[1]**former** ['fɔːmə], *s.* 1. der Bildner, Gestalter; 2. die Form, Schablone; (*Av.*) der Spant.

[2]**former,** *adj.* vorig, früher; vorhergehend, vorherig; ehemalig; erst(erwähnt), jene(r, –s) (*of two*); ***in — times,*** vormals. **formerly,** *adv.* ehemals, vormals, ehedem, früher.

formic ['fɔːmik], *adj.* ameisensauer; ***— acid,*** die Ameisensäure. **formicary,** *s.* der Ameisenhaufen. **formication** [–'keiʃən], *s.* (*Med.*) das Ameisenlaufen.

formidable ['fɔːmidəbl], *adj.* furchtbar, schrecklich; ungeheuer, gewaltig.

forming ['fɔːmiŋ], *s.* (*Tech.*) die Formgebung, Verformung, Fassonierung; das Bilden, Formen. **formless,** *adj.* formlos, gestaltlos. **formlessness,** *s.* die Formlosigkeit.

formula ['fɔːmjulə], *s.* (*pl.* **-e** [–liː], **–s**) die Formel; (*Med.*) das Rezept, die Vorschrift. **formulate** [–leit], *v.t.* formulieren, darlegen, klarlegen. **formulation** [–'leiʃən], *s.* die Formulierung, Fassung.

fornicate ['fɔːnikeit], *v.i.* Unzucht treiben, huren. **fornication** [–'keiʃən], *s.* die Unzucht, Hurerei. **fornicator,** *s.* der Hurer, Hurenbock.

forsake [fə'seik], *irr.v.t.* entsagen (*Dat.*), aufgeben; (*a p.*) verlassen, im Stich lassen, (*coll.*) sitzen lassen. **forsaken,** *adj.* einsam, verlassen.

forsook [fə'suk], *imperf. of* **forsake.**

forsooth [fə'suːθ], *adv.* (*obs. now only iron.*) fürwahr, wahrlich, traun.

forswear [fɔː'swɛə], *irr.v.t.* 1. entsagen (*Dat.*), aufzugeben versprechen; ***— his company,*** seinen Umgang meiden; 2. (*obs.*) unter Eid verleugnen, abschwören, eidlich ableugnen; ***— o.s.,*** meineidig werden, einen Meineid leisten. **forsworn, 1.** *p.p. of* **forswear. 2.** *adj.* meineidig.

fort [fɔːt], *s.* das Fort, Festungswerk, die Festung, Feste, Schanze; (*Hist. esp. Am.*) Handelsniederlassung.

forte ['fɔːti], **1.** *adv* (*Mus.*) laut. **2.** *s.* die Stärke, starke Seite, ausgesprochene Fähigkeit.

forth [fɔːθ], *adv.* (*of time*) fort, weiter, von . . . an *or* ab, fortan; (*of place*) her, vor, hervor; heraus, hinaus; draußen; ***from this time —,*** von jetzt an, hinfort, künftighin; ***and so —,*** und so fort *or* weiter; ***back and —,*** hin und her; ***come —,*** hervortreten; ***set —,*** (*v.t.*) darlegen, klarlegen; (*v.i.*) eine Reise antreten.

forth|coming, *adj.* bevorstehend; im Erscheinen begriffen (*of books*); (*fig.*) (*of a p.*) zuvorkommend, entgegenkommend; ***be —,*** erscheinen, eintreten, zum Vorschein kommen, sich zeigen, erfolgen, in die Wege geleitet werden. **–right, 1.** *adj.* gerade, offen. **2.** *adv.* geradeaus. **–rightness,** *s.* die Offenheit, Geradheit. **–with** [–'wiθ], *adv.* sogleich, sofort, ohne weiteres.

fortieth ['fɔːtiiθ], **1.** *num. adj.* vierzigst. **2.** *s.* der *or* die *or* das Vierzigste; das Vierzigstel.

fortification [fɔːtifi'keiʃən], *s.* 1. das (Ver)stärken; die (Be)festigung; Befestigungskunst; 2. (*oft. pl.*) das Festungswerk, die Befestigung(sanlage), Festung. **fortifier** ['fɔːtifaiə], *s.* das Stärkungsmittel. **fortify** [–fai], *v.t.* befestigen (*also fig.*); (ver)stärken; anreichern (*foodstuffs etc.*), ermutigen (*a p.*), bestärken, bekräftigen, erhärten; ***— o.s. against,*** sich wappnen gegen.

fortitude ['fɔːtitjuːd], *s.* die Seelenstärke, Standhaftigkeit, der Mut.

fortnight ['fɔːtnait], *s.* vierzehn Tage; ***this day —,*** heute über 14 Tage *or* in 14 Tagen; ***a — ago,*** heute vor 14 Tagen; ***Sunday —,*** Sonntag über 14 Tage *or* in 14 Tagen; ***this —,*** seit 14 Tagen; ***a —'s holiday,*** ein vierzehntägiger Urlaub. **fortnightly, 1.** *adj.* vierzehntägig. **2.** *adv.* alle vierzehn Tage. **3.** *s.* die Halbmonatsschrift.

fortress ['fɔ:tris], *s.* die Festung.

fortuitous [fɔ:'tjuitəs], *adj.* zufällig. **fortuitousness, fortuity,** *s.* der Zufall, die Zufälligkeit, das Ungefähr.

fortunate ['fɔ:tʃənit], *adj.* glücklich; günstig, glückverheißend. **fortunately,** *adv.* glücklicherweise, zum Glück.

fortune ['fɔ:tʃun], *s.* 1. das Glück; der Glücksfall, glücklicher Zufall; ***be the architect of one's own –,*** seines Glückes Schmied sein; ***bad –,*** see ***ill –***; ***– favours the bold,*** dem Mutigen lächelt das Glück; ***good –,*** das Glück; ***by good –,*** glücklicherweise, zum Glück; ***with good –,*** wenn man Glück hat; ***ill –,*** das Unglück; ***make one's –,*** sein Glück machen; ***seek one's –,*** sein Glück suchen; ***try one's –,*** sein Glück versuchen; ***wheel of –,*** das Glücksrad; 2. das Geschick, Schicksal; (*Myth.*) Fortuna (*f.*), die Glücksgöttin; ***tell –s,*** wahrsagen; (aus den) Karten lesen, die Karten legen; ***have one's – told,*** sich (*Dat.*) wahrsagen lassen; ***turn of –,*** die Schicksalswende, der Glückswechsel; 3. das Vermögen, der Reichtum; ***come into a –,*** ein Vermögen erben; ***make a –,*** sich (*Dat.*) ein Vermögen erwerben; ***marry a –,*** reich heiraten, eine reiche Frau heiraten, eine reiche Partie machen; ***spend a (small) – on,*** ein (kleines) Vermögen ausgeben für.

fortune| hunter, *s.* der Mitgiftjäger. **--teller,** *s.* der (die) Wahrsager(in). **--telling,** *s.* das Wahrsagen.

forty ['fɔ:ti], **1.** *num. adj.* vierzig; (*coll.*) ***– winks,*** das Nickerchen, Schläfchen. **2.** *s.* die Vierzig; ***the forties,*** die Vierziger(jahre); (*Naut.*) ***the roaring forties,*** stürmische Gegend (zwischen dem 40. und 50. Breitengrad).

forum ['fɔ:rəm], *s.* das Forum; (*fig.*) Tribunal, Gericht.

forward ['fɔ:wəd], **1.** *adj.* 1. vorn (befindlich), vorder, vorgerückt, vorwärts gerichtet; vorgerückt, vorgeschritten; (*Footb.*) ***– pass,*** die Vorlage; 2. (*coll.*) vorschnell, voreilig, vorlaut, naseweis; (*Bot. etc.*) frühreif, frühzeitig; 3. (*Comm.*) auf Zeit *or* spätere Lieferung (*as contract*); ***– deal,*** das Termingeschäft; ***– quotation,*** der Preis im Termingeschäft. **2.** *adv.* vorwärts; weiter, fort; ***from this time –,*** von jetzt an; ***bring –,*** vorwärtsbringen; früher beginnen lassen; vorbringen, beibringen (*argument etc.*); einbringen (*a law etc.*); (*Comm.*) vortragen, übertragen; (*Comm.*) ***brought*** or ***carried –,*** der Übertrag; ***go –,*** fortschreiten; (*fig.*) ***push o.s. –,*** sich hervortun; ***look – to,*** entgegensehen (*Dat.*). **3.** *v.t.* fördern, beschleunigen; begünstigen; (weiter)befördern, versenden, spedieren; nachschicken (*a letter*). **4.** *s.* (*Footb.*) der Stürmer; ***– line,*** die Stürmerreihe.

forwarder ['fɔ:wədə], *s.* der Nachsender; Spediteur. **forwarding,** *s.* die Versendung, Spedition; ***– agent,*** der Spediteur, Transporteur; ***– charges,*** Versandspesen (*pl.*); ***– note,*** der Frachtbrief, Speditionsauftrag. **forwardness,** *s.* der Eifer; die Frühreife, Frühzeitigkeit; Voreiligkeit, Keckheit, Dreistigkeit. **forwards,** *adv. See* **forward, 2**; ***backwards and –,*** hin und her.

fossa ['fɔsə], *s.* (*pl.* **-e** [–sai]) (*Anat.*) die Grube, Höhlung.

fosse [fɔs], *s.* der Graben; (*Anat.*) *see* **fossa.**

fossil [fɔsl], **1.** *adj.* ausgegraben, fossil, versteinert; (*fig.*) verknöchert, rückständig, veraltet. **2.** *s.* das Fossil, die Versteinerung; (*coll.*) rückständige *or* verknöcherte Person. **fossiliferous** [–si'lifərəs], *adj.* fossilienhaltig. **fossilization** [–lai'zeiʃən], *s.* die Versteinerung, Fossil(ien)bildung. **fossilize, 1.** *v.t.* versteinern. **2.** *v.i.* sich versteinern; (*fig.*) verknöchern.

fossorial [fɔ'sɔ:riəl], *adj.* (*Zool.*) grabend, Grab–.

foster ['fɔstə], *v.t.* nähren, pflegen, aufziehen; (*fig.*) hegen, begünstigen, fördern, anregen, beleben, günstig sein (*Dat.*). **foster|-brother,** *s.* der Pflegebruder. **--child,** *s.* das Pflegekind. **fosterer,** *s.* der Pflegevater; die Amme; (*fig.*) der Förderer. **foster-father,** *s.* der Pflegevater. **fosterling,** *s.* das Pflegekind, Pflegling, (*fig.*) der Schützling. **foster|-mother,** *s.* die Pflegemutter. **--parent,** *s.* der Pflegevater, die Pflegemutter; *pl.* Pflegeeltern (*pl.*).

fought [fɔ:t], *imperf., p.p. of* **fight.**

foul [faul], **1.** *adj.* schmutzig, unrein, verschmutzt; (*fig.*) widerwärtig, widerlich, abscheulich, ekelhaft, garstig, anrüchig, verrucht, unzüchtig, zotig; (*Spt.*) regelwidrig, unfair, unredlich, unehrlich; (*Typ.*) voll(er) Korrekturen; ***fall – of him,*** bei ihm Anstoß erregen, mit ihm in Kollision geraten; (*Naut.*) ***run – of,*** festfahren auf (*Acc.*); ***– air,*** schlechte Luft, (*Min.*) gebrauchte Wetter (*pl.*); ***the anchor is –,*** der Anker ist unklar; ***– bottom,*** schlechter (Anker)grund; bewachsener Boden (*of ship*); ***– breath,*** übelriechender Atem; ***– chimney,*** verrußter Schornstein; (*Typ.*) ***– copy,*** vielfach korrigiertes Konzept; ***– deed,*** die Schandtat; ***– fiend,*** böser Feind, der Teufel; ***– gun-barrel,*** verschmiertes *or* verschmutztes Rohr; ***– language,*** gemeine *or* schmutzige Reden (*pl.*), Zoten (*pl.*); ***by fair means or –,*** komme wie es wolle; ***– play,*** unsauberes Spiel; (*fig.*) unredliche Machenschaften (*pl.*), verräterische Handlung; (*Typ.*) ***– proof,*** unkorrigierter Abzug; ***– shore,*** unreine Küste; (*fig.*) ***– tongue,*** böse Zunge, loses Maul; ***– water,*** trübes *or* verdorbenes Wasser; ***– weather,*** schlechtes Wetter; ***– wind,*** widriger Wind. **2.** *v.t.* 1. beschmutzen, verschmutzen; (*fig.*) besudeln; 2. anstoßen, anfahren, ansegeln, anrennen (gegen *or* an (*Acc.*)) (*of ships*); verwickeln (*the anchor*); verstopfen, (ver)sperren, hemmen; (*Spt.*) regelwidrig behindern; ***– the points,*** an der Weiche entgleisen. **3.** *v.i.* sich verwickeln (*of anchor*), sich festfahren (*of ship*); (*Spt.*) unfair spielen. **4.** *s.* der Zusammenstoß, (*Spt.*) regelwidriger Stoß *or* Schlag, der Regelverstoß.

fouling ['fauliŋ], *s.* die Verunreinigung, Beschmutzung; (*Naut.*) der Bewuchs, Anwuchs (*on ship's hull*); ***anti--*** (***paint***), die Unterwassergleitfarbe.

foul-mouthed, *adj.* ein loses Maul habend, schmutzige Reden führend. **foulness,** *s.* der Schmutz, die Unreinheit, Trübheit; (*fig.*) Gemeinheit, Schlechtigkeit, Falschheit (*of intentions*).

[1]**found** [faund], *imperf., p.p. of* **find.**

[2]**found,** *v.t.* gründen, den Grund legen von, errichten; stiften, ins Leben rufen, einrichten; (*fig.*) stützen, bauen (***on,*** auf (*Acc.*)); ***be –ed on,*** beruhen auf (*Dat.*); ***well--ed,*** gut begründet.

[3]**found,** *v.t.* (*Metall.*) gießen.

foundation [faun'deiʃən], *s.* 1. (*Build.*) der Grund, die Grundlage, Grundmauer, das Fundament; der Unterbau, die Bettung, Fundierung (*of a road etc.*), das Grundmauerwerk (*of a wall*); (*Dressm. etc.*) die Unterlage, das Steifleinen; ***to its very –s,*** bis in die Grundfesten; 2. die Gründung, Grundlegung, Einrichtung, Errichtung, Stiftung; 3. (*fig.*) Grundlage, Basis; ***moral –,*** sittliche Unterlage; ***the rumour has no –,*** das Gerücht entbehrt jeder Grundlage; 4. die Anstalt, Stiftung, das Stift; die Schenkung, das Stipendium; ***pious –,*** milde Stiftung.

foundationer [faun'deiʃənə], *s.* der Stipendiat. **foundation| garment,** *s.* das Korsett, Korselett, Mieder, die Korsage. **--plate,** *s.* die Grundplatte, Sohle. **--scholar,** *s.* der Freischüler, Stiftsschüler. **--school,** *s.* die Stiftsschule. **--stone,** *s.* der Grundstein; (*fig.*) die Grundlage, Basis, das Fundament.

[1]**founder** ['faundə], *s.* der Gründer, Stifter; ***–'s day,*** der Stiftergedenktag; (*Comm.*) ***–'s shares,*** Gründeraktien (*pl.*).

[2]**founder,** *s.* (*Metall.*) der Schmelzer, Gießer.

[3]**founder,** *v.i.* (*Naut.*) sinken, untergehen; (*fig.*) mißlingen, fehlschlagen, scheitern, zerschellen, zusammenbrechen; (ein)stürzen, einfallen (*as buildings*); steif werden, lahmen (*of a horse*).

foundling ['faundliŋ], *s.* der Findling, das Findelkind. **foundling-hospital,** *s.* das Findelhaus.

foundry ['faundri], *s.* die Gießerei, (Schmelz)hütte.

fount [faunt], *s.* 1. (*Poet.*) *see* **fountain**; 2. (*Typ.*) die Schrift(sorte), der (Schrift)satz, Schriftguß.

fountain ['fauntin], *s.* die Quelle (*also fig.*), der Springbrunnen, das Wasserwerk; (*fig.*) der Ursprung, die Herkunft. **fountain|-head,** *s.* (*fig.*) der Urquell, Ursprung, (eigentliche) Quelle. **--pen,** *s.* die Füllfeder.

four [fɔ:], **1.** *num. adj.* vier; ***the – corners of the earth,*** die entlegensten Gegenden der Erde; ***– figures,*** vierstellige Zahl. **2.** *s.* die Vier; (*Rowing*) der Vierer (*boat*), die Vierermannschaft; ***in –s,*** zu vieren; ***on all –s,*** auf allen vieren; ***be on all –s with,*** genau entsprechen (*Dat.*); ***carriage and –,*** der Vierspänner. *For clock times see under* **eight.**

four|-barrelled, *adj.* Vierlings–. **--cornered,** *adj.* viereckig. **--edged,** *adj.* vierkantig. **--engined,** *adj.* viermotorig. **--flusher,** *s.* (*sl.*) der Schwindler, Großtuer, Mogler. **–fold,** *adj.* vierfach, vierfältig. **--footed,** *adj.* vierfüßig. **--handed,** *adj.* (*Mus.*) vierhändig. **--in-hand, 1.** *s.* der Vierspänner, das Viergespann. **2.** *adv.* ***drive –,*** vierspännig fahren. **--legged,** *adj.* vierbeinig. **–part,** *adj.* (*Mus.*) vierstimmig. **–penny** [–pəni], *adj.* im Wert von 4 Pence; (*coll.*) ***give him a – one,*** ihm eine herunterhauen. **--poster,** *s.* das Himmelbett. **–score,** *adj.* achtzig. **--seater,** *s.* der Viersitzer.

foursome ['fɔ:səm], *s.* (*Golf*) das Viererspiel; (*fig.*) die Gesellschaft (*of persons*) *or* der Satz (*of things*) von vier(en).

four|square, *adj.* viereckig, vierkantig, quadratisch; (*fig.*) fest, standhaft. **--stroke,** *adj.* Viertakt–.

fourteen ['fɔ:ti:n], **1.** *num. adj.* vierzehn. **2.** *s.* die Vierzehn. **fourteenth, 1.** *num. adj.* vierzehnt. **2.** *s.* der *or* die *or* das Vierzehnte; das Vierzehntel. **fourth, 1.** *num. adj.* viert; ***– form,*** die Tertia (*school*). **2.** *s.* der *or* die *or* das Vierte; das Viertel; (*Mus.*) die Quarte. **fourthly,** *adv.* viertens, zum vierten.

four|-wheel, *adj.* ***– drive,*** der Vierradantrieb. **--wheeled,** *adj.* vierräd(e)rig. **--wheeler,** *s.* vierrädriger Wagen, die Droschke.

fowl [faul], **1.** *s.* das Haushuhn; (*obs.*) der Vogel; *pl.* das Geflügel, Federvieh, Hühner (*pl.*); ***barn-door –,*** das Haushuhn. **2.** *v.i.* Vögel fangen *or* schießen. **fowler,** *s.* der Vogelfänger, Vogelsteller. **fowling,** *s.* der Vogelfang, die Vogeljagd, das Vogelstellen. **fowling-piece,** *s.* die Vogelflinte. **fowl|-pest,** *s.* die Hühnerpest, Geflügelpest. **--run,** *s.* der Auslauf (für Hühner).

[1]**fox** [fɔks], **1.** *s.* der Fuchs; (*fig.*) Schlaukopf, Schlaumeier; ***set the – to keep the geese,*** den Bock zum Gärtner machen; (*Prov.*) ***with –es one must play the –,*** mit den Wölfen muß man heulen. **2.** *v.t.* (*sl.*) täuschen, hintergehen, überlisten.

[2]**fox,** *v.i.* stockfleckig werden (*of books, paper*).

fox|-brush, *s.* der Fuchsschwanz. **--earth,** *s.* der Fuchsbau.

foxed [fɔkst], *adj.* stockfleckig; *see* [2]**fox.**

fox|glove, *s.* (*Bot.*) der Fingerhut. **--hole,** *s.* der Fuchsbau; (*Mil.*) das Schützenloch; (*fig.*) Schlupfloch, der Schlupfwinkel. **–hound,** *s.* der Fuchshund. **--hunt(ing),** *s.* die Fuchsjagd. **--terrier,** *s.* der Foxterrier. **–trot,** *s.* der Foxtrott. **foxy,** *adj.* 1. (*fig.*) verschlagen, gerissen, schlau, listig; 2. fuchsig, rotbraun.

foyer ['fwæjei, 'fɔiei], *s.* die Wandelhalle, der Wandelgang, das Foyer.

fracas ['frækɑ:], *s.* der Lärm, Aufruhr, Spektakel.

fraction ['frækʃən], *s.* das Bruchstück, der Bruchteil; (*Math.*) Bruch; (*coll.*) das Stückchen, bißchen; ***vulgar*** or ***simple –,*** gemeiner Bruch; ***by a – of an inch,*** um ein Haar; ***representative –,*** der Maßstab (*on maps*). **fractional,** *adj.* (*Geol., Chem.*) gebrochen, fraktionär, fraktioniert, (*Math. etc.*) Bruch–, Teil–; (*coll.*) minimal, unbedeutend; ***– distillation,*** fraktionierte Destillation. **fractionate** [–eit], *v.t.* (*Chem.*) fraktionieren.

fractious ['frækʃəs], *adj.* zänkisch, mürrisch, verdrießlich, reizbar, widerspenstig, störrisch, widerborstig. **fractiousness,** *s.* die Reizbarkeit, Zanksucht, Widerspenstigkeit.

fracture ['fræktʃə], **1.** *s.* (*Med.*) der (Knochen)bruch, die Fraktur; Bruch(fläche), Bruchstelle. **2.** *v.t.* (zer)brechen; ***– one's leg,*** sich (*Dat.*) das Bein brechen; ***–d skull,*** der Schädelbruch. **3.** *v.i.* zerbrechen, zersplittern.

fragile ['frædʒail], *adj.* zerbrechlich, brüchig; (*fig.*) gebrechlich, hinfällig, schwach, zart. **fragility** [frə'dʒiliti], *s.* die Zerbrechlichkeit, Brüchigkeit; (*fig.*) Gebrechlichkeit, Hinfälligkeit, Schwäche, Zartheit.

fragment ['frægmənt], *s.* das Bruchstück, Fragment, der Brocken. **fragmental** [–'mentl], *adj.* (*Geol.*) Trümmer–. **fragmentary,** *adj.* fragmentarisch, bruchstückartig; abgebrochen, unvollständig. **fragmentation** [–'teiʃən], *s.* die Zersplitterung, Zertrümmerung; (*Mil.*) Splitterwirkung; ***– bomb,*** die Splitterbombe.

fragrance, fragrancy ['freigrəns(i)], *s.* der Wohlgeruch, Duft, das Aroma. **fragrant,** *adj.* wohlriechend, duftend, duftig, aromatisch; ***be – of*** or ***with,*** duften von.

[1]**frail** [freil], *s.* der Binsenkorb.

[2]**frail,** *adj.* schwach, zart, gebrechlich; zerbrechlich, hinfällig; vergänglich; sündhaft. **frailness,** *s.* die Schwäche, Schwachheit, Gebrechlichkeit, Zerbrechlichkeit. **frailty,** *s. See* **frailness**; (*fig.*) (moralische) Schwäche, der Fehltritt.

fraise [freiz], *s.* 1. (*Fort.*) das Pfahlwerk; 2. (*Tech.*) die Bohrfräse.

frame [freim], **1.** *v.t.* 1. bilden, formen; einrichten, anpassen (*to, Dat.*); 2. einrahmen, einfassen; 3. (*fig.*) zusammenfügen, zusammensetzen; ausdrücken, aussprechen; entwerfen, erfinden, ersinnen, schmieden; 4. (*sl.*) verleumden, intrigieren gegen, hereinlegen. **2.** *v.i.* (*obs.*) sich anlassen, sich anschicken. **3.** *s.* 1. der Rahmen, das Gerüst, Gestell, Gehäuse, der Bock; die Einfassung, Einrahmung; (*Shipb., Av.*) das Spant, Gerippe, (*Typ.*) (Setz)regal, (*Films*) Teilbild, Einzelbild, (*T.V.*) Bildfeld, der Raster; der Körperbau, die Form, Figure, Gestalt; (*Hort.*) ***forcing-–,*** der Treibkasten, Frühbeetkasten; ***spectacle –,*** das Brillengestell; ***window –,*** der Fensterrahmen; 2. (*fig.*) das Gebilde, Gefüge, System, der Bau, Zustand, die (An)ordnung, Einrichtung, Verfassung; ***– of mind,*** die Geistesverfassung; Gemütsverfassung, Stimmung; ***– of reference,*** das Bezugssystem.

frame|-aerial, *s.* die Rahmenantenne. **--house,** *s.* das Holzhaus, Fachwerkhaus. **--saw,** *s.* die Spannsäge. **--up,** *s.* (*sl.*) die Machenschaft, abgekartetes Spiel. **–work,** *s.* das Gerüst, Gerippe, Gestell; (*Carp.*) Gebälk, Fachwerk, Riegelwerk; (*fig.*) System, die Einrichtung, der Rahmen, Bau. **framing,** *s.* die Einrahmung, Einfassung; (*fig.*) Entwerfung, Gestaltung.

France [frɑ:ns], *s.* Frankreich (*n.*).

franchise ['fræntʃaiz], *s.* (*Pol.*) das Wahlrecht, Stimmrecht; (*Hist.*) Vorrecht, die Gerechtsame; (*Comm.*) Konzession, das Privileg.

Franciscan [fræn'siskn], **1.** *adj.* Franziskaner–. **2.** *s.* der Franziskaner(mönch).

Franco– ['fræŋkou], *adj. pref.* französisch; ***–German,*** deutsch-französisch.

Franconia [fræŋ'kouniə], *s.* (*Geog.*) Franken (*n.*). **Franconian, 1.** *adj.* fränkisch, (*Hist.*) salisch. **2.** *s.* der Franke (die Fränkin).

francophile ['fræŋkofail], **1.** *adj.* franzosenfreundlich. **2.** *s.* der Franzosenfreund. **francophobe** [–foub], *s.* der Franzosenfeind.

frangibility [frændʒi'biliti], *s.* die Zerbrechlichkeit. **frangible,** *adj.* zerbrechlich.

Frank [fræŋk], *s. See* **Franconian, 2.**

[1]**frank,** *adj.* frei(mütig), aufrichtig, offen(herzig).

[2]**frank, 1.** *s.* (*obs.*) portofreier Brief; der Frankovermerk. **2.** *v.t.* portofrei versenden, frankieren; (von Zahlung) befreien.

frankincense ['fræŋkinsens], *s.* der Weihrauch.

Frankish ['fræŋkiʃ], *adj. See* **Franconian, 1.**

franklin ['fræŋklin], *s.* (*Hist.*) der Freisasse, kleiner Gutsbesitzer.

frankly ['fræŋkli], *adv.* frei (heraus), offen (gestanden), rückhaltlos. **frankness,** *s.* die Offenheit, Freimütigkeit.

frantic ['fræntik], *adj.* rasend, ungestüm, wild, außer sich (***with***, vor (*Dat.*)); (*coll.*) ***be in a – hurry,*** es schrecklich eilig haben.

frap [fræp], *v.t.* (*Naut.*) zurren.

fraternal [frə'tə:nl], *adj.* brüderlich, Bruder–, Brüder–, Bruderschafts–. **fraternity,** *s.* die Brüderlichkeit; Bruderschaft, Verbindung, Vereinigung. **fraternization** [frætənai'zeiʃən], *s.* **1.** die Verbrüderung; 2. (*Mil. coll.*) freundschaftlicher Verkehr (mit den Besiegten). **fraternize,** *v.i.* **1.** sich verbrüdern; 2. (*Mil. coll.*) (mit den Besiegten) freundschaftlich verkehren.

fratricidal [frætri'saidl], *adj.* brudermörderisch; (*fig.*) sich gegenseitig zerstörend. **fratricide** ['frætrisaid], *s.* **1.** der Brudermord; 2. Brudermörder.

fraud [frɔ:d],*s.***1.** der Betrug, Schwindel (***against***, an (*Dat.*)), die Unterschlagung; 2. (*coll.*) der Betrüger, Schwindler. **fraudulence, fraudulency** ['frɔ:djuləns(i)], *s.* die Betrügerei. **fraudulent,** *adj.* betrügerisch; – ***conversion,*** die Veruntreuung, Unterschlagung.

fraught [frɔ:t], *pred. adj.* (*Poet.*) beladen; versehen (***with***, mit), voll (von); – ***with danger,*** gefahrvoll; – ***with meaning,*** bedeutungsvoll, bedeutungsschwer.

[1]**fray** [frei], *s.* die Rauferei, Schlägerei; ***eager for the –,*** kampflustig.

[2]**fray, 1.** *v.t.* abreiben, durchreiben, abnutzen, ausfransen. **2.** *v.i.* sich abnutzen *or* ausfransen.

frazzle [fræzl], *s.* (*sl.*) die Erschöpfung; ***to a –,*** bis zur völligen Erschöpfung.

freak [fri:k], *s.* die Laune, Grille, drolliger Einfall; – (***of nature***), das Monstrum, die Mißgeburt, Mißbildung. **freakish,** *adj.* grotesk, wunderlich; launenhaft, grillenhaft.

freckle [frekl], **1.** *s.* die Sommersprosse; das Fleckchen. **2.** *v.t.* sprenkeln, tüpfeln. **3.** *v.i.* Sommersprossen bekommen. **freckled,** *adj.* sommersprossig; fleckig, gesprenkelt.

Frederic(k) ['fredərik], *s.* Friedrich (*m.*).

free [fri:], **1.** *adj.* 1. frei, befreit, verschont (***of, from***, von), gesichert, immun (***from***, gegen); 2. frei, selbständig, unabhängig; 3. ungebunden, uneingeschränkt, ungehemmt, unbehindert, ungezwungen, zwanglos; 4. kostenlos, unentgeltlich; 5. (*Chem.*) nicht gebunden; 6. (*fig.*) frei(mütig), offenherzig; lose, zügellos, dreist, derb, (allzu) frei.

(a) (*with nouns*) – ***agent,*** unabhängige Person; ***carriage –,*** Fracht bezahlt; – ***church,*** die Freikirche; – ***city,*** die Freistadt; – ***delivery,*** portofreie Zustellung; – ***enterprise,*** freie Wirtschaft; – ***and unencumbered estate,*** unbelastetes *or* hypothekenfreies Erbgut; – ***fight,*** allgemeine Schlägerei; (*Comm.*) – ***gift,*** die Gratisprobe; ***have a – hand,*** freie Hand haben; (*Spt.*) – ***kick,*** der Freistoß; – ***labour,*** unorganisierte Arbeiterschaft; – ***library,*** öffentliche Lesehalle, die Volksbücherei; – ***list,*** die Liste der Empfänger von Freikarten *or* Freiexemplaren; – ***liver,*** der Schlemmer; – ***love,*** freie Liebe; – ***and easy manner,*** zwangloses *or* ungeniertes *or* ungezwungenes Benehmen; – ***pass,*** die Freikarte; – ***passage,*** (*Naut.*) freie Überfahrt; (*on land*) freier *or* unbehinderter Durchgang; – ***place,*** die Freistelle; – ***play,*** (*Tech.*) der Spielraum, (*fig.*) die Handlungsfreiheit; – ***port,*** der Freihafen; ***post –,*** franko; – ***quarters,*** das Freiquartier; ***have the – run,*** nach Belieben aus und eingehen können (***of***, in (*Dat.*)); – ***school,*** die Freischule; (*fig.*) – ***scope,*** freie Hand; – ***state,*** der Freistaat; (*swimming*) – ***style,*** der Freistil; – ***translation,*** freie Übersetzung; (*Tech.*) – ***travel,*** toter Gang; – ***verse,*** freier Vers; (*Pol.*) – ***vote,*** die Abstimmung ohne Fraktionszwang; – ***will,*** die Willensfreiheit; ***of one's own – will,*** aus freiem Willen; (*Naut.*) – ***wind,*** raumer Wind.

(b) (*with verbs*) ***you are – to do it,*** es steht dir frei, es zu tun; ***get one's hand –,*** die Hand freibekommen; ***make – with him,*** sich (*Dat.*) ihm gegenüber zuviel erlauben *or* herausnehmen, sich (*Dat.*) Freiheiten gegen ihn erlauben; ***make – with a th.,*** mit etwas schalten und walten, etwas wie sein Eigentum behandeln; ***set –,*** befreien, freilassen, entlassen, auf freien Fuß setzen.

(c) (*with preps.*) – ***from care,*** sorgenfrei; – ***from danger,*** ungefährdet; – ***from error,*** fehlerfrei; – ***from fear,*** furchtlos; – ***of charge,*** gebührenfrei, spesenfrei, kostenlos; ***make him – of a city,*** ihm das Bürgerrecht verleihen; – ***of debt,*** schuldenfrei; – ***of duty,*** zollfrei; ***be – of the harbour,*** aus dem Hafen heraus sein; (*Comm.*) – ***on board,*** frei Schiff; (*Comm.*) – ***on rail,*** frei Eisenbahn; – ***with one's money,*** freigebig, großzügig.

2. *adv.* (*also sl.* ***for –***) frei, kostenlos.

3. *v.t.* befreien, entlassen, auf freien Fuß setzen, freilassen, freimachen; – ***from,*** befreien *or* erlösen von; – ***from acid,*** entsäuern, neutralisieren; – ***of,*** entlasten von.

free|board, *s.* (*Naut.*) das Freibord. **–booter,** *s.* der Freibeuter. **–born,** *adj.* freigeboren. **freedman,** *s.* Freigelassene(r).

freedom ['fri:dəm], *s.* die Freiheit; Unabhängigkeit, Selbstbestimmung; das Freisein, Befreitsein (***from***, von); Vorrecht, Privileg; Nutznießungsrecht, freie Benutzung (***of***, *Gen.*), freier Zutritt (zu); die Freimütigkeit, Ungezwungenheit; – ***of a city,*** das Bürgerrecht; – ***of a company,*** das Meisterrecht; – ***of the press,*** die Pressefreiheit; – ***of the seas,*** die Freiheit der Meere; – ***from wear and tear,*** die Verschleißfestigkeit; – ***of (the) will,*** die Willensfreiheit.

free|-for-all, *s.* (*sl.*) 1. allgemeine Schlägerei; 2. offenes Spiel. **–hand,** *adj.* freihändig; – ***drawing,*** das Freihandzeichnen. **--handed,** *adj.* freigebig, großzügig. **–hold,** *s.* freier Grundbesitz; (*Hist.*) das Freisassengut, Freilehen; – ***residence,*** die Eigentumswohnung. **–holder,** *s.* der Grundbesitzer; (*Hist.*) Freisasse. **–lance, 1.** *s.* freier Schriftsteller; (*Mil.*) der Freischärler, Söldner; (*fig.*) Unabhängige(r), Parteilose(r). **2.** *v.i.* freiberuflich tätig sein. **3.** *adj.* freiberuflich tätig, selbständig, unabhängig. **4.** *adv.* auf eigene Faust, ohne Parteibindung.

freely ['fri:li], *adv.* frei, bereitwillig, ohne Zwang; reichlich, im Überfluße; vertraulich, freimütig; ***bleed –,*** reichlich *or* stark bluten; ***drink –,*** stark trinken; ***speak –,*** offen reden, (sich (*Dat.*)) kein Blatt vor den Mund nehmen; ***translate –,*** frei übersetzen.

free|man, *s.* freier Mann; der Ehrenbürger; Wahlberechtigte(r); der Meister (*of a guild*). **–martin,** *s.* unfruchtbare Kuh. **–mason,** *s.* der Freimaurer. **–masonry,** *s.* die Freimaurerei. **--spoken,** *adj.* offen, freimütig. **–stone,** *s.* der Sandstein. **--stone,** *adj.* Freistein– (*plum etc.*). **–thinker,** *s.* der Freidenker, Freigeist. **–thinking,** *s.* die Freidenkerei, Freigeisterei. **--trade,** *s.* der Freihandel. **–way,** *s.* (*Am.*) die Autobahn. **--wheel, 1.** *s.* der Freilauf. **2.** *v.i.* mit Freilauf fahren. **--wheeling,** *s.* der Freilauf. **--will, 1.** *adj.* freiwillig. **2.** *s.* ***See free will.***

freeze [fri:z], **1.** *v.t.* zum Gefrieren bringen (*water*); erfrieren lassen (*living beings*); tief kühlen (*food*); (*fig.*) erstarren *or* schaudern machen; (*Comm.*) sperren, blockieren, stoppen; (*coll.*) – ***him out,*** ihn hinausdrängen *or* ausschließen *or* ausschalten (***of***, aus). **2.** *v.i.* (ge)frieren, zu Eis werden; einfrieren, zufrieren (*as a pond*), (*fig.*) eisig werden, erstarren; – ***to death,*** erfrieren; (*coll.*) – ***on to,*** festhalten an (*Acc.*); – ***up,*** vereisen. **3.** *s.* (*Comm.*) der Stillstand, Stopp. **freezer,** *s.* die Gefriermaschine, Tiefkühltruhe. **freezing, 1.** *adj.* eisig. **2.** *s.* **1.** das Gefrieren, Einfrieren; ***below –(-point),*** unter dem Gefrierpunkt; 2. (*Comm.*) das Sperren, Stoppen.

freight [freit], **1.** *s.* die Fracht, Ladung; (*esp. Am.*) das Frachtgut; Frachtgeld, die Frachtgebühr, der Frachtlohn; (*Naut.*) das Heuergeld; ***bill of –,*** der Frachtbrief; – ***out*** (– ***home***), die Hinfracht (Rückfracht). **2.** *v.t.* befrachten, beladen (*a ship*); verfrachten, befördern (*goods*); verheuern (*a ship for* *transport*). **freightage** [–tidʒ], *s.* die Schiffsladung, Fracht; der Transport; das Frachtgeld, die Frachtgebühr.

freight|-car, *s.* (*Am.*) der Güterwagen. **--carrier,** *s.* das Güterflugzeug. **freighter,** *s.* der Verfrachter; Befrachter; Frachtdampfer. **freight|-train,** *s.* (*Am.*) der Güterzug. **--yard,** *s.* (*Am.*) der Güterbahnhof.

French [frentʃ], **1.** *adj.* französisch; ***she is* –,** sie ist Französin; – ***bean,*** die Feuerbohne, welsche Bohne; – ***Canadian,*** frankokanadisch; – ***chalk,*** die Schneiderkreide, das Federweiß; – ***horn,*** das Waldhorn; ***take* – *leave,*** sich heimlich drücken; – ***polish,*** die Möbelpolitur; – ***roll,*** das (Weiß)-brötchen, Franzbrot; – ***seam,*** die Rechts-Links-Naht; – ***window,*** die Verandatür, das Flügelfenster. **2.** *s.* **1.** ***the* –,** Franzosen (*pl.*); 2. (*language*) das Französisch(e). **French|man** [–mən], *s.* der Franzose. **–woman,** *s.* die Französin.

frenetic [frə'netik], *adj.* rasend, wahnsinnig.

frenzied ['frenzid], *adj.* wahnsinnig, rasend. **frenzy,** *s.* der Wahnsinn, die Raserei, (*coll.*) wilde Aufregung.

frequency ['fri:kwənsi], *s.* 1. die Häufigkeit; – ***curve,*** die Häufigkeitskurve; 2. (*Phys.*) die Frequenz, Schwingungszahl; ***audio* –,** die Tonfrequenz; ***high* –,** die Hochfrequenz; (*Rad.*) **--*changer*** or ***converter,*** der Frequenzwandler; (*Rad.*) – ***response,*** die Frequenztreue, Frequenzwiedergabe; (*Rad.*) – ***selection,*** die Grobeinstellung.

frequent, 1. ['fri:kwənt], *adj.* häufig (wiederholt *or* wiederkehrend); ***be* –,** häufig vorkommen; – ***visitor,*** fleißiger *or* regelmäßiger Besucher. **2.** [fri'kwent], *v.t.* häufig *or* regelmäßig besuchen, frequentieren. **frequentative** [fri'kwentətiv], **1.** *adj.* (*Gram.*) frequentativ. **2.** *s.* (*Gram.*) das Frequentativum. **frequenter** [fri'kwentə], *s.* fleißiger *or* regelmäßiger Besucher. **frequently** ['fri:kwəntli], *adv.* häufig, öfters, oft.

fresco ['freskou], **1.** *s.* die Freskomalerei, das Fresko(gemälde). **2.** *v.t.* in Fresko malen.

fresh [freʃ], **1.** *adj.* 1. frisch, neu; verschieden, anders; – ***arrival,*** der Neuankömmling, Neuling; (*fig.*) ***break* – *ground,*** etwas (ganz) Neues unternehmen; – ***news,*** die Neuigkeit; 2. ungesalzen (*as butter*); süß, trinkbar (*as water*); erfrischend, kühl, rein (*as air*); munter, blühend, lebhaft (*as complexion*); – ***water,*** das Süßwasser; ***in the* – *air,*** im Freien; 3. (*sl.*) frech, keck, vorlaut, anmaßend, dreist. **2.** *s.* das Oberwasser (*of a river*), die Frühe, Kühle (*of the morning*). **freshen, 1.** *v.t.* auffrischen, erfrischen, beleben. **2.** *v.i.* frisch werden; ***the wind* –*s,*** der Wind nimmt zu. **fresher,** *s.* (*coll.*) *see* **freshman. freshet** [–it], *s.* die Überschwemmung, Flut, das Hochwasser. **freshman,** *s.* (*Univ.*) der Fuchs. **freshness,** *s.* die Frische; Neuheit, Unerfahrenheit. **freshwater,** *adj.* Süßwasser–.

[1]**fret** [fret], **1.** *v.t.* abreiben, aufreiben, verzehren, anfressen, zerfressen, aushöhlen; kräuseln (*the surface of water etc.*); (*fig.*) ärgern, reizen, aufregen; – ***o.s.,*** *see* **2. 2.** *v.i.* sich ärgern *or* quälen, sich (*Dat.*) Sorgen machen; – ***and fume,*** vor Wut schäumen (***over, at,*** über (*Acc.*)). **3.** *s.* die Aufregung; der Ärger, Verdruß; (*coll.*) ***be on the* –,** aufgeregt *or* nervös sein.

[2]**fret, 1.** *v.t.* gitterförmig verzieren. **2.** *s.* das Gitterwerk, verflochtene Verzierung.

[3]**fret,** *s.* (*usu. pl.*) der Bund, die Griffleiste (*of a guitar etc.*).

fretful ['fretful], *adj.* ärgerlich, mürrisch, verdrießlich, reizbar. **fretfulness,** *s.* der Unmut, die Verdrießlichkeit, Reizbarkeit.

fret|saw, *s.* die Laubsäge. **–work,** *s.* die Laubsägearbeit; durchbrochene Arbeit.

friability [fraiə'biliti], *s.* die Sprödigkeit, Brüchigkeit, Bröckligkeit, Zerreibbarkeit. **friable,** *adj.* mürbe, mulmig, spröde, brüchig, bröcklig, zerreibbar.

friar ['fraiə], *s.* der Mönch, Klosterbruder; ***Austin Friar,*** der Augustiner; ***Black Friar,*** der Dominikaner; ***Grey Friar,*** der Franziskaner; ***White Friar,*** der Karmeliter; **–*'s balsam,*** der Wundbalsam; (*Bot.*) **–*'s cowl,*** die Mönchskappe. **friary,** *s.* das (Mönchs)kloster.

fricassee [frikə'si:], **1.** *s.* das Frikassee. **2.** *v.t.* frikassieren; –***d veal,*** das Kalbsfrikassee.

fricative ['frikətiv], *s.* (*Phonet.*) der Reibelaut.

friction ['frikʃən], *s.* die Reibung (*also fig.*); (*Med.*) Einreibung, das Frottieren; (*fig.*) die Schwierigkeit, Mißhelligkeit, Spannung, Reiberei. **frictional,** *adj.* Reibungs–. **friction|-clutch,** *s.* die Reibungskupplung. **--drive,** *s.* der Friktionsantrieb. **--gear,** *s.* das Reibrädergetriebe. **--primer,** *s.* der Abreißzünder. **--wheel,** *s.* das Friktionsrad.

Friday ['fraidi], *s.* der Freitag; (*coll.*) ***girl* –,** das Mädchen für alles, Aschenbrödel; ***Good* –,** der Karfreitag.

fridge [fridʒ], *s.* (*coll.*) der Kühlschrank, Eisschrank.

fried [fraid], *imperf., p.p. of* [2]**fry.**

friend [frend], *s.* der (die) Freund(in); Bekannte(r); der Helfer, Förderer; ***Friends,*** Quäker (*pl.*); ***be* –*s with,*** befreundet sein mit; ***bosom* –,** der Busenfreund; (*fig.*) – ***at court,*** einflußreicher Gönner; ***a* – *in need is a* – *indeed,*** in der Not erkennt man seine Freunde; (*Parl.*) ***my honourable* –,** der verehrte Herr Vorredner; (*Law*) ***my learned* –,** mein verehrter Herr Kollege; ***make a* –,** einen Freund gewinnen; ***make* –*s with,*** sich befreunden mit, Freundschaft schließen mit.

friendless ['frendlis], *adj.* freundlos. **friendlessness,** *s.* die Freundlosigkeit. **friendliness,** *s.* die Freundlichkeit, freundschaftliche Gesinnung, das Wohlwollen. **friendly,** *adj.* freundlich; freundschaftlich (gesinnt), wohlwollend, hilfsbereit, geneigt; ***Friendly Islands,*** die Freundschaftsinseln; (*Spt.*) – ***match,*** das Freundschaftsspiel; – ***nation*** or ***power,*** befreundete Macht; – ***neutrality,*** wohlwollende Neutralität; – ***society,*** die Unterstützungskasse; ***be on* – *terms with,*** auf freundschaftlichem Fuße stehen mit; – ***turn,*** der Freundschaftsdienst. **friendship,** *s.* die Freundschaft; Freundschaftlichkeit, freundschaftliche Gesinnung.

frieze [fri:z], *s.* (*Archit., Weav.*) der Fries.

frigate ['frigət], *s.* die Fregatte. **frigate-bird,** *s.* (*Am.*) der Pracht-Fregattvogel (*Fregata magnificens*).

fright [frait], **1.** *s.* der Schreck(en), das Entsetzen; (*fig.*) die Fratze, Scheuche, das Schreckbild, Scheusal; (*coll.*) ***get a* –,** einen Schreck bekommen; (*coll.*) ***look a perfect* –,** einfach verboten aussehen; ***take* –,** see ***get a* –**; (*of horses*) scheu werden. **2.** *v.t.* (*Poet.*) *see* **frighten. frighten,** *v.t.* erschrecken, in Furcht *or* Schrecken versetzen; – ***away*** or ***off,*** verscheuchen; – ***him into doing it,*** ihn durch Schrecken dazu treiben; – ***him out of his wits,*** ihn furchtbar erschrecken; – ***him to death,*** ihn zu Tode erschrecken, ihn in Todesangst versetzen. **frightening,** *adj.* erschreckend. **frightened,** *adj.* erschreckt; ***be* – *of,*** sich fürchten vor (*Dat.*). **frightful,** *adj.* schrecklich, gräßlich, furchtbar, fürchterlich, entsetzlich. **frightfully,** *adv.* schrecklich; (*coll.*) äußerst, höchst. **frightfulness,** *s.* die Schrecklichkeit; der Greuel, Greueltaten (*pl.*).

frigid ['fridʒid], *adj.* kalt, frostig, eisig; (*Med.*) frigid, gefühllos; (*fig.*) kühl, abstoßend (*manner*); – ***zone,*** kalte Zone. **frigidity** [–'dʒiditi], *s.* die Kälte, Frostigkeit; (*Med.*) Frigidität.

frill [fril], **1.** *s.* die Halskrause, Handkrause, Rüsche; (Papier)krause; *pl.* (*fig.*) der Tand, Schmuck; die Ziererei. **2.** *v.t.* kräuseln; mit einer Krause schmücken. **3.** *v.i.* (*Phot.*) sich kräuseln. **frillies,** *pl.* (*coll.*) feine Damenunterwäsche. **frilling,** *s.* das Kräuseln; Krausen (*pl.*), der Stoff zu Rüschen. **frilly,** *adj.* gekräuselt.

fringe [frindʒ], **1.** *s.* 1. die Franse, der Besatz; Rand, Saum, die Einfassung; 2. (*fig.*) Randzone, der Randbezirk, äußerer Rand; – ***benefits,*** Nebenbezüge (*pl.*), zusätzliche Vergütung; 3. (*coll.*) die Ponyfrisur. **2.** *v.t.* mit Fransen besetzen; (*fig.*) umsäumen, einsäumen.

frippery ['fripəri], **1.** *s.* der Flitterkram, Plunder, Tand. **2.** *adj.* wertlos, nichtig, geringfügig, Flitter–.

Frisian ['fri:zjən], **1.** *adj.* friesisch. **2.** *s.* 1. der Friese (die Friesin), der (die) Friesländer(in); 2. (*language*) das Friesisch(e).

frisk [frisk], **1.** *v.i.* hüpfen und springen, herumhüpfen. **2.** *v.t.* (*sl.*) absuchen, durchsuchen. **3.** *s.* das Hüpfen und Springen, der Freudensprung. **friskiness,** *s.* die Munterkeit, Lebendigkeit. **frisky,** *adj.* munter, lustig, lebhaft, ausgelassen.

frit [frit], **1.** *s.* die Glas(schmelz)masse, Fritte. **2.** *v.t.* schmelzen, fritten (*glass*).

fritillary [fri'tiləri], *s.* (*Bot.*) die Schachbrettblume; (*Ent.*) der Argusfalter.

fritter ['fritə], **1.** *s.* (*oft. pl.*) (*Cul.*) gebackener Eierteig; ***apple –s,*** Apfelscheiben in Eierteig gebacken. **2.** *v.t.* zerschneiden; zerstückeln; (*usu.*) – ***away,*** verzetteln, vertrödeln, vergeuden.

frivol [frivl], *v.t.* (*coll.*) – ***away,*** vertändeln, verplempern. **frivolity** [–'vɔliti], *s.* die Leichtfertigkeit, Frivolität; Wertlosigkeit, Nichtigkeit. **frivolous,** *adj.* (*of a th.*) nichtig, wertlos, geringfügig; (*of excuse, argument etc.*) nicht stichhaltig, ungenügend, unbegründet; (*of a p.*) leichtfertig, leichtsinnig, frivol.

frizz [friz], **1.** *v.t.* kräuseln (*hair*). **2.** *v.i.* sich kräuseln, kraus werden. **3.** *s.* gekräuseltes Haar.

frizzle [frizl], **1.** *v.i.* zischen. **2.** *v.t.* rösten.

frizzly ['frizli], **frizzy,** *adj.* kraus, gekräuselt.

fro [frou], *adv.* (*only in*) ***to and –,*** hin und her, auf und ab.

frock [frɔk], **1.** *s.* das Kleid; Kinderröckchen; die Kutte (*of monks*); der Kittel; (*collect.*) Priesterstand. **2.** *v.t.* in einen Rock kleiden; (*fig.*) mit einem Amt bekleiden (*a priest etc.*). **frock-coat,** *s.* der Gehrock, (*coll.*) Bratenrock.

[1]**frog** [frɔg], *s.* (*Mil.*) der Schnurbesatz, die Quaste; der Degenhalter (*on belt*); das Kreuzungsstück, Herzstück (*of railway line*); die Gabel, der Strahl (*of hoof*).

[2]**frog,** *s.* 1. (*Zool.*) der Frosch (*also Mus. of violin bow*); (*coll.*) ***have a – in one's throat,*** heiser sein; 2. (*pej.*) der Franzose.

frog|-bit, *s.* (*Bot.*) der Froschbiß. **--eater,** *s.* (*pej.*) *see* [2]**frog,** 2. **-hopper,** *s.* (*Ent.*) die Schaumzirpe. **-man** [–mən], *s.* (*Mil.*) der Kampfschwimmer. **-march,** *v.t.* (*coll.*) (mit dem Kopf nach unten) fortschleppen. **--spawn,** *s.* der Froschlaich.

frolic ['frɔlik], **1.** *s.* lustiger Streich, der Spaß, die Posse; Lustbarkeit, Ausgelassenheit. **2.** *v.i.* Possen treiben, scherzen, spaßen, tollen, ausgelassen sein. **frolicsome** [–səm], *adj.* lustig, fröhlich, vergnügt, ausgelassen. **frolicsomeness,** *s.* die Lustigkeit, Ausgelassenheit.

from [frɔm], *prep.* 1. von; (*place*) . . . her, von . . . weg, von . . . aus; aus, aus . . . heraus; (*time*) von . . . an, seit; ***apart –,*** abgesehen von; ***– the beginning,*** vom Anfang an; ***– a child,*** von Kindheit an; ***– day to day,*** täglich, von Tag zu Tag; ***defend –,*** schützen vor (*Dat.*); ***descend –,*** abstammen von; ***I am far – thinking,*** ich bin weit davon entfernt zu denken, es liegt mir fern zu denken; ***far – the truth,*** weit von der Wahrheit entfernt; ***– first to last,*** von A bis Z; ***hide s.th. – him,*** (vor) ihm etwas verbergen; ***keep him – doing s.th.,*** ihn abhalten *or* hindern etwas zu tun; ***live – hand to mouth,*** von der Hand in den Mund leben; ***come – school,*** aus der Schule kommen; ***take s.th. – him,*** ihm etwas wegnehmen; ***– time to time,*** von Zeit zu Zeit, gelegentlich; ***where are you –?*** wo stammen Sie her? ***– above,*** (*adv.*) von oben herab; ***– afar,*** von weither, aus der Ferne; ***– before,*** (*prep.*) aus der Zeit vor (*Dat.*); ***– behind,*** (*adv.*) von hinten, (*prep.*) hinter (*Dat.*) . . . hervor; ***– below*** or ***beneath,*** (*adv.*) von unten; (*prep.*) unter (*Dat.*) . . . hervor *or* heraus; ***– between,*** zwischen (*Dat.*) . . . hervor; ***– beyond,*** (*adv., prep.*) von jenseits; ***– on high,*** aus der Höhe, von oben; ***– out of,*** aus . . . heraus; ***– over,*** (*prep.*) von jenseits . . . her; ***– under,*** (*prep.*) unter (*Dat.*) . . . hervor; ***– within,*** von innen (her(aus)); ***– without,*** von außen (her); 2. (*fig.*) wegen, infolge von; nach, gemäß, in betreff; ***– my own experience,*** aus eigener Erfahrung; ***die – exposure,*** durch Erfrieren sterben; ***to judge – his appearance,*** seinem Aussehen nach; ***– life,*** nach dem Leben; ***drawn – nature,*** nach der Natur gezeichnet; ***– my point of view,*** von meinem Standpunkt aus; ***suffer –,*** leiden an (*Dat.*); ***– what you have told me,*** nach dem, was Sie mir gesagt haben.

frond [frɔnd], *s.* der Wedel (*of fern*). **frondage** [–idʒ], *s.* das Blattwerk. **frondescence** [–'desəns], *s.* die Zeit der Blattbildung. **frondescent,** *adj.* blattbildend. **frondiferous** [–'difərəs], *adj.* laubtragend, wedeltragend. **frondose,** *adj.* wedeltragend, dicht belaubt.

front [frʌnt], **1.** *s.* 1. (*Archit.*) die Vorderseite, Fassade; 2. vorderer Teil; (*fig.*) ***come to the –,*** in den Vordergrund treten, hervortreten, sich auszeichnen; ***in –,*** davor, an die *or* der Spitze; ***in – of,*** vor (*Dat.*), gegenüber; ***to the –,*** nach vorn, voraus, voran; 3. die Frontpromenade (*at the seaside*); 4. (*Mil.*) Front; ***at the –,*** an der Front; 5. die Hemdbrust, das Vorhemd (*of shirt etc.*); 6. (*Poet.*) die Stirn; 7. falsches Haar; 8. (*fig.*) (*Pol.*) die Front, Organisation, (*coll.*) Fassade, äußerer Schein, (*coll.*) der Strohmann, das Aushängerschild; 9. (*coll.*) die Keckheit, Frechheit, Unverfrorenheit; ***show a bold –,*** mit kecker Stirn auftreten; 10. (*Meteor.*) ***cold –,*** die Einbruchsfront, Kaltluftfront; ***warm –,*** die Aufgleitfront, Warmluftfront. **2.** *attrib. adj.* Vorder–; (*Parl.*) ***– bench,*** die Ministerbank; ***– door,*** die Haustür; ***– elevation,*** die Vorderansicht; ***– garden,*** der Vorgarten; (*Mil.*) ***– line,*** die Kampffront; ***– page,*** die Vorderseite; ***--page,*** aktuell, wichtig (*of news*); ***– room,*** das Vorderzimmer; ***– row,*** die Vorderreihe, erste Reihe; ***– view,*** die Vorderansicht; (*Phonet.*) ***– vowel,*** der Vorderzungenlaut; ***--wheel drive,*** der Vorderradantrieb. **3.** *v.t.* gegenüberstehen *or* gegenüberliegen (*Dat.*); (*a p.*) gegenübertreten (*Dat.*), Trotz *or* die Stirn bieten (*Dat.*). **4.** *v.i.* die Front haben *or* mit der Front liegen (***on to,*** nach); (*Mil.*) ***eyes –!*** Augen geradeaus!

frontage ['frʌntidʒ], *s.* (*Archit.*) die Vorderfront, Frontbreite, Frontlänge; (*Mil.*) Frontbreite, der Frontabschnitt; ***– line,*** die Baufluchtlinie. **frontal,** **1.** *adj.* Vorder–, Front–; (*Anat.*) Stirn–; ***– attack,*** der Frontalangriff; ***– bone,*** das Stirnbein. **2.** *s.* (*Archit.*) die Fassade; (*Eccl.*) Altardecke.

frontier ['frʌntiə], *s.* die Grenze; *pl.* (*fig.*) der Grenzbereich. **frontiersman,** *s.* (*Am.*) der Grenzansiedler, Grenzbewohner.

frontispiece ['frʌntispi:s], *s.* (*Archit.*) die Vorderseite; (*Typ.*) das Titelbild, Titelkupfer. **frontlet** [–lit], *s.* das Stirnband; die Stirn (*of animals*).

frost [frɔst], **1.** *s.* 1. der Frost; ***2 degrees of –,*** zwei Grad Kälte; ***ground –,*** der Bodenfrost; ***hoar –,*** der Rauhreif; 2. (*sl.*) der Mißerfolg, Fehlschlag. **2.** *v.t.* mit Reif überziehen (*as a window*); (*Cul.*) glasieren, mit Zuckerguß überziehen; mattieren (*glass*). **frost|-bite,** *s.* das Erfrieren, die Frostbeule; der Frostschaden. **-bitten,** *adj.* erfroren. **frosted,** *adj.* bereift; mit Zuckergruß (überzogen), glasiert; ***– glass,*** das Milchglas, Mattglas. **frostiness,** *s.* der Frost, eisige Kälte; (*fig.*) die Frostigkeit. **frosting,** *s.* (*Cul.*) die Zuckerglasur; das Mattschleifen (*of glass*). **frosty,** *adj.* eisig, eiskalt, frostig; (*fig.*) eisig, frostig.

froth [frɔθ], **1.** *s.* der (Ab)schaum, die Blume (*of beer*); (*fig.*) Nichtigkeit, Seichtigkeit; (*coll.*) Schaumschlägerei. **2.** *v.t.* schaumig *or* schäumend machen, zu Schaum schlagen. **3.** *v.i.* schäumen, Schaum schlagen (*also fig.*). **frothiness,** *s.* das Schäumen, der Schaum; (*fig.*) die Nichtigkeit, Leerheit, Hohlheit, Seichtigkeit, Schaumschlägerei. **frothing,** *s.* die Schaumbildung. **frothy,** *adj.* schäumend, schaumig, schaumartig; moussierend; leer, nichtig, phrasenhaft (*of utterance*).

froward ['frouəd], *adj.* (*obs.*) widerspenstig, eigensinnig, trotzig. **frowardness,** *s.* der Eigensinn, Trotz, die Eigensinnigkeit, Widerspenstigkeit.

frown [fraun], **1.** *s.* das Stirnrunzeln; finsterer Blick. **2.** *v.t.* durch finstere Blicke ausdrücken; – ***him into silence,*** ihn durch finstere Blicke zum Schweigen bringen. **3.** *v.i.* die Stirn runzeln, finster dreinsehen; (*fig.*) – ***upon,*** mißbilligen, mit Mißfallen ansehen, finster *or* scheel ansehen.

frowst [fraust], *s.* (*coll.*) muffige *or* stickige Luft, der Muff, Mief. **frowstiness,** *s.* die Muffigkeit. **frowsty,** *adj.* muffig, moderig, ranzig.

frowziness ['frauzinis], *s.* 1. *See* **frowstiness**; 2. die Schlampigkeit. **frowzy,** *adj.* 1. *See* **frowsty**; 2. schlampig, schmutzig, unordentlich.

froze [frouz], *imperf. of* **freeze. frozen,** *adj.* gefroren; zugefroren (*as a pond*), eingefroren (*as pipes*); (*fig. Comm.*) eingefroren, festliegend, nicht verwertbar; – ***capital,*** eingefrorenes Kapital; – ***to death,*** erfroren; – ***expression,*** frostiger *or* teilnahmsloser Ausdruck; – ***food,*** tiefgekühlte Lebensmittel; – ***meat,*** das Gefrierfleisch; – ***ocean,*** das Eismeer; – ***over*** or ***up,*** zugefroren.

fructiferous [frʌk'tifərəs], *adj.* fruchttragend. **fructification** [–fi'keiʃən], *s.* die Befruchtung, Fruchtbildung. **fructify** ['frʌktifai], **1.** *v.t.* befruchten, fruchtbar machen (*also fig.*). **2.** *v.i.* Früchte tragen (*also fig.*). **fructose,** *s.* der Fruchtzucker.

frugal [fru:gl], *adj.* genügsam; spärlich, mäßig, frugal; sparsam (***of,*** mit *or* in (*Dat.*)). **frugality** [–'gæliti], *s.* die Genügsamkeit, Mäßigkeit, Sparsamkeit.

frugivorous [fru:'dʒivərəs], *adj.* (*Zool.*) von Früchten lebend, fruchtfressend.

fruit [fru:t], *s.* die Frucht (*also fig.*); Früchte (*pl.*), das Obst; (*fig. usu. pl.*) die Folge, Wirkung, das Ergebnis, Resultat, der Ertrag, Gewinn, Nutzen; (*B.*) die Nachkommenschaft; ***bear –,*** Frucht bringen, Früchte tragen; (*fig.*) Nutzen gewähren; ***dried –,*** das Backobst, Dörrobst; ***–s of the earth,*** die Früchte der Erde; ***the – of all my endeavours,*** das Ergebnis aller meiner Bemühungen; ***fresh –,*** rohes Obst; ***stewed –,*** das Kompott.

fruitage ['fru:tidʒ], *s.* das Tragen (*of fruit trees*); die Fruchternte. **fruitarian** [–'tɛəriən], *s.* der Rohköstler. **fruit|-bearing,** *adj.* fruchttragend. **--cake,** *s.* englischer Kuchen. – **cocktail,** *s.* gemischtes Obst. **--drop,** *s.* das Fruchtbonbon. **fruiterer,** *s.* der Obsthändler. **fruitful,** *adj.* fruchtbar; (*fig.*) ergiebig, ergebnisreich, ertragreich, reich (***of, in,*** in (*Dat.*)). **fruitfulness,** *s.* die Fruchtbarkeit (*also fig.*). **fruition** [fru'iʃən], *s.* der (Voll)genuß; die Erfüllung, ersehnter Erfolg, das Ergebnis. **fruitless,** *adj.* unfruchtbar; (*fig.*) fruchtlos, vergeblich, unnütz. **fruitlessness,** *s.* (*fig.*) die Fruchtlosigkeit. **fruit| machine,** *s.* (*coll.*) der Spielautomat. – **pulp,** *s.* das Fruchtfleisch. **--salad,** *s.* der Obstsalat. **--tree,** *s.* der Obstbaum. **fruity,** *adj.* fruchtartig; würzig (*of wine, also fig.*); (*sl.*) saftig (*as a joke*); klangvoll (*as a voice*).

frumentaceous [fru:mən'teiʃəs], *adj.* Getreide–, getreideartig. **frumenty** ['fru:mənti], *s.* süßer Weizenbrei.

frump [frʌmp], *s.* (*coll.*) altmodisch gekleidetes Frauenzimmer; ***old –,*** alte Schachtel. **frumpish,** *adj.* altmodisch (gekleidet).

frustrate [frʌs'treit], *v.t.* vereiteln, verhindern; durchkreuzen, zuschanden *or* zunichte machen; – ***his hopes,*** ihn in seinen Erwartungen täuschen. **frustrated,** *adj.* enttäuscht, vereitelt; (*Psych.*) gehemmt, verkrampft. **frustration** [–'treiʃən], *s.* die Vereitelung; Enttäuschung; (*Psych.*) Gehemmtheit, Verkrampfung.

frustum ['frʌstəm], *s.* (*Geom.*) der Stumpf.

[1]**fry** [frai], **1.** *v.t.* in der Pfanne braten; ***fried egg,*** das Spiegelei, Setzei; ***fried potatoes,*** Bratkartoffeln. **2.** *s.* Gebratene(s); das Gekröse, Kaldauen (*pl.*).

[2]**fry,** *s.* die Fischbrut, der Fischrogen, junge Fische; (*coll.*) ***small –,*** das Kindervolk; (*sl.*) unbedeutende Leute.

frying-pan, *s.* die Bratpfanne; ***out of the – into the fire,*** aus dem *or* vom Regen in die Traufe.

fuchsia ['fju:ʃə], *s.* (*Bot.*) die Fuchsie.

fuddle [fʌdl], **1.** *v.t.* berauschen; (*fig.*) verwirren. **2.** *v.i.* sich betrinken. **fuddled,** *adj.* (*coll.*) angeheitert, angesäuselt.

fuddy-duddy ['fudidʌdi], *s.* (*coll.*) (*usu.* ***old –***) alter Kauz, der Rückschrittler.

[1]**fudge** [fʌdʒ], *s.* (*Cul.*) weiches Zuckerwerk.

[2]**fudge, 1.** *v.i.* schwindeln, mogeln. **2.** *v.t.* (zurecht)-pfuschen, fälschen, frisieren. **3.** *s.* die Täuschung, der Schwindel, das Blech, Flausen (*pl.*).

fuel ['fju:əl], **1.** *s.* die Feuerung, das Heizmaterial, der Brennstoff; (*Motor. etc.*) Kraftstoff, Treibstoff, Betriebsstoff, (*sl.*) Sprit; (*fig.*) ***add – to the flames,*** Öl ins Feuer gießen; – ***gas,*** das Heizgas; – ***gauge,*** die Benzinuhr, der Kraftstoffmesser; – ***level,*** der Treibstoffstand; – ***oil,*** das Brennöl, Heizöl. **2.** *v.i.* Brennstoff einnehmen, (*Motor. etc.*) tanken, (*ships*) bunkern.

fug [fʌg], *s.* (*sl.*) stickige Luft, muffiger Geruch, der Mief.

fugacious [fju'geiʃəs], *adj.* flüchtig, vergänglich. **fugacity** [–'gæsiti], *s.* die Flüchtigkeit, Vergänglichkeit.

fugal [fju:gl], *adj.* (*Mus.*) Fugen–, fugenartig.

fuggy ['fʌgi], *adj.* (*sl.*) stickig, muffig.

fugitive ['fju:dʒitiv], **1.** *adj.* fliehend; geflohen, entflohen; flüchtig, vergänglich, kurzlebig, vorübergehend, unbeständig; – ***colour,*** lichtempfindliche Farbe; – ***to light,*** unecht gegen Licht. **2.** *s.* der Flüchtling, Ausreißer.

fugleman ['fju:glmən], *s.* (*Mil., rare*) der Flügelmann; (*fig.*) (Wort)führer, Sprecher; Sekundant, rechte Hand.

fugue [fju:g], *s.* die Fuge.

fulcrum ['fʌlkrəm], *s.* der Drehpunkt, Hebepunkt, Gelenkpunkt, Auflagepunkt, Stützpunkt.

fulfil [ful'fil], *v.t.* erfüllen, vollziehen, vollbringen; ausführen, befolgen (*instructions*), befriedigen, zufriedenstellen (*requirements*), nachkommen (*Dat.*) (*obligation*). **fulfilment,** *s.* die Erfüllung, Vollziehung, Ausführung, Befriedigung.

fulgency ['fʌldʒənsi], *s.* (*Poet.*) der Glanz. **fulgent,** *adj.* glänzend. **fulgurant** ['fʌlgjərənt], *adj.* funkelnd, aufblitzend. **fulgurate** [–reit], *v.i.* glänzen, blitzen, aufleuchten.

fuliginous [fju'lidʒinəs], *adj.* rußig, verrußt, Ruß–; rauchig.

[1]**full** [ful], **1.** *adj.* voll (***of,*** von), (an)gefüllt (mit); (*also coll.* – ***up***) (voll) besetzt (*as a room*); (*coll.*) (*of a p.*) gesättigt, satt; voll, dick, rund, plump (*shape*); weit, groß (*of clothes*); stark, schwer (*of wine*); stark, kräftig, satt (*light, colour etc.*), voll, stark, mächtig (*sound*); (*fig.*) ganz, vollständig, unverkürzt; ausführlich, weitläufig, eingehend; (*relationship*) leiblich, echt, rein; – ***age,*** die Mündigkeit, Volljährigkeit; ***of – age,*** mündig, volljährig; – ***amount,*** ganzer Betrag; (*Artil.*) – ***charge,*** die Gefechtsladung; – ***citizen,*** der Vollbürger; – ***consent,*** volle Zustimmung; (*Law*) – ***costs,*** sämtliche Kosten; ***in – cry,*** laut bellend (*of hounds*), (*fig.*) mit großer Begeisterung; ***in – daylight,*** am hellichten Tag; – ***description,*** ausführliche Beschreibung; – ***dress,*** der Gesellschaftsanzug, (*Mil.*) Paradeanzug, die Gala; – ***employment,*** die Vollbeschäftigung; – ***face,*** das Bildnis mit zugewandtem Gesicht, (*Typ.*) fette Schrift; – ***gallop,*** gestreckter Galopp; – ***hour,*** ganze *or* geschlagene Stunde; – ***intent,*** feste Absicht; (*fig.*) ***at – length,*** ausführlich, eingehend; – ***load,*** die Vollbelastung, Vollast; das Gesamtgewicht; – ***meal,*** vollständige Mahlzeit; – ***moon,*** der Vollmond; – ***pay,*** voller (Arbeits)lohn, volles Gehalt; – ***powers,*** unumschränkte Vollmacht; – ***professor,*** der Ordinarius; ***under – sail,*** (*Naut.*) alles bei, (*fig.*) mit vollen Segeln; – ***scale,*** natürliche Größe; (***at***) – ***speed,*** (*Motor.*) (mit) Vollgas, (*Naut.*) (mit) Volldampf; (*coll.*) im Galopp, spornstreichs; – ***statement,*** eingehender *or* ausführlicher Bericht; – ***steam ahead,*** Volldampf voraus; – ***stop,*** der Punkt; (*fig.*) ***come to a – stop,*** plötzlich stillstehen, ins Stocken geraten; ***in – strength,*** in voller Stärke; (*coll.*) ***in – swing,*** in vollem Gang; – ***throttle,*** das Vollgas;

(*Spt.*) – *time*, volle Spielzeit; – *toss*, direkter Wurf; – *value*, der Ersatzwert; *in* – *view* (*of*), gerade gegenüber (*Dat.*); *have one's hands* –, vollauf zu tun haben; *be – of o.s.*, von sich eingenommen sein. **2.** *adv.* völlig, vollkommen, gänzlich, ganz; genau, direkt, gerade; (*Poet.*) gar, sehr; *look him – in the face*, ihm gerade ins Gesicht sehen; (*Poet.*) – *many a*, gar manche; (*Poet.*) – *nigh*, fast, beinahe; – *well*, sehr gut *or* wohl. **3.** *s.* die Fülle, Genüge; (*fig.*) das Ganze, höchstes Maß, der Höhepunkt; *at the* –, auf dem Höhepunkt; *at the – of the tide*, beim höchsten Wasserstand; – *of the moon*, der Vollmond; *in* –, vollständig, ungekürzt; (*Comm.*) per Saldo; *write out in* –, ausschreiben; *pay in* –, voll bezahlen; (*Comm.*) *acquittance in* –, die Generalquittung; *to the* –, vollständig, vollkommen, in vollem Maße, reichlich.

²**full,** *v.t.* walken (*cloth*).

full|-back, *s.* (*Footb.*) der Verteidiger, (*Rugby*) Schlußmann. **--blooded,** *adj.* vollblütig, echtblütig, (*coll.*) kräftig. **--blown,** *adj.* in voller Blüte, voll aufgeblüht, (*coll.*) ausgesprochen, total. **--bodied,** *adj.* (*of wine*) stark, schwer, (*fig.*) mächtig, kräftig. **--bottomed,** *adj.* breit; – *wig*, die Allongeperücke. **--dress,** *adj.* formell, Gala–; (*coll.*) wichtig; – *rehearsal*, die Generalprobe.

fuller [ˈfulə], *s.* der (Tuch)walker; *–'s earth*, die Bleicherde; (*Bot.*) *–'s teasel* or *weed*, die Weberkarde. **fullery,** *s.* die Walkmühle, Walke(rei).

full|-faced, *adj.* mit rundem Gesicht, pausbackig; (*Typ.*) fett; (*of a portrait*) mit zugewandtem Gesicht. **--fledged,** *adj.* (*Orn.*) flügge; (*fig.*) voll entwickelt, Voll–. **--grown,** *adj.* ausgewachsen; voll entwickelt, voll erwachsen.

fulling [ˈfuliŋ], *s.* das Walken; – *mill*, *see* **fullery.**

full|-length, *adj.* in Lebensgröße, lebengroß; – *film*, abendfüllender Film. **--mouthed,** *adj.* (*Vet.*) mit vollem Gebiß; (*of hounds*) laut bellend; (*fig.*) starktönend.

fullness [ˈfulnis], *s.* die Fülle, der Reichtum; die Vollständigkeit; Dicke, Weite, Plumpheit; – *of the heart*, die Fülle des Herzens; *in the – of time*, (*B.*) da die Zeit erfüllt war; (*coll.*) zur rechten Zeit.

full|-page, *adj.* ganzseitig. **--rigged,** *adj.* vollgetakelt. **--scale,** *adj.* gründlich, vollständig. **--size,** *adj.* lebensgroß, in Lebensgröße. **--time,** *adj.* hauptamtlich; – *job*, ganztägige Beschäftigung. **--track(ed),** *adj.* Vollketten– (*vehicle*). **--wave,** *adj.* (*Elec.*) Doppelweg–.

fully [ˈfuli], *adv.* voll, völlig, gänzlich, ausführlich; – *automatic*, vollautomatisch; – *entitled*, vollberechtigt; – *fashioned*, mit Paßform (*stockings*); – *twenty seconds*, volle zwanzig Sekunden.

fulmar [ˈfulmə], *s.* (*Orn.*) der Eissturmvogel (*Fulmarus glacialis*).

fulminate [ˈfʌlmineit], **1.** *v.i.* donnern, krachen; detonieren, explodieren; (*fig.*) losdonnern, wettern. **2.** *v.t.* zur Explosion bringen; (*fig.*) schleudern (*censures*). **3.** *s.* das Knallpulver; (*Chem.*) knallsaures Salz; – *of mercury*, das Knallquecksilber. **fulminating,** *adj.* Knall–, knallend; – *powder*, das Knallpulver. **fulmination** [–ˈneiʃən], *s.* das Donnern, der Knall; das Explodieren; (*fig.*) der Bannstrahl, Fluch. **fulminatory** [–nətəri], *adj.* donnernd, Droh–. **fulminic** [fʌlˈminik], *adj.* knallsauer; – *acid*, die Knallsäure.

fulsome [ˈfulsəm], *adj.* widerlich, widerwärtig, abstoßend, ekelhaft; übertrieben, übermäßig, geschmacklos. **fulsomeness,** *s.* die Widerlichkeit, Ekelhaftigeit, Geschmacklosigkeit.

fumble [fʌmbl], **1.** *v.i.* umhertasten, umhertappen; – *for*, tappen nach; – *with*, (herum)fummeln an (*Dat.*). **2.** *v.t.* ungeschickt handhaben *or* behandeln, nicht (auf)fangen, fallen lassen (*a ball etc.*). **fumbling,** *adj.* tappend; täppisch, linkisch.

fume [fju:m], **1.** *s.* (*usu. pl.*) der Dunst, Dampf, Rauch, Schwaden; (*fig.*) die Aufwallung, Aufregung; *in a* –, in Wut, aufgebracht. **2.** *v.t.* (aus)räuchern. **3.** *v.i.* dampfen, rauchen, dunsten; (*fig.*) toben, wüten, aufgebracht sein; – *with rage*, vor Wut kochen.

fumigate [ˈfju:migeit], *v.t.* ausräuchern, durchräuchern. **fumigation** [–ˈgeiʃən], *s.* die (Aus)räucherung.

fumitory [ˈfju:mitəri], *s.* (*Bot.*) der Erdrauch, Lerchensporn.

fun [fʌn], *s.* der Scherz, Spaß; *it is* –, es macht Spaß; *it is great* –, es ist ein Hauptspaß; (*coll.*) *he is great* –, er ist sehr amüsant; *for* –, zum *or* aus Spaß; *for the – of the thing*, des Spaßes wegen, spaßeshalber; *have good* –, sich ausgezeichnet amüsieren; *in* –, im *or* zum Scherz; *make – of* or *poke – at him*, sich über ihn lustig machen, ihn zum besten haben.

function [ˈfʌŋkʃən], **1.** *s.* 1. die Funktion (*also Math.*); das Wirken; die Aufgabe, Obliegenheit; (Amts)tätigkeit, das Amt, amtliche Pflicht, der Dienst, Beruf; *natural* –, die Notdurft; 2. die Veranstaltung, Feier, Zeremonie. **2.** *v.i.* fungieren, tätig sein, amtieren; (*Tech.*) arbeiten, wirksam sein, funktionieren. **functional,** *adj.* 1. formell, repräsentativ; amtlich, dienstlich; zweckmäßig, zweckhaft, funktionell, Funktions–; – *building*, der Zweckbau; – *disease*, die Funktionsstörung. **functionalism,** *s.* die Zweckmäßigkeit, Zweckhaftigkeit; der Zweckstil, die Sachlichkeit. **functionary,** *s.* Beamte(r), der Funktionär.

fund [fʌnd], **1.** *s.* (*Comm.*) die Geldsumme, der Fonds, das Kapital; (*fig.*) die Fülle, der Vorrat, Schatz, Grundstock (*of*, an (*Dat.*)); *pl.* Gelder (*pl.*), Geldmittel (*pl.*); fundierte Staatspapiere *or* Staatsschulden (*pl.*), öffentlicher Fonds; (*coll.*) *in –s*, (gut) bei Kasse; *out of –s*, mittellos; *sufficient –s*, genügende Deckung; *without –s in hand*, ohne Deckung; *–s on hand*, flüssige Mittel; *original –s*, das Stammkapital; *sinking* –, der Schuldentilgungsfonds; *trust* –, der Treuhandfonds. **2.** *v.t.* in Staatspapieren anlegen (*money*); fundieren (*floating debt*).

fundament [ˈfʌndəmənt], *s.* das Gesäß; der After; (*fig.*) Unterbau, das Fundament. **fundamental** [–ˈmentl], **1.** *adj.* grundlegend, als Grundlage dienend (*to*, für); Grund–, grundsätzlich, wesentlich, tiefgreifend, ursprünglich, elementar, Haupt–, Wesens–; – *data*, grundlegende Tatsachen; – *idea*, der Grundbegriff; (*Math. etc.*) – *law*, der Hauptsatz; – *science*, die Hauptwissenschaft; – *tone*, der Grundton; – *truths*, Grundwahrheiten. **2.** *s.* 1. (*Mus.*) der Grundton, Grundakkord; 2. (*Elec.*) die Grundwelle; 3. *pl. See* **fundamentals. fundamentalism,** *s.* (*Eccl.*) der Buchstabenglaube. **fundamentally,** *adv.* im Grunde, im wesentlichen. **fundamentals,** *pl.* Grundlagen, Grundzüge, Grundbegriffe, Grundwahrheiten, (*coll.*) Hauptsachen (*pl.*).

funeral [ˈfju:nərəl], **1.** *s.* die Beerdigung, Bestattung, das Begräbnis, Leichenbegängnis; feierliche Beisetzung; (*coll.*) *that's your (own)* –, das ist dein eigener Schaden. **2.** *adj.* Begräbnis–, Grab–, Leichen–, Trauer–; – *expenses*, Bestattungskosten (*pl.*); – *march*, der Trauermarsch; – *oration*, die Leichenpredigt; – *pile*, der Scheiterhaufen; – *procession*, der Leichenzug; – *service*, der Trauergottesdienst; – *urn*, die Totenurne. **funereal** [–ˈniəriəl], *adj.* Beerdigungs–, Trauer–, Leichen–; traurig, trübe, düster, klagend.

fungi [ˈfʌŋgai], *pl. of* **fungus.**

fungible [ˈfʌndʒibl], *adj.* (*Law*) vertretbar, ersetzbar.

fungicidal [fʌndʒiˈsaidl], *adj.* pilztötend. **fungicide** [ˈfʌndʒisaid], *s.* pilztötendes Mittel. **fungoid** [ˈfʌŋgɔid], **fungous** [ˈfʌŋgəs], *adj.* pilzartig, schwammartig, schwammig; *fungoid spores*, der Mehltau. **fungus** [ˈfʌŋgəs], *s.* (*pl.* **-i** [ˈfʌŋgai], **-uses**) der Pilz, Schwamm; Schimmelpilz, Schmarotzerpilz; (*Med.*) schwammartiger Auswuchs, krankhafte Geschwulst.

funicular [fju:ˈnikjulə], *adj.* Seil–, Band–, Strang–; – *railway*, die (Draht)seilbahn.

funk [fʌŋk], **1.** *v.i.* in Angst geraten; (*Am.*) – *out*, sich drücken. **2.** *v.t.* Angst haben *or* sich fürchten vor (*Dat.*), sich drücken von. **3.** *s.* der Bammel, große Angst; der Feigling, Angsthase; *blue* –, die Mordsangst, Heidenangst; *be in a (blue)* –,

Dampf *or* mächtigen Bammel haben (***about***, vor (*Dat.*)). **funk-hole,** *s.* (*sl.*) der Heldenkeller, Schlupfwinkel, das Schlupfloch, der Unterstand. **funky,** *adj.* feige, bange.

funnel [fʌnl], **1.** *s.* der Trichter; (*of volcano*) Schlot; (*of blast furnace*) Mund; (*Found.*) das Gußloch; die Abzugsröhre, der Rauchfang, Schlot; (*of a ship etc.*) Schornstein. **2.** *v.t.* (*fig.*) zusammenbringen, konzentrieren (***into***, auf (*Acc.*)). **funnel-shaped,** *adj.* trichterförmig.

funny ['fʌni], *adj.* komisch; drollig, spaßhaft, ulkig; (*coll.*) ***feel –***, sich unbehaglich fühlen; (*coll.*) ***I came over –***, es wurde mir elend; (*coll.*) ***– business,*** der Schwindel, zweideutige S. **funny-bone,** *s.* der Musikantenknochen.

fur [fəː], **1.** *s.* der Pelz; Balg, das Fell; der Pelzmantel; *pl.* das Pelzwerk, Rauchwaren (*pl.*); der Belag (*on the tongue*); Kesselstein (*of a boiler*); (*coll.*) ***make the – fly,*** Unruhe stiften. **2.** *v.t.* mit Pelz füttern *or* besetzen. **3.** *v.i.* sich mit Belag *or* Kesselstein überziehen.

furbelow ['fəːbilou], **1.** *s.* die Falbel; (*fig.*) der Staat, Putz. **2.** *v.t.* mit Falbeln besetzen.

furbish ['fəːbiʃ], *v.t.* polieren, blank putzen; ***– up,*** aufputzen, herrichten.

furcate ['fəːkeit], *adj.* gabelförmig, gegabelt. **furcation** [–'keiʃən], *s.* die Gabelung.

furious ['fjuəriəs], *adj.* wütend, rasend; (*fig.*) wild, unbändig, ungestüm. **furiousness,** *s.* die Wut, Raserei, das Ungestüm.

furl [fəːl], *v.t.* zusammenrollen, festmachen, beschlagen (*sails*), aufrollen (*a flag*); (*Naut.*) ***–ing line,*** das Beschlagzeising.

furlong ['fəːlɔŋ], *s.* die Achtelmeile (= *201 Meter*).

furlough ['fəːlou], **1.** *s.* der Urlaub; ***on –,*** auf Urlaub. **2.** *v.t.* beurlauben.

furnace ['fəːnis], *s.* der Ofen, Brennofen, Schmelzofen; Heizkessel; ***blast –,*** der Hochofen; (*B.*) ***the fiery –,*** der Feuerofen; (*coll.*) ***like a –,*** wie im Backofen.

furnish ['fəːniʃ], *v.t.* 1. versehen, versorgen, ausrüsten, ausstatten (***with***, mit); 2. möblieren, ausstatten, einrichten (*rooms, houses etc.*); ***–ed rooms,*** möblierte Zimmer; 3. beschaffen, verschaffen, gewähren, (dar)bieten, liefern; ***– proof,*** (den) Beweis liefern *or* führen. **furnisher,** *s.* der Lieferant; Möblierer. **furnishing,** *s.* die Einrichtung, Ausstattung, (*pl.*) das Mobiliar, Möbel (*pl.*), Einrichtungsgegenstände (*pl.*); (*Tech.*) das Zubehör.

furniture ['fəːnitʃə], *s.* (*no pl.*) 1. Möbel (*pl.*), das Mobiliar, der Hausrat; 2. (*Naut.*) die Ausrüstung, Betakelung; das Sattelzeug, Geschirr (*of a horse*); (*Tech.*) Zubehör. **furniture|-polish,** *s.* die Möbelpolitur. **--remover,** *s.* der Möbelspediteur. **--van,** *s.* der Möbelwagen.

furore [fju'rɔːri], *s.* die *or* das Furore, das Aufsehen.

furred [fəːd], *adj.* mit Pelz besetzt *or* verbrämt (*clothes*), mit Kesselstein belegt (*boiler*), belegt (*tongue*). **furrier** ['fʌriə], *s.* der Kürschner; Pelzhändler.

furrow ['fʌrou], **1.** *s.* (*Agr.*) die Furche, (*Tech.*) Rille, Rinne, Nut(e); (*on skin*) Furche, Runzel. **2.** *v.t.* pflügen (*land*), durchfurchen (*the waves*), runzeln, furchen (*brow etc.*); (*Tech.*) riefen, riffeln, auskehlen, aushöhlen. **furrowed,** *adj.* gefurcht, durchfurcht, runzelig.

furry ['fəːri], *adj.* Pelz–, aus Pelz; pelzartig.

further ['fəːðə], **1.** *adj.* weiter, ferner, entfernter; weiter, zusätzlich; ***till – notice,*** bis auf weiteres; ***till – orders,*** bis auf weiteren Befehl; ***– particulars,*** nähere Einzelheiten, Nähere(s). **2.** *adv.* weiter, ferner, mehr; weiterhin, außerdem, überdies; ***no –,*** nicht weiter; ***nothing –?*** weiter nichts? sonst noch was? **3.** *v.t.* fördern, unterstützen.

furtherance ['fəːðərəns], *s.* die Förderung, Unterstützung; ***in – of,*** um . . . zu fördern, zur Förderung von. **further|more,** *adv.* ferner, überdies, außerdem. **-most,** *adj.* weitest, fernst. **furthest,** **1.** *adj.* weitest, fernst. **2.** *adv.* am weitesten.

furtive ['fəːtiv], *adj.* verstohlen, heimlich, unbemerkt (*of actions*); (hinter)listig, hinterhältig, verschlagen (*of a p.*). **furtiveness,** *s.* die Verstohlenheit; Hinterhältigkeit.

furuncle ['fjuərʌŋkl], *s.* der Furunkel.

fury ['fjuəri], *s.* 1. die Raserei, Wut; Heftigkeit, das Ungestüm; ***in a –,*** rasend, wütend; (*coll.*) ***like –,*** wie toll; 2. (*fig.*) unbändiges Weib, die Xantippe; (*Myth.*) ***the Furies,*** die Furien, Rachegöttinnen, Erinnyen, Eumeniden.

furze [fəːz], *s.* (*Bot.*) der Stechginster, Gaspeldorn (*Ulex*).

fuse [fjuːz], **1.** *v.t.* 1. verschmelzen (*also fig.*); 2. (*Artil. etc.*) Zünder anbringen an (*Dat.*); 3. (*Elec.*) absichern; 4. (*Comm.*) fusionieren; (*fig.*) vereinigen, vermischen, zusammenbringen. **2.** *v.i.* schmelzen, zerfließen, zusammenschmelzen; (*Elec.*) durchbrennen; (*fig.*) zusammenfließen, sich vereinigen, eins werden. **3.** *s.* 1. der Zünder, (*obs.*) die Lunte; Zündschnur, das Leitfeuer; ***– cap,*** die Zünderkappe, das Zündhütchen; 2. (*Elec.*) die Sicherung, der Schmelzeinsatz; ***the – has blown,*** die Sicherung ist durchgebrannt; ***– box,*** der Sicherungskasten; ***– wire,*** der Abschmelzdraht, Sicherungsdraht.

fusee [fjuː'ziː], *s.* 1. (*Horol.*) die Schnecke; 2. (*obs.*) das Windfeuerzeug, Streichholz.

fuselage ['fjuːzəlɑːʒ], *s.* (*Av.*) der Rumpf.

fusibility [fjuːzi'biliti], *s.* die Schmelzbarkeit. **fusible** ['fjuːzibl], *adj.* schmelzbar, schmelzflüssig.

fusil ['fjuːzil], *s.* (*Her.*) die Raute.

fusilier [fjuːzi'liə], *s.* der Füsilier. **fusilade** [–'leid], **1.** *v.t.* beschießen (*a place*), erschießen, füselieren (*a p.*). **2.** *s.* das Gewehrfeuer, die Salve; (*fig.*) der Hagel (*of stones etc.*).

fusing ['fjuːziŋ], *s.* das Schmelzen, die Einschmelzung; ***– point,*** der Schmelzpunkt. **fusion** ['fjuːʒən], *s.* das Schmelzen; der Zusammenfluß; (*fig.*) Zusammenschluß, die Verschmelzung; Fusion.

fuss [fʌs], **1.** *s.* der Lärm, das Getue, Wesen, übertriebene Geschäftigkeit; ***make a – about,*** viel Aufhebens machen um. **2.** *v.i.* sich aufregen, viel Aufhebens machen (***about, over***, um). **fussiness,** *s.* die Geschäftigkeit; übertriebene Umständlichkeit. **fuss-pot,** *s.* (*coll.*) der Umstandskrämer, Wichtigtuer. **fussy,** *adj.* kleinlich, pedantisch, umständlich; geschäftig.

fustian ['fʌstiən], **1.** *s.* 1. der Barchent; 2. (*fig.*) Schwulst, Bombast. **2.** *adj.* 1. barchen; 2. (*fig.*) schwülstig, hochtrabend; minderwertig.

fustigate ['fʌstigeit], *v.t.* prügeln. **fustigation** [–'geiʃən], *s.* die Prügelstrafe.

fustiness ['fʌstinis], *s.* muffiger Geruch, der Modergeruch. **fusty,** *adj.* muffig, moderig; (*fig.*) veraltet, verstaubt.

futile ['fjuːtail], *adj.* leer, nichtig, unnütz; nutzlos, aussichtslos, zwecklos, wirkungslos, wertlos; unzulänglich. **futility** [–'tiliti], *s.* die Nichtigkeit, Leerheit, Unzulänglichkeit; Zwecklosigkeit, Nutzlosigkeit, Sinnlosigkeit, Wertlosigkeit.

futtock ['fʌtək], *s.* der Auflanger, Sitzer; *pl.* (*Naut.*) Püttings(wanten) (*pl.*).

future ['fjuːtʃə], **1.** *adj.* (zu)künftig, Zukunfts–; (*Comm.*) Termin–; (*Gram.*) ***– tense,*** das Futurum. **2.** *s.* die Zukunft; (*Gram.*) das Futurum; *pl.* (*Comm.*) Termingeschäfte (*pl.*), Terminwaren (*pl.*); (*Gram.*) ***– perfect,*** das Futurum exactum; ***in –,*** in Zukunft; ***for*** or ***in the –,*** künftig(hin), für die *or* in der Zukunft. **3.** *v.t.* (*Comm.*) ***– a guarantee,*** die Garantie übergeben. **futurism,** *s.* (*Art*) der Futurismus. **futurist(ic)** [–rist (–'ristik)], *adj.* (*Art*) futuristisch. **futurity** [–'tjuəriti], *s.* die Zukunft, das Zukünftige; *pl.* zukünftige Ergebnisse (*pl.*).

fuze, *see* **fuse.**

fuzz [fʌz], **1.** *v.i.* zerfasern, sich auflösen. **2.** *s.* 1. flaumiges Haar, die Fussel; der Flaum (*on fruit*); 2. (*pej.*) (*collect.*) die Polizei. **fuzziness,** *s.* die Struppigkeit (*as hair*), (*fig.*) Verschwommenheit, Undeutlichkeit. **fuzzy,** *adj.* flaumig, flockig, faserig; kraus, struppig, zottig (*hair*); (*fig.*) ver-

wischt, verschwommen. **fuzzy-wuzzy,** *s.* (*coll.*) der Krauskopf, Wuschelkopf.
Fyen ['fju:ən], *s.* (*Geog.*) Fünen (*n.*).
fylfot ['filfɔt], *s.* das Hakenkreuz.

G

G, g [dʒi:], *s.* das G, g (*also Mus.*); ***G clef,*** der Violinschlüssel, G-Schlüssel; ***G flat,*** das Ges, ges; ***G major,*** G-Dur; ***G minor,*** g-Moll; ***G sharp,*** das Gis, gis; (*coll.*) ***G-string,*** der Lendenschurz, (*striptease*) letzte Hülle. (*See Index of Abbreviations.*)
gab [gæb], *s.* das Geschwätz, Geplauder; (*vulg.*) ***stop your –!*** halt deinen Schnabel! ***gift of the –,*** ein tüchtiges Mundwerk.
gabardine, *see* **gaberdine,** 2.
gabble [gæbl], **1.** *v.i.* schnattern (*as geese*); schwatzen, plappern, in den Bart reden, hastig *or* unverständlich sprechen. **2.** *s.* das Geschnatter; Geschwätz; undeutliches Sprechen. **gabbler,** *s.* der Schwätzer, das Plappermaul.
gaberdine, *s.* 1. ['gæbədi:n], (*Hist.*) der Kittel; Kaftan (*of Jews*); 2. [–'di:n] der *or* die Gabardine, der Gabardinemantel.
gabion ['geibiən], *s.* der Schanzkorb. **gabionade** [–'neid], *s.* die Schanzkorbbefestigung.
gable [geibl], *s.* der Giebel. **gabled,** *adj.* gegiebelt, Giebel–. **gable|-end,** *s.* die Giebelwand. **--window,** *s.* das Giebelfenster.
gaby ['geibi], *s.* der Trottel, Tropf.
[1]**gad!** [gæd], *int.* ***by –!*** meiner Treu!
[2]**gad,** **1.** *v.i.* ***– about,*** umherstreifen, sich umhertreiben. **2.** *s.* ***be on the –,*** see ***– about.*** **gad|-about,** *s.* der Bummler, Pflastertreter. **–fly,** *s.* die Viehbremse, Biesfliege; (*fig.*) lästiger Kerl, der Störenfried.
gadget ['gædʒit], *s.* die Vorrichtung, der Apparat, (kleines) Gerät; (*coll.*) das Ding(sda).
Gael [geil], *s.* (schottischer) Kelte. **Gaelic,** **1.** *adj.* gälisch. **2.** *s.* das Gälisch (*language*).
gaff [gæf], *s.* der Fischhaken (*for salmon*); (*Naut.*) die Gaffel; (*sl.*) der Unfug; (*sl.*) ***blow the –,*** petzen, pfeifen, alles verplaudern.
gaffe [gæf], *s.* der Schnitzer, Mißgriff.
gaffer ['gæfə], *s.* (*coll.*) Alte(r), das Väterchen; der Gevatter; Aufseher, Vorarbeiter, Chef.
gag [gæg], **1.** *v.t.* knebeln; (*fig.*) mundtot machen. **2.** *v.i.* (*Theat.*) improvisieren, extemporieren. **3.** *s.* 1. der Knebel; (*fig.*) die Knebelung; (*Parl.*) der Debattenschluß; 2. (*Theat.*) extemporierte Einschaltung, die Improvisation; (*coll.*) alter Witz, der Ulk; Schwindel.
gaga ['gɑ:gɑ:], *adj.* (*sl.*) meschugge.
[1]**gage** [geidʒ], **1.** *s.* das (Unter)pfand, die Bürgschaft; ***throw down the –,*** den Fehdehandschuh hinwerfen. **2.** *v.t.* verpfänden.
[2]**gage,** (*Am.*) *see* **gauge.**
gaggle [gægl], **1.** *v.i.* schnattern, gackern. **2.** *s.* – (*of geese*), die Schar Gänse.
gaiety ['geiəti], *s.* die Heiterkeit, Lustigkeit, Fröhlichkeit, der Frohsinn; die Festlichkeit, Lustbarkeit.
gaily ['geili], *adv.* lustig, heiter, fröhlich; *see* **gay.**
gain [gein], **1.** *s.* 1. der Gewinn, Vorteil, Nutzen (*to,* für), die Ausbeute (*from, Gen.*); (*Comm.*) (*usu. pl.*) der Profit, Einnahmen (*pl.*); ***clear –,*** der Reingewinn; 2. die Steigerung, Zunahme, (*Rad.*) Verstärkung; (*Rad.*) ***--control,*** die Lautstärkeregelung; der Verstärkungsregler. **2.** *v.t.* gewinnen; bekommen, erhalten, erwerben, erlangen (*from,* von); ankommen an *or* in (*Dat.*), erreichen; ***– the day,*** den Sieg erringen *or* davontragen, obsiegen; ***– the ear of,*** Gehör finden bei; ***– one's ends,*** seinen Zweck erreichen; ***– by force,*** erzwingen; ***– ground,*** (an) Boden gewinnen; (*fig.*) Fuß fassen, um sich greifen, sich durchsetzen; ***– the upper hand,*** die Oberhand gewinnen; ***– one's living,*** seinen Lebensunterhalt verdienen; ***– over,*** für sich gewinnen (*a p.*); ***– possession,*** Besitz ergreifen; ***– speed,*** schneller werden; ***– time,*** Zeit gewinnen. **3.** *v.i.* 1. (an Wert) gewinnen, im Ansehen steigern, Vorteil haben, Einfluß *or* Boden gewinnen; 2. vorgehen (*of clocks*); 3. ***– on,*** (*in a race*) einholen, aufholen; näherkommen (*Dat.*); (*as influence etc.*) übergreifen auf (*Acc.*), sich ausbreiten über (*Acc.*). **gainer,** *s.* der Gewinner; ***be the – by,*** gewinnen durch. **gainful,** *adj.* einträglich, gewinnbringend, vorteilhaft, ertragreich. **gainings,** *pl.* der Profit, Gewinne (*pl.*), Einkünfte (*pl.*).
gainsay [gein'sei], *irr.v.t.* widersprechen (*a p.*) (*Dat.*); bestreiten, leugnen (*a th.*).
gait [geit], *s.* die Haltung, Gehweise, der Gang, (*of horse*) die Gangart.
gaiter ['geitə], *s.* die Gamasche.
gal [gæl], *s.* (*coll.*) *see* **girl.**
gala ['gɑ:lə], **1.** *s.* die Festlichkeit, Feier. **2.** *adj.* festlich, Fest–, Gala–.
galactic [gə'læktik], *adj.* (*Astr.*) Milchstraßen–. **galactometer** [gælək'tɔmitə], *s.* die Milchwaage, der Milchmesser.
galantine ['gælənti:n], *s.* (*Cul.*) die Sülzplatte.
galanty show [gə'lænti], *s.* das Schattenspiel.
Galatians [gə'leiʃənz], *pl.* (*B.*) Galater (*pl.*).
galaxy ['gæləksi], *s.* 1. die Milchstraße; 2. (*fig.*) glänzende Versammlung.
galbanum ['gælbənəm], *s.* das Galbanharz.
[1]**gale** [geil], *s.* frischer *or* heftiger Wind, steife Brise; ***moderate –,*** harter Wind; ***fresh –,*** stürmischer Wind; ***strong –,*** der Sturmwind; ***whole –,*** schwerer Sturm.
[2]**gale,** *s.* periodische Renten– *or* Pacht– *or* Mietzahlung.
galena [gə'li:nə], *s.* der Bleiglanz, Galenit.
Galilee ['gælili:], *s.* Galiläa (*n.*); (*B.*) ***Sea of –,*** der See Genezareth.
galilee, *s.* (*Archit.*) die (Dom)vorhalle.
[1]**gall** [gɔ:l], *s.* 1. (*Med.*) die Galle; ***– bladder,*** die Gallenblase; 2. (*fig.*) die Bitterkeit, Bosheit, Erbitterung; 3. (*coll.*) Frechheit.
[2]**gall,** *s.* (*Bot.*) der Gallapfel; ***--fly,*** die Gallwespe.
[3]**gall,** **1.** *s.* 1. das Wundreiben; wund(gerieben)e Stelle, (*coll.*) der Wolf; 2. (*fig.*) Ärger, die Erbitterung. **2.** *v.t.* wundreiben; (*fig.*) quälen, peinigen, ärgern, belästigen, reizen.
gallant ['gælənt], **1.** *adj.* tapfer, mutig; brav, ritterlich, höflich, zuvorkommend; galant, Liebes–; prächtig, stattlich. **2.** *s.* der Galan, Kurmacher. **gallantry,** *s.* die Tapferkeit, der (Helden)mut; Edelmut, die Ritterlichkeit; Artigkeit, Zuvorkommenheit, Höflichkeit (*to women*).
galleon ['gæliən], *s.* (*Hist.*) die Galeone, Gallione.
galleria [gælə'riə], *s.* (*Geog.*) der Galleriewald.
gallery ['gæləri], *s.* die Galerie (*also Theat.*), Säulenhalle; Empore (*of a church*); (*Fort.*) bedeckter Gang, der Minengang; (*Min.*) Stollen, die Strecke; ***picture-–,*** die Gemäldegalerie; ***play to the –,*** nach Effekt haschen.
galley ['gæli], *s.* 1. (*Hist.*) die Galeere; 2. (*Naut.*) das Langboot; 3. (*Naut.*) die Schiffsküche, Kombüse; 4. (*Typ.*) das Setzschiff. **galley|(-proof),** *s.* (*Typ.*) der Bürstenabzug. **--slave,** *s.* der Galeerensklave, Galeerensträfling.
gallic ['gælik], *adj.* ***– acid,*** die Gallussäure.
Gallic, *adj.* gallisch. **Gallican,** *adj.* gallikanisch, französisch-katholisch. **Gallicism** ['gælisizm], *s.* der Gallizismus. **Gallicize** [–saiz], *v.t.* französieren.

gallimaufry [gæli'mɔ:fri], *s.* der Mischmasch, das Durcheinander.
gallinaceous [gæli'neiʃəs], *adj.* hühnerartig.
galling ['gɔ:liŋ], *adj.* (*usu. fig.*) ärgerlich, verdrießlich; *see* ³**gall.**
gallinule ['gælinju:l], *s.* (*Orn.*) (*Am.*) *see* **moorhen.**
galliot ['gæliət], *s.* kleine Galeere.
gallipot ['gælipɔt], *s.* der Apothekertopf, Salbentopf.
gallivant ['gælivænt], *v.i.* (*coll.*) sich herumtreiben, umherflanieren.
gallon ['gælən], *s.* die Gallone (= *4.54 Liter*; *Am.* = *3.78 Liter*).
galloon [gə'lu:n], *s.* die Tresse, Borte, Litze.
gallop ['gæləp], **1.** *s.* der Galopp; *full* –, gestreckter Galopp; (*fig.*) größte Eile; *at a* –, im Galopp. **2.** *v.i.* galoppieren; lossprengen (*at*, auf (*Acc.*)); (*fig.*) hasten, eilen; *–ing consumption,* galoppierende Schwindsucht. **3.** *v.t.* galoppieren lassen, in Galopp setzen (*a horse*). **gallopade** [–'peid], *s.* die Galoppade (*dance*).
Gallophile ['gælofail], *s.* der Franzosenfreund. **Gallophobe** [–foub], *s.* der Franzosenhasser.
gallows ['gælouz], *pl.* (*usu. sing. constr.*) der Galgen; *– bird,* der Galgenvogel, Galgenstrick; *– tree,* der Galgen.
gall-stone, *s.* der Gallenstein.
Gallup poll ['gæləp], *s.* die Meinungsforschung, Meinungsumfrage, Meinungsbefragung.
galoot [gə'lu:t], *s.* (*sl.*) der Tölpel, roher Kerl.
galop ['gæləp, gə'lɔp], *s.* der Galopp (*dance*).
galore [gə'lɔ:], *adv.* (*coll.*) in Hülle und Fülle, in Menge, mehr als genug.
galosh [gə'lɔʃ], *s.* (*usu. pl.*) der Überschuh, Gummischuh, die Galosche.
galumph [gə'lʌmf], *v.i.* (*coll.*) einherstolzieren.
galvanic [gæl'vænik], *adj.* galvanisch; *– electricity,* die Berührungselektrizität. **galvanism** ['gælvənizm], *s.* der Galvanismus, die Berührungselektrizität. **galvanize** ['gælvənaiz], *v.t.* 1. galvanisieren; verzinken; *–d iron,* verzinktes Eisen(blech); 2. (*fig.*) beleben, anspornen, wecken (*into*, zu). **galvanometer** [–'nɔmitə], *s.* das Galvanometer.
gambit ['gæmbit], *s.* (*Chess*) das Gambit; (*fig.*) erster Schritt.
gamble [gæmbl], **1.** *v.i.* um Geld *or* um hohen Einsatz *or* um Hasard spielen, spekulieren; *– on,* wetten auf (*Acc.*); (*coll.*) *you can – on it,* darauf können Sie Gift nehmen; (*fig.*) *– with,* aufs Spiel setzen. **2.** *v.t.* *– away,* verspielen. **3.** *s.* das Glücksspiel, Hasardspiel; (*fig.*) gewagtes Unternehmen, das Wagnis. **gambler,** *s.* der Spieler. **gambling,** *s.* das Spielen (um Geld), Wetten; *– den,* die Spielhölle.
gamboge [gæm'bu:ʒ], *s.* das Gummigutt.
gambol [gæmbl], **1.** *s.* der Luftsprung, Freudensprung. **2.** *v.i.* Luftsprünge machen, herumspringen, herumhüpfen.
game [geim], **1.** *s.* 1. das Spiel, die Partie; *– of chance,* das Glücksspiel, Hasardspiel; *– of skill,* das Geschicklichkeitsspiel; *give* or *throw up the –,* das Spiel aufgeben; *on one's –,* in Form; *play the –,* nach den Regeln spielen, mit ehrlichen Mitteln kämpfen; *play a good –,* gut spielen; (*fig.*) *play a losing –,* bestimmt verlieren; 2. der Scherz, Spaß, die Belustigung; *make – of,* auslachen, zum besten haben (*a p.*), ins Lächerliche ziehen (*a th.*); 3. (*coll.*) der Plan, Schlich, geheime Absicht; *give the – away,* den Plan verraten; *beat him at his own –,* ihn mit seinen eignen Waffen schlagen; (*coll.*) *the – is up,* das Spiel ist aus, alles ist verloren; *the – is not worth the candle,* die S. lohnt die Mühe nicht; *what's his* (*little*) *–?* was führt er im Schilde? (*fig.*) *play a double –,* ein Doppelspiel treiben; 4. (*Hunt.*) jagdbare Tiere, das Wild; *big –,* das Großwild; (*coll.*) *fair –,* das Freiwild; 5. *pl.* (*at school*) der Sport. **2.** *v.i.* (um Geld) spielen. **3.** *adj.* **1.** (*coll.*) mutig, unerschrocken, entschlossen; bereit (*for*, zu); *die –,* tapfer sterben; *he is – for anything,* er ist zu allem bereit *or* für alles zu haben; **2.** (*coll.*) verletzt, lahm (*of arm or leg*).
game|-bag, *s.* die Jagdtasche. **--bird,** *s.* der Jagdvogel. **--cock,** *s.* der Kampfhahn. **-keeper,** *s.* der Förster; Wildhüter. **--laws,** *pl.* Wildschutzgesetze (*pl.*). **--licence,** *s.* der Jagdschein.
gameness ['geimnis], *s.* (*coll.*) die Ausdauer, Entschlossenheit; der Mut, Schneid.
game-preserve, *s.* der Wildpark. **games-master,** *s.* der Sportlehrer. **gamester** [–stə], *s.* der (die) Spieler(in) (um Geld).
gamete [gæ'mi:t], *s.* (*Biol.*) der Gamet, die Gamete, Keimzelle.
game|-tenant, *s.* der Jagdpächter. **--warden,** *s.* der Jagdaufseher. **gamey** [–i], *adj.* angegangen, mit Wildgeschmack (*of food*).
gamin ['gæmɛ̃], *s.* der Straßenjunge.
gaminess ['geiminis], *s.* der Wildgeschmack, Wildgeruch.
gaming ['geimiŋ], *s.* das Spiel(en) (um Geld); *– table,* die Spielbank.
gamma rays ['gæmə], *pl.* Gammastrahlen (*pl.*).
gammer ['gæmə], *s.* (*obs.*) das Mütterchen, Gevatterin.
¹**gammon** ['gæmən], **1.** *s.* doppelter Gewinn (*at backgammon*); (*fig.*) der Betrug, Schwindel, Humbug, Unsinn. **2.** *v.t.* doppelt schlagen (*at backgammon*); (*fig.*) betrügen, anführen, foppen.
²**gammon, 1.** *s.* geräucherter Schinken. **2.** *v.t.* räuchern und einsalzen (*ham*).
gamp [gæmp], *s.* (*coll.*) der Regenschirm.
gamut ['gæmət], *s.* (*Mus.*) die (Grund)tonleiter; der Stimmumfang; (*fig.*) Umfang, Bereich, die Stufenleiter, Skala.
gamy, *adj. See* **gamey.**
gander ['gændə], *s.* der Gänserich; (*Prov.*) *what is sauce for the goose is sauce for the –,* was dem einen recht ist, ist dem andern billig.
gang [gæŋ], **1.** *s.* die Bande, Rotte, Sippschaft; (*of workmen*) Kolonne, Abteilung, der Trupp; (*of tools*) Satz. **2.** *v.i.* *– together* or *up,* sich zusammenrotten. **gang-condenser,** *s.*(*Elec.*) der Mehrfachkondensator. **ganged,** *adj.* (*Tech.*) Einkopf–. **ganger,** *s.* der Werkführer, Vorarbeiter.
gangling ['gæŋgliŋ], *adj.* (*coll.*) hochgewachsen, hoch aufgeschossen.
ganglion ['gæŋgliən], *s.* (*pl.* **-s** *or* **-lia**) (*Anat.*) der Nervenknoten; (*Med.*) das Überbein; (*fig.*) der Mittelpunkt, Knotenpunkt.
gang-plank, *s.* der Laufsteg; (*Naut.*) Landungssteg.
gangrene ['gæŋgri:n], **1.** *s.* (*Med.*) der Brand; (*fig.*) die Fäulnis. **2.** *v.t.* brandig machen. **3.** *v.i.* brandig werden. **gangrenous** [–grinəs], *adj.* brandig.
gangster ['gæŋstə], *s.* (bewaffneter) Verbrecher.
gangway ['gæŋwei], **1.** *s.* der Durchgang; (*Theat. etc.*) Gang; (*Naut.*) das Fallreep, die Fallreepspforte, Fallreepstreppe; der Laufgang, Gangbord, die Laufplanke; (*Parl.*) der Quergang; (*Min.*) die Strecke; (*Parl.*) *members below the –,* Wilden (*pl.*). **2.** *int.* Durchgang *or* Platz bitte!
gannet ['gænit], *s.* (*Orn.*) der Baßtölpel (*Morus bassanus*).
gantry ['gæntri], *s.* die Faßunterlage, das Faßlager (*for barrels*), die Kranbahn (*of crane*); (*Railw.*) *signal –,* die Signalbrücke.
gaol [dʒeil], **1.** *s.* das Gefängnis. **2.** *v.t.* ins Gefängnis werfen. **gaol|-bird,** *s.* (*coll.*) der Gewohnheitsverbrecher, (*sl.*) Knastschieber. **--break,** *s.* der Ausbruch aus dem Gefängnis. **--breaker,** *s.* der Ausbrecher. **gaoler,** *s.* der Gefängnisaufseher. **gaol-fever,** *s.* der Flecktyphus. *Also* **jail.**
gap [gæp], *s.* die Öffnung, Lücke, Spalte, Kluft, der Spalt, Riß, Sprung, die Scharte; (*Mil.*) Bresche (*in the line*), Gasse (*in minefield*); (*Geog.*) Schlucht, Kluft, der Durchbruch; (*coll.*) (*of time*) die Unterbrechung, Leere, Lücke; (*fig.*) (*coll.*) Abweichung, der Unterschied; *air-–,* der Luft-

spalt; ***spark*--**, die Funkstrecke; (*fig.*) ***fill a* –**, eine Lücke ausfüllen; ***stop a* –**, ein Loch zustopfen.

gape [geip], *v.i.* (*of a p.*) den Mund aufsperren *or* aufreißen, (*coll.*) gähnen; (*fig.*) starren, gaffen, glotzen; (*of a th.*) sich öffnen *or* spalten, klaffen, gähnen, offen stehen; ***stand gaping***, Maulaffen feil halten. **gapes,** *pl.* (*Vet.*) die Schnabelsperre. **gaping, 1.** *adj.* starrend, (*coll.*) gähnend; klaffend. **2.** *s.* das Starren, (*coll.*) Gähnen.

garage ['gærɑ:ʒ, –ridʒ], **1.** *s.* die Garage; Autowerkstatt. **2.** *v.t.* (in eine Garage) einstellen; (in einer Garage) unterbringen.

garb [gɑ:b], *s.* das Gewand, die Kleidung; Tracht; (*fig.*) Hülle, Form, der Mantel.

garbage ['gɑ:bidʒ], *s.* (*esp. Am.*) der (Küchen)-abfall, Müll; (*fig.*) Dreck, Auswurf, Ausschuß; (*Am.*) – ***can,*** der Kehrichtkasten, Müllkasten; – ***chute,*** der Müllschlucker.

garble [gɑ:bl], *v.t.* 1. verstümmeln, entstellen; 2. (*obs.*) sichten, (aus)sieben, auslesen.

garboard (strake) ['gɑ:bəd (streik)], *s.* (*Naut.*) der Kielgang.

garden [gɑ:dn], **1.** *s.* der Garten; *pl.* Gartenanlagen (*pl.*); ***botanical –s,*** botanischer Garten; ***market –,*** die (Handels)gärtnerei; ***nursery –,*** die Baumschule. **2.** *v.i.* im Garten arbeiten; Gartenbau treiben. **garden city,** *s.* die Gartenstadt. **gardener,** *s.* der (die) Gärtner(in).

gardenia [gɑ:'di:niə], *s.* (*Bot.*) die Gardenie.

gardening ['gɑ:dniŋ], *s.* der Gartenbau; die Gärtnerei, Gartenarbeit. **garden| mould,** *s.* die Blumentopferde. – **party,** *s.* das Gartenfest. – **path,** *s.* der Gartenweg; (*coll.*) ***lead him up the –,*** ihn auf den Holzweg führen. – **produce,** *s.* Gartengewächse (*pl.*), Gartenerzeugnisse (*pl.*), Gartengemüse (*pl.*). – **roller,** *s.* die Gartenwalze. – **shears,** *pl.* die Heckenschere. – **suburb,** *s.* die Gartenvorstadt. **--warbler,** *s.* (*Orn.*) die Gartengrasmücke (*Sylvia borin*). – **white,** *s.* (*Ent.*) der Weißling.

gargantuan [gɑ:'gæntjuən], *adj.* riesig, ungeheuer.

gargle [gɑ:gl], **1.** *v.i.* gurgeln, (den Hals *or* Mund) ausspülen. **2.** *s.* das Mundwasser.

gargoyle ['gɑ:gɔil], *s.* der Wasserspeier.

garish ['gɛəriʃ], *adj.* grell, blendend; prunkend, auffallend. **garishness,** *s.* die Grellheit, Grelle; das Prunken.

garland ['gɑ:lənd], **1.** *s.* 1. der Kranz; das Blumengewinde, Laubgewinde, (*also Archit.*) die Girlande; 2. (*fig.*) der Ehrenpreis, die Siegespalme; 3. (*of verses etc.*) Blumenlese. **2.** *v.t.* bekränzen.

garlic ['gɑ:lik], *s.* der Knoblauch.

garment ['gɑ:mənt], *s.* das Kleid(ungsstück), Gewand; (*fig.*) die Decke, Hülle.

garner ['gɑ:nə], **1.** *s.* der Getreideboden, Getreidespeicher; (*fig.*) Speicher, die Kornkammer. **2.** *v.t.* aufspeichern (*also fig.*), (*fig.*) ansammeln.

garnet ['gɑ:nit], *s.* der Granat.

garnish ['gɑ:niʃ], *v.t.* 1. (*Poet.*) (ver)zieren, schmücken, (*Cul.*) garnieren; 2. (*Law*) vorladen, zitieren. **garnishing,** *s.* (*Cul.*) die Garnierung. **garnishment,** *s.* 1. der Zierat, Schmuck, die Verzierung; 2. (*Law*) gerichtliche Vorladung, die Zitierung; Beschlagnahme einer Forderung.

garniture ['gɑ:nitʃə], *s.* der Schmuck, die Verzierung, Ausstattung; Garnitur; das Zubehör.

garret ['gærət], *s.* die Dachstube, Bodenkammer.

garrison ['gærisn], **1.** *s.* die Garnison, Besatzung; der Standort; ***in –,*** in Garnison; – ***commander,*** der Standortskommandant; – ***town,*** die Garnisonstadt. **2.** *v.t.* belegen, besetzen, mit einer Besatzung versehen (*a town*); in Garnison legen (*troops*).

garrotte [gə'rɔt], **1.** *s.* die Garrotte, Erdrosselung. **2.** *v.t.* garrottieren, erdrosseln.

garrulity [gə'ru:liti], *s.* die Schwatzhaftigkeit, Geschwätzigkeit. **garrulous** ['gæruləs], *adj.* schwatzhaft, geschwätzig, redselig.

garter ['gɑ:tə], **1.** *s.* das Strumpfband, der Sockenhalter; ***Order of the Garter,*** der Hosenbandorden; ***Knight of the Garter,*** der Ritter des Hosenbandordens. **2.** *v.t.* 1. mit dem Strumpfband binden; 2. mit dem Hosenbandorden ehren.

garth [gɑ:θ], *s.* (*obs.*) der Hofgarten, Klosterhof.

gas [gæs], **1.** *s.* 1. das Gas; Leuchtgas; (*Mil.*) (*also* ***poison –***) der Kampfstoff, das (Gift)gas; 2. (*Am. coll.*) Benzin, der Kraftstoff; (*coll.*) ***step on the –,*** Gas geben. **2.** *v.t.* mit Gas vergiften, vergasen. **3.** *v.i.* (*sl.*) schwatzen, faseln.

gas|-bag, *s.* die Gaszelle (*of airships*); (*coll.*) der Schwätzer, Windbeutel. **--bracket,** *s.* der Gasarm. **--burner,** *s.* der Gasbrenner. **--carbon,** *s.* die Retortenkohle. **--chamber,** *s.* die Gaskammer. – **coal,** *s.* die Fettkohle.

Gascon [gæskn], **1.** *s.* der (die) Gaskogner(in). **2.** *adj.* gaskonisch. **gasconade** [–'neid], **1.** *s.* die Prahlerei, Aufschneiderei. **2.** *v.i.* prahlen, aufschneiden. **Gascony,** *s.* die Gaskogne.

gas|-cooker, *s.* der Gasherd. **--cylinder,** *s.* die Gasflasche. **--detector,** *s.* der Gasanzeiger. **--engine,** *s.* der Gasmotor. **gaseous** ['geisiəs, –ziəs], *adj.* gasförmig, gasartig. **gas|-fire,** *s.* die Gasheizung. **--fired,** *adj.* Gas– (*boiler etc.*). **-fitter,** *s.* der Gasinstallateur. **--fittings,** *pl.* Gasarmaturen (*pl.*). – **gangrene,** *s.* der Gasbrand.

gash [gæʃ], **1.** *v.t.* tief ins Fleisch schneiden (*Dat.*); aufschneiden, aufschlitzen. **2.** *s.* klaffende Wunde, tiefe Schnittwunde; der Schmiß, die Schmarre; Spalte, tiefer Riß.

gas-holder, *s.* (*Tech.*) der Gasometer; (*Chem.*) die Gasglocke. **gasify** ['gæsifai], **1.** *v.t.* in Gas verwandeln, vergasen. **2.** *v.i.* zu Gas werden. **gas-jet,** *s.* der Gasbrenner; die Gasflamme.

gasket ['gæskit], *s.* 1. die Dichtung, der Verdichtungsring; 2. (*Naut.*) das Seising, Zeising.

gas|light, *s.* das Gaslicht, die Gasbeleuchtung; Gaslampe; (*Phot.*) – ***paper,*** das Gaslichtpapier. **--main,** *s.* das Gasrohr, die Gasleitung. **-man,** *s.* (*coll.*) der Gaskassierer. **--mantle,** *s.* der Glühstrumpf. **-mask,** *s.* die Gasmaske. **-meter,** *s.* der Gasmesser, die Gasuhr.

gasoline ['gæsəli:n], *s.* der Gasäther, das Gasolin; (*Am.*) Benzin. **gasometer** [–'ɔmitə], *s.* der Gasbehälter, Gasometer.

gasp [gɑ:sp], **1.** *s.* das Keuchen, Ringen nach Luft, schweres Atmen; ***be at one's last –,*** in den letzten Zügen liegen. **2.** *v.t.* – ***out,*** ausatmen, aushauchen (*one's life*), hervorstoßen, seufzend äußern (*words etc.*). **3.** *v.i.* nach Luft ringen, schwer atmen, keuchen, schnaufen; – ***for breath,*** nach Luft schnappen. **gasper,** *s.* (*sl.*) billige Zigarette, der Sargnagel.

gas|-pipe, *s.* das Gasrohr. **--pliers,** *pl.* die Gasrohrzange. **--ring,** *s.* der Gaskocher, Gasbrenner. **gassed** [gæst], *adj.* gaskrank, gasvergiftet, vergast. **gassing,** *s.* 1. das Vergasen, die Vergasung; 2. (*Tech.*) Gasentwicklung, das Gasen; 3. (*sl.*) Schwatzen. **gas| station,** *s.* (*Am.*) die Tankstelle. **--stove,** *s.* der Gasofen, Gasherd. **--supply,** *s.* die Gasversorgung, Gaszufuhr. **gassy,** *adj.* 1. gasig, gashaltig; 2. (*sl.*) geschwätzig. **gas tar,** *s.* der Steinkohlenteer.

gastric ['gæstrik], *adj.* gastrisch, Magen–; – ***juice,*** der Magensaft; – ***ulcer,*** die Magengeschwür. **gastritis** [–'traitis], *s.* der Magenkatarrh. **gastroenteritis** [–trouentə'raitis], *s.* der Magen-Darm-Katarrh.

gastronome ['gæstrənoum], **gastronomer** [gæs'trɔnəmə], *s.* der Feinschmecker. **gastronomic(al)** [–'nɔmik(l)], *adj.* feinschmeckerisch. **gastronomist** [–'trɔnəmist], *s.* *See* **gastronome. gastronomy** [–'trɔnəmi], *s.* die Kochkunst; Feinschmeckerei.

gas| turbine, *s.* die Gasturbine. – **warfare,** *s.* chemischer Krieg. **-works,** *pl.* (*sing. constr.*) das Gaswerk, die Gasanstalt.

gat [gæt], *s.* (*Am.*) (*sl.*) der Revolver.

gate [geit], **1.** *s.* 1. das Tor, die Pforte; (*of locks*) das Schleusentor; (*Railw.*) die Sperre, Schranke; (*Phot.*) das Filmfenster; (*fig.*) der Zugang, Weg;

2. (*Spt.*) die Besucherzahl; eingenommenes Eintrittsgeld. **2.** *v.t.* (*Univ. sl.*) den Ausgang verbieten (*Dat.*); *he was –d*, er bekam Ausgangsverbot.

gate|-crash, 1. *v.t.* (*coll.*) uneingeladen mitmachen. **2.** *v.i.* (*coll.*) uneingeladen kommen. **--crasher,** *s.* der Eindringling, ungebetener Gast. **-house,** *s.* das Torhaus, Pförtnerhaus. **--keeper,** *s.* der Pförtner; (*Railw.*) Bahnwärter. **--legged table,** *s.* der Klapptisch. **-man,** *s. See* **--keeper. --money,** *s.* eingenommenes Eintrittsgeld. **-post,** *s.* der Torpfosten; (*coll.*) *between you and me and the –*, unter vier Augen. **-way,** *s.* der Torweg, die Einfahrt; (*fig.*) der Zugang, das (Eingangs)tor.

gather ['gæðə], **1.** *v.t.* 1. (an)sammeln, aufsammeln, einsammeln, anhäufen, zusammenhäufen (*things*), versammeln, zusammenbringen (*persons*), ernten (*corn etc.*), pflücken, lesen (*flowers etc.*); (*Bookb.*) zusammentragen (*sheets*); *– breath*, zu Atem kommen; *– dust*, staubig werden; (*B.*) *be –ed to one's fathers*, zu seinen Vätern versammelt werden; *– in*, einbringen, einsammeln; *– him in one's arms*, ihn in die Arme schließen; *– speed*, schneller werden; *– strength*, zu Kräften kommen; *– together*, versammeln; *– o.s. together*, sich zusammennehmen; *– up*, aufsammeln, zusammennehmen, auflesen; (*Naut.*) *– way*, in Fahrt kommen (*also fig.*); 2. (*fig.*) schließen, folgern (*from*, aus); 3. gewinnen, erwerben, einziehen (*information etc.*); 4. (*Dressm.*) zusammenziehen, raffen, (an)krausen, in Falten legen, aufreihen. **2.** *v.i.* 1. sich (ver)sammeln, sich ansammeln, sich häufen, zusammenkommen, sich zusammenziehen; 2. sich vergrößern, größer werden, anwachsen, ansteigen; *– to a head*, (*Med.*) eitern, reifen, (*fig.*) zur Reife kommen. **3.** *s.* die Falte.

gathering ['gæðəriŋ], *s.* 1. das (Ver)sammeln; die Versammlung; (Menschen)ansammlung; 2. (*Dressm.*) das Kräuseln, Aufreihen; 3. (*Med.*) Eitern, Geschwür; (*Bookb.*) die Lage.

gatling gun ['gætliŋ], *s.* das Revolvergeschütz.

gauche [gouʃ], *adj.* linkisch, taktlos. **gaucheness, gaucherie** [–əri], *s.* die Ungeschicklichkeit, Taktlosigkeit.

gaud [gɔ:d], *s.* der Putz, Schmuck, Tand, Flitter, Prunk, Pomp. **gaudiness,** *s.* geschmackloser Putz, prunkhafte Aufmachung, der Flitterstaat. **gaudy,** *adj.* prunkhaft, aufgeputzt; bunt, grell.

gauge [geidʒ], **1.** *v.t.* abmessen; (ab)eichen, justieren; (*fig.*) (ab)schätzen, beurteilen, taxieren (*by*, nach). **2.** *s.* 1. das (Normal)maß, Eichmaß; (*Railw.*) die Spurweite; (*of stockings*) das Maschenzahlmaß; *broad –*, die Breitspur; *narrow –*, die Schmalspur; *standard –*, die Normalspur, Regelspur; (*Naut.*) *have the weather –*, zu Luv liegen; 2. der Messer, (An)zeiger, das Meßgerät, die Lehre; (*fig.*) der Maßstab; *oil –*, der Ölstandzeiger; *pressure –*, das Manometer, der Druckmesser, die Drucklehre; *rain –*, der Niederschlagsmesser; *wind –*, das Windmeßgerät, der Windstärkenmesser. **gauger,** *s.* der Eichmeister. **gauging-rod,** *s.* das Eichmaß, der Eichstab.

gault [gɔ:lt], *s.* (*Geol.*) der Flammenmergel, Gault.

gaunt [gɔ:nt], *adj.* mager, hager, dürr.

[1]**gauntlet** ['gɔ:ntlit], *s.* der (Stulpen)handschuh, Panzerhandschuh, Fechthandschuh, Reithandschuh; (*fig.*) Fehdehandschuh; *throw down the –*, den Fehdehandschuh hinwerfen; *take up the –*, den Fehdehandschuh aufnehmen.

[2]**gauntlet,** *s. run the –*, Spießruten laufen.

gauntry ['gɔ:ntri], *see* **gantry.**

gauze [gɔ:z], *s.* die Gaze, der Flor; Schleier; *wire –*, das Drahtgewebe. **gauzy,** *adj.* gazeartig, florartig.

gave [geiv], *imperf. of* **give.**

gavel [gævl], *s.* der Hammer (*of an auctioneer*).

gavotte [gə'vɔt], *s.* (*Mus.*) die Gavotte.

gawk [gɔ:k], *s.* der Tölpel; Einfaltspinsel. **gawkiness,** *s.* die Ungeschicklichkeit, Tölpelhaftigkeit. **gawky,** *adj.* tölpelhaft, linkisch, schlaksig.

gawp [gɔ:p], *v.i.* (*sl.*) gaffen, glotzen.

gay [gei], *adj.* 1. heiter, lustig, fröhlich (*of a p.*), bunt, lebhaft, glänzend, strahlend (*as colours*); (*coll.*) vergnügungssüchtig, lebenslustig, flott; ausschweifend, liederlich; 2. (*sl.*) warm, (*pred. only*) homo. **gayness,** *s. See* **gaiety.**

gaze [geiz], **1.** *v.i.* starren (*at*, (*up*)*on*, auf (*Acc.*)); *– at*, anblicken, anstarren. **2.** *s.* fester *or* starrer Blick; das Anstarren.

gazebo [gæ'zi:bou], *s.* der Aussichtsturm, Aussichtspunkt.

gazelle [gə'zel], *s.* (*Zool.*) die Gazelle.

gazette [gə'zet], **1.** *s.* das Amtsblatt, der Staatsanzeiger; die Zeitung. **2.** *v.t.* amtlich bekanntgeben; *he has been –d captain*, seine Ernennung zum Hauptmann ist im Amtsblatt bekanntgegeben.

gazetteer [gæzə'tiə], *s.* geographisches Lexikon, das Ortslexikon.

gear [giə], **1.** *s.* 1. (*Tech.*) das Getriebe, Zahnrad, Triebwerk; (*Motor.*) der Gang, (*Cycl.*) die Übersetzung; *bevel –*, das Kegelrad; *change –*, schalten; *change into bottom –*, den ersten Gang einschalten; *differential –*, das Ausgleichsgetriebe; *high-speed –*, das Schnellganggetriebe, Schonganggetriebe; *be in –*, im Eingriff stehen (*with*, mit), eingreifen (in (*Acc.*)) (*of wheels*), (*Motor.*) eingerückt sein; *low –*, (*Motor.*) erster Gang, (*Cycl.*) kleine Übersetzung; *put in –*, einschalten; *spur –*, das Stirnrad; *out of –*, im Leerlauf, außer Eingriff, ausgerückt; (*fig.*) *throw out of –*, in Unordnung bringen, stören; *transmission –*, das Übersetzungsgetriebe; 2. (*Naut.*) das Seezeug, Gerät, Geschirr; (*harness*) (Pferde)geschirr, Sielenzeug; (*coll.*) Zeug. **2.** *v.t.* mit Getriebe versehen; (*fig.*) anpassen, angleichen (*to*, *Dat. or* an (*Acc.*)), einstellen (auf (*Acc.*)); *– down*, untersetzen; *– up*, übersetzen. **3.** *v.i.* ineinandergreifen; (*fig.*) *– with*, zusammenpassen zu.

gear|box, *s.* (*Motor.*) das Getriebe(gehäuse). **-case,** *s.* (*Cycl.*) der Kettenschützer. **--change,** *s.* die Gangschaltung. **gearing,** *s.* (*Tech.*) die Verzahnung, das Triebwerk, Getriebe; (*Cycl.*) die Übersetzung. **gear|-lever,** *s.* die Gangschaltung, der Schalthebel. **– ratio,** *s.* die Übersetzung, das Übersetzungsverhältnis. **--shift,** *s. See* **--lever. -wheel,** *s.* das Zahnrad, Getrieberad.

gee! [dʒi:], *int.* (*coll.*) Donnerwetter! nanu! *– ho!* or *– up!* hott! hottehü! **gee-gee,** *s.* (*nursery talk*) das Hottehü.

geese, *pl. of* **goose.**

geezer ['gi:zə], *s.* (*sl.*) alter Tropf.

Geiger counter ['gaigə], *s.* der Geigerzähler.

gel [dʒel], *v.i.* gel(atin)ieren. **gelatin(e)** ['dʒeləti:n], *s.* (tierische) Gallerte, das Gallert. **gelatinize** [dʒə'lætinaiz], **1.** *v.t.* gel(atin)ieren lassen. **2.** *v.i.* gel(atin)ieren. **gelatinous** [–'lætinəs], *adj.* gallertartig.

geld [geld], *reg. & irr.v.t.* verschneiden, kastrieren. **gelding,** *s.* das Verschneiden; der Wallach, Schnittling.

gelid ['dʒelid], *adj.* eiskalt. **gelidity** [dʒə'liditi], *s.* die Eis(es)kälte.

gelignite ['dʒelignait], *s.* das Gelatinedynamit.

gem [dʒem], **1.** *s.* der Edelstein; die Gemme; (*fig.*) Perle, das Juwel, Prachtstück, Glanzstück. **2.** *v.t.* mit Edelsteinen besetzen.

geminate, 1. ['dʒemineit], *v.t.* (*v.i.* sich) verdoppeln. **2.** [–nit], *adj.* gepaart, verdoppelt, Doppel–, Zwillings–. **gemination** [–'neiʃən], *s.* die Verdoppelung, Gemination; (*Gram.*) Konsonantenverdoppelung. **Gemini** ['dʒeminai], *pl.* (*Astr.*) die Zwillinge, Kastor und Pollux.

gemma ['dʒemə], *s.* (*pl.* **-mae** [–mai]) (*Bot.*) die Blattknospe, Gemme. **gemmate** [–eit], *adj.* knospentragend, knospentreibend. **gemmation** [–'meiʃən], *s.* die Knospenbildung, Knospung. **gemmiferous** [–'mifərəs], **gemmiparous** [–'mipərəs], *adj. See* **gemmate.**

gen [dʒen], *s.* (*sl.*) die Auskunft, Anweisungen (*pl.*).

gendarme ['ʒɔndɑ:m], *s.* der Landjäger, Gendarm.

gender ['dʒendə], *s.* (*Gram.*) das Geschlecht, Genus.

gene [dʒi:n], *s.* (*Biol.*) das Gen, die Erbeinheit.

genealogical [dʒi:niə'lɔdʒikl], *adj.* genealogisch,

Abstammungs–, Stamm–; – *tree,* der Stammbaum. **genealogist** [–'ælədʒist], *s.* der Genealoge. **genealogize** [–'ælədʒaiz], *v.i.* Ahnenforschung (be)treiben. **genealogy** [–'ælədʒi], *s.* die Geschlechterforschung, Familienforschung, Genealogie; der Stammbaum; die Abstammung, Geschlechterfolge.

general ['dʒenərəl], **1.** *adj.* 1. allgemein, gemeinsam, gemeinschaftlich, Gemeinschafts–; allgemein verbreitet *or* gebräuchlich, üblich, durchgängig; allumfassend, uneingeschränkt, unbegrenzt; unbestimmt, vage, unspezifisch, annähernd, ungefähr; – ***approbation,*** ungeteilter Beifall; – ***cargo,*** gemischte Fracht, das Stückgut; – ***dealer,*** der Krämer, Gemischtwarenhändler; – ***education,*** unspezialisierte Erziehung; – ***election,*** allgemeine Wahlen (*pl.*); – ***hospital,*** allgemeines Krankenhaus; – ***idea,*** ungefähre Vorstellung; ***in*** –, im allgemeinen; ***of*** – ***interest,*** von allgemeinem Interesse; ***have a*** – ***invitation,*** ein für allemal eingeladen sein; – ***practice,*** übliches Verfahren; – ***practitioner,*** praktischer Arzt; – ***readers,*** das große Lesepublikum; ***as a*** – ***rule,*** in den meisten Fällen, meistens, üblicherweise; – ***servant,*** das Mädchen für alles; – ***store,*** die Gemischtwarenhandlung; ***in*** – ***terms,*** im großen und ganzen, ganz im allgemeinen; 2. Haupt–, General–; ***governor*** –, der Generalgouverneur; ***General Headquarters,*** Großes Hauptquartier; – ***manager,*** der Generaldirektor; ***General Post Office,*** das Hauptpostamt; ***General Staff,*** der Generalstab. **2.** *s.* 1. (*rare*) das Allgemeine, die Allgemeinheit; ***caviare to the*** –, Kaviar fürs Volk; 2. (*Mil.*) der General, (*fig.*) Feldherr; 3. (*Eccl.*) Obere(r), das Ordensoberhaupt; 4. (*coll.*) *see* – ***servant.***

generalissimo [dʒenərə'lisimou], *s.* der Oberbefehlshaber, oberster Heerführer, der Generalissimus. **generality** [–'ræliti], *s.* 1. (*oft. pl. constr.*) die Allgemeinheit, Mehrzahl, größter Teil; 2. (*only sing.*) die Unbestimmtheit, Vagheit; (*also pl. constr.*) allgemeine Äußerung; allgemeines Prinzip, die Regel; ***speak in generalities,*** sich in allgemeinen Äußerungen ergehen. **generalization** [–lai'zeiʃən], *s.* die Verallgemeinerung. **generalize** ['dʒenərəlaiz], **1.** *v.i.* allgemeine Schlüsse ziehen, allgemeine Äußerungen machen, Verallgemeinerungen anstellen, allgemein werden. **2.** *v.t.* allgemein anwenden, verallgemeinern; (*Phil.*) generalisieren, induzieren, Allgemeines ableiten aus. **generally,** *adv.* (*coll.*) meistens, in den meisten Fällen, gewöhnlich; – ***speaking,*** im allgemeinen, im großen und ganzen, im Grunde genommen. **generalship,** *s.* der Generalsrang, die Feldherrnwürde; Feldherrnkunst, Kriegführung; (*fig.*) Strategie, Führung, Leitung.

generate ['dʒenəreit], *v.t.* erzeugen, hervorbringen, entwickeln; (*Biol.*) zeugen; (*Math.*) bilden, erzeugen; (*fig.*) verursachen, hervorrufen, bewirken. **generating,** *adj.* erzeugend; – ***plant,*** die Stromerzeugungsanlage; – ***station,*** das Kraftwerk, Elektrizitätswerk. **generation** [–'reiʃən], *s.* 1. die Generation, das Menschenalter; ***people of one's (own)*** –, die Altersgenossen; ***rising*** –, heranwachsende Generation; 2. die Erzeugung, Hervorbringung, Entwicklung; (*Biol.*) Zeugung, Fortpflanzung. **generative** [–rətiv], *adj.* zeugend, Zeugungs–, Fortpflanzungs–, generativ, fruchtbar; – ***power,*** die Zeugungskraft. **generator,** *s.* (*Elec.*) der Stromerzeuger, die Dynamomaschine; (*Math.*) Erzeugende; (*Mus.*) der Grundton; (*Tech.*) Generator, Entwickler; (*Biol.*) (Er)zeuger; (*Am., Motor.*) *see* **dynamo**; – ***gas,*** das Verbrauchergas.

generic [dʒə'nerik], *adj.* generisch, Gattungs–; generell, typisch; – ***name,*** die Gattungsname.

generosity [dʒenə'rɔsiti], *s.* der Edelmut, die Großmut; Großzügigkeit, Freigebigkeit. **generous** ['dʒenərəs], *adj.* edelmütig, großmütig, großzügig, freigebig; üppig, ausgiebig, reichlich; (*as wine*) gehaltvoll, vollmundig.

genesis ['dʒenisis], *s.* die Genese, Entstehung, das Werden; der Ursprung, die Herkunft; (*B.*) ***Genesis,*** erstes Buch Mosis.

genet ['dʒenit], *s.* (*Zool.*) die Genette, Ginsterkatze.

genetic [dʒə'netik], *adj.* genetisch, Entstehungs–, Entwicklungs–, entwicklungsgeschichtlich, Erb–. **genetics,** *pl.* (*sing. constr.*) die Erblehre, Vererbungslehre, Genetik.

Geneva [dʒə'ni:və], *s.* Genf (*n.*); – ***Convention,*** Genfer Konvention. **Genevese** [dʒenə'vi:z], **1.** *adj.* Genfer–. **2.** *s.* der (die) Genfer(in).

genial ['dʒi:niəl], *adj.* (*of a p.*) freundlich, herzlich, heiter, munter, lustig; belebend, anregend; (*of climate*) mild, warm; (*obs.*) genial, Genie–. **geniality** [–'æliti], *s.* die Freundlichkeit, Herzlichkeit; (*of climate*) Wärme, Milde.

genital ['dʒenitl], *adj.* Zeugungs–, Geschlechts–. **genitals,** *pl.* Genitalien, Geschlechtsteile (*pl.*).

genitival [dʒeni'taivl], *adj.* genitivisch, Genitiv–. **genitive** ['dʒenitiv], *s.* der Genitiv, Wesfall.

genius ['dʒi:niəs], *s.* 1. (*pl.* **-es**) genialer Mensch, das Genie; 2. (*no pl.*) (*of a p.*) die (Natur)anlage, (natürliche) Begabung, geniale *or* schöpferische Kraft, die Genialität, das Geniale; (*of an age, nation etc.*) eigener Charakter, das Charakteristische, die Eigentümlichkeit, (innewohnender) Geist, der Genius; ***man of*** –, *see* 1; ***his*** – ***does not lie in that direction,*** dazu hat er keine Anlage; – ***of the age,*** der Zeitgeist; 3. (*pl.* **genii** [–iai]) Genius, Schutzgeist, Dämon; ***evil*** –, böser Genius; ***good*** –, der Schutzgeist.

Genoa ['dʒenouə], *s.* Genua (*n.*).

genocide ['dʒenəsaid], *s.* der Völkermord, Rassenmord.

Genoese [dʒeno'i:z], **1.** *adj.* genuesisch, Genueser–. **2.** *s.* der (die) Genueser(in).

genre [ʒɑ̃r], *s.* das Genre, die Gattung, Art, Form, der Stil; – ***painting,*** die Genremalerei.

gent [dʒent], *s.* (*coll.*) feiner Herr. **genteel** [–'ti:l], *adj.* vornehm, elegant, fein; vornehmtuend, affektiert. **genteelness,** *s.* die Vornehmheit, Eleganz; Vornehmtuerei.

gentian ['dʒenʃən], *s.* (*Bot.*) der Enzian; ***yellow*** –, die Bitterwurz.

gentile ['dʒentail], **1.** *s.* der Heide (die Heidin); der Nichtjude (die Nichtjüdin). **2.** *adj.* heidnisch; nichtjüdisch.

gentility [dʒen'tiliti], *s.* die Vornehmheit, feine Lebensart; *see also* **genteelness.**

gentle [dʒentl], *adj.* sanft, mild, zart, leicht, lind, weich, leise, (*of horse etc.*) fromm; ***of*** – ***birth*** or ***blood,*** von vornehmer Herkunft; – ***reader!*** geneigter Leser! – ***sex,*** zartes Geschlecht; – ***slope,*** leichter Abhang. **gentlefolk(s),** *pl.* vornehme Leute.

gentleman ['dʒentlmən], *s.* der Herr; Mann von Stand, vornehmer *or* gesellschaftsfähiger Mann, der Ehrenmann; –***-at-arms,*** der Leibgardist; – ***of the bedchamber,*** königlicher Kammerjunker; ***country*** –, der Landedelmann; ***fine*** –, feiner Herr; – ***of private means,*** (wohlhabender) Rentner; –***'s agreement,*** stillschweigendes Übereinkommen, die Vereinbarung auf Treu und Glauben; –***'s*** –, der (Kammer)diener; ***gentlemen!*** meine Herren! ***too much of a*** – ***to (do etc.),*** zu sehr Ehrenmann als daß . . .; ***he is no*** –, er hat keine Lebensart.

gentleman|-driver, *s.* (*Motor.*) der Herrenfahrer. **–-farmer,** *s.* der Gutsbesitzer und Landwirt. **–like,** *adj. See* **gentlemanly. gentlemanliness,** *s.* die Vornehmheit, feine Lebensart, vornehme Art *or* Haltung, die Bildung. **gentlemanly,** *adj.* vornehm, fein, ehrenhaft; gebildet, wohlgesittet. **gentleman-rider,** *s.* der Herrenreiter.

gentleness ['dʒentlnis], *s.* die Milde, Güte, Sanftheit, Sanftmut, Zartheit.

gentlewoman ['dʒentlwumən], *s.* vornehme Dame, die Dame von Stand.

gently ['dʒentli], *adv. See* **gentle**; – ***does it!*** sachte!

gentry ['dʒentri], *s.* niederer Adel, der Landadel, besitzende Stände (*pl.*); (*coll.*) Leute (*pl.*), die Sippschaft, Gesellschaft; (*coll.*) ***long-fingered*** –, Langfinger (*pl.*), (Taschen)diebe (*pl.*).

genuflect ['dʒenjuflekt], *v.i.* (*esp. Eccl.*) die Knie beugen. **genuflection, genuflexion** [–'flekʃən], *s.* die Kniebeugung.

genuine ['dʒenjuin], *adj.* echt, wahr, wirklich; echt, unverfälscht; (*of a p.*) aufrichtig, lauter. **genuineness,** *s.* die Echtheit, Wahrheit; Unverfälschtheit.

genus ['dʒi:nəs], *s.* (*pl.* **genera** ['dʒenərə]) die Gattung; (*fig.*) Art, Sorte, Klasse.

geocentric [dʒio'sentrik], *adj.* geozentrisch.

geode ['dʒi:oud], *s.* die Druse, der Adlerstein.

geodesic(al) [dʒiə'di:sik(l)], *adj. See* **geodetic(al). geodesy** [–'ɔdisi], *s.* die Geodäsie, Erdmessung. **geodetic(al)** [–'detik(l)], *adj.* geodätisch. **geognosy** [–'ɔgnəsi], *s.* die Erdschichtenkunde, Geologie.

geographer [dʒi'ɔgrəfə], *s.* der Geograph. **geographic(al)** [dʒiə'græfik(l)], *adj.* geographisch. **geography,** *s.* die Erdkunde, Geographie; Erdbeschreibung.

geologic(al) [dʒiə'lɔdʒik(l)], *adj.* geologisch. **geologist** [–'ɔlədʒist], *s.* der Geologe. **geology** [–'ɔlədʒi], *s.* die Geologie.

geomancer ['dʒiomænsə], *s.* der Erdwahrsager. **geomancy,** *s.* die Erdwahrsagung.

geometer [dʒi'ɔmitə], *s.* 1. (*obs.*) der Mathematiker; 2. (*Ent.*) die Spannerraupe. **geometric(al)** [dʒiə'metrik(l)], *adj.* geometrisch. **geometry,** *s.* die Geometrie, Raumlehre; ***plane* –,** die Geometrie der Ebene, Planimetrie; ***solid* –,** die Stereometrie; **– *set*,** das Reißzeug.

geophysical [dʒio'fizikl], *adj.* geophysikalisch. **geophysics,** *pl.* (*sing. constr.*) die Geophysik.

George [dʒɔ:dʒ], *s.* Georg (*m.*).

georgette [dʒɔ:'dʒet], *s.* der Seidenkrepp.

Georgia ['dʒɔ:dʒə], *s.* 1. (*U.S.S.R.*) Georgien (*n.*); 2. (*U.S.A.*) Georgia (*n.*). **Georgian, 1.** *adj.* 1. (*Hist.*) georgianisch; 2. (*U.S.S.R.*) georgi(ni)sch; 3. (*U.S.A.*) georginisch. **2.** *s.* 1. (*U.S.S.R.*) der (die) Georgier(in); (*language*) das Georgisch(e); 2. (*Hist.*) der (die) Georgianer(in).

geranium [dʒə'reiniəm], *s.* (*Bot.*) der Storchschnabel, die Geranie.

gerfalcon ['dʒə:fɔ:(l)kn], *s.* (*Orn.*) der G(i)erfalke (*Falco rusticolus*).

geriatrician [dʒeriə'triʃən], *s.* der Facharzt für Greisenkrankheiten. **geriatrics** [–'ætriks], *pl.* (*sing. constr.*) die Geriatrie, Lehre (und Forschung) von Alterskrankheiten.

germ [dʒə:m], *s.* der Keim, die Bazille, Bakterie; (*fig.*) der Keim, Ansatz, Ursprung; **– *carrier*,** der Bazillenträger; **– *warfare*,** der Bakterienkrieg.

german ['dʒə:mən], *adj.* (*following noun*) lieblich, ersten Grades.

German, 1. *s.* 1. Deutsche(r); ***the* –*s*,** die Deutschen; 2. (*language*) das Deutsch(e); ***he speaks* – *well*,** er spricht gut Deutsch. **2.** *adj.* deutsch; **– *clock*,** die Schwarzwalduhr; **– *Confederation*,** Deutscher Bund (1815–66); **– *measles*,** Röteln (*pl.*); **– *Ocean*,** die Nordsee; **– *silver*,** das Neusilber; **– *steel*,** der Schmelzstahl; **– *tinder*,** der Zündschwamm; **– *toys*,** Nürnberger Spielsachen (*pl.*); **– *type*,** die Frakturschrift.

germane [dʒə:'mein], *adj.* gehörig, passend (*to*, zu), angemessen (*Dat.*); einschlägig, betreffend.

Germanic [dʒə'mænik], **1.** *adj.* germanisch. **2.** *s.* (*language*) das Germanische. **Germanism** ['dʒə:mənizm], *s.* der Germanismus, deutsche Spracheigenheit. **Germanophile** [–'mænofail], **1.** *adj.* deutschfreundlich. **2.** *s.* Deutschfreundliche(r). **Germanophobe** [–'mænofoub], *s.* der Deutschenhasser. **Germanophobia** [–'foubiə], *s.* der Deutschenhaß. **Germany** ['dʒə:məni], *s.* Deutschland (*n.*).

germ-free, *adj.* keimfrei, steril. **germicidal** [dʒə:mi'saidl], *adj.* keimtötend. **germicide** ['dʒə:misaid], *s.* keimtötendes Mittel.

germinal ['dʒə:minl], *adj.* Keim–, Bakterien–; (*usu. fig.*) Anfangs–, unentwickelt. **germinant,** *adj.* keimend, sprossend. **germinate** [–neit], *v.i.* keimen, sprossen; (*fig.*) aufgehen, sich entwickeln.

germination [–'neiʃən], *s.* das Keimen, Sprossen, Sprießen.

gerontocracy [dʒerɔn'tɔkrəsi], *s.* die Greisenherrschaft.

gerrymander ['dʒerimændə], *v.t.* (*Pol. esp. Am.*) durch unlautere Mittel beeinflussen (*elections*); (*fig.*) (zum eigenen Vorteil) verdrehen, willkürlich zurechtmachen.

gerund ['dʒerənd], *s.* (*Gram.*) das Gerundium. **gerundial** [–'rʌndiəl], *adj.* Gerundial–. **gerundival** [–'daivl], *adj.* gerundivisch, Gerundiv–. **gerundive** [–'rʌndiv], *s.* das Gerundiv(um).

gestate [dʒes'teit], *v.i.* (*Med.*) (im Mutterleib) tragen. **gestation** [–'teiʃən], *s.* die Schwangerschaft, (*of beasts*) Trächtigkeit.

gesticulate [dʒes'tikjuleit], *v.i.* sich lebhaft bewegen, gestikulieren, (*coll.*) (mit den Händen) herumfuchteln. **gesticulation** [–'leiʃən], *s.* das Gebärdenspiel. **gesticulative** [–lətiv], **gesticulatory** [–lətəri], *adj.* gebärdenhaft, gestikulierend. **gesture** ['dʒestʃə], **1.** *s.* die Gebärde, (*usu. fig.*) Geste; das Gebärdenspiel. **2.** *v.i. See* **gesticulate.**

get [get], **1.** *irr.v.t.* 1. erhalten, bekommen, (*coll.*) kriegen; gewinnen, erwerben, erzielen, erlangen, erringen, verdienen, sich (*Dat.*) aneignen *or* verschaffen; besorgen, verschaffen (*for, Dat.*); **– *it ready*,** es fertigmachen; 2. (*with inf.*) veranlassen, bewegen, dahin *or* dazu bringen; **– *him to come*,** ihn veranlassen zu kommen; **– *him to talk*,** ihn zum Sprechen bewegen *or* bringen; 3. (*with p.p.*) lassen; **– *one's hair cut*,** sich (*Dat.*) die Haare schneiden lassen; **– *one's hands wet*,** die Hände naß machen; **– *you gone!*** mach dich fort! pack dich! 4. (*coll.*) müssen; (*coll.*) ***he has got to come*,** er muß kommen; 5. (*coll.*) (*perf. only*) haben; (*coll.*) ***he has got my pencil*,** er hat meinen Bleistift.

(a) (*with nouns*) **– *the better of him*,** ihn ausstechen *or* besiegen, die Oberhand über ihn gewinnen; (*sl.*) **– *the boot*,** den Laufpaß bekommen, fliegen; **– *the dinner* (*ready*),** das Mittagessen fertigmachen *or* herrichten; **– *a glimpse of*,** nur flüchtig zu sehen bekommen; (*sl.*) **– *his goat*,** ihn auf die Palme bringen, ihn fuchtig machen; (*sl.*) **– *a big hand*,** reichen Beifall ernten; **– *the upper hand*,** die Oberhand gewinnen; **– *help*,** Hilfe holen; **– *hold of*,** zu fassen kriegen, erwischen; (*fig.*) **– *a hold on*** or ***over*,** in seine Macht *or* unter seinen Einfluß bekommen; **– *possession of*,** in Besitz nehmen, Besitz ergreifen von; (*coll.*) **– *the sack*,** an die Luft gesetzt werden; **– *a sight of*,** zu Gesicht bekommen; **– *the start of*,** zuvorkommen (*Dat.*); (*fig.*) **– *wind of*,** wittern, Wind bekommen von; (*sl.*) **– *the wind up*,** Angst *or* Bammel kriegen, Dampf bekommen; **– *the worst of it*** or ***of the bargain*,** den kürzeren ziehen; **– *a woman with child*,** eine Frau schwängern.

(b) (*with advs.*) (*coll.*) **– *across*,** verständlich machen, klarmachen; **– *away*,** wegbringen, fortschaffen; **– *back*,** zurückerhalten, wiederbekommen; **– *one's own back*,** sich rächen; **– *clear*,** klarwerden über (*Acc.*); **– *down*,** hinunterbringen, herunterholen, (*food*) hinunterschlucken; (*a p.*) auf die Nerven fallen (*Dat.*); **– *in*,** hineinbringen, hineintun, hineinschieben, (*money due*) eintreiben, (*crops*) einbringen; (*coll.*) **– *one's hand in*,** sich üben; ***hardly* – *a word in edgeways*,** kaum ein Wort anbringen *or* einwerfen können; **– *off*,** wegbringen, wegschaffen; (*clothes*) ausziehen, ablegen; losmachen, loskriegen (*lid etc.*), lernen (*a task*); **– *on*,** anziehen (*clothes*); (*coll.*) **– *a move on*,** sich beeilen; **– *out*,** herausbringen, herausholen; (*a book*) herausbringen, (*a secret*) herausbekommen; **– *over*,** hinter sich (*Dat.*) haben, ein Ende machen (*Dat.*); **– *through*,** durchbringen, durchbekommen; **– *through to him*,** ihm zum Bewußtsein bringen; **– *together*,** zusammenbringen, zusammenstellen; **– *up*,** veranstalten, einrichten, organisieren, zustandebringen, ins Werk setzen; zurechtmachen, herausputzen, aufbessern, ausstaffieren, (*book*) ausstatten, (*laundry*) waschen und bügeln, (*a rôle*) einstudieren, einpauken; (*coll.*) erfinden, konstruieren; (*coll.*) (*from sleep*) aufwecken; **– *steam up*** or **– *up steam*,** Dampf aufmachen, (*coll.*) in Schwung kommen; **– *the wind up*,** *see under* **(a).**

(c) (*coll. or sl. idiomatic usage*) ***you – me wrong,*** du verstehst mich falsch; ***he got it at last,*** endlich kapierte er (es); ***you'll – it hot, you'll – what's coming to you,*** du wirst dein Fett bekommen; ***I'll – you for it,*** ich werde dich schon packen; ***it –s me,*** es geht über meine Begriffe; ***come and – it!*** das Essen ist auf dem Tisch; ***– it into one's head,*** es sich (*Dat.*) in den Kopf setzen.
2. *irr.v.i.* 1. (an)kommen, gelangen, sich begeben (*to a place*); ***– home,*** nach Hause kommen, zu Hause ankommen; ***– as far as Mars,*** bis nach Mars gelangen; 2. (*with adj.*) werden; ***– better,*** besser werden; sich erholen; (*coll.*) ***– busy!*** mach dich an die Arbeit! (*coll.*) ***– clear,*** entwischen; ***– dressed,*** sich anziehen; ***– drunk,*** sich betrinken; ***– even with him,*** es ihm heimzahlen; ***– excited,*** sich aufregen *or* ereifern (***about, over,*** über (*Acc.*)); ***– married,*** (sich ver)heiraten; ***– ready,*** sich fertig machen; ***– rid of,*** loswerden; ***– tired,*** ermüden, müde werden; ***– used to,*** sich gewöhnen an (*Acc.*); 3. (*with inf. or pr. p.*) beginnen, dahin kommen, dazu übergehen.
(a) (*with advs.*) ***– about*** or ***around,*** unter die Leute kommen, (*as rumour etc.*) sich verbreiten; (*coll.*) ***– across,*** wirken, Wirkung *or* Erfolg haben, Eindruck machen, einschlagen, ankommen; ***– along,*** weiterkommen, vorwärtskommen, Fortschritte machen; ***– along well together,*** sich gut vertragen, miteinander gut auskommen; ***– along on £5 a week,*** mit 5 Pfd. in der Woche auskommen; ***– along!*** geh weiter! beeile dich! mach' dich fort! ***– along with you!*** red' doch keinen Unsinn! hör' doch auf! ***– away,*** entkommen, davonkommen; wegkommen; ***there's no getting away from it,*** davon kann man nicht loskommen; (*coll.*) ***– away with,*** Erfolg haben mit; ungestraft ausführen; (*coll.*) ***– away with it,*** ungestraft davonkommen; ***– back,*** zurückkommen; (*sl.*) ***– back at,*** abrechnen mit, sich rächen an (*Dat.*); ***– behind,*** zurückbleiben; ***– by,*** durchkommen, (*coll.*) sich durchschwindeln; ***– down,*** herunterkommen, heruntersteigen, (*from horse etc.*) absteigen; (*coll.*) ***– down to,*** sich (heran)machen an (*Acc.*); (*coll.*) ***– down to business*** or ***to brass tacks,*** zur S. kommen; ***– in,*** einsteigen (*a vehicle*), hineingehen, hineinkommen (*a building*), gewählt werden (*parliament*); (*coll.*) ***– in with,*** in (enge) Beziehungen treten zu, vertraut werden mit; ***– near,*** nahekommen (*Dat.*); ***– off,*** aussteigen, absteigen (*from a vehicle*); (*coll.*) aufbrechen, abreisen; davonkommen, entkommen; (*coll.*) freigesprochen werden (*as a culprit*); (*coll.*) einschlafen; (*sl.*) ***tell him where to – off,*** ihm die Leviten lesen; (*sl.*) ***– off with,*** anbändeln mit; (*coll.*) ***– off lightly*** or ***cheaply,*** mit einem blauen Auge davonkommen; ***– on,*** einsteigen (*a vehicle*); (*fig.*) vorwärtskommen, Fortschritte machen; ***– on!*** nur weiter! ***– on in the world,*** es zu etwas bringen; ***be getting on (in life),*** älter werden; ***be getting on for 60,*** sich den 60ern nähern, auf die 60er zugehen; ***– on well with him,*** sich gut mit ihm vertragen, mit ihm gut auskommen; ***– out,*** aussteigen (*from a vehicle*), hinauskommen (*from a building*); durchsickern (*as news etc.*); ***– out!*** mach' dich fort! (*sl.*) hör' auf! was für Unsinn! ***– over,*** hinüberkommen, herüberkommen; ***– round,*** sich dazu entschließen, endlich dazu kommen (*with inf.*); ***– through,*** durchkommen (*also in examinations*), das Ziel erreichen; (*Tele.*) verbunden werden, Anschluß bekommen; ***– through to him,*** bei ihm Anklang finden, bei ihm ankommen; ***– together,*** zusammenkommen, sich versammeln, (*fig.*) sich einigen, einig werden; ***– up,*** aufstehen (*from a chair, from bed*); (*of wind*) sich erheben, aufkommen, (*of sea*) stürmisch werden.
(b) (*with preps.*) ***– across the road,*** (quer) über die Straße gehen; ***– across the river,*** den Fluß überqueren; ***– at,*** erreichen, herankommen an (*Acc.*), (*fig.*) ermitteln, herausfinden (*facts*); (*sl.*) beeinflussen, bestechen; (*sl.*) aufs Korn nehmen, veräppeln; ***what are you getting at?*** worauf zielst du hin? ***are you getting at me?*** gilt mir diese Stichelei? ***– in(to),*** (hinein)kommen in (*Acc.*), (*coll.*) steigen in (*Acc.*) (*clothes*); ***– into debt,*** in Schulden geraten, Schulden machen; ***– into a habit,*** eine Gewohnheit annehmen; (*sl.*) ***what's got into him?*** was ist mit ihm los? ***– off,*** absteigen von (*horse etc.*), aussteigen aus (*vehicle*), heruntergehen von (*wall etc.*), weggehen von (*lawn etc.*); ***– on,*** aufsteigen auf (*Acc.*) (*horse etc.*), einsteigen in (*Acc.*) (*vehicle*), sich stellen auf (*Acc.*); ***– on one's feet,*** sich erheben; ***– out of,*** herauskommen *or* hinauskommen aus, heraussteigen aus; (*coll.*) sich davor drücken (***doing,*** zu tun); ***– out of bed on the wrong side,*** mit dem linken Fuß zuerst aufstehen; ***– out of one's depth,*** den Boden unter den Füßen verlieren (*also fig.*); ***– out of the habit of swearing,*** sich (*Dat.*) das Fluchen abgewöhnen; ***– out of hand,*** sich der Kontrolle entziehen; ***– over,*** steigen *or* klettern über (*Acc.*); (*fig.*) hinwegkommen über (*Acc.*), überwinden (*difficulties*), sich erholen von, überstehen (*loss, illness*); ***– round,*** (*fig.*) herumkommen um, umgehen (*difficulties*); (*coll.*) um den Bart gehen (*a p., Dat.*), herumkriegen; ***– through,*** kommen durch, gehen durch; bestehen (*examination*); fertig werden mit (*work*), verschwenden, vergeuden, verzetteln (*a fortune etc.*); ***– to,*** erreichen, kommen nach.

get|-at-able [-'ætəbl], *adj.* (*coll.*) erreichbar (*of a th.*), zugänglich (*of a p. or place*). **-away,** *s.* (*coll.*) das Entkommen; ***make one's –,*** auf und davon gehen, sich aus dem Staube machen. **--together,** *s.* (*coll.*) zwanglose Zusammenkunft, zwangloses Treffen. **--up,** *s.* (*coll.*) der Anzug, Putz, Staat, die Ausstaffierung; (*of a book etc.*) Aufmachung, Ausstattung, (*of a drama*) Inszenierung.

gewgaw ['gju:gɔ:], *s.* die Nichtigkeit, Lappalie; das Spielzeug, der Tand.

geyser ['gi:zə], *s.* 1. der Geiser, (heiße) Springquelle; 2. der Badeofen; Warmwasserapparat.

ghastliness ['gɑ:stlinis], *s.* gräßliches Aussehen, die Gräßlichkeit; Leichenblässe, Totenblässe. **ghastly,** *adj., adv.* geisterhaft, gespenstisch; totenblaß, leichenblaß, totenbleich; gräßlich, grausig, schauderhaft; (*coll.*) entsetzlich, furchtbar, haarsträubend.

gherkin ['gə:kin], *s.* die Pfeffergurke, Essiggurke.

ghetto ['getou], *s.* das Getto, Judenviertel.

ghost [goust], *s.* 1. der Geist, das Gespenst, die Spuk; ***give up the –,*** den Geist aufgeben; ***Holy Ghost,*** Heiliger Geist; ***lay a –,*** einen Geist bannen; 2. (*fig.*) die Spur, der Anflug, Schatten; ***not a*** or ***the – of a chance,*** nicht die geringste Aussicht; 3. (*T.V.*) (*also* ***– image***) der Geist, das Geisterbild. **ghostlike, ghostly,** *adj.* gespenstisch, gespensterhaft, geisterhaft. **ghost|-story,** *s.* die Gespenstergeschichte, Geistergeschichte. **– town,** *s.* verlassene *or* entvölkerte Stadt. **– writer,** *s.* anonymer Verfertiger (*of speeches etc*).

ghoul [gu:l], *s.* leichenverzehrender Dämon, der Ghul. **ghoulish,** *adj.* ghulenhaft, leichenschänderisch; (*fig.*) greulich, grausig.

giant ['dʒaiənt], **1.** *s.* der Riese. **2.** *adj.* riesenhaft, riesig; ***– star,*** der Riesenstern. **giantess,** *s.* die Riesin.

gibber ['dʒibə], *v.i.* kauderwelsch sprechen. **gibberish,** *s.* das Geschnatter, Kauderwelsch.

gibbet ['dʒibit], **1.** *s.* der Galgen; Kranbalken (*of a crane*). **2.** *v.t.* (auf)hängen, henken.

gibbosity [gi'bɔsiti], *s.* die Wölbung; der Buckel, Höcker. **gibbous** ['gibəs], *adj.* gewölbt; buckelig; ***the – moon,*** der Mond zwischen Vollmond und Halbmond.

gibe [dʒaib], **1.** *s.* der Spott, die Stichelei. **2.** *v.i.* spotten (***at,*** über (*Acc.*)). **3.** *v.t.* verspotten, verhöhnen.

giblets ['dʒiblits], *pl.* das Gänseklein, Innereien (*pl.*).

giddiness ['gidinis], *s.* 1. der Schwindel, die Schwindeligkeit; 2. (*fig.*) Unbesonnenheit, der Leichtsinn; die Unbeständigkeit, Flatterhaftigkeit. **giddy,** *adj.* 1. (*pred.*) schwind(e)lig; taumelnd (***with,*** vor (*Dat.*)); ***I am*** or ***feel –,*** mir ist schwind(e)lig; 2. (*attrib.*) (*of a p.*) unbeständig; unbesonnen, leichtsinnig, leichtfertig, flatterhaft; (*height etc.*) schwindelnd, schwindelerregend; (*coll.*) albern, absurd.

gift [gift], **1.** *s.* 1. die Gabe, das Geschenk; das Geben, Schenken; die Schenkung, Zuwendung; ***deed of –***, die Schenkungsurkunde; ***make a – of***, schenken; (*coll.*) ***it's a –***, es ist geschenkt; ***I wouldn't have it as a –***, das nehme ich nicht geschenkt; 2. (*Law*) das Verleihungsrecht, Patronatsrecht; ***the living is in his –***, er hat die Pfründe zu verleihen *or* zu vergeben; 3. (*fig.*) die Gabe, Begabung, das Talent; (*coll.*) ***– of the gab***, ein tüchtiges Mundwerk; ***– of tongues***, die Sprachbegabung; (*B.*) das Zungenreden. **2.** *v.t.* beschenken. **gifted,** *adj.* begabt, talentiert. **gift-horse,** *s.* ***look a – in the mouth***, einem geschenkten Gaul ins Maul sehen.

gig [gig], *s.* 1. zweirädriger, offener Einspänner; 2. (*Naut.*) das Kommandantenboot; leichtes Ruderboot; 3. (*Tech.*) die Rauhmaschine; 4. (*sl.*) das Engagement.

gigantic [dʒai'gæntik], *adj.* riesenhaft, gigantisch; riesig, ungeheuer.

giggle [gigl], **1.** *v.i.* kichern. **2.** *s.* das Gekicher.

gigolo ['dʒigəlou], *s.* der Eintänzer.

[1]**gild** [gild], *irr.v.t.* vergolden; (*fig.*) zieren, schmücken, verschönern; beschönigen; ***– the pill***, die Pille versüßen.

[2]**gild,** *see* **guild.**

gilded ['gildid], *adj.* vergoldet, golden; (*fig.*) verschönt, beschönigt. **gilding,** *s.* die Vergoldung; Goldauflage; (*fig.*) Verschönerung, Beschönigung.

[1]**gill** [gil], *s.* (*usu. pl.*) (*Ichth.*) die Kieme; (*Orn.*) der Kehllappen; die Lamelle (*of mushrooms*); (*coll.*) das Doppelkinn; ***--slit***, die Kiemenspalte.

[2]**gill** [gil], *s.* (*dial.*) die Bergschlucht.

[3]**gill** [dʒil], *s.* die Viertelpinte (= *0.14 litre*, (*Am.*) = *0.12 litre*).

gillie ['gili], *s.* (*Scots*) der Jagdbegleiter, Bursche, Diener.

gillyflower ['dʒiliflauə], *s.* (*Bot.*) die Levkoje.

[1]**gilt** [gilt], *s.* junge Sau.

[2]**gilt, 1.** *See* [1]**gild. 2.** *adj.* vergoldet; (*Bookb.*) ***– edges***, der Goldschnitt. **3.** *s.* die Vergoldung; ***take the – off the gingerbread***, der S. den Reiz nehmen. **gilt-edged,** *adj.* mit Goldschnitt; (*coll.*) prima, erstklassig; (*Comm.*) ***– securities***, mündelsichere Papiere.

gimbals ['dʒimbəlz], *pl.* (*Naut.*) kardanische Aufhängung, Kardanringe (*pl.*).

gimcrack ['dʒimkræk], (*coll.*) **1.** *adj.* wertlos, nichtig. **2.** *s.* der Flitter, Tand, Plunder.

gimlet ['gimlit], *s.* der Handbohrer, Vorbohrer.

gimmick ['gimik], *s.* (*coll.*) der Kniff, Dreh. **gimmicky,** *adj.* (*sl.*) kniff(e)lig; knallig.

gimp [gimp], *s.* die Gimpe, Borte, Besatzschnur.

[1]**gin** [dʒin], *s.* der Wachholderschnaps, Genever; (*coll.*) ***– palace***, großaufgemachtes Wirtshaus, feudales Lokal.

[2]**gin, 1.** *s.* das Hebezeug, die Winde; (*Min.*) Fördermaschine, der Göpel; ***cotton--***, die Egreniermaschine. **2.** *v.t.* egrenieren, entkörnen (*cotton*).

[3]**gin, 1.** *s.* der Fallstrick, die Schlingenfalle. **2.** *v.t.* mit einer Schlinge fangen, verstricken.

ginger ['dʒindʒə], **1.** *s.* der Ingwer; (*colour*) das Rötlichgelb, Gelblichbraun; (*sl.*) der Rotkopf; (*fig.*) (*sl.*) der Mumm, Schneid. **2.** *v.t.* (*coll.*) ***– up***, anfeuern, aufpulvern, aufrütteln, auffrischen. **ginger| ale, – beer,** *s.* das Ingwerbier. **-bread,** *s.* der Pfefferkuchen, Lebkuchen.

gingerly ['dʒindʒəli], *adv.* behutsam, sachte; zimperlich.

gingersnap ['dʒindʒəsnæp], *s.* das Ingwerkeks. **gingery,** *adj.* Ingwer–; scharf gewürzt; rötlich.

gingham ['giŋəm], *s.* der Gingan(g).

gingivitis [dʒindʒi'vaitis], *s.* die Zahnfleischentzündung.

gippo ['dʒipou], *s.* (*sl.*) die Soße.

gipsy ['dʒipsi], **1.** *s.* der (die) Zigeuner(in); die Zigeunersprache. **2.** *adj.* zigeunerhaft, Zigeuner–. **gipsy|-moth,** *s.* (*Ent.*) der Schwammspinner. **--rose,** *s.* (*Bot.*) Wilde Skabiose. **--winch,** *s.* (*Naut.*) die Verholwinde, das Verholspill.

giraffe [dʒi'rɑ:f], *s.* die Giraffe.

girandole ['dʒirəndoul], *s.* (verzierter) Armleuchter; (*Firew.*) die Feuergarbe, das Feuerrad.

[1]**gird** [gə:d], *reg. & irr.v.t.* (*Poet.*) gürten (*dress etc.*); umgürten (*a p.*); (*fig. usu. pass.*) umgeben, umschließen; ***– o.s. for the fray***, sich zur Schlacht gürten (*also fig.*); (*fig.*) ***– up one's loins***, sich rüsten; ***– on***, umgürten, umlegen, anlegen (*sword etc.*).

[2]**gird, 1.** *v.i.* (*obs.*) sticheln, spotten, schmähen (***at***, über (*Acc.*)). **2.** *s.* (*obs.*) der Spott, die Stichelei.

girder ['gə:də], *s.* der Träger, (Trag)balken, Tragbaum, die Stütze; (*Av.*) der Holm.

[1]**girdle** [gə:dl], **1.** *s.* der Gürtel, Gurt; (*esp. Am.*) Hüfthalter; (*fig.*) Ring, Umfang; die Einfassung (*of a gem*). **2.** *v.t.* umgürten, umgeben, einschließen; ringeln (*trees*).

[2]**girdle,** *s.* (*dial. esp. Scots*) das Röstblech; ***– cake*** der Röstkuchen.

girl [gə:l], *s.* das Mädchen; (*coll.*) Mädel; Dienstmädchen; (*coll.*) die Liebste, der Schatz; ***shop –***, das Ladenmädchen. **girl guide,** *s.* die Pfadfinderin. **girlhood,** *s.* Mädchenjahre (*pl.*), die Mädchenzeit; Mädchenhaftigkeit. **girlish,** *adj.* mädchenhaft. **girlishness,** *s.* die Mädchenhaftigkeit, das Mädchenhafte. **girl| scout,** *s.* (*Am.*) *see* **– guide.**

girt [gə:t], *imperf., p.p. of* **gird.**

girth [gə:θ], **1.** *s.* der Sattel(gurt); (*fig.*) Umfang; ***in –***, an Umfang. **2.** *v.t.* gürten (*a horse*); (*also* ***– up***) festschnallen, aufschnallen (*a saddle*).

gist [dʒist], *s.* der Hauptpunkt, Hauptinhalt, Kern, das Wesentliche.

give [giv], **1.** *irr.v.t.* geben (***him s.th.*** or ***s.th. to him***, ihm etwas); übergeben, überreichen, überlassen, übertragen, übermitteln; hergeben, opfern; schenken, verleihen, erteilen; zuteilen, zuweisen, zuschreiben; gewähren, (ver)gönnen, angedeihen lassen; (*a song etc.*) vortragen, zum besten geben, (*a groan, sigh etc.*) von sich geben, (*medicine*) eingeben, verabreichen, (*the sacrament*) spenden, austeilen, (*a blow*) versetzen, (*a prize*) zuerkennen, zusprechen, verteilen.

(a) (*with nouns*) ***– attention to***, achtgeben auf (*Acc.*); ***– battle***, es zu einer Schlacht kommen lassen (***to***, mit); ***– a wide berth***, (*Naut.*) weit abhalten, gut frei halten (***to***, von); (*fig.*) aus dem Weg gehen (*Dat.*), einen Bogen machen (um); ***– birth to***, gebären, zur Welt bringen; (*fig.*) hervorbringen, entstehen lassen, Veranlassung geben zu; (*sl.*) ***– him the boot***, ihn hinausschmeißen; ***– the bridle to***, die Zügel schießen lassen (*Dat.*); ***– chase to***, nachjagen (*Dat.*), verfolgen; ***– credit to***, Glauben schenken *or* beimessen (*Dat.*); ***– a cry***, aufschreien; ***– the details***, die Einzelheiten angeben; ***– him his due***, ihm Gerechtigkeit widerfahren lassen, ihm das Seinige zukommen lassen; ***– ear to***, Gehör schenken (*Dat.*), anhören; ***– effect to***, in Kraft treten lassen, Kraft verleihen (*Dat.*); ***– ground***, nachgeben, zurückweichen, sich zurückziehen; (*coll.*) ***– a hand***, mithelfen, mit anpacken; ***– him one's hand***, ihm die Hand geben *or* reichen; ***– heed to***, Beachtung schenken (*Dat.*), beachten; ***– help***, Hilfe leisten *or* gewähren (***to***, *Dat.*); ***– judgement***, ein Urteil abgeben *or* fällen *or* sprechen; ***– a jump***, aufspringen; ***– a knock***, anklopfen; ***– a laugh***, auflachen; ***– lectures***, Vorlesungen halten (***on***, über (*Acc.*)); ***– lessons***, Unterricht erteilen; ***– him the lie***, ihm Lügen strafen; ***– the lie to s.th.***, etwas als unwahr erweisen; ***– one's life***, sein Leben widmen *or* opfern *or* (hin)geben (***for***, *Dat.*); (*coll.*) ***– him a lift***, ihn (im Auto) mitnehmen, ihn mitfahren lassen; ***– him a look***, ihm einen Blick zuwerfen, ihn anblicken; ***– one's mind to***, sich befleißigen (*Gen.*), sich widmen (*Dat.*); ***– one's name***, seinen Namen nennen; ***– notice of***, anmelden; ***– him notice***, ihn kündigen; ***– him notice of***, ihn benachrichtigen von, ihm ankündigen *or* berichten (*Acc.*); ***– offence***, Anstoß *or* Ärgernis erregen (***to***, bei); ***– pain***, weh tun; ***– him***

a piece of one's mind, ihm ordentlich die Meinung sagen; – ***place,*** Platz machen (***to,*** für *or Dat.*), ersetzt werden (von); – ***pleasure,*** Vergnügen bereiten, Spaß *or* Freude machen (***to,*** *Dat.*); – ***point to,*** Gewicht *or* Nachdruck verleihen (*Dat.*); – ***one's reasons,*** seine Gründe angeben; – ***him my kindest regards!*** bestellen Sie ihm herzliche Grüße von mir! ich lasse ihn herzlich grüßen; (*fig.*) – (***free***) ***rein to,*** freien Lauf lassen (*Dat.*), freies Spiel geben (*Dat.*), die Zügel schießen lassen (*Dat.*); – ***rise to,*** veranlassen, verursachen, herbeiführen, hervorrufen, bewirken, aufkommen lassen, Anlaß geben zu; (*sl.*) – ***him the sack,*** ihn an die Luft setzen, ihn fliegen lassen; (*coll.*) – ***him the slip,*** ihm entkommen; – ***a start,*** zusammenfahren; – ***tongue,*** (*of hounds*) Laut geben, anschlagen; (*fig.*) sich äußern; – ***a toast,*** einen Toast ausbringen; – ***trouble,*** Mühe machen; – ***vent to,*** freien Lauf lassen (*Dat.*); – ***voice to,*** Ausdruck verleihen (*Dat.*), äußern; – ***way,*** (*of a p.*) nachgeben, nachlassen, zurückweichen, sich zurückziehen; Platz machen (müssen), weichen (***to,*** *Dat.*); (*of a th.*) zusammenbrechen, einstürzen; – ***way to despair,*** sich der Verzweiflung hingehen; – ***one's word,*** sein Wort verpfänden.

(b) (*with advs.*) – ***away,*** hergeben, weggeben, verschenken; (*prizes*) verteilen, (*a bride*) übergeben; (*coll.*) verraten; – ***o.s. away,*** sich bloßstellen, sich (*Dat.*) eine Blöße geben; (*coll.*) – ***the show away,*** den ganzen Schwindel aufdecken, das Geheimnis verraten; – ***back,*** zurückgeben; – ***forth,*** von sich geben; – ***in,*** einreichen; – ***in one's name,*** sich eintragen *or* einschreiben lassen; – ***off,*** ausströmen, ausstrahlen, abgeben, von sich geben; – ***out,*** ausgeben, verteilen, austeilen; bekanntmachen, bekanntgeben, verkünden, ankündigen; *see also* – ***off***; – ***o.s. out to be,*** sich ausgeben für; – ***over,*** übergeben, überlassen (***to,*** *Dat.*); – ***o.s. over to,*** verfallen (*Dat.*), sich ergeben (*Dat.*); – ***up,*** aufgeben, preisgeben; abstehen von, verzichten auf (*Acc.*); – ***o.s. up,*** sich freiwillig stellen, sich ergeben; – ***o.s. up for lost,*** sich für verloren halten; – ***o.s. up to,*** sich hingeben (*Dat.*).

2. *irr.v.i.* 1. spenden (***to,*** *Dat.*); 2. nachgeben, nachlassen, weichen; (*of a p.*) versagen, schlapp werden; (*of a th.*) federn, elastisch sein; – ***in,*** sich geschlagen geben, klein beigeben; nachgeben (***to,*** *Dat.*), einwilligen (in (*Acc.*)); – ***out,*** ausgehen, versiegen, zu Ende gehen, zur Neige gehen; (*coll.*) – ***over,*** aufhören; – ***up,*** (es) aufgeben, nicht mehr weiter wollen, sich geschlagen geben; 3. sich anpassen (***to,*** *Dat. or* an (*Acc.*)); 4. (*of road, door etc.*) führen, (*as window*) hinausgehen (***into, on to,*** in *or* auf (*Acc.*)).

3. *s.* (*coll.*) das Nachgeben; die Biegsamkeit, Elastizität.

give-and-take, *s.* der *or* das Kompromiß, der Ausgleich; (Gedanken)austausch, (Meinungs)austausch.

given [givn], **1.** *p.p. of* **give. 2.** *adj.* 1. (*attrib.*) bestimmt, festgesetzt, festgelegt, (*also Math.*) gegeben; 2. (*pred.*) ergeben, geneigt, veranlagt (***to,*** *Dat.*); ***I am – to understand,*** man hat mir zu verstehen gegeben. **giver,** *s.* der Geber, Spender; (*Comm.*) Aussteller, Trassant.

gizzard [ˈgizəd], *s.* (*Orn.*) der Muskelmagen; (*coll.*) ***it sticks in my –,*** es ist mir zuwider; es liegt mir schwer im Magen.

glabrous [ˈgleibrəs], *adj.* kahl, glatt, unbehaart.

glacial [ˈgleiʃəl, ˈglæsiəl], *adj.* (*Geog.*) Eis–, Gletscher–; (*Geol.*) eiszeitlich, Eiszeit–; (*Chem.*) – ***acetic acid,*** die Eisessigsäure; – ***detritus,*** der Glazialschutt; – ***epoch,*** das Diluvium, (quartäre) Eiszeit. **glaciated** [–ʃieitid, –sieitid], *adj.* vereist, vergletschert. **glacier** [ˈglæsiə], *s.* der Gletscher.

glacis [ˈgleisis], *s.* (*Geol.*) flache Abdachung; (*Mil.*) das Glacis.

glad [glæd], *adj.* 1. (*pred.*) froh, erfreut (***of, at,*** über (*Acc.*)); ***be – of heart,*** frohen Herzens sein; ***I am – of it,*** ich freue mich darüber, das freut mich; ***I should be – to know,*** ich möchte gern wissen; ***I am – to see,*** es freut mich zu sehen, ich sehe gern, zu meiner Freude sehe ich; ***I am – to say,*** es freut mich sagen zu dürfen, zu meiner Freude kann ich sagen; 2. (*attrib.*) heiter, fröhlich, vergnügt; freudig, erfreulich, angenehm; (*sl.*) ***the – eye,*** verliebter *or* einladender Blick; (*sl.*) ***give him the – hand,*** ihm die Hand des Willkomms reichen; (*sl.*) – ***rags,*** die Sonntagskluft; – ***tidings,*** frohe Nachricht. **gladden,** *v.t.* erfreuen.

glade [gleid], *s.* die Lichtung, Schneise.

gladiator [ˈglædieitə], *s.* der Gladiator. **gladiatorial** [–əˈtɔ:riəl], *adj.* gladiatorisch; – ***fights,*** Gladiatorenkämpfe.

gladiola [glædiˈoulə], **gladiolus,** *s.* (*pl.* **-uses, -i** [–lai]) (*Bot.*) die Gladiole.

gladly [ˈglædli], *adv.* gern, mit Freuden. **gladness,** *s.* die Freude, Fröhlichkeit. **gladsome** [–səm], *adj.* (*Poet.*) freudig, fröhlich; erfreulich.

glair [glɛə], **1.** *s.* das Eiweiß. **2.** *v.t.* mit Eiweiß bestreichen.

glaive [gleiv], *s.* (*Poet.*) das (Breit)schwert.

glamor, (*Am.*) *see* **glamour.**

glamorize [ˈglæməraiz], *v.t.* anpreisen, verherrlichen. **glamorous,** *adj.* bezaubernd. **glamour** [–mə], *s.* der Zauber, das Blendwerk; bezaubernde Schönheit, bezaubernder Glanz; ***it casts a – over,*** es bezaubert, es schlägt . . . in seinen Bann; ***--girl,*** die Reklameschönheit.

[1]**glance** [glɑ:ns], **1.** *s.* 1. flüchtiger Blick; ***at a –, at*** (***the***) ***first –,*** auf den ersten Blick; ***take a – at,*** flüchtig ansehen; 2. das (Auf)leuchten, (Auf)blitzen, der Schimmer, Schein, Lichtstrahl; 3. das Abprallen; (*Crick. etc.*) der Streifschlag. **2.** *v.i.* flüchtig blicken (***at,*** auf (*Acc.*)); (auf)leuchten, (auf)blitzen; – ***aside,*** abprallen, abrutschen, abgleiten; – ***at,*** einen flüchtigen Blick werfen auf (*Acc.*), flüchtig anblicken; (*fig.*) anspielen auf (*Acc.*), streifen, kurz berühren; – ***off,*** abschwenken, abschweifen; *see also* – ***aside***; – ***over,*** überfliegen, flüchtig überblicken (*pages etc.*).

[2]**glance,** *s.* (*Min.*) der Glanz, die Blende; – ***coal,*** die Glanzkohle; ***lead –,*** der Bleiglanz.

gland [glænd], *s.* (*Anat.*) die Drüse; (*Tech.*) Dichtung, Stopfbuchse.

glandered [ˈglændəd], *adj.* rotzig, rotzkrank (*of horses*). **glanders,** *pl.* (*sing. constr.*) der Rotz, die Rotzkrankheit (*of horses*).

glandular [ˈglændjulə], *adj.* drüsenartig, drüsig, Drüsen–.

glans [glænz], *s.* (*Anat.*) die Eichel.

glare [glɛə], **1.** *s.* 1. grelles Licht, blendender Glanz; 2. wilder *or* durchbohrender Blick. **2.** *v.i.* 1. grell leuchten, blendend strahlen, glänzen, blenden; 2. (*of a p.*) durchdringend blicken, stieren, starren; – ***at,*** anstarren. **3.** *v.t.* – ***defiance,*** ein trotziges Gesicht machen. **glaring,** *adj.* blendend, grell; aufdringlich, schreiend (*as colours*); (*fig.*) schamlos, eklatant, schreiend, unverhüllt, offenkundig; – ***sun,*** pralle Sonne.

glass [glɑ:s], **1.** *s.* das Glas; Trinkglas, Wasserglas; (*amount*) Glas(voll); Glasgefäß; Glasdach, der Glaskasten, Gewächshäuser (*pl.*); der Spiegel; das Uhrglas; Stundenglas; Wetterglas, das *or* der Barometer; die Lupe, das Vergrößerungsglas; *pl.* die Brille, (Augen)gläser (*pl.*); das Fernglas, Opernglas; ***pair of –es,*** die Brille; – ***after –,*** ein Glas nach dem andern; ***broken –,*** Glasscherben (*pl.*); ***cut –,*** geschliffenes Glas; ***looking--,*** der Spiegel; ***magnifying--,*** das Vergrößerungsglas; ***pane of –,*** die Fensterscheibe; ***spun –,*** die Glaswolle, Glaswatte; ***stained –,*** buntes Glas; ***a – too much,*** ein Trunk über den Durst; ***a – of wine,*** ein Glas Wein. **2.** *adj.* gläsern, Glas–; – ***door,*** die Glastür; – ***eye,*** das Glasauge; – ***fibre,*** *see* **fibreglass.**

glass|-blower, *s.* der Glasbläser. **--cutter,** *s.* der Glasschleifer, Glasschneider (*also tool*); Glaserdiamant. **glassful,** *s.* das Glasvoll. **glasshouse,** *s.* 1. das Treibhaus, Gewächshaus; ***people in –s shouldn't throw stones,*** wer im Glashaus sitzt, soll nicht mit Steinen werfen; 2. (*Mil.*) (*sl.*) Militärgefängnis. **glassiness,** *s.* das Glasige, die Glätte,

Klarheit; (*of eyes*) Glasigkeit. **glass|paper,** *s.* das Glaspapier. **-ware,** *s.* das Glas(geschirr). **-works,** *pl.* die Glashütte. **glassy,** *adj.* gläsern, glasartig; glasig, starr (*as eye*); klar, glatt (*as water*).

Glauber('s) salt [ˈglɔ:bə(z)], *s.* das Natriumsulphat, schwefelsaures Natrium.

glaucoma [glɔ:ˈkoumə], *s.* grüner Star, das Glaukom. **glaucous** [ˈglɔ:kəs], *adj.* bläulich grün.

glaze [gleiz], **1.** *v.t.* verglasen, mit Glasscheiben versehen; glasieren (*a cake etc.*); lasieren (*paintings*); glätten, satinieren (*paper etc.*). **2.** *v.i.* 1. gläsern *or* glasig werden; 2. leblos erscheinen. **3.** *s.* der Glanz, die Glätte, Politur; (*Cul.*) Glasur; (*Tech.*) Schmelze, Lasur, (*paper*) Satinierung; (*of eye*) Glasigkeit, der Schleier. **glazed,** *adj.* Glas-, verglast; (*as eyes*) glasig, verschleiert; (*Tech.*) poliert, geglättet, glatt, (*paper*) satiniert; (*Cul.*) glasiert; (*paintings*) lasiert. **glazer,** *s.* der Glasierer; Feinschleifer. **glazier** [ˈgleizjə], *s.* der Glaser; **-'s diamond,** der Glaserdiamant. **glazing,** *s.* das Verglasen; (*Tech.*) Polieren, die Politur, (*paintings*) Lasur, Lasierung, (*china etc.*) das Glasieren, die Glasur, (*paper*) Satinierung, Satinage.

gleam [gli:m], **1.** *s.* der Lichtstrahl, Schein, Schimmer, Glanz; **– *of hope,*** der Hoffnungsstrahl, Schimmer von Hoffnung. **2.** *v.i.* glänzen, scheinen, schimmern; leuchten, strahlen.

glean [gli:n], **1.** *v.t.* nachlesen; auflesen; (*fig.*) (ein)sammeln, zusammenbringen, auflesen (*information etc.*); **– *from,*** erfahren von, schließen aus. **2.** *v.i.* Ähren lesen. **gleaner,** *s.* der Ährenleser; (*fig.*) Sammler. **gleaning,** *s.* das Ährenlesen, (*fig.*) Sammeln, Zusammentragen; (*usu. pl.*) die Nachlese, (*fig.*) das Gesammelte.

glebe [gli:b], *s.* (*Poet.*) die Scholle, der Boden; (*Eccl.*) **– *land,*** der Pfarracker, das Pfarrland.

glede [gli:d], *s.* (*Orn.*) die Gabelweihe, Roter Milan (*Milvus milvus*).

glee [gli:], *s.* 1. die Freude, Fröhlichkeit, Heiterkeit; ***malicious*** or ***wicked* –,** die Schadenfreude; 2. das Tafellied, der Rundgesang, Wechselgesang; **– *club,*** der Gesangverein. **gleeful,** *adj.* fröhlich, vergnügt, heiter, froh, lustig. **gleeman,** *s.* (*obs.*) fahrender Sänger, der Spielmann.

glen [glen], *s.* enges Tal, die Bergschlucht. **glengarry** [-ˈgæri], *s.* schottische Mütze.

glib [glib], *adj.* schlagfertig, zungenfertig; leichtfertig, oberflächlich; **– *tongue,*** geläufige Zunge. **glibness,** *s.* die Zungenfertigkeit, Schlagfertigkeit; Leichtfertigkeit.

glide [glaid], **1.** *v.i.* gleiten, sanft dahinfließen *or* dahingleiten; (*Av.*) im Gleitflug niedergehen; segeln, einen Gleitflug machen. **2.** *s.* (*Danc.*) die Glissade, der Schleifschritt; (*Av.*) Gleitflug; (*Phonet.*) Gleitlaut; (*Mus.*) das (Ver)binden. **glider,** *s.* das Segelflugzeug, der Gleiter; Segelflieger. **gliding,** *s.* das Segelfliegen, der Segelflug; (*of powered plane*) Gleitflug; (*Av.*) **– *ratio,*** die Gleitzahl.

glimmer [ˈglimə], **1.** *v.i.* glimme(r)n; schimmern, flimmern, flackern. **2.** *s.* 1. der Schimmer (*also fig.*); das Glimmen, Flackern; **– *of hope,*** der Hoffnungsschimmer; (*coll.*) ***not a – of an idea,*** kein Schimmer; 2. (*Geol.*) der Glimmer.

glimpse [glimps], **1.** *s.* flüchtiger (An)blick (***of,*** *Gen.*) *or* Einblick (in (*Acc.*)); der Schimmer, Lichtblick; ***catch*** or ***get a – of,*** nur flüchtig zu sehen bekommen. **2.** *v.i.* flüchtig blicken (***at,*** auf (*Acc.*)). **3.** *v.t.* einen Blick erhaschen von, flüchtig sehen, plötzlich erblicken.

glint [glint], **1.** *v.i.* glänzen, schimmern, funkeln, glitzern. **2.** *s.* der Schimmer, Glanz, (Licht)schein, Lichtstrahl.

glissade [gliˈsɑ:d], **1.** *s.* (*Mount.*) die Abfahrt, (*Danc.*) Glissade, der Schleifschritt. **2.** *v.i.* (*Mount.*) abrutschen, abfahren, (*Danc.*) gleiten.

glisten [glisn], (*obs.*) **glister** [ˈglistə], *v.i. See* **glitter.**

glitter [ˈglitə], **1.** *v.i.* glitzern, glänzen, funkeln, schimmern, flimmern, gleißen; (*fig.*) strahlen, glänzen; ***all is not gold that –s,*** es ist nicht alles Gold, was glänzt. **2.** *s.* das Funkeln, Gefunkel; der Glanz, Schimmer; (*fig.*) Glanz, die Pracht. **glittering,** *adj.* glänzend, glitzernd; prächtig.

gloaming [ˈgloumiŋ], *s.* die Dämmerung, das Zwielicht.

gloat [glout], *v.i.* anglotzen, anstieren, gierig anblicken ((***up***) ***on,*** *Acc.*); **– *over,*** sich weiden an (*Dat.*), sich hämisch freuen über (*Acc.*). **gloating, 1.** *s.* die Schadenfreude, hämische Lust. **2.** *adj.* schadenfroh, hämisch.

global [gloubl], *adj.* weltumfassend, weltumspannend, Welt-; (*fig.*) umfassend, Gesamt-. **globate** [-beit], *adj.* kugelförmig, kugelrund. **globe, 1.** *s.* die Kugel; Erdkugel, Erde, der Erdball, (*Geog.*) Globus; die Lampenglocke; ***habitable* –,** bewohnbarer Erdkreis. **2.** *v.t., v.i.* zusammenballen.

globe|-flower, *s.* die Trollblume. **--trotter,** *s.* der Welt(en)bummler.

globose [ˈgloubous], *adj. See* **globular. globosity** [-ˈbɔsiti], *s.* die Kugelform, Kugelförmigkeit. **globular** [ˈglɔbjulə], *adj.* kugelförmig, rundlich. **globule(t)** [ˈglɔbjul(it)], *s.* das Kügelchen.

glomerate [ˈglɔmərit], *adj.* knäuelförmig, geknäuelt, (zusammen)geballt. **glomeration** [-ˈreiʃən], *s.* die (Zusammen)ballung.

gloom [glu:m], **1.** *s.* das Dunkel, die Dunkelheit, Düsternis; (*fig.*) Düsterkeit, Schwermut, gedrückte Stimmung, der Trübsinn. **2.** *v.i.* trüb *or* düster aussehen, finster brüten, schwermütig *or* mürrisch blicken. **3.** *v.t.* verdunkeln, verdüstern. **gloominess,** *s. See* **gloom** (*usu. fig.*). **gloomy,** *adj.* finster, dunkel, düster, trüb (*also fig.*); (*fig.*) schwermütig, trübsinnig; hoffnungslos.

glorification [glɔ:rifiˈkeiʃən], *s.* die Verherrlichung, (*Eccl.*) Verklärung, Lobpreisung. **glorify** [ˈglɔ:rifai], *v.t.* verherrlichen, rühmen, preisen; (*Eccl.*) lobpreisen, verklären, verehren.

gloriole [ˈglɔ:rioul], *s.* der Heiligenschein, Glorienschein, die Strahlenkrone.

glorious [ˈglɔ:riəs], *adj.* glorreich, ruhmreich, ruhmvoll; herrlich, prächtig, strahlend; (*coll.*) großartig, köstlich. **glory, 1.** *s.* 1. der Ruhm, die Ehre; Herrlichkeit, Pracht, der Glanz; 2. (*Eccl.*) *see* **glorification** (*Eccl.*); 3. *See* **gloriole**; (*fig.*) Nimbus. **2.** *v.i.* (*obs.*) sich freuen, frohlocken (***in,*** über (*Acc.*)); (*obs.*) stolz sein (auf (*Acc.*)), sich rühmen (*Gen.*).

glory-hole, *s.* (*sl.*) die Rumpelkammer.

[1]**gloss** [glɔs], **1.** *s.* die Glosse, Erklärung, Erläuterung, erklärende Anmerkung, Randbemerkung; (*coll.*) irreführende Deutung. **2.** *v.t.* kommentieren, erklären, auslegen; **– (*over*),** (hin)wegdeuten, hinweggehen über (*Acc.*).

[2]**gloss, 1.** *s.* 1. der (Preß)glanz; **– *paint,*** der Glanzlack; 2. (*fig.*) der Anstrich, Firnis, äußerer Schein. **2.** *v.t.* glänzend machen, polieren; (*fig.*) **– *over,*** beschönigen, übertünchen, bemänteln, vertuschen.

glossary [ˈglɔsəri], *s.* das Glossar, Spezialwörterbuch.

glossiness [ˈglɔsinis], *s.* die Glätte, Politur, der Glanz. **glossy,** *adj.* glänzend, glatt, poliert; (*coll.*) **– *magazine,*** die Illustrierte, großaufgemachte und bebilderte Zeitschrift (meistens im Farbdruck).

glottal [glɔtl], *adj.* (*Phonet.*) Stimmritzen-; **– *stop,*** der Knacklaut, harter Einsatz. **glottic,** *adj.* (*Anat.*) *see* **glottal. glottis,** *s.* die Stimmritze.

glove [glʌv], *s.* der Handschuh; ***a pair of –s,*** ein Paar Handschuhe; ***fit like a –,*** wie angegossen passen; ***be hand in – with him,*** mit ihm (in böser Absicht) zusammenarbeiten; (*fig.*) ***take the –s off,*** ernst machen, derb werden, unsanft vorgehen; ***take up the –,*** den Fehdehandschuh aufnehmen; ***throw down the –,*** den Fehdehandschuh hinwerfen (***to,*** *Dat.*), herausfordern (*Acc.*). **glover,** *s.* der Handschuhmacher.

glow [glou], **1.** *s.* die Glut, das Glühen, Leuchten; (*fig.*) Brennen, (Er)glühen, die Hitze, Röte; Wärme, das Wohlbehagen; (*coll.*) ***all of a* –** or ***in a* –,** glühend, gerötet. **2.** *v.i.* glühen; leuchten, strahlen, glänzen (*as colours*); (*fig. of a p.*) brennen, (er)glühen (***with,*** vor (*Dat.*)).

glower ['glauə], **1.** *s.* finsterer Blick. **2.** *v.i.* finster blicken *or* aussehen; – *at*, finster anblicken. **glowering,** *adj.* finster, verdrießlich, grollend.

glowing ['glouiŋ], *adj.* glühend, brennend, leuchtend, glänzend, strahlend; (*fig. coll.*) feurig, begeistert. **glow-worm,** *s.* der Leuchtkäfer, das Glühwürmchen.

gloze ['glouz], **1.** *v.t.* – (*over*), *see* [1]**gloss, 2. 2.** *v.i.* (*obs.*) schmeicheln.

glucose ['glu:kous], *s.* die Glukose, Glykose, Dextrose, der Traubenzucker.

glue [glu:], **1.** *s.* der (Tischler)leim. **2.** *v.t.* leimen, kleben (*to*, an (*Acc.*)); (*fig.*) heften (auf (*Acc.*)). **glue-pot,** *s.* der Leimtiegel. **gluey** [-i], *adj.* klebrig, leimig.

glum [glʌm], *adj.* mißmutig, verdrossen, verdrießlich, mürrisch, sauer, finster.

glumaceous [glu:'meiʃəs], *adj.* spelzblütig, Spelzen–. **glumal** [glu:ml], *adj.* spelzig. **glume,** *s.* (*Bot.*) die Spelze.

glumness ['glʌmnis], *s.* die Verdrießlichkeit, der Mißmut.

glumose ['glu:mous], **glumous,** *adj. See* **glumaceous.**

glut [glʌt], **1.** *v.t.* (über)sättigen, überladen, überfüllen; (*Comm.*) überschwemmen; (*fig.*) sättigen, stillen, befriedigen. **2.** *s.* die (Über)sättigung, Überladung; (*Comm.*) Überfüllung, das Überangebot; der Überfluß, Übermaß (*of*, an (*Dat.*)), (*of money*) Überhang.

gluteal ['glu:tiəl], *adj.* (*Anat.*) Gesäß–, Glutäal–.

gluten ['glu:tən], *s.* der Kleber, das Gluten. **glutinous,** *adj.* leimig, klebrig.

glutton [glʌtn], *s.* der Fresser, Schlemmer; (*Zool.*) Vielfraß; (*fig.*) Schwelger, Unersättliche(r), Gierige(r); – *for work*, arbeitswütiger Mensch. **gluttonous,** *adj.* gefräßig, unersättlich; (*fig.*) gierig (*of, for*, nach). **gluttony,** *s.* die Gefräßigkeit, Unersättlichkeit; Völlerei, Schlemmerei.

glycerin(e) ['glisərin], *s.* das Glyzerin.

glyph [glif], *s.* (*Archit.*) die Rille, Furche, Glyphe; (*Archaeol.*) Glypte, Steinfigur. **glyptic** ['gliptik], *adj.* Steinschneide–. **glyptograph** [–ptəgrɑ:f], *s.* die Gemme, geschnittener Stein. **glyptography** [–'tɔgrəfi], *s.* die Glyptik, Steinschneidekunst; Gemmenkunde.

gnarl [nɑ:l], *s.* der Knorren. **gnarled,** *adj.* knorrig.

gnash [næʃ], *v.t.* – *one's teeth*, mit den Zähnen knirschen.

gnat [næt], *s.* die Mücke; Schnake; *–-bite*, der Mückenstich.

gnaw [nɔ:], **1.** *v.t.* nagen an (*Dat.*), zernagen; (*as acid etc.*) zerfressen; (*fig.*) zermürben, aufreiben. **2.** *v.i.* nagen (*at, on*, an (*Dat.*)), (*as acid etc.*) sich einfressen (*into*, in (*Acc.*)).

gneiss [nais], *s.* (*Geol.*) der Gneis.

[1]**gnome** [noum], *s.* der Zwerg, Kobold, Troll, Gnom.

[2]**gnome,** *s.* der Sinnspruch, Denkspruch, Aphorismus, die Sentenz. **gnomic,** *adj.* aphoristisch, gnomisch; – *poetry*, die Spruchdichtung.

gnomish ['noumiʃ], *adj.* zwerg(en)haft, gnomenhaft.

gnomon ['noumən], *s.* der Sonnen(uhr)zeiger; (*Math.*) Gnomon.

gnosis ['nousis], *s.* die Gnosis, mystische *or* tiefe religiöse Erkenntnis. **gnostic** ['nɔstik], **1.** *adj.* gnostisch; mystisch, esoterisch, okkult. **2.** *s.* der Gnostiker. **gnosticism** ['nɔstisizm], *s.* der Gnostizismus.

gnu [nu:], *s.* (*Zool.*) das Gnu.

go [gou], **1.** *irr.v.i.* gehen, laufen, fahren, reisen; verkehren (*of vehicles*), in Gang *or* Betrieb sein, funktionieren (*of engines*); fortgehen, abgehen, abreisen, dahingehen, sich begeben, sich (fort)-bewegen, sich rühren; vergehen, verstreichen, verfließen (*of time*), in Umlauf sein, kursieren, sich verbreiten (*as rumours*), lauten (*of documents*); sich entwickeln, seinen Verlauf nehmen, verlaufen, sich gestalten (*of events*); (*coll.*) ausgehen, ausfallen, Erfolg haben, gelingen; sich erstrecken, reichen; gelten, gültig sein, angenommen werden; ***be -ing to, see*** **(f)** *below*; ***a week to –***, noch eine Woche; (*coll.*) – ***all out***, alles daransetzen, alle Anstrengungen machen; ***all systems –***, alles klar; ***as far as that -es***, an und für sich; was das anlangt; bis zu einem gewissen Grade; ***let –***, fahren lassen, loslassen; ***let it – at that***, es dabei bewenden lassen; ***it only -es to show***, es dient nur als Beweis dazu; ***as the story -es***, wie man sich erzählt; ***as things –***, unter den Umständen; ***as times –***, wie die Zeiten nun einmal sind; ***how -es the time***, wie spät ist es? ***who -es there?*** wer da? ***here -es!*** nun los! ***there he -es again!*** da fängt er schon wieder an! ***-ing, -ing, gone!*** zum ersten, zum zweiten, zum dritten!

(a) (*with nouns*) – ***bail for***, bürgen für, Bürgschaft leisten *or* Bürge sein für; (*coll.*) – ***Dutch***, halbe halbe machen; – ***halves***, teilen (***with***, mit; ***in***, *Acc.*), halbpart machen (***in***, bei); (*sl.*) – ***the whole hog***, aufs Ganze gehen, alles daransetzen; (*coll.*) – ***the pace***, schnell gehen; (*fig.*) ein flottes Leben führen; – ***shares***, teilen; – ***one's way***, seines Weg(e)s gehen; – ***a long way***, weit *or* lange (aus)-reichen; – ***a long way towards***, wesentlich beitragen zu.

(b) (*with adjs.*) (*coll.*) – ***bad***, schlecht werden, verderben; – ***blind***, erblinden; (*sl.*) – ***broke***, Bankrott machen; (*sl.*) – ***bust***, ruiniert sein; ***be -ing cheap***, billig zu haben sein; – ***easy***, es sich (*Dat.*) bequem machen, sich nicht überanstrengen; – ***easy with***, sparsam umgehen mit; (*fig.*) – ***far***, es weit bringen; – ***far towards***, see – ***a long way towards***; – ***hard***, schlimm *or* übel ergehen (***with***, *Dat.*); ***I – hot and cold***, mir wird heiß und kalt; – ***hungry***, hungern; – ***mad***, verrückt werden; – ***native***, verwildern; – ***short of***, entbehren; – ***sick***, sich krank melden; – ***steady***, sich vorsichtig verhalten, vorsichtig gehen; (*coll.*) einen festen Freund haben; (*coll.*) ***be -ing strong***, noch auf den Beinen sein; – ***unheeded***, unbeachtet bleiben; – ***unpunished***, davonkommen; (*sl.*) – ***west***, zunichte werden, in die Binsen gehen, flötengehen; – ***wrong***, (*of a p.*) fehlgehen, sich irren; auf die schiefe Bahn *or* auf Abwege geraten; (*of machines*) nicht richtig funktionieren, (*as plans*) fehlschlagen, schiefgehen.

(c) (*with advs.*) – ***aboard***, an Bord gehen, sich einschiffen; – ***about***, (*Naut.*) wenden, lavieren; (*coll.*) umherfahren, umhergehen; – ***abroad***, ins Ausland gehen *or* reisen; – ***ahead***, vorwärtsgehen; weitergehen, weiterschreiten, weitermachen, fortfahren; – ***ahead!*** vorwärts! weiter! – ***along***, weitergehen; (*coll.*) – ***along (with you)!*** sei nicht so dumm! (*fig.*) – ***along with***, einverstanden sein mit, seine Unterstützung zuteil werden lassen (*Dat.*); – ***amiss***, schiefgehen; – ***astray***, sich verirren; verloren gehen; – ***away***, weggehen, abreisen; – ***back***, zurückgehen; (*coll.*) – ***back on***, zurücknehmen, nicht halten (*one's word*), im Stich lassen (*a p.*); – ***back to***, zurückgehen *or* zurückgreifen auf (*Acc.*); – ***by***, vorbeigehen, vorübergehen; (*as time*) verfließen, vergehen, verstreichen; – ***down***, hinuntergehen, herabgehen; zu Boden fallen *or* gehen (*from a blow*), (*fig.*) unterliegen (*in conflict*) (***before***, *Dat.*); nachlassen, sich legen (*as wind*), sinken, fallen (*as prices*), untergehen, sinken (*ship, sun etc.*), geschluckt werden, hinunterrutschen (*food*); (*coll.*) Wirkung haben, Glauben *or* Anklang *or* Annahme finden, ankommen (***with***, bei), geglaubt *or* geschluckt werden (von); (*coll.*) die Universität verlassen, sich exmatrikulieren lassen; – ***down in history***, in die Geschichte eingehen; – ***down to posterity***, auf die Nachwelt kommen; – ***down with flu***, an Grippe daniederliegen; (*coll.*) ***that won't – down with me***, das kannst du mir nicht weismachen *or* aufbinden, das lasse ich mir nicht gefallen; – ***far***, weit gehen; weit reichen; (*fig.*) viel gelten (***with***, bei); es weit bringen; – ***forth***, hervorgehen; – ***forward***, vorwärts gehen, vorrücken; fortschreiten; – ***in***, hineingehen; (*Crick.*) zum Schlagen drankommen; (*coll.*) – ***in for***, betreiben, sich befassen mit, sich legen auf (*Acc.*), sich widmen (*Dat.*); – ***in for an examination***, ein Examen machen; – ***in with***, sich assoziieren mit; – ***off***, fortgehen, weggehen;

(*actor*) abgehen; (*gun etc.*) losgehen, explodieren; (*fig.*) (*of events*) sich entwickeln, vonstatten gehen; (*coll.*) (*as food*) sich verschlechtern, schlecht werden, (*as pain*) nachlassen; – ***off into hysterics,*** einen hysterischen Anfall bekommen; – ***off to sleep,*** einschlafen; – ***off without a hitch,*** reibungslos vonstatten gehen, tadellos klappen; – ***on,*** vorwärts gehen, weitergehen; (*fig.*) fortfahren (***doing,*** zu tun); daraufhin *or* anschließend anfangen (***to do,*** zu tun), (*of events*) vor sich gehen, fortdauern, weiterbestehen; (*coll.*) losfahren (***at,*** auf (*Acc.*)), herziehen (über (*Acc.*)), schimpfen (mit); (*of clothes*) sich anziehen lassen, sich benehmen *or* aufführen; – ***on!*** see – ***ahead!*** and – ***along! don't – on about it!*** hör' auf damit! ***be –ing on for,*** gehen auf (*Acc.*), sich nähern (*Dat.*); – ***out,*** hinausgehen; (*as news*) verbreitet werden; (*as fire*) ausgehen, erlöschen; (*coll.*) aus der Mode kommen, unmodern werden; ***my heart –es out to him,*** mein Herz schlägt ihm entgegen; – ***out on strike,*** streiken; – ***out to service,*** in Stellung gehen; – ***over,*** übergehen ((***in***)***to,*** in (*Acc.*)), (*fig.*) übergehen, übertreten (***to,*** zu); (*sl.*) Erfolg haben, wirken; (*sl.*) – ***over big,*** ein Bombenerfolg sein; – ***round,*** (*fig.*) (zu)reichen, genügen, (für alle) ausreichen; (*coll.*) einen Besuch machen (***to,*** bei *or Dat.*), vorbeikommen (bei); (*coll.*) – ***slow,*** bummeln (*of workers*); (*sl.*) – ***straight,*** keine krummen Sachen mehr machen; – ***straight on,*** geradeaus gehen; – ***through,*** durchgehen, angenommen werden, Annahme finden (*of a proposal*); – ***through with,*** durchhalten mit *or* in (*Dat.*), durchsetzen, durchführen, zu Ende führen; (*obs.*) – ***to!*** wohlan! – ***together,*** (*of things*) sich (miteinander) vertragen, zusammenpassen; – ***under,*** untergehen, (*fig.*) unterliegen, zugrunde gehen; – ***up,*** hinaufgehen, aufsteigen; errichtet werden (*as building*); ***prices are –ing up,*** die Preise steigen; – ***up to town,*** in die Stadt (*or esp.* nach London) fahren; (*coll.*) – ***up*** (***to the University***), die Universität beziehen; – ***without,*** verzichten, Verzicht üben *or* leisten.

(d) (*with preps.*) – ***about,*** sich befassen mit, in Angriff nehmen, sich machen an (*Acc.*); – ***about one's business,*** sich um seine eigenen Angelegenheiten kümmern; – ***about one's work,*** sich an die Arbeit machen; ***that's the wrong way to – about it,*** Sie fangen das verkehrt an; – ***against,*** ziehen wider *or* gegen (*the enemy*); (*fig.*) zuwiderhandeln (*Dat.*) (*instructions*), zuwiderlaufen, widerstreben (*Dat.*) (*desires*); – ***against the grain,*** (mir) gegen den Strich gehen, (mir im Innersten) widerstreben; ***the decision will – against him,*** die Entscheidung wird zu seinen Ungunsten ausfallen; – ***at,*** (*a p.*) angreifen, losgehen auf (*Acc.*); (*a th.*) (energisch) anpacken, in Angriff nehmen; (*fig.*) – ***behind his back,*** ihn hintergehen; – ***beyond,*** hinausgehen über (*Acc.*), überschreiten; – ***by air,*** mit dem Flugzeug fahren, fliegen; – ***by train,*** mit dem Zug fahren; – ***by the instructions,*** sich an die Weisungen halten, sich nach den Weisungen richten; – ***by the name of . . .,*** unter dem Namen . . . bekannt sein, den Namen . . . führen; (*sl.*) – ***down the drain,*** flötengehen, zum Fenster hinaus geschmissen werden; – ***for,*** holen gehen; (*fig.*) betrachtet werden als, gehalten werden für, gelten für *or* als; (*coll.*) losgehen *or* (los)stürzen auf (*Acc.*), sich bemühen um, streben nach; (*sl.*) schwärmen für, verschossen *or* verknallt sein in (*Acc.*); – ***for a walk,*** spazierengehen, einen Spaziergang machen; – ***for a drive,*** spazierenfahren, ausfahren; (*coll.*) – ***for nothing,*** nichts gelten *or* fruchten, wirkungslos sein; (*coll.*) ***that –es for me too,*** das lasse ich gelten *or* mir gefallen; – ***in fear,*** in ständiger Angst leben; – ***in rags,*** in Lumpen herumlaufen; – ***into,*** hineingehen *or* eintreten in (*Acc.*); (*fig.*) ergreifen (*business, politics etc.*); (*Math.*) enthalten sein in (*Dat.*), gehen in (*Acc.*); (*coll.*) untersuchen, erforschen, eingehen auf (*Acc.*), sich befassen mit; (*coll.*) – ***into holes,*** Löcher bekommen; – ***into mourning,*** Trauerkleider anlegen; – ***into partnership,*** sich assoziieren; – ***into a trance,*** in Ekstase geraten; – ***on,*** sich halten an (*Acc.*); (*coll.*) – ***on the dole,*** stempeln gehen; – ***on an errand,*** einen Gang tun; – ***on foot,*** zu Fuß gehen; – ***on horseback,*** reiten, zu Pferd gehen; – ***on a journey,*** eine Reise unternehmen; – ***on the parish,*** der Gemeinde zur Last fallen; – ***on one's way,*** sich auf den Weg machen; – ***out of business,*** das Geschäft aufgeben; – ***out of fashion,*** aus der Mode kommen, unmodern werden; – ***out of print,*** vergriffen sein; (*fig.*) – ***out of one's way,*** keine Mühe scheuen; sich bemühen *or* einsetzen; – ***over,*** überschreiten, überqueren; (*fig.*) besichtigen (*a house etc.*), (über)prüfen, untersuchen (*accounts etc.*), überarbeiten, (nochmals) durchgehen *or* durchsehen *or* durchlesen; (*Mil. coll.*) – ***over the top,*** aus dem Schützengraben steigen; – ***through,*** durchmachen, erleiden (*an ordeal*), erleben (*several editions*); (*coll.*) durchlesen, prüfen, durchsehen (*papers etc.*), durchsuchen (*a drawer, luggage etc.*); (*sl.*) durchbringen (*a fortune*); – ***to,*** sich wenden an (*Acc.*), greifen zu; (*as a bequest*) übergehen *or* zufallen an (*Acc.*); – ***to bed,*** schlafengehen; (*sl.*) – ***to blazes,*** zur Hölle *or* zum Teufel gehen; – ***to court*** or ***to law,*** sich ans Gericht wenden, vor Gericht gehen; (*Parl.*) – ***to the country,*** Neuwahlen ausschreiben, sich an das Volk appellieren; (*coll.*) – ***to the dogs,*** auf den Hund kommen, vor die Hunde gehen; – ***to great expense,*** sich in Unkosten stürzen; – ***to pieces,*** (*of a th.*) in Stücke gehen; (*coll.*) (*of a p.*) zusammenbrechen, zugrunde gehen; (*sl.*) – ***to pot,*** kaputt gehen; – ***to sea,*** Seemann werden, zur See gehen (*of a p.*), absegeln, in See stechen (*of a ship*); – ***to a lot of trouble,*** sich (*Dat.*) viel Mühe geben; (*coll.*) – ***to the wall,*** an die Wand gedrückt werden; – ***to war,*** Krieg beginnen; – ***to waste,*** verlorengehen, vergeudet werden, verkommen, verwildern; – ***to work,*** an die Arbeit gehen; – ***to wrack and ruin,*** untergehen, zugrunde gehen; – ***through fire and water,*** durchs Feuer gehen; – ***up,*** hinaufgehen (*road etc.*), hinaufsteigen (*hill, ladder etc.*); (*Mil.*) – ***up the line,*** an die Front gehen; – ***with,*** (*of a p.*) gehen mit, begleiten; (*fig.*) übereinstimmen mit, sich halten an (*Acc.*), es halten mit; (*coll.*) verkehren mit; (*of a th.*) passen zu, zusammenpassen mit; ***things – well with him,*** es steht gut mit ihm; – ***with child,*** schwanger sein; – ***with young,*** trächtig sein; – ***without,*** entbehren, verzichten auf (*Acc.*), auskommen ohne; ***that –es without saying,*** das versteht sich von selbst, das ist selbstverständlich.

(e) (*with pres. p.*) – ***begging,*** betteln gehen (*of a p.*), (*coll.*) umsonst zu haben sein (*of a th.*); – ***limping from the room,*** hinkend aus dem Zimmer gehen; – ***motoring,*** eine Autofahrt machen.

(f) (*going with inf.*) ***be –ing to do,*** im Begriff sein zu tun, sich anschicken zu tun, (bald) tun werden *or* wollen; ***I was just –ing to say,*** ich wollte gerade sagen; ***he thought he was –ing to die,*** er glaubte er würde sterben; ***what is –ing to be done?*** was wird man tun müssen? was soll nun geschehen?

2. *irr.v.t.* (*coll.*) – ***one better than,*** überbieten, übertreffen; (*coll.*) – ***it!*** nur los! immer zu! (*coll.*) – ***it*** (***strong***), entschlossen auftreten, drauflosgehen; (*coll.*) – ***it alone,*** es allein machen.

3. *s.* **1.** (*coll.*) das Gehen, der Gang; ***on the –,*** in Bewegung; **2.** (*coll.*) der Versuch; ***from the word –,*** von Anfang an; ***have a – at,*** einen Versuch machen mit, probieren; **3.** die Mode; der Schneid, Schwung, Schmiß; Schluck; die Abmachung; ***be all*** or ***quite the –,*** Furore machen, große Mode *or* der letzte Schrei sein; ***it's a –!*** abgemacht! ***make a – of,*** erfolgreich sein mit; ***it's no –!*** es ist nichts zu machen, das geht nicht, es ist zwecklos; **4.** (*Univ. sl.*) die Prüfung; ***Great Go,*** die Hauptprüfung; ***Little Go,*** das Vorexamen, die Aufnahmeprüfung.

goad [goud], **1.** *s.* der Stachelstock, Treibstock; (*fig.*) Stachel, Ansporn, Antrieb. **2.** *v.t.* (*usu. fig., oft.* – ***on***) anstacheln, (an)treiben, aufstacheln, (auf)reizen.

go-ahead, 1. *s.* (*coll.*) ***get the –,*** freie Bahn bekommen. **2.** *adj.* fortschrittlich, modern; unternehmend, unternehmungslustig, aufstrebend, strebsam.

goal [goul], *s.* das Ziel, der Endpunkt; Bestimmungsort; (*Footb.*) das Tor; der Torschuß; (*fig.*) das Ziel, der (End)zweck, Zielpunkt; (*obs.*) das Mal, Grenzmal; ***get*** or ***score a –***, ein Tor machen. **goalie, goal|-keeper,** *s.* der Torwart, Tormann. **--kick,** *s.* der Torstoß. **--post,** *s.* der Torpfosten. **--scorer,** *s.* der Torschütze.

goat [gout], *s.* die Ziege, Geiß; (*Astr.*) der Steinbock; (*coll.*) Narr, Tölpel; ***he--***, der Ziegenbock; (*sl.*) ***get his –***, ihn ärgern, ihn fuchtig machen; (*coll.*) ***play the –***, sich übermütig benehmen; (*B.*) ***the sheep and the –s***, die Schafe und die Böcke. **goatee** [–'ti:], *s.* der Ziegenbart, Spitzbart. **goat-herd,** *s.* der Ziegenhirt. **goatish,** *adj.* bockig; (*fig.*) geil. **goat-moth,** *s.* der Weidenbohrer. **goat's-beard,** *s.* (*Bot.*) der Ziegenbart, Geißbart, Bocksbart. **goat|skin,** *s.* das Ziegenfell, Ziegenleder. **–sucker,** *s.* (*Orn.*) der Ziegenmelker (*Caprimulgus europaeus*). **--willow,** *s.* (*Bot.*) die Salweide.

gob [gɔb], *s.* 1. (*vulg.*) der Speichel, Schleimauswurf; 2. (*vulg.*) die Fratze; 3. (*Min.*) taubes Gestein; 4. (*Am. sl.*) die Blaujacke.

gobbet ['gɔbit], *s.* das Stück (Fleisch), der Bissen.

gobble [gɔbl], **1.** *v.t.* (*usu. – up*) gierig verschlingen. **2.** *v.i.* (*of turkeys*) kollern.

gobbledygook ['gɔbldigu:k], *s.* (*coll.*) das Kauderwelsch.

gobbler ['gɔblə], *s.* 1. der Truthahn, Puter; 2. Fresser, Vielfraß.

go-between, *s.* der Vermittler, Unterhändler, Mittelsmann, Makler.

goblet ['gɔblit], *s.* der Kelch, Becher, Pokal.

goblin ['gɔblin], *s.* der Kobold.

goby ['goubi], *s.* (*Ichth.*) die Grundel.

go|-by, *s.* (*coll.*) ***give him the –***, ihn ignorieren *or* schneiden. **--cart,** *s.* der Gängelwagen, Laufwagen (*for toddlers*); (*obs.*) Kinderwagen; Handwagen.

god [gɔd], *s.* der Gott, die Gottheit; der Abgott, Götze; ***a sight for the –s***, ein Anblick für Götter; (*sl.*) ***ye –s!*** heiliger Strohsack! **God,** *s.* Gott (*m.*); ***– the Father***, Gott Vater; ***the Lord –***, Gott der Herr; ***Almighty*** – or ***– the Almighty***, Gott der Allmächtige; ***for –'s sake***, um Gottes willen; ***– forbid!*** Gott bewahre! *or* behüte! ***good –!*** ach du lieber Gott! ***– grant***, gebe Gott; ***– help him!*** Gott stehe ihm bei! ***so help me –!*** so wahr mir Gott helfe! ***– knows***, weiß Gott; ***thank –!*** Gott sei Dank! ***–'s truth***, die reine Wahrheit; ***– willing***, so Gott will; ***would to –***, Gott gebe, woll(t)e Gott.

god|child, *s.* das Patenkind. **–daughter,** *s.* die Patentochter.

goddess ['gɔdis], *s.* die Göttin.

god|father, *s.* der Taufzeuge, Pate, Patenonkel; ***stand – to***, Pate stehen bei. **--fearing,** *adj.* gottesfürchtig. **--forsaken,** *adj.* (*coll.*) gottverlassen, elend, erbärmlich. **--given,** *adj.* von Gott gesandt. **-head,** *s.* die Gottheit.

godless ['gɔdlis], *adj.* gottlos. **godlike,** *adj.* gottähnlich, göttlich. **godliness,** *s.* die Frömmigkeit, Gottesfurcht. **godly,** *adj.* fromm, gottesfürchtig.

god|mother, *s.* die (Tauf)patin, Patentante. **–parents,** *pl.* Taufzeugen (*pl.*). **gods,** *s.* (*sing. constr.*) (*Theat. sl.*) der Olymp. **god|send,** *s.* die Gottesgabe, der Glücksfall, unverhoffter Fund, wahrer Segen. **–son,** *s.* der Patensohn. **--speed,** *s.* das Lebewohl, der Scheidegruß; ***wish him –***, ihm eine glückliche Reise wünschen.

godwit ['gɔdwit], *s.* (*Orn.*) die Uferschnepfe.

goer ['gouə], *s.* der Geher, Läufer. **goes** [gouz], *see* **go.**

goffer ['gɔfə], **1.** *v.t.* kräuseln, plissieren, gaufrieren. **2.** *s.* die Falte, das Plissee.

go-getter, *s.* (*coll.*) der Draufgänger.

goggle [gɔgl], *v.i.* stieren, glotzen. **goggle-eyed,** *adj.* glotzäugig. **goggles,** *pl.* die Schutzbrille; (*sl.*) Brille.

going ['gouiŋ], **1.** *adj.* gehend; im Gange *or* Betrieb; ***be –*** (*with inf.*), *see under* **go, 1. (f)**; ***– concern***, gutgehendes *or* blühendes Geschäft; ***the greatest scoundrel –***, der größte Schurke, den es gibt. **2.** *s.* das (Weg)gehen; der Weggang, die Abfahrt, Abreise; (*fig.*) Bodenbeschaffenheit; ***– back***, das Zurück(gehen); (*fig.*) ***there's no – back***, ein Zurück(weichen) ist unmöglich, das Los ist gefallen; ***the – was rough***, es war ein beschwerlicher Weg; (*fig. coll.*) ***it was tough –***, es war eine arge Schinderei; (*fig.*) ***while the – is good***, solange es noch möglich *or* angängig ist. **goings-on,** *pl.* das Verfahren, Benehmen; Treiben, Techtelmechtel.

goitre ['gɔitə], *s.* der Kropf. **goitrous** [–rəs], *adj.* Kropf–, kropfartig, strumös.

gold [gould], **1.** *s.* das Gold; Goldmünzen (*pl.*), (*fig.*) das Geld, der Reichtum; (*colour*) das Goldgelb; (*Prov.*) ***all is not – that glitters***, es ist nicht alles Gold, was glänzt; ***as good as –***, sehr artig, kreuzbrav; ***with a heart of –***, gutherzig; ***worth its weight in –***, unschätzbar, unbezahlbar. **2.** *adj.* Gold–, golden; goldfarben, goldgelb; (*Geog. obs.*) ***Gold Coast***, die Goldküste; ***– foil***, *see* **gold-leaf**; ***– plate***, das Goldgeschirr, Tafelgold.

gold|-beater, *s.* der Goldschläger; ***–'s skin***, die Goldschlägerhaut. **–crest,** *s.* (*Orn.*) das Wintergoldhähnchen (*Regulus regulus*). **--digger,** *s.* der Goldgräber. **--dust,** *s.* der Goldstaub.

golden [gouldn], *adj.* *See* **gold, 2**; ***– age***, goldenes Zeitalter; (*Orn.*) ***– eagle***, der Steinadler (*Aquila chrysaetus*); ***– mean***, goldener Mittelweg; ***– opinions***, hohe Anerkennung; ***– opportunity***, günstige Gelegenheit; (*Orn.*) ***– oriole***, der Pirol (*Oriolus oriolus*); (*Orn.*) ***– pheasant***, der Goldfasan (*Chrysolophus pictus*); (*Orn.*) (***Am. Eurasian***) ***– plover***, der Goldregenpfeifer (*Charadrius apricarius*); (*Bot.*) ***– rod***, die Goldrute; (*Math., fig.*) ***– rule***, goldene Regel; (*Math.*) ***– section***, goldener Schnitt; ***– wedding***, goldene Hochzeit.

gold|finch, *s.* (*Orn.*) (***Am. European –***) der Stieglitz, Distelfink (*Carduelis carduelis*). **–fish,** *s.* der Goldfisch. **–hammer,** *s.* (*Orn.*) die Goldammer (*Emberiza citrinella*).

goldilocks ['gɔldilɔks], *s.* 1. (*Bot.*) goldgelber Hahenfuß; 2. (*coll.*) das Goldköpfchen.

gold|-leaf, *s.* das Blattgold, die Goldfolie. **--mine,** *s.* die Goldgrube (*also fig.*). **--plated,** *adj.* vergoldet. **--rush,** *s.* der Goldrausch. **--size,** *s.* der Goldgrund. **–smith,** *s.* der Goldschmied.

golf [gɔlf], *s.* das Golf(spiel); ***play –, go –ing***, Golf spielen; ***– club***, der Golfschläger; Golfklub; ***– links***, der Golfplatz. **golfer,** *s.* der Golfspieler.

golliwog ['gɔliwɔg], *s.* die Negerpuppe.

golly! ['gɔli], *int.* (*coll.*) Donnerwetter!

gonad ['gɔnæd], *s.* (*Biol.*) die Gonade, Keimdrüse, Geschlechtsdrüse.

gondola ['gɔndələ], *s.* die Gondel (*also Av.*). **gondolier** [–'liə], *s.* der Gondelführer, Gondoliere.

gone [gɔn], **1.** *p.p. of* **go**; ***he has –***, er ist gegangen; ***he is –***, er ist fort *or* weg *or* verschwunden; ***all his money is –***, sein ganzes Geld ist weg; ***it is – midnight***, Mitternacht ist vorbei; ***a year has – since . . .***, ein Jahr ist vergangen, seitdem . . .; ***be –! get you –!*** geh! pack dich! ***I must be –***, ich muß fort. **2.** *adj.* ***– is –***, hin ist hin; ***dead and –***, tot und dahin; (*sl.*) ***be – on***, versessen sein auf (*Acc.*), vernarrt *or* verknallt sein in (*Acc.*); ***far –***, weit vorgeschritten *or* vorgerückt. **goner** ['gɔnə], *s.* (*sl.*) ein Mann des Todes; hoffnungslos verlorene S.

gonfalon ['gɔnfələn], *s.* das Banner.

gong [gɔŋ], **1.** *s.* der Gong. **2.** *v.t.* durch Gongschlag stoppen.

goniometer [gouni'ɔmitə], *s.* der Winkelmesser.

gonococcus ['gɔnəkɔkəs], *s.* (*pl.* **-cci**) der Gonokokkus. **gonorrhoea** [–'riə], *s.* die Gonorrhö(e), der Tripper.

good [gud], **1.** *adj.* (*comp.* ***better***, *sup.* ***best***) 1. gut; (*as children*) artig, brav; freundlich, lieb(enswürdig); 2. (*Law*) rechtskräftig, (rechts)gültig, (*as reasons*) annehmbar, begründet, berechtigt, stichhaltig, triftig; 3. (*Comm.*) sicher, zuverlässig, kreditfähig, zahlungsfähig; 4. tugendhaft, fromm; redlich, rechtschaffen; 5. tüchtig, fähig, geschickt, bewährt;

6. (*of a th.*) günstig, vorteilhaft, geeignet, zuträglich, zufriedenstellend, angenehm; genügend, ausreichend, angemessen, angebracht, zweckmäßig, passend, schicklich, richtig; gründlich, reichlich, nützlich, wertvoll, heilsam, tauglich, brauchbar; (*of food*) frisch; 7. (*coll.*) ordentlich, beträchtlich, beachtlich, ansehnlich, erheblich, gehörig, ziemlich.

(a) (*with nouns*) ***– old age,*** hohes Alter; ***on – authority,*** aus guter Quelle; ***the – book,*** die Bibel; ***– breeding,*** die Wohlerzogenheit, feine Lebensart; ***– cheer,*** gute Laune *or* Stimmung; ***be – company,*** ein guter Gesellschafter sein; ***– day!*** guten Tag! ***a – deal,*** ziemlich viel; ***– debts,*** sichere Schulden; ***in – earnest,*** in vollem Ernst; ***is this egg still –?*** ist das Ei noch frisch? ***in – faith,*** auf Treu und Glauben; ***– fellowship,*** die Kameradschaftlichkeit; ***– form,*** guter Ton; ***Good Friday,*** der Karfreitag; ***– God!*** see ***– Lord! – gracious!*** du meine Güte! ach du liebe Zeit! ***a – half,*** reichlich die Hälfte; ***– health,*** das Wohlbefinden; ***a – hour,*** eine ganze *or* volle Stunde; ***– humour,*** gute Laune; ***– looks,*** die Schönheit, gutes Aussehen; ***– Lord!*** du großer Gott! ***– luck,*** das Glück; ***a – many,*** ziemlich viele; ***– measure,*** reichliches Maß; ***I have a – mind,*** ich hätte wohl Lust; ***– news,*** erfreuliche Nachricht; ***– night!*** gute Nacht! ***take in – part,*** nicht übelnehmen, gut aufnehmen; ***have a – press,*** gute Aufnahme in der Presse finden; ***Good Samaritan,*** (*B.*) barmherziger Samariter, (*fig.*) der Helfer in der Not; ***that makes – sense,*** das ist sehr vernünftig; ***a – share,*** beträchtlicher Anteil; ***– temper,*** die Gutmütigkeit; ***have a – time,*** sich amüsieren; ***in – time,*** zur rechten Zeit, bei Zeiten; ***be in – train,*** günstig stehen; ***– turn,*** die Gefälligkeit; ***a – while,*** ziemlich lange; ***his – wife,*** seine liebe Frau; ***– will,*** das Wohlwollen; (*Comm.*) der Geschäftswert; ***– word,*** freundliches Wort; ***put in a – word,*** ein gutes Wort einlegen.

(b) (*with verbs*) ***be as – as,*** auf dasselbe hinauslaufen wie; ***enough is as – as a feast,*** allzuviel ist ungesund; ***as – as gold,*** kreuzbrav; ***he gives as – as he gets,*** er bleibt nichts schuldig; ***be as – as one's word,*** sein Wort halten, völlig zuverlässig sein; ***be so – as*** or ***be – enough,*** sei so gütig (***to do,*** zu tun); ***hold –,*** noch gelten, gültig bleiben, sich bewähren; ***make –,*** (*v.t.*) ersetzen, vergüten (*a loss*), wiedergutmachen, Ersatz leisten für (*damage*), halten, erfüllen, sich halten an (*Acc.*) (*a promise*), rechtfertigen, geltend machen, durchsetzen (*a claim*); (*v.i.*) (*coll.*) Erfolg haben, sich durchsetzen *or* bewähren; ***stand –,*** see ***hold –; stand – for,*** haften *or* bürgen für.

(c) (*with preps.*) ***– at,*** geschickt *or* bewandert in (*Dat.*); ***– for,*** gut gegen *or* für (*disease etc.*), zuträglich (*Dat.*); (*coll.*) fähig *or* geneigt zu, gewachsen (*Dat.*); (*Comm.*) (*of a debtor*) gut für, (*of a cheque*) über den Betrag von; (*coll.*) ***– for you!*** (*usu. iron.*) ich gratuliere! das spricht für dich! ***– for nothing,*** nichtsnutzig, unbrauchbar; ***what is it – for?*** wozu wird es gebraucht?

2. *adv.* (*coll.*) ***he as – as insulted me,*** er hat mich so gut wie beleidigt *or* mich praktisch beleidigt; (*coll.*) ***– and proper,*** gehörig, tüchtig; (*coll.*) ***– and ready,*** ganz *or* durchaus fertig.

3. *s.* 1. Gute(s), das Wohl; (*Phil.*) Gut(e); ***the common –,*** das Gemeinwohl; ***do –,*** Gutes tun; ***do him –,*** ihm guttun *or* wohltun; ***for the – of all,*** zum Besten von allen; ***a power for –,*** eine Kraft zum Guten; ***be all to the –,*** zum Guten ausschlagen; (*coll.*) ***be up to no –,*** nichts Gutes im Schilde führen; 2. (*fig.*) der Wert, Nutzen, Vorteil; ***be no*** (or ***not much***) ***–,*** nichts (*or* nichts viel) taugen; ***it is no*** (or ***not much***) ***–,*** es hat keinen (*or* wenig) Sinn *or* Zweck, es ist zwecklos, es nützt nichts (***doing,*** zu tun); (*oft. iron.*) ***much – may it do you!*** wohl bekomm's! ***do no –,*** nichts nützen; ***for –*** (***and all***), ein für allemal, endgültig; ***for your own –,*** zu deinem eigenen Vorteil; ***to the –,*** obendrein, extra; (*Comm.*) auf die Kreditseite, als Nettogewinn; ***what – will it do?*** was hat es für einen Wert? was nützt es? ***what – will it do you?*** was wird es dir helfen? 3. (*collect.*) die Guten, Rechtschaffenen; 4. *pl.* (*Law*) bewegliches Vermögen, (*Comm.*) (Handels)güter (*pl.*), (Handels)waren (*pl.*), die (Handels)ware; Fracht, das Frachtgut; ***consumer –s,*** Konsumgüter, Verbrauchsgüter (*pl.*); ***dry –s,*** Kurzwaren, Schnittwaren (*pl.*); ***soft –s,*** Stoffe, Textilien (*pl.*); ***–s and chattels,*** das Hab und Gut, bewegliches Vermögen; (*sl.*) ***be the –s,*** das Wahre *or* Richtige sein; (*sl.*) ***deliver the –s,*** den Erwartungen entsprechen, das Versprochene erfüllen; (*coll.*) ***by –s,*** per Fracht, mit dem Güterzug.

good|-bye, 1. *s.* das Lebewohl. **2.** *int.* leb(e) wohl! auf Wiedersehen. **--for-nothing, 1.** *s.* der Nichtsnutz, Taugenichts. **2.** *adj.* nichtsnutzig, unbrauchbar. **--hearted,** *adj.* gutherzig, gutmütig. **--humoured,** *adj.* gut aufgelegt *or* gestimmt, aufgeräumt. **goodish,** *adj.* (*coll.*) leidlich, annehmbar; ziemlich, ansehnlich, beträchtlich. **goodliness,** *s.* die Anmut, Gefälligkeit. **good-looking,** *adj.* gut aussehend, hübsch. **goodly,** *adj.* schön, anmutig, gefällig, stattlich; beträchtlich, beachtlich, ansehnlich. **good|man** [–mən], *s.* (*obs.*) der Hausherr, Ehemann. **--natured,** *adj.* gutmütig, gefällig.

goodness [ˈgudnis], *s.* die Güte, (Vor)trefflichkeit; das Gute; die Frömmigkeit, Tugend, Rechtschaffenheit, Redlichkeit; Güte, Gütigkeit, Freundlichkeit; ***– gracious!*** du lieber Himmel! du meine Güte! ***– knows!*** weiß der Himmel! ***my –!*** ach je! ***in the name of –,*** um Himmels willen; ***for – sake!*** um Gottes willen! ***thank –!*** Gott sei Dank! ***I wish to –,*** wollte Gott. **goods,** *pl. See* **good, 3.,** 4.; ***– train,*** der Güterzug; ***– traffic,*** der Güterverkehr. **good|-tempered,** *adj.* gut gelaunt; gutartig, gutmütig. **–wife,** *s.* (*obs.*) die Hausfrau. **goody, 1.** *adj.* (*oft.* –––) (*coll.*) frömmelnd, prüde, zimperlich. **2.** *s.* (*coll.*) 1. der Tugendbold; 2. (*usu. pl.*) (*coll.*) Süßigkeiten (*pl.*), das Zuckerwerk, der *or* das Bonbon.

goof [gu:f], *s.* (*sl.*) der Tropf. **goofy,** *adj.* (*sl.*) blöd, albern, doof.

goop [gu:p], *s.* (*sl.*) der Flegel, Lümmel.

goosander [gu:ˈsændə], *s.* (*Orn.*) der Gänsesäger, Großer Säger (*Mergus merganser*).

goose [gu:s], *s.* (*pl.* **geese** [gi:s]) die Gans; (*fig.*) der Narr, Dummkopf; ***Mother Goose,*** Frau Holle; ***all his geese are swans,*** er übertreibt; (*coll.*) ***cook his –,*** ihm den Garaus machen; ***kill the – that lays the golden egg,*** die Gans schlachten, die goldene Eier legt; (*Orn.*) ***pink-footed –,*** die Kurzschnabelgans (*Anser brachyrhynchus*); ***not say bo(o) to a –,*** ein Hasenfuß sein, den Mund nicht auftun können; ***roast –,*** der Gänsebraten; ***wild-– chase,*** unsinnige Verfolgung, zweckloses Unternehmen.

gooseberry [ˈguzbəri], *s.* die Stachelbeere; (*coll.*) ***play –,*** den Anstandswauwau spielen; ***--fool,*** der Stachelbeerkrem.

goose|flesh, *s.* (*fig.*) die Gänsehaut. **--foot,** *s.* (*Bot.*) der Gänsefuß. **goosegog** [ˈguzgɔg], *s.* (*sl.*) *see* **gooseberry.**

goose|-grass, *s.* (*Bot.*) das Klebkraut, Gänsekraut. **--pimples,** *pl. See* **--flesh. --quill,** *s.* der Gänsekiel, die Gänsefeder. **--step,** *s.* (*Mil.*) der Paradeschritt, Stechschritt.

Gordian [ˈgɔ:diən], *adj.* ***cut the – knot,*** den gordischen Knoten durchhauen.

¹**gore** [gɔ:], **1.** *s.* der Zwickel, Keil, das Keilstück, die Gehre, Bahn; dreieckiges Stück. **2.** *v.t.* mit Zwickel versehen, keilförmig zuschneiden; ***–d skirt,*** der Bahnenrock, Glockenrock.

²**gore,** *s.* (geronnenes) Blut.

³**gore,** *v.t.* durchbohren, aufspießen (*with horns*).

gorge [gɔ:dʒ], **1.** *s.* 1. die Gurgel, Kehle, der Schlund; ***my – rises,*** mir wird schlecht *or* übel (***at,*** bei); 2. (*Geog.*) die (Berg)schlucht, der Hohlweg; 3. (*Archit.*) die Hohlleiste, Hohlkehle; (*Fort.*) (Festungs)kehle. **2.** *v.t.* gierig verschlingen; vollpfropfen; ***– o.s.,*** sich vollfressen. **3.** *v.i.* fressen, sich vollstopfen.

gorgeous [ˈgɔ:dʒəs], *adj.* prächtig, glänzend, prachtvoll, blendend. **gorgeousness,** *s.* die Pracht, der Glanz, Prunk.

gorget [ˈgɔ:dʒit], *s.* der Halsschmuck, das Hals-

band; Halstuch, Brusttuch; (*Orn.*) der Kehlfleck; (*obs. Mil.*) die Halsberge.
Gorgon ['gɔ:gən], *s.* (*Myth.*) die Gorgo, Meduse; (*fig.*) schreckliche Frau.
gorilla [gə'rilə], *s.* der Gorilla.
gormandize ['gɔ:məndaiz], *v.i.* fressen, prassen, schlemmen. **gormandizing,** *s.* die Schlemmerei, Prasserei.
gorse [gɔ:s], *s.* (*Bot.*) der Stechginster, Gaspeldorn (*Ulex*).
gory ['gɔ:ri], *adj.* blutig, blutbefleckt.
gosh! [gɔʃ], *int.* Donnerwetter!
goshawk ['gɔshɔ:k], *s.* (*Orn.*) der Hühnerhabicht (*Accipiter gentilis*).
gosling ['gɔzliŋ], *s.* das Gänschen, junge Gans.
go-slow, *s.* der Bummelstreik.
gospel ['gɔspəl], *s.* das Evangelium (*also fig.*); (*fig.*) die Lehre; ***take for*** or ***as*** –, für bare Münze nehmen; – ***truth,*** buchstäbliche Wahrheit. **gospeller,** *s.* der Wanderprediger; (*coll.*) ***hot*–**–, religiöser Eiferer.
gossamer ['gɔsəmə], *s.* Sommerfäden, Marienfäden (*pl.*); (*coll.*) der Altweibersommer, das Mariengarn; dünne Gaze.
gossip ['gɔsip], **1.** *s.* 1. die Klatschbase; 2. der Klatsch, das Geschwätz; die Plauderei (*in newspapers*); – ***column,*** die Klatschspalte. **2.** *v.i.* schwatzen, klatschen, tratschen. **gossipy,** *adj.* geschwätzig, klatschsüchtig.
gossoon [gɔ'su:n], *s.* (*Irish*) der Bursche, Diener.
got [gɔt], *imperf., p.p. of* **get.**
Goth [gɔθ], *s.* (*Hist.*) der Gote.
Gotham ['goutəm], *s.* Schilda, Krähwinkel (*n.*); ***wise man of*** –, **Gothamite,** *s.* der Schildbürger, Krähwinkler.
Gothic ['gɔθik], **1.** *adj.* 1. gotisch; – ***architecture,*** gotischer Baustil, die Gotik; – ***letters,*** gotische Schrift, die Fraktur; 2. (*fig.*) barbarisch. **2.** *s.* (*language*) das Gotisch(e).
gotten [gɔtn], (*Am.*) *p.p. of* **get.**
gouge [gaudʒ], **1.** *s.* das Hohleisen, der Hohlmeißel, Hohlbeitel, die Gutsche. **2.** *v.t.* (– ***out***) ausmeißeln, aushöhlen; herausdrücken (*eyes*).
gourd [guəd], *s.* der (Flaschen)kürbis; die Kürbisflasche.
gourmand ['guəmənd], **1.** *adj.* 1. feinschmeckerisch; 2. gefräßig. **2.** *s.* 1. der Feinschmecker; 2. starker Esser. **gourmet** [–mei], *s.* der Feinschmecker, Weinkenner.
gout [gaut], *s.* die Gicht, das Zipperlein, Podagra. **goutiness,** *s.* die Anlage zur Gicht. **gouty,** *adj.* gichtisch (veranlagt).
govern ['gʌvən], **1.** *v.t.* regieren (*also Gram.*), beherrschen; verwalten, lenken, leiten, bestimmen; (*Tech.*) regeln, regulieren, steuern; (*Law*) als Präzedenzfall dienen für, (*fig.*) beherrschen, kontrollieren, zügeln, im Zaume halten. **2.** *v.i.* regieren, herrschen. **governable,** *adj.* lenkbar, leitbar, regierbar; (*Tech.*) regulierbar, steuerbar; (*fig.*) lenksam, folgsam. **governance,** *s.* (*usu. fig.*) die Herrschaft, Beherrschung, Kontrolle (*of,* über (*Acc.*)). **governess,** *s.* die Hauslehrerin, Gouvernante, Erzieherin. **governing,** *adj.* herrschend, leitend, Vorstands–; (*fig.*) Leit–; – ***body,*** die Leitung, Direktion, der Vorstand, Verwaltungsrat; – ***principle,*** der Leitsatz.
government ['gʌvnmənt], *s.* 1. die Regierung (*also Pol.*), Führung, Leitung, Verwaltung; Kontrolle, Beherrschung, Herrschaft (*of,* über (*Acc.*)); Regierungsbezirk; ***central*** –, die Zentralregierung; ***local*** –, die Lokalverwaltung; ***military*** –, die Militärverwaltung; ***parliamentary*** –, die Parlamentsregierung; ***petticoat*** –, das Weiberregiment; – ***control,*** die Bewirtschaftung; – ***grant,*** staatliche Unterstützung; – ***loan,*** die Staatsanleihe; – ***office,*** die Verwaltungskanzlei, Staatsstelle; – ***official,*** Staatsbeamte(r); – ***property,*** das Landeseigentum; – ***securities,*** Staatspapiere (*pl.*); 2. (*Gram.*) die Rektion. **governmental** [–'mentl], *adj.* Regierungs–, Staats–.
governor ['gʌvənə], *s.* 1. der Statthalter, Gouverneur (*of a province etc.*); (*Mil.*) (Festungs)kommandant; (*Comm.*) Direktor, Leiter, Präsident, Vorstand, Vorsitzende(r), (*coll.*) Chef; (*sl.*) Vater, Alte(r), alter Herr; Erzieher, Hauslehrer; Herrscher, Regent; *pl.* das Kuratorium (*of a school*); 2. (*Tech.*) der Regler, Regulator. **governor general,** *s.* der Generalgouverneur (*of dominions*). **governorship,** *s.* die Statthalterschaft.
gowan ['gauən], *s.* (*Scots*) das Gänseblümchen.
gowk [gauk], *s.* (*Scots*) der Kuckuck; (*fig.*) Tölpel, Einfaltspinsel.
gown [gaun], *s.* das (Damen)kleid; (*Law, Univ.*) Amtsgewand, der Talar; ***town and*** –, Stadt und Universität, Philister und Akademiker. **gownsman,** *s.* der Student.
grab [græb], **1.** *v.t.* ergreifen, fassen, packen, (*coll.*) grapsen, schnappen; (*fig.*) an sich reißen, sich (*Dat.*) aneignen, einheimsen. **2.** *v.i.* haschen, greifen, schnappen, grapsen (*at,* nach). **3.** *s.* 1. plötzlicher Griff, das Grapsen; ***make a*** – ***at,*** grapsen nach; 2. (*Tech.*) der Greifer, die Klaue, Kranschaufel. **grabber,** *s.* Habsüchtige(r), Habgierige(r). **grab|-hook,** *s.* der Greifhaken. **--line, --rope,** *s.* die Fangleine, Sicherheitsleine.
grace [greis], **1.** *s.* 1. die Gunst, Gnade, Huld, das Wohlwollen; göttliche Gnade, die Barmherzigkeit; ***act of*** –, der Gnadenakt; ***by the*** – ***of God,*** von Gottes Gnaden; ***by*** – ***of the Senate,*** durch Senatsbeschluß; (*Law*) ***by way of*** –, auf dem Gnadenweg; ***the year of*** –, das Jahr des Heils; ***be in his bad*** –***s,*** bei ihm in Ungnade sein; ***be in his good*** –***s,*** in seiner Gunst stehen, bei ihm gut sein; 2. die Anmut, Charme, Grazie, der (Lieb)reiz; Anstand, die Schicklichkeit; ***airs and*** –***s,*** die Vornehmtuerei; ***have the*** – ***to do,*** anständigerweise tun, den Anstand haben zu tun; ***with a bad*** or ***ill*** –, unwillig, ungern, widerwillig; ***with a good*** –, gern, (bereit)willig, mit guter Miene; 3. (*Law, Comm.*) der (Zahlungs)aufschub, die Frist, Wartezeit; ***days of*** –, Respekttage; ***a day's*** –, ein Tag Aufschub; 4. das Tischgebet; ***say*** –, das Tischgebet sprechen; 5. (*Myth.*) ***the Graces,*** die Grazien; 6. (*as title*) ***your Grace,*** Euer Gnaden. **2.** *v.t.* schmücken, zieren; (be)ehren, auszeichnen.
graceful ['greisful], *adj.* anmutig, hold, zierlich, graziös; geziemend, taktvoll. **gracefulness,** *s.* die Anmut, Grazie, Zierlichkeit. **graceless,** *adj.* gottlos, verworfen, verdorben; unverschämt, taktlos, schamlos. **grace-note,** *s.* (*Mus.*) die Verzierung.
gracious ['greiʃəs], *adj.* gütig, freundlich, wohlwollend; herablassend, gnädig, huldvoll (*of rulers*); barmherzig (*of God*); (*obs.*) anmutig, reizvoll; – ***me! good***(*ness*) –***!*** du meine Güte! lieber Himmel! **graciousness,** *s.* die Gnade, Huld, Freundlichkeit, Güte; Anmut, der (Lieb)reiz.
gradate [grə'deit], **1.** *v.t.* abstufen, abtönen, aufeinander abstimmen, gegeneinander absetzen. **2.** *v.i.* sich abstufen, stufenweise übergehen. **gradation** [–'deiʃən], *s.* der Stufengang, die Stufenfolge; Abstufung (*of colours etc.*); (*Gram.*) der Ablaut.
grade [greid], **1.** *s.* der Grad, Rang; die Stufe, Klasse; (*of ground*) das Gefälle, die Steigung; Neigung; (*Comm.*) der Gütegrad, die Güteklasse, Güte, Qualität, Sorte; (*Am.*) (Schul)klasse; (*Am.*) – ***crossing,*** der Bahnübergang; (*Am.*) – ***school,*** die Grundschule, Volksschule; (*coll.*) ***he is on the down*** –, er ist im Abstieg, mit ihm geht's bergab; (*coll.*) ***on the up*** –, im Aufstieg; (*coll.*) ***make the*** –, sich durchsetzen, Erfolg haben. **2.** *v.t.* abstufen; einteilen, ordnen, sortieren; – ***up,*** aufkreuzen, veredeln (*cattle*).
gradient ['greidiənt], *s.* die Steigung, das Gefälle; die Neigung, geneigte Fläche, schiefe Ebene; ***temperature*** –, der Temperaturgradient.
gradual ['grædjuəl], *adj.* stufenweise fortschreitend; allmählich. **gradually,** *adv.* allmählich, nach und nach.
graduate, **1.** ['grædjueit], *v.t.* 1. in Grade einteilen, mit einer Skala versehen, eichen, einteilen, graduieren; abstufen, staffeln (*taxes*); 2. (*Chem.*) gradie-

ren, titrieren. **2.** [–eit], *v.i.* **1.** sich abstufen *or* staffeln, allmählich übergehen; 2. (*Univ.*) promovieren; (*Am.*) *– from school,* die Schule absolvieren. **3.** [–it], *s.* Graduierte(r). **graduated,** *adj.* abgestuft, gestaffelt (*as taxes*), graduiert, eingeteilt (*as a vessel*). **graduation** [–'eiʃən], *s.* 1. das Abstufen, Staffeln, die Abstufung, Staffelung; (*Chem.*) Gradierung; Gradeinteilung, Graduierung; der Teilstrich (*on a vessel*); 2. (*Univ.*) Promovierung, Promotion, (*Am.*) das Absolvieren.

[1]**graft** [grɑ:ft], **1.** *v.t.* pfropfen (***on,*** auf (*Acc.*)); (*Med.*) transplantieren, verpflanzen; (*fig.*) übertragen ((***up***)***on, in,*** auf (*Acc.*)), einimpfen, einpflanzen (*Dat.*). **2.** *s.* 1. das Pfropfreis; die Pfropfstelle; 2. (*Med.*) Transplantation, Gewebeverpflanzung; das Transplantat, verpflanztes Gewebe.

[2]**graft,** **1.** *s.* (*coll.*) die Schieberei, Bestechung, Korruption; das Bestechungsgeld, Schmiergeld. **2.** *v.i.* (*sl.*) schieben.

Grail [greil], *s.* der Gral; ***Knight of the Holy –,*** der Gralsritter; ***legend of the Holy –,*** die Gralssage.

grain [grein], **1.** *s.* 1. das Korn, Getreide; Samenkorn, Körnchen (*of sand, salt etc.*); 2. (*measure*) Gran, Grän; (*fig.*) die Spur, das Stückchen, winziges Teilchen, bischen; (*fig.*) ***not a – of hope,*** nicht die geringste Hoffnung; 3. die (Längs)faser, Faserung, (*of wood*) Maserung, Ader; (*Phot.*) Körnigkeit; Faserrichtung, der Strich; (*fig.*) das Gefüge, Gewebe, Wesen, die Natur; (*fig.*) ***against the –,*** wider den Strich, widerwillig; ***dyed in the –,*** in der Wolle gefärbt. **2.** *v.t.* körnen, granulieren; masern, ädern, marmorieren (*wood*); krispeln, narben (*leather*).

gram [græm], *s.* das Gramm.

gramarye ['græməri], *s.* (*obs.*) die Zauberkunst.

gramercy! ['græməsi], *int.* (*obs.*) vielen Dank!

graminaceous [græmi'neiʃəs], **gramineous** [–'miniəs], *adj.* grasartig. **graminivorous** [–'nivərəs], *adj.* grasfressend.

grammalogue ['græmələg], *s.* (*shorthand*) das Sigel, Kürzel.

grammar ['græmə], *s.* die Grammatik; ***that is good*** (***bad***) ***–,*** das ist grammatisch richtig (falsch); ***– school,*** höhere Schule, das Gymnasium, (*Hist.*) die Lateinschule. **grammarian** [grə'mɛəriən], *s.* der Grammatiker. **grammatical** [grə'mætikl], *adj.* grammatisch, grammatikalisch.

gramme, *s. See* **gram.**

gramophone ['græməfoun], *s.* das Grammophon, der Plattenspieler; ***– pick-up,*** der Tonabnehmer; ***– record,*** die Schallplatte, Grammophonplatte.

grampus ['græmpəs], *s.* der Butzkopf, Schwertwal; (*coll.*) ***blow like a –,*** wie eine Maschine schnaufen.

granary ['grænəri], *s.* der Kornspeicher, Getreidespeicher, (*fig.*) die Kornkammer.

grand [grænd], **1.** *adj.* 1. groß, erhaben, würdevoll; imposant, grandios, eindrucksvoll; vornehm, stattlich, prächtig, (*coll.*) großartig, glänzend, herrlich; wichtig, bedeutend, gewaltig; 2. Haupt–, Groß–; ***– duchess,*** die Großherzogin; ***– duchy,*** das Großherzogtum; ***– duke,*** der Großherzog; ***Russian – duke,*** russischer Großfürst; ***Grand Fleet,*** die Hochseeflotte; ***– jury,*** großes Geschworenengericht; ***– opera,*** große Oper; ***– piano,*** der Flügel; ***– tour,*** die Kavaliersreise; ***– vizier,*** der Großwesir. **2.** *s.* 1. (*coll.*) der Flügel; ***baby –,*** der Salonflügel; ***concert –,*** der Konzertflügel; 2. (*sl.*) (*Am.*) tausend Dollar.

grandad ['grændæd], *s. See* **grand-dad. grandam,** *s.* (*obs.*) die Großmutter, altes Mütterchen. **grand|child,** *s.* der (die) Enkel(in), das Enkelkind. **--dad,** *s.* (*coll.*) der Großpapa, Opa. **--daughter,** *s.* die Enkelin. **--ducal,** *adj.* großherzoglich.

grandee [græn'di:], *s.* der Grande, Magnat (*in Spain*).

grandeur ['grændjə], *s.* die Größe, Hoheit, Würde, Herrlichkeit, Pracht; (*fig.*) Vornehmheit, Erhabenheit, Großartigkeit.

grandfather ['græn(d)fɑ:ðə], *s.* der Großvater; ***– clock,*** (große) Standuhr.

grandiloquence [græn'diləkwəns], *s.* das Pathos, die (Rede)schwulst, Großsprecherei. **grandiloquent,** *adj.* hochtrabend, schwülstig; großsprecherisch.

grandiose ['grændious], *adj.* großartig, grandios, hochtrabend, pompös, prunkvoll.

grand|ma, –mamma, *s.* (*coll.*) die Großmama, Oma. **Grand-Master,** *s.* der Großmeister, Hochmeister. **grand|mother,** *s.* die Großmutter; (*coll.*) ***go teach your – to suck eggs,*** lehre du mich nur die Welt kennen! **--nephew,** *s.* der Großneffe. **--niece,** *s.* die Großnichte. **–pa,** *s.* (*coll.*) *see* **--dad. –parent,** *s.* der Großvater, die Großmutter; *pl.* Großeltern (*pl.*). **–sire,** *s.* (*obs.*) der Großvater; (*of animals*) Ahnherr. **–son,** *s.* der Enkel. **–stand,** *s.* die Haupttribüne; (*Spt.*) (*coll.*) ***– finish,*** packende Entscheidung.

grange [greindʒ], *s.* der Meierhof.

graniferous [græ'nifərəs], *adj.* körnertragend.

granite ['grænit], **1.** *s.* der Granit. **2.** *or* **granitic** [–'nitik], *adj.* granitartig, Granit–.

grannie, granny ['græni], *s.* (*coll.*) die Oma; ***– knot,*** der Altweiberknoten.

grant [grɑ:nt], **1.** *v.t.* 1. bewilligen, gewähren, gestatten, vergönnen; (*Law*) überlassen, übertragen, überweisen, verleihen; ***Heaven – that,*** gebe der Himmel, daß; ***– his life,*** ihm das Leben schenken; ***– permission,*** Erlaubnis geben *or* erteilen; ***– a request,*** eine Bitte erfüllen, einer Bitte nachkommen *or* stattgeben, einem Ansuchen Folge leisten; 2. zugeben, zugestehen, einräumen; ***take for –ed,*** als erwiesen *or* selbstverständlich annehmen, voraussetzen; ***–ed that,*** angenommen *or* zugegeben *or* gesetzt, daß; ***–ing this to be true,*** angenommen, dies wäre wahr. **2.** *s.* 1. die Bewilligung, Gewährung; 2. (*Law*) Erteilung, Verleihung (***to,*** an (*Acc.*)), Überweisung, Übertragung (***to,*** auf (*Acc.*)); übertragene *or* bewilligte S., (*esp.*) die Unterstützung, Subvention, der Zuschuß; ***government –,*** der Staatszuschuß; ***--in-aid,*** die Notunterstützung; ***student's –,*** die Studienbeihilfe. **grantee** [–'ti:], *s.* (*Law*) Begünstigte(r), Privilegierte(r), der Konzessionär. **grantor,** *s.* (*Law*) der Verleiher, Zedent.

granular ['grænjulə], *adj.* körnig, gekörnt, granuliert; ***– ore,*** das Graupenerz. **granulate** [–leit], *v.t.* körnen, granulieren. **granulated,** *adj.* körnig, granuliert. **granulation** [–'leiʃən], *s.* das Körnen, Granulieren; die Kornbildung, Kristallbildung, Körnigkeit, (*Med.*) Granulation. **granule,** *s.* das Körnchen. **granulous,** *adj. See* **granular.**

grape [greip], *s.* 1. die Weinbeere, (Wein)traube; ***bunch of –s,*** die Weintraube; 2. *pl.* (*Vet.*) Mauke. **grape|fruit,** *s.* die Pampelmuse. **–shot,** *s.* die Kartätsche. **--stone,** *s.* der Weinbeerkern. **--sugar,** *s.* der Traubenzucker. **--vine,** *s.* der Weinstock; (*coll.*) nichtamtliche Meldung, das Gerücht, die Flüsterpropaganda.

graph [grɑ:f], **1.** *s.* graphische Darstellung, das Kurvenblatt, Schaubild, Diagramm; (*esp. Math.*) die Kurve; ***– paper,*** das Millimeterpapier. **2.** *v.t.* graphisch darstellen. **graphic(al)** ['græfik(l)], *adj.* graphisch, zeichnerisch; diagrammatisch; (*fig.*) anschaulich, lebendig (geschildert), getreu.

graphite ['græfait], *s.* der Graphit, das Reißblei, die Temperkohle. **graphitic** [–'fitik], *adj.* graphitisch, graphitartig, Graphit–.

graphology [græ'fɔlədʒi], *s.* die Handschriftendeutung, Graphologie.

grapnel ['græpnəl], *s.* (*Naut.*) der Dregganker, die Dragge, Dregge; der Enterhaken; (*Build.*) die (Greif)klaue, das Ankereisen, der Anker.

grapple [græpl], **1.** *v.t.* (*Naut.*) mit Enterhaken fassen, entern; (*Build.*) verankern, verklammern. **2.** *v.i.* sich raufen, miteinander ringen, handgemein werden; sich festhalten *or* klammern (***with,*** an (*Dat.*)); (*fig.*) ***– with,*** ringen *or* kämpfen mit, sich auseinandersetzen mit, anpacken, ernstlich in Angriff nehmen. **3.** *s.* der Enterhaken; das Greifzeug, der Greifer. **grappling|-hook, --iron,** *s.* der Enterhaken.

grasp [grɑ:sp], **1.** *v.t.* packen, fassen, (er)greifen; (*fig.*) verstehen, begreifen, (er)fassen; ***– the nettle,***

die Schwierigkeit anpacken. **2.** *v.i.* – *at,* greifen nach, (*fig.*) streben *or* trachten nach; – ***at a straw,*** sich an einen Strohhalm klammern. **3.** *s.* der Griff; die Reichweite; (*fig.*) der Bereich, die Macht, Gewalt; der Besitz, die Kontrolle, Herrschaft; Fassungskraft, das Verständnis; ***be beyond his –,*** seine Fassungskraft übersteigen; ***have a – of,*** beherrschen; ***no – of,*** kein Verständnis für; ***have within his –,*** in Reichweite haben, (*fig.*) Gewalt haben über (*Acc.*). **grasping,** *adj.* (*fig.*) habgierig, geizig.

grass [gra:s], **1.** *s.* 1. das Gras, der Rasen; das Grasland, die Weide, Wiese; ***at –,*** auf der Weide; ***go to –,*** zur Weide gehen; (*coll.*) sich (von der Arbeit) zurückziehen; ***put*** or ***turn out to –,*** auf die Weide treiben, (*coll.*) entlassen, abschieben; ***not let the – grow under one's feet,*** unverzüglich ans Werk gehen, nicht lange zögern; 2. (*sl.*) das Hasch(isch). **2.** *v.t.* 1. mit Gras bedecken; 2. auf dem Rasen bleichen (*flax*); 3. abschießen (*a bird*). **3.** *v.i.* (*sl.*) pfeifen, petzen; – ***on him,*** ihn verpetzen *or* verpfeifen.

grass|-cloth, *s.* das Grasleinen, Nesseltuch. **--green,** *adj.* grasgrün. **--grown,** *adj.* mit Gras bewachsen. **–hopper,** *s.* (*Ent.*) die Heuschrecke, der Grashüpfer. **grassiness,** *s.* der Grasreichtum. **grass|land,** *s.* die Wiese, Weide. **--roots,** **1.** *pl.* (*fig.*) die Quelle, Wurzel. **2.** *adj.* (*fig.*) volksverbunden, aus dem Volk. **--snake,** *s.* die Ringelnatter. **--widow,** *s.* die Strohwitwe. **--widower,** *s.* der Strohwitwer. **grassy,** *adj.* grassig, grasbedeckt, grasreich.

[1]**grate** [greit], **1.** *s.* der (Feuer)rost, Herd, Kamin; das (Kamin)gitter. **2.** *v.t.* vergittern; ***–d window,*** das Gitterfenster.

[2]**grate,** **1.** *v.t.* abschaben, (zer)reiben; (*fig.*) beleidigen, verletzen; – ***one's teeth,*** mit den Zähnen knirschen. **2.** *v.i.* knarren, knirschen; (*fig.*) zuwider sein, weh tun (*on*, *Dat.*); – ***on the ear,*** das Ohr beleidigen; – ***on the nerves,*** auf die Nerven gehen.

grateful ['greitful], *adj.* dankbar, erkenntlich (*to*, *Dat.*); (*of a th.*) erfreulich, angenehm, zusagend, wohltuend. **gratefulness,** *s.* die Dankbarkeit; Annehmlichkeit.

grater ['greitə], *s.* das Reibeisen, die Raspel.

graticule ['grætikju:l], *s.* das Fadenkreuz; Gitter, Netz.

gratification [grætifi'keiʃən], *s.* 1. die Befriedigung, Zufriedenstellung; Genugtuung (*at*, über (*Acc.*)); Freude, das Vergnügen, der Genuß; 2. das Trinkgeld, die Belohnung, Gratifikation. **gratify** ['grætifai], *v.t.* befriedigen, zufriedenstellen; willfahren (*Dat.*), entgegenkommen (*Dat.*), gefällig sein (*Dat.*); erfreuen; ***be gratified at,*** sich freuen über (*Acc.*). **gratifying,** *adj.* erfreulich.

[1]**grating** ['greitiŋ], *s.* das Gitter(werk), der Rost, die Vergitterung; (*Naut.*) Gräting.

[2]**grating,** *adj.* knirschend, kratzend, mißtönend.

gratis ['gra:tis], *adv.* unentgeltlich, umsonst.

gratitude ['grætitju:d], *s.* die Dankbarkeit, Erkenntlichkeit; ***in – for,*** aus Dankbarkeit für; ***a debt of –,*** eine Dankesschuld; ***owe him a debt of –,*** ihm zu (großem) Dank verpflichtet sein.

gratuitous [grə'tjuitəs], *adj.* freiwillig, unverlangt, unaufgefordert, ohne Gegenleistung, unentgeltlich; unbegründet, unberechtigt, unverdient; grundlos, mutwillig.

gratuity [grə'tjuiti], *s.* die Belohnung, das Trinkgeld, (kleines) Geldgeschenk, die Gratifikation.

gravamen [grə'veimən], *s.* das Belastende, der Beschwerdepunkt, Beschwerdegrund.

[1]**grave** [greiv], *adj.* ernst(haft), gesetzt, würdevoll, feierlich; ernst, wichtig, schwer(wiegend), bedenklich; gedämpft, tief (*as sound*).

[2]**grave,** *s.* das Grab, der Grabhügel; ***have one foot in the –,*** mit einem Fuß im Grabe stehen; ***turn in one's –,*** sich im Grabe umdrehen.

[3]**grave,** *reg. & irr.v.t.* (*Poet.*) meißeln, schnitzen; (*fig.*) eingraben, einprägen.

[4]**grave,** *v.t.* (*Naut.*) kalfatern.

[5]**grave** [gra:v], *s.* (*Phonet.*) (*also* – ***accent***) der Gravis.

grave|-clothes, *pl.* das Totengewand. **--digger,** *s.* der Totengräber.

gravel [grævl], **1.** *s.* der Kies; (*Med.*) Grieß. **2.** *v.t.* 1. mit Kies bedecken; 2. (*fig.*) verwirren. **gravelly,** *adj.* kiesig. **gravel|-pit,** *s.* die Kiesgrube. **–stone,** *s.* der Kieselstein.

graven [greivn], **1.** *p.p. of* [3]**grave.** **2.** *adj.* – ***image,*** das Götzenbild.

graver ['greivə], *s.* 1. der Grabstichel, Stechmeißel; 2. (*Poet.*) Bildhauer, Bildschnitzer.

graves [greivz], *pl. See* [2]**greaves.**

grave|stone, *s.* der Grabstein. **–yard,** *s.* der Friedhof.

gravid ['grævid], *adj.* schwanger. **gravidity** [–'viditi], *s.* die Schwangerschaft.

gravimeter [græ'vimitə], *s.* der Dichtigkeitsmesser, Schweremesser. **gravimetric** [–'metrik], *adj.* Gewichts–, gewichtsanalytisch.

graving|-dock, *s.* das Trockendock; *see* [4]**grave.** **--tool,** *s.* der Grabstichel; *see* [3]**grave.**

gravitate ['græviteit], *v.i.* gravitieren, (hin)streben, (hin)neigen, hingezogen werden (*to*(*wards*), zu), angezogen werden (von). **gravitation** [–'teiʃən], *s.* die Schwerkraft; (*fig.*) Tendenz, Neigung, der Hang. **gravitational,** *adj.* Gravitations–, Schwere–.

gravity ['græviti], *s.* 1. das Gewicht; die Schwerkraft, (Erd)schwere; ***centre of –,*** der Schwerpunkt; ***force of –,*** die Schwerkraft; ***law of –,*** das Gesetz der Schwere; ***specific –,*** spezifisches Gewicht; 2. (*fig.*) die Wichtigkeit, der Ernst; die Ernsthaftigkeit, Feierlichkeit, Würde; Tiefe (*of sound*).

gravy ['greivi], *s.* das Bratenfett, der Fleischsaft, die Tunke, Soße. **gravy-boat,** *s.* die Sauciere.

gray, (*Am.*) *see* **grey.**

grayling ['greiliŋ], *s.* (*Ichth.*) die Äsche.

[1]**graze** [greiz], **1.** *v.t.* abgrasen, abweiden; grasen *or* weiden lassen. **2.** *v.i.* grasen, weiden.

[2]**graze,** **1.** *v.t.* streifen, leicht berühren; abschürfen. **2.** *s.* der Querschläger, Streifschuß; (*Med.*) die Abschürfung, Schramme.

grazier ['greiziə], *s.* der Viehzüchter, Viehmäster. **grazing,** *s.* das Weiden; Weideland, die Weide, Trift.

grease [gri:s], **1.** *s.* das Fett, Schmalz; (*Tech.*) Schmiermittel, die Schmiere; der Schweiß (*of wool*); (*Vet.*) die Mauke; ***in –,*** in Feist (*of deer*); ***in the –,*** ungereinigt (*of wool*). **2.** *v.t.* einfetten; (ein)ölen, schmieren; (*unintentionally*) beschmieren; – ***a cake-tin,*** eine Backform ausstreichen; (*fig.*) – ***his palm,*** ihn schmieren, ihm Schmiergeld bezahlen; ***like –d lightning,*** wie ein geölter Blitz.

grease|-box, *s.* die Schmierbüchse. **--gun,** *s.* die Schmierspritze, Schmierpistole. **--paint,** *s.* die (Bühnen)schminke. **--proof,** *adj.* fettdicht; – ***paper,*** das Butterbrotpapier. **greaser,** *s.* die Schmiervorrichtung, der Schmiernippel; (*Naut.*) Schmierer. **grease-spot,** *s.* der Fettfleck. **greasiness,** *s.* die Schmierigkeit, Fettigkeit. **greasy,** *adj.* schmierig; fettig, ölig, fetthaltig, fettartig; glitschig, schlüpfrig (*of the ground*); – ***pole,*** eingefetteter Kletterbaum.

great [greit], **1.** *adj.* groß, bedeutend, wichtig, hervorragend, beträchtlich; ungeheuer, mächtig; vornehm, berühmt, überragend, prächtig, stattlich, erhaben, imponierend; hochherzig, großmütig; (*coll.*) herrlich, ausgezeichnet, wunderbar, glänzend, großartig, famos; (*only pred.*) (*coll.*) geschickt, bewandert (*at*, in (*Dat.*)); ***she is – on the piano,*** sie spielt glänzend Klavier; – ***age,*** hohes Alter; – ***attraction,*** die Hauptzugnummer; (*Orn.*) – ***auk,*** der Riesenalk (*Alca impennis*); (*coll.*) – ***big,*** ungeheuer groß, Mords–; ***Great Britain,*** Großbritannien; – ***circle,*** der Großkreis; ***Great Dane,*** die Dogge; ***a – deal,*** sehr viel; ***in – detail,*** in allen Einzelheiten; ***in – favour with,*** in hoher Gunst bei; – ***friend,*** intimer Freund; (*Univ. sl.*) ***Great Go,*** das Schlußexamen; – ***hall,*** der Hauptsaal; ***a – many,***

eine große Anzahl, sehr viele; ***it is no – matter,*** es macht nicht viel aus; ***the – powers,*** die Großmächte; ***– Scot(t)!*** Großer Gott! ***– toe,*** große Zehe; ***the Great War,*** Erster Weltkrieg; ***a – while,*** eine lange Zeit, recht lange; ***– with young,*** trächtig, **2.** (*collect.*) ***the –*** (*coll. –s*), die Großen, Vornehmen (*pl.*).

great|coat, *s.* der Wintermantel. **--grandchild,** *s.* das Urenkelkind. **--granddaughter,** *s.* die Urenkelin. **--grandfather,** *s.* der Urgroßvater. **--grandparents,** *pl.* Urgroßeltern (*pl.*). **--grandson,** *s.* der Urenkel. **--great-grandfather,** *s.* der Ururgroßvater. **--hearted,** *adj.* hochherzig, großmütig. **greatly,** *adv.* in hohem Maß *or* Grad, überaus, sehr, höchst; weitaus, bei weitem. **greatness,** *s.* die Größe, das Ausmaß; die Bedeutung, Stärke, Gewalt; Prominenz, Erhabenheit, Herrlichkeit. **Greats,** *pl.* (*Oxford Univ.*) das Schlußexamen (in der klassischen Philologie).

[1]**greaves** [gri:vz], *pl.* (*Hist.*) Beinschienen (*pl.*).

[2]**greaves,** *pl.* Fettgrieben, (Talg)grieben (*pl.*).

grebe [gri:b], *s.* (*Orn.*) der Taucher (*Podicipitidae*).

Grecian ['gri:ʃən], *adj.* (klassisch) griechisch. **Greece** [gri:s], *s.* Griechenland (*n.*).

greed [gri:d], *s.* die (Hab)gier, Habsucht. **greediness,** *s.* die Gier(igkeit), Gefräßigkeit; *see also* **greed. greedy,** *adj.* (be)gierig (***of, for,*** nach *or* auf (*Acc.*)); habsüchtig, habgierig; gefräßig.

Greek [gri:k], **1.** *adj.* griechisch; ***– Orthodox Church,*** Griechisch-katholische Kirche. **2.** *s.* **1.** der Grieche (die Griechin); 2. (*language*) das Griechisch(e); (*coll.*) ***that's all – to me,*** das sind mir böhmische Dörfer, das kommt mir spanisch vor.

green [gri:n], **1.** *adj.* grün; (*fig.*) frisch; unreif (*as fruit*); (*coll.*) unreif, unerfahren; ***– in one's memory,*** noch in frischem Andenken; ***– old age,*** rüstiges Greisenalter; ***– belt,*** der Grüngürtel, das Parkgelände; ***– cheese,*** unreifer Käse; der Kräuterkase; (*coll.*) ***– fingers,*** gärtnerische Begabung; (*fig.*) ***give the – light to,*** grünes Licht geben (*Dat.*) (*a p. or th.*); ***– with envy,*** gelb vor Neid. **2.** *s.* 1. das Grün, grüne Farbe; 2. die Grünfläche, Wiese, der Grasplatz, Anger, Rasen; (*Golf*) das Grün; ***bowling –,*** die Kegelwiese; ***putting –,*** das Grün; ***village –,*** der Dorfanger; 3. (*fig.*) die (Jugend)frische, Lebenskraft; 4. das Laub; *pl.* Blattgemüse, Grünzeug, Grüne(s).

greenback ['gri:nbæk], *s.* (*Am.*) (*sl.*) die Banknote, das Papiergeld. **greenery,** *s.* das Laub(werk), Grün. **green|finch,** *s.* (*Orn.*) der Grünfink, Grünling (*Chloris chloris*). **-fly,** *s.* (*Ent.*) die Blattlaus. **--fodder,** *s.* das Grünfutter, Futterpflanzen (*pl.*). **-gage,** *s.* die Reineclaude. **-grocer,** *s.* der Obst- und Gemüsehändler. **-grocery,** *s.* 1. (*oft. pl.*) Obst- und Gemüsewaren (*pl.*), der Grünkram; 2. die Obst- und Gemüsehandlung. **-horn,** *s.* (*coll.*) der Grünschnabel, unerfahrener Junge, der Einfaltspinsel. **-house,** *s.* das Gewächshaus, Treibhaus. **greenish,** *adj.* grünlich. **Greenland,** *s.* Grönland (*n.*). **greenness,** *s.* das Grün(e); (*fig.*) die Frische; Unreife; (*sl.*) Unerfahrenheit. **green|room,** *s.* (*Theat.*) das Künstlerzimmer. **-shank,** *s.* (*Orn.*) der Grünschenkel (*Tringa nebularia*). **--sickness,** *s.* die Bleichsucht. **-stick,** *adj.* (*Med.*) Grünholz–, Knick– (*fracture*). **-stuff,** *s.* grünes Gemüse, der Grünkram; das Grünfutter (*for animals*). **-sward,** *s.* der Rasen. **-wood,** *s.* belaubter Wald.

[1]**greet** [gri:t], *v.i.* (*Scots*) weinen, klagen.

[2]**greet,** *v.t.* (be)grüßen; grüßend empfangen. **greeting,** *s.* die Begrüßung; der Gruß; ***–s telegram,*** das Glückwunschtelegramm.

gregarious [gri'gɛəriəs], *adj.* in Herden *or* Scharen lebend, Herden–; gesellig. **gregariousness,** *s.* das Zusammenleben in Herden; die Geselligkeit.

gremlin ['gremlin], *s.* (*sl.*) der Kobold, böser Geist.

grenade [grə'neid], *s.* die (Hand)granate. **grenadier** [grenə'diə], *s.* der Grenadier.

grenadine ['grənədi:n], *s.* 1. (*Weav.*) die Grenadine; 2. (*Cul.*) der Grenadin, gespickte Fleischschnitte.

gresorial [grə'sɔ:riəl], *adj.* Stelz–, (*Orn.*) Schreit–.

grew [gru:], *imperf. of* **grow.**

grey [grei], **1.** *adj.* 1. grau; ***Grey Friar,*** der Franziskanermönch, Kapuziner; ***– horse,*** der Grauschimmel; (*coll.*) ***the – mare is the better horse,*** die Frau führt das Regiment *or* hat die Hosen an; (*coll.*) ***– matter,*** graue Substanz, der Verstand, die Grütze; (*Am.*) ***– partridge,*** *see* **partridge**; 2. grau(haarig), ergraut, altersgrau; 3. trübe, düster. **2.** *s.* 1. das Grau, graue Farbe; 2. der Grauschimmel (*horse*). **3.** *v.i.* grau werden, ergrauen.

grey|beard, *s.* der Graubart. **--haired,** *adj.* grauhaarig. **--headed,** *adj.* grauköpfig. **-hen,** *s.* (*Orn.*) das Birkhuhn, Haselhuhn (*Lyrurus tetrix*). **-hound,** *s.* das Windspiel, der Windhund; ***--racing,*** das Hunderennen. **greyish,** *adj.* fahlgrau, graulich, gräulich. **greylag (goose),** *s.* (*Orn.*) die Graugans, Wildgans (*Anser anser*). **greyness,** *s.* graue Farbe, das Grau(e). **greywacke** [–wækə], *s.* (*Geol.*) die Grauwacke.

grid [grid], *s.* das Gitter (*also Rad.*); (*Elec.*) Überland(leitungs)netz; (*maps*) Gitter(netz); (*Rad.*) ***– bias,*** die Gittervorspannung; (*Rad.*) ***control –,*** das Steuergitter; ***– reference,*** die Planquadratangabe (*maps*); (*Rad.*) ***screen –,*** das Schirmgitter; *see also* **gridiron. griddle,** *s.* (*dial.*) das Kuchenblech. **grid|iron,** *s.* 1. der Bratrost; 2. (*Naut.*) die Balkenroste; 3. (*Am. Footb.*) das Spielfeld. **--leak,** *s.* (*Rad.*) der Gitterwiderstand.

grief [gri:f], *s.* der Kummer, Schmerz, Gram, das Leid; ***come to –,*** zu Schaden *or* Fall kommen, ein schlimmes Ende nehmen (*of a p.*); versagen, fehlschlagen, (*coll.*) kaputtgehen (*of a th.*). **grief-stricken,** *adj.* kummervoll.

grievance ['gri:vəns], *s.* die Beschwerde, der Verdruß, Groll, das Ressentiment; der Grund zur Klage, Mißstand, Übelstand; ***nurse a –,*** einen Groll hegen; ***redress a –,*** einem Übelstand abhelfen. **grieve, 1.** *v.t.* kränken, betrüben, bekümmern; Kummer bereiten (*Dat.*), wehtun (*Dat.*). **2.** *v.i.* sich grämen *or* härmen, bekümmert sein (***over, about,*** über (*Acc.*)). **grievous,** *adj.* schmerzlich, kränkend, bedrückend, bitter; schlimm, arg, schwer, schrecklich; (*Law*) ***– bodily harm,*** schwere Körperverletzung. **grievousness,** *s.* das Drückende, Schmerzliche, der Druck, die Bitterkeit.

[1]**griffin** ['grifin], *s.* (*Her., Myth.*) der Greif.

[2]**griffin,** *s.* der Neuling, Neuankömmling.

griffon ['grifən], *s.* 1. der Affenpinscher; 2. *See* [1]**griffin. griffon-vulutre,** *s.* (*Orn.*) der Gänsegeier (*Gyps fulvus*).

grig [grig], *s.* (*dial.*) 1. die Grille, das Heimchen; 2. der Sandaal.

grill [gril], **1.** *v.t.* 1. auf dem Rost braten, rösten; 2. (*fig.*) quälen, plagen; (*sl.*) ins Verhör nehmen. **2.** *v.i.* braten, schmoren. **3.** *s.* 1. der Bratrost; Rostbraten; 2. *See* **grill-room.**

grillage ['grilidʒ], *s.* das Gitterwerk, Pfahlrost. **grille** [gril], *s.* das Türgitter; Sprechgitter, Gitterfenster.

grilling ['griliŋ], *s.* (*sl.*) scharfes Verhör. **grill-room,** *s.* der Grillroom.

grilse [grils], *s.* junger Lachs.

grim [grim], *adj.* grimmig; schrecklich, grausam, hart; ***– humour,*** der Galgenhumor; ***– truth,*** grausame Wahrheit.

grimace [gri'meis], **1.** *s.* die Grimasse, Fratze. **2.** *v.i.* Grimassen schneiden.

grimalkin [gri'mælkin], *s.* die Katze.

grime [graim], **1.** *s.* der Schmutz, Dreck, Ruß. **2.** *v.t.* besudeln, beschmutzen. **griminess,** *s.* die Schmutzigkeit, der Schmutz.

grimness ['grimnis], *s.* die Grimmigkeit, Schrecklichkeit, Grausamkeit, Härte.

grimy ['graimi], *adj.* schmutzig, rußig.

grin [grin], **1.** *v.i.* grinsen, feixen; ***– and bear it,*** gute Miene zum bösen Spiel machen. **2.** *s.* das Grinsen.

grind [graind], **1.** *irr.v.t.* zerstoßen, zerstampfen, (zer)mahlen, zerreiben, zerkleinern, zermalmen; schleifen, wetzen (*knife etc.*); (*fig.*) quälen, schinden; ***have an axe to –,*** eigennützige Zwecke verfolgen; – ***a barrel-organ,*** einen Leierkasten drehen; – ***colours,*** Farben reiben; – ***the face of the poor,*** die Armen bedrücken *or* ausnützen *or* ausbeuten; – ***to powder,*** zermalmen; – ***roughly,*** schroten; – ***one's teeth,*** mit den Zähnen knirschen; – ***down,*** feinmahlen (*corn etc.*), abwetzen (*knife etc.*); (*fig.*) unterdrücken; – ***out,*** mühsam herunterleiern (*music etc.*). **2.** *irr.v.i.* 1. sich mahlen *or* schleifen lassen; knirschend reiben, knirschen (***on, against,*** an (*Dat.*)); 2. (*sl.*) ochsen, büffeln, schuften. **3.** *s.* (*sl.*) die Plackerei, Schinderei; das Ochsen, Büffeln. **grinder,** *s.* der Schleifer; Backenzahn, Mahlzahn; (*Tech.*) die Schleifmaschine; das Mahlwerk; (*sl.*) der Einpauker. **grinding, 1.** *s.* das Mahlen; Schleifen; Knirschen. **2.** *adj.* knirschend; (*fig.*) mühsam, bedrückend, zermürbend. **grindstone,** *s.* der Wetzstein, Schleifstein; (*coll.*) ***keep one's nose to the –,*** sich abschinden *or* dahinterklemmen.

grip [grip], **1.** *s.* 1. der Griff, das Anpacken, (Er)greifen; ***at –s,*** handgemein, im Kampf; ***come to –s,*** handgemein werden, (*fig.*) sich auseinandersetzen; (*Motor.*) ***tyre –,*** die Griffigkeit der Reifen; 2. der Händedruck; (*of sword etc.*) (Hand)griff, (*of rifle*) Kolbenhals; (*coll.*) die Haarspange, Haarklemme; 3. (*fig.*) Herrschaft, Gewalt (***on, of,*** über (*Acc.*)); (*fig.*) ***in the – of,*** in den Klauen von; (*fig.*) ***have a – on,*** in der Gewalt haben; Verständnis haben für; (*fig.*) ***lose one's – on,*** den Halt *or* die Herrschaft verlieren über (*Acc.*); 4. (*coll.*) *see* **gripsack. 2.** *v.t.* 1. ergreifen, (an)fassen, (an)packen; festhalten; 2. (*fig.*) in der Gewalt haben; in Spannung halten, fesseln. **3.** *v.i.* fassen, Halt finden, halten (*as an anchor*); (*fig.*) fesseln, packen.

gripe [graip], **1.** *v.t.* 1. (*obs.*) *see* **grip, 2.**; 2. (*usu. fig.*) betrüben, (be)drücken; (*Med.*) zwicken, Bauchgrimmen verursachen (*Dat.*); ***be –d,*** Bauchschmerzen haben; 3. zurren, seefest machen (*boats*). **2.** *v.i.* 1. zugreifen, zupacken; 2. (*Med.*) Bauchgrimmen verursachen; 3. (*Naut.*) luvgierig sein; 3. (*sl.*) murren, meckern. **3.** *s.* 1. *See* **grip, 1.**; 2. *pl.* (*Med.*) die Kolik, das Bauchgrimmen. **griper,** *s.* (*sl.*) der Meckerfritze. **griping, 1.** *adj.* 1. drückend, zwickend, nagend (*as pain*); 2. (*Naut.*) luvgierig. **2.** *s.* (*sl.*) das Meckern.

gripping ['gripiŋ], *adj.* (*fig.*) ergreifend, packend, fesselnd, spannend.

gripsack ['gripsæk], *s.* (*Am.*) die Reisetasche.

griskin ['griskin], *s.* (*Cul.*) der Schweinsrücken, das Rippenstück, die Karbonade.

grisliness ['grizlinis], *s.* die Grausigkeit, Gräßlichkeit, Schauerlichkeit. **grisly,** *adj.* schrecklich, entsetzlich, schauerlich, grausig, gräßlich.

Grisons ['grisənz], *s.* (*Geog.*) Graubünden (*n.*).

grist [grist], *s.* das Mahlgut, Mahlkorn; (*Brew.*) Malzschrot; ***that's – to his mill,*** das ist Wasser auf seine Mühle; ***bring – to the mill,*** Vorteil *or* Nutzen bringen, einträglich sein.

gristle [grisl], *s.* der Knorpel; (*fig.*) ***in the –,*** unentwickelt, im Entstehen. **gristly,** *adj.* knorpelig.

grit [grit], **1.** *s.* 1. der Kies, Grieß, grober Sand; (*Min.*) der Grus, Sandstein; 2. (*coll.*) die (Charakter)festigkeit, (*coll.*) der Mumm; die Entschlossenheit, der Mut; 3. *pl.* die Grütze; das Schrot, grobes Hafermehl. **2.** *v.i.* knirschen. **3.** *v.t.* – ***one's teeth,*** mit den Zähnen knirschen. **grittiness,** *s.* sandige *or* kiesige Beschaffenheit. **gritty,** *adj.* kiesig, sandig.

[1]**grizzle** [grizl], *s.* das Grau, graue Farbe.

[2]**grizzle,** *v.i.* (*coll.*) nörgeln, quengeln, murren.

grizzled [grizld], *adj.* grau(haarig), ergraut. **grizzly, 1.** *adj.* grau, gräulich. **2.** *s.* (*also* – ***bear***) der Graubär.

groan [groun], **1.** *v.i.* stöhnen, ächzen; knarren, knacken (*as furniture*). **2.** *v.t.* unter Stöhnen hervorbringen. **3.** *s.* das Stöhnen, Ächzen; Murren.

groat [grout], *s.* (*obs.*) der Grot (= *2 pence*).

groats [grouts], *pl.* die (Hafer)grütze.

grocer ['grousə], *s.* der Kolonialwarenhändler, Krämer; ***–'s shop,*** das Kolonialwarengeschäft.

grocery, *s.* 1. der Kolonialwarenladen; Kolonialwarenhandel; 2. (*oft. pl.*) Kolonialwaren (*pl.*).

grog [grɔg], *s.* der Grog; (*sl.*) – ***blossom,*** die Schnapsnase. **grogginess,** *s.* (*coll.*) die (Be)trunkenheit; Wackeligkeit, Taumeligkeit. **groggy,** *adj.* (*coll.*) betrunken, angetrunken, beschwipst; (*Boxing*) angeschlagen; taumelig, wackelig, schwach auf den Beinen; steif, abgejagt (*as horses*); (*sl.*) anfällig, kränklich.

groin [grɔin], **1.** *s.* 1. (*Anat.*) die Leiste(ngegend); 2. (*Archit.*) der Grat, die Rippe. **2.** *v.t.* mit Rippen *or* Gurten versehen; ***–ed ceiling,*** gerippte Decke; ***–ed vault,*** das Kreuzgewölbe.

grommet ['grʌmit], *s.* 1. der Gummi(dichtungs)ring; die Öse; 2. (*Naut.*) der Taukranz.

groom [gru:m], **1.** *s.* 1. der Stallknecht, Pferdeknecht, Reitknecht; 2. Bräutigam (bei der Trauung); 3. (*obs.*) Diener; – ***in waiting,*** diensttuender Kammerjunker; – ***of the chamber,*** königlicher Kammerdiener. **2.** *v.t.* warten, pflegen, striegeln, besorgen (*horses*); (*coll., fig.*) vorbereiten; ***well-–ed,*** gepflegt. **groomsman,** *s.* der Beistand des Bräutigams (*at the wedding*).

groove [gru:v], **1.** *s.* 1. die Nut(e), Rinne, Furche, Hohlkehle, Auskehlung, (*gramophone record*) Rille, *pl.* Züge (*of a gun*); 2. (*fig.*) die Routine, Schablone, das Fahrwasser, gewohnter Gang, gewohntes Geleise; ***be*** or ***stay in a –,*** immer in demselben Geleise bleiben. **2.** *v.t.* auskehlen, aushöhlen, falzen, nuten, riffeln, riefeln, rillen.

grope [group], **1.** *v.t.* tasten nach; – ***one's way,*** sich dahintasten. **2.** *v.i.* tasten, tappen (***for,*** nach); – ***about,*** herumtappen.

grosbeak ['grousbi:k], *s.* (*Orn.*) der Kernbeißer (*Coccothraustes coccothraustes*); (*Am.*) ***cardinal –,*** der Kardinal(vogel) (*Richmondena cardinalis*); ***pine –,*** der Hakengimpel (*Pinicola enucleator*); (*Am.*) ***rose-breasted –,*** der Rosengimpel (*Hedymeles ludovicianus*); ***sociable –,*** *see* **weaverbird.**

gross [grous], **1.** *adj.* 1. sehr dick, massiv, plump, fett, feist (*figure*); 2. derb, grob, roh, unfein (*manners*); schwerfällig, stumpf (*mind*); 3. ungeheuerlich, schreiend, schwer (*error etc.*); – ***error,*** schwerer Fehler; – ***misrepresentation,*** grobe Entstellung; 4. (*Comm.*) Brutto–, Roh–; – ***amount,*** die Gesamtsumme, der Bruttobetrag; – ***earnings,*** Bruttoeinnahmen (*pl.*), der Rohertrag; – ***tonnage,*** der Bruttotonnengehalt; – ***weight,*** das Bruttogewicht. **2.** *s.* das Gros, 12 Dutzend; ***in the –,*** im (großen und) ganzen, in Bausch und Bogen. **grossly,** *adv.* in hohem Grad, ungeheuer. **grossness,** *s.* die Derbheit, Grobheit, Unfeinheit, Roheit, Gemeinheit, Schwerfälligkeit, Plumpheit.

grotesque [grou'tesk], *adj.* grotesk, wunderlich, bizarr, absurd, lächerlich, phantastisch. **grotesqueness,** *s.* das Groteske, Absurde, die Absurdität, Lächerlichkeit.

grotto ['grɔtou], *s.* die Felsenhöhle, Grotte.

grouch [grautʃ], (*Am. sl.*) **1.** *v.i.* *See* [2]**grouse. 2.** *s.* *See* **grouser.**

[1]**ground** [graund], **1.** *imperf., p.p. of* **grind. 2.** – ***coffee,*** gemahlener Kaffee; – ***glass,*** matt(geschliffen)es Glas, (*Phot.*) die Mattscheibe.

[2]**ground, 1.** *s.* 1. der Grund; (Erd)boden, die Erde; ***below (the) –,*** unter der Erde; ***to the –,*** zu Boden, zur Erde; (*coll.*) ***down to the –,*** von Grund aus, gründlich, in jeder Hinsicht, vollständig, durchaus, absolut, ganz und gar; ***break new –,*** ein Brachfeld umpflügen *or* umbrechen, (*fig.*) neues Gebiet erschließen; ***cut the – from under his feet,*** ihm den Boden unter den Füßen wegziehen, ihn in die Enge treiben; (*fig.*) ***fall*** (or ***be dashed***) ***to the –,*** ins Wasser fallen, fehlschlagen, scheitern; ***strike to the –,*** zu Boden schlagen; ***till the –,*** Land bestellen; 2. der Meeresgrund, Meeresboden; (*Naut.*) ***take the –,*** stranden, auflaufen; 3. das Gelände, Gebiet, Ländereien (*pl.*), die Strecke, Fläche; (*fig.*) Stellung, der Standpunkt, Standort; ***fishing –,*** das Fischereigebiet; ***rising –,*** die Steigung, Anhöhe; ***cover much –,*** (*of a th.*) sich weithin strecken; (*of a p.*) gut weiterkommen, eine

weite Strecke zurücklegen; (*fig.*) umfassend sein; ***cover old –***, ein altes Gebiet behandeln; ***gain –***, sich durchsetzen, (an) Boden gewinnen, um sich greifen; ***gain – (up)on him***, ihm Boden abgewinnen; ***give –***, *see* ***lose –***; ***go over the –***, besprechen, überlegen, (*coll.*) durchackern; ***go over old – (again)***, Bekanntes wiederholen; ***hold one's –***, sich *or* die Stellung behaupten, (*fig.*) auf seine Meinung beharren; ***lose –***, weichen, (an) Boden verlieren; ***maintain*** or ***stand one's –***, see ***hold one's –***; ***shift one's –***, den Standpunkt ändern, umschwenken; 4. der Grundsitz, Grund und Boden, das Grundstück; *pl.* (Garten)anlagen (*pl.*); ***in its own –s***, auf eignem Grund und Boden; 5. (*oft. pl.*) (*Spt.*) der Spielplatz; ***football –***, der Fußballplatz; 6. (*Paint.*) der Untergrund, Fond, die Unterlage, Grundfarbe, Grundierung; 7. (*fig.*) (*oft. pl.*) Grundlage, Basis, Ursache, Veranlassung, der (Beweg)grund; ***on the –(s) that***, mit der Begründung, daß; ***on the –(s) of***, wegen, auf Grund (*Gen.*); ***on political –s***, aus politischen Gründen *or* Rücksichten; 8. (*Rad., Elec.*) die Erde, der Erd(an)schluß; 9. *pl.* der (Boden)satz; ***coffee –s***, der Kaffeesatz.
2. *v.t.* 1. auf den Boden stellen *or* setzen; hinlegen, niederstellen, niedersetzen, niederlegen; (*Naut.*) stranden lassen, auf Strand setzen; (*Av.*) am Starten verhindern, Startverbot erteilen, abstellen; 2. (*Paint.*) vorfärben, grundieren; 3. (*Elec.*) erden; 4. (*fig.*) stützen, gründen (***on, in***, auf (*Acc.*)), begründen (in (*Dat.*)), aufbauen (auf (*Dat.*)); ***be –ed in***, gestützt *or* gegründet sein auf (*Acc.*), verwurzelt sein *or* wurzeln in (*Dat.*); 5. einweisen (***in***, in (*Acc.*)), in den Anfangsgründen (*Gen.*) unterrichten; ***be well –ed***, gute Vorkenntnisse haben.
3. *v.i.* (*Naut.*) stranden, auflaufen.

groundage ['graundidʒ], *s.* Hafengebühren (*pl.*), das Ankergeld. **ground|-alert,** *s.* (*Mil. etc.*) die Alarmbereitschaft. **--angling,** *s.* das Grundangeln. **--attack,** *s.* (*Av.*) der Tiefangriff. **--bait,** *s.* der Grundköder. **--bass,** *s.* (*Mus.*) der Grundbaß. **--cherry,** *s.* die Zwergkirsche. **--clearance,** *s.* die Bodenfreiheit (*of vehicles*). **--coat,** *s.* der Grundanstrich. **--colour,** *s.* die Grundfarbe, Grundierung. **--communication,** *s.* (*Av.*) der Boden-zu-Bord-Verkehr. **--connection,** *s.* (*Elec.*) die Erdung, der Erd(an)schluß. **--crew,** *s.* *See* **--staff** (*Av.*).

grounded ['graundid], *adj.* *See* **ground, 2.** **grounder,** *s.* (*Crick.*) (*coll.*) der Bodenball.

ground|-floor, *s.* das Erdgeschoß, Parterre; ***on the –***, im Erdgeschoß; (*fig. coll.*) ***get in on the –***, von Anfang an dabeisein. **--frost,** *s.* der Bodenfrost. **--game,** *s.* (*Hunt.*) das Niederwild.

grounding ['graundiŋ], *s.* 1. (*Build.*) das Fundament, der Unterbau; 2. (*Paint.*) die Grundierung, Grundfarbe; 3. (*Naut.*) das Stranden, Auflaufen; 4. (*fig.*) die Einführung, der Anfangsunterricht.

ground|-ivy, *s.* (*Bot.*) der Gundermann, die Gundelrebe. **--landlord,** *s.* der Grundeigentümer. **groundless,** *adj.* grundlos, unbegründet. **ground-level,** *s.* die Bodennähe.

groundling ['graundliŋ], *s.* (*Ichth.*) der Gründling (*also Theat. obs.*).

ground|-mechanic, *s.* (*Av.*) der Wart. **--nut,** *s.* die Erdnuß. **--panel,** *s.* (*Av.*) das Fliegertuch. **--plan,** *s.* der Grundriß. **--plate,** *s.* die Grundplatte, Schwelle, Sohle. **--rent,** *s.* der Bodenzins.

groundsel ['graundsəl], *s.* 1. (*Bot.*) das Kreuzkraut; 2. (*Archit.*) *see* **ground-plate.**

groundsman ['graundzmən], *s.* der Platzwart.

ground|-speed, *s.* (*Av.*) die Geschwindigkeit über Grund. **--staff,** *s.* (*Av.*) das Bodenpersonal; (*Spt.*) Platzpersonal. **--swell,** *s.* die Grundsee, Dünung. **--troops,** *pl.* Erdtruppen (*pl.*). **--water,** *s.* das Grundwasser. **--wave,** *s.* die Bodenwelle. **-work,** *s.* (*Build.*) das Fundament, der Unterbau; (*Paint. etc.*) Grund; (*fig.*) die Grundlage(n) (*pl.*).

group [gru:p], **1.** *s.* die Gruppe; (*fig.*) der Kreis; (*Av.*) das Geschwader; ***– captain***, der Oberst der Luftwaffe. **2.** *v.t.* gruppieren, zusammenstellen, anordnen; einordnen (***with***, mit). **grouping,** *s.* die Gruppierung, Gruppenbildung, Anordnung, Einordnung in Gruppen.

[1]**grouse** [graus], *s.* (*pl.* –) (*Orn.*) ***black –***, das Birkhuhn (*Lyrurus tetrix*); ***red –***, schottisches Moorhuhn, das Schneehuhn (*Lagopus scoticus*).

[2]**grouse, 1.** *v.i.* (*coll.*) murren, grollen, nörgeln, meckern. **2.** *s.* (*coll.*) ***have a – against***, einen Groll haben gegen. **grouser,** *s.* der Nörgler, Griesgram. **grousing,** *s.* das Murren, Meckern, die Nörgelei, Quengelei.

[1]**grout** [graut], **1.** *s.* 1. das Schrotmehl; 2. dünner Mörtel. **2.** *v.t.* mit Mörtel überziehen, ausfüllen, verstopfen (*cracks*).

[2]**grout, 1.** *v.t.* aufwühlen (*of pigs*). **2.** *v.i.* (in der Erde) wühlen.

grove [grouv], *s.* das Gehölz, die Waldung, (*Poet.*) der Hain.

grovel [grɔvl], *v.i.* am Boden kriechen; (*fig.*) sich erniedrigen, kriechen. **groveller,** *s.* der Speichellecker, Kriecher. **grovelling, 1.** *adj.* (*fig.*) unterwürfig, kriecherisch, kriechend; niedrig, unwürdig. **2.** *s.* die Kriecherei, Speichelleckerei.

grow [grou], **1.** *irr.v.i.* 1. wachsen, gedeihen; ***– in favour***, an Gunst zunehmen; ***– out of***, herauswachsen aus; (*fig.*) entwachsen (*Dat.*); *see also* ***– from***; ***– out of one's clothes***, aus den Kleidern wachsen; ***– together***, verwachsen, zusammenwachsen; ***– up***, aufwachsen; heranwachsen; 2. sich entwickeln, werden (***into***, zu); ***– angry***, böse werden; ***– to be***, werden; ***– better***, sich bessern; ***– fond of***, lieb gewinnen; ***– less***, sich vermindern; ***– obsolete***, veralten; ***– old***, altern, alt werden; ***– pale***, verblassen, verbleichen; ***– poor***, verarmen; ***– worse***, sich verschlimmern; ***– from***, sich entwickeln *or* entstehen *or* erwachsen aus, folgen *or* kommen *or* eine Folge sein von; ***– into a habit***, zur Gewohnheit werden; ***it –s on me***, es wird mir immer lieber *or* vertrauter, ich gewinne es lieb; es wird mir zur zweiten Natur, ich gewöhne mich daran; ***the conviction grew on him***, er kam mehr und mehr zu der Überzeugung; ***– out of use***, außer Gebrauch kommen. **2.** *irr.v.t.* (an)bauen, züchten, ziehen; ***– a beard***, sich (*Dat.*) einen Bart wachsen lassen.

grower ['grouə], *s.* 1. wachsende Pflanze; 2. der Pflanzer, Züchter, Produzent. **growing,** *adj.* wachsend, zunehmend; ***– pains***, Wachtumsschmerzen (*pl.*); (*fig.*) Anfangsschwierigkeiten (*pl.*).

growl [graul], **1.** *s.* das Knurren, Brummen; Rollen (*of thunder*). **2.** *v.i.* knurren, brummen; rollen (*as thunder*); (*fig.*) murren, grollen; ***– at***, anknurren, anbrummen. **growler,** *s.* knurriger Hund; (*fig.*) der Brummbär.

grown [groun], **1.** *p.p. of* **grow. 2.** *adj.* erwachsen; ***– man***, Erwachsene(r); ***full–*** or ***fully –***, ausgewachsen; ***– over with***, bewachsen *or* überwachsen mit. **grown-up,** (*coll.*) **1.** *adj.* erwachsen. **2.** *s.* Erwachsene(r).

growth [grouθ], *s.* 1. der Wuchs, das Wachstum; (*Bot.*) der Zuwachs; 2. (*fig.*) die Vergrößerung, Vermehrung, Entwickling; Zunahme, der Anstieg, das Wachsen, Werden; 3. (*Med.*) Gewächs, die Wucherung.

groyne [grɔin], *s.* die Buhne, der Wellenbrecher.

[1]**grub** [grʌb], *s.* die Made, Raupe; (*coll.*) schmutzige *or* schlampige P.; (*sl.*) der Fraß, das Futter, Fressalien (*pl.*).

[2]**grub, 1.** *v.i.* (*coll.*) graben, wühlen; (*sl.*) futtern; (*coll.*) ***– along***, sich abplagen *or* abmühen. **2.** *v.t.* ***– up***, ausjäten, ausgraben, ausroden; (*fig.*) aufstöbern, ausknobeln.

grubbiness ['grʌbinis], *s.* (*coll.*) die Schmutzigkeit, Schlampigkeit. **grubby,** *adj.* (*coll.*) schlampig, schmutzig, schmierig.

grub-screw, *s.* die Stiftschraube, der Gewindestift.

grudge [grʌdʒ], **1.** *v.t.* mißgönnen, neiden (*a th.*); ***– him his good fortune***, ihm sein Glück mißgönnen, ihn um sein Glück beneiden; ***– giving***, widerwillig *or* ungern geben; ***– no pains***, sich (*Dat.*)

keine Mühe verdrießen lassen; – ***the time,*** sich (*Dat.*) die Zeit nicht gönnen. **2.** *s.* die Mißgunst, der Groll, Widerwille; ***bear him a –, have a – against him,*** ihm übelwollen, ihm böse sein, ihm grollen. **grudging,** *adj.* mißgünstig, neidisch; widerwillig, ungern gegeben. **grudgingly,** *adv.* widerwillig, ungern.

gruel ['gruəl], *s.* der Haferschleim; (*coll.*) ***get one's –,*** sein(en) Teil *or* sein Fett kriegen. **gruelling,** *adj.* (*coll.*) anstrengend, strapaziös.

gruesome ['gru:səm], *adj.* schauerlich, grausig, grauenhaft. **gruesomeness,** *s.* die Grausigkeit, Schauerlichkeit, Scheußlichkeit.

gruff [grʌf], *adj.* mürrisch; barsch, schroff, bärbeißig; rauh (*voice*). **gruffness,** *s.* die Grobheit, Schroffheit, Barschheit; (*of voice*) Rauheit, Heiserkeit.

grumble [grʌmbl], **1.** *v.i.* murren, brummen, nörgeln (***at,*** über (*Acc.*)); (g)rollen (*as thunder*). **2.** *s.* das Murren, Brummen; (G)rollen. **grumbler,** *s.* der Nörgler, (*coll.*) Brummbär. **grumbling,** *s.* das Gebrumm, Gemurre.

grume [gru:m], *s.* der Blutklumpen.

grummet, *see* **grommet.**

grumous ['gru:məs], *adj.* klumpig, geronnen (*of blood*).

grumpiness ['grʌmpinis], *s.* (*coll.*) die Verdrießlichkeit. **grumpy,** *adj.* (*coll.*) mürrisch, verdrießlich.

grunt [grʌnt], **1.** *v.i.* grunzen. **2.** *s.* das Grunzen.

gruyère [gru'jɛə], *s.* der Schweizerkäse.

gryphon ['grifən], *see* **¹griffin.**

guana ['gwɑ:nə], *s.* (*Zool.*) der Leguan.

guano ['gwɑ:nou], *s.* der Guano, Vogeldünger.

guarantee [gærən'ti:], **1.** *s.* 1. die Bürgschaft, Garantie, Sicherheit (***of,*** für); Gewähr(leistung), Versicherung, Zusicherung; Kaution, das Pfand; 2. der Bürge, Garant, Gewährsmann. **2.** *v.t.* garantieren, gewährleisten; (sich ver)bürgen für, Garantie leisten für; sichern, schützen (***against,*** vor (*Dat.*) *or* gegen); sicherstellen, verbürgen. **guarantor,** *s. See* **guarantee, 1,** 2. **guaranty** ['gærənti], *s. See* **guarantee, 1,** 1.

guard [gɑ:d], **1.** *v.t.* (be)schützen, bewachen, wachen über (*Acc.*), (be)hüten; bewahren, beschirmen, sichern (***from, against,*** vor (*Dat.*)); (*fig.*) – ***one's tongue,*** seine Zunge beherrschen *or* bezähmen *or* im Zaum halten. **2.** *v.i.* – ***against,*** auf der Hut sein *or* sich hüten *or* schützen *or* sich in Acht nehmen vor (*Dat.*), Vorkehrungen treffen gegen. **3.** *s.* 1. die Wacht, Hut, Wachsamkeit; Bewachung, Wache, Aufsicht; ***advance(d) –,*** die Vorhut; ***keep –,*** Wache halten; ***mount –,*** Wache stehen; ***come off –,*** von der Wache kommen; ***on –,*** auf Wache; ***go on –,*** die Wache beziehen; auf Wache ziehen; ***rear–,*** die Nachhut; 2. der Wächter, Wärter, Aufseher; (*Mil.*) die Wache, Wachmannschaft; der (Wach)posten; (*Railw.*) Schaffner; (*Am.*) Bahnwärter; ***frontier –,*** die Grenzwache (*troops*), der Grenzwächter (*sentry*); ***home –,*** die Bürgerwehr; – ***of honour,*** die Ehrenwache; ***life –,*** die Schwimmwache, Rettungsmannschaft; ***post –s,*** Posten ausstellen; 3. (*Boxing, Fenc.*) die Abwehrstellung, Deckung, Parade; ***off one's –,*** unachtsam, unbedacht; ***throw him off his –,*** ihn überraschen; ***be on one's –,*** sich hüten *or* vorsehen, auf der Hut sein; ***put him on his –,*** ihn warnen; 4. die Schutzvorrichtung, das Schutzgitter; Stichblatt (*of a sword*); (*fig.*) die Vorsichtsmaßnahme; ***fire–,*** das Kamingitter; 5. ***the Guards*** (*pl.*), die Garde, das Gardekorps, Garderegiment.

guard|-chain, *s.* die Sicherheitskette. **--commander,** *s.* wachhabender Offizier, Wachhabende(r). **--dog,** *s.* der Wachhund. **--duty,** *s.* der Wachdienst. **guarded,** *adj.* gesichert, geschützt, bewacht, beaufsichtigt; (*fig.*) vorsichtig, behutsam; ***in – terms,*** vorsichtig. **guardedness,** *s.* die Vorsicht, Behutsamkeit. **guard-house,** *s.* (*Mil.*) die Wache, das Wachlokal.

guardian ['gɑ:diən], **1.** *s.* der Wächter, Hüter, Wärter, Verwahrer, Kustos; (*Law*) Kurator, Vormund; – ***of the poor,*** der Armenpfleger; ***board of –s,*** das Armenamt. **2.** *adj.* schützend, Schutz–; ***--angel,*** der Schutzengel. **guardianship,** *s.* der Schutz, die Obhut; (*Law*) Vormundschaft.

guard|-rail, *s.* das Schutzgeländer; (*Railw.*) die Leitschiene. **--room,** *s.* (*Mil.*) die Wachstube; Arrestzelle. **guardsman,** *s.* (*Mil.*) der Gardist.

gubernatorial [gjubənə'tɔ:riəl], *adj.* (*Am.*) Gouverneurs–, Regierungs–.

¹gudgeon ['gʌdʒən], *s.* (*Ichth.*) der Gründling; (*fig.*) Einfaltspinsel.

²gudgeon, *s.* der Zapfen, Bolzen; (*Naut.*) die Ruderöse; – ***pin,*** der Kolbenbolzen.

guelder-rose ['geldə], *s.* (*Bot.*) der Wasserahorn, Schneeball.

Guelph [gwelf], *s.* (*Hist.*) der Welfe.

guerdon [gə:dn], **1.** *s.* (*Poet.*) der Lohn, die Belohnung. **2.** *v.t.* belohnen.

guer(r)illa [gə'rilə], *s.* 1. der Freischärler, Partisan, Guerillakämpfer; 2. (*usu.* – ***war(fare)***) Kleinkrieg, Partisanenkrieg, Guerillakrieg.

guess [ges], **1.** *v.t.* 1. (er)raten, (ab)schätzen; 2. sich (*Dat.*) denken, ahnen, vermuten; (*Am. coll.*) denken, glauben, meinen, annehmen. **2.** *v.i.* – ***at,*** schätzen, eine Schätzung *or* Mutmaßung machen über (*Acc.*); (*coll.*) ***keep him –ing,*** ihm zu raten geben. **3.** *s.* die Schätzung, Vermutung, Mutmaßung; (*coll.*) ***anybody's –,*** reine Vermutung; ***by –,*** schätzungsweise, aufs Geratewohl; ***a good –,*** gut geraten *or* geschätzt; ***make a –,*** raten, schätzen. **guess|-rope,** *s. See* **guest-rope. -work,** *s.* die Mutmaßung, Vermutung(en (*pl.*)); ***by –,*** see ***by guess.***

guest [gest], *s.* der Gast (***at,*** bei); (*Bot., Zool.*) Parasit, Einmieter, Kommensale; ***he is my –,*** er ist bei mir zu Gast; – ***of honour,*** der Ehrengast; ***paying –,*** der Pensionär. **guest|-house,** *s.* das Fremdenheim, die Pension. **--room,** *s.* das Fremdenzimmer. **--rope,** *s.* (*Naut.*) (zweite) Vertäuleine *or* Schlepptrosse.

guff [gʌf], *s.* (*sl.*) der Quatsch.

guffaw [gʌ'fɔ:], **1.** *s.* schallendes Gelächter. **2.** *v.i.* laut (auf)lachen *or* brüllen.

Guiana [gi'ɑ:nə], *s.* (*obs.*) *see* **Guyana.**

guidable ['gaidəbl], *adj.* lenkbar, leitbar, lenksam. **guidance,** *s.* die Führung, Leitung; (*fig.*) Anleitung, Orientierung, Unterweisung, Lenkung, Beratung, Belehrung; ***for his –,*** zu seiner Orientierung.

guide [gaid], **1.** *s.* 1. der Leiter, Führer; Bergführer; Fremdenführer, Reiseführer, Reisebegleiter; (*fig.*) Berater, Ratgeber; 2. (*fig.*) Anhalt(spunkt), leitendes Prinzip, die Richtschnur; 3. (*textbook*) Einführung, der Wegweiser (***to,*** in (*Acc.*)), Leitfaden, das Lehrbuch, Handbuch (*Gen.*); 4. (*guidebook*) der (Reise)führer (***to,*** durch); 5. (*Tech.*) die Führung(svorrichtung), Leitöse, das Leitauge. **2.** *v.t.* den Weg zeigen (*Dat.*), führen, (ge)leiten, lenken (*a p.*), lenken (*events*), bestimmen (*actions*); (*fig.*) (an)leiten, beraten, belehren.

guide-book, *s.* der (Reise)führer (***to,*** durch). **guided,** *adj.* gelenkt, gesteuert; – ***missile,*** ferngelenktes Geschoß, der Fernlenkkörper. **guide|-line,** *s.* (*fig.*) die Richtlinie, Richtschnur, der Leitfaden. **--rail,** *s.* die Führungsschiene. **--rope,** *s.* das Schlepptau (*balloons*). **guiding,** *adj.* leitend, Lenk–; – ***star,*** der Leitstern.

guidon [gaidn], *s.* die Standarte, der Wimpel.

guild [gild], *s.* (*Hist.*) die Gilde, Zunft, Innung; Vereinigung, der Verein. **guildhall,** *s.* (*Hist.*) das Zunfthaus, Innungshaus; Rathaus, die Stadthalle.

guile [gail], *s.* die Tücke, (Arg)list. **guileful,** *adj* tückisch, (arg)listig, (be)trügerisch. **guileless,** *adj* arglos, aufrichtig, offen. **guilelessness,** *s.* die Arglosigkeit, Aufrichtigkeit.

guillemot ['gilimɔt], *s.* (*Orn.*) die (Trottel)lumme (*Uria aalge*).

guillotine ['gilәti:n], **1.** *s.* 1. das Fallbeil, die Guillotine; (Papier)schneidemaschine; 2. (*Parl.*) Befristung der Abstimmung. **2.** *v.t.* (mit dem Fallbeil) hinrichten, guillotinieren.

guilt [gilt], *s.* die Schuld; (*Law*) Strafbarkeit, Straffälligkeit; ***incur*** –, straffällig werden. **guiltiness,** *s.* die Schuld(igkeit), das Schuldbewußtsein, Schuldgefühl. **guiltless,** *adj.* schuldlos, unschuldig (*of*, an (*Dat.*)); (*fig.*) ***be – of,*** nichts wissen von, nicht kennen, unberührt sein von, unkundig sein (*Gen.*). **guilty,** *adj.* schuldig (*of, Gen.*); schuldbewußt, schuldbeladen; strafbar, verbrecherisch; ***– conscience,*** schlechtes Gewissen; (*Law*) ***find him –,*** ihn für schuldig erklären; ***find him not –,*** ihn für unschuldig erklären; ***be found – on a charge,*** einer Anklage für schuldig befunden werden; (*Law*) ***plead (not) –,*** sich (nicht) schuldig bekennen (***to doing***, getan zu haben).

guinea ['gini], *s.* die Guinee. **guinea|-fowl,** *s.* das Perlhuhn. **--pig,** *s.* 1. das Meerschweinchen; 2. (*fig.*) Versuchskaninchen.

guise [gaiz], *s.* die Form, Gestalt, das Aussehen, äußere Erscheinung; (*fig.*) der Mantel, Vorwand, die Maske, Verkleidung. **guiser,** *s.* (*Scots*) Vermummte(r).

guitar [gi'tɑ:], *s.* die Gitarre.

gulch [gʌltʃ], *s.* (*Am.*) die (Berg)schlucht.

gules [gju:lz], *s.* (*Her.*) das Rot.

gulf [gʌlf], *s.* (*Geog.*) der Golf, Meerbusen; Abgrund, Schlund, die Schlucht; (*fig.*) Kluft; ***Gulf Stream,*** der Golfstrom.

[1]**gull** [gʌl], *s.* (*Orn.*) die Möwe (*Laridae*); ***common –,*** die Sturmmöwe (*Larus canus*); ***herring –,*** die Silbermöwe (*L. argentus*); ***lesser black-backed –,*** die Heringsmöwe (*L. fuscus*); ***greater black-backed –,*** die Mantelmöwe (*L. marinus*); ***black-headed –,*** die Lachmöwe (*L. ridibundus*); ***great black-headed –,*** die Fischmöwe (*L. ichthyaëtus*).

[2]**gull, 1.** *s.* der Tölpel, Tollpatsch, Gimpel. **2.** *v.t.* übertölpen, übers Ohr hauen, hineinlegen, prellen.

gullet ['gʌlit], *s.* 1. (*Anat.*) die Speiseröhre, der Schlund; (*coll.*) die Kehle, Gurgel; 2. (*Tech.*) der Graben, Kanal, Einstich, Durchstich, die Wasserrinne; 3. (*Tech.*) (*of saw*) (Ein)schweifung.

gullibility [gʌli'biliti], *s.* die Einfältigkeit, Leichgläubigkeit. **gullible** ['gʌlibl], *adj.* einfältig, leichtgläubig.

gully ['gʌli], *s.* der Wasserlauf, die (Wasser)rinne; Ablaufrinne, der Abzugskanal; Sinkkasten, Absturzschacht.

gulp [gʌlp], **1.** *v.t.* (*oft.* ***– down***) (gierig) hinunterschlucken; (*fig.*) (ver)schlucken, verschlingen. **2.** *v.i.* schlucken, würgen. **3.** *s.* der Schluck, das Schlucken; ***at one –,*** auf einen Zug.

[1]**gum** [gʌm], *s.* (*oft. pl.*) das Zahnfleisch.

[2]**gum, 1.** *s.* 1. das Gummi, der Kautschuk; Klebstoff, die Gummilösung; (*philately*) Gummierung; (*Bot.*) der Gummifluß, das Pflanzenharz; 2. der *or* das Gummibonbon, (*Am. coll.*) der Kaugummi; *pl.* (*Am. sl.*) Gummi(über)schuhe (*pl.*). **2.** *v.t.* kleben, gummieren; ***– down,*** aufkleben, zukleben; (*sl. fig.*) ***– up the works,*** lästig *or* hinderlich sein. **gum-arabic,** *s.* das Gummiarabikum.

gum|boil, *s.* das Zahngeschwür; *see* [1]**gum.** **--elastic,** *s.* der Kautschuk, das Gummielastikum. **--juniper,** *s.* (*Bot.*) der Sandarak. **--kino,** *s.* das Kino(gummi). **gummy,** *adj.* gummiartig, klebrig, zäh(flüssig).

gumption ['gʌmpʃən], *s.* (*coll.*) der Mutterwitz, Mumm, die Grütze, Initiative, Schlagfertigkeit.

gum|-resin, *s.* das Gummiharz. **-shoe, 1.** *s.* 1. (*Am.*) der Gummi(über)schuh; 2. (*Am. sl.*) Spitzel, Spion. **2.** *v.i.* (*Am. sl.*) schleichen, leise gehen. **--tree,** *s.* der Gummibaum; (*Austral.*) Eukalyptus; (*sl.*) ***up a –,*** in der Klemme.

gun [gʌn], **1.** *s.* 1. die Feuerwaffe, Schußwaffe; das Gewehr; Geschütz, die Kanone; ***anti-aircraft –,*** die Flugzeugabwehrkanone, Flakkanone; (*coll.*) ***big –,*** hohes Tier, große Kanone; ***blow great –s,*** heulen, toben (*of the wind*); ***jump the –,*** (*Spt.*) zu früh starten; (*coll. fig.*) sich übereilen; ***machine--,*** das Maschinengewehr; (*sl.*) ***son of a –,*** der (Teufels)kerl; (*fig.*) ***stick to one's –s,*** nicht weichen, fest bleiben; 2. (*Hunt.*) der Schütze, Jagdgast. **2.** *v.t.* (*coll.*) schießen auf (*Acc.*); ***– down,*** erschießen. **3.** *v.i.* (*sl.*) ***be gunning for,*** verfolgen; sich bemühen um, auf der Jagd sein nach.

gun|-barrel, *s.* der Gewehrlauf; das Geschützrohr. **-boat,** *s.* das Kanonenboot. **--carriage,** *s.* die Lafette. **-cotton,** *s.* die Schieß(baum)wolle, Kollodiumwolle, Nitrozellulose. **-crew,** *s.* die Geschützbedienung. **--deck,** *s.* das Batteriedeck. **--dog,** *s.* der Jagdhund. **--drill,** *s.* das Geschützexerzieren. **--emplacement,** *s.* die Geschützbettung. **-fire,** *s.* das Artilleriefeuer. **--flashes,** *pl.* das Mündungsfeuer. **--layer** [-leiə], *s.* der Richtkanonier. **--licence,** *s.* der Waffenschein. **-man** [-mən], *s.* bewaffneter Räuber. **--metal,** *s.* das Kanonenmetall, der Geschützguß.

gunner ['gʌnə], *s.* der Kanonier, Artillerist; (*tank, machine-gun*) Schütze, (*Av.*) Bordschütze. **gunnery,** *s.* das Geschützwesen, die Artillerie(wissenschaft); (*Naut.*) ***– officer,*** der Artillerieoffizier.

gun|-pit, *s.* der Geschützbunker, Geschützstand, die Geschützstellung. **--port,** *s.* (*Naut., Hist.*) die Stückpforte. **-powder,** *s.* das Schießpulver; ***– plot,*** die Pulververschwörung (5. Nov. 1605). **--room,** *s.* (*Naut.*) die Kadettenmesse; (*Hunt.*) der Gewehrraum. **--runner,** *s.* der Waffenschmuggler. **--running,** *s.* der Waffenschmuggel. **-shot,** *s.* der Gewehrschuß; Kanonenschuß; die Schußweite; ***within –,*** in Schußweite; ***– wound,*** die Schußwunde. **--shy,** *adj.* (*Hunt.*) schußscheu. **-sight,** *s.* das Visier. **-smith,** *s.* der Büchsenmacher. **-stock,** *s.* der Gewehrschaft, Gewehrkolben.

gunter ['gʌntə], *s.* (*usu.* ***– rig***) (*Naut.*) die Gleittakelung, Schiebetakelung.

gun-turret, *s.* (*tanks*) der Geschützturm, (*Av.*) die Kanzel.

gunwale [gʌnl], *s.* (*Naut.*) der Schandeckel; (*on row-boats*) das Strombord, Dollbord.

gurgle [gə:gl], **1.** *v.i.* (*as water*) murmelnd rieseln, gurgeln, (*as infants*) glucksen. **2.** *or* **gurgling,** *s.* das Gemurmel, Gurgeln; Glucksen.

gurnard ['gə:nəd], **gurnet** ['gə:nit], *s.* (*Orn.*) grauer Knurrhahn (*Trigla hirundo*).

gush [gʌʃ], **1.** *v.i.* 1. (hervor)strömen, hervorquellen, hervorbrechen, stürzen, sich ergießen (***from***, aus); ***– out*** or ***forth,*** entströmen (***from***, *Dat.*); 2. (*coll.*) schwärmen, sich überschwenglich ausdrücken. **2.** *s.* 1. der Guß, Strom; (*fig.*) Erguß, Schwall, die Flut; 2. (*coll.*) Schwärmerei, Überschwenglichkeit. **gusher,** *s.* (*Am.*) die Springquelle; (*esp.*) Ölquelle. **gushiness,** *s.* (*coll.*) *see* **gush, 2.,** 2. **gushing,** *adj.* 1. (über)strömend, (über)sprudelnd; 2. (*coll.*) *see* **gushy. gushy,** *adj.* (*coll.*) schwärmerisch, überschwenglich, überspannt.

gusset ['gʌsit], **1.** *s.* (*Dressm.*) der Zwickel, Keil; (*Tech.*) das Eckblech, Winkelstück. **2.** *v.t.* (*Dressm.*) mit einem Zwickel versehen; (*Tech.*) mit einem Eckblech verbinden.

gust [gʌst], *s.* der (Wind)stoß, die Bö.

gustation [gʌs'teiʃən], *s.* der Geschmack(ssinn), das Geschmacksvermögen. **gustatory** ['gʌstətəri], *adj.* Geschmacks–.

gustiness ['gʌstinis], *s.* die Böigkeit.

gusto ['gʌstou], *s.* (*coll.*) 1. besondere Neigung *or* Vorliebe, die Lust, der Genuß; 2. Schwung, Eifer; ***with –,*** eifrig, bereitwillig, herzlich gern.

gusty ['gʌsti], *adj.* böig; windig, stürmisch.

gut [gʌt], **1.** *s.* 1. (*Anat.*) der Darm(kanal); *pl.* das Eingeweide, Gedärm(e); *pl.* (*sl.*) das Innere, (*fig.*) wahrer Gehalt, wesentlicher Inhalt; 2. *pl.* (*sl.*) die Unerschrockenheit, Widerstandskraft; Kraft und Saft, der Schneid, Mumm. **2.** *v.t.* ausweiden, ausnehmen; (*fig.*) ausleeren; ***the house was gutted (by fire)***, das Haus war völlig ausgebrannt.

gutta-percha [gʌtə'pə:tʃə], *s.* die Guttapercha.

gutter ['gʌtə], **1.** *s.* der Straßengraben, Rinnstein, die (Straßen)rinne, Gosse; (*Build.*) Dachrinne, Traufrinne, Abflußrinne; das Ablaufrohr, der Ausguß; (*Tech.*) die Rille, Hohlkehle; (*fig.*) ***she picked him up out of the –,*** sie las ihn aus der Straße *or* Gosse auf. **2.** *v.t.* furchen, rillen, riefen, aushöhlen. **3.** *v.i.* **1.** rinnen, triefen; 2. (ab)laufen, tropfen (*as a candle*). **guttering,** *s. See* **gutter, 1.** (*Build.*). **gutter|-press,** *s.* die Schmutzpresse. **–snipe,** *s.* der Gassenjunge.

guttural [ˈgʌtərəl], **1.** *adj.* Kehl–, guttural. **2.** *s.* der Kehllaut.

gutty [ˈgʌti], *s.* (*sl.*) der Golfball.

[1]**guy** [gai], **1.** *s.* die Vogelscheuche, der Popanz; (*sl.*) (*esp. Am.*) Kerl, Bursche; (*sl.*) ***wise*** **–**, ganz Kluge(r). **2.** *v.t.* lächerlich machen, verulken, foppen.

[2]**guy, 1.** *s.* (*Naut.*) der Backstag, das Geitau; (Ab)-spannseil, Haltetau. **2.** *v.t.* befestigen, verankern.

Guyana [gaiˈænə], *s.* Guyana (*n.*).

guy-rope, *s.* die Spannschnur.

guzzle [gʌzl], **1.** *v.i.* unmäßig trinken *or* essen; saufen; fressen. **2.** *v.t.* gierig trinken *or* essen; saufen; fressen, verschlingen. **guzzler,** *s.* der Säufer; Fresser, Schlemmer, Prasser.

gybe [dʒaib], **1.** *v.t.* (*Naut.*) übergehen lassen, durchkaien (*sail*). **2.** *v.i.* sich umlegen, giepen.

gym [dʒim], *s.* (*coll.*) *see* **gymnastics, gymnasium**; **–** ***shoes,*** Turnschuhe (*pl.*). **gymkhana** [–ˈkɑːnə], *s.* das Sportfest, die Sportveranstaltung. **gymnasium** [–ˈneiziəm], *s.* (*pl.* **-s, -sia**) die Turnhalle, Sporthalle. **gymnast** [ˈdʒimnæst], *s.* der Turner. **gymnastic** [–ˈnæstik], *adj.* gymnastisch, turnerisch, Turn–. **gymnastics,** *pl.* Leibesübungen (*pl.*), das Turnen, die Turnkunst, (*also fig.*) Gymnastik.

gymno– [ˈdʒimnou], *pref.* (*Bot., Zool.*) nackt. **–carpous** [–ˈkɑːpəs], *adj.* nacktfrüchtig. **–sperm,** *s.* nacktsamige Pflanze, der Nacktsamer. **–spermous** [–ˈspəːməs], *adj.* nacktsamig.

gynaecological [gainikəˈlɔdʒikl], *adj.* gynäkologisch. **gynaecologist** [–ˈkɔlədʒist], *s.* der Frauenarzt, Gynäkologe. **gynaecology** [–ˈkɔlədʒi], *s.* die Frauenheilkunde, Gynäkologie.

gynocracy [gaiˈnɔkrəsi], *s.* die Weiberherrschaft.

[1]**gyp** [dʒip], *s.* (*sl.*) (*Univ.*) der Diener.

[2]**gyp,** *v.t.* (*sl.*) beschwindeln.

gyps(e)ous [ˈdʒips(i)əs], *adj.* gipsartig, gipshaltig, Gips–. **gypsum,** *s.* der Gips.

gypsy, *see* **gipsy.**

gyrate [dʒaiˈreit], *v.i.* kreisen, wirbeln, sich drehen. **gyration** [–ˈreiʃən], *s.* die Kreisbewegung, Drehung; (*of a shell*) Windung. **gyratory** [ˈdʒairətəri], *adj.* sich drehend, wirbelnd, (*of shell*) sich spiralig windend, (*of traffic*) Rund–, Kreis–.

gyr falcon (*Am.* **gyrfalcon**), *s. See* **gerfalcon.**

gyro [ˈdʒairo], *s.* der Kreisel. **gyro|-compass,** *s.* der Kreiselkompaß. **–plane,** *s.* der Tragschrauber, Hubschrauber, das Drehflügelflugzeug, Windmühlenflugzeug.

gyroscope [ˈdʒairoskoup], *s.* der Kreisel, die Kreiselvorrichtung, das Gyroskop. **gyroscopic** [–ˈskɔpik], *adj.* Kreisel–; **–** ***stabilizer,*** der Stabilisierkreisel.

gyves [dʒaivz], *pl.* (Fuß)fesseln (*pl.*).

H

H, h [eitʃ], *s.* das H, h. *See Index of Abbreviations.*

ha! [hɑː], *int.* ha!

habeas corpus [ˈheibiəsˈkɔːpəs], *s.* (*Law*) ***writ of*** **–**, der Vorführungsbefehl.

haberdasher [ˈhæbədæʃə], *s.* der Kurzwarenhändler. **haberdashery,** *s.* Kurzwaren (*pl.*); das Kurzwarengeschäft.

habergeon [ˈhæbədʒən], *s.* (*Hist.*) das Panzerhemd.

habiliments [həˈbilimənts], *pl.* die (Amts)kleidung, Festkleidung.

habit [ˈhæbit], **1.** *s.* **1.** die (An)gewohnheit; Beschaffenheit, Verfassung, Disposition; Konstitution; (*Bot.*) Wachstumsart; (*Zool.*) Lebensweise; **–** ***of mind,*** die Sinnesart, Geistesverfassung, geistige Beschaffenheit *or* Disposition; ***break o.s. of a*** **–**, sich (*Dat.*) etwas abgewöhnen; ***from*** **–**, aus Gewohnheit; ***be in the*** **–**, gewöhnt sein, pflegen (***of doing***, zu tun); ***fall*** or ***get into the*** **–** ***of swearing,*** sich (*Dat.*) das Fluchen angewöhnen; ***fall into bad*** **–*s***, schlechte Gewohnheiten annehmen, in schlechte Gewohnheiten verfallen; ***get out of the*** **–** ***of swearing,*** sich (*Dat.*) das Fluchen abgewöhnen; 2. (*obs.*) die Tracht, Kleidung, (*esp.*) Ordenskleidung; ***riding*–**–, das Reitkleid, Reitkostüm. **2.** *v.t.* (*obs.*) kleiden.

habitable [ˈhæbitəbl], *adj.* bewohnbar. **habitableness,** *s.* die Bewohnbarkeit. **habitant,** *s.* **1.** der Einwohner, Bewohner; 2. Kanadier französischer Abstammung. **habitat** [–tæt], *s.* die Heimat, der Fundort; (*Bot.*) Standort, (*Zool.*) das Wohngebiet. **habitation** [–ˈteiʃən], *s.* das Wohnen; die Wohnung, der Wohnsitz; Wohnort, Aufenthalt(sort).

habitual [həˈbitjuəl], *adj.* gewohnt, üblich, ständig; gewohnheitsmäßig, Gewohnheits–. **habituate** [–eit], *v.t.* gewöhnen (*to*, an (*Acc.*)). **habituation** [–ˈeiʃən], *s.* die Gewöhnung (***to***, an (*Acc.*)). **habitude** [ˈhæbitjuːd], *s.* die (An)gewohnheit, Veranlagung. **habitué** [–ei], *s.* ständiger Besucher, der Stammgast.

hachure [hæˈʃuə], *s.* (*usu. pl.*) die Schraffe, Schraffierung, Schraffur (*on maps*).

[1]**hack** [hæk], **1.** *s.* **1.** das Mietpferd; Gebrauchspferd, gewöhnliches (Reit)pferd, der Gaul; 2. (*fig.*) Lohnschreiber, literarischer Tagelöhner; 3. der Gelegenheitsarbeiter, Tagelöhner. **2.** *adj.* Miet(s)–, Lohn–, gemietet; **–** ***lawyer,*** der Winkeladvokat; **–** ***saying,*** abgedroschene Redensart; **–** ***writer,*** der Lohnschreiber. **3.** *v.t.* abnutzen, abdreschen. **4.** *v.i.* ein Reitpferd mieten; im Schritt reiten.

[2]**hack, 1.** *v.t.* (zer)hacken; (*Footb.*) mit dem Fuß stoßen. **2.** *v.i.* **1.** kurz husten; ***–ing cough,*** trockener Husten; 2. **–** ***at,*** einhauen auf (*Acc.*), herumhacken auf (*Dat.*), hacken nach. **3.** *s.* **1.** die Kerbe, Einkerbung, der Einschnitt; 2. Hieb; (*Footb.*) Fußtritt.

hackle [hækl], **1.** *v.t.* hecheln. **2.** *s.* **1.** die Hechel; 2. (*of a cock*) (lange) Nackenfedern (*pl.*); (*fig.*) ***with his –s up,*** angriffslustig, kampflustig.

hackney [ˈhækni], **1.** *s.* gewöhnliches Reitpferd, das Mietpferd, der Gaul. **2.** *adj.* Lohn–, Miet(s)–; **–** ***carriage,*** die Mietskutsche, Droschke, der Fiaker. **3.** *v.t.* abnutzen. **hackneyed,** *adj.* abgenutzt, abgegriffen. abgedroschen, alltäglich, banal.

hacksaw [ˈhæksɔː], *s.* die Metallsäge; *see* [2]**hack.**

had [hæd], *imperf., p.p. of* **have.**

haddock [ˈhædək], *s.* der Schellfisch.

haemal [ˈhiːməl], *adj.* Blut–. **haematin,** *s.* das Hämatin. **haematite** [–tait], *s.* (*Min.*) der Roteisenstein. **haematuria** [–ˈtjuəriə], *s.* (*Med.*) das Blutharnen. **haemoglobin** [–ˈgloubin], *s.* roter Blutfarbstoff, das Hämoglobin. **haemoleucocyte** [–ˈljuːkəsait], *s.* weißes Blutkörperchen. **haemophilia** [–ˈfiliə], *s.* die Bluterkrankheit, Hämophilie. **haemophiliac,** *s.* an Hämophilie Leidende(r).

haemorrhage [ˈheməridʒ], *s.* die Blutung, der Blutsturz. **haemorrhoids** [–rɔidz], *pl.* Hämorrhoiden (*pl.*).

haft [hɑːft], **1.** *s.* das Heft, der Griff, Stiel. **2.** *v.t.* mit einem Heft versehen.

hag [hæg], *s.* häßliches altes Weib.

haggard [ˈhægəd], **1.** *adj.* **1.** hager, abgehärmt; verstört; 2. (*Hunt.*) (*of falcon*) wild, ungezähmt. **2.** *s.* ungezähmter Falke.

haggis [ˈhægis], *s.* (*Scots*) der Fleischpudding.

haggle [hægl], *v.i.* feilschen, knickern, schachern, markten (***about, over***, um); (*coll.*) streiten, zanken.

hagiographa [hægi'ɔgrəfə], *pl.* Hagiographen (*pl.*). **hagiographer,** *s.* der Verfasser von Heiligenlegenden. **hagiography,** *s.* die Lebensbeschreibung der Heiligen. **hagiolatry** [–'ɔlətri], *s.* die Heiligenverehrung. **hagiology** [–'ɔlədʒi], *s.* (die Literatur über) Heiligenlegenden; das Heiligenverzeichnis.

hag-ridden, *adj.* (von Alpdrücken) verfolgt *or* gequält.

Hague [heig], *s.* (*Geog.*) ***the –,*** Den Haag (*m.*).

hah! [hɑ:], *int. See* **ha!**

ha-ha ['hɑ:hɑ:], *s.* versenkter Grenzgraben.

[1]**hail** [heil], **1.** *v.t.* anrufen, ansprechen; (*Naut.*) zurufen (*Dat.*); ***--fellow-well-met,*** vertraut, auf vertrautem Fuß, auf du und du. **2.** *v.i.* 1. (*esp. Naut.*) rufen, sich melden; (be)grüßen, bewillkommnen; 2. ***– from,*** (her)kommen *or* (her)stammen von *or* aus, abstammen von. **3.** *s.* der (Zu)ruf; Gruß; ***within –,*** in Hörweite *or* Rufweite. **4.** *int.* (*Poet.*) Heil! Glück zu!

[2]**hail,** **1.** *s.* der Hagel (*also fig.*). **2.** *v.i.* hageln; ***it is –ing,*** es hagelt. **3.** *v.t.* ***– down,*** (nieder)hageln lassen ((***up***)***on,*** auf (*Acc.*)). **hail|stone,** *s.* das Hagelkorn, die Schloße. **–storm,** *s.* das Hagelwetter.

hair [hɛə], **1.** *s.* (einzelnes) Haar; das Haar, Haare (*pl.*); ***–'s breadth,*** *see* **hairbreadth**; (*fig.*) ***by a –,*** um Haaresbreite; ***do one's —,*** sich frisieren, sich (*Dat.*) die Haare machen; ***false –,*** falsche Haare; ***a fine head of –,*** schöner Haarwuchs; (*sl.*) ***he gets in my –,*** ich kann ihn nicht ausstehen; (*sl.*) ***get him by the short –s,*** ihn unter der Fuchtel haben; (*sl.*) ***keep your – on!*** immer mit der Ruhe! ***let one's – down,*** die Haare herunterlassen; (*fig.*) sich ungeniert benehmen; ***put one's – up,*** sich (*Dat.*) die Haare aufstecken; ***split –s,*** Haarspalterei treiben; ***his – stood on end,*** ihm standen die Haare zu Berge; (*coll.*) ***take a – of the dog that bit you,*** den Kater in Alkohol ersäufen; ***tear one's –,*** sich die Haare ausraufen; ***not touch*** or ***harm a – of his head,*** ihm kein Haar krümmen; ***to a –,*** haargenau, aufs Haar; ***without turning a –,*** ohne mit der Wimper zu zucken.

hair|breadth, **1.** *s.* die Haaresbreite; ***by*** or ***within a –,*** um ein Haar, ums Haar, um Haaresbreite. **2.** *adj.* ***– escape,*** das Entkommen mit genauer *or* knapper Not. **–brush,** *s.* die Haarbürste, Frisierbürste. **--clippers,** *pl.* die Haarschneidemaschine. **-cut,** *s.* der Haarschnitt; (*coll.*) ***have a –,*** sich (*Dat.*) die Haare schneiden lassen. **--do,** *s.* (*coll.*) die Frisur. **–dresser,** *s.* der Friseur (die Friseuse), der (die) Haarschneider(in). **–dressing,** *s.* das Haarschneiden, Frisieren. **--dryer,** *s.* der Fön. **--dye,** *s.* das Haarfärbemittel.

haired [hɛəd], *adj.* behaart; (*as suff.*) –haarig. **hair-grass,** *s.* (*Bot.*) das Straußgras, die Schmiele. **hairiness,** *s.* die Behaartheit, Haarigkeit. **hairless,** *adj.* haarlos, unbehaart, ohne Haare, kahl.

hair|line, **1.** *s.* der Haaransatz; (*Opt. etc.*) Haarstrich, Faden. **2.** *adj.* haarfein (*crack etc.*). **--mattress,** *s.* die Roßhaarmatratze. **--net,** *s.* das Haarnetz. **--oil,** *s.* das Haaröl. **–pin,** *s.* die Haarnadel; ***– bend,*** scharfe Kurve *or* Biegung. **--raising,** *adj.* haarsträubend, aufregend. **--restorer,** *s.* das Haarwuchsmittel. **--shirt,** *s.* härenes Hemd. **--sieve,** *s.* das Haarsieb. **--slide,** *s.* die Haarspange. **--splitting,** **1.** *adj.* haarspalterisch, spitzfindig. **2.** *s.* die Haarspalterei, Wortklauberei. **--spring,** *s.* (*Horol.*) die Unruhfeder. **--trigger,** *s.* der Stecher, das Stechschloß (*of a gun*). **--wash,** *s.* das Haarwasser.

hairy ['hɛəri], *adj.* haarig, behaart.

hake [heik], *s.* (*Ichth.*) der Hechtdorsch, Seehecht.

halation [hæ'leiʃən], *s.* (*Phot.*) der Lichthof; die Lichthofbildung; ***no –,*** lichthoffrei.

halberd ['hælbəd], *s.* (*Hist.*) die Hellebarde. **halberdier** [–'diə], *s.* der Hellebardier.

halcyon ['hælsiən], **1.** *s.* (*Myth.*) der Eisvogel. **2.** *adj.* friedlich, ruhig; ***– days,*** glückliche Tage.

[1]**hale** [heil], *adj.* gesund, kräftig, rüstig; ***– and hearty,*** gesund und munter.

[2]**hale,** *v.t.* (*obs.*) ziehen, schleppen.

half [hɑ:f], **1.** *s.* (*pl.* **halves** [hɑ:vz]) 1. die Hälfte; ***a litre and a –,*** anderthalb Liter; (*coll.*) ***his better –,*** seine Ehehälfte, seine Frau; ***not good enough by –,*** lange nicht gut genug; ***do by halves,*** nur halb tun; ***too clever by –,*** viel zu gescheit, überklug; ***in –*** or ***halves,*** entzwei; ***cut in –,*** entzweischneiden; ***cut into halves,*** in zwei Hälften teilen; ***go halves with him in it,*** es mit ihm teilen, dabei mit ihm halbpart machen; 2. (*Spt.*) Spielhälfte, Halbzeit; 3. (*Univ.*) das Halbjahr, Semester; 4. (*Law*) die Seite, Partei; 5. (*Footb.*) ***centre –,*** der Mittelläufer; (*Footb.*) ***left –,*** linker Läufer. **2.** *adj.* halb; ***– the amount,*** halb soviel, die Hälfte; (*coll.*) ***that's – the battle,*** damit ist die S. schon halb getan *or* gewonnen; (*obs.*) ***– a crown*** or ***a – crown,*** eine halbe Krone; (*coll.*) ***six of one and – a dozen of the other,*** dasselbe in grün; ***– an hour*** or ***a – hour,*** eine halbe Stunde; ***– knowledge,*** das Halbwissen; ***have – a mind,*** beinahe (*or* nicht übel) Lust haben, fast geneigt sein; ***at – the price,*** zum halben Preise; ***a – truth,*** nur die halbe Wahrheit. **3.** *adv.* zur Hälfte, halb(wegs), nahezu, beinahe, fast; ***– as long again,*** anderthalbmal so lang; um die Hälfte länger; ***– dead,*** halbtot; ***– empty,*** zur Hälfte leer; ***I – wish,*** ich wünsche beinahe *or* fast; ***not –,*** nicht annähernd, lange (*or* bei weitem) nicht; (*coll.*) ***not –!*** durchaus nicht! (ganz und) gar nicht! (*coll.*) ***not – bad,*** gar nicht übel; (*sl.*) ***I don't – like him,*** ich bin ihm herzlich zugetan; (*sl.*) ***he didn't – carry on,*** er schimpfte gar nicht übel; (*sl.*) ***are you coming? not –!*** kommst du mit? Und ob! (*sl.*) ***were you pleased? not –!*** hast du dich gefreut? Und wie! ***– past twelve,*** halb eins.

half|-and-half, *adv.* zu gleichen Teilen. **--back,** *s.* (*Footb.*) der Läufer. **--baked,** *adj.* halbgar; (*fig.*) unerfahren, unreif (*a p.*), unverdaut; halbfertig (*plan etc.*). **--binding,** *s.* der Halb(franz)band, Halblederband. **--blood,** *s.* das Halbblut. **--blooded,** *adj.* halbbürtig, Halbblut–. **--bound,** *adj.* in Halbband gebunden. **--breed,** *s.* der Mischling. **--brother,** *s.* der Stiefbruder. **--calf,** *s.* der Halbfranzband. **--caste,** **1.** *adj.* halbbürtig. **2.** *s.* der Mischling. **--cloth,** *s.* das Halbleinen. **--cock,** *s.* die Vorderrast (*rifle*); (*fig.*) (***at***) ***–,*** vorzeitig, überstürzt. **--deck,** *s.* das Halbdeck. **--hearted,** *adj.* lau, gleichgültig, kleinmütig, zaghaft. **--heartedness,** *s.* die Gleichgültigkeit, Zaghaftigkeit. **--holiday,** *s.* freier Nachmittag. **--hourly,** **1.** *adj.* halbstündig. **2.** *adv.* halbstündlich, jede halbe Stunde. **--leather,** *s.* das Halbleder. **--length,** *adj.* in Halbfigur; ***– portrait,*** das Brustbild. **--life,** *adj.* (*Phys.*) Halbwert–. **--light,** *s.* das Halblicht. **--mast,** *s.* der Halbmast; ***at –,*** halbstocks, halbmast. **--measure,** *s.* die Halbheit, der *or* das Kompromiß. **--moon,** *s.* der Halbmond. **--mourning,** *s.* die Halbtrauer. **--pay,** *s.* halber Sold, das Ruhegehalt; (*Mil.*) ***on –,*** außer Dienst, zur Disposition.

halfpenny ['heipəni], **1.** *s.* (*pl.* **-pence** [–pəns]) halber Penny, das Halbpennystück; ***a penny –, three halfpence,*** anderthalb Penny. **2.** *adj.* einen halben Penny wert. **halfpennyworth,** *s.* der Wert eines halben Penny; für einen halben Penny.

half|-seas-over, *pred. adj.* (*coll.*) beschwipst. **--sister,** *s.* die Stiefschwester. **--sovereign,** *s.* (*obs.*) das 50-Pence-Stück. **--time,** *s.* (*Footb.*) die Halbzeit. **--tone,** *s.* 1. (*Mus.*) der Halbton; 2. (*etching*) die Autotypie. **--track(ed),** *adj.* Halbketten–. **--volley,** *s.* der Halbflugball. **–way,** **1.** *adv.* halbwegs, auf halbem Weg. **2.** *adj.* auf halbem Weg gelegen; (*fig.*) ***– house,*** die Zwischenstufe, Zwischenstation, der *or* das Kompromiß. **--wit,** *s.* Blöde(r). **--witted,** *adj.* blöd, albern, nicht recht gescheit. **--yearly,** *adj., adv.* halbjährlich.

halibut ['hælibət], *s.* (*Ichth.*) der Heilbutt.

halide ['hælaid], *s.* (*Chem.*) das Halogenid.

halitosis [hæli'tousis], *s.* der Mundgeruch.

hall [hɔ:l], *s.* 1. die (Fest)halle, der (Fest)saal; 2. Vorraum, Vorsaal, die Vorhalle, Diele, der (Haus)flur, das Vestibül; ***servants' –,*** die Bedientenstube;

3. der Gang, Korridor; 4. Landsitz, das Herrenhaus; 5. (*Univ.*) Studentenheim, (*in colleges*) der Speisesaal; (*Hist.*) das Zunfthaus, Innungshaus, Logenhaus, Stammhaus, der Sitz; ***town* –,** das Rathaus; (*Univ.*) ***I shall not go to – tonight,*** ich werde heute abend nicht im Speisesaal (des College) essen.

hallelujah [hæli'lu:jə], *s.*, *int.* (das) (H)alleluja.

halliard, *see* **halyard.**

hallmark ['hɔ:lmɑ:k], **1.** *s.* der Feingehaltsstempel; (*fig.*) Stempel, das Gepräge, Merkmal, Kennzeichen. **2.** *v.t.* stempeln (*also fig.*), (*fig.*) das Gepräge geben (*Dat.*), kennzeichnen.

hallo [hʌ'lou], **1.** *int.* hallo! **2.** *s.* der Halloruf.

halloo [hə'lu:], **1.** *v.i.* (hallo) rufen; (*Hunt.*) nach den Hunden rufen; (*fig.*) schreien; ***not – before one is out of the wood,*** den Tag nicht vor dem Abend loben, nicht zu früh triumphieren. **2.** *int.* (*Hunt.*) hallo! **3.** *s.* (*Hunt.*) das Hallo.

hallow ['hælou], *v.t.* heiligen, weihen. **Hallowe'en** [–'i:n], *s.* der Abend vor Allerheiligen (31. Okt.). **Hallowmas,** *s.* (das) Allerheiligen(fest) (1. Nov.)

hallstand ['hɔ:lstænd], *s.* der Schirmständer, Garderobenständer.

hallucination [həlu:si'neiʃən], *s.* die Sinnestäuschung, Halluzination, Wahnvorstellung.

halo ['heilou], *s.* der Glorienschein, Heiligenschein; (*Astr.*) Hof; (*Phot.*) Lichthof; (*fig.*) Nimbus.

halogen ['hælədʒən], *s.* (*Chem.*) das Halogen, der Salzbildner. **halogenation** [–'neiʃən], *s.* die Halogenierung, Salzbildung. **halogenous** [hə'lɔdʒinəs], *adj.* salzbildend, halogen. **haloid** [–ɔid], **1.** *adj.* salzähnlich. **2.** *s.* das Halogensalz.

[1]**halt** [hɔ:lt], **1.** *v.i.* (an)halten, haltmachen, stehenbleiben. **2.** *v.t.* anhalten (lassen), haltmachen lassen, zum (An)halten bringen. **3.** *s.* der Halt, die Rast, Marschpause; (*Railw.*) (Bedarfs)haltestelle; (*usu. fig.*) ***call a* –,** Einhalt gebieten (*Dat.*); ***come to a* –,** zum Stehen *or* Stillstand kommen, stehenbleiben, haltmachen, (an)halten.

[2]**halt, 1.** *adj.* (*Poet.*) lahm, hinkend. **2.** *v.i.* (*obs.*) hinken; schwanken, zögern.

halter ['hɔ:ltə], **1.** *s.* die *or* der *or* das Halfter; (*fig.*) der Strick. **2.** *v.t.* (an)halftern (*a horse*); erhängen (*a p.*).

halting ['hɔ:ltiŋ], *adj.* hinkend, schleppend, zögernd, unschlüssig, unsicher.

halve [hɑ:v], *v.t.* 1. halbieren, zu gleichen Hälften teilen; 2. um die Hälfte verringern, auf die Hälfte reduzieren. **halves,** *pl. of* **half.**

halyard ['hæljəd], *s.* (*Naut.*) das Fall.

ham [hæm], **1.** *s.* 1. der Schinken; 2. (*Anat.*) Hinterschenkel, die Gesäßbacke; 3. (*sl.*) (*Theat.*) der Schmierenschauspieler; schlechtes Spiel; (*coll.*) (*radio*) –, der Radio-Amateur. **2.** *adj.* (*sl.*) (*esp. Theat.*) schlecht, stümperhaft, dilettantisch.

hamadryad [hæmə'draiæd], *s.* die Waldnymphe.

hamburger ['hæmbə:gə], *s.* die Hackfleischpastete deutsches Beefsteak.

hame [heim], *s.* (*usu. pl.*) das Kum(me)t.

Hamelin ['hæmlin], *s.* (*Geog.*) Hameln (*n.*).

ham|-fisted, --handed, *adj.* (*sl.*) ungeschickt, linkisch.

hamlet ['hæmlit], *s.* der Weiler, Flecken, das Dörfchen.

hammer ['hæmə], **1.** *s.* der Hammer; (*Tech.*) das Hammerwerk; ***sledge* –,** der Vorschlaghammer; (*coll.*) ***– and tongs,*** wild drauflos, mit aller Kraft; ***come under the* –,** unter den Hammer kommen, versteigert werden; (*Spt.*) ***throwing the* –,** das Hammerwerfen. **2.** *v.t.* hämmern, (mit dem Hammer) schlagen; bearbeiten (*metal*) (*into*, zu); (*coll.*) verdreschen, verprügeln, (*Spt.*) vernichtend schlagen; ***– in,*** einschlagen (*a nail*); (*fig.*) einhämmern, einprägern; (*fig.*) ***– it into him,*** es ihm einhämmern *or* einbleuen *or* eintrichtern; ***– out,*** schmieden, (durch Hämmern) formen (*metal*); (*fig.*) (her)ausarbeiten, ersinnen, erdenken; klarlegen; (*Comm.*) ***be –ed,*** für zahlungsunfähig erklärt werden. **3.** *v.i.* hämmern; ***– away at,*** herumhämmern auf (*Dat.*); (*fig.*) herumarbeiten an (*Dat.*), sich abmühen mit.

hammer|-beam, *s.* (*Build.*) der Stichbalken. **--blow,** *s.* der Hammerschlag. **--cloth,** *s.* die Kutschsitzdecke. **–head,** *s.* (*Ichth.*) der Hammerhai.

hammock ['hæmək], *s.* die Hängematte.

[1]**hamper** ['hæmpə], *s.* der Packkorb, Eßkorb, Frühstückskorb.

[2]**hamper,** *v.t.* 1. verstricken, verwickeln (*in*, in (*Acc.*)); 2. (*usu. fig.*) (be)hindern, hemmen.

hamshackle ['hæmʃækl], *v.t.* fesseln.

hamster ['hæmstə], *s.* (*Zool.*) der (Gold)hamster.

hamstring ['hæmstriŋ], **1.** *s.* die Kniefleсhse. **2.** *irr.v.t.* die Kniefleсhsen zerschneiden (*Dat.*); (*fig.*) lähmen.

hand [hænd], **1.** *s.* 1. die Hand; der Vorderfuß (*of animals*); ***note of* –,** der Handwechsel, Handschuldschein; ***by show of –s,*** durch Aufheben der Hände; ***sleight of* –,** der Kunstgriff; ***in the turn of a* –,** im Handumdrehen; ***–s off!*** Hände weg! laß die Hände davon! ***–s up!*** Hände hoch! 2. die Handschrift, Unterschrift; 3. (*Horol.*) der Zeiger; 4. die Handbreite (= 4 Zoll); 5. Seite; 6. (*usu. pl.*) der Arbeiter; Mann, Matrose; ***all –s on deck!*** alle Mann an Deck! ***the ship was lost with all –s,*** das Schiff ging mit Mann und Maus unter; 7. (*Cards*) das Blatt, Karten (*pl.*); 8. das Büschel, Bündel (*fruit etc.*).

(a) (*with adjs.*) (*sl.*) ***give him a big* –,** ihm Beifall klatschen; ***at first* –,** aus erster Hand; ***be a good – at,*** geübt *or* geschickt sein in (*Dat.*), sich verstehen auf (*Acc.*), Geschicklichkeit *or* Veranlagung haben zu *or* für; ***write a good* –,** eine schöne Handschrift haben; ***with a heavy* –,** (be)drückend, mit großer Strenge, erbarmungslos; ***lend a helping* –,** eine hilfreiche Hand leisten; ***with a high* –,** selbstherrlich, rücksichtslos, willkürlich, anmaßend, hochmütig; ***an iron* –,** eiserne Zucht; ***be an old* –,** ein alter Praktikus sein, gründlich bewandert sein (*at*, in (*Dat.*)); ***with one's own* –,** mit eigner Hand; ***the upper* –,** die Oberhand; (*Cards*) ***a wretched* –,** ein schlechtes Blatt, schlechte Karten.

(b) (*with verbs*) ***ask for her* –,** um sie anhalten, um ihre Hand bitten; ***tie him up*** or ***bind him – and foot,*** ihn an Händen und Füßen fesseln; ***be – and*** or ***in glove with,*** auf vertrautem Fuße stehen mit, ein Herz und eine Seele sein mit; ***bear a* –,** anfassen, mithelfen; Hilfe leisten (*Dat.*), zur Hand gehen (*Dat.*); ***change –s,*** in andere Hände kommen *or* übergehen; (*coll.*) ***not do a –'s turn,*** keinen Finger rühren; (*coll.*) ***get one's – in,*** sich einarbeiten, in Übung kommen; ***have a – in,*** die Hand im Spiele haben bei, beteiligt sein an (*Dat.*); ***have one's –s full,*** alle Hände voll zu tun haben; (*coll.*) ***hold one's* –,** sich zurückhalten, sich nicht einmischen; ***hold o.s. in* –,** sich beherrschen; (*fig.*) ***join –s,*** sich verbünden; ***keep one's – in,*** in Übung bleiben; ***keep a tight – on,*** streng im Zaum halten; ***lay one's –(s) on,*** habhaft werden (*Gen.*); ***lay –s on,*** ergreifen, (an)fassen, anpacken; (*coll.*) erhalten; ***lay –s on o.s.,*** Hand an sich legen; ***lend a* –,** helfen (*with*, bei); ***play into each other's –s,*** sich (*Dat.*) in die Hände spielen; (*coll.*) ***put one's – on,*** finden; ***put one's – to,*** in Angriff nehmen; ***shake –s,*** sich (*Dat.*) die Hände geben; ***show one's* –,** seine Karten aufdecken (*also fig.*); ***throw in one's* –,** (*Cards*) sein Blatt wegwerfen, (*fig.*) aufgeben, sich zurückziehen; ***throw up one's –s,*** eine verzweifelte Gebärde machen; ***try one's – at,*** versuchen; ***wash one's –s of,*** nichts mehr zu tun haben wollen mit (*a p.*), seine Hände in Unschuld waschen in (*Dat.*) (*an affair*); ***win –s down,*** spielend gewinnen.

(c) (*with preps.*) ***at* –,** zur Hand, bereit, bei der Hand; (***near***) ***at* –,** (*place*) nahe, (*time*) nahe bevorstehend; ***at the –(s) of,*** seitens *or* von seiten (*Gen.*); ***by* –,** mit der Hand; durch Boten; ***bring up by* –,** mit der Flasche nähren (*a child*); ***by the – of,*** vermittelst, durch; ***shake him by the* –,** ihm die Hand geben *or* reichen; ***take by the* –,** bei der Hand nehmen; ***from – to* –,** von Hand zu Hand;

from – to mouth, aus der Hand in den Mund; ***in –,*** in der Hand, unter Kontrolle; (*Comm.*) ***cash in –,*** der Kassenbestand, Barbestand; ***have in –,*** unter den Händen haben; ***– in –,*** Hand in Hand; (*fig.*) ***go – in – with,*** Schritt halten mit; ***matter in –,*** vorliegende Angelegenheit; ***put in –,*** in Ausführung *or* Arbeit nehmen; ***take in –,*** unternehmen, übernehmen; ***it is in his –s,*** es liegt in seiner Hand; ***take one's life in one's –,*** sein Leben aufs Spiel setzen; ***fall into his –s,*** ihm in die Hände fallen; ***take the law into one's own –s,*** sich (*Dat.*) selbst Recht verschaffen; ***take it off his –s,*** es ihm abnehmen; ***on –,*** vorrätig, auf Lager, verfügbar; (*fig.*) bevorstehend; ***on either –,*** zu beiden Seiten; ***on every –,*** auf jeder Seite; ***be on his –s,*** ihm zur Last fallen; ***have on one's –s,*** am *or* auf dem Halse haben; ***on the one –,*** auf der einen Seite, einerseits; ***on the other –,*** auf der anderen Seite, ander(er)seits; ***on the right –,*** rechter Hand; ***out of –,*** im Handumdrehen, kurzerhand, unverzüglich, auf der Stelle; außer Kontrolle, unbändig; ***climb – over –,*** Hand über Hand klettern; (*fig.*) ***– over fist,*** Zug um Zug, in rascher Folge, rasch nacheinander; ***to –,*** zur Hand, bereit; (*Comm.*) ***your letter to –,*** im Besitz Ihres Schreibens; ***come to –,*** einlaufen, eintreffen, einlangen, zum Vorschein kommen; ***under one's –,*** eigenhändig unterschrieben; ***with one's own –,*** eigenhändig.

2. *v.t.* (über)reichen, übergeben, aushändigen; (*Naut.*) beschlagen, festmachen (*sail*); (*sl.*) ***one must – it to him,*** man muß ihm Anerkennung zollen, das muß man ihm lassen; ***– down,*** herunterlangen, herunterreichen; (*as inheritance*) hinterlassen, vererben (*to, Dat.*); ***– down to posterity,*** der Nachwelt überliefern; ***– in,*** einreichen (*petition*), einliefern, aufgeben, abgeben (*a th.*); (*Rugby footb.*) ***– off,*** mit der Hand abwehren; ***– on,*** weitergeben, weiterreichen (*to, Dat. or* an (*Acc.*)); überliefern (*to, Dat.*); ***– out,*** austeilen (*to*, an (*Acc.*)); ***– over,*** hergeben, aushändigen, überlassen, abgeben (*to, Dat.*), abtreten (an (*Acc.*)); ***– round,*** herumreichen; ***– up,*** hinaufreichen, hinauflangen.

hand|bag, *s.* die (Damen)handtasche. **–ball,** *s.* der Handball. **–bell,** *s.* die Tischglocke, Schelle. **–bill,** *s.* gedruckter Zettel, das Flugblatt, der Reklamezettel. **–book,** *s.* das Handbuch. **–breadth,** *s.* die Handbreite. **–cart,** *s.* die Handkarre, der Handkarren. **–cuff, 1.** *s.* (*usu. pl.*) die Handschelle, Handfessel. **2.** *v.t.* Handschellen anlegen (*Dat.*), fesseln.

-handed ['hændid], *adj. suff.* –händig. **handful,** *s.* die Handvoll; (*coll.*) ***he is a –,*** er ist ein ungezogenes Kind, er macht mir sehr zu schaffen.

hand|-gallop, *s.* kurzer Galopp. **--grenade,** *s.* die Handgranate. **–hold,** *s.* der Halt, Handgriff.

handicap ['hændikæp], **1.** *s.* **1.** die Vorgabe, das Handikap; 2. Ausgleichsrennen; 3. (*fig.*) die (Vor)belastung, Erschwerung, Benachteiligung, Behinderung, das Hindernis (*to*, für). **2.** *v.t.* (*Spt.*) mit Vorgabe belegen; extra belasten (*a horse*); (*fig.*) hemmen, (be)hindern, belasten, beeinträchtigen, benachteiligen. **handicapped,** *adj.* benachteiligt, behindert (*also Med., Psych.*).

handicraft ['hændikrɑ:ft], *s.* das Gewerbe, (Kunst)handwerk. **handicraftsman,** *s.* der Handwerker.

handily ['hændili], *adv. See* **handy. handiness,** *s.* (*of a p.*) die Gewandtheit; (*of a th.*) Handlichkeit, Bequemlichkeit, Zweckmäßigkeit. **handiwork,** *s.* das Werk, die Arbeit, Schöpfung; (*rare*) Handarbeit.

handkerchief ['hæŋkətʃif], *s.* das Taschentuch.

handle [hændl], **1.** *v.t.* anfassen, befühlen; handhaben, hantieren mit; führen, lenken, leiten; behandeln, sich beschäftigen *or* befassen mit; (*Comm.*) handeln *or* Handel treiben mit. **2.** *v.i.* (*Motor. etc.*) ***– well,*** sich gut fahren. **3.** *s.* der Griff, Stiel; die Kurbel (*on a spindle*); der Henkel (*of a vessel*); Schwengel (*of a pump*); (*fig.*) die Handhabe, der Vorwand; ***crank –,*** der Kurbelgriff; ***door –,*** der Türgriff, Türdrücker, die Türklinke; (*coll.*) ***a – to one's name,*** ein Titel vor dem Namen; (*sl.*) ***fly off the –,*** aus dem Häuschen geraten. **handlebar,** *s.* (*Cycl.*) die Lenkstange.

handler, *s.* (*esp.*) ***dog–,*** der Hundeführer. **handling,** *s.* 1. die Handhabung, Führung (*of tools etc.*), Behandlung, Darstellung (*of a theme*); 2. (*Comm.*) Beförderung; ***– charges,*** Umschlag(s)spesen (*pl.*).

hand|-made, *adj.* mit der Hand gemacht; ***– paper,*** das Büttenpapier. **–maid(en),** *s.* (*B.*) die Dienerin, Magd; (*fig.*) der Gehilfe, Handlanger. **--me-downs,** *pl.* (*sl.*) gebrauchte Kleidung, alte Erbstücke. **--operated,** *adj.* handbedient, Hand–. **--out,** *s.* (*sl.*) 1. die Erklärung (*for the press etc.*); der Werbezettel; die Spende (*of money etc.*), (*oft. iron.*) Liebesgabe, das Gnadenbrot. **--picked,** *adj.* (*coll.*) für den Zweck ausgewählt. **–rail,** *s.* das Geländer. **–saw,** *s.* die Handsäge.

handsel ['hæn(d)səl], **1.** *s.* 1. das Neujahrsgeschenk, Begrüßungsgeschenk; Angeld, Handgeld; 2. (*fig.*) der Vorgeschmack. **2.** *v.t.* 1. zum ersten Mal gebrauchen *or* versuchen, dem Gebrauch einweihen; 2. Handgeld geben (*Dat.*).

hand|set, *s.* (*Tele.*) der Hörer. **–shake,** *s.* der Händedruck.

handsome ['hænsəm], *adj.* 1. hübsch, schön, stattlich; 2. großzügig, freigebig, nobel; (*Prov.*) ***– is that – does,*** edel ist wer edel handelt; 3. ansehnlich, beträchtlich. **handsomeness,** *s.* 1. die Schönheit, Stattlichkeit; 2. Großzügigkeit, Großmütigkeit; 3. Ansehnlichkeit, Beträchtlichkeit.

hand|spike, *s.* die Brechstange; (*Naut., Artil.*) Handspake, der Hebebaum. **–spring,** *s.* (*Gymn.*) der Handstandüberschlag. **–stand,** *s.* (*Gymn.*) der Handstand. **--to-hand,** *adj.* Mann gegen Mann; ***– fighting,*** der Nahkampf. **–wheel,** *s.* das Stellrad, Kurbelrad. **–writing,** *s.* die (Hand)schrift.

handy ['hændi], *adj.* zur Hand, bei der Hand, leicht erreichbar, schnell greifbar; bequem, handlich; (*of a p.*) gewandt, geschickt; (*of a boat*) wendig; ***come in –,*** nützlich sein, zustatten kommen. **handyman,** *s.* der Mann für alles.

hang [hæŋ], **1.** *irr.v.t.* hängen (*on, to, from*, an (*Acc.*)), aufhängen (an (*Dat.*)); einhängen (*doors*); behängen (*a room with pictures*); hängen lassen (*one's head etc.*); ***– fire,*** (*Artil.*) nachbrennen; (*fig.*) (*of a p.*) sich nicht entschließen können, zögern, (*of a th.*) zurückbleiben, auf sich warten lassen; ***– out the washing,*** die Wäsche aufhängen; ***– up,*** aufhängen (*one's coat etc.*); (*Tele., coll.*) (den Hörer) einhängen *or* auflegen; ***well hung,*** (*of game*) gut abgehangen. **2.** *reg.v.t.* (er)hängen, henken (*a p.*); ***– it!*** zum Teufel *or* Henker! ***I'll be –ed if,*** ich will mich hängen lassen, wenn.

3. *reg.v.i.* gehängt *or* gehenkt werden (*of a p.*); (*coll.*) ***let it go –,*** sich (*Dat.*) den Teufel darum kümmern.

4. *irr.v.i.* hangen, (*now usu.*) hängen (*on, by*, an (*Dat.*)), herabhängen, baumeln; schweben; ***– by a thread,*** an einem Faden hängen; ***– in the balance,*** in der Schwebe *or* noch unentschieden sein; **(a)** (*with preps.*) ***– about,*** herumlungern *or* sich herumtreiben in (*Dat.*) (*a place*); sich hängen an (*Acc.*) (*a p.*); (*fig.*) ***– on,*** hängen an (*Dat.*), abhängen von, beruhen auf (*Dat.*); ***– on his words,*** an seinen Worten hängen; ***time is –ing on my hands,*** die Zeit ist mir lang; ***– over,*** sich beugen *or* neigen über (*Acc.*), hängen *or* schweben über (*Dat.*); **(b)** (*with advs.*) ***– about,*** faulenzen, umherlungern; ***– back,*** zögern, zaudern, sich sträuben *or* zurückhalten; ***– down,*** herab– *or* herunterhängen; ***– on,*** festhalten, sich (fest)klammern (*to*, an (*Dat.*)); (*coll.*) ausharren, nicht nachlassen; ***– on!*** (*coll.*) halt (dich) fest! (*fig.*) laß nicht los! gib nicht auf! ***– out,*** ausgehängt sein, heraushängen; (*sl.*) wohnen; ***– together,*** zusammenhalten (*of persons*), zusammenhängen (*of things*); (*Tele.*) ***– up,*** den Hörer einhängen.

5. *s.* 1. der Abhang, die Neigung, Senkung; (*of clothes etc.*) der Sitz, Fall; 2. (*coll.*) die Bedeutung, der Sinn; (*coll.*) ***get the – of a th.,*** etwas herausbekommen, hinter etwas kommen; (*sl.*) ***I don't give a –,*** mir ist es schnuppe.

hangar ['hæŋə], *s.* (*Av.*) die Flugzeughalle; der Schuppen.

hangdog ['hæŋdɔg], **1.** *s.* der Galgenvogel, Galgenstrick. **2.** *adj.* – *look,* die Galgenmiene, der Armesünderblick. **hanger,** *s.* 1. der Aufhänger, Haken, Henkel; 2. die Schlaufe (*on coats etc.*); 3. der Kleiderbügel; 4. Hirschfänger. **hanger-on,** *s.* (*coll.*) der Anhänger, Mitläufer, Schmarotzer. **hangfire,** *s.* (*Artil.*) die Nachzündung.

hanging ['hæŋiŋ], **1.** *s.* das (Auf)hängen; Erhängen; ***execution by*** –, Hinrichtung durch den Strang; ***a – matter,*** etwas das zum Galgen führt. **2.** *adj.* Hänge–, (herab)hängend. **hangings,** *pl.* die Wandbekleidung, der Wandbehang, Vorhänge (*pl.*), Tapeten (*pl.*).

hang|man, *s.* der Henker. **–nail,** *s.* (*Med.*) der Niednagel. **––out,** *s.* (*sl.*) der Stammplatz. **–over,** *s.* 1. (*coll.*) der Überbleibsel, Überrest; 2. (*sl.*) Kater, Katzenjammer.

hank [hæŋk], *s.* 1. der *or* das Knäuel, der Wickel, das Bund; (*fig.*) die Strähne (*of hair etc.*); 2. (*Naut.*) der Sauger, Legel.

hanker ['hæŋkə], *v.i.* verlangen, sich sehnen (***after, for,*** nach), begehren (*Acc.*). **hankering,** *s.* das Verlangen, die Sehnsucht.

hanky ['hæŋki], *s.* (*coll.*) *see* **handkerchief.**

hanky-panky [hæŋki'pæŋki], *s.* (*coll.*) der Hokuspokus, Schwindel.

Hanover ['hænouvə], *s.* Hannover (*n.*). **Hanoverian** [–'vɛəriən], **1.** *adj.* (*Geog.*) hannover(i)sch, hannöver(i)sch, (*Hist.*) hannoveranisch. **2.** *s.* der (die) Hannoveraner(in).

Hanse [hæns], *s.* (*Hist.*) die Hansa, Hanse. **Hanseatic** [–i'ætik], *adj.* hansisch, hanseatisch, Hanse–, Hanseaten–.

hansel, *see* **handsel.**

hansom ['hænsəm], *s.* zweirädrige Droschke.

hap [hæp], (*obs.*) **1.** *v.i.* sich ereignen. **2.** *s.* zufälliges Ereignis, der Glücksfall, Zufall. **haphazard, 1.** *s.* der Zufall, das Geratewohl. **2.** *adj.* zufällig, wahllos. **hapless,** *adj.* unselig, glücklos, unglücklich. **haply,** *adv.* (*obs.*) vielleicht, von ungefähr.

ha'p'orth ['heipəθ], *see* **halfpennyworth.**

happen [hæpn], *v.i.* sich ereignen, geschehen, zustandekommen, vorkommen, vorfallen, (*coll.*) passieren; sich (zufällig) ergeben, sich (gerade) treffen; ***I –ed to read,*** ich las zufällig; ***as it –s,*** wie es sich trifft; – ***upon,*** (durch Zufall) stoßen auf (*Acc.*) *or* treffen; – ***to him,*** mit ihm geschehen, aus ihm werden, ihm zustoßen *or* (*coll.*) passieren. **happening,** *s.* das Ereignis, Vorkommnis, der Vorfall.

happily ['hæpili], *adv.* zum Glück, glücklich(erweise). **happiness,** *s.* 1. das Glück; die Glückseligkeit; 2. Trefflichkeit, glückliche Wahl; 3. die Gewandtheit, Geschicklichkeit. **happy,** *adj.* 1. glücklich; beglückt, erfreut (***at, about,*** über (*Acc.*)), zufrieden (mit); – ***in his friendship,*** froh über seine Freundschaft; ***I am – to know,*** ich freue mich zu wissen; – ***hunting ground(s),*** ewige Jagdgründe; ***many – returns of the day,*** viel Glück zum Geburtstag; 2. trefflich, erfreulich; treffend, passend, gewandt, geschickt; – ***dispatch,*** legaler Selbstmord; – ***retort,*** passende *or* treffende Entgegnung; – ***thought,*** trefflicher Gedanke. **happy-go-lucky,** *adj.* unbekümmert, sorglos.

Hapsburg ['hæpsbə:g], *s.* (*Hist.*) der (die) Habsburger(in).

harangue [hə'ræŋ], **1.** *v.t.* eine Ansprache halten an (*Acc.*), eine Rede schwingen vor (*Dat.*). **2.** *v.i.* eine Ansprache halten, eine Rede schwingen. **3.** *s.* die Ansprache, feierliche Rede.

harass ['hærəs, hə'ræs], *v.t.* dauernd belästigen, aufreiben, quälen, plagen, beunruhigen, stören (*also Mil.*); (*Mil.*) ***–ing fire,*** das Störfeuer. **harassment,** *s.* die Beunruhigung, Belästigung.

harbinger ['hɑ:bindʒə], **1.** *s.* der Vorbote, Vorläufer. **2.** *v.t.* ankünd(ig)en.

harbour ['hɑ:bə], **1.** *s.* der Hafen; (*fig.*) Zufluchtsort, Unterschlupf. **2.** *v.t.* beherbergen; Schutz *or* Obdach gewähren (*Dat.*); (*fig.*) hegen (*feelings etc.*); – ***a criminal,*** einen Verbrecher verbergen. **3.** *v.i.* im Hafen ankern *or* anlegen. **harbourage** [–ridʒ], *s.* die Unterkunft, Herberge, Zuflucht, der Schutz, das Obdach; Unterkommen im Hafen. **harbour|-dues,** *pl.* Hafengebühren (*pl.*). **––master,** *s.* der Hafenmeister.

hard [hɑ:d], **1.** *adj.* 1. hart, fest; (*coll.*) – ***cash,*** das Hartgeld, Metallgeld; klingende Münze; – ***core,*** das Unterfutter, die Schotterlage (*of roads*); (*fig.*) der Kern, das Herz, Innerste; – ***currency,*** harte Währung; (*Am.*) – ***pan,*** der Ortstein; (*fig.*) die Grundlage; – ***and fast rule,*** ausnahmslos gültige *or* absolut bindende Regel; – ***soap,*** die Kernseife; 2. schwer (zu bewältigen(d) *or* verstehen(d)), schwierig, mühsam, anstrengend; angestrengt, angespannt, intensiv; heftig, kräftig; ***drive a – bargain,*** aufs äußerste feilschen; – ***case,*** schwieriger *or* (besonders) harter Fall; (*Law*) eine Härte; ***a – death,*** ein schwerer Tod; – ***drinker,*** heftiger Trinker, der Säufer; – ***labour,*** die Zwangsarbeit; – ***times,*** schlimme Zeiten; ***for – wear,*** unverwüstlich; – ***work,*** schwere Arbeit; – ***worker,*** fleißiger Arbeiter; – ***to deal with,*** schwer auszukommen *or* umzugehen mit; – ***to digest,*** schwerverdaulich; ***he is – to please,*** er ist sehr anspruchsvoll *or* schwer zu befriedigen; – ***of hearing,*** schwerhörig; 3. streng, drückend, schlimm, ungünstig, unbillig, ungerecht, hartherzig, gefühllos, unbarmherzig, unbeugsam, grausam; ***the – facts,*** die unumstößlichen Tatsachen; ***no – feelings!*** nichts für ungut! (*coll.*) – ***lines,*** großes Pech, ein hartes Los; (*coll.*) – ***luck,*** das Unglück, Pech; – ***winter,*** strenger Winter; ***be – on him,*** hart *or* streng gegen ihn sein, ihm hart zusetzen; 4. karg, geizig; 5. herb, sauer, rauh (*as liquor*); 6. kalkhaltig (*of water*).

2. *adv.* 1. heftig, stark, mächtig, wuchtig; ***bear – upon,*** hart treffen; ***die –,*** ein zähes Leben haben; ***drink –,*** übermäßig trinken; ***go – with,*** schlecht ergehen (*Dat.*); (*coll.*) ***hold –,*** festhalten; ***look – at,*** fest *or* scharf ansehen; ***rain –,*** heftig *or* stark regnen; 2. fleißig, tüchtig; – ***at work,*** fleißig bei *or* an der Arbeit; ***try –,*** mit aller Kraft versuchen, sein Äußerstes tun; ***work –,*** tüchtig *or* fleißig *or* hart arbeiten; 3. mit Mühe, schwer, sauer; – ***pressed,*** hart *or* schwer bedrängt, in großer Bedrängnis; ***be – put to it,*** es sich (*Dat.*) sauer werden lassen, in großer Verlegenheit sein; 4. nahe, dicht; – ***by,*** nahe *or* dicht (da)bei, ganz in der Nähe (von); – ***on his heels,*** ihm hart *or* dicht auf den Fersen.

3. *s.* 1. (*Naut.*) festes Uferland, die Landestelle; 2. (*coll.*) die Zwangsarbeit, Zuchthausstrafe.

hard|bitten, *adj.* hartnäckig, verbissen. **–board,** *s.* die Hart(faser)platte. **––boiled,** *adj.* hart(gekocht) (*egg*); (*fig. coll.*) hartgesotten, abgebrüht, (kalt)berechnend, unsentimental, realistisch. **––earned,** *adj.* sauer erworben.

harden [hɑ:dn], **1.** *v.t.* härten, hart *or* härter machen; (*fig.*) stählen, abhärten (***against,*** gegen); gewöhnen (***to,*** an (*Acc.*)); verhärten, (be)stärken; gefühllos machen. **2.** *v.i.* hart werden; (*fig.*) sich verhärten *or* verfestigen, erstarren; sich abhärten, unempfindlich werden; (*Comm.*) steigen, anziehen, sich festigen, fest werden (*of prices*). **hardener,** *s.* (*Metall.*) der Härter, das Härtemittel. **hardening, 1.** *s.* das Härten. **2.** *adj.* Härte–.

hard|-featured, *adj.* mit harten Gesichtszügen. **––fisted,** *adj.* geizig, knauserig. **––headed,** *adj.* nüchtern, praktisch, realistisch. **––hearted,** *adj.* hartherzig, gefühllos, grausam.

hardihood ['hɑ:dihud], *s.* die Kühnheit, Unerschrockenheit; Dreistigkeit. **hardiness,** *s.* die Widerstandsfähigkeit, Ausdauer; Körperkraft, Rüstigkeit.

hardly ['hɑ:dli], *adv.* 1. kaum, schwerlich, fast *or* wohl nicht; – ***ever,*** fast nie; 2. eben gerade, mit Mühe, mühsam, schwer; hart, streng.

hard-mouthed, *adj.* hartmäulig.

hardness ['hɑ:dnis], *s.* 1. die Härte, Festigkeit; 2. Strenge, Hartherzigkeit, Gefühllosigkeit, Unbeugsamkeit, Hartnäckigkeit; 3. Schwierigkeit, Mühsamkeit, Beschwerlichkeit.

hardship ['hɑ:dʃip], *s.* die Härte, Not, Bedrängnis; Mühsal, das Ungemach.

hard|tack, *s.* der Schiffswieback. **--up,** *pred. adj.* in (Geld)not, auf dem trockenen, nicht bei Kasse; – ***for,*** in Verlegenheit *or* schlimm dran um. **-ware,** *s.* Metallwaren, Eisenwaren (*pl.*). **-wearing,** *adj.* verschleißfest. **-wood,** *s.* das Hartholz. **--working,** *adj.* fleißig.

hardy ['hɑ:di], *adj.* abgehärtet, robust, kräftig; kühn verwegen; (*plants*) winterfest; – ***annual,*** winterannuelle Pflanze; (*fig. coll.*) periodisch wiederkehrendes Problem.

hare [hɛə], *s.* der Hase; – ***and hounds,*** die Schnitzeljagd; ***mad as a March –,*** total verrückt; ***run with the – and hunt with the hounds,*** es mit beiden Parteien halten.

hare|bell, *s.* (*Bot.*) rundblättrige Glockenblume. **-brained,** *adj.* unbesonnen, gedankenlos, zerfahren. **-lip,** *s.* die Hasenscharte.

harem ['hɛərəm, hɑ:'ri:m], *s.* der Harem.

hare's-foot, *s.* (*Bot.*) der Ackerklee.

haricot ['hærikou], *s.* das Hammelragout; – ***bean,*** die Dörrbohne, welsche Bohne.

hark [hɑ:k], **1.** *v.i.* horchen; – ***back,*** nach der Fährte zurückgehen (*of hounds*); (*fig.*) zurückkommen, zurückgehen, zurückgreifen (***to,*** auf (*Acc*)). **2.** *int.* horch! hör zu!

harlequin ['hɑ:likwin], *s.* der Hanswurst, Harlekin, Kasperl. **harlequinade** [–'neid], *s.* das Possenspiel.

harlot ['hɑ:lət], *s.* die Dirne, Hure. **harlotry,** *s.* die Hurerei.

harm [hɑ:m], **1.** *s.* der Schaden, Nachteil, das Leid, Unrecht; Übel, Böse(s); ***do no –,*** nicht(s) schaden; ***do him –,*** ihm schaden; ***mean no –,*** es nicht böse meinen, nichts Böses im Sinne haben; ***keep out of –'s way,*** die Gefahr meiden, in Sicherheit bleiben. **2.** *v.t.* schädigen, verletzen; schaden (*Dat.*), Schaden *or* Leid zufügen (*Dat.*); ***not – a hair of his head,*** ihm kein Haar krümmen. **harmful,** *adj.* nachteilig, schädlich (***to,*** für *or Dat.*). **harmless,** *adj.* harmlos, unschädlich, ungefährlich; schuldlos, arglos.

harmonic [hɑ:'mɔnik], **1.** *adj.* (*Mus., Math.*) harmonisch; übereinstimmend, zusammenstimmend; – ***proportion,*** harmonische Reihe. **2.** *s.* (*Mus.*) der Oberton; (*Phys.*) die Oberwelle, Unterschwingung. **harmonica,** *s.* die (Mund)harmonika. **harmonics,** *pl.* (*sing. constr.*) (*Mus.*) die Harmonielehre, Harmonik.

harmonious [hɑ:'mouniəs], *adj.* harmonisch, wohlklingend; (*fig.*) zusammenstimmend; einträchtig. **harmoniousness,** *s.* der Wohlklang; die Eintracht; Übereinstimmung, der Einklang.

harmonist ['hɑ:mənist], *s.* der Harmonielehrer; (*Eccl.*) Harmoniker. **harmknium** [–'mounjəm], *s.* das Harmonium.

harmonization [hɑ:mənai'zeiʃən], **s.** die Harmonisierung. **harmonize** ['hɑ:mənaiz], **1.** *v.i.* harmonieren; übereinstimmen, in Einklang sein (***with,*** mit), passen (zu), zusammenstimmen, zusammenpassen, zueinander passen. **2.** *v.t.* 1. (*Mus.*) harmonisieren, mehrstimmig setzen; 2. (*fig.*) in Übereinstimmung *or* Einklang bringen, aufeinander abstimmen, ausgleichen. **harmony,** *s.* **1.** (*Mus.*) die Harmonie, der Wohlklang; Zusammenklang, Akkord; die Harmonielehre; ***sing in –,*** mehrstimmig singen; ***close*** (or ***open***) ***–,*** enger (*or* weiter) Satz; ***two-part –,*** zweistimmiger Satz; **2.** (*fig.*) das Gleichmaß, Ebenmaß; die Übereinstimmung, Eintracht, der Einklang.

harness ['hɑ:nis], **1.** *s.* das Geschirr; (*obs.*) der Harnisch, die Rüstung; (*fig.*) ***be in –,*** mitten in der Arbeit stehen; (*fig.*) ***die in –,*** in den Sielen sterben; ***parachute –,*** das Gurtwerk. **2.** *v.t.* anschirren, anspannen, vorspannen; spannen (***to,*** an (*Acc.*)); (*fig.*) einspannen (***to,*** in (*Acc.*)); nutzbar machen (*natural forces*).

harp [hɑ:p], **1.** *s.* die Harfe; ***Jew's--,*** die Maultrommel. **2.** *v.i.* Harfe spielen, harfen; (*fig. coll.*) ***– on,*** immer wieder berühren *or* betonen, herumreiten auf (*Dat.*); (*fig.*) ***be always –ing on the same string,*** immer dieselbe Leier anstimmen. **harper, harpist,** *s.* der (die) Harfner(in), Harfenist(in).

harpoon [hɑ:'pu:n], **1.** *s.* die Harpune. **2.** *v.t.* harpunieren.

harpsichord ['hɑ:psikɔ:d], *s.* der Kielflügel, das Cembalo.

harpy ['hɑ:pi], *s.* (*Myth.*) die Harpyie; (*fig.*) raubgieriger Mensch.

harquebus ['hɑ:kwibəs], **s.** (*Hist.*) die Büchse. **harquebusier** [–'siə], *s.* der Büchsenschütze.

harridan ['hæridən], *s.* alte Vettel.

harrier ['hæriə], *s.* 1. (*Hunt.*) der Hasenhund; 2. (*Orn.*) die *or* der Weihe (*Circus*); 3. (*Spt.*) der Geländeläufer.

harrow ['hærou], **1.** *s.* die Egge. **2.** *v.t.* 1. eggen; 2. (*fig.*) quälen, martern. **harrowing,** *adj.* herzzerreißend, qualvoll, schmerzlich, schrecklich.

harry ['hæri], *v.t.* verheeren, verwüsten, (aus)plündern, ausrauben (*a land*); ausnehmen, rauben (*a nest*); verfolgen, quälen (*a p.*).

harsh [hɑ:ʃ], *adj.* rauh, hart (*touch*); herb, sauer (*taste*); grell (*sound, colour*); (*fig.*) streng, barsch, schroff, unsanft, grausam. **harshness,** *s.* die Rauheit, Herbheit; (*fig.*) Härte.

hart [hɑ:t], *s.* der Hirsch; – ***of ten,*** der Zehnender.

hartebeest ['hɑ:təbi:st], *s.* (*Zool.*) der Kama.

harts|horn, *s.* (*Chem.*) das Hirschhorn. **-tongue,** *s.* (*Bot.*) die Hirschzunge, der Zungenfarn.

harum-scarum ['hɛərəm'skɛərəm], (*coll.*) **1.** *adj.* wild, unbändig; fahrig, gedankenlos, leichtsinnig, flatterhaft, zerfahren. **2.** *s.* fahrige Person; der Wildfang.

harvest ['hɑ:vist], **1.** *s.* die Ernte; Erntezeit; (*fig.*) der Gewinn, Ertrag. **2.** *v.t.* ernten; abernten (*field*); (*fig.*) sammeln, sparen, haushalten mit; aufsparen, aufspeichern. **3.** *v.i.* die Ernte einbringen *or* einholen. **harvest-bug,** *s.* die Grasmilbe. **harvester,** *s.* 1. der (die) Erntearbeiter(in), Schnitter(in); 2. die Mähmaschine, Erntemaschine; 3. *See* **harvest bug. harvest|-festival,** *s. See* **--thanksgiving. --home,** *s.* das Erntefest. **--mite,** *s. See* **--bug. --moon,** *s.* der Vollmond im Herbste. **--mouse,** *s.* die Zwergmaus. **--thanksgiving,** *s.* das Erntedankfest. **--tick,** *s. See* **--bug.**

has [hæz], *3rd sing. pres. indic. of* **have. has-been,** *s.* (*coll.*) Ausgespielte(r), Ausrangierte(r), Gestrige(r); Überholte(s), Vergangene(s).

hash [hæʃ], **1.** *s.* das Haschee, Faschierte(s), Gehackte(s); (*fig.*) der Mischmasch, Wirrwarr, heilloses Durcheinander; Wiederaufgewärmte(s), (*coll.*) alter Kohl; (*sl.*) ***make a – of,*** verpfuschen, verpatzen; (*sl.*) ***settle his –,*** ihm einen Strich durch die Rechnung machen, ihn erledigen *or* abtun. **2.** *v.t.* haschieren, zerhacken; – ***up an old story,*** eine alte Geschichte aufwärmen.

hashish ['hæʃiʃ], *s.* das Haschisch.

haslet ['hæslit], *s.* das (Schweins)geschlinge, Innereien (*pl.*).

hasn't [hæznt] = ***has not.***

hasp [hɑ:sp], **1.** *s.* das Schließband, die Haspe, Spange; Haspel. Spule (*for yarn*), Docke (*of yarn*). **2.** *v.t.* mit einer Haspe verschließen, zuhaken.

hassle [hæsl], *s.* (*Am. sl.*) der Streit, Zank; Ärger.

hassock ['hæsək], **s.** das Kniekissen, Betkissen.

hast [hæst], (*obs.*) *2nd sing. pres. indic. of* **have.**

hastate ['hæsteit], *adj.* (*Bot.*) spießförmig.

haste [heist], **1.** *s.* die Hast, Eile; Hastigkeit, Übereilung; ***make –,*** sich beeilen; ***in –,*** in Eile, eilig; (*Prov.*) ***more – less speed,*** Eile mit Weile. **2.** *v.i.* (*Poet.*) *see* **hasten, 2. hasten** [heisn], **1.** *v.t.* beschleunigen, antreiben. **2.** *v.i.* eilen, sich beeilen. **hastily,** *adv. See* **hasty. hastiness,** *s.* die Hastigkeit, Übereilung; Voreiligkeit, Eilfertigkeit, Hitze, Ungeduld, das Ungestüm. **hasty,** *adj.* hastig, eilig; eilfertig, voreilig, übereilt, überstürzt; hitzig, ungestüm. **hasty-pudding,** *s.* der Mehlpudding, Mehlbrei.

hat [hæt], *s.* der Hut; (*fig.*) ***cardinal's –,*** die Kardinalswürde; (*fig.*) ***– in hand,*** respektvoll, demütig, unterwürfig; (*sl.*) ***bad –***, übler Kunde; ***beat into a cocked –***, in Stücke schlagen, total fertigmachen; (*coll.*) ***my –!*** was Sie sagen! ***raise one's –***, den Hut abnehmen; (*fig.*) ***take off*** or ***raise one's – to him***, ihm Beifall *or* Bewunderung *or* Anerkennung zollen; ***go round with the –***, ***pass*** or ***send round the –***, freiwillige Beiträge sammeln; (*coll.*) ***talk through one's –***, faseln, Kohl reden, kohlen; ***top –***, der Zylinder; ***touch one's – to him***, ihn grüßen; (*coll.*) ***under one's –***, geheim, für sich. **hat|-block,** *s.* die Hutform. **–box,** *s.* die Hutschachtel.

[1]**hatch** [hætʃ], **1.** *v.t.* ausbrüten (*eggs*); (*fig.*) aushecken, ersinnen. **2.** *v.i.* (aus dem Ei) auskriechen *or* ausschlüpfen, ausgebrütet werden; (*fig.*) sich entwickeln. **3.** *s.* die Brut, Hecke.

[2]**hatch,** *s.* die Halbtür; (*Naut.*) Luke, Lukentür, der Lukendeckel; Einstieg (*of tanks etc.*); das Servierfenster; ***under –es***, unter Deck; (*coll.*) in Arrest.

[3]**hatch,** *v.t.* schraffieren, stricheln, (mit Linien) schattieren.

hatchery ['hætʃəri], *s.* der Brutplatz, die Brutanstalt.

hatchet ['hætʃit], *s.* das Beil; ***bury the –***, das Kriegsbeil begraben. **hatchet-face,** *s.* scharfgeschnittenes Gesicht.

[1]**hatching** ['hætʃiŋ], *s.* das (Aus)brüten, Ausschlüpfen; (*fig.*) Aushecken (*of a plot*); die Brut.

[2]**hatching,** *s.* die Schraffierung, Schraffur.

hatchment ['hætʃmənt], *s.* (*Her.*) das Wappenschild eines Verstorbenen, Totenschild.

hatchway ['hætʃwei], *s.* die Luke(nöffnung).

hate [heit], **1.** *s. See* **hatred. 2.** *v.t.* hassen, verabscheuen; (*coll.*) nicht ausstehen können, nicht mögen. **hateful,** *adj.* verhaßt; hassenswert, widerlich, abscheulich. **hatefulness,** *s.* die Verhaßtheit, Widerlichkeit.

hatless ['hætlis], *adj.* ohne Hut, barhäuptig. **hatpin,** *s.* die Hutnadel.

hatred ['heitrid], *s.* der Haß (***of, against, towards***, gegen *or* auf (*Acc.*)), Abscheu (vor (*Dat.*)); die Feindschaft.

hatstand ['hætstænd], *s.* der Hutständer, die Hutablage. **hatter,** *s.* der Hutmacher; ***mad as a –***, völlig übergeschnappt. **hat-trick,** *s.* (*Crick.*) drei Erfolge des Werfes hintereinander; (*fig.*) drei Siege *or* glückliche Treffer hintereinander.

haughtiness ['hɔ:tinis], *s.* der Hochmut, die Überheblichkeit, Arroganz. **haughty,** *adj.* hochmütig, überheblich, arrogant.

haul [hɔ:l], **1.** *s.* 1. kräftiger Zug; ***short –***, kurzer Transportweg; 2. der Fischzug; (*fig.*) Fang, Gewinn, die Beute; (*sl.*) ***make a –***, Beute machen. **2.** *v.t.* ziehen, zerren, schleppen; (*Naut.*) anholen; befördern, transportieren; (*Min.*) fördern; ***– down***, niederholen, streichen (*flag*); (*Naut.*) ***– in***, einholen; (*Naut.*) ***– off***, verholen; (*coll.*) ***– him over the coals***, ihn abkanzeln, ihm eine Standpauke halten; ***– up***, (*Naut.*) aufholen, aufwinden, aufziehen; (*fig.*) zur Verantwortung ziehen, ausschimpfen, abkanzeln. **3.** *v.i.* ziehen, zerren (***at, on***, an (*Dat.*)); ***– (to) the wind***, an den Wind gehen; ***– round***, umspringen (*of wind*).

haulage ['hɔ:lidʒ], *s.* der Transport, die Spedition, Beförderung; (*Min.*) Förderung; Transportkosten (*pl.*); ***– contractor***, der Fuhrwerksunternehmer. **hau(i)er,** *s.* (*Min.*) der Schlepper; (*Comm.*) Fuhrmann, Spediteur.

haulm [hɔ:m], *s.* der Halm, Stengel.

haunch [hɔ:ntʃ], *s.* (*Anat.*) die Hüfte, der Schenkel (*of a horse*); die Keule (*of venison*), Lende, das Lendenstück (*of beef*).

haunt [hɔ:nt], **1.** *v.t.* häufig besuchen, immer wieder aufsuchen; heimsuchen, belästigen, plagen, verfolgen; (*of ghosts*) spuken *or* umgehen in (*Dat.*); ***the place is –ed***, hier spukt es; ***–ed by memories***, durch Erinnerungen geplagt. **2.** *s.* häufig besuchter Ort *or* Aufenthalt, der Lieblingsplatz; das Lager (*of animals*), der Schlupfwinkel (*of robbers etc.*). **haunted,** *adj.* verwunschen, gespenstig, Geister–.

Hausa ['hauzə], *s.* **1.** der Haussa; *pl.* Haussa (*pl.*), das Haussavolk; 2. (*language*) Haussa.

hautboy ['oubɔi], *s.* (*obs.*) die Hoboe.

Havana [hə'vænə], *s.* Havanna (*n.*).

have [hæv, həv], **1.** *irr.v.t.* haben, besitzen; erhalten, erlangen, bekommen; (erfahren) haben.

(a) (*with nouns*) ***– a baby***, ein Kind bekommen *or* zur Welt bringen; ***– breakfast***, frühstücken; ***– the care of***, Sorge tragen für– ***– a care!*** vorgesehen! passen Sie auf! ***– a cigar***, eine Zigarre rauchen; ***– a cigar!*** nehmen Sie eine Zigarre! ***– a cup of tea***, eine Tasse Tee trinken; (*coll.*) ***– a down on him***, Groll gegen ihn hegen; ***– food***, essen, Essen einnehmen, Speise zu sich nehmen; ***– the 'flu***, an Grippe leiden; ***now you – it!*** Sie haben es jetzt getroffen! ***– it from him***, von ihm erfahren haben; ***– it your own way!*** meinetwegen! wie du willst! (*coll.*) ***let him – it***, es ihm gehörig geben *or* sagen; ***he will – it that***, er behauptet daß; ***as (good) luck would – it***, glücklicherweise; ***rumour has it***, es geht das Gerücht, man munkelt; ***– the kindness to . . .***, seien Sie so freundlich, zu . . .! ***– a look at a th.***, sich (*Dat.*) etwas ansehen; ***– a lot to do***, viel zu tun haben; ***– a mind***, Lust haben; ***– no doubt***, nicht zweifeln; ***– no French***, Französisch nicht können; ***– no news***, keine Nachricht bekommen; ***we shall – rain***, wir werden Regen bekommen; ***– one's say***, seine Meinung ausdrücken; ***– a good time***, es schön *or* gut haben, viel Spaß haben; ***– a try***, einen Versuch machen (***at***, mit), versuchen, (aus)probieren; ***you – my word for it***, ich gebe Ihnen mein Wort darauf.

(b) (*with advs.*) ***– back***, zurückbekommen; ***– him in for dinner***, ihn zum Abendessen einladen; (*coll.*) ***– it in for him***, Groll gegen ihn hegen; ***– on***, anhaben, tragen (*coat*), aufhaben (*hat*); (*coll.*) ***– him on***, ihn zum besten haben; (*coll.*) ***– it out with him***, es mit ihm ausfechten, sich mit ihm auseinandersetzen; (*coll.*) ***– him up***, ihn vor Gericht ziehen *or* bringen (***for***, wegen).

(c) (*with p.p.*) ***– one's hair cut***, sich (*Dat.*) die Haare schneiden lassen; ***I won't – it, I'm not having it***, ich lasse mich nicht darauf ein; ***I will not – it discussed***, ich dulde nicht, daß es besprochen wird; ***– done!*** laß das! hör auf! ***– done with it***, damit fertig sein, damit nichts mehr zu schaffen haben; (*sl.*) ***he's had it***, den hat's erwischt, es ist aus mit ihm, er ist erledigt; (*sl.*) ***you've been had***, man hat dich beschummelt *or* hereingelegt *or* angeschmiert; ***he had three horses shot under him***, ihm wurden drei Pferde unter dem Leibe erschossen.

(d) (*with inf.*) müssen; ***he has to go***, er muß gehen; ***you – but to speak the truth***, Sie brauchen nur die Wahrheit zu sagen; ***it has to be done***, es muß getan werden.

(e) (*with Acc. and inf.*) mögen, sollen; ***I will*** or ***would – you know***, Sie sollen wissen; ich möchte, daß Sie wissen; nehmen Sie zur Kenntnis; ***what would you – me do?*** was soll ich tun? ***– him come in!*** er soll hereinkommen.

(f) (*with preps.*) ***– about one***, bei sich haben; ***he has your happiness at heart***, den Glück liegt ihm am Herzen; ***– by heart***, auswendig können; ***– in keeping***, in Verwahr(ung) haben, verwahren, aufbewahren; ***I – it in mind***, ich behalte es im Gedächtnis; (*sl.*) ***– s.th. on him***, belastendes Material gegen ihn haben; (*coll.*) ***– nothing on him***, ihm weit unterlegen sein, gegen ihn nicht ankommen *or* aufkommen können.

2. *irr.v.i.* ***– at***, zielen auf (*Acc.*), sich hermachen über (*Acc.*), anpacken, angreifen; ***– at you!*** nimm dich in acht! sieh dich vor! ***you had best go***, du wirst gut daran tun, zu gehen; ***you had better go***, am besten gehst du; (*sl.*) ***you better had***, das wäre das beste; (*coll.*) ***I had rather you didn't***, ich möchte viel lieber, du tätest es nicht.

3. *irr.v.aux.* haben (*with v.t., v.r.*), sein (*with v.i.*); ***he has been***, er ist gewesen; ***he has come***, er ist gekommen; ***you – done it, haven't you?*** Sie haben es getan, nicht wahr? ***he hasn't washed***, er hat sich nicht gewaschen; (*coll.*) ***I – got***, ich habe *or* besitze.

4. *s.* (*usu. pl.*) ***the –s and the ––nots***, die Besitzenden und die Habenichtse, die Reichen und die Armen.

haven [heivn], *s.* der Hafen; (*usu. fig. oft.* – *of rest*) das Asyl, die Freistätte, der Zufluchtsort.

haven't [hævnt] = *have not.*

haversack [ˈhævəsæk], *s.* der Brotbeutel, die Provianttasche; – *ration*, die Marschverpflegung.

having [ˈhæviŋ], **1.** *See* **have.** **2.** *s.* das Eigentum, die Habe, der Besitz.

havoc [ˈhævək], *s.* die Verwüstung, Verheerung, Zerstörung; *cause* –, Verheerung anrichten; *make* – *of, play* – *with* or *among*, verwüsten, verheeren, zerstören, vernichten.

[1]**haw** [hɔː], *s.* (*Bot.*) die Hagebutte, Mehlbeere.

[2]**haw,** *s.* (*Vet.*) entzündete Nickhaut.

[3]**haw,** *v.i. only in hum and* –, zögernd sprechen, sich räuspern.

hawfinch [ˈhɔːfintʃ], *s.* (*Orn.*) der Kernbeißer (*Coccothraustes coccothraustes*).

[1]**hawk** [hɔːk], *v.t.* verhökern, feilbieten, (*also fig.*) hausieren mit.

[2]**hawk,** *v.i.* sich räuspern; – *up*, aushusten.

[3]**hawk, 1.** *s.* der Falke, Habicht; (*fig.*) Gauner. **2.** *v.i.* mit Falken beizen *or* jagen.

[1]**hawker** [ˈhɔːkə], *s.* der Falkenjäger.

[2]**hawker,** *s.* der Hausierer, Straßenhändler, Höker. **hawk-eyed,** *adj.* scharfsichtig, falkenäugig. **hawking,** *s.* die Falkenbeize. **hawk|-moth,** *s.* der Schwärmer. **--nosed,** *adj.* mit einer Habichtsnase. **hawk's|-beard,** *s.* (*Bot.*) der Pippau. **--bill,** *s.* die Karettschildkröte. **hawkweed,** *s.* (*Bot.*) das Habichtskraut.

hawse [hɔːz], *s.* (*Naut.*) (*--hole*) die Klüse. **hawse-pipe,** *s.* das Klüsenrohr. **hawser,** *s.* die Trosse, das Kabeltau.

hawthorn [ˈhɔːθɔːn], *s.* (*Bot.*) der Weißdorn, Rotdorn, Mehldorn, Hagedorn.

hay [hei], **1.** *s.* das Heu; *make* –, Heu machen; (*sl.*) *hit the* –, pennen; (*Prov.*) *make* – *while the sun shines*, das Eisen schmieden, solange es heiß ist. **2.** *v.i.* Heu machen. **hay|-box,** *s.* die Kochkiste. **-cock,** *s.* der Heuschober, Heuhaufen. **--fever,** *s.* das Heufieber, der Heuschnupfen. **-loft,** *s.* der Heuboden. **-maker,** *s.* der Heumacher. **-making,** *s.* das Heumachen. **-mow, -rick,** *s. See* **-cock.** **-seed,** *s.* 1. der Grassame; 2. (*Am. sl.*) Bauerntölpel. **-stack,** *s. See* **-cock.** **-wire,** *adj.* (*sl.*) *go* –, (*of a th.*) durcheinander geraten, kaputtgehen, schiefgehen; (*of a p.*) rabiat werden.

hazard [ˈhæzəd], **1.** *s.* die Gefahr, das Wagnis, Risiko; der Zufall, das Ungefähr; Glückspiel, (eine Art) Würfelspiel; (*Golf*) das Hindernis; *at all* –*s*, auf alle Fälle; *at the* – *of one's life*, unter Einsatz seines Lebens, unter Lebensgefahr; *run a* –, (damit) ein Wagnis auf sich nehmen, sich in ein Wagnis stürzen, sich auf ein Wagnis einlassen; *at whatever* –, auf jede Gefahr hin; (*Bill.*) *losing* –, der Verläufer; (*Bill.*) *winning* –, der Treffer. **2.** *v.t.* dem Zufall aussetzen, aufs Spiel setzen, wagen, riskieren; zu sagen wagen. **hazardous,** *adj.* gewagt, gefährlich, riskant.

[1]**haze** [heiz], **1.** *s.* leichter Nebel, der Dunst(schleier), Höhenrauch; (*fig.*) die Trübung, Unklarheit; Verwirrung. **2.** *v.i.* (*usu. fig.*) – *over*, sich trüben.

[2]**haze,** *v.t.* durch schwere Arbeit bestrafen; (*Am. sl.*) schinden, schikanieren.

hazel [heizl], **1.** *s.* der Hasel(nuß)strauch. **2.** *adj.* nußbraun. **hazel|nut,** *s.* die Haselnuß. **-tree,** *s. See* **hazel, 1.**

haziness [ˈheizinis], *s.* die Nebeligkeit, Dunstigkeit, Diesigkeit; (*fig.*) Nebelhaftigkeit, Verschwommenheit, Unschärfe, Unbestimmtheit, Unklarheit. **hazy,** *adj.* dunstig, diesig, neblig; (*fig.*) unklar, unscharf, undeutlich, unbestimmt, verschwommen, verworren, nebelhaft.

H-bomb [ˈeitʃbɔm], *s.* die Wasserstoffbombe.

he [hiː], **1.** *pers. pron.* er; (*before rel. clause*) der(jenige); – *who*, wer. **2.** *s.* männliches Wesen (*esp.* Tier), das Männchen.

head [hed], **1.** *s.* 1. der Kopf; (*high style*) das Haupt; (*Art*) Kopfbild; – *of hair*, der Haarwuchs; –*s or tails?* Kopf oder Schrift? *crowned* –*s*, gekrönte Häupter; (*Prov.*) *you cannot put an old* – *on young shoulders*, Jugend hat keine Tugend; (*coll.*) *swelled* –, der Größenwahn; 2. (*fig.*) die Spitze, führende Stellung; *at the* – *of the army*, an der Spitze der Armee; *at the* – *of the table*, oben am Tisch; 3. vorderes *or* oberes Ende; (*of a ship*) der Bug, das Vorderteil; (*of land*) die Landspitze, das Vorgebirge; (*of river*) die Quelle; (*of a bed*) das Kopfende; (*of stairs*) oberer Absatz; (*of axe*) die Klinge; (*of mast*) der Topp; (*of abscess*) die Durchbruchstelle; (*on beer etc.*) Schaumkrone, der Schaum; 4. (An)führer, Vorsteher, Vorstand, Leiter, Chef, (*of school*) der (die) Dirketor(in), (*of tribe*) das Oberhaupt, der Häuptling; – *of the church*, das Oberhaupt der Kirche; – *of the department*, der Abteilungsleiter; *civic* –*s*, Stadtälteste (*pl.*); 5. der Höhepunkt, die Krise, Entscheidung; 6. der Hauptpunkt, (Haupt)abschnitt, die Abteilung; (*see also* **heading**) Rubrik, Überschrift, der Titelkopf; Rechnungsposten; –*s of the charges*, Klagepunkte (*pl.*); –*s of a discourse*, Hauptpunkte einer Abhandlung (*pl.*); 7. (*Tech.*) die Säule(nhöhe), Gefällhöhe, Fallhöhe, das Gefälle (*of water*), die Druckhöhe, der Druck (*of steam*); 8. (*no pl.*) (einzelne) P.; das Stück (*of cattle*); *40* – *of cattle*, 40 Stuck Vieh; 9. (*fig.*) der Kopf, Verstand.

(a) (*with verbs*) *gather* –, überhandnehmen, zu Kräften kommen; *give him his* –, ihm freien Lauf lassen; *give a horse his* –, einem Pferde die Zügel schießen lassen; (*coll.*) *have a* –, Schädelbrummen *or* einen Brummschädel haben; *let him have his* –, ihm seinen Willen lassen; *keep one's* –, die Fassung bewahren, nicht den Kopf verlieren; *keep one's* – *above water*, sich über Wasser halten (*also fig.*); *lose one's* –, geköpft werden; (*fig.*) den Kopf verlieren; *not make* – *or tail of it*, daraus nicht klug werden können; *puzzle one's* – *over it*, sich (*Dat.*) den Kopf darüber zerbrechen; *my* – *spins* or *swims*, es schwindelt mir; *turn one's* –, sich umdrehen; *turn his* –, ihm den Kopf verdrehen.

(b) (*with preps.*) (*Naut.*) *down by the* –, vorlastig; *by* – *and shoulders*, an den Haaren, gewaltsam; (*Spt.*) *by a* –, um eine Kopflänge; *by a short* –, um eine Nasenlänge; *from* – *to foot*, von Kopf (*or* oben) bis Fuß (*or* unten), von Scheitel bis zur Sohle; *it runs in my* –, es geht mir im Kopfe herum; *get into one's* –, sich (*Dat.*) einprägen; *put s.th. into his* –, ihm etwas in den Kopf setzen; *take s.th. into one's* –, sich (*Dat.*) etwas in den Kopf setzen; (*coll.*) *off one's* –, verrückt, übergeschnappt; (*coll.*) *I can do it on my* –, es ist für mich eine Spielerei; *on this* –, in diesem Punkt, in dieser Hinsicht; *have it on one's* –, dafür verantwortlich sein, es auf dem Gewissen haben; (*sl.*) *knock it on the* –, es vereiteln *or* zugrunde richten; *out of one's own* –, aus eigenem Denken, von sich aus; *not be able to get it out of one's* –, es sich (*Dat.*) nicht aus dem Sinne schlagen können; *over his* –, über dem Kopf (*of roof*); über seinem Haupte (*impending evil*); (*fig.*) über seinen Kopf hinweg (*of remarks*), über seinem Begriffsvermögen (*of ideas*); *be promoted over his* –, ihn (bei der Beförderung) überspringen; – *over ears*, bis über die Ohren, ganz und gar, völlig, gänzlich; – *over heels*, Hals über Kopf; *per* –, pro Kopf *or* P.; *bring to a* –, zur Entscheidung bringen; *come to a* –, (*of abscess*) eitern, aufbrechen; (*fig.*) zur Entscheidung kommen, sich zuspitzen; *go to his* –, ihm in den (*as a cold*) *or* zu (*as success*) Kopf steigen.

(c) (*with advs.*) – *foremost*, *see* **headfirst**; (*coll.*) *bite* or *snap his* – *off*, ihn fressen; (*coll.*) *talk his* – *off*, ihm ein Loch in den Bauch reden; (*coll.*) *talk one's* – *off*, unaufhörlich losschwatzen; *put one's* –*s together*, sich berat(schlag)en.

2. *v.t.* 1. (an)führen, befehligen (*an army etc.*), leiten; steuern, lenken (*ship*), treiben, richten (*group, flock*), an der Spitze stehen (*Gen.*), als erster stehen auf (*Dat.*) (*a list*); 2. vorangehen, vorausgehen (*Dat.*), hinter sich lassen; 3. mit einem Kopfe *or* (*Typ.*) Titel versehen; 4. (*Dat.*) den Weg verstellen (*Dat.*), entgegentreten (*Dat.*),

sich entgegenstellen (*Dat.*); – *off*, ablenken, abwehren, abdrängen; (*Footb.*) mit dem Kopfe stoßen.
3. *v.i.* Richtung nehmen (*for*, nach), zugehen, losgehen, lossteuern (auf (*Acc.*)), (*Naut.*) Kurs haben (nach), liegen (auf (*Acc.*)); (*Am.*) entspringen (*of a river*); (*Naut.*) ***how does she –?*** was liegt an?
4. *adj.* 1. erst, oberst, führend, Ober–, Haupt–; – ***clerk,*** erster Kommis *or* Buchführer, der Bürovorsteher; – ***office,*** das Hauptbüro; – ***waiter,*** der Ober(kellner); 2. Vorder–, Kopf–, Spitzen–; 3. Gegen–; – ***sea,*** die Gegensee; – ***wind,*** der Gegenwind.

head|ache, *s.* Kopfschmerzen (*pl.*), das Kopfweh; (*coll.*) Kopfzerbrechen, schwieriges Problem. **–band,** *s.* die Kopfbinde; (*Archit.*) Kopfleiste. **–board,** *s.* das Kopfbrett (*of bed*). **–dress,** *s.* der Kopfputz, Kopfschmuck.

-headed ['hedid], *adj. suff.* –köpfig; ***cool––,*** kaltblütig; ***hot––,*** hitzköpfig, ungestüm; ***long––,*** schlau. **header,** *s.* 1. (*Archit.*) der Schlußstein, Binder(stein); 2. (*Tech.*) Rohrverbinder, das Sammelrohr; 3. (*Spt.*) der Hechtsprung, Kopfsprung; ***take a –,*** einen Kopfsprung machen; 4. (*Footb.*) der Kopfball.

head|fast, *s.* (*Naut.*) die Bugleine. **–first,** *adv.* kopfüber; (*fig. coll.*) Hals über Kopf. **–gear,** *s.* die Kopfbedeckung. **––hunter,** *s.* der Kopfjäger.

headiness ['hedinis], *s.* das Berauschende, die Stärke (*of wine*); (*fig.*) das Ungestüm, die Unbesonnenheit.

heading ['hediŋ], *s.* 1. (*Typ.*) der Titel(kopf), die Rubrik, Überschrift; (*fig.*) der Punkt, das Thema; 2. (*Tech.*) Kopfstück, Kopfteil, Kopfende; 3. (*Naut. etc.* der Steuerkurs, Kompaßkurs; die (Fahrt)richtung; 4. (*of barrels*) das Bodenstück, der (Faß)boden; die Bodmung, Ausbödung; 5. (*Min.*) der Querschlag, Quertrieb, Stollen; 6. (*Footb.*) das Kopfspiel; 7. (*Build.*) – ***course,*** die Binderschicht.

head|lamp, *s. See* **–light. –land,** *s.* das Vorgebirge, die Landspitze, Landzunge; (*Agr.*) der Rain. **headless,** *adj.* ohne Kopf, kopflos; führerlos. **head|light,** *s.* (*Motor.*) der Scheinwerfer, (*Naut.*) das Mastlicht, Topplicht. **–line,** *s.* (*Typ.*) die Schlagzeile, Kopfzeile. **–long, 1.** *adj.* jäh, ungestüm; (*fig.*) unbesonnen, überstürzt, stürmisch, wild. **2.** *adv.* kopfüber, mit dem Kopfe voran; (*fig.*) Hals über Kopf, unbedachtsam, unbesonnen, unüberlegt, hastig. **–man,** *s.* der Häuptling, Führer; Vorarbeiter, Vorsteher. **–master,** *s.* der Direktor, Rektor (*of school*). **–mastership,** *s.* die Direktorstelle. **–mistress,** *s.* die Direktorin, Schulleiterin. **––money,** *s.* das Kopfgeld. **––on,** *adj.* direkt gegeneinander *or* aufeinander; – ***collision,*** frontaler Zusammenstoß. **–phone,** *s.* der Kopfhörer. **–piece,** *s.* (*Hist.*) der Helm; (*Typ.*) die Kopfleiste; Zierleiste; (*of harness*) der Stirnriemen; (*coll.*) Verstand, Kopf. **–quarters,** *pl.* (*oft. sing. constr.*) (*Mil.*) das Hauptquartier; (*Comm.*) die Hauptgeschäftsstelle, der Hauptsitz, die Zentrale; (*coll.*) der Aufenthaltsort; ***at –,*** im Hauptquartier. **––resistance,** *s.* (*Av.*) der Stirnwiderstand. **–rest,** *s.* die Kopflehne. **–room,** *s.* (*Archit.*) lichte Höhe. **–sail,** *s.* das Fockmastsegel. **–set,** *s.* (*Tele.*) der Kopfhörer. **headship** ['hedʃip], *s.* führende *or* leitende Stellung, oberste Leitung; *see also* **headmastership.**

headsman ['hedzmən], *s.* der Scharfrichter, Henker; (*Min.*) Schlepper.

head|spring, *s.* 1. (*usu. fig.*) die (Haupt)quelle, der Ursprung; 2. (*Gymn.*) Kopfstandüberschlag. **–stall,** *s.* das Kopfstück, der Stirnriemen (*of a bridle*). **–stock,** *s.* (*Tech.*) der Spindelstock. **–stone,** *s.* der Grabstein; (*Archit.*) Eckstein, Schlußstein. **–strong,** *adj.* starrköpfig, halsstarrig, eigenwillig, eigensinnig. **––voice,** *s.* die Kopfstimme. **–water,** *s.* (*usu. pl.*) der Oberlauf, Zuflußgewässer (*pl.*) (*of river*). **–way,** *s.* (*Naut.*) die Geschwindigkeit, Fahrt voraus; (*fig.*) das Vorwärtskommen, der Fortschritt, Forschritte (*pl.*); *see also* **–room**; ***make –,*** vorankommen, vorwärtskommen, Fortschritte machen. **––work,** *s.* die Kopfarbeit, Denkarbeit, geistige Arbeit.

heady ['hedi], *adj.* berauschend (*of liquor*); ungestüm, übereilt, unüberlegt, unbesonnen, jäh, hitzig.

heal [hi:l], **1.** *v.t.* heilen, kurieren (*of*, von); (*fig.*) beilegen (*quarrel*), ausgleichen, versöhnen (*contradictions*). **2.** *v.i.* (*usu.* – ***up*** or ***over***) (zu)heilen. **healer,** *s.* der Heiler; (*fig.*) das Heilmittel; ***time is a great –,*** die Zeit heilt viele Wunden. **healing, 1.** *adj.* heilsam, Heil(ungs)–; (*fig.*) versöhnend. **2.** *s.* die Heilung.

health [helθ], *s.* 1. die Gesundheit; ***bad*** or ***poor –,*** die Kränklichkeit; ***good –,*** das Wohlbefinden; ***public –,*** öffentliche Gesundheitspflege; ***public – officer,*** Beamte(r) des Gesundheitsamtes; ***in the best of –,*** bei bester Gesundheit; – ***insurance,*** die Krankenversicherung; – ***resort,*** das Bad, der Kurort; 2. das Heil, Wohl; der Toast; ***drink his –,*** auf sein Wohl *or* seine Gesundheit trinken; ***here's to the – of*** . . ., . . . soll leben! es lebe . . .! (ein) Prosit . . . (*Dat.*)! ***your good –!*** auf Ihr Wohl! **healthful, health-giving,** *adj.* gesund(heitsfördernd), heilsam. **healthiness,** *s.* das Wohlbefinden, die Gesundheit. **healthy,** *adj.* gesund; *see also* **healthful.**

heap [hi:p], **1.** *s.* der Haufe(n); (*coll.*) –(*s*), der Haufen, die Menge; (*coll.*) ***struck all of a –,*** ganz platt *or* verblüfft; ***in –s,*** haufenweise; (*coll.*) ***–s of time,*** eine Menge *or* viel Zeit; (*coll.*) ***–s of times,*** viele *or* unzählige Male, sehr oft; (*coll.*) ***–s worse,*** sehr viel schlimmer. **2.** *v.t.* häufen; (*coll.*) anfüllen, beladen, (*fig.*) überschütten, überhäufen (***with,*** mit); – ***coals of fire on his head,*** feurige Kohlen auf sein Haupt sammeln; ***–ed spoonful,*** gehäufter Löffelvoll; – ***up,*** anhäufen, aufhäufen, aufstapeln.

hear [hiə], **1.** *irr.v.t.* hören; zuhören (*Dat.*), anhören; (*Law*) verhören, vernehmen (*a witness*), verhandeln (*a case*); abhören (*lessons etc.*); ***make o.s. –d,*** sich (*Dat.*) Gehör verschaffen, sich vernehmbar machen; – ***mass,*** an der Messe teilnehmen; – ***him out,*** ihn ausreden lassen. **2.** *irr.v.i.* hören, zuhören; Nachricht bekommen, erfahren (***of, about,*** von *or* über); ***let me – how*** . . ., laß mich wissen, wie . . .; ***let me – from you,*** laß von dir hören; ***I will not – of it,*** ich will nichts davon wissen *or* hören; – ***say,*** sagen hören; – ***tell of it,*** davon sprechen hören; ***–! –!*** hört! hört! **heard** [hə:d], *imperf., p.p. of* **hear. hearer** [–rə], *s.* der (Zu)hörer.

hearing ['hiəriŋ], *s.* 1. das Hören, Gehör; Hörvermögen, der Gehörsinn; ***hard of –,*** schwerhörig; ***in my –,*** in meiner Gegenwart; ***out of –,*** außer Hörweite; ***within –,*** in Hörweite; – ***aid,*** das Hörgerät, der Hörapparat; 2. das (An)hören; 3. Gehör, die Audienz; ***gain*** or ***obtain a –,*** sich (*Dat.*) Gehör verschaffen, angehört werden; ***give*** or ***grant him a –,*** ihn anhören; 4. (*Law*) das Verhör, die Vernehmung, Voruntersuchung; Verhandlung; (*Law*) ***fix a –,*** einen Termin anberaumen.

hearken [hɑ:kn], (*Poet.*) *v.i.* hören, horchen, lauschen (***to,*** auf (*Acc.*)); (*fig.*) – ***to,*** Beachtung schenken (*Dat.*).

hearsay ['hiəsei], *s.* das Hörensagen, Gerede; ***by –,*** vom Hörensagen; – ***evidence,*** das Zeugnis vom Hörensagen.

hearse [hə:s], *s.* der Leichenwagen, die Bahre. **hearse-cloth,** *s.* das Leichentuch, Bahrtuch.

heart [hɑ:t], *s.* 1. das Herz (*also fig.*); (*fig.*) die Seele, das Inner(st)e, Wesentliche, der Kern; ***the – of the matter,*** der Kern der S., des Pudels Kern; – ***of oak,*** das Eichenkernholz; (*fig.*) ***–s of oak,*** englische Matrosen; 2. der Mut, die Energie; das Mitgefühl; Gemüt; ***change of –,*** der Gesinnungswechsel; 3. der Schatz, das Herzchen; 4. (*Cards*) Herz, die Herzkarte; *pl.* Herzfarbe; ***king of –s,*** der Herzkönig; ***ten of –s,*** die Herzzehn.
(a) (*with verbs*) ***his – is in his work,*** er ist mit dem Herzen bei der Arbeit; ***my – was in my mouth,*** ich war in atemloser Spannung, ich war zu Tode erschrocken; ***bless my –!*** ach du lieber Himmel! ***break his –,*** ihm das Herz brechen; ***it does my – good,*** es freut mich im Grunde meiner Seele; ***eat one's – out,*** sich vor Kummer verzehren; ***my – fails me,*** see ***lose –***; ***my – goes out to him,*** ich

fühle mit ihm; (*coll.*) ***have a –,*** Erbarmen haben; ***have no –,*** kein Mitgefühl haben; ***have the –,*** es über das Herz bringen (*to do*, zu tun); ***lose –,*** den Mut verlieren; ***lose one's – to,*** sein Herz verlieren an (*Acc.*); ***open one's – to him,*** ihm sein Herz ausschütten; ***set one's – on,*** sein Herz hängen an (*Acc.*); ***set his – at rest,*** ihn beruhigen; ***take –,*** Mut fassen, sich (*Dat.*) ein Herz fassen; ***wear one's – on one's sleeve,*** seine Gefühle zur Schau tragen, das Herz auf der Zunge haben; ***it wrings my –,*** es schmerzt mich tief.
(b) (*with preps.*) ***after one's*** (*etc.*) ***own –,*** ganz nach Wunsch; ***at –,*** im Grunde (des Herzens), in Wahrheit; ***have at –,*** auf dem Herzen haben, von Herzen wünschen; ***by –,*** auswendig; ***from one's –,*** von Herzen, frisch von der Leber weg; ***in his –*** (***of –s***), im Grunde seines Herzens; ***I could not find it in my –,*** ich konnte es nicht übers Herz bringen; ***in good –,*** in gutem Zustande, fruchtbar (*of land*); ***in the – of,*** inmitten, mitten in; ***in the very – of,*** im Innersten von; ***it goes to my –,*** es geht mir zu Herzen; ***take to –,*** sich (*Dat.*) zu Herzen nehmen; ***to one's –'s content,*** nach Herzenslust; ***– to –,*** offen und ehrlich; ***with all my –,*** herzlich gern, von *or* mit ganzem Herzen, mit Leib und Seele; ***with a heavy –,*** schweren Herzens.

heart|ache, *s.* der Kummer, Gram. **--attack,** *s.* der Herzanfall. **-beat,** *s.* der Herzschlag. **-break,** *s.* der Herzenskummer, das Herzeleid. **--breaking,** *adj.* herzzerbrechend, niederdrückend. **--broken,** *adj.* gebrochenen Herzens, untröstlich. **-burn,** *s.* das Sodbrennen. **--burning,** *s.* (*oft. pl.*) der Groll, Neid. **--disease,** *s.* das Herzleiden, die Herzkrankheit.

-hearted ['hɑ:tid], *adj. suff.* -herzig. **hearten** [-n], *v.t.* aufmuntern, ermuntern, ermutigen, anfeuern. **heartening,** *adj.* herzerquickend. **heart|-failure,** *s.* der Herzschlag. **-felt,** *adj.* tiefempfunden, herzlich, innig, aufrichtig.

hearth [hɑ:θ], *s.* der Herd; Schmiedeherd, das Schmiedefeuer; (*fig.*) Heim. **hearth|-rug,** *s.* der Kaminvorleger. **--stone,** *s.* die Herdplatte, der Herd; weicher Scheuerstein.

heartily ['hɑ:tili], *adv.* herzlich, innig, aufrichtig, von Herzen; tüchtig, kräftig, herzhaft; (*coll. fig.*) herzlich, vollkommen, ganz und gar. **heartiness,** *s.* die Herzlichkeit, Innigkeit, Aufrichtigkeit; Herzhaftigkeit, Stärke (*of appetite*); Wärme (*of feelings*); Kraft, Frische.

heartless ['hɑ:tlis], *adj.* herzlos, gefühllos, grausam. **heartlessness,** *s.* die Herzlosigkeit.

heart|-rending, *adj.* herzzerreißend. **--searchings,** *pl.* Nöte (*pl.*), die Beklemmung.

heart's-ease, heartsease, *s.* (*Bot.*) das Stiefmütterchen.

heart|-shaped, *adj.* herzförmig. **--sick,** *adj.* (*fig.*) tief betrübt, kummervoll, verzagt, verzweifelt, schwermütig. **-some** [-səm], *adj.* (*Scots*) erfrischend, ermunternd, erheiternd, belebend. **--sore,** *adj.* *See* **--sick.** **--strings,** *pl.* (*fig.*) das Herz, innerste Seele. **--throb,** *s.* 1. der Herzschlag; 2. (*coll.*) Schwarm. **-wood,** *s.* das Kernholz.

hearty ['hɑ:ti], **1.** *adj.* herzlich, innig, tiefempfunden, aufrichtig (*as feelings*); gesund, stark, kräftig, tüchtig (*as appetite*); kernig, herzhaft, nahrhaft. **2.** *s.* (*coll.*) der Naturbursche, Sportler.

heat [hi:t], **1.** *s.* 1. die Hitze (*also fig.*); (*Phys.*) Wärme; ***latent –,*** gebundene Wärme; ***red –,*** die Glühhitze; ***degree of –,*** der Wärmegrad; 2. (*fig.*) die Erhitzung, Heftigkeit, Leidenschaft, das Feuer, Ungestüm; die Erregung, der Zorn, Eifer; (*fig.*) ***in the – of the moment,*** in der Hitze des Gefechts; 3. (*of animals*) die Brunst, Brunft, Brunftzeit, Läufigkeit; ***on –,*** brünstig, in der Brunst; 4. (*Spt.*) der Vorlauf, das Ausscheidungsrennen; Einzelrennen, einzelner Lauf; ***dead –,*** unentschiedenes *or* totes Rennen; ***final –,*** letzte Ausscheidungsrunde. **2.** *v.t.* heiß machen; heizen (*stove etc.*); erhitzen (*also fig.*). **3.** *v.i.* heiß werden, (*also fig.*) sich erhitzen.

heater ['hi:tə], *s.* der Heizkörper, die Heizanlage, Heizvorrichtung; der Bolzen (eines Plätteisens); (*Rad.*) Heizfaden.

heath [hi:θ], *s.* die Heide, das Heideland; (*Bot.*) Heidekraut.

heathen [hi:ðn], **1.** *s.* der Heide (die Heidin). **2.** *adj.* heidnisch, Heiden-. **heathendom** [-dəm], *s.* das Heidentum. **heathenish,** *adj.* (*usu. fig.*) heidnisch, barbarisch, roh, ungesittet. **heathenism,** *s.* das Heidentum; (*fig.*) die Barbarei.

heather ['heðə], *s.* (*Bot.*) das Heidekraut, die Erika. **heather|-bell,** *s.* (*Bot.*) die Glockenheide, Sumpfheide. **--mixture,** *adj.* (*Text.*) gesprenkelt.

heating ['hi:tiŋ], *s.* die Heizung; Beheizung; (*of engine*) das Heißlaufen; ***– element,*** elektrischer Heizkörper; ***– surface,*** die Heizfläche.

heat|proof, --resisting, *adj.* hitzbeständig. **--spot,** *s.* das Hitzebläschen. **-stroke,** *s.* der Sonnenstich, Hitzschlag. **--wave,** *s.* die Hitzwelle.

heave [hi:v], **1.** *v.t.* 1. (*reg.*) emporheben, hochheben; ***– a sigh,*** einen Seufzer ausstoßen; 2. (*reg. or irr.*) (*Naut.*) (ein)hieven, aufwinden; (*Naut., coll.*) werfen, schleudern; ***– the anchor,*** den Anker lichten *or* (*Navy only*) hieven; ***– the lead,*** das Lot werfen; ***– the log,*** loggen; ***–*** (***a ship***) ***down,*** kielholen; ***– overboard,*** über Bord werfen. **2.** *v.i.* 1. (*reg.*) sich heben (und senken), (an)schwellen, wogen, sich empordrängen; ***her breast –d,*** ihr Busen wogte; 2. (*reg.*) Brechreiz haben, sich übergeben wollen; 3. (*irr.*) (*Naut.*) getrieben werden, treiben (*as ships*); ***– away! – ho!*** zieh! hiev! ***– in sight,*** (*Naut.*) in Sicht kommen, (*coll.*) auftauchen, aufkreuzen; ***– to,*** beidrehen, beilegen, stoppen. **3.** *s.* das (Hoch)heben, Hochziehen, Aufwinden; Sichheben, Anschwellen, (*of the breast*) Schwellen, Wogen; (*Geol.*) die Verwerfung, Verschiebung; (*coll.*) das Werfen, Schleudern, der Wurf.

heaven [hevn], *s.* 1. (*no art., no pl.*) der Himmel, das Himmelreich; (*fig.*) die Vorsehung, Gott (*m.*); das Paradies, die Seligkeit, himmliches Glück; ***in –,*** im Himmel; ***thank –(s)!*** Gott sei Dank! ***– forbid!*** Gott behüte! ***go to –,*** in den Himmel kommen *or* eingehen; ***move – and earth,*** Himmel und Hölle in Bewegung setzen; 2. (*with art. and usu. pl.*) der Himmel, das Himmelszelt, Himmelsgewölbe, Firmament; (*fig.*) Klima, die Zone; ***the –s,*** die himmlischen Mächte; ***good –s!*** (du) lieber Himmel!

heaven-born, *adj.* vom Himmel stammend, himmlisch. **heavenliness,** *s.* das Himmlische, (*fig.*) die Herrlichkeit, Köstlichkeit. **heavenly,** *adj.* Himmels-, himmlisch (*also fig.*); (*fig.*) göttlich; erhaben; (*coll.*) köstlich, herrlich, wunderbar. **heaven-sent,** *adj.* vom Himmel gesandt. **heavenward** [-wəd], **1.** *adj.* gen Himmel gerichtet. **2.** *or* **heavenwards,** *adv.* gen Himmel, himmelwärts.

heavier ['heviə], *comp. adj.,* **heaviest,** *sup. adj.,* **heavily,** *adv.* *See* **heavy. heaviness,** *s.* die Schwere, Last, das Gewicht, der Druck; die Schwerfälligkeit, Schläfrigkeit; ***– of spirit,*** Bedrücktheit, Schwermut.

heavy ['hevi], **1.** *adj.* schwer; massiv, massig, schwergebaut, wuchtig; heftig, gewaltig, stark (*as storm etc.*); (*fig.*) schwerfällig, unbeholfen, träge, schläfrig, benommen, matt; niedergeschlagen, bedrückt, betrübt, trübe, finster, düster; schwerverdaulich (*as food*); klitschig, pappig (*as dough*); unwegsam, aufgeweicht (*as ground*); drückend, dunstig (*as atmosphere*); dröhnend (*as sound*); ergiebig, reich (*as crops*); schwierig, beschwerlich, mühsam, ermüdend (*as work*); (*fig.*) ***– book,*** langweiliges Buch; ***– cavalry,*** schwere Reiterei; ***– cloud,*** dicke Wolke; ***– drinker,*** starker Trinker; ***– expenses,*** drückende Kosten; ***– eyes,*** müde Augen; ***– father,*** gestrenger Vater; ***– features,*** grobe Gesichtszüge; (*Mil.*) ***– fire,*** das Dauerfeuer; ***– frost,*** strenger Frost; ***have a – hand,*** plump sein; ***with a – heart,*** schweren Herzens; ***– industry,*** die Schwerindustrie; ***– news,*** traurige Nachricht(en); ***– oil,*** das Schweröl; ***– rain,*** heftiger Regen; ***– with sleep,*** schlaftrunken; ***– swell,*** die Bullendünung; ***– type,*** der Fettdruck; ***– water,*** schweres Wasser, das Schwerwasser; ***– with young,*** trächtig. **2.** *adv.*

(*esp. in compounds*) schwer–. **3.** *s.* 1. (*Mil.*) (*usu. pl.*) schwere Kavallerie *or* Artillerie; 2. (*Spt.*) der Schwergewichtler; 3. (*sl.*) schwerer Junge; 4. (*Comm.*) Schwerindustrieaktien (*pl.*); 5. (*coll.*) das Starkbier.

heavy|-armed, *adj.* schwerbewaffnet. **–-duty,** *adj.* Hochleistungs–. **–-handed,** *adj.* plump, ungeschickt, unbeholfen. **–-hearted,** *adj.* betrübt, bekümmert, bedrückt, niedergeschlagen. **–-laden,** *adj.* schwerbeladen. **–weight,** *s.* (*Spt.*) das Schwergewicht (*über 175 Pfund*); der Schwergewichtler; (*coll.*) einflußreiche P., Prominente(r).

hebdomadal [heb'dɔmədl], *adj.* wöchentlich, Wochen–; (*Oxford*) – ***council,*** höchste akademische Behörde.

hebetate ['hebiteit], *v.t.* abstumpfen. **hebetude** [–tju:d], *s.* (geistige) Stumpfheit, die Verblödung.

Hebrew ['hi:bru:], **1.** *adj.* hebräisch. **2.** *s.* 1. der (die) Hebräer(in); 2. (*language*) das Hebräisch; (*B.*) ***Epistle to the –s,*** der Hebräerbrief.

hecatomb ['hekətu:m], *s.* die Hekatombe.

heckle [hekl], *v.t.* 1. hecheln (*flax etc.*); 2. (*Pol.*) störende Fragen stellen (*Dat.*). **heckler,** *s.* störender Fragesteller, der Zwischenrufer.

hectare ['hektɛə], *s.* das Hektar.

hectic ['hektik], **1.** *adj.* 1. (*Med.*) hektisch, auszehrend, schwindsüchtig; fieberrot; 2. (*coll.*) fieberhaft, rastlos, erregt, aufregend. **2.** *s.* die Auszehrung, Schwindsucht; Fieberröte.

hectogram(me) ['hektəgræm], *s.* das Hektogramm. **hectograph, 1.** *s.* der Hektograph. **2.** *v.t.* vervielfältigen, hektographieren. **hectolitre,** *s.* das Hektoliter.

hector ['hektə], **1.** *s.* der Prahler, Aufschneider, Eisenfresser, Raufbold. **2.** *v.t.* einschüchtern, tyrannisieren. **3.** *v.i.* prahlen, aufschneiden, renommieren, großtun.

he'd [hiəd, hi:d], (*coll.*) = ***he had, he would.***

heddle [hedl], **1.** *s.* (*usu. pl.*) die Litze, Helfe. **heddle-hook,** *s.* die Einziehnadel. **2.** *v.t.* einziehen.

hedge [hedʒ], **1.** *s.* 1. die Hecke, der Heckenzaun; 2. (*Comm.*) die Gegendeckung. **2.** *v.t.* 1. einzäunen, einfriedigen, einhegen; – ***about*** or ***in,*** umgeben, umzingeln, einengen, einsperren, absperren; 2. (*fig.*) (durch Gegendeckung) sichern. **3.** *v.i.* 1. Hecken anlegen; sich (nach allen Seiten) sichern *or* decken; 2. (*coll.*) sich nicht festlegen, sich vorsichtig ausdrücken, ausweichen, sich winden.

hedge|-clippers, *pl.* die Heckenschere. **–hog, 1.** *s.* der Igel; (*Mil.*) die Igelstellung. **2.** *v.i.* (*Mil.*) sich einigeln. **–-hop,** *v.i.* (*Av. sl.*) tief fliegen, heckenspringen. **–hopper,** *s.* (*Av. sl.*) der Tiefflieger. **–row,** *s.* die Baumhecke. **–sparrow,** *s.* (*Orn.*) die Heckenbraunelle (*Prunella modularis*).

hedonic [hi'dɔnik], *adj.* hedon(ist)isch. **hedonism** ['hi:dənizm], *s.* der Hedonismus. **hedonist** ['hi:dənist], **1.** *s.* der (die) Hedonist(in). **2.** *adj. See* **hedonic.**

heed [hi:d], **1.** *v.t.* beachten; achten *or* achtgeben auf (*Acc.*). **2.** *v.i.* aufpassen, achtgeben. **3.** *s.* die Aufmerksamkeit, Hut, Acht, Sorgfalt; ***give*** or ***pay –,*** *see* **1**; ***take –,*** *see* **2**; sich in acht nehmen; ***take no – of,*** in den Wind schlagen. **heedful,** *adj.* achtsam, aufmerksam (*of,* auf (*Acc.*)); behutsam, vorsichtig, sorgfältig. **heedfulness,** *s.* die Achtsamkeit, Vorsicht, Behutsamkeit. **heedless,** *adj.* achtlos, unachtsam, unbesonnen (*of,* auf (*Acc.*)), unbekümmert (um), ungeachtet (*Gen.*). **heedlessness,** *s.* die Unachtsamkeit, Sorglosigkeit, Unbesonnenheit.

hee-haw ['hi:hɔ:], **1.** *v.i.* iahen. **2.** *s.* das Iah.

[1]**heel** [hi:l], **1.** *s.* 1. die Ferse, Hacke; der Absatz (*on shoe etc.*); Fuß, das Ende (*of mast etc.*); ***Achilles' –,*** die Achillesferse; ***at*** or ***on his –s,*** ihm auf den Fersen, dicht hinter ihm; ***close at –,*** dicht hinterher; (*coll.*) ***cool one's –s,*** lange warten (müssen); ***down at –, out at –s,*** zerlumpt, verwahrlost, verkommen, heruntergekommen, schäbig; ***kick one's –s,*** see ***cool one's –s***; ***lay by the –s,*** erwischen; ***show a clean pair of –s, take to one's –s,*** sich aus dem Staub machen, ausreißen, Fersengeld geben; (***to***) ***–!*** bei Fuß! (*to a dog*); ***bring to –,*** zur Strecke bringen, gefügig machen, unterkriegen; ***turn on one's –,*** sich kurz umdrehen, kehrtmachen; 2. (*sl.*) der Schurke, verräterischer Schuft. **2.** *v.t.* 1. mit Absätzen *or* Hacken versehen (*shoes*), Fersen anstricken in (*Acc.*) (*socks*); (*Am. sl.*) ***be well–-ed,*** in der Wolle sitzen; 2. (*Rugby footb.*) mit der Ferse stoßen.

[2]**heel, 1.** *v.i.* (*also* – ***over***) sich auf die Seite legen; (*Naut.*) krängen. **2.** *s.* die Krängung.

heel|ball, *s.* das Schusterwachs, Polierwachs. **–piece,** *s.* der Absatzfleck, das Absatzstück, (*of armour*) Fersenstück. **–plate,** *s.* die Kolbenplatte (*of rifle*). **–tap,** *s.* (*coll.*) die Neige, letzter Rest; ***no –s!*** ausgetrunken!

heft [heft], **1.** *s.* (*Am.*) das Gewicht, der Umfang, die Schwere, Bedeutung. **2.** *v.t.* (*Am.*) (hoch)heben, emporheben; anheben, abwiegen, abschätzen.

hefty ['hefti], *adj.* (*coll.*) kräftig (gebaut), muskulös, stramm; (*sl.*) groß, mächtig.

hegemony [hi'gemәni], *s.* die Hegemonie, Oberherrschaft; Vormachtstellung, Führung.

hegira ['hedʒirə], *s.* die Hedschra.

heifer ['hefə], *s.* die Färse, junge Kuh.

heigh! [hei], *int.* he! hei! **heigh-ho!** *int.* heisa! heißa!

height [hait], *s.* die Höhe; (Körper)größe; (*of land*) Erhebung, Anhöhe, der Hügel; (*fig.*) Höhepunkt, Gipfel; ***be at its –,*** den Höhepunkt erreichen; ***10 inches in –,*** 10 Zoll hoch; ***in the – of fashion,*** nach der neuesten Mode; ***twice the – of,*** doppelt so hoch wie; ***– of the barometer,*** der Barometerstand; ***– of folly,*** der Gipfel der Torheit; ***what is your –?*** wie groß sind Sie? **heighten, 1.** *v.t.* 1. höher machen, erhöhen; 2. (*fig.*) betonen, hervorheben; vergrößern, verstärken, vermehren, heben, steigern. **2.** *v.i.* (an)steigen, sich erhöhen, zunehmen, wachsen, höher werden.

heinous ['heinəs], *adj.* abscheulich, fürchterlich, gräßlich, verrucht, verhaßt, hassenswert. **heinousness,** *s.* die Abscheulichkeit, Verruchtheit.

heir [ɛə], *s.* der Erbe (*to, Gen.*); ***– apparent,*** gesetzmäßiger (Thron)erbe; ***–-at-law,*** der Intestaterbe; ***– general,*** der Universalerbe; ***– presumptive,*** mutmaßlicher (Thron)erbe; ***– to the throne,*** der Thronerbe, Thronfolger; ***be – to,*** erben. **heirdom** [–dəm], *s.* die Erbschaft, das Erbe. **heiress,** *s.* (reiche) Erbin. **heirloom,** *s.* das Erbstück. **heirship,** *s.* die Erbschaft, das Erbrecht.

held [held], *imperf., p.p. of* **hold.**

heliacal ['hi:liəkl, hi'laiəkl], *adj.* hel(iakal)isch, Sonnen–. **helianthus** [hi:li'ænθəs], *s.* (*Bot.*) die Sonnenblume.

helical ['helikl], *adj.* schneckenförmig, schraubenförmig, Schrauben–; ***– gear,*** das Schneckengetriebe; ***– gearwheel,*** das Schneckenrad.

helicopter ['helikɔptə], *s.* (*Av.*) der Hubschrauber.

heliocentric [hi:lio'sentrik], *adj.* (*Astr.*) heliozentrisch. **heliochromy** ['hi:liəkroumi], *s.* die Farbphotographie. **heliograph** ['hi:liəgra:f], **1.** *s.* der Heliograph, Spiegeltelegraph. **2.** *v.t.* heliographieren. **heliography** [–'ɔgrəfi], *s.* die Heliographie, Spiegeltelegraphie. **heliogravure** [–grə'vjuə], *s.* die Heliogravüre, Photogravüre. **heliotrope** ['hi:liətroup], **1.** *s.* 1. (*Min.*) das Heliotrop, der Chalzedon; 2. (*Bot.*) die Sonnenblume; 3. Malvenfarbe. **2.** *adj.* malvenfarbig. **heliotype** ['hi:liətaip], *s.* der Lichtdruck.

heliport ['helipɔ:t], *s.* der Hubschrauber-Landeplatz.

helium ['hi:liəm], *s.* das Helium.

helix ['hi:liks], *s.* (*pl.* **-es, -ices** ['helisi:z]) die Schneckenlinie, Spirallinie; (*Archit.*) Schnecke; (*Anat.*) Ohrleiste, Knorpelleiste (*of ear*).

he'll [hiəl], (*coll.*) = ***he will.***

hell [hel], *s.* die Hölle; (*oh,*) ***–!*** zum Teufel! ***to – with . . .,*** zum Teufel mit . . .; ***what the – . . .?*** was zum Teufel . . .? (*coll.*) *--for-leather,* wie der Teufel; *gambling –,* die Spielhölle; (*coll.*) *be in a – of a rage,* eine Mordswut haben; (*coll.*) *– of a row,* höllischer Lärm, der Höllenspektakel; (*coll.*) *like –,* wie der Teufel, wie wild; (*sl.*) *give him –,* ihm die Hölle heiß machen; *go to –,* zur Hölle fahren; (*fig.*) zum Teufel gehen, sich zum Teufel scheren; *all –'s let loose,* der Teufel ist los; (*sl.*) *kick up* or *raise –,* Krawall machen, einen Mordskrach schlagen.

hell|-bent, *adj.* (*coll.*) erpicht, versessen (*on, after,* auf (*Acc.*)). **--broth,** *s.* der Hexentrank. **–cat,** *s.* die Hexe, (*fig.*) der Drache.

hellebore ['helibɔ:], *s.* (*Bot.*) der Nieswurz.

hell|fire, *s.* das Höllenfeuer. **–hound,** *s.* der Höllenhund, abscheulicher Mensch. **hellish,** *adj.* höllisch, teuflisch, abscheulich. **hellishness,** *s.* die Abscheulichkeit.

hello! [he'lou], *int.* hallo!

[1]**helm** [helm], *s.* (*obs., Poet.*) *see* **helmet.**

[2]**helm,** *s.* das Steuer(rad), Ruder (*also fig.*), die Pinne; *at the –,* am Ruder (*also fig.*); *– down!* Ruder in Lee! *put the – hard over,* das Ruder in Hartlage legen; *carry lee –* (*weather –*), leegierig (luvgierig) sein; *starboard the –!* Steuerbord das Ruder!

helmet ['helmit], *s.* der Helm; (*Fenc.*) die Fechtmaske; *crash –,* der Sturzhelm; *diving –,* der Taucherhelm; *spiked –,* die Pickelhaube; *steel –,* der Stahlhelm; *tropical –,* der Tropenhelm. **helmeted,** *adj.* behelmt.

helminth ['helminθ], *s.* der Eingeweidewurm.

helmsman ['helmzmən], *s.* der Rudergast, Rudergänger.

helot ['helət], *s.* der Helote, Sklave. **helotry,** *s.* das Helotentum, die Sklaverei.

help [help], **1.** *v.t.* 1. (*a p.*) helfen (*Dat.*), beistehen (*Dat.*), Hilfe leisten (*Dat.*); (*a th.*) nachhelfen (*Dat.*), fördern, unterstützen, beitragen zu; (*at table*) *– him to,* ihm verhelfen zu *or* vorlegen *or* auftun *or* geben *or* servieren; *can I – you?* kann ich Ihnen behilflich sein? *so – me God!* so wahr mir Gott helfe! *– o.s.,* sich bedienen, zugreifen, zulangen; (*coll.*) *– o.s. to,* sich (*Dat.*) aneignen, sich (*Dat.*) zu eigen machen; *– forward* or *on,* weiterhelfen (*Dat.*), fördern, unterstützen; *– him on with his coat,* ihm in seinen Mantel helfen; *– him off with his coat,* ihm den Mantel ablegen helfen; *– on,* see *– forward*; *– out,* aushelfen (*Dat.*), aus der Not helfen (*Dat.*); *– him out of a difficulty,* ihm aus einer Schwierigkeit heraushelfen; *– him over a difficulty,* ihm über eine Schwierigkeit hinweghelfen; 2. abhelfen (*Dat.*), helfen bei, lindern, ändern, (ver)hindern; *I cannot – it,* ich kann nichts dafür, ich kann es nicht ändern; *I cannot – laughing* or *but laugh,* ich kann nicht umhin zu lachen, ich muß doch lachen; *I cannot – my looks,* ich kann nichts für mein Aussehen; *it can't be –ed,* dem ist nicht abzuhelfen, es ist nicht zu ändern, es läßt sich nicht ändern; *you cannot – being jealous,* man kommt nicht um die Eifersucht herum; *don't be any slower than you can –,* arbeite nicht langsamer als nötig ist; (*coll.*) *I cannot – myself,* ich kann nicht anders. **2.** *v.i.* helfen, dienen (*to,* zu). **3.** *s.* 1. die Hilfe, Unterstützung, der Beistand; die Abhilfe, Hilfeleistung; das Hilfsmittel; *with* or *by the – of,* mit Hilfe von; *give –,* Abhilfe schaffen, Hilfe bringen; *there is no – for it,* da ist nicht zu helfen, es läßt sich nicht ändern; 2. (*coll.*) die Aushilfe, Stütze, der Gehilfe (die Gehilfin); *daily –,* das Tagmädchen; *holiday –,* die Ferienaushilfe; *lady –,* die Stütze der Hausfrau; *mother's –,* das Kinderfräulein.

helper ['helpə], *s.* der (die) Helfer(in), der Gehilfe (die Gehilfin), die Hilfe, der Beistand. **helpful,** *adj.* hilfreich, behilflich; nützlich, dienlich (*to, Dat.*); *be –,* nützen. **helpfulness,** *s.* die Dienstlichkeit, Nützlichkeit (*of a th.*), Hilfsbereitschaft (*of a p.*).

helping, 1. *s.* 1. die Hilfe(leistung), das Helfen; 2. (*at table*) die Portion. **2.** *adj.* hilfreich, helfend; *give him a – hand,* ihm unter die Arme greifen. **helpless,** *adj.* hilflos; (*coll. of a p.*) unselbständig, hoffnungslos unpraktisch; (*coll.*) *–ly drunk,* bis zur Hilflosigkeit *or* über alle Maßen betrunken. **helplessness,** *s.* die Hilflosigkeit. **helpmate, helpmeet,** *s.* der Gehilfe, die Gehilfin; Gattin.

helter-skelter ['heltə'skeltə], **1.** *adv.* holterdiepolter, Hals über Kopf, ungestüm. **2.** *s.* die Rutschbahn.

helve [helv], **1.** *s.* der Stiel, Griff; *throw the – after the hatchet,* die Flinte ins Korn werfen. **2.** *v.t.* mit einem Stiel versehen.

[1]**hem** [hem], **1.** *s.* der Saum. **2.** *v.t.* (um)säumen; (*fig.*) *– in,* einschließen, umgeben, umringen, umzingeln.

[2]**hem, 1.** *v.i.* sich räuspern; *– and haw,* in der Rede stocken, mit der Sprache nicht herauswollen. **2.** *int.* hm!

hematite, *etc. See* **haematite** *etc.*

hemicycle ['hemisaikl], *s.* der Halbkreis. **hemidemisemiquaver,** *s.* die Vierundsechzigstelnote. **hemiplegia** [–'pli:dʒə], *s.* einseitige Lähmung. **hemipteron** [he'miptərɔn], *s.* (*pl.* **-ptera**) (*Ent.*) der Halbflügler. **hemisphere,** *s.* die Halbkugel, Hemisphäre; (*Anat.*) Großhirnhälfte. **hemispherical,** *adj.* halbkug(e)lig. **hemistich** [–stik], *s.* der Halbvers.

hemlock ['hemlɔk], *s.* (*Bot.*) der Schierling; (*fig.*) Giftbecher, Schierlingstrank. **hemlock|-fir, --spruce,** *s.* die Hemlocktanne, Schierlingstanne.

hemorrhage *etc. See* **haemorrhage** *etc.*

hemp [hemp], *s.* (*Bot.*) der Hanf, die Hanffaser; (*fig.*) das Henkerseil; (*sl.*) Haschisch. **hempen,** *adj.* hänfen, hanfen, Hanf–.

hemstitch ['hemstitʃ], **1.** *s.* der Hohlsaum(stich). **2.** *v.t.* mit Hohlsaum nähen.

hen [hen], **1.** *s.* die Henne, das Huhn (*fowl*); Weibchen (*of all birds*); (*sl.*) die Frau; *–'s egg,* das Hühnerei. **henbane,** *s.* das Bilsenkraut; (*fig.*) Gift.

hence [hens], **1.** *adv.* 1. (*of place*) (*Poet.*) (*also from –*) von hier, von hinnen, hinweg, fort; 2. (*of time*) von jetzt an; *a short time –,* binnen kurzen; *six months –,* in *or* binnen *or* nach sechs Monaten; 3. (*consequence*) hieraus, daraus, daher, deshalb, deswegen, folglich. **2.** *int.* (*Poet.*) fort! hinweg! **hence|forth, –forward,** *adv.* von nun an, von jetzt ab, künftig, fernerhin, fortan, hinfort.

henchman ['hentʃmən], *s.* (*obs.*) der Knappe, Page; (*fig.*) Gefolgsmann, Anhänger, (*Pol.*) Konjunkturritter, feiler Parteigänger.

hen-coop, *s.* der Hühnerstall.

hendecagon [hen'dekəgən], *s.* das Elfeck. **hendecasyllabic** [–si'læbik], **1.** *adj.* elfsilbig. **2.** *s.* elfsilbiger Vers.

hendiadys [hen'daiədis], *s.* (*Metr.*) das Hendiadys.

hen|-harrier, *s.* (*Orn.*) die Kornweihe (*Circus cyanus*). **--house,** *s. See* **--coop.**

henna ['henə], *s.* (*Bot.*) der Hennastrauch; die Henna(farbe).

hen|-party, *s.* (*coll.*) der Kaffeeklatsch, das Kaffeekränzchen; die Damengesellschaft. **–peck,** *v.t.* (*coll.*) unter dem Pantoffel haben; *–ed husband,* der Pantoffelheld. **--roost,** *s.* die Hühnerstange; *see also* **--coop.**

hepatic [hi'pætik], *adj.* Leber–.

heptagon ['heptəgən], *s.* das Siebeneck. **heptagonal** [–'tægənl], *adj.* siebeneckig. **heptahedron** [–'hi:drən], *s.* das Heptaeder, Siebenflach. **heptarchy** ['heptɑ:ki], *s.* die Heptarchie. **heptateuch** [–tju:k], *s.* (*B.*) der Heptateuch.

her [hə:], **1.** *pers. pron.* (*Acc.*) sie; (*Dat.*) ihr; (*of ships*) ihn, es (*Dat.* ihm); (*of the moon*) (*Poet.*) ihn (*Dat.* ihm); *to* or *for –,* ihr. *For examples see* **him.** **2.** *poss. adj.* ihr *etc.* (sein *etc. if the noun referred to is masc. or neut.*). *See* **his. 3.** *refl. pron.* sich. *See* **him.**

herald ['herəld], **1.** *s.* der Herold; (*fig.*) Verkünder, Vorläufer, (Vor)bote; *College of Heralds,* das Heroldsamt. **2.** *v.t.* (feierlich) verkünden, ankündigen; *– in,* (feierlich) einführen. **heraldic** [hə'rældik], *adj.* heraldisch, Wappen–. **heraldry,**

s. die Wappenkunde, Heraldik; (*collect.*) das Wappen, der Wappenschild.

herb [hə:b], *s.* das Kraut, Gewächs, die Pflanze; (*Cul.*) das Gewürzkraut. **herbaceous** [-'beiʃəs], *adj.* kraut(art)ig, Kraut-; laubblattartig; – ***border,*** die Blumenrabatte. **herbage** [-bidʒ], *s.* **1.** (*collect.*) Kräuter (*pl.*), das Laub(werk), Blätterwerk, Gras; die Weide, Trift; **2.** (*Law*) das Weiderecht. **herbal, 1.** *s.* das Pflanzenbuch, Kräuterbuch. **2.** *adj.* Kräuter-, Pflanzen-. **herbalist,** *s.* der Kräuterkenner; Kräutersammler, Kräuterhändler. **herbarium** [-'bεəriəm], *s.* das Herbarium, die Pflanzensammlung. **herb-bennet,** *s.* (*Bot.*) die Nelkenwurz. **herbivorous** [-'bivərəs], *adj.* pflanzenfressend. **herborize** [-əraiz], *v.i.* Pflanzen sammeln, botanisieren. **herb|-robert,** *s.* (*Bot.*) Stinkender Storchschnabel, das Ruprechtskraut. **--tea,** *s.* der Kräutertee.

herculean [hə:'kju:liən], *adj.* Herkules-, übermenschlich, herkulisch.

herd [hə:d], **1.** *s.* die Herde; (*fig.*) der Haufe(n); ***the common*** –, die große Masse, der Pöbel; – ***of deer,*** das Rudel Hochwild; – ***instinct,*** der Herdentrieb. **2.** *v.t.* hüten (*cattle*); zusammentreiben. **3.** *v.i.* in Herden gehen; – ***together,*** zusammenhausen (*of men*). **herdsman,** *s.* der Hirt.

here [hiə], *adv.* (*place*) hier, an diesem Orte *or* (*fig.*) dieser Stelle; (*time*) zu diesem Zeitpunkt; (*fig.*) in diesem Falle; (*with verbs of motion*) (hier)her; ***be*** –, anwesend *or* da sein; ***belong*** –, hierher gehören; – ***below,*** hienieden; ***bring*** –, hierherbringen; – ***goes!*** also los! – ***and there,*** hier und da; hin und wieder; ***that's neither – nor there,*** das ist sinnlos *or* zwecklos, das gehört nicht zur S.; ***it was Lady B.*** –, ***Lady B. there,*** es hieß Lady B. hinten und vorn; – ***there and everywhere,*** überall; (*sl.*) ***this – chap,*** dieser Kerl hier; –***'s to you!*** auf dein Wohl! – ***today and gone tomorrow,*** flüchtig und vergänglich.

here|about(s), *adv.* hier herum. **-after, 1.** *adv.* nachher, hernach, künftig(hin), zukünftig, in Zukunft, von jetzt an; im (zu)künftigen Leben. **2.** *s.* die Zukunft; das Jenseits, (zu)künftiges Leben. **-by,** *adv.* hierdurch, dadurch.

hereditable [hi'reditəbl], *adj.* *See* **heritable. hereditament** [heri'ditəmənt], *s.* (*Law*) das Erbgut. **hereditary,** *adj.* (*Law*) erblich, Erb-, vererbt; (*of disease etc.*) vererbbar, angeboren, ererbt. **heredity,** *s.* die Erblichkeit, Vererbung.

here|in, *adv.* hierin. **-inafter,** *adv.* hiernach, nachstehend, im folgenden, unten. **-of,** *adv.* hiervon. **-on,** *adv.* hierauf, hierüber.

heresiarch [he'ri:ziɑ:k], *s.* der Erzketzer. **heresy** ['herəsi], *s.* die Ketzerei, Irrlehre, Häresie. **heretic** ['herətik], *s.* der Ketzer. **heretical** [hi'retikl], *adj.* ketzerisch.

here|to, *adv.* hierzu. **-tofore** [-'fɔ:], *adv.* ehemals, vorhin, vordem, bis jetzt. **-under,** *adv.* *See* **-inafter. -upon,** *adv.* hierauf, darauf(hin). **-with,** *adv.* hiermit, hierdurch.

heriot ['heriət], *s.* (*obs. Law*) der Hauptfall.

heritable ['heritəbl], *adj.* erbfähig; erblich, vererbbar, Erb-, sich vererbend. **heritage** [-tidʒ], *s.* die Erbschaft, das Erbe, Erbgut. **heritor,** *s.* (*Law*) der Erbe.

hermaphrodite [hə:'mæfrədait], *s.* der Zwitter; (*Bot.*) die Zwitterpflanze; (*fig.*) das Zwitterding, Zwitterwesen. **hermaphroditism,** *s.* die Zwitterbildung, Zwittrigkeit.

hermeneutic [hə:mi'nju:tik], *adj.* erklärend, auslegend. **hermeneutics,** *pl.* (*sing. constr.*) die Hermeneutik.

hermetic [hə:'metik], *adj.* luftdicht, hermetisch; –***ally sealed,*** luftdicht abgeschlossen.

hermit ['hə:mit], *s.* der Einsiedler, Eremit, Klausner. **hermitage** [-tidʒ], *s.* die Einsiedelei, Klause. **hermit-crab,** *s.* der Einsiedlerkrebs.

hernia ['hə:niə], *s.* der Bruch. **hernial,** *adj.* Bruch-.

hero ['hiərou], *s.* der Held; die Hauptperson (*in drama etc.*); (*Myth.*) der Halbgott, Heros; – ***worship,*** der Heroenkultus, die Heldenverehrung.

Herod ['herəd], *s.* (*B.*) Herodes (*m.*); ***out-herod*** – alles überbieten.

heroic [hi'rouik], *adj.* heldenhaft, heldenmütig; – ***age,*** das Heldenzeitalter; – ***couplet,*** heroisches Reimpaar; – ***deed,*** die Heldentat; – ***metre,*** heroisches Versmaß; (*Classics*) der Hexameter, (*French*) Alexandriner, (*English*) Blankvers; – ***poem,*** das Heldengedicht; – ***verse,*** epische Dichtung. **heroics,** *pl.* Überschwenglichkeiten (*pl.*), das Pathos; ***go off into*** –, schwärmen.

heroin ['herouin], *s.* (*Chem.*) das Heroin.

heroine ['herouin], *s.* die Heldin; (*Myth.*) Halbgöttin. **heroism,** *s.* der Heldenmut, das Heldentum; der Heroismus, Heldengeist.

heron ['herən], *s.* (*Orn.*) der Reiher (*Ardea cinerea*). **heronry,** *s.* der Reiherstand.

herpes ['hə:pi:z], *s.* (*Med.*) die Flechte. **herpetic** [-'petik], *adj.* flechtenartig, Flechten-.

herpetology [hə:pə'tɔlədʒi], *s.* die Reptilienkunde.

herring ['heriŋ], *s.* der Hering; ***grilled*** –, der Brathering; ***kippered*** –, der Räucherhering; ***pickled*** –, der Matjeshering; Rollmops; ***red*** –, der Bück(l)ing; (*fig.*) das Ablenkungsmanöver.

herring|bone, 1. *s.* das Grätenmuster; der Grätenstich (*sewing*); Grätenschritt (*skiing*). **2.** *v.t.* mit Grätenstich nähen. **3.** *adj.* fischgrätenartig, Fischgräten-. **--gull,** *s.* (*Orn.*) die Silbermöwe (*Larus argentatus*). **--pond,** *s.* (*coll.*) Atlantischer Ozean.

hers [hə:z], *poss. pron.* (*pred.*) ihr; der *or* die *or* das ihr(ig)e; ***a friend of*** –, eine ihrer Freundinnen, eine Freundin von ihr. **herself** [hə:'self], *pron.* **1.** (*emph.*) (sie *or* ihr) selbst; **2.** (*refl.*) sich. *For examples see* **himself.**

he's [hi:z], (*coll.*) = ***he is*** or ***he has.***

hesitance, hesitancy ['hezitəns(i)], *s.* die Unschlüssigkeit, das Zögern. **hesitant,** *adj.* zögernd, zaudernd, unschlüssig. **hesitate** [-teit], *v.i.* zögern, zaudern, unschlüssig sein, Bedenken tragen. **hesitation** [-'teiʃən], *s.* das Zögern, Zaudern, die Unschlüssigkeit, das Bedenken; ***without any*** –, ohne jedes Bedenken; ***have no*** –, kein Bedenken tragen (***in doing,*** zu tun). **hesitative** [-tətiv], *adj.* *See* **hesitant.**

Hesse [hes], *s.* (*Geog.*) Hessen (*n.*). **Hessian** ['hesiən], **1.** *s.* der Hesse (die Hessin). **2.** *adj.* hessisch; – ***boots,*** Reitstiefel (*pl.*). **hessian,** *s.* (grobes) Sackzeug.

hetero- ['hetərou], *pref.* fremd, anders, verschieden. **heterochthonous** [-'ɔkθənəs], *adj.* fremd, nicht ursprünglich. **heteroclite** [-klait], **1.** *s.* unregelmäßiges Wort. **2.** *adj.* unregelmäßig (flektiert), anomal. **heterodox,** *adj.* irrgläubig, andersgläubig, heterodox. **heterodoxy,** *s.* der Irrglaube, die Andersglaubigkeit, Heterodoxie, abweichende Meinung. **heterodyne** [-dain], *adj.* (*Rad.*) Überlagerungs-. **heterogeneity** [-dʒi'ni:iti], *s.* die Ungleichartigkeit, Ungleichförmigkeit, Uneinheitlichkeit, Verschiedenartigkeit. **heterogeneous** [-'dʒi:njəs], *adj.* ungleichartig, verschiedenartig, grundverschieden, fremdartig, heterogen; (*Math.*) – ***number,*** gemischte Zahl. **heteromorphic** [-'mɔ:fik], **heteromorphous** [-'mɔ:fəs], *adj.* verschiedengestaltig. **heterosexual,** *adj.* heterosexuell.

hetman ['hetmən], *s.* der Kosakenführer, ukrainischer Befehlshaber.

het-up ['het'ʌp], *adj.* (*sl.*) aufgeregt, unruhig.

heuristic [hjuə'ristik], *adj.* heuristisch, wegweisend, richtunggebend.

hew [hju:], *reg. or irr. v.t.* hauen, hacken; behauen (*masonry*); – ***one's way,*** sich (*Dat.*) einen Weg bahnen; – ***to*** or ***in pieces,*** zerhauen, in Stücke hauen. **hewer,** *s.* der (Be)hauer; (*Min.*) Häuer; –***s of wood and drawers of water,*** (*B.*) Holzhauer und Wasserträger; (*coll. fig.*) Arbeitssklaven (*pl.*). **hewn,** *p.p. of* **hew.**

hexachord ['heksəkɔ:d], *s.* (*Mus.*) der *or* das Hexachord, große Sexte. **hexagon,** *s.* das Sechseck. **hexagonal** [-'sægənl], *adj.* sechseckig. **hexahedral** [-'hi:drəl], *adj.* hexaedrisch, sechsflächig.

hexahedron, *s.* das Hexaeder, Sechsflach, der Würfel. **hexameter** [–'sæmitə], *s.* (*Metr.*) der Hexameter, Sechsfüßler. **hexapod,** *s.* (*Zool.*) der Sechsfüß(l)er.

hey! [hei], *int.* he! hei! – *presto!* sieh mal! und da haben Sie's!

heyday ['heidei], *s.* der Höhepunkt, Gipfelpunkt, die Blüte(zeit), Vollkraft, Hochflut, der Überschwang, Sturm (*of passion*).

hi! [hai], *int.* he! heda! ei!

hiatus [hai'eitəs], *s.* die Lücke, Kluft, der Spalt; (*Gram.*) Hiatus.

hibernate ['haibəneit], *v.i.* Winterschlaf halten, überwintern; (*fig.*) abgeschlossen leben, sich vergraben. **hibernation** [–'neiʃən], *s.* der Winterschlaf, die Überwinterung.

hibiscus [hi'biskəs], *s.* (*Bot.*) der Eibisch.

hiccough, hiccup ['hikʌp], **1.** *s.* (*usu. pl.*) der Schlucken, Schluckauf. **2.** *v.i.* den Schlucken haben.

hick [hik], **1.** *s.* (*Am. sl.*) der Lümmel, Tölpel. **2.** *adj.* ländlich, provinziell; ungehobelt, tölpelhaft.

hickory ['hikəri], *s.* das Hickoryholz.

hid [hid], *imperf. of* [1]**hide. hidden, 1.** *p.p. of* [1]**hide. 2.** *adj.* heimlich, versteckt, verborgen.

[1]**hide** [haid], **1.** *irr.v.t.* verbergen, verheimlichen (*from, Dat. or* vor (*Dat.*)), verstecken (vor (*Dat.*)); – *from view,* dem Blick entziehen; *clouds – the moon,* Wolken bedecken den Mond. **2.** *irr.v.i.* sich verbergen *or* verstecken; *--and-seek* (*Am. --and-go-seek, --and coop*), das Versteckspiel; *play (at) --and-seek,* Versteck spielen.

[2]**hide,** *s.* (*obs.*) die Hufe (= *60–100 acres or 24–40 ha.*).

[3]**hide, 1.** *s.* die (Tier)haut, das Fell; (*coll.*) *save one's own –,* die eigene Haut retten; (*coll.*) *thick –,* dickes Fell. **2.** *v.t.* (*coll.*) prügeln.

hide|-away, *s.* (*coll.*) der Versteckplatz. **-bound,** *adj.* mit eng anschließender Haut *or* Rinde; (*usu. fig.*) kleinlich, borniert, eng(herzig); *be – by tradition,* im Bann der Überlieferung stecken.

hideous ['hidiəs], *adj.* entsetzlich, häßlich, schrecklich, abscheulich, gräßlich, scheußlich. **hideousness,** *s.* die Häßlichkeit, Abscheulichkeit, Scheußlichkeit.

hide-out, *s.* (*coll.*) das Versteck, der Schlupfwinkel.

[1]**hiding,** *s.* das Verbergen, Verstecken; *be in –,* sich versteckt halten; – *place, see* **hide-out.**

[2]**hiding,** *s.* (*coll.*) die Tracht Prügel.

hie [hai], *v.i.* (*also – o.s.*) (*Poet.*) eilen.

hierarch ['haiərɑ:k], *s.* der Hierarch, Oberpriester. **hierarchic(al)** [–'rɑ:kik(l)], *adj.* hierarchisch. **hierarchy,** *s.* 1. die Hierarchie, Priesterherrschaft; 2. (*fig.*) Rangordnung; Beamtenhierarchie. **hieratic(al)** [–'rætik(l)], *adj.* priesterlich, Priester–. **hierocracy** [–'rɔkrəsi], *s.* die Priesterherrschaft.

hieroglyph ['haiərɔglif], *s.* die Hieroglyphe, symbolisches Schriftzeichen. **hieroglyphic** [–'glifik], *adj.* hieroglyphisch; geheimnisvoll, rätselhaft; unleserlich. **hieroglyphics,** *pl.* Hieroglyphen (*pl.*), ägyptische Bilderschrift; (*coll.*) unleserliches Gekritzel.

hierophant ['haiərofænt], *s.* der Oberpriester.

hi-fi ['haifai], *s.* (*adj.*) (*coll.*) (mit) getreue(r) Tonwiedergabe; das Hi-Fi-Gerät.

higgle [higl], *v.i.* feilschen, handeln, knickern, schachern. **higgledy-piggledy** ['higldi'pigldi], **1.** *adj., adv.* kunterbunt, drunter und drüber, durcheinander, planlos. **2.** *s.* das Durcheinander.

high [hai], **1.** *adj.* hoch; hoch(gelegen), hoch(stehend), erhaben, vornehm; (*in rank*) Hoch–, Haupt–, Ober–; angesehen, bedeutend, wichtig; groß, stark, kräftig, heftig; übertrieben, extrem; (*as meat*) abgehangen, angegangen, pikant; (*voice, tone*) laut, stark, lärmend, schrill; – *altar,* der Hochaltar; – *antiquity,* fernes *or* tiefes Altertum; – *birth,* hohe Geburt; *High Church,* die Hochkirche; – *colour,* lebhafte *or* blühende Farbe; – *command,* das Oberkommando; – *commendation,* großes Lob; *High Commissioner,* der Gesandte (der Dominien) in London; *High Court,* oberster Gerichtshof; – *dive,* das Turmspringen; – *explosive,* der Sprengstoff; – *farming,* intensive Bewirtschaftung; *in – feather,* in gehobener Stimmung; – *frequency,* die Hochfrequenz; *High German,* das Hochdeutsch; *with a – hand,* hochmütig, hochfahrend, willkürlich, rücksichtslos; (*coll.*) *get on one's – horse,* sich aufs hohe Roß setzen; (*coll.*) – *jinks,* ausgelassene Fröhlichkeit; – *jump,* der Hochsprung; – *life,* vornehme Welt; – *living,* das Wohlleben; *High Mass,* das Hochamt; – *noon,* hoch am Mittag; – *priest,* der Oberpriester; (*Jew.*) Hohepriester, Hoher Priester; (*fig.*) der Hohepriester, Prophet; – *school,* höhere Schule; (*Am.*) die Mittelschule; (*riding*) Hohe Schule; – *sea,* hochgehende See; – *seas,* offenes Meer, hohe See; – *spirits,* gehobene Stimmung; – *standing,* guter Ruf; hohes Niveau; – *summer,* der Hochsommer; (*Univ.*) – *table,* der Speisetisch der Graduierten; – *tea* (*approx.* =) das Abendessen mit kalter Platte; – *tension,* die Hochspannung; – *tide,* das Hochwasser, die Flut; höchster Wasserstand; – *time,* höchste Zeit; (*coll.*) – *old time,* der Heidenspaß; – *Tory,* extremer Konservativer; – *treason,* der Hochverrat; – *voltage* see – *tension*; – *water* see – *tide*; – *wind,* starker Wind; – *words,* heftige *or* zornige Worte; – *and dry,* gestrandet, aufgelaufen; (*fig.*) auf dem trockenen; – *and mighty,* hochmütig, hochfahrend, anmaßend, arrogant. **2.** *adv.* hoch, in die Höhe; stark, heftig, in hohem Grad; *pay –,* teuer zahlen; *play –,* mit hohem Einsatz spielen; *run –,* hochgehen (*of waves*); heftig werden (*of feelings*); *search – and low,* überall *or* an allen Ecken und Enden suchen; *stand –,* in gutem Rufe stehen. **3.** *s.* 1. (*Meteor.*) das Hoch(druckgebiet); 2. der Höchststand; 3. *on –,* droben; im Himmel.

high|-altitude flying, *s.* der Höhenflug. **--angle fire,** *s.* das Steilfeuer. **--angle gun,** *s.* das Steilfeuergeschütz. **--backed,** *adj.* mit hoher Lehne (*chair*). **-ball,** *s.* (*sl.*) der Highball. **-born,** *adj.* hochgeboren, von hoher Geburt. **-bred,** *adj.* vornehm, von edlem Blut. **-brow, 1.** *adj.* (bewußt) intellektuell. **2.** *s.* Intellektuelle(r). **High|-Church,** *adj.* hochkirchlich, hochanglikanisch. **--Churchman,** *s.* der Hochkirchler. **high|-class,** *adj.* hochwertig, erstklassig. **--day,** *s.* der Festtag, Freudentag.

higher ['haiə], *comp. adj.* höher; obere, Ober–; höher(entwickelt), differenzierter; – *criticism,* historische (Bibel)kritik; – *education,* fortgeschrittene Schulausbildung, die Hochschulbildung. **highest** [–ist], **1.** *sup. adj.* höchst, oberst; *at its –,* auf dem Höhepunkt; – *bidder,* Meistbietende(r). **2.** *sup. adv.* am höchsten.

high|-explosive, *adj.* Brisanz–, Spreng–. **-falutin(g)** [–fə'lu:tin], *adj.* (*sl.*) bombastisch, hochtrabend. **--fidelity,** *adj., s.* (*Rad. etc.*) *see* **hi-fi. --flier,** *s.* (*coll.*) der Schwärmer, Draufgänger. **--flown,** *adj.* überspannt, hochtrabend, aufgeblasen, überschwenglich, schwülstig. **--flying,** *adj.* (*fig.*) ehrgeizig, hochfliegend. **--frequency,** *adj.* Hochfrequenz–. **--grade,** *adj.* hochgradig, hochwertig, Qualitäts–; Vergütungs– (*steel*). **--handed,** *adj.* anmaßend, willkürlich, gewaltsam. **--handedness,** *s.* die Willkür, Anmaßung. **--hat,** *adj.* (*sl.*) hochnäsig. **--heeled,** *adj.* mit hohen Absätzen. **-land** [–lənd], **1.** *s.* das Hochland, Bergland; *the* (*Scottish*) *Highlands,* schottisches Hochland. **2.** *adj.* hochländisch, Hochland–; schottisch. **-lander,** *s.* der Hochlander, Bergschotte. **-light, 1.** *s.* 1. (*Art etc.*) das Schlaglicht; 2. (*fig.*) der Höhepunkt. **2.** *v.t.* betonen, hervorheben.

highly ['haili], *adv.* hoch, höchst, sehr, in hohem Grad; – *coloured,* sehr bunt, lebhaft; (*fig.*) übertrieben; – *flavoured,* stark gewürzt, pikant; – *gifted,* hochbegabt; – *placed,* hochgestellt; (*fig.*) – *strung,* überempfindlich, nervös, überspannt; *speak – of,* anerkennend *or* lobend sprechen von; *think – of,* viel halten von.

high|-minded, *adj.* hochherzig, großherzig.

--mindedness, *s.* die Großherzigkeit. **--necked,** *adj.* hochgeschlossen (*dress*).

highness ['hainis], *s.* 1. die Höhe; 2. (*fig.*) Vornehmheit, Erhabenheit; (*rank*) Hoheit; ***His Royal Highness,*** Seine Königliche Hoheit; 3. pikanter Geschmack, der Stich (*of food*).

high|-octane, *adj.* klopffest (*petrol*). **--pass filter,** *s.* (*Rad.*) die Kondensatorkette. **--pitched,** *adj.* steil (*of roof*); in hoher Tonlage (*of sound*). **--pressure,** *adj.* (*Tech.*) Hochdruck–; (*fig. coll.*) konzentriert, energisch; (*Meteor.*) – ***area,*** das Hoch(druckgebiet); (*coll.*) – ***salesmanship,*** intensive Verkaufsmethoden (*pl.*). **--priced,** *adj.* teuer, kostspielig (*goods*); hochstehend (*shares etc.*). **--principled,** *adj.* von hohen Grundsätzen. **--priority,** *adj.* Dringlichkeits–. **-road,** *s.* die Landstraße; Hauptverkehrsstraße; (*fig.*) ***the – to success,*** der sichere Weg zum Erfolg. **--sounding,** *adj.* hochtönend, hochklingend, hochtrabend. **--speed,** *adj.* Schnell– (*as railw.*); Schnell(dreh)– (*as steel*); schnell laufend, von großer Geschwindigkeit. **--spirited,** *adj.* munter, lebhaft; feurig (*as horse*). **-spot,** *s.* (*coll.*) der Hauptpunkt, die Hauptsache. **--stepper,** *s.* hochtrabendes Pferd. **--stepping,** *adj.* hochtrabend (*horse, also fig.*).

hight [hait], *p.p.* (*obs.*) genannt.

high|-tension, *adj.* (*Elec.*) Hochspannungs–; (*Rad.*) Anoden–. **--toned,** *adj.* erhaben, hochgesinnt. **--up,** *s.* (*sl.*) hohes Tier. **--water,** *adj.* Hochwasser–; – ***mark,*** das Hochwasserstandzeichen; (*fig.*) der Höhepunkt, Gipfel, Höchststand. **-way,** *s.* öffentliche Straße; die Landstraße, Hauptstraße, Chaussee; (*fig.*) bester *or* direkter Weg; – ***code,*** die Straßenverkehrsordnung; – ***robbery,*** der Straßenraub. **-wayman,** *s.* der Straßenräuber. **--wing,** *adj.* (*Av.*) hochdeckig; – ***aircraft,*** der Hochdecker.

hijack ['haidʒæk], *v.t.* überfallen und berauben (*vehicle*), entführen (*aircraft*). **hijacker,** *s.* der (die) (Luft)pirat(in).

hike [haik], 1. *v.i.* wandern. 2. *s.* die Wanderung. **hiker,** *s.* der (Fuß)wanderer. **hiking,** *s.* das Wandern.

hilarious [hi'lɛəriəs], *adj.* vergnügt, heiter, fröhlich, lustig, ausgelassen. **hilarity** [hi'læriti], *s.* die Heiterkeit, Fröhlichkeit, Lustigkeit, Ausgelassenheit.

hill [hil], *s.* der Hügel; Berg, die Anhöhe, Steigung; (*fig.*) ***be over the –,*** über den Berg sein; ***up – and down dale,*** über Berg und Tal; ***as old as the –s,*** uralt. **hill|billy,** *s.* (*coll.*) der Hinterwälder. **--climb,** *s.* (*Motor.*) die Bergfahrt. **hilliness,** *s.* die Hügeligkeit. **hillock** [–ək], *s.* kleiner Hügel, das Hügelchen. **hill|side,** *s.* der Bergabhang. **-top,** *s.* die Bergspitze. **hilly,** *adj.* hügelig.

hilt [hilt], *s.* der Griff, das Heft; ***up to the –,*** bis ans Heft; (*fig.*) ganz und gar, durch und durch.

him [him], 1. *pers. pron.* (*Acc.*) ihn, den(jenigen); (*Dat.*) ihm, dem(jenigen); ***to*** or ***for –,*** ihm; ***she gave – the book,*** sie gab ihm das Buch; (*coll.*) ***it's*** or ***that's –,*** er ist es. 2. *refl. pron.* sich; ***he looked about –,*** er sah um sich. **himself** [–'self], *pron.* 1. (*emph.*) (er *or* ihn *or* ihm) selbst; ***it is he –,*** er ist es selbst; ***he – did it, he did it –,*** er selbst hat es *or* er hat es selbst getan; ***I sent him the money for –,*** ich schickte ihm das Geld für ihn selbst; 2. (*refl.*) sich (selbst); ***he is a big boy now and can wash –,*** er ist schon ein großer Junge und kann sich (selbst) waschen; ***by –,*** allein, für sich, von selbst, ohne Hilfe; ***he works by –,*** er arbeitet für sich; ***he works for –,*** er arbeitet für sich selbst, er ist selbständig; (*coll.*) ***he is – again,*** er ist wieder der alte; (*coll.*) ***he is not –,*** er ist nicht ganz beisammen, er ist nicht auf der Höhe; ***he is beside –,*** er ist außer sich; ***he came to –,*** er kam zu sich; ***he repeats –,*** er wiederholt sich; ***he talks to –,*** er redet vor sich hin; ***he thinks to –,*** er denkt bei sich; ***he thinks – clever,*** er hält sich für klug.

[1]**hind** [haind], *s.* die Hindin, Hirschkuh.

[2]**hind,** *s.* (*Scots*) der Knecht, Bauer, Tagelöhner.

[3]**hind,** *adj.* hinter, Hinter–; – ***leg,*** das Hinterbein; – ***quarters,*** die Hinterhand (*of a horse*); das Hinterteil, Hinterviertel (*pl.*); (*coll.*) das Gesäß.

hinder ['hində], 1. *v.t.* hindern (***from,*** an (*Dat.*)), abhalten (von), zurückhalten (vor (*Dat.*)), aufhalten, stören (*a p.*). 2. *v.i.* hinderlich sein.

hind(er)most ['haind(ə)moust], *sup. adj. See* [3]**hind**; hinterst, letzt; ***the devil take the hindmost,*** den letzten beißen die Hunde.

hindrance ['hindrəns], *s.* das Hindernis (***to,*** für), die Behinderung.

hindsight ['haindsait], *s.* die Erkenntnis hinterher, Einsicht die zu spät kommt; ***with the benefit of –,*** im Rückblick.

Hindu [hin'du:], *s.* der Hindu. **Hindustani** [–'stɑ:ni], 1. *adj.* Hindostani–, hinduistisch. 2. *s.* (*language*) das Hind(ostan)i.

hinge [hindʒ], 1. *s.* die Angel (*of a door etc.*); das Scharnier (*of a box etc.*); Gelenk(band); (*philately*) der Klebefalz; (*fig.*) springender Punkt, der Angelpunkt, Wendepunkt; ***off the –s,*** aus den Angeln *or* Fugen. 2. *v.t.* mit Scharnieren versehen, (*door etc.*) einhängen; (*fig.*) abhängig machen (***on,*** von). 3. *v.i.* (*fig.*) sich drehen (***on,*** um), ankommen (auf (*Acc.*)), abhängen (von). **hinged,** *adj.* (auf– *or* zusammen)klappbar. **hinge-pin,** *s.* der Drehzapfen.

hinny ['hini], *s.* der Maulesel.

hint [hint], 1. *v.t.* andeuten. 2. *v.i.* einen Wink geben; eine Andeutung machen (***at,*** von), anspielen (auf (*Acc.*)). 3. *s.* der Wink, Fingerzeig; die Andeutung (***of,*** von; ***as to,*** über (*Acc.*)), Anspielung (***at,*** auf (*Acc.*)); ***broad –,*** der Wink mit dem Zaunpfahl; ***drop*** or ***give him a –,*** ihm einen Wink geben; ***take a –,*** einen Wink verstehen, es sich (*Dat.*) gesagt sein lassen; ***throw out a –,*** zu verstehen geben, merken lassen.

hinterland ['hintəlænd], *s.* das Hinterland.

[1]**hip** [hip], *s.* (*Bot.*) die Hagebutte.

[2]**hip,** *v.t.* bedrücken, trübsinnig machen, traurig stimmen.

[3]**hip,** *s.* (*Anat.*) die Hüfte, Lende, (*Build.*) der Walm, Ecksparren; (*coll.*) ***have him on the –,*** ihn in der Gewalt haben; (*B.*) ***smite – and thigh,*** erbarmungslos vernichten.

hip|-bath, *s.* das Sitzbad. **-bone,** *s.* das Hüftbein. **--flask,** *s.* die Reiseflasche. **--joint,** *s.* das Hüftgelenk.

[1]**hipped** [hipt], *adj.* mit . . . Hüften; (*Build.*) Walm–.

[2]**hipped, hippish,** *adj.* 1. trübsinnig, bedrückt, schwermütig; 2. (*Am.*) erpicht, versessen (***on,*** auf (*Acc.*)).

hippo ['hipou], *s.* (*coll.*) *see* **hippopotamus. hippocampus** [–o'kæmpəs], *s.* (*Ichth.*) das Seepferdchen. **hippodrome** [–ədroum], *s.* die Rennbahn, Reitbahn. **hippogriff, hippogryph** [–grif], *s.* das Flügelroß, Musenroß. **hippophagy** [–'pɔfədʒi], *s.* das Essen von Pferdefleisch. **hippopotamus** [–ə'pɔtəməs], *s.* das Nilpferd, Flußpferd.

hip|-rafter, *s.* der Gratsparren. **--roof,** *s.* das Walmdach. **-shot,** *adj.* (lenden)lahm.

hircine ['hə:sain], *adj.* bockig, Bocks–; (*fig.*) übelriechend, stinkend.

hire ['haiə], 1. *v.t.* mieten; dingen, in Dienst nehmen, anstellen (*a p.*), (an)heuern (*sailors*); – ***out,*** vermieten; – ***o.s.*** (***out***), sich verdingen *or* anheuern (***as,*** als; ***to,*** bei); ***–d hand*** or ***man,*** der Lohnarbeiter (*esp. on farms*). 2. *s.* die Miete, der Mietspreis, (Arbeits)lohn; ***for –,*** zu vermieten; ***on –,*** mietweise; zu vermieten; ***have*** or ***take on –,*** mieten; ***let out on –,*** vermieten. **hireling,** 1. *s.* der Mietling. 2. *adj.* feil, käuflich. **hire-purchase,** *s.* das Abzahlungskauf, Ratenkauf; – ***system,*** das Abzahlungssystem.

hirsute ['hə:sju:t], *adj.* haarig, behaart, struppig, zottig; rauhhaarig, borstig.

his [hiz], 1. *poss. pron.* sein(e), seines; der *or* die *or* das sein(ig)e; ***a book of –,*** eins seiner Bücher, eins von seinen Büchern; ***it is –,*** es gehört ihm. 2. *poss.*

adj. sein(e); ***he has hurt – finger,*** er hat sich (*Dat.*) den Finger verletzt.

hispid ['hispid], *adj.* (*Bot., Zool.*) borstig, rauh(haarig).

hiss [his], **1.** *v.i.* zischen. **2.** *v.t.* (*Theat.*) auszischen, auspfeifen; ***–ed off the stage,*** ausgepfiffen. **3.** *s.* das Zischen, Gezisch; (*Phonet.*) der Zischlaut.

hist! [hist], *int.* (*obs.*) st! still!

histogram ['histogræm], *s.* das Staffelbild, Histogramm. **histology** [–'tɔlədʒi], *s.* (*Med.*) die Gewebslehre. **histolysis** [–'tɔlisis], *s.* der Gewebszerfall.

historian [his'tɔ:riən], *s.* der Geschicht(s)schreiber, Historiker. **historic** [–'tɔrik], *adj.* historisch, geschichtlich bedeutend. **historical,** *adj.* historisch, geschichtlich, Geschichts–. **historicity** [–'risiti], *s.* die Geschichtlichkeit. **historiographer** [–'ɔgrəfə], *s.* amtlicher Geschicht(s)schreiber. **historiography,** *s.* (amtliche) Geschicht(s)schreibung.

history ['histəri], *s.* die Geschichte; Darstellung *or* Schilderung (des Geschehens), Entwicklung(sgeschichte), der Werdegang; (*without art.*) die Geschichte, Geschichtswissenschaft; (*coll.*) Vergangenheit; ***ancient –,*** die Geschichte des Altertums; (*coll.*) alte Geschichte, abgetane S.; (*coll.*) ***have a –,*** eine Vergangenheit haben; ***make –,*** Geschichte machen; ***universal –,*** die Weltgeschichte; ***– book,*** das Geschichtsbuch; ***– piece,*** historisches Gemälde.

histrionic [histri'ɔnik], *adj.* schauspielerisch, Schauspiel(er)–; theatralisch. **histrionics,** *pl.* die Schauspielkunst; (*fig.*) Schauspielerei, Effekthascherei.

hit [hit], **1.** *irr.v.t.* schlagen; anschlagen, anstoßen (***on, against,*** an (*Acc.*)); treffen (*the mark etc.*); (*coll.*) ***– it*** (or ***the nail on the head***), (den Nagel auf den Kopf) treffen; ***– one's head on*** or ***against the door,*** mit dem Kopf gegen die Tür stoßen; ***– him back,*** ihn wieder schlagen; ***– him below the belt,*** (*Boxing*) ihm einen Tiefschlag versetzen; (*fig.*) ihm unfair begegnen; ***– him a blow,*** ihm einen Schlag versetzen; ***be hard –,*** schwer getroffen sein (***by,*** durch); (*sl.*) ***– the hay,*** pennen; (*coll.*) ***– off,*** richtig *or* überzeugend *or* treffend darstellen *or* schildern; (*coll.*) ***– it off,*** glänzend auskommen, sich ausgezeichnet vertragen (***with,*** mit); (*Am. sl.*) ***– town,*** in die Stadt ankommen. **2.** *irr.v.i.* schlagen, treffen; ***– against,*** stoßen gegen; ***– (up)on,*** zufällig treffen *or* finden; kommen *or* verfallen *or* stoßen auf (*Acc.*); ***– out,*** um sich schlagen; ***– or miss,*** aufs Geratewohl, auf gut Glück. **3.** *s.* 1. der Schlag, Stoß; Hieb, Streich, Stich; ***direct –,*** der Volltreffer; 2. (*fig.*) glücklicher Zufall, der Glücksfall, Treffer, Erfolg, (*Theat. etc.*) Hit, (Spitzen)schlager; treffende Bemerkung, glücklicher Einfall, gute Idee; (*coll.*) ***make a –,*** einen Treffer erzielen, (*fig.*) gut anschlagen, auf einen grünen Zweig kommen.

hit|-and-miss, *adj.* zufällig, unbeabsichtigt, unvorsätzlich; (*pred. only*) blindlings, auf gut Glück, aufs geratewohl. **--and-run,** *adj.* ***– driver,*** flüchtiger Fahrer; (*Av.*) ***– raid,*** der Einbruchsangriff, Stippangriff.

hitch [hitʃ], **1.** *s.* der Ruck, Zug; (*Naut.*) Stek, Stich, Knoten; (*fig.*) das Hindernis, die Stockung, Störung, toter Punkt; der Haken; ***there is a – in the business,*** das Ding hat einen Haken; ***without a –,*** reibungslos, ohne die geringste Störung. **2.** *v.t.* 1. ruckartig ziehen, rücken; 2. festmachen, befestigen, (*horse etc.*) anschirren, anspannen; (*sl.*) ***get –ed,*** heiraten; ***– up,*** hochziehen. **3.** *v.i.* 1. hinken, humpeln; 2. hängenbleiben, stocken, sich verfangen, sich festhaken; 3. (*sl.*) per Anhalter fahren. **hitch|-hike,** *v.i.* per Anhalter fahren. **--hiker,** *s.* (*coll.*) der Anhalter.

hither ['hiðə], **1** *adv.* hierher; ***– and thither,*** hin und her, auf und ab. **2.** *adj.* diesseitig. **hitherto,** *adv.* bisher, bis jetzt. **hitherward** [–wəd], *adv.* (*obs.*) *see* **hither.**

hit|-or-miss, *adj. See* **--and-miss. – parade,** *s.* die Hitparade. **– record, – song,** *s.* der Hit, (Spitzen)schlager.

Hittite ['hitait], **1.** *s.* (*B.*) der (die) Hethiter(in). **2.** *adj.* hethitisch.

hive [haiv], **1.** *s.* der Bienenkorb, Bienenstock; (*fig.*) Sammelpunkt, Brennpunkt; ***– of bees,*** das Bienenvolk, der Bienenschwarm. **2.** *v.t.* 1. in den Stock tun *or* bringen; 2. (*Comm.*) ***– off,*** abtreten (*contracts etc.*). **3.** *v.i.* in den Stock fliegen; (*fig.*) zusammenwohnen, hausen (***with,*** mit).

hives [haivz], *pl.* der Nesselausschlag; die Halsbräune.

ho! [hou], *int.* ho! holla! ***– there!*** holla! wer da?

hoar [hɔ:], *adj.* (*Poet.*) weiß(grau); grau bereift; (*fig.*) altersgrau, ehrwürdig.

hoard [hɔ:d], **1.** *s.* der Vorrat, Schatz, Hort. **2.** *v.t.* (*also* ***– up***) anhäufen, aufhäufen, sammeln; hamstern, horten, sparen, zurücklegen. **3.** *v.i.* Vorräte sammeln, hamstern.

[1]**hoarding** ['hɔ:diŋ], *s.* das Anhäufen, Sammeln, Hamstern.

[2]**hoarding,** *s.* der Bauzaun, Bretterzaun; die Reklamewand, Litfaßsäule.

hoar-frost, *s.* der (Rauh)reif. **hoariness,** *s.* das Weißgrau; (*fig.*) die Ehrwürdigkeit.

hoarse [hɔ:s], *adj.* heiser, rauh; krächzend. **hoarseness,** *s.* die Heiserkeit.

hoary ['hɔ:ri], *adj. See* **hoar**; grauhaarig, ergraut.

hoax [houks], **1.** *s.* die Täuschung, der Schwindel, Schabernack; die Flunkerei, Fopperei; (Zeitungs)ente. **2.** *v.t.* zum besten haben, zum Narren halten, foppen, anführen, einen Bären aufbinden (*Dat.*).

hob [hɔb], *s.* 1. der Kaminabsatz; 2. die Nabe (*of wheel*); der Pflock (*as target*).

hobble [hɔbl], **1.** *v.i.* humpeln; hinken. **2.** *v.t.* fesseln (*a horse*). **3.** *s.* 1. das Hinken, Humpeln; 2. die Verlegenheit, Patsche.

hobbledehoy ['hɔbldihɔi], *s.* der Taps, Schlaks, linkischer Bursche.

hobble-skirt, *s.* enger Rock, der Humpelrock.

hobby ['hɔbi], *s.* (*fig.*) das Steckenpferd, die Liebhaberei. **hobby-horse,** *s.* 1. das Steckenpferd, Schaukelpferd; 2. (*fig.*) *see* **hobby.**

hobgoblin [hɔb'gɔblin], *s.* der Kobold; Popanz, das Schreckgespenst.

hobnail ['hɔbneil], *s.* (grober) Schuhnagel, der Hufnagel. **hobnailed,** *adj.* mit groben Nägeln beschlagen, genagelt.

hobnob [hɔb'nɔb], *v.i.* (*coll.*) zusammen kneipen; vertraulich plaudern, intim sein, verkehren.

hobo ['houbou], *s.* (*Am. sl.*) der Landstreicher.

[1]**hock** [hɔk], **1.** *s.* das Sprunggelenk, die Hachse. **2.** *v.t.* die KniefIechsen zerschneiden (*Dat.*).

[2]**hock,** *s.* der Rheinwein.

[3]**hock, 1.** *s.* (*sl.*) das Pfand; ***in –,*** verpfändet (*of a th.*), im Kittchen (*of a p.*). **2.** *v.t.* (*sl.*) verpfänden.

hockey ['hɔki], *s.* das Hockey(spiel).

hocus ['houkəs], *v.t.* betrügen, täuschen; betäuben, berauschen (*a p.*); fälschen, mischen (*wine etc.*). **hocuspocus** [–'poukəs], *s.* der Hokuspokus, Schwindel, Betrug, die Gaukelei.

hod [hɔd], *s.* 1. die Tragmulde, der Mörteltrog, das Steinbrett; 2. der Kohleneimer.

hodge-podge ['hɔdʒpɔdʒ], *s. See* **hotchpotch.**

hodiernal [hɔdi'ə:nl], *adj.* heutig, gegenwärtig.

hodman ['hɔdmən], *s.* der Mörtelträger, Ziegelträger; (*fig.*) Tagelöhner, Handlanger.

hodometer [hɔ'dɔmitə], *s.* der Schrittzähler, Wegmesser.

hoe [hou], **1.** *s.* die Hacke. **2.** *v.t.* hacken, aufbrechen, lockern (*ground*), behacken, jäten (*weeds*).

hog [hɔg], **1.** *s.* 1. das (Schlacht)schwein; der Keiler; 2. (*Tech.*) die Rührschaufel; 3. (*Naut.*) Aufbucht; 4. (*fig.*) Sau, der Schweinehund; Schmutzfink, das Ferkel; (*sl.*) ***go the whole –,*** seine S. gründlich machen, alles daransetzen, reinen Tisch machen, aufs Ganze gehen. **2.** *v.t.* 1. stutzen (*mane*); 2. (*sl.*) an sich reißen, erraffen, wegschnappen; 3. (*Naut.*) ***– down,*** fieren.

hogback ['hɔgbæk], *s.* (langer) Gebirgskamm. **hog-**

get [-it], *s.* einjähriges Schaf. **hoggish,** *adj.* (*fig.*) schweinisch, saugrob, säuisch, gemein, gefräßig. **hoggishness,** *s.* die Schweinerei; Gefräßigkeit.

hogmanay ['hɔgmənei], *s.* (*Scots*) das *or* der Silvester.

hog-mane, *s.* gestutzte Mähne. **hog's-back,** *s. See* **hogback. hogshead,** *s.* das Oxhoft (*etwa 240 Liter*); großes Faß. **hog|-tie,** *v.t.* fesseln, binden. **-wash,** *s.* das Spülwasser; (*vulg.*) der Saufraß; das Gewäsch.

hoi(c)k [hɔik], *v.t.* (*Av.*) ruckweise hochziehen.

hoist [hɔist], **1.** *v.t.* 1. hochwinden, hochziehen; 2. (*Naut.*) heißen, hissen; – ***out a boat,*** ein Boot aussetzen. **2.** *p.p.* (*obs.*) – ***with one's own petard,*** in seiner eigenen Falle gefangen, den eigenen Ränken zum Opfer gefallen. **3.** *s.* 1. (*Tech.*) der Aufzug, die Winde, das Hebezeug; 2. (*Naut.*) der Heiß (*of sail*), die Tiefe (*of flag*). **hoisting-engine,** *s.* das Hebewerk; (*Min.*) die Fördermaschine.

hoity-toity ['hɔiti'tɔiti], **1.** *adj.* hochmütig, hochnäsig; übermütig, mutwillig, auslassen. **2.** *int.* potztausend!

hokey-pokey ['houki'pouki], *s.* (*coll.*) das Speiseeis.

hokum ['houkəm], *s.* (*coll.*) der Schwindel, die Übertreibung, der Unsinn, leeres Geschwätz; (*Theat.*) kitschige Aufmachung, das Theatermätzchen.

hold [hould], **1.** *irr.v.t.* 1. halten, festhalten; gefangenhalten (*a p.*); 2. behalten, behaupten (*a position*) (*also Mil.*); 3. enthalten, fassen (*as a container*); 4. anhalten, aufhalten; zurückhalten, abhalten; aufrechterhalten, beibehalten; 5. (*fig.*) haben, vertreten, behaupten (*opinions etc.*), der Meinung sein (daß), betrachten (als), halten (für), (*Law*) dafürhalten, entscheiden; 6. besitzen, in Besitz haben, (*an office*) innehaben, bekleiden.
(a) (*with nouns*) – ***the audience,*** die Zuhörer in Spannung halten; (*sl.*) ***be left -ing the baby,*** den Kopf hinhalten (müssen); – ***one's breath,*** den Atem anhalten; – ***a brief for,*** eintreten für; (*coll.*) – ***a candle to him,*** sich mit ihm messen, mit ihm einen Vergleich aushalten; – ***a conversation,*** eine Unterredung führen; – ***counsel,*** sich beraten; (*Naut.*) – ***a course,*** einen Kurs beibehalten; – ***the floor,*** see – ***the stage;*** – ***one's ground,*** see – ***one's own;*** (*fig.*) – ***one's hand,*** sich zurückhalten; – ***one's head high,*** stolz auftreten; (*sl.*) – ***your horses!*** keine Übereilung! sachte! (*coll.*) – ***the line,*** am Apparat bleiben; (*Comm.*) – ***the market,*** den Markt beherrschen; – ***a meeting,*** eine Versammlung abhalten; – ***one's own,*** sich behaupten, standhalten; – ***one's peace,*** den Mund halten; – ***shares,*** Aktien besitzen; – ***the stage,*** im Mittelpunkt stehen; – ***one's stomach in,*** den Bauch einziehen; – ***sway,*** herrschen, vorherrschen; – ***one's tongue,*** see – ***one's peace;*** (*coll.*) – ***your tongue!*** halt's Maul! – ***water,*** wasserdicht sein; (*fig.*) stichhalten, stichhaltig sein.
(b) (*with adjs. or advs.*) – (***o.s.***) ***aloof,*** sich abseits halten; – ***back,*** zurückhalten; verschweigen (*the truth*); – ***cheap,*** gering achten; – ***dear,*** liebhaben; – ***down,*** niederhalten, unterdrücken; (*coll.*) behalten, sich halten in (*Dat.*) (*a job*); – ***o.s. erect,*** sich gerade halten; – ***forth,*** bieten, in Aussicht stellen (*hopes*); – ***in,*** zurückhalten, im Zaum halten; – ***o.s. in,*** sich beherrschen; den Bauch einziehen; – ***off,*** fernhalten, abhalten, abwehren; – ***out,*** ausstrecken, hinhalten, bieten (*hands etc.*); machen (*offer*); gewähren (*hope*); geben (*promise*); – ***out prospects of,*** in Aussicht stellen; – ***over,*** verschieben, aufschieben; – ***him responsible,*** ihn als verantwortlich betrachten; – ***tight!*** Achtung! fest anhalten! – ***up,*** (her)zeigen; hochhalten, aufrecht halten, stützen; (*fig.*) hinstellen; (*coll.*) überfallen (und ausrauben); (*coll.*) aufhalten, hindern; – ***up to derision,*** dem Spott preisgeben *or* aussetzen; – ***up as an example,*** als Beispiel hinstellen; – ***up one's hand,*** sich melden (*at school*); – ***up one's hands,*** die Hände hochheben, sich ergeben; – ***up one's head,*** den Kopf hochhalten; – ***up the traffic,*** den Verkehr behindern.
(c) (*with preps.*) – ***in check,*** in Schach halten; – ***in contempt,*** verachten; – ***in esteem,*** wertschätzen, achten; – ***o.s. in readiness,*** sich bereit halten; – ***in suspense,*** im Zweifel lassen; – ***of no*** or ***little account,*** geringschätzen; – ***him to his promise*** or ***word,*** ihn beim Wort halten; – ***to ransom,*** gegen Lösegeld festhalten.
2. *irr.v.i.* halten, festhalten; (*Tech.*) angreifen, fassen (*as a wheel*), binden, halten (*as gum*); aushalten, standhalten, sich halten; andauern, fortdauern; (*fig.*) gültig sein; gelten, sich bewähren; – ***back,*** sich zurückhalten (***from doing,*** zu tun); – ***forth,*** sich ergehen, eine Rede schwingen (*on,* über (*Acc.*)); – ***good,*** gelten (*of,* von); gültig *or* in Kraft bleiben, sich bestätigen *or* bewähren; (*sl.*) – ***hard!*** halt! warte mal! – ***off,*** sich zurückhalten *or* fernhalten (***from doing,*** zu tun); ausbleiben; – ***on,*** (sich) festhalten; (*fig.*) durchhalten, aushalten, weitermachen; (*coll.*) am Apparat bleiben; (*sl.*) wärte! hör auf! – ***out,*** aushalten, durchhalten, sich behaupten (***against,*** gegen); (*coll.*) – ***out for,*** bestehen auf (*Dat.*); (*sl.*) – ***out on him,*** ihm etwas vorenthalten *or* verheimlichen; – ***together,*** zusammenhalten; – ***true,*** see – ***good;*** – ***up,*** stehenbleiben; sich aufrecht halten; – ***with,*** übereinstimmen mit; einverstanden sein mit, billigen (*views*).
3. *s.* 1. der Halt, Griff; (*fig.*) die Macht, Gewalt (***on, over,*** über (*Acc.*)), der Einfluß (auf (*Acc.*)); ***catch*** or ***lay*** or ***seize*** or ***take – of,*** ergreifen, (er)fassen; ***get – of,*** erwischen, kommen zu; ***get a – on him,*** ihn unter seinen Einfluß bekommen; ***have – of,*** in Händen haben; (*fig.*) ***have a firm – of*** or ***on,*** beherrschen, meistern; ***keep – of,*** festhalten; ***let go one's –,*** loslassen, fahren lassen; ***take a strong – on,*** beeindrucken, Eindruck machen auf (*Acc.*); 2. (*Naut.*) der Schiffsraum, Frachtraum, Laderaum; 3. (*obs.*) die Haft, der Gewahrsam; 4. (*obs.*) befestigter Platz; das Lager, Versteck (*of a beast*); 5. (*Mus.*) Aushaltezeichen, die Fermate.

hold|-all, *s.* der Behälter, das Necessaire. **--back,** *s.* das Hindernis. **holder,** *s.* 1. (*a p.*) Haltende(r); der Inhaber, Besitzer, (*of lease*) Pächter, (*Spt.*) Träger; 2. (*a th.*) Halter, Griff (*of pen etc.*), die Fassung (*of lamp*); der Behälter; ***cigarette –,*** die Zigarettenspitze. **holdfast,** *s.* die Klammer, Zwinge, Spannkluppe, der Kloben, Klemmhaken, Klemmbock; (*fig.*) (fester) Halt, die Stütze. **holding, 1.** *adj.* (*Mil.*) – ***attack,*** der Fesselungsangriff; – ***capacity,*** das Fassungsvermögen; (*Comm.*) – ***company,*** die Dachgesellschaft; (*Naut.*) – ***ground,*** der Ankergrund. **2.** *s.* 1. das (Fest)halten; Abhalten, die Abhaltung; 2. das Pachtgut, der Grundbesitz, das Guthaben; 3. *pl.* (*Comm.*) der Bestand, Besitz, Anteil. **hold|-over,** *s.* der Rest, das Überbleibsel. **--up,** *s.* 1. (*coll.*) (räuberischer) Überfall; 2. die Störung, Stockung; ***traffic –,*** die Verkehrsstockung, Verkehrsstauung.

hole [houl], **1.** *s.* das Loch, die Öffnung; Höhle, der Bau (*of animals*); (*sl.*) die Klemme, Patsche; ***full of –s,*** durchlöchert; (*coll.*) ***pick –s in,*** bekritteln, zerpflücken. **2.** *v.t.* 1. durchlöchern; 2. (*Spt.*) ins Loch spielen, einlochen (*ball*). **3.** *v.i.* in die Höhle gehen (*of animals*). **hole|-and-corner,** *adj.* (*coll.*) heimlich, versteckt, unter der Hand; zweifelhaft, anrüchig; – ***business,*** zweifelhaftes *or* anrüchiges Geschäft, das Winkelgeschäft; die Quetsche; ***do in a – way,*** unter der Hand *or* hintenherum tun. **--board,** *s.* (*Weav.*) das Lesebrett. **--gauge,** *s.* die Lochlehre.

holiday ['hɔlidei], *s.* der Feiertag; freier Tag, der Ruhetag; *pl.* Ferien (*pl.*), der Urlaub; ***half –,*** freier Nachmittag; ***be on –,*** in den Ferien sein, Ferien haben; ***go on –*** or ***on one's –s,*** in die Ferien gehen; ***we have a – today,*** wir haben heute frei; – ***course,*** der Ferienkurs. **holidaymaker,** *s.* der Sommerfrischler, Ferienreisende(r).

holiness ['houlinəs], *s.* die Heiligkeit (*also title*).

holla ['hɔlə], **1.** *s.* der Halloruf. **2.** *v.i.* hallo rufen. **3.** *v.t.* laut (aus)rufen.

Holland ['hɔlənd], *s.* Niederlande (*pl.*), Holland (*n.*).

holland, *s.* ungebleichte Leinwand.

hollands [ˈhɔləndz], *s.* der Wacholderschnaps.

holler [ˈhɔlə], *v.i., v.t.* (*sl.*) schreien, brüllen. **hollo,** *see* **holla.**

hollow [ˈhɔlou], **1.** *adj.* 1. hohl, Hohl–; tiefliegend (*eyes*), eingefallen (*cheeks*); 2. dumpf (*sound*); 3. (*fig.*) hohl, leer, nichtssagend, wertlos, gehaltlos. **2.** *adv.* (*coll.*) *beat –*, glatt aus dem Felde schlagen. **3.** *s.* die Vertiefung, Einsenkung, Mulde, Grube, das Tal, der Hohlweg; das Loch, die Höhle, der Hohlraum, die (Aus)höhlung; (*Tech.*) Nut, Rinne, Hohlkehle; *– of the hand,* die hohle Hand; (*fig.*) *have in the – of one's hand,* völlig in seiner Gewalt haben; *– of the knee,* die Kniekehle. **4.** *v.t.* (*– out*) hohl machen, aushöhlen; auskehlen.

hollow|-cheeked, *adj.* hohlwangig. **–-eyed,** *adj.* hohläugig. **–-ground,** *adj.* hohlgeschliffen. **hollowness,** *s.* die Hohlheit; Dumpfheit (*of sound*); (*fig.*) Leerheit, Wertlosigkeit; Unredlichkeit, Falschheit. **hollow-ware,** *s.* Hohlwaren (*pl.*), das Kochgeschirr.

holly [ˈhɔli], *s.* (*Bot.*) die Stechpalme; *– oak, see* **holm-oak.**

hollyhock [ˈhɔlihɔk], *s.* (*Bot.*) die Stockrose.

holm [houm], *s.* der Werder, flaches Uferland. **holm-oak,** *s.* (*Bot.*) immergrüne Eiche, Steineiche (*Quercus ilex*).

holocaust [ˈhɔləkɔ:st], *s.* das Brandopfer; (*fig.*) verheerende Katastrophe, der Massenmord.

holograph [ˈhɔləgrɑ:f], *adj.* (*s.*) eigenhändig geschrieben(e Urkunde).

holster [ˈhoulstə], *s.* die Pistolenhalfter.

holt [hoult], *s.* 1. der Otterbau; 2. (*Poet.*) das Gehölz, der Hain.

holus-bolus [ˈhouləsˈbouləs], *adv.* im ganzen, alles auf einmal.

holy [ˈhouli], *adj.* heilig; *Holy Bible,* die Heilige Schrift; *– day,* kirchlicher Festtag; *Holy Father,* der Papst; *Holy Ghost,* Heiliger Geist; *Holy of Holies,* das Allerheiligste; (*sl.*) *– Joe,* der Pfaffe; *Holy Land,* das Heilige Land; *Holy Office,* die Inquisition; *– orders,* geistlicher Stand, das Priesteramt; *take – orders,* Geistlicher werden; *Holy Spirit,* see *Holy Ghost*; *Holy Roman Empire,* Heiliges Römisches Reich (Deutscher Nation); (*coll.*) *– terror,* der Quälgeist; *Holy Thursday,* der Himmelfahrtstag; (*R.C.*) Gründonnerstag; *– water,* das Weihwasser; *Holy Week,* die Karwoche, Passionswoche; *Holy Writ,* Heilige Schrift.

holystone [ˈhoulistoun], **1.** *s.* der Scheuerstein. **2.** *v.t.* (*Naut.*) scheuern, schrubben.

homage [ˈhɔmidʒ], *s.* die Huldigung; (*Hist.*) Lehenspflicht; *do* or *pay* or *render –,* huldigen (*to, Dat.*).

home [houm], **1.** *s.* 1. die Heimat; der Wohnort, Heimat(s)ort, das Zuhause; (Eltern)haus, Heim, die Wohnung; (*fig.*) Familie, der Familienkreis, Hausstand; *at –,* zu Hause, daheim; in der Heimat, im Lande; der Empfangstag; (*fig.*) in seinem Element, ungezwungen; *be at –,* zu sprechen sein; Empfangstag haben; (*fig.*) *be at – in,* vertraut sein mit, bewandert sein in; *make o.s. at –,* tun als ob man zu Hause wäre, es sich (*Dat.*) bequem machen; *at – to no one,* für niemand zu sprechen; *away from –, not at –,* nicht zu Hause, abwesend, verreist; *– is –, there is no place like –,* eigner Herd ist Goldes wert; 2. das Heim, Asyl, die Anstalt, Pflegestätte (*for sick, aged etc.*); *– for girls,* das Mädchenheim; 3. das Ziel, Mal (*in games*).

2. *adj.* 1. häuslich; inländisch, (ein)heimisch, inner, Inlands–, Innen–; *– affairs,* innere Angelegenheiten, die Innenpolitik; *– circle,* der Familienkreis; *– comforts,* häusliche Gemütlichkeit; *– consumption,* einheimischer Verbrauch; *– counties,* die Gegend um London; *– defence,* die Bürgerwehr; *– farm,* die Hauptfarm; *– game,* das Heimatspiel; *– guard,* see *– defence*; *– gymnastics,* die Zimmergymnastik; *– journey,* die Rückreise, Rückfahrt, Heimreise; *– market,* der Inlandsmarkt, Binnenmarkt; *– mission,* innere Mission; *Home Office,* das Ministerium des Innern; *– port,* der Heimathafen, Einsatzhafen; *– rule,* die Selbstregierung, Autonomie; *Home Secretary,* der Innenminister, Minister des Innern; (*Railw.*) *– signal,* das Einfahrt(s)signal; (*Spt.*) *– stretch,* die Zielstrecke; *– thrust,* treffender Hieb, der Treffer; *– town,* die Heimatstadt; *– trade,* der Binnenhandel; 2. (*fig.*) derb, treffend; *– truth,* ungeschminkte Wahrheit, die Binsenwahrheit.

3. *adv.* heim, nach Hause; daheim, zu Hause; (*fig.*) am Ziel; nachdrücklich; *be – soon,* bald zu Hause sein; (*fig.*) *bring s.th. – to him,* ihm etwas klarmachen *or* zu Gemüte führen; (*fig.*) *come – to him,* ihn treffen *or* nahe berühren, ihm nahegehen *or* klarwerden; *drive a nail –,* einen Nagel fest einschlagen; *drive a th. – to him,* ihm etwas nachdrücklich *or* gründlich einprägen; *go –,* nach Hause gehen, (*fig.*) seine Wirkung tun; *the thrust has gone –,* der Hieb hat gesessen; *press – an attack,* einen Angriff wirkungsvoll vortragen; *press – one's point,* seinen Standpunkt durchsetzen; *push the bolt –,* den Riegel vorschieben; *return –,* nach Hause zurückkehren; *see him –,* ihn nach Hause begleiten; *strike –,* Eindruck machen, wirken, seine Wirkung tun; ins Ziel treffen, sitzen; *welcome –!* willkommen zu Hause! (*sl.*) *nothing to write – about,* nichts Aufregendes *or* Besonderes.

4. *v.i.* (*Av.*) sich einpeilen, (automatisch) zusteuern (*on to,* auf (*Acc.*)).

home|-baked, *adj.* hausbacken. **–bound,** *adj.* auf der Heimreise (befindlich). **–-brewed,** *adj.* selbstgebraut. **–-coming,** *s.* die Heimkehr. **–felt,** *adj.* tiefempfunden. **–land,** *s.* die Heimat, das Heimatland, Vaterland. **homeless,** *adj.* heimatlos; obdachlos. **homelike,** *adj.* behaglich, heimisch, anheimelnd.

homeliness [ˈhoumlinis], *s.* 1. die Häuslichkeit, Gemütlichkeit; Einfachheit, Schlichtheit; 2. (*Am.*) Reizlosigkeit, Unschönheit. **homely,** *adj.* 1. heimisch, behaglich, gemütlich, anheimelnd, einfach, schlicht; *– cooking,* die Hausmannskost; 2. (*Am.*) reizlos, unschön, unansehnlich, nicht hübsch.

home|-made, *adj.* selbstgemacht, hausgemacht; inländisch; *– bread,* hausbackenes Brot. **–sick,** *adj.* heimwehkrank; *he is –,* er hat Heimweh. **–sickness,** *s.* das Heimweh. **–spun, 1.** *adj.* zu Hause gesponnen; (*fig.*) einfach, schlicht. **2.** *s.* grober Wollstoff. **–stead,** *s.* das Gehöft; Eigenheim mit Garten; (*Am.*) die Heimstätte.

homeward [ˈhoumwəd], **1.** *adv.* heimwärts, nach Hause; (*Naut.*) *– bound,* auf der Rückreise (begriffen). **2.** *adj.* heimwärts gerichtet, Heim–; *– journey,* die Heimreise. **homewards,** *adv.* *See* **homeward, 1.**

home-work, *s.* die Heimarbeit; (*school*) Hausaufgabe, Hausarbeit.

homicidal [hɔmiˈsaidl], *adj.* mörderisch. **homicide** [ˈhɔmisaid], *s.* 1. der Totschlag, Mord, (*Law*) die Tötung; *– squad,* die Mordkommission; 2. (*a p.*) der Mörder.

homiletic [hɔmiˈletik], *adj.* homiletisch. **homiletics,** *pl.* die Kanzelberedsamkeit, Homiletik.

homily [ˈhɔmili], *s.* die Homilie, Predigt; (*fig.*) Moralpredigt.

homing [ˈhoumiŋ], **1.** *adj.* heimkehrend; (*Av.*) *– device,* das Zielfluggerät; *– instinct,* das Heimkehrvermögen; *– loft,* der Heimatschlag; *– pigeon,* die Brieftaube. **2.** *s.* der Rückflug (*of pigeons*); (*Av.*) Zielflug, die Zielpeilung.

hominy [ˈhɔmini], *s.* (*Am.*) das Maismehl; der Maisbrei.

homoeopath [ˈhoumiopæθ], *s.* der Homöopath. **homoeopathic** [–ˈpæθik], *adj.* homöopathisch.

homogeneity [hɔmodʒiˈni:iti], *s.* die Gleichartigkeit, Gleichförmigkeit, Einheitlichkeit. **homogeneous** [–ˈdʒi:niəs], *adj.* gleichartig, gleichförmig, einheitlich, homogen. **homogenesis** [–ˈdʒenisis], *s.* (*Biol.*) die Homogenese. **homogenize** [həˈmɔdʒənaiz], *v.t.* homogenisieren. **homogenous** [həˈmɔdʒinəs], *adj.* (*Bot.*) homostyl.

homologous [həˈmɔləgəs], *adj.* homolog, (*Math.*) übereinstimmend, (*Biol.*) (morphologisch) gleichwertig, (*Chem.*) (strukturell) ähnlich, (*Gram.*)

gleichnamig, gleichlautend. **homologue** ['hɔmə-lɔg], *s.* das Homolog. **homology** [hə'mɔlədʒi], *s.* die Übereinstimmung, Gleichwertigkeit, (strukturelle) Ähnlichkeit. **homomorphic** [–'mɔ:fik], *adj.* gleichgestaltig.

homonym ['hɔmənim], *s.* das Homonym, gleichlautendes Wort. **homonymous** [hə'mɔniməs], *adj.* homonym, gleichlautend. **homoptera** [hə-'mɔptərə], *pl.* (*Ent.*) Gleichflügler (*pl.*). **homosexual** [–'seksjuəl], **1.** *adj.* homosexuell. **2.** *s.* Homosexuelle(r).

homunculus [ho'mʌŋkjuləs], *s.* der Homunkulus; das Menschlein; der Zwerg, Knirps.

hone [houn], **1.** *s.* der Schleifstein, Wetzstein, Abziehstein. **2.** *v.t.* abziehen, schärfen (*razors*).

honest ['ɔnist], *adj.* redlich, ehrlich, rechtschaffen, aufrichtig; (*obs.*) ehrbar, sittsam, tugendhaft; echt; ***earn*** or ***turn an – penny,*** sich ehrlich durchschlagen; ***make an – woman of her,*** sie zur ehrbaren Frau machen. **honest|-to-God, --to-goodness,** *adj.* (*coll.*) echt, wirklich, bieder. **honesty,** *s.* 1. die Ehrlichkeit, Redlichkeit, Aufrichtigkeit, Rechtschaffenheit; (*Prov.*) – ***is the best policy,*** ehrlich währt am längsten; 2. (*Bot.*) Mondviole.

honey ['hʌni], *s.* 1. der Honig; 2. (*fig.*) die Süßigkeit, Lieblichkeit; 3. (*coll.*) das Herzchen, der Schatz, Liebling. **honey|-bag,** *s.* der Honigmagen, die Honigblase. **--bear,** *s.* der Wickelbär. **--bee,** *s.* die Honigbiene. **--buzzard,** *s.* (*Orn.*) der Wespenbussard (*Pernis apivorus*). **–comb, 1.** *s.* die (Honig)wabe, Honigscheibe; (*fig.*) das Waffelmuster; (*Elec.*) – ***coil,*** die Wabenwicklung. **2.** *v.t.* (wabenartig) durchlöchern. **–combed,** *adj.* zellig; löcherig; durchlöchert. **–dew,** *s.* der Honigtau, Blatthonig; süßlicher Tabak. **honeyed** [–d], *adj.* honigsüß (*usu. fig.*). **honey|moon, 1.** *s.* Flitterwochen (*pl.*), die Hochzeitsreise. **2.** *v.i.* die Flitterwochen verbringen. **–mooner,** *s.* Hochzeitsreisende(r). **--sac,** *s. See* **--bag. –suckle,** *s.* (*Bot.*) das Geißblatt.

honied, *adj. See* **honeyed.**

honk [hɔŋk], **1.** *s.* der Schrei der Wildgans. **2.** *v.t.* schreien (*of geese*); (*Motor. coll.*) hupen.

honky-tonk ['hɔŋkitɔŋk], *s.* (*sl.*) die Spelunke.

honor, (*Am.*) *see* **honour.**

honorarium [ɔnə'rɛəriəm], *s.* (*pl.* **-ia** *or* **-s**) das Ehrengehalt, Honorar.

honorary ['ɔnərəri], *adj.* ehrend; Ehren–, ehrenamtlich; (*Univ.*) – ***degree,*** der Ehrengrad; – ***member,*** das Ehrenmitglied; – ***post,*** das Ehrenamt; – ***secretary,*** ehrenamtlicher Schriftführer.

honorific [ɔnə'rifik], **1.** *adj.* ehrend, Ehren–. **2.** *s.* der Titel, ehrendes Wort.

honour ['ɔnə], **1.** *s.* 1. die Ehre; ***affair of –,*** der Ehrenhandel, die Ehrensache; ***code of –,*** der Ehrenkodex; ***court of –,*** das Ehrengericht; ***maid of –,*** die Ehrendame, Hofdame; (*esp. Am.*) Brautjungfer; ***man of –,*** der Ehrenmann; ***point of –,*** die Ehrensache; ***word of –,*** das Ehrenwort; ***do – to him,*** ihm zur Ehre gereichen; ***have the – to inform,*** die Ehre haben *or* sich beehren mitzuteilen; ***an – to his profession,*** eine Zierde seines Berufs; ***there is – among thieves,*** eine Krähe hackt der andern die Augen nicht aus; – ***to whom – is due,*** Ehre, wem Ehre gebührt; ***in his –,*** ihm zu Ehren; ***in – bound,*** moralisch verpflichtet; (***up***)***on my –!*** auf mein (Ehren)wort! bei meiner Ehre! ***put him on his –,*** ihn an der Ehre packen; ***to his –,*** see ***in his –***; ***be on one's –,*** moralisch verpflichtet sein; ***with –,*** glorreich, ehrenvoll; 2. die Verehrung, Hochachtung, Ehrerbietung, Ehrenbezeigung, Ehrenerweisung, Ehrung, Auszeichnung; 3. das Ansehen, guter Ruf *or* Namen; 4. das Ehrgefühl; ***sense of –,*** das Ehrgefühl; 5. (Euer *or* Ew.) Ehrwürden *or* Gnaden (*in titles*); 6. *pl.* (*Univ.*) das Studium *or* die Prüfung höherer Ordnung; ***–s degree,*** (akademischer) Grad höherer Ordnung (in einem Spezialfach); 7. *pl.* (*Cards*) Honneurs (*pl.*); ***–s are easy,*** die Honneurs (*or fig.*) Vorteile sind gleich verteilt; ***do the –s,*** die Honneurs machen. **2.** *v.t.* 1. Ehre erweisen (*Dat.*), (ver)ehren, in Ehren halten; beehren (***with,*** mit); ehren, auszeichnen, verherrlichen; 2. (*Comm.*) honorieren, akzeptieren, einlösen (*a cheque etc.*).

honourable ['ɔnərəbl], *adj.* ehrenvoll, achtbar, rühmlich; ehrenhaft, ehrlich, redlich; ehrenwert (*in titles*); (*Mil.*) – ***discharge,*** ehrenvoller Abschied; (*Parl.*) ***the – gentleman, my – friend,*** der Herr Vorredner; ***Right Honourable,*** Hochwohlgeboren (*title*).

hooch [hu:tʃ], *s.* (*sl.*) (illegaler) Schnaps, der Fusel.

hood [hud], **1.** *s.* die Haube, Schutzhaube (*also Motor.*); Kapuze, Kappe; (*Motor.*) das Verdeck, die Plane; (*Univ.*) der Überwurf. **2.** *v.t.* mit einer Kappe *or* Haube *etc.* bedecken. **hooded,** *adj.* mit einer Kappe, (*fig.*) verhüllt; (*Orn.*) – ***crow,*** die Nebelkrähe (*Corvus cornix*).

hoodlum ['hu:dləm], *s.* (*sl.*) der Strolch, Rowdy, Gangster.

hoodoo ['hu:du:], *s.* (*coll.*) der Unheilbringer; das Pech, Mißgeschick.

hoodwink ['hudwiŋk], *v.t.* die Augen verbinden (*Dat.*); (*usu. fig.*) täuschen, blenden, hintergehen.

hooey ['hu:i], *s.* (*sl.*) der Quatsch.

hoof [hu:f], **1.** *s.* (*pl.* **hooves** [hu:vz]) der Huf, die Klaue, Schale (*of deer*); (*sl.*) der Fuß; ***on the –,*** lebend (*of cattle*). **2.** *v.t.* (*sl.*) – ***it,*** zu Fuß gehen; (*sl.*) – ***out,*** hinausschmeißen. **hoofed** [–t], *adj.* behuft; – ***animal,*** das Huftier.

hoo-ha ['hu:hɑ:], *s.* (*sl.*) der Tamtam, das Getue.

hook [huk], **1.** *s.* 1. der Haken, die Klammer; der Widerhaken; ***crochet –,*** die Häkelnadel; ***fish –,*** der Angelhaken; ***grappling –,*** der Staken; ***picture –,*** der Bilderhaken; ***reaping –,*** die Sichel; ***–s and eyes,*** Haken und Ösen; (*coll.*) ***by – or by crook,*** auf Biegen oder Brechen, gleichgültig wie, so oder so; (*sl.*) ***on one's own –,*** auf eigene Faust; (*coll.*) ***off the –,*** von der Stange (*clothes*); nicht eingehängt (*phone*); (*sl.*) ***go off the –s,*** verrückt werden, überschnappen; (*sl.*) ***sling*** or ***take one's –,*** sich aus dem Staube machen, durchbrennen, türmen; (*coll.*) –, ***line and sinker,*** Stumpf und Stiel, mit Leib und Seele; 2. (*Mus.*) (Noten)schwanz, das Fähnchen; 3. (*Boxing*) der Haken, Seitenschlag. **2.** *v.t.* 1. zuhaken (*dress etc.*), einhaken, festhaken; angeln, fangen (*fish, also fig.*); (*sl.*) klauen, mausen, stibitzen; 2. (*Spt.*) von der Außenseite schlagen (*ball*), (*Boxing*) einen Haken versetzen (*Dat.*), in die Seite schlagen; 3. (*sl.*) – ***it,*** abhauen, türmen. **3.** *v.i.* (– ***on***) sich einhaken *or* festhaken; (*sl.*) – ***up,*** heiraten.

hookah ['hukə], *s.* die Huka.

hooked [hukt], *adj.* krumm, gekrümmt, hakenförmig. **hooker,** *s.* 1. (*Naut.*) der Huker, (*coll.*) alter Kahn; 2. (*Rugby footb.*) (ein) Stürmer der vorderen Reihe. **hook|nose,** *s.* die Hakennase. **--up,** *s.* (*coll.*) der Anschluß, die Anordnung, Schaltung, (*Rad.*) Zusammenschaltung, Ringsendung; (*fig.*) das Übereinkommen, der Zusammenschluß.

hooky ['huki], *s.* (*sl.*) (*only in*) ***play –,*** schwänzen.

hooligan ['hu:ligən], *s.* der (Straßen)lümmel, Radaubruder, Rowdy. **hooliganism,** *s.* das Rowdytum.

[1]**hoop** [hu:p], **1.** *s.* der Reifen, Ring, das Band; der Reif (*of dress*); **--iron,** das Bandeisen. **2.** *v.t.* abbinden, mit Reifen belegen (*a cask*).

[2]**hoop,** *see* **whoop.**

hooped [hu:pt], *adj.* gereift; – ***petticoat,*** der Reifrock.

[1]**hooper** ['hu:pə], *s.* der Böttcher, Küfer, Faßbinder.

[2]**hooper,** *s. See* **whooper.**

hoopla ['hu:plɑ:], *s.* das Ringwerfen.

hoopoe ['hu:pu:], *s.* (*Orn.*) der Wiedehopf (*Upupa epops*).

hooray [hu'rei], *see* **hurrah.**

hoot [hu:t], **1.** *v.i.* schreien (*also of owls*), heulen, johlen; (*coll.*) sich vor Lachen (fast) platzen; (*Motor.*) tuten, hupen; – ***at,*** auspfeifen, auszischen (*a p.*), auslachen, verspotten (*ideas etc.*). **2.** *s.* das Geschrei, Geheul; (*Motor.*) Tuten, Hupen;

I don't care a* – or *two –s, mir ist es völlig schnuppe *or* piepe, ich mache mir nicht die Bohne daraus. **hooter,** *s.* die Sirene, Dampfpfeife, (*Motor.*) Hupe. **hoots!** *int.* (*Scots*) ach was!

Hoover ['hu:və], (*reg. trade mark*) **1.** *s.* der Staubsauger. **2.** *v.t., v.i.* absaugen, mit den Staubsauger reinigen.

hooves [hu:vz], *pl. of* **hoof.**

[1]**hop** [hɔp], **1.** *s.* 1. der Sprung, Hüpfer, Hopser; (*Spt.*) *–, **step and jump,*** der Dreisprung; (*sl.*) ***be on the –,*** dauernd herumrennen; (*sl.*) ***catch on the –,*** erwischen, ertappen; (*sl.*) ***keep him on the –,*** ihm keine (Rast und) Ruhe lassen; 2. (*coll.*) kurze Strecke, (*esp. Av.*) kurzer Flug; 3. (*sl.*) der Tanz, Schwof. **2.** *v.i.* hüpfen, hopsen, springen; (*coll.*) ***– off,*** sich aufmachen, weggehen; ***– on, – over,*** *see* **3.**; (*sl.*) ***– it,*** verschwinden, verduften. **3.** *v.t.* springen über (*Acc.*); (*coll.*) springen auf (*Acc.*) (*train etc.*).

[2]**hop, 1.** *s.* der Hopfen; Hopfenzapfen, die Hopfenblüte. **2.** *v.t.* hopfen (*beer*). **3.** *v.i.* Hopfen ernten *or* pflücken. **hop-back,** *s.* (*Brew.*) der Hopfenseiher.

hope [houp], **1.** *s.* die Hoffnung, Zuversicht, das Vertrauen (***of,*** auf (*Acc.*)); ***there is no – for him*** or ***he is past*** (***all***) ***–,*** für ihn gibt es keine Hoffnung mehr, er ist ein hoffnungsloser Fall; ***set one's –s on,*** seine Hoffnung setzen auf (*Acc.*); ***hold out –*(*s*) *to him,*** ihm Hoffnungen machen. **2.** *v.t., v.i.* hoffen (***for,*** auf (*Acc.*)); ***– against hope,*** hoffen wo nichts (mehr) zu hoffen ist, wenig *or* geringe Hoffnung haben, auf die bloße Möglichkeit hoffen; ***it is to be –d,*** es ist zu hoffen; ***– for the best,*** das Beste hoffen; ***I – not,*** das will ich nicht hoffen; ***I – so,*** das hoffe ich, hoffentlich.

hopeful ['houpful], **1.** *adj.* hoffnungsvoll, zuversichtlich; vielversprechend; ***be – of,*** Hoffnung setzen auf (*Acc.*). **2.** *s.* (*oft.* ***young*** –) vielversprechender Jüngling. **hopefulness,** *s.* die Hoffnungsfreudigkeit. **hopeless,** *adj.* hoffnungslos, aussichtlos, verzweifelt; unverbesserlich. **hopelessness,** *s.* die Hoffnungslosigkeit.

hop|-kiln, *s.* die Hopfendarre. **--o'-my-thumb,** *s.* der Zwerg, Knirps, Däumling, Dreikäsehoch. **hopper,** *s.* 1. (*Ent.*) der Hüpfer, die Käsemade; 2. (*Tech.*) der (Füll)trichter, (Füll)rumpf, Kornkasten; das Fallbodenfahrzeug; 3. der (die) Hopfenpflücker(in). **hop-picker,** *s. See* **hopper,** 3. **hopping (mad),** *adj.* (*coll.*) wütend. **hop|-pole,** *s.* die Hopfenstange. **–scotch,** *s.* das Tempelhüpfen, Himmel-und-Hölle(-Spiel). **--yard,** *s.* das Hopfenfeld.

Horace ['hɔris], *s.* Horaz (*m.*).

horary ['hɔ:rəri], *adj.* Stunden–, stündlich.

Horatian [hə'reiʃən], *adj.* horazisch.

horde [hɔ:d], **1.** *s.* die Horde, der Haufen, die Bande. **2.** *v.i.* ***– together,*** sich zusammenscharen.

horizon [hə'raizn], *s.* der Horizont, Gesichtskreis (*also fig.*); (*Naut.*) die Kimm; ***artificial –,*** der Kreiselhorizont; ***rational –,*** geozentrischer Horizont; ***sensible –,*** scheinbarer Horizont.

horizontal [hɔri'zɔntl], **1.** *adj.* waagerecht, horizontal, Horizont–; (*Tech.*) liegend; (*Gymn.*) ***– bar,*** das Reck; ***– line,*** die Längslinie; ***– projection*** or ***section,*** der Grundriß. **2.** *s.* (*Math.*) die Waag(e)-rechte.

hormone ['hɔ:moun], *s.* das Hormon, der Wirkstoff.

horn [hɔ:n], **1.** *s.* 1. das Horn (*of beasts, also substance and Mus.*); (*usu. pl.*) Geweih; (*Chem.*) Keratin, der Hornstoff; (*Ent.*) Fühler, das Fühlhorn; 2. (*Motor.*) die Hupe; (*fig.*) ***draw in one's –s,*** gelindere Saiten aufziehen; ***be on the –s of a dilemma,*** sich in einer Zwickmühle *or* verzwickten Lage befinden; (*Mus.*) ***French –,*** das Waldhorn; ***– of plenty,*** das Füllhorn; 3. (*gramophone etc.*) der (Schall)trichter; 4. (*Hist.*) das Trinkhorn; 5. (*fig.*) der Flügel, Arm, Vorsprung. **2.** *v.i.* (*sl.*) ***– in,*** sich eindrängen (***on,*** in (*Acc.*)), sich unverschämt vordrängen.

horn|beam, *s.* (*Bot.*) die Weißbuche, Hainbuche. **–bill,** *s.* (*Orn.*) der Nashornvogel. **–blende,** *s.* die Hornblende.

horned [hɔ:nd], *adj.* Horn–, gehörnt; ***– cattle,*** das Hornvieh; (*Orn.*) ***– grebe,*** der Ohrentaucher (*Colymbus auritus*); (*Orn.*) ***– lark,*** die Ohrentaube (*Otocoris alpestris*); ***– mine,*** die Bleikappenmine.

hornet ['hɔ:nit], *s.* die Hornisse; ***bring a –s' nest about one's ears,*** in ein Wespennest stechen.

horn|pipe, *s.* (*Mus., Hist.*) die Hornpfeife; (*Naut.*) der Seemannstanz. **--rimmed,** *adj.* Horn– (*spectacles*). **horny,** *adj.* hornig, hörnern, Horn–, hornartig; (*of hands*) schwielig.

horologe ['hɔ:rəlɔdʒ], *s.* der Zeitmesser, Stundenmesser, die Sonnen– *or* Sand– *or* Wasseruhr *etc.* **horology** [hɔ'rɔlədʒi], *s.* 1. die Zeitmessung; 2. Uhrmacherkunst.

horoscope ['hɔrəskoup], *s.* das Horoskop; ***cast a –,*** ein Horoskop stellen.

horrendous [hɔ'rendəs], *adj. See* **horrible.**

horrible ['hɔribl], *adj.* entsetzlich, schrecklich, furchtbar, fürchterlich, abscheulich, scheußlich, gräßlich, schauerlich, grausig.

horrid ['hɔrid], *adj.* (*coll.*) *see* **horrible.**

horrific [hɔ'rifik], *adj.* schreckenerregend. **horrify** ['hɔrifai], *v.t.* erschrecken, entsetzen, empören.

horror ['hɔrə], *s.* das Entsetzen, Grausen, der Schreck(en), Abscheu, Schauder (***of,*** vor (*Dat.*)), Widerwille (gegen); (*oft. pl.*) Schrecken, Greuel; (*coll.*) (*of a p.*) das Scheusal, (*of a th.*) scheußliches Ding; ***scenes of –,*** Schreckensszenen; ***–s of war,*** die Kriegsgreuel; (*coll.*) ***the –s,*** kaltes Grausen, das Grauen. **horror|-film,** *s.* der Gruselfilm. **--stricken, --struck,** *adj.* von Grau(s)en *or* Schrecken gepackt.

hors d'oeuvre [ɔ:'də:vr], *s.* die Vorspeise.

horse [hɔ:s], **1.** *s.* 1. das Pferd, Roß, der Gaul; Hengst, Wallach; (*coll.*) ***a dark –,*** unbeschriebenes Blatt; ***flog a dead –,*** sich vergeblich anstrengen; ***don't look a gift – in the mouth,*** einem geschenkten Gaul sieht man nicht ins Maul; (*coll.*) ***come off one's high –,*** klein beigeben; (*coll.*) ***get on one's high –,*** sich aufs hohe Roß setzen; ***lead –,*** das Handpferd; ***pack--,*** das Saumpferd; ***saddle –,*** das Reitpferd; ***wild –s will not . . .,*** nicht vier Pferde werden . . ., keine Kraft der Welt wird . . .; ***back the wrong –,*** auf die falsche Karte setzen; ***give a – its head,*** einem Pferde die Zügel schießen lassen; (*sl.*) ***hold your –s!*** nicht so rasch! ***as strong as a –,*** stark wie ein Gaul; ***put the cart before the –,*** das Pferd beim Schwanze aufzäumen, eine S. verkehrt anfangen *or* angehen *or* anpacken; (*coll.*) ***straight from the –'s mouth,*** aus bester Quelle; (*Mil.*) ***to –!*** zu Pferde! aufgesessen! aufsitzen! (*Mil.*) ***sound to –,*** zum Aufsitzen blasen; ***take –,*** reiten, sich zu Pferde setzen, aufsitzen; 2. (*Mil.*) (*collect.*) die Reiterei, Kavallerie; ***light –,*** leichte Kavallerie; ***master of the –,*** der Stallmeister; 3. (*Tech.*) das Gestell, der Bock, Ständer; ***clothes –,*** der Kleiderständer; (*Gymn.*) ***vaulting –,*** das Pferd. **2.** *v.t.* mit Pferd(en) versehen; bespannen (*vehicle*); (*fig.*) auf dem Rücken tragen; decken, beschälen (*a mare*).

horse|-artillery, *s.* reitende Artillerie. **–back,** *s.* ***on –,*** zu Pferde, beritten; ***be*** or ***go on –,*** reiten. **--bean,** *s.* die Saubohne. **--block,** *s.* der Aufsteigeblock. **--box,** *s.* der Pferde(transport)wagen. **--breaker,** *s.* der Bereiter, Zureiter. **--breeding,** *s.* die Pferdezucht. **--brush,** *s.* die Kardätsche. **--chestnut,** *s.* (*Bot.*) die Roßkastanie. **--cloth,** *s.* die Pferdedecke, Schabracke. **--collar,** *s.* das Kum(me)t. **--coper,** *s. See* **--dealer.**

horsed [hɔ:st], *adj.* bespannt (*vehicle*), beritten (*a p.*).

horse|-dealer, *s.* der Pferdehändler. **--doctor,** *s.* (*coll.*) der Roßarzt. **--drawn,** *adj.* Pferde–, bespannt. **--droppings,** *pl.* der Pferdemist, Pferdepillen (*pl.*). **–flesh,** *s.* 1. das Pferdefleisch; 2. (*collect., sl.*) Pferde (*pl.*). **–fly,** *s.* die (Pferde)bremse. **–guards,** *pl.* berittene Garde; englisches Gardekavallerieregiment. **–hair,** *s.* das Roßhaar, Schweifhaar. **--laugh,** *s.* (*coll.*) wieherndes Gelächter. **--leech,** *s.* der Pferdeegel.

horseman ['hɔ:smən], *s.* (erfahrener) Reiter. **horsemanship,** *s.* die Reitkunst.

horse|meat, *s. See* **–flesh,** 1. **–play,** *s.* derber Scherz, rauher Spaß, die Rauferei. **–pond,** *s.* die Pferdeschwemme. **–power,** *s.* (*Tech.*) die Pferdestärke. **–-race, –-racing,** *s.* das Pferderennen. **–-radish,** *s.* der Meerrettich. **– sense,** *s.* (*coll.*) gesunder Menschenverstand. **–shoe, 1.** *s.* das Hufeisen. **2.** *adj.* hufeisenförmig, Hufeisen–. **–-show,** *s.* die Pferdeschau. **–tail,** *s.* 1. der Pferdeschwanz, Roßschweif; 2. (*Bot.*) Schachtelhalm. **–whip, 1.** *s.* die Reitgerte, Reitpeitsche. **2.** *v.t.* mit der Reitgerte schlagen. **–woman,** *s.* (erfahrene) Reiterin.

horsiness ['hɔ:sinis], *s.* 1. der Stallgeruch; 2. (*fig.*) die Pferdeliebhaberei. **horsy,** *adj.* 1. pferdenärrisch, Rennsport liebend; jockeimäßig, stallknechtmäßig; 2. nach dem Stall riechend.

hortative ['hɔrtətiv], **hortatory** [–təri], *adj.* (er)mahnend, Ermahnungs–.

horticultural [hɔ:ti'kʌltʃərəl], *adj.* Garten(bau)–, gärtnerisch. **horticulture** ['hɔ:tikʌltʃə], *s.* der Gartenbau, die Garten(bau)kunst, Gärtnerei. **horticulturist,** *s.* der Garten(bau)künstler, Gärtner.

hosanna [hou'zænə], *s.* das Hosianna, der Lobgesang.

hose [houz], **1.** *s.* 1. (*collect.*) (*pl. constr.*) (lange) Strümpfe (*pl.*); (*Hist.*) das Beinkleid, die Kniehose; 2. (*pl.* **-s**) der Schlauch; ***garden –,*** der Gartenschlauch. **2.** *v.t.* mit einem Schlauch bespritzen. **hosepipe,** *s.* die Schlauchleitung.

hosier ['houzjə], *s.* der Strumpfhändler, Wirkwarenhändler; Strumpfwirker. **hosiery,** *s.* Strumpfwaren, Wirkwaren, Strickwaren, Trikotwaren (*pl.*).

hospice ['hɔspis], *s.* die Herberge, das Hospiz.

hospitable ['hɔspitəbl], *adj.* gast(freund)lich (*to,* gegen), gastfrei (*as a house*); (*fig.*) aufgeschlossen (*to,* Dat.), empfänglich, aufnahmebereit (für) (*ideas etc.*).

hospital ['hɔspitl], *s.* 1. das Krankenhaus, (Ho)spital, die Klinik, (*Mil.*) das Lazarett; ***she is in –,*** sie liegt im Krankenhaus; ***walk the –s,*** klinische Ausbildung durchmachen; ***– fever,*** der Flecktyphus; ***– nurse,*** die (Kranken)schwester, Krankenpflegerin; (*Mil.*) ***– orderly,*** der Sanitäter; ***– ship,*** das Lazarettschiff; ***Hospital Sunday,*** der Sonntag für Krankenhauskollekte; ***– train,*** der Lazarettzug; 2. (*obs.*) das Hospiz; wohltätige Stiftung.

hospital(l)er ['hɔspitələ], *s.* (*Hist.*) der Johanniter(ritter), barmherziger Bruder.

hospitality [hɔspi'tæliti], *s.* die Gastfreiheit, Gastlichkeit, Gastfreundschaft.

hospitalization [hɔspitəlai'zeiʃən], *s.* (*Am.*) die Einlieferung ins Krankenhaus; der Krankenhausaufenthalt. **hospitalize** ['hɔspitəlaiz], *v.t.* in einem Krankenhaus unterbringen, in ein Krankenhaus einliefern.

[1]**host** [houst], *s.* der (Gast)wirt; Gastgeber, Hausherr; (*Bot.*) die Wirtspflanze, (*Biol.*) der Wirt, das Wirtstier; ***reckon without one's –,*** die Rechnung ohne den Wirt machen.

[2]**host,** *s.* (*Poet.*) das (Kriegs)heer; (*coll.*) die Schar, Masse, (Un)menge, Unzahl; ***Lord of Hosts,*** der Herr der (himmlischen) Heerscharen; ***– of questions,*** eine Unmenge Fragen; ***he is a – in himself,*** er kann soviel wie hundert andere, er ersetzt eine ganze Schar.

Host, *s.* (*R.C.*) die Hostie.

hostage ['hɔstidʒ], *s.* der *or* die Geisel; (*fig.*) das (Unter)pfand; ***be held as –,*** als Geisel festgehalten sein; ***give –s to fortune,*** sich Gefahren aussetzen.

hostel [hɔstl], *s.* die Herberge; ***student's –,*** das Studentenheim; ***youth –,*** die Jugendherberge. **hostelry,** *s.* (*obs.*) das Gasthaus, Wirtshaus.

hostess ['houstis], *s.* die Wirtin; Gastgeberin, Hausfrau; (*coll.*) Empfangsdame, bezahlte Tanzpartnerin; (*Av.*) (*also* ***air –***) die Stewardeß, Flugbegleiterin.

hostile ['hɔstail], *adj.* feindlich, Feindes–; feindlich gesinnt, feindselig (*to,* gegen), abhold, abgeneigt (*Dat.*). **hostility** [–'tiliti], *s.* die Feindschaft, Feindlichkeit, Feindseligkeit (*to,* gegen); (*fig.*) Gegnerschaft. **hostilities,** *pl.* (*Mil.*) Feindseligkeiten (*pl.*).

hostler ['ɔslə], *see* **ostler.**

hot [hɔt], **1.** *adj.* heiß; erhitzt; (*fig.*) hitzig, feurig, eifrig (*of a p.*); (*coll.*) geil, lüstern (*of a p.*); (*coll.*) gestohlen, geschmuggelt; (*as spices*) beißend, scharf (gewürzt); ***– air,*** die Heißluft; (*sl.*) leeres Geschwätz, blauer Dunst; (*Comm.*) ***– bills,*** kürzlich emittierte Papiere; ***sell*** or ***go like – cakes,*** wie warme Semmeln abgehen; ***– dinner,*** warmes Essen; (*coll.*) ***– dog,*** heißes Würstchen (im aufgeschnittenen Brötchen); (*sl.*) ***a – favourite,*** hoher Favorit; ***– fight,*** heißes *or* heftiges Gefecht; (*Pol. coll.*) ***– line,*** heißer Draht; ***– jazz,*** die Swingmusik; (*Hunt.*) ***– scent,*** frische Fährte; (*Am. sl.*) ***– seat,*** elektrischer Stuhl; ***– spring,*** die Thermalquelle; (*sl.*) ***– stuff,*** großartige S.; forscher Kerl (*also of a girl*); ***– temper,*** hitziges *or* feuriges Temperament; ***– water,*** das Heißwasser; (*coll.*) ***get into – water,*** in des Teufels Küche kommen, sich in die Nesseln setzen (***with,*** bei), es zu tun kriegen (mit); ***– wire,*** (*Tech.*) der Hitzdraht; (*Pol. coll.*) *see* ***– line***; ***I am –,*** mir ist heiß; (*coll.*) ***– and bothered,*** aufgeregt, in Aufregung; ***get – under the collar,*** sich ereifern; aufgebracht *or* erregt werden; ***it got too – for him,*** ihm wurde der Boden (unter den Füßen) zu heiß; (*coll.*) ***give it him –,*** ihm gründlich einheizen; ***make it – for him,*** ihm die Hölle heiß machen; ***– from the press,*** frisch von der Presse; ***– on his heels,*** ihm dicht auf den Fersen. **2.** *v.t.* (*coll.*) ***– up,*** aufwärmen (*food*); (*fig. coll.*) zuspitzen, antreiben, anspornen. **3.** *v.i.* (*fig. coll.*) ***be hotting up,*** sich zuspitzen.

hot|bed, *s.* das Mistbeet; (*fig.*) die Brutstätte. **–-blooded,** *adj.* (*fig.*) heißblütig, leidenschaftlich, temperamentvoll.

hotchpotch ['hɔtʃpɔtʃ], *s.* der Mischmasch, das Durcheinander; (*Cul.*) Eintopfgericht, die Gemüsesuppe.

hotel [hou'tel], *s.* das Hotel, Gasthaus, der Gasthof, die Gaststätte; ***– register,*** das Fremdenbuch.

hot|-foot, *adv.* schnellen Schrittes, schleunigst, schnurstracks. **–head,** *s.* der Heißsporn, Hitzkopf. **–headed,** *adj.* hitzköpfig, ungestüm, unbesonnen. **–headedness,** *s.* das Ungestüm, die Unbesonnenheit. **–house,** *s.* das Treibhaus; (*fig.*) die Brutstätte.

hotness ['hɔtnis], *s.* die Hitze; (*fig.*) Hitzigkeit; (*of spices*) Schärfe.

hot|-plate, *s.* die Heizplatte. **–-pot,** *s.* *See* **hotchpotch** (*Cul.*). **–-press, 1.** *s.* die Heißpresse. **2.** *v.t.* heiß pressen *or* plätten, (*fabric*) dekatieren, (*paper*) satinieren. **–spur,** *s.* (*obs.*) *see* **–head. –-short,** *adj.* (*Metall.*) rotbrüchig. **–-tempered,** *adj.* heftig, hitzig.

Hottentot ['hɔtəntɔt], **1.** *s.* 1. der Hottentotte (die Hottentottin); 2. (*language*) das Hottentottische. **2.** *adj.* hottentottisch.

hotter ['hɔtə], *comp. adj.*, **hottest,** *sup. adj.* *See* **hot. hot-water,** *adj.* ***– bottle,*** die Wärmflasche; ***– heating (system),*** die Warmwasserheizung.

hough [hɔk], *see* [1]**hock.**

hound [haund], **1.** *s.* der Jagdhund, Spürhund, Hetzhund; Rüde; ***follow the –s, ride to –s,*** an der Parforcejagd teilnehmen; ***pack of –s,*** die Meute; (*Spt.*) ***hare and –s,*** die Schnitzeljagd. **2.** *v.t.* (*usu. fig.*) jagen, hetzen; (*fig.*) ***–ed by,*** geradezu verfolgt von; ***– him (on),*** ihn antreiben *or* vorwärtsdrängen. **hounds,** *pl.* (*Naut.*) Mastbacken (*pl.*).

hour [auə], *s.* die Stunde (*duration*), (Tages)zeit (*point of time*); (*R.C.*) ***the –s,*** das Stundengebet, Offizium; (*Myth.*) ***the Hours,*** die Horen (*pl.*); ***at all –s,*** zu jeder Tages– und Nachtzeit; ***for –s, – after –,*** stundenlang; ***by the –,*** stundenweise; ***half an –,*** eine halbe Stunde; ***a quarter of an –,*** eine Viertelstunde; ***three-quarters of an –,*** dreiviertel Stunde(n); ***man of the –,*** der Mann des Tages; ***question of the –,*** die Tagesfrage; ***– of death,*** die Todesstunde; ***keep early –s,*** früh schlafen gehen; ***at the eleventh –,*** im letzten Augenblick, kurz vor Toresschluß; ***in an evil –,*** zu einer ungünstigen Zeit; ***the last –,*** die Todesstunde; ***keep late –s,*** nachts lange aufbleiben; ***keep regular –s,*** ein ordentliches Leben führen; ***the small –s (of the night),*** frühe Morgenstunden, die Stunden nach Mitternacht; ***till the small–s,*** bis nach Mitternacht; ***an –'s walk from here,*** eine (Weg)stunde entfernt; ***working –s,*** Dienststunden (*pl.*), die Arbeitszeit.

hour|-glass, *s.* das Stundenglas, die Sanduhr. **--hand,** *s.* der Stundenzeiger.

houri ['huəri], *s.* die Huri.

hourly ['auəli], *adj., adv.* stündlich; – ***wage,*** der Stundenlohn.

house, I. [haus], *s.* I. das Haus (*also Astrol.*); die Wohnung; der Haushalt; (*obs.*) – ***of call,*** die Herberge; – ***of cards,*** das Kartenhaus (*also fig.*); (*obs.*) – ***of correction,*** die Besserungsanstalt; ***House of God,*** das Gotteshaus; – ***and home,*** Haus und Hof; ***neither – nor home,*** weder Dach noch Fach; – ***of ill fame,*** das Bordell; – ***of mourning,*** das Trauerhaus; ***keep –,*** haushalten, den Haushalt führen (*for, Dat.*); ***keep the –,*** das Haus hüten; ***keep open –,*** ein gastfreies Haus führen; (*fig.*) ***put*** or ***set one's – in order,*** seine Angelegenheiten in Ordnung bringen; (*Prov.*) ***my – is my castle,*** mein Haus ist meine Burg; (*coll.*) ***like a – on fire,*** mit Windeseile, wie wild; – ***collection,*** die Haussammlung; 2. (*fig.*) das Geschlecht, die Dynastie, Fürstenfamilie; 3. (*Comm.*) das Geschäftshaus, Handelshaus, die Firma; 4. (*Parl.*) das Parlament, Abgeordnetenhaus, die Kammer; ***House of Commons,*** das Unterhaus; ***House of Lords,*** das Oberhaus; (*Am.*) ***House of Representatives,*** das Abgeordnetenhaus, Repräsentantenhaus; ***constitute a –,*** eine beschlußfähige Anzahl Mitglieder aufweisen; ***enter the House,*** Mitglied des Parlaments werden; ***the House rises,*** die Sitzung endet; 5. das Pensionshaus (*school*); 6. (*Theat.*) Publikum, Zuhörer (*pl.*), Zuschauer (*pl.*); ***bring down the –,*** stürmischen Beifall finden, das Publikum hinreißen; ***poor*** or ***small –,*** schlecht besetztes Haus.
2. [hauz], *v.t.* (*a p.*) Wohnraum zur Verfügung stellen (*Dat.*), unterbringen; (*a th.*) unter Dach (und Fach) *or* in Sicherheit bringen, verwahren; (*Naut.*) festigen, zurren; (*of buildings etc.*) als Behausung dienen (*Dat.*), beherbergen.
3. [hauz], *v.i.* hausen, wohnen.

house|-agent, *s.* der Häusermakler. **-boat,** *s.* das Wohnboot, Hausboot. **-breaker,** *s.* der Einbrecher. **-breaking,** *s.* der Einbruch. **-coat,** *s.* der Morgenrock, das Hauskleid. **--flag,** *s.* die Reedereiflagge. **-fly,** *s.* die Stubenfliege. **houseful,** *s.* das Hausvoll.

house|hold, I. *s.* der Haushalt, die Familie; ***Royal Household,*** die Hofhaltung. **2.** *adj.* häuslich, Haus–, Familien–; – ***bread,*** gewöhnliches Brot; – ***expenses,*** Haushaltungskosten; – ***gods,*** Hausgötter, Penaten (*pl.*); – ***jam,*** billige Marmelade; – ***linen,*** das Weißzeug; – ***medicine,*** die Hausarznei; – ***soap,*** die Haushaltsseife; – ***troops,*** Gardetruppen (*pl.*), die Leibgarde; – ***washing,*** die Hauswäsche; – ***words,*** Alltagsworte, geflügelte Worte. **-holder,** *s.* der Haushaltsvorstand, Hausherr, Wohnungsinhaber.

house|-hunting, *s.* (*coll.*) die Wohnungssuche. **-keeper,** *s.* die Haushälterin, Wirtschafterin, Hausfrau. **-keeping, I.** *adj.* Haushaltungs–; – ***money,*** das Haushaltsgeld, Wirtschaftsgeld. **2.** *s.* die Haushaltsführung, Haushaltung, Hauswirtschaft. **--leek,** *s.* (*Bot.*) die Hauswurz, Dachwurz. **-maid,** *s.* das Hausmädchen, Stubenmädchen; ***–'s knee,*** die Kniescheibenentzündung. **-man** [-mən], *s.* (*coll.*) der Anstaltsarzt. **--martin,** *s.* (*Orn.*) die Mehlschwalbe (*Delichon urbica*). **-master,** *s.* der Leiter eines Pensionshauses (*school*). **--painter,** *s.* der Anstreicher. **--party,** *s.* der Logierbesuch im Landhaus. **--physician,** *s.* der Anstaltsarzt. **--proud,** *adj.* in der Haushaltung peinlich sorgfältig. **--room,** *s.* ***give – to,*** ins Haus nehmen (*a p.*), Platz *or* Raum machen für (*a th.*); (*coll.*) ***I wouldn't give it –,*** ich würde es nicht geschenkt nehmen. **--sparrow,** *s.* (*Orn.*) der Haussperling (*Passer domesticus*). **--surgeon,** *s.* der Anstaltschirurg. **--to-house,** *adj.* – ***fighting,*** der Häuserkampf; – ***search,*** die Haussuchung. **-top,** *s.* ***proclaim from the –s,*** öffentlich verkünden. **--trained,** *adj.* stubenrein. **--warming,** *s.* die Einzugsfeier, das Einstandsfest. **-wife,** *s.* I. die Hausfrau, Wirtschafterin; 2. (*coll.*) ['hʌzif] der Nähbeutel, das Nähzeug. **-wifely,** *adv.* hausfraulich. **-work,** *s.* die Hausarbeit, Haushaltsarbeiten (*pl.*).

housing ['hauziŋ], *s.* I. das Wohnen, Hausen; die Wohngelegenheit, Unterkunft, Behausung; Unterbringung, Beherbergung, Wohnbeschaffung; – ***estate,*** die (Wohn)siedlung; – ***shortage,*** die Wohnungsnot; 2. (*Comm.*) die Lagerung, das Lagern; Lagergeld, die Lagermiete; 3. (*Naut.*) Häsung, der Zurring; (*Tech.*) das Gerüst, Gehäuse; (*harness*) die Schabracke, Satteldecke.

hove [houv], *imperf., p.p. of* **heave**; ***the ship was*** or ***lay – to,*** das Schiff wurde beigedreht *or* beigelegt.

hovel [hɔvl], *s.* der Schuppen, elende Hütte.

hoveller ['hɔvlə], *s.* der Berger (*of wrecks*).

hover ['hɔvə], *v.i.* (in der Luft) schweben; (*fig.*) schwanken, zögern; (*fig.*) – ***about*** or ***round,*** sich herumtreiben. **hovercraft,** *s.* das Luftkissenfahrzeug.

how [hau], *adv.* wie, auf welche Weise, in welcher Art; – ***do you do?*** guten Tag; – ***do you know?*** woher weißt du das? – ***are you?*** wie geht es Ihnen? – ***is*** or ***comes it that?*** (*Am. coll.* – ***come?***), wie kommt es (dazu), daß; ***it depends on –,*** es hängt davon ab, wie; ***do it – you can,*** mach es so gut du kannst; (*sl.*) ***and –!*** und wie! (*coll.*) ***here's –!*** auf Ihr Wohl! (*sl.*) ***all you know –,*** so gut du kannst; – ***like him!*** das sieht ihm ähnlich! (*coll.*) – ***now?*** wie geht's? – ***many,*** wieviel, wie viele; – ***much is it?*** wieviel (*or coll.* was) kostet es? wieviel macht es? ***know – to do,*** zu tun verstehen, tun können; ***he does not know – to say it,*** er weiß nicht, wie er es sagen soll.

howbeit [hau'bi:it], **I.** *adv.* (*obs.*) nichtsdestoweniger, wie dem auch sei. **2.** *conj.* (*B.*) – (***that***), wenngleich.

howdah ['haudə], *s.* der Sitz auf Elefanten.

how|-d'ye-do [–djə'du:], *s.* (*coll.*) die Patsche, verflixte Lage, schöne Bescherung. **—ever, I.** *adv.* I. wie auch immer, wenn auch noch so; ***all mistakes – small,*** alle noch so kleinen Fehler; – ***it may be,*** wie dem auch sei; – ***he may try,*** und wenn er es auch noch so sehr versucht, soviel er es auch versuchen mag; 2. jedoch, dennoch, indes, aber. **2.** *conj.* (*obs.*) gleichwohl.

howitzer ['hauitsə], *s.* die Haubitze.

howl [haul], **I.** *v.i.* heulen, brüllen, schreien; laut klagen; (*coll.*) weinen; (*Rad.*) pfeifen, summen. **2.** *v.t.* – ***down,*** niederschreien (*a p.*). **3.** *s.* das Heulen, Gebrüll, Geheul; (*Rad.*) Pfeifen, der Heulton. **howler,** *s.* (*coll.*) grober Schnitzer; ***schoolboy –,*** die Schülerweisheit. **howling,** *adj.* I. heulend, brüllend; 2. (*coll.*) schaurig, entsetzlich, fürchterlich; 3. (*sl.*) enorm, kolossal, gewaltig.

howsoever [hausou'evə], *adv.* auf welche Art auch immer, wie (sehr) auch immer.

[1]**hoy** [hɔi], *s.* (*Naut.*) der Leichter, das Leichterschiff.

[2]**hoy!** *int.* holla! hallo! he! (*Naut.*) ahoi!

hoyden [hɔidn], *s.* ausgelassenes Mädchen, der Wildfang.

hub [hʌb], *s.* die Nabe (*of a wheel*); (*fig.*) der Angelpunkt, Mittelpunkt.

hubbub ['hʌbʌb], *s.* der Lärm, das Getöse, der Tumult, Wirrwarr.

hubby ['hʌbi], *s.* (*coll.*) *see* **husband.**

hubris ['hju:bris], *s.* die Hybris, Selbstüberhebung.

huckaback ['hʌkəbæk], *s.* der Drell.

huckle [hʌkl], *s.* die Hüfte. **huckle|berry,** *s.* (*Bot., Am.*) die Bickbeere, Blaubeere, Heidelbeere. **-bone,** *s.* der Hüftknochen; Fußknöchel, das Sprungbein.

huckster ['hʌkstə], **1.** *s.* der Höker, Krämer. **2.** *v.i.* hökern; schachern.

huddle [hʌdl], **1.** *v.i.* sich (zusammen)drängen; – ***together,*** sich zusammenkauern; – ***up,*** sich schmiegen (***to,*** an (*Acc.*)). **2.** *v.t.* unordentlich durcheinanderwerfen. **3.** *s.* (*coll.*) ***go into a*** –, die Köpfe zusammenstecken.

[1]**hue** [hju:], *s.* (*only in*) – ***and cry,*** das Zetergeschrei; (*fig.*) die Hetze; ***raise a – and cry,*** Zeter und Mordio *or* Zetergeschrei erheben (***about,*** gegen), mit lautem Geschrei verfolgen (***after,*** *Acc.*); einen Steckbrief erlassen.

[2]**hue,** *s.* die Farbe, Färbung, Tönung, der (Farb)ton, das Kolorit. **hued,** *adj.* gefärbt, farbig (*esp. as suff.*).

huff [hʌf], (*coll.*) **1.** *s.* der Ärger, die Mißstimmung; ***be in a*** –, gekränkt sein, sich beleidigt fühlen. **2.** *v.t.* herfahren über (*Acc.*), grob anfahren; scharf anfassen, beleidigen; (*Draughts*) blasen, pusten. **3.** *v.i.* sich beleidigt fühlen, beleidigt sein. **huffiness,** *s.* das Übelnehmen, die Gereiztheit, Ärgerlichkeit; (*obs.*) Anmaßung, Aufgeblasenheit. **huffish,** *adj. See* **huffy. huffishness,** *s. See* **huffiness. huffy,** *adj.* übelnehmerisch, verärgert; (*obs.*) anmaßend, aufgeblasen.

hug [hʌg], **1.** *v.t.* umarmen, an sich drücken; (*fig.*) festhalten an (*Dat.*); (*fig.*) – ***o.s.,*** sich schmeicheln; – ***the wind*** (***coast***), sich nahe *or* dicht an den Wind (die Küste) halten. **2.** *s.* die Umarmung; der Griff (*in wrestling*).

huge [hju:dʒ], *adj.* sehr groß, riesig, ungeheuer, riesengroß. **hugely,** *adv.* ungemein, gewaltig. **hugeness,** *s.* ungeheure Größe, die Riesenhaftigkeit.

hugger-mugger ['hʌgəmʌgə], **1.** *adj., adv.* (*coll.*) unordentlich; (*obs.*) heimlich, verstohlen. **2.** *s.* das Sammelsurium.

Huguenot ['hju:gənou], **1.** *s.* der Hugenotte (die Hugenottin). **2.** *adj.* hugenottisch.

hulk [hʌlk], *s.* 1. (*Naut.*) der *or* die Hulk *or* Holk; 2. der Klumpen, Klotz, schwerfällige Masse; ungeschlachter Mensch. **hulking,** *adj.* schwerfällig, ungeschlacht, plump (*of p.*).

hull [hʌl], **1.** *s.* 1. (*Bot.*) die Hülse, Schale; 2. (*Naut., Av.*) der Rumpf; – ***down,*** (*Naut.*) weit entfernt, gerade sichtbar; (*Mil.*) in Rampenstellung (*of tanks*). **2.** *v.t.* 1. schälen, enthülsen; 2. den Schiffsrumpf (*Gen.*) treffen *or* durchschießen.

hullabaloo [hʌləbə'lu:], *s.* (*coll.*) der Lärm, Tumult, Spektakel, Klamauk.

hullo! [hʌ'lou], *int.* hallo!

hum [hʌm], **1.** *v.i.* summen, brummen; murmeln; – ***and haw,*** in der Rede stocken, verlegen stottern; – ***and haw about a th.,*** mit der Sprache nicht herausrücken, nicht anbeißen wollen; (*sl.*) ***make things*** –, die S. in Schwung bringen, Leben in die Bude bringen. **2.** *v.t.* summen (*a tune*). **3.** *s.* das Summen, Brummen, Dröhnen, Gebrumme, Gesumme (*of insects etc.*); Gemurmel (*of conversation*); (*Rad.*) ***mains*** –, der Netzbrumm. **4.** *int.* hm!

human ['hju:mən], **1.** *adj.* menschlich, Menschen–; – ***being,*** der Mensch; – ***nature,*** menschliche Natur, die Menschlichkeit; ***the – race,*** die Menschheit, das Menschengeschlecht; ***to err is*** –, Irren ist menschlich. **2.** *s.* (*coll.*) der Mensch.

humane [hju:'mein], *adj.* 1. menschenfreundlich, wohlwollend, human; – ***killer,*** die Schlachtmaske; ***Humane Society,*** die Lebensrettungsgesellschaft; 2. humanistisch; – ***learning,*** humanistische Bildung.

humanism ['hju:mənizm], *s.* der Humanismus, Humanitätsglaube. **humanist,** *s.* der (die) Humanist(in). **humanistic** [–'nistik], *adj.* humanistisch. **humanitarian** [–mæni'tɛəriən], **1.** *s.* der (die) Menschenfreund(in). **2.** *adj.* menschenfreundlich, Humanitäts–. **humanitarianism,** *s.* die Menschenfreundlichkeit, Nächstenliebe. **humanities** [–'mænitiz], *pl.* klassische Philologie; ***modern*** –, neuere Sprachen und Literatur, Geisteswissenschaften (*pl.*). **humanity** [–'mæniti], *s.* 1. das Menschsein, menschliche Natur; 2. die Menschheit, das Menschengeschlecht, Menschen (*pl.*); 3. die Menschlichkeit, Menschenliebe, Humanität, menschliches Gefühl; 4. (*Scots Univ.*) lateinische Philologie. **humanization** [–nai'zeiʃən], *s.* die Vermenschlichung, Humanisierung. **humanize,** *v.t.* humanisieren, zivilisieren, menschlich *or* gesittet machen; vermenschlichen, als Menschen vorstellen. **humankind,** *s.* das Menschengeschlecht, die Menschheit. **humanly,** *adv. See* **human, 1**; – ***possible,*** menschenmöglich; – ***speaking,*** menschlich gesehen, nach menschlichem Ermessen.

humble [hʌmbl], **1.** *adj.* bescheiden, demütig, anspruchslos; niedrig, gering, ärmlich, dürftig; ***of – birth,*** von niedriger Geburt; ***in my – opinion,*** nach meiner unmaßgeblichen Meinung; ***eat – pie,*** Abbitte tun, zu Kreuze kriechen, sich erniedrigen; ***my – self,*** meine Wenigkeit; ***your – servant,*** Ihr ergebener. **2.** *v.t.* erniedrigen, demütigen. **humble-bee,** *s.* die Hummel. **humbleness,** *s.* die Niedrigkeit (*of birth etc.*); Demut, Unterwürfigkeit.

humbug ['hʌmbʌg], **1.** *s.* (*coll.*) 1. der Schwindel, Betrug, Humbug, die Schwindelei, Täuschung; 2. der Unsinn, Quatsch, Mumpitz; 3. Schwindler, Aufschneider, Schaumschläger; 4. der *or* das Pfefferminzbonbon. **2.** *v.t.* beschwindeln, übervorteilen, zum besten haben, foppen; – ***him out of s.th.,*** ihn um etwas prellen *or* betrügen.

humdinger ['hʌmdiŋə], *s.* (*sl.*) tolle S.; der Mordskerl.

humdrum ['hʌmdrʌm], *adj.* alltäglich, langweilig, eintönig, fade.

humeral ['hju:mərəl], *adj.* (*Anat.*) Schulter–, Oberarmknochen–, Humerus–. **humerus,** *s.* das Oberarmbein.

humid ['hju:mid], *adj.* feucht, naß. **humidifier** [–'midifaiə], *s.* der Anfeuchter. **humidify,** *v.t.* anfeuchten, befeuchten, benetzen. **humidity** [–'miditi], *s.* die Feuchtigkeit, der Feuchtigkeitsgehalt.

humiliate [hju:'milieit], *v.t.* erniedrigen, demütigen. **humiliating,** *adj.* demütigend, kränkend, erniedrigend. **humiliation** [–'eiʃən], *s.* die Demütigung, Erniedrigung.

humility [hju:'militi], *s.* die Demut, Bescheidenheit.

humming ['hʌmiŋ], **1.** *adj.* summend, brummend, Brumm–; (*coll.*) lebhaft, kräftig, gewaltig. **2.** *s.* das Summen, Brummen. **humming|-bird,** *s.* der Kolibri. **--top,** *s.* der Brummkreisel.

hummock ['hʌmək], *s.* kleiner Hügel.

humor, (*Am.*) *see* **humour.**

humoral ['hju:mərəl], *adj.* (*obs. Anat.*) humoral, Humoral–.

humoresque [hju:mə'resk], *s.* die Humoreske.

humorist ['hju:mərist], *s.* der Humorist; (*coll.*) Spaßvogel. **humorous** ['hju:mərəs], *adj.* humorvoll, humoristisch; spaßhaft, komisch, lustig, heiter. **humorousness,** *s.* die Spaßhaftigkeit, Lustigkeit, das Spaßige.

humour ['hju:mə], **1.** *s.* 1. die Gemütsverfassung, Gemütsart; Stimmung, Laune; ***in the – for,*** aufgelegt zu; ***in a good*** (***bad***) –, gut (schlecht) aufgelegt *or* gelaunt, bei guter (schlechter) Laune; ***out of*** –, verstimmt, schlecht aufgelegt, mißgelaunt; 2. der Humor, die Komik, das Komische; ***sense of*** –, der (Sinn für) Humor; 3. (*obs.*) der (Körper)saft, die Flüssigkeit. **2.** *v.t.* willfahren (*Dat.*), den Willen tun *or* lassen (*Dat.*), gewähren lassen. **humoured,** *adj. suff.* –gelaunt, –aufgelegt. **humourless,** *adj.* humorlos. **humoursome** [–səm], *adj.* (*rare*) drollig, launisch.

humous ['hju:məs], *adj.* humusreich, Humus–; *see* **humus.**

hump [hʌmp], **1.** *s.* 1. der Höcker, Buckel; (*fig. coll.*) ***be over the*** –, über den Berg sein; 2. (*coll.*) der Ärger, üble Laune; (*coll.*) ***have the*** –, üble Laune haben, verdrießlich sein; (*coll.*) ***give him the*** –, ihm auf die Nerven gehen. **2.** *v.t.* 1. krümmen; – ***one's back,*** einen Buckel machen; 2. (*coll.*) auf den Rücken nehmen, auf dem Rücken tragen. **hump|-**

back, *s.* Bucklige(r). **–backed,** *adj.* bucklig (*of a p.*). **humped,** *adj.* bucklig, höckerig (*of a th.*).
humph! ['hʌmf], *int.* hm!
humpty-dumpty ['hʌmpti'dʌmpti], *s.* kleine dicke P., der Stöpsel.
humpy ['hʌmpi], *adj.* 1. *See* **humped**; 2. (*as road*) holperig; 3. (*coll.*) **humpbacked.**
humus ['hju:məs], *s.* der Humus.
Hun [hʌn], *s.* (*Hist.*) der Hunne (die Hunnin); (*sl.*) Deutsche(r).
hunch [hʌntʃ], **1.** *s.* 1. *See* **hump**; 2. (*coll.*) das Vorgefühl, die (Vor)ahnung, der Verdacht, Animus. **2.** *v.t.* krümmen; *–ed up,* hockend, kauernd. **hunchback,** *s. See* **humpback.**
hundred ['hʌndrəd], **1.** *num. adj.* hundert; ***a*** or ***one – people,*** (ein) hundert Leute; ***several – men,*** mehrere hundert Mann; (*coll.*) ***a – and one things to do,*** hunderterlei zu tun. **2.** *s.* 1. das Hundert; ***by the –,*** hundertweise, zu Hunderten; ***–s and –s,*** Hunderte und aber Hunderte; (*fig.*) ***– per cent,*** hundertprozentig, vollständig, echt; ***–s and thousands,*** Zuckerkügelchen (*pl.*); ***–s of times,*** hundertemale; 2. (*Hist.*) der Bezirk, die Hundertschaft. **hundredth, 1.** *num. adj.* hundertst. **2.** *s.* der *etc.* Hundertste (*ordinal*); das Hundertstel (*fraction*). **hundredweight,** *s.* der Zentner (*Engl. 112 lb. = 50 kg.*; *Am. 100 lb. = 45 kg.*); ***metric –,*** deutscher Zentner.
hung [hʌŋ], *imperf., p.p. of* **hang, 1., 4.**
Hungarian [hʌŋ'gɛəriən], **1.** *s.* 1. der (die) Ungar(in); 2. (*language*) das Ungarisch. **2.** *adj.* ungarisch. **Hungary** ['hʌŋgəri], *s.* Ungarn (*n.*).
hunger ['hʌŋgə], **1.** *s.* der Hunger (*also fig.*); (*fig.*) Durst, die Begierde, das Verlangen (***for, after,*** nach); ***die of –,*** Hungers *or* an Hunger sterben, verhungern; (*Prov.*) ***– is the best sauce,*** Hunger ist der beste Koch. **2.** *v.i.* (*usu. fig.*) hungern, dürsten, sich sehnen (***after,*** nach). **hunger-strike,** *s.* der Hungerstreik. **hungriness,** *s.* der Hunger, die Hungrigkeit. **hungry,** *adj.* hungrig (*also fig.*); (*fig.*) dürstend, begierig (***for,*** nach); (*as soil*) unergiebig, unfruchtbar; ***be*** or ***feel –,*** hungrig sein, Hunger haben; ***go –,*** hungern; ***– forties,*** die Hungerjahre 1840–50; ***– as a bear*** or ***a hunter,*** hungrig wie ein Wolf.
hunkydory ['hʌŋki'dɔ:ri], *adj.* (*Am. sl.*) erstklassig, prima.
Hunnish ['hʌniʃ], *adj.* (*Hist.*) hunnisch; (*fig.*) barbarisch.
hunt [hʌnt], **1.** *v.t.* jagen, hetzen; (*a p.*) nachstellen (*Dat.*), nachsetzen (*Dat.*), verfolgen; (*territory*) durchstöbern, absuchen; (*dogs, horses etc. for hunting*) jagen mit; (*fig.*) (*also* ***– out, – up***) ausfindig machen, aufspüren, nachspüren, aufstöbern. **2.** *v.i.* 1. jagen, Jagd machen (***for, after,*** auf (*Acc.*)); (*fig.*) suchen, forschen, streben (***for,*** nach); 2. (*Tech.*) oszillieren, pendeln. **3.** *s.* die Jagd, (*for foxes etc.*) Hetzjagd; (*fig.*) das Jagen, die Suche (***for,*** nach), Verfolgung (*Gen.*); die Jagdgesellschaft; das Jagdrevier. **hunter,** *s.* 1. der Jäger; Jagdhund; das Jagdpferd; 2. (*Ent.*) die Jagdspinne; 3. (*Horol.*) Doppelkapseluhr.
hunting ['hʌntiŋ], *s.* das Jagen, die (Hetz)jagd, (*Poet.*) das Weidwerk; (*fig.*) die Suche, Nachstellung, Verfolgung; (*Tech.*) das Oszillieren, Pendeln, die Pendelschwingung. **--box,** *s. See* **--lodge. --crop,** *s.* die Jagdpeitsche. **--ground,** *s.* das Jagdgebiet, Jagdrevier; (*fig.*) ***happy –,*** ewige Jagdgründe. **--horn,** *s.* das Jagdhorn, Jägerhorn, Hifthorn. **--lodge,** *s.* die Jagdhütte, das Jagdhäuschen.
huntress ['hʌntris], *s.* (*usu. Myth. or fig.*) die Jägerin.
huntsman ['hʌntsmən], *s.* der Jäger, (*Poet.*) Jägersmann, Weidmann. **huntsmanship,** *s.* die Jägerei. **huntswoman,** *s.* die Jägerin.
hurdle [hə:dl], **1.** *s.* 1. die Hürde (*also Spt., fig.*); 2. das Reisiggeflecht, Weidengeflecht; (*Mil.*) die Faschine, der Schanzkorb; (*Min.*) Rätter, das Gitter; 3. (*Spt., fig.*) Hindernis; (*fig.*) die Schwierigkeit. **2.** *v.t.* (*also* ***– off***) mit Hürden einschließen *or* umgeben, umzäunen. **3.** *v.i.* Hürden *or* Hindernisse überspringen; (*Spt.*) Hürdenlauf *or* Hürdenrennen betreiben; an einem Hürdenlauf *or* Hürdenrennen teilnehmen, ein Hürdenrennen machen. **hurdler,** *s.* der (die) Hürdenläufer(in). **hurdle|-race,** *s.* das Hürdenrennen, der Hürdenlauf. **--work,** *s.* das Flechtwerk.
hurdy-gurdy ['hə:digə:di], *s.* der Leierkasten, die Drehorgel, Drehleier.
hurl [hə:l], *v.t.* schleudern, (*fig.*) ausstoßen (*as insults*); ***– defiance,*** den Fehdehandschuh hinwerfen (***at,*** *Dat.*). **hurling,** *s.* (irisches) Hurling(spiel).
hurly-burly ['hə:libə:li], *s.* der Tumult, Wirrwarr, Sog, das Getümmel.
hurra(h) [hə'rɑ:], **1.** *int.* hurra! ***– for!*** es lebe . . . (hoch)! **2.** *s.* der Hurraruf, das Hurra(geschrei).
hurricane ['hʌrikən], *s.* der Orkan, Hurrikan, Wirbelsturm; (*fig.*) Wirbel. **hurricane|-deck,** *s.* das Sturmdeck. **--lamp,** *s.* die Sturmlaterne.
hurried ['hʌrid], *adj.* eilig, hastig, gehetzt; übereilt, flüchtig. **hurry, 1.** *v.t.* (*a p.*) (zur Eile) (an)treiben *or* drängen, (*a th.*) (*also coll.* ***– up***) beschleunigen, vorwärtstreiben, eilig befördern, eilig verrichten. **2.** *v.i.* (*oft.* ***– up***) eilen, sich beeilen, hasten; ***– away,*** davoneilen, forteilen; ***– back,*** zurückeilen; ***– off,*** see ***– away***; ***– on,*** sich eilig weiterbewegen; ***– on to,*** zueilen (*Dat.*); ***– over,*** eilig *or* flüchtig hinweggehen über (*Acc.*), schnell erledigen. **3.** *s.* die Hast, Eile; das Hasten, Eilen, der Drang; ***there is no –,*** es hat keine Eile; ***be in a –,*** Eile *or* es eilig haben; (*coll.*) ***that won't happen in a –,*** das wird nicht so schnell *or* leicht *or* bald geschehen.
hurst [hə:st], *s.* das Gehölz, der Hain.
hurt [hə:t], **1.** *irr.v.t.* verletzen, verwunden; weh(e) tun (*Dat.*), schmerzen; schaden (*Dat.*), Schaden zufügen (*Dat.*); (*a th.*) beschädigen; (*feelings*) verletzen, kränken; ***feel –,*** sich gekränkt fühlen; ***not – a hair of his head,*** ihm kein Haar krümmen; ***be – at,*** sich verletzt fühlen von *or* wegen. **2.** *irr.v.i.* weh(e) tun, schmerzen; (*coll.*) Schaden anrichten, schaden, zu Schaden kommen; (*coll.*) ***that won't –,*** das schadet *or* tut nichts. **3.** *s.* die Verletzung, Verwundung; der Schaden, Nachteil, die Beschädigung. **hurter,** *s.* (*Tech.*) der Stoßring. **hurtful,** *adj.* schädlich, schädigend, nachteilig, verderblich (***to,*** für). **hurtfulness,** *s.* die Schädlichkeit.
hurtle [hə:tl], *v.i.* (an)stoßen, (an)prallen; sausen, stürzen, (p)rasseln (***against,*** auf *or* an (*Acc.*)).
husband ['hʌzbənd], **1.** *s.* der (Ehe)mann, Gatte, Gemahl; ***ship's –,*** der Schiffsagent. **2.** *v.t.* haushälterisch *or* sparsam umgehen mit, haushalten mit. **husbandless,** *adj.* unverheiratet, ohne Gatten. **husbandman,** *s.* der Landmann, Landwirt. **husbandry,** *s.* der Ackerbau, die Landwirtschaft; ***animal –,*** die Tierzucht.
hush [hʌʃ], **1.** *int.* still! pst! **2.** *s.* die Stille; (*fig.*) Flaute. **3.** *v.t.* zum Schweigen bringen; (*fig.*) besänftigen, beruhigen, beschwichtigen; ***– up,*** geheimhalten, totschweigen, vertuschen. **4.** *v.i.* still sein *or* werden. **hushaby!** ['hʌʃəbai], *int.* eiapopeia! **hushed,** *adj.* still, lautlos. **hush|-hush,** *adj.* (*coll.*) geheimtuerisch; heimlich, Geheim–. **--money,** *s.* das Schweigegeld.
husk [hʌsk], **1.** *s.* die Hülse, Schale, Schote; (*fig.*) äußere Form. **2.** *v.t.* enthülsen.
huskiness ['hʌskinis], *s.* die Rauheit, Heiserkeit. **husky, 1.** *adj.* 1. hülsig, schalig, (*as voice*) rauh, heiser, belegt; 2. (*coll.*) kräftig, stämmig. **2.** *s.* 1. der Eskimo; Eskimohund; die Eskimosprache; 2. (*coll.*) der Kraftmeier.
hussar [hu'zɑ:], *s.* der Husar.
hussy ['hʌsi, –zi], *s.* das Weibsbild, Flittchen; (*coll.*) die Blage, freche Göre, der Fratz.
hustings ['hʌstiŋz], *pl.* (*usu. sing. constr.*) (*Hist.*) die Rednerbühne; Wahl(bühne).
hustle [hʌsl], **1.** *v.t.* drängen, stoßen; ***– s.th. through,*** etwas energisch vorantreiben *or* durchsetzen. **2.** *v.i.* 1. sich (durch)drängen, sich einen Weg bahnen; 2. (*Am.*) unermüdlich arbeiten, arbeitsam

sein, sich rühren, sich tüchtig umtun; 3. (*sl. esp. Am.*) abgaunern. 3. *s.* das Gedränge, Getriebe, der (Hoch)betrieb; (*Am.*) die Betriebsamkeit, der Schwung, Hochdruck. **hustler,** *s.* 1. (*coll.*) der Brausekopf, Himmelsstürmer; 2. (*sl.*) Schwindler.

hut [hʌt], 1. *s.* die Hütte; (*Mil.*) Baracke; ***mountain* –**, die Schutzhütte, Alpenhütte. 2. *v.t.* (*Mil.*) in Baracken unterbringen.

hutch [hʌtʃ], *s.* der Kasten, Trog (*for coal etc.*); die Hütte, der Verschlag, Stall (*for small animals*).

hutment ['hʌtmənt], *s.* das Barackenlager.

huzza [hu'zɑ:], 1. *int.* heisa! heißa! hussa! juchhe! 2. *s.* das Jauchzen, der Hurraruf. 3. *v.i.* hurra rufen, jauchzen. 4. *v.t.* zujauchzen (*Dat.*).

hyacinth ['haiəsinθ], *s.* die Hyazinthe.

hyaline ['haiəlin], *adj.* glasartig, glasklar, glasig, gläsern, durchsichtig; – ***quartz,*** der Glasquarz. **hyalite** [–lait], *s.* (*Min.*) der Hyalit, Glasopal. **hyaloid,** *adj. See* **hyaline**; – (***membrane***), die Glashaut (*of the eye*).

hybrid ['haibrid], 1. *adj.* hybrid(isch), bastardartig, Bastard–, Misch–, Zwitter–. 2. *s.* der Mischling, Bastard, der *or* die Hybride, die Zwitterbildung. **hybridism,** *s.* die Bastardierung, Kreuzung. **hybridity** [–'briditi], *s.* die Mischbildung, Zwitterbildung, Hybridenbildung. **hybridize** [–aiz], *v.t.* kreuzen, bastardieren, hybridisieren.

hydra ['haidrə], *s.* (*Myth.*) die Hydra; (*Zool.*) der Süßwasserpolyp. **hydra-headed,** *adj.* vielköpfig, hydraköpfig.

hydrangea [hai'dreindʒə], *s.* (*Bot.*) die Hortensie.

hydrant ['haidrənt], *s.* der Hydrant, Feuerhahn.

hydrate ['haidreit], 1. *s.* (*Chem.*) das Hydrat. 2. *v.t.* hydratisieren. **hydrated,** *adj.* wasserhaltig, hydrathaltig.

hydraulic [hai'drɔ:lik], *adj.* hydraulisch; – ***brake,*** die Öldruckbremse; – ***cement,*** der (Unter)wassermörtel; – ***engine,*** die Wasserkraftmaschine; – ***engineering,*** der Wasserbau; – ***power,*** die Wasserkraft; – ***press,*** hydraulische Presse, die Wasserdruckpresse; – ***pressure,*** der Flüssigkeitsdruck. **hydraulics,** *pl.* (*sing. constr.*) die Hydraulik.

hydriodic [haidri'ɔdik], *adj.* (*Chem.*) jodwasserstoffsauer; – ***acid,*** die Jodwasserstoffsäure.

hydro ['haidrou], 1. *s.* (*coll.*) *see* ***hydropathic establishment.*** 2. *pref.* Wasser–. **hydro|carbon,** *s.* (*Chem.*) der Kohlenwasserstoff. **–carbonaceous,** *adj.* kohlenwasserstoffhaltig. **–cephalic,** *adj.* wasserköpfig. **–cephalus** [–'sefələs], *s.* der Wasserkopf, die Gehirnwassersucht. **–chlorate,** *s. See* **–chloride. –chloric,** *adj.* (*Chem.*) salzsauer; – ***acid,*** der Chlorwasserstoff, die Salzsäure. **–chloride,** *s.* das Chlorhydrat. **–cyanic,** *adj.* blausauer, Zyanwasserstoff–; – ***acid,*** die Blausäure, Zyanwasserstoffsäure. **–dynamic,** *adj.* hydrodynamisch. **–dynamics,** *pl.* (*sing. constr.*) die Wasserdrucklehre, Hydrodynamik. **–electric,** *adj.* hydroelektrisch; – ***generating station,*** das Wasserkraftwerk. **–-extract,** *v.t.* entwässern, zentrifugieren, trockenschleudern. **–foil,** *s.* (*Av.*) der Tragflügel, die Tragfläche, Gleitfläche.

hydrogen ['haidrədʒən], *s.* der Wasserstoff; – ***bomb,*** die Wasserstoffbombe; – ***peroxide,*** das Wasserstoffsuperoxyd; – ***sulphide,*** der Schwefelwasserstoff. **hydrogenation** [–'neiʃən], *s.* die Hydrierung; – ***plant,*** die Hydrieranlage. **hydrogenize** [–'drɔdʒənaiz], *v.t.* hydrieren, (*oil*) härten. **hydrogenous** [–'drɔdʒənəs], *adj.* wasserstoffhaltig, Wasserstoff–.

hydrographic [haidro'græfik], *adj.* hydrographisch; ***Hydrographic Department,*** nautische Abteilung der Kriegsmarine (*in England*). **hydrography** [–'drɔgrəfi], *s.* die Gewässerbeschreibung, Hydrographie. **hydrology** [–'drɔlədʒi], *s.* die Hydrologie, Gewässerkunde. **hydrolyse** ['haidrəlaiz], *v.t.* hydrolysieren. **hydrolysis** [–'drɔləsis], *s.* die Hydrolyse. **hydrometer** [–'drɔmitə], *s.* das *or* der Hydrometer, die Senkwaage, der Dichtigkeitsmesser. **hydrometric** [–o'metrik], *adj.* hydrometrisch. **hydropathic** [–o'pæθik], *adj.* hydropathisch, Wasserbehandlungs–; – ***establishment,*** die Wasserheilanstalt. **hydropathy** [–'drɔpəθi], *s.* die Wasserheilkunde, Wasserkur. **hydrophobia** [–'foubiə], *s.* die Wasserscheu; (*Med.*) Tollwut. **hydrophobic** [–'foubik], *adj.* wasserscheu. **hydrophone,** *s.* das Unterwasserhorchgerät. **hydropic** [–'drɔpik], *adj.* wassersüchtig.

hydro|plane, *s.* (*Naut.*) das Gleitboot; Tiefenruder (*of submarines*); (*Av.*) Wasserflugzeug; die Gleitfläche (*of seaplane*). **–quinone** [–'kwainoun], *s.* (*Phot.*) das Hydrochinon. **–sphere,** *s.* die Hydrosphäre. **–static,** *adj.* hydrostatisch, Wasser–; – ***balance,*** die Wasserwaage; – ***pressure,*** der Wasserdruck. **–statics,** *pl.* (*sing. constr.*) die Hydrostatik. **–therapy,** *s.* die Wasserheilkunde, Wasserbehandlung.

hydrous ['haidrəs], *adj.* wasserhaltig.

hydroxide [hai'drɔksaid], *s.* (*Chem.*) das Hydroxyd, Hydrat.

hyena [hai'i:nə], *s.* die Hyäne.

hygiene ['haidʒi:n], *s.* die Gesundheitspflege, Hygiene. **hygienic** [–'dʒi:nik], *adj.* gesundheitlich, hygienisch; – ***measures,*** Gesundheitsmaßnahmen (*pl.*). **hygienics,** *pl.* (*sing. constr.*) die Gesundheitslehre.

hygro– ['haigrou], *adj. pref.* Feuchtigkeits–. **hygrometer** [–'grɔmitə], *s.* der (Luft)feuchtigkeitsmesser. **hygrometric** [–'metrik], *adj.* hygrometrisch. **hygroscope,** *s.* der Feuchtigkeitszeiger. **hygroscopic** [–'skɔpik], *adj.* hygroskopisch, wasserziehend.

hymen ['haimen], *s.* 1. (*Anat.*) das Jungfernhäutchen; 2. (*Poet.*) die Ehe; (*Myth.*) der Hymen, Gott der Ehe. **hymeneal** [–'niəl], 1. *adj.* hochzeitlich, Hochzeits–. 2. *s.* das Hochzeitslied. **hymenopter** [–'nɔptə], *s.* (*Ent.*) der Hautflügler. **hymenopterous,** *adj.* Hautflügler–.

hymn [him], 1. *s.* das Kirchenlied, geistliches Lied; die Hymne, der Hymnus, Lobgesang. 2. *v.t.* (lob)preisen (*Dat.*). **hymnal** [–nl], 1. *adj.* hymnisch. 2. *or* **hymn-book,** *s.* das Gesangbuch. **hymnic** [–nik], *adj. See* **hymnal, 1. hymnody** [–nədi], *s.* das Hymnensingen, der Hymnengesang; (*collect.*) Hymnen (*pl.*). **hymnology** [–'nɔlədʒi], *s.* die Hymnologie, Hymnendichtung.

hyoid ['haiɔid], *adj.* (*Anat.*) – ***bone,*** das Zungenbein.

hyper– ['haipə], *pref.* über–, übermäßig. **hyperaesthesia,** *s.* nervöse Reizbarkeit, die Überempfindlichkeit. **hyperbola** [–'pə:bələ], *s.* (*Math.*) die Hyperbel. **hyperbole** [–'pə:bəli], *s.* (*fig.*) die Übertreibung, Hyperbel. **hyperbolic** [–'bɔlik], *adj.* (*Math.*) Hyperbel–. **hyperbolical,** *adj.* (*fig.*) übertreibend, hyperbolisch. **hyperborean** [–'bɔ:riən], 1. *adj.* hyperboreisch, nördlich. 2. *s.* der Hyperboreer.

hyper|catalectic, *adj.* (*Metr.*) überzählig. **–critical,** *adj.* übermäßig *or* allzu kritisch, allzuscharf kritisierend; peinlich genau. **–(metr)opia,** *s.* die Weitsichtigkeit. **–sarcosis,** *s.* wildes Fleisch. **–sensitive,** *adj.* überempfindlich (*to,* gegen). **–tension,** *s.* (*Med.*) der Bluthochdruck, die Hypertonie. **–trophy** [–'pə:trəfi], *s.* die Überentwicklung, Hypertrophie, übermäßiges Wachstum.

hyphen [haifn], 1. *s.* der Bindestrich; das Divis. 2. *or* **hyphenate** [–neit], *v.t.* mit Bindestrich schreiben; –***d name,*** der Doppelname.

hypnoid ['hipnɔid], *adj.* schlafähnlich. **hypnosis** [–'nousis], *s.* die Hypnose. **hypnotic** [–'nɔtik], 1. *adj.* hypnotisch, schlaffördernd, einschläfernd. 2. *s.* 1. Hypnotisierte(r); 2. das Betäubungsmittel, Schlafmittel, Einschläferungsmittel. **hypnotism** [–nətizm], *s.* der Hypnotismus. **hypnotist,** *s.* der Hypnotiseur. **hypnotize** [–taiz], *v.t.* hypnotisieren; (*fig.*) fesseln, faszinieren.

hypo, 1. ['haipə], *pref.* unter–, unterhalb. 2. ['haipou], *s.* (*abbr. for* ***sodium hyposulphite***) unterschwefligsaures Natron, das Natriumthiosulfat, (*Phot.*) Fixiersalz. **hypochlorous,** *adj.* unterchlorig.

hypochondria [haipə'kɔndriə], *s.* die Hypochondrie. **hypochondriac** [–iæk], 1. *adj.* hypochondrisch, schwermütig. 2. *s.* der Hypochonder.

hypocrisy [hi'pɔkrisi], *s.* die Heuchelei, Scheinheiligkeit. **hypocrite** ['hipəkrit], *s.* Scheinheilige(r), der (die) Heuchler(in). **hypocritical** [–'kritikl], *adj.* heuchlerisch; scheinheilig.

hypodermic [haipə'də:mik], **1.** *adj.* subkutan; – ***injection,*** hypodermatische Einspritzung; – ***syringe,*** die Spritze. **2.** *s.* (*coll.*) *see* – ***syringe.*** **hypodermis,** *s.* (*Anat.*) das Hypoderm, Unterhautsgewebe.

hypogastrium [haipə'gæstriəm], *s.* die Unterbauchgegend.

hypogeal [haipə'dʒiəl], **hypogean, hypogeous,** *adj.* unterirdisch (wachsend *or* lebend).

hypostasis [hai'pɔstəsis], *s.* 1. (*Log.*) die Grundlage, Unterlage, das Zugrundeliegende, die Hypostase; 2. (*Med.*) Blutstauung, Blutsenkung, Hypostasie. **hypostasize** [–saiz], **hypostatize,** *v.t.* (*Log.*) vergegenständlichen, hypostasieren.

hypo|sulphate, *s.* unterschwefelsaures Salz. **–sulphite,** *s.* unterschwefligsaures Salz; *see* **hypo, 2.**

hypotactic [haipə'tæktik], *adj.* unterordnend. **hypotaxis** [–'tæksis], *s.* die Unterordnung.

hypotenuse [h(a)i'pɔtənju:z], *s.* die Hypotenuse.

hypothec [h(a)i'pɔθik], *s.* (*Scots*) die Hypothek. **hypothecary,** *adj.* Hypotheken–, hypothekarisch, pfandrechtlich. **hypothecate** [–keit], *v.t.* verpfänden, verschreiben, hypothekarisieren.

hypothesis [hai'pɔθəsis], *s.* (*pl.* **-theses** [–si:z]) die Voraussetzung, Annahme, Vermutung, Hypothese. **hypothetical** [–pə'θetikl], *adj.* hypothetisch, mutmaßlich, angenommen.

hypsometer [hip'sɔmitə], *s.* das Höhenmesser; das Siedethermometer. **hypsometric(al)** [–'metrik(l)], *adj.* Höhen–, hypsometrisch. **hypsometry,** *s.* die Höhenmessung.

hyssop ['hisəp], *s.* (*Bot.*) der Ysop.

hysterectomy [histə'rektəmi], *s.* (*Surg.*) die Gebärmutterentfernung.

hysteresis [histə'ri:sis], *s.* (*Elec.*) die Hysterese.

hysteria [his'tiəriə], *s.* die Hysterie. **hysteric(al)** [–'terik(l)], *adj.* hysterisch; – ***crying,*** der Weinkrampf; – ***laughter,*** der Lachkrampf. **hysterics,** *pl.* die Hysterie, hysterischer Zustand, hysterischer Anfall; ***go into*** or ***have a fit of*** –, hysterische Anfälle bekommen.

hysterocele ['histərəsi:l], *s.* der Gebärmutterbruch. **hysterotomy** [–'rɔtəmi], *s.* (*Surg.*) der Kaiserschnitt.

I

[1]**I, i** [ai], *s.* das I, i. *See Index of Abbreviations.*

[2]**I,** *pers. pron.* ich; ***it is*** –, ich bin es; – ***say!*** hören Sie mal!

iamb ['aiæmb], *s.* der Jambus. **iambic** [–'æmbik], **1.** *adj.* jambisch. **2.** *s.* (*usu. pl.*) *see* **iamb. iambus** [–'æmbəs], *s. See* **iamb.**

Iberian [ai'biəriən], **1.** *s.* der (die) Iberer(in). **2.** *adj.* iberisch.

ibex ['aibeks], *s.* (*Zool.*) der Steinbock.

ibidem [i'baidem], *adv.* ebenda.

ibis ['aibis], *s.* (*pl.* **ibes** [–i:z]) (*Orn.*) der Ibis, Brauner Sichler (*Plegadis falcinellus*).

ice [ais], **1.** *s.* das Eis; die Eisschicht, Eisdecke; das (Speise)eis, Gefrorene(s); (*on cakes etc.*) der Zuckerguß, die (Zucker)glasur; ***broken*** –, Eisstollen (*pl.*), (*Cul.*) Eisstücke (*pl.*); ***drifting*** or ***floating*** –, das Treibeis; ***pack*** –, das Packeis; ***sheet*** –, das Glatteis; (*fig.*) ***break the*** –, das Eis brechen; (*coll.*) ***cut no*** –, nichts ausrichten, keine Wirkung haben, keinen Eindruck machen, nicht ziehen (***with,*** bei); (*fig.*) ***put on*** –, sicherstellen; (*fig.*) ***skate on thin*** –, ein heikles Thema berühren. **2.** *v.t.* 1. mit Eis bedecken, in Eis verwandeln, gefrieren machen; 2. (*Cul.*) überzuckern, mit Zuckerguß überziehen, glasieren (*cakes*); 3. kühlen (*wine*). **3.** *v.i.* (– ***up***) gefrieren, eineisen, vereisen.

ice|-age, *s.* die Eiszeit. **--axe,** *s.* der Eispickel. **–berg,** *s.* (schwimmender) Eisberg. **--boat,** *s.* der Segelschlitten. **--bound,** *adj.* eingefroren, eingeeist (*ship*), zugefroren (*harbour*). **--box,** *s.* der Eisschrank. **--breaker,** *s.* der Eisbrecher. **--cap,** *s.* der Kontinentalgletscher, das Inlandeis, die Eisdecke. **--cold,** *adj.* eiskalt. **--cream,** *s.* das (Speise)eis, Gefrorene(s); – ***cone,*** die Eistüte; – ***parlour,*** die Eisdiele.

iced [aist], *adj.* 1. eisgekühlt (*wine*); 2. (*Cul.*) überzuckert, mit Zuckerguß überzogen (*cakes*).

ice|-fall, *s.* der Gletscherabbruch. **--ferns,** *pl.* Eisblumen (*pl.*). **--field,** *s.* das Eisfeld. **--floe,** *s.* die Treibscholle, Eisscholle. **--foot,** *s.* der Eisgürtel. **--hockey,** *s.* das Eishockey.

Iceland ['aislənd], *s.* Island (*n.*). **Icelander,** *s.* der (die) Isländer(in). **Icelandic** [–'lændik], **1.** *adj.* isländisch. **2.** *s.* (*language*) das Isländisch(e).

ice|-pail, *s.* der Eiskübel, Weinkühler. **--plant,** *s.* Eiskraut. **--rink,** *s.* die (Kunst)eisbahn.

ichneumon [ik'nju:mən], *s.* (*Zool.*) das *or* der Ichneumon. **ichneumon-fly,** *s.* die Schlupfwespe.

ichor ['aikɔ:], *s.* (*Myth.*) das Götterblut; (*Med.*) Blutwasser, die Jauche. **ichorous** [–ərəs], *adj.* blutwässerig, eiterähnlich.

ichthyology [ikθi'ɔlədʒi], *s.* die Fischkunde, Zoologie der Fische. **ichthyophagous** [–'ɔfəgəs], *adj.* fisch(fr)essend. **ichthyosaurus** [–o'sɔ:rəs], *s.* der Ichthyosaurus.

icicle ['aisikl], *s.* der Eiszapfen.

icily ['aisili], *adv. See* **icy. iciness,** *s.* eisige Kälte, die Eiskälte; (*fig.*) Kälte, Frostigkeit, Zurückhaltung.

icing ['aisiŋ], *s.* 1. (*Av.*) die Vereisung; 2. (*Cul.*) der Zuckerguß, Beguß, die Glasur; – ***sugar,*** der Puderzucker, Staubzucker.

icon ['aikɔn], *s.* das Abbild; Christusbild, Heiligenbild. **iconoclasm** [–'kɔnəklæzm], *s.* die Bilderstürmerei. **iconoclast** [–'kɔnəklæst], *s.* der Bilderstürmer. **iconoclastic** [–'klæstik], *adj.* bilderstürmend, Bilderstürmer–. **iconography** [–'nɔgrəfi], *s.* die Bildniskunde; Bildersammlung. **iconolatry** [–'nɔlətri], *s.* die Bilderverehrung, Bilderanbetung. **iconology** [–'nɔlədʒi], *s. See* **iconography.**

icosahedron [aikɔsə'hi:drən], *s.* der Zwanzigflächner, das Ikosaeder.

ictus ['iktəs], *s.* der Starkton, Iktus, die Arsis, rhythmischer Akzent.

icy ['aisi], *adj.* eisig; (*fig.*) kalt, frostig; – ***cold,*** eiskalt.

id [id], *s.* (*Psych.*) das Es.

I'd [aiəd], (*coll.*) = ***I would, I should*** or ***I had.***

idea [ai'diə], *s.* die Idee, Vorstellung, der Begriff; Gedanke, Einfall, Plan, die Absicht; (*coll.*) Ansicht, Meinung, Vorstellung, Ahnung; ***form an – of,*** sich (*Dat.*) vorstellen, sich (*Dat.*) einen Begriff machen von; ***I have an – that,*** ich denke *or* meine daß; mir kommt es vor, als ob; ***have little*** (or ***no***) – ***of,*** wenig (*or* keine) Ahnung haben von; (*coll.*) ***that's the*** –, darum dreht's sich; (*coll.*) ***what's the –?*** was soll das (heißen *or* bedeuten)? (*coll.*) ***the very –!*** denk' dir nur!

ideal [ai'diəl], **1.** *adj.* 1. ideal, vollkommen, vollendet; wünschenswert, mustergültig, vorbildlich; 2. (*Phil.*) ideell, nicht wirklich, eingebildet; 3. gedanklich, Gedanken–, Ideen–; 4. (*Math.*) uneigentlich, ideell. **2.** *s.* das Ideal, Vorbild, Wunschbild, Zielbild. **idealism,** *s.* der Idealismus. **idealist,** *s.* der (die) Idealist(in). **idealistic** [–'listik], *adj.* idealistisch. **ideality** [–'æliti], *s.*

idealer Zustand. **idealization** [-lai'zeiʃən], *s.* die Idealisierung, (*Phil.*) Ideenbildung. **idealize, 1.** *v.t.* idealisieren; verklären, veredeln, vergeistigen. **2.** *v.i.* Ideale bilden.

ideation [aidi'eiʃən], *s.* die Ideenbildung(sfähigkeit), Vorstellung(sfähigkeit). **ideational,** *adj.* Ideenbildungs-, Vorstellungs-.

idée fixe ['idei'fi:ks], *s.* fixe Idee.

idem ['aidem], *adj.* derselbe, dasselbe, dieselbe.

identical [ai'dentikl], *adj.* derselbe, dasselbe, dieselbe; identisch, (genau) gleich, gleichbedeutend, übereinstimmend; (*Geom.*) deckungsgleich, kongruent; – ***twins,*** eineiige Zwillinge. **identicalness,** *s.* die Identität, Übereinstimmung.

identifiable [ai'dentifaiəbl], *adj.* feststellbar, identifizierbar. **identification** [-fi'keiʃən], *s.* 1. die Identifizierung, Feststellung, Bestimmung; Erkennung; – ***light,*** das Kennlicht; – ***mark,*** das Erkennungszeichen; – ***parade,*** die Gegenüberstellung, Konfrontierung; 2. die Gleichsetzung, Gleichmachung, völlige Übereinstimmung; 3. Legitimation, der Ausweis; – ***card,*** der Personalausweis, die Kennkarte; – ***papers,*** die Legitimation, der Personalausweis, (*Austr.*) Identitätsausweis. **identify,** *v.t.* 1. identifizieren, die Identität (*or Biol., Bot. etc.* Art) feststellen von, erkennen; 2. ausweisen, legitimieren (*a p.*); 3. als identisch betrachten, gleichsetzen (***with,*** *Dat.*); – ***o.s. with,*** sich solidarisch erklären mit, sich anschließen an (*Acc.*), sich einsetzen für.

identity [ai'dentiti], *s.* die Identität, völlige Gleichheit; Individualität; ***mistaken*** –, die Personenverwechslung; ***prove one's*** –, sich legitimieren *or* ausweisen. **identity|-card,** *s.* der (Personal)ausweis. **--disk,** *s.* die Erkennungsmarke.

ideogram ['idiəgræm], **ideograph** [-grɑ:f], *s.* das Begriffszeichen.

ideological [aidiə'lɔdʒikl], *adj.* ideologisch. **ideologist** [-'ɔlədʒist], *s.* unpraktischer Theoretiker, der Schwärmer. **ideology** [-'ɔlədʒi], *s.* (*Phil.*) die Begriffslehre, Ideenlehre, Ideologie; (*coll.*) Denkungsart, Denkweise, Vorstellungswelt; Schwärmerei, reine Theorie.

ides [aidz], *pl.* die Iden.

idiocy ['idiəsi], *s.* (*Med.*) der Blödsinn, die Idiotie, Demenz; (*coll.*) Torheit, der Blödsinn.

idiom ['idiəm], *s.* die Spracheigentümlichkeit, idiomatische Redewendung; charakteristische Sprachstruktur; die Mundart, der Dialekt, das Idiom; (*fig.*) die Eigentümlichkeit, persönlicher Stil. **idiomatic(al)** [-'mætik(l)], *adj.* idiomatisch, spracheigentümlich; sprachrichtig.

idiopathic [idio'pæθik], *adj.* (*Med.*) idiopathisch.

idioplasma [idio'plæzmə], *s.* (*Med.*) die Erbmasse.

idiosyncrasy [idio'siŋkrəsi], *s.* abnorme Wesenseigenheit, die Idiosynkrasie, charakteristische Eigenart, eigene Naturanlage; besondere Empfindlichkeit, krankhafte Abneigung. **idiosyncratic** [-'krætik], *adj.* idiosynkratisch.

idiot ['idiət], *s.* (*Med.*) Schwachsinnige(r), Blödsinnige(r), Geistesschwache(r), der (die) Idiot(in); (*coll.*) der Narr, Dummkopf. **idiotic** [-'ɔtik], *adj.* (*usu. fig.*) blödsinnig, idiotisch, einfältig, dumm.

idle [aidl], **1.** *adj.* 1. (*of a p.*) träge, faul, arbeitsscheu; müßig, untätig, unbeschäftigt; – ***fellow,*** der Faulenzer, Faulpelz; – ***hour,*** die Mußestunde; (*Prov.*) ***Satan finds mischief for – hands,*** Müßiggang ist aller Laster Anfang; 2. (*of a th.*) eitel, leer, hohl, wertlos, nichtig, zwecklos, unnütz; – ***fears,*** grundlose *or* unbegründete Besorgnis; – ***talk,*** leeres Geschätz *or* Gewäsch; – ***threat,*** leere Drohung; – ***words,*** unnütze Worte; 3. (*Tech.*) stillstehend, außer Betrieb; leerlaufend; – ***motion,*** der Leergang, Leerlauf; – ***wheel,*** das Leerlaufrad, Spannrad, Umlenkrad, Zwischenrad, Leitrad; 4. (*Comm.*) – ***capital,*** totes *or* unproduktives Kapital; ***lie*** –, brach liegen (*of land*). **2.** *v.i.* 1. faulenzen; 2. (*Tech.*) ***be idling,*** leerlaufen. **3.** *v.t.* – ***away one's time,*** seine Zeit vertändeln *or* müßig hinbringen. **idleness,** *s.* die Faulheit, Trägheit; Untätigkeit, der Müßiggang; die Zwecklosigkeit, Bedeutungslosigkeit, Nichtigkeit, Unfruchtbarkeit.

idler ['aidlə], *s.* 1. der Faulenzer, Müßiggänger; 2. *See* ***idle wheel.*** **idling,** *s.* 1. das Nichtstun, Faulenzen; 2. (*Tech.*) der Leerlauf.

idol [aidl], *s.* der Götze, das Götzenbild, Idol; (*fig.*) der Abgott. **idolater** [ai'dɔlətə], *s.* der Götzendiener, (*fig.*) Vergötterer, Anbeter, Verehrer. **idolatress,** *s.* die Götzendienerin. **idolatrous,** *adj.* götzendienerisch, Götzen-; (*fig.*) abgöttisch. **idolatry,** *s.* der Götzendienst, die Götzenanbetung, Abgötterei; (*fig.*) Anbetung, Vergötterung. **idolization** [-ai'zeiʃən], *s.* die Götzendienerei, Abgötterei, (*fig.*) Vergötterung. **idolize,** *v.t.* vergöttern, abgöttisch verehren *or* anbeten.

idyll ['idil], *s.* die Idylle, das Schäfergedicht, Hirtengedicht; (*fig.*) Idyll. **idyllic** [(a)i'dilik], *adj.* idyllisch (*also fig.*).

if [if], **1.** *conj.* wenn, falls, im Falle daß; wenn auch, wiewohl, wofern; (*introducing indirect question*) ob; ***fifty – a day,*** mindestens fünfzig Jahre alt; – ***any,*** höchstens *or* wenn überhaupt einer; ***as*** –, als ob, als wenn; ***even*** –, selbst wenn, wenn auch *or* überhaupt; – ***not,*** wo *or* wenn nicht; – ***so,*** in diesem *or* dem Fall, gegebenenfalls. **2.** *s.* das Wenn; ***without –s or ans*** or ***buts,*** ohne Wenn und Aber.

igloo ['iglu:], *s.* die Schneehütte.

igneous ['igniəs], *adj.* feurig, glühend; (*Geol.*) Eruptiv-.

ignis fatuus ['ignis'fætjuəs], *s.* (*pl.* **ignes fatui** ['igni:z'fætjuai]) das Irrlicht, (*fig.*) Blendwerk, Trugbild.

ignite [ig'nait], **1.** *v.t.* anzünden, entzünden, in Brand setzen; (*Chem.*) bis zur Verbrennung erhitzen. **2.** *v.i.* sich entzünden, Feuer fangen. **ignition** [-'niʃən], *s.* das Anzünden, Entzünden, die Entzündung; (*Chem.*) Erhitzung; (*Motor.etc.*) Zündung. **ignition|-charge,** *s.* die Zündladung. **--coil,** *s.* die Zündspule. **--key,** *s.* der Zündschlüssel. **--spark,** *s.* der Zündfunke. **--timing,** *s.* die Zündfolge.

ignoble [ig'noubl], *adj.* unedel, unwürdig, niedrig, gemein. **ignobleness,** *s.* die Unwürdigkeit, Gemeinheit, Niedrigkeit.

ignominious [igno'miniəs], *adj.* schmählich, schimpflich, schändlich, schmachvoll, entehrend. **ignominiousness, ignominy** ['ignəmini], *s.* die Schmach, Schande, der Schimpf; die Schändlichkeit, Niederträchtigkeit.

ignoramus [ignə'reiməs], *s.* Unwissende(r), der (die) Ignorant(in).

ignorance ['ignərəns], *s.* die Unwissenheit; Unkenntnis; ***plead*** –, Unkenntnis vorschützen. **ignorant,** *adj.* 1. unwissend, unkundig; ***be – of,*** nicht wissen, nicht kennen, nichts wissen von, unbekannt sein mit; – ***of the world,*** ohne Weltkenntnis; 2. ungebildet.

ignore [ig'nɔ:], *v.t.* nicht beachten, unbeachtet lassen, keine Notiz nehmen von, ignorieren; (*Law*) verwerfen, als unbegründet abweisen.

iguana [i'gwɑ:nə], *s.* (*Zool.*) gemeiner Leguan.

ileum ['iliəm], *s.* (*Anat.*) der Krummdarm.

ilex ['aileks], *s.* (*Bot.*) die Stechpalme; *see also* **holm-oak.**

iliac ['iliæk], *adj.* (*Anat.*) Darmbein-.

Iliad ['iliæd], *s.* die Ilias, Iliade.

ilk [ilk], *adj.* (*only in*) ***of that*** –, desselben Namens, (*coll.*) derselben Art, des- *or* der- *or* ihresgleichen.

I'll [aiəl], (*coll.*) = ***I shall*** or ***I will.***

ill [il], **1.** *adj.* 1. schlimm, schlecht; böse, bösartig, feindlich; übel, unheilvoll, widrig, ungünstig; – ***blood,*** böses Blut; – ***breeding,*** die Ungezogenheit; – ***effect,*** schlimme Auswirkung, üble Wirkung, unangenehme Folge; – ***feeling,*** die Abneigung, Unfreundlichkeit, üble Gesinnung; ***with an – grace,*** unwillig, widerwillig; – ***health,*** schlechte Gesundheit, die Kränklichkeit, Unpäßlichkeit, das Unwohlsein; – ***humour,*** schlechte Laune; – ***luck,*** das Unglück; ***as – luck would have it,*** unglücklicherweise; – ***management,*** die Mißwirtschaft; – ***nature,*** die Bösartigkeit, Böswilligkeit; – ***repute,*** schlechter Ruf; – ***turn,*** schlimmer *or* böser Streich; – ***usage,*** schlechte Behandlung; (*Prov.*) – ***weeds grow apace,*** Unkraut vergeht *or* verdirbt nicht; – ***will,*** das Übelwollen, die Feindschaft, Abneigung, der Groll; ***bear him – will,*** einen Groll gegen ihn haben, auf ihn schlecht zu sprechen sein; (*Prov.*) ***it's an – wind that blows nobody any good,*** des einen Unglück ist des andern Glück; 2. (*pred. only*) krank, unwohl; ***be taken –, fall –,*** krank werden. **2.** *adv.* 1. schlecht, böse, unrecht; schlimm, übel; nicht gut, ungünstig; ***accord – with,*** schlecht passen zu; ***it becomes him –,*** es steht ihm schlecht an; – ***at ease,*** befangen (***with,*** gegenüber), unbehaglich; ***fare*** or ***go – with,*** übel ergehen (*Dat.*), schlecht stehen um *or* mit; ***speak – of,*** schlecht *or* Schlimmes reden über; ***take –,*** übelnehmen; 2. kaum, schwerlich; – ***afford,*** nicht leisten können, nicht auf sich nehmen können; ***he can – bear it,*** er kann es schwerlich *or* kaum *or* nicht gut ertragen. **3.** *s.* das Übel, Böse(s); (*oft. pl.*) Unglück, Mißgeschick.

ill|-adapted, *adj.* ungeeignet, schlecht passend (***to,*** für). **--advised,** *adj.* 1. schlecht beraten; 2. nicht ratsam; 3. unbesonnen, unüberlegt, unklug. **--affected,** *adj.* übelgesinnt (***to(wards),*** gegen). **--assorted,** *adj.* zusammengewürfelt, schlecht zusammenpassend.

illation [i'leiʃən], *s.* der Schluß, die Folgerung. **illative, 1.** *adj.* folgernd, schließend, Schluß–. **2.** *s.* (*Gram.*) der Schlußsatz.

ill|-behaved, *adj.* ungezogen, unartig. **--bred,** *adj.* ungebildet, unhöflich. **--conditioned,** *adj.* schlecht beschaffen, schadhaft, in schlechtem Zustand; bösartig. **--considered,** *adj. See* **--advised,** 3. **--contrived,** *adj.* schlecht geplant. **--disposed,** *adj.* übelgesinnt, unfreundlich, nicht gewogen (***to(wards),*** *Dat.*).

illegal [i'li:gl], *adj.* ungesetzlich, widerrechtlich, gesetzwidrig, rechtswidrig, unrechtmäßig, verboten, illegal. **illegality** [–'gæliti], *s.* die Ungesetzlichkeit, Widerrechtlichkeit, Gesetzwidrigkeit, Rechtswidrigkeit, Unrechtmäßigkeit, Illegalität.

illegibility [iledʒi'biliti], *s.* die Unleserlichkeit. **illegible** [i'ledʒibl], *adj.* unleserlich.

illegitimacy [ili'dʒitimisi], *s.* 1. die Unehelichkeit; 2. Unrechtmäßigkeit, Unechtheit, Ungültigkeit. **illegitimate,** *adj.* 1. unehelich, außerehelich, illegitim; 2. rechtswidrig, unrechtmäßig, widerrechtlich.

ill|-fated, *adj.* unglücklich, unselig, ungünstig. **--favoured,** *adj.* häßlich, unschön, ungestalt. **--founded,** *adj.* unbegründet. **--gotten,** *adj.* unrechtmäßig *or* unredlich erworben. **--humoured,** *adj.* verärgert, übelgelaunt.

illiberal [i'libərəl], *adj.* knauserig, karg; engherzig, engstirnig, beschränkt. **illiberality** [–'ræliti], *s.* die Knauserei, Kargheit; Engherzigkeit, Engstirnigkeit, Beschränktheit.

illicit [i'lisit], *adj.* unerlaubt, verboten, rechtswidrig, gesetzwidrig; unzulässig; – ***sale,*** der Schwarzkauf; – ***trade,*** der Schwarzhandel, Schleichhandel; – ***work,*** die Schwarzarbeit.

illimitable [i'limitəbl], *adj.* unermeßlich, unbegrenzbar, grenzenlos.

illiteracy [i'litərəsi], *s.* die Ungelehrtheit, Ungebildetheit, Unwissenheit; das Analphabetentum. **illiterate, 1.** *adj.* ungelehrt, ungebildet, unwissend; analphabetisch. **2.** *s.* Ungebildete(r), Unwissende(r); der (die) Analphabet(in).

ill|-judged, *adj.* unbesonnen, unklug. **--mannered,** *adj.* unhöflich, unmanierlich. **--matched,** *adj.* schlecht zusammenpassend. **--natured,** *adj.* boshaft, bösartig; böswillig.

illness ['ilnis], *s.* die Krankheit, Unpäßlichkeit, das Leiden, Unwohlsein.

illogical [i'lɔdʒikl], *adj.* unlogisch; folgewidrig; vernunftwidrig. **illogicality** [–'kæliti], *s.* die Unlogik, das Vernunftwidrige.

ill|-omened, *adj.* von böser Vorbedeutung, Unglücks–. **--starred,** *adj.* unglücklich, unheilvoll, von Unglück verfolgt. **--tempered,** *adj.* schlecht gelaunt, verdrießlich, verärgert, mürrisch. **--timed,** *adj.* unpassend, ungelegen. **--treat,** *v.t.* mißhandeln. **--treatment,** *s.* die Mißhandlung.

illume [i'lju:m], *v.t.* (*Poet.*) erleuchten, aufhellen. **illuminate** [–ineit], *v.t.* 1. beleuchten, erleuchten, erhellen; festlich beleuchten, illuminieren (*street etc.*); 2. bunt ausmalen, kolorieren (*a manuscript*); (*Typ.*) ***–d capital,*** die Initiale; ***–d manuscript,*** die Bilderhandschrift; 3. (*fig.*) aufklären, aufhellen; erleuchten. **illuminati** [–i'nɑ:ti], *pl.* (*Eccl.*) Illuminaten (*pl.*). **illuminating,** *adj.* (*esp. fig.*) aufschlußreich, erleuchtend. **illumination** [–'neiʃən], *s.* 1. die Beleuchtung, Erleuchtung; Festbeleuchtung, Illumination; 2. Kolorierung; 3. (*Phot.*) Lichtstärke, Helligkeit; 4. (*fig.*) Aufklärung, Erleuchtung. **illumine,** *v.t.* (*Poet.*) *see* **illuminate.**

illusion [i'l(j)u:ʒən], *s.* die Sinnestäuschung, Einbildung, Illusion; Wahnvorstellung, das Trugbild, Blendwerk; ***optical –,*** optische Täuschung. **illusionist,** *s.* der Zauberkünstler. **illusive,** *adj.* täuschend, trügerisch, illusorisch. **illusiveness,** *s.* die Täuschung, Trüglichkeit. **illusory,** *adj. See* **illusive.**

illustrate ['iləstreit], *v.t.* 1. erläutern, erklären; veranschaulichen; 2. illustrieren (*a book*). **illustration** [–'streiʃən], *s.* 1. die Erläuterung, Erklärung, Veranschaulichung; das Beispiel; 2. (*in a book*) die Abbildung, Illustration. **illustrative** [–treitiv, i'lʌstrətiv], *adj.* erklärend, erläuternd; ***be – of,*** veranschaulichen, ins rechte Licht rücken; – ***material,*** das Anschauungsmaterial. **illustrator,** *s.* der Illustrator; Erläuterer.

illustrious [i'lʌstriəs], *adj.* berühmt, ruhmreich; erhaben, erlaucht, ausgezeichnet. **illustriousness,** *s.* die Berühmtheit; Erlauchtheit.

I'm [aim], (*coll.*) = ***I am.***

image ['imidʒ], **1.** *s.* 1. das Bild, Bildnis, bildliche Darstellung; ***graven –,*** das Götzenbild; (*Rad.*) – ***interference,*** das Wellenecho; – ***worship,*** der Götzendienst, Bilderdienst; 2. das Abbild, Ebenbild; ***the very – of his father,*** das Ebenbild seines Vaters; 3. das Vorstellungsbild, geistiges Bild, die Vorstellung; 4. Verkörperung, Erscheinungsform; 5. das Standbild, die Bildsäule; 6. Metapher, bildlicher Ausdruck. **2.** *v.t.* 1. abbilden, bildlich *or* anschaulich darstellen; 2. widerspiegeln; 3. verkörpern, symbolisieren. **imagery,** *s.* 1. das Bildwerk, Bilder (*pl.*); 2. die Bildersprache, bildliche Sprache *or* Darstellung.

imaginable [i'mædʒinəbl], *adj.* vorstellbar, denkbar; erdenklich; ***the finest weather –,*** das denkbar schönste Wetter. **imaginary,** *adj.* eingebildet, nur in der Vorstellung vorhanden, nur gedacht, Schein–, Phantasie–; (*Math.*) fingiert, imaginär; – ***weakness,*** eingebildete Schwäche. **imagination** [–'neiʃən], *s.* 1. die Einbildung, Vorstellung, das Denkvermögen; ***I was at your side in (my) –,*** ich stand im Geiste dir zur Seite; 2. die Einbildungskraft, Vorstellungskraft, Phantasie, der Ideenreichtum; ***his suggestions lack –,*** seine Vorschläge sind ideenarm. **imaginative,** *adj.* erfinderisch; ideenreich; phantasievoll, phantasiereich; – ***faculty,*** die Einbildungskraft. **imagine,** *v.t.* sich (*Dat.*) einbilden *or* vorstellen *or* denken; (*coll.*) glauben, vermuten, annehmen; ***just –!*** denken Sie (sich) nur!

imago [i'mɑ:gou], *s.* die Imago, vollentwickeltes Insekt.

imbalance [im'bæləns], *s.* (*fig.*) die Unausgeglichenheit, Unausgewogenheit.

imbecile ['imbisi:l], **1.** *adj.* schwachsinnig, blödsinnig, geistesschwach; (*coll.*) närrisch, blöd. **2.** *s.* Schwachsinnige(r); (*coll.*) der Narr. **imbecility** [–'siliti], *s.* der Schwachsinn, Blödsinn, die Geistesschwäche; (*coll.*) Dummheit, Blödheit; der Unsinn, Blödsinn.

imbibe [im'baib], *v.t.* einsaugen, aufsaugen; (*fig.*) geistig *or* in sich aufnehmen, sich (*Dat.*) zu eigen machen; (*coll.*) trinken.

imbricate ['imbrikeit], **1.** *adj.* dachziegelartig,

schuppenartig. **2.** *v.t.* dachziegelartig übereinanderlegen, schuppenartig anordnen. **3.** *v.i.* dachziegelartig übereinanderliegen.

imbroglio [im'brouliou], *s.* die Verwick(e)lung, Verwirrung, der Wirrwarr; (*Pol.*) verwickelte Lage, ernste Schwierigkeit.

imbrue [im'bru:], *v.t.* benetzen, (durch)tränken (***in, with***, mit); (*usu. fig.*) baden, eintauchen (in (*Dat.*)).

imbue [im'bju:], *v.t.* durchtränken, einweichen; (*usu. fig.*) erfüllen, durchdringen (***with***, mit *or* von).

imitable ['imitəbl], *adj.* nachahmbar. **imitate** [–eit], *v.t.* nachahmen; nachmachen, nachbilden, nachschaffen; kopieren, imitieren; – ***him in everything***, ihm alles nachmachen; ***not to be –d***, unnachahmlich. **imitated,** *adj.* künstlich, unecht. **imitation** [–'teiʃən], **1.** *s.* die Nachahmung; Nachgeahmte(s), Nachgemachte(s), die Nachbildung, Kopie, Fälschung, Imitation; ***in – of***, nach dem Muster *or* Vorbild (*Gen.*), als Nachahmung von. **2.** *attrib. adj.* unecht, künstlich, Kunst–; – ***leather***, das Kunstleder; – ***stone***, der Straß, unechter Diamant. **imitative** [–tətiv], *adj.* nachbildend, nachahmend; nachgemacht, nachgeahmt, nachgebildet; – ***word***, lautmalerisches *or* lautnachahmendes Wort.

immaculate [i'mækjulit], *adj.* unbefleckt; makellos, rein; (*fig.*) fleckenlos, fehlerfrei; ***Immaculate Conception***, Unbefleckte Empfängnis. **immaculateness,** *s.* die Unbeflecktheit, Reinheit.

immanence ['imənəns], *s.* das Innewohnen, die Immanenz. **immanent,** *adj.* innewohnend, immanent.

immaterial [imə'tiəriəl], *adj.* 1. unkörperlich, stofflos, körperlos, immateriell; 2. (*fig.*) unwesentlich, unbedeutend, unwichtig, nebensächlich, gleichgültig; (*coll.*) ***be – to me***, mir gleichgültig *or* einerlei sein. **immateriality** [–'æliti], *s.* 1. die Unstofflichkeit, Unkörperlichkeit; 2. (*fig.*) Unwesentlichkeit, Gleichgültigkeit.

immature [imə'tjuə], *adj.* unreif, unausgereift, unentwickelt. **immaturity,** *s.* die Unreife, Unfertigkeit.

immeasurable [i'meʒərəbl], *adj.* unermeßlich, unermeßbar, grenzenlos. **immeasurableness,** *s.* die Unermeßlichkeit.

immediacy [i'mi:diəsi], *s.* 1. die Unmittelbarkeit, Direktheit; 2. Unverzüglichkeit. **immediate,** *adj.* 1. (*space*) unmittelbar, umliegend, angrenzend, nächstgelegen; (*time*) unmittelbar (bevorstehend), nächst; – ***circle***, enger Kreis; – ***heir***, nächster Erbe; – ***vicinity***, nächste Umgebund; 2. augenblicklich, unverzüglich, sofortig; – ***plans***, augenblickliche Pläne; – ***steps***, Sofortmaßnahmen (*pl.*). **immediately, 1.** *adv.* sogleich, sofort, augenblicklich, unverzüglich, auf der Stelle; – ***after***, unmittelbar darauf. **2.** *conj.* sobald (als).

immemorial [imə'mɔ:riəl], *adj.* un(vor)denklich, uralt; ***from time –***, seit unvordenklichen Zeiten.

immense [i'mens], *adj.* unermeßlich, ungeheuer. **immensity,** *s.* die Unermeßlichkeit, Unendlichkeit; ungeheure Größe, gewaltige Ausdehnung.

immensurability [imenʃərə'biliti], *s.* die Unermeßlichkeit. **immensurable** [–'menʃərəbl], *adj.* unermeßbar, unermeßlich.

immerse [i'mə:s], *v.t.* 1. untertauchen, eintauchen; 2. (*fig.*) (*usu.* – ***o.s.***) (sich) vertiefen *or* versenken (***in***, in (*Acc.*)) (*a book etc.*), (sich) verstricken *or* verwickeln (***in***, in (*Acc.*)) (*problems, debt etc.*). **immersion** [i'mə:ʃən], *s.* 1. das Untertauchen, Eintauchen; – ***heater***, der Tauchsieder; 2. (*fig.*) das Vertieftsein, die Versenkung, Versunkenheit; 3. (*Astr.*) Immersion; 4. (*Eccl.*) Immersionstaufe.

immigrant ['imigrənt], **1.** *s.* der Einwanderer (die Einwanderin). **2.** *adj.* einwandernd. **immigrate** [–eit], *v.i.* einwandern (***into***, in (*Acc.*)). **immigration** [–'greiʃən], *s.* die Einwanderung.

imminence ['iminəns], *s.* nahes Bevorstehen; bevorstehendes Unheil, drohende Gefahr. **imminent,** *adj.* unmittelbar bevorstehend, drohend.

immiscible [i'misibl], *adj.* unvermischbar.

immitigable [i'mitigəbl], *adj.* nicht zu besänftigen(d) *or* lindern(d), unstillbar.

immobile [i'moubail], *adj.* unbeweglich, ortsfest. **immobility** [–'biliti], *s.* die Unbeweglichkeit. **immobilization** [–bilai'zeiʃən], *s.* (*Med.*) die Immobilisierung, Ruhigstellung; (*Comm.*) Einziehung. **immobilize,** *v.t.* unbeweglich machen, festlegen; (*Med.*) immobilisieren, ruhigstellen; (*Comm.*) aus dem Umlauf ziehen, einziehen (*specie*); immobil machen (*troops*).

immoderate [i'mɔdərit], *adj.* unmäßig, übermäßig, maßlos, übertrieben, extrem. **immoderation** [–'reiʃən], *s.* die Unmäßigkeit, Maßlosigkeit, das Übermaß.

immodest [i'mɔdist], *adj.* unbescheiden, unverschämt, anmaßend, aufdringlich, frech; unsittlich, unkeusch, unzüchtig, schamlos, unanständig. **immodesty,** *s.* die Unbescheidenheit, Unverschämtheit, Anmaßung, Aufdringlichkeit, Frechheit; Unkeuschheit, Unsittlichkeit, Unzüchtigkeit, Unanständigkeit, Schamlosigkeit.

immolate ['imoleit], *v.t.* opfern, zum Opfer bringen, als Opfer darbringen (*also fig.*). **immolation** [–'leiʃən], *s.* das Opfer, die Opferung (*also fig.*); ***self-–***, die Selbstaufopferung.

immoral [i'mɔrəl], *adj.* unmoralisch, unsittlich, sittenlos. **immorality** [–'ræliti], *s.* die Unsittlichkeit, Sittenlosigkeit.

immortal [i'mɔ:tl], **1.** *adj.* unsterblich; ewig, unvergänglich. **2.** *s.* Unsterbliche(r). **immortality** [–'tæliti], *s.* die Unsterblichkeit; (*fig.*) ewiger Ruhm. **immortalize** [–təlaiz], *v.t.* unsterblich machen, verewigen. **immortelle** [–'tel], *s.* (*Bot.*) die Immortelle, Strohblume.

immovability [imu:və'biliti], *s.* die Unbewegbarkeit, (*fig.*) Unerschütterlichkeit. **immovable** [–'mu:vəbl], *adj.* unbeweglich (*also Law*), bewegungslos, unbewegt, fest, unerschütterlich; unveränderlich. **immovables,** *pl.* (*Law*) Liegenschaften, Immobilien (*pl.*).

immune [i'mju:n], *adj.* geschützt, gefeit (***to, from, against***, gegen); (*Med.*) immun (gegen), unempfänglich (für). **immunity,** *s.* die Befreiung, Freiheit (***from***, von); (*Med.*) Immunität (gegen), Unempfänglichkeit (für); (*Law*) (*oft. pl.*) das Privileg, Sonderrecht; – ***from taxation***, die Steuerfreiheit. **immunization** [–ai'zeiʃən], *s.* die Immunisierung, Impfung (***against***, gegen). **immunize** ['imjunaiz], *v.t.* (*Med.*) unempfänglich *or* immun machen, immunisieren (***against***, gegen).

immure [i'mjuə], *v.t.* einmauern, vermauern, einschließen, einsperren, einkerkern; (*fig.*) – ***o.s.***, sich abschließen *or* vergraben.

immutability [imju:tə'biliti], *s.* die Unveränderlichkeit, Unwandelbarkeit. **immutable** [–'mju:təbl], *adj.* unveränderlich, unwandelbar.

¹imp [imp], *s.* das Teufelchen, der Kobold; (*coll.*) Schelm, Schlingel, Knirps, Racker, Fratz.

²imp, *v.t.* (*fig.*) beflügeln, beschwingen.

impact, 1. [im'pækt], *v.t.* zusammenpressen, einklemmen, einkeilen. **2.** ['impækt], *s.* 1. der (Zusammen)stoß, Zusammenprall, Anprall; (*Artil.*) Aufprall, Aufschlag, Einschlag; ***point of –***, der Auftreffpunkt; 2. (*fig., coll.*) der Einfluß, die (Ein)wirkung.

impair [im'pεə], *v.t.* verschlimmern, verschlechtern, beeinträchtigen, schädigen; schwächen, schmälern, entkräften, verringern, vermindern. **impairment,** *s.* die Verschlechterung, Beeinträchtigung, Schädigung, Schwächung.

impale [im'peil], *v.t.* 1. pfählen, aufspießen; (*fig.*) durchbohren; 2. (*Her.*) durch einen senkrechten Pfahl verbinden. **impalement,** *s.* 1. die Pfählung, Aufspießung; Durchbohrung; 2. (*Her.*) Verbindung zweier Wappen in einem Schild.

impalpable [im'pælpəbl], *adj.* unfühlbar, äußerst fein; (*fig.*) unfaßbar, kaum faßlich, unmerklich.

impanel, *see* **empanel.**

impart [im'pɑ:t], *v.t.* geben, verleihen, gewähren, zuteilen, erteilen, zukommen lassen; (*fig.*) enthüllen, kundtun, mitteilen (***to***, *Dat.*).

impartial [im'pɑːʃl], *adj.* unparteiisch, unvoreingenommen, unbefangen. **impartiality** [-ʃi'æliti], *s.* die Unparteilichkeit, Unbefangenheit, Unvoreingenommenheit.

impartment [im'pɑːtmənt], *s.* die Mitteilung, Enthüllung, Weitergabe.

impassable [im'pɑːsəbl], *adj.* unwegsam, nicht befahrbar (*as roads*), unüberschreitbar, unübersteigbar (*as an obstacle*).

impasse ['impæs], *s.* die Sackgasse; das Stocken, völliger Stillstand.

impassibility [impæsi'biliti], *s.* die Unempfindlichkeit (*to*, für), Gefühllosigkeit (gegen). **impassible,** *adj.* empfindungslos, unempfindlich (*to*, für), gefühllos (gegen).

impassioned [im'pæʃənd], *adj.* leidenschaftlich (erregt), feurig.

impassive [im'pæsiv], *adj.* gefühllos, leidenschaftslos, teilnahm(s)los; unempfindlich, ungerührt, unbeweglich. **impassiveness, impassivity** [-'siviti], *s.* die Unempfindlichkeit, Ungerührtheit; Gefühllosigkeit, Leidenschaftslosigkeit.

impaste [im'peist], **1.** *v.t.* Farben dick auftragen auf (*Acc.*), impastieren, pastos malen. **impasto,** *s.* dickes Auftragen der Farbe; das Impasto, dick aufgetragene Farbe.

impatience [im'peiʃəns], *s.* die Ungeduld; Unduldsamkeit (*of*, gegen), der Unwille (*at, with*, über (*Acc.*)). **impatient,** *adj.* ungeduldig (*at, of, with*, über (*Acc.*)); unduldsam (*of*, gegen), ungehalten (über (*Acc.*)); begierig (*for*, nach); *be – of*, nicht dulden *or* ertragen können.

impawn [im'pɔːn], *v.t.* verpfänden.

impeach [im'piːtʃ], *v.t.* beschuldigen, anklagen (*of*, *Gen.*); des Hochverrats *or* Amtsmißbrauchs unter Anklage stellen (*an official*); angreifen, anfechten, in Zweifel ziehen, in Frage stellen; tadeln, herabsetzen (*motives etc.*). **impeachable,** *adj.* anfechtbar, angreifbar, bestreitbar (*motives etc.*), anklagbar (*a p.*). **impeachment,** *s.* (öffentliche) Anklage (wegen Amtsmißbrauchs *or* Hochverrats); die Beschuldigung, Verklagung (*of a p.*), Infragestellung, Anfechtung, Herabsetzung; *– of a witness,* die Zurückweisung eines Zeugen wegen Unglaubwürdigkeit.

impeccability [impekə'biliti], *s.* die Unfehlbarkeit, Fehlerlosigkeit. **impeccable** [-'pekəbl], *adj.* unfehlbar, sünd(en)los; (*coll.*) tadellos, einwandfrei.

impecuniosity [impəkjuːni'ɔsiti], *s.* der Geldmangel. **impecunious** [-'kjuːniəs], *adj.* mittellos, geldlos, arm.

impedance [im'piːdəns], *s.* (*Elec.*) der Scheinwiderstand, die Impedanz.

impede [im'piːd], *v.t.* (be)hindern, aufhalten (*a p.*); verhindern, erschweren (*a th.*).

impediment [im'pedimənt], *s.* **1.** das Hindernis, die Verhinderung; (*Law*) das Ehehindernis; **2.** (*Med.*) die Funktionsstörung; *– in one's speech,* der Sprachfehler. **impedimenta** [-'mentə], *pl.* (*Mil.*) das Gepäck; der Troß.

impel [im'pel], *v.t.* (an)treiben, vorwärtstreiben, drängen, (*fig.*) bewegen, zwingen (*to*, zu). **impellent, 1.** *s.* die Triebkraft. **2.** *attrib. adj.* Trieb–.

impend [im'pend], *v.i.* hängen, schweben (*over*, über (*Dat.*)); (*fig.*) bevorstehen, drohen. **impending,** *adj.* überhangend; (*fig.*) bevorstehend, drohend.

impenetrability [impenitrə'biliti], *s.* die Undurchdringlichkeit; (*fig.*) Unerforschlichkeit, Unergründlichkeit. **impenetrable** [-'penitrəbl], *adj.* undurchdringlich (*to*, für); (*fig.*) unerforschlich, unergründlich; unempfindlich (für), unempfänglich (gegen), unzugänglich (*Dat.*).

impenitence [im'penitəns], *s.* die Unbußfertigkeit, Verstocktheit. **impenitent,** *adj.* unbußfertig, verstockt, reuelos.

imperative [im'perətiv], **1.** *adj.* befehlend, gebieterisch, Befehls–, gebietend; dringend (notwendig), bindend, unumgänglich, zwingend; (*Gram.*) *– mood,* der Imperativ, die Befehlsform. **2.** *s.* das Gebot, Geheiß; (*Gram.*) *see – mood.*

imperceptibility [impəsepti'biliti], *s.* die Unwahrnehmbarkeit, Unmerklichkeit. **imperceptible** [-'septibl], *adj.* unbemerkbar, unwahrnehmbar (*to*, für); unmerklich, unmerkbar, verschwindend klein.

imperfect [im'pəːfikt], **1.** *adj.* **1.** unvollkommen; unvollständig, unvollendet; mangelhaft, fehlerhaft; *– rhyme,* unreiner Reim; 2. (*Gram.*) *– tense,* das Imperfekt(um). **2.** *s.* (*Gram.*) *see – tense.* **imperfection** [-'fekʃən], *s.* die Unvollkommenheit, Fehlerhaftigkeit, Mangelhaftigkeit; der Mangel, Fehler; (*fig.*) die Schwäche.

imperforate [im'pəːfərit], *adj.* undurchbohrt, undurchlöchert, ohne Öffnung; ungezähnt (*postage-stamps*).

imperial [im'piəriəl], **1.** *adj.* kaiserlich, Kaiser–, Reichs–; (*Hist.*) Weltreichs– (*of Gt. Britain*); gebietend, (ober)herrschaftlich, souverän; herrlich, stattlich; (*Hist.*) *– city,* freie Reichsstadt; (*Hist.*) *Imperial Diet,* deutscher Reichstag; *– eagle,* der Kaiseradler; *– pint,* gesetzliches (englisches) Flüssigkeitsmaß (= *0.57 l.*); (*Hist.*) *– preference,* Zollvergünstigungen innerhalb des britischen Weltreiches. **2.** *s.* **1.** Kaiserlicher (Soldat); 2. das Imperial(papier) (*22 × 32 in.*); 3. der Knebelbart, Zwickelbart; 4. die Imperiale, das Wagenverdeck; 5. der Gepäckkasten (*of a coach*).

imperialism [im'piəriəlizm], *s.* die Kaiserherrschaft; der Imperialismus, die Weltherrschaft, Weltmachtpolitik. **imperialist, 1.** *s.* Kaiserliche(r), Kaiserlichgesinnte(r); der Imperialist. **2.** *adj.* 1. kaiserlich, kaisertreu; 2. *or* **imperialistic** [-'listik], *adj.* imperialistisch.

imperil [im'peril], *v.t.* gefährden.

imperious [im'piəriəs], *adj.* 1. gebieterisch, herrschsüchtig, herrisch, anmaßend; 2. zwingend, dringend (*as necessity*). **imperiousness,** *s.* 1. die Herrschsucht, Anmaßung, herrisches Wesen; 2. die Dringlichkeit.

imperishable [im'periʃəbl], *adj.* unvergänglich, unzerstörbar.

impermanence [im'pəːmənəns], *s.* die Unbeständigkeit, Wandelbarkeit. **impermanent,** *adj.* unbeständig, vorübergehend.

impermeability [impəːmiə'biliti], *s.* die Undurchlässigkeit, Undurchdringlichkeit. **impermeable,** *adj.* undurchdringlich (*to*, für), undurchlässig; wasserdicht.

impermissible [impə'misibl], *adj.* unstatthaft, unzulässig.

impersonal [im'pəːsənl], *adj.* unpersönlich; (*Gram.*) unpersönlich (*verb*), unbestimmt (*pronoun*). **impersonality** [-'næliti], *s.* die Unpersönlichkeit.

impersonate [im'pəːsəneit], *v.t.* verkörpern, personifizieren; sich ausgeben als; (*Theat.*) darstellen. **impersonation** [-'neiʃən], *s.* die Verkörperung, Personifizierung; Darstellung. **impersonator,** *s.* (*Theat.*) der Darsteller, Imitator.

impertinence [im'pəːtinəns], *s.* 1. die Frechheit, Unverschämtheit, Ungebührlichkeit, Ungehörigkeit; 2. (*rare*) Belanglosigkeit. **impertinent,** *adj.* 1. frech, unverschämt, ungebührlich, ungehörig, unangebracht; 2. (*rare*) belanglos, nebensächlich.

imperturbability [impətəːbə'biliti], *s.* die Gelassenheit, Unerschütterlichkeit, der Gleichmut. **imperturbable** [-'təːbəbl], *adj.* gelassen, unerschütterlich.

impervious [im'pəːviəs], *adj.* undurchdringlich (*to*, für), undurchlässig; (*fig.*) unzugänglich (*to*, für *or* *Dat.*), unwegsam; *– to water,* wasserdicht. **imperviousness,** *s.* die Undurchdringlichkeit; (*fig.*) Unzugänglichkeit.

impetigo [impə'taigou], *s.* (*Med.*) die Impetigo.

impetuosity [impetju'ɔsiti], *s.* die Heftigkeit, das Ungestüm. **impetuous** [im'petjuəs], *adj.* ungestüm, heftig.

impetus ['impətəs], *s.* die Triebkraft, Stoßkraft,

der Impuls; (*fig.*) Antrieb, Anstoß; ***give a fresh –,*** neuen Antrieb geben.

impiety [im'paiəti], *s.* die Gottlosigkeit; Pietätlosigkeit, Ehrfurchtslosigkeit.

impinge [im'pindʒ], *v.i.* stoßen ((***up***)***on***, an (*Acc.*) *or* gegen), zusammenstoßen (mit); fallen (*of light*) (auf (*Acc.*)); (*fig.*) verstoßen (gegen); eindringen, eingreifen (in (*Acc.*)), einwirken (auf (*Acc.*)). **impingement,** *s.* der Stoß ((***up***)***on***, gegen), Zusammenstoß (mit); Übergriff, Eingriff (in (*Acc.*)), die Einwirkung (auf (*Acc.*)).

impious ['impiəs], *adj.* gottlos, ruchlos; ehrfurchtslos, pietätlos.

impish ['impiʃ], *adj.* (*fig.*) schelmisch.

implacability [implækə'biliti], *s.* die Unversöhnlichkeit, Unerbittlichkeit. **implacable** [–'plækəbl], *adj.* unversöhnlich, unerbittlich.

implant [im'plɑ:nt], *v.t.* (*fig.*) einpflanzen, einimpfen, einprägen (***in***, *Dat.*).

implausible [im'plɔ:zibl], *adj.* unglaubwürdig, unwahrscheinlich.

implement, 1. ['implimənt], *s.* 1. das Gerät, Werkzeug, Zubehör; 2. (*Scots Law*) die Ausführung, Erfüllung. **2.** [–ment], *v.t.* ausführen, durchführen, erfüllen, vollenden, zur Ausführung bringen, in Wirkung setzen, (*as a guarantee*) in Anspruch nehmen.

implicate ['implikeit], *v.t.* verwickeln, hineinziehen (***in***, in (*Acc.*)); in Verbindung *or* Zusammenhang bringen (***with***, mit); (*fig.*) in sich schließen, mit einbegreifen (*a th.*). **implication** [–'keiʃən], *s.* die Verwick(e)lung, das Einbegriffensein; stillschweigende Folgerung, die Folge, Begleiterscheinung; tieferer Sinn, eigentliche Bedeutung; ***marriage and all its –s,*** die Ehe und alles, was sie mit sich bringt; ***by –,*** stillschweigend, ohne weiteres, als selbstverständliche Folgerung.

implicit [im'plisit], *adj.* unbeschränkt, unbedingt, blind; mit inbegriffen, einbegriffen, stillschweigend (inbegriffen). **implicitly,** *adv.* unbedingt; stillschweigend, ohne weiteres, implizite. **implicitness,** *s.* die Unbeschränktheit, Unbedingtheit; das Mitinbegriffensein.

implied [im'plaid], *adj.* mit inbegriffen, stillschweigend verstanden; *see* **imply.**

implore [im'plɔ:], *v.t.* anflehen, flehentlich bitten, beschwören (*a p.*), flehen, bitten (***for***, um). **imploring,** *adj.* flehentlich, flehend.

imply [im'plai], *v.t.* mitenthalten, einbegreifen, in sich schließen; bedeuten, besagen, zu verstehen geben, durchblicken lassen, andeuten; ***that may be implied from,*** das ergibt sich aus, das ist zu erschließen aus.

impolite [impo'lait], *adj.* unhöflich, grob. **impoliteness,** *s.* die Unhöflichkeit, Grobheit.

impolitic [im'pɔlitik], *adj.* unklug, unüberlegt, unvernünftig.

imponderable [im'pɔndərəbl], **1.** *adj.* (*usu. fig.*) unwägbar. **2.** *s.* (*usu. pl.*) Imponderabilien (*pl.*).

import, 1. [im'pɔ:t], *v.t.* 1. (*Comm.*) einführen, importieren; 2. (*rare*) bedeuten, besagen, mit sich bringen; betreffen, angehen, von Wichtigkeit sein für. **2.** [–'pɔ:t], *v.i.* (*rare*) von Wichtigkeit sein, Bedeutung haben. **3.** ['impɔ:t], *s.* 1. (*Comm.*) die Einfuhr, der Import; (*usu. pl.*) Einfuhrartikel, Importwaren (*pl.*); ***– duty,*** der Einfuhrzoll; 2. der Sinn, die Bedeutung; Wichtigkeit, Tragweite.

importance [im'pɔ:təns], *s.* die Wichtigkeit, Bedeutsamkeit, Bedeutung, der Wert, Belang, Einfluß, das Gewicht; (*coll.*) die Wichtigtuerei; ***man of –,*** der Mann von Bedeutung, einflußreicher Mann. **important,** *adj.* wichtig, bedeutsam, erheblich; bedeutend, wesentlich (***to***, für); einflußreich; (*coll.*) wichtigtuerisch.

importation [impɔ:'teiʃən], *s.* die (Waren)einfuhr; eingeführter Artikel. **importer** [–'pɔ:tə], *s.* der Einfuhrhändler, Importhändler, Importeur.

importunate [im'pɔ:tjunit], *adj.* lästig, zudringlich, aufdringlich.

importune [impɔ:'tju:n], *v.t.* belästigen, behelligen, dringend *or* anhaltend bitten. **importunity,** *s.* die Zudringlichkeit, Aufdringlichkeit.

impose [im'pouz], **1.** *v.t.* 1. auferlegen, aufbürden ((***up***)***on***, *Dat.*) (*on a th. or a p.*), aufdrängen, aufbinden, anhängen ((***up***)***on***, *Dat.*) (*on a p.*); ***– a tax on,*** besteuern; 2. (*Typ.*) ausschießen. **2.** *v.i.* imponieren, beeindrucken; ***– upon,*** zu sehr beanspruchen, mißbrauchen; (*coll.*) betrügen, täuschen, hintergehen, anschmieren; ***be easily –d upon,*** sich leicht täuschen lassen; ***not to be –d upon,*** sich nichts vormachen lassen; ***– upon his good nature,*** seine Gutherzigkeit ausnützen *or* mißbrauchen. **imposing,** *adj.* imponierend, eindrucksvoll, imposant.

imposition [impə'ziʃən], *s.* 1. (*Eccl.*) das Auflegen (*of hands*); 2. (*Comm. etc.*) die Auferlegung, Aufbürdung (*of taxes*); Steuer, Abgabe, Auflage; 3. Strafarbeit (*in schools*); 4. Zumutung, schamloses Ausnützen; ***an – on his good nature,*** ein Mißbrauch seiner Gutherzigkeit; 5. die Übervorteilung, Täuschung; 6. (*Typ.*) Formeinrichtung, das Ausschießen.

impossibility [impɔsi'biliti], *s.* die Unmöglichkeit. **impossible** [–'pɔsibl], *adj.* unmöglich, ausgeschlossen, undurchführbar, undenkbar; (*coll. of a p.*) unausstehlich, unerträglich.

impost ['impɔst], *s.* 1. die Abgabe, Auflage, Steuer; 2. (*Archit.*) der Kämpfer; 3. (*Spt.*) (*sl.*) das Gewicht (*horse-racing*).

impostor [im'pɔstə], *s.* der Betrüger, Schwindler. **imposture** [–tʃə], *s.* der Betrug, Schwindel.

impotence, impotency ['impətəns(i)], *s.* das Unvermögen, die Unfähigkeit; (*Med.*) Impotenz, Zeugungsunfähigkeit; (*fig.*) Gebrechlichkeit, Hinfälligkeit, Schwäche. **impotent,** *adj.* unfähig; (*Med.*) impotent, zeugungsunfähig; (*fig.*) gebrechlich, hinfällig, kraftlos, machtlos, hilflos, schwach.

impound [im'paund], *v.t.* einpferchen, einsperren, einschließen; (*Law*) in gerichtliche Verwahrung nehmen, mit Beschlag belegen.

impoverish [im'pɔvəriʃ], *v.t.* arm machen; erschöpfen, aussaugen (*land*); ***be –ed,*** verarmen. **impoverishment,** *s.* die Verarmung; Erschöpfung (*of soil*).

impracticability [impræktikə'biliti], *s.* die Undurchführbarkeit; Unlenksamkeit, Hartnäckigkeit; Ungangbarkeit, Unwegsamkeit (*of roads*). **impracticable,** *adj.* unausführbar, undurchführbar, untunlich; widerspenstig, unlenksam, hartnäckig; unwegsam, ungangbar (*as roads*).

imprecate ['imprikeit], *v.t.* herabwünschen, herbeiwünschen (*misfortune*) (***upon***, auf (*Acc.*)); ***– curses on,*** verwünschen, verfluchen. **imprecation** [–'keiʃən], *s.* die Verwünschung, der Fluch. **imprecatory,** *adj.* verwünschend, Verwünschungs–.

impregnability [impregnə'biliti], *s.* die Unüberwindlichkeit, Unbezwingbarkeit. **impregnable,** *adj.* uneinnehmbar, unbezwinglich, unüberwindlich; (*fig.*) unerschütterlich (***to***, gegenüber).

impregnate, 1. ['impregneit], *v.t.* 1. schwängern, schwanger machen; (*Bot.*) befruchten; 2. (*Chem.*) sättigen, imprägnieren; (*fig.*) durchtränken, durchdringen, erfüllen. **2.** [–'pregnit], *adj.* geschwängert, schwanger, befruchtet; (*fig.*) durchtränkt (***with***, mit), voll (von). **impregnation** [–'neiʃən], *s.* die Schwängerung; Befruchtung; Sättigung, Imprägnierung; Durchdringung.

impresario [imprə'sɑ:riou], *s.* der Impresario.

imprescriptible [impri'skriptibl], *adj.* (*Law*) unveräußerlich (*rights etc.*).

impress, 1. [im'pres], *v.t.* 1. (auf)drücken, eindrücken, abdrücken, (ein)prägen (***on***, auf (*Acc.*)); 2. (*fig.*) verleihen, aufdrücken (***upon***, *Dat.*), (*a p.*) einprägen, einschärfen, nahelegen ((***up***)***on***, *Dat.*), (*a p.*) erfüllen, durchdringen (***with***, mit); ***the urgency was –ed on my mind,*** die dringende Eile wurde mir eingeschärft *or* nahegelegt; ***–ed with the necessity,*** von der Notwendigkeit durchdrungen; 3. beeindrucken, Eindruck machen auf (*Acc.*); ***be favourably –ed by,*** einen guten Eindruck erhalten von; *-ed by the idea,* durch den Gedanken beeindruckt; 4. pressen (*seamen*); 5. beschlagnahmen (*goods*). **2.** ['impres], *s.* der Abdruck, Stempel, die Prägung; (*fig.*) das Gepräge, Merkmal. **impressible** [-'presibl], *adj. See* **impressionable.**

impression [im'preʃən], *s.* 1. *See* **impress, 2.**; 2. (*fig.*) der Eindruck, die (Ein)wirkung (*on,* auf (*Acc.*)); (*coll.*) Vermutung, dunkle Erinnerung; *give the – of being,* den Eindruck hinterlassen zu sein; *give* or *leave the wrong –,* den falschen Eindruck vermitteln; *I am under the –,* ich habe den Eindruck, ich hege die Vermutung, es schwebt mir dunkel vor; 3. (*Dentistry*) der Gebißabdruck; 4. (*Typ.*) (Ab)druck, Abzug, (*of a book*) (unveränderte) Auflage; *new –,* der Neudruck, neue Auflage.

impressionable [im'preʃənəbl], *adj.* empfänglich (*to,* für), beeindruckbar, leicht zu beeindrucken(d), leicht bestimmbar (durch). **impressionism,** *s.* (*Art*) der Impressionismus. **impressionist,** *s.* der Impressionist. **impressionistic** [-'nistik], *adj.* impressionistisch.

impressive [im'presiv], *adj.* eindrucksvoll, eindringlich, ergreifend, imponierend. **impressiveness,** *s.* Eindrucksvolle(s), Ergreifende(s).

impressment [im'presmənt], *s.* 1. (*Naut.*) das Pressen, gewaltsame Anwerbung (*of seamen*); 2. (*Comm.*) die Beschlagnahme, Requirierung (*of goods*).

imprest ['imprest], *s.* der Staatsvorschuß.

imprimatur [impri'meitə], *s.* die Druckbewilligung, Druckerlaubnis.

imprint, 1. [im'print], *v.t.* (auf)drücken, aufprägen, aufpressen (*on,* auf (*Acc.*)), eindrücken (in (*Acc.*)), (*fig.*) einprägen (in (*Acc.*)). **2.** ['imprint], *s.* 1. der Abdruck, Stempel; (*fig.*) Eindruck, das Gepräge; 2. (*Typ.*) der Druckvermerk, die Verlagsangabe, das Impressum.

imprison [im'prizn], *v.t.* einkerkern, einsperren, ins Gefängnis stecken, verhaften; (*fig.*) einschließen, einsperren, festhalten. **imprisonment,** *s.* die Verhaftung, Einkerkerung, Inhaftierung; Haft, Gefangenschaft, Freiheitsstrafe, Gefängnisstrafe; *false –,* ungesetzliche Haft; *– before trial,* die Untersuchungshaft.

improbability [imprɔbə'biliti], *s.* die Unwahrscheinlichkeit, Unglaubwürdigkeit. **improbable** [-'prɔbəbl], *adj.* unwahrscheinlich, unglaubwürdig.

improbity [im'proubiti], *s.* die Unredlichkeit, Unehrlichkeit.

impromptu [im'prɔmptju:], **1.** *adj., adv.* unvorbereitet, aus dem Stegreif, improvisiert. **2.** *s.* das Stegreifgedicht; (*Mus.*) Impromptu, die Improvisation.

improper [im'prɔpə], *adj.* 1. ungeeignet, untauglich, unpassend (*to,* für); 2. unzulässig; unschicklich, ungehörig, unanständig; 3. (*Math.*) *– fraction,* unechter Bruch.

impropriate, 1. [im'prouprieit], *v.t.* (*Eccl.*) (an Laien) zur Nutznießung übertragen. **2.** [-iit], *adj.* (einem Laien) übertragen. **impropriation** [-'eiʃən], *s.* das Übertragen an Laien; einem Laien übertragene Pfründe. **impropriator** [-eitə], *s.* weltlicher Pfründenbesitzer.

impropriety [imprə'praiəti], *s.* 1. die Untauglichkeit, Ungeeignetheit, Unangebrachtheit; 2. Unschicklichkeit, Ungehörigkeit; 3. ungehörige Bemerkung, Ungehörige(s).

improvable [im'pru:vəbl], *adj.* verbesserungsfähig, verbesserlich, bildsam; (*of land*) kultivierbar, kulturfähig, anbaufähig. **improve, 1.** *v.t.* 1. verbessern, vervollkommnen, ausbauen, erhöhen, verstärken, vergrößern, vermehren, aufbessern, anreichern, veredeln, verfeinern, meliorisieren (*land*); 2. benutzen, ausnützen, sich (*Dat.*) zunutze machen; *– the occasion,* gleich eine Predigt halten; *– the shining hour,* seine Zeit vorteilhaft ausnützen. **2.** *v.i.* besser werden, sich (ver)bessern, sich vervollkommnen, Fortschritte machen; steigen, anziehen (*prices*); sich erholen (*health*); *– (up)on,* überbieten, übertreffen; *not to be –d upon,* unübertrefflich; *– on acquaintance,* bei näherer Bekanntschaft gewinnen. **3.** *s.* (*coll.*) *on the –,* auf dem Wege der Besserung.

improvement [im'pru:vmənt], *s.* 1. die (Ver)besserung, Vervollkommnung; *– in health,* die Besserung der Gesundheit; 2. die Ausnutzung, Nutzanwendung, vorteilhafte Anwendung; 3. die Veredelung, Verfeinerung, Aufbesserung, Ausbildung; *– in prices,* die Kursaufbesserung, Preissteigung; *– of the soil,* die Bodenverbesserung, Melioration; 4. der Fortschritt, Gewinn ((*up*)*on,* gegenüber). **improver,** *s.* 1. der Verbesserer; 2. (*Comm.*) Volontär; 3. das Verbesserungsmittel.

improvidence [im'prɔvidəns], *s.* die Unbedachtsamkeit, Unvorsichtigkeit; Sorglosigkeit, der Leichtsinn. **improvident,** *adj.* unvorsichtig, unbedacht(sam), achtlos, sorglos, unbekümmert, leichtsinnig.

improving [im'pru:viŋ], *adj.* förderlich, heilsam, gedeihlich, wohltätig.

improvisation [imprəvai'zeiʃən], *s.* die Stegreifdichtung; unvorbereitete Veranstaltung, die Improvisation (*also Mus.*). **improvisator** [-'prɔvizeitə], *s.* der Improvisator, Stegreifdichter. **improvise** ['imprəvaiz], *v.t., v.i.* aus dem Stegreif *or* ohne Vorbereitung tun (reden, sprechen, spielen, dichten), improvisieren, extemporieren; im Handumdrehen einrichten; (*coll.*) aus dem Boden stampfen, aus dem Ärmel schütteln. **improvised,** *adj.* improvisiert, extemporiert, unvorbereitet, Stegreif–; behelfsmäßig, Behelfs–.

imprudence [im'pru:dəns], *s.* die Unklugheit, Unvorsichtigkeit. **imprudent,** *adj.* unklug, unvorsichtig, unüberlegt, übereilt.

impudence ['impjədəns], *s.* die Unverschämtheit, Frechheit. **impudent,** *adj.* unverschämt, frech.

impugn [im'pju:n], *v.t.* anfechten, bestreiten, in Zweifel ziehen; bekämpfen, angreifen, antasten. **impugnable,** *adj.* bestreitbar, anfechtbar. **impugnment,** *s.* die Bestreitung, Anfechtung, Widerlegung; der Einwand.

impulse ['impʌls], *s.* 1. der (An)stoß, Antrieb, die Triebkraft; 2. (*fig.*) Triebkraft, der Anreiz, (An)trieb, Drang, Impuls, die Anregung; Regung, Anwandlung, Eingebung; *act on the – of the moment,* einer augenblicklichen Eingebung *or* Regung folgen; *on an –,* auf einen Antrieb hin; *on –,* impulsiv; 3. (*Elec.*) der (Spannungs- *or* Strom)stoß. **impulsion** [-'pʌlʃən], *s. See* **impulse,** 1., 2. **impulsive** [im'pʌlsiv], *adj.* (an)treibend, Trieb–; (*usu. fig.*) impulsiv, gefühlsbeherrscht, leicht erregbar, triebhaft. **impulsiveness,** *s.* die Erregbarkeit, Impulsivität.

impunity [im'pju:niti], *s.* die Straflosigkeit, Straffreiheit; *with –,* ungestraft.

impure [im'pjuə], *adj.* unrein, schmutzig; nicht rein, verfälscht; (*fig.*) unkeusch, unzüchtig; unsauber (*as motives*), gemischt, nicht einheitlich (*as style*). **impurity,** *s.* die Unreinheit, Unreinlichkeit; Unkeuschheit; *pl.* fremde Bestandteile (*pl.*), Beimischungen (*pl.*), die Verunreinigung, der Schmutz.

imputable [im'pju:təbl], *adj.* zuzuschreiben(d), zuzurechnen(d), beizumessen(d) (*to, Dat.*). **imputation** [-'teiʃən], *s.* 1. die Zuschreibung, Zurechnung, Beimessung, Beilegung; 2. Anschuldigung, Beschuldigung, Bezichtigung; *– on his character,* der Makel auf seinem Charakter. **impute,** *v.t.* anrechnen, zurechnen, zuschreiben, beimessen, zur Last legen (*to, Dat.*). **imputed,** *adj.* unterstellt, zugeschrieben; abgeleitet, veranschlagt.

in [in], **1.** *prep.* **(a)** (*situation*) in, an, auf (*Dat.*), innerhalb (*Gen.*); *– the country,* auf dem Lande; *blind – one eye,* auf einem Auge blind; *– the rain,* in *or* bei Regen; *– the sky,* am Himmel; *– the street,* auf der Straße; *– town,* in der Stadt; **(b)** (*movement in space*) see **into**; *break – two,* entzweibrechen; *he put it – his pocket,* er steckte es in seine Tasche; **(c)** (*time*) in, an, unter (*Dat.*), während (*Gen.*), binnen, bei, zu; *– the afternoon,* nachmittags; – ***the beginning,*** am Anfang; – ***conclusion,*** schließlich; – ***due course,*** zu seiner *or* rechter Zeit; – ***the daytime,*** bei Tage, während des Tages; – ***1870,*** im Jahre 1870; – ***the evening,*** abends, am Abend; – ***January,*** im Januar; – ***the meantime,*** inzwischen, mittlerweile, unterdessen; – ***the reign of,*** unter der Regierung (*Gen.*); – ***time,*** mit der Zeit; rechtzeitig; zur rechten Zeit; – ***10 years(') time,*** nach 10 Jahren; – ***bad weather,*** bei schlechtem Wetter; – ***a week,*** in acht Tagen; nach acht Tagen; – ***the last 10 years,*** der letzten 10 Jahre; **(d)** (*fig. situation*) in, an, auf, unter (*Dat.*), bei; – ***an accident,*** bei einem Unfall; (*Mil.*) – ***arms,*** unter Waffen; – ***the army,*** beim Heer; ***be – cash,*** bei Kasse sein; – ***the circumstances,*** unter den Umständen; – ***his defence,*** zu seiner Verteidigung; – ***good health,*** in *or* bei guter Gesundheit; – ***his honour,*** ihm zu Ehren; ***be – liquor,*** unter Alkohol sein; – ***obedience to,*** aus Gehorsam gegen; – ***remembrance of,*** zum Andenken an (*Acc.*); – ***the press,*** im Druck, unter der Presse; – ***search of,*** auf der Suche nach; – ***his sleep,*** im Schlaf; – ***Shakespeare,*** bei Sh.; **(e)** (*condition, circumstance*) in (*Dat.*), auf (*Acc.*), mit; ***infant – arms,*** der Säugling, das Brustkind, Baby; – ***any case,*** auf jeden Fall; – ***contempt,*** aus Verachtung; – ***debt,*** verschuldet; – ***doubt,*** im Zweifel; – ***dozens,*** dutzendweise; – ***German,*** auf deutsch; – ***groups,*** gruppenweise; – ***a hurry,*** eilig; – ***this manner*** or ***way,*** auf diese Weise, in dieser Weise; – ***particular,*** im besonderen; – ***praise of,*** zum Lobe von; – ***print,*** im Druck, gedruckt; – ***ruins,*** zerstört; – ***short,*** kurz (gesagt); – ***stock,*** vorrätig; – ***truth,*** in der Tat, wahrhaftig; – ***no way,*** auf keine Weise, in keiner Weise, keineswegs, durchaus nicht; ***dressed – white,*** weißgekleidet; – ***a word,*** mit einem Wort, in aller Kürze; – ***writing,*** schriftlich; **(f)** (*relation*) in, an (*Dat.*), in bezug auf (*Acc.*), nach, gemäß; – ***answer to,*** in Beantwortung (*Gen.*), als Antwort auf (*Acc.*); – ***appearance,*** dem Anschein *or* Äußeren nach; – ***body and mind,*** am Körper und im Gemüt; – ***as*** or ***so far as,*** insoweit als; – ***all likelihood*** or ***probability,*** aller Wahrscheinlichkeit nach; – ***number,*** an Zahl; – ***my opinion,*** nach meiner Meinung, meiner Meinung nach, meines Erachtens; – ***respect of . . .,*** was . . . betrifft *or* anbelangt; – ***size,*** an Größe; – ***stature,*** von Figur; – ***turn,*** der Reihe nach; **(g)** (*number, amount*) in (*Dat.*), aus, von, zu; – ***all,*** im ganzen; ***one – ten,*** einer *etc.* unter zehn; ***a woman – a million,*** eine Frau wie man sie unter einer Million nicht findet; (*obs.*) ***a shilling – the pound,*** 5 Prozent; **(h)** (*participation*) ***have a hand – it,*** daran beteiligt sein, es mitmachen; (*coll.*) ***he's not – it,*** er zählt nicht mit; ***there's money – it,*** dabei ist viel Geld zu verdienen; ***there's nothing – it,*** es ist nichts daran, es hat keinen Wert; es lohnt sich nicht, es springt nichts dabei heraus; es ist nichts dabei, es ist ja ganz einfach; es ist kein großer Unterschied, (*Spt.*) es ist noch unentschieden; ***there's something – it,*** es steckt etwas dahinter; ***take part – it,*** daran teilnehmen; (*coll.*) ***he's not got it – him,*** er hat nicht das Zeug dazu; **(i)** (*with many v.i.*) *e.g.* ***abound –, believe –, engage –, originate –, participate –, persist –, rejoice –, trust –,*** *etc.*; *see the verb*; **(j)** (*with gerunds*) 1. *render with inf. clause*: ***I have much pleasure – informing you,*** es freut mich, Ihnen mitteilen zu können; 2. bei *with n. inf.*: – ***crossing the road,*** beim Überqueren der Straße; 3. mit *with n. inf.*: ***I passed the time – sleeping,*** ich brachte die Zeit mit Schlafen hin; 4. bei *or* mit *with noun derivative of the verb*: – ***making this contribution,*** mit der Leistung dieses Beitrags; – ***selling the house,*** beim Verkauf des Hauses; **(k)** (*other idioms*) – ***order to do,*** um zu tun; – ***that he agreed,*** weil er *or* insofern als er einwilligte.

2. *adv.* **(a)** innen, drinnen; **(b)** (*with verbs of movement as sep. pref.*) herein–, hinein–; **(c)** da, (an)gekommen; zu Hause; (*Pol.*) an der Macht; (*Spt.*) am Spiel, am Schlagen; (*coll.*) in Mode; (*coll.*) ***the fire has stayed*** or ***is –,*** das Feuer brennt noch; ***the harvest is –,*** die Ernte ist eingebracht; ***be – for,*** zu erwarten or befürchten haben; (*coll.*) ***be – for it,*** schön in der Patsche *or* Klemme sitzen; ***be – for an examination,*** sich für eine Prüfung gemeldet haben; ***break –,*** abrichten, bändigen (*horse*); ***breed –,*** sich durch Inzucht fortpflanzen; ***come –!*** herein! ***he came –,*** er kam herein; (*coll.*) ***fall – with,*** übereinstimmen mit; ***go –,*** hineingehen, eintreten; (*coll.*) ***go – for,*** betreiben, sich beschäftigen mit; ***keep –,*** nachsitzen lassen (*in school*); ***keep – with him,*** auf gutem Fuße mit ihm bleiben; ***keep one's hand –,*** in Übung bleiben; ***rub –,*** einreiben; ***show him –!*** führen Sie ihn herein! – ***and out,*** hin und her; ***year – year out,*** jahraus, jahrein; (*Prov.*) – ***for a penny, – for a pound,*** wer A sagt, muß auch B sagen; (*coll.*) ***throw –,*** als Zugabe geben.

3. *s.* (*Pol.*) ***the –s,*** die Regierungspartei; (*coll.*) ***the –s and outs,*** alles was drum und dran ist, die Winkel und Ecken, alle Einzelheiten *or* Feinheiten *or* Besonderheiten.

inability [inə'biliti], *s.* die Unfähigkeit, das Unvermögen; *see* **unable.**

inaccessibility [inəksesi'biliti], *s.* die Unzugänglichkeit (*to*, für), Unerreichbarkeit, Unnahbarkeit. **inaccessible** [–'sesibl], *adj.* unerreichbar, unzugänglich, unnahbar (*to*, für *or Dat.*).

inaccuracy [in'ækjərəsi], *s.* die Ungenauigkeit; der Fehler, Irrtum. **inaccurate,** *adj.* ungenau; falsch, irrig.

inaction [in'ækʃən], *s.* die Untätigkeit. **inactive** [–tiv], *adj.* untätig; träge, müßig, passiv; (*Chem. etc.*) unwirksam, träge; (*Mil.*) nicht aktiv, außer Dienst; (*Comm.*) unbelebt, lustlos, flau. **inactivity** [–'tiviti], *s.* die Untätigkeit; Trägheit; (*Comm.*) Unbelebtheit, Flauheit, Lustlosigkeit.

inadaptability [inədæptə'biliti], *s.* die Unanwendbarkeit (*to*, für *or* auf (*Acc.*)). **inadaptable** [–'dæptəbl], *adj.* unanwendbar (*to*, auf (*Acc.*)), untauglich (für).

inadequacy [in'ædəkwəsi], *s.* die Unzulänglichkeit, Unangemessenheit. **inadequate,** *adj.* ungenügend, unzulänglich, unangemessen, unzureichend.

inadmissibility [inədmisi'biliti], *s.* die Unzulässigkeit. **inadmissible** [–'misibl], *adj.* unzulässig, unstatthaft.

inadvertence, inadvertency [inəd'və:təns(i)], *s.* die Unachtsamkeit, Nachlässigkeit, Fahrlässigkeit; der Irrtum, das Versehen. **inadvertent,** *adj.* unachtsam, nachlässig, fahrlässig; unbeabsichtigt, unabsichtlich; versehentlich, irrtümlich. **inadvertently,** *adv.* aus Versehen, versehentlich, unbeabsichtigt.

inadvisability [inədvaizə'biliti], *s.* die Unratsamkeit. **inadvisable** [–'vaizəbl], *adj.* unratsam, nicht empfehlenswert.

inalienability [ineiliənə'biliti], *s.* die Unveräußerlichkeit. **inalienable** [–'eiliənəbl], *adj.* unveräußerlich, unübertragbar.

inalterable [in'ɔ:ltərəbl], *adj.* unveränderlich, unabänderlich.

inamorata [inæmə'rɑ:tə], *s.* die Verliebte; das Liebchen. **inamorato** [–tou], *s.* der Verliebte, Liebhaber.

inane [i'nein], *adj.* leer, nichtig, fade; geistlos, sinnlos, albern.

inanimate [in'ænimit], *adj.* leblos, unbeseelt; (*Comm.*) unbelebt, flau.

inanition [inæ'niʃən], *s.* (*Med.*) die Schwäche, Entkräftung.

inanity [i'næniti], *s.* die Trivialität, Sinnlosigkeit, Leere, Nichtigkeit; Hohlheit, Albernheit, Geistlosigkeit; *pl.* fades *or* leeres Geschwätz.

inapplicability [in'æplikə'biliti], *s.* die Unanwendbarkeit. **inapplicable,** *adj.* unanwendbar, nicht zutreffend (*to*, auf (*Acc.*)), ungeeignet, unbrauchbar, untauglich (für).

inapposite [in'æpəzit], *adj.* unangemessen, unangebracht, unpassend (*to*, für).

inappreciable [inə'pri:ʃiəbl], *adj.* unmerklich, unbedeutend, unwichtig.

inapprehensible [inæpri'hensibl], *adj.* unbegreiflich, unfaßbar, unfaßlich, undenkbar.
inapproachable [inə'proutʃəbl], *adj.* unnahbar, unzugänglich; (*coll.*) einzig dastehend, konkurrenzlos.
inappropriate [inə'proupriit], *adj.* ungeeignet, unpassend (*to*, *for*, für), unangemessen, ungehörig (*Dat.*). **inappropriateness,** *s.* die Unangemessenheit, Ungehörigkeit.
inapt [in'æpt], *adj.* 1. unpassend, ungeeignet, unangemessen; 2. unbegabt, ungeschicklich, ungeschickt (*at*, bei). **inaptitude** [–itju:d], *s.* die Unbegabtheit, Ungeschicklichkeit, Ungeschicktheit. **inaptness,** *s.* 1. die Ungeeignetheit, Untauglichkeit (*for*, zu), Unangemessenheit (für); 2. *See* **inaptitude.**
inarch [in'ɑ:tʃ], *v.t.* (*Hort.*) absaugen, ablaktieren.
inarticulate [inɑ:'tikjulit], *adj.* unartikuliert; undeutlich, unverständlich (*of speech*); (*Zool.*) ungegliedert; – *with rage*, sprachlos vor Wut. **inarticulateness,** *s.* die Undeutlichkeit, Unverständlichkeit; Sprachlosigkeit; (*Zool.*) Ungegliedertheit.
inartistic [inɑ:'tistik], *adj.* unkünstlerisch; ohne Kunstverständnis, kunstfremd.
inasmuch [inəz'mʌtʃ], *conj.* – *as*, da (ja), in Anbetracht der Tatsache daß.
inattention [inə'tenʃən], *s.* die Unaufmerksamkeit, Unachtsamkeit (*to*, gegenüber), Nichtbeachtung, Gleichgültigkeit (gegen). **inattentive** [–tiv], *adj.* unaufmerksam, unachtsam (*to*, gegenüber), nachlässig, achtlos, gleichgültig (gegen). **inattentiveness,** *s.* die Unaufmerksamkeit.
inaudibility [inɔ:di'biliti], *s.* die Unhörbarkeit. **inaudible** [–'ɔ:dibl], *adj.* unhörbar.
inaugural [in'ɔ:gjərəl], *adj.* Einweihungs–, Einführungs–, Eröffnungs–; – *speech*, die Antrittsrede. **inaugurate** [–reit], *v.t.* einweihen, (feierlich) eröffnen (*building etc.*) *or* einführen *or* einsetzen (*a p.*); (*fig.*) beginnen, ins Leben rufen, einleiten (*an era etc.*). **inauguration** [–'reiʃən], *s.* die Einweihung, feierliche Eröffnung (*of building, meeting*), Amtseinsetzung, Amtseinführung (*of a p.*); (*fig.*) der Anfang, Beginn, das Beginnen; (*Am.*) *Inauguration Day*, der Amtsantrittstag des Präsidenten. **inaugurator** [–reitə], *s.* der Einführer. **inauguratory,** *adj. See* **inaugural.**
inauspicious [inɔ:'spiʃəs], *adj.* ungünstig, unglücklich, unheilvoll, von böser Vorbedeutung. **inauspiciousness,** *s.* üble Vorbedeutung; die Ungünstigkeit.
inboard ['inbɔ:d], **1.** *adv.* binnenbords, im Schiff. **2.** *attrib. adj.* (*Naut.*) Innen–; – *engine*, der Innenbordmotor; Einbaumotor.
inborn ['inbɔ:n], *adj.* angeboren (*in*, *Dat.*).
inbreathe [in'bri:ð], *v.t.* einhauchen.
inbred ['inbred], *adj.* angeboren, ererbt; (*fig.*) tief eingewurzelt.
inbreed [in'bri:d], *irr.v.t.* durch Inzucht züchten. **inbreeding,** *s.* die Inzucht.
incalculability [in'kælkjulə'biliti], *s.* die Unberechenbarkeit, Unbestimmbarkeit. **incalculable,** *adj.* unberechenbar, unbestimmbar, nicht abzuschätzen(d), unermeßlich, unmeßbar; (*of a p.*) unberechenbar, unzuverlässig.
incandescence [inkæn'desəns], *s.* das Weißglühen, die Weißglut. **incandescent,** *adj.* (weiß)glühend, leuchtend, Glüh–; – *mantle*, der Glühstrumpf.
incantation [inkæn'teiʃən], *s.* die Beschwörung; Beschwörungsformel, der Zauberspruch.
incapability [inkeipə'biliti], *s.* die Unfähigkeit, Untauglichkeit (*of*, zu). **incapable** [–'keipəbl], *adj.* unfähig, untauglich, nicht fähig *or* imstande (*of*, zu); (*of a p.*) unfähig, untüchtig; *drunk and* –, hilflos betrunken.
incapacitate [inkə'pæsiteit], *v.t.* 1. untauglich *or* ungeeignet *or* unfähig machen (*for*, für); 2. (*Law*) für (rechts)unfähig erklären. **incapacitation** [–'teiʃən], *s.* 1. das Unfähigmachen; 2. (*Law*) die Aberkennung der Rechtsfähigkeit, Disqualifikation. **incapacity,** *s.* 1. die Unfähigkeit, Untauglichkeit (*for*, zu); 2. (*Law*) Rechtsunfähigkeit.
incapsulate [in'kæpsjuleit], *v.t.* einkapseln; (*Gram.*) einschachteln. **incapsulation** [–'leiʃən], *s.* die Einkapselung, (*Gram.*) Einschachtelung.
incarcerate [in'kɑ:səreit], *v.t.* 1. einkerkern, einsperren; 2. (*Med.*) einklemmen. **incarceration** [–'reiʃən], *s.* 1. die Einkerkerung, Einsperrung; 2. (*Med.*) Einklemmung.
incarnadine [in'kɑ:nədain], *adj.* (*Poet.*) fleischfarben.
incarnate, **1.** [in'kɑ:nit], *adj.* fleischgeworden; (*fig.*) verkörpert, personifiziert; eingefleischt, leibhaftig; *God* –, Gott in Menschengestalt; *devil* –, leibhaftiger Teufel. **2.** [–neit], *v.t.* mit Fleisch bekleiden; (*fig.*) verwirklichen, verkörpern, versinnbildlichen, konkret darstellen. **incarnation** [–'neiʃən], *s.* die Fleischwerdung, Menschwerdung; (*fig.*) Verkörperung, Personifikation, der Inbegriff.
incautious [in'kɔ:ʃəs], *adj.* unvorsichtig, unbedacht, sorglos. **incautiousness,** *s.* die Unvorsichtigkeit.
incendiarism [in'sendjərizm], *s.* 1. die Brandstiftung; 2. (*fig.*) Aufwiegelung. **incendiary,** **1.** *adj.* 1. Brand–; – *bomb*, die Brandbombe; – *fires*, Brandstiftungen; 2. (*fig.*) aufrührerisch, aufwieglerisch. **2.** *s.* 1. der Brandstifter; 2. (*coll. Mil.*) die Brandbombe; 3. (*fig.*) der Aufruhrstifter, Aufwiegler, Hetzer, Agitator.
[1]**incense** ['insens], **1.** *s.* der Weihrauch, das Räucherwerk; – *burner*, die Räucherbüchse. **2.** *v.t.* beweihräuchern; mit Weihrauch *or* Duft erfüllen, durchduften.
[2]**incense** [in'sens], *v.t.* erzürnen, in Wut bringen (*with*, durch).
incentive [in'sentiv], **1.** *adj.* anreizend, anspornend, antreibend, anregend, ermutigend, aufmunternd (*to*, zu). **2.** *s.* der Anreiz, Antrieb, Ansporn (*to*, zu).
incept [in'sept], **1.** *v.i.* (*Univ.*) anerkannt werden, sich habilitieren. **2.** *v.t.* (*Biol.*) einnehmen, in sich aufnehmen. **inception** [–'sepʃən], *s.* 1. die Gründung, Eröffnung, das Beginnen; der Beginn, Anfang; 2. (*Biol.*) die Aufnahme; 3. (*Univ.*) Anerkennung, Qualifikation, Promotion (zum Doktor), Habilitation. **inceptive,** *adj.* beginnend, anfangend, Anfangs–; (*Gram.*) inchoativ; – *proposition*, der Vordersatz; – *verb*, das Inchoativ(um). **inceptor,** *s.* (*Univ.*) der Promovent.
incertitude [in'sə:titju:d], *s.* die Unsicherheit, Unbestimmtheit, Ungewißheit; Unschlüssigkeit, Unentschlossenheit.
incessancy [in'sesənsi], *s.* die Unablässigkeit, Unaufhörlichkeit. **incessant,** *adj.* unaufhörlich, unablässig, stetig, fortgesetzt.
incest ['insest], *s.* die Blutschande. **incestuous** [in'sestjuəs], *adj.* blutschänderisch.
inch [intʃ], **1.** *s.* der Zoll (= *2.54 cm.*); (*fig.*) die Kleinigkeit, das bißchen; – *by* –, Zoll für Zoll, Schritt für Schritt, ganz langsam, allmählich; *by –es*, zollweise, allmählich, nach und nach; *flog him within an – of his life*, ihn fast zu Tode prügeln; *every* –, jeder Zoll, durch und durch, (*usu. of a p.*) vom Scheitel bis zur Sohle; *not yield an* –, nicht einen Zoll weichen; *give him an – and he'll take an ell*, gibt man ihm den kleinen Finger, so nimmt er die ganze Hand; *2 –es of rain*, 2 Zoll Regen; *two-– plank*, zweizölliges Brett; *s.o. of his –es*, jemand von seiner Größe *or* Figur *or* Gestalt *or* seinem Wuchs. **2.** *v.i.* – (*o.s.*) *forward*, sich langsam *or* vorsichtig *or* Schritt für Schritt vorwärtsbewegen.
inchoate [in'kouit], *adj.* anfangend, beginnend, eben angefangen, Anfangs–; unvollkommen, unfertig, rudimentär. **inchoateness,** *s.* die Unvollständigkeit, Unfertigkeit; das Anfangsstadium. **inchoative,** **1.** *adj.* (*Gram.*) inchoativ; *see also* **inchoate.** **2.** *s.* (*Gram.*) das Inchoativ(um).
incidence ['insidəns], *s.* 1. das Vorkommen, Aufkommen, Auftreten, Eintreten; 2. die Ausdehnung, Ausbreitung, Verbreitung, Wirkweite, das

Wirkungsgebiet; – ***of taxation,*** die Steuerbelastung, Verteilung der Steuerlast; 3. (*Phys.*) der Einfall; ***angle of*** –, der Einfall(s)winkel.

incident ['insidənt], **1.** *adj.* 1. vorkommend (*to*, bei *or* in (*Dat.*)); eigen (*Dat.*), zugehörig (zu), verknüpft, verbunden (mit); (*Law*) als Nebenumstand zugehörig; 2. (*Phys.*) auffallend, einfallend; 3. (*Math.*) ineinanderliegend; ***be*** –, ineinanderliegen. **2.** *s.* 1. der Vorfall, (Neben)umstand, (zufälliges) Ereignis, (*esp. Pol.*) der Zwischenfall; 2. (*Law*) die Nebensache, Nebensächlichkeit.

incidental [insi'dentl], *adj.* zufällig, gelegentlich; nebensächlich, beiläufig, Neben–; – ***to,*** gehörend *or* gehörig zu, verbunden mit; ***be – to,*** gehören zu; ***be – upon,*** folgen auf (*Acc.*), auftreten nach; – ***expenses,*** Nebenausgaben, Nebenspesen; – ***images,*** Nachbilder; – ***music,*** die Begleitmusik. **incidentally,** *adv.* beiläufig, gelegentlich, nebenbei; übrigens, außerdem, nebenbei bemerkt. **incidentals,** *pl.* Nebenumstände, Begleitumstände; (*Comm.*) Nebenausgaben, Nebenspesen (*pl.*).

incinerate [in'sinəreit], *v.t.* zu Asche verbrennen, einäschern. **incineration** [–'reiʃən], *s.* die Einäscherung, Feuerbestattung. **incinerator,** *s.* der Verbrennungsofen.

incipience, incipiency [in'sipiəns(i)], *s.* der Anfang, Beginn, das Beginnen; Anfangsstadium. **incipient,** *adj.* beginnend, anfangend, Anfangs–.

incise [in'saiz], *v.t.* einschneiden in (*Acc.*), aufschneiden; (*stones*) einschnitzen, eingravieren; **–*d wound,*** die Schnittwunde. **incision** [–'siʒən], *s.* der Einschnitt, (*Surg.*) Schnitt. **incisive** [–siv], *adj.* einschneidend; (*fig.*) schneidend, scharf, durchdringlich, ausdrucksvoll; beißend, sarkastisch. **incisiveness,** *s.* (beißende) Schärfe. **incisor** [–zə], *s.* (*Anat., Zool.*) der Schneidezahn. **incisorial** [–si'zɔːriəl], **incisory** [–zəri], *adj.* schneidend, Schneide(zahn)–.

incitation [insai'teiʃən], *s.* die Anreizung, Anregung, der Antrieb, Anreiz, Ansporn. **incite** [in'sait], *v.t.* anreizen, antreiben, anspornen, anstacheln; aufmuntern, aufreizen, aufstacheln, aufwiegeln (*to*, zu); (*Med.*) anregen, stimulieren. **incitement,** *s.* die Anreizung, Aufreizung, Anregung (*to*, zu); der Antrieb, Ansporn.

incivility [insi'viliti], *s.* die Unhöflichkeit, Grobheit.

incivism ['insivizm], *s.* die Unbürgerlichkeit.

in-clearing [in'kliəriŋ], *s.* der Gesamtbetrag der zu zahlenden Schecks, Abrechnungsbetrag.

inclemency [in'klemənsi], *s.* die Rauheit, Unfreundlichkeit, Härte, Unbill (*of weather*). **inclement,** *adj.* rauh, unfreundlich.

inclinable [in'klainəbl], *adj.* geneigt, (hin)neigend. **inclination** [inkli'neiʃən], *s.* 1. (*fig.*) die Neigung, Vorliebe, Anlage, der Hang (***to(wards)***, zu), die Zuneigung (***for***, zu); 2. (*of respect*) Verbeugung, Neigung; 3. (*Math., Phys.*) Neigung, Schräge, Schrägstellung, der Abhang; (*of magnet*) die Inklination.

incline, 1. [in'klain], *v.i.* 1. sich neigen, abfallen (***to(wards)***, nach); 2. (*fig.*) (hin)neigen, geneigt sein, eine Neigung haben (zu); eine Neigung zeigen (zu), dazu neigen, sich nähern (*Dat.*); – ***to red,*** ins Rötliche spielen; 3. (*in respect*) sich verbeugen *or* verneigen. **2.** [–'klain], *v.t.* 1. neigen, beugen, senken (*one's head*); (*fig.*) – ***one's ear to,*** sein Ohr leihen (*Dat.*); 2. (*fig.*) geneigt machen, veranlassen, bewegen (***to***, zu), (*with inf.*) lassen, machen. **3.** ['inklain], *s.* schiefe Ebene, die Neigung, der Abhang. **inclined,** *adj.* 1. geneigt; schief abschüssig; 2. (*fig.*) aufgelegt (***for, to***, zu), gewogen (*Dat.*); (*coll.*) ***I don't feel*** –, ich habe keine Lust (dazu).

inclose *etc. See* **enclose.**

include [in'kluːd], *v.t.* einschließen, umgeben; (*fig.*) umfassen, enthalten, in sich begreifen *or* einschließen; (*fig.*) einschließen, einrechnen (***in***, in (*Acc.*)), rechnen (***among***, zu *or* unter (*Acc.*)). **included,** *adj.* eingeschlossen, umfaßt; (*fig.*) mit eingeschlossen *or* inbegriffen; ***two sides and the – angle,*** zwei Seiten und der eingeschlossene Winkel; ***not*** –, nicht mit inbegriffen; ***fares*** –, einschließlich Fahrgeld, Fahrgeld eingeschlossen *or* inbegriffen. **including,** *prep.* einschließlich (*Gen.*), mit Einschluß (*Gen. or* von), (*follows Acc.*) eingeschlossen.

inclusion [in'kluːʒən], *s.* die Einschließung, Umschließung, Umfassung; (*fig.*) Einschließung, Einbeziehung, der Einschluß (***in***, in (*Acc.*)), die Zugehörigkeit (zu); (*Min.*) der Einschluß; ***with the – of,*** mit Einschluß von. **inclusive** [–siv], *adj.* (*fig.*) umschließend, umfassend; einschließend, enthaltend (***of***, *Acc.*); einschließlich, mitgerechnet, inklusive, alles inbegriffen; ***from Monday to Wednesday*** –, von Montag bis Mittwoch einschließlich; ***be – of,*** umfassen, enthalten, in sich einschließen; – ***terms,*** Preise einschließlich Licht und Bedienung. **inclusiveness,** *s.* das Miteinbegriffensein.

incoercible [inkou'əːsibl], *adj.* unbezwingbar.

incognito [in'kɔgnitou, –'niːtou], **1.** *adv.* unter fremdem Namen; unerkannt, inkognito. **2.** *s.* das Inkognito.

incognizance [in'kɔgnizəns], *s.* das Nichterkennen, Nichtwissen; die Unkenntnis. **incognizant,** *adj.* nicht erkennend *or* wissend (***of***, *Acc.*), unbekannt (mit); ***be – of,*** nicht (er)kennen *or* wissen.

incoherence, incoherency [inkou'hiərəns(i)], *s.* die Zusammenhangslosigkeit; Unvereinbarkeit, Nichtübereinstimmung; Inkonsequenz, der Widerspruch. **incoherent,** *adj.* unzusammenhängend, zusammenhang(s)los; unvereinbar, nicht übereinstimmend, widerspruchsvoll, inkonsequent.

incombustible [inkəm'bʌstibl], *adj.* unverbrennbar.

income ['inkəm], *s.* das Einkommen, Einkünfte (*pl.*) (***from***, aus); ***additional*** –, Nebeneinkünfte (*pl.*); ***assessed*** –, steuerpflichtiges Einkommen; ***big*** –, hohes Einkommen; ***earned*** –, das Einkommen durch Arbeit; ***exempted*** –, steuerfreies Einkommen; ***unearned*** –, das Einkommen aus Vermögen; –***-tax,*** die Einkommensteuer; –***-tax return,*** die (Einkommen)steuererklärung.

incomer ['inkʌmə], *s.* Hereinkommende(r), der Ankömmling; Zugezogene(r), der Einwanderer; Eindringling; (*Law*) neuer Eigentümer; der Nachfolger, Neueintretende(r) (*to post*). **incoming, 1.** *adj.* hereinkommend (*as tide*); neueintretend, nachfolgend (*as tenant*); eingehend, einlaufend (*as payment*); ankommend (*as phone call, traffic etc.*); – ***supplies,*** Warenzugänge (*pl.*). **2.** *s.* der Eintritt, das Eintreffen; (*usu. pl.*) Einkünfte (*pl.*) (*money*), Eingänge (*pl.*) (*goods*).

incommensurability [inkəmensjərə'biliti], *s.* die Unvergleichbarkeit; (*Math.*) Inkommensurabilität. **incommensurable** [–'mensjərəbl], *adj.* nicht vergleichbar, untereinander nicht meßbar, unverhältnismäßig, unvereinbar, (*Math.*) inkommensurabel. **incommensurate** [–'mensjərit], *adj.* unvereinbar (***to, with***, mit), unangemessen (*Dat.*); ***be – with,*** nicht entsprechen (*Dat.*); *see also* **incommensurable.**

incommode [inkə'moud], *v.t.* belästigen, behindern; lästig *or* beschwerlich fallen (*Dat.*). **incommodious,** *adj.* unbequem, lästig, beschwerlich (*to, Dat. or* für).

incommunicability [inkəmjuːnikə'biliti], *s.* die Unmitteilbarkeit. **incommunicable** [–'mjuːnikəbl], *adj.* unmitteilbar, unausdrückbar. **incommunicative,** *adj.* nicht mitteilsam, verschlossen, zurückhaltend.

incommutable [inkə'mjuːtibl], *adj.* unveränderlich, unabänderlich; unvertauschbar, unaustauschbar.

incomparability [inkɔmpərə'biliti], *s.* die Unvergleichbarkeit (***to, with***, mit). **incomparable** [–'kɔmpərəbl], *adj.* unvergleichlich, einzigartig; nicht vergleichbar *or* zu vergleichen(d) (***to, with***, mit). **incomparableness,** *s.* die Unvergleichlichkeit, Einzigartigkeit.

incompatibility [inkəmpæti'biliti], *s.* die Unvereinbarkeit, Unverträglichkeit, Widersprüchlichkeit, der Widerspruch. **incompatible** [–'pætibl], *adj.* unvereinbar, widersprüchlich, einander widersprechend; (*Med.*; *also as a character*) unverträglich; *be* –, sich widersprechen, kollidieren; unverträglich sein.

incompetence [in'kɔmpitəns], *s.* die Unfähigkeit, Untüchtigkeit, Unzulänglichkeit, Untauglichkeit. **incompetency,** *s.* (*Law*) (*of a p.*) die Nichtzuständigkeit, Inkompetenz, (*of evidence*) Unzulässigkeit, Ungültigkeit. **incompetent,** *adj.* unfähig, untüchtig; untauglich, unzulänglich, unzureichend; (*Law*) unbefugt, unzuständig, inkompetent (*of a p.*), unzulässig, ungültig (*as evidence*).

incomplete [inkəm'pli:t], *adj.* unvollendet, unvollständig, mangelhaft, lückenhaft, unvollkommen. **incompleteness,** *s.* die Unvollständigkeit, Unvollkommenheit.

incomprehensibility [inkɔmprihensi'biliti], *s.* die Unbegreiflichkeit. **incomprehensible** [–'hensibl], *adj.* unbegreiflich, unverständlich, unfaßbar.

incompressibility [inkəmpresi'biliti], *s.* die Nichtzusammendrückbarkeit. **incompressible,** *adj.* nicht zusammendrückbar.

incomputable [inkəm'pju:təbl], *adj.* unberechenbar, nicht errechenbar.

inconceivability [inkənsi:və'biliti], *s.* die Unvorstellbarkeit, Unbegreiflichkeit, Unfaßbarkeit. **inconceivable,** *adj.* unvorstellbar, undenkbar, unfaßbar, unbegreiflich (*to*, für).

inconclusive [inkən'klu:siv], *adj.* nicht überzeugend, ohne Beweiskraft, nicht entscheidend, ergebnislos. **inconclusiveness,** *s.* der Mangel an Beweiskraft, die Ergebnislosigkeit.

incongruence [in'kɔŋgruəns], **incongruity** [inkəŋ'gruiti], *s.* die Nichtübereinstimmung, Unvereinbarkeit, Unangemessenheit; Ungereimtheit, Widersinnigkeit; das Mißverhältnis; (*Math.*) die Inkongruenz. **incongruous** [in'kɔŋgruəs], *adj.* nicht übereinstimmend *or* zueinanderpassend, widerspruchsvoll; unvereinbar (*with*, mit); ungereimt, widersinnig; unangemessen, unpassend; (*Math.*) nicht kongruent.

inconsequence [in'kɔnsikwəns], *s.* 1. die Folgewidrigkeit, Inkonsequenz, Zusammenhangslosigkeit; 2. Belanglosigkeit, Irrelevanz. **inconsequent,** *adj.* 1. folgewidrig, inkonsequent, unlogisch, unzusammenhängend; 2. belanglos, irrelevant. **inconsequential** [–'kwenʃəl], *adj.* belanglos, unwichtig, irrelevant, nicht zur S. gehörig.

inconsiderable [inkən'sidərəbl], *adj.* unbedeutend, unwichtig, geringfügig, unbeträchtlich, belanglos.

inconsiderate [inkən'sidərit], *adj.* rücksichtslos (*towards*, gegen); unbesonnen, unüberlegt, unbedacht(sam). **inconsiderateness,** *s.* die Rücksichtslosigkeit, Unbesonnenheit, Unbedachtsamkeit.

inconsistency [inkən'sistənsi], *s.* 1. die Unvereinbarkeit, Folgewidrigkeit, Inkonsequenz; innerer Widerspruch; 2. (*of a p.*) die Veränderlichkeit, Unbeständigkeit, Unstetigkeit, der Wankelmut. **inconsistent,** *adj.* 1. unvereinbar, nicht übereinstimmend, folgewidrig, einander widersprechend; 2. ungereimt, widersinnig, inkonsequent; 3. unstet, unbeständig, wankelmütig.

inconsolable [inkən'souləbl], *adj.* untröstlich.

inconspicuous [inkən'spikjuəs], *adj.* unauffällig, unmerklich. **inconspicuousness,** *s.* die Unauffälligkeit.

inconstancy [in'kɔnstənsi], *s.* die Unbeständigkeit, Veränderlichkeit, Unstetigkeit, der Wankelmut; (*between sexes*) die Untreue, Treulosigkeit. **inconstant,** *adj.* unbeständig, veränderlich, unstet, wankelmütig; untreu, treulos.

incontestable [inkən'testibl], *adj.* unstreitig, unbestritten, unbestreitbar, unumstößlich, unwiderleglich, unwidersprechlich.

incontinence [in'kɔntinəns], *s.* die Unenthaltsamkeit, Unmäßigkeit, Zügellosigkeit, Ausschweifung, (*esp.*) Unkeuschheit; das Nicht(zurück)haltenkönnen, (*Med.*) der Harnfluß. **incontinent,** *adj.* unenthaltsam, unmäßig, ausschweifend, zügellos, (*esp.*) unkeusch; nicht imstande zu halten (*also Med.*), unaufhörlich, ununterbrochen; *be – of,* nicht halten können.

incontrovertible [inkɔntrə'və:tibl], *adj.* unbestreitbar, unstreitig, unbestritten, unumstößlich.

inconvenience [inkən'vi:niəns], 1. *s.* die Unannehmlichkeit, Unbequemlichkeit, Schwierigkeit; Lästigkeit, Beschwerlichkeit. 2. *v.t.* lästig sein, zur Last fallen, Unannehmlichkeiten bereiten (*Dat.*), belästigen. **inconvenient,** *adj.* unbequem, lästig, beschwerlich; unpassend, ungelegen (*to*, für).

inconvertibility [inkənvə:ti'biliti], *s.* die Unverwandelbarkeit; (*Comm.*) Nichteinlösbarkeit, Nichtumsetzbarkeit, Nichtkonvertierbarkeit. **inconvertible** [–'və:tibl], *adj.* unverwandelbar; (*Comm.*) nicht einlösbar, nicht umsetzbar, unkonvertierbar.

incorporate, 1. [in'kɔ:pərit], *adj.* einverleibt (*in*(*to*), in (*Acc.*)), vereinigt, verbunden (mit); (*Law, Comm.*) inkorporiert; *– body,* die Körperschaft. 2. [–reit], *v.t.* verbinden, vereinigen (*with, into,* mit), einverleiben (*Dat.*), aufnehmen (*into,* in (*Acc.*)) (*as member*), eingemeinden (*towns*); (*Law*) Körperschaftsrechte verleihen (*Dat.*), als Körperschaft eintragen, registrieren, inkorporieren; (*fig.*) enthalten, in sich schließen; *–d society,* eingetragener Verein. 3. [–reit], *v.i.* sich zusammenschließen *or* vereinigen *or* verbinden (*with,* mit). **incorporation** [–'reiʃən], *s.* die Aufnahme, Einverleibung (*into,* in (*Acc.*)); Vereinigung, enge Verbindung; (*of towns*) die Eingemeindung; (*Law*) Inkorporation, Körperschaftsbildung, Eintragung in das Vereinsregister; *certificate of –,* die Korperationsurkunde.

incorporeal [inkɔ:'pɔ:riəl], *adj.* unkörperlich, unstofflich, geistig, immateriell. **incorporeality** [–ri'æliti], **incorporeity** [–'ri:iti], *s.* die Unkörperlichkeit, Körperlosigkeit, Immaterialität.

incorrect [inkə'rekt], *adj.* unrichtig, fehlerhaft, ungenau; unwahr, irrig, irrtümlich, falsch; ungehörig, unschicklich (*as behaviour*). **incorrectness,** *s.* die Unrichtigkeit, Fehlerhaftigkeit, Ungenauigkeit; Unwahrheit.

incorrigibility [inkɔridʒi'biliti], *s.* die Unverbesserlichkeit (*of a p.*), Unausrottbarkeit (*of a fault*). **incorrigible** [–'kɔridʒibl], *adj.* unverbesserlich; unausrottbar.

incorruptibility [inkərʌpti'biliti], *s.* die Unverderblichkeit; (*fig.*) Unbestechlichkeit. **incorruptible,** *adj.* unverderblich; (*fig.*) unverderbbar, unverführbar, redlich, (*esp.*) unbestechlich.

increase, 1. [in'kri:s], *v.i.* sich vergrößern *or* erhöhen *or* steigern *or* vermehren, stärker *or* größer werden, zunehmen, (an)wachsen (*in,* an (*Dat.*)); (*fig.*) steigen (*as prices*); *–d demand,* der Mehrbedarf, die Bedarfszunahme. 2. [–'kri:s], *v.t.* vermehren, vergrößern, verstärken, erhöhen, steigern. 3. ['inkri:s], *s.* das Zunehmen, (An)wachsen, Steigen, die Zunahme, der Zuwachs, das Wachstum, die Vergrößerung, Vermehrung, Verstärkung, Erhöhung, Steigerung; der Mehrbetrag, Gewinn; (*coll.*) die (Lohn- *or* Gehalts)zulage; *on the –,* im Zunehmen *or* Wachsen; *– in the bank rate,* die Heraufsetzung des Diskontsatzes; *– in the population,* der Bevölkerungszuwachs; *– in price,* die Preissteigerung; *– in speed,* die Geschwindigkeitszunahme; *– in* or *of trade,* der Aufschwung des Handels; *– in wages,* die Lohnerhöhung; *– on last year's figures,* der Fortschritt gegenüber den Vorjahrszahlen. **increasingly,** *adv.* immer mehr, mehr und mehr, in zunehmendem Maße.

incredibility [inkredi'biliti], *s.* die Unglaublichkeit, Unglaubhaftigkeit. **incredible** [–'kredibl], *adj.* unglaubhaft, unwahrscheinlich; unglaublich.

incredulity [inkri'dju:liti], *s.* die Ungläubigkeit, der Skeptizismus; Unglaube. **incredulous** [in'kredjuləs], *adj.* ungläubig, skeptisch.

increment ['inkrimənt], *s.* die Zunahme, der Zuwachs; (Mehr)ertrag, Gewinn; (*Math.*) positives Differential; *– value,* der Wertzuwachs;

unearned – tax, die Wertzuwachssteuer. **incremental** [–'mentl], *adj.* Zuwachs–.

incriminate [in'krimineit], *v.t.* (eines Vergehens) beschuldigen, belasten. **incrimination** [–'neiʃən], *s.* die Anschuldigung, Beschuldigung, Belastung.

incrustation [inkrʌs'teiʃən], *s.* die Bekrustung, Inkrustation, Krustenbildung; Kruste; (*Geol.*) Inkrustation, (*on walls*) Verkleidung, der Belag, (*on boilers*) Kesselstein.

incubate ['iŋkjubeit], **1.** *v.t.* ausbrüten. **2.** *v.i.* brüten. **incubation** [–'beiʃən], *s.* das Brüten; die Ausbrütung, (*Med.*) Inkubation; (*Med.*) *– period,* die Inkubation(szeit). **incubator,** *s.* der Brutapparat, Brutschrank (*eggs, bacteria*), Brutkasten (*premature infants*).

incubus ['iŋkjəbəs], *s.* der Alp, das Alpdrücken; (*fig.*) bedrückende Last.

inculcate ['inkʌlkeit], *v.t.* einschärfen, einprägen (*in,* (*up*)*on, Dat.*). **inculcation** [–'keiʃən], *s.* die Einschärfung.

inculpate ['inkʌlpeit], *v.t.* beschuldigen, anklagen. **inculpation** [–'peiʃən], *s.* die Beschuldigung; der Vorwurf, Tadel. **inculpatory** [in'kʌlpətəri], *adj.* beschuldigend, Anklage–.

incumbency [in'kʌmbənsi], *s.* 1. die Amtsführung; Amtszeit; der Amtsbereich; 2. Pfründenbesitz; 3. (*fig.*) das Obliegen. **incumbent, 1.** *adj.* sich stützend, lastend, drückend ((*up*)*on,* auf (*Acc.*)); (*Bot.*) aufliegend, (*Geol.*) überlagernd; (*fig.*) zufallend, obliegend ((*up*)*on, Dat.*); *it is – on me,* es ist meine Pflicht, es liegt mir ob. **2.** *s.* der Pfründeninhaber, Pfründenbesitzer, Amtsinhaber.

incunabula [inkju'næbjulə], *pl.* Wiegendrucke, Inkunabeln (*pl.*).

incur [in'kə:], *v.t.* sich (*Dat.*) zuziehen, auf sich laden, geraten in (*Acc.*); *– debts,* Schulden machen; *– danger,* sich einer Gefahr aussetzen; *– a fine,* sich (*Dat.*) eine Geldstrafe zuziehen; *– a loss,* einen Verlust erleiden; *– obligations,* Verpflichtungen eingehen.

incurability [inkjuərə'biliti], *s.* die Unheilbarkeit; (*fig.*) Unverbesserlichkeit. **incurable** [–'kjuərəbl], **1.** *adj.* unheilbar; (*fig.*) unverbesserlich. **2.** *s.* Unheilbare(r).

incurious [in'kjuəriəs], *adj.* gleichgültig, uninteressiert, nicht neugierig.

incursion [in'kə:ʃən], *s.* (feindlicher) Einfall, der Vorstoß, Streifzug; (*fig.*) das Eindringen, der Einbruch, Eingriff, Übergriff.

incurve [in'kə:v], *v.t.* (nach innen) krümmen, (ein)biegen.

incuse [in'kju:z], **1.** *adj.* eingeprägt, eingehämmert. **2.** *v.t.* prägen. **3.** *s.* die (Auf)prägung.

indanthrene [in'dænθri:n], *s.* das Indanthren.

indebted [in'detid], *adj.* verschuldet; (*fig.*) verbunden, verpflichtet; *be – to him for s.th.,* ihm für etwas zum Dank verpflichtet sein. **indebtedness,** *s.* die Verschuldung, Schulden (*pl.*); (*fig.*) die Verpflichtung, Dankesschuld.

indecency [in'di:sənsi], *s.* die Unanständigkeit. **indecent,** *adj.* unanständig, anstößig; *– assault,* die Unzucht, Schändung, Notzucht; *– exposure,* die Exhibition.

indecipherable [indi'saifərəbl], *adj.* unentzifferbar, unleserlich.

indecision [indi'siʒən], *s.* die Unentschlossenheit, Unschlüssigkeit. **indecisive** [–'saisiv], *adj.* nicht entscheidend, unentschieden (*as a battle*), unbestimmt, unsicher, ungewiß (*as outlines*); (*of a p.*) unschlüssig, schwankend. **indecisiveness,** *s.* die Unentschiedenheit; Unbestimmtheit, Unsicherheit, Ungewißheit.

indeclinable [indi'klainəbl], *adj.* undeklinierbar.

indecorous [in'dekərəs], *adj.* unschicklich, ungehörig, unziemlich, unanständig. **indecorousness, indecorum** [indi'kɔ:rəm], *s.* die Unschicklichkeit, Ungehörigkeit, Unziemlichkeit.

indeed [in'di:d], **1.** *adv.* 1. (*emph., usu. following*) in der Tat, wirklich, tatsächlich; *thank you very much –!* vielen herzlichen Dank! 2. (*unemphatic preceding*) freilich, allerdings, zwar, ja. **2.** *int.* ach wirklich! ich danke! was Sie sagen! nicht möglich!

indefatigability [indifætigə'biliti], *s.* die Unermüdlichkeit, Unverdrossenheit. **indefatigable** [–'fætigəbl], *adj.* unermüdlich, unverdrossen.

indefeasibility [indifi:zi'biliti], *s.* die Unantastbarkeit, Unverletzlichkeit (*of a title*), Unveräußerlichkeit (*of property*). **indefeasible** [–'fi:zibl], *adj.* unverletzlich, unwiderruflich, unantastbar; unveräußerlich.

indefectible [indi'fektibl], *adj.* unvergänglich, nicht verfallend; (*fig.*) unfehlbar.

indefensibility [indifensi'biliti], *s.* die Unhaltbarkeit. **indefensible** [–'fensibl], *adj.* unhaltbar (*also fig.*), nicht zu verteidigen(d); (*fig.*) unentschuldbar, ungerechtfertigt.

indefinable [indi'fainəbl], *adj.* unbestimmbar, undefinierbar, unerklärbar. **indefinite** [in'definit], *adj.* unbestimmt (*also Gram.*), unbegrenzt, unklar, undeutlich, verschwommen. **indefiniteness,** *s.* die Unbestimmtheit, Unklarheit.

indelibility [indeli'biliti], *s.* die Unauslöschlichkeit. **indelible** [–'delibl], *adj.* unauslöschlich; unvertilgbar, unvergänglich, unvergeßlich; *– ink,* die Kopiertinte; *– pencil,* der Tintenstift.

indelicacy [in'delikəsi], *s.* der Mangel an Zartgefühl, die Taktlosigkeit; Unfeinheit, Unanständigkeit. **indelicate,** *adj.* ohne Zartgefühl, taktlos; unfein, unanständig.

indemnification [indemnifi'keiʃən], *s.* 1. die Entschädigung, Schadloshaltung, Sicherstellung; 2. Entschädigung, Vergütung, Ersatzleistung, das Abstandsgeld. **indemnify** [in'demnifai], *v.t.* 1. entschädigen, schadlos halten (*for,* für), sicherstellen (*from, against,* gegen); 2. vergüten, gutmachen, entschädigen für (*a loss*). **indemnity** [–'demniti], *s.* 1. die Entschädigung, Vergütung, Schadloshaltung, Sicherstellung; (*Law*) Straflosigkeit, Indemnität; *act of –,* der Indemnitätsbeschluß; *letter of –,* die Ausfallbürgschaft; 2. der Schadenersatz, das Abstandsgeld, die Abfindung(ssumme).

indemonstrable [in'demənstrəbl], *adj.* unbeweisbar, unerweislich.

indent, 1. [in'dent], *v.t.* 1. einschneiden (*also Geol.*), einzahnen, (ein)kerben, auszacken; 2. (*Typ.*) einrücken (*a line*); 3. (*Law*) genaue Abschrift(en) ausfertigen *or* anfertigen von (*a document*); abschließen (*a contract*). **2.** [–'dent], *v.i.* eine Forderung stellen; (*Mil.*) requirieren; *– on him for a th.,* bei ihm eine S. bestellen, von ihm eine S. verlangen *or* anfordern *or* einfordern. **3.** ['indent], *s.* 1. der Einschnitt, die Kerbe, Einkerbung, Auszackung; 2. (*Law*) der Vertrag, Kontrakt; 3. (*Comm.*) Auslandsauftrag, die Warenbestellung; (*Mil.*) (amtliche) Requisition; 4. (*Typ.*) der Einzug, die Einrückung. **indentation** [–'teiʃən], *s.* 1. *See* **indent, 3,** 1, 4; 2. (eingedruckte) Vertiefung. **indented** [in'dentid], *adj.* 1. gezahnt, (ein)gekerbt, (aus)gezackt, zackig, (*Her.*) gezackt; 2. (*Law*) kontraktlich gebunden *or* verpflichtet; 3. (*Typ.*) eingerückt, eingezogen. **indention** [in'denʃən], *s.* *See* **indent, 3,** 1, 4.

indenture [in'dentʃə], **1.** *s.* 1. die Vertragsurkunde, der Vertrag, Kontrakt; (*esp.*) Lehrvertrag, Lehrbrief; (*Law*) amtliches Verzeichnis; *take up one's –,* die Lehrzeit beenden, ausgelernt haben; 2. *See* **indent, 3,** 1; **indentation,** 2. **2.** *v.t.* verdingen, in die Lehre geben, kontraktlich binden, vertraglich verpflichten.

independence [indi'pendəns], *s.* 1. die Unabhängigkeit (*of, from,* von), Selbständigkeit; 2. hinreichendes Auskommen. **independency,** *s.* (*Eccl.*) der Independentismus; unabhängiger Staat. **independent, 1.** *adj.* unabhängig (*of,* von), selbständig; (*Pol.*) parteilos; *– axle,* die Schwingachse; *– clause* der Hauptsatz; *– fire,* das Schützenfeuer, Schnellfeuer, Einzelfeuer; *– income* or *means,* eignes Vermögen; *man of – means,* der Rentner, Privatier; *– suspension,* die Einzelaufhängung; *– television,* kommerzielles Fernsehen; (*Math.*) *– variable,* unabhängige Veränderliche; *be –,* auf eigenen

Füßen stehen (*of p.*), für sich bestehen (*of th.*). **2.** *s.* (*Eccl.*) der Independent, (*Pol.*) Unabhängige(r). **independently,** *adv.* *act* –, eigenmächtig *or* auf eigene Faust handeln.

indescribability [indiskraibə'biliti], *s.* die Unbeschreiblichkeit. **indescribable** [–'skraibəbl], *adj.* unbeschreiblich.

indestructibility [indistrʌkti'biliti], *s.* die Unzerstörbarkeit. **indestructible** [–'strʌktibl], *adj.* unzerstörbar.

indeterminable [indi'tə:minəbl], *adj.* unbestimmbar, undefinierbar. **indeterminate** [–nit], *adj.* unbestimmt, ungewiß, unklar; unentschieden, ergebnislos; (*Gram.*) unbetont. **indeterminateness,** *s.* die Unbestimmtheit. **indetermination** [–'neiʃən], *s.* die Unschlüssigkeit, Unentschlossenheit.

index ['indeks], **1.** *s.* (*pl.* **-es, indices** ['indisi:z]) 1. der Zeiger; 2. (*Anat.*) Zeigefinger; 3. das Inhaltsverzeichnis, Register (*of a book*); (*R.C.*) der Index; *card* –, die Kartei, Kartothek; 4. (*Math.*) (*pl. only* **indices**) der Exponent, die Hochzahl, Kennziffer; – *of a logarithm,* die Kennziffer *or* Charakteristik eines Logarithmus; – *of refraction,* der Brechungsexponent; 5. (*Tech., Comm.*) die Vergleichsziffer, Meßziffer, Meßzahl, der Index; *cost-of-living*–, der Lebenshaltungsindex; – *of intelligence,* die Intelligenzmeßzahl; 6. (*Typ.*) das Unterscheidungszeichen, Handzeichen; 7. (*fig.*) (An)zeichen (*of,* für, von *or Gen.*), der Hinweis (*to,* auf (*Acc.*)), Wegweiser, Fingerzeig (für). **2.** *v.t.* mit einem Inhaltsverzeichnis versehen (*a book*), in ein Verzeichnis aufnehmen, registrieren.

index|-card, *s.* die Karteikarte. **–-finger,** *s.* der Zeigefinger. **indexing,** *s.* das Ordnen, Registrieren. **index-number,** *s.* die Meßziffer, Indexziffer, Indexzahl, der Index; (*Motor.*) polizeiliches Kennzeichen.

India ['indiə], *s.* Indien (*n.*); *Further* –, Hinterindien (*n.*). **Indiaman** [–mən], *s.* der Ostindienfahrer. **Indian, 1.** *s.* 1. (*Asian*) der (die) Inder(in), (*Am.*) (*also American* or *Red* –) Indianer(in); 2. (*language*) das Indianisch. **2.** *adj.* (*Asian*) indisch, (*Am.*) indianisch; – *club,* die (Schwing)keule; – *corn,* der Mais; (*Hist.*) – *Empire,* Britisch-Indisches Reich; – *file,* der Gänsemarsch; – *hemp,* das Haschisch; – *ink,* (chinesische) (Auszieh)-tusche; – *summer,* der Nachsommer, Spätsommer, Altweibersommer.

India| Office, *s.* (*Hist.*) das Reichsamt für Indien. **– paper,** *s.* das Dünndruckpapier, Chinapapier. **indiarubber, 1.** *s.* (*substance*) das Gummi, der Kautschuk; (*eraser*) der Radiergummi. **2.** *adj.* Gummi–.

indicate ['indikeit], *v.t.* anzeigen, angeben, bezeichnen; andeuten, hinweisen *or* hindeuten auf (*Acc.*); (*Med.*) indizieren, anzeigen, erfordern; *be –d,* angezeigt *or* indiziert sein; (*fig., coll.*) erforderlich *or* angebracht sein; *–d horsepower,* indizierte Pferdestärke. **indication** [–'keiʃən], *s.* der Hinweis (*of,* auf (*Acc.*)); die Anzeige, Angabe, Andeutung (über (*Acc.*)), das (An)zeichen, Kennzeichen; (*Med.*) Symptom, die Indikation; *give – of,* (an)zeigen; *there is every –,* alles deutet darauf hin.

indicative [in'dikətiv], **1.** *adj.* hinweisend, andeutend, anzeigend; (*Comm.*) indikativisch, Indikativ–; *be – of,* anzeigen, (hin)deuten auf (*Acc.*). **indicator** ['indikeitə], *s.* der Anzeiger; (*Tech.*) Zeiger, Messer, Indikator, (*Motor.*) Winker, (*Tele.*) Zeigerapparat; (*Tele.*) *–board,* der Klappenschrank. **indicatory,** *adj.* – *of,* hinweisend auf (*Acc.*), anzeigend, andeutend.

indices ['indisi:z], *pl. of* **index.**

indict [in'dait], *v.t.* (*Law*) anklagen, verklagen (*for,* wegen); (*fig.*) beschuldigen. **indictable,** *adj.* anklagbar, verklagbar; – *offence,* das Kriminalverbrechen. **indictment,** *s.* (formelle) Anklage, die Anklageschrift; Anklageverfügung, der Anklagebeschluß.

indifference [in'difərəns], *s.* 1. (*of a p.*) die Gleichgültigkeit, Teilnahm(s)losigkeit, Interesselosigkeit, Apathie (*to,* gegen), Unbekümmertheit (um); Unparteilichkeit, Neutralität; 2. (*of a th.*) Unwichtigkeit, Bedeutungslosigkeit (*to,* für); *it is a matter of* –, es ist unwichtig *or* belanglos; 3. die Mittelmäßigkeit. **indifferent,** *adj.* 1. (*of a p.*) gleichgültig, teilnahm(s)los, interesselos (*to,* gegen); unparteiisch; 2. (*of a th.*) unwichtig, unwesentlich, belanglos (*to,* für); 3. nebensächlich, (mittel)-mäßig, leidlich; 4. (*Chem.*) indifferent, neutral.

indigence ['indidʒəns], *s.* die Bedürftigkeit, Armut, Not.

indigene ['indidʒi:n], *s.* Eingeborene(r); einheimisches Tier; einheimische Pflanze. **indigenous** [in'didʒinəs], *adj.* eingeboren, einheimisch (*to,* in (*Dat.*)), (*esp. Bot.*) bodenständig; (*fig.*) angeboren.

indigent ['indidʒənt], *adj.* bedürftig, arm, mittellos.

indigested [indi'dʒestid], *adj.* unverdaut. **indigestibility** [–i'biliti], *s.* die Unverdaulichkeit. **indigestible,** *adj.* unverdaulich, schwerverdaulich (*also fig.*). **indigestion** [–tʃən], *s.* die Verdauungsstörung, Verdauungsschwäche. **indigestive,** *adj.* schwer verdaulich.

indignant [in'dignənt], *adj.* entrüstet, empört, aufgebracht, ungehalten (*at,* über (*Acc.*)). **indignation** [–'neiʃən], *s.* die Entrüstung, Empörung, Ungehaltenheit, der Unwille; – *meeting,* die Protestversammlung. **indignity,** *s.* schimpfliche Behandlung, die Schmach, Beleidigung, Demütigung.

indigo ['indigou], **1.** *s.* der Indigo. **2.** *adj.* Indigo–, indigofarben. **indigo blue, 1.** *s.* das Indigoblau, Indigotin. **2.** *adj.* indigoblau. **indigotin** [–gətin], *s. See* **indigo blue, 1.**

indirect [indi'rekt], *adj.* indirekt, mittelbar; (*fig.*) nicht gerade, schief, krumm; (*Mil.*) – *fire,* das Steilfeuer; – *means,* Umwege, Umschweife (*pl.*); (*Gram.*) – *object,* das Dativobjekt; (*Gram.*) – *question,* abhängiger Fragesatz; (*Rad.*) – *ray,* reflektierte Welle; (*Gram.*) – *speech,* indirekte Rede; – *tax,* die Verbrauchssteuer, indirekte Steuer.

indiscernible [indi'sə:nibl], *adj.* nicht wahrnehmbar, unmerklich; nicht unterscheidbar.

indiscipline [in'disiplin], *s.* die Disziplinlosigkeit; der Mangel an Disziplin.

indiscoverable [indis'kʌvərəbl], *adj.* unentdeckbar, nicht feststellbar.

indiscreet [indis'kri:t], *adj.* taktlos, indiskret; unklug; unbesonnen, unüberlegt, unbedacht(sam). **indiscretion** [–'kreʃən], *s.* die Taktlosigkeit, Unbesonnenheit, (*esp. Pol.*) Indiskretion, der Vertrauensbruch; die Unklugheit, Unbedachtsamkeit, Unvorsichtigkeit.

indiscriminate [indis'kriminit], *adj.* unterschiedslos, wahllos, kritiklos. **indiscriminately,** *adv.* wahllos, ohne Unterschied, unterschiedslos, aufs Geratewohl. **indiscrimination** [–'neiʃən], *s.* die Unterschiedslosigkeit, Kritiklosigkeit. **indiscriminative,** *adj.* (*of a p.*) keinen Unterschied machend, kritiklos, blind.

indispensability [indispensə'biliti], *s.* die Unentbehrlichkeit, Unerläßlichkeit. **indispensable** [–'spensəbl], *adj.* unentbehrlich, unerläßlich, unbedingt notwendig (*to, for,* für); (*Mil.*) unabkömmlich.

indispose [indis'pouz], *v.t.* abgeneigt machen (*to,* zu), untauglich machen (*for,* zu). **indisposed,** *adj.* (*usu. pred.*) 1. unpäßlich, unwohl; 2. abgeneigt (*to, Dat.*), eingenommen (gegen). **indisposition** [–pə'ziʃən], *s.* die Unpäßlichkeit, das Unwohlsein; die Abneigung, Abgeneigtheit (*to*(*wards*), gegen).

indisputability [indispju:tə'biliti], *s.* die Unstreitigkeit, Unbestreitbarkeit. **indisputable** [–'pju:təbl], *adj.* unbestreitbar, unbestritten, unstreitig.

indissolubility [indisəlju'biliti], *s.* die Unauflöslichkeit, (*fig.*) Unzertrennbarkeit, Unzerstörbarkeit. **indissoluble** [–'səljubl], *adj.* unauflöslich, unauflösbar; (*Chem.*) unlöslich; (*fig.*) unzertrennlich, unzerstörbar.

indistinct [indis'tiŋkt], *adj.* unklar, undeutlich, verworren, verschwommen. **indistinctness,** *s.* die

Undeutlichkeit, Verworrenheit, Verschwommenheit, Unklarheit.

indistinguishable [indis'tiŋgwiʃəbl], *adj.* ununterscheidbar, nicht zu unterscheiden(d).

indite [in'dait], *v.t.* (*obs.*) (nieder)schreiben, abfassen.

individual [indi'vidjuəl], **1.** *adj.* einzeln, Einzel–, persönlich, individuell; besonder, eigentümlich, persönlich, charakteristisch; – ***case,*** der Einzelfall; – ***credit,*** der Personalkredit; – ***income,*** das Privateinkommen; – ***psychology,*** die Individualpsychologie. **2.** *s.* das Einzelwesen, Individuum, die Einzelperson; (*coll.*) Person, der Mensch; ***private*** –, der Privatmann, die Privatperson. **individualism,** *s.* der Individualismus; die Eigentümlichkeit, Eigenart; Eigenwilligkeit. **individualist,** *s.* der (die) Individualist(in). **individualistic** [–'listik], *adj.* individualistisch. **individuality** [–'æliti], *s.* die Individualität, Persönlichkeit; persönliche Eigenart, das Kennzeichen. **individualization** [–ai'zeiʃən], *s.* die Individualisierung, Einzelbetrachtung. **individualize, 1.** *v.t.* individualisieren, einzeln darstellen *or* herausheben; im einzelnen betrachten, charakterisieren, kennzeichnen. **2.** *v.i.* ins Einzelne gehen. **individually,** *adv.* einzeln betrachtet *or* genommen, jeder *etc.* für sich; – ***and collectively,*** einzeln und insgesamt.

indivisibility [indivizi'biliti], *s.* die Unteilbarkeit. **indivisible** [–'vizibl], *adj.* unteilbar.

Indo|-China [indou–], *s.* Hinterindien (*n.*). **--Chinese, 1.** *s.* 1. der Indochinese (die Indochinesin); 2. (*language*) das Sinotibetisch. **2.** *adj.* indochinesisch, hinterindisch.

indocile [in'dousail], *adj.* ungelehrig, unbändig, unlenksam. **indocility** [indo'siliti], *s.* die Ungelehrigkeit, Unbändigkeit.

indoctrinate [in'dɔktrineit], *v.t.* unterweisen, belehren, schulen (***in,*** in (*Dat.*)), erfüllen, durchdringen (***with,*** mit). **indoctrination** [–'neiʃən], *s.* die Belehrung, Schulung, Unterweisung.

Indo|-European, --Germanic, 1. *s.* das Indogermanisch. **2.** *adj.* indogermanisch.

indolence ['indələns], *s.* die Trägheit, Indolenz; (*Med.*) Schmerzlosigkeit. **indolent,** *adj.* träge, lässig, indolent; schmerzlos (*as a tumour*).

indomitable [in'dɔmitəbl], *adj.* unbezwinglich, unbezähmbar. **indomitableness,** *s.* die Unbezähmbarkeit.

indoor ['indɔ:], *adj.* Haus–, Zimmer–; – ***aerial,*** die Zimmerantenne; – ***game,*** das Zimmerspiel; – ***relief,*** die Anstaltspflege; – ***swimming-pool,*** das Hallenbad. **indoors** [–'dɔ:z], *adv.* im Hause, zu Hause; ins Haus.

indorse *etc. See* **endorse.**

indubitable [in'dju:bitəbl], *adj.* zweifellos, fraglos, unzweifelhaft, gewiß, sicher. **indubitableness,** *s.* die Unzweifelhaftigkeit, Fraglosigkeit, Zweifellosigkeit, Gewißheit.

induce [in'dju:s], *v.t.* herbeiführen, hervorrufen, auslösen, bewirken, verursachen (*a th.*); bewegen, veranlassen, überreden, dahinbringen, verleiten (*a p.*); (*Elec.*) induzieren, durch Induktion hervorrufen; (*Log.*) induzieren, durch Induktion ableiten *or* schließen; ***–d current,*** der Induktionsstrom. **inducement,** *s.* die Veranlassung; der Anlaß, Beweggrund, Anreiz (***to,*** zu).

induct [in'dʌkt], *v.t.* (*Eccl.*) einsetzen, einführen; (*Mil.*) einberufen, einziehen; (*fig.*) geleiten, führen (***into,*** zu *or* in (*Acc.*)), einführen, einweihen (***in,*** in (*Acc.*)). **inductance,** *s.* (*Elec.*) die Induktivität, Selbstinduktion; Induktanz, induktiver (Schein)-widerstand.

inductile [in'dʌktail], *adj.* (*Metall.*) un(aus)dehnbar. **inductility** [–'tiliti], *s.* die Un(aus)dehnbarkeit.

induction [in'dʌkʃən], *s.* (*Eccl.*) die Einführung, Einsetzung, (*Mil.*) Einberufung; Anführung (*of proof etc.*); (*Phys., Log.*) Induktion, (*Log.*) der Induktionsschluß; (*fig.*) die Herbeiführung, Auslösung; (*Elec.*) – ***coil,*** der Induktionsapparat, Funkeninduktor; (*Elec.*) – ***current,*** der Induktionsstrom; (*Mil.*) – ***order,*** der Gestellungsbefehl, Einberufungsbefehl; – ***pipe,*** das Einlaßrohr. **inductive** [–tiv], *adj.* verleitend, führend (***to,*** zu); (*Log.*) induktiv, hergeleitet; (*Elec.*) Induktions–. **inductor,** *s.* (*Elec.*) der Induktionsapparat, Induktor; die Induktionsspule, Drosselspule.

indulge [in'dʌldʒ], **1.** *v.t.* 1. nachgeben (*Dat.*), gefällig sein (*Dat.*), nachsichtig sein gegen, gewähren lassen (*a p.*); – ***him in s.th.,*** ihm etwas nachsehen, ihm in etwas (*Dat.*) willfahren; – ***o.s.,*** sich gehen lassen, sich ergehen, sich nicht zurückhalten, schwelgen (***in,*** in (*Dat.*)), sich gütlich tun (an (*Dat.*)), sich hingeben (*Dat. or* an (*Acc.*)); 2. verwöhnen, verzärteln (*a child*); 3. nachgeben (*Dat.*), sich ergeben (*Dat.*), frönen (*Dat.*) (*a th.*); – ***one's desires,*** seinen Wünschen frönen *or* nachhängen, sich seinen Wünschen hingeben. **2.** *v.i. See* – ***o.s.***; (*coll.*) gern trinken, ein Trinker sein.

indulgence [in'dʌldʒəns], *s.* 1. das Nachsehen, die Nachsicht, Duldung, Schonung (***to, of,*** gegenüber), Verwöhnung, Verzärtelung (*of children*); 2. Befriedigung (***of,*** *Gen.*), das Frönen (*Dat.*), Schwelgen (in (*Dat.*)); 3. Wohlleben, Genußleben, der Genuß; 4. die Gunst(bezeigung); 5. (*R.C.*) der Ablaß; 6. (*Comm.*) (Zahlungs)aufschub, die Stundung. **indulgent,** *adj.* nachsichtig, schonend (***to,*** gegen), mild, nachgiebig.

indurate ['indjureit], **1.** *v.t.* hart machen, härten; (*fig.*) verhärten, abhärten, abstumpfen (***to, against,*** gegen). **2.** *v.i.* hart *or* fest werden, sich verhärten; (*fig.*) abstumpfen, sich abhärten, abgehärtet werden. **induration** [–'reiʃən], *s.* die (Ver)-härtung, das Hartwerden; (*fig.*) die Verstocktheit, Gefühllosigkeit, Härte; (*Med.*) Verhärtung, Schwiele.

Indus ['indəs], *s.* (*Geog.*) der Indus.

industrial [in'dʌstriəl], *adj.* gewerblich, gewerbetreibend, Gewerbe–, Industrie–, industriell; – ***accident,*** der Betriebsunfall; – ***administration,*** die Betriebswirtschaft; – ***alcohol,*** denaturierter Sprit; – ***association,*** der Fachverband; – ***court,*** das Schlichtungsamt; – ***exhibition,*** die Gewerbeausstellung; – ***relations,*** das Verhältnis zwischen Arbeitgeber und Arbeitnehmer; – ***revolution,*** industrielle Revolution; – ***school,*** die Gewerbeschule; (*Hist.*) Besserungsanstalt; – ***town,*** die Industriestadt, Fabrikstadt; – ***worker,*** der Industriearbeiter, Fabrikarbeiter.

industrialism [in'dʌstriəlizm], *s.* die Industriearbeit, der Industrialismus. **industrialist,** *s.* Industrielle(r). **industrialization** [–lai'zeiʃən], *s.* die Industrialisierung. **industrialize,** *v.t.* industrialisieren.

industrious [in'dʌstriəs], *adj.* fleißig, arbeitsam, betriebsam, emsig. **industriousness,** *s.* der Fleiß, die Emsigkeit.

industry ['indəstri], *s.* 1. das Gewerbe, die Industrie, der Industriezweig; 2. die Betriebsamkeit, der Fleiß.

indwell [in'dwel], *v.i.* (*fig.*) – ***in,*** wohnen in (*Dat.*), innewohnen (*Dat.*). **indwelling,** *adj.* innewohnend; (*Med.*) Dauer–, Verweil–.

inebriate, 1. [in'i:briit], *adj.* betrunken, berauscht. **2.** [–iit], *s.* der Trunkenbold. **3.** [–ieit], *v.t.* betrunken machen, (*fig.*) trunken machen, berauschen. **inebriated** [–ieitid], *adj. See* **inebriate, 1. inebriation** [–'eiʃən], **inebriety** [ini'braiiti], *s.* die Trunkenheit, der Rausch.

inedible [in'edibl], *adj.* ungenießbar, nicht eßbar.

inedited [in'editid], *adj.* ohne Änderung herausgegeben, nicht redigiert.

ineffable [in'efəbl], *adj.* unaussprechlich, unbeschreiblich. **ineffableness,** *s.* die Unaussprechlichkeit.

ineffaceable [ini'feisəbl], *adj.* unauslöschlich, unauslöschbar.

ineffective [ini'fektiv], *adj.* 1. unwirksam, wirkungslos, fruchtlos, erfolglos; 2. untauglich, unfähig. **ineffectiveness,** *s.* 1. die Unwirksamkeit, Wirkungslosigkeit, Erfolglosigkeit; 2. Untauglichkeit.

ineffectual [ini'fektjuəl], *adj. See* **ineffective;**

schwach, kraftlos. **ineffectuality** [-ju'æliti], *s. See* **ineffectiveness**; die Schwäche, Kraftlosigkeit, Nutzlosigkeit.

inefficacious [inefi'keiʃəs], *adj.* unwirksam, wirkungslos, erfolglos. **inefficacy** [in'efikəsi], *s.* die Unwirksamkeit, Wirkungslosigkeit, Erfolglosigkeit, Unzulänglichkeit.

inefficiency [ini'fiʃənsi], *s.* die Unfähigkeit, Unzulänglichkeit, Untauglichkeit, (*coll.*) Schlamperei; Wirkungslosigkeit, Erfolglosigkeit. **inefficient,** *adj.* (leistungs)unfähig, untauglich, unzulänglich; (*coll.*) schlampig; unwirksam, unfruchtbar, wirkungslos.

inelastic [ini'læstik], *adj.* nicht elastisch, (*fig.*) unbeugsam, starr, nicht anpassungsfähig. **inelasticity** [-'tisiti], *s.* die Unbeugsamkeit, Starrheit, der Mangel an Anpassungsfähigkeit.

inelegance, inelegancy [in'eligəns(i)], *s.* die Geschmacklosigkeit, Unfeinheit, Uneleganz. **inelegant,** *adj.* unelegant, geschmacklos, unfein.

ineligibility [inelidʒi'biliti], *s.* die Unwählbarkeit; Untauglichkeit. **ineligible** [-'elidʒibl], *adj.* unwählbar; (*fig.*) untauglich, nicht in Betracht *or* Frage kommend, ungeeignet.

ineluctable [ini'lʌktəbl], *adj.* unvermeidlich, unabwendbar, unausweichbar, unentrinnbar.

inept [i'nept], *adj.* albern, abgeschmackt; ungeeignet, unangemessen, unpassend, ungehörig, ungeschickt. **ineptitude** [-itju:d], **ineptness,** *s.* die Albernheit, Abgeschmacktheit, Ungeeignetheit (*for*, zu), Ungeschicklichkeit, Ungehörigkeit.

inequality [ini'kwɔliti], *s.* die Ungleichheit (*also Math.*), Verschiedenheit, Verschiedenartigkeit; Unebenheit (*of surface*); Ungerechtigkeit.

inequitable [in'ekwitəbl], *adj.* ungerecht, unbillig. **inequity,** *s.* die Ungerechtigkeit, Unbilligkeit.

ineradicable [ini'rædikəbl], *adj.* unausrottbar, unvertilgbar.

inert [i'nə:t], *adj.* träge, leblos, inaktiv; indifferent, edel (*of gases*); untätig, unwirksam; (*fig.*) schwerfällig, stumpf. **inertia** [-'nə:ʃə], *s.* die Trägheit (*also fig.*), (*Phys.*) das Beharrungsvermögen, Trägheitsmoment. **inertness,** *s.* die Trägheit, Untätigkeit, Inaktivität, Passivität.

inescapable [inis'keipəbl], *adj.* unvermeidlich, unentrinnbar, unabwendbar.

inessential [ini'senʃəl], **1.** *adj.* unwesentlich, unbedeutend, unwichtig. **2.** *s.* Unwesentliche(s), die Nebensache.

inestimable [in'estiməbl], *adj.* unschätzbar.

inevitability [inevitə'biliti], *s.* die Unvermeidlichkeit. **inevitable** [-'evitəbl], *adj.* unvermeidlich, unumgänglich.

inexact [inig'zækt], *adj.* ungenau. **inexactitude** [-itju:d], **inexactness,** *s.* die Ungenauigkeit.

inexcusability [inikskju:zə'biliti], *s.* die Unverzeihlichkeit, Unentschuldbarkeit. **inexcusable** [-'skju:zəbl], *adj.* unverzeihlich, unentschuldbar; unverantwortlich.

inexhaustibility [inigzɔ:sti'biliti], *s.* die Unerschöpflichkeit; Unermüdlichkeit. **inexhaustible** [-'zɔ:stibl], *adj.* unerschöpflich, unermüdlich. **inexhaustive,** *adj.* unerschöpflich.

inexorability [ineksərə'biliti], *s.* die Unerbittlichkeit. **inexorable** [-'eksərəbl], *adj.* unerbittlich.

inexpediency [iniks'pi:diənsi], *s.* die Unzweckmäßigkeit, Undienlichkeit. **inexpedient,** *adj.* unangemessen, ungeeignet, unpassend; unzweckmäßig, undienlich, unvorteilhaft, unklug, nicht ratsam.

inexpensive [iniks'pensiv], *adj.* nicht teuer, wohlfeil, billig. **inexpensiveness,** *s.* die Wohlfeilheit, Billigkeit.

inexperience [iniks'piəriəns], *s.* die Unerfahrenheit. **inexperienced,** *adj.* unerfahren; (*Naut.*) unbefahren.

inexpert [in'ekspə:t], *adj.* ungeübt (*in*, in (*Dat.*)), ungeschickt, unbeholfen. **inexpertness,** *s.* die Ungeübtheit; Ungeschicktheit, Unbeholfenheit.

inexpiable [in'ekspiəbl], *adj.* unsühnbar, unversöhnlich.

inexplicability [ineksplikə'biliti], *s.* die Unerklärlichkeit. **inexplicable** [-'plikəbl], *adj.* unerklärlich, unbegreiflich, unfaßlich.

inexplicit [iniks'plisit], *adj.* unklar, undeutlich ausgedrückt. **inexplicitness,** *s.* die Unklarheit, undeutliche Ausdrucksweise.

inexpressibility [inikspresi'biliti], *s.* die Unaussprechlichkeit, Unbeschreiblichkeit. **inexpressible** [-'presibl], *adj.* unaussprechlich, unbeschreiblich, unsagbar, unsäglich. **inexpressibles,** *pl.* (*coll. obs.*) Beinkleider (*pl.*).

inexpressive [iniks'presiv], *adj.* ausdruckslos, nichtssagend. **inexpressiveness,** *s.* die Ausdruckslosigkeit.

inexpugnable [iniks'pju:nəbl], *adj.* unüberwindlich, unbezwinglich.

in extenso [ineks'tensou], *adv.* ausführlich, vollständig.

inextinguishable [iniks'tiŋgwiʃəbl], *adj.* un(aus)löschbar, (*fig.*) unauslöschlich.

in extremis [iniks'treimis], *adv.* in äußerster Not.

inextricable [in'ekstrikəbl], *adj.* unentwirrbar, un(auf)lösbar; (*fig.*) verschlungen, verworren, hoffnungslos verwirrt.

infallibility [infæli'biliti], *s.* die Unfehlbarkeit. **infallible** [-'fælibl], *adj.* unfehlbar; untrüglich, verläßlich, zuverlässig.

infamous ['infəməs], *adj.* verrufen, berüchtigt (***for***, wegen); niederträchtig, schändlich, ehrlos. **infamy,** *s.* die Ehrlosigkeit, Schande; Schändlichkeit, Niederträchtigkeit, Niedertracht.

infancy ['infənsi], *s.* frühes Kindesalter, das Säuglingsalter, frühe Kindheit; (*Law*) die Minderjährigkeit, Unmündigkeit, (*fig.*) Kindheit, der Anfang, das Anfangsstadium; (*fig.*) ***be still in its –,*** noch in den Kinderschuhen stecken.

infant ['infənt], **1.** *s.* der Säugling, das Brustkind, Baby; (*under 7 yrs.*) kleines Kind, das Kleinkind; (*Law*) Unmündige(r), Minderjährige(r). **2.** *adj.* Säuglings–; Kindes–, Kinder–, Kleinkind–, Kindheits–; (*also fig.*) noch klein, jung, kindlich, unentwickelt; (*Law*) unmündig, minderjährig; – ***baptism,*** die Kindertaufe; ***Infant Jesus,*** das Jesuskind; – ***mortality,*** die Säuglingssterblichkeit; – ***school,*** die Kleinkinderschule, der Kindergarten; – ***welfare,*** die Säuglingsfürsorge.

infanta [in'fæntə], *s.* die Infantin. **infante** [-tə], *s.* der Infant.

infanticide [in'fæntisaid], *s.* 1. der Kindesmord, Kindermord; 2. der (die) Kindesmörder(in), Kindermörder(in).

infantile ['infəntail], *adj.* (*Med.*) kindlich, jugendlich, Kindes–, Kinder–, Kindheits–; (*coll.*) kindisch, infantil; (*fig.*) unentwickelt, Anfangs–; – ***disease,*** die Kinderkrankheit; – ***paralysis,*** die Kinderlähmung. **infantilism** [in'fæntilizm], *s.* der Infantilismus. **infantine,** *adj.* (*rare*) *see* **infantile.**

infantry ['infəntri], *s.* die Infanterie, (*obs.*) das Fußvolk. **infantryman** [-mən], *s.* der Infanterist, (*obs.*) Fußsoldat, (*sl.*) Landser.

infarct ['infɑ:kt], *s.* (*Med.*) der Infarkt. **infarction** [-'fɑ:kʃən], *s.* die Infarzierung, Infarktbildung.

infatuate [in'fætjueit], *v.t.* betören, verblenden (***with***, durch). **infatuated,** *adj.* betört, verblendet, vernarrt (***with***, in (*Acc.*)). **infatuation** [-'eiʃən], *s.* die Betörung, Verblendung (***with***, durch); Vernarrtheit (***for***, in (*Acc.*)).

infect [in'fekt], *v.t.* anstecken (*also fig.*), infizieren; verderben, verpesten, vergiften (*air etc.*), (*fig.*) (ungünstig) beeinflussen, packen, mitreißen (*with enthusiasm etc.*); ***become -ed,*** sich anstecken *or* infizieren. **infection** [-'fekʃən], *s.* die Ansteckung, Infizierung; der Infektionsstoff, Infektionsträger, Ansteckungskeim; die Infektionskrankheit, Seuche; ***catch the –,*** angesteckt werden. **infectious** [-'fekʃəs], *adj.* übertragbar, ansteckend, Infektions–, infektiös; – ***disease,*** die Infektionskrankheit; – ***enthusiasm,*** ansteckende Begeisterung. **infectiousness,** *s.* die Übertragbarkeit, Ansteckungsfähigkeit.

infelicitous [infi'lisitəs], *adj.* unangebracht, unpassend, unglücklich (gewählt). **infelicity,** *s.* die Unglückseligkeit, das Unglück; die Ungeeignetheit, Unangemessenheit; unpassende Bemerkung, ungeeigneter Ausdruck; – ***of style,*** der Stilmangel.

infer [in'fə:], *v.t.* schließen, folgern, herleiten, ableiten (***from,*** aus); schließen lassen auf (*Acc.*), erkennen lassen; (*coll.*) annehmen, vermuten. **inferable** ['infərəbl], *adj.* zu folgern(d), zu schließen(d), ableitbar (***from,*** aus). **inference** ['infərəns], *s.* der (Rück)schluß, die Folgerung (***from,*** aus); (*coll.*) Annahme, Hypothese. **inferential** [–'renʃəl], *adj.* Folgerungs–, Schluß–; folgernd, gefolgert. **inferentially,** *adv.* durch Schlußfolgerung.

inferior [in'fiəriə], **1.** *adj.* unter, Unter–, niedriger, tiefer (stehend), weiter unten gelegen (*in position*); geringer, schwächer, tieferstehend (***to,*** als), untergeordnet (*Dat.*) (*in rank*); minderwertig, mittelmäßig, zweitklassig, unbedeutend, gering (*in quality*); ***be – to him,*** ihm untergeordnet sein, ihm nachstehen, hinter ihm zurückstehen (***in,*** in *or* an (*Dat.*)); ***be – to none,*** keinem etwas nachgeben; (*Law*) – ***court,*** das Untergericht; – ***goods,*** minderwertige Waren. **2.** *s.* (*in performance*) Geringere(r), Schwächere(r), Tieferstehende(r); (*in rank*) Untergegebene(r), Untergeordnete(r); ***be his – in,*** ihm nachstehen in (*Dat.*). **inferiority** [–ri'ɔriti], *s.* die Untergeordnetheit, Unterlegenheit, geringerer Stand *or* Wert *etc.*; geringere Zahl *or* Menge *etc.*; (*coll.*) die Minderwertigkeit, Inferiorität; – ***complex,*** der Minderwertigkeitskomplex.

infernal [in'fə:nl], *adj.* Höllen–, höllisch; teuflisch; (*coll.*) verflucht; ***the – fires,*** das höllische Feuer; – ***machine,*** die Höllenmaschine; – ***regions,*** die Unterwelt. **inferno,** *s.* die Hölle; (*fig.*) das Flammenmeer.

infertile [in'fə:tail], *adj.* unfruchtbar, steril. **infertility** [–'tiliti], *s.* die Unfruchtbarkeit.

infest [in'fest], *v.t.* heimsuchen, verheeren, plagen; (*fig.*) überschwemmen; ***–ed with,*** überschwemmt von. **infestation** [–'teiʃən], *s.* die Heimsuchung, Verheerung, Plage; Überschwemmung.

infeudation [infju:'deiʃən], *s.* (*Hist.*) die Belehnung, die Zehntverleihung.

infidel ['infidəl], **1.** *adj.* ungläubig, heidnisch. **2.** *s.* Ungläubige(r), der Heide, Nichtchrist.

infidelity [infi'deliti], *s.* (eheliche) Untreue, der Ehebruch (***to,*** gegen); Treubruch, die Treuelosigkeit.

infield ['infi:ld], *s.* dem Hofe naheliegendes Ackerland; (*Spt.*) das Innenfeld; (*Crick.*) nahestehende Fänger.

infighting ['infaitiŋ], *s.* (*Boxing*) der Nahkampf (*also fig.*).

infiltrate ['infiltreit], **1.** *v.t.* eindringen lassen, allmählich einführen (***into,*** in (*Acc.*)); durchtränken, durchsetzen, durchdringen (***with,*** mit); (*fig. esp. Mil.*) einsickern in (*Acc.*), durchsickern durch; ***–d with,*** durchtränkt von. **2.** *v.i.* (*fig.*) durchsickern, einsickern, allmählich eindringen (***into,*** in (*Acc.*)). **infiltration** [–'treiʃən], *s.* das Durchsickern, Einsickern, allmähliches Eindringen; die Durchtränkung, Durchdringung, Infiltration.

infinite ['infinit], **1.** *adj.* unendlich, endlos; grenzenlos, unbegrenzt; (*fig.*) zahllos, unzählig, ungeheuer. **2.** *s.* das Unendliche, unendlicher Raum (*space*), die Endlosigkeit (*time*); (*Math.*) unendliche Zahl *or* Größe. **infinitely,** *adv.* (*fig. coll.*) unendlich, außerordentlich.

infinitesimal [infini'tesiml], **1.** *adj.* unendlich klein; (*coll.*) winzig (klein); – ***calculus,*** die Infinitesimalrechnung. **2.** *s.* (*Math.*) infinitesimale Größe.

infinitival [infini'taivl], *adj.* infinitivisch, Infinitiv–. **infinitive** [in'finitiv], *s.* die Nennform, der Infinitiv.

infinitude [in'finitju:d], *s.* die Unendlichkeit, Unbegrenztheit, Unermeßlichkeit; unendliche Größe *or* Menge *or* Zahl. **infinity,** *s.* **1.** *See* **infinitude**; 2. (*Math.*) unendliche Größe, das Unendliche; ***to –,*** bis ins Unendliche; ***approach –,*** sich dem Unendlichen nähern.

infirm [in'fə:m], *adj.* kraftlos, schwach, gebrechlich; – ***of purpose,*** unentschlossen, willensschwach. **infirmary,** *s.* das Krankenhaus, Spital. **infirmity,** *s.* die (Alters)schwäche, Gebrechlichkeit, Kränklichkeit; das Gebrechen, Leiden; (*fig.*) die Schwachheit, (menschliche) Schwäche; – ***of purpose,*** die Charakterschwäche, Unentschlossenheit.

infix [in'fiks], **1.** *v.t.* befestigen, hineintreiben, (*fig.*) einpflanzen, einprägen (***in,*** *Dat.*); (*Gram.*) einfügen. **2.** *s.* (*Gram.*) die Einfügung, das Infix.

inflame [in'fleim], **1.** *v.t.* (*Med.*) entzünden; (*fig.*) entflammen, entfachen (*feelings etc.*), erregen, erhitzen (*a p.*); ***–d with rage,*** wutentbrannt. **2.** *v.i.* sich entzünden; (*fig.*) sich erhitzen, entbrennen (***with,*** vor (*Dat.*)).

inflammability [inflæmə'biliti], *s.* die Brennbarkeit, Entzündlichkeit; (*fig.*) Erregbarkeit. **inflammable,** *adj.* brennbar, feuergefährlich, leicht entzündlich; (*fig.*) leicht erregbar, hitzig, jähzornig; – ***matter,*** der Zündstoff.

inflammation [inflə'meiʃən], *s.* (*Med.*) die Entzündung; (*fig.*) Aufregung, Erregung. **inflammatory** [in'flæmətəri], *adj.* (*Med.*) Entzündungs–; (*fig.*) aufreizend, aufhetzend, aufrührerisch; – ***speech,*** die Hetzrede.

inflatable [in'fleitəbl], *adj.* aufblasbar; – ***boat,*** das Schlauchboot. **inflate,** *v.t.* aufblasen, aufblähen (*also fig.*), aufpumpen (*tyres*); (*fig.*) hochtreiben (*prices*). **inflated,** *adj.* aufgeblasen, aufgebläht; (*fig.*) aufgeblasen, hochmütig (*of a p.*), schwulstig, hochtrabend (*style*), inflatorisch (*prices*); ***be – with,*** sich aufblähen vor (*Dat.*). **inflation** [–'fleiʃən], *s.* die Aufblähung; (*fig.*) Aufgeblasenheit; Schwulstigkeit; (*Comm.*) Inflation. **inflationary,** *adj.* Inflations–, inflationistisch, inflatorisch. **inflator,** *s.* die Luftpumpe.

inflect [in'flekt], *v.t.* biegen; (*Gram.*) beugen, abwandeln, flektieren, (*Mus.*) modulieren. **inflection** [–'flekʃən], *s.* die Biegung; (*Gram.*) Beugung, Flexion; Modulation (*of the voice*); (*Gram.*) Flexionsendung, Flexionsform; (*Gram.*) Flexionslehre. **inflectional,** *adj.* Flexions–; – ***language,*** flektierende Sprache.

inflexibility [infleksi'biliti], *s.* die Unbiegsamkeit, (*fig.*) Unbeugsamkeit. **inflexible** [–'fleksibl], *adj.* unbiegsam, starr; (*fig.*) unbeugsam, fest, unerbittlich, unerschütterlich, unbeweglich (*of a p.*).

inflexion, *see* **inflection.**

inflict [in'flikt], *v.t.* auferlegen ((***up***)***on,*** *Dat.*), verhängen (*punishment*) (***on,*** über (*Acc.*)), beibringen (*a defeat*) ((***up***)***on,*** *Dat.*), zufügen (*injuries*) (***on,*** *Dat.*); – ***o.s.*** (***up***)***on him,*** sich ihm aufbürden *or* aufdrängen. **infliction** [–'flikʃən], *s.* 1. die Auferlegung, Verhängung; Zufügung, Beibringung; 2. Last, Plage.

inflorescence [inflɔ'resəns], *s.* der Blütenstand, Blüten (*pl.*); (*fig.*) das Aufblühen, die Blüte.

inflow ['inflou], *s.* der Zufluß, Zulauf, Zustrom (*also Comm.*); das Einfließen, Einströmen.

influence ['influəns], **1.** *s.* der Einfluß, die Einwirkung ((***up***)***on, over,*** auf (*Acc.*); ***with,*** bei); Macht (über (*Dat.*)); bestimmender Faktor; ***sphere of –,*** der Machtbereich, die Interessensphäre; (*coll.*) ***under the –,*** betrunken. **2.** *v.t.* Einfluß ausüben auf (*Acc.*), einwirken auf (*Acc.*), beeinflussen; bewegen, hinlenken, bestimmen; – ***him for good,*** ihn zum Guten hinlenken. **influential** [–'enʃəl], *adj.* einflußreich, von (großem) Einfluß (***on,*** auf (*Acc.*); ***in,*** in (*Dat.*)).

influenza [influ'enzə], *s.* die Grippe, Influenza.

influx ['inflʌks], *s.* 1. das Einfließen, Einströmen; der Zufluß, Zustrom, (*of a river*) das Einmünden, die Mündung; 2. (*Comm.*) Zufuhr, Einfuhr; (*fig.*) das Eindringen, der Andrang.

inform [in'fɔːm], **1.** *v.t.* 1. benachrichtigen, verständigen, in Kenntnis setzen, unterrichten (*of*, von), informieren (über (*Acc.*)); – ***him of it***, es ihm mitteilen *or* bekanntgeben, ihm davon Mitteilung machen; ***keep o.s. -ed***, sich auf dem laufenden halten; 2. (*Poet.*) durchdringen, erfüllen, beseelen (***with***, mit). **2.** *v.i.* Anzeige erstatten; – ***against***, denunzieren, anzeigen, angeben.

informal [in'fɔːml], *adj.* 1. zwanglos, ungezwungen, ohne Förmlichkeit, nicht formell, unzeremoniell; 2. formlos, formwidrig. **informality** [–'mæliti], *s.* 1. die Ungezwungenheit, Zwanglosigkeit; 2. Formlosigkeit, Formwidrigkeit, der Formfehler.

informant [in'fɔːmənt], *s.* 1. der Berichterstatter, Einsender, Gewährsmann; 2. Denunziant, Angeber.

information [infə'meiʃən], *s.* 1. (*no pl.*) die Nachricht, Meldung, Mitteilung, Auskunft, Auskünfte (*pl.*), Informationen (*pl.*), der Bescheid, Aufschluß (***about, on***, über (*Acc.*)); die Belehrung, Unterweisung, Benachrichtigung; ***for your –***, zu Ihrer Kenntnisnahme; ***gather –***, sich erkundigen, Erkundigungen einholen; ***I have no –***, ich bin nicht unterrichtet; ***Ministry of Information***, das Aufklärungsministerium; 2. (*Law*) (*with pl.*) die Anklage, Anzeige; ***file*** or ***lodge – against***, Anzeige erstatten *or* Klage erheben gegen.

information|-bureau, --centre, --office, *s.* die Auskunftsstelle, Auskunftei, das Auskunftsbüro. **--service,** *s.* der Nachrichtendienst.

informative [in'fɔːmətiv], *adj.* (*of a p.*) mitteilsam; (*of a th.*) belehrend, lehrreich, instruktiv. **informed,** *adj.* unterrichtet, informiert. **informer,** *s.* der Angeber, Denunziant; ***common –***, der Spitzel.

infra ['infrə], *adv.* (weiter) unten; (*coll.*) – ***dig***, unter der Würde, unwürdig; ***--red***, infrarot, ultrarot.

infract [in'frækt], *v.t.* brechen, verletzen. **infraction** [–'frækʃən], *s.* die Verletzung, Übertretung.

infrangibility [infrændʒi'biliti], *s.* die Unzerbrechlichkeit; (*fig.*) Unverletzlichkeit. **infrangible** [–'frændʒibl], *adj.* unzerbrechlich; (*fig.*) unverletzlich.

infrequency [in'friːkwənsi], *s.* die Seltenheit; Spärlichkeit. **infrequent,** *adj.* selten; spärlich.

infringe [in'frindʒ], **1.** *v.t.* übertreten, verletzen (*laws*), verstoßen gegen. **2.** *v.i.* – (*up*)*on*, übergreifen auf (*Acc.*), eingreifen in (*Acc.*), verletzen, beeinträchtigen. **infringement,** *s.* der Eingriff, Übergriff (***on***, in (*Acc.*)), die Übertretung, Verletzung; der Verstoß (***of***, gegen), Übergriff (auf (*Acc.*)), Eingriff (in (*Acc.*)).

infuriate [in'fjuərieit], *v.t.* wütend machen, in Wut versetzen. **infuriated,** *adj.* wütend, rasend. **infuriating,** *adj.* (gerade) zu ärgerlich; (*pred. only*) zum Verrücktwerden, (*coll.*) um die (glatten) Wände *or* an den (glatten) Wänden hochzugehen *or* hochzuklettern, um junge Hunde zu kriegen. **infuriation** [–'eiʃən], *s.* die Wut.

infuse [in'fjuːz], **1.** *v.t.* begießen, aufgießen (*tea etc.*); (*Chem., Pharm.*) einweichen, ziehen lassen; (*fig.*) einträufeln, einflößen, eingeben (***into***, *Dat. or* in (*Acc.*)); durchdringen, durchtränken, erfüllen (***with***, mit). **2.** *v.i.* ziehen (*as tea*). **infuser,** *s.* das Tee-Ei.

infusible [in'fjuːzibl], *adj.* unschmelzbar (*metals*).

infusion [in'fjuːʒən], *s.* das Eingießen, Ziehenlassen, Einweichen; der Aufguß, die Infusion; (*fig.*) Einflößung; der Zustrom, Zufluß; die Beimischung, der Beigeschmack, Anstrich.

infusoria [infju'zɔːriə], *pl.* Wimpertierchen, Aufgußtierchen, Infusorien (*pl.*). **infusorial,** *adj.* Infusorien–; – ***earth***, die Kieselgur. **infusorian,** *s.* das Wimpertierchen, Aufgußtierchen, Infusorium.

ingathering ['ingæðəriŋ], *s.* (*Poet., B.*) das Einernten, die Einsammlung.

ingenious [in'dʒiːniəs], *adj.* geistreich, erfinderisch, klug (*of a p.*); sinnreich, sinnvoll, klug angelegt, kunstvoll (*of a th.*).

ingénue [onʒei'nuː], *s.* naives *or* unschuldiges *or* schlichtes Mädchen; (*Theat.*) die Naive.

ingenuity [indʒi'njuiti], *s.* der Scharfsinn, die Erfindungsgabe, Findigkeit (*of a p.*); das Sinnreiche (*of a th.*).

ingenuous [in'dʒenjuəs], *adj.* 1. aufrichtig, freimütig, treuherzig, offen(herzig), unbefangen; 2. naiv, arglos, schlicht, bieder. **ingenuousness,** *s.* 1. die Offenheit, Aufrichtigkeit, Offenherzigkeit, Treuherzigkeit, der Freimut; 2. die Biederkeit, Arglosigkeit, Unbefangenheit, Schlichtheit.

ingest [in'dʒest], *v.t.* einnehmen, zu sich nehmen (*nourishment*). **ingestion** [–tʃən], *s.* die Nahrungsaufnahme, Einnahme.

ingle [iŋgl], *s.* (*obs.*) der Herd, Kamin, das Kaminfeuer; – ***nook***, die Kaminecke.

inglorious [in'glɔːriəs], *adj.* unrühmlich, schimpflich, schändlich.

ingoing ['ingouiŋ], **1.** *s.* das Eintreten, der Antritt. **2.** *adj.* eintretend, antretend.

ingot ['iŋgət], *s.* der Barren (*gold etc.*), Stab, Zain, Block (*steel etc.*). **ingot|-mould,** *s.* die Gießform, Gußform, Kokille. **--steel,** *s.* der Flußstahl.

ingrain, 1. ['ingrein *as attrib.*, in'grein *as pred.*], *adj.* in der Wolle gefärbt. **2.** *v.t.* *See* **engrain. ingrained,** *adj.* (*fig.*) tief verwurzelt, eingewurzelt, eingefleischt.

ingrate ['ingreit], (*obs.*) **1.** *adj.* undankbar. **2.** *s.* Undankbare(r).

ingratiate [in'greiʃieit], *v.t.* (*usu.* – ***o.s.***) in Gunst setzen, (sich) beliebt machen, (sich) einschmeicheln (***with***, bei). **ingratiating,** *adj.* gewinnend, einnehmend, einschmeichelnd. **ingratiation** [–'eiʃən], *s.* die Einschmeichelung, Liebedienerei.

ingratitude [in'grætitjuːd], *s.* die Undankbarkeit, der Undank.

ingredient [in'griːdiənt], *s.* der Bestandteil, die Zutat.

ingress ['ingres], *s.* das Eintreten, der Eintritt (***into***, in (*Acc.*)) (*also Astr.*); Zutritt, das Eintrittsrecht (***into***, zu); der Eingang, Zugang, die Eingangstür.

ingrowing ['ingrouiŋ], *adj.* ins Fleisch *or* einwärts wachsend. **ingrown** [in'groun], *adj.* eingewachsen.

inguinal ['ingwinl], *adj.* (*Anat.*) Leisten–.

ingurgitate [in'gəːdʒiteit], *v.t.* hinunterschlucken, hinunterschlingen, verschlingen (*also fig.*).

inhabit [in'hæbit], *v.t.* wohnen in (*Dat.*), bewohnen. **inhabitable,** *adj.* bewohnbar.

inhabitancy [in'hæbitənsi], *s.* ständiger Aufenthalt; das Wohnrecht. **inhabitant,** *s.* der Bewohner, Einwohner. **inhabitation** [–'teiʃən], *s.* das (Be)wohnen, die Bewohnung.

inhalant [in'heilənt], *s.* (*Med.*) das Inhalationsmittel. **inhalation** [inhə'leiʃən], *s.* 1. die Einatmung, Inhalation; 2. *See* **inhalant. inhale,** *v.t.* einatmen, (*Med.*) inhalieren. **inhaler,** *s.* 1. Einatmende(r); 2. (*Med.*) der Inhalationsapparat, Inhalator, Atmungsansatz.

inharmonious [inhɑː'mouniəs], *adj.* unharmonisch, mißtönend; (*fig.*) uneinig. **inharmoniousness,** *s.* der Mißklang, die Disharmonie; (*fig.*) Uneinigkeit.

inhaul ['inhɔːl], *s.* (*Naut.*) der Niederholer.

inhere [in'hiə], *v.i.* anhaften, eigen sein, innewohnen (***in***, *Dat.*), enthalten sein (in (*Dat.*)) (*a th. only*). **inherence, inherency,** *s.* das Anhaften, Innewohnen, Verwurzeltsein, (*Phil.*) die Inhärenz. **inherent,** *adj.* anhaftend, angeboren, eigen, innewohnend (***in***, *Dat.*), von Natur gehörig (zu), unzertrennlich (von); ***be – in the blood***, im Blut liegen; – ***right***, unveräußerliches Recht.

inherit [in'herit], **1.** *v.t.* (er)erben. **2.** *v.i.* erben, erbberechtigt sein. **inheritable,** *adj.* erblich, Erb–, vererbbar (*of a th.*); erbfähig, erbberechtigt (*of a p.*). **inheritance,** *s.* die Hinterlassenschaft, Erbschaft, das Erbteil, Erbgut, Erbe; Erbrecht, die Vererbung; (*Biol., fig.*) Vererbung; ***by –***, erblich, durch Vererbung, im Erbgang. **inherited,** *adj.* ererbt. **inheritor,** *s.* der Erbe. **inheritress, inheritrix,** *s.* die Erbin.

inhibit [in'hibit], *v.t.* hemmen; hindern (*from*, an (*Dat.*)), zurückhalten (von); (*obs.*) verbieten, untersagen (*from doing*, zu tun). **inhibition** [–'biʃən], *s.* die Hemmung (*also Psych.*), (*Law*) der Einhalt, das Inhibitorium. **inhibitory,** *adj.* hemmend, Hemmungs–, (ver)hindernd; (*Law*) inhibierend.

inhospitable [inhɔs'pitəbl], *adj.* nicht gastfreundlich; (*fig*) unwirtlich, ungastlich, unfreundlich. **inhospitality** [–'tæliti], *s.* die Ungast(freund)-lichkeit; (*fig.*) Unwirtlichkeit, Ungastlichkeit.

inhuman [in'hju:mən], *adj.* unmenschlich, grausam, gefühllos. **inhumanity** [–'mæniti], *s.* die Unmenschlichkeit.

inhumation [inhju'meiʃən], *s.* die Beerdigung, das Begräbnis. **inhume** [in'hju:m], *v.t.* beerdigen, begraben.

inimical [i'nimikl], *adj.* feindlich, schädlich, nachteilig (*to*, *Dat.*), feindselig (gegen).

inimitable [in'imitəbl], *adj.* unnachahmlich, unvergleichlich, einzigartig. **inimitableness,** *s.* die Unnachahmlichkeit.

iniquitous [i'nikwitəs], *adj.* unbillig, ungerecht; schändlich, frevelhaft, boshaft. **iniquity,** *s.* die Ungerechtigkeit, Widerrechtlichkeit; Schändlichkeit, Frevelhaftigkeit, Schlechtigkeit; Schandtat, der Frevel.

initial [i'niʃəl], **1.** *adj.* anfänglich, ursprünglich, Anfangs–, Ausgangs–; (*Phonet.*) Ansatz–, anlautend; (*Tech.*) – *reading*, die Nulleinstellung. **2.** *s.* der Anfangsbuchstabe (*of word*), die Initiale (*of name, on MSS.*). **3.** *v.t.* mit den Initialen unterzeichnen, paraphieren.

initiate, 1. [i'niʃieit], *v.t.* (*a th.*) anfangen, beginnen, einleiten, in Gang setzen, ins Leben rufen, (*Pol.*) als erste(r) beantragen; (*a p.*) einführen, einweihen (*in*, in (*Acc.*)); *be –d*, entstehen. **2.** [–ʃiit], *s.* Eingeweihte(r); der Anfänger, Neuling. **initiation** [–'eiʃən], *s.* die Einweihung, Einführungszeremonie, feierliche Aufnahme *or* Einführung, (*fig.*) Einleitung, der Beginn.

initiative [i'niʃiətiv], **1.** *adj.* einleitend, einführend, Einführungs–, anfänglich. **2.** *s.* erster Anstoß *or* Schritt, die Anregung; Initiative, der Unternehmungsgeist; (*Parl.*) das Antragsrecht; (*Pol.*) die Volksinitiative; *take the –*, die ersten Schritte tun, die Initiative ergreifen; *on one's own –*, aus eigenem Antrieb *or* eigener Initiative. **initiator** [–eitə], *s.* der Beginner, Anreger, Urheber. **initiatory,** *adj.* einweihend, Einweihungs–; *see also* **initiative, 1.**

inject [in'dʒekt], *v.t.* (*Med.*) einspritzen, injizieren; (*sl. drugs*) schießen; (*Tech.*) ausspritzen (*a vessel*) (*with*, mit), einspritzen (*oil etc.*); (*fig.*) einimpfen, einflößen (*fear etc.*), einführen, hereinbringen (*new ideas etc.*), einwerfen (*remarks etc.*); (*Med.*) – *his arm*, eine Einspritzung in seinen Arm machen. **injection** [–'dʒekʃən], *s.* die Einspritzung, Injektion; (*sl. drugs*) der Schuß; das Eingespritzte; – *syringe*, die Injektionsspritze, Klistierspritze. **injector,** *s.* die Strahlpumpe, Einspritzdüse.

injudicious [indʒu'diʃəs], *adj.* unverständig, unklug, unbesonnen, unüberlegt. **injudiciousness,** *s.* die Unverständigkeit, Unklugheit.

injunction [in'dʒʌŋkʃən], *s.* die Einschärfung, ausdrücklicher Befehl; (*Law*) gerichtliche Verfügung, gerichtliches Verbot, richterlicher Befehl, das Unterlassungsgebot; *give strict –s*, dringend einschärfen (*to*, *Dat.*).

injure ['indʒə], *v.t.* beschädigen, verletzen (*a th.*), (*fig.*) beeinträchtigen, schädigen, schaden; verletzen, verwunden (*a p.*); (*fig.*) unrecht tun (*Dat.*), kränken; – *one's head*, sich den Kopf verletzen *or* verwunden; *the –d party*, Geschädigte(r); *–d vanity*, gekränkte Eitelkeit. **injurious** [–'dʒuəriəs], *adj.* verderblich, schädlich, nachteilig (*to*, für); beleidigend, schmähend, Schmäh–, boshaft (*as language*); ungerecht; *be – to*, schaden (*Dat.*); – *to health*, gesundheitschädlich.

injury ['indʒəri], *s.* (*Med.*) die Verletzung, Verwundung, Wunde; (*to a th.*) Beschädigung, der Schaden; (*fig.*) die Beleidigung, Kränkung, Schädigung, Ungerechtigkeit, das Unrecht; *that adds insult to –*, zum Schaden hat man noch den Spott; – *to the head*, die Kopfverletzung; *personal –*, die Körperverletzung.

injustice [in'dʒʌstis], *s.* die Ungerechtigkeit, das Unrecht; *do him an –*, ihm unrecht tun.

ink [iŋk], **1.** *s.* die Tinte; *as black as –*, pechschwarz, kohl(raben)schwarz; *Indian –*, chinesische Tusche; *printer's –*, die Druckerschwärze. **2.** *v.t.* mit Tinte schwärzen *or* beschmieren *or* beklecksen; einfärben (*types*); – *in*, tuschieren (*outline*).

ink-bottle, *s.* die Tintenflasche. **inker,** *s. See* **inking-roller. ink-eraser,** *s.* der Tintengummi. **inkiness,** *s.* die Schwärze. **inking-roller,** *s.* die Auftragwalze, Farbwalze.

inkling ['iŋkliŋ], *s.* (dunkle) Ahnung, die Andeutung; *have an – of*, dunkel ahnen; *get an – of*, Wind bekommen von.

ink|-pad, *s.* das Farbkissen, Stempelkissen. **--pencil,** *s.* der Tintenstift. **--pot,** *s.* das Tintenfaß. **–stand,** *s.* das Schreibzeug; *see* **--pot. --well,** *s.* (eingelassenes) Tintenfaß. **inky,** *adj.* tintig, mit Tinte beschmiert, tintenschwarz; (*fig.*) – (*black*), pech(raben)schwarz.

inlaid ['inleid], *adj.* eingelegt, Einlege–, Mosaik–; – *floor*, der Parkett(fuß)boden; – *woodwork*, die (*or Austr.* das) Holzmosaik; – *work*, die Einlegearbeit.

inland ['inlənd], **1.** *adj.* inländisch, einheimisch, Landes–, Inland(s)–; binnenländisch, Binnen–; – *bill*, der Inlandwechsel; – *duty*, die Landessteuer; der Binnenzoll; – *navigation*, die Binnenschiffahrt; – *produce*, Landeserzeugnisse, Landesprodukte (*pl.*); – *revenue*, Staatsabgaben, Steuereinnahmen (*pl.*); – *sea*, der Binnensee; – *trade*, der Binnenhandel; – *waterways*, die Binnengewässer. **2.** [*also* –'lænd], *adv.* landeinwärts, im Landesinnern, ins Innere des Landes. **3.** *s.* das Binnenland, Inland, Landesinnere. **inlander,** *s.* der (die) Binnenländer(in).

in-law ['inlɔ:], *s.* (*coll.*) angeheiratete(r) Verwandte(r).

inlay, 1. [in'lei], *v.t.* einlegen, auslegen, täfeln, furnieren. **2.** ['inlei], *s.* die Einlegearbeit, Intarsie; das Furnier; (*Dentistry*) die Plombe. **inlaying,** *s.* das Einlegen; die Täfelung, eingelegte Arbeit.

inlet ['inlet], *s.* der Einlaß, Eingang (*also Anat.*), die Einfahrt, der Zugang (*also fig.*); (*of coast*) kleine Bucht. **inlet-valve,** *s.* das Einlaßventil.

in-line ['in'lain], *attrib. adj.* Reihen– (*of engines*).

inly ['inli], *adv.* (*Poet.*) innerlich, innig, heimlich.

inlying ['inlaiiŋ], *adj.* inner, Innen–.

inmate ['inmeit], *s.* der Insasse (die Insassin), der Hausgenosse (die Hausgenossin); der (die) Mitbewohner(in).

inmost ['inmoust], *adj.* innerst, (*fig.*) geheimst, innigst, verborgenst.

inn [in], *s.* **1.** der Gasthof, das Gasthaus, Wirtshaus, die Gaststätte, Wirtschaft, Schenke; **2.** *Inns of Court*, die (Gebäude der) Advokateninnungen und Rechtsschulen (in London).

Inn, *s.* (*Geog.*) der Inn.

innards ['inədz], *s.* (*coll.*) das Innere.

innate [i'neit], *adj.* angeboren, eigen (*in*, *Dat.*); (*Med.*) kongenital. **innately,** *adv.* von Natur (aus). **innateness,** *s.* das Angeborensein.

inner ['inə], *adj.* inner, inwendig, Innen–; (*fig.*) geheim, verborgen, innerlich; – *diameter*, lichte Weite; – *man*, die Seele; (*coll.*) der Magen; – *meaning*, verborgener Sinn; (*Cycl., Motor.*) – *tube*, der (Luft)schlauch; – *voice*, die Stimme des Gewissens. **innermost,** *adj.* innerst, (*fig.*) tiefst, innigst.

innervate [i'nə:veit], *v.t.* Nervenkraft zuführen (*Dat.*) (*organs*); (*fig.*) beleben, anregen. **innervation** [–'veiʃən], *s.* die Innervation; Nervenverteilung; (*fig.*) Belebung, Anregung.

innings ['iniŋz], *pl.* (*Crick.*) das Am-Spiel-Sein,

Dransein; Spiel, die Spielzeit; (*fig.*) ***have one's –,*** an der Macht sein, am Ruder sein; (*fig.*) ***have had a good –,*** das ganze (lange) Leben es schön gehabt haben.

innkeeper ['inki:pə], *s.* der (die) Gastwirt(in), Schenkwirt(in).

innocence ['inəsəns], *s.* die Unschuld (*of,* an (*Dat.*)), Schuldlosigkeit, Arglosigkeit, Harmlosigkeit, (Herzens)einfalt. **innocent, 1.** *adj.* unschuldig, schuldlos (***of,*** an (*Dat.*)); harmlos, unschädlich (*as drugs etc.*); arglos, naiv; (*coll.*) – ***of,*** frei von, ohne, (*following noun*) bar (*Gen.*). **2.** *s.* Unschuldige(r), Arglose(r); (*B.*) ***Massacre of the Innocents,*** Bethlehemitischer Kindermord, (*Parl.*) (*sl.*) die Nichterledigung der Tagesordnung am Sessionsende; ***Innocents' Day,*** das Fest der Unschuldigen Kinder (*Dec. 28*).

innocuous [i'nɔkjuəs], *adj.* unschädlich, harmlos, ungefährlich. **innocuousness,** *s.* die Unschädlichkeit, Harmlosigkeit.

innominate [i'nɔmineit], *adj.* namenlos, unbenannt; – ***bone,*** das Becken, Hüftbein.

innovate ['inoveit], *v.i.* Neuerungen vornehmen *or* einführen. **innovation** [–'veiʃən], *s.* die Neuerung. **innovator,** *s.* der Neuerer, Umgestalter.

innoxious [i'nɔkʃəs], *adj.* unschädlich.

innuendo [inju'endou], *s.* (*pl.* **-es**) (versteckte) Andeutung *or* Anspielung (***at,*** auf (*Acc.*)); Stichelei, Anzüglichkeit; Unterstellung, Bezichtigung; (*Law*) Auslegung eines (verleumderischen) Ausdrucks.

innutritious [inju'triʃəs], *adj.* nicht nahrhaft, ohne Nährwert.

inobservance [inəb'zə:vəns], *s.* die Nichtbeachtung, Nichteinhaltung, Unaufmerksamkeit, Unachtsamkeit (*of,* gegen).

inoculate [i'nɔkjuleit], *v.t.* (*Med.*) impfen (*a p.*) (***for,*** gegen), einimpfen (*serum*) (***into,*** *Dat.*); (*fig.*) – ***him with s.th.,*** ihm etwas einimpfen. **inoculation** [–'leiʃən], *s.* die Einimpfung (*of serum; also fig.*); Impfung.

inodorous [in'oudərəs], *adj.* geruchlos.

inoffensive [inə'fensiv], *adj.* harmlos, gutartig, einwandfrei, unschädlich. **inoffensiveness,** *s.* die Harmlosigkeit, Unschädlichkeit.

inofficious [inə'fiʃəs], *adj.* (*Law*) gegen natürliche Pflichten.

inoperable [in'ɔpərəbl], *adj.* nicht praktizierbar (*as plans*), (*Surg.*) nicht operierbar. **inoperative,** *adj.* unwirksam, ungültig.

inopportune [in'ɔpətju:n], *adj.* ungelegen, unangemessen, unangebracht, unzeitgemäß, unzeitig. **inopportuneness,** *s.* die Unangemessenheit.

inordinate [in'ɔ:dinit], *adj.* 1. unmäßig, übermäßig; 2. regellos, ungeregelt, unregelmäßig, ungeordnet; unbeherrscht, zügellos. **inordinateness,** *s.* 1. die Unmäßigkeit, Übermäßigkeit; 2. Unregelmäßigkeit, Regellosigkeit; Zügellosigkeit.

inorganic [inɔ:'gænik], *adj.* unorganisch; (*Chem.*) anorganisch.

inosculate [in'ɔskjuleit], **1.** *v.t.* (*Anat.*) verbinden, vereinigen (***with,*** mit) (*also fig.*), einmünden lassen, einfügen (***into,*** in (*Acc.*)). **2.** *v.i.* ineinander münden, (*also fig.*) eng verbunden sein, in Verbindung stehen, sich verbinden, sich eng berühren. **inosculation** [–'leiʃən], *s.* (*Anat.*) die Ineinandermündung, Anastomose; (*also fig.*) Einfügung, Vereinigung, enge Verbindung.

in-patient, *s.* der (die) Anstaltspatient(in).

in-phase, *adj.* (*Elec.*) gleichphasig; – ***component,*** die Wirkkomponente.

input ['input], *s.* (*Tech., Rad.*) die Eingangsenergie, Leistungsaufnahme, zugeführte Energie *or* Leistung; (*Rad.*) – ***amplifier,*** der Vorverstärker; (*Rad.*) – ***circuit,*** der Eingangskreis; (*Rad.*) – ***impedance,*** die Gitterkreisimpedanz; (*Rad.*) – ***terminals,*** der Speisepunkt.

inquest ['inkwest], *s.* gerichtliche Untersuchung; ***coroner's –,*** die Leichenschau.

inquietude [in'kwaiətju:d], *s.* die Unruhe, Ruhelosigkeit; (*usu. fig.*) Beunruhigung, Besorgtheit.

inquire [in'kwaiə], **1.** *v.i.* (nach)fragen, sich erkundigen (***about,*** über (*Acc.*); ***of, from,*** bei); – ***within,*** Näheres im Hause; – ***after,*** fragen nach, sich erkundigen nach; ***much –d after,*** viel gefragt, sehr gesucht; – ***into a th.,*** eine S. untersuchen *or* erforschen. **2.** *v.t.* sich erkundigen nach, fragen nach, erfragen; – ***the way,*** sich nach dem Wege erkundigen; – ***his name,*** nach seinem Namen fragen. **inquirer,** *s.* Untersuchende(r), (Nach)-fragende(r). **inquiring,** *adj.* forschend, fragend, wißbegierig, neugierig.

inquiry [in'kwaiəri], *s.* die Erkundigung, (An)frage, Nachfrage (***for,*** nach); Untersuchung, Prüfung, (Nach)forschung (***into,*** *Gen.*); ***make inquiries,*** Erkundigungen einziehen (***about,*** über (*Acc.*); ***of him,*** bei ihm); ***on –,*** auf Nachfrage, nach Erkundigung. **inquiry-office,** *s.* die Auskunftsstelle.

inquisition [inkwi'ziʃən], *s.* gerichtliche Untersuchung; (*R.C.*) das Ketzergericht, die Inquisition; (*fig.*) Nachforschung (***into,*** über (*Acc.*)).

inquisitive [in'kwizitiv], *adj.* neugierig (***about,*** auf (*Acc.*)), wißbegierig. **inquisitiveness,** *s.* die Neugier(de), Wißbegierde.

inquisitor [in'kwizitə], *s.* (*Law*) der Untersuchungsrichter, Untersuchungsbeamte(r), (*R.C.*) Inquisitor. **inquisitorial** [–'tɔ:riəl], *adj.* Untersuchungs–, (*R.C.*) Inquisitions–; (*fig.*) forschend, neugierig.

inroad ['inroud], *s.* (feindlicher) Einfall (***in,*** in (*Acc.*)), der Angriff, Überfall ((***up***)***on,*** auf (*Acc.*)); (*fig.*) Eingriff (***in***(***to***), (***up***)***on,*** in (*Acc.*)), Übergriff (auf (*Acc.*)); *pl.* das Eindringen (*of disease etc.*) (***on,*** in (*Acc.*)), die Inanspruchnahme (***on,*** *Gen.*) (*a th.*).

inrush ['inrʌʃ], *s.* der Zustrom, das (Her)einströmen.

insalubrious [insə'lu:briəs], *adj.* ungesund, gesundheitsschädlich. **insalubrity,** *s.* die Ungesundheit.

insane [in'sein], *adj.* geisteskrank, wahnsinnig, irrsinnig; (*fig.*) unsinnig, verrückt.

insanitary [in'sænitəri], *adj.* ungesund, gesundheitsschädlich.

insanity [in'sæniti], *s.* die Geisteskrankheit, der Irrsinn, Wahnsinn; (*fig.*) die Unsinnigkeit, Verrücktheit, Sinnlosigkeit.

insatiability [inseiʃiə'biliti], *s.* die Unersättlichkeit. **insatiable,** (*Poet.*) **insatiate** [–eit], *adj.* unersättlich, unstillbar.

inscribe [in'skraib], *v.t.* einschreiben, aufschreiben; eintragen, einschreiben (*one's name etc.*) (***in,*** in (*Acc.*)); zueignen, widmen (*a book etc.*) (***to,*** *Dat.*); (*Geom.*) einbeschreiben, einzeichnen (*a figure*); (*fig.*) einprägen (***on,*** *Dat.*); (*Geom.*) ***–d circle,*** einbeschriebener Kreis, der Inkreis; (*Comm.*) ***–d stock,*** Namensaktien (ohne Besitzerschein) (*pl.*).

inscription [in'skripʃən], *s.* die Einschreibung, Eintragung; Inschrift, Aufschrift, Beschriftung; (*Geom.*) Einbeschreibung, Einzeichnung; Zueignung, Widmung; (*Comm.*) (Registrierung von) Namensaktien (*pl.*).

inscrutability [inskru:tə'biliti], *s.* die Unerforschlichkeit, Unergründlichkeit. **inscrutable** [–'skru:təbl], *adj.* unerforschlich, unergründlich; rätselhaft, unverständlich.

insect ['insekt], *s.* das Kerbtier, Insekt. **insecticide** [–'sektisaid], *s.* das Insektenvertilgungsmittel, Insektenpulver, Insektizid, Schädlingsbekämpfungsmittel. **insectifuge** [–'sektifju:dʒ], *s.* das Insektenvertreibungsmittel. **insectivore** [–'sektivɔ:], *s.* (*Zool.*) der Insektenfresser. **insectivorous** [–'tivərəs], *adj.* insektenfressend. **insect-powder,** *s. See* **insecticide.**

insecure [insi'kjuə], *adj.* unsicher, ungewiß, ungesichert. **insecurity,** *s.* die Unsicherheit, Ungewißheit.

inseminate [in'semineit], *v.t.* (*Biol.*) befruchten, schwängern; (*fig.*) einpflanzen (***in,*** in (*Acc.*)), einprägen, einimpfen (*Dat.*). **insemination** [–'neiʃən], *s.* die Befruchtung; ***artificial –,*** künstliche Befruchtung.

insensate [in'senseit], *adj.* empfindungslos, gefühllos; unsinnig, unvernünftig.

insensibility [insensi'biliti], *s.* 1. die Bewußtlosigkeit, Ohnmacht; 2. Gleichgültigkeit, Gefühllosigkeit (*to*, gegen), Unempfänglichkeit, Unempfindlichkeit (für); (*fig.*) Stumpfheit, der Stumpfsinn. **insensible,** *adj.* 1. bewußtlos, ohnmächtig; 2. unempfindlich, empfindungslos, gefühllos; unempfänglich (*of, to*, für), gleichgültig (gegen); ***not – of,*** sich (*Dat.*) im klaren über (*Acc.*), sich (*Dat.*) bewußt (*Gen.*); 3. (*rare*) unmerklich, kaum wahrnehmbar.

insensitive [in'sensitiv], *adj.* unempfindlich (*to*, gegen), unempfänglich (*to*, für). **insensitiveness,** *s.* (*usu. fig.*) die Empfindungslosigkeit, Gefühllosigkeit, Unempfänglichkeit. **insensitivity** [–'tiviti], *s.* die Unempfindlichkeit.

insentience [in'senʃiəns], *s.* die Empfindungslosigkeit, Gefühllosigkeit; Leblosigkeit. **insentient,** *adj. See* **insensate.**

inseparability [insepərə'biliti], *s.* die Untrennbarkeit, Unzertrennlichkeit. **inseparable** [–'sepərəbl], *adj.* untrennbar (*also Gram.*), unzertrennlich. **inseparables,** *pl.* (*coll.*) unzertrennliche Freunde.

insert, 1. [in'sə:t], *v.t.* einsetzen, einlassen, einführen; einschalten, einfügen, einwerfen (*coin in slot*), stecken (*key in lock*), einrücken (lassen), aufgeben (lassen) (*advertisement*). **2.** ['insə:t], *s.* die Einlage, Beilage (*in a book etc.*), Einfügung, Einschaltung, der Einsatz, Zusatz. **insertion** [–'sə:ʃən], *s.* 1. das Einsetzen, Einlassen, Einführen, die Einsetzung, Einführung, Einschaltung, Einfügung, Eintragung; 2. das Eingefügte, der Einsatz, Zusatz; das Inserat, die (Zeitungs)-anzeige; 3. der Einwurf (*of coin*).

inset ['inset], **1.** *s.* der Einsatz, die Einlage, der Eckeinsatz (*in a picture*), das Nebenbild, die Nebenkarte (*in an atlas*); das Einströmen (*of the tide*). **2.** *v.t.* einsetzen, einlegen.

inshore ['in'ʃɔ:], **1.** *adv.* an *or* nahe der Küste; küsteneinwärts, zur Küste hin; ***– of the ship,*** zwischen dem Schiff und der Küste. **2.** *adj.* Küsten–.

inside, 1. ['insaid], *adj.* inner, inwendig, Innen–; ***– callipers,*** der Lochzirkel; ***– diameter,*** lichte Weite, der Innendurchmesser; (*coll.*) ***– information,*** direkte Informationen (*pl.*), die Nachricht aus erster Hand; (*Footb.*) ***– left,*** der Linksinnen-(stürmer). **2.** [–'said], *adv.* im Innern, drinnen; ins Innere, nach innen; (*coll.*) ***– of,*** innerhalb von, in weniger als. **3.** [–'said], *prep.* innerhalb, im Innern (von *or Gen.*). **4.** ['insaid, –'said], *s.* die Innenseite, innere Seite, das Innere; (*coll.*) der Magen, Leib; (*coll.*) Innensitze (*pl.*), Innenplätze (*pl.*) (*of vehicle*); (*coll.*) ***the – of a week,*** nahezu eine Woche, nicht mehr als eine Woche; ***– out,*** das Innere nach außen; ***turn s.th. – out,*** etwas völlig umkrempeln; (*coll.*) ***know s.th. – out,*** etwas inund auswendig kennen. **insider** [–'saidə], *s.* (*coll.*) Eingeweihte(r); Innenstehende(r).

insidious [in'sidiəs], *adj.* hinterlistig, hinterhältig, verräterisch, heimtückisch; (*Med.*) tückisch, schleichend; ***– agitation,*** die Wühlarbeit. **insidiousness,** *s.* die Hinterlist, Heimtücke.

insight ['insait], *s.* die Einsicht, der Einblick (*into*, in (*Acc.*)), das Verständnis (von); der Scharfblick.

insignia [in'signiə], *pl.* Abzeichen, Insignien (*pl.*).

insignificance [insig'nifikəns], *s.* die Bedeutungslosigkeit, Belanglosigkeit, Unerheblichkeit, Unwichtigkeit, Geringfügigkeit. **insignificant,** *adj.* unbedeutend, unwichtig, unerheblich, belanglos, nichtssagend, bedeutungslos; geringfügig, verächtlich.

insincere [insin'siə], *adj.* unaufrichtig, falsch, heuchlerisch. **insincerity** [–'seriti], *s.* die Unaufrichtigkeit, Falschheit, Heuchelei.

insinuate [in'sinjueit], *v.t.* 1. zu verstehen geben, vorsichtig beibringen, einflüstern (*to, Dat.*), merken lassen (*Acc.*); 2. anspielen auf (*Acc.*), andeuten; 3. langsam hineinbringen *or* einschmuggeln (*into*, in); ***– o.s.,*** sich einschmeicheln (*into*, bei). sich einschleichen *or* einschmuggeln *or* hineinwinden, unbemerkt eindringen (*into*, in (*Acc.*)). **insinuating,** *adj.* einschmeichelnd, einnehmend. **insinuation** [–'eiʃən], *s.* 1. die Einflüsterung, versteckte Andeutung *or* Anspielung; 2. leises Eindringen, das Sich-Einschleichen, die Einschmeichelung.

insipid [in'sipid], *adj.* unschmackhaft, geschmacklos; (*fig.*) fad(e), schal, abgeschmackt. **insipidity** [–'piditi], **insipidness,** *s.* die Unschmackhaftigkeit, Fadheit; Abgeschmacktheit, Geschmacklosigkeit.

insist [in'sist], *v.i.* ***– (up)on,*** bestehen auf (*Dat.*), beharren auf (*Dat.*), dringen auf (*Acc.*), ausdrücklich verlangen; Gewicht legen auf (*Acc.*), hervorheben, betonen, geltend machen. **insistence,** *s.* das Beharren (*on*, bei), Bestehen (auf (*Dat.*)); der Nachdruck, die Eindringlichkeit. **insistent,** *adj.* beharrlich, eindringlich, nachdrücklich.

insobriety [inso'braiiti], *s.* die Unmäßigkeit, Trunkenheit.

insofar ['insoufɑ:], *adv.* insoweit (*as*, als), in dem Maße (wie).

insole ['insoul], *s.* die Einlegesohle, Brandsohle.

insolence ['insələns], *s.* die Unverschämtheit, Frechheit; Überheblichkeit, Anmaßung. **insolent,** *adj.* unverschämt, frech; überheblich, anmaßend.

insolubility [insɔlju'biliti], *s.* 1. die Un(auf)löslichkeit; 2. (*fig.*) Unlösbarkeit. **insoluble,** *adj.* 1. un(auf)löslich; 2. (*fig.*) unlösbar, unerklärbar.

insolvency [in'sɔlvənsi], *s.* die Zahlungsunfähigkeit, der Konkurs, Bankrott. **insolvent, 1.** *adj.* zahlungsunfähig, bankrott, insolvent; ***– estate,*** die Konkursmasse. **2.** *s.* zahlungsunfähiger Schuldner.

insomnia [in'sɔmniə], *s.* die Schlaflosigkeit.

insomuch ['insoumʌtʃ], *adv.* dermaßen, dergestalt (*that*, daß), insofern (*as*, als).

insouciance [in'su:siəns], *s.* die Sorglosigkeit. **insouciant,** *adj.* sorglos, unbekümmert.

inspect [in'spekt], *v.t.* besichtigen, besehen, untersuchen, prüfen, inspizieren (*things*), beaufsichtigen, mustern (*persons*). **inspection** [–'spekʃən], *s.* die Besichtigung, Durchsicht, Untersuchung, Prüfung, Inspizierung, Aufsicht; (*Mil.*) der Appell; (*Comm.*) ***for your –,*** zur Ansicht *or* Durchsicht. **inspection|-copy,** *s.* das Prüfungsexemplar (*of book*). **--lamp,** *s.* die Ableuchtlampe.

inspector [in'spektə], *s.* Aufsichtsbeamte(r), der Inspektor, Aufseher; ***customs –,*** der Zollaufseher; ***police –,*** der Polizeikommissar; ***– general,*** der Oberinspektor; ***– of schools,*** der Schulinspektor. **inspectoral,** *adj.* Aufsichts–, Inspektions–, Inspektor(en)–. **inspectorate** [–rit], *s.* die Aufsichtsbehörde; der Aufsichtsbezirk. **inspectorship,** *s.* das Inspektorat, Inspektoramt; die Aufsicht.

inspiration [inspi'reiʃən], *s.* 1. (*Med.*) das Atemholen, Einatmen, die Einatmung; 2. (*fig.*) Eingebung, Begeisterung; ***divine –,*** göttliche Eingebung *or* Erleuchtung; ***at the – of,*** auf Veranlassung von; (*coll.*) ***on the – of the moment,*** durch einen plötzlichen Einfall. **inspirational,** *adj.* eingegeben, Begeisterungs–. **inspirator** ['inspireitə], *s.* (*Med.*) der Inhalator, Inspirierapparat. **inspiratory** [–'reitəri], *adj.* (*Med.*) (Ein)atmungs–.

inspire [in'spaiə], *v.t.* 1. (*Med.*) inhalieren, einatmen; 2. (*fig.*) eingeben, einflößen (*in, Dat.*), auslösen, erwecken (in (*Dat.*)); begeistern, anfeuern (*a p.*); ***– him with,*** ihn erfüllen *or* beseelen mit; ***–d by the government,*** durch die Regierung veranlaßt; ***the –d word,*** das (von Gott) eingegebene *or* inspirierte Wort. **inspiring,** *adj.* begeisternd, belebend.

inspirit [in'spirit], *v.t.* anfeuern, beleben, beseelen, ermutigen.

inspissate [in'spiseit], *v.t.* verdicken, eindicken, eindampfen, einkochen. **inspissated** [–'seitidl, *adj.* (*fig.*) undurchdringlich, undurchsichtig. **inspissation** [–'seiʃən], *s.* die Verdickung, Eindampfung.

instability [instə'biliti], *s.* mangelnde Festigkeit, die Instabilität; (*fig.*) Unbeständigkeit, Wankelmütigkeit; Unsicherheit, Labilität; *see* **unstable.**

install [in'stɔ:l], *v.t.* 1. einsetzen, einweisen, bestallen (*a p.*) (*in*, in (*Acc.*)) (*an office*); 2. anlegen, anbringen, aufstellen, einbauen, einrichten, installieren, montieren (*apparatus*). **installation** [–stə'leiʃən], *s.* 1. die Bestallung, Einsetzung (*of a p.*); 2. Aufstellung, Anbringung, Einrichtung, Installierung, Montage, der Einbau (*of equipment*); 3. die Einrichtung, Anlage, Installation.

instalment [in'stɔ:lmənt], *s.* 1. die Rate, Abzahlung, Teilzahlung, Ratenzahlung, Abschlagszahlung; (Teil)lieferung (*of a book etc.*), Fortsetzung (*of a serial*); ***by –s,*** ratenweise, in Raten; in Lieferungen; ***first –,*** die Anzahlung; ***– plan,*** die Ratenzahlung; 2. *See* **installation,** 1.

instance ['instəns], **1.** *s.* 1. (besonderer) Fall, das Beispiel; ***another – of,*** ein zweites Beispiel für; ***for –,*** zum Beispiel; ***in this –,*** in diesem (einzelnen) Fall; 2. (*rare*) das Ansuchen, Ersuchen, inständige Bitte; ***at the – of our friend,*** auf Ansuchen *or* Veranlassung unseres Freundes; 3. (*Law*) die Instanz; ***in the first –,*** an erster Stelle, in erster Linie; das erstemal, zuerst; ***Court of first –,*** das Gericht erster Instanz; ***in the last –,*** letzten Endes, letztlich. **2.** *v.t.* als Beispiel anführen, zitieren, erwähnen.

instant ['instənt], **1.** *adj.* 1. sofortig, augenblicklich, unverzüglich, unmittelbar; ***– coffee,*** der Pulverkaffee; 2. (*usu. abbr. inst.*) gegenwärtig, laufend, dieses Monats; ***on the 10th –,*** am zehnten dieses *or* laufenden Monats; 3. inständig, anhaltend (*of prayer*). **2.** *s.* der Augenblick, Zeitpunkt, Moment; ***in an –,*** sofort, augenblicklich, im Nu; ***the – he spoke,*** sobald er sprach; ***this –,*** sofort, in diesem Augenblick; ***at that –,*** in dem Augenblick.

instantaneous [instən'teiniəs], *adj.* augenblicklich, unverzüglich, sofortig; gleichzeitig (*of two events*); momentan, Augenblicks–, Moment–; ***his death was –,*** er war auf der Stelle tot; (*Phot.*) ***– shutter,*** der Momentverschluß. **instantaneously,** *adv.* sofort, sogleich, unverzüglich, augenblicklich, im Nu.

instantly, *adv. See* **instantaneously.**

instead [in'sted], *adv.* dafür, statt dessen; ***– of,*** an Stelle von, (an)statt (*Gen.*); ***– of me,*** statt meiner, an meiner Statt *or* Stelle; ***– of writing,*** (an)statt zu schreiben; ***be – of,*** eintreten *or* stehen *or* gelten für.

instep ['instep], *s.* der Spann, Rist; (*coll.*) ***be high in the –,*** die Nase hoch tragen.

instigate ['instigeit], *v.t.* anreizen, aufreizen, aufhetzen, antreiben (*a p.*) (***to do,*** zu tun); anstiften. **instigation** [–'geiʃən], *s.* die Anstiftung, Aufreizung, Aufhetzung, das Antreiben, Betreiben; der Antrieb, Ansporn; ***at*** or ***on the – of,*** auf Betreiben (*Gen.*). **instigator,** *s.* der (die) (Auf)hetzer(in), Anstifter(in) (***of,*** zu *or Gen.*).

instil(l) [in'stil], *v.t.* eintröpfeln, einträufeln, (*fig.*) einflößen, beibringen (***into,*** *Dat.*). **instillation** [–'leiʃən], **instil(l)ment,** *s.* das Eintröpfeln, (*fig.*) Einflößen, die Einflößung.

instinct, 1. [in'stiŋkt], *pred. adj.* erfüllt, angeregt, belebt, durchdrungen (***with,*** von). **2.** ['instiŋkt], *s.* der Instinkt, (Natur)trieb, die Naturanlage; angeborene Tendenz, natürliche Neigung, instinktives Gefühl (***for,*** für); ***by –,*** instinktiv, von Natur (aus); ***act on –,*** instinktiv *or* instinktmäßig *or* aus Instinkt handeln; ***– of self-preservation,*** der Selbsterhaltungstrieb. **instinctive** [in'stiŋktiv], *adj.* instinktmäßig, triebmäßig, unwillkürlich, instinktiv.

institute ['institju:t], **1.** *v.t.* einrichten, errichten, stiften, gründen, ins Leben rufen, in Gang setzen; (*Eccl.*) einführen, einsetzen (***into,*** in (*Acc.*)); anstellen, einleiten (*inquiry, comparison etc.*), anordnen, verordnen, einführen, festsetzen (*regulations etc.*). **2.** *s.* 1. gelehrte Gesellschaft, der Verein, das Institut, die Anstalt, Einrichtung, Institution; das Institutsgebäude; 2. (*obs.*) (*usu. pl.*) Statut, Grundgesetz, der Grundsatz, die Grundregel, Grundlehre; ***Justinian's –s,*** Justinians Institutionen.

institution [insti'tju:ʃən], *s.* 1. die Einrichtung, Errichtung, Anordnung, Stiftung, Gründung; Verordnung, Satzung, das Gesetz, Statut; 2. Institut, die Stiftung, Anstalt, Gesellschaft, (öffentliche) Einrichtung; ***benevolent –,*** milde Stiftung, die Wohltätigkeitseinrichtung; ***educational –,*** die Erziehungsanstalt; 3. (*Eccl.*) die Einführung, Einsetzung. **institutional,** *adj.* Institut(ions)–, Anstalts–; institutionsmäßig. **institutor** ['institju:tə], *s.* der Stifter, Gründer, Errichter, Einrichter, Anordner; (*Eccl.*) Einsetzer, einführende(r) Geistliche(r).

instruct [in'strʌkt], *v.t.* unterrichten, unterweisen, ausbilden, anleiten, belehren (***in,*** in (*Dat.*)); informieren, anweisen, beauftragen; (*Law*) instruieren. **instruction** [–'strʌkʃən], *s.* 1. die Unterweisung, Anweisung, Belehrung, Anleitung; Lehre, der Unterricht; (*Mil.*) die Ausbildung, Instruktion; ***course of –,*** der Lehrgang; 2. *pl.* die Vorschrift, (An)weisung, Verhaltungsmaßregel, Anordnung, der Auftrag, (*Law*) die Instruktion; ***according to –s,*** den Weisungen entsprechend; ***contrary to –s,*** gegen ausdrückliche Weisung; ***–s for use,*** die Gebrauchsanweisung. **instructional,** *adj.* erzieherisch, Erziehungs–, Lehr–; Ausbildungs–, Unterrichts–; (*Mil.*) Übungs–; *see also* **instructive**; ***– film,*** der Lehrfilm. **instructive,** *adj.* belehrend, lehrreich. **instructor,** *s.* der Lehrer, Erzieher; (*Mil.*) Ausbilder, Instruktor; (*Am.*) Dozent; ***driving –,*** der Fahrlehrer; ***flying –,*** der Fluglehrer. **instructress,** *s.* die Lehrerin, Erzieherin.

instrument ['instrumənt], **1.** *s.* 1. das Werkzeug (*also fig.*), Instrument (*also Mus.*); (Meß)gerät, der Apparat, (technische) Vorrichtung; ***–-board,*** die Schalttafel, das Armaturenbrett; ***chosen –,*** auserwähltes Rüstzeug; ***musical –,*** das Musikinstrument; 2. (*Law*) die Urkunde, das Dokument; (*Comm.*) ***– payable to bearer,*** das Inhaberpapier; 3. (*fig.*) (*of a th.*) das (Hilfs)mittel, (*of a p.*) Werkzeug, der Handlanger. **2.** *v.t.* instrumentieren.

instrumental [instru'mentl], *adj.* 1. als Mittel *or* Werkzeug dienend, dienlich, förderlich, behilflich; (*Gram.*) ***– case,*** der Instrumental(is); ***be –,*** behilflich sein (***in doing,*** zu tun); ***be – to(wards),*** beitragen zu, mitwirken bei, veranlassen, bewirken; ***he was – in finding a house for us,*** er setzte es durch, daß eine Wohnung für uns gefunden wurde; 2. (*Mus.*) Instrumental–; ***– music,*** die Instrumentalmusik; 3. (*Tech.*) Instrumenten–; ***– error,*** der Fehler des Apparats. **instrumentalist,** *s.* (*Mus.*) der Instrumentspieler. **instrumentality** [–'tæliti], *s.* die Mitwirkung, Mithilfe; Vermittlung; ***by the – of,*** durch Vermittlung von, (ver)mittels (*Gen.*). **instrumentation** [–'teiʃən], *s.* (*Mus.*) die Instrumentierung.

insubordinate [insə'bɔ:dinit], *adj.* widersetzlich, widerspenstig, aufsässig, ungehorsam, unbotmäßig. **insubordination** [–'neiʃən], *s.* die Widersetzlichkeit, Widerspenstigkeit, Unbotmäßigkeit, der Ungehorsam, (*Mil.*) die Gehorsamsverweigerung, Auflehnung, Meuterei, Insubordination.

insubstantial [insəb'stænʃəl], *adj.* unkörperlich, immateriell, unwirklich, nicht stofflich; (*fig.*) gebrechlich, hinfällig, unwesentlich, unmaßgeblich. **insubstantiality** [–ʃi'æliti], *s.* die Unkörperlichkeit, Nicht-Stofflichkeit.

insufferable [in'sʌfərəbl], *adj.* unerträglich, unausstehlich, unleidlich.

insufficiency [insə'fiʃənsi], *s.* die Unzulänglichkeit, Unfähigkeit, Untauglichkeit; (*Comm.*) ***– of assets,*** mangelnde Deckung. **insufficient,** *adj.* unzulänglich, unzureichend, ungenügend; (*Law*) rechtsungültig.

insufflation [insə'fleiʃən], *s.* (*R.C.*) das Anhauchen, (*Med.*) Einblasen.

insular ['insjələ], *adj.* insular, Insel–; (*fig.*) abgeschlossen, engstirnig, beschränkt. **insularity** [–'læriti], *s.* insulare Lage; (*fig.*) die Beschränktheit, Abgeschlossenheit, Engstirnigkeit, beschränkter Horizont.

insulate ['insjəleit], *v.t.* isolieren (*also Elec.*),

absondern. **insulating,** *adj.* isolierend, Isolier–; – ***tape,*** das Isolierband. **insulation** [–ˈleiʃən], *s.* die Isolierung (*also Elec.*), Absonderung, Abtrennung; (*Elec.*) Isolation; der Isolierstoff. **insulator,** *s.* (*Elec.*) der Isolator, Nichtleiter.

insulin [ˈinsjəlin], *s.* das Insulin.

insult, 1. [ˈinsʌlt], *s.* die Beleidigung (***to,*** für), Beschimpfung, Ehrenkränkung (*Gen.*); ***swallow an*** –, eine Beleidigung einstecken. **2.** [inˈsʌlt], *v.t.* beleidigen, beschimpfen. **insulting** [inˈsʌltiŋ], *adj.* beleidigend, beschimpfend, Schmäh–; (*of a p.*) unverschämt, anmaßend; – ***language,*** Schimpfworte (*pl.*).

insuperability [insju:pərəˈbiliti], *s.* die Unüberwindlichkeit. **insuperable** [–ˈsju:pərəbl], *adj.* unüberwindlich; unübersteigbar (*as a barrier*).

insupportable [insəˈpɔ:təbl], *adj.* unerträglich, unausstehlich; (*as a claim*) nicht zu rechtfertigen(d).

insurability [inʃuərəˈbiliti], *s.* die Versicherungsfähigkeit, Versicherbarkeit. **insurable** [–ˈʃuərəbl], *adj.* versicherungsfähig, versicherbar; – ***value,*** der Versicherungswert.

insurance [inˈʃuərəns], *s.* die Versicherung, Assekuranz; ***take out an*** –, eine Versicherung eingehen, sich versichern lassen; ***unemployment*** –, die Arbeitslosenversicherung. **insurance| agent,** *s.* der Versicherungsagent. – **broker,** *s.* der Assekuranzmakler. – **company,** *s.* die Versicherungsgesellschaft. – **policy,** *s.* der Versicherungsschein, die Police. – **premium,** *s.* die Versicherungsprämie.

insure [inˈʃuə], **1.** *v.t.* versichern; (*fig.*) sichern, verbürgen, sicherstellen (***against,*** gegen); ***–d party,*** der Versicherungsnehmer. **2.** *v.i.* sich versichern lassen, eine Versicherung abschließen. **insurer,** *s.* der Versicherer; *pl.* die Versicherungsgesellschaft.

insurgence, insurgency [inˈsə:dʒəns(i)], *s.* der Aufruhr, Aufstand, die Auflehnung, Rebellion. **insurgent, 1.** *adj.* aufständisch, aufrührerisch. **2.** *s.* Aufständische(r), der Aufrührer, Rebell.

insurmountable [insəˈmauntəbl], *adj.* unübersteigbar, (*fig.*) unüberwindlich.

insurrection [insəˈrekʃən], *s.* der Aufstand, Aufruhr, die Rebellion, Empörung. **insurrectionary, 1.** *adj.* aufrührerisch, aufständisch. **2.** *or* **insurrectionist,** *s. See* **insurgent, 2.**

insusceptibility [insəseptiˈbiliti], *s.* die Unempfänglichkeit, Unzugänglichkeit (*to,* für). **insusceptible** [–ˈseptibl], *adj.* unempfänglich (***to, of,*** für), unzugänglich (*Dat.*); ungeeignet (für *or* zu), unfähig (zu); – ***of pity,*** mitleidslos.

intact [inˈtækt], *adj.* unberührt, unangerührt; unversehrt, unverletzt.

intaglio [inˈtɑ:ljou], *s.* 1. das Intaglio, die Gemme; eingravierte Verzierung; 2. (*Typ.*) der Tiefdruck, das Tiefdruckverfahren.

intake [ˈinteik], *s.* das Einnehmen, Ansaugen; die Aufnahme, der Zustrom; (*Tech.*) Einlaß, die Einlaßöffnung; – ***of breath,*** der Atemzug; – ***of food,*** die Nahrungsaufnahme; (*Motor.*) – ***valve,*** die Einlaßklappe.

intangibility [intændʒiˈbiliti], *s.* die Unkörperlichkeit, Un(be)fühlbarkeit, Nichtgreifbarkeit. **intangible** [–ˈtændʒibl], *adj.* unkörperlich, nicht greifbar, unfühlbar; (*fig.*) unfaßbar, unbestimmt, vage; – ***assets,*** immaterielle Aktiven.

integer [ˈintidʒə], *s.* (*Math.*) das Ganze, ganze Zahl. **integral** [–grəl], **1.** *adj.* ganz, vollständig; integriert; (*Math.*) ganz(zahlig), Integral–, (*fig.*) wesentlich; – ***calculus,*** die Integralrechnung; – ***part,*** wesentlicher Bestandteil; – ***whole,*** vollständiges Ganzes. **2.** *s.* (*Math.*) das Integral; Ganze, die Ganzheit. **integrant,** *adj.* integrierend; wesentlich.

integrate [ˈintigreit], **1.** *v.t.* 1. ergänzen, vervollständigen; 2. eingliedern, einbeziehen, zusammenfassen (***into,*** in (*Acc.*)), (*Math.*) integrieren. **2.** *v.i.* integriert werden, sich (zu einem Ganzen) zusammenschließen. **integration** [–ˈgreiʃən], *s.* 1. die Ergänzung, Vervollständigung; 2. Eingliederung *or* Einbeziehung (in ein Ganzes), Integration; (*Math.*) Integrierung; (*Pol.*) Rassenintegration.

integrity [inˈtegriti], *s.* 1. die Ganzheit, Vollständigkeit; (*Math.*) Ganzzahligkeit; 2. (*fig.*) Unversehrtheit, Reinheit, Lauterkeit, Echtheit; Rechtschaffenheit, Unbescholtenheit, Redlichkeit, Ehrlichkeit.

integument [inˈtegjumənt], *s.* (*Anat.*) die Decke, Hülle, (Deck)haut.

intellect [ˈintilekt], *s.* der Verstand, Intellekt, die Urteilskraft, Denkfähigkeit; (*coll.*) kluger Kopf, *pl.* die Intelligenz. **intellection** [–ˈlekʃən], *s.* das Verstehen, Begreifen; der Gedanke, Begriff. **intellectual** [–ˈlektjuəl], **1.** *adj.* verstandesmäßig, intellektuell, gedanklich, geistig, Verstandes–, Geistes–; (*of a p.*) vernünftig, klug, intelligent; – ***power(s),*** die Geisteskraft, Verstandeskraft. **2.** *s.* Intellektuelle(r), Gebildete(r), der Verstandesmensch; Kopfarbeiter. **intellectuality** [–tjuˈæliti], *s.* die Verstandesmäßigkeit, Geistigkeit; (*of a p.*) Geisteskraft, Verstandeskraft, Intelligenz.

intelligence [inˈtelidʒəns], *s.* 1. (*no pl.*) der Verstand, Scharfsinn, die Intelligenz, Denkfähigkeit, Auffassungsgabe, Klugkeit, Einsicht, das Verständnis; 2. (*esp. Mil.*) die Nachricht, Mitteilung, Kunde, Auskunft; (*Mil., Pol.*) der Nachrichtendienst; 3. (*with pl.*) verständiges *or* vernünftiges Wesen.

intelligence|-department, *s.* (*Mil.*) das Nachrichtenamt, geheimer Nachrichtendienst, der Geheimdienst, die Spionageabteilung. **–-office,** *s.* (*Am.*) das Auskunftsbüro. **–-officer,** *s.* (*Mil.*) der Nachrichtenoffizier. – **quotient,** *s.* der Intelligenzquotient. **intelligencer,** *s.* der Kundschafter, Geheimagent, Spion. **intelligence|-service,** *s.* der Abwehrdienst. – **test,** *s.* die Intelligenzprüfung.

intelligent [inˈtelidʒənt], *adj.* intelligent, gescheit, scharfsinnig, aufgeweckt, klug, begabt; verstandesbegabt, vernünftig, verständnisvoll, einsichtsvoll. **intelligentsia** [–ˈdʒentsiə], *s.* gebildete (Ober)schicht, die Intelligenz, Intellektuelle (*pl.*).

intelligibility [intelidʒiˈbiliti], *s.* die Verständlichkeit. **intelligible** [–ˈtelidʒibl], *adj.* verständlich, klar, deutlich (*to, Dat. or* für).

intemperance [inˈtempərəns], *s.* die Unmäßigkeit, Ausschweifung, (*esp.*) Trunksucht. **intemperate** [–rit], *adj.* unmäßig, ausschweifend, zügellos, ungezügelt, unbeherrscht, (*esp.*) trunksüchtig.

intend [inˈtend], *v.t.* beabsichtigen, vorhaben, im Sinne haben, bezwecken, bedacht sein auf (*Acc.*), planen, wollen; meinen, sagen wollen (***by,*** mit); bestimmen (***for,*** für *or* zu); ***as –ed,*** wie beabsichtigt; ***–ed as,*** gemeint als; ***the picture is –ed to be me,*** das Bild soll ich sein *or* soll mich darstellen; ***was your rudeness –ed?*** war deine Unhöflichkeit Absicht?

intendancy [inˈtendənsi], *s.* die Oberaufsicht, Intendantur. **intendant,** *s.* der Vorsteher, Verwalter, Oberaufseher, Intendant.

intended [inˈtendid], **1.** *adj.* geplant, beabsichtigt; absichtlich; (*coll.*) (zu)künftig; – ***husband,*** Verlobte(r), der Zukünftige. **2.** *s.* (*coll.*) Zukünftige(r), Verlobte(r), der Bräutigam, die Braut. **intending,** *adj.* angehend; – ***purchaser,*** der Reflektant.

intense [inˈtens], *adj.* stark, heftig, intensiv; sehnlichst (*as desires*), kräftig, tief (*as colour*), (an)gespannt, angestrengt (*as effort*); (*coll.*) empfindsam, überspannt. **intenseness,** *s. See* **intensity**; die Empfindsamkeit, Gefühlsbetontheit, Überspannung; Anstrengung, Anspannung.

intensification [intensifiˈkeiʃən], *s.* die Verstärkung (*also Phot.*), Steigerung, Verschärfung. **intensifier** [inˈtensifaiə], *s.* (*Phot.*) der Verstärker. **intensify** [–fai], **1.** *v.t.* verstärken (*also Phot.*), verschärfen, steigern. **2.** *v.i.* sich steigern *or* verstärken.

intensity [inˈtensiti], *s.* die Heftigkeit, Stärke,

Fülle, Tiefe, Größe, (hoher) Grad; (*Phys.*) der Stärkegrad, die Dichte, Intensität, (*Elec.*) Stromstärke, Feldstärke, (*Phot.*) Dichtigkeit; *see also* **intenseness**; – ***of feeling,*** die Tiefe des Gefühls; – ***of light,*** die Lichtstärke; – ***of sound,*** die Tonstärke. **intensive,** *adj.* stark, intensiv; steigernd, (*Gram.*) verstärkend, Verstärkungs–.

intent [in'tent], **1.** *adj.* gespannt, gerichtet, eifrig bedacht, erpicht, versessen ((***up***)***on***, auf (*Acc.*)), eifrig beschäftigt (mit); gespannt, aufmerksam. **2.** *s.* die Absicht, der Vorsatz, das Vorhaben; der Zweck, Plan, das Ziel; der Sinn, wahre Bedeutung; (*Law*) ***proof of*** –, der Beweis der Vorsätzlichkeit; ***to all –s and purposes,*** durchaus, ganz und gar, in jeder Hinsicht; eigentlich, im Grunde, in Wirklichkeit, praktisch (genommen); ***to do with*** –, absichtlich tun; ***with – to do,*** in der Absicht zu tun; ***with evil*** –, in böser Absicht.

intention [in'tenʃən], *s.* die Absicht, der Vorsatz, Plan, Zweck, das Vorhaben, Ziel; *pl.* (*coll.*) Heiratsabsichten (*pl.*); ***with the – of doing,*** in der Absicht zu tun; ***it is my*** –, ich habe die Absicht, es ist meine Absicht; ***with the best –s,*** in bester Absicht. **intentional,** *adj.* absichtlich, vorsätzlich, mit Fleiß; zweckbestimmt, beabsichtigt. **–intentioned,** *adj. suff.* –gesinnt.

intentness [in'tentnis], *s.* gespannte Aufmerksamkeit, der Eifer; – ***of purpose,*** die Zielstrebigkeit.

inter [in'tə:], *v.t.* beerdigen, begraben.

inter- ['intə], *pref.* (da)zwischen, (dar)unter, Zwischen–; einander, gegenseitig, wechselseitig, Wechsel–.

1**interact** ['intəækt], *s.* das Zwischenspiel, der Zwischenakt.

2**interact** [intə'ækt], *v.i.* aufeinander (ein)wirken, einander *or* sich gegenseitig beeinflussen. **interaction** [–'ækʃən], *s.* die Wechselwirkung, gegenseitige Beeinflussung. **interactive,** *adj.* wechselwirkend, aufeinander einwirkend.

inter-allied [intərə'laid], *adj.* (*Pol.*) interalliiert.

interbreed [intə'bri:d], **1.** *irr.v.t.* kreuzen, durch Kreuzung züchten. **2.** *irr.v.i.* sich kreuzen. **interbreeding,** *s.* die Kreuzung.

intercalary [intə'kæləri], *adj.* eingeschaltet, eingeschoben; – ***day,*** der Schalttag. **intercalate** [–'tə:kəleit], *v.t.* einschalten, einschieben, einfügen. **intercalation** [–'leiʃən], *s.* die Einschaltung, Einschiebung, Einfügung, (*Geol.*) Einschließung, Einlagerung; Einlage.

intercede [intə'si:d], *v.t.* sich verwenden, sich ins Mittel legen, Fürsprache einlegen (***with,*** bei; ***for,*** für). **interceder,** *s.* der Fürsprecher, Vermittler.

intercept, 1. [intə'sept], *v.t.* abfangen (*also Av.*), auffangen (*a blow etc.*), abhören, ablauschen (*a message*), unterschlagen (*letters*); (*coll.*) aufschnappen; hemmen, (be)hindern, aufhalten, versperren, unterbrechen, abschneiden (*also Av.*); (*Math.*) einschließen, abschneiden. **2.** ['intəsept], *s.* (*Math.*) der Abschnitt. **interception** [–'sepʃən], *s.* das Auffangen, Aufhalten, Abfangen; die Versperrung, Unterbrechung, Hemmung; (*Av.*) – ***flight,*** der Sperrflug. **interceptor** [–'septə], *s.* der Auffänger, Abfänger; (*Av.*) – (***plane***), der Abfangjäger; – ***service,*** der Horchdienst, Abhördienst.

intercession [intə'seʃən], *s.* die Fürbitte, Fürsprache, Vermittlung; ***make*** –, sich verwenden, Fürsprache einlegen (***to,*** bei; ***for,*** für); ***service of*** –, der Fürbittegottesdienst. **intercessor** [–'sesə], *s.* der Fürsprecher, Vermittler. **intercessory,** *adj.* fürsprechend, Fürsprech–, vermittelnd.

interchange, 1. [intə'tʃeindʒ], *v.t.* miteinander *or* untereinander austauschen, auswechseln; vertauschen, austauschen, abwechseln lassen (***with,*** mit). **2.** [–'tʃeindʒ], *v.i.* (ab)wechseln. **3.** ['intətʃeindʒ], *s.* der Umtausch, Austausch; die Vertauschung, Auswechslung; – ***of ideas,*** der Gedankenaustausch. **interchangeability** [–ə'biliti], *s.* die Auswechselbarkeit, Vertauschbarkeit. **interchangeable,** *adj.* auswechselbar, austauschbar, vertauschbar; (miteinander) abwechselnd.

intercollegiate [intəkə'li:dʒiit], *adj.* zwischen den Colleges.

intercolonial [intəkə'louniəl], *adj.* interkolonial.

intercom ['intəkɔm], *s.* (*coll.*) die Wechselsprechanlage, (*Av.*) Eigenverständigung, der Bordverkehr.

intercommunicate [intəkə'mju:nikeit], *v.i.* miteinander in Verbindung stehen, untereinander verkehren. **intercommunication** [–'keiʃən], *s.* gegenseitiger Verkehr, gegenseitige Verbindung *or* Verständigung; – ***system,*** *see* **intercom.**

interconnect [intəkə'nekt], **1.** *v.t.* untereinander *or* miteinander verbinden. **2.** *v.i.* untereinander verbunden sein *or* werden, sich untereinander verbinden. **interconnection** [–'nekʃən], *s.* gegenseitige Verbindung.

intercostal [intə'kɔstl], *adj.* (*Anat.*) Zwischenrippen–.

intercourse ['intəkɔ:s], *s.* der Verkehr, Umgang (***with,*** mit); (*Comm.*) Geschäftsverkehr, Handelsverbindungen (*pl.*); (***sexual***) –, der Geschlechtsverkehr.

intercross [intə'krɔs], **1.** *v.i.* sich *or* einander kreuzen (*as lines*). **2.** *v.t.* einander kreuzen lassen.

intercurrent [intə'kʌrənt], *adj.* dazwischenkommend, dazukommend, (*Med.*) nebenherlaufend, hinzutretend.

interdepend [intədi'pend], *v.i.* voneinander abhängen. **interdependence, interdependency,** *s.* gegenseitige Abhängigkeit. **interdependent,** *adj.* gegenseitig *or* voneinander abhängig; (*fig.*) eng zusammenhängend, ineinandergreifend.

interdict, 1. [intə'dikt], *v.t.* untersagen, verbieten (***to,*** *Dat.*), (*R.C.*) mit dem Interdikt belegen; – ***him from a th.,*** ihm eine S. verbieten, ihn von einer S. ausschließen. **2.** ['intədikt], *s.* das Verbot, (*R.C.*) Interdikt. **interdiction** [–'dikʃən], *s.* das Verbieten, Untersagen; Verbot, der Kirchenbann. **interdictory** [–'diktəri], *adj.* Verbots–, Untersagungs–; verbietend.

interdigital [intə'didʒitl], *adj.* zwischen den Fingern *or* Zehen (liegend). **interdigitate** [–teit], *v.i.* ineinandergreifen, verflochten sein.

interest ['intərest], **1.** *v.t.* 1. interessieren (***in,*** für); Interesse *or* Teilnahme erwecken *or* gewinnen *or* erregen (***in,*** an (*Dat.*)); – ***o.s. in,*** Anteil nehmen an (*Dat.*), sich interessieren für; sich (*Dat.*) angelegen sein lassen; 2. anziehen, reizen, fesseln, einnehmen, (*esp. Comm.*) beteiligen (***in,*** an (*Dat.*)), gewinnen (für); 3. angehen, betreffen; ***your reproaches do not – me,*** deine Vorwürfe gehen mich nichts an. **2.** *s.* 1. das Interesse (***in,*** an (*Dat.*) *or* für), die (An)teilnahme (an (*Dat.*)); ***have no – for him,*** ihn nicht interessieren; ***lose*** –, das Interesse verlieren; ***take an*** (or (***a***) ***great***) – ***in,*** sich (sehr) interessieren für; 2. (*esp. Comm.*) die Beteiligung, der Anteil (***in,*** an (*Dat.*)), (*Law*) das Anrecht (auf (*Acc.*)); ***have an – in,*** beteiligt sein an (*Dat.*) *or* bei; ***shipping –s,*** Reedereigeschäfte (*pl.*); 3. der Vorteil, Nutzen, Gewinn; ***the common*** –, das allgemeine Beste, der allgemeine Vorteil; ***be in*** or ***to his*** –, in seinem Interesse liegen, zu seinem Vorteil sein; 4. der Einfluß, die Macht (***with,*** bei); 5. Wichtigkeit, Bedeutung (***to,*** für); ***be of small*** –, von geringer Bedeutung sein; 6. (*Comm.*) (*no pl.*) der Zins, Zinsen (*pl.*); (*coll.*) der Zinsfuß, Zinssatz; ***arrears of*** –, Zinsrückstände (*pl.*); – ***on arrears,*** Verzugszinsen (*pl.*); ***bear*** –, sich verzinsen, verzinslich sein, Zinsen tragen; ***bearing no*** –, unverzinslich; ***compound*** –, Zinseszinsen (*pl.*); – ***due,*** fällige Zinsen, Passivzinsen (*pl.*); ***ex*** –, ohne Zinsen; ***invest one's money at*** –, sein Geld verzinslich anlegen; ***lend on*** or ***at*** –, Geld auf Zinsen ausleihen; ***payment of*** –, die Zinszahlung; ***simple*** –, Kapitalzinsen (*pl.*); ***with*** –, mit Zinsen; (*coll.*) in verstärktem Maße.

interested ['intərestid], *adj.* 1. interessiert (***in,*** an (*Dat.*)), voreingenommen, eigennützig; ***be – in,*** sich interessieren für; 2. beteiligt (***in,*** an (*Dat.*) *or* bei); ***the – parties,*** die Beteiligten, Interessenten. **interestedly,** *adv.* mit Interesse; in interessanter Weise. **interestedness,** *s.* das Beteiligtsein; die

Voreingenommenheit, der Eigennutz. **interesting,** *adj.* interessant, fesselnd, anziehend; unterhaltend; (*coll.*) ***in an – condition,*** in anderen Umständen.

interface ['intəfeis], *s.* die Zwischenfläche, Grenzfläche. **interfacial** [–'feiʃəl], *adj.* (Zwischen)-flächen–; – ***angle,*** der Flächenwinkel.

interfere [intə'fiə], *v.i.* sich einmischen *or* einmengen (***in,*** in (*Acc.*)), dazwischentreten, sich ins Mittel legen, einschreiten, eingreifen; – ***with,*** stören, hindern, beeinträchtigen, in Konflikt geraten mit; störend beeinflussen, störend einwirken auf (*Acc.*). **interference,** *s.* das Dazwischentreten; die Einmischung (***in,*** in (*Acc.*)), der Eingriff (***with,*** in (*Acc.*)), die Beeinträchtigung; (*Rad.*) Interferenz, Störung, das Störgeräusch; (*Rad.*) ***elimination of –,*** die Entstörung.

interflow ['intəflou], *s.* das Ineinanderfließen.

interfuse [intə'fju:z], *v.t.* (miteinander) vermischen; durchdringen, durchsetzen (***with,*** mit). **interfusion** [–'fju:ʒən], *s.* die Vermischung, Durchdringung, Durchsetzung.

interglacial [intə'gleiʃəl], *adj.* (*Geol.*) interglazial.

interim ['intərim], **1.** *s.* die Zwischenzeit; einstweilige Regelung, (*Hist.*) das Interim; ***in the –,*** bis auf weiteres, unterdessen, einstweilig, einstweilen, mittlerweile, vorläufig, in der Zwischenzeit. **2.** *adj.* einstweilig, vorläufig, interimistisch, Interims–, Zwischen–; – ***balance,*** die Zwischenbilanz; – ***dividend,*** die Abschlagsdividende; – ***injunction,*** einstweilige Verfügung; – ***report,*** vorläufiger Bericht.

interior [in'tiəriə], **1.** *adj.* inner, Innen–, innerlich, inwendig; (*Geog.*) binnenländisch, Binnen–; (*Math.*) – ***angle,*** der Innenwinkel; – ***decorator,*** der Innenarchitekt. **2.** *s.* der Innenraum, die Innenseite, das Innere; (*Geog.*) Innere, Binnenland; (*Phot.*) die Innenaufnahme; (*Am.*) ***Department of the Interior,*** das Innenministerium.

interject [intə'dʒekt], *v.t.* einwerfen, dazwischenwerfen (*a remark*), (*fig.*) einschalten, einschieben, hinzufügen (*a parenthesis*). **interjection** [–'dʒekʃən], *s.* der Einwurf; Ausruf, (*Gram.*) die Interjektion. **interjectional, interjectory,** *adj.* dazwischengeworfen, eingeschaltet, eingeschoben; Ausruf–, ausrufartig.

interlace [intə'leis], **1.** *v.t.* (miteinander) verflechten *or* verweben *or* verschlingen; (*also fig.*) durchweben, durchflechten, einweben, einflechten (***with,*** mit); (*fig.*) (ver)mischen, vermengen. **2.** *v.i.* sich verflechten *or* kreuzen; (*Archit.*) ***interlacing arches,*** verschränkte Bogen, Kreuzbogen (*pl.*).

interlard [intə'lɑ:d], *v.t.* (*fig.*) spicken, durchsetzen (***with,*** mit).

interleave [intə'li:v], *v.t.* durchschießen (*a book*). **interleaved,** *adj.* durchschossen.

interline [intə'lain], *v.t.* zwischenzeilig schreiben, einfügen (*a word*); (*Typ.*) zwischensetzen, durchschießen. **interlinear** [–'liniə], *adj.* zwischenzeilig (geschrieben), zwischengeschrieben; Interlinear–; (*Typ.*) – ***space,*** der Durchschuß.

interlink [intə'liŋk], *v.t.* verketten.

interlock [intə'lɔk], **1.** *v.i.* ineinandergreifen, sich ineinanderschließen. **2.** *v.t.* zusammenschließen, ineinanderschachteln, verschränken; ineinanderhaken, (miteinander) verzahnen.

interlocution [intəlo'kju:ʃən], *s.* die Unterredung, das (Zwie)gespräch. **interlocutor** [–'kju:tə], *s.* der (die) Gesprächspartner(in). **interlocutory** [–'lɔkjutəri], *adj.* 1. gesprächsweise, in Gesprächsform, Gesprächs–; 2. (*Law*) vorläufig, Zwischen–; – ***decree*** die Zwischenentscheidung.

interlope [intə'loup], *v.i.* (*rare*) sich eindrängen *or* dazwischendrängen; (*obs.*) den Markt aufkaufen, verbotenen Handel treiben. **interloper** ['intəloupə], *s.* der Eindringling; (*obs.*) Schleichhändler, Winkelmakler.

interlude ['intəlju:d], *s.* (*Mus.*) das Zwischenspiel (*also fig.*), Intermezzo, (*Theat.*) die Pause; (*fig.*) Zwischenzeit.

intermarriage [intə'mæridʒ], *s.* 1. die Heirat zwischen Mitgliedern verschiedener Gruppen; 2. Heirat innerhalb einer Gruppe. **intermarry,** *v.i.* 1. untereinander heiraten; 2. innerhalb der Gruppe heiraten.

intermaxillary [intəmæk'siləri], *adj.* – ***bone,*** der Zwischenkiefer(knochen).

intermediary [intə'mi:diəri], **1.** *adj.* dazwischen befindlich, Zwischen–; verbindend, Verbindungs–; vermittelnd. **2.** *s.* der Vermittler, (*Comm.*) Zwischenhändler; (*of a th.*) die Zwischenform, das Mittelding; Hilfsmittel, die Vermittlung. **intermediate** [–diit], **1.** *adj.* *See* **intermediary**; indirekt, mittelbar; ***be – between,*** liegen (in der Mitte) zwischen; – ***examination,*** die Zwischenprüfung; (*England*) erste Universitätsprüfung; (*Am.*) – ***school,*** die Mittelschule; – ***stage,*** das Zwischenstadium; (*Log.*) – ***terms,*** Mittelglieder, innere Glieder (*pl.*); – ***trade,*** der Zwischenhandel. **2.** *s.* 1. der Verbindungsmann, Vermittler; das Zwischenglied, die Zwischenform; 2. *See* – ***examination.***

interment [in'tə:mənt], *s.* die Beerdigung, Bestattung, Beisetzung.

intermezzo [intə'metzou], *s.* das Intermezzo, Zwischenspiel.

interminable [in'tə:minəbl], *adj.* endlos, unendlich, grenzenlos; (*coll.*) langwierig. **interminableness,** *s.* die Endlosigkeit, Grenzenlosigkeit.

intermingle [intə'miŋgl], **1.** *v.t.* vermischen. **2.** *v.i.* sich vermischen.

intermission [intə'miʃən], *s.* das Aussetzen, Unterbrechen, die Unterbrechung, Aussetzung, (*also Theat.*) Pause; ***without –,*** unaufhörlich, unausgesetzt, ohne Unterlaß, unablässig.

intermit [intə'mit], **1.** *v.t.* aussetzen mit, aussetzen lassen, (zeitweilig) unterbrechen. **2.** *v.i.* vorübergehend aufhören, aussetzen. **intermittence,** *s.* vorübergehende Unterbrechung, zeitweiliges Versagen *or* Aussetzen. **intermittent,** *adj.* aussetzend, diskontinuierlich, unterbrochen; ***be –,*** aussetzen, periodisch unterbrochen werden; (*Elec.*) – ***current,*** intermittierender Strom; (*Med.*) – ***fever,*** das Wechselfieber; (*Naut.*) – ***light,*** das Blinkfeuer.

intermix [intə'miks], **1.** *v.t.* vermischen, untermischen. **2.** *v.i.* sich mischen. **intermixture** [–tʃə], *s.* das (Ver)mischen, die (Ver)mischung; Mischung, das Gemisch; die Beimischung, der Zusatz.

intern, 1. [in'tə:n], *v.t.* internieren. **2.** ['intə:n], *s.* der Pflichtassistent *or* Hilfsarzt im Krankenhaus.

internal [in'tə:nl], *adj.* inner, innerlich, inwendig; einheimisch, inländisch, Innen–, Binnen–; intern; (*Pol.*) – ***affairs,*** innere Angelegenheiten; (*Geom.*) – ***angle,*** der Innenwinkel; ***–-combustion engine,*** der Verbrennungsmotor; – ***diameter,*** lichte Weite; (*Anat.*) – ***ear,*** das Innenohr; – ***evidence,*** innerer Beweis; – ***injury,*** innere Verletzung; – ***loan,*** die Inlandsanleihe; (*Anat.*) – ***organs,*** innere Organe; – ***pressure,*** der Innendruck; – ***revenue,*** Staatseinkünfte (*pl.*); (*Metr.*) – ***rhyme,*** der Binnenreim; – ***trade,*** der Binnenhandel. **internals,** *pl.* (*coll.*) innere Organe.

international [intə'næʃənl], **1.** *adj.* international, zwischenstaatlich; – ***exhibition,*** die Weltausstellung; – ***language,*** die Weltsprache; – ***law,*** das Völkerrecht; – ***money-order,*** die Auslandspostanweisung; – ***relations,*** zwischenstaatliche Beziehungen. **2.** *s.* 1. (*Pol.*) die Internationale; 2. (*Spt.*) internationaler Spieler. **internationalism,** *s.* der Internationalismus. **internationality** [–'næliti], *s.* überstaatlicher Charakter. **internationalize,** *v.t.* internationalisieren, unter internationale Kontrolle stellen.

internecine [intə'ni:sain], *adj.* sich gegenseitig zerstörend, Vernichtungs–, mörderisch.

internee [intə:'ni:], *s.* Internierte(r). **internment,** *s.* die Internierung; – ***camp,*** das Internierungslager.

interpellate [in'tə:pileit], *v.t.* (*Parl.*) eine Anfrage richten an (*Acc.*). **interpellation** [–'leiʃən], *s.* der Einspruch, die Einrede; Anfrage, Interpellation.

interpenetrate [intə'penitreit], **1.** *v.i.* sich gegenseitig durchdringen. **2.** *v.t.* durchsetzen, durchdringen. **interpenetration** [–'treiʃən], *s.* gegenseitige Durchdringung.

interplanetary [intə'plænitəri], *adj.* interplanetar(isch).

interplay ['intəplei], *s.* die Wechselwirkung, gegenseitige Beeinflussung, wechselseitiges Spiel, das Ineinandergreifen (*of forces*).

interpolate [in'tə:poleit], *v.t.* einschalten, einfügen, einschieben, dazwischenschalten, (*also Math.*) interpolieren. **interpolation** [–'leiʃən], *s.* 1. die Interpolation, Interpolierung (*also Math.*), Einschiebung, Einschaltung; 2. das Einschiebsel, die Textfälschung.

interposal [intə'pouzl], *s. See* **interposition. interpose, 1.** *v.t.* dazwischenstellen, dazwischenlegen, dazwischensetzen, dazwischenschalten, einwerfen, einflechten (*a remark etc.*), vorbringen, einlegen (*veto*). **2.** *v.i.* sich ins Mittel legen, vermitteln (***between***, zwischen), dazwischentreten, dazwischenkommen, (*in speaking*) (sich) unterbrechen. **interposition** [-pə'ziʃən], *s.* das Dazwischentreten, Eingreifen; die Einfügung; Vermittlung.

interpret [in'tə:prit], *v.t.* 1. auslegen, erklären, deuten, (*also Mus.*) interpretieren; 2. verdolmetschen, übersetzen; 3. darstellen, wiedergeben (*a role*). **interpretation** [–'teiʃən], *s.* 1. die Auslegung, Auswertung, Erklärung, Deutung; 2. Verdolmetschung, (mündliche) Übersetzung; 3. (*Mus., Theat.*) die Interpretation, Darstellung, Wiedergabe. **interpretative,** *adj.* erklärend, erläuternd, deutend, auslegend. **interpreter,** *s.* 1. der Dolmetscher; 2. Ausleger, Darsteller.

interregnum [intə'regnəm], *s.* die Zwischenregierung, Übergangsregierung, (*fig.*) Unterbrechung.

interrelated [intəri'leitid], *adj.* untereinander zusammenhängend. **interrelation(ship)** [–'leiʃən(ʃip)], *s.* gegenseitige Beziehung, die Wechselbeziehung.

interrogate [in'terəgeit], **1.** *v.t.* (be)fragen, ausfragen; (*Law*) vernehmen, verhören. **2.** *v.i.* Fragen stellen. **interrogation** [–'geiʃən], *s.* das Befragen, die Befragung, Frage; (*Law*) das Verhör, Ausfragen, die Vernehmung; *--mark,* das Fragezeichen; (*Mil.*) – ***officer,*** der Vernehmungsoffizier. **interrogative** [intə'rɔgətiv], **1.** *adj.* fragend, Frage–. **2.** *s.* das Fragewort. **interrogator,** *s.* der Frager, Fragesteller. **interrogatory** [intə'rɔgətəri], **1.** *adj.* fragend, Frage–. **2.** *s.* die Fragestellung, (*Law*) gerichtliches Verhör.

interrupt [intə'rʌpt], **1.** *v.t.* unterbrechen; aufhalten, verhindern, stören; – ***him,*** ihm in die Rede fallen; ***don't let me – you,*** lassen Sie sich durch mich nicht stören. **2.** *v.i.* unterbrechen, stören; ***please don't –!*** bitte, stören Sie nicht! **interrupted,** *adj.* unterbrochen; (*Elec.*) diskontinuierlich. **interruptedly,** *adv.* mit Unterbrechung. **interrupter,** *s.* der Unterbrecher (*also Tech.*), Störer; die Fliehbacke (*of a fuse*). **interruption** [–'rʌpʃən], *s.* die Unterbrechung, Stockung, Hemmung, Störung; ***without –,*** ohne Unterbrechung, ununterbrochen.

intersect [intə'sekt], **1.** *v.t.* (durch)schneiden, kreuzen. **2.** *v.i.* sich (ver)schneiden *or* überschneiden *or* durchschneiden *or* kreuzen. **intersecting,** *adj.* (*Geom.*) Schnitt–; – ***line,*** die Schnittlinie; – ***plane,*** die Schnittebene. **intersection** [–'sekʃən], *s.* die Durchschneidung; (*Geom.*) Verschneidung, Durchdringung, der (Durch)schnitt; Schnittpunkt, die Schnittlinie; (*esp. Am.*) (*Railw. etc.*) (Straßen)kreuzung; – ***of the axes,*** der Nullpunkt des Koordinatensystems; ***point of –,*** der Schnittpunkt.

interspace, 1. ['intəspeis], *s.* der Zwischenraum. **2.** [–'speis], *v.t.* Raum lassen zwischen (*Dat.*).

intersperse [intə'spə:s], *v.t.* einstreuen, einmengen (***among***, zwischen (*Acc.*)), vermischen, untermengen, durchsetzen (***with***, mit). **interspersion** [–'spə:ʃən], *s.* die Einstreuung.

interstate ['intəsteit], *adj.* (*Am.*) zwischenstaatlich.

interstice [in'tə:stis], *s.* der Zwischenraum, Spalt, die Spalte, Lücke. **interstitial** [–'stiʃəl], *adj.* zwischenräumlich.

intertwine [intə'twain], **1.** *v.t.* verflechten, verschlingen; ***be –d,*** sich ineinanderschlingen. **2.** *v.i.* sich verflechten *or* verschlingen, verflochten sein.

interval ['intəvl], *s.* (*in space*) der Abstand (*also fig.*), Zwischenraum; (*in time*) die Zwischenzeit, (*also Theat.*) Pause; (*Mus.*) das Intervall, der Tonabstand; ***at –s,*** (*space, time*) in Abständen; (*time*) ab und zu, dann und wann; ***at frequent –s,*** öfters wiederholt; in häufigen Abständen; ***lucid –s,*** lichte Augenblicke; (*Rad.*) – ***signal,*** das Pausenzeichen.

intervene [intə'vi:n], *v.i.* dazwischenkommen, dazwischentreten, hinzukommen, dazwischenliegen; (*of events*) sich (unerwarteterweise) ereignen, plötzlich eintreten, dazwischenkommen, vorfallen; (*of a p.*) sich einmischen (***in***, in (*Acc.*)), sich verwenden (***on behalf of,*** für), sich ins Mittel legen, vermitteln (***between***, zwischen (*Dat.*)), (*Med.*) operieren, eingreifen, intervenieren. **intervention** [–'venʃən], *s.* das Dazwischentreten, Dazwischenkommen; (*of a p.*) die Einmischung, Vermittlung; (*Med.*) der Eingriff, die Intervention; ***armed –,*** bewaffnete Intervention.

interview ['intəvju:], **1.** *s.* die Zusammenkunft, Unterredung; Besprechung (zu Pressezwecken), das Interview. **2.** *v.t.* (als Berichterstatter) befragen, interviewen; ein Interview *or* eine Zusammenkunft haben mit. **interviewer,** *s.* befragender Berichterstatter, der Befrager, Interviewer.

interweave [intə'wi:v], **1.** *irr.v.t.* durchweben, durchflechten, verflechten, verweben (***with***, mit); miteinander verweben *or* verflechten. **2.** *irr.v.i.* sich verweben *or* verflechten. **interwoven,** *adj.* verflochten.

intestacy [in'testəsi], *s.* das Fehlen eines Testaments. **intestate, 1.** *adj.* ohne Testament; – ***succession,*** die Intestaterbfolge. **2.** *s.* der Erblasser ohne Testament.

intestinal [in'testinəl], *adj.* Eingeweide–, Darm–. **intestine, 1.** *adj.* inner, einheimisch; – ***war,*** der Bürgerkrieg. **2.** *s.* (*usu. pl.*) Eingeweide (*pl.*), das Gedärm(e); ***large –,*** der Dickdarm; ***small –,*** der Dünndarm.

intimacy ['intiməsi], *s.* die Vertraulichkeit, Vertrautheit, Innigkeit, Intimität, vertrauter Umgang; intime *or* geschlechtliche Beziehungen (*pl.*); ***be on terms of –,*** auf vertrautem Fuße stehen.

[1]**intimate** ['intimit], **1.** *adj.* innig, vertraut, intim, vertraulich; (*fig.*) eng, nah (*contact*), genau, gründlich (*knowledge*); ***on – terms,*** auf vertrautem Fuße. **2.** *s.* Vertraute(r), der (die) Busenfreund(in).

[2]**intimate** ['intimeit], *v.t.* andeuten, zu verstehen geben; nahelegen, bekanntmachen, mitteilen, kundtun, ankündigen. **intimation** [–'meiʃən], *s.* die Andeutung, der Wink, Fingerzeig, das Anzeichen; die Ankündigung, Anzeige, Bezeigung.

intimidate [in'timideit], *v.t.* einschüchtern, bange machen, abschrecken. **intimidation** [–'deiʃən], *s.* die Einschüchterung. **intimidatory,** *adj.* einschüchternd.

into ['intu], *prep.* in (*Acc.*), in . . . hinein; ***bribe – secrecy,*** durch Bestechung zum Schweigen bringen; ***cheat – accepting,*** durch List zur Annahme bewegen; ***come – property,*** zu Vermögen kommen; ***convert – money,*** zu Geld machen; ***develop –,*** werden zu; ***dip –,*** flüchtig durchlesen, überfliegen (*a book*); ***4 divides – 12 three times,*** 4 geht in 12 dreimal; ***get – debt,*** in Schulden geraten; ***get – a habit,*** eine Gewohnheit annehmen; ***grow –,*** werden zu; ***be led – error,*** zum Irrtum verleitet werden; ***look –,*** prüfen, untersuchen; ***make – jam,*** zu Marmelade verarbeiten; ***marry –,*** einheiraten in (*Acc.*); ***put – execution,*** ausführen; ***put – shape,*** in Form bringen; ***put – writing,*** schriftlich niederlegen; ***turn – money,*** zu Geld machen; ***turn – ridicule,*** lächerlich machen.

intolerable [in'tɔlərəbl], *adj.* unerträglich, unausstehlich. **intolerableness,** *s.* die Unerträglichkeit, Unausstehlichkeit.

intolerance [in'tɔlərəns], *s.* die Unduldsamkeit (*of,* gegen). **intolerant,** *adj.* unduldsam, unnachsichtig (*of,* gegen), intolerant; *be – of,* nicht gelten lassen.

intonate ['intəneit], *v.t. See* **intone. intonation** [–'neiʃən], *s.* (*Mus.*) das Anstimmen, die Tongebung, der Tonansatz; (*Eccl.*) liturgisches Singen, das Psalmodieren, die Intonation; (*Phonet.*) der Tonfall, die Satzmelodie, Sprachmelodie. **intone** [in'toun], *v.t.* anstimmen, intonieren; liturgisch singen, psalmodieren, rezitieren; modulieren.

in toto [in'toutou], *adv.* im ganzen *or* gesamten.

intoxicant [in'tɔksikənt], **1.** *s.* berauschendes Getränk. **2.** *adj.* berauschend. **intoxicate** [–keit], *v.t.* berauschen (*also fig.*), (*fig.*) betören. **intoxicated,** *adj.* berauscht (*also fig.*), betrunken, (*fig.*) trunken (*by, with,* von); *be – with,* sich berauschen an (*Dat.*). **intoxication** [–'keiʃən], *s.* die Betrunkenheit, (*also fig.*) Berauschung, Trunkenheit, der Rausch.

intractability [intræktə'biliti], *s.* die Unlenksamkeit, Widerspenstigkeit, Störrigkeit, Halsstarrigkeit, Starrsinnigkeit. **intractable** [in'træktəbl], *adj.* 1. unlenksam, widerspenstig, eigensinnig, störrig, halsstarrig, unbändig; 2. schwer zu bearbeiten(d) *or* handhaben(d) (*of materials*). **intractableness,** *s. See* **intractability.**

intrados [in'treidɔs], *s.* (*Archit.*) innere Wölbung, die Leibung.

intramural [intrə'mjuərəl], *adj.* 1. innerhalb der Mauern (einer Stadt, Universität, Anstalt) vorkommend; 2. (*Anat.*) intramural.

intransigence [in'trænsidʒəns], *s.* die Unnachgiebigkeit, Kompromißlosigkeit, Unversöhnlichkeit. **intransigent, 1.** *adj.* unversöhnlich, unnachgiebig, kompromißlos. **2.** *s.* starrer Parteimann, der Starrkopf.

intransitive [in'trɑ:nsitiv], **1.** *adj.* (*Gram.*) nichtzielend, intransitiv. **2.** *s.* das Intransitiv(um).

intravenous [intrə'vi:nəs], *adj.* (*Med.*) intravenös, endovenös.

intrepid [in'trepid], *adj.* unerschrocken, unverzagt, furchtlos. **intrepidity** [–'piditi], *s.* die Unerschrockenheit, Furchtlosigkeit.

intricacy ['intrikəsi], *s.* die Verwick(e)lung, Komplikation, Verworrenheit, Schwierigkeit; Kompliziertheit, Feinheit, (*coll.*) Kniffligkeit. **intricate** [–it], *adj.* verwickelt, verworren, kompliziert, verschlungen, verzweigt; schwierig, knifflig, ausgeklügelt.

intrigue [in'tri:g], **1.** *s.* das Ränkespiel, die Intrige, Machenschaft; der Liebeshandel, das (Liebes)-verhältnis, (geheime) Liebschaft; die Verwicklung, Knotenschürzung (*of a drama*); *pl.* Machenschaften, Schliche, Umtriebe, Ränke (*pl.*). **2.** *v.i.* Ränke schmieden, intrigieren. **3.** *v.t.* (*coll.*) faszinieren, gefangennehmen, fesseln. **intriguer,** *s.* der Ränkeschmied, Intrigant. **intriguing,** *adj.* ränkevoll, arglistig, intrigierend; (*coll.*) fesselnd, faszinierend, spannend.

intrinsic [in'trinsik], *adj.* inner(lich), (*fig.*) wahr, wirklich, wesentlich, eigentlich.

introduce [intrə'dju:s], *v.t.* (*a th.*) einführen, hineinbringen, hereinbringen, einfügen (*into,* in (*Acc.*)), (*a p.*) bekannt machen (*to,* mit), vorstellen (*Dat.*) (*to another p.*), bekannt machen (mit), einführen (in (*Acc.*)) (*to a th.*); einbringen (*a bill*); aufbringen (*fashions etc.*); einleiten, eröffnen (*a book, sentence etc.*); zur Sprache bringen, vorbringen, anschneiden (*a topic*); (*Med. etc.*) einführen, einlassen.

introduction [intrə'dʌkʃən], *s.* die Einführung (*also Med.*); das Vorstellen, Bekanntmachen, die Vorstellung; Einleitung, Vorrede, das Vorwort (*of a book*); die Anleitung, der Leitfaden (*to a subject*); *letter of –,* das Empfehlungsschreiben. **introductory,** *adj.* einleitend, Einleitungs–; *– remarks,* Vorbemerkungen (*pl.*).

introit ['introit], *s.* der Introitus, das Eingangslied (der Messe).

intromission [intrə'miʃən], *s.* 1. die Einführung, Zulassung; 2. (*Scots Law*) unbefugte Einmischung. **intromit,** *v.i.* 1. (hin)einführen, einfügen (*into,* in (*Acc.*)), zulassen (zu); 2. (*Scots Law*) sich unbefugterweise einmischen (*in,* in (*Acc.*)).

introspection [intrə'spekʃən], *s.* die Selbstprüfung, Selbstbeobachtung, Innenschau. **introspective** [–tiv], *adj.* beschaulich, selbstprüfend, nach innen gekehrt *or* schauend.

introversion [intrə'və:ʃən], *s.* das Einwärtskehren, (*also fig.*) Nachinnengerichtetsein; (*Psych.*) die Introvertiertheit, Introversion. **introversive** [–siv], *adj.* nach innen gerichtet. **introvert, 1.** [–'və:t], *v.t.* nach innen richten (*thoughts etc.*); einwärts kehren. **2.** ['intrəvə:t], *s.* Introvertierte(r).

intrude [in'tru:d], **1.** *v.i.* sich eindrängen (*into,* in (*Acc.*)); sich aufdrängen ((*up*)*on, Dat.*), lästig fallen (*Dat.*), stören. **2.** *v.t.* eindrängen, einzwängen (*into,* in (*Acc.*)), aufzwingen, aufdrängen ((*up*)*on, Dat.*). **intruder,** *s.* der Eindringling, Störenfried, Aufdringliche(r), ungebetener Gast; (*Av.*) der Einbruchsflieger. **intrusion** [–'tru:ʒən], *s.* 1. das Eindrängen, Einzwängen, Eindringen; Aufdrängen; die Aufdringlichkeit, Zudringlichkeit; 2. (*Law*) Besitzentziehung, Besitzstörung; 3. (*Geol.*) Intrusion. **intrusive** [–siv], *adj.* aufdringlich, zudringlich, lästig (*of a p.*), eingedrungen (*of a th.*), (*Geol.*) intrusiv. **intrusiveness,** *s.* die Zudringlichkeit, Aufdringlichkeit.

intubation [intju'beiʃən], *s.* (*Med.*) das Einführen einer Röhre (*of,* in (*Acc.*)).

intuition [intju'iʃən], *s.* unmittelbare Erkenntnis *or* Anschauung, die Intuition. **intuitive** [in'tjuitiv], *adj.* unmittelbar erfaßt, anschaulich, intuitiv; *– faculty,* das Anschauungsvermögen.

intumescence [intju'mesəns], *s.* das Anschwellen, die Aufblähung; Geschwulst, Anschwellung; (*fig.*) Schwülstigkeit, der Schwulst. **intumescent,** *adj.* geschwulstig, anschwellend.

inundate ['inʌndeit], *v.t.* überschwemmen, überfluten (*also fig.*). **inundation** [–'deiʃən], *s.* die Überschwemmung, Überflutung, Flut.

inure [in'juə], *v.t.* gewöhnen (*to,* an (*Acc.*)); (*fig.*) abhärten (gegen). **inurement,** *s.* die Gewöhnung, Abhärtung.

inutility [inju'tiliti], *s.* die Nutzlosigkeit.

invade [in'veid], *v.t.* einfallen *or* eindringen in (*Acc.*), angreifen, anfallen, überfallen; (*fig.*) überlaufen, befallen, antasten (*rights*). **invader,** *s.* der Angreifer, Eindringling.

[1]**invalid** ['invəlid], **1.** *s.* Kränkliche(r), Gebrechliche(r), Kranke(r); (*Mil.*) der Invalide. **2.** *adj.* 1. krank, kränklich, gebrechlich, leidend; 2. Kranken–; *– chair,* der Rollstuhl; *– diet,* die Krankenkost. **3.** *v.t.* (*usu. pass.*) auf die Invalidenliste setzen, als Invalide entlassen; *be –ed out of the army,* wegen Invalidität aus dem Dienst ausscheiden.

[2]**invalid** [in'vælid], *adj.* (rechts)ungültig, null und nichtig; (*fig.*) hinfällig; *make* or *render –, see* **invalidate.**

invalidate [in'vælideit], *v.t.* entkräften, ungültig erklären *or* machen, umstoßen, außer Kraft setzen. **invalidation** [–'deiʃən], *s.* die Entkräftung, Ungültigsprechung.

invalidism ['invəlidizm], *s.* dauernde Kränklichkeit, (*esp. Mil.*) die Invalidität.

invalidity [invə'liditi], *s.* die Ungültigkeit, Invalidität, Nichtigkeit, Hinfälligkeit.

invaluable [in'væljuəbl], *adj.* unschätzbar, unbezahlbar.

invariability [invɛəriə'biliti], *s.* die Unveränderlichkeit. **invariable** [in'vɛəriəbl], **1.** *adj.* unveränderlich (*also Math.*), (*Math.*) konstant, invariabel. **2.** *s.* (*Math.*) die Konstante, unveränderliche Größe. **invariably,** *adv.* unveränderlich, beständig.

invasion [in'veiʒən], *s.* das Eindringen, der Einfall, Einbruch (*of,* in (*Acc. or Dat.*)); (*Mil.*) die Invasion (*of, Gen.*), der Überfall, Angriff (auf (*Acc.*)); (*fig.*) Eingriff, plötzliches Auftreten, das Hereinbrechen (*of,* in (*Acc.*)). **invasive** [-siv], *adj.* (*rare*) angreifend, Angriffs–, Invasions–; eindringend, aufdringlich, eingreifend.

invective [in'vektiv], **1.** *s.* die Schmähung, Schmährede, Schmähschrift, Beschimpfung. **2.** *adj.* schmähend, schimpfend, Schmäh–.

inveigh [in'vei], *v.i.* – ***against,*** herziehen über (*Acc.*), losziehen gegen, schimpfen *or* schelten über *or* auf (*Acc.*).

inveigle [in'veigl, in'vi:gl], *v.t.* verlocken, verleiten, verführen (***into,*** zu), locken (in (*Acc.*)). **inveiglement,** *s.* die Verlockung, Verführung, Verleitung.

invent [in'vent], *v.t.* 1. erfinden; 2. erdenken, ersinnen, erdichten. **invention** [–'venʃən], *s.* 1. das Erfinden, Erdichten, die Erfindung; 2. Erfindung, Erdichtung, Fiktion, das Märchen; 3. die Erfindungsgabe, Phantasie; 4. (*R.C.*) ***Invention of the Cross,*** die Kreuzauffindung. **inventive,** *adj.* erfinderisch, erfindungsreich (*of,* in (*Dat.*)), schöpferisch, phantasievoll, originell. **inventiveness,** *s.* die Erfindungsgabe. **inventor,** *s.* der Erfinder.

inventory ['invəntri], **1.** *s.* der (Waren)bestand, Lagerbestand, das Inventar, Bestandsverzeichnis, die Bestandsliste; Inventur, Bestandsaufnahme; ***draw up an –, take –,*** Inventur machen, inventarisieren. **2.** *v.t.* inventarisieren.

inverse, 1. [in'və:s], *adj.* (*also Math.*) umgekehrt, entgegengesetzt; (*Math.*) reziprok, invers; (*Elec.*) – ***current,*** der Gegenstrom; – ***function,*** die Umkehrfunktion; – ***proportion,*** umgekehrtes Verhältnis; ***in the – ratio,*** umgekehrt. **2.** ['invə:s], *s.* die Umkehrung, das Gegenteil, (*Math.*) Reziproke(s), Umgekehrte(s), die Inverse. **inversion** [–'və:ʃən], *s.* (*Math., Mus., Log.*) die Umkehrung, (*Gram., Chem., Psych.*) Inversion.

invert, 1. [in'və:t], *v.t.* umdrehen, umkehren, umwenden, (*Gram.*) umstellen, (*Mus.*) versetzen, umkehren, (*Chem. etc.*) invertieren. **2.** ['invə:t], *s.* (*Psych.*) Homosexuelle(r). **3.** ['invə:t], *adj.* (*Chem.*) durch Inversion umgewandelt; – ***sugar,*** der Invertzucker.

invertebrate [in'və:tibreit], **1.** *adj.* wirbellos; (*fig.*) ohne Rückgrat, haltlos. **2.** *s.* wirbelloses Tier.

inverted [in'və:tid], *adj.* 1. umgekehrt, umgestellt; (*Archit.*) – ***arch,*** umgekehrter Bogen; – ***commas,*** Anführungszeichen, (*coll.*) Gänsefüßchen (*pl.*); (*Av.*) – ***flight,*** der Rückenflug; (*Mus.*) – ***interval,*** umgekehrtes Intervall; (*Mus.*) – ***mordent,*** der Pralltriller; 2. (*Psych.*) invertiert, pervers, homosexuell.

invest [in'vest], **1.** *v.t.* 1. bekleiden, bedecken (***with,*** mit) (*also fig.*), kleiden (in (*Acc.*)); (*fig.*) einkleiden (***with,*** in (*Acc.*)), schmücken, zieren (mit); 2. belehnen, ausstatten (***with,*** mit), einsetzen (***in,*** in (*Acc.*)); 3. (*Comm.*) anlegen, investieren, (*coll.*) hineinstecken (*money*) (***in,*** in (*Dat.*)); ***–ed capital,*** das Anlagekapital; 4. (*Mil.*) einschließen, belagern, zernieren. **2.** *v.i.* (*coll.*) – ***in,*** Geld ausgeben für (*a new car etc.*).

investigate [in'vestigeit], **1.** *v.t.* erforschen, ergründen, untersuchen. **2.** *v.i.* nachforschen (*Dat.*), Untersuchungen anstellen. **investigation** [–'geiʃən], *s.* die Erforschung, Untersuchung (***of, into,*** *Gen.*); ***on –,*** bei näherer Untersuchung. **investigator,** *s.* der Forscher, Untersucher.

investiture [in'vestitʃə], *s.* die Investitur, Amtseinsetzung, Bestallung, Belehnung; (*fig.*) Ausstattung, Bekleidung.

investment [in'vestmənt], *s.* 1. (*Mil.*) die Belagerung, Einschließung; 2. (*Comm.*) Investierung, das Anlegen (*of money*); die (Geld)anlage, Kapitalanlage; – ***account,*** das Einlagekonto; ***make an –,*** Geld anlegen; 3. *See* **investiture. investor,** *s.* der Kapitalanleger.

inveteracy [in'vetərəsi], *s.* das Eingewurzeltsein, die Unausrottbarkeit; (*Med.*) Hartnäckigkeit.

inveterate, *adj.* eingewurzelt, unausrottbar; (*Med.*) hartnäckig; (*of a p.*) eingefleischt, Gewohnheits–, Erz–.

invidious [in'vidiəs], *adj.* 1. gehässig, boshaft, verhaßt; 2. abfällig, abschätzig. **invidiousness,** *s.* 1. die Gehässigkeit; 2. Abfälligkeit.

invigilate [in'vidʒileit], *v.i.* die Aufsicht führen. **invigilation** [–'leiʃən], *s.* die Aufsichtsführung. **invigilator,** *s.* Aufsichtsführende(r).

invigorate [in'vigəreit], *v.t.* kräftigen, stärken; (*fig.*) beleben. **invigoration** [–'reiʃən], *s.* die Kräftigung, Stärkung, Belebung.

invincibility [invinsi'biliti], *s.* die Unbezwinglichkeit, Unbesiegbarkeit, Unüberwindlichkeit. **invincible** [in'vinsibl], *adj.* unüberwindlich, unbezwinglich, unbesiegbar.

inviolability [invaiələ'biliti], *s.* die Unverletzlichkeit, Unverbrüchlichkeit (*of an oath etc.*). **inviolable** [–'vaiələbl], *adj.* unverletzlich, unverbrüchlich, heilig. **inviolate** [–'vaiəlit], *adj.* unverletzt, unversehrt, unentweiht, unberührt.

invisibility [invizi'biliti], *s.* die Unsichtbarkeit. **invisible** [in'vizibl], *adj.* unsichtbar (*to,* für); ***it is –,*** es ist nicht zu sehen, es läßt sich nicht sehen; – ***exports,*** unsichtbare Exporte; – ***ink,*** die Geheimtinte; – ***mending,*** das Kunststopfen.

invitation [invi'teiʃən], *s.* 1. die Einladung (***to,*** an (*Acc.*) (*a p.*); ***to a meal,*** zum Essen); Aufforderung; Anlockung, Verlockung; 2. (*Comm.*) Ausschreibung. **invite** [in'vait], *v.t.* einladen; auffordern, verlocken, verführen, ermutigen; herausfordern (*danger, criticism*); (*Comm.*) ausschreiben; – ***him in,*** ihn hereinbitten; – ***him to a meal,*** ihn zum Essen einladen; – ***questions,*** Fragen erbitten, zu Fragen anregen. **inviting,** *adj.* einladend, verlockend, anziehend.

invocation [invə'keiʃən], *s.* das Anrufen; die Anrufung; Beschwörung; Beschwörungsformel. **invocatory** [in'vɔkətəri], *adj.* anrufend, anflehend, Bitt–; – ***prayer,*** das Bittgebet.

invoice ['invɔis], **1.** *s.* die Faktura, (Waren)rechnung; ***as per –,*** laut Faktura; – ***clerk,*** der Fakturist. **2.** *v.t.* fakturieren, in Rechnung stellen; ***as –d,*** laut Faktura.

invoke [in'vouk], *v.t.* 1. anrufen, anflehen; appellieren an (*Acc.*) (*a p.*), zitieren, beschwören (*spirits*), erflehen, flehen um (*help etc.*); 2. (*fig.*) zitieren, anführen (*as evidence, in confirmation etc.*).

involucre [invə'lju:kə], *s.* die Hülle, (*Bot.*) der Außenkelch.

involuntariness [in'vɔləntərinis], *s.* die Unfreiwilligkeit, Unwillkürlichkeit. **involuntary,** *adj.* unfreiwillig, unwillkürlich, unabsichtlich.

involute ['invəlju:t], **1.** *adj.* (*Bot.*) eingerollt, (*fig.*) verwickelt. **2.** *s.* (*Geom.*) die Evolvente. **involution** [-'lju:ʃən], *s.* 1. (*Math.*) die Involution, Potenzierung; 2. (*Bot. etc.*) Einrollung, Einschrumpfung, Rückbildung, Regression; 3. das Einhüllen, Einwickeln; (*fig.*) die Verwick(e)lung.

involve [in'vɔlv], *v.t.* 1. verwickeln, hineinziehen (*a p.*) (*in,* in (*Acc.*)) (*in difficulties etc.*); – ***o.s.*** or ***get –d in,*** verwickelt werden in (*Acc.*); 2. verwirren, komplizieren (*a th.*); 3. (*fig.*) zur Folge haben, nach sich ziehen, mit sich bringen, in sich schließen, umfassen, enthalten, einschließen, einbegreifen, einbeziehen; ***it –s hard work,*** dazu gehört harte Arbeit; 4. (*obs.*) einhüllen, einwickeln. **involved,** *adj.* 1. verworren, verwickelt; 2. einbegriffen; ***be –,*** in Frage kommen, auf dem Spiel stehen; 3. verwickelt (*also fig.*) (*in,* in (*Acc.*)); – ***in debt,*** verschuldet. **involvement,** *s.* 1. die Verwick(e)lung (*in,* in (*Acc.*)), Beschäftigung (mit); 2. Schwierigkeit, Verlegenheit.

invulnerability [invʌlnərə'biliti], *s.* die Unverwundbarkeit; (*fig.*) Unanfechtbarkeit. **invulnerable** [–'vʌlnərəbl], *adj.* unverwundbar; (*fig.*) unangreifbar, unanfechtbar.

inward ['inwəd], **1.** *adj.* inner, innerlich, inwendig, Innen–; (*fig.*) geistig, seelisch. **2.** *adv.* einwärts, nach innen, ins Innere. **3.** *s.* (*fig.*) das Innere. **inwardly,** *adv.* innerlich, im Innern; (*fig.*)

unbemerkt, im stillen, leise, für sich. **inwardness,** *s.* innere Natur, die Innerlichkeit. **inwards,** *adv. See* **inward, 2.**

inweave [in'wi:v], *irr.v.t.* einweben (*into*, in (*Acc.*)), (*fig.*) einflechten (*in(to)*, in (*Acc.*)), verflechten (*with*, mit).

inwrought ['inrɔ:t], *adj.* hineingearbeitet, verwoben (*in(to)*, in (*Acc.*)), verarbeitet, verflochten; geschmückt (*with*, mit).

iodic [ai'ɔdik], *adj.* Jod–, jodsauer. **iodide** ['aiədaid], *s.* das Jodid, die Jodverbindung; – *of nitrogen*, das Jodstickstoff. **iodine** ['aiədi:n], *s.* das Jod; *tincture of* –, die Jodtinktur. **iodism** ['aiədizm], *s.* die Jodvergiftung. **iodize** ['aiədaiz], *v.t.* (*Phot.*) mit Jod behandeln, jodieren. **iodoform** [ai'oudəfɔ:m], *s.* das Jodoform.

iolite ['aiəlait], *s.* (*Geol.*) der Iolith.

ion ['aiən], *s.* das Ion.

Ionian [ai'ouniən], **1.** *s.* der (die) Ionier(in). **2.** *adj.* (*esp. Archit.*), **Ionic** [ai'ɔnik], *adj.* ionisch.

ionization [aiənai'zeiʃən], *s.* die Ionisierung. **ionize** ['aiənaiz], **1.** *v.t.* ionisieren. **2.** *v.i.* sich in Ionen spalten. **ionosphere** [ai'ɔnəsfiə], *s.* die Ionosphäre.

iota [ai'outə], *s.* das Iota, Jota; (*fig.*) Tüpfelchen, Tüttelchen.

ipecacuanha [ipə'kækjuænə], *s.* (*Bot.*) die Brechwurz(el), Kopfbeere.

ipso facto ['ipsou'fæktou], *adv.* gerade dadurch.

Iran [i'rɑ:n], *s.* Iran (*n. or m.*). **Iranian** [–'reiniən], **1.** *s.* der (die) Iranier(in). **2.** *adj.* iranisch.

Iraq [i'rɑ:k], *s.* Irak (*n. or m.*). **Iraqi** [–i], **1.** *s.* der (die) Iraker(in). **2.** *adj.* irakisch.

irascibility [iræsi'biliti], *s.* die Reizbarkeit, der Jähzorn. **irascible** [i'ræsibl], *adj.* reizbar, jähzornig.

irate [ai'reit], *adj.* erzürnt, zornig.

ire ['aiə], *s.* (*Poet.*) der Zorn, die Wut. **ireful,** *adj.* (*Poet.*) zornig, wütend.

Ireland ['aiələnd], *s.* Irland (*n.*).

iridescence [iri'desəns], *s.* das Schillern. **iridescent,** *adj.* schillernd, irisierend.

iridium [i'ridiəm], *s.* das Iridium.

iris ['aiəris], *s.* 1. (*Anat.*) der Regenbogen, die Regenbogenhaut; (*Phot.*) – ***diaphragm,*** die Irisblende; 2. (*Bot.*) die Schwertlilie.

Irish ['aiəriʃ], **1.** *adj.* ir(länd)isch; – ***Free State,*** der Irische Freistaat; (*coll.*) – ***bull,*** der Unsinn; – ***stew,*** das Eintopfgericht. **2.** ***the*** –, Iren, Irländer (*pl.*). **Irishism,** *s.* irische (Sprach)eigentümlichkeit. **Irish|man** [–mən], *s.* der Ire, Irländer. **–woman,** *s.* die Irin, Irländerin.

irk [ə:k], *v.t.* (*usu. imp.*) ärgern, verdrießen; (*Poet.*) ermüden. **irksome** [–səm], *adj.* lästig, verdrießlich, beschwerlich. **irksomeness,** *s.* die Lästigkeit, Verdrießlichkeit, Beschwerlichkeit.

iron ['aiən], **1.** *s.* 1. das Eisen; ***cast*** –, das Gußeisen, der Grauguß; ***corrugated*** –, das Wellblech; ***pig*** –, das Roheisen; (*fig.*) ***with a rod of*** –, mit eiserner Hand; ***have too many –s in the fire,*** sich mit vielerlei zugleich befassen, zuviel auf seinen Schultern haben; ***sheet*** –, das Blecheisen, Eisenblech; ***soldering*** –, der Lotkolben; ***strike while the – is hot,*** das Eisen schmieden solange es heiß ist, zuschlagen solange das Eisen heiß ist; ***will of*** –, eiserner Wille; ***wrought*** –, das Schmiedeeisen, Schweißeisen; 2. Bügeleisen, Plätteisen; 3. der Golfschläger; 4. eisernes Werkzeug; 5. *pl.* Beinschienen (*pl.*), (*Hist.*) Fesseln (*pl.*); ***in –s,*** in Ketten *or* Fesseln *or* Eisen, (*Med.*) in (Bein)schienen, (*Naut.*) nicht wendefähig, im Wind; ***put him in –s,*** ihm Fußschellen anlegen, ihn in Fesseln legen. **2.** *adj.* eisern, Eisen–; (*fig.*) unbeugsam, fest (*as will*); ***the – age,*** die Eisenzeit; – ***cross,*** Eisernes Kreuz; (*Pol.*) – ***curtain,*** eiserner Vorhang; (*obs.*) – ***horse,*** (*Cycl.*) das Stahlroß, (*Railw.*) Dampfroß; – ***lung,*** eiserne Lunge; – ***ration,*** eiserne Ration. **3.** *v.t.* bügeln, plätten; (*fig.*) – ***out,*** ausgleichen, beseitigen (*difficulties etc.*).

iron|-bound, *adj.* eisenbeschlagen; felsig (*as a coast*). **--casting,** *s.* der Eisenguß; das Eisengußstück. **–clad, 1.** *adj.* (*Naut.*) gepanzert; eisenbewehrt, eisenverkleidet; (*fig.*) starr, streng, unumstößlich. **2.** *s.* das Panzerschiff. **--fisted,** *adj.* geizig, geldgierig. **--founder,** *s.* der Eisengießer. **--foundry,** *s.* die Eisengießerei. **--grey,** *adj.* eisengrau. **--handed,** *adj.* unerbittlich, streng, grausam. **--hearted,** *adj.* hartherzig.

ironic(al) [ai'rɔnik(l)], *adj.* spöttelnd, spöttisch, ironisch.

ironing ['aiəniŋ], *s.* 1. das Plätten, Bügeln; 2. die Wäsche zum Bügeln, ungeplättete Wäsche. **ironing-board,** *s.* das Plättbrett, Bügelbrett.

iron|master, *s.* der Eisenhüttenbesitzer. **–monger,** *s.* der Eisen(waren)händler. **–mongery,** *s.* Eisenwaren (*pl.*); die Eisen(waren)handlung. **--mould,** *s.* der Rostfleck. **--ore,** *s.* das Eisenerz. **--pyrites,** *s.* der Schwefelkies. **–sides,** *pl.* (*Hist.*) Cromwells Reiterei. **--smelting,** *s.* die Eisenverhüttung. **–smith,** *s.* der Eisenschmied. **–stone,** *s.* der Eisenstein. **–ware,** *s.* Eisenwaren (*pl.*). **–work,** *s.* die Eisenkonstruktion. **–works,** *pl.* (*sing. constr.*) die Eisenhütte, das Eisenwerk.

irony ['airəni], *s.* die Ironie.

Iroquois ['irəkwɔiz], **1.** *s.* der Irokese (die Irokesin). **2.** *adj.* irokesisch.

irradiance, irradiancy [i'reidiəns(i)], *s.* das (Aus)strahlen; der Strahlenglanz. **irradiate** [–ieit], *v.t.* bestrahlen, belichten, erleuchten (*a th. with light*); ausstrahlen, verbreiten (*light*); (*Med.*) bestrahlen; (*fig.*) aufklären, Licht werfen auf (*Acc.*); aufheitern, verklären. **irradiation** [–i'eiʃən], *s.* das Strahlen, Leuchten; der (Licht)strahl; (*Med.*) die Bestrahlung, Durchleuchtung; (*Opt.*) Irradiation; (*fig.*) Aufklärung, Erleuchtung.

irrational [i'ræʃənl], **1.** *adj.* sinnlos, unsinnig, unlogisch, vernunftwidrig; (*Math., Phil.*) irrational. **2.** *s.* (*Math.*) irrationale Größe. **irrationalism,** *s.* (*Phil.*) der Irrationalismus. **irrationality** [–'næliti], *s.* die Unvernunft, Vernunftlosigkeit, Vernunftwidrigkeit; (*Math.*) Irrationalität.

irreclaimable [iri'kleiməbl], *adj.* unwiderruflich, unwiederbringlich; unverbesserlich, nicht kulturfähig (*of land*).

irrecognizable [i'rekəgnaizəbl], *adj.* nicht erkennbar, nicht wiederzuerkennen(d).

irreconcilability [irekənsailə'biliti], *s.* die Unversöhnlichkeit, Unvereinbarkeit (*to, with,* mit). **irreconcilable** [–'rekənsailəbl], *adj.* unversöhnlich, unvereinbar (*to, with,* mit); (*of statements*) widerstreitend, gegensätzlich.

irrecoverable [iri'kʌvərəbl], *adj.* unwiederbringlich (verloren), unersetzlich, nicht wiedergutzumachen(d), (*as debt*) uneintreibbar. **irrecoverableness,** *s.* die Unersetzlichkeit, Unwiederbringlichkeit.

irredeemable [iri'di:məbl], *adj.* 1. nicht rückkaufbar *or* wiederkaufbar, nicht einlösbar (*as paper currency*), nicht tilgbar, unkündbar (*as loans*); 2. (*fig.*) unverbesserlich, hoffnungslos; 3. unersetzlich.

irredentism [iri'dentizm], *s.* (*Pol.*) der Irredentismus. **irredentist, 1.** *s.* Irredentist. **2.** *adj.* irredentistisch.

irreducible [iri'dju:sibl], *adj.* nicht reduzierbar, nicht zu vermindern(d); nicht verwandelbar, unveränderbar; ***the – minimum,*** das Allergeringste, Mindestmaß (*of*, an (*Dat.*)).

irrefragability [irefrəgə'biliti], *s.* die Unwiderleglichkeit, Unumstößlichkeit. **irrefragable** [i'refrəgəbl], *adj.* unwiderleglich, unumstößlich.

irrefrangible [iri'frændʒibl], *adj.* (*Law*) unübertretbar, unumstößlich, unverletzlich; (*Opt.*) unbrechbar.

irrefutability [irifju:tə'biliti, irefjutə'biliti], *s.* die Unwiderlegbarkeit. **irrefutable** [iri'fju:təbl, i'refjutəbl], *adj.* unwiderleglich, unwiderlegbar.

irregular [i'regjulə], *adj.* unregelmäßig (*also Gram.*), regellos, regelwidrig; uneben, ungleichmäßig, ungleichförmig, uneinheitlich (*as a surface*), ungeregelt, unstet, unordentlich (*of conduct*),

(*Mil.*) irregulär. **irregularity** [–'læriti], *s.* 1. die Unregelmäßigkeit (*also Gram.*), Uneinheitlichkeit, Ungleichförmigkeit, Ungleichmäßigkeit, Unebenheit; Regellosigkeit, Regelwidrigkeit; Unordnung, Unordentlichkeit, Ausschweifung, Abweichung von der Norm, abnormer Zustand; 2. der Fehler, Verstoß, das Vergehen; 3. (*R.C.*) kanonisches Hindernis.

irrelevance, irrelevancy [i'reləvəns(i)], *s.* die Belanglosigkeit, Unerheblichkeit; Unanwendbarkeit (*to*, auf (*Acc.*)). **irrelevant,** *adj.* nicht zur S. gehörig, ohne Beziehung (*to*, zu); belanglos, ohne Belang, unerheblich (*to*, für); unanwendbar (*to*, auf (*Acc.*)).

irrelievable [iri'li:vəbl], *adj.* nicht abzuhelfen(d), nicht abzustellen(d).

irreligion [iri'lidʒən], *s.* der Unglaube, die Gottlosigkeit, Religionslosigkeit, Religionsfeindlichkeit, Gottvergessenheit. **irreligious,** *adj.* irreligiös, ungläubig, gottlos, religionslos, religionsfeindlich, gottvergessen. **irreligiousness,** *s.* die Religionslosigkeit, Irreligiosität.

irremediable [iri'mi:diəbl], *adj.* unheilbar; (*fig.*) unabänderlich, nicht wiedergutzumachen(d).

irremissible [iri'misibl], *adj.* unverzeihlich (*fault*), unerläßlich (*duty*).

irremovable [iri'mu:vəbl], *adj.* nicht entfernbar *or* abnehmbar, unbeweglich; unabsetzbar (*from office etc.*).

irreparable [i'repərəbl], *adj.* unersetzlich, unwiederbringlich; nicht wiederherstellbar, nicht wiedergutzumachen(d).

irrepealable [iri'pi:ləbl], *adj.* unwiderruflich.

irreplaceable [iri'pleisəbl], *adj.* unersetzbar, unersetzlich.

irrepressibility [iripresi'biliti], *s.* die Unbezähmbarkeit, Ununterdrückbarkeit. **irrepressible** [–'presibl], *adj.* ununterdrückbar, nicht zu unterdrücken(d), un(be)zähmbar, unbändig.

irreproachable [iri'proutʃəbl], *adj.* untadelig, einwandfrei, unbescholten. **irreproachableness,** *s.* die Untadeligkeit, Unbescholtenheit.

irresistibility [irizisti'biliti], *s.* die Unwiderstehlichkeit. **irresistible** [–'zistibl], *adj.* unwiderstehlich, unaufhaltsam.

irresolute [i'rezəlju:t], *adj.* unschlüssig, unentschlossen, schwankend, zögernd. **irresoluteness, irresolution** [–'lju:ʃən], *s.* die Unentschlossenheit, Unschlüssigkeit.

irresolvable [iri'zɔlvəbl], *adj.* un(auf)lösbar, un(auf)löslich.

irrespective [iri'spektiv], *adj.* – ***of,*** ohne Rücksicht auf (*Acc.*), abgesehen von, unabhängig von, ungeachtet (*Gen.*).

irresponsibility [irispɔnsi'biliti], *s.* (*of an action*) die Unverantwortlichkeit, (*of a p. or action*) Verantwortungslosigkeit, (*Med., Law*) Unzurechnungsfähigkeit. **irresponsible** [–'spɔnsibl], *adj.* unverantwortlich (*of an action*), verantwortungslos (*of a p. or action*), (*Law*) unzurechnungsfähig.

irresponsive [iri'spɔnsiv], *adj.* teilnahm(s)los, gleichgültig, verständnislos (*to*, gegenüber), unempfänglich (für); ***be – to,*** nicht reagieren auf (*Acc.*).

irretentive [iri'tentiv], *adj.* unfähig zu behalten, schwach (*of memory*).

irretraceable [iri'treisəbl], *adj.* nicht zurückzuverfolgen(d) (*path etc.*), nicht rückgängig zu machen(d) (*steps*).

irretrievable [iri'tri:vəbl], *adj.* unwiederbringlich, unersetzlich, unersetzbar; nicht wiedergutzumachen(d).

irreverence [i'revərəns], *s.* die Unehrerbietigkeit, Respektlosigkeit. **irreverent,** *adj.* unehrerbietig, geringschätzig, respektlos (***towards***, gegenüber).

irreversibility [irivə:si'biliti], *s.* die Unwiderruflichkeit, Unabänderlichkeit, (*Tech.*) Irreversibilität. **irreversible** [–'və:sibl], *adj.* unwiderruflich, unabänderlich; (*Tech.*) nicht umkehrbar, irreversibel.

irrevocability [irevəkə'biliti], *s.* die Unwiderruflichkeit. **irrevocable** [i'revəkəbl], *adj.* unwiderruflich, unumstößlich, unabänderlich.

irrigable ['irigəbl], *adj.* bewässerungsfähig (*as land*). **irrigate** [–geit], *v.t.* bewässern, berieseln, mit Wasser versorgen (*land*); (*Med.*) (aus)spülen. **irrigation** [–'geiʃən], *s.* die Bewässerung, Berieselung, (*Med.*) Spülung. **irrigational,** *adj.* Bewässerungs–, Berieselungs–.

irritability [iritə'biliti], *s.* die Reizbarkeit; Gereiztheit, krankhafte Erregbarkeit. **irritable** ['iritəbl], *adj.* reizbar; gereizt, nervös, (*coll.*) grantig.

irritancy ['iritənsi], *s.* (*Scots law*) die Verwirkung, Nichtigmachung, Ungültigmachung; Nichtigkeitsklausel.

[1]**irritant** ['iritənt], 1. *adj.* Reiz–. 2. *s.* das Reizmittel, der Reizstoff.

[2]**irritant,** *adj.* (*Scots law*) verwirkend, annulierend.

irritate ['iriteit], *v.t.* reizen (*also Med.*), (ver)ärgern, erzürnen; (*Med.*) entzünden; ***be –d,*** verärgert *or* erzürnt sein (*at, with, by*, über (*Acc.*)). **irritating,** *adj.* ärgerlich, lästig, störend; aufreizend, provozierend; (*Med.*) schmerzlich. **irritation** [–'teiʃən], *s.* die Verärgerung, der Ärger (*at, over*, über (*Acc.*)); (*Med.*) Reiz, die Reizung, Entzündung. **irritative** [–tətiv], *adj.* reizend, Reiz–; aufreizend, provozierend.

irruption [i'rʌpʃən], *s.* das Hereinbrechen, Eindringen; der Einbruch, Einfall. **irruptive** [–tiv], *adj.* (her)einbrechend; (*Geol.*) intrusiv.

is [iz], *3rd pers. sing. pres. indic. of* **be,** ist, wird; ***it – I,*** ich bin es; ***it – not for me,*** es geziemt mir nicht (*to*, zu); ***there – no man who,*** es gibt keinen Menschen, der . . .; ***that – to say,*** das heißt; ***how – it that?*** woher kommt es, daß? ***how – she?*** wie geht es ihr? wie befindet sie sich?

Isaac ['aizək], *s.* (*B.*) Isaak (*m.*).

Isaiah [ai'zaiə], *s.* (*B.*) 1. Isaias, Jesaia(s) (*m.*); 2. das Buch Jesaia(s).

Iscariot [is'kæriət], *s.* (*B.*) Ischariot (*m.*).

ischial ['iskiəl], **ischiatic** [–i'ætik], *adj.* Sitzbein–, Gesäß–. **ischium,** *s.* das Sitzbein, Gesäßbein.

Ishmael ['iʃmeil], *s.* (*B.*) Ismael (*m.*). **Ishmaelite** [–ait], *s.* der Ismaelit.

isinglass ['aiziŋglɑ:s], *s.* die Hausenblase; der Fischleim.

Islam ['izləm], *s.* der Islam. **Islamic** [–'læmik], *adj.* islam(it)isch.

island ['ailənd], *s.* 1. die Insel; 2. (*Motor.*) Verkehrsinsel. **islander,** *s.* der (die) Inselbewohner(in). **isle** [ail], *s.* die Insel, (*Poet.*) das Eiland. **islet** [–lit], *s.* das Inselchen, kleine Insel.

ism [izm], *s.* (*coll.*) der Ismus, bloße Theorie.

isn't [iznt], (*coll.*) = ***is not.***

iso– ['aisou], *pref.* gleich–. **iso|bar,** *s.* die Isobare. **–chromatic,** *adj.* gleichfarbig, isochrom(atisch); (*Phot.*) orthochromatisch. **isogamous** [ai'sɔgəməs], *adj.* isogam. **isogenous** [ai'sɔdʒinəs], *adj.* isogen.

isolate ['aisəleit], *v.t.* absondern (***from***, von); (*Med., Elec.*) isolieren; (*Chem.*) rein darstellen; (*fig.*) abschließen, abdichten. **isolated,** *adj.* isoliert, (ab)gesondert; vereinzelt, Einzel–. **isolation** [–'leiʃən], *s.* die Abschließung, (*esp. Med.*) Absonderung, Isolierung; – ***hospital,*** das Krankenhaus für ansteckende Krankheiten. **isolationism,** *s.* (*Pol.*) die Isolationspolitik, der Isolationismus. **isolationist,** *s.* der Anhänger der Isolationspolitik.

isomeric [aiso'merik], *adj.* isomer, gleichteilig. **isomorphic** [–'mɔ:fik], *adj.* isomorph, gleichgestaltig. **isomorphism,** *s.* die Gleichgestaltigkeit, Strukturgleichheit.

isosceles [ai'sɔsili:z], *adj.* gleichschenk(e)lig.

isotherm ['aisoθə:m], *s.* die Isotherme. **isothermal** [–'θə:ml], *adj.* isotherm(isch). **isotope** ['aisotoup], *s.* das Isotop. **isotype** ['aisotaip], *s.* (*Stat.*) das Schaubild.

Israel ['izreil], *s.* (*B., Geog.*) Israel (*n.*). **Israeli** [–'reili], 1. *s.* der Israeli. 2. *adj.* israelisch. **Israelite**

[-rəlait], **1.** *s.* (*B.*) der (die) Israelit(in). **2.** *adj.* israelitisch.

issuable ['iʃuəbl], *adj.* auszugeben(d), emittierbar. **issuance,** *s.* (*Am.*) die Ausgabe, Verteilung, Erteilung, Austeilung, (*Comm.*) Emission.

issue ['iʃu:], **1.** *v.t.* 1. ausgeben, erlassen, erteilen, ergehen lassen (*instructions etc.*), ausliefern, aussenden (*goods*); 2. (*Comm.*) in Umlauf setzen, emittieren, ausgeben (*bills etc.*), ausstellen, ausfertigen (*cheques etc.*), auflegen (*loans*); 3. (*books*) publizieren, veröffentlichen, herausgeben; 4. (*Mil.*) verteilen, ausgeben (*rations, equipment*); – ***him with,*** ihn beliefern *or* ausstatten *or* versehen mit. **2.** *v.i.* 1. herauskommen, hervorkommen, herausgehen, hervorgehen, herausbrechen, hervorbrechen, herausströmen, herausfließen (***from,*** aus); (*esp. Law*) herstammen, herkommen, herrühren, entspringen (von); 2. end(ig)en, zu einem Ergebnis kommen, resultieren (***in,*** in (*Dat.*)), auslaufen (in (*Acc.*)). **3.** *s.* 1. das Ausgeben, Erteilen, Erlassen, der Erlaß (*of instructions etc.*); 2. (*Comm.*) die Ausgabe, Emission (*of bills, money etc.*), Auflegung (*of loans*), Ausstellung, Ausfertigung (*of cheques etc.*); ***bank of –,*** die Notenbank; 3. (*books*) die Veröffentlichung, (Her)ausgabe, Publikation; 4. (*Mil.*) Ausgabe, Verteilung (*of rations etc.*); 5. das Herausgehen, Herauskommen (*of a p.*); der Abfluß, Abzug (*of liquid*), (*Med.*) Ausfluß, Abgang (*of blood, pus etc.*); 6. die Öffnung, Mündung, der Ausgang; 7. (*fig.*) Ausgang, Schluß, das Ergebnis, Resultat; ***bring to an –,*** zur Entscheidung bringen; ***force an –,*** eine Entscheidung erzwingen; ***in the –,*** schließlich; 8. (*esp. Law*) die Meinungsverschiedenheit, Streitfrage, der Streitpunkt, Streitfall; (*esp. Pol.*) Angelpunkt, Sachverhalt, die Kernfrage, das Problem; (*Law*) ***– in fact,*** die Tatsachenfrage; ***– in law,*** die Rechtsfrage; ***– at stake,*** das zur Rede stehende Problem; ***be at – with him,*** mit ihm im Streit liegen; mit ihm uneinig sein; anders denken als er; ***join – with him,*** sich mit ihm auf einen Streit einlassen; gegenteiliger Ansicht sein als er; ***live –,*** aktuelle Frage; ***point at –,*** umstrittener Punkt; ***raise the whole –,*** den ganzen Sachverhalt anschneiden; ***the real –,*** das eigentliche Problem; ***side –,*** nebensächlicher Punkt; 9. die Nachkommenschaft, Nachkommen (*pl.*), Abkömmlinge (*pl.*), (Leibes)erben (*pl.*); ***die without –,*** ohne direkte Erben sterben; 10. die (Neu)auflage (*of a book*), Nummer (*of a periodical*).

issue-department, *s.* die Emissionsabteilung, Notenausgabestelle. **issueless,** *adj.* ohne Nachkommen. **issuer,** *s.* der (die) Emittent(in), Aussteller(in), Ausgeber(in).

isthmus ['is(θ)məs], *s.* die Landenge, der Isthmus; (*Anat.*) die Enge, Vereng(er)ung.

it [it], **1.** *pron.* (*Nom.*) er, es, sie; (*Acc.*) ihn, es, sie; (*Dat.*) ihm, ihr; (*refl. after prep.*) sich; **(a)** (*as Nom.*) ***– is I,*** ich bin es; ***how is – with you?*** wie steht es mit dir? ***from what has been said – follows*** or ***– is clear,*** aus dem Gesagten folgt *or* wird klar; ***– is not your fault,*** Ihre Schuld ist es nicht; **(b)** (*as Acc.*) ***confound –!*** zum Teufel (damit)! ***you must face –,*** du mußt es ausbaden; ***you must fight –,*** du mußt dagegen kämpfen; (*coll.*) ***foot –,*** zu Fuß gehen; tanzen; (*sl.*) ***go –!*** nur zu! (*coll.*) ***lord –,*** den Herrn spielen (***over,*** bei); ***I take – that . . .,*** ich nehme an, daß . . .; **(c)** (*with preps.*) ***at –,*** daran, darüber, dazu; ***by –,*** dadurch, dabei; ***for –,*** dafür, deswegen; ***there's nothing for – but . . .,*** es bleibt nichts übrig als . . .; ***there's no remedy for –,*** da ist kein Mittel dagegen; ***from –,*** davon; ***in –,*** darin; ***of –,*** davon, darüber; (*coll.*) ***have a fine time of -,*** sich köstlich amüsieren; ***to –,*** dazu; daran; ***with –,*** damit; (*sl.*) auf Draht; ***power carries responsibility with –,*** die Macht bringt Verantwortung mit sich. **2.** *s.* (*sl.*) die Höhe, der Gipfel; ***for cheek you really have –,*** deine Frechheit ist doch der Gipfel *or* die Höhe; ***she certainly has –,*** sie hat ein gewisses Etwas.

Italian [i'tæljən], **1.** *s.* 1. der (die) Italiener(in); 2. (*language*) das Italienisch(e). **2.** *adj.* italienisch.

italic [i'tælik], *adj.* kursiv. **italicize** [-lisaiz], *v.t.* kursiv *or* in Kursivschrift drucken. **italics,** *pl.* die Kursivschrift, Schrägschrift; ***in –,*** kursiv (gedruckt), in Schrägdruck.

Italy ['itəli], *s.* Italien (*n.*); ***North –,*** Oberitalien (*n.*).

itch [itʃ], **1.** *s.* das Jucken, Kribbeln; (*Med.*) die Krätze; (*coll.*) das Verlangen, Gelüst(e); ***– of desire,*** der Sinnenkitzel. **2.** *v.i.* jucken, kribbeln; (*coll.*) dürsten, gelüsten (***for,*** nach); ***I –,*** es juckt mich; ***my fingers – to do it,*** es juckt mir in den Fingern, es zu tun. **itchiness,** *s.* der Juckreiz. **itching, 1.** *s.* das Jucken; (*coll.*) Verlangen, Gelüst(e). **2.** *adj.* juckend; (*coll.*) lüstern, begierig. **itchy,** *adj. See* **itching, 2.**

item ['aitəm], **1.** *s.* einzelner Punkt *or* Gegenstand; (*Comm.*) der Posten, die Buchung; Zeitungsnotiz. **2.** *v.t.* notieren, vermerken. **3.** *adv.* (*obs.*) ebenso, desgleichen. **itemize** [-aiz], *v.t.* (einzeln) aufzählen *or* angeben *or* aufführen *or* verzeichnen, spezifizieren, detaillieren.

iterance, iterancy ['itərəns(i)], *s. See* **iteration. iterate** [-reit], *v.t.* wiederholen. **iteration** [-'reiʃən], *s.* die Wiederholung. **iterative** [-rətiv], *adj.* sich wiederholend, (*Gram.*) iterativ.

itinera(n)cy [ai'tinərə(n)si], *s.* das Umherwandern, Umherreisen, Umherziehen. **itinerant,** *adj.* (herum)reisend, umherziehend, Wander–; ***– judge,*** herumziehender Richter; ***– preacher,*** der Wanderprediger; ***– scholar,*** fahrender Schüler. **itinerary, 1.** *s.* die Reiseroute, der Reiseweg; Reiseplan; Reisebericht, die Reisebeschreibung. **2.** *adj.* Reise–. **itinerate** [-reit], *v.i.* (*rare*) (umher)reisen.

its [its], *poss. pron.* sein, ihr; dessen, deren.

it's [its], (*coll.*) = ***it is.***

itself [it'self], *pron.* (*emphatic*) selbst; (*refl.*) sich (selbst); ***by –,*** für sich (allein); ***in –,*** an sich; ***of –,*** von selbst; ***she is innocence –,*** sie ist die Unschuld selbst.

I've [aiv], (*coll.*) = ***I have.***

ivied ['aivid], *adj.* mit Efeu bedeckt *or* bewachsen, efeuumrankt.

ivory ['aivəri], **1.** *s.* das Elfenbein; Elfenbeinweiß; (*sl.*) ***the ivories,*** Zähne; Würfel; Klaviertasten; Billardkugeln; ***vegetable –,*** die Steinnuß. **2.** *adj.* elfenbeinern, Elfenbein–; (*fig.*) ***– tower,*** elfenbeinerner Turm.

ivy ['aivi], *s.* (*Bot.*) der Efeu.

izard ['izəd], *s.* (*Zool.*) die (Pyrenäen)gemse.

J

J [dʒei], *s.* das J, j. *See Index of Abbreviations.*

jab [dʒæb], **1.** *s.* (*coll.*) der Stoß, Stich; (*Med. sl.*) die Spritze, (Schutz)impfung, Einspritzung; (*Boxing*) linker Gerader. **2.** *v.t.* (*coll.*) (hinein)stoßen; (hinein)stechen (***into,*** in (*Acc.*)). **3.** *v.i.* stoßen, stechen.

jabber ['dʒæbə], **1.** *v.i.* (*coll.*) schnattern, plappern, quasseln, schwatzen. **2.** *s.* (*coll.*) das Geschnatter, Geplapper, Gequassel, Geschwätz.

jabot ['ʒæbou], *s.* das Jabot, die Brustkrause, Rüsche.

Jack [dʒæk], *s.* Hans (*m.*); (*coll.*) ***– Frost,*** der Winter, Frost, Reif; ***– and Jill,*** Hans und Grete; ***– Ketch,*** der Henker; (*coll.*) ***before you could say – Robinson,*** im Nu, im Handumdrehen; ***– Sprat,*** der Dreikäsehoch; (*coll.*) ***– Tar,*** die Teerjacke; ***Yellow –,*** das Gelbfieber.

[1]**jack, 1.** *s.* 1. (*Cards*) der Bube; ***– of all trades,*** Hans Dampf in allen Gassen, der Allerweltskerl; ***every man –,*** jede Menschenseele; 2. (*Tech.*) die Winde,

Hebevorrichtung, der (Wagen)heber; (*obs.*) Bratenwender; (*Tele.*) die Klinke; das Gestell, der (Säge)bock; Stiefelknecht; ***lifting* –**, der Wagenheber; 3. (*Bowls*) die Zielkugel; 4. (*Ichth.*) junger Hecht; 5. (*Am.*) der Esel; 6. (*of small animals*) das Männchen. **2.** *v.t.* (– *up*) hochheben, hochwinden; aufwinden; (*coll.*) in die Höhe treiben, hochtreiben, antreiben (*prices etc.*); (*sl.*) **– *in*** or ***up,*** aufgeben, hinschmeißen.

[2]**jack,** *s.* (*Naut.*) die Gösch, Bugflagge; ***Union Jack,*** englische Nationalflagge.

jackal ['dʒækɔːl], *s.* der Schakal; (*fig.*) Handlanger, Helfershelfer.

jackanapes ['dʒækəneips], *s.* der Naseweis, Schlingel, Schelm; Geck, Laffe, Affenschwanz.

jackass ['dʒækæs], *s.* männlicher Esel; (*fig.*) der Esel, Dummkopf; (*Orn.*) ***laughing* –,** der Riesenkönigsfischer (*Dacelo gigas*).

jack|boots, *pl.* Kanonenstiefel, (hohe) Wasserstiefel (*pl.*). **–daw,** *s.* (*Orn.*) die Dohle (*Corvus monedula*).

jacket ['dʒækit], *s.* das Jackett, die Jacke; (*Tech.*) der Mantel, das Mantelrohr, die Muffe, Umhüllung; (*on a book*) der Schutzumschlag; (*of plants*) die (Schutz)hülle, Hülse, Schale; ***potatoes in their –s,*** Pellkartoffeln (*pl.*); (*coll., fig.*) ***dust his* –,** ihn durchprügeln; ***water* –,** der Kühl(wasser)-mantel.

jack|-in-office, *s.* wichtigtuender Beamter, der Wichtigtuer. **--in-the-box,** *s.* das Schachtelmännchen. **–knife, 1.** *s.* (großes) Klappmesser. **2.** *v.i.* (*coll.*) zusammenklappen. **--leg,** *adj.* (*Am.*) Winkel– (*as lawyer*). **--o'-lantern,** *s.* das Irrlicht. **–plane,** *s.* der Schropphobel, Schrubbhobel. **–pot,** *s.* (*poker*) der Jackpot; (*coll.*) großer Gewinn; (*coll.*) ***hit the* –,** großen Dusel haben. **–screw,** *s.* die Hebeschraube, Hebespindel. **–snipe,** *s.* (*Orn.*) die Zwergschnepfe (*Lymnocryptes minimus*). **--staff,** *s.* der Göschstock. **--towel,** *s.* das Rollhandtuch.

Jacob ['dʒeikəb], *s.* Jakob (*m.*); ***–'s ladder,*** (*Bot.*) die Himmelsleiter; (*Naut.*) Jakobsleiter, Strickleiter. **Jacobean** [dʒækə'biən], *adj.* (*Hist.*) der Zeit Jakobs I.; (*furniture*) Dunkeleiche–. **Jacobin** ['dʒækəbin], *s.* (*Hist.*) der Jakobiner. **Jacobite** ['dʒækəbait], *s.* (*Hist.*) der Jakobit.

jactation [dʒæk'teiʃən], *s.* (*Med.*) das Durchschütteln des Körpers.

jactitation [dʒækti'teiʃən], *s.* 1. (*Law*) falsche Behauptung; **– *of marriage,*** die Unterschiebung eines Ehestandes; 2. (*Med.*) *see* **jactation.**

[1]**jade** [dʒeid], *s.* der Nierenstein, Beilstein; das Jadegrün.

[2]**jade, 1.** *s.* die (Schind)mähre, (*coll.*) Kracke; (*sl.*) das Weibsbild. **2.** *v.t.* abschinden, (*fig.*) abhetzen, ermüden. **jaded,** *adj.* abgemattet, erschöpft; übersättigt, abgestumpft.

jag [dʒæg], **1.** *s.* (*coll.*) die Zacke, Kerbe, der Zacken; Stich. **2.** *v.t.* (ein)kerben, (aus)zacken; stechen. **jagged** [–id], *adj.* zackig, (aus)gezackt. **jaggedness,** *s.* die Zackigkeit.

jaguar ['dʒægjuə], *s.* der Jaguar.

jail, *see* **gaol.**

jalap ['dʒæləp], *s.* die Jalap(p)enwurzel, Purgierwinde.

jalop(p)y [dʒə'lɔpi], *s.* (*sl. esp. Am.*) die Klapperkiste.

[1]**jam** [dʒæm], *s.* die Marmelade; (*sl.*) ***have all the* –,** die Rosinen aus dem Kuchen haben.

[2]**jam, 1.** *v.t.* (hinein)zwängen, festklemmen, einklemmen; (*Tech.*) verstopfen, versperren; (*Rad.*) blockieren, stören; (*coll.*) **– *on the brakes,* – *the brakes on,*** mit voller Kraft bremsen. **2.** *v.i.* eingeklemmt sein, (sich ver)klemmen, sich festfressen, festsitzen, stocken, (*of a gun*) Ladehemmung haben. **3.** *s.* das Quetschen, Klemmen, Einzwängen; die Stockung, Stauung, das Gedränge; die Ladehemmung (*of a gun*); (*sl.*) Klemme; ***traffic* –,** die Verkehrsstockung.

Jamaica [dʒə'meikə], *s.* Jamaika (*n.*). **Jamaican, 1.** *s.* der (die) Jamaikaner(in), Jamaiker(in). **2.** *adj.* jamaikanisch, jamaikisch.

jamb [dʒæm], *s.* der (Tür)pfosten.

jamboree [dʒæmbə'riː], *s.* das Pfadfindertreffen; (*coll.*) der Heidenspaß.

James [dʒeimz], *s.* Jacob (*m.*).

jamming ['dʒæmiŋ], *s.* (*Tech.*) die (Ver)klemmung, Hemmung, Stockung; (*Rad.*) das Stören, die Störung; **– *station,*** der Störsender.

jammy ['dʒæmi], *adj.* (*sl.*) erstklassig; spielend leicht.

jangle [dʒæŋgl], **1.** *v.i.* mißtönend (er)klingen, schrillen, kreischen; klirren. **2.** *v.t.* mißtönend erklingen lassen; klirren mit (*keys etc.*). **3.** *s.* der Mißklang. **jangling, 1.** *adj.* mißtönend, schrill. **2.** *s. See* **jangle, 3.**

janissary ['dʒænisəri], *s. See* **janizary.**

janitor ['dʒænitə], *s.* der Pförtner.

janizary ['dʒænizəri], *s.* der Janitschar; (*fig.*) das Werkzeug der Tyrannei.

jankers ['dʒæŋkəz], *pl.* (*sing. constr.*) (*Mil. sl.*) der Lagerarrest.

January ['dʒænjuəri], *s.* der Januar.

Jap [dʒæp], **1.** *s.* (*pej.*) der Japs. **2.** *adj.* (*pej.*) japanisch.

Japan [dʒə'pæn], *s.* Japan (*n.*).

japan, 1. *s.* der Japanlack; lackierte Arbeit. **2.** *v.t.* schwarz lackieren.

Japanese [dʒæpə'niːz], **1.** *s.* der (die) Japaner(in); (*language*) das Japanisch(e). **2.** *adj.* japanisch.

japanned [dʒə'pænd], *adj.* schwarz lackiert. **japanning,** *s.* das Lackieren.

jape [dʒeip], **1.** *s.* der Spott; Spaß, Scherz. **2.** *v.i.* spotten (***at,*** über (*Acc.*)). **3.** *v.t.* foppen, zum Narren halten, zum besten haben.

[1]**jar** [dʒɑː], *s.* der Krug, Topf, die Kruke, Kanne; (*for jam*) das Glas; ***Leyden* –,** Leidener Flasche.

[2]**jar, 1.** *v.i.* knarren, kreischen, schnarren, rasseln; (*fig.*) in schreiendem Gegensatz stehen (***with,*** zu); **– *on his nerves,*** ihm auf die Nerven gehen; **– *(up)on the ear,*** das Ohr beleidigen *or* unangenehm berühren; **– *on his feelings,*** seine Gefühle verletzen, seinen Gefühlen weh tun; ***the colours* –,** die Farben beißen sich. **2.** *v.t.* erschüttern, rütteln. **3.** *s.* 1. das Knarren, Knirschen, Kreischen, der Mißton; 2. (*fig.*) (Wider)streit, die Mißhelligkeit; 3. der Stoß, Schlag, Schock.

jargon ['dʒɑːgən], *s.* das Kauderwelsch; die Berufssprache, Zunftsprache, Standessprache, der Jargon.

jargonelle [dʒɑːgə'nel], *s.* die Frühbirne.

jarring ['dʒɑːriŋ], **1.** *adj.* kreischend, knarrend; mißtönend; **– *note,*** der Mißton. **2.** *s. See* [2]**jar, 3.**

jasmine ['dʒæzmin], *s.* der Jasmin.

jasper ['dʒæspə], *s.* der Jaspis.

jaundice ['dʒɔːndis], *s.* 1. (*Med.*) die Gelbsucht; 2. (*fig.*) der Neid. **jaundiced,** *adj.* 1. gelbsüchtig; 2. (*fig.*) scheel(süchtig), neidisch, voreingenommen.

jaunt [dʒɔːnt], **1.** *v.i.* umherstreifen, lustwandeln. **2.** *s.* der Ausflug, die Wanderung, Vergnügungsfahrt, Spritztour. **jauntiness,** *s.* die Munterkeit, Lebhaftigkeit, Frische, flottes Wesen. **jaunting-car,** *s.* (*Irish*) zweirädriger Wagen. **jaunty,** *adj.* munter, lebhaft, flott; schmuck, elegant.

Java ['dʒɑːvə], *s.* Java (*n.*). **Javanese** [–'niːz], **1.** *s.* der (die) Javaner(in). **2.** *adj.* javanisch.

javelin ['dʒævlin], *s.* der Wurfspieß, (*Spt.*) Speer; ***throwing the* –,** das Speerwerfen.

jaw [dʒɔː], **1.** *s.* der Kiefer, Kinnbacken; (*usu. pl.*) das Maul; der Rachen, Schlund; (*sl.*) das Maul, die Fresse; (*coll.*) das Geschwätz, Getratsche, der Tratsch; (*Tech.*) die Backe, Klaue; ***–s of death,*** der Todesrachen; (*sl.*) ***hold your –!*** halt das Maul! **2.** *v.t.* (*coll.*) ausschimpfen, anranzen, anschnauzen, abkanzeln (*a p.*). **3.** *v.i.* schwatzen, tratschen.

jaw|bone, *s.* der Kinnbacken(knochen), Kieferknochen, die Kinnlade. **--breaker,** *s.* zungenbrecherisches Wort. **--coupling,** *s.* die Klauenkupplung.

jay [dʒei], *s.* (*Orn.*) der (Eichel)häher (*Garrulus glandarius*); (*fig.*) Schwätzer; (*sl.*) Tölpel. **jay|-walker,** *s.* verkehrswidriger *or* unvorsichtiger Fußgänger. **--walking,** *s.* verkehrswidrige Straßenüberquerung.

jazz [dʒæz], **1.** *s.* der Jazz, die Jazzmusik. **2.** *v.t.* (– *up*) (*sl.*) aufmöbeln, aufpulvern. **jazz-band,** *s.* die Jazzkapelle. **jazzy,** *adj.* (*fig.*) heraufgedonnert, herausgeputzt, auffallend, schreiend.

jealous ['dʒeləs], *adj.* 1. eifersüchtig, neidisch (*of,* auf (*Acc.*)); 2. argwöhnisch, mißtrauisch (*of,* gegen); 3. eifrig bedacht (*of,* auf (*Acc.*)), besorgt (*of, over,* um). **jealously,** *adv.* eifrig, sorgfältig. **jealousy,** *s.* die Eifersucht; der Neid (*of, towards,* auf (*Acc.*)); Argwohn, die Besorgnis; ***petty jealousies,*** Eifersüchteleien (*pl.*).

jean [dʒi:n], *s.* der Baumwollköper. **jeans,** *pl.* die Niethose, Jeans (*pl.*).

jeep [dʒi:p], *s.* (*Mil.*) der Geländewagen.

[1]**jeer** [dʒiə], *s.* (*usu. pl.*) (*Naut.*) die Falltakel.

[2]**jeer, 1.** *v.i.* sich lustig machen, spotten (*at,* über (*Acc.*)); – ***at,*** verhöhnen, verspotten, lächerlich machen. **2.** *s.* (*usu. pl.*) der Spott, Hohn, die Stichelei, Spötterei. **jeering, 1.** *adj.* höhnisch, spöttisch. **2.** *s.* die Verhöhnung, Verspottung; *see also* **jeer, 2.**

Jehovah [dʒə'houvə], *s.* (*B.*) Jehova (*m.*); ***–'s Witnesses,*** Bibelforscher (*pl.*), (eine) Bibelforschersekte.

Jehu ['dʒi:hju:], *s.* (*hum.*) der Schnellfahrer; Kutscher.

jejune [dʒi'dʒu:n], *adj.* unfruchtbar, mager (*of land*), (*fig.*) geistlos, nüchtern, trocken, fade. **jejuneness,** *s.* (*fig.*) die Nüchternheit, Trockenheit, Fadheit.

jellied ['dʒelid], *adj.* in Gelee; gallertartig. **jellify** [–ifai], *v.i.* *See* **jelly, 2. jelly, 1.** *s.* die Sülze, Gallerte, das Gelee, Gallert; (*coll.*) ***beat him into a –,*** ihn zu Mus hauen. **2.** *v.i.* gelieren, Gelee bilden; gerinnen, erstarren, sich verdicken. **3.** *v.t.* zum Gelieren bringen, erstarren lassen. **jelly|-fish,** *s.* die Qualle, Meduse. **--like,** *adj.* gallertartig. **--roll,** (*Am.*) *see* **Swiss roll.**

jemmy ['dʒemi], *s.* das Brecheisen.

jennet ['dʒenit], *s.* kleines spanisches Pferd.

jenny ['dʒeni], *s.* 1. das Weibchen (*of small animals*); 2. die Jennyspinnmaschine, der Jennywebstuhl; Laufkran. **jenny|-ass,** *s.* die Eselin. **--wren,** *s.* (weiblicher) Zaunkönig.

jeopardize ['dʒepədaiz], *v.t.* gefährden, aufs Spiel setzen, in Frage stellen. **jeopardy** [–i], *s.* die Gefahr, Gefährdung; (*Law*) ***double –,*** zwiefache Straffälligkeit; (*Law*) ***former –,*** früheres Strafverfahren in gleicher S.

jerboa [dʒə:'bouə], *s.* die Springmaus.

jeremiad [dʒerə'maiæd], *s.* das Klagelied, die Wehklage, Jeremiade.

[1]**jerk** [dʒə:k], **1.** *s.* 1. plötzlicher Stoß, der Ruck, Zug, Sprung, Satz, Schwung, Wurf, (*Med.*) Krampf, die Zuckung; ***with a –,*** plötzlich, mit einem Ruck; ***by –s,*** stoßweise, sprungweise, ruckweise; (*sl.*) ***put a – in it,*** tüchtig herangehen, energisch anpacken; (*coll.*) ***physical –s,*** Leibesübungen (*pl.*); 2. (*Am. sl.*) übler Kerl. **2.** *v.t.* ruckweise ziehen *or* reißen (an (*Dat.*)); rücken, stoßen; schleudern, schnellen. **3.** *v.i.* (zusammen)-zucken, auffahren.

[2]**jerk,** *v.t.* in Streifen schneiden und an der Sonne trocknen (*beef*).

jerkin ['dʒə:kin], *s.* (*Hist.*) das Wams; ***leather –,*** das Koller.

jerkiness ['dʒə:kinis], *s.* die Sprunghaftigkeit, Ruckartigkeit.

[1]**jerky** ['dʒə:ki], *adj.* sprungartig, ruckartig, stoßartig, sprunghaft, krampfhaft.

[2]**jerky,** *s.* (*Am.*) das Pökelfleisch, die Charaque.

jerry ['dʒeri], *s.* 1. (*sl.*) das Nachtgeschirr; 2. (*pej.*) der Deutsche. **jerry|-builder,** *s.* der Bauspekulant. **--building,** *s.* unsolide Bauart. **--built,** *adj.* unsolid gebaut; – ***house,*** die Bruchbude. **–can,** *s.* (*sl.*) der Benzinbehälter.

jersey ['dʒə:zi], *s.* die Strickjacke; – ***cloth,*** der Jersey, Trikotstoff; ***Jersey cow,*** das Jersey-Rind.

jess [dʒes], *s.* (*usu. pl.*) der Wurfriemen um den Fuß des Falken.

jessamine ['dʒesəmin], *s.* *See* **jasmine.**

jest [dʒest], **1.** *s.* der Scherz, Spaß, Witz; die Zielscheibe des Scherzes; ***in –,*** im Scherz *or* Spaß, scherzweise; ***make a –,*** scherzen (*of,* über (*Acc.*)). **2.** *v.i.* scherzen, spaßen, Witze machen, Scherz treiben. **jester,** *s.* der Spaßmacher, Spaßvogel, Witzbold; (*Hist.*) (Hof)narr, Hanswurst, Possenreißer; ***king's –,*** der Hofnarr. **jesting,** *s.* das Scherzen, Spaßen, der Scherz; ***no – matter,*** keine S. zum Spaßen. **jestingly,** *adv.* scherzweise.

Jesu ['dʒi:zju:], *s.* (*Poet.*) Jesus (*m.*).

Jesuit ['dʒezjuit], **1.** *s.* der Jesuit. **2.** *adj.* jesuitisch; (*fig.*) spitzfindig, schlau, listig, verschlagen. **Jesuitical** [–'itikl], *adj.* *See* **Jesuit, 2.**

Jesus ['dʒi:zəs], *s.* Jesus (*m.*); – ***Christ,*** Jesus Christus.

[1]**jet** [dʒet], **1.** *v.i.* ausspritzen, ausströmen, hervorsprudeln. **2.** *v.t.* auswerfen, ausspeien. **3.** *s.* 1. (*of liquid*) der Strahl, Strom; (*of gas*) die Stichflamme; ***– of flame,*** der Feuerstrahl; ***– of water,*** der Wasserstrahl; 2. (*Tech.*) die Röhre, Düse, das Strahlrohr; (*coll.*) *see* ***– plane***; (*Av.*) ***– engine,*** der Düsenmotor, das Strahltriebwerk; – ***liner,*** das Düsenverkehrsflugzeug; ***– plane,*** das Düsenflugzeug; ***--propelled,*** Düsen–, Strahl(trieb)–, mit Strahlantrieb *or* Düsenantrieb; – ***propulsion,*** der Düsenantrieb, Strahlantrieb, Rückstoßantrieb.

[2]**jet,** *s.* der Gagat, Jett, die Pechkohle; ***–(-black),*** pechschwarz, kohlschwarz, (kohl)rabenschwarz.

jetsam ['dʒetsəm], *s.* (*Naut.*) das Seewurfgut; (*fig.*) unnützes Zeug; ***flotsam and –,*** treibendes Wrack– und Strandgut; (*fig.*) die niederen Elemente des Lebens.

jet-stream, *s.* (*Meteor.*) die Strahlströmung.

jettison ['dʒetisn], *v.t.* über Bord werfen (*cargo*); im Notwurf abwerfen (*bombs*); (*fig.*) abwerfen, wegschlagen, sich entledigen (*Gen.*).

jetty ['dʒeti], *s.* der Hafendamm, die Mole, der Landungssteg, Pier, die Landungsbrücke, Anlegebrücke.

Jew [dʒu:], *s.* der Jude (die Jüdin); ***--baiting,*** die Judenhetze, Judenverfolgung; ***–'s harp,*** die Maultrommel; ***the Wandering –,*** der Ewige Jude.

jewel ['dʒuəl], *s.* das Juwel, der Edelstein; (*in a watch*) Stein; (*fig.*) das Kleinod, die Perle, der Schatz. **jewel(l)er,** *s.* der Juwelier. **jewel(le)ry,** *s.* der Schmuck, das Geschmeide; Juwelen (*pl.*), Edelsteine (*pl.*), Schmucksachen (*pl.*).

Jewess ['dʒu:es], *s.* die Jüdin. **Jewish** [–iʃ], *adj.* jüdisch, Juden–. **Jewry** [–ri], *s.* das Judentum, die Judenschaft; (*Hist.*) das Judenviertel.

[1]**jib** [dʒib], *s.* (*Naut.*) der Klüver; ***flying –,*** der Außenklüver; (*coll.*) ***the cut of his –,*** sein Aussehen, seine äußere Erscheinung.

[2]**jib,** *s.* der Ausleger, Kranbalken (*of crane*).

[3]**jib,** *v.i.* scheuen (*at,* vor (*Dat.*)) (*also fig.*), bocken, störrisch sein (*of horses*); (*fig.*) stehenbleiben, innehalten (*at,* vor (*Dat.*)), sich widersetzen, widerstreben (*Dat.*). **jibber,** *s.* bockiges Pferd.

jib-door, *s.* die Tapetentür.

jibe, *see* **gibe.**

jiff(y) ['dʒif(i)], *s.* (*coll.*) der Augenblick; (*coll.*) ***in a –,*** im Nu.

[1]**jig** [dʒig], **1.** *s.* (*Mus.*) die Gigue. **2.** *v.i.* eine Gigue tanzen; (*coll.*) hopsen, hüpfen.

[2]**jig, 1.** *s.* (*Tech.*) die Einstellvorrichtung, Spannvorrichtung, Schablone, das Montagegestell; (*Min.*) der Setzkasten, die (Sieb)setzmaschine, das Setzsieb. **2.** *v.t.* (*Min.*) waschen, scheiden, setzen (*ore*).

jigger ['dʒigə], *s.* (*Naut.*) 1. die Handtalje; 2. das Hecksegel; 3. (*Min.*) *see* [2]**jig** (*Min.*); der Erzscheider, Siebsetzer; 4. (*Angling*) Torpedospinner; 5. (*coll.*) das Ding(sda).

jiggered ['dʒigəd], *adj.* (*coll.*) ***I'm –! I'll be –!*** hol' mich der Teufel!

jiggery-pokery ['dʒigəri'poukəri], *s.* (*coll.*) der Humbug, Schwindel, Hokuspokus.

jigsaw ['dʒigsɔ:], *s.* 1. die Laubsäge, Spaltsäge; 2. (*also* – ***puzzle***) das Zusammensetzspiel, Puzzelspiel, Mosaikspiel.

jiggle [dʒigl], *v.t.* (*coll.*) rütteln, wackeln.

jilt [dʒilt], **1.** *s.* die Kokette. **2.** *v.t.* sitzenlassen (*of the man*), den Laufpaß geben (*Dat.*) (*of the girl*).

jiminy! ['dʒimini], *int.* (*obs.*) ***by –!*** bei Gott!

jimjams ['dʒimdʒæmz], *pl.* (*sl.*) das Delerium, der Säuferwahnsinn; Schauder, das Gruseln.

jimmy ['dʒimi], (*Am.*) *see* **jemmy.**

jimp [dʒimp], *adj.* (*Scots*) schlank, zierlich; spärlich, knapp.

jingle [dʒiŋgl], **1.** *v.i.* klingeln (*bells*), klimpern (*coins*), klirren (*keys*), rasseln (*chain*); (*fig.*) gleichlauten, staben (*as rhymes*). **2.** *v.t.* klingeln *or* klimpern *etc.* lassen. **3.** *s.* 1. das Geklingel, Gebimmel (*bells*), Geklirr, die Klimperei, das Gerassel; (*fig.*) Reimgeklingel, Wortgeklingel; 2. (*T.V. etc.*) Werbelied.

jingo ['dʒiŋgou], **1.** *s.* der Hurrapatriot, Säbelraßler, Chauvinist. **2.** *int.* ***by –!*** alle Wetter! **jingoism,** *s.* der Hurrapatriotismus, Chauvinismus. **jingoistic** [–'istik], *adj.* chauvinistisch.

jink [dʒiŋk], **1.** *v.t.* (*coll.*) ausweichen (*Dat.*). **2.** *v.i.* (*coll.*) entweichen.

jinks [dʒiŋks], *pl.* ***high –,*** übermütige Laune, ausgelassene Lustigkeit.

jinx [dʒiŋks], *s.* (*sl.*) der Unglücksrabe, Pechvogel; ***put a – on,*** verhexen.

jitterbug ['dʒitəbʌg], **1.** *s.* der (die) Swingtänzer(in). **2.** *v.i.* Swing tanzen.

jitters ['dʒitəz], *pl.* (*sl.*) die Angst. **jittery,** *adj.* (*sl.*) ängstlich, nervös.

jiu-jitsu, *see* **ju-jitsu.**

jive [dʒaiv], **1.** *s.* die Swingmusik. **2.** *v.i.* Swingmusik spielen; Swing tanzen.

Joan [dʒoun], *s.* Johanna (*f.*); – ***of Arc,*** die Jungfrau von Orleans; ***Pope –,*** die Päpstin Johanna.

Job [dʒoub], *s.* (*B.*) Hiob (*m.*); ***the Book of –,*** das Buch Hiob; ***the patience of –,*** die Engelsgeduld; ***–'s comforter,*** der Hiobströster, schlechter Tröster.

¹job [dʒɔb], **1.** *s.* ein Stück Arbeit, die Stückarbeit, Akkordarbeit; (*coll.*) Beschäftigung, Stellung, Stelle, der Beruf, Posten; das Geschäft, der Auftrag, die Aufgabe; (*printing*) Akzidenz(arbeit); (*coll.*) das Profitgeschäft, der Kuhhandel, die Schiebung; (*sl.*) krumme S., schräges Ding (*of criminals*); (*coll.*) ***that was a –!*** das war ein schweres Stück Arbeit! ***know one's –,*** seine S. *or* sein Handwerk verstehen; ***what a –!*** das ist ja rein zum Verzweifeln! ***a bad –,*** eine schlimme S.; ***make the best of a bad –,*** retten was zu retten ist; ***make a good – of it,*** es ordentlich machen; (*coll.*) ***it is a good –,*** es ist ein wahres Glück; ***a good – of work,*** eine gute Leistung; (*coll.*) ***and a good – too,*** und recht so; ***odd –s,*** Gelegenheitsarbeiten (*pl.*); (*coll.*) ***put-up –,*** abgekartete S.; (*coll.*) ***soft –,*** angenehme Arbeit; ***by the –,*** nach Leistung *or* Stückzahl, auf *or* im *or* in Akkord; (*coll.*) ***on the –,*** auf dem Posten; ***out of a –,*** arbeitslos, stellungslos. **2.** *v.i.* in Akkord arbeiten; Makler sein, wuchern, schachern, spekulieren. **3.** *v.t.* (– ***out***) vermieten, ausmieten (*horses*), in Akkord vergeben, (weiter)-vergeben (*work*), durch Schiebung befördern (*a p.*).

²job, 1. *v.t., v.i.* stechen, stoßen (***at,*** nach). **2.** *s.* der Stoß, Stich, Schlag.

jobation [dʒo'beiʃən], *s.* die Strafpredigt, Standpauke.

jobber ['dʒɔbə], *s.* der Effektenhändler, Zwischenhändler, Börsenspekulant; Schieber; Akkordarbeiter, Gelegenheitsarbeiter. **jobbery,** *s.* die Schiebung, Veruntreuung, Unterschlagung; Mißwirtschaft, Korruption, der Amtsmißbrauch.

jobbing, *s.* die Akkordarbeit; der Effektenhandel, das Maklergeschäft, die Börsenspekulation; Schiebung; – ***cobbler,*** der Flickschuster; – ***printer,*** der Akzidenzdrucker; – ***work,*** die Akkordarbeit; (*Typ.*) Akzidenzarbeit.

job|-horse, *s.* das Mietpferd. **– lot,** *s.* der Gelegenheitsankauf; ***sell as a –,*** im Ramsch verkaufen. **–-master,** *s.* der Pferdevermieter, Mietwagenbesitzer. **–-printer,** *s.* der Akzidenzdrucker. **– work,** *s.* die Akkordarbeit; (*Typ.*) der Akzidenzdruck.

Jock [dʒɔk], *s.* (*coll.*) der Schotte; schottischer Soldat.

jockey ['dʒɔki], **1.** *s.* der Jockei. **2.** *v.t.* betrügen, prellen (***out of,*** um); verleiten, hineintreiben (***into,*** zu).

jockstrap ['dʒɔkstræp], *s.* das Suspensorium.

jocose [dʒou'kous], *adj.* spaßhaft, scherzhaft, heiter, lustig, drollig. **jocoseness,** *s.* die Scherzhaftigkeit, Spaßhaftigkeit, Lustigkeit.

jocular ['dʒɔkjulə], *adj.* lustig, heiter, scherzend, spaßig. **jocularity** [–'læriti], *s.* die Lustigkeit, Heiterkeit, der Humor. **jocund** [–kənd], *adj.* fröhlich, munter, lustig. **jocundity** [–'kʌnditi], *s.* die Lustigkeit, Fröhlichkeit, Munterkeit.

jodhpurs ['dʒɔdpəz], *pl.* die Reithose.

jog [dʒɔg], **1.** *v.t.* (auf)rütteln, schütteln; (an)stoßen, schubsen; – ***his memory,*** seinem Gedächtnis nachhelfen, sein Gedächtnis auffrischen. **2.** *v.i.* – ***along*** or ***on,*** dahinschlendern, dahintrotten, weitertraben, (*fig.*) gemütlich fortfahren, weiterkommen, fortwursteln; ***things – along as usual,*** die Dinge nehmen ihren Lauf. **3.** *s.* der Stoß, das Stoßen.

joggle [dʒɔgl], **1.** *v.t.* 1. leicht schütteln *or* rütteln; 2. (*Carp.*) federn und nuten, (*Tech.*) verzahnen, kröpfen, verschränken, zusammenfügen, (*Min.*) verzehren. **2.** *v.i.* sich schütteln, wackeln. **3.** *s.* (*Carp.*) die Verbindung auf Nut und Feder, (*Tech.*) Verzahnung.

jog-trot, 1. *s.* leichter Trab *or* Trott; (*fig.*) der Schlendrian, Alltagstrott. **2.** *adj.* (behaglich) schlendernd; (*fig.*) alltäglich, eintönig.

John [dʒɔn], *s.* Johann(es) (*m.*); – ***the Baptist,*** Johannes der Täufer; – ***Bull,*** der Stockengländer; ***feast of St. –,*** das Johannisfest; ***Knight of St. –,*** der Johanniter(ritter).

johnny ['dʒɔni], *s.* (*coll.*) der Kerl, Bursche.

join [dʒɔin], **1.** *v.t.* verbinden (*also Geom.*), vereinigen, zusammenfügen (***to,*** mit), sich vereinigen *or* verbinden mit, stoßen zu; (*of a p.*) sich anschließen an (*Acc.*), sich gesellen zu, eintreten in (*Acc.*), beitreten (*Dat.*); angrenzen an (*Acc.*) (*territory*), münden in (*Acc.*) (*tributary*); – ***the army,*** ins Heer eintreten; Soldat werden; – ***battle,*** den Kampf aufnehmen, die Schlacht beginnen; – ***company with,*** sich anschließen (*Dat.*); – ***forces,*** sich zusammenschließen; – ***hands,*** sich (*Dat.*) die Hand *or* Hände reichen; (*fig.*) zusammengehen, gemeinsam S. machen (***with,*** mit); – ***issue with,*** sich auf einen Streit einlassen mit, nicht übereinstimmen mit; – ***the majority,*** sich der Mehrheit anschließen; – ***in marriage,*** verheiraten, vermählen (***with,*** mit); – ***one's regiment,*** zu seinem Regiment stoßen; – ***a ship,*** sich einschiffen *or* an Bord begeben. **2.** *v.i.* (*persons, things*) zusammenkommen, sich verbinden, sich vereinigen; (*things only*) anstoßen, sich berühren, aneinandergrenzen; – ***in,*** teilhaben *or* teilnehmen an (*Dat.*), sich beteiligen an (*Dat.*); mitmachen; – ***in his praise,*** in seinem Lob einstimmen; (*coll.*) – ***up,*** Soldat werden; ***I – with you in thinking,*** ich stimme mit Ihnen überein, ich teile Ihre Ansicht (***that,*** daß). **3.** *s.* die Verbindung(sstelle), Verbindungslinie, Fuge, Naht.

joinder ['dʒɔində], *s.* (*Law*) die Vereinigung.

joiner ['dʒɔinə], *s.* der Tischler, Schreiner; ***–'s bench,*** die Hobelbank. **joinery,** *s.* das Tischlerhandwerk, die Tischlerarbeit.

joint [dʒɔint], **1.** *s.* 1. (*Carp.*) die Verbindung, Fuge; Verbindungsart, der Verband, (*Anat., Tech.*) das

Gelenk, (*Bot.*) der Gelenkknoten, das Blattgelenk; ***ball and socket –***, das Kugelgelenk; (*Carp.*) ***dowel –***, der Holzdübel; (*Carp.*) ***halved –***, das Blatt; ***mitre –***, die Gehrung; ***out of –***, ausgerenkt, verrenkt; (*fig.*) aus den Fugen; ***put one's arm out of –***, sich (*Dat.*) den Arm verrenken; (*fig.*) ***put his nose out of –***, ihn aus der Fassung bringen; ihn ausstechen; ***riveted –***, die Nietung; ***soldered –***, die Lötnaht; ***universal –***, das Kardangelenk; 2. das Fleischstück, der Braten, die Keule (*of meat*); ***cold –***, kalter Braten; 3. (*Geol.*) der Riß, die Kluft, (Quer)spalte; 4. (*sl.*) Bude, der Laden; das Lokal, die Kneipe, Spelunke; 5. (*sl. drugs*) der Joint. **2.** *v.t.* verbinden, zusammenfügen; (*Carp.*) verzapfen. **3.** *attrib. adj.* vereint, verbunden, (*esp. Law*) gemeinschaftlich, gemeinsam, Mit–; (*Law*) ***– and several,*** gesamtschuldnerisch; ***– and several obligation,*** die Gesamtverbindlichkeit, Gesamtverpflichtung; ***– account,*** gemeinschaftliches Konto, das Metakonto, Gemeinschaftskonto, Konsortialkonto; ***– action,*** gemeinsames Vorgehen; ***– authorship,*** gemeinsame Verfasserschaft; (*Univ.*) ***Joint Board,*** vereinigter (Prüfungs)-ausschuß; ***– business*** or ***concern,*** das Partizipationsgeschäft; ***– capital,*** das Gesellschaftskapital, Gesamtkapital; ***– heir,*** der Miterbe; ***during their – lives,*** solange sie beide (*or* alle) am Leben sind; ***– ownership,*** das Miteigentum; ***– plaintiff,*** der Mitkläger; ***– proprietor,*** der Teilhaber; ***– stock,*** das Aktienkapital; ***–-stock company,*** die Aktiengesellschaft; ***– tenancy,*** der Mitbesitz, die Mitpacht; ***– tenant,*** der Mitpächter.

jointed ['dʒɔintid], *adj.* gegliedert, (*Bot.*) knotig gegliedert; ***– doll,*** die Gliederpuppe. **jointer,** *s.* (*Carp.*) der Schlichthobel, (*Build.*) das Fugeisen. **jointing,** *s.* das Verbinden, Zusammenfügen. **jointly,** *adv.* gemeinschaftlich; ***– and severally,*** gesamtschuldnerisch, (*coll.*) samt und sonders. **jointure** [–tʃə], **1.** *s.* das Leibgedinge, Wittum. **2.** *v.t.* ein Wittum aussetzen. (*Dat*).

joist [dʒɔist], **1.** *s.* der (Quer)balken, Streckbalken, (Quer)träger. **2.** *v.t.* mit Balken belegen.

joke [dʒouk], **1.** *s.* der Witz; Scherz, Spaß; ***crack a –***, einen Witz reißen; ***play a practical – on him,*** ihm einen Streich spielen; ***see*** or ***take a –***, einen Spaß verstehen; (*coll.*) ***it's no –***, es ist keine Kleinigkeit. **2.** *v.i.* scherzen, spaßen; Witze machen. **3.** *v.t.* necken, hänseln (*about,* wegen), sich lustig machen über (*Acc.*). **joker,** *s.* der Spaßmacher, Spaßvogel, Witzbold; (*Cards*) Joker. **joking, 1.** *s.* das Scherzen, Spaßen; ***– apart!*** Scherz beiseite! **2.** *adj.* scherzhaft, spaßhaft.

jollier ['dʒɔliə], *comp. adj.*, **jolliest,** *sup. adj. See* **jolly.**

jollification [dʒɔlifi'keiʃən], *s.* die Lustbarkeit, fröhliches Fest. **jolliness, jollity,** *s.* die Lustigkeit, Fröhlichkeit, Munterkeit. **jolly, 1.** *adj.* lustig, fröhlich, munter, vergnügt, fidel; (*coll.*) beschwipst, angeheitert; (*sl.*) (*usu. iron.*) famos, herrlich, schön. **2.** *adv.* (*coll.*) sehr; ***– good, – well,*** großartig, famos; ***you'll – well have to,*** du mußt wohl oder übel, du kannst gar nicht anders. **3.** *v.t.* (*usu.* ***– along***) schmeicheln (*Dat.*), schöntun (*Dat.*), um den Bart gehen (*Dat.*); hänseln, aufziehen. **4.** *s.* (*sl.*) der Marinesoldat.

jolly-boat, *s.* (*Naut.*) die Jolle. **Jolly-Roger,** *s.* die Piratenflagge.

jolt [dʒoult], **1.** *v.t.* stoßen, (auf)rütteln. **2.** *v.i.* rütteln, schütteln (*esp. of vehicle*). **3.** *s.* der Stoß, Ruck. **jolting,** *s.* das Rütteln, Schütteln, Gerüttel. **jolty,** *adj.* (*coll.*) holperig (*road etc.*), ruckartig (*movement*).

Jonah ['dʒounə], *s.* (*B.*) Jonas (*m.*); (*fig.*) der Unglücksrabe.

jonquil ['dʒɔŋkwil], *s.* die Jonquille.

Jordan [dʒɔ:dn], *s.* (*river*) Jordan (*m.*); (*country*) Jordanien (*n.*). **Jordanian** [–'deiniən], **1.** *adj.* jordanisch. **2.** *s.* der (die) Jordanier(in).

jorum ['dʒɔ:rəm], *s.* der Trinkkrug, Humpen.

Joshua ['dʒɔʃjuə], *s.* (*B.*) Josua (*m.*).

joss [dʒɔs], *s.* chinesischer Götze.

josser ['dʒɔsə], *s.* (*sl.*) der Kerl, Bursche.

joss|-house, *s.* (*coll.*) chinesischer Tempel. **–-stick,** *s.* der Räucherstock, Räucherstab.

jostle [dʒɔsl], **1.** *v.t.* anrennen, anrempeln, stoßen gegen *or* an (*Acc.*). **2.** *v.i.* rempeln, stoßen (*against,* gegen), zusammenstoßen, sich dränge(l)n (*with,* mit).

jot [dʒɔt], **1.** *s.* das Jota, bißchen, der Deut. **2.** *v.t.* (*usu.* ***– down***) aufnotieren, flüchtig hinwerfen *or* niederschreiben, kurz vermerken. **jotter,** *s.* das Notizbuch, Schreibheft, die Kladde. **jotting,** *s.* kurze Notiz, der Vermerk.

journal [dʒə:nl], *s.* 1. das Tagebuch, Journal; die Zeitschrift, Zeitung, das Tageblatt; (*Naut.*) Logbuch; 2. (*Tech.*) der Wellenzapfen. **journalese** [–'li:z], *s.* der Zeitungsstil. **journalism,** *s.* der Journalismus, das Zeitungswesen. **journalist,** *s.* der (die) Zeitungsschriftsteller(in), Journalist(in). **journalistic** [–'listik], *adj.* journalistisch, Zeitungs–.

journey ['dʒə:ni], **1.** *s.* die Reise; ***day's –***, die Tagereise; ***two days' –***, zweitägige Reise; ***ten mile –***, eine Reise von 10 Meilen; ***double –***, die Hin- und Rückreise; ***return –***, die Rückreise; ***go on*** or ***undertake a –***, verreisen, eine Reise machen *or* unternehmen. **2.** *v.i.* reisen.

journeyman ['dʒə:nimən], *s.* der (Handwerks)-geselle; ***– baker,*** der Bäckergeselle.

joust [dʒaust], **1.** *s.* das Turnier. **2.** *v.i.* tournieren. **jousting,** *s.* das Turnier(spiel).

Jove [dʒouv], *s.* Jupiter, Zeus (*m.*); ***by –!*** Donnerwetter!

jovial ['dʒouviəl], *adj.* lustig, heiter, munter, vergnügt, aufgeräumt. **joviality** [–'æliti], *s.* die Lustigkeit, Heiterkeit, Munterkeit, der Frohsinn.

jowl [dʒaul], *s.* die Wange, Backe; das Unterkinn, der Unterkiefer; (*Zool.*) die Wamme, (*Orn.*) der Kehllappen, (*Ichth.*) die Kopfpartie; (*coll.*) ***cheek by –***, dicht beieinander, Seite an Seite.

joy [dʒɔi], **1.** *s.* die Freude (*at,* über (*Acc.*); *in, of,* an (*Dat.*)); Fröhlichkeit, das Vergnügen, Entzücken; ***tears of –***, Freudentränen; ***it gives me great –***, es macht *or* bereitet mir große Freude; ***dance*** or ***jump*** or ***leap for –***, vor Freude hüpfen; ***wish him – of,*** ihm gratulieren *or* Glück wünschen zu. **2.** *v.i.* (*Poet.*) sich freuen, entzückt sein (*in,* über (*Acc.*)). **joyful,** *adj.* froh, freudig, erfreulich (*as news*), froh, freudig, erfreut (*as a p.*); ***be –***, sich freuen. **joyfulness,** *s.* die Fröhlichkeit, Freudigkeit. **joyless,** *adj.* freudlos (*of a p.*), unerfreulich (*of a th.*). **joylessness,** *s.* die Freudlosigkeit. **joyous,** *adj. See* **joyful. joyousness,** *s. See* **joyfulness. joy|-ride,** *s.* die Lustfahrt; Schwarzfahrt. **–-stick,** *s.* (*Av.*) der (Steuer)knüppel.

jubilance, jubilancy ['dʒu:biləns(i)], *s. See* **jubilation. jubilant,** *adj.* jubelnd, frohlockend. **jubilate, 1.** [–leit], *v.i.* jubeln, jauchzen, frohlocken. **2.** [–'lɑ:ti], *s.* der 3. Sonntag nach Ostern; 100. Psalm, Jubilate. **jubilation** [–'leiʃən], *s.* das Jauchzen, Entzücken, Frohlocken, der Jubel.

jubilee ['dʒu:bili:], *s.* 50jähriges Jubiläum; (*R.C.*) das Jubeljahr, Ablaßjahr; die Jubelfeier, das Jubelfest, der Jubel; ***silver –***, 25jähriges Jubiläum; ***diamond –***, 60jähriges Jubiläum.

Judah ['dʒu:də], *s.* (*B.*) Judä(a) (*m.*). **Judaic(al)** [–'deiik(l)], *adj.* jüdisch. **Judaism** [–deiizm], *s.* das Judentum, jüdische Religion. **Judean** [–'diən], **1.** *s.* der Judäer. **2.** *adj.* judäisch.

judge [dʒʌdʒ], **1.** *s.* der Richter (*also B. and fig.*) (*of,* über (*Acc.*)); (*Spt.*) Schiedsrichter; Kenner, Sachverständige(r); (*B.*) ***Book of Judges,*** das Buch der Richter; ***be a – of,*** sich verstehen auf (*Acc.*); ***– of wine,*** der Weinkenner; ***I am no – of these things,*** darüber kann ich nicht beurteilen *or* habe ich kein Urteil; ***as God is my –!*** so wahr mir Gott helfe! ***sober as a –***, vollkommen nüchtern; ***Judge Advocate,*** der Kriegsgerichtsrat; ***Judge Advocate General,*** der Chef des Heeresjustizwesens. **2.** *v.i.* urteilen, sich (*Dat.*) ein Urteil bilden (*by, from,* nach; *of,* über (*Acc.*)), schließen, folgern (*by, from,* aus). **3.** *v.t.* (*Law*) ein Urteil fällen *or* Recht sprechen über (*Acc.*), entscheiden; beurteilen, einschätzen (*by*, nach); schließen (*from*, aus); halten (*to be*, für), betrachten (*to be*, als).

judg(e)ment ['dʒʌdʒmənt], *s.* 1. (*Law*) das Urteil, der Urteilsspruch, gerichtliche Entscheidung; – ***by default***, das Versäumnisurteil; ***error of*** –, das Fehlurteil; ***give*** –, entscheiden, ein Urteil sprechen; ***pass*** or ***pronounce*** –, ein Urteil fällen, urteilen (*on*, über (*Acc.*)); ***sit in*** –, zu Gericht sitzen ((***up***)***on***, über (*Acc.*)); 2. (*fig.*) die Urteilskraft, Einsicht, der Verstand, das Verständnis; Urteil, die Beurteilung, Meinung, Ansicht; Urteilsbildung; ***act with*** –, mit Verständnis handeln; ***in my*** –, meines Erachtens, nach meiner Ansicht; ***man of*** (***sound***) –, urteilsfähiger *or* einsichtsvoller Mann; ***use one's*** –, nach bestem Ermessen handeln; 3. das Strafgericht, göttliches Gericht; ***day of*** – or ***the last*** –, das Jüngste Gericht. **judg(e)ment| day,** *s.* (*Eccl.*) Jüngster Tag. **--seat,** *s.* der Richterstuhl.

judicature ['dʒu:dikətʃə], *s.* der Gerichtshof, (*collect.*) Richter (*pl.*); die Rechtspflege, Rechtsprechung, Justizgewalt, richterliche Gewalt; das Richteramt; ***the Supreme Court of Judicature***, das Oberlandesgericht.

judicial [dʒu:'diʃəl], *adj.* gerichtlich, richterlich, Gerichts–, Richter–, (*fig.*) kritisch; – ***error***, der Justizirrtum; – ***murder***, der Justizmord; – ***procedure***, das Gerichtsverfahren; – ***proceedings***, Gerichtsverhandlungen; – ***sale***, gerichtliche Veräußerung; – ***separation***, die Trennung von Tisch und Bett; – ***system***, das Gerichtswesen. **judiciary,** 1. *s.* das Gerichtssystem, Gerichtswesen; die Justizgewalt, richterliche Gewalt; (*collect.*) die Richterschaft, Richter (*pl.*). 2. *adj.* richterlich, gerichtlich.

judicious [dʒu:'diʃəs], *adj.* verständnisvoll, verständig, vernünftig, klug, weise, einsichtsvoll, wohlüberlegt, sinnvoll, zweckentsprechend. **judiciousness,** *s.* die Vernünftigkeit, Klugheit, Einsicht.

jug [dʒʌg], 1. *s.* 1. der Krug, die Kanne; 2. (*sl.*) das Loch, Kittchen. 2. *v.t.* 1. (*Cul.*) schmoren, dämpfen; ***jugged hare***, der Hasenpfeffer; 2. (*sl.*) einlochen, ins Kittchen stecken. **jugful,** *s.* der Krugvoll.

juggernaut ['dʒʌgənɔ:t], *s.* der Moloch, blutrünstiger Götze, (*fig.*) unwiderstehliche Gewalt; (*Motor. coll.*) der Fernlaster.

juggins ['dʒʌginz], *s.* (*sl.*) der Tröttel, Tropf.

juggle [dʒʌgl], 1. *v.i.* gaukeln, Kunststücke machen, jonglieren; (*fig.*) falsches Spiel treiben, täuschen, irreführen; – ***with facts***, Tatsachen verfälschen; – ***with words***, Worte manipulieren, mit Worten spielen. 2. *v.t.* jonglieren mit, Kunststücke machen mit; (*fig.*) frisieren (*accounts etc.*), betrügen (***out of***, um). 3. *s.* die Taschenspielerei, Gaukelei, das Kunststück; der Schwindel, Hokuspokus. **juggler,** *s.* der Jongleur, Taschenspieler, Zauberkünstler; Gaukler, Betrüger. **jugglery, juggling,** *s.* das Jonglieren; die Gaukelei, Taschenspielerei.

Jugoslav *etc., see* **Yugoslav** *etc.*

jugular ['dʒʌgjələ], *adj.* Kehl–, Gurgel–; – ***vein***, die Halsader, Drosselader. **jugulate** [–leit], *v.t.* (*fig.*) erdrosseln, abwürgen, unterdrücken.

juice [dʒu:s], *s.* der Saft; (*fig.*) Gehalt, Inhalt, das Wesen(tliche); (*sl.*) (*Motor.*) der Sprit, (*Elec.*) Strom; (*sl.*) ***stew in one's own*** –, im eigenen Fett schmoren. **juiciness** [–sinis], *s.* die Saftigkeit; (*fig., coll.*) Würzigkeit. **juicy,** *adj.* saftig; (*fig., coll.*) würzig, spannend.

ju-jitsu [dʒu:'dʒitsu:], *s.* das Jiu-Jitsu.

ju-ju ['dʒu:dʒu:], *s.* das Tabu, der Fetisch, Zauber.

jujube ['dʒu:dʒu:b], *s.* (*Bot.*) die Brustbeere; (*Med.*) Brustbeerentablette.

juke-box ['dʒu:k-], *s.* der Musikautomat.

julep ['dʒu:lep], *s.* (*Am.*) der Julep, Julap, das Kühlgetränk.

Julian ['dʒu:liən], *adj.* julianisch.

July [dʒu'lai], *s.* der Juli.

jumble [dʒʌmbl], 1. *v.t.* (*also* – ***up*** or ***together***) zusammenwerfen, durcheinanderwerfen, durcheinanderbringen, in Unordnung bringen; ***be*** or ***get –d up***, durcheinanderkommen, durcheinandergeraten, durcheinandergebracht sein *or* werden, in Unordnung sein *or* kommen *or* geraten. 2. *s.* 1. das Durcheinander, die Unordnung, Verwirrung, der Wirrwarr, Mischmasch; 2. (*coll.*) Ramsch, Trödel, altes Zeug, Ramschwaren (*pl.*); – ***sale***, der Ramschverkauf.

jumbo ['dʒʌmbou], 1. *s.* (*coll.*) *see* **elephant**; (*coll. fig.*) der Riese. 2. *attrib. adj.* Riesen–.

jump [dʒʌmp], 1. *s.* der Sprung, Satz; (*Spt.*) die Sprunghöhe, Sprungweite; (*Spt.*) das Hindernis; (*Av.*) der (Fallschirm)absprung; (*of a th.*) das Emporschnellen, (*of a p.*) Auffahren, Zusammenfahren, (*also pl.*) nervöses Zucken; (*Spt.*) ***broad*** or ***long*** –, der Weitsprung; (*Spt.*) ***high*** –, der Hochsprung; (*sl.*) ***be for the high*** –, es ausbaden *or* auslöffeln müssen; ***give a*** –, (*of a p.*) auffahren; – ***in price***, die Preissteigerung; ***make*** or ***take a*** –, einen Sprung machen; ***running*** –, der Sprung mit Anlauf; (*Spt.*) ***take the*** –, das Hindernis nehmen. 2. *v.t.* (hinweg)springen über (*Acc.*), überspringen (*an obstacle*); (*fig., coll.*) auslassen, überspringen; (*Cul.*) schwenken; (*sl.*) – ***bail***, ausreißen und die Kaution verfallen lassen; (*Min.*) – ***a claim***, einen fremden Schurf widerrechtlich in Besitz nehmen; – ***the gun***, (*Spt.*) zu früh starten; (*fig., coll.*) vorgreifen; – ***the queue***, sich vordränge(l)n; – ***the rails***, entgleisen; (*sl.*) – ***the train***, auf den Zug aufspringen. 3. *v.i.* springen; hüpfen; (*fig.*) (plötzlich) (an)steigen (*as prices*), (*of a p.*) auffahren, in die Höhe fahren; – ***for joy***, vor Freude hüpfen; (*coll.*) ***see which way the cat –s***, sehen wie der Hase läuft; ***my heart –ed into my mouth***, ich bekam Herzklopfen; **(a)** (*with advs.*) – ***about***, herumhüpfen, umherhüpfen; – ***clear of***, wegspringen von; – ***down***, abspringen, herunterspringen; – ***in***, einspringen; – ***off***, abspringen; – ***up***, aufspringen; **(b)** (*with preps.*) (*fig.*) – ***at***, mit beiden Händen greifen nach, sich stürzen auf (*Acc.*); – ***at the idea***, den Gedanken (mit Begeisterung) aufgreifen; – ***at*** or ***to conclusions***, voreilige Schlüsse ziehen; (*coll.*) – ***down his throat***, ihm über den Mund fahren, ihn anfahren *or* anschnauzen; – ***from one th. to another***, Gedankensprünge machen; (*fig.*) – ***on***, stürzen auf (*Acc.*); (*coll.*) – ***on the bandwagon***, mitlaufen; (*coll.*) – ***on him***, ihm auf die Bude rücken *or* aufs Dach steigen; – ***on a horse***, (auf ein Pferd) aufsitzen; (*coll.*) – ***on the idea***, an der Idee kein gutes Haar lassen, über die Idee den Stab brechen; – ***out of one's skin***, aus der Haut fahren; – ***over***, (hinweg)springen über (*Acc.*).

jumper ['dʒʌmpə], *s.* 1. der Springer; (*Tech.*) Steinbohrer, Stoßbohrer; (*Elec.*) Schaltdraht; (*Ent.*) die Käsemade; (*garment*) der Schlüpfer, Pullover, Pulli, die Strickjacke.

jumpiness ['dʒʌmpinis], *s.* (*coll.*) die Nervosität. **jumping,** *s.* das Springen; Hüpfen; ***--bean***, springende Bohne; ***--board***, das Sprungbrett; ***--jack***, der Hampelmann; ***--mouse***, die Hüpfmaus; ***--off point***, die Absprungstelle, (*Av.*) der Abflugpunkt; (*coll., fig.*) Ausgangspunkt; ***--pole***, die Sprungstange; ***--spider***, die Springspinne. **jumpy,** *adj.* (*coll.*) nervös, unruhig.

junction ['dʒʌŋkʃən], *s.* die Verbindung, Zusammenfügung, Vereinigung; (*Geom.*) Berührung, der Berührungspunkt; (*Railw.*) Knotenpunkt; Anschlußbahnhof; (*of roads*) die (Weg)kreuzung; der Treffpunkt, Zusammenkunftsort. **junction|-box,** *s.* (*Elec.*) die Abzweigdose, Anschlußdose, der Kabelkasten. **--line,** *s.* (*Railw.*) die Verbindungsbahn.

juncture ['dʒʌŋktʃə], *s.* das Zusammentreffen (*of events*); (*fig.*) der Stand *or* die Lage der Dinge, die Krisis, kritischer Zeitpunkt *or* Augenblick; (*obs.*) die Verbindung, Naht, Fuge, das Verbindungsstück, Gelenk; ***at this*** –, an dieser Stelle, in diesem Augenblick, zu diesem Zeitpunkt.

June [dʒu:n], *s.* der Juni.

jungle [dʒʌŋgl], *s.* der *or* das (*or Austr.* die)

Dschungel, das Sumpfdickicht, der Sumpfwald; (*fig.*) das Dickicht, die Wildnis.

junior ['dʒu:niə], **1.** *adj.* jünger (*to*, als), untergeordnet, nachfolgend; (*Spt.*) – ***champion,*** der Juniorenmeister, Jugendmeister; (*Am. Univ.*) – ***class,*** dritter Jahrgang; – ***clerk,*** zweiter Buchhalter; – ***department,*** see – ***school***; – ***forms,*** die Klassen bis zur Tertia; – ***lawyer,*** der Rechtspraktikant, Gerichtsreferendar; – ***partner,*** jüngerer Teilhaber; – ***school,*** die Unterstufe; – ***year,*** *see* – ***class***; ***Smith*** –, Schmidt der Jüngere, der jüngere Schmidt. **2.** *s.* der (die) Jüngere (*usu.* der Sohn); Untergeordnete(r); (*Am. Univ.*) der Student des dritten Jahrgangs; (*Am. coll.*) Kleine(r); ***he is my – by some years,*** er ist einige Jahre jünger als ich. **juniority** [–'ɔriti], *s.* geringeres Alter, das Jüngersein; untergeordnete Stellung.

juniper ['dʒu:nipə], *s.* der Wacholder(baum).

[1]**junk** [dʒʌŋk], *s.* (*Naut.*) die Dschunke, Dschonke.

[2]**junk,** *s.* **1.** die Ausschußware, der Ausschuß, das Altmaterial, Altwaren (*pl.*), der Trödel, Kram, Plunder, Kitsch, wertloses Zeug, das Gerümpel, der Schund, Abfälle (*pl.*); 2. (*Naut.*) altes Tauwerk, (*sl.*) zähes Pökelfleisch. **junk|-dealer,** *s.* der Altwarenhändler, Trödler. **--heap,** *s.* (*sl.*) der Abfallplatz; Autofriedhof. **--shop,** *s.* der Trödelladen, Ramschladen.

junket ['dʒʌŋkit], **1.** *s.* 1. dicke Milch, der Quark; 2. (*coll.*) die Festlichkeit, Feier, das Fest. **2.** *v.i.* schmausen, ein Fest feiern. **junketing,** *s.* (*oft. pl.*) die Schmauserei, Lustigkeit, Belustigung.

junkie ['dʒʌŋki], *s.* (*sl.*) Rauschgiftsüchtige(r).

junta ['dʒʌntə], *s.* die Ratsversammlung, (spanische) Junta. **junto,** *s.* die Clique, der Klüngel.

Jurassic [dʒu'ræsik], *adj.* (*Geol.*) Jura–.

juridical [dʒu'ridikl], *adj.* Rechts–, gerichtlich, Gerichts–.

jurisdiction [dʒuəris'dikʃən], *s.* die Rechtsprechung; Gerichtsbarkeit, Oberaufsicht, Gerichtshoheit, Zuständigkeit; der Gerichtsbezirk, Verwaltungsbezirk; ***have – over,*** zuständig sein für; ***come under the – of,*** unter die Zuständigkeit fallen von.

jurisprudence [dʒuəris'pru:dəns], *s.* die Rechtskunde, Rechtswissenschaft. **jurisprudential** [–'denʃəl], *adj.* rechtswissenschaftlich.

jurist ['dʒuərist], *s.* Rechtskundige(r), Rechtsgelehrte(r); (*Am.*) der Jurist, Rechtsanwalt.

juror ['dʒuərə], *s.* (*Law*) Geschworene(r); der Preisrichter (*of competitions*). **jury** [–ri], *s.* (*Law*) Geschworenen (*pl.*), die Geschworenenbank; Jury, Preisrichter (*pl.*), der Preisrichterausschuß, das Preisgericht (*in competitions*); ***foreman of the*** –, der Geschworenenobmann; ***grand*** –, die Anklagejury; ***petty*** –, die Urteilsjury; ***trial by*** –, die Schwurgerichtsverhandlung.

jury|-box, *s.* die Geschworenenbank. **–man,** *s. See* **juror** (*Law*).

jury|-mast, *s.* der Notmast. **--rigged,** *adj.* behelfsmäßig getackelt.

[1]**just** [dʒʌst], *adj.* 1. gerecht, billig, unparteiisch (*to*, gegen); 2. genau, richtig, recht, wahr; (*Mus.*) (ton)rein; – ***proportions,*** richtiges Maß; 3. berechtigt, gerechtfertigt, (wohl)begründet, (wohl)verdient, rechtmäßig, angemessen, gehörig; ***my – right,*** mein volles Recht; 4. (*B.*) redlich, rechtschaffen.

[2]**just,** *adv.* gerade, eben; genau; soeben, gerade (noch), ganz knapp, mit knapper Not; nur, bloß; (*before imper.*) mal, doch, nur; (*coll.*) wirklich, eigentlich; (*coll.*) einfach, geradezu; – ***a bit,*** nur ganz wenig; – ***as,*** (*degree*) ebenso wie, (*time*) gerade als; – ***as large,*** ebenso groß; – ***as well,*** genau so gut; ***that's – enough,*** das reicht gerade hin; – ***for fun,*** bloß zum Spaß; – ***a moment!*** einen Augenblick, bitte! wart' einmal! nur nicht so eilig! – ***now,*** soeben, eben erst; gerade jetzt, jetzt gerade; ***that's – it!*** das ist es (ja) gerade *or* eben; ***that's – right,*** das ist gerade recht, das paßt gerade; ***that's – the point,*** darauf kommt es gerade an; – ***the thing,*** gerade das Richtige; – ***let me see!*** laß mal sehen, zeig einmal her! – ***so!*** ganz recht! jawohl! – ***then,*** gerade in dem Moment; – ***there,*** genau dort.

justice ['dʒʌstis], *s.* 1. die Gerechtigkeit (*to*, gegenüber), Billigkeit, Rechtlichkeit, Rechtmäßigkeit, Berechtigung; – ***was done,*** der Gerechtigkeit wurde Genüge getan; ***do – to him*** or ***do him*** –, ihm Gerechtigkeit widerfahren lassen; ***do o.s.*** –, sich nichts abgeben lassen; ***do – to a dish,*** einer Speise tüchtig zusprechen; ***in – to him,*** um ihm gerecht zu werden; ***with*** –, mit Recht; 2. (*Law*) die Rechtsprechung, Rechtspflege, das Recht, Justizwesen; Gericht; der Richter; ***court of*** –, der Gerichtshof; ***High Court of Justice,*** das Reichsgericht; ***Lord Chief Justice,*** der Lord Oberrichter; – ***of the peace,*** der Friedensrichter, Laienrichter; ***administer*** –, Recht sprechen; ***see – done to him,*** ihm Recht verschaffen; ***in*** –, von Rechts wegen; ***bring to*** –, vor den Richter bringen, gerichtlich belangen. **justiceship,** *s.* das Richteramt.

justiciable [dʒʌs'tiʃiəbl], *pred. adj.* der Gerichtsbarkeit unterworfen. **justiciary, 1.** *s.* der Gerichtshalter, Rechtsprecher; (*Scots*) ***High Court of Justiciary,*** oberstes Kriminalgericht. **2.** *adj.* gerichtlich.

justifiability [dʒʌstifaiə'biliti], *s.* die Entschuldbarkeit, Rechtmäßigkeit. **justifiable** ['dʒʌstifaiəbl], *adj.* zu rechtfertigen(d), berechtigt, rechtmäßig. **justification** [–fi'keiʃən], *s.* 1. die Rechtfertigung, Berechtigung; ***in – of,*** zur Rechtfertigung von *or* (*Gen.*); 2. (*Typ.*) die Ausschließung, Justierung. **justificatory** [–fikeitəri], *adj.* rechtfertigend, Rechtfertigungs–.

justifier ['dʒʌstifaiə], *s.* 1. der Rechtfertiger; 2. (*Typ.*) Justierer. **justify,** *v.t.* 1. rechtfertigen (*to*, ***before***, vor (*Dat.*) *or* gegenüber); (*Theol.*) freisprechen, lossprechen; ***be justified in doing,*** berechtigt sein zu tun; ***the end justifies the means,*** der Zweck heiligt die Mittel; 2. (*Typ.*) ausschließen, justieren.

justly ['dʒʌstli], *adv.* mit Recht, richtig, einwandfrei, gerechterweise, verdientermaßen; *see* [1]**just**. **justness,** *s.* die Gerechtigkeit, Billigkeit; Richtigkeit, Genauigkeit.

jut [dʒʌt], **1.** *v.i.* (– ***out***) hervorstehen, hervorragen, hinausragen, vorspringen, ausbauchen. **2.** *s.* der Vorsprung.

jute [dʒu:t], *s.* (*Bot.*) die Jutepflanze; Jute(faser).

Jute, *s.* (*Hist.*) der Jüte. **Jutish,** *adj.* jütisch. **Jutland** ['dʒʌtlənd], *s.* Jütland (*n.*); ***Battle of*** –, die Skagerrakschlacht.

jut-window, *s.* das Erkenfenster.

juvenescence [dʒu:və'nesəns], *s.* die Verjüngung, das Jungwerden; ***well of*** –, der Jungbrunnen. **juvenescent,** *adj.* sich verjüngend; unentwickelt, unreif.

juvenile ['dʒu:vənail], **1.** *adj.* jung, jugendlich, Jugend–; – ***court,*** das Jugendgericht; – ***delinquency,*** die Jugendkriminalität; – ***delinquent,*** jugendlicher Verbrecher; – ***wear,*** die Kleidung für Jugendliche. **2.** *s.* Jugendliche(r). **juvenilia** [–'niliə], *pl.* Jugendwerke (*pl.*). **juvenility** [–'niliti], *s.* das Jungsein, die Jugendlichkeit; jugendliche Unreife; jugendlicher Leichtsinn; *pl.* Kindereien, Jugendtorheiten (*pl.*).

juxtapose [dʒʌkstə'pouz], *v.t.* nebeneinanderstellen. **juxtaposition** [–pə'ziʃən], *s.* die Nebeneinanderstellung.

K

K, k [kei], *s.* das K, k. *See Index of Abbreviations.*

Kaffir ['kæfə], *s.* (*pej.*) der (die) Kaffer(in).

kale [keil], *s.* der Winterkohl, Krauskohl; (*Scots*) *--yard,* der Gemüsegarten, Küchengarten; *--yard school,* schottische Heimatdichtung.

kaleidoscope [kə'laidəskoup], *s.* das Kaleidoskop. **kaleidoscopic** [–'skɔpik], *adj.* kaleidoskopisch, (*fig.*) bunt durcheinandergewürfelt.

kali ['keili], *s.* (*Bot.*) das Salzkraut.

Kalmu(c)k ['kælmʌk], *s.* der Kalmücke (die Kalmückin).

kangaroo [kæŋgə'ru:], *s.* das Känguruh. **kangaroo court,** *s.* unrechtmäßiges Gericht.

Kantian ['kæntiən], **1.** *adj.* kantisch. **2.** *s.* der Kantianer.

kaolin ['keiəlin], *s.* das Kaolin, die Porzellanerde.

kapok ['keipɔk], *s.* das Haar des Kapokbaums, die Pflanzenfaser.

karma ['kɑ:mə], *s.* das Schicksal.

kayak ['kaiæk], *s.* der *or* das Kajak, das Paddelboot.

kedge [kedʒ], **1.** *s.* (*--anchor*) der Warpanker. **2.** *v.t.* warpen, verholen (*a ship*).

kedgeree ['kedʒəri:], *s.* (indisches) Gericht aus Reis, Fisch und Eiern.

keel [ki:l], **1.** *s.* der Kiel; (*Poet.*) das Schiff; *on an even –,* auf ebenem Kiel; (*fig.*) ruhig, ausgeglichen. **2.** *v.i.* *– over,* umschlagen, umkippen, kieloben liegen, kentern; (*fig., coll.*) kopfüber stürzen, umstürzen. **3.** *v.t.* *– over,* kieloben legen, umlegen, umkippen. **keelage** [–idʒ], *s.* das Kielgeld, Hafengebühren (*pl.*).

keeled, *adj.* (*Bot.*) kielförmig. **keelhaul,** *v.t.* kielholen (lassen); (*fig.*) abkanzeln. **keelson,** *s.* (*Am.*) *see* **kelson.**

[1]**keen** [ki:n], **1.** *s.* (irische) Totenklage. **2.** *v.i.* (weh)klagen. **3.** *v.t.* (weh)klagen um, beklagen.

[2]**keen,** *adj.* 1. scharf (geschliffen); (*fig.*) scharf (*eyesight*), fein (*hearing*), scharfsinnig (*wits*); *– perception of,* feines Gefühl für; 2. (*fig.*) (*of a p.*) scharf, erpicht (*on, about* or *for,* auf (*Acc.*)), lebhaft interessiert (*on,* an (*Dat.*)), begierig (nach); eifrig, lebhaft, begeistert, einsatzfreudig, leidenschaftlich; *– huntsman,* der Jagdfreund; (*coll.*) *as – as mustard,* wild versessen *or* toll (*on,* auf (*Acc.*)), Feuer und Flamme (für); *be – on swimming,* ein eifriger *or* begeisterter *or* leidenschaftlicher Schwimmer sein; *– to go out,* Lust haben auszugehen; *I am not very –,* ich habe wenig Lust; 3. durchdringend (*as a glance*), beißend (*as wit, frost*), schneidend, streng (*as cold*), stark, groß (*as appetite, delight*), heftig, bitter (*as pain, sorrow*), lebhaft, eingehend (*as interest, desire, attention*), stark, lebhaft, heiß (*as contest, competition*).

keen|-edged, *adj.* scharf geschliffen, mit scharfer Schneide. **--eyed,** *adj.* scharfsichtig. **keenly,** *adv.* (*fig.*) heftig, sehr; *– interested,* sehr interessiert. **keenness,** *s.* die Schärfe; Heftigkeit, Bitterkeit; der Eifer; Scharfsinn; *– of hearing,* die Feinhörigkeit; *– of sight,* die Scharfsichtigkeit. **keen-witted,** *adj.* scharfsinnig.

keep [ki:p], **1.** *irr.v.t.* 1. halten, aufbewahren; (*fig.*) (be)halten, (be)wahren; sich halten *or* behaupten in *or* auf (*Dat.*); (fest)halten, bewachen; (auf)bewahren, aufheben; 2. vorenthalten, verheimlichen (*s.th. from him,* ihm etwas); 3. (*fig.*) (*a p.*) erhalten, unterhalten, ernähren; 4. beobachten, befolgen (*laws etc.*); feiern, abhalten (*a festival*); 5. verfolgen, einhalten, innehalten (*a course*); 6. hüten (*one's bed etc.*); 7. (*Comm.*) führen (*goods in stock, ledger etc.*), auf Lager haben.

(a) (*with nouns*) *– an appointment,* eine Verabredung einhalten; *– one's balance,* sein *or* das Gleichgewicht wahren *or* (be)halten; *– the ball rolling,* die S. im Gang halten; *– boarders* or *lodgers,* Kostgänger *or* (Unter)mieter (bei sich) haben; (*coll.*) *– body and soul together,* Leib und Seele zusammenhalten; (*sl.*) *– cave,* Schmiere stehen; (*coll.*) *– your chin up!* Kopf hoch! *– Christmas,* das Weihnachtsfest begehen, Weihnachten feiern; *– him company,* ihm Gesellschaft leisten; *– company with him,* mit ihm verkehren, mit ihm Beziehungen unterhalten; *– one's (own) counsel,* seine Absicht für sich behalten, verschwiegen sein; *– one's distance,* Abstand halten; *– your distance!* bleib mir vom Leibe! *– an eye on,* im Auge behalten; *– faith with him,* ihm die Treue halten; *have a family to –,* eine Familie unterhalten *or* ernähren müssen; *– one's feet,* sich auf den Füßen halten; (*Footb.*) *– goal,* das Tor hüten; *– one's ground,* standhalten; *– guard,* Wache stehen *or* halten; *– a guard over one's tongue,* seine Zunge im Zaume halten; *– one's hand in,* in *or* bei Übung bleiben; *– one's head,* kaltes Blut bewahren, den Kopf nicht verlieren; *– hold of,* festhalten; *– a (firm) hold on,* in seiner Macht *or* unter seinem Einfluß halten; *– late hours,* spät zu Bett gehen, spät aufbleiben; *– house,* die Haushalt *or* Wirtschaft führen (*for, Dat.*); (*coll.*) *– a stiff upper lip,* sich nicht unterkriegen lassen, sich (*Dat.*) nichts anmerken lassen, die Ohren steif halten; *– a look-out,* Ausschau halten; *– a (good) look-out for,* auf der Hut sein vor (*Dat.*); *– one's mind on one's work,* sich der Arbeit befleißigen, sich von der Arbeit nicht ablenken lassen; *– a mistress,* eine Geliebte haben, sich (*Dat.*) eine Mätresse halten; *– pace,* Schritt halten, mitgehen, mitkommen (*with,* mit); *– the peace,* die öffentliche Sicherheit wahren; (*coll.*) *– the pot boiling,* see *– the ball rolling*; *– him (a) prisoner,* ihn gefangenhalten; *– one's promise,* see *– one's word*; *– a record,* Aufzeichnungen machen, Buch führen (*of,* über (*Acc.*)); *– a tight rein over,* im Zaume halten; *– one's room,* das Zimmer hüten; *– one's seat,* sitzenbleiben; *– a secret,* ein Geheimnis bewahren; *– it (a) secret,* es geheimhalten; *– servants,* Bediente haben *or* halten; *– (a) shop,* ein Geschäft *or* einen Laden besitzen; *– silence,* schweigen; still *or* ruhig sein, Stillschweigen beobachten; (*sl.*) *– tabs on,* kontrollieren, überwachen; *– one's temper,* sich beherrschen; *– time,* (*of clocks*) richtig gehen, (*Mus.*) Takt halten; (*coll.*) *– track of,* (laufend) verfolgen; *– watch,* Wache stehen; aufpassen, achtgeben (*on, over,* auf (*Acc.*)); *– one's word,* sein Wort *or* Versprechen halten.

(b) (*with adjs.*) *– him advised,* see *– him informed*; *– it dark,* es verschweigen; *– dry!* vor Nässe zu schützen! *– going,* (*a th.*) in Gang halten, (*a p.*) aufrechthalten, über Wasser halten; *– him informed* or (*coll.*) *posted,* ihn auf dem laufenden halten; *– him short (of money),* ihm wenig Geld geben; *– him waiting,* ihn warten lassen.

(c) (*with advs.*) *– apart,* getrennt halten; *– away,* fernhalten; *– back,* weghalten, zurückhalten (*from,* von), (*fig.*) geheimhalten, vorenthalten (*from, Dat.*); *– down,* unterdrücken, niederdrücken, nicht aufkommen lassen, (*fig.*) beschränken (*to,* auf (*Acc.*)), (*prices*) drücken; *– in,* anhalten (*one's breath*), nicht ausgehen lassen (*a fire*), nachsitzen lassen (*a pupil*); *– off,* fernhalten, weghalten, abweisen, abwehren, nicht näherkommen lassen; *– on,* anbehalten (*clothes*), aufbehalten (*hat*), anlassen, brennen lassen (*a light*), (*coll.*) beibehalten (*employee*); (*sl.*) *– your hair* or *shirt on!* nur immer mit der Ruhe! *– out,* nicht hereinlassen, ausschließen; *– up,* aufrechterhalten, nicht sinken lassen; (*fig.*) unterhalten (*correspondence, a fire etc.*), stehen lassen (*type*), nicht zu Bett gehen lassen (*a p.*); *– up appearances,* den Schein wahren; (*coll.*) *– your chin up!* immer feste auf die Weste! (*coll.*) *– one's end up,* sich behaupten, seinen Mann stehen; durchhalten, gut abschneiden; *– one's spirits up,* den Mut nicht sinken lassen; (*coll.*) *– it up,* nicht nachlassen, nicht schlappmachen, es immer weitermachen; *– it up!* immer zu! nur weiter! (*coll.*) *– up one's German,* sein Deutsch nicht einrosten lassen.

(d) (*with preps.*) *– at,* festhalten an (*Dat.*), verweilen bei (*a th.*), (*coll.*) drängen, belästigen, an-

halten (***about***, um) (*a p.*); – ***at a distance,*** von sich fernhalten; – ***at work,*** dauernd beschäftigen; zur Arbeit anhalten; – ***for later,*** für später aufheben; – ***from coming,*** verhindern *or* davon abhalten zu kommen; – ***from danger,*** vor Gefahr schützen; – ***it from him,*** es ihm verschweigen *or* verheimlichen *or* vorenthalten; – ***in one's own hands,*** selbst verwalten; – ***in mind,*** im Gedächtnis behalten, daran denken, nicht vergessen; – ***him in money,*** ihm dauernd Geld zukommen lassen, ihn mit Geld versorgen; – ***in repair,*** in gutem Zustand erhalten; – ***in suspense,*** im Zweifel *or* ungewissen lassen, hinhalten (*a p.*), unentschieden *or* in der Schwebe lassen (*a th.*), (*Comm.*) nicht akzeptieren, Not leiden lassen; – ***in view,*** im Auge behalten; – ***on £5 a week,*** von 5 Pfund in der Woche ernähren; – ***on the boil,*** im *or* am Kochen halten, (*fig.*) in Wallung *or* im Gang halten; – ***out of sight,*** verborgen halten; – ***to o.s.,*** für sich behalten; – ***o.s. to o.s.,*** für sich bleiben; – ***him to his promise,*** ihn zu seinem Wort halten; (*sl.*) – ***it under one's hat,*** es hinter den Spiegel stecken.
2. *irr.v.i.* sich halten (*of food etc.*), bleiben, verweilen (*of a p. in a place*), weiter– (*with verb of activity*); (*coll.*) – ***going,*** weitergehen, weitermachen; (*coll.*) ***how are you –ing?*** wie geht's (Ihnen)? (*coll.*) ***the matter will –,*** die S. eilt nicht *or* hat Zeit.
(a) (*with advs.*) – ***abreast,*** Schritt halten, fortschreiten (***of,*** mit); – ***aloof,*** sich abseits halten (***from,*** von); – ***away,*** sich fernhalten, wegbleiben (***from,*** von), fernbleiben (*Dat.*); – ***clear of,*** meiden, sich fernhalten von, aus dem Weg gehen (*Dat.*); – ***dark about,*** hinterm Berg halten mit; – ***down,*** sich geduckt halten; – ***in,*** sich versteckt halten; – ***in with him,*** es gut mit ihm halten; – ***off,*** sich fernhalten *or* abseits halten, fernbleiben; – ***on,*** fortfahren, weitermachen; ***it kept on raining,*** es regnete unaufhörlich *or* (immer) weiter; (*coll.*) – ***on at him,*** an ihm dauernd herumnörgeln, ihn immer wieder drängen; – ***out,*** draußen bleiben; – ***quiet,*** sich ruhig verhalten; – ***up,*** sich aufrecht erhalten, hoch bleiben; Schritt halten; ***prices are –ing up,*** die Preise behaupten sich; – ***up with,*** Schritt halten mit, (*fig.*) es gleichtun (*Dat.*).
(b) (*with preps.*) – ***at,*** festhalten an (*Dat.*), beharren *or* verweilen bei; (*coll.*) belästigen, drängen (*a p.*); ***be unable to – from,*** (*neg. only*) nicht umhin können (***doing,*** zu tun); – ***in good health,*** gesund bleiben; – ***in sight,*** in Sicht(weite) bleiben; – ***in touch with,*** Fühlung behalten mit, in Verbindung *or* Berührung bleiben mit; – ***off the grass!*** Betreten des Rasens verboten! – ***out of danger,*** sich außer Gefahr halten; – ***out of debt,*** sich schuldenfrei erhalten; – ***out of mischief,*** keine bösen Streiche machen; – ***out of sight,*** sich nicht sehen *or* blicken lassen, außer Sicht bleiben, sich verbergen; – ***to,*** (sich) halten an (*Acc.*), festhalten an (*Dat.*), bleiben bei, befolgen; – ***to the left!*** links fahren! halten Sie sich links! (*coll.*) – ***to o.s.,*** für sich bleiben; – ***to one's word,*** sein Wort halten.
3. *s.* 1. der (Lebens)unterhalt, die Kost, Verpflegung (*of a p.*), Unterhaltskosten (*pl.*) (*of animals*); ***earn one's –,*** den Unterhalt verdienen; 2. der Hauptturm, Bergfried, das Burgverlies (*Austr.* Burgverließ); 3. (*coll.*) ***for –s,*** auf *or* für immer; ***play for –s,*** mit zurückbehaltenem Gewinn spielen.

keeper ['ki:pə], *s.* 1. (*usu. in compounds*) der Inhaber, Besitzer (*of a hotel etc.*); 2. Hüter, Wächter, Aufseher, (*of prisoners, animals etc.*) Wärter, (*of collections, museums*) Kustos, Verwalter, Verwahrer, Bewahrer; – ***of the archives,*** der Archivar; – ***of the Great Seal,*** der Großsiegelbewahrer; – ***of manuscripts,*** der Direktor der Handschriftenabteilung; – ***of the Privy Purse,*** der Intendant der königlichen Zivilliste; 3. (*Tech.*) der Halter, Schutzring, (*of a magnet*) Anker.

keep-fit, *attrib. adj.* Trimm-dich-.

keeping ['ki:piŋ], **1.** *adj.* haltbar, dauerhaft; – ***apples,*** Daueräpfel (*pl.*). **2.** *s.* 1. die Verwahrung, Aufsicht, Pflege, Obhut, (*of fruit etc.*) das Lagern, (*of prisoners etc.*) der Gewahrsam; ***in safe –,*** in Verwahrung, in guter Obhut; 2. der Unterhalt, die Nahrung; 3. Übereinstimmung, der Einklang; ***be in*** (***out of***) – ***with,*** (nicht) stimmen *or* passen zu, (nicht) übereinstimmen mit *or* in Einklang stehen mit.

keepsake ['ki:pseik], *s.* das Andenken; ***as a –,*** zum *or* als Andenken.

kef [kef], *s.* der (Haschisch)rausch; süßes Nichtstun.

keg [keg], *s.* das Fäßchen, kleines Faß.

kelp [kelp], *s.* der Seetang; das Kelp, die Seetangasche.

kelpie ['kelpi], *s.* (*Scots*) der Wassergeist.

kelson ['kelsən], *s.* das Kielschwein.

ken [ken], **1.** *s.* der Gesichtskreis, die Sicht(weite); (*fig.*) das Wissen, der Wissensbereich, Horizont; ***beyond*** or ***out of one's –,*** außerhalb des Gesichtskreises; ***within one's –,*** innerhalb des Gesichtskreises. **2.** *v.t.* (*Scots*) wissen, kennen.

[1]**kennel** [kenl], **1.** *s.* 1. die Hundehütte, der Hundestall; *pl.* der Hundezwinger, (*Hunt.*) die Stallung (*for pack of hounds*); 2. Meute, Koppel (*hounds*). **2.** *v.i.* (*fig.*) in einem Loch hausen, in einer elenden Behausung liegen. **3.** *v.t.* in einem Hundestalle unterbringen.

[2]**kennel,** *s.* die Gosse, Rinne, der Rinnstein.

kentledge ['kentlidʒ], *s.* (*Naut.*) das Ballasteisen.

Kenya ['kenjə, 'ki:njə], *s.* Kenia (*n.*). **Kenyan, 1.** *s.* der (die) Kenianer(in). **2.** *adj.* kenianisch.

kept [kept], **1.** *imperf., p.p. of* **keep. 2.** *adj.* – ***woman,*** die Mätresse.

kerb [kə:b], *s.* die Bordkante, Straßenkante; – ***market,*** inoffizielle *or* schwarze Börse. **kerbstone,** *s.* der Randstein, Bordstein, Prellstein.

kerchief ['kə:tʃif], *s.* das Kopftuch, Halstuch; (*Poet.*) Taschentuch.

kerf [kə:f], *s.* die Kerbe, Schnittbreite (*of a saw*).

kermes ['kə:miz], *s.* (*Ent.*) der Kermes, die Kermesschildlaus; (*collect.*) Kermeskörner (*pl.*), der Kermesfarbstoff.

kermis ['kə:mis], *s.* die Kirmes, Kirchweih.

kernel [kə:nl], *s.* der Kern (*of nuts etc.*; *also fig.*), das Korn (*of oats etc.*); (*fig.*) Wesen, Innerste(s).

kerosene ['kerəsi:n], *s.* das Kerosin, Leuchtöl, Brennöl.

kersey ['kə:zi], *s.* grobes Wollzeug.

kestrel ['kestrəl], *s.* (*Orn.*) der Turmfalke (*Falco tinnunculus*).

ketch [ketʃ], *s.* die Ketsch, der Besankutter.

ketchup ['ketʃəp], *s.* kalte pikante Soße.

kettle [ketl], *s.* der Kessel; (*coll.*) ***a pretty – of fish!*** eine schöne Bescherung! **kettle|-drum,** *s.* die Kesselpauke. **--drummer,** *s.* der Paukenschläger. **--holder,** *s.* der Anfasser.

key [ki:], **1.** *s.* 1. der Schlüssel; (*R.C.*) ***power of the –s,*** die Schlüsselgewalt; ***turn the –,*** abschließen; ***keep under lock and –,*** unter Schloß und Riegel halten; 2. (*fig.*) der Schlüssel, die Lösung; 3. Übersetzung; Unterlage; Zeichenerklärung; 4. (*Mus.*) Tonart; ***speak in a high –,*** in hohem Tone sprechen; 5. (*fig.*) der Einklang, die Übereinstimmung; ***in – with,*** in Einklang mit; 6. (*Tech.*) der Keil, Vorsteckbolzen; Schraubenschlüssel; die Taste (*piano etc.*), Klappe (*flute etc.*), (*Tele.*) der Schalter. **2.** *v.t.* befestigen; (– ***in*** or ***on***) festkeilen; (*coll.*) – ***up,*** anfeuern (***to,*** zu); (*coll.*) ***all –ed up,*** erregt, (hoch)gespannt. **3.** *adj.* Schlüssel–; – ***man,*** die Hauptperson; unentbehrlicher Arbeiter.

key|board, *s.* die Tastatur (*typewriter etc.*), Klaviatur (*piano*); – ***instrument,*** das Tasteninstrument; – ***music,*** die Musik für Tasteninstrumente. **--bugle,** *s.* das Klapphorn. **keyed,** *adj.* mit Tasten *or* Klappen; – ***instrument,*** das Tasteninstrument; ***six-- flute,*** die Flöte mit sechs Klappen. **keyhole,** *s.* das Schlüsselloch; – ***saw,*** die Stichsäge, Lochsäge. **keyless,** *adj.* ohne Schlüssel; – ***watch,*** die Remontoiruhr. **key|note,** *s.* der Grundton (*also fig.*), (*fig.*) die Grundstimmung, der Hauptgedanke, Grundgedanke. **--ring,** *s.* der Schlüsselring. **--signature,** *s.* (*Mus.*) die (Tonart)-vorzeichnung. **-stone,** *s.* der Schlußstein; (*fig.*) Grundpfeiler, die (Haupt)stütze, Grundlage, das A und O. **--way,** *s.* die (Keil)nut. **-word,** *s.* das Schlüsselwort, Stichwort.

khaki ['kɑ:ki], **1.** *adj.* staubfarbig, graugelb. **2.** *s.* das Khaki.

^{1}**khan** [kɑ:n], *s.* der Tatarenfürst.

^{2}**khan,** *s.* die Karawanserei.

Khedive [ki'di:v], *s.* der Khedive.

kibbutz [ki'buts], *s.* (*pl.* **-im** [-'im]) der Kibbuz.

kibe [kaib], *s.* eiternde Frostbeule.

kibosh ['kaibɔʃ], *s.* (*sl.*) der Mumpitz, Quatsch, das Blech, höherer Blödsinn; (*sl.*) ***put the – on,*** den Garaus machen (*Dat.*), (*a p.*) fertigmachen, erledigen.

kick [kik], **1.** *v.t.* (mit dem Fuße) stoßen *or* treten, einen Fußtritt geben (*Dat.*), (*Footb.*) kicken; (*sl.*) ***– the bucket,*** ins Gras beißen; ***– him downstairs,*** ihn die Treppe hinunterwerfen; ***– a goal,*** ein Tor schießen; ***– one's heels,*** ungeduldig *or* müßig warten (müssen); (*coll.*) ***– him out,*** ihn hinausschmeißen; ***– up one's heels,*** ausschlagen, sich hemmungslos benehmen; (*coll.*) ***– up a dust,*** viel Staub aufwirbeln; (*coll.*) ***– up a row,*** Radau schlagen, Spektakel machen. **2.** *v.i.* mit den Füßen stoßen, (*of animals*) hinten ausschlagen; stoßen (*firearms*), hochfliegen (*of balls*), (*fig.*) sich auflehnen *or* (mit Händen und Füßen) wehren (*at, against,* gegen); ***– against the pricks,*** wider den Stachel löcken; ***– off,*** (*Footb.*) anstoßen, (*coll.*) den ersten Stoß machen, das Spiel beginnen; (*fig.*) ***– over the traces,*** über die Stränge schlagen, über die Schnur hauen. **3.** *s.* 1. der Fußtritt, Stoß mit dem Fuß; ***get more –s than halfpence,*** wenig Dank ernten, mehr Prügel als Lob ernten; (*sl.*) ***get the –,*** 'rausfliegen, den Laufpaß bekommen; 2. der Rückstoß (*of a gun*), (*coll.*) Schwung, Mumm, die Stoßkraft, Energie, Wirkung (*of a drink*); (*sl.*) ***get a – out of,*** viel Spaß haben an (*Dat.*); (*sl.*) ***he does it for –s,*** er macht's bloß um den Kitzel; 3. (*Footb.*) der Schuß; ***free –,*** der Freistoß; ***goal –,*** der Torstoß; ***penalty –,*** der Elfmeter.

kick-off, *s.* (*Footb.*) der Anstoß, (*coll.*) Start.

kickshaw ['kikʃɔ:], *s.* die Schleckerei, Delikatesse.

kick-starter, *s.* (*Motor.*) der Tretanlasser.

^{1}**kid** [kid], **1.** *s.* 1. das Zicklein, die Kitze; (*material*) das Ziegenleder; 2. (*sl.*) Gör, der Bengel; ***– brother,*** junger Bruder. **2.** *v.i.* zickeln. **3.** *adj.* ziegenledern; ***– gloves,*** Glacéhandschuhe (*pl.*); (*fig.*) ***handle with – gloves,*** mit Glacéhandschuhen anfassen, rücksichtsvoll behandeln.

^{2}**kid, 1.** *s.* (*sl.*) der Ulk, Bluff. **2.** *v.t.* (*coll.*) hereinlegen, zum Narren haben, verkohlen, nasführen; ***– him,*** ihm weismachen; ***you're kidding,*** Sie scherzen. **kidding,** *s.* das Foppen, Aufziehen; der Ulk, Bluff.

kiddy ['kidi], *s.* (*coll.*) das Gör.

kidnap ['kidnæp], *v.t.* entführen, rauben, stehlen (*child etc.*). **kidnapper,** *s.* der Kinderdieb, Menschenräuber. **kidnapping,** *s.* der Kinderraub, Menschenraub.

kidney ['kidni], *s.* die Niere; (*fig.*) (*coll.*) Art, Sorte, der Schlag. **kidney|-bean,** *s.* die Schminkbohne, französische Bohne. **--machine,** *s.* künstliche Niere. **--shaped,** *adj.* nierenförmig.

Kiev ['ki:ef], *s.* Kiew (*n.*).

kilderkin ['kildəkin], *s.* das Fäßchen (= *18 gallons or 82 l.*).

kill [kil], **1.** *v.t.* töten, erschlagen, umbringen; schlachten (*cattle*); (*fig.*) zerstören, vernichten, unterdrücken, ersticken; dämpfen, übertönen (*sound*); unwirksam machen, ausgleichen, neutralisieren (*colours*); totmachen (*a play etc.*); streichen (*an entry*), ungültig machen, für ungültig erklären, widerrufen, stornieren, (*Parl.*) zu Fall bringen (*a bill*); (*Tenn.*) ***– the ball,*** den Ball töten; ***– two birds with one stone,*** zwei Fliegen mit einer Klappe schlagen; (*fig.*) ***– the fatted calf,*** einen Begrüßungsschmaus veranstalten; (*coll.*) ***dressed up*** (***fit***) ***to –,*** todschick angezogen, aufgedonnert; ***– time,*** die Zeit totschlagen; ***– with kindness,*** mit Güte überwältigen; ***– off,*** abschlachten (*cattle*); ausrotten, vertilgen, beseitigen; (*coll.*) abmurksen. **2.** *s.* 1. die Tötung; 2. (Jagd)beute. **killer,** *s.* der Mörder, Totschläger; ***– whale,*** der Schwertwal. **killing, 1.** *adj.* 1. mörderisch; 2. (*coll.*) überwältigend, unwiderstehlich, zum Kaputtlachen. **2.** *s.* das Töten. **kill|-joy,** *s.* der Störenfried, Spielverderber. **--or-cure,** *attrib. adj.* drastisch (*remedy*).

kiln [kiln], *s.* der Brennofen, Röstofen, die Darre. **kiln-dry,** *v.t.* darren, dörren.

kilo ['ki:lou], *s.* (*coll.*) *see* **kilogram.**

kilo|cycle ['kilə-], *s.* das Kilohertz. **-gram(me),** *s.* das Kilo(gramm). **-litre,** *s.* das Kiloliter. **-metre,** *s.* der Kilometer. **-watt,** *s.* das Kilowatt.

kilt [kilt], **1.** *s.* das Schottenröckchen. **2.** *v.t.* fälteln, in senkrechte Falten legen; aufschürzen. **kilted,** *adj.* 1. Schottenrock *or* Faltenrock tragend; 2. senkrecht gefaltet, plissiert.

kimono [ki'mounou], *s.* japanischer Schlafrock.

kin [kin], *s.* (*usu. pl. constr.*) die (Bluts)verwandtschaft; Verwandte(r), Verwandte (*pl.*); die Familie, Sippe, das Geschlecht; ***next of –,*** nächste(r) Verwandte(r), die nächsten Verwandten.

^{1}**kind** [kaind], *adj.* gut, gütig, freundlich, wohlwollend, liebenswürdig (*to,* gegenüber *or* zu); ***– to animals,*** tierlieb; ***be – enough to*** or ***be so – as to*** . . ., seien Sie so freundlich *or* gut *or* haben Sie die Güte zu . . .; ***– regards,*** freundliche Grüße (*to,* an (*Acc.*)); ***send one's – regards to him,*** ihn freundlich grüßen lassen.

^{2}**kind,** *s.* 1. die Art, Gattung, Sorte; Klasse, das Geschlecht; ***all of a –,*** alle von derselben Art (*with,* wie); ***all –s of people, people of all –s,*** alle (möglichen) Arten von Menschen, allerlei Menschen, Menschen jeder Art; ***every – of*** . . ., see ***all –s of*** . . .; ***nothing of the –,*** nichts dergleichen; (*as exclamation*) mitnichten! ***something of the –,*** etwas derartiges; ***this – of p.,*** diese Art (von) Mensch; (*coll.*) ***these – of people,*** diese Art Leute; ***this – of th.,*** derartiges; ***what – of p. is he?*** was für ein Mensch ist er? welche Art (von) Mensch ist er? 2. die Natur, Beschaffenheit, Art und Weise; (*sl.*) ***– of,*** sozusagen, gleichsam; (*sl.*) ***I – of promised,*** ich versprach halb und halb; ***difference in degree rather than in –,*** mehr ein Unterschied des Grades als der S.; 3. (*Eccl.*) die Gestalt; 4. Waren (*pl.*), Naturalien (*pl.*); ***in –,*** in Waren, in Natura; (*fig.*) ***repay in –,*** mit gleicher Münze zurückzahlen; ***taxes paid in –,*** Naturalabgaben (*pl.*).

kindergarten ['kindəgɑ:tn], *s.* der Kindergarten.

kind-hearted, *adj.* gutherzig, gütig.

kindle [kindl], **1.** *v.t.* anzünden, entzünden (*also fig.*), (*fig.*) entflammen, anfeuern, erregen; ***– a fire,*** ein Feuer anmachen. **2.** *v.i.* sich entzünden, Feuer fangen; (*fig.*) entbrennen, entflammen, sich erhitzen *or* erregen. **kindler,** *s.* (*fig.*) der Aufwiegler, Unheilstifter, Brandstifter.

kindliness ['kaindlinis], *s.* *See* **kindness,** 1.

kindling ['kindliŋ], *s.* das Anbrennholz, Anmachholz.

kindly ['kaindli], **1.** *adj.* gütig, freundlich, liebenswürdig, gnädig, wohlwollend, wohltätig; gutartig, günstig (*of climate etc.*). **2.** *adv.* freundlich, liebenswürdig; freundlicherweise, freundlichst, gütigst, (*oft. iron.*) gefälligst; ***– give it to me,*** bitte geben Sie es mir! ***take it – of him,*** ihm verbunden sein; ***take – to,*** sich hingezogen fühlen zu, sich befreunden mit, geneigt sein (*Dat.*), liebgewinnen; ***thank you –!*** herzlichen Dank!

kindness ['kaindnis], *s.* 1. die Güte, Freundlichkeit, das Wohlwollen; 2. die Gefälligkeit, Wohltat, der Gefallen.

kindred ['kindrid], **1.** *s.* die (Bluts)verwandtschaft, (*pl. constr.*) Verwandte (*pl.*), die Verwandtschaft. **2.** *adj.* (bluts)verwandt, (*fig.*) verwandt, gleichartig, ähnlich; ***– spirit,*** der Gesinnungsgenosse.

kinema ['kinəmə], *s.* *See* **cinema.**

kinetic [k(a)i'netik], *adj.* kinetisch. **kinetics,** *pl.* (*sing. constr.*) die Kinetik, Bewegungslehre.

king [kiŋ], **1.** *s.* der König (*also Cards, Chess*); (*Draughts*) die Dame; (*B.*) ***Book of Kings,*** das Buch der Könige. **2.** *v.t.* zum König machen. **3.** *v.i.* – ***it,*** den König spielen. **king|-craft,** *s.* die Regierungskunst, das Herrschertalent. **--cup,** *s.* (*Bot.*) der Hahnenfuß.

kingdom ['kiŋdəm], *s.* das Königreich; (*Bot., Zool.*) Reich; ***animal –,*** das Tierreich; ***vegetable –,*** das Pflanzenreich; ***the – of God*** or ***Heaven,*** das Reich Gottes, Himmelreich; (*B.*) ***thy – come,*** dein Reich komme; (*coll.*) ***--come,*** das Jenseits.

king|fisher, *s.* (*Orn.*) der Eisvogel (*Alcedo atthis*). **-like,** *adj. See* **kingly. kingliness,** *s.* das Königliche, Majestätische. **kingly,** *adj.* königlich, majestätisch. **king|-of-arms,** *s.* der Wappenkönig. **-pin,** *s.* (*Motor.*) der Achsschenkelbolzen, Drehbolzen, Achszapfen; (*fig.*) (*a p.*) Hauptvertreter, die Hauptperson, (*a th.*) das Hauptelement, die Hauptsache, Hauptstütze. **--post,** *s.* (*Archit.*) die Dachstuhlsäule, Firstsäule, Giebelsäule.

King's| bench, *s.* das Oberhofgericht. – **Counsel,** *s.* der Kronanwalt. **king's| English,** *s.* das reine Englisch. – **evidence,** *s.* der Hauptzeuge; ***turn –,*** Kronzeuge werden. – **evil,** *s.* Skrofeln (*pl.*). – **highway,** *s.* die (öffentliche) Landstraße. **kingship,** *s.* die Königswürde, das Königtum. **king-size,** *adj.* (*coll.*) überdurchschnittlich groß. **King's Speech,** *s.* die Thronrede.

kink [kiŋk], **1.** *s.* die Kink, Schleife (*in rope*), der Knick (*in wire*); (*fig. coll.*) die Schrulle, Grille, der Klaps, Vogel, Sparren. **2.** *v.i.* Schleifen bilden. **3.** *v.t.* verknoten, knicken.

kinkajou ['kiŋkədʒu:], *s.* (*Zool.*) der Wickelbär.

kinky ['kiŋki], *adj.* (*usu. fig. coll.*) schrullenhaft, überspannt.

kino ['ki:nou], *s.* das Kino(harz), Kinogummi.

kinsfolk ['kinzfouk], *pl.* Verwandte (*pl.*), die Verwandtschaft. **kinship** [–ʃip], *s.* die (Bluts)verwandtschaft, das Verwandtschaftsverhältnis (***to, with,*** mit). **kins|man** [–mən], *s.* (Bluts)verwandte(r). **-woman,** *s.* die (Bluts)verwandte.

kiosk ['kiɔsk], *s.* der Kiosk; Verkaufsstand, Verkaufspavillon; ***telephone –,*** die Fernsprechzelle.

kip [kip], **1.** *v.i.* (*also* ***– down***) (*sl.*) pennen. **2.** *s.* (*sl.*) die Penne.

kipper ['kipə], **1.** *s.* der Räucherhering, Bückling; Hakenlachs. **2.** *v.t.* einsalzen und räuchern.

kirk [kə:k], *s.* (*Scots*) die Kirche; ***the Kirk,*** Schottische Nationalkirche; – ***session,*** das Kollegium der Kirchenältesten.

kirtle [kə:tl], *s.* (*obs.*) das Wams, der Frauenrock.

kiss [kis], **1.** *v.t.* küssen; (*fig. esp. Bill.*) leicht berühren; (*sl.*) – ***the dust,*** ins Gras beißen; – ***him good night,*** ihm einen Gutenachtkuß geben; – ***him good-bye,*** ihm einen Abschiedskuß geben; – ***his hand,*** ihm die Hand küssen, ihm einen Handkuß geben; – ***one's hand to him,*** ihm eine Kußhand zuwerfen; – ***and make*** (***it***) ***up,*** sich wieder vertragen; – ***the rod,*** sich ergeben, sich fügen. **2.** *s.* der Kuß; ***blow*** or ***throw him a –,*** ihm eine Kußhand zuwerfen. **kissing,** *s.* das Küssen. **kissing|-crust,** *s.* der Anstoß am Brote. **--gate,** *s.* das Schwinggatter. **kiss|-me-quick,** *s.* (*coll.*) die Schmachtlocke. **--of-life,** *s.* die Mund-zu-Mund-Beatmung. **--proof,** *adj.* kußecht.

kit [kit], *s.* 1. der Eimer, Zuber, die Wanne, Bütte, das Fäßchen, Tönnchen; 2. die Werkzeugtasche, der Werkzeugkasten; das Handwerkszeug, Arbeitsgerät; 3. (*Mil., coll.*) Gepäck, die Ausrüstung. **kit-bag,** *s.* der Seesack.

kitcat ['kitkæt], *adj.* – ***portrait,*** das Brustbild.

kitchen ['kitʃin], *s.* die Küche. **kitchener,** *s.* der (Patent)kochherd; Küchenmeister (*in monasteries*). **kitchenette** [–'net], *s.* die Kochnische, Kleinküche. **kitchen|-garden,** *s.* der Gemüsegarten, Küchengarten. **--maid,** *s.* die Küchenmagd. **--midden,** *s.* (*Archaeol.*) der Muschelhaufen, Abfallhaufen, Kjökkenmöddinger (*pl.*). **--range,** *s.* der Kochherd. **-ware,** *s.* das Küchengeschirr.

kite [kait], *s.* 1. (*Orn.*) der Gabelweih(e), (Roter) Milan (*Milvus milvus*); 2. der (Papier)drache; (*Av. sl.*) die Kiste, Mühle; ***fly a –,*** einen Drachen steigen lassen; (*Comm.*) Wechselreiterei betreiben; (*fig. coll.*) einen Versuchsballon loslassen; 3. (*sl.*) der Gauner, Halunke; 4. (*Comm.*) (*coll.*) Gefälligkeitswechsel, Kellerwechsel, Reitwechsel. **kite|-balloon,** *s.* der Fesselballon. **--flying,** *s.* (*Comm.*) die Wechselreiterei; (*fig.*) das Sondieren, Loslassen eines Versuchsballons.

kith [kiθ], *s.* (*only in*) – ***and kin,*** Verwandte und Bekannte.

kitten [kitn], **1.** *s.* das Kätzchen. **2.** *v.i.* Junge werfen (*of cats*). **kittenish** ['kitəniʃ], *adj.* kätzchenhaft, (*fig.*) verspielt, spielerisch.

kittiwake ['kitiweik], *s.* (*Orn.*) (*Am.* ***blacklegged –***) die Dreizehenmöwe (*Rissa tridactyla*).

kittle [kitl], *adj.* (*coll.*) kitzlig, heikel, schwer zu behandeln(d) (*of a th.*), unberechenbar (*of a p.*); (*Scots*) – ***cattle,*** unsicher.

kitty ['kiti], *s.* 1. (*Cards etc.*) die (Sammel)kasse, (*coll.*) gemeinsame Kasse; 2. *See* **kitten.**

kiwi ['ki:wi:], *s.* der Kiwi, Schnepfenstrauß.

klepto|mania [klepto'meiniə], *s.* die Kleptomanie, Stehlsucht, der Stehltrieb. **-maniac,** *s.* der Kleptomane (die Kleptomanin).

knack [næk], *s.* (*coll.*) die Fertigkeit, Geschicklichkeit, ausgesprochenes Geschick (***of,*** in *or* mit); der Kunstgriff, Kniff; ***have the – of a th.,*** den Kniff einer S. heraushaben, etwas weghaben.

knacker ['nækə], *s.* der Abdecker, Pferdeschlächter; (*coll.*) Abbruchunternehmer. **knackered,** *adj.* (*vulg.*) völlig fertig *or* erschöpft, abgehetzt, marode. **knackery,** *s.* die Abdeckerei.

knag [næg], *s.* der Knorren, Knoten, Knast. **knaggy,** *adj.* knorrig, knotig.

knap [næp], *s.* die Spitze, Kuppe (*of a hill*); kleiner Hügel.

knapsack ['næpsæk], *s.* der Tornister, Rucksack, Ranzen.

knapweed ['næpwi:d], *s.* (*Bot.*) die Flockenblume.

knar [nɑ:], *s. See* **knag.**

knave [neiv], *s.* der Schuft, Schurke, Spitzbube; (*Cards*) Bube. **knavery,** *s.* die Gaunerei, Schurkerei, Büberei; der Schelmenstreich. **knavish,** *adj.* (spitz)bübisch, schurkisch; – ***trick,*** der Bubenstreich.

knead [ni:d], *v.t.* durchkneten (*dough*); (*fig.*) kneten, massieren; formen, bilden (***into,*** zu); – ***in,*** verkneten; – ***together,*** miteinander verkneten. **kneading,** *s.* das Kneten; – ***trough,*** der Backtrog.

knee [ni:], *s.* das Knie; die Fußwurzel (*of animals*), das Fußwurzelgelenk (*of birds*); (*Tech.*) das Kniestück, die Kröpfung; ***bow the – to,*** das Knie beugen vor (*Dat.*); ***bring him to his –s,*** ihn in *or* auf die Knie zwingen; ***housemaid's –,*** entzündetes Knie; ***on one's –s,*** kniend; ***on bended –, on one's bended –s,*** kniefällig; ***go on one's –s,*** auf die Knie sinken, niederknien (***to,*** vor (*Dat.*)), (*fig.*) kniefällig bitten; ***on the –s of the gods,*** im Schoße der Götter.

knee|-bending, *s.* die Kniebeuge. **--boots,** *pl.* Schaftstiefel, Kanonenstiefel, Kniestiefel (*pl.*). **--breeches,** *pl.* die Kniehose. **-cap,** *s.* 1. (*Anat.*) die Kniescheibe; 2. (*of harness*) das Knieleder. **kneed,** *suff.* ***knock--,*** X-beinig; (*fig.*) ***weak--,*** schwach, nachgiebig. **knee|-deep,** *adj.* knietief (*as snow*), bis an die Knie (*in snow etc.*). **--joint,** *s.* das Kniegelenk (*also Tech.*).

kneel [ni:l], *reg. & irr.v.i.* (– ***down***) knien, auf den Knien liegen; hinknien, niederknien, das Knie beugen (***to,*** vor (*Dat.*)). **kneeler,** *s.* das Kniekissen.

knee|-pan, *s. See* **--cap,** 1. **knees-bend,** *s.* die Kniebeuge. **knee-timber,** *s.* das Knieholz, Krummholz.

knell [nel], **1.** *s.* die Totenglocke, das Grabgeläute; (*fig.*) die Todeswarnung; düsterer Klang. **2.** *v.i.* (*obs.*) läuten. **3.** *v.t.* (durch Läuten) verkünden.

knelt [nelt], *imperf., p.p. of* **kneel.**

knew [nju:], *imperf. of* **know.**

knickerbockers ['nikəbɔkəz], *pl.* (*Hist.*) die Kniehose; *a pair of –*, eine Kniehose; (*obs.*) *see* **knickers.**

knickers ['nikəz], *pl.* der (Damen)schlüpfer, die Schlupfhose; *a pair of –*, eine Schlupfhose.

knick-knack ['niknæk], *s.* der Tand, Schnickschnack, Nippes (*pl.*), die Nippsache; *pl.* der Trödelkram, das Drum und Dran.

knife [naif], **1.** *s.* (*pl.* **knives** [naivz]) das Messer; *– and fork,* das (Eß)besteck; (*coll.*) *have one's – in him, get one's – into him,* ihm übelwollen, ihn gefressen haben; *war to the –,* der Krieg *or* Kampf bis aufs Messer. **2.** *v.t.* erstechen, erdolchen; (*fig. sl.*) in den Rücken fallen (*Dat.*), abschießen. **knife|-board,** *s.* das Messerputzbrett; (*fig. coll.*) die Doppelsitzbank. **--edge,** *s.* die Messerschneide; (*Tech.*) Waageschneide; (*fig.*) Schneide, haarscharfer Rand. **--edged,** *adj.* messerscharf. **--grinder,** *s.* (hausierender) Scherenschleifer. **--rest,** *s.* das Messerbänkchen.

knight [nait], **1.** *s.* der Ritter (*also title*); (*Chess*) Springer; (*fig.*) (*Poet.*) Kavalier, Beschützer, Kämpe; *--at-arms,* bewaffneter Ritter; *– of the road,* der Straßenräuber; Handlungsreisende(r). **2.** *v.t.* zum Ritter schlagen.

knightage ['naitidʒ], *s.* (*collect.*) die Ritterschaft, das Verzeichnis der Ritter. **knight|-errant,** *s.* fahrender Ritter. **--errantry,** *s.* fahrendes Rittertum. **knighthood,** *s.* der Ritterstand, die Ritterwürde; (*collect.*) Ritter (*pl.*), die Ritterschaft; (*fig.*) Ritterlichkeit, das Rittertum. **knight-hospitaller,** *s.* der Johanniter(ritter), Maltheser(ritter). **knightliness,** *s.* die Ritterlichkeit. **knightly,** *adj.* ritterlich; Ritter–. **knight-service,** *s.* (*Hist.*) das (Ritter)lehen, der Ritterdienst.

knit [nit], **1.** *reg. & irr. v.t.* stricken; (*Tech.*) wirken; (*fig.*) (*also Med.*) verbinden, zusammenfügen; (*fig.*) vereinigen, (ver)knüpfen; *– up,* zusammenfügen; abschließen (*argument*); *– the brows,* die Brauen zusammenziehen, die Stirn runzeln. **2.** *irr.v.i.* stricken; (*fig.*) (*– together*) sich verbinden. **knitted,** *adj.* Strick–; *– goods,* Strickwaren, Wirkwaren, Trikotwaren (*pl.*). **knitter,** *s.* der (die) Stricker(in). **knitting,** *s.* das Stricken; Strickzeug; die Strickarbeit, Strickerei; *--machine,* die Strickmaschine; *--needle,* die Stricknadel; *--wool,* das Strickgarn. **knitwear,** *s. See knitted goods.*

knives [naivz], *pl. See* **knife.**

knob [nɔb], *s.* der Knopf, Knauf, Griff; Knorren, Knoten, Buckel, Klumpen, Auswuchs; (*coll.*) das Stückchen (*of sugar etc.*); (*sl.*) die Birne, der Kürbis; (*sl.*) *with –s on,* und wie! **knobbed** [–d], **knobby,** *adj.* knorrig, knotig, buck(e)lig. **knobkerrie,** *s.* der Knüppel.

knock [nɔk], **1.** *v.i.* klopfen (*also of engines*), stoßen, schlagen, prallen (*against*, gegen); (*coll.*) *– about,* sich herumtreiben, bummeln, herumzigeunern; *– against,* zusammenstoßen gegen; (*coll.*) zufällig stoßen auf (*Acc.*) (*a th.*) *or* treffen (*a p.*); (*coll.*) *– off,* aufhören, Schluß machen (*with*, mit); Feierabend machen, die Arbeit einstellen; *– together,* aneinanderstoßen; *– under,* nachgeben, sich geschlagen geben, klein beigeben; *– up against,* zusammenstoßen mit; (*fig.*) zufällig treffen, in den Weg laufen (*Dat.*).
2. *v.t.* klopfen, stoßen, schlagen; *– (at) the door,* an die Tür klopfen; *– one's head,* mit dem Kopf stoßen (*against*, gegen).
(a) (*with advs.*) *– about,* umherstoßen, arg zurichten (*a th.*), böse mitnehmen, arg zusetzen (*a p.*); (*sl.*) *– back,* heruntergießen (*a drink*); *– down,* niederschlagen, niederwerfen, zu Boden strecken, umstoßen; überfahren (*with a vehicle*), einreißen, abbrechen (*buildings etc.*), (*fig.*) vernichten, zunichte machen; stark drücken (*prices*), zuschlagen, zusprechen (*to, Dat.*) (*at auctions*); *– in,* einschlagen; *– off,* abbrechen (*also Typ.*), abschlagen, (*coll.*) schnell erledigen *or* abwickeln, aus dem Ärmel schütteln, schnell hinwerfen; aufhören mit; (*coll.*) abrechnen, abziehen (*from price*); (*sl.*) klauen, mitgehen heißen; (*sl.*) absetzen, abstoßen, an den Mann bringen (*sale*); *– out,* herausarbeiten; (*Boxing, fig.*) kampfunfähig machen, schlagen, besiegen, außer Gefecht bringen, zur Strecke bringen, (*coll.*) erschöpfen; *– over,* umwerfen; überfahren; *– together,* zusammenbasteln, behelfsmäßig zusammenbauen; *– up,* in die Höhe schlagen; wecken; (*coll.*) erschöpfen, fertigmachen; (*coll.*) schnell entwerfen; *–ed up,* (*coll.*) ermüdet, erschöpft, ermattet, abgespannt; (*vulg.*) schwanger.
(b) (*with preps.*) *– against,* stoßen gegen; *– into his head,* ihm einhämmern *or* einprägen; (*coll.*) *– him into the middle of next week,* ihn völlig fertigmachen; *– into shape,* Form *or* Gestalt geben (*Dat.*), gestalten; *– two rooms into one,* zwei Räume zusammenlegen; *– off the price,* von dem Preise abziehen; *– on the head,* niederschlagen (*a p.*), ein Ende machen (*Dat.*), erledigen, vereiteln (*a th.*); (*fig.*) *– the bottom out of,* den Boden entziehen (*Dat.*), zunichte machen.
3. *s.* der Schlag, Stoß; das Anklopfen, Pochen (*at the door*).

knock|-about, *adj.* lärmend, unstet, ruhelos; strapazierfähig (*of clothes*); *– act,* die Clownszene; *– farce,* das Radaustück. **--down,** *adj.* (*coll.*) niederschmetternd, überwältigend; *– price,* der Mindestpreis, äußerster Preis.

knocker ['nɔkə], *s.* 1. der Klopfer, Klopfende(r); *--up,* der Wecker (*a p.*); 2. der Türklopfer; (*sl.*) *up to the –,* famos; 3. (*sl.*) der Miesmacher, Kritikaster; Nörgler.

knock|-kneed, *adj.* X-beinig, (*fig.*) hinkend, lahm. **--knees,** *pl.* X-Beine (*pl.*). **--out,** **1.** *adj.* entscheidend, k.-o.– (*as a blow*), (*Spt.*) Ausscheidungs–. **2.** *s.* (*Boxing*) der Niederschlag, Knockout, K.-o.; (*fig.*) entscheidender Schlag; (*sl.*) *he's* or *it's a –,* er (es) ist unwiderstehlich.

[1]**knoll** [noul], *s.* kleiner Hügel, die Kuppe.

[2]**knoll,** **1.** *s.* (*obs.*) das Geläut(e). **2.** *v.t.* (*obs.*) (zu Grabe) läuten.

knop [nɔp], *s.* (*of yarn*) die Noppe; (*obs.*) (Blumen)-knospe; (*obs.*) der Knopf, Knauf.

[1]**knot** [nɔt], **1.** *s.* 1. der Knoten, (*Naut.*) Stich, Stek; *granny('s) –,* falscher Knoten; *true-lover's –,* der Liebesknoten; *cut the –,* den Knoten durchhauen; *tie a –,* einen Knoten machen; (*fig.*) *tie o.s. into –s,* sich in Widersprüche verwickeln; 2. (*Naut.*) der Knoten, die Seemeile in der Stunde; 3. der (Ast)-knorren, Ast(knoten) (*in wood*); 4. die Schleife, Docke (*of yarn*); 5. (*Mil. etc.*) Epaulette, das Achselstück; 6. (*fig.*) die Schwierigkeit, Verwicklung, der Kern(punkt) (*of a problem*); 7. die Gruppe, der Haufen, der *or* das Knäuel (*of people etc.*). **2.** *v.t.* (ver)knoten, knüpfen, (*fig.*) verwickeln, verwirren, verheddern; *– together,* zusammenknoten. **3.** *v.i.* sich zu (einem) Knoten schürzen, (einen) Knoten bilden.

[2]**knot,** *s.* (*Orn.*) der Knutt, Isländischer Strandläufer (*Calidris canutus*).

knot|-grass, *s.* (*Bot.*) der Knöterich. **--hole,** *s.* das Astloch (*in wood*). **knotted,** *adj.* geknüpft, verknotet (*as cord*); (*fig.*) verwickelt, verschlungen; *see also* **knotty.** **knotty,** *adj.* knotig, knorrig (*as wood*); (*fig.*) schwierig, verwickelt, verzwickt. **knotwork,** *s.* die Knüpfarbeit.

knout [naut], **1.** *s.* die Knute. **2.** *v.t.* die Knute geben (*Dat.*), mit der Knute schlagen.

know [nou], **1.** *irr.v.t.* wissen, sich bewußt sein (*Gen.*); kennen, vertraut sein mit (*a p. or th.*), erkennen (*for*, als), unterscheiden (*from*, von), erleben, erfahren; *he –s it,* er weiß es; *he –s him,* er kennt ihn; *– him to be,* erkennen ihn als; wissen, daß er ist; (*coll.*) *not – him from Adam,* keine Ahnung haben, wer er ist; *– how to do,* zu tun verstehen; *– how to swim,* schwimmen können; *as well as he –s how,* mit Einsatz seines ganzen Könnens; *– what to do,* wissen was zu tun ist; (*coll.*) *– what's what,* sich auskennen; *before you – where you are,* ehe man sich's versieht, im Handumdrehen; *– which side one's bread is buttered,* auf seinen Vorteil bedacht sein; *– by heart,* auswendig wissen *or* können; *– by name,* dem Namen nach kennen; *– by sight,* von Ansehen kennen; *– thyself!* erkenne dich selbst!

(a) (*with nouns*) (*iron.*) – ***all the answers,*** aber auch alles wissen, überall Bescheid wissen (wollen); – ***one's mind,*** sich im klaren sein; wissen, was man will; (*sl.*) – ***one's onions,*** wissen, wo Barthel den Most holt; ***have –n better days,*** bessere Tage gesehen haben; (*coll.*) – ***the ropes,*** sich gut auskennen, gut Bescheid wissen; (*coll.*) – ***a thing or two,*** sich auskennen, Bescheid wissen (***about,*** in (*Dat.*) (*subject, topic*) *or* mit (*a th.*)); – ***the way,*** den Weg kennen *or* wissen; – ***one's way about,*** sich auskennen *or* zurechtfinden.
(b) (*with verbs*) ***come to –,*** erfahren; ***come to be –n,*** bekannt werden; ***get to –,*** kennenlernen; ***let him –,*** ihn wissen lassen, ihn verständigen; ***make –n,*** bekannt machen; ***I have never –n him lie,*** meines Wissens hat er niemals gelogen.
2. *irr.v.i.* wissen (***about, of,*** um *or* von), (*coll.*) im Bilde sein (***about,*** über (*Acc.*)); – ***better than to do,*** nicht so dumm sein, als zu tun; so viel Verstand haben zu wissen, daß man nicht tut; ***there is no –ing,*** man kann nicht wissen; ***not that I – of,*** nicht, daß ich wüßte; (*coll.*) ***I –,*** ich weiß es; selbstverständlich; (*coll.*) ***you –? don't you –?*** nicht wahr? nämlich, verstehen Sie.
3. *s.* (*coll. only in*) ***be in the –,*** im Bilde sein, gut orientiert sein, eingeweiht sein, Bescheid wissen.

knowable ['nouəbl], *adj.* (er)kennbar, kenntlich. **know|-all,** *s.* (*sl.*) der (Alles)besserwisser, Schlaumeier, gelehrtes Haus. **--how,** *s.* (*sl.*) die (Sach)kenntnis, Erfahrung, praktisches Wissen.

knowing ['nouiŋ], *adj.* schlau, gerieben, durchtrieben, verschmitzt; einsichtig, scharfsinnig, geschickt, klug, verständig; – ***look,*** verständnisvoller Blick; (*coll.*) – ***one,*** der Schlauberger. **knowingly,** *adv.* wissentlich, absichtlich, vorsätzlich. **knowingness,** *s.* die Schlauheit, Klugheit.

knowledge ['nɔlidʒ], *s.* (*only sing.*) das Wissen, Kenntnisse (*pl.*) (*of, Gen. or in* (*Dat.*)); die Kenntnis, Kunde; Bekanntschaft, Erfahrung (***of,*** mit); ***come to his –,*** ihm zu Ohren *or* zur Kenntnis kommen; ***be common –,*** allgemein bekannt sein; ***extensive –,*** ausgebreitete Kenntnisse (*pl.*); (*Law*) ***have carnal – of,*** geschlechtlichen Umgang haben mit; ***out of all –,*** so daß man es nicht wiedererkennt; ***tree of –,*** der Baum der Erkenntnis; (***not***) ***to my –,*** (nicht) soviel ich weiß; ***to the best of my –*** (***and belief***), meines Wissens, nach bestem Wissen (und Gewissen); ***working –,*** nützliche *or* verwertbare Kenntnisse; ***without my –,*** ohne mein Wissen. **knowledgeable,** *adj.* kenntnisreich.

known [noun], *adj.* bekannt, anerkannt; ***well-–,*** (wohl)bekannt (***for,*** durch; ***as,*** als).

knuckle [nʌkl], **1.** *s.* der Knöchel, das (Finger)-gelenk; Kniestück (*of veal*), Eisbein (*of pork*); (*fig.*) ***near the –,*** gerade noch möglich, bis nahe an die Grenzen des Anständigen; (*fig.*) ***rap on*** or ***over the –s,*** der Verweis. **2.** *v.t.* mit den Knöcheln pressen *or* reiben. **3.** *v.i.* – ***down to,*** sich eifrig machen an (*Acc.*); – ***down under,*** – ***under to,*** sich beugen (*Dat.*) *or* vor (*Dat.*) *or* unter (*Acc.*), nachgeben (*Dat.*), sich unterwerfen (müssen) (*Dat.*). **knuckle|-bones,** *s.* das Knöchelspiel. **--duster,** *s.* der Schlagring. **--joint,** *s.* (*Anat.*) das (Knöchel- *or* Finger)gelenk, (*Tech.*) die Gliederfuge.

knurl [nə:l], **1.** *v.t.* rändeln, kordeln, riffeln. **2.** *s.* der Knorren, Ast, Knoten.

knut [nʌt], *s.* der Stutzer, Geck, Zierbengel.

koala (bear) [kou'ɑ:lə], *s.* der Beutelbär, Koala.

kope(c)k ['koupek], *s.* die Kopeke.

kopje ['kɔpi], *s.* (*S. Africa*) kleiner Hügel, die Anhöhe.

Koran [kɔ:'rɑ:n], *s.* der Koran.

Korea [kɔ'riə], *s.* Korea (*n.*). **Korean, 1.** *s.* **1.** der (die) Koreaner(in); 2. (*language*) das Koreanisch(e). **2.** *adj.* koreanisch.

kosher ['kouʃə], *adj.* (*Jew.*) koscher, rein (*of meat*); (*sl. esp. Am.*) echt, tauglich.

ko(w)tow [kau'tau], **1.** *s.* (chinesische) demütige Ehrenbezeigung, der Kotau. **2.** *v.i.* Kotau machen (***to,*** vor (*Dat.*)); (*fig.*) sich unterwürfig zeigen (*Dat.*), kriechen, sich ducken (vor (*Dat.*)).

kraal [krɑ:l], *s.* der Kral, die Umzäunung, das Hottentottendorf.

Kremlin ['kremlin], *s.* der Kreml.

kudos ['kju:dɔs], *s.* (*sl.*) der Ruf, Ruhm, Preis, das Ansehen, die Ehre.

kukri ['kukri], *s.* der Ghurkadolch.

kulak ['ku:læk], *s.* der Großbauer.

Kuwait [ku'weit], *s.* Kuwait (*n.*). **Kuwaiti, 1.** *s.* der (die) Kuwaiter(in). **2.** *adj.* kuwaitisch.

kyanize ['kaiənaiz], *v.t.* kyanisieren, mit Sublimat tränken.

kyle [kail], *s.* (*Scots*) die Meerenge, der Sund.

L

L, l [el], *s.* das L, l. *See Index of Abbreviations.*

¹la [lɑ:], *s.* (*Mus.*) die sechste Silbe der Solmisation.

²la! *int.* (*obs.*) sieh (da)! –, –*!* na, na!

laager ['lɑ:gə], **1.** *s.* das Burenlager, die Wagenburg. **2.** *v.t.* (*v.i.*) (sich) lagern.

lab [læb], *s.* (*abbr. for* **laboratory**) (*coll.*) das Labor.

label [leibl], **1.** *s.* 1. der Zettel, das Etikett, (Anhänge)-schildchen, die (Aufklebe)marke; (*fig.*) Etikette, Aufschrift, Beschriftung, Bezeichnung, Kennzeichnung; 2. (*Her.*) der Turnierkragen; 3. (*Archit.*) die Kranzleiste. **2.** *v.t.* mit einem Zettel *or* einer Aufschrift versehen, etikettieren, beschriften; (*fig.*) bezeichnen (***as,*** als), stempeln (zu).

labia ['leibiə], *pl. of* **labium. labial, 1.** *adj.* Lippen–, labial. **2.** *s.* der Lippenlaut, Labial(laut). **labialize** [–laiz], *v.t.* labialisieren. **labiate** [–ieit], **1.** *adj.* lippenförmig; (*Bot.*) lippenblütig. **2.** *s.* der Lippenblüter.

labile ['leibail], *adj.* labil, unsicher; (*Chem.*) unbeständig. **lability** [læ'biliti], *s.* die Labilität.

labio ['leibiou], *pref.* Lippe(n)–. **labium,** *s.* (*Anat.*) die (Scham)lippe.

labor, (*Am.*) *see* **labour.**

laboratory [lə'bɔrətəri, (*Am.*) 'læbrətəri], *s.* das Laboratorium, Labor; die Werkstatt, Werkstätte; – ***assistant,*** der (die) Laborant(in).

laborious [lə'bɔ:riəs], *adj.* 1. mühselig, mühsam, mühevoll; 2. arbeitsam, fleißig (*of a p.*); 3. (*fig.*) schwer(fällig), schleppend. **laboriousness,** *s.* 1. die Mühsal, Mühseligkeit; 2. Arbeitsamkeit, Emsigkeit, der Fleiß; 3. (*fig.*) die Schwerfälligkeit.

labour ['leibə], **1.** *s.* 1. (schwere) Arbeit; die Mühe, Anstrengung, Beschwerde; – ***camp,*** die Arbeitslager; ***Labour Exchange,*** das Arbeitsamt, der Arbeitsnachweis; ***hard –,*** die Zwangsarbeit; ***9 months'*** (***imprisonment with***) ***hard –,*** 9 Monate Zuchthaus; ***have one's – for one's pains,*** sich umsonst abmühen; ***lost –,*** vergebliche Mühe; – ***of love,*** gern getane Arbeit; ***manual –,*** körperliche Arbeit; – ***market,*** der Arbeitsmarkt; – ***shortage,*** der Mangel an Arbeitskräften; ***skilled –,*** Facharbeiter (*pl.*); 2. (*Med.*) Wehen (*pl.*), die Entbindung; ***be in –,*** in den Wehen liegen; 3. Arbeitskräfte (*pl.*), Arbeiter (*pl.*), die Arbeiterschaft, der Arbeiterstand; ***Labour Day,*** der Tag der Arbeit; ***Labour Party,*** die Arbeiterpartei. **2.** *v.i.* 1. arbeiten (***at,*** an (*Dat.*)), sich anstrengen, sich bemühen, sich abmühen, sich (*Dat.*) (alle *or* viel) Mühe geben (***for,*** um); 2. sich mühsam bewegen; (*Naut.*) schlingern, stampfen; – ***under,*** zu kämpfen haben mit, zu leiden haben unter, kranken an (*Dat.*); –

under a delusion or *misapprehension*, sich im Irrtum befinden. **3.** *v.t.* – *an argument*, das Argument umständlich darlegen; – *the point*, auf den Punkt ausführlich eingehen.

laboured ['leibəd], *adj.* mühsam, gezwungen, schwerfällig; – *breath*, schwerer Atem. **labourer,** *s.* (ungelernter) Arbeiter; *agricultural* –, der Landmann, Landarbeiter; *casual* –, der Gelegenheitsarbeiter. **labouring,** *adj.* arbeitend; werktätig, handwerksmäßig, Arbeits–, Arbeiter–; – *classes*, die Arbeiterbevölkerung. **labourite,** *s.* (*coll.*) der Anhänger *or* Abgeordnete der Arbeiterpartei. **labour-saving, 1.** *adj.* arbeitsparend. **2.** *s.* die Arbeitsersparnis.

labret ['læbrit], *s.* der Lippenpflock.

laburnum [lə'bə:nəm], *s.* (*Bot.*) der Goldregen.

labyrinth ['læbərinθ], *s.* das Labyrinth, der Irrgang, Irrgarten; (*fig.*) das Gewirr. **labyrinthine** [–'rinθain], *adj.* labyrinthisch; (*fig.*) verwickelt, wirr, verworren.

[1]**lac** [læk], *s.* der Gummilack.

[2]**lac,** *s.* das Hunderttausend (Rupien).

lace [leis], **1.** *s.* **1.** (geklöppelte) Spitze, Spitzen (*pl.*); (*on uniform etc.*) die Litze, Tresse, Borte, Schnur; **2.** der Schnürsenkel, das Schnürband, der Schuhriemen. **2.** *v.t.* **1.** (zu)schnüren, zusammenschnüren, festschnüren, (*with corset*) einschnüren; (*thread through an eye*) (durch)fädeln, (durch)ziehen (*through*, durch), einfädeln, einziehen (in (*Acc.*)); mit Spitzen besetzen, verbrämen; *–d boots*, Schnürstiefel (*pl.*); **2.** (*coll.*) mit Spirituosen versetzen; *coffee –d with brandy*, der Kaffee mit einem Schuß Branntwein; **3.** (*coll.*) durchprügeln. **3.** *v.i.* sich schnüren (lassen), ein Schnürkorsett tragen; (*as shoes*) zum Schnüren sein.

Lacedaemon [læsi'di:mən], *s.* Lakedämon, Lazedämon (*n.*). **Lacedaemonian** [–di'mouniən], **1.** *s.* der (die) Lakedämonier(in), Lazedämonier(in). **2.** *adj.* lakedämonisch, lazedämonisch.

lace|-maker, *s.* der Spitzenklöppler. **–-paper,** *s.* das Spitzenpapier, Papierspitzen (*pl.*). **–-pillow,** *s.* das Klöppelkissen.

lacerate ['læsəreit], *v.t.* zerreißen, zerfleischen; (*fig.*) verletzen (*feelings etc.*); *–d wound*, die Rißwunde. **laceration** [–'reiʃən], *s.* die Zerreißung, Zerfleischung; der Riß, die Fleischwunde, Rißwunde; (*fig.*) Verletzung.

lacertian [læ'sə:ʃən], **lacertine** [–tain], *adj.* eidechsenartig, Eidechsen–.

lacework ['leiswə:k], *s.* die Spitzenarbeit, Klöppelarbeit; das Spitzenmuster, Filigran(muster).

laches ['lætʃiz], *s.* (*Law*) fahrlässiges Versäumnis, der Verzug.

lachrymal ['lækriml], *adj.* Tränen–. **lachrymator** [–meitə], *s.* (*Mil.*) das Tränengas, der Augenreizstoff. **lachrymatory** [–'meitəri], **1.** *s.* das Tränengefäß. **2.** *adj.* augenreizend, tränenerregend. **lachrymose,** *adj.* tränenreich, weinerlich, rührselig.

lacing ['leisiŋ], *s.* **1.** das (Ver)schnüren; **2.** Schnürband, der Schnürsenkel.

lack [læk], **1.** *v.t.* fehlen an (*Dat.*), nicht haben, entbehren, dringend benötigen; *they – water*, Wasser fehlt ihnen, es fehlt ihnen an Wasser; *he –s perseverance*, es mangelt ihm an Ausdauer; *he –s nothing in perseverance*, er läßt es nicht an Ausdauer fehlen. **2.** *v.i.* (*only pres. p.*) *see* **lacking. 3.** *s.* der Mangel, die Knappheit (*of*, an (*Dat.*)), Ermangelung, das Fehlen (von); *for – of*, aus Mangel an (*Dat.*); *there was no – of*, es fehlte nicht an (*Dat.*); – *of money*, der Geldmangel; *for – of time*, aus Zeitmangel; *water was the chief* –, hauptsächlich fehlte es an Wasser.

lackadaisical [lækə'deizikl], *adj.* (*coll.*) schmachtend; energielos, schlapp, schlaff.

lackey ['læki], **1.** *s.* der Lakai; (*coll. fig.*) Speichellecker, Kriecher. **2.** *v.i.* unterwürfig dienen *or* aufwarten, den Lakai *or* Schranzen machen (*for*, *Dat.*).

lacking ['lækiŋ], *adj. be* –, fehlen, Mangel leiden (*in*, an (*Dat.*)); (*coll.*) einfältig *or* blöde sein. **lack-lustre,** *adj.* glanzlos, matt.

laconic [lə'kɔnik], *adj.* lakonisch, kurz und bündig; einsilbig, kurz angebunden, wortkarg. **laconicism** [–nisizm], **laconism** ['lækənizm], *s.* treffende Kürze, knappe *or* gedrängte Redeweise, die Wortkargheit, der Lakonismus.

lacquer ['lækə], **1.** *v.t.* lackieren. **2.** *s.* **1.** der Lack, (Lack)firnis; **2.** (*also* –*-work*) die Lackarbeit.

lacrosse [lə'krɔs], *s.* das Lacrosse (*kanadisches Nationalballspiel*).

lactate ['lækteit], **1.** *s.* das Laktat; – *of*, milchsauer. **2.** *v.i.* Milch absondern. **lactation** [–'teiʃən], *s.* die Milchabsonderung, Milchbildung; das Säugen, Stillen. **lacteal** [–tiəl], *adj.* milchig, Milch–. **lacteals,** *pl.* (*Anat.*) Lymphgefäße (*pl.*). **lactic,** *adj.* (*Chem.*) Milch–, milchsauer; – *acid*, die Milchsäure; – *fermentation*, die Milchgärung. **lactometer** [–'tɔmitə], *s.* die Milchwaage. **lactose,** *s.* der Milchzucker.

lacuna [lə'kju:nə], *s.* (*pl.* **-ae**) die Lücke; (*Anat.*, *Bot.*) Grube, Vertiefung, der Zwischenraum, Hohlraum, Spalt. **lacunar** [–nɑ:], **1.** *s.* (*Archit.*) die Kassettendecke. **2.** *or* **lacunary** [–nəri], *adj.* lückenhaft.

lacy ['leisi], *adj.* Spitzen–; spitzenartig.

lad [læd], *s.* der Junge, Knabe, Bursche, Jüngling; (*coll.*) lustiger Geselle.

ladder ['lædə], **1.** *s.* die Leiter; (*fig.*) Stufenleiter; Laufmasche (*in stockings*); (*Naut.*) *accommodation* –, die Fallreeptreppe; *rope* –, die Strickleiter; *step* –, die Treppenleiter; – *to fame*, der Weg zur Berühmtheit; (*fig.*) *get one's foot on the* –, einen Anfang machen. **2.** *v.i.* Laufmaschen bekommen. **3.** *v.t.* Laufmaschen machen in (*Acc.*). **ladder-proof,** *adj.* maschenfest.

lade [leid], *v.t.* befrachten, beladen (*a ship etc.*), verfrachten, verladen (*goods*); schöpfen (*water etc.*). **laden,** *adj.* beladen (*also fig.*), (*fig.*) belastet, bedrückt.

la-di-da [lɑ:di'dɑ:], *adj.* (*hum.*) geziert, affektiert.

ladies ['leidiz], *pl. of* **lady**; *–' man*, *see* **lady's man.**

lading ['leidiŋ], *s.* das (Ver)laden, Befrachten; die Ladung, Fracht; *bill of* –, der Frachtbrief, das Konnossement.

ladle [leidl], **1.** *s.* der Schöpflöffel, Kochlöffel; (*Tech.*) die Schöpfkelle; (*of waterwheel*) Schaufel. **2.** *v.t.* schöpfen, auslöffeln.

lady ['leidi], **1.** *s.* die Dame; (*as title*) Lady; (*obs. or coll.*) Frau, Gattin, Gemahlin; (*Poet.*) Herrin, Geliebte; (*Theat.*) *leading* –, die Hauptdarstellerin, erste Liebhaberin; *my* –, gnädige Frau (*usu. servants to titled mistress*); *not a* or *no* –, keine feine Dame; *Our (Blessed) Lady*, die Mutter Gottes, Unsere Liebe Frau; *our sovereign* –, unsere königliche Gebieterin; (*coll.*) *your good* –, Ihre Frau Gemahlin; *Church of Our Lady*, die Marienkirche, Frauenkirche; *young* –, (gnädiges) Fräulein; (*coll.*) die Freundin, der Schatz, die Verlobte; *ladies!* meine Damen! (*coll.*) *ladies* (*sing. constr.*), die Damentoilette. **2.** *attrib. adj.* – *doctor*, die Ärztin; – *friend*, die Freundin; – *help*, die Stütze der Hausfrau; – *mayoress*, die Gemahlin des Oberbürgermeisters.

lady|bird, *s.* (*Ent.*) die Marienkäfer. **–-chapel,** *s.* die Marienkapelle. **Lady-Day,** *s.* Mariä Verkündigung (*25th March*). **lady|-fern,** *s.* der Frauenfarn. **–-in-waiting,** *s.* königliche Kammerfrau, die Hofdame. **–-killer,** *s.* der Herzensbrecher, Schürzenjäger, Weiberheld. **–like,** *adj.* damenhaft. **–love,** *s.* die Geliebte.

lady's bedstraw, *s.* (*Bot.*) das Labkraut.

ladyship ['leidiʃip], *s.* gnädige Frau, gnädiges Fräulein (*as title*).

lady's|-laces, *s.* (*Bot.*) das Mariengras. – **maid,** *s.* die Kammerzofe. – **man,** *s.* der Damenheld, Salonheld. **–-mantle,** *s.* (*Bot.*) der Frauenmantel. **-smock** (*or* **ladysmock**) ['leidismɔk], *s.* (*Bot.*) das Wiesenschaumkraut.

lady's-slipper, *s.* (*Bot.*) der Frauenschuh.
laevulose ['li:vjəlous], *s.* der Fruchtzucker.
[1]**lag** [læg], **1.** *v.i.* **1.** (*oft.* – *behind*) zaudern, zögern, langsam gehen, zurückbleiben, nicht mitkommen, sich (*Dat.*) Zeit lassen; – *behind him,* hinter ihm zurückbleiben, ihm nachstehen *or* nachhinken; 2. (*Elec.*) nacheilen (*in phase*). **2.** *s.* die Verzögerung, das Zurückbleiben; (*Tech.*) die Laufzeit, der Zeitabstand; (*Av.*) die Rücktrift; (*Elec.*) (negative) Phasenverschiebung, die Nacheilung.
[2]**lag, 1.** *v.t.* (*sl.*) ins Loch stecken. **2.** *s.* (*sl.*) (*oft. old* –) der Knastschieber.
[3]**lag, 1.** *s.* die Daube. **2.** *v.t.* verkleiden, verschalen, mit Dauben belegen (*a boiler etc.*).
lagan ['lægən], *s.* (*Naut.*) versenktes Wrackgut.
lager ['lɑ:gə], *s.* das Lagerbier.
laggard ['lægəd], **1.** *adj.* zögernd, langsam, saumselig, lässig, träge. **2.** *s.* Saumselige(r), der Zauderer, Nachzügler, (*coll.*) Schlappschwanz.
[1]**lagging** ['lægiŋ], **1.** *adj.* zögernd, zaudernd. **2.** *s.* das Zögern, Zaudern, Zurückbleiben.
[2]**lagging,** *s.* das Verschalen, Verkleiden; die Verschalung, Verkleidung.
lagoon [lə'gu:n], *s.* die Lagune.
laic ['leiik], **1.** *s.* der Laie. **2.** *or* **laical,** *adj.* weltlich, laienhaft, Laien–. **laicize** [–isaiz], *v.t.* verweltlichen, säkularisieren.
laid [leid], **1.** *imperf., p.p. of* **lay. 2.** *adj.* (*sl.*) – *off,* arbeitslos; – *out,* (geschmackvoll) angelegt (*as a garden*); angelegt, angewandt (*as money*); (*coll.*) – *up,* bettlägerig (*with,* infolge von); aufgehäuft, angesammelt (*as a stock*); abgetakelt (*as a boat*); – *paper,* gestreiftes *or* geripptes Papier.
lain [lein], *p.p. of* [2]**lie, 2.**
lair [lɛə], *s.* das Lager (*of animals*).
laird [lɛəd], *s.* (*Scots*) der Gutsherr.
laissez-faire [leisei'fɛə], *s.* wirtschaftlicher Liberalismus; (*fig.*) das Gehenlassen, die Gleichgültigkeit.
laity ['leiiti], *s.* (*pl. constr.*) Laien (*pl.*), der Laienstand.
[1]**lake** [leik], *s.* der (Binnen)see; *on the* –, am See; *Lake District,* das Seengebiet (von Cumberland und Westmorland); *–-dwellers,* Pfahlbaubewohner (*pl.*); *–-dwellings,* Pfahlbauten (*pl.*); – *poets,* Dichter der englischen Seeschule.
[2]**lake,** *s.* roter Farbstoff, das Kokkusrot.
lakh, *see* [2]**lac.**
Lallans ['lælənz], *s.* das Tieflandschottisch(e).
lam [læm], **1.** *v.t.* (*sl.*) verdreschen, vermöbeln, verbleuen. **2.** *v.i.* (*sl.*) – *into,* drauflosschlagen auf (*Acc.*). **3.** *s.* (*sl.*) *on the* –, beim Abhauen *or* Türmen.
lama ['lɑ:mə], *s.* der Lama. **lamasery,** *s.* der Lamakloster.
lamb [læm], **1.** *s.* das Lamm; (*Cul.*) junges Hammelfleisch ; *with* –, trächtig (*of sheep*); (*fig.*) *like a* –, sanft wie ein Lamm. **2.** *v.i.* (ab)lammen; *–ing time,* die Lammzeit.
lambaste ['læmbæst], *v.t.* (*sl.*) *see* **lam, 1**; (*fig.*) herunterputzen.
lambency ['læmbənsi], *s.* das Strahlen, Funkeln, Züngeln. **lambent,** *adj.* strahlend, züngelnd, flackernd, funkelnd (*of light; also fig.*).
lambkin ['læmkin], *s.* das Schäfchen, Lämmchen. **lamb|like,** *adj.* (*fig.*) sanft, lammfromm. **–skin,** *s.* das Lammfell; Schafleder.
lamb's| lettuce, *s.* (*Bot.*) der Feldsalat. **– tails,** *pl.* (*coll.*) Haselkätzchen; Weidenkätzchen (*pl.*). **–-wool,** *s.* die Schafwolle, Lammwolle.
lame [leim], **1.** *adj.* lahm, hinkend (*in,* auf (*Dat.*)); (*fig.*) unbefriedigend, fehlerhaft, mangelhaft; (*coll.*) – *duck,* der Versager, die Niete, krankes Huhn, der Pechvogel; (*Comm.*) Zahlungsunfähige(r), fauler Kunde; – *excuse,* faule Ausrede; – *verse,* hinkender Vers. **2.** *v.t.* lähmen, lahm schlagen.
lamella [læ'melə], *s.* das Plättchen, Blättchen, die Lamelle. **lamellar, lamellate(d)** ['læmileit(id)], *adj.* blätterig, lamellenartig.
lameness ['leimnis], *s.* die Lahmheit, (*fig.*) Mangelhaftigkeit, Schwäche.
lament [lə'ment], **1.** *v.t.* beklagen, bejammern, betrauern, beweinen. **2.** *v.i.* (weh)klagen, jammern, trauern (*for, over,* um). **3.** *s.* die (Weh)klage, der Jammer; das Klagelied. **lamentable** ['læməntəbl], *adj.* bedauerlich, beklagenswert; kläglich, jammervoll, jämmerlich, erbärmlich, elend. **lamentation** [læmen'teiʃən], *s.* die Wehklage; (*B.*) *Lamentations,* Klagelieder Jeremiä (*pl.*). **lamented,** *adj.* betrauert; *the late* –, kürzlich Verstorbene(r).
lamina ['læminə], *s.* das Plättchen, die Schuppe; (*Bot.*) Blattfläche; (*Geol.*) dünne Schicht. **laminar,** *adj.* in Plättchen, blätterig. **laminate, 1.** [–eit], *v.t.* (*Metall.*) auswalzen, strecken; (*Elec.*) lamellieren; (*Text.*) laminieren. **2.** [–eit], *v.i.* sich blättern. **3.** [–it], *adj. See* **laminar. laminated,** *adj.* lamellenförmig, in Schichten, blätterig. **lamination** [–'neiʃən], *s.* **1.** das Strecken, die Laminierung, Schichtung; **2.** das Plättchen; (Transformator)blech.
Lammas ['læməs], *s.* (*also* – *day,* – *tide*) Petri Kettenfeier (*1st August*).
lammergeier, lammergeyer ['læməgaiə], *s.* (*Orn.*) der Bartgeier (*Gypaëtus barbatus*).
lamp [læmp], *s.* die Lampe; Ampel; (*fig.*) Leuchte, das Licht. **lamp|-black,** *s.* der Lampenruß, Gasruß, Kienruß, Ölruß, das Rußschwarz, Lampenschwarz. **–-chimney, –-glass,** *s.* der (Lampen)zylinder. **–-holder,** *s.* die (Lampen)fassung. **–light,** *s.* das Lampenlicht. **–-lighter,** *s.* der Laternenanzünder. **–-oil,** *s.* das Brennöl, Leuchtöl.
lampoon [læm'pu:n], **1.** *s.* die Schmähschrift, Satire. **2.** *v.t.* eine Schmähschrift machen auf (*Acc.*) *or* richten gegen, verunglimpfen. **lampooner,** *s.* der Verfasser einer Schmähschrift.
lamp-post, *s.* der Laternenpfahl; (*coll.*) *between you,* (*and*) *me and the* –, unter uns (gesagt).
lamprey ['læmpri], *s.* (*Ichth.*) das Neunauge.
lamp-shade, *s.* der Lampenschirm, die Lampenglocke.
lanate ['læneit], *adj.* wollig, Woll–.
lance [lɑ:ns], **1.** *s.* die Lanze, der Speer. **2.** *v.t.* (mit einer Lanze) durchbohren; (*Surg.*) (mit einer Lanzette) aufschneiden. **lance|-bucket,** *s.* der Lanzenschuh. **–-corporal,** (*sl.*) **–-jack,** *s.* Gefreite(r). **lanceolate** [–iəleit], *adj.* lanzettförmig, (*esp. Bot.*) lanzettlich.
lancer ['lɑ:nsə], *s.* der Ulan; *pl.* (*sing. constr.*) (*dance*) Lanciers (*pl.*).
lancet ['lɑ:nsit], *s.* die Lanzette; – *arch,* der Spitzbogen; – *window,* das Spitzbogenfenster.
land [lænd], **1.** *s.* das Land; der Grund und Boden, Landbesitz, Grundbesitz, das Grundstück, *pl.* Güter (*pl.*), Ländereien (*pl.*); *pl.* (*Tech.*) (*of gun barrel*) Felder (*pl.*); (*fig.*) das Reich, Gebiet; *by* –, zu Lande; (*Scots*) – *of the leal,* der Himmel; – *of the living,* das Reich der Lebenden; (*Naut.*) *make* (*the*) –, Land sichten; – *of Nod,* der Schlaf; *ploughed* –, bebauter Acker; (*fig.*) *see how the* – *lies,* wissen woher der Wind weht, wissen wie der Hase läuft. **2.** *v.t.* landen, an Land bringen, ausschiffen (*troops etc.*), ans Land bringen (*fish*), löschen, ausladen (*cargo*), absetzen, niedersetzen (*a passenger*); (*fig. coll.*) versetzen, verpassen (*a blow*), gewinnen, kriegen, erringen, sich holen, schnappen, (*Spt.*) ans Ziel bringen; – *him in a difficulty,* ihn in eine Klemme bringen *or* verwickeln; (*coll.*) – *o.s. in, be –ed in,* hineingeraten in (*Acc.*); – *him with,* ihm aufhalsen. **3.** *v.i.* landen, aussteigen, sich ausschiffen, an Land gehen (*at,* in (*Dat.*)) (*of passengers*), anlegen (*of ships*), (*fig.*) ans Ziel kommen, ankommen, gelangen; – *on one's head,* auf den Kopf fallen; (*Av.*) – *on instruments,* eine Blindlandung machen.
land-agent, *s.* der Gütermakler, Grundstückmakler.
landau ['lændɔ:], *s.* der Landauer; *state* –, die

Staatskutsche. **landaulet** [–'let], *s.* der Halblandauer.

land|-bank, *s.* die Bodenkreditanstalt, Grundkreditbank, Hypothekenbank. **--breeze,** *s.* der Landwind.

landed ['lændid], *adj.* Land–, Grund–; – ***gentry,*** niederer Landadel; – ***interest,*** (*collect.*) Grundbesitzer (*pl.*); – ***nobility,*** der Landadel; – ***property,*** das Grundeigentum, der Grundbesitz, Ländereien (*pl.*); – ***proprietor,*** der Grundbesitzer, Grundeigentümer.

land|fall, *s.* (*Naut.*) die Landsichtung, Landkennung, (*Av.*) Landung. **--fighting,** *s.* der Erdkampf. **--forces,** *pl.* Landstreitkräfte (*pl.*). **--girl,** *s.* die Erntearbeiterin, Erntehelferin. **--grabber,** *s.* der Landraffer, Landschnapper. **–grave,** *s.* (*Hist.*) der Landgraf. **–holder,** *s.* der Gutsbesitzer, Grundeigentümer.

landing ['lændiŋ], *s.* 1. das Landen, die Landung (*passengers, aircraft*), das Anlegen (*ships*), Ausladen, Löschen (*goods*), die Ausschiffung (*troops*); (*Av.*) ***blind*** –, die Blindlandung; (*Av.*) ***forced*** –, die Notlandung; (*Av.*) ***pancake*** –, die Durchsacklandung; (*Av.*) ***rough*** –, die Bumslandung; (*Av.*) ***make a safe*** –, glücklich landen; 2. der (Treppen)absatz (*of stairs*); 3. (*Min.*) das Füllort.

landing|-apron, *s.* das Schleppsegel (*for seaplanes*). **--charges,** *pl.* die Löschgebühr. **--craft,** *s.* das Landungsboot. **--deck,** *s.* das Flugdeck. **--field,** *s. See* **--ground. --gear,** *s.* (*Av.*) das Fahrwerk, Fahrgestell. **--ground,** *s.* (*Av.*) der Landeplatz. **--light,** *s.* (*Av.*) das Landelicht. **--net,** *s.* der Hamen, Ketscher. **--party,** *s.* das Landungskommando. **--place,** *s.* (*Naut.*) der Anlegeplatz, Landeplatz. **--stage,** *s.* die Landungsbrücke, der Landungssteg. **--strip,** *s.* (*Av.*) die Landebahn, das Rollfeld. **--wheel,** *s.* (*Av.*) das Laufrad.

land|-jobber, *s.* der Gütermakler, Grundbesitzspekulant. **–lady,** *s.* die Wirtin. **--league,** *s.* (*Hist.*) (irische) Landliga. **landless,** *adj.* grundbesitzlos, ohne Grundbesitz. **land|-locked,** *adj.* vom Lande eingeschlossen, landumschlossen. **–lord,** *s.* 1. der Gutsherr, Grundbesitzer, Grundeigentümer; 2. Hauseigentümer, Hausbesitzer, Hausherr; 3. Hauswirt; (Gast)wirt. **–lubber,** *s.* (*Naut.*) die Landratte. **–mark,** *s.* der Grenzstein, das Grenzzeichen, (*fig.*) der Markstein, das Wahrzeichen, der Wendepunkt. – **measure,** *s.* das Flächenmaßsystem. **–mine,** *s.* (*Mil.*) die Flattermine; (*Av.*) Fallschirmbombe. **–owner,** *s.* der Grundbesitzer, Gutsbesitzer. **–owning,** *adj.* grundbesitzend. **–rail,** *s.* (*Orn.*) der Wachtelkönig, Wiesenknarrer, die Wiesenralle (*Crex crex*). – **reform,** *s.* die Bodenreform. – **register,** *s.* das Grundbuch. **Land-Rover,** *s.* (*registered trade name*) der Geländewagen, geländegängiger Wagen.

landscape ['læn(d)skeip], *s.* die Landschaft; *--gardening,* die Landschaftsgärtnerei; *--painter,* der Landschaftsmaler.

land|-shark, *s.* (*Naut.*) (*sl.*) der Halsabschneider; (*Am.*) *see* **--grabber. –slide,** *s.* (*Geol.*) der Erdrutsch; (*fig. Pol.*) Zusammenbruch, Umsturz, Umschwung; politische Umwälzung, überwältigender (Wahl)sieg. **–slip,** *s.* der Erdrutsch, Bergsturz.

landsman ['lændzmən], *s.* der Landbewohner.

land|-surveyor, *s.* der Landvermesser. **--tax,** *s.* die Grundsteuer. **landward** [–wəd], *adj.* land(ein)wärts gelegen. **landward(s),** *adv.* land(ein)wärts, (nach) dem Lande zu.

lane [lein], *s.* der Heckenweg, Pfad (*in the country*); die Gasse, das Gäßchen (*in towns*); der Durchhau, die Schneise (*in a wood*); das Spalier (*of persons*); (*fig.*) (*Naut.*) die (Fahrt)route, der Dampferweg; die Durchfahrt (*in ice*), Sperrlücke (*in minefield*); (*Spt.*) Bahn; (*Motor.*) Fahrbahn; ***air*** –, die Flugschneise ; ***it is a long – that has no turning,*** selbst der längste Weg *or* Tag hat einmal ein Ende.

lang syne ['læŋ'zain], (*Scots*) **1.** *adv.* lange her, einst, längst, vor langer Zeit. **2.** *s.* ***auld*** –, längst vergangene Zeit.

language ['læŋgwidʒ], *s.* 1. die Sprache; 2. Worte (*pl.*), Reden (*pl.*); die Ausdrucksweise, Sprechweise, Diktion; Terminologie, Phraseologie, der Stil; ***bad*** –, Schimpfworte, ordinäre Ausdrücke (*pl.*); ***strong*** –, Kraftausdrücke (*pl.*), derbe Sprache.

languid ['læŋgwid], *adj.* schlaff, matt, erschöpft; lau, träge, schleppend; (*Comm.*) flau. **languidness,** *s.* die Mattigkeit, Schlaffheit, Erschöpfung; Trägheit, Lauheit, Flauheit. **languish,** *v.i.* matt *or* schwach *or* schlaff werden, erschlaffen, ermatten, erlahmen (*as interest*); dahinsiechen, dahinwelken; (ver)schmachten; sich sehnen *or* härmen (***for,*** nach); daniederliegen (*as trade*). **languishing,** *adj.* ermattend, erschlaffend, erlahmend; (dahin)siechend, (ver)schmachtend; sehnsuchtsvoll, sehnsüchtig, schmachtend (*glances etc.*); (*Comm.*) lau, flau.

languor ['læŋgə], *s.* die Ermüdung, Müdigkeit, Schwäche, Abspannung, Abgespanntheit, Mattigkeit, Schlaffheit, Trägheit, Stumpfheit, Lauheit, Flauheit. **languorous,** *adj.* matt, schlaff, schwach; träge, lau, stumpf; schmachtend, sehnsüchtig; drückend, schwül.

lank [læŋk], *adj.* schlaff, schlapp; mager, dünn; (*of hair etc.*) strähnig, (*of plants*) hoch aufgeschossen. **lankiness,** *s.* (*usu. of a p.*) die Schlacksigkeit. **lankness,** *s.* die Schlaffheit, Schlappheit; Magerkeit, Dünnheit. **lanky,** *adj.* (*usu. of a p.*) schlacksig, (lang) aufgeschossen.

lanner ['lænə], *s.* (weiblicher) Würgfalke *or* Blaufußfalke. **lanneret** [–'ret], *s.* männlicher Würgfalke *or* Blaufußfalke.

lanoline ['lænəlin], *s.* das Lanolin, (Schaf)wollfett.

lansquenet ['lænskənet], *s.* (*Hist.*) der Landsknecht.

lantern ['læntən], *s.* die Laterne; der Laternenraum (*of lighthouse*); (*Archit.*) durchbrochenes Türmchen, der Dachaufsatz; ***Chinese*** –, der Lampion; ***dark*** –, die Blendlaterne; ***magic*** –, der Projektionsapparat. **lantern|-jawed,** *adj.* hohlwangig. **--jaws,** *pl.* eingefallene Wangen (*pl.*). **--lecture,** *s.* der Lichtbildervortrag. **--slide,** *s.* das Lichtbild, Diapositiv, die Lichtbildplatte.

lanyard ['lænjəd], *s.* (*Naut.*) das Taljereep; die Schnur, Schleife, Schlinge.

Laos [laus], *s.* Laos (*n.*). **Laotian** ['lauʃən], **1.** *s.* der Laote (die Laotin). **2.** *adj.* laotisch.

[1]**lap** [læp], *s.* der Schoß; ***in the – of the gods,*** im Schoß der Götter.

[2]**lap, 1.** *v.t.* 1. falten, (ein)hüllen, (ein)wickeln, einschlagen (*in,* in (*Acc.*)); übereinanderlegen (*boards etc.*); (*fig.*) einschließen, einhüllen, umhüllen, umgeben, betten (***in,*** in (*Acc.*)); 2. (*Spt.*) überrunden. **2.** *v.i.* (– ***over***) vorstehen, hinübergreifen, hineinragen (***into, on to,*** in *or* auf (*Acc.*)). **3.** 1. (*Bookb.*) der Falz; 2. (*Text.*) Wickel, die Wick(e)lung, Windung; 3. der Vorstoß, übergreifende Kante; 4. (*Spt.*) die Runde, der Lauf.

[3]**lap, 1.** *s.* das Auflecken, Plätschern, Anschlagen. **2.** *v.t.* auflecken (*of animals*); plätschern an (*Acc.*) *or* gegen (*of water*); (*coll.*) – ***up,*** verschlingen, verzehren. **3.** *v.i.* plätschern, lecken.

lap-dog, *s.* der Schoßhund.

lapel [lə'pel], *s.* der (Rock)aufschlag, Revers.

lapidary ['læpidəri], **1.** *adj.* Stein–, Lapidar–; – ***style,*** wuchtiger Stil. **2.** *s.* der Steinschneider. **lapidate** [–deit], *v.t.* steinigen. **lapidation** [–'deiʃən], *s.* die Steinigung.

lapis lazuli [læpis'læzjulai], *s.* der Lasurstein.

lap-joint, 1. *s.* die Überlappung(sverbindung). **2.** *v.t.* überlappen.

Lapland ['læplənd], *s.* Lappland (*n.*). **Laplander, Lapp,** *s.* der (die) Lappe, Lappländer(in).

lappet ['læpit], *s.* der Zipfel (*of a coat*); Lappen (*of skin*).

lapse [læps], **1.** *s.* 1. das Dahingleiten, Hinabgleiten, (Ab)sinken, Verfallen; 2. (*fig.*) Abfallen, Abweichen, Abgehen, (*esp. Eccl.*) der Abfall, (*esp. moral*) die Entgleisung, das Versäumnis, Vergehen, der Fehltritt; Mißgriff, Lapsus, kleiner Fehler *or* Irrtum, das Versehen; 3. (*of time*) der Verlauf, Ablauf, die Zeitspanne; (*Law*) der Verfall, das Erlöschen (*of laws*), der Heimfall (*of inheritance*). **2.** *v.i.* 1. dahingleiten, (hin)abgleiten, absinken, verfallen, geraten (***into***, in (*Acc.*)), (*esp. Eccl.*) abfallen (***from***, von); 2. verstreichen, verfließen, verlaufen (*as time*); 3. straucheln, einen Fehltritt tun, entgleisen (*morally*); 4. (*Law*) verfallen, erlöschen (*as laws*), heimfallen (*inheritance*) (***to***, an (*Acc.*)).

lapwing ['læpwiŋ], *s.* (*Orn.*) der Kiebitz (*Vanellus vanellus*).

larboard ['lɑ:bəd], *s.* (*Naut.*) (*obs.*) das Backboard.

larcenist ['lɑ:sənist], *s.* der Dieb. **larceny,** *s.* der Diebstahl.

larch [lɑ:tʃ], *s.* (*Bot.*) die Lärche.

lard [lɑ:d], **1.** *s.* das Schweinefett, Schmalz. **2.** *v.t.* spicken (*meat, also fig.*); (*coll.*) einfetten. **lardaceous** [–'deiʃəs], *adj.* (*Med.*) fettartig, speckartig.

larder ['lɑ:də], *s.* die Speisekammer, der Speiseschrank. **larding-needle,** *s.* die Spicknadel. **lardon** [–n], **lardoon** [–'du:n], *s.* der Speckstreifen.

large [lɑ:dʒ], *adj.* groß; beträchtlich, bedeutend; ausgedehnt, umfassend, weitgehend; (*obs.*) großzügig, hochherzig, großmütig; ***as – as life,*** in Lebensgröße; ***at –,*** auf freiem Fuß; (*fig.*) im ganzen *or* allgemeinen, als Ganzes, in der Gesamtheit; ***talk at –,*** in den Tag hineinreden; ***treat*** (*a thing*) ***at –,*** (eine S.) ausführlich besprechen; ***world at –,*** gesamte Welt; ***by and –,*** im großen und ganzen; ***on the – side,*** etwas zu weit (*of clothes*); ***– intestine,*** der Dickdarm; ***– meal,*** reichliche Mahlzeit.

large|-boned, *adj.* starkknochig. **--hearted,** *adj.* großherzig, großmütig, großzügig. **--limbed,** *adj.* starkgliederig. **largely,** *adv.* reichlich; in großem Umfange, weitgehend, zum großen Teil, großenteils, größtenteils. **large|-minded,** *adj.* weitherzig, großdenkend, tolerant, aufgeschlossen, vorurteilslos. **--mindedness,** *s.* die Vorurteilslosigkeit, Weitherzigkeit, Toleranz. **largeness,** *s.* die Größe, Weite, Ausdehnung, der Umfang; (*obs.*) die Großzügigkeit, Freigebigkeit. **large|-scale,** *adj.* Groß–, Massen–; (*map*) in großem Maßstab; (*fig.*) groß(angelegt), umfangreich. **--sized,** *adj.* großen Formats, Groß–. **largess(e)** [–'dʒes], *s.* die Freigebigkeit; Gabe, Schenkung. **largish** [–dʒiʃ], *adj.* ziemlich groß.

lariat ['læriət], *s.* der *or* das Lasso.

[1]**lark** [lɑ:k], *s.* (*Orn.*) die (Feld)lerche (*Alauda arvensis*); ***rise with the –,*** mit den Hühnern aufstehen.

[2]**lark, 1.** *s.* (*coll.*) der Spaß, Ulk, Jux, Feez; ***what a –!*** zum Schießen! ***have a –,*** seinen Spaß haben. **2.** *v.i.* (***– about***) tolle Streiche machen, Possen treiben.

larkspur ['lɑ:kspə:], *s.* (*Bot.*) der Rittersporn.

larrikin ['lærikin], *s.* (*Austral. sl.*) der Raufbold, Lümmel.

larrup ['lærəp], *v.t.* (*sl.*) verdreschen, vermöbeln.

larva ['lɑ:və], *s.* die Larve, Puppe. **larval,** *adj.* Larven–, Raupen–.

laryngeal [læ'rindʒiəl], *adj.* Kehlkopf–. **laryngitis** [–'dʒaitis], *s.* die Kehlkopfentzündung. **laryngophone** [–'riŋgəfoun], *s.* das Kehlkopfmikrophon. **laryngoscope** [–'riŋgəskoup], *s.* (*Med.*) der Kehlkopfspiegel. **larynx** ['læriŋks], *s.* der Kehlkopf.

lascar ['læskə], *s.* indischer Matrose.

lascivious [lə'siviəs], *adj.* lüstern, geil, wollüstig; lasziv. **lasciviousness,** *s.* die Geilheit, Lüsternheit.

laser ['leizə], *s.* der Laserstrahl.

[1]**lash** [læʃ], **1.** *s.* 1. der Peitschenhieb; die Prügelstrafe; Peitschenschnur; (*fig.*) Geißel, Rute; 2. *See* **eyelash. 2.** *v.t.* peitschen; peitschen an (*Acc.*), schlagen gegen (*of water*); peitschen mit (*its tail, of an animal*); (*fig.*) geißeln, verspotten; treiben (*into*, zu); ***– o.s. into a fury,*** sich in Wut hineinsteigern. **3.** *v.i.* ***– down,*** herabstürzen, niederprasseln (*of rain*); ***– out,*** (hinten) ausschlagen (*as a horse*); (*fig.*) wild um sich schlagen; ausbrechen (***into***, in (*Acc.*)).

[2]**lash,** *v.t.* festmachen, (fest)binden (***to, on,*** an (*Dat.*)), (*Naut.*) laschen, zurren.

lasher ['læʃə], *s.* der Überfall (*of water*); das Wehr.

[1]**lashing** ['læʃiŋ], *s.* 1. das Peitschen, Geißeln; die Auspeitschung, Tracht Prügel; 2. *pl.* (*sl.*) die Fülle (***of***, an (*Dat.*)), Menge, Massen (*pl.*) (von).

[2]**lashing,** *s.* das Festmachen, Anbinden; (*Naut.*) der Zurring, das Zeising, Seising; Sorrtau, Rödeltau, Bändsel; ***square –,*** der Bockschnürbund.

lass [læs], *s.* (*Scots, coll.*) das Mädchen; (*Poet.*) die Liebste, der Schatz. **lassie,** *s.* (*Scots*) kleines Mädchen, das Mädel.

lassitude ['læsitju:d], *s.* die Müdigkeit, Mattigkeit, Mattheit, Schlaffheit, Abspannung, Abgespanntheit.

lasso [læ'su:], **1.** *s.* der *or* das Lasso. **2.** *v.t.* mit dem Lasso fangen.

[1]**last** [lɑ:st], **1.** *adj.* 1. letzt; vorig, vergangen; ***in the – analysis,*** letzten Endes; ***the – hope,*** die einzig übrigbleibende Hoffnung; ***the Last Judgement,*** Jüngstes Gericht; ***be on one's – legs,*** auf dem letzten Loch pfeifen; ***to the – man,*** bis auf den letzten Mann; ***– Monday*** or ***Monday –,*** letzten *or* vorigen Montag; ***– meal,*** die Henkersmahlzeit; ***– night,*** gestern abend; ***– but one,*** vorletzt; ***the – post,*** der Zapfenstreich; ***– sacrament,*** das Sterbesakrament; ***for the – time,*** zum letzten Mal; ***the – two,*** die beiden letzten; ***– but two,*** drittletzt; 2. äußerst, höchst; ***of the – importance,*** von der äußersten *or* höchsten Wichtigkeit; ***the – thing in . . .,*** das Neueste auf dem Gebiet von . . .; 3. am wenigsten erwartet *or* geeignet. **2.** *s.* ***the –,*** der *or* die *or* das Letzte *or* Hinterste; (*Poet.*) das Ende; der Tod; ***at –,*** endlich, schließlich, zuletzt; ***at long –,*** zu guter Letzt; ***breathe one's –,*** den letzten Atem aushauchen, den Geist aufgeben; ***hear*** (***see***) ***the – of,*** nichts mehr hören (sehen) von; ***look one's – on,*** den letzten Blick werfen auf (*Acc.*); ***to the –,*** bis zum Ende *or* Schluß *or* äußersten. **3.** *adv.* zuletzt, zum letzten Mal; als letzte(r, -s), an letzter Stelle; ***– (but) not least,*** nicht zuletzt, nicht zum wenigsten; ***– of all,*** ganz zuletzt, (*fig.*) zu allerletzt, nicht zum wenigsten.

[2]**last, 1.** *v.i.* (an)dauern, fortdauern, anhalten, bestehen, währen; (sich) halten (*as colour*); (*also coll.* ***– out***) (hin)reichen, ausreichen. **2.** *v.t.* so lange dauern *or* leben wie, überdauern, überleben; (*with Dat. of p.*) ausreichen für, hinreichen für, genügen (*Dat.*); ***he won't – the winter,*** er überlebt den Winter nicht; ***it will – us the whole week,*** es wird uns für die ganze Woche ausreichen; (*coll.*) ***– him out,*** ebenso lange aushalten wie er, länger aushalten als er.

[3]**last,** *s.* der Leisten; ***put on the –,*** über den Leisten schlagen; (*fig.*) ***stick to one's –,*** bei seinem Leisten bleiben.

[4]**last,** *s.* ***– of herrings,*** 12 Faß Heringe; ***– of wheat,*** (etwa) 3000 l. Weizen; ***– of wool,*** (etwa) 2000 kg. Wolle.

lasting ['lɑ:stiŋ], *adj.* (aus)dauernd, dauerhaft; anhaltend, haltbar; nachhaltig, beständig. **lastingness,** *s.* die Dauerhaftigkeit, Haltbarkeit, Beständigkeit, Nachhaltigkeit.

latch [lætʃ], **1.** *s.* die Klinke, der Drücker, Schnäpper, das Sicherheitsschloß, Schnappschloß; ***on the –,*** (nur) eingeklinkt. **2.** *v.t.* einklinken, zuklinken, zuschließen. **3.** *v.i.* sich klinken lassen, (sich) einklinken, einschnappen; (*coll.*) ***– on to,*** sich anschließen an (*Acc.*), sich zugesellen (*Dat.*) (*a p.*), die Gedanken lenken *or* verlegen auf (*Acc.*), erfassen (*ideas*).

latchet ['lætʃit], *s.* (*B.*) der Schuhriemen.

latchkey ['lætʃki:], *s.* der Schnappschloßschlüssel, (*coll.*) Haus(tür)schlüssel; ***– child,*** das Schlüsselkind.

late [leit], **1.** *adj.* 1. spät; zu spät, verspätet; Spät–, vorgerückt; ***be –,*** sich verspäten, Verspätung haben; zu spät kommen, spät dran sein; zurück *or* rückständig sein; ***be – in developing,*** sich spät entwickeln; ***at a – hour,*** zu später Stunde, sehr spät; 2. verstorben, selig; ***my – brother,*** mein seliger *or* verstorbener Bruder; 3. früher, ehemalig, einstig, vormalig; ***– owner,*** früherer *or* ehemaliger Besitzer; ***of – years,*** seit einigen Jahren, in den letzten Jahren; 4. jüngst; ***– news,*** neueste Nachrichten. **2.** *adv.* spät; ***as – as yesterday,*** noch *or* erst gestern; ***come –,*** zu spät kommen; ***– in the day,*** spät am Tage, zu später Stunde; (*coll.*) reichlich spät, fast zu spät; ***better – than never,*** lieber spät als gar nicht; ***of –,*** kürzlich, neulich, in letzter Zeit, seit einiger Zeit; ***– of London,*** früher wohnhaft in L.; ***stay up –,*** bis spät in die Nacht aufbleiben.

latecomer [ˈleitkʌmə], *s.* der Spätling, Nachzügler, Zuspätgekommene(r), Zuspätkommende(r).

lateen sail [læˈti:n], *s.* das Lateinsegel.

late-fee, *s.* die Strafgebühr für Verspätung; der Portozuschlag nach Postschluß.

lately [ˈleitli], *adv.* kürzlich, vor kurzem, neulich, jüngst, unlängst.

latency [ˈleitənsi], *s.* das Verborgensein, die Verborgenheit, Latenz.

lateness [ˈleitnis], *s.* die Verspätung, spätes Kommen; späte Entwicklung; ***– of the hour,*** späte *or* vorgerückte Stunde.

latent [ˈleitənt], *adj.* verborgen, versteckt; unentwickelt, schlafend, latent; (*Chem.*) gebunden; ***– heat,*** die Umwandlungswärme; (*Psych.*) ***– period,*** die Latenzzeit, das Latenzstadium.

later [ˈleitə], *comp. adj. or adv. See* **late**; ***– on,*** später(hin); ***sooner or –,*** früher oder später, über kurz oder lang.

lateral [ˈlætərəl], **1.** *adj.* seitlich, Seiten–, Neben–, Quer–; ***– axis,*** die Querachse; ***– branch,*** die Seitenlinie (*of a family*); (*Av.*) ***– controls,*** die Quersteuerung; ***– deviation*** or ***error,*** seitliche Abweichung; ***– pressure,*** der Seitendruck; ***– thrust,*** der Querschub. **2.** *s.* (*Bot.*) der Seitenzweig.

latest [ˈleitist], *sup. adj. or adv. See* **late**; ***at (the) –,*** spätestens; ***the –,*** das Neueste; ***the – fashions,*** die neuesten Moden.

latex [ˈleiteks], *s.* der Milchsaft, (*esp.*) die Gummimilch.

lath [lɑ:θ], *s.* die Latte, Leiste, (*Build.*) der Putzträger; ***as thin as a –,*** spindeldürr.

lathe [leið], *s.* die Drehbank; (*of a loom*) Lade, der Schlag; ***–-hand,*** der Dreher; ***turn on a –,*** drechseln.

lather [ˈlæðə], **1.** *s.* der (Seifen)schaum; – (*of sweat*), schäumiger Schweiß; (*fig. coll.*) die Erregung; ***get into a –,*** (*v.i.*) ganz aus dem Häuschen sein *or* geraten; (*v.t.*) ganz aus dem Häuschen bringen, in die Wolle bringen. **2.** *v.i.* schäumen. **3.** *v.t.* einseifen; (*sl.*) verbleuen, vermöbeln. **lathering,** *s.* das Einseifen; Schäumen; (*sl.*) die Tracht Prügel. **lathery,** *adj.* schaumig.

lathing [ˈlɑ:θiŋ], **lath-work,** *s.* das Lattenwerk.

Latin [ˈlætin], **1.** *s.* 1. das Latein, Lateinisch(e); ***dog –,*** das Küchenlatein; ***thieves' –,*** die Gaunersprache; 2. (*Hist.*) der Latiner, Römer; (*coll.*) Romane. **2.** *adj.* Latein–, lateinisch; (*Hist.*) latinisch, römisch; (*coll.*) romanisch; ***– Quarter,*** das Quartier Latin. **Latin-American, 1.** *s.* der Lateinamerikaner. **2.** *adj.* lateinamerikanisch. **Latinism,** *s.* der Latinismus.

latish [ˈleitiʃ], *adj.* (*coll.*) etwas spät.

latitude [ˈlætitju:d], *s.* 1. (*Geog.*) die Breite; *pl.* Breiten (*pl.*), der Himmelsstrich; ***degree of –,*** der Breitengrad; 2. (*fig.*) die (Bewegungs)freiheit, der Spielraum; (*rare*) Umfang, die Ausdehnung, (Reich)weite. **latitudinal** [–ˈtju:dinl], *adj.* Breiten–.

latitudinarian [lætitju:diˈnɛəriən], **1.** *adj.* weitherzig, duldsam, (*esp. Eccl.*) freisinnig, freidenkerisch. **2.** *s.* der Freidenker, Freigeist. **latitudinarianism,** *s.* (*Eccl.*) die Duldsamkeit, Toleranz; Freigeisterei, Freidenkerei.

latrine [ləˈtri:n], *s.* (*oft. pl.*) der Abort, das Klosett, die Latrine.

latten [lætn], *s.* (*obs.*) das Messingblech, messingähnliches Blech.

latter [ˈlætə], *adj.* 1. letzt(genannt); ***the –,*** der *or* die *or* das letztere; letztere(r, -s); diese(r, -s) (*of two*); 2. (*attrib.*) (*Poet.*) ***the – days,*** die jüngste Zeit, neuere Zeiten; ***the – end,*** der Tod; (*obs.*) ***– grass,*** zweite Mahd, das Grummet; ***the – years of his life,*** seine letzten *or* späteren Lebensjahre. **latter-day,** *adj.* jüngst; ***Latter-Day Saints,*** Mormonen (*pl.*). **latterly,** *adv.* kürzlich, neuerdings, in letzter Zeit.

lattice [ˈlætis], **1.** *s.* das Gitter(werk), Gatter; die Gittertür. **2.** *v.t.* vergittern. **lattice|-bridge,** *s.* die Gitterbrücke. **–-window,** *s.* das Gitterfenster. **–work, latticing,** *s.* das Gitterwerk, die Vergitterung.

Latvia [ˈlætviə], *s.* Lettland (*n.*). **Latvian, 1.** *s.* 1. der Lett (die Lettin); 2. (*language*) das Lettisch(e). **2.** *adj.* lettisch.

laud [lɔ:d], **1.** *v.t.* (*Poet.*) loben, preisen, rühmen. **2.** *s.* (*rare*) der Preis, das Lob; Loblied, Preislied, der Lobgesang, Preisgesang, die Lobeshymne. **laudability** [–əˈbiliti], *s.* die Löblichkeit. **laudable,** *adj.* löblich, lobenswert.

laudanum [ˈlɔ:dənəm], *s.* die Opiumtinktur, das Laudanum.

laudation [lɔ:ˈdeiʃən], *s.* das Lob, die Belobigung. **laudatory** [ˈlɔ:dətəri], *adj.* lobend, preisend.

laugh [lɑ:f], **1.** *v.i.* lachen; ***– at,*** belachen (*a th.*), lachen *or* sich lustig machen über (*Acc.*) (*a th. or p.*), auslachen (*a p.*); ***– at him to his face, – in his face,*** ihm ins Gesicht lachen; ***– away,*** draufloslachen; ***– away!*** lach' nur zu! ***– up one's sleeve,*** sich (*Dat.*) ins Fäustchen lachen; ***he will – on the other side of his face,*** ihm wird das Lachen vergehen; (*Prov.*) ***he –s best who –s last,*** wer zuletzt lacht, lacht am besten. **2.** *v.t.* ***– a bitter laugh,*** bitter lachen; ***– away,*** durch Lachen vertreiben; ***– down,*** gründlich auslachen, durch Verlachen zum Schweigen bringen; ***– off,*** sich lachend hinwegsetzen über (*Acc.*); ***– out of,*** durch (Ver)lachen abbringen von (*a p.*); (*fig.*) ***– out of court,*** restlos lächerlich machen (*a th.*); ***– to scorn,*** verhöhnen, verspotten. **3.** *s.* das Lachen, Gelächter; die Lache; ***broad –,*** lautes Gelächter; ***burst into a tremendous –,*** eine gewaltige Lache aufschlagen; ***get the – of one's life,*** lachen wie nie zuvor (im Leben); ***have a good – at,*** sich recht lustig machen über (*Acc.*); ***have the – of him,*** über ihn triumphieren; (*Prov.*) ***the – is always against the loser,*** wer den Schaden hat, braucht für den Spott nicht zu sorgen; ***have the – on one's side,*** die Lacher auf seiner Seite haben; ***the – was against him,*** die Lacher waren auf der anderen Seite; ***raise a –,*** Lachen erregen; ***with a –,*** lachend.

laughable [ˈlɑ:fəbl], *adj.* lächerlich, lachhaft. **laughing,** *adj.* lachend, (*fig.*) strahlend; ***it is no – matter,*** es ist nicht zum Lachen. **laughing|-gas,** *s.* das Lachgas. **–-jackass,** *s.* (*Orn.*) der Riesenkönigsfischer (*Dacelo gigas*). **–-stock,** *s.* der Gegenstand des Gelächters, die Zielscheibe des Spottes.

laughter [ˈlɑ:ftə], *s.* das Gelächter; ***roars of –,*** schallendes Gelächter; ***–-loving,*** fröhlich, vergnügt.

[1]**launch** [lɔ:ntʃ], **1.** *v.t.* schleudern (*a spear etc.*), vom Stapel lassen (*a ship*; *also fig.*), lancieren (*a torpedo*), abschießen (*a rocket*), aussetzen (*a ship's boat*); (*fig.*) in Tätigkeit *or* Gang setzen, loslassen (*threats etc.*); (*of ship*) ***be –ed,*** vom Stapel gehen; ***– an attack,*** angreifen, einen Angriff ansetzen; ***– into eternity,*** ins Jenseits befördern; ***– him into*** or ***on*** (*a career etc.*), ihm einen Start geben in (*Acc.*). **2.** *v.i.* (*also* ***– out, – forth***) sich stürzen, sich hineinbegeben; sich verbreiten, ergehen, ausschweifen (*into*, in (*Acc.*)), beginnen, unternehmen. **3.** *s.* der Stapellauf (*for ships*); (*coll.*) Start, Abschuß.

[2]**launch,** *s.* (*Naut.*) die Barkasse; (***motor***) ***–,*** das Motorboot.

launching|-cradle, *s.* das Ablaufgerüst. **–-pad,**

– platform, *s.* die Abschußrampe. **––tube,** *s.* das Ausstoßrohr. **––ways,** *pl.* die Bettung, Helling.

launder ['lɔːndə], **1.** *v.t.* waschen (und bügeln) (*clothes*). **2.** *v.i.* Wäsche bereiten (*of a p.*), sich (gut) waschen lassen (*of clothes etc.*). **launderette** [–'ret], *s.* der Mietwaschsalon, die Schnellwäscherei. **laundress** [–dris], *s.* die Wäscherin, Waschfrau. **laundry** [–dri], *s.* **1.** die Wäscherei, Waschanstalt; (*in a house*) Waschküche; **2.** Wäsche.

laureate ['lɔriət], **1.** *adj.* lorbeergekrönt, lorbeerbekränzt. **2.** *s.* gekrönter Dichter; der Hofdichter. **laureateship,** *s.* die Hofdichterwürde.

laurel ['lɔrəl], *s.* der Lorbeer(baum); (*fig.*) (*usu. pl.*) Lorbeeren (*pl.*), der Ruhm, die Ehre, Anerkennung; ***gain*** or ***win one's –s,*** Lorbeeren ernten; ***look to one's –s,*** auf seinen Ruhm bedacht sein; ***rest on one's –s,*** auf seinen Lorbeeren ausruhen; ***– wreath,*** der Lorbeerkranz, die Lorbeerkrone.

lava ['lɑːvə], *s.* die Lava.

lavatory ['lævətəri], *s.* der Waschraum, die Toilette, das Klosett; ***public –,*** die Bedürfnisanstalt.

lave [leiv], **1.** *v.t.* (*Poet.*) waschen, baden; bespülen (*as waves*). **2.** *v.i.* sich waschen *or* baden; spülen (***against,*** an (*Acc.*)).

lavender ['lævində], *s.* (*Bot.*) der Lavendel.

lavish ['læviʃ], **1.** *adj.* freigebig, verschwenderisch (***of, in,*** mit); (über)reichlich; ***be – in one's promises,*** mit Versprechungen um sich werfen. **2.** *v.t.* verschwenden, vergeuden; ***– favours on,*** mit Gunstbezeigungen überhäufen. **lavishness,** *s.* die (Über)reichlichkeit; Verschwendung, verschwenderische Freigebigkeit.

law [lɔː], *s.* **1.** das Gesetz; (*oft. pl.*) Recht(system); die Rechtswissenschaft, Rechtskunde, Rechtsgelehrsamkeit, Rechte (*pl.*), Jura (*pl.*); **2.** juristische Laufbahn, der Juristenberuf; **3.** das Gebot, der Befehl, die Vorschrift, Regel; Gesetzmäßigkeit; **4.** (*Hunt.*) der Vorsprung.
(a) (*with nouns*) ***– days,*** der Fälligkeitstermin; (*Naut.*) zugestandene Löschtage; ***–s of the game,*** Spielregeln (*pl.*); ***– of inheritance,*** das Erbrecht; ***– of the land,*** das Landesrecht, Gesetze des Landes (*pl.*); (*fig.*) ***– of the Medes and Persians,*** unabänderliches Recht; ***– of nations,*** das Völkerrecht; ***– of nature,*** das Naturgesetz; ***– and order,*** Recht und Ordnung; ***– of the pendulum,*** das Pendelgesetz; ***workman's compensation –,*** das Arbeiterunfallversicherungsgesetz.
(b) (*with adjs.*) ***civil –,*** das Zivilrecht, bürgerliches Recht; ***commercial –,*** das Handelsrecht; ***common –,*** das Gewohnheitsrecht; ***criminal –,*** das Strafrecht; ***divine –,*** göttliches Gesetz; ***ecclesiastical –,*** das Kirchenrecht; ***ex post facto –,*** rückwirkendes Gesetz; ***international –,*** das Völkerrecht; ***natural –,*** (*Pol.*) das Naturrecht, (*Biol. etc.*) Naturgesetz, wissenschaftliches Gesetz; ***statute –,*** gesetzliches Recht; ***substantive –,*** materielles Recht; ***sumptuary –,*** das Aufwandgesetz.
(c) (*with verbs*) ***be –,*** (das) Gesetz sein, dem Gesetz entsprechen, mit dem Gesetz übereinstimmen; ***be a – unto o.s.,*** sich über alle Konvention hinwegsetzen; ***possession is nine points of the –,*** sei im Besitze und du wohnst im Recht; ***be in the –,*** Jurist sein; ***become –,*** (zum) Gesetz werden; (*Hunt.*) ***give a hare good –,*** einem Hasen einen Vorsprung gewähren; ***go in for –,*** Jura studieren; ***go to –,*** den Rechtsweg beschreiten, zu *or* vor Gericht gehen; ***go to – with him,*** (*coll.*) ***have the – on him,*** ihn belangen *or* verklagen; ***necessity knows no –,*** Not kennt kein Gebot; ***lay down the –,*** selbstherrlich verfahren, gebieterisch auftreten; ***pass into –,*** see ***become –***; ***practise –,*** als Rechtsanwalt praktizieren; ***read*** or ***study –,*** Jura studieren; ***take the – into one's own hands,*** sich (*Dat.*) selbst Recht verschaffen.
(d) (*with preps.*) ***according to –,*** von Rechts wegen, dem Gesetz entsprechend; ***at –,*** vor Gericht, gerichtlich; ***be at –,*** einen Prozeß führen, prozessieren; ***by –,*** gesetzlich, von Rechts wegen; ***good in –,*** rechtsgültig; ***doctor of –(s),*** Doktor der Rechte; ***due process of –,*** ordentliches Rechtsverfahren; ***contrary to –,*** rechtswidrig; ***under the –,*** auf Grund des Gesetzes, nach dem Gesetz; ***under Scottish –,*** nach schottischem Recht *or* Gesetz.

law|-abiding, *adj.* friedlich, ordnungsliebend, den Gesetzen folgend, an die Gesetze haltend; ***be –,*** die Gesetze befolgen, sich friedlich benehmen; ***– citizens,*** friedliche Bürger. **––breaker,** *s.* der Gesetzesübertreter. **––breaking,** *s.* die Gesetzesüberschreitung. **––charges,** *pl.* Prozeßkosten, Gerichtsgebühren (*pl.*). **––court,** *s.* der Gerichtshof. **lawful,** *adj.* gesetzlich, gesetzmäßig, legal, rechtmäßig, legitim; gültig, erlaubt; ***– age,*** gesetzliches Mindestalter, die Majorennität, Volljährigkeit; ***– children,*** eheliche *or* legitime Kinder; ***– marriage,*** gültige Heirat; ***– ruler,*** rechtmäßiger Herrscher. **lawfulness,** *s.* die Gesetzlichkeit, Rechtmäßigkeit, Legalität, Gültigkeit. **law-giver,** *s.* der Gesetzgeber.

law(ks)! [lɔː(ks)], *int.* (*obs.*) herrje!

lawless ['lɔːlis], *adj.* gesetzlos; gesetzwidrig, unrechtmäßig; (*fig.*) zügellos. **lawlessness,** *s.* die Gesetzlosigkeit; Zügellosigkeit. **law-lords,** *pl.* Mitglieder des Oberhauses in richterlicher Funktion. **law-merchant,** *s.* (*Law*) das Handelsrecht.

[1]**lawn** [lɔːn], *s.* der Batist, das Linon.

[2]**lawn,** *s.* der Rasen(platz). **lawn|-mower,** *s.* der Rasenmäher. **––roller,** *s.* die Rasenwalze. **––tennis,** *s.* das (Lawn)tennis.

law|-officer, *s.* der Rechtsberater der Regierung. **– school,** *s.* (*Univ.*) juristische Fakultät. **–suit,** *s.* der (Zivil)prozeß, Rechtshandel, die Klage; ***carry on a –,*** einen Prozeß führen.

lawyer ['lɔːjə], *s.* der (Rechts)anwalt, Rechtsbeistand, Sachwalter; Jurist, Rechtsgelehrte(r).

lax [læks], *adj.* lose, locker, schlaff (*also fig.*); (*fig.*) vag(e), unklar; (nach)lässig, lax; offen, weich (*of bowels*). **laxative** [–ətiv], **1.** *adj.* stuhl(gang)fördernd, abführend. **2.** *s.* das Abführmittel. **laxity,** (*usu. fig.*) *or* **laxness,** (*usu. lit.*) *s.* die Lockerheit, Schlaffheit, Ungenauigkeit, Lässigkeit, Laxheit.

[1]**lay** [lei], *adj.* weltlich, Laien–; (*fig.*) nicht fachmännisch, laienhaft; ***– habit,*** weltliche Kleidung; ***– preacher,*** der Laienprediger.

[2]**lay,** *s.* (*Poet.*) das Lied.

[3]**lay,** *imperf. of* [2]**lie.**

[4]**lay, 1.** *s.* (*coll.*) die Lage; (*sl.*) das Unternehmen, Betätigungsfeld, die Beschäftigung; der Schlag (*of rope*); (*fig.*) ***– of the land,*** die Lage der Dinge. **2.** *irr.v.t.* legen (*also eggs*), setzen, (hin)stellen, niederlegen; wetten, (ein)setzen (*a sum of money*); richten (*a gun*); bannen (*ghosts*); löschen (*dust*); mäßigen, lindern, besänftigen, beruhigen (*fears etc.*); zerstreuen, unterdrücken (*doubts*); schlagen, belegen (*a rope*).
(a) (*with adjs.*) ***– bare,*** bloßlegen, (*fig.*) aufdecken, offen darlegen; ***– low,*** zu Fall bringen, fällen, (zu Boden) stürzen, (*fig.*) demütigen, erniedrigen; ***– open,*** see ***– bare***; ***– o.s. open to,*** sich aussetzen (*Dat.*); ***– waste,*** verwüsten, verheeren.
(b) (*with nouns*) ***– an ambush,*** einen Hinterhalt legen; ***– the blame (up)on him,*** ihm die Schuld zuschieben *or* zuschreiben; ***– claim to,*** Anspruch erheben *or* machen auf (*Acc.*), in Anspruch nehmen; ***– the cloth,*** den Tisch decken; ***– eyes on,*** erblicken; ***– a fire,*** ein Feuer anlegen; ***– hands on,*** (an)fassen, ergreifen, in Besitz nehmen (*a th.*), erwischen (*a p.*); ***– hands on o.s.,*** Hand an sich legen; ***– one's heads together,*** die Köpfe zusammenstecken; ***– hold of,*** see ***– hands on***; ***– plans,*** Pläne ersinnen *or* festlegen; ***– a plot,*** ein Komplott schmieden; ***– siege to,*** belagern, (*fig.*) bestürmen (*a p.*); ***– stress on,*** Gewicht *or* Nachdruck legen auf (*Acc.*), betonen; ***– the table,*** den Tisch decken; ***– a tax on,*** eine Steuer auferlegen (*Dat.*); ***– a trap,*** eine Falle stellen; ***– a wager,*** eine Wette machen.
(c) (*with advs.*) ***– aside,*** beiseitelegen, zurücklegen (*money*); ***– by,*** zurücklegen, sparen (*money etc.*); aufbewahren, aufspeichern; ***– s.th. by for a rainy day,*** einen Notgroschen zurücklegen; ***– down,*** hinlegen; niederlegen (*a post*), aufgeben (*hope etc.*), hinterlegen, bar bezahlen (*money*); einlagern, einlegen (*wine*); opfern, hingeben (*one's life*); auf-

stellen, vorschreiben, festlegen (*rules*); anführen (*reasons*); entwerfen, anlegen, aufzeichnen (*plans*); bauen (*road, railway*); auf Stapel legen (*a ship*); – ***down one's arms,*** die Waffen niederlegen; – ***down the law,*** selbstherrlich auftreten; – ***o.s. down,*** sich niederlegen; – ***it down that,*** behaupten *or* die Behauptung aufstellen daß, vorschreiben; – ***down one's tools,*** streiken; – ***in,*** sich (*Dat.*) anlegen, einlegen, einkaufen, anschaffen, sich eindecken mit, aufspeichern; – ***off,*** abstechen; (*coll.*) entlassen (*workers*), einstellen (*work*); – ***on,*** auftragen (*colours*); anlegen (*water, gas etc.*); auferlegen (*taxes*); (*sl.*) – ***it on,*** zuschlagen; zu viel des Guten tun, übertreiben, dick auftragen; – ***out,*** auslegen, ausbreiten, zur Schau stellen, ausstellen; aufbahren (*a corpse*); auslegen, ausgeben (*money*); anlegen (*a garden, money*); entwerfen, aufreißen, abstecken, trassieren, planieren; (*sl.*) zu Boden strecken, k.o.-schlagen; – ***o.s. out;*** sich sehr anstrengen *or* bemühen, sich (*Dat.*) große Mühe geben; – ***over,*** belegen, bedecken, überziehen (***with,*** mit); (*Naut.*) – ***to,*** beidrehen mit; – ***up,*** aufsparen, aufspeichern, aufbewahren, zurücklegen; abtakeln, auflegen (*a ship*); einstellen (*a vehicle*); brachliegen lassen (*land*); ans Bett fesseln (*usu. pass.*); ***be laid up with,*** daniederliegen an (*Dat.*).

(d) (*with preps.*) – ***at his door,*** ihm zur Last legen, ihm in die Schuhe schieben; – ***before him,*** ihm vorlegen *or* zur Ansicht geben; – ***by the heels,*** zur Strecke bringen, erwischen, kaltstellen; – ***in ashes,*** einäschern (*a town etc.*); – ***to his charge,*** ihm zur Last legen; – ***to rest,*** zur letzten Ruhe geleiten, bestatten; – ***him under an obligation,*** ihm eine Verpflichtung auferlegen.

3. *irr.v.i.* legen (*of hens*); wetten; decken (*the table for s.o.*); – ***about one,*** um sich schlagen, drauflosschlagen, tüchtig dreinschlagen; (*sl.*) – ***into,*** verdreschen, draufloshauen auf (*Acc.*); sich eifrig machen an (*Acc.*), energisch anpacken; (*sl.*) – ***off,*** es lassen, damit aufhören; (*Naut.*) beidrehen.

lay-about, *s.* (*coll.*) der Faulenzer, Tagedieb, Gammler.

lay brother, *s.* der Laienbruder.

lay|-by, *s.* der Park- und Rastplatz. **--days,** *pl.* (*Naut.*) Liegetage (*pl.*), die Liegezeit.

[1]**layer** ['leiə], *s.* **1.** die Leg(e)henne; ***be a good –,*** gut legen, viele Eier legen; 2. (*Artil.*) der Richtkanonier; 3. (*Railw.*) ***plate –,*** der Schienenleger.

[2]**layer,** **1.** *s.* die Schicht, Lage; (*Hort.*) der Ableger, Absenker, Setzling, das Senkreis. **2.** *v.t.* überlagern; (*Hort.*) absenken. **3.** *v.i.* niederliegen, sich legen (*of corn*).

layette [lei'et], *s.* die Babyausstattung, Babywäsche.

lay figure, *s.* die Gliederpuppe; (*fig.*) der Strohmann.

laying ['leiiŋ], *s.* 1. das (Eier)legen; ***hens past –,*** Hennen, die nicht mehr legen; 2. (*Artil.*) das Richten; 3. (*Build.*) Verputzen *or* Bewerfen mit Mörtel; 4. – ***of cables,*** die Kabelverlegung.

layman ['leimən], *s.* der Laie; (*coll.*) Nichtfachmann.

lay|-off, *s.* (vorübergehende) Entlassung. **-out,** *s.* die Anordnung, Planung, Gruppierung, Linienführung; Skizze, Anlage, der Plan, Entwurf, das Arbeitsschema; (*Typ.*) Layout, der Satzspiegel, die Aufmachung. **--shaft,** *s.* (*Tech.*) die Vorgelegewelle.

lazaret(to) [læzə'ret(ou)], *s.* 1. (*Hist.*) (***--house***) das Lazarett, Spital; 2. (*Naut.*) die Isolierstation, Quarantäneanstalt.

laze [leiz], **1.** *v.i.* faulenzen, nichts tun. **2.** *v.t.* – ***away,*** verbummeln, vertändeln. **laziness,** *s.* die Faulheit, Trägheit. **lazy,** *adj.* faul, träge. **lazy|-bones,** *s.* (*coll.*) der Faulpelz. **--tongs,** *pl.* die Gelenkzange.

[1]**lea** [li:], *s.* (*Poet.*) die Au(e), Flur, Wiese, das Weideland.

[2]**lea,** *s.* das Lea (*wool = 80 yds.* (*approx. 73 m.*); *cotton, silk = 120 yds.* (*approx. 110 m.*); *hemp = 300 yds.* (*approx. 274 m.*)).

leach [li:tʃ], *v.t.* auslaugen, durchsickern lassen.

[1]**lead** [led], **1.** *s.* 1. das Blei; (***black***) **–,** der Graphit; Bleistift; ***red –,*** der Mennig, die Mennige; der Rotstift; ***white –,*** das Bleiweiß; 2. (*Naut.*) das Lot, Senkblei; ***heave the –,*** loten, das Lot auswerfen; (*sl.*) ***swing the –,*** sich drücken; 3. die (Bleistift)mine, der Bleistift; 4. (*Typ.*) Durchschuß; *pl.* Durchschußlinien (*pl.*), die Bleifassung; 5. *pl.* (*Build.*) Bleiplatten (*pl.*), das Bleidach; das Fensterblei (*of windows*); ***under –s,*** unter Bleiverschluß. **2.** *v.t.* verbleien, mit Blei überziehen; plombieren; in Blei fassen (*windows*); (*Typ.*) durchschießen.

[2]**lead** [li:d], **1.** *irr.v.t.* führen, leiten; den Weg zeigen (*Dat.*), lenken; an der Spitze stehen von, anführen, befehligen; bewegen, veranlassen, verleiten, verführen, dahin bringen (***to,*** zu); (*Cards*) anspielen, ausspielen; (*Mus.*) vorspielen, vorsingen; – ***him captive,*** ihn gefangen abführen; – ***the dance,*** den Tanz anführen; (*coll.*) – ***him a*** (***fine***) ***dance,*** ihm viele Scherereien bereiten, ihm gehörig zu schaffen machen; – ***him a dog's life,*** ihm das Leben sauer machen; (*Scots law*) – ***evidence,*** bezeugen; – ***the fashion,*** die Mode angeben; – ***the field,*** die Führung haben, an der Spitze des Feldes liegen, das Feld anführen; – ***a sedentary life,*** eine sitzende Lebensweise führen; – ***the way,*** vorangehen.

(a) (*with advs.*) – ***astray,*** verleiten, verführen, irreführen; – ***off,*** ableiten, abführen; (*coll.*) beginnen, eröffnen; – ***on,*** verlocken; (*fig.*) aufmuntern, ermutigen; – ***out,*** hinausführen.

(b) (*with preps.*) – ***him by the hand,*** ihn an der Hand führen; – ***him by the nose,*** ihn an der Nase herumführen; – ***him into thinking,*** ihn veranlassen *or* dahin bringen zu glauben, ihn auf den Gedanken bringen; (*coll.*) – ***him up the garden*** (***path***), ihn anführen, ihn hinters Licht führen.

2. *irr.v.i.* vorangehen, als Erste(r) *or* Anführer sein, den Weg bahnen; führen (***to,*** zu *or* nach); (*Cards*) die Vorhand haben, ausspielen; (*Boxing*) zum Angriff übergehen; – ***off,*** anfangen, beginnen; (*Bill. etc.*) anstoßen; – ***out of,*** in Verbindung stehen mit (*as rooms*); (*fig.*) – ***to,*** führen zu, bewirken, ergeben, hervorbringen (*trouble etc.*); – ***up to,*** einleiten, führen *or* übergehen *or* überleiten zu, hinführen auf (*Acc.*).

3. *s.* 1. die Führung, Leitung; (*Hunt.*) das Vorangehen, (*Spt.*) der Vorsprung, die Führung; (*Cards*) das Anspielen, der Anwurf, die Vorhand; (*Boxing*) der Angriffsschlag; (*aiming*) Vorhalt; ***have the –,*** die Führung haben; (*Cards*) die Vorhand haben, ausspielen; (*dice etc.*) den ersten Wurf haben, anwerfen; ***take a –,*** vorhalten (*aiming*); ***take the –,*** die Führung übernehmen, an die Spitze kommen, sich an der Spitze setzen, (*fig.*) vorangehen; 2. (*fig.*) der Fingerzeig, Hinweis, Anhaltspunkt; ***give a –,*** einen Fingerzeig geben, mit gutem Beispiel vorangehen; 3. (*for dogs*) die Leine; (*Elec.*) Leitung(sschnur), der Leitungsdraht, Leiter; ***on the –,*** an der Leine (*of a dog*); 4. (*Elec.*) die Voreilung (*of phase*); 5. (*Theat.*) Hauptrolle, führende Rolle; der (die) Hauptdarsteller(in).

leaden [ledn], *adj.* bleiern, Blei–; (*usu. fig.*) bleiern, schwerfällig, träg(e), stumpf; (*colour*) bleigrau, bleifarben, trüb, düster, glanzlos.

leader ['li:də], *s.* 1. der Führer, Leiter, Erste(r), Vorangehende(r); Anführer, Befehlshaber; (*Parl.*) Vormann, Verhandlungsleiter; (*Mus.*) Konzertmeister, erster Geiger (*orchestra*), der Chorführer (*choir*); ***band –,*** der Kapellmeister; (*Mil.*) ***section –,*** der Zugführer; 2. der Leitartikel (*in newspaper*); – ***writer,*** der Leitartikler; 3. das Vorderpferd, Leitpferd; 4. der Haupttrieb, Leittrieb (*of a plant*); 5. (*Comm. coll.*) Lockartikel, die Zugware; 6. (*Med. coll.*) Sehne; 7. (*Build.*) das Leitungsrohr, Fallrohr. **leadership,** *s.* die Führerschaft; Führung, Leitung; – ***principle,*** das Führerprinzip.

lead-in ['li:din], *s.* (*Rad.*) der Zuleitungsdraht, die (Antennen)zuleitung, Niederführung.

leading ['li:diŋ], **1.** *adj.* führend, leitend; herrschend, tonangebend, wegweisend; Haupt–, erst, hervorragend; (*Elec.*) voreilend; (*Naut.*) raum, günstig (*of wind*); – ***article,*** der Leitartikel (*in newspaper*); *see also* **leader,** 5; (*Law*) – ***case,*** der Präzedenzfall; (*Av.*) – ***edge,*** die Leitkante, Profilvorderkante, Nasenleiste (*of wings*), Vorderkante, Blattnase (*of propeller, rotor etc.*); (*Theat.*) – ***lady,*** die Hauptdarstellerin, erste Liebhaberin; – ***light,*** (*Naut.*) das Richtfeuer, Kursfeuer; (*coll. fig.*) die Leuchte; (*Theat.*) – ***man,*** der Hauptdarsteller, erster Liebhaber; – ***men,*** führende Geister; (*Mus.*) – ***note,*** der Leitton, große Septime; – ***question,*** die Suggestivfrage; – ***seaman,*** der Obermatrose. **2.** *s.* die Führung, Leitung, Lenkung. **leading|-rein,** *s.* der Leitzügel. **--strings,** *pl.* das Gängelband, die Führungsleine; (*fig.*) ***be in –,*** am Gängelband geführt werden, noch in den Kinderschuhen stecken; ***have*** or ***keep in –,*** am Gängelband führen.

lead|-line ['led–], *s.* die Lotleine. **--pencil,** *s.* der Bleistift. – **poisoning,** *s.* die Bleivergiftung. **--shot,** *s.* Bleikugeln (*pl.*). **leadsman,** *s.* (*Naut.*) der Lotgast, Handloter.

leaf [li:f], **1.** *s.* (*pl.* **leaves** [li:vz]) das Blatt (*plant or book*); (*Tech.*) der Flügel (*door*), die Klappe, Platte, das Einlegebrett (*table*), die Aufziehklappe (*bridge*); das Blättchen, Plättchen, die Folie, Lamelle (*of metal*); das Blatt (*of spring*); (*Poet.*) Laub, Blattwerk; ***in –,*** belaubt; ***come into –,*** Blätter entwickeln, ausschlagen; (*fig.*) ***take a – out of his book,*** ihn nachahmen, ihm nacheifern, seinem Beispiel folgen, sich (*Dat.*) ihn zum Muster nehmen; ***over the –,*** auf dem nächsten Blatt; ***turn over the –,*** umblättern, das Blatt umschlagen; ***turn over the leaves of a book,*** ein Buch durchblättern; (*fig.*) ***turn over a new –,*** sich bessern, ein neues Leben anfangen. **2.** *adj.* Blatt–, Blätter–. **3.** *v.t.* – ***through,*** durchblättern (*a book*).

leafage ['li:fidʒ], *s.* Blätter (*pl.*), das Laub, Blätterwerk. **leaf|-brass,** *s.* die Messingfolie. **--bud,** *s.* die Blattknospe. **leafed,** *adj.* beblättert; (*as suff.*) -blättrig. **leaf|-gilding,** *s.* die Blattgoldvergoldung. **--gold,** *s.* das Buchbindergold, Blattgold. **--green, 1.** *s.* das Blattgrün, Chlorophyll. **2.** *adj.* blattgrün, laubgrün. **leafiness,** *s.* die Belaubung, Belaubtheit. **leafless,** *adj.* blattlos, blätterlos, unbelaubt; entblättert.

leaflet ['li:flit], *s.* **1.** (*Bot.*) das Blättchen; **2.** (*fig.*) Flugblatt, die Broschüre, der Prospekt. **leaf|-mould,** *s.* die Lauberde. **--sight,** *s.* das Klappvisier (*of rifle*). **--spring,** *s.* die Blattfeder. **--stalk,** *s.* der Blattstiel. **--table,** *s.* der Klapptisch, Ausziehtisch. **--tobacco,** *s.* der Blättertabak, Rohtabak. **--valve,** *s.* das Klappenventil. **--work,** *s.* (*Archit.*) das Blattwerk, Laubwerk, die Blattverzierung. **leafy,** *adj.* belaubt, laubreich, Laub–.

[1]**league** [li:g], *s.* (*Poet.*) die Meile (*usu.* = *approx. 3 Engl. miles (4.8 km.)*).

[2]**league, 1.** *s.* das Bündnis, der Bund, Verband, Verein, (*also Hist., Footb.*) die Liga; ***League of Nations,*** der Völkerbund. **2.** *v.t.* – ***o.s.,*** sich verbünden. **leaguer,** *s.* Verbündete(r), der Bundesgenosse.

leak [li:k], **1.** *s.* das Leck, durchsickernde Flüssigkeit; das Loch, der Riß, undichte Stelle; (*Elec.*) die Ableitung, der Verluststrom; Stromverluste (*pl.*); (*fig.*) das Durchsickern (*of news etc.*); ***spring a –,*** ein Leck bekommen; (*Elec.*) – ***current,*** der Verluststrom; (*Rad.*) ***grid –,*** – ***resistance,*** der Gitterwiderstand. **2.** *v.i.* lecken, leck *or* undicht sein, ein Leck haben, Wasser durchlassen (*of a vessel*); (*also* – *out*) auslaufen, durchsickern, ausströmen (*of liquid*), entweichen (*of gas*); (*fig.*) – ***out,*** durchsickern, bekannt werden (*as news*). **3.** *v.t.* (*coll.*) durchsickern lassen (*news*).

leakage ['li:kidʒ], *s.* das Lecken, Auslaufen, Durchsickern (*see also* **leak, 1**); (*Comm.*) die Leckage; (*fig.*) das Durchsickern; der Schwund, Abgang, Verlust, die Abnahme. **leakiness,** *s.* die Undichtigkeit, Durchlässigkeit. **leaking, leaky,** *adj.* leck, undicht, durchlässig.

leal [li:l], *adj.* (*Scots*) treu; ***land o' the –,*** der Himmel, das Paradies, Land der Seligen.

[1]**lean** [li:n], **1.** *irr.v.i.* **1.** sich lehnen (***against,*** an (*Acc.*) *or* gegen), stützen (***on,*** auf (*Acc.*)); schief stehen, sich beugen *or* neigen; lehnen (***against,*** an (*Dat.*)); – ***forward,*** sich vornüber neigen; – ***out,*** sich hinauslehnen; – ***out of the window,*** sich aus dem Fenster beugen; (*coll.*) – ***over backwards,*** sich (*Dat.*) (gegen seine Neigung) alle erdenkliche Mühe geben; **2.** (*fig.*) (hin)neigen (***to(wards),*** zu), zuneigen (*Dat.*), eine Vorliebe zeigen (für), bevorzugen (*Acc.*); **3.** (*fig.*) sich verlassen (***on,*** auf (*Acc.*)); – ***on his help,*** sich auf seine Hilfe verlassen. **2.** *irr.v.t.* lehnen, stützen (***against,*** gegen *or* an (*Acc.*)); (***up***)***on,*** auf (*Acc.*)); (*fig.*) – ***one's ear to,*** das Ohr neigen nach. **3.** *s.* die Neigung (***towards,*** nach); ***on the –,*** geneigt, schief.

[2]**lean, 1.** *adj.* mager, hager (*a p.*), mager (*as meat*); (*fig.*) mager, dürftig, dürr; unfruchtbar, unergiebig; (*Tech.*) – ***mixture,*** das Spargemisch; (*coll.*) ***have a – time,*** eine magere Zeit durchmachen. **2.** *s.* das Magere (*of meat*).

leaning ['li:niŋ], **1.** *adj.* sich neigend, geneigt, schief; – ***tower,*** schiefer Turm. **2.** *s.* (*usu. fig.*) die Neigung (***towards,*** zu), Vorliebe (für).

leanness ['li:nnis], *s.* die Magerkeit (*also fig.*).

leant [lent], *imperf., p.p. of* [1]**lean.**

lean-to, 1. *s.* der Anbau; das Pultdach, der Schuppen mit Pultdach. **2.** *adj.* angebaut, Anbau–; – ***roof,*** das Pultdach.

leap [li:p], **1.** *irr.v.i.* springen, hüpfen, (*as flames*) auflodern, (*as water*) hochschießen, emporschießen; – ***at,*** sich stürzen auf (*Acc.*); – ***at the chance,*** die Gelegenheit beim Schopfe fassen *or* mit beiden Händen ergreifen *or* packen; – ***for joy,*** vor Freude hüpfen; – ***into fame,*** mit einem Schlag berühmt werden; – ***into flame,*** aufflammen, entflammen; – ***to a conclusion,*** voreilig einen Schluß ziehen; – ***to the eye,*** ins Auge springen; ***look before you –!*** erst besinn's, dann beginn's! **2.** *irr.v.t.* springen *or* hinwegsetzen über (*Acc.*), überspringen; springen lassen (*a horse*); (*of male animals*) decken, bespringen (*the female*). **3.** *s.* der Sprung, Satz; ***take a –,*** einen Sprung tun *or* machen; (*fig.*) – ***in the dark,*** der Sprung ins Ungewisse; (*fig.*) ***by –s (and bounds),*** sprunghaft, sprungweise, in gewaltigen Sprüngen, in großen Sätzen.

leap-frog, 1. *s.* das Bockspringen; der Bocksprung. **2.** *v.i.* (*v.t.*) bockspringen (über (*Acc.*)).

leapt [lept], *imperf., p.p. of* **leap.**

leap-year, *s.* das Schaltjahr.

learn [lə:n], **1.** *irr.v.t.* (er)lernen; erfahren (***from,*** von), ersehen (aus); (*coll. but incorrect*) *see* **teach;** – ***by heart*** or ***rote,*** auswendig lernen; – ***to swim,*** schwimmen lernen; – ***German,*** Deutsch lernen; – ***how to do it,*** lernen wie man es macht; – ***the truth,*** die Wahrheit erfahren; – ***the violin,*** die Violine spielen lernen. **2.** *irr.v.i.* lernen; erfahren, hören (***of,*** von); ***I – from his letter,*** ich habe aus seinem Brief ersehen.

learned ['lə:nid], *adj.* gelehrt; erfahren, bewandert (***in,*** in (*Dat.*)); ***the – professions,*** die gelehrten Berufe; (*Parl.*) ***my – friend,*** mein gelehrter Herr Kollege. **learner,** *s.* der Lehrling, Schüler, Anfänger. **learning,** *s.* das (Er)lernen; die Gelehrtheit, Gelehrsamkeit; ***a little – is a dangerous thing,*** Halbbildung ist schlimmer als Unbildung; ***the new –,*** der Humanismus. **learnt** [lə:nt], *imperf., p.p. of* **learn.**

lease [li:s], **1.** *s.* die Verpachtung, Vermietung (***to,*** an (*Acc.*)); Pacht, Miete; der Mietvertrag, Pachtbrief; die Pachtzeit, Mietzeit; das Mietverhältnis; Pachtgrundstück, der Pachtbesitz; ***let (out) on –,*** verpachten, vermieten, in Pacht geben; ***take on –,*** ***take a – of,*** pachten, mieten, in Pacht nehmen; (*fig.*) – ***of life,*** die Lebensfrist, Lebensdauer; (*fig.*) ***a new – of life,*** neues Leben, neue Lebenszuversicht. **2.** *v.t.* pachten, mieten; (*also* – ***out***) verpachten, vermieten (***to,*** an (*Acc.*)).

lease|hold, 1. *s.* die Pacht(ung); der Pachtbesitz, das Pachtgrundstück. **2.** *adj.* gepachtet, Pacht–; – ***estate,*** das Pachtgut; – ***residence,*** die Wohnung auf Zeitpacht. **-holder,** *s.* der Pächter. **--lend act,** *s.* (*Pol.*) das Pacht– und Leihgesetz.

leash [liːʃ], **1.** *s.* **1.** die Koppelleine, der Koppelriemen (*for dogs*); (*fig.*) ***hold in –,*** im Zügel halten; 2. (*Hunt.*) die Koppel (*of dogs*), drei Hunde. **2.** *v.t.* (zusammen)koppeln.

leasing [ˈliːsiŋ], *s.* (*B.*) das Lügen; die Lüge.

least [liːst], **1.** *sup. adj.* geringst, kleinst, mindest, wenigst; (*Math.*) ***– common multiple,*** kleinstes gemeinsames Vielfaches. **2.** *sup. adv.* am wenigsten; ***– of all,*** am allerwenigsten; ***last*** (***but***) ***not –,*** nicht zum wenigsten; ***not –,*** nicht am wenigsten; (*Prov.*) ***– said, soonest mended,*** Reden ist Silber, Schweigen Gold. **3.** *s.* das Geringste, Mindeste; ***to say the – of it,*** gelinde *or* milde gesagt; ***the – said, the better,*** see ***– said, soonest mended***; ***at*** (***the***) ***–,*** wenigstens, mindestens, zum mindesten; ***at the very –,*** allermindestens; ***not in the*** (***very***) ***–,*** nicht im geringsten, durchaus nicht, keineswegs.

leather [ˈleðə], **1.** *s.* das Leder; (*sl.*) die Haut, das Fell; der (Fuß)ball; *pl.* die Lederhose, Reithose; Ledergamaschen (*pl.*), das Lederzeug; (*coll.*) ***hell for –,*** wie wild, wie der Teufel; (*of shoes*) ***upper –,*** das Oberleder. **2.** *adj.* ledern, Leder–. **3.** *v.t.* mit Leder überziehen; (*coll.*) das Fell gerben (*Dat.*), verdreschen, versohlen. **4.** *v.i.* (*coll.*) ***– away,*** schuften (***at***, an (*Dat.*)). **leatherette** [–ˈret], *s.* die Lederimitation, das Kunstleder. **leathern,** *adj.* (*obs.*) ledern, Leder–. **leatherneck,** *s.* (*Am. sl.*) der Marineinfanterist. **leathery,** *adj.* lederartig, zäh.

[1]**leave** [liːv], *s.* die Erlaubnis, Bewilligung, der Abschied; (*also* ***– of absence***) Urlaub; ***man on –,*** der Urlauber; ***ticket of –,*** das Entlassungszeugnis; ***ask – of him,*** ihn um Erlaubnis bitten; ***I beg – to contradict,*** darf ich so frei sein, zu widersprechen; ***grant him –,*** ihn beurlauben; ***have –,*** Urlaub haben; ***go on –,*** auf Urlaub gehen, Urlaub nehmen; den Urlaub antreten; ***take*** (***one's***) ***–,*** Abschied nehmen (***of,*** von), sich empfehlen (*Dat.*); ***take French –,*** sich französisch empfehlen; ***take – of one's senses,*** den Verstand verlieren; ***by your –,*** mit Verlaub; (*coll.*) ***without a by your –,*** ohne zu fragen.

[2]**leave,** **1.** *irr.v.t.* hinterlassen (*also a p.*), vermachen (*only a th.*) (***s.th. to him*** or ***him s.th.,*** ihm etwas) (*after death*); zurücklassen (*a p. or a th.*); übriglassen, liegenlassen, stehenlassen (*only a th.*); lassen, bestehen *or* bleiben lassen, belassen; verlassen, abreisen *or* weggehen von; im Stich lassen, aufgeben; überlassen, anheimstellen, freistellen (***to,*** *Dat.*); ***be left,*** übrigbleiben; ***to be left till called for,*** postlagernd; (*coll.*) ***– go,*** fahren lassen, loslassen.

(a) (*with nouns*) ***– one's card,*** seine Visitenkarte abgeben; ***– one's hat,*** den Hut liegenlassen; ***we left the house,*** wir verließen das Haus; ***– an impression,*** einen Eindruck hinterlassen *or* zurücklassen; ***– much to be desired,*** viel zu wünschen übriglassen; ***– a scar,*** eine Narbe zurücklassen; ***– school,*** von der Schule abgehen; ***– the service,*** aus dem Heere ausscheiden; ***– no stone unturned,*** nichts unversucht lassen; ***– things as they are,*** die Dinge so lassen, wie sie sind; ***– one's umbrella,*** den Regenschirm stehenlassen; ***– word,*** sagen lassen, Bescheid hinterlassen.

(b) (*with adjs.*) (*coll.*) ***– me alone,*** laß mich in Ruhe *or* ungestört, stören Sie mich nicht; (*coll.*) ***– a th. alone,*** etwas nicht berühren; ***– severely alone,*** vollkommen ignorieren; ***this –s me cold,*** das läßt mich kalt; ***– one's children comfortably off,*** seine Kinder in gesicherten Verhältnissen zurücklassen; ***– undone,*** unterlassen; ***– nothing undone,*** alles tun, nichts unversucht lassen; ***– him wondering,*** ihn im Zweifel *or* im unklaren darüber lassen.

(c) (*with preps.*) ***– it at that,*** es (so) gut sein lassen, es dabei (bewenden) lassen; ***– Kiel for Berlin,*** von K. nach B. abreisen; ***– London for the country,*** von L. aufs Land reisen; ***– in the lurch,*** im Stich lassen; ***– the church on one's left,*** die Kirche links liegen lassen; ***I – it to you to . . .,*** ich überlasse es Ihnen, zu . . .; ***– nothing to chance,*** nichts dem Zufall überlassen; ***I – that entirely to you*** or ***to your discretion,*** das steht in Ihrem Ermessen, ich gebe Ihnen völlig freie Hand; ***– him to himself,*** ihn sich (*Dat.*) selbst überlassen; ***I am left with the impression,*** es hinterläßt bei mir den Eindruck.

(d) (*with advs.*) ***– about,*** herumliegen lassen; ***– behind,*** zurücklassen, hinterlassen; liegen *or* stehen lassen; hinter sich (*Dat.*) lassen; ***– off,*** aufhören mit (*speaking etc.*); einstellen (*work*); ablegen (*clothes*); aufgeben, unterlassen (*habits*); ***– off crying!*** laß das Weinen! ***– out,*** auslassen, weglassen; ***– over,*** übriglassen; ***be left over,*** übrigbleiben.

2. *irr.v.i.* abreisen, fortgehen (***for,*** nach); (*of train etc.*) abfahren; (*of employee*) gehen, austreten, die Stellung *or* den Posten aufgeben; (*coll.*) ***– off,*** aufhören; ***– on a journey,*** eine Reise antreten.

leaved [liːvd], *adj. suff.* –blätt(e)rig; –flügelig (*as a door*); *see* **leaf.**

leaven [levn], **1.** *s.* der Sauerteig, die Hefe; (*coll.*) das Gärmittel, Ferment, der Beigeschmach. **2.** *v.t.* säuern; (*fig.*) durchsetzen, durchdringen, erfüllen.

leaves [liːvz], *pl. of* **leaf.**

leave|-taking, *s.* das Abschiednehmen, der Abschied. **--train,** *s.* (*Mil.*) der Urlauberzug. **leaving,** **1.** *adj.* ***– certificate,*** das Abgangszeugnis. **2.** *s.* **1.** das Verlassen, Hinterlassen; *see* [2]**leave**; 2. *pl.* Überbleibsel, Reste (*pl.*).

Lebanese [lebəˈniːz], **1.** *s.* der Libanese (die Libanesin). **2.** *adj.* libanesisch. **Lebanon** [ˈlebənən], *s.* der Libanon.

lecher [ˈlɛtʃə], *s.* der Wüstling. **lecherous,** *adj.* wollüstig, geil. **lechery,** *s.* die Wollust, Geilheit, Unzüchtigkeit.

lectern [ˈlektəːn], *s.* das Lesepult; (*Eccl.*) Chorpult.

lectionary [ˈlekʃənəri], *s.* (*Eccl.*) das Kollektenbuch, Lektionar.

lecture [ˈlektʃə], **1.** *s.* der Vortrag, (*Univ.*) die Vorlesung (***on,*** über (*Acc.*)); (*coll.*) Strafpredigt, der Verweis; ***attend –s,*** Vorlesungen *or* ein Kolleg hören; (*coll.*) ***cut a –,*** eine Vorlesung schwänzen; ***give a –,*** einen Vortrag *or* eine Vorlesung halten; ***read him a –,*** ihn abkanzeln, ihm die Leviten lesen *or* eine Strafpredigt halten. **2.** *v.i.* einen Vortrag *or* Vorträge *or* (*Univ.*) eine Vorlesung *or* Vorlesungen halten, (*Univ.*) lesen (***on,*** über (*Acc.*); ***to,*** vor (*Dat.*)). **3.** *v.t.* (*coll.*) den Text *or* die Leviten lesen, eine Lektion erteilen, eine Moralpredigt *or* Strafpredigt halten (*Dat.*).

lecture| hall, *s.* der Vortragssaal; *see also* **– room.** **– notes,** *pl.* (*Univ.*) das Kollegheft. **lecturer,** *s.* Vortragende(r); (***university***) –, der Dozent, außerordentlicher Professor. **lecture room,** *s.* (*Univ.*) der Hörsaal. **lectureship,** *s.* die Dozentenstelle, außerordentliche Professur.

led [led], **1.** *imperf., p.p. of* [2]**lead.** **2.** *adj.* ***– captain,*** der Schmarotzer, Speichellecker; ***– horse,*** das Handpferd.

ledge [ledʒ], *s.* der *or* das Sims, die Brüstung; vorstehender Rand, vorspringende Kante; (*Naut.*) das (Felsen)riff, die Felsbank; (*Mount.*) Leiste, das Gesims; (*Min.*) Lager, die Schicht, Ader.

ledger [ˈledʒə], *s.* 1. (*Comm.*) das Hauptbuch; 2. (*Archit.*) der Querbalken, Sturz. **ledger-line,** *s.* (*Mus.*) die Hilfslinie.

lee [liː], **1.** *s.* der Schutz; (*Naut.*) die Lee(seite); ***under the – of the shore,*** im Schutz der Küste. **2.** *adj.* (*Naut.*) Lee–. **lee-board,** *s.* das (Seiten)-schwert.

[1]**leech** [liːtʃ], *s.* (*Zool.*) der Blutegel; (*fig.*) Blutsauger, Wucherer; (*fig.*) ***stick like a –,*** wie eine Klette festhängen.

[2]**leech,** *s.* (*Naut.*) das Liek, Leik.

leek [liːk], *s.* (*Bot.*) der Lauch, Porree.

leer [liə], **1.** *s.* boshafter Seitenblick. **2.** *v.i.* boshaft schielen, Seitenblicke werfen (***at,*** nach). **leery,** *adj.* schlau, gerieben, gerissen.

lees [liːz], *pl.* die Hefe, der Bodensatz; (*fig.*) Abhub; ***drain to the –,*** bis zur Neige leeren.

leet [liːt], *s.* (*Scots*) die (Kandidaten)liste.

leeward [ˈliːwəd], [(*Naut.*) ˈluːəd], **1.** *adv.* (*Naut.*) leewärts, nach Lee, unter dem Winde; ***drift*** or ***drive to –,*** abtreiben; ***fall to –,*** (vom Winde) abfallen. **2.** *adj.* vom Winde geschützt; (*Naut.*) Lee–.

Leeward Islands ['li:wəd], *pl.* (*Geog.*) Inseln unter dem Winde.

leeway ['li:wei], *s.* die Abtrift, der Abtrieb, Leeweg; (*fig.*) Rückschritt, Rückstand, die Rückständigkeit; (*Naut.*) ***make* –,** stark abtreiben; (*fig.*) ***make up* (*the* or *for*) –,** Versäumtes nachholen, (Rückstand) aufholen.

[1]**left** [left], **1.** *s.* die Linke (*also Pol., Boxing*), linke Hand *or* Seite, (*Mil.*) linker Flügel; ***on the* –,** links, zur Linken, linkerhand, zu linker Hand; ***on my* –,** mir zur Linken, zu meiner Linken; ***to the* –,** nach links; ***the first on*** or ***to the* –,** die erste (Straße) links; ***keep to the* –,** sich links halten, links ausweichen, (*traffic*) links fahren. **2.** *adj.* link; ***on the* – *hand,*** linker Hand. **3.** *adv.* (nach) links, zur Linken; (*Mil.*) ***– turn!*** linksum!

[2]**left,** *imperf., p.p. of* [2]**leave.**

left|-hand, *attrib. adj.* Links–, link; (*Motor.*) ***–-drive,*** die Linkssteuerung. **–-handed,** *adj.* linkshändig (*of a p.*), mit der linken Hand (*blow*); (*Tech.*) linksläufig, linksgängig; (*fig.*) linkisch, ungeschickt; fragwürdig, zweifelhaft; ***– compliment,*** zweifelhaftes Kompliment; ***– marriage,*** die Ehe zur linken Hand, morganatische Ehe; ***– person,*** der Linkshänder, (*coll.*) Linkser; ***– rotation,*** die Linksdrehung; ***– screw,*** linksgängige Schraube. **–-handedness,** *s.* die Linkshändigkeit. **–-hander,** *s.* (*Boxing*) die Linke; (*coll.*) der Linkser. **leftist,** *s.* (*Pol.*) Linksradikale(r).

left|-luggage office, *s.* die Gepäckaufbewahrung(sstelle). **–-off,** *attrib. adj.* abgelegt (*clothes*). **–-overs,** *pl.* (*coll.*) der (Speise)rest.

left|-wing, *adj.* (*Pol.*) linkradikal. **–-winger,** *s.* (*Footb.*) der Linksaußen; (*Pol. coll.*) *see* **leftist.**

leg [leg], **1.** *s.* das Bein (*also of trousers, stockings, chair, table*), die Keule (*of mutton etc.*); der Schenkel (*of compasses etc.*); Schaft (*of boots*); Abschnitt, die Etappe (*of journey*); (*Naut.*) (Teil)strecke (*in regatta, also Av.*), der Schlag (*tacking*); ***bandy* –*s,*** O-Beine; ***wooden* –,** der Stelzfuß, die Prothese; ***on one's* –*s,*** auf den Beinen; (*coll.*) (*of speaker*) stehend; (*coll.*) ***be on one's last* –*s,*** auf *or* aus dem letzten Loch pfeifen; ***get on one's hind* –*s,*** sich erheben, sich auf die Hinterbeine stellen; ***give him a – up,*** ihm hinaufhelfen *or* auf die Beine helfen; (*fig.*) ihm beistehen; (*fig.*) ***not have a – to stand on,*** jeglicher Grundlage entbehren, (*of a p.*) nicht die geringste Aussicht haben; (*coll.*) ***pull his* –,** ihn zum Narren halten; (*coll.*) ***shake a* –,** das Tanzbein schwingen; (*coll.*) ***show*** or ***shake a –!*** hurtig! mach schnell! heraus aus den Federn! ***stretch one's* –*s,*** einen Spaziergang machen, sich (*Dat.*) die Beine vertreten; ***take to one's* –*s,*** Fersengeld geben; ***walk one's* –*s off,*** sich (*Dat.*) die Beine ablaufen; ***walk him off his* –*s,*** ihn todmüde machen. **2.** *v.i.* (*sl.*) ***– it,*** sich auf die Beine *or* Socken machen.

legacy ['legəsi], *s.* das Vermächtnis (*also fig.*), die Erbschaft, das Legat; (*fig.*) ***– of . . .,*** Erb–, überkommen. **legacy|-duty,** *s.* die Erbschaftssteuer. **–-hunter,** *s.* der Erbschleicher.

legal [li:gl], *adj.* gesetzlich, rechtlich; gesetzmäßig, rechtsgültig, rechtskräftig; Rechts–, juristisch; ***– adviser,*** der Rechtsberater, Rechtsbeistand; ***– aid,*** die Rechtshilfe; ***– decision,*** gerichtliches *or* rechtskräftiges Urteil; ***– documents,*** Aktenstücke; ***– force,*** die Rechtskraft, Rechtswirksamkeit; ***– heir,*** der Rechtsnachfolger; ***– procedure,*** der Rechtsweg; ***– proceedings,*** das Rechtsverfahren; ***take – proceedings,*** see ***take – steps***; ***– profession,*** der Juristenberuf; ***– remedy,*** das Rechtsmittel; ***– separation,*** die Ehetrennung; ***take – steps,*** gerichtlich vorgehen; ***– system,*** das Rechtssystem; ***– tender,*** gesetzliches Zahlungsmittel.

legality [li'gæliti], *s.* die Gesetzlichkeit, Rechtsgültigkeit; Gesetzmäßigkeit, Rechtmäßigkeit. **legalization** [li:gəlai'zeiʃən], *s.* gerichtliche Beglaubigung; die Legalisierung, gesetzliche Bestätigung *or* Anerkennung. **legalize** ['li:gəlaiz], *v.t.* rechtskräftig machen, legalisieren; als gesetzlich anerkennen, amtlich beglaubigen *or* bestätigen.

[1]**legate** ['legət], *s.* päpstlicher Gesandter, der Legat.

[2]**legate** [li'geit], *v.t.* (testamentarisch) vermachen (*to, Dat.*). **legatee** [legə'ti:], *s.* der Vermächtnisnehmer, Erbe (die Erbin), der (die) Legatar(in).

legation [li'geiʃən], *s.* die Gesandtschaft; das Gesandtschaftsgebäude; die Botschaft, Delegation, Mission.

legato [li'gɑ:tou], *adv.* (*Mus.*) gebunden.

legator [li'geitə], *s.* der (die) Erblasser(in), Testator(in).

leg|-bail, *s.* (*coll.*) ***give* –,** Fersengeld geben. **–-break,** *s.* (*Crick.*) der Ball mit Effekt nach links.

legend ['ledʒənd], *s.* 1. die Legende, Heiligengeschichte; Sage, Wundergeschichte, das Märchen; 2. die Inschrift, Umschrift (*on coins*); der Text (*to illustrations*). **legendary,** *adj.* sagenhaft, legendenhaft, legendär.

legerdemain ['ledʒədəmein], *s.* die Taschenspielerei, Taschenspielerkunst; Gaukelei, das Kunststück.

legged ['legid], *adj. suff.* –beinig. **legging,** *s.* (*usu. pl.*) hohe Gamasche. **leg-guard,** *s.* (*Crick.*) die Beinschiene. **leggy,** *adj.* (*coll.*) langbeinig.

Leghorn ['leghɔ:n], *s.* (*Geog.*) Livorno (*n.*).

legibility [ledʒi'biliti], *s.* die Leserlichkeit, Lesbarkeit. **legible** ['ledʒibl], *adj.* (gut) lesbar *or* leserlich; deutlich, kenntlich.

legion ['li:dʒən], *s.* (*Mil.*) die Legion; (*fig.*) große Menge, die Unzahl; ***Royal British Legion,*** britischer Frontkämpferverband; ***Legion of Honour,*** (französische) Ehrenlegion; ***Foreign Legion,*** die Fremdenlegion. **legionary,** *s.* (*Hist.*) der Legionär, Legionssoldat; Fremdenlegionär.

legislate ['ledʒisleit], *v.i.* Gesetze geben. **legislation** [–'leiʃən], *s.* die Gesetzgebung. **legislative** [–lətiv], **1.** *adj.* gesetzgebend. **2.** *s. See* **legislature.** **legislator,** *s.* der Gesetzgeber. **legislature** [–leitʃə], *s.* gesetzgebende Gewalt *or* Versammlung, die Legislative.

legitimacy [li'dʒitiməsi], *s.* die Gesetzmäßigkeit, Rechtmäßigkeit, Legitimität; (*fig.*) Berechtigung, Rechtfertigung, Gültigkeit, Richtigkeit (*of conclusions etc.*); Ehelichkeit (*of children*). **legitimate** **1.** [–mit], *adj.* gesetzlich, legitim, gesetzmäßig, rechtmäßig (*ruler etc.*); wohlbegründet, berechtigt, folgerichtig, einwandfrei (*as arguments*); ehelich (geboren), legitim (*of child*); ***– drama,*** echtes Drama. **2.** [–meit], *v.t. See* **legitimize.** **legitimation** [–'meiʃən], *s.* die Gültigkeitserklärung; Legitimation, der Ausweis; das Gültigmachen, die Legitimierung; Ehelicherklärung (*of a child*). **legitimatize** [–taiz], *v.t. See* **legitimize.** **legitimist,** *s.* der Legitimist. **legitimize,** *v.t.* für gesetzlich *or* (rechts)gültig erklären, legitimieren; für berechtigt erklären, rechtfertigen; für ehelich erklären (*child*); ***–d child,*** das Brautkind.

legless ['leglis], *adj.* beinlos, ohne Beine. **leg|-of-mutton,** *adj.* keulenförmig; ***– sail,*** das Schratsegel; ***– sleeve,*** der Keulenärmel, Gigot. **–-pull(ing),** *s.* (*coll.*) die Neckerei, Fopperei. **–-show,** *s.* (*sl.*) die Beinschau, Fleischschau.

legume ['legju:m], *s.* (*oft. pl.*) die Hülse, Hülsenfrucht. **leguminous** [–'gju:minəs], *adj.* Hülsen–, hülsentragend; hülsenartig, erbsenartig, bohnenartig.

leisure ['leʒə (*Am. also* 'li:ʒə)], **1.** *s.* die Muße, Freizeit, freie Zeit; ***at* –,** unbeschäftigt, frei; ohne Hast, mit Muße; ***at your* –,** wenn es Ihnen beliebt, wenn Sie Zeit haben, wenn es Ihnen gerade paßt, bei passender Gelegenheit, gelegentlich. **2.** *adj.* müßig, Muße–; ***– hour,*** freie Stunde, die Mußestunde; ***– time,*** freie Zeit, die Freizeit. **leisured,** *adj.* frei, unbeschäftigt; ***– classes,*** wohlhabende *or* begüterte Klassen. **leisureliness,** *s.* die Ruhe, Gemächlichkeit. **leisurely, 1.** *adj.* ruhig, gemächlich. **2.** *adv.* ohne Hast, mit Ruhe, gemütlich, gemächlich.

leit-motif ['laitmoti:f], *s.* (*Mus.*) das Leitmotiv.

leman ['lemən], *s.* (*obs.*) Liebste(r), Geliebte(r); die Buhlerin, Buhle, Mätresse.

lemma ['lemə], *s.* (*pl.* **-ta** [-'mɑ:tə]) das Lemma, der Hilfssatz, Lehnsatz; das Stichwort, die Überschrift.

lemon ['lemən], **1.** *s.* 1. die Zitrone; Zitronenfarbe, das Zitronengelb; ***salts of –,*** das Kleesalz; 2. (*sl.*) (*of a th.*) die Niete, der Versager; (*of a p.*) Spielverderber, das Mädchen zum Abgewöhnen. **2.** *adj.* zitronengelb. **lemonade** [-'neid], *s.* die (Zitronen)limonade, der Zitronensaft.

lemon|-cheese, --curd, *s.* die Zitronenkrem. **--juice,** *s.* der Zitronensaft. **--peel,** *s.* die Zitronenschale. **--sole,** *s.* (*Ichth.*) die Rotzunge. **--squash,** *s.* der Zitronensaft, das Zitronenwasser. **--squeezer,** *s.* die Zitronenpresse. **--yellow, 1.** *s.* das Zitronengelb. **2.** *adj.* zitronengelb.

lemur ['li:mə], *s.* (*Zool.*) der Maki, Lemur(e).

lend [lend], *irr.v.t.* ausleihen, verleihen (*to*, an (*Acc.*)), leihen (*Dat.*); (*fig.*) gewähren, leisten (*aid*), schenken (*an ear*), hergeben (*one's name*) (*to*, *Dat.*); ***– a hand,*** mit Hand anlegen, behilflich sein (***with,*** bei); ***– o.s. to,*** sich hergeben zu; ***– itself to,*** sich eignen zu *or* für. **lender,** *s.* der Verleiher. **lending-library,** *s.* die Leihbibliothek.

length [leŋθ], *s.* die Länge (*also Racing*); (lange) Strecke, die Weite, Entfernung; (Zeit)dauer (*of time*); ***at –,*** in der ganzen Länge; ausführlich, in allen Einzelheiten; endlich, schließlich, zuletzt; ***at full –,*** der Länge nach, in voller Länge; ***at great –,*** sehr ausführlich; ***at arm's –,*** in angemessener Entfernung; (*fig.*) ***keep him at arm's –,*** sich (*Dat.*) ihn vom Leibe halten; ***full –,*** in Lebensgröße; ***fall full –,*** der Länge nach hinfallen; ***100 cm. in –,*** 100 cm. lang; ***overall –, – over all,*** die Baulänge, Gesamtlänge; ***go (to) the – of saying,*** so weit gehen, zu sagen; ***go to any –s,*** alles daransetzen, vor nichts zurückschrecken; ***go to all –s,*** aufs Ganze gehen; ***go to desperate –s,*** verzweifelt weit gehen; ***go to great*** or ***extreme –s,*** bis zum Äußersten gehen, sehr weit gehen, sich sehr bemühen.

lengthen ['leŋθən], **1.** *v.t.* verlängern, ausdehnen; dehnen (*syllables*). **2.** *v.i.* sich verlängern, sich ausdehnen, länger werden; ***– out,*** sich in die Länge ziehen. **lengthening, 1.** *s.* die Verlängerung. **2.** *attrib. adj.* Verlängerungs–, Ansatz–. **lengthiness,** *s.* die Langatmigkeit, Weitschweifigkeit, Langwierigkeit. **lengthways, lengthwise,** *adv.* der Länge nach. **lengthy,** *adj.* sehr lang; langatmig, langwierig, weitschweifig; ***have a – talk with him,*** sich mit ihm länger unterhalten.

leniency ['li:niənsi], *s.* die Milde, Nachsicht. **lenient,** *adj.* mild(e), nachsichtig, schonend, sanft, gelind(e) (*to*(***wards***), gegen(über)).

lenitive ['lenitiv], **1.** *adj.* lindernd, besänftigend. **2.** *s.* das Beruhigungsmittel, Linderungsmittel. **lenity,** *s.* (*rare*) *see* **leniency.**

lens [lenz], *s.* die Linse, Optik; ***concave –,*** die Zerstreuungslinse; ***convex –,*** die Sammellinse; ***contact –,*** das Haftglas, die Haftschale; (*Phot.*) ***supplementary –,*** die Vorsatzlinse.

lent [lent], *imperf.*, *p.p. of* **lend.**

Lent, *s.* die Fastenzeit; (*obs.*) Fasten (*pl.*); ***keep –,*** fasten; ***– lily,*** gelbe Narzisse; (*Univ.*) ***– term,*** das Frühjahrstrimester. **Lenten,** *adj.* Fasten–; ***– fare,*** fleischlose *or* magere Kost.

lenticular [len'tikjulə], *adj.* linsenartig, Linsen–.

lentil ['lentil], *s.* die Linse.

leonine ['liənain], *adj.* löwenartig, Löwen–.

Leonine, *adj.* ***– verse,*** leoninischer Vers.

leopard ['lepəd], *s.* der Leopard, Panther; ***a – cannot change its spots,*** man kann nicht aus seiner Haut heraus. **leopardess,** *s.* das Leopardenweibchen.

leper ['lepə], *s.* Aussätzige(r), Leprakranke(r).

lepidoptera [lepi'dɔptərə], *pl.* Schmetterlinge (*pl.*). **lepidopterous,** *adj.* Schmetterlings–.

leporine ['lepərain], *adj.* Hasen–.

leprechaun ['leprikɔ:n], *s.* (*Irish*) der Kobold.

leprosy ['leprəsi], *s.* der Aussatz, die Lepra. **leprous,** *adj.* aussätzig, leprakrank.

Lesbian ['lezbiən], **1.** *s.* (*Hist.*) der (die) Lesbier(in); (*fig.*) die Lesbierin, Tribade. **2.** *adj.* lesbisch (*also fig.*). **Lesbianism,** *s.* lesbische Liebe, die Tribadie.

lese-majesty [li:z'mædʒisti], *s.* die Majestätsbeleidigung; der Hochverrat.

lesion ['li:ʒən], *s.* 1. (*Med.*) die Verletzung; krankhafte Veränderung (*of an organ or tissue*); 2. (*Law*) die Schädigung.

less [les], **1.** *comp. adj.* kleiner, geringer, weniger; ***more haste – speed,*** eile mit Weile; ***no – a person than,*** kein Geringerer als. **2.** *comp. adv.* weniger, in geringerem Maße; ***– and –,*** immer weniger; ***more or –,*** mehr oder weniger; ***none the –,*** nichtsdestoweniger; ***nothing – than,*** alles eher als, zumindest, nichts weniger als; ***no – than,*** ebensogut wie; ***much –*** or ***still –,*** noch viel weniger, geschweige denn; ***the – the better,*** je weniger desto besser; ***the – so as,*** um so weniger als. **3.** *prep.* abzüglich (*Gen.*), minus. **4.** *s.* eine kleinere Zahl *or* Menge, ein geringeres Maß; ***I cannot sell it for –,*** ich kann es nicht billiger abgeben; ***in – than no time,*** im Handumdrehen; ***little – than,*** so gut wie, nicht viel weniger als.

lessee [le'si:], *s.* der (die) Pächter(in), Mieter(in).

lessen [lesn], **1.** *v.t.* verkleinern, verringern, vermindern; schmälern, herabsetzen; mildern (*pain*). **2.** *v.i.* kleiner *or* geringer werden, abnehmen, sich vermindern *or* verringern. **lesser,** *attrib. adj.* kleiner, geringer, unbedeutender; ***the – evil*** or ***– of two evils,*** das kleinere Übel.

lesson [lesn], *s.* 1. die Aufgabe, Lektion; (Lehr)stunde, Unterrichtsstunde; *pl.* Stunden (*pl.*), der Unterricht; ***give –s,*** Stunden geben, Unterricht erteilen; ***have*** or ***take –s with,*** Stunden *or* Unterricht nehmen bei; ***music –,*** die Musikstunde; 2. die Lehre, Vorschrift; (*fig.*) Warnung, der Denkzettel (*to*, für); ***let this be a – to you*** or ***teach you a –,*** lassen Sie sich das zur Warnung dienen; 3. (*Eccl.*) die Lesung, Lektion.

lessor ['lesɔ:], *s.* der (die) Vermieter(in), Verpächter(in).

lest [lest], *conj.* 1. (*followed by* ***should***) damit nicht, daß nicht; aus Furcht daß; ***– you should not understand me,*** damit du mich recht verstehst; ***– he understands,*** damit er nicht versteht; 2. (*followed by expressions of fear*) daß; ***fear –,*** fürchten daß.

[1]**let** [let], **1.** *irr.v.t.* 1. lassen, (*with Dat.*) zulassen, gestatten, erlauben; 2. (herein– *or* hinaus)lassen; 3. vermieten, verpachten (*a house etc.*) (*to*, an (*Acc.*)); ***– rooms,*** Zimmer vermieten; 4. ***– blood,*** zur Ader lassen.

(a) (*with adjs.*) ***– alone,*** in Ruhe *or* Frieden lassen, nicht belästigen (*a p.*), unberührt lassen, nicht anrühren *or* berühren, stehen *or* sein lassen, sich nicht mischen in (*Acc.*) *or* beschäftigen mit (*a th.*); (*fig. coll.*) geschweige denn, ganz zu schweigen von; ***– well alone,*** (es) gut sein lassen, sich nicht (unnötig) einmischen; ***– loose,*** loslassen.

(b) (*aux. with inf.*) ***– be,*** see ***– alone***; ***– it come to this,*** es darauf ankommen lassen; ***– o.s. be deceived,*** sich täuschen lassen; ***– fall,*** fallen lassen (*also fig.*); (*Geom.*) fällen (***on***, auf (*Acc.*)); ***– fly,*** abschießen; (*fig.*) von sich geben, loslassen; ***– fly at him,*** auf ihn schießen; (*coll. fig.*) ihm (tüchtig *or* energisch) zusetzen, gegen ihn grob werden; ***– go,*** gehen lassen; in Freiheit setzen; fahren lassen, loslassen; vergeben (*goods*); ***– o.s. go,*** sich gehen lassen; ***– it go at that,*** es dabei bewenden lassen; (*sl.*) ***– go of,*** loslassen; ***– him have,*** ihm zukommen lassen; ***– me (help),*** erlauben Sie mir; ***– him know,*** ihn wissen lassen; ***– pass,*** fahren lassen; ***– things slide,*** die Dinge gehen *or* ihren Lauf nehmen lassen; ***– an opportunity slip,*** die Gelegenheit entgehen lassen.

(c) (*aux. as imper.*) ***– x = 10,*** nehmen wir an, x gleich 10; ***– us go! –'s go!*** gehen wir! ***– us suppose,*** nehmen wir an; ***– me see*** or ***think!*** einen Augenblick! ***– him try,*** so mag er *or* er soll es nur versuchen.

(d) (*with preps.*) – ***him into the house,*** ihn in das Haus (herein)lassen; (*fig.*) – ***him into the secret,*** ihn in das Geheimnis einweihen, ihn ins Vertrauen ziehen; – ***him off a promise,*** ihn von einem Versprechen entbinden; – ***him off a punishment,*** ihm eine Strafe erlassen, ihn von einer Strafe befreien; – ***him over the house,*** ihm gestatten, das Haus zu besichtigen; – ***him out of the house,*** ihn aus dem Haus herauslassen.
(e) (*with advs.*) – ***down,*** herablassen, herunterlassen; (*fig. coll.*) – ***him down,*** ihn enttäuschen *or* im Stich lassen; – ***him down gently,*** ihn glimpflich behandeln; – ***in,*** hereinlassen, (hin)einlassen; Zutritt gestatten (*Dat.*); (*Dressm. etc.*) einlassen, einfügen, einsetzen; (*coll.*) – ***him in for,*** ihm einbrocken *or* aufhalsen; ihn hereinlegen *or* bringen um; – ***o.s. in for,*** sich (*Dat.*) aufhalsen *or* aufbürden lassen; (*coll.*) – ***him in on,*** ihn (in Vertrauen) wissen lassen, ihn einweihen in (*Acc.*), ihn aufklären über (*Acc.*); – ***off,*** abschießen, losschießen, abfeuern; (*fig.*) vom Stapel lassen, loslassen; – ***off steam,*** Dampf ablassen, (*fig.*) sich (*Dat.*) Luft machen; (*coll.*) – ***him off,*** ihm die Strafe erlassen, bei ihm ein Auge zudrücken; ihn davonkommen lassen; ***be – off lightly,*** leichten Kaufes davonkommen; – ***out,*** herauslassen; auslassen (*a dress*); ausplaudern (*a secret*); vermieten, verpachten, vergeben (*rooms etc.*).
2. *irr.v.i.* vermietet werden, sich vermieten (*at, for,* für); ***house to –,*** Haus zu vermieten; – ***on,*** (*coll.*) vorgeben, tun als ob; (*sl.*) plaudern, schwatzen; (*sl.*) – ***up,*** nachlassen, aufhören; (*sl.*) – ***up on,*** ablassen von.

[2]let, 1. *v.t.* (*obs.*) (be)hindern. **2.** *s.* (*Tenn.*) das Let, ungültiger Anschlag; (*Law*) ***without – or hindrance,*** ohne Hinderung, völlig unbehindert.

let-down, *s.* (*coll.*) die Enttäuschung, Ernüchterung.

lethal [li:θl], *adj.* tödlich, todbringend, Todes–; – ***chamber,*** die Todeskammer.

lethargic(al) [lə'θɑ:dʒik(l)], *adj.* schlafsüchtig, lethargisch; (*fig.*) träge, stumpf, teilnahmslos. **lethargy** ['leθədʒi], *s.* (*Med.*) die Schlafsucht, Lethargie; (*fig.*) Interesselosigkeit, Teilnahmslosigkeit, Stumpfheit.

Lethe ['li:θi], *s.* die Lethe; (*fig.*) Vergessenheit.

let-off, *s.* (*coll.*) ungestraftes Davonkommen.

Lett [let], *s., adj. See* **Latvian.**

letter ['letə], **1.** *s.* 1. der Buchstabe; (*Typ.*) die Letter, Type, Schrift; – ***of the law,*** der Buchstabe des Gesetzes; (*Typ.*) ***black –,*** die Fraktur, gotische Schrift; ***capital –,*** der Großbuchstabe; ***dead –,*** toter Buchstabe, unwirksames Gesetz; ***in – and spirit,*** dem Buchstaben und Inhalt nach; (*Typ.*) ***proof before –s,*** Abzug vor der Schrift; (*Typ.*) ***roman –s,*** die Antiqua; ***small –,*** der Kleinbuchstabe; ***to the –,*** buchstäblich; 2. der Brief, das Schreiben, die Zuschrift, Mitteilung (*to,* an (*Acc.*)); – ***of acceptance,*** das Akzept; – ***of advice,*** der Avisbrief; – ***of application,*** das Bewerbungsschreiben; – ***of attorney,*** die Vollmacht; – ***of condolence,*** der Beileidsbrief; – ***of credit,*** der Kreditbrief; – ***of introduction*** or ***recommendation,*** der Empfehlungsbrief, das Empfehlungsschreiben; ***by –,*** brieflich, schriftlich; ***covering –,*** das Begleitschreiben; ***dead –,*** unzustellbarer Brief; ***–s patent,*** die Patenturkunde; ***prepaid –,*** frankierter Brief; ***red–– day,*** der Festtag, Glückstag, Freudentag; ***registered –,*** eingeschriebener Brief; 3. *pl.* (schöne) Literatur; die Bildung, Gelehrsamkeit; ***man of –s,*** Gelehrte(r), der Schriftsteller, Literat; ***republic of –s,*** die gelehrte *or* literarische Welt. **2.** *v.t.* mit Buchstaben bezeichnen; beschriften (*drawings*); betiteln, mit Lettern *or* Titel versehen.

letter|-balance, *s.* die Briefwaage. **--book,** *s.* das Briefkopierbuch, der Briefordner. **--box,** *s.* der Briefkasten. **--card,** *s.* der Kartenbrief. **--case,** *s.* die Brieftasche; (*Typ.*) der Setzkasten. **lettered,** *adj.* 1. gelehrt, (wissenschaftlich) gebildet; 2. beschriftet, betitelt. **letter|-file,** *s.* der Briefordner. **--founder,** *s.* der Schriftgießer. **--head,** *s.* (gedruckter) Briefkopf.

lettering ['letəriŋ], *s.* die Bezeichnung mit Buchstaben; Beschriftung (*of drawings*); Aufschrift, der Aufdruck; (*Art*) das Schriftschreiben. **letter|-lock,** *s.* das Buchstabenschloß, Vexierschloß. **--perfect,** *adj.* auf den Buchstaben genau. **–press,** *s.* der Druck, Text; – ***printing,*** der Pressendruck, Buchdruck; (*obs.*) die Kopierpresse. **--rack,** *s.* der Briefhalter, Briefständer. **--weight,** *s.* der Briefbeschwerer. **--writer,** *s.* der Briefschreiber, Briefsteller.

lettuce ['letis], *s.* der Lattich; ***garden –,*** der (Garten)salat, Kopfsalat.

let-up, *s.* (*coll.*) das Nachlassen; die Pause, Unterbrechung.

leucocyte ['lju:kəsait], *s.* weißes Blutkörperchen. **leucoma** [–'koumə], *s.* die Hornhauttrübung, das Leukom. **leucorrhœa** [–'riə], *s.* die Leukorrhö(e), der Weißfluß. **leukæmia** [–'ki:miə], *s.* die Leukämie, Weißblütigkeit.

levant [li'vænt], *v.i.* (*coll.*) durchbrennen, durchgehen.

Levant, *s.* die Levante. **Levantine** [li'væntain, 'levəntain], **1.** *s.* der (die) Levantiner(in). **2.** *adj.* levant(in)isch.

levator [li'veitə], *s.* (*Anat.*) der Hebemuskel.

[1]levee ['levi], **1.** *s.* (*Am.*) der Uferdamm, Schutzdamm, Deich. **2.** *v.t.* eindämmen (*a river*).

[2]levee, *s.* (*Hist.*) das Lever, der Morgenempfang; die Levee, der Empfang, die Audienz.

level [levl], **1.** *s.* 1. die Horizontalebene, Waagerechte, waagerechte Fläche; ***datum –,*** die Bezugsebene; (*coll.*) ***dead –,*** gerade Ebene, (*fig.*) die Eintönigkeit; 2. gleiche Höhe *or* Stufe, dasselbe Niveau; (*Med.*) der Spiegel; (*fig.*) die Höhe, das Niveau, der Grad, Stand; (*fig.*) ***find one's –,*** den Platz einnehmen, der einem zukommt; ***find its –,*** sich ausgleichen; – ***of prices,*** das Preisniveau, der Stand der Preise; ***oil –,*** der Ölstand; (*coll.*) ***on the –,*** ehrlich, offen, vertrauenswürdig; (*fig.*) ***on a – with,*** auf gleicher Höhe *or* Stufe mit; ***sea –,*** der Meeresspiegel, die Meereshöhe; ***water –,*** der Wasserstand; 3. (*Tech.*) die Wasserwaage, Libelle; (*Build.*) das Richtscheit; (*Min.*) die Sohle, der Stollen. **2.** *v.t.* waagerecht *or* eben machen, ebnen, planieren, nivellieren (*ground*); einebnen, dem Erdboden gleichmachen; (*fig.*) auf die gleiche Stufe stellen, auf den gleichen Stand *or* aufs gleiche Niveau bringen, ausgleichen, gleichmachen, gleichmäßig machen; zielen, richten (*a weapon*) (*at, against,* auf (*Acc.*)); richten (*criticism etc.*) (gegen); – ***down,*** (herab)drücken, herabsetzen (*as wages*), hinunterdrücken, hinabschrauben, nach unten ausgleichen; – ***off,*** ebnen, planieren, eben machen; (*Av.*) abfangen; – ***up,*** auf gleiche Höhe bringen; hinaufschrauben, erhöhen (*as wages*), nach oben ausgleichen; – ***with*** or ***to the ground,*** dem Erdboden gleichmachen. **3.** *adj.* waagerecht, horizontal; eben, gerade, flach; (*fig.*) gleich, gleichmäßig, ausgeglichen (*of style*); (*coll.*) ***do one's – best,*** sein möglichstes tun; (*Railw.*) – ***crossing,*** schienengleicher Übergang; – ***race,*** ausgeglichenes Rennen; (*Phonet.*) – ***stress,*** gleichstarke *or* schwebende Betonung; – ***with,*** in gleicher Höhe mit, (*fig.*) auf gleicher Höhe *or* Stufe mit; ***draw – with,*** einholen, in gleiche Linie kommen mit.

level-headed, *adj.* verständig, vernünftig, nüchtern, klarblickend. **levelling,** *s.* das Planieren, die Nivellierung; (*Gram.*) Angleichung, Analogiebildung; – ***instrument,*** das Nivellierinstrument; (*Artil.*) – ***mechanism,*** die Horizontierung; – ***screw,*** die Stellschraube.

lever ['li:və], **1.** *s.* der Hebel (*also fig.*); Hebebaum, das Brecheisen, die Brechstange; (*Horol.*) der Anker; ***hand –,*** der Griffhebel; (*Phys.*) – ***of the first order,*** zweiarmiger Hebel; (*Phys.*) – ***of the second order,*** einarmiger Hebel. **2.** *v.t.* mit einem Hebel heben *or* bewegen. **leverage** [–ridʒ], *s.* die Hebelanordnung, Hebelübersetzung, das Hebelverhältnis; die Hebelwirkung, Hebelanwendung; Hebelkraft, (*fig.*) das (Druck)mittel, der Einfluß;

– *escapement*, die Ankerhemmung; – *watch*, die Ankeruhr.

leveret ['levərit], *s.* junger Hase, das Häschen.

leviathan [li'vaiəθən], *s.* (*B.*) der Leviathan; das Seeungeheuer, (*fig.*) Ungetüm, der Riese, Koloß.

levigate ['levigeit], *v.t.* zerreiben, zerstoßen, pulverisieren, abschlämmen. **levigation** [–'geiʃən], *s.* die Zerreibung.

levitate ['leviteit], **1.** *v.t.* schweben lassen. **2.** *v.i.* frei schweben; leicht werden. **levitation** [–'teiʃən], *s.* das Schweben.

levity ['leviti], *s.* die Leichtfertigkeit, Sorglosigkeit, der Leichtsinn; die Flüchtigkeit; *with* –, leichtfertig.

levulose, *see* **laevulose.**

levy ['levi], **1.** *v.t.* erheben (*taxes*); ausheben (*troops*); anfangen, führen (*war*); auferlegen (*a fine*) ((*up*)*on*, *Dat.*). **2.** *s.* die Erhebung (*of taxes*), der Beitrag, die Umlage; (*Mil.*) Aushebung, das Aufgebot; ausgehobene Truppen (*pl.*); *capital* –, die Kapitalabgabe, Vermögenssteuer.

lewd [lju:d], *adj.* liederlich, unzüchtig. **lewdness,** *s.* die Unzüchtigkeit, Liederlichkeit.

lewis ['lu:is], *s.* der (Stein)keil.

lexical ['leksikl], *adj.* lexikalisch, Lexikon–. **lexicographer** [–'kɔgrəfə], *s.* der Wörterbuchverfasser, Lexikograph. **lexicologist** [–'kɔlədʒist], *s.* der Wortforscher. **lexicology** [–'kɔlədʒi], *s.* die Wortkunde. **lexicon,** *s.* das Wörterbuch, Lexikon.

Leyden [leidn], *s.* (*Geog.*) Leiden (*n.*); (*Elec.*) – *jar*, Leidener Flasche.

liability [laiə'biliti], *s.* 1. die Verantwortlichkeit, Verantwortung; *accept* or *incur* –, Verantwortlichkeit übernehmen; 2. (*Comm.*) die Verpflichtung, Obligation, Verbindlichkeit; Haftbarkeit, Haftpflicht, Haftung; *insurance against* –, die Haftpflichtversicherung; *joint* –, die Gesamthaftung; *limited* –, beschränkte Haftpflicht; *discharge* or *meet one's liabilities*, seinen Verbindlichkeiten nachkommen; – *to military service*, die Wehrpflicht; 3. das Ausgesetztsein, Unterworfensein (*to*, *Dat.*), der Hang, die Neigung (zu); 4. *pl.* (*Comm.*) Schulden (*pl.*), Belastungen (*pl.*), Passiva (*pl.*), der Schuldposten, die Schuldenmasse.

liable ['laiəbl], *adj.* 1. ausgesetzt, unterworfen (*to*, *Dat.*); *be* – *to*, unterworfen *or* ausgesetzt sein (*Dat.*), unterliegen (*Dat.*), neigen zu; – *to be forgotten*, in Gefahr sein, vergessen zu werden; *difficulties are* – *to occur*, Schwierigkeiten treten leicht auf, mit Schwierigkeiten muß gerechnet werden; *he is* – *to kill himself*, er neigt zum Selbstmord, er zeigt selbstmörderische Absichten *or* Tendenzen; *be* – *to prosecution*, sich strafbar machen, strafrechtliche Verfolgung zu gewärtigen haben; 2. verpflichtet (*for*, zu), verantwortlich (für), (*Comm.*) haftbar, haftpflichtig; *be* – *for*, haften für; *this price is* – *to discount*, von diesem Preis geht ein Rabatt ab; – *to duty*, zollpflichtig; – *for military service*, wehrpflichtig.

liaise [li'eiz], *v.i.* (*coll.*) eine Verbindung herstellen *or* aufnehmen *or* aufrechthalten (*with*, mit). **liaison** [–n], *s.* die Verbindung, Fühlung, Zusammenarbeit; (*Phonet.*) Bindung; (*coll.*) Liebschaft, das (Liebes)verhältnis. **liaison-officer,** *s.* der Verbindungsoffizier.

liana [li'ɑ:nə], *s.* die Schlingpflanze, Liane.

liar ['laiə], *s.* der (die) Lügner(in).

Lias ['laiəs], *s.* (*Geol.*) der *or* die Lias, schwarzer Jura.

libation [lai'beiʃən], *s.* das Trankopfer.

libel ['laibəl], **1.** *s.* (*Law*) die Klageschrift; Schmähschrift; (*coll.*) Verleumdung, Verunglimpfung, Beleidigung; (*coll.*) *it is an absolute* –, es ist ein wahrer Hohn (*on*, auf (*Acc.*)) *or* Beleidigung (für) *or* Entstellung *or* Verzerrung (*Gen.*); *action for* –, die Verleumdungsklage. **2.** *v.t.* (*Law*) eine Klageschrift einreichen gegen; schriftlich verleumden; (*coll.*) beschimpfen, verunglimpfen; entstellen, verzerren. **libellant,** *s.* (*Law*) der (die) Kläger(in).

libellee [–'li:], *s.* (*Law*) Beklagte(r). **libeller,** *s.* der (die) Urheber(in) einer Verleumdung, Verfasser(in) einer Schmähschrift. **libellous,** *adj.* Verleumdungs–, verleumderisch, Schmäh–.

liberal ['libərəl], **1.** *adj.* 1. freigebig, großzügig (*of*, mit); – *donation*, großzügige Spendung; 2. ansehnlich, beträchtlich, reichlich (bemessen); – *meal*, reichliches Mahl; 3. offen, frei(sinnig), vorurteilslos, weitherzig, aufgeklärt, aufgeschlossen, fortschrittlich, freiheitlich (*as views*); – *arts*, freie *or* schöne Künste, Geisteswissenschaften (*pl.*); – *education*, die Allgemeinbildung, allgemeine Bildung; – *interpretation*, ungezwungene *or* weitherzige Auslegung; – *profession*, freier Beruf; 4. (*Pol.*) liberal. **2.** *s.* Freisinnige(r), (*usu. Pol.*) Liberale(r).

liberalism ['libərəlizm], *s.* die Aufgeklärtheit, der Freisinn, (*usu. Pol.*) Liberalismus. **liberalistic** [–'listik], *adj.* liberal gesinnt. **liberality** [–'ræliti], *s.* die Freigebigkeit, Großzügigkeit; Unvoreingenommenheit, Vorurteilslosigkeit, Freisinnigkeit, Unbefangenheit, Unparteilichkeit.

liberate ['libəreit], *v.t.* befreien (*from*, von); freigeben, freilassen (*slaves*); (*Chem.*) freimachen, entbinden, ausscheiden; (*Chem.*) *be* –*d*, auftreten. **liberation** [–'reiʃən], *s.* die Befreiung (*from*, von), Freilassung (aus); (*Chem.*) das Freiwerden, Freimachen. **liberator,** *s.* der Befreier.

Liberia [lai'biəriə], *s.* Liberia (*n.*). **Liberian, 1.** *s.* der (die) Liberier(in), Liberianer(in). **2.** *adj.* liberisch, liberianisch.

libertarian [libə'tɛəriən], **1.** *adj.* (*Phil.*) indeterministisch. **2.** *s.* der Indeterminist. **libertarianism,** *s.* der Indeterminismus.

libertinage ['libətinidʒ], *s.* *See* **libertinism. libertine, 1.** *s.* der Wüstling; (*Hist.*) (römischer) Freigelassener; der Freidenker. **2.** *adj.* liederlich, ausschweifend; freidenkerisch. **libertinism,** *s.* die Liederlichkeit, Ausschweifung.

liberty ['libəti], *s.* die Freiheit, Ungebundenheit; (*usu. pl.*) das (Vor)recht, Sonderrecht, Privileg(ium); die Erlaubnis, freie Wahl; der Freibezirk, die (Stadt)freiheit; (*coll.*) die Ungehörigkeit, Ungebührlichkeit, Frechheit; *at* –, in Freiheit, frei; (*fig.*) *be at* –, freie Hand haben, die Erlaubnis haben, dürfen; *you are at* –, es steht Ihnen frei; *be at* – *to disclose*, enthüllen dürfen; *set at* –, befreien, freilassen, in Freiheit setzen; – *of conscience*, die Glaubensfreiheit, Gewissensfreiheit; – *of the press*, die Pressefreiheit; *religious* –, die Religionsfreiheit; *take the* –, sich (*Dat.*) die Freiheit (heraus)nehmen; *take liberties*, sich (*Dat.*) Freiheiten herausnehmen *or* gestatten *or* erlauben (*with*, gegen); *take liberties with the facts*, mit den Tatsachen willkürlich umgehen.

liberty-man, *s.* der Matrose auf Urlaub.

libidinous [li'bidinəs], *adj.* unzüchtig, wollüstig, lüstern, geil. **libido** ['libidou], *s.* (*Psych.*) der Geschlechtstrieb, die Libido.

Libra ['laibrə], *s.* (*Astr.*) die Waage.

librarian [lai'brɛəriən], *s.* der (die) Bibliothekar(in); *chief* –, der Bibliotheksdirektor. **librarianship,** *s.* das Amt eines Bibliothekars. **library** ['laibrəri], *s.* die Bibliothek, Bücherei; das Bibliotheksgebäude; die Buchreihe, Bücherreihe; *circulating* or *lending* –, die Leihbibliothek; *free* –, die Volksbücherei; *reference* –, die Handbibliothek, Präsenzbibliothek.

librate ['laibreit], *v.i.* schwanken, schwingen, pendeln, sich im Gleichgewicht halten.

librettist [li'bretist], *s.* der Librettoschreiber, Textdichter. **libretto,** *s.* das Libretto, Textbuch, der (Opern)text.

Libya ['libiə], *s.* Libyen (*n.*). **Libyan, 1.** *s.* 1. der (die) Libyer(in); 2. (*language*) das Libysch(e). **2.** *adj.* libysch.

lice, *pl.* *See* **louse.**

licence ['laisəns], *s.* 1. die Erlaubnis, Bewilligung, amtliche Genehmigung; die Konzession, Lizenz; der Erlaubnisschein, (Zulassungs)schein; *dog* –, die Hundesteuer(marke); *driving* –, der Führerschein; ***gun–-***, der Waffenschein; ***special –***, die Sonder-Eheerlaubnis; ***take out a –***, sich (*Dat.*) eine Konzession beschaffen; ***wireless –***, die Radiogebühr; (*Motor.*) (*Am.*) – ***plate***, *see* **number-plate**; 2. die (Handlungs)freiheit; Zügellosigkeit, Ausschweifung; ***poetic –***, dichterische Freiheit.

license ['laisəns], **1.** *v.t.* amtlich genehmigen *or* zulassen, bewilligen, konzessionieren (*things*); freigeben (*a play*); ermächtigen (*a p.*); ***–d victualler***, konzessionierter Gastwirt. **2.** *s.* (*Am.*) *see* **licence. licensee** [–'si:], *s.* der Konzessionsinhaber, Lizenznehmer; konzessionierter Gastwirt. **licenser,** *s.* der Konzessionserteiler, Lizenzgeber. **licentiate** [–'senʃieit], *s.* der Lizenziat.

licentious [lai'senʃəs], *adj.* zügellos, zuchtlos, ausschweifend; sittenlos, unsittlich, unzüchtig, liederlich. **licentiousness,** *s.* die Zügellosigkeit, Zuchtlosigkeit, Ausschweifung, Liederlichkeit, Unzüchtigkeit.

lichen ['laikən], *s.* (*Bot., Med.*) die Flechte.

lich-gate ['litʃ–], *s.* das Friedhofstor.

lick [lik], **1.** *v.t.* (ab)lecken, belecken; (*fig.*) lecken an (*Dat.*); (*sl.*) verhauen, verdreschen, verprügeln; besiegen, schlagen; übertreffen, hinter sich (*Dat.*) lassen; (*fig.*) – ***his boots,*** ihm den Staub von den Schuhen lecken, vor ihm kriechen; – ***the dust,*** ins Gras beißen; (*sl.*) ***that –s everything,*** das ist die Höhe *or* der Gipfel; (*sl.*) ***it –s me how . . .***, es geht über meine Begriffe *or* da komme ich nicht mehr mit, wie . . .; (*coll.*) – ***into shape,*** (die richtige) Gestalt *or* Form geben (*Dat.*); (*fig.*) zurechtbiegen, zustutzen. **2.** *v.i.* züngeln (*of flames*). **3.** *s.* 1. das Lecken; (*coll.*) ***a – and a promise,*** die Katzenwäsche; (*fig.*) schlampige Arbeit; – ***of paint,*** flüchtiger Anstrich; 2. (*sl.*) das Tempo, der Hetz; (*sl.*) ***at a tremendous –***, mit rasender Hast. **licker,** *s.* der Lecker; (*Tech.*) Öler.

lickerish ['likəriʃ], *adj.* naschhaft, leckerig; (be)gierig, lüstern (***after, for,*** nach).

licking ['likiŋ], *s.* 1. das Lecken; 2. (*sl.*) Dresche (*pl.*), die Tracht Prügel, Schmiere; (*Spt.*) Niederlage. **lickspittle,** *s.* der Speichellecker.

licorice, *see* **liquorice.**

lictor ['liktə], *s.* der Amtsdiener.

lid [lid], *s.* der Deckel (*also sl.* = ***hat***); das (Augen)lid; (*sl.*) ***put the – on it,*** (der S.) die Krone aufsetzen, dem Faß den Boden ausschlagen.

lido ['li:dou], *s.* das Strandbad.

¹lie [lai], **1.** *s.* die Lüge; ***tell –s*** or ***a –***, lügen; ***give him the –***, ihn Lügen strafen, ihn als Lügner hinstellen; ***give the – to a th.***, etwas als unwahr erweisen; ***white –***, die Notlüge. **2.** *v.i.* lügen; (*of a th.*) täuschen, irreführen, trügen; ***the figures don't –***, die Zahlen trügen nicht; – ***like a book,*** lügen wie gedruckt; – ***in one's throat*** or ***teeth,*** das Blaue vom Himmel herunterlügen; – ***to him,*** ihn anlügen *or* belügen, ihm vorlügen.

²lie, 1. *s.* die Lage; (*of animals*) das Versteck, Lager; (*fig.*) – ***of the land,*** die Lage der Dinge.
2. *irr.v.i.* liegen, ruhen, liegenbleiben; gelegen sein, sich befinden (*of places*); sich lagern, gelagert sein; existieren, bestehen; sich legen *or* stützen *or* lehnen (***on,*** auf (*Acc.*), ***against,*** an (*Acc.*)); führen, verlaufen (*as roads*); (*Law*) anhängig *or* zulässig sein (*appeal etc.*); (*Prov.*) ***as one makes one's bed, so one must –***, wie man sich bettet, so liegt man; (*Prov.*) ***let sleeping dogs –***, laß den Hund begraben sein.
(a) (*with advs.*) – ***about,*** umherliegen; – ***by,*** unbenutzt liegen, stilliegen, brachliegen; (*sl.*) – ***doggo,*** sich nicht rühren, sich verborgen halten; – ***down,*** sich hinlegen *or* niederlegen; ***take it lying down,*** klein beigeben, keinen Widerstand leisten, es sich (*Dat.*) gefallen lassen, ohne weiteres hinnehmen; – ***hard*** or ***heavy on,*** schwer lasten auf (*Dat.*); – ***idle,*** see – ***by***; – ***in,*** im Wochenbett liegen, in den Wochen sein, in die Wochen kommen; (*coll.*) sich (tüchtig) ausschlafen; – ***low,*** sich versteckt halten, sich nicht verraten, sich abwartend verhalten; (*Naut.*) – ***off,*** vom Lande abhalten; – ***open to,*** ausgesetzt sein, unterliegen (*Dat.*); – ***over,*** aufgeschoben werden, liegenbleiben; (*Naut.*) – ***to,*** beigedreht liegen, beiliegen; – ***up,*** das Bett hüten.
(b) (*with preps.*) – ***at anchor,*** vor Anker liegen; ***this –s at his door,*** er trägt die Schuld daran, die Schuld fällt auf ihn *or* liegt bei ihm, das wird ihm zur Last gelegt; – ***at death's door,*** am Rande des Grabes liegen; – ***at full length,*** ausgestreckt daliegen; – ***at his mercy,*** seiner Willkür preisgegeben sein; – ***at the root of the matter,*** der S. zugrunde liegen; ***her talents do not – in that direction,*** dazu hat sie kein Talent; ***as far as in me –s,*** soweit es an mir liegt *or* in meinen Kräften steht; – ***in prison,*** im Gefängnis sitzen; – ***in state,*** auf dem Paradebett *or* feierlich aufgebahrt liegen; – ***in wait for him,*** ihm auflauern; – ***on my conscience,*** schwer auf meinem Gewissen lasten; – (***heavy***) ***on my stomach,*** mir schwer im Magen liegen; – ***on my hands,*** (unbenutzt *or* unverkauft) bei mir liegenbleiben; (*Law*) – ***on him,*** ihm obliegen; (*Naut.*) – ***to the east,*** Ost anliegen; – ***under,*** unterliegen (*Dat.*); – ***under an imputation,*** angeschuldigt *or* beschuldigt sein (***of,*** *Gen.*); – ***under the necessity,*** genötigt sein; – ***under sentence of death,*** zum Tode verurteilt (worden) sein; – ***under*** (***the***) ***suspicion,*** unter (dem) Verdacht stehen (***of,*** *Gen.*; ***of doing,*** getan zu haben); (*B.*) – ***with,*** liegen *or* schlafen bei; beischlafen, beiwohnen (*Dat.*); ***it –s with him,*** es liegt an *or* bei ihm, es steht bei ihm.

lie-abed, *s.* der (die) Langschläfer(in).

lief [li:f], *adv.* (*obs.*) gern; ***I had*** or ***would as – go as stay,*** ich ginge ebenso gern wie ich bliebe; ***I had as – die as go,*** ich würde lieber sterben als gehen.

Liège [li'eiʒ], *s.* (*Geog.*) Lüttich (*n.*).

liege [li:dʒ], **1.** *adj.* lehnspflichtig, Lehns–; – ***lord,*** der Lehnsherr. **2.** *s.* der Lehnsmann, Vasall; Lehnsherr.

lien [liən], *s.* (*Law*) das Zurückbehaltungsrecht, Pfandrecht (***on,*** auf (*Acc.*)).

lieu [lju:], *s.* ***in – of,*** anstatt (*Gen.*), an Stelle von *or* (*Gen.*); ***in –***, stattdessen.

lieutenancy [lef'tenənsi, *Nav. and Am.* lu:'tenənsi], *s.* der Leutnantsrang; die Statthalterschaft. **lieutenant,** *s.* (*Mil.*) der Oberleutnant, (*Nav.*) Kapitänleutnant; Statthalter, Stellvertreter; ***first –***, der Oberleutnant; ***lord –***, der Vertreter des Königs; ***second –***, der Leutnant. **lieutenant|-colonel,** *s.* der Oberstleutnant. **–-commander,** *s.* (*Nav.*) der Korvettenkapitän. **–-general,** *s.* der Generalleutnant. **–-governor,** *s.* der Unterstatthalter.

life [laif], *s.* (*pl.* **lives** [laivz]) 1. das Leben; Lebenserscheinungen (*pl.*), das Lebewesen; lebenspendende *or* belebende Kraft, die Lebenskraft; (*fig.*) Lebendigkeit, Lebhaftigkeit, das Temperament; menschliches Leben *or* Tun und Treiben, das Menschenleben; die Lebensart, Lebensweise, Lebensführung, der Lebenswandel; die Lebenszeit, Lebensdauer; der Lebenslauf, die Lebensbeschreibung; 2. (*Art*) lebendes Modell, die Natur; 3. (*Insur.*) auf Lebenszeit Versicherte(r).
(a) (*with nouns*) – ***and death struggle,*** der Kampf auf Leben und Tod; ***a matter of – and death,*** eine S. auf Leben und Tod *or* von entscheidender Bedeutung; ***acceptance of –***, die Lebensbejahung; ***expectation of –***, mutmaßliche Lebensdauer; ***escape with – and limb,*** mit einem blauen Auge davonkommen; ***with great sacrifice of –***, mit schweren Verlusten an Menschenleben; – ***and soul of the party,*** die Seele der Gesellschaft.
(b) (*with adjs.*) ***animal –***, das Tierleben; ***have a charmed –***, kugelfest *or* unverwundbar sein; – ***to come,*** zukünftiges Leben, das Leben nach dem Tode; ***early –***, die Jugend; ***in early –***, in jungen Jahren; – ***everlasting,*** ewiges Leben; ***full of –***, voller Leben; ***high –***, das Leben der vornehmen Klassen; ***as large as –***, lebensgroß, in voller Lebensgröße; ***low –***, das Leben der unteren Schichten; ***marine –***, das Leben im Meer; ***married –***, das Eheleben; ***still –***, das Stilleben; ***this –***, das irdische Leben.
(c) (*with verbs*) ***give – to,*** beleben; ***lay down one's –***

for, sein Leben hingeben für; ***lead a good –,*** einen guten Lebenswandel führen; ***they lost their lives,*** sie verloren ihr Leben, sie kamen ums Leben; ***many lives were lost,*** viele Menschenleben sind zu beklagen; ***put – into,*** see ***give – to***; ***risk one's –,*** sein Leben aufs Spiel setzen; ***many lives were saved,*** viele Menschen wurden gerettet *or* kamen mit dem Leben davon; ***see –,*** das Leben genießen *or* kennenlernen; ***seek his –,*** ihm nach dem Leben trachten; ***take his*** (or ***one's own***) ***–,*** ihm (*or* sich) das Leben nehmen; ***take one's – in one's hands,*** sein Leben riskieren.
(d) (*with preps.*) ***for –,*** fürs (ganze) Leben; lebenslänglich, auf Lebenszeit; ***imprisonment for –,*** lebenslängliche Freiheitsstrafe; ***not for the – of me,*** nicht um alles in der Welt; um keinen Preis; absolut nicht; beim besten Willen nicht; ***have no regard for human –,*** rücksichtslos über Menschenleben hinweggehen; ***run for one's –*** or ***for dear –,*** aus Leibeskräften *or* ums (liebe) Leben davonlaufen; ***drawn from –,*** nach dem lebenden Modell *or* dem Leben *or* der Natur gezeichnet; ***early in –,*** in jungen Jahren; ***in danger of one's –,*** in Todesgefahr; ***go in danger of one's –,*** in ständiger Lebensgefahr schweben; ***have the time of one's –,*** sich glänzend amüsieren; ***bring to –,*** wieder zum Bewußtsein bringen; ***come to –,*** wieder zur Besinnung kommen; (*fig.*) Interesse zeigen, aufleben, aufwachen; ***to the –,*** nach dem Leben, naturgetreu; (*obs.*) ***upon*** (or ***'pon***) ***my –!*** so wahr ich lebe! ***enter upon –,*** in die Welt eintreten.

life|-and-death, *attrib. adj.* auf Leben und Tod. **--annuity,** *s.* die Leibrente. **--assurance,** *s.* die Lebensversicherung. **-belt,** *s.* der Rettungsring. **--blood,** *s.* (*fig.*) das Herzblut. **-boat,** *s.* das Rettungsboot. **--expectancy,** *s.* mutmaßliche Lebensdauer. **--giving,** *adj.* belebend, lebenspendend. **-guard,** *s.* der Rettungsschwimmer. **--guard,** *s.* die Leibwache. **Life Guards,** *pl.* die Garde, das Gardekorps. **life|-imprisonment,** *s.* lebenslängliche Freiheitsstrafe. **--insurance,** *s.* *See* **--assurance. – interest,** *s.* lebenslänglicher Nießbrauch. **--jacket,** *s.* die Schwimmweste.

lifeless ['laiflis], *adj.* leblos, tot; unbelebt, (*fig.*) ohne Leben, schwunglos, fad, schlaff; (*Comm.*) lustlos. **lifelessness,** *s.* (*usu. fig.*) die Leblosigkeit, Schwunglosigkeit.

life|like, *adj.* lebenswahr, naturgetreu. **--line,** *s.* die Rettungsleine; Signalleine (*of diver*); (*fig.*) lebenswichtige Verbindung, die Lebensader; der Rettungsanker; (*palmistry*) die Lebenslinie. **-long,** *adj.* lebenslänglich. **--membership,** *s.* lebenslängliche Mitgliedschaft. **--preserver,** *s.* 1. der Rettungsgürtel, die Schwimmweste; 2. der Bleistock, Totschläger.

lifer ['laifə], *s.* (*sl.*) lebenslänglicher Zuchthäusler.

life|-raft, *s.* das Rettungsfloß. **--saving, 1.** *s.* die Lebensrettung. **2.** *adj.* lebensrettend, Rettungs-. **--sentence,** *s.* das Urteil auf lebenslänglichen Kerker. **--size(d),** *adj.* lebensgroß, in Lebensgröße. **– span,** *s.* die Lebensdauer. **--strings,** *pl.* (*Poet.*) der Lebensfaden. **--subscription,** *s.* einmaliger Beitrag auf Lebenszeit. **--table,** *s.* die Sterblichkeitstabelle. **-time, 1.** *s.* die Lebenszeit, Lebensdauer; ***once in a –,*** einmal im Leben. **2.** *adj.* lebenslänglich, auf Lebenszeit. **--work,** *s.* das Lebenswerk.

lift [lift], **1.** *v.t.* (auf)heben, emporheben, erheben, hochheben; ausmachen (*potatoes etc.*); (*sl.*) klemmen, klauen, mausen; ***– down,*** herunterholen; ***– up one's eyes,*** die Augen erheben *or* emporrichten, aufblicken; ***have one's face –ed,*** sich (*Dat.*) die Runzeln entfernen lassen; ***not – a finger,*** keinen Finger rühren; ***– one's hand against,*** sich auflehnen gegen, die Hand erheben gegen; ***– up one's voice,*** die Stimme erheben. **2.** *v.i.* sich heben; aufsteigen, sich zerstreuen (*as mist*). **3.** *s.* 1. das (Hoch)heben, Aufheben; (Hoch)steigen; Hochhalten, aufrechte Haltung; (*Tech.*) die Steighöhe, Förderhöhe, (*of a valve etc.*) Hubhöhe, der Hub; (*Av.*) Auftrieb; (*fig.*) Aufschwung, die Erhebung; 2. der Fahrstuhl, Aufzug; das Hebewerk, Fördergerät; 3. (*coll.*) ***give him a –,*** ihn mitfahren lassen; (*fig.*) ihm beistehen *or* helfen.

lifter ['liftə], *s.* (*Tech.*) die Knagge, der Nocken, Stößel. **lifting,** *s.* das Heben; ***– force,*** die Hebekraft; (*Av.*) Hubkraft; Tragkraft, Auftriebkraft, der Auftrieb; ***– jack,*** die Wagenwinde, der Wagenheber.

ligament ['ligəmənt], *s.* das Band, die Sehne, Flechse.

ligate [lai'geit], *v.t.* (*esp. Med.*) verbinden; unterbinden, abbinden, abschnüren (*artery*). **ligation** [-'geiʃən], *s.* das Verbinden; Abbinden, Unterbinden.

ligature ['ligətʃə], *s.* das Band, die Binde, der Verband; die Unterbindung (*of artery*); (*Typ.*) Ligatur, (*Mus.*) Bindung.

[1]**light** [lait], **1.** *s.* 1. das Licht, die Helligkeit, der Schein; das Licht, die Lichtquelle; Beleuchtung, Lampe, Kerze; ***by the – of,*** beim Schein von; ***get out of the –,*** aus dem Licht gehen; ***in a good –,*** gut beleuchtet, (*fig.*) in günstigem Licht; (*fig.*) ***in the – of,*** unter Heranziehung *or* Berücksichtigung von, in *or* im Hinblick auf (*Acc.*), angesichts (*Gen.*); ***put it in its true –,*** es ins rechte Licht rücken; ***stand in one's own –,*** sich (*Dat.*) selbst im Licht stehen; (*fig.*) sich (*Dat.*) selbst schaden; ***throw*** or ***shed – (up)on,*** Licht werfen auf (*Acc.*); 2. das Sonnenlicht, Tageslicht, der Tag; ***bring to –,*** ans Licht *or* an den Tag bringen; ***come to –,*** ans Licht *or* an den Tag kommen; ***see the –,*** das Licht der Welt erblicken; zum ersten Male aufgeführt werden (*of plays*); 3. der Lichtzutritt, Lichteinlaß, die Fensteröffnung; 4. (*Naut.*) das (Leucht)feuer, der Leuchtturm; ***flashing –,*** das Blitzfeuer, Blinkfeuer, Drehfeuer; ***harbour –,*** das Hafenfeuer; ***masthead –,*** das Topplicht; ***navigation –,*** das Feuer; ***pierhead –,*** das Molenfeuer; ***revolving –,*** das Drehfeuer; 5. das Feuer; ***give him a –,*** ihm Feuer geben; ***put a – to,*** anzünden; ***strike a –,*** Feuer schlagen; 6. (*fig.*) die Einsicht, Erkenntnis, Aufklärung, Erleuchtung; (*fig.*) ***I saw the –,*** mir ging ein Licht auf; 7. (*fig.*) Eingebungen (*pl.*), geistige Fähigkeiten (*pl.*); ***according to his –s,*** nach dem Maß seiner Einsicht, so gut er es versteht; 8. die Leuchte (*a p.*); 9. (*Art*) hellere Teile (*pl.*). **2.** *adj.* licht, hell; ***– blue,*** hellblau. **3.** *irr.v.t.* 1. anzünden (*a fire or lamp*); ***– a cigar,*** sich (*Dat.*) eine Zigarre anzünden; 2. beleuchten, erleuchten (*a room etc.*); ***– him upstairs,*** ihm nach oben leuchten; ***– up,*** hell beleuchten, (*fig.*) beleben, aufhellen, aufleuchten lassen, aufheitern. **4.** *irr.v.i.* sich entzünden (*of fire etc.*); (*usu.* ***– up***) hell werden, sich erhellen; (*fig.*) aufleuchten (*as the face*); ***– up,*** die Beleuchtung einschalten; (*coll.*) (sich) (*Dat.*) eine Pfeife (*etc.*) anzünden.

[2]**light,** *adj.* leicht, nicht schwer, unschwer; flott, flink, behende (*as movements*); leichtfertig, sorglos, oberflächlich (*character etc.*); locker (*of bread, soil etc.*); leicht verdaulich (*of food*); unbeladen, leer (*of ships etc.*); leicht zu tun *or* ertragen; ***make – of,*** sich (*Dat.*) nichts machen aus, auf die leichte Schulter nehmen; ***– car,*** das Kleinauto; ***hold in – esteem,*** geringachten; (*Typ.*) ***– face,*** magere Schrift; (*coll.*) ***– fingers,*** lange Finger (*pl.*); ***– of foot,*** leichtfüßig; ***with a – heart,*** leichten Herzens; ***– in the head,*** wirr im Kopf; ***– infantry,*** leichtbewaffnete Infanterie; ***– literature,*** die Unterhaltungsliteratur; ***no – matter,*** keine Kleinigkeit; ***– metal,*** das Leichtmetall; ***– music,*** die Unterhaltungsmusik; ***– punishment,*** milde Strafe; ***– railway,*** die Kleinbahn; ***– reading,*** see ***– literature***; ***– touch,*** leise Berührung; ***– weight,*** das Mindergewicht, Untergewicht.

[3]**light,** *v.i.* (*obs.*) (ab)steigen (***from,*** von); ***– on,*** fallen auf (*Acc.*), sich niederlassen auf (*Dat.*); stoßen *or* geraten auf (*Acc.*), zufällig treffen.

light-armed, *adj.* leicht bewaffnet.

[1]**lighten** [laitn], **1.** *v.i.* 1. hell(er) werden, sich aufhellen; 2. blitzen; ***it –s,*** es blitzt. **2.** *v.t.* beleuchten, erleuchten, erhellen.

[2]**lighten, 1.** *v.t.* leichter machen; (*Naut.*) leichtern,

lichten, löschen; (*fig.*) erleichtern, aufheitern. **2.** *v.i.* leichter werden.

[1]**lighter** ['laitə], *s.* 1. der Anzünder; 2. das Feuerzeug.

[2]**lighter,** *comp. adj.* leichter.

[3]**lighter,** *s.* (*Naut.*) der Leichter, Lichter, Prahm, das Leichterschiff, Lichterschiff. **lighterage** [-ridʒ], *s.* das Leichtergeld, Lichterkosten (*pl.*), die Löschgebühr. **lighterman,** *s.* der Leichterschiffer, Löscher.

lighter-than-air, *attrib. adj.* . . . leichter als Luft, . . . mit natürlichem Auftrieb.

light|-fingered, *adj.* langfingerig, diebisch; geschickt. **--footed,** *adj.* flink, leichtfüßig, schnellfüßig. **--handed,** *adj.* leicht belastet, unbeschwert, mit leeren Händen; (*Naut.*) leicht bemannt. **--headed,** *adj.* wirr im Kopf, schwindlig, benommen; (*fig.*) unbesonnen, leichtfertig. **--headedness,** *s.* die Benommenheit; Unbesonnenheit. **--hearted,** *adj.* leichten Herzens, sorglos, leichtbeschwingt, wohlgemut, fröhlich. **--heartedness,** *s.* der Frohsinn, die Sorglosigkeit. **--heavyweight,** *s.* (*Boxing*) der Leichtgewichtler (*less than 175 lb.*). **--horse,** *s.* leichte Reiterei. **-house,** *s.* der Leuchtturm; – ***man,*** der Leuchtturmwächter.

lighting ['laitiŋ], **1.** *s.* 1. das Anzünden, Entzünden; 2. die Beleuchtung; Beleuchtungsanlage; 3. (*Art*) Lichtverteilung. **2.** *adj.* Licht–. **lighting-up time,** *s.* die Zeit eintretender Dunkelheit.

lightly ['laitli], *adv.* (*see* [2]**light**) leicht; mühelos; oberflächlich, obenhin; leichthin, unbesonnen, leichtfertig, flüchtig; ***not – to be ignored,*** nicht leichthin zu ignorieren; ***take –,*** auf die leichte Achsel nehmen; ***think – of,*** geringschätzen; ***treat –,*** als unerheblich behandeln.

light-minded, *adj.* leichtsinnig, leichtfertig, gedankenlos.

lightness ['laitnis], *s.* die Leichtheit, Leichtigkeit; Leichtfertigkeit, der Leichtsinn; die Flinkheit, Behendigkeit, Gewandtheit, Zierlichkeit, Grazie (*of movement*); Leichtverdaulichkeit (*of food*); Milde (*of punishment etc.*).

lightning ['laitniŋ], **1.** *s.* der Blitz; ***forked –,*** der Linienblitz, Zickzackblitz; ***like –, quick as –,*** wie der Blitz, blitzartig, blitzschnell; ***like greased –,*** wie geschmiert; ***struck by –,*** (*of a p.*) vom Blitz erschlagen, (*of tree etc.*) vom Blitz getroffen; ***the – struck the house,*** der Blitz schlug in das Haus (ein); ***summer –,*** das Wetterleuchten. **2.** *adj.* blitzschnell; ***with – speed,*** mit Blitzesschnelle; (*fig.*) ***– strike,*** der Überraschungsstreik, Blitzstreik. **lightning|-arrester, --conductor, --rod,** *s.* der Blitzableiter.

light|-o'-love, *s.* (*obs.*) die Trulle, das Flittchen. **-proof,** *adj.* lichtdicht.

lights [laits], *pl.* die Lunge (*as animal food*).

lightship ['laitʃip], *s.* das Leuchtschiff, Feuerschiff.

lightsome ['laitsəm], *adj.* leicht, flink, behend, zierlich, graziös; fröhlich, wohlgemut. **lightweight, 1.** *s.* (*Boxing*) der Leichtgewichtler (*under 135 lb.*); (*fig.*) unbedeutender Mensch. **2.** *adj.* leicht(wiegend), Leicht–.

ligneous ['ligniəs], *adj.* holzartig, holzig, Holz–. **lignify** [–fai], *v.t.* (*v.i.*) (sich) in Holz verwandeln, verholzen. **lignite** [–nait], *s.* die Braunkohle.

lignum-vitae ['lignəm'vaiti], *s.* das Guajakholz, Pockholz.

ligula ['ligjulə], *s.* (*Ent.*) die Ligula; *see also* **ligule. ligular, ligulate** [–eit], *adj.* zungenförmig. **ligule,** *s.* (*Bot.*) die Ligula, das Blatthäutchen (*of grasses*), Strahlenblütchen, Zungenblütchen (*of flowers*).

likable, *see* **likeable.**

[1]**like** [laik], **1.** *adj.* gleich (*Dat.*), wie; ähnlich (*Dat.*). **(a)** (*attrib.*) ***of – extent,*** von gleicher Ausdehnung, ebenso groß; ***in – manner,*** in gleicher *or* dergleichen Weise, auf gleiche Weise, gleichermaßen, ebenso; (*Prov.*) ***– father, – son,*** der Apfel fällt nicht weit vom Stamm; (*Prov.*) ***– master, – man,*** wie der Herr, so der Knecht ***– sum,*** ähnliche Summe; (*Math.*) ***– terms,*** gleichnamige Gliede (*pl.*).
(b) (*pred.*) ***as – as two peas,*** ähnlich wie ein Ei dem andern; ***it is – hearing one's own voice,*** man hört gleichsam seine eigene Stimme; ***I feel – coming,*** ich habe Lust zu kommen, ich möchte *or* würde gern kommen; ***look –,*** so aussehen als ob; ***it looks – rain,*** es sieht nach Regen aus; ***nothing*** or ***not anything – as good as,*** lange nicht *or* nicht annähernd *or* bei weitem nicht so gut wie; ***there is nothing – . . .,*** es geht nichts über . . . (*Acc.*); (*coll.*) ***something –,*** etwa; (*sl.*) ***that is something –,*** das läßt sich hören; ***what is he –?*** wie ist er? wie sieht er aus?
(c) (*with following object*) ***that is just – him,*** das sieht ihm ähnlich; ***they are – each other,*** sie sind einander ähnlich; ***die – a hero,*** wie ein Held sterben; ***he is – that,*** er ist nun einmal so; ***a th. – that,*** so etwas, derartiges; ***don't talk – that!*** red, nicht so! ***a man – that,*** so ein Mann.
(d) (*obs.*) (*with inf. expressed or understood*) ***he is – to die,*** er wird wahrscheinlich sterben; (*obs.*) ***'tis – enough!*** es ist wohl glaublich.
2. *adv.* (so) wie, in der Art wie, in gleichem Maße wie; ***– all prophets he is . . .,*** er ist, gleich allen Propheten, . . .; ***she cannot cook – my mother,*** sie kann nicht kochen wie meine Mutter; (*coll.*) ***hurry – anything*** or ***– mad*** or ***– the dickens,*** eilen wie verrückt *or* besessen; (*sl.*) ***rant – the devil,*** lärmen wie verteufelt; (*coll.*) ***as – as not,*** höchst wahrscheinlich.
3. *s.* der *or* die *or* das Gleiche; ***his –*** or (*coll.*) ***the –s of him,*** seinesgleichen; ***their –*** or (*coll.*) ***the –s of them,*** ihresgleichen; ***the –*** or (*coll.*) ***the –s of it,*** so etwas; ***the – of these people,*** dergleichen wie diese Leute; (*coll.*) ***the –s of me,*** unsereiner, meine Wenigkeit; ***and the*** or (*coll.*) ***such –,*** und dergleichen; ***– attracts –,*** gleich und gleich gesellt sich gern.

[2]**like, 1.** *v.t.* gern haben *or* sehen, (gern) mögen, (gut) leiden können, lieben; ***– well,*** gern mögen; ***– better,*** lieber mögen; ***– best,*** am liebsten mögen; ***how do you – it?*** wie findest du es? wie gefällt es dir? ***as you – it,*** wie es euch gefällt; ***– pancakes,*** Pfannkuchen gern essen; ***do you – skating?*** laufen Sie gern Schlittschuh? ***do you – my hat?*** gefällt Ihnen mein Hut? ***I do not – to interrupt,*** ich unterbreche nur ungern; ***I do not – it mentioned,*** ich habe nicht gern, daß es erwähnt wird; (*iron.*) ***I – that,*** das ist aber die Höhe; ***I – her,*** ich mag sie gern (leiden); ***I should*** (***very much***) ***– to know,*** ich möchte *or* würde (sehr) gern wissen; ***I should – you to be here,*** ich hätte gern, daß Sie hier wären; ***make o.s. –d,*** sich beliebt machen (***with,*** bei). **2.** *v.i.* wollen; (***just***) ***as you –,*** wie es Ihnen beliebt, wie Sie wollen, ganz nach Belieben. **3.** *s.* die Neigung, Vorliebe; ***–s and dislikes,*** Neigungen und Abneigungen.

likeable ['laikəbl], *adj.* liebenswürdig, liebenswert, reizend, angenehm. **liked,** *adj.* beliebt.

likelihood ['laiklihud], *s.* die Wahrscheinlichkeit; ***in all –,*** aller Wahrscheinlichkeit *or* allem Anschein nach; ***there is a strong*** or ***every – of,*** es ist sehr wahrscheinlich daß; ***there is little – of,*** es ist kaum wahrscheinlich daß.

likely ['laikli], **1.** *adj.* wahrscheinlich, voraussichtlich; in Frage kommend, geeignet; (*coll.*) vielversprechend, aussichtsreich; (*iron.*) kaum glaubhaft; ***it is – he will come, he is – to come,*** er kommt wahrscheinlich *or* voraussichtlich, es ist wahrscheinlich daß er kommt; ***most – candidate,*** der scheinbar geeignetste Bewerber; ***he is the most – to win,*** er hat die größte Aussicht zu gewinnen. **2.** *adv.* (*usu.* ***most*** or ***very –***) ***he is most – to win,*** er wird höchstwahrscheinlich gewinnen; ***not –,*** schwerlich, kaum; ***as – as not,*** sehr wahrscheinlich.

like|-minded, *adj.* gleichgesinnt; ***be – with,*** derselben Meinung sein wie, übereinstimmen mit. **--mindedness,** *s.* die Gleichgesinntheit.

liken [laikn], *v.t.* vergleichen (*to,* mit).

likeness ['laiknis], *s.* die Ähnlichkeit, Gleichheit; das Bild, Porträt; ***have one's – taken,*** sich malen or photographieren lassen; *in the – of,* in Gestalt (*Gen.*), mit dem Anschein (*Gen.*).

likewise ['laikwaiz], *adv.* ebenso, desgleichen, gleichfalls, ebenfalls, auch.

liking ['laikiŋ], *s.* das Gefallen, die Zuneigung; Neigung, Vorliebe, der Geschmack; *have a – for,* Gefallen haben an (*Dat.*), eine Zuneigung haben zu, gern haben; *take a – to,* Gefallen finden an (*Dat.*), eine Zuneigung fassen zu, liebgewinnen; *is it to your –?* ist es nach Ihrem Geschmack? sagt es Ihnen zu? *too fast for my –,* mir zu schnell.

lilac ['lailək], **1.** *s.* (*Bot.*) (spanischer) Flieder; (*colour*) das Lila, die Lilafarbe. **2.** *adj.* lilafarben, Lila–.

liliaceous [lili'eiʃəs], *adj.* Lilien–, lilienartig.

lilt [lilt], **1.** *s.* fröhliches Lied; rhythmischer Schwung. **2.** *v.t., v.i.* fröhlich singen, trällern; *–ing gait* or *step,* federnder *or* wiegender Gang.

lily ['lili], *s.* die Lilie; *– of the valley,* das Maiglöckchen. **lily|-livered,** *adj.* bangbüxig, benaut, memmenhaft, weibisch. **--white,** *adj.* lilienweiß.

[1]**limb** [lim], *s.* das Glied; (*of a tree*) der (Haupt)ast; (*fig.*) Arm, Teil, Ausläufer; *pl.* Gliedmaßen (*pl.*); *artificial –,* die Prothese, das Ersatzglied; (*sl.*) *– of the law,* der Rechtsverdreher; *escape with life and –,* mit einem blauen Auge davonkommen; (*coll.*) *out on a –,* in einer gefährlichen Lage, sehr im Nachteil; *tear – from –,* in Stücke zerreißen.

[2]**limb,** *s.* (*Astr.*) der Rand; (*Bot.*) Blattrand (*of moss*), (Kelch)saum, Limbus (*of flowers*); (*Math.*) Limbus, Teilkreis. **limbate** [–beit], *adj.* gerandet, gesäumt.

limbed [limd], *adj. suff.* –gliedrig.

[1]**limber** ['limbə], *adj.* biegsam, schmiegsam, geschmeidig, gelenkig, wendig.

[2]**limber, 1.** *s.* die Protze (*of gun-carriage*). **2.** *v.t.* (*– up*) aufprotzen. **3.** *v.i.* (*fig.*) *– up,* Vorbereitungsübungen machen.

limbers ['limbəz], *pl.* (*Naut.*) der Wasserlauf, Wasserlauflöcher (*pl.*) (*of kelson*).

limbo ['limbou], *s.* die Vorhölle; (*fig.*) Rumpelkammer; Vergessenheit; (*sl.*) das Kittchen.

[1]**lime** [laim], **1.** *s.* (*Chem., Min. etc.*) der Kalk; Vogelleim; *slaked –,* gelöschter Kalk. **2.** *v.t.* mit Kalk düngen; mit Vogelleim bestreichen.

[2]**lime,** *s.* die Linde; der Lindenbaum.

[3]**lime,** *s.* die Limone, Limonelle, Zitronelle, Limette.

lime|-burner, *s.* der Kalkbrenner. **–juice,** *s.* der Limonensaft, Limonellensaft. **--kiln,** *s.* der Kalkofen. **–light,** *s.* das Kalklicht; (*Theat.*) der Scheinwerfer; (*fig.*) das Rampenlicht, Licht der Öffentlichkeit; *in the –,* unter Scheinwerferlicht; (*fig.*) im Brennpunkt *or* Mittelpunkt des Interesses; (*fig.*) *bring into the –, throw the – on,* in helles Licht rücken; (*fig.*) *disappear from the –,* aus dem Interesse verschwinden.

limen ['laimen], *s.* (*Psych.*) die Reizschwelle, Empfindungsgrenze.

limerick ['limərik], *s.* fünfzeiliger Schüttelreimvers.

lime|stone, *s.* der Kalkstein. **--twig,** *s.* die Leimrute. **--wash, 1.** *s.* die Kalktünche. **2.** *v.t.* kalken, tünchen. **–water,** *s.* das Kalkwasser, die Kalklösung.

limey ['laimi], *s.* (*Am. sl.*) der Engländer, (*esp.*) englischer Matrose.

liminal ['liminl], *adj.* (*Psych.*) Schwellen–.

limit ['limit], **1.** *s.* die Grenze, Schranke, Beschränkung; Grenzlinie, der Endpunkt, das Ziel; (*Math.*) der Grenzwert; (*Comm.*) äußerster Preis, der Mindestbetrag; Höchstpreis, die Preisgrenze; spätester Zeitpunkt, die Gültigkeitsdauer; *there is a – to everything,* alles hat seine Grenzen; *set –s to,* Grenzen setzen (*Dat.*); (*coll.*) *that's the* (*absolute*) *–!* da hört doch alles auf! das ist wirklich die Höhe *or* der Gipfel *or* unerhört! (*coll.*) *he is the –!* er ist ohnegleichen *or* einfach unmöglich! (*Am.*) *off –s,* Zutritt verboten; *within –s,* in Grenzen, maßvoll; *without –,* ohne Grenze *or* Schranken. **2.** *v.t.* begrenzen, beschränken, einschränken (*to,* auf (*Acc.*)). **limitation** [–'teiʃən], *s.* die Beschränkung, Begrenzung, Einschränkung; (*Law*) Verjährung(sfrist); (*fig.*) Grenze; *know one's –s,* seine Grenzen kennen. **limitative** [–tətiv], *adj.* (*Am.*) beschränkend, einschränkend.

limited ['limitid], *adj.* beschränkt, begrenzt, eingeschränkt (*to,* auf (*Acc.*)); *– edition,* begrenzte Auflage; *– liability,* beschränkte Haftung; *–* (*liability*) *company,* die Gesellschaft mit beschränkter Haftung; *– monarchy,* konstitutionelle Monarchie; *– partnership,* die Kommanditgesellschaft; (*Am.*) *–* (*train*), der Luxus-Schnellzug. **limiting,** *adj.* begrenzend, einschränkend. **limitless,** *adj.* grenzenlos, schrankenlos.

limn [lim], *v.t.* (*Poet.*) malen, zeichnen, darstellen, abbilden. **limner** ['limnə], *s.* der Porträtmaler.

limnetic [lim'netik], *adj.* Süßwasser–. **limnology** [–'nɔlədʒi], *s.* die Seenkunde.

limonite ['laimənait], *s.* der Limonit, Brauneisenstein.

limousine [limə'zi:n], *s.* die Limousine.

[1]**limp** [limp], **1.** *v.i.* hinken (*also fig.*); humpeln (*with,* infolge). **2.** *s.* das Hinken; *walk with a –,* hinken, lahmen.

[2]**limp,** *adj.* schlaff, biegsam; (*fig.*) schlapp, kraftlos.

limpet ['limpit], *s.* die Napfschnecke; (*fig.*) *like a –,* wie eine Klette; (*Naut.*) *– mine,* die Haftmine.

limpid ['limpid], *adj.* hell, klar, durchsichtig. **limpidity** [–'piditi], **limpidness,** *s.* die Klarheit, Durchsichtigkeit.

limy ['laimi], *adj.* kalkhaltig, kalkig, Kalk–; leimig, klebrig.

linage ['lainidʒ], *s.* die Zeilenzahl (*of a page*); das Zeilenhonorar.

linchpin ['lintʃpin], *s.* die Lünse, der Achsnagel.

linden ['lindən], *s.* (*Poet.*) die Linde.

[1]**line** [lain], *v.t.* füttern (*clothes*); (*Tech.*) ausfüttern, auskleiden, belegen; (*coll.*) *– one's pocket,* Geld machen.

[2]**line, 1.** *s.* 1. die Linie, der Strich; richtunggebende Linie, die Richtung; *– of bearing,* die Peillinie; *– of demarcation,* die Trennungslinie; *– of direction,* die Richtungslinie; Bauflucht(linie); (*Artil.*) *– of elevation,* verlängerte Seelenlänge, die Seelenachsenlinie; *– of fire,* die Schußlinie, Schußrichtung; *– of latitude,* der Breitenkreis; *– of longitude,* der Längenkreis; *– of sight,* die Blickrichtung, Visierlinie, Schußlinie; *– of vision,* die Gesichtsachse; (*Press*) *below the –,* unter dem Strich; (*Archit.*) *building –,* die Bauflucht; *date –,* die Datumsgrenze; (*coll.*) *draw a* or *the – at,* haltmachen vor (*Dat.*), nicht mehr mitmachen, die Grenze ziehen bei, nicht dulden, ablehnen; *isobaric –s,* Isobaren (*pl.*); *rhumb –,* die Loxodrome; 2. (*of the face*) der Zug, die Runzel, Falte, Furche; 3. die Reihe (*of trees etc.*); (*Naut.*) *– abreast,* die Dwarslinie; (*Naut.*) *– ahead* or *astern,* die Kiellinie; *– of hills,* die Reihe *or* Kette von Hügeln; *be in – with,* übereinstimmen mit; *bring into –,* ins Einvernehmen *or* in Einklang bringen (*with,* mit); *come* or *fall into – with,* sich anpassen (*Dat.*); *fall in – with,* sich decken mit; *form a –,* in Linie antreten, sich einreihen; *in – with,* in Übereinstimmung *or* im Einklang mit; *keep in –,* in Reih und Glied bleiben; (*fig.*) bei der Stange bleiben; *ship of the –,* das Linienschiff; *toe the –,* in Linie antreten; (*usu. fig.*) sich der Parteilinie unterwerfen, linientreu sein, (*sl.*) spuren; seinen Verpflichtungen nachkommen; 4. (*Typ.*) die Zeile, (*Metr.*) der Vers; (*T.V.*) die Bildzeile, Abtastzeile; (*coll.*) das Briefchen; *pl.* die Strafarbeit (*at school*), (*Theat.*) Rolle; *– upon –,* Zeile auf Zeile; (*coll.*) *drop him a –,* ihm ein paar Zeilen schreiben; (*Theat.*) *forget one's –s,* steckenbleiben; *marriage –s,* der Trauschein; *read between the –s,* zwischen den Zeilen lesen; (*Theat.*) *study one's –s,* seine Rolle (ein)studieren; 5. (*esp. Naut.*) die Leine, Schnur, das Seil, Tau, Kabel, der Draht; die Wäscheleine; Angelschnur; *clothes –,* die Wäscheleine; *fishing –,* die Angelleine, Angelschnur; (*fig. coll.*) *hook, – and sinker,* mit allem Drum und Dran;

6. die (Abstammungs)linie, Familie, der Stamm, das Geschlecht; ***male* –,** der Mannesstamm; 7. (*Mil.*) die Front, Kampflinie, vorderste Stellung; – ***of battle,*** die Schlachtlinie; – ***of defence,*** die Verteidigungslinie; ***all along the* –,** an der ganzen Front, (*fig.*) auf der ganzen Linie; ***go up the* –,** an die Front gehen, nach vorn gehen; ***the* –,** die Linientruppen (*pl.*); 8. (*Elec.*) die Leitung; (*Tele.*) der Nummernanschluß; (*coll.*) ***get a – on,*** eine Information erhalten über (*Acc.*); (*Tele.*) ***hold the* –,** am Apparat bleiben; (*Elec.*) ***overhead* –,** die Freileitung; (*Tele.*) ***the – is engaged,*** die Leitung ist besetzt; 9. (*Comm.*) das (Interessen)-gebiet, Tätigkeitsfeld, Fach, der (Geschäfts)-zweig, die Branche; – ***of business,*** der Geschäftszweig, die Branche; (*coll.*) – ***of country,*** see . . . ***in my* –** (*fig.*); ***that is not in my* –,** (*Comm.*) das führe *or* erzeuge ich nicht; (*fig.*) das liegt mir nicht, das schlägt nicht in mein Fach; (*coll.*) ***the building* –,** die Baubranche, das Baufach; 10. (*Comm.*) der Posten, die Partie; (*coll.*) ***a cheap – in gents' hosiery,*** eine preiswerte Partie Herrenstrümpfe; (*coll.*) ***he has quite a* –,** er ist recht zungenfertig; 11. (*fig.*) (*oft. pl.*) richtunggebendes Verhalten *or* Verfahren, die Art und Weise, Methode; Grundlage, Richtschnur; das Muster; *pl.* Grundsätze, Richtlinien, Prinzipien (*pl.*); – ***of argument,*** die Beweisführung; – ***of conduct,*** das Verhalten, die Lebensführung; – ***of resistance,*** die Widerstandslinie; ***–s of action,*** taktische Möglichkeiten; ***–s of his policy,*** Grundlinien seiner Politik; ***along these –s,*** nach diesen Grundsätzen; ***hard and fast –s,*** strenge Grenzlinien; ***in the – of,*** nach Art von; ***on broad –s,*** auf breiter Grundlage; ***on the –s of,*** nach dem Muster von; ***on these –s,*** auf diese Weise, in diesem Sinne; ***take the – of least resistance,*** den Weg des geringsten Widerstandes einschlagen; ***take a strong* –,** energisch vorgehen; ***take one's own* –,** eigene Wege gehen, nach eigener Methode vorgehen; (*coll.*) ***take the – that,*** die Ansicht *or* den Standpunkt vertreten daß; ***work on the wrong –s,*** nach einer falschen Methode *or* falschen Richtlinien arbeiten; 12. die Route, (Verkehrs)linie, Eisenbahnlinie, Strecke; (*Railw.*) das Geleise, Gleis, die Schiene, der Schienenstrang; – ***of march,*** die Marschroute; ***–s of communication,*** die Etappe, rückwärtige Verbindungen; ***air* –,** die Luftverkehrslinie; Luftverkehrsgesellschaft; ***bus* –,** die Autobusgesellschaft; (*Railw.*) ***come off the –(s),*** entgleisen; (*Railw.*) ***double* –,** zweigleisige Bahnlinie; (*Railw.*) ***down* –,** die Strecke von London; ***main* –,** die Hauptlinie; ***passengers must not cross the –!*** das Überschreiten der Geleise ist verboten! ***railway* –,** die Bahnlinie; der Schienenstrang; (*Railw.*) ***up* –,** die Strecke nach London; 13. (*Art*) die Linienführung; *pl.* der Riß, Entwurf, Plan; die Umrißlinie (*of a ship etc.*); 14. *pl.* (*coll.*) ***hard –s,*** hartes Los, das Pech.

2. *v.t.* lini(i)eren, zeichnen; (durch)furchen; ***hundreds –d the streets,*** Hunderte säumten die Straßen; ***streets –d with trees,*** Straßen von Bäumen eingefaßt *or* (ein)gesäumt; ***the troops –d the streets,*** die Soldaten bildeten an den Straßen Spalier; ***they –d the streets with troops,*** man stellte Soldaten den Straßen entlang auf; – ***in,*** einzeichnen; – ***off,*** abgrenzen; – ***out,*** entwerfen, skizzieren; – ***through,*** durchstreichen; – ***up,*** in Linie aufstellen (*troops*); (*coll.*) zusammenstellen, einordnen (*things*).

3. *v.i.* – ***up,*** sich in einer Reihe *or* in Linie aufstellen; Schlange stehen; (*fig.*) sich zusammenschließen.

lineage ['liniidʒ], *s.* das Geschlecht, die Familie, der Stamm; die Abstammung, Abkunft. **lineal** [–əl], *adj.* geradlinig, direkt, in direkter Linie; – ***descendant,*** direkter Nachkomme; – ***descent,*** geradlinige Abstammung.

lineament ['liniəmənt], *s.* (*usu. pl.*) der (Gesichts)-zug.

linear ['liniə], *adj.* Linien–, linear, geradlinig, Längen–; linienförmig, strichförmig, fadenförmig; (*Bot.*) linealisch; – ***equation,*** lineare Gleichung, die Gleichung ersten Grades; – ***expansion,*** die Längenausdehnung; – ***measure,*** das Längenmaß(system); – ***numbers,*** Linearzahlen; – ***perspective,*** die Linearperspektive. **lineation** [–'eiʃən], *s.* Striche, Linien (*pl.*), die Linienführung.

line|-drawing, *s.* die Federzeichnung, Stiftzeichnung. **--engraving,** *s.* (der Stich in) Linienmanier (*f.*). **--fishing,** *s.* die Angelfischerei. **--frequency,** *s.* (*T.V.*) die Zeilenfrequenz. **–man,** *s.* (*Tele.*) der Leitungsmann, Störungssucher.

linen ['linin], **1.** *s.* die Leinwand (*product*); das Leinen (*raw material*); (*coll.*) die (Unter)wäsche; das Weißzeug; ***dirty* –,** schmutzige Wäsche (*also fig.*); ***wash one's dirty – in public,*** seine schmutzige Wäsche vor aller Welt ausbreiten; ***change of* –,** Wäsche zum Wechseln; ***change one's* –,** reine Wäsche anziehen. **2.** *adj.* leinen, Leinwand–; – ***paper,*** das Leinenpapier; – ***thread,*** der Leinenzwirn.

linen|-basket, *s.* der Wäschekorb. **--draper,** *s.* der Weißwarenhändler. **–fold,** *s.* (*Archit.*) die Faltenverzierung. **--goods,** *pl.* Leinenwaren (*pl.*). **--press,** *s.* der Wäscheschrank.

¹liner ['lainə], *s.* der Passagierdampfer, Überseedampfer, das Linienschiff; ***air–*–,** das Verkehrsflugzeug.

²liner, *s.* (*Tech.*) das Futter, die Ausfütterung; Buchse, Einlage, das Einlegestück; (*Artil.*) der Einstecklauf, das Einlegerohr; *see* **¹line.**

linesman ['lainzmən], *s.* 1. (*Railw.*) der Streckenarbeiter; 2. (*Spt.*) Linienrichter.

¹ling [liŋ], *s.* (*Ichth.*) der Leng, Langfisch.

²ling, *s.* (*Bot.*) das Heidekraut, gemeine Binsenheide.

linger ['liŋgə], *v.i.* sich hinziehen, sich in die Länge ziehen; noch fortleben, fortdauern, (noch) (ver)weilen, sich (lange) aufhalten, (*of invalids*) dahinsiechen; (*coll.*) zögern, zaudern; schlendern; ***the impression still –s in my mind,*** ich kann mich des Eindrucks nicht erwehren.

lingerie ['lɛ̃ʒəri], *s.* die Damenunterwäsche.

lingering ['liŋgəriŋ], *adj.* fortdauernd; – ***disease,*** langwierige *or* schleichende Krankheit; – ***hope,*** noch verbleibende Hoffnung; – ***sound,*** nachklingender Ton; – ***taste,*** nachwirkender *or* nachhaltender Geschmack.

lingo ['liŋgou], *s.* (*coll.*) das Kauderwelsch; der (Fach)jargon, die Fremdsprache.

lingual ['liŋgwəl], **1.** *adj.* Zungen–. **2.** *s.* der Zungenlaut. **linguist,** *s.* Sprachkundige(r); der Sprachforscher, Linguist; ***I am not a good* –,** ich bin nicht sprachgewandt. **linguistic** [–'gwistik], *adj.* sprachwissenschaftlich, Sprach(en)–, sprachlich. **linguistics,** *pl.* (*sing. constr.*) die Sprachwissenschaft, Linguistik.

liniment ['linimənt], *s.* das Einreibemittel.

lining ['lainiŋ], *s.* (*of clothes*) das Futter, die (Aus)-fütterung; der Futterstoff; (*Tech.*) die Verkleidung, Auskleidung, Verblendung, Ausmauerung; ***brake* –,** der Bremsbelag; (*Prov.*) ***every cloud has a silver* –,** selbst der schlechteste Tag hat ein Ende.

¹link [liŋk], **1.** *s.* das (Ketten)glied; Getriebeglied, Gelenk(stück), die Kulisse; (*fig.*) das (Binde)glied, die Verbindung; ***connecting* –,** das Bindeglied; ***cuff* –,** der Manschettenknopf; (*fig.*) ***missing* –,** fehlendes Glied in der Kette, unbekannte Zwischenstufe; (*Tech.*) – ***motion,*** die Kulissensteuerung. **2.** *v.t.* verketten, (*fig.*) (*also* – ***up***) verbinden (***with,*** mit), anschließen (an (*Acc.*)); – ***arms,*** sich einhaken; ***–ed atoms,*** gebundene Atome. **3.** *v.i.* (*also* – ***up***) sich verbinden (***with,*** mit), sich anschließen (an (*Acc.*)).

²link, *s.* (*obs.*) die Pechfackel.

linkage ['liŋkidʒ], *s.* die Verkettung, Verknüpfung, Verbindung; (*Tech.*) das Gestänge; (*Elec., Biol.*) die Kopplung.

link|-boy, --man, *s.* (*obs.*) der Fackelträger.

links [liŋks], *pl.* grasbewachsene Küstendünen (*pl.*); (*usu. sing. constr.*) der Golf(spiel)platz.

linn [lin], *s.* (*Scots*) der Wasserfall; Teich, Tümpel.
linnet ['linit], *s.* (*Orn.*) der Hänfling (*Carduelis cannabina*).
lino ['lainou], *s.* das Lineoleum; *--cut*, der Linolschnitt. **linoleum** [li'nouliəm], *s.* das Linoleum. **linotype** [-taip], *s.* die Zeilengießmaschine.
linseed ['linsi:d], *s.* der Leinsamen; *- cake*, der Leinkuchen, Ölkuchen; *- oil*, das Leinöl.
linsey-woolsey ['linzi'wulzi], *s.* das Wolle-und-Baumwolle-Mischzeug, Halbwollzeug; (*fig. coll.*) der Schund, billiges Zeug.
lint [lint], *s.* (*Surg.*) die Charpie, Zupfleinwand.
lintel [lintl], *s.* der Sturz (*of door or window*), Oberbalken, die Oberschwelle.
lion ['laiən], *s.* der Löwe (*also fig.*); (*fig.*) Held; (*coll.*) Prominente(r), die Größe; *literary -*, der Modeschriftsteller; *make a - of him*, ihn zum Helden des Tages machen; *put one's head into the -'s mouth*, sich in die Höhle des Löwen wagen; *-'s share*, der Löwenanteil; *-s of a place*, die Sehenswürdigkeiten (eines Ortes); *twist the -'s tail*, dem Löwen auf den Schwanz treten. **lioness,** *s.* die Löwin. **lion|-hearted,** *adj.* löwenherzig, unverzagt. **--hunter,** *s.* (*fig.*) der Prominentenjäger. **lionize,** *v.t.* die Sehenswürdigkeiten besichtigen (*a place, Gen.*); *- him*, ihn zum Helden des Tages machen.
lip [lip], **1.** *s.* 1. die Lippe (*also Bot.*); der Rand (*of hollow, dish, wound etc.*), die Tülle (*of jug*); *bite one's -*, sich auf die Lippen beißen; *hang on his -s*, an seinem Mund hängen; *from his own -s*, aus seinem eigenen Mund; *keep a stiff upper -*, unverzagt bleiben, das Kinn *or* die Ohren steif halten; *smack one's -s*, die Lippen lecken; *not a word passed my -s*, kein Wort kam über meine Lippen; 2. (*sl.*) die Unverschämtheit, Frechheit; *none of your -!* keine Unverschämtheiten! **2.** *v.t.* mit den Lippen berühren; (*fig.*) bespülen, spülen an (*Acc.*).
lipped [lipt], *adj.* 1. (*as suff.*) (*esp. Bot.*) -lippig; (*fig.*) -randig; 2. (*as attrib.*) (*of a vessel*) mit einer Tülle *or* einem Ausguß.
lip|-read, *irr.v.t., v.i.* von den Lippen ablesen. **--reading,** *s.* das Lippenlesen, Ablesen von den Lippen. **-salve,** *s.* die Lippensalbe. **--service,** *s.* der Lippendienst, die Lippenfrömmigkeit, Augendienerei. **-stick,** *s.* der Lippenstift.
liquate [li'kweit], *v.t.* (*Metall.*) (aus)seigern, abseigern. **liquation** [-ʃən], *s.* die (Aus)seigerung; *- furnace*, der Seigerofen.
liquefaction [likwi'fækʃən], *s.* die Verflüssigung, Schmelzung; Verdichtung (*of gas*). **liquefiable** ['likwifaiəbl], *adj.* schmelzbar. **liquefy** ['likwifai], **1.** *v.t.* schmelzen; verflüssigen; verdichten (*gas*); *liquefied gas*, das Flüssiggas. **2.** *v.i.* sich verflüssigen, flüssig werden. **liquescent** [li'kwesənt], *adj.* sich verflüssigend.
liqueur [li'kə:], *s.* der Likör.
liquid ['likwid], **1.** *adj.* flüssig, Flüssigkeits-; (*fig.*) (*of sound*) fließend, dahinströmend, wohltönend, sanft, (*Phonet.*) liquid, palatal(isiert); (*as eyes*) hell, klar; (*Comm.*) flüssig, liquid, sofort fällig (*as debts*), sofort realisierbar (*of securities*); (*fig.*) unbeständig, schwankend; *- air*, flüssige Luft; *- measure*, das Flüssigkeitsmaß; (*Phonet.*) *- sound*, die Liquida. **2.** *s.* die Flüssigkeit; (*Phonet.*) Liquida, der Liquidlaut.
liquidate ['likwideit], *v.t.* bezahlen, begleichen, abtragen, tilgen, löschen (*debts*); saldieren, abrechnen (*account*); abwickeln, auflösen, liquidieren (*business etc.*); gegen bar verkaufen, flüssig machen (*securities*); (*fig.*) beseitigen, ausrotten (*a th.*), (*coll.*) beseitigen, umbringen (*a p.*). **liquidation** [-'deiʃən], *s.* die Tilgung, Bezahlung (*of debts*), Saldierung, Abrechnung (*of accounts*), Auflösung, Abwicklung, Liquidierung (*of a business*); der Abverkauf gegen bar, das Flüssigmachen (*of securities*); (*fig.*) die Beseitigung; *go into -*, sich auflösen, in Liquidation treten; *- proceedings*, das Konkursverfahren. **liquidator,** *s.* der Liquidator. **liquidity** [-'kwiditi], *s.* die Flüssigkeit, flüssiger Zustand.
liquor ['likə], **1.** *s.* die Flüssigkeit; (*Dye.*) Lauge. Flotte; (*Cul.*) Brühe; geistiges Getränk; *be in -, be the worse for -*, betrunken sein. **2.** *v.t.* einweichen.
liquorice ['likəris], *s.* das Süßholz, die Lakritze.
lisle [lail], *s.* der Flor, das Florgarn; die Florware.
lisp [lisp], **1.** *v.t., v.i.* lispeln, mit der Zunge anstoßen. **2.** *s.* das Lispeln. **lisping, 1.** *adj.* lispelnd. **2.** *s.* das Gelispel.
lissom(e) ['lisəm], *adj.* geschmeidig, biegsam; beweglich, flink. **lissom(e)ness,** *s.* die Geschmeidigkeit, Flinkheit.
[1]**list** [list], **1.** *s.* die Liste, das Verzeichnis; *- of contents*, das Inhaltsverzeichnis; *draw up a -, make a -*, eine Liste aufstellen; (*Naut.*) *crew -*, die Musterrolle; *price -*, die Preisliste; *- of subscribers*, die Zeichnungsliste, Subskriptionsliste. **2.** *v.t.* (in eine Liste) eintragen, (in einer Liste) verzeichnen; registrieren, aufzählen, aufzeichnen.
[2]**list, 1.** *s.* 1. die Gewebeleiste, Webkante, das Salband; der Rand, Saum; 2. *pl.* (*Hist.*) Schranken (*pl.*); (*fig.*) *enter the -s*, in die Schranken treten, in den Kampf eingreifen. **2.** *v.t.* mit Salleisten beschlagen (*a door*).
[3]**list, 1.** *s.* (*Naut.*) die Schlagseite. **2.** *v.i.* Schlagseite haben.
[4]**list,** *imp. v.t., v.i.* (*obs.*) belieben (*Dat.*), gefallen (*Dat.*), gelüsten, wünschen, wollen.
[5]**list,** *v.i.* (*obs.*) horchen, hören (*to*, auf (*Acc.*)).
listen ['lisn], *v.i.* horchen, lauschen, hören (*to*, auf (*Acc.*)) (*a p. or th.*), zuhören (*Dat.*), Gehör schenken (*Dat.*), anhören (*Acc.*) (*a p.*); *- for*, aufpassen auf (*Acc.*), horchend abwarten; *- in*, Rundfunk *or* Radio hören; *- in on a conversation*, eine Unterredung mithören; *- in to a play*, ein Stück im Radio anhören; (*fig.*) *- to him*, seinem Rat folgen; *- to advice*, Ratschläge beachten; *- to reason*, Vernunft annehmen. **listener,** *s.* der Zuhörer, Horcher, Lauscher; (Rundfunk)hörer; (*Prov.*) *-s never hear good of themselves*, ein Horcher an der Wand, hört seine eigne Schand'. **listening|(-in),** *s.* das Rundfunkhören. **--post,** *s.* (*Mil.*) der Horchposten. **--service,** *s.* der Abhördienst.
listless ['listlis], *adj.* gleichgültig, teilnahmslos; interesselos, lustlos, schwunglos, schlaff, träge, flau. **listlessness,** *s.* die Gleichgültigkeit, Teilnahmslosigkeit, Schlaffheit.
list price, *s.* der Katalogpreis. **lists** [lists], *pl. See* [2]**list.**
lit [lit], *imperf., p.p. of* [1]**light**; (*sl.*) *- up*, besoffen, illuminiert.
litany ['litəni], *s.* die Litanei (*also fig.*).
liter (*Am.*), *see* **litre.**
literacy ['litərəsi], *s.* die Lese- und Schreibfähigkeit; das Buchwissen, geistige Bildung; *- test*, die Prüfung der Lese- und Schreibkenntnisse.
literal ['litərəl], *adj.* wortgetreu, wörtlich; (*of a p.*) prosaisch, nüchtern, pedantisch; (*fig.*) buchstäblich, förmlich, eigentlich; *- sense*, eigentliche Bedeutung; *- translation*, wörtliche Übersetzung; *- truth*, nüchterne *or* ungeschminkte Wahrheit. **literally,** *adv.* wörtlich, Wort für Wort; (*fig.*) buchstäblich.
literary ['litərəri], *adj.* schriftstellerisch, literarisch; Literatur-, Literar-; *- activity*, schriftstellerische Tätigkeit; *- historian*, der Literarhistoriker; *- history*, die Literaturgeschichte; *- language*, die Schriftsprache; *- man*, der Schriftsteller, Literat; *- property*, geistiges Eigentum; *- career*, schriftstellerische Laufbahn.
literate ['litərit], **1.** *adj.* des Lesens und Schreibens kundig; gelehrt, (literarisch) gebildet. **2.** *s.* des Lesens und Schreibens Kundige(r); Gelehrte(r), (literarisch) Gebildete(r). **literati** [-'rɑ:ti], *pl.* Literaten, Gelehrte (*pl.*). **literature** [-rətʃə], *s.* das Schrifttum, die Literatur; *history of -*, die Literaturgeschichte; *light -*, die Unterhaltungsliteratur; *legal -*, juristische Fachliteratur.
litharge ['liθɑ:dʒ], *s.* (*Chem.*) die Bleiglätte, Bleiasche.
lithe [laið], *adj.* geschmeidig, wendig; schlank,

graziös. **litheness,** *s.* die Geschmeidigkeit. Wendigkeit. **lithesome** [–səm], *adj. See* **lithe.**

lithium ['liθiəm], *s.* (*Chem.*) das Lithium.

lithochromatic [liθəkrə'mætik], *adj.* Buntdruck–, Farbendruck–. **lithograph** ['liθəgrɑ:f], **1.** *s.* der Steindruck. **2.** *v.t., v.i.* lithographieren. **lithographer** [li'θɔgrəfə], *s.* der Lithograph. **lithographic** [liθə'græfik], *adj.* Steindruck–, lithographisch; – ***paper,*** das Lithographierpapier, Steindruckpapier; – ***print,*** der Steindruck. **lithography** [li'θɔgrəfi], *s.* die Lithographie, das Steindruckverfahren. **lithology** [li'θɔlədʒi], *s.* die Gesteinskunde. **lithophyte** ['liθəfait], *s.* (*Bot.*) die Steinpflanze. **lithotomy** [li'θɔtəmi], *s.* (*Surg.*) der (Blasen)steinschnitt.

Lithuania [liθju'einiə], *s.* Litauen (*n.*). **Lithuanian, 1.** *s.* 1. der (die) Litauer(in); 2. (*language*) das Litauische. **2.** *adj.* litauisch.

litigant ['litigənt], **1.** *adj.* prozeßführend; prozeßsüchtig. **2.** *s.* Prozeßführende(r), streitende Partei. **litigate** [–eit], **1.** *v.i.* prozessieren. **2.** *v.t.* prozessieren *or* streiten um. **litigation** [–'geiʃən], *s.* der Rechtsstreit, Prozeß. **litigious** [li'tidʒəs], *adj.* prozeßsüchtig, streitsüchtig; – ***person,*** der Querulant. **litigiousness,** *s.* die Streitsucht, Prozeßsucht.

litmus ['litməs], *s.* das Lackmus; – ***paper,*** das Lackmuspapier, Reagenzpapier; – ***solution,*** die Lackmustinktur; ***showing acid reaction to –,*** lackmussauer.

litotes [lai'touti:z], *s.* die Litotes, Übertreibung.

litre ['li:tə], *s.* das *or* der Liter.

litter ['litə], **1.** *s.* 1. die Tragbahre, (*Hist.*) Sänfte; 2. Streu (*for animals*); zerstreute *or* herumliegende Dinge (*pl.*), der Abfall; 3. die Unordnung, das Durcheinander; ***in a –,*** in Unordnung; 4. der Wurf (*of pigs*). **2.** *v.t.* (*animals*) (*oft.* – ***down***) Streu aufschütten für, einstreuen; (*stables, plants*) mit Streu bedecken, einstreuen; unordentlich herumliegen in *or* auf (*Dat.*), unordentlich bestreuen (*a place*); ***lie –ed about,*** verstreut *or* unordentlich herumliegen. **3.** *v.i.* Junge werfen (*of pigs*). **litter-lout,** *s.* der Umweltverschmutzer.

little [litl], **1.** *adj.* klein, Klein–; unbeträchtlich, unbedeutend, gering(fügig) (*of degree*), kurz (*of time, distance etc.*); wenig (*of amount*); ***but –,*** nur wenig; ***so this is your – game,*** also darauf willst du hinaus; – ***hope,*** wenig Hoffnung; (*coll.*) – ***Mary,*** der Magen; ***Little Masters,*** die Kleinmeister (*German engravers*); – ***minds,*** kleine Geister; ***no – trouble,*** viel *or* nicht wenig Mühe; – ***or no,*** wenig oder gar kein; – ***one,*** ein Kleines, das Wurm; ***the – ones,*** die Kleinen *or* Kinder; – ***things,*** Kleinigkeiten, Nebensächlichkeiten; ***a – way,*** eine kurze Strecke (Weges); ***his – ways,*** seine Eigenheiten *or* Eigentümlichkeiten; ***a – while,*** eine kleine Weile. **2.** *adv.* (nur) wenig, kaum, nicht im geringsten; ***be it ever so –,*** sei es auch noch so wenig; ***he – knows*** or – ***does he know that*** . . ., er hat kaum eine *or* hat nicht die geringste Ahnung daß . . .; ***in – less than a year,*** in nicht viel weniger als einem Jahr. **3.** *s.* Weniges, die Kleinigkeit, das bißchen; ***a –,*** etwas, ein wenig, ein bißchen, eine Kleinigkeit; ***not a –,*** nicht wenig; ***after a –,*** nach kurzer Zeit; – ***by –,*** allmählich, nach und nach; ***for a –,*** für kurze Zeit; – ***or nothing,*** wenig oder (gar) nichts.

little auk [ɔ:k], *s.* (*Orn.*) kleiner Krabbentaucher (*Plautus alle*). **Little-Englander,** *s.* der Gegner der imperialistischen Politik Englands. **littleness,** *s.* die Kleinheit; Geringfügigkeit; Kleinlichkeit, Engstirnigkeit. **little office,** *s.* (*R.C.*) marianische Tagzeiten (*pl.*). **Little| Red Riding Hood,** *s.* das Rotkäppchen. – **Russian,** *s.* der (die) Ukrainer(in), der Kleinrusse (die Kleinrussin). **little theatre,** *s.* Kammerspiele (*pl.*), die Kleinbühne, Experimentierbühne.

littoral ['litərəl], **1.** *adj.* Küsten–, Ufer–, Strand–. **2.** *s.* das Uferland, Küstenland, Litorale.

liturgical [li'tə:dʒikl], *adj.* liturgisch. **liturgy** ['litədʒi], *s.* die Liturgie.

[1]**live** [liv], **1.** *v.i.* leben, Leben haben, am Leben bleiben; wohnen, sich aufhalten (***at,*** in (*Dat.*)); (*also* – ***on***) fortleben, weiterleben; (*fig. of ship in storm*) sich halten; sich (er)nähren (***on,*** von; ***by,*** durch), (*fig.*) leben auf Kosten (***on,*** *Gen.*), zehren (von); – ***a bachelor,*** als Junggeselle leben; – ***and learn,*** man lernt nie aus; – ***and let –,*** leben und leben lassen; – ***by writing,*** sich (*Dat.*) durch Schriftstellerei den Lebensunterhalt verdienen *or* bestreiten; – ***by one's wits,*** mit Schlauheit durchs Leben kommen; – ***down,*** überwinden; – ***in,*** am Arbeitsplatz wohnen; – ***in clover,*** in der Wolle sitzen, leben wie Gott in Frankreich; – ***in luxury,*** ein üppiges Leben führen; – ***on bread,*** von Brot leben; – ***on one's capital,*** von seinem Kapital zehren; – ***on one's income,*** in den Grenzen seines Einkommens leben; – ***on nothing,*** von der Luft leben; ***they – on bad terms,*** sie vertragen sich schlecht; – ***on one's wife('s money),*** auf Kosten *or* von den Einkünften seiner Frau leben; – ***through a crisis,*** eine Krise durchmachen *or* durchleben; – ***to a great age,*** ein hohes Alter erreichen; – ***to o.s.,*** für sich leben; ***you will – to regret it,*** du wirst es noch bereuen; – ***to see,*** erleben; – ***up to one's principles,*** seinen Grundsätzen gemäß leben; – ***with,*** zusammenleben mit, wohnen bei; – ***with a woman,*** mit einer Frau in wilder Ehe leben. **2.** *v.t.* verleben, führen (*a life etc.*); (im Leben) verwirklichen *or* zum Ausdruck bringen; – ***a good life,*** ein tadelloses Leben führen; – ***down,*** durch die Lebensweise widerlegen *or* überwinden *or* in Vergessenheit geraten lassen.

[2]**live** [laiv], *attrib. adj.* 1. lebend, lebendig; (*fig.*) wirklich, richtig; (*coll.*) lebhaft, voll Leben, tätig, energisch, rührig (*of a p.*), wichtig, aktuell (*of issues*); – ***bait,*** lebender Köder; – ***weight,*** das Lebendgewicht; 2. scharf (*as bombs*); (*Elec.*) stromführend, eingeschaltet; ungebraucht (*as matches*); glühend (*as embers*); – ***wire,*** stromführender Draht, (*coll.*) rühriger Mensch; 3. (*Rad., T.V.*) Original–, Direkt–, unmittelbar übertragen; – ***broadcast,*** die Live-Sendung; 4. (*Tech.*) – ***load,*** die Nutzlast; 5. (*Mech.*) – ***steam,*** der Frischdampf.

-lived [livd], *adj. suff.* –lebig.

livelihood ['laivlihud], *s.* der (Lebens)unterhalt, das Auskommen; ***make a*** or ***one's –, earn one's –,*** sein Brot verdienen. **liveliness,** *s.* die Munterkeit, Lebhaftigkeit, Lebendigkeit.

livelong ['livlɔŋ], *adj.* (*Poet.*) (*only in*) ***the – day,*** den lieben langen Tag.

lively ['laivli], *adj.* lebhaft, munter, voll Leben (*of a p.*); lebendig, lebensvoll, lebenswahr, eindrucksvoll (*description etc.*); lebhaft, kräftig (*feelings, colours*); stark, fest, eifrig (*as faith, hope*); aufregend (*time etc.*); – ***interest,*** lebhaftes Interesse; (*coll.*) ***a – time,*** aufregende Zeiten (*pl.*); – ***wine,*** schäumender Wein.

liven ['laivən], (*coll.*) (*usu.* – ***up***) **1.** *v.i.* aufleben, lebendig werden, sich beleben. **2.** *v.t.* lebendig machen, beleben, aufmuntern.

[1]**liver** ['livə], *s.* Lebende(r); (*only in*) ***fast –,*** der Lebemann; ***good –,*** der Schlemmer; ***loose –,*** liederlicher Mensch.

[2]**liver,** *s.* die Leber; ***–-complaint,*** die Leberkrankheit. **liver|-coloured,** *adj.* rötlich braun, leberfarbig. **–-fluke,** *s.* der Leberegel.

liveried ['livərid], *adj.* in Livree, livriert.

liverish ['livəriʃ], *adj.* (*coll.*) leberleidend; mürrisch, griesgrämig. **liver|-rot,** *s.* die Leberegelseuche. **–wort,** *s.* das Leberblümchen.

livery ['livəri], *s.* 1. die Livree, Dienstkleidung; Amtstracht (*of guild etc.*); (*Poet.*) das Gewand, Kleid; ***in –,*** *see* **liveried**; (*Zool.*) ***winter –,*** das Winterkleid; 2. (*Law*) die Übergabe, Übertragung; ***sue for –,*** die Übergabe eines Besitzes ersuchen; 3. (*obs.*) Versorgung mit Kleidung und Nahrung; Futterlieferung; ***at –,*** in Futter (*of horses*).

livery|-company, *s.* wahlfähige Zunft. **–man,** *s.* 1. das Zunftmitglied; 2. der Mietstallbesitzer. **–-servant,** *s.* livrierter Diener. **–-stable,** *s.* die Mietstallung.

lives [laivz], *pl. of* **life.**

livestock ['laivstɔk], *s.* lebendes Inventar, der Viehbestand, das Vieh.

livid ['livid], *adj.* bleifarben, blaugrau; fahl, bleich, leichenblaß, aschgrau (*with*, vor (*Dat.*)). **lividness,** *s.* die Fahlheit, Bleichheit, Leichenblässe.

living ['liviŋ], **1.** *adj.* lebend; lebendig; brennend, glühend; zeitgenössisch; gewachsen (*as rock*); (*fig.*) lebensecht, (natur)getreu (*of likeness*); ***the* –**, die Lebenden (*pl.*); ***in the land of the* –**, im Reiche der Lebendigen; **– *death,*** trostloses Leben; ***no man* –**, kein Sterblicher; **– *memory,*** das Menschengedenken; ***while* –**, bei Lebzeiten. **2.** *s.* 1. das Leben; **– *conditions,*** Lebensbedingungen (*pl.*); **– *space,*** der Lebensraum; ***standard of* –**, der Lebensstandard; 2. die Lebensweise, der Lebensstil; ***good*** or ***high* –**, das Wohlleben, üppige Lebensweise; 3. der (Lebens)unterhalt, das Auskommen; **– *wage,*** das Existenzminimum; ***earn one's* –, *work for one's* –**, seinen Lebensunterhalt *or* sein Brot verdienen; ***make a* –**, sich ernähren *or* sein Auskommen haben (***out of,*** von); 4. (*Eccl.*) die Pfründe.

living-room, *s.* das Wohnzimmer.

Livonia [li'vouniə], *s.* Livland (*n.*). **Livonian, 1.** *s.* 1. der (die) Livländer(in); 2. (*language*) das Livisch(e). **2.** *adj.* livländisch.

Livy ['livi], *s.* Livius (*m.*).

lixiviate [lik'sivieit], *v.t.* auslaugen. **lixiviation** [–'eiʃən], *s.* die Auslaugung.

lizard ['lizəd], *s.* die Eidechse; (*coll.*) ***lounge* –**, der Salonlöwe.

lizzie ['lizi], *s.* (*sl.*) die Karre, Kiste.

llama ['lɑ:mə], *s.* (*Zool.*) das Lama.

lo! [lou], *int.* (*Poet.*) siehe! **– *and behold,*** und siehe da!

loach [loutʃ], *s.* (*Ichth.*) die Schmerle.

load [loud], **1.** *s.* 1. die Last, Ladung, Fracht; (*fig.*) Bürde; (*also cart*-–) Fuhre, Wagenladung, (*of hay*) das Fuder; (*Naut.*) **– *displacement,*** die Ladeverdrängung; **– *on ground,*** der Bodendruck; (*Naut.*) **– (*water-*)*line,*** die Lade(wasser)linie; ***a – is taken off my mind,*** mir ist ein Stein vom Herzen genommen; ***axle* –**, der Achsdruck; (*sl.*) ***get a – of this!*** hör mal gut zu! paß mal auf! 2. (*Mech., Elec.*) die Belastung, Arbeitsleistung; **– *capacity,*** die Tragfähigkeit, Ladefähigkeit; (*Elec.*) Belastbarkeit, Leistungsaufnahme; ***breaking* –**, die Bruchfestigkeit; ***peak* –**, die Belastungsspitze; ***permissible* –**, die Höchstbelastung; ***safe* –**, zulässige Belastung; ***useful* –**, die Nutzlast; 3. *pl.* (*coll.*) die Unmenge, Unmasse, Massen (*pl.*), Haufen (*pl.*). **2.** *v.t.* 1. beladen (*vehicle*), (auf)laden (*goods*); laden (*guns*); **– *film in the camera,*** den Film in den Apparat einlegen; 2. (*fig.*) (*with work etc.*) überladen, überlasten; (*with cares etc.*) belasten, beschweren, bedrücken; (*with gifts etc.*) überschütten, überhäufen; 3. **– *dice,*** Würfel fälschen *or* beschweren; (*fig.*) **– *the dice,*** etwas zu seinen Gunsten auslegen. **3.** *v.i.* (**– *up***) (*of a p.*) aufladen, (*of vehicle*) (ein)laden, Ladung einnehmen (***for,*** nach); (*Comm.*) stark kaufen.

loaded ['loudid], *adj.* 1. beladen, belastet; 2. (*fig.*) beschwert; (*sl.*) steinreich; (*sl.*) besoffen; **– *stomach,*** überladener Magen; 3. **– *cane,*** der Bleistock, Totschläger; **– *dice,*** falsche Würfel (*pl.*); **– *wine,*** verfälschter *or* verschnittener Wein. **loader,** *s.* der (Ver)lader, Auflader; Lader (*of gun*); ***breech* –**, der Hinterlader. **loading,** *s.* 1. das (Auf)laden; die Ladung, Last; **– *and unloading,*** das Laden und Löschen; (*Naut.*) **– *berth,*** die Ladestelle; **– *platform,* – *ramp,*** die (Ver)laderampe; (*Artil.*) **– *tray,*** die Ladeschale, der Ladetisch; 2. (*Tech.*) die Belastung; **– *limit,*** die Belastungsgrenze; 3. (*fig.*) die Beschwerung.

loadstar, *see* **lodestar.**

loadstone ['loudstoun], *s.* der Magneteisenstein; (*fig.*) Magnet.

[1]**loaf** [louf], *s.* (*pl.* **loaves** [louvz]) 1. der Laib (Brot), das Brot; **– *of sugar,*** der Zuckerhut; **– *sugar,*** der Hutzucker; ***half a – is better than no bread,*** etwas ist besser als gar nichts; 2. (*sl.*) die Bohne, Birne, Rübe, der Dez; (*sl.*) ***use your –!*** sei gescheit! nimm dich zusammen!

[2]**loaf, 1.** *v.i.* (*oft.* **– *about,* – *around***) herumlungern, bummeln, faulenzen. **2.** *v.t.* **– *away,*** vertrödeln, verbummeln (*time*). **loafer,** *s.* der Müßiggänger, Bummler, Drückeberger.

loam [loum], *s.* der Lehm(boden); (*obs.*) Ton. **loamy,** *adj.* lehmig, Lehm–, lehmhaltig.

loan [loun], **1.** *s.* die Anleihe (***on,*** auf (*Acc.*)), das Darlehen (***to,*** an (*Acc.*)), die Leihgabe (*for exhibition*); das (Ver)leihen; die Ausleihung; Darlehnung, Entlehnung; ***government* –**, die Staatsanleihe; ***public* –**, öffentliche Anleihe; ***have the – of,*** borgen, leihen, geliehen haben *or* bekommen; ***as a* –, *on* –**, leihweise; (*Comm.*) als Anleihe; ***ask for the – of,*** leihweise erbitten; (*Comm.*) ***take up a* –**, eine Anleihe aufnehmen. **2.** *v.t.* verleihen (***to,*** *Dat.*). **loanable,** *adj.* verleihbar. **loan|-society,** *s.* die Darlehnskasse. **--word,** *s.* das Lehnwort.

loath [louθ], *pred. adj.* abgeneigt, unwillig, nicht willens (***to do,*** zu tun; ***for him to do,*** daß er tut); ***I am – to do it,*** ich tue es ungern, ich habe keine Lust, es zu tun; ***I am – for him to do it,*** ich bin dagegen, daß er es tut; ***nothing* –**, durchaus nicht abgeneigt.

loathe [louð], *v.t.* mit Ekel ansehen, sich (*Dat. or Acc.*) ekeln *or* Ekel empfinden vor (*Dat.*); verabscheuen, (*coll.*) nicht leiden können, nicht gern tun *or* haben. **loathing,** *s.* der Widerwille, Ekel, Abscheu (***at,*** vor (*Dat.*)). **loathingly,** *adv.* mit Ekel *or* Abscheu *or* Widerwillen. **loathsome,** *adj.* ekelhaft, eklig, widerlich, abscheulich, ekelerregend, verhaßt. **loathsomeness,** *s.* die Ekelhaftigkeit, Widerlichkeit, Abscheulichkeit.

loaves [louvz], *pl. of* [1]**loaf.**

lob [lɔb], **1.** *s.* (*Tenn.*) der Hoch(flug)ball, Lob(ball), (*Crick.*) Wurf von unten. **2.** *v.t.* (*Tenn.*) hoch zurückschlagen, (*Crick.*) von unten werfen. **3.** *v.i.* (*Tenn.*) lobben, einen Lobball schlagen.

lobate ['loubeit], *adj.* (*Bot.*) *see* **lobed. lobation** [–'beiʃən], *s.* (*Bot.*) die Lappenbildung.

lobby ['lɔbi], **1.** *s.* die Vorhalle, Wandelhalle, der Vorraum, Vorsaal, das Vorzimmer, Foyer, der Wandelgang, (breiter) Korridor; (*Pol.*) die Interessen(ten)gruppe; (*Parl.*) ***division* –**, der Abstimmungssaal. **2.** *v.t.* bearbeiten, zu beeinflussen suchen, beeinflussen (*a delegate etc.*). **3.** *v.i.* sich außerhalb des Verhandlungssaals beraten; im geheimen arbeiten, intrigieren, antichambrieren. **lobbyist,** *s.* (*esp. Am.*) bezahlter Agent, der die Abgeordneten zu beeinflussen sucht.

lobe [loub], *s.* der Lappen; **– *of the ear,*** das Ohrläppchen. **lobed,** *adj.* lappig, gelappt (*Bot. etc.*).

lobelia [lou'bi:liə], *s.* die Lobelie.

lobster ['lɔbstə], *s.* der Hummer; **– *pot,*** die Hummerfalle; ***red as a* –**, puterrot, krebsrot.

lobular ['lɔbjulə], *adj.* (*Med.*) lappenförmig, Lobulär–. **lobule** [–ju:l], *s.* das Läppchen.

lobworm ['lɔbwə:m], *s.* der Köderwurm.

local [loukl], **1.** *adj.* örtlich, Orts–, Stadt–, lokal, Lokal–; **– *anaesthetic,*** örtliche Betäubung; **– *authority,*** die Ortsbehörde, Stadtbehörde; **– *branch,*** die Ortsgruppe, der Ortsverband, örtliche Zweigstelle *or* Niederlassung; **– *call,*** das Ortsgespräch; **– *colour,*** das Lokalkolorit; **– *custom,*** ortsüblicher Brauch; **– *declination,*** die Ortsmißweisung (*of compass needle*); **– *doctor,*** ortsansässiger *or* hiesiger Arzt; **– *expression,*** ortsgebundener Ausdruck; **– *government,*** die Gemeindeverwaltung, Kommunalverwaltung; **– *inflammation,*** örtliche Entzündung; **– *inhabitant,*** Ortsansässige(r); **– *news,*** Lokalnachrichten (*pl.*); **– *option,*** der Ortsentscheid; **– *patriotism,*** der Lokalpatriotismus; **– *service,*** der Nahverkehr (*trains, buses*); **– *situation,*** örtliche Lage; **– *time,*** die Ortszeit; **– *traffic,*** der Ortsverkehr, Nahverkehr; **– *train,*** der Nahverkehrszug, Personenzug. **2.** *s.* der Lokalzug; lokale Nachricht; Ortsbewohner, Ortsansässige(r); (*coll.*) das Ortsgasthaus.

locale [lou'kɑːl], *s.* der Schauplatz.

localism ['loukəlizm], *s.* **1.** örtliche (Sprach)eigentümlichkeit; **2.** (*fig.*) enger Horizont, die Borniertheit. **locality** [–'kæliti], *s.* der Ort, die Örtlichkeit, Ortschaft; örtliche Lage; ***sense of –,*** der Ortssinn, Orientierungssinn. **localization** [–lai'zeiʃən], *s.* örtliche Bestimmung *or* Beschränkung, die Lokalisierung, Festlegung. **localize,** *v.t.* (örtlich) beschränken, lokalisieren (***to***, auf (*Acc.*)); (örtlich) bestimmen *or* festlegen.

locate [lou'keit], *v.t.* örtlich feststellen *or* festlegen, ausfindig machen; die Grenzen abstecken; (einen bestimmten Platz) zuweisen (*Dat.*), (an einen bestimmten Ort) verlegen, einordnen; (*Navig.*) orten, einpeilen; (*coll.*) (auf)finden, ermitteln; (*coll.*) ***be –d,*** gelegen sein, liegen; wohnhaft sein. **location** [–'keiʃən], *s.* die Lage, Stelle, der Platz, Standort; die Lokalisierung, örtliche Feststellung *or* Festlegung; (*coll.*) das (Auf)finden; die Niederlassung, Siedlung; (*Law*) Vermietung, Verpachtung; (*Am.*) Grenzbestimmung, Abmessung (*of land*); (*Am.*) abgestecktes Stück Land; (*Films*) der Standort einer Außenaufnahme; ***on –,*** auf Außenaufnahme.

locative ['lɔkətiv], **1.** *adj.* (*Gram.*) Orts–, Lokativ–. **2.** *s.* der Ortsfall, Lokativ, Lokalis.

loch [lɔx], *s.* (*Scots*) der (Binnen)see; Meeresarm, enge Bucht.

loci ['lousai], *pl. of* **locus.**

[1]**lock** [lɔk], *s.* die Locke; Flocke (*of wool*); *pl.* (*Poet.*) das Haar.

[2]**lock, 1.** *s.* **1.** das Schloß, der Verschluß; (*coll.*) ***–, stock, and barrel,*** in Bausch und Bogen, mit Stumpf und Stiel; ***under – and key,*** unter Schloß und Riegel; 2. die Schleuse(nkammer) (*of canal*); 3. (*Wrestling*) Fesselung; (*fig.*) Stockung, Verstopfung, Stauung; 4. der Einschlag (*of wheels*). **2.** *v.t.* **1.** zuschließen, abschließen (*a door etc.*); einschließen (***in***, in (*Acc.*)), verschließen (in (*Dat.*)) (*a p. or th.*); (um)schließen, fest (umfassen) (***in***, in (*Acc.*)), verschließen (in (*Dat.*)) (*in one's arms etc.*); ***– the door against him,*** ihm die Tür verschließen; ***– the stable door after the horse has bolted,*** den Brunnen zudecken, wenn das Kind ertrunken ist; ***– in,*** einschließen, einsperren; ***– out,*** aussperren; ***– up,*** verschließen, abschließen, zuschließen (*a th.*), einschließen, einsperren (*a p.*); sperren (*as frost a river*); fest anlegen (*funds*); (*Typ.*) schließen; 2. mit Schleusen versehen (*a canal*), (durch)schleusen (*a ship*); ***– up,*** stromaufwärts durchschleusen (*ship*); 3. sperren, hemmen (*a wheel*). **3.** *v.i.* (sich) schließen (lassen); gehemmt *or* gesperrt werden; ineinandergreifen (*as gearwheels*).

lockage ['lɔkidʒ], *s.* **1.** das (Durch)schleusen (*of ships*); 2. Schleusensystem, die Schleusenanlage, Schleußen (*pl.*); 3. das Schleusengeld, die Schleusengebühr; 4. Schleusenhöhe, das Schleusengefälle.

locker ['lɔkə], *s.* verschließbarer Schrank, das Schließfach, das *or* der Spind; ***in Davy Jones's –,*** ertrunken.

locket ['lɔkit], *s.* das Medaillon.

lock|-gate, *s.* das Schleusentor. **–jaw,** *s.* die Kieferklemme, der Trismus. **–-keeper,** *s.* der Schleusenwärter. **–nut,** *s.* die Kontermutter, Gegenmutter. **–-out,** *s.* die Aussperrung. **–smith,** *s.* der Schlosser. **–-stitch,** *s.* der Steppstich. **–-up, 1.** *s.* **1.** der Tor(es)schluß; 2. feste (Kapitals)-anlage; 3. (*coll.*) verschließbare Mietgarage; (*coll.*) der Karzer. **2.** *attrib. adj.* verschließbar.

[1]**loco** ['loukou], *adj.* (*sl.*) übergeschnappt, plemplem.

[2]**loco,** *s.* (*coll.*) die Lok.

locomotion [loukə'mouʃən], *s.* die Ortsveränderung, Fortbewegung(sfähigkeit). **locomotive** [–tiv], **1.** *adj.* der freien *or* spontanen Ortsveränderung fähig, fortbewegungsfähig, sich fortbewegend; freibeweglich (*as bivalves*); ***– engine,*** die Lokomotive; ***– power,*** die Fortbewegungsfähigkeit. **2.** *s.* die Lokomotive. **locomotor** [–tə], *s.* der Triebwagen; (*Med.*) ***– ataxia,*** die Rückenmarksschwindsucht, Rückenmarksdarre.

locum (tenens) ['loukəm ('tiːnənz)], *s.* der (die) Stellvertreter(in).

locus ['loukəs], *s.* (*pl.* **loci** [–sai]) der Ort, die Stelle; (*Math.*) geometrischer Ort.

locust ['loukəst], *s.* die Heuschrecke; (*Bot.*) Kassiaschote; Karobe. **locust-tree,** *s.* die Robinie, falsche Akazie (*Robinia pseudoacacia*); der Johannisbrotbaum (*Ceratonia siliqua*).

locution [lɔ'kjuːʃən], *s.* der Ausdruck, die Redewendung, Redensart; Sprechweise, Redeweise.

lode [loud], *s.* (*Min.*) der Gang, die Ader; der Entwässerungsgraben, Abzugsgraben. **lodestar,** *s.* der Polarstern; (*fig.*) Leitstern.

lodestone, *see* **loadstone.**

lodge [lɔdʒ], **1.** *v.t.* **1.** beherbergen, aufnehmen, einquartieren, unterbringen (*a p.*); einlagern (*goods*); 2. einzahlen, hinterlegen, deponieren (*money*); (*fig.*) übertragen (***with***, *Dat. or* auf (*Acc.*)), in Verwahrung geben (bei), anvertrauen (*Dat.*); 3. einreichen (*a complaint*), einbringen, einlegen, erheben (*a protest*), (Klage *or* Beschwerde) führen (***against***, gegen; ***with***, bei); ***– information against,*** Anzeige erstatten gegen, anzeigen; 4. hineintreiben, hineinstoßen (***in***, in (*Acc.*)), ans Ziel bringen (*a missile*). **2.** *v.i.* logieren, zur Miete *or* in Untermiete wohnen; übernachten, einkehren (***with***, bei); steckenbleiben, sitzenbleiben, festsitzen (*as a bullet*). **3.** *s.* das Häuschen, Jagdhaus, Forsthaus; Pförtnerhaus, die Portierwohnung; (*Freem.*) Loge.

lodg(e)ment ['lɔdʒmənt], *s.* **1.** (*Law*) die Hinterlegung, Einzahlung, Deponierung (*of money*), Einlegung, Einreichung (*of claim*), Erhebung (*of complaint*); 2. das Hängenbleiben, Steckenbleiben, Sitzenbleiben, Festsetzen; 3. die Anhäufung, Ansammlung; 4. (*Mil.*) Verschanzung, befestigte Stellung.

lodger ['lɔdʒə], *s.* der (die) (Unter)mieter(in). **lodging,** *s.* das Wohnen, Logieren; die Wohnung, der Wohnsitz; ***night's –,*** das Logis, Nachtquartier, Obdach, die Unterkunft; *pl.* die (Miets)wohnung, möbliertes Zimmer. **lodging-house,** *s.* das Logierhaus, die Pension; ***common –,*** die Herberge.

loess ['louis], *s.* (*Geol.*) der Löß.

loft [lɔft], **1.** *s.* der Boden, Speicher; das Dachgeschoß, der Dachboden, die Dachkammer; ***hanging –,*** der Hängeboden. **2.** *v.t.* hochschlagen (*ball*). **loftiness,** *s.* die Höhe; (*fig.*) Erhabenheit; der Hochmut. **lofty,** *adj.* hoch(ragend), sich auftürmend; (*fig.*) erhaben, hehr, edel; hochmütig.

log [lɔg], **1.** *s.* **1.** der (Holz)klotz, unbehauenes Holz, das Scheit; ***like a –,*** wie ein Klotz; ***– cabin*** or ***hut,*** das Blockhaus, die Blockhütte; 2. (*Naut. etc.*) das Schiffsjournal, Tagebuch, Log. **2.** *v.t.* (*Naut.*) loggen, zurücklegen (*distance*); ins Logbuch eintragen.

logan ['lougən], *s.* (*Geol.*) der Wagstein.

loganberry ['lougənberi], *s.* die Logan-Beere (*Kreuzung von Himbeere und Brombeere*).

logarithm ['lɔgəriðm], *s.* der Logarithmus. **logarithmic** [–'riθmik], *adj.* logarithmisch; ***– tables,*** Logarithmentafeln (*pl.*).

logbook ['lɔgbuk], *s.* (*Naut.*) das Logbuch, Schiffsjournal; (*Av.*) Bordbuch; (*Motor.*) Fahrtenbuch; (*coll.*) Reisetagebuch.

loggerhead ['lɔgəhed], *s.* (*obs.*) der Dummkopf, Schafskopf; ***be at*** or ***fall to –s,*** sich in die Haare kriegen, sich in den Haaren liegen; ***be at –s with,*** in den Haaren liegen mit.

logic ['lɔdʒik], *s.* die Logik; (*fig.*) Folgerichtigkeit. Überzeugungskraft. **logical,** *adj.* logisch, folgerichtig, konsequent. **logician** [–'dʒiʃən], *s.* der Logiker.

logistic [lɔ'dʒistik], *adj.* Rechen–; (*Mil.*) logistisch. **logistics,** *pl.* (*sing. constr.*) der Logikkalkül; (*Mil.*) das Verpflegungswesen, die Logistik.

logogram ['lɔgəgræm], *s.* (*shorthand*) das Wortzeichen, die Sigle. **logomachy** [–ˈgɔməki], *s.* die Wortklauberei, Silbenstecherei.

log|-roll, 1. *v.i.* sich gegenseitig in die Hände arbeiten. **2.** *v.t.* durch Kuhhandel durchbringen. **--rolling,** *s.* der Kuhhandel. **--wood,** *s.* das Kampescheholz, Blauholz.

loin [lɔin], *s.* 1. (*usu. pl.*) die Lende; das Lendenstück (*of meat*); ***roast –,*** der Lendenbraten; ***– of veal,*** der Kalbsnierenbraten; 2. *pl.* (*fig., B.*) die Zeugungskraft. **loin-cloth,** *s.* das Lendentuch.

loiter [ˈlɔitə], **1.** *v.i.* bummeln, schlendern; ***– about,*** herumschlendern. **2.** *v.t.* ***– away,*** verbummeln, vertrödeln. **loiterer,** *s.* der Müßiggänger, Bummler, Faulenzer. **loitering,** *s.* das Herumstehen, Faulenzen.

loll [lɔl], **1.** *v.i.* sich nachlässig lehnen *or* bequem hinstrecken (***upon,*** auf (*Acc.*)), sich rekeln *or* fläzen (auf (*Dat.*)); ***– out,*** heraushängen (*as the tongue*). **2.** *v.t.* (***– out***) heraushängen lassen (*tongue*).

lollipop [ˈlɔlipɔp], *s.* der *or* das Lutschbonbon; *pl.* Bonbons, Süßigkeiten (*pl.*).

lollop [ˈlɔləp], *v.i.* (*coll.*) schwerfällig gehen, watscheln.

lolly [ˈlɔli], *s.* 1. (*coll.*) der *or* das Lutschbonbon; 2. (*sl.*) die Pinke-pinke, Moneten (*pl.*).

Lombardy [ˈlɔmbədi], *s.* die Lombardei.

lone [loun], *attrib. adj.* (*Poet.*) einsam; ***play a – hand,*** für sich *or* auf eigene Faust arbeiten. **loneliness,** *s.* die Einsamkeit, Verlassenheit. **lonely, lonesome,** *adj.* einsam, verlassen. **lonesomeness,** *s. See* **loneliness.**

[1]**long** [lɔŋ], **1.** *adj.* lang (*of space*); lang(dauernd) (*of time*); (*fig.*) (allzu *or* übermäßig) lang, langwierig; (*fig.*) ***– arm,*** weitreichende Macht; (*fig.*) ***as broad as it is –,*** eins wie das andere; (*coll.*) ***not by a – chalk,*** bei weitem nicht; (*Comm.*) ***– date,*** der Wechsel auf lange Sicht; ***pull a – face,*** ein langes Gesicht machen; ***– finger,*** der Mittelfinger; ***– firm,*** die Schwindelfirma; (*Am. sl.*) ***– green,*** das Papiergeld; ***have a – head,*** umsichtig *or* schlau sein; (*obs.*) ***– hundred,*** hundertzwanzig, das Großhundert; ***– journey,*** weite Reise; (*Spt.*) ***– jump,*** der Weitsprung; (*fig.*) ***it is a – lane that has no turning,*** alles muß sich einmal ändern; ***– measure,*** das Längenmaß; ***– memory,*** weitreichendes Gedächtnis; ***– odds,*** schlechte Chance; ***it is – odds he . . .,*** ich möchte hundert gegen eins wetten, daß er . . .; (*Typ.*) ***– primer,*** die Korpus(schrift); ***in the – run,*** auf die Dauer, am Ende, im Endergebnis, letztlich, zuletzt, schließlich; ***– service,*** langjährige Dienstzeit; ***– side,*** die Längsseite; ***– sight,*** die Weitsicht; (*fig.*) der Weitblick; ***of – standing,*** alt(hergebracht), langjährig; (*Cards*) ***– suit,*** lange Farbe; ***for a – time,*** seit langem, schon lange; ***– vacation,*** große Ferien (*pl.*); ***take a – view,*** von höherer Warte aus betrachten; ***– way round,*** großer Umweg; ***for a – while,*** see ***– time***; ***– years of waiting,*** langwierige Jahre des Wartens. **2.** *adv.* lang(e) (*of time*); ***– ago,*** vor langer Zeit; ***not – ago,*** (erst *or* noch) vor kurzem, kürzlich, unlängst; ***all day –,*** den ganzen Tag; ***as – as,*** solange (wie); (voraus)gesetzt daß; ***as – ago as,*** schon; ***be –,*** lange dazu brauchen ((*in*) ***coming,*** (um) zu kommen); ***don't be –!*** mach schnell! ***not – before,*** kurz vorher; ***it was not – before,*** es dauerte nicht lange bis; ***– since,*** see ***– ago***; ***so – as,*** see ***as – as***; (*coll.*) ***so – !*** bis dahin! auf Wiedersehen! **3.** *s.* die Länge; lange Zeit; (*Mus.*) lange Note; (*Metr.*) lange Silbe; ***before –*** (*Poet.* ***ere –***), binnen kurzem, bald; ***for –,*** lange; ***that is the – and the short of it,*** das ist das ganze Geheimnis *or* die ganze Geschichte; ***the – and the short of it is,*** um es kurz zu sagen, kurzum; ***take –,*** lange brauchen.

[2]**long,** *v.i.* verlangen, sich sehnen (***for,*** nach); ***I – to see you,*** ich sehne mich danach *or* mich verlangt (danach), dich zu sehen; ***the –ed-for rest,*** die ersehnte Ruhe.

long|boat, *s.* großes Beiboot, das Großboot. **–bow** [–bou], *s.* der Langbogen; (*coll.*) ***draw the –,*** aufschneiden, angeben, übertreiben. **--clothes,** *pl.* das Tragkleid(chen). **--continued,** *adj.* lange dauernd. **--dated,** *adj.* (*Comm.*) langsichtig (*bill*). **--delayed,** *adj.* lange verzögert. **--distance,** *adj.* (*Spt.*) Langstrecken–, Dauer–; (*Tele., Motor. etc.*) Fern–. **--drawn(-out),** *adj.* (*fig.*) ausgedehnt, lang hin(aus)gezogen, langatmig.

longe, *see* [2]**lunge.**

long-eared, *adj.* langohrig; (*Orn.*) ***– owl,*** die Waldohreule (*Asio otus*).

longer [ˈlɔŋgə], *comp. adj., adv.* länger, mehr; ***no –,*** nicht mehr *or* länger; ***no – ago than yesterday,*** erst gestern; ***not any –,*** see ***no –.***

longeron [ˈlɔndʒərɔn], *s.* (*Av.*) der Rumpf(längs)-holm.

longest [ˈlɔŋgist], **1.** *sup. adj.* längst. **2.** *sup. adv.* am längsten; ***at the –,*** längstens, spätestens.

longevity [lɔnˈdʒeviti], *s.* die Langlebigkeit.

long|hand, *s.* die Kurrentschrift; ***in –,*** mit der Hand geschrieben. **--headed,** *adj.* langköpfig, langschädelig; (*fig.*) umsichtig, schlau, gescheit. **–horn,** *s.* langhörniges Rind.

longing [ˈlɔŋiŋ], **1.** *adj.* sehnsüchtig, schmachtend. **2.** *s.* die Sehnsucht, das Verlangen (***for,*** nach).

longish [ˈlɔŋiʃ], *adj.* ziemlich *or* etwas lang, länglich.

longitude [ˈlɔndʒitju:d], *s.* (geographische) Länge; ***degree of –,*** der Längengrad. **longitudinal** [–ˈtju:dinl], *adj.* (*Geog.*) Längen–; (*Geom. etc.*) Längs–. **longitudinally,** *adv.* der Länge nach.

long|-legged, *adj.* langbeinig. **–lived,** *adj.* langlebig. **--playing,** *adj.* Langspiel– (*record*). **--range,** *adj.* weittragend, Fernkampf– (*gun*), (*Av.*) Langstrecken–, (*Rad.*) Weit–, weitreichend, (*fig.*) auf weite Sicht (*planning*). **–shoreman,** *s.* der Hafenarbeiter, Schauermann. **--sighted,** *adj.* weitsichtig, fernsichtig; (*fig.*) weitblickend, scharfsichtig, umsichtig; (*Comm.*) langsichtig. **--sightedness,** *s.* die Weitsicht(igkeit); (*fig.*) der Weitblick. **--standing,** *adj.* alt(hergebracht). **--suffering, 1.** *adj.* langmütig. **2.** *s.* die Langmut. **--term,** *adj.* (*Comm.*) langfristig, auf lange Sicht.

longueur [lɔ̃ˈgə:], *s.* (*oft. pl.*) (*fig.*) die Länge, langweilige Stelle.

long|ways, *adv.* der Länge nach. **--winded,** *adj.* (*usu. fig.*) langatmig, weitschweifig, langweilig. **--windedness,** *s.* die Langatmigkeit, Weitschweifigkeit. **–wise,** *adv. See* **–ways.**

[1]**loo** [lu:], **1.** *s.* das Luspiel. **2.** *v.t.* (beim Luspiel) alle Stiche machen.

[2]**loo,** *s.* (*sl.*) der Lokus, das Klo.

loofah [ˈlu:fə], *s.* der Luffaschwamm.

look [luk], **1.** *v.i.* 1. (*of p.*) schauen, blicken, (hin)-sehen, (*coll.*) gucken (***at*** *or* ***on,*** auf (*Acc.*) *or* nach); 2. (*of p. and th.*) aussehen, scheinen; 3. (*of th.*) liegen, sehen, gerichtet sein (***towards,*** nach).

(a) (*with adjs. etc.*) (*coll.*) ***– alive!*** see ***– sharp! things – bad,*** die Lage sieht schlecht aus; ***– before you leap!*** erst wägen dann wagen! erst besinn's, dann beginn's! ***– one's best,*** vorteilhaft aussehen, sich am besten zeigen; (*fig.*) ***– black,*** (*of th.*) finster *or* düster aussehen, (*of p.*) düster blicken; ***– blank,*** verblüfft *or* verständnislos dreinsehen; (*fig.*) (*of p.*) ***– blue,*** traurig *or* trübe dreinschauen; ***– like,*** aussehen wie, den Anschein haben; ***it –s like rain,*** es sieht nach Regen aus; ***I – like missing the train,*** es sieht so aus, als ob ich den Zug verpasse; ***– much better for,*** besser aussehen infolge; ***– here!*** passen Sie auf! hören Sie mal! ***– the other way,*** wegblicken (*of p.*), nach der anderen Richtung zeigen (*of th.*); ***– the part,*** danach aussehen; ***– and see!*** überzeugen Sie sich! (*coll.*) ***– sharp! – smart!*** nun aber los! ***– small,*** klein aussehen, (*fig. of a p.*) entlarvt werden; (*coll.*) ***– you!*** sieh! sehen Sie mal!

(b) (*with advs.*) ***– about,*** sich umsehen (***for,*** nach); (*fig.*) ***– ahead,*** Vorsorge treffen; ***– back,*** sich umsehen, (*fig.*) zurückblicken (***on,*** auf (*Acc.*)); ***after that he never –ed back,*** danach hielt er nicht mehr ein; ***– down,*** herabsehen, heruntersehen; die Augen niederschlagen; (*fig.*) herabsehen, herabblicken (***on,*** auf (*Acc.*)); ***– forward to s.th.,*** etwas (*Dat.*) erwartungsvoll entgegensehen, sich auf eine S. freuen; ***– in,*** vorsprechen, einen kurzen

Besuch machen ((*up*)*on*, bei); – *on*, zuschauen, zusehen (*at*, bei); – *out*, (*a p.*) hinaussehen (*through*, *of*, *at*, aus *or* zu); (*coll.*) sich vorsehen, aufpassen; (*a th.*) einen Ausblick haben *or* gewähren (*on*, auf (*Acc.*) *or* nach); – *out!* Vorsicht! Achtung! gib acht! – *out for*, ausschauen *or* Ausschau halten *or* sich umsehen nach; (*coll.*) gefaßt sein *or* sich gefaßt machen auf (*Acc.*); – *round*, sich umsehen; – *up*, (hin)aufblicken, (hin)aufsehen, (hin)aufschauen; (*coll. Comm.*) sich bessern, einen Aufschwung nehmen; (*of prices, trade*) steigen, anziehen; – *up to*, als Muster ansehen, aufblicken zu.
(c) (*with preps.*) – ***about one***, um sich sehen, sich umsehen; – ***after***, nachsehen, nachblicken (*Dat.*); (*fig.*) aufpassen *or* achten auf (*Acc.*); sorgen für, sich kümmern um; – ***at***, ansehen, anblicken, anschauen, betrachten; – ***at the facts***, die Tatsachen beachten *or* ins Auge fassen; ***to – at him you would think . . .***, dem Ausschauen nach würde man von ihm meinen . . .; (*coll.*) ***he wouldn't – at it***, er wollte nichts davon wissen; – ***down one's nose at***, ein verdrießliches Gesicht machen über (*Acc.*); – ***for***, suchen (nach), sich umsehen nach; (*fig.*) entgegensehen (*Dat.*), erwarten; – ***into***, (hinein)sehen *or* (hinein)blicken in (*Acc.*); (*fig.*) nachgehen (*Dat.*), untersuchen, prüfen; – ***on***, ansehen, betrachten; (*of windows etc.*) (hinaus)gehen auf (*Acc.*); – ***on the bright side (of things)***, das Leben von der heiteren Seite nehmen; – ***over***, blicken über (*Acc.*); – ***through***, sehen *or* blicken durch; (hin)durchsehen durch; (*fig.*) hinwegsehen über (*Acc.*), ignorieren, wie Luft behandeln (*a p.*); – ***to***, aufpassen *or* achten *or* achthaben *or* bedacht sein auf (*Acc.*), sich kümmern um; zählen *or* sich verlassen auf (*Acc.*) (*a p.*) (***for***, wegen); rechnen mit, erwarten, erhoffen (*results etc.*); (*of buildings*) gerichtet sein nach, liegen nach; – ***to it that . . .!*** achte darauf *or* sieh zu *or* sorge dafür, daß . . .! – ***upon***, see – ***on***.
(d) (*with nouns*) ***he doesn't – his age***, man sieht ihm sein Alter nicht an; – ***a fool***, wie ein Narr aussehen; (*coll*) – ***a sight***, einen lächerlichen Anblick darbieten.
2. *v.t.* – ***daggers at***, mit Blicken durchbohren; – ***death in the face***, dem Tod ins Angesicht sehen; – ***him in the eye*** or ***face***, ihm in die Augen *or* ins Gesicht sehen; – ***a gift horse in the mouth***, einem geschenkten Gaul ins Maul sehen; – ***one's last at***, zum letztenmal ansehen; (*with advs.*) – ***out***, (her)aussuchen; – ***over***, (über)prüfen, durchsehen, durchgehen (*a th.*), mustern (*a p.*); – ***through***, durchsehen, durchlesen, durchblättern (*book etc.*), mit Blicken durchbohren (*a p.*); – ***up***, nachschlagen, nachsuchen (*in a book*); (*coll.*) aufsuchen, einen kurzen Besuch machen bei (*a p.*); – ***him up and down***, ihn von oben bis unten mustern.
3. *s.* 1. der Blick (*at*, auf (*Acc.*) *or* nach); ***cast a – at***, einen Blick werfen auf (*Acc.*); (*coll.*) ***have a – at***, sich (*Dat.*) ansehen; ***have a good –***, genau *or* richtig nachsehen; ***have a good – at***, genau *or* prüfend ansehen; (*coll.*) ***have a – round***, sich (*Dat.*) mal umschauen; ***if –s could kill***, wenn Blicke töten könnten; 2. das Aussehen, die Miene, der Gesichtsausdruck; ***hang-dog –***, die Galgenmiene; ***I do not like the –*** (*coll.* ***–s***) ***of it***, es gefällt mir gar nicht; ***wear a – of***, aussehen wie.

looker ['lukə], *s.* 1. der (die) Beschauer(in), Schauende(r); 2. (*usu.* ***good–***) gut aussehende P., fescher Kerl. **looker-on**, *s.* der (die) Zuschauer(in) (***at***, bei).

look-in, *s.* (*coll.*) die Aussicht, (Gewinn)chance; ***not get a –***, keine Chance haben.

looking ['lukiŋ], *adj. suff.* –aussehend. **looking-glass**, *s.* der Spiegel.

look-out, *s.* 1. (*also* – ***post***) der Aussichtspunkt, Beobachtungsstand, Ausguck, (*Naut.*) das Krähennest; 2. (*also* – ***man***) der Wächter, Beobachtungsposten, die Wache; 3. Aussicht, der Ausblick (***over***, über (*Acc.*)); 4. (*coll.*) die Ausschau, Wacht; ***be on the –***, Ausschau halten (***for***, nach); (*fig.*) ***keep a*** (***good***) – ***for***, auf der Hut sein vor (*Dat.*), (scharf) aufpassen auf (*Acc.*); 5. (*coll.*) Aussichten (*pl.*); (*coll.*) ***poor –***, schlechte Aussichten; (*coll.*) ***that's your*** (***own***) –, darum mußt du dich selbst kümmern, das ist deine Angelegenheit *or* Sache.

looks [luks], *pl.* (*only in*) ***good –***, die Schönheit, Stattlichkeit.

[1]**loom** [lu:m], *s.* 1. der Webstuhl, die Webmaschine; 2. (*Elec.*) der Isolierschlauch.

[2]**loom, 1.** *v.i.* undeutlich erscheinen *or* auftauchen, undeutlich sichtbar werden, (drohend) aufragen; (*fig.*) – ***large***, sich drohend auftürmen *or* erheben. **2.** *s.* (*usu. Naut.*) (undeutliches) Sichtbarwerden *or* Auftauchen.

[1]**loon** [lu:n], *s.* (*Am. Orn.*) *see* **diver.**

[2]**loon,** *s.* der Tölpel, Lümmel; (*Scots*) Bursche, Bengel.

loony ['lu:ni], **1.** *s.* (*coll.*) Verrückte(r). **2.** *adj.* übergeschnappt, plemplem. **loony-bin,** *s.* (*sl.*) die Klapsmühle.

[1]**loop** [lu:p], **1.** *s.* die Schlinge, Schleife; Schlaufe, Öse; (*of a river*) Windung, Schleife; (*Railw.*) *see* – ***line***; (*Av.*) der Überschlag, das *or* der Looping; (*Av.*) ***loop the –***, einen Looping drehen; – ***antenna***, die Rahmenantenne; – ***knot***, einfacher Knoten; – ***line***, die Schleife(nabzweigung); – ***stitch***, die Masche. **2.** *v.t.* in Schleifen *or* in eine Schleife legen, schlingen, eine Schlinge machen in (*Acc.*); (*Av.*) – ***the loop***, *see under* **1**; – ***back***, zurückbinden; – ***up***, aufbinden, aufstecken (*hair*), aufschürzen (*dress*). **3.** *v.i.* Schleifen *or* eine Schleife machen, sich winden, eine Schlinge bilden.

[2]**loop,** *s.* (*Metall.*) die Luppe, der Deul.

looper ['lu:pə], *s.* (*Ent.*) die Spannerraupe; (*Sew.-mach.*) der Schlaufenfadenführer. **loophole** [–houl], **1.** *s.* (*Fort.*) die Schießscharte, der Sehschlitz, das Guckloch; (*fig.*) das Schlupfloch, die Ausflucht, der Ausweg, die Hintertür; – ***in the law***, die Lücke des Gesetzes. **2.** *v.t.* mit Schießscharten versehen.

loopy ['lu:pi], *adj.* (*sl.*) übergeschnappt, verrückt.

loose [lu:s], **1.** *adj.* 1. los(e), frei; ***break –***, losbrechen, abbrechen (*of a th.*), ausreißen, ausbrechen (*from prison*); ***come*** or ***get –***, sich losmachen; losgehen; ***let –***, loslassen; Luft machen (*Dat.*) (*feelings*); 2. locker, schlaff, weit (*as a dress*), lose hängend, fliegend (*as hair*); unverpackt, lose *or* nicht verpackt (*of goods*); ***hang –***, schlaff hängen; ***work –***, sich lockern (*as a screw etc.*); – ***bowels***, flüssiger Stuhlgang; – ***change***, das Kleingeld; – ***collar***, loser Kragen; (*Elec.*) – ***contact***, der Wackelkontakt; (*fig.*) – ***ends***, Kleinigkeiten (*pl.*); (*coll.*) ***at a – end***, ohne feste Beschäftigung; – ***ice***, offenes Eis; – ***leaf***, versetzbares Blatt (*in note-book*); – ***money***, see – ***change***; ***he has a screw –***, bei ihm ist eine Schraube los; – ***soil***, lockerer Boden; – ***tongue***, lose Zunge; – ***tooth***, loser *or* lockerer Zahn; 3. einzeln, zusammenhang(s)los, verstreut; (*fig.*) unklar, unbestimmt, unlogisch, ungenau (*ideas etc.*); – ***talk***, gewissenloses Gerede; – ***thinking***, unklares *or* wirres Denken; – ***translation***, freie Übersetzung; 4. liederlich, locker (*of p.*); (*coll.*) – ***fish***, lockerer Vogel; (*coll.*) ***play fast and – with***, Schindluder treiben mit. **2.** *v.t.* lösen, befreien, freimachen (***from***, von); losmachen, losbinden, (*knot etc.*) lösen, aufmachen, aufbinden; loslassen, freilassen, laufen lassen; – ***one's hold of*** or ***on***, loslassen, fahren lassen; – ***off***, losschießen, abschießen, abfeuern (*a shot etc.*). **3.** *v.i.* den Anker lichten, absegeln. **4.** *s.* (*sl.*) ***go on the –***, sumpfen.

loose|-box, *s.* (*Railw.*) der Stallabteil. **–-leaf,** *adj.* – ***binder***, der Schnellhefter; – ***note-book***, das Einlegeheft. **loosen** [lu:sn], **1.** *v.t.* losmachen, freimachen, losbinden (*a string etc.*); locker machen, (auf)lockern (*earth*); öffnen (*bowels*); lösen (*tongue, cough*). **2.** *v.i.* sich lösen *or* lockern, locker werden. **looseness,** *s.* die Lockerheit, Schlaffheit; (*fig.*) Unklarheit, Ungenauigkeit; Laxheit, Liederlichkeit; (*Med.*) der Durchfall.

loosestrife ['lu:sstraif], *s.* (*Bot.*) der Weiderich, das Pfennigkraut.

loot [lu:t], **1.** *v.i.* plündern. **2.** *v.t.* plündern (*town* etc.), ausplündern (*a p.*), erbeuten (*goods*). **3.** *s.* die (Kriegs)beute, das Raubgut; *see also* **looting. looter,** *s.* der Plünderer. **looting,** *s.* die Plünderung.

[1]**lop** [lɔp], *v.t.* beschneiden, (zu)stutzen (*trees*); – ***off,*** abhauen, abschneiden.

[2]**lop, 1.** *v.t.* herabhängen lassen. **2.** *v.i.* schlaff herunterhängen; – ***about,*** herumlungern.

lope [loup], **1.** *v.i.* mit leichten Schritten gehen *or* (*of horse*) kantern. **2.** *s.* leichter Kanter.

lop|-eared, *adj.* mit Hängeohren. **--ears,** *pl.* Hängeohren (*pl.*).

loppings [ˈlɔpiŋz], *pl.* abgehauene Zweige (*pl.*). **lopping-shears,** *pl.* die Baumschere.

lopsided [lɔpˈsaidid], *adj.* nach einer Seite hängend, schief; gekrängt, unsymmetrisch; (*fig.*) einseitig.

loquacious [louˈkweiʃəs], *adj.* geschwätzig, redselig, schwatzhaft. **loquaciousness, loquacity** [–ˈkwæsiti], *s.* die Geschwätzigkeit, Redseligkeit, Schwatzhaftigkeit.

lord [lɔːd], **1.** *s.* 1. der Herr, Gebieter; ***the –s of creation,*** die Herren der Schöpfung; 2. (*Poet.*) der Gemahl, Eheherr; ***my – and master,*** mein Herr und Gebieter; 3. der Feudalherr, Lehensherr; – ***of the manor,*** der Grundherr; 4. der Peer, Adlige(r); der Lord (*as title*); (*Parl.*) ***the –s,*** das Oberhaus; ***–s spiritual*** (***temporal***), geistliche (weltliche) Mitglieder des Oberhauses; (*coll.*) ***drunk as a –,*** voll wie eine Strandkanone; ***the House of Lords,*** das Oberhaus; ***live like a –,*** wie ein Fürst leben; ***my Lord!*** gnädiger Herr! Mylord! 5. (*coll.*) der Magnat; 6. ***the Lord,*** Gott der Herr; ***the Lord's Day,*** der Tag des Herrn; ***good Lord!*** du lieber Gott! ach Gott! ***the Lord of Hosts,*** der Herr der Heerscharen, Herr Zebaoth; ***Our Lord,*** Christus; ***the Lord's Prayer,*** das Vaterunser; ***the Lord's Supper,*** heiliges Abendmahl; ***in the year of Our Lord,*** im Jahre des Herrn; (*coll.*) ***Lord knows where,*** weiß Gott wo, weiß der Himmel wo. **2.** *v.i.* (*coll.*) – ***it,*** den großen Herrn spielen, gebieterisch auftreten; – ***it over,*** sich als Herr aufspielen gegenüber, herumkommandieren.

Lord| Advocate, *s.* (*Scots*) der Generalstaatsanwalt. **– Chamberlain,** *s.* der Haushofmeister. – **Chief Justice,** *s.* der Lordoberrichter. – **High Commissioner,** *s.* der Oberkommissar. – **Lieutenant,** *s.* der Vizekönig, Gouverneur; Vertreter des Königs (*of a country*).

lordliness [ˈlɔːdlinis], *s.* die Hoheit, Würde, Vornehmheit; Pracht, der Glanz; die Großmut, Großzügigkeit; Anmaßung, der Hochmut. **lordling,** *s.* das Herrchen. **lordly,** *adj.* vornehm, edel, großmütig, großzügig; prächtig, großartig; stolz, herrisch, anmaßend, gebieterisch, hochmütig.

Lord| Mayor, *s.* der Oberbürgermeister; ***–'s Show,*** der Festzug des neuerwählten Oberbürgermeisters von London. – **President,** *s.* der Präsident des Geheimen Staatsrats. – **Privy Seal,** *s.* der Lordsiegelbewahrer. – **Protector,** *s.* (*Hist.*) der Reichsverweser. – **Provost,** *s.* (*Scots*) der Oberbürgermeister.

lords-and-ladies, *see* **cuckoo-pint.**

lordship [ˈlɔːdʃip], *s.* die Herrschaft; (*Hist.*) das Herrschaftsgebiet; (*as address*) ***Your Lordship,*** Euer Gnaden.

lore [lɔː], *s.* die Lehre, Kunde, Überlieferung, überliefertes Wissen.

lorgnette [lɔːˈnjet], *s.* die Lorgnette, Stielbrille.

loricate [ˈlɔrikeit], *adj.* (*Zool.*) gepanzert, Panzer–.

lorn [lɔːn], *adj.* (*obs.*) einsam, verlassen.

Lorraine [loˈrein], *s.* Lothringen (*n.*).

lorry [ˈlɔri], *s.* das Lastauto, der Last(kraft)wagen; (*Railw.*) die Lore, Lori; (*Build., Min.*) der Kipper; ***lorried infantry,*** motorisierte Infanterie.

lose [luːz], **1.** *irr.v.t.* 1. verlieren; verwirken, einbüßen, kommen um, verlustig gehen (*Gen.*), verlegen; 2. vergeuden, verschwenden (*time etc.*); 3. zurückbleiben, nachgehen (*as a watch*); 4. loswerden, befreit werden von (*headache etc.*); 5. verpassen, versäumen (*train etc.*).

(a) (*with nouns*) ***I lost his answer in the noise,*** ich überhörte *or* mir entging seine Antwort bei dem Lärm; – ***one's bearings,*** sich verirren, die Orientierung verlieren; – ***colour,*** abfärben; (*fig.*) – ***the day,*** den Kampf verlieren; – ***face,*** den guten Ruf verlieren; – ***all fear,*** alle Furcht ablegen; – ***ground,*** (an) Boden verlieren, (zurück)weichen; (*fig.*) (an) Einfluß verlieren (***with,*** bei); – ***one's hair,*** das Haar verlieren; – ***one's head,*** enthauptet *or* geköpft werden, (*fig.*) den Kopf verlieren; – ***heart,*** den Mut sinken lassen; – ***one's heart to,*** sein Herz verlieren an (*Acc.*); (*Av.*) – ***height,*** absacken; – ***one's hold of,*** loslassen, fahren lassen; – ***one's labour,*** sich (*Dat.*) unnütze Mühe geben, sich (*Acc.*) umsonst plagen; – ***one's life,*** sein *or* das Leben verlieren; – ***one's mind,*** den Verstand verlieren; – ***a minute a day,*** täglich eine Minute nachgehen; – ***an opportunity,*** sich (*Dat.*) eine Gelegenheit entgehen lassen, eine Gelegenheit vorbeigehen lassen; – (***one's***) ***patience,*** die Geduld verlieren; – ***sight of,*** aus den Augen verlieren; – ***one's temper,*** heftig *or* wütend *or* hitzig *or* ärgerlich werden, in Zorn geraten; – ***no time,*** keine Zeit verlieren; – ***one's voice,*** heiser werden; – ***one's way,*** sich verirren.

(b) (*causative*) um den Verlust bringen, bringen um; kosten; ***that will – you your job,*** das wird dich um deine Stellung bringen.

(c) (*passive*) ***be lost,*** verlorengehen (*also of a ship*); verschwinden (*of a th.*); sich verirrt haben, (*also fig.*) sich nicht mehr zurechtfinden (*of a p.*); untergehen, den Tod finden (*of a p.*); ***be lost in,*** versunken *or* vertieft sein in (*Dat.*); ***be lost to,*** bar sein (*Gen.*), nicht mehr empfindlich sein für; ***be lost upon,*** keinen Eindruck machen *or* keine Wirkung ausüben auf (*Acc.*), erfolglos sein bei; ***it won't be lost upon him,*** das wird er sich schon merken.

(d) (*refl.*) – ***o.s.,*** den Weg verlieren, sich verirren; sich verlieren (*also fig.*) (***in,*** in (*Dat.*)).

2. *irr.v.i.* verlieren (***in,*** an (*Dat.*)); Verluste *or* Einbuße erleiden (***by,*** durch); geschlagen werden, den kürzeren ziehen; nachgehen (*as a watch*); (*Spt.*) – ***to a team,*** einer Mannschaft unterliegen; ***what I – on the swings I gain on the roundabouts,*** ich halte mich schadlos.

loser [ˈluːzə], *s.* der (die) Verlierer(in), Verlierende(r); ***be a – by,*** Schaden *or* Einbuße erleiden durch; ***come off a –,*** den kürzeren ziehen. **losing,** *adj.* verlierend; (*Comm.*) verlustbringend, unrentabel; – ***game,*** aussichtsloses Unternehmen; (*Bill.*) – ***hazard,*** der Verläufer. **losings,** *pl.* (Spiel)verluste (*pl.*).

loss [lɔs], *s.* der Verlust, Nachteil, Schaden (***to,*** für), die Einbuße, der Ausfall, Abgang (***in,*** an (*Dat.*)); (*Insur.*) Schadensfall; ***at a –,*** mit *or* unter Verlust; ***be at a – for,*** verlegen *or* in Verlegenheit sein um; ***be at a – to . . .,*** nicht . . . können; – ***of appetite,*** die Appetitlosigkeit; – ***of blood,*** der Blutverlust; (*Mil.*) ***combat –es,*** Gefechtsausfälle (*pl.*); (*coll.*) ***dead –,*** totaler Verlust; ***cut one's –es,*** weitere Verluste verhüten; – ***of memory,*** die Amnesie; – ***of power,*** der Leistungsabfall; – ***of time,*** der Zeitverlust; – ***through shrinkage,*** die Zehrung.

lost [lɔst], *adj.* verloren(gegangen), (da)hin; zugrunde gegangen; verirrt; verschwunden; verschwendet, vergeudet; ***give up as*** or ***for –,*** verloren geben; – ***cause,*** aussichtslose S.; – ***heat,*** die Abwärme; – ***motion,*** toter Gang, der Leerlauf; – ***property office,*** (*Am.*) – ***and found,*** das Fundbüro; *see also* **lose, 1. (c).**

lot [lɔt], **1.** *s.* 1. das Los (*also fig.*); (*fig.*) Geschick, Schicksal; ***by –,*** durch Losen, durch das Los; ***cast*** or ***draw –s,*** losen (***for,*** um); ***it falls to my –,*** es fällt mir (das Los) zu; ***throw in one's – with,*** das Los teilen mit; 2. (*Comm.*) der Posten, die Partie; ***in –s,*** partienweise, in Einzelposten; 3. (*of land*) das Stück Land, die Parzelle; ***building –,*** der Bauplatz, die Baustelle; 4. (*coll.*) die Menge, Masse, ganze Gruppe *or* Gesellschaft, der Haufen; (*coll.*) ***the –,*** alle(s), das Ganze; ***is that the –?*** ist das alles? sind das alle? ***a – more,*** viel *or* beträchtlich mehr; ***a – of, –s of,*** eine Menge *or* Masse, ein

Haufen; sehr viel(e); ***the whole –***, die ganze Sippschaft; 5. (*sl.*) der Kerl; ***bad –***, fauler Kunde. **2.** *v.t.* (*– **out***) 1. durch Los zuteilen *or* zuweisen; 2. (*land*) in Parzellen teilen, parzellieren.

loth, *adv. See* **loath.**

lotion ['louʃən], *s.* das Waschmittel, Hautwasser; ***shaving –***, das Rasierwasser.

lottery ['lɔtəri], *s.* die Lotterie; (*fig.*) das Lotteriespiel, die Glückssache. **lottery-ticket,** *s.* das Lotterielos.

lotto ['lɔtou], *s.* das Lotto(spiel).

lotus ['loutəs], *s.* der Lotos, die Lotusblume; der Lotusklee, Steinklee, Hornklee. **lotus-eater,** *s.* der Lotosesser, Genüßling.

loud [laud], *adj.* laut; lärmend, geräuschvoll; (*fig.*) schreiend, grell, aufdringlich, auffallend (*as colours*). **loudness,** *s.* die Lautheit, der Lärm; (*Rad.*) die Lautstärke; (*fig.*) das Schreiende, Auffallende. **loudspeaker,** *s.* (*Rad.*) der Lautsprecher.

lough [lɔx], *s.* (*Irish*) der See; Meerbusen, Meeresarm.

lounge [laundʒ], **1.** *s.* 1. die Diele, Halle, der Gesellschaftsraum, das Foyer; 2. die Chaiselongue. **2.** *v.i.* müßiggehen, faulenzen, lungern; sich rekeln, faul herumliegen; *– **about***, herumlungern. **3.** *v.t.* *– **away***, vertrödeln (*one's time*). **lounge|-chair,** *s.* der Klubsessel. **--coat,** *s.* der Sakko. **--lizard,** *s.* (*sl.*) der Salonlöwe. **lounger,** *s.* der Faulenzer, Müßiggänger. **lounge-suit,** *s.* der Straßenanzug.

lour [lauə], *v.i.* drohend *or* finster blicken ((***up***)***on***, ***at***, auf (*Acc.*)); (*fig.*) düster werden, sich verfinstern (*of sky*); finster aussehen, drohen (*of events*). **louring,** *adj.* düster, finster, drohend.

louse [laus], **1.** *s.* (*pl.* **lice** [lais]) die (Kopf)laus. **2.** *v.t.* (*sl.*) *– **up***, vermurksen, verderben. **lousiness** [-zinis], *s.* die Verlaustheit; (*fig. sl.*) Lausigkeit, Gemeinheit. **lousy** [-zi], *adj.* verlaust; (*fig. sl.*) lausig, gemein; ***be – with money***, im Geld schwimmen.

lout [laut], *s.* der Tölpel, Lümmel. **loutish,** *adj.* tölpelhaft, lümmelhaft, flegelhaft. **loutishness,** *s.* die Tölpelhaftigkeit.

louver, louvre ['lu:və], *s.* 1. (*Archit.*) durchbrochenes Türmchen, das Dachfenster; 2. der Kühlschlitz, Lüftungsschieber.

lovable ['lʌvəbl], *adj.* liebenswürdig, liebenswert. **lovableness,** *s.* die Liebenswürdigkeit.

lovage ['lʌvidʒ], *s.* (*Bot.*) das Liebstückel.

love [lʌv], **1.** *s.* 1. die Liebe (***of, for, to***(***wards***), zu); ***– of one's country***, die Vaterlandsliebe; ***– of glory***, die Ruhmsucht; ***–'s labours lost***, verlorene Liebesmüh; ***be in – with***, verliebt sein in (*Acc.*); ***fall in – with***, sich verlieben in (*Acc.*); ***for*** (***the***) ***– of***, aus Liebe zu; ***for the – of God***, um Gottes willen; ***give my – to your sister***, grüße deine Schwester herzlich von mir; ***make – to***, den Hof machen (*Dat.*), hofieren; ***not for – or money***, nicht für Geld und gute Worte; ***play for –***, um die Ehre spielen; ***send one's – to***, herzlich grüßen lassen; ***there is no – lost between them***, sie haben für einander nichts übrig; 2. die Liebschaft; 3. der Schatz, das Liebchen; (*coll.*) ***a – of a dress***, ein allerliebstes Kleid; ***my –***, mein Liebes; 4. der Amor, Liebesgott; 5. (*Tenn.*) null, nichts; ***– all!*** beide null! ***four*** (***to***) ***–***, vier gegen nichts. **2.** *v.t.* lieben, liebhaben (*a p.*), lieben, gern haben *or* mögen; Gefallen *or* Vergnügen finden an (*Dat.*) (*a th.*); (*coll.*) ***– doing*** or ***to do***, gern tun, mit Vergnügen tun. **3.** *v.i.* lieben.

love|-affair, *s.* die Liebschaft, das Liebesverhältnis, der Liebeshandel. **--apple,** *s.* (*obs.*) die Tomate. **--bird,** *s.* (*Orn.*) der Sperlingspapagei. **--child,** *s.* das Kind der Liebe, uneheliches Kind. **--game,** *s.* (*Tenn.*) das Nullspiel. **--in-a-mist,** *s.* (*Bot.*) das Kapuzinerkraut. **--in-idleness,** *s.* (*Bot.*) das Stiefmütterchen. **--knot,** *s.* der Liebesknoten, die Liebesschleife.

loveless ['lʌvlis], *adj.* lieblos. **love|-letter,** *s.* der Liebesbrief. **--lies-bleeding,** *s.* (*Bot.*) Roter Fuchsschwanz. **loveliness,** *s.* die Lieblichkeit, der Reiz, die Schönheit; (*coll.*) Herrlichkeit; Köstlichkeit. **love|lock,** *s.* die Schmachtlocke. **--lorn,** *adj.* vom Liebchen verlassen; in Liebeskummer schmachtend. **lovely,** *adj.* allerliebst, lieblich, entzückend, reizend, wunderschön; (*coll.*) herrlich, köstlich. **love|-making,** *s.* das Lieben, Hofieren, Hofmachen, Kurmachen. **--match,** *s.* die Liebesheirat. **--philtre, --potion,** *s.* der Liebestrank.

lover ['lʌvə], *s.* der Liebhaber, Geliebte(r), Liebste(r), *pl.* Liebende (*pl.*), das Liebespaar; ***–'s knot***, *see* **love-knot. love|-set,** *s.* (*Tenn.*) die Nullpartie. **-sick,** *adj.* liebeskrank. **--song,** *s.* das Liebeslied. **--story,** *s.* die Liebesgeschichte. **--token,** *s.* das Liebeszeichen, Liebespfand.

loving ['lʌviŋ], *adj.* liebend, Liebes-, zärtlich, liebevoll; *– **care***, liebevolle Fürsorge; *– **kindness***, das Wohlwollen, die Barmherzigkeit, Herzensgüte; ***in – memory***, in liebendem Gedenken (***of***, an (*Acc.*)); (*in letters*) ***your – mother***, deine dich liebende Mutter. **loving-cup,** *s.* der Liebesbecher, Freundschaftsbecher, Umtrunkbecher.

[1]**low** [lou], **1.** *adj., adv.* 1. niedrig; tief, nieder (*of rank*); ***bring him –***, ihn zu Fall bringen; ***lay –***, besiegen, stürzen; demütigen; (*sl.*) ***lie –***, sich versteckt halten; (*fig.*) nichts unternehmen, abwarten; nichts verraten; *– **birth***, niedere Geburt; *– **bow***, tiefe Verneigung; *– **frequency***, (*Elec.*) die Niederfrequenz, (*Rad.*) Tonfrequenz; (*Motor.*) *– **gear***, erster Gang; *– **ground***, das Tiefland; *– **life***, das Leben der unteren Stände; *– **pressure***, der Niederdruck, Unterdruck, (*Meteor.*) Tiefdruck; (*Elec.*) *– **tension***, die Niederspannung; (*fig.*) ***be in – water***, auf dem trocknen sitzen, schlecht bei Kasse sein; ***the sun is – on the horizon***, die Sonne steht tief am Horizont; 2. schwach, leise (*as sound etc.*); 3. seicht (*as water*); *– **tide***, *– **water***, niedrigste Ebbe, das Niedrigwasser; 4. niedergeschlagen, gedrückt (*as the spirits*); ***feel –***, in gedrückter Stimmung sein, sich krank fühlen; *– **spirits***, die Niedergeschlagenheit, Gedrücktheit, gedrückte Stimmung; 5. mäßig, billig, wohlfeil (*of price*); ***be –***, niedrig stehen; 6. gemein, gewöhnlich, ordinär, vulgär, niederträchtig, roh (*of p.*); *– **comedy***, der Schwank, das Possenspiel; 7. tief ausgeschnitten (*as a dress*); *– **neck***, tiefer Ausschnitt; 8. gering(schätzig), ungünstig, minderwertig (*of opinion etc.*); *– **opinion***, geringe Meinung; 9. knapp; (*coll.*) ***be running –***, zur Neige gehen, knapp werden; ***the sands are running –***, die Zeit *or* es geht zu Ende. **2.** *adv.* 1. tief; *– **down***, tief unten; ***fall –***, tief fallen; 2. leise (*of sound*).

[2]**low,** **1.** *v.i.* brüllen, muhen. **2.** *s.* das Brüllen, Muhen.

low|-born, *adj.* von niedriger Geburt, aus niederem Stande. **--bred,** *adj.* unfein, ordinär, ungebildet, gemein. **--brow,** **1.** *adj.* geistig anspruchslos. **2.** *s.* geistig Anspruchslose(r), der Spießer. **Low| Church,** *s.* puritanische Richtung der anglikanischen Kirche. **--church,** *adj.* puritanisch (gesinnt). **– Countries,** *pl.* die Niederlande. **low-down,** **1.** *adj.* (*coll.*) niederträchtig; gemein; *– **trick***, die Gemeinheit. **2.** *s.* (*sl.*) unverblümte Wahrheit, wahre Tatsachen (*pl.*).

[1]**lower** ['louə], **1.** *comp. adj.* 1. tiefer, niedriger; 2. (*only attrib.*) unter, nieder; Unter-; (*Typ.*) *– **case***, der Unterkasten; Kleinbuchstaben; *– **classes***, untere *or* niedere Klassen; *– **deck***, das Unterdeck; ***Lower House***, das Unterhaus; ***the – regions***, die Hölle, Unterwelt; *– **school***, die Unterstufe; *– **sixth***, die Unterprima. **2.** *comp. adv.* tiefer; leiser (*of sound*).

[2]**lower,** **1.** *v.t.* niederlassen, herunterlassen, herablassen; niederholen, streichen (*flag*), fieren, zu Wasser bringen *or* setzen (*boats*); niederschlagen, senken, sinken lassen (*the eyes*); (*fig.*) herabsetzen, mäßigen, verringern, abschwächen; erniedrigen (*a p., also Mus.*); senken, ermäßigen, herabsetzen (*prices*); drücken (*records*); *– **o.s.***, sich herablassen *or* demütigen; *– **one's voice***, leise(r) sprechen. **2.** *v.i.* sinken, fallen, sich senken, heruntergehen; (*fig.*) sinken, abnehmen, sich verringern *or* vermindern *or* mäßigen.

[3]**lower** ['lauə], *see* **lour.**

Lower|Austria, *s.* Niederösterreich (*n.*). – **Egypt,** *s.* Unterägypten (*n.*).

lowermost ['louəmoust], **1.** *adj.* niedrigst. **2.** *adv.* am niedrigsten. **lowest** ['louist], *sup. adj.* tiefst, unterst; – ***bidder,*** Mindestbietende(r); (*Math.*) – ***common multiple,*** kleinstes gemeinsames Vielfaches.

Low German, *s.* 1. das Niederdeutsch; 2. Plattdeutsch.

lowland ['loulənd], *s.* das Tiefland, die Niederung; ***the Lowlands,*** das schottische Tiefland. **Lowlander,** *s.* der Tieflandschotte.

Low Latin, *s.* das Spätlatein.

lowliness ['loulinis], *s.* die Bescheidenheit, Demut; Einfachheit; Niedrigkeit (*of station*). **lowly,** *adj.* niedrig, gering; demütig, bescheiden, einfach.

low-lying, *adj.* flach. **Low Mass,** *s.* stille Messe. **low|-minded,** *adj.* niedrig *or* gemein gesinnt. **--necked,** *adj.* tief ausgeschnitten (*dress*).

lowness ['lounis], *s.* die Niedrigkeit, Tiefe (*of sound, price etc.*); – ***of spirits,*** die Niedergeschlagenheit.

low|-pass filter, *s.* (*Rad.*) die Spulenkette, Hochfrequenz-Sperrkette. **--pitched,** *adj.* schwach geneigt, flach (*as a roof*); tief(tönend) (*as a sound*). **--pressure,** *adj.* (*Tech.*) Unterdruck–, (*Meteor.*) Tiefdruck–. **--spirited,** *adj.* gedrückt, niedergeschlagen, verzagt, mutlos. **Low Sunday,** *s.* Weißer Sonntag. **low|-temperature,** *adj.* (*Tech.*) Ur–. **--tension, --voltage,** *adj.* Niederspannungs–, Schwachstrom–; (*Rad.*) – ***battery,*** die Heizbatterie. **--water mark,** *s.* niedrigster Wasserstand; (*fig.*) der Tiefstand, Tiefpunkt. **--wing monoplane,** *s.* der Tiefdecker.

loyal ['lɔiəl], *adj.* 1. (*Pol.*) treu(ergeben), loyal; – ***demonstration,*** patriotische Kundgebung; – ***toast,*** der Trinkspruch auf Herrscher und Herrscherhaus; 2. (*fig.*) (ge)treu (***to,*** *Dat.*); 3. zuverlässig, rechtschaffen, bieder, redlich. **loyalist,** *s.* Treugesinnte(r). **loyalty,** *s.* die Treue, Loyalität (***to,*** zu *or* gegen).

lozenge ['lɔzindʒ], *s.* (*Geom., Her.*) die Raute, der Rhombus; (*Med.*) die Pastille, Tablette. **lozenge-shaped,** *adj.* rautenförmig.

lubber ['lʌbə], *s.* der Lümmel, Flegel, Tölpel, Tolpatsch; (*Naut.*) unbefahrener Seemann; (*also* ***land--***) die Landratte. **lubber-line,** *s.* der Steuerstrich (*of a compass*). **lubberly,** *adj.* tölpelhaft, plump, tolpatschig.

lubricant ['l(j)u:brikənt], *s.* das Schmiermittel. **lubricate** [–keit], *v.t.* schmieren, ölen. **lubrication** [–'keiʃən], *s.* das Schmieren, Ölen, die Einschmierung, Einölung. **lubricator** [–keitə], *s.* der Öler, die Schmierbüchse.

lubricity [l(j)u:'brisiti], *s.* die Schlüpfrigkeit; Unbeständigkeit (*of fortune*); (*fig.*) Lüsternheit, Geilheit.

luce [l(j)u:s], *s.* (ausgewachsener) Hecht.

lucency ['l(j)u:sənsi], *s.* der Glanz. **lucent,** *adj.* glänzend, leuchtend, klar.

Lucerne [lu:'sə:n], *s.* Luzern; ***Lake of –,*** der Vierwaldstättersee.

lucid ['l(j)u:sid], *adj.* (*usu. fig.*) klar, deutlich; (*Poet.*) hell, licht, glänzend, leuchtend; – ***intervals,*** lichte Augenblicke; – ***mind,*** heller Geist. **lucidity** [–'siditi], **lucidness,** *s.* (*usu. fig.*) die Klarheit, Deutlichkeit, Verständlichkeit; Klarheit, Helligkeit (*of mind*).

Lucifer ['lu:sifə], *s.* (*Myth.*) Luzifer (*m.*).

lucifer, *s.* (*obs.*) das Streichholz.

luciferous [l(j)u:'sifərəs], *adj.* leuchtend, lichtspendend. **lucifugous** [–'sifəgəs], *adj.* lichtscheu.

luck [lʌk], *s.* das Glück, Schicksal, Geschick; der Zufall, die (Schicksals)fügung; ***bad –,*** das Unglück, (*coll.*) Pech; (*coll.*) ***be down on one's –,*** vom Glück verlassen *or* vom Pech verfolgt sein, an seinem Glück verzagen; ***keep it for –,*** es als Glückbringer behalten; ***good –,*** das Glück, (*coll.*) Schwein; ***by good –,*** glücklicherweise; ***with (good) –,*** wenn man Glück hat, glücklichenfalls; ***good –!*** viel Glück! (*coll.*) ***hard –,*** see ***bad –***; ***as – would have it,*** wie es der Zufall *or* das Schicksal (haben) wollte, (un)glücklicherweise; ***ill –,*** see ***bad –***; ***be in –,*** Schwein haben; ***just my –!*** so geht es mir immer! ***be out of –,*** Pech haben; ***piece of –,*** großes Glück; ***run of good –,*** andauerndes Glück; (*coll.*) ***tough –!*** see ***worse –! try one's –,*** sein Glück versuchen; (*coll.*) ***worse –!*** Pech! leider!

luckily ['lʌkili], *adv.* zum Glück, glücklicherweise; – ***for him,*** zu seinem Glück. **luckiness,** *s.* das Glück. **luckless,** *adj.* erfolglos, glücklos, unglücklich. **lucklessness,** *s.* die Erfolglosigkeit, Glücklosigkeit, das Unglück. **lucky,** *adj.* glücklich; glückbringend, günstig, Glücks–; ***be –,*** Glück haben; – ***bag, – dip,*** der Glückstopf; – ***dog*** or ***fellow,*** der Glückspilz; – ***for him!*** er kann von Glück reden *or* sagen! – ***hit,*** der Zufallstreffer, (*fig.*) Glücksfall.

lucrative ['l(j)u:krətiv], *adj.* einträglich, gewinnbringend, rentabel. **lucre** ['l(j)u:kə], *s.* der Gewinn, Vorteil; die Profitgier, Gewinnsucht, Habsucht; (*sl.*) ***filthy –,*** Moneten (*pl.*), das Blech, der Kies, das Moos.

lucubrate ['l(j)u:kju:breit], *v.i.* bei Nachtlicht arbeiten. **lucubration** [–'breiʃən], *s.* gelehrte Nachtarbeit; (*usu. pl.*) gelehrte Abhandlungen.

ludicrous ['l(j)u:dikrəs], *adj.* lächerlich, absurd, albern; drollig, possierlich. **ludicrousness,** *s.* die Lächerlichkeit; Possierlichkeit.

ludo ['l(j)u:dou], *s.* Mensch ärgere dich nicht (*n.*).

lues ['lu:i:z], *s.* die Syphilis.

luff [lʌf], **1.** *s.* (*Naut.*) die Luv(seite), Windseite; das Vorliek (*of sail*). **2.** *v.t.* an den Wind bringen (*ship*). **3.** *v.i.* (– ***up***) anluven, aufluven.

[1]**lug** [lʌg], *v.t.* (*sl.*) schleppen, schleifen, zerren; (*fig.*) – ***in,*** an den Haaren herbeiziehen.

[2]**lug,** *s.* (*Tech.*) der Henkel, das Öhr; der Ansatz, Zapfen, die Zinke, Knagge, Warze; (*Scots or sl.*) das Ohr.

[3]**lug,** *see* **lugsail.**

luge [lu:ʒ], **1.** *s.* der Schlitten. **2.** *v.i.* rodeln.

luggage ['lʌgidʒ], *s.* (*no pl.*) das Gepäck; ***free –,*** das Freigepäck; ***heavy –,*** großes Gepäck; ***light –,*** das Handgepäck; ***register the –,*** das Gepäck aufgeben.

luggage|-carrier, *s.* (*Cycl.*) der Gepäckträger. **--grid,** *s.* (*Motor.*) die Kofferbrücke. **--insurance,** *s.* die Reisegepäckversicherung. **--locker,** *s.* das Gepäckschließfach. **--office,** *s.* die Gepäckabfertigung(sstelle), der Gepäckschalter. **--rack,** *s.* (*Railw.*) das Gepäcknetz. **--train,** *s.* der Güterzug. **--van,** *s.* der Gepäckwagen.

lugger ['lʌgə], *s.* (*Naut.*) der Lugger, Logger. **lugsail,** *s.* das Luggersegel.

lugubrious [lu'gju:briəs], *adj.* traurig, kummervoll. **lugubriousness,** *s.* die Traurigkeit, das Traurige.

lugworm ['lʌgwə:m], *s.* der Köderwurm.

Luke [lu:k], *s.* (*B.*) (das Buch) Lukas.

lukewarm ['lu:kwɔ:m], *adj.* lau(warm); angewärmt, (*fig.*) lau, gleichgültig. **lukewarmness,** *s.* die Lauwärme; (*fig.*) Lauheit, Gleichgültigkeit.

lull [lʌl], **1.** *v.t.* einschläfern, einlullen; (*fig.*) beschwichtigen, beruhigen, überreden (*a p.*) (***into,*** zu); – ***to sleep,*** einschläfern. **2.** *v.i.* sich beruhigen, sich legen, nachlassen (*of wind*). **3.** *s.* die Ruhepause, Stille (*also fig.*); vorübergehende Windstille, die Flaute; (*fig.*) Stockung; – ***in the conversation,*** die Gesprächspause.

lullaby ['lʌləbai], *s.* das Wiegenlied, Schlummerlied, Schlaflied.

lumbago [lʌm'beigou], *s.* der Hexenschuß.

lumbar ['lʌmbə], *adj.* (*Anat.*) Lenden–, lumbal; – ***puncture,*** die Lumbalpunktion.

[1]**lumber** ['lʌmbə], **1.** *s.* 1. das Gerümpel, der Plunder, (Trödel)kram; 2. (*esp. Am.*) behauenes Bauholz, das Nutzholz. **2.** *v.t.* (– ***up***) überladen, belasten, vollstopfen (*a room etc.*).

[2]**lumber,** *v.i.* poltern, rumpeln; (– ***along***) sich hinschleppen *or* schwerfällig fortbewegen. **lumbering,** *adj.* rumpelnd, polternd; schwerfällig, plump, schleppend.

lumber|jack, *s.* der Holzarbeiter, Holzfäller.

--jacket, *s.* der Lumberjack. **–man,** *s. See* **–jack.** **--mill,** *s.* die Sägemühle. **--room,** *s.* die Rumpelkammer. **–yard,** *s.* der Holzplatz.

lumen ['lju:mən], *s.* die Lichteinheit, das Lumen.

luminary ['l(j)u:minəri], *s.* leuchtender Körper, der Lichtkörper, (*Astr.*) Himmelskörper; (*fig.*) die Leuchte (*a p.*). **luminescence** [–'nesəns], *s.* die Lichterregung, Lichtausstrahlung. **luminescent** [–'nesənt], *adj.* lichterregend, lichtausstrahlend. **luminosity** [–'nɔsiti], *s.* die Helligkeit, Lichtstärke; das Leuchten, der Glanz. **luminous** [–nəs], *adj.* leuchtend, strahlend, glänzend, Leucht–; (*fig.*) hell, klar, licht; lichtvoll; *– dial,* das Leuchtzifferblatt; *– paint,* die Leuchtfarbe; *– ray,* der Lichtstrahl.

lump [lʌmp], **1.** *s.* 1. der Klumpen, Knollen; *a – came in my throat,* mir war die Kehle wie zugeschnürt; *– of gold,* der Goldklumpen; 2. das Stück; *– sugar,* der Würfelzucker; *two –s of sugar,* zwei Stück Zucker; 3. (*Metall.*) die Luppe, der Deul; 4. (*Med.*) die Beule, Schwellung; 5. (*fig.*) Masse, Gesamtheit; *in the –,* in Bausch und Bogen, im ganzen; (*coll.*) *all of a –,* alles auf einmal; *– sum,* die Pauschalsumme; 6. (*coll.*) grober *or* plumper Mensch. **2.** *v.t.* (*– together*) zusammenwerfen, in einen Topf *or* auf einen Haufen werfen, über einen Kamm scheren; zusammenfassen, pauschalieren (*under,* unter (*Dat.*)); (*sl.*) *if you don't like it you can – it,* wenn dir's nicht paßt, mußt du dich (wohl oder übel) damit abfinden.

lumper ['lʌmpə], *s.* der Hafenarbeiter, Löscharbeiter.

lumpish ['lʌmpiʃ], *adj.* klotzig, schwerfällig, unbeholfen, plump; stumpf, träge, stur. **lumpy,** *adj.* klumpig; unruhig, bewegt (*of sea*).

lunacy ['lu:nəsi], *s.* der Irrsinn, Wahnsinn; (*Law*) die Unzurechnungsfähigkeit; (*coll.*) Verrücktheit, große Dummheit.

lunar ['l(j)u:nə], *adj.* Mond–; (*fig.*) blaß, schwach; *– caustic,* der Höllenstein; *– month,* der Mondmonat.

lunatic ['lu:nətik], **1.** *adj.* geisteskrank, geistesgestört, wahnsinnig, irrsinnig; (*coll.*) verrückt, blödsinnig. **2.** *s.* Geistesgestörte(r), Irrsinnige(r), Wahnsinnige(r); *– asylum,* die Irrenanstalt; (*coll.*) *– fringe,* Übereifrige, Extremisten (*pl.*).

lunation [l(j)u:'neiʃən], *s.* der Mondumlauf, synodischer Monat.

lunch [lʌntʃ], **1.** *s.* der Lunch, das Mittagessen; zweites Frühstück, das Gabelfrühstück. **2.** *v.i.* zu Mittag essen. **lunch-counter,** *s.* die Imbißstube. **luncheon** ['lʌntʃən], *s.* formelle Mittagsmahlzeit; *– basket,* der Speisekorb. **lunch-hour,** *s.* die Mittagspause.

lune [l(j)u:n], *s.* (*Geom.*) halbmondförmige Figur. **lunette** [–'net], *s.* (*Archit.*) das Halbkreisfeld, Bogenfeld, die Lünette; (*Fort.*) Brillschanze.

lung [lʌŋ], *s.* (*Anat.*) der Lungenflügel; *pl.* die Lunge; (*fig.*) Grünfläche (*of towns*); *have good –s,* eine kräftige Stimme haben; *inflammation of the –s,* die Lungenentzündung.

[1]**lunge** [lʌndʒ], **1.** *s.* (*Fenc., Gymn.*) der Ausfall; Stoß, Angriff. **2.** *v.i.* ausfallen, einen Ausfall machen (*at,* gegen); *– out,* ausschlagen (*at,* auf (*Acc.*)).

[2]**lunge, 1.** *s.* die Longe, Laufleine. **2.** *v.t.* longieren.

lung|fish, *s.* der Lungenfisch. **–wort,** *s.* das Lungenkraut.

[1]**lupin(e)** ['lu:pin], *s.* (*Bot.*) die Lupine, Wolfsbohne.

[2]**lupine** ['l(j)u:pain], *adj.* wölfisch, Wolfs–.

lupus ['l(j)u:pəs], *s.* der Lupus, die Hauttuberkulose.

[1]**lurch** [lə:tʃ], *s.* (*only in*) *leave in the –,* im Stiche lassen.

[2]**lurch, 1.** *s.* (*Naut.*) das Überholen, plötzliches Schlingern *or* Umlegen *or* Rollen; (*fig.*) der Ruck; das Taumeln, Torkeln. **2.** *v.i.* schlingern (*of ships*); taumeln, torkeln (*of persons*).

lurcher ['lə:tʃə], *s.* der Spürhund.

lure [ljuə], **1.** *s.* der Köder, die Lockspeise (*also fig.*); (*fig.*) der Reiz, Zauber. **2.** *v.t.* ködern, (an)locken; (*fig.*) verlocken, verführen (*into,* zu).

lurid ['ljuərid], *adj.* helleuchtend, grell (*of colours*); (*fig.*) gespenstisch, unheimlich, grausig; (*Bot.*) fahlgelb.

lurk [lə:k], **1.** *v.i.* lauern, auf der Lauer liegen; (*fig.*) sich verstecken, sich versteckt halten, verborgen liegen. **2.** *s. on the –,* auf der Lauer. **lurking, 1.** *s.* das Verstecken, Lauern, die Lauer; *--place,* das Versteck, der Hinterhalt, Schlupfwinkel. **2.** *adj.* versteckt, heimlich, schlummernd.

Lusatia [lu:'seiʃə], *s.* die Lausitz. **Lusatian, 1.** *s.* der (die) Lausitzer(in). **2.** *adj.* lausitzisch.

luscious ['lʌʃəs], *adj.* saftig; lecker, köstlich; übersüß, süßlich. **lusciousness,** *s.* die Saftigkeit; Köstlichkeit, Leckerheit; Süße, Süßigkeit, Süßlichkeit.

lush [lʌʃ], *adj.* saftig, üppig (*of plants*); (*fig.*) überladen (*with,* mit), überreich (an (*Dat.*)). **lushness,** *s.* die Üppigkeit; Überladenheit.

lust [lʌst], **1.** *s.* sinnliche Begierde, die Wollust, Sinnlichkeit; (*fig.*) Gier, Sucht, das Gelüste, leidenschaftliches Verlangen (*after, of, for,* nach). **2.** *v.i.* begehren (*for, after, Acc.*), verlangen (nach); gelüsten (*imp., Acc. of p.*) (nach).

luster, (*Am.*) *see* **lustre.**

lustful ['lʌstful], *adj.* lüstern, wollüstig, geil. **lustfulness,** *s.* die Lüsternheit, Geilheit.

lustiness ['lʌstinis], *s.* die Rüstigkeit, Stärke, Energie, Lebenskraft.

lustral ['lʌstrəl], *adj.* Reinigungs–, Weih–. **lustrate** [–eit], *v.t.* reinigen. **lustration** [–'treiʃən], *s.* die Reinigung; (*Eccl.*) das Reinigungsopfer.

lustre ['lʌstə], *s.* 1. der Glanz (*also Min. and fig.*), Schein, Schimmer; 2. Kronleuchter; 3. (*fabric*) Lüster. **lustreless,** *adj.* glanzlos, matt.

lustring ['lʌstriŋ], *s.* der Glanztaft, Lustrin. **lustrous,** *adj.* glänzend, strahlend (*also fig.*), leuchtend.

lustrum ['lʌstrəm], *s.* das Lustrum, Jahrfünft.

lusty ['lʌsti], *adj.* rüstig, (tat)kräftig; energisch, frisch, lebhaft.

lutanist ['l(j)u:tənist], *s.* der Lautenspieler.

[1]**lute** [l(j)u:t], *s.* (*Mus.*) die Laute; *rift in the –,* die Verstimmung.

[2]**lute, 1.** *s.* 1. der Kitt; 2. Dichtungsring. **2.** *v.t.* 1. verkitten; 2. dichten.

lutestring ['l(j)u:tstriŋ], *s. See* **lustring.**

Lutheran ['lu:θərən], **1.** *s.* der Lutheraner. **2.** *adj.* luther(an)isch. **Lutheranism,** *s.* das Luthertum.

luting ['l(j)u:tiŋ], *s. See* [2]**lute, 1.**

lutist ['l(j)u:tist], *s. See* **lutanist.**

luxate [lʌk'seit], *v.t.* ausrenken, verrenken. **luxation** [–ʃən], *s.* die Verrenkung.

luxe [lʌks], *s.* (*only in*) *de –,* Luxus–, Pracht–.

Luxembourg ['lʌksəmbə:g], *s.* Luxemburg (*n.*).

luxuriance, luxuriancy [lʌg'zjuəriəns(i)], *s.* die Üppigkeit, Fülle, der Überfluß, Reichtum (*of,* an (*Dat.*)). **luxuriant,** *adj.* üppig, wuchernd, (*fig.*) reich, fruchtbar; überschwenglich, verschnörkelt, schwülstig, blütenreich (*as style*). **luxuriate** [–eit], *v.i.* üppig leben *or* wachsen *or* gedeihen, wuchern; sich ergehen, schwelgen (*in,* in (*Dat.*)). **luxurious,** *adj.* schwelgerisch, genußsüchtig, verschwenderisch (*a p.*), üppig, prächtig, luxuriös, Luxus– (*of furniture etc.*). **luxuriousness,** *s. See* **luxury,** 1.

luxury ['lʌkʃəri], *s.* 1. der Luxus, Überfluß, das Wohlleben; die Üppigkeit, Pracht, der Aufwand; *live in –,* im Überfluß leben; *in the lap of –,* im Schoß des Glückes; 2. (*oft. pl.*) der Luxusartikel, das Genußmittel.

lyceum [lai'siəm], *s.* das Lyzeum; die Bildungsanstalt; literarische Gesellschaft; (*Am.*) die Volkshochschule.

lychnis ['liknis], *s.* (*Bot.*) die Lichtnelke.

lycopodium [laikə'poudiəm], *s.* der Bärlapp; *– powder,* der Bärlappsamen.

lye [lai], **1.** *s.* die Lauge. **2.** *v.t.* mit Lauge behandeln.

¹lying ['laiiŋ], **1.** *adj.* lügnerisch, lügenhaft, verlogen. **2.** *s.* das Lügen. *See* **¹lie.**

²lying, 1. *adj.* liegend. **2.** *s.* das Liegen; – ***in state,*** öffentliche Aufbahrung. *See* **²lie. lying|-in,** *s.* das Wochenbett, Kindbett; – ***hospital,*** die Entbindungsanstalt. **--to,** *s.* (*Naut.*) das Beiliegen.

lymph [limf], *s.* (*Anat.*) die Lymphe, das Blutwasser; (*Med.*) der Impfstoff; (*Poet.*) das Quellwasser. **lymphatic** [–'fætik], **1.** *adj.* lymphatisch, Lymph–; (*fig.*) blutlos, schlapp; – ***gland,*** der Lymphknoten; – ***system,*** das Lymphgefäßsystem. **2.** *s.* (*usu. pl.*) das Lymphgefäß. **lymphocyte** [–əsait], *s.* das Lymphkörperchen.

lynch [lintʃ], *v.t.* lynchen. **lynch-law,** *s.* die Lynchjustiz, Volksjustiz.

lynx [liŋks], *s.* der Luchs. **lynx-eyed,** *adj.* luchsäugig.

Lyons ['laiənz, 'li:ɔ̃], *s.* Lyon (*n.*).

lyre ['laiə], *s.* die Leier, (*Antiqu.*) Lyra. **lyre-bird,** *s.* der Leierschwanz.

lyric ['lirik], **1.** *adj.* lyrisch. **2.** *s.* lyrisches Gedicht; *pl.* die Lyrik; (*Mus.*) der (Lied)text. **lyrical,** *adj.* lyrisch, liedartig. **lyricism** [–sizm], *s.* lyrischer Stil *or* Charakter; der Gefühlsausdruck. **lyricist,** *s.* der (Schlager)texter. **lyrist,** *s.* lyrischer Dichter, der Lyriker.

lysol ['laisəl], *s.* das Lysol.

M

M, m [em], *s.* das M, m. *See Index of Abbreviations.*

ma [mɑ:], *s.* (*coll.*) *See* **mam(m)a.**

ma'am [mæm], *s.* *See* **madam.**

macabre [mə'kɑ:br], *adj.* schrecklich, grauenhaft, grausig, gruselig.

macaco [mə'keikou], *s.* (*Zool.*) der Maki, Lemur.

macadam [mə'kædəm], **1.** *s.* der Schotter; die Schotterdecke. **2.** *adj.* Schotter–. **macadamize,** *v.t.* makadamisieren, beschottern.

macaroni [mækə'rouni], *s.* die Makkaroni (*oft. pl.*). **macaronic** [–'rɔnik], *adj.* makkaronisch, gemischtsprachig (*poetry*).

macaroon [mækə'ru:n], *s.* die Makrone.

macaw [mə'kɔ:], *s.* 1. (*Orn.*) der Keilschwanzsittich; 2. (*Bot.*) Macawbaum, die Macahubapalme.

Maccabee [mækə'bi:], *s.* (*B.*) der Makkabäer. **Maccabean,** *adj.* makkabäisch.

¹mace [meis], *s.* der Amtsstab; (*Hist.*) Streitkolben, die (Kriegs)keule; – ***bearer,*** der Zepterträger.

²mace, *s.* die Muskatblüte.

Macedonia [mæsi'douniə], *s.* Mazedonien (*n.*). **Macedonian, 1.** *s.* der Mazedonier. **2.** *adj.* mazedonisch.

macerate ['mæsəreit], *v.t.* einweichen, aufweichen, erweichen; entkräften, abzehren, ausmergeln, abhärmen, kasteien. **maceration** [–'reiʃən], *s.* die Einweichung; (*fig.*) Entkräftung, Abzehrung, Ausmergelung, Abhärmung, Kasteiung.

Machiavellian [mækiə'veliən], *adj.* machiavellistisch.

machicolation [mætʃikə'leiʃən], *s.* (*Fort.*) die Pechnasenreihe, Gußlochreihe, der Gußerker.

machinate ['mækineit], *v.i.* Ränke schmieden, intrigieren. **machination** [–'neiʃən], *s.* die Machenschaft; Anstiftung, Anzettelung; (*usu. pl.*) Machenschaften, Umtriebe, Ränke (*pl.*). **machinator,** *s.* der Ränkeschmied, Intrigant.

machine [mə'ʃi:n], **1.** *s.* die Maschine; Vorrichtung, der Mechanismus, Apparat; (*coll.*) das Fahrrad, Flugzeug *etc.*; (*fig.*) der Apparat, die Maschinerie (*of government etc.*). **2.** *v.t.* maschinell bearbeiten.

machine|-gun, 1. *s.* das Maschinengewehr. **2.** *v.t.* mit dem Maschinengewehr beschießen. **--made,** *adj.* maschinell hergestellt, Fabrik–, Maschinen–.

machinery [mə'ʃi:nəri], *s.* die Maschinerie, Apparatur, der Mechanismus, das (Trieb)werk, Getriebe; Maschinen (*pl.*); (*fig.*) *see* **machine** (*fig.*).

machine|-shop, *s.* die Maschinenwerkstatt. **--tool,** *s.* die Werkzeugmaschine. **–twist,** *s.* die Nähmaschinenseide. **machinist,** *s.* der Maschinenbauer; Maschinenschlosser, (*also Theat.*) Maschinist.

Mach number [mɑ:k], *s.* die Mach-Zahl.

macintosh, *see* **mackintosh.**

mackerel ['mækərəl], *s.* die Makrele. **mackerel|-shark,** *s.* der Heringshai. **--sky,** *s.* der Schäfchenhimmel.

mackintosh ['mækintɔʃ], *s.* der Regenmantel.

mackle [mækl], **1.** *v.t.* (*Typ.*) schmitzen, doppelt drucken, duplieren; ***–d sheets,*** der Ausschuß. **2.** *s.* (*Typ.*) der Schmitz, Doppeldruck, verwischter Druck; der Makel, (Schand)fleck.

macrocosm ['mækrəkɔzm], *s.* das Weltall, der Makrokosmos.

macron ['mækrən], *s.* das Längezeichen.

macula ['mækjulə], *s.* der Klecks, (Schmutz)fleck; (*Astr.*) Sonnenfleck. **macular,** *adj.* fleckig, gefleckt. **maculation** [–'leiʃən], *s.* die Befleckung, Beschmutzung; (*Bot. Zool.*) Musterung, Zeichnung.

mad [mæd], *adj.* verrückt, wahnsinnig, toll, irre; (*Vet.*) tollwütig; (*fig.*) verrückt, sinnlos, unsinnig; (*coll.*) überspannt; wütend (***at, about,*** über *or* auf (*Acc.*)); wild, verrückt, erpicht, versessen (***on, about,*** auf (*Acc.*)), vernarrt (in (*Acc.*)); wahnsinnig, rasend, außer sich (***with,*** vor (*Dat.*)); ***drive him –,*** ihn um den Verstand bringen; ***it's enough to drive you –,*** es ist zum Verrücktwerden; ***go –,*** verrückt werden; (*coll.*) ***as – as a hatter*** or ***a March hare,*** ganz übergeschnappt; (*coll.*) ***like –,*** wie toll *or* verrückt.

Madagascan [mædə'gæskən], **1.** *s.* der Madagasse (die Madagassin). **2.** *adj.* madagassisch. **Madagascar,** *s.* Madagaskar (*n.*).

madam ['mædəm], *s.* gnädige Frau, gnädiges Fräulein.

madcap ['mædkæp], **1.** *s.* der Wildfang. **2.** *adj.* ausgelassen, übermütig. **madden** [mædn], **1.** *v.t.* rasend *or* toll machen. **2.** *v.i.* rasend werden. **maddening,** *adj.* aufreizend; ***it is –,*** es ist zum Verrücktwerden.

¹madder ['mædə], *comp. adj. See* **mad.**

²madder, *s.* (*Bot.*) der Krapp; Krappfarbstoff, die Färberröte.

maddest ['mædist], *sup. adj. See* **mad.**

made [meid], **1.** *imperf., p.p. of* **make. 2.** *adj.* gemacht; gebaut, hergestellt, zusammengesetzt; – ***in England,*** in England hergestellt; – ***ground,*** neu gewonnenes Land; – ***man,*** gemachter Mann; – ***to measure,*** nach Maß; – ***up,*** fertig, Fertig–, Konfektions– (*clothes*); zusammengestellt, Fabriks– (*articles*); (*fig.*) erfunden, erdichtet, erdacht (*story*), geschminkt (*complexion*); – (***up***) ***of,*** bestehend aus.

mad|-headed, *adj.* (*fig.*) wahnsinnig, tollköpfig. **–house,** *s.* das Irrenhaus; (*fig.*) Tollhaus, Narrenhaus. **madly,** *adv.* wie toll *or* verrückt; (*coll.*) schrecklich, wahnsinnig. **madman,** *s.* Verrückte(r), Tolle(r), Wahnsinnige(r). **madness,** *s.* die Verrücktheit, Tollheit, der Wahnsinn; (*coll.*) die Narrheit, Torheit.

madrepore ['mædrəpɔ:], *s.* die Steinkoralle.

madrigal ['mædrigəl], *s.* das Madrigal.

maelstrom ['meilstrəm], *s.* der Wirbel, Strudel, Sog.

Mae West ['mei'west], *s.* aufblasbare Schwimmweste.

mafficking ['mæfikiŋ], *s.* der Siegestaumel, patriotische Ausgelassenheit, das Johlen.
magazine [mægə'zi:n], *s.* 1. das Magazin (*also of rifle*), Warenlager, die Niederlage, (*usu.*) das Pulvermagazin, Munitionslager; 2. (illustrierte) Zeitschrift. **magazine-rifle,** *s.* das Schnellfeuergewehr, Mehrladegewehr.
magdalen ['mægdəlin], *s.* die Büßerin, reuige Sünderin.
mage [meidʒ], *s.* (*obs.*) der Magier.
magenta [mə'dʒentə], **1.** *s.* das Magenta(rot), Fuchsin. **2.** *adj.* magentarot.
maggot ['mægət], *s.* die Made, Larve; (*fig.*) Grille, Schrulle. **maggoty,** *adj.* madig; (*fig.*) grillenhaft, schrullig.
magi ['meidʒai], *pl. of* **magus.**
magic ['mædʒik], **1.** *s.* die Magie, Zauberei; Zauberkraft, der Zauber; (*coll.*) das Wunder. **2.** *adj.* magisch, zauberisch, Zauber–; (*Rad.*) – ***eye,*** die Abstimmglimmröhre; – ***lantern,*** die Zauberlaterne; Laterna magica; ***under a – spell,*** verzaubert; – ***wand,*** der Zauberstab. **magical,** *adj. See* **magic, 2**; zauberhaft, bezaubernd. **magician** [–'dʒiʃən], *s.* der Zauberer, Magier, Schwarzkünstler; Zauberkünstler, Taschenspieler.
magisterial [mædʒis'tiəriəl], *adj.* richterlich, obrigkeitlich; (*fig.*) maßgebend; gebieterisch, herrisch, diktatorisch, anmaßend.
magistracy ['mædʒistrəsi], *s.* obrigkeitliches Amt; die Magistratur, Obrigkeit; obrigkeitliche Beamten (*pl.*). **magistral,** *adj.* (*Pharm.*) eigens verschrieben, nicht offizinell. **magistrate** [–eit], *s.* obrigkeitlicher *or* richterlicher Beamter; der Friedensrichter, Polizeirichter.
magma ['mægmə], *s.* das Magma, dünnflüssiger Brei; (*Geol.*) der Glutbrei.
magnanimity [mægnə'nimiti], *s.* die Großmut, der Edelmut; die Großmütigkeit, Edelmütigkeit. **magnanimous** [–'næniməs], *adj.* großmütig, edelmütig, hochherzig.
magnate ['mægneit], *s.* der Magnat.
magnesia [mæg'ni:ziə], *s.* die Magnesia, das Magnesiumoxyd; – ***hydrate,*** die Bittererde; – ***limestone,*** der Bitterkalk, Dolomit. **magnesium,** *s.* das Magnesium.
magnet ['mægnit], *s.* der Magnet (*also fig.*). **magnetic** [–'netik], *adj.* magnetisch; (*fig.*) fesselnd, anziehend; – ***compass,*** der Magnetkompaß, die Bussole; – ***course,*** mißweisender Kurs; – ***declination,*** – ***variation,*** die Mißweisung; – ***deviation,*** die Fehlweisung; – ***needle,*** die Magnetnadel; – ***tape,*** das Tonband. **magnetics,** *pl.* (*sing. constr.*) die Lehre vom Magnetismus. **magnetism,** *s.* der Magnetismus; (*fig.*) die Anziehungskraft. **magnetization** [–ai'zeiʃən], *s.* die Magnetisierung. **magnetize,** *v.t.* magnetisieren; (*fig.*) anziehen, fesseln.
magneto [mæg'ni:tou], *s.* magnetelektrische Maschine; der Magnetapparat, Magnetzünder, (Zünd)magnet. **magneto|-electric,** *adj.* magnetelektrisch. **--generator,** *s.* der Kurbelinduktor.
magnetron ['mægnətrɔn], *s.* das Magnetron.
Magnificat [mæg'nifikæt], *s.* der Lobgesang (Mariens).
magnification [mægnifi'keiʃən], *s.* (*Opt.*) die Vergrößerung(sstärke); (*Rad.*) Verstärkung; (*fig.*) Verherrlichung.
magnificence [mæg'nifisəns], *s.* die Großartigkeit, Herrlichkeit, Pracht, der Glanz. **magnificent,** *adj.* herrlich, prachtvoll, prächtig, glänzend; (*coll.*) ausgezeichnet, großartig.
magnifier ['mægnifaiə], *s.* das Vergrößerungsglas. **magnify,** *v.t.* vergrößern (*also fig.*); (*fig.*) übertreiben; (*obs.*) verherrlichen; ***–ing glass,*** das Vergrößerungsglas, die Lupe.
magniloquence [mæg'niləkwəns], *s.* die Großsprecherei; der Bombast, Schwulst. **magniloquent,** *adj.* großsprecherisch, prahlerisch, ruhmredig; bombastisch, schwülstig, hochtrabend.
magnitude ['mægnitju:d], *s.* die Größe (*also Math., Astr.*), der Umfang, das Ausmaß; die Wichtigkeit, Bedeutung; (*fig.*) ***of the first –,*** von äußerster Wichtigkeit.
magnolia [mæg'nouliə], *s.* die Magnolie.
magnum ['mægnəm], *s.* große Flasche (*2 quarts*).
magpie ['mægpai], *s.* (*Orn.*) die Elster (*Pica pica*); (*fig.*) der (die) Schwätzer(in), das Plappermaul; (*coll.*) zweiter Ring von außen (*of a target*).
magus ['meigəs], *s.* (*pl.* **magi** [–dʒai]) der Magier, Zauberer; (*Antiqu.*) (persischer) Zauberpriester; (*B.*) ***the (three) Magi,*** die (drei) Weisen aus dem Morgenlande, die Heiligen Drei Könige.
Magyar ['mægjɑ:], **1.** *s.* der Madjar, Ungar. **2.** *adj.* madjarisch, ungarisch.
maharaja [mɑ:hə'rɑ:dʒə], *s.* indischer Großfürst. **maharani** [–ni:], *s.* die Gemahlin eines indischen Großfürsten.
mahlstick, *s. See* **maulstick.**
mahogany [mə'hɔgəni], *s.* der Mahagonibaum; das Mahagoni(holz); ***have one's feet under his –,*** bei ihm zu Tisch sein, seine Gastfreundschaft genießen.
Mahomet [mə'hɔmit], *s.* Mohammed (*m.*).
mahout [mə'haut], *s.* der Elefantentreiber.
maid [meid], *s.* (junges) Mädchen; das (Dienst)mädchen, die Hausangestellte, Magd; (*Poet.*) Jungfrau; – ***of honour,*** die Hofdame, Ehrendame; (*Am.*) Brautführerin, Brautjungfer; ***Maid of Orleans,*** die Jungfrau von Orleans; (*coll.*) ***old –,*** alte Jungfer; ***--of-all-work,*** das Mädchen für alles.
maiden [meidn], **1.** *s.* 1. das Mädchen, die Jungfrau; 2. (*Hist.*) Guillotine. **2.** *adj.* 1. jungfräulich, mädchenhaft, Mädchen–, unverheiratet; – ***aunt,*** unverheiratete Tante; – ***name,*** der Mädchenname; 2. (*fig.*) Jungfern–, Antritts–, Erstlings–; – ***race,*** das Jungfernrennen; – ***speech,*** die Jungfernrede, Erstlingsrede; – ***voyage,*** die Jungfernfahrt; 3. (*Crick.*) – ***over,*** der Spielsatz ohne Läufe.
maiden|hair, *s.* (*Bot.*) das Frauenhaar, Venushaar. **-head,** *s.* (*Anat.*) das Jungfernhäutchen, Hymen; (*fig.*) *see* **maidenhood. maidenhood,** *s.* die Jungfräulichkeit, Jungfernschaft, Unberührtheit. **maidenlike,** *adj. See* **maidenly. maidenliness,** *s.* die Mädchenhaftigkeit, Jungfräulichkeit. **maidenly,** *adj.* mädchenhaft; züchtig, sittsam, jungfräulich. **maidservant,** *s.* das (Dienst)mädchen.
¹**mail** [meil], *s.* der Panzer, die Plattenrüstung; (*also* ***chain–-***) der Kettenpanzer; ***coat of –,*** das Panzerhemd; (*Poet.*) der Harnisch.
²**mail, 1.** *s.* die Post, der Postdienst, das Postwesen; der Postversand; Postsachen, Postsendungen (*pl.*); ***air–-,*** die Luftpost; ***by –,*** per Post; ***by return (of) –,*** postwendend, umgehend. **2.** *v.t.* (*esp. Am.*) zur Post geben, mit der Post (ver)schicken, absenden, aufgeben. **mailable,** *adj.* postversandfähig.
mail|-bag, *s.* der Briefbeutel. **--box,** *s.* (*Am.*) *see* **letter-box. --cart,** *s.* der Handwagen. **--coach,** *s.* die Postkutsche.
mailed [meild], *adj.* gepanzert; *see* ¹**mail**; (*fig.*) – ***fist,*** die Waffengewalt; Gewaltanwendung.
mailing ['meiliŋ], *s.* der Postversand; – ***list,*** die Adressenkartei. **mail|man,** *s.* (*Am.*) *see* **postman. --order,** *s.* die Postbestellung; ***--firm,*** das Versandhaus, Postversandgeschäft. **--train,** *s.* der Postzug. **--van,** *s.* der Postwagen.
maim [meim], *v.t.* verstümmeln, lähmen; zum Krüppel schlagen; verkrüppeln (*also fig.*). **maimed,** *adj.* verstümmelt.
¹**main** [mein], **1.** *adj.* (*only attrib.*) hauptsächlich, wichtigst, Haupt–; (*Mil.*) – ***body,*** das Hauptkorps, Gros; ***have an eye to the – chance,*** an seinen eigenen Vorteil denken; (*Gram.*) – ***clause,*** der Hauptsatz; – ***deck,*** das Hauptdeck; ***by – force*** or ***strength,*** mit bloßer *or* aller *or* nackter Gewalt, mit voller Kraft; (*Naut.*) – ***hatch,*** die Großluke; (*Railw.*) – ***line,*** die Hauptstrecke, Hauptlinie; – ***road,*** die Hauptverkehrsstraße; – ***street,*** die Hauptstraße (*esp. Am. as name*); – ***thing,*** die Hauptsache. **2.** *s.* 1. der Hauptpunkt, Hauptteil,

die Hauptsache; ***in the –***, in der Hauptsache, hauptsächlich, zum größten Teil, größtenteils; 2. (*Tech.*) die Hauptleitung (*Elec., water, gas*), das Hauptrohr (*water, gas*), Hauptkabel (*Elec.*); *pl.* (*coll. Elec.*) (Strom)netz; ***connected to the –s,*** mit Netzanschluß; ***–s voltage,*** die Netzspannung; 3. (*coll.*) die Gewalt, Kraft; (*only in*) ***with might and –,*** mit aller *or* voller Gewalt *or* Macht.

[2]**main,** *s.* (*Poet.*) hohe See, das weite Meer.

Main [main], *s.* (*Geog.*) der Main.

main|-brace, *s.* (*Naut.*) die Brasse der Großrahe. **–land,** *s.* das Festland. **mainly,** *adv.* hauptsächlich, größtenteils, zum größten Teil, vornehmlich. **mainmast,** *s.* der Großmast. **mains,** *pl. See* [1]**main, 2,** 2. **main|sail** [–səl], *s.* (*Naut.*) das Großsegel. **--sheet,** *s.* (*Naut.*) der Großschot. **–spring,** *s.* die Hauptfeder (*of clock etc.*); (*fig.*) (Haupt)triebfeder, treibende Kraft. **–stay,** *s.* (*Naut.*) das Großstag; (*fig.*) die Hauptstütze.

maintain [mein'tein], *v.t.* 1. instandhalten, (aufrecht)erhalten, beibehalten, (be)wahren (*a th.*); ***– life,*** das Leben erhalten; ***– one's reputation,*** seinen guten Ruf wahren; 2. unterhalten, versorgen, mit Lebensunterhalt versehen, alimentieren (*a p.*); 3. (*fig.*) unterhalten, weiterführen; 4. (*fig.*) behaupten, verfechten, verteidigen (*an opinion*); ***– one's ground,*** seine Stellung behaupten, standhalten; (*fig.*) sich behaupten. **maintainable,** *adj.* (*fig.*) verfechtbar, haltbar, gerechtfertigt, zu rechtfertigen(d). **maintainer,** *s.* der Versorger, Erhalter; (*fig.*) Verfechter.

maintenance ['meintinəns], *s.* 1. das Beibehalten; die (Aufrecht)erhaltung, Instandhaltung; (*Tech.*) Wartung; ***cost of –,*** die Instandhaltungskosten (*pl.*); ***– and repair,*** die Unterhaltung und Instandsetzung; ***– man,*** der Wartungsmonteur; 2. die Ernährung, Beköstigung, der Unterhalt; ***– grant,*** der Unterhaltszuschuß; 3. die Behauptung, Verfechtung; (*Law*) widerrechtliche Unterstützung (*of a party*).

main|top, *s.* (*Naut.*) der Großmars. **--topgallant–,** *pref.* (*Naut.*) Großbram–. **--topmast,** *s.* (*Naut.*) die Großstenge. **--topsail** [–səl], *s.* das Großmarssegel. **--yard,** *s.* (*Naut.*) die Großrah(e).

maison(n)ette [meizə'net], *s.* kleines Eigenheim, das Einfamilienhaus.

maize [meiz], *s.* der Mais, (*Austr.*) Kukuruz.

majestic [mə'dʒestik], *adj.* majestätisch, würdevoll, erhaben. **majesty** ['mædʒisti], *s.* die Majestät, Würde, Erhabenheit, Hoheit; (*of royalty*) Majestät, königliche Hoheit; ***Your Majesty,*** Eure Majestät.

majolica [mə'jɔlikə], *s.* die Majolika.

major ['meidʒə], **1.** *s.* 1. (*Mil.*) der Major; 2. (*Law*) Mündige(r), Volljährige(r); 3. (*Log.*) der Obersatz, Oberbegriff; 4. (*Univ., esp. Am.*) das Hauptfach. **2.** *attrib. adj.* 1. größer; (*Geom.*) ***– axis,*** die Hauptachse; ***– offender,*** Hauptschuldige(r); ***– part,*** größter Teil; (*Log.*) ***– premiss,*** der Obersatz; ***the – prophets,*** die größeren Propheten; ***– repair,*** größere Reparatur; 2. (*Mus.*) ***C –,*** C-Dur; ***– key,*** die Durtonart; ***– third,*** große Terz; 3. älter (*of two brothers*); ***Smith –,*** Smith der Ältere. **3.** *pred. adj.* mündig, majorenn, volljährig. **4.** *v.i.* (*Am.*) ***– in,*** im *or* als Hauptfach studieren.

Majorca [mə'dʒɔ:kə], *s.* Mallorca (*n.*).

major|-domo [–'doumou], *s.* (*Hist.*) der Hausmeier; Haushofmeister. **--general,** *s.* der Generalmajor.

majority [mə'dʒɔriti], *s.* 1. die Mehrheit; Mehrzahl, Überzahl; ***the – of cases,*** die Mehrzahl der Fälle; ***join the –,*** zu den Vätern versammelt werden; ***– principle,*** das Majoritätsprinzip; ***two-thirds –,*** die Zweidrittelmehrheit; ***vast –,*** überwiegende Anzahl; ***– (of) vote(s),*** die Stimmenmehrheit; 2. (*Law*) die Volljährigkeit, Mündigkeit; ***attain one's –,*** mündig werden; 3. (*Mil.*) die Majorsstelle, der Majorsrang.

majuscule ['mædʒəskju:l], *s.* großer (Anfangs)-buchstabe, der Versal(buchstabe).

makar ['mæka:], *s.* (*Scots*) der Dichter.

make [meik], **1.** *irr.v.t.* 1. machen, (er)schaffen; (er)bauen, erzeugen, verfertigen, anfertigen, fabrizieren, fertigstellen, herstellen (***of, from, out of,*** aus); 2. verarbeiten, formen, bilden (***into,*** in (*Acc.*)); 3. lassen (***do,*** tun), zwingen (***do,*** zu tun), nötigen (***act,*** zum Handeln) (*a p.*); 4. bewirken, verursachen, herbeiführen, mit sich bringen, ergeben, sich belaufen auf (*Acc.*); 5. gewinnen, zusammenbringen, zustandebringen; 6. ernennen zu.

(a) (*with nouns*) ***– allowance for,*** in Anschlag bringen, in Betracht ziehen; (*Comm.*) ***– an allowance,*** Rabatt gewähren; ***– amends for,*** Ersatz leisten für, ersetzen, wiedergutmachen; ***– the acquaintance of,*** kennenlernen, bekannt werden mit; ***– arrangements,*** Verabredungen *or* Vorkehrungen treffen; ***– an attempt,*** einen Versuch anstellen; ***– the bed,*** das Bett machen; ***– a change,*** eine Abwechslung sein; ***– a choice,*** eine Wahl treffen; (*Elec.*) ***– contact,*** den Strom schließen; ***– a decision,*** eine Entscheidung fällen; ***that –s a difference,*** das ist etwas (ganz) anderes; ***that –s no difference,*** das macht nichts (aus), das ist gleich(gültig); ***– no doubt,*** keinen Zweifel hegen (***of,*** über (*Acc.*)); ***– an effort,*** sich bemühen *or* anstrengen, sich (*Dat.*) Mühe geben; ***– one's escape,*** entweichen, entwischen; ***– an example of,*** ein Beispiel statuieren an (*Dat.*); ***– excuses,*** Ausflüchte gebrauchen; ***– faces,*** Gesichter schneiden; ***– a fool of o.s.,*** sich blamieren; ***– a fortune,*** sich (*Dat.*) ein Vermögen erwerben; ***– friends with,*** sich anfreunden mit; ***– fun of,*** sich lustig machen über (*Acc.*); ***– haste,*** sich beeilen; ***not – head or tail of,*** nicht daraus klug werden; ***– headway,*** Fortschritte machen, vorankommen; ***– inquiries,*** Erkundigungen einziehen (***of,*** bei; ***about,*** über (*Acc.*)); ***– (heavy) inroads on,*** (stark) in Anspruch nehmen; ***– a bad job of,*** verpatzen; ***– a good job of,*** ordentlich machen; ***– a journey,*** eine Reise unternehmen; (*Naut.*) ***– the land,*** Land sichten; ***– a loss,*** einen Verlust erleiden; ***– love,*** den Hof machen (***to,*** *Dat.*); ***– mention of,*** erwähnen; ***– a mess of,*** verpfuschen; ***– a name for o.s.,*** sich (*Dat.*) einen Namen machen; ***– objections,*** Einwände erheben; ***– payment,*** Zahlung leisten; ***– peace,*** Frieden schließen; ***– plans,*** Pläne schmieden; ***– a point of s.th.,*** sich (*Dat.*) etwas angelegen sein lassen; ***– a port,*** einen Hafen anlaufen; ***– a present of,*** als Geschenk geben; ***– provision,*** sorgen (***for,*** für); Vorkehrungen treffen (***against,*** gegen); ***it –s pleasant reading,*** es bietet angenehme Lektüre; ***– (a) reply,*** Antwort geben, erwidern; ***– room,*** Platz machen; ***– a rule,*** eine Regel aufstellen; ***– a sacrifice,*** ein Opfer bringen; ***– sail,*** das Segel setzen; ***– shift,*** sich behelfen; ***– a speech,*** eine Rede halten; ***– a stay,*** sich aufhalten; ***– tea,*** Tee bereiten; ***they – good teachers,*** sie geben gute Lehrer ab; ***– trouble,*** (*of a p.*) Unheil anstiften *or* anrichten; (*of a th.*) Schwierigkeiten bereiten; ***– war upon,*** Krieg führen mit; ***– way,*** vorwärtskommen; ***– heavy weather of,*** viel Wind machen um.

(b) (*with double objects*) ***– it one's business,*** es sich (*Dat.*) zur Aufgabe machen; ***they made him their chief,*** sie machten ihn zu ihrem Anführer; ***he was made colonel,*** er wurde zum Obersten gemacht *or* ernannt; ***I – the distance 100 yards,*** ich schätze die Entfernung auf 100 Yard; ***she made him an ideal partner,*** sie erwies sich als eine ideale Partnerin für ihn; ***– it a rule,*** es sich (*Dat.*) zur Regel machen; ***what do you – the time?*** wie spät ist es? ***I – it 3 o'clock,*** ich habe 3 Uhr.

(c) (*with adjs.*) ***– the best of,*** die beste Seite abgewinnen (*Gen.*), sich abfinden *or* zufriedengeben mit; ***– the best of a bad job,*** gute Miene zum bösen Spiel machen; ***– fast,*** befestigen; ***– itself felt,*** sich fühlbar machen; ***– good,*** wiedergutmachen, ersetzen, Ersatz leisten für, vergüten; rechtfertigen, geltend machen, bestätigen, als berechtigt erweisen, nachweisen, begründen (*a claim*); glücklich bewerkstelligen (*one's escape*); ***– good one's position,*** seine Stellung ausbauen; ***– good a promise,*** ein Versprechen erfüllen, einem Versprechen nachkommen; ***– good one's word,*** Wort halten; ***– known,*** ver-

kündigen, bekanntgeben, bekanntmachen; – ***o.s. known,*** sich zu erkennen geben; – ***light*** or ***little of,*** auf die leichte Schulter nehmen, sich (*Dat.*) nichts machen aus, wenig halten von; – ***the most of,*** nach Kräften ausnützen, ins beste Licht stellen; – ***much of,*** viel Wesens machen von, große Stücke halten auf (*Acc.*); (*coll.*) – ***o.s. scarce,*** sich aus dem Staube machen; – ***sure,*** sich vergewissern, sich (*Dat.*) Gewißheit verschaffen (***of,*** über (*Acc.*); ***that,*** ob); – ***o.s. understood,*** sich verständlich machen.
(d) I. (*with inf.* (*active without to*)) – ***them agree,*** sie zur Übereinstimmung bringen; ***she made me do this,*** sie zwang mich dazu; – ***it do,*** – ***do with it,*** es genug sein lassen, sich damit behelfen *or* zufrieden geben; ***your attitude –s me feel that . . .,*** dein Verhalten läßt mich vermuten *or* annehmen *or* glauben, daß . . .; (*coll.*) – ***things hum,*** alles in Schwung bringen; – ***s.th. last,*** sich (*Dat.*) etwas einteilen, so daß man damit auskommt; – ***the passage read as follows,*** die Stelle folgendermaßen formulieren, der Stelle folgenden Wortlaut geben; – ***him sit down,*** ihn zum Sitzen nötigen; (*fig.*) – ***him smart,*** ihn büßen lassen; 2. (*pass. with to* (*also ellipt.*)) ***he was made to do it,*** er wurde gezwungen *or* genötigt, es zu tun; ***I won't be made to*** (*go*), auf keinen Fall lasse ich mich zwingen (zu gehen).
(e) (*with advs.*) – ***out,*** ausstellen (*cheque*), anfertigen, aufstellen (*list*); (*coll.*) verstehen, klug werden aus (*a p.*), erkennen, feststellen, herausbekommen (*a th.*), entziffern (*handwriting*), begreifen (*meaning*), beweisen, darstellen, glaubhaft machen, (als glaubwürdig) hinstellen (*a case*); – ***o.s. out to be,*** sich stellen als; – ***over,*** übergeben, vermachen, übertragen (***to,*** *Dat.*); – ***up,*** ersetzen, wiedergutmachen, vergüten (***to,*** *Dat.*); einholen, nachholen (*lost ground*); vervollständigen, ergänzen, zum Abschluß bringen (*s.th. incomplete*), zusammensetzen, zusammenstellen (*a group*); bilden, ausmachen (*a whole etc.*); sich (*Dat.*) ausdenken, erfinden (*a story*); ausarbeiten (*a speech*); aufstellen, anfertigen (*a list etc.*); verpacken, verschnüren (*a parcel*); schüren (*a fire*); beilegen (*quarrel etc.*); ausgleichen (*accounts*); zusammennähen, anfertigen (*dresses etc.*); herrichten, ausstaffieren, zurechtmachen, schminken (*one's face*); umbrechen (*type into pages*); ***be made up of,*** bestehen *or* sich zusammensetzen aus; (*coll.*) – ***it up*** (***with him***), sich (mit ihm) aussöhnen; – ***up one's mind,*** sich entschließen.
2. *irr.v.i.* gehen, führen, sich begeben *or* wenden, sich anschicken, den Versuch machen; (*as tide etc.*) eintreten, einsetzen, (an)steigen; – ***believe,*** vorgeben, vorschützen; – ***as if*** or ***though to do,*** (so) tun als wenn *or* ob; – (***so***) ***bold,*** sich (*Dat.*) die Freiheit nehmen, sich erdreisten; – ***free with,*** frei schalten *or* walten mit (*a th.*), sich (*Dat.*) Freiheiten anmaßen *or* sich (*Dat.*) Freiheiten *or* zuviel herausnehmen gegenüber (*a p.*); – ***merry,*** sich belustigen, fröhlich *or* lustig sein.
(a) (*with preps.*) – ***after,*** folgen, nachlaufen, nachjagen (*Dat.*), verfolgen; – ***at,*** losgehen *or* sich stürzen auf (*Acc.*); – ***for,*** lossteuern *or* zugehen auf (*Acc.*), sich aufmachen *or* begeben nach (*a place*); (*Naut.*) Kurs haben auf (*Acc.*); (*fig.*) dienlich sein für, beitragen zu, fördern, bewirken, herbeiführen; (*coll.*) – ***of,*** halten *or* sich (*Dat.*) eine Vorstellung machen von; ***what do you – of it?*** was denken Sie darüber? – ***towards,*** zugehen auf (*Acc.*), sich nähern (*Dat.*).
(b) (*with advs.*) – ***away,*** sich fortmachen *or* davonmachen; – ***away with,*** um die Ecke bringen, beseitigen (*a p.*), mitnehmen (*a th.*), durchbringen, vergeuden (*one's money*); – ***off,*** sich auf und davon machen, sich aus dem Staube machen, ausreißen; – ***off with,*** durchgehen *or* durchbrennen mit; (*coll.*) – ***out,*** abschneiden, fertigwerden, vorankommen; – ***out to be,*** vorgeben zu sein, sich stellen als ob man sei; – ***up,*** sich zurechtmachen *or* putzen *or* (*esp.*) schminken; – ***up for,*** ersetzen, Ersatz leisten für (*expenses*); wiedergutmachen, wettmachen, aufholen, ausgleichen (*loss*); (*coll.*) – ***up to,*** scharwenzeln um, den Hof machen (*Dat.*), um den Bart gehen (*Dat.*); – ***up to him for,*** ihn entschädigen für.
3. *s.* die Form, Fasson, der Schnitt; Bau, das Gefüge, die Bauart, (Mach)art, Ausfertigung, Ausführung, Fassung, Type, Marke, Mache, das Produkt, Erzeugnis, Fabrikat; die Fabrikation, Herstellung, Anfertigung; (*Elec.*) ***at –,*** geschlossen; (*sl.*) ***be on the –,*** auf Gewinn zielen, auf Profit aus *or* hinter dem Geld her sein.

make|-believe, I. *s.* die Verstellung, Heuchelei, der (An)schein, Vorwand. **2.** *adj.* verstellt, geheuchelt; dem Anschein nach, scheinbar, angeblich, vorgeblich. **--contact,** *s.* (*Elec.*) der Schließkontakt. **--fast,** *s.* (*Naut.*) der Poller, Vertäupfahl. **maker,** *s.* der Hersteller, Verfertiger, Fabrikant; (*Eccl.*) Schöpfer, Gott; ***boiler –,*** der Kesselschmied; ***peace –,*** der Friedensstifter. **make|-ready,** *s.* (*Typ.*) die Zurichtung. **-shift, I.** *s.* der Notbehelf. **2.** *adj.* behelfsmäßig, Not–, Behelfs–, Aushilfs–. **--up,** *s.* die Ausstaffierung, Kostümierung, Aufmachung, Zusammensetzung, Struktur, Verfassung, Ausstattung, Verpackung; Erfindung; (*Typ.*) der Umbruch; (*coll.*) die Schminke. **--weight,** *s.* der Zusatz, die Zulage, Zugabe; (*fig.*) der Ausgleich, Lückenbüßer, das Anhängsel, fünftes Rad am Wagen; der Ersatz, Notbehelf.

making ['meikiŋ], *s.* das Machen, die Erzeugung; Verfertigung, Herstellung, Fabrikation; ***that was the – of him,*** das hat sein Glück gemacht; ***in the –,*** in Arbeit, im Bau *or* Entstehen *or* Werden, in der Entwicklung; ***it is of my own –,*** ich habe es selbst gemacht; ***he has the –s of . . .,*** er hat das Zeug zu . . .; ***go to the – of,*** ausmachen, zustandebringen.

Malachi ['mæləkai], *s.* (*B.*) Maleachi (*m.*).

malachite ['mæləkait], *s.* der Malachit, Kupferspat.

maladjusted [mælə'dʒʌstid], *adj.* (*Psych.*) milieugestört, entfremdet. **maladjustment,** *s.* das Mißverhältnis, schlechte Einstellung *or* Anpassung.

maladministration [mælədmini'streiʃən], *s.* schlechte Verwaltung, die Mißwirtschaft.

maladroit [mælə'drɔit], *adj.* ungeschickt, linkisch, taktlos. **maladroitness,** *s.* die Ungeschicklichkeit, Taktlosigkeit; das Ungeschick.

malady ['mælədi], *s.* die Krankheit.

Malagasy [mælə'gæsi], **I.** *s.* der Madagasse (die Madagassin). **2.** *adj.* madagassisch.

malaise [mæ'leiz], *s.* die Unpäßlichkeit, das Unwohlsein, Unbehagen.

malapert ['mæləpə:t], *adj.* (*obs.*) unverschämt, vermessen, vorlaut, naseweis.

malapropism ['mæləprɔpizm], *s.* die Wortverwechslung, Wortentstellung, Wortverdrehung.

malapropos [mælæprə'pou], *adv.* zur Unzeit, unangebracht, ungelegen.

malar ['meilə], *adj.* (*Anat.*) Backen–.

malaria [mə'lɛəriə], *s.* die Malaria, das Sumpffieber. **malarial, malarious,** *adj.* Malaria–.

Malawi [mə'lɑ:wi:], *s.* Malawi (*n.*). **Malawian, I.** *s.* der (die) Malawier(in). **2.** *adj.* malawisch.

Malay [mə'lei], **I.** *s.* I. der Malaie (die Malaiin); 2. (*language*) das Malaiisch(e). **2.** *adj.* malaiisch. **Malaysia** [–ziə], *s.* Malaysia (*n.*). **Malaysian, I.** *s.* der (die) Malaysier(in). **2.** *adj.* malaysisch.

malcontent ['mælkəntɛnt], **I.** *adj.* mißvergnügt, verstimmt, unzufrieden. **2.** *s.* Mißvergnügte(r), Unzufriedene(r), der Rebell.

Maldives ['mɔ:ldivz], *pl.* Malediven (*pl.*). **Maldivian** [–'diviən], **I.** *s.* der (die) Malediver(in). **2.** *adj.* maledivisch.

male [meil], **I.** *s.* der Mann; das Männchen (*of birds etc.*). **2.** *adj.* männlich; – ***child,*** der Knabe; – ***cousin,*** der Vetter; – ***issue,*** männlicher Nachkomme, (*also pl.*) männliche Nachkommen(schaft); – ***nurse,*** der Krankenpfleger; – ***screw,*** die Schraube(nspindel); – ***voice,*** die Männerstimme.

malediction [mæli'dikʃən], *s.* die Verwünschung, der Fluch. **maledictory** [–təri], *adj.* Verwünschungs–.

malefactor ['mælifæktə], *s.* der Übeltäter, Missetäter.

maleficent [mə'lefisənt], *adj.* bösartig; nachteilig, schädlich (*to*, für *or Dat.*).

malevolence [mə'levələns], *s.* die Böswilligkeit, Feindseligkeit; Bosheit, Mißgunst, böser Wille, feindselige Einstellung (*to(wards)*, gegen). **malevolent,** *adj.* böswillig, feindselig, feindlich gesinnt (*to(wards)*, gegen), (*of a th.*) widrig, mißgünstig.

malfeasance [mæl'fi:zəns], *s.* gesetzwidrige *or* strafbare Handlung, die Gesetzesübertretung, Missetat. **malfeasant, 1.** *adj.* gesetzwidrig. **2.** *s.* der (die) Missetäter(in).

malformation [mælfɔ:'meiʃən], *s.* die Mißbildung. **malformed** [–'fɔ:md], *adj.* mißgebildet, mißgestaltet, verunstaltet.

Mali ['mɑ:li], *s.* Mali (*n.*). **Malian, 1.** *s.* der (die) Malier(in). **2.** *adj.* malisch.

malic ['mælik], *adj.* (*Chem.*) apfelsauer; – ***acid,*** die Apfelsäure.

malice ['mælis], *s.* die Bosheit, Böswilligkeit, Gehässigkeit; (Heim)tücke, Arglist; der Groll; (*Law*) böse Absicht, böser Vorsatz; (*Law*) ***with – aforethought*** or ***prepense,*** mit bösem Vorbedacht, vorsätzlich; ***bear him –,*** ihm grollen. **malicious** [mə'liʃəs], *adj.* boshaft, arglistig, gehässig, (heim)tückisch, hämisch, schadenfroh; (*Law*) böswillig, vorsätzlich; – ***glee,*** die Schadenfreude. **maliciousness,** *s.* die Böswilligkeit, Gehässigkeit, Boshaftigkeit, Arglist, (Heim)tücke.

malign [mə'lain], **1.** *adj.* schädlich, verderblich, unheilvoll, unheilbringend; *see also* **malignant**; (*Med.*) bösartig. **2.** *v.t.* verleumden, verlästern, beschimpfen.

malignancy [mə'lignənsi], *s.* die Bosheit, Boshaftigkeit, Böswilligkeit, Feindseligkeit (*of a p.*), Widrigkeit, Ungunst (*of events*); (*Med.*) Bösartigkeit. **malignant, 1.** *adj.* boshaft, böswillig, gehässig, feindselig; (*Med.*) bösartig. **2.** *s.* Übelgesinnte(r). **malignity,** *s.* böser Wille, erbitterte Feindschaft; (*of events*) *see* **malignancy.**

Malines [mæ'li:n], *s.* (*Geog.*) Mecheln (*n.*).

malinger [mə'liŋgə], *v.i.* Krankheit vortäuschen, simulieren, sich krank stellen, sich drücken. **malingerer,** *s.* der Simulant, Drückeberger.

mall [mɔ:l], *s.* 1. der Schlegel; 2. schattiger Weg.

mallard ['mæləd], *s.* (*Orn.*) die Stockente (*Anas platyrhynchos*).

malleability [mæliə'biliti], *s.* die Schmiedbarkeit, Hämmerbarkeit; Verformbarkeit, Dehnbarkeit, Streckbarkeit; (*fig.*) Geschmeidigkeit, Gefügigkeit. **malleable** ['mæliəbl], *adj.* (kalt) schmiedbar, hämmerbar; verformbar, dehnbar, streckbar; (*fig.*) gefügig, geschmeidig; – ***cast iron,*** der Temperguß.

malleolar [mə'li:ələ], *adj.* (*Anat.*) Knöchel–.

mallet ['mælit], *s.* der Holzhammer, Schlegel; (*Min.*) Fäustel, Schlägel; (*Spt.*) Schläger, das Schlagholz.

mallow ['mælou], *s.* (*Bot.*) die Malve, Käsepappel.

malm [mɑ:m], *s.* kalkreicher Lehmboden.

malmsey ['mɑ:mzi], *s.* der Malvasier.

malnutrition [mælnju'triʃən], *s.* schlechte Ernährung, die Unterernährung.

malocclusion [mælə'klu:ʒən], *s.* (*Dentistry*) die Gebißanomalie.

malodorous [mæl'oudərəs], *adj.* übelriechend.

malpractice [mæl'præktis], *s.* die Übeltat, strafbare Handlung; der Amtsmißbrauch, das Amtsvergehen; (*Med.*) verkehrte Behandlung, die Pfuscherei.

malt [mɔ:lt], **1.** *s.* das Malz. **2.** *v.t.* malzen, mälzen; ***–ed milk,*** die Malzmilch. **3.** *v.i.* zu Malz werden.

Malta ['mɔ:ltə], *s.* Malta (*n.*). **Maltese** [–'ti:z], **1.** *s.* 1. der (die) Malteser(in); 2. (*language*) das Maltesisch(e). **2.** *adj.* maltesisch; – ***cross,*** das Malteserkreuz.

malt-house, *s.* die Mälzerei. **malting,** *s.* das Malzen, Mälzen. **malt-kiln,** *s.* die Malzdarre. **maltose,** *s.* der Malzzucker, die Maltose.

maltreat [mæl'tri:t], *v.t.* schlecht behandeln, mißhandeln. **maltreatment,** *s.* die Mißhandlung, schlechte Behandlung.

maltster ['mɔ:ltstə], *s.* der Mälzer. **malty,** *adj.* malzhaltig, malzig, Malz–.

malversation [mælvə'seiʃən], *s.* das Amtsvergehen, der Amtsmißbrauch, Unterschleif, die Veruntreuung.

mamilla [mə'milə], *s.* die Brustwarze. **mamillary** ['mæmiləri], *adj.* Brustwarzen–. **mamilliform** [–ifɔ:m], *adj.* brustwarzenförmig.

[1]**mam(m)a** [mə'mɑ:], *s.* die Mama, Mutti.

[2]**mamma** ['mæmə], *s.* (*pl.* **-mae**) (*Anat.*) die Brust.

mammal [mæml], *s.* das Säugetier, der Säuger. **mammalia** [–'meiliə], *pl.* Säugetiere (*pl.*). **mammalian** [–'meiliən], *adj.* Säugetier–.

mammary ['mæməri], *adj.* Brust–, Milch–; (*Zool.*) Euter–.

mammon ['mæmən], *s.* der Mammon, Reichtum, das Geld, irdische Güter (*pl.*). **mammonism, mammon-worship,** *s.* der Mammondienst, die Geldgier.

mammoth ['mæməθ], **1.** *s.* das Mammut. **2.** *adj.* ungeheuer, riesenhaft, riesig, Riesen–.

mammy ['mæmi], *s.* 1. (*coll.*) *see* **mam(m)a**; 2. (*Am.*) farbiges Kindermädchen, schwarze Amme.

man [mæn], **1.** *s.* (*pl.* **men** [men]) 1. der Mann; – ***about town,*** der Lebemann, Salonheld; ***--at-arms,*** der Reiter, bewaffneter (und berittener) Soldat; – ***of conscience,*** gewissenhafter Mensch; ***Man Friday,*** treuer Knecht; – ***of genius,*** das Genie; – ***of honour,*** der Ehrenmann; – ***of letters,*** der Literat, Schriftsteller; – ***of mark,*** bedeutende Persönlichkeit; – ***of many parts,*** vielseitiger Mensch; – ***of straw,*** der Strohmann; – ***in the street,*** der Mann von der Straße, der gemeine *or* einfache Mann, der Durchschnittsmensch; – ***in a thousand,*** außergewöhnlicher Mensch; – ***and wife,*** Mann und Frau; – ***of many words,*** der Schwätzer; – ***of the world,*** der Mann der Welt, Weltmann; ***be one's own –,*** sein eigner Herr sein; ***best –,*** der Beistand des Bräutigams; ***be the – for s.th.,*** der passende *or* richtige Mann für etwas sein; ***a Cambridge –,*** einer, der in Cambridge studiert (hat); ***feel a new –,*** sich wie neugeboren fühlen; ***my good –!*** mein lieber Herr! ***inner –,*** innerer Mensch; ***little –,*** kleiner Kerl, der Knirps; ***medical –,*** der Arzt, Hausarzt; (*coll.*) ***my old –,*** mein Alter; ***show yourself a –!*** zeige, daß du ein Mann bist! ***her young –,*** ihr Freund *or* Schatz; 2. der Mensch, die Person, menschliches Wesen; ***any –,*** jedermann, irgend jemand; ***between – and –,*** von Mensch zu Mensch; – ***for –,*** Mann für Mann; ***no – alive,*** kein Sterblicher; ***per –,*** pro Person; ***to a –,*** bis auf den letzten Mann; 3. die Menschen (*pl.*), die Menschheit, das Menschengeschlecht; (*B.*) ***the fall of –,*** der Sündenfall; ***rights of –,*** Menschenrechte (*pl.*); 4. (*Hist.*) der Lehnsmann; 5. Diener, Arbeiter; 6. (*in address*) (*coll.*) Menschenskind; – ***alive!*** Mensch(enskind)! 7. (*Draughts etc.*) der (Dame)stein, die Figur; 8. *pl.* (*Mil.*) Soldaten, Matrosen, Gemeine (*pl.*), die Mannschaft. **2.** *v.t.* bemannen (*with troops, sailors*); besetzen (*trench etc.*); – ***o.s.,*** sich ermannen; – ***the yards,*** die Rahen zum Salut bemannen.

manacle ['mænəkl], **1.** *s.* (*usu. pl.*) die Handfessel, Handschelle. **2.** *v.t.* Handschellen anlegen (*Dat.*), fesseln.

manage ['mænidʒ], **1.** *v.t.* 1. führen, leiten, verwalten (*a business etc.*); bewirtschaften (*an estate etc.*); vorstehen (*Dat.*), beaufsichtigen, dirigieren, regulieren; 2. handhaben, umgehen mit (*tool, weapon etc.*); (*fig.*) bewerkstelligen, zustande bringen, es einrichten *or* fertigbringen *or* zuwege bringen, (*coll.*) deichseln, einfädeln, managen (*a th.*); (*coll.*) wissen umzugehen mit *or* zu behandeln, fertig werden mit, für sich gewinnen, herumkriegen, gefügig machen (*a p.*); ***I can – it,*** ich kann es bewältigen; ***I can – him,*** ich kann es mit ihm aufnehmen. **2.** *v.i.* 1. den Haushalt *or* Betrieb *or* das Geschäft führen, wirtschaften; 2. auskommen (*with*, mit); (*coll.*) es schaffen *or* einrichten, fertigbringen; ***he -d to get away***, es gelang ihm zu entkommen, er kam eben noch weg; ***I cannot - to come***, es ist mir nicht möglich zu kommen; - ***very well*** or ***nicely***, gut auskommen, ganz gut fertig werden.

manageable ['mænidʒəbl], *adj.* (*of a th.*) handlich, leicht zu handhaben; (*of a p.*) lenksam, fügsam, folgsam, willfährig, gelehrig; (*of a vehicle*) lenksam, manövrierbar. **manageableness,** *s.* die Handlichkeit; Lenksamkeit.

management ['mænidʒmənt], *s.* 1. die Verwaltung, Direktion, Geschäftsleitung, Betriebsführung, der Vorstand, das Direktorium; ***industrial -***, die Betriebswirtschaft; ***under new -!*** Geschäftsübernahme! 2. (*of estate*) die Bewirtschaftung; 3. kluge Handlungsweise *or* Taktik, die Manipulation; 4. Behandlung, Handhabung. **manager,** *s.* der Geschäftsführer, Betriebsleiter, Direktor, Vorsteher; Verwalter; (*Theat., film etc.*) Regisseur, Intendant; (*of film stars, artists etc.*) Manager; ***general -***, der Generaldirektor; ***good -***, guter Wirtschafter *or* Verwalter *or* Haushalter; ***hotel -***, der Hoteldirektor; ***works -***, der Betriebsleiter; ***board of -s***, das Direktorium; (*of a school etc.*) Kuratorium. **manageress,** *s.* die Geschäftsführerin, Direktorin, Vorsteherin, Leiterin. **managerial** [-'dʒiəriəl], *adj.* Leitungs-, Verwaltungs-, Direktions-; (*fig.*) managerhaft, herrisch; ***in - capacity***, in leitender Stellung. **managing,** *adj.* geschäftsführend, leitend; bevormundend (*of character*); - ***director***, der Betriebsdirektor, das Vorstandsmitglied; ***joint - director***, geschäftsführender Teilhaber.

man-ape, *s.* der Menschenaffe.

Manchu [mæn'tʃu:], **1.** *s.* 1. der Mandschu; 2. (*language*) das Mandschu. **2.** *adj.* mandschurisch, Mandschu-. **Manchuria** [-riə], *s.* die Mandschurei. **Manchurian,** *adj. See* **Manchu, 2.**

manciple ['mænsipl], *s.* (*obs.*) der Ökonom, Verwalter, Wirtschafter.

mandamus [mæn'deiməs], *s.* (*Law*) das Mandat an ein untergeordnetes Gericht.

mandarin ['mændərin], *s.* 1. der Mandarin; 2. *See* **mandarine.**

mandarin-duck, *s.* (*Orn.*) die Mandarinenente (*Anas galericulata*). **mandarine** [-rin], *s.* (*Bot.*) die Mandarine, Zwergapfelsine.

mandatary ['mændətəri], *s.* (*Law*) (Prozeß)bevollmächtigte(r), der Mandatar. **mandate, 1.** [-deit], *s.* das Mandat, die (Prozeß)vollmacht, (*Law*) Bevollmächtigung, der (Vertretungs)auftrag; (*Pol.*) das (Völkerbunds)mandat; Mandat(sgebiet); (*fig. Poet.*) die Verordnung, Verfügung, der Befehl, Auftrag, Erlaß, das Geheiß. **2.** [-'deit], *v.t.* einem Mandat unterstellen; ***-d territory***, das Mandatsgebiet. **mandator** [-'deitə], *s.* (*Law*) der Vollmachtgeber, Auftraggeber, Mandant. **mandatory, 1.** *adj.* zwangsweise, verbindlich, obligatorisch, pflichtgemäß, Pflicht-; (*Pol.*) Mandatar-. **2.** *s.* der Mandatarstaat; *see also* **mandatary.**

mandible ['mændibl], *s.* die Kinnlade, der Kinnbacken, Unterkiefer(knochen).

mandolin ['mændəlin], *s.* die Mandoline.

mandragora [mæn'drægərə], **mandrake** ['mændreik], *s.* (*Bot.*) der Alraun, die Alraune, Alraunwurzel.

mandrel, mandril ['mændril], *s.* der Dorn, Drehstift, die Docke, Welle, Spindel.

mandrill ['mændril], *s.* (*Zool.*) der Mandrill.

mane [mein], *s.* die Mähne.

man|-eater, *s.* der Menschenfresser. **--eating,** *adj.* menschenfressend.

mane-comb, *s.* der Striegel. **maned,** *adj.* gemähnt, Mähnen-.

manège [mæ'neʒ], *s.* die Reitschule, Reitbahn; Manege, Dressierkunst, Reitkunst; das Zureiten, Schulreiten.

manes ['meini:z], *pl.* Manen (*pl.*).

maneuver, (*Am.*) *see* **manœuvre.**

manful ['mænful], *adj.* mannhaft, entschlossen, tapfer. **manfulness,** *s.* die Mannhaftigkeit, Entschlossenheit, Tapferkeit.

manganate ['mæŋgəneit], *s.* mangansaures Salz. **manganese** [-ni:z], *s.* das Mangan.

mange [meindʒ], *s.* die Räude.

mangel-wurzel ['mæŋgl'wə:zl], *s.* die Runkelrübe, der Mangold.

manger ['meindʒə], *s.* die Krippe, der Futtertrog; ***dog in the -***, der Neidhammel, Neidhart.

manginess ['meindʒinis], *s.* die Räudigkeit.

[1]**mangle** [mæŋgl], **1.** *s.* die Mange(l), Wäscherolle. **2.** *v.t.* mangeln, rollen (*clothes*).

[2]**mangle,** *v.t.* zerreißen, zerfetzen, zerfleischen, zerstückeln; (*fig.*) verstümmeln, entstellen.

mango ['mæŋgou], *s.* der Mangobaum; die Mango(pflaume).

mangold ['mæŋgould], *s. See* **mangel-wurzel.**

mangrove ['mæŋgrouv], *s.* der Mangrove(n)baum, die Mangrove.

mangy ['meindʒi], *adj.* räudig, krätzig; (*sl. fig.*) schäbig, lausig.

man|-handle, *v.t.* durch Menschenkraft (allein) bewegen *or* befördern; (*fig. a p.*) gewaltsam anpacken, rauh behandeln, mißhandeln. **-hole,** *s.* die Einsteigeöffnung, das Mannloch; - ***cover***, der Schachtdeckel.

manhood ['mænhud], *s.* menschliche Natur, das Menschentum; die Männlichkeit, Mannhaftigkeit, Mannesehre, der Mannesmut; das Mannesalter; (*collect.*) Männer (*pl.*); - ***suffrage***, das Männerwahlrecht.

man|-hour, *s.* die Arbeitsstunde pro Mann. **--hunt,** *s.* die Menschenjagd.

mania ['meiniə], *s.* der Wahn(sinn), die Raserei, Besessenheit; Manie; (*fig.*) Leidenschaft (*for*, für), Sucht (nach), Verrücktheit (auf (*Acc.*)), Manie, der Fimmel. **maniac** [-niæk], **1.** *adj.* wahnsinnig, rasend, manisch. **2.** *s.* Wahnsinnige(r), Verrückte(r), Irre(r). **maniacal** [mə'naiəkl], *adj. See* **maniac, 1. manic** ['mænik], *adj.* manisch, besessen; ***--depressive***, manisch-depressiv.

manicure ['mænikjuə], **1.** *s.* die Handpflege, Nagelpflege, Maniküre. **2.** *v.t.* maniküren. **manicurist** [-rist], *s.* die Maniküre, Handpflegerin.

manifest ['mænifest], **1.** *adj.* offenbar, offenkundig, augenscheinlich, handgreiflich, deutlich; ***make -***, offenbaren, kundtun, klarlegen, klarstellen. **2.** *v.t.* offenbaren, verkünden, bekunden, kundtun, (deutlich) (an)zeigen, darlegen, manifestieren; ***be -ed***, sich zeigen. **3.** *v.i.* öffentlich auftreten; erscheinen, sich zeigen *or* offenbaren (*of ghost*). **4.** *s.* (*Naut.*) das Ladungsverzeichnis, der Frachtbrief. **manifestation** [-'teiʃən], *s.* die Offenbarung, Kundgebung, Bekanntmachung, Äußerung, Darlegung; (Geister)erscheinung. **manifesto** [-'festou], *s.* öffentliche Bekanntmachung *or* Erklärung, das Manifest.

manifold ['mænifould], **1.** *adj.* mannigfaltig, mannigfach, mehrfach, vielfach, vielfältig, (*indecl.*) vielerlei; vielförmig, verschiedenartig; (*Tech.*) Vielfach-, Vielzweck-, Mehrzweck-. **2.** *v.t.* vervielfältigen. **3.** *s.* (*Tech.*) die Sammelleitung. **manifold|-paper,** *s.* das Durchschlagpapier.

manikin ['mænikin], *s.* das Männlein, der Zwerg, Knirps; (*registered trade name*) - ***cigar***, das *or* der (*coll.* die) Zigarillo.

Manila [mə'nilə], *s.* 1. die Manilazigarre; 2. der Manilahanf; - ***paper***, das Manilapapier.

maniple ['mænipl], *s.* (*R.C.*) die Manipel, (*Hist., Mil.*) der Manipel.

manipulate [mə'nipjuleit], *v.t.* behandeln, handhaben, hantieren mit; (*Comm.*) (künstlich) beeinflussen (*the market*); (*coll.*) zurechtstutzen, frisieren, deichseln. **manipulation** [-'leiʃən], *s.* (kunstgerechte) Handhabung *or* Behandlung *or* Bearbeitung; (*Comm.*) Manipulation, (künstliche) Beeinflussung; (*coll.*) der Kniff, Kunstgriff; (*oft. pl.*) die Manipulation, das Manöver, Machenschaften (*pl.*). **manipulative** [–lətiv], *adj.* Handhabungs–, Manipulations–. **manipulator,** *s.* der Bearbeiter, Handhaber. **manipulatory,** *adj.* *See* **manipulative.**

mankind [mæn'kaind], *s.* die Menschheit, das Menschengeschlecht; (*collect.*) Menschen (*pl.*), der Mensch. **manlike,** *adj.* menschenähnlich; (*of a woman*) männisch, männerhaft, unweiblich. **manliness,** *s.* die Männlichkeit, Mannhaftigkeit. **manly,** *adj.* männlich, mannhaft; Mannes–, Männer–. **man-made,** *adj.* künstlich.

manna ['mænə], *s.* (*B.*) die *or* das Manna.

mannequin ['mænikin], *s.* die Vorführdame, das *or* der Mannequin; – ***parade***, die Modenschau.

manner ['mænə], *s.* 1. die Art, Weise, Art und Weise; ***adverb of*** –, das Umstandswort der Art und Weise; ***after the – of,*** nach (der) Art von; ***all – of things,*** alles mögliche; ***by all – of means,*** auf alle Fälle, schlechterdings; ***by no – of means,*** keineswegs, auf keinen Fall, durchaus nicht, unter gar keinen Umständen; ***in a*** –, in gewisser Hinsicht, gewissermaßen, gleichsam; ***in a – of speaking,*** sozusagen; ***in like*** or ***the same*** –, in gleicher Weise, ebenso; ***in such a*** –, auf solche Weise, derart; ***in this*** –, in dieser *or* auf diese Weise; ***as to the – born,*** als ob es (ihm) angeboren wäre; ***what – of means?*** was für . . .? 2. das Verhalten, Betragen, Auftreten (*of a p.*); 3. der Stil, die Stilart, Manier (*of art*); ***in the grand*** –, mit würdevollem Gehabe.

mannered ['mænəd], *adj.* 1. gekünstelt, geziert, manieriert; 2. (*in compounds*) gesittet, geartet; *e.g.* ***ill-***–, ungeraten, ungezogen; ***well-***–, artig, brav, gut erzogen. **mannerism** [–rizm], *s.* die Manieriertheit, Geziertheit, Gespreiztheit, Verschrobenheit, Unnatürlichkeit, Künstelei (*of behaviour*), eigenartige Wendung (*in speech*); (*Art*) der Manierismus. **mannerless,** *adj.* unmanierlich, ohne Manieren. **mannerliness,** *s.* die Manierlichkeit, Höflichkeit, gutes Benehmen. **mannerly,** *adj.* gesittet, höflich, manierlich. **manners** [–z], *pl.* das Benehmen, Manieren (*pl.*), (gute) Umgangsformen (*pl.*), Sitten (*pl.*); Sitten (und Gebräuche) (*pl.*); ***it is bad*** –, es schickt *or* gehört sich nicht; ***he has no*** –, er hat keine Manieren; ***comedy of*** –, die Sittenkomödie; ***other times other*** –, andere Zeiten andere Sitten.

manning ['mæniŋ], *s.* die Bemannung, Besetzung. **mannish,** *adj.* (*usu. of a woman*) männisch, männerhaft, unweiblich, unfraulich.

manoeuvrability [mənu:vrə'biliti], *s.* die Manövrierfähigkeit. **manoeuvrable** [–'nu:vrəbl], *adj.* manövrierbar, manövrierfähig; (*fig.*) beweglich, wendig. **manoeuvre** [–'nu:və], 1. *s.* das Manöver; *pl.* (*Mil.*) große Truppenübung, (*Naut.*) Flottenübung; (*fig.*) taktische Bewegung, die Schwenkung; der Kunstgriff, Schachzug, die Finte, List. 2. *v.i.* manövrieren; (*fig.*) geschickt zu Werke gehen. 3. *v.t.* manövrieren lassen; (*fig.*) geschickt handhaben; – ***o.s. into a position,*** sich durch Geschick in eine Lage bringen, sich (*Dat.*) eine Lage verschaffen.

man-of-war, *s.* das Kriegsschiff; (*Orn.*) ***magnificent – bird,*** der Pracht-Fregattvogel (*Fregata magnificens*).

manometer [mæ'nɔmitə], *s.* das Manometer, der (Dampf)druckmesser.

manor ['mænə], *s.* das Rittergut, Landgut; ***lord of the*** –, der Gutsherr. **manor-house,** *s.* das Herrschaftshaus, herrschaftliches Schloß, der Herrensitz, das Herrenhaus. **manorial** [mə'nɔ:riəl], *adj.* herrschaftlich, Herrschafts–, Ritterguts–.

manpower ['mænpauə], *s.* das Menschenmaterial, der Menschenbestand, Personalbestand, Arbeitskräfte (*pl.*); (*Mil.*) die Kriegsstärke; (*rare*) Menschenkraft, Arbeitsleistung.

mansard ['mænsɑ:d], *s.* (*also* ––***roof***) das Mansardendach.

manse [mæns], *s.* (*Scots*) das Pfarrhaus.

manservant ['mænsə:vənt], *s.* der Diener, Bediente(r).

mansion ['mænʃən], *s.* (herrschaftliches) Wohnhaus; *pl.* der Häuserblock mit größeren Einzelwohnungen. **mansion-house,** *s.* das Herrenhaus; ***the Mansion-House,*** die Amtswohnung des Londoner Oberbürgermeisters.

manslaughter ['mænslɔ:tə], *s.* (*Law*) fahrlässige Tötung, der Totschlag.

mantel [mæntl], *s.* (*also* ***–piece, –shelf***) der *or* das Kaminsims, das Kamingesims, die Kamineinfassung.

mant(e)let ['mæntlit], *s.* (*Mil.*) die Schutzwehr, schußsicherer Schild.

mantilla [mæn'tilə], *s.* die Mantille, spanischer Schleier *or* Umhang.

mantis ['mæntis], *s.* (*Ent.*) die Gottesanbeterin.

mantle [mæntl], 1. *s.* ärmelloser Mantel, der Umhang, Überwurf; (*fig.*) Schutzmantel, die Hülle, Umhüllung; (*also* ***gas***––) der Glühstrumpf; (*Tech.*) Formmantel. 2. *v.t.* bedecken, überziehen, einhüllen; (*fig.*) verbergen, verhüllen. 3. *v.i.* (*Poet.*) sich überziehen, bedeckt werden; (*fig.*) rot werden, erröten (*of the face*).

mantrap ['mæntræp], *s.* die Fußangel.

manual ['mænjuəl], 1. *adj.* manuell, Hand–; (*Law*) eigenhändig; – ***aid,*** tätige Beihilfe; – ***alphabet,*** die Fingersprache; (*Mil.*) – ***exercise,*** die Griffübung; – ***labour,*** see – ***work***; – ***press,*** die Handpresse; ***sign*** –, eigenhändige Unterschrift; – ***training,*** der Werkunterricht; – ***work,*** körperliche Arbeit, die Handarbeit. 2. *s.* 1. das Handbuch, der Leitfaden, die Vorschrift; 2. das Manual (*of an organ*).

manufactory [mænju'fæktəri], *s.* (*obs.*) das Fabrikgebäude, die Fabrik.

manufacture [mænju'fæktʃə], 1. *s.* 1. die Herstellung, Erzeugung, Verfertigung, Fabrikation; 2. das Erzeugnis, Industrieprodukt, Fabrikat, die (Fertig)ware, der Artikel. 2. *v.t.* herstellen, erzeugen, anfertigen, verfertigen, fabrizieren (***out of,*** aus), verarbeiten (***into,*** zu); ***–d article,*** der Fabriksartikel, die Fabrikware, das Fabrikat; ***–d goods,*** Manufakturwaren, Fertigwaren (*pl.*). **manufacturer,** *s.* 1. der Hersteller, Erzeuger, Anfertiger; 2. (*Comm.*) Fabrikant, Fabrikbesitzer, Industrielle(r). **manufacturing,** *adj.* 1. Fabrik–, Industrie–; – ***town,*** die Fabrikstadt, Industriestadt; 2. Herstellungs–, Produktions–, Fabrikations–; – ***expenses,*** die Gestehungskosten; – ***process,*** das Herstellungsverfahren.

manumission [mænju'miʃən], *s.* die Freilassung (*of slaves*). **manumit** [–'mit], *v.t.* freilassen.

manure [mə'njuə], 1. *s.* der Dünger, das Düngemittel, der Mist; ***liquid*** –, die Jauche. 2. *v.t.* düngen.

manuscript ['mænjuskript], 1. *s.* die Handschrift, das Manuskript; (*of an author*) Autorenmanuskript, die Urschrift; (*Typ.*) Satzvorlage, Druckvorlage. 2. *adj.* handschriftlich, handgeschrieben.

many ['meni], 1. *adj.* (*before pl.*) viel(e), (*before sing.*) manche(r, -s), manch eine(r, -s); – ***another,*** manch anderer; ***as*** –, ebenso viel; ***as – as you like,*** so viele Sie wollen; ***as – as 10,*** nicht weniger als 10; – ***fewer,*** viel weniger; – ***a man,*** mancher (Mann); (*Prov.*) – ***hands make light work,*** viele Hände machen bald ein Ende; (*Prov.*) – ***men,*** – ***minds,*** viele Köpfe, viele Sinne; – ***a one,*** manch einer; ***in – respects,*** in viel(fach)er Hinsicht; – ***a time,*** schon oft, schon des öfteren; – ***and – a time,*** gar manches Mal, zu wiederholten Malen; – ***is the time,*** gar manches Mal; ***like so – ants,*** wie ein Haufen Ameisen; ***in so – words,*** ausdrücklich; ***too – by half,*** um die Hälfte zuviel; ***one too*** –, einer zu viel; ***be (one) too – for me,*** mir überlegen sein; ***in – ways,*** see ***in – respects.*** 2. *s.* (*pl. constr.*) die große Masse, der große Haufen; ***a good (great)*** –, eine ziemliche (große) Menge, (*as attrib.*) ziemlich (sehr) viele.

many|-coloured, *adj.* vielfarbig, bunt. **––cornered,** *adj.* vieleckig. **––sided,** *adj.* vielseitig (*also fig.*). **––sidedness,** *s.* die Vielseitigkeit.

map [mæp], 1. *s.* die (Land)karte; Geländekarte, das Meßtischblatt; – ***of the heavens,*** die Himmelskarte,

Sternkarte; – *of the town*, der Stadtplan; – *of the world*, die Weltkarte; (*coll.*) *off the* –, abgelegen, unzugänglich, gottverlassen; (*fig.*) so gut wie nicht vorhanden, bedeutungslos; (*fig.*) *wipe off the* –, dem Erdboden gleichmachen, ausradieren; (*coll.*) *on the* –, beachtenswert, von Bedeutung; *put on the* –, Geltung verschaffen (*Dat.*), zur Geltung bringen. **2.** *v.t.* kartographisch darstellen; kartographisch vermessen *or* aufnehmen; auf einer Karte eintragen *or* abbilden *or* verzeichnen; (*fig.*) – *out*, genau aufzeichnen, entwerfen, vorausplanen, ausarbeiten; aufteilen (*one's time*).

map|-case, *s.* das Kartenfutteral, der Kartenbehälter. **--exercise,** *s.* (*Mil.*) das Planspiel.

maple [meipl], *s.* der (Feld)ahorn. **maple-sugar,** *s.* der Ahornzucker.

mapping ['mæpiŋ], *s.* die Kartenaufnahme, Kartographie, das Kartenzeichnen. **map-reading,** *s.* das Kartenlesen.

maquis ['mæki], *pl.* (*Mil.*) Maquisarden (*pl.*).

mar [mɑ:], *v.t.* von Nachteil sein (*Dat.*), (be)-schädigen, beeinträchtigen; stören, verderben, vereiteln; *make or* –, Glück oder Verderben bringen (*Dat.*).

marabou ['mærəbu:], *s.* (*Orn.*) der Marabu, Kropfstorch (*Leptoptilus*).

marasmic [mə'ræzmik], *adj.* (*Med.*) marastisch, marantisch, entkräftet, Schwäche–. **marasmus,** *s.* die Entkräftung, Abzehrung, (Alters)schwäche, körperlicher Zerfall, der Kräfteverfall, Marasmus.

marathon ['mærəθən], **1.** *s.* (*Spt.*) der Langstreckenlauf, (*also fig.*) Dauerlauf; (*fig.*) Dauerwettkampf. **2.** *adj.* Dauer–.

maraud [mə'rɔ:d], *v.i.* plündern, marodieren. **marauder,** *s.* der Plünderer, Mordbrenner, Marodeur.

marble ['mɑ:bl], **1.** *s.* 1. der Marmor; (*Art*) das Marmorkunstwerk; 2. die Murmel, der Schneller, Klicker (*toy*); *pl.* das Murmelspiel; *play (at) –s*, Murmeln spielen. **2.** *adj.* marmorn, Marmor–; (*fig.*) steinhart; marmorweiß. **3.** *v.t.* marmorieren. **marble-paper,** *s.* marmoriertes Papier. **marbling,** *s.* die Marmorierung.

[1]**march** [mɑ:tʃ], **1.** *s.* die Grenze, Mark; *pl.* (umstrittenes) Grenzgebiet. **2.** *v.i.* grenzen (*upon*, an (*Acc.*)), zusammenstoßen (*with*, mit).

[2]**march, 1.** *s.* der Marsch (*also Mus.*); Vormarsch (*on*, auf (*Acc.*)); Tagesmarsch; Marschschritt; (*fig.*) das Vorwärtsschreiten, der Fortschritt, (Fort)gang, (Ab)lauf, die Entwicklung; *dead* –, der Totenmarsch; *line of* –, die Marschlinie; – *past*, der Parademarsch, Vorbeimarsch; *slow* –, langsamer Parademarsch; *steal a – on him*, ihm überrunden *or* zuvorkommen, ihm den Rang ablaufen *or* ein Schnippchen schlagen. **2.** *v.i.* marschieren, ziehen; (*fig.*) vorwärtsschreiten; *time –es on*, die Zeit schreitet fort; – *off*, abrücken; – *at ease!* ohne Tritt marsch! – *past*, (im Paradeschritt) vorbeimarschieren an (*Dat.*); *quick –!* Abteilung marsch! **3.** *v.t.* marschieren lassen, abführen (*troops*); im Marsch zurücklegen (*distance*); – *off*, abführen.

March, *s.* der März; – *hare*, der Märzhase.

marching ['mɑ:tʃiŋ], *adj.* Marsch–; – *order*, die Marschausrüstung; – *orders*, der Marschbefehl; (*coll. fig.*) Laufpaß; *be under – orders*, Marschbefehl haben; – *song*, das Marschlied.

marchioness ['mɑ:ʃənis], *s.* die Marquise, Markgräfin.

marchpane ['mɑ:tʃpein], *s. See* **marzipan.**

mare [mɛə], *s.* die Stute. **mare's| nest,** *s.* (*fig.*) Gemseneier (*pl.*), die Zeitungsente **--tail,** *s.* (*Bot.*) der Tannenwedel; *pl.* Wolkenstreifen, Federwolken (*pl.*).

margaric [mɑ:'gærik], *adj.* (*Chem.*) Margarin–. **margarine** [–gə'ri:n, –dʒə'ri:n], *s.* die Margarine.

[1]**marge** [mɑ:dʒ], *s.* (*Poet.*) der Rand, Saum.

[2]**marge,** (*coll.*) *see* **margarine.**

margin ['mɑ:dʒin], **1.** *s.* 1. der Rand; (*Typ.*) (Seiten)rand; *in the* –, am Rande, nebenstehend; *on the* –, auf dem Rande, an der Grenze; 2. der Spielraum; (*Comm.*) (*also profit* –) die Verdienstspanne, Gewinnspanne, Handelsschere; der Überschuß; (*fig.*) *leave a* –, Spielraum lassen; *leave no* – (*of profit*), keinen Überschuß gewähren, keinen Gewinn abwerfen; (*fig.*) *by a narrow* –, mit knapper Not; – *of safety*, der Sicherheitsfaktor; 3. (*St. Exch.*) die Deckung, Hinterlegungssumme, Einschlußzahlung, Marge; 4. (*Spt.*) der Vorsprung, Abstand. **2.** *v.t.* 1. umranden, säumen; 2. mit Rand(bemerkungen) versehen, am Rand vermerken; 3. (*Comm.*) decken.

marginal ['mɑ:dʒinl], *adj.* 1. auf dem *or* am Rande, Rand–, Grenz–; – *case*, der Grenzfall; – *inscription*, die Umschrift (*on coins*); – *note*, die Randbemerkung; 2. Mindest–; – *profit*, das Gewinnminimum, die Rentabilitätsgrenze. **marginalia** [–'neiliə], *pl.* Randbemerkungen (*pl.*).

margrave ['mɑ:greiv], *s.* der Markgraf. **margraviate** [–greiviət], *s.* die Markgrafschaft. **margravine** [–grə'vi:n], *s.* die Markgräfin.

marguerite [mɑ:gə'ri:t], *s.* (*Bot.*) die Margerite, großes Maßlieb.

marigold ['mærigould], *s.* (*Bot.*) die Ringelblume.

marijuana [mɑ:ri'hwɑ:nə], *s.* das Marihuana.

marina [mə'ri:nə], *s.* das Jachtbassin.

marinade [mæri'neid], *s.* die Marinade, Essigsoße. **marinate** ['mærineit], *v.t.* marinieren, sauer einmachen.

marine [mə'ri:n], **1.** *adj.* Meer(es)–, See–; – *cable*, das Seekabel; – *engine*, der Bootsmotor, die Schiffsmaschine; – *insurance*, die Schiffahrtsversicherung; – *station*, der Hafenbahnhof; – *stores*, Schiffsgegenstände (*pl.*). **2.** *s.* 1. der Seesoldat; *pl.* Seetruppen (*pl.*), die Marineinfanterie; (*coll.*) *tell that to the –s!* das mach' einem andern weis! 2. die Marine; *mercantile* –, die Handelsmarine.

mariner ['mærinə], *s.* der Seemann, Matrose; *–'s compass*, der Schiffskompaß, die Bussole.

mariolatry [mæri'ɔlətri], *s.* die Marienvergötterung, der Madonnenkult.

marionette [mæriə'net], *s.* die Drahtpuppe, Marionette; (*fig.*) Puppe, Figur.

marital ['mæritl], *adj.* ehelich, Ehe–; – *rights*, das Gattenrecht; – *status*, das Familienstand.

maritime ['mæritaim], *adj.* 1. See–, Schiffahrts–, Seehandel treibend; – *affairs*, Schiffahrtsangelegenheiten (*pl.*), das Seewesen; – *court*, das Seeamt; – *law*, das Seerecht; – *nations*, seehandeltreibende Nationen; – *powers*, Seemächte; 2. (*esp. Bot., Zool.*) Meer(es)–, Strand–, am Strand gelegen *or* lebend.

marjoram ['mɑ:dʒərəm], *s.* (*Bot.*) der Marjoran, Meiran.

Mark [mɑ:k], *s.* (*B.*) Markus (*m.*); (*Tristan legend*) (König) Marke.

[1]**mark,** *s.* die (deutsche) Mark (*currency*).

[2]**mark, 1.** *s.* 1. die Bezeichnung, Markierung, das Mal, (An)zeichen; die Marke, das (Merk)zeichen; *distinctive or distinguishing* –, das Kennzeichen, Unterscheidungszeichen; *laundry* –, das Wäschezeichen; – *of mouth*, die Kennung, Bohne (*of horses*); – *of origin*, das Herkunftszeichen; *trade* –, die Schutzmarke, Handelsmarke; 2. (*fig.*) das (Kenn)zeichen, Gepräge, Merkmal, der Stempel; – *of confidence*, der Vertrauensbeweis; – *of favour*, die Gunstbezeigung; *man of* –, ein Mann von Bedeutung, markante Persönlichkeit; – *of respect*, das Zeichen der Hochachtung; *leave one's – upon*, seinen Stempel aufdrücken (*Dat.*), seine Spur hinterlassen auf (*Dat.*); *make one's* –, sich (*Dat.*) einen Namen machen; 3. das Schriftzeichen, Kreuz (*as signature*); 4. die Narbe, Schwiele, Strieme, Kerbe, der Einschnitt; 5. die Zielscheibe, das Ziel, Mal; *easy* –, leichtes Ziel; (*sl.*) leichter Kauf, leichte Beute; *hit the* –, (ins Schwarze) treffen; *miss one's* –, fehlschießen, vorbeischießen, (*fig.*) sein Ziel verfehlen, (*coll.*) danebenhauen; (*fig.*) *overshoot the* –, über das Ziel hinausschießen, über die Stränge schlagen, zu weit gehen; *quite beside* or *far from the* –, nicht zur S. gehörig, fehl

am Platz, unangebracht; ***up to the –,*** der Aufgabe gewachsen, den Anforderungen genügend, den Erwartungen entsprechend; (*coll.*) (*of health*) auf der Höhe; ***wide of the –,*** weit vom Ziel, am Ziel vorbei, (*fig.*) irrig, verfehlt, (*coll.*) danebengehauen; ***within the –,*** innerhalb der erlaubten Grenzen, berechtigt; 6. (*Spt.*) die Startlinie; ***get off the –,*** starten; 7. (*Naut. etc.*) die Bake, das Leitzeichen; 8. (*Tech.*) Modell, die Type; 9. (*oft. pl.*) Zensur, Note, der Punkt, das Zeugnis (*at school*); ***bad*** or ***poor –s,*** schlechte Note, schlechtes Zeugnis; ***full –s,*** höchste Punkte, beste Note. **2.** *v.t.* 1. (be)zeichnen, kennzeichnen, charakteristisch *or* kennzeichnend *or* ein Zeichen sein für; zum Ausdruck bringen, hervorheben, auszeichnen; (*Comm.*) festsetzen, notieren (lassen); Zeichen hinterlassen auf (*Dat.*); (*fig.*) bestimmen, auswählen (*for*, für); (*fig.*) ***be –ed by,*** im Zeichen stehen (***with***, *Gen.*); ***– with a hot iron,*** brandmarken; ***– an occasion,*** zum Anlaß nehmen; ***– time,*** (*Mil.*) auf der Stelle treten; (*fig.*) nicht vom Fleck kommen; sich abwartend verhalten; ***– down,*** (*Comm.*) im Preis herabsetzen (*goods*); vormerken, bestimmen (***for***, für) (*a p.*); ***– off,*** abgrenzen, abstecken, (*Geom. etc.*) abtragen; abstreichen (*on a list*); (*fig.*) (aus)scheiden, absondern, trennen; ***– out,*** abgrenzen, abstecken (*ground*), bezeichnen; (*fig.*) bestimmen, ausersehen (***for***, für *or* zu); (*Comm.*) ***– up,*** im Preis heraufsetzen, erhöhen; 2. achtgeben auf (*Acc.*), beachten, sich (*Dat.*) merken; anmerken, vermerken, notieren; ***– my words!*** nimm das zur Kenntnis! 3. zensieren, bewerten, korrigieren (*school-work*); 4. (*Spt.*) decken (*opponent*); aufschreiben, notieren, markieren (*score*). **3.** *v.i.* aufpassen, achtgeben; ***– you!*** wohlgemerkt! passen Sie auf!

marked [mɑːkt], *adj.* 1. markiert, ge(kenn)zeichnet; ***– cheque,*** bestätigter Wechsel; ***– coin,*** abgestempelte Münze; 2. ausgeprägt, markant, auffällig, auffallend, deutlich, merklich, ausdrücklich; ***– attention,*** gespannte Aufmerksamkeit; ***– progress*** merklicher Fortschritt; 3. gebrandmarkt, verrufen; ***– man,*** Gebrandmarkte(r). **marker,** *s.* der Aufschreiber, Notierer (*in games*); Anzeiger (*at target-practice*); (*Bill.*) Markör; (*Mil.*) Flügelmann; (*Naut., Av.*) das Sichtzeichen; (*Av.*) der Beleuchter (*plane*); (*also* ***book –***) das Lesezeichen, Merkzeichen.

market [ˈmɑːkit], **1.** *s.* 1. der Marktplatz, die Markthalle; ***to –,*** auf den Markt; 2. der Markt; ***be on the –,*** (zum Verkauf) angeboten werden; ***come into the –,*** auf den Markt kommen; ***drug in*** (*Am.* ***on***) ***the –,*** unverkäufliche Ware, der Ladenhüter; ***glut the –,*** den Markt überschwemmen; ***hold the –,*** den Markt beherrschen; ***place*** or ***put on the –,*** auf den Markt bringen; ***sell in the open –*** freihändig verkaufen; 3. (*St. Exch.*) der Geldmarkt, Handelsverkehr, die Wirtschaftslage, Börse; (*coll.*) ***play the –,*** an der Börse spekulieren; ***rig the –,*** die Kurse in die Höhe treiben; 4. der Marktwert, Marktpreis, Marktpreise (*pl.*); 5. der Absatz, Handelsbereich, das Absatzgebiet; ***find a – for,*** an den Mann bringen; ***meet with a ready –*** schnellen *or* guten Absatz finden; ***open new –s,*** neue Handelsbeziehungen anbahnen; 6. die Nachfrage (***for***, nach), der Bedarf (an (*Dat.*)); ***be in the – for,*** Bedarf haben an (*Dat.*). **2.** *v.i.* einkaufen; auf dem Markt handeln. **3.** *v.t.* auf dem Markt verkaufen, auf den Markt bringen, Absatz finden für.

marketable [ˈmɑːkitəbl], *adj.* verkäuflich, gangbar, marktfähig, marktgängig; (*St. Exch.*) börsenfähig. **market|-day,** *s.* der Markttag. **--garden,** *s.* der Gemüsegarten, Handelsgarten. **--gardener,** *s.* der Handelsgärtner, Gemüsegärtner. **--gardening,** *s.* die Handelsgärtnerei, Gemüsegärtnerei. **--hall,** *s.* die Markthalle. **marketing,** *s.* 1. der Marktbesuch, das Einkaufen; ***do one's –,*** seine Einkäufe machen; 2. (*Comm.*) die Marktversorgung, Absatzpolitik; ***– organization,*** die Absatzorganisation, Marktvereinigung. **market|-place,** *s.* der Marktplatz. **--price,** *s.* der Marktpreis; (*St. Exch.*) Kurs(wert). **--quotation,** *s.* (*St. Exch.*) die Börsennotierung. **--report,** *s.* der Handelsbericht; (*St. Exch.*) Börsenbericht. **--research,** *s.* die Marktforschung. **--rigging,** *s.* (*sl.*) die Kurstreiberei. **--town,** *s.* der Marktflecken, die Kreisstadt. **--value,** *s.* der Verkehrswert, Kaufwert.

marking [ˈmɑːkiŋ], *s.* die Kennzeichnung, Markierung; (*Zool. etc.*) Zeichnung, Musterung; (*Mus.*) Bezeichnung; (*of examinations*) das Korrigieren, Zensieren, die Bewertung. **marking|-awl,** *s.* die Reißahle. **--ink,** *s.* die Wäschetinte. **--thread,** *s.* das Zeichengarn (*sewing*), die Schlagschnur (*painting*).

marksman [ˈmɑːksmən], *s.* der Scharfschütze, Meisterschütze. **marksmanship,** *s.* die Schießkunst.

marl [mɑːl], **1.** *s.* der Mergel. **2.** *v.t.* mit Mergel düngen, mergeln.

marline [ˈmɑːlin], *s.* die Marlleine. **marlinespike,** *s.* der Marlspieker.

marly [ˈmɑːli], *adj.* mergelhaltig, merg(e)lig.

marmalade [ˈmɑːməleid], *s.* die Orangenmarmelade.

marmoreal [mɑːˈmɔːriəl], *adj.* marmorartig, marmorn, Marmor–.

marmoset [ˈmɑːməzet], *s.* (*Zool.*) das Seidenäffchen.

marmot [ˈmɑːmət], *s.* (*Zool.*) das Murmeltier, der Hamster.

[1]**maroon** [məˈruːn], *adj.* kastanienbraun, rotbraun.

[2]**maroon,** **1.** *s.* der Maron(neger), Buschneger; (*Hist.*) entlaufener Negersklave. **2.** *v.t.* (zur Strafe) an einer öden Küste *or* Insel aussetzen; (*fig.*) einsam und hilflos verlassen. **3.** *v.i.* (*Am.*) herumlungern; an einem einsamen Platz zelten.

[3]**maroon,** *s.* der Kanonenschlag, das Signalfeuerwerk.

marplot [ˈmɑːplɔt], *s.* der Störenfried, Unheilstifter, Spaßverderber, Spielverderber.

marque [mɑːk], *s.* das Kaperschiff; (*Naut.*) ***letter(s) of –,*** der Kaperbrief.

marquee [mɑːˈkiː], *s.* großes Zelt.

marquess, ***see*** **marquis.**

marquetry [ˈmɑːkitri], *s.* die Marketerie, Intarsia, Einlegearbeit.

marquis [ˈmɑːkwis], *s.* der Marquis. **marquisate** [–ət], *s.* das Marquisat, die Marquiswürde.

marred [mɑːd], *imperf., p.p. of* **mar.**

marriage [ˈmæridʒ], *s.* die Ehe, der Ehestand; die Eheschließung, Heirat, Hochzeit, Vermählung, Trauung (***to***, mit); (*fig.*) Vermählung, enge Verbindung; ***ask for her (hand) in –,*** um sie anhalten; ***by –,*** angeheiratet; ***related by –,*** verschwägert; ***by his first –,*** aus seiner ersten Ehe; ***civil –,*** standesamtliche Trauung; ***companionate –,*** die Kameradschaftsehe; ***consummate the –,*** den Eheakt vollziehen; ***contract (a) –,*** die Ehe eingehen; ***– of convenience,*** die Zweckheirat, Geldheirat, Verstandesheirat, Vernunftehe; ***give her in –,*** sie verheiraten; ***morganatic –,*** die Ehe zur linken Hand; ***take her in –,*** sie heiraten; ***– by proxy,*** die Ferntrauung.

marriageable [ˈmæridʒəbl], *adj.* heiratsfähig, mannbar; ***– age,*** die Ehemündigkeit. **marriage|-articles,** *pl.* der Ehevertrag. **--bed,** *s.* das Ehebett. **--broker,** *s.* der Heiratsvermittler. **--ceremony,** *s.* die Eheschließung, Trauung. **--certificate,** *s.* *See* **--lines. --contract,** *s.* *See* **--articles. --licence,** *s.* (standes)amtliche Eheerlaubnis. **--lines,** *pl.* der Trauschein. **--portion,** *s.* die Mitgift. **--rites,** *pl.* Hochzeitsbräuche (*pl.*). **--service,** *s.* kirchliche Trauung. **--settlement,** *s.* die Vermögensübertragung durch Ehevertrag. **--vow,** *s.* das Ehegelöbnis.

married [ˈmærid], *adj.* verheiratet, vermählt; (*Law*) verehelicht; ehelich, Ehe–; (*fig.*) eng *or* innig verbunden; ***newly –,*** neuvermählt; ***– life,*** das Eheleben; ***– man,*** der Ehemann; ***– people,*** Eheleute; ***– state,*** der Ehestand.

[1]**marrow** [ˈmærou], *s.* das (Knochen)mark; (*fig.*)

das Mark, der Kern, Innerste(s), Wesentlichste(s); (*fig.*) ***to the* –**, bis aufs Mark, bis ins Innerste.

²**marrow,** *s.* (*also* ***vegetable*** –) der Eierkürbis.

marrow|-bone, *s.* der Markknochen. **–fat,** *s.* die Markerbse. – **squash,** *s.* (*Am.*) *see* ²**marrow. marrowy,** *adj.* markig, kernig.

¹**marry** ['mæri], **1.** *v.t.* heiraten, sich verheiraten *or* vermählen mit (*one's partner*), verheiraten, vermählen (*son or daughter*) (***to***, mit *or* an (*Acc.*)), verheiraten, trauen (*as the priest*); (*fig.*) eng verbinden *or* zusammenfügen (***to, with,*** mit); (*Naut.*) spleißen, splissen (*ropes*); ***be married to,*** verheiratet sein mit; ***get married to,*** sich verheiraten mit; ***at last get married,*** endlich unter die Haube kommen; – ***off,*** verheiraten, unter die Haube bringen. **2.** *v.i.* (sich ver)heiraten; – ***beneath one's station,*** eine Mißheirat schließen; – ***for love,*** aus Liebe heiraten; (*Prov.*) – ***in haste and repent at leisure,*** schnell gefreit wird meist bereut.

²**marry!** *int.* (*obs.*) wahrlich! traun! fürwahr!

marsh [mɑːʃ], *s.* der Sumpf, Morast, das Sumpfland.

marshal ['mɑːʃəl], **1.** *s.* der Marschall; Zeremonienmeister, Festordner; (*Am.*) Vollstreckungsbeamte(r), Bezirkspolizeichef, Gerichtsvollzieher; (*Av.*) ***air*** –, der General der Luftwaffe; (*Am.*) ***city*** –, der Polizeidirektor; (*Mil.*) ***field*** –, der (General)-feldmarschall. **2.** *v.t.* (an)ordnen, einordnen; aufstellen (*troops*); ordnungsgemäß aufstellen, ordnen (*ideas*); feierlich (hinein)führen (***into,*** in (*Acc.*)); zusammenstellen (*trains*). **marshalling yard,** *s.* der Verschiebebahnhof, Rangierbahnhof.

marsh|-fever, *s.* die Malaria, das Sumpffieber. **--gas,** *s.* das Sumpfgas, Grubengas. **--harrier,** *s.* (*Orn.*) der Rohrweihe (*Circus æruginosus*). **--hawk,** *s.* (*Am.*) *see* **hen-harrier.**

marshiness ['mɑːʃinis], *s.* die Sumpfigkeit.

marsh|-mallow, *s.* (*Bot.*) gemeiner Eibisch, die Althee, Stockrose. **–mallow,** *s.* der Lederzucker. **--marigold,** *s.* die Sumpfdotterblume. **--sandpiper,** *s.* (*Orn.*) der Teichwasserläufer (*Tringa stagnatilis*). **--titmouse,** *s.* (*Orn.*) die Sumpfmeise (*Parus palustris*). **--warbler,** *s.* (*Orn.*) der Sumpf-Rohrsänger (*Acrocephalus palustris*). **marshy,** *adj.* sumpfig, bruchig; – ***ground,*** der Sumpfboden, Bruchboden.

marsupial [mɑː'sjuːpiəl], **1.** *s.* das Beuteltier. **2.** *adj.* Beuteltier–; – ***pouch,*** der Brutsack. **marsupium,** *s.* (*Zool.*) die Bauchtasche, Bauchfalte; der Brutbeutel, Eierbeutel; (*Bot.*) Fruchtbeutel.

mart [mɑːt], *s.* (*Poet.*) der Markt(platz), Handelsplatz; (*coll.*) Auktionsraum.

martagon ['mɑːtəgən], *s.* (*Bot.*) der Türkenbund.

marten ['mɑːtin], *s.* (*Zool.*) der Marder.

martial ['mɑːʃəl], *adj.* kriegerisch, soldatisch, militärisch, Kriegs–, Militär–; – ***bearing,*** soldatische Haltung; – ***law,*** das Kriegsrecht, Standrecht; ***state of – law,*** der Belagerungszustand; – ***music,*** die Militärmusik; – ***spirit,*** der Kampfesmut, die Kampfesfreude.

martin ['mɑːtin], *s.* (*Orn.*) ***house*** –, die Mehlschwalbe, Hausschwalbe (*Delichon urbica*); ***sand–***, die Uferschwalbe (*Riparia riparia*).

martinet [mɑːti'net], *s.* strenge(r) Vorgesetzte(r), der Zuchtmeister.

martingale ['mɑːtiŋgeil], *s.* der Sprungriemen (*of harness*); (*Naut.*) das Stampfstag.

Martinmas ['mɑːtinməs], *s.* der Martinstag (*11 Nov.*).

martyr ['mɑːtə], **1.** *s.* der (die) Märtyrer(in), der Blutzeuge; (*fig.*) das Opfer; ***be a – to gout,*** von Gicht (ständig) geplagt werden; ***be a – in the cause of*** or ***a – to science,*** ein Opfer der Wissenschaft sein, sein Leben im Dienst der Wissenschaft opfern; ***make a – of o.s.,*** sich aufopfern. **2.** *v.t.* zum Märtyrer machen, zu Tode martern, den Martertod erleiden lassen; (*fig.*) martern, quälen, peinigen. **martyrdom** [–dəm], *s.* das Martyrium, Märtyrertum, der Märtyrertod; (*fig.*) Marterqualen (*pl.*). **martyrize,** *v.t.* martern, quälen, peinigen, foltern. **martyrolatry** [–'rɔlətri], *s.* die Märtyrerverehrung, der Märtyrerkult. **martyrology** [–'rɔlədʒi], *s.* das Märtyrologium, Märtyrerbuch, die Geschichte der Märtyrer, Märtyrergeschichten (*pl.*).

marvel ['mɑːvəl], **1.** *s.* das Wunder(ding), (etwas) Wunderbares; ***it is a – to me,*** es ist ein Wunder für mich; (*coll.*) ***he is a*** –, er ist ein unglaublicher Mensch. **2.** *v.i.* staunen, sich (ver)wundern (***at,*** über (*Acc.*)). **marvellous,** *adj.* wunderbar, erstaunlich; (*fig.*) unglaublich, unfaßbar, (*coll.*) phantastisch, fabelhaft. **marvel-of-Peru,** *s.* (*Bot.*) die Wunderblume, falsche Jalape. **marvelous,** (*Am.*) *see* **marvellous.**

Marxism ['mɑːksizm], *s.* der Marxismus. **Marxist, 1.** *s.* der Marxist. **2.** *adj.* marxistisch.

Mary ['mɛəri], *s.* Maria (*f.*).

marzipan [mɑːzi'pæn], *s.* das Marzipan.

mascara [mæs'kɑːrə], *s.* die Wimperntusche.

mascot ['mæskət], *s.* der Talisman; der (die) Glücksbringer(in); (*Motor.*) ***radiator*** –, die Kühlerfigur.

masculine ['mæskjulin], **1.** *adj.* männlich (*also Gram., Metr.*), (*Metr.*) stumpf; Männer–, Herren–; (*of woman*) unweiblich. **2.** *s.* (*Gram.*) das Maskulinum. **masculinity** [–'liniti], *s.* die Männlichkeit, Mannhaftigkeit.

mash [mæʃ], **1.** *s.* der Brei, breiige Masse, das Mus, Gemisch, (*coll.*) der Mischmasch, Mansch; (*Brew.*) die Maische; (*fodder*) das Mengfutter; (*coll.*) der Kartoffelbrei, Quetschkartoffeln (*pl.*). **2.** *v.t.* zerquetschen, zerstoßen, (zer)stampfen; (*Brew.*) (ein)maischen; ***–ed potatoes,*** der Kartoffelbrei, das Kartoffelpüree; ***–ed through a sieve,*** durchgesiebt, durchgeseiht; ***–(ing) tub,*** der Maischbottich.

masher ['mæʃə], *s.* (*obs.*) der Weiberheld.

mashie ['mæʃi], *s.* (eine Art) Golfschläger (*m.*).

mask [mɑːsk], **1.** *s.* 1. die Maske, Larve; ***death*** –, die Totenmaske; ***fencing-***–, die Fechtmaske; ***gas-***–, die Gasmaske; (*fig.*) ***throw off the*** –, die Maske fallen lassen; 2. das Maskenkostüm, die Verkleidung, Maskerade; 3. (*a p.*) Maskierte(r), Vermummte(r), die Maske; 4. (*fig.*) der Schein, Vorwand, Schirm, Deckmantel, die Verkleidung, Verkappung, Verhüllung, Hülle; (*fig.*) ***under the – of,*** unter dem Deckmantel *or* Schutz (*Gen.*). **2.** *v.t.* 1. maskieren, verkleiden, vermummen; ***–ed ball,*** der Maskenball; 2. (*fig.*) verschleiern, verhüllen, verbergen, verdecken; 3. (*Mil.*) tarnen; ***–ed battery,*** maskierte *or* verdeckte Batterie. **masker,** *s.* der Maskenspieler, Maskentänzer, die Maske.

masochism ['mæzəkizm], *s.* der Masochismus. **masochist,** *s.* der Masochist.

mason [meisn], **1.** *s.* 1. der Maurer; Steinhauer, Steinmetz; 2. Freimaurer. **2.** *v.t.* mauern. **masonic** [mə'sɔnik], *adj.* freimaurerisch, Freimaurer–. **masonry,** *s.* 1. die Steinmetzarbeit; Maurerei, Maurerarbeit, das Maurerhandwerk; 2. Mauerwerk; ***bound*** –, das Quaderwerk; 3. die Freimaurerei.

masque [mɑːsk], *s.* das Maskenspiel. **masquerade** [mɑːskə'reid], **1.** *s.* der Maskenball, Maskenzug, das Maskenfest; die Maskerade, Verkleidung, Vermummung, das Maskenkostüm; (*fig.*) die Verstellung, (*coll.*) Schauspielerei, das Theater. **2.** *v.i.* (*fig.*) maskiert gehen, eine Maske tragen; (*fig.*) sich verstellen, sich ausspielen *or* ausgeben (***as,*** als). **masquerader,** *s.* der Maskierer; (*fig.*) Versteller, Vortäuscher.

¹**mass** [mæs], *s.* (*R.C., Mus.*) die Messe; – ***for the dead,*** die Seelenmesse; ***attend*** or ***go to*** –, zur Messe gehen; ***say*** –, die Messe lesen.

²**mass, 1.** *s.* die Masse (*also Phys.*); großer Haufen, große Ansammlung *or* Anhäufung, große Menge *or* (An)zahl, die Unzahl, Unmenge; Allgemeinheit (*of people*); Gesamtheit, Ganzheit, der Hauptteil, größerer Teil, die Mehrzahl (*of things*); ***the***

-es, die (breite) Masse, der Pöbel; (*coll.*) ***be a – of,*** bedeckt sein mit, voll sein von; ***– of cloud,*** die Wolkenmasse; ***– of fire,*** das Feuermeer; ***in the –,*** im allgemeinen, im großen und ganzen. **2.** *v.t.* (an)häufen, aufhäufen, (an)sammeln, zusammentragen, zusammenstellen; (*Mil.*) zusammenziehen, konzentrieren. **3.** *v.i.* sich (an)sammeln *or* (an)häufen, sich zusammenziehen *or* zusammenballen, Massen bilden. **4.** *attrib. adj.* Massen–; ***– action,*** die Massenwirkung; ***– media,*** Massenmedien (*pl.*); ***– meeting,*** die Massenversammlung; ***– production,*** die Massenherstellung, Serienproduktion.

massacre ['mæsəkə], **1.** *s.* das Gemetzel, Blutbad, der Massenmord. **2.** *v.t.* niedermetzeln.

massage ['mæsɑ:ʒ], **1.** *s.* das Massieren, die Massage. **2.** *v.t.* massieren. **masseur** [–'sə:], *s.* der Masseur. **masseuse** [–'sə:z], *s.* die Masseuse.

massif ['mæsif], *s.* die Bergmasse, der Gebirgsstock.

massive ['mæsiv], *adj.* massiv, massig, sehr groß, schwer, Massen–; (*fig.*) mächtig, gediegen, wuchtig, klotzig. **massiveness,** *s.* die Mächtigkeit, mächtiges Ausmaß, die Schwere, Wucht, Gediegenheit.

¹**mast** [mɑ:st], *s.* die Mast, das Mastfutter.

²**mast,** *s.* der Mast; ***aerial –,*** der Antennenmast, Antennenturm; ***at half—,*** auf Halbmast; ***mooring –,*** der Ankermast; ***topgallant –,*** die Bramstenge; ***sail before the –,*** Matrose sein, zur See fahren. **masted,** *adj.* bemastet; (*as suff.*) –mastig, *e.g.* ***three—,*** dreimastig; ***three— vessel,*** der Dreimaster.

master ['mɑ:stə], **1.** *s.* 1. der Herr, Eigentümer, Besitzer; Hausherr; Herrscher, Gebieter; ***be – of,*** beherrschen; ***be – of the situation,*** Herr der Lage sein; ***be – in one's own house,*** der Herr im Hause sein; ***be – of one's time,*** über seine Zeit verfügen können; ***be one's own –,*** sein eigner Herr sein; ***like – like man,*** wie der Herr so der Knecht; ***make o.s. – of,*** beherrschen, sich (*Dat.*) erwerben; 2. der Vorsteher, Leiter, Direktor, Betriebsmeister, Werkmeister; Meister, Arbeitgeber, Dienstherr, Chef, Prinzipal; 3. (*titles*) ***– of ceremonies,*** der Conférencier, Zeremonienmeister; ***– of the horse,*** der Oberstallmeister; ***– of (the) hound,*** oberster Jagdleiter; ***– of the lodge,*** der Meister vom Stuhl; ***– of the revels,*** der Leiter der Hoflustbarkeiten; ***– of the rolls,*** der Oberarchivar, Direktor des Staatsarchivs; 4. der Kapitän (*of a merchant-vessel*); 5. Lehrer, Studienrat (*in schools*), Rektor (*of some colleges*), (*Univ.*) Magister; ***Master of Arts,*** der Magister der philosophischen Fakultät; ***second*** or ***senior –,*** der Oberstudienrat; 6. der (Handwerks)-meister, Lehrmeister (*of a trade*); 7. junger Herr (*before Christian names*); 8. der Vituose, großer Maler; ***old –,*** der Renaissancemaler; das Renaissancegemälde. **2.** *v.t.* Meister sein *or* werden in (*Dat.*), Meisterschaft erlangen in (*Dat.*) (*an art*), mächtig sein (*Gen.*), beherrschen (*a language*), meistern, bewältigen (*a problem*); Herr werden *or* sein über (*Acc.*), sich zum Herrn machen über (*Acc.*), Macht *or* Gewalt haben über (*Acc.*), unterwerfen, besiegen (*a p.*); (be)zähmen, bändigen (*passion etc.*). **3.** *attrib. adj.* Meister–; Haupt–; führend.

master|-at-arms, *s.* (*Nav.*) der Stabwachtmeister, Schiffsprofos. **--builder,** *s.* der Baumeister. **--carpenter,** *s.* der Zimmermeister. **--clock,** *s.* die Normaluhr, Kontrolluhr. **--compass,** *s.* der Mutterkompaß. **--copy,** *s.* die Originalkopie. **masterful,** *adj.* 1. herrschsüchtig, herrisch, gebieterisch; despotisch, tyrannisch, eigenmächtig; 2. *See* **masterly. master|-gunner,** *s.* (*Naut.*) der Feldwebelleutnant, (*Am. Mil.*) Oberkanonier. **--key,** *s.* der Hauptschlüssel.

masterless ['mɑ:stəlis], *adj.* herrenlos. **masterliness,** *s.* die Meisterhaftigkeit, Meisterschaft, das Meisterhafte. **masterly,** *adj.* meisterhaft; ***– performance,*** das Meisterwerk, meisterhafte Leistung.

master|-mariner, *s.* der (Schiffs)kapitän. **–mind,** *s.* führender Geist, überlegener Kopf. **–piece,** *s.* das Meisterwerk, Meisterstück. **--sergeant,** *s.* (*Am.*) der Stabsfeldwebel. **mastership,** *s.* 1. die Herrschaft, Macht, Gewalt (***over,*** über (*Acc.*)); Meisterschaft (***of,*** in (*Dat.*)), vollkommene Beherrschung (*Gen.*); 2. das Lehramt, Vorsteheramt, leitende Stellung. **master|singer,** *s.* (*Hist.*) der Meistersinger. **--stroke,** *s.* der Meisterzug, das Meisterstück; (*fig.*) Glanzstück, Bravourstück, genialer Streich. **--tailor,** *s.* der Schneidermeister. **--tape,** *s.* die Originalaufnahme.

mastery ['mɑ:stəri], *s.* die Herrschaft, Gewalt, Macht (***of, over,*** über (*Acc.*)); der Vorrang, die Oberhand, Überlegenheit, Meisterschaft (***in, of,*** in (*Dat.*)), Beherrschung (***of,*** *Gen.*) (*language etc.*), Bezähmung, Bändigung (***of,*** *Gen.*) (*passions etc.*); ***– of the air,*** die Beherrschung der Luft; ***gain the –,*** die Oberhand gewinnen (***over,*** über (*Acc.*)).

masthead ['mɑ:sthed], *s.* der Mars, Topp, Mastkorb; ***– light,*** das Topplicht.

mastic ['mæstik], *s.* der Mastix; das Mastixharz; der (Stein)kitt, Mastixzement.

masticate ['mæstikeit], *v.t.* (zer)kauen. **mastication** [–'keiʃən], *s.* das (Zer)kauen. **masticator,** *s.* die Knetmaschine, Mahlmaschine. **masticatory,** *adj.* Kau–.

mastiff ['mæstif], *s.* der Bullenbeißer, Mastiff, englische Dogge.

mastitis [mæs'taitis], *s.* die Brustdrüsenentzündung, (*Vet.*) Euterentzündung.

mastodon ['mæstədən], *s.* der Urelefant, das Mastodon.

mastoid ['mæstɔid], **1.** *adj.* brust(warzen)förmig; ***– process,*** *see* **2. 2.** *s.* (*Anat.*) der Warzenfortsatz; *also coll. for* **mastoiditis** [–'daitis], *s.* die Warzenfortsatzentzündung, Mittelohrentzündung.

masturbate ['mæstəbeit], *v.i.* onanieren. **masturbation** [–'beiʃən], *s.* die Onanie, Selbstbefleckung.

¹**mat** [mæt], **1.** *s.* die Matte, Fußdecke, der Läufer, Vorleger, Abtreter; (*on table*) Untersatz, Untersetzer; (*fig.*) verfilzte Masse, das Gestrüpp, Geflecht, Gewirr; ***beer –,*** der Bierdeckel; (*sl.*) ***be on the –,*** in der Tinte sitzen, zur Rechenschaft gezogen werden, es ausbaden müssen. **2.** *v.t.* mit Matten bedecken *or* belegen; ineinanderflechten, verflechten, verfilzen; ***matted hair,*** wirres *or* verfilztes Haar. **3.** *v.i.* (*usu.* ***– together***) sich verfilzen *or* verflechten, ineinanderwachsen.

²**mat, 1.** *adj.* matt, mattiert, glanzlos. **2.** *v.t.* mattieren, mattschleifen.

matador ['mætədɔ:], *s.* der Matador; (*Cards*) Haupttrumpf.

¹**match** [mætʃ], *s.* das Zündholz, Streichholz; (*Hist.*) Zündpapier, der Zündstock, die Zündschnur, Lunte.

²**match, 1.** *s.* 1. der *etc.* Gleiche *or* Ebenbürtige; das Gegenstück; ***be (more than) a – for,*** gewachsen sein (*Dat.*); ***exact –,*** genaue Bemusterung; ***find one's –, meet one's –,*** seinen Mann finden; ***his –,*** seinesgleichen; 2. die Heirat, (*a p.*) (Heirats)-partie; ***good –,*** gute Partie; ausgezeichnetes Paar; ***ill-assorted –,*** schlecht zusammenpassendes Ehepaar; 3. der Wettkampf, das Wettspiel, Treffen, die Partie; ***boxing –,*** der Boxkampf; ***football –,*** das Fußball(wett)spiel; Fußballtreffen; ***wrestling –,*** der Ringkampf. **2.** *v.t.* 1. ehelich verbinden, passend verheiraten (***to, with,*** mit); 2. (*only pass. constr.*) sich messen mit, es aufnehmen mit, ebenbürtig *or* gewachsen sein (*Dat.*); 3. vergleichen (***with,*** mit), im Gegensatz stellen, ausspielen (***against,*** gegen); 4. anpassen, zusammenpassen, passend machen, abmustern; passen zu, entsprechen (*Dat.*); Passendes *or* Gleiches finden zu; ***be well -ed,*** gut zusammenpassen *or* zueinander passen, gut ausgeglichen sein; ***this colour is hard to –,*** zu dieser Farbe läßt sich schwer etwas Passendes finden; ***I know nothing to – it,*** ich kenne seinesgleichen nicht. **3.** *v.i.* zusammenpassen, übereinstimmen (***with,*** mit), gleich sein (*Dat.*), entsprechen (*Dat.*); ***envelopes to –,*** dazu passende Umschläge.

match|-board, *s.* das Riemenbrett, verzinktes *or* genutetes Holzbrett. **--boarding,** *s.* die Riemenwand. **–box,** *s.* die Zündholzschachtel. **--head,** *s.* die Zündholzmasse.

matching [ˈmætʃiŋ], **1.** *adj.* (dazu) passend; – *colours,* aufeinander abgestimmte Farben; (*Elec.*) – *condenser,* der Abgleichkondensator. **2.** *s.* die Anpassung. **matchless,** *adj.* unvergleichlich, unübertrefflich, ohnegleichen, einzig dastehend.

match|lock, *s.* (*Hist.*) das Luntenschloß, die Lunten(schloß)muskete. **–-maker,** *s.* der (die) Ehestifter(in), Ehevermittler(in). **–making,** *s.* die Ehevermittlung, Heiratsvermittlung. **–stalk, –stick,** *s.* (verbranntes) Streichhölzchen. **–wood,** *s.* Holzsplitter (*pl.*), das Kleinholz; *make – of, reduce to –,* in tausend Splitter zerbrechen, Kleinholz machen aus, kurz und klein schlagen.

[1]**mate** [meit], **1.** *s.* 1. der Gefährte, Genosse, Kamerad; 2. Gehilfe, Handlanger, die Hilfe, Hilfskraft (*at work*); 3. der Gatte (die Gattin), Gemahl(in); das Männchen (Weibchen) (*of birds*); 4. das Gegenstück (*of th.*); 5. (*Naut.*) der Maat, Steuermann; *cook's –,* der Kochsmaat; *gunner's –,* der Hilfskanonier. **2.** *v.t.* verheiraten, vermählen, verbinden; (*animals*) paaren, gatten; (*things*) einander anpassen. **3.** *v.i.* (sich ver)heiraten, sich (ehelich) verbinden, (*animals*) sich paaren *or* gatten.

[2]**mate, 1.** *s.* das Matt (*chess*). **2.** *v.t.* matt setzen.

maté [ˈmætei], *s.* 1. der Matebaum; 2. Mate, Paraguaytee.

material [məˈtiəriəl], **1.** *s.* 1. das Material, der (Roh)stoff, die Substanz; der Werkstoff, (Grund)bestandteil, Bestandteile (*pl.*), Elemente (*pl.*); (*fig.*) (*oft. pl.*) das Material, Materialien, Unterlagen, Gegebenheiten (*pl.*) (*for,* zu); *building –s,* Baustoffe (*pl.*); *cleaning –s,* das Putzzeug; *raw –,* der Rohstoff; *raw –s,* Materialien (*pl.*); *writing –s,* das Schreibgerät; 2. der Stoff, das Zeug, Gewebe. **2.** *adj.* materiell, substantiell, physisch, körperlich, stofflich, Material–, real, Real–, sachlich, Sach–; (*fig.*) leiblich, materialistisch, weltlich, irdisch; (*Law*) erheblich, einschlägig, unentbehrlich; (*coll.*) unumgänglich, ausschlaggebend, wichtig, wesentlich (*to,* für); – *goods,* Sachgüter.

materialism [məˈtiəriəlizm], *s.* der Materialismus. **materialist, 1.** *s.* der Materialist. **2.** *or* **materialistic** [–ˈlistik], *adj.* materialistisch. **materiality** [–iˈæliti], *s.* die Körperlichkeit, Stofflichkeit; (*fig.*) (*also Law*) (Ge)wichtigkeit, Wesentlichkeit, Erheblichkeit, Bedeutung.

materialization [mətiəriəlaiˈzeiʃən], *s.* die Materialisation (*of spirits*); Veranschaulichung, Versinnlichung, Verkörperung. **materialize** [məˈtiəriəlaiz], **1.** *v.t.* verkörpern, versinnlichen; realisieren, verwirklichen. **2.** *v.i.* sich verwirklichen *or* verkörpern *or* realisieren (*in,* in (*Dat.*)), zum Abschluß *or* zustande kommen; sichtbar werden, Tatsache *or* Wirklichkeit werden, feste Gestalt annehmen; (*of spirits*) sichtbar werden, (in körperlicher Form) erscheinen.

materially [məˈtiəriəli], *adv.* (*Phil.*) materiell; physisch, körperlich, stofflich; (*coll.*) wesentlich, erheblich, beträchtlich.

materia medica [məˈtiəriəˈmedikə], *s.* die Arzneimittellehre; Arzneimittel (*pl.*).

matériel [mæteriˈel], *s.* Erfordernisse (*pl.*), die Ausrüstung, das Rüstzeug, Material.

maternal [məˈtə:nl], *adj.* mütterlich, Mütter–; mütterlicherseits; – *love,* die Mutterliebe; – *mortality,* die Müttersterblichkeit; – *uncle,* der Onkel mütterlicherseits. **maternity,** *s.* die Mutterschaft; – *centre,* die Mütterberatungsstelle; – *hospital,* die Entbindungsanstalt.

matey [ˈmeiti], **1.** *adj.* (*coll.*) kameradschaftlich, familiär. **2.** *s.* (*as address*) Freund, Kamerad.

mathematical [mæθəˈmætikl], *adj.* mathematisch; – *instruments,* das Reißzeug. **mathematician** [–məˈtiʃən], *s.* der Mathematiker. **mathematics,** *pl.* (*sing. constr.*) die Mathematik.

matin [ˈmætin], **1.** *adj.* (*Poet.*) Morgen–, früh. **2.** *s.* (*R.C.*) die Frühmesse, Matutin; *pl.* (*C. of E.*) der Frühgottesdienst. **matinée** [–ei], *s.* (*Theat.*) die Nachmittagsvorstellung.

mating [ˈmeitiŋ], *s.* die Paarung; – *season,* die Paarungszeit.

matrass [ˈmætrəs], *s.* der Distillierkolben.

matriarch [ˈmeitria:k], *s.* die Stam(mes)mutter. **matriarchal,** *adj.* mutterrechtlich, matriarchalisch. **matriarchy,** *s.* die (Stam)mutterherrschaft; das Mutterrecht.

matric [məˈtrik], *s.* (*coll.*) *see* **matriculation.**

matrices [ˈmeitrisi:z], *pl. of* **matrix.**

matricidal [ˈmeitrisaidl], *adj.* muttermörderisch, Muttermord–. **matricide,** *s.* 1. der Muttermord; 2. der (die) Muttermörder(in).

matriculate [məˈtrikjuleit], **1.** *v.t.* (*Univ.*) immatrikulieren. **2.** *v.i.* sich immatrikulieren (lassen). **matriculation** [–ˈleiʃən], *s.* (*Univ.*) die Immatrikulation, (*also – examination*) Zulassungsprüfung, das Abitur (*at school*).

matrimonial [mætriˈmouniəl], *adj.* ehelich, Ehe–, Heirats–; – *agency,* das Ehevermittlungsbüro. **matrimonially,** *adv.* – *inclined,* heiratslustig. **matrimony** [ˈmætriməni], *s.* die Ehe, der Ehestand; *holy –,* der Stand der heiligen Ehe; *join in –,* trauen.

matrix [ˈmeitriks], *s.* (*pl.* **–ices** [–isi:z]) (*Anat.*) die Gebärmutter, (*Biol.*) der Nährboden, Mutterboden (*also fig.*), die Gewebeschicht, Grundsubstanz; (*Min.*) das Ganggestein, die Gangart; (*Tech.*) Matrize, Hohlform, Gießform, Schablone, der Prägestempel, Prägestock, das Gesenk; (*Math.*) die Matrix.

matron [ˈmeitrən], *s.* die Matrone, würdige Dame, ältere (verheirate) Frau; die Hausmutter, Aufseherin, Wärterin, Vorsteherin (*of hostel*), Oberschwester, Oberin (*of hospital*). **matronly,** *adj.* matronenhaft, mütterlich; (*fig.*) gesetzt, würdig.

matt, *see* [2]**mat. matted,** *imperf., p.p. of* [1]**mat, 2.**

matter [ˈmætə], **1.** *s.* 1. der Stoff, das Material, (*also Phil., Phys.*) die Materie, Substanz, Masse, der Körper; (*coll.*) *grey –,* der Mutterwitz; *mind and –,* Geist und Materie; 2. der Inhalt, Gehalt, Gegenstand; 3. die Sache, Angelegenheit; *in the – of,* bezüglich (*Gen.*); *it's a – of common knowledge,* es ist allgemein bekannt; *it is a – for congratulation,* es ist zu begrüßen; – *of consequence,* wichtige Angelegenheit; *a – of course,* die Selbstverständlichkeit, ausgemachte S.; *a – of fact,* die Tatsache; (*Law*) der Tatbestand; *as a – of fact,* in der Tat, in Wirklichkeit, tatsächlich; *the – in hand,* die vorliegende Angelegenheit; *it's a – of indifference to me,* es ist mir ganz einerlei *or* völlig gleichgültig; *no laughing –,* nichts zum Lachen; *it's a – of life and death,* es geht um Leben und Tod; *be a – of £7,* auf etwa sieben Pfund kommen; *a – of moment,* etwas von Belang; *personal –,* persönliche Angelegenheit; – *of taste,* die Geschmackssache; *a – of time,* eine Frage der Zeit; *a – of 10 years,* ungefähr *or* etwa zehn Jahre; *for that –,* übrigens, überhaupt, schließlich, was das betrifft *or* anbelangt; *no –!* es macht nichts (aus)! *no – how long,* ohne Rücksicht darauf *or* ungeachtet wie lange; *no – whether,* es spielt keine Rolle ob; *no – which,* was auch immer, einerlei was; *s.th. is the –,* es ist etwas los *or* vorgefallen *or* nicht in Ordnung; *what –?* was liegt daran? *what's the –?* was ist los? wo fehlt's? was gibt's? was geht vor? *what's the – with you?* was fehlt dir? was ist mit dir los? *is anything the – with you?* fehlt dir was? ist dir nicht wohl? (*coll.*) *that's what the – is,* da liegt der Hund begraben; 4. *pl.* (*no art.*) Dinge, Umstände (*pl.*); *as –s stand,* (so) wie die Dinge liegen *or* die S. steht, nach Lage der Dinge, unter den gegebenen Umständen; *to make –s worse,* was die S. noch schlimmer macht; *not mince –s,* kein Blatt vor den Mund nehmen; 5. (*Typ.*) der (Schrift)satz, das Manuskript; *dead –,* der Ablegesatz; *printed –,* die Drucksache; *standing –,* der Stehsatz; 6. (*Med.*) der Eiter. **2.** *v.i.* von Bedeutung sein (*to,* für), daran gelegen sein, darauf ankommen (*Dat.*); *it does not –,* es macht nichts aus; *what does it –?* was macht *or* tut das? *it –s little,* es ist ziemlich einerlei.

matter|-of-course, *adj.* selbstverständlich. **–-of-fact,** *adj.* sachlich, prosaisch, nüchtern.

matting ['mætiŋ], *s.* das Material zu Matten *or* Läufern, (*collect.*) die Matte, Matten (*pl.*).

mattins ['mætinz], *see* **matin, 2.**

mattock ['mætək], *s.* die Hacke, Haue, der Karst.

mattress ['mætrəs], *s.* die Matratze; ***hair –,*** die Roßhaarmatratze; ***spring –,*** die Sprungfedermatratze; ***– cover,*** der Matratzenschoner.

maturate ['mætjureit], *v.i.* 1. (*Med.*) eitern; 2. (*Psych.*) zur Reife kommen. **maturation** [–'reiʃən], *s.* 1. die (Aus)reifung, Eiterung; 2. das Reifen, Reifwerden. **maturative** [mə'tjuərətiv], *adj.* 1. zum Eitern bringend; 2. zur Reife bringend.

mature [mə'tjuə], **1.** *adj.* reif, vollentwickelt; (*fig.*) wohl überlegt, durchdacht, reiflich (erwogen); (*Comm.*) abgelaufen, fällig. **2.** *v.t.* reifen, zur Reife *or* Vollendung bringen, vollenden, ausreifen lassen. **3.** *v.i.* reifen, reif werden, ausreifen, heranreifen; (*Comm.*) fällig werden, verfallen. **matured,** *adj.* ausgereift (*plan*); abgelagert (*wine*); fällig (*bill*). **maturity** [–riti], *s.* 1. die Reife; 2. Fälligkeit, Verfall(s)zeit (*of a bill*); ***at*** or ***on –,*** bei Verfall (*of a bill*).

matutinal [mə'tju:tinəl], *adj.* morgendlich, früh, Morgen–.

maudlin ['mɔ:dlin], *adj.* weinselig, benebelt; weinerlich, rührselig, gefühlvoll.

maul [mɔ:l], **1.** *s.* der Schlegel. **2.** *v.t.* mißhandeln, durchprügeln; beschädigen, zerzausen, (*as an animal*) zerfleischen, zerreißen; rücksichtslos anfassen, übel zurichten, traktieren, herunterreißen (*by criticism*); ***badly –ed,*** schwer angeschlagen (*as troops*). **mauling,** *s.* rohe Behandlung.

maulstick ['mɔ:lstik], *s.* der Malerstock.

maunder ['mɔ:ndə], *v.i.* gedankenlos schlendern, dösen; faseln, kindisch schwätzen, vor sich hin reden. **maundering,** *s.* das Gefasel, Geschwätz.

maundy ['mɔ:ndi], *s.* (*R.C.*) die Fußwaschung. **maundy-money,** *s.* die Almosenverteilung am Gründonnerstag. **Maundy-Thursday,** *s.* der Gründonnerstag.

Mauritania [mɔ:ri'teiniə], *s.* Mauretanien (*n.*). **Mauritanian, 1.** *s.* der (die) Mauretanier(in). **2.** *adj.* mauretanisch.

mausoleum [mɔ:sə'liəm], *s.* das Mausoleum, Grabmal.

mauve [mouv], **1.** *s.* die Malvenfarbe. **2.** *adj.* hellviolett, malvenfarbig, mauve.

maverick ['mævərik], *s.* (*Am.*) das Vieh ohne Brandzeichen; Kalb ohne Muttertier; (*fig.*) der Außenseiter, Einzelgänger (*esp. Pol.*).

mavis ['meivis], *s.* (*Poet.*) die Singdrossel.

maw [mɔ:], *s.* der (Tier)magen; (*fig.*) Rachen, Schlund.

mawkish ['mɔ:kiʃ], *adj.* rührselig, gefühlsselig; süßlich. **mawkishness,** *s.* die Gefühlsduselei; Süßlichkeit.

maxilla [mæk'silə], *s.* der Kiefer, Kinnbacken, die Kinnlade. **maxillary, 1.** *adj.* Kiefer–, Kinnbacken–. **2.** *s.* der (Ober)kieferknochen.

maxim ['mæksim], *s.* die Maxime, Sentenz, der Gemeinspruch; Grundsatz.

maximal ['mæksiml], *adj.* Maximal–, Höchst–. **maximum, 1.** *s.* das Maximum, Höchstmaß, der Höhepunkt; Höchstwert (*also Math.*), Höchststand; (*Comm.*) Höchstpreis, Höchstbetrag; die Höchstzahl, Höchstgrenze; (*Math.*) (*of a curve*) der Scheitel; ***– thermometer,*** das Maximalthermometer. **2.** *adj.* höchst, größt, Höchst–, Maximal–; ***– load,*** (*Tech.*) die Bruchlast, Bruchbelastung, Höchstbeanspruchung, (*Elec.*) Höchstbelastung; ***– price,*** der Höchstpreis; ***– wages,*** der Spitzenlohn.

[1]**may** [mei], *aux. v.* (*only pres.*; *imperf.* ***might***) mag, kann, darf; (*as pl.*) mögen, können, dürfen; *aux. forming subj.*: ***you – well ask,*** du kannst gut fragen; ***you might as well ask,*** du könntest sowieso fragen; ***you might as well have asked,*** du hättest ebensogut fragen können; ***be that as it –,*** es mag sein wie es will; ***you – be right,*** du magst recht haben; ***he – come today,*** er kommt vielleicht heute; ***come what –,*** komme, was da wolle; ***– he go?*** darf er gehen? ***it might happen,*** es könnte geschehen; ***it might have happened,*** es hätte geschehen können; ***– it please your Majesty,*** Euer Majestät mögen geruhen; ***I am afraid he – not return,*** ich fürchte, er kehrt nicht zurück; ***I was afraid he might not return,*** ich fürchtete, daß er nicht zurückkehren würde.

[2]**may,** *s.* (*Bot.*) die Weißdornblüte.

May, *s.* der Mai, (*Poet., fig.*) Lenz, die Blütezeit, Jugend.

maybe ['meibi:], *adv.* vielleicht, möglicherweise.

mayday ['meidei], *s.* (*Naut.*) das (Funk)notsignal.

May|-day, *s.* erster Mai. **--flower,** *s.* die Maiblume; (*Am.*) der Primelstrauch. **--fly,** *s.* die Eintagsfliege.

mayhap ['meihæp], *adv.* (*obs.*) *see* **maybe.**

mayhem ['meihem], *s.* (*Law*) die Körperverletzung.

mayonnaise [meijə'neiz], *s.* die Mayonnaise.

mayor [mɛə], *s.* der Bürgermeister; ***Lord Mayor,*** der Oberbürgermeister. **mayoral** [–rəl], *adj.* Bürgermeister–, bürgermeisterlich. **mayoralty,** *s.* das Bürgermeisteramt; die Amtsdauer des Bürgermeisters. **mayoress** [–res], *s.* die Bürgermeisterfrau (*as wife*); Bürgermeisterin (*in her own right*); ***Lady Mayoress,*** die Frau Oberbürgermeister.

maypole ['meipoul], *s.* der Maibaum.

mazarine [mæzə'ri:n], *adj.* dunkelblau.

maze [meiz], **1.** *s.* der Irrgarten, das Labyrinth; (*fig.*) die Verwirrung, Bestürzung; ***be in a –,*** bestürzt *or* verwirrt sein. **2.** *v.t.* (*obs.*) (*esp. p.p.*) verblüffen, verwirren.

mazurka [mə'zə:kə], *s.* die Masurka.

mazy ['meizi], *adj.* labyrinthisch, verwickelt; wirr, verwirrt.

me [mi:], **1.** *pers. pron.* (*Acc.*) mich; (*Dat. also to –*) mir; (*coll. nom.*) ich; ***dear –!*** du meine Güte! ***poor –,*** ich Arme(r); ***do it for me,*** tu es meinetwegen! ***give – your hand,*** reiche mir die Hand! ***not for the life of –,*** beileibe nicht, nicht um alles in der Welt; (*coll.*) ***it's –,*** ich bin's. **2.** *refl. pron.* ***I looked about –,*** ich sah mich um.

[1]**mead** [mi:d], *s.* der Met.

[2]**mead,** (*Poet.*) *see* **meadow.**

meadow ['medou], *s.* die Wiese, Flur, Matte, der Anger. **meadow|-bunting,** *s.* (*Orn.*) die Wiesenammer (*Emberiza cioides*). **--grass,** *s.* das Rispengras. **--pipit,** *s.* (*Orn.*) der Wiesenpieper (*Anthus pratensis*). **--saffron,** *s.* die Herbstzeitlose. **-sweet,** *s.* das Mehlkraut. **meadowy,** *adj.* Wiesen–, wiesenartig, wiesenreich.

meager, (*Am.*) *see* **meagre.**

meagre ['mi:gə], *adj.* arm(selig), ärmlich, dürftig, kärglich; unfruchtbar, dürr (*soil etc.*); mager (*persons*). **meagreness,** *s.* die Dürftigkeit, Ärmlichkeit, Armseligkeit; Dürre; Magerkeit.

[1]**meal** [mi:l], *s.* das Essen, Mahl, die Mahlzeit; ***eat*** or ***have a –,*** eine Mahlzeit zu sich nehmen; ***make a – of,*** verzehren, sich gütlich tun an (*Dat.*); ***square –,*** reichliche Mahlzeit; ***take one's –s,*** essen, seine Mahlzeiten nehmen; (*coll.*) ***–s on wheels,*** rollender Essenzustelldienst.

[2]**meal,** *s.* (grobes) Mehl, (*Scots*) das Hafermehl, (*Am.*) Maismehl.

mealies ['mi:liz], *pl.* der Mais (*in S. Africa*).

mealiness ['mi:linis], *s.* die Mehligkeit.

meal|-ticket, *s.* (*Am.*) das Essensbon; (*fig.*) die Geldquelle. **– time,** *s.* die Essenszeit.

mealy ['mi:li], *adj.* mehlig, mehlartig, mehlhaltig; staubbedeckt; blaß. **mealy-mouthed,** *adj.* zurückhaltend, kleinlaut, leisetretend, sanftzüngig, glattzüngig, heuchlerisch.

[1]**mean** [mi:n], *adj.* 1. gering, unbedeutend; ***no – achievement,*** keine geringe Leistung; ***no – artist,*** ein Künstler von gewisser Bedeutung, ein nicht zu unterschätzender Künstler; 2. gemein, niederträchtig, schäbig, kleinlich; 3. geizig, knauserig, filzig, knickerig; 4. niedrig (*rank etc.*); 5. ärmlich, armselig, erbärmlich (*as streets*).

[2]**mean, 1.** *adj.* mittlere(r, -s), Mittel–; mittelmäßig; (*Math.*) durchschnittlich, Durchschnitts–; – ***annual temperature,*** mittlere Jahreswärme, das Wärmejahresmittel; (*Av.*) – ***chord,*** die Profilsehne; (*Stat.*) – ***deviation,*** durchschnittliche Streuung; (*Phys.*) – ***life,*** die Halbwertzeit; – ***sea level,*** mittlerer Meeresspiegel, die Normalnull; – ***number,*** die Durchschnittszahl, der Mittelwert; (*Astr.*) – ***time,*** mittlere (Sonnen)zeit; (*Math.*) – ***term,*** das Innenglied; – ***value,*** der Mittelwert. **2.** *s.* die Mitte, (arithmetisches) Mittel, das Mittelmaß, der Mittelwert, Durchschnitt; die Durchschnittszahl; *pl. See* **means**; ***geometrical*** –, geometrisches Mittel; ***golden*** or ***happy*** –, goldener Mittelweg; ***strike a*** –, einen Mittelwert errechnen; (*fig.*) einen Mittelweg finden.

[3]**mean, 1.** *irr.v.t.* 1. vorhaben, beabsichtigen, gedenken, im Auge haben; willens *or* entschlossen *or* gesonnen sein (*to do,* zu tun), wollen (tun); – ***business,*** Ernst machen, es ernst meinen; – ***no harm,*** es nicht böse meinen; – ***mischief,*** Böses im Sinne haben; ***I did not – to . . .,*** es war nicht meine Absicht zu . . .; ***I meant him to stay,*** ich wollte, daß er bleiben sollte; ***without –ing it,*** ohne es zu wollen; 2. meinen, sagen wollen, im Sinne haben; ***I – to say,*** ich will sagen; ***I – what I say,*** ich spaße nicht, ich mein's wie ich's sage; ***he –s it for our own good,*** er meint es gut mit uns; ***say what one –s,*** sagen, was man im Sinne hat; ***you don't – it,*** das kann nicht dein Ernst sein, dir ist nicht Ernst damit; ***what do you – by this?*** was meinen Sie damit *or* wollen Sie damit sagen? ***what do you – by coming?*** was fällt dir ein, daß du kommst? 3. bedeuten, zu bedeuten haben (*to,* für); – ***all the world,*** alles bedeuten (*to, Dat.*); ***this –s war,*** dies bedeutet *or* heißt Krieg; 4. (*esp. pass.*) bestimmen, ausersehen (*for,* zu); ***he was meant to be a doctor,*** er war zum Arzt bestimmt; ***they were meant for each other,*** sie waren für einander bestimmt. **2.** *irr.v.i.* – ***well*** (***ill***), es gut (schlecht) meinen (*by,* mit), wohl (übel) gesinnt sein (*Dat.*).

meander [mi'ændə], **1.** *v.i.* sich winden *or* schlängeln; ziellos umherirren, mäandern. **2.** *s.* (*usu. pl.*) das Labyrinth, der Irrweg, die Windung; (*Archit.*) die Grecborte, gewundenes Zierband, der Mäander, Mäanderlinien (*pl.*). **meandering, 1.** *adj.* gewunden, geschlängelt, schlängelnd; umherirrend. **2.** *s.* das Schlängeln; Umherirren.

meaning ['mi:niŋ], **1.** *s.* die Bedeutung, der Sinn; ***with*** –, bedeutungsvoll; ***what's the – of all this?*** was soll dies alles heißen *or* bedeuten? ***with the same*** –, mit derselben Bedeutung. **2.** *adj.* bedeutsam, bedeutungsvoll; ***well*** –, wohlwollend. **meaningful,** *adj.* bedeutungsvoll, bedeutsam. **meaningless,** *adj.* bedeutungslos; ausdruckslos. **meaningly,** *adv.* bedeutungsvoll.

meanly ['mi:nli], *adv.* schlecht, schäbig, armselig, niedrig; ärmlich. **meanness,** *s.* die Niedrigkeit, Ärmlichkeit, Armseligkeit; Gemeinheit, Niederträchtigkeit; Knauserigkeit.

means [mi:nz], *pl.* 1. (*sing. and pl. constr.*) das Mittel, der Weg (*to an end*); – ***of communication,*** das Verkehrsmittel; – ***of transport,*** Verkehrsmittel, Beförderungsmittel (*pl.*); ***by – of,*** durch, mittels, vermittels(t); ***by all*** –, auf alle Fälle, schlechterdings; ***by any*** –, auf irgendwelche Weise, überhaupt; ***not by any*** –, ***by no*** (***manner of***) –, auf keinen Fall, keineswegs, durchaus nicht, ganz gewiß nicht; ***by fair*** –, im Guten, in Güte; ***by foul*** –, im Bösen, mit Gewalt; ***by some – or*** (***an***)***other,*** auf die eine oder andere Weise; ***by this*** or ***these*** –, hierdurch, dadurch; ***ways and*** –, Mittel und Wege; 2. (*pl. constr.*) Hilfsmittel, (Geld)mittel (*pl.*), das Vermögen, Einkommen, Verhältnisse (*pl.*); – ***test,*** der Bedürftigkeitsnachweis; ***beyond one's*** –, über seine Verhältnisse; ***within one's*** –, seinen Verhältnissen entsprechend; ***man of*** (***independent***) –, bemittelter Mann.

meant [ment], *imperf., p.p. of* [3]**mean.**

mean|time, -while, 1. *s.* die Zwischenzeit; ***in the*** –, *see* **2. 2.** *adv.* inzwischen, unterdessen, mittlerweile.

measled [mi:zld], *adj.* finnig (*as pigs*). **measles,** *pl.* (*sing. constr.*) (*Med.*) Masern (*pl.*); (*Vet.*) Finnen (*pl.*); (*Med.*) ***German*** –, Röteln (*pl.*). **measly,** *adj.* (*Med.*) maserkrank, (*Vet.*) finnig; (*sl.*) erbärmlich, elend, schäbig, lumpig.

measurable ['meʒərəbl], *adj.* meßbar; (*fig.*) absehbar.

measure ['meʒə], **1.** *s.* 1. das Maß (*also fig.*); – ***of capacity,*** das Hohlmaß; ***cubic*** –, das Raummaß, Körpermaß; ***dry*** –, das Trockenmaß; ***liquid*** –, das Flüssigkeitsmaß; ***solid*** –, see ***cubic*** –; ***square*** –, ***superficial*** –, das Flächenmaß; ***make to*** –, nach Maß arbeiten (*clothes*); ***take his*** –, ihm Maß nehmen (*for,* zu); (*fig.*) sich (*Dat.*) über ihn ein Urteil bilden, ihn einschätzen *or* taxieren; 2. das Meßgerät, Meßinstrument; Maßsystem; die Maßeinheit; (*Arith.*) ***common*** –, gemeinsamer Teiler; ***tape*** –, *see* **measuring-tape**; 3. der Maßstab, das Verhältnis; ***be a – of,*** als Maßstab dienen (*Dat.*); 4. (*Metr.*) das Versmaß, Metrum, (*Mus.*) Zeitmaß, der Takt; ***tread a*** –, tanzen, sich im Takt drehen; 5. (*fig.*) das Ausmaß, richtiges Maß, vernünftige Grenzen; ***beyond*** –, über alle Maßen; ***in some*** or ***a certain*** –, gewissermaßen, in gewissem Maße, bis zu einem gewissen Grade; ***in*** (***a***) ***great*** –, in großem Maßen, großenteils; ***set –s*** or ***set a – to,*** Grenzen *or* Maß und Ziel setzen (*Dat.*); 6. (*fig.*) der Schritt, die Maßregel, Maßnahme; ***coercive –s,*** Zwangsmaßnahmen (*pl.*); ***temporary*** –, vorübergehende Maßnahme; ***take –s,*** Maßnahmen treffen, Maßregeln ergreifen; ***take legal –s,*** den Rechtsweg einschlagen; 7. (*Poet.*) die Weise, Melodie. **2.** *v.t.* 1. messen (*also fig.*), abmessen, ausmessen (*material etc.*), (*Surv.*) vermessen; (*fig.*) – ***one's length,*** der Länge nach hinfallen; – ***swords,*** die Degen kreuzen; (*fig.*) sich messen (*with,* mit); – ***him for a suit,*** ihm zu einem Anzug Maß nehmen; ***be*** or ***get –d for a suit,*** sich (*Dat.*) zu einem Anzug Maß nehmen lassen; – ***the length of,*** der Länge nach ausmessen; – ***him with one's eyes,*** ihn von oben bis unten messen; 2. (*fig.*) ermessen, abwägen, abschätzen (*by,* an (*Dat.*)), beurteilen (nach). **3.** *v.i.* messen, einen Umfang haben von; (*coll.*) – ***up,*** die Ansprüche erfüllen (*to,* für); ***it –s 2 ft.,*** es ist zwei Fuß lang.

measured ['meʒəd], *adj.* 1. (ab)gemessen (*also fig.*); – ***mile,*** amtlich gemessene Meile; 2. (*fig.*) regelmäßig, gleichmäßig, maßvoll, gemäßigt; ***with – steps,*** gemessenen Schrittes; ***speak in – terms,*** sich maßvoll ausdrücken. **measureless,** *adj.* unermeßlich, unbeschränkt.

measurement ['meʒəmənt], *s.* 1. das Messen, die (Ver)messung, Abmessung; 2. Maßmethode; (Maß)einheit (*also Math.*); Größe, Abmessungen (*pl.*), Ausmaße (*pl.*), (*usu. pl.*) (*for clothes*) das Maß.

measuring ['meʒəriŋ], *s.* das Messen, die (Ver)messung; die Meßkunst. **measuring|-glass,** *s.* das Meßglas, Mensurglas. **--instrument,** *s.* das Meßinstrument. **--tape,** *s.* das Meßband, Maßband, Bandmaß.

meat [mi:t], *s.* das Fleisch; (*obs.*) die Speise, Nahrung; (*fig.*) der Gehalt, Inhalt, die Substanz; (*Scots*) ***butcher*** –, das Fleisch; ***canned*** or ***tinned*** –, das Büchsenfleisch; ***frozen*** –, das Gefrierfleisch; ***minced*** –, Gehackte(s), das Hackfleisch; ***pickled*** –, das Pökelfleisch; ***potted*** –, eingemachtes Fleisch; ***preserved*** –, die Fleischkonserve; ***roast*** –, der Braten; – ***and drink,*** Speise und Trank; ***it is – and drink to me,*** es ist mir eine Wonne *or* ein großer Genuß (*with inf.*); (*Prov.*) ***one man's – is another man's poison,*** des einen Tod ist des andern Brot.

meat|-ball, *s.* das Fleischklößchen. **--chopper,** *s.* das Hackmesser. **--jack,** *s.* der Bratenwender. **meatless,** *adj.* fleischlos. **meat|-pie,** *s.* die Fleischpastete. **--safe,** *s.* der Speiseschrank, Fliegenschrank.

meatus [mi:'eitəs], *s.* (*Anat.*) der Gang, Kanal.

meaty ['mi:ti], *adj.* fleischig, fleischartig; (*fig.*) kernig, markig, gehaltvoll.

mechanic [mə'kænik], *s.* der Mechaniker, Machinist, Monteur, (*Motor.*) Autoschlosser; (*obs.*)

Handwerker; (*Av.*) ***flight*** –, der Bordwart. **mechanical,** *adj.* Maschinen–, mechanisch, maschinell; automatisch, selbsttätig; (*fig.*) automatisch, unwillkürlich, unbewußt, gewohnheitsmäßig, routinemäßig, maschinenmäßig, handwerksmäßig, geistlos; (*Tech.*) – ***effect,*** der Nutzaffekt; – ***engineer,*** der Maschinen(bau)-techniker; – ***engineering,*** der Maschinenbau; – ***equivalent of heat,*** mechanisches Wärmeäquivalent; – ***properties,*** Fertigkeitseigenschaften (*pl.*). **mechanically,** *adv.* mechanisch, maschinell, maschinenmäßig; –***-minded,*** technisch begabt *or* veranlagt.

mechanician [mekə'niʃən], *s.* (*obs.*) der Mechaniker; (*Naut.*) Maschinenmaat. **mechanics** [mi'kæniks], *pl.* (*sing. constr.*) die Mechanik, Bewegungslehre; (*coll.*) der Mechanismus, mechanische Einzelheiten (*pl.*); ***practical*** –, die Maschinenlehre. **mechanism** ['mekənizm], *s.* der Mechanismus, (mechanische) Vorrichtung, das (Trieb)werk; (*fig.*) die Maschine (*of government etc.*); (*Phil.*) mechanistische Auffassung. **mechanist** ['mekənist], *s.* (*obs.*) der Mechaniker; (*Phil.*) mechanistischer Denker. **mechanistic,** *adj.* (*Phil.*) mechanistisch. **mechanization** [–ai'zeiʃən], *s.* die Mechanisierung; (*Mil.*) Motorisierung. **mechanize** ['mekənaiz], *v.t.* mechanisieren; (*Mil.*) motorisieren; (*Mil.*) –***d division,*** die Panzergrenadierdivision.

meconic [me'kɔnik], *adj.* (*Chem.*) mohnsauer, Mekon–; – ***acid,*** die Mohnsäure, Mekonsäure. **meconium** [–'kouniəm], *s.* (*Med.*) das Kindspech; (*obs.*) Opium, der Mohnsaft.

medal [medl], *s.* die Medaille, Denkmünze, Schaumünze; (*Mil. etc.*) Ehrenmedaille, Ehrenauszeichnung, das Ehrenabzeichen, der Orden. **medallion** [mə'dæljən], *s.* (große) Denkmünze *or* Schaumünze, das Medaillion. **medal(l)ist,** *s.* der (die) Inhaber(in) einer Ehrenmedaille.

meddle [medl], *v.i.* sich (unberufen *or* ungefragt) befassen *or* abgeben *or* einlassen (***with,*** mit), sich (ein)mischen (***in,*** in (*Acc.*)), (*coll.*) herumspielen, herumhantieren, zu schaffen haben (***with,*** mit). **meddler,** *s.* Unbefugte(r), Zudringliche(r), der Naseweis. **meddlesome,** *adj.* zudringlich, aufdringlich, naseweis, vorwitzig, lästig. **meddlesomeness,** *s.* die Zudringlichkeit, Aufdringlichkeit. **meddling, 1.** *s.* (unerwünschte) Einmischung. **2.** *adj. See* **meddlesome.**

Mede [mi:d], *s.* der (die) Meder(in); (*fig.*) ***law of the –s and Persians,*** unabänderliches Recht.

[1]**media** ['mi:diə], *pl. of* **medium.**

[2]**media,** *s.* (*Phonet.*) stimmhafter Verschlußlaut, die Media.

medi(a)eval [medi'i:vl], *adj.* mittelalterlich. **medi(a)evalism,** *s.* die Mittelalterlichkeit, der Geist des Mittelalters; die Vorliebe für das *or* der Hang zum Mittelalter. **medi(a)evalist,** *s.* der Kenner *or* Forscher des Mittelalters.

medial ['mi:diəl], **1.** *adj.* mittlere(r, -s), Mittel–; (*Math.*) Durchschnitts–; (*Phonet.*) inlautend; – ***sound,*** der Inlaut. **2.** *s. See* [2]**media. medially,** *adv.* in der Mitte liegend; (*Phonet.*) im Inlaut.

median ['mi:diən], **1.** *adj.* (*Math., Stat., Med.*) Mittel–, mittlere(r, -s), median, Zentral–; – ***line,*** (*Anat.*) die Mittellinie, Medianlinie; (*Math.*) Mittellinie, Halbierungslinie; – ***point,*** (*Geom.*) der Mittelpunkt *or* Schnittpunkt der Winkelhalbierenden; (*Stat.*) *see* **2**; – ***section,*** der Mittelschnitt. **2.** *s.* (*Stat.*) die Mediane, der Mittelwert.

mediant ['mi:diənt], *s.* (*Mus.*) die Mediante.

mediate, 1. ['mi:dieit], *v.t.* vermitteln. **2.** [–ieit], *v.i.* vermitteln, den Vermittler spielen (***between,*** zwischen (*Dat.*)); einen mittleren Standpunkt einnehmen, ein Bindeglied bilden. **3.** [–iət], *adj.* mittelbar, indirekt; Mittel–, mittlere(r, -s), dazwischenkommend; (*Hist.*) nicht souverän *or* reichsunmittelbar. **mediation** [–'eiʃən], *s.* die Vermittlung; Fürsprache, Fürbitte; (*Math.*) Interpolation, Zwischenschaltung; (*Mus.*) melodische Mittelfigur.

mediative ['mi:diətiv], *adj. See* **mediatorial. mediatize, 1.** *v.t.* (*Hist.*) mediatisieren, der Landeshoheit unterwerfen, landsässig machen (*a ruler*), einverleiben (*territory*). **2.** *v.i.* die Reichsunmittelbarkeit verlieren, mediatisiert werden.

mediator ['mi:dieitə], *s.* der Vermittler, Unterhändler, Fürsprecher; (*Theol.*) Mittler. **mediatorial** [–ə'tɔ:riəl], **mediatory** [–ətəri], *adj.* vermittelnd, Vermittler–; (*Theol.*) Mittler–. **mediatrix** [–'eitriks], *s.* die Vermittlerin, Unterhändlerin, Fürsprecherin.

medic ['medik], *s.* (*coll.*) der Arzt, Mediziner; Medizinstudent. **medical, 1.** *adj.* ärztlich, medizinisch, Kranken–, Heil–, (*Mil.*) Sanitäts–; – ***advice,*** ärztliches Rat; – ***attendant,*** der Hausarzt; – ***board,*** die Sanitätskommission; (*Mil.*) – ***corps,*** die Sanitätstruppe; – ***examination,*** ärztliche Untersuchung; – ***jurisprudence,*** die Gerichtsmedizin; (*coll.*) – ***man,*** der Arzt, Mediziner; – ***officer,*** (*Mil.*) der Sanitätsoffizier; (*school etc.*) Schularzt, Fürsorgearzt; – ***officer of health,*** der Amtsarzt, Bezirksarzt; (*Mil.*) – ***orderly,*** der Sanitäter; – ***practitioner,*** praktischer Arzt; – ***service,*** der Gesundheitsdienst, die Staatskrankenkasse; – ***science,*** die Medizin, Heilkunde; – ***student,*** der (die) Medizinstudent(in), Mediziner(in); – ***superintendent,*** der Chefarzt.

medicament [me'dikəmənt], *s.* das Heilmittel, Arzneimittel, die Arznei. **medicate** ['medikeit], *v.t.* mit Arzneistoffen imprägnieren; medizinisch behandeln; –***d soap,*** die Medizinalseife. **medication** [–'keiʃən], *s.* medizinische Behandlung, die Verordnung *or* das Verabreichen von Medikamenten; die Imprägnierung mit *or* Beimischung von Arzneistoffen. **medicative** ['medikətiv], **medicatory** ['medikətəri], *adj.* heilend, heilkräftig, heilsam.

medicinal [me'disinl], *adj.* medizinisch, heilkräftig, heilsam, Heil–; – ***herbs,*** Heilkräuter, Arzneikräuter; – ***properties,*** Heilkräfte; – ***spring,*** die Heilquelle. **medicine** ['medsin], *s.* **1.** die Arznei, Medizin; –***-chest,*** der Arzneischrank, die Hausapotheke; **2.** die Heilkunde, Heilkunst, Medizin; ***forensic*** –, die Gerichtsmedizin; ***student of*** –, der Medizinstudent, Mediziner; – ***ball,*** der Medizinball; **3.** (*primitive tribes*) die Medizin, der Zauber; –***-man,*** der Zauberer, Medizinmann. **medico** ['medikou], *s.* (*coll.*) der Arzt.

medieval, *see* **mediaeval.**

mediocre ['mi:dioukə], *adj.* mittelmäßig, zweitklassig. **mediocrity** [–'ɔkriti], *s.* die Mittelmäßigkeit; mäßige Begabung; unbedeutender Mensch, der Dutzendmensch.

meditate ['mediteit], **1.** *v.i.* nachdenken, nachsinnen, grübeln ((***up***)***on,*** über (*Acc.*)); – ***on*** überlegen. **2.** *v.t.* im Sinne haben, vorhaben; überlegen, erwägen, bedenken. **meditation** [–'teiʃən], *s.* das Nachdenken, (Nach)sinnen; (*Eccl.*) die Andacht, fromme Betrachtung; ***book of –s,*** das Erbauungsbuch; –***s on death,*** Betrachtungen über den Tod. **meditative,** *adj.* nachdenklich, grübelnd, nachsinnend. **meditativeness,** *s.* die Nachdenklichkeit, das Sinnen, Grübeln.

Mediterranean [meditə'reiniən], **1.** *s.* das Mittelmeer. **2.** *adj.* Mittelmeer–.

medium ['mi:diəm], **1.** *adj.* mittlere(r, -s), Mittel–, Durchschnitts–; – ***paper,*** das Medianpapier; – ***price,*** der Durchschnittspreis; – ***quality,*** die Sekundaqualität; – ***size,*** die Mittelgröße; ***of – size,*** mittelgroß; (*Rad.*) – ***wave,*** die Mittelwelle, mittlere Wellenlänge. **2.** *s.* (*pl.* **-s** *and* **media**) die Mitte, der Mittelweg, das Mittelglied, Mittelding, (*Log.*) der Mittelsatz; das (Hilfs)mittel, Werkzeug, die Vermittlung, (*also spiritualism*) das Medium; der Träger, (vermittelnder) Stoff, (*Phys.*) das Agens, (*Biol.*) der Nährboden; (*fig.*) das Lebenselement, Milieu, die Umgebung, Lebensbedingungen (*pl.*); ***by*** or ***through the – of,*** vermittels (*Gen.*), durch (die) Vermittlung von. **mediumistic** [–'mistik], *adj.* Medium– (*spiritualism*). **medium-sized,** *adj.* mittelgroß.

medlar ['medlə], *s.* (*Bot.*) die Mispel.

medley ['medli], **1.** *s.* das Gemisch, Durcheinander, der Mischmasch, (*Mus.*) das Potpourri. **2.** *adj.* gemischt.
medulla [mə'dʌlə], *s.* das Rückenmark, (Knochen)-mark. **medullary,** *adj.* Mark–, markig, markhaltig.
meed [mi:d], *s.* (*Poet.*) die Belohnung, der Lohn, Preis.
meek [mi:k], *adj.* sanft(mütig), mild, gütig, hold; demütig, bescheiden; ***as – as a lamb,*** lammfromm. **meekness,** *s.* die Milde, Sanftmut; Demut, Bescheidenheit.
meerschaum ['miəʃəm], *s.* der Meerschaum; (*also* ***--pipe***), die Meerschaumpfeife.
¹**meet** [mi:t], **1.** *irr.v.t.* 1. begegnen (*Dat.*), (an)treffen, stoßen (auf (*Acc.*)); ***– him at the station,*** ihn vom Bahnhof abholen; ***be met,*** empfangen werden; ***come (go) to –,*** entgegenkommen (entgegengehen) (*Dat.*); ***– one another*** or ***each other,*** sich treffen, einander begegnen; (*coll.*) ***– my wife!*** gestatten Sie, daß ich Ihnen meine Frau vorstelle! (*coll.*) ***pleased to – you!*** sehr erfreut, Sie kennenzulernen *or* Ihre Bekanntschaft zu machen! ***well met!*** gut *or* schön, daß wir uns treffen! 2. münden in (*Acc.*); 3. (*fig.*) entgegentreten (*Dat.*), zusammentreffen *or* zusammenstoßen mit, entgegenkommen (*Dat.*) (*views, opinions etc.*); ***– competition,*** dem Wettbewerb entgegentreten; ***– his eye,*** ihm ins Auge fallen, seinen Blick erwidern; ***– the eye,*** auffallen (*of a th.*); ***there's more to it than –s the eye,*** da steckt (etwas) mehr dahinter; ***he met his fate,*** das Schicksal ereilte ihn; ***– one's fate calmly,*** seinem Schicksal gelassen entgegensehen; ***– one's match,*** seinen Mann finden; ***– one's reward,*** den Lohn erhalten; ***– trouble half-way,*** Maßnahmen gegen (etwaige) Unannehmlichkeiten treffen; ***– him half-way,*** ihm auf halbem Wege entgegenkommen; 4. antworten auf (*Acc.*), entgegnen (*Dat.*); 5. widerlegen (*objections etc.*); 6. entsprechen (*Dat.*), nachkommen (*Dat.*), befriedigen, erfüllen (*wishes, obligations etc.*); ***– the case,*** das Problem lösen, dem Zweck entsprechen; ***– all contingencies,*** gegen alle unvorhergesehenen Fälle gewappnet werden; ***the supply –s the demand,*** das Angebot entspricht der Nachfrage; ***in order to – your demands,*** um Ihren Forderungen nachzukommen; ***– the exigencies of the case,*** den Umständen gerecht zu werden; 7. decken, begleichen, einlösen, honorieren (*bill*); tragen, bestreiten (*expenses*).
2. *irr.v.i.* sich (*Dat.*) *or* einander begegnen, sich treffen, sich kennenlernen; zusammentreffen, zusammentreten, zusammenkommen, sich versammeln; sich vereinigen *or* verbinden, in Beziehung *or* Berührung kommen, sich berühren; zusammenstoßen, aneinandergeraten (*as enemies*); ***make both ends –,*** sich nach der Decke strecken, sich einrichten, (mit seinen Einkünften) auskommen; ***– with,*** (*sl.*) ***– up with,*** (zufällig) stoßen auf (*Acc.*), zufällig treffen; erleiden, erfahren, erleben; ***– with an accident,*** verunglücken, einen Unfall erleiden; ***– with approval,*** gebilligt werden, Beifall finden; ***– with a denial,*** bestritten *or* verneint werden (*of a statement*); ***– with difficulties,*** auf Schwierigkeiten stoßen; ***– with a good reception,*** gut aufgenommen werden; ***– with a refusal,*** abgewiesen werden, eine abschlägige Antwort bekommen; ***– with success,*** Erfolg haben.
3. *s.* das (Zusammen)treffen; Jagdtreffen.
²**meet,** *adj.* (*obs.*) passend, geeignet; schicklich.
meeting ['mi:tiŋ], *s.* die Begegnung, Zusammenkunft, das Zusammentreffen; die Versammlung, Sitzung, Tagung, Konferenz; Versammlungsteilnehmer (*pl.*); der Zusammenfluß (*of rivers*); (*Spt.*) das Treffen; Stelldichein, Rendezvous; ***at a –,*** auf einer Sitzung; ***call a – for 10 a.m.,*** eine Versammlung auf 10 Uhr einberufen; (*Spt.*) ***race –,*** der Renntag.
meeting|-house, *s.* das Andachtshaus, Bethaus (*of Quakers*). **--place,** *s.* der Treffpunkt, Sammelplatz, Versammlungsort. **--point,** *s.* der Treffpunkt, Berührungspunkt. **--room,** *s.* der Sitzungssaal.
mega|cephalic ['megəse'fælik], **–cephalous** [–'sefələs], *adj.* großköpfig, makrozephal. **–cycle,** *s.* (*Rad.*) das Megahertz. **–lith** [–liθ], *s.* der Megalith, großer Steinblock. **–lithic** [–'liθik], *adj.* megalithisch.
megalo|cardia [megələ'kɑ:diə], *s.* (*Med.*) die Herzerweiterung. **–cephalic** [–se'fælik], *adj.* *See* **megacephalic.** **–mania,** *s.* der Größenwahn.
megaphone ['megəfoun], *s.* das Megaphon, Sprachrohr, der Schalltrichter.
megass [mə'gæs], *s.* die Bagasse.
megatherium [megə'θiəriəm], *s.* das Riesenfaultier.
megger ['megə], *s.* (*Elec.*) (*coll.*) der Isolationsmesser.
megilp [mə'gilp], *s.* der Leinölfirnis.
megohm ['megoum], *s.* (*Elec.*) das Megohm.
megrim ['mi:grim], *s.* (*Med.*) die Migräne; (*coll.*) Grille, der Spleen; *pl.* die Schwermut, Melancholie; (*Vet.*) der Koller.
meiosis [mai'ousis], *s.* (*Rhet.*) die Litotes, (*Biol.*) Reduktionsteilung.
melancholia [melən'kouliə], *s.* die Schwermut, Melancholie, der Trübsinn. **melancholiac,** *s.* *See* **melancholic, 2.** **melancholic** [–'kɔlik], **1.** *adj.* schwermütig, melancholisch. **2.** *s.* der Melancholiker. **melancholy** ['melənkəli], **1.** *s.* die Melancholie; Schwermut, Niedergeschlagenheit, der Trübsinn. **2.** *adj.* schwermütig, trübsinnig, melancholisch; düster, traurig, betrübend.
mélange [me'lɑ̃ʒ], *s.* die Mischung, das Gemisch.
melanism ['melənizm], **melanosis** [–'nousis], *s.* (*Med.*) der Melanismus, die Melanose, Dunkelfärbigkeit, Schwarzsucht.
mêlée ['melei], *s.* das Handgemenge, (*fig.*) Gewoge, Hin und Her.
meliorate ['mi:liəreit], *v.t.* (ver)bessern, veredeln. **melioration** [–'reiʃən], *s.* die (Ver)besserung, Veredelung.
melliferous [me'lifərəs], *adj.* honigtragend. **mellifluence** [–fluəns], *s.* der Honigfluß; (*fig.*) das Dahinfließen, die Lieblichkeit. **mellifluent** (*obs.*), **mellifluous,** *adj.* (*fig.*) honigsüß; lieblich, einschmeichelnd, dahinfließend.
mellow ['melou], **1.** *adj.* reif, saftig, weich, mürbe (*of fruit*); sanft, zart, lieblich (*in tone*); lieblich (*as wine*); (aus)gereift (*as age*); (*fig.*) heiter, freundlich; (*sl.*) angeheitert, benebelt. **2.** *v.t.* weich *or* mürbe machen; (aus)reifen, zur Reife bringen, reifen lassen; (*fig.*) erweichen, mildern, sänftigen. **3.** *v.i.* mild *or* weich *or* mürbe *or* reif werden; (*fig.*) sich abklären. **mellowness,** *s.* die Reife, Mürbheit (*of fruit*); Milde, Sanftheit, Weichheit, Gereiftheit.
melodic [me'lɔdik], **melodious** [–'loudiəs], *adj.* melodisch, wohlklingend. **melodiousness,** *s.* der Wohlklang.
melodist ['melədist], *s.* der (die) Liedersänger(in); der Melodiker, Liederkomponist.
melodrama ['melədrɑ:mə], *s.* das Melodrama; Volksstück; (*fig.*) die Sensation. **melodramatic** [–drə'mætik], *adj.* melodramatisch; (*fig.*) sensationell.
melody ['melədi], *s.* die Melodie, (Sing)weise, Tonfolge; der Wohlklang, Wohllaut; das Lied, der Gesang.
melon ['melən], *s.* die Melone.
melt [melt], **1.** *v.t.* schmelzen, zerlassen; (zer)fließen *or* (zer)schmelzen lassen (***into,*** in (*Acc.*)); (*fig.*) verschmelzen *or* verschwimmen lassen (*colour etc.*), weich machen, rühren (*persons*); ***– down,*** einschmelzen, zusammenschmelzen. **2.** *v.i.* (zer)schmelzen, flüssig werden; (*fig.*) sich auflösen, verschwinden, zergehen (*clouds etc.*); aufgehen, übergehen (***into,*** in (*Acc.*)); auftauen (*of persons*); ***– in the mouth,*** auf der Zunge schmelzen; ***– into tears,*** in Tränen zerfließen, zu Tränen gerührt werden; ***– away,*** dahinschmelzen, zergehen, zusammenschmelzen, dahinschwinden. **melting,** **1.** *adj.* schmelzend, Schmelz–; rührend, weich, mitleidig, sanft; ***– point,*** der Schmelzpunkt; ***– pot,***

der Schmelztiegel; (*fig.*) ***be in the – pot,*** in völliger Umgestaltung begriffen sein; (*fig.*) ***put into the – pot,*** gänzlich ummodeln, von Grund auf ändern. **2.** *s.* das Schmelzen, die Verschmelzung.

member ['membə], *s.* das Mitglied; (*Anat., Math., fig.*) Glied; der (Einzel)teil; (*Anat.*) die Gliedmaße; – (***of parliament***), Abgeordnete(r). **membered,** *adj.* gegliedert; (*as suff.*) –gliedrig. **membership,** *s.* der Mitgliedschaft, Zugehörigkeit; Mitgliederschaft, Mitgliederzahl. **membership|-card,** *s.* die Mitgliedskarte. **--fee,** *s.* der Mitgliedsbeitrag.

membrane ['membrein], *s.* das Häutchen, die Membran(e); (*Bot.*) – ***of a cell,*** die Zellwand; ***mucous –,*** die Schleimhaut. **membran(e)ous** [–'breinəs], *adj.* häutig, häutchenartig, Membran–.

memento [mə'mentou], *s.* (*pl.* **-(e)s**) das Erinnerungszeichen, Andenken (*of,* an (*Acc.*)); – ***mori,*** die Todesmahnung.

memo ['memou], *s.* (*coll.*) die Notiz, der Vermerk; *see* **memorandum.**

memoir ['memwɑ:], *s.* die Denkschrift, der Bericht; (wissenschaftliche) Abhandlung (***on,*** über (*Acc.*)); *pl.* Memoiren, Denkwürdigkeiten, (Lebens)erinnerungen, Aufzeichnungen (*pl.*).

memorabilia [memərə'biliə], *pl.* Denkwürdigkeiten (*pl.*).

memorable ['memərəbl], *adj.* denkwürdig, merkwürdig, erinnerungswert. **memorableness,** *s.* die Denkwürdigkeit, Merkwürdigkeit.

memorandum [memə'rændəm], *s.* (*pl.* **-da**) der Vermerk, die Notiz (*of,* über (*Acc.*)); (*Pol.*) das Memorandum, die Denkschrift, Eingabe; (*Law*) Aufzeichnung, das Merkblatt; Protokoll, die Urkunde; (*Comm.*) Nota, Rechnung. **memorandum-book,** *s.* das Notizbuch, Manual, Memorial, die Kladde.

memorial [mə'mɔ:riəl], **1.** *adj.* zum Andenken (dienend), Gedächtnis–, Gedenk–; – ***service,*** die Gedenkfeier; – ***stone,*** der Denkstein. **2.** *s.* das Denkmal, Ehrenmal; Gedenkzeichen; die Denkschrift (***to,*** für), das Andenken (an (*Acc.*)); (*Law*) die Bittschrift, Eingabe (an (*Acc.*)); ***as a*** or ***in –,*** zum Andenken. **memorialist,** *s.* der Unterzeichner einer Bittschrift, Bittsteller. **memorialize,** *v.t.* eine Bittschrift *or* Denkschrift einreichen bei; feiern, eine Gedenkfeier abhalten für, erinnern an (*Acc.*).

memoriam [mə'mɔ:riəm], *s.* ***in –,*** die Denkschrift.

memorization [memərai'zeiʃən], *s.* das Auswendiglernen. **memorize** ['meməraiz], *v.t.* im Gedächtnis behalten, auswendig lernen; (*obs.*) zur Erinnerung aufzeichnen.

memory ['meməri], *s.* das Gedächtnis, die Erinnerungskraft; Erinnerung, das Andenken (***of,*** an (*Acc.*)); ***commit to –,*** auswendig lernen, dem Gedächtnis einprägen; ***call to –,*** sich erinnern an (*Acc.*), sich (*Dat.*) ins Gedächtnis zurückrufen; ***that has escaped my –,*** das ist mir *or* meinem Gedächtnis entfallen; ***by*** or ***from –,*** auswendig, aus dem Gedächtnis; ***in the – of man,*** seit Menschengedenken; ***in – of,*** zum Andenken an (*Acc.*); ***of blessed –,*** seligen Andenkens; ***if my – serves me right,*** wenn ich mich recht erinnere *or* entsinne; ***within living –,*** noch in Erinnerung vieler Lebenden.

men [men], *pl. of* **man.**

menace ['menis], **1.** *s.* drohende Gefahr (***to,*** für), die (Be)drohung (*Gen.*). **2.** *v.t.* (*a p.*) drohen (*Dat.*), bedrohen (***with,*** mit), androhen (*Dat.*) (***with,*** *Acc.*); (*a th.*) gefährden. **menacing,** *adj.* drohend, bedrohlich.

ménage ['menɑ:ʒ], *s.* der Haushalt, die Haushaltung.

menagerie [mə'nædʒəri], *s.* die Menagerie, Tierschau.

mend [mend], **1.** *v.t.* reparieren, ausbessern, wiederherstellen; flicken (*clothes*); (*obs.*) berichtigen, besser machen, (ver)bessern; – ***one's efforts,*** seine Anstrengungen verdoppeln; – ***a fire,*** das Feuer schüren; – ***one's pace,*** den Schritt beschleunigen; – ***stockings,*** Strümpfe stopfen; – ***one's ways,*** sich bessern; (*Prov.*) ***least said, soonest –ed,*** durch viel Reden wird hier nicht geholfen. **2.** *v.i.* besser werden, sich bessern; genesen; ***be –ing,*** auf dem Wege der Besserung sein. **3.** *s.* die Ausbesserung, ausgebesserte Stelle; ***be on the –,*** see ***be –ing.***

mendacious [men'deiʃəs], *adj.* lügnerisch, lügenhaft, verlogen. **mendacity** [–'dæsiti], *s.* die Lügenhaftigkeit, Verlogenheit.

mendicancy ['mendikənsi], *s.* die Bettelei, das Betteln; *see also* **mendicity. mendicant, 1.** *adj.* bettelnd; Bettel–; (*R.C.*) – ***order,*** der Bettelorden. **2.** *s.* der (die) Bettler(in); (*R.C.*) der Bettelmönch.

mendicity [–'disiti], *s.* die Bettelarmut, der Bettelstand; *see also* **mendicancy**; ***reduce to –,*** an den Bettelstab bringen.

mending ['mendiŋ], *s.* 1. das (Aus)bessern, Flicken; ***invisible –,*** das Kunststopfen; – ***wool,*** das Stopfgarn; 2. (*collect.*) Kleider, Strümpfe *etc.*, die geflickt werden müssen.

menfolk ['menfouk], *pl.* Mannsleute (*pl.*), (*coll.*) Mannsbilder (*pl.*).

menhaden [men'heidn], *s.* (*Ichth.*) der Bunker.

menhir ['meniə], *s.* der Druidenstein, Hünenstein.

menial ['mi:niəl], **1.** *adj.* gemein, niedrig, knechtisch; Gesinde–; – ***offices,*** niedrige Dienste. **2.** *s.* der (die) Diener(in), der Knecht, die Magd; *pl.* das Gesinde.

meningeal [me'nindʒiəl], *adj.* (*Anat.*) Hirnhaut–. **meninges** [–dʒi:z], *pl.* Hirnhäute (*pl.*). **meningitis** [–'dʒaitis], *s.* die Hirnhautentzündung. **meningocele** [me'niŋgosi:l], *s.* der Hirnhautbruch.

meniscus [me'niskəs], *s.* (*pl.* **-i** [–'nisai]) (*Opt.*) konvex-konkave Linse, das Meniskenglas; (*Anat.*) die Gelenkscheibe, der Gelenkzwischenknorpel.

menopause ['menopɔ:z], *s.* Wechseljahre (*pl.*), das Klimakterium, (*coll.*) kritisches Alter.

menses ['mensi:z], *pl. See* **menstruation.**

menstrual ['menstruəl], *adj.* monatlich, Monats–; (*Med.*) Menstruations–. **menstruate** [–eit], *v.i.* menstruieren; (*coll.*) die Regel haben. **menstruation** [–'eiʃən], *s.* die Menstruation, der Monatsfluß, (*coll.*) die Regel.

mensurability [menʃərə'biliti], *s.* die Meßbarkeit. **mensurable** ['menʃərəbl], *adj.* meßbar. **mensuration** [–'reiʃən], *s.* das Abmessen, die (Ver)messung, Abmessung; (*Math.*) Meßkunst.

mental [mentl], *adj.* geistig, Geistes–; (*coll.*) geisteskrank; – ***ability,*** geistige Fähigkeit; – ***age,*** geistiges Alter; – ***arithmetic,*** das Kopfrechnen; – ***case,*** Geisteskranke(r); – ***deficiency,*** der Schwachsinn, geistige Minderwertigkeit; – ***derangement*** or ***disease*** or ***disorder,*** der Irrsinn, die Geisteskrankheit, Geistesstörung; – ***hospital,*** die Nervenklinik, Irrenanstalt; – ***patient,*** see – ***case;*** – ***power,*** die Geisteskraft; – ***reservation,*** der Gedankenvorbehalt, geheimer Vorbehalt; – ***state,*** der Geisteszustand. **mentality** [–'tæliti], *s.* die Geistesrichtung, Denkungsart, Denkweise, Mentalität, Gesinnung.

menthol ['menθɔl], *s.* das Menthol.

mention ['menʃən], **1.** *s.* die Erwähnung; ***honourable –,*** ehrenvolle Erwähnung; ***make – of,*** erwähnen. **2.** *v.t.* erwähnen; ***as –ed above,*** wie oben erwähnt; ***not to –,*** geschweige denn, abgesehen von; ***don't – it!*** bitte sehr! gern geschehen! es hat nichts zu sagen! ***not worth –ing,*** nicht der Rede wert. **mentionable,** *adj.* erwähnenswert.

mentor ['mentɔ:], *s.* treuer Ratgeber, der Berater, Mentor.

menu ['menju:], *s.* die Speisenfolge, das Menü; die Speisekarte.

mephitic [me'fitik], *adj.* verpestet, giftig; – ***air,*** die Stickluft, faule Ausdünstung.

mercantile ['mə:kəntail], *adj.* Handels–, handeltreibend, kaufmännisch; – ***classes,*** handeltreibende Klassen, der Kaufmannsstand; – ***law,*** das Handelsrecht; – ***marine,*** die Handelsmarine; –

system or *theory, see* **mercantilism**; – *town,* die Handelsstadt. **mercantilism,** *s.* der Merkantilismus, das Merkantilsystem.

mercenarily ['mə:sənərili], *adv.* für Geld, um Lohn, aus Gewinnsucht. **mercenariness,** *s.* die Gewinnsucht; Käuflichkeit, Feilheit. **mercenary,** **1.** *adj.* feil, käuflich; gewinnsüchtig; – *marriage,* die Geldheirat; – *soldiers,* Söldner(truppen), gedungene Soldaten. **2.** *s.* der Söldner.

mercer ['mə:sə], *s.* (*obs.*) der Seidenhändler, Textilhändler. **mercerize,** *v.t.* merzerisieren (*cotton*). **mercery,** *s.* (*obs.*) Seidenwaren, Schnittwaren (*pl.*); das Schnittwarengeschäft.

merchandise ['mə:tʃəndaiz], **1.** *s.* (*no pl.*) Waren, Handelsgüter (*pl.*); *article of* –, die Ware. **2.** *v.t.* (*Am.*) verkaufen; Werbung machen für (*goods*).

merchant ['mə:tʃənt], **1.** *s.* der Kaufmann, (Groß)-händler; *city* –, der Kaufherr; Krämer; *the* –*s,* die Kaufmannschaft, Handelskreise (*pl.*); *wholesale* –, der Großkaufmann; *retail* –, der Kleinhändler, Einzelhändler; –*'s clerk,* der Handlungsgehilfe; (*sl.*) *speed* –, rücksichtsloser Fahrer. **2.** *adj.* Handels–, Kaufmanns–; (*Hist.*) – *adventurer,* kaufmännischer Übersee-Spekulant; – *fleet,* die Kauffahrteiflotte; – *marine* or *navy,* die Handelsmarine; – *prince,* der Handelsmagnat, reicher Kaufherr; – *service,* die Handelsschiffahrt; *see also* – *marine.* **merchantman,** *s.* das Handelsschiff, Kauffahrteischiff.

merciful ['mə:siful], *adj.* barmherzig, mitleidvoll (*to,* gegen), gnädig (*Dat.*) (*as God*). **mercifully,** *adv.* (*also coll.*) erfreulicherweise. **mercifulness,** *s. See* **mercy. merciless,** *adj.* unbarmherzig, erbarmungslos, schonungslos, hartherzig, grausam. **mercilessness,** *s.* die Unbarmherzigkeit, Schonungslosigkeit, Grausamkeit.

mercurial [mə:'kjuəriəl], **1.** *adj.* Quecksilber–, quecksilberartig, quecksilberhaltig; (*fig.*) quecksilb(e)rig, lebhaft, beweglich, unbeständig. **mercurialism,** *s.* die Quecksilbervergiftung. **mercurialize,** *v.t.* mit Quecksilber behandeln. **mercuric,** *adj.* Quecksilber–; – *chloride,* das Sublimat; – *fulminate,* das Knallquecksilber. **mercurous** ['mə:kjərəs], *adj.* Quecksilber–; – *chloride,* das Kalomel.

mercury ['mə:kjəri], *s.* 1. (*Myth., Astr.*) der Merkur; (*fig.*) Bote; 2. das Quecksilber; – *column,* die Quecksilbersäule; *the* – *is rising,* das Barometer steigt.

mercy ['mə:si], *s.* die Barmherzigkeit, das Mitleid, Erbarmen; die Gnade; (*coll.*) Wohltat, der Segen, glückliche Fügung; *at his* –, ihm auf Gnade und Ungnade ausgeliefert, in seiner Gewalt; *at the* – *of,* preisgegeben (*Dat.*) (*waves etc.*); *beg for* –, um Gnade flehen; (*coll.*) *it is a* – *that* . . ., es ist ein Segen *or* eine wahre Wohltat, daß . . .; *Lord have* – *upon us!* Herr, erbarme Dich unser! *sister of* –, barmherzige Schwester; *throw o.s. on his* –, sich ihm auf Gnade und Ungnade ergeben; – *on us!* Gott sei uns gnädig! *have* – *on him,* sich seiner erbarmen; (*coll.*) *for* –*'s sake!* um Gottes willen! barmherziger Himmel! (*iron.*) *leave to the tender mercies of,* der rauhen Behandlung von . . . ausliefern; *show* – *to him* or *show him* –, see *have* – *on him*; *show no* –, keine Gnade walten lassen; *small* –, wenig Rücksicht; *be thankful for small mercies,* sich mit wenigem zufrieden geben; *without* –, ohne Gnade.

mercy|-killing, *s.* der Gnadentod, die Euthanasie. **–-seat,** *s.* der Gnadenstuhl (Gottes).

[1]**mere** [miə], *s.* der Weiher, kleiner See.

[2]**mere,** *adj.* bloß, nichts als; allein(ig), völlig, rein, lauter; *a* – *child,* (noch) ein reines Kind; – *form,* bloße Formsache; *no* – *imitator,* kein bloßer *or* nicht nur Nachahmer; (*coll.*) *for a* – *song,* um einen Pappenstiel. **merely,** *adv.* nur, bloß, lediglich. **merest** [–rist], *sup. adj. the* – *chance,* der reinste Zufall.

meretricious [meri'triʃəs], *adj.* buhlerisch; (*fig.*) verführerisch, trügerisch, unecht, kitschig.

merganser [mə:'gænsə], *s.* (*Orn.*) (*Am.*) *see* **goosander**; *hooded* –, der Kappensäger (*Lophodytes cucullatus*); *red-breasted* –, der Mittelsäger (*Mergus serrator*).

merge [mə:dʒ], **1.** *v.t.* verschmelzen (*in,* mit), einverleiben (*Dat.*), aufgehen lassen (*in,* in (*Dat.*)); (*Law*) aufheben, tilgen; (*Comm.*) fusionieren; *be* –*d in,* aufgehen in (*Dat.*). **2.** *v.i.* sich verschmelzen (*in,* mit), aufgehen (in (*Dat.*)). **mergence,** *s.* das Verschmelzen (*into,* mit), Aufgehen (*in,* in (*Dat.*)). **merger** [–ə], *s.* (*Law*) das Aufgehen; die Verschmelzung, der Verschmelzungsvertrag; (*Comm.*) Zusammenschluß, die Fusion, Fusionierung (*of firms*), Zusammenlegung (*of resources*).

mericarp ['merikɑ:p], *s.* (*Bot.*) die Teilfrucht.

meridian [mə'ridiən], **1.** *s.* (*Geog.*) der Meridian, die Mittagslinie, der Mittagskreis, Längenkreis; (*Astr.*) Kulminationspunkt; (*fig.*) Höhepunkt, Gipfel; die Blüte(zeit); (*Poet.*) der Mittag, die Mittagszeit. **2.** *adj.* Mittags–, mittäglich; (*fig.*) höchst; – *altitude,* die Mittagshöhe. **meridional,** **1.** *adj.* mittäglich, südlich. **2.** *s.* der Südländer.

meringue [mə'ræŋ], *s.* das Baiser, Schaumgebäck, die Meringe.

merino [mə'ri:nou], *s.* (*pl.* **-s**) das Merinoschaf. **merino-wool,** *s.* die Merinowolle.

merit ['merit], **1.** *s.* das Verdienst; der Wert, die Vortrefflichkeit, der Vorzug; *pl.* (*Law*) Hauptpunkte (*pl.*); *inquire into the* –*s of a case,* der Sache auf den Grund gehen; *on its* (*own*) –*s,* an und für sich, dem wesentlichen Inhalt nach; *rest* or *stand on its own* –*s,* nach dem eigentlichen Wert beurteilt werden; *on the* –*s of the case,* nach Lage der Dinge; *make a* – *of,* sich (*Dat.*) zum Verdienst anrechnen, sich (*Dat.*) zugute tun auf (*Acc.*); *in order of* –, nach Verdienst *or* Leistung geordnet; *Order of Merit,* der Verdienstorden. **2.** *v.t.* verdienen. **merited,** *adj.* (wohl)verdient. **meritocracy** [–'tɔkrəsi], *s.* die Leistungsgesellschaft. **meritorious** [–'tɔ:riəs], *adj.* verdienstlich. **meritoriousness,** *s.* die Verdienstlichkeit.

merle [mə:l], *s.* (*Poet.*) die Amsel.

merlin ['mə:lin], *s.* (*Orn.*) der Zwergfalke, Merlin (*Falco columbarius*).

merlon ['mə:lən], *s.* (*Hist.*) die Mauerzacke, Schartenbacke, der Zinnenzahn.

mermaid ['mə:meid], *s.* die Seejungfer, Wassernixe. **merman,** *s.* der Nix, Wassermann; (*Myth.*) Triton.

Merovingian [mero'vindʒiən], **1.** *s.* der Merowinger. **2.** *adj.* merowingisch.

merrily ['merili], *adv.* lustig, munter, fröhlich. **merriment,** *s.* die Fröhlichkeit, Munterkeit, Lustigkeit; Belustigung, Lustbarkeit. **merriness,** *s.* die Heiterkeit, der Frohsinn.

merry ['meri], *adj.* lustig, vergnügt, heiter, munter, fröhlich; scherzhaft, ergötzlich, spaßhaft; (*coll.*) angeheitert, beschwipst; *Merry Christmas!* fröhliche Weihnachten! *as* – *as a cricket,* kreuzfidel; *Merry England,* das fröhliche (Alt)england; *make* –, vergnügt sein, sich belustigen; sich lustig machen (*over,* über (*Acc.*)); *the more the merrier,* je mehr desto besser.

merry|-andrew, *s.* der Hanswurst, Spaßmacher. **–-go-round,** *s.* das Karussell; (*fig.*) der Wirbel. **–-making,** *s.* die Belustigung, Lustbarkeit, das Fest. **–-thought,** *s.* das Gabelbein, Wunschbein (*of poultry*).

mésalliance [me'zæljɑ̃s], *s.* die Mißheirat.

meseems [mi'si:mz], *imp.v.* (*obs.*) mir scheint, mich dünkt.

mesenteric [mesen'terik], *adj.* Gekrös–. **mesentery** ['mesəntəri], *s.* das Gekröse.

mesh [meʃ], **1.** *s.* die Masche; *pl.* das Netzwerk, Geflecht; (*Tech.*) die Maschenweite; (*fig.*) Schlingen, Stricke (*pl.*); (*Tech.*) *in* –, im Eingriff (*of gears*). **2.** *v.t.* im Netz fangen; (*Tech.*) einkuppeln, einrücken, ineinandergreifen lassen (*gear-wheels*); (*fig.*) umstricken, verstricken, umgarnen. **3.** *v.i.* ineinandergreifen, eingreifen (*of gears*). **mesh-connection,** *s.* (*Elec.*) die Dreieckschaltung. **meshed,** *adj. suff. close-* or *fine*–, engmaschig. **mesh-work,** *s.* das Netzwerk, Geflecht, Maschen (*pl.*).

mesmeric [mez'merik], *adj.* hypnotisch, heilmagnetisch. **mesmerism** ['mezmərizm], *s.* tierischer Magnetismus, der Heilmagnetismus. **mesmerist** ['mezmərist], *s.* der Hypnotiseur, Heilmagnetiseur. **mesmerization** [–rai'zeiʃən], *s.* die Heilmagnetisierung. **mesmerize** ['mezməraiz], *v.t.* hypnotisieren; (*fig.*) fesseln, faszinieren.

mesne [mi:n], *adj.* (*Law*) Mittel–, Zwischen–, dazwischentretend; – ***lord,*** der Afterlehnsherr; – ***interest,*** der Zwischenzins; – ***process,*** der Nebenprozeß.

meso– ['mesou], *pref.* mittel–, Mittel–, Zwischen–. **mesolithic** [–'liθik], *adj.* mesolithisch, mittelsteinzeitlich.

Mesopotamia [mesəpə'teimiə], *s.* Mesopotamien (*n.*). **Mesopotamian,** *adj.* mesopotamisch.

meso|thorax, *s.* (*Ent.*) der Mittelbrustring. **–zoic** [–'zouik], **1.** *s.* (*Geol.*) das Mesozoikum. **2.** *adj.* mesozoisch.

mess [mes], **1.** *s.* 1. (*coll.*) die Unordnung, das Durcheinander; der Schmutz, die Schweinerei; (*fig.*) Klemme, Patsche; ***in a –,*** in Verwirrung *or* Unordnung (*of th.*), in der Patsche (*of p.*); ***get into a –,*** in die Klemme geraten; ***make a –,*** Schmutz machen; ***make a – of,*** verderben, verpatzen, verhunzen, verpfuschen; 2. (*Mil.*) die Messe, der Regimentstisch, das Kasino; (*Naut.*) die Back(mannschaft); ***officer's –,*** das Offizierskasino; 3. (*rare*) die Speise, das Gericht, der Mischmasch; (*B.*) – ***of pottage,*** das Linsengericht; (*fig.*) der Mischmasch, unappetitliches Gericht. **2.** *v.t.* (*also – up*) beschmutzen, beschmieren; in Verwirrung *or* Unordnung bringen, verderben. **3.** *v.i.* 1. gemeinsam essen (***with,*** mit); (*Naut.*) – ***together,*** Messe führen, zu einer Back gehören; 2. (*coll.*) – ***about*** or ***around,*** sich zu schaffen machen (***with,*** mit), herumpfuschen, herumfummeln, herumpüttieren (an (*Dat.*)); herummurksen, herumschludern.

message ['mesidʒ], *s.* die Botschaft; Nachricht, Mitteilung, der Bescheid, Bericht; (*fig.*) die Botschaft, bedeutsame Mitteilung (*of a poet etc.*); *pl.* (*Scots*) Einkäufe, Besorgungen (*pl.*); ***bear a –,*** eine Botschaft überbringen; ***go on*** or ***deliver*** or ***take a –,*** eine Botschaft ausrichten; ***send him a –,*** ihm eine Mitteilung zukommen lassen, ihn benachrichtigen; ***radio –,*** die Funkmeldung, Funkmitteilung; ***telephone –,*** telephonische Nachricht. **message|-blank,** *s.* (*Mil.*) die Meldekarte. **--centre,** *s.* (*Mil.*) der Meldekopf, die Melde(sammel)stelle.

messenger ['mesindʒə], *s.* der Bote, (*esp. Mil.*) Kurier, (*Mil.*) Meldeläufer; ***express*** or ***special –,*** der Eilbote; ***by –,*** durch Boten. **messenger|-boy,** *s.* der Laufbursche, Botenjunge, Ausläufer. **--cable,** *s.* (*Naut.*) das Kabelar. **--dog,** *s.* der Meldehund. **--pigeon,** *s.* die Brieftaube.

Messiah [mi'saiə], *s.* der Messias, Heiland, Erlöser. **Messianic** [mesi'ænik], *adj.* messianisch.

messiness ['mesinis], *s.* die Unordnung, Verwirrung; Unordentlichkeit, Schmutzigkeit.

messing ['mesiŋ], *s.* (*Mil.*) die Verpflegung. **mess|-jacket,** *s.* (*Mil.*) blaue (Abend)jacke. **–mate,** *s.* (*Mil.*) der Tischgenosse, Meßkamerad, (*Naut.*) Backgenosse; (*coll.*) Kamerad.

Messrs. ['mesəz], *pl.* (die) Herren (*before two or more names*), (die) Firma (*as address of a firm*).

mess|-sergeant, *s.* (*Mil.*) der Küchenunteroffizier, (*coll.*) Küchenbulle. **–tin,** *s.* das Kochgeschirr, Eßgeschirr.

messuage ['meswidʒ], *s.* (*Law*) das Anwesen, Wohnhaus mit Grundstück.

messy ['mesi], *adj.* unordentlich, unsauber, schmutzig.

mestiza [mes'ti:zə], *s.* die Mestizin. **mestizo** [–zou], *s.* (*pl.* **-s**) der Mestize.

met [met], *imperf., p.p. of* [1]**meet.**

meta– ['metə], *pref.* Meta–, Zwischen–, Mit–, Um–.

metabasis [me'tæbəsis], *s.* (*Med.*) die Veränderung; (*Rhet.*) der Übergang.

metabolic [metə'bɔlik], *adj.* veränderlich, wandelbar; (*Med.*) Stoffwechsel–. **metabolism** [mə'tæbəlizm], *s.* die Formveränderung, Verwandlung; (*Med.*) der Stoffwechsel; (*Bot.*) die Umsetzung; (*Chem.*) der Metabolismus.

metacarpal [metə'kɑ:pl], *adj.* Mittelhand–. **metacarpus,** *s.* (*pl.* **-pi** [–pai]) die Mittelhand, (*of animals*) das Vordermittelfuß.

metacentre ['metəsentə], *s.* (*Tech.*) das Metazentrum, der Schwankpunkt.

metage ['mi:tidʒ], *s.* amtliches Messen (*esp. of coal*); das Meßgeld, Waagegeld.

meta|genesis, *s.* der Generationswechsel, die Metagenese. **–genetic,** *adj.* metagenetisch.

metal [metl], **1.** *s.* das Metall; (*glassmaking*) die Glasmasse; (*for roads etc.*) Beschotterung, Kiesfüllung, der Schotter; *pl.* (*Railw.*) das Gleis, Geleise, Schienen (*pl.*); ***base –,*** unedles Metall; ***crude –,*** das Rohmetall; (*Railw.*) ***run off the –s,*** entgleisen. **2.** *v.t.* mit Metall überziehen, (*roads etc.*) beschottern; ***metalled road,*** die Schotterstraße.

metaled, metaling, metalize, (*Am.*) *see* **metalled, metalling, metallize.**

metallic [mə'tælik], *adj.* Metall–, metallen, metallisch; – ***currency,*** das Hartgeld, die Metallwährung; – ***lustre,*** der Metallglanz; – ***oxide,*** das Metalloxyd; – ***voice,*** metallene Stimme. **metalliferous** [metə'lifərəs], *adj.* metallhaltig, metallreich, metallführend; – ***vein,*** die Erzader, der Erzgang. **metalline** ['metəlain], *adj.* Metall–, metallisch, metallhaltig. **metalling** ['metəliŋ], *s.* die Beschotterung (*of roads etc.*), (*Railw.*) Schienenlegung. **metallization** [metəlai'zeiʃən], *s.* die Metallisierung. **metallize** ['metəlaiz], *v.t.* metallisieren. **metalloid** ['metəlɔid], **1.** *adj.* metalloidisch, metallähnlich, metallartig. **2.** *s.* das Metalloid, Nichtmetall.

metallurgic(al) [metə'lə:dʒik(l)], *adj.* metallurgisch, Hütten–. **metallurgist** [–'tælədʒist], *s.* der Metallurg(e), Hüttenkundige(r). **metallurgy** [–'tælədʒi], *s.* die Metallurgie, Hüttenkunde, das Hüttenwesen.

metal|-plating, *s.* die Plattierung. **--work,** *s.* die Metallarbeit. **–worker,** *s.* der Metallarbeiter.

metamorphic [metə'mɔ:fik], *adj.* gestaltverändernd, umgestaltend, Umwandlungs–; (*Geol.*) metamorph. **metamorphism,** *s.* die Umgestaltung, Umwandlung, Metamorphose; (*Geol.*) der Metamorphismus. **metamorphose** [–fouz], **1.** *v.t.* verwandeln, umgestalten ((***in***)***to,*** in (*Acc.*)), umbilden (in (*Acc.*) *or* zu). **2.** *v.i.* sich verwandeln. **metamorphosis** [–'mɔ:fəsis], *s.* (*pl.* **-ses** [–si:z]) die Umwandlung, Verwandlung, Gestaltveränderung, Metamorphose.

metaphor ['metəfə], *s.* die Metapher, bildlicher *or* übertragener Ausdruck. **metaphoric(al)** [–'fɔrik(l)], *adj.* bildlich, figürlich, übertragen, metaphorisch.

metaphrase ['metəfreiz], *s.* wörtliche Übertragung *or* Übersetzung. **metaphrastic** [–'fræstik], *adj.* umschreibend.

meta|physical, *adj.* metaphysisch, abstrakt, übersinnlich. **–physician,** *s.* der Metaphysiker. **–physics,** *pl.* (*sing. constr.*) die Metaphysik.

metaphysis [me'tæfəsis], *s.* (*Anat.*) die Metaphyse.

metaplasia [metə'pleiziə], *s.* (*Biol.*) die Metaplasie. **metaplasis** [–'tæpləsis], *s.* (*Biol.*) das Stadium der Entwicklungsreife.

metastasis [me'tæstəsis], *s.* (*Biol.*) der Stoffwechsel, Substanzwechsel; (*Geol.*) die Gesteinartverwandlung; (*Med.*) der Tochterherd, die Tochtergeschwulst, Metastase; (*Rhet.*) Metastase.

metatarsal [metə'tɑ:sl], *adj.* Mittelfuß–. **metatarsus,** *s.* der Mittelfuß, (*of animals*) Mittel(hinter)fuß.

metathesis [me'tæθəsis], *s.* die Lautversetzung, (Buchstaben)umstellung, Metathese.

métayage ['meteiɑ:ʒ], *s.* die Halbpacht.

mete [mi:t], **1.** *v.t.* (*Poet.*) messen; – ***out,*** zumessen (*punishment*) (*to, Dat.*). **2.** *s.* das Maß, die Grenze; ***–s and bounds,*** Maß und Ziel.

metempsychosis [metəmpsi'kousis], *s.* die Seelenwanderung.

meteor ['mi:tiə], *s.* der *or* das Meteor, die Sternschnuppe; (*fig.*) Lufterscheinung. **meteoric** [–ti'ɔrik], *adj.* meteorisch, Meteor–; (*fig.*) meteorartig, plötzlich, flüchtig. **meteorite** [–rait], *s.* der Meteorstein.

meteorological [mi:tiərə'lɔdʒikl], *adj.* meteorologisch, Wetter–; – ***conditions,*** Witterungsverhältnisse (*pl.*); – ***observatory,*** die Wetterwarte; – ***office,*** das Amt für Wetterdienst; – ***report,*** der Wetterbericht. **meteorologist** [–'rɔlədʒist], *s.* der Meteorologe. **meteorology** [–'rɔlədʒi], *s.* die Meteorologie, Wetterkunde.

[1]**meter** ['mi:tə], **1.** *s.* der Messer, Zähler, das Zählwerk, Meßgerät; ***gas –,*** die Gasuhr; ***parking –,*** die Parkuhr. **2.** *v.t.* messen.

[2]**meter,** (*Am.*) *see* **metre.**

methane ['mi:θein], *s.* das Sumpfgas, Grubengas, Methan, der Kohlenwasserstoff.

methinks [mi'θiŋks], *v.imp.* (*obs.*) *see* **meseems.**

method ['meθəd], *s.* die Methode, Art und Weise, das Verfahren, der Prozeß; die Arbeitsweise, Lehrweise; Denkmethode; das System, die Anordnung, der Plan. **methodic(al)** [mə'θɔdik(l)], *adj.* methodisch, systematisch, planmäßig, folgerecht.

Methodism['meθədizm], *s.* (*Eccl.*) der Methodismus. **Methodist, 1.** *s.* (*Eccl.*) der Methodist. **2.** *adj.* Methodisten–, methodistisch.

methodize ['meθədaiz], *v.t.* planmäßig ordnen. **methodology** [–'dɔlədʒi], *s.* die Methodenlehre, Unterrichtsmethodik.

methought, *imperf. of* **methinks.**

methyl ['meθil], *s.* das Methyl; – ***alcohol,*** der Methylalkohol, Holzgeist, das Methanol. **methylate** [–eit], *v.t.* mit Methyl mischen, denaturieren; ***–d spirit,*** denaturierter Spiritus, der Methylalkohol, Brennspiritus. **methylene** [–i:n], *s.* das Methylen. **methylic** [mi'θilik], *adj.* Methyl–.

meticulous [mə'tikjuləs], *adj.* übergenau, peinlich genau, penibel.

métier ['metiei], *s.* das Gewerbe; (*usu. fig.*) Fach, (Spezial)gebiet.

metonymy [me'tɔnimi], *s.* die Begriffsvertauschung, Metonymie.

metope ['metoup], *s.* (*Archit.*) das Zwischenfeld, Schmuckfeld.

metre ['mi:tə], *s.* 1. das (*coll. oft.* der) Meter; 2. (*Metr.*) das Versmaß, Silbenmaß, Metrum.

metric ['metrik], *adj.* metrisch, Maß–; – ***analysis,*** die Maßanalyse; – ***hundredweight,*** der Zentner; – ***system,*** das Dezimalsystem. **metrical,** *adj.* (*Metr.*) metrisch, rhythmisch, periodisch, Vers–. **metrication** [–'keiʃən], *s.* der Übergang zum Dezimalsystem. **metrics,** *pl.* (*sing. constr.*) die Metrik, Verslehre.

metro ['metrou], *s.* (*coll.*) die Untergrundbahn.

metronome ['metrənoum], *s.* (*Mus.*) das Metronom, der Taktmesser, Tempogeber.

metropolis [mə'trɔpəlis], *s.* die Hauptstadt, Metropole. **metropolitan** [metrə'pɔlitən], **1.** *adj.* 1. hauptstädtisch; 2. (*Eccl.*) Metropolitan–. **2.** *s.* 1. der (die) Hauptstadtbewohner(in), Großstadtbewohner(in), Großstädter(in); 2. (*Eccl.*) der Erzbischof, Metropolit.

mettle [metl], *s.* der (Grund)stoff, das Wesen; (*fig.*) die Naturanlage, Naturkraft; Rassigkeit, Herzhaftigkeit, der Eifer, Enthusiasmus, Mut, das Feuer; ***be on one's –,*** alle Kräfte anspannen, sein möglichstes tun; ***put him on his –,*** ihn zur Aufbietung aller Kräfte ansporen, ihn auf die Probe stellen. **mettled, mettlesome,** *adj.* feurig, mutig, rassig.

Meuse [mə:z], *s.* Maas (*f.*).

[1]**mew** [mju:], **1.** *s.* das Miauen. **2.** *v.i.* miauen.

[2]**mew, 1.** *s.* der (Mauser)käfig. **2.** *v.i.* (sich) mausern. **3.** *v.t.* (*obs.*) abwerfen (*plumage*); (*also* – ***up***), abschließen, einsperren.

[3]**mew (gull),** *s.* (*Am.*) *see* ***common gull.***

mewl [mju:l], *v.i.* wimmern, quäken.

mews [mju:z], *pl.* 1. königlicher Marstall; 2. (*sing. constr.*) die Stallung, Stallgasse.

Mexican ['meksikən], **1.** *s.* der (die) Mexikaner(in). **2.** *adj.* mexikanisch. **Mexico** [–kou], *s.* Mexiko (*n.*).

mezzanine ['mezəni:n], *s.* der Halbstock, das Halbgeschoß, Zwischengeschoß, Mezzanin, Entresol.

mezzo|-soprano ['metsousə'prɑ:nou], *s.* der Mezzosopran; die Mezzosopransängerin. **–tint,** *s.* der Kupferstich in Schabmanier.

mho [mou], *s.* (*Elec.*) das Siemens.

mi [mi:], *s.* (*Mus.*) die dritte Silbe der Solmisation.

miaow [mi'au], *see* [1]**mew.**

miasma [mai'æzmə], *s.* (*Med.*) der Krankheitsstoff, Ansteckungsstoff. **miasmal, miasmatic** [–'mætik], *adj.* miasmatisch, ansteckend.

mica ['maikə], *s.* der Glimmer; – ***schist,*** – ***slate,*** der Glimmerschiefer. **micaceous** [–'keiʃəs], *adj.* Glimmer–, glimmerartig.

mice [mais], *pl. of* **mouse.**

Michaelmas ['mikəlməs], *s.* das Michaelsfest, Michaelis; ***at –,*** zu Michaelis; – ***daisy,*** die Strandaster; – ***Day,*** der Michaelistag; – ***term,*** das Herbstsemester.

mickle [mikl], *adj.* (*Scots*) groß, viel.

microbe ['maikroub], *s.* die Mikrobe, der Mikroorganismus, das Kleinlebewesen. **microbial** [–'kroubiəl], *adj.* Mikroben–.

micro– ['maikrou], *pref.* klein, Klein–.

micro|cephalic [–sə'fælik], **–cephalous** [–'sefələs], *adj.* kleinköpfig.

microcosm ['maikrəkɔzm], *s.* der Mikrokosmos, die Welt im Kleinen.

micro|farad, *s.* (*Elec.*) das Mikrofarad. **–film,** *s.* der Mikrofilm. **–meter** [–'krɔmitə], *s.* die Mikrometerschraube, (Feinmeß)schraub(lehr)e; *see also* **micron. ––microfarad,** *s.* (*Elec.*) das Picofarad.

micron ['maikrɔn], *s.* das Mikrometer, Mikron.

micro-organism, *s. See* **microbe.**

microphone ['maikrəfoun], *s.* das Mikrophon.

microscope ['maikrəskoup], *s.* das Mikroskop. **microscopic** [–'skɔpik], *adj.* mikroskopisch; (*fig.*) verschwindend klein. **microscopical,** *adj.* mikroskopisch. **microscopy** [–'krɔskəpi], *s.* die Mikroskopie.

microsome ['maikrəsoum], *s.* das Klebekorn, Mikrosom.

micro|spore, *s.* die Mikrospore, Kleinspore. **–structure,** *s.* das Kleingefüge. **–wave,** *s.* (*Rad.*) die Mikrowelle.

micturate ['miktjureit], *v.i.* Harn lassen, urinieren. **micturition** [–'riʃən], *s.* der Harndrang, Urindrang.

mid [mid], *attrib. adj.* in der Mitte (*Gen.*), Mittel–; ***in – air,*** mitten in der Luft; ***in – career,*** in vollem Lauf; – ***May,*** Mitte Mai; ***in – ocean,*** auf offenem Meer.

midday ['middei], **1.** *s.* der Mittag. **2.** *adj.* Mittags–, mittäglich; – ***meal,*** das Mittagessen.

midden [midn], *s.* die Müllgrube, der Misthaufen; (*Archaeol.*) Kehrichthaufen.

middle [midl], **1.** *s.* die Mitte; das Mittelstück, mittlerer Teil; (*of the body*) der Gürtel, die Taille, Hüftlinie; ***in the – of his speech,*** mitten in seiner Rede; ***in the – of July,*** Mitte Juli; (*coll.*) ***knock him into the – of next week,*** ihn völlig fertigmachen. **2.** *attrib. adj.* mittlere(r, -s), Mittel–; – ***age,*** mittleres Alter; ***the Middle Ages,*** das Mittelalter; – ***class(es),*** der Mittelstand; – ***course,*** der Mittelweg; – ***distance,*** (*Phot. etc.*) der Mittelgrund; (*Spt.*) die Mittelstrecke; – ***ear,*** das Mittelohr;

Middle East, Mittlerer Osten; *Middle English,* das Mittelenglisch; – *finger,* der Mittelfinger; *Middle High German,* das Mittelhochdeutsch; – *rhyme,* der Binnenreim; (*Log.*) – *term,* das Mittelglied; (*Naut.*) – *watch,* die Hundewache; *Middle West,* der Mittelwesten.

middle|-aged, *adj.* von mittlerem Alter. **–brow, 1.** *adj.* (*coll.*) geistig mittelmäßig. **2.** *s.* geistiger Durchschnittsmensch. **–-class,** *adj.* Mittelstands–. **–-distance,** *adj.* (*Spt.*) Mittelstrecken–. **–man,** *s.* (*Comm.*) der Zwischenhändler, Makler; die Mittelsperson; *–'s profit,* der Zwischengewinn. **–-of-the-road,** *adj.* (*coll.*) neutral, unabhängig. **–-size(d),** *adj.* von mittlerer Größe. **–weight,** *s.* (*Spt.*) das Mittelgewicht (*under 160 lb.*); der Mittelgewichtler.

middling ['midliŋ], **1.** *adj.* mittelmäßig, Mittel–, Durchschnitts–; (*coll.*) leidlich. **2.** *adv.* (*coll.*) leidlich, ziemlich. **3.** *s.* (*Comm.*) (*usu. pl.*) die Ware mittlerer Qualität, die Mittelsorte, (*esp.*) das Mittelmehl.

middy ['midi], *s.* (*coll.*) *see* **midshipman.**

midge [midʒ], *s.* die Mücke.

midget ['midʒit], **1.** *s.* der Zwerg, Knirps; (etwas) Winziges. **2.** *adj.* Zwerg–, Kleinst–, Miniatur–.

midinette [midi'net], *s.* (Pariser) Ladenmädchen.

mid|land [–lənd], **1.** *s.* (*usu. pl.*) das Mittelland; *the Midlands,* Mittelengland. **2.** *adj.* binnenländisch. **–night, 1.** *s.* die Mitternacht. **2.** *adj.* Mitternachts–, mitternächtig; *burn the – oil,* bis spät in die Nacht arbeiten. **–rib,** *s.* (*Bot.*) die Mittelrippe. **–riff,** *s.* (*coll.*) das Zwerchfell. **–shipman,** *s.* der Seekadett. **–ships,** *adv.* mittschiffs.

midst [midst], *s.* die Mitte; (*only with preps.*) *e.g. from our –,* aus unserer Mitte; *in our –,* mitten unter uns; *in the – of,* mitten unter (*Dat.*), inmitten (*Gen.*).

mid|stream, *s.* die Strommitte. **–-stream,** *adv.* in der Mitte des Stroms. **–summer, 1.** *s.* der Hochsommer. **2.** *adj.* hochsommerlich, Hochsommer–; – *day,* der Johannistag (*24 Juni*), die Sommersonnenwende; *Midsummer Night's Dream,* der Sommernachtstraum; (*coll.*) – *madness,* heller Wahnsinn. **–-Victorian,** *adj.* kennzeichnend für die 60er und 70er Jahre (des 19. Jahrhunderts). **–way,** *adv.* auf halbem Wege, mitten auf dem Wege. **–week(ly),** *adj., adv.* in der Mitte der Woche. **Midwest,** *s. See Middle West.* **mid|wife,** *s.* die Hebamme, Geburtshelferin. **–wifery** [–wifəri], *s.* der Hebammendienst, die Geburtshilfe. **–winter,** *s.* die Mitte des Winters; (*Astr.*) Wintersonnenwende.

mien [mi:n], *s.* (*Poet.*) die Haltung, das Auftreten, Gebaren.

[1]**might** [mait], *imperf. of* [1]**may.**

[2]**might,** *s.* die Macht, Gewalt; Kraft, Stärke; *with all one's –, with – and main,* mit voller Kraft, mit aller Gewalt, aus Leibeskräften; – *is right,* Gewalt geht vor Recht. **mightily,** *adv.* mächtig, kräftig, mit Gewalt; (*coll.*) gewaltig, riesig, sehr. **mightiness,** *s.* die Macht, Gewalt; (*coll.*) Größe; (*coll.*) *high and –,* die Hochmütigkeit, Hochnäsigkeit. **mighty, 1.** *adj.* mächtig, gewaltig, heftig; (*coll.*) riesig, groß. **2.** *adv.* (*coll.*) (*before adj. or adv.*) kolossal, riesig, ungeheuer.

mignonette [minjə'net], *s.* (*Bot.*) die Reseda, Resede.

migraine ['mi:grein], *s.* die Migräne.

migrant ['maigrənt], **1.** *s.* 1. (*Orn.*) der Zugvogel; (*Zool.*) das Wandertier; (*Orn.*) *accidental –,* der Irrgast; *local –,* der Strichvogel; *partial –,* der Teilzieher; 2. der (Aus)wanderer. **2.** *adj.* Zug–, Wander–. **migrate** [–'greit], *v.i.* (fort)ziehen, (aus)wandern (*to,* nach); übersiedeln, umziehen. **migration** [–'greiʃən], *s.* (*Orn.*) der Vogelzug; (*Zool. and peoples*) Zug; das Fortziehen, die Wanderung; (*Chem., Phys., Geol.*) Wanderung; *seasonal –,* periodische Wanderung; – *of peoples,* die Völkerwanderung; *right of free –,* die Freizügigkeit. **migratory** ['maigrətəri], *adj.* (aus)wandernd, umherziehend; nomadisch, Zug–; – *animals,* Wandertiere; – *birds,* Zugvögel; – *worker,* der Wanderarbeiter.

mikado [mi'ka:dou], *s.* der Mikado, Kaiser von Japan.

mike [maik], (*coll.*) *see* **microphone.**

milage, *see* **mileage.**

Milan [mi'læn], *s.* Mailand (*n.*). **Milanese** [milə'ni:z], **1.** *s.* der (die) Mailänder(in). **2.** *adj.* mailändisch.

milch [miltʃ], *adj.* milchgebend. **milch-cow,** *s.* die Milchkuh (*also fig.*); *look on him as a –,* ihn als melkende Kuh betrachten.

mild [maild], *adj.* mild, sanft, gelind(e), freundlich, angenehm (*weather, character*); leicht (*disease, cigar*); warm, lind (*weather*); mäßig, glimpflich (*punishment*); *to put it –ly,* gelinde gesagt.

mildew ['mildju:], **1.** *s.* der Meltau, Schimmel; Brand (*in grain*); Moder, Moderflecke (*pl.*), Stockflecke (*pl.*) (*in paper or cloth*); *spot of –,* der Moderfleck, Stockfleck. **2.** *v.t.* verschimmeln; *be –ed,* verschimmelt sein. **3.** *v.i.* schimmelig *or* moderig *or* brandig *or* stockig werden.

mildness ['maildnis], *s.* die Milde, Sanftheit; (*of character*) Sanftmut. **mild|-steel,** *s.* der Flußstahl, schweißbarer Stahl. **–-tempered,** *adj.* sanftmütig.

mile [mail], *s.* die Meile; *statute –,* englische Meile (= *1609.3 Meter*); *nautical* or *geographical –,* die Seemeile (= *1853.2 Meter*); – *after – of* or *–s and –s of ruins,* meilenweite Ruinen; *for –s,* meilenweit; *from –s,* meilenweit her; *miss by a –,* (meilen)weit verfehlen, hoffnungslos danebentreffen. **mileage** [–idʒ], *s.* 1. die Meilenlänge *or* Meilenzahl; 2. das Kilometergeld. **mile-post,** *s.* der Meilenstein. **miler,** *s.* (*Spt.*) der Meilenläufer, Mittelstreckenläufer. **milestone,** *s.* der Meilenstein, (*fig.*) Markstein.

milfoil ['milfɔil], *s.* (*Bot.*) die Schafgarbe.

miliaria [mili'ɛəriə], *s.* (*Med.*) Frieseln (*pl.*), das Frieselfieber. **miliary** ['miliəri], *adj.* hirsekornförmig; – *fever, see* **miliaria**; – *gland,* die Hirsedrüse.

militancy ['militənsi], *s.* der Kriegsgeist, Kampfgeist; Kampf, Kriegszustand. **militant, 1.** *adj.* kämpfend, kriegführend, streitend; kriegerisch, kampflustig, streitbar. **2.** *s.* der Kämpfer, Streiter.

militarily ['militərili], *adv.* in militärischer Hinsicht. **militarism,** *s.* der Militarismus. **militarist,** *s.* der Militarist. **militaristic** [–'ristik], *adj.* militaristisch, kriegerisch.

military ['militəri], **1.** *adj.* militärisch, Militär–; Kriegs–, Heeres–; – *academy,* die Kriegsschule; – *age,* militärpflichtiges Alter; – *attaché,* der Militärattaché; – *authorities,* Militärbehörden (*pl.*); – *band,* die Militärkapelle; – *code,* das Militärstrafgesetz(buch); – *court,* das Militärgericht, Kriegsgericht; *Military Cross,* das Militär(verdienst)kreuz; – *dictatorship,* die Militärdiktatur; – *district,* der Wehrkreis; – *equipment,* die Heeresausrüstung; – *forces,* die Wehrmacht; – *government,* die Militärregierung, Besatzungsbehörde; – *intelligence,* der (Heeres)nachrichtendienst, Abwehrdienst, die Abwehr; Feindnachrichten (*pl.*); – *law,* das Kriegsrecht, Standrecht; – *man,* der Offizier; – *matters,* das Wehrwesen; – *outfitter,* der Militärschneider; – *police,* die Militärpolizei, Feldpolizei; – *property,* das Heeresgut; – *science,* die Wehrwissenschaft; – *service,* der Heeresdienst, Militärdienst, Wehrdienst; (*un*)*fit for – service,* militär(un)tauglich; *universal* (*compulsory*) – *service,* allgemeine Wehrpflicht *or* Dienstpflicht; – *service book,* der Wehrpaß; – *song,* das Soldatenlied; – *stores,* das Kriegsmaterial, der Kriegsbedarf; – *tribunal,* das Kriegsgericht. **2.** *s.* (*pl. constr.*) das Militär, Soldaten, Truppen (*pl.*); *call in the –,* das Militär zu Hilfe rufen.

militate ['militeit], *v.i.* sprechen (*against,* gegen), widerstreiten (*Dat.*) (*a p.*); entgegentreten, entgegenwirken (*Dat.*) (*a th.*). **militation** [–'teiʃən], *s.* der Kampf, Konflikt, Widerstreit.

militia [mi'liʃə], *s.* die Miliz, Landwehr, Bürgerwehr. **militiaman** [–mən], *s.* der Milizsoldat.

milk [milk], **1.** *s.* die Milch; (*fig.*) – ***and honey,*** Milch und Honig, die Überfülle, der Überfluß; ***skim(med)*** –, die Magermilch; ***full cream*** or ***rich*** –, die Vollmilch; (*coll.*) ***it's no use crying over spilt*** –, hin ist hin, geschehene Dinge sind nicht zu ändern; – ***of human kindness,*** die Milch der frommen Denkungsart; – ***of magnesia,*** die Magnesiamilch; – ***of sulphur,*** die Schwefelmilch. **2.** *v.t.* melken; (*sl.*) schröpfen, rupfen (*a p.*), anzapfen (*phone etc.*); (*coll.*) – ***the bull*** or ***pigeon*** or ***ram,*** den Mohren weißwaschen (wollen).

milk|-and-water, **1.** *s.* seichtes Gewäsch, die Seichtheit, Weichlichkeit. **2.** *attrib. adj.* saft- und kraftlos, seicht, weichlich, zimperlich. **--bar,** *s.* die Milch(trink)halle. **--can,** *s.* die Milchkanne. **--diet,** *s.* die Milchkost. **milker,** *s.* 1. der (die) Melker(in); 2. die Milchkuh. **milk|-fever,** *s.* das Milchfieber. **--float,** *s.* der Milchwagen. **milkiness,** *s.* die Milchigkeit, Milchartigkeit, Milchähnlichkeit. **milking,** *s.* das Melken; – ***machine,*** die Melkmaschine.

milk|-jug, *s.* der Milchtopf. **–maid,** *s.* die Milchmagd, Kuhmagd, das Milchmädchen. **–man** [–mən], *s.* der Milchmann, Milchhändler. **--round,** *s.* die Runde des Milchmannes. **--shake,** *s.* das Milchmischgetränk. **–sop,** *s.* das Muttersöhnchen, der Schlappschwanz, Weichling. **--sugar,** *s.* der Milchzucker, die Laktose. **--tooth,** *s.* der Milchzahn. **–weed,** *s.* (*Bot.*) die Wolfsmilch. **--white,** *adj.* milchweiß. **–wort,** *s.* (*Bot.*) die Kreuzblume. **milky,** *adj.* milchig, milchartig; (*fig.*) milchweiß, (*of gems*) wolkig; ***Milky Way,*** die Milchstraße.

[1]**mill** [mil], **1.** *s.* die Mühle; Fabrik, das Werk, (*esp.*) (***spinning***-)–, die Spinnerei; das Hammerwerk, Hüttenwerk, (*Mint.*) Prägewerk; ***rolling***-–, das Walzwerk; (*coll.*) ***go through the*** –, eine harte Schule durchmachen; (*coll.*) ***put him through the*** –, ihn in eine harte Schule schicken; ***that is grist to his*** –, das ist Wasser auf seine Mühle. **2.** *v.t.* mahlen (*grain*), (aus)walzen (*paper, metal*), walken (*cloth*), fräsen (*wood*), prägen (*money*), rändeln (*coins*); ***–ed edge,*** die Rändelung. **3.** *v.i.* (*coll.*) sich schlagen, raufen; sich im Kreise bewegen (*of cattle*); (*coll.*) – ***around,*** zwecklos umherirren.

[2]**mill,** *s.* (*Am.*) das Tausendstel (= *1/10-Cent*).

mill|board, *s.* starke Pappe, der Pappdeckel. **--dam,** *s.* das Mühlwehr.

millenarian [milə'nɛəriən], **1.** *adj.* tausendjährig; (*Eccl.*) zum tausendjährigen Reich (Christi) gehörig. **2.** *s.* der Chiliast. **millenarianism,** *s.* der Chiliasmus. **millenary** [mi'lenəri], **1.** *adj.* tausendjährig, Jahrtausend–. **2.** *s.* die Tausendjahrfeier, Jahrtausend feier; das Jahrtausend.

millennial, [mi'leniəl], *adj.* tausendjährig. **millennium,** *s.* das Jahrtausend; die Jahrtausendfeier, Tausendjahrfeier; (*Eccl.*) tausendjähriges Reich Christi; (*fig.*) das Zeitalter des Glücks und Friedens.

millepede ['milipi:d], *s.* der Tausendfuß, Tausendfüß(l)er.

miller ['milə], *s.* der Müller (*also Ent.*).

millesimal [mi'lesiml], **1.** *adj.* tausendst; tausendfach. **2.** *s.* das Tausendstel.

millet ['milit], *s.* die Hirse. **millet grass,** *s.* das Flattergras, die Waldhirse.

mill|-hand, *s.* der Mühlenarbeiter, (*esp.*) der (die) Spinnereiarbeiter(in). **--hopper,** *s.* der Mühltrichter, Mühlrumpf.

milli|ammeter [mili'æmi:tə], *s.* das Milliampermeter. **–amp(ere),** *s.* das Milliampere. **milliard** ['miliəd], *s.* die Millarde (= 10^9). **milli|gram(me),** *s.* das Milligram. **–metre,** *s.* das Millimeter.

milliner ['milinə], *s.* die Putzmacherin, Modistin; ***man***-–, der Putzmacher. **millinery,** *s.* Putzwaren, Modewaren (*pl.*); das Modewarengeschäft.

[1]**milling** ['miliŋ], *s.* das Mahlen; (*esp.*) (*Tech.*) Walken, Fräsen, Rändeln; *see* [1]**mill, 2.**

[2]**milling,** *adj. See* [1]**mill, 3**; – ***crowd,*** drängende *or* wogende Menschenmenge.

milling-machine, *s.* die Fräsmaschine; das Rändelwerk.

million ['miljən], *s.* die Million; *3* –(*s*), 3 Millionen; *10* – ***inhabitants,*** 10 Millionen Einwohner; ***be worth 2*** ***–s,*** 2 Millionen Pfund besitzen; ***by the*** –, nach Millionen; (*coll.*) ***–s of people were there,*** eine Unmenge *or* Unmasse Menschen war da. **millionaire** [–'nɛə], *s.* der Millionär. **millionairess,** *s.* die Millionärin. **millionfold,** *adj.* millionenfach, millionenfältig. **millionth,** **1.** *adj.* millionst. **2.** *s.* das Millionstel.

millipede, *see* **millepede.**

mill|-owner, *s.* der Mühlenbesitzer; (*esp.*) Spinnereibesitzer. **--pond,** *s.* der Mühlteich. **--race,** *s.* der Mühlgraben, das Mühlgerinne, der Flutgang, Fluder.

Mills| bomb, – **grenade** [milz], *s.* die (Eier)handgranate.

mill|stone, *s.* der Mühlstein; ***lower*** or ***nether*** or ***under*** –, der Bodenstein; ***running*** or ***upper*** –, der Lauferstein; (*fig.*) ***be between two*** ***–s,*** von zwei Seiten her unter Druck stehen. **–stream,** *s.* das Mühlbach, Mühlgerinne. **–wheel,** *s.* das Mühl(en)rad. **–wright,** *s.* der Mühlenbauer.

milt [milt], **1.** *s.* (*Anat.*) die Milz; (*Ichth.*) Milch. **2.** *v.t.* befruchten (*the spawn*). **milter,** *s.* der Milch(n)er.

mime [maim], **1.** *s.* 1. der Mimus, die Gebärde, das Gebärdenspiel; 2. der Mime, Gebärdenspieler. **2.** *v.i.* als Mime auftreten. **3.** *v.t.* mimen, mimisch darstellen.

mimeograph ['mimiəgrɑ:f], **1.** *s.* der Vervielfältigungsapparat. **2.** *v.t.* vervielfältigen.

mimesis [mai'mi:sis], *s.* die Nachahmung; (*Zool. etc.*) Mimikry. **mimetic** [–'metik], *adj.* nachahmend, mimetisch; (*Phonet.*) lautmalend.

mimic ['mimik], **1.** *s.* der Nachahmer, Nachäffer, Imitator. **2.** *v.t.* nachahmen, nachäffen. **3.** *adj.* nachahmend, mimisch; nachgeahmt, Schein–; (*rare*) Schauspiel–. **mimicking, mimicry** [–kri], *s.* das Nachahmen, die Nachäffung, Mimik; (*Zool. etc.*) Mimikry.

mimosa [mi'mouzə], *s.* (*Bot.*) die Mimose, echte Akazie.

minacious [mi'neiʃəs], *adj. See* **minatory.**

minaret ['minəret], *s.* das Minarett.

minatory ['minətəri], *adj.* drohend, bedrohlich.

mince [mins], **1.** *v.t.* 1. zerhacken, zerstückeln, kleinschneiden; – ***meat,*** Fleisch hacken; ***–d meat,*** das Hackfleisch, Gehackte(s); 2. (*fig.*) mildern, beschönigen; – ***one's words,*** affektiert *or* geziert sprechen; ***not – matters or one's words,*** kein Blatt vor den Mund nehmen; – ***one's steps,*** (einher)trippeln. **2.** *v.i.* sich geziert benehmen, zimperlich tun; trippeln. **3.** *s. See* ***–d meat.***

mince|meat, *s.* (eine Art) Pastetenfüllung aus gemischtem Dörrobst; (*coll.*) ***make – of,*** keinen guten Faden lassen an (*Dat.*). **--pie,** *s.* (eine Art) (Weihnachts)pastete. **mincer,** *s. See* **mincing-machine.**

mincing ['minsiŋ], **1.** *s.* 1. das (Klein)hacken, Zerschneiden; 2. (*fig.*) die Ziererei. **2.** *adj.* (*fig.*) geziert, affektiert, zimperlich. **mincing-machine,** *s.* die Fleischhackmaschine, der Fleischwolf.

[1]**mind** [maind], **1.** *v.t.* 1. achten *or* achtgeben *or* merken auf (*Acc.*); sich in acht nehmen *or* sich hüten *or* auf der Hut sein vor (*Dat.*); – ***the door,*** auf die Tür achtgeben; – ***your head!*** achte auf deinen Kopf! (*coll.*) – ***one's P's and Q's,*** sich ganz gehörig in acht nehmen; – ***the step!*** Achtung Stufe! 2. sorgen für, sehen nach, sich kümmern um; – ***one's own business,*** sich um seine eigenen Angelegenheiten kümmern; – ***the baby,*** auf das Kind aufpassen; ***don't*** or ***never – me!*** lassen Sie sich nicht stören! ***never – him!*** kümmere dich nicht um ihn! 3. (*usu. neg. or inter.*) sich (*Dat.*) etwas machen aus, etwas einzuwenden haben gegen, sich stoßen an (*Dat.*), nicht gern sehen; ***I don't – the rain,*** ich

mache mir nichts aus dem Regen; ***do you – my smoking?*** haben Sie etwas dagegen *or* stört es Sie, wenn ich rauche? (*coll.*) ***I don't – saying,*** ich möchte wohl behaupten; 4. (*obs.*) sich erinnern an (*Acc.*), in Erinnerung haben; erinnern, mahnen (*a p.*) (*of*, an (*Acc.*)). **2.** *v.i.* achthaben, aufpassen; ***– you!*** wohlgemerkt! ***– you write to me!*** vergiß nicht *or* denk daran, an mich zu schreiben! sieh zu, daß du an mich schreibst! ***never –!*** es macht nichts (aus)! es hat nichts zu sagen! es tut nichts! laß gut sein! mach dir nichts daraus! ***I don't –!*** meinetwegen! es macht mir nichts aus! ich habe nichts dagegen! (*coll.*) ***I shouldn't –,*** ich wäre nicht abgeneigt; ***I don't – if I do,*** wenn ich bitten darf; ***would you –?*** würden Sie so freundlich sein?

2**mind,** *s.* 1. der Geist, Verstand; das Gemüt, die Gesinnung, Seele; ***the –'s eye,*** geistiges Auge, die Einbildungskraft; ***absence of –,*** die Geistesabwesenheit; ***it was a weight off my –,*** mir fiel ein Stein vom Herzen; ***it came into my –,*** es kam mir in den Sinn; ***cast one's – back,*** sich im Geiste zurückversetzen (*to*, nach); ***close one's – to,*** sich verschließen gegen; ***cross*** or ***enter his –,*** ihm in den Sinn kommen; ***frame of –,*** die Gesinnung, Stimmung, Geistesverfassung, Gemütsverfassung; ***give one's – to,*** sich befleißigen (*Gen.*); ***have an open –,*** unvoreingenommen *or* unbeeinflußt sein (***on, about,*** in (*Dat.*)); ***have it in –,*** es beherzigen, sich (*Dat.*) es zu Gemüte führen; ***have on one's –,*** auf dem Herzen haben; ***I shall have it off my –,*** ich brauche nicht mehr daran zu denken; ***in his right –,*** bei vollem Verstand; ***in my –'s eye,*** im Geiste; ***leave an impression on his –,*** einen Eindruck bei ihm hinterlassen; ***lie (heavy) on his –,*** ihn bedrücken; ***lose one's –,*** den Verstand verlieren; ***many men many –s,*** viele Köpfe viele Sinne; ***out of his –,*** nicht recht bei Trost *or* Sinnen *or* Verstand, verrückt; ***presence of –,*** die Geistesgegenwart; ***out of sight out of –,*** aus den Augen aus dem Sinn; ***put out of one's –,*** sich (*Dat.*) aus dem Sinn schlagen; ***read his –,*** seine Gedanken lesen; ***that will relieve my –,*** das beruhigt *or* erleichtert mein Gewissen; ***things of the –,*** geistige Dinge; ***the workings of the –,*** der Gedankenvorgang, die Vorstellungsweise; 2. die Absicht, das Vorhaben, der Wille, Sinn; ***have a – of one's own,*** wissen was man will; ***know one's own –,*** seine eigene Meinung haben; ***make up one's own –,*** sich entschließen, zu dem Schluß *or* der Überzeugung kommen, sich (*Dat.*) klarwerden (***about,*** über (*Acc.*)); ***set one's – on,*** seinen Sinn richten auf (*Acc.*); ***I have it in – to go,*** ich beabsichtige *or* ich habe die Absicht *or* ich habe es vor, zu gehen; 3. die Meinung, Ansicht, Überzeugung, Neigung, Lust; ***alter one's –,*** see ***change one's –; there can be no two –s about it,*** es kann keine geteilte Meinung darüber geben; ***be of his*** or ***the same –,*** einer Meinung mit ihm *or* seiner Meinung sein; ***change one's –,*** sich anders besinnen; ***give him a (good) piece of one's –,*** ihm ordentlich *or* gründlich die Meinung sagen; ***have a (no) –,*** (keine) Lust haben, (nicht) geneigt *or* willens sein; ***have half a – to go,*** beinahe Lust haben zu gehen; ***in my –,*** nach meiner Meinung, meines Erachtens; ***be in two –s,*** mit sich im unklaren sein, geteilter Meinung *or* unschlüssig sein, schwanken (***about,*** über (*Acc.*)); ***of one –,*** einmütig; ***speak one's –,*** seine Meinung äußern, freimütig sein, frei herausreden; ***to my –,*** see ***in my –***; 4. die Erinnerung, das Gedächtnis; ***bear*** or ***keep in –,*** berücksichtigen, denken an (*Acc.*), eingedenk sein (*Gen.*), im Gedächtnis *or* Auge behalten, nicht vergessen; ***bring back*** or ***call to –,*** sich erinnern an (*Acc.*), sich (*Dat.*) ins Gedächtnis zurückrufen; ***put him in – of,*** ihn erinnern an (*Acc.*); ***time out of –,*** seit undenklichen Zeiten.

minded ['maindid], *adj.* geneigt, gewillt, gesonnen (*with inf.*); (*as suff.*) gesinnt; ***air-–,*** flugbegeistert; ***evil-–,*** böse gesinnt; ***narrow-–,*** engstirnig, beschränkt. **mindedness,** *s.* (*only in compounds*) die Neigung, Gesinnung; ***air-–,*** die Flugbegeisterung; ***evil-–,*** die Boshaftigkeit; ***narrow-–,*** die Engstirnigkeit, Beschränktheit. **minder,** *s.* der Wärter, Aufseher. **mindful,** *adj.* aufmerksam, achtsam (***of,*** auf (*Acc.*)), eingedenk (*Gen.*); ***be – of,*** achten auf (*Acc.*). **mindfulness,** *s.* die Aufmerksamkeit, Achtsamkeit. **mindless,** *adj.* 1. achtlos, unachtsam, ohne Rücksicht (***of,*** auf (*Acc.*)), uneingedenk (*Gen.*), unbekümmert, unbesorgt (um); 2. geistlos, geistesarm, stumpfsinnig, blöde. **mindlessness,** *s.* die Geistlosigkeit, Geistesarmut, Blödigkeit, der Stumpfsinn.

1**mine** [main], **1.** *poss. pron.* der *or* die *or* das mein(ig)e, ***a book of –,*** eines meiner Bücher, ein Buch von mir; ***this boy of –,*** mein Sohn hier, dieser mein Sohn; ***this house is –,*** dieses Haus gehört mir; ***me and –,*** ich und die Mein(ig)en. **2.** *poss. adj.* (*obs.*) *see* **my**; ***– host,*** der Herr Wirt.

2**mine, 1.** *s.* 1. (*Min.*) das Bergwerk, die Grube, Zeche; *pl.* (*Comm.*) die Montanindustrie, der Bergbau; 2. (*fig.*) die Fundgrube (***of,*** an (*Dat.*)); ***– of information,*** reicher Wissensschatz; 3. (*Mil., Naut.*) die Mine; ***anti-tank –,*** die Tankmine; ***contact –,*** die Tretmine; ***floating –,*** die Treibmine; ***spring a –,*** eine Mine springen lassen. **2.** *v.t.* 1. gewinnen, abbauen (*ore*); graben in (*Dat.*) (*ground*) (***for,*** nach); 2. (*fig.*) unterminieren, untergraben; 3. (*Mil., Naut.*) mit Minen belegen, verminen. **3.** *v.i.* minieren; schürfen, graben (***for,*** nach); sich vergraben *or* eingraben (*of animals*).

mine|-crater, *s.* der Sprengtrichter, Minentrichter. **--detector,** *s.* das Minensuchgerät. **--field,** *s.* das Minenfeld, die Minensperre. **--layer,** *s.* (*Naut.*) der Minenleger. **miner,** *s.* 1. der Bergmann, Bergarbeiter, Bergknappe, Grubenarbeiter, Kumpel; ***–s' association,*** die Knappschaft; ***–'s lamp,*** die Grubenlampe; 2. (*Mil.*) Mineur.

mineral ['minərəl], **1.** *s.* 1. das Mineral; 2. *pl.* das Mineralwasser. **2.** *adj.* mineralisch, Mineral–; (*Chem.*) anorganisch; ***– deposit,*** die (Erz)lagerstätte; ***– kingdom,*** das Mineralreich, Steinreich; ***– oil,*** das Erdöl, Mineralöl; ***– spring,*** die Mineralquelle, der Heilbrunnen; ***– tar,*** der Bergteer; ***– water,*** das Mineralwasser. **mineralize,** *v.t.* vererzen; (*Chem.*) versteinern, mit anorganischem Stoff durchsetzen. **mineralogical** [–'lɔdʒikl], *adj.* mineralogisch. **mineralogist** [–'rælədʒist], *s.* der Mineraloge. **mineralogy** [–'rælədʒi], *s.* die Mineralogie, Mineralienkunde.

mine|-sweeper, *s.* das Minenräumboot, der Minenräumer. **--thrower,** *s.* der Minenwerfer.

minever, *see* **miniver.**

mingle [miŋgl], **1.** *v.t.* (ver)mischen, (ver)mengen. **2.** *v.i.* sich vermischen *or* vereinigen *or* verbinden (***with,*** mit), (*fig.*) sich (ein)mischen (***in,*** in (*Acc.*)), sich mischen *or* begeben (***among, with,*** unter (*Acc.*)).

mingy ['mindʒi], *adj.* (*sl.*) knickerig, knauserig, filzig.

miniature ['minitʃə], **1.** *s.* die Miniatur; das Miniaturbild; ***in –,*** im kleinen. **2.** *adj.* Klein–, im kleinen; ***– camera,*** die Kleinbildkamera, Kleinkamera; ***– lamp-holder,*** die Mignonfassung; ***– rifle shooting,*** das Kleinkaliberschießen. **miniaturist,** *s.* der Miniatur(en)maler.

minify ['minifai], *v.t.* verkleinern, vermindern.

minikin ['minikin], **1.** *adj.* winzig; (*fig.*) geziert, affektiert. **2.** *s.* kleine Stecknadel.

minim ['minim], *s.* 1. (*Mus.*) halbe Note; 2. (*Pharm.*) der Tropfen, das Sechzigstel Drachme; (*fig.*) Winzige(s), das Tüttelchen.

minimal ['miniml], *adj.* minimal, kleinst, geringst, mindest. **minimization** [–ai'zeiʃən], *s.* die Reduzierung auf das Minimum. **minimize,** *v.t.* auf das Mindestmaß zurückführen, auf ein Minimum bringen; verkleinern, möglichst klein darstellen; unterschätzen, herabsetzen. **minimum, 1.** *s.* (*pl.* **-a**) das Minimum, Mindestmaß, der Mindestbetrag; (*Comm.*) ***at a –,*** sehr niedrig; ***existence –,*** das Existenzminimum. **2.** *adj. See* **minimal**; ***– wage,*** der Mindestlohn. **minimus,** *s.* (*school sl.*) der Jüngste (von drei Brüdern).

mining ['mainiŋ], *s.* der Bergbau, das Bergwesen; ***open-cast –,*** der Tagebau; ***– engineer,*** der Bergbauingenieur; ***– equipment,*** das Gezähe; ***– industry,*** die Bergbauindustrie, Montanindustrie.

minion ['minjən], *s.* 1. der Günstling, Liebling; – *of the law,* der Gerichtsvollzieher, Häscher; 2. (*Typ.*) die Kolonel(schrift).
minister ['ministə], **1.** *s.* 1. (*Eccl.*) Geistliche(r), der Pfarrer, Priester; 2. (*Pol.*) (Staats)minister; 3. Gesandte(r), (*obs.*) das Werkzeug, der Gehilfe, Diener. **2.** *v.i.* 1. – *to,* dienen (*Dat.*), helfen (*Dat.*), dienlich *or* behilflich *or* nützlich sein (*Dat.*); – *to his wants,* für seine Bedürfnisse sorgen; 2. (*Eccl.*) als Geistlicher wirken, ministrieren. **3.** *v.t.* darreichen, spenden (*the sacrament*).
ministerial [minis'tiəriəl], *adj.* 1. (*Eccl.*) priesterlich, geistlich; 2. (*Pol.*) ministeriell, Minister–; – *benches,* Sitze der Regierungspartei; 3. *be – to,* dienen (*Dat.*); *be – to the needs,* die Bedürfnisse befriedigen.
ministrant ['ministrənt], **1.** *adj.* dienend, dienstbar (*to, Dat.*). **2.** *s.* der Meßdiener, Ministrant. **ministration** [–'treiʃən], *s.* 1. die Hilfe (*to,* für), der Dienst (*Dat.*); 2. (*Eccl.*) die Pfarrtätigkeit, priesterlicher Beruf; *pl.* kirchliche Amtsübungen (*pl.*). **ministrative** [–trətiv], 1. *adj.* helfend, dienend; 2. (*Eccl.*) ministrierend. **ministry** [–tri], *s.* 1. (*Eccl.*) kirchliches *or* geistliches Amt, kirchlicher *or* priesterlicher *or* geistlicher Beruf; (*collect.*) die Geistlichkeit, Priesterschaft; 2. (*Pol.*) der Ministerposten, das Ministeramt; Ministerium, Kabinett.
minium ['miniəm], *s.* die Mennige.
miniver ['minivə], *s.* das Feh, Grauwerk.
mink [miŋk], *s.* der Nerz, Nörz; das Nerzfell.
minnesinger ['minəsiŋə], *s.* der Minnesänger. **minnesong,** *s.* das Minnelied, der Minnesang.
minnow ['minou], *s.* (*Ichth.*) die Elritze.
minor ['mainə], **1.** *adj.* 1. kleiner, geringer, weniger, jünger; unbedeutend, geringfügig, klein; *Asia Minor,* Kleinasien; – *clergy,* niedere Geistlichkeit; *of – importance,* von zweitrangiger Bedeutung; – *operation,* leichte Operation; – *planets,* die Planetoiden, Asteroiden; – *prophets,* kleine Propheten; *Hobson –,* der jüngere Hobson; 2. (*Log.*) Neben–, Unter–; – *point,* die Nebensache; – *premiss,* der Untersatz; 3. (*Mus.*) Moll–; *A–*–, a-Moll; – *chord,* der Mollakkord; – *key,* die Molltonart; – *mode,* das Moll(geschlecht); – *scale,* die Molltonleiter; – *third,* kleine Terz. **2.** *s.* 1. Minderjährige(r), Unmündige(r); 2. (*Log.*) der Untersatz; 3. (*Mus.*) das Moll, die Molltonart, der Mollakkord; 4. (*Am.*) das Nebenfach.
Minorca [mi'nɔ:kə], *s.* Menorca (*n.*).
Minorite ['minərait], *s.* der Minorist, Franziskaner.
minority [mai'nɔriti], *s.* 1. (*Law*) die Minderjährigkeit, Unmündigkeit; 2. Minderheit, Minderzahl; (*Pol.*) Minorität; – *report,* der Bericht der Minderheit (eines Ausschusses).
minster ['minstə], *s.* das Münster, die Stiftskirche, Klosterkirche, Kathedrale.
minstrel ['minstrəl], *s.* (*Hist.*) der (Minne)sänger, Spielmann, fahrender Musikant; (*Poet.*) Sänger, Dichter, Barde; *Negro –s,* die Negersänger. **minstrelsy,** *s.* die Spielmannsdichtung, der Minnegesang; (*Poet.*) die Dichtkunst; Musikantentruppe.
¹**mint** [mint], *s.* (*Bot.*) die Minze; (*Am.*) – *julep,* der Pfefferminzlikör; – *sauce,* saure Minztunke.
²**mint, 1.** *s.* die Münze; Münzstätte, Münzanstalt; (*fig.*) Quelle, Fundgrube; *a – of money,* großer Haufen Geld. **2.** *adj.* unbeschädigt; – *condition,* wie neu, tadellos erhalten. **3.** *v.t.* prägen (*also fig.*), münzen, schlagen (*money*). **mintage,** *s.* die Prägung (*also fig.*), das Münzen; geprägtes Geld; die Münzgebühr.
minuend ['minjuend], *s.* (*Math.*) der Minuend(us).
minuet [minju'et], *s.* (*Mus.*) das Menuett.
minus ['mainəs], **1.** *prep.* weniger, minus; (*coll.*) ohne. **2.** *adj.* negativ, Minus–; – *quantity,* negative Größe; (*coll.*) *he is a – quantity,* er zählt überhaupt nicht; – *sign,* das Minuszeichen. **3.** *adv.* minus, unter null; *the temperature is – 10 degrees,* wir haben 10 Grad Kälte. **4.** *s.* das Minus(zeichen); negative Größe.

minuscule ['minəskju:l], **1.** *s.* die Minuskel, kleiner (Anfangs)buchstabe. **2.** *adj.* winzig, sehr klein.
¹**minute** ['minit], **1.** *s.* 1. die Minute; (*fig.*) der Augenblick, kurze Zeit; *at the last –,* im letzten Augenblick; *for a –,* eine Minute (lang); (*coll.*) *just a –,* einen Augenblick, ich komme sofort; *only 10 –s on foot,* man geht nur 10 Minuten; (*coll.*) *the – that,* sobald; *to the –,* auf die Minute; (*coll.*) *up to the –,* hypermodern; 2. (*Comm. etc.*) kurzer Entwurf, das Konzept; Memorandum, die Notiz, der Protokolleintrag; *pl.* der Sitzungsbericht, das (Verhandlungs)protokoll; *keep the –s,* das Protokoll führen; *make a – of,* zu Protokoll nehmen, notieren, vermerken; *read the –s,* den Sitzungsbericht verlesen. **2.** *v.t.* zu Protokoll nehmen, protokollieren, notieren, vermerken.
²**minute** [mai'nju:t], *adj.* 1. sehr klein, winzig; 2. peinlich genau, sorgfältig, minuziös.
minute|-book, ['minit–], *s.* das Protokollbuch. **–-gun,** *s.* das Minutengeschütz. **–-hand,** *s.* der Minutenzeiger.
minutely [mai'nju:tli], *adv.* umständlich, peinlich genau, eingehend, ausführlich. **minuteness,** *s.* 1. die Kleinheit, Winzigkeit; 2. Umständlichkeit, Exaktheit, (peinliche) Genauigkeit.
minutiae [mi'nju:ʃii:], *pl.* Einzelheiten (*pl.*).
minx [miŋks], *s.* (*coll.*) ausgelassenes Mädchen, der Frechdachs; Wildfang, die Range.
Miocene ['maiəsi:n], *adj.* (*Geol.*) miozän, Miozän–.
miracle ['mirəkl], *s.* das Wunder; Wunderwerk, die Wundertat; *work –s,* Wunder wirken *or* tun; (*coll.*) *next door to a –,* ans Wunderbare grenzend. **miracle-play,** *s.* das Mirakelspiel.
miraculous [mi'rækjuləs], *adj.* Wunder–; wunderbar; übernatürlich. **miraculously,** *adj.* (wie) durch ein Wunder. **miraculousness,** *s.* das Wunderbare; Übernatürliche.
mirage ['mirɑ:ʒ], *s.* die Luftspiegelung, Fata Morgana; (*fig.*) Täuschung, der Wahn, das Luftbild.
mire ['maiə], **1.** *s.* der Schlamm, Sumpf; Kot, Dreck; (*coll.*) *be deep in the –,* tief in der Tinte *or* Klemme *or* Patsche sitzen; (*fig.*) *drag through the –,* verunglimpfen, durch den Dreck ziehen. **2.** *v.t.* (*usu. pass.*) im Sumpf festhalten; (*fig.*) in Schwierigkeiten bringen *or* verwickeln *or* stürzen; beschmutzen, besudeln.
mirror ['mirə], **1.** *s.* der Spiegel; (*fig.*) das Vorbild, Muster, Spiegelbild; *hold up the – to,* den Spiegel vorhalten (*Dat.*); *concave –,* der Hohlspiegel; *convex –,* der Vollspiegel; – *finish,* der Hochglanz; – *image,* das Spiegelbild; – *sight,* das Spiegelvisier; – *symmetry,* die Spiegelbildlichkeit; – *writing,* die Spiegelschrift. **2.** *v.t.* (wider)spiegeln, abspiegeln; *be –ed,* sich spiegeln.
mirth [mə:θ], *s.* der Frohsinn, die Freude, Fröhlichkeit, Heiterkeit. **mirthful,** *adj.* fröhlich, heiter. **mirthfulness,** *s.* die Fröhlichkeit. **mirthless,** *adj.* freudlos.
miry ['maiəri], *adj.* schlammig, sumpfig; dreckig, kotig.
misadventure [misəd'ventʃə], *s.* der Un(glücks)fall, das Mißgeschick; *death by –,* der Unfall mit tödlichem Ausgang.
misadvise [misəd'vaiz], *v.t.* schlecht *or* falsch beraten.
misalignment [misə'lainmənt], *s.* (*Tech.*) der Flucht(ungs)fehler.
misalliance [misə'laiəns], *s.* die Mißheirat.
misanthrope ['misənθroup], *s.* der Misanthrop, Menschenfeind. **misanthropic(al)** [–'θrɔpik(l)], *adj.* menschenfeindlich, misanthropisch. **misanthropist** [–'ænθrəpist], *s.* *See* **misanthrope. misanthropy** [–'ænθrəpi], *s.* der Menschenhaß, die Menschenfeindlichkeit.
misapplication [misæpli'keiʃən], *s.* falsche Anwendung *or* Verwendung; der Mißbrauch. **misapply** [–ə'plai], *v.t.* falsch anbringen *or* anwenden; mißbrauchen, zu unerlaubten Zwecken verwenden.
misapprehend [misæpri'hend], *v.t.* mißverstehen.

misapprehension [–'henʃən], *s.* das Mißverständnis, falsche Auffassung; ***be*** or ***labour under a –,*** sich in einem Irrtum befinden; ***be under no – as to . . .***, sich (*Dat.*) völlig klar sein über . . . (*Acc.*).

misappropriate [misə'prouprieit], *v.t.* sich (*Dat.*) unrechtmäßig *or* widerrechtlich aneignen, unterschlagen. **misappropriation** [–pri'eiʃən], *s.* widerrechtliche *or* unrechtmäßige Aneignung, die Unterschlagung, Veruntreuung.

misarrange [misə'reindʒ], *v.t.* schlecht *or* falsch (an)ordnen. **misarrangement,** *s.* schlechte *or* falsche (An)ordnung.

misbecome [misbi'kʌm], *irr.v.t.* sich nicht schicken *or* ziemen für, schlecht (an)stehen (*Dat.*).

misbegotten [misbi'gɔtən], *adj.* unehelich; (*fig.*) ekelhaft, scheußlich; unnatürlich.

misbehave [misbi'heiv], *v.i.* (*also – o.s.*) sich schlecht benehmen; sich vergehen, sich ungebührlich betragen. **misbehaviour** [–jə], *s.* schlechtes Betragen *or* Benehmen, die Ungezogenheit, (*Mil.*) schlechte Führung, die Ungebühr, ungebührliches Benehmen.

misbelief [misbi'li:f], *s.* der Irrglaube. **misbeliever** [–'li:və], *s.* Irrgläubige(r), der (die) Ketzer(in).

miscalculate [mis'kælkjəleit], **1.** *v.t.* falsch (ab)schätzen *or* (be)rechnen *or* beurteilen. **2.** *v.i.* sich verrechnen *or* verzählen. **miscalculation** [–'leiʃən], *s.* falsche Rechnung, die Fehlrechnung, der Rechenfehler; falsches Urteil.

miscall [mis'kɔ:l], *v.t.* falsch *or* zu Unrecht (be)nennen; (*dial.*) beschimpfen.

miscarriage [mis'kæridʒ], *s.* das Mißlingen, Fehlschlagen, Mißglücken; Verlorengehen (*of a letter etc.*); der Fehlschlag; (*Med.*) die Fehlgeburt; ***– of justice,*** die Rechtsbeugung, das Fehlurteil. **miscarry,** *v.i.* mißlingen, fehlschlagen, mißglücken, scheitern (*of plans*); verlorengehen (*as letters*); (*Med.*) eine Fehlgeburt haben, abortieren.

miscast [mis'kɑ:st], *irr.v.t.* unpassend besetzen (*a play*), eine unpassende Rolle zuteilen (*Dat.*) (*a p.*); ***he is – in this rôle,*** die Rolle paßt nicht für ihn. **miscasting,** *s.* unpassende Besetzung.

miscegenation [misidʒə'neiʃən], *s.* die Rassenmischung.

miscellanea [misə'leiniə], *pl.* vermischte Schriften, Miszellen (*pl.*). **miscellaneous** [–iəs], *adj.* gemischt, vermischt; mannigfaltig, vielseitig, verschiedenartig. **miscellaneousness,** *s.* die Gemischtheit; Mannigfaltigkeit, Vielseitigkeit. **miscellany** [–'seləni], *s.* das Gemisch; der Sammelband, die Sammlung.

mischance [mis'tʃɑ:ns], *s.* das Mißgeschick, der Unfall; ***by –,*** durch einen unglücklichen Zufall, unglücklicherweise.

mischief ['mistʃif], *s.* das Unheil, der Schaden; die Ursache des Unheils, der Übelstand; die Zwietracht; der Unfug, Possen (*pl.*); ***be up to –,*** see ***get into –***; ***do –,*** Unheil anrichten; ***do him*** (***a***) ***–,*** ihm Schaden zufügen; ***do s.th. out of –,*** etwas aus Mutwillen tun; ***get into –,*** etwas anstellen, Unfug machen; ***keep out of –,*** brav sein, auf keine schlimmen Gedanken kommen; ***make –,*** Zwietracht säen; ***mean*** or ***intend –, be bent on –,*** auf Unheil sinnen, Böses im Schilde führen; ***the – is that . . .***, das Unglück ist daß . . .. **mischief|-maker,** *s.* der Störenfried, Unheilstifter. **–-making,** *s.* das Unheilstiften, Intrigieren.

mischievous ['mistʃivəs], *adj.* schädlich, nachteilig, verderblich; boshaft, schadenfroh; mutwillig, schelmisch. **mischievousness,** *s.* die Schädlichkeit, Nachteiligkeit, Verderblichkeit; Bosheit, Mutwilligkeit, der Mutwille, die Schalkhaftigkeit.

miscible ['misibl], *adj.* mischbar.

misconceive [miskən'si:v], **1.** *v.t.* mißverstehen, falsch auffassen. **2.** *v.i.* eine irrige Meinung haben (*of,* von). **misconception** [–'sepʃən], *s.* das Mißverständnis, falsche Auffassung.

misconduct, 1. [mis'kɔndʌkt], *s.* schlechtes Benehmen *or* Betragen, der Fehltritt; (*esp.*) unerlaubter geschlechtlicher Verkehr, der Ehebruch. **2.** [miskən'dʌkt], *v.t.* schlecht führen *or* verwalten; ***– o.s.*** sich schlecht aufführen *or* betragen *or* benehmen; einen Fehltritt begehen.

misconstruction [miskən'strʌkʃən], *s.* die Mißdeutung, irrige Auslegung; ***put a – on,*** eine falsche Auslegung geben (*Dat.*). **misconstrue** [–'stru:], *v.t.* mißdeuten, falsch auslegen, mißverstehen.

miscount [mis'kaunt], **1.** *v.t.* falsch (be)rechnen *or* zählen. **2.** *v.i.* sich verrechnen. **3.** *s.* die Verrechnung, der Rechenfehler, falsche Zählung.

miscreant ['miskriənt], **1.** *s.* der Bösewicht, Schurke. **2.** *adj.* schurkisch, gemein, ruchlos.

miscue [mis'kju:], **1.** *s.* (*Bill.*) der Kicks, Fehlstoß. **2.** *v.i.* einen Fehlstoß machen, kicksen.

misdate [mis'deit], **1.** *s.* falsches Datum. **2.** *v.t.* falsch datieren.

misdeal [mis'di:l], **1.** *irr.v.i.* (*v.t.*) (Karten) vergeben *or* falsch verteilen. **2.** *s.* das Vergeben.

misdeed [mis'di:d], *s.* die Missetat, das Vergehen.

misdemean [misdi'mi:n], *v.t.* ***– o.s.,*** sich schlecht aufführen. **misdemeanant,** *s.* (*Law*) der (die) Missetäter(in), Straffällige(r). **misdemeanour,** *s.* (*Law*) (strafbares) Vergehen, das Delikt, die Übertretung.

misdirect [misdi'rekt], *v.t.* irreleiten, falsch unterrichten (*a p.*), falsch belehren (*the jury*), falsch adressieren (*a letter*); (*fig.*) falsch anbringen *or* verwenden; ***– one's aim,*** schlecht zielen. **misdirection** [–'rekʃən], *s.* das Irreführen, Irreleiten; die Irreführung, Irreleitung, (*Law*) unrichtige (Rechts)belehrung; falsche Auskunft *or* Adresse *or* Verwendung.

misdoing [mis'du:iŋ], *s.* die Missetat, das Vergehen.

misdoubt [mis'daut], *v.t.* (*obs.*) bezweifeln, zweifeln an (*Dat.*); mißtrauen (*Dat.*), in Verdacht haben.

mise-en-scène ['mi:zɑ̃'sen], *s.* die Inszenierung, das Bühnenbild; (*fig.*) die Umgebung, Umwelt.

misemploy [misem'plɔi], *v.t.* schlecht anwenden, mißbrauchen. **misemployment,** *s.* schlechte Anwendung, der Mißbrauch.

miser ['maizə], *s.* der Geizhals, Geizige(r), der Filz, Knicker.

miserable ['mizərəbl], *adj.* elend, armselig, ärmlich, kläglich, beklagenswert, jämmerlich, erbärmlich; verächtlich, nichtswürdig, schlecht; unglücklich, traurig.

Miserere [mizə'riəri], *s.* (*Mus.*) das Miserere, der Bußpsalm, 51. Psalm.

misericord [mi'zerikɔ:d], *s.* 1. das Trinkrefektorium (*in monasteries*); 2. die Miserikordie (*for support when standing*); 3. der Dolch für den Gnadenstoß.

miserliness ['maizəlinis], *s.* der Geiz, die Knauserei, Knickerei, Knick(e)rigkeit. **miserly,** *adj.* geizig, knauserig, knick(e)rig, filzig.

misery ['mizəri], *s.* das Elend, die Not, Trübsal.

misfeasance [mis'fi:zəns], *s.* (*Law*) der Amtsmißbrauch, pflichtwidrige Handlung.

misfire [mis'faiə], **1.** *v.i.* (*Artil.*) versagen; (*Motor.*) aussetzen, fehlzünden; (*coll. of plan etc.*) nicht klappen. **2.** *s.* (*Artil.*) der Versager; (*Motor.*) die Fehlzündung.

misfit ['misfit], *s.* nichtpassendes Stück (*clothing etc.*); (*fig.*) der Einzelgänger, Eigenbrötler.

misfortune [mis'fɔ:tjun], *s.* das Unglück, Mißgeschick, der Unglücksfall.

misgive [mis'giv], **1.** *irr.v.t.* (*only in*) ***my mind*** or ***heart –s me,*** mir ahnt nichts Gutes, ich habe ein banges Vorgefühl *or* das unangenehme Gefühl. **2.** *irr.v.i.* (*Scots*) scheitern, fehlgehen. **misgiving,** *s.* böse Ahnung, die Befürchtung, Besorgnis, der Zweifel; ***have –s,*** Bedenken tragen.

misgovern [mis'gʌvən], *v.t.* schlecht regieren. **misgovernment,** *s.* schlechte Regierung *or* Verwaltung.

misguidance [mis'gaidəns], *s.* die Irreleitung, Verleitung. **misguide,** *v.t.* irreführen, verleiten; ***in a –d moment,*** in einem unbedachten Augenblick.

mishandle [mis'hændl], *v.t.* mißhandeln; (*fig.*) schlecht handhaben, (*coll.*) verkorksen.

mishap ['mishæp], *s.* der Unfall, das Unglück.
mishear [mis'hiə], *irr.v.t.* (*v.i.*) (sich) verhören, falsch hören.
mishit ['mishit], *s.* (*coll.*) der Fehlschlag, Fehltreffer.
mishmash ['miʃmæʃ], *s.* der Mischmasch.
misinform [misin'fɔ:m], *v.t.* falsch unterrichten *or* belehren. **misinformation** [–fə'meiʃən], *s.* falsche Auskunft *or* Angabe, falscher Bericht.
misinterpret [misin'tə:prit], *v.t.* mißdeuten, falsch deuten *or* auslegen *or* verstehen. **misinterpretation** [–'teiʃən], *s.* die Mißdeutung, falsche Auslegung.
misjudge [mis'dʒʌdʒ], *v.t.* falsch *or* ungerecht beurteilen, verkennen, mißdeuten; – *the distance*, die Entfernung falsch schätzen. **misjudg(e)ment,** *s.* irriges Urteil, das Fehlurteil; die Verkennung, Mißdeutung, falsche Beurteilung, Über– *or* Unterschätzung.
mislay [mis'lei], *irr.v.t.* verlegen.
mislead [mis'li:d], *irr.v.t.* irreführen, irreleiten; (*fig.*) verführen, verleiten (*into doing*, zu tun); täuschen; *be misled*, sich verleiten lassen; getäuscht werden. **misleading,** *adj.* irreführend, täuschend; *be* –, täuschen.
mismanage [mis'mænidʒ], *v.t.* schlecht führen *or* verwalten; unsachgemäß behandeln. **mismanagement,** *s.* schlechte Verwaltung, die Mißwirtschaft.
misnomer [mis'noumə], *s.* falsche Benennung, irrtümliche Bezeichnung; unpassender Name, (*Law*) der Namensirrtum.
misogamist [mi'sɔgəmist], *s.* der Ehefeind. **misogamy,** *s.* die Ehescheu.
misogynist [mi'sɔdʒinist], *s.* der Weiberfeind, Misogyn. **misogynous,** *adj.* weiberfeindlich. **misogyny** [–ni], *s.* der Weiberhaß.
misplace [mis'pleis], *v.t.* verlegen, an die falsche Stelle legen *or* setzen; (*fig.*) falsch *or* übel anbringen (*confidence*). **misplaced,** *adj.* übel angebracht, unangebracht, unberechtigt. **misplacement,** *s.* das Verstellen, Versetzen, (*fig.*) falsches Anbringen.
misprint, 1. [mis'print], *v.t.* verdrucken, falsch drucken. **2.** ['misprint], *s.* der Druckfehler.
misprision [mis'priʒən], *s.* (*Law*) das Vergehen, (Pflicht)versäumnis; die Nichtanzeige, Unterlassung der Anzeige (*of a crime*).
misprize [mis'praiz], *v.t.* unterschätzen, geringschätzen, mißachten, verachten.
mispronounce [misprə'nauns], *v.t., v.i.* falsch aussprechen. **mispronunciation** [–nʌnsi'eiʃən], *s.* falsche Aussprache.
misquotation [miskwou'teiʃən], *s.* falsche Anführung, falsches Zitat. **misquote** [–'kwout], *v.t.* falsch zitieren *or* anführen.
misread [mis'ri:d], *irr.v.t.* falsch lesen *or* deuten, mißdeuten.
misrepresent [misrepri'zent], *v.t.* falsch *or* ungenau darstellen, verdrehen, entstellen. **misrepresentation** [–'teiʃən], *s.* falsche *or* ungenaue Darstellung *or* Angabe, falsches Bild, die Verdrehung.
misrule [mis'ru:l], **1.** *s.* schlechte Regierung, die Mißregierung; Unordnung, der Tumult, Aufruhr. **2.** *v.t.* schlecht regieren.
¹**miss** [mis], *s.* **1.** (*as title*) *Miss*, Fräulein, Miß; *Miss England*, die Schönheitskönigin von E.; 2. (*coll.*) der Backfisch, das (Schul)mädchen.
²**miss, 1.** *v.t.* 1. (ver)missen, entbehren; *we – him very much*, er fehlt uns sehr, wir vermissen ihn sehr; 2. verfehlen, nicht treffen; sich (*Dat.*) entgehen lassen, versäumen, verfehlen, verpassen; – *one's aim*, das Ziel verfehlen; (*coll.*) – *the boat* or *bus*, die Chance verpassen; – *one's chance*, see – *one's opportunity*; – *fire*, *see* **misfire**; – *one's footing*, ausrutschen, ausgleiten, fehltreten; (*coll.*) – *one's guess*, falsch tippen; (*coll.*) – *the mark*, danebenschießen; – *one's opportunity*, die (günstige) Gelegenheit vorübergehen lassen *or* verpassen *or* versäumen; – *school*, die Schule versäumen; – *one's step*, see – *one's footing*; – *the train*, den Zug verpassen *or* versäumen; – *one's way*, den Weg verfehlen; 3. entgehen (*Dat.*), entkommen (*Dat.*), vermeiden; *he just –ed being killed*, er ist gerade dem Tod entgangen; 4. nicht bekommen, verlustig gehen (*Gen.*); 5. nicht begreifen *or* verstehen (*also of a joke*); – *the point*, das Wesentliche nicht begreifen; 6. überhören (*a remark*); 7. (*also* – *out*) überspringen, übergehen, auslassen. **2.** *v.i.* 1. (*Shooting*) nicht treffen; 2. – *out*, leer ausgehen; – *out on*, verpassen, versäumen. **3.** *s.* 1. das Verpassen, Verfehlen; (*coll.*) *feel the – of*, vermissen; (*coll.*) *give him a –*, ihn übergehen *or* umgehen *or* meiden; (*coll.*) *give it a –*, es vermeiden, davon ablassen; 2. der Fehlschuß, Fehlstoß; (*Prov.*) *a – is as good as a mile*, verfehlt ist verspielt; *near –*, die Nächsttreffer.
missal [misl], *s.* (*R.C.*) das Meßbuch, Missal(e).
missel(-thrush) [misl], *s.* (*Orn.*) die Misteldrossel (*Turdus viscivorus*).
misshapen [mis'ʃeipən], *adj.* ungestalt(et), mißgestalt(et), unförmig.
missile ['misail (*Am.* misl)], **1.** *s.* das (Wurf)geschoß; *guided –*, das Fernlenkgeschoß, ferngesteuertes Raketengeschoß. **2.** *adj.* Wurf–, Schleuder–.
missing ['misiŋ], *adj.* abwesend, fehlend, ausbleibend, nicht zu finden(d), (*Comm.*) abgängig; (*Mil.*) verschollen, vermißt; *be –*, fehlen (*also with imp. subject*); vermißt werden; *be reported –*, als vermißt gemeldet werden; – *link*, fehlendes Glied, die Zwischenstufe.
mission ['miʃən], *s.* 1. (*Pol.*) die Gesandtschaft, Botschaft; 2. (*Mil.*) der (Einsatz)auftrag, Kampfauftrag, die (Kampf)aufgabe, (*Av.*) der Einsatz, Feindflug; 3. (*fig.*) (– *in life*) Lebenszweck, die Bestimmung, (innerer) Beruf; 4. (*Eccl.*) die Mission, Sendung; Mission(sgesellschaft); das Missionshaus, die Missionsstation; *foreign –* äußere Mission; *home –*, innere Mission; *on a –*, in einer Mission. **missionary, 1.** *adj.* Missions–; – *society*, die Missionsgesellschaft; – *zeal*, der Bekehrungseifer. **2.** *s.* der (die) Missionar(in).
missis, *see* **missus.**
missive ['misiv], *s.* das Sendschreiben, Missiv.
misspell [mis'spel], *irr.v.t.* falsch buchstabieren *or* schreiben. **misspelling,** *s.* falsche Buchstabierung, orthographischer Fehler.
misspend [mis'spend], *irr.v.t.* falsch verwenden, verschwenden, vertun, vergeuden.
misstate [mis'steit], *v.t.* falsch angeben. **misstatement,** *s.* falsche Angabe.
missus ['misiz], *s.* (*coll.*) die (Ehe)frau; (*as address*) gnädige Frau (*written Mrs.*). **missy,** *s.* (*coll.*) kleines Fräulein.
mist [mist], **1.** *s.* der Nebel, Dunst; (*coll.*) (*on glass*) Beschlag, Hauch; (*fig.*) Schleier; *Scotch –*, der Sprühregen, starker Nebel; (*fig.*) *in a –*, verdutzt, verwirrt, irre. **2.** *v.t.* umnebeln, umwölken. **3.** *v.i.* (*usu.* – *over*) neblig werden; (*fig.*) (*also – over*) sich trüben.
mistakable [mis'teikəbl], *adj.* verkennbar, (leicht) zu verwechseln(d), mißzuverstehen(d). **mistake, 1.** *irr.v.t.* verwechseln (*th. or p.*) (*for*, mit); (fälschlich) halten (für); verkennen (*a p.*); mißverstehen, sich irren in (*Dat.*), falsch verstehen (*a th.*); – *the* or *one's way*, den Weg verfehlen, sich verlaufen *or* verirren. **2.** *irr.v.i.* (*usu. pass.*) sich irren *or* täuschen *or* versehen *or* verrechnen. **3.** *s.* der Irrtum, Fehler (*of doing*, zu tun); das Versehen, Mißverständnis; *by –*, irrtümlich, versehentlich, aus Versehen; (*coll.*) *and no –!* bestimmt! sicher(lich)! unzweifelhaft! ohne Zweifel! zweifelsohne! *in – for*, an Stelle (*Gen.*); *make a –*, sich irren; (*coll.*) *make no – (about it)!* darauf kannst du dich verlassen! (*sl.*) darauf kannst du Gift nehmen! *my –*, ein Irrtum von mir. **mistaken,** *adj.* irrig, irrtümlich, verfehlt, falsch, mißverstanden; im Irrtum (befangen); *be –*, sich irren *or* versehen, (*usu.*) sich versehen haben (*in*, in (*Dat.*)), im Irrtum sein (über (*Acc.*)); – *ideas*, falsche Ideen; – *identity*, die Personenverwechslung.

Mister ['mistə], *s.* (*as title*) (*normally written* ***Mr.***) Herr; (*Pol.*) – ***Speaker,*** Herr Vorsitzender.

mistime [mis'taim], *v.t.* zur Unzeit *or* unpassenden Zeit tun; die Zeit falsch einteilen für; einen falschen Zeitpunkt wählen für. **mistimed,** *adj.* unzeitig, unangebracht.

mistiness ['mistinis], *s.* die Nebligkeit, Dunstigkeit; (*fig.*) Verschwommenheit, Unklarheit, Trübheit.

mistletoe ['misltou], *s.* die Mistel.

mistook [mis'tuk], *imperf. of* **mistake.**

mistral ['mistrəl], *s.* der Mistral.

mistranslate [mistrɑ:ns'leit], *v.t.* falsch übersetzen. **mistranslation** [–'leiʃən], *s.* falsche Übersetzung.

mistress ['mistris], *s.* 1. die Herrin; Gebieterin; Meisterin, Besitzerin; – ***of the robes,*** oberste Kammerfrau; ***she remained – of herself,*** sie wußte sich zu beherrschen; 2. die Hausfrau, Frau des Hauses; 3. Lehrerin; ***English –,*** die Englischlehrerin; ***form –,*** die Klassenlehrerin; 4. die Geliebte, Mätresse.

mistrial [mis'traiəl], *s.* (*Law*) fehlerhaft geführter Prozeß.

mistrust [mis'trʌst], **1.** *v.t.* mißtrauen (*Dat.*), nicht trauen (*Dat.*). **2.** *s.* das Mißtrauen, der Argwohn (***of,*** gegen). **mistrustful,** *adj.* mißtrauisch, argwöhnisch (***of,*** gegen); ***be – of,*** mißtrauen (*Dat.*).

misty ['misti], *adj.* neblig, dunstig; (*fig.*) verschwommen, trüb, unklar.

misunderstand [misʌndə'stænd], *irr.v.t.* mißverstehen; sich irren in (*Dat.*). **misunderstanding,** *s.* das Mißverständnis; die Mißhelligkeit, Uneinigkeit. **misunderstood** [–'stud], *adj.* mißverstanden.

misusage [mis'ju:zidʒ], *s.* die Mißhandlung, verkehrte Behandlung; der Mißbrauch, unsachgemäßer Gebrauch. **misuse, 1.** [–'ju:z], *v.t.* mißbrauchen, unsachgemäß gebrauchen, falsch anwenden *or* verwenden; mißhandeln, schlecht behandeln. **2.** [–'ju:s], *s. See* **misusage.**

[1]**mite** [mait], *s.* (*Zool.*) die Milbe, Made.

[2]**mite,** *s.* der Heller, Deut; das Scherflein; (*coll.*) bißchen, (kleines) Stückchen; (*coll.*) kleines Ding *or* Wesen, kleines Würmchen (*of a child*).

miter, (*Am.*) *see* **mitre.**

mitigate ['mitigeit], *v.t.* mildern, mäßigen (*punishment*); lindern, beschwichtigen, stillen (*pain, grief etc.*); besänftigen, beruhigen (*anger etc.*). **mitigation** [–'geiʃən], *s.* die Milderung, Linderung, Besänftigung, Erleichterung, Abschwächung; (*Law*) ***plead in –,*** für Strafmilderung plädieren. **mitigatory,** *adj.* mildernd, lindernd, mäßigend, besänftigend, beruhigend.

mitosis [mai'tousis], *s.* (*Biol.*) die Zellteilung, Mitose.

mitrailleuse [mitrai'ə:z], *s.* die Mitrailleuse, Kugelspritze.

[1]**mitre** ['maitə], **1.** *s.* die Bischofsmütze, Mitra, Inful; (*fig.*) Bischofswürde, der Bischofshut. **2.** *v.t.* mit der Bischofswürde bekleiden, infulieren.

[2]**mitre, 1.** *s.* (*Tech.*) die Gehrung, Gehre. **2.** *v.t.* gehren. **mitre|-block,** *s.* die Gehrungslade. **--cut,** *s.* der Gehr(ungs)schnitt. **--gear,** *s.* der Kegel(an)trieb. **--joint,** *s.* der Stoß auf Gehrung, Gehrstoß, die Gehrfuge. **--square,** *s.* das Gehrmaß, Gehrdreieck. **--wheel,** *s.* das Kegelrad.

mitt [mit], *s.* (*sl.*) die Pfote, Tatze, Flosse; der Spitzenhalbhandschuh, Pulswärmer. **mitten,** *s.* der Fausthandschuh, Fäustling; (*sl.*) ***get*** (***give***) ***the –,*** einen Korb bekommen (geben). **mittens,** *pl.* (*coll.*) Boxhandschuhe (*pl.*).

mittimus ['mitiməs], *s.* (*Law*) der Haftbefehl; (*coll.*) Laufpaß, blauer Brief.

mix [miks], **1.** *v.t.* (ver)mischen, vermengen (***with,*** mit); (*ingredients*) (*also* – ***up***) anrühren, zusammenmischen, (durcheinander)mischen; (*Weav.*) melieren; (*drinks*) mixen; – ***up,*** tüchtig *or* gründlich mischen, (*coll.*) völlig durcheinanderbringen, verwirren; (*coll.*) verwechseln (***with,*** mit); ***be –ed up with*** or ***in,*** verwickelt sein in (*Acc.*). **2.** *v.i.* sich vermischen, sich mischen (lassen); (*fig.*) sich vertragen; verkehren, Umgang haben (***with,*** mit; ***in,*** in (*Dat.*)). **3.** *s.* die Mischung; (*coll.*) Verwirrung, das Durcheinander.

mixed [mikst], *adj.* gemischt, vermischt, Misch–; (*of fabric*) meliert; (*coll.*) verschiedenartig, bunt, zusammengewürfelt; (*coll.*) (*also* – ***up***) konfus, verwirrt; ***ready –,*** anstrichfertig (*of paint*); – ***bathing,*** das Familienbad; – ***blood,*** gemischte Abstammung; ***man of – blood,*** der Mischling, das Halbblut; – ***cargo,*** die Stückgutladung; – ***company,*** bunte *or* gemischte Gesellschaft; (*Tenn.*) – ***doubles,*** gemischtes Doppel(spiel); ***I heard it with – feelings,*** ich hörte es mit gemischten Gefühlen; als ich es hörte, war es mir unbehaglich zumute; – ***grill,*** der Mixed Grill, gebratenes Mischgericht; – ***marriage,*** die Mischehe; – ***metaphor,*** gemischte Metapher; – ***pickles,*** pikant eingemachtes Gemüse, Mixpickles (*pl.*); – ***school,*** die Gemeinschaftsschule, Koedukationsschule.

mixer ['miksə], *s.* der Mischer, die Mischmaschine; (*Rad.*) das Mischgerät, Mischpult; der Mischverstärker; ***cocktail –,*** der Mixer; ***concrete –,*** das Betonmischwerk; (*coll.*) ***good –,*** geselliger Mensch; ***kitchen –,*** der Mixer, Mixquirl. **mixture** [–tʃə], *s.* das (Ver)mischen, Vermengen, die (Ver)mischung; Mischung, das Gemisch, (*Weav.*) meliertes Tuch, (*Chem.*) das Gemisch, Gemenge, (*Pharm.*) die Mixtur. **mix-up,** *s.* (*coll.*) 1. das Durcheinander, der Wirrwarr; 2. das Handgemenge, die Schlägerei.

miz(z)en [mizn], *s.* (*Naut.*) der Besan. **miz(z)en|-mast,** *s.* der Besanmast; (*on square-riggers*) Kreuzmast. **--sail,** *s.* das Besansegel. **--topsail,** *s.* das Kreuz(mars)segel.

mizzle [mizl], **1.** *v.i.* fein regnen, rieseln, nieseln. **2.** *s.* der Staubregen, Sprühregen.

mnemonic [ne'mɔnik], **1.** *adj.* Gedächtnis–, mnemotechnisch. **2.** *s.* die Gedächtnishilfe. **mnemonics,** *pl.* (*sing. constr.*), **mnemotechny** [nemou'tekni], *s.* die Gedächtniskunst, Mnemotechnik.

mo [mou], *s.* (*coll.*) das Momentchen, der *or* das Nu.

moan [moun], **1.** *s.* das Stöhnen. **2.** *v.i.* stöhnen, ächzen; (*coll.*) (weh)klagen, jammern.

moat [mout], *s.* der Burggraben, Festungsgraben, Stadtgraben. **moated,** *adj.* mit einem Wassergraben umgeben.

mob [mɔb], **1.** *s.* das Gesindel, der Pöbel(haufen), lärmende Menge, die Menschenmenge. **2.** *v.t.* lärmend herfallen über (*Acc.*) *or* bedrängen *or* anfallen.

mob-cap, *s.* die Morgenhaube.

mobile ['moubail], *adj.* (leicht) beweglich; (*fig.*) veränderlich, unstet; (*Mil.*) mobil, motorisiert; – ***library,*** die Wanderbücherei; – ***warfare,*** der Bewegungskrieg. **mobility** [–'biliti], *s.* die Beweglichkeit.

mobilization [moubilai'zeiʃən], *s.* (*Mil.*) die Mobilmachung; (*Comm.*) Flüssigmachung; (*fig.*) Aktivierung, Mobilisierung. **mobilize** ['moubilaiz], **1.** *v.t.* mobilmachen; (*Comm.*) flüssigmachen, in Umlauf setzen; (*fig.*) mobilisieren, einsetzen, daransetzen. **2.** *v.i.* (*Mil.*) mobilmachen.

mob-law, *s.* die Lynchjustiz, das Faustrecht. **mobocracy** [–'ɔkrəsi], *s.* (*coll.*) die Pöbelherrschaft.

moccasin ['mɔkəsin], *s.* der Mokassin, Indianerschuh; (*Zool.*) die Mokassinschlange, der Kupferkopf.

mocha ['moukə], *s.* 1. der Mokka(kaffee); 2. (*Min.*) Mochastein, heller Chalzedon.

mock [mɔk], **1.** *v.t.* verspotten, verlachen, verhöhnen; necken, narren, aufziehen; nachahmen, nachäffen; spotten (*Gen.*), trotzen (*Dat.*), Trotz bieten (*Dat.*). **2.** *v.i.* spotten, spötteln, sich lustig machen (***at,*** über (*Acc.*)). **3.** *s.* der Spott, Hohn, die Verhöhnung; Nachahmung; ***make a – of,*** verhöhnen, zum Gespött machen, lächerlich machen. **4.** *attrib. adj.* nachgemacht, Schein–; Schwindel–; – ***fight,*** das Scheingefecht; – ***hare,*** falscher Hase; – ***king,*** der Schattenkönig; – ***modesty,*** vorgetäuschte Sittsamkeit; – *sun,* die Nebensonne; – *trial,* der Scheinprozeß.

mocker ['mɔkə], *s.* der (die) Spötter(in), der Spottvogel. **mockery,** *s.* der Spott, Hohn, die Spötterei (*of,* über (*Acc.*)), Verhöhnung, das Gespött; der Schein, das Blendwerk, die Farce, Gaukelei, das Possenspiel; *make a – of,* verhöhnen, zum Gespött machen; *turn into –,* Spott *or* sein Gespött treiben mit. **mock-heroic,** *adj.* komisch-heroisch. **mocking, 1.** *adj.* spöttisch, höhnisch, Spott–. **2.** *s.* das Gespött, der Spott, Hohn. **mocking-bird,** *s.* die Spottdrossel. **mock-up,** *s.* (*coll.*) das Modell (in natürlicher Größe).

modal [moudl], *adj.* die Art und Weise *or* die Form betreffend; durch Umstände bedingt; modal; – *verb,* modales Hilfszeitwort. **modality** [–'dæliti], *s.* die Modalität, Art und Weise, Ausführungsart.

mode [moud], *s.* 1. die (Art und) Weise, Methode; 2. (*coll.*) der Brauch, die Sitte, Mode; *be all the –,* modern *or* ganz Mode sein; 3. (*Mus.*) die Tongattung, Tonart, das Tongeschlecht; *major –,* das Durgeschlecht; 4. (*Gram.*) der Modus; 5. die (Erscheinungs)form, Beschaffenheit.

model [mɔdl], **1.** *s.* 1. das Muster, Vorbild; *after* or *on the – of,* nach dem Vorbild von *or* (*Gen.*); – *of truthfulness,* das Muster der Wahrhaftigkeit; 2. das Modell, die Nachbildung; *working –,* das Arbeitsmodell; 3. das Modell; *act as –,* Modell stehen (*to, for, Dat.*); *artist's –,* lebendes Modell; 4. die Vorlage, das Muster, (*fig.*) Urbild, der Urtyp; 5. das *or* der Mannequin, die Vorführdame (*for dresses*). **2.** *v.t.* 1. modellieren; 2. Form geben (*Dat.*); (*fig.*) formen, bilden, gestalten, modeln (*after, on,* nach); – *o.s. on,* sich ein Muster nehmen an (*Dat.*); 3. vorführen (*dresses*). **3.** *v.i.* Modell stehen. **4.** *adj.* 1. Modell–; – *railway,* die Modelleisenbahn; 2. (*fig.*) vorbildlich, musterhaft, Muster–; – *farm,* die Musterwirtschaft; – *husband,* der Mustergatte.

modeler, modeling, (*Am.*) *see* **modeller, modelling.**

modeller ['mɔdlə], *s.* der Modellierer. **modelling,** *s.* 1. das Modellieren, die Modellierkunst; 2. (*fig.*) Formgebung, Formung; 3. (*of artist's model*) das Modellstehen; (*of mannequin*) das (Kleider)-vorführen.

moderate, 1. ['mɔdərət], *adj.* mäßig, gemäßigt, mild; niedrig, angemessen, vernünftig (*price*), bescheiden (*demand*), mittelmäßig. **2.** [–rət], *s.* Gemäßigte(r). **3.** [–reit], *v.t.* mäßigen, mildern, lindern, beruhigen, einschränken. **4.** [–reit], *v.i.* abnehmen, nachlassen, sich mäßigen *or* beruhigen. **moderateness** [–rətnis], *s.* die Mäßigkeit, Gemäßigtheit, Milde; Mittelmäßigkeit; Angemessenheit. **moderation** [–'reiʃən], *s.* 1. die Mäßigung; Mäßigkeit, das Maß(halten); *in –,* mit Maß, mäßig; 2. *pl.* erste Universitätsprüfung (*at Oxford*). **moderator** [–reitə], *s.* 1. (*Scots*) Vorsitzende(r) der schottischen Kirche; 2. (*Univ.*) der Prüfungskommissar für die Universitätsprüfung (*Oxford*) *or* Universitätsprüfung in Mathematik (*Cambridge*); 3. (*Tech.*) der Regler, Dämpfer, die Reaktionsbremse.

modern ['mɔdən], **1.** *adj.* modern, neu(zeitlich), jetzig; – *history,* neue(re) Geschichte; – *languages,* neuere Sprachen; – *side,* die Realabteilung (*of school*); – *times,* die Neuzeit; – *writer,* moderner Schriftsteller. **2.** *s. the –s,* die Neueren (*pl.*). **modernism,** *s.* die Neuerung, moderner Ausdruck; moderne Richtung, moderne Ansichten (*pl.*); (*Eccl.*) der Modernismus. **modernity** [–'də:niti], *s.* Moderne(s), die Modernität, Neuzeitlichkeit. **modernization** [–ai'zeiʃən], *s.* die Modernisierung. **modernize,** *v.t.* modernisieren, erneuern. **modernness,** *s. See* **modernity.**

modest ['mɔdist], *adj.* bescheiden; maßvoll, mäßig, anspruchslos; anständig, sittsam. **modesty,** *s.* die Bescheidenheit, Anspruchslosigkeit; Sittsamkeit, der Anstand.

modicum ['mɔdikəm], *s.* (ein) wenig, (ein) bißchen, kleine Menge, (*fig.*) das Körnchen.

modifiable ['mɔdifaiəbl], *adj.* abänderlich, (ab)-änderungsfähig, modifizierbar. **modification** [–fi'keiʃən], *s.* die Abänderung, Veränderung, Umänderung, Abwandlung, Modifikation (*to,* an (*Dat.*)); Einschränkung, nähere Bestimmung; Umstellung; (*Gram.*) der Umlaut; (*Biol.*) nichterbliche Abänderung. **modify** [–fai], **1.** *v.t.* abändern, abwandeln; modifizieren; einschränken, näher bestimmen; mildern, beschränken, mäßigen; (*Gram.*) umlauten. **2.** *v.i.* abgeändert *or* abgewandelt *or* modifiziert werden; (*Gram.*) umgelautet werden.

modish ['moudiʃ], *adj.* modisch, nach der Mode. **modiste** [–'di:st], *s.* die Modistin.

modulate ['mɔdjuleit], **1.** *v.t.* regulieren, abstimmen, abmessen, abtönen, abstufen, anpassen. **2.** *v.i.* (*Mus.*) modulieren (*to,* nach), übergehen, die Tonart wechseln. **modulation** [–'leiʃən], *s.* die Tongebung, der Tonfall (*of the voice*); die Anpassung, Regelung; (*Rad.*) Abstimmung, (*Mus., Rad.*) Modulation. **modulator,** *s.* (*Rad.*) der Modulator, die Modulatorröhre, Modulationsröhre.

module ['mɔdju:l], *s.* das Verhältnismaß, die Maßeinheit, der Modul (*also Archit.*), Model. **modulus** [–jələs], *s.* (*pl.* **-li**) (*Math.*) der Modul, konstanter Koeffizient.

Mogul ['mougʌl], *s.* der Mogul; (*fig.*) Magnat, hoher Herr; – *Empire,* das Reich der Mogulen.

mohair ['mouhɛə], *s.* das Angoraziegenhaar, der Mohär; Mohärstoff.

Mohammed [mou'hæmid], *s.* Mohammed (*m.*). **Mohammedan, 1.** *s.* der (die) Mohammedaner(in). **2.** *adj.* mohammedanisch. **Mohammedanism,** *s.* der Mohammedanismus, Islam.

Mohican ['mouikən], *s.* der Mohikaner.

moiety ['mɔiəti], *s.* der Teil; die Hälfte.

moil [mɔil], **1.** *v.i.* sich abplacken *or* abquälen *or* schinden. **2.** *s.* die Plackerei, Schinderei.

moire [mwɑ:], *s.* 1. der Mohr, Wasserglanz (*on material*); 2. (*also – antique*) geflammter *or* gewässerter Stoff, der Moiréstoff, der *or* das Moiré. **moiré** [–'rei], **1.** *s.* 1. *See* **moire,** 1; 2. wolkenartiger Schimmer (*on metal*). **2.** *adj.* moiriert, geflammt, gewässert.

moist [mɔist], *adj.* feucht; naß; – *sugar,* der Sandzucker; – *steam,* der Naßdampf. **moisten** [mɔisn], *v.t.* anfeuchten, befeuchten. **moistness, moisture** ['mɔistʃə], *s.* die Feuchtheit, Feuchtigkeit, Nässe.

moke [mouk], *s.* (*sl.*) der Esel.

molar ['moulə], **1.** *adj.* (zer)malmend; – *tooth,* der Backenzahn. **2.** *s.* der Backenzahn, Mahlzahn.

molasses [mə'læsiz], *pl.* (*sing. constr.*) die Melasse; der Zuckersyrup.

mold, (*Am.*) *see* **mould.**

Moldavia [mɔl'deiviə], *s.* die Moldau. **Moldavian, 1.** *adj.* moldauisch, Moldau–. **2.** *s.* der (die) Moldauer(in).

molder, (*Am.*) *see* **moulder.**

[1]**mole** [moul], *s.* das Muttermal, der Leberfleck.

[2]**mole,** *s.* (*Zool.*) der Maulwurf.

[3]**mole,** *s.* die Mole, der Hafendamm.

[4]**mole,** *s.* (*Vet.*) das Mondkalb.

molecular [mə'lekjulə], *adj.* molekular, Molekular–. **molecule** ['mɔlikju:l], *s.* das Molekül, die Molekel.

mole|-hill, *s.* der Maulwurfshaufen; (*coll.*) *make a mountain out of a –,* aus einer Mücke einen Elefanten machen. **-skin,** *s.* das Maulwurfsfell; Englischleder.

molest [mo'lest], *v.t.* belästigen; lästig *or* zur Last *or* beschwerlich fallen (*Dat.*). **molestation** [–'teiʃən], *s.* die Belästigung.

mollification [mɔlifi'keiʃən], *s.* die Besänftigung, Beruhigung, Beschwichtigung. **mollify** ['mɔlifai], *v.t.* besänftigen, beruhigen, beschwichtigen; mildern, lindern; erweichen (*wax etc.*).

mollusc ['mɔləsk], *s.* (*pl.* **-a** [–'lʌskə]) das Weichtier, die Molluske. **molluscoid** [–'lʌskɔid], *adj.* molluskenartig. **molluscous** [–ˈlʌskəs], *adj.* Weichtier–, Mollusken–; (*fig.*) weichlich, schwammig, wabbelig.

mollycoddle [ˈmɔlikɔdl], **1.** *s.* der Weichling, Schlappschwanz; das Muttersöhnchen. **2.** *v.t.* verhätscheln, verzärteln.

Moloch [ˈmoulɔk], *s.* der Moloch, (*fig.*) menschenfressendes Ungeheuer.

molt, (*Am.*) *see* **moult.**

molten [ˈmoultən], *adj.* geschmolzen, (schmelz)-flüssig; – ***mass,*** die Schmelze.

molybdate [məˈlibdeit], *s.* molybdänsaures Salz, das Molybdat. **molybdenum** [–dənəm], *s.* das Molybdän. **molybdic,** *adj.* Molybdän–, molybdänsauer.

moment [ˈmoumənt], *s.* 1. der Augenblick, Moment, Zeitpunkt; ***at the*** –, gerade jetzt *or* damals, im Augenblick; ***at this*** –, in dem Augenblick; ***come here this –!*** komm sofort! ***at the last*** –, im letzten Augenblick; ***the – he had done it,*** sobald er es getan hatte; ***the*** (***very***) ***– that,*** gerade als; ***for the*** –, gerade jetzt; ***in a*** –, sogleich, sofort, auf der Stelle; ***one –! half a –!*** (nur) einen Augenblick! 2. die Wichtigkeit, Tragweite, Bedeutung, der Belang (***to,*** für); ***it is of no great*** –, es ist ohne Belang; 3. (*Phys.*) das Moment; – ***of a force,*** das Kraftmoment, Moment einer Kraft; – ***of a force about a point,*** das Drehungsmoment einer Kraft; – ***of inertia,*** das Trägheitsmoment; – ***of resistance,*** das Widerstandsmoment.

momentarily [ˈmoumənṭərili], *adv.* vorübergehend, für einen Augenblick nur. **momentary,** *adj.* augenblicklich, momentan; flüchtig, vorübergehend, vergänglich.

momentous [məˈmentəs], *adj.* (ge)wichtig, bedeutend, folgenschwer. **momentousness,** *s.* die Wichtigkeit, Bedeutung, Tragweite.

momentum [məˈmentəm], *s.* (*Phys.*) die Bewegungsgröße, der Impuls; (*Tech.*) bewegende Kraft, die Triebkraft; (*coll.*) Wucht, Stoßkraft, der Schwung, Impuls; ***gather*** –, (an) Stoßkraft gewinnen.

monachism [ˈmɔnəkizm], *s.* das Mönch(s)tum, Mönchswesen.

Monaco [ˈmɔnəkou], *s.* Monaco (*n.*).

monad [ˈmɔnæd], *s.* (*Phil.*) die Monade; (*Biol.*) organische Einheit, einzelliger Organismus, der Einzeller; (*Chem.*) einwertiges Element. **monadelphous** [–nəˈdelfəs], *adj.* (*Bot.*) monadelphisch, einbrüderig. **monadic** [–ˈnædik], *adj.* (*Math.*) einstellig, eingliedrig; (*Phil.*) Monaden–, monadisch. **monadism** [ˈmɔnədizm], *s.* die Monadenlehre, Monadologie.

monandrous [mɔˈnændrəs], *adj.* (*Bot.*) einmännig, mit nur einem Staubgefäß. **monanthous** [–θəs], *adj.* (*Bot.*) einblütig.

monarch [ˈmɔnək], *s.* der (die) Monarch(in), (Allein)herrscher(in). **monarchal** [məˈnɑ:kl], **monarchic(al)** [məˈnɑ:kik(l)], *adj.* monarchisch, Monarchie–; monarchistisch, monarchiefreundlich. **monarchism,** *s.* der Monarchismus. **monarchist, 1.** *s.* der (die) Monarchist(in). **2.** *attrib. adj.* monarchistisch. **monarchy** [–ki], *s.* die Monarchie.

monastery [ˈmɔnəstri], *s.* das (Mönchs)kloster. **monastic** [məˈnæstik], *adj.* klösterlich, Mönchs–; (*fig.*) weltabgewandt, abgeschlossen. **monasticism** [–ˈnæstisizm], *s.* das Klosterleben, Mönch(s)-tum; die Askese.

Monday [ˈmʌndi], *s.* der Montag; ***on*** –, am Montag; ***on –(s)***, montags; (*sl.*) ***Black*** –, der Schulanfang.

Monegasque [ˈmɔnəgæsk], **1.** *s.* der Monegasse (die Monegassin). **2.** *adj.* monegassisch.

monetary [ˈmʌnitri], *adj.* Geld–, Finanz–, Münz–, Währungs–; – ***crisis,*** die Geldkrise, Währungskrise; – ***standard,*** der Münzfuß; – ***unit,*** die Währungseinheit. **monetize,** *v.t.* zu Münzen prägen, in Umlauf setzen (*coin*).

money [ˈmʌni], *s.* das Geld; ***call*** –, Geld auf Abruf; (*coll.*) ***coin*** –, Geld wie Heu verdienen; ***demand*** –, das Tagesgeld; (*coll.*) – ***for jam,*** guter Profit bei wenig Mühe; ***make*** –, reich werden, gut verdienen (***by,*** durch *or* bei); ***public*** –, öffentliche Gelder; ***ready*** –, bares Geld; ***short of*** –, knapp an Geld, schlecht *or* nicht bei Kasse; ***–'s worth,*** der Geld(es)wert; ***his*** (***full***) ***–'s worth,*** etwas Vollwertiges für sein Geld.

money|-bag, *s.* der Geldbeutel. **--bags,** *pl.* (*coll.*) das Geld, der Reichtum; steinreicher Mensch, der Geldsack. **--box,** *s.* die Sparbüchse. **--changer,** *s.* der Geldwechsler, Geldmakler. **moneyed** [–d], *adj.* vermögend, reich; – ***classes,*** besitzende Klassen, Kapitalisten; – ***interest,*** die Finanz(welt). **money|-grubber,** *s.* der Geizhals, Geldraffer. **--grubbing,** *adj.* geldgierig, geldraffend. **–lender,** *s.* der Geldverleiher. **--making, 1.** *adj.* gewinnbringend, einträglich. **2.** *s.* der Gelderwerb. **--market,** *s.* der Geldmarkt, die Börse. **--matters,** *pl.* Geldangelegenheiten (*pl.*). **--order,** *s.* die Zahlungsanweisung. **--transaction,** *s.* das Geldgeschäft, Effektivgeschäft.

monger [ˈmʌŋgə], *s.* (*usu. in compounds*) der Krämer, Händler; ***fish–,*** der Fischhändler; ***news–,*** der Neuigkeitskrämer; ***scandal–,*** die Klatsche, das Lästermaul; ***sensation–,*** der Sensationsmacher, Sensationsschmied; ***war–,*** der Kriegshetzer.

Mongol [ˈmɔŋgɔl], *s.* der Mongole (die Mongolin); *pl.* (*collect.*) Mongoliden. **Mongolia** [–ˈgouliə], *s.* die Mongolei. **Mongolian** [–ˈgouliən], *adj.* mongolisch; (*Ethn.*) mongolid. **Mongolism,** *s.* (*Med.*) der Mongolismus, mongoloide Idiotie. **mongoloid** [–ɔid], *adj.* mongolenartig, mongolenähnlich, mongoloid.

mongoose [ˈmɔŋgu:s], *s.* (*Zool.*) der Mungo.

mongrel [ˈmʌŋgrəl], **1.** *s.* der Mischling (*of men*), Bastard, das Kreuzungsprodukt (*animals*); (*coll.*) der Köter, die Promenadenmischung (*dog*), das Zwischending (*a th.*). **2.** *adj.* Misch–, Bastard–.

monism [ˈmɔnizm], *s.* (*Phil.*) der Monismus. **monist,** *s.* der Monist. **monistic** [–ˈnistik], *adj.* monistisch.

monition [mɔˈniʃən], *s.* die (Er)mahnung, Warnung; (*Law*) Vorladung.

monitor [ˈmɔnitə], **1.** *s.* 1. der (Er)mahner, Warner; 2. (*esp.*) Klassenordner, Lehrgehilfe (*in school*); 3. die Warnung, das Warnzeichen; 4. (*Tech., esp. Rad.*) der Überwachungstechniker; Abhörer; das Abhörgerät; 5. (*Naut.*) der Monitor, Küstenpanzer; 6. (*Zool.*) Waran. **2.** *v.t.* (*Rad. etc.*) abhören, überwachen. **monitorial** [–ˈtɔ:riəl], *adj. See* **monitory, 1**; (*in schools*) Klassenordner–, Monitor–. **monitorship,** *s.* die Stellung des Klassenordners. **monitory** [–tri], **1.** *adj.* (er)-mahnend, warnend, Mahn–. **2.** *s.* (*Eccl.*) das Ermahnungsschreiben.

monk [mʌŋk], *s.* 1. der Mönch; 2. (*Typ.*) die Schmierstelle. **monkery,** *s.* das Mönchswesen, Mönch(s)tum; Klosterleben; (*collect.*) Mönche (*pl.*).

monkey [ˈmʌŋki], **1.** *s.* 1. der Affe (*also fig.*); (*coll.*) ***little*** –, der Schlingel, kleiner Strolch; 2. (*sl.*) fünfhundert Pfund *or* Dollar; 3. (*Tech.*) die Ramme, der Rammblock, Rammklotz, Fallblock, Fallhammer, Hammerbär; 4. (*sl.*) ***get one's – up,*** fuchtig werden, in Wut geraten; (*sl.*) ***get*** or ***put his – up,*** ihn in Wut *or* auf die Palme bringen. **2.** *v.i.* (*coll.*) – ***about,*** Schabernack *or* Possen treiben, Dummheiten machen; – (***about***), herumpfuschen (***with,*** an (*Dat.*)), herumspielen, herumfummeln, leichtsinnig umgehen (mit). **3.** *v.t.* nachäffen.

monkey|-business, *s.* (*coll.*) der Unfug. **--engine,** *s.* die Rammaschine. **--gland,** *s.* die Verjüngungsdrüse. **--house,** *s.* das Affenhaus. **--jacket,** *s.* die Matrosenjacke. **–nut,** *s.* die Erdnuß. **--puzzle,** *s.* (*Bot.*) die Schuppentanne, Araukarie. **--tricks,** *pl.* Narrenspossen (*pl.*). **--wrench,** *s.* der Engländer, Franzose, Universal(schrauben)schlüssel.

monkish [ˈmʌŋkiʃ], *adj.* mönchisch, klösterlich.

monk's-hood, *s.* (*Bot.*) der Eisenhut.

mono– [ˈmɔnou, –ə], *pref.* ein–.

monobasic [mɔnəˈbeisik], *adj.* (*Chem.*) einbasig.

monocarpic [mɔnə'kɑ:pik], *adj.* nur einmal fruchtend. **monocarpous,** *adj.* einfrüchtig.
monochromatic [mɔnəkrə'mætik], *adj.* einfarbig, monochrom. **monochrome** ['mɔnəkroum], *s.* einfarbiges Gemälde.
monocle ['mɔnəkl], *s.* das Einglas, Monokel.
monoclinal [mɔnə'klainl], *adj.* (*Geol.*) mit nur einer Neigungsfläche. **monoclinic** [–'klinik], *adj.* (*Min.*) monoklin, mit drei ungleichwertigen Achsen.
monocoque ['mɔnəkɔk], *s.* (*Av.*) der Stromlinienrumpf.
monocotyledon [mɔnəkɔti'li:dn], *s.* einkeimblättrige Pflanze.
monocular [mɔ'nɔkjulə], *adj.* einäugig; für ein Auge.
monodactylous [mɔnə'dæktiləs], *adj.* (*Zool.*) einzehig.
monody ['mɔnədi], *s.* die Monodie, der Einzelgesang.
monogamous [mɔ'nɔgəməs], *adj.* monogam. **monogamy** [–mi], *s.* die Einehe, Monogamie.
monogram ['mɔnəgræm], *s.* das Monogramm.
monograph ['mɔnəgrɑ:f], *s.* die Monographie.
monolith ['mɔnəliθ], *s.* der Monolith, einzeln bearbeiteter Steinblock.
monologue ['mɔnəlɔg], *s.* der Monolog, das Selbstgespräch.
monomania [mono'meiniə], *s.* fixe Idee, die Zwangsvorstellung, Monomanie. **monomaniac** [–iæk], *s.* der *or* die Monomane.
monometallism [mono'metəlizm], *s.* einheitliche Währung.
monomial [mɔ'noumiəl], **1.** *s.* (*Math.*) einfache Größe. **2.** *adj.* monomisch, eingliedrig.
monophase ['mɔnəfeiz], *adj.* (*Elec.*) einphasig, Einphasen–.
monoplane ['mɔnəplein], *s.* (*Av.*) der Eindecker; ***high-wing*** –, der Hochdecker; ***low-wing*** –, der Tiefdecker.
monopolist [mə'nɔpəlist], *s.* der Monopolist, Alleinhersteller, Alleinhändler. **monopolize,** *v.t.* monopolisieren; für sich allein in Anspruch nehmen, allein beherrschen, an sich reißen, mit Beschlag belegen. **monopoly,** *s.* das Alleinverkaufsrecht, Alleinherstellungsrecht, die Monopolstellung; das Monopol (***of,*** auf (*Acc.*)); (*fig.*) ausschließliches Recht (auf (*Acc.*)), alleiniger Besitz (von), die Alleinherrschaft (über (*Acc.*)).
monorail ['mɔnəreil], **1.** *adj.* einschienig. **2.** *s.* die Einschienenbahn.
monosyllabic [mɔnəsi'læbik], *adj.* einsilbig. **monosyllable** ['mɔnəsiləbl], *s.* einsilbiges Wort; ***in –s,*** einsilbig.
monotheism ['mɔnəθi:izm], *s.* der Monotheismus. **monotheist,** *s.* der Monotheist. **monotheistic** [–'istik], *adj.* monotheistisch.
monotone ['mɔnətoun], *s.* gleichbleibender Ton, eintönige Wiederholung, die Eintönigkeit; Einfarbigkeit; (*fig.*) *see* **monotony. monotonous** [mə'nɔtənəs], *adj.* eintönig, monoton; (*fig.*) einförmig, langweilig. **monotony** [mə'nɔtəni], *s.* (*fig.*) die Eintönigkeit, Monotonie; Einförmigkeit, ewiges Einerlei.
monotype ['mɔnətaip], *s.* die Monotype(setzmaschine).
monoxide [mɔ'nɔksaid], *s.* das Monoxyd.
monozygotic [mɔnəzai'gɔtik], *adj.* (*Biol.*) eineiig.
monsoon [mɔn'su:n], *s.* der Monsun; ***dry*** –, der Wintermonsun; ***wet*** –, der Sommermonsun, Regenmonsun.
monster ['mɔnstə], **1.** *s.* 1. das Ungeheuer, Scheusal; – ***of ugliness,*** der Ausbund von Häßlichkeit, wahres Scheusal; 2. die Mißbildung, Mißgestalt, Mißgeburt, das Mostrum. **2.** *adj.* ungeheuer(lich), enorm, riesengroß, Riesen–.
monstrance ['mɔnstrəns], *s.* die Monstranz.
monstrosity [mɔn'strɔsiti], *s.* die Ungeheuerlichkeit; Mißgestalt, Mißbildung, das Ungeheuer.
monstrous ['mɔnstrəs], *adj.* 1. ungeheuer, riesig, riesenhaft, enorm; 2. mißgestalt(et), unförmig, ungestalt, unnatürlich, widernatürlich; ungeheuerlich, fürchterlich, gräßlich, entsetzlich, scheußlich, abscheulich, schrecklich; 3. (*coll.*) haarsträubend, absurd. **monstrousness,** *s.* die Ungeheuerlichkeit, Entsetzlichkeit, Abscheulichkeit.
montage [mɔn'tɑ:ʒ], *s.* die Zusammensetzung, Aufstellung, Montage (*film etc.*).
month [mʌnθ], *s.* der Monat; ***this last*** –, seit vier Wochen; ***this day*** –, heute in einem Monat; ***by the*** –, (all)monatlich; ***for –s,*** monatelang; ***once a*** –, einmal im Monat; (*coll.*) – ***of Sundays,*** unabsehbare Zeit; ***give a –'s notice,*** mit vierwöchentlicher Wirkung kündigen. **monthly, 1.** *adj.* monatlich, Monats–. **2.** *adv.* monatlich, jeden Monat. **3.** *s.* 1. die Monatsschrift; 2. *pl.* (*coll.*) monatliche Regel.
monticule ['mɔntikju:l], *s.* die Erhebung, das Hügelchen.
monument ['mɔnjumənt], *s.* das Denkmal (*also fig.*), Grabmal (***to,*** für). **monumental** [–'mentl], *adj.* Denkmal–, Grabmal–, Gedenk–; (*fig.*) hervorragend, monumental, kolossal, gewaltig, überdimensional; – ***mason,*** der Friedhofssteinmetz.
moo [mu:], **1.** *v.i.* muhen (*of cows*). **2.** *s.* das Muhen.
mooch [mu:tʃ], *v.i.* (*sl.*) (*also* – ***around*** or ***about***) sich herumtreiben, herumlungern; – ***along,*** einherlatschen.
moo-cow, *s.* (*nursery talk*) die Muhkuh.
[1]**mood** [mu:d], *s.* (*Gram., Log.*) der Modus, die Aussageweise; ***subjunctive*** –, die Möglichkeitsform, der Konjunktiv; ***verb of*** –, see ***modal verb.***
[2]**mood,** *s.* die Gefühlslage, Stimmung, Laune; ***in a melancholy*** –, niedergeschlagen; ***be in the*** (***no***) –, (nicht) aufgelegt sein, (keine) Lust haben (***for,*** zu); ***when the – is on me,*** wenn ich in der Stimmung bin; ***man of –s,*** launischer Mensch. **moodiness,** *s.* die Launenhaftigkeit; Verdrießlichkeit, Verstimmtheit, üble Laune. **moody,** *adj.* launisch, launenhaft; schwermütig, niedergeschlagen; übelgelaunt, verstimmt, verdrießlich.
moon [mu:n], **1.** *s.* der Mond; (*fig., Poet.*) Monat; ***cry for the*** –, Unmögliches verlangen; ***full*** –, der Vollmond; ***face like a full*** –, das Vollmondgesicht; ***new*** –, der Neumond; ***old*** –, abnehmender Mond; ***once in a blue*** –, nur alle Jubeljahre (einmal); ***there is a*** (***no***) –, der Mond scheint (nicht). **2.** *v.i.* (*coll.*) – ***about,*** umherschweifen, herumlungern. **3.** *v.t.* (*coll.*) – ***away one's time,*** die Zeit vertrödeln.
moon|beam, *s.* der Mondstrahl. **–calf,** *s.* das Mondkalb; (*fig.*) der Einfaltspinsel, Tölpel. **–light, 1.** *adj.* mondhell, Mondlicht–, Mondschein–; (*coll.*) – ***flit,*** heimliches Ausziehen bei Nacht. **2.** *s.* das Mondlicht, der Mondschein. **–lit,** *adj.* mondhell. **–rise,** *s.* der Mondaufgang. **–shine,** *s.* 1. *See* **–light, 2**; 2. (*fig.*) leerer Schein, der Schwindel; Unsinn, das Gefasel; 3. (*Am.*) geschmuggelter Alkohol. **–shiner,** *s.* (*Am.*) der Alkoholschmuggler. **–stone,** *s.* der Mondstein, echter Adular. **–struck,** *adj.* mondsüchtig, besessen. **moony,** *adj.* (*coll.*) zerstreut, verträumt.
Moor [muə], *s.* der Mohr, Maure.
[1]**moor,** *s.* das Moor, (*oft. pl.*) Hochmoor, Heideland, die Bergheide.
[2]**moor, 1.** *v.t.* (*Naut.*) vertäuen, vermuren, anlegen; festmachen; ***be –ed,*** *see* **2. 2.** *v.i.* vertäut *or* festgemacht liegen, festmachen, sich vermuren. **moorage** [–ridʒ], *s.* der Liegeplatz, die Vertäuung.
moor|cock, *s.* männliches Teichhuhn. **–hen,** *s.* weibliches Teichhuhn (*Gallinula chloropus*).
mooring ['muəriŋ], *s.* das Festmachen, Vertäuen; (*oft. pl.*) die Vertäuung; der Liegeplatz. **mooring|-buoy,** *s.* die Hafenboje. **–mast,** *s.* (*Av.*) der Ankermast. **--post,** *s.* der Vertäuungspfahl. **--rope,** *s.* die Halteleine.
Moorish ['muəriʃ], *adj.* maurisch.
moorland ['muələnd], *s.* das Heidemoor(land).

moose [mu:s], *s.* (*Zool.*) amerikanischer Elch; das Elen(tier).

moot [mu:t], **1.** *v.t.* erörtern, zur Diskussion stellen, aufwerfen, anschneiden (*a problem*). **2.** *adj.* strittig, umstritten, zweifelhaft, zu erörtern(d). **3.** *s.* (*Hist.*) die Volks(gerichts)versammlung, (*Law*) Erörterung; (*fig.*) Tagung, das Lagertreffen.

[1]**mop** [mɔp], **1.** *s.* der Scheuerlappen, Wischlappen; Staubbesen; (*Naut.*) Schrubber, Dweil; (*fig.*) Wust (*of hair*). **2.** *v.t.* (auf)wischen; (ab)wischen; (*sl.*) – ***the floor with him,*** mit ihm Schlitten fahren; – ***up,*** aufwischen; (*Mil.*) (*coll.*) niedermachen, gefangennehmen (*stragglers*), säubern (*an area*); (*sl.*) verschlucken (*food*), (*fig.*) schlucken (*profit etc.*). **3.** *v.i.* (*Mil.*) – ***up,*** (vom Feinde) säubern.

[2]**mop, 1.** *v.i.* – ***and mow,*** Grimassen *or* Gesichter schneiden. **2.** *s.* ***–s and mows,*** Grimassen.

[3]**mop,** *s.* der Jahrmarkt.

mope [moup], **1.** *v.i.* niedergeschlagen *or* schwermütig *or* teilnahmslos sein, den Kopf hängen lassen, Trübsal blasen. **2.** *v.t.* (*only pass.*) ***be –d,*** entmutigt *or* niedergeschlagen *or* betrübt sein. **3.** *s.* der Kopfhänger, Trübsalbläser; (*coll.*) ***the –s,*** der Trübsinn, heulendes Elend.

moped [′mouped], *s.* das Moped, Mofa.

moper [′moupə], *s. See* **mope, 3.**

mop-head, *s.* (*coll.*) der Krauskopf, Strubelkopf, Wuschelkopf.

mopish [′moupiʃ], *adj.* niedergeschlagen, lustlos, betrübt, trübsinnig, trübselig, griesgrämig, verdrießlich. **mopishness,** *s.* der Trübsinn, die Lustlosigkeit, Niedergeschlagenheit, Verdrießlichkeit, Griesgrämigkeit.

moppet [′mɔpit], *s.* (*coll.*) das Püppchen (*also fig.*), die Krabbe.

mopping-up operation, *s.* (*Mil.*) die Säuberungsaktion.

moquette [mo′ket], *s.* das Mokett, Plüschgewebe.

moraine [mo′rein], *s.* die (Gletscher)moräne.

moral [′mɔrəl], **1.** *adj.* 1. moralisch, sittlich, Moral–, Sitten–; – ***character,*** die Charakterfestigkeit; – ***law,*** das Sittengesetz; – ***obligation,*** moralische Verpflichtung; – ***philosophy,*** die Sittenlehre, Moralphilosophie; – ***right,*** auf dem Sittengesetz gegründetes Recht; – ***sense,*** das Sittlichkeitsgefühl, sittliches Empfinden; 2. sittenstreng, sittenrein, tugendhaft, sittsam; – ***weeklies,*** moralische Wochenschriften; 3. vernunftgemäß, innerlich (gefestigt), charakterlich; – ***courage,*** sittliche Entschlossenheit; – ***pressure,*** moralischer Druck; – ***support,*** innerliche Unterstützung; – ***victory,*** moralischer Sieg; 4. – ***certainty,*** voraussichtliche *or* zuversichtliche Gewißheit. **2.** *s.* 1. die Nutzanwendung, Lehre (*of a story etc.*); ***draw the – from,*** die Lehre ziehen aus; 2. sittlicher Standpunkt *or* Grundsatz; ***point the –,*** den sittlichen Standpunkt betonen; 3. *pl.* die Sittlichkeit, Moral, Sitten (*pl.*), sittliches Verhalten; 4. *pl.* (*sing. constr.*) (*Phil.*) die Sittenlehre, Ethik.

morale [mo′rɑ:l], *s.* die Moral, geistig-seelische Verfassung *or* Haltung, (*esp. Mil.*) der (Kampf)-geist.

moralist [′mɔrəlist], *s.* 1. der Sittenlehrer, Sittenrichter, Sittenprediger; 2. Ethiker. **morality** [–′ræliti], *s.* 1. sittliches Verhalten, moralische Grundsätze (*pl.*), die Moral, Sittlichkeit, Tugendhaftigkeit; 2. Sittenlehre, Ethik; 3. Sittenpredigt; 4. (*also* – ***play***) Moralität. **moralize, 1.** *v.i.* moralisieren, moralische Betrachtungen anstellen, sittenpredigen (***about, on,*** über (*Acc.*)). **2.** *v.t.* 1. sittlich veredeln *or* beeinflussen, versittlichen; 2. eine Moral ziehen aus, moralisch auslegen.

morass [mo′ræs], *s.* der Morast, Sumpf; (*fig.*) die Wirrnis.

moratorium [mɔrə′tɔ:riəm], *s.* die Stundung, das Stillhalteabkommen, Moratorium, der Zahlungsaufschub.

Moravia [mə′reiviə], *s.* Mähren (*n.*). **Moravian, 1.** *s.* 1. der Mähre(r) (die Mähr(er)in); 2. (*language*) das Mährisch(e). **2.** *adj.* mährisch; – ***Brethren,*** die Brüdergemeine, Herrnhüter (*pl.*).

morbid [′mɔ:bid], *adj.* krankhaft, pathologisch; (*coll.*) grausig, schauerlich; – ***anatomy,*** pathologische Anatomie.

morbidezza [mɔ:bi′detsə], *s.* (*Art*) die Zartheit der Fleischfarben.

morbidity [mɔ:′biditi], *s.* die Krankhaftigkeit; (*Stat.*) Erkrankungsziffer. **morbidness** [′mɔ:bidnis], *s.* die Krankhaftigkeit.

mordancy [′mɔ:dənsi], *s.* (beißende) Schärfe, das Beißende. **mordant, 1.** *adj.* beißend, ätzend (*also fig.*); brennend, fressend; (*fig.*) sarkastisch. **2.** *s.* die Beize, das Beizmittel, Ätzwasser.

mordent [′mɔ:dənt], *s.* (*Mus.*) der Pralltriller.

more [mɔ:], **1.** *comp. adj.* mehr; noch (mehr), weitere (*pl.*); ***no – money,*** kein Geld mehr; ***not a word –,*** kein Wort mehr; ***–'s the pity!*** leider Gottes! ***some – water,*** noch etwas Wasser; ***some – people,*** noch einige Leute; ***ten – miles*** or ***miles –,*** noch *or* weitere zehn Meilen. **2.** *adv.* mehr; weiter, wieder(um); (*in forming comp. adj. and adv.*) –er; – ***often,*** öfter; – ***silently,*** stiller, ruhiger; – ***and –,*** immer mehr; ***the – so,*** um so mehr (***as,*** als; ***because,*** da); – ***or less,*** mehr oder weniger, einigermaßen, ungefähr; – ***so,*** in größerem *or* höherem Maße; – ***than anxious,*** übereifrig, äußerst begierig; (*coll.*) ***make – of a th. than it is,*** eine S. übertreiben *or* aufbauschen; ***once –,*** noch einmal; ***never –,*** nie(mals) wieder; ***say no –,*** nichts mehr sagen; ***be no –,*** tot sein; ***no –*** or ***not any – than,*** ebensowenig wie; ***no – will I,*** ich auch nicht; – ***than repay,*** überreichlich bezahlen; ***and – than that, and what is –,*** und was noch wichtiger ist, und (was) noch mehr (ist), und überdies; ***the – the merrier,*** je mehr desto besser; – ***to the point*** or ***purpose,*** zweckmäßiger. **3.** *s.* das Mehr; ***see – of,*** öfter sehen.

moreen [mo′ri:n], *s.* moirierter Wollstoff.

[1]**morel** [mo′rel], *s.* (*Bot.*) Schwarzer Nachtschatten.

[2]**morel,** *s.* (*Bot.*) die Morchel; *see also* **morello.**

morello [mo′relou], *s.* (*Bot.*) die Morelle, Sauerweichsel.

moreover [mɔ:′rouvə], *adv.* überdies, außerdem, übrigens, weiter, ferner, noch dazu.

morganatic [mɔ:gə′nætik], *adj.* morganatisch.

morgue [mɔ:g], *s.* das Leichenhaus, die Leichenhalle.

moribund [′mɔribʌnd], *adj.* im Sterben (liegend), sterbend.

morion [′mɔriən], *s.* (*Hist.*) die Sturmhaube.

Mormon [′mɔ:mən], *s.* der Mormone (die Mormonin). **Mormonism,** *s.* das Mormonentum.

morn [mɔ:n], *s.* (*Poet.*) der Morgen.

morning [′mɔ:niŋ], **1.** *s.* der Morgen, Vormittag; ***the – after,*** (*adv.*) am Morgen darauf, am darauffolgenden Morgen; (*prep.*) am Morgen nach; (*coll.*) ***the – after the night before,*** der Katzenjammer, Kater; ***in the –,*** morgens, des Morgens, am Morgen; (*coll.*) morgen (früh), am nächsten *or* andern Morgen; ***early in the –,*** früh morgens, früh am Morgen; ***on Monday –,*** am Montagmorgen; ***one –,*** eines Morgens; ***this –,*** heute morgen *or* früh; ***tomorrow –,*** morgen früh; ***yesterday –,*** gestern morgen *or* früh. **2.** *attrib. adj.* Morgen–, Vormittags–, Früh–; – ***break,*** die Frühpause; – ***call,*** der Vormittagsbesuch; – ***coat,*** der Cut(away); (***early***) – ***cup of tea,*** eine Tasse Tee vor dem Aufstehen; – ***dress,*** schwarzer Rock mit gestreifter Hose; – ***paper,*** die Morgenzeitung; – ***performance,*** die Vormittagsvorstellung; – ***prayer,*** das Morgengebet; – ***prayers,*** der Frühgottesdienst; – ***room,*** das Frühstückszimmer; – ***sickness,*** morgendliche Übelkeit; – ***suit,*** see – ***dress***; (*Naut.*) – ***watch,*** die Frühwache.

Moroccan [mə′rɔkən], **1.** *s.* der (die) Marokkaner(in). **2.** *adj.* marokkanisch. **Morocco** [–kou], *s.* Marokko (*n.*).

morocco, 1. *adj.* Saffian–. **2.** *s.* der Saffian, Maroquin, das Saffianleder.

moron [′mɔ:rɔn], *s.* Schwachsinnige(r); (*coll.*) der Idiot, Trottel.

morose [mə′rous], *adj.* mürrisch, grämlich, verdrießlich. **moroseness,** *s.* die Grämlichkeit, Verdrießlichkeit.

morpheme ['mɔ:fi:m], *s.* (*Gram.*) das Morphem.

morphia ['mɔ:fiə], **morphine** [–fi:n], *s.* das Morphium. **morphinism,** *s.* die Morphinsucht, der Morphinismus.

morphological [mɔ:fə'lɔdʒikl], *adj.* (*Gram.*) morphologisch, Form–. **morphology** [–'fɔlədʒi], *s.* die Morphologie; Formenlehre.

morris(-dance) ['mɔris–], *s.* der Moriskentanz.

morris-tube, *s.* der Einsatzlauf.

morrow ['mɔrou], *s.* (*Poet.*) folgender *or* morgiger Tag; ***on the – of,*** am Tage *or* (in der Zeit) unmittelbar nach.

morse [mɔ:s], *s.* (*obs.*) das Walroß.

Morse, **1.** *v.i., v.t.* morsen. **2.** *adj.* – ***alphabet,*** – ***code,*** das Morse-Alphabet, die Morseschrift.

morsel [mɔ:sl], *s.* der Bissen; Brocken, das Stückchen, bißchen; der Leckerbissen.

1**mort** [mɔ:t], *s.* (*Hunt.*) das (Hirsch)totsignal.

2**mort,** *s.* (*dial.*) die Menge.

mortal [mɔ:tl], **1.** *adj.* 1. sterblich; 2. vergänglich, irdisch, menschlich; (*coll.*) ***in all my – days,*** mein Leben lang; (*coll.*) ***two – hours,*** zwei endlose *or* geschlagene Stunden; 3. todbringend, tödlich (***to,*** für), Tod(es)–; – ***agony,*** der Todeskampf; – ***combat,*** der Kampf auf Leben und Tod; – ***foe,*** der Todfeind; – ***fright,*** die Todesangst; – ***hatred,*** tödlicher Haß; – ***hour,*** die Todesstunde; – ***offence,*** tödliche Beleidigung; – ***sin,*** die Todsünde; – ***wound,*** tödliche Verletzung, die Todeswunde; 4. (*coll.*) absolut, menschenmöglich, vorstellbar, mordsmäßig, Mords–; (*coll.*) – ***hurry,*** die Mordseile; (*coll.*) ***of no – use,*** absolut zwecklos. **2.** *s.* Sterbliche(r); (*coll.*) der Mensch, Kerl. **mortality** [–'tæliti], *s.* 1. die Sterblichkeit; 2. (*also – rate*) Sterblichkeitsziffer. **mortally,** *adv.* tödlich.

1**mortar** ['mɔ:tə], *s.* 1. (*Mil.*) der Mörser, Minenwerfer, Granatwerfer; 2. (*Chem.*) Mörser, die Reibschale.

2**mortar,** *s.* (*Build.*) der Mörtel, Speis, die Speise.

mortar-board, *s.* das Mörtelbrett; (*coll.*) viereckige Akademikermütze.

mortgage ['mɔ:gidʒ], **1.** *s.* 1. (*also – **bond*** or ***deed***) die Pfandurkunde, Pfandverschreibung, der Pfandbrief, Hypothekenbrief; 2. die Hypothek; ***borrow on –,*** auf Hypothek leihen; ***lend on –,*** auf Hypothek (ver)leihen; ***raise a –,*** eine Hypothek aufnehmen (***on,*** auf (*Acc.*)). **2.** *v.t.* 1. verpfänden (***to,*** an (*Acc.*)) (*also fig.*); 2. hypothekarisch *or* mit einer Hypothek belasten, eine Hypothek aufnehmen auf (*Acc.*). **mortgagee** [–'dʒi:], *s.* der Hypothekengläubiger, Hypothekar. **mortgager, mortgagor** [–'dʒɔ:], *s.* der Hypothekenschuldner.

mortician [mɔ:'tiʃən], *s.* (*Am.*) der Leichenbestatter.

mortification [mɔ:tifi'keiʃən], *s.* 1. (*Med.*) der Brand, die Nekrose; 2. (*fig.*) Kasteiung (*of the flesh*); 3. Demütigung, Kränkung; 4. (*coll.*) der Ärger, Verdruß. **mortify** ['mɔ:tifai], **1.** *v.t.* 1. (*Med.*) absterben lassen, brandig machen; 2. (*fig.*) abtöten, kasteien (*the flesh*); 3. demütigen, kränken; (*coll.*) ***deeply mortified,*** tief gekränkt. **2.** *v.i.* absterben, brandig werden.

mortise ['mɔ:tis], **1.** *s.* das Zapfenloch, Stemmloch, die Nut; – ***and tenon,*** Nut und Zapfen. **2.** *v.t.* einzapfen (***into,*** in (*Acc.*)), nuten, verschwalben, verzapfen. **mortise|-chisel,** *s.* der Stemmeißel, Stechbeitel, Lochbeitel. **--joint,** *s.* die Zapfenverbindung. **--lock,** *s.* das (Ein)steckschloß.

mortmain ['mɔ:tmein], *s.* (*Law*) tote Hand; der Besitz der toten Hand, unveräußerliches Gut; ***alienation in –,*** die Veräußerung an die tote Hand.

mortuary ['mɔ:tjuəri], **1.** *adj.* Toten–, Leichen–; – ***chapel,*** die Begräbniskapelle. **2.** *s.* die Totenhalle, Leichenhalle.

mosaic [mo'zeiik], **1.** *adj.* Mosaik–. **2.** *s.* das Mosaik.

Mosaic, *adj.* (*B.*) mosaisch.

moschatel [mɔskə'tel], *s.* (*Bot.*) das Bisamkraut, Moschuskraut.

Moscow ['mɔskou], *s.* Moskau (*n.*).

Moselle [mo'zel], *s.* 1. die Mosel; 2. der Moselwein.

Moslem ['mɔzləm], **1.** *s.* der (die) Muselman(in), Muslim(e), der Moslem (die Moslime). **2.** *adj.* muselmanisch, moslem(in)isch, mohammedanisch.

mosque [mɔsk], *s.* die Moschee.

mosquito [mɔs'ki:tou], *s.* (*pl.* **-es**) der Moskito. **mosquito|-bite,** *s.* der Moskitostich. **--net,** *s.* das Moskitonetz.

moss [mɔs], *s.* (*Bot.*) das Moos; (*esp. Scots*) (Torf)-moor, der Morast; Torf. **moss|-clad, --grown,** *adj.* bemoost, moosbewachsen. **--hag,** *s.* das Moorbruch, der Torfboden. **mossiness,** *s.* die Moosbedeckung, Bemoostheit. **moss|-rose,** *s.* die Moosrose. **--troopers,** *pl.* (*Hist.*) Grenzräuber, Wegelagerer (*pl.*). **mossy,** *adj.* moosig, bemoost, moosbewachsen, Moos–.

most [moust], **1.** *sup. adj.* (*before sing. subject*) meist; größt; (*before pl. subject*) die meisten, die Mehrzahl von, fast alle; ***for the – part,*** größtenteils, meistenteils, zum größten Teil; in den meisten Fällen; ***have the – need of,*** am meisten *or* dringendsten brauchen; – ***men,*** die meisten Menschen. **2.** *adv.* meist(ens), am meisten; (*before adj. or adv.*) höchst, äußerst, überaus; (*to form sup. of adj. or adv.*) –(e)st; ***--favoured nation clause,*** die Meistbegünstigungsklausel; – ***happy,*** überaus glücklich; – ***important,*** wichtigst; – ***of all,*** am allermeisten; – ***probably,*** höchstwahrscheinlich. **3.** *s.* (*as sing.*) das Meiste, Höchste, Äußerste; (*as pl. with pl. constr.*) die meisten; ***at*** (***the***) –, höchstens, allenfalls, bestenfalls; ***make the – of,*** möglichst gut *or* aufs beste ausnutzen, den größten Nutzen ziehen aus, ins beste Licht stellen; – ***of the rest,*** fast alle übrigen; – ***of the time,*** die meiste Zeit. **mostly,** *adv.* meistens, größtenteils, meistenteils, hauptsächlich, in der Hauptsache, im wesentlichen.

mote [mout], *s.* das Stäubchen; (*B.*) der Splitter.

motel [mou'tel], *s.* das Kraftfahrerhotel, Motel.

motet [mou'tet], *s.* die Motette.

moth [mɔθ], *s.* der Nachtfalter, Spinner, die Eule; (Kleider)motte. **moth|-ball,** *s.* die Mottenkugel; ***put in –s,*** einmotten (*also fig.*). **--eaten,** *adj.* mottenzerfressen, von Motten angefressen; (*sl.*) (*fig.*) veraltert.

1**mother** ['mʌðə], **1.** *s.* die Mutter; (*Orn.*) ***Mother Carey's chicken,*** die Sturmschwalbe (*Hydrobates pelagicus*); ***Mother Superior,*** die Oberin, Äbtissin; ***a –'s heart,*** das Mutterherz; ***–s' help,*** das Kinderfräulein, die Stütze (der Hausfrau); ***–s' meeting,*** die Sitzung des Hausfrauenvereins; ***every –'s son,*** jeder(mann). **2.** *attrib. adj.* Mutter–; – ***church,*** die Mutterkirche; – ***country,*** das Mutterland, Vaterland, Heimatland; ***Mother Earth,*** Mutter Erde; – ***love,*** die Mutterliebe; – ***ship,*** das Mutterschiff; Begleitschiff; – ***tongue,*** die Muttersprache; – ***wit,*** der Mutterwitz. **3.** *v.t.* an Kindes Statt annehmen; bemuttern, wie eine Mutter sorgen für; (*fig.*) – ***it on him,*** es ihm zuschreiben.

2**mother,** *s.* (*also – **of vinegar***) die Essigmutter; – ***batch,*** die Grundmischung; – ***of salt,*** die Salzsohle.

mothercraft ['mʌðəkrɑ:ft], *s.* die Mutterkunde. **motherhood,** *s.* die Mutterschaft. **mother-in-law,** *s.* die Schwiegermutter. **motherless,** *adj.* mutterlos. **motherliness,** *s.* die Mütterlichkeit.

mother-liquor, *s.* die Mutterlauge, Endlauge.

motherly ['mʌðəli], *adj.* mütterlich.

mother|-of-pearl, *s.* die Perlmutter, das Perlmutt. **--substance,** *s.* hefiger Rückstand. **mothery,** *adj.* trübe, hefig.

mothy ['mɔθi], *adj.* vermottet, voller Motten; *see also* **moth-eaten.**

motif [mou'ti:f], *s.* das Leitmotiv, der Leitgedanke.

motile ['moutail], *adj.* bewegungsfähig, frei beweglich. **motility** [–'tiliti], *s.* die Bewegungsfähigkeit, selbständiges Bewegungsvermögen.

motion ['mouʃən], **1.** *s.* 1. die Bewegung, der Gang, Bewegungsvorgang; – ***of the hand,*** der Wink; – ***of***

the head, das Zeichen mit dem Kopf; ***alternating –,*** die Hin- und Herbewegung; ***free –,*** der Spielraum; ***idle –,*** der Leerlauf, Leergang; ***oscillatory –,*** schwingende Bewegung; ***perpetual –,*** beständige Bewegung; ***put*** or ***set in –,*** in Gang bringen, in Bewegung setzen; ***slow –,*** die Zeitlupe (*film*); ***in slow –,*** in Zeitlupe(ntempo); 2. der Antrieb, die Regung; 3. (*Parl. etc.*) der Antrag; ***bring forward*** or ***put*** or ***propose a –,*** einen Antrag stellen; ***carry a –,*** einen Antrag durchbringen; ***the – was carried,*** der Antrag ging durch *or* wurde angenommen; ***the – was lost,*** der Antrag wurde abgelehnt; ***the – was put to the meeting,*** der Antrag wurde der Versammlung zur Abstimmung vorgelegt; ***second a –,*** einen Antrag unterstützen; 4. (*Anat.*) der Stuhl(gang). **2.** *v.t.* (zu)winken (*Dat.*), anweisen, (durch einen Wink) zu verstehen geben (*Dat.*) *or* auffordern. **3.** *v.i.* winken (***with,*** mit; ***to,*** *Dat.*), zuwinken (*Dat.*).

motionless ['mouʃənlis], *adj.* bewegungslos, regungslos, unbeweglich. **motion|-picture,** *s.* der Film. **--study,** *s.* die Bewegungsstudie, Rationalisierungsstudie.

motivate ['moutiveit], *v.t.* begründen, motivieren; hervorrufen, herbeiführen, anregen, verursachen, der Beweggrund sein für. **motivation** [-'veiʃən], *s.* die Begründung, Motivierung. **motive, 1.** *s.* das Motiv, der Beweggrund, Antrieb (***for,*** zu); *see also* **motif. 2.** *adj.* Trieb-, Motiv-, bewegend, treibend; ***– nerve,*** der Bewegungsnerv, motorischer Nerv; ***– power,*** die Triebkraft, Antriebskraft, bewegende Kraft. **3.** *v.t.* (*usu. pass.*) *see* **motivate. motiveless,** *adj.* grundlos. **motivity** [-'tiviti], *s.* die Bewegungskraft, Bewegungsfähigkeit.

motley ['mɔtli], **1.** *adj.* (bunt)scheckig, bunt; (*fig.*) bunt, verschiedenartig; kunterbunt, durcheinander. **2.** *s.* buntes Gemisch, das Durcheinander.

motor ['moutə], **1.** *s.* 1. der Motor, die Kraftmaschine, Antriebsmaschine; 2. das Auto(mobil), der (Kraft)wagen. **2.** *attrib. adj.* 1. bewegend, (an)treibend, Bewegungs-, motorisch; 2. Motor-, Auto-. **3.** *v.i.* (im Auto) fahren. **4.** *v.t.* (im Auto) transportieren.

motor|-accident, *s.* der Autounfall. **--ambulance,** *s.* der Krankenwagen. **– bicycle,** (*coll.*) **-bike,** *s.* *See* **-cycle, 1. -boat,** *s.* das Motorboot. **-boating,** *s.* der Motorbootsport; (*Elec.*) das Blubbern. **-bus,** *s.* der Autobus. **motorcade** [-keid], *s.* (*esp. Am.*) die Autokolonne. **motor|car,** *s.* der Kraftwagen, das Kraftfahrzeug, Auto(mobil), (*coll.*) der Wagen. **-coach,** *s.* der Verkehrskraftwagen. **-cycle, 1.** *s.* das Motorrad, Kraftrad; (*Mil.*) Krad. **2.** *v.i.* motorradfahren. **-cyclist,** *s.* der Motorradfahrer. **--driven,** *adj.* mit Motorantrieb. **--engine,** *s.* die Kraftmaschine. **--generator,** *s.* (*Elec.*) der Generator. **--horn,** *s.* die Hupe.

motorial [mo'tɔ:riəl], *adj.* bewegend, Bewegungs-, motorisch.

motoring ['moutəriŋ], *s.* das Autofahren; Automobilwesen; der Autosport; ***school of –,*** die Fahrschule. **motorist,** *s.* der Kraftfahrer, Autofahrer. **motorization** [-rai'zeiʃən], *s.* die Motorisierung. **motorize,** *v.t.* motorisieren (*esp. Mil.*).

motor| launch, *s.* die Motorbarkasse. **– lorry,** *s.* der Lastkraftwagen, das Lastauto. **-man,** *s.* (*Elec., Railw.*) der Wagenführer. **--mechanic,** *s.* der Autoschlosser. **– oil,** *s.* das Treiböl, Motorenöl. **– pump,** *s.* die Kraftfahrspritze (*fire brigade*). **--road,** *s.* die Autobahn. **– scooter,** *s.* der Motorroller, das Mota. **– ship,** *s.* das Motorschiff. **--show,** *s.* die Auto(mobil)ausstellung. **--spirit,** *s.* das Benzin. **– torpedo-boat,** *s.* das E-Boot, Schnellboot. **– tractor,** *s.* der Schlepper, Traktor, Trecker. **– transport,** *s.* der Kraftwagentransport. **– truck,** *s.* der Elektrokarren. **– van,** *s.* der Lieferwagen. **– vehicle,** *s.* das Kraftfahrzeug. **-way,** *s.* die Autobahn.

mottle [mɔtl], *v.t.* sprenkeln, melieren, masern, marmorieren. **mottled,** *adj.* gefleckt, gesprenkelt, meliert.

motto ['mɔtou], *s.* (*pl.* **-(e)s**) der Wahlspruch, Sinnspruch, das Motto.

moujik, *see* **muzhik.**

[1]**mould** [mould], **1.** *s.* der Schimmel, Moder; Schimmelpilz; ***iron--,*** der Rostfleck, Stockfleck. **2.** *v.i.* schimm(e)lig werden, (ver)schimmeln.

[2]**mould,** *s.* die Gartenerde, lockere Erde, der Humus(boden).

[3]**mould, 1.** *s.* 1. die Form (*also fig.*), Hohlform, Gießform, Gußform; ***casting –,*** die Gußform; ***firing –,*** die Brennform; 2. die Preßform, Matrize, Kokille, Schablone, das (Form)modell, Gesenk; 3. (*Cul.*) die Puddingform; 4. der Guß, das Gußstück; 5. (*Archit.*) das *or* der Sims, die Leiste, Hohlkehle; 6. (*fig.*) das Muster, Vorbild; 7. der Charakter, Bau, die Natur, Art, Beschaffenheit, das Wesen. **2.** *v.t.* formen (*also fig.*), gießen (*candles*), kneten (*dough*); (*fig.*) bilden, gestalten, Form *or* Gestalt geben (*Dat.*) (***on,*** nach dem Muster von; ***into,*** zu). **mould-candle,** *s.* gegossene Kerze.

[1]**moulder** ['mouldə], *s.* der Former, Gießer, (*fig.*) Bildner.

[2]**moulder,** *v.i.* (*also* ***– away***) vermodern, (zu Staub) zerfallen, zerbröckeln. **mouldiness,** *s.* die Schimm(e)ligkeit; (*sl.*) Schlechtigkeit, Schäbigkeit.

moulding ['mouldiŋ], *s.* 1. das Formen, Modellieren, die Formgebung, Formung; 2. (*Archit.*) das *or* der Sims, das Gesims, der Fries, die (Zier)-leiste, Kehlung. **moulding|-board,** *s.* das Formbrett, Knetbreet. **--clay,** *s.* die Formerde. **– composition,** *s.* die Preßmasse, der Preßstoff. **--machine,** *s.* die Formmaschine; (*Carp.*) Kehl(hobel)maschine. **--plane,** *s.* der Kehlhobel. **--press,** *s.* die Formpresse. **--sand,** *s.* der Formsand. **--wax,** *s.* das Modellierwachs, Bossierwachs.

mould-loft, *s.* (*Shipb.*) der Mallboden, Schnürboden.

mouldy ['mouldi], *s.* schimm(e)lig, verschimmelt, Schimmel-; (*sl.*) fad, mies.

moult [moult], **1.** *v.i.* (sich) mausern, sich häuten. **2.** *v.t.* abstoßen, abwerfen, verlieren (*feathers*). **moulting,** *s.* das Mausern; die Mauser(ung); Häutung.

[1]**mound** [maund], *s.* 1. der Erdhügel, Erdwall, Damm; 2. (*also* ***burial –***) Grabhügel, Tumulus; 3. Haufen, Berg (*of rubbish etc.*).

[2]**mound,** *s.* (*Her.*) der Reichsapfel.

[1]**mount** [maunt], *s.* (*Poet.*) der Berg; (*without art. in geog. names*) ***Mount*** (*usu. abbr.* ***Mt.***) ***Etna,*** der Ätna; (*B.*) ***Mount of Olives,*** der Ölberg; ***Sermon on the Mount,*** die Bergpredigt.

[2]**mount, 1.** *s.* 1. der Träger, das Gestell, Gehäuse, die Fassung, (*Artil.*) Lafette; (*for pictures*) der Aufziehkarton, (*for postage stamps*) Klebefalz; (*microscope*) Objektträger; 2. das Reittier, (*esp. Mil.*) Reitpferd. **2.** *v.t.* 1. besteigen (*mountain, horse, throne, bicycle etc.*); ersteigen, hinaufgehen (*stairs etc.*); 2. mit einem Pferd versehen (*a p.*); beritten machen (*troops*); ***be -ed,*** zu Pferde sitzen; 3. stellen, setzen, errichten (***on,*** auf (*Acc.*)), aufstellen, hochsetzen (auf (*Dat.*)); ***be -ed on,*** hochsitzen auf (*Dat.*); 4. (*Mil. etc.*) in Stellung bringen (*a gun*); (*of the officer*) ***– a guard,*** Posten aufstellen; (*of sentry*) ***– guard,*** auf Wache ziehen; ***– the trenches,*** die Schützengräben beziehen; ***be -ed with,*** bestückt sein mit (*of a ship*), führen, haben (*guns*); 5. montieren, aufstellen, zusammenbauen (*machinery etc.*); 6. inszenieren, in Szene setzen (*a play*); 7. aufkleben, aufziehen (*picture etc.*), einkleben (*postage stamps*), fassen (*gems*), (*microscope*) präparieren, fixieren. **3.** *v.i.* 1. (empor)steigen; (hin)aufsteigen (***to,*** zu); aufsitzen, aufs Pferd steigen (*on horseback*); (*Mil.*) ***– !*** aufgesessen! (*coll.*) (*also* ***– on***) steigen auf (*Acc.*) (*a th.*), besteigen (*horse*); 2. (*coll.*) (*also* ***– up***), wachsen, zunehmen, sich auftürmen *or* vermehren; ***– up to,*** sich belaufen auf (*Acc.*), betragen.

mountain ['mauntin], *s.* der Berg; (*fig.*) die Masse, der Haufen; *pl.* Berge (*pl.*), das Gebirge; ***a range of -s,*** ein Gebirge; ***-s high,*** berg(e)hoch, turmhoch; ***make a – out of a molehill,*** aus einer Mücke einen Elefanten machen.

mountain| air, *s.* die Höhenluft. – **artillery,** *s.* die Gebirgsartillerie. – **ash,** *s.* (*Bot.*) die Eberesche. – **chain,** *s.* die Gebirgskette, der Höhenzug.

mountaineer [maunti'niə], **1.** *s.* der Bergsteiger, Hochtourist; Bergbewohner. **2.** *v.i.* Berge steigen, bergsteigen, Bergpartien machen. **mountaineering, 1.** *s.* das Bergsteigen. **2.** *attrib. adj.* Bergsteig–.

mountainous ['mauntinəs], *adj.* bergig, gebirgig, Gebirgs–; (*fig.*) berg(e)hoch, gewaltig, riesig.

mountain| pasture, *s.* die Alp, Alpentrift. – **railway,** *s.* die Gebirgsbahn. – **range,** *s. See* – **chain.** – **ridge,** *s.* der Gebirgskamm, das Joch. – **scenery,** *s.* die Gebirgslandschaft. – **sickness,** *s.* die Höhenkrankheit. –**side,** *s.* der Bergabhang. –**-top,** *s.* die Bergspitze, der Gipfel.

mountebank ['mauntibæŋk], *s.* der Marktschreier, Quacksalber, Kurpfuscher.

mounted ['mauntid], *adj.* 1. beritten, zu Pferde; 2. (*Artil.*) in Stellung (gebracht); 3. (*Tech.*) montiert, zusammengebaut, aufgestellt; 4. (*Phot. etc.*) aufgezogen; (*jewels*) (ein)gefaßt. **mounting,** *s.* 1. die Montage, Aufstellung, Installation, der Einbau; 2. die Befestigung, Einbettung, Aufhängung, (*of jewels*) (Ein)fassung; 3. Fassung, Garnitur, Armatur, der Rahmen, das Gestell, (*Artil.*) die Lafette.

mourn [mɔ:n], **1.** *v.t.* trauern um, betrauern (*a p.*), beklagen (*one's lot*). **2.** *v.i.* trauern (***for, over,*** um), Trauer anlegen. **mourner,** *s.* Leidtragende(r). **mournful,** *adj.* trauervoll, traurig, düster, Trauer–; klagend. **mournfulness,** *s.* die Traurigkeit, Düsterheit.

mourning ['mɔ:niŋ], **1.** *adj.* Trauer–. **2.** *s.* die Trauer(kleidung); die Trauer, das Trauern; ***be in –,*** Trauer haben; ***go into –,*** Trauer anlegen (***for,*** um); ***go out of –,*** Trauer ablegen. **mourning|-band,** *s.* der Trauerstreifen. –**-border,** *s.* der Trauerrand. –**-crape,** *s.* der Trauerflor. –**-paper,** *s.* das Briefpapier mit Trauerrand.

mouse [maus], **1.** *s.* (*pl.* **mice** [mais]) 1. die Maus; (***as***) ***quiet as a –,*** mäuschenstill; 2. (*sl.*) blaues Auge. **2.** *v.i.* mausen, Mäuse fangen. **mouse|-deer,** *s.* (*Zool.*) das Moschustier. –**-ear,** *s.* (*Bot.*) das Mausöhrlein, Habichtskraut, Hornkraut. –**-hole,** *s.* das Mauseloch. **mouser,** *s.* mäusefressendes Tier, der Mäusefänger. **mouse|-tail,** *s.* (*Bot.*) der Mäuseschwanz. –**trap,** *s.* die Mausefalle.

mousing ['mauziŋ], *s.* (*Naut.*) der Mausknoten, die Mausing, (Stag)maus; (*Weav.*) die Hemmung, Sperrvorrichtung.

moustache [mə'stɑ:ʃ], *s.* der Schnurrbart; – ***cup,*** die Barttasse.

mousy ['mausi], *adj.* 1. mauseartig; 2. mausfarbig, mausgrau; 3. mäuschenstill; (*fig.*) furchtsam, ängstlich, verzagt, schüchtern, blöde, hausbacken.

[1]**mouth** [mauθ], *s.* (*pl.* **-s** [mauðz]) 1. der Mund; (*of beasts*) das Maul, der Rachen, die Schnauze; (*Hunt.*) ***give –,*** Laut geben; ***keep one's – shut,*** den Mund halten; ***make –s*** or ***a –,*** ein schiefes Gesicht *or* Maul ziehen (***at,*** über (*Acc.*)); ***stop his –,*** ihm den Mund stopfen; ***down in the –,*** niedergeschlagen, kopfhängerisch; ***be in everybody's –,*** in aller Leute Munde sein; ***put the words in his –,*** ihm die Worte in den Mund legen; ***by word of –,*** mündlich; ***take the words out of his –,*** ihm die Worte aus dem Munde nehmen; (*of horse*) ***with a hard –,*** hartmäulig; 2. die Mündung (*of river, cannon*); Öffnung (*of bag, well etc.*); der Eingang (*of cave*); 3. die Gicht, das Loch (*of furnace*); 4. Mundstück (*of wind-instrument*).

[2]**mouth** [mauð], **1.** *v.t.* in den Mund nehmen (*food*); affektiert *or* gespreizt (aus)sprechen (*words*). **2.** *v.i.* den Mund vollnehmen; salbungsvoll *or* geschwulstig *or* affektiert reden; Gesichter schneiden. **mouthed** [–d], *adj. suff.* –mäulig; *see* **foul, open.**

mouthful ['mauθful], *s.* der Mundvoll, Bissen; (*sl.*) ***say a –,*** eine wichtige Äußerung machen. **mouth|-organ,** *s.* die Mundharmonika. –**piece,** *s.* (*Mus.*) das Mundstück; (*of phone*) der Schalltrichter, die Sprechmuschel; (*of harness*) das Gebiß; (*fig.*) das Sprachrohr, der Wortführer. –**wash,** *s.* das Mundwasser.

movable ['mu:vəbl], *adj.* beweglich, lose, verschiebbar, verstellbar; – ***property,*** *see* **movables. movableness,** *s.* die Beweglichkeit. **movables,** *pl.* Mobilien (*pl.*), bewegliche Habe.

move [mu:v], **1.** *v.t.* 1. fortbewegen, fortrücken, fortschieben, forttragen, fortziehen; 2. entfernen, fortbringen, fortschaffen; 3. in Gang bringen, in Bewegung setzen (*a th.*); – ***on,*** vorwärts treiben (*crowds*); 4. bewegen, (an)treiben, anreizen, veranlassen (*a p.*) (***to,*** zu); – ***him to anger,*** ihn erzürnen; 5. (*fig.*) rühren, ergreifen (*a p.*); ***be –d to pity,*** zu Mitleid gerührt sein; 6. erregen, anregen, aufregen, erwecken (*feelings*); 7. vorschlagen, vorbringen, (*Parl.*) beantragen, einen Antrag stellen auf (*Acc.*); – ***an amendment,*** einen Abänderungsantrag einbringen *or* stellen. **2.** *v.i.* 1. sich bewegen, sich regen, sich rühren; – ***round,*** sich umdrehen; – ***up and down,*** auf- und abgehen; 2. sich fortbewegen, (ab)marschieren, aufbrechen, abziehen, (um)ziehen (***to,*** nach); – ***about,*** umherziehen; – ***away,*** fortziehen, sich fortbewegen, sich entfernen, davongehen; – ***in,*** einziehen; – ***into new rooms,*** eine neue Wohnung beziehen; (*coll.*) – ***off,*** sich davonmachen; (*coll.*) – ***on,*** weitergehen; – ***out,*** ausziehen; 3. verkehren; – ***in good society,*** in guter Gesellschaft verkehren; 4. (*Chess etc.*) ziehen, einen Zug machen; 5. (*fig.*) fortschreiten, weitergehen (*as time*); 6. vorgehen, Schritte tun (*in a matter*); 7. (*Parl.*) – ***for,*** einen Antrag stellen auf (*Acc.*), beantragen. **3.** *s.* 1. die (Fort)bewegung, der Aufbruch, Umzug; (*sl.*) ***get a – on,*** sich rühren *or* beeilen; ***make a –,*** aufbrechen; ***on the –,*** in Bewegung; auf dem Marsch, im Abzug; 2. (*Chess etc.*) der Zug; ***whose – is it?*** wer ist am Ziehen? 3. der Schritt, die Maßnahme; ***make the first –,*** den ersten Schritt tun.

moveable, *see* **movable.**

movement ['mu:vmənt], *s.* 1. die Bewegung; ***freedom of –,*** die Freizügigkeit; (*Comm.*) ***upward – in prices,*** das Steigen der Preise; 2. die Beförderung, der Transport (*of goods, troops etc.*); 3. die (Gemüts)bewegung, (Er)regung (*of emotions*); 4. Entwicklung, das Fortschreiten, der Gang (*of events*); Fortgang (*of narrative, drama etc.*); 5. Takt, das Zeitmaß, Tempo (*of music*); der Rhythmus, rhythmische Bewegung (*of verse*); 6. (*Mus.*) der Satz; 7. das Gehwerk (*of a watch*); 8. (*fig.*) der Schwung, Fluß, die Lebendigkeit, das Leben, Feuer; 9. (*Eccl., Pol. etc.*) die (Massen)bewegung, Massenbestrebung, Richtung; 10. (*Med.*) – ***of the bowels,*** der Stuhlgang; 11. *pl.* (*fig.*) das Tun, Handeln; Schritte, Maßnahmen (*pl.*), die Tätigkeit; ***watch his –s,*** ihm auflauern.

mover ['mu:və], *s.* 1. der Anstifter, Anreger, Urheber; (*Tech.*) die Triebkraft (*also fig.*), bewegende Kraft, der Antrieb; ***prime –,*** (*Tech.*) der Antriebsmotor, Hauptantrieb; (*fig.*) Anstifter, Urheber; 2. (*Parl. etc.*) der Antragsteller; 3. (*coll., Am.*) Möbelspediteur.

movie ['mu:vi], (*Am.*) **1.** *s.* der Film. **2.** *attrib. adj.* Film–, Kino–, Lichtspiel–. **movies,** *pl.* (*Am.*) das Kino, die Kinovorstellung, Filmvorführung; das Filmwesen.

moving ['mu:viŋ], **1.** *adj.* 1. beweglich, (sich) bewegend, treibend, Trieb–; (*Elec.*) – ***coil,*** die Schwingspule, Drehspule; treibende Kraft, die Triebkraft; – ***pictures,*** *see* **movies**; – ***spirit,*** anregender Geist, der Führer; – ***staircase,*** die Rolltreppe; 2. (*fig.*) rührend; packend, eindringlich. **2.** *s.* das Umziehen; – ***day,*** der Umzugstag.

[1]**mow** [mou], *s.* die Getreidegarbe, der Heuhaufen, Schober, Feim(en), die Feime; der Getreideboden, die Banse (*in barn*).

[2]**mow,** *reg. & irr.v.t.* mähen, schneiden (*grass*), abmähen (*field*); – ***down,*** niedermähen (*usu. fig.*). **mower,** *s.* der (die) Mäher(in), Schnitter(in); die Mähmaschine. **mowing,** *s.* das Mähen, die

Mahd; --*machine*, die Mähmaschine. **mown,** *adj. See* ²**mow.**

much [mʌtʃ], **1.** *adj.* viel; – *ado about nothing*, viel Lärm um nichts; *he is too – for me*, ich bin ihm nicht gewachsen. **2.** *adv.* sehr; (*before comp.*) viel, weit; (*before sup.*) weitaus; bei weitem; fast, beinahe, ungefähr, ziemlich, annähernd; – *less*, viel weniger . . .; geschweige denn . . .; – *more likely*, viel wahrscheinlicher; – *the most likely*, bei weitem das Wahrscheinlichste; (*coll.*) *not* –, wohl kaum (*as reply*); – *obliged*, sehr verbunden; – *too* –, viel zu sehr. **(a)** (*with as*) – *as* (*if*), etwa wie *or* etwa als wenn; – *as it was*, ziemlich dasselbe; *as – as*, so viel wie; *that is as – as to say*, das heißt mit anderen Worten, das soll so viel heißen wie; *he went on as – as to say*, er fuhr fort als wenn er sagen wollte; *he said as* –, das war (ungefähr) der Sinn seiner Worte; *I thought as* –, das habe ich mir (eben) gedacht; *as – again.* noch einmal soviel. **(b)** (*with so*) (*ever*) *so – better*, sehr viel besser; *so – the better*, um so besser; *so – the better for*, um so viel besser für; *so – the best*, bei weitem das beste; *not so – as*, nicht einmal; *without so – as*, ohne auch nur; *so – for his appearance*, soweit sein Äußeres; *so – for the present*, genug für diesmal; *so – so*, und zwar so sehr. **3.** *s.* das Viel (*of*, von), Besondere(s); *not come to* –, nicht viel dabei herauskommen; *make – of*, viel Wesens machen um *or* von; *think – of*, viel halten von; *not – of a scholar*, kein großer Gelehrter; *so* or *this* or *that – is certain*, so viel ist gewiß; *too – of a good thing*, des Guten zuviel.

muchly [ˈmʌtʃli], *adv.* (*sl.*) sehr, besonders, äußerst. **muchness,** *s.* (*coll.*) die Größe, große Menge; (*coll.*) *much of a* –, praktisch dasselbe, (so) ziemlich einerlei.

mucilage [ˈmju:silidʒ], *s.* der Pflanzenschleim; Klebstoff. **mucilaginous** [–ˈlædʒinəs], *adj.* schleimig, schleimhaltig; klebrig.

muck [mʌk], **1.** *s.* der Dung, Mist (*also fig.*); (*coll.*) Kot, Unrat, Schmutz, Dreck (*also fig.*); (*sl.*) *make a – of*, verhunzen, verpfuschen, verpatzen. **2.** *v.t.* düngen, misten; (*usu.* – *up*) besudeln, beschmutzen; (*fig.*) verpfuschen. **3.** *v.i.* (*sl.*) – *about*, herumlungern. **mucker,** *s.* (*sl.*) (schwerer) Sturz, (*fig.*) der Reinfall; (*esp. Am.*) Schuft, Außenseiter; (*sl.*) *come a* –, stürzen, (*fig.*) reinfallen.

muck|-heap, *s.* der Misthaufen. **--rake,** *s.* die Mistgabel, Mistharke. **-raker,** *s.* (*fig. coll.*) der Sensationsmacher, Korruptionsaufdecker. **-worm,** *s.* der Mistkäfer. **mucky,** *adj.* (*coll.*) schmutzig, dreckig.

mucous [ˈmju:kəs], *adj.* schleimig; – *membrane*, die Schleimhaut. **mucus,** *s.* der Schleim.

mud [mʌd], *s.* der Schlamm, Schlick; Schmutz, Kot, Dreck; (*coll.*) *as clear as* –, klar wie Kloßbrühe; *drag in the* –, in den Schmutz ziehen; (*fig.*) *throw – at*, mit Schmutz bewerfen; *stick in the* –, im Schlamme steckenbleiben (*also fig.*). **mud-bath,** *s.* das Schlammbad, Moorbad. **muddiness,** *s.* die Schlammigkeit, Schmutzigkeit.

muddle [mʌdl], **1.** *v.t.* verwirren, in Verwirrung bringen, konfus machen, benebeln (*a p.*), in Unordnung bringen, durcheinanderbringen (*a th.*); (*also – up*), verwechseln, durcheinanderwerfen, durcheinanderbringen. **2.** *v.i.* – *on*, weiterwursteln; – *through*, mit mehr Glück als Verstand *or* recht und schlecht durchkommen, sich mit Mühe und Not *or* mit Ach und Krach durchbringen, sich durchwursteln. **3.** *s.* die Verwirrung, Verworrenheit; Unordnung, das Durcheinander, der Wirrwarr; (*of a p.*) *be in a* –, verwirrt *or* in Verwirrung sein; *make a – of it*, es durcheinanderbringen *or* verpfuschen *or* vermasseln. **muddle|-head,** *s.* der Wirrkopf. **--headed,** *adj.* wirr(köpfig), verworren; benebelt. **--headedness,** *s.* die Wirrköpfigkeit, Wirrheit. **muddler,** *s.* der Pfuscher, Wirrkopf.

muddy [ˈmʌdi], **1.** *adj.* schlammig, trüb (*of water*), schmutzig; (*fig.*) verschwommen, verworren, unklar, konfus (*as style*). **2.** *v.t.* trüben; beschmutzen.

mud|-flat, *s.* der Schlickboden, die Schlickstrecke; *pl.* Watten (*pl.*). **--floor,** *s.* der Lehm(fuß)boden. **-guard,** *s.* (*Motor.*) das Schutzblech, der Kotflügel. **-lark,** *s.* (*fig.*) der Schmutzfink. **--pie,** *s.* der Sandkuchen. **--slinger,** *s.* (*coll.*) der Verleumder. **--slinging,** *s.* (*coll.*) die Verleumdung. **--wall,** *s.* die Lehmwand.

¹**muff** [mʌf], **1.** *s.* (*sl.*) der Tropf, Tölpel, Stümper; *make a – of*, *see* **2.** **2.** *v.t.* verpfuschen; fallen lassen, ungeschickt schlagen (*ball*).

²**muff,** *s.* (*Tech.*) die Muffe. **muffetee** [–əˈti:], *s.* (*dial.*) der Pulswärmer.

muffin [ˈmʌfin], *s.* flacher, runder Kuchen. **muffineer** [–ˈniə], *s.* der Salzstreuer, Zuckerstreuer.

muffle [mʌfl], **1.** *v.t.* (*also – up*) umwickeln, umhüllen, einwickeln, einhüllen; (*fig.*) dämpfen (*drum etc.*), unterdrücken (*curse*). **2.** *s.* der Schalldämpfer; (*Tech.*) die Muffel; – *furnace*, der Muffelofen. **muffled,** *adj.* bewickelt, umhüllt; (*fig.*) dumpf, gedämpft. **muffler,** *s.* wollenes Halstuch, der Schal; (*Tech.*) Auspufftopf, Schalldämpfer; Dämpfer (*of a piano*).

mufti [ˈmʌfti], *s.* der Mufti, mohammedanischer Rechtsgelehrter; (*Mil.*) der Zivilanzug; *in* –, in Zivil(kleidung).

¹**mug** [mʌg], *s.* die Kanne; der Krug, Becher.

²**mug,** **1.** *s.* 1. (*sl.*) der Schnabel, das Maul; die Fresse, Fratze; 2. (*sl.*) der Tropf, Tölpel, Stümper. **2.** *v.i.* (*sl.*) ochsen, büffeln. **3.** *v.t.* 1. (*usu.* – *up*) einpauken; 2. (*sl.*) überfallen und ausrauben.

mugginess [ˈmʌginis], *s.* die Schwüle, Schwülheit; Dumpfigkeit, Muffigkeit.

muggins [ˈmʌginz], *s.* (*coll.*) der Tölpel.

muggy [ˈmʌgi], *adj.* schwül; dumpfig, muffig.

mugwort [ˈmʌgwə:t], *s.* (*Bot.*) der Beifuß.

mugwump [ˈmʌgwʌmp], *s.* (*Am., Pol.*) der Einzelgänger, Unabhängige(r), Wilde(r); (*fig.*) hohes Tier.

mujik, *see* **muzhik.**

mulatto [mjuˈlætou], **1.** *s.* (*pl.* **-es**) der Mulatte (die Mulattin). **2.** *adj.* Mulatten–.

mulberry [ˈmʌlbəri], *s.* die Maulbeere; der Maulbeerbaum.

mulch [mʌltʃ], *s.* die Mistbedeckung, Strohbedeckung, Strohmatte.

mulct [mʌlkt], **1.** *s.* die Geldstrafe. **2.** *v.t.* mit Geldstrafe belegen.

¹**mule** [mju:l], *s.* 1. das Maultier, der Maulesel; 2. (*Bot., Zool.*) Mischling, Bastard; 3. (*Tech.*) die Mulemaschine, Jennymaschine, der Schlepper, Traktor, Trecker; 4. (*fig.*) störrischer Mensch.

²**mule,** *s.* der Pantoffel, Hausschuh.

muleteer [mju:ləˈtiə], *s.* der Maultiertreiber. **mule-track,** *s.* der Saumpfad.

muliebrity [mju:liˈebriti], *s.* die Weiblichkeit, Fraulichkeit, Frauenhaftigkeit.

mulish [ˈmju:liʃ], *adj.* (*fig.*) eigensinnig, störrisch. **mulishness,** *s.* der Eigensinn, die Störrigkeit.

¹**mull** [mʌl], *s.* der (*or* das) Mull.

²**mull,** **1.** *v.t.* verpfuschen, einen Bock schießen bei. **2.** *v.i.* (*sl.*) – *over*, grübeln über (*Acc.*). **3.** *s. make a – of*, *see* **1.**

³**mull,** *v.t.* aufglühen und würzen (*wine etc.*); *-ed ale*, das Warmbier; *-ed claret*, der Glühwein.

⁴**mull,** *s.* (*Scots*) das Vorgebirge.

mullein [ˈmʌlin], *s.* (*Bot.*) das Wollkraut.

muller [ˈmʌlə], *s.* (*Art*) der Reibstein.

¹**mullet** [ˈmʌlit], *s.* (*Ichth.*) die Meerbarbe, Meeräsche.

²**mullet,** *s.* (*Her.*) das Spornrädchen.

mulligatawny [mʌligəˈtɔ:ni], *s.* gewürzte Suppe.

mulligrubs [ˈmʌligrʌbz], *s.* (*sl.*) das Bauchweh, Bauchgrimmen; üble Laune.

mullion [ˈmʌliən], *s.* der Mittelpfosten (*of a window*). **mullioned,** *adj.* mit Mittelpfosten, durch Längspfosten geteilt.

mullock [ˈmʌlək], *s.* (*dial.*) taube Gestein (*gold-mining*); der Schutt.
multangular [mʌlˈtæŋgjulə], *adj.* vielwinklig.
multeity [mʌlˈti:iti], *s.* die Vielheit.
multi- [ˈmʌlti], *pref.* viel–, mehr–, Mehrfach–.
multi|-coloured, *adj.* bunt, vielfarbig. **--engined,** *adj.* mehrmotorig.
multifarious [mʌltiˈfɛəriəs], *adj.* mannigfaltig. **multifariousness,** *s.* die Mannigfaltigkeit.
multi|form, *adj.* vielförmig, vielgestaltig. **–graph,** *s.* der Vervielfältigungsapparat. **–lateral,** *adj.* vielseitig. **–millionaire,** *s.* mehrfacher Millionär.
multiparity [mʌltiˈpæriti], *s.* die Vielgeburt. **multiparous** [–ˈtipərəs], *adj.* mehrgebärend.
multi|partite, *adj.* vielfach geteilt. **–phase,** *adj.* mehrphasig; – ***current,*** der Mehrphasenstrom.
multiple [ˈmʌltipl], **1.** *adj.* vielfach, mehrfach, mannigfaltig; (*Math., Med.*) multipel; (*Elec.*) – ***connection,*** die Vielfachschaltung; – ***demand,*** der Mehrbedarf; *--**lens camera,*** der Reihenbildapparat; (*Chem.*) – ***proportions,*** multiple Proportionen; – ***stores,*** das Zweiggeschäft, der Filialbetrieb; – ***telegraphy,*** die Mehrfachtelegraphie. **2.** *s.* das Vielfache; ***least common –,*** kleinstes gemeinsames Vielfaches.
multiplex [ˈmʌltipleks], *adj.* (*Elec. etc.*) vielfach, mehrfach, Mehrfach–.
multipliable [ˈmʌltiplaiəbl], *adj.* multiplizierbar, zu vervielfältigen(d). **multiplicand** [–pliˈkænd], *s.* der Multiplikand. **multiplication** [–pliˈkeiʃən], *s.* die Vervielfachung, Vermehrung; (*Math.*) Multiplikation; – ***sign,*** das Malzeichen, Multiplikationszeichen; – ***table,*** das Einmaleins. **multiplicity** [–ˈplisiti], *s.* die Vielfältigkeit, Vielfalt, Mannigfaltigkeit; Vielheit, Vielzahl, Menge.
multiplier [ˈmʌltiplaiə], *s.* der Vermehrer, Verstärker, Vervielfacher; (*Math.*) Multiplikator. **multiply, 1.** *v.t.* vermehren (*also Bot., Zool.*); vervielfachen, vervielfältigen; (*Math.*) multiplizieren (***by,*** mit). **2.** *v.i.* sich vermehren; zunehmen, sich verbreiten *or* ausbreiten. **multiplying,** *adj.* Vergrößerungs–, Verstärk–; (*Math.*) Multiplikations–.
multi|purpose, *adj.* Mehrzweck–. **–stage,** *adj.* Mehrstufen– (*rocket*). **–stor(e)y,** *adj.* Hochhaus–; – ***car-park,*** die Hochgarage. **–syllable,** *adj.* vielsilbig.
multitude [ˈmʌltitju:d], *s.* große Zahl, die Menge; Vielheit; Menschenmenge; ***the –,*** der große Haufen, der Pöbel. **multitudinous** [–ˈtju:dinəs], *adj.* zahlreich, mannigfach.
multi|valent [–ˈveilənt], *adj.* (*Chem.*) mehrwertig. **–valve, 1.** *adj.* (*Zool.*) vielschalig, (*Rad.*) mehrröhrig. **2.** *s.* vielschalige Muschel.
multure [ˈmʌltʃə], *s.* das Mahlgeld.
[1]**mum** [mʌm], *adj.* still (wie ein Mäuschen), lautlos; (*coll.*) ***keep –,*** den Mund halten; ***–'s the word!*** kein Wort darüber! *–!* pst! still!
[2]**mum,** *see* [2]**mummy.**
mumble [mʌmbl], **1.** *v.t., v.i.* murmeln, mummeln, nuscheln. **2.** *s.* das Gemurmel, Gemummel.
mumbo jumbo [ˈmʌmbouˈdʒʌmbou], *s.* (*coll.*) der Popanz; Hokuspokus.
mummer [ˈmʌmə], *s.* Vermummte(r), die Maske; (*obs.*) der Komödiant, Schauspieler. **mummery,** *s.* der Mummenschanz, die Pantomime, Maskerade, Verstellung.
mummification [mʌmifiˈkeiʃən], *s.* die Einbalsamierung, Mumifizierung, Mumifikation. **mummify** [ˈmʌmifai], **1.** *v.t.* mumifizieren. **2.** *v.i.* vertrocknen, verdorren (*usu. fig.*).
[1]**mummy** [ˈmʌmi], *s.* die Mumie; (*coll.*) ***beat to a –,*** windelweich *or* breiweich schlagen.
[2]**mummy,** *s.* (*coll.*) die Mutti, Mama.
mump [mʌmp], *v.i.* betteln; schwindeln; greinen. **mumpish,** *adj.* verdrießlich, grämlich, mürrisch, übelgelaunt. **mumps,** *pl.* (*sing. constr.*) (*Med.*) der Ziegenpeter; (*coll.*) ***in the –,*** übler Laune.
munch [mʌntʃ], *v.t., v.i.* geräuschvoll *or* schmatzend kauen.
mundane [ˈmʌndein], *adj.* weltlich, irdisch, Welt–.
Munich [ˈmju:nik], *s.* München (*n.*).
municipal [mju:ˈnisipl], *adj.* städtisch; Stadt–, Gemeinde–, Kommunal–; – ***election,*** die Gemeindewahl; – ***rates,*** Gemeindesteuern, Stadtabgaben (*pl.*). **municipality** [–ˈpæliti], *s.* der Stadtbezirk, die Stadt mit Selbstverwaltung; Stadtbehörde, Stadtverwaltung, Stadtobrigkeit, der Stadtrat. **municipalize** [–pəlaiz], *v.t.* verstadtlichen; die Obrigkeitsgewalt verleihen (*Dat.*).
munificence [mju:ˈnifisəns], *s.* die Freigebigkeit, Großzügigkeit. **munificent,** *adj.* freigebig, großmütig.
muniment [ˈmju:nimənt], *s.* die (Rechts)urkunde; Urkundensammlung. **muniment-room,** *s.* das Archiv.
munition [mjuˈniʃən], **1.** *s.* (*usu. pl.*) die Munition, Rüstung, das Kriegsmaterial, der Kriegsvorrat; – ***factory,*** die Rüstungsfabrik; – ***worker,*** der Munitionsarbeiter. **2.** *v.t.* mit Munition versehen.
mural [ˈmjuərəl], **1.** *adj.* Mauer–, Wand–. **2.** *s.* (*also* – ***painting***) das Wandgemälde.
murder [ˈmə:də], **1.** *s.* der Mord (***of,*** an (*Dat.*)), die Ermordung (*Gen.*); (*fig.*) Vernichtung, Verhunzung, das Totschlagen; ***commit –,*** Mord begehen; (*coll.*) ***the –'s out,*** nun kommt die Wahrheit heraus; (*coll.*) ***cry blue –,*** Zeter und Mordio schreien; – ***story,*** die Mordgeschichte. **2.** *v.t.* (er)morden; (*fig.*) verschandeln, verhunzen, entstellen; (*coll.*) radebrechen (*a language*). **murderer,** *s.* der Mörder. **murderess,** *s.* die Mörderin. **murderous,** *adj.* mörderisch, Mord–; todbringend, tödlich; blutig, blutdürstig; – ***intent,*** die Mordabsicht.
mure [mjuə], *v.t.* (*obs.*) einmauern, einpferchen; einsperren.
murex [ˈmjuəreks], *s.* (*pl.* **-es, murices** [–risi:z]) (*Zool.*) die Stachelschnecke.
muriate [ˈmjuərieit], *s.* (*Chem.*) salzsaures Salz; – ***of lead,*** das Bleihornerz; – ***of lime,*** der Chlorkalk. **muriatic** [–iˈætik], *adj.* salzsauer; – ***acid,*** die Salzsäure.
murk [mə:k], *s.* die Dunkelheit, Düsterheit; dicker Nebel. **murkiness,** *s. See* **murk**; die Nebligkeit, Dunstigkeit. **murky,** *adj.* dunkel, finster, trüb, düster; (*of fog*) undurchdringlich, dicht.
murmur [ˈmə:mə], **1.** *s.* das Murmeln, Rauschen (*of water, wind*), Gemurre, Gemurmel, Murren (*of discontent*); (*Med.*) Rasseln, Geräusch. **2.** *v.i.* murmeln, rauschen; murren (***against,*** gegen); leise *or* undeutlich sprechen, murmeln. **3.** *v.t.* murmelnd *or* undeutlich sagen. **murmurous,** *adj.* murmelnd; murrend.
murphy [ˈmə:fi], *s.* (*Irish*) die Kartoffel.
murrain [ˈmʌrin], *s.* die Viehseuche, Maul– und Klauenseuche.
murre [mə:], *s.* (*Orn.*) (*Am.*) die Lumme (*Uria*); ***Atlantic –,*** *see* **guillemot.**
muscadel [mʌskəˈdel], (*obs.*) **muscadine** [ˈmʌskədin], *s. See* **muscatel. muscat** [ˈmʌskət], *s.* die Muskatellertraube. **muscatel** [–ˈtel], *s.* 1. die Muskatellertraube; 2. der Muskatellerwein.
muscle [mʌsl], **1.** *s.* der Muskel; (*fig.*) die Muskelkraft; *pl.* (*coll.*) das Muskelfleisch, Muskeln (*pl.*); ***without moving a –,*** ohne mit der Wimper zu zucken. **2.** *v.i.* (*sl.*) – ***in,*** sich rücksichtslos eindrängen. **muscle-bound,** *adj.* mit Muskelkater.
muscoid [ˈmʌskɔid], *adj.* moosartig, Moos–. **muscology** [–ˈkɔlədʒi], *s.* die Mooskunde.
Muscovite [ˈmʌskəvait], *s.* der (die) Moskowiter(in). **Muscovy** [–vi], *s.* (*Hist.*) Rußland (*n.*).
muscular [ˈmʌskjulə], *adj.* Muskel–; muskulös, muskelstark, kräftig; – ***atrophy,*** der Muskelschwund; – ***strength,*** die Muskelkraft. **muscularity** [–ˈlæriti], *s.* die Muskelstärke, Muskelkraft, der Muskelbau. **musculature** [–lətʃə], *s.* die Muskulatur.
[1]**muse** [mju:z], *s.* die Muse.
[2]**muse, 1.** *s.* ***in a –,*** in Gedanken versunken. **2.** *v.i.* (nach)sinnen, nachdenken, grübeln (***on,*** über (*Acc.*)).

musette [mju:'zet], *s.* kleiner Dudelsack.
museum [mju:'ziəm], *s.* das Museum, die Sammlung; das Museumsgebäude, die Gemäldegalerie.
[1]**mush** [mʌʃ], *s.* 1. das Mus, der Brei; (*Am.*) Maismehlbrei; 2. (*fig. sl.*) die Gefühlsduselei; 3. (*Rad. coll.*) das (Knister)geräusch.
[2]**mush,** *v.i.* (*Am.*) durch den Schnee waten *or* stapfen; mit einem Hundeschlitten fahren.
mushroom ['mʌʃru:m], **1.** *s.* 1. der Champignon; eßbarer Pilz; ***grow like –s,*** wie Pilze aus der Erde schießen; 2. (*fig.*) der Emporkömmling. **2.** *adj.* (*fig.*) eben aufgetaucht, plötzlich entstanden *or* emporgeschossen; kurzlebig, Eintags–. **3.** *v.i.* Pilze sammeln; (*fig.*) sich (pilzartig) breitschlagen (*bullet*).
mushy ['mʌʃi], *adj.* 1. breiartig, breiig, weich; 2. (*fig. sl.*) gefühlsduselig.
music ['mju:zik], *s.* 1. die Musik, Tonkunst; Komposition, das Musikstück; Noten (*pl.*), Musikalien (*pl.*); ***have you brought any –?*** haben Sie Noten mitgebracht? ***copy –,*** Noten abschreiben; (*coll.*) ***face the –,*** die Folgen tragen, dafür geradestehen, die Suppe auslöffeln; der Gefahr ins Gesicht sehen; ***Master of the Queen's Music,*** königlicher Hofkapellmeister; ***play from –,*** vom Blatt spielen; ***set to –,*** in Musik setzen, vertonen; 2. (*fig.*) die Melodie, der Wohlklang, Wohllaut; ***his news was – to my ears,*** seine Nachricht war Musik in meinen Ohren.
musical ['mju:zikl], **1.** *adj.* musikalisch, Musik–; wohlklingend; – ***box,*** die Spieldose; – ***chairs,*** die Reise nach Jerusalem, Stuhlpolonaise; – ***comedy,*** komisches Singspiel, das Musical; – ***glasses,*** die Glasharmonika; – ***instrument,*** das Musikinstrument; – ***pitch,*** die Tonhöhe; – ***setting,*** die Vertonung. **2.** *s. See – comedy.* **musicality** [–'kæliti], *s.* der Wohlklang; die Musikalität.
music|-book, *s.* das Notenheft. **--case,** *s.* die Notenmappe. **--hall,** *s.* das Variété(theater); (*Rad.*) buntes Programm.
musician [mju'ziʃən], *s.* der Musiker; ***she is a good –,*** sie ist sehr musikalisch; sie spielt *or* singt gut. **musicianship,** *s.* musikalisches Können.
music|-master, *s.* der Musiklehrer. **--paper,** *s.* das Notenpapier. **--room,** *s.* das Musikzimmer. **--shop,** *s.* die Musikalienhandlung. **--stand,** *s.* der Notenständer, das Notenpult. **--stool,** *s.* der Klavierstuhl. **--teacher,** *s.* der (die) Musiklehrer(in).
musing ['mju:ziŋ], **1.** *adj.* nachdenklich, in Gedanken versunken, sinnend, träumerisch. **2.** *s.* das Grübeln, Nachdenken, Nachsinnen; (*oft. pl.*) die Betrachtung, Träumerei.
musk [mʌsk], *s.* 1. der Moschus, Bisam; 2. Moschusgeruch; 3. (*Bot.*) die Moschuspflanze. **musk-deer,** *s.* das Moschustier.
musket ['mʌskit], *s.* die Muskete, Flinte. **musketeer** [–'tiə], *s.* der Musketier. **musketry** [–ri], *s.* die Schießkunst; Schießübung, der Schießunterricht; – ***fire,*** das Handgewehrfeuer; – ***instructor,*** der Schießlehrer.
musk|-ox, *s.* der Moschusochse. **--rat,** *s.* die Bisamratte. **--rose,** *s.* die Moschusrose. **musky** [–i], *adj.* nach Moschus riechend.
Muslim ['mʌzlim], *see* **Moslem.**
muslin ['mʌzlin], *s.* der Musselin.
musquash ['mʌskwɔʃ], *s.* (*Zool.*) die Bisamratte, (*usu. of fur*) der Bisam.
muss [mʌs], **1.** *s.* (*Am.*) das Durcheinander, die Unordnung; das Gerümpel, der Plunder. **2.** *v.t.* (*usu.* – ***up***) vermasseln, vermurksen.
mussel [mʌsl], *s.* die (Mies)muschel.
[1]**must** [mʌst], **1.** *irr.v.aux.* müssen (*only pres. and past tenses*); (*with neg.*) dürfen (*only pres. tense*); ***I (he) –,*** ich (er) muß(te); ***I (he) – not,*** ich (er) darf nicht; ***he – have heard it,*** er muß es gehört haben (*with reference to past time*); ***if he was in the next room he – have heard it,*** wenn er im Nebenzimmer war, hätte er es hören müssen (*dependent on hypothesis*). **2.** *s.* das Muß; ***it is a –,*** es ist völlig unerläßlich *or* unbedingt erforderlich.
[2]**must,** *s.* der Most.
[3]**must,** *s.* der Moder, die Modrigkeit, Muffigkeit.
mustachio [mus'tɑ:ʃou], (*obs.*) *see* **moustache.**
mustang ['mʌstæŋ], *s.* der Mustang, halbwildes Präriepferd.
mustard ['mʌstəd], *s.* 1. der Senf (*also Bot.*), Mostrich; 2. (*sl.*) schneidiger Kerl; (*of a th.*) etwas Rassiges. **mustard|-gas,** *s.* das Gelbkreuz(gas), Yperit. **--plaster,** *s.* das Senfpflaster. **--poultice,** *s.* die Senfpackung. **--seed,** *s.* der Senfsame; (*B.*) ***grain of –,*** das Senfkorn.
muster ['mʌstə], **1.** *s.* 1. (*Mil.*) das Sammeln, Antreten, der Appell; (*fig.*) ***pass –,*** Zustimmung finden, für tauglich gelten *or* erachtet werden (***with,*** bei); 2. das Zusammenkommen, die Versammlung; 3. das Aufgebot. **2.** *v.t.* 1. (*Mil., fig.*) mustern, versammeln, zusammenrufen, antreten lassen (*troops etc.*); – ***troops into service,*** Soldaten einziehen; – ***troops out of service,*** Soldaten entlassen *or* ausmustern; 2. (*also* – ***up***) aufbringen, zusammenbringen, auftreiben, sammeln; (*fig.*) zusammennehmen, zusammenraffen (*courage etc.*). **3.** *v.i.* sich einfinden *or* (ver)sammeln, zusammenkommen, (*Mil.*) antreten. **muster-roll,** *s.* die Stammrolle.
mustiness ['mʌstinis], *s.* die Muffigkeit. **musty,** *adj.* muffig, mod(e)rig, schimm(e)lig; (*fig.*) fad(e).
mutability [mju:tə'biliti], *s.* die Veränderlichkeit; (*fig.*) Unbeständigkeit, Wankelmütigkeit; (*Biol.*) Mutationsfähigkeit. **mutable** ['mju:təbl], *adj.* veränderlich; (*fig.*) wankelmütig, unbeständig; (*Biol.*) mutationsfähig.
mutant ['mju:tənt], *s.* (*Biol.*) die Variante, der Abweicher. **mutate** [–'teit], **1.** *v.t.* verändern; (*Gram.*) umlauten. **2.** *v.i.* sich ändern; (*Gram.*) umlauten; (*Biol.*) mutieren. **mutated** [–'teitid], *adj.* (*Gram.*) umgelautet; – ***vowel,*** der Umlaut. **mutation** [–'teiʃən], *s.* 1. die (Ver)änderung, der Wechsel; die Umwandlung, Umformung (*of energy*); 2. (*Biol.*) Mutation; 3. das Mutationsprodukt; 4. (*Gram.*) der Umlaut; 5. (*Mus.*) – ***stop,*** das Obertonregister. **mutational,** *adj.* Änderungs–, Mutations–. **mutative** [–tətiv], *adj.* sich ändernd, veränderlich; (*Biol., Gram.*) mutativ.
mute [mju:t], **1.** *adj.* stumm (*also Phonet.*), sprachlos, wortlos; lautlos, schweigend, still; (*Orn.*) – ***swan,*** der Höckerschwan (*Cygnus olor*); – ***vowel,*** der Verschlußvokal. **2.** *s.* 1. Stumme(r); 2. (*Theat.*) der Statist; 3. (*Mus.*) Dämpfer, die Sordine; 4. (*Phonet.*) der Verschlußlaut. **3.** *v.t.* (*Mus.*) dämpfen. **muteness,** *s.* die Stummheit, Schweigsamkeit, Lautlosigkeit.
mutilate ['mju:tileit], *v.t.* verstümmeln; (*fig.*) verballhornen (*text*). **mutilation** [–'leiʃən], *s.* die Verstümmelung.
mutineer [mju:ti'niə], *s.* der Meuterer. **mutinous** ['mju:tinəs], *adj.* meuterisch; rebellisch, aufständisch, aufrührerisch. **mutiny** ['mju:tini], **1.** *s.* die Meuterei; Auflehnung, Rebellion, der Aufstand, Aufruhr. **2.** *v.i.* meutern.
mutism ['mju:tizm], *s.* die Stummheit.
mutt [mʌt], *s.* (*Am. sl.*) der Tölpel, Schafskopf.
mutter ['mʌtə], **1.** *v.t.* murmeln. **2.** *v.i.* murmeln; (*fig.*) murren (***at,*** über (*Acc.*); ***against,*** gegen). **muttering,** *s.* das Gemurmel; (*oft. pl.*) Gemunkel.
mutton [mʌtn], *s.* das Hammelfleisch; – ***chop,*** das Hammelrippchen, Hammelkotelett; – ***chop whiskers,*** der Kotelettenbart; (*coll.*) ***dead as –,*** mausetot; ***leg of –,*** die Hammelkeule. **muttonhead,** *s.* (*coll.*) der Schafskopf.
mutual ['mju:tʃuəl], *adj.* 1. gegenseitig, wechselseitig; – ***aid,*** gegenseitige Hilfe; (*coll.*) – ***admiration society,*** die Gesellschaft zur gegenseitigen Bewunderung; ***by – consent,*** durch gegenseitige Übereinkunft; – ***effect,*** die Wechselwirkung; – ***insurance (company),*** die Versicherung(sgesellschaft) auf Gegenseitigkeit; ***on – terms,*** zu gegenseitigem Vorteil; 2. (*coll. but incorrect*) gemeinsam; ***our – friend,*** unser gemeinsamer Freund. **mutuality** [–'æliti], *s.* die Gegenseitigkeit.
muzhik, muzjik ['mu:ʒik], *s.* der Muschik.

muzzle [mʌzl], **1.** *s.* 1. das Maul, die Schnauze; 2. die (Rohr)mündung (*of a gun*); 3. der Maulkorb (*for a dog*). **2.** *v.t.* 1. einen Maulkorb anlegen (*Dat.*); 2. (*fig.*) den Mund stopfen (*Dat.*), zum Schweigen bringen, mundtot machen, knebeln (*press etc.*). **muzzle|-loader,** *s.* der Vorderlader. **--velocity,** *s.* die Mündungsgeschwindigkeit.

muzzy ['mʌzi], *adj.* (*coll.*) duselig, beduselt, benebelt; verschwommen, unklar.

my [mai], *poss. adj.* mein(e); – ***head is aching,*** mir tut der Kopf weh; (*coll.*) ***oh –!*** du lieber Gott! du meine Güte! – ***eye!*** potztausend!

myalgia [mai'ældʒiə], *s.* der Muskelrheumatismus.

mycelium [mai'si:liəm], *s.* das Pilzgeflecht, Myzel. **mycetology** [–si'tɔlədʒi], **mycology** [–'kɔlədʒi], *s.* die Pilzkunde. **mycosis** [–'kousis], *s.* die Pilzkrankheit, Mykose.

myelitis [maiə'laitis], *s.* die Rückenmarksentzündung. **myeloid** ['maiəlɔid], *adj.* Rückenmark–.

myocarditis [maiəka:'daitis], *s.* die Herzmuskelentzündung. **myocyte** ['maiəsait], *s.* die Muskelzelle.

myology [mai'ɔlədʒi], *s.* die Muskellehre, Muskelkunde.

myoma [mai'oumə], *s.* (*pl.* **-s, -ta** [–mətə]) die Muskelgeschwulst, das Myom.

myope ['maioup], *s.* Kurzsichtige(r). **myopia** [–'oupiə], *s.* die Kurzsichtigkeit (*also fig.*). **myopic** [–'ɔpik], *adj.* kurzsichtig. **myopy,** *s. See* **myopia.**

myosis [mai'ousis], *s.* die Pupillenverengerung, Myose, Miosis.

myosotis [maiə'soutis], *s.* (*Bot.*) das Vergißmeinnicht.

myriad ['miriəd], **1.** *s.* die Myriade, Unzahl, unzählige Menge. **2.** *adj.* zahllos, unzählig.

myriapod ['miriəpɔd], *s.* der Tausendfüß(l)er.

myrmidon ['mə:midən], *s.* der Helfershelfer, Gefolgsmann, Scherge, Häscher; – ***of the law,*** der Vollstrecker der Gerechtigkeit.

myrrh [mə:], *s.* (*Bot.*) die Myrrhe, Süßdolde.

myrtle [mə:tl], *s.* (*Bot.*) die Myrte.

myself [mai'self], *pron.* 1. (*emph.*) (ich) selbst; ***I saw it –,*** ich sah es selbst *or* mit eigenen Augen; ***I – am doubtful,*** persönlich *or* was mich betrifft, bin ich skeptisch; 2. (*refl.*) mich, mir; ***I have hurt –,*** ich habe mich verletzt *or* mir weh getan.

Mysore ['maisɔ:], *s.* (*Geog.*) Maisur (*n.*).

mysterious [mis'tiəriəs], *adj.* geheimnisvoll, unerklärlich, rätselhaft, mysteriös, schleierhaft. **mysteriousness,** *s.* die Unerklärlichkeit, Rätselhaftigkeit, das Geheimnisvolle, Rätselhafte.

mystery ['mistəri], *s.* 1. das Geheimnis, Rätsel (***to,*** für); 2. der Schleier des Geheimnisses, (geheimnisvolles) Dunkel, die Rätselhaftigkeit, Unerklärlichkeit; Heimlichtuerei; 3. (*Eccl.*) das Mysterium; 4. *pl.* die Geheimlehre, Mysterien (*pl.*).

mystery|-monger, *s.* der Geheimniskrämer. **--novel,** *s.* der Detektivroman. **--play,** *s.* (*Hist.*) das Mysterienspiel. **--ship,** *s.* die U-Boot-Falle. **--trip,** *s.* die Fahrt ins Blaue.

mystic ['mistik], **1.** *adj.* mystisch, esoterisch, mysteriös, geheim, dunkel, schleierhaft. **2.** *s.* (*Eccl.*) der (die) Mystiker(in); (*fig.*) Schwärmer(in), Mystizist(in). **mystical,** *adj.* symbolisch, sinnbildlich, mystisch, intuitiv; *see also* **mystic, 1. mysticism** [–sizm], *s.* die Mystik, der Mystizismus.

mystification [mistifi'keiʃən], *s.* die Täuschung, Irreführung, Verblüffung, Fopperei, Mystifikation. **mystified** ['mistifaid], *adj.* verblüfft. **mystify** ['mistifai], *v.t.* hinters Licht führen, irreführen, täuschen, anführen, foppen, mystifizieren, (*esp. pass.*) verblüffen, verwirren, irremachen.

myth [miθ], *s.* 1. der Mythus, Mythos, die Mythe, Sage, Heldensage, Göttersage; 2. (*coll.*) das Märchen, die Fabel, Erfindung, Erdichtung. **mythical,** *adj.* 1. mythisch, sagenhaft; 2. (*fig.*) fiktiv, erfunden, erdichtet.

mythological [miθə'lɔdʒikl], *adj.* mythologisch, sagenhaft, fabelhaft. **mythologist** [–'θɔlədʒist], *s.* der Mythologe. **mythologize** [–'θɔlədʒaiz], *v.t.* mythologisieren. **mythology** [–'θɔlədʒi], *s.* die Mythologie, Götter– und Heldensagen (*pl.*). **mythop(o)eic** [–'pi:ik], **mythopoetic** [–pou'etik], *adj.* mythenbildend.

myx(o)edema [miksə'di:mə], **myxoma** [mik'soumə], *s.* die Schleimgeschwulst, das Myxödem, Myxom. **myxomatosis** [–mə'tousis], *s.* die Myxomatose. **myxomycete** [–'maisi:t], *s.* (*Bot.*) der Schleimpilz.

N

N, n [en], *s.* das N, n; (*Math.*) 6^n (***six to the nth***), sechs hoch n; (*coll.*) ***to the*** n^{th} ***degree,*** im höchsten Grade. *See Index of Abbreviations.*

nab [næb], *v.t.* (*coll.*) erwischen, schnappen.

nabob ['neibɔb], *s.* der Nabob, (*fig.*) Krösus.

nacelle [næ'sel], *s.* die Motorgondel (*of aeroplane*), Gondel (*of airship*), der Ballonkorb (*of balloon*).

nacre ['neikə], *s.* die Perlmutter, das Perlmutt. **nacr(e)ous** [–kr(i)əs], *adj.* perlmutterartig, Perlmutter–; – ***lustre,*** der Perlenglanz.

nadir ['neidiə], *s.* (*Astr.*) der Nadir, Fußpunkt; (*fig.*) tiefster Stand, der Tiefstand, Nullpunkt.

naevus ['ni:vəs], *s.* das Muttermal.

[1]**nag** [næg], *s.* kleines Pferd, (*coll.*) der Gaul, Klepper.

[2]**nag, 1.** *v.t.* keifen *or* nörgeln *or* meckern mit. **2.** *v.i.* nörgeln, meckern, quengeln (***at,*** mit). **nagging, 1.** *s.* die Nörgelei, das Meckern, Gekeife, Quengeln. **2.** *adj.* nörgelnd, nörglig, (*fig. of pain*) bohrend, nagend.

naiad ['naiæd], *s.* die Najade, Wassernymphe.

nail [neil], **1.** *s.* der Nagel (*on fingers etc., also of metal*); (*of animals also*) die Kralle, Klaue; (*Naut.*) der Spieker; ***drive a – into,*** einen Nagel einschlagen in (*Acc.*); ***a – in his coffin,*** ein Nagel zu seinem Sarg; (*coll.*) ***on the –,*** auf der Stelle, unverzüglich; ***pay on the –,*** bar zahlen; ***wire –,*** der Drahtstift; ***as hard as –s,*** stahlhart. **2.** *v.t.* nageln; (*Naut.*) verspiekern; benageln, mit Nägeln beschlagen (*boots etc.*); (*fig.*) (*coll.*) festhalten, zur Strecke bringen (*a p.*); (*fig.*) – ***a lie,*** eine Lüge festnageln; – ***down,*** zunageln (*a box etc.*); – ***him down to,*** ihn festnageln auf (*Acc.*); – ***one's eyes on,*** die Augen heften auf (*Acc.*); – ***to the cross,*** ans Kreuz schlagen, kreuzigen; (*fig.*) – ***to the spot,*** auf dem Fleck festnageln; – ***up,*** zunageln, festnageln, vernageln.

nail|-brush, *s.* die Nagelbürste. **--clippers,** *pl.* die Nagelzange. **nailer,** *s.* der Nagelschmied; (*sl.*) Prachtkerl, die Kanone. **nail|-file,** *s.* die Nagelfeile. **--head,** *s.* der Nagelkopf. **--scissors,** *pl.* die Nagelschere. **--varnish,** *s.* die Nagelpolitur.

nainsook ['neinsuk], *s.* (eine Art) Musselin (*m.*).

naissant ['neisənt], *adj.* (*Her.*) hervorkommend.

naïve [nai'i:v], (*also* **naive**), *adj.* unbefangen, naiv, ungekünstelt. **naïveté** [–tei], (*also* **naïvety** [–ti], **naivety**), *s.* die Unbefangenheit, Naivität.

naked ['neikid], *adj.* 1. nackt, unbekleidet, bloß, unbedeckt; ***with the – eye,*** mit bloßem *or* unbewaffnetem Auge; ***with – fists,*** mit bloßer Faust; (*Bot.*) ***Naked Lady,*** die Herbstzeitlose; – ***sword,*** blankes Schwert; ***strip –,*** ganz ausziehen; 2. hilflos, schutzlos, wehrlos; 3. kahl, unbeschützt, offen; 4. unverhüllt; – ***facts,*** ungeschminkte *or* nackte Tatsachen; – ***truth,*** unverblümte *or* offene *or* nackte *or* einfache *or* reine Wahrheit; 5. entblößt (*of*, von). **nakedness,** *s.* die Nacktheit, Blöße; (*fig.*) Kahlheit; Offenheit.

namable, *see* **nameable.**

namby-pamby ['næmbi'pæmbi], *adj.* (*coll.*) sentimental, süßlich, verweichlicht, geziert.

name [neim], **1.** *s.* 1. der Name, die Benennung, Bezeichnung, der Titel; ***by* –,** mit Namen, namens; namentlich, dem Namen nach; ***call by* –,** beim *or* mit Namen rufen; ***call him* –*s*,** ihn beschimpfen; ***Christian* –,** der Taufname, Vorname; ***family* –,** der Familienname; ***give one's* –,** seinen Namen nennen; ***give it a* –!** heraus damit! ***not have a penny to one's* –,** nicht einen Groschen haben; ***in the* – *of*,** im Namen von, um . . . (*Gen.*) willen; ***in* – *only*,** nur dem Namen nach; ***in one's own* –,** in eigenem Namen; ***issue a ticket in the* – *of John*,** eine Karte auf den Namen John ausstellen; ***know by* –,** (nur) dem Namen nach kennen; ***mention by* –,** mit Namen nennen, namentlich erwähnen; ***don't mention* –*s*!** werden Sie nicht persönlich! ***put one's* – *down for*,** sich bewerben um; sich vormerken lassen für (*library book etc.*); ***reduce to a* –,** auf einen bloßen Namen bringen; ***send in one's* –,** sich (an)melden; ***under*** or ***by the* – *of Smith*,** unter dem Namen Smith; ***what is your* –?** wie heißen Sie? ***what's in a* –?** was bedeutet schon ein Name? 2. guter Name, der Ruhm, Ruf, die Berühmtheit; berühmte Person; ***give a dog a bad* –** (***and hang him***), ihn ein für allemal abtun; ***he has a bad* –,** er hat einen schlechten Ruf; ***have a* – *for being* . . .,** (*with noun*) im Rufe . . . (*Gen.*) stehen, (*with adj.*) im Rufe stehen, . . . zu sein; verschrien sein als . . .; ***make a* – *for o.s.*, *make one's* –,** sich (*Dat.*) einen Namen machen; 3. die Sippe, Familie, Linie, das Geschlecht. **2.** *v.t.* 1. nennen (*a p.*), benennen (*a th.*) (***after***, nach); anführen, erwähnen (*a th.*); mit Namen nennen, namhaft machen (*a p.*); 2. ernennen, bestimmen (*to*, *for*, zu); 3. festsetzen, bestimmen, angeben (*a date*); 4. (*Parl.*) zur Ordnung rufen, von der Sitzung ausschließen (*a deputy*).

nameable ['neiməbl], *adj.* (be)nennbar. **namebrand,** *s.* der Markenartikel. **named,** *adj.* genannt, namens; erwähnt. **name-day,** *s.* der Namenstag; (*Comm.*) Skontrierungstag, Skontrotag. **nameless,** *adj.* 1. namenlos, anonym; 2. unbekannt, nicht berühmt, unerwähnt; 3. unaussprechlich, unsäglich, unbeschreiblich. **namelessness,** *s.* die Namenlosigkeit, Anonymität. **namely,** *adv.* nämlich. **name|-part,** *s.* die Titelrolle. **–plate,** *s.* das Türschild; das Firmenschild. **–sake,** *s.* der Namensvetter. **naming,** *s.* die Namengebung.

nancy(-boy) ['nænsi–], *s.* 1. (*coll.*) Homosexuelle(r); 2. der Weichling.

nanism ['neinizm], *s.* der Zwergwuchs, Nanismus.

nankeen [næŋ'ki:n], *s.* der Nanking(stoff); *pl.* Nankinghosen (*pl.*).

nanny ['næni], *s.* (*coll.*) das Kindermädchen, die Kinderpflegerin. **nanny-goat,** *s.* (*coll.*) die Ziege, Geiß.

[1]**nap** [næp], **1.** *s.* das Schläfchen, (*coll.*) Nickerchen; ***take a* –,** ein Schläfchen halten, ein Nickerchen machen, sich aufs Ohr legen. **2.** *v.i.* schlummern, einnicken; ***catch him napping*,** ihn überraschen *or* überrumpeln.

[2]**nap, 1.** *s.* die Noppe, Pole. **2.** *v.t.* noppen.

[3]**nap,** *s.* (*Cards*) Napoleon; (*horse-racing*) (*also* – ***selection***) die Voraussage, Ausrechnung; (*Cards*) ***go* –,** Stiche für alle Karten ansagen; (*fig.*) alles aufs Spiel *or* auf eine Karte setzen (***on***, für); (*fig.*) – ***hand*,** gute Gewinnchancen.

napalm ['neipɑ:m], *s.* das Napalm; – ***bomb*,** die Napalmbombe.

nape [neip], *s.* (*usu.* – ***of the neck***) der Nacken, das Genick.

napery ['neipəri], *s.* (*Scots*) das Tischzeug, Leinenzeug, Weißzeug.

naphtha ['næfθə], *s.* das Erdöl, Steinöl, Leuchtöl. **naphthalene, naphthalin(e)** [–lin], *s.* das Naphthalin.

napkin ['næpkin], *s.* 1. (*also* ***table*–**) das Mundtuch, die Serviette; 2. Windel (*for baby*); 3. (*Am.*) Monatsbinde (*for women*). **napkin-ring,** *s.* der Serviettenring.

napless ['næplis], *adj.* ungenoppt, glatt; fadenscheinig.

napped [næpt], *adj.* rauh, haarig, filzig (*fabric*).

nappy ['næpi], (*coll.*) *s.* die Windel.

narcissism ['nɑ:sisizm], *s.* der Narzißmus, Autoerotismus, krankhafte Selbstbewunderung.

narcissus [nɑ:'sisəs], *s.* (*Bot.*) die Narzisse.

narcosis [nɑ:'kousis], *s.* die Narkose. **narcotic** [–'kɔtik], **1.** *adj.* einschläfernd, betäubend, narkotisch. **2.** *s.* 1. das Betäubungsmittel, Einschläferungsmittel, Narkotikum, Rauschgift; 2. (*a p.*) Rauschgiftsüchtige(r). **narcotism** ['nɑ:kətizm], *s.* narkotischer Zustand. **narcotize** ['nɑ:kətaiz], *v.t.* narkotisieren, betäuben.

nard [nɑ:d], *s.* (*Bot.*) die Narde; Nardensalbe.

nargileh ['nɑ:gilə], *s.* die Nargileh, Wasserpfeife.

[1]**nark** [nɑ:k], *s.* (*sl.*) der Spitzel.

[2]**nark, 1.** *s.* (*sl.*) der Meckerer, Spielverderber. **2.** *v.t.*, *v.i.* (ver)ärgern.

narrate [nə'reit], *v.t.* erzählen. **narration** [–'reiʃən], *s.* die Erzählung; das Erzählen. **narrative** ['nærətiv], **1.** *adj.* erzählend, Erzählungs–. **2.** *s.* die Erzählung, Geschichte; Schilderung, Darstellung, der Bericht. **narrator,** *s.* der Erzähler.

narrow ['nærou], **1.** *adj.* 1. eng, schmal; ***bring into a* – *compass*,** kurz zusammenfassen; – ***gauge*,** die Schmalspur; ***within* – *limits*,** in engen Grenzen; – ***pass*,** der Hohlweg, Engpaß; – ***seas*, *see* 4,** 2; 2. (*fig.*) beschränkt, eingeschränkt; ***in* – *circumstances*,** in beschränkten Verhältnissen; 3. knapp; ***have a* – *escape*** or (*coll.*) ***squeak*,** mit knapper Not entkommen; – ***finish*,** knappe Entscheidung; – ***majority*,** knappe Mehrheit; 4. (*of a p. or opinions*) engherzig, engstirnig, borniert, kleinlich. **2.** *v.t.* 1. verenge(r)n, schmäler *or* enger machen; 2. beschränken, einschränken; 3. einengen, beengen; 4. (*knitting*) abnehmen (*stitches*). **3.** *v.i.* 1. sich verengen, schmäler *or* enger werden; 2. (*knitting*) (Maschen) abnehmen. **4.** *s.* 1. der Engpaß; 2. (*usu. pl.*) die Meerenge.

narrow-gauge, *adj.* schmalspurig. **narrowly,** *adv.* nur eben, mit Mühe *or* knapper Not. **narrow|-minded,** *adj.* engherzig, engstirnig. **–-mindedness,** *s.* die Engherzigkeit, Borniertheit. **narrowness,** *s.* 1. die Enge, Schmalheit; 2. Beschränktheit, Engherzigkeit.

narwhal ['nɑ:wəl], *s.* der Narwal.

nasal [neizl], **1.** *adj.* Nasen–, (*Phonet.*) Nasal–; näselnd (*sound*); – ***bone*,** das Nasenbein; – ***twang*,** das Näseln. **2.** *s.* der Nasallaut. **nasality** [–'zæliti], *s.* die Nasalität. **nasalization** [–ai'zeiʃən], *s.* die Nasalierung, nasale Aussprache. **nasalize, 1.** *v.i.* durch die Nase sprechen, näseln; (*Phonet.*) nasalieren. **2.** *v.t.* nasalieren. **nasally,** *adv.* durch die Nase, als Nasallaut.

nascent ['neisənt], *adj.* entstehend, wachsend, werdend; (*Chem.*) freiwerdend, naszierend; – ***state*,** der Entstehungszustand.

nastiness ['nɑ:stinis], *s.* die Schmutzigkeit; Unflätigkeit, Schlüpfrigkeit; Ekelhaftigkeit, Ekligkeit, Widerlichkeit; (*coll.*) Gemeinheit, Gehässigkeit, Bosheit.

nasturtium [nə'stə:ʃəm], *s.* die Kapuzinerkresse.

nasty ['nɑ:sti], *adj.* 1. unangenehm, abstoßend, garstig; widerlich, eklig, ekelhaft; schmutzig, schlüpfrig, unflätig; 2. böse, schlimm, ernst, schwer (*as accident*); 3. gemein, niederträchtig, boshaft, hämisch, gehässig (*to*, gegen); (*coll.*) – ***one*,** treffende *or* böse Bemerkung; (*sl.*) – ***piece of work*,** übler Kunde (*of p.*).

natal [neitl], *adj.* Geburts–; – ***day*,** der Geburtstag. **natality** [nə'tæliti], *s.* die Geburtenziffer.

natant ['neitənt], *adj.* schwimmend. **natation** [nə'teiʃən], *s.* das Schwimmen. **natatorial** [–'tɔ:riəl], **natatory** [–təri], *adj.* Schwimm–.

nation ['neiʃən], *s.* die Nation, das Volk; ***League of***

Nations, der Völkerbund; – *state,* der Nationalstaat; *United Nations,* Vereinte Nationen.

national ['næʃənl], **1.** *adj.* national, National–, Volks–, Landes–; öffentlich, staatlich, Staats–; völkisch, vaterländisch; – *anthem,* die Nationalhymne; – *assembly,* die Nationalversammlung; – *character,* der Volkscharakter; – *characteristics,* völkische Eigenart; – *costume,* die Landestracht; – *debt,* die Staatsschuld; – *flag,* die Nationalflagge; *National Health Service,* staatlicher Gesundheitsdienst; – *income,* das Volkseinkommen; – *insurance,* die Sozialversicherung; – *mourning,* die Volkstrauer; – *park,* das Naturschutzgebiet, der Nationalpark; – *product,* das Sozialprodukt; – *service,* der Militärdienst, Wehrdienst; *National Socialism,* der Nationalsozialismus; (*Footb.*) – *team,* die Nationalelf; – *trust,* der Ausschuß für Naturschutzgebiete. **2.** *s.* Staatsangehörige(r); *pl.* Landsleute.

nationalism ['næʃənəlizm], *s.* der Nationalismus; das Nationalbewußtsein, Nationalgefühl. **nationalist, 1.** *s.* der Nationalist. **2.** *or* **nationalistic** [–'listik], *adj.* nationalistisch, nationalbewußt. **nationality** [–'næliti], *s.* 1. die Staatsangehörigkeit, Staatszugehörigkeit, Nationalität; 2. der Nationalcharakter, nationale Eigenart; 3. der Patriotismus, das Nationalgefühl, Nationalbewußtsein; 4. nationale Einheit *or* Unabhängigkeit. **nationalization** [–ai'zeiʃən], *s.* die Nationalisierung, Verstaatlichung. **nationalize,** *v.t.* verstaatlichen, nationalisieren. **nationally,** *adv.* in nationaler Hinsicht.

nationhood ['neiʃənhud], *s.* nationale Einheit *or* Unabhängigkeit. **nation-wide,** *adj.* allgemein.

native ['neitiv], **1.** *adj.* 1. Landes–, inländisch, (ein)heimisch; – *rock,* gewachsener Fels; 2. eingeboren, Eingeborenen–; – *quarter,* das Eingeborenenviertel; (*coll.*) *go* –, verwildern; 3. Geburts–, heimatlich, Heimat–, Vater–, Mutter–; – *country,* das Vaterland; – *language,* die Muttersprache; – *place,* der Geburtsort; – *town,* die Heimatstadt, Vaterstadt; 4. (*fig.*) natürlich, angeboren (*to, Dat.*), ursprünglich, naturhaft, urwüchsig; 5. gediegen (*as metals*). **2.** *s.* 1. Eingeborene(r); 2. Einheimische(r), das Landeskind; *a – of Hanover,* geborener Hannoveraner; 3. (*Bot.*) einheimische Pflanze; (*Zool.*) einheimisches Tier; 4. künstlich gezüchtete Auster.

nativity [nə'tiviti], *s.* 1. die Geburt; (*Eccl.*) Geburt Christi; – *play,* das Christfestspiel, Krippenspiel; 2. (*Astrol.*) die Nativität.

natron ['neitrən], *s.* kohlensaures Natron.

natter ['nætə], **1.** *v.i.* (*sl.*) schwatzen, plaudern. **2.** *s.* (*sl.*) das Gerede, der Schwatz; *have a* –, einen Schwatz halten (*about,* über (*Acc.*)).

natterjack ['nætədʒæk], *s.* (*Zool.*) die Kreuzkröte.

natty ['næti], *adj.* (*coll.*) nett, schmuck, zierlich.

natural ['nætʃərəl], **1.** *adj.* 1. natürlich, Natur–; naturgemäß, naturbedingt; physisch, real, normal, üblich, selbstverständlich; – *colour,* die Naturfarbe, Eigenfarbe; *come* –, ganz selbstverständlich sein (*to, Dat.*); *die a – death,* eines natürlichen Todes sterben; – *forces,* Naturkräfte (*pl.*); – *gas,* das Erdgas; – *history,* die Naturgeschichte; – *law,* das Naturgesetz; (*esp. Scots*) – *philosopher,* der Naturwissenschaftler, Physiker; – *philosophy,* die Naturphilosophie, Naturwissenschaft, Physik; – *religion,* die Naturreligion; – *resources,* Naturschätze (*pl.*); – *science,* die Naturwissenschaft; – *selection,* natürliche Zuchtwahl; 2. angeboren, eigen (*to, Dat.*); – *disposition,* das Naturell, die Charaktereigentümlichkeit; – *frequency,* die Eigenfrequenz; – *oscillation,* die Grundschwingung, Eigenschwingung; 3. (*fig.*) natürlich, ungekünstelt, ungezwungen, naturhaft, urwüchsig; 4. unehelich, außerehelich (*of children*); 5. (*Mus.*) ohne Vorzeichen, – *key,* die C-Dur-Tonart. **2.** *s.* 1. Blödsinnige(r), Schwachsinnige(r), der Idiot; 2. (*coll.*) Naturbursche, von Natur (aus) befähigte P. *or* geeignete S., sofortiger Erfolg (*p. or th.*); 3. (*Mus.*) weiße Taste (*piano*), der Ton ohne Vorzeichen; das Auflösungszeichen.

naturalism ['nætʃərəlizm], *s.* 1. (*Art*) der Naturalismus; 2. die Naturhaftigkeit. **naturalist,** *s.* 1. der Naturforscher, Naturaliensammler; 2. Tierhändler; 3. Tierausstopfer, Tierpräparator; 4. (*Art, Phil.*) Naturalist. **naturalistic** [–'listik], *adj.* (*Art, Phil.*) naturalistisch. **naturalization** [–ai'zeiʃən], *s.* die Naturalisierung, Einbürgerung. **naturalize,** *v.t.* 1. naturalisieren, einbürgern (*a p.*); (*Bot., Zool.*) akklimatisieren, heimisch machen; *become –d,* sich naturalisieren lassen (*of p.*); (*Bot. etc.*) sich akklimatisieren, heimisch werden; 2. (*fig.*) einführen, verbreiten. **naturally,** *adv.* natürlich; von Natur (aus), naturgemäß, instinktmäßig; auf natürlichem Wege; (*fig.*) ohne Schwierigkeit, von selbst, natürlich(erweise), selbstverständlich. **naturalness,** *s.* die Natürlichkeit, Naturhaftigkeit, Ursprünglichkeit, Urwüchsigkeit; (*fig.*) Natürlichkeit, Ungekünsteltheit, Ungezwungenheit, Selbstverständlichkeit.

nature ['neitʃə], *s.* 1. (*without art.*) die Natur (*also fig. and personified as fem.*); *all* –, die ganze Natur; (*Art*) *from* –, nach der Natur; *beauties of* –, die Schönheit der Natur(erscheinungen); *law of* –, das Naturgesetz; *in a state of* –, im Naturzustand, (*coll., hum.*) nackt; *pay one's debt to* –, der Natur seinen Tribut zahlen; *return to* –, die Rückkehr zur Natur; 2. (*oft. with indef. art. or poss.*) die (Eigen)art, Natur(anlage), Charakteranlage, Veranlagung, der Charakter, das Wesen, Naturell; *by* –, von Natur; *good* –, die Gutherzigkeit, Gutmütigkeit; *human* –, menschliche Natur; *in his* –, seiner Natur nach; *be second – with him,* ihm zur zweiten Natur geworden sein; 3. (*with def. art.*) die Art, Sorte, Form, Beschaffenheit; *in the – of,* in Form *or* nach Art (*Gen.*), gleichsam als; *in the – of the case* or *of things,* wie die Umstände nun einmal liegen, nach Lage der Dinge; *of this* –, dieser Art.

natured ['neitʃəd], *adj. suff.* geartet, –artig; *good-–,* gutmütig. **nature|-lover,** *s.* der Naturliebhaber. **–-myth,** *s.* der Naturmythus. **–-printing,** *s.* der Naturselbstdruck. **–-study,** *s.* die Naturkunde. **–-worship,** *s.* die Naturanbetung.

naught [nɔ:t], *pred. adj., s.* (*Poet.*) nichts; *bring to* –, zum Scheitern bringen; *come to* – nichts daraus werden; *set at* –, sich hinwegsetzen über (*Acc.*), außer acht lassen, für nichts achten, in den Wind schlagen; *see also* **nought.**

naughtiness ['nɔ:tinis], *s.* die Ungezogenheit, Unartigkeit. **naughty,** *adj.* unartig, ungezogen.

nausea ['nɔ:siə], *s.* 1. der Brechreiz, die Übelkeit; 2. Seekrankheit; 3. (*fig.*) der Ekel. **nauseate** [–ieit], **1.** *v.i.* Ekel empfinden, sich ekeln (*at,* vor (*Dat.*)). **2.** *v.t.* Übelkeit erregen (*Dat.*), anekeln, mit Ekel erfüllen (*a p.*); (*rare*) mit Ekel zurückweisen (*food etc.*); *be –d,* sich ekeln, Ekel empfinden (*at,* vor (*Dat.*)). **nauseating, nauseous,** *adj.* ekelerregend, ekelhaft, eklig, widerlich. **nauseousness,** *s.* die Ekelhaftigkeit, Widerlichkeit.

nautical ['nɔ:tikl], *adj.* nautisch, See(fahrts)–, Schiffs–; – *almanac,* nautisches Jahrbuch; – *chart,* die Seekarte; – *day,* das Etmal; – *mile,* die Seemeile.

nautilus ['nɔ:tiləs], *s.* (*Zool.*) der Nautilus, das Schiffsboot.

naval [neivl], *adj.* (Kriegs)marine–, Flotten–; Schiffs–, See–; – *aerodrome,* der Seeflughafen; – *agreement,* das Flottenabkommen; – *air arm,* die Marineluftwaffe; – *airplane,* das Marineflugzeug; – *architect,* der Schiffsbauingenieur; – *architecture,* die Schiffsbaukunst; – *attaché,* der Marine-Attaché; – *base,* der Flottenstützpunkt; – *battle,* die Seeschlacht; – *cadet,* der Seekadett; – *college,* die Seekadettenschule; – *conference,* die Flottenkonferenz; – *disarmament,* die Flottenabrüstung; – *dockyard,* die Marinewerft; – *engagement,* see – *battle*; – *estimates,* der Marineetat; – *forces,* Marinestreitkräfte (*pl.*), die Seemacht; – *officer,* der Marineoffizier; – *port,* der Kriegshafen; – *power,* die Seemacht; – *prestige,* die Seegeltung; – *station,* der Kriegshafen; – *warfare,* der Seekrieg.

[1]**nave** [neiv], *s.* das Hauptschiff, Mittelschiff.

[2]**nave,** *s.* die (Rad)nabe.

navel [neivl], *s.* (*Anat.*) der Nabel; (*fig.*) die Mitte, das Zentrum. **navel-string,** *s.* die Nabelschnur.

navicert ['nævisə:t], *s.* der Warenpaß, Geleitschein.

navicular [nə'vikjulə], **1.** *adj.* bootförmig, nachenförmig. **2.** *s.* (*Vet.*) das Kahnbein.

navigability [nævigə'biliti], *s.* die Schiffbarkeit, (Be)fahrbarkeit (*of waterway*), Lenkbarkeit (*of aircraft*), Fahrtüchtigkeit (*of vehicle*). **navigable** ['nævigəbl], *adj.* schiffbar, (be)fahrbar; – ***balloon,*** lenkbares Luftschiff. **navigate** ['nævigeit], **1.** *v.t.* befahren (*river etc.*); durchfliegen (*the air*); steuern (*also fig.*), lenken (*ship, aircraft etc.*). **2.** *v.i.* segeln, schiffen, zu Schiff fahren; steuern, orten (*to*, nach). **navigation** [–'geiʃən], *s.* die Schiffahrt, der Schiffsverkehr; die Steuermannskunst, Schiffahrtskunde, Navigation; (*Hist.*) ***Navigation Act,*** die Navigationsakte; ***aerial –,*** die Luftfahrtskunst; ***celestial –,*** astronomische Navigation; – ***channel,*** das Fahrwasser; – ***laws,*** Schiffahrtsgesetze (*pl.*); – ***light,*** die Positionslampe, das Kennlicht; – ***officer,*** der Navigationsoffizier. **navigator** ['nævigeitə], *s.* der Seefahrer; Steuermann; (*Av.*) Navigationsoffizier, (*coll.*) Franz.

navvy ['nævi], *s.* der Erdarbeiter, Streckenarbeiter; ***steam –,*** der Löffelbagger, Schipper.

navy ['neivi], *s.* die Kriegsmarine, (Kriegs)flotte; – ***bill,*** die Flottenvorlage, Flottennovelle; – ***blue,*** marineblau; – ***list,*** die Marinerangordnung.

nawab [nə'wɑ:b], *s.* indischer Fürst.

nay [nei], **1.** *adv.* 1. (*obs.*) (*as reply*) nein; ***say (him) –,*** (ihm) die Zustimmung verweigern; 2. (*as reservation*) nein vielmehr, ja sogar. **2.** *s.* 1. (*obs.*) abschlägige Antwort; 2. (*Parl.*) die Neinstimme, das Nein.

naze [neiz], *s.* die Landspitze, das Vorgebirge.

neap [ni:p], **1.** *s.* (*also* **––tide**) die Nippflut. **2.** *v.i.* niedriger werden (*of tides*). **3.** *v.t.* (*usu. pass.*) ***be –ed,*** wegen Nippflut nicht durchkommen (*of ships*).

Neapolitan [niə'pɔlitən], **1.** *s.* der (die) Neapolitaner(in). **2.** *adj.* neapolitanisch.

near [niə], **1.** *attrib. adj.* 1. nahe(gelegen), naheliegend; ***Near East,*** Naher Osten; – ***future,*** nahe Zukunft; – ***hit,*** der Nächsttreffer; – ***miss,*** der Fehltreffer; 2. (*fig.*) nahe (verwandt); eng befreundet, vertraut; 3. genau, wortgetreu (*as a translation*); 4. (*esp. comp. and sup.*) kurz, gerade (*as the way*); ***–est way,*** nächster *or* kürzester Weg; 5. knapp; – ***escape,*** knappes Entrinnen; – ***race,*** knappes Rennen; (*coll.*) ***a – thing!*** um ein Haar! 6. knickerig, knauserig (*of a p.*); 7. link (*of vehicles and animals*); ***the – horse,*** das Sattelpferd; ***the – side,*** die Sattelseite, linke Seite (*of road, horse, vehicle etc.*); ***the – wheeler,*** das Stangensattelpferd; 8. – ***beer,*** das Dünnbier; – ***silk,*** die Halbseide. **2.** *adv.* 1. nahe, in der Nähe, dicht heran (*in place*), nahe bevorstehend (*in time*); – ***at hand,*** dicht dabei, in der nächsten Nähe (*of place*), nahe bevorstehend, vor der Tür (*of time*); – ***by,*** in der Nähe; ***draw –,*** heranrücken (*to*, an (*Acc.*)), sich nähern (*Dat.*); ***Christmas draws –,*** es geht auf Weihnachten zu; ***far and –,*** überall, weit und breit; ***sail – the wind,*** hoch *or* hart am Winde segeln; 2. (*coll.*) nahezu, beinahe, fast; ***not – so big as,*** see **nearly.** **3.** *prep.* nahe an (*Dat.*) *or* bei, in der Nähe *or* unweit (*Gen.*) *or* von; – ***Christmas,*** nahe an Weihnachten; ***come*** or ***go – (to) doing,*** beinahe *or* fast tun; ***no –er doing,*** nicht näher daran zu tun; – ***fulfilment,*** der Erfüllung nahe; ***lie – his heart,*** ihm nahegehen. **4.** *v.t.* näherkommen (*Dat.*); – (or ***be –ing) completion,*** der Vollendung entgegengehen.

near-by ['niəbai], *adj.* nahe(gelegen). **nearly** [–li], *adv.* 1. fast, beinahe, annähernd; ***not –,*** bei weitem nicht, nicht annähernd; noch lange nicht; ***for – 12 hours,*** fast 12 Stunden lang; 2. (*rare*) nahe, eng; ***it – concerns me,*** es geht mich nahe an; ***they are – related,*** sie sind nahe verwandt. **nearness,** *s.* 1. die Nähe; 2. (*fig.*) Vertrautheit, Innigkeit; 3. nahe Verwandtschaft; 4. (*coll.*) die Knickerigkeit, Knauserigkeit; 5. Genauigkeit. **near|-sighted,** *adj.* kurzsichtig. **––sightedness,** *s.* die Kurzsichtigkeit.

[1]**neat** [ni:t], *adj.* 1. reinlich; ordentlich, sauber; zierlich, niedlich, nett; 2. rein, unverdünnt (*of liquor*); 3. (*coll.*) geschickt, treffend.

[2]**neat,** *s.* das Rind, der Ochse; (*usu. collect., pl. constr.*) das Rindvieh; ***–'s-foot oil,*** das Klauenfett.

neath [ni:θ], *prep.* (*Poet.*) see **beneath.**

neatness ['ni:tnis], *s.* 1. die Nettigkeit, Ordentlichkeit, Sauberkeit; Zierlichkeit, Niedlichkeit; 2. (*coll.*) Geschicklichkeit.

neb [neb], *s.* (*Scots*) der Schnabel, die Schnauze; Spitze.

nebula ['nebjulə], *s.* (*pl.* **-lae** [-li:]) (*Astr.*) der Nebel(fleck). **nebular,** *adj.* Nebel(fleck)–, Nebular–. **nebulosity** [–'lɔsiti], *s.* 1. die Nebligkeit; 2. (*fig.*) Nebelhaftigkeit, Undeutlichkeit, Verschwommenheit. **nebulous,** *adj.* 1. wolkig, wolkenartig, neblig, (*Astr.*) Nebel–; 2. (*fig.*) undeutlich, unbestimmt, verschwommen, nebelhaft.

necessarily ['nesisərili], *adv.* notwendig(erweise), unbedingt, durchaus. **necessary, 1.** *adj.* notwendig, (durchaus) nötig, erforderlich, unentbehrlich (*to, for*, für); unumgänglich, unvermeidlich, zwangsläufig, notgedrungen, (not)gezwungen; ***it is – that I should go,*** es ist notwendig, daß ich gehe; ***it is – to go,*** man muß unbedingt gehen; ***absolutely –,*** unumgänglich notwendig; – ***evil,*** notwendiges Übel; ***if –,*** nötigenfalls. **2.** *s.* 1. das Bedürfnis, Erfordernis; *pl.* (*Law*) notwendiger Unterhalt; ***necessaries of life,*** Lebensbedürfnisse (*pl.*); (*sl.*) ***the –,*** das nötige Geld; (*coll.*) ***do the –,*** das Notwendige tun; 2. (*Comm.*) der Bedarfsartikel.

necessitarian [nəsesi'tɛəriən], **1.** *s.* der Determinist. **2.** *adj.* deterministisch.

necessitate [nə'sesiteit], *v.t.* 1. erfordern, notwendig *or* nötig machen; 2. nötigen, zwingen (*a p.*).

necessitous [nə'sesitəs], *adj.* bedürftig, arm, notleidend (*a p.*), dürftig, armselig, ärmlich.

necessity [nə'sesiti], *s.* 1. die Notwendigkeit, Unumgänglichkeit, Unvermeidlichkeit; ***of –, as a –,*** notwendig(erweise), notgedrungen; ***no – for,*** durchaus nicht nötig, daß; 2. der Zwang; ***be under the – of doing,*** sich gezwungen sehen, zu tun; 3. dringendes Bedürnis, die Not(lage), Armut, Bedürftigkeit, der Notstand; 4. die Zwangslage, Not; ***in case of –,*** im Notfall; (*Prov.*) – ***is the mother of invention,*** Not macht erfinderisch; (*Prov.*) – ***knows no law,*** Not kennt kein Gebot; ***make a virtue of –,*** aus der Not eine Tugend machen; 5. *pl.* Bedarfsartikel (*pl.*), Bedarfsgegenstände (*pl.*).

neck [nek], **1.** *s.* 1. der Hals (*also of a bottle*), Nacken; das Genick; (*Spt., fig.*) – ***and –,*** Kopf an Kopf; (*coll.*) – ***and crop,*** mit Stumpf und Stiel, ganz und gar; ***break one's –,*** sich (*Dat.*) das Genick brechen; ***break the – of a th.,*** das Schwerste an einer S. überstehen *or* hinter sich bringen *or* haben; ***crane one's –,*** sich (*Dat.*) den Hals verrenken *or* ausrecken; (*sl.*) ***get it in the –,*** eins aufs Dach *or* auf den Hut kriegen, einen Wischer *or* sein Fett kriegen; (*sl.*) ***give him a pain in the –,*** ihn anekeln; – ***or nothing,*** auf Biegen oder Brechen, auf jede Gefahr hin; (*as attrib. adj.*) blind, verzweifelt; ***risk one's –,*** sein Leben aufs Spiel setzen; ***save one's –,*** seine Haut retten; ***stick one's – out,*** Kopf und Kragen riskieren, die eigene *or* seine Haut zu Markte tragen; ***take by the –,*** beim Kragen fassen; (*sl.*) ***be out on one's –,*** 'rausgeworfen werden; ***be up to one's – in work,*** bis über die Ohren in der Arbeit stecken; ***win by a –,*** um eine *or* mit Halslänge gewinnen; 2. das Nackenstück (*of meat*); 3. die Landenge, Engpaß (*of land*); – ***of land,*** die Landzunge; 4. der Ausschnitt (*of a dress*); 5. (*Tech.*) die Verbindungsröhre; 6. (*sl.*) Schnoddrigkeit. **2.** *v.i.* (*sl.*) liebeln, flirten, schmusen, knutschen.

neck|-band, *s.* der Halsbund. **––bone,** *s.* der Halswirbel. **––cloth,** *s.* (*obs.*) das Halstuch, die Krawatte. **necked,** *adj. suff.* –halsig, –nackig. **necker-**

chief [–ətʃif], *s.* das Halstuch. **necking,** *s.* (*sl.*) die Liebelei, der Flirt, das Geschmuse, Geknutsche. **necklace** [–lis], **necklet** [–lit], *s.* das Halsband, die Halskette, der Halsschmuck. **neck|-line,** *s.* der Ausschnitt (*of dress*). **--mould(ing),** *s.* (*Archit.*) der Säulenhals. **--plate,** *s.* der Ringkragen (*of armour*). **-tie,** *s.* die Halsbinde, Krawatte, der Schlips. **-wear,** *s.* Krawatten, Kragen (*pl.*).

necrology [ne'krɔlədʒi], *s.* das Sterberegister, die Totenliste.

necromancer ['nekromænsə], *s.* der Schwarzkünstler, Zauberer, Geisterbeschwörer. **necromancy,** *s.* die Geisterbeschwörung, Schwarzkunst.

necropolis [ne'krɔpəlis], *s.* der Friedhof, Begräbnisplatz.

necrosis [ne'krousis], *s.* die Nekrose, der Brand.

nectar ['nektə], *s.* der Nektar; (*Myth.*) Göttertrank. **nectarean** [–'tεəriən], **nectareous** [–'tεəriəs], *adj.* Nektar–; (*fig.*) süß, köstlich. **nectarine** [–ri:n], *s.* die Nektarine. **nectary** [–ri], *s.* (*Bot.*) die Honigdrüse, das Honiggefäß, Nektarium.

neddy ['nedi], *s.* (*coll.*) der Esel.

née [nei], *adj.* geborene; ***Mrs. Smith, – Miller,*** Frau Smith, geb. Miller.

need [ni:d], **1.** *s.* 1. die Notwendigkeit, (dringender) Grund; ***be no – for*** . . ., nicht nötig sein, daß . . .; ***there is no –,*** es ist kein Grund vorhanden (***for,*** daß); ***have no – for,*** keinen Grund haben zu; ***have – of, be*** or ***stand in – of,*** nötig haben, brauchen, benötigen; 2. das Bedürfnis (***of, for,*** nach), der Bedarf, Mangel (an (*Dat.*)); ***feel the – for*** or ***of,*** vermissen; 3. die Not(lage), Notdurft, Armut, Bedrängnis, der Notstand, das Elend; ***in case of –, if – arise*** or ***be,*** nötigenfalls, im Notfall; ***in –,*** in Not; ***a friend in – is a friend indeed,*** Freunde erkennt man in der Not. **2.** *v.t.* 1. nötig haben, benötigen, brauchen, Bedarf haben an (*Dat.*), bedürfen (*Gen.*); 2. erfordern. **3.** *v. aux.* müssen, brauchen; ***what – I care?*** was brauche ich danach zu fragen? ***it –ed saying,*** es mußte (einmal) gesagt werden.

needful ['ni:dful], **1.** *adj.* notwendig, nötig, erforderlich (***for, to,*** für). **2.** *s.* das Nötige; (*sl.*) das nötige Geld. **neediness,** *s.* die Armut, Bedürftigkeit.

needle [ni:dl], **1.** *s.* die Nadel; (*Archit.*) der Obelisk; ***darning-–,*** die Stopfnadel; ***pine –,*** die Fichtennadel, Tannennadel; ***gramophone –,*** die Grammophonnadel; ***hypodermic –,*** die Injektionskanüle; ***knitting-–,*** die Stricknadel; ***sewing-–,*** die Nähnadel; ***– of a balance,*** das Zünglein an der Waage; ***– of the compass,*** die Magnetnadel; ***– of rock,*** die Felszinne; ***–'s eye,*** das Nadelöhr; ***as sharp as a –,*** haarscharf; (*sl.*) ***get the –,*** eine Wut kriegen; (*Theat.*) Lampenfieber bekommen; ***look for a – in a haystack,*** sich mit nutzlosem Suchen abmühen. **2.** *v.t.* 1. mit der Nadel arbeiten an (*Dat.*); durchstechen; ***– one's way through,*** sich durchschlängeln; 2. (*sl.*) reizen, ärgern, aufbringen. **3.** *v.i.* sich winden.

needle|-bath, *s.* die Dusche, Brause. **--case,** *s.* die Nadelbüchse. **--galvanometer,** *s.* das Zeigergalvanometer. **--gun,** *s.* das Zündnadelgewehr. **--maker,** *s.* der Nadler. **--point (lace),** *s.* die Nadelspitze.

needless ['ni:dlis], *adj.* unnötig, überflüssig; ***– to say,*** selbstverständlich. **needlessness,** *s.* die Unnötigkeit, Überflüssigkeit.

needle|-telegraph, *s.* der Zeigertelegraph. **--threader,** *s.* der Einfädler. **-woman,** *s.* die Näherin. **-work,** *s.* die Handarbeit, Näherei, Stickerei.

needn't [ni:dnt], (*coll.*) = ***need not.***

needs [ni:dz], *adv.* (*coll.*) (*only with* ***must***) notwendigerweise, unbedingt, ausgerechnet, durchaus, schlechterdings; ***– must when the devil drives,*** Not bricht Eisen; ***if you – must do it,*** wenn du es unbedingt tun willst.

needy ['ni:di], *adj.* arm, bedürftig, notleidend.

ne'er [nεə], (*Poet.*) *see* **never. ne'er-do-well, 1.** *s.* der Taugenichts. **2.** *adj.* nichtsnutzig.

nefarious [nə'fεəriəs], *adj.* schändlich, ruchlos, verrucht. **nefariousness,** *s.* die Ruchlosigkeit, Bosheit.

negate [ni'geit], *v.t.* 1. verneinen, leugnen; 2. negieren. **negation,** *s.* das Verneinen, die Verneinung, Leugnung, Negierung, (*Log.*) Negation; Null, das Nichts.

negative ['negətiv], **1.** *adj.* 1. verneinend, negierend, abschlägig (*as answer*); 2. (*Phot., Elec., Math., Med.*) negativ; (*Math.*) ***– sign,*** das Minuszeichen, negatives Vorzeichen; 3. ergebnislos, unfruchtbar (*as criticism*). **2.** *s.* 1. die Verneinung, (*Gram.*) das Verneinungswort; ***in the –,*** verneinend; ***answer in the –,*** verneinen; 2. verneinende Stimme, der Einspruch, das Veto; 3. (*Elec., Phot.*) Negativ. **3.** *v.t.* 1. verneinen, negieren; 2. ablehnen, verwerfen; 3. widerlegen, neutralisieren, unwirksam machen.

negatron ['negətrɔn], *s.* das Negatron.

neglect [ni'glekt], **1.** *s.* 1. die Vernachlässigung, Hintansetzung; 2. das Übergehen, Übersehen, Außerachtlassen; die Mißachtung; 3. Nachlässigkeit; Unterlassung, das Versäumnis; ***– of duty,*** die Pflichtvergessenheit; 4. Verwahrlosung. **2.** *v.t.* 1. vernachlässigen, hintanstellen, hintansetzen; 2. versäumen, verfehlen, unterlassen (*a duty etc.*); 3. übergehen, übersehen, mißachten, außer acht lassen (*precaution*). **neglected,** *adj.* verwahrlost. **neglectful,** *adj.* nachlässig, unachtsam; ***be – of,*** vernachlässigen, außer acht lassen. **neglectfulness,** *s.* die Nachlässigkeit, Unachtsamkeit.

negligé ['negliʒei], *s.* das Negligé, Hauskleid, Morgenkleid.

negligence ['neglidʒəns], *s.* 1. die Nachlässigkeit, Unachtsamkeit; 2. (*Law*) Fahrlässigkeit; ***contributory –,*** das Mitverschulden; ***gross –,*** grobe Fahrlässigkeit. **negligent,** *adj.* 1. unachtsam, nachlässig, gleichgültig (***of,*** gegen); ***be – of,*** vernachlässigen; ***– of duty,*** pflichtvergessen; 2. (*Law*) fahrlässig. **negligible,** *adj.* nicht zu beachten(d), unbedeutend, unwesentlich, nebensächlich, geringfügig.

negotiability [nigouʃiə'biliti], *s.* die Verkäuflichkeit, Umsetzbarkeit; Indossierbarkeit, Börsenfähigkeit; Handelsfähigkeit, Verwertbarkeit, Übertragbarkeit. **negotiable** [ni'gouʃiəbl], *adj.* 1. übertragbar, verkäuflich, umsetzbar, verwertbar, begebbar, börsenfähig; ***– instrument,*** begebbare Urkunde; ***not –,*** nur zur Verrechnung; 2. (*fig.*) gangbar, befahrbar (*as road*), übersteigbar, überwindbar (*as obstacle*).

negotiate [ni'gouʃieit], **1.** *v.t.* 1. zustande bringen, vermitteln, herbeiführen, abschließen (*treaty, loan etc.*); 2. verhandeln über (*Acc.*); begeben (*cheque etc.*); 3. (*fig.*) setzen über (*Acc.*), nehmen, übersteigen, überwinden (*obstacle*). **2.** *v.i.* verhandeln, unterhandeln (***with,*** mit). **negotiation** [–ʃi'eiʃən], *s.* 1. das (Ver)handeln, Aushandeln, Unterhandeln; 2. (*usu. pl.*) die Verhandlung, Unterhandlung; ***enter into –s,*** in Verhandlungen eintreten; 3. die Vermittlung; 4. Begebung (*of a bill*); (*Comm.*) ***mode of –,*** die Begebungsform; 5. (*fig.*) die Überwindung (*of obstacles*). **negotiator,** *s.* der Unterhändler, Vermittler.

Negress ['ni:gres], *s.* die Negerin. **Negro** [–rou], **1.** *s.* (*pl.* **-oes**) der Neger. **2.** *adj.* Neger–; ***– minstrels,*** die Negersänger. **Negroid** [–rɔid], *adj.* negerartig, negroid, negrid.

negus ['ni:gəs], *s.* der Glühwein.

Negus, *s.* der König von Abessinien.

neigh [nei], **1.** *v.i.* wiehern. **2.** *s.* das Wiehern.

neighbor, (*Am.*) *see* **neighbour.**

neighbour ['neibə], **1.** *s.* der (die) Nachbar(in); (*esp. B.*) Nächste(r), der Mitmensch. **2.** *adj.* Nachbar–, angrenzend, benachbart. **3.** *v.t.* (an)stoßen *or* (an)grenzen an (*Acc.*). **4.** *v.i.* grenzen (***upon,*** an (*Dat.*)). **neighbourhood** [–hud], *s.* 1. die Nachbarschaft, Nähe (*also fig.*); Gegend, Umgebung; ***in the – of,*** in der Umgebung *or* Nähe von; (*coll.*) etwa, um

(. . . herum), ungefähr; 2. Nachbarn (*pl.*). **neighbouring,** *adj.* Nachbar–, benachbart, angrenzend. **neighbourliness,** *s.* gutes nachbarliches Verhältnis, die Geselligkeit. **neighbourly,** *adj.* nachbarlich; gesellig, freundlich.

neighing ['neiiŋ], *s.* das Gewieher.

neither ['naiðə, 'ni:ðə], **1.** *adj., pron.* kein (von beiden); – *of us,* keiner von uns beiden; – *way* or – *of the ways,* keiner von den beiden Wegen; *beer or wine? –!* Bier oder Wein? keins von beiden! **2.** *adv.* – . . . *nor,* weder . . . noch; (*coll.*) (*emph. neg.*) *no* or *nor* or *not* . . . –, doch (auch) nicht. **3.** *conj.* (*after neg. clause*) ebensowenig, auch nicht, noch auch; *I cannot come, – can he,* ich kann nicht kommen, er auch nicht.

Nejd [nedʒd], *s.* (*Geog.*) das Nedschd.

nematode ['nemətoud], **nematoid,** *s.* der Fadenwurm. **nematophore** [–tofɔ:], *s.* das Nesseltier.

nemesis ['neməsis], *s.* (*fig.*) die Vergeltung.

nenuphar ['nenjufə], *s.* (*Bot.*) weiße Seerose.

neolith ['niəliθ], *s.* jungsteinzeitliches Gerät. **neolithic** [–'liθik], *adj.* jungsteinzeitlich; – *period,* das Neolithikum.

neologism [ni'ɔlədʒizm], **neology,** *s.* sprachliche Neubildung, die Sprachneuerung, neuer Ausdruck; (*Theol.*) die Neuerung, rationalistische Ansicht.

neon ['niɔn], *s.* (*Chem.*) das Neon; – *lamp* or *light,* die Neonlampe; – *sign,* die Neonreklame.

neophyte ['niəfait], *s.* Neubekehrte(r), Neugetaufte(r), der (die) Novize; (*fig.*) der Neuling, Anfänger.

neoplasm ['niəplæzm], *s.* (*Med.*) die Geschwulstbildung, das Gewächs. **neoplasticism** [–'plæstisizm], *s.* der Neoplastizismus. **Neo-Platonism** [–'pleitənizm], *s.* der Neuplatonismus.

neoteric [niə'terik], *adj.* modern, neuzeitlich. **neozoic** [–'zouik], *adj.* (*Geol.*) neozoisch.

nepenthe [nə'penθi], *s.* der Zaubertrank.

nephew ['nefju, 'nevju:], *s.* der Neffe.

nephology [ne'fɔlədʒi], *s.* die Wolkenkunde.

nephrite ['nefrait], *s.* der Nephrit, Beilstein. **nephritic** [–'fritik], *adj.* Nieren–. **nephritis** [–'fraitis], *s.* die Nierenentzündung.

nepotism ['nepətizm], *s.* der Nepotismus; die Vetternwirtschaft.

Neptune ['neptju:n], *s.* der Neptun.

nereid ['niəriid], *s.* die Nereide, Wassernymphe.

nervation [nə:'veiʃən], *s.* (*Bot., Zool.*) die Äderung, Nervatur.

nerve [nə:v], **1.** *s.* 1. der Nerv; (*Anat.*) die Nervenfaser, das Nervenbündel; (*Poet.*) die Sehne; (*coll.*) *a bundle of –s,* ein Nervenbündel; *get on his –s,* ihm auf die Nerven fallen; *strain every –,* die allergrößten Anstrengungen machen, alle Nerven *or* Sehnen anspannen; 2. (*fig.*) die Kraft, (Seelen)-stärke, der (Wage)mut; *lose one's –,* den Mut verlieren; 3. (*Bot.*) die Rippe, Ader; 4. (*coll.*) Unverfrorenheit, Unverschämtheit, Frechheit; *of all the –!* so eine Unverschämtheit! *have the –,* die Unverschämtheit haben; 5. *pl.* die Nervenschwäche, Nervosität; *fit of –s,* nervöse Erregung, der Nervenschock. **2.** *v.t.* kräftigen, stärken, ermutigen; – *o.s.,* sich aufraffen *or* zusammenraffen, Mut fassen.

nerve|-cell, *s.* die Nervenzelle. **--centre,** *s.* das Nervenzentrum (*also fig.*). **nerved,** *adj.* nervig (*also Bot.*); (*Bot.*) gerippt, –ad(e)rig. **nerveless,** *adj.* 1. kraftlos, schlapp (*also fig.*); 2. (*Bot.*) ohne Rippen *or* Adern *or* Nerven. **nerve|-racking,** *adj.* nervenaufreibend. **--strain,** *s.* die Nervenüberanstrengung.

nervine ['nə:vain], **1.** *adj.* nervenstärkend. **2.** *s.* nervenstärkendes Mittel.

nervous ['nə:vəs], *adj.* 1. nervös, erregbar, gereizt; – *excitement,* nervöse Erregtheit; 2. furchtsam, befangen, ängstlich; 3. Nerven–; – *breakdown,* der Nervenzusammenbruch; – *system,* das Nervensystem; 4. (*rare*) sehnig, markig, nervig, kräftig; gediegen, kraftvoll. **nervousness,** *s.* 1. die Nervenschwäche, Nervosität; 2. Ängstlichkeit, Befangenheit; 3. (*rare*) Nervigkeit, Stärke. **nervy,** *adj.* 1. (*coll.*) nervös, erregbar; 2. (*Am. sl.*) unverfroren, frech, dreist.

nescience ['nesiəns], *s.* das Nichtwissen, die Unwissenheit. **nescient,** *adj.* unwissend (*of,* in (*Dat.*)).

ness [nes], *s.* das Vorgebirge.

nest [nest], **1.** *s.* 1. das Nest; *build* or *make one's –,* nisten; (*fig.*) *feather one's –,* sich bereichern, sein Schäfchen ins Trockene bringen; *mare's –,* die Zeitungsente; 2. die Brut (*of young*); *take a –,* ein Nest ausnehmen; 3. (*fig.*) die Brutstätte; 4. der Satz, die Serie (*of boxes etc.*). **2.** *v.i.* 1. nisten, horsten, sich niederlassen *or* einnisten; 2. Nester ausnehmen. **3.** *v.t.* 1. (wie im Nest) legen *or* setzen *or* einpacken; 2. ineinanderlegen, ineinanderpacken.

nest-egg, *s.* 1. das Nestei; 2. (*fig.*) der Notpfennig, Spargroschen. **nester,** *s.* der Brutvogel. **nesting-box,** *s.* der Nistkasten.

nestle [nesl], **1.** *v.i.* 1. sich einnisten; 2. sich (an)-schmiegen (*against, on, close to,* an (*Acc.*)); – *down,* sich behaglich niederlassen. **2.** *v.t.* schmiegen, drücken (*one's head etc.*) (*against,* an (*Acc.*)). **nestling** ['nes(t)liŋ], *s.* der Nestling; – *feather,* die Nestfeder.

[1]**net** [net], **1.** *s.* 1. das Netz, Maschenwerk; 2. der Tüll, Musselin; 3. (*fig.*) das Netz(werk); 4. die Falle, Schlinge, der Fallstrick, das Garn. **2.** *v.t.* 1. mit Netz fangen (*fish etc.*); 2. mit einem Netze abfischen (*a river,* in einem Flusse); 3. (*Tenn.*) ins Netz schlagen (*the ball*); 4. knüpfen, in Filet arbeiten. **3.** *v.i.* Filet arbeiten.

[2]**net, 1.** *adj.* netto, Rein–; – *amount,* der Reinbetrag; – *cash,* netto Kasse, ohne Abzug gegen bar; – *cost,* der Grundpreis; – *load,* die Nutzlast; – *price,* der Nettopreis; – *proceeds* or *profit,* die Nettoeinnahme, der Nettoertrag, Reingewinn; – *weight,* das Nettogewicht, Eigengewicht; – *yield,* der Nettoertrag, Nettoerlös. **2.** *v.t.* 1. netto einbringen *or* eintragen *or* ergeben; 2. netto verdienen.

netball ['netbɔ:l], *s.* das Netzballspiel.

nether ['neðə], *adj.* nieder, unter; – *lip,* die Unterlippe; – *regions,* – *world,* die Unterwelt.

Netherlander ['neðələndə], *s.* (*rare*) der (die) Niederländer(in). **Netherlands,** *pl.* Niederlande (*pl.*).

nethermost ['neðəmoust], *adj.* niedrigst, unterst.

netting ['netiŋ], *s.* 1. das Netzstricken, die Filetarbeit; das Netz(werk), Geflecht; 2. die Netzfischerei, das Fangen mit einem Netz.

nettle [netl], **1.** *s.* die Nessel; *dead-–,* die Taubnessel; *stinging –,* die Brennessel. **2.** *v.t.* 1. mit *or* an Nesseln brennen; 2. (*usu. fig.*) ärgern, wurmen; *be –d,* geärgert sein (*at,* über (*Acc.*)). **nettle-rash,** *s.* der Nesselausschlag, das Nesselfieber.

network ['netwə:k], *s.* 1. das Geflecht, Netzwerk, Maschenwerk; 2. (*fig.*) Netz (*roads, railways etc.*), (*Rad.*) Sendernetz, die Sendergruppe.

neum(e) [nju:m], *s.* (*Mus.*) die Neume.

neural ['njuərəl], *adj.* Nerven–.

neuralgia [njuə'rældʒə], *s.* der Nervenschmerz, die Neuralgie. **neuralgic,** *adj.* neuralgisch.

neurasthenia [njuərəs'θi:niə], *s.* die Nervenschwäche, Neurasthenie. **neurasthenic, 1.** *adj.* nervenschwach. **2.** *s.* der Neurastheniker.

neuration [njuə'reiʃən], *s.* (*Zool.*) die Äderung, das Geäder; (*Anat.*) Nervensystem, die Nervenanordnung.

neuritis [njuə'raitis], *s.* die Nervenentzündung.

neurologist [njuə'rɔlədʒist], *s.* der Nervenarzt, Neurologe. **neurology,** *s.* die Nerven(krankheits)-lehre, Neurologie.

neuropath ['njuərəpæθ], *s.* Nervenleidende(r), Nervenkranke(r). **neuropathic** [–'pæθik], *adj.* nervenleidend, nervenkrank. **neuropathist** [–'rɔpəθist], *s. See* **neurologist. neuropathy** [–'rɔpəθi], *s.* das Nervenleiden.

neuropter [njuə'rɔptə], *s.* (*Ent.*) der Netzflügler.

neuropterous, *adj.* netzflügelig; – *fly, see* **neuropter.**

neurosis [njuə'rousis], *s.* (*pl.* **neuroses** [–si:z]) die Neurose, Nervenkrankheit, Nervenstörung. **neurotic** [–'rɔtik], **1.** *adj.* 1. neurotisch, nervenkrank, nervenleidend, (*coll.*) nervös; 2. Nerven–. **2.** *s.* 1. Nervenkranke(r); 2. das Nervenmittel.

neuter ['nju:tə], **1.** *adj.* 1. (*Bot., Zool.*) geschlechtslos; – ***cat,*** verschnittener Kater; 2. (*Gram.*) sächlich (*of nouns*), intransitiv (*of verbs*). **2.** *s.* 1. kastriertes Tier; 2. (*Gram.*) das Neutrum, Intransitivum.

neutral ['nju:trəl], **1.** *adj.* 1. neutral, parteilos, unparteiisch; 2. gleichgültig, unbeteiligt (*of a p.*); 3. indifferent, unausgesprochen, unbestimmt, farblos (*of a th.*); (*Elec.*) – ***conductor,*** der Nulleiter; – ***equilibrium,*** indifferentes Gleichgewicht; – ***gear,*** der Leerlauf(gang), die Ruhelage; (*Phys.*) – ***line,*** die Neutrale, Nullinie, Indifferenzzone; – ***point,*** der Nullpunkt; – ***position,*** die Nullstellung, Ruhestellung. **2.** *s.* 1. Neutrale(r), Parteilose(r), Unparteiische(r) (*of a p.*); 2. (*Pol.*) neutraler Staat; Angehörige(r) eines neutralen Staates; 3. (*Motor. coll.*) die Ruhelage. **neutralism,** *s.* der Neutralismus, die Neutralitätspolitik. **neutrality** [–'træliti], *s.* die Neutralität, Parteilosigkeit; ***armed*** –, bewaffnete Neutralität.

neutralization [nju:trəlai'zeiʃən], *s.* 1. die Neutralisierung, Ausgleichung; 2. (*Chem.*) Neutralisation; 3. (*Pol.*) Neutralitätserklärung; 4. (*Mil.*) Lahmlegung. **neutralize** ['nju:trəlaiz], *v.t.* 1. neutralisieren, ausgleichen, unwirksam machen; – ***each other,*** sich gegenseitig aufheben; 2. (*Pol.*) für neutral erklären; 3. (*Mil.*) niederkämpfen, niederhalten.

névé ['nevei], *s.* der Firn.

never ['nevə], *adv.* nie(mals), nimmer(mehr); nicht im geringsten, auf keine Weise, überhaupt *or* durchaus *or* (ganz und) gar nicht; – ***fear!*** nur nicht bange! (*coll.*) ***well, I –!*** nein, so was! – ***mind!*** macht *or* tut nichts! hat nichts zu sagen! laß gut sein! mach dir nichts draus! – ***to be forgotten,*** unvergeßlich; – ***say die!*** nur nicht ängstlich! (*coll.*) – ***so . . . as to,*** doch nicht so . . . um zu; – ***so much,*** auch noch so sehr *or* viel; – ***so much as,*** sogar nicht, (noch) nicht einmal; ***were it – so good,*** mag es auch noch so gut sein.

never|-ceasing, *adj.* unaufhörlich. **--ending,** *adj.* unaufhörlich, ohne Ende. **--failing,** *adj.* unfehlbar; nie versagend. **–more,** *adv.* nie wieder, nimmermehr. **--never,** *s.* (*sl.*) ***buy on the –,*** auf Stottern kaufen. **nevertheless** [–ðəles], *conj.* nichtsdestoweniger, dennoch, dessen ungeachtet. **never-tiring,** *adj.* unverdrossen, unermüdlich.

nevus, *see* **naevus.**

new [nju:], **1.** *adj.* (*of a th.*) neu, unbekannt (*to, Dat.*), ungewohnt (für), (*of a p.*) nicht vertraut (mit), unerfahren, ungeübt (in (*Dat.*)), neuerschienen (*book*); neuentdeckt, bisher unbekannt (*facts etc.*); unerforscht (*ground*); modern; – ***birth,*** die Wiedergeburt; – ***bread,*** frisches Brot; – ***brooms sweep clean,*** neue Besen kehren gut; – ***building,*** der Neubau; – ***generation,*** junge Generation, der Nachwuchs; – ***ground,*** das Neuland (*also fig.*); ***turn over a – leaf,*** sich bessern, ein neues Leben beginnen; ***the – learning,*** die Renaissance; – ***moon,*** der Neumond; – ***publication,*** die Neuerscheinung; ***New Style,*** Gregorianische Zeitrechnung, Neuer Stil; ***New Testament,*** Neues Testament; ***New World,*** Neue Welt; ***nothing –,*** nichts Neues.

new|-born, *adj.* neugeboren, eben geboren. **–comer,** *s.* der Ankömmling; (*fig.*) Neuling.

newel ['njuəl], *s.* die Spindel (*of winding stair*); der Treppenpfosten (*of banister*).

New England, *s.* Neuengland (*n.*). **new|-fangled,** *adj.* (*coll.*) neuerungssüchtig; (neu)modisch. **--fledged,** *adj.* flügge geworden, (*fig.*) neugebacken.

Newfoundland ['nju:fəndlənd], *s.* Neufundland (*n.*).

New Guinea, *s.* Neuguinea (*n.*).

newish ['nju:iʃ], *adj.* (*coll.*) ziemlich neu. **new-laid,** *adj.* frisch(gelegt); – ***eggs,*** frische Eier. **newly,** *adv.* jüngst, kürzlich, neulich; – ***married,*** neuvermählt; – ***rich,*** neureich; Neureiche(r); (*coll.*) --***weds,*** Neuvermählte (*pl.*). **new-mown,** *adj.* frisch gemäht. **newness,** *s.* das Neue, die Neuheit.

news [nju:z], *pl.* (*sing. constr.*) die Nachricht (***of,*** über (*Acc.*)), Neuigkeiten (*pl.*), Neue(s); (*Rad.*) der Nachrichtendienst; ***it is – to me,*** es ist mir neu; ***in the –,*** in allen Zeitungen; ***be in the –,*** von sich reden machen; ***what's the –?*** was gibt's Neues? ***a piece of –,*** eine Neuigkeit; ***no – is good –,*** keine Nachricht ist auch eine Nachricht; ***we have had –,*** wir haben erfahren *or* gehört.

news| agency, *s.* die Nachrichtenagentur. **–agent,** *s.* der Zeitungshändler. **--boy,** *s.* der Zeitungsjunge, Zeitungsausträger. – **broadcast, –cast,** *s.* die Nachrichtensendung. **–caster,** *s.* (*Rad.*) der Nachrichtensprecher. **--editor,** *s.* der Nachrichtenredakteur. **--flash,** *s.* (*coll. esp. Rad.*) die Kurznachricht. – **item,** *s.* die Zeitungsnotiz. **--letter,** *s.* das Rundschreiben, Informationsblatt. **–monger,** *s.* die Neuigkeitskrämer.

New South Wales, *s.* Neusüdwales (*n.*).

news|paper, *s.* die Zeitung; – ***advertisement,*** die Zeitungsannonce, Zeitungsanzeige, das Inserat; – ***announcement,*** die Pressenotiz; – ***cutting,*** der Zeitungsausschnitt; – ***man,*** der Journalist; Zeitungsverkäufer; – ***report,*** der Pressebericht, der Zeitungsnachricht; – ***reporter,*** der Berichterstatter; – ***wrapper,*** das Kreuzband. **–print,** *s.* das Zeitungspapier. **–reader,** *s. See* **–caster. –reel,** *s.* die Wochenschau (*film*). **–room,** *s.* das Zeitschriftenzimmer (*of library*), der Nachrichtenraum (*press, radio etc.*). – **summary,** *s.* Nachrichten in Kurzfassung. **--theatre,** *s.* das Aktualitätenkino. **–vendor,** *s.* der Zeitungsverkäufer. **–worthy,** *adj.* ***be –,*** Publikationswert haben.

newt [nju:t], *s.* (*Zool.*) der Wassermolch.

New Year, *s.* Neues Jahr; ***after the –,*** nach Neujahr; ***–'s Day,*** der Neujahrstag; ***–'s Eve,*** der Silvester; ***–'s greetings,*** der Neujahrswunsch.

New Zealand [–'zi:lənd], *s.* Neuseeland (*n.*).

next [nekst], **1.** *adj.* nächst, nächststehend, nächstfolgend; – ***best,*** zweitbest; ***be the – best th. to,*** fast so gut sein wie; ***the – day,*** am folgenden Tag, am Tage darauf; ***in the – few days,*** in den nächsten Tagen; – ***door,*** nebenan, im nächsten Haus; – ***door but one,*** zwei Häuser *or* Türen weiter; (*fig.*) – ***door to,*** fast, beinahe; ***that is – door to felony,*** das grenzt an Verbrechen; – ***in importance,*** nächstwichtigst; – ***in size,*** nächstgrößer, nächstkleiner; (***the***) – ***moment,*** im nächsten Augenblick; – ***but one,*** übernächst; – ***time,*** das nächste Mal, in Zukunft, ein andermal, künftighin; ***week after –,*** übernächste Woche; ***what –?*** was (sonst) noch? (*iron.*) sonst noch was? was denn noch alles? **2.** *prep.* zunächst *or* gleich nach; gleich neben (*Dat.*); – ***your skin,*** auf dem Leibe. **3.** *adv.* das nächste Mal, zunächst; (gleich) darauf, nächstens, demnächst; an nächster Stelle; – ***after,*** gleich nach; – ***before,*** direkt vor; – ***to,*** direkt neben, dicht bei (*place*), gleich nach (*time*); – ***to in importance, most important – to,*** nächstwichtigst nach; – ***to impossible,*** nahezu unmöglich; – ***to nothing,*** fast gar nichts; ***for – to nothing,*** fast umsonst. **4.** *s.* der *or* die *or* das Nächste; ***to be continued in our –,*** Fortsetzung folgt.

next-of-kin, *s.* nächste(r) Verwandte(r), (*collect.*) nächste Angehörige (*pl.*).

nexus ['neksəs], *s.* die Verbindung, Verknüpfung, der Zusammenhang, Nexus.

nib [nib], *s.* die (Feder)spitze; ***cocoa –s,*** Kakaokörnchen (*pl.*).

nibble [nibl], **1.** *v.t.* knabbern an (*Dat.*), abbeißen, abnagen; anbeißen (*as fish*). **2.** *v.i.* – ***at,*** nagen *or* knabbern an (*Dat.*); (*fig.*) bekritteln. **3.** *s.* 1. das Knabbern, Nagen; 2. der Happen, kleiner Bissen.

nibs [nibz], *pl.* (*sing. constr.*) (*coll.*) ***his –,*** seine Hoheit.

Nice [ni:s], *s.* (*Geog.*) Nizza (*n.*).

nice [nais], *adj.* 1. wählerisch, heikel (*about*, in (*Dat.*)); – ***point***, kitzliger *or* heikler Punkt; 2. lecker, schmackhaft, wohlschmeckend (*of food*); 3. peinlich genau, gewissenhaft, sorgfältig; 4. fein, scharf, ausgebildet; – ***discernment***, scharfes Beurteilungsvermögen; – ***distinction***, feiner Unterschied; 5. (*coll.*) nett, artig; ***not*** –, unanständig; 6. freundlich, gütig (***to***, zu *or* gegen); 7. (*coll.*) hübsch, nett, schön, niedlich, angenehm; – ***and fat***, schön *or* hübsch dick; – ***and warm***, angenehm warm; – ***mess!*** schöne Bescherung! **nicely,** *adv.* (*coll.*) fein, ausgezeichnet; ***beg –!*** Schön! (*to a dog*); ***do*** –, ausgezeichnet sein *or* passen; ***he is doing*** –, es geht ihm besser, er macht Fortschritte; ***talk – to him***, ihm gute Worte geben. **niceness,** *s.* 1. die Genauigkeit, Feinheit; 2. Verwöhntheit; 3. Niedlichkeit, Annehmlichkeit.

nicety ['naisiti], *s.* 1. die Feinheit, Schärfe; 2. peinliche Genauigkeit, Spitzfindigkeit; ***to a*** –, bis aufs Haar, aufs genaueste; 3. *pl.* Feinheiten, kleine Unterschiede (*pl.*); ***not stand upon niceties***, es nicht so genau nehmen, (*coll.*) fünf gerade sein lassen.

niche [nitʃ], *s.* die Nische; (*fig.*) passender Ort, der Platz.

Nick [nik], *s.* (*coll.*) ***Old*** –, der Deibel, Kuckuck.

nick, 1. *s.* 1. der Einschnitt, die Kerbe, Einkerbung; 2. hoher Wurf (*of dice*); 3. (*sl.*) das Polizeirevier; 4. ***in the – of time***, gerade im rechten Augenblick *or* zur rechten Zeit. **2.** *v.t.* 1. (ein)kerben; 2. (*sl.*) (er)fassen, erwischen, ertappen; 3. (*sl.*) klauen.

nickel [nikl], **1.** *s.* 1. das Nickel; 2. (*Am. coll.*) Fünfcentstück, der Nickel. **2.** *adj.* Nickel–, vernickelt. **3.** *v.t.* vernickeln. **nickel|odeon** [–ə'loudiən], *s.* (*Am. coll.*) der Musikautomat. **--plating,** *s.* die Vernickelung.

nicker ['nikə], *v.i.* (*Scots*) wiehern.

nick-nack, *see* **knick-knack.**

nickname ['nikneim], **1.** *s.* der Spitzname. **2.** *v.t.* einen Spitznamen geben (*Dat.*), mit Spitznamen bezeichnen.

nicotian [ni'kouʃiən], *adj.* Tabak(s)–. **nicotine** ['nikəti:n], *s.* das Nikotin. **nicotinism** ['nikətinizm], die Nikotinvergiftung.

nict(it)ate ['nik(ti)teit], *s.* (mit den Augenlidern) blinzeln; (*Orn.*) ***nict(it)ating membrane***, die Nickhaut, Blinzhaut.

nide [naid], *s.* die Brut (*of pheasants*).

nidificate ['nidifikeit], **nidify** ['nidifai], *v.i.* nisten.

nidus ['naidəs], *s.* das Nest, die Brutstätte; (*fig.*) der Sitz, die Lagerstätte.

niece [ni:s], *s.* die Nichte.

niello [ni'elou], *s.* der Schwarzschmelz; ***work in*** –, niellieren.

niff [nif], **1.** *s.* (*sl.*) das Gestänk. **2.** *v.i.* (*sl.*) stinken.

nifty ['nifti], *adj.* (*sl.*) schmuck, fesch, pfundig.

niggard ['nigəd], **1.** *s.* der Geizhals, Knicker, Knauser, Filz. **2.** *adj.* geizig, knauserig, knickerig, sparsam (***of***, mit). **niggardliness,** *s.* der Geiz, die Knauserei. **niggardly,** *adj. See* **niggard, 2.**

nigger ['nigə], *s.* (*pej.*) der Neger, Schwarze(r); ***the – in the woodpile***, der wirkliche Grund, der Hase im Pfeffer.

niggle [nigl], *v.i.* nörgeln; herumtüfteln, sich in Einzelheiten verlieren. **niggling, niggly,** *adj.* pedantisch, kleinlich; krittelig, nörglig.

nigh [nai], (*Poet.*) **1.** *adv.* nahe; (*usu.* ***well*** –) beinahe, fast; ***draw*** –, sich nähern (***to***, *Dat.*), heranrücken (an (*Acc.*)). **2.** *prep.* nahe bei, neben.

night [nait], *s.* die Nacht, der Abend; (*fig.*) die Dunkelheit; – ***after*** –, jeden Abend, Nacht für Nacht; ***all*** – (***long***), die ganze Nacht (hindurch); ***at*** –, nachts, abends; ***late at*** –, spät abends; ***the – before***, am vorhergehenden Abend; ***the – before last***, vorgestern abend; ***by*** –, ***during the*** –, ***in the*** –, bei Nacht, nachts, des Nachts; ***at dead of*** –, in tiefer Nacht, mitten in der Nacht; ***on a dark*** –, in einer dunklen Nacht; ***on the – of Jan. 1st***, am Abend des 1. Jan.; (*Theat.*) ***first*** –, die Erstaufführung, Premiere; ***good –!*** gute Nacht! guten Abend! ***have a good*** –, gut schlafen; ***last*** –, gestern abend; in der vergangenen Nacht; ***make a – of it***, die ganze Nacht durchmachen, bis in die Morgenstunden durchfeiern, sich (*Dat.*) die Nacht um die Ohren schlagen; ***have a – out***, abends ausgehen; ***over*** –, über Nacht; ***stay the*** –, übernachten (***at***, in (*Dat.*); ***with***, bei); ***tomorrow*** –, morgen abend.

night|-bird, *s.* der Nachtvogel; (*fig.*) Nachtschwärmer. **-cap,** *s.* die Schlafmütze, (*fig.*) der Schlummertrunk. **--clothes,** *pl.* das Nachtzeug. **--club,** *s.* das Nachtlokal, der Nachtklub. **-dress,** *s.* das Nachthemd (*for women*). **-fall,** *s.* das Dunkelwerden, der Einbruch der Nacht. **-gown,** *s. See* **-dress. -hawk,** *s.* (*Am.*) (*Orn.*) ***common*** –, der Nachtfalke (*Chordeiles minor*). **nightie,** *s.* (*coll.*) *see* **nightdress.**

nightingale ['naitiŋgeil], *s.* (*Orn.*) die Nachtigall (*Luscinia megarhynchos*).

night|jar, *s.* (*Orn.*) der Ziegenmelker, die Nachtschwalbe (*Caprimulgus europaeus*). **--long, 1.** *adj.* eine ganze Nacht dauernd. **2.** *adv.* die ganze Nacht hindurch. **nightly, 1.** *adj.* nächtlich, Nacht–. **2.** *adv.* jede Nacht, (all)nächtlich.

nightmare ['naitmɛə], *s.* das Alpdrücken, böser Traum; (*fig.*) der Alpdruck, das Angstgefühl; Schreckgespenst. **nightmarish** [–riʃ], *adj.* beängstigend, erschreckend.

night|-porter, *s.* der Nachtportier. **--school,** *s.* die Abendschule, Fortbildungsschule. **-shade,** *s.* (*Bot.*) der Nachtschatten. **--shift,** *s.* die Nachtschicht. **-shirt,** *s.* das Nachthemd (*for men*). **-soil,** *s.* der Abtrittsdünger. **-stool,** *s.* der Nachtstuhl. **--time,** *s.* die Nacht(zeit). **--watch,** *s.* die Nachtwache. **--watchman,** *s.* der Nachtwächter. **--wear,** *s.* das Nachtzeug. **-work,** *s.* die Nachtarbeit. **nighty,** *s.* (*coll.*) *see* **nightdress.**

nigrescence [nai'gresəns], *s.* das Schwarzwerden; die Dunkelheit. **nigrescent,** *adj.* schwärzlich.

nihilism ['naiilizm], *s.* der Nihilismus. **nihilist, 1.** *s.* der Nihilist. **2.** *or* **nihilistic** [–'listik], *adj.* nihilistisch.

nil [nil], *s.* das Nichts, die Null; (*Footb. etc.*) ***three*** (***goals to***) –, drei zu null; – ***return***, die Fehlanzeige.

Nile [nail], *s.* der Nil.

nilgai ['nilgai], *see* **nylg(h)au.**

nimble [nimbl], *adj.* flink, behende, hurtig, flott, gewandt. **nimble|-fingered,** *adj.* geschickt; langfingerig. **--footed,** *adj.* leichtfüßig. **nimbleness,** *s.* die Behendigkeit, Gewandtheit. **nimble-witted,** *adj.* geistig beweglich, schlagfertig.

nimbus ['nimbəs], *s.* der Heiligenschein, Nimbus; (*Meteor.*) die Regenwolke.

nimiety [ni'maiiti], *s.* (*rare*) das Übermaß, die Überfülle.

niminy-piminy ['nimini'pimini], *adj.* etepetete, zimperlich, geziert, affektiert.

nincompoop ['ninkəmpu:p], *s.* (*coll.*) der Einfaltspinsel, Dussel.

nine [nain], **1.** *num. adj.* neun; – ***days' wonder***, die Sensation, das Ereignis des Tages; ***have – lives***, ein zähes Leben haben; ***possession is – points of the law***, sei im Besitze und du wohnst im Recht; – ***times out of ten***, im allgemeinen. **2.** *s.* die Neun; (*Cards*) – ***of hearts***, die Herzneun; (*coll.*) ***to the –s***, vollkommen, im höchsten Maße; ***dressed up to the –s***, aufgedonnert; *for clock time see under* **eight. ninefold,** *adj.* neunfach.

ninepin ['nainpin], *s.* der Kegel; *pl.* (*sing. constr.*) das Kegelspiel; ***play*** (***at***) ***–s***, Kegel schieben, kegeln; ***fall over like –s***, wie Kegel umpurzeln.

nineteen ['nain'ti:n], **1.** *num. adj.* neunzehn. **2.** *s.* die Neunzehn; ***talk – to the dozen***, das Blaue vom Himmel herunterreden. **nineteenth, 1.** *num. adj.* neunzehnt; (*Golf*) – ***hole***, die Bar im Klubhaus. **2.** *s.* das Neunzehntel. **nineties** [–tiz], *pl.* die neuziger Jahre. **ninetieth** [–tiəθ], **1.** *num. adj*, neunzigst. **2.** *s.* das Neunzigstel. **ninety** [–ti]. **1.** *num. adj.* neunzig. **2.** *s.* die Neunzig.

Nineveh ['ninivə], *s.* Nineve (*n.*).

ninny ['nini], *s.* (*coll.*) der Einfaltspinsel, Tropf, das Kamel.

ninth [nainθ], **1.** *num. adj.* neunt. **2.** *s.* das Neuntel; (*Mus.*) die None. **ninthly,** *adv.* neuntens, zum neunten.

[1]**nip** [nip], **1.** *v.t.* 1. kneifen, kneipen, zwicken, klemmen; – ***off,*** abzwicken, abkneifen; 2. durch Frost beschädigen *or* zerstören *or* töten; – ***in the bud,*** im Keime ersticken; 3. (*coll.*) klauen. **2.** *v.i.* 1. zwicken; 2. schneiden, beißen (*as wind*); 3. (*sl.*) sich schnell bewegen, flitzen; (*sl.*) – ***in,*** hineinschlüpfen, sich hineindrängen *or* hineinschieben. **3.** *s.* 1. das Kneifen, Zwicken; 2. der Zwick, Biß, Knick (*of a rope*); 3. Frostbrand; – ***in the air,*** frostige Luft; 4. (*coll.*) (*Am.*) – ***and tuck,*** in schnellem Wechsel, in hartem Kampf.

[2]**nip, 1.** *s.* das Schlückchen (*of brandy etc.*). **2.** *v.i.* (*v.t.*) nippen (an (*Dat.*)).

nipper [ˈnipə], *s.* 1. (*coll.*) der Dreikäsehoch, Kiekindiewelt; 2. der Schneidezahn (*of a horse*); 3. die Kralle, Schere (*of a crab*); 4. (*Naut.*) das Seising; 5. *pl.* die Kneifzange, der Kneifer; (*sl.*) Handschellen (*pl.*).

nipping [ˈnipiŋ], *adj.* beißend, schneidend.

nipple [nipl], *s.* die Brustwarze, Zitze; der Sauger, Lutscher, das Gummihütchen (*of a baby's bottle*); (*Tech.*) der Nippel. **nipple|-shield,** *s.* das Warzenhütchen. **–wort,** *s.* (*Bot.*) das Warzenkraut.

nippy [ˈnipi], **1.** *adj.* 1. (*coll.*) schnell, flink, behende; 2. (*of wind, cold etc.*) *see* **nipping. 2.** *s.* (*sl.*) die Kellnerin.

nisi [ˈnaisai], *conj.* (*Law*) ***decree –,*** vorläufiges Scheidungsurteil; (*Law*) ***court of – prius,*** das Grafschaftsgericht für Zivilklagen.

nit [nit], *s.* die Nisse, Niß, das Lausei.

niter, (*Am.*) *see* **nitre.**

nitrate [ˈnaitreit], **1.** *s.* das Nitrat, salpetersaures Salz; ***silver –, – of silver,*** salpetersaures Silber. **2.** *v.t.* nitrieren, mit Salpetersäure behandeln. **nitre** [–tə], *s.* der Salpeter. **nitric** [–trik], *adj.* salpetersauer, Salpeter–; – ***acid,*** die Salpetersäure; – ***oxide,*** das Stick(stoff)oxyd. **nitrify** [–trifai], *v.t.* (*v.i.*) (sich) in Salpeter verwandeln. **nitrite** [–trait], *s.* das Nitrit, salpetrigsaures Salz.

nitro-cellulose [ˈnaitrou–], *s.* die Schießbaumwolle, das Kollodium, Pyroxylin.

nitrogen [ˈnaitrədʒən], *s.* der Stickstoff; – ***monoxide,*** das Stickstoffoxydul, Lachgas. **nitrogenize** [–ˈtrɔdʒənaiz], *v.t.* mit Stickstoff sättigen. **nitrogenized, nitrogenous** [–ˈtrɔdʒənəs], *adj.* stickstoffhaltig.

nitro|-glycerine, *s.* das Nitroglyzerin, Sprengöl. **–-hydrochloric** *or* **–-muriatic acid,** *s.* das Königswasser, Goldscheidewasser, die Salpetersalzsäure.

nitrous [ˈnaitrəs], *adj.* salpetrig; – ***acid,*** salpetrige Säure; – ***gases,*** nitrose Gase; – ***oxide,*** see ***nitrogen monoxide.***

nitwit [ˈnitwit], *s.* (*coll.*) der Nichtswisser, Nichtskönner, Dummkopf.

[1]**nix** [niks], *s.* (*sl.*) nichts, niemand.

[2]**nix,** *s.* der Nix, Wassergeist. **nixie,** *s.* 1. die (Wasser)nixe; 2. (*Am.*) unbestellbarer Brief.

no [nou], **1.** *adj.* kein; ***on – account,*** auf keinen Fall; – ***good books,*** keine guten Bücher; ***that is – concern of yours,*** das geht Sie nichts an; (*Typ.*) – ***date,*** ohne Jahr; ***there is – denying,*** es läßt sich nicht leugnen; – ***doubt,*** ohne Zweifel, zweifelsohne; ***to – end,*** vergebens, zwecklos; – ***end of trouble,*** unendliche Mühe, nichts als Unannehmlichkeiten; (*coll.*) ***he's – end of a fellow,*** er ist ein Kerl wie noch nie; – ***flowers,*** Blumenspenden dankend verbeten; (*coll.*) ***it's – go,*** das geht nicht; – ***gratuities!*** Trinkgeldablösung! ***there is – knowing,*** man kann nicht *or* nie wissen; – ***man,*** niemand; – ***mean writer,*** ein bedeutender Schriftsteller; ***by – means,*** auf keine Weise, keineswegs; ***and – mistake,*** sicherlich, tatsächlich, ohne Zweifel; (*Comm.*) – ***obligation,*** ohne jegliche Verpflichtung; – ***one,*** keiner; – ***one man,*** nicht einer; – ***parking,*** Parkverbot; – ***Popery!*** kein Pfaffentum! – ***such thing(s),*** nichts dergleichen; – ***thoroughfare!*** Durchgang *or* Durchfahrt gesperrt! ***at – time,*** nie; ***in – time,*** im Handumdrehen, sehr bald, in kürzester Zeit; – – ***trumps!*** ohne Trumpf! ***of – use,*** nutzlos, ohne Nutzen, zwecklos; – ***wonder,*** kein Wunder. **2.** *adv.* 1. (*as neg. reply*) nein; 2. nicht; – ***better than,*** nicht *or* um nichts besser als; – ***longer ago than last Friday,*** erst vorigen Freitag; – ***more,*** (*amount*) nichts mehr; (*time*) nicht mehr, nie wieder; – ***more than,*** ebensowenig wie; – ***more of your nonsense!*** kein Unsinn mehr! – ***more will I,*** ich auch nicht; ***be – more,*** tot sein; – ***sooner . . . than,*** kaum . . . als; ***whether or – he comes, whether he comes or –,*** ob er kommt oder nicht. **3.** *s.* das Nein; die Weigerung, Absage; (*Parl.*) Gegenstimme; ***the –es,*** die Stimmen wider; ***the –es have it,*** die Mehrheit ist dagegen.

Noah [ˈnouə], *s.* (*B.*) Noah (*m.*); ***–'s ark,*** die Arche Noah(s) *or* Noä.

nob [nɔb], *s.* 1. (*sl.*) (= ***head***) der Dez; 2. (*sl.*) feines Aas, hohes Tier.

nobble [nɔbl], *v.t.* 1. (*sl.*) für sich gewinnen, bestechen; 2. übervorteilen, betrügen; 3. stehlen, mausen.

nobby [ˈnɔbi], *adj.* (*sl.*) noblig, pikfein.

nobiliary [noˈbiliəri], *adj.* Adels–; – ***particle,*** das Adelsprädikat.

nobility [noˈbiliti], *s.* 1. der Adel(sstand); (*collect.*) hoher Adel, Adlige (*pl.*); – ***and gentry,*** hoher und niedriger Adel; 2. (*fig.*) die Hoheit, Erhabenheit, Vornehmheit, Würde, der Adel; – ***of mind,*** vornehme Gesinnung; – ***of soul,*** der Seelenadel, die Seelengröße.

noble [noubl], **1.** *adj.* adlig, Adels–; (*fig.*) edel, vornehm, erhaben, erlaucht; groß(mütig); prächtig, ausgezeichnet, vortrefflich, herrlich; ***the – art,*** das Boxen; – ***metal,*** das Edelmetall. **2.** *s.* 1. (hohe(r)) Adlige(r), der Edelmann; 2. (*Hist.*) (Rose)nobel (*gold coin*).

noble|man [–mən], *s.* (hoher) Adliger. **–-minded,** *adj.* edelgesinnt, edeldenkend, hochherzig. **–(-minded)ness,** *s.* der Edelsinn, Edelmut, edle Gesinnung. **–woman,** *s.* die Adlige, Edelfrau.

nobody [ˈnoubədi], **1.** *pron.* niemand, keiner; – ***else,*** sonst niemand *or* keiner, niemand anders; ***–'s business,*** das worum sich keiner kümmert; (*coll.*) ein Problem, das sich nicht bewältigen läßt. **2.** *s.* (*fig.*) (*with indef. art.*) unbedeutender Mensch, die Null; ***they are just nobodies,*** sie sind ganz gewöhnliche Menschen, sie sind keine besonderen Leute.

nock [nɔk], **1.** *s.* die Kerbe, der Einschnitt (*of arrow*). **2.** *v.t.* einkerben.

no|-claims bonus, *s.* (*Insur.*) die Prämie bei Schadensfreiheit. **– confidence,** *s.* (*Parl.*) ***vote of –,*** das Mißtrauensvotum.

noctambulant [nɔkˈtæmbjulənt], *adj.* nachtwandelnd, schlafwandelnd. **noctambulist,** *s.* der Nachtwandler, Schlafwandler.

nocturn [ˈnɔktə:n], *s.* (*R.C.*) die Nachtmette. **nocturnal** [–ˈtə:nl], *adj.* nächtlich, Nacht–. **nocturne,** *s.* (*Mus.*) das Notturno, (*Art*) Nachtstück.

nocuous [ˈnɔkjuəs], *adj.* schädlich, giftig.

nod [nɔd], **1.** *v.t.* nicken mit, durch Nicken andeuten; – ***assent,*** beistimmend nicken, durch Kopfnicken zustimmen; – ***one's head,*** mit dem Kopfe nicken. **2.** *v.i.* 1. nicken, sich neigen; – ***to him,*** ihm zunicken; 2. (*fig.*) unachtsam sein, schlummern; – ***off,*** einnicken, einschlafen, einschlummern. **3.** *s.* das (Kopf)nicken; der Wink; ***a – is as good as a wink,*** ein kurzer *or* sanfter Wink genügt; ***a – is as good as a wink to a blind horse,*** er *etc.* läßt sich durch nichts umstimmen; (*coll.*) ***Land of Nod,*** der Schlaf; (*sl.*) ***on the –,*** auf Borg.

nodal [noudl], *adj.* Knoten–; (*Phys.*) – ***line,*** die Schwingungslinie; (*Phys.*) – ***point,*** der Schwingungspunkt, (*fig.*) Knotenpunkt.

nodding [ˈnɔdiŋ], **1.** *s.* das Nicken. **2.** *adj.* nickend; (*fig.*) – ***acquaintance,*** oberflächliche Bekanntschaft; oberflächliche(r) Bekannte(r); ***be on – terms with,*** nur vom Grüßen kennen.

noddle [nɔdl], *s.* (*sl.*) der Dez, die Birne, Rübe.

node [noud], *s.* der Knoten; (*Med.*) Gichtknoten, das Knötchen; (*Phys.*) der Schwingungsknoten. **nodose** [–ous], *adj.* Knoten–, knotig, knorrig. **nodosity** [–'dɔsiti], *s.* knotige Beschaffenheit; (*Med.*) der Knoten, das Knötchen, die Schwellung.

nodular ['nɔdjulə], *adj.* knötchenartig, knotig, Knoten–. **nodule** [–ju:l], *s.* das Knötchen, Klümpchen; (*Geol.*) die Niere, Putze.

nodus ['noudəs], *s.* (*fig.*) die Schwierigkeit, Verwick(e)lung.

Noel [nou'el], *s.* das Weihnachtsfest.

nog [nɔg], **1.** *v.t.* mit Holznägeln befestigen; (*Build.*) mit Holz einfassen *or* ausmauern. **2.** *s.* der Holznagel, Holzpflock, Holzbolzen, Holzklotz, Holm.

noggin ['nɔgin], *s.* kleiner (hölzerner) Krug; ein Flüssigkeitmaß (= ¼ *pint*).

no|-good, 1. *adj.* (*coll.*) nichtsnutzig, nichtswürdig. **2.** *s.* der Nichtsnutz, Taugenichts. **–how,** *adv.* (*sl.*) keineswegs, durchaus nicht; ***look –,*** nach nichts aussehen.

noil [nɔil], *s.* der Kämmling, die Kurzwolle.

noise [nɔiz], **1.** *s.* 1. der Lärm, das Geräusch, Getöse, Geschrei; (*Rad.*) Fremdgeräusch; (*fig.*) ***make a –,*** viel Aufhebens machen, Aufsehen erregen, von sich reden machen; (*coll.*) ***hold your –!*** halt das Maul! (*sl.*) ***big –,*** großes *or* hohes Tier. **2.** *v.t.* ***– abroad,*** als Gerücht verbreiten, aussprengen (*rumour*); ***be –d abroad,*** als Gerücht umlaufen, ruchbar werden. **noise abatement,** *s.* die Geräuschunterdrückung. **noiseless,** *adj.* geräuschlos, still. **noiselessness,** *s.* die Geräuschlosigkeit, Stille. **noise| level,** *s.* 1. die Geräuschkulisse, der Geräuschpegel; 2. (*Rad.*) Störpegel, Störspiegel, Rauscheffekt. **– suppression,** *s.* (*Rad.*) die Entstörung. **noisiness,** *s.* das Geräusch, Getöse, der Lärm.

noisome ['nɔisəm], *adj.* schädlich, ungesund; ekelhaft, widerlich. **noisomeness,** *s.* die Schädlichkeit, Widerlichkeit.

noisy ['nɔizi], *adj.* geräuschvoll, lärmend; (*fig.*) schreiend, laut, grell, auffallend.

noli-me-tangere ['noulaimi:'tændʒəri], *s.* (*Bot.*) das Springkraut, Rührmichnichtan.

nolle prosequi ['nɔli'prɔsəkwi], *s.* die Zurücknahme der Klage, Aufgabe des Prozesses (*by plaintiff*); Einstellung des Verfahrens (*by prosecutor*).

nomad ['noumæd], **1.** *adj.* nomadisch, Nomaden–. **2.** *s.* der Nomade (die Nomadin). **nomadic** [–'mædik], *adj. See* **nomad, 1**; (*fig.*) unstet. **nomadism,** *s.* das Nomadentum, Nomadenleben.

no-man's land, *s.* das Niemandsland.

nom-de-|guerre ['nɔmdə'gɛə], *s.* der Deckname. **–plume** [–'plu:m], *s.* der Schriftstellername.

nomenclature [nou'menklətʃə], *s.* 1. die Terminologie, das Benennungssystem, Namenverzeichnis, (*collect.*) Namen, Bezeichnungen (*pl.*); 2. die Fachsprache, Nomenklatur, Namengebung.

nominal ['nɔminl], *adj.* 1. (*Gram.*) nominal, Nominal–; 2. namentlich, Namen–, Nenn–; ***– amount,*** der Nennbetrag; ***– capital,*** das Grundkapital, Stammkapital; ***– roll,*** die Namenliste; ***– value,*** der Nennwert; 3. nominell, nur dem Namen nach, angeblich; ***– fine,*** nominelle Geldstrafe; ***– rank,*** der Titularrang; ***– rent,*** geringe Miete; ***– sum,*** die Nominalsumme.

nominalism ['nɔminlizm], *s.* (*Phil.*) der Nominalismus.

nominate ['nɔmineit], *v.t.* 1. ernennen (*to*, zu), einsetzen (in (*Acc.*)); 2. (*Parl.*) zur Wahl vorschlagen, als Kandidaten aufstellen. **nomination** [–'neiʃən], *s.* 1. die Ernennung, Berufung (*to*, zu), Einsetzung (in (*Acc.*)); 2. (*Parl.*) Aufstellung, Nominierung; ***– day,*** der Wahlvorschlagstermin.

nominative ['nɔminətiv], **1.** *adj.* (*Gram.*) Nominativ–. **2.** *s.* der Werfall, Nominativ. **nominator** [–eitə], *s.* der Ernenner. **nominee** [–'ni:], *s.* Vorgeschlagene(r), Ernannte(r).

non- [nɔn], *pref.* nicht, Nicht–, un–. **non-acceptance,** *s.* die Annahmeverweigerung, Nichtannahme.

nonage ['nounidʒ], *s.* die Minderjährigkeit, Unmündigkeit.

nonagenarian [nounədʒi'nɛəriən], **1.** *s.* Neunzig(jährig)e(r). **2.** *adj.* neunzigjährig.

non|-aggression, *adj.* Nichtangriffs–. **--alcoholic,** *adj.* alkoholfrei. **--appearance, --attendance,** *s.* das Nichterscheinen, Ausbleiben. **--belligerent,** *adj.* nicht kriegführend.

nonce [nɔns], *s.* (*only in*) ***for the –,*** für dies eine Mal, nur für diesen Fall, einstweilen. **nonce-word,** *s.* das Gelegenheitswort, die Augenblicksbildung.

nonchalance ['nɔnʃələns], *s.* die Nachlässigkeit, Gleichgültigkeit. **nonchalant,** *adj.* (nach)lässig, gleichgültig; unbekümmert.

non|-collegiate, *adj.* keinem College angehörig. **--combatant, 1.** *s.* der Nichtkämpfer. **2.** *adj.* am Kampf nicht beteiligt. **--commissioned,** *adj.* nicht bevollmächtigt, unbestallt; (*esp. Mil.*) ***– officer,*** der Unteroffizier. **–committal, 1.** *adj.* nicht bindend, unverbindlich; zurückhaltend. **2.** *s.* freie Hand, die Unverbindlichkeit. **–compliance,** *s.* die Nichteinhaltung, Nichterfüllung, Nichtbefolgung (***with***, von), Zuwiderhandlung (gegen); Weigerung. **– compos (mentis),** *adj.* (*Law*) unzurechnungsfähig. **--conductor,** *s.* (*Elec. etc.*) der Nichtleiter. **–conformist, 1.** *s.* (*Eccl.*) der Dissident, Nonkonformist; (*fig.*) Widerspruchsgeist. **2.** *adj.* (*Eccl.*) nonkonformistisch; (*fig.*) nicht übereinstimmend. **–conformity,** *s.* (*Eccl.*) der Dissens, freikirchliche Gesinnung; (*fig.*) die Nichtübereinstimmung (***with***, mit), mangelnde Anpassung (*to*, an (*Acc.*)). **--contributory,** *adj.* beitragsfrei. **--cooperation,** *s.* (*Pol.*) passiver Widerstand. **--cooperative,** *adj.* die Mitarbeit verweigernd. **--creasing,** *adj.* knitterfrei. **--crystalline,** *adj.* unkristallinisch. **--delivery,** *s.* die Nichtbestellung.

nondescript ['nɔndiskript], *adj.* unklassifizierbar, schwer beschreibbar; unbestimmt, nichtssagend.

none [nʌn], **1.** *pron.* (*usu. pl. constr.*) kein; ***– but the best,*** nichts als das *or* nur das allerbeste; ***– but fools act like that,*** nur Narren tun so was; ***– more so than I,*** keiner mehr als ich; ***it was – other than my wife,*** es war niemand anders *or* keine andere als meine Frau; ***we – of us trust him,*** keiner von uns traut ihm; ***she will have – of me,*** sie will von mir nichts wissen; ***I cannot lend you money, I have –,*** ich kann dir kein Geld borgen, ich habe keins; ***it is – of the best,*** es ist keins von den besten, es ist keineswegs gut; ***– of that,*** nichts dergleichen; ***it's – of your business,*** es geht dich nichts an; ***– of your tricks!*** (unter)laß deine Späße! **2.** *adv.* keineswegs, in keiner Weise, nicht im geringsten; ***– too soon,*** keineswegs zu früh, beinahe zu spät, im allerletzten Augenblick; ***– too good,*** nicht gerade gut; ***– the better for it,*** deshalb nicht (im geringsten) besser daran; ***– the less,*** nichtsdestoweniger; ***– the wiser,*** um nichts klüger, (genau) so klug *or* schlau wie zuvor.

non|-effective, 1. *adj.* wirkungslos, ohne Wirkung; (*Mil.*) dienstuntauglich. **2.** *s.* (*Mil.*) Dienstuntaugliche(r). **--ego,** *s.* (*Phil.*) das Nicht-Ich. **–entity,** *s.* (*Phil.*) das Nichtsein; Nichtseiende(s); (*coll.*) unbedeutender Mensch, die Null.

nones [nounz], *pl.* Nonen (*pl.*); (*R.C.*) das Mittagsoffizium.

non-essential, 1. *adj.* unwesentlich, nicht unbedingt notwendig. **2.** *s.* unwesentliche S., die Nebensache; (*usu. pl.*) nicht lebensnotwendige Güter (*pl.*).

nonesuch ['nʌnsʌtʃ], *s.* 1. (*rare*) das Muster, Unvergleichliche(s), die S. *or* P. ohnegleichen; 2. (*Bot.*) Brennende Liebe; 3. (*Bot.*) der Nonpareilleapfel.

nonet [nou'net], *s.* (*Mus.*) das Nonett.

non|-existence, *s.* das Nicht(da)sein, Nichtvorhandensein. **--existent,** *adj.* nicht existierend *or* vorhanden. **--expendable,** *adj.* (*esp. Mil.*)

Nichtverbrauchs–, Gebrauchs–. **--feasance,** *s.* (*Law*) pflichtwidrige Unterlassung. **--ferrous,** *adj.* Nichteisen–, nicht eisenhaltig. **--fiction,** **1.** *adj.* nicht erzählend; – *book,* das Sachbuch. **2.** *s.* nichterzählende Werke (*pl.*), die Sachliteratur. **--freezing,** *adj.* kältebeständig. **--fulfilment,** *s.* die Nichterfüllung. **--halating,** *adj.* (*Phot.*) lichthoffrei. **--inductive,** *adj.* (*Elec.*) induktionsfrei. **--inflammable,** *s.* feuersicher, nicht feuergefährlich. **--intervention,** *s.* (*Pol.*) die Nichteinmischung. **--iron,** *adj.* bügelfrei. **--juror,** *s.* der Eidesverweigerer. **--laddering,** *adj.* maschenfest.

nonliquet [nɔn'likwit], *s.* (*Law*) der Urteilsausfall wegen mangelnden Beweises. **non|-luminous,** *adj.* nicht leuchtend. **--magnetic,** *adj.* nichtmagnetisch, antimagnetisch. **--malignant,** *adj.* (*Med.*) nicht bösartig, gutartig. **--member,** *s.* das Nichtmitglied. **--metallic,** *adj.* Nichtmetall–; – *element,* das Metalloid. **--negotiable,** *adj.* (*Comm.*) nicht übertragbar; – *cheque,* der Verrechnungsscheck. **--observance,** *s.* die Nichtbeachtung, Nichterfüllung.

nonpareil [nɔnpə'rel], **1.** *s.* 1. Unvergleichliche(s), noch nicht Dagewesene(s); 2. (*Typ.*) die Nonpareille(schrift). **2.** *adj.* unvergleichlich, ohnegleichen. **non|-party,** *adj.* nicht parteigebunden, überparteilich. **--payment,** *s.* die Nicht(be)zahlung. **--performance,** *s.* die Nichterfüllung, Nichtvollziehung. **-placet,** *s.* (*Law*) die Verweigerung der Zustimmung.

nonplus [nɔn'plʌs], *v.t.* in Verlegenheit bringen *or* setzen, in die Enge treiben, verwirren, verblüffen. **nonplussed,** *adj.* verblüfft, verdutzt.

non|-productive, *adj.* unproduktiv. **--professional,** *adj.* nicht berufsmäßig. **--profitmaking,** *adj.* gemeinnützig. **--representational,** *adj.* (*Art*) gegenstandslos, abstrakt. **--resident,** **1.** *adj.* nicht ansässig, abwesend, (*of a member*) auswärtig. **2.** *s.* Nichtansässige(r); *dining room for -s,* der Speisesaal für Passanten. **--returnable,** *adj.* (*bottle, package etc.*) Einweg–, verloren. **--reversible,** *adj.* nicht umkehrbar. **--rigid,** *adj.* (*airship*) unstarr.

nonsense ['nɔnsəns], *s.* der Unsinn; die Widersinnigkeit; *–!* Unsinn! Blödsinn! Quatsch! dummes Zeug! *stand no –,* sich (*Dat.*) nichts gefallen lassen, nicht mit sich spaßen lassen; *talk –,* Unsinn reden; *make – of,* Unsinn machen aus; – *verse,* Klapphornverse (*pl.*). **nonsensical** [–'sensikl], *adj.* unsinnig, sinnlos, absurd, albern.

non| sequitur [–'sekwitə:], *s.* der Trugschluß, irrige Folgerung. **--sexual,** *adj.* geschlechtslos. **--skid,** *adj.* rutschsicher. **--smoker,** *s.* der Nichtraucher, (*coll.*) (*Railw.*) das Nichtraucherabteil. **--smoking,** *adj.* Nichtraucher–. **--stop,** *adj.* durchgehend (*train etc.*), ohne Zwischenlandung, Dauer–, Nonstop– (*plane*), pausenlos, ununterbrochen (*performance etc.*). **-such,** *s. See* **nonesuch.**

nonsuit ['nɔnsju:t], **1.** *s.* (*Law*) die Zurücknahme einer Klage (*by the plaintiff*), Abweisung *or* Sistierung einer Klage (*by the court*). **2.** *v.t.* abweisen, sistieren, nicht stattgeben (*a case*); zur Aufgabe der Klage veranlassen (*the plaintiff*).

non|-taxable, *adj.* steuerfrei, nicht besteuerbar. **--transferable,** *adj.* nicht übertragbar. **--U** [–'ju:], *adj.* (*coll.*) nicht vornehm, plebejisch. **--union,** *adj.* (*of workers*) nicht organisiert. **--valent,** *adj.* (*Chem.*) nullwertig. **--voter,** *s.* der (die) Nichtwähler(in). **--voting,** *adj.* nicht stimmberechtigt.

[1]**noodle** [nu:dl], *s.* (*coll.*) der Dussel, Trottel; (*sl.*) die Birne, der Dez.

[2]**noodle,** *s.* (*esp. Am.*) die Nudel.

nook [nuk], *s.* das Versteck, der (Schlupf)winkel; *every – and cranny,* alle Ecken.

noon [nu:n], **1.** *s.* (*also -day, -tide*) der Mittag, die Mittagszeit; *at –,* zu Mittag. **2.** *attrib. adj.* mittägig, Mittags–.

noose [nu:s], **1.** *s.* die Schleife, Schlinge; (*fig.*) *put one's head into a –,* in die Falle gehen. **2.** *v.t.* schlingen (*a rope*) (*round,* um); mit einer Schlinge fangen (*an animal*).

nor [nɔ:], *conj.* (*after neg.*) noch; auch nicht; – *I* (*n*)*either,* ich auch nicht; *neither . . . – . . .,* weder . . . . noch . . . .

norm [nɔ:m], *s.* die Norm, Regel, Richtschnur, das Muster; (*Stat.*) die Durchschnittsleistung.

normal ['nɔ:məl], **1.** *adj.* 1. normal, Normal–, regelrecht; – *school,* das Lehrerseminar; – *time,* die Einheitszeit; 2. (*Geom.*) senkrecht. **2.** *s.* 1. das Normale, der Normalstand, Normaltyp, Normalwert; üblicher Zustand; 2. (*Geom.*) die Normale, Senkrechte. **normalcy** [–si], **normality** [–'mæliti], *s.* die Normalität, Regelmäßigkeit, der Normal(zu)stand. **normalization** [–ai'zeiʃən], *s.* die Normalisierung; Normierung, Normung. **normalize,** *v.t.* normalisieren; normieren, normen. **normally,** *adv.* normalerweise.

Norman ['nɔ:mən], **1.** *s.* der Normanne (die Normannin). **2.** *adj.* normannisch. **Normandy** [–di], *s.* die Normandie.

Norse [nɔ:s], **1.** *adj.* 1. skandinavisch; 2. norwegisch. **2.** *s.* das Norwegisch(e) (*language*); *Old –,* das Altnordisch(e). **Norseman,** *s.* (*Hist.*) der Nordländer.

north [nɔ:θ], **1.** *s.* der Norden, (*Poet.*) Nord; *the North,* die Nordstaaten (*of U.S.A.*); *to the – of,* nördlich von; *magnetic –,* magnetisch Nord: *true –,* geographisch Nord; – *by east,* Nord zu Ost. **2.** *adv.* nördlich (*of,* von); *go –,* nach Norden gehen; – *and south,* von Norden nach Süden; in nordsüdlicher Richtung. **3.** *adj.* nördlich, Nord–; *North Atlantic Treaty,* der Nordatlantikpakt; *North Britain,* Schottland; *the North Country,* Nordengland; *--countryman,* der Nordengländer; *North Pole,* der Nordpol; *North Sea,* die Nordsee; *North Star,* der Polarstern; – *wind,* der Nordwind, (*Poet.*) Nord.

north|-east, **1.** *s.* der Nordost(en); – *by east,* Nordost zu Ost. **2.** *adj.* Nordost–. **3.** *adv.* nordöstlich (*of,* von). **--easter,** *s.* der Nordostwind. **--easterly,** **1.** *adv.* nordöstlich. **2.** *adj.* nordöstlich, Nordost–. **--eastern,** *adj.* nordöstlich. **--eastward,** **1.** *adv., adj.* nordöstlich. **2.** *s.* nordöstliche Richtung.

northerly ['nɔ:ðəli], **1.** *adj.* nördlich, nach Norden (*course*), von Norden (*wind*). **2.** *adv.* im *or* nach Norden. **northern,** *attrib. adj.* nördlich, Nord–; *Northern China,* Nordchina; – *lights,* das Nordlicht. **northerner,** *s.* der Nordländer. **northernmost,** *adj.* nördlichst.

northing ['nɔ:θiŋ], *s.* nördliche Richtung, der Kurs *or* die Entfernung nach Norden. **northman,** *s.* der Skandinavier, Nordländer. **northward,** **1.** *s.* nördliche Gegend *or* Richtung. **2.** *adj.* nördlich (*of, from,* von). **northward(s),** *adv.* nordwärts.

north|-west, --wester, --westerly, --western, --westward, *for forms see under* **--east.**

Norway ['nɔ:wei], *s.* Norwegen (*n.*). **Norwegian** [–'wi:dʒən], **1.** *s.* 1. der (die) Norweger(in); 2. (*language*) das Norwegisch(e). **2.** *adj.* norwegisch.

nose [nouz], **1.** *s.* 1. die Nase (*also fig.*); *cut off one's – to spite one's face,* sich ins eigene Fleisch schneiden; *follow one's –,* immer der Nase nach gehen; *have a good – for,* eine feine Nase (*or coll.*) einen (guten) Riecher haben für; *hold one's –,* sich (*Dat.*) die Nase zuhalten; *lead him by the –,* ihn an der Nase herumführen; *look down one's – at,* die Nase rümpfen über (*Acc.*); *pay through the –,* tüchtig zahlen *or* bluten müssen; *pick one's –,* in der Nase bohren; *poke* or *put* or *thrust one's – into,* seine Nase stecken in (*Acc.*); *put his – out of joint,* ihn ausstechen *or* aus dem Sattel heben; *not see beyond one's –,* die Hand vor den Augen nicht sehen können; (*fig.*) beschränkt *or* kurzsichtig sein; *snap his – off,* ihn hart anfahren; *speak through one's –,* näseln, durch die Nase sprechen; *turn up one's – at,* die Nase rümpfen über (*Acc.*); *under his* (*very*) *–,* ihm direkt vor der Nase; 2. offenes Ende, die Öffnung, Mündung; 3. Schnauze, Spitze, der Schnabel; 4. (*Av.*) die Rumpfspitze, der Bug, (*Naut.*) Bug; 5. das Kopfteil (*of a shell*); 6. der Geruch (*of tea, hay etc.*); 7. (*sl.*) Spion, Spitzel. **2.** *v.i.* schnuppern, schnüffeln; – ***about,*** herumschnüffeln; (*coll.*) – ***around,*** herumspähen. **3.** *v.t.* 1. riechen, wittern, spüren; – ***out,*** ausspüren, aufspüren, ausfindig machen; 2. beriechen, beschnüffeln; 3. mit der Nase stoßen an (*Acc.*); 4. – ***one's way,*** schrittweise vorangehen.

nose|-bag, *s.* der Futterbeutel, Freßbeutel. **--band,** *s.* der Nasenriemen. **--bleed(ing),** *s.* das Nasenbluten. **nosed,** *adj. suff.* -nasig. **nose|-dive, 1.** *s.* (*Av.*) der Sturzflug. **2.** *v.i.* (*Av.*) einen Sturzflug machen; (*fig.*) stürzen. **-gay,** *s.* der Blumenstrauß. **--heavy,** *adj.* (*Naut.*) buglastig; (*Av.*) vorderlastig, kopflastig. **--piece,** *s.* 1. das Objektivende, der Revolver (*of a microscope*); 2. *See* **--band. noser,** *s.* der Kopfwind.

nosey ['nouzi], *adj.* 1. (*coll.*) neugierig; – ***Parker,*** der Topfgucker, Pottkieker; 2. muffig (*as hay*); aromatisch (*as tea*).

nosing ['nouziŋ], *s.* (*Build.*) hervorstehende Kante.

nosology [nɔ'zɔlɔdʒi], *s.* die Krankheitslehre.

nostalgia [nɔs'tældʒiə], *s.* die Sehnsucht, das Heimweh(gefühl) (*for,* nach). **nostalgic,** *adj.* Heimweh-, sehnsüchtig.

nostril ['nɔstril], *s.* das Nasenloch; die Nüster (*of animals*).

nostrum ['nɔstrəm], *s.* das Geheimmittel, (*fig.*) Heilmittel.

nosy, *see* **nosey.**

not [nɔt], *adv.* nicht; – ***a,*** kein(e); – ***a few,*** nicht wenige; – ***at all,*** keineswegs, durchaus nicht; – ***at home,*** ausgegangen, nicht zu sprechen; – ***but that,*** obwohl; ***I could – but think,*** ich konnte nicht umhin zu denken; ***certainly –,*** gewiß nicht, nicht doch; (*sl.*) – ***half!*** und wie! (*coll.*) – ***I,*** ich denke nicht daran; – ***if I know it,*** nicht wenn es nach mir geht; – ***that I know,*** nicht als ob *or* nicht daß ich wüßte; ***is it –?*** (*coll.* ***isn't it?***) nicht wahr? – ***long ago,*** vor kurzer Zeit; (*Scots Law*) – ***proven,*** unbewiesen; ***more often than –,*** in den meisten Fällen; ***I think –,*** ich glaube es nicht; – ***too good,*** es dürfte besser sein; – ***(as) yet,*** noch nicht, zur Zeit nicht.

notability [noutə'biliti], *s.* die Bedeutung, Merkwürdigkeit, Bemerkenswerte(s); *see also* **notable, 2.**

notable ['noutəbl], **1.** *adj.* 1. bemerkenswert, beachtenswert, merkwürdig, denkwürdig; 2. ansehnlich, beträchtlich; 3. angesehen, hervorragend; 4. (*Chem.*) merklich, feststellbar. **2.** *s.* angesehene Person, die Standesperson. **notably,** *adv.* 1. *See* **notable, 1**; 2. besonders, insbesondere, obendrein, vor allem andern; hauptsächlich, vorwiegend, vorzugsweise, speziell, vorzüglich, vornehmlich, ausnehmend.

notarial [no'tɛəriəl], *adj.* notariell, Notariats-; notariell beglaubigt. **notary** ['noutəri], *s.* (*also* – ***public***) der Notar.

notation [no'teiʃən], *s.* die Bezeichnung, Schreibung; (*Mus.*) Notation, (Noten)schrift; (*rare*) Aufzeichnung; ***arithmetical –,*** das Zahlensystem; ***unit of –,*** die Maßeinheit.

notch [nɔtʃ], **1.** *s.* die Kerbe, Scharte, Nut(e), der Einschnitt, Ausschnitt; die Kimme (*on gun*); ***take him down a –,*** ihn demütigen. **2.** *v.t.* (ein)kerben, einschneiden; (*Carp.*) falzen, nuten; (*coll.*) – ***up,*** gewinnen, erwerben (*points etc.*).

note [nout], **1.** *s.* 1. die Anmerkung, Bemerkung, der Vermerk; die Anweisung, Mitteilung; (*usu. pl.*) Aufzeichnung, Notiz; ***compare –s,*** sich berat(schlag)en, Gedanken austauschen; ***make*** or ***take a – of,*** notieren, aufschreiben, sich (*Dat.*) vormerken; ***speak without –s,*** frei sprechen; ***take –s,*** sich (*Dat.*) Notizen machen; 2. ein paar Zeilen, das Zettelchen, Billett, (*Comm.*) die Rechnung, Nota; Banknote, der Schein; (*Comm.*) ***advice –,*** die Versandanzeige; – ***of exchange,*** der Kurszettel; ***exchange of –s,*** der Notenaustausch (*of diplomats*); – ***of hand, promissory –,*** der Schuldschein, Schuldbrief, die Schuldverschreibung; ***treasury –,*** der Schatzschein; 3. (*Typ.*) – ***of exclamation,*** das Ausrufungszeichen; – ***of interrogation,*** das Fragezeichen; 4. (*Mus.*) die Note, Taste; ***strike the –s,*** die Tasten anschlagen; 5. der Ton, Klang; Gesang (*of birds*); (*fig.*) Ton, die Tonart; (*fig.*) ***strike the right –,*** den rechten Ton anschlagen; 6. das (Kenn)zeichen, Merkmal; (*fig.*) Ansehen, der Ruf, die Bedeutung, Wichtigkeit; ***man of –,*** der Mann von Ruf *or* Ansehen; ***nothing of –,*** nichts von Bedeutung; 7. die Kenntnisnahme, Beachtung; ***take – of,*** sich (*Dat.*) merken, zur Kenntnis nehmen; berücksichtigen; ***worthy of –,*** beachtenswert. **2.** *v.t.* 1. bemerken, beachten, Kenntnis nehmen von; 2. (*also* – ***down***) aufschreiben, aufzeichnen, verzeichnen, niederschreiben, notieren; 3. (*Comm.*) buchen, anschreiben; – ***a bill,*** einen Wechsel protestieren.

note|-book, *s.* das Taschenbuch, Notizbuch. **-case,** *s.* die Brieftasche. **noted,** *adj.* berühmt, bekannt; berüchtigt (*for,* wegen). **notedly,** *adv.* besonders; deutlich, ausgesprochen. **note|-paper,** *s.* das Briefpapier. **-worthy,** *adj.* bemerkenswert, beachtenswert.

nothing ['nʌθiŋ], **1.** *pron., s.* 1. nichts; das Nichts; – ***at all,*** gar nichts; – ***but,*** – ***except,*** nichts außer, nur, lediglich; – ***else than,*** nichts anderes als, sonst *or* weiter nichts als; – ***if not stupid,*** überaus dumm; – ***important,*** nichts Wichtiges; – ***much,*** nichts Bedeutendes; – ***to what . . .,*** nichts gegen das, was . . ., nichts im Vergleich zu dem, was . . .; ***be –,*** ohne Bedeutung sein (***to,*** für), nichts im Vergleich sein (zu); ***be as –,*** nichts bedeuten; ***it is – to him,*** es geht ihn nichts an; ***there is – for it but,*** es bleibt nichts übrig als; ***there is – in it,*** das hat nichts auf sich; ***there is – like,*** es geht nichts über (*Acc.*); ***come to –,*** mißlingen, zunichte *or* zu Wasser werden; ***it will come to –,*** daraus wird nichts; (*coll.*) – ***doing,*** nichts zu machen, es geht nicht; ***feel like – on earth,*** sich hundeelend fühlen; ***for –,*** umsonst, vergebens; (*price*) umsonst, unentgeltlich; ***not for – that,*** nicht umsonst daß; ***he is good for –,*** er ist zu nichts zu gebrauchen; ***I can make – of it,*** ich weiß damit nichts anzufangen, ich kann daraus nicht klug werden; (*coll.*) ***neck or –,*** auf Biegen oder Brechen; ***to say – of,*** geschweige denn; ***to –,*** in *or* zu nichts; ***next to –,*** fast nichts; (*Prov.*) – ***venture – have,*** frisch gewagt ist halb gewonnen; 2. die Kleinigkeit, (*Math.*) Null (*also fig. of p.*); *pl.* Nichtigkeiten (*pl.*). **2.** *adv.* keineswegs, in keiner Weise, durchaus nicht; – ***like finished,*** in keiner Weise vollendet, längst nicht fertig; – ***like so . . .,*** bei weitem nicht so . . .; – ***loath,*** durchaus nicht abgeneigt; – ***short of,*** geradezu, wirklich. **nothingness,** *s.* das Nichts, Nichtsein; die Nichtigkeit.

notice ['noutis], **1.** *s.* 1. die Anzeige, Notiz, kurzer Bericht (*in a newspaper*), die Nachricht, Meldung, Ankündigung, Bekanntgabe, Mitteilung, der Bescheid; die Besprechung (*of book, play etc.*); ***–s of births, marriages and deaths,*** Geburts-, Trauungs- und Todesanzeigen; ***give – that,*** (hiermit) bekanntmachen; ***give – of,*** ankündigen, anzeigen, bekanntgeben; ***give – of appeal,*** Berufung einlegen; ***have – of,*** Kenntnis haben von; ***receive –,*** Nachricht bekommen; 2. die Kündigung(sfrist) (*to leave*), Warnung; – ***to quit,*** die Kündigung; ***at a day's –,*** innerhalb eines Tages; ***at a moment's –,*** zu jeder Zeit, jederzeit, fristlos; ***at short –,*** innerhalb kurzer Zeit, kurzfristig; ***give him (his) –,*** ihm kündigen (*for,* zu); ***give him a week's –,*** eine Woche vorher *or* mit achttägiger Frist kündigen; ***give him very short –,*** ihm wenig Zeit lassen, ihn sehr spät benachrichtigen; ***he was given – to quit,*** ihm wurde gekündigt; ***till*** or ***until further –,*** bis auf weiteres; 3. die Aufmerksamkeit, Beachtung; ***–!*** zur Beachtung! Bekanntmachung! ***to avoid –,*** um Aufsehen zu vermeiden; ***beneath his –,*** unter seiner Würde; ***bring to his –,*** ihm zur Kenntnis bringen; ***come into –,*** Aufmerksamkeit erregen; ***come under his –,*** ihm bekanntwerden; ***escape –,*** unbeachtet *or* unbemerkt bleiben; ***take –,*** aufachten (*as a child*); Notiz *or* Kenntnis nehmen (*of,* von), achtgeben auf (*Acc.*), Beachtung schenken (*Dat.*), bemerken, beachten; ***take no – of,*** unbeachtet lassen, nicht achten auf (*Acc.*), sich nicht kümmern um, ignorieren; ***worthy of –,*** der Beachtung wert, beachtungswert. **2.** *v.t.* 1. feststellen, wahrnehmen, beobachten; 2. bemerken, erwähnen, anzeigen; 3. besprechen (*a book*); 4. Notiz nehmen von, beachten, anerkennen, mit Aufmerksamkeit behandeln (*a p.*).

noticeable [ˈnoutisəbl], *adj.* wahrnehmbar, merklich, bemerkbar; sichtbar, ins Auge fallend, auffällig; bemerkenswert. **notice-board,** *s.* schwarzes Brett, die Anschlagtafel.

notifiable [ˈnoutifaiəbl], *adj.* meldepflichtig. **notification** [–fiˈkeiʃən], *s.* die Anzeige, Ankündigung, Bekanntmachung, Mitteilung, Meldung. **notify,** *v.t.* anzeigen, bekanntgeben, melden, kundtun, amtlich mitteilen (***s.th. to him,*** ihm etwas), benachrichtigen, in Kenntnis setzen (***him of,*** ihn von *or* über (*Acc.*)).

notion [ˈnouʃən], *s.* 1. der Begriff, Gedanke, die Vorstellung, Idee (*of*, von); ***airy –s,*** leere Einfälle; ***I have a – that . . .,*** ich denke mir *or* bilde mir ein, daß . . .; ***I had no*** (or ***not the slightest*** or ***vaguest***) ***– that . . .,*** ich hatte keine (*or* nicht die leiseste) Ahnung, daß . . .; ***put –s into his head,*** ihm den Kopf vollmachen; 2. die Meinung, Ansicht; (*coll.*) ***he hasn't a –,*** darüber weiß er absolut nichts; 3. die Absicht, Neigung (***of doing,*** zu tun); 4. *pl.* (*Am.*) Kurzwaren, Galanteriewaren (*pl.*). **notional,** *adj.* 1. Begriffs–, begrifflich, gedanklich, spekulativ; 2. imaginär, nur gedacht, eingebildet; 3. (*Am.*) phantastisch, launenhaft.

notoriety [noutəˈraiəti], *s.* 1. die Offenkundigkeit, allgemeine Bekanntheit, das Berüchtigtsein; ***unenviable –,*** traurige *or* nicht beneidenswerte Berühmtheit; 2. weitbekannte Persönlichkeit. **notorious** [noˈtɔːriəs], *adj.* 1. allgemein bekannt, allbekannt, offenkundig; 2. berüchtigt, nur zu bekannt (***for,*** wegen); 3. (*only attrib.*) notorisch.

notwithstanding [nɔtwiðˈstændiŋ], **1.** *prep.* ungeachtet, unbeschadet (*Gen.*), trotz (*Gen. or Dat.*); ***– that,*** dessenungeachtet. **2.** *conj.* ***– that,*** obgleich. **3.** *adv.* trotzdem, dennoch, nichtsdestoweniger.

nougat [ˈnʌgit, ˈnuːgɑː], *s.* der Nugat.

nought [nɔːt], *s.* (*Math.*) die Null; ***bring to –,*** zerstören, zunichte machen, zum Scheitern bringen; ***come to –,*** fehlschlagen, zunichte werden; zu Wasser werden; ***set at –,*** unbeachtet lassen, sich hinwegsetzen über (*Acc.*), nicht achten, beiseite schieben, in den Wind schlagen; *see also* **naught.**

noumenon [ˈnaumənən], *s.* (*Phil.*) bloße Idee, reines Gedankending, das Ding an sich, Noumenon.

noun [naun], *s.* das Hauptwort, Nennwort, Substantiv; ***proper –,*** der Eigenname.

nourish [ˈnʌriʃ], **1.** *v.t.* (er)nähren (***on,*** von); (*fig.*) nähren (***with,*** mit), erhalten, unterhalten; pflegen, hegen (*feelings etc.*). **2.** *v.i.* nähren, nahrhaft sein. **nourishing,** *adj.* nahrhaft, Nähr–. **nourishment,** *s.* die Ernährung; Nahrung (*also fig.*), das Nahrungsmittel; ***take –,*** Nahrung zu sich nehmen.

nous [naus], *s.* (*Phil.*) der Verstand; (*sl.*) Mutterwitz, die Grütze.

nova [ˈnouvə], *s.* (*Astr.*) neuer Stern.

Nova Scotia [–ˈskouʃiə], *s.* Neuschottland (*n.*).

[1]**novel** [ˈnɔvəl], *s.* der Roman; ***psychological –,*** der Bildungsroman; ***– with a purpose,*** der Tendenzroman; ***short –,*** die Novelle.

[2]**novel,** *adj.* neu(artig), ungewöhnlich.

novelette [nɔvəˈlet], *s.* der Groschenroman, kitschiger Roman. **novelist** [ˈnɔvəlist], *s.* der (die) Romanschriftsteller(in).

novelty [ˈnɔvəlti], *s.* die Neuheit; Neuartigkeit, Neuerung; *pl.* Neuheiten, Modeartikel, Scherzartikel (*pl.*); ***the –,*** das (Aller)neueste, Ungewöhnliche.

November [noˈvembə], *s.* der November.

novercal [noˈvəːkl], *adj.* stiefmütterlich.

Novgorod [ˈnɔvgərɔd], *s.* Nowgorod (*n.*).

novice [ˈnɔvis], *s.* der Neuling, Anfänger; (*Eccl.*) Novize (die Novizin).

novitiate [noˈviʃiət], *s.* (*Eccl.*) die Probezeit, das Noviziat; die Lehr(lings)zeit.

now [nau], **1.** *adv.* nun, jetzt, gegenwärtig, soeben; dann, darauf(hin), damals, zu jener Zeit; ***– –!*** or ***come –!*** nur ruhig! sachte, sachte! ***– and again,*** von Zeit zu Zeit, dann und wann, hin und wieder; ab und zu, gelegentlich, zuweilen; ***before –,*** schon früher, schon einmal, ehedem; ***by –,*** mittlerweile; (*coll.*) ***how –?*** nun, was gibt's? ***– if,*** wenn nun aber; ***just –,*** gerade jetzt, soeben; ***– at last*** or ***length,*** jetzt endlich; (***every***) ***– and then,*** see ***– and again;*** ***– then,*** nun also, wohlan; ***– this – that,*** bald dies, bald das; ***up to*** or ***till –,*** bis jetzt; ***what is it –?*** was gibt's schon wieder? **2.** *conj.* ***–*** (***that***), da nun, nun da, jetzt wo. **3.** *s.* das Jetzt. **nowadays** [–ədeiz], *adv.* heutzutage.

noway(s) [ˈnouwei(z)], *adv.* in keiner Weise, keineswegs.

nowhere [ˈnou(h)wɛə], *adv.* nirgends, nirgendwo, nirgendwohin; (*sl.*) ***be –,*** nicht in Betracht kommen, ganz unten durch sein; (*coll.*) ***– near,*** bei weitem nicht, nicht annähernd.

nowise [ˈnouwaiz], *see* **noway(s).**

noxious [ˈnɔkʃəs], *adj.* schädlich, verderblich. **noxiousness,** *s.* die Schädlichkeit.

nozzle [nɔzl], *s.* die Düse; Mündung, Ausgußröhre (*of a hose*); Tülle, Schneppe, der Ausguß (*of vessels*); (*sl.*) der Zinken, die Schnauze.

nuance [ˈnjuãs], *s.* 1. die Abtönung, Abstufung, Schattierung; 2. feiner Unterschied, die (Bedeutungs)nuance.

nub, nubble [nʌb(l)], *s.* der Klumpen, Auswuchs, Knopf, das Knötchen; (*fig.*) springender Punkt.

Nubian [ˈnjuːbiən], **1.** *s.* der (die) Nubier(in). **2.** *adj.* nubisch.

nubile [ˈnjuːbil], *adj.* heiratsfähig, mannbar (*of females*). **nubility** [–ˈbiliti], *s.* die Heiratsfähigkeit, Mannbarkeit.

nuclear [ˈnjuːkliə], *adj.* kernförmig, Kern–; ***– attack,*** atomarer Angriff; ***– charge,*** die Kernladung; (*Pol.*) ***– deterrent,*** atomare Abschreckung; ***– energy,*** die Kernenergie, Atomenergie; ***– fission,*** die Kernspaltung; ***– physicist,*** der Atomphysiker, Kernphysiker; ***– physics,*** die Kernphysik; ***– plant,*** see ***– power station;*** ***– power,*** die Atomkraft; ***– power station,*** das Atomkraftwerk; ***– reaction,*** die Kernreaktion; ***– reactor,*** der Kernreaktor; ***– research,*** die Atomkernforschung; ***– test,*** der Atomwaffenversuch, Kernwaffenversuch; ***– war(fare),*** der Atomkrieg; ***– warhead,*** der Atomsprengkopf; ***– weapons,*** atomare Waffen, Atomwaffen (*pl.*).

nucleus [ˈnjuːkliəs], *s.* (*pl.* **-lei** [–liai]) der Kern (*also fig.*); (*Bot.*) Samenkern; (*Biol.*) Zellkern; (*Phys.*) Atomkern; (*Opt.*) Kernschatten; (*fig.*) Mittelpunkt, Grundstock.

nude [njuːd], **1.** *adj.* nackt, bloß; (*Law*) nichtig, ungültig. **2.** *s.* die Nacktheit, nackter Zustand; (*Art*) nackte Figur, der Akt.

nudge [nʌdʒ], **1.** *s.* leichter (Rippen)stoß. **2.** *v.t.* leise anstoßen, einen Rippenstoß geben (*Dat.*).

nudism [ˈnjuːdizm], *s.* die Nachtkultur, Freikörperkultur. **nudist,** *s.* der (die) Nudist(in). **nudity** [–diti], *s.* die Nacktheit, Blöße; (*fig.*) Dürftigkeit, Armut.

nugatory [ˈnjuːgətəri], *adj.* wertlos, wirkungslos, bedeutungslos, unwirksam, unbedeutend, eitel, leer, nichtig, albern.

nugget [ˈnʌgit], *s.* der (Gold)klumpen.

nuisance [ˈnjuːsəns], *s.* der Skandal, Unfug, Mißstand, das Ärgernis; die Unannehmlichkeit, Lästigkeit, Ungelegenheit; (***of a p.***) der Quälgeist, die Plage, Pest, lästiger Mensch; ***abate a –,*** einen Mißstand beseitigen, einen Unfug abstellen; ***be a –,*** lästig fallen *or* werden (***to,*** *Dat.*); ***commit no –!*** Verunreinigung dieses Ortes verboten! ***make a – of o.s.,*** sich lästig machen; ***public –,*** öffentliches Ärgernis; die Störung der öffentlichen Ordnung; ***what a –!*** wie ärgerlich! wie unangenehm! **nuisance-raid,** *s.* (*Av.*) der Störflug.

null [nʌl], **1.** *pred. adj,* nichtig, ungültig; wertlos, nichtssagend, gehaltlos, leer; – ***and void,*** null und nichtig. **nullification** [–ifi'keiʃən], *s.* die Aufhebung, Vernichtung, Ungültigmachung, Nichtigkeitserklärung. **nullify** [–ifai], *v.t.* ungültig machen, aufheben, vernichten, (für) null und nichtig erklären. **nullity** [–iti], *s.* (*esp. Law*) die Nichtigkeit, Ungültigkeit; ***decree of –,*** die Annullierung der Ehe; ***suit of –,*** die Nichtigkeitsklage.

numb [nʌm], **1.** *adj.* erstarrt, starr, empfindungslos (***with,*** vor (*Dat.*)); (*fig.*) stumpf, betäubt. **2.** *v.t.* starr machen, erstarren lassen, (*fig.*) abstumpfen, betäuben.

number ['nʌmbə], **1.** *s.* 1. die Zahl, Ziffer, Nummer, das Zahlzeichen; ***by –s,*** nummernweise; ***cardinal –,*** die Grundzahl; ***consecutive –s,*** laufende Nummern; (*Tele.*) – ***engaged,*** besetzt; ***even –,*** gerade Zahl; ***odd –,*** ungerade Zahl; ***ordinal –,*** die Ordnungszahl; (*coll.*) ***his – is up,*** seine Stunde ist geschlagen; – ***one,*** die eigene P., der eigene Vorteil; (*as attrib.*) erstklassig; (*nursery talk*) kleines Geschäft; (*nursery talk*) – ***two,*** großes Geschäft; (*Mil. sl.*) ***a – nine,*** eine Abführpille; – ***10,*** die Amtswohnung des englischen Premierministers; 2. die Anzahl; (*of persons*) Menge, Schar; ***in –,*** an Zahl, der Zahl nach; ***in large –s,*** in großen Mengen; ***in round –s,*** in runder Zahl, rund; ***a great – of,*** sehr viele; ***a – of,*** mehrere, eine Anzahl (*Gen.*); ***the – of times,*** die vielen Male; ***three times the –,*** dreimal so viel; ***by force of –s,*** durch Übermacht; ***one of their –,*** einer aus ihren Reihen; ***–s of times,*** zu wiederholten Malen; ***times out of –, times without –,*** unzählige Male; 3. (*Gram.*) der Numerus; ***plural –,*** die Mehrzahl; ***singular –,*** die Einzahl; 4. das Heft, die Lieferung, Nummer (*of a work*); ***back –,*** die Zeitung älteren Datums; (*coll.*) der Ladenhüter, Mensch mit veralteten Ansichten; ***published in –s,*** in Lieferungen erschienen; 5. (*Metr.*) das Versmaß, Silbenmaß, der Rhythmus. **2.** *v.t.* 1. (zusammen)zählen, numerieren (*houses etc.*); ***the seats are –ed,*** die Plätze sind numeriert; 2. (dazu)zählen, (dazu)rechnen (***among,*** unter (*Acc.*) *or* zu); 3. betragen, zählen, sich belaufen auf (*Acc.*); 4. (*Mil. fig.*) – (***off***), abzählen; ***my hours are –ed,*** meine Stunden sind gezählt.

numbering ['nʌmbəriŋ], *s.* die Numerierung. **numberless,** *adj.* zahllos, unzählig. **number-plate,** *s.* (*Motor.*) das Nummernschild. **Numbers,** *pl.* (*sing. constr.*) (*B.*) Numeri (*m. pl.*) (4. Buch Mose).

numbness ['nʌmnis], *s.* die Erstarrung, Starrheit; Betäubung.

numerable ['nju:mərəbl], *adj.* zählbar. **numeracy** [–əsi], *s.* das Rechenkenntnis. **numeral, 1.** *adj.* Zahl(en)–. **2.** *s.* das Zahlzeichen, die Grundzahl, Ziffer, Nummer; (*Gram.*) das Zahlwort. **numerate** [–eit], *adj.* rechenkundig. **numeration** [–'reiʃən], *s.* das Zählen, Rechnen, die Zählkunst, Rechenkunst; (Auf)zählung, Numerierung. **numerative** [–ətiv], *adj.* Zahl(en)–. **numerator** [–eitə], *s.* der Zähler (*of a fraction*).

numerical [nju:'merikl], *adj.* zahlenmäßig, Zahl(en)–, Nummern–, numerisch; – ***order,*** die Zahlenordnung; – ***value,*** der Zahlenwert; – ***majority,*** zahlenmäßige Mehrheit. **numerically,** *adv.* zahlenmäßig, an Zahl, der Zahl nach, in Zahlen.

numerous ['nju:mərəs], *adj.* zahlreich; ***–ly attended,*** stark besucht. **numerousness,** *s.* die Menge, Anzahl, große Zahl.

numismatic [nju:miz'mætik], *adj.* numismatisch, Münz(en)–. **numismatics,** *pl.* (*sing. constr.*) die Münzkunde. **numismatist** [–'mizmətist], *s.* der Münzenkenner.

nummulite ['nʌmjəlait], *s.* der Nummulit, Kalkmünzstein.

numskull ['nʌmskʌl], *s.* (*coll.*) der Dummkopf, Tölpel, Tropf.

nun [nʌn], *s.* die Nonne, Klosterfrau, Schwester; (*Orn.*) Blaumeise (*Parus caeruleus*). **nun-buoy,** *s.* (*Naut.*) die Spitztonne.

nunciature ['nʌnʃətjuə], *s.* (*R.C.*) die Nunziatur. **nuncio** [–ʃiou], *s.* (*R.C.*) der Nunzius.

nuncupative ['nʌnkjəpeitiv], *adj.* mündlich; (*Law*) – ***will,*** mündliche letztwillige Verfügung.

nunnery ['nʌnəri], *s.* das Nonnenkloster.

nuptial ['nʌpʃəl], *adj.* Hochzeits–, Ehe–, Trauungs–; – ***bed,*** das Brautbett; – ***chamber,*** das Brautgemach; (*Ent.*) die Hochzeitskammer. **nuptials,** *pl.* die Hochzeit.

Nuremberg ['njuərəmbə:g], *s.* Nürnberg (*n.*).

nurse [nə:s], **1.** *s.* 1. die Krankenschwester, Krankenpflegerin, Krankenwärterin; ***male –,*** der Krankenpfleger, Krankenwärter; ***trained –,*** die (Kranken)-schwester; 2. die Amme, Kinderwärterin, Kinderfrau, das Kindermädchen; ***children's –,*** das Kindermädchen; ***wet –,*** die Amme; ***put (out) to –,*** in Pflege geben; 3. (*fig.*) die Nährmutter. **2.** *v.t.* 1. säugen, stillen, die Brust geben (*Dat.*) (*an infant*); 2. pflegen, warten (*the sick etc.*); durch schonende Behandlung kurieren, auskurieren (*a cold etc.*); 3. schonen, hätscheln (*an injury, one's voice etc.*); – ***one's leg,*** das eine Bein über das andere schlagen; 4. auf den Schoß nehmen (*child, doll etc.*); 5. aufziehen, großziehen (*also fig.*), (*fig.*) nähren, hegen, pflegen, fördern (*plants, growth etc.*); – ***a grievance,*** einen Groll hegen; 6. sparsam verwalten, schonend umgeben mit (*resources etc.*).

nurseling, *see* **nursling.**

nursemaid ['nə:smeid], *s.* das Kindermädchen.

nursery ['nə:səri], *s.* 1. die Kinderstube, das Kinderzimmer; 2. (*Hort.*) die Pflanzschule, Baumschule, Samenschule; 3. (*fig.*) Pflanzstätte, Zuchtstätte. **nursery| cannon,** *s.* (*Bill.*) die Karambolageserie. **--governess,** *s.* das Kinderfräulein. **–man** [–mən], *s.* der Kunstgärtner, Handelsgärtner, Pflanzenzüchter. **--rhyme,** *s.* der Kinderreim, das Kinderlied. **--school,** *s.* der Kindergarten. – **slopes,** *pl.* (*skiing*) Anfängerhügel, (*coll.*) Idiotenhügel (*pl.*). – **stakes,** *s.* das Rennen für Zweijährige (*horse-racing*).

nursing ['nə:siŋ], *s.* 1. das Stillen, Säugen; 2. (*also sick-–*) die Krankenpflege. **nursing|-bottle,** *s.* die Saugflasche. **--home,** *s.* die (Privat)klinik. – **mother,** *s.* stillende Mutter.

nursling ['nə:sliŋ], *s.* der Säugling; Pflegling, das Pflegekind; (*fig.*) der Schützling, Liebling.

nurture ['nə:tʃə], **1.** *s.* die Nahrung; Ernährung, das Nähren; (*fig.*) die Pflege, Erziehung. **2.** *v.t.* (er)nähren; (*fig.*) erziehen, aufziehen.

nut [nʌt], **1.** *s.* 1. die Nuß; (*sl.*) ***be –s on,*** versessen sein auf (*Acc.*), verschossen *or* vernarrt sein in (*Acc.*); ***crack –s,*** Nüsse knacken; (*fig.*) ***a hard*** or ***tough – to crack,*** ein harte Nuß; (*sl.*) ***–s!*** Quatsch! (*coll.*) ***not for –s,*** überhaupt nicht; (*sl.*) ***go –s,*** überschnappen, verrückt werden; 2. (*Tech.*) die (Schrauben)mutter; 3. der Frosch (*on a violinbow*); 4. (*coll.*) Geck, Zierbengel; 5. (*sl.*) die Birne; ***off one's –,*** verrückt; 6. *pl.* die Nußkohle. **2.** *v.i.* Nüsse sammeln *or* pflücken.

nutant ['nju:tənt], *adj.* (*Bot.*) überhängend. **nutation** [–'teiʃən], *s.* (*Bot., Astr.*) die Nutation, (*Med.*) unwillkürliches *or* krankhaftes Nicken.

nut|-brown, *adj.* nußbraun. **--butter,** *s.* die Nußbutter. **–cracker,** *s.* (*Orn.*) der Tannenhäher (*Nucifraga caryocatactes*); *pl.* der Nußknacker. **--gall,** *s.* der Gallapfel. **–hatch,** *s.* (*Orn.*) der Kleiber (*Sitta europæa*). **–meg,** *s.* die Muskatnuß.

nutria ['nju:triə], *s.* der Biberrattenpelz.

nutrient ['nju:triənt], **1.** *adj.* nährend, nahrhaft; Nähr–, Ernährungs–. **2.** *s.* der Nährstoff. **nutriment,** *s.* die Nahrung, das Nahrungsmittel.

nutrition [nju:'triʃən], *s.* die Ernährung; der Ernährungsvorgang. **nutritionist,** *s.* der Diätetiker, Ernährungssachverständige(r). **nutritious,** *adj.* nahrhaft, nährend. **nutritiousness,** *s.* die Nahrhaftigkeit. **nutritive** ['nju:tritiv], *adj. See* **nutrient, 1. nutritiveness,** *s. See* **nutritiousness.**

nut|shell, *s.* die Nußschale; (*usu. fig.*) ***in a –,*** in nuce, mit einem Wort, in aller Kürze, in wenigen Worten. **--tree,** *s.* der Haselnußbaum. **nutty,** *adj.* 1. Nuß–, nußartig; 2. nußreich; 3. (*fig.*) würzig, pikant; 4. (*sl.*) – ***on,*** *see* **nut, 1,** 1.

nux vomica [nʌks'vɔmikə], *s.* die Brechnuß; (*Bot.*) der Brechnußbaum.

nuzzle [nʌzl], **1.** *v.t.* mit der Schnauze aufwühlen (*of pigs*), mit dem Kopf reiben an (*Dat.*); (*fig.*) liebkosen, hätscheln (*as children*). **2.** *v.i.* schnüffeln, stöbern, mit der Schnauze wühlen (*in*, in (*Dat.*); *for*, nach); die Schnauze stecken (*into*, in (*Acc.*)), den Kopf drücken (an (*Acc.*)), sich (an)schmiegen *or* drücken (*against*, an (*Acc.*)).

Nyasaland [nai'æsəlænd], *s.* (*obs.*) Njassaland (*n.*).

nyctalopia [niktə'loupiə], *s.* die Nachtblindheit.

nylg(h)au ['nilgɔ:], *s.* die Nilgauantilope.

nylon ['nailɔn], *s.* das Nylon; *pl.* (*coll.*) Nylonstrümpfe (*pl.*).

nymph [nimf], *s.* 1. die Nymphe; 2. (*Ent.*) Larve, Puppe. **nymphal,** *adj.* (*Ent.*) Puppen–. **nymphean** [–'fiən], *adj.* nymphish. **nymph-like,** *adj.* nymphenhaft.

nymphomania [nimfə'meiniə], *s.* die Mannstollheit. **nymphomaniac,** *s.* mannstolles Weib.

nystagmus [nis'tægməs], *s.* das Augenzittern.

O

O, o [ou], **1.** *s.* das O, o; (*Math.*) die Null; *see Index of Abbreviations.* **2.** *int.* (*when followed by another word without intervening punctuation*) ach! – *yes!* jawohl! – *no!* Gott bewahre! *see also* **oh.**

o' [ə], *abbr.* = *of*, *e.g. one o'clock.*

oaf [ouf], *s.* der Dummkopf, Einfaltspinsel, Lümmel, Dämel, Däm(e)lack. **oafish,** *adj.* dumm, einfältig, tölpelhaft, dämlich.

oak [ouk], **1.** *s.* die Eiche, der Eich(en)baum; das Eichenholz; Eichenlaub; (*Univ.*) *sport one's –*, nicht zu sprechen sein, die Tür verschließen; *the Oaks*, das Fohlenrennen zu Epsom (*horse-racing*). **2.** *adj.* eichen, Eichen–.

oak|-apple, *s.* der Gallapfel. **--beauty,** *s.* (*Ent.*) der Eichenspanner. **oaken,** *adj.* (*Poet.*) *see* **oak, 2. oak|-gall,** *s. See* **--apple. --tree,** *s.* die Eiche, der Eich(en)baum.

oakum ['oukəm], *s.* das Werg; *pick –*, Werg zupfen.

oar [ɔ:], **1.** *s.* 1. das Ruder (*also fig.*); (*Naut.*) der (Boots)riemen; *bank of –s*, die Ruderbank; *pull a good –*, gut rudern; *put one's – in*, seine Hand im Spiele haben, seinen Senf dazugeben; *rest on one's –s*, aufhören zu rudern; (*fig.*) auf seinen Lorbeeren ausruhen; *ship the –s*, die Riemen einlegen; 2. (*Spt.*) der Ruderer. **2.** *v.t.*, *v.i.* (*Poet.*) rudern. **oared** [ɔ:d], *adj. suff.* mit Rudern, –ruderig. **oarlock,** *s.* (*Am.*) *see* **rowlock. oarsman** ['ɔ:zmən], *s.* der Ruderer. **oarsmanship,** *s.* die Ruderkunst. **oarswoman,** *s.* die Ruderin.

oasis [ou'eisis], *s.* (*pl.* **oases** [–si:z]) die Oase.

oast [oust], *s.* die (Hopfen)darre. **oast-house,** *s.* das Darrhaus, die Hopfendarre.

oat [out], *s.* (*usu. pl.*) der Hafer; *false –*, der Wiesenhafer; (*porridge*) *–s*, Haferflocken (*pl.*); *sow one's wild –s*, sich (*Dat.*) die Hörner ablaufen. **oatcake,** *s.* der Haferkuchen. **oaten,** *adj.* Hafer–; *– pipe*, die Hirtenpfeife.

oath [ouθ], *s.* 1. der Eid, Schwur; *– of allegiance*, der Treueid, Fahneneid; *false –*, der Falscheid, Meineid; *– of fealty*, der Lehnseid; *– of office, official –*, der Amtseid, Diensteid; *administer* or *tender an* or *the – to him, put him on his –*, ihn schwören lassen, ihn vereidigen, ihm den Eid abnehmen; *swear an –*, einen Eid ablegen *or* leisten, schwören (*on, to*, auf (*Acc.*)); *take the –*, den Eid leisten; *I will take my – that . . .*, ich beschwöre *or* will darauf schwören, daß . . .; *by (an) –*, eidlich, durch Eidschwur; *in lieu of (an) –*, an Eides Statt, eidesstattlich; *on (one's)* or *under (an) –*, unter Eid, eidlich verpflichtet; *under the – of secrecy*, unter dem Siegel der Verschwiegenheit; *upon my –!* das kann ich beschwören! 2. der Fluch, die Verwünschung; *utter an –*, fluchen. **oath|-breaking,** *s.* der Eidbruch. **--taking,** *s.* die Eidesleistung (*to*, auf (*Acc.*)).

oatmeal ['outmi:l], *s.* das Hafermehl, die Hafergrütze.

Obadiah [oubə'daiə], *s.* (*B.*) (das Buch) Obadja.

obbligato [ɔbli'gɑ:tou], **1.** *s.* (*pl.* **-s**) (*Mus.*) selbständige Begleitstimme. **2.** *adj.* selbständig geführt.

obduracy ['ɔbdjurəsi], *s.* die Verstocktheit, Halsstarrigkeit. **obdurate** [–ət], *adj.* verstockt, halsstarrig, unbeugsam.

obedience [ə'bi:diəns], *s.* 1. der Gehorsam (*to*, gegen); *– from one's children*, Gehorsam von seiten seiner Kinder; *absolute –*, der Kadavergehorsam; 2. (*fig.*) die Abhängigkeit (*to*, von), Unterwerfung (unter (*Acc.*)); *in – to*, (*a th.*) entsprechend, gemäß (*Dat.*), im Verfolg (*Gen.*); (*a p.*) auf Verlangen *or* unter dem Druck von; 3. (*Eccl.*) die Obedienz, Gehorsamspflicht, (*also fig.*) Herrschaft, Obrigkeit; 4. (*obs.*) Ehrfurchtsbezeigung. **obedient,** *adj.* gehorsam (*to, Dat.*); unterwürfig, ergeben, folgsam (*Dat.*), (*fig.*) abhängig (von); *your – servant*, Ihr sehr ergebener.

obeisance [o'beisəns], *s.* 1. die Verbeugung; *make one's – to*, sich verbeugen vor (*Dat.*); 2. die Huldigung, Ehrerbietung; *make* or *do* or *pay – to*, huldigen (*Dat.*).

obelisk ['ɔbəlisk], *s.* 1. (*Archit.*) der Obelisk, die Spitzsäule; 2. (*Typ.*) *see* **obelus. obelize** [–laiz], *v.t.* (*Typ.*) als fragwürdig bezeichnen. **obelus** [–ləs], *s.* (*pl.* **-li** [–lai]) der Obelus, das Kreuz.

obese [ou'bi:s], *adj.* beleibt, fettleibig, korpulent. **obeseness, obesity** [–iti], *s.* die Beleibtheit, Fettleibigkeit, Korpulenz.

obey [o'bei], **1.** *v.t.*, *v.i.* (*a p.*) gehorchen, folgen (*Dat.*). **2.** *v.t.* (*command*) Folge leisten (*Dat.*), befolgen; *– orders*, Befehle ausführen.

obfuscate ['ɔbfʌskeit], *v.t.* verdunkeln, (*fig.*) trüben, verwirren. **obfuscation** [–'keiʃən], *s.* die Verdunk(e)lung, Trübung; (*fig.*) Verwirrung, Betäubung, Benebelung.

obit ['ɔbit], *s.* (*obs.*) die Seelenmesse, Todesgedenkfeier. **obituary** [ə'bitjuəri], **1.** *s.* die Todesanzeige, der Nachruf, Nekrolog. **2.** *adj.* Todes–; *– notice*, die Todesanzeige.

1**object** [əb'dʒekt], **1.** *v.t.* 1. vorhalten, vorwerfen (*to, Dat.*); 2. (*fig.*) einwenden, vorbringen (*to*, gegen). **2.** *v.i.* 1. Einspruch erheben, Einwendungen machen, protestieren (*to*, gegen); 2. etwas einwenden, etwas dagegen haben (*to my smoking*, wenn ich rauche).

2**object** ['ɔbdʒikt], *s.* 1. der Gegenstand, das Objekt, Ding; *money (is) no –*, Geld ist Nebensache *or* spielt keine Rolle; *salary no –*, auf Gehalt wird nicht gesehen; 2. das Ziel, der Zweck, die Absicht; *make it one's –*, es sich (*Dat.*) zum Ziel setzen, es sich (*Dat.*) zur Aufgabe machen; *what is his –?* was bezweckt er? 3. (*Gram.*) das Objekt. **object-glass,** *s. See* **objective, 2,** 1.

objectify [əb'dʒektifai], *v.t.* vergegenständlichen, objektivieren.

objection [əb'dʒekʃən], *s.* die Einwendung, der Einwand, Einspruch, Einwurf, das Bedenken (*to*, gegen); der Widerwille, die Abneigung, Beanstandung; *have no –s*, nichts dagegen haben, nichts auszusetzen *or* einzuwenden haben; *make* or *raise an –*, einen Einwand erheben (*to*, gegen); *right of –*, das Einspruchsrecht; *take – to*, Einspruch *or* Protest erheben gegen; *no – to a married man*, verheiratete Bewerber nicht ausgeschlossen. **objectionable,** *adj.* 1. nicht einwandfrei, unannehmbar, unzulässig; 2. anstößig, unangenehm (*to*, für *or Dat.*).

objective [ɔb'dʒektiv], **1.** *adj.* 1. objectiv, konkret, wirklich, gegenständlich; 2. objektiv, sachlich, unpersönlich, vorurteilslos; 3. (*Gram.*) – *case*, der Objektsfall; – *genitive*, objectiver Genitiv; 4. (*Mil.*) – *point*, das (Operations)ziel, Angriffsziel. **2.** *s.* 1. (*Phot.*) das Objektiv, die Objektivlinse; 2. (*Gram.*) der Objektsfall; 3. (*Mil., fig.*) das Reiseziel, (End)ziel, Operationsziel. **objectiveness, objectivity** [–'tiviti], *s.* die Objektivität.

object-lens, *see* **objective, 2,** 1.

objectless ['ɔbdʒiktlis], *adj.* 1. gegenstandslos; 2. ziellos, zwecklos. **object-lesson,** *s.* 1. die Anschauungsstunde, der Anschauungsunterricht; 2. (*fig.*) lehrreiches *or* anschauliches Beispiel.

objector [ɔb'dʒektə], *s.* der Gegner, Widersacher; *conscientious* –, der Kriegsdienstverweigerer.

objurgate ['ɔbdʒə:geit], *v.t.* tadeln, schelten. **objurgation** [–'geiʃən], *s.* der Tadel. **objurgatory** [–'dʒə:gətəri], *adj.* tadelnd.

[1]**oblate** [ou'bleit], *adj.* abgeplattet.

[2]**oblate** ['ɔbleit], *s.* (*R.C.*) der Laienbruder, die Laienschwester.

oblateness [ou'bleitnis], *s.* die Abplattung.

oblation [ɔb'leiʃən], *s.* das Opfer, die Opfergabe. **oblatory** ['ɔblətəri], *adj.* Opfer–.

obligate ['ɔbligeit], *v.t.* (*usu. pass.*) 1. verpflichten; 2. (*Law*) zwingen, nötigen. **obligation** [–'geiʃən], *s.* 1. die Verbindlichkeit, Verpflichtung, Obliegenheit (*to*, gegenüber); *be* or *lie under an* –, verbunden *or* zu Dank verpflichtet sein (*to*, *Dat.*); *incur an* –, eine Verbindlichkeit eingehen; *lay* or *put him under an* –, ihn verpflichten; *meet one's* –*s*, seinen Verpflichtungen nachkommen; *of* –, obligatorisch; (*Eccl.*) *days of* –, strenge Fasttage; *without* –, unverbindlich, freibleibend; 2. (*Comm.*) die Schuldverschreibung, Obligation. **obligatory** [ɔ'bligətəri], *adj.* verbindlich, bindend, verpflichtend, obligatorisch ((*up*)*on*, für).

oblige [ə'blaidʒ], **1.** *v.t.* 1. nötigen, zwingen; *be* –*d to go*, gehen müssen; 2. verpflichten, verbinden; *be* –*d to him*, ihm verbunden *or* zu Dank verpflichtet sein, es ihm zu verdanken haben; – *him*, ihm gefällig sein, ihm dienen *or* einen Gefallen tun; – *me by asking him*, wollen Sie die Güte haben *or* so freundlich sein, ihn zu fragen? *to* – *you*, Ihnen zu Gefallen; *much* –*ed!* sehr verbunden! *anything to* – (*you*)*!* wenn ich Ihnen damit einen Gefallen tun kann! **2.** *v.i.* 1. (*coll.*) zur Unterhaltung beitragen (*with*, mit *or* durch), etwas zum besten geben; – *with a song*, ein Lied zum besten geben; 2. (*Comm.*) erwünscht sein; *early reply will* –, *please* – *with an early reply*, um baldige Antwort wird gebeten.

obligee [ɔbli'dʒi:], *s.* (*Law*) der (Obligations)-gläubiger, Forderungsberechtigte(r). **obligement** [ə'blaidʒmənt], *s.* der Gefallen, die Gefälligkeit.

obliging [ə'blaidʒiŋ], *adj.* verbindlich, gefällig, zuvorkommend, entgegenkommend, dienstfertig. **obligingness,** *s.* die Gefälligkeit, Zuvorkommenheit. **obligor** [ɔbli'gɔ:], *s.* (*Law*) der (Obligations)-schuldner.

oblique [o'bli:k], *adj.* 1. schief, schräg; – *angle*, schiefer Winkel; (*Artil.*) – *fire*, das Schrägfeuer; 2. (*fig.*) mittelbar, indirekt, versteckt; – *glance*, der Seitenblick; 3. heimtückisch, unaufrichtig; 4. (*Gram.*) abhängig, indirekt; – *case*, abhängiger Fall; – *speech*, indirekte Rede. **obliqueness,** *s.* 1. *See* **obliquity**; 2. (*fig.*) die Unaufrichtigkeit, Unredlichkeit.

obliquity [o'blikwiti], *s.* 1. die Schrägheit, Schiefe, schiefe Lage *or* Richtung, die Schrägstellung; (*Astr.*) Schiefe; 2. (*fig.*) Schiefheit, Unregelmäßigkeit; 3. Verirrung, der Abweg, das Vergehen.

obliterate [o'blitəreit], *v.t.* auslöschen, ausradieren, (ver)tilgen; entwerten (*stamps*); (*fig.*) verwischen, vernichten. **obliteration** [–'reiʃən], *s.* die Auslöschung, das Verwischen; (*fig.*) die Vernichtung, Vertilgung.

oblivion [o'bliviən], *s.* 1. die Vergeßlichkeit; *act of* –, der Gnadenerlaß, Straferlaß, die Amnestie; 2. die Vergessenheit; *commit to* –, der Vergessenheit überlassen; *fall* or *sink into* –, in Vergessenheit geraten. **oblivious,** *adj.* vergeßlich; *be* – *of*, vergessen; *be* – *to*, blind sein gegen. **obliviousness,** *s.* die Vergeßlichkeit.

oblong ['ɔblɔŋ], **1.** *adj.* länglich; (*Geom.*) rechteckig. **2.** *s.* das Rechteck.

obloquy ['ɔbləkwi], *s.* 1. die Schmähung, Verleumdung; 2. Schande, Schmach, schlechter Ruf, der Verruf.

obnoxious [əb'nɔkʃəs], *adj.* 1. gehässig, anstößig, abscheulich; 2. verhaßt (*to*, *Dat.*); 3. (*obs.*) preisgegeben, unterworfen, ausgesetzt (*to*, *Dat.*). **obnoxiousness,** *s.* 1. die Anstößigkeit, Verhaßtheit; 2. (*of a p.*) Gehässigkeit.

oboe ['oubou], *s.* die Oboe. **oboist,** *s.* der Oboist.

obscene [ɔb'si:n], *adj.* schlüpfrig, zotig, unzüchtig, obszön. **obscenity** [–'seniti], *s.* die Schlüpfrigkeit, Unzüchtigkeit; *pl.* Zoten (*pl.*).

obscurant [ɔb'skjuərənt], *s.* der Obskurant, Finsterling, Dunkelmann, Bildungsfeind. **obscurantism** [–'ræntizm], *s.* der Obskurantismus, Bildungshaß, die Kulturfeindlichkeit, Verdummung. **obscurantist** [–'ræntist], **1.** *s.* *See* **obscurant. 2.** *adj.* obskurantistisch, kulturfeindlich.

obscuration [ɔbskjuə'reiʃən], *s.* (*Astr.*) die Verdunkelung.

obscure [ɔb'skjuə], **1.** *adj.* 1. dunkel, finster, düster, trübe; 2. (*fig.*) dunkel, unklar, unverständlich, undeutlich; 3. unberühmt, unbekannt, unbedeutend, unauffällig, unscheinbar; obskur; 4. verborgen, abgelegen. **2.** *v.t.* 1. verdunkeln, verfinstern, trüben; 2. (*fig.*) undeutlich *or* unverständlich machen; 3. verbergen, in den Schatten stellen. **3.** *s.* (*Poet.*) *see* **obscurity.**

obscurity [ɔb'skjuəriti], *s.* 1. die Finsternis, Dunkelheit, das Dunkel; 2. (*fig.*) die Undeutlichkeit, Unklarheit, Unverständlichkeit, Dunkelheit; 3. Verborgenheit, Unbekanntheit; *retire into* –, sich vom öffentlichen Leben zurückziehen; 4. die Niedrigkeit (*of birth*); *be lost in* –, vergessen sein.

obsecration [ɔbsi'kreiʃən], *s.* flehentliche Bitte, die Beschwörung; (*Eccl.*) das Bittgebet, die Bittformel.

obsequies ['ɔbsikwiz], *pl.* das Leichenbegängnis, die Leichenfeier.

obsequious [əb'si:kwiəs], *adj.* unterwürfig, kriecherisch, kriechend, knechtisch, servil. **obsequiousness,** *s.* die Unterwürfigkeit, Servilität, Kriecherei.

observable [əb'zə:vəbl], *adj.* 1. zu beachten(d), bemerkbar, merklich, wahrnehmbar; 2. bemerkenswert. **observance,** *s.* 1. die Beobachtung, Befolgung, Innehaltung, Einhaltung (*of laws etc.*); 2. Vorschrift, Regel, Sitte, (herkömmlicher) Brauch, das Herkommen; 3. Feiern, die Heilighaltung; 4. Ordensregel, Observanz.

observant [əb'zə:vənt], *adj.* 1. beobachtend, befolgend (*of*, *Acc.*), haltend auf (*Acc.*); *be* – *of*, halten auf (*Acc.*), befolgen; 2. aufmerksam, achtsam, wachsam (*of*, auf (*Acc.*)). **observation** [ɔbzə'veiʃən], *s.* 1. die Beobachtung, Wahrnehmung; *fall under his* –, von ihm bemerkt werden; *keep under* –, beobachten *or* überwachen (lassen); 2. die Beobachtungsgabe, das Beobachtungsvermögen; 3. *See* **observance**; 4. die Äußerung, Bemerkung (*on*, über (*Acc.*)); *make an* –, eine Bemerkung machen.

observation|-balloon, *s.* der Fesselballon. **–-car,** *s.* (*Railw.*) der Aussichtswagen. **–-plane,** *s.* das Aufklärungsflugzeug. **–-port,** *s.* die Sehklappe. **–-post,** *s.* die Beobachtungsstelle, der Beobachtungsstand. **–-tower,** *s.* der Aussichtsturm. **–-ward,** *s.* die Beobachtungsstation.

observatory [əb'zə:vətəri], *s.* die Sternwarte, Wetterwarte.

observe [əb'zə:v], **1.** *v.t.* 1. beobachten, wahrnehmen, feststellen, bemerken; 2. äußern, bemerken, sagen; 3. halten, feiern (*holidays*); 4. be(ob)achten, befolgen, einhalten, innehalten (*rules*); – *the proprieties*, die Anstandsregeln beachten; – ***silence,*** Stillschweigen bewahren. **2.** *v.i.* Beobachtungen *or* Bemerkungen machen, sich äußern ((***up***)***on***, über (*Acc.*)). **observer,** *s.* 1. der Beobachter, Zuschauer; 2. Befolger (*of rules*); 3. (*Av.*) Beobachter; (*Mil.*) Luftspäher; (*Mil.*) – ***corps,*** der Flugmeldedienst.

obsess [ɔb'sɛs], *v.t.* quälen, heimsuchen, verfolgen; ***–ed with*** or ***by,*** besessen von. **obsession** [–'seʃən], *s.* fixe Idee, die Besessenheit, der Verfolgungswahn; (*Med.*) die Zwangsvorstellung.

obsidian [ɔb'sidiən], *s.* (*Geol.*) der Obsidian, Feuerkiesel.

obsolescence [ɔbsə'lesəns], *s.* das Veralten. **obsolescent,** *adj.* veraltend.

obsolete ['ɔbsəli:t], *adj.* 1. veraltet, außer Gebrauch, überholt; 2. abgenutzt, verbraucht; 3. (*Biol.*) unvollkommen entwickelt, rudimentär. **obsoleteness,** *s.* 1. das Veraltetsein, die Verbrauchtheit; 2. (*Biol.*) unvollkommene Entwicklung.

obstacle ['ɔbstəkl], *s.* das Hindernis (***to***, für), die Sperre. **obstacle-race,** *s.* das Hindernisrennen.

obstetric(al) [ɔb'stetrik(l)], *adj.* geburtshilflich, Geburts–, Entbindungs–. **obstetrician** [–'triʃən], *s.* der Geburtshelfer. **obstetrics,** *pl.* (*sing. constr.*) die Geburtshilfe.

obstinacy ['ɔbstinəsi], *s.* die Hartnäckigkeit (*also fig. of disease, struggle etc.*), Halsstarrigkeit, Unbeugsamkeit, der Eigensinn, Starrsinn. **obstinate** [–nit], *adj.* hartnäckig (*also fig,*), halsstarrig, starrsinnig, eigensinnig, störrisch.

obstreperous [ɔb'strepərəs], *adj.* 1. lärmend, geräuschvoll, überlaut; 2. widerspenstig, ungebärdig, tobend. **obstreperousness,** *s.* das Lärmen, Toben, die Widerspenstigkeit.

obstruct [ɔb'strʌkt], **1.** *v.t.* 1. versperren, blockieren (*the way etc.*); verstopfen; 2. aufhalten, nicht durchlassen, behindern, hemmen, lahmlegen (*traffic*); 3. (*fig.*) verhindern, vereiteln. **2.** *v.i.* (*Parl. etc.*) Obstruktion treiben. **obstruction** [–kʃən], *s.* 1. die Verstopfung (*also Med.*), Versperrung, Hemmung, Behinderung; 2. das Hindernis (***to***, für). **obstructionism,** *s.* die Obstruktionspolitik. **obstructionist, 1.** *s.* der Obstruktionist. **2.** *adj.* Obstruktions–. **obstructive** [–tiv], **1.** *adj.* (*usu. fig.*) hinderlich (***of, to,*** für); ***be –,*** sich sträuben; ***be – to,*** behindern. **2.** *s.* das Hindernis, Hemmnis; *see also* **obstructionist. obstructiveness,** *s.* die Hinderlichkeit; Obstruktion.

obtain [ɔb'tein], **1.** *v.t.* erlangen, erreichen, bekommen, erhalten, erwerben, erzielen, sich (*Dat.*) verschaffen *or* besorgen; – ***by entreaty,*** erbitten; – ***by flattery,*** (sich (*Dat.*)) erschmeicheln; – ***expert opinion,*** ein Gutachten einholen; – ***the prize,*** den Preis gewinnen; – ***the victory,*** den Sieg davontragen; – ***one's wish,*** seinen Willen durchsetzen; ***further information may be –ed from,*** Näheres erfährt man von. **2.** *v.i.* bestehen, (vor)herrschen, in Gebrauch sein, üblich sein, Geltung haben, anerkannt werden, sich behaupten. **obtainable,** *adj.* erreichbar, zu erlangen(d), erhältlich (***at***, bei). **obtainment,** *s.* (*rare*) die Erlangung.

obtrude [ɔb'tru:d], **1.** *v.t.* aufdrängen, aufdringen, aufnötigen, aufzwingen ((***up***)***on,*** *Dat.*); – ***o.s.*** (***up***)***on,*** *see* **2. 2.** *v.i.* sich aufdrängen ((***up***)***on,*** *Dat.*), zudringlich sein *or* werden. **obtruder,** *s.* Aufdringliche(r).

obtrusion [ɔb'tru:ʒən], *s.* 1. das Aufdrängen, Aufdringen, die Aufnötigung; 2. (etwas) Aufgezwungenes. **obtrusive** [–siv], *adj.* (*a p.*) aufdringlich, zudringlich, (*a th.*) aufdringlich, sich aufdrängend. **obtrusiveness,** *s.* die Aufdringlichkeit.

obturate ['ɔbtjureit], *v.t.* verstopfen, zustopfen; abdichten, verschließen. **obturation** [–'reiʃən], *s.* die Abdichtung, Verschließung; (*of a gun*) Liderung. **obturator,** *s.* die Schließvorrichtung, Abdichtungsvorrichtung, Verschlußvorrichtung, der Verschluß; (*Anat.*) Schließmuskel; (*of a gun*) Liderungsring.

obtuse [ɔb'tju:s], *adj.* **1.** (*Geom.*) stumpf; – ***angle,*** stumpfer Winkel; 2. (*fig.*) dumpf (*as pain*); 3. (*of a p.*) beschränkt, stumpfsinnig. **obtuseness,** *s.* 1. die Stumpfheit; 2. Stumpfsinnigkeit, Beschränktheit.

obverse ['ɔbvə:s], **1.** *adj.* 1. dem Betrachter zugewandt, Vorder–; 2. (*Bot.*) umgekehrt. **2.** *s.* 1. die Vorderseite, Bildseite, der Avers (*of a coin*); 2. das Gegenstück, die andere Seite; 3. (*Log.*) umgekehrter Schluß. **obversely** [–'və:sli], *adv.* umgekehrt. **obversion** [–'və:ʃən], *s.* (*Log.*) die Umkehrung.

obviate ['ɔbvieit], *v.t.* 1. vorbeugen (*Dat.*), zuvorkommen (*Dat.*), begegnen (*Dat.*); abwenden; verhindern, verhüten; 2. erübrigen, überflüssig *or* unnötig machen; 3. beseitigen, aus dem Wege räumen (*difficulties*). **obviation** [–'eiʃən], *s.* das Vorbeugen, die Abwendung, Beseitigung; Verhütung, Erübrigung.

obvious ['ɔbviəs], *adj.* handgreiflich, augenfällig, augenscheinlich, offensichtlich, klar, deutlich, offenbar, unverkennbar; ***be –,*** einleuchten, auf der Hand liegen, in die Augen springen; ***the – thing,*** das Naheliegendste; ***an – ruse,*** eine durchsichtige List. **obviousness,** *s.* die Augenscheinlichkeit, Augenfälligkeit, Offensichtlichkeit, Unverkennbarkeit, Deutlichkeit.

occasion [ə'keiʒən], **1.** *s.* 1. die Veranlassung, der Anlaß, Grund (***for***, zu), die Ursache (*Gen.*); ***there is no – for,*** es besteht kein Grund zu; ***be the – of, give – to,*** Anlaß *or* den Anstoß geben zu, veranlassen, hervorrufen; ***have – to do,*** Grund haben zu tun; 2. (günstige) Gelegenheit (***for***, für *or* zu); ***as – serves,*** wenn sich die Gelegenheit (dar)bietet; ***for the –,*** eigens zu diesem Zweck; ***on –,*** bei Gelegenheit, wenn nötig, gelegentlich; ***on the – of,*** anläßlich *or* gelegentlich (*Gen.*); ***on this –,*** bei dieser Gelegenheit; ***be equal*** or ***rise to the –,*** sich der Lage gewachsen zeigen; 3. (*coll.*) das Ereignis, die Veranstaltung; ***celebrate the –,*** das Ereignis feiern. **2.** *v.t.* veranlassen, verursachen, bewirken, zeitigen.

occasional [ə'keiʒənl], *adj.* 1. zufällig, gelegentlich; – ***showers*** or ***rain,*** vereinzelte Regenfälle; 2. Gelegenheits–; – ***poems,*** Gelegenheitsgedichte; – ***furniture,*** das Kleinmöbel. **occasionally,** *adv.* gelegentlich, bei Gelegenheit, dann und wann.

Occident ['ɔksidənt], *s.* (*Poet.*) der Westen, das Abendland. **Occidental** [–'dentl], *adj.* abendländisch, westlich.

occipital [ɔk'sipitl], *adj.* Hinterhaupt(s)–. **occiput** ['ɔksipət], *s.* das Hinterhaupt, der Hinterkopf.

occlude [ɔ'klu:d], *v.t.* 1. verschließen, abschließen, verstopfen; 2. (*Chem.*) okkludieren, adsorbieren. **occlusion** [–ʒən], *s.* 1. die Verschließung, der Verschluß; die Verstopfung; 2. (*Chem.*) Okklusion, Adsorption; 3. (*Meteor.*) Okklusion; 4. (*Dentistry*) Okklusion, der Biß; ***normal –,*** der Normalbiß; ***abnormal –,*** die Bißanomalie. **occlusive** [–siv], *adj.* verschließend, Verschluß–; – ***pessary,*** das Okklusivpessar.

occult [ɔ'kʌlt], **1.** *adj.* verborgen, versteckt, geheim(nisvoll), magisch, okkult, Geheim–; ***the –,*** okkulte Wissenschaft, Geheimnisvolle(s). **2.** *v.t.* verdecken, verbergen; (*Astr.*) verdunkeln, verfinstern. **3.** *v.i.* (vorübergehend) verschwinden, verdeckt werden; (*Naut.*) ***–ing light,*** das Blinkfeuer. **occultation** [–'teiʃən], *s.* (*Astr.*) die Verfinsterung; Verdeckung, (vorübergehendes) Verschwinden. **occultism,** *s.* der Okkultismus, die Geheimlehre.

occupancy ['ɔkjupənsi], *s.* 1. (*Law*) die Besitznahme, Besitzergreifung; 2. Inanspruchnahme, das Innehaben, der Besitz. **occupant,** *s.* 1. der Besitzer, Inhaber; 2. Insasse (*of a vehicle*), Bewohner (*of a house*); 3. (*Law*) Besitzergreifer.

occupation [ɔkju'peiʃən], *s.* 1. der Besitz, das Innehaben; 2. (*Law*) die Besitznahme, Besitzergreifung; 3. (*Mil.*) Besetzung; ***army of –,*** das Besatzungsheer, die Okkupationsarmee; – ***troops,*** die Besatzung, Besatzungstruppen (*pl.*); 4. der Beruf, das Gewerbe, die Beschäftigung; ***by –,*** von Beruf; ***without –,*** beschäftigungslos. **occupational,** *adj.* beruflich, Berufs–; – ***disease,*** die Berufskrankheit; – ***hazard,*** das Berufsrisiko, (*coll.*) notwendiges Risiko; – ***therapy,*** die Beschäftigungstherapie; – ***training,*** die Fachausbildung.

occupier [ˈɔkjupaiə], *s.* der Bewohner, Inhaber, Besitzer, (*of land*) Pächter. **occupy,** *v.t.* 1. in Besitz nehmen, Besitz ergreifen von; 2. (*Mil.*) besetzen; 3. innehaben, besitzen; 4. einnehmen, ausfüllen, in Anspruch nehmen (*space*); 5. bewohnen (*a house*); 6. (*fig.*) innehaben, bekleiden (*a position, post etc.*); 7. dauern, in Anspruch nehmen (*time*); 8. beschäftigen (*attention etc.*); – ***o.s., be occupied,*** sich beschäftigen (***with, in,*** mit).

occur [əˈkə:], *v.i.* 1. vorkommen, sich finden (***in,*** bei); 2. sich ereignen, vorfallen, eintreten; 3. zustoßen (***to,*** *Dat.*) (*a p.*); 4. (*fig.*) einfallen (*an idea etc.*) (***to,*** *Dat.*). **occurrence** [əˈkʌrəns], *s.* 1. das Vorkommen, Auftreten; ***of frequent –,*** häufig vorkommend; 2. das Vorkommnis, Ereignis, der Vorfall, Vorgang.

ocean [ˈouʃən], *s.* das (Welt)meer, der Ozean; – ***liner,*** der Passagierdampfer; (*coll.*) ***–s of,*** Riesenmengen *or* Unmengen von. **ocean-going,** *adj.* Hochsee–. **Oceania** [ouʃiˈeiniə], *s.* (*Geog.*) Ozeanien (*n.*). **oceanic** [ouʃiˈænik], *adj.* Meer(es)–, Ozean–, ozeanisch.

oceanographer [ouʃiəˈnɔgrəfə], *s.* der Ozeanograph, Meereskundler, Meeresforscher. **oceanographic(al)** [–əˈgræfik(l)], *adj.* meereskundlich. **oceanography,** *s.* die Meereskunde.

ocellate(d) [ˈɔsəleit(id)], *adj.* (*Bot., Zool. etc.*) mit Augenflecken *or* Punktaugen versehen. **ocellus** [ouˈseləs], *s.* (*Zool.*) das Punktauge, die Ozelle.

ocelot [ˈousəlɔt], *s.* (*Zool.*) die Pardelkatze, der Ozelot.

ocher, (*Am.*) *see* **ochre.**

ochlocracy [ɔkˈlɔkrəsi], *s.* die Pöbelherrschaft.

ochre [ˈoukə], *s.* der Ocker; ***red –,*** der Roteisenocker; ***yellow –,*** gelber (Eisen)ocker, das Ockergelb. **ochr(e)ous** [ˈoukr(i)əs], *adj.* ockerhaltig, Ocker–.

o'clock [əˈklɔk], *s.* (die) Uhr (*in clock time*), *e.g. one –,* ein Uhr; (*obs.*) ***what – is it?*** wieviel Uhr ist es?

octagon [ˈɔktəgən], *s.* (*Geom.*) das Achteck. **octagonal** [–ˈtægənəl], *adj.* achteckig, achtseitig, achtkantig. **octahedral** [–ˈhi:drəl], *adj.* achtflächig, Oktaeder–. **octahedron** [–ˈhi:drən], *s.* das Oktaeder, Achtflach, der Achtflächner.

octane [ˈɔktein], *s.* (*Chem.*) das Oktan; ***high-– fuel,*** der Superkraftstoff; (*Motor.*) – ***rating,*** die Oktanzahl, der Klopffestigkeitsgrad.

octant [ˈɔktənt], *s.* der Oktant, Achtelkreis.

octave [ˈɔktiv], *s.* 1. (*Mus.*) die Oktave; 2. (*Eccl.*) achter Tag, achttägige Feier.

octavo [ɔkˈteivou], *s.* 1. (*Typ.*) das Oktav(format); 2. der Oktavband. **2.** *adj.* Oktav–.

octennial [ɔkˈteniəl], *adj.* achtjährig, achtjährlich.

octet [ɔkˈtet], *s.* (*Mus.*) das Oktett.

octillion [ɔkˈtiliən], *s.* 1. die Oktillion, eine Million zur achten Potenz; 2. (*Am.*) die Quadrilliarde, ein Tausend zur neunten Potenz.

octo– [ˈɔktə], *pref.* acht–; *see below.*

October [ɔkˈtoubə], *s.* der Oktober.

octodecimo [ɔktəˈdesimou], *s.* 1. (*Typ.*) das Oktodez(format); 2. der Oktodezband.

octogenarian [ɔktədʒiˈnɛəriən], **1.** *adj.* achtzigjährig. **2.** *s.* Achtzigjährige(r).

octopod [ˈɔktəpɔd], *s.* (*Zool.*) der Krake, Achtfüßler. **octopus** [–pəs], *s.* 1. der Seepolyp, Kopffüßer, Krake, achtfüßiger Tintenfisch; 2. (*fig.*) Polyp.

octoroon [ɔktəˈru:n], *s.* (*Ethn.*) der Mischling von Weißen und Quarteronen.

octo|syllabic, *adj.* achtsilbig. **–syllable,** *s.* das Wort *or* der Vers von acht Silben.

octroi [ˈɔktrwɑ:], *s.* (*Hist.*) kommunale Abgabe.

ocular [ˈɔkjulə], **1.** *adj.* 1. Augen–; – ***inspection,*** der Augenschein, die Okularinspektion; 2. augenscheinlich, augenfällig, sichtbar; – ***demonstration,*** sichtbarer Beweis. **2.** *s.* das Okular. **ocularist,** *s.* der Augenarzt.

odd [ɔd], *adj.* 1. ungerade (*of numbers*); – ***number,*** ungerade Zahl; 2. einzeln, vereinzelt (*of a set*); – ***glove,*** einzelner Handschuh; ***3 – volumes,*** 3 Einzelbände; 3. etwas über, einige (*before numbers*), und einige (darüber), und etliche (*after numbers*); ***50 –,*** einige 50; ***50 lb. –,*** etwas über 50 Pfund; 4. übrig(bleibend), überschüssig, überzählig, restlich; ***still some – money,*** noch etwas Geld übrig; ***the – pennies,*** die übrigen Pennies; (*Whist*) – ***trick,*** letzter *or* dreizehnter Stich; (*coll.*) – ***man out,*** Zurückgewiesene(r); 5. Gelegenheits–, gelegentlich; – ***jobs,*** die Gelegenheitsarbeit; (*coll.*) häusliche Reparaturen; ***at – moments,*** dann und wann, gelegentlich, zwischendurch; 6. seltsam, sonderbar, wunderlich; – ***fellow*** or ***fish,*** wunderlicher Kauz; ***an – way of doing things,*** eine seltsame *or* ungewöhnliche Art und Weise zu handeln.

oddity [ˈɔditi], *s.* 1. wunderlicher Kauz, der Sonderling, das Original; 2. die Wunderlichkeit, Seltsamkeit, Eigenartigkeit. **oddly,** *adv.* seltsam(erweise), sonderbar(erweise), auf seltsame Weise; – ***enough,*** höchst merkwürdig, merkwürdigerweise. **oddments,** *pl.* 1. Reste, Überbleibsel (*pl.*); 2. Ramschwaren (*pl.*). **oddness,** *s.* die Seltsamkeit, Sonderbarkeit, Wunderlichkeit.

odds [ɔdz], *pl.* (*oft. sing. constr.*) 1. ungleiche Dinge; – ***and ends,*** allerlei Kleinigkeiten, Überreste, Abfälle; 2. die Ungleichheit, der Unterschied; (*sl.*) ***there's not much – between them,*** sie sind einander so ziemlich gleich; (*coll.*) ***what's the –?*** was macht es aus? was schadet es? was tut's? ***what – is it to you?*** was geht es dich an? ***it makes no –,*** es macht nichts (aus); 3. der Streit, die Uneinigkeit; ***at –,*** im Streit, uneinig, uneins; 4. der Vorteil, das Übergewicht, die Überlegenheit, Übermacht; ***the – are on his side*** or ***in his favour,*** der Vorteil liegt auf seiner Seite; ***the – are against him,*** er ist im Nachteil; ***against tremendous –,*** gegen große Überzahl *or* Überlegenheit *or* Übermacht; 5. (*Spt.*) die Vorgabe; ***give him –,*** ihm etwas vorgeben; ***take –,*** sich (*Dat.*) vorgeben lassen; 6. ungleiche Wette, die Wahrscheinlichkeit, (Gewinn)chance; ***the – are ten to one,*** die Chancen stehen zehn zu eins; ***the – are that,*** (*sl.*) ***it's – on that,*** es ist sehr wahrscheinlich, daß; ***lay*** (***the***) ***–,*** eine ungleiche Wette eingehen (***with,*** mit); ***by long –,*** gegen die Wahrscheinlichkeit.

ode [oud], *s.* die Ode.

odious [ˈoudiəs], *adj.* verhaßt; abscheulich; widerlich, abstoßend, ekelhaft. **odiousness,** *s.* die Verhaßtheit; Widerwärtigkeit, Abscheulichkeit; Widerlichkeit.

odium [ˈoudiəm], *s.* 1. die Verhaßtheit, der Haß; 2. Vorwurf, Tadel, Schimpf, Makel; ***bring – upon,*** verhaßt *or* unbeliebt machen.

odometer [ouˈdɔmitə], *s.* der Kilometerzähler, Wegmesser.

odontalgia [ɔdɔnˈtældʒiə], *s.* der Zahnschmerz. **odontic** [–ˈdɔntik], *adj.* Zahn–. **odontology** [–ˈtɔlədʒi], *s.* die Zahnheilkunde.

odor, (*Am.*) *see* **odour.**

odorant [ˈoudərənt], **odoriferous** [–ˈrifərəs], **odorous,** *adj.* wohlriechend, duftend.

odour [ˈoudə], *s.* der Geruch (*also fig.*); Wohlgeruch, Duft; – ***of sanctity,*** der Geruch der Heiligkeit; ***be in bad –,*** in schlechtem Rufe stehen (***with,*** bei). **odourless,** *adj.* geruchlos, geruchfrei.

Odyssey [ˈɔdisi], *s.* die Odyssee; (*fig.*) Irrfahrt.

œcology, *see* **ecology.**

œcumenical [i:kjuˈmenikl], *adj.* ökumenisch.

œdema [i:ˈdi:mə], *s.* das Ödem, die Wassergeschwulst.

Oedipus [ˈi:dipəs], *m.* Ödipus (*m.*).

o'er [ˈoə], (*Poet.*) *see* **over.**

œsophagus [iˈsɔfəgəs], *s.* die Speiseröhre.

œstrous [ˈi:strəs], *adj.* (*Med.*) östrisch, östral, Östrus–; (*Zool.*) Brunst–. **œstrum, œstrus,** *s.* die Brunst, Brünstigkeit, das Brunststadium.

œuvre [ˈə:vrə], *s.* das Œuvre, (Lebens)werk.

of [ɔv, əv], *prep.* 1. *serves to express Gen. lacking in*

English: may lead to ambiguity, e.g. ***love – children,*** *is* **(a)** *poss. Gen. as in* ***love for sweets*** *(in German always Gen. of article and noun doing the possessing), and* **(b)** *objective Gen. as in* ***her love – children*** *(German uses prep. usu.* für *or* zu); **(c)** *partitive Gen., e.g.* ***a glass – wine*** *(in German not translated:* ein Glas Wein); 2. *expresses various relationships, e.g. origin, cause etc., basically rendered by* von, *though other preps. are commonly used: for such idiomatic usages see the characteristic word of the idiom in question.*

off [ɔf], **1.** *adv.* 1. (*position*) entfernt, weg, von hier; ***far –,*** weit entfernt, weit weg; ***a great way –,*** sehr weit von hier; 2. (*direction*) fort, weg, davon (*with verbs of movement usu. as sep. pref.*); ***– like a shot,*** auf und davon; ***be – (with you)!*** fort (mit dir)! ***get –,*** davonkommen; (*sl.*) ***get – with her,*** mit ihr anbändeln; ***see him –,*** ihn zur Reise begleiten, ihn fortbegleiten; 3. (*separation*) ab (*usu. sep. pref.*); ***break –,*** abbrechen (*also fig.*); ***cool –,*** abkühlen; (*coll.*) ***fall –,*** zurückgehen, abnehmen; (*Naut.*) ***pay –,*** abhalten; ***take –,*** ablegen, ausziehen (*coat etc.*), abnehmen (*hat*); (*coll.*) nachäffen; 4. (*cessation*) aus(geschaltet), ab(geschaltet), abgesperrt (*as water, gas etc.*); ***turn –,*** abdrehen, abstellen; 5. (*completion*) zu Ende, gänzlich, aus–; (*coll.*) (*of goods*) ***be –,*** nicht mehr vorrätig sein, aus *or* alle sein; (*coll.*) ***the affair is –,*** die S. ist aus; (*sl.*) ***come –,*** gelingen; ***drink –,*** ganz austrinken; ***kill –,*** ausrotten; ***pass –,*** vorübergehen, vergehen; ***sell –,*** ausverkaufen; 6. (*time*) ***– and on,*** dann und wann, ab und zu; mit Unterbrechungen; 7. (*coll.*) nicht mehr frisch (*as meat*), (*fig.*) nicht wohl; 8. ***well –,*** wohlhabend, gut situiert, (*also fig.*) gut daran; ***how is he – for . . .?*** wie ist er daran in Beziehung auf (*Acc.*) . . .? 9. frei; ***take a day –,*** sich (*Dat.*) einen Tag freinehmen.

2. *prep.* 1. (*movement*) fort *or* weg von, von (. . . weg *or* . . . herunter); ***fall –,*** herunterfallen von; ***keep – the grass,*** das Betreten des Rasens ist verboten; 2. (*position*) weg von, von . . . ab; ***– one's balance,*** aus dem Gleichgewicht; ***– centre,*** nicht genau ausgerichtet; (*coll.*) ***– colour,*** unpäßlich, nicht auf der Höhe; ***go – one's head,*** den Kopf verlieren; ***a yard – me,*** ein(en) Meter von mir; ***street – Cheapside,*** die Seitenstraße *or* Nebenstraße von Cheapside; ***– form,*** nicht in Form, nicht auf der Höhe; ***never – one's legs,*** immer auf den Beinen; (*Am.*) ***– limits,*** Zutritt verboten; ***– the map,*** am Ende der Welt; ***– the point,*** nicht zur S. gehörig, belanglos; ***two miles – the road,*** zwei Meilen von der Straße ab; 3. (*coll.*) frei von; ***– duty,*** nicht im Dienst, dienstfrei; (*coll.*) ***be – smoking,*** nicht mehr rauchen; ***– work,*** außer Arbeit; 4. (*Naut.*) auf der Höhe von, (quer) vor (*Dat.*); ***– Portsmouth,*** auf der Höhe von Portsmouth; ***– shore,*** vor der Küste.

3. *adj.* recht (*of vehicles etc.*); (*Crick.*) rechts vom Schläger; ***– beat,*** der Auftakt; ***– day,*** freier Tag; (*coll.*) der Tag wo alles schief geht; ***– season,*** stille *or* tote Saison; ***– side,*** rechte Seite (*of a horse etc.*, (*Crick.*) *of batsman*).

offal ['ɔfəl], *s.* der (Fleisch)abfall, geringe Fischsorte; (*fig.*) der Ausschuß, Schund.

off|-beat, *adj.* (*coll.*) ausgefallen, extravagant. **--centre,** *adj.* verrutscht. **--chance,** *s.* schwache *or* entfernte Möglichkeit, geringe Aussicht; (*coll.*) ***on the –,*** aufs Geratewohl. **--colour,** *adj.* unwohl, nicht auf der Höhe. **--cut,** *s.* Abgeschnittene(s). **--drive,** *s.* (*Crick.*) der Schlag nach rechts.

offence [ə'fens], *s.* 1. der Anstoß, das Ärgernis, die Beleidigung, Kränkung; ***cause*** or ***give –,*** Anstoß *or* Ärgernis erregen (*to,* bei); beleidigen, kränken; ***no – (meant)!*** nichts für ungut! ***take – at,*** Anstoß nehmen an (*Dat.*), sich beleidigt *or* gekränkt fühlen über (*Acc.*), übelnehmen; 2. (*Law*) das Vergehen, der Verstoß, die Übertretung, strafbare Handlung (***against,*** gegen); ***commit an – against,*** sich vergehen an (*Dat.*); 3. (*Mil.*) der Angriff, die Offensive; ***weapons of –,*** Angriffswaffen.

offend [ə'fend], **1.** *v.t.* 1. beleidigen, verletzen (*the eye, ear etc.*); 2. ärgern, erzürnen, kränken (*Acc.*), Anstoß erregen bei, zu nahe treten (*Dat.*); ***be –ed,*** aufgebracht *or* gekränkt sein (***at,*** über (*Acc.*); ***by,*** durch (*a th.*)); sich gekränkt *or* beleidigt fühlen (***with,*** durch (*a p.*)). **2.** *v.i.* sich vergehen, verstoßen, sündigen (***against,*** an (*Dat.*)), Anstoß erregen. **offender,** *s.* der Verbrecher, Missetäter; ***first –,*** nicht Vorbestrafte(r).

offense, (*Am.*) *see* **offence.**

offensive [ə'fensiv], **1.** *adj.* 1. widerwärtig, widerlich, ekelhaft (*to* (*Dat.*)); beleidigend, anstößig, anstoßerregend; 2. (*Mil. etc.*) offensiv, Angriffs–. **2.** *s.* die Offensive, der Angriff; (*fig. Pol.*) die Bewegung; ***be on the –,*** in der Offensive sein; ***assume*** or ***take the –,*** zum Angriff übergehen, die Offensive ergreifen. **offensiveness,** *s.* das Beleidigende, die Anstößigkeit; Widerlichkeit, Widerwärtigkeit, Ekelhaftigkeit.

offer ['ɔfə], **1.** *v.t.* 1. anbieten, (dar)bieten, hinhalten, zur Verfügung stellen; ***– battle,*** sich kampfbereit stellen; (*Univ.*) ***– German as principal subject,*** Deutsch als Hauptfach wählen; ***– one's hand,*** die Hand reichen (*to, Dat.*); (*fig.*) ***– one's hand (in marriage),*** die Hand (zur Heirat) anbieten; ***– one's reasons,*** seine Gründe vorbringen; ***– resistance,*** Widerstand leisten; ***– one's services,*** seine Dienste anbieten; ***– a suggestion,*** einen Vorschlag machen; ***– violence,*** gewalttätig werden; Gewalt antun (*to, Dat.*); ***an opportunity will – itself,*** eine Gelegenheit wird sich bieten; 2. (*Comm.*) (zum Verkauf) anbieten, offerieren (*goods*), bieten (*sum of money*); 3. (*also* ***– up***) darbringen, opfern; ***– up a prayer,*** ein Gebet darbringen; ***– (up) a sacrifice,*** ein Opfer darbringen. **2.** *v.i.* sich (dar)bieten, sich zeigen; sich erbieten, sich bereit erklären, sich anschicken, Anstalten *or* Miene machen (*to,* zu). **3.** *s.* das Anerbieten, Angebot, (*Comm.*) Offert, die Offerte; ***– of marriage,*** der Heiratsantrag; ***on –,*** zum Verkauf angeboten.

offering ['ɔfəriŋ], *s.* 1. das Angebot, Anerbieten; 2. die Spende; 3. (*Eccl.*) Darbringung; Opferung; das Opfer.

offertory ['ɔfətəri], *s.* 1. die Kollekte, (*R.C.*) Opferung, das Offertorium; 2. (Geld)opfer, Opfergeld.

off|-hand, **1.** *adv.* aus dem Stegreif, auf der Stelle, unvorbereitet, auf (den ersten) Anhieb, ohne weiteres. **2.** *or* **--handed,** *adj.* ungezwungen, lässig, so leichthin, ganz beiläufig.

office ['ɔfis], *s.* 1. (öffentliches *or* staatliches) Amt, der Posten, die Stellung; ***be in –,*** ein öffentliches Amt bekleiden; im Ministerium sein (*minister*), an der Regierung sein (*cabinet*); (*Pol.*) ***come into –, enter upon –,*** das Amt antreten, ins Ministerium kommen; ***hold*** or ***fill an –,*** ein Amt bekleiden; ***resign (one's) –,*** vom Amt zurücktreten, sein Amt niederlegen; ***take –,*** das Amt übernehmen *or* antreten; 2. (*fig.*) die Pflicht, Aufgabe, Funktion; 3. der (Liebes)dienst, die Gefälligkeit, Dienstleistung, Verrichtung; ***do him a kind –,*** ihm einen guten Dienst erweisen; ***through the good –s of,*** durch die gütige Vermittlung von; 4. die Amtsstube, Kanzlei, Dienststelle, das Geschäftszimmer, Kontor; ***go to the –,*** ins Büro gehen; ***booking –,*** der Fahrkartenschalter; ***inquiry –,*** das Auskunftsbüro; ***life –,*** die Lebensversicherungsgesellschaft; ***lost-property –,*** das Fundbüro; ***post –,*** das Postamt; ***record –,*** das Archiv; 5. (*Parl.*) das Amtsgebäude, Ministerium, (Ministerial)amt; ***Foreign Office,*** das Außenministerium; ***Holy Office,*** die Inquisition; ***Home Office,*** das Innenministerium; ***War Office,*** das Kriegsministerium; 6. (*Eccl.*) das Offizium, der Gottesdienst; ***– for the dead,*** der Totengottesdienst; ***perform the last –s to him,*** ihm die letzte Ehre erweisen; ***divine –,*** katholischer Gottesdienst; 7. *pl.* Wirtschaftsräume, Küchenräume, Geschäftsräume, Verwaltungsgebäude, Nebengebäude, Stallungen (*pl.*) 8. (*Am., Med.*) *see* **consulting room.**

office|-bearer, *s.* der Amtsinhaber, Funktionär. **--block,** *s.* das Bürogebäude. **--boy,** *s.* der Laufbursche, Bürodiener. **– building,** *s.* das Bürohaus. **– clerk,** *s.* der Handlungsgehilfe, Kontorist. **– equipment,** *s.* die Büroeinrichtung. **--holder,** *s. See* **--bearer. --hours,** *pl.* die Geschäftszeit,

Dienststunden (*pl.*). **--hunter,** *s.* der Postenjäger.

officer ['ɔfisə], **1.** *s.* 1. Beamte(r); ***police –,*** der Polizist, Schutzmann; 2. (*Mil.*) der Offizier; ***commanding –,*** der Befehlshaber, Kommandeur; (*Mil.*) ***duty –,*** der Offizier vom Dienst; (*Naut.*) ***petty –,*** der Maat; (*Mil.*) ***warrant –,*** der Feldwebelleutnant; 3. (*of club, society etc.*) der Funktionär, das Vorstandsmitglied. **2.** *v.t.* (*usu. pass.*) Offiziere stellen (*Dat.*), mit Offizieren versehen; ***be –ed by,*** befehligt werden von.

official [ə'fiʃəl], **1.** *adj.* 1. amtlich, Amts–, Dienst–; ***through – channels,*** auf dem Instanzenweg *or* Dienstweg; ***– duties,*** Amtspflichten; Amtshandlungen; ***– report,*** amtlicher Bericht, amtliche Meldung; ***– residence,*** die Amtswohnung; ***–stamps,*** die Dienstmarke; 2. offiziell, formell (*dinner etc.*). **2.** *s.* (Staats)beamte(r). **officialdom** [–dəm], *s.* das Beamtentum, der Beamtenstand. **officialese** [–'li:z], *s.* die Behördensprache, Amtssprache. **officialism,** *s.* 1. Amtsmethoden (*pl.*); 2. amtliche Pedanterie, die Paragraphenreiterei, der Amtsschimmel, Bürokratismus. **officially,** *adv.* offiziell, formell.

officiant [ə'fiʃiənt], *s.* amtierender Geistlicher. **officiate** [–eit], *v.i.* amtieren; fungieren (*as*, als); ***– at a wedding,*** den Traugottesdienst abhalten.

officinal [ɔfi'sainl], *adj.* offizinell, Arznei–.

officious [ə'fiʃəs], *adj.* 1. zudringlich, aufdringlich, übertrieben dienstfertig; 2. (*Pol.*) halbamtlich, offiziös. **officiousness,** *s.* übertriebene Dienstfertigkeit, aufdringlicher Diensteifer, die Zudringlichkeit.

offing ['ɔfiŋ], *s.* der Seeraum, die Räumte; ***in the –,*** auf offener See; (*fig.*) in einiger Entfernung, in Sicht. **offish,** *adj.* (*coll.*) zurückhaltend, reserviert, unnahbar, kühl, steif.

off|-licence, *s.* der Ausschank über die Straße (*Austr.* Gasse). **--peak,** *adj.* nicht auf dem Höchststand, außerhalb der Spitzen(belastungs)zeit; (*Elec.*) ***– tariff,*** der Nachtstromtarif. **–print,** *s.* der Sonder(ab)druck, Separatdruck. **–scourings,** *pl.* der Kehricht, (*esp. fig.*) Abschaum, Auswurf.

offset, 1. ['ɔfset], *s.* 1. der Ausgleich; 2. (*Comm.*) die Verrechnung; 3. (*Build.*) der Mauerabsatz, Mauervorsprung; 4. (*Bot.*) Ausläufer, Ableger, Absenker; 5. (*Tech.*) die Kröpfung; 6. (*Elec.*) (Ab)zweigleitung; 7. (*Surv.*) Ordinate; 8. (*Min.*) der Querschlag; 9. (*Typ.*) Offsetdruck; 10. (*fig.*) Seitenzweig, die Seitenlinie, Abzweigung. **2.** ['ɔfset], *adj.* (*Typ.*) Offset–. **3.** [ɔf'set], *v.t.* 1. ausgleichen, aufwiegen; 2. (*Build.*) absetzen; 3. (*Tech.*) kröpfen; 4. (*Typ.*) in Offsetverfahren drucken; 5. (*fig.*) wettmachen.

off|shoot, *s.* 1. der Sprößling, Ausläufer, Ableger, Absenker, Nebensproß; 2. (*fig.*) Ausläufer, die Abzweigung; 3. Seitenlinie, der Seitenzweig. **–shore,** *adj.* küstenabgewandt; ***– wind,*** der Landwind. **–side,** *s.* (*Spt.*) das Abseits. **–spring,** *s.* (*only sing.*) die Nachkommenschaft, Nachkommen (*pl.*); der Nachkomme, Nachkömmling, Abkömmling; (*fig.*) die Frucht, das Ergebnis. **--stage,** *adj.* hinter der Bühne (befindlich). **--the-record,** *adj.* nicht für die Öffentlichkeit bestimmt, inoffiziell, vertraulich.

oft [ɔft], *adv.* (*Poet., except as pref.*) oft. **often** [ɔfn, 'ɔftən], *adv.* oft, öfters, oftmals, häufig; ***ever so –,*** sehr oft, immer wieder; ***as – as not, more – than not,*** meistens, des öfteren.

ogee [ou'dʒi:], *s.* die Kehlleiste, Glockenleiste, der S-Bogen, das Karnies; ***– arch,*** der Eselsrücken.

ogival [o'dʒaivl], *adj.* Spitzbogen–, Ogival–. **ogive** ['oudʒaiv], *s.* (gotischer) Spitzbogen; die Gratrippe (*of a vault*).

ogle [ougl], **1.** *v.t.* liebäugeln mit, kokett *or* zärtlich anblicken. **2.** *v.i.* liebäugeln, Augen machen. **3.** *s.* liebäugelnder *or* verliebter Blick. **ogler,** *s.* Liebäugelnde(r).

ogre ['ougə], *s.* der Oger, Menschenfresser, (menschenfressendes) Ungeheuer. **ogress** [–gris], *s.* die Menschenfresserin, weibliches Ungeheuer.

oh! [ou], *int.* ach! *See* **o, 2.**

ohm [oum], *s.* das Ohm. **ohmmeter,** *s.* das Ohmmeter, der Widerstandsmesser.

oho! [o'hou], *int.* oho! aha!

oil [ɔil], **1.** *s.* das Öl; (*Am.*) Petroleum, Erdöl; ***crude –,*** das Rohöl; ***essential*** or ***volatile –s,*** flüchtige *or* ätherische Öle; ***fatty*** or ***fixed –s,*** fette Öle; (*coll.*) ***burn the midnight –,*** bis spät in die Nacht arbeiten; ***mineral –,*** das Mineralöl; ***vegetable –,*** das Pflanzenöl; ***– of vitriol,*** die Schwefelsäure; (*fig.*) ***pour – on troubled waters,*** Öl auf die Wogen schütten *or* gießen, die Gemüter beruhigen; (*fig.*) ***pour*** or ***throw – on the flames,*** Öl ins Feuer gießen; ***strike –,*** Erdöl entdecken; (*fig.*) Glück haben; 2. *pl.* die Ölmalerei; ***paint in –s,*** in Öl malen. **2.** *v.t.* (ein)-ölen, einfetten; schmieren; (*fig.*) ***– his palm,*** ihn schmieren *or* bestechen; ***a well –ed tongue,*** ein gutes Mundwerk; (*fig.*) ***– the wheels,*** den Karren schmieren.

oil|-bearing, *adj.* ölhaltig. **--brake,** *s.* die Öldruckbremse. **--burning,** *adj.* Ölfeuerungs–. **--cake,** *s.* der Ölkuchen, Leinkuchen. **--can,** *s.* der Öler, die Ölkanne. **–cloth,** *s.* das Wachstuch. **--colour,** *s.* die Ölfarbe. **oiler,** *s.* der Öler, die Ölkanne. **oil|-feed,** *s.* die Ölzufuhr. **--field,** *s.* das Petroleumfeld, Erdölfeld. **--fired,** *adj. See* **--burning. –fuel,** *s.* das Treiböl, Heizöl. **--gauge,** *s.* der Ölstandsmesser, Ölstandsanzeiger. **--gland,** *s.* (*Orn.*) die Bürzeldrüse.

oiliness ['ɔilinis], *s.* 1. die Öligkeit, Fettigkeit; 2. (*fig.*) salbungsvolles Wesen, die Schlüpfrigkeit, Speichelleckerei, Schmeichelei. **oil|-lamp,** *s.* die Petroleumlampe. **--level,** *s.* der Ölstand. **–man,** *s.* der Ölhändler. **--painting,** *s.* 1. die Ölmalerei; 2. das Ölgemälde. **--rig,** *s.* die Bohrinsel. **–skin,** *s.* das Öltuch, die Ölleinwand; *pl.* das Ölzeug. **--slick,** *s.* der Ölschlick. **–stone,** *s.* der Ölstein. **--tanker,** *s.* das Öltankschiff. **--well,** *s.* die Ölquelle, der Petroleumbrunnen. **oily,** *adj.* 1. ölig, ölhaltig, Öl–; fettig, schmierig; 2. (*fig.*) schmeichlerisch, glattzungig, salbungsvoll.

ointment ['ɔintmənt], *s.* die Salbe; ***a fly in the –,*** ein Haar in der Suppe.

old [ould], **1.** *adj.* 1. alt; ***– age,*** hohes Alter, das Greisenalter; (*coll.*) ***– boy, – chap, – fellow,*** alter Knabe, altes Haus; (*coll.*) ***– fogy,*** alter Knacker; ***grow –,*** altern; ***have grown – in vice,*** in Laster ergraut sein; ***– gold,*** das Mattgold; ***have an – head on young shoulders,*** altklug sein; ***as – as the hills,*** uralt; ***– maid,*** alte Jungfer; (*coll.*) ***the – man,*** der Alte, Chef, Prinzipal, Kapitän; (*coll.*) ***– man,*** alter Freund; (*sl.*) ***my – man,*** mein Alter, mein Mann; ***– moon,*** abnehmender Mond; ***– woman,*** altes Waschweib (*of men*); (*sl.*) ***my – woman,*** meine Alte, meine Frau; 2. abgenutzt, verbraucht; ***– clothes,*** (ab)getragene Kleider; (*sl.*) ***– hat,*** abgedroschen, verstaubt; 3. altertümlich, früher, veraltet; ***– boy,*** früherer Schüler; ***– country,*** das Heimatland, Mutterland (*of emigrant*); (*Art*) ***the Old Masters,*** die Alten Meister; ***a politician of the – school,*** ein Politiker der alten Schule, traditionsgebundener Politiker; (*coll.*) ***– school tie,*** die Traditionsgebundenheit, das Zugehörigkeitsgefühl; ***– style,*** Alter Stil (*calendar*); ***the good – times,*** die gute alte Zeit; 4. ***– hand,*** alter Hase *or* Praktikus; ***– offender,*** vielfach Vorbestrafte(r); (*coll.*) ***– salt,*** alter Seebär; (*sl.*) ***– sweat,*** altgedienter Soldat; 5. (*coll.*) ***any – thing,*** eine x-beliebige S.; (*coll.*) ***a high – time,*** eine glänzende Zeit; (*coll.*) ***any – way,*** auf jede Weise, in x-beliebiger Weise. **2.** *s.* ***of –,*** ehedem, von jeher, vor *or* seit alters; ***times of –,*** alte Zeiten.

old|-age, *adj.* Alters–; ***– pension,*** die Altersrente. **--clothes man,** *s.* der Trödler. **olden,** *adj.* (*Poet.*) alt. **Old English,** *s.* Altenglisch (*n.*). **older,** *comp. adj.* älter. **oldest,** *sup. adj.* ältest. **old|-established,** *adj.* alt(hergebracht). **--fashioned,** *adj.* altmodisch. **Old Glory,** *s.* (*coll.*) das Sternenbanner. **oldish,** *adj.* ältlich. **Old| Man's Beard,** *s.* (*Bot.*) das Greisenhaar. **– Nick,** *s.* (*coll.*) der Teufel. **oldsquaw,** *s.* (*Am.*) *see* ***long-tailed duck.*** **oldster,** *s.* (*coll.*) ältlicher Herr, alter Knabe.

old|-time, *adj.* aus alter Zeit. **--timer,** *s.* alt(erfahren)er Mensch; alteingesessener Bewohner; langjähriges Mitglied. – **wives' tale,** *s.* das Ammenmärchen. **--world,** *adj.* altmodisch, rückständig, altväterisch.

oleaginous [ouli'ædʒinəs], *adj.* ölig, ölhaltig, fettig.

oleander [ouli'ændə], *s.* (*Bot.*) der Oleander.

oleate ['oulieit], **1.** *adj.* ölsauer. **2.** *s.* ölsaures Salz. **oleograph** [–ogra:f], *s.* der Öldruck.

olfactory [ɔl'fæktəri], *adj.* Geruchs–; – ***nerve,*** der Geruchsnerv.

oligarch ['ɔliga:k], *s.* der Oligarch. **oligarchic(al)** [–'ga:kik(l)], *adj.* oligarchisch. **oligarchy,** *s.* die Oligarchie.

oligocene ['ɔligosi:n], *adj.* (*Geol.*) oligozän.

olive ['ɔliv], **1.** *s.* 1. die Olive (*fruit*); 2. der Ölbaum; (*B.*) ***Mount of Olives,*** der Ölberg; 3. das Olivgrün. **2.** *adj.* olivgrün. **olive|-branch,** *s.* der Ölzweig (*also fig.*). **--oil,** *s.* das Olivenöl. **--tree,** *s.* der Ölbaum.

olla podrida ['ɔləpə'dri:də], *s.* (*fig.*) der Mischmasch.

Olympiad [ə'limpiæd], *s.* die Olympiade. **Olympian** [–piən], **1.** *s.* der Olympier. **2.** *adj.* olympisch, göttlich. **Olympic,** *adj.* olympisch; ***Olympic Games,*** Olympische Spiele, die Olympiade.

ombre ['ɔmbə], *s.* (*Cards*) das Lomber(spiel).

omelet(te) ['ɔmlit], *s.* der Eierkuchen, das Omelett; ***you cannot make an – without breaking eggs,*** um etwas zu erreichen, muß man die Opfer in Kauf nehmen; wo gehobelt wird, da fallen Späne.

omen ['oumən], **1.** *s.* das Vorzeichen, Omen, die Vorbedeutung. **2.** *v.t.* vorhersagen, prophezeien, ahnen lassen, verkünden, deuten auf (*Acc.*); ***ill--ed,*** verhängnisvoll, unheilvoll.

omentum [o'mentəm], *s.* (*pl.* **-ta**) (*Anat.*) das Darmnetz.

ominous ['ɔminəs], *adj.* unheilvoll, verhängsnisvoll, schicksalsschwer, von übler Vorbedeutung; drohend, bedenklich. **ominousness,** *s.* das Ominöse, üble Vorbedeutung.

omissible [o'misibl], *adj.* auslaßbar, auszulassen(d). **omission** [–'miʃən], *s.* die Auslassung, Weglassung, Unterlassung (*also Theol.*), das Versäumnis; ***sin of –,*** die Unterlassungssünde.

omit [o'mit], *v.t.* 1. auslassen, weglassen, fortlassen (***from,*** aus *or* von); übergehen; 2. unterlassen, versäumen (***doing*** or ***to do it,*** es zu tun).

omnibus ['ɔmnibʌs], **1.** *s.* 1. der (Omni)bus, Autobus; 2. Sammelband, die Sammlung. **2.** *attrib.* Sammel–, Mantel–.

omnifarious [ɔmni'fɛəriəs], *adj.* Allerlei–, vielseitig; – ***knowledge,*** das Wissen von allerlei Art. **omnifariousness,** *s.* die Vielseitigkeit, Mannigfaltigkeit.

omnipotence [ɔm'nipətəns], *s.* die Allmacht. **omnipotent,** *adj.* allmächtig, allgewaltig.

omnipresence [ɔmni'prezəns], *s.* die Allgegenwart. **omnipresent,** *adj.* allgegenwärtig.

omniscience [ɔm'nisiəns], *s.* die Allwissenheit. **omniscient,** *adj.* allwissend.

omnium ['ɔmniəm], *s.* (*Comm.*) die Gesamtsumme, der Gesamtwert; die Generalschuldverschreibung. **omnium-gatherum** [–'gæðərəm], *s.* (*coll.*) das Sammelsurium, bunte *or* gemischte Gesellschaft.

omnivorous [ɔm'nivərəs], *adj.* alles verschlingend *or* fressend.

omophagous [o'mɔfəgəs], *adj.* rohes Fleisch fressend.

omoplate ['ouməpleit], *s.* (*Anat.*) das Schulterblatt.

omphalic [ɔm'fælik], *adj.* Nabel–. **omphalocele** [–əsi:l], *s.* der Nabelbruch. **omphalos** ['ɔmfəlɔs], *s.* 1. (*Antiqu.*) der Schildbuckel; 2. (*fig.*) Mittelpunkt, Nabel.

on [ɔn], **1.** *prep.* (*situation*) auf (*Dat.*), an (*Dat.*), in (*Dat.*); (*direction*) auf (*Acc.*) . . . hin, an (*Acc.*), zu, (*fig.*) auf (*Acc.*) . . . hin, bei, aus, nach, unter. **(a)** (*before nouns*) ***payment – account,*** die Akontozahlung; – ***account of,*** wegen; – ***the air,*** in Betrieb; – ***the alert,*** see – ***one's guard***; – ***analysis,*** bei näherer Untersuchung; ***with a lady – his arm,*** eine Dame am Arme führend; – ***my arrival,*** gleich nachdem ich ankam, gleich nach meiner Ankunft; – ***good authority,*** aus guter Quelle; – (***an***) ***average,*** im Durchschnitt; ***swear – the Bible,*** auf die *or* bei der Bibel schwören; – ***board,*** an Bord; – ***bread and water,*** bei Wasser und Brot; – ***call,*** auf Abruf; – ***the coast,*** an der Küste; ***be – the committee,*** zum Ausschuß gehören; – ***these conditions,*** unter diesen Bedingungen; – ***further consideration,*** bei *or* nach reiflicher Überlegung; – ***the continent,*** auf dem Kontinent; – ***the contrary,*** im Gegenteil; – ***demand,*** auf Antrag; (*coll.*) – ***the dot,*** auf die Minute; – ***duty,*** im Dienst; ***a box – the ear,*** eine Ohrfeige; – ***earth,*** auf Erden; – ***entering,*** beim Eintritt *or* Eintreten; – ***the eve of,*** unmittelbar vor (*Dat.*); (*coll.*) – ***the fence,*** neutral, unentschlossen; ***the ring – her finger,*** der Ring an ihrem Finger; – ***fire,*** in Brand, in Flammen; – ***the first of April,*** am ersten April; – ***or before the first of April,*** bis zum ersten April; – ***foot,*** zu Fuß; – ***all fours,*** auf allen vieren; – ***one's guard,*** auf der Hut; – ***half-pay,*** auf Halbsold; – ***hand,*** auf Lager; – ***the right*** (***hand***), zur Rechten; – ***hearing the news,*** als er (*etc.*) die Nachricht hörte; – ***my honour,*** bei meiner Ehre; – ***horseback,*** zu Pferd; – ***a journey,*** auf einer Reise; – ***his knees,*** kniend; ***fall – one's knees,*** auf die Knie fallen; – ***leave,*** auf Urlaub; – ***the left*** (***hand***), zur Linken; ***loss – loss,*** Verlust auf *or* über Verlust, ein Verlust nach dem andern; – ***Monday,*** am Montag; – ***Mondays,*** montags; – ***the morning of,*** am Morgen des; – ***an optimistic note,*** in zuversichtlicher Weise; – ***this occasion,*** bei dieser Gelegenheit; – ***my part,*** meinerseits; – ***penalty of death,*** bei Todesstrafe; – ***the piano,*** auf dem Klavier; – ***principle,*** grundsätzlich; – ***publication,*** gleich nach Erscheinen; – ***purpose,*** absichtlich, mit Absicht; – ***receipt,*** nach *or* bei Empfang; – ***the river,*** am Flusse; (*coll.*) – ***the run,*** auf der Flucht; – ***sale,*** zum Verkauf, verkäuflich; ***profit – sales,*** Gewinn beim Absatz; – ***the shore,*** am Ufer; (*Footb.*) – ***side,*** im Spiele; – ***this side,*** auf dieser Seite; – ***the spot,*** auf der Stelle; (*Mil.*) – ***the staff,*** im Stabe; – ***an empty stomach,*** mit einem leeren Magen; – ***strike,*** im Ausstand; (*Am.*) – ***a sudden,*** plötzlich, auf einmal; – ***suspicion,*** auf Verdacht (hin); – ***tap,*** im Anstich; – ***my theory,*** nach meiner Theorie; – ***time,*** pünktlich, zur festgesetzten Zeit; – ***tour,*** auf Reisen; – ***the wall,*** an der Wand; – ***the whole,*** im ganzen.

(b) (*after nouns*) ***the agreement –,*** das Abkommen über (*Acc.*); ***the attack –,*** der Angriff auf (*Acc.*); ***a curse – him!*** Fluch über ihn! ***lay hands –,*** Hand legen an (*Acc.*); ***an increase – last year,*** eine Steigerung gegen letztes Jahr; ***a lecture –,*** ein Vortrag über (*Acc.*); ***a joke – me,*** ein Scherz auf meine Kosten; ***the march –,*** der Marsch auf (*Acc.*); ***have pity – me!*** habt Mitleid mit mir! ***revenge*** or ***vengeance –,*** Rache an (*Dat.*).

(c) (*after adjs.*) (*coll.*) ***gone –,*** verschossen in (*Acc.*); ***keen –,*** erpicht auf (*Acc.*); ***mad –,*** wild *or* versessen auf (*Acc.*).

(d) (*with verbs*) ***agree –,*** sich einigen über (*Acc.*); (*coll.*) ***this is – me,*** dies geht auf meine Rechnung; (*coll.*) ***this is a new one – me,*** da bin ich überfragt; ***bestow*** or ***confer –,*** verleihen (*Dat.*); ***call –,*** besuchen; auffordern; ***frown –,*** böse ansehen; ***go – an errand,*** eine Besorgung machen; (*coll.*) ***have you a match – you?*** haben Sie Streichhölzer bei sich? (*coll.*) ***have nothing – him,*** vor ihm nichts voraus haben; gegen ihn nichts ankönnen; ihm nichts vorzuhalten haben; ***live – air,*** von (der) Luft leben; ***set one's heart –,*** sein Herz hängen an (*Acc.*); ***meditate –,*** nachdenken über (*Acc.*); ***smile –,*** anlächeln; ***shut the door –,*** die Tür verschließen (*Dat.*); ***start – a journey,*** eine Reise antreten; (*sl.*) ***he tells – me,*** er verpetzt *or* verrät mich; (*coll.*) ***it tells – him,*** es nimmt ihn sichtlich mit; ***turn the key –,*** einschließen; ***turn one's back –,*** den Rücken zukehren (*Dat.*); ***throw – the floor,*** auf den Boden werfen; ***write –,*** schreiben über (*Acc.*).

2. *adv.* (*position*) darauf; an, auf; (*direction away*) vorwärts, heran, weiter, weiter–, fort–; (*direction* *towards*) an, herbei; *– and –,* immer weiter; *– and off,* hin und wieder, ab und zu; *far –,* weit vorgerückt; *later –,* später; *and so –,* und so weiter; *from that time –,* seit jener Zeit; *the brake is –,* die Bremse ist angezogen; *the switch is –,* es ist eingeschaltet; *the water is –,* das Wasser läuft *or* ist an; *what's – today?* was ist heute los? (*Theat.*) was wird heute gegeben? (*coll.*) *you're – next,* jetzt kommst du daran; *I can't get my boots –,* ich kann meine Stiefel nicht anziehen; *have one's coat –,* den Mantel anhaben; *with his hat –,* mit dem Hut auf; *time marches –,* die Zeit schreitet vorwärts; (*coll.*) *get –,* Fortschritte machen; *it's getting – for six,* es geht auf sechs Uhr zu; *go –,* weitergehen, fortfahren, (*coll.*) weitermachen; *he went – whistling,* er pfiff weiter; *collide head –,* frontal zusammenstoßen; *look –,* zuschauen; (*sl.*) *be – to a th.,* Kenntnis haben von einer S.; (*sl.*) *he's always – at me,* er setzt mir dauernd zu.

onager ['ɔnəgə], *s.* wilder Esel, der Onager.

onanism ['ounɔnizm], *s.* 1. Coitus interruptus (*m.*); 2. die Onanie, Selbstbefleckung, Selbstbefriedigung.

once [wʌns], **1.** *adv.* 1. einmal; ein einziges Mal; *– or twice,* ein paarmal, einige Male; *– (and) for all,* ein für allemal; *– in a while,* gelegentlich, zuweilen; (*coll.*) *– in blue moon,* alle Jubeljahre einmal; *more than –,* mehrmals, mehrere Male; *– more,* noch einmal; *a cousin – removed,* ein Vetter zweiten Grades; (*Prov.*) *– bitten, twice shy,* gebranntes Kind scheut das Feuer; 2. einst, vormals, ehedem; *– upon a time,* einmal; 3. dereinst. **2.** *s. at –,* (so)gleich, sofort; zugleich, zu gleicher Zeit, auf einmal; *all at –,* mit einem Male, plötzlich; alle gleichzeitig; *for –,* für diesmal, ausnahmsweise; *for – in a way,* einmal zur Abwechslung; *this –,* dieses eine Mal. **3.** *conj.* sobald, wenn erst *or* einmal; *– there, we shall . . .,* sind wir einmal da, so werden wir . . .

once-over, *s.* (*sl.*) flüchtige Überprüfung *or* Durchsicht.

oncoming ['ɔnkʌmiŋ], *adj.* herankommend, entgegenkommend; *– traffic,* der Gegenverkehr.

one [wʌn, wɔn], **1.** *num. adj.* ein; *twenty-–,* einundzwanzig; *– hundred,* hundert; *– thousand,* tausend; *– p. in a hundred,* jeder hundertste; *– and a half,* anderthalb, ein(und)einhalb; (*sl.*) *be – up on him,* ihm (ein wenig) voraus sein; *for clock time see under* **eight.**
2. *dem. adj.* eine(r, -s), eins; (*emph.*) einzig; *all –,* ganz gleich, alles eins, einerlei, ein und dasselbe; *– and all,* alle zusammen, samt und sonders, ausnahmslos; *– another,* einander; *at –,* einig; *– after another, – by –,* einer nach dem andern; *– day, – of these days,* eines Tages; *I for –,* ich zum Beispiel; *on the – hand,* einerseits; (*coll.*) *– in the eye,* der Wischer, Denkzettel; *all in –,* alles in einem, miteinander, zusammen, zugleich; *as – man,* alle wie einer; *– more song,* noch ein Lied; *– thing or another,* dies und jenes; *for – thing,* zunächst einmal; *– of these works,* eines dieser Werke; *– or two,* einige; *– too many,* einer zuveil; *– and the same,* ein und derselbe; *– with another,* eins ins andere gerechnet, im Durchschnitt.
3. *indef. pron.* 1. (irgend)eine(r), (irgend)ein; jemand; *– Mr. Smith,* ein gewisser Herr Schmidt; *each –,* jede(r, -s), eine jede, ein jeder *or* jedes; *many a –,* manche(r, -s), manch eine(r, -s); *no –,* keiner, niemand; *such a –,* ein solcher, so einer; *such –s,* solche; *– or other,* einer oder der andere; *the – who,* derjenige der; *the –s who,* diejenigen die; *this –,* dieser; *these –s,* diese; *that –,* jener; *those –s,* jene; *which –?* welcher? *which –s?* welche? *like – lost,* wie ein Verlorener; *I am not – to . . .,* ich bin kein Mann, der . . .; *be – of a party,* dabei sein; *your view is the right –,* Ihre Ansicht ist die richtige; *the great –s of the earth,* die Großen der Erde; *my little –s,* meine Kleinen, meine Kinder; *a sly –,* ein Schlauberger; 2. man; *– knows,* man weiß; *it drives – mad,* es macht einen verrückt; *–'s impression was,* der Eindruck, den man bekam, war; *lose –'s life,* das Leben verlieren; *it gives – a shock,* es gibt einem einen Stoß; *cry –'s eyes out,* sich (*Dat.*) die Augen ausweinen; *take –'s meals,* das Essen einnehmen.
4. *s.* die Eins, der Ein(s)er; *a row of –s,* eine Reihe Einsen; (*coll.*) *take care of number –,* für sich selbst sorgen.

one|-act play, *s.* der Einakter. **--armed,** *adj.* einarmig; (*coll.*) *– bandit,* der Spielautomat. **--eyed,** *adj.* einäugig. **--handed,** *adj.* einhändig. **--horse,** *adj.* einspännig; (*sl.*) dürftig, zweitrangig. **--legged,** *adj.* einbeinig. **--man show,** *s.* (*coll.*) der Einmannbetrieb; (*fig.*) die Einzelleistung.

oneness ['wʌnnis], *s.* 1. die Einheit, Gleichheit, Identität, Nämlichkeit; 2. Einigkeit, Übereinstimmung, Harmonie.

one|-night stand, *s.* (*Theat.*) einmaliges Gastspiel. **--off,** *adj.* (*Tech.*) *– production,* die Einzel(stück)-fertigung. **--price shop,** *s.* das Einheitspreisgeschäft.

oner ['wɔnə], *s.* (*sl.*) 1. die Kanone (*at,* in (*Dat.*)) (*person*); 2. das Mordsding, die Prachtleistung; 3. krasse Lüge; 4. wuchtiger Schlag.

onerous ['ɔnərəs], *adj.* lästig, beschwerlich, drückend (*to,* für). **onerousness,** *s.* die Lästigkeit, Beschwerlichkeit, Last.

oneself [wʌn'self], **1.** *refl. pron.* sich (selbst *or* selber). **2.** *emph. pron.* (sich) selbst *or* selber. **one|-sided,** *adj.* einseitig (*also fig.*); (*fig.*) parteiisch, voreingenommen. **--sidedness,** *s.* die Einseitigkeit. **--storied,** *adj.* einstöckig. **--time,** *attrib. adj.* einstig, früher. **--track,** *adj.* eingleisig, einspurig; (*fig.*) einseitig, beschränkt, verbohrt. **--way,** *adj.* Einbahn- (*traffic*), Einweg- (*switch, tap etc.*).

onion ['ʌnjən], *s.* die Zwiebel; (*sl.*) *he knows his –s,* er versteht sein Geschäft.

onlooker ['ɔnlukə], *s.* der (die) Zuschauer(in) (*at,* bei).

only ['ounli], **1.** *adj.* einzig, alleinig; *one and –,* einzigst. **2.** *adv.* 1. nur, bloß, allein; *if –,* wenn nur; *not – . . ., but . . .,* nicht nur . . ., sondern (auch) . . .; 2. erst; *– after,* erst nachdem; *– just,* eben erst *or* gerade, kaum; *– yesterday,* erst gestern. **3.** *conj.* nur daß, jedoch. **only-begotten,** *adj.* (*B.*) eingeboren.

on-off switch, *s.* der Ein-Aus-Schalter.

onomastic [ɔnə'mæstik], *adj.* Namens–. **onomasticon,** *s.* das Namenverzeichnis.

onomatopœia [ɔnəmætə'piə], *s.* die Tonmalerei, Wortmalerei, Lautmalerei, Lautnachahmung, Onomatopöie. **onomatopœic** [–'piik], **onomatopoetic** [–pou'etik], *adj.* lautnachahmend, onomatopoetisch.

on|rush, *s.* der Ansturm, Vorstoß, das Vordrängen. **-set,** *s.* der Angriff, Anfall; (*fig.*) Ansatz, Anlauf, Anfang, Beginn, (*Med.*) Anfall, Ausbruch. **-slaught** [–slɔ:t], *s.* der Angriff, Ansturm. **--the-spot,** *attrib. adj.* (*Law*) *– investigation,* der Lokaltermin.

ontogenesis [ɔnto'dʒenisis], *s.* die Ontogenese. **ontology** [ɔn'tɔlədʒi], *s.* die Ontologie.

onus ['ounəs], *s.* die Last, Verpflichtung, Verantwortung; *– of proof,* die Beweislast.

onward ['ɔnwəd], **1.** *adv.* vorwärts, weiter, (*time*) von . . . an. **2.** *adj.* fortschreitend. **onwards,** *adv.* *See* **onward, 1.**

onyx ['ɔniks], *s.* der Onyx.

oodles ['u:dəlz], *pl.* (*sl.*) Unmengen (*pl.*).

oof [u:f], *s.* (*sl.*) das Moos, Blech, der Kies, Zaster, Knöpfe (*pl.*), Moneten (*pl.*).

oogamous [ou'ɔgəməs], *adj.* (*Biol.*) oogam; *– reproduction,* die Oogamie. **oogenesis** [ouə'dʒenisis], *s.* die O(v)ogenese, Eientwicklung.

oolite ['ouəlait], *s.* der Oolith, Rogenstein; (*Geol.*) Dogger. **oolitic** [–'litik], *adj.* Oolith–.

oomph [u:mf], *s.* (*sl.*) der Sex-Appeal.

oosperm ['ouəspə:m], *s.* (*Biol.*) befruchtetes Ei, die Zygote. **oospore** [–spɔ:], *s.* befruchtete Eizelle.

ooze [u:z], **1.** *v.i.* (durch)sickern; triefen (*with,* von); (*fig.*) *– away,* (dahin)schwinden; (*fig.*) *– out,* durchsickern. **2.** *s.* 1. der Schlamm, Matsch,

Schlick; 2. (*Tan.*) die Lohbrühe; 3. der (Ab)fluß, durchgesickerte Flüssigkeit. **oozy** [-i], *adj.* schlammig, schlick(er)ig; schleimig, schmierig.

opacity [o'pæsiti], *s.* 1. die Undurchsichtigkeit; 2. Deckkraft, Deckfähigkeit (*of paint*); 3. (*fig.*) Dunkelheit, Unverständlichkeit.

opal ['oupəl], *s.* der Opal; – ***glass,*** das Milchglas, Alabasterglas, Opalglas. **opalesce** [–'les], *v.i.* opalisieren, schillern. **opalescence,** *s.* das Schillern, Opalisieren, die Opaleszenz. **opalescent,** *adj.* opalisierend, bunt schillernd. **opaline** [–ain], **1.** *adj.* Opal–. **2.** *s. See* ***opal glass.***

opaque [o'peik], **1.** *adj.* 1. undurchsichtig, undurchdringlich, undurchlässig; (*Med.*) – ***meal,*** die Kontrastmahlzeit; 2. deckfähig (*as paint*); – ***colour,*** die Deckfarbe; 3. (*fig.*) unverständlich, unklar, dunkel. **2.** *s.* das Dunkel, Dunkle(s). **opaqueness,** *s. See* **opacity.**

open ['oupən], **1.** *adj.* 1. offen(stehend), geöffnet, auf; ***a little*** –, klaffend (*as door*); ***with – arms,*** mit offenen Armen; (*fig.*) – ***book,*** offener Mensch; – ***bowels,*** offener Leib, der Stuhlgang; ***break*** –, aufbrechen, erbrechen; ***with – doors,*** mit offenen Türen; ***keep one's eyes*** –, die Augen offenhalten; ***with one's eyes*** –, mit offenen Augen; – ***fire-place,*** – ***hearth,*** offener Herd; – ***hand,*** freigebige Hand; – ***house,*** gastfreies Haus; (*Mil.*) – ***order,*** geöffnete *or* aufgelöste Ordnung; – ***sight,*** das Balkenvisier (*of gun*); ***over – sights,*** über Kimme und Korn; – ***steam,*** direkter Dampf; ***throw*** –, aufreißen (*a door*); zugängig machen, eröffnen; – ***vat,*** die Wanne; – ***warfare,*** die Bewegungskrieg; 2. unbedeckt, bloß, offenliegend, frei; – ***air,*** freie Luft; ***in the – air,*** im Freien, unter freiem Himmel; – ***boat,*** das Boot ohne Verdeck; – ***field,*** freies Feld; ***in the – sea,*** auf hoher See; – ***spaces,*** ungebautes Gelände; ***on the – street,*** auf offener Straße; – ***working,*** *see* **open-face**; ***keep the day*** or ***date*** –, sich (*Dat.*) den Tag freihalten; ***lay*** –, aufdecken, klarlegen; 3. zugänglich (*to,* für) (*also fig.*); offen(herzig), aufrichtig, aufgeschlossen (*to,* für); ***be – to conviction,*** mit sich reden lassen; ***be – to discussion,*** zur Diskussion stehen; ***be – to an offer,*** mit sich handeln lassen; ***it is – to him to do,*** es steht ihm frei zu tun; ***be – with him,*** offen mit ihm reden; 4. offenkundig, offenbar, öffentlich; – ***access,*** die Freihand (*library*); – ***championship,*** die Amateurmeisterschaft; – ***competition,*** freier Wettbewerb; ***in – court,*** öffentlich, vor Gericht; – ***lecture,*** öffentliche Vorlesung; – ***letter,*** offener Brief; – ***market,*** freier Markt, der Freiverkehr; – ***scholarship,*** offenes Stipendium; – ***season,*** die Jagdzeit; – ***session,*** öffentliche Sitzung; – ***shop,*** offener Betrieb; ***throw*** –, ausschreiben (*to competition*); 5. offenbleibend, unentschieden; – ***question,*** offene *or* noch unentschiedene Frage; – ***verdict,*** unentschiedener Urteilsspruch; 6. unterworfen, ausgesetzt (*to, Dat.*); – ***to criticism,*** nicht frei von Schuld; ***lay o.s. – to criticism,*** sich der Kritik aussetzen; ***be – to doubt*** or ***question,*** anfechtbar sein, Zweifel (*Dat.*) unterliegen; 7. eisfrei (*as a harbour*); – ***ice,*** fahrbares Eis; – ***water,*** eisfreies Gewässer; – ***weather,*** frostfreier Winter; 8. (*Comm.*) laufend; – ***account,*** das Kontokorrent(konto), laufendes Konto; – ***cheque,*** der Barscheck; 9. durchbrochen, durchlöchert; 10. (*Mus.*) – ***harmony,*** weiter Satz; – ***note,*** der Grundton; – ***string,*** leere Saite; 11. (*Typ.*) – ***matter,*** lichter *or* weit durchschossener Satz.

2. *v.t.* öffnen, aufmachen; aufschlagen (*a book, eyes*), entkorken (*a bottle*); eröffnen (*fire, debate, parliament, account, shop etc.*), mitteilen, enthüllen (*thoughts, feelings*); (*Naut.*) in Sicht bekommen; – ***a case,*** einen Prozeß eröffnen; – ***a correspondence,*** einen Briefwechsel anknüpfen; – ***the door to,*** die Tür öffnen (*Dat.*) (*a p.*) (*N.B. to let him in*); (*fig.*) Tür und Tor öffnen (*Dat.*), Gelegenheit geben zu, ermöglichen (*a th.*); – ***the door for,*** die Tür öffnen (*Dat.*) (*a p.*) (*N.B. because he cannot*); – ***his eyes,*** ihm die Augen öffnen (*to,* für); – ***one's heart,*** sein Herz ausschütten *or* aufschließen; (*fig.*) – ***one's mouth,*** es ausplaudern, nicht reinen Mund halten; – ***negotiations,*** Verhandlungen beginnen *or* anknüpfen; – ***a way,*** (sich (*Dat.*)) einen Weg bahnen; – ***out,*** ausbreiten, entfalten; – ***up,*** erschließen (*country etc.*).

3. *v.i.* 1. sich öffnen *or* auftun, aufgehen; offen sein *or* haben (*as shops*); aufblühen (*as flowers*); – ***to him,*** ihm die Tür öffnen; – ***out,*** sich ausdehnen *or* ausbreiten *or* erweitern, (*fig.*) sich aussprechen, mitteilsam werden; (*Motor.*) (*coll.*) Vollgas geben; – ***up,*** sich zeigen *or* auftun; (*coll. of a p.*) aus sich herausgehen; (*of guns*) das Feuer eröffnen; 2. beginnen, anfangen; (*Theat.*) – ***with Hamlet,*** die Spielzeit mit Hamlet eröffnen; 3. sich erschließen *or* zeigen (*to one's view*), (*Naut.*) in Sicht kommen; 4. führen, (hinaus)gehen (*as rooms etc.*) (***into,*** nach; ***on*** (***to***), auf (*Acc.*)).

4. *s.* freie Luft, das Freie *or* freie Feld *or* offene Meer; ***in the*** –, im Freien, unter freiem Himmel, auf freier Flur; (*fig.*) ***come into the*** –, offen reden (***with,*** über (*Acc.*)), kein Hehl machen (aus).

open|-air, *adj.* Freilicht–, Freiluft–, im Freien. **--and-shut,** *adj.* ***it is an – case,*** das Ergebnis steht von vornherein fest. **--ended,** *adj.* 1. (*Elec.*) leer laufend, offen; 2. (*fig.*) unbegrenzt. **opener,** *s.* der Öffner (*p. or instrument*), Eröffner (*of a debate*). **open|-eyed,** *adj.* mit offenen Augen (***to,*** für), wachsam. **--face,** *adj.* (*Min.*) – ***working,*** der Tag(e)bau. **--handed,** *adj.* freigebig. **--hearted,** *adj.* offen(herzig), aufrichtig. **--hearth,** *adj.* – ***furnace,*** der Siemens-Martin-Ofen; – ***process,*** das Martinverfahren.

opening ['oup(ə)niŋ], **1.** *adj.* Anfangs–, Eröffnungs–, einleitend; – ***price,*** der Eröffnungskurs, Anfangskurs; – ***remarks,*** die Eingangsworte; – ***speech,*** die Eröffnungsrede. **2.** *s.* 1. das Öffnen; die Eröffnung (*of a shop, parliament, game of chess etc.*), Erschließung (*of a country*); 2. Öffnung, Mündung, das Loch, der Riß, Spalt; Durchlaß, Durchgang; die Bresche; (*Am.*) lichte Stelle, Lichtung (*in a wood*); 3. (*Comm.*) der Absatzweg, Markt; günstige Aussicht; die Gelegenheit (***for,*** für); 4. der Anfang, Beginn, einleitender Teil.

openly ['oupənli], *adv.* offen, freimütig, unverhohlen; öffentlich. **open|-minded,** *adj.* vorurteilslos, unbefangen, unvoreingenommen, aufgeschlossen. **--mindedness,** *s.* die Vorurteilslosigkeit, Unvoreingenommenheit, Aufgeschlossenheit. **--mouthed,** *adj.* mit aufgesperrtem Munde; gaffend; (*of a vessel*) mit weiter Öffnung. **openness,** *s.* 1. die Offenheit; 2. Offenherzigkeit, Aufgeschlossenheit. **openwork,** *s.* durchbrochene Arbeit.

opera ['ɔpərə], *s.* die Oper; Opernmusik, Opern (*pl.*); – ***bouffe, comic*** –, komische Oper; ***grand*** –, große Oper.

operable ['ɔpərəbl], *adj.* (*Med.*) operierbar; (*fig.*) durchführbar.

opera|-cloak, *s.* der Abendmantel. **--glass,** *s.* (*usu. pl.*) das Opernglas. **--hat,** *s.* der Klapphut. **--house,** *s.* das Opernhaus, die Oper. – **singer,** *s.* der (die) Opernsänger(in).

operate ['ɔpəreit], **1.** *v.i.* 1. (ein)wirken, eine Wirkung haben (***on,*** auf (*Acc.*)); 2. tätig *or* wirksam sein, arbeiten, funktionieren; 3. (*Surg., Mil.*) operieren (***on,*** *Acc.*); (*Surg.*) ***be –d on,*** operiert werden; 4. (*Comm.*) spekulieren. **2.** *v.t.* bewirken; in Gang *or* Betrieb bringen; handhaben, regulieren, hantieren, betätigen (*a business etc.*); bedienen (*signals*).

operatic [ɔpə'rætik], *adj.* Opern–, opernhaft.

operating ['ɔpəreitiŋ], *adj.* 1. (*Med.*) Operations–; – ***room,*** der Operationssaal; – ***surgeon,*** der Operateur; – ***table,*** der Operationstisch; – ***theatre,*** see – ***room***; 2. (*Tech., Comm.*) Betriebs–; – ***costs,*** Betriebs(un)kosten (*pl.*); – ***instructions,*** die Betriebsanweisung, Bedienungsvorschriften (*pl.*); – ***time,*** die Arbeitszeit, (*Elec.*) Schaltzeit; – ***voltage,*** die Betriebsspannung.

operation [ɔpə'reiʃən], *s.* 1. (*Med., Mil., Math.*) die Operation; (*Med.*) (chirurgischer) Eingriff; – ***for appendicitis,*** die Blinddarmoperation; – ***on the leg,*** die Beinoperation; – ***on my father,*** die Operation meines Vaters; ***undergo an*** –, sich einer Operation unterziehen; 2. (*Mil.*) das Unternehmen, der Einsatz, die Kampfhandlung; ***scene*** or ***theatre of –s***, der Kriegsschauplatz, das Einsatzgebiet, Operationsgebiet; 3. (*Math.*) die Ausführung; 4. das Wirken, die Wirkung (*on*, auf (*Acc.*)); 5. (*esp. Law*) Geltung, Wirksamkeit; ***by – of***, kraft (*Gen.*); ***come into –***, wirksam werden, in Kraft treten; (*Tech.*) in Gang kommen; 6. (*esp. Tech.*) der Vorgang, (Arbeits)gang, (Arbeits)-prozeß, die Arbeitsweise, Prozedur, das Verfahren; ***building –s***, Bauarbeiten (*pl.*); 7. der Betrieb, Gang, Lauf, die Tätigkeit (*of machines*), Handhabung, Bedienung, Betätigung (*by machine-minders*); (*Tele.*) ***automatic –***, der Selbstwählverkehr; ***continuous –***, der Tag- und Nachtbetrieb; ***in –***, in Betrieb *or* Kraft; 8. (*Comm.*) der Betrieb, die Unternehmung, (*St. Exch.*) Spekulation.

operational [ɔpəˈreiʃənl], *adj.* 1. (*Tech.*) Betriebs–, Arbeits–, Funktions–; 2. (*Mil.*) Operations–, Einsatz–; einsatzbereit; ***– headquarters***, der Führungsstab; ***– order***, die Einsatzanweisung; ***– readiness***, die Einsatzbereitschaft; ***– training***, einsatzmäßige Ausbildung.

operative [ˈɔpərətiv], **1.** *adj.* 1. wirkend, tätig (eingreifend); praktisch, wirksam; ***become –***, in Kraft treten, wirksam werden; ***make –***, in Kraft treten lassen; ***– cause***, springender Punkt; ***– word***, entscheidendes Wort; 2. (*Tech.*) Betriebs–, betriebsfähig; 3. (*Med.*) Operations–, operativ. **2.** *s.* der (Fabrik)arbeiter, Handwerker, Mechaniker; (*Am.*) Agent.

operator [ˈɔpəreitə], *s.* 1. Wirkende(r); 2. (*Med.*) operierender Arzt, der Operateur; 3. (*Films*) Kameramann; (*Tele.*) der (die) Telephonist(in), das Fräulein vom Amt; der (die) Telegraphist(in); ***crane –***, der Kranführer; ***machine –***, der Machinist; ***wireless –***, der Funker; 4. (*Comm.*) der Unternehmer, Produzent; (*St. Exch.*) Spekulant.

opercular [oˈpə:kjulə], **operculate(d)** [–leit(id)], *adj.* (*Bot.*) deckeltragend, Deckel–, (*Ichth.*) Kiemendeckel–. **operculum** [–ləm], *s.* (*Bot.*) der Deckel, (*Ichth.*) Kiemendeckel.

operetta [ɔpəˈretə], *s.* die Operette, leichte Oper.

operose [ˈɔpərous], *adj.* mühsam, mühselig, beschwerlich. **operoseness,** *s.* die Mühsamkeit, Mühseligkeit, Beschwerlichkeit.

ophicleide [ˈɔfiklaid], *s.* (*Mus.*) die Ophikleide.

ophidian [oˈfidiən], **1.** *s.* die Schlange. **2.** *adj.* schlangenartig, Schlangen–. **ophiolater** [–ˈɔlətə], *s.* der Schlangenanbeter. **ophiolatry** [–ˈɔlətri], *s.* der Schlangenkult, die Schlangenanbetung, Ophiolatrie.

ophite [ˈɔfait], *s.* (*Geol.*) der Ophit, Schlangenstein, Serpentin. **ophitic** [ɔˈfitik], *adj.* Ophit–, serpentinartig.

ophthalmia [ɔfˈθælmiə], *s.* die Augenentzündung, Bindehautentzündung, Ophthalmie. **ophthalmic,** *adj.* Augen–; augenkrank. **ophthalmitis** [ɔfθəlˈmaitis], *s. See* **ophthalmia. ophthalmological** [–məˈlɔdʒikl], *adj.* augenärztlich, ophthalmologisch. **ophthalmologist** [–ˈmɔlədʒist], *s.* der Augenarzt, Ophthalmologe. **ophthalmology** [–ˈmɔlədʒi], *s.* die Augenheilkunde, Ophthalmologie. **ophthalmoscope** [–məskoup], *s.* der Augenspiegel, das Ophthalmoskop.

opiate [ˈoupieit], **1.** *adj.* einschläfernd, betäubend (*also fig.*). **2.** das Schlafmittel, Betäubungsmittel, Opiat; (*fig.*) Beruhigungsmittel.

opine [oˈpain], *v.i.* (*obs.*) meinen, der Meinung sein, dafürhalten.

opinion [əˈpinjən], *s.* 1. die Meinung, Ansicht, (*usu. pl.*) Überzeugung (*of, about*, über (*Acc.*)); ***be of the –***, der Meinung *or* Ansicht sein; ***form an – of***, sich (*Dat.*) eine Meinung bilden von; ***have*** or ***hold an –***, eine Ansicht vertreten *or* hegen; ***have a high – of***, eine hohe Meinung haben von; ***have no (high) – of***, nicht viel *or* nichts halten von; ***have the courage of one's –s***, zu seiner Meinung stehen; ***in my –***, meiner Meinung nach, nach meiner Meinung, meines Erachtens; ***incline to the –***, zu der Ansicht neigen; ***remain of the –***, der Ansicht bleiben; ***matter of –***, die Ansichtssache, Geschmack(s)sache; ***public –***, öffentliche Meinung; 2. das Gutachten, Urteil (*on*, über (*Acc.*)); ***get another*** or ***a second –***, das Gutachten eines anderen einholen.

opinionated [əˈpinjəneitid], *adj.* von sich eingenommen, eigensinnig, starrsinnig, eigenwillig. **opinionatedness,** *s.* der Eigensinn, Starrsinn, Eigenwille, die Voreingenommenheit. **opinionative,** *adj. See* **opinionated.**

opisometer [ɔpiˈsɔmitə], *s.* der Kurvenmesser.

opium [ˈoupiəm], *s.* das Opium. **opium-eater,** *s.* der Opiumesser. **opiumism,** *s.* die Opiumsucht; Opiumvergiftung.

opopanax [əˈpɔpənæks], *s.* das Gummiharz, der *or* das (Opo)panaxgummi.

opossum [əˈpɔsəm], *s.* die Beutelratte, das Opossum.

oppidan [ˈɔpidən], **1.** *s.* 1. der Externe, nicht in der Schulanstalt wohnender Stadtschüler (*at Eton*); 2. (*rare*) der (die) Städter(in), Stadtbewohner(in). **2.** *adj.* in der Stadt wohnend, auswärtig.

oppilate [ˈɔpileit], *v.t.* (*Med.*) verstopfen. **oppilation** [–ˈleiʃən], die Verstopfung.

opponency [ɔˈpounənsi], *s.* (*rare*) die Gegnerschaft. **opponent, 1.** *s.* der (die) Gegner(in), (*Spt.*) Gegenspieler(in); der Widersacher, Konkurrent. **2.** *adj.* gegnerisch, entgegengesetzt (*to, Dat.*); (*rare*) gegenüberliegend, gegenüberstehend, entgegengestellt, Gegen–.

opportune [ˈɔpətju:n], *adj.* gelegen, gut angebracht, günstig, passend; rechtzeitig. **opportunely,** *adv.* zu gelegener Zeit, im richtigen *or* passenden Augenblick. **opportuneness,** *s.* die Rechtzeitigkeit, passende Gelegenheit, günstiger Zeitpunkt *or* Augenblick.

opportunism [ɔpəˈtju:nizm], *s.* der Opportunismus, (*coll.*) die Gesinnungslumperei. **opportunist, 1.** *s.* der (die) Opportunist(in). **2.** *or* **opportunistic** [–ˈnistik], *adj.* opportunistisch.

opportunity [ɔpəˈtju:niti], *s.* (günstige) Gelegenheit (***of doing, to do***, zu tun); günstiger Zeitpunkt; die Möglichkeit, Chance; *pl.* Möglichkeiten (*pl.*) (***for***, für *or* zu); ***at*** or ***on the first –***, bei der ersten Gelegenheit; ***miss the –***, die Gelegenheit verpassen; ***an – presents itself***, eine Gelegenheit bietet sich; ***seize*** or ***take the –***, die Gelegenheit ergreifen.

oppose [əˈpouz], *v.t.* 1. bekämpfen, entgegentreten (*Dat.*), angehen gegen; sich widersetzen (*Dat.*), ablehnend gegenüberstehen (*Dat.*), widerstehen (*Dat.*); 2. im Wege stehen (*Dat.*), zuwiderlaufen (*Dat.*), hemmen; 3. entgegensetzen, entgegenstellen (*to, with, Dat.*). **opposed,** *adj.* 1. feindlich (*to*, gegen), feind, abgeneigt, abhold, zuwider (*Dat.*) (*a p.*); entgegengesetzt (*to, Dat.*) (*a th.*); 2. gegensätzlich, Gegen–. **opposing,** *adj.* 1. entgegengesetzt, zusammenstoßend, konfliktierend; 2. widerstreitend, (sich) widersetzend *or* widersprechend, unvereinbar (*ideas etc.*); 3. gegnerisch, opponierend, Gegen– (*forces etc.*).

opposite [ˈɔpəzit], **1.** *adj.* 1. gegenüberstehend, gegenüberliegend (*to, Dat.*), Gegen–; (*Geom.*) ***– angles***, Scheitelwinkel (*pl.*); ***be – to***, gegenüberstehen (*Dat.*) (*also fig.*), gegenüberliegen (*Dat.*); (*fig.*) grundverschieden sein von; ***on the – side to***, auf der gegenüberliegenden Seite von; 2. entgegengesetzt, gegensätzlich; ***in an*** or ***the – direction***, in entgegengesetzter Richtung; (*Math.*) ***of – sign***, ungleichnamig; 3. (grund)verschieden, andere(r, -s) (***to, from***, zu *or* von); ***– sex***, anderes Geschlecht; 4. (*esp. Spt. etc.*) gegnerisch, Gegen–; (*coll.*) ***– number***, der Partner, Mitspieler; Gegenspieler, Widersacher, Gegner; das Gegenstück, entsprechendes Stück, die Entsprechung, das Pendant; 5. (*Bot.*) gegenständig, opponiert. **2.** *adv.* gegenüber. **3.** *prep.* gegenüber (*Dat.*); (*Spt. etc.*) ***play – him***, als Partner(in) von ihm spielen. **4.** *s.* das Gegenteil, der Gegensatz; ***just the –, the very –***, das gerade Gegenteil.

opposition [ɔpəˈziʃən], *s.* 1. der Widerstand, das Widerstreben (*to*, gegen); ***be in –***, (*Pol.*) der Opposition angehören, (*Astr.*) in Opposition stehen (*to*, zu), (*fig.*) Opposition machen (gegen);

encounter or *meet with* –, auf Widerstand stoßen; *offer* –, Widerstand leisten; 2. der Gegensatz (zu); *act in – to his wishes,* seinen Wünschen zuwiderhandeln; 3. der Widerstreit, Widerspruch (*to, with,* mit); 4. das Gegenüberstehen, Gegenüberliegen, die Gegenüberstellung; – *of the thumb,* die Gegenstellung *or* Opponierbarkeit des Daumens; 5. (*Pol.*) die Gegenpartei, Opposition; – *party,* die Opposition(spartei); 6. (*Astr.*) die Opposition, Gegenstellung, der Gegenschein; 7. (*Comm.*) die Konkurrenz.

oppositive [ə'pɔzitiv], *adj.* (*rare*) gegnerisch, gegensätzlich, entgegengesetzt.

oppress [o'pres], *v.t.* 1. unterdrücken, niederdrücken, niederhalten; 2. bedrücken, beklemmen (*spirits*). **oppression** [–ʃən], *s.* 1. die Unterdrückung, Vergewaltigung; 2. der Druck, die Schwere, Härte, Bedrängnis; 3. Niedergeschlagenheit, Beklemmung, Bedrücktheit, trübe Stimmung. **oppressive,** *adj.* 1. niederdrückend, (be)drückend; 2. drückend, schwül (*weather*); 3. tyrannisch, grausam (*as ruler*). **oppressiveness,** *s.* die Schwüle, der Druck. **oppressor,** *s.* der Tyrann, Unterdrücker, Bedrücker.

opprobrious [ə'proubriəs], *adj.* 1. schimpflich, schändlich, schmählich; 2. ehrenrührig, Schimpf–, Schmäh–. **opprobrium,** *s.* Schimpf und Schande, der Schimpf, Schmach, die Schande; Schmähung.

oppugn [ə'pju:n], *v.t.* bestreiten, anfechten, in Frage stellen, für falsch erklären.

opsimath ['ɔpsimæθ], *s.* (*rare*) lerneifriger Greis. **opsimathy** [–i], *s.* 1. das Studium im Alter; 2. spät erworbene Kenntnisse.

opsonic [ɔp'sɔnik], *adj.* (*Med.*) Opsonin–. **opsonin** ['ɔpsənin], *s.* das Opsonin, der Blutserumstoff.

opt [ɔpt], *v.i.* sich entscheiden, optieren (*for,* für), die Wahl treffen, wählen (*between,* zwischen (*Dat.*)); (*coll.*) – *out,* sich drücken. **optative** [–ətiv], **1.** *adj.* Wunsch–; – *mood, see* **2. 2.** *s.* (*Gram.*) der Optativ, die Wunschform.

optic ['ɔptik], **1.** *adj.* Seh–, Augen–; – *nerve,* der Sehnerv; – *thalamus,* der Sehhügel. **2.** *s.* (*coll.*) das Auge. **optical,** *adj.* optisch. **optician** [–'tiʃən], *s.* der Optiker. **optics,** *pl.* (*sing. constr.*) die Optik.

optimal ['ɔptiml], *adj.* optimal.

optimism ['ɔptimizm], *s.* der Optimismus, die Fortschrittsgläubigkeit, Zuversichtlichkeit. **optimist,** *s.* der Optimist. **optimistic(al)** [–'mistik(l)], *adj.* optimistisch, zuversichtlich, hoffnungsfroh.

optimum ['ɔptiməm], **1.** *s.* 1. das Beste, der Bestfall, günstigster Fall; 2. der Bestwert, das Optimum. **2.** *adj.* bestmöglich, Best–, günstigst, optimal.

option ['ɔpʃən], *s.* 1. die Wahl(möglichkeit), freie Wahl *or* Entscheidung, die Entscheidungsfreiheit; *at your* –, nach Wahl; *leave it to his* –, es ihm freistellen; 2. gebotene Möglichkeit, die Alternative; *have no* –, keine Wahl haben, keine andere Möglichkeit haben (*but to do,* als zu tun); *with the – of a fine,* mit dem Recht, eine Geldstrafe (anstatt Haft) zu wählen; 3. (*Comm.*) das Vorkaufsrecht; Optionsrecht, befristetes Kaufangebot; (*St. Exch.*) das Prämiengeschäft; *he gave me the – on the house,* er gab mir das Haus an Hand; *have the – on a purchase,* einen Kauf an Hand haben; 4. (*Univ.*) wahlfreies Fach. **optional,** *adj.* freistehend, freigestellt, anheimgestellt; beliebig, wahlfrei, fakultativ, nicht pflichtmäßig; (*Motor. etc.*) – *extra(s),* die Extraausstattung, das Sonderzubehör (auf Wunsch); (*Univ.*) – *subject,* das Wahlfach.

opulence, opulency ['ɔpjuləns(i)], *s.* 1. die (Über)-fülle, Üppigkeit, der Reichtum, Überfluß (*of,* an (*Dat.*)); 2. (*coll.*) Wohlstand, Luxus. **opulent,** *adj.* 1. üppig, reich(lich); 2. (*coll.*) vermögend, wohlhabend.

opuntia [o'pʌnʃiə], *s.* (*Bot.*) die Opuntie.

opus ['oupəs], *s.* das Werk, Opus; *magnum* –, das Hauptwerk. **opuscule** [o'pʌskjul], *s.* kleine Arbeit, die Studie, das Werkchen, Opusculum.

[1]**or** [ɔ:], *s.* (*Her.*) das Gold.

[2]**or** [ɔ:, ə], *conj.* oder; (*after neg.*) noch; *either* . . . – . . ., entweder . . . oder . . .; – *else,* sonst, wenn nicht; *not fame – riches (either),* kein Ruhm noch Reichtum, nicht Ruhm und auch nicht Reichtum; *one – two,* einige; *a tree – two,* einige Baume.

orach ['ɔritʃ], *s.* (*Bot.*) Wilder Spinat, die Melde.

oracle ['ɔrəkl], *s.* 1. das Orakel, der Orakelspruch, die Weissagung; (*coll.*) *work the* –, hinter den Kulissen *or* auf krummen Wegen arbeiten; 2. (*fig.*) (unfehlbare) Autorität. **oracular** [o'rækjulə], *adj.* 1. orakelhaft, Orakel–; 2. maßgebend (*of a p.*); 3. (*fig.*) zweideutig, rätselhaft, schwer verständlich, dunkel.

oral ['ɔ:rəl], *adj.* 1. mündlich; – *examination,* mündliche Prüfung; 2. (*Anat.*) Mund–; – *cavity,* die Mundhöhle; – *vaccine,* der Schluckimpfstoff.

[1]**Orange** ['ɔrindʒ], *s.* (*Hist*) Oranien; *House of* –, das Haus Oraniens.

[2]**Orange,** *s.* der Oranje (*river*); (*Hist.*) – *Free State,* der Oranjefreistaat.

orange, **1.** *s.* 1. die Apfelsine, Orange; 2. der Orangenbaum; 3. die Orangefarbe. **2.** *adj.* 1. Orange(n)–; 2. orange(n)farbig. **orangeade** ['ɔrin'dʒeid], *s.* die Orangeade. **orange|-blossom,** *s.* die Orangenblüte. **--coloured,** *adj.* orangenfarbig, rötlich gelb. **--peel,** *s.* die Apfelsinenschale. **orangery** [–ri], *s.* die Orangerie. **orange-stick,** *s.* der Nagelreiniger.

orang|-outang [ou'ræŋju:tæŋ], **--utan** [–u:tæn], *s.* der Orang-Utan.

orate [ɔ:'reit], *v.i.* (*coll.*) (lange) Reden halten, immerzu reden (*on,* über (*Acc.*)). **oration** [o'reiʃən], *s.* (feierliche) Rede; (*Gram.*) die Rede. **orator** ['ɔrətə], *s.* der Redner. **oratorical** [ɔrə'tɔrikl], *adj.* rednerisch, Redner–; rhetorisch, oratorisch.

oratorio [ɔrə'tɔ:riou], *s.* (*Mus.*) das Oratorium.

oratory ['ɔrət(ə)ri], *s.* 1. die Beredsamkeit, Redekunst, Rhetorik; (*coll.*) *mere* –, bloßes Gerede; 2. (*R.C.*) die (Privat)kapelle, der Andachtsraum.

orb [ɔ:b], *s.* 1. die Kugel; 2. (*Her.*) der Reichsapfel; 3. (*Poet.*) Himmelskörper; 4. (*Poet.*) das Auge, der Augapfel. **orbicular** [–'bikjulə], *adj.* kugelrund, kreisrund, kreisförmig, ringförmig. **orbiculate** [–'bikjuleit], *adj.* (*Bot.*) kugelrund, gerundet.

orbit ['ɔ:bit], *s.* 1. (*Anat.*) die Augenhöhle; 2. (*Astr.*) (Planeten)bahn, Umlaufbahn; 3. (*fig.*) der (Macht)bereich, die Einflußsphäre, das (Wirkungs)gebiet. **orbital,** *adj.* Augenhöhlen–; – *cavity,* die Augenhöhle.

orc(a) ['ɔ:k(ə)], *s.* der Schwertwal, Butzkopf.

Orcadian [ɔ:'keidiən], *s.* der (die) Bewohner(in) der Orkneyinseln.

orchard ['ɔ:tʃəd], *s.* der Obstgarten.

orchestic [ɔ:'kestik], *adj.* Tanz–. **orchestics,** *s.* (*sing. constr.*) die Tanzkunst, Orchestik.

orchestra ['ɔ:kistrə], *s.* 1. das Orchester; 2. (*Theat.*) der Orchesterraum; – *stalls* (*Am. seats*), das Parkett. **orchestral** [–'kestrəl], *adj.* Orchester–. **orchestrate** [–reit], *v.t., v.i.* orchestrieren, instrumentieren. **orchestration** [–'treiʃən], *s.* die Orchestrierung, Instrumentierung.

orchid ['ɔ:kid], *s.* die Orchidee. **orchidaceous** [–'deiʃəs], *adj.* Orchideen–.

orchis ['ɔ:kis], *s.* 1. (*Anat.*) die Hode; 2. (*Bot.*) das Knabenkraut; *see also* **orchid. orchitis** [–'kaitis], *s.* die Hodenentzündung.

orcin(ol) ['ɔ:sin(ɔl)], *s.* (*Chem.*) das Orzin.

ordain [ɔ:'dein], *v.t.* 1. fügen, bestimmen (*as God*); (*fig.*) festsetzen, anordnen, verfügen; 2. (*Eccl.*) ordinieren, weihen (*as,* zu).

ordeal [ɔ:'diəl], *s.* 1. schwere Prüfung, die Heimsuchung; (*fig.*) Qual, Pein; 2. (*Hist.*) (Feuer)-probe (*also fig.*), das Gottesurteil.

order ['ɔ:də], **1.** *v.t.* 1. in Ordnung bringen, ordnen, regulieren, einrichten (*things*); 2. befehlen (*a p., Dat.*; *an attack etc., Acc.*); beauftragen (*a p.*), anordnen (*a th.*); *he –ed the ship to be sunk,* er befahl, das Schiff zu versenken; 3. beordern, schicken (*a p.*) (*to,* nach); – *about,* herumkommandieren, hin und her schicken, schurigeln, schikanieren; – *out,* hinausweisen; 4. verordnen,

anordnen (*as a doctor*) (*a p., Dat.*; *a th., Acc.*); **5.** (*Comm.*) bestellen (*goods*); – ***in advance,*** im voraus bestellen, vorausbestellen; 6. (*Mil.*) – ***arms!*** Gewehr ab!
2. *s.* 1. der Befehl (*also Mil.*), Erlaß, die Verfügung, Weisung, Vorschrift, Verordnung; – ***in council,*** der Kabinettserlaß; – ***to pay,*** der Zahlungsbefehl, die Zahlungsanweisung; (*Mil.*) ***at the*** –, Gewehr bei Fuß; ***by*** –, auf Befehl; ***by – of,*** auf Befehl *or* Verordnung *or* (*Comm.*) im Auftrage *or* auf Order von; ***by – of the courts,*** auf Gerichtsbeschluß; ***citation in –s,*** besondere Erwähnung; ***disobedience of –s,*** der Ungehorsam; ***doctor's –s,*** ärztliche Anordnung; ***give –s*** or ***the*** or ***an*** –, Befehl geben (***for it to be done,*** es zu tun); ***marching –s,*** der Marschbefehl; (*coll.*) Laufpaß; ***on the –(s) of,*** auf Befehl (von); ***sailing –s,*** die Reiseinstruktionen; (*coll.*) ***tall*** –, schwierige Aufgabe, arge Zumutung; ***till further –s,*** bis auf weitere Befehle; ***be under –s,*** Befehl haben; ***warning*** –, der Vorbefehl, das Ankündigungskommando;
2. (*Comm.*) die Bestellung, Order, der Auftrag; ***banker's*** –, der Zahlungsauftrag an die Bank; ***your esteemed*** –, Ihr geschätzter Auftrag; ***cancel an – (for s.th.),*** (etwas) abbestellen, eine Bestellung rückgängig machen; ***give*** or ***place an – for,*** bestellen, eine Bestellung machen *or* aufgeben für, in Auftrag geben (***with,*** bei); ***money*** –, die Postanweisung (für größere Beträge bis £50), Zahlungsanweisung; ***postal*** –, die Postanweisung (für kleinere Beträge); ***take an – for,*** einen Auftrag erhalten auf (*Acc.*); ***on*** –, bestellt, in Bestellung; ***as per*** –, laut Bestellung; ***to*** –, (*Mil.*) (wie) auf Befehl, befehlsgemäß, auftragsgemäß; (*Comm.*) auf Bestellung, an Order; ***make to*** –, nach Maß *or* auf Bestellung herstellen *or* anfertigen;
3. geordneter Zustand, die Ordnung; ***law and*** –, Ruhe und Ordnung; ***love of*** –, die Ordnungsliebe; ***in (good)*** –, in Ordnung, wohlbehalten, in gutem Zustand; ***keep*** –, die Ordnung aufrechterhalten, Ordnung halten; ***keep in*** –, in Ordnung halten, instand halten; beaufsichtigen; ***out of*** –, (*Med.*) gestört, angegriffen; (*Tech.*) defekt; ***put*** or ***set in*** –, in Ordnung bringen, ordnen; ***in (good) running*** –, betriebsfertig; ***in – that,*** damit; ***in – to . . .,*** um zu . . .;
4. die Reihenfolge, Anordnung; – ***of firing,*** die Zündfolge (*of engines*); – ***of magnitude,*** das Größenverhältnis; – ***of merit*** or ***precedence,*** die Rangordnung; – ***of succession,*** die Reihenfolge, der Ablauf; ***in alphabetical*** –, alphabetisch geordnet; ***invert*** or ***reverse the*** –, die Reihenfolge umkehren; ***word*** –, die Wortfolge, (Satz)stellung; ***in*** –, der Reihe nach, in der richtigen Reihenfolge; ***out of*** –, in Unordnung, außer der Reihenfolge;
5. die (Geschäfts)ordnung; *–! –!* zur Sache *or* Ordnung! – ***of the day,*** (*Mil.*) der Tagesbefehl, (*Parl.*) die Tagesordnung; (*fig.*) ***be the – of the day,*** an der Tagesordnung sein; ***pass to the – of the day,*** zur Tagesordnung übergehen; ***standing –s,*** feststehende Geschäftsordnung; ***in*** –, (*Parl. etc.*) zulässig, gemäß der Geschäftsordnung; (*coll.*) am Platze; ***not in*** –, ordnungswidrig, nicht zur Geschäftsordnung; (*Parl.*) ***out of*** –, unzulässig, gegen die Geschäftsordnung; ***call to*** –, der Ordnungsruf; ***he was called to*** –, er wurde zur Ordnung gerufen; ***rise to (a point of)*** –, zur Geschäftsordnung sprechen, beantragen daß zur Geschäftsordnung gesprochen wird;
6. (*Mil.*) die Aufstellung; – ***of battle,*** die Schlachtordnung, (*Nav.*) Gefechtsformation; (*Mil.*) ***close*** –, geschlossene Ordnung; ***extended*** –, ***open*** –, geöffnete Ordnung; – ***of march,*** die Marschordnung; ***in skirmishing*** –, ausgeschwärmt;
7. die Gattung, Art, Sorte, Klasse, Ordnung; (*Archit.*) ***Doric*** –, dorische Säulenordnung;
8. die Stellung, der Rang, Grad; ***of a high*** –, hochgradig; ***the lower –s,*** die untere Gesellschaftsschicht;
9. der (Ritter)orden; das Ordenszeichen; ***Order of the Garter,*** der Hosenbandorden; – ***of knighthood,*** der Ritterorden; ***Order of Merit,*** der Verdienstorden; (*Am.*) ***Order of the Purple Heart,*** das Verwundetenabzeichen;
10. religiöser Orden;
11. (*Mil.*) die Uniform, Ausrüstung; ***marching*** –, die Marschausrüstung;
12. *pl.* geistlicher Stand; ***holy –s,*** der geistlicher Stand; ***be in –s,*** Geistlicher sein; ***take –s,*** Geistlicher werden.

order|-book, *s.* das Bestellbuch, Auftragsbuch. **--clerk,** *s.* der Auftragsbuchhalter. **--form,** *s.* der Bestellzettel, Bestellschein. **orderless,** *adj.* unordentlich, ohne Ordnung.

orderliness ['ɔ:dəlinis], *s.* 1. die Regelmäßigkeit, Ordnung; 2. (*of a p.*) Ordnungsliebe, Ordentlichkeit. **orderly, 1.** *adj.* 1. planmäßig, regelmäßig, ordnungsgemäß, methodisch, geregelt, (wohl)geordnet, ordentlich; 2. (*of a p.*) friedlich, ordnungsliebend; 3. (*Mil.*) diensttuend, diensthabend, Ordonnanz–. **2.** *s.* 1. die Ordonnanz; 2. der (Offiziers)bursche; (*Mil.*) ***hospital*** or ***medical*** –, der Krankenwärter, Lazarettgehilfe.

orderly|-book, *s.* (*Mil.*) das Parolebuch. **--duty,** *s.* die Ordonnanz. **--officer,** *s.* der Offizier vom Dienst, Ordonnanzoffizier, diensttuender Offizier. **--room,** *s.* (*Mil.*) das Geschäftszimmer, die Schreibstube, Dienststube; – ***sergeant,*** der (Bataillons)schreiber.

order-paper, *s.* das Sitzungsprogramm, Programm der Tagesordnung, die Tagesordnung.

[1]**ordinal** ['ɔ:dinl], **1.** *adj.* Ordnungs–, Ordinal–. **2.** *s.* (*also* – ***numeral,*** – ***number***) die Ordnungszahl, Ordinalzahl.

[2]**ordinal,** *s.* (*Eccl.*) das Ordinale, Ritual (für die Ordinierung). **ordinance,** *s.* 1. die Verordnung, Verfügung; 2. (*Eccl.*) (festgesetzter) Brauch, der Ritus.

ordinarily ['ɔ:dinərili], *adv.* üblicherweise, normalerweise, gewöhnlich. **ordinariness,** *s.* 1. die Gewöhnlichkeit, Alltäglichkeit, Mittelmäßigkeit; 2. das Normale. **ordinary, 1.** *adj.* 1. gewöhnlich, üblich, normal; alltäglich, Alltags–, mittelmäßig, Durchschnitts–; 2. regelmäßig, ständig, ordentlich; – ***debts,*** Buchschulden (*pl.*); ***judge*** –, festangestellter Richter; – ***member,*** ordentliches Mitglied; – ***seaman,*** der Leichtmatrose; – ***share,*** die Stammaktie. **2.** *s.* 1. das Gewöhnliche, Übliche, Normale; ***out of the*** –, ungewöhnlich, außergewöhnlich, ausgefallen; ***nothing out of the*** –, nichts Ungewöhnliches; 2. (*obs.*) gemeinsame Tafel, fester Mittagstisch; (*esp. Am.*) die Gaststätte; 3. (*Hist.*) das Hochrad; 4. die Meßordnung, das Ordinarium; 5. (*Eccl.*) der (Erz)bischof; 6. (*Law*) ordentlicher Richter; 7. ***in*** –, von Amts wegen; ***chaplain in – to the King,*** der Hauskaplan *or* Hofkaplan des Königs; ***physician in*** –, der Leibarzt, Hausarzt.

ordinate ['ɔ:dinit], *s.* (*Geom.*) die Ordinate.

ordination [ɔ:di'neiʃən], *s.* die Ordinierung, Priesterweihe.

ordnance ['ɔ:dnəns], *s.* (*only sing.*) die Artillerie, Geschütze (*pl.*); ***piece of*** –, schweres Geschütz; ***Army Ordnance Corps,*** das Zeugkorps; (*Am.*) ***Ordnance Department,*** das Zeugamt, Waffenamt, die Feldzeugmeisterei; ***Director-General of the Ordnance,*** der Generalfeldzeugmeister.

ordnance|-datum, *s.* (*Surv.*) mittlere Höhe über Normalnull. **--depot,** *s.* das Feldzeugdepot, Artilleriedepot. **--map,** *s.* die Generalstabskarte, das Meßtischblatt. **--survey,** *s.* amtliche Landesvermessung.

ordure ['ɔ:djuə], *s.* der Kot, Schmutz, Unflat.

ore [ɔ:], *s.* das Erz; (*Poet.*) Metall.

organ ['ɔ:gən], *s.* 1. das Organ (*also Anat., fig.*), Werkzeug (*also fig.*), Hilfsmittel; (menschliche) Stimme; ***sense*** –, das Sinnesorgan; 2. (*Mus.*) die Orgel; ***American*** –, das Harmonium; 3. (*fig.*) der Träger, das Sprachrohr, die Zeitung; – ***of public opinion,*** der Träger der öffentlichen Meinung. **organ-builder,** *s.* der Orgelbauer.

organdie ['ɔ:gəndi], *s.* der Organdy.

organ|-gallery, *s.* *See* **--loft. --grinder,** *s.* der Leierkastenmann.

organic [ɔ:'gænik], *adj.* 1. organisch; – ***chemistry,***

organische Chemie; (*Chem.*) – ***analysis,*** die Elementaranalyse; 2. (*fig.*) zusammenhängend, (systematisch) geordnet, organisiert; 3. (*Law*) konstitutionell, grundlegend, Grund–; – ***law,*** das Grundgesetz. **organism** ['ɔ:gənizm], *s.* 1. der Organismus (*also fig.*), das Lebewesen; 2. (*fig.*) Gefüge, die Struktur.

organist ['ɔ:gənist], *s.* der (die) Organist(in).

organization [ɔ:gən(a)i'zeiʃən], *s.* 1. die Organisierung, Einrichtung, Gliederung, (Aus)gestaltung, Anordnung; 2. Organisation, Körperschaft, Gesellschaft, der Verband; 3. Organismus, das System, Gefüge; 4. (*coll.*) der Verwaltungsapparat. **organizational,** *adj.* Organisations–, organisatorisch. **organize** ['ɔ:gənaiz], **1.** *v.t.* 1. organisieren, anordnen, ausbauen, aufbauen, (planmäßig) gliedern; 2. einrichten, veranstalten, arrangieren. **2.** *v.i.* sich organisieren. **organizer,** *s.* der Organisator.

organ|-loft, *s.* der Orgelchor. **--recital,** *s.* das Orgelkonzert. **--screen,** *s.* der Orgellettner. **--stop,** *s.* das Orgelregister.

organzine ['ɔ:gənzi:n], *s.* das *or* der Organsin.

orgasm ['ɔ:gæzm], *s.* 1. der Orgasmus; 2. (*fig.*) heftige Erregung, höchste Wallung.

orgiastic [ɔ:dʒi'æstik], *adj.* zügellos, orgienhaft. **orgy** ['ɔ:dʒi], *s.* 1. die Orgie, Schwelgerei, Ausschweifung; 2. Sauferei, das Saufgelage.

oriel ['ɔ:riəl], *s.* der Erker.

Orient ['ɔ:riənt], *s.* 1. das Morgenland, der Orient; 2. (*Poet.*) Osten, Morgen. **orient, 1.** *adj.* (*Poet.*) 1. aufgehend, aufsteigend; 2. strahlend, leuchtend, glänzend. **2.** *v.t.* 1. orientieren, orten, die Lage *or* Richtung bestimmen von; (*fig.*) – ***o.s.,*** sich orientieren *or* zurechtfinden, sich unterrichten *or* informieren; 2. nach Osten richten, osten (*a church*). **Oriental** [–'entl], *s.* der Orientale (die Orientalin). **oriental,** *adj.* östlich, orientalisch, morgenländisch; – ***scholar,*** *see* **Orientalist. Orientalist** [–'entəlist], *s.* der Orientalist, Orientforscher. **orientate** [–eit], *v.t.* *See* **orient, 2. orientation** [–'teiʃən], *s.* 1. die Orientierung, Ortung, Richtungsbestimmung, Ausrichtung; 2. Richtung, Anlage; 3. Ostung (*of a church*); 4. der Orientierungssinn.

orifice ['ɔrifis], *s.* die Mündung, Öffnung.

oriflamme ['ɔriflæm], *s.* die Fahne; (*fig.*) das Wahrzeichen, Fanal.

origin ['ɔridʒin], *s.* 1. der Ursprung, die Quelle; – ***of species,*** der Ursprung der Arten; 2. die Entstehung, Herkunft, Abstammung; ***date of*** –, das Entstehungsdatum; 3. (*Comm.*) Provenienz; 4. (*Math.*) der Koordinatennullpunkt; – ***of a force,*** der Angriffspunkt einer Kraft.

original [ə'ridʒinəl], **1.** *adj.* 1. ursprünglich, Ur–, original, Original–; – ***binding,*** der Originaleinband; – ***cause,*** die Grundursache; – ***inhabitants,*** Ureinwohner (*pl.*); – ***position,*** die Ausgangsstellung; – ***research,*** selbständige Forschung; – ***sin,*** die Erbsünde; – ***state,*** der Anfangszustand; – ***text,*** der Urtext; 2. originell, neu(artig), einzigartig, unabhängig, selbständig; (*of a p.*) erfinderisch, schöpferisch; – ***genius,*** das Originalgenie, der Schöpfergeist; – ***thinker,*** selbständiger *or* unabhängiger *or* schöpferischer Denker. **2.** *s.* 1. das Original (*also of p.*), Urbild, die Urschrift, Urform, Urfassung, der Urtext; 2. (*Bot., Zool.*) Urtypus, die Stammform, Wildart; 3. (*coll. of a p.*) das Unikum; 4. (*Art*) Modell, die Vorlage. **originality** [–'næliti], *s.* 1. die Originalität, Ursprünglichkeit, Echtheit; 2. Eigenart, Eigentümlichkeit; 3. Neuheit, Neuartigkeit, Unabhängigkeit, Selbständigkeit; (*of a p.*) schöpferische Kraft. **originally,** *adv.* ursprünglich, anfangs, zuerst, von Anfang an.

originate [ə'ridʒineit], **1.** *v.t.* hervorbringen, ins Leben rufen, den Grund legen zu. **2.** *v.i.* 1. entstehen, entspringen (***from,*** aus), seinen Ursprung *or* seine Ursache haben (in (*Dat.*)), herstammen (von *or* aus), ausgehen (von); 2. beginnen (***with, in,*** bei), ausgehen (von). **origination** [–'neiʃən], *s.* 1. die Hervorbringung, (Er)schaffung, Entstehung; 2. Abstammung, Herkunft, der Ursprung. **originative** [–ətiv], *adj.* schöpferisch. **originator,** *s.* 1. der Urheber, Schöpfer, Hervorbringer, Begründer; 2. Schaffende(r).

oriole ['ɔ:rioul], *s.* (*Orn.*) ***golden*** –, der Pirol, die Goldamsel (*Oriolus oriolus*).

orison ['ɔrizən], *s.* (*Poet.*) das Gebet.

orlop ['ɔ:ləp], *s.* (*Naut.*) das Orlopdeck.

ormolu ['ɔ:məlu:], *s.* das Malergold, Muschelgold, die Goldbronze.

ornament ['ɔ:nəmənt], **1.** *s.* 1. der Schmuck, Putz, Zierat, das Ornament, die Verzierung; (*fig.*) Zier(de) (*of p.*) (***to,*** für *or Gen.*); *pl.* der Schmuck, Schmucksachen (*pl.*); ***by way of*** –, zur *or* als Verzierung. **2.** *v.t.* verzieren, schmücken. **ornamental** [–'mentl], *adj.* zierend, Zier–, schmückend, dekorativ; – ***plant,*** die Zierpflanze. **ornamentation** [–'teiʃən], *s.* die Ornamentierung, Verzierung, Ausschmückung.

ornate [ɔ:'neit], *adj.* reich geziert *or* geschmückt, (*of style*) überladen. **ornateness,** *s.* reicher Schmuck, die Überladenheit.

ornithological [ɔ:niθə'lɔdʒikl], *adj.* ornithologisch. **ornithologist** [–'θɔlədʒist], *s.* der Ornithologe. **ornithology** [–'θɔlədʒi], *s.* die Vogelkunde, Ornithologie. **ornithomancy** [–'naiθəmænsi], *s.* die Vogelwahrsagung, Ornithomantie. **ornithopter** [–'θɔptə], *s.* (*Av.*) der Schwingenflügler. **ornithorhynchus** [–θo'riŋkəs], *s.* (*Zool.*) das Schabeltier.

orography [ɔ'rɔgrəfi], *s.* die Geomorphologie. **orology** [ɔ'rɔlədʒi], *s.* die Gebirgskunde.

orotund ['ɔ:rotʌnd], *adj.* klangvoll, volltönend (*of the voice*), bombastisch, schwülstig, pompös (*of style*). **orotundity** [–'tʌnditi], *s* der Bombast.

orphan ['ɔ:fən], **1.** *s.* die Waise, das Waisenkind. **2.** *adj.* verwaist; – ***child,*** das Waisenkind. **3.** *v.t.* (*usu. pass.*) ***be*** –***ed,*** Waise werden, verwaisen. **orphanage** [–idʒ], *s.* 1. das Waisenhaus; 2. die Verwaistheit, das Verwaistsein.

Orphic ['ɔ:fik], *adj.* orphisch; (*fig.*) geheimnisvoll, mystisch.

orphrey ['ɔ:fri], *s.* die Goldborte, Goldstickerei.

orpiment ['ɔ:pimənt], *s.* das Rauschgelb.

orpine ['ɔ:pin], *s.* (*Bot.*) die Fetthenne, das Johanniskraut.

orrery ['ɔrəri], *s.* das Planetarium.

orris ['ɔris], *s.* die Schwertlilie; – ***root,*** die Veilchenwurzel.

orthochromatic [ɔ:θoukrə'mætik], *adj.* orthochromatisch, farb(wert)richtig.

orthoclase ['ɔ:θoukleiz], *n.* (*Geol.*) der Orthoklas.

orthodox ['ɔ:θədɔks], *adj.* 1. rechtgläubig, altgläubig, strenggläubig, orthodox; ***Orthodox Church,*** griechischkatholische Kirche; 2. (*fig.*) üblich, althergebracht, konventionell, landläufig, anerkannt. **orthodoxy,** *s.* die Rechtgläubigkeit, Strenggläubigkeit, Orthodoxie.

orthoepist [ɔ:'θouipist], *s.* der Aussprachelehrer. **orthoepy,** *s.* richtige Aussprache.

orthogonal [ɔ:'θɔgənl], *adj.* rechtwinklig.

orthographic(al) [ɔ:θou'græfik(l)], *adj.* 1. orthographisch; 2. (*Surv.*) senkrecht. **orthography** [–'θɔgrəfi], *s.* die Rechtschreibung.

orthopaedic [ɔ:θə'pi:dik], *adj.* orthopädisch. **orthopaedist,** *s.* der Orthopäde. **orthopaedy** ['ɔ:θəpi:di], *s.* die Orthopädie.

orthoptera [ɔ:'θɔptərə], *pl.* (*Ent.*) Geradflügler (*pl.*).

ortolan ['ɔ:tələn], *s.* (*Orn.*) die Fettammer, Gartenammer, der Ortolan (*Emberiza hortulana*).

orts [ɔ:ts], *pl.* (*obs.*) der Abfall, (Über)reste, Überbleibsel (*pl.*).

oscillate ['ɔsileit], **1.** *v.i.* 1. schwingen, pendeln, oszillieren; 2. (*fig.*) (hin– und her)schwanken. **2.** *v.t.* ins Schwingen bringen. **oscillating,** *adj.* Schwing(ungs)–, Pendel–; – ***circuit,*** der Schwing(ungs)kreis. **oscillation** [–'leiʃən], *s.* 1. die Schwingung; ***damped*** –, gedämpfte Welle; ***natural***

–, die Eigenschwingung; 2. (*fig.*) die Schwankung, das Schwanken. **oscillator,** *s.* der Oszillator. **oscillatory** [–lətəri], *adj.* schwingend, Schwingungs–, oszillierend.

oscillogram [əˈsiləgræm], *s.* das Oszillogramm. **oscillograph,** *s.* (*cathode ray*) –, der (Kathodenstrahl)oszillograph. **oscilloscope,** *s.* das Oszilloskop.

oscular [ˈɔskjulə], *adj.* 1. (*Math.*) oskulär; 2. (*coll.*) Kuß–, küssend, sich berührend. **osculate** [–leit], **1.** *v.i.* sich eng berühren, oskulieren; ***osculating circle,*** der Schmiegungskreis. **2.** *v.t.* küssen. **osculation** [–ˈleiʃən], *s.* 1. das Küssen, der Kuß; 2. (*Math.*) die Berührung höherer Ordnung; ***point of –,*** der Berührungspunkt. **osculatory** [–lətəri], *adj.* 1. Kuß–; 2. (*Math.*) oskulierend.

osier [ˈouziə], *s.* die Korbweide. **osier-bed,** *s.* die Weidenpflanzung.

osmic [ˈɔzmik], *adj.* (*Chem.*) Osmium–. **osmium,** *s.* das Osmium.

osmosis [ɔzˈmousis], *s.* die Osmose.

osmund [ˈɔzmənd], *s.* der Rispenfarn.

osprey [ˈɔspri], *s.* 1. (*Orn.*) der Fischadler (*Pandion haliaetus*); 2. (*coll.*) Federschmuck, die Reiherfeder.

osseous [ˈɔsiəs], *adj.* knöchern, Knochen–. **ossicle** [–ikl], *s.* das Knöchelchen. **ossification** [–fiˈkeiʃən], *s.* die Verknöcherung, Knochenbildung. **ossified** [ˈɔsifaid], *adj.* verknöchert (*also fig.*), (*fig.*) erstarrt, starr.

ossifrage [ˈɔsifridʒ], *s. See* **osprey.**

ossify [ˈɔsifai], **1.** *v.t.* verknöchern (*also fig.*). **2.** *v.i.* verknöchern (*also fig.*), (*fig.*) erstarren. **ossuary** [–juəri], *s.* das Beinhaus, der Karner.

Ostend [ɔsˈtend], *s.* Ostende (*n.*).

ostensible [ɔsˈtensibl], *adj.* vorgeblich, angeblich, vorgeschoben, scheinbar. **ostensive,** *adj.* anschaulich, darstellend; *see also* **ostensible. ostensory,** *s.* (*Eccl.*) die Monstranz.

ostentation [ɔstenˈteiʃən], *s.* 1. die Schaustellung; 2. Prahlerei, das Gepränge. **ostentatious,** *adj.* 1. prahlend, prahlerisch, großtuerisch; 2. demonstrativ, ostentativ, auffällig. **ostentatiousness,** *s.* die Prahlerei, Großtuerei.

osteoblast [ˈɔstiəblæst], *s.* der Knochenbildner, die Knochenbildungszelle. **osteology** [–ˈɔlədʒi], *s.* die Knochenlehre, Knochenkunde. **osteoma** [–ˈouməl], *s.* die Knochengeschwulst, das Osteom. **osteomalacia** [–məˈleiʃiə], *s.* die Knochenerweichung. **osteomyelitis** [–maiəˈlaitis], *s.* die Knochenmarksentzündung, Myelomatose. **osteopath** [–pæθ], *s.* der Osteopath. **osteosclerosis** [–skləˈrousis], *s.* die Knochenverhärtung. **osteotomy** [–ˈɔtəmi], *s.* die Knochenresektion, Osteotomie.

ostler [ˈɔslə], *s.* der Stallknecht.

ostracism [ˈɔstrəsizm], *s.* (*Hist.*) das Scherbengericht; (*fig.*) die Verbannung, Ächtung. **ostracize** [–saiz], *v.t.* ausstoßen, verbannen, ächten, verfemen.

ostrich [ˈɔstritʃ], *s.* der Strauß. **ostrich|-egg,** *s.* das Straußenei. **– policy,** *s.* die Vogel-Strauß-Politik.

Ostrogoth [ˈɔstrəgɔθ], *s.* der Ostgote.

other [ˈʌðə], **1.** *adj.* ander, sonstig, weiter, übrig; anders (***than,*** als), verschieden (von); ***the – day,*** vor einigen Tagen, vor einiger Zeit, neulich, kürzlich; ***every – day,*** einen Tag um den andern, alle zwei Tage, jeden zweiten Tag; ***on the – hand,*** and(e)rerseits, hingegen; ***the – morning,*** neulich morgens; ***– things being equal,*** bei sonst gleichen Bedingungen; ***none – than,*** kein anderer als; ***not – than,*** nicht anders als, nur; ***any p. – than yourself,*** jeder außer dir. **2.** *pron.* der *or* die *or* das andere; ***each –,*** einander; ***no – than,*** kein anderer als; ***one after the –,*** einer nach dem andern; ***one or – of them,*** der eine oder andere von ihnen; ***somebody or –,*** irgend jemand, irgendwer; ***some day*** or ***time or –,*** eines Tages, irgendeinmal; ***some way or –,*** irgendwie, auf irgendeine Weise; ***the ten –s,*** die zehn anderen, die anderen zehn; ***and some –s,*** und noch einige (andere); (*coll.*) ***some fool or –,*** irgendwelcher Narr. **3.** *adv.* anders (***than,*** als).

otherwise [ˈʌðəwaiz], *adv.* anders (***than,*** als); sonst, im übrigen; andernfalls; anderweitig; ***not – than,*** nicht anders als, genau so wie; ***the benefits or –,*** die Vor– oder Nachteile; ***rather pleased than –,*** eher zufrieden als nicht *or* als das Gegenteil; ***be – engaged,*** anderweitig beschäftigt sein, anders vorhaben; ***he is ill, – he would be here,*** er ist krank, sonst *or* andernfalls wäre er hier.

other|worldliness, *s.* die Jenseitigkeit. **--worldly,** *adj.* jenseitig, Jenseits–.

otiose [ouʃiˈous], *adj.* 1. unnütz, überflüssig, zwecklos, nutzlos, fruchtlos; 2. (*rare*) müßig. **otiosity** [–ˈɔsiti], *s.* 1. die Zwecklosigkeit, Nutzlosigkeit; 2. Muße, der Müßiggang.

otology [oˈtɔlədʒi], *s.* die Ohrenheilkunde. **otoscope** [ˈoutəskoup], *s.* der Ohr(en)spiegel.

otter [ˈɔtə], *s.* 1. der Otter; Otterpelz; 2. (*Nav.*) das Minenräumgerät. **otter|-dog, --hound,** *s.* der Otterhund.

Ottoman [ˈɔtəmən], **1.** *s.* der Osmane, Türke. **2.** *adj.* osmanisch, türkisch.

ottoman, *s.* die Ottomane, das Sofa, Sitzpolster.

oubliette [u:bliˈet], *s.* das Verlies.

ouch! [autʃ], *int.* au(tsch)!

[1]**ought** [ɔ:t], *s.* (*coll.*) die Null.

[2]**ought,** *v.aux.* (*only pres. & imp.*) sollte; ***I – to go,*** ich sollte (eigentlich) gehen; ***it – to be done,*** es sollte getan werden, es sollte geschehen; ***he – to have gone,*** er hätte gehen sollen; ***you – to know,*** du solltest *or* müßtest wissen; ***if she had done as she –,*** hätte sie gehandelt wie sie sollte.

[1]**ounce** [auns], *s.* die Unze (= *28½ g; gold, silver etc. = 31 g*); ***by the –,*** nach (dem) Gewicht; ***half an –,*** ein Lot; (*fig.*) ***not an – of truth,*** nicht ein Körnchen Wahrheit.

[2]**ounce,** *s.* 1. der Irbis (*panthera uncia*); 2. (*Poet.*) der Luchs.

our [ˈauə], *poss. adj.* unser; (*coll.*) ***Our Father,*** das Vaterunser; ***Our Lady,*** die Mutter Gottes; ***in the year of – Lord,*** im Jahre des Herrn. **ours** [–z], *poss. pron.* unser, der *or* die *or* das unsrige *or* unsere; ***a friend of –,*** ein Freund von uns, einer von unseren Freunden; ***in this world of –,*** in dieser unserer Welt; ***it became – after his death,*** wir erwarben es nach seinem Tod; ***that's –,*** das gehört uns. **ourself** [–ˈself], *emph. pron. **we –,*** wir selbst (*editorial language*); Wir Höchstselbst (*of a king*). **ourselves** [–ˈselvz], **1.** *emph. pron. pl.* wir selbst (*Nom.*), uns selbst (*Dat., Acc.*); ***of –,*** aus unserm eigenen Antriebe, von selbst. **2.** *refl. pron.* (*Acc., Dat.*) uns (selbst).

ousel, *see* **ouzel.**

oust [aust], *v.t.* 1. ausstoßen, vertreiben, entfernen, verdrängen (***from,*** aus); entheben, entsetzen (***from office,*** des Amtes); 2. (*Law*) berauben (***of,*** *Gen.*).

out [aut], **1.** *adv.* 1. (*movement*) hinaus, hinaus–, heraus, heraus–, (*with nouns*) Aus–; (*fig.*) aus, entgegen; 2. (*position*) (*usu. with **to be***) draußen; nicht zu Hause, ausgegangen, nicht daheim, fort, verreist; außer dem Hause, im Freien; (*Naut.*) auf See; (*Mil.*) im Felde; (*of plants*) in Blüte; (*of a joint*) verrenkt; (*of fire, light*) aus, erloschen; (*of library book*) ausgeliehen; (*coll.*) unter *or* im Streik; nicht mehr im Dienst *or* Ministerium *or* Amt *or* am Ruder *or* Spiel; völlig erschöpft, verbraucht, (*Boxing*) ausgezählt, kampfunfähig; aus der Mode, vorbei, vorüber, vergangen, abgelaufen, zu Ende; fehlerhaft, im Irrtum (befangen), auf dem Holzweg; hörbar, laut; offen, frei, ohne Zurückhaltung, enthüllt, entdeckt, offenbar; gesellschaftsfähig, ballfähig (*of a girl*).

(a) (*with nouns*) ***have an evening –,*** am Abend ausgehen; ***the best thing –,*** das Beste, was es gibt; das Beste in der Welt; ***voyage –,*** die Ausreise, Hinreise; ***way –,*** der Ausgang, (*fig.*) Ausweg; ***some way –,*** in einiger Entfernung vom Ufer.

(b) (*with verbs*) (*for obvious meanings see the relevant verb*); ***be*** (***far*** or ***quite***) ***–,*** (mächtig) auf dem

Holzwege sein, sich (sehr) irren *or* im Irrtum befinden; ***blue is quite –,*** blau ist völlig aus der Mode; ***the calculation is –,*** die Berechnung ist fehlerhaft *or* stimmt nicht; ***the batsman is –,*** der Schläger ist nicht mehr im Spiel; ***the book is just –,*** das Buch ist soeben erschienen; ***before many days were –,*** ehe viele Tage verstrichen waren; ***my hand is –,*** ich bin außer Übung; ***– of the business,*** aus dem Geschäfte ausgetreten; ***– of business,*** nicht mehr geschäftstätig; ***be £10 –,*** um £10 ärmer sein, £10 eingebüßt haben; ***the secret is –,*** das Geheimnis ist entdeckt; ***the tide is –,*** es ist Ebbe; ***his time is –,*** seine Lehrzeit ist vorüber; ***come –,*** (*coll. of workers*) streiken, in den Streik treten; (*of a young girl*) in die Gesellschaft eingeführt werden, ballfähig werden; ***cry –,*** laut ausrufen; ***find –,*** entdecken, ausfindig machen; ***go – for a walk,*** einen Spaziergang machen; ***hear him –,*** ihn bis zum Ende *or* ganz anhören; (*coll.*) ***have it – with him,*** sich mit ihm gründlich auseinandersetzen; ***have a tooth –,*** sich (*Dat.*) einen Zahn ziehen lassen; ***hold –,*** entgegenhalten; (*fig.*) standhalten; ***keep –,*** nicht einlassen; (*fig.*) sich nicht einmischen; ***look –,*** aufpassen; ***read –,*** vorlesen; laut lesen; ***ring –,*** laut tönen; ***see him –,*** ihn hinausbegleiten; ***see it –,*** es bis zu Ende mitmachen; ***speak –!*** heraus damit! ***tire –,*** vollständig erschöpfen; ***turn him –,*** ihm die Tür weisen; ***blood will –,*** Blut setzt sich durch, Blut bricht sich Bahn; (*fig.*) ***murder will –,*** die Sonne bringt es an den Tag.

(c) (*with preps.*) ***– at elbows,*** (*fig.*) (*of clothes*) schäbig, abgetragen, (*of a p.*) heruntergekommen, auf den Hund gekommen; ***be (all) – for,*** auf der Suche *or* Jagd sein nach, hinter . . . her sein; sich einsetzen für, erpicht *or* bedacht *or* versessen sein auf (*Acc.*), abzielen auf (*Acc.*), trachten nach; ***– of,*** aus, aus . . . heraus; außerhalb *or* entfernt von; außer(halb); nicht in (*Dat.*), nicht gemäß, nicht in Übereinstimmung mit; abstammend von, . . . als Mutter, gezeugt aus; ***by X – of Y,*** dessen Vater X, dessen Mutter Y ist (*horses, dogs etc.*); (*with noun to give attrib. adj. phrase*) ***– of bounds,*** verboten; ***– of breath,*** atemlos, außer Atem; ***– of date,*** veraltet; ***– of doors,*** im Freien; ***– of fear,*** aus Furcht; ***– of drawing,*** nicht richtig gezeichnet, verzeichnet; ***– of fashion,*** aus der Mode; ***– of focus,*** unscharf; (*Prov.*) ***– of the frying-pan into the fire,*** aus dem Regen in die Traufe; ***– of hand,*** sofort, unverzüglich, auf der Stelle; außer Zucht, unbeherrscht; ***get – of hand,*** über die Stränge schlagen; ***– of humour,*** schlecht gelaunt; ***– of joint,*** aus den Fugen (geraten); ***be – of keeping with,*** nicht übereinstimmen mit, nicht passen zu; ***be – of love with,*** nicht mehr leiden mögen; ***– of his mind,*** verrückt, außer sich; ***– of money,*** nicht bei Kasse; ***times – of number,*** unzählige Male; ***– of order,*** außer der Reihenfolge, in Unordnung; (*Parl. etc.*) unzulässig; (*Med.*) gestört; (*Tech.*) defekt; ***– of pity,*** aus Mitleid; (*Footb.*) ***– of play,*** aus dem Spiel, tot; ***– of pocket,*** see ***– of money;*** ***– of practice,*** außer Übung; ***– of print,*** vergriffen; ***– of all proportion,*** in keinem Verhältnis; ***it is – of the question,*** es ist ausgeschlossen, es kommt nicht in Frage; ***– of reach,*** außer Reichweite, unerreichbar, unzugänglich; (*fig.*) ***be – of the running,*** nicht mehr in Frage kommen; ***– of sight,*** außer Sicht; (*Prov.*) ***– of sight, – of mind,*** aus den Augen, aus dem Sinn; (*coll.*) ***be – of sorts,*** unpäßlich *or* nicht recht auf dem Damm sein; ***– of temper,*** schlecht gelaunt; ***nine – of ten,*** neun von zehn; ***– of town,*** verreist; ***– of training,*** außer Übung; ***– of tune,*** verstimmt (*also fig.*); ***play – of tune,*** unrein spielen; ***– of the way,*** abseits gelegen, abgelegen; (*fig.*) ausgefallen, abwegig, ungewöhnlich; ***be – of the way,*** aus dem Wege sein, nicht auf dem Wege liegen; ***get – of the way,*** aus dem Weg gehen; (*fig.*) ***go – of one's way,*** sich (*Dat.*) besondere Mühe geben, keine Mühe scheuen; ***keep – of the way,*** sich abseits halten; ***put – of the way,*** aus dem Wege schaffen (*a th.*), um die Ecke bringen (*a p.*); ***take him – of his way,*** ihn einen Umweg machen lassen; (*fig.*) ***– of the wood,*** überm Berg; ***– of work,*** arbeitslos; (*with verb*) (*coll.*) ***be – of . . ., . . .*** nicht (mehr) haben, ohne . . . sein, entbehren, (*Comm.*) nicht vorrätig haben; (*sl.*) ***be – of it,*** keine Chance haben; ***cheat – of,*** betrügen *or* prellen um; (*coll.*) ***feel – of it,*** sich (*Dat.*) abgehängt vorkommen; ***make*** or ***manufacture – of,*** herstellen *or* verfertigen aus; ***be – to do,*** darauf ausgehen *or* aus sein zu tun.

(d) (*with advs.*) ***– and about,*** auf den Beinen; ***– and away,*** bei weitem; ***– there,*** da draußen.

2. *s.* 1. (*Typ.*) die Auslassung, Leiche; 2. (*coll.*) der Ausweg, die Entschuldigung; 3. *pl.* (*Parl.*) Opposition(smitglieder) (*pl.*); 4. ***the ins and –s,*** alle Einzelheiten, Winkelzüge; Windungen (*of a road etc.*).

3. *adj.* auswärtig.

out|-and-out, 1. *adj.* absolut, Erz–. **2.** *adv.* ganz (und gar), durch und durch, durchaus, völlig, gründlich, ausgesprochen. **--and-outer,** *s.* (*sl.*) 1. Hundertprozentige(r), Waschechte(r), der Hauptkerl, Mordskerl; 2. famose S., etwas ganz Typisches. **-back,** *s.* (*Austral.*) der Busch. **-balance,** *v.t.* überwiegen, übertreffen. **-bid,** *irr.v.t.* überbieten. **-board,** *adj.* Außenbord–. **-brave,** *v.t.* 1. Trotz bieten (*Dat.*); 2. an Glanz *or* Tapferkeit übertreffen. **-break,** *s.* der Ausbruch. **-building,** *s.* das Nebengebäude. **-burst,** *s.* der Erguß, Ausbruch. **-cast, 1.** *adj.* vertrieben, verbannt, verwiesen, ausgestoßen, verstoßen. **2.** *s.* 1. Ausgestoßene(r), Vetriebene(r), Verbannte(r), Verstoßene(r); 2. (*Tech.*) der Ausschuß. **-class,** *v.t.* weit überlegen sein (*Dat.*), weit übertreffen. **-come,** *s.* das Ergebnis, Resultat, die Folge; ***be the – of,*** entspringen (*Dat.*). **-crop, 1.** *s.* 1. das Anstehen, Zutageliegen; der Ausbiß; 2. (*fig.*) das Zutagetreten, Zutagekommen. **2.** *v.i.* anstehen, ausbeißen, zutage liegen *or* treten. **-cry,** *s.* 1. das Geschrei; 2. der Aufschrei, Entrüstungsschrei. **--dated,** *adj.* überholt, veraltet, altmodisch, unmodern. **--distance,** *v.t.* weit überholen, weit hinter sich (*Dat.*) (zurück)lassen; (*fig.*) überflügeln. **-do,** *irr.v.t.* es zuvortun (*Dat.*), übertreffen, ausstechen.

out|door, *adj.* Außen–, im Freien, außer dem Hause; ***– department,*** der Ausschank über die Gasse; ***– dress,*** der Ausgehanzug; ***– relief,*** die Unterstützung außerhalb des Armenhauses; ***– sports,*** Spiele im Freien; ***– temperature,*** die Außentemperatur; ***– work,*** die Außenarbeit. **-doors,** *adv.* draußen, im Freien.

outer ['autə], **1.** *adj.* äußer, Außen–; ***– man,*** äußerer Mensch; ***– space,*** der Weltraum; ***– wall,*** die Umfassungsmauer; ***– world,*** die Außenwelt. **2.** *s.* äußerer Ring (*of target*). **outermost,** *adj.* äußerst.

out|face, *v.t.* 1. aus der Fassung bringen; 2. Trotz bieten (*Dat.*), Herr werden (*Gen.*). **-fall,** *s.* der Ausfluß, Abfluß, Ableitungskanal. **-field,** *s.* 1. (*Spt.*) das Außenfeld; 2. (*fig.*) unbestimmtes Gebiet. **-fielder,** *s.* der Spieler im Außenfeld.

outfit ['autfit], **1.** *s.* 1. die Ausrüstung, Ausstattung; 2. (*coll.*) Einrichtung; 3. (*sl.*) Belegschaft, Mannschaft, Gesellschaft, der (Personen)kreis. **2.** *v.t.* ausrüsten, ausstatten, versorgen. **outfitter,** *s.* 1. der Ausrüstungslieferant, Ausstatter; 2. Modehändler, das Konfektionsgeschäft; 3. der Händler.

out|flank, *v.t.* überflügeln, umgehen; ***–ing movement,*** die Umgehung. **-flow,** *s.* der Ausfluß. **-go,** *see* **-going, 2.** *pl.* **-going, 1.** *adj.* abgehend (*post*), abfahrend, abgehend (*train etc.*), zurückgehend (*tide*), ausziehend (*tenant*), abtretend, ausscheidend (*representative*). **2.** *s.* 1. das Ausgehen; 2. *pl.* (Geld)auslagen, (Gesamt)ausgaben (*pl.*). **-grow,** *irr.v.t.* 1. schneller wachsen *or* größer werden als, hinauswachsen über (*Acc.*), über den Kopf wachsen (*Dat.*) (*a p.*); 2. herauswachsen aus, zu groß werden für (*garments*); 3. entwachsen (*Dat.*) (*one's toys etc.*); (mit der Zeit) ablegen *or* überwinden (*habits*); 4. ***– one's strength,*** zu schnell wachsen. **-growth,** *s.* 1. der Auswuchs, die Exkreszenz; 2. das Ergebnis, Nebenprodukt. **-haul,** *s.* (*Naut.*) der Ausholer. **--herod,** *v.t.* (an Brutalität) übertreffen. **-house,** *s.* das Nebengebäude, der Anbau, Schuppen.

outing ['autiŋ], *s.* der Ausflug, die Partie; ***go on an –,*** einen Ausflug machen.
outlandish [aut'lændiʃ], *adj.* 1. fremdartig, seltsam, ausgefallen; 2. abgelegen; 3. rückständig.
outlast [aut'lɑ:st], *v.t.* überdauern, überleben.
outlaw ['autlɔ:], **1.** *s.* Geächtete(r), Vogelfreie(r). **2.** *v.t.* (*Hist.*) ächten, für vogelfrei erklären, in Acht und Bann tun; (*fig.*) verfemen, verpönen; ausschließen, verbieten. **outlawry** [–ri], *s.* die Acht, Ächtung, Verfemung.
outlay ['autlei], *s.* die (Geld)auslage(n), Ausgabe(n) (*on*, für).
outlet ['autlit], *s.* 1. der Ausgang, Ausfluß, Auslauf, Austritt, Ausguß, Auslaß, Abfluß, Ablaß, Abzug, die Abzugsrinne, (Abzugs)öffnung; Abflußmöglichkeit; 2. (*Comm.*) das Absatzgebiet, der Absatzmarkt; 3. (*Elec.*) Anschluß(punkt), die Steckdose; 4. (*fig.*) das Ventil, Betätigungsfeld; (*fig.*) ***find an – for,*** Luft machen *or* Ausdruck geben können (*Dat.*). **outlet|-pipe,** *s.* das Abflußrohr, Abzugsrohr. **–-valve,** *s.* das Auslaßventil.
outline ['autlain], **1.** *s.* 1. der Umriß, die Umrißlinie, Kontur; 2. (*fig.*) der Entwurf, die Skizze; 3. (*fig.*) der Auszug, Abriß, Grundzüge (*pl.*); 4. *pl.* Umrisse, Konturen (*pl.*), die Silhouette, (*fig.*) Hauptlinien, Hauptzüge (*pl.*). **2.** *v.t.* 1. umreißen, skizzieren, im Umriß darstellen; 2. (*fig.*) in groben Zügen darstellen, einen Überblick geben über (*Acc.*); 3. ***be –d against,*** sich (scharf) abheben von *or* abzeichnen gegen.
outlive [aut'liv], *v.t.* überleben, überdauern.
outlook ['autluk], *s.* 1. die Aussicht, der Ausblick; 2. Ausguck, die Warte; 3. (*fig.*) der Standpunkt, die Einstellung, (Lebens)auffassung, (Welt)anschauung.
out|lying, *adj.* am Rande *or* abseits liegend, abgelegen; Außen–, auswärtig. **–manœuvre,** *v.t.* durch geschicktes Manövrieren überlisten, an Geschick überlegen sein (*Dat.*). **–march,** *v.t.* schneller marschieren als. **–match,** *v.t.* übertreffen, überflügeln. **–mode,** *v.t.* (*usu. pass.*) aus der Mode bringen. **–moded,** *adj.* überholt, veraltet, unmodern. **–number,** *v.t.* an Zahl übertreffen, zahlenmäßig überlegen sein (*Dat.*); ***be –d,*** in der Minderheit sein.
out-of|-date, *adj.* veraltet, altmodisch, unzeitgemäß. **–-pocket,** *adj.* – ***expenses,*** Barauslagen (*pl.*). **–-the-way,** *adj.* (*fig.*) ungewöhnlich, ausgefallen.
out|pace, *v.t.* überholen, hinter sich lassen, schneller vorwärtskommen als. **–-patient,** *s.* ambulanter Patient; ***–'s department,*** die Poliklinik, Ambulanz; – ***treatment,*** ambulante Behandlung. **–point,** *v.t.* an Punktzahl übertreffen, nach Punkten schlagen. **–post,** *s.* der Vorposten. **–pouring,** *s.* (*usu. fig.*) der Erguß, Ausbruch.
output ['autput], *s.* die Produktion, Arbeitsleistung; Ausbeute, der Ausstoß, Ertrag, das Rendement; (*Min.*) Förderquantum, die Fördermenge; ***actual –,*** die Nutzleistung; ***normal –,*** die Nennleistung; (*Rad.*) – ***valve,*** die Endverstärkerröhre; (*Rad.*) – ***voltage,*** die Ausgangsspannung.
outrage ['autreidʒ], **1.** *v.t.* 1. schmählich behandeln, freveln an (*Dat.*), sich vergehen an (*Dat.*); mißhandeln, verschandeln, Gewalt antun (*Dat.*) (*also fig.*), schänden; 2. (*fig.*) (grob) verstoßen gegen *or* verletzen, mit Füßen treten (*feelings etc.*), schockieren, beleidigen (*a p.*). **2.** *s.* 1. die Gewalttat; Greueltat, Ausschreitung, der Greuel, Exzeß; 2. Frevel (*on*, an (*Dat.*)), grobes Vergehen (gegen), grobe Verletzung, (*esp. fig.*) die Vergewaltigung (*Gen.*). **outrageous** [–'reidʒəs], *adj.* frevelhaft, abscheulich, empörend, unerhört, unverschämt, schmählich, schändlich. **outrageousness,** *s.* 1. die Frevelhaftigkeit, Schändlichkeit, Abscheulichkeit; 2. Unverschämtheit.
outrange [aut'reindʒ], *v.t.* an Schußweite übertreffen.
outré ['u:trei], *adj.* überspannt, übertrieben, extravagant, outriert.
out|reach, *v.t.* übertreffen, übersteigen, hinausreichen über (*Acc.*), weiter reichen als. **–ride,** *irr.v.t.* 1. schneller reiten als; 2. (*Naut.*) trotzen (*Dat.*), abreiten, ausreiten (*storm*). **–rider,** *s.* der Vorreiter. **–rigger,** *s.* 1. (*Naut.*) der Ausleger; 2. (*Artil.*) Holm, Längsträger; 3. das Auslegerboot.
outright [aut'rait], *adv.* 1. gerade heraus, ohne Vorbehalt, unverblümt; ***laugh –,*** laut auflachen; 2. gänzlich, völlig, ganz und gar, total; sogleich, auf der Stelle; rundweg, unverwandt; ***kill –,*** auf der Stelle töten; ***refuse –,*** rundweg ablehnen; ***sell –,*** ganz verkaufen.
out|rival, *v.t.* übertreffen, überflügeln, ausstechen; überbieten (*in*, in *or* an (*Dat.*)). **–run,** *irr.v.t.* schneller laufen als, (im Laufen) übertreffen; (*fig.*) hinausgehen über (*Acc.*), hinter sich lassen, übersteigen, vorauseilen (*Dat.*). **–runner,** *s.* der (Vor)läufer, Vorreiter. **–sell,** *v.t.* sich besser *or* teurer verkaufen als.
outset ['autset], *s.* der Anfang, Beginn; ***from the –,*** von Anfang an.
outshine [aut'ʃain], *irr.v.t.* überstrahlen, in den Schatten stellen.
outside ['aut'said], **1.** *s.* 1. das Äußere, die Außenseite; Oberfläche, äußere Erscheinung; ***from the –,*** von außen, von der Außenseite; ***on the – of the bus,*** außen auf dem Autobus; 2. (*fig.*) das Äußerste; ***at the*** (***very***) ***–,*** (aller)höchstens; 3. (*Footb. etc.*) – ***right,*** der Rechtsaußen. **2.** *adj.* 1. äußer, Außen–; – ***diameter,*** äußere Weite; – ***edge,*** die Außenkante; – ***seat,*** der Außensitz; 2. außenstehend, von außen kommend, extern; – ***activities,*** außerberufliche Beschäftigung; – ***broker,*** der Winkelmakler; – ***influences,*** äußere Einflüsse; – ***interference,*** die Einmischung von außen; – ***opinion,*** die Ansicht der Außenstehenden; 3. äußerst (*as price*). **3.** *adv.* 1. (von) außen; 2. draußen; – ***of,*** außerhalb (*Gen.*); (*sl.*) ***get – of,*** verspeisen, sich (*Dat.*) einverleiben; 3. nach außen, heraus, hinaus; 4. (*sl.*) außer, ausgenommen. **4.** *prep.* außerhalb, jenseits (*Gen.*). **outsider,** *s.* 1. Nichteingeweihte(r), der Nichtfachmann; 2. Außenstehende(r), Fernstehende(r), (*also racing*) der Außenseiter.
out|size, **1.** *s.* große Weite, die Übergröße, ungewöhnliche Größe (*of clothes*). **2.** *adj.* übergroß. **–skirts,** *pl.* nähere Umgebung, das Randgebiet, die Peripherie. **–smart,** *v.t.* (*sl.*) überlisten, übers Ohr hauen.
outspoken [aut'spoukən], *adj.* 1. freimütig, offen(herzig); 2. (*fig.*) ungeschminkt, unverblümt, (kraß) realistisch. **outspokenness,** *s.* 1. die Offenheit, Offenherzigkeit, Freimut, Freimütigkeit; 2. Ungeschminktheit, Unverblümtheit, (krasser) Realismus.
outstanding [aut'stændiŋ], *adj.* 1. hervorstechend, (*Comm.*) offenstehend, ausstehend; – ***debts,*** Außenstände (*pl.*); 2. (*esp. fig.*) hervorragend, auffallend, prominent; – ***event,*** das Hauptereignis.
out|stay, *v.t.* länger bleiben als; – ***one's welcome,*** länger bleiben als dem Wirt lieb ist. **–stretch,** *v.t.* ausstrecken. **–strip,** *v.t.* überholen, hinter sich lassen; (*fig.*) übertreffen, überflügeln. **–talk,** *v.t.* in Grund und Boden reden, an Zungenfertigkeit übertreffen. **–vote,** *v.t.* überstimmen.
outward ['autwəd], **1.** *adj.* 1. äußer, Außen–, äußerlich; ***–form,*** die Erscheinungsform; 2. nach außen; – ***passage,*** die Hinreise. **2.** *adv.* nach auswärts, nach außen; ***–-bound,*** auf der Ausreise *or* Hinreise. **outwardly,** *adv.* (nach) außen, äußerlich (betrachtet), nach außen hin. **outwards,** *adv. See* **outward, 2.**
out|weigh, *v.t.* 1. schwerer sein als, (an Gewicht) übertreffen; 2. (*esp. fig.*) aufwiegen, überwiegen; wichtiger *or* bedeutender *or* wertvoller sein als. **–wit,** *v.t.* überlisten, übertölpeln, übers Ohr hauen.
outwork ['autwə:k], **1.** *s.* 1. (*usu. pl.*) (*Fort.*) das Außenwerk, Bollwerk; 2. (*Comm.*) die Heimarbeit. **2.** [–'wə:k], *v.t.* länger *or* schneller *or* besser *or* mehr arbeiten als.

outworn [aut'wɔ:n], *adj.* abgenutzt, verbraucht; abgetragen (*as clothes*); (*usu. fig.*) überholt, veraltet (*as beliefs*).

ouzel ['u:zl], *s.* (*Orn.*) ***ring* –**, die Ringdrossel (*Turdus torquatus*); ***water* –**, die Wasseramsel (*Cinclus cinclus*).

oval ['ouvl], **1.** *adj.* oval, eirund. **2.** *s.* das Oval.

ovarian [o'vɛəriən], *adj.* Eierstock(s)–. **ovary** ['ouvəri], *s.* 1. (*Anat.*) der Eierstock; 2. (*Bot.*) Fruchtknoten.

ovate ['ouveit], *adj.* eirund, (*Bot.*) eiförmig.

ovation [o'veiʃən], *s.* der Beifallssturm, die Huldigung, Ehrenbezeigung, Ovation.

oven ['ʌvən], *s.* der Backofen, die Backröhre; (*Tech.*) der Ofen. **oven-bird,** *s.* der Töpfervogel.

over ['ouvə], **1.** *adv.* (*in v. compounds*) über–; über (. . . hin), herüber, hierher; drüben, hinüber, darüber (. . . hin); (*in v. compounds*) (her)um–; (*in adj. compounds*) übermäßig, allzu–, über–; (*of amount*) mehr, darüber (. . . hinaus); (*remainder*) übrig, über; (*of time*) zu Ende, vorüber, vorbei, aus; – ***and above,*** außerdem, obendrein, überdies, noch dazu; – ***and* – (*again*),** immer wieder; – ***again,*** noch einmal; – ***against,*** gegenüber, (*fig.*) im Gegensatz zu; ***all* –**, über und über, ganz und gar; überall, allenthalben; ***be all* – *with,*** aus, vorbei *or* vorüber sein mit; ***all* – (*and done with*),** total erledigt; (*coll.*) ***that's him all* –**, das sieht ihm ähnlich; (*coll.*) ***come all* – *goose-pimples,*** ein kribbliges Gefühl am ganzen Körper empfinden; (*coll.*) ***get it* – *with,*** es los werden, damit fertig werden; ***fifty times* –**, fünfzigmal hintereinander; ***(all) the world* –**, durch die ganze *or* in der ganzen Welt.
(*with verbs*) (*coll.*) ***ask him* –**, ihn einladen; ***boil* –**, überkochen; (*Comm.*) ***carried* –**, der Übertrag; ***covered (all)* –**, (ganz) bedeckt; ***deliver* –**, ausliefern, zustellen (*to, Dat.*); ***fall* –**, umfallen; ***go* – *to,*** überlaufen *or* übergehen zu; ***hand* –**, übergeben; ***have (left)* –**, übrig haben; ***lean* –**, sich neigen *or* beugen *or* lehnen; ***make* –**, übertragen (*to, Dat. or* an (*Acc.*)), vermachen (*Dat.*); ***read* –**, (nochmals) durchlesen; ***run* –**, überfließen; ***see* –**, siehe nächste Seite! siehe umstehend! ***talk* –**, gründlich besprechen; ***think* –**, überlegen, nachdenken über (*Acc.*); ***turn* –**, (her)umdrehen; ***please turn* –!** bitte wenden!
2. *prep.* (*position*) über (*Dat.*), jenseits, auf der anderen Seite von *or* (*Gen.*); (*movement*) über (*Acc.*) (. . . hin *or* (hin)weg); (*fig.*) bei, über (*Dat.*); wegen, über (*Acc.*); vor (*Dat.*); mehr als, über (*Acc.*); während, über (*Acc.*); ***preference* – *all others,*** der Vorzug vor allen andern.
(a) (*with nouns*) ***all* – *Europe,*** durch ganz Europa; ***from all* – *Europe,*** aus allen Teilen Europas; – ***the fire,*** beim (Kamin)feuer; – ***a glass of wine,*** bei einem Glas Wein; – ***our heads,*** über unsere(n) Köpfe(n); (*fig.*) über unsern Verstand *or* Horizont; über unsere Köpfe hinweg; – ***one's signature,*** über seiner Unterschrift, unter seinem Namen, selbst unterzeichnet; – ***a year,*** mehr *or* länger als *or* über ein Jahr; – ***many years,*** viele Jahre hindurch.
(b) (*with verbs*) ***be* – *him,*** über ihm stehen; (*sl.*) ***be all* – *him,*** an ihm einen Narren gefressen haben; (*coll.*) ***get* – *it,*** darüber hinwegkommen, es überwinden *or* überstehen; ***go* – *one's notes,*** seine Notizen durchgehen; ***reign* –**, herrschen über (*Acc.*); ***show us* – *your house,*** führen Sie uns in Ihrem Hause herum; ***spread* – *a series of years,*** auf einige Jahre verteilen.
3. *s.* 1. (*Artil.*) der Weitschuß; 2. (*Crick.*) Wechsel, Satz von sechs Würfen.

over|abound, *v.i.* im Überfluß vorhanden sein. **–abundance,** *s.* der Überfluß (*of,* an (*Dat.*)). **–abundant,** *adj.* überreich(lich), übermäßig.

over|act, *v.t., v.i.* (*Theat.*) übertrieben spielen, überspielen; (*fig.*) übertreiben, des Guten zuviel tun. **–active,** *adj.* übermäßig geschäftig *or* tätig. **–activity,** *s.* übermäßige Geschäftigkeit *or* Tätigkeit.

over|all, 1. *adj.* Gesamt–. **2.** *s.* 1. (*usu. pl.*) der Schutzkittel, Arbeitsanzug, das Überkleid; 2. (*Mil.*) (*only pl.*) Galahosen. **--ambitious,** *adj.* allzu ehrgeizig. **--anxious,** *adj.* überängstlich. **–arch,** *v.t.* überwölben. **–arm,** *adj.* Hand-über-Hand– (*swimming*), über die Schulter (*bowling*). **–awe,** *v.t.* einschüchtern.

overbalance [ouvə'bæləns], **1.** *v.t.* überwiegen; aus dem Gleichgewicht bringen, umkippen, umstoßen. **2.** *v.i.* das Gleichgewicht verlieren, umkippen, überkippen. **3.** *s.* das Übergewicht.

overbear [ouvə'bɛə], *irr.v.t.* 1. überwältigen, überwinden; 2. überwiegen; 3. unterdrücken, niederdrücken. **overbearance,** *s.* die Anmaßung. **overbearing,** *adj.* herrisch, anmaßend, hochfahrend.

over|blow, *irr.v.i.* (*Mus.*) überblasen. **–blown,** *adj.* verblüht, ausgeblüht.

over|board, *adv.* über Bord; (*sl.*) ***go* –**, sich überschlagen. **–brim, 1.** *v.i.* überfließen, überlaufen (***with,*** von). **2.** *v.t.* überfließen *or* überlaufen lassen. **–build,** *irr.v.t.* überbauen, zu dicht (be)bauen. **–burden,** *v.t.* überladen, überlasten, überbürden.

over|call, *v.i.* (*Cards*) überbieten. **--careful,** *adj.* allzu sorgfältig *or* gewissenhaft. **–cast, 1.** *irr.v.t.* 1. überziehen, bedecken, bewölken, umwölken; 2. (*sewing*) umnähen, (um)säumen. **2.** *adj.* 1. bedeckt, bewölkt, trüb (*as sky*); 2. überwendlich genäht (*as seam*). **--cautious,** *adj. See* **--careful. –charge, 1.** *v.t.* 1. überladen, überfüllen; 2. überfordern (*a p.*); zuviel verlangen von. **2.** *s.* 1. der Überdruck, die Über(be)lastung; 2. (*Comm.*) Überforderung, Überteuerung. **–cloud, 1.** *v.t.* bewölken, trüben, (*esp. fig.*) umwölken, verdüstern. **2.** *v.i.* sich bewölken *or* beziehen, (*fig.*) sich trüben.

overcoat ['ouvəkout], *s.* der Überrock, Überzieher.

overcome [ouvə'kʌm], **1.** *irr.v.t.* überwältigen, übermannen, besiegen (*a p.*); (*fig.*) überwinden, Herr werden (*Gen.*); – ***temptation,*** der Versuchung widerstehen; ***be* – *with rage,*** von Wut hingerissen sein. **2.** *irr.v.i.* den Sieg davontragen, siegen.

over|compensation, *s.* (*Psych.*) die Überkompensation. **--confidence,** *s.* allzu großes Selbstvertrauen, die Vermessenheit. **--confident,** *adj.* allzu selbstsicher, überheblich, vermessen. **–credulous,** *adj.* allzu leichtgläubig. **–crop,** *v.t.* zugrunde wirtschaften, Raubbau treiben mit (*land*). **–crowd,** *v.t.* überfüllen. **–crowding,** *s.* die Überfüllung. **–develop,** *v.t.* (*esp. Phot.*) überentwickeln.

over|do, *irr.v.t.* 1. zu weit treiben, übertreiben; – ***it,*** zu weit gehen, es zu arg treiben; sich überanstrengen; 2. zu sehr kochen *or* braten (*meat etc.*). **–done,** *adj.* übergar (*meat etc*).

overdose ['ouvə'dous], **1.** *s.* zu starke Dosis. **2.** *v.t.* eine zu starke Dosis geben (*Dat.*).

over|draft, *s.* die Überziehung (*of an account*); überzogener Betrag. **–draw, 1.** *irr.v.t.* 1. überspannen, übertreiben; 2. überziehen (*an account*). **2.** *v.i.* sein Konto überziehen.

over|dress, 1. *v.t.* übertrieben *or* unzweckmäßig anziehen. **2.** *v.i.* sich übertrieben kleiden, sich zu sehr aufputzen *or* schmücken. **–drink,** *v.i.* übermäßig trinken.

overdrive ['ouvə'draiv], **1.** *s.* (*Motor.*) der Schnellgang, Schongang. **2.** *irr.v.t.* 1. zu weit treiben, übertreiben; 2. abschinden, abhetzen, überanstrengen.

overdue [ouvə'dju:], *adj.* verfallen, überfällig (*bill*); ***be* –**, Verspätung haben (*trains etc.*), vermißt werden, ausgeblieben sein (*ships*).

over|eager, *adj.* übereifrig. **–eagerness,** *s.* der Übereifer.

overeat [ouvə'i:t], *v.i.* zuviel essen, sich überessen.

over-emotional, *adj.* zu leicht erregbar.

over|emphasis, *s.* allzu starke Betonung, zu großer Nachdruck. **–emphasize,** *v.t.* übermäßig betonen, zu großen Nachdruck legen auf (*Acc.*).

over|enthusiasm, *s.* übermäßige Begeisterung. **–enthusiastic,** *adj.* übermäßig begeistert.

over|estimate, 1. [–eit], *v.t.* überschätzen, zu hoch bewerten. **2.** [–ət], *s.* die Überbewertung. **–estimation,** *s.* die Überschätzung.

over|excitable, *adj.* allzu reizbar. **–excite,** *v.t.*

übermäßig aufregen, überreizen. **-excitement,** *s.* übergroße Aufregung.

over|exert, *v.t.* überanstrengen. **-exertion,** *s.* die Überanstrengung. **-expose,** *v.t.* allzu viel aussetzen (***to***, *Dat.*); (*Phot.*) überbelichten.

overfall ['ouvəfɔ:l], *s.* die Sturzsee; (*of locks*) der Überlauf.

over|-fatigue, **1.** *s.* die Übermüdung. **2.** *v.t.* übermüden, überanstrengen. **-fault,** *s.* (*Geol.*) überliegende Falte, die Deckfalte. **-feed,** *irr.v.t.* überfüttern.

over|flow, **1.** *s.* die Überschwemmung, Überflutung; (*fig.*) der Überschuß; (*Tech.*) Überlauf; – ***meeting,*** die Parallelversammlung; – ***pipe,*** das Überlaufrohr. **2.** *v.t.* überfluten, überschwemmen; – ***the banks,*** austreten, über die Ufer treten; – ***the brim,*** über den Rand fließen *or* laufen (*of liquid*); – ***the glass,*** das Glas überlaufen lassen (*of p. filling*); (*fig.*) – ***the room,*** das Zimmer bis zum Bersten füllen, im Zimmer nicht mehr Platz finden (*of crowd*). **3.** *v.i.* 1. überströmen (*also fig.*), überfließen, überlaufen (***with,*** von), (*fig.*) überquellen; 2. sich ergießen (***into,*** in (*Acc.*)). **-flowing,** **1.** *adj.* überlaufend, überfließend; (*fig.*) überströmend, übersprudelnd. **2.** *s.* das Überfließen; ***full to –,*** zum Überlaufen voll; (*fig.*) bis zum Bersten voll, bis auf den letzten Platz besetzt.

overfold ['ouvəfould], *s.* (*Geol.*) überkippte Falte.

over|fond, *adj.* überzärtlich. **-generous,** *adj.* allzu freigebig.

over|grow, **1.** *irr.v.t.* 1. überwachsen, überwuchern; bewachsen; 2. hinauswachsen über (*Acc.*), zu groß werden für. **2.** *irr.v.i.* zu groß werden. **-grown,** *adj.* 1. überwachsen, überwuchert; 2. zu groß gewachsen.

over|hand, *adj.* 1. den Handrücken nach oben gekehrt; *see also* **-arm**; (*Tenn.*) – ***service,*** der Überhandaufschlag; 2. (*sewing*) überwendlich; – ***knot,*** einfacher Knoten.

overhang [ouvə'hæŋ], **1.** *irr.v.t.* überhängen; (über)hängen *or* hervorragen *or* hervorstehen über (*Acc.*). **2.** *irr.v.i.* überhängen, hervorragen, hervorstehen. **3.** *s.* ['ouvə–] der Vorsprung, Überhang.

over-hasty, *adj.* überstürzt, übereilt, übereilig.

overhaul ['ouvə'hɔ:l], **1.** *v.t.* 1. einholen, (*Naut.*) überholen; 2. überprüfen, reparieren, überholen, in Ordnung bringen. **2.** *s.* die Überholung, Überprüfung, gründliche Reparatur.

overhead ['ouvə'hed], **1.** *adv.* (dr)oben. **2.** *adj.* oberirdisch, über der Erde (befindlich) (*as cables etc.*); – ***cable,*** die Freileitung, Oberleitung, das Luftkabel; – ***expenses,*** laufende Unkosten; – ***railway,*** die Hochbahn. **3.** *pl. See* – ***expenses.***

overhear [ouvə'hiə], **1.** *irr.v.t.* zufällig hören, mithören, belauschen. **2.** *irr.v.i.* mithören, lauschen.

over|heat, **1.** *v.t.* überheizen. **2.** *v.i.* zu heiß werden. **-heated,** *adj.* überheizt; warmgelaufen (*of an engine*).

over|indulge, **1.** *v.t.* zu nachsichtig behandeln (*a p.*), frönen (*Dat.*), huldigen (*Dat.*), nachgeben (*Dat.*) (*a habit*). **2.** *v.i.* sich zu sehr ergehen (***in,*** in (*Dat.*)). **-indulgence,** *s.* 1. zu große Schonung *or* Nachsicht; 2. übermäßiger Genuß. **-indulgent,** *adj.* allzu nachsichtig.

over-issue, **1.** *s.* die Mehrausgabe, Papiergeldinflation. **2.** *v.t.* zuviel ausgeben (*notes etc.*).

over|joyed, *adj.* außer sich vor Freude, hocherfreut, entzückt (***at,*** über (*Acc.*)). **-laden,** *adj.* überbelastet, überladen. **-laid,** *imperf., p.p. of* **-lay. -lain,** *p.p. of* **-lie.**

overland ['ouvə'lænd], **1.** *adj.* (Über)land–; – ***route,*** der Landweg. **2.** *adv.* über Land, zu Lande, auf dem Landweg.

over|lap, **1.** *v.i.* ineinander *or* aufeinander übergreifen, (*fig.*) sich (teilweise) decken, sich überschneiden. **2.** *v.t.* sich überschneiden mit, (teilweise) zusammenfallen mit, hinübergehen *or* sich erstrecken über (*Acc.*), übergreifen in *or* auf (*Acc.*). **3.** *s.* das Übergreifen, Überschneiden (***on,*** auf (*Acc.*)), Zusammenfallen, die Überschneidung; (*Tech.*) Überlappung. **-lapping,** *adj.* aufeinander *or* ineinander übergreifend, einander überschneidend; sich deckend, (teilweise) zusammenfallend.

overlay ['ouvə'lei], **1.** *irr.v.t.* überziehen, überlagern, belegen, bedecken. **2.** *s.* die Bedeckung; Auflage, der Überzug; das Tischdeckchen; die Auflegemaske; Planpause.

overleaf [ouvə'li:f], *adv.* umstehend, umseitig.

over|leap, *irr.v.t.* überspringen, springen über (*Acc.*). **-lie,** *irr.v.t.* 1. liegen auf (*Dat.*); 2. (*Geol.*) überlagern; 3. durch Daraufliegen ersticken *or* erdrücken (*a child*). **-load,** **1.** *v.t.* überladen, überlasten, überbelasten. **2.** *s.* die Überbelastung, Überbeanspruchung.

overlong [ouvə'lɔŋ], *adj.* allzu lang(e).

overlook [ouvə'luk], *v.t.* 1. übersehen, hinwegsehen über (*Acc.*), nicht beachten; 2. überblicken, hinabblicken auf (*Acc.*), Ausblick *or* Aussicht haben auf *or* über (*Acc.*); 3. beaufsichtigen, überwachen.

over|lord, *s.* der Ober(lehns)herr. **-lordship,** *s.* die Oberherrschaft.

overly ['ouvəli], *adv.* (*Am.*) übertrieben, übermäßig.

over|man, *s.* (*Min.*) der Aufseher, Steiger. **-mantel,** *s.* der Kaminaufsatz, Kaminsims. **-master,** *v.t.* bemeistern, bezwingen, übermannen, überwältigen. **-mastering,** *adj.* überwältigend, hinreißend.

overmuch [ouvə'mʌtʃ], *adv.* allzuviel, allzusehr, übermäßig.

overnight ['ouvənait], **1.** *adv.* 1. über Nacht, die Nacht über, während der Nacht; 2. am Abend zuvor, am Vorabend. **2.** *adj.* 1. von einer Nacht; – ***case,*** der Handkoffer; – ***stop,*** der Aufenthalt von (nur) einer Nacht; 2. des Vorabends.

overpass ['ouvəpɑ:s], *s.* die (Straßen)überführung.

over|pay, *irr.v.t.* zu hoch bezahlen, überreichlich belohnen. **-payment,** *s.* die Über(be)zahlung.

over|-particular, *adj.* zu genau. **--peopled,** *adj.* übervölkert.

over|persuade, *v.t.* gegen den eigenen Willen überreden; ***be -d,*** sich ungern überreden lassen. **-pitch,** *v.t.* 1. zu weit werfen; 2. (*fig.*) übertreiben. **-play,** *v.t., v.i. See* **-act**; – ***one's hand,*** zu weit gehend.

overplus ['ouvəplʌs], *s.* der Mehrbetrag, Überschuß.

over|populate, *v.t.* übervölkern. **-power,** *v.t.* überwältigen. **-pressure,** *s.* die Überbürdung.

overprint ['ouvə'print], **1.** *v.t.* 1. überdrucken; 2. (*Phot.*) überkopieren. **2.** *s.* erweiteter Aufdruck (*on stamps*).

over|produce, *v.t., v.i.* im Übermaß herstellen. **-production,** *s.* die Überproduktion. **-proof,** *adj.* überprozentig (*spirits*).

over|rate, *v.t.* überschätzen. **-reach,** *v.t.* überlisten, übervorteilen; – ***o.s.,*** zu weit gehen, sich übernehmen, sich (*Dat.*) zuveil zumuten. **-ride,** *irr.v.t.* 1. (*fig.*) umstoßen, aufheben, über den Haufen werfen, rücksichtslos hinweggehen *or* sich hinwegsetzen über (*Acc.*); hinüberreichen über (*Acc.*), sich schieben über (*Acc.*); 2. zuschanden reiten (*a horse*). **-riding,** *adj.* (*fig.*) überwiegend, überragend, allergrößt. **-ripe,** *adj.* überreif.

over|rule, *v.t.* 1. verwerfen, umstoßen, aufheben, beiseitesetzen, zurückweisen; überstimmen (*a p.*); 2. die Oberhand gewinnen über (*Acc.*). **-ruling,** *adj.* beherrschend, übermächtig.

overrun ['ouvə'rʌn], **1.** *irr.v.t.* 1. überlaufen, überrennen, überschwemmen, sich verbreiten über (*Acc.*), herfallen über (*Acc.*), einfallen in (*Acc.*); ***be – with,*** wimmeln von (*mice etc.*); 2. (*fig.*) um sich greifen in (*Dat.*), sich breitmachen in (*Dat.*), grassieren in (*Dat.*); (*of plants*) überwuchern; 3. hinauslaufen *or* hinausgehen über (*Acc.*), überschreiten; 4. (*Typ.*) umbrechen. **2.** *irr.v.i.* 1. zu weit gehen; 2. (*Typ.*) umbrechen. **3.** *s.* 1. das Überlaufen *etc.*, der Einfall, die Überschreitung; 2. (*Typ.*) der Umbruch.

over|sea, *adj.* überseeisch, Übersee–. **-seas,** *adv.* in *or* nach Übersee.

over|see, *irr.v.t.* beaufsichtigen, überwachen. **–seer,** *s.* 1. der Aufseher, Vorarbeiter; 2. (*Hist.*) Armenpfleger. **–sensitive,** *adj.* überempfindlich. **–set,** *irr.v.t.* umwerfen, umstürzen. **–sew,** *irr.v.t.* überwendlich nähen. **–-sexed,** *adj.* geschlechtlich überreizt. **–shadow,** *v.t.* überschatten, beschatten, verdunkeln; (*fig.*) in den Schatten stellen. **–shoe,** *s.* der Überschuh. **–shoot,** *irr.v.t.* hinausschießen über (*Acc.*); – *o.s.* or ***the mark,*** übers Ziel hinausschießen, des Guten zuviel tun, zu weit gehen. **–shot,** *adj.* oberschlächtig.

over|sight, *s.* 1. das Versehen; ***by an –,*** aus Versehen; 2. die Aufsicht. **–simplify,** *v.t., v.i.* radikal vereinfachen. **–size(d),** *adj.* übergroß, übermäßig groß. **–skirt,** *s.* der Oberrock. **–sleep,** *irr.v.t., irr.v.r.* sich *or* die Zeit verschlafen. **–sleeves,** *pl.* Ärmelschoner (*pl.*). **–spend, 1.** *irr.v.t.* überschreiten (*one's income*). **2.** *irr.v.i.* (*also* – *o.s.*) zuviel ausgeben, sich übermäßig verausgaben. **–spill,** *s.* der (Bevölkerungs)überschuß. **–-staffed,** *adj.* mit Personal überbesetzt.

over|state, *v.t.* zu hoch angeben, zu stark betonen, übertreiben, übertrieben ausdrücken; – ***one's case,*** in seinen Behauptungen zu weit gehen. **–statement,** *s.* die Übertreibung. **–stay,** *v.t.* überschreiten (*time*); – ***one's welcome,*** länger bleiben als erwünscht ist. **–steer,** *v.i.* (*Motor.*) zu wenig Spiel bei der Lenkung haben. **–step,** *v.t.* (*usu. fig.*) überschreiten. **–stock,** *v.t.* 1. überbeliefern; 2. überhäufen, überfüllen.

over|strain, 1. *v.t.* überanstrengen; (*fig.*) überspannen. **2.** *s.* die Überanstrengung. **–strained,** *adj.* (*fig.*) überspannt, überspitzt. **–strung,** *adj.* 1. kreuzseitig (*piano*); 2. (*fig.*) überanstrengt, überreizt. **–subscribe,** *v.t.* überzeichnen. **–subtle,** *adj.* allzu raffiniert. **–-supply, 1.** *s.* das Überangebot, der Überfluß, zu reiche Zufuhr. **2.** *v.t.* überreichlich versehen.

overt [ˈouvəːt], *adj.* offen(kundig); (*Law*) – ***act,*** äußerer Tatbestand.

over|take, *irr.v.t.* 1. überholen (*also Motor.*), einholen; 2. (*fig.*) überfallen, überraschen. **–task,** *v.t.* überbürden, zu stark in Anspruch nehmen, überfördern. **–tax,** *v.t.* 1. zu hoch besteuern; 2. (*fig.*) überbürden, überfordern, zu sehr in Anspruch nehmen; – ***one's strength,*** zu hohe Anforderungen an seine Gesundheit stellen, sich (*Dat.*) zuviel zumuten.

overthrow [ˈouvəˈθrou], **1.** *irr.v.t.* umwerfen, umstürzen, umstoßen, niederreißen, vernichten; stürzen (*government*), besiegen, niederwerfen (*enemy*). **2.** *s.* 1. der (Um)sturz; die Vernichtung, Zerstörung, (*Mil.*) Niederlage; 2. (*Crick.*) zu weit zurückgeworfener Ball.

over|time, 1. *s.* Überstunden (*pl.*); die Mehrarbeit; – (*pay*), der Überstundenzuschlag; ***work –,*** Überstunden machen. **2.** *adv.* über die Zeit hinaus; ***work –,*** nach Arbeitsschluß weiterarbeiten. **–tire,** *v.t.* übermüden.

overtly [ouˈvəːtli], *adv.* offen(kundig), öffentlich.

over|tone, *s.* 1. (*Mus.*) der Oberton; 2. *pl.* (*fig.*) Assoziationen, Nebenbedeutungen (*pl.*). **–top,** *v.t.* überragen, übertreffen. **–tower,** *v.i.* überragen. **–train,** *v.t.* übermäßig trainieren. **–trump,** *v.t.* übertrumpfen (*also fig.*).

overture [ˈouvətʃə], *s.* 1. (*Mus.*) die Ouvertüre; 2. (*fig.*) Einleitung, das Vorspiel; (formeller) Vorschlag, der Antrag, das Angebot; ***make –s to,*** sich mit dem Vorschlag wenden an (*Acc.*); – ***of marriage,*** der Heiratsantrag.

overturn [ˈouvəˈtəːn], **1.** *v.t.* 1. umkehren, umwerfen, umstoßen, umstürzen, umkippen; 2. stürzen (*government*). **2.** *v.i.* umschlagen, umfallen, umkippen; (*Naut.*) kentern. **3.** *s.* der (Um)sturz.

over|valuation, *s.* die Überschätzung, Überbewertung. **–value,** *v.t.* überschätzen, überbewerten, zu hoch einschätzen. **–weening,** *adj.* eingebildet, anmaßend. **–weight, 1.** *s.* das Übergewicht. **2.** *v.t.* überladen, überlasten.

over|whelm, *v.t.* 1. (*usu. fig.*) überhäufen, überschütten, verschütten, (unter sich) begraben; 2. überwältigen, übermannen. **–whelming,** *adj.* überwältigend.

overwind [ouvəˈwaind], *irr.v.t.* zu weit aufziehen (*a watch*).

over|work, 1. *v.t.* überarbeiten, mit Arbeit überlasten. **2.** *v.i.* sich überarbeiten. **3.** *s.* die Überarbeitung, übermäßig viel Arbeit. **–wrought,** *adj.* überarbeitet; (*fig.*) überreizt.

oviduct [ˈouvidʌkt], *s.* der Eileiter, die Muttertrompete. **oviform,** *adj.* eiförmig. **oviparous** [–ˈvipərəs], *adj.* eierlegend. **oviposit** [–ˈpɔzit], *v.i.* Eier legen (*of insects*). **ovipositor** [–ˈpɔzitə], *s.* die Legeröhre, der Legebohrer. **ovisac** [–sæk], *s.* der Eiersack.

ovogenesis [ouvəˈdʒenisis], *s.* die Eibildung. **ovoid** [ˈouvɔid], *adj.* eiförmig.

ovular [ˈouvjulə], *adj.* Ei–, ovulär, Ovular–. **ovulate** [–eit], *v.i.* ovulieren. **ovulation** [–ˈleiʃən], *s.* die Eiausstoßung, der Eiaustritt. **ovule** [ˈouvjuːl], *s.* (*Zool.*) unbefruchtetes Ei. **ovum** [ˈouvəm], *s.* (*pl.* **ova**) die Eizelle, das Ei.

owe [ou], **1.** *v.t.* 1. schuldig sein, schulden (*to, Dat.*); – ***him a grudge,*** gegen ihn einen Groll hegen; 2. Schulden haben bei, die Bezahlung schuldig sein (*Dat.*), schulden (*Dat.*) (*for,* für); 3. (*fig.*) verpflichtet sein, verdanken, zu verdanken haben (***it to him*** or ***him it,*** es ihm). **2.** *v.i.* Schulden haben; die Bezahlung schuldig sein *or* schulden (*for,* für). **owing,** *pred. adj.* 1. geschuldet; ***be –,*** zu zahlen sein (*to,* an (*Acc.*)), noch offenstehen; ***have –,*** ausstehen haben; 2. – *to,* infolge von *or* (*Gen.*), wegen (*Gen.*), vermöge (*Gen.*), dank (*Dat.*); ***be – to,*** herrühren von, zurückzuführen sein auf (*Acc.*), verursacht sein durch, zu verdanken *or* zuzuschreiben sein (*Dat.*).

owl [aul], *s.* die Eule; der Uhu, Kauz. **owlet** [–it], *s.* junge Eule. **owlish,** *adj.* 1. eulenhaft; 2. (*fig.*) dumm.

[1]**own** [oun], *adj.* (*only after poss. pron. or Gen. noun*) eigen; selbst; ***make one's – clothes,*** sich (*Dat.*) die Kleider selbst machen; ***God's – country,*** Land von Gottes Gnaden; ***with my*** (*his etc.*) – ***eyes,*** mit eigenen Augen; ***be one's – master,*** sein eigener Herr sein; ***the King's Own,*** das Leibregiment; ***countess in her – right,*** geborene Gräfin; ***truth for its – sake,*** die Wahrheit um ihrer selbst willen; ***my – self,*** ich selbst; (*coll.*) ***get one's – back,*** sich rächen (*on,* an (*Dat.*)), es heimzahlen (*Dat.*); ***hold one's –,*** sich halten, standhalten, seine Stellung behaupten (*also fig.*); ***have for one's –,*** sein eigen nennen; ***come into one's –,*** zu seinem Rechte kommen; (*fig. coll.*) zur Geltung kommen; ***a house of his –,*** sein eigenes Haus; ***have a way of one's –,*** eine eigene Art haben; (***all***) ***on one's –,*** allein; ***left on one's –,*** sich (*Dat.*) selbst überlassen; (*coll.*) ***on one's –,*** aus eigenem Antrieb, von selbst; von sich aus, unabhängig, selbständig, ohne fremde Hilfe; auf eigene Verantwortung *or* Faust.

[2]**own, 1.** *v.t.* 1. besitzen; 2. bekennen, anerkennen, zugeben, (ein)gestehen, zugestehen, einräumen; – ***o.s. defeated,*** sich geschlagen bekennen; ***it must be –ed that,*** man muß zugeben daß. **2.** *v.i.* sich bekennen (*to,* zu); ***he –ed to being,*** er gestand zu sein; (*coll.*) – ***up,*** gestehen, beichten; – ***up to s.th.,*** etwas offen zugeben *or* bekennen. **owned,** *adj.* gehörig (*by, Dat.*), im Besitz (von); (*oft. as suff.*) *e.g.* ***state-–,*** im Staatsbesitz.

owner [ˈounə], *s.* der Eigentümer, Besitzer; ***at –'s risk,*** auf eigene Gefahr. **owner|-driver,** *s.* der Selbstfahrer. **–-occupier,** *s.* der Eigenheimbesitzer. **ownership,** *s.* 1. das Eigentumsrecht; 2. der Besitz.

ox [ɔks], *s.* (*pl.* **oxen**) der Ochse, das Rind.

oxalate [ˈɔksəleit], *s.* oxalsaures Salz. **oxalic** [–ˈsælik], *adj.* oxalsauer; – ***acid,*** die Oxalsäure, Klee(salz)säure.

ox|-eye, *s.* das Ochsenauge; (*Bot.*) – ***daisy,*** großes Maßlieb, die Marienblume. **–-hide,** *s.* die Ochsenhaut; das Rindsleder.

oxidate [ˈɔksideit], *v.t., v.i. See* **oxidize, 1. oxidation** [–ˈdeiʃən], *s. See* **oxidization. oxide**

['ɔksaid], *s.* das Oxyd, die Sauerstoffverbindung; ***ferrous* –**, das Eisenoxydul. **oxidization** [-idai'zeiʃən], *s.* die Oxydierung, Oxydation. **oxidize** ['ɔksidaiz], **1.** *v.t.* oxydieren, mit Sauerstoff verbinden. **2.** *v.i.* oxydieren.

ox|lip, *s.* hohe Schlüsselblume. **--tail,** *s.* der Ochsenschwanz. **--tongue,** *s.* die Ochsenzunge.

oxy-acetylene [ɔksiə'setəlin], *adj.* Sauerstoff-Azetylen–; – ***burner,*** der Brennschneider, Schneidbrenner; – ***welding,*** autogene Schweißung, das Autogenschweißen.

oxygen ['ɔksidʒən], *s.* der Sauerstoff; – ***apparatus,*** der Sauerstoffapparat; – ***starvation,*** der Sauerstoffmangel. **oxygenate** [-eit], *v.t.* oxydieren, mit Sauerstoff verbinden *or* behandeln *or* anreichern *or* sättigen. **oxygenator,** *s.* der Sauerstofferzeuger. **oxy-hydrogen,** *adj.* Hydrooxygen–; – ***blowpipe,*** das Knallgasgebläse; – ***gas,*** das Knallgas; – ***light,*** Drummondsches Licht.

oxymoron [ɔksi'mɔ:rən], *s.* das Oxymoron. **oxytone** [–toun], *s.* das Oxytonon.

oyer ['ɔiə], *s.* (*Hist.*) das Verhör; die Untersuchung; (*Law*) – ***and terminer,*** das Hören und Entscheiden.

oyez [ou'jez], *int.* (*Hist.*) hört (zu)!

oyster ['ɔistə], *s.* die Auster; (*fig.*) ***like an –***, zugeknöpft. **oyster|-bed,** *s.* die Austernbank. **--catcher,** *s.* (*Orn.*) der Austernfischer (*Haematopus ostralegus*). **--farm,** *s.* der Austernpark.

ozokerit(e) [o'zɔkərait], *s.* (*Geol.*) der Ozokerit, das Erdwachs, Bergwachs.

ozone ['ouzoun], *s.* das Ozon. **ozonic** [–'zɔnik], *adj.* Ozon–, ozonisch, ozonhaltig. **ozoniferous** [–o'nifərəs], *adj.* ozonerzeugend. **ozonize** ['ouzənaiz], *v.t.* 1. mit Ozon behandeln; 2. in Ozon verwandeln. **ozonizer,** *s.* der Ozonerzeuger.

P

P, p [pi:], *s.* das P, p; (*coll.*) ***mind one's P's and Q's,*** sich ganz gehörig in acht nehmen. *See Index of Abbreviations.*

pa [pɑ:], *s. See* **papa.**

pabulum ['pæbjuləm], *s.* die Nahrung.

paca ['pækə], *s.* (*Zool.*) das Paka.

[1]**pace** [peis], **1.** *s.* 1. der Schritt; ***make*** or ***take a –***, einen Schritt tun *or* machen; 2. die Gangart, der Paßgang (*of horse*); ***put a horse through its –s,*** ein Pferd alle Gangarten machen lassen; (*fig.*) ***put him through his –s,*** ihn auf Herz und Nieren prüfen; 3. das Tempo; (*coll.*) ***go the –***, schnell gehen; (*fig.*) ein flottes Leben führen; ***keep –***, Schritt halten (***with,*** mit) (*also fig.*); ***set the –***, Schrittmacher sein, (*fig.*) das Tempo angeben; (*coll.*) ***stand the –***, das Tempo durchhalten; ***at a great –***, sehr schnell, in raschem Tempo. **2.** *v.i.* 1. (einher)schreiten; 2. (*of horse*) im Paßgang gehen. **3.** *v.t.* 1. abschreiten (*a room etc.*); 2. im Paßgang gehen lassen (*a horse*); 3. (*Spt.*) Schritt machen für; (*fig.*) das Tempo bestimmen von.

[2]**pace** ['peisi], *prep.* (*Liter.*) mit Erlaubnis von *or* (*Gen.*).

paced [peist], *adj.* 1. (*Spt.*) mit Schrittmacher gelaufen *or* gefahren; 2. (*as suff.*) ***slow-–***, langsam schreitend; (*fig.*) ***thorough-–***, durchtrieben, Erz–. **pacemaker,** *s.* der Schrittmacher; ***act as –***, Schritt machen (***to, for,*** *Dat.*) (*also fig.*). **pacer,** *s.* 1. Schreitende(r); 2. (*horse*) der Paßgänger; 3. (*Spt.*) *see* **pacemaker. pace|setter,** *s.* (*fig.*) *see* **–maker.**

pacha, *see* **pasha.**

pachyderm ['pækidə:m], *s.* (*pl.* **-s** *or* **-ata**) (*Zool.*) der Dickhäuter. **pachydermatous** [–'də:mətəs], *adj.* (*Zool.*) dickhäutig, Dickhäuter–. **pachydermous** [–'də:məs], *adj.* (*Bot.*) dickwandig.

pacifiable ['pæsifaiəbl], *adj.* zu beruhigen(d) *or* befriedigen(d). **pacific** [pə'sifik], *adj.* 1. friedlich, friedfertig, friedliebend; 2. versöhnlich, Friedens–; 3. (*Geog.*) ***Pacific (Ocean),*** Stiller *or* Großer *or* Pazifischer Ozean, der Pazifik; ***Pacific Islands,*** Pazifische Inseln; ***Pacific states,*** die Pazifikstaaten; ***Pacific (standard) time,*** die Pazifik-Normalzeit. **pacificate** [pə'sifikeit], *v.t. See* **pacify. pacification** [–fi'keiʃən], *s.* 1. die Beschwichtigung, Besänftigung, Beruhigung; 2. Befriedung; Versöhnung, Frieden(s)stiftung, der Friedensvertrag.

pacifier ['pæsifaiə], *s.* der Frieden(s)stifter; (*Am.*) *See* **dummy 1,** 2. **pacifism,** *s.* der Pazifismus. **pacifist, 1.** *s.* der Pazifist. **2.** *adj.* pazifistisch. **pacify,** *v.t.* 1. beruhigen, beschwichtigen, besänftigen; 2. den Frieden bringen (*Dat.*), befrieden (*a country*); 3. stillen (*hunger etc.*).

pack [pæk], **1.** *s.* 1. der Pack(en), das Päckchen, Paket, Bündel, (*esp. of cigarettes etc.*) die Packung; 2. (*Mil.*) der Rucksack, Tornister; 3. Ballen (*of wool etc.*) (= *240 lb.*), Sack (*of flour*) (= *280 lb.*); 4. (*coll.*) Haufen, die Menge (*of things*); – ***of lies,*** ein Haufen Lügen; – ***of nonsense,*** lauter Unsinn; 5. (*coll.*) die Bande, Rotte, das Pack (*of thieves*); ***the whole – of them,*** das ganze Lumpenpack; 6. die Meute, Koppel (*of hounds*); das Rudel (*of wolves, submarines*); 7. Spiel (*of cards*); 8. (*Med.*) die Packung; 9. (*Rugby Footb.*) Stürmer (*pl.*). **2.** *v.t.* 1. verpacken, (ein)packen, zusammenpacken; 2. fest zusammenpacken, zusammenpressen; ***–ed like sardines,*** wie die Heringe (gepreßt); 3. vollpacken, (voll)stopfen; (*Theat.*) ***–ed house,*** volles Haus; 4. (*Med.*) einpacken; 5. (*Tech.*) (ab)dichten, lidern; 6. in Dosen einmachen, eindosen, konservieren (*fish, fruit etc.*); 7. beladen, bepacken (*beasts*); 8. zu einem Päckchen zusammenlegen (*cards*); 9. (*sl.*) (*usu.* – ***off***) fortschicken; 10. (*sl.*) verabreichen können (*a punch*); (bei sich) tragen (*a pistol*). **3.** *v.i.* 1. (*oft.* – ***up***) packen, seine Sachen einpacken; 2. sich packen (lassen) (*as goods*); 3. sich zusammenscharen *or* zusammenballen; 4. (*coll.*) ***send him –ing,*** ihn hinausschmeißen *or* fortjagen; 5. (*sl.*) – ***(it) in,*** sich geschlagen geben, die Flinte ins Korn werfen; (*sl.*) – ***(it) up,*** aufhören; (*sl.*) – ***up,*** sterben, verrecken (*of an engine etc.*).

package ['pækidʒ], **1.** *s.* 1. die Packung, das Paket; 2. (*Comm.*) die Verpackung, Emballage. **2.** *v.t.* (*Comm.*) (ver)packen, paketieren. **package deal,** *s.* das Kopplungsgeschäft.

pack|-animal, *s.* das Lasttier, Saumtier. **--cloth,** *s.* die Packleinwand. **--drill,** *s.* (*Mil.*) das (Straf)-exerzieren mit Gepäck. **packer,** *s.* 1. der (Ver)-packer; 2. die Packmaschine. **packet** [–it], *s.* 1. das Paket, Päckchen; 2. (*also* ***--boat***) das Paketboot, der Postdampfer; 3. (*sl.*) ***catch*** or ***stop a –***, einer Kugel in den Weg laufen. **pack|-horse,** *s.* 1. das Packpferd, Lastpferd, Saumpferd; 2. (*fig.*) Lasttier. **--ice,** *s.* das Packeis.

packing ['pækiŋ], *s.* 1. das Packen; ***do one's –***, packen; 2. die Verpackung; 3. Füllung, Packung, das Packmaterial, Füllmaterial, Stopfmaterial; 4. (*Tech.*) die (Ab)dichtung, Liderung; das Dichtungsmaterial.

packing|-bush, *s.* die Stopfbuchse. **--case,** *s.* die Packkiste. **--house,** *s.* (*Am.*) die Konservenfabrik. **--needle,** *s.* die Packnadel. **--paper,** *s.* das Packpapier. **--ring,** *s.* der Dicht(ungs)ring. **--sheet,** *s.* das Packtuch. **--thread,** *s. See* **pack-thread.**

pack|-saddle, *s.* der Saumsattel, Packsattel. **--thread,** *s.* der Bindfaden, Packzwirn. **--train,** *s.* die Tragtierkolonne.

pact [pækt], *s.* der Vertrag, Pakt.

[1]**pad** [pæd], **1.** *s.* 1. (*obs.*) der Weg, die Straße; 2. (*sl.*) die Bude. **2.** *v.i.* (*sl.*) – ***along,*** dahintrotten. **3.** *v.t.* (*sl.*) – ***it*** or ***the hoof,*** auf Schusters Rappen gehen.

[2]**pad, 1.** *s.* 1. das Polster, Kissen, der Wulst, Bausch; 2. die Unterlage; 3. Pfote, der (Fuß)-ballen (*of dog etc.*); 4. (*Crick.*) die Beinschiene; 5. (*also* **writing--**) der (Schreib)block, Briefblock; 6. (*rocketry*) (*also* **launching--**) die (Abschuß)-rampe. **2.** *v.t.* 1. (aus)polstern, ausstopfen, wattieren; ***padded cell,*** die Gummizelle; 2. (*fig.*) (*also* **– *out***) aufbauschen (*a sentence*). **padding,** *s.* 1. das (Aus)polstern, Wattieren; die Polsterung, Wattierung; (Polster)füllung, Watte; 2. (*fig.*) leere Phrasen, leeres Beiwerk *or* Füllwerk, die Schwafelei, das Zeilenfüllsel, Geschreibsel.

paddle [pædl], **1.** *v.i., v.t.* paddeln (*a boat*); (*fig.*) – ***one's own canoe,*** allein weiterkommen, selbständig vorwärtskommen, auf eigenen Füßen stehen. **2.** *v.i.* planschen, plätschern, (herum)paddeln (*in water*); watscheln (*as a toddler*). **3.** *s.* 1. das Paddel; *see* **paddle-board**; 2. (*Tech.*) die Rührstange, das Rührholz, Rührscheit; 3. ***have a –,*** *see* **2.**

paddle|-board, *s.* die (Rad)schaufel. **--box,** *s.* der Radkasten. **--steamer,** *s.* der Raddampfer. **--wheel,** *s.* das Schaufelrad. **paddling,** *s.* 1. das Paddeln; 2. Planschen, Plätschern; – ***pool,*** das Planschbecken.

[1]**paddock** [ˈpædək], *s.* 1. die (Pferde)koppel, das Gehege; 2. (*Racing*) der Sattelplatz.

[2]**paddock,** *s.* 1. (*Scots*) der Frosch; 2. (*obs.*) die Kröte.

[1]**paddy** [ˈpædi], *s.* der Reis (auf dem Halm), ungeschälter Reis.

[2]**paddy,** *s.* (*coll.*) der Wutanfall, Wutausbruch.

paddy wagon, *s.* (*Am.*) grüne Minna.

padlock [ˈpædlɔk], **1.** *s.* das Vorhängeschloß, Vorlegeschloß. **2.** *v.t.* mit Vorhängeschloß verschließen.

pad-nag, *s.* 1. der Paßgänger; 2. Klepper, Gaul.

padre [ˈpɑːdri], *s.* (*coll.*) Militärgeistliche(r), der Kaplan.

paean [ˈpiːən], *s.* das Siegeslied, Triumphlied, der Päan; – ***of praise,*** das Loblied, der Lobgesang, die Lobrede, Lobeserhebung.

paederast [ˈpedəræst], *s.* der Päderast. **paederasty** [–i], *s.* die Knabenliebe, Päderastie.

paediatrician [piːdiəˈtriʃən], *s.* der (die) Kinderarzt (–ärztin). **paediatrics** [–iˈætriks], *pl.* (*sing. constr.*) die Kinderheilkunde, Pädiatrie.

pagan [ˈpeigən], **1.** *adj.* heidnisch. **2.** *s.* der Heide (die Heidin). **paganism,** *s.* das Heidentum.

[1]**page** [peidʒ], **1.** *s.* 1. die (Buch)seite; 2. (*fig.*) das Buch, Blatt, die Episode, Chronik; ***–s of history,*** die Tafeln der Geschichte. 3. *v.t.* paginieren.

[2]**page, 1.** *s.* 1. (*Hist.*) der Page, Edelknabe; 2. (*also* ***--boy***) der Page, Hoteldiener, Boy; (*Am.*) Laufbursche, Amtsbote. **2.** *v.t.* (durch Pagen) holen *or* suchen *or* ausrufen lassen.

pageant [ˈpædʒənt], *s.* historischer Aufzug, der Festzug, großartiges Schauspiel *or* Schaustück. **pageantry,** *s.* 1. das (Schau)gepränge, der Prunk, Pomp, Aufwand; 2. (*fig.*) leerer Schein.

paginal [ˈpædʒinl], *adj.* Seiten–. **paginate** [–neit], *v.t.* paginieren. **pagination** [–ˈneiʃən], *s.* die Paginierung, Seitenzählung.

paging [ˈpeidʒiŋ], *s. See* **pagination.**

pagoda [pəˈgoudə], *s.* die Pagode. **pagoda-tree,** *s.* die Sophora; ***shake the –,*** in Indien sein Glück machen.

paid [peid], **1.** *imperf., p.p. of* **pay. 2.** *adj.* frei! franko! (*on letters etc.*); – ***for,*** (schon) bezahlt; – ***in,*** eingezahlt; – ***up,*** abgezahlt, abgetragen (*debts*). **paid-up,** *attrib. adj.* – ***capital,*** das Einlagekapital; – ***membership,*** eingetragene Mitgliedschaft.

pail [peil], *s.* der Eimer, Kübel. **pailful,** *s.* der Eimervoll.

paillasse [ˈpæljæs], *s.* der Strohsack, die (Stroh)-matratze.

pain [pein], **1.** *s.* 1. der Schmerz, Schmerzen (*pl.*), die Pein; ***be in*** or ***suffer –,*** leiden, Schmerzen haben; ***he is*** or ***he gives me a – in the neck,*** er geht mir auf die Nerven; 2. *pl.* (*Med.*) (Geburts)wehen (*pl.*); 3. (*mental*) das Leid, Leiden, der Kummer; ***give*** or ***cause him –,*** ihm Kummer machen; ***hear with –,*** mit Wehmut hören; 4. *pl.* (*fig.*) die Mühe, Bemühungen (*pl.*); ***be at*** or ***take –s, go to great –s,*** sich bemühen, sich (*Dat.*) Mühe geben; ***for my*** (***his etc.***) ***–s,*** als Belohnung; ***spare no –s,*** keine Mühe scheuen; 5. (*obs.*) die Strafe; (***up***)***on*** or ***under – of death,*** bei Todesstrafe; ***upon – of my displeasure,*** bei Verlust meines Wohlwollens. **2.** *v.t.* 1. weh tun (*Dat.*), schmerzen, Schmerzen bereiten (*Dat.*); 2. (*fig.*) schmerzlich berühren. **pained,** *adj.* schmerzvoll; – ***expression,*** der Ausdruck des Schmerzes.

painful [ˈpeinful], *adj.* 1. schmerzlich, schmerzhaft; 2. (*fig.*) peinlich, mühsam; – ***effort,*** mühsame Anstrengung; – ***scene,*** peinliche Szene. **painfully,** *adv.* (*also coll.*) – ***accurate,*** peinlich genau. **painfulness,** *s.* 1. die Schmerzhaftigkeit; 2. Peinlichkeit, Schmerzlichkeit. **pain-killer,** *s.* schmerzstillendes Mittel, die Schmerztablette. **painless,** *adj.* 1. schmerzlos; 2. (*fig.*) mühelos. **painlessness,** *s.* die Schmerzlosigkeit. **pain-reliever,** *s.* schmerzlinderndes Mittel.

painstaking [ˈpeinzteikiŋ], **1.** *adj.* 1. sorgfältig, gewissenhaft, unverdrossen; 2. arbeitsam, rührig, fleißig, emsig. **2.** *s.* die Mühe, Sorgfalt.

paint [peint], **1.** *v.t.* 1. malen (*a picture*); – ***his portrait,*** ihn malen; – ***from nature,*** nach der Natur malen; 2. (an)streichen, tünchen (*a wall etc.*), bemalen (*an article*); – ***in,*** bemalen; – ***out,*** übermalen; (*coll.*) – ***the town red,*** Radau machen, auf die Pauke hauen; 3. schminken (*the face*); 4. aufstreichen, (aus)pinseln (*as with iodine*); 5. (*fig.*) ausmalen, schildern, darstellen, beschreiben. **2.** *v.i.* 1. malen; – ***from nature,*** nach der Natur malen; 2. sich schminken *or* anmalen. **3.** *s.* 1. die Farbe; 2. Anstrichfarbe, Tünche, der Anstrich (*of a wall etc.*); ***coat of –,*** der (Farb)anstrich; ***fresh as –,*** schmuck, frisch und munter; ***wet –!*** frisch gestrichen! 3. die Schminke; 4. (*Med.*) Tinktur.

paint|-box, *s.* der Malkasten, Tuschkasten. **--brush,** *s.* der Malerpinsel, Tuschpinsel, Anstrichpinsel.

painted lady, *s.* (*Ent.*) der Distelfalter.

[1]**painter** [ˈpeintə], *s.* 1. der (die) (Kunst)maler(in); – ***in watercolours,*** der Aquarellmaler; – ***in oils,*** der Ölmaler; ***–'s colic,*** die Bleikolik, Malerkrankheit; 2. der (Dekorations)maler, Anstreicher.

[2]**painter,** *s.* (*Naut.*) die Fangleine, das Bootstau; (*coll.*) ***cut the –,*** seinen eignen Weg gehen, sich (von den andern) loslösen (*esp. Pol.*).

painting [ˈpeintiŋ], *s.* 1. das Malen, die Malerei; – ***on glass,*** die Glasmalerei; – ***in oils,*** die Ölmalerei; 2. das Gemälde; ***the – in oils,*** das Ölgemälde; 3. die Malerarbeit, Malerarbeiten (*pl.*), die Bemalung, der Anstrich; 4. (*Med.*) die Pinselung; 5. das Schminken.

paint|-remover, *s.* das Abbeizmittel. **-work,** *s. See* **painting,** 3.

pair [pɛə], **1.** *s.* 1. das Paar (*in German oft. omitted*); ***carriage and –,*** der Zweispänner; – ***of boots,*** das Paar Stiefel; ***two –s of boots,*** zwei Paar Stiefel; – ***of compasses,*** der Zirkel; – ***of drawers*** or ***pants,*** die Unterhose; – ***of horses,*** das Gespann Pferde; – ***of scales,*** die Waage; – ***of scissors*** die Schere; ***two –s of scissors,*** zwei Scheren; – ***of spectacles*** or ***glasses,*** die Brille; – ***of steps,*** die Trittleiter; – ***of tongs,*** die Zange; – ***of trousers,*** die Hose; 2. der *or* das *or* die andere (von einem Paar), das Gegenstück; 3. (Ehe)paar. **2.** *v.t.* 1. paaren (*animals*); 2. (*also* – ***off***) in Paaren *or* paarweise anordnen. **3.** *v.i.* 1. sich paaren (*animals, also fig.*); sich begatten (*animals*); 2. (*fig.*) zusammenpassen; 3. – ***off,*** zu zweien gehen, sich paarweise anschließen; (*coll.*) heiraten (*with, Acc.*). **pairing,** *s.* die Paarung. **pair-oar,** *s.* der Zweier (*rowing*).

pajamas, *see* **pyjamas.**

Pakistan [pɑːkiˈstɑːn], *s.* Pakistan (*n.*). **Pakistani** [–i], **1.** *s.* der (die) Pakistaner(in). **2.** *adj.* pakistanisch.

pal [pæl], **1.** *s.* (*coll.*) der Kamerad, Genosse,

(Busen)freund, Spezi. **2.** *v.i.* – ***up,*** sich anfreunden, Freundschaft schließen (***to, with,*** mit).

palace [ˈpæləs], *s.* der Palast, das (Residenz)schloß, Palais.

paladin [ˈpælədin], *s.* der Paladin.

palaeographer [pæliˈɔgrəfə], *s.* der Paläograph. **palaeography,** *s.* die Handschriftenkunde, Paläographie. **palaeolithic** [–oˈliθik], **1.** *adj.* altsteinzeitlich. **2.** *s.* die Altsteinzeit, ältere Steinzeit, das Paläolithikum. **palaeologist** [–ˈɔlədʒist], *s.* der Paläologe, Altertumskundige(r). **palaeology,** *s.* die Paläologie, Altertumskunde. **palaeontologist** [–ɔnˈtɔlədʒist], *s.* der Paläontologe. **palaeontology,** *s.* die Paläontologie, Versteinerungskunde. **palaeozoic** [–əˈzouik], **1.** *adj.* paläozoisch. **2.** *s.* das Paläozoikum.

palanquin [ˈpælənkiːn], *s.* der Palankin, Tragsessel, die Sänfte.

palatable [ˈpælətəbl], *adj.* 1. schmackhaft, wohlschmeckend; 2. (*fig.*) angenehm, annehmbar, zusagend.

palatal [ˈpælətl], **1.** *adj.* Palatal–, Gaumen–. **2.** *s.* der Gaumenlaut, Palatal(laut). **palatalize,** *v.t.* (*Phonet.*) palatalisieren.

palate [ˈpælit], *s.* 1. der Gaumen; ***cleft –,*** die Gaumenspalte, der Wolfsrachen; ***hard –,*** der Vordergaumen; ***soft –,*** der Hintergaumen; 2. (*fig.*) der Geschmack(ssinn); 3. (*fig.*) Geschmack, das Gefallen (***for,*** an (*Dat.*)).

palatial [pəˈleiʃəl], *adj.* 1. palastartig, Palast–; 2. prächtig, Luxus–.

Palatinate [pəˈlætinət], *s.* die (Rhein)pfalz.

Palatine [ˈpælətain], *adj.* pfälzisch, Pfalz–; ***Count –,*** der Pfalzgraf.

palatine, 1. *adj.* (*Anat.*) Gaumen–. **2.** *s.* der Gaumenknochen.

palaver [pəˈlɑːvə], **1.** *s.* die Besprechung, Unterredung, (*coll.*) das Geschwätz, Gewäsch, endlose Rederei. **2.** *v.i.* unterhandeln; (*coll.*) schwatzen, quasseln. **3.** *v.t.* (*coll.*) beschwatzen (*a p.*).

^{1}**pale** [peil], **1.** *adj.* blaß, bleich, fahl; schwach, matt (*light*); hell (*colour*); – ***ale,*** helles Bier; – ***blue,*** das Hellblau; blaßblau, hellblau; ***as – as a ghost,*** kreidebleich, totenbleich; ***turn*** or ***grow –,*** *see* **2**; abblassen (*as colours*). **2.** *v.i.* 1. erblassen, erbleichen, bleich *or* blaß werden; 2. (*fig.*) verblassen (***beside,*** vor (*Dat.*)).

^{2}**pale,** *s.* 1. der Pfahl (*also Her.*); die Einpfahlung, Einfriedung; 2. (*fig.*) (enge) Grenzen, Schranken (*pl.*); (*Hist.*) der Bereich, Bezirk, das Gebiet; (*coll.*) ***beyond the –,*** jenseits der Grenzen des Erlaubten; ***English Pale,*** der englische Bezirk (*in Ireland*); ***within the – of the church,*** im Schoß der Kirche.

pale|face, *s.* das Bleichgesicht, Angehörige(r) der weißen Rasse. **–-faced,** *adj.* blaß, von bleichem Gesicht. **paleness,** *s.* die Bleichheit, Blässe, Farblosigkeit.

paleo–, *see* **palaeo–.**

Palestine [ˈpælistain], *s.* Palästina (*n.*). **Palestinian** [–ˈtiniən], **1.** *adj.* palästinisch. **2.** *s.* der (die) Palästinier(in).

paletot [ˈpælətou], *s.* der Überrock, Mantel.

palette [ˈpælit], *s.* 1. der Farbenteller, die Palette; 2. (*fig.*) Farbenskala. **palette-knife,** *s.* der *or* die Spachtel, das Palettmesser, Streichmesser.

palfrey [ˈpɔːlfri], *s.* der Zelter.

palimpsest [ˈpælimpsest], *s.* der *or* das Palimpsest.

palindrome [ˈpælindroum], *s.* das Palindrom.

paling [ˈpeiliŋ], *s.* das Pfahlholz, der Zaunpfahl; (*also pl.*) Lattenzaun, Pfahlzaun, das Staket.

palingenesis [pælinˈdʒenisis], *s.* die Wiedergeburt, Palingenese.

palinode [ˈpælinoud], *s.* die Palinodie, (dichterischer) Widerruf.

palisade [pæliˈseid], **1.** *s.* das Staket, der Schanzpfahl, die Pfahlsperre, Palisade. **2.** *v.t.* verschanzen, mit einer Palisade befestigen.

^{1}**pall** [pɔːl], **1.** *s.* 1. das Bahrtuch, Leichentuch, Sargtuch; 2. (*Her.*) die Deichsel; *see also* **pallium**; 3. (*fig.*) der Mantel, die Decke, Hülle; – ***of smoke,*** die Rauchwolke. **2.** *v.t.* 1. mit einem Bahrtuch bedecken; 2. (*fig.*) verhüllen, umhüllen, einhüllen.

^{2}**pall, 1.** *v.i.* 1. jeden Reiz verlieren (***on,*** für), ermüdend wirken (auf (*Acc.*)), kalt lassen (*Acc.*), langweilen (*Acc.*); 2. langweilig *or* schal *or* fad(e) werden. **2.** *v.t.* 1. (über)sättigen; 2. verderben, unschmackhaft machen.

palladium [pəˈleidiəm], *s.* 1. das Palladium (*also Chem.*); 2. (*fig.*) der Schutz, Hort.

^{1}**pallet** [ˈpælit], *s.* das Strohbett, Strohlager, die Pritsche.

^{2}**pallet,** *s.* 1. das Streichmesser (*pottery*); 2. (*Horol.*) die Hemmung, der Sperrkegel, Spindellappen; 3. (*Tech.*) die Klaue, (*organ*) Sperrklappe; 4. Palette (*for moving goods*); *see also* **palette.**

palliasse, *see* **paillasse.**

palliate [ˈpælieit], *v.t.* 1. lindern; 2. (*fig.*) bemänteln, beschönigen. **palliation** [–ˈeiʃən], *s.* 1. die Linderung, Erleichterung; 2. (*fig.*) Bemäntelung, Beschönigung; ***in – of,*** als Entschuldigung für. **palliative** [–liətiv], **1.** *adj.* 1. lindernd, Linderungs–; 2. (*fig.*) bemäntelnd, beschönigend. **2.** *s.* das Linderungsmittel.

pallid [ˈpælid], *adj.* bleich, blaß. **pallidness,** *s. See* **pallor.**

pallium [ˈpæliəm], *s.* 1. (*Eccl.*) das Pallium; 2. Altartuch, Meßtuch, Hostientuch, die Palla; 3. (*Antiqu.*) der Philosophenmantel; 4. (*Zool.*) Mantel.

pallor [ˈpælə], *s.* die Blässe.

pally [ˈpæli], *adj.* (*coll.*) kameradschaftlich, freundschaftlich; befreundet (***with,*** mit).

^{1}**palm** [pɑːm], *s.* 1. (*also* ***–-tree***) die Palme; 2. (*fig.*) Siegespalme, Krone, der Triumph, Sieg; ***bear*** or ***win the –,*** den Sieg erringen; ***give the –,*** den Preis zuerkennen (***to,*** *Dat.*); ***yield the –,*** sich geschlagen geben (***to,*** *Dat.*).

^{2}**palm, 1.** *s.* 1. (*also* ***– of the hand***) die Handfläche, hohle *or* flache Hand; (*coll.*) ***grease his –,*** ihn bestechen *or* schmieren; (*coll.*) ***have an itching –,*** eine offene Hand haben; 2. die Vorderfußsohle (*of apes*); 3. (*obs.*) Handbreit (*as measure*); 4. Innenhand(fläche) (*of glove*); ***sailmaker's –,*** der Segelmacherhandschuh; 5. die Schaufel (*of antlers or anchor*); 6. das Blatt (*of oar*). **2.** *v.t.* 1. (mit der Handfläche) berühren, betasten; 2. in der hohlen Hand verbergen, in der Hand verschwinden lassen; 3. – ***a th.*** (***off***) ***on him,*** ihm etwas andrehen *or* aufhängen *or* anhängen; – ***o.s. off as,*** sich ausgeben als.

palmaceous [pælˈmeiʃəs], *adj.* palmenartig, Palmen–.

palmar [ˈpælmə], *adj.* Handflächen–, Hohlhand–. **palmate(d),** *adj.* handförmig.

palm-grease, *s.* (*coll.*) das Schmiergeld, Bestechungsgeld.

palm-house, *s.* das Palmenhaus.

palmiped [ˈpælmiped], **1.** *adj.* (*Orn.*) schwimmfüßig. **2.** *s.* der Schwimmfüßer.

palmist [ˈpɑːmist], *s.* der Chiromant, der (die) Handwahrsager(in). **palmistry,** *s.* die Chiromantie, Handlesekunst.

palmitic [pælˈmitik], *adj.* – ***acid,*** die Palmitinsäure.

palm|-leaf, *s.* das Palmenblatt, der Palmwedel. **–-oil,** *s.* die Palmbutter; (*coll.*) *see* **–-grease. Palm Sunday,** *s.* der Palmsonntag. **palmy,** *adj.* 1. (*Poet.*) palmenreich; 2. (*coll.*) glorreich, glücklich; – ***days,*** die Glanzzeit, Blütezeit.

palp [pælp], *s.* (*pl.* **-i**) der Fühler, Taster, das Fühlhorn.

palpability [pælpəˈbiliti], *s.* 1. die Fühlbarkeit, Greifbarkeit, Tastbarkeit; 2. (*fig.*) Offensichtlichkeit, Handgreiflichkeit. **palpable,** *adj.* 1. fühlbar, greifbar, (ab)tastbar; 2. (*fig.*) handgreiflich, offensichtlich, augenfällig, deutlich.

palpate [ˈpælpeit], *v.t.* (*Med.*) betasten, abtasten, befühlen, palpieren. **palpation** [–ˈpeiʃən], *s.* das Betasten, Abtasten, die Palpation.

palpebral ['pælpəbrəl], *adj.* Augenlid-.
palpitate ['pælpiteit], *v.i.* 1. heftig klopfen, unregelmäßig schlagen (*as the heart*); 2. beben, zittern (*with*, vor (*Dat.*)). **palpitation** [-'teiʃən], *s.* (*also pl.*) (*Med.*) das Herzklopfen.
palpus ['pælpəs], *s. See* **palp.**
palsied ['pɔ:lzid], *adj.* gelähmt, (*fig.*) zitterig, gebrechlich, hinfällig. **palsy, 1.** *s.* die Lähmung, der Schlagfluß; (*B.*) *sick of the –*, Gichtbrüchige(r). **2.** *v.t.* lähmen.
palter ['pɔ:ltə], *v.i.* zweideutig handeln (*with*, an (*Dat.*) *or* gegen), Spiegelfechterei *or* sein Spiel treiben (mit), feilschen *or* knickern (mit).
paltriness ['pɔ:ltrinis], *s.* die Kleinlichkeit, Armseligkeit, Erbärmlichkeit. **paltry,** *adj.* kleinlich, dürftig, fipsig; armselig, erbärmlich, fadenscheinig, unbedeutend, wertlos; *– excuse*, lahme *or* lumpige Entschuldigung.
palud(in)al [pə'lju:d(in)l], *adj.* sumpfig, Sumpf-.
pampas [pæmpəs], *pl.* Pampas (*pl.*). **pampas-grass,** *s.* das Pampasgras.
pamper ['pæmpə], *v.t.* verwöhnen, verzärteln, (ver)hätscheln, verpimpeln (*a child etc.*), frönen (*Dat.*), willfahren (*Dat.*) (*desires*).
pamphlet ['pæmflit], *s.* die Flugschrift, Broschüre. **pamphleteer** [-'tiə], *s.* der Flugschriftenschreiber.
[1]**pan** [pæn], **1.** *s.* 1. die Pfanne; *frying –*, die Bratpfanne; 2. die Pfanne, Schale, Schüssel, der Tiegel, Napf, das Gefäß, Becken; *lavatory –*, das Klosettbecken; *pots and –s*, das Kochgeschirr; *warming –*, die Wärmpfanne; 3. (*of scales*) die (Waag)schale; 4. *hard –*, der Ortstein, (*fig.*) Boden, feste Unterlage; 5. (*coll., fig.*) *flash in the –*, unerwarteter und vorübergehender Erfolg. **2.** *v.t.* 1. (*also – out*) (im Setzkasten) waschen (*gold-bearing gravel*), auswaschen (*gold*); 2. (*sl.*) scharf kritisieren (*a p.*). **3.** *v.i.* 1. Gold waschen; 2. *– out*, (*of gold-bearing gravel*) ergiebig sein; (*fig., coll.*) (*also – out well*) Erfolg haben, einschlagen, gut (aus)gehen, sich bewähren.
[2]**pan-,** *pref.* All-, Pan-; *–Europe*, das Pan-Europa; *–German*, alldeutsch.
[3]**pan, 1.** *v.t.* (*Phot.*) schwenken. **2.** *v.i.* panoramieren.
panacea [pænə'siə], *s.* das Allheilmittel, Universalmittel.
panache [pæ'næʃ], *s.* 1. der Federbusch; 2. (*fig.*) Prunk, die Prahlerei, Großtuerei.
panada [pə'nɑ:də], *s.* der Semmelbrei.
Panama ['pænəmɑ:], *s.* Panama (*n.*); *– Canal*, der Panamakanal; *– hat*, der Panamahut. **Panamanian** [-'meiniən], **1.** *s.* der (die) Panamaer(in), ((*Austr.*) Panamener(in)). **2.** *adj.* panamaisch. ((*Austr.*) panamenisch).
pancake ['pænkeik], **1.** *s.* der Pfannkuchen, flacher Eierkuchen; *Pancake* (*Tues*)*day*, die Fastnacht; (*as*) *flat as a –*, flach wie ein Brett; (*Av.*) *– (landing)*, die Sacklandung, Bumslandung. **2.** *v.i.* (*Av.*) sacklanden, bumslanden, durchsacken.
panchromatic [pænkrə'mætik], *adj.* (*Phot.*) panchromatisch.
pancratic [pæn'krætik], *adj.* 1. (*Antiqu.*) athletisch, Pankration-; 2. (*Opt.*) pankratisch; 3. (*fig.*) vollkommen. **pancratium** [-'kreiʃiəm], *s.* (*Antiqu.*) das Pankration, der Allkampf.
pancreas ['pænkriəs], *s.* die Bauchspeicheldrüse. **pancreatic** [-ri'ætik], *adj.* Bauchspeichel-; *– juice*, der Bauchspeichel.
panda ['pændə], *s.* der Katzenbär, Panda; (*police*) *– car*, (zweifarbiger) Streifenwagen.
pandects ['pændekts], *pl.* Pandekten (*pl.*).
pandemic [pæn'demik], **1.** *adj.* 1. (*Med.*) (ganz) allgemein verbreitet, pandemisch; 2. allgemein, generell. **2.** *s.* (*Med.*) pandemische Seuche, die Pandemie.
pandemonium [pændi'mouniəm], *s.* 1. (*Antiqu.*) die Hölle, Lästerstätte, das Pandämonium; 2. (*coll.*) der Höllenlärm, Höllenspektakel.
pander ['pændə], **1.** *s.* 1. der Kuppler, Zuhälter; (*fig.*) Handlanger; 2. die Verführung. **2.** *v.t.* verkuppeln. **3.** *v.i.* (*fig.*) *– to his ambition*, seinem Ehrgeiz Vorschub leisten, seinen Ehrgeiz unterstützen *or* stärken; ihn in seinem Ehrgeiz bestärken.
pane [pein], *s.* 1. die (Fenster)scheibe; 2. rechteckiges Feld *or* Fach; 3. die Füllung (*of a door*); 4. Pinne, Finne (*of a hammer*).
panegyric [pæni'dʒirik], **1.** *s.* die Lobrede, Lobpreisung, Lobschrift, Lobeserhebung (*on*, auf (*Acc.*)). **2.** *or* **panegyrical,** *adj.* lobpreisend, lobredend, Lob(es)-. **panegyrist,** *s.* der Lobredner. **panegyrize** ['pænidʒiraiz], *v.t., v.i.* lobpreisen, verherrlichen.
panel [pænl], **1.** *s.* 1. vertieftes, viereckiges Feld *or* Fach; die Tafel, Platte, Füllung (*of a door*); 2. das Einsatzstück (*of a dress*); 3. (*Elec.*) die Schalttafel; *instrument –*, das Armaturenbrett; 4. (*Archit.*) die Täfelung, getäfelte Wandbekleidung, das Paneel; 5. (*Av.*) (*also ground-–*) Grundtuch, Fliegertuch; 6. (*Law*) die Geschworenenliste (*of a jury*), Geschworenen (*pl.*); 7. das Forum, Podium, Gremium, der Ausschuß; *advisory –*, beratender Ausschuß; 8. die Liste, das Verzeichnis (der Krankenkassenärzte); *on the –*, zur Kassenpraxis zugelassen. **2.** *v.t.* täfeln, paneelieren; *panelled ceiling*, getäfelte Decke.
panel|-discussion, *s.* (*Rad., T.V.*) das Podiumsgespräch. **–-doctor,** *s.* der Kassenarzt. **– game,** *s.* (*Rad. etc.*) der Quiz. **panelling,** *s.* die Täfelung, das Tafelwerk, Getäfel, die Paneelierung. **panellist,** *s.* (*Rad. etc.*) der Diskussionsteilnehmer. **panel|-patient,** *s.* der Kassenpatient. **–-saw,** *s.* die Paneelsäge. **–-work,** *s.* das Tafelwerk.
pang [pæŋ], *s.* 1. stechender Schmerz, der Stich; 2. (*fig.*) aufschießende Pein *or* Qual *or* Angst; *–s of conscience* or *remorse*, Gewissensbisse (*pl.*), das Reuegefühl.
pangolin [pæŋ'goulin], *s.* (*Zool.*) der Pangolin, das Schuppentier.
panhandle ['pænhændl], *v.i.* (*Am. coll.*) betteln, schnorren.
[1]**panic** ['pænik], *s.* (*Bot.*) die Kolbenhirse.
[2]**panic, 1.** *adj.* panisch, fassungslos, verzweifelt. **2.** *s.* die Panik, panischer Schrecken, die Bestürzung; *in –*, von Schrecken ergriffen, panikartig. **3.** *v.i.* 1. von Schrecken ergriffen werden; 2. sich hinreißen lassen (*into doing*, zu tun). **panicky,** *adj.* (*coll.*) überängstlich.
panicle ['pænikl], *s.* (*Bot.*) die Rispe.
panic|-monger, *s.* der Bangemacher. **–-stricken, –-struck,** *adj.* von Schrecken ergriffen.
paniculate(d) [pæ'nikjuleit(id)], *adj.* (*Bot.*) rispenartig, rispenförmig.
panjandrum [pæn'dʒændrəm], *s.* 1. der Wichtigtuer, Bonze, großes Tier; 2. die Wichtigtuerei.
pannage ['pænidʒ], *s.* 1. die Buchmast, Eichelmast; 2. das Mastgeld; 3. Mastrecht.
pannier ['pæniə], *s.* 1. der Tragkorb, die Kiepe; 2. der Reifrock; 3. Aufwärter (*in the Inns of Court*).
pannikin ['pænikin], *s.* das (Trink)kännchen.
[1]**panning** ['pæniŋ], *s.* (*Films etc.*) das Schwenken, die Panoramierung; *– shot*, der Schwenk.
[2]**panning,** *s.* die Goldwäsche.
panoplied ['pænəplid], *adj.* 1. vollständig gerüstet; 2. geschmückt. **panoply,** *s.* 1. vollständige Rüstung; 2. (*fig.*) der Schmuck.
panorama [pænə'rɑ:mə], *s.* das Panorama, die Gesamtansicht; der Rundblick, (*fig.*) vollständiger Überblick (*of*, über (*Acc.*)). **panoramic** [-'ræmik], *adj.* Panorama-; (*fig.*) umfassend; *– lens*, das Weitwinkelobjektiv; *– view*, der Rundblick.
pansy ['pænzi], *s.* (*Bot.*) das Stiefmütterchen; 2. (*sl.*) der Zierbengel, Gigerl.
pant [pænt], **1.** *v.i.* 1. schwer atmen, keuchen, schnaufen, schnauben; *– for breath*, nach Luft schnappen; 2. (*fig.*) lechzen, dürsten (*after, for*, nach); (*coll.*) *be –ing for a drink*, großen Durst haben. **2.** *s.* das Keuchen, Schnaufen.
pantaloon ['pæntəlu:n], *s.* 1. der Hanswurst,

dummer August; 2. *pl.* das Beinkleid, Pantalons (*pl.*).

pantechnicon [pæn'teknikən], *s.* 1. der Möbelspeicher; 2. (*also* – *van*) Möbelwagen.

pantheism ['pænθiizm], *s.* der Pantheismus. **pantheist,** *s.* der Pantheist. **pantheistic** [–'istik], *adj.* pantheistisch.

pantheon ['pænθiən], *s.* die Ruhmeshalle, Gedächtnishalle, der Ehrentempel; (*Antiqu.*) das Pantheon.

panther ['pænθə], *s.* der Panther, Leopard (*Panthera pardus*), Jaguar (*P. onca*); ***American* –,** der Puma, Kuguar (*P. concolor*). **pantheress,** *s.* weiblicher Panther.

panties ['pæntiz], *pl.* (*coll.*) das Höschen, der Schlüpfer.

pantile ['pæntail], *s.* die Dachpfanne, der Pfannenziegel.

panto ['pæntou], *s.* (*coll.*) *see* **pantomime,** 2.

pantograph ['pæntəgrɑ:f], *s.* 1. (*Mech.*) der Storchschnabel; 2. (*Elec.*) Scherenstromabnehmer.

pantomime ['pæntəmaim], *s.* 1. das Gebärdenspiel, Mienenspiel; (*Hist.*) die Pantomime; 2. Weihnachtsrevue, revueartiges Märchenspiel. **pantomimic** [–'mimik], *adj.* pantomimisch.

pantry ['pæntri], *s.* die Speisekammer, Anrichte; (*Naut.*) der Anrichteraum.

pants [pænts], *pl.* die Unterhose; ***a pair of* –,** eine Unterhose; (*coll.*) die Hose; (*sl.*) ***kick in the* –,** der Tritt in den Hintern.

[1]**pap** [pæp], *s.* 1. die Brustwarze; 2. der Kegel, runde Hügel.

[2]**pap,** *s.* der (Kinder)brei, Papp, das Mus.

papa [pə'pɑ:], *s.* der Papa, Vati.

papacy ['peipəsi], *s.* 1. das Papsttum; 2. die Papstherrschaft. **papal,** *adj.* päpstlich; – ***crown,*** die Papstkrone; (*Hist.*) – ***states,*** der Kirchenstaat.

papaveraceous [pəpeivə'reiʃəs], **papaverous** [pə'peivərəs], *adj.* mohnartig, Mohn–.

papaw [pə'pɔ:], **papaya** [–'peijə], *s.* der Melonenbaum.

paper ['peipə], **1.** *s.* 1. (*no pl.*) das Papier; ***brown* –,** das Packpapier; ***carbon* –,** das Kohlenpapier; ***commit to* –,** zu Papier bringen; ***kraft* –,** see **brown** –; ***on* –,** auf dem Papier, theoretisch; ***put pen to* –,** zur Feder greifen; ***silver* –,** das Silberpapier; ***tissue* –,** das Seidenpapier; ***tracing* –,** das Pauspapier; ***waste* –,** das Altpapier; 2. (*also* ***wall–***–) die Tapete; 3. (*collect.*) (*Comm.*) Aktien, Wechsel, Wertpapiere, Effekten (*pl.*); (*also* ***––money***) das Papiergeld; 4. die Zeitung, das Blatt; ***daily* –,** die Tageszeitung, das Tageblatt; 5. der Aufsatz, Vortrag, (wissenschaftliche) Abhandlung (***on,*** über (*Acc.*)); ***read a* –,** einen Vortrag halten (***on,*** über (*Acc*)); 6. (*Univ. etc.*) schriftliche Prüfung, der Fragebogen, die Prüfungsarbeit; 7. das Heft, Büchlein, Päckchen, der Brief (*of pins etc.*); – ***of patterns,*** das Musterbuch, die Musterkarte; 8. (*only pl.*) amtliche Papiere, Ausweispapiere, Personalien (*pl.*), die Legitimation, der Ausweis; ***send in one's –s,*** den Abschied nehmen; 9. (*only pl.*) (*Law*) Briefschaften, Schriftstücke, (amtliche) Unterlagen, Dokumente, Akten (*pl.*). **2.** *adj.* 1. papieren, Papier–; (*Comm.*) – ***cover,*** die Papierdeckung; – ***credit,*** offener Wechselkredit; – ***currency*** or ***money,*** das Papiergeld; 2. dünn; leicht; 3. – ***army,*** ein Heer auf dem Papier; – ***war,*** der Federkrieg, Pressekrieg, die Pressefehde. **3.** *v.t.* 1. (*usu.* – ***up***) in Papier verpacken; 2. tapezieren (*a room*); 3. (*sl.*) (*Theat.*) durch Freikarten füllen.

paper|back, *s.* das Buch im Pappband, Paperback. **––bag,** *s.* die Tüte. **–board,** *s.* die Pappe. **–boy,** *s.* der Zeitungsjunge. **––carriage,** *s.* der (Schreibmaschinen)wagen. **––chase,** *s.* die Schnitzeljagd. **––clip,** *s.* die Heftklammer, Büroklammer. **––cutter,** *s.* die Papierschneidemaschine. **––fastener,** *s. See* **––clip. –hanger,** *s.* der Tapezierer. **papering,** *s.* das Tapezieren. **paper|-knife,** *s.* das Papiermesser, Falzbein. **–mill,** *s.* die Papierfabrik. **–weight,** *s.* 1. der Briefbeschwerer; 2. (*Boxing*) das Papiergewicht. **papery,** *adj.* papierartig, papierähnlich, (papier)dünn.

papier-mâché ['pæpjei'mæʃei], *s.* das Papiermaché.

papilionaceous [pəpiljə'neiʃəs], *adj.* 1. Schmetterlings–; 2. (*Bot.*) schmetterlingsblütig.

papilla [pə'pilə], *s.* die Papille, Warze, das Wärzchen. **papillary,** *adj.* warzenartig, Papillar–. **papillate, papillose** [–ous], *adj.* warzig; *see also* **papillary.**

papism ['peipizm], *s.* der Papismus. **papist,** *s.* der Papist, Römling. **papistic(al)** [pə'pistik(l)], *adj.* papistisch. **papistry** [–ri], *s.* die Papisterei, der Papismus.

papoose [pə'pou:s], *s.* das Indianerkind; (*coll.*) kleines Kind.

pappus ['pæpəs], *s.* (*pl.* **pappi**), (*Bot.*) die Haarkrone.

pappy ['pæpi], *adj.* breiig, breiartig, pappig, pampig, musartig.

papula ['pæpjulə], *s.* (*pl.* **papulae**) *see* **papule. papular,** *adj.* Knötchen–. **papule** [–ju:l], *s.* das Bläschen, Knötchen, die Pustel, Papel.

papyrus [pə'pairəs], *s.* (*pl.* **papyri** [–ai]) 1. (*Bot.*) der Papyrus, die Papyrusstaude; 2. Papyrusrolle.

par [pɑ:], *s.* 1. die Gleichheit, Gleichwertigkeit, Ebenbürtigkeit; (*sl.*) ***not up to* –, *below* –,** nicht auf der Höhe (*of health*); (*fig.*) ***be on a* –,** vergleichbar sein, sich (*Dat.*) die Waage halten; (*fig.*) ***be on a* – *with,*** gleich *or* ebenbürtig *or* gewachsen sein (*Dat.*), entsprechen (*Dat.*); ***put him on a* – *with,*** ihn gleichstellen (*Dat.*); 2. (*Comm.*) das Pari, der Nennwert; ***at* –,** pari, zum Nennwert; ***above* –,** über Pari; ***below*** or ***under* –,** unter Pari; – ***of exchange,*** die Wechselparität, der Parikurs; 3. (*Golf*) die Einheit.

para– ['pærə], *pref.* 1. abnorm, anomal; 2. ähnlich, neben.

parable ['pærəbl], *s.* die Parabel, das Gleichnis.

parabola [pə'ræbələ], *s.* (*Math.*) die Parabel. **parabolic** [pærə'bɔlik], *adj.* (*Math.*) parabolisch, Parabol–. **parabolical,** *adj.* parabolisch, gleichnishaft, allegorisch. **paraboloid,** *s.* das Paraboloid.

parachute ['pærəʃu:t], **1.** *s.* der Fallschirm; – ***cords,*** Fangleinen (*pl.*); – ***harness,*** der Fallschirmgurt; – ***jump,*** der Fallschirmabsprung; – ***mine,*** die Luftmine; – ***troops,*** Fallschirmtruppen (*pl.*). **2.** *v.i.* 1. mit Fallschirm abspringen; 2. (wie) mit einem Fallschirm schweben. **parachutist,** *s.* der Fallschirmspringer; (*Mil.*) Fallschirmjäger.

paraclete ['pærəkli:t], *s.* (*Theol.*) der Fürsprecher.

parade [pə'reid], **1.** *s.* 1. (*Mil.*) die Parade, der Vorbeimarsch (***before,*** vor (*Dat.*)); der Appell, das Antreten; ***on* –,** marschierend; 2. der Aufmarsch, (Um)zug; 3. (*fig.*) die Vorführung, das (Zur)schaustellung; (*fig.*) ***make a* – *of,*** prunken *or* Staat machen mit, zur Schau stellen; 4. (*street*) die Promenade, Esplanade; 5. (*Fenc.*) Parade, das Parieren. **2.** *v.t.* 1. paradieren *or* vorbeimarschieren lassen; antreten *or* aufmarschieren lassen (*troops*); 2. (*fig.*) protzen *or* prunken mit, zur Schau tragen; 3. (*coll.*) – ***the streets,*** auf der Straße auf und ab gehen. **3.** *v.i.* 1. (*Mil.*) antreten, aufmarschieren; (*also Pol. etc.*) paradieren, (vorbei)marschieren; 2. (*fig., coll.*) sich breit machen.

parade-ground, *s.* der Paradeplatz.

paradigm ['pærədaim], *s.* das Muster, Beispiel, Paradigma. **paradigmatic** [–dig'mætik], *adj.* paradigmatisch, typisch, beispielhaft.

paradisaic(al) [pærədi'zaiik(l)], *adj.* paradiesisch. **paradise** ['pærədais], *s.* das Paradies (*also fig.*); der Himmel; ***in* –,** im Paradiese; ***bird of* –,** der Paradiesvogel; ***fool's* –,** (verhängnisvoller) Irrtum; ***live in a fool's* –,** sich (*Dat.*) Illusionen hingeben.

parados ['pærədɔs], *s.* die Rückenwehr, Rückendeckung.

paradox ['pærədɔks], *s.* widersprüchliche Behauptung, der Widerspruch, das Paradox(on). **paradoxic(al)** [–'dɔksik(l)], *adj.* paradox, widersinnig, widersprüchlich.

paradrop ['pærədrɔp], *v.t.* (mit einem Fallschirm) abwerfen (*goods*) *or* absetzen (*men*).

paraffin ['pærəfin], *s.* das Paraffin; – ***heater*** or ***stove,*** (transportierbarer) Ölofen; – ***oil,*** das Paraffinöl, Leuchtpetroleum; – ***wax,*** das Paraffin.
paragon ['pærəgən], *s.* 1. das Muster, Vorbild; der Musterknabe; – ***of perfection,*** der Inbegriff aller Vollkommenheiten; – ***of virtue,*** das Muster von Tugend; 2. (*Typ.*) die Text.
paragraph ['pærəgra:f], *s.* 1. der Absatz, Abschnitt, Paragraph; 2. kurzer Zeitungsartikel; 3. (*Typ.*) das Absatzzeichen. **paragrapher, paragraphist,** *s.* der Kleinartikelschreiber.
Paraguay ['pærugwai], *s.* 1. der Paraguay (*river*); 2. Paraguay (*n.*) (*state*). **Paraguayan** [–'gwaiən], **1.** *s.* der (die) Paraguayer(in). **2.** *adj.* paraguayisch.
parakeet ['pærəki:t], *s.* der (Halsband)sittich.
paralipomena [pærəli'pɔminə], *pl.* Ergänzungen, Nachträge (*pl.*).
parallactic [pærə'læktik], *adj.* parallaktisch. **parallax** ['pærəlæks], *s.* die Parallaxe.
parallel ['pærəlel], **1.** *adj.* 1. parallel (*to, **with,*** zu *or* mit); (*Gymn.*) – ***bars,*** der Barren; (*Elec.*) – ***connection,*** die Parallelschaltung, Nebeneinanderschaltung; – ***ruler,*** das Parallellineal; 2. (*fig.*) gleich(gerichtet), gleichlaufend, gleichlautend, entsprechend, ähnlich; – ***case,*** der Parallelfall; (*fig.*) ***on – lines,*** in der gleichen Richtung. **2.** *s.* 1. die Parallele (*also fig.*), Parallellinie; ***draw a – between,*** einen Vergleich anstellen *or* eine Parallele ziehen zwischen (*Dat.*), vergleichen mit; (*Elec.*) ***in –,*** parallel(geschaltet), nebeneinander(geschaltet); 2. (*Geog.*) der Parallelkreis, Breitenkreis; – ***of latitude,*** der Breitenkreis; 3. (*fig.*) die Parallelität, Übereinstimmung, Ähnlichkeit; 4. Entsprechung, das Gegenstück, der Vergleich; ***without –,*** ohnegleichen. **3.** *v.t.* 1. (*usu. fig.*) als gleich *or* ähnlich hinstellen; 2. in Einklang bringen, vergleichen (***with,*** mit); ***be –ed to,*** sich vergleichen lassen mit, nicht zurückstehen hinter (*Dat.*), entsprechen (*Dat.*); 3. ein Gegenstück *or* etwas Entsprechendes *or* Gleichartiges finden zu, angleichen; 4. gleichkommen (*Dat.*), entsprechen (*Dat.*).
parallelism ['pærəlelizm], *s.* der Parallelismus, die Parallelität (*also fig.*); (*fig.*) Ähnlichkeit, Übereinstimmung. **parallelogram** [–'leləgræm], *s.* das Parallelogram.
paralogism [pə'rælədʒizm], *s.* der Trugschluß, Fehlschluß.
paralysation [pærəlai'zeiʃən], *s.* 1. die Lähmung; 2. (*fig.*) Lahmlegung. **paralyse** ['pærəlaiz], *v.t.* 1. lähmen, paralysieren; 2. (*fig.*) lahmlegen. **paralysis** [pə'rælisis], *s.* 1. die Lähmung, Paralyse; 2. (*fig.*) Lahmlegung. **paralytic** [–'litik], **1.** *adj.* gelähmt, paralytisch. **2.** *s.* der Paralytiker, Gelähmte(r).
paralyze, (*Am.*) *see* **paralyse.**
parameter [pæ'ræmitə], *s.* (*Math.*) der Parameter.
paramilitary [pærə'militəri], *adj.* halbmilitärisch, militärähnlich.
paramount ['pærəmaunt], **1.** *adj.* oberst, übergeordnet, höchst, (*fig.*) vorherrschend, überragend, ausschlaggebend; ***be –,*** über alles gehen, an erster Stelle stehen, ausschlaggebend sein; ***be – to,*** höher stehen als, wichtiger sein als. **2.** *s.* (***lord –***) der Oberlehnsherr. **paramountly,** *adv.* vornehmlich, vor allem.
paramour ['pærəmuə], *s.* der Liebhaber, Geliebte(r).
paranoia [pærə'nɔiə], *s.* die Paranoia. **paranoic,** *adj.* paranoisch. **paranoid** ['pærənɔid], *adj.* paranoid.
parapet ['pærəpit], *s.* 1. (*Mil.*) die Brustwehr; 2. (*Archit.*) das (Schutz)geländer, die Brückenmauer; Brüstung.
paraph ['pærəf], *s.* der Namenszug, Handzug; Paraph, die Paraphe, der Schnörkel (*of signature*).
paraphernalia [pærəfə'neiliə], *pl.* 1. (*Law*) das Paraphernalgut; 2. (*coll.*) (*sing. constr.*) Zubehör, Drum und Dran.
paraphrase ['pærəfreiz], **1.** *s.* die Umschreibung, Paraphrase, freie Wiedergabe. **2.** *v.t., v.i.* umschreiben, frei wiedergeben. **paraphrastic** [–'fræstik], *adj.* umschreibend, paraphrastisch.
paraplegia [pærə'pli:dʒiə], *s.* die Querschnittslähmung, Paraplexie, Paraplegie.
parasite ['pærəsait], *s.* der Schmarotzer (*also fig.*), Parasit; (*coll.*) Nassauer (*of persons*). **parasitic** [–'sitik], *adj.* schmarotzend, Schmarotzer–, parasitisch, parisitär; (*Elec.*) – ***current,*** der Wirbelstrom, Kriechstrom; (*Av.*) – ***drag,*** schädlicher (Luft)widerstand; (*Rad.*) – ***noise,*** das Störgeräusch, Fremdgeräusch. **parasitical** [–'sitikl], *adj. See* **parasitic. parasitism,** *s.* das Schmarotzertum, der Parasitismus; (*fig.*) das Schmarotzen.
parasol ['pærəsɔl], *s.* der Sonnenschirm.
paratactic [pærə'tæktik], *adj.* beigeordnet, parataktisch. **parataxis,** *s.* die Nebenordnung, Beiordnung.
parathyroid [pærə'θairɔid], *s.* (*also* – ***gland***) die Nebenschilddrüse.
paratroops ['pærətru:ps], *pl.* Fallschirmjäger, Luftlandetruppen (*pl.*).
paratyphoid [pærə'taifɔid], *s.* der Paratyphus.
paravane ['pærəvein], *s.* (*Naut.*) das Bugschutzgerät (*against mines*).
parboil ['pa:bɔil], *v.t.* 1. halb kochen, aufkochen lassen, ankochen, abbrühen; 2. (*fig.*) überhitzen.
parbuckle ['pa:bʌkl], **1.** *s.* das Jolltau. **2.** *v.t.* (*Naut.*) mit Jolltau heben.
parcel [pa:sl], **1.** *s.* 1. das Paket, Päckchen, Bündel; 2. die Parzelle (*of land*); 3. (*Comm.*) der Posten, die Partie; 4. (*obs.*) (*only in*) ***part and – of,*** wesentliches Bestandteil von. **2.** *v.t.* 1. (*usu.* – ***out***) abteilen, aufteilen, austeilen, verteilen; parzellieren (*land*); 2. (*also* – ***up***) (ver)packen, einpacken, zusammenpacken (*goods*); 3. (*Naut.*) (be)schmarten (*rope*). **3.** *adv.* (*obs.*) teilweise, halb–. **parcelling,** *s.* 1. die Einteilung; 2. (*Naut.*) Schmarting. **parcel|-office,** *s.* die Gepäckabfertigung(sstelle). **– post,** *s.* die Paketpost.
parcenary ['pa:sinəri], *s.* (*Law*) der Mitbesitz (durch Erbschaft). **parcener,** *s.* der Miterbe.
parch [pa:tʃ], **1.** *v.t.* dörren, austrocknen; ***be –ed with thirst,*** vor Durst verschmachten; ***–ed corn,*** gerösteter Mais; ***–ed lips,*** trockene Lippen. **2.** *v.i.* vertrocknen, eintrocknen. **parching,** *adj.* sengend (*heat*), brennend (*thirst*).
parchment ['pa:tʃmənt], *s.* das Pergament, die (Pergament)urkunde.
pard [pa:d], *s.* (*sl.*) der Partner, Kumpel.
pardon [pa:dn], **1.** *s.* 1. die Verzeihung, Vergebung; ***I beg your –,*** (*as implied question*) wie bitte? (*as apology*) entschuldigen *or* verzeihen Sie! ***ask*** or ***beg his –,*** ihn um Entschuldigung *or* Verzeihung bitten; ***a thousand –s,*** ich bitte tausendmal um Verzeihung; 2. die Begnadigung; Amnestie, der Straferlaß; ***general –,*** die Amnestie; 3. (*Eccl.*) der Ablaß. **2.** *v.t.* 1. verzeihen (*Dat.*), vergeben (*Dat.*), entschuldigen (*a p.*); – ***me!*** verzeihen *or* entschuldigen Sie! 2. die Strafe erlassen (*Dat.*), das Leben schenken (*Dat.*), begnadigen. **pardonable,** *adj.* verzeihlich (*mistake*), läßlich (*sin*). **pardoner,** *s.* (*Hist.*) der Ablaßkrämer.
pare [pɛə], *v.t.* (be)schneiden (*nails etc.*); schälen (*apples etc.*); – ***away*** or ***off,*** abschneiden; (*Tech.*) abschälen, abschaben; (*fig.*) – ***down,*** beschränken, einschränken, beschneiden.
paregoric [pærə'gɔrik], **1.** *adj.* schmerzstillend. **2.** *s.* das Linderungsmittel.
parenchyma [pə'renkimə], *s.* (*Anat.*) das Parenchym, Grundgewebe; (*Bot.*) Zellgewebe.
parent ['pɛərənt], **1.** *s.* 1. der Elternteil; Vater, die Mutter; *pl.* Eltern (*pl.*); 2. (*Zool.*) das Muttertier, (*Bot.*) die Mutterpflanze; 3. (*fig.*) Ursache, Quelle, der Urheber, Ursprung. **2.** *adj.* (*Biol.*) Mutter– (*also fig.*); (*fig.*) Ur–, (*Comm.*) Stamm–, Dach–; – ***cell,*** die Mutterzelle; – ***company,*** das Stammhaus; – ***form,*** die Urform, Urgestalt; – ***organization,*** die Dachorganisation; (*Naut.*) – ***ship,*** das Mutterschiff, Begleitschiff; (*Mil.*) – ***unit,*** der Stammtruppenteil.

parentage ['pεərəntidʒ], *s.* 1. die Abkunft, Abstammung, Familie; 2. Elternschaft; 3. (*fig.*) Herkunft, der Ursprung. **parental** [pə'rentl], *adj.* elterlich, Eltern–; – *roof,* das Elternhaus.

parenthesis [pə'renθəsis], *s.* (*pl.* **-theses** [–θəsi:z]) 1. die Einschaltung, Parenthese, der Einschub; *in –, by way of –,* beiläufig, nebenbei; 2. (*Typ.*) (*usu. pl.*) (runde) Klammern; *put in parentheses,* einklammern. **parenthesize,** *v.t.* 1. einschalten, einflechten; 2. (*Typ.*) einklammern. **parenthetic(al)** [pærən'θetik(l)], *adj.* 1. eingeschaltet, eingeflochten; 2. (*Typ.*) eingeklammert.

parenthood ['pεərənthud], *s.* die Elternschaft. **parentless,** *adj.* elternlos, verwaist. **parent-teacher association,** *s.* der Elternbeirat.

paresis ['pærəsis], *s.* (*Med.*) die Parese. **paretic** [–'retik], *adj.* paretisch, Parese–, Lähmungs–.

par excellence [pɑ:'ekselɑ̃s], *adv.* schlechthin, vor allen anderen, im wahren Sinne des Wortes.

parget ['pɑ:dʒit], **1.** *s.* der Bewurf, Stuck, (Wand)-putz. **2.** *v.t.* verputzen. **parget(t)ing,** *s.* die Stuckarbeit, Stuckverzierung.

parhelion [pɑ:'hi:liən], *s.* die Nebensonne, Gegensonne, das Parhelium.

pariah [pə'raiə], *s.* 1. der Paria; 2. (*fig.*) Ausgestoßene(r), Entrechtete(r), Rechtlose(r), Verachtete(r).

Parian ['pεəriən], *adj.* (*Geog.*) parisch.

parietal [pə'riətl], **1.** *adj.* (*Anat.*) parietal. **2.** *s.* (– *bone*) das Scheitelbein.

paring ['pεəriŋ], **1.** *s. See* **pare**; 1. das Abschneiden, Abschaben, Schälen; 2. *pl.* Schnitzel, Späne, Schabsel (*pl.*); Schalen (*pl.*) (*of potatoes etc.*). **2.** *attrib. adj.* Schab–, Schäl–.

pari passu ['pæri'pæsju:], *adv.* gleichzeitig, gleichlaufend.

Paris ['pæris], *s.* Paris (*n.*); *plaster of –,* gebrannter Gips.

parish ['pæriʃ], **1.** *s.* 1. das Kirchspiel, der Pfarrbezirk, Sprengel; 2. (*collect.*) die Gemeinde, Gemeindemitglieder (*pl.*); *come* or *go on the –,* der Gemeinde zur Last fallen; *be on the –,* der Gemeinde zur Last liegen. **2.** *attrib. adj.* 1. Pfarr–, Kirchen–; – *church,* die Pfarrkirche; – *clerk,* der Küster; – *priest,* der Ortspfarrer; – *register,* das Kirchenbuch; 2. Gemeinde–; – *council,* der Gemeinderat; *–-pump politics,* die Kirchturmpolitik; – *relief,* die Gemeindeunterstützung. **parishioner** [pə'riʃənə], *s.* das Pfarrkind, Gemeindemitglied.

Parisian [pə'riziən], **1.** *s.* der Pariser. **2.** *adj.* parisisch, Pariser–. **Parisienne** [–i'en], *s.* die Pariserin.

parisyllabic [pærisi'læbik], *adj.* gleichsilbig.

parity ['pæriti], *s.* 1. die Gleichheit, Gleichberechtigung; – *of esteem with,* gleiche Würdigung wie; 2. (*Comm.*) die Parität, der Umrechnungskurs, Pariwert; *at –,* pari, zu Pari.

park [pɑ:k], **1.** *s.* 1. der Park, die Parkanlage, das Parkgelände, öffentliche Anlage; *national –,* das Naturschutzgebiet; 2. (*Motor.*) der Parkplatz; 3. (*Mil.*) die Sammelstelle, der Fuhrpark, Geschützpark. **2.** *v.t.* 1. (*Motor.*) abstellen, parken; 2. (*Mil.*) lagern, deponieren; 3. (*coll.*) abstellen lassen; (*sl.*) – *o.s.,* sich setzen *or* niederlassen. **3.** *v.i.* parken.

parkin ['pɑ:kin], *s.* der Honigkuchen, Pfefferkuchen.

parking ['pɑ:kiŋ], *s.* das Parken; – *light,* das Standlicht; – *meter,* die Parkuhr; – *place* (*Am. lot*), der Parkplatz; – *problem,* das Parkproblem; – *space,* die Parklücke; (*coll.*) – *ticket,* polizeiliche Vorladung (wegen verkehrswidrigen Parkens); *no –!* Parkverbot! Parken verboten!

park|-keeper, *s.* der Parkaufseher. **–land,** *s.* leichtbewaldetes Grasland. **parky,** *adj.* (*coll.*) kalt, windig, ungeschützt.

parlance ['pɑ:ləns], *s.* die Redeweise; *in common –,* wie man sich gewöhnlich ausdrückt, auf gut deutsch; *in legal –,* juristisch ausgedrückt.

parley ['pɑ:li], **1.** *v.i.* (*Mil.*) verhandeln, unterhandeln, parlamentieren. **2.** *v.t.* (*sl.*) parlieren. **3.** *s.* 1. die Unterhandlung, Unterredung; 2. (*esp. Mil.*) (Waffenstillstands)verhandlungen (*pl.*); (*Hist.*) *beat* or *sound a –,* Schamade schlagen.

parliament ['pɑ:ləmənt], *s.* das Parlament; *act of –,* der Parlamentsbeschluß, das Reichsgesetz; *enter* or *get into* or *go into –,* ins Parlament gewählt werden; *in –,* im Parlament; *member of –,* das Parlamentsmitglied, Abgeordnete(r). **parliamentarian** [–'tεəriən], **1.** *s.* 1. der Parlamentarier; 2. (*Hist.*) Parlamentsanhänger. **2.** *adj.* parlamentarisch. **parliamentarianism,** *s.* der Parlamentarismus. **parliamentary** [–'mentəri], *adj.* Parlaments–, parlamentarisch, (*fig.*) höflich; – *language,* höfliche Redensart; – *roll,* das Verzeichnis der Stimmberechtigten; – *secretary,* der Parlamentssekretär.

parlor, (*Am.*) *see* **parlour.**

parlour ['pɑ:lə], *s.* das Wohnzimmer, gute Stube, der Salon; das Empfangszimmer, Besuchszimmer, Sprechzimmer; Gästezimmer (*in inns*); *beauty-–,* der Schönheitssalon; *ice-cream –,* die Eisdiele.

parlour|-car, *s.* (*Am.*) der Salonwagen. **–-game,** *s.* das Gesellschaftsspiel. **–-maid,** *s.* das Stubenmädchen.

parlous ['pɑ:ləs], *adj.* (*obs.*) gefährlich, (*coll.*) furchtbar, schlimm, kritisch.

Parmesan [pɑ:mi'zæn], *adj.* parmesanisch, Parmesan–; – (*cheese*), der Parmesankäse.

Parnassian [pɑ:'næsiən], *adj.* parnassisch, (*fig.*) poetisch, dichterisch. **Parnassus,** *s.* (*Antiqu.*) der Parnaß.

parochial [pə'roukiəl], *adj.* 1. Pfarr–, Gemeinde–, Kirchspiel–; 2. (*fig.*) eng(herzig), beschränkt, begrenzt, provinzlerisch; – *point of view,* enger Horizont; – *politics,* die Kirchturmpolitik. **parochialism,** *s.* 1. die Engherzigkeit, Engstirnigkeit, Beschränktheit, Spießigkeit; 2. Kirchturmpolitik.

parodist ['pærədist], *s.* der Verfasser von Parodien. **parody** [–di], **1.** *s.* die Parodie (*of, auf* (*Acc.*)), Parodierung (*Gen.*); (*fig.*) Entstellung, Verzerrung. **2.** *v.t.* parodieren.

parol [pə'roul], *s.* (*Law*) mündliche Erklärung; *by –,* mündlich.

parole [pə'roul], **1.** *s.* 1. (*esp. Mil.*) das Ehrenwort; *on –,* auf Ehrenwort; 2. (*Law*) bedingte Haftentlassung, (bedingter) Straferlaß; – *board,* die Kommission für Haftentlassungen; *put* or *release on –,* bedingt entlassen; 3. (*Mil.*) die Parole, Losung, das Losungswort, Erkennungswort, Kennwort. **2.** *v.t.* 1. auf Ehrenwort verpflichten; 2. (*Law*) bedingt entlassen.

paronym ['pærənim], *s.* stammverwandtes Wort, die Lehnübersetzung, das Paronym(on). **paronymic, paronymous** [–'rɔniməs], *adj.* stammverwandt, lehnübersetzt.

paroquet ['pærəket], *s. See* **parakeet.**

parotid [pə'rɔtid], *adj.* – *gland,* die Ohrspeicheldrüse.

paroxysm ['pærəksizm], *s.* der (Krampf)anfall, Paroxysmus (*also fig.*); – *of laughter,* der Lachanfall. **paroxysmal** [–'sizməl], *adj.* krampfartig.

paroxytone [pə'rɔksitoun], *s.* das Paroxytonon.

parpen ['pɑ:pən], *s.* der Tragstein, Binder.

parquet [pɑ:'ket], **1.** *s.* das Parkett (*also Theat.*); [*also* 'pɑ:kei] der Parkett(fuß)boden. **2.** *v.t.* parkettieren. **parquetry** ['pɑ:kitri], *s.* die Parkettarbeit, getäfelter Fußboden.

parr [pɑ:], *s.* junger Lachs, der Sälmling.

parricidal [pæri'saidl], *adj.* vatermörderisch, muttermörderisch. **parricide** ['pærisaid], *s.* 1. der Vatermörder, Muttermörder, Elternmörder; Landesverräter; 2. Vatermord, Muttermord, Elternmord; Landesverrat.

parrot ['pærət], **1.** *s.* der Papagei; (*fig.*) Nachschwätzer; *repeat –-fashion,* gedankenlos nachplappern. **2.** *v.t.* nachplappern.

parry ['pæri], **1.** *s.* 1. (*Fenc.*) die Parade; 2. Abwehrbewegung, der Fangstoß. **2.** *v.t., v.i.* parieren, abwehren.

parse [pɑ:z], *v.t.* grammatisch zerlegen *or* zergliedern *or* analysieren *or* definieren.

Parsee [ˈpɑ:ˈsi:], *s.* 1. der Parse; 2. (*language*) das Parsi(k).

parsimonious [pɑ:siˈmouniəs], *adj.* 1. sparsam, karg (*of*, mit); 2. knauserig, knickerig. **parsimoniousness, parsimony** [ˈpɑ:siməni], *s.* die Sparsamkeit, Kargheit, Knauserei; Knauserigkeit.

parsley [ˈpɑ:sli], *s.* die Petersilie.

parsnip [ˈpɑ:snip], *s.* der Pastinak, die Pastinake; Pastinakwurzel; (*coll.*) ***fine words butter no –s***, mit Worten allein ist nicht geholfen.

parson [pɑ:sn], *s.* (*coll.*) der Pfarrer, Pastor, Geistliche(r); (*coll.*) ***–'s nose***, der Bürzel. **parsonage,** *s.* 1. das Pfarrhaus; 2. die Pfarre.

part [pɑ:t], **1.** *s.* 1. der *or* das Teil; das Stück, Glied; ***be – and parcel of***, ein wesentlicher Bestandteil sein von; ***component*** or ***constituent –***, der Bestandteil; ***form a – of***, einen Teil bilden von; ***a great – of***, ein großer Teil von; ***for the greater –***, größtenteils, in den meisten Fällen; ***in –***, teilweise, zum Teil; in gewissem Grade; ***in large –***, zum großen Teil; ***payment in –***, die Teilzahlung, Abschlagzahlung; ***private*** or ***privy –s***, Schamteile, Geschlechtsteile (*pl.*); ***– of speech***, der Redeteil, die Wortklasse; 2. (*oft. pl.*) die Gegend, der Bezirk; ***from all –s***, von allen Ecken und Enden; ***in foreign –s***, im Auslande; ***in these –s***, hierzulande, in dieser Gegend; 3. der Anteil, die Beteiligung; ***be art and – in***, Anteil haben an (*Dat.*); ***take – in***, teilnehmen an (*Dat.*); 4. die Partei, Seite; ***for my –***, was mich (an)betrifft, meinerseits, ich für meinen Teil; ***on the – of***, von seiten, seitens (*Gen.*); ***on my –***, meinerseits; ***take his –***, seine Partei ergreifen; ***take in good*** (***bad***) ***–***, gut (übel) aufnehmen; 5. die Lieferung (*of a book*); ***in –s***, in Lieferungen; 6. (*Theat., fig.*) die Rolle; ***act a –***, eine Rolle spielen; ***play a –***, eine Rolle spielen (*also fig.*), (*fig.*) von Bedeutung sein; ***play one's –***, seinen Teil dazu beitragen; ***take a –***, eine Rolle übernehmen; 7. die Obliegenheit, Aufgabe, Schuldigkeit, Pflicht, (*coll.*) Sache; ***it is not my –***, es ist nicht meine Pflicht (***to do***, zu tun); ***do one's –***, seine Schuldigkeit *or* das Seinige tun; 8. (*Mus.*) die Einzelstimme, Partie, das Einzelinstrument; 9. *pl.* (geistige) Fähigkeiten *or* Anlagen (*pl.*), das Talent; ***he is a man of*** (***many***) ***–s***, er ist ein fähiger Kopf, er ist vielseitig begabt. **2.** *adv.* teils, teilweise, zum Teil. **3.** *v.t.* 1. (zer)teilen; 2. trennen (***from***, von), abgrenzen (gegen); ***– company with***, sich trennen von; (*fig.*) anderer Meinung sein als; 3. (*Chem.*) scheiden; 4. scheiteln (*the hair*). **4.** *v.i.* sich trennen (*as roads*); auseinandergehen, scheiden; sich lösen, (entzwei)brechen, zerreißen; ***– from***, sich trennen *or* scheiden von, Abschied nehmen von (*a p.*); ***– with***, aufgeben, fahren lassen, loswerden; verkaufen; sich für immer trennen von; ***–*** (***as***) ***friends***, als Freunde auseinandergehen; ***– with one's money***, mit dem Geld herausrücken.

partake [pɑ:ˈteik], *irr.v.i.* teilnehmen, teilhaben (***in***, an (*Dat.*)); ***– of***, etwas an sich (*Dat.*) haben von; ***– of a meal***, eine Mahlzeit einnehmen *or* zu sich nehmen. **partaker,** *s.* der Teilnehmer, Teilhaber (***of***, an (*Dat.*)).

parterre [pɑ:ˈtɛə], *s.* 1. das Blumenbeet; 2. (*Theat.*) Parterre.

parthenogenesis [pɑ:θənoˈdʒenisis], *s.* die Parthenogenese, (*Zool.*) Jungfernzeugung; (*Bot.*) Jungfernfrüchtigkeit.

Parthian [ˈpɑ:θiən], **1.** *s.* der (die) Parther(in). **2.** *adj.* parthisch; ***– shot***, der Partherpfeil, (*fig.*) spitzige Bemerkung beim Abgehen.

partial [ˈpɑ:ʃəl], *adj.* 1. partiell, unvollständig, Halb–, Teil–; ***– acceptance***, bedingte Annahme; ***– bond***, der Teilschuldschein; ***– eclipse***, partielle Verfinsterung; ***– fraction***, der Partialbruch; ***– success***, der Halberfolg; 2. parteiisch, eingenommen (***to***, für), einseitig; ***be – to***, sehr gerne haben, eine besondere Vorliebe haben für. **partiality** [–ʃiˈæliti], *s.* 1. die Parteilichkeit, Voreingenommenheit; 2. besondere Vorliebe (***to, for***, für). **partially,** *adv.* zum Teil, teilweise.

participance, participancy [pɑ:ˈtisipəns(i)], *s.* die Teilnahme, Teilhaftigkeit. **participant,** *s.* der (die) Teilnehmer(in) (***in***, an (*Dat.*)). **participate** [–peit], *v.i.* teilhaben, teilnehmen, sich beteiligen, beteiligt sein (***in***, an (*Dat.*)). **participating,** *adj.* 1. (*Comm.*) gewinnberechtigt, Gewinnbeteiligungs–; 2. (*of a p.*) (mit) beteiligt. **participation** [–ˈpeiʃən], *s.* 1. die Mitwirkung, Teilnahme, Beteiligung (***in***, an (*Dat.*)); 2. (Gewinn)beteiligung, Teilhaberschaft. **participator,** *s.* *See* **participant.**

participial [pɑ:tiˈsipiəl], *adj.* (*Gram.*) partizipial. **participle** [ˈpɑ:tisipl], *s.* das Partizip(ium), Mittelwort.

particle [ˈpɑ:tikl], *s.* 1. das Teilchen, Stückchen, bißchen; (*coll.*) ***not a – of***, kein bißchen *or* Fünkchen *or* keine Spur von; 2. (*Phys.*) das Stoffteilchen, Körperchen; 3. (*Gram.*) die Partikel.

parti-coloured [pɑ:tiˈkʌləd], *adj.* bunt, verschiedenfarbig.

particular [pəˈtikjulə], **1.** *adj.* 1. einzeln, individuell, speziell, besonder; ***nothing –***, nichts Besonderes; ***for no – reason***, aus keinem besonderen Grund; 2. sonderbar, außergewöhnlich, eigentümlich; 3. umständlich, peinlich, genau, wählerisch; heikel, eigen; ***be – about***, es genau nehmen mit, Wert legen auf (*Acc.*); ***not be too –***, es nicht zu genau nehmen, nicht zu wählerisch sein; ***he is not – to a day***, es kommt ihm auf einen Tag nicht an. **2.** *s.* 1. einzelner Punkt, besonderer Umstand, die Einzelheit; ***in –***, insbesondere, im besonderen, besonders, vornehmlich; ***argue from the general to the –***, vom Allgemeinen auf das Besondere schließen; ***on this –***, in diesem Punkt; 2. *pl.* *See* **particulars.**

particularism [pəˈtikjulərizm], *s.* 1. der Partikularismus, die Kleinstaaterei; 2. Sonderbestrebung. **particularity** [– læriti], *s.* 1. die Genauigkeit, Ausführlichkeit, Umständlichkeit; 2. Besonderheit, Eigentümlichkeit, besonderer Umstand, besondere Bewandtnis. **particularization** [–ləraiˈzeiʃən], *s.* die Einzelbehandlung, Detailschilderung. **particularize, 1.** *v.t.* einzeln *or* umständlich anführen, ausführlich angeben, partikularisieren, spezifizieren, eingehend darstellen, besonders hervorheben. **2.** *v.i.* ins einzelne gehen, auf Einzelheiten eingehen. **particularly,** *adv.* besonders, insbesondere, im besonderen, vorzüglich, hauptsächlich, ausdrücklich; (***more***) ***– as***, um so mehr als; ***most –***, höchst angelegentlich; ***not –***, nicht sonderlich. **particulars,** *pl.* Einzelheiten, nähere Umstände (*pl.*), nähere Auskunft, Nähere(s); (*of a p.*) Personalien (*pl.*); ***for – apply within***, Näheres hierbei; ***for – apply to . . ., further – from . . .***, Näheres (erfährt man) bei . . .; ***enter*** or ***go into –***, *see* **particularize, 2.**

parting [ˈpɑ:tiŋ], **1.** *attrib. adj.* 1. Scheide–, Abschieds–; ***– breath***, letzter Atemzug; ***– kiss***, der Abschiedskuß; (*fig.*) ***– shot***, spitzige Bemerkung beim Abgehen; 2. Trennungs–; (*Tech.*) ***– tool***, der Geißfuß. **2.** *s.* 1. das Teilen, die Teilung; 2. Trennung, das Scheiden, der Abschied; ***at –***, beim Weggehen *or* Abschied; 3. der Scheitel, die Trennlinie (*of hair*); 4. Gabelung (*of roads*); ***– of the ways***, die Wegscheide, (*fig.*) der Scheideweg; 5. (*Chem.*) die Scheidung; 6. (*Naut.*) der Bruch, das (Zer)reißen.

1**partisan** [ˈpɑ:tizən], *s.* (*Hist.*) die Partisane, Hellebarde.

2**partisan** [pɑ:tiˈzæn], *s.* 1. der Anhänger, Parteigenosse, Parteigänger; ***– spirit***, der Parteigeist; 2. (*Mil.*) der Freischärler, Partisan. **partisanship,** *s.* 1. das Parteigängertum, die Parteianhängerschaft, lebhafte Parteinahme; 2. die Parteiwirtschaft, Cliquenwirtschaft.

partite [ˈpɑ:tait], *adj.* 1. (*Bot.*) geteilt; 2. (*as suff.*) –teilig.

partition [pɑ:ˈtiʃən], **1.** *s.* 1. die (Ver)teilung, Zerteilung, Aufteilung; 2. (*Math.*) Zerlegung; 3. Trennung, Absonderung; 4. Abteilung, der Verschlag, das Fach (*of cupboard etc.*), die Scheidewand (*also Bot.*); – ***wall***, die Brandmauer, Zwischenmauer. **2.** *v.t.* (ver)teilen, aufteilen; – ***off***, abteilen, abtrennen.

partitive ['pɑːtitiv], **1.** *adj.* 1. Teil–, teilend; 2. (*Gram.*) partitiv. **2.** *s.* (*Gram.*) das Partitivum.

partlet ['pɑːtlit], *s.* (*Hist.*) die Halskrause; ***Dame Partlet***, Frau Kratzfuß.

partly ['pɑːtli], *adv.* teils, zum Teil, in gewissem Grade; – ***closed***, teilweise geschlossen. **part-music,** *s.* mehrstimmige (Vokal)musik.

partner ['pɑːtnə], **1.** *s.* 1. der (die) Teilnehmer(in) (***in***, an (*Dat.*)); der Genosse (die Genossin); 2. (*Comm.*) der Teilhaber, Gesellschafter, Kompagnon, Associé, Sozius; ***limited*** –, der Kommanditist; ***senior*** –, älterer Teilhaber; ***sleeping*** ((*Am.*) ***silent***) –, stiller Teilhaber; 3. (*Spt. etc.*) der (die) Mitspieler(in), (Spiel)partner(in), (Tanz)partner(in); ***be –s***, zusammenspielen; 4. der Gatte (die Gattin), Lebenskamerad(in); 5. (*Naut.*) Fischungen (*pl.*). **2.** *v.t.* (*Spt. etc.*) als Partner spielen mit. **partnership,** *s.* 1. (offene) Handelsgesellschaft, die Genossenschaft; ***limited*** –, die Kommanditgesellschaft; ***deed of*** –, der Gesellschaftsvertrag; ***take him into*** –, ihn als Teilhaber aufnehmen; 2. die Mitbeteiligung, Teilhaberschaft (***in***, an (*Dat.*)); ***enter into*** –, sich assoziieren (***with***, mit); 3. (*Spt. etc.*) die Partnerschaft.

part|-owner, *s.* der (die) Miteigentümer(in). **–-payment,** *s.* die Teilzahlung, Abschlagzahlung; ***in*** –, auf Abschlag.

partridge ['pɑːtridʒ], *s.* (*Orn.*) das Rebhuhn (*Perdix perdix*).

part|-singing, *s.* mehrstimmiger Gesang. **–-song,** *s.* mehrstimmiges Lied. **–-time,** *adj.* nicht vollzeitig; – ***work***, die Nebenbeschäftigung, Halbtagsbeschäftigung; – ***worker***, (*coll.*) ***part-timer***, der Kurzarbeiter, Halbtagsarbeiter, (Aus)hilfsarbeiter.

parturient [pɑː'tjuəriənt], *adj.* gebärend, kreißend, (*fig.*) schwanger. **parturition** [–'riʃən], *s.* das Gebären, Kreißen, die Entbindung, Niederkunft.

party ['pɑːti], **1.** *s.* 1. (*Pol., Law*) die Partei; 2. (*Law*) streitender Teil; (*Comm.*) der Teilnehmer, Teilhaber, Interessent, Beteiligte(r) (***to***, an (*Dat.*)); ***be*** (***a***) – ***to***, beteiligt sein *or* teilnehmen an (*Dat.*) *or* bei, zu tun haben mit; ***the parties concerned***, die Beteiligten *or* Betroffenen; (*Comm.*) ***contracting*** or ***interested*** –, der Kontrahent; ***offended*** –, beleidigter Teil; ***third*** –, der Dritte; 3. (*Mil.*) das Kommando, die Abteilung; 4. (*Spt. etc.*) Partie, Gruppe, Gesellschaft; ***hunting*** –, die Jagdgesellschaft; ***make one of the*** –, sich der Gesellschaft anschließen; 5. (*social*) die Party, Gesellschaft, (geselliges) Beisammensein; ***give*** or ***throw a*** –, eine Party *or* Gesellschaft geben; ***bottle*** –, die Bottleparty; ***tea*** –, die Teegesellschaft; ***go to a*** –, eingeladen sein; 6. (*hum.*) der Kerl, Mensch, Kunde, das Individuum. **2.** *attrib. adj.* Partei–; – ***boss***, der Parteibonze; – ***dress***, das Gesellschaftskleid; – ***line***, (*Pol.*) offizielles Parteiprogramm, Parteidirektiven (*pl.*); (*Tele.*) der Sammelanschluß; ***follow the – line***, Parteidiziplin halten; – ***machinery***, die Parteiorganisation; – ***man***, der Parteimann, linientreues Parteimitglied; – ***politics***, die Parteipolitik; – ***spirit***, der Parteigeist; (*Archit.*) – ***wall***, die Brandmauer, gemeinsame Mauer; die Scheidewand.

parvenu ['pɑːvənjuː], *s.* der Emporkömmling, Parvenü, Neureiche(r).

parvis ['pɑːvis], *s.* (*Archit.*) der Vorhof.

paschal ['pæskəl], *adj.* Passah–, Oster–.

pasha ['pæʃə], *s.* der Pascha.

pasque-flower ['pɑːsk–], *s.* die Küchenschelle, Osterblume.

pasquinade [pæskwi'neid], *s.* die Schmähschrift, das Pasquill.

[1]**pass** [pɑːs], *s.* der (Eng)paß, das Gebirgsjoch; der Durchgang, (Zu)gang, Weg; (*Naut.*) Kanal, die Durchfahrt.

[2]**pass,** **1.** *s.* 1. der (Reise)paß, Personalausweis, Passierschein; 2. (*Mil.*) Urlaubsschein; ***be on*** –, auf Urlaub sein; 3. (*Theat., Railw.*) die Freikarte; 4. (*fig.*) kritischer Zustand, kritische Lage; ***at a desperate*** –, in einer verzweifelten Lage; ***things have come to such a*** –, die Dinge haben sich derart zugespitzt; 5. (*Fenc.*) der Stoß, Ausfall; 6. (*Footb. etc.*) das Zuspiel(en); 7. Passen (*cards*); 8. Streichen, die Bestreichung (*mesmerism*); 9. das Bestehen, (gutes) Durchkommen (*in examinations*); 10. (*coll.*) ***make a – at her***, ihr gegenüber deutlich werden.

2. *v.i.* 1. sich (fort)bewegen; (fort)gehen, (fort)schreiten, ziehen, fahren, fließen; 2. vergehen, vorübergehen, dahingehen, verschwinden, verstreichen, zu Ende gehen (*of time etc.*); 3. vor sich gehen, vorfallen, passieren, geschehen, sich ereignen *or* abspielen *or* zutragen (*of events*); 4. durchgehen, bewilligt werden (*of a bill*); 5. durchkommen, bestehen (*in an examination*); 6. geduldet werden, unanbestandet bleiben, hingehen, angehen; 7. Eingang finden, in Umgang *or* gangbar sein, (als gültig) anerkannt werden; 8. (*Fenc.*) ausfallen; 9. (*Footb.*) zupassen; 10. (*Cards*) passen.

(a) (*as inf. with v.*) ***bring to*** –, bewirken, herbeiführen; ***come to*** –, geschehen; ***let*** –, (vorüber)gehen *or* vorbeigehen lassen; ***let it –!*** das soll hingehen! ***let – unpunished***, unbestraft lassen.

(b) (*with adv.*) – ***away***, vorbei– *or* vorübergehen, vergehen, dahinschwinden; (*fig.*) sterben, verscheiden; – ***by***, see – ***away***; (*fig.*) (*of time*) ablaufen, vergehen, verfließen; – ***in***, hineingehen, hineingelassen werden; – ***off***, vorübergehen, vor sich gehen, vonstatten gehen, ablaufen, sich abwickeln; – ***on***, vorwärtsgehen, weitergehen, fortschreiten, fortrücken; übergehen (***to***, zu); (*fig.*) sterben, verscheiden; – ***out***, hinausgehen; (*coll.*) ohnmächtig werden, umkippen; – ***over***, übergehen (***into***, in (*Acc.*)), hinübergehen (– ***to***, auf (*Acc.*)).

(c) (*with prep.*) ***words –ed between them***, Worte wurden zwischen ihnen gewechselt; – ***beyond***, hinausgehen über (*Acc.*), überschreiten; – ***by***, vorbei– or vorübergehen an (*Dat.*); – ***for*** or ***as***, gehalten *or* angesehen *or* angenommen werden für, gelten für *or* als; – ***from . . . into***, übergehen von . . . in (*Acc.*); – ***over***, übergehen, keine Notiz nehmen von; – ***through***, gehen *or* reisen durch; dringen durch; (*fig.*) durchmachen, erleben, erfahren; – ***through my mind***, mir durch den Kopf gehen; – ***to***, übertragen werden *or* übergehen auf (*Acc.*), fallen *or* kommen *or* gelangen an (*Acc.*).

3. *v.t.* 1. vorbeigehen, –fahren, –reiten *etc.* an (*Dat.*), (*also Motor.*) überholen; 2. hinausgehen über (*Acc.*), überschreiten, übersteigen, übertreffen, durchschreiten, durchqueren, durchschneiden, passieren (*a limit*); 3. fahren *or* gleiten *or* hinübergehen lassen (*over s.th.*), hindurchleiten, hindurchgehen lassen (*through s.th.*); 4. verbringen, zubringen, vertreiben (*time*); 5. in Verkehr bringen, in Umlauf bringen *or* setzen, verausgaben; 6. weitergeben, (weiter)reichen; 7. (*Parl. etc.*) durchsetzen, genehmigen, (als gültig) anerkennen, gelten lassen, billigen (*a proposal*), verabschieden (*a bill*); 8. bestehen (*an examination*), durchlassen, bestehen lassen (*an examinee*); 9. (*Footb.*) zuspielen.

(a) (*with nouns*) – ***the bounds of moderation***, die Grenzen der Mäßigung überschreiten; (*sl.*) – ***the buck***, sich der Verantwortung entziehen; – ***the butter, please!*** bitte reichen Sie mir die Butter! ***he has –ed the chair***, er ist Vorsitzender gewesen; – ***a cheque***, einen Scheck einlösen; ***that –es my comprehension***, das geht über meinen Verstand *or* meine Begriffe; – ***criticism on***, Kritik üben an (*Dat.*); – ***one's eye over***, flüchtig überblicken; – ***one's hand over***, mit der Hand fahren über (*Acc.*); – ***the hat round***, freiwillige Beiträge sammeln; ***the bill has –ed the house***, der Gesetzentwurf ist vom Parlament verabschiedet worden; – ***judgement***, sein Urteil abgeben (***on***, über (*Acc.*)); – ***muster***, Zustimmung finden (***with***, bei); (*fig.*) die Prüfung bestehen; – ***an opinion***, seine Meinung äußern *or* aussprechen (***on***, über (*Acc.*)); – ***sentence***, das Urteil fällen (***on***, über (*Acc.*)); (*coll.*) – ***the time of***

day (*with him*), (ihn) grüßen; – *a vote of thanks*, im Namen aller Anwesenden den Dank aussprechen; – *water*, Wasser lassen.
(b) (*with preps.*) – *for clearance*, zur Einfuhr freigeben (*into*, nach); – *for military service*, für diensttauglich erklären; – *in review*, vorbeimarschieren lassen, (*also fig.*) Revue passieren lassen; – *through a filter*, durch ein Sieb passieren *or* streichen; – *through a lock*, durchschleusen (*a ship*); – *to his account*, ihm in Rechnung stellen *or* bringen.
(c) (*with advs.*) – *away*, vertreiben (*time*); – *by*, übergehen; übersehen, unbeachtet lassen; – *in*, einlassen (*a p.*), einreichen, einhändigen (*a th.*); – *off*, ausgeben (*as*, *for*, als); – *on*, weiterleiten, weiterschicken, weitergeben (*to*, an (*Acc.*)); – *over*, weitergeben, überreichen, übertragen (*to*, an (*Acc.*)); übergehen (*a p.*), auslassen (*a th.*); hingehen lassen (*a misdemeanour*); – *over in silence*, stillschweigend hingehen lassen *or* übergehen; – *round*, herumreichen, herumgehen lassen; (*sl.*) – *up*, vorübergehen lassen, aufgeben, verzichten auf (*Acc.*), sich (*Dat.*) entgehen lassen.

passable ['pɑ:səbl], *adj.* 1. gangbar, befahrbar, passierbar (*road etc.*), überquerbar (*obstacle*); 2. (*Comm.*) gangbar, gültig; 3. (*fig., coll.*) annehmbar, erträglich, leidlich, passabel.

passage ['pæsidʒ], **1.** *s.* 1. die (Durch)fahrt, (Durch)reise; 2. Seereise, Überfahrt; – *home*, die Rückfahrt, Heimreise; *book one's* –, die Schiffskarte lösen; *work one's* – (*out*), die Überfahrt durch Arbeit an Bord verdienen; 3. der Durchzug (*of birds*); *bird of* –, der Durchzügler; 4. (*Tech.*) der Durchgang, Durchlaß; *air* –, der Luftkanal; 5. (*fig.*) das Durchgehen, Durchkommen, Inkrafttreten, die Annahme (*of a bill*); 6. (*Archit.*) Flur, der Gang, Korridor; Verbindungsgang, Weg; 7. (*fig.*) Verlauf, Ablauf (*of time*); 8. Übergang, Übertritt (*from*, von; *to*, zu *or* in (*Acc.*)); 9. Passus, die Stelle (*in a book*); (*fig.*) *purple* –, die Glanzstelle; 10. (*Mus.*) die Passage, der Lauf; 11. (*Anat.*) *urinary* –, Harnwege (*pl.*); 12. – *of arms*, der Waffengang. **2.** *v.i.* seitwärts reiten; sich seitwärts bewegen (*as a horse*).

passage|-money, *s.* das Überfahrtsgeld. **-way,** *s.* der Korridor, Durchgang.

passant ['pæsənt], *adj.* (*Her.*) schreitend.

pass|-book, *s.* das Bankbuch, Kontogegenbuch. **--cheque,** *s.* der Passierschein. – **degree,** *s.* (*Univ.*) unterster akademischer Grad.

passé(e) ['pɑ:sei], *adj.* vergangen, veraltet, überholt, altmodisch; (*of a woman*) verblüht, verblichen.

passement [pæs'mã], *s.* die Tresse, Borte. **passementerie** [–təri:], *s.* Posamentierwaren (*pl.*).

passenger ['pæsindʒə], **1.** *s.* 1. der Fahrgast, Passagier, Reisende(r), (*Av.*) der Fluggast; 2. (*coll.*) Schmarotzer, Drückeberger. **2.** *attrib. adj.* Passagier–; – *cabin*, die Passagierkabine; – *flight*, der Passagierflug; – *list*, die Passagierliste; – *pigeon*, die Wandertaube; – *traffic*, der Personenverkehr; – *train*, der Personenzug; – *transport*, die Personenbeförderung.

passe-partout ['pæsəpɑ:'tu], *s.* der Papierrahmen; – *frame*, der Wechselrahmen; – *binding* (*reel*), die Klebestreifenrolle.

passer-by ['pɑ:sə'bai], *s.* (*pl.* **passers-by**) Vorübergehende(r), der (die) Passant(in).

passerine ['pæsərin], **1.** *adj.* (*Orn.*) Sperlings–, sperlingartig; Sitzfüßler–. **2.** *s.* der Sitzfüßler.

pass-examination, *s.* (*Univ.*) unterste akademische Abschlußprüfung.

passibility [pæsi'biliti], *s.* (*Theol.*) die Leidensfähigkeit. **passible** [–ibl], *adj.* leidensfähig.

passim ['pæsim], *adv.* hie und da, an verschiedenen Orten.

passing ['pɑ:siŋ], **1.** *adj.* 1. vorübergehend, vorbeigehend; 2. (*fig.*) vorübergehend, flüchtig, beiläufig. **2.** *adv.* (*obs.*) sehr, überaus. **3.** *s.* das Vorbeigehen, Durchgehen; *in* –, im Vorbeigehen, (*fig.*) nebenher, beiläufig; (*Motor.*) *no* –! Überholen verboten! 2. das Inkrafttreten, die Annahme (*of a bill*); 3. das Bestehen (*of examination*); 4. (Ver)schwinden, Dahinschwinden, Hinscheiden.

passing|-bell, *s.* die Totenglocke, Sterbeglocke. **--note,** *s.* (*Mus.*) die Durchgangsnote.

passion ['pæʃən], *s.* 1. die Leidenschaft; Wut, der Zorn, heftiger (Gefühls)ausbruch; *in a* –, in Wut; *fly into a* –, in Wut geraten; *with* –, leidenschaftlich; 2. heiße Liebe, heftige Neigung, die Vorliebe (*for*, für); Begierde, das Verlangen (nach); *be a* – *with him*, seine Leidenschaft sein; *become a* – *with him*, ihm zur Leidenschaft werden; *have a* – *for*, eine Vorliebe *or* Schwäche haben für; – *for gambling*, die Spielwut; 3. (*Eccl.*) das Leiden, die Passion (*of Christ*).

passional ['pæʃənəl], *s.* das Passionsbuch, die Passional. **passionate** [–it], *adj.* 1. leidenschaftlich; 2. heftig, hitzig, feurig, jähzornig. **passionateness,** *s.* die Leidenschaftlichkeit, Heftigkeit. **passion| flower,** *s.* die Passionsblume. – **fruit,** *s.* eßbare Passionsblume. **passionless,** *adj.* leidenschaftslos. **Passion|-play,** *s.* das Passionspiel. – **Sunday,** *s.* der Sonntag Judika. – **Week,** *s.* die Karwoche, Stille Woche.

passive ['pæsiv], *adj.* 1. leidend, duldend, widerstandslos, teilnahm(s)los, untätig, willensträge, passiv; – *resistance*, passiver Widerstand; 2. (*Gram.*) passiv(isch), Leide–; – *verb*, intransitives Zeitwort; – *voice*, die Leideform, das Passiv(um); 3. (*Comm.*) untätig, nicht zinstragend. **passiveness, passivity** [–'siviti], *s.* die Passivität, Teilnahm(s)losigkeit, Ergebung, Widerstandslosigkeit.

pass|-key, *s.* der Hauptschlüssel, Drücker. **--mark,** *s.* ausreichende Note (*in examinations*).

Passover ['pɑ:souvə], *s.* 1. das Passah; 2. Osterlamm, Osteropfer.

passport ['pɑ:spɔ:t], *s.* 1. der (Reise)paß; 2. (*fig.*) Geleitbrief, die Empfehlung (*to*, für), der Zugang, Weg(öffner) (zu). **passport|-office,** *s.* die Paßstelle. **--photograph,** *s.* das Paßbild.

password ['pɑ:swɔ:d], *s.* das Losungswort, die Losung, Parole.

past [pɑ:st], **1.** *adj.* 1. vergangen, ehemalig; *for some time* –, seit einiger Zeit; 2. vorig, früher; – *master*, (*freemasonry*) ehemaliger Meister vom Stuhl; (*fig.*) wahrer Meister (*in*, *of*, in (*Dat.*), unübertroffener Kenner (*Gen.*); 3. (*Gram.*) Vergangenheits–; – *participle*, das Mittelwort der Vergangenheit; – *tense*, die Vergangenheit; 4. (*pred. only*) vorbei, vorüber. **2.** *s.* 1. die Vergangenheit, das Vergangene; *in the* –, früher, ehemals; *have a* –, ein Vorleben haben; 2. (*Gram.*) die Vergangenheit(sform). **3.** *prep.* (*time*) nach; (*space*) an (*Dat.*) . . . vorbei *or* vorüber; (*fig.*) über (*Acc.*) . . . hinaus; – *all belief*, unglaublich; *be* – *his comprehension*, über seine Begriffe gehen; *be* – *one's best* or *prime*, sich auf dem absteigenden Ast befinden; – *cure* or *help*, unheilbar; (*Comm.*) – *due*, überfällig; – *hope*, hoffnungslos; *he is* – *praying for*, an ihm ist Hopfen und Malz verloren, ihm ist nicht mehr zu helfen; (*coll.*) *I wouldn't put it* – *him*, das traue ich ihm glatt *or* ohne weiteres zu; – *saving*, rettungslos verloren; – *all shame*, ohne jede Scham, völlig schamlos; *half* – *twelve*, halb eins; *a quarter* – *twelve*, (ein) Viertel nach zwölf, (ein) Viertel eins. **4.** *adv.* vorbei, vorüber, dahin.

pasta ['pæstə], *s.* Nudeln, Teigwaren (*pl.*).

paste [peist], **1.** *s.* 1. (*Cul.*) der Teig; 2. Klebstoff, Kleister; 3. die Paste (*as fish*––, *tooth*––); 4. der Straß, künstlicher Edelstein. **2.** *v.t.* 1. kleben, kleistern; bekleben (*with*, mit); – (*up*), (auf)kleben, ankleben (*a notice*) (*on*, an *or* auf (*Acc.*)); – *up*, zukleben (*a hole*); 2. (*sl.*) verprügeln; (*sl.*) – *him one*, ihm eine kleben.

pasteboard ['peistbɔ:d], **1.** *s.* 1. die Pappe, der Karton; 2. (*coll.*) die Visitenkarte, Spielkarte. **2.** *attrib. adj.* 1. Papp–, aus Pappe; 2. (*fig.*) unecht, Schein–, Kitsch–.

pastel [pæstl], *s.* 1. der Pastellstift; 2. die Pastellfarbe; – ***shades,*** Pastelltöne (*pl.*); 3. die Pastellmalerei; 4. das Pastell(bild); 5. (*Dye.*) Waidblau. **pastel(l)ist,** *s.* der Pastellmaler.

paste-pot, *s.* der Kleistertopf.

pastern ['pæstən], *s.* die Fessel (*of horse*). **pastern-joint,** *s.* das Fesselgelenk.

pasteurization ['pɑ:stərai'zeiʃən], *s.* die Pasteurisierung. **pasteurize,** *v.t.* pasteurisieren, entkeimen, haltbar machen.

pastiche [pæs'ti:ʃ], *s.* die Nachahmung, das Flickwerk, Machwerk.

pastille ['pæstil], *s.* 1. das Räucherkerzchen; 2. (*Med.*) Plätzchen, die Pastille.

pastime ['pɑ:staim], *s.* der Zeitvertreib, die Kurzweil, Belustigung; ***as a –,*** zum Zeitvertreib.

pastiness ['peistinis], *s.* 1. die Teigigkeit, Breiigkeit; 2. kränkliches *or* bleiches Aussehen. **pasting,** *s.* (*sl.*) die Dresche, Tracht Prügel.

pastor ['pɑ:stə], *s.* der Pfarrer, Pastor; Seelsorger, Seelenhirt. **pastoral, 1.** *adj.* 1. Hirten–, Schäfer–, ländlich; – ***play,*** das Schäferspiel; – ***poet,*** der Idyllendichter; – ***poetry,*** die Hirtendichtung, Schäferdichtung; 2. (*Eccl.*) seelsorgerisch, Pastoral–; – ***duties,*** geistliche Pflichten; – ***letter,*** der Hirtenbrief; (*Eccl.*) – ***staff,*** der Krummstab. **2.** *s.* 1. das Hirtengedicht, Idyll; 2. (*Eccl.*) der Hirtenbrief; 3. ländliche Szene, ländliches Bild. **pastorale** [–'rɑ:l], *s.* (*Mus.*) das Pastorale. **pastorate,** *s.* das Pfarramt, Seelsorgeamt, Pastorat; Pastoren (*pl.*).

pastry ['peistri], *s.* 1. der Teig; ***flaky –,*** der Blätterteig; ***short –,*** der Mürbeteig; 2. das Gebäck, Backwerk; Pasteten, Torten (*pl.*). **pastry|-board,** *s.* das Teigbrett. **–cook,** *s.* der Feinbäcker, Konditor.

pasturage ['pɑ:stjəridʒ], *s.* 1. das Weiden; 2. Grasfutter, Viehfutter, Weidegras; 3. *See* **pasture, 1. pasture, 1.** *s.* die Weide, Trift, Wiese, das Weideland, Grasland. **2.** *v.t.* weiden (*cattle*), abweiden (*grassland*). **3.** *v.i.* grasen, weiden. **pastureland,** *s. See* **pasture, 1.**

[1]**pasty** ['pæsti], *s.* die Fleischpastete.

[2]**pasty** ['peisti], *adj.* 1. teigig, brei(art)ig, pappig; 2. (*coll.*) (*also* **–*faced***) bleich, kränklich.

[1]**pat** [pæt], *attrib. adj., adv.* passend, zutreffend, gelegen, parat, zur Hand; ***answer –,*** schlagfertig *or* prompt antworten; ***very –,*** eben *or* gerade recht, rechtzeitig, geeignet; ***have*** or ***know it off –,*** es (wie) am Schnürchen haben *or* können; ***stand –,*** (*poker*) aus der Hand spielen, (*coll.*) am alten festhalten, bei seinem Entschluß bleiben.

[2]**pat, 1.** *s.* 1. der Klaps, leichter Schlag, der Taps; (*of feet*) das Getrappel, Patschen, Tapsen; 2. Stückchen, Klümpchen (*of butter*). **2.** *v.t.* einen Klaps geben (*Dat.*), leicht schlagen; tätscheln; (*fig.*) – (***o.s.***) ***on the back,*** (sich) beglückwünschen. **3.** *v.i.* klopfen, patschen, tapsen. **pat-a-cake,** *s.* backe-backe-Kuchen.

patch [pætʃ], **1.** *s.* 1. der Lappen, Flicken (*for repair*); – ***pocket,*** aufgesetzte Tasche; (*coll.*) ***be not a – on,*** sich nicht messen können an (*Dat.*), gar nicht zu vergleichen sein mit; 2. der Fleck, das Stück(chen) (*of land*); der Fleck(en) (*of colour etc.*); ***cabbage –,*** das Kohlbeet; (*coll.*) ***strike a bad –,*** eine Pechsträhne haben; ***in –es,*** stellenweise; ***–es of fog,*** neblige Stellen; (*fig.*) ***purple –,*** die Glanzstelle; 3. das Pflaster; Schönheitspflästerchen; 4. (*Mil.*) Tuchabzeichen; 5. die Augenbinde. **2.** *v.t.* flicken, ausbessern; – ***up,*** zusammenflicken; (*fig.*) zusammenschustern, zusammenstoppeln, zusammenstumpern; (*coll.*) schlichten, beilegen (*a quarrel*). **patchiness,** *s.* (*fig.*) die Unregelmäßigkeit, Uneinheitlichkeit, Ungleichmäßigkeit.

patchouli [pæ'tʃu:li], *s.* (*Bot.*) das Patschuli.

patchwork ['pætʃwə:k], *s.* 1. die Flickerei, das Flickwerk; – ***quilt,*** die Flickendecke; 2. (*fig.*) Zusammengestoppelte(s), schachbrettartiges Muster. **patchy,** *adj.* 1. voller Flicken; 2. (*fig.*) zusammengestoppelt; fleckig; 3. (*coll.*) ungleichmäßig, unregelmäßig, uneinheitlich.

pate [peit], *s.* (*coll.*) der Schädel, Kopf.

pâté ['pætei], *s.* die Pastete.

-pated ['peitid], *adj. suff.* –köpfig.

patella [pæ'telə], *s.* (*Anat.*) die Kniescheibe. **patellar,** *adj.* Kniescheiben–.

paten ['pætən], *s.* (*Eccl.*) der Hostienteller.

patency ['peitənsi], *s.* 1. die Offenkundigkeit; 2. (*Anat.*) das Offensein.

[1]**patent** ['peit(ə)nt], *adj.* offen(kundig), offensichtlich, allgemein bekannt, zugänglich; ***as is – from,*** wie erhellt aus.

[2]**patent, 1.** *adj.* patentiert, durch Patent *or* gesetzlich geschützt, Patent–, Marken–, (*coll.*) patent, großartig; – ***fastener,*** der Druckknopf; – ***fuel,*** Briketts, Preßkohlen (*pl.*); – ***law,*** das Patentrecht; – ***leather,*** das Glanzleder; – (***leather***) ***boot,*** der Lackstiefel; ***letters –,*** die Privilegsurkunde, Bestallungsurkunde; der Freibrief, das Patent; – ***medicine,*** die Markenarznei; – ***office,*** das Patentamt. **2.** *s.* der Patentbrief, das Patent, Privileg(ium), die Bestallung(surkunde), (*fig.*) der Freibrief; ***take out a – for,*** ein Patent nehmen auf (*Acc.*); ***apply for a –,*** ein Patent anmelden; – ***applied for,*** Patent angemeldet; – ***of nobility,*** der Adelsbrief. **3.** *v.t.* gesetzlich schützen, patentieren (lassen). **patentable,** *adj.* patentierbar, patentfähig. **patentee** [–'ti:], *s.* der Patentinhaber.

patently ['peit(ə)ntli], *adv.* ***it is – clear*** or ***obvious,*** es liegt klar auf der Hand. *See* [1]**patent.**

pater ['peitə], *s.* (*coll.*) der Vater, alter Herr. **paterfamilias** [–fæ'mi:liəs], *s.* der Hausvater, Familienvater, das Familienoberhaupt.

paternal [pə'tə:nəl], *adj.* väterlich; – ***grandmother,*** die Großmutter väterlicherseits. **paternalism,** *s.* väterliche Fürsorge. **paternalist(ic)** [–list (–'listik)], *adj.* fürsorglich, väterlich sorgend. **paternity,** *s.* 1. die Vaterschaft; 2. (*fig.*) Herkunft, Urheberschaft.

paternoster ['peitənɔstə], *s.* 1. das Vaterunser; 2. der Rosenkranz; 3. – ***pump,*** die Kettenpumpe; – ***wheel,*** das Kettenwerk, Eimerwerk.

path [pɑ:θ], *s.* (*pl.* **-s** [pɑ:ðz]) der (Fuß)weg, Pfad; (*fig.*) Weg (*also Elec.*), die Bahn (*also of comets etc.*); ***beaten –,*** ausgetretener Weg (*also fig.*); ***bridle –,*** der Reitweg; – ***of duty,*** der Weg der Pflicht; ***tow(ing) –,*** der Treidelweg.

pathetic [pə'θetik], *adj.* 1. rührend, ergreifend, erschütternd, pathetisch; (*Liter.*) – ***fallacy,*** die Vermenschlichung der Natur; 2. kläglich, armselig, bemitleidenswert.

pathfinder ['pɑ:θfaində], *s.* der Pfadfinder; (*Av.*) Zielbeleuchter; (*fig.*) Bahnbrecher, Vorläufer. **pathless,** *adj.* pfadlos, unwegsam, ungebahnt.

pathogenic [pæθə'dʒenik], **pathogenous** [–'θɔdʒinəs], *adj.* krankheitserregend. **pathological,** *adj.* pathologisch, krankhaft. **pathologist** [–'θɔlədʒist], *s.* der Pathologe. **pathology** [–'θɔlədʒi], *s.* 1. die Krankheitslehre, Pathologie; 2. Krankheitserscheinungen (*pl.*).

pathos ['peiθɔs], *s.* 1. das Pathos, Ergreifende(s); 2. die Gefühlsbewegung, Gefühlserregung, Ergriffenheit.

pathway ['pɑ:θwei], *s.* der Weg, Pfad, die Bahn (*also fig.*).

patience ['peiʃəns], *s.* 1. die Geduld; Ausdauer, Beharrlichkeit; Nachsicht, Langmut; ***my – is at an end,*** jetzt reißt mir die Geduld; ***have –,*** Geduld üben, sich gedulden; ***have no – with,*** nicht ausstehen *or* leiden können; ***the – of Job,*** die Engelsgeduld; ***lose*** (***all*** or ***one's***) – ***with,*** ungehalten werden über (*Acc.*); ***out of – with,*** aufgebracht über (*Acc.*); 2. (*Cards*) die Patience, das Geduldspiel.

[1]**patient** ['peiʃənt], *adj.* geduldig, duldsam, nachsichtig (***towards, with,*** gegen); langmütig, ausharrend, ausdauernd, beharrlich; ***be – of,*** geduldig ertragen; (*fig.*) zulassen.

[2]**patient,** *s.* der (die) Patient(in), Kranke(r).

patina ['pætinə], *s.* 1. der Edelrost, die Patina; 2. (*fig.*) ehrwürdiges Aussehen.

patio ['pætiou], *s.* der Lichthof, die Terasse, Veranda.

patois ['pætwɑ:], *s.* die Mundart.

patriarch ['peitriɑ:k], *s.* 1. der Patriarch, Erzvater; 2. (*Eccl.*) Oberbischof; 3. (*fig.*) Altmeister, ehrwürdiger Alter. **patriarchal** [–'ɑ:kl], *adj.* 1. patriarchalisch; 2. (*fig.*) ehrwürdig. **patriarchate,** *s.* (*Eccl.*) das Patriarchat. **patriarchy,** *s.* patriarchalische Regierungsform.

patrician [pə'triʃən], **1.** *adj.* 1. patrizisch; Patrizier–; 2. (*fig.*) aristokratisch. **2.** *s.* der Patrizier. **patriciate** [–ieit], *s.* das Patriziat; (*collect.*) Patrizier (*pl.*).

patricidal [pætri'saidl], *adj.* vatermörderisch. **patricide** ['pætrisaid], *s.* 1. der Vatermord; 2. der (die) Vatermörder(in).

patrimonial [pætri'mouniəl], *adj.* ererbt, Erb–. **patrimony** ['pætriməni], *s.* 1. väterliches Erbgut *or* Erbteil; 2. (*Eccl.*) das Kirchengut, Patrimonium.

patriot ['pei–, 'pætriət], *s.* der Patriot, Vaterlandsfreund. **patriotic** [–'ɔtik], *adj.* vaterländisch, patriotisch. **patriotism,** *s.* die Vaterlandsliebe, der Patriotismus.

patristic [pə'tristik], *adj.* patristisch. **patristics,** *pl.* (*sing. constr.*) die Patristik.

patrol [pə'troul], **1.** *s.* 1. der Spähtrupp, Stoßtrupp, die Patrouille, Streife; – ***boat,*** das (Küsten)-wachschiff; – ***car,*** der Streifenwagen; – ***plane,*** das Überwachungsflugzeug; (*Am.*) – ***wagon,*** *see* **prison-van**; 2. die Runde, das Patrouillieren; ***on*** –, im Wachdienst *or* Überwachungsdienst. **2.** *v.i.* die Runde machen, patrouillieren. **3.** *v.t.* durchstreifen, abpatrouillieren. **patrolman,** *s.* (*Am.*) der Streifenpolizist.

patron ['peitrən], *s.* 1. der Schutzherr, Patron; 2. Beschützer, Gönner, Förderer, Wohltäter, Mäzen; 3. (*Eccl.*) Kirchenpatron; (*also* – ***saint***) Schutzheilige(r); 4. (*Comm.*) der Kunde (die Kundin), Klient.

patronage ['pætrənidʒ], *s.* 1. die Begünstigung, Förderung, Protektion, Gönnerschaft, der Schutz; 2. das Mäzenatentum; 3. (*Eccl.*) Patronat(srecht), Besetzungsrecht, Pfründenverleihungsrecht; 4. (*Comm.*) die Kundschaft, der Besucherkreis.

patroness ['peitrənes], *s.* 1. die Schutzherrin, Patronin; 2. Gönnerin, Förderin, Beschützerin; 3. (*Eccl.*) Schutzheilige.

patronization ['pætrənai'zeiʃən], *s.* 1. die Begünstigung, Förderung; 2. Unterstützung, regelmäßiger Besuch. **patronize,** *v.t.* 1. beschützen, begünstigen, fördern, unterstützen; 2. mit Herablassung *or* gönnerhaft behandeln (*other people*); 3. (*Comm.*) Kunde *or* Stammgast sein bei, (*esp. Theat.*) regelmäßig besuchen. **patronizer,** *s.* 1. der Beschützer, Gönner, Förderer; 2. regelmäßiger Besucher. **patronizing,** *adj.* gönnerhaft, herablassend; – ***air,*** die Gönnermiene.

patronymic [pætrə'nimik], **1.** *adj.* patronymisch. **2.** *s.* der Geschlechtsname, Familienname.

patten [pætn], *s.* 1. der Holzschuh, Stelzschuh; 2. (*Archit.*) Säulenfuß, Sockel.

1**patter** ['pætə], **1.** *v.i.* platschen, prasseln, klatschen (*as rain*); – ***along,*** trippeln, trappeln; – ***down,*** niederplatschen. **2.** *s.* das Platschen, Prasseln (*of rain*), Trippeln, Getrappel (*of feet*).

2**patter, 1.** *v.t.* (her)plappern, schnattern. **2.** *s.* 1. die Gaunersprache, der Jargon, das Rotwelsch; 2. Geplapper; 3. die Mundfertigkeit. **patter-song,** *s.* schnell gesungenes Lied.

pattern ['pætən], **1.** *s.* 1. das Muster, Vorbild; ***according to –, on the – of*** nach dem Muster *or* Vorbild von; 2. die Vorlage, Vorzeichnung; 3. (*Tech.*) das Gußmodell, Probemodell, die Schablone; 4. (*Dressm. etc.*) das Schnittmuster; ***dress –,*** der Schnitt; ***needlework –,*** das Stickmuster; ***paper*** –, das Schnittmuster; 5. (*Weav.*) das Dessin, die Musterung; 6. (*Comm.*) das Muster, die (Waren)-probe; 7. das Modell, Probestück, Musterstück; 8. (*fig.*) der Plan, die Anlage; ***always*** (***on*** or ***of***) ***the same –,*** immer die gleiche Art *or* Methode. **2.** *attrib. adj.* vorbildlich, musterhaft, Muster–. **3.** *v.t.* 1. nachbilden, formen (***after,*** nach); 2. sich (*Dat.*) ein Beispiel nehmen (***on,*** an (*Dat.*)).

pattern|-bombing, *s.* (*Av.*) der Reihenwurf, die Belegung mit einem Bombenteppich. **–-book,** *s.* das Musterbuch. **patterned,** *adj.* gemustert. **pattern-maker,** *s.* 1. der Musterzeichner; 2. Modellmacher, Modellschlosser, Modelleur.

patty ['pæti], *s.* das Pastetchen. **patty-pan,** *s.* das Pastetenblech.

patulous ['pætjuləs], *adj.* ausgedehnt, ausgebreitet.

paucity ['pɔ:siti], *s.* geringe Anzahl *or* Menge, die Wenigkeit, der Mangel.

Paul [pɔ:l], *s.* Paul(us) (*m.*); ***rob Peter to pay –,*** ein Loch aufzureißen, um ein anderes zuzustopfen; – ***Pry,*** Hans Dampf in allen Gassen.

1**Pauline** ['pɔ:lain], *adj.* paulinisch.

2**Pauline** ['pɔ:li:n], *s.* Pauline (*f.*).

paunch [pɔ:ntʃ], *s.* 1. der (Dick)bauch, Wanst; 2. (*Zool.*) Pansen. **paunchiness,** *s.* die Dickbäuchigkeit. **paunchy,** *adj.* dickbäuchig, beleibt.

pauper ['pɔ:pə], **1.** *s.* Arme(r), der Almosenempfänger; (*Law*) unter Armenrecht Klagende(r). **2.** *attrib. adj.* Armen–. **pauperism,** *s.* (dauernde) Armut, allgemeine Verarmung, die Massenarmut, der Pauperismus. **pauperization** [–rai'zeiʃən], *s.* die Verarmung. **pauperize,** *v.t.* (bettel)arm *or* zum Bettler machen, in Armut bringen.

pause [pɔ:z], **1.** *s.* 1. die Pause, Unterbrechung, der Stillstand, das Innehalten, Zögern; ***give him –,*** ihm zu denken geben, ihn zögern *or* innehalten lassen; ***make a –,*** innehalten, pausieren; ***without a –,*** ohne Unterbrechung; 2. (*Typ.*) der Gedankenstrich; 3. (*Metr.*) Absatz, die Zäsur; 4. (*Mus.*) Fermate. **2.** *v.i.* 1. innehalten, stehenbleiben, anhalten, pausieren; warten, zögern; 2. verweilen (***upon,*** bei); – ***upon a note,*** einen Ton aushalten.

pavage ['peividʒ], *s.* 1. die (Be)pflasterung, das Pflastern; 2. Pflastergeld.

pavan [pæ'væn], *s.* die Pavane.

pave [peiv], *v.t.* pflastern; (*fig.*) – ***the way,*** den Weg ebnen *or* bahnen *or* bereiten (***for,*** *Dat.* (*a p.*); für *or* zu (*a th.*)). **pavement,** *s.* das (Straßen)pflaster; der Fußsteig, Bürgersteig, Gehweg, das Trottoir; (*Am.*) die Fahrbahn; – ***artist,*** der Pflastermaler; ***crazy –,*** das Mosaikpflaster. **paver,** *s.* der Pflasterer, Steinsetzer; (*Am.*) Straßenbetonmischer.

pavilion [pə'viljən], *s.* 1. großes Zelt; 2. (*Her.*) das Wappenzelt; 3. (*Archit.*) der Pavillon, das Gartenhäuschen; 4. Ausstellungsgebäude. **pavilion-roof,** *s.* (*Archit.*) das Zeltdach.

paving ['peiviŋ], *s.* das Pflastern, die Pflasterung; das Straßenpflaster. **paving-stone,** *s.* der Pflasterstein.

pavio(u)r ['peivjə], *s. See* **paver.**

pavonine ['pævənain], *adj.* pfauen(schwanz)artig.

paw [pɔ:], **1.** *s.* 1. die Pfote, Tatze; 2. (*sl.* = ***hand***) Pfote. **2.** *v.i.* scharren, stampfen (*as horse*). **3.** *v.t.* (*sl.*) derb *or* ungeschickt anfassen, angrapschen, betatschen, betätcheln, fummeln an (*Dat.*); – ***the air,*** in die Luft schlagen; – ***the ground,*** auf den Boden stampfen *or* scharren.

pawl [pɔ:l], *s.* der Sperrhaken, die Sperrklinke.

1**pawn** [pɔ:n], *s.* 1. (*Chess*) der Bauer; 2. (*fig.*) die Schachfigur, der Strohmann.

2**pawn, 1.** *s.* das Pfand, die Verpfändung; das Pfandobjekt, Pfandstück; ***in –,*** verpfändet, versetzt; ***put*** or ***give in –,*** verpfänden, versetzen. **2.** *v.t.* verpfänden (*also fig.*), versetzen. **pawn|-broker,** *s.* der Pfandleiher. **–broking,** *s.* das (Pfand)leihgeschäft. **pawnee,** *s.* der Pfandnehmer, Pfandinhaber. **pawner,** *s.* der Verpfänder, Pfandleiher, Pfandschuldner. **pawn|shop,** *s.* das Pfandhaus, Leihhaus, die Pfandleihe. **–-ticket,** *s.* der Pfandschein.

pax [pæks], **1.** *s.* (*Eccl.*) die Reliquientafel. **2.** *int.* (*sl.*) Friede! Waffenstillstand!

1**pay** [pei], **1.** *irr.v.t.* 1. zahlen (*what one owes*), bezahlen, begleichen (*a bill*), bezahlen (*a p.*); – ***away,*** see – ***out***; – ***back,*** zurückzahlen, zurückerstatten; – ***cash*** (***down***), bar bezahlen; – ***the costs,*** die Kosten tragen; – ***one's debts,*** seine Schulden (be)zahlen; (*fig.*) – ***one's debt to nature,*** sterben; – ***down,*** bar zahlen; – ***the fare,*** für die Fahrt zahlen; – ***in,*** einzahlen; – ***interest on,*** verzinsen; – ***off,*** voll bezahlen, ab(be)zahlen, tilgen (*debts*); entlohnen, auszahlen, abmustern (*a crew*); (*Naut.*) laufen lassen, ausgeben (*a rope*); – ***out,*** auszahlen, auslegen; (*Naut.*) (aus)stecken, fieren, (langsam) schießen lassen (*rope etc.*); – ***the penalty of,*** sühnen; – ***the piper,*** die Zeche bezahlen, die Kosten tragen; die Suppe auslöffeln, der Dumme sein; – ***a sum of money,*** einen Betrag entrichten; – ***up,*** voll bezahlen; voll einzahlen (*shares*); – ***wages,*** löhnen, Lohn auszahlen; – ***one's way,*** seinen Verbindlichkeiten nachkommen; auf eigenen Füßen stehen, ohne Zuschuß auskommen, genug zum Leben verdienen, für seinen Unterhalt aufkommen (können); sich bezahlt machen, auf seine Kosten kommen; 2. (*fig.*) belohnen, vergelten, entschädigen; – ***him back in his own coin,*** ihm mit gleicher Münze heimzahlen, Gleiches mit Gleichem vergelten; – ***him out for,*** ihm heimzahlen; 3. geben, schenken, erweisen, widmen, zollen, abstatten; – ***attention,*** Aufmerksamkeit schenken (***to,*** *Dat.*), achtgeben (auf (*Acc.*)); – ***a call on,*** einen Besuch machen bei; – ***him a compliment,*** ihm ein Kompliment machen; – ***him the compliment,*** ihm die Ehre erweisen (***of doing,*** zu tun); – (***one's***) ***court,*** seine Aufwartung *or* den Hof machen (***to,*** *Dat.*); – ***heed,*** see – ***attention;*** – ***homage,*** huldigen (***to,*** *Dat.*), Ehre erweisen (*Dat.*); – ***regard to,*** beachten; – ***one's respects to him,*** sich ihm empfehlen; ihm einen Anstandsbesuch machen; – ***a visit,*** besuchen, einen Besuch machen; (*sl.*) mal austreten. **2.** ***irr.v.i.*** 1. zahlen, Zahlung leisten (***for,*** für); – ***by cheque,*** per Scheck zahlen; – ***through the nose,*** tüchtig zahlen *or* bluten müssen, schwer draufzahlen; – ***for,*** die Kosten tragen *or* aufbringen für; (*fig.*) büßen; – ***for the seat,*** den Platz bezahlen; ***he had to – dearly for it,*** es kam ihm teuer zu stehen; – ***towards,*** beitragen *or* beisteuern zu; 2. sich bezahlt machen, sich lohnen *or* rentieren; ***it –s hand over fist,*** es macht sich glänzend bezahlt; – ***off,*** (*coll.*) sich bezahlt machen, sich lohnen *or* rentieren; (*Naut.*) abfallen, vom Winde abhalten. **3.** *s.* die Bezahlung; das Gehalt, der (Arbeits)lohn; Sold, die Löhnung, Besoldung; (*fig.*) Belohnung; ***in his –,*** bei ihm beschäftigt; ***additional –,*** die Gehaltszulage; ***rise in –,*** die Gehaltserhöhung; (*Mil.*) ***on half –,*** zur Disposition gestellt.

²**pay,** *reg.v.t.* (*Naut.*) (ein)schmieren, teeren, verpechen, auspichen.

payable [ˈpeiəbl], *adj.* 1. (ein)zahlbar (***to,*** an (*Acc.*)); 2. fällig, abgelaufen (*as bills*); 3. (*Min.*) ertragreich, ergiebig, rentabel.

pay|-as-you-earn, *s.* der Lohnsteuerabzug. **–book,** *s.* (*Mil.*) das Soldbuch. **–box,** *s.* die Kasse. **--cheque,** *s.* der Lohnscheck, Gehaltsscheck. **--clerk,** *s.* Lohnbüroangestellte(r); (*Mil.*) der Rechnungsführer. **--day,** *s.* der Zahltag; (*Mil.*) Löhnungstag.

payee [peiˈiː], *s.* (*Comm.*) der (Zahlungs)empfänger, Wechselinhaber, Präsentant. **payer,** *s.* 1. der (Aus)zahler; 2. Trassat, Bezogene(r) (*of a cheque*). **paying,** *adj.* lohnend, einträglich, rentabel; – ***concern*** or (*fig.*) ***proposition,*** einträgliches Geschäft; – ***guest,*** der (die) Pensionär(in); – ***ore,*** das Scheideerz. **pay|load,** *s.* die Nutzlast. **–master,** *s.* (*Mil.*) der Zahlmeister; (*fig.*) Zahler, Unterstützer.

payment [ˈpeimənt], *s.* 1. die (Be)zahlung, Auszahlung; Einzahlung; Abtragung, Entrichtung (*of debt*); Einlösung (*of a cheque*); ***against –,*** gegen Bezahlung; – ***by instalments,*** die Ratenzahlung; ***as – for,*** see ***in – of;*** ***make – for,*** bezahlen; – ***in advance,*** die Vorauszahlung; – ***in cash,*** die Barzahlung; – ***of duty,*** die Verzollung; – ***in kind,*** die Naturalleistung, Sachleistung; ***in – of,*** zum Ausgleich von; – ***on account,*** die Abschlagszahlung, Akontozahlung; ***on – of,*** gegen Bezahlung von, nach Eingang von; 2. der Lohn, Sold, die Löhnung, Entlohnung, Besoldung; 3. (*fig.*) Belohnung.

paynim [ˈpeinim], *s.* (*obs.*) der Heide (die Heidin).

pay|-off, *s.* (*coll.*) die Vergeltung, Heimzahlung. **--office,** *s.* das Lohnbüro, die Zahlstelle, das Rechnungsamt. **--packet,** *s.* die Lohntüte. **--parade,** *s.* (*Mil.*) der Löhnungsappell. **--roll,** *s.* der Gesamtbetrag, der Löhne; die Löhnungsliste; ***be on the –,*** angestellt *or* beschäftigt sein. **--sheet,** *s.* die Lohnliste, Zahlliste. **--slip,** *s.* der Gehaltsstreifen.

pea [piː], *s.* die Erbse; ***green –s,*** Schoten (*pl.*); ***sweet –,*** Spanische Wicke; ***as like as two –s,*** wie ein Ei dem anderen; ***as easy as shelling –s,*** kinderleicht; ***--green,*** erbsengrün, maigrün.

peace [piːs], **1.** *s.* 1. der Friede(n); ***at –,*** in Frieden, im Friedenszustand; (*fig.*) gestorben; ***breach of the –,*** die Ruhestörung; (*Mil.*) – ***establishment,*** der Friedensbestand, die Friedensstärke; ***justice of the –,*** der Friedensrichter; ***the King's –,*** der Landfrieden, öffentliche Sicherheit; ***keep the –,*** die öffentliche Sicherheit wahren; ***make –,*** Frieden schließen; 2. die Ruhe, Friedlichkeit, Eintracht; – ***of mind,*** die Seelenruhe, Gemütsruhe; ***at – with,*** in Eintracht mit; ***have no –,*** keine Ruhe haben; ***hold one's –,*** schweigen, sich ruhig verhalten; ***in –*** (***and quiet***), ungestört, in Ruhe (und Frieden); ***leave him in –,*** ihn in Ruhe *or* Frieden lassen; ***make – between,*** versöhnen; ***make one's – with,*** sich aussöhnen mit. **2.** *int.* still! sei(d) ruhig!

peaceable [ˈpiːsəbl], *adj.* 1. friedliebend, friedfertig; 2. ruhig, ungestört, friedlich. **peaceful,** *adj.* friedlich, ruhig. **peacefulness,** *s.* die Friedlichkeit. **peace|-loving,** *adj.* *See* **peaceable.** **--maker,** *s.* der Frieden(s)stifter. **--offering,** *s.* 1. das Sühnopfer; 2. der Versöhnungsdienst, die Genugtuung. **–time,** *s.* die Friedenszeit; ***in –,*** im Frieden, in Friedenszeiten. – **treaty,** *s.* der Friedensvertrag.

¹**peach** [piːtʃ], *s.* der Pfirsich; (*sl.*) ***a – of a . . .,*** ein prächtiger *or* prachtvoller *or* pfundiger . . ., ein(e) Pracht– *or* Pfunds–.

²**peach,** *v.i.* (*sl.*) angeben; – ***on him,*** ihn denunzieren *or* angeben *or* verraten.

peach|-colour, *s.* die Pfirsichfarbe. **--coloured,** *adj.* pfirsichfarben.

peacher [ˈpiːtʃə], *s.* (*sl.*) der Angeber, Denunziant.

peachick [ˈpiːtʃik], *s.* junger Pfau.

peachy [ˈpiːtʃi], *adj.* (*sl.*) prachtvoll, fabelhaft, prima.

pea|cock, *s.* der Pfau; – ***blue,*** pfauenblau; – ***butterfly,*** das Tagpfauenauge. **–hen,** *s.* die Pfauhenne. **--jacket,** *s.* (*Naut.*) die Pijacke, Matrosenjacke.

¹**peak** [piːk], **1.** *s.* 1. der Gipfel (*also fig.*), die Spitze, (*fig.*) Höhe, der Höhepunkt; (*Math.*) Scheitel(punkt), Scheitelwert (*of a curve*); 2. (*Tech. etc.*) die Hauptbelastung(szeit), Stoßzeit; 3. (*Naut.*) Piek, (Gaffel)nock (*of a sail*); 4. der (Mützen)schirm (*of a cap*). **2.** *v.i.* emporragen. **3.** *v.t.* 1. nach oben schieben, senkrecht heben; 2. (*Naut.*) toppen.

²**peak,** *v.i.* – ***and pine,*** dahinsiechen, sich abhärmen (***over,*** über (*Acc.*)).

peaked [piːkt], *adj.* spitz (zulaufend), Spitz–. **peak|-hour,** *s.* die Stunde des Hochbetriebs. **--load,** *s.* (*Elec.*) die Spitzenbelastung. **--output,** *s.* das Produktionsmaximum, die Maximalleistung. **--power,** *s.* die Spitzenleistung. **--season,** *s.* die Hochkonjunktur. **--traffic,** *s.* die Verkehrsspitze, der Spitzenverkehr. **--value,** *s.* der Höchstwert, Maximalwert.

¹**peaky** [ˈpiːki], *adj.* zugespitzt; *see also* **peaked.**

²**peaky,** *adj.* (*coll.*) kränklich, abgehärmt.

peal [piːl], **1.** *s.* 1. das Geläute; 2. Glockenspiel; 3. (*fig.*) Geschmetter, Getöse, der Schall, Krach; – ***of applause,*** der Beifallssturm; – ***of laughter,*** schallendes Gelächter; – ***of thunder,*** der Donnerschlag. **2.** *v.i.* erschallen, schmettern; (*fig.*) tönen, dröhnen. **3.** *v.t.* 1. läuten (*bells*); ertönen *or* erschallen lassen; 2. (*fig.*) laut verkünden.

pea|nut, *s.* die Erdnuß; – ***butter,*** die Erdnußbutter; (*sl.*) – ***politics,*** politisches Intrigenspiel. **--pod,** *s.* die Erbsenhülse.

pear [pɛə], *s.* die Birne.

pearl [pəːl], **1.** *s.* 1. die Perle (*also fig.*); ***cast –s before swine,*** Perlen vor die Säue werfen; 2. (*colour*) das Perlgrau; ***--grey,*** perlgrau; ***--white,***

perlweiß; 3. (*Typ.*) die Perl(schrift). **2.** *attrib. adj.* Perl(en)–, Perlmutter–. **3.** *v.i.* perlen, tropfen, Perlen bilden.

pearl|-barley, *s.* Perlgraupen (*pl.*). **--button,** *s.* der Perlmutterknopf. **--diver, --fisher,** *s.* der Perlenfischer. **--oyster,** *s.* die Perlmuschel. **pearly,** *adj.* Perl(en)–, perlenartig; perlmutterartig, perlweiß; perlenreich; – ***gates,*** zwölf Himmelstüren; – ***lustre,*** der Perlenglanz.

pear|-shaped, *adj.* birnenförmig. **--tree,** *s.* der Birnbaum.

peasant ['pezənt], **1.** *s.* der Bauer, Landmann, Landarbeiter. **2.** *attrib. adj.* bäuerlich, Bauern–; – ***boy,*** der Bauernjunge; – ***proprietor,*** bäuerlicher Grundbesitzer; – ***woman,*** die Bäuerin, Bauersfrau. **peasantry,** *s.* Bauern (*pl.*), die Bauernschaft, der Bauernstand, das Landvolk.

pease [pi:z], *pl.* (*obs.*) Erbsen (*pl.*); – ***pudding,*** der Erbsenbrei.

pea|shooter, *s.* das Blasrohr, Pustrohr. **–soup,** *s.* die Erbsensuppe. **–souper,** *s.* (*coll.*) dichter Nebel, die Waschküche.

peat [pi:t], *s.* der Torf. **peat|-bog,** *s.* das Torfmoor. **--cutter,** *s.* der Torfstecher. **peaty,** *adj.* torfartig, Torf–; vertorft, torfig.

pebble [pebl], *s.* 1. der Kiesel(stein); ***he is not the only – on the beach,*** man ist auf ihn allein nicht angewiesen; man kann auch ohne ihn auskommen; 2. (*Min.*) der Achat, Bergkristall. **pebbly,** *adj.* kieselig, Kiesel–.

peccability [pekə'biliti], *s.* die Sündhaftigkeit. **peccable** ['pekəbl], *adj.* sündig, sündhaft. **peccadillo** [–'dilou], *s.* leichte Sünde, gering(fügig)es Vergehen. **peccancy** ['pekənsi], *s.* 1. die Sündhaftigkeit; 2. (*Med.*) Faulheit. **peccant,** *adj.* 1. sündigend, sündig, schuldig; 2. (*Med.*) faul.

peccary ['pekəri], *s.* das Nabelschwein, Pekari.

[1]**peck** [pek], *s.* 1. der Viertelscheffel (= 9 *liter*); 2. (*fig.*) die Menge, der Haufen (*of trouble etc.*).

[2]**peck, 1.** *s.* 1. das Picken, Hacken; 2. die Delle, Einbuchtung; 3. (*coll.*) flüchtiger Kuß. **2.** *v.i.* picken (*at,* nach) (*as a bird*); hacken, hauen (*with a tool*); – ***at one's food,*** an dem Essen knabbern *or* herumpicken, zimperlich essen. **2.** *v.t.* picken, hacken; – ***up the ground,*** den Boden aufhacken. **pecker,** *s.* 1. die Hacke, Haue, Picke; 2. (*sl.*) Nase; (*sl.*) ***keep one's – up,*** den Mut nicht sinken lassen, den Kopf hochhalten, sich nicht kleinkriegen lassen. **peckish,** *adj.* (*coll.*) hungrig.

pecten ['pektən], *s.* 1. (*Anat.*) die Kammhaut; 2. (*Zool.*) Kammuschel.

pectic ['pektik], *adj.* Pektin–. **pectin,** *s.* das Pektin.

pectinate ['pektinət], *adj.* kammförmig, kammartig, Kamm–.

pectoral ['pektərəl], **1.** *adj.* Brust–. **2.** *s.* 1. (*Med.*) das Brustmittel, Hustenmittel; 2. (*Her.*) der Brustschild; 3. (*Eccl.*) das Pektorale, (*R.C.*) Brustkreuz; 4. (*Ichth.*) die Brustflosse.

peculate ['pekjuleit], **1.** *v.t.* unterschlagen, veruntreuen. **2.** *v.i.* sich (*Dat.*) Unterschlagungen zuschulden kommen lassen. **peculation** [–'leiʃən], *s.* die Unterschlagung, Veruntreuung, der Unterschleif. **peculator,** *s.* der Betrüger, Veruntreuer, Kassendieb.

peculiar [pi'kju:liə], **1.** *adj.* 1. eigen(tümlich) (*to, Dat.*); 2. absonderlich, eigen(artig), seltsam; (*coll.*) verdreht, nicht recht gescheit. **2.** *s.* 1. eigner Besitz, das Sondereigentum; 2. ausschließliches Recht, Sondervorrecht. **peculiarity** [–li'æriti], *s.* 1. die Eigenheit, Besonderheit; 2. Eigentümlichkeit, Eigenartigkeit, Seltsamkeit. **peculiarly,** *adv.* besonders, vornehmlich.

pecuniary [pi'kju:niəri], *adj.* geldlich; Geld–, pekuniär.

pedagogic(al) [pedə'gɔdʒik(l)], *adj.* erzieherisch, Erziehungs–, pädagogisch. **pedagogics,** *pl.* (*sing. constr.*) die Pädagogik. **pedagogue** ['pedəgɔg], *s.* 1. der Pädagoge, Erzieher, Schulmeister; 2. (*fig.*) Pedant, Schulfuchs. **pedagogy** ['pedəgɔgi], *s.* die Unterrichtsmethode

pedal [pedl], **1.** *s.* das Pedal, der Fußhebel; die Tretkurbel; (*Mus.*) ***soft*** (***loud***) –, das Piano–(Forte)pedal; (*fig.*) ***apply the soft –,*** einen sanften Ton anschlagen. **2.** *v.i.* 1. radfahren; 2. das Pedal treten. **3.** *v.t.* 1. fahren (*a cycle*); 2. treten. **4.** *attrib. adj.* Pedal–; – ***bin,*** der Treteimer; – ***cycle,*** das Fahrrad; (*organ*) – ***board,*** die Pedalklaviatur; (*organ*) – ***coupler,*** die Pedalkoppel; (*organ*) – ***key,*** die Pedaltaste; – ***note,*** (*organ*) der Pedalton, (*wind instrument*) Grundton.

pedant ['pedənt], *s.* der Pedant, Schulfuchs, Kleinigkeitskrämer. **pedantic** [pi'dæntik], *adj.* schulmeisterlich, pedantisch, kleinlich. **pedantry,** *s.* die Pedanterie, Kleinlichkeit.

pedate ['pedeit], *adj.* (*Zool.*) fußförmig.

peddle ['pedl], **1.** *v.t.* hausieren mit; (*fig.*) handeln mit, hausieren gehen mit, verkloppen. **2.** *v.i.* 1. hausieren gehen, hökern; 2. (*fig.*) sich mit Kleinigkeiten abgeben. **peddler,** *s.* (*Am.*) *see* **pedlar. peddling, 1.** *adj.* (*fig.*) kleinlich, nichtig, geringfügig, unbedeutend. **2.** *s.* der Hausierhandel.

pederast(y), *see* **paederast(y).**

pedestal ['pedəstl], *s.* 1. (*Archit.*) das Postament, Fußgestell, Piedestal, der Sockel, Säulenfuß; (*fig.*) ***place*** or ***set on a –,*** idealisieren, vergöttern; 2. (*Tech.*) Untersatz, das Fundament; 3. (*fig.*) die Grundlage, Basis.

pedestrian [pi'destriən], **1.** *adj.* zu Füß (gehend); Fuß–; – ***crossing,*** der Fußgängerüberweg; – ***traffic,*** der Fußgängerverkehr; 2. (*fig.*) alltäglich, prosaisch, langweilig, schwunglos. **2.** *s.* der Fußgänger. **pedestrianism,** *s.* 1. das Fußreisen, Wandern; 2. (*fig.*) die Alltäglichkeit, Schwunglosigkeit, prosaische Art.

pediatric, *see* **paediatric.**

pedicel ['pedisəl], *s.* *See* **pedicle. pedicellate(d)** [–'seleit(id)], *adj.* *See* **pediculate, 1. pedicle** [–ikl], *s.* (*Bot.*) der Blütenstiel, Blütenstengel; (*Med., Zool.*) Stiel, das Stielchen. **pediculate** [pə'dikjulət], **1.** *adj.* gestielt. **2.** *s.* (*Zool.*) der Armflosser. **pedicule,** *s.* *See* **pedicle.**

pedicure ['pedikjuə], *s.* 1. die Fußpflege; 2. der (die) Fußpfleger(in).

pedigree ['pedigri:], *s.* der Stammbaum, (*fig.*) die Herkunft, Abkunft; – ***horse,*** das Zuchtpferd.

pediment ['pedimənt], *s.* (*Archit.*) das Giebelfeld, der (Zier)giebel.

pedlar ['pedlə], *s.* der Hausierer (*of,* mit). **pedlary,** *s.* 1. *See* **peddling, 2.**; 2. Hausierwaren (*pl.*).

pedometer [pe'dɔmitə], *s.* der Schrittmesser, Schrittzähler.

peduncle [pe'dʌŋkl], *s.* (*Bot.*) der Blüten(stand)-stiel; (*Zool., Anat.*) Stiel, Träger. **peduncular** [–kjulə], **pedunculate** [–kjulət], *adj.* gestielt, Stiel–.

pee [pi:], *v.i.* (*coll.*) pinkeln.

peek [pi:k], **1.** *v.i.* (*coll.*) gucken. **2.** *s.* flüchtiger Blick. **peek-a-boo,** *s.* das Versteckspiel, Guck-Guck-Spiel.

[1]**peel** [pi:l], **1.** *v.t.* schälen, entrinden; – ***off,*** abschälen; (*sl.*) ausziehen, abstreifen (*one's clothes*); (*coll.*) ***keep one's eyes –ed,*** scharf aufpassen. **2.** *v.i.* 1. (*also* – ***off***) sich (ab)schälen, sich abblättern; abbröckeln, sich abschuppen; (*sl.*) sich ausziehen; 2. (*Av.*) – ***off,*** abdrehen, ausscheren. **3.** *s.* die Schale, Rinde.

[2]**peel,** *s.* der Brotschieber, die Backschaufel.

[1]**peeler** ['pi:lə], *s.* 1. das Schälmesser, die Schälmaschine; 2. (*sl.*) Entkleidungskünstlerin.

[2]**peeler,** *s.* (*obs.*) der Schutzmann.

peeling ['pi:liŋ], *s.* (*oft. pl.*) die Schale, Rinde, Haut.

peen [pi:n], *s.* die Pinne, Finne (*of hammer*).

[1]**peep** [pi:p], **1.** *v.i.* piep(s)en. **2.** *s.* das Piep(s)en; (*coll.*) ***there wasn't a – from him,*** er sagte kein Wort.

[2]**peep, 1.** *v.i.* 1. gucken, lugen, neugierig *or* verstohlen blicken; – ***at,*** angucken, begucken; 2. (*also* – ***forth*** or ***out***) hervorgucken, sich zeigen, zum

Vorschein kommen (*from*, aus). **2.** *v.t.* – *out one's head,* den Kopf hervorstecken. **3.** *s.* verstohlener Blick; *have* or *take a* –, heimlich zusehen; *have* or *take a* – *at,* heimlich ansehen; – *of day,* der Tagesanbruch.

peep-bo ['pi:pbou], *s. See* **peek-a-boo. peeper,** *s.* (*usu. pl.*) (*sl.*) das Auge. **peep-hole,** *s.* das Guckloch, der Sehschlitz, Sehspalt. **peeping Tom,** *s.* heimlicher Beobachter, der Schnüffler. **peep|-show,** *s.* der Guckkasten. **--sight,** *s.* das Lochvisier.

[1]**peer** [piə], *v.i.* 1. blicken, schauen, gucken, spähen (*into*, in (*Acc.*)); – *at*, (sich (*Dat.*)) genau ansehen, in Augenschein nehmen, begucken; 2. (*Poet.*) erscheinen, sich zeigen.

[2]**peer,** *s.* 1. Gleiche(r), Gleichrangige(r); Ebenbürtige(r); *be the* – *of,* den Vergleich aushalten mit; *he has no* –, keiner kommt ihm gleich; *one's* –(*s*), seinesgleichen; *without a* –, unvergleichlich, ohnegleichen; 2. hoher Adliger, (*Britain*) der Peer, (*France*) Pair. **peerage** [–ridʒ], *s.* 1. höherer Adelsstand, der Hochadel; 2. hoher Adelsrang, die Peerswürde; 3. der Adelskalender. **peeress,** *s.* die Gemahlin eines Peers; – *in her own right,* hohe Adlige, die Trägerin der Peerswürde. **peerless,** *adj.* unvergleichlich, ohnegleichen, beispiellos, einzigartig. **peerlessness,** *s.* die Unvergleichlichkeit.

peeve [pi:v], *v.t.* ärgern, reizen. **peeved, peevish,** *adj.* verdrießlich, mürrisch, grämlich, ärgerlich, verärgert (*at, about,* über (*Acc.*)). **peevishness,** *s.* die Verdrießlichkeit, Grämlichkeit.

peewit, *see* **pewit.**

peg [peg], **1.** *s.* 1. der (Holz)pflock, Zapfen, Dübel; Holznagel, (Holz)stift; *take him down a* – (*or two*), ihm einen Dämpfer aufsetzen, ihn herabwürdigen *or* demütigen; *come down a* – (*or two*), einen Pflock (*or* einige Pflöcke) zurückstecken; *be a square* – *in a round hole,* am falschen Platz stehen; 2. der Haken (*for hat and coat*); (*Mil. sl.*) *on the* –, angezeigt; (*coll.*) *off the* –, von der Stange, fertiggekauft; 3. die (Wäsche)klammer (*for washing*); 4. der Wirbel (*of violin etc.*); 5. (*fig.*) der Grund, Vorwand, das Mittel zum Zweck; 6. (*sl.*) der Schluck (Schnaps). **2.** *v.t.* 1. festpflöcken, anpflöcken; 2. (fest)klammern (*washing*); – *out the clothes* or *washing,* die Wäsche (zum Trocknen) aufhängen; 3. (*Tech.*) (an)nageln, (an)stiften, dübeln; – *down,* festnageln (*to*, auf (*Acc.*)); 4. begrenzen, einschränken, einengen; 5. (stabil)halten, stützen, festlegen (*prices*); 6. – *out,* abstecken (*a claim*); (*fig.*) – *out one's claim,* seine Ansprüche vorbringen *or* darlegen. **3.** *v.i.* 1. – *away,* emsig weiterarbeiten, drauflosarbeiten (*at*, an (*Dat.*)); 2. (*sl.*) – *out,* krepieren.

pegamoid ['pegəmɔid], *s.* das Kunstleder.

peg|-board, *s.* gelochte Hartplatte. **--leg,** *s.* (*coll.*) das Holzbein. **--top,** *s.* der Kreisel.

peignoir ['peinwɑ:], *s.* der Frisiermantel.

pejorative [pi'dʒɔrətiv], *adj.* verschlechternd, verschlimmernd, herabsetzend.

Peking [pi:'kiŋ], *s.* Peking (*n.*).

pekoe ['pi:kou], *s.* der Pekoetee.

pelage ['pelidʒ], *s.* (*Zool.*) die Hautbedeckung.

pelagian [pe'leidʒən], **pelagic** [–'lædʒik], *adj.* Hochsee–, ozeanisch.

pelargonium [pelə'gouniəm], *s.* (*Bot.*) die Pelargonie.

pelerine ['pelərі:n], *s.* die Pelerine, der Umhang.

pelf [pelf], *s.* (*sl.*) (schnöder) Mammon, Moneten (*pl.*).

pelican ['pelikən], *s.* (*Orn.*) der Pelikan, die Kropfgans (*Pelecanus*).

pelisse [pe'li:s], *s.* langer (Damen– *or* Kinder– *or* Husaren)mantel.

pellet ['pelit], *s.* 1. die Pille, das Kügelchen; 2. (*for gun*) Schrotkorn, die Schrotkugel.

pellicle ['pelikl], *s.* das Häutchen; der Belag, Überzug. **pellicular** [–'likjulə], *adj.* Häutchen–, membranartig.

pellitory ['pelitəri], *s.* (*Bot.*) 1. das Glaskraut; 2. die Bertramkamille.

pell-mell ['pel'mel], **1.** *adj.* 1. kunterbunt, unordentlich; 2. übereilt. **2.** *adv.* 1. unterschiedslos; 2. durcheinander, wie Kraut und Rüben; 3. Hals über Kopf, blindlings. **3.** *s.* das Durcheinander, der Wirrwarr.

pellucid [pe'lju:sid], *adj.* durchsichtig, durchscheinend; (*fig.*) klar. **pellucidity** [–'siditi], **pellucidness,** *s.* die Durchsichtigkeit, Klarheit.

pelmet ['pelmit], *s.* die (Vorhangs)falbel, der Gardinenstangenüberzug.

Peloponnesian [peləpə'ni:ziən], **1.** *s.* der (die) Peloponneser(in). **2.** *adj.* peloponnesisch. **Peloponnesus** [–'ni:səs], *s.* Peloponnes (*m.*).

pelorus [pə'lɔ:rəs], *s.* (*Naut.*) die Peilscheibe.

[1]**pelt** [pelt], **1.** *v.t.* bewerfen; (*fig.*) bestürmen, bombardieren; – *him with stones,* Steine nach ihm werfen. **2.** *v.i.* (nieder)prasseln; –*ing rain,* der Platzregen. **3.** *s.* 1. das Prasseln; 2. (*fig.*) (*at*) *full* –, in höchster Eile.

[2]**pelt,** *s.* der Pelz, das Fell, rohe Haut. **peltry,** *s.* Pelze, Häute, ungegerbte Felle (*pl.*); Pelzwaren (*pl.*), das Rauchwerk. **peltry-man,** *s.* der Rauchwarenhändler, Kürschner. **pelt-wool,** *s.* die Sterblingswolle.

pelvic ['pelvik], *adj.* Becken–. **pelvis,** *s.* (*Anat.*) das Becken.

pem(m)ican ['pemikən], *s.* harter Fleischkuchen, das Dauerfleisch, der Pemmikan.

[1]**pen** [pen], **1.** *s.* 1. die (Schreib)feder; – *and ink,* das Schreibzeug; –*and-ink drawing,* die Federzeichnung; *put* or *set* – *to paper,* die Feder ansetzen; *take up one's* –, die Feder ergreifen; 2. (*fig.*) die Schreibart, der Stil; 3. die Schriftstellerei. **2.** *v.t.* (nieder)schreiben, aufschreiben; verfassen, abfassen.

[2]**pen, 1.** *s.* 1. die Hürde, Koppel, das Gehege; der Pferch, Verschlag, (Hühner)stall; 2. (*Naut.*) U-Boot-Bunker; 3. (*for toddlers*) Laufstall, das Ställchen. **2.** *v.t.* (*also* – *in*) einpferchen, einschließen, einsperren.

[3]**pen,** *s.* weiblicher Schwan.

penal ['pi:nl], *adj.* 1. Straf–; – *code,* das Strafgesetz(buch); – *colony,* die Strafkolonie; – *law,* das Strafgesetz, Strafrecht; – *reform,* die Reform des Strafrechts; – *servitude,* die Zuchthausstrafe; 2. strafbar, sträflich. **penalization** [–ai'zeiʃən], *s.* 1. die Bestrafung; 2. (*fig.*) Belastung. **penalize,** *v.t.* 1. als strafbar erklären, mit einer Strafe belegen; 2. (*fig.*) belasten, benachteiligen.

penalty ['penlti], *s.* 1. (gesetzliche) Strafe; *on* or *under* – *of,* bei Strafe von; *on* – *of death,* bei Todesstrafe; *under* – *of death,* zur Todesstrafe verurteilt; *severe penalties for smoking,* auf Rauchen stehen strenge Strafbestimmungen; 2. (*fig.*) der Nachteil, Fluch; *pay the* – *of one's folly,* seine Torheit büßen müssen; 3. (*Spt.*) der Strafpunkt, die Strafe; (*Footb.*) – *area,* der Strafraum, Elfmeterraum; (*Footb.*) – *kick,* der Strafstoß, Elfmeter.

penance ['penəns], *s.* die Buße; *do* –, Buße tun.

pence [pens], *pl. of* **penny.**

penchant ['pɑ̃ʃɑ̃], *s.* der Hang, die Neigung (*for*, zu), Vorliebe (für).

pencil [pensl], **1.** *s.* 1. der Bleistift; *in* –, mit Bleistift, in Blei; *coloured* –, der Farbstift; *indelible* –, der Tintenstift; *lead* –, der Bleistift; *propelling* –, der Drehstift; *red* –, der Rotstift; 2. (*Tech. etc.*) der Stift; 3. (*Opt. etc.*) das Strahlenbüschel, Strahlenbündel; 4. (*obs.*) der Pinsel. **2.** *v.t.* 1. zeichnen, entwerfen; 2. mit Bleistift schreiben *or* (an)zeichnen *or* anstreichen. **pencil-case,** *s.* das Schüleretui. **pencilled** [–sild], *adj.* 1. mit Bleistift geschrieben *or* (an)gezeichnet; 2. (*Opt.*) büschelig, gebündelt; 3. (*fig.*) fein gestrichelt. **pencil|-shaped,** *adj.* büschelförmig. **--sharpener,** *s.* der Bleistiftspitzer.

pendant ['pendənt], *s.* 1. das (Ohr)gehänge, Anhängsel; 2. die Hängelampe, der Hängeleuchter; 3. (*Archit.*) Hängeschmuck; 4. (*fig.*) Anhang, das

Seitenstück, Gegenstück, Pendant. **pendent,** *adj.* 1. (herab)hängend, überhängend, Hänge–; 2. (*fig.*) angehängt, beigefügt; 3. *See* **pending, 1. pendentive** [–'dentiv], *s.* (*Archit.*) der Strebebogen, das Pendentif. **pending, 1.** *adj.* 1. (*fig.*) bevorstehend; 2. unentschieden, schwebend, anhängig, in der Schwebe. **2.** *prep.* während; bis (zu); – *further instructions,* bis auf weiteres.

pendulate ['pendjuleit], *v.i.* 1. pendelartig schwingen, pendeln, baumeln; 2. (*fig.*) schwanken, Schwankungen unterworfen sein. **penduline** [–lin], *adj.* (*Orn.*) hängend (*as a nest*). **pendulous,** *adj.* (herab)hängend, pendelnd, schwebend; – *motion,* die Pendelbewegung. **pendulum,** *s.* 1. das Pendel; – *wheel,* die Unruhe (*of clock*); 2. (*fig.*) die Pendelbewegung (*of opinion etc.*).

penetrability [penitrə'biliti], *s.* die Durchdringbarkeit, Durchdringlichkeit. **penetrable** ['penitrəbl], *adj.* durchdringbar, durchdringlich, (*fig.*) erfaßbar. **penetralia** [–'treiliə], *pl.* 1. Allerheiligste(s); 2. (*fig.*) das Privatleben, intime Geheimnisse (*pl.*).

penetrate ['penitreit], **1.** *v.t.* 1. durchdringen, erfüllen (*with,* mit); 2. eindringen in (*Acc.*), durchdringen; 3. (*fig.*) erforschen, ergründen, erfassen, durchschauen. **2.** *v.i.* eindringen ((*in*)*to,* in (*Acc.*)), durchdringen (zu), vordringen ((bis) zu). **penetrating,** *adj.* 1. durchdringend (*also fig.*), eindringend; 2. (*fig.*) scharfsinnig, eindringlich. **penetration** [–'treiʃən], *s.* 1. das Durchdringen (*into, Gen.*), Eindringen (in (*Acc.*)); *peaceful* –, die Einflußnahme (*of,* auf) (*Acc.*)), friedliche Durchdringung (*Gen.*); 2. (*Mil. etc.*) der Durchbruch (*of, Gen.*), Einbruch, das Vordringen (in (*Acc.*)); 3. (*Artil.*) Eindringungsvermögen, die Tiefenwirkung, Durchschlagskraft; 4. (*fig.*) Einsicht, der Scharfsinn. **penetrative,** *adj.* Eindringungs–; *see also* **penetrating.**

pen|-feather, *s.* die Schwungfeder. **–-friend,** *s.* der (die) Brieffreund(in).

penguin ['peŋgwin], *s.* (*Orn.*) der Pinguin.

pen-holder, *s.* der Federhalter.

penicillate [peni'silit], *adj.* pinselförmig, bündelartig.

penicillin [peni'silin], *s.* das Penizillin.

peninsula [pə'ninsjulə], *s.* die Halbinsel; *Iberian Peninsula,* die Pyrenäenhalbinsel. **peninsular,** *adj.* halbinselförmig; Halbinsel–; *Peninsular War,* der Peninsularkrieg (1808–14).

penis ['pi:nis], *s.* der Penis, männliches Glied; (*Zool.*) die Rute.

penitence ['penitəns], *s.* die Reue, Buße. **penitent, 1.** *adj.* reuig, bußfertig. **2.** *s.* 1. Bußfertige(r), Büßende(r), der (die) Büßer(in); 2. (*R.C.*) das Beichtkind. **penitential** [–'tenʃəl], **1.** *adj.* reuig, reuevoll, reumütig, bußfertig, Buß–. **2.** *s.* das Bußbuch. **penitentiary** [–'tenʃəri], **1.** *adj.* 1. Buß–; 2. Besserungs–. **2.** *s.* 1. (*esp. Am.*) das Gefängnis, Zuchthaus; die Besserungsanstalt, Korrektionsanstalt; 2. (*R.C.*) der Bußpriester, Beichtvater.

penknife ['pennaif], *s.* das Taschenmesser. **penmanship,** *s.* die Schreibkunst, Kalligraphie, das Schönschreiben. **pen-name,** *s.* der Schriftstellername.

pennant ['penənt], *s.* 1. (*Naut.*) der Wimpel, Stander; 2. das Fähnchen.

penniform ['penifɔ:m], *adj.* federförmig, kielförmig.

penniless ['penilis], *adj.* ohne (einen Pfennig) Geld, arm, mittellos.

pennon ['penən], *s.* (*Mil.*) das (Lanzen)fähnchen, Fähnlein, der Wimpel.

penny ['peni], *s.* (*pl.* **pennies,** *collect.* **pence**) (*also new* –) (englischer) Penny; (*Am. coll.*) das Eincentstück; (*fig.*) der Pfennig, Heller, die Kleinigkeit; *in for a – in for a pound,* wer A sagt, muß auch B sagen; *he hasn't a – to his name* or *to bless himself with,* er hat keinen roten Heller; (*coll.*) *has the – dropped?* ist der Groschen gefallen? *to the last* –, bis auf den letzten Heller; *take care of the pence and the pounds will take care of themselves,* wer den Pfennig nicht ehrt, ist des Talers nicht wert; *turn an honest* –, ehrlich sein Brot verdienen; *a pretty* –, eine schöne Summe; (*coll.*) *spend a* –, austreten müssen; *a – for your thoughts!* sprich's doch heraus! *not worth a* –, keinen Heller wert.

penny|-a-liner, *s.* der Skribent, Zeilenschinder. **–-dreadful,** *s.* der Schauerroman, Hintertreppenroman. **–-farthing bicycle,** *s.* (*Hist.*) das Hochrad. **–-in-the-slot machine,** *s.* der Verkaufsautomat. **–-royal,** *s.* (*Bot.*) die Poleiminze. **–weight,** *s.* 1/20 Unze (= *1.55 g.*). **–-wise,** *adj.* sparsam im kleinen; *be – and pound-foolish,* am unrechten Ende sparen. **–wort,** *s.* (*Bot.*) das Nabelkraut. **–worth,** *s.* der Pfennigwert; *a – of sweets,* für einen Penny Bonbons.

penological [pi:nə'lɔdʒikl], *adj.* strafrechtlich, Strafrechts–, kriminalkundlich. **penologist** [–'nɔlədʒist], *s.* der Strafrechtler. **penology** [–'nɔlədʒi], *s.* die Strafrechtslehre, Kriminalstrafkunde.

pen|-pal, *s. See* **–-friend. –-pusher,** *s.* (*coll.*) der Schreiberling, Bürohengst.

pensile ['pensail], *adj.* Hänge–, (herab)hängend, schwebend.

1**pension** ['pãsjɔ̃], *s.* die Pension, das Fremdenheim, Pensionat.

2**pension** ['penʃən], **1.** *s.* das Ruhegehalt, die Pension, Rente, das Jahrgeld, Kostgeld; *old-age* –, die Altersversorgung; *on* –, in Pension, in Ruhestand; *retire on* –, in Pension *or* in den Ruhestand gehen; *retiring* –, das Ruhegehalt. **2.** *v.t.* ein Jahrgeld geben (*Dat.*); – *off,* in den Ruhestand versetzen, mit Ruhegehalt entlassen, pensionieren. **pensionable,** *adj.* pensionsberechtigt (*a p.*), pensionsfähig (*age*). **pensionary, pensioner,** *s.* der Ruhegehaltsempfänger, Pensionär.

pensive ['pensiv], *adj.* 1. nachdenklich, gedankenvoll, sinnend; 2. tiefsinnig, ernst, schwermütig. **pensiveness,** *s.* 1. die Nachdenklichkeit; 2. Tiefsinnigkeit, Schwermut, der Tiefsinn.

penstock ['penstɔk], *s.* das Schützenwehr, Schütz.

pent [pent], *adj.* 1. (*also – up*) eingepfercht, eingeschlossen; 2. (*fig.*) – *up,* verhalten, zurückgehalten (*as anger etc.*).

pentacle ['pentəkl], *s.* der Drudenfuß, Fünfstern, das Pentagramm.

pentad ['pentæd], *s.* 1. der Zeitraum von 5 Jahren, das Jahrfünft; 2. die Zahl 5; 3. (*Chem.*) fünfwertiges Element.

pentagon ['pentəgən], *s.* das Fünfeck; (*Am.*) *the Pentagon,* das Pentagon. **pentagonal** [–'tægənl], *adj.* fünfeckig, fünfkantig, fünfseitig. **pentagram,** *s. See* **pentacle. pentagrid,** *s.* (*Rad.*) die Fünfgitterröhre. **pentahedral** [–'hi:drəl], *adj.* fünfflächig. **pentahedron** [–'hi:drən], *s.* das Fünfflach, Pentaeder. **pentameter** [–'tæmitə], *s.* (*Metr.*) der Pentameter. **Pentateuch** [–tju:k], *s.* (*B.*) der Pentateuch. **pentathlon** [–'tæθlən], *s.* (*Spt.*) der Fünfkampf.

Pentecost ['pentikɔst], *s.* das Pfingstfest, Pfingsten (*Austr., Swiss oft. pl.*). **Pentecostal** [–'kɔstl], *adj.* Pfingst–, pfingstlich.

penthouse ['penthaus], *s.* 1. das Schutzdach, Wetterdach; 2. die Dachwohnung (eines Hochhauses).

pentode ['pentoud], *s.* (*Rad.*) die Dreigitterröhre, Fünfpolröhre.

pentstemon [pent'sti:mən], *s.* (*Bot.*) der Bartfaden.

penult [pe'nʌlt], *s.* vorletzte Silbe. **penultimate** [–timit], *adj.* vorletzt.

penumbra [pe'nʌmbrə], *s.* der Halbschatten. **penumbral,** *adj.* halbdunkel, Halbschatten–.

penurious [pe'njuəriəs], *adj.* 1. dürftig, ärmlich; karg; 2. geizig, knauserig, filzig. **penury** ['penjuri], *s.* 1. die Armut, Not; 2. Knappheit, der Mangel (*of,* an (*Dat.*)).

pen-wiper, *s.* der Tintenwischer.

peon [piən], *s.* 1. (*India*) der Bote, Schutzmann;

2. (*Latin Am.*) Tagelöhner, Leibeigene(r). **peonage,** *s.* die Leibeigenschaft, Dienstbarkeit.

peony ['piəni], *s.* die Pfingstrose, Bauernrose, Päonie.

people [pi:pl], **1.** *s.* 1. (*collect., pl. constr.*) Leute, Menschen (*pl.*), die Bevölkerung; – ***of quality,*** die vornehme Gesellschaft; ***he of all*** –, ausgerechnet er, er vor allen anderen; ***country*** –, Landbewohner (*pl.*), die Landbevölkerung; ***the little*** –, die Feen(welt); ***many*** –, manche (Leute); 2. (*after poss. pron., pl. constr.*) (gemeines) Volk, Untertanen (*pl.*), die Dienerschaft, das Gefolge; die Familie, Verwandte (*pl.*), Angehörige (*pl.*); 3. (*after def. art., also sing. constr.*) das Volk, die große Masse, die Nation, Wählerschaft, Wähler (*pl.*), Bürger (*pl.*); ***the Scottish*** –, die Schotten; ***the*** – ***of Israel,*** das Volk Israel; 4. (*impers.*) man; ***what will*** – ***say?*** was wird man sagen? **2.** *v.t.* bevölkern, besiedeln (***with,*** mit).

pep [pep], **1.** *s.* (*sl.*) der Schwung, Schmiß, Elan, Mumm; – ***pill,*** die Aufputschpille; – ***talk,*** der Ermahnungszuspruch, Ermunterungszuspruch. **2.** *v.t.* – ***up,*** anfeuern, beleben, aufputschen.

pepper ['pepə], **1.** *s.* der Pfeffer. **2.** *v.t.* 1. pfeffern; 2. bestreuen, sprenkeln; 3. (*fig.*) beschießen, bewerfen (*with missiles*), überhäufen (*with questions etc.*); 4. durchprügeln. **3.** *v.i.* – ***away at,*** losschießen auf (*Acc.*).

pepper|-and-salt, *adj.* gelblich-grauweiß. **--box, --caster,** *s.* der Pfefferstreuer. **-corn,** *s.* das Pfefferkorn. **-mint,** *s.* 1. die Pfefferminze; 2. das Pfefferminz(plätzchen). **--pot,** *s. See* **--box. peppery,** *adj.* 1. pfefferig, gepfeffert; 2. (*fig.*) beißend, scharf; 3. (*of a p.*) jähzornig, heftig, hitzig.

peppy ['pepi], *adj.* (*sl.*) schwungvoll, schmissig, forsch.

pepsin ['pepsin], *s.* das Pepsin. **peptic,** *adj.* 1. verdauungsfördernd; 2. Verdauungs–; – ***gland,*** die Labdrüse; – ***ulcer,*** das Magengeschwür. **peptone,** *s.* das Pepton, verdauter Eiweißstoff.

per [pə:], **1.** *prep.* pro; per, mit, für, durch, laut, gemäß; (*Comm.*) ***as*** –, laut, gemäß; (*coll.*) ***as*** – ***usual,*** wie sonst *or* gewöhnlich; – ***annum,*** pro Jahr, jährlich; – ***bearer,*** durch Überbringer; – ***capita,*** pro Kopf *or* Person; (*attrib.*) Kopf–; – ***cent,*** pro *or* vom Hundert; *see* **percent**; (*Comm.*) – ***contra,*** als Gegenforderung, auf der Gegenseite; (*coll.*) umgekehrt, im Gegenteil; – ***diem,*** täglich, pro Tag; – ***pound,*** das Pfund; (*Comm.*) – ***pro.,*** per Prokura, in Vertretung *or* im Auftrag (von); – ***rail,*** per Bahn; – ***se,*** für sich, an (und für) sich; – ***second,*** in der *or* pro Sekunde. **2.** *pref.* (*Chem.*) Per–, Über–.

peradventure [perəd'ventʃə], **1.** (*obs.*) *adv.* von ungefähr, vielleicht; ***if*** –, wenn etwa *or* zufällig. **2.** *s.* die Ungewißheit, der Zweifel.

perambulate [pə'ræmbjuleit], **1.** *v.t.* 1. durchwandern, durchschreiten; 2. bereisen, besichtigen, abschreiten (*boundaries etc.*). **2.** *v.i.* umherwandern, umhergehen. **perambulation** [–'leiʃən], *s.* 1. die Durchwanderung, Besichtigung; 2. Inspektionsreise, Grenzbegehung. **perambulator,** *s.* der Kinderwagen.

perceivable [pə'si:vəbl], *adj.* wahrnehmbar, merkbar, merklich, vernehmlich, spürbar. **perceive,** *v.t.* 1. wahrnehmen, (be)merken, gewahr werden; (ver)spüren, empfinden; 2. erkennen, begreifen, einsehen.

percent [pə'sent], **1.** *s.* das Prozent. **2.** *adj.* prozentig. **percentage,** *s.* 1. der Prozentsatz, Prozente (*pl.*); 2. (*Comm.*) die Provision, Tantieme; 3. (*coll.*) der (An)teil (***of,*** an (*Dat.*)). **percentile** [–tail], *adj.* (*Stat.*) Prozent–.

percept ['pə:sept], *s.* (*Phil.*) wahrgenommener Gegenstand. **perceptibility** [–i'biliti], *s.* die Wahrnehmbarkeit. **perceptible** [–'septibl], *adj.* wahrnehmbar, vernehmlich, bemerkbar, merklich, fühlbar, spürbar.

perception [pə'sepʃən], *s.* 1. die Wahrnehmung, Empfindung; 2. das Empfindungsvermögen; 3. intuitive Erkenntnis, die Vorstellung, der Begriff. **perceptive** [–tiv], *adj.* 1. wahrnehmend, Wahrnehmungs–; 2. (*of a p.*) einsichtsvoll, scharfsichtig, tiefblickend, erkenntnisreich, auffassungsfähig. **perceptiveness, perceptivity** [–'tiviti], *s.* 1. das Wahrnehmungsvermögen, Auffassungsvermögen; 2. der Scharfsinn.

[1]**perch** [pə:tʃ], *s.* (*Ichth.*) der (Fluß)barsch.

[2]**perch, 1.** *s.* 1. die (Sitz)stange, Hühnerstange; 2. (*fig.*) (sicherer) Sitz; (*coll.*) ***fall off one's*** –, vom Stengel fallen; (*coll.*) ***knock him off his*** –, ihn verdrängen *or* aus dem Sattel heben; (*sl.*) ***take one's*** –, sich setzen; 3. die Rute (= *5.03 m.*); 4. der Langbaum (*of a wagon*); 5. (*Naut.*) die Spiere, das Stangenseezeichen. **2.** *v.i.* sitzen (***on,*** auf (*Dat.*)); sich setzen *or* niederlassen (auf (*Acc.*)); (*fig.*) hoch sitzen. **3.** *v.t.* (*fig.*) setzen; ***be*** –***ed,*** sitzen; – ***o.s.,*** sich setzen.

perchance [pə'tʃɑ:ns], *adv.* (*Poet.*) vielleicht, zufällig, von ungefähr.

perchlorate [pə:'klɔ:rit], *s.* überchlorsaures Salz. **perchloric,** *adj.* überchlorig; – ***acid,*** die Überchlorsäure.

percipience [pə'sipiəns], *s.* das Wahrnehmen, Wahrnehmungsvermögen. **percipient, 1.** *adj.* 1. wahrnehmend, Wahrnehmungs–; 2. scharfsichtig. **2.** *s.* der (die) Wahrnehmer(in).

percolate ['pə:kəleit], **1.** *v.i.* durchsickern (*also fig.*), durchsintern, durchlaufen. **2.** *v.t.* durchsickern lassen, durchseihen, filtern, filtrieren, kolieren. **percolation** [–'leiʃən], *s.* das Durchsickern, Durchseihen. **percolator,** *s.* der Filtriertrichter; Kaffeefilter.

percuss [pə'kʌs], *v.t.* (*Med.*) beklopfen, perkutieren. **percussion** [–'kʌʃən], *s.* 1. die Erschütterung, der Schlag, Stoß; – ***borer,*** der Stoßbohrer; – ***cap,*** das Zündhütchen; die Sprengkapsel; – ***fuse,*** der Aufschlagzünder; 2. (*Med.*) das Beklopfen, die Perkussion; 3. (*Mus.*) das Schlagzeug; – ***instrument,*** das Schlaginstrument. **percussive,** *adj.* schlagend, Schlag–, stoßend, Stoß–.

perdition [pə'diʃən], *s.* 1. (*Eccl.*) ewige Verdammnis; 2. das Verderben.

perdu(e) [pə:'dju:], *adj., adv.* auf der Lauer, im Hinterhalt; verborgen, versteckt.

perdurability [pə'djuərə'biliti], *s.* lange Dauer, die Dauerhaftigkeit. **perdurable,** *adj.* 1. sehr dauerhaft, unverwüstlich; 2. immerwährend, lange dauernd.

peregrinate ['perəgrineit], *v.i.* wandern, umherreisen. **peregrination** [–'neiʃən], *s.* 1. die Wanderschaft, das Wandern, Umherreisen; 2. die Reise, Wanderung. **peregrinatory** [–'neitəri], *adj.* Wander–, Reise–. **peregrin(e)** [–grin], *s.* (*Orn.*) (– ***falcon***) der Wanderfalke (*Falco peregrinus*).

peremptoriness [pə'remptərinis], *s.* 1. die Entschiedenheit, Endgültigkeit; 2. gebieterische Art, herrische Manier. **peremptory,** *adj.* 1. endgültig, entscheidend, entschieden, unbedingt, peremptorisch; 2. herrisch, gebieterisch, energisch, diktatorisch.

perennial [pə'reniəl], **1.** *adj.* 1. das ganze Jahr dauernd; 2. (*Bot.*) überdauernd, winterhart, perennierend; 3. immerwährend, (immer)dauernd, anhaltend, beständig, Dauer–. **2.** *s.* perennierende Pflanze.

[1]**perfect** ['pə:fikt], **1.** *adj.* 1. vollkommen, vollendet, fehlerlos, makellos, tadellos, perfekt, vortrefflich, vorzüglich; ***make*** –, vervollkommnen; – ***circle,*** vollkommener Kreis; (*Mus.*) – ***pitch,*** absolutes Gehör; 2. vollkommen ausgebildet, vollständig, gänzlich, (*Math.*) ganz; – ***number,*** ganze Zahl; 3. gründlich unterrichtet, ausgebildet, bewandert (***in,*** in (*Dat.*)); ***practice makes*** –, Übung macht den Meister; 4. (*coll.*) rein, komplett (*nonsense etc.*); – ***fool,*** kompletter Narr; 5. (*Mus.*) – ***cadence,*** der Ganzschluß; 6. (*Gram.*) – ***participle,*** das Partizipium der Vergangenheit. **2.** *s.* (*Gram.*) (*also* – ***tense***) das Perfekt(um).

[2]**perfect** [pə'fekt], *v.t.* vollenden, zur Vollendung

bringen, vervollständigen, vervollkommnen; ausbilden; – *o.s. in,* sich vervollkommnen in (*Dat.*).

perfectibility [pəfekti'biliti], *s.* die Vervollkommnungsfähigkeit. **perfectible** [–'fektibl], *adj.* vervollkommnungsfähig.

perfection [pə'fekʃən], *s.* die Vollendung, Vervollkommnung; Vollkommenheit, (Vor)trefflichkeit, Vorzüglichkeit, Fehlerlosigkeit; ***to –,*** vollkommen, vortrefflich, meisterhaft, in hoher Vollendung; ***bring to –,*** vollenden, zur Vollendung bringen, vervollkommnen; ***counsel of –,*** der Rat des Weisen. **perfectionist,** *s.* der Perfektionist (*also Phil., Eccl.*).

perfective [pə'fektiv], *adj.* (*Gram.*) perfektivisch.

perfectly ['pə:fiktli], *adv. See* [1]**perfect, 1**; (*coll.*) ganz, gänzlich, völlig, geradezu.

perfervid [pə'fə:vid], *adj.* glühend, heiß, innig, inbrünstig.

perfidious [pə'fidiəs], *adj.* treulos, verräterisch, heimtückisch, falsch, hinterlistig. **perfidiousness,** *s.* die Treulosigkeit, Falschheit, Tücke, Hinterlist, Perfidie. **perfidy** ['pə:fidi], *s.* der Treubruch, Verrat; *see also* **perfidiousness.**

perfoliate [pə:'foulieit], *adj.* (*Bot.*) durchwachsen.

perforate, 1. ['pə:fəreit], *v.t.* durchbohren, durchschlagen, durchlöchern, lochen, perforieren. **2.** [–eit], *v.i.* 1. Löcher schlagen; 2. durchdringen, eindringen, sich hineinbohren (*into,* in (*Acc.*)). **3.** [–it], *adj.* 1. durchlöchert; 2. (*Her.*) durchbrochen. **perforation** [–'reiʃən], *s.* 1. die Durchbohrung, Durchlochung, Durchlöcherung; ***– of the stomach,*** der Magendurchbruch; 2. die Lochung, Perforierlinie (*as on stamps*); 3. Öffnung, das Loch. **perforator** [–eitə], *s.* der Locher, die Lochzange.

perforce [pə'fɔ:s], *adv.* gezwungen(ermaßen), notwendigerweise, notgedrungen.

perform [pə'fɔ:m], **1.** *v.t.* 1. machen, tun, leisten, bewerkstelligen, verrichten; ausführen, durchführen, vollbringen, vollziehen, vollstrecken; ***– miracles,*** Wunder wirken; 2. erfüllen, nachkommen (*Dat.*) (*obligation*); 3. (*Mus., Theat.*) aufführen, vortragen, geben, spielen. **2.** *v.i.* 1. (*Theat. etc.*) auftreten, spielen, vortragen; 2. funktionieren. **performable,** *adj.* 1. ausführbar, durchführbar; 2. (*Theat. etc.*) aufführbar.

performance [pə'fɔ:məns], *s.* 1. die Ausführung, Ausübung, Verrichtung, Vollziehung, Vollbringung, Vollstreckung, Erfüllung; 2. (*Theat.*) Vorstellung, Aufführung (*of a play etc.*), schauspielerische Leistung, die Darstellung (*of a character*); 3. Arbeit, Tat, Leistung; ***promises without –,*** Worte ohne Taten, Versprechungen ohne Erfüllung; 4. (*Motor. etc.*) die Leistung. **performer,** *s.* 1. Ausführende(r), der Vollzieher, Verrichter; 2. (*Theat. etc.*) Schauspieler, Darsteller; Künstler, Virtuose. **performing,** *attrib. adj.* dressiert, abgerichtet (*as dogs etc.*).

perfume ['pe:fju:m], **1.** *s.* 1. der Wohlgeruch, Duft; 2. das Parfüm, Parfum, der Riechstoff. **2.** *v.t.* parfümieren, durchduften. **perfumed,** *adj.* parfümiert, wohlriechend. **perfumer** [–'fju:mə], *s.* der Parfümeriehändler, Parfümeur. **perfumery** [–'fju:məri], *s.* 1. die Parfümerie; 2. das Parfümeriegeschäft.

perfunctoriness [pə'fʌŋktərinis], *s.* die Nachlässigkeit, Flüchtigkeit, Oberflächlichkeit. **perfunctory,** *adj.* 1. nachlässig, oberflächlich, flüchtig; 2. mechanisch, gewohnheitsmäßig; ***in a – manner,*** beiläufig, obenhin.

perfuse [pə'fju:z], *v.t.* 1. begießen, besprengen; 2. durchschwemmen, durchtränken, durchsetzen. **perfusion** [–ʒən], *s.* die Begießung, Durchtränkung, Durchströmung.

pergola ['pə:gələ], *s.* offener Laubengang.

perhaps [pə'hæps], *adv.* vielleicht, möglicherweise.

peri ['piəri], *s.* die Peri, Fee, Elfe.

perianth ['periænθ], *s.* (*Bot.*) die Blütenhülle.

pericarditis [perikɑ:'daitis], *s.* (*Med.*) die Herzbeutelentzündung. **pericardium** [–'kɑ:diəm], *s.* (*Anat.*) der Herzbeutel.

pericarp ['perikɑ:p], *s.* (*Bot.*) die Fruchthülle.

perichondritis [perikɔn'draitis], *s.* (*Med.*) die Knorpelhautentzündung. **perichondrium** [–'kɔndriəm], *s.* (*Anat.*) die Knorpelhaut.

perigee ['peridʒi:], *s.* (*Astr.*) die Erdnähe.

perigynous [pə'ridʒinəs], *adj.* (*Bot.*) mittelständig, perigyn.

perihelion [peri'hi:liən], *s.* (*Astr.*) die Sonnennähe.

peril ['peril], *s.* die Gefahr; ***at your (own) –,*** auf Ihre (*or* eigene) Gefahr *or* Verantwortung, auf Ihr Risiko; ***in – of one's life,*** in Lebensgefahr; ***the yellow –,*** die gelbe Gefahr. **perilous,** *adj.* gefährlich, gefahrvoll.

perimeter [pə'rimitə], *s.* 1. (*Geom., fig.*) der Umkreis; 2. (*fig.*) Peripherie; 3. (*Mil.*) die Vorpostenlinie.

perineum [peri'niəm], *s.* (*Anat.*) der Damm, das Mittelfleisch.

period ['piəriəd], **1.** *s.* 1. die Periode, Umlaufszeit, der Umlauf, Kreislauf, regelmäßige Wiederkehr; 2. die Periode, Zeit(spanne), der Zeitabschnitt, Zeitraum; (*coll.*) ***for a –,*** für einige Zeit; ***for a – of,*** auf die Dauer von; ***incubation –,*** die Reifezeit, Inkubationszeit; (*Spt.*) ***– of extra time,*** die Spielverlängerung; ***– of office,*** die Amtsdauer, Amtszeit; ***– of transition,*** die Übergangszeit; 3. das Zeitalter; ***dress of the –,*** die Kleidung des Tages, zeitgenössische Tracht; 4. (*Rhet.*) die Pause, der Absatz; 5. (*Typ.*) der Punkt; 6. (*Elec. etc.*) die Schwing(ungs)dauer; 7. (Lehr)stunde, Unterrichtsstunde (*in school*); 8. (*Gram.*) der Gliedersatz, das Satzgefüge; 9. (*oft. pl.*) (*also* ***monthly –***) die Periode, Menstruation, (*coll.*) Regel. **2.** *attrib. adj.* ***– furniture,*** das Stilmöbel; ***– novel,*** zeitgeschichtlicher Roman; ***– piece,*** das Museumstück; ***– play,*** historisches (Theater)-stück.

periodic [piəri'ɔdik], *adj.* 1. periodisch (*also Gram.*), regelmäßig wiederkehrend; ***– motion,*** der Kreislauf; 2. (*Gram.*) wohlgefügt. **periodical, 1.** *adj.* 1. *See* **periodic**; 2. Zeitschriften–. **2.** *s.* die Zeitschrift. **periodicity** [–ɔ'disiti], *s.* die Periodizität.

periosteum [peri'ɔstiəm], *s.* (*Anat.*) die Knochenhaut, das Periost. **periostitis** [–ɔs'taitis], *s.* die Knochenhautentzündung. **periostosis** [–ɔs'tousis], *s.* die Knochenhautgeschwulst, Exostose.

peripatetic [peripə'tetik], **1.** *adj.* peripatetisch, umherziehend, Wander–. **2.** *s.* der Peripatetiker.

peripheral [pə'rifərəl], *adj.* peripherisch, Rand–. **periphery,** *s.* die Peripherie; (*fig.*) der Rand, die Grenze.

periphrasis [pe'rifrəsis], *s.* (*pl.* **-es** [–si:z]), die Umschreibung. **periphrastic** [–'fræstik], *adj.* umschreibend, periphrastisch.

periscope ['periskoup], *s.* das Periskop, Sehrohr, der Beobachtungsspiegel.

perish ['periʃ], *v.i.* 1. umkommen, sterben, (*sl.*) krepieren (***with,*** vor (*Dat.*)), untergehen, eingehen, zugrunde gehen (***by,*** durch *or* an (*Dat.*)); 2. verwelken, verfallen, absterben. **perishable, 1.** *adj.* 1. vergänglich; 2. leicht verderblich, nicht haltbar (*as goods etc.*). **2.** *s.* ***–s,*** leicht verderbliche Waren (*pl.*). **perishableness,** *s.* 1. leichte Verderblichkeit (*of goods*); 2. die Vergänglichkeit. **perished,** *adj.* verwelkt, verdorben; (*coll.*) ***be – (with cold),*** schwach *or* hilflos *or* zitternd vor Kälte sein; (*coll.*) ***be – with fright,*** vor Schrecken fast umkommen. **perisher,** *s.* (*sl.*) der Hundsfott. **perishing,** *adj., adv.* (*coll.*) grimmig (*as cold*); (*sl.*) verflixt.

peristalsis [peri'stælsis], *s.* die Peristaltik. **peristaltic,** *adj.* peristaltisch, wurmförmig.

peristyle ['peristail], *s.* (*Archit.*) der Säulengang.

peritoneum [peri'touniəm], *s.* (*Anat.*) das Bauchfell. **peritonitis** [–tə'naitis], *s.* (*Med.*) die Bauchfellentzündung.

periwig ['periwig], *s.* die Perücke.

periwinkle ['periwiŋkl], *s.* 1. die Uferschnecke; 2. (*Bot.*) das Immergrün, Singrün.

perjure ['pə:dʒə], *v.t.* ***– o.s.,*** einen Meineid leisten, eidbrüchig *or* meineidig werden. **perjurer,** *s.* Meineidige(r). **perjurious** [–ˈdʒuəriəs], *adj.* meineidig, eidbrüchig. **perjury,** *s.* der Meineid, (*Law*) fahrlässiger Falscheid.

[1]**perk** [pə:k], *s.* (*coll.*) (*abbr. of* **perquisite**) die Nebeneinnahme, zusätzliche Sozialleistung.

[2]**perk, 1.** *v.i.* sich brüsten, die Nase hochtragen; (*coll.*) – ***up,*** sich wieder erholen, in Stimmung kommen. **2.** *v.t.* putzen, schmücken; – ***o.s.,*** sich aufputzen; – ***up,*** emporrecken; – ***up one's ears,*** die Ohren spitzen. **perkiness,** *s.* 1. der Übermut, die Keckheit, das Selbstbewußtsein; 2. die Munterkeit, Lebhaftigkeit. **perky,** *adj.* 1. keck, übermütig, selbstbewußt; 2. lebhaft, munter.

perm [pə:m], **1.** *s.* (*coll.*) die Dauerwelle. **2.** *v.t.* Dauerwellen machen in (*Acc.*).

permanence [ˈpə:mənəns], *s.* 1. die (Fort)dauer, das Beharren, die Ständigkeit; 2. Beständigkeit, Dauerhaftigkeit (*of colours etc.*); ***have no* –,** nicht von Dauer sein. **permanency** [–i], *s.* 1. *See* **permanence**; 2. (*coll.*) ***a* –,** feste Anstellung, die Dauerstellung. **permanent,** *adj.* (be)ständig, (fort)dauernd, fortwährend, bleibend, anhaltend, nachhaltig, dauerhaft, Dauer–; ortsfest, bodenständig; – ***abode,*** fester Wohnsitz; – ***appointment,*** die Lebensstellung; – ***committee,*** ständiger Ausschuß; (*Artil.*) – ***emplacement,*** ortsfeste Stellung; – ***magnet,*** der Dauermagnet, Permanentmagnet; (*Pol.*) – ***secretary,*** ständiger Staatssekretär; – ***wave,*** die Dauerwelle; (*Railw.*) – ***way,*** die Gleisanlage, der Oberbau, Bahnkörper.

permanganate [pəˈmæŋgəneit], *s.* das Permanganat; – ***of potash,*** übermangansaures Kali.

permeability [pə:miəˈbiliti], *s.* 1. die Durchdringbarkeit, Durchlässigkeit; 2. spezifische magnetische Leitfähigkeit. **permeable** [ˈpə:miəbl], *adj.* durchdringbar, durchlässig (***to,*** für). **permeance,** *s.* magnetischer Leitwert. **permeate** [ˈpə:mieit], **1.** *v.t.* durchdringen. **2.** *v.i.* dringen (***into,*** in (*Acc.*)), durchsickern (***through,*** durch), sich verbreiten (***among,*** unter (*Dat.*)). **permeation** [–ˈeiʃən], *s.* das Durchdringen, Eindringen.

permissible [pəˈmisibl], *adj.* erlaubt, zulässig, statthaft. **permission** [–ˈmiʃən], *s.* die Erlaubnis, Bewilligung, Genehmigung, Zulassung; ***ask his –, ask him for –,*** ihn um Erlaubnis bitten; ***he gave*** (***his***) –, er gab mir Erlaubnis. **permissive,** *adj.* 1. zulassend, gestattend; 2. gestattet, zugelassen, zulässig; 3. – ***society,*** freizügige Gesellschaft.

[1]**permit** [pəˈmit], **1.** *v.t.* erlauben, gestatten (*a th., Acc.; a p., Dat.*); zulassen, dulden (*a th.*); ***he was permitted to go,*** er durfte gehen, ihm wurde gestattet *or* erlaubt zu gehen, man erlaubte ihm zu gehen; – ***o.s. a th.,*** sich (*Dat.*) etwas erlauben *or* gönnen. **2.** *v.i.* es erlauben; ***circumstances permitting, if circumstances* –,** wenn es die Umstände erlauben; ***time permitting, if time –s,*** wenn es die Zeit erlaubt; ***weather permitting,*** bei günstiger Witterung; – ***of,*** zulassen; – ***of no exception,*** keine Ausnahme zulassen.

[2]**permit** [ˈpə:mit], *s.* der Zulassungsschein, Erlaubnisschein, Ausweis, Passierschein, die Genehmigung, Ein– *or* Ausreisebewilligung, Ein– *or* Ausfuhrerlaubnis, der Bezugschein, die Lizenz.

permutation [pə:mjuˈteiʃən], *s.* 1. (*Math.*) die Permutation, Versetzung, Umsetzung; 2. Vertauschung, der Austausch. **permute** [–ˈmju:t], *v.t.* permutieren, vertauschen, umsetzen.

pernicious [pəˈniʃəs], *adj.* 1. schädlich, verderblich, nachteilig (***to,*** *Dat.*); 2. (*Med.*) bösartig.

pernickety [pəˈnikəti], *adj.* (*coll.*) 1. heikel, kitz(e)lig; 2. (*of a p.*) pedantisch, kleinlich, wählerisch, pinselig (***about,*** mit).

perorate [ˈperəreit], *v.i.* 1. eine Rede schließen; 2. (*fig.*) hochtrabend reden. **peroration** [–ˈreiʃən], *s.* der Redeschluß, zusammenfassender Schluß, die Schlußerörterung.

peroxide [pəˈrɔksaid], *s.* das Superoxyd, Hyperoxyd.

perpendicular [pə:pənˈdikjulə], **1.** *adj.* 1. senkrecht, lotrecht; (*Archit.*) – ***style,*** englische Spätgotik; 2. rechtwink(e)lig (***to,*** auf (*Dat.*)); 3. sehr steil, aufrecht. **2.** *s.* 1. die Senkrechte, das Lot, der *or* das Perpendikel; ***raise a* –,** ein Lot errichten (***on,*** auf (*Dat.*)); ***let fall a* –,** ein Lot fällen; ***out of*** (***the***) –, schief, nicht senkrecht *or* lotrecht; 2. (*Tech.*) das Richtscheit, Senklot, die Senkwaage. **perpendicularity** [–ˈlæriti], *s.* senkrechte Richtung.

perpetrate [ˈpə:pitreit], *v.t.* verüben, begehen (*a crime etc.*); (*coll.*) machen; verbrechen (*a pun etc.*). **perpetration** [–ˈtreiʃən], *s.* die Verübung, Begehung. **perpetrator,** *s.* der Begeher, Verüber, Täter, Frevler.

perpetual [pəˈpetjuəl], *adj.* 1. unaufhörlich, andauernd, fortwährend, immerwährend, beständig, stet, ewig, ununterbrochen; – ***calendar,*** immerwährender Kalender; – ***motion,*** das Perpetuum mobile; 2. lebenslänglich, unabsetzbar; 3. (*Comm.*) unablösbar, unkündbar; 4. (*Bot.*) ausdauernd, immerblühend; 5. (*coll.*) häufig, wiederholt, ständig. **perpetuate** [–eit], *v.t.* verewigen, fortbestehen lassen, immerwährend fortsetzen. **perpetuation** [–ˈeiʃən], *s.* die Verewigung, Fortdauer, endlose Fortsetzung. **perpetuity** [pə:piˈtjuiti], *s.* 1. unaufhörliches Bestehen, (ununterbrochene) Fortdauer, die Unaufhörlichkeit, Ewigkeit; ***in*** or ***to* –,** auf ewig, für immer, in alle Ewigkeit; 2. lebenslängliche Rente.

perplex [pəˈpleks], **1.** *v.t.* verwirren, verblüffen, bestürzt machen. **2.** *v.i.* Verwirrung stiften. **perplexed,** *adj.* verwirrt, verlegen, verblüfft, verdutzt, bestürzt. **perplexing,** *adj.* verwirrend, verblüffend. **perplexity,** *s.* 1. die Verwirrung, Bestürzung, Verlegenheit; 2. Verworrenheit, Verwick(e)lung, Verwick(e)lungen (*pl.*).

perquisite [ˈpə:kwizit], *s.* 1. (*usu. pl.*) Akzidenzien, Sporteln, Nebeneinkünfte, Nebeneinnahmen, Nebenbezüge (*pl.*), der Nebenverdienst; 2. (*Law*) Selbsterworbene(s); 3. (*coll.*) persönliches Vorrecht.

perron [ˈperən], *s.* (*Archit.*) der Beischlag; die Freitreppe.

perry [ˈperi], *s.* der Birn(en)most.

persecute [ˈpə:sikju:t], *v.t.* 1. verfolgen; 2. belästigen, quälen, plagen, drangsalieren. **persecution** [–ˈkju:ʃən], *s.* die Verfolgung; – ***mania,*** der Verfolgungswahn. **persecutor,** *s.* der Verfolger.

perseverance [pə:siˈviərəns], *s.* die Standhaftigkeit, Beharrlichkeit, Ausdauer; das Beharren, Verharren. **perseverant,** *adj.* beharrlich.

perseverate [pəˈsevəreit], *v.i.* (*Psych.*) spontan auftreten, (*also fig.*) ständig wiederkehren. **perseveration** [–ˈreiʃən], *s.* ständige Wiederkehr, dauernde Wiederholung.

persevere [pə:siˈviə], *v.i.* beharren, ausharren (***in,*** bei), festhalten (an (*Dat.*)), nicht nachgeben *or* nachlassen, standhaft fortfahren *or* weiterarbeiten (***with,*** mit). **persevering,** *adj.* beharrlich, standhaft.

Persia [ˈpə:ʃə], *s.* Persien (*n.*). **Persian, 1.** *s.* 1. der (die) Perser(in); 2. (*language*) das Persisch(e). **2.** *adj.* persisch; – ***blind,*** die Jalousie; – ***cat,*** die Angorakatze; – ***lamb,*** das Persianerfell; – ***rug,*** der Perserteppich.

persiflage [ˈpə:siflɑ:ʒ], *s.* die Verspottung, Spötterei, Spöttelei, Persiflage.

persimmon [pəˈsimən], *s.* die Dattelpflaume.

persist [pəˈsist], *v.i.* 1. beharren (***in,*** bei *or* auf (*Dat.*)), verharren, bleiben (bei), bestehen (auf (*Dat.*)), hartnäckig fortfahren (***in doing,*** zu tun), beharrlich weiterarbeiten (***with,*** an (*Dat.*)); 2. fortdauern, andauern, fortbestehen. **persistence, persistency,** *s.* 1. das Beharren (***in,*** bei), hartnäckiges Fortfahren (in (*Dat.*)), das Fortdauern, Andauern, wiederholtes Vorkommen; 2. (*Phys.*) die Fortwirkung, Nachwirkung, Beharrung; 3. (*of a p.*) Ausdauer, Beharrlichkeit, Hartnäckigkeit, Festigkeit. **persistent,** *adj.* 1. beharrlich, hartnäckig; 2. dauernd, nachhaltig; anhaltend, ständig.

person [pə:sn], *s.* 1. die Person, der Mensch, das

Individuum, (Einzel)wesen; ***any* –**, irgend jemand; ***fictitious* –, *– at law***, juristische Person; ***in* –**, persönlich, selbst; ***in one's own* –**, in eigener Person; ***no* –**, niemand; ***not a* –**, keine Seele; ***have respect of –s***, die Person ansehen; 2. der Körper, das Äußere; ***carry on one's* –**, an *or* bei sich tragen; 3. (*Theat. etc.*) die Gestalt, Rolle, der Charakter. **personable,** *adj.* gutaussehend, ansehnlich, stattlich. **personage,** *s.* 1. die Standesperson, (hohe) Persönlichkeit; 2. (*Theat.*) die Figur, Rolle, der Charakter.

personal ['pə:sənl], *adj.* 1. persönlich, individuell, eigen, Privat–; **–** ***account***, das Privatkonto; (*Law*) **–** ***action***, die Forderungsklage; **–** ***allowance***, der Freibetrag; **–** ***best***, see **–** ***record*** (*Spt.*); (*Tele.*) **–** ***call***, das Gespräch mit Voranmeldung; **–** ***column***, persönliche Anzeigen (*pl.*); **–** ***effects***, das Privateigentum, das Mobiliarvermögen; **–** ***liberty***, persönliche Freiheit; **–** ***letter***, vertraulicher Brief; **–** ***life***, das Privatleben; **–** ***matter***, die Privatsache; **–** ***opinion***, eigene Meinung; **–** ***pronoun***, persönliches Fürwort, das Personalpronomen; **–** ***property***, see **–** ***effects***; **–** ***record***, der Personalbogen; (*Spt.*) persönliche Bestzeit *or* Bestleistung; (*Comm.*) **–** ***share***, die Namensaktie; **–** ***status***, der Personenstand; 2. äußer; **–** ***appearance***, körperliches Aussehen; (*Theat.*) persönliches Auftreten; **–** ***charms***, äußere Reize (*pl.*); **–** ***hygiene***, die Körperpflege; 3. anzüglich (*remarks*); ***become* –**, anzüglich werden; **–** ***remarks***, anzügliche Bemerkungen.

personality [pə:sə'næliti], *s.* 1. die Person, Persönlichkeit; **–** ***cult***, der Personenkult; ***split* –**, gespaltene Persönlichkeit; 2. die Individualität; 3. *pl.* Anzüglichkeiten, anzügliche Bemerkungen (*pl.*).

personalization ['pə:sənəlai'zeiʃən], *s.* die Personifizierung. **personalize,** *v.t.* personifizieren; persönlich nehmen (*a remark*).

personally ['pə:snəli], *adv.* persönlich; ***sign* –**, eigenhändig unterschreiben. **personalty,** *s.* (*Law*) das Privateigentum, bewegliches Eigentum.

personate ['pə:səneit], **1.** *v.t.* 1. darstellen; 2. sich fälschlich ausgeben für, (fälschlich) vorstellen *or* verkörpern, nachahmen. **2.** *v.i.* eine Rolle spielen. **personation** [–'neiʃən], *s.* 1. die Darstellung; 2. Nachahmung, (fälschliches) Ausgeben.

personification [pəsənifi'keiʃən], *s.* die Verkörperung, Personifizierung. **personify** [–'sɔnifai], *v.t.* 1. personifizieren; 2. verkörpern, versinnbildlichen.

personnel [pə:sə'nəl], *s.* das Personal, die Belegschaft; (*Mil.*) Mannschaften (*pl.*), (*Naut.*) die Besatzung; **–** ***division***, die Personalabteilung; **–** ***manager***, der Personalchef.

perspective [pə'spektiv], **1.** *adj.* perspektivisch, Perspektiv–. **2.** *s.* 1. die Perspektiv, Bildweite; ***in (true)* –**, perspektivisch richtig, in richtiger Perspektive; 2. perspektivische Ansicht, perspektivisch richtige Darstellung *or* Zeichnung; 3. die Fernsicht, Aussicht, Fernschau; (*fig.*) Aussicht, der Ausblick; (*fig.*) ***he has no* –**, er hat keinen Blick für die relative Bedeutung der Dinge.

perspex ['pə:speks], *s.* (*registered trade name*) das Plexiglas.

perspicacious [pə:spi'keiʃəs], *adj.* scharfsichtig, weitsichtig, scharfsinnig. **perspicacity** [–'kæsiti], *s.* der Scharfblick, Scharfsinn, die Scharfsichtigkeit.

perspicuity [pə:spi'kjuiti], *s.* die Deutlichkeit, Klarheit, Verständlichkeit. **perspicuous** [–'spikjuəs], *adj.* klar, deutlich, (leicht) verständlich.

perspiration [pə:spi'reiʃən], *s.* 1. der Schweiß; 2. das Schwitzen, Transpirieren; (*fig.*) die Ausdünstung. **perspire** [–'paiə], **1.** *v.i.* 1. schwitzen, transpirieren; 2. ausdünsten. **2.** *v.t.* ausschwitzen, ausdünsten.

persuade [pə'sweid], *v.t.* überzeugen (***of***, von), überreden, bereden (***to do, into doing***, zu tun); **–** ***o.s.***, sich (*Dat.*) einreden *or* einbilden; ***be –d***, überzeugt sein (***of***, von), sich überreden lassen. **persuasion** [–ʒən], *s.* 1. die Überredung; ***power of* –**, die Überredungsgabe, Überredungskunst, (*of a th.*) Überzeugungskraft; 2. die Überzeugung, feste Meinung, fester Glaube; 3. (*Eccl.*) die Sekte, Glaubensrichtung; 4. (*coll.*) Art, Sorte. **persuasive** [–siv], *adj.* 1. überredend; 2. überzeugend. **persuasiveness,** *s.* 1. überzeugende Kraft; 2. (*of a p.*) die Überredungsgabe.

pert [pə:t], *adj.* keck, vorlaut, schnippisch, naseweis.

pertain [pə'tein], *v.i.* gehören (***to***, zu), angehören, zukommen (*Dat.*), betreffen (*Acc.*); ***–ing to***, betreffend.

pertinacious [pə:ti'neiʃəs], *adj.* 1. beharrlich, standhaft; 2. hartnäckig. **pertinaciousness, pertinacity** [–'næsiti], *s.* 1. die Standhaftigkeit, Beharrlichkeit; 2. Hartnäckigkeit.

pertinence, pertinency ['pə:tinəns(i)], *s.* die Angemessenheit, Gemäßheit, Eignung (***to***, für); Schicklichkeit. **pertinent,** *adj.* gehörig (***to***, zu), passend, schicklich (für), angemessen (*Dat.*); treffend, einschlägig, zweckdienlich; ***be* – *to***, Bezug haben auf (*Acc.*). **pertinents,** *pl.* (*esp. Scots*) das Zubehör.

pertness ['pə:tnis], *s.* die Keckheit, vorlautes *or* schnippisches Wesen.

perturb [pə'tə:b], *v.t.* beunruhigen, stören, verwirren. **perturbable,** *adj.* ***easily* –**, leicht aus der Fassung zu bringen(d). **perturbation** [pə:tə'beiʃən], *s.* die Störung (*also Astr.*), Beunruhigung, Verwirrung, Bestürzung, Unruhe. **perturbed,** *adj.* beunruhigt (***by***, durch; ***about***, wegen; ***at***, über (*Acc.*)).

Peru [pə'ru:], *s.* Peru (*n.*).

peruke [pə'ru:k], *s.* die Perücke.

perusal [pə'ru:zl], *s.* das Durchlesen, Durchsehen, die Durchsicht; ***for* –**, zur Einsicht. **peruse,** *v.t.* durchsehen, durchlesen.

Peruvian [pə'ru:viən], **1.** *s.* der (die) Peruaner(in). **2.** *adj.* peruanisch; **–** ***bark***, die Chinarinde.

pervade [pə'veid], *v.t.* durchdringen, erfüllen, durchziehen. **pervasion** [–ʒən], *s.* die Durchdringung. **pervasive** [–siv], *adj.* 1. durchdringend; 2. (*fig.*) immer gegenwärtig, überall vorhanden.

perverse [pə'və:s], *adj.* 1. verkehrt, Fehl– (*of a th.*); 2. verderbt, entartet; 3. verstockt, störrisch, widerspenstig; eigensinnig; 4. (*Med. etc.*) pervers, widernatürlich. **perverseness,** *s.* der Eigensinn, die Widerspenstigkeit, Halsstarrigkeit, Verstocktheit. **perversion** [–ʃən], *s.* 1. die Umkehrung, Verdrehung, Entstellung; 2. Entartung, Verderbtheit; 3. (*esp. Eccl.*) Verirrung; 4. (*Med., Psych.*) Perversion. **perversity,** *s.* die Verkehrtheit, Widernatürlichkeit, Perversität; *see also* **perverseness. perversive,** *adj.* 1. verderblich (***of***, für); 2. entartend, verderbend, verdrehend.

pervert, 1. [pə'və:t], *v.t.* 1. verkehren; 2. verdrehen, entstellen (*meaning etc.*); 3. verführen, verderben (*a p.*). **2.** ['pə:və:t], *s.* 1. (*Eccl.*) Abtrünnige(r); 2. (*also* ***sex(ual)*** –) perverser Mensch. **perverted** [pə'və:tid], *adj.* 1. verkehrt, falsch, anomal; 2. verderbt, entartet; ***be*** or ***become* –**, entarten; 3. (*Med. etc.*) pervers.

pervious ['pə:viəs], *adj.* 1. durchlässig (***to***, für); 2. (*fig.*) offen, zugänglich (für). **perviousness,** *s.* die Durchlässigkeit (***to***, für).

peseta [pi'seitə], *s.* die Peseta.

pessary ['pesəri], *s.* das Pessar, der Scheidenring, Mutterring.

pessimism ['pesimizm], *s.* der Pessimismus; die Kopfhängerei, Schwarzseherei. **pessimist, 1.** *s.* der Pessimist, Schwarzseher. **2.** *or* **pessimistic** [–'mistik], *adj.* pessimistisch (***about***, über (*Acc.*)).

pest [pest], *s.* 1. die Pest, Seuche, Plage; (*obs.*) **–** ***house***, das Spital für Pestkranke; 2. der Schädling; **–** ***control***, die Schädlingsbekämpfung; 3. (*coll.*) lästiger Mensch; lästige S.

pester ['pestə], *v.t.* 1. plagen, quälen, ärgern; ***be –ed with***, geplagt werden von; 2. zusetzen (*Dat.*), belästigen, bedrängen; **–** ***him for money***, ihn unentwegt um Geld angehen.

pesticide ['pestisaid], *s.* das Schädlingsbekämpfungsmittel.

pestiferous [pes'tifərəs], *adj. See* **pestilent**; (*coll.*) lästig, ärgerlich, beschwerlich.

pestilence ['pestiləns], *s.* die Seuche, Pest(ilenz). **pestilent, pestilential** [–'lenʃəl], *adj.* 1. Pest–, pestartig; 2. verpestend, ansteckend; 3. (*fig.*) schädlich, verderblich; 4. (*coll.*) widerlich, ekelhaft; 5. lästig.

pestle [pesl], *s.* 1. die Mörserkeule, Stampfe, der Stößel; (*Chem.*) das Pistill.

pestology [pes'tɔlədʒi], *s. See* **pest control.**

[1]**pet** [pet], **1.** *s.* 1. gezähmtes *or* zahmes Tier, das Lieblingstier, Haustier; 2. (*coll.*) der Liebling, gehätscheltes Kind, das Schoßkind; (*coll.*) ***be a – and*** . . ., sei gut *or* sei so lieb *or* nett und . . .. **2.** *attrib. adj.* Lieblings–; Schoß–; – ***aversion,*** höchster *or* größter Greuel; – ***dog,*** der Schoßhund; – ***mistake,*** (ihm *etc.*) eigentümliches Versehen, der Gewohnheitsfehler; – ***name,*** der Kosename; – ***theory,*** die Lieblingstheorie. **3.** *v.t.* (ver)hätscheln. **4.** *v.i.* (*coll.*) sich abküssen, knutschen.

[2]**pet,** *s.* schlechte *or* üble Laune, der Verdruß, Ärger, Unwille; ***in a –,*** verdrießlich, verärgert, schlecht gelaunt; ***take (the) – at,*** sich ärgern über (*Acc.*), übelnehmen.

petal [petl], *s.* das Blumenblatt. **petal(l)ed, petalous,** *adj.* mit Blumenblättern (versehen), blumenblätt(e)rig.

petard [pə'tɑ:d], *s.* (*Hist.*) die Petarde, Sprengbüchse; ***be hoist with one's own –,*** in die Grube fallen, die man andern gegraben hat; den eigenen Ränken zum Opfer fallen.

peter ['pi:tə], *v.i.* (*coll.*) – ***out,*** zu Ende gehen, sich verlieren *or* erschöpfen *or* totlaufen; zerrinnen, versickern, abflauen, allmählich aufhören.

Peter, *s.* Peter, Petrus (*m.*); (*coll.*) ***rob – to pay Paul,*** ein Loch aufreißen, um ein anderes zuzustopfen; ***St. –,*** der heilige Petrus; ***St. –'s (Church),*** die Peterskirche, Petrikirche; ***–'s pence,*** der Peterspfennig.

petiolar ['petioulə], *adj.* Blattstiel–. **petiolate** [–leit], *adj.* gestielt. **petiole,** *s.* (*Bot.*) der Blattstiel; (*Zool.*) Stiel.

petite [pə'ti:t], *adj.* zierlich, niedlich.

petition [pə'tiʃən], **1.** *s.* die Bitte (***for,*** um), Eingabe, Bittschrift, Denkschrift, Petition, das Gesuch; (*Law*) die Klage, der Antrag (***for,*** auf (*Acc.*)); (*Law*) ***Petition of Right,*** die Klage gegen den Souverän; – ***for clemency,*** das Gnadengesuch; ***file a – for divorce,*** eine Scheidungsklage einreichen; ***file a – in bankruptcy,*** Konkurs anmelden. **2.** *v.t.* einen Antrag stellen bei, eine Bittschrift einreichen bei, bitten, ersuchen, angehen (***for,*** um). **3.** *v.i.* einen Antrag stellen (***for,*** auf (*Acc.*)); eine Bittschrift einreichen, ersuchen, bitten (um); – ***for divorce,*** die Scheidung beantragen. **petitioner,** *s.* der Bittsteller, Antragsteller; (*Law*) Kläger auf Ehescheidung.

petit| mal [pəti'mæl], *s.* leichte Epilepsie. – **point,** [–'pwæ], *s.* der Perlstich; die Perlstichstickerei.

Petrarch ['petrɑ:k], *s.* Petrarka (*m.*).

petrel ['petrəl], *s.* (*Orn.*) (*also* ***storm–***), die Sturmschwalbe (*Hydrobatus pelagicus*); (*fig.*) ***stormy –,*** der Unruhestifter, unruhiger Geist.

petrifaction [petri'fækʃən], *s.* 1. die Versteinerung; 2. *pl.* Fossilien (*pl.*). **petrify** ['petrifai], **1.** *v.t.* 1. versteinern; 2. (*fig.*) starr machen, bestürzen; ***petrified with,*** starr *or* wie gelähmt vor (*Dat.*). **2.** *v.i.* zu Stein werden, sich versteinern.

petrograph ['petrogrɑ:f], *s.* die Fels(en)inschrift, Felszeichnung.

petrol ['petrəl], *s.* das Benzin, der Kraftstoff, Treibstoff; – ***lighter,*** das Feuerzeug; – ***pump,*** die Zapfsäule; – ***station,*** die Tankstelle. **petroleum** [pi'trouliəm], *s.* das Erdöl, Petroleum; – ***ether,*** der Petroläther; – ***jelly,*** die Vaseline, das Vaselin.

petrology [pe'trɔlədʒi], *s.* die Gesteinskunde, Petrographie.

petrous ['petrəs], *adj.* steinhart, steinig, felsig; (*Anat.*) – ***bone,*** das Felsenbein.

petticoat ['petikout], **1.** *s.* 1. der (Frauen)unterrock; (*coll.*) ***in –s,*** in Kinderröckchen; 2. (*coll.*) das Frauenzimmer, Weibsbild. **2.** *attrib. adj.* Weiber–, Frauen–; – ***government,*** das Weiberregiment; (*Law*) ***–hold,*** das Kunkellehen.

pettifog ['petifɔg], *v.i.* Schliche *or* Kniffe anwenden, schikanieren. **pettifogger,** *s.* der Winkeladvokat, Rechtsverdreher, Rabulist. **pettifogging, 1.** *adj.* 1. schikanös, rabulistisch; 2. (*coll.*) armselig, lumpig. **2.** *s.* die Rabulistik, Schikanen (*pl.*), Rechtskniffe (*pl.*).

pettiness ['petinis], *s.* die Kleinlichkeit (*of character*), Geringfügigkeit (*of a th.*).

petting ['petiŋ], *s.* (*coll.*) das Knutschen; – ***party,*** die Knutscherei.

pettish ['petiʃ], *adj.* empfindlich, launisch, mürrisch, verdrießlich. **pettishness,** *s.* die Empfindlichkeit, Launenhaftigkeit, Verdrießlichkeit.

pettitoes ['petitouz], *pl.* Schweinsfüße (*pl.*).

petty ['peti], *adj.* 1. klein, gering(fügig), unbedeutend, unwesentlich, unwichtig; – ***cash,*** kleine Ausgaben (*pl.*), geringfügige Beträge (*pl.*); die Handkasse; – ***goods,*** see – ***wares;*** – ***jury,*** kleine Jury; – ***larceny,*** kleiner Diebstahl; – ***offence,*** das Vergehen, geringfügige Verfehlung; – ***officer,*** der Maat, Unteroffizier; – ***prince,*** der Duodezfürst; – ***sessions,*** die Gerichtsverhandlung ohne Geschworene; – ***wares,*** Kurzwaren (*pl.*); 2. (*of character*) kleinlich.

petulance ['petjuləns], *s.* die Gereiztheit, Verdrießlichkeit, Ungeduld, der Mutwille. **petulant,** *adj.* ungeduldig, verdrießlich, mutwillig, launenhaft, schmollend, mürrisch.

petunia [pi'tju:niə], *s.* (*Bot.*) die Petunie.

pew [pju:], *s.* der Kirchenstuhl, Kirchensitz; (*sl.*) Stuhl, Sitz; (*sl.*) ***take a –!*** nehmen Sie Platz! setzen Sie sich! **pewage,** *s.* die Kirchenstuhlmiete.

pewit ['pi:wit], *s.* (*Orn.*) der Kiebitz (*Vanellus vanellus*).

pewter ['pju:tə], **1.** *s.* 1. das Hartzinn, Britanniametall; 2. (*collect.*) Zinngerät, Zinngefäß; 3. (*sl.*) der Preispokal. **2.** *adj.* zinnern, Zinn–. **pewterer,** *s.* der Zinngießer.

phaeton [feitn], *s.* der Phaeton, vierrädriger Zweispänner.

phaged(a)ena [fædʒə'di:nə], *s.* fressendes Geschwür. **phagocyte** ['fægəsait], *s.* die Phagozyte, Freßzelle.

phalange ['fælændʒ], *s.* 1. die Phalanx; 2. *pl.* (*Anat.*) Phalangen (*pl.*). **phalanger,** *s.* (*Zool.*) der Kletterbeutler. **phalanx,** *s.* (*pl.* **-es** or **-nges** [fə'lændʒiz]) die Phalanx; (*fig.*) Schlachtreihe, geschlossene Front *or* Reihe; ***in –, –ed,*** in Reihen aufgestellt, geschlossen.

phalarope ['fæləroup], *s.* (*Orn.*) ***grey*** (***Am. red***) –, das Thorshühnchen (*Phalaropus fulicarius*); ***red-necked*** (***Am. northern***) –, das Odinshühnchen (*Ph. lobatus*).

phallic ['fælik], *adj.* phallisch. **phallus,** *s.* (*pl.* **-li** [–ai]) der Phallus, männliches Glied.

phantasm ['fæntæzm], *s.* 1. das Trugbild, Hirngespinst, Wahngebilde; 2. Gespenst, die (Geister)-erscheinung.

phantasmagoria [fæntəzmə'gɔ:riə], *s.* das Blendwerk, Truggebilde, Gaukelbilder (*pl.*). **phantasmagoric,** *adj.* trügerisch, gaukelhaft, traumhaft.

phantasmal [fæn'tæzməl], *adj.* 1. geisterhaft, gespensterhaft; 2. eingebildet, unwirklich, trügerisch, illusorisch, Phantasie–.

phantom ['fæntəm], **1.** *s.* 1. das Gespenst, die Erscheinung, der Geist; 2. das Hirngespinst, Wahngebilde, Trugbild, Phantom; 3. (*fig.*) der Schatten, Schein. **2.** *attrib. adj.* Schein–, Geister–, gespenstisch; (*Elec.*) – ***circuit,*** die Viererleitung; – ***ship,*** das Geisterschiff.

Pharaoh ['fɛərou], *s.* (*B.*) Pharao (*m.*).

pharisaic(al) [færi'zeiik(l)], *adj.* pharisäisch, heuchlerisch, selbstgerecht, scheinheilig. **pharisaism,** *s.* das Pharisäertum, die Scheinheiligkeit. **Pharisee** ['færisi:], *s.* 1. der Pharisäer; 2. (*fig.*) Heuchler, Selbstgerechte(r), Scheinheilige(r).

pharmaceutical [fɑːməˈsjuːtikl], *adj.* pharmazeutisch, arzneikundlich, Apotheker–, Apotheken–; – ***chemist,*** der Apotheker. **pharmaceutics,** *pl.* (*sing. constr.*) die Arzneiwissenschaft, Pharmazeutik. **pharmacist** [ˈfɑːməsist], *s.* der Pharmazeut, Apotheker.

pharmacological [fɑːməkəˈlɔdʒikl], *adj.* pharmakologisch. **pharmacologist** [–ˈkɔlədʒist], *s.* der Pharmakologe. **pharmacology** [–ˈkɔlədʒi], *s.* die Arzneimittellehre. **pharmacopoeia** [–kəˈpiə], *s.* amtliches Arzneibuch.

pharmacy [ˈfɑːməsi], *s.* 1. die Arzneimittelkunde, Apothekerkunst; 2. Apotheke.

pharos [ˈfɛərəs], *s.* (*obs.*) der Leuchtturm.

pharyng(e)al [fæˈrindʒ(i)əl], *adj.* Kehlkopf–, Rachen(kopf)–, Schlund(kopf)–. **pharyngitis** [–ˈdʒaitis], *s.* (*Med.*) der Rachenkatarrh. **pharyngoscope** [–ˈriŋgəskoup], *s.* der Schlundspiegel. **pharynx** [ˈfæriŋks], *s.* (*pl.* **-es, -nges** [–ˈrindʒiːz]) der Schlund(kopf), die Rachenhöhle.

phase [feiz], **1.** *s.* 1. (*Astr., Elec.*) die Phase; (*Elec.*) – ***difference*** or ***shift,*** die Phasenverschiebung; – ***lag,*** die Phasennacheilung; – ***lead,*** die Phasenvoreilung; ***in*** –, phasengleich; ***out of*** –, in der Phase verschoben; 2. (*fig.*) das Stadium, die (Entwicklungs)stufe, Etappe. **2.** *v.t.* 1. (*Elec.*) synchronisieren, in Phase bringen; 2. (*fig.*) (in Phasen) einteilen; – ***out,*** abwickeln.

pheasant [feznt], *s.* (*Orn.*) (*Am.* ***ring-necked*** –) der Fasan (*Phasianus colchicus*); – ***shooting,*** die Fasanenjagd. **pheasantry,** *s.* die Fasanerie.

phenacetin [fəˈnæsitin], *s.* das Phenazetin.

phenate [ˈfiːneit], *s.* die Phenolverbindung. **phenic,** *adj.* karbolsauer; – ***acid,*** *see* **phenol. phenobarbitone** [–ouˈbɑːbitoun], *s.* das Phenobarbital, Luminal.

phenol [ˈfiːnɔl], *s.* die Karbolsäure, das Phenol. **phenolate** [–eit], *s.* – ***of,*** *see* **phenic.**

phenomena [fiˈnɔmənə], *pl. of* **phenomenon. phenomenal,** *adj.* 1. (*Phil.*) phänomenal, Erscheinungs–; 2. (*coll.*) außerordentlich, erstaunlich, einzigartig, großartig, fabelhaft. **phenomenalism,** *s.* (*Phil.*) der Phänomenalismus. **phenomenological** [–əˈlɔdʒikl], *adj.* phänomenologisch. **phenomenon,** *s.* (*pl.* **-mena**) 1. das Phänomen, die Erscheinung; 2. (*fig.*) wahres Wunder; das Wunderkind.

phenyl [ˈfiːnil], *s.* das Phenyl. **phenylene,** *s.* das Phenylen. **phenylic** [–ˈnilik], *adj.* Phenyl–, karbolsauer; – ***acid,*** die Karbolsäure, das Phenol.

phew! [fjuː], *int.* puh!

phial [ˈfaiəl], *s.* das Fläschchen, die Phiole, Ampulle.

philander [fiˈlændə], *v.i.* tändeln, schäkern, flirten. **philanderer,** *s.* der Courmacher, Hofmacher, Schäkerer, Schürzenjäger, Schwerenöter.

philanthropic(al) [filənˈθrɔpik(l)], *adj.* menschenfreundlich, philanthropisch. **philanthropist** [–ˈlænθrəpist], *s.* der Menschenfreund, Philanthrop. **philanthropy** [–ˈlænθrəpi], *s.* die Menschenliebe.

philatelic [filəˈtelik], *adj.* Briefmarken–. **philatelist** [–ˈlætəlist], *s.* der Markensammler. **philately** [–ˈlætəli], *s.* die Briefmarkenkunde, das Briefmarkensammeln.

philharmonic [filhɑːˈmɔnik], *adj.* musikliebend, philharmonisch.

philhellenic [ˈfilhəˈlenik], *adj.* griechenfreundlich.

Philippians [fiˈlipiənz], *pl.* (*sing. constr.*) (*B.*) der Brief an die Philipper, Philipperbrief.

philippic [fiˈlipik], *s.* die Philippika, Strafrede, Brandrede, Schmährede, (*coll.*) Standpauke.

philippina [filiˈpiːnə], *s.* das Vielliebchen.

Philippine [ˈfilipiːn], **1.** *s.* der (die) Philippiner(in), Filipino. **2.** *adj.* philippinisch; – ***Islands*** *or* **Philippines,** *pl.* Philippinen (*pl.*).

philistine [ˈfilistain], **1.** *s.* der Philister, Spießer, Spießbürger. **2.** *adj.* spießig, spießbürgerlich, spießerisch, philisterhaft, philiströs. **philistinism** [–stinizm], *s.* das Spieß(bürg)ertum, Philistertum, die Philisterei.

philological [filəˈlɔdʒikl], *adj.* sprachwissenschaftlich, philologisch. **philologist** [–ˈlɔlədʒist], *s.* der Sprachwissenschaftler, Sprachforscher, Philologe. **philology** [–ˈlɔlədʒi], *s.* die Sprachwissenschaft, Philologie.

philosopher [fiˈlɔsəfə], *s.* der Philosoph; ***natural*** –, der Naturforscher; –***s' stone,*** der Stein der Weisen. **philosophic(al)** [–ləˈsɔfik(l)], *adj.* philosophisch; (*fig.*) einsichtig, weise; beherrscht, mäßig. **philosophize,** *v.i.* philosophieren. **philosophy** [–fi], *s.* 1. die Philosophie, Weltweisheit; ***moral*** –, die Moralphilosophie, Ethik; ***natural*** –, die Naturwissenschaft; 2. die Weltanschauung, Lebensanschauung.

philter (*Am.*), *see* **philtre.**

philtre [ˈfiltə], *s.* der Liebestrank, Zaubertrank.

phiz [fiz], *s.* (*sl.*) die Visage.

phlebitis [fləˈbaitis], *s.* die Venenentzündung. **phlebotomize** [–ˈbɔtəmaiz], **1.** *v.t.* zur Ader lassen (*a p.*). **2.** *v.i.* eine Ader öffnen. **phlebotomy** [–mi], *s.* der Aderlaß.

phlegm [flem], *s.* 1. (*Med.*) der Schleim; 2. (*fig.*) das Phlegma, die Stumpfheit, (geistige) Trägheit, Gleichgültigkeit, Gemütsruhe, der Gleichmut. **phlegmatic** [–ˈmætik], *adj.* (*fig.*) phlegmatisch, träge, stumpf, gleichmütig, gleichgültig. **phlegmon** [ˈflegmən], *s.* (*Med.*) die Phlegmone, Zellgewebsentzündung.

phlogistic [flɔˈdʒistik], *adj.* (*Med.*) entzündlich.

phlox [flɔks], *s.* (*Bot.*) die Flammenblume.

phobia [ˈfoubiə], *s.* die Angst, der Angstzustand, krankhafte Furcht *or* Scheu.

Phoenicia [fiˈniːʃə], *s.* Phönikien (*n.*).

phoenix [ˈfiːniks], *s.* (*Myth.*) der Phönix.

phon [fɔn], *s.* (*Phys.*) das Phon.

[1]**phone** [foun], *s.* (*Phonet.*) das Phonem, der Individuallaut.

[2]**phone, 1.** *s.* (*coll.*) das Telephon, der Fernsprecher; ***be on the*** –, Telephonanschluß haben; am Apparat sein; ***be wanted on the*** –, am Telephon verlangt werden; (*coll.*) – ***book,*** das Fernsprechbuch. **2.** *v.t.* anrufen, telephonieren. **3.** *v.i.* telephonieren; – ***for the doctor,*** den Arzt anrufen.

phoneme [ˈfouniːm], *s. See* [1]**phone. phonetic** [fəˈnetik], *adj.* Laut–, phonetisch; – ***spelling,*** die Lautschrift. **phonetician** [founəˈtiʃən], *s.* der Phonetiker. **phonetics** [fəˈnetiks], *pl.* (*sing. constr.*) die Phonetik. **phonic,** *adj.* Laut–, akustisch, lautlich.

phon(e)y [ˈfouni], **1.** *adj.* (*sl.*) unecht, falsch, fingiert, nicht koscher; – ***war,*** der Sitzkrieg. **2.** *s.* (*sl.*) (*a p.*) der Schwindler, fauler Kunde; (*a th.*) der Schwindel, fauler Zauber.

phonogram [ˈfounəgræm], *s.* das Lautzeichen. **phonograph,** *s.* (*obs.*) der Phonograph, die Sprechmaschine. **phonology** [foˈnɔlədʒi], *s.* die Lautlehre.

phosgene [ˈfɔzdʒiːn], *s.* das Phosgen, Chlorkohlenoxyd.

phosphate [ˈfɔsfeit], *s.* 1. das Phosphat, phosphorsaures Salz; – ***of,*** phosphorsauer; 2. (*Agr.*) das Kali. **phosphide** [–faid], *s.* die Phosphorverbindung; – ***of iron,*** das Phosphoreisen. **phosphite,** *s.* phosphorigsaures Salz.

phosphor [ˈfɔsfə], *attrib. adj.* Phosphor–. **phosphorate** [–reit], *v.t.* (*usu. p.p.*) phosphorisieren, phosphatieren. **phosphoresce** [–ˈres], *v.i.* phosphoreszieren, (nach)leuchten. **phosphorescence** [–ˈresns], *s.* die Phosphoreszenz, das Nachleuchten; – ***of the sea,*** das Meeresleuchten. **phosphorescent,** *adj.* phosphoreszierend. **phosphoric** [–ˈfɔrik], *adj.* Phosphor–, phosphorig; – ***acid,*** die Phosphorsäure. **phosphorous,** *adj.* phosphorig(sauer), phosphorhaltig. **phosphorus,** *s.* der Phosphor; – ***necrosis,*** der Knochenbrand. **phosphuretted** [–retid], *adj.* mit Phosphor verbunden; – ***hydrogen,*** der Phosphorwasserstoff.

photo [ˈfoutou], *s.* (*coll.*) *see* **photograph.**

photo|cell, *s.* die Photozelle, lichtempfindliche Zelle. **–copy,** **1.** *s.* die Photokopie, Lichtpause. **2.** *v.t.* photokopieren. **--electric,** *adj.* photoelektrisch; *– cell, see* **–cell**; elektrisches Auge. **--engraving,** *s.* die Buchdruckätzung, Photogravüre. **--finish,** *s.* (*Spt.*) die Entscheidung durch Zielphotographie. **--flash,** *s.* das Blitzlicht.

photogenic [foutə'dʒenik], *adj.* bildwirksam, photogen. **photogrammetry** [–'græmətri], *s.* das Meßbildverfahren.

photograph ['foutəgrɑ:f], **1.** *s.* das Lichtbild, die Photographie; *take a –,* photographieren, eine Aufnahme machen. **2.** *v.t.* photographieren, aufnehmen, (*coll.*) knipsen. **3.** *v.i.* photographieren, photographiert werden; *– well,* sich gut photographieren lassen. **photographer** [fə'tɔgrəfə], *s.* der Photograph. **photographic** [–'græfik], *adj.* 1. photographisch, Bild–; *– interpretation,* die Lichtbildauswertung; 2. (*fig.*) naturgetreu; *– memory,* bildliches Gedächtnis. **photography** [fə'tɔgrəfi], *s.* die Photographie.

photo|gravure, *s.* die Photogravüre, Heliogravüre, der Kupfertiefdruck. **–lithograph,** *s.* der Photolithograph. **–lithography,** *s.* die Photolithographie.

photometer [fou'tɔmitə], *s.* der Belichtungsmesser, Licht(stärke)messer. **photometric** [–'metrik], *adj.* photometrisch.

photomicrograph [foutou'maikrəgrɑ:f], *s.* die Mikrophotographie.

photon ['foutɔn], *s.* das Photon, Lichtquant.

photosphere ['foutousfiə], *s.* (*Astr.*) die Photosphäre. **photostat** [–stæt], **1.** *s.* die Photokopie, Lichtpause. **2.** *v.t.* photokopieren, ablichten. **photo|-survey,** *s.* die Geländeaufnahme. **--telegraphy,** *s.* die Bildtelegraphie. **–type,** *s.* 1. die Lichtdruckplatte; Phototypie; 2. der Lichtdruck.

phrase [freiz], **1.** *s.* 1. die Redensart, (Rede)wendung, der Ausdruck; *– book,* die Sammlung von Redewendungen; 2. (*Gram.*) der Wortkomplex, die Wortverbindung; 3. (*Mus.*) der Satz, das Melodieglied. **2.** *v.t.* 1. in Worte fassen, ausdrücken, nennen; 2. (*Mus.*) phrasieren. **phrasemonger,** *s.* der Phrasendrescher. **phraseology** [–i'ɔlədʒi], *s.* die Redeweise, Ausdrucksweise, Phraseologie. **phrasing,** *s.* 1. *See* **phraseology**; 2. (*Mus.*) die Phrasierung.

phrenetic [frə'netik], *adj.* frenetisch, wahnsinnig, rasend, toll.

phrenic ['frenik], *adj.* Zwerchfell–.

phrenological [frenə'lɔdʒikl], *adj.* phrenologisch. **phrenologist** [–'nɔlədʒist], *s.* der Phrenologe. **phrenology** [–'nɔlədʒi], *s.* die Schädellehre, Phrenologie.

phthisical ['tizikl], *adj.* schwindsüchtig. **phthisis** ['θaisis], *s.* die Schwindsucht.

phut [fʌt], *adv.* (*sl.*) *go –,* futsch *or* kaputt gehen.

phylactery [fi'læktəri], *s.* 1. (*Jew.*) der Gebetriemen; 2. (*fig.*) religiöse Selbstgefälligkeit.

phylloxera [filɔk'siərə], *s.* (*Ent.*) die Reblaus.

phylogeny [fai'lɔdʒəni], *s.* (*Biol.*) die Stammesgeschichte.

physic ['fizik], **1.** *s.* 1. (*obs.*) die Arzneikunde, Heilkunst; 2. (*coll.*) die Arznei, das Heilmittel. **2.** *v.t.* Arznei geben (*Dat.*), herumdoktern an (*Dat.*), kurieren (*a p.*).

physical ['fizikl], *adj.* 1. physikalisch, naturwissenschaftlich, Natur–; *– geography,* physikalische Geographie; *– science,* die Naturwissenschaft; 2. körperlich, Körper–; *– capacity,* körperliche Fähigkeit; *– condition,* der Gesundheitszustand; *– culture,* die Körperpflege; *– education,* die Körperkultur, Leibeserziehung; *– fitness,* körperliche Tüchtigkeit *or* Tauglichkeit; *– force,* rohe Gewalt; (*Pol.*) bewaffnete Macht; *– impossibility,* absolute Unmöglichkeit; (*coll.*) *– jerks,* Leibesübungen (*pl.*); *– strength,* die Körperkraft; *– training,* körperliche Ertüchtigung, Leibesübungen (*pl.*), das Turnen.

physician [fi'ziʃən], *s.* der Arzt; (*B.*) *–, heal thyself!* Arzt, hilf dir selber!

physicist ['fizisist], *s.* der Physiker. **physics** [–iks], *pl.* (*sing. constr.*) die Physik.

physiognomist [fizi'ɔnəmist], *s.* der Mienendeuter, Physiognom(iker). **physiognomy,** *s.* 1. die Physiognomie, Gesichtsbildung, Gesichtszüge (*pl.*); (*fig.*) äußere Erscheinung, charakteristische Gestalt; 2. die Physiognomik, Mienenkunde.

physiography [fizi'ɔgrəfi], *s.* physikalische Geographie, die Naturbeschreibung.

physiological [fiziə'lɔdʒikl], *adj.* physiologisch. **physiologist** [–'ɔlədʒist], *s.* der Physiologe. **physiology** [–'ɔlədʒi], *s.* die Physiologie.

physio|therapist [fizio'θerəpist], *s.* physikalischer Therapeut. **–therapy,** *s.* physikalische Heilkunde.

physique [fi'zi:k], *s.* der Körperbau, die Körperbeschaffenheit.

phytography [fai'tɔgrəfi], *s.* die Pflanzenbeschreibung. **phytophagous** [–'tɔfəgəs], *adj.* pflanzenfressend.

pi [pai], *s.* (*Math.*) das Pi, Ludolfsche Zahl.

pianissimo [piə'nisimou], *adv.* (*Mus.*) sehr leise. **pianist** ['piənist], *s.* der (die) Klavierspieler(in), Pianist(in).

[1]**piano** [pi'ɑ:nou], *adv.* (*Mus.*) leise.

[2]**piano** [pi'ænou], *s.* das Klavier; *at the –,* am Klavier; *cottage –,* see *upright –*; *grand –,* der Flügel; *on the –,* auf dem Klavier; *upright –,* das (Wand)klavier, Pianino; *– duet,* vierhändiges Spiel; *– recital,* der Klaviervortrag; *– score,* der Klavierauszug; *– stool,* der Klavierstuhl.

pianoforte [pi'ænou'forti], *s.* 1. (*Hist.*) das Hammerklavier; 2. *See* [2]**piano.** **pianola** [piə'noulə], *s.* das Pianola.

piaster, (*Am.*) *see* **piastre.**

piastre [pi'æstə], *s.* der Peso (*Spanish*), Gersch (*Turkish*).

piazza [pi'ætsə], *s.* 1. (*Italian*) der Platz, Hof; 2. (*Am.*) Balkon, die Veranda.

pibroch ['pi:brɔx], *s.* die Kriegsmusik *or* Kampfmusik (auf dem Dudelsack).

pica ['paikə], *s.* (*Typ.*) die Cicero(schrift).

picador ['pikadɔ:], *s.* der Pikador.

Picardy ['pikədi], *s.* Pikardie (*f.*).

picaresque [pikə'resk], *adj.* Abenteuer–, Schelmen–; *– novel,* der Schelmenroman. **picaroon** [–'ru:n], *s.* der Seeräuber, Korsar.

piccalilli [pikə'lili], *s.* das Essiggemüse.

piccaninny [pikə'nini], *s.* das Negerkind; (*coll.*) Kind, Gör.

piccolo ['pikəlou], *s.* die Pikkoloflöte.

[1]**pick** [pik], *s.* 1. die Spitzhacke, Picke, der Pickel; 2. Eispickel; 3. Zahnstocher; 4. (*Mus.*) das Plektron.

[2]**pick,** **1.** *v.t.* 1. hacken (*a hole*), aufhacken (*ground*); (ab)pflücken, sammeln (*flowers*); scheiden (*ore*); rupfen (*poultry*); zupfen, ausfasern (*wool, oakum*); abnagen (*a bone*); abkratzen (*a scab*); (*coll.*) *have a bone to – with him,* mit ihm ein Hühnchen zu rupfen haben; *– his brains,* seine Kentnisse ausbeuten; (*fig.*) *– holes in,* etwas am Zeug flicken (*Dat.*), etwas auszusetzen haben an (*Dat.*), bekritteln; *– a lock,* ein Schloß erbrechen; *– one's nose,* (sich (*Dat.*)) in der Nase bohren; *– off,* (ab)pflücken, (*fig.*) (einzeln) abschießen; *– to pieces,* zerpflücken, zerreißen; (*fig.*) herunterreißen, herziehen über (*Acc.*)); *– his pocket,* ihn bestehlen, seine Tasche plündern; *– one's teeth,* in den Zähnen (herum)stochern; 2. (*fig.*) (sorgsam) aussuchen, (sorgfältig) auswählen; *– one's company,* in seinem Umgang wählerisch sein; *– over,* durchsuchen; *– a quarrel,* Streit *or* Händel suchen, einen Streit vom Zaune brechen; *– one's way,* sich (*Dat.*) mühsam einen Weg suchen; *– one's words,* seine Worte wählen; 3. *– out,* auswählen, aussuchen; sondern, scheiden, trennen; hervorheben (*a pattern*); (*fig.*) erkennen, ausmachen (*with the eye*), herausfinden, herausbekommen (*meaning*), nach Gehör spielen (*a melody*); 4. *– up,* aufhacken (*ground*); aufheben, aufnehmen, in die Hand nehmen; aufnehmen (*stitches*), mitnehmen (*pas-*

sengers); (*coll.*) abholen (*a p.*), fassen, ergreifen (*a fugitive*), stoßen auf (*Acc.*), auftreiben, erstehen, ergattern, aufgabeln (*a bargain etc.*), sich (*Dat.*) angewöhnen *or* aneignen (*a habit*), (mühsam) zusammenbringen *or* erlernen, aufschnappen (*a language*), empfangen, auffangen (*radio signal*), anleuchten (*by searchlight*), zufällig kennenlernen (*a p.*) *or* erfahren, mitbekommen, mitkriegen (*a fact*); – ***up cheap*** (or ***for a song***), (spott)billig erstehen; – ***up courage***, Mut fassen; – ***up a living***, sich mühsam durchschlagen; – ***o.s. up***, aufstehen, (wieder) hochkommen, sich erheben; – ***up speed***, auf Touren kommen. **2.** *v.i.* 1. häppchenweise *or* wie ein Spatz essen; – ***and choose***, wählerisch sein; – ***at***, picken *or* zupfen an (*Dat.*), (*food*) wie ein Spatz essen; 2. (*coll.*) mausen, stibitzen; 3. – ***on***, sich entscheiden für, aussuchen, herausangeln (*a th.*); etwas am Zeug flicken (*Dat.*), herumhacken auf (*Dat.*), nicht in Ruhe lassen (*a p.*); 4. (*coll.*) – ***up***, auf Touren kommen (*of motor*); sich erholen, wieder hochkommen (*of health*), wieder in Gang kommen (*as trade etc.*). **3.** *s.* die (Aus)wahl, Auslese, die Besten (*pl.*); – ***of the bunch*** or ***basket***, das Beste von allen.

pick|-a-back, *adv.* huckepack; ***carry him*** –, ihn huckepack tragen. **–axe,** *s.* die Breithacke, Spitzhacke, Picke, (*Min.*) (Keil)haue. **picked** [pikt], *adj.* (aus)erlesen, ausgesucht; – ***troops***, Kerntruppen (*pl.*).

pickerel [ˈpikərəl], *s.* junger Hecht.

picket [ˈpikit], **1.** *s.* 1. der (Holz)pfahl, Pflock; Zeltpflock, Hering; (*Surv.*) Absteckpfahl; 2. (Latten)zaun; 3. (*Mil.*) Vorposten, die Feldwache; 4. (***strike***) –, der Streikposten. **2.** *v.t.* einzäunen, einpfählen (*a space*), anpflocken (*an animal*); mit Streikposten besetzen, durch Streikposten blockieren, Streikposten aufstellen vor (*Dat.*) (*a factory*); (*Mil.*) befestigen, sichern, verpalisadieren. **3.** *v.i.* 1. (als) Streikposten stehen; 2. (*Mil.*) auf Wache stehen.

picking [ˈpikiŋ], *s.* 1. das Pflücken; Lesen; Zupfen; 2. *pl.* (zweifelhafte) Nebeneinkünfte (*pl.*), (unehrlicher) Gewinn; 3. *pl.* Überreste, Überbleibsel (*pl.*), die Nachlese.

pickle [pikl], **1.** *s.* 1. die (Salz)lake, Essigbrühe, (saure) Würztunke; (*coll.*) ***in*** –, in Bereitschaft; 2. (*Metall.*) die Beize, das Abbeizmittel; 3. (*usu. pl.*) Pickles (*pl.*), Eingepökelte(s); ***mixed –s***, sauer eingelegtes Gemüse, Mixpickles (*pl.*); 4. (*coll.*) die Patsche; (*coll.*) ***be in a*** –, in der Patsche sitzen; 5. (*coll.*) der Trotzkopf, Wildfang. **2.** *v.t.* 1. (ein)pökeln, einsalzen, sauer *or* in Essig einlegen, marinieren; 2. (*Metall.*) (ab)beizen. **pickled,** *adj.* 1. gepökelt, eingesalzen, mariniert, Essig–, Salz–, Pökel–; – ***cucumber***, die Essiggurke, saure Gurke; – ***herring***, der Salzhering; 2. (*sl.*) berotzt.

pick|-lock, *s.* 1. der Dietrich; 2. Einbrecher. **--me-up,** *s.* (*coll.*) die (Magen)stärkung. **-pocket,** *s.* der Taschendieb. **--up,** *s.* 1. der Tonabnehmer, die Schalldose, Abtastdose (*record player etc.*); 2. (*sl.*) die Nutte, Flitsche, das Flittchen.

picnic [ˈpiknik], **1.** *s.* das Picknick, die Landpartie, Mahlzeit im Freien; (*sl.*) ***no*** –, keine leichte S. **2.** *v.i.* picknicken, im Freien essen. **picnicker,** *s.* der Picknickteilnehmer, Ausflügler.

picquet, *see* **picket** (*Mil.*).

picric [ˈpikrik], *adj.* Pikrin–.

Pict [pikt], *s.* der Pikte.

pictograph [ˈpiktəgrɑːf], *s.* 1. das Begriffszeichen, Bilderschriftzeichen; 2. bildliche Darstellung, das Bildsymbol, Bilddiagramm, die Bildstatistik.

pictorial [pikˈtɔːriəl], **1.** *adj.* 1. Maler–, malerisch; 2. illustriert, Bilder– (*edition*); – ***advertising***, die Bildwerbung; 3. (*fig.*) bildhaft. **2.** *s.* die Illustrierte.

picture [ˈpiktʃə], **1.** *s.* 1. das Gemälde, Bild; (*fig.*) ***be in the*** –, im Bild *or* auf dem laufenden bleiben *or* sein; (*fig.*) ***come into the*** –, in Erscheinung treten; (*fig.*) ***keep him in the*** –, ihn auf dem laufenden halten; (*coll.*) ***not in the*** –, ohne Belang, (*Spt.*) nicht placiert; (*fig.*) ***put him in the*** –, ihn ins Bild setzen; ***sit for one's*** –, sich malen lassen; ***she is a perfect*** –, sie ist zum Malen schön; ***the dress is a*** –, das Kleid ist ein Gedicht; 2. (*in a book*) die Abbildung, Illustration; 3. (*Phot.*) Aufnahme, Photographie; (*T.V. etc.*) das Bild; 4. (*also* ***motion*** –) der Film; (*coll.*) ***the –s***, das Kino, die Kinovorstellung; ***go to the –s***, ins Kino gehen; ***on the –s***, beim Film; 5. (*fig.*) das Abbild, Ebenbild; 6. (*fig.*) die Schilderung, anschauliche Darstellung, (*coll.*) Verkörperung, das Urbild, Sinnbild; ***be*** or ***look the – of health***, blühend aussehen, von Gesundheit strotzen; ***form a – of***, sich (*Dat.*) ein Bild *or* eine Vorstellung machen von. **2.** *v.t.* abbilden, darstellen, (*fig.*) schildern, ausmalen; – (***to o.s.***), sich (*Dat.*) ein Bild machen von, sich (*Dat.*) vorstellen *or* ausmalen.

picture|-book, *s.* das Bilderbuch. **--card,** *s.* (*Cards*) das Bild, die Bildkarte. **--frame,** *s.* der Bilderrahmen. **--gallery,** *s.* die Gemäldegalerie. **--goer,** *s.* der (die) Kinobesucher(in). **--hat,** *s.* breitkrempiger (Damen)hut. **--house, --palace,** *s.* das Lichtspieltheater, Kino. **--postcard,** *s.* die Ansichtskarte. **--puzzle,** *s.* das Vexierbild, Bilderrätsel. **--rail,** *s.* die Bilderleiste.

picturesque [piktʃəˈresk], *adj.* pittoresk, malerisch. **picturesqueness,** *s.* das Malerische, malerische Schönheit.

picture|-theatre, *s. See* **--house. --transmission,** *s.* die Bildübertragung, der Bildfunk. **--writing,** *s.* die Bilderschrift.

piddle [pidl], *v.i.* (*vulg.*) pinkeln, schiffen. **piddling,** *adj.* (*sl.*) belanglos, fipsig, lumpig.

pidgin [ˈpidʒin], *s.* 1. (*sl.*) die Sache, Angelegenheit; 2. – (***English***), das Pidgin-Englisch, die Verkehrssprache zwischen Europäern und Ostasiaten.

[1]**pie** [pai], *s.* die Pastete; Torte; ***as easy as*** –, kinderleicht, ein Kinderspiel; – ***in the sky***, goldene Berge, leere Versprechungen; ***eat humble*** –, Abbitte tun, zu Kreuze kriechen; ***have a finger in the*** –, die Hand im Spiele haben.

[2]**pie,** *s. See* **magpie.**

[3]**pie,** *s.* (*Typ.*) Zwiebelfische (*pl.*); (*fig.*) ***printer's*** –, der Wirrwarr, die Verwirrung, das Durcheinander; ***make – of***, verwirren, durcheinanderbringen.

piebald [ˈpaibɔːld], *adj.* bunt, (bunt)scheckig, gescheckt; – ***horse***, die Schecke.

piece [piːs], **1.** *s.* 1. das Stück; (*coll.*) ***say one's*** –, seine Meinung sagen; – ***of advice***, der Rat(schlag); – ***of bread and butter***, das Butterbrot; – ***of folly***, die Torheit; – ***of furniture***, das Mobelstück; – ***of*** (***good***) ***luck***, der Glücksfall, glücklicher Zufall; – ***of impudence***, die Unverschämtheit; – ***of land***, das Grundstück; ***give him a – of one's mind***, ihm ordentlich die Meinung sagen; – ***of news***, die Neuigkeit, Nachricht; – ***of paper***, das Blatt Papier; – ***of wallpaper***, die Rolle Tapete; – ***of work***, das Stück Arbeit; ***by the*** –, stückweise; – ***by*** –, Stück für Stück; ***in –s***, in Stücke zerbrochen, in Stücken, entzwei, (*coll.*) kaputt; ***fall in –s***, zerfallen, in Stücke fallen; ***tear in –s***, zerreißen; (*fig.*) (***all***) ***of a*** –, aus einem Guß, gleichmäßig; von derselben Art (***with***, wie), übereinstimmend, eins (mit); ***to –s***, in Stücke, auseinander; (*fig.*) ***all to –s***, ganz zerrüttet, völlig erledigt *or* fertig; ***break to –s***, zerbrechen; ***come*** or ***fall to –s***, in Scherben *or* Stücke gehen; (*fig.*) ***go to –s***, zusammenbrechen, zerrüttet werden; (*fig.*) ***pick*** or ***pull to –s***, zerpflücken; ***take to –s***, zerlegen, auseinandernehmen; ***tear to –s***, zerreißen, in Stücke reißen; 2. das (Musik)stück, (Theater)stück, Gemälde; – ***of music***, das Musikstück; – ***of poetry***, das Gedicht; 3. das (Geld)stück; – ***of money***, das Geldstück; 4. das Geschütz, die Kanone, Flinte; 5. (*Chess*) (Schach)figur, (*draughts etc.*) der Stein; 6. (*sl.*) das Weibsbild, Weibsstück; 7. (*coll.*) Stück Weg, die Wegstrecke. **2.** *v.t.* anstücken (*a dress*), ein Stück aufsetzen auf (*Acc.*) *or* ansetzen an (*Acc.*) *or* einsetzen in (*Acc.*), stückeln, flicken; (*usu.*) – ***together***, zusammensetzen, zusammenstücke(l)n, (*also fig.*) zusammenstellen.

pièce de résistance [pjes də reizisˈtɑ̃s], *s.* 1. die

Hauptsache, das Hauptereignis; 2. (*of meal*) Hauptgericht.

piece|-goods, *pl.* Schnittwaren, Meterwaren; Stückwaren, Manufakturwaren (*pl.*). **-meal,** *adv.* stückweise, Stück für Stück, einzeln. **--rate,** *s.* der Akkordsatz, Stücklohn. **--wages,** *pl.* der Akkordlohn, Stücklohn. **-work,** *s.* die Akkordarbeit; *be on* -, im Akkord arbeiten. **-worker,** *s.* der Akkordarbeiter.

pied [paid], *adj. See* **piebald**; - *piper* (*of Hamelin*), der Rattenfänger von Hameln; - *wagtail,* (*Orn.*) die Bachstelze (*Motacilla alba*).

pied-à-terre [pjeidæ'tɛə], *s.* das Absteigequartier.

Piedmont ['pi:dmənt], *s.* Piemont (*n.*). **Piedmontese** [-'ti:z], **1.** *s.* der Piemontese (die Piemontesin). **2.** *adj.* piemontesisch.

pier [piə], *s.* der (Brücken)pfeiler; Hafendamm, Kai, die Mole, Anlegestelle, Landebrücke, der Landungssteg, Ausladeplatz, Löschplatz. **pierage,** *s.* das Kaigeld.

pierce ['piəs], **1.** *v.t.* 1. durchstechen, durchbohren, durchlöchern; anstechen (*a cask*); 2. (*fig.*) durchdringen; (*fig.*) - *him to the heart,* ihm ins Herz schneiden; 3. durchschauen, ergründen (*mystery etc.*); 4. (*esp. Mil.*) durchstoßen, eindringen in (*Acc.*). **2.** *v.i.* eindringen (*into,* in (*Acc.*)), bohren, stechen, dringen (*through,* durch). **piercing,** *adj.* schneidend, scharf, durchdringend; - *cold,* schneidende Kälte; - *cry,* gellender *or* durchdringender Schrei; - *glance,* durchdringender Blick; - *pain,* stechender Schmerz.

pier|-glass, *s.* der Pfeilerspiegel, großer Wandspiegel. **-head,** *s.* der Molenkopf.

pierrette [piə'ret], *s.* die Kabarettspielerin. **pierrot** ['piərou], *s.* der Kabarettspieler (in Harlekintracht).

pietism ['paiətizm], *s.* der Pietismus. **pietist,** *s.* der Pietist. **pietistic** [-'tistik], *adj.* pietistisch. **piety** ['paiəti], *s.* 1. die Frömmigkeit, Gottesfurcht; 2. Pietät (*to*(*wards*), gegenüber (*Dat.*)), Ehrfurcht (vor (*Dat.*)), Anhänglichkeit (an (*Acc.*)); *filial* -, kindliche Liebe.

piffle [pifl], *s.* (*coll.*) der Quatsch, Unsinn, das Geschwätz. **piffling,** *adj.* belanglos, fipsig; albern.

pig [pig], **1.** *s.* 1. das Schwein; Ferkel; *buy a - in a poke,* die Katze im Sack kaufen; *make a - of o.s.,* sich wie ein Ferkel benehmen; *sucking* -, das Spanferkel; 2. (*Metall.*) die Mulde (*of lead*), Massel, der Rohblock, Barren (*of iron*). **2.** *v.i.* 1. ferkeln, frischen; 2. (*coll.*) - *it,* zusammengepfercht hausen.

pigeon ['pidʒin], *s.* die Taube; *-'s milk,* das Mückenfett; 2. (*sl.*) die Sache, Angelegenheit; (*sl.*) *that's your* -, das ist Ihre Sache. **pigeon|-breasted,** *adj.* hühnerbrüstig. **--fancier,** *s.* der Taubenzüchter. **-hole, 1.** *s.* das (Schub)fach, Ablegefach. **2.** *v.t.* 1. ablegen; 2. einordnen, klassifizieren; 3. (*fig.*) beiseitelegen, zurückstellen, die Erledigung von ... hinausschieben, zu den Akten legen, auf Eis stellen, auf die lange Bank schieben (*plans etc.*), abstempeln, einordnen (*a p.*). **--livered,** *adj.* (*coll.*) bangbüxig. **--toed,** *adj.* mit einwärts gerichteten Füßen.

piggery ['pigəri], *s.* 1. der Schweinestall; 2. (*fig.*) die Schweinerei. **piggish,** *adj.* 1. schweinisch; 2. (*fig.*) gemein, gierig. **piggy,** *s.* (*coll.*) das Schweinchen, Ferkelchen. **piggyback,** *adv. See* **pick-a-back. pig|headed,** *adj.* dickköpfig, störrisch, eigensinnig. **-headedness,** *s.* die Störrigkeit. **--iron,** *s.* das Roheisen, Masseleisen. **--lead,** *s.* das Muldenblei. **piglet,** *s.* das Schweinchen, Ferkel.

pigment ['pigmənt], **1.** *s.* 1. der Farbstoff, die Farbe; 2. (*Biol.*) das Pigment. **2.** *v.t.* färben, pigmentieren. **pigmental** [-'mentl], **pigmentary,** *adj.* Pigment-. **pigmentation** [-'teiʃən], *s.* die Färbung.

pigmy, *see* **pygmy.**

pig|nut, *s.* die Erdnuß. **-skin,** *s.* 1. das Schweinsleder; 2. (*sl.*) der Sattel. **-sticker,** *s.* 1. der Sauspieß; 2. (*sl.*) Hirschfänger, das (Fang)messer. **-sticking,** *s.* die Wildschweinjagd, Sauhatz. **-sty,** *s.* der Schweinestall (*also fig.*). **-tail,** *s.* der Zopf. **-wash,** *s.* das Schweinefutter.

pi-jaw ['paidʒɔ:], **1.** *s.* (*sl.*) die Standpauke, Gardinenpredigt. **2.** *v.t.* die Leviten lesen (*Dat.*), anschnauzen.

[1]**pike** [paik], *s.* (*Ichth.*) der Hecht.

[2]**pike,** *s.* (*Mil.*) der Spieß, die Pike.

[3]**pike,** *s. See* **turnpike.**

pikelet ['paiklit], *s.* runder Teekuchen.

pikeman ['paikmən], *s.* 1. (*Mil.*) der Pikenier, Pikenträger; 2. (*obs.*) Zolleinnehmer; 3. (*Min.*) Hauer. **piker,** *s.* (*Am. sl.*) vorsichtiger Spieler, der Knacker. **pikestaff,** *s.* der Pikenschaft; *as plain as a* -, sonnenklar.

pilaster [pi'læstə], *s.* der Pilaster, Wandpfeiler, Stützpfeiler.

Pilate ['pailət], *s.* (*B.*) Pilatus (*m.*).

pilch [piltʃ], *s.* der Babyschlüpfer.

pilchard ['piltʃəd], *s.* (*Ichth.*) die Sardine.

[1]**pile** [pail], **1.** *s.* 1. der Haufen, Stoß, Stapel; *put in a* -, (auf)stapeln, aufschichten; 2. (*also funeral* -) der Scheiterhaufen; 3. der Gebäudekomplex, großes Gebäude, hohes Bauwerk; 4. (*Elec.*) die Säule; *atomic* -, der Atommeiler, die Atomsäule; *galvanic* -, galvanische Säule; 5. (*coll.*) der Haufen, die Masse, (große) Menge, (*esp.*) die Stange *or* der Haufen Geld; (*sl.*) *make one's* -, sein Glück machen; (*coll.*) *-s of money,* Geld wie Heu; *make a - of money,* eine Stange Geld verdienen. **2.** *v.t.* 1. zusammensetzen (*arms*); 2. bedecken, überladen, überhäufen (*table*) (*with,* mit); (*coll.*) - *it on,* übertreiben; (*coll.*) - *on the agony,* es auf die Spitze treiben, die Erwartung aufs höchste spannen; 3. (*also* - *up*) (auf)häufen, aufschichten, (auf)-stapeln; (*fig.*) aufspeichern; (*coll.*) - *the car up,* den Wagen zu Bruch *or* zu Schrot fahren. **3.** *v.i.* 1. (*coll.*) stürzen, sich drängen; (*sl.*) - *in,* hineindrängen, scharenweise besteigen; - *out,* scharenweise aussteigen; 2. - *up,* sich anhäufen *or* aufhäufen *or* auftürmen, (*also fig.*) sich ansammeln; (*sl.*) (*Av.*) Bruch machen.

[2]**pile, 1.** *s.* 1. der Pfahl, Pfeiler; - *driver,* die Ramme, Rammaschine, der Rammer, Rammklotz; - *dwelling,* der Pfahlbau; 2. das Brückenjoch; 3. (*Her.*) der Spitzpfahl. **2.** *v.t.* verpfählen, unterpfählen.

[3]**pile, 1.** *s.* 1. weiche Behaarung, der Flaum, die Daune (*of animals*); 2. der Flor (*of carpet*), Pol, Felbel (*of velvet*). **2.** *adj. suff. double--,* doppelflorig; *three--,* dreifach gewebt. **pileous** [-iəs], *adj.* (*Bot.*) behaart, haarig, flaumig.

piles [pailz], *pl.* Hämorrhoiden (*pl.*).

pile-up, *s.* (*Motor. coll.*) die Karambolage.

pilfer ['pilfə], *v.t.* klauen, mausen, stibitzen. **pilferage,** *s. See* **pilfering. pilferer,** *s.* der Dieb, Langfinger. **pilfering,** *s.* kleiner Diebstahl, die Dieberei, Mauserei, das Mausen, Stibitzen.

pilgrim ['pilgrim], *s.* der Pilger, Wallfahrer; (*Hist.*) *the Pilgrim Fathers,* die Pilgerväter. **pilgrimage, 1.** *s.* 1. die Wallfahrt, Pilgerfahrt (*to,* nach); *place of* -, der Wallfahrtsort; 2. (*fig.*) beschwerliche Reise, das Erdenleben. **2.** *v.i.* wallfahr(t)en, pilgern.

pill [pil], **1.** *s.* 1. die Pille, Tablette; (*Med. coll.*) *be on the* -, die Pille nehmen; *gild the* -, die bittere Pille versüßen *or* verzuckern; (*coll.*) *swallow a bitter* -, in den sauren Apfel beißen; 2. (*sl.*) die Kugel; 3. (*sl.*) der Ball; (*sl.*) *game of -s,* die Partie Billard; 4. *pl.* (*vulg.*) Eier (*pl.*). **2.** *v.t.* (*sl.*) durchfallen lassen, ablehnen (*a candidate*).

pillage ['pilidʒ], **1.** *s.* die (Aus)plünderung, der Raub. **2.** *v.t., v.i.* (aus)plündern, (aus)rauben, brandschatzen.

pillar ['pilə], **1.** *s.* 1. die Säule, der Pfeiler, Ständer, Träger; *from - to post,* von Pontius zu Pilatus; - *of smoke,* die Rauchsäule; 2. (*fig.*) die Stütze. **2.** *v.t.* mit Pfeilern stützen *or* schmücken. **pillar-box,** *s.* (freistehender) Briefkasten. **pillared,** *adj.* 1. von Pfeilern gestützt, mit Säulen geschmückt; 2. säulenförmig.

pill-box, *s.* 1. die Pillenschachtel; 2. (*Mil.*) der Bunker, Unterstand.

pillion ['piliən], *s.* 1. der Damensattel; 2. das Sattelkissen; 3. der Sozius(sitz) (*on motor-cycle*); *ride –,* auf dem Sozius (mit)fahren. **pillion|-passenger, --rider,** *s.* der Sozius. **--seat,** *s.* der Soziussitz.

pillory ['piləri], **1.** *s.* der Pranger (*also fig.*); *in the –,* am Pranger. **2.** *v.t.* 1. an den Pranger stellen; 2. (*fig.*) anprangern, dem Spott aussetzen.

pillow ['pilou], **1.** *s.* 1. das Kopfkissen; *lace –,* das Klöppelkissen; *take counsel of one's –,* die S. beschlafen; 2. (*Tech.*) der Pfühl (*of a plough*), das (Zapfen)lager, die Lagerschale, Pfanne. **2.** *v.t.* auf ein Kissen legen; *– up,* hoch betten, mit Kissen stützen.

pillow|-case, *s.* der Kissenbezug. **--fight,** *s.* die Kissenschlacht. **--lace,** *s.* Klöppelspitzen (*pl.*). **--slip,** *s. See* **--case.**

pilose ['pailous], *adj.* haarig, behaart. **pilosity** [–'lɔsiti], *s.* die Behaartheit.

pilot ['pailət], **1.** *s.* 1. (*Naut.*) der Lotse, Pilot; 2. das Segelhandbuch; 3. (*Av.*) der Flugzeugführer, Pilot; (*Av.*) *automatic –,* der Selbststeurer, das Selbststeuergerät; 4. (*fig.*) der Führer, Wegweiser, Leiter. **2.** *v.t.* 1. (*Naut.*) lotsen, steuern; 2. (*Av.*) steuern, lenken; 3. (*fig.*) führen, lenken, leiten, als Wegweiser dienen für. **pilotage,** *s.* 1. das Lotsen; 2. Lotsengeld; 3. (*fig.*) die Leitung, Führung.

pilot| balloon, *s.* der Probeballon. **--boat,** *s.* das Lotsenboot. **– burner,** *s.* der Sparbrenner, die Zündflamme. **--cloth,** *s.* dunkelblauer Fries. **--engine,** *s.* die Leerfahrtlokomotive. **--flag,** *s.* die Lotsenflagge. **– lamp,** *s.* (*Elec.*) die Kontrollampe. **pilotless,** *adj.* führerlos, unbemannt (*plane*). **pilot| light,** *s. See* **– burner, – lamp.** **--officer,** *s.* der Fliegerleutnant. **– scheme,** *s.* das Versuchsprojekt.

pilous ['pailəs], *adj. See* **pilose.**

pilule ['pilju:l], *s.* kleine Pille.

pimento [pi'mentou], *s.* der Nelkenpfeffer, Piment.

pimp [pimp], **1.** *s.* der Kuppler, Zuhälter. **2.** *v.i.* kuppeln.

pimpernel ['pimpənel], *s.* (*Bot.*) die Pimpernelle.

pimple [pimpl], *s.* die Pustel, Finne, der Pickel. **pimpled, pimply,** *adj.* voll(er) Pusteln, pustelig, finnig, pick(e)lig.

pin [pin], **1.** *s.* 1. die (Steck)nadel; *–s and needles,* das Kribbeln, Ameisenlaufen; *on –s and needles,* (wie) auf glühenden Kohlen; (*coll.*) *I don't care two –s,* es ist mir piepe *or* wurst *or* schnuppe; *not worth a –,* keinen Deut *or* Pfifferling wert; 2. die Zwecke, Pinne; *drawing –,* der Reißnagel, die Zwecke; 3. der Dübel, Stift, Pflock (*of wood*), Bolzen, Zapfen (*of metal*); *crank –,* der Kurbelzapfen; *dowel –,* der Dübel, Diebel; *firing –,* der Schlagbolzen; *hinge –,* der Angeldorn, Scharniernagel; *retaining –,* der Schlüsselbolzen; *split –,* der Federsplint; 4. *hair–,* die Haarnadel; *safety –,* die Sicherheitsnadel; 5. *rolling –,* das Rollholz, Nudelholz, die Nudelwalze; 6. (*Mus.*) der Wirbel; 7. Kegel (*at ninepins*); 8. *pl.* (*sl.*) Beine, Stelzen (*pl.*); (*coll.*) *knock him off his –s,* ihn umschmeißen. **2.** *v.t.* 1. feststecken, festmachen, befestigen (*to, on,* an (*Acc.*)); *– one's faith* or *hopes on,* sein ganzes Vertrauen setzen auf (*Acc.*), fest bauen auf (*Acc.*); (*coll.*) *– on,* zuschieben, anhängen (*Dat.*); *– up,* aufstecken, hochstecken; 2. (*fig.*) festhalten (*to, against,* an (*Dat.*)), drücken, pressen (gegen *or* an (*Acc.*)), heften (an (*Acc.*)); 3. *– down,* festhalten (*to,* an (*Dat.*)); zurückführen, festlegen, festnageln (auf (*Acc.*)), zuschreiben, beimessen (*Dat.*); binden (an (*Acc.*)); in die Enge treiben, verpflichten; (*Mil.*) fesseln (*enemy*).

pinafore ['pinəfɔ:], *s.* die Schürze, das Lätzchen.

pin-ball machine, *s.* das Spielautomat.

pince-nez [pɛ̃s'nei], *s.* der Kneifer, Klemmer.

pincer-movement ['pinsə–], *s.* (*Mil.*) die Umklammerung. **pincers,** *pl.* 1. die (Kneif)zange; *pair of –,* die Zange; 2. (*Med.*) Pinzette; 3. (*of crab*) Krebsschere, Krabbenschere.

pinch [pintʃ], **1.** *v.t.* 1. kneifen, zwicken, quetschen, (ein)klemmen, drücken; *– off,* abzwicken, abkneifen; 2. (*sl.*) klauen, klemmen; 3. (*Naut.*) hart an den Wind bringen; 4. (*sl.*) (*usu. pass.*) verhaften, schnappen, einspunden; (*sl.*) *get –ed,* geschnappt werden. **2.** *v.i.* 1. drücken, kneifen, zwicken; (*fig.*) *know where the shoe –es,* wissen wo der Schuh drückt; 2. (*fig.*) geizen, knausern (*on,* mit), sich nichts vergönnen, darben; (*coll.*) *– and scrape,* sich (*Dat.*) alles vom Munde absparen; 3. (*Naut.*) hart an den Wind segeln. **3.** *s.* 1. das Kneifen, Zwicken, (Ein)klemmen; der Kniff, Druck; 2. die Prise (*of salt etc.*); (*fig.*) *with a – of salt,* mit Vorbehalt; 3. (*fig.*) Notlage, der Druck; (*coll.*) *at a –,* zur Not, im Notfall, notfalls, wenn alle Stricke reißen.

pinchbeck ['pintʃbek], **1.** *s.* der Tombak, das Talmi. **2.** *adj.* 1. Talmi–; 2. (*fig.*) unecht, nachgemacht; minderwertig.

pinched [pintʃt], *adj.* 1. zusammengedrückt, eingeklemmt; 2. (*fig.*) abgezehrt, abgemagert, abgehärmt, ausgemergelt (*features*), bedrückt, beschränkt (*circumstances*); (*fig.*) *be – for,* knapp sein an (*Dat.*), wenig . . . haben (*time, room, money etc.*); *be – for money,* knapp bei Kasse sein; (*fig.*) *– with cold,* erstarrt vor Kälte; *– with hunger,* halb verhungert.

pincushion ['pinkuʃən], *s.* das Nadelkissen.

[1]**pine** [pain], *s.* die Kiefer, Föhre, Pinie.

[2]**pine,** *v.i.* 1. sich grämen *or* abhärmen (*over,* über (*Acc.*)); 2. schmachten, sich sehnen (*for,* nach); 3. *– away,* verschmachten, vor Gram vergehen, dahinwelken.

pineal ['painiəl], *adj.* *– gland,* die Zirbeldrüse, Epiphyse.

pine|apple, *s.* die Ananas. **--beauty,** *s.* (*Ent.*) der Kiefernfalter. **--cone,** *s.* der (Kiefern)zapfen. **--marten,** *s.* (*Zool.*) der Baummarder. **--needle,** *s.* die Kiefernnadel. **pinery,** *s.* 1. die Kiefernpflanzung; 2. das Ananas(treib)haus. **pine|-tree,** *s. See* [1]**pine.** **-wood,** *s.* 1. das Kiefernholz; 2. der Kiefernwald.

pin-feather, *s.* die Stoppelfeder.

pinfold ['pinfould], *s.* (*obs.*) die Viehhürde.

ping [piŋ], **1.** *v.i.* pfeifen, schwirren (*as bullets*). **2.** *s.* das Schwirren. **ping-pong,** *s.* das Tischtennis.

pin|-head, *s.* der (Steck)nadelkopf. **--hole,** *s.* 1. das Nadelloch, Nagelloch; 2. (*Phot.*) kleines Loch; *– camera,* die Lochkamera.

pinic ['pi:nik], *adj.* *– acid,* die Pininsäure.

[1]**pinion** ['pinjən], **1.** *s.* 1. die Flügelspitze; 2. (*also – feather*) die Schwungfeder, Flugfeder; 3. (*Poet.*) der Flügel, Fittich, die Schwinge. **2.** *v.t.* 1. beschneiden, stutzen (*wing*); die Flügel stutzen (*Dat.*) (*bird*); 2. (*fig.*) binden, fesseln (*hands etc.*); die Hände fesseln (*Dat.*) (*a p.*).

[2]**pinion,** *s.* (*Tech.*) das Ritzel, der Drehling; *– drive,* der Ritzelantrieb; *– gear,* das Getriebe.

[1]**pink** [piŋk], **1.** *adj.* blaßrot, rosarot, rosig; *rose –,* rosenrot; *salmon –,* lachsfarben. **2.** *s.* 1. das Blaßrot, Rosa; 2. (*Hunt.*) roter Jagdrock; (*fig.*) der Gipfel, höchster Grad, die Höhe, Krone; *the – of perfection,* die höchste Vollendung, das Muster der Vollkommenheit; (*coll.*) *in the – (of condition),* in bester Verfassung, in Hochform.

[2]**pink,** *s.* (*Naut.*) die Pinke, das Heckboot.

[3]**pink,** *v.t.* 1. auszacken, kunstvoll ausschneiden; 2. durchbohren, durchlöchern, durchstechen.

[4]**pink,** *v.i.* (*Motor.*) klopfen.

pinking|-iron, *s.* das Auszackeisen. **--scissors, --shears,** *pl.* die Zackenschere.

pinkish ['piŋkiʃ], *adj.* rötlich, blaßrosa. **pinkness,** *s.* das Rosa(rot), die Rosafarbe, Röte.

pin-money, *s.* das Nadelgeld; (*fig.*) geringfügige Belohnung.

pinna ['pinə], *s.* (*pl.* **-e** *or* **-s**) 1. (*Anat.*) die Ohrmuschel; 2. (*Bot.*) Fieder; 3. (*Zool.*) Flosse; 4. (*Bot.*) Feder, der Flügel.

pinnace ['pinəs], *s.* die Pinasse, Barkasse, das Beiboot, Großboot.

pinnacle ['pinəkl], *s.* 1. (*Archit.*) der Spitzturm, die Fiale, Zinne; 2. Felsspitze; 3. (*fig.*) Spitze, der Gipfel, Höhepunkt.

pinnate ['pineit], *adj.* federartig, federförmig, Feder–; (*Bot.*) fiederförmig, gefiedert. **pinnatiped** [–'nætiped], **pinnigrade, pinniped, 1.** *s.* der Schwimmfüßer. **2.** *adj.* schwimmfüßig. **pinnule** [–ju:l], *s.* 1. das Federchen; 2. (*Zool.*) Flößchen, Flössel; 3. (*Bot.*) Fiederblättchen.

pinny ['pini], *s.* (*coll.*) *see* **pinafore.**

pin|-point, 1. *s.* die Nadelspitze; – ***bombing,*** gezielter Bombenwurf; – ***target,*** das Punktziel. **2.** *v.t.* 1. genau zielen nach; 2. (*fig.*) (haar)genau bestimmen *or* festlegen; ins Auge fassen, ein Schlaglicht werfen auf (*Acc.*), hervorheben, klar hervortreten lassen. **–prick,** *s.* der Nadelstich (*also fig.*); (*fig.*) (*oft. pl.*) die Stichelei, spitze Bemerkung. **––stripe,** *s.* der Nadelstreifen.

pint [paint], *s.* der Schoppen (= *0.57 l., Am. 0.47 l.*).

pin|-table, *s.* das Spielautomat. **–tail,** *s.* (*also* – ***duck***) die Spießente (*Ansa acuta*).

pintle [pintl], *s.* 1. der (Dreh)bolzen, Achsnagel; 2. (*Artil.*) Protznagel, Spannagel; ***––eye,*** der Protzring; ***––hook,*** der Protzhaken; 3. (*Naut.*) Ruderhaken, Fingerling.

pinto ['pintou], *s.* geschecktes Pferd, der Scheck, die Schecke.

pin-up, *s.* (*coll.*) (*also* – ***girl***) das Pin-up-girl, die Illustriertenschönheit.

pioneer [paiə'niə], **1.** *s.* 1. (*Mil.*) der Pionier(soldat); 2. (*fig.*) Pionier, Bahnbrecher, Vorkämpfer, Wegbereiter (***of,*** *Gen. or* in (*Dat.*)). **2.** *v.i.* bahnbrechende Arbeit leisten, den Weg bahnen. **3.** *v.t.* Bahn brechen (*Dat.*), den Weg bahnen für, bahnbrechende Arbeit leisten für, vorangehen mit.

pious ['paiəs], *adj.* fromm, gottesfürchtig; (*fig.*) – ***hopes,*** fromme Wünsche.

¹pip [pip], *s.* 1. das Auge (*cards*), der Punkt (*dice*); 2. (*Mil.*) Stern (als Rangabzeichen); 3. Leuchtfleck (*radar*); 4. (kurzer) Ton (*time-signal etc.*).

²pip, *s.* der (Obst)kern (*of apples etc.*).

³pip, *s.* 1. der Pips (*in fowls*); 2. (*coll.*) der Ärger, Unmut; (*coll.*) ***give him the –,*** ihm auf die Nerven gehen; ***have the –,*** schlechter Laune sein.

⁴pip, 1. *v.t.* (*coll.*) 1. schlagen, überlisten; – ***at the post,*** direkt vorm Ziel überrumpeln; 2. durchfallen lassen. **2.** *v.i.* (*coll.*) durchfallen.

pipe [paip], **1.** *s.* 1. (*Mus.*) die Pfeife, Einhandflöte, einfache Flöte; ***–s of Pan,*** die Panflöte, Bündelflöte; 2. (*also* ***tobacco*** –) die (Tabaks)pfeife; – ***of peace,*** die Friedenspfeife (*also fig.*); (*coll.*) ***put that in your – and smoke it,*** laß dir das gesagt sein; 3. das Rohr, die Röhre, (Rohr)leitung (*gas etc.*); 4. das Piep(s)en (*of birds*); 5. (*obs.*) die Pipe (= *105 gallons,* = *477 l.*) (*of wine*); 6. *pl.* (*Mus.*) der Dudelsack; 7. *pl.* (*coll.*) Luftwege (*pl.*). **2.** *v.i.* 1. auf der Pfeife spielen; 2. pfeifen (*as the wind*), zirpen (*of insects*), piepen (*of birds*), piepsen, quieken (*of persons*); (*coll.*) – ***in,*** dazwischenreden; (*sl.*) – ***down,*** die Schnauze halten; – ***up,*** (*coll.*) das Wort ergreifen; (*Naut.*) zunehmen (*of wind*). **3.** *v.t.* 1. (*Naut.*) zusammenpfeifen, durch Pfeifensignal zusammenrufen (*the crew*) *or* empfangen (*the admiral*); 2. paspelieren, mit Schnur besetzen (*a dress*); 3. mit Röhren *or* Rohrleitungen versehen (*a house*), leiten (*gas etc.*); 4. (*Hort.*) absenken.

pipe|-bend, *s.* das Rohrknie. **––bowl,** *s.* der Pfeifenkopf. **––burst,** *s.* der Rohrbruch. **––clay,** *s.* 1. der Pfeifenton, Töpferton; 2. (*Mil. coll.*) die Schniegelei, der Kommiß. **––clip,** *s.* die Rohrschelle. **––dream,** *s.* der Wunschtraum. **pipeful,** *s.* die Pfeifevoll (*of tobacco*). **pipe|line,** *s.* 1. die Rohrleitung, (*esp.*) Ölleitung; 2. (*fig. coll.*) der Informationsweg. – **major,** *s.* der Musikmeister (der Dudelsackkapelle). **piper,** *s.* der (Dudelsack)-pfeifer; ***pay the –,*** die Kosten tragen, die Zeche bezahlen, der Dumme sein; ***he who pays the – calls the tune,*** wer bezahlt, hat zu bestimmen. **pipe|-rack,** *s.* der Pfeifenständer. **––stem,** *s.* der Pfeifenstiel.

pipette [pi'pet], *s.* die Pipette, der Stechheber.

pipe|work, *s. See* **piping, 3,** 2. **––wrench,** *s.* die Rohrzange. **piping, 1.** *adj.* 1. pfeifend, schrill; 2. friedlich, idyllisch; ***the – times of yore,*** die guten alten Zeiten. **2.** *adv.* – ***hot,*** siedend heiß. **3.** *s.* 1. das Pfeifen, Piepen; Dudelsackspielen; 2. Röhren (*pl.*), die Rohrleitung, Röhrenanlage; 3. der Schnurbesatz, die Paspel, Litze, Biese.

pipit ['pipit], *s.* (*Orn.*) der Pieper (*Anthus*).

pipkin ['pipkin], *s.* irdenes Töpfchen.

pippin ['pipin], *s.* der Pippinapfel.

pip-squeak, *s.* (*sl.*) der Wichtigtuer; (*Mil. sl.*) Leutnant.

piquancy ['pikənsi], *s.* 1. die Würze, Schärfe, Pikantheit, das Pikante; 2. (*fig.*) angenehmer Reiz. **piquant,** *adj.* 1. würzig, scharf, pikant; 2. (*fig.*) reizvoll, reizend.

pique [pi:k], **1.** *s.* der Groll, Unwille, Ärger, die Verstimmung, Gereiztheit, Pikiertheit; ***in a fit of –,*** in plötzlicher Verstimmung; ***take a – against,*** auf der Pike haben. **2.** *v.t.* verstimmen, erzürnen, (auf)reizen, kränken, ärgern; – ***o.s. on,*** sich (*Dat.*) etwas einbilden auf (*Acc.*), sich brüsten mit.

piqué ['pi:kei], *s.* der Pikee.

piqued [pi:kt], *adj.* pikiert, verärgert (***at,*** über (*Acc.*)).

piquet [pi'ket], *s.* (*Cards*) das Pikett.

piracy ['pairəsi], *s.* 1. die Seeräuberei, Piraterie, Freibeuterei; 2. (*fig.*) literarischer Diebstahl, das Plagiat, die Copyrightverletzung, Patentverletzung; der Raubdruck, unbefugter Nachdruck (*of books*), die Raubpressung (*of gramophone records*). **pirate** [–ət], **1.** *s.* 1. der Seeräuber, Pirat; 2. das Piratenschiff, Seeräuberschiff; 3. (*fig.*) unrechtmäßiger Nachdrucker; 4. konkurrierender Privatomnibus; 5. inoffizieller Radiosender. **2.** *v.t.* (*fig.*) plagiieren; ohne Erlaubnis nachdrucken (*books*) *or* nachpressen (*records*). **piratical** [–'rætikl], *adj.* 1. (see)räuberisch, Seeräuber–; 2. (*fig.*) unerlaubt (nachgedruckt), Raub–; – ***edition,*** unerlaubter Nachdruck, der Raubdruck; – ***printer,*** der Nachdrucker.

pirouette [piru'et], **1.** *s.* die Pirouette, Kreisdrehung. **2.** *v.i.* pirouettieren.

pis-aller [pi:'zælei], *s.* die Notlösung.

piscary ['piskəri], *s.* ***common of –,*** die Fischereigerechtigkeit, das Fischereirecht. **piscatorial** [–'tɔ:riəl], **piscatory** [–təri], *adj.* Fischer(ei)–, Fisch–.

Pisces ['paisi:z], *pl.* (*Astr.*) Fische (*pl.*).

pisciculture ['piskikʌltʃə], *s.* die Fischzucht.

piscina [pi'si:nə, –'sainə], *s.* 1. das Wasserbecken, der Schwimmteich; 2. Fischbehälter; 3. (*Eccl.*) das Abspülbecken.

piscivorous [pis'kivərəs], *adj.* fischfressend.

pisé ['pi:zei], *s.* 1. die Stampfmasse, Stampferde, der Pisee; 2. Piseebau, Stampfbau.

pish! [piʃ], *int.* (*obs.*) pfui!

pisiform ['pisifɔ:m], *adj.* Erbsen–, Bohnen–.

piss [pis], **1.** *s.* (*vulg.*) der Harn, die Pisse, Schiffe. **2.** *v.i.* harnen, pissen, schiffen, seichen. **3.** *v.t.* pissen in (*Acc.*), bepissen.

pistachio [pis'tɑ:ʃiou], *s.* (*Bot.*) die Pistazie; – ***nut,*** die Pistazienmandel.

pistil ['pistil], *s.* (*Bot.*) der Stempel, das Pistill. **pistillate,** *adj.* mit Stempel(n); (*Bot.*) weiblich.

pistol [pistl], **1.** *s.* die Pistole. **2.** *v.t.* mit der Pistole (er)schießen. **pistol|-gallery,** *s.* die Pistolenschießbude. **––grip,** *s.* der Pistolengriff. **––shot,** *s.* der Pistolenschuß; ***within –,*** in Pistolenschußweite.

piston ['pistən], *s.* der Kolben. **piston|-displacement,** *s.* die Kolbenverdrängung, der Hubraum. **––engine,** *s.* der Kolbenmotor. **––head,** *s.* der Kolbenboden. **––rod,** *s.* die Kolbenstange, Pleuelstange. **––stroke,** *s.* der Kolbenhub.

¹pit [pit], **1.** *s.* 1. die Grube, Einsenkung, Vertiefung, das Loch; – ***of the stomach,*** die Magengrube; 2. (*Min.*) die (Kohlen)grube, Zeche, das (Kohlen)-bergwerk, der Schacht, Stollen; 3. die Fallgrube, Falle (*also fig.*); 4. der Abgrund (*also fig.*); ***the bottomless –,*** der Höllenschlund; 5. (*Hist.*) der Hahnenkampfplatz; 6. (*Comm.*) die (Getreide)-börse; 7. (*Motor.*) Box; 8. (*Med.*) (Blatter)narbe; 9. (*Theat.*) das Parterre. **2.** *v.t.* 1. vergraben, eingraben, einmieten (*potatoes etc.*); 2. (*Med.*) mit Narben zeichnen; ***pitted with smallpox,*** blatternarbig; 3. (*fig.*) feindlich gegenüberstellen (***against,*** *Dat.*), ausspielen (gegen); – ***one's strength against,*** seine Kraft aufbieten gegen *or* messen mit. **3.** *v.i.* 1. sich senken *or* aushöhlen; 2. (*Med.*) eine Delle *or* Grube bilden.

[2]**pit,** *s.* (*Am.*) *see* **stone** (*of fruit*).

pit-a-pat ['pitə'pæt], **1.** *adv.* ticktack (*as the heart*), klippklapp, tripptrapp (*as the feet*). **2.** *s.* das Trippeln, Getrippel, Getrappel.

[1]**pitch** [pitʃ], **1.** *s.* das Pech; (***as***) ***black as –,*** pech-(raben)schwarz. **2.** *v.t.* verpichen, teeren.

[2]**pitch, 1.** *s.* 1. der Wurf, (Vor)stoß; 2. Aufschlag, Aufprall (*of a ball*); 3. (*Naut.*) das Stampfen; 4. die Flughöhe (*of bird of prey, arrow*); 5. (*Build.*) Neigung, (Dach)schräge, Abdachung, das Gefälle (*of roof*); (*Archit.*) – ***of an arch,*** die Bogenhöhe; 6. (*Tech.*) die Steigung, Ganghöhe (*of screw*); Gradteilung, Zahnteilung, Kettenteilung (*of cog*); Schränkung, der Schrank (*of saw*); 7. (Stärke)grad, die Höhe, Stufe; (*fig.*) Höhepunkt, Gipfel, äußerster Punkt; (*fig.*) ***at the highest –,*** auf der Höhe; ***to the highest –,*** aufs äußerste; 8. (*Mus.*) die Tonhöhe; Stimmung (*of an instrument*); ***difference in*** or ***of –,*** der Tonunterschied; ***sense of –,*** das Tonbewußtsein; ***perfect*** or ***absolute –,*** absolutes Gehör; ***standard –,*** die Normaltonhöhe; ***sustain the –,*** den Ton halten; ***true to –,*** tonrein; 9. (*Spt.*) das (Spiel)-feld; 10. der Stand (*of a trader*); (*coll.*) ***queer his –,*** ihm einen Strich durch die Rechnung machen, ihm ins Handwerk pfuschen.
2. *v.t.* 1. werfen, schleudern (*a missile*); 2. (auf)-laden (*hay etc.*); 3. aufschlagen (*tent*), aufstellen (*ladder etc.*); errichten, anlegen (*camp*), einschlagen, einstecken, feststecken, befestigen (*pegs etc.*); 4. beschottern, pflastern (*a road*); 5. (*Mus.*) die Tonhöhe festsetzen *or* anschlagen für, anstimmen, stimmen (*an instrument*); – ***the voice*** (***high***), (hoch) anstimmen; (*fig.*) – ***one's hopes high,*** die Hoffnungen hoch schrauben; 6. (*fig.*) festsetzen, festlegen, ansetzen, abstimmen (***at, on,*** auf (*Acc.*)); 7. ***-ed battle,*** regelrechte Schlacht.
3. *v.i.* 1. aufschlagen, aufprallen (*of a ball*); 2. stampfen (*of a ship*); 3. (kopfüber) (hin)fallen *or* (hin)stürzen ((***up***)***on,*** auf (*Acc.*)); 4. (*fig. coll.*) verfallen ((***up***)***on,*** auf (*Acc.*)), sich entscheiden (für); 5. abfallen, sich neigen *or* senken (*as a roof*); 6. (*coll.*) – ***in,*** kräftig ans Werk gehen, sich ins Zeug legen, tüchtig einhauen; – ***into,*** herfallen über (*Acc.*), tüchtig einhauen auf (*Acc.*) (*a p.*) *or* in (*Acc.*) (*a meal etc.*).

pitch|-and-toss, *s.* Kopf oder Wappen (*game*); (*fig.*) ***play – with,*** leichtfertig umgehen mit. **--angle,** *s.* (*Archit.*) der Fallwinkel, Steigungswinkel. **--black,** *adj.* pechschwarz. **-blende,** *s.* (*Min.*) die Pechblende, das Uranpecherz. **--dark,** *adj.* stockdunkel.

[1]**pitcher** ['pitʃə], *s.* (*baseball*) der Werfer; ***–'s box,*** das (Ab)wurfmal.

[2]**pitcher,** *s.* der (Wasser)krug; (*Prov.*) ***little –s have long ears,*** kleine Pötte haben große Ohren; (*Prov.*) ***the – goes often to the well but is broken at last,*** der Krug geht so lange zum Brunnen bis er bricht.

pitch|fork, 1. *s.* die Heugabel, Mistgabel. **2.** *v.t.* (*coll.*) rücksichtslos werfen, lancieren, gewaltsam drängen. **--pine,** *s.* (*Bot.*) die Pechkiefer. **--pipe,** *s.* (*Mus.*) die Stimmpfeife. **--shot,** *s.* (*golf*) der Steilschlag. **pitchy,** *adj.* 1. pechig, teerig, pechartig, teerartig; 2. pechschwarz.

pit-coal, *s.* die Steinkohle.

piteous ['pitiəs], *adj.* kläglich, erbärmlich, jämmerlich; rührend, mitleiderregend, herzzerreißend.

pitfall ['pitfɔ:l], *s.* die (Fall)grube, Falle (*also fig.*); (*usu. fig.*) der Irrtum.

pith [piθ], *s.* 1. (*Bot.*) das Mark (*also fig.*); die Seele (*of feather, also fig.*); (*fig.*) der Kern, das Innerste, Wesen(tliche), die Quintessenz; 2. Kraft, Stärke, Energie; 3. Bedeutung, das Gewicht, der Nachdruck.

pit-head, *s.* 1. (*Min.*) die Schachtöffnung, Tagöffnung, Schachtmündung, (Schacht)kaue; 2. das Förderhaus, Fördergerüst, Füllort; – ***baths,*** die Waschkaue; – ***price,*** der Preis frei Grube, Preis ab Schacht.

pithecanthropus [piθi'kænθrəpəs], *s.* der Javamensch.

pith-helmet, *s.* der Tropenhelm. **pithiness,** *s.* 1. die Markigkeit; 2. (*fig.*) Kernigkeit, Prägnanz, Kraft, Stärke. **pithy,** *adj.* 1. (*Bot.*) markig, markreich; 2. (*fig.*) markig, kernig, prägnant, gehaltvoll, inhaltsschwer; – ***saying,*** der Kernspruch.

pitiable ['pitiəbl], *adj.* bedauernswert, bejammernswert; *see also* **piteous**; (*fig.*) *see* **pitiful** (*coll.*). **pitiful,** *adj.* 1. mitleidig, mitleid(s)voll, mitfühlend; *see also* **piteous**; 2. (*usu. coll. fig.*) elend, armselig, dürftig, läppisch. **pitifulness,** *s.* die Jämmerlichkeit, Erbärmlichkeit; (*fig.*) Armseligkeit, Dürftigkeit. **pitiless,** *adj.* erbarmungslos, unbarmherzig, mitleidslos. **pitilessness,** *s.* die Unbarmherzigkeit, Härte.

pit|-man, *s.* der Grubenarbeiter, Schachtarbeiter, Bergmann, Kumpel. **--mouth,** *s.* die Grubeneinfahrt.

piton [pi'tɔn], *s.* der Kletterhaken; – ***hammer,*** der Kletterhammer.

pit|-pony, *s.* das Grubenpferd. **--prop,** *s.* die Holzstütze, der Grubenstempel. **--saw,** *s.* die Schrotsäge, Brettsäge.

pittance ['pitəns], *s.* 1. kleine Portion, kleiner Anteil, (kleines) bißchen; 2. armseliges Auskommen, der Hungerlohn.

pitted ['pitid], *adj.* 1. (*Tech.*) narbig, ausgehöhlt; 2. (*Bot.*) getüpfelt.

pitter-patter ['pitə'pætə], *adv., s. See* **pit-a-pat.**

pitting [pitiŋ], *s.* (*Tech.*) die Körnung, das Körnen, Angefressensein, der Lochfraß.

pituitary [pi'tjuitəri], *adj.* schleimabsondernd, Schleim–; – ***gland,*** der Hirnanhang, die Hypophyse.

pity ['piti], **1.** *s.* 1. das Mitleid, Mitgefühl; Erbarmen; ***feel – for, take – on,*** Mitleid haben mit; ***have – on,*** Erbarmen haben mit; ***for –'s sake,*** um Gottes *or* Himmels willen; 2. der Jammer; ***the – of it is . . .,*** es ist nur schade daß . . ., der (einzige) Nachteil (dabei) ist . . .; ***it is a*** (***great***) ***–,*** es ist (sehr) schade; ***it is a thousand pities,*** es ist jammerschade; ***what a –!*** wie schade! (*coll.*) ***more's the –,*** um so schlimmer. **2.** *v.t.* bemitleiden, Mitleid haben mit, bedauern; (*in scorn*) ***you are to be pitied*** or ***I – you if . . .,*** du kannst mir leid tun, wenn . . .. **pitying,** *adj.* mitleidsvoll, mitleidig.

pivot ['pivət], **1.** *s.* 1. der Drehpunkt, (Dreh)zapfen; die Achse, Spindel; 2. Angel; 3. (*Mil.*) der Flügelmann; 4. (*fig.*) Angelpunkt. **2.** *v.i.* sich drehen (*on,* um) (*also fig.*). **3.** *v.t.* drehbar lagern; ***be -ed on,*** *see* **2.** (*also fig.*). **4.** *adj.* Gelenk–, Dreh–, Schwenk–; – ***arm,*** der Schwenkarm; – ***industry,*** die Schlüsselindustrie. **pivotal,** *adj.* 1. Angel–, Zapfen–; – ***point,*** der Angelpunkt; 2. (*usu. fig.*) Haupt–, Schlüssel–, Kardinal–, zentral, lebenswichtig; – ***question,*** entscheidende Frage.

pixie, pixy ['piksi], *s.* der Elf, die Fee, das Wichtelmännchen.

pizzle [pizl], *s.* die Rute, der (Ochsen)ziemer.

placability [plækə'biliti], *s.* die Versöhnlichkeit, Nachgiebigkeit. **placable** ['plækəbl], *adj.* versöhnlich, nachgiebig. **placableness,** *s. See* **placability.**

placard ['plækɑ:d], **1.** *s.* der Anschlag(zettel), das Plakat. **2.** *v.t.* mit Plakaten bekleben (*wall*), anschlagen, durch Anschläge bekanntgeben (*announcement*).

placate [plə'keit], *v.t.* versöhnen, besänftigen, beschwichtigen. **placation** [–'keiʃən], *s.* die Versöhnung, Besänftigung, Beschwichtigung.

place [pleis], **1.** *s.* 1. der Platz (*also Spt.*), Ort, die Stelle (*also Math.*), Stätte; 2. Ortschaft, Stadt, der Wohnort, Aufenthaltsort; (*esp. in the country*) Wohnsitz, Landsitz, das Anwesen; (*coll.*) Haus, die Wohnung, Wohnstätte; 3. der Sitz, (Sitz)-platz; 4. Posten, das Amt, die (An)stellung, (Arbeits)stelle; 5. (*fig.*) Aufgabe, Pflicht; 6. (*fig.*) Stelle, Lage; 7. (*opp. to time*) der Raum; 8. (*Theat.*) Ort, Schauplatz.
(a) (*with adj.*) (*coll.*) ***every –***, überall; (*coll.*) ***no –***, nirgends; ***no – for***, nicht der (geeignete) Ort für; ***native –***, der Heimatort; ***sore –***, wunde Stelle.
(b) (*with noun*) ***decimal –***, die (Dezimal)stelle; ***– of amusement***, die Vergnügungsstätte; ***– of assembly***, der Treffpunkt; ***– of business***, der Geschäftssitz; (*Naut.*) ***– of call***, der Anlaufhafen; ***– of delivery***, der Erfüllungsort; ***– of destination***, der Bestimmungsort; ***– of employment***, der Arbeitsplatz, die Arbeitsstelle, Arbeitsstätte; ***– of interest***, die Sehenswürdigkeit; ***– of issue***, der Ausstellungsort; ***– of refuge***, der Zufluchtsort; (*fig.*) ***– in the sun***, der Platz an der Sonne; ***– of worship***, das Gotteshaus.
(c) (*with verb*) ***change –s***, den Platz tauschen; ***find one's –***, sich zurechtfinden; ***give – to***, Platz machen für *or* (*Dat.*), ersetzt werden von; (*coll.*) ***go –s***, Sehenswürdigkeiten besuchen, Vergnügungstätten aufsuchen; (*sl.*) es weit bringen; ***it is not his –***, es ist nicht seines Amts (*to do*, zu tun); ***know one's –***, wissen, was sich geziemt; wissen, wohin man gehört; ***take –***, sich ereignen, stattfinden, eintreten; ***take your –s!*** nehmen Sie ihre Plätze (ein)! setzen Sie sich! ***take his –***, seine Stelle einnehmen, ihn vertreten; ***take the – of***, an die Stelle treten von, ersetzen.
(d) (*with prep.*) (*coll.*) ***at his –***, bei ihm (zu Hause); ***at this –***, hier; ***from – to –***, von Ort zu Ort; ***in –***, am (richtigen) Platz; (*fig.*) am Platz, angebracht; ***in – of***, (an)statt, an Stelle von *or* (*Gen.*), als Ersatz für; ***in –s***, an gewissen *or* verschiedenen Stellen, stellenweise; ***in its –***, an seinem Platz, an Ort und Stelle; ***in their –s***, auf ihren Plätzen (*of persons*); (*fig.*) ***in his –***, an seiner Stelle, in seiner Lage; (*fig.*) ***keep him in his –***, ihn in seinen Grenzen halten; (*fig.*) ***put him in his –***, ihn in die Schranken weisen; (*fig.*) ***put o.s. in his –***, sich in seine Lage versetzen; ***in another –***, anderswo, an anderer Stelle; (*Parl.*) im Oberhaus; ***in the first –***, zuerst, erstens, an erster Stelle; gleich von Anfang an, in erster Linie, von vornherein, überhaupt; ***his heart is in the right –***, er hat sein Herz auf dem *or* am rechten Fleck; ***the right man in the right –***, der rechte Mann an der rechten Stelle; ***in some – (or other)***, irgendwo; ***in the wrong –***, am unrichtigen Ort, an der falschen Stelle; ***of that –***, dortig; ***of this –***, hiesig(en Ortes); ***out of –***, nicht am richtigen Platz, am unrechten Ort; (*fig.*) fehl am Platz, unangebracht; (*coll.*) ***all over the –***, überall.
2. *v.t.* 1. stellen, legen, setzen; ***– confidence in***, Vertrauen setzen in (*Acc.*), Vertrauen haben zu; ***– under confinement***, in Haft nehmen; ***– at his disposal***, ihm zur Verfügung stellen; ***– beyond (a) doubt***, über allen Zweifel erheben; ***– in order***, ordnen; ***– on record***, (schriftlich) festhalten, aufzeichnen; 2. (*Comm.*) anlegen, investieren (*money*), absetzen (*goods*), erteilen, vergeben (*contract*); ***– to account***, in Rechnung stellen, auf Rechnung bringen; (*Comm.*) ***– to his credit***, ihm gutschreiben; ***– an order***, eine Bestellung machen *or* aufgeben; 3. (*a p.*) eine (An)stellung beschaffen *or* vermitteln (*Dat.*), anstellen, in ein Amt einsetzen, unterbringen; 4. (*Spt.*) placieren; (*usu. pass.*) ***be –d***, sich (unter den drei Ersten) placieren; 5. (*coll.*) näher bestimmen, festlegen, festsetzen, identifizieren, einordnen, unterbringen.

placebo [plə'si:bou], *s.* (*Med.*) das Suggestionsmittel, Beruhigungsmittel.

place|-card, *s.* die Platzkarte, Tischkarte. **--hunter,** *s.* der Stellenjäger. **--hunting,** *s.* die Stellenjägerei. **--kick,** *s.* (*Spt.*) der Abstoß, Freistoß; (*Rugby Footb.*) Torschuß. **–man,** *s.* der Futterkrippenpolitiker.

placement ['pleismənt], *s.* 1. (*Comm.*) das Placieren, die Anlage, Unterbringung (*of money*); 2. Einstellung (*of worker*), Vermittling (*of work*); ***– service***, die Stellenvermittlung; ***– test***, die Einstufungsprüfung.

place-name, *s.* der Ortsname.

placenta [plə'sentə], *s.* 1. der Mutterkuchen, Fruchtkuchen, die Nachgeburt; 2. (*Bot.*) Samenleiste. **placental,** *adj.* Mutterkuchen–.

placer ['pleisə], *s.* (*Min.*) erzhaltige Stelle.

placet ['pleisit], *s.* die Jastimme, Zustimmung.

placid ['plæsid], *adj.* sanft, mild, friedlich, (seelen)-ruhig, gelassen. **placidity** [–'siditi], *s.* die Milde, Sanftheit, (Gemüts)ruhe, Gelassenheit.

placing ['pleisiŋ], *s.* 1. die Lage, Stellung, Haltung; 2. (*Spt.*) der Platz.

placket ['plækit], *s.* 1. (*Dressm.*) der Schlitz; 2. die Tasche (*in woman's skirt*).

plagiarism ['pleidʒiərizm], *s.* das Plagiat, literarischer Diebstahl. **plagiarist,** *s.* der Plagiator. **plagiarize, 1.** *v.i.* ein Plagiat begehen, plagiieren. **2.** *v.t.* plagiieren. **plagiary,** *s.* *See* **plagiarism.**

plague [pleig], **1.** *s.* 1. die Pest, Seuche; 2. (*fig.*) Plage, Heimsuchung, Geißel; (*a*) ***– on it!*** hol's der Teufel! zum Kuckuck damit! 3. (*coll.*) die Plage, Qual, (*of a p.*) der Quälgeist. **2.** *v.t.* 1. plagen, quälen; 2. (*coll.*) lästig fallen (*Dat.*), belästigen. **plague-spot,** *s.* 1. die Pestbeule; 2. (*fig.*) der Schandfleck. **plagu(e)y,** *adj.* (*coll.*) verwünscht, verflixt.

plaice [pleis], *s.* (*Ichth.*) die Scholle.

plaid [plæd], **1.** *s.* der *or* das Plaid, das Plaidtuch. **2.** *adj.* bunt kariert.

plain [plein], **1.** *adj.* 1. einfach, schlicht; ***– clothes***, der Zivilanzug, das Zivil; ***--clothes man*** or ***officer***, Kriminalbeamte(r), der Geheimpolizist; ***– cooking***, bürgerliche Küche; ***under – cover***, unauffällig; ***– fare***, die Hausmannskost; ***– living***, einfache Lebensweise; ***– postcard***, gewöhnliche Postkarte; (*fig.*) ***– sailing***, leichte Aufgabe, klare *or* einfache S.; ***– tea***, Tee und Gebäck; 2. unverziert, schmucklos, ungemustert; einfarbig, unkoloriert; ***– knitting***, das Glattstricken, Rechtsstricken; ***– paper***, unliniiertes Papier; ***– sewing***, das Weißnähen; 3. flach, eben, glatt; 4. unscheinbar, unansehnlich, unschön, nicht hübsch (*as the face*); 5. klar, deutlich, unmißverständlich, einleuchtend, offenbar, offen(kundig); ***as – as can be*** or ***as a pikestaff***, sonnenklar, so klar wie nur etwas; ***be – with him***, mit ihm offen reden; ***make – to him***, ihm deutlich zu verstehen geben; ***– dealing***, die Offenheit, Ehrlichkeit, Redlichkeit; ***in – English***, rund *or* gerade heraus, auf gut deutsch; ***in – language***, (*post*) unverschlüsselt; (*coll.*) ohne Umschweife; ***– speaking*** or ***talk***, offene Meinungsäußerung, unverblümte Redeweise; ***in – terms***, see ***in – English***; ***– text***, der Klartext; ***– truth***, nackte *or* ungeschminkte Wahrheit; 6. rein, nackt, bar (*nonsense etc.*). **2.** *adv.* 1. klar, deutlich; 2. (*coll.*) ***– stupid***, ausgesprochen dumm. **3.** *s.* die Ebene, das Flachland; *pl.* die Prärie, Steppe.

plainly ['pleinli], *adv.* offenbar, offensichtlich, unverkennbar. **plainness,** *s.* 1. die Ebenheit; 2. (*of a p.*) Unansehnlichkeit; 3. Einfachheit, Schlichtheit; 4. Klarheit, Deutlichkeit; 5. Offenheit, Redlichkeit.

plainsman ['pleinzmən], *s.* der Präriebewohner, Steppenbewohner.

plain|-song, *s.* gregorianische Kirchenmusik; einstimmiger Choralgesang. **--spoken,** *adj.* offen, freimütig; ***he is quite –***, er nimmt kein Blatt vor den Mund.

plaint [pleint], *s.* 1. (*Poet.*) die Klage; 2. (*Law*) Klageschrift, Beschwerde. **plaintiff,** *s.* (*Law*) der Kläger. **plaintive,** *adj.* klagend, traurig, wehmütig, kläglich, Klage–. **plaintiveness,** *s.* die Kläglichkeit, Traurigkeit.

plait [plæt], **1.** *s.* der Zopf, die Flechte (*of hair*);

das Geflecht (*of straw*). **2.** *v.t.* flechten. **plaited,** *adj.* geflochten. **plaiting,** *s.* das Flechten; Geflecht.

plan [plæn], **1.** *s.* 1. der Plan, Entwurf, die Anlage; ***according to*** –, planmäßig; ***make*** ***–s,*** Pläne schmieden; 2. die Absicht, das Vorhaben, Projekt; 3. Vorgehen, Verfahren, die Methode, der Weg; 4. (*Surv., Tech.*) (Grund)riß, die (Maß)-zeichnung; 5. (*coll.*) Idee. **2.** *v.t.* 1. einen Plan entwerfen zu *or* für, planen, entwerfen; 2. systematisch ausarbeiten, im voraus festlegen; 3. (*fig.*) planen, im Sinn haben, beabsichtigen.

planchet ['plæntʃit], *s.* die (Münz)platte.

[1]**plane** [plein], **1.** *adj.* eben (*also Math.*), flach; (*Tech.*) plan, Plan–; – ***mirror,*** der Planspiegel. **2.** *s.* 1. (ebene) Fläche, die Ebene; (*Artil.*) – ***of direction,*** die Visierebene; – ***of projection,*** die Projektionsebene; – ***geometry,*** (ebene) Geometrie; – ***sailing,*** das Plansegeln; – ***table,*** der Meßtisch; ***inclined*** –, schiefe Ebene, geneigte Fläche; ***on the upward*** –, ansteigend, im Anstieg; ***vertical*** –, senkrechte Ebene, die Vertikalebene; 2. (*fig.*) die Stufe, Sphäre, das Niveau, der Bereich; ***on the same – as,*** auf demselben Niveau wie; 3. (*Min.*) die Förderstrecke. **3.** *v.t.* 1. planieren, schlichten, ebnen, glätten; 2. (*Typ.*) bestoßen.

[2]**plane,** *s.* (*Bot.*) (*also* ***--tree***) (ahornblättrige) Platane.

[3]**plane, 1.** *s.* (*Carp.*) der Hobel. **2.** *v.t.* (ab)hobeln.

[4]**plane, 1.** *s.* 1. (*Av.*) die Tragfläche; 2. (*coll.*) das Flugzeug. **2.** *v.i.* 1. (*Av.*) gleiten, segeln; 2. (*sailing*) sich (ab)heben.

planer ['pleinə], *s.* 1. die Hobelmaschine; 2. (*Typ.*) das Streichbrett, Klopfholz.

planet ['plænit], *s.* der Planet, Wandelstern. **planetarium** [–'tɛəriəm], *s.* das Planetarium. **planetary,** *adj.* 1. planetarisch, Planeten–; 2. (*fig.*) unstet, umherirrend. **planetoid,** *s.* der Planetoid.

plangency ['plændʒənsi], *s.* die Tonstärke, Tonfülle. **plangent,** *adj.* (laut)tönend, schallend, durchdringend.

planimeter ['plænimi:tə], *s.* der Flächenmesser. **planimetry** [–'nimitri], *s.* die Planimetrie.

planish [plæniʃ], *v.t.* glätten, planieren, (ab)-schlichten; glatthämmern, hammerstrecken (*metal*); ***–ing hammer,*** der Schlichthammer.

plank [plæŋk], **1.** *s.* 1. die Planke, Bohle, Diele, das Brett; ***walk the*** –, ertränkt werden; 2. (*fig.*) die Stütze, der Halt, (*esp. Pol. coll.*) parteipolitischer Grundsatz, der Programmpunkt. **2.** *v.t.* mit Planken *or* Bohlen belegen, dielen, verschalen; beplanken (*ship*); (*sl.*) – ***down,*** hinschmeißen, (bar) auf den Tisch legen (*money*). **plank bed,** *s.* die Pritsche. **planking,** *s.* (*Naut.*) die Beplankung; (*Carp.*) Verschalung, Bekleidung, der Belag; (*collect.*) Planken (*pl.*).

plankton ['plæŋktən], *s.* das Plankton.

planless ['plænlis], *adj.* planlos. **planned,** *adj.* geplant; – ***economy,*** die Planwirtschaft. **planner,** *s.* der Plänemacher. **planning,** *s.* das Planen, die Planung; ***economic*** –, die Bewirtschaftung; ***family*** –, die Familienplanung.

plant [plɑ:nt], **1.** *s.* 1. die Pflanze, das Gewächs; Wachstum; 2. Werk, die Fabrik(anlage), (Betriebs)anlage, der Betrieb; 3. das Betriebsmaterial, Gerät, Inventar, die Apparatur, Maschinerie, technische Einrichtung, Gerätschaften (*pl.*); 4. (*sl.*) der Polizeispitzel, Spion; 5. (*sl.*) ausgemachter Schwindel, der Kniff, die Falle, Mache. **2.** *v.t.* 1. pflanzen, anpflanzen, einpflanzen; bepflanzen (*ground*); – ***out,*** verpflanzen, umpflanzen; 2. aufpflanzen, aufstellen (*flag etc.*); 3. fest setzen *or* stellen auf (*Acc.*) (*one's foot etc.*); (*coll.*) versetzen, verpassen (*a blow*); 4. (*fig.*) errichten, anlegen, gründen (*colony*), ansiedeln (*colonists*); 5. postieren (*a p.*); – ***o.s.,*** sich hinpflanzen *or* hinstellen; 6. einprägen, einimpfen (*in,* in (*Acc.*)); 7. (*sl.*) als Spion aufstellen; 8. (*sl.*) (ein)-schmuggeln, heimlich unterbringen; (*sl.*) – ***on him,*** ihm aufhalsen *or* andrehen, bei ihm einschmuggeln.

plantain ['plæntin], *s.* 1. (*Bot.*) der Wegerich; 2. (*also* ***--tree***) der Pisang(baum), die Paradiesfeige.

plantar ['plæntə], *adj.* Fußsohlen–.

plantation [plæn'teiʃən], *s.* 1. die (An)pflanzung, Schonung; Plantage; 2. Ansiedlung.

planter ['plɑ:ntə], *s.* 1. der Pflanzer, Plantagenbesitzer; 2. Siedler; 3. die Sämaschine.

plantigrade ['plæntigreid], **1.** *adj.* auf den Fußsohlen gehend. **2.** *s.* (*Zool.*) der Sohlengänger.

plaque [plæk], *s.* die Schmuckplatte, Agraffe, Gedenktafel. **plaquette** [–'ket], *s.* die Plakette.

[1]**plash** [plæʃ], *v.t.* ineinanderflechten, zu einer Hecke flechten (*twigs*).

[2]**plash, 1.** *v.i., v.t.* plätschern, platschen, klatschen (*in,* mit *or* auf (*Dat.*)). **2.** *s.* 1. die Pfütze, Lache, der Pfuhl; 2. das Plätschern. **plashy,** *adj.* 1. plätschernd, platschend; 2. patschig, schlammig, matschig.

plasm [plæzm], **plasma,** *s.* 1. das (Proto)plasma; 2. Blutplasma. **plasm(at)ic** [–('mæt)ik], *adj.* Plasma–, (proto)plasmatisch.

plaster ['plɑ:stə], **1.** *s.* 1. (*Med.*) das Pflaster; ***sticking*** –, das Heftpflaster; 2. (*Build.*) der Mörtel, (Ver)putz, Stuck, Bewurf; – ***of Paris,*** gebrannter Gips. **2.** *v.t.* 1. (*Med.*) bepflastern, ein Pflaster legen auf (*Acc.*); 2. (*Build.*) (*also* – ***over***) verputzen, bewerfen, vergipsen, (über)tünchen; 3. (*sl.*) überschütten, überhäufen (***with,*** mit).

plaster|board, *s.* die Faserzementplatte. **--cast,** *s.* 1. der Gipsabdruck, Gipsabguß; 2. (*Med.*) Gipsverband. **plastered,** *adj.* (*sl.*) blau, besoffen. **plasterer,** *s.* der Gipsarbeiter, Stuckarbeiter. **plastering,** *s.* die Stuckarbeit, Stukkatur; der Bewurf, (Ver)putz.

plastic ['plæstik], **1.** *adj.* 1. plastisch, biegsam, modellierbar, (ver)formbar, knetbar; – ***art,*** bildende Kunst; – ***compound,*** der Preßstoff, Kunststoff; 2. (*fig.*) gestaltungsfähig, bildungsfähig, bildsam, (um)formbar; 3. formgebend, bildend, gestaltend; – ***surgery,*** plastische Chirurgie; 4. deutlich (hervortretend), anschaulich; (*fig.*) – ***effect,*** die Tiefenwirkung. **2.** *s.* der Preßstoff, Kunststoff; – ***bomb,*** die Plastikbombe; – ***raincoat,*** die Regenhaut.

plasticine ['plæstisi:n], *s.* die Knetmasse, das Plastilin.

plasticity [plæs'tisiti], *s.* 1. die Knetbarkeit, (Ver)-formbarkeit, Bildsamkeit; 2. (*fig.*) Bildhaftigkeit, Anschaulichkeit; 3. Bildungsfähigkeit, Gestaltungsfähigkeit, Plastizität. **plasticize** ['plæstisaiz], *v.t.* (*v.i.*) knetbar *or* formbar machen (*or* werden), plasti(fi)zieren.

plastron ['plæstrən], *s.* 1. die Brustplatte (*armour*); (*Fenc.*) das Schutzleder, Schutzpolster; 2. (*Dressm. etc.*) der Hemdeinsatz, Brusteinsatz.

[1]**plat** [plæt], *s. See* [1]**plot.**

[2]**plat,** *see* **plait.**

[3]**plat** [plæ], *s.* das Gericht, die Speise.

plate [pleit], **1.** *s.* 1. der Teller; – ***of soup,*** der Teller Suppe; ***soup--,*** der Suppenteller; (*coll.*) ***have enough on one's*** –, genug auf den Schultern haben; (*coll.*) ***he has everything on a*** –, alles fällt ihm in den Schoß; ***take the – round,*** den Sammelteller herumreichen; 2. die Platte (*also Phot.*), Scheibe, Metallplatte, Metalltafel; das (Tür)schild; ***name-*** –, das Namenschild; ***steel*** –, die Panzerplatte, Stahlplatte; 3. (*Tech.*) das Blech; 4. (*Tech.*) der Deckel, das Blatt, die Lamelle; ***baffle*** –, die Schlingerwand; 5. (*Bot., Zool.*) das Blättchen, Plättchen; 6. (*Rad.*) die Anode, (*Elec.*) Elektrode; ***electro--,*** das Galvano; 7. die Dachplatte, Schwelle; 8. (*Typ.*) Druckplatte, Stereotypplatte, der Stich; 9. die Illustration, (Bild)tafel (*in a book*); ***book--,*** das Exlibris; 10. das Goldgeschirr, Silbergeschirr, Tafelgeschirr; 11. (*Spt.*) der Preis, Pokal; das Pokalrennen; 12. (*coll.*) künstliches Gebiß; ***dental*** –, die Gaumenplatte, Zahnplatte. **2.** *v.t.* 1. plattieren, dublieren, überziehen; 2. panzern (*a ship*); 3. (*Typ.*) stereotypieren.

plate-armour, *s.* 1. (*Naut.*) die Plattenpanzerung; 2. (*Mil., Hist.*) der Plattenpanzer.

plateau [plæ'tou], *s.* (*pl.* **-x** *or* **-s** [-z]) die Hochebene, das Plateau.

plate| basket, *s.* der Besteckkorb. – **circuit,** *s.* (*Rad.*) der Anodenkreis. **--cover,** *s.* der Schüsseldeckel. **plated,** *adj.* plattiert, dubliert, metallüberzogen, versilbert, vergoldet, verchromt; *electro--*, galvanisch versilbert. **plateful,** *s.* der Tellervoll. **plate| glass,** *s.* das Spiegelglas, Tafelglas. **--holder,** *s.* (*Phot.*) die (Platten)kassette. **--layer,** *s.* (*Railw.*) der Schienenleger, Streckenarbeiter. **--mark,** *s. See* **hallmark.**

platen ['plætən], *s.* 1. der (Druck)tiegel, die Druckplatte; 2. (*also --roller*) Walze (*of typewriter*).

plate|-powder, *s.* das Putzpulver. **--rack,** *s.* das Tellergestell, Tellerbrett. **--warmer,** *s.* der Tellerwärmer, Schüsselwärmer.

platform ['plætfɔ:m], *s.* 1. die Plattform, Rampe, Terrasse; 2. (*Railw.*) der Bahnsteig; Perron (*of a tramcar*); 3. (*Artil.*) Geschützdamm, die Bettung; 4. (Redner)bühne, Tribüne, das Podium (*in halls etc.*); 6. (*fig.*) öffentliches Forum, (*esp. Pol.*) das Parteiprogramm, parteipolitischer Standpunkt.

platform|-car, *s.* (*Railw.*) offener Güterwagen. **--scale,** *s.* die Brückenwaage. **--stage,** *s.* (*Theat.*) die Plattformbühne. **--ticket,** *s.* die Bahnsteigkarte.

plating ['pleitiŋ], *s.* 1. (*Metall.*) die Plattierung; 2. (*Naut.*) Panzerung, Panzerplatten (*pl.*).

platinic [plæ'tinik], *adj.* Platin-. **platiniferous** [-'nifərəs], *adj.* platinhaltig. **platinize** ['plætinaiz], *v.t.* platinieren, mit Platin überziehen. **platinotype,** *s.* der Platindruck. **platinum** ['plætinəm], *s.* das Platin; – *blonde,* die Platinblonde.

platitude ['plætitju:d], *s.* die Seichtheit, Plattheit, der Gemeinplatz. **platitudinarian** [-di'nεəriən], *s.* der Phrasendrescher, Schwätzer. **platitudinize** [-'tju:dinaiz], *v.i.* sich in Phrasen ergehen, quatschen, seichen. **platitudinous** [-'tju:dinəs], *adj.* seicht, nichtssagend, abgedroschen, phrasenhaft.

Plato ['pleitou], *s.* Platon (*m.*). **platonic** [plə'tɔnik], *adj.* platonisch, seelisch, rein geistig, unsinnlich; (*coll.*) harmlos (*of friendship etc.*). **Platonist** ['pleitənist], *s.* der Platoniker.

platoon [plə'tu:n], *s.* 1. (*Mil.*) der Zug; – *commander,* der Zugführer; – *firing,* – *volleys,* das Pelotonfeuer; 2. das Aufgebot (*of police*).

platter ['plætə], *s.* (*obs. or Am.*) die Schüssel, Servierplatte.

platypus ['plætipʌs], *s.* das Schnabeltier. **platyrrhine** [-rain], **1.** *adj.* breitnasig. **2.** *s.* (*Zool.*) die Breitnase.

plaudit ['plɔ:dit], *s.* (*usu. pl.*) lauter Beifall, das Beifallsklatschen, der Beifallssturm.

plausibility [plɔ:zi'biliti], *s.* 1. die Wahrscheinlichkeit, Glaubwürdigkeit; 2. einnehmendes Wesen, gefälliges Äußere(s) (*of a p.*). **plausible** ['plɔ:zibl], *adj.* 1. annehmbar, glaubhaft, plausibel, nicht unwahrscheinlich, einleuchtend (*as reason*); 2. äußerlich gefällig, einnehmend, gewinnend (*of a p.*).

play [plei], **1.** *s.* 1. das Spiel; (*fig.*) – *of colours,* das Farbenspiel; *at* –, beim Spiel(en); *fair* (*foul*) –, ehrliches (falsches) Spiel; *see fair* –, für (ein) ehrliches Spiel sorgen; *in* –, im Spiel (*of ball*); 2. das Glücksspiel (*cards, dice etc.*); 3. der Scherz, Spaß, Zeitvertreib, die Spielerei, Kurzweil, Unterhaltung; – *on words,* das Wortspiel; (*said*) *in* –, in Scherz (gesagt); 4. (*Theat.*) das Schauspiel, (Theater- *or* Bühnen)stück, Drama; *at the* –, im Theater; 5. (*Tech., also fig.*) der Spielraum, die Bewegungsfreiheit; (*fig.*) Bewegung, Tätigkeit, der Gang; *in full* –, in vollem Gang; *bring into* –, in Gang bringen, in Bewegung setzen; (*fig.*) zur Geltung *or* Anwendung bringen; *come into* –, in Gang kommen; (*fig.*) ins Leben gerufen werden, mitzuspielen beginnen; *give free* or *full* – *to,* freien Lauf lassen (*Dat.*); *make* – *with,* Effekt machen mit, ausnutzen, breittreten.
2. *v.i.* 1. spielen (*also Mus., Theat., fig.*), (*Mus.*) musizieren, (*Theat.*) agieren, auftreten; 2. scherzen, spaßen; 3. sich tummeln, sich spielerisch bewegen, (umher)springen, (umher)hüpfen, flattern, schwirren, gaukeln, (*as light*) flackern, hin- und herschießen; 4. (*as colours*) spielen, schillern; 5. (*Tech.*) freies Spiel *or* freien Spielraum haben; 6. im Gange *or* Betrieb sein (*as a fountain*); 7. (*Chess*) *white to* –, Weiß ist am Zug.
(a) (*with advs.*) – *fair,* ehrlich *or* fair spielen, (*fig.*) ehrliches Spiel treiben; – *fast and loose,* zum Narren *or* besten halten, ein zweideutiges Spiel treiben; – *safe,* auf Nummer Sicher gehen; – *up,* tüchtig spielen, sich anstrengen; (*coll.*) sich lästig machen (*on, Dat.*); (*coll.*) – *up to him,* ihm um den Bart gehen; sich ihm anbiedern.
(b) (*with preps.*) – *at chess* or *football, see under* **3**; – *at soldiers,* Soldaten spielen; (*coll.*) – *at being a gardener,* Gärtnerei nur nebenbei betreiben, sich nur flüchtig mit der Gärtnerei abgeben; – *at sight,* see – *from sight*; *two can* – *at that game,* das kann ein anderer auch; – *by ear,* nach dem Gehör spielen; – *for love,* um die Ehre spielen; – *for safety,* see – *safe*; – *for time,* auf Zeit spielen; – *from memory,* nach dem Gedächtnis spielen; – *from sight,* vom Blatt spielen; – *into his hands,* ihm in die Hände spielen; – *on,* gerichtet sein auf (*Acc.*), (*water*) bespritzen, anspritzen, (*light*) bestrahlen, anstrahlen; – *on his feelings,* seine Gefühle ausnutzen; – *on words,* in Wortspielen reden; – *round the idea,* mit dem Gedanken spielen; (*Mus.*) – *to,* vorspielen (*Dat.*); – *to the gallery,* nach Effekt haschen; (*fig.*) – *with,* herumfingern an (*Dat.*) (*trinket etc.*), sein Spiel treiben mit, scherzen *or* tändeln mit (*a p.*).
3. *v.t.* 1. spielen (*game, drama, rôle, piece of music*); (*Theat.*) darstellen (*rôle*), aufführen (*drama*); 2. ausspielen (*card*), ziehen (*chessman etc.*); 3. (*jet of water, beam of light*) spielen lassen (*on,* auf (*Dat.*)), richten, lenken (auf (*Acc.*)).
(a) (*with nouns*) – *the ball,* (*esp. Crick.*) den Ball schlagen; (*sl.*) – *ball,* mitmachen, mitwirken, sich betätigen; zusammenarbeiten, zueinanderhalten; – *one's best* or *hardest,* nach besten Kräften spielen; – *billiards,* Billard spielen; – *him at billiards,* mit ihm *or* gegen ihn Billard spielen; (*fig.*) – *one's cards well,* seine Möglichkeiten gut ausnutzen; (*sl.*) – *it cool,* untertreiben, sich zurückhaltend ausdrücken *or* verhalten; – *the devil* or *old Harry with,* arg mitspielen (*Dat.*), Schindluder treiben mit; – *ducks and drakes with,* verschwenden, vergeuden, zum Fenster hinauswerfen; – *him false,* ein falsches Spiel mit ihm treiben; *his memory* –*ed him false,* sein Gedächtnis ließ ihn im Stich *or* täuschte ihn; (*fig.*) – *second fiddle,* eine Nebenrolle spielen; – *a fish,* einen Fisch auszappeln lassen; – *the fool,* Possen treiben; – *football,* Fußball spielen; – *his school at football,* gegen seine Schule Fußball spielen; (*fig.*) – *the game,* fair spielen, sich an die Regeln halten; sich anständig benehmen, ehrlich sein, mit ehrlichen Mitteln kämpfen; – *a losing game,* bestimmt verlieren, ohne Aussicht sein; (*coll.*) – *gooseberry,* den Anstandswauwau spielen; – *havoc with,* durcheinanderbringen, auf den Kopf stellen, verwüsten, verheeren; (*sl.*) – *hell,* (vor Wut) aus der Haut fahren; (*sl.*) – *hell with,* (*a th.*) see – *havoc*; (*a p.*) arg mitspielen (*Dat.*); (*sl.*) – *the horses,* bei Pferderennen wetten; – *a hose on,* eine Spritze lenken *or* richten auf (*Acc.*); – *a trick on him,* ihm einen Streich spielen; – *truant,* (die Schule) schwänzen.
(b) (*with advs.*) – *him in,* ihn mit Musik hineinbegleiten; – *down,* in den Hintergrund rücken, vernachlässigen; – *off,* entscheiden, zur Entscheidung bringen (*a game*); ausspielen (*against,* gegen); – *him out,* ihn mit Musik hinausbegleiten; (*fig. coll.*) *be* –*ed out,* ausgespielt haben, erledigt *or* fertig sein; (*coll.*) – *up,* aufbauschen, an die große Glocke hängen (*a th.*), reizen, ärgern (*a p.*).

playable ['pleiəbl], *adj.* 1. spielbar, zu spielen(d) (*ball or music*), zum Spielen geeignet (*ground*); 2. (*Theat.*) aufführbar, bühnengerecht. **play|-actor,** *s.* (*obs.*) der Schauspieler (*also fig.*). **-back,** *s.* das Abspielen (*of tape-recording*). **-bill,** *s.* der

Theaterzettel. **–book,** *s.* (*Theat.*) das Textbuch. **–boy,** *s.* (*coll.*) der Lebemann, (reicher) Nichtsnutz.

player ['pleiə], *s.* 1. der (die) Spieler(in); 2. (*Spt.*) (Berufs)spieler; 3. (*Theat.*) Schauspieler; 4. (*Tech.*) automatischer Antrieb, der Steuermechanismus (*of player piano*); – ***piano,*** elektrisches Klavier.

playfellow ['pleifelou], *s.* der (die) Spielkamerad(in).

playful ['pleiful], *adj.* spielerisch; spaßig, neckisch, launig, mutwillig. **playfulness,** *s.* die Spaßigkeit, der Mutwille.

play|goer, *s.* der Theaterbesucher. **–ground,** *s.* der Spielplatz (*also fig.*), (*of school*) Schulhof. **–house,** *s.* (*obs.*) das Schauspielhaus.

playing ['pleiiŋ], *s.* das Spielen; (*Mus.*) ***to the – of,*** unter dem Spiel von. **playing|-card,** *s.* die Spielkarte. **--field,** *s.* der Spielplatz, Sportplatz. **--time,** *s.* die Spielzeit (*of tape, record*).

playlet ['pleilit], *s.* kurzes Schauspiel. **play|mate,** *s. See* **–fellow. --off,** *s.* (*Spt.*) das Entscheidungsspiel, der Stichkampf. **–pen,** *s.* das Laufgitter, der Laufstall, (*coll.*) das Ställchen.

playsome ['pleisəm], *adj.* (*obs.*) übermütig, ausgelassen.

play|thing, *s.* das Spielzeug; *pl.* Spielsachen (*pl.*). **–time,** *s.* die Freizeit, (*at school*) Pause. **–wright,** *s.* der Schauspieldichter, Bühnenschriftsteller, Bühnenautor, Dramatiker.

plea [pli:], *s.* 1. (*Law*) der Einspruch, (Rechts)einwand, die Einrede; – ***of guilty,*** das Schuldgeständnis, Schuldbekenntnis; – ***in bar,*** peremptorische Einrede; – ***for annulment,*** die Nichtigkeitsklage; ***put in*** or ***enter a –,*** eine Einrede erheben; ***make a –,*** Einspruch erheben; 2. die Ausrede, Entschuldigung, der Vorwand; (*coll.*) ***on*** or ***under the – of,*** unter dem Vorwand (*Gen.*); 3. dringende Bitte (***for,*** um), das Gesuch; (*coll.*) ***put in a – for,*** eifrig befürworten.

plead [pli:d], **1.** *v.i.* 1. (*Law*) plädieren, vor Gericht reden, Beweisgründe vorbringen; – ***(not) guilty,*** sich (für *or* als) (nicht) schuldig bekennen; 2. eine dringende Bitte vorbringen, inständig bitten, flehen (***for,*** um); – ***with him,*** ihn anflehen, sich bei ihm einsetzen *or* verwenden (***for,*** für); 3. (*fig.*) sprechen (***for,*** für). **2.** *v.t.* 1. vertreten, verteidigen, sich einsetzen für (*a cause*); 2. als Beweis(grund) *or* Entschuldigung anführen, sich berufen auf (*Acc.*), vorschützen; – ***ignorance,*** Unwissen vorschützen. **pleadable,** *adj.* rechtsgültig, triftig. **pleader,** *s.* der Anwalt, Verteidiger, Fürsprecher. **pleading, 1.** *s.* 1. das Plädieren, Plädoyer, gerichtliche Verhandlungen; Aussagen der Prozeßparteien (*pl.*); die Verteidigung, Fürsprache; (*coll.*) ***special –,*** einseitige Beweisführung, die Sophisterei; 2. (*fig.*) das Bitten, Flehen (***for,*** um). **2.** *adj.* flehend, bittend, inständig.

pleasance ['plezəns], *s.* (*Poet.*) das Vergnügen, die Wonne, der Genuß. **pleasant,** *adj.* 1. angenehm, erfreulich, wohltuend; – ***odour,*** der Wohlgeruch; – ***taste,*** der Wohlgeschmack; 2. (*of a p.*) freundlich, liebenswürdig. **pleasantness,** *s.* 1. die Annehmlichkeit; 2. Freundlichkeit. **pleasantry** [–ri], *s.* 1. der Scherz, Spaß, Witz; 2. die Lustigkeit, Heiterkeit.

please [pli:z], **1.** *v.imp., v.i.* gefallen, befriedigen, angenehm sein, Anklang finden; ***–!*** bitte sehr! wenn ich bitten darf, gefälligst, mit Verlaub; ***if you –,*** wenn es Ihnen recht ist, wenn Sie nichts dagegen haben, wenn ich bitten darf; ***he insulted me, if you –,*** er beschimpfte mich, stellen Sie sich vor *or* man denke sich; ***as you –,*** wie es Ihnen beliebt, wie Sie wollen *or* wünschen; – ***God,*** so Gott will. **2.** *v.t.* 1. gefallen, (eine) Freude bereiten, zusagen, gefällig sein (*Dat.*), erfreuen; ***be –d with,*** befriedigt sein von, Vergnügen haben an (*Dat.*), Gefallen finden an (*Dat.*); ***I am –d to say,*** ich freue mich *or* es freut mich *or* ich bin erfreut, sagen zu können; ***I was –d with it, it –d me,*** es gefiel mir; ***I shall be –d,*** es wäre mir ein Vergnügen; 2. befriedigen, zufriedenstellen; ***anxious to –,*** dienstbeflissen; ***hard to –,*** schwer zufriedenzustellen *or* zu befriedigen; – ***o.s.,*** tun (und lassen) wie man will; ***just to – me,*** mir zuliebe, nur aus Gefälligkeit für mich; 3. (*usu. pass.*) für richtig halten, (*formal or iron.*) belieben, geruhen, die Güte haben; ***the king has been –d to grant,*** Seine Majestät hat geruht zu gewähren. **pleased,** *adj.* erfreut (***at,*** über (*Acc.*)), zufrieden (***with,*** mit); ***as – as Punch,*** quietschvergnügt; ***only too – to help,*** mit dem größten Vergnügen helfen. **pleasing,** *adj.* gefällig, angenehm.

pleasurable ['pleʒərəbl], *adj.* angenehm, wohltuend, reizend.

pleasure ['pleʒə], *s.* 1. das Vergnügen, die Freude (***in,*** an (*Dat.*)), der Genuß; ***do me the –,*** tun Sie mir den Gefallen (***of coming,*** zu kommen); ***for the – of it,*** aus reinem Vergnügen; ***give him much –,*** ihm viel Spaß machen; ***have the – of doing,*** das Vergnügen haben, zu tun; ***take – in,*** Freude *or* Vergnügen finden an (*Dat.*); ***take – in (doing),*** seine Freude daran haben (zu tun); ***it's a –!*** es ist mir ein Vergnügen! ***take one's –,*** sich amüsieren; ***with –!*** mit Vergnügen! 2. (*after poss. pron.*) das Belieben, Gutdünken; ***at one's –,*** nach Belieben; ***it is our –,*** wir geruhen (*of royalty*); ***what is your –?*** womit kann ich dienen? was steht zu Diensten? (*Law*) ***during Her Majesty's –,*** auf Lebenszeit.

pleasure|-boat, *s.* der Vergnügungsdampfer. **--ground,** *s.* der Vergnügungspark. **--loving, --seeking,** *adj.* vergnügungssüchtig. **--trip,** *s.* der Ausflug, die Vergnügungsreise.

pleat [pli:t], **1.** *v.t.* fälteln, plissieren; ***–ed skirt,*** der Faltenrock. **2.** *s.* die Falte, das Plissee.

plebeian [pli'biən], **1.** *adj.* plebejisch, gemein, pöbelhaft. **2.** *s.* der (die) Plebejer(in). **plebeianism,** *s.* das Plebejertum.

plebiscite ['plebisit], *s.* (*Pol.*) die Volksabstimmung, der Volksentscheid. **plebs,** *s.* 1. (*Rom. Hist.*) die Plebs; 2. (*coll.*) der Plebs, Pöbel, (niederes) Volk.

plectrum ['plektrəm], *s.* 1. das Plektron, Schlagstäbchen, der Schlagring; 2. (*Orn.*) Sporn.

pledge [pledʒ], **1.** *s.* 1. das (Unter)pfand, die Bürgschaft, Sicherheit, Garantie, (*Hist.*) das Faustpfand, (*obs.*) die Bürge, der *or* die Geisel; ***as a – for, in – of,*** als Pfand für; ***be in –,*** verpfändet sein; ***hold in –,*** als Pfand in Händen haben; ***put in –,*** verpfänden, versetzen; ***take out of –,*** einlösen; 2. (verbindliches) Versprechen, das Gelübde, Ehrenwort, (feste) Zusage *or* Versicherung; (*coll.*) ***sign*** or ***take the –,*** Abstinenzler werden; (*fig.*) ***under the – of,*** unter dem Siegel (*Gen.*); 3. (*fig.*) ***– of love,*** das Pfand der Liebe; 4. der Trinkspruch, Toast. **2.** *v.t.* 1. verpfänden (***to,*** *Dat. or* an (*Acc.*)), zum Pfand geben, als Sicherheit geben *or* stellen *or* hinterlegen (*Dat.*); – ***one's word,*** sein Ehrenwort geben; 2. – ***o.s.,*** geloben, sich verpflichten; – ***one's support,*** sich zur Unterstützung verpflichten; – ***him to secrecy,*** ihn zum Schweigen verpflichten; 3. – ***him,*** auf sein Wohl *or* seine Gesundheit trinken, ihm zutrinken. **pledgeable,** *adj.* verpfändbar. **pledgee** [–'dʒi:], *s.* der Pfandnehmer, Pfandgläubiger, Pfandinhaber. **pledg(e)-or** [–'dʒɔ:], **pledger,** *s.* der Pfandgeber, Pfandschuldner, Verpfänder.

Pleiad ['plaiæd], *s.* (*fig.*), **Pleiades** [–ədi:z], *pl.* (*Astr.*) das Siebengestirn.

Pleistocene ['plaistəsi:n], *s.* das Eiszeitalter, Diluvium, Pleistozän.

plenary ['pli:nəri], *adj.* 1. voll(ständig), Voll–, Plenar–; – ***session,*** die Plenarsitzung, Vollversammlung; 2. uneingeschränkt, unbeschränkt, voll(kommen); – ***indulgence,*** vollkommener Ablaß; – ***power,*** unbeschränkte Vollmacht.

plenipotentiary [plenipə'tenʃəri], **1.** *adj.* 1. bevollmächtigt; 2. unbeschränkt, unumschränkt, absolut. **2.** *s.* Bevollmächtigte(r), Gesandte(r) mit unbeschränkter Vollmacht.

plenish ['pleniʃ], *v.t.* (*Scots*) (auf)füllen. **plenishing,** *s.* (*oft. pl.*) das Hausgerät, die Hauseinrichtung, Wohnungsausstattung, das Mobiliar.

plenitude ['plenitju:d], *s.* 1. die Vollkommenheit,

Vollständigkeit; 2. Fülle, der Überfluß; Reichtum (*of*, an (*Dat.*)).

plenteous ['plentiəs], *adj.* (*Poet.*) reich(lich) (*in*, an (*Dat.*)), ausreichend, hinreichend. **plenteousness,** *s. See* **plenty. plentiful,** *adj.* reich, ergiebig; reichlich *or* im Überfluß vorhanden. **plentifulness,** *s. See* **plenty.**

plenty ['plenti], **1.** *s.* die Fülle, Menge, der Reichtum, Überfluß (*of*, an (*Dat.*)); ***horn of –,*** das Füllhorn; ***in –,*** im Überfluß; ***– to do,*** vollauf zu tun; ***– of money,*** eine Menge *or* viel Geld; ***– of room,*** reichlich Platz; ***– of time,*** viel Zeit; ***– of times,*** viele Male. **2.** *adv.* (*coll.*) reichlich, massenhaft, allerhand, vollauf; (*coll.*) ***– more,*** noch viel(e).

plenum ['pli:nəm], *s.* 1. (*Pol.*) die Vollversammlung, das Plenum; 2. (vollkommen) ausgefüllter Raum; ***– heating,*** die Umwälzheizung; ***– ventilation,*** die Durchlüftung.

pleonasm ['pliənæzm], *s.* der Pleonasmus. **pleonastic** [–'næstik], *adj.* überflüssig, pleonastisch.

plethora ['pleθərə], *s.* 1. (*Med.*) der Blutandrang; 2. (*fig.*) das Zuviel, Übermaß, die Überfülle (*of*, an (*Dat.*)). **plethoric** [–'θɔrik], *adj.* 1. vollblütig, vollsaftig; 2. (*fig.*) überreich, übervoll, überladen.

pleura ['pluərə], *s.* das Brustfell, Rippenfell. **pleural,** *adj.* Brustfell–. **pleurisy** [–risi], *s.* die Rippenfellentzündung, Brustfellentzündung. **pleurocarpous** [–ou'kɑ:pəs], *adj.* (*Bot.*) seitenfrüchtig. **pleuro-pneumonia,** *s.* (*Vet.*) die Brustseuche.

pleximeter [plek'simitə], *s.* der Plessimeter. **plexor** ['pleksə], *s.* der Perkussionshammer.

plexus ['pleksəs], *s.* 1. das (Nerven)geflecht; ***solar –,*** das Sonnengeflecht, der Solarplexus; 2. (*fig.*) das Netz(werk), Flechtwerk, der Komplex.

pliability [plaiə'biliti], *s.* die Biegsamkeit, Geschmeidigkeit. **pliable** ['plaiəbl], *adj.* 1. biegsam, geschmeidig; 2. (*fig.*) nachgiebig, fügsam, gefügig, anstellig, schmiegsam. **pliancy,** *s. See* **pliability. pliant,** *adj. See* **pliable.**

plica ['plaikə] (*pl.* **-cæ** ['plaisi:]), *s.* 1. die Hautfalte; 2. (*Med.*) der Weichselzopf. **plicate(d)** [–'keit(id)], *adj.* (*Bot., Zool.*) gefaltet, faltig. **plication** [–'keiʃən], *s.* die Falte, Faltung, Faltenbildung, Falten (*pl.*).

pliers ['plaiəz], *pl.* die (Draht)zange; ***pair of –,*** die Zange; ***flat-nosed –,*** die Flachzange, Plattzange; ***round-nosed –,*** die Rundzange.

[1]**plight** [plait], *s.* (schlimmer) Zustand; (traurige *or* unangenehme) Lage, die Zwangslage, Misere; ***hopeless –,*** hoffnungslose Lage.

[2]**plight,** **1.** *v.t.* (*Poet.*) verpfänden; ***– one's faith*** or (*obs.*) ***troth,*** Treue schwören (*to*, *Dat.*); versprechen, verloben; ***–ed lovers,*** Verlobte (*pl.*); ***–ed troth,*** gelobte Treue. **2.** *s.* (*obs.*) feierliche Verpflichtung, die Verlobung.

Plimsoll line ['plimsəl], *s.* (*Naut.*) die Höchstlademarke. **plimsolls,** *pl.* Turnschuhe (*pl.*).

plinth [plinθ], *s.* die Säulenplatte, Sockelplatte, Plinthe, der Sockel.

Pliny ['plini], *s.* Plinius (*m.*).

Pliocene ['plaiəsi:n], *s.* das Pliozän.

plod [plɔd], **1.** *v.i.* 1. mühsam *or* schwerfällig gehen, sich hinschleppen; 2. (*fig.*) sich abplacken *or* abplagen *or* abmühen; (*coll.*) schuften, büffeln, ochsen (*at*, an (*Dat.*)). **2.** *v.t.* ***– one's way,*** sich mühsam dahinschleppen. **plodder,** *s.* (*fig.*) das Arbeitstier, der Büffler. **plodding,** **1.** *adj.* 1. schwerfällig, mühsam; 2. (*fig.*) arbeitsam, unverdrossen (arbeitend). **2.** *s.* das Schuften, Büffeln, die Plackerei.

plonk [plɔŋk], **1.** *s.* (*sl.*) der Rachenputzer (*wine*). **2.** *v.t.* (*sl.*) hinschmeißen, hinhauen.

plop [plɔp], **1.** *v.i.* plumpsen. **2.** *v.t.* plumpsen lassen. **3.** *s.* der Plumps, das Plumpsen. **4.** *int.* plumps!

plosive ['plousiv], **1.** *s.* (*Phonet.*) der Verschlußlaut. **2.** *adj.* Verschluß–.

[1]**plot** [plɔt], *s.* das Stück *or* der Flecken Land, der Grundstück, die Parzelle; ***building –,*** der Bauplatz; ***vegetable –,*** die Gemüseecke.

[2]**plot,** **1.** *s.* 1. das Komplott, der Anschlag; die Verschwörung, Intrige; ***lay a –,*** ein Komplott schmieden; 2. die Fabel, Handlung (*of a play etc.*). **2.** *v.t.* anstiften, anzetteln, heimlich planen, es absehen auf (*Acc.*), abzielen auf (*Acc.*). **3.** *v.i.* Ränke *or* ein Komplott schmieden, intrigieren, sich verschwören.

[3]**plot,** **1.** *v.t.* 1. einen Plan *or* eine Zeichnung machen von; 2. (*Math.*) graphisch darstellen; 3. (*Mil., Naut.*) (in einen Plan *or* auf eine Seekarte) einzeichnen (*position, course*). **2.** *s.* 1. graphische Darstellung, das Diagramm; 2. (*Mil.*) der Zielort; 3. (*Naut., radar*) Standort, die Position.

plotter ['plɔtə], *s.* der (die) Anstifter(in), Intrigant(in), Verschwörer(in), der Ränkeschmied. **plotting,** *s.* 1. das Ränkeschmieden, Intrigieren; 2. das Planzeichnen; ***– paper,*** das Zeichenpapier, Millimeterpapier; ***– scale,*** der Zeichenmaßstab.

plough [plau], **1.** *s.* 1. der Pflug; (*fig.*) ***put one's hand to the –,*** Hand ans Werk legen; ***under –,*** das Ackerland; 2. das Ackerland; 3. (*Carp.*) der Nuthobel, Falzhobel, Kehlhobel; 4. (*Astr.*) ***the Plough,*** Großer Bär, der Wagen; 5. (*sl.*) das Durchfallen, der Mißerfolg. **2.** *v.t.* 1. (um)pflügen; (*fig.*) ***– back,*** wieder in das Geschäft stecken (*profit*); ***– in,*** unterpflügen; ***– up,*** umpflügen (*land*); (*fig.*) ***– a lonely furrow,*** allein seinen Weg gehen; 2. (*fig.*) (durch)furchen (*the sea*); (*fig.*) ***– one's way,*** sich (*Dat.*) einen Weg bahnen; 3. (zer)furchen (*the brow etc.*); 4. (*sl.*) durchfallen lassen; ***be –ed,*** durchfallen, (durch)rasseln, versieben. **3.** *v.i.* 1. (*fig.*) sich vorwärtsarbeiten *or* (durch)arbeiten (***through***, durch); (*coll.*) ***– through a book,*** ein Buch durchackern; 2. sich stürzen (***into***, in (*Acc.*) (*work*), auf (*Acc.*) (*meal*)).

plough|-boy, *s.* der Ackerknecht. **--horse,** *s.* das Ackerpferd. **ploughing,** *s.* das Pflügen. **plough|-land,** *s.* das Ackerland. **–man** [–mən], *s.* der Pflüger, Acker(s)mann. **–share,** *s.* die Pflugschar. **–tail,** *s.* der Pflugsterz.

plover ['plʌvə], *s.* (*Orn.*) ***golden –,*** der Goldregenpfeifer (*Pluvialis apricarius*); ***ringed –,*** der Sandregenpfeifer, Halsbandregenpfeifer (*Charadrius hiaticula*).

plow, (*Am.*) *see* **plough.**

ploy [plɔi], *s.* 1. (*dial.*) die Beschäftigung, das Unternehmen, Vorgehen, Verfahren; 2. (*coll.*) der Kniff, die Schikane, Praktiken (*pl.*).

pluck [plʌk], **1.** *v.t.* 1. (ab)pflücken, abbrechen (*flowers*); 2. rupfen (*birds*); 3. ausreißen, auszupfen (*wool etc.*); 4. zupfen, zerren (***by***, an (*Dat.*)); (*fig.*) ***– up courage,*** Mut fassen; 5. (*sl.*) rupfen, ausnehmen, ausplündern (*a p.*); 6. (*sl.*) durchfallen *or* durchrasseln lassen; (*usu. pass.*) ***be –ed,*** durchfallen, durchrasseln, durchfliegen. **2.** *v.i.* zupfen, zerren (***at***, an (*Dat.*)), greifen (nach). **3.** *s.* 1. das Pflücken, Zupfen, Zerren, Rupfen; 2. Innereien (*pl.*), das Geschlinge (*of animal*); 3. (*coll.*) der Mut, Schneid, die Schneidigkeit. **pluckiness,** *s.* (*coll.*) der Mut, die Beherztheit. **plucky,** *adj.* 1. (*coll.*) mutig, beherzt, schneidig; 2. (*Phot.*) scharf.

plug [plʌg], **1.** *s.* 1. der Pflock, Stöpsel, Pfropf(en), Zapfen, Spund, Döbel; 2. (*Dentistry*) die (Zahn)plombe; 3. (*Elec.*) der Stecker; 4. Priem (*of tobacco*); 5. (*also* ***spark(ing)––***) die Zündkerze; 6. (*sl.*) die Befürwortung, (ständige) Reklame. **2.** *v.t.* 1. (*also* ***– up***) verstopfen, zustopfen, (zu)pfropfen, zustöpseln; 2. plombieren (*teeth*); 3. verspunden (*cask*); 4. (*sl.*) ***– him,*** ihn anschießen *or* erschießen; 5. (*Elec.*) ***– in,*** einstecken, anschließen, einschalten; 6. (*sl.*) ***– it,*** es befürworten *or* anpreisen, dafür Reklame machen. **3.** *v.i.* (*sl.*) ***– along*** or ***away,*** sich placken, schuften, ochsen (***at***, an (*Dat.*)).

plug|-adaptor, *s.* der Umstecker. **--box, --contact,** *s. See* **--socket. –hole,** *s.* das Spundloch, Spülloch. **--socket,** *s.* die Steckdose, der Steckkontakt. **--ugly,** *s.* (*Am. sl.*) der Raufbold, Straßenlümmel, Rowdy.

plum [plʌm], *s.* 1. die Pflaume, Zwetschge, (*obs.*) Rosine; 2. (*coll., fig.*) das Beste, der Leckerbissen, die Rosine; (*coll.*) ***take all the –s***, sich (*Dat.*) die Rosinen aus dem Kuchen klauben; 3. (*sl.*) hübsches Stück Geld, £100,000.

pluma [ˈplu:mə], *s.* (*pl.* **-mae**) (*Orn.*) die Schwungfeder. **plumaceous** [–ˈmeiʃəs], *adj.* schwungfederartig. **plumage** [–idʒ], *s.* das Gefieder, Federkleid; ***adult –***, das Alterskleid.

plumb [plʌm], **1.** *s.* das Senkblei, Lot(blei); ***out of –***, aus dem Lot, nicht (mehr) senkrecht. **2.** *adj.* 1. senkrecht, lotrecht; 2. (*Min.*) seiger. **3.** *adv.* 1. senkrecht; 2. g(e)rade, g(e)rade(n)wegs, genau; 3. (*sl.*) schier, total, komplett, glatt, richtig(gehend). **4.** *v.t.* 1. lotrecht machen; 2. (*Naut.*) (ab)loten; 3. (*fig.*) sondieren, ergründen. **5.** *v.i.* klempnern, Röhre legen.

plumbago [plʌmˈbeigou], *s.* 1. das Reißblei, der Graphit; 2. (*Bot.*) die Bleiwurz. **plumbeous** [ˈplʌmbiəs], *adj.* bleiartig; bleifarbig.

plumber [ˈplʌmə], *s.* der Klempner, Spengler, Installateur, Rohrleger. **plumbic** [–bik], *adj.* (*Chem.*) Blei–; ***– acid***, das Bleisuperoxyd. **plumbiferous** [–ˈbifərəs], *adj.* bleihaltig.

plumbing [ˈplʌmiŋ], *s.* 1. die Klempnerarbeit, Installateurarbeit; 2. Rohrleitung, Röhren (*pl.*).

plumbism [ˈplʌmbizm], *s.* die Bleivergiftung.

plumb|-line, *s.* die Lotleine, Senkschnur. **--rule,** *s.* die Setzwaage, das Richtscheit.

plum|-cake, *s.* der Rosinenkuchen. **– duff,** *s.* der Rosinenpudding.

plume [plu:m], **1.** *s.* 1. die Feder; ***borrowed –s***, fremde Federn; 2. der Federbusch (*on helmet*); 3. (*Bot.*) Pappus, das Haarbüschel; 4. (*fig.*) die Fahne, der Streifen (*of smoke etc.*). **2.** *v.t.* 1. aufplustern (*feathers*); ***– itself***, sich aufplustern (*of birds*); 2. mit Federn schmücken; (*fig.*) ***– o.s.***, sich etwas einbilden (*on*, auf (*Acc.*)), sich brüsten (mit). **plumed,** *adj.* 1. gefiedert; 2. mit Federn geschmückt; ***– hat***, der Federhut.

plummet [ˈplʌmit], **1.** *s.* 1. das Senkblei, Senklot, die Setzwaage, Lotleine; 2. (*Angling*) der (Blei)senker; 3. (*fig.*) das Bleigewicht. **2.** *v.i.* abstürzen.

plummy [ˈplʌmi], *adj.* 1. pflaumenartig; 2. (*coll.*) ausgezeichnet, prima.

plumose [ˈplu:mous], *adj.* 1. gefiedert; 2. (*Bot.*) flaumig, haarfaserig, federig.

[1]**plump** [plʌmp], **1.** *adj.* dick, fett, rund(lich), drall, pummelig; ***– cheeks***, Pausbacken (*pl.*). **2.** *v.t.* (*also – **out** or **up***) aufschwemmen, aufschwellen, dick machen, runden.

[2]**plump,** **1.** *v.t.* plumpsen *or* fallen lassen. **2.** *v.i.* plump hinfallen, hinplumpsen; ***– down***, hinunterplumpsen; (*coll.*) ***– for***, ohne Bedenken stimmen *or* entscheiden für; (*coll.*) ***– out with***, herausplatzen mit. **3.** *adv.* plumps, rundweg, glattweg, geradeheraus, unverblümt. **4.** *adj.* glatt, plump. **5.** *s.* der Plumps, jäher Fall.

[1]**plumper** [ˈplʌmpə], *s.* 1. (*Pol.*) ungeteilte Wahlstimme; 2. (*sl.*) glatte *or* (faust)dicke Lüge.

[2]**plumper,** **1.** *s.* der Bausch. **2.** *comp. adj. See* [1]**plump, 1. plumpness,** *s.* die Rundlichkeit, Rundheit, Dicke, Drallheit, Pausbackigkeit.

plum|-pudding, *s.* der Plumpudding, Weihnachtspudding. **--tart,** *s.* die Zwetschgentorte. **--tree,** *s.* der Pflaumenbaum.

plumulaceous [plu:mjuˈleiʃəs], *adj.* daunig, flaumartig. **plumule** [ˈplu:mju:l], *s.* 1. (*Bot.*) die Blattanlage, Sproßknospe; 2. (*Orn.*) Flaumfeder, Daunenfeder. **plumy** [ˈplu:mi], *adj.* 1. federartig; 2. gefiedert, befiedert.

plunder [ˈplʌndə], **1.** *s.* 1. der Raub, die (Kriegs)beute; 2. (*sl.*) der Gewinn, Rebbach. **2.** *v.t.* plündern (*a country etc.*), rauben (*a th.*), ausplündern, ausrauben (*a p.*), berauben (*of, Gen.*). **plunderer,** *s.* der Plünderer, Räuber, Beutemacher.

plunge [plʌndʒ], **1.** *v.t.* 1. (ein)tauchen, untertauchen, (ver)senken (*into water etc.*); stoßen (*a sword etc.*); stecken (*one's hand*); 2. (*fig.*) stürzen, treiben, versetzen. **2.** *v.i.* 1. untertauchen (***into***, in (*Dat.*)), (ein)tauchen, sich werfen, (sich) stürzen (in (*Acc.*)); ***– into the room***, ins Zimmer stürzen *or* stürmen; 2. (*fig.*) sich stürzen (***into***, in (*Acc.*)) (*debt etc.*); 3. steil abfallen (*as cliffs*); 4. springen und ausschlagen (*as a horse*); stampfen (*as a ship*); 5. (*sl.*) spekulieren, es wagen. **3.** *s.* 1. das (Unter)tauchen, Eintauchen; der Sturz; ***take a –***, einen (Kopf)sprung ins Wasser machen; 2. das Ausschlagen (*of a horse*); 3. (*fig.*) Wagnis; ***take the –***, den entscheidenden Schritt tun, ein Wagnis auf sich nehmen, es wagen. **plunge-bath,** *s.* das Tauchbad. **plunger,** *s.* 1. der Taucher; 2. (*usu. Tech.*) Tauchkolben, Tauchbolzen; 3. (*sl.*) wilder Spekulant, der Glücksspieler, Hasardeur.

plunk [plʌŋk], **1.** *s.* 1. (*Am.*) der Plumps; 2. (*Am. sl.*) Dollar. **2.** *v.t.* hinschmeißen, hinhauen. **3.** *v.i.* plump hinfallen, hinplumpsen.

pluperfect [plu:ˈpə:fikt], *s.* (*also – **tense***) das Plusquamperfekt(um), die Vorvergangenheit.

plural [ˈpluərəl], **1.** *s.* die Mehrzahl, der Plural. **2.** *adj.* Plural–, pluralisch; ***– number***, *see* **1**; ***– vote***, ***– voting***, das Mehrstimmenwahlrecht, die Pluralwahl. **pluralism,** *s.* 1. (*Eccl.*) der Besitz mehrerer Pfründen; 2. (*Phil.*) der Pluralismus. **pluralist,** *s.* der Inhaber mehrerer Pfründen. **plurality** [pluˈræliti], *s.* 1. die Mehrheit, Mehrzahl; 2. Vielheit, Vielzahl; große Anzahl *or* Menge; ***– of gods***, die Vielgötterei; ***– of wives***, die Vielweiberei; 3.(*Eccl.*) der Besitz mehrerer Pfründen. **pluralize,** **1.** *v.t.* die Mehrzahl bilden von, in den Plural setzen. **2.** *v.i* (*Eccl.*) mehrere Pfründen innehaben.

plus [plʌs], **1.** *prep.* und, plus, (*esp. Comm.*) zuzüglich (*Gen.*); (*coll.*) mit. **2.** *adj.* 1. Mehr–, Extra–, extra; 2. (*Math., Elec.*) positiv. **3.** *s.* 1. das Plus, Mehr, der Überschuß; 2. (*Typ.*) (*also – **sign***) das Plus(zeichen). **plus-fours,** *pl.* die Golfhose, Pumphose, Knickerbockerhose.

plush [plʌʃ], **1.** *s.* der Plüsch. **2.** *adj.* (*coll., fig.*) feudal, luxuriös. **plushy,** *adj.* plüschartig.

plutarchy [ˈplu:tɑ:ki], **plutocracy** [–ˈtɔkrəsi], *s.* die Geldherrschaft; (*collect.*) Geldaristokratie. **plutocrat** [–təkræt], *s.* der Kapitalist, Geldprotz. **plutocratic** [–təˈkrætik], *adj.* Geld–, auf Geldbesitz aufgebaut.

Plutonian [plu:ˈtouniən], *adj.* plutonisch, Pluto–. **Plutonic** [–ˈtɔnik], *adj.* (*Geol.*) plutonisch, vulkanisch. **Plutonism** [ˈplu:tənizm], *s.* (*Geol.*) der Plutonismus. **plutonium,** *s.* (*Chem.*) das Plutonium.

pluvial [ˈplu:viəl], *adj.* regnerisch, Regen–. **pluviometer** [–ˈɔmitə], *s.* der Regenmesser. **pluvious,** *adj. See* **pluvial.**

[1]**ply** [plai], **1.** *v.t.* 1. (fleißig) handhaben, emsig umgehen mit, emsig gebrauchen *or* anwenden; ***– one's needle***, die Nadel emsig führen; 2. (fleißig) ausüben *or* betreiben (*one's business*); 3. ***– him with***, ihn ständig versehen *or* versorgen mit, ihn überhäufen mit, ihm zusetzen mit, ihm wiederholt anbieten *or* aufdrängen; ***– him with drinks***, ihn mit Getränken traktieren. **2.** *v.i.* regelmäßig fahren *or* verkehren; ***– for hire***, auf Kunden warten; (*Naut.*) ***– to windward***, aufkreuzen, lavieren.

[2]**ply,** *s.* 1. die Falte (*of cloth*), Strähne (*of rope*), Lage, Schicht (*of timber*). **plywood,** *s.* das Sperrholz.

pneuma [ˈnju:mə], *s.* die Seele, der Geist, Atem, Lebenshauch.

pneumatic [nju:ˈmætik], **1.** *adj.* 1. pneumatisch, Luft–; ***– action***, pneumatische Traktur (*of organ*); ***– tyre***, der Luftreifen; 2. (*Zool.*) lufthaltig; 3. Luftdruck–, Preßluft–; ***– brake***, die Druckluftbremse; ***– drill***, der Preßluftbohrhammer. **2.** *s.* der Luftreifen. **pneumatics,** *pl.* (*sing. constr.*) die Pneumatik.

pneumatocele [ˈnju:mətousi:l], *s.* (*Med.*) der Lungenbruch, die Luftgeschwulst. **pneumatocyst** [–sist], *s.* (*Zool.*) der Luftsack, die Luftblase.

pneumatology [nju:məˈtɔlədʒi], *s.* (*Theol.*) die Lehre vom Heiligen Geist; Dämonenlehre.

pneumectomy [nju:ˈmektəmi], *s.* (*Med.*) die Lungenresektion. **pneumonectomy** [–məˈnektəmi], *s.* (*Med.*) die Lobektomie. **pneumonia** [–ˈmouniə], *s.* die Lungenentzündung; ***bronchial –***, die Bronchopneumonie; ***double –***, doppelseitige Lungenentzündung. **pneumonic** [–ˈmɔnik], *adj.* Lungen(entzündungs)–.

po [pou], *s.* (*coll.*) das Pott.

[1]**poach** [poutʃ], **1.** *v.t.* 1. wildern in (*Dat.*) (*private land*); unbefugt fangen *or* jagen, räubern (*protected game*); 2. zertreten, zertrampeln, aufwühlen, aufweichen (*ground*); 3. (*coll.*) durch unerlaubte Mittel erreichen, sich (*Dat.*) unrechtmäßig verschaffen (*advantage etc.*). **2.** *v.i.* 1. wildern, Wilddieberei treiben; 2. matschig werden (*of ground*); 3. (*fig.*) ***– on,*** unbefugt eindringen in (*Acc.*), übergreifen auf (*Acc.*); ***– on his preserves,*** ihm ins Gehege kommen.

[2]**poach,** *v.t.* pochieren, ohne Schale kochen (*eggs*); ***–ed egg,*** verlorenes Ei.

poacher [ˈpoutʃə], *s.* der Wilderer, Wilddieb. **poaching,** *s.* das Wildern, die Wild(dieb)erei.

pochard [ˈpoutʃəd], *s.* (*Orn.*) (*Am.* ***common –***) die Tafelente (*Aythya ferina*).

pochette [pɔˈʃət], *s.* das Handtäschchen.

pock [pɔk], *s.* (*usu. pl.*) (*Med.*) die Pocke, Blatter.

pocket [ˈpɔkit], **1.** *s.* 1. die Tasche; ***be £1 in –,*** £1 in die Tasche gesteckt haben, sich um £1 bereichern (*by,* durch); ***have him in one's –,*** ihn in der Tasche haben, mit ihm fertig werden; ***be £1 out of –,*** £1 verloren *or* draufgezahlt haben; ***put one's hand in one's –,*** die Hand in die Tasche stecken; (*fig.*) in die Tasche greifen, Geld ausgeben; ***put one's pride in one's –,*** klein beigeben; (*fig.*) ***line one's –,*** schwer verdienen; 2. (*Geol.*) der Einschluß, das Erznest; 3. (*Bill.*) Loch, der Beutel, die Tasche; 4. der Sack (*of hops, wool etc.*); 5. (*Av.*) (*also* ***air-–***) die Fallbö, das Luftloch; 6. (*Mil.*) ***– of resistance,*** das Widerstandsnest. **2.** *v.t.* 1. in die Tasche stecken, einstecken; 2. (*Bill.*) in den Beutel treiben; 3. (*fig.*) sich (*Dat.*) aneignen, einheimsen (*profits*), einstecken, hinnehmen, auf sich sitzen lassen (*insult etc.*); ***– one's pride,*** see ***put one's pride in one's –.***

pocket|-battleship, *s.* der Westentaschenkreuzer. **–book,** *s.* das Taschenbuch, Notizbuch. **–-borough,** *s.* (*Hist.*) winziger Wahlflecken. **–-edition,** *s.* die Taschenausgabe. **pocketful,** *s.* die Taschevoll. **pocket| handkerchief,** *s.* das Taschentuch. **–knife,** *s.* das Taschenmesser. **–-money,** *s.* das Taschengeld. **–-size,** *adj.* in Taschenformat. **–-torch,** *s.* die Taschenlampe.

pock|mark, *s.* die Pockennarbe. **–marked,** *adj.* pockennarbig.

pod [pɔd], **1.** *s.* 1. (*Bot.*) die Schote, Hülse, Schale; 2. (*Ent.*) der Kokon. **2.** *v.i.* Schoten ansetzen. **3.** *v.t.* ausschoten, enthülsen (*peas*).

podagra [pɔˈdægrə], *s.* das Podagra, die (Fuß)gicht.

podgy [ˈpɔdʒi], *adj.* (*coll.*) untersetzt, rundlich, pummelig.

podium [ˈpoudiəm], *s.* das Podium, das *or* der Podest.

poem [ˈpouim], *s.* das Gedicht. **poesy,** *s.* (*Poet.*) die Poesie, Dichtkunst. **poet,** *s.* der Dichter; ***– laureate,*** der Hofdichter, (lorbeer)gekrönter Dichter; ***minor –,*** der Dichter zweiten Ranges. **poetaster** [–iˈtæstə], *s.* der Reimschmied, Dichterling. **poetess,** *s.* die Dichterin. **poetic** [–ˈetik], *adj.* dichterisch, poetisch; ***– diction,*** die Dichtersprache; ***– justice,*** dichterische Gerechtigkeit; ***– licence,*** dichterische Freiheit. **poetical** [–ˈetikl], *adj.* 1. Vers–, in Versen; 2. phantasievoll, erdichtet. **poeticize** [–ˈetisaiz], *see* **poetize. poetics** [–ˈetiks], *pl.* (*sing. constr.*) die Poetik. **poetize, 1.** *v.i.* dichten. **2.** *v.t.* in Verse setzen *or* bringen, in Versen ausdrücken *or* darstellen, dichterisch verherrlichen. **poetry** [–itri], *s.* 1. die Dichtkunst, Poesie, Dichtung; 2. (*collect.*) Dichtungen, Gedichte, Dichtwerke (*pl.*); 3. (*fig.*) dichterisches Gefühl.

pogrom [ˈpougrəm], *s.* der Pogrom, die Judenverfolgung, Judenhetze.

poignancy [ˈpɔinjənsi], *s.* 1. das Scharfe, die Schärfe (*also fig.*); 2. (*fig.*) Schmerzlichkeit, Bitterkeit. **poignant,** *adj.* 1. scharf, beißend, stechend; 2. (*fig.*) bitter (*grief, regret*), brennend (*interest*), bissig (*wit etc.*), schmerzlich, rührend, erschütternd, ergreifend.

point [pɔint], **1.** *s.* 1. die Spitze (*of needle, pencil, tongue etc.*); ***at the – of the bayonet,*** mit blanker Waffe; ***– of the compass,*** der Kompaßstrich; ***on the – of the nose,*** auf der Nasenspitze; ***at the – of the revolver,*** mit vorgehaltenem Revolver; (*fig.*) ***at the – of the sword,*** unter Zwang; ***not put too fine a – on it,*** es nicht zu gerade gewählt ausdrücken; 2. der Punkt, Fleck, Ort, (bestimmte) Stelle; ***– of contact,*** der Berührungspunkt, Tangentialpunkt; ***– of destination,*** der Bestimmungsort; ***– of impact,*** der Aufschlagpunkt, Auftreffpunkt; ***– of intersection,*** der Schnittpunkt; ***– of origin,*** der Herkunftsort, Ursprungsort; ***– of no return,*** der Punkt, von dem es kein Zurück mehr gibt; ***at many –s,*** an vielen Stellen; 3. (*Typ.*) der Punkt, das Punktzeichen; 4. (*Math.*) Komma; 5. (*fig.*) die Absicht, der (End)zweck, das Ziel; ***carry*** or ***gain*** or ***make*** or ***prove one's –,*** seinen Kopf durchsetzen, seine Absicht *or* sein Ziel erreichen; ***there's no – in going,*** es hat keinen Zweck zu gehen; ***there's not much – in it,*** es hat wenig Sinn *or* wenig an sich; ***see no – in going,*** es für unnötig halten, zu gehen; 6. entscheidendes Stadium, (kritischer) Zeitpunkt *or* Augenblick; ***at the – of death,*** im Sterben, dem Tode nahe; ***– of time,*** der Zeitpunkt, Augenblick; ***at this –,*** in diesem Augenblick; ***on the – of going,*** im Begriff zu gehen; ***to the – of,*** bis an die Grenze von; 7. die (Teil)frage, Einzelheit, der Abschnitt; ***– of interest,*** interessante Einzelheit; die Sehenswürdigkeit; (*Parl.*) ***– of order,*** die Verfahrensfrage, Frage der Geschäftsordnung; ***at all –s,*** in jeder Hinsicht, ganz und gar; ***a case in –,*** typischer Fall, einschlägiges Beispiel; ***cite as a case in –,*** als Begründung anführen; ***the case in –,*** vorliegender Fall; ***in many –s,*** in vielerlei Hinsicht; 8. besondere Eigenschaft, charakteristischer Zug; ***– for –,*** Punkt für Punkt verglichen; ***the –s of a horse,*** die hervorstechenden Merkmale eines Pferdes; ***good –s,*** gute Seiten; ***strong –,*** die Stärke (*of character*); ***weak –,*** wunder Punkt, schwache Seite, die Blöße (*of character*); 9. die Pointe (*of a joke*), wesentlicher *or* springender Punkt, der Kernpunkt, die Hauptfrage, Kernfrage, Hauptsache, das Wesentliche *or* Entscheidende, (besonderer) Wert; ***– by –,*** Punkt für Punkt; ***– of honour,*** die Ehrensache, (unbedingte) Satisfaktion (*by a duel etc.*); ***– of view,*** der Standpunkt, Gesichtspunkt; ***from this – of view,*** von diesem Standpunkt aus (gesehen); ***– at issue,*** strittiger Punkt, die Streitfrage; ***small –,*** unwichtige S.; ***argue the – with,*** sich auseinandersetzen mit; ***that's the*** (***whole***) ***–!*** darauf kommt es an! darum geht es! das ist es ja *or* gerade! (*coll.*) ***you have a –!*** da haben Sie (vielleicht) was! ***make a –*** (***of going***) or ***make it a –*** (***to go***), es sich (*Dat.*) angelegen sein lassen, es sich (*Dat.*) zum Prinzip *or* zur Aufgabe machen, Wert darauf legen (zu gehen); ***make a – of it,*** darauf bestehen; ***make the – that,*** hervorheben *or* die Feststellung machen, daß; ***strain a –,*** zu weit gehen; ***stretch a –,*** es nicht allzu genau nehmen, ein übriges tun, eine Ausnahme machen, ein Auge zudrücken; ***beside the –,*** unwichtig, unerheblich, nicht zur S. gehörig, abwegig; ***wander from the –,*** von der S. abschweifen; ***in – of,*** in Hinsicht auf (*Acc.*), hinsichtlich *or* betreffs (*Gen.*); ***in – of fact,*** tatsächlich; ***off the –,*** nicht zur S. (gehörig); unzutreffend; ***to the –,*** zur S. (gehörig), sachdienlich, sachgemäß, zutreffend; ***come to the –,*** zur S. kommen; ***keep to the –,*** bei der S. bleiben; 10. der Nachdruck, das Gewicht; ***give – to,*** Nachdruck verleihen (*Dat.*); 11. der Grad, die Stufe; ***boiling –,*** der Seidepunkt; ***freezing –,*** der Gefrierpunkt; ***up to a –,*** bis zu einem gewissen Grade; ***to bursting –,*** zum Bersten; ***when it came to the –,*** als es so weit war, als es darauf ankam; 12. (*Spt., fig.*) der Punkt; ***give –s to,*** vorgeben (*Dat.*); überlegen sein (*Dat.*), über-

treffen; ***possession is nine –s of the law,*** sei im Besitze und du wohnst im Recht; ***victory on –s,*** der Punktsieg; ***win on –s,*** nach Punkten gewinnen; ***yield a – to,*** recht geben (*Dat.*); 13. (*Geog.*) die Landspitze, Landzunge; ***cardinal –s,*** die (vier) Himmelsgegenden; 14. (*Tech.*) der Griffel, Grabstichel, die Radiernadel, Ahle; (*lace*) Nähspitze, Nadelspitze; 15. (*Hunt.*) Sprosse, das (Geweih)-ende; 16. (*Elec.*) der Steckkontakt; 17. *pl.* (*Railw.*) Weichen (*pl.*).
2. *v.t.* 1. zuspitzen, (an)spitzen; 2. (*fig.*) bekräftigen, unterstreichen; ***– a moral,*** eine Lehre ziehen, moralische Betrachtungen anstellen; 3. ausfüllen (*brick-work*); 4. richten (***at,*** auf (*Acc.*)); ***– one's finger,*** mit dem Finger zeigen *or* deuten (***at,*** auf (*Acc.*)); (*scorn*) ***– the finger,*** mit Fingern zeigen (***at,*** auf (*Acc.*)); 5. ***– out,*** zeigen, aufmerksam machen auf (*Acc.*), hinweisen auf (*Acc.*); darlegen, ausführen, auseinandersetzen, erklären, klarmachen, aufzeigen, aufdecken; ***as (was) –ed out before,*** wie bereits ausgeführt; ***I –ed it out to him,*** ich machte ihn darauf aufmerksam.
3. *v.i.* 1. mit dem Finger *or* mit Fingern zeigen; 2. zeigen, (hin)deuten, (hin)weisen (***at, to,*** auf (*Acc.*)); ***– towards,*** liegen nach (*as a house etc.*); 3. (*Hunt.*) vorstehen (*of hounds*); 4. (*Naut.*) hart am Wind segeln.

point-blank, 1. *adj.* schnurgerade; ***at – range,*** in Kernschußweite; ***– refusal,*** glatte Abfuhr; ***– shot,*** der Kernschuß. **2.** *adv.* (*fig.*) direkt, geradezu, geradeheraus, unverhohlen, schlankweg, rundweg.

point d'appui [pwændæ'pwi:], *s.* (*Mil.*) der Stützpunkt, Rückhaltspunkt.

point-duty, *s.* der Verkehrsdienst; ***– policeman,*** der Verkehrspolizist. **pointed,** *adj.* 1. zugespitzt, spitz(ig); ***– arch,*** der Spitzbogen; 2. (*fig.*) deutlich, zutreffend; 3. beißend, anzüglich. **pointedly,** *adv.* beabsichtigt. **pointedness,** *s.* 1. die Spitzigkeit; 2. (*fig.*) Schärfe, Deutlichkeit. **pointer,** *s.* 1. der Zeiger, Zeigestock, Zeigestab; 2. (*Hunt.*) Vorstehhund, Hühnerhund; 3. (*coll.*) Fingerzeig, Tip, Wink. **pointing,** *s.* 1. das Zuspitzen; 2. Zeigen; 3. (*Build.*) die Fugenausfüllung, Fugenverstreichung; 4. Interpunktion. **point lace,** *s.* genähte Spitzen (*pl.*). **pointless,** *adj.* 1. stumpf; 2. (*fig.*) gehaltlos, nichtssagend; 3. zwecklos, sinnlos. **pointlessness,** *s.* (*fig.*) die Sinnlosigkeit, Zwecklosigkeit. **point-to-point (race),** *s.* das Querfeldeinrennen.

poise [pɔiz], **1.** *s.* 1. das Gleichgewicht, die Schwebe(haltung), der Schwebezustand; 2. die (Körper)-haltung, (*fig.*) Ausgeglichenheit. **2.** *v.t.* im Gleichgewicht halten, balancieren; ***be –d,*** im Gleichgewicht ruhen; (*fig.*) ausgeglichen sein. **3.** *v.i.* schweben, in der Schwebe sein.

poison [pɔizn], **1.** *s.* das Gift; ***hate like –,*** tödlich hassen; ***slow –,*** schleichendes Gift. **2.** *v.t.* vergiften (*also fig.*); ***–ed finger,*** infizierter Finger. **poisoner,** *s.* der (die) Giftmörder(in), Giftmischer(in). **poison|-fang,** *s.* der Giftzahn. **--gas,** *s.* das Giftgas, der Kampfstoff. **poisoning,** *s.* 1. die Vergiftung; 2. der Giftmord. **poisonous,** *adj.* 1. giftig, Gift–; ***– snake,*** die Giftschlange; 2. (*coll.*) widerlich, ekelhaft. **poison-pen,** *s.* der (die) anonyme Verfasser(in) verleumderischer Briefe.

[1]**poke** [pouk], *s.* (*obs.*) die Tasche, der Beutel; (*Scots*) die Tüte; ***buy a pig in a –,*** eine Katze im Sack kaufen.

[2]**poke, 1.** *s.* der Stoß, Puff, Knuff. **2.** *v.t.* 1. stoßen, puffen; ***– him in the ribs,*** ihm einen Rippenstoß geben; ***– his eye out,*** ihm das Auge ausschlagen; 2. schüren (*the fire*); 3. vorstrecken, vorstecken (*head etc.*); ***– fun at,*** sich lustig machen über (*Acc.*), aufziehen; (*fig.*) ***– one's nose into,*** die Nase stecken in (*Acc.*). **3.** *v.i.* (herum)tappen, tasten; ***– about,*** herumschnüffeln.

poke-bonnet, *s.* der Kiepenhut, die Schute.

[1]**poker** ['poukə], *s.* 1. der Feuerhaken, das Schüreisen; ***as stiff as a –,*** steif wie ein Brett; 2. (*Studs. sl.*) der Pedell.

[2]**poker,** *s.* (*Cards*) das Poker.

[3]**poker,** *s.* (*Am.*) das Schreckgespenst, der Popanz.

poker|-faced, *adj.* mit Pokergesicht. **--work,** *s.* die Brandmalerei.

poky ['pouki], *adj.* (*coll.*) 1. eng, dumpf(ig); 2. erbärmlich, dürftig, lumpig.

Poland ['poulənd], *s.* Polen (*n.*).

polar ['poulə], **1.** *adj.* 1. (*Geog.*) Polar–; (*Phys.*) polar; ***– air,*** arktische Kaltluft; ***– axis,*** die Polarachse; ***– bear,*** der Eisbär; ***– circle,*** der Polarkreis; (*Astr.*) ***– distance,*** der Polabstand; ***– regions,*** das Polargebiet; ***– sea,*** das Eismeer; ***– star,*** der Polarstern; 2. (*fig.*) genau entgegengesetzt. **2.** *s.* (*Geom.*) die Polare. **polarity** [–'læriti], *s.* 1. die Polarität; 2. (*fig.*) Gegensätzlichkeit, Wechselbeziehung. **polarization** [–rai'zeiʃən], *s.* die Polarisation. **polarize,** *v.t.* polarisieren.

polder ['pouldə], *s.* der Koog.

[1]**pole** [poul], *s.* 1. (*Astr., Geog., Elec.*) der Pol; (*Astr.*) ***altitude of the –,*** die Polhöhe; (*Elec.*) ***like (unlike) –s,*** gleich(namig)e (ungleiche *or* entgegengesetzte) Pole; (*Elec.*) ***– reversal,*** die Umpolung; 2. (*fig.*) der Gegenpol, entgegengesetztes Extrem; ***–s apart,*** himmelweit verschieden.

[2]**pole, 1.** *s.* 1. die Stange, der Pfahl, Stab, Pfosten; die Deichsel (*of a cart*); ***curtain –,*** die Gardinenstange; (*Naut.*) ***under bare –s,*** vor Topp und Takel; (*sl.*) ***up the –,*** klapsig, plemplem; 2. (*obs.*) die Rute (= *5.03 m.*). **2.** *v.t.* mit einer Stange treiben, staken (*as a boat*), mit Stangen stützen (*hops etc.*).

Pole, *s.* der Pole (die Polin).

pole|-axe, 1. *s.* 1. die Streitaxt; 2. (*Naut.*) das Enterbeil; Schlächterbeil. **2.** *v.t.* 1. (mit einem Beil) schlachten (*animals*); 2. erschlagen. **–cat,** *s.* der Iltis.

polemic [pə'lemik], **1.** *adj.* streitsüchtig, streitlustig, polemisch, Streit–. **2.** *s.* 1. der Polemiker; 2. Meinungsstreit; (*usu. pl.*) die Polemik, das Wortgefecht.

polenta [pɔ'lentə], *s.* der Maisbrei.

pole|-star, *s.* 1. der Polarstern; 2. (*fig.*) Leitstern. **--vault, 1.** *s.* der Stabhochsprung. **2.** *v.i.* stabhochspringen. **--vaulting,** *s.* das Stabspringen.

police [pə'li:s], **1.** *s.* die Polizei; (*pl. constr.*) Polizisten (*pl.*). **2.** *v.t.* polizeilich überwachen, unter Polizeigewalt halten, Polizei stationieren in (*Dat.*), in Ordnung halten.

police|-constable, *s.* *See* **–man. --court,** *s.* das Polizeigericht. **--dog,** *s.* der Polizeihund. **--force,** *s.* die Polizei. **--inquiry,** *s.* polizeiliche Untersuchung. **--inspector,** *s.* der Polizeikommissar. **–man** [–mən], *s.* Polizeibeamte(r), der Schutzmann, Polizist; *pl.* Schutzleute, die Polizei. **--officer,** *s.* Polizeibeamte(r). **--raid,** *s.* die Razzia. **--record,** *s.* das Strafregister. **--state,** *s.* der Polizeistaat, totalitärer Staat. **--station,** *s.* die Polizeiwache, das Polizeirevier. **--surgeon,** *s.* der Gerichtsarzt. **--trap,** *s.* (*Motor.*) die Autofalle. **–woman,** *s.* die Polizistin.

[1]**policy** ['pɔlisi], *s.* 1. die Politik, politischer Grundsatz, politische Linie; ***domestic –,*** die Innenpolitik; ***foreign –,*** die Außenpolitik; 2. (*fig.*) die Zweckmäßigkeit; ***from motives of –,*** aus kluger Rücksicht; 3. die Taktik, Methode, das Verfahren; ***honesty is the best –,*** ehrlich währt am längsten.

[2]**policy,** *s.* (*Comm.*) die (Versicherungs)police, der Versicherungsschein. **policy-holder,** *s.* der Policeinhaber.

polio(myelitis) ['pouliou(maiə'laitis)], *s.* spinale Kinderlähmung.

polish ['pɔliʃ], **1.** *s.* 1. die Glätte, Politur, der (Hoch)glanz; 2. das Bohnerwachs, die Schuhcreme, Wichse; 3. (*fig.*) der Glanz, Schliff, die Vollkommenheit. **2.** *v.t.* 1. glätten, polieren; wichsen (*leather*), putzen (*shoes*), bohnern (*floors*), abschleifen, glanzschleifen, abschmirgeln (*metal*); 2. (*fig.*) abschleifen, (aus)feilen, verfeinern; (*sl.*) ***– off,*** erledigen, abtun, abmurksen (*a p.*), verputzen (*food*), hinhauen (*work*); (*coll.*) ***– up,*** aufpolieren, (*fig.*) auffrischen, aufbessern (*knowledge*). **3.** *v.i.*

glatt *or* blank werden, glänzend werden, sich putzen lassen.

Polish ['pouliʃ], **1.** *adj.* polnisch. **2.** *s.* das Polnisch(e) (*language*).

polished ['pɔliʃt], *adj.* 1. glatt, poliert; 2. (*fig.*) gesittet, fein, elegant (*as manners*). **polisher,** *s.* 1. der Polierer, Schleifer (*a p.*); 2. die Politur, das Glanzmittel; 3. die Polierbürste, Polierscheibe. **polishing,** *s.* das Polieren; – ***brush,*** die Glanzbürste, Polierbürste; – ***powder,*** das Putzpulver.

polite [pə'lait], *adj.* 1. höflich, artig (*to*, gegen); 2. fein, verfeinert, vornehm, gebildet; – ***literature,*** schöne Literatur. **politeness,** *s.* 1. die Höflichkeit, Artigkeit; 2. Vornehmheit, feine Sitten (*pl.*).

politic ['pɔlitik], *adj.* staatsklug, diplomatisch, politisch, (welt)klug, berechnend; ***body*** –, der Staat(skörper).

political [pə'litikl], *adj.* 1. politisch; – ***economist,*** der Volkswirtschaftler; – ***economy,*** die Volkswirtschaft, Nationalökonomie; – ***science,*** die Staatswissenschaft; 2. staatskundig, staatsmännisch, Staats–; – ***prisoner,*** Staatsgefangene(r); – ***system,*** das Regierungssystem. **politician** [pɔli'tiʃən], *s.* der Staatsmann, Politiker.

politics ['pɔlitiks], *pl.* (*also sing. constr.*) 1. die Politik, Staatskunst; ***enter*** –, ins politische Leben eintreten; (*coll.*) ***practical*** –, durchführbar; ***talk*** –, politisieren; 2. die Staatswissenshaft; 3. (partei)-politische Gesinnung *or* Richtung.

polity ['pɔliti], *s.* 1. politische Ordnung, die Verfassung, Regierungsform, Staatsform; 2. der Staat, das Gemeinwesen.

polka ['pɔlkə], *s.* die Polka; – ***dot,*** das Punktmuster (*of fabric*).

[1]**poll** [poul], **1.** *s.* 1. die Wahl, Abstimmung, Stimmabgabe; ***heavy*** (***poor*** or ***light***) –, starke (geringe) Wahlbeteiligung; 2. die Stimmenzählung; 3. der Wahlort; ***go to the –s,*** zur Wahl gehen; 4. die Stimmenzahl, das Wahlergebnis; 5. (*also* ***public opinion*** –) die Meinungsumfrage. **2.** *v.t.* 1. in die Wahlliste eintragen; 2. auf sich vereinigen, erhalten (*votes*). **3.** *v.i.* wählen, (ab)stimmen, die Stimme abgeben.

[2]**poll, 1.** *v.t.* köpfen, stutzen, kappen (*plant*), die Hörner stutzen (*Dat.*) (*cattle*). **2.** *adj.* hornlos (*cattle*); (*Law*) ***deed*** –, die Urkunde eines einzigen Rechtsgeschäfts. **3.** *s.* (*obs.*) 1. der Schädel, (Hinter)kopf; 2. die Person; (*Law*) ***challenge to the –s,*** die Ablehnung eines Geschworenen.

[3]**poll** [pɔl], *s.* (*sl.*) *the –, collect. pl. of* **pollman**; – ***degree,*** das Bakkalaureat (*Cambridge Univ.*).

[4]**poll,** *s.* (*coll.*) der Papagei.

pollack ['pɔlək], *s.* (*Ichth.*) der Pollack.

pollard ['pɔləd], **1.** *s.* 1. gekappter Baum; 2. hornloses Tier; der Hirsch, der Hörner abgeworfen hat; 3. die Kleie. **2.** *v.t.* kappen, stutzen (*tree*). **3.** *adj.* gekappt, gestutzt.

poll-book, *s.* die Wahlliste, Wählerliste; *see* [1]**poll.**

pollen ['pɔlən], *s.* der Pollen, Blütenstaub; – ***grain,*** das Blütenstaubkorn. **pollenization** [–ai'zeiʃən], *s. See* **pollination. pollenize,** *see* **pollinate. pollinate** [–ineit], *v.t.* bestäuben. **pollination** [–i'neiʃən], *s.* die Bestäubung.

polling ['pouliŋ], *s.* das Wählen, Abstimmen; die Wahl, Abstimmung; *–****-booth,*** die Wahlzelle; *–****-day,*** der Wahltag; *–****-district,*** der Wahlbezirk; *–****-officer,*** der Wahlprotokollführer; *–****-station,*** das Wahllokal; *see* [1]**poll.**

pollman ['pɔlmən], *s.* der Kandidat für das Bakkalaureat (*Cambridge Univ.*); *see* [3]**poll.**

pollock, *see* **pollack.**

pollster ['poulstə], *s.* (*coll.*) der Meinungsforscher; *see* [1]**poll.**

poll-tax, *s.* das Kopfgeld, die Kopfsteuer; *see* [2]**poll.**

pollute [pə'lju:t], *v.t.* 1. beflecken, besudeln; 2. verunreinigen, beschmutzen; 3. (*fig.*) entweihen; verderben. **pollution** [–lju:ʃən], *s.* 1. die Befleckung, Besudelung, Verunreinigung; ***environmental*** –, die Umweltverschmutzung; 2. (*fig.*) die Entweihung; 3. (*Physiol.*) Pollution.

polo ['poulou], *s.* das Polo(spiel); ***water*** –, der Wasserball, das Wasserballspiel; – ***neck,*** der Rollkragen; –(*-****neck***) ***shirt,*** das Polohemd.

polonaise [pɔlə'naiz], *s.* die Polonaise.

polony [pə'louni], *s.* die Bologneser (Wurst).

poltroon [pɔl'tru:n], *s.* der Feigling, die Memme. **poltroonery,** *s.* die Feigheit.

poly- ['pɔli], *pref.* viel, Viel–, Poly–.

polyandrian [pɔli'ændriən], **polyandrous,** *adj.* (*Bot.*) vielmännig. **polyandry** [–ri], *s.* die Vielmännerei.

polyanthus [pɔli'ænθəs], *s.* (*Bot.*) die Tuberose.

polybasic [pɔli'beisik], *adj.* mehrbasig.

polycarpous [pɔli'kɑ:pəs], *adj.* aus vielen Fruchtblättern.

poly|chromatic, *adj.* vielfarbig, bunt. **–chrome, 1.** *s.* 1. die Vielfarbigkeit; 2. mehrfarbige Plastik. **2.** *adj.* vielfarbig, bunt. **polychromy** ['pɔlikroumi], *s.* der Vielfarbendruck, vielfarbige Darstellung.

polyclinic ['pɔliklinik], *s.* die Klinik für alle Krankheiten.

polygamist [pɔ'ligəmist], *s.* der (die) Polygamist(in). **polygamous,** *adj.* polygam(isch). **polygamy,** *s.* die Polygamie, Vielehe.

polyglot ['pɔliglɔt], **1.** *adj.* vielsprachig, Polyglotten–. **2.** *s.* der Polyglotte (*a p.*), die Polyglotte (*book*).

polygon ['pɔligən], *s.* das Vieleck, Polygon. **polygonal** [pə'ligənl], *adj.* polygonal, vieleckig.

polyhedral [pɔli'hi:drəl], *adj.* polyedrisch, vielflächig. **polyhedron,** *s.* das Polyeder, Vielflach.

polyhistor [pɔli'histɔ:], **polymath** ['pɔlimæθ], *s.* der Polyhistor, Universalgelehrte(r).

polymerism ['pɔlimərizm], *s.* (*Biol., Chem.*) die Polymerie.

polymorphic [pɔli'mɔ:fik], *adj. See* **polymorphous. polymorphism,** *s.* die Vielgestaltigkeit, der Polymorphismus. **polymorphous,** *adj.* verschiedengestaltig, vielgestaltig, polymorph.

Polynesia [pɔli'ni:ʒə], *s.* (*Geog.*) Polynesien (*n.*). **Polynesian, 1.** *s.* der (die) Polynesier(in). **2.** *adj.* polynesisch.

polynomial [pɔli'noumiəl], **1.** *adj.* vielgliederig, polynomisch. **2.** *s.* (*Math.*) das Polynom.

polyp ['pɔlip], *s.* 1. (*Zool.*) der Polyp, das Hydrozoon; 2. (*Med.*) der Polyp. **polypary,** *s.* der Polypenstock. **polype,** *s. See* **polyp.**

polyphase ['pɔlifeiz], *adj.* mehrphasig; – ***current,*** der Drehstrom.

polyphonic [pɔli'fɔnik], *adj.* vielstimmig, mehrstimmig, kontrapunktisch, polyphon(isch).

polypite ['pɔlipait], *s.* (*Zool.*) der Einzelpolyp.

polypod ['pɔlipɔd], *s.* der Vielfüßer.

polypodium [pɔli'poudiəm], *s.* (*Bot.*) der Tüpfelfarn.

polypoid ['pɔlipɔid], *adj.* polypenartig; *see* **polyp.**

polypore ['pɔlipɔ:], **polyporus** [–'lipərəs], *s.* (*Bot.*) der Löcherpilz.

polypous ['pɔlipəs], *adj.* (*Zool., Med.*) Polypen–. **polypus,** *s.* (*pl.* **-pi** [–pai]) (*Med.*) der Polyp.

polystyrene [pɔli'staiərin], *s.* (*Chem.*) das Polystyrol.

poly|syllabic, *adj.* mehrsilbig, vielsilbig. **–syllable,** *s.* vielsilbiges Wort.

polytechnic [pɔli'teknik], **1.** *adj.* polytechnisch. **2.** *s.* technische Fachschule.

polytheism ['pɔliθi:izm], *s.* die Vielgötterei. **polytheistic** [–'istik], *adj.* polytheistisch.

polythene ['pɔliθi:n], *s.* (*Chem.*) das Polyäthylen.

polyvalence [pɔli'veiləns], *s.* (*Chem.*) die Mehrwertigkeit. **polyvalent,** *adj.* mehrwertig.

polyzoa [pɔli'zouə], *pl.* die Moostierchengattung.

pomace ['pʌmis], *s.* (Apfel)trester (*pl.*).

pomade [pə'meid, –'mɑ:d], **1.** *s.* die Pomade, das Haarfett. **2.** *v.t.* mit Pomade einreiben.

pome [poum], *s.* 1. die Kernfrucht; 2. (*Hist.*) der Reichsapfel.

pomegranate ['pɔmigrænit], *s.* der Granatapfel(baum).
Pomerania [pɔmə'reiniə], *s.* Pommern (*n.*). **Pomeranian, 1.** *s.* der (die) Pommer(in); – (*dog*), der Spitz. **2.** *adj.* pommer(i)sch.
pomiculture ['poumikʌltʃə], *s.* die Obstbaumzucht.
pommel [pʌml], **1.** *s.* 1. der Knauf (*of a sword*); 2. Sattelknopf (*of a saddle*). **2.** *v.t.* schlagen; puffen, knuffen.
pomology [pou'mɔlədʒi], *s.* die Obst(bau)kunde.
pomp [pɔmp], *s.* der Pomp, Prunk, die Pracht, das Gepränge.
Pompeii [pɔm'pei(i)], *s.* Pompeji (*n.*).
pom-pom ['pɔmpɔm], *s.* die Flugabwehrmaschinenkanone, das Schnellfeuergeschütz.
pompon ['pɔmpɔn], *s.* das Büschel, die Quaste, Troddel.
pomposity [pɔm'pɔsiti], *s.* die Prahlerei, Pomphaftigkeit, der Prunk, Bombast. **pompous** ['pɔmpəs], *adj.* prunkvoll, pomphaft, pompös; wichtigtuend, großspurig, aufgeblasen, prahlerisch (*of p.*), hochtrabend, bombastisch, schwülstig (*as style*).
ponce [pɔns], *s.* (*sl.*) der Zuhälter, Loddel.
poncho ['pɔntʃou], *s.* 1. der Poncho; 2. Regenumhang.
pond [pɔnd], *s.* der Teich, Weiher, Tümpel; *horse*-–, die Schwemme. **pondage** [–idʒ], *s.* die Wassermenge, das Fassungsvermögen.
ponder ['pɔndə], **1.** *v.t.* erwägen, bedenken, nachdenken über (*Acc.*), grübeln (*on, over*, über (*Acc.*)). **ponderability** [–rə'biliti], *s.* (*Phys.*) die Wägbarkeit. **ponderable,** *adj.* wägbar. **ponderation** [–'reiʃən], *s.* das Wägen, Wiegen. **pondering,** *s.* das Nachdenken, Erwägen. **ponderosity** [–'rɔsiti], *s.* 1. das Gewicht, die Schwere; 2. (*fig.*) Gewichtigkeit, Schwerfälligkeit, Plumpheit. **ponderous,** *adj.* 1. schwer, wuchtig, massig; 2. (*fig.*) schwerfällig, plump. **ponderousness,** *see* **ponderosity.**
pondweed ['pɔndwi:d], *s.* das Laichkraut.
pone [poun], *s.* (*Am.*) das Maisbrot.
pong [pɔŋ], **1.** *v.i.* (*sl.*) stinken. **2.** *s.* (*sl.*) der Mief.
pongee [pɔn'dʒi:], *s.* chinesische Seide.
poniard ['pɔniəd], **1.** *s.* der Dolch. **2.** *v.t.* erdolchen.
pontiff ['pɔntif], *s.* 1. der Hohepriester; 2. Papst. **pontifical** [–'tifikl], **1.** *adj.* 1. (ober)priesterlich; 2. bischöflich; 3. päpstlich. **2.** *s.* 1. das Pontifikale; 2. *pl.* bischöfliche Amtstracht, Pontifikalien (*pl.*). **pontificate** [–'tifikeit], **1.** *s.* das *or* der Pontifikat. **2.** *or* **pontify** [–tifai], *v.i.* sich (*Dat.*) Unfehlbarkeit anmaßen, mit dreister Selbstverständlichkeit auftreten, sich autoritativ gebärden.
Pontine ['pɔntain], *adj.* (*Geog.*) pontinisch.
pontoneer, pontonier [pɔntə'niə], *s.* (*Mil.*) der Brückenbauingenieur.
¹**pontoon** [pɔn'tu:n], *s.* (*Mil.*) der Ponton, Brückenkahn; – ***bridge,*** die Schiff(s)brücke.
²**pontoon,** *s.* (*Cards*) das Vingt-et-un.
pony ['pouni], *s.* 1. das Pony, Kleinpferd, kleines Pferd; 2. kleines Bierglas; 3. (*sl.*) £25 Sterling; 4. (*Am. sl.*) die Eselsbrücke, Klatsche. **pony|-engine,** *s.* kleine Rangierlokomotive. **–tail,** *s.* der Pferdeschwanz (*hair-style*).
poodle [pu:dl], *s.* der Pudel.
pooh! [pu:], *int.* pah! ach was! **pooh-pooh,** *v.t.* über die Achsel ansehen, geringschätzig behandeln *or* abtun, die Nase rümpfen über (*Acc.*).
¹**pool** [pu:l], **1.** *s.* 1. der Tümpel, Pfuhl, Teich, Weiher; 2. die Pfütze, Lache; – ***of blood,*** die Blutlache; 3. das (Schwimm)becken, Bassin. **2.** *v.t.* (*Min.*) schrämen.
²**pool, 1.** *s.* 1. der (Spiel)einsatz, gemeinsame Spielkasse; 2. (*Comm.*) die Interessengemeinschaft, der Ring, das Kartell; 3. gemeinsamer Fonds, gemeinsame Kasse; 4. (*Bill.*) das Poulespiel; 5. ***football*** –, der Fußballtoto. **2.** *v.t.* 1. zusammentun, zusammenwerfen; 2. verteilen, aufteilen (*profits*); 3. (*fig.*) vereinigen, zusammenfassen.
poop [pu:p], **1.** *s.* (*Naut.*) das Heck, Hinterteil; (*obs.*) die Achterhütte, Kampanie; – ***deck,*** das Achterdeck. **2.** *v.t.* über das Heck schlagen (*Dat.*) (*of waves*); ***be –ed,*** eine Sturzsee von hinten bekommen, (*fig.*) gefährlich getroffen sein; (*sl.*) fertig *or* erledigt *or* ausgepumpt sein.
poor ['puə, pɔ:], **1.** *adj.* 1. arm, bedürftig, mittellos; 2. dürftig, kümmerlich, ärmlich, armselig, erbärmlich; ***make but a – shift,*** sich kümmerlich behelfen; 3. (*fig.*) arm (*in*, an (*Dat.*)), schlecht, schwach, mangelhaft, unzulänglich, unzureichend; – ***consolation,*** schlechter *or* schwacher Trost; ***a – head for . . .,*** keinen Kopf *or* wenig Begabung für . . .; – ***health,*** schwache Gesundheit; ***a – look-out,*** traurige *or* schlechte Aussichten; – ***me!*** ich Arme(r)! ***have a – night,*** eine unruhige Nacht verbringen; ***have a – opinion of,*** wenig halten *or* eine geringe Meinung haben von; ***in my – opinion,*** meiner unmaßgeblichen Meinung nach; (*B.*) – ***in spirit,*** arm im Geist; (*sl.*) – ***fool,*** armer Tropf; – ***visibility,*** unsichtiges Wetter; 4. mager, unfruchtbar, unergiebig, dürr (*as soil*); – ***crop,*** unergiebige Ernte. **2.** *s.* (*collect.*) ***the –,*** die Armen; (*B.*) ***the – in spirit,*** die da geistlich arm sind.
poor|-box, *s.* die Armenbüchse, Almosenbüchse. **–-house,** *s.* das Armenhaus. **–-law,** *s.* das Armengesetz, öffentliches Fürsorgerecht. **poorly, 1.** *adv.* 1. dürftig, armselig; – ***off,*** schlimm daran; 2. (*fig.*) mangelhaft, schwach, schlecht; ***think – of,*** nicht viel halten von. **2.** *pred. adj.* unwohl, unpäßlich. **poorness,** *s.* 1. (*fig.*) die Armut, der Mangel (*of*, an (*Dat.*)); 2. die Ärmlichkeit, Dürftigkeit, Armseligkeit; 3. Unfruchtbarkeit (*of soil*); Unergiebigkeit (*of ore*). **poor|-rate,** *s.* die (Gemeinde)armensteuer. **–-relief,** *s.* die Armenfürsorge. **–-spirited,** *adj.* verzagt, mutlos, kleinmütig.
¹**pop** [pɔp], **1.** *s.* 1. der Paff, Knall; (*coll.*) ***have a – at,*** schießen nach; 2. (*coll.*) die Brause; ***ginger –,*** das Ingwerbier; 3. (*sl.*) ***in –,*** verpfändet. **2.** *adv.* plötzlich, mit einem Knall; ***go –,*** knallen, platzen. **3.** *int.* paff! klatsch! futsch! **4.** *v.i.* 1. knallen, (los)platzen, losgehen; aufplatzen; 2. (*coll.*) flitzen, huschen; – ***along,*** forthuschen; – ***in,*** hereinplatzen, auf einen Sprung kommen; – ***off,*** abhauen, sich aus dem Staub machen; einnicken; (*sl.*) abkratzen, hops gehen; – ***out,*** einen Sprung hinaus machen (*of a p.*), plötzlich herausspringen (*of a th.*); – ***up,*** plötzlich auftauchen, aufkreuzen. **5.** *v.t.* 1. rösten (*corn*); 2. knallen lassen (*a cork*); 3. (*sl.*) verpfänden; 4. (*coll.*) – ***the kettle on,*** schnell Wasser aufsetzen; (*coll.*) – ***a letter in the post,*** einen Brief in den Kasten stecken; 5. – ***off 10 rabbits,*** 10 Kaninchen abknallen; 6. (*coll.*) – ***the question,*** einen Heiratsantrag machen.
²**pop,** *s.* (*coll.*) (*also* – ***music***) volkstümliche Musik; – ***group,*** die Beatgruppe; – ***song,*** der Schlager, die Schnulze; – ***singer,*** der (die) Schlagersänger(in).
popcorn ['pɔpkɔ:n], *s.* der Röstmais, Puffmais.
pope [poup], *s.* der Papst. **popedom,** *s.* das Papsttum. **popery,** *s.* die Papisterei, das Pfaffentum.
pop|-eyed, *adj.* glotzäugig. **–-gun,** *s.* die Knallbüchse.
popinjay ['pɔpindʒei], *s.* der Geck, Laffe, Fatzke.
popish [poupiʃ], *adj.* papistisch, Pfaffen–.
poplar ['pɔplə], *s.* die Pappel.
poplin ['pɔplin], *s.* die Popeline.
popliteal [pɔp'litiəl], *adj.* Kniekehlen–; – ***space,*** die Kniekehle.
poppet ['pɔpit], *s.* 1. (*Naut.*) der Schlittenständer; 2. (*coll.*) das Püppchen, Täubchen; 3. (*Tech.*) (*also* ***–-head***) die Docke (*of a lathe*); (*also* ***–-valve***) das Tellerventil.
popping ['pɔpiŋ], *s.* das Knallen, Knattern. **popping-crease,** *s.* (*Crick.*) die Schlagmallinie.
popple ['pɔpl], **1.** *v.i.* Wellen schlagen. **2.** *s.* leichter Wellenschlag *or* Wellengang.
poppy ['pɔpi], *s.* der Mohn; ***opium –,*** der Schlafmohn; ***Poppy Day,*** der Waffenstillstandstag, (englischer) Heldengedenktag (*11 Nov.*). **poppy|-**

cock, *s.* (*sl.*) der Quatsch, Unsinn. **–head,** *s.* die Mohnkapsel.
popshop ['pɔpʃɔp], *s.* (*sl.*) das Pfandhaus.
popsy ['pɔpsi], *s.* (*sl.*) das Mädel.
populace ['pɔpjuləs], *s.* (gemeines) Volk, der große Haufen, der Pöbel.
popular ['pɔpjulə], *adj.* 1. Volks–, volkstümlich, volksmäßig, volksnah; (*Pol.*) – ***front,*** die Volksfront; – ***government,*** die Volksherrschaft; – ***sovereignty,*** die Volkssouveränität; – ***tradition,*** volkstümliche Überlieferung; 2. populär, gemeinverständlich, leichtfaßlich; – ***science,*** die Popularwissenschaft; – ***song,*** der Schlager; – ***writer,*** vielgelesener Schriftsteller; 3. allgemein, weitverbreitet, (allgemein) beliebt (***with,*** bei); ***make o.s.*** –, sich beliebt machen (***with,*** bei); 4. – ***edition,*** die Volksausgabe; ***at – prices,*** zu volkstümlichen Preisen. **popularity** [–'læriti], *s.* die Volkstümlichkeit, Beliebtheit, Volksgunst, Popularität (***with,*** bei; ***among,*** unter (*Dat.*)). **popularize,** *v.t.* 1. gemeinverständlich *or* volkstümlich darstellen, popularisieren; 2. in den weitesten Kreisen verbreiten, unter das Volk bringen, populär machen.
populate ['pɔpjuleit], *v.t.* bevölkern, besiedeln. **population** [–'leiʃən], *s.* 1. die Bevölkerung, Einwohnerschaft; 2. Bevölkerungszahl, (Gesamt)-zahl, Einwohnerzahl. **populous,** *adj.* dicht bevölkert *or* besiedelt, volkreich. **populousness,** *s.* die Bevölkerungsdichte.
porbeagle ['pɔ:bi:gl], *s.* (*Ichth.*) der Heringshai.
porcelain ['pɔ:slin], **1.** *s.* das Porzellan. **2.** *adj.* Porzellan–; – ***clay,*** das Kaolin, die Porzellanerde.
porch [pɔ:tʃ], *s.* 1. der Vorbau, überdachte Vorhalle; 2. (*Am.*) die Veranda.
porcine ['pɔ:sain], *adj.* Schwein(e)–, schweineartig.
porcupine ['pɔ:kjupain], *s.* 1. das Stachelschwein; 2. (*Tech.*) die Kammwalze, Hechelmaschine.
1**pore** [pɔ:], *s.* (*Anat.*) die Pore; (*fig.*) ***at every –,*** am ganzen Körper.
2**pore,** *v.i.* (*usu.* – *over*) fleißig *or* eifrig studieren, brüten *or* hocken über (*Dat.*).
pork [pɔ:k], *s.* das Schweinefleisch. **pork-butcher,** *s.* der Schweineschlächter. **porker,** *s.* das Mastschwein, Mastferkel. **pork pie,** *s.* die Schweinefleischpastete; ***pork-pie hat,*** runder Filzhut.
pornographic [pɔ:nə'græfik], *adj.* Schmutz–, obszön, zotig. **pornography** [–'nɔgrəfi], *s.* die Pornographie, Schmutzliteratur.
porosity [pɔ:'rɔsiti], *s.* die Durchlässigkeit, Porosität. **porous** ['pɔ:rəs], *adj.* durchlässig, porös.
porphyritic [pɔ:fi'ritik], *adj.* Porphyr–. **porphyry** ['pɔ:firi], *s.* der Porphyr.
porpoise ['pɔ:pəs], *s.* das Meerschwein, der Tümmler.
porridge ['pɔridʒ], *s.* der Haferbrei, die Hafergrütze.
porrigo [pə'raigou], *s.* (*Med.*) der Grind.
porringer ['pɔrindʒə], *s.* der Suppennapf.
1**port** [pɔ:t], *s.* 1. der Hafen; – ***of call,*** der Zwischenhafen, Anlegehafen, Anlaufhafen; ***call at a –,*** einen Hafen anlaufen; – ***of clearance*** or ***departure,*** der Abgangshafen; ***clear a –,*** aus einem Hafen auslaufen; – ***of delivery*** or ***discharge,*** der Löschhafen; – ***of destination,*** der Bestimmungshafen; – ***of entry,*** der Einfahrtshafen, Einlaufhafen; ***free*** –, der Freihafen; ***Port of London Authority,*** die Londoner Hafenbehörde; – ***of registry,*** der Heimatshafen; – ***of transhipment,*** der Umschlaghafen; – ***charges,*** – ***dues,*** die Hafengebühren (*pl.*); 2. der Hafenplatz, die Hafenstadt; 3. (*fig.*) Zuflucht.
2**port,** *s.* 1. das Tor, die Pforte; 2. (*Naut.*) Ladepforte, Pfortluke, das Schießloch; 3. (*Tech.*) die (Ventil)öffnung, der Abzug; ***exhaust*** –, der Auspuffkanal, Auslaßabzug.
3**port, 1.** *s.* (*Naut.*) das Backbord; die Backbordseite; ***on the – beam,*** an Backbord dwars; ***on the – bow,*** Backbord voraus; ***on the – quarter,*** an Backbord achteraus *or* achtern; ***have a list to –,*** Backbordschlagseite haben; ***on the – tack,*** mit Backbordhalsen. **2.** *v.t.* Backbord nehmen (*the helm*); – ***the helm!*** Backbord das Ruder! **3.** *adj.* (*Naut.*) Backbord–; (*Av.*) link.
4**port,** *s.* der Portwein.
5**port, 1.** (*obs.*) die (Körper)haltung, das Benehmen. **2.** *v.t.* (*Mil.*) schräg vorm Körper halten (*arms*).
portable ['pɔ:təbl], *adj.* tragbar, transportierbar, fahrbar, Reise–; (*fig.*) handlich, beweglich; – ***railway,*** die Feldbahn; – ***typewriter,*** die Reiseschreibmaschine; – ***radio,*** der Kofferradio.
portage ['pɔ:tidʒ], **1.** *s.* 1. das Tragen, (*of canoes etc.*) Umsetzen; 2. der Transport; 3. das Rollgeld, die Fracht, Zustellungsgebühr, Transportkosten (*pl.*), der Botenlohn; 4. die Tragstelle, Portage (*between navigable waters*). **2.** *v.t.* umsetzen, transportieren (*a canoe*).
portal [pɔ:tl], **1.** *s.* 1. das Portal, der (Haupt)eingang, das Haupttor; 2. (*Poet.*) Tor, die Pforte, (*fig.*) der Eingang. **2.** *adj.* (*Anat.*) – ***vein,*** die Pfortader.
portamento [pɔ:tə'mentou], *s.* (*Mus.*) das Portament, Hinübergleiten.
portcullis [pɔ:t'kʌlis], *s.* das Fallgatter.
Porte [pɔ:t], *s.* ***Sublime –,*** Hohe Pforte.
portend [pɔ:'tend], *v.t.* vorbedeuten, vorhersagen, verkündigen; anzeigen, (hin)deuten auf (*Acc.*). **portent** ['pɔ:tent], *s.* 1. die Vorbedeutung, Voraussage; 2. schlimmes Vorzeichen *or* Anzeichen; 3. das Wunder. **portentous** [–'tentəs], *adj.* 1. unheilvoll, unheilverkündend, verhängnisvoll; 2. (*coll.*) furchtbar, ungeheuer, gewaltig.
1**porter** ['pɔ:tə], *s.* der Pförtner, Portier.
2**porter,** *s.* der (Gepäck)träger, Dienstmann; Packträger, Lastträger.
3**porter,** *s.* das Porterbier.
porterage ['pɔ:təridʒ], *s.* der Botenlohn, die Zustellungsgebühr.
portfire ['pɔ:tfaiə], *s.* (*Hist.*) die Zündrute, Lunte.
portfolio [pɔ:t'fouliou], *s.* 1. die Aktentasche, Mappe; 2. (*Pol.*) das (Minister)portefeuille; ***without –,*** ohne Geschäftsbereich; 3. (*Comm.*) das (Wechsel)portfeuille.
porthole ['pɔ:thoul], *s.* (*Naut.*) das (Lüftungs)-fenster, Bullauge.
portico ['pɔ:tikou], *s.* die Säulenhalle.
portière [pɔ:'tjɛə], *s.* der Türvorhang.
portion ['pɔ:ʃən], **1.** *s.* 1. der *or* das Teil, das Quantum, die Menge, der Anteil (***of,*** an (*Dat.*)); 2. die Portion (*of food*); 3. das (*or Law* der) Erbteil, das Heiratsgut, die Aussteuer, Mitgift; ***legal –,*** der *or* das Pflichtteil. **2.** *v.t.* 1. einteilen; – ***out,*** austeilen, aufteilen, verteilen (***to,*** unter (*Acc.*)); (*fig.*) zuteilen, zuteil werden lassen; 2. (*also* – ***off***) aussteuern, ausstatten (*a daughter*) (***with,*** mit). **portionless,** *adj.* ohne Aussteuer.
portliness ['pɔ:tlinis], *s.* 1. die Behäbigkeit, Beleibtheit; 2. Würde, Stattlichkeit. **portly,** *adj.* 1. (wohl)beleibt, behäbig; 2. würdevoll, stattlich, ansehnlich.
portmanteau [pɔ:t'mæntou], *s.* (*pl.* **-x** [–z]) der Handkoffer; – ***word,*** das Schachtelwort, Mischwort.
portrait ['pɔ:trit], *s.* 1. das Porträt, Bild(nis); ***paint his –,*** ihn malen; ***take his –,*** ihn photographieren; 2. (*fig.*) die Beschreibung, Darstellung, Schilderung. **portraitist, portrait| painter,** *s.* der Porträtmaler. – **painting, portraiture** [–tʃə], *s.* 1. die Porträtmalerei; 2. (*fig.*) Schilderung, Darstellung, das Bild.
portray [pɔ:'trei], *v.t.* 1. (ab)malen, abbilden, nachbilden, porträtieren; 2. (*fig.*) schildern, darstellen. **portrayal,** *s.* das Abmalen, die Abbildung, (*usu. fig.*) Darstellung, Schilderung.
Portugal ['pɔ:tjugəl], *s.* Portugal (*n.*). **Portuguese** [–'gi:z], **1.** *s.* 1. der Portugiese (die Portugiesin); 2. (*language*) das Portugiesisch(e). **2.** *adj.* portugiesisch.
pose [pouz], **1.** *s.* die Pose (*also fig.*), Positur, Haltung, Stellung. **2.** *v.t.* 1. (auf)stellen (*assertion*); 2. aufwerfen (*question*); 3. zurechtstellen, in

Positur setzen. **3.** *v.i.* **1.** sich in Positur setzen (*for*, für) (*a picture*); Modell stehen (*for*, *Dat.*) (*a p.*); 2. (*fig.*) posieren, figurieren, auftreten, sich ausgeben (*as*, als). **poser,** *s.* (*coll.*) verblüffende Frage, harte Nuß. **poseur** [–ˈzə:], *s.* der Wichtigtuer.

posh [pɔʃ], **1.** *adj.* (*sl.*) elegant, piekfein, todschick; nobel, erstklassig, tipptopp. **2.** *v.t.* (*sl.*) – ***o.s. up,*** sich aufdonnern.

posit [ˈpɔzit], *v.t.* voraussetzen, postulieren, als Voraussetzung hinstellen.

position [pəˈziʃən], **1.** *s.* 1. die Stellung, der Stand(ort), die Lage; 2. Sachlage, Situation, der (Zu)stand; ***awkward –,*** verzwickte Lage; ***financial –,*** Vermögensverhältnisse (*pl.*), die Finanzlage; ***be in a – to,*** in der Lage sein zu; ***in my –,*** in meiner Lage; 3. soziale Stellung, der Rang, Stand; 4. das Amt, der Posten, die Stellung; ***hold a –,*** eine Stellung innehaben, ein Amt bekleiden; 5. (*fig.*) der Standpunkt, die (Ein)stellung, Behauptung; ***define one's –,*** seinen Standpunkt klarmachen; ***take up a – on,*** Stellung nehmen zu; 6. (*Naut.*) die Position, der Schiffsort; 7. (*Mil.*) die Stellung; 8. (*Mus.*) Lage. **2.** *v.t.* 1. in die richtige Stellung *or* Lage bringen, (richtig) hinstellen; 2. (*Mil.*) stationieren.

positional [pəˈziʃənl], *adj.* Stellungs–. **position|-finder,** *s.* das Ortungsgerät. **--finding,** *s.* die Ortung. **--light,** *s.* das Positionslicht. – **report,** *s.* die Standortmeldung.

positive [ˈpɔzitiv], **1.** *s.* 1. ausdrücklich, bestimmt, (fest)stehend, ausgemacht, vorgeschrieben; – ***offer,*** festes Angebot; – ***order,*** ausdrücklicher Befehl; 2. einwandrei, unumstößlich, unzweifelhaft, unwiderruflich, sicher; ***proof –, – proof,*** sicherer *or* unwiderlegbarer Beweis; ***be – about,*** überzeugt sein von, (absolut) sicher sein (*Gen.*); 3. (*of a p.*) selbstherrlich, selbstsicher, überzeugt, rechthaberisch, hartnäckig; – ***theology,*** die Dogmatik; 4. (*Math., Gram., Elec., Med.*) positiv; (*Gram.*) – ***degree,*** der Positiv, die Grundstufe; (*Elec.*) – ***electrode,*** die Anode; – ***quantity,*** positive Größe; (*Gram.*) – ***statement,*** bejahende Aussage; 5. (*Phil.*) positiv, tatsächlich, wirklich, gegeben, empirisch; 6. (*coll.*) vollkommen, komplett, absolut. **2.** *s.* 1. (*Gram.*) der Positiv, die Grundstufe; ***answer in the –,*** eine bejahende *or* zustimmende Antwort geben; 2. (*Phot.*) das Positiv. **positively,** *adv.* unbedingt, absolut; ausdrücklich, durchaus. **positiveness,** *s.* 1. die Bestimmtheit, Wirklichkeit; 2. (*fig.*) Gewißheit, Hartnäckigkeit. **positivism,** *s.* (*Phil.*) der Positivismus.

positron [ˈpɔzitrɔn], *s.* das Positron.

posse [ˈpɔsi], *s.* das Aufgebot; die Schar, der Trupp; – ***comitatus,*** der Landsturm.

possess [pəˈzes], *v.t.* besitzen, im Besitz haben, (inne)haben (*a th.*); sich bemächtigen (*Gen.*), beherrschen, in der Gewalt haben (*a p.*); – ***o.s. of,*** sich (*Dat.*) aneignen *or* zu eigen machen, sich bemächtigen (*Gen.*); – ***one's soul in patience,*** sich n Geduld fassen; – ***a woman,*** eine Frau besitzen *or* genießen. **possessed,** *adj.* besessen; ***be – of,*** besitzen, im Besitz sein von; ***become – of,*** in den Besitz kommen (*Gen.*); ***be – with,*** besessen *or* eingenommen *or* erfüllt sein von; ***a man –,*** ein Besessener.

possession [pəˈzeʃən], *s.* 1. der Besitz; ***have – of, be in – of,*** besitzen, sich im Besitz befinden (*Gen.*), im Besitz sein (*Gen.*) (*of a p.*); ***be in the – of,*** gehören (*Dat.*), besessen sein *or* im Besitz sein von (*of a th.*); ***take – of,*** Besitz ergreifen von, in Besitz nehmen (*a th.*), sich bemächtigen (*Gen.*) (*a p.*); ***vacant –,*** sofort zu beziehen (*of houses*); ***the person in –,*** der Besitzer; ***rejoice in the – of,*** glücklicher Besitzer sein (*Gen.*); 2. das Besitztum, *pl.* Besitzungen (*pl.*); ***British –s,*** englische Besitzungen; 3. (*fig.*) die Besessenheit (*by an idea*).

possessive [pəˈzesiv], **1.** *adj.* 1. (*Gram.*) besitzanzeigend; – ***adjective,*** (verbundenes) Personalpronomen; – ***case,*** der Genitiv; – ***pronoun,*** besitzanzeigendes Fürwort, (unverbundenes) Possessivpronomen; 2. besitzgierig (*of a p.*); – ***instinct,*** der Sinn für Besitz. **2.** *s.* 1. der Genitiv, Besitzfall; 2. das Possessivpronomen, besitzanzeigendes Fürwort. **possessiveness,** *s.* die Besitzgier.

possessor [pəˈzesə], *s.* der (die) Besitzer(in), Inhaber(in). **possessory,** *adj.* Besitz–.

posset [ˈpɔsit], *s.* heißes Würzgetränk.

possibility [pɔsiˈbiliti], *s.* 1. die Möglichkeit (*of, Gen.*; ***of doing,*** zu tun); ***by any –,*** auf irgendeine Weise; ***not by any –,*** keineswegs; ***there is no –,*** es besteht keine Möglichkeit (***of doing,*** zu tun; ***of his doing,*** daß er tut); 2. etwas Mögliches; ***human –,*** das Menschenmögliche; ***within the range of –,*** im Bereich des Möglichen; 3. *pl.* Entwicklungsmöglichkeiten, Fähigkeiten (*pl.*). **possible** [ˈpɔsibl], *adj.* 1. möglich; ***if –,*** womöglich, wenn (irgend) möglich; 2. denkbar, eventuell, etwaig; ***best – way*** or ***best way –,*** denkbar bester Weg; 3. (*coll.*) leidlich, erträglich. **possibly,** *adv.* vielleicht, möglicherweise; ***if I – can,*** wenn ich irgend kann; ***I cannot – come,*** ich kann unmöglich *or* auf keinen Fall kommen; ***how can I –?*** wie kann ich nur? ***is it not – right?*** ist es nicht etwa richtig?

possum [ˈpɔsəm], *s.* (*Zool.*) die Beutelratte; (*coll.*) ***play –,*** sich unschuldig *or* krank *or* tot stellen; äußerst vorsichtig sein.

[1]**post** [poust], **1.** *s.* der Pfahl, Posten, die Stange; (*Naut.*) der Steven; (***as***) ***deaf as a –,*** stocktaub; ***be beaten*** or ***pipped at the –,*** kurz vorm Ziel geschlagen werden; ***be left at the –,*** nicht starten, zurückbleiben; ***from pillar to –,*** von Pontius zu Pilatus; (*Spt.*) ***starting –,*** die Startlinie; (*Spt.*) ***finishing*** or ***winning –,*** das Ziel, die Ziellinie. **2.** *v.t.* (*also* – ***up***) anschlagen, ankleben (*a notice*), bekanntgeben, bekanntmachen (*a fact*); – ***the wall with bills,*** die Mauer mit Zetteln bekleben; – ***no bills!*** Zettelankleben verboten! – ***as missing,*** als vermißt melden.

[2]**post,** **1.** *s.* 1. (*esp. Mil.*) der Posten, Platz, Standort; ***at one's –,*** auf seinem Posten; (*Mil.*) ***last –,*** der Zapfenstreich; 2. der Stand(platz), Platz, die Stelle, Station; ***trading –,*** die Handelsniederlassung; 3. (*of a p.*) die Stelle, (An)stellung, der Posten, das Amt. **2.** *v.t.* 1. (*esp. Mil.*) aufstellen, postieren (*sentry*), stationieren (*troops*); 2. (*usu. pass.*) ernennen (*to a rank*).

[3]**post,** **1.** *s.* 1. die Post; ***by –,*** mit der *or* durch die Post; ***by today's –,*** mit der heutigen Post; ***by return of –,*** umgehend, postwendend; 2. das Postamt; 3. die Postzustellung, Postaustragung; 4. Postsachen, Postsendungen (*pl.*); 5. (*Hist.*) die Postkutsche; 6. der Kurier, Eilbote; 7. großes Briefpapierformat (*20″ × 16″*); 8. ***general –,*** das Blindekuhspiel (*game*); (*fig.*) allgemeiner Platzwechsel. **2.** *v.t.* 1. zur Post bringen *or* geben, in den Briefkasten stecken *or* werfen; 2. mit der *or* durch die Post schicken; 3. (*Comm.*) eintragen, übertragen (*item in ledger*); – ***up,*** ins reine schreiben; – ***forward,*** vortragen, transportieren; 4. (*coll. usu. pass.*) informieren; *see* **posted. 3.** *v.i.* 1. (*Hist.*) mit der Post(kutsche) fahren; 2. (*fig.*) eilig reisen, eilen. **4.** *adv.* (*obs.*) eilig, in Eile; ***ride –,*** Kurier reiten; ***travel –,*** mit der Post(kutsche) reisen.

[4]**post–,** *pref.* nach–, Nach–.

postage [ˈpoustidʒ], *s.* das Porto, die Postgebühr, Postspesen (*pl.*); – ***due,*** das Strafporto, die Nachgebühr; – ***stamp,*** die Briefmarke, das Postwertzeichen; ***pay the – on,*** frankieren, freimachen. **postal,** *adj.* Post–, postalisch; – ***collection,*** die Leerung, das Abholen der Post; – ***delivery,*** die Postzustellung; – ***district,*** der Postzustellbezirk; – ***order,*** die Postanweisung (unter £50); – ***rates,*** der Posttarif; – ***reply coupon,*** der Rückantwortschein; – ***tuition,*** der Fernunterricht; ***Postal Union,*** der Weltpostverein.

post|-bag, *s.* 1. der Postbeutel; 2. (*fig.*) Briefschaften (*pl.*). **--box,** *s.* der Briefkasten. **–card,** *s.* die Postkarte; ***picture –,*** die Ansichtskarte. **--chaise,** *s.* (*Hist.*) die Postkutsche.

post|-date, *v.t.* nachdatieren (*a letter*), später *or* nachträglich datieren (*an event*). **--diluvial,** *adj.* nacheiszeitlich. **--diluvian,** *adj.* nachsintflutlich.

posted [ˈpoustid], *adj.* (*fig.*) informiert; ***keep him –,*** ihn auf dem laufenden halten.

post-entry, *s.* 1. (*Comm.*) nachträgliche Buchung *or* Eintragung; 2. (*Spt.*) die Nachnennung.

poster ['poustə], *s.* das Plakat, der Anschlag.

poste restante ['poust'restãt], **1.** *adv., adj.* postlagernd. **2.** *s.* – (***counter***), die Briefausgabe.

posterior [pɔs'tiəriə], **1.** *adj.* später (*time*), hinter, Hinter– (*space*); ***be – to,*** später sein als, folgen auf (*Acc.*) (*time*); kommen nach *or* hinter (*Dat.*), folgen (*Dat.*) (*space*). **2.** *s.* der Hintere, das Hinterteil; (*coll.*) Gesäß. **posteriori,** *see* **a posteriori. posteriority** [–ri'ɔriti], *s.* das Spätersein, späteres Eintreten. **posterity** [–'teriti], *s.* 1. die Nachkommenschaft; 2. Nachwelt.

postern ['pɔstən], *s.* (*also* – ***gate***) die Hintertür, Seitentür, Nebentür; (*Mil. Hist.*) Ausfallpforte.

post|fix, *s.* (*Gram.*) das Suffix. **--free,** *adj., adv.* franko, portofrei. **-graduate, 1.** *s.* der Jungakademiker, Graduierte(r). **2.** *adj.* vorgeschritten, Doktoranden–. **--haste,** *adv.* in großer Eile, eiligst, schnellstens.

posthumous ['pɔstjuməs], *adj.* nachgeboren, hinterlassen (*child*), nachgelassen, postum (*writings*); – ***fame,*** der Nachruhm.

postil ['pɔstil], *s.* die Randbemerkung, Glosse, (*Eccl.*) Postille.

postil(l)ion [pɔs'tiliən], *s.* (*Hist.*) der Postkutscher.

post-impressionism, *s.* der Nachimpressionismus.

posting ['poustiŋ], *s.* 1. das Aufgeben (*of letters*); 2. (*Hist.*) Reisen mit der Postkutsche; 3. Aufstellen, Postieren (*of sentries*), die Stationierung (*of troops*); 4. das Anschlagen (*of notice*); 5. (*Comm.*) die Eintragung, Übertragung (*of ledger-entries*).

postliminy [poust'limini], *s.* die Wiederherstellung des früheren Rechtzustandes, Wiedergewinnung der Rechte.

post|man, *s.* der Briefträger, Postbote. **-mark, 1.** *s.* der Poststempel. **2.** *v.t.* (ab)stempeln. **-master,** *s.* der Postmeister, Postamtsvorsteher; (*obs.*) ***Postmaster General,*** der Reichspostminister.

post| meridian, *adj.* Nachmittags–, nachmittägig. **--meridiem,** *adv.* nachmittags, abends.

postmistress ['poustmistris], *s.* die Postmeisterin, Postamtsvorsteherin.

post|-mortem [–'mɔ:təm], **1.** *adj.* nach dem Tode eintretend *or* stattfindend. **2.** *s.* – (***examination***), die Leichenöffnung, Leichenschau. **--natal,** *adj.* nach der Geburt (stattfindend). **--nuptial,** *adj.* nach der Hochzeit (stattfindend). **--obit, 1.** *adj.* (*Law*) nach dem Tode in Kraft *or* Wirkung tretend. **2.** *s.* – (***bond***), nach dem Tode fälliger Schuldschein.

post|-office, *s.* das Postamt, die Post; ***general –,*** das Hauptpostamt, die Hauptpost; – ***box,*** das Postschließfach; – ***clerk,*** Postbeamte(r); – ***savings bank,*** die Postsparkasse. **--paid,** *adj.* frankiert, freigemacht.

postpone [pous(t)'poun], *v.t.* 1. aufschieben, verschieben, hinausschieben (***till,*** auf (*Acc.*)); 2. nachstellen, zurückstellen, unterordnen (*to, Dat.*). **postponement,** *s.* der Aufschub, die Verschiebung, Zurückstellung.

post|position, *s.* 1. die Nachstellung; 2. (*Gram.*) nachgestellte Präposition. **-positive,** *adj.* nachgestellt. **-prandial,** *adj.* nach dem Essen, nach Tisch; – ***nap,*** das Nachmittagsschläfchen. **-script,** *s.* die Nachschrift (*to a letter*), der Nachtrag, Nachhang (*to a book*).

postulant ['pɔstjulənt], *s.* (*Eccl.*) der Bewerber (um Aufnahme in einen religiösen Order).

postulate ['pɔstjuleit], **1.** *s.* (*Log.*) das Postulat, die (Grund)voraussetzung. **2.** *v.t.* 1. fordern; 2. (als gegeben) voraussetzen. **postulation** [–'leiʃən], *s.* 1. das Gesuch, die Forderung; 2. unentbehrliche Annahme.

posture ['pɔstʃə], **1.** *s.* 1. die (Körper)haltung, Positur, Stellung; 2. Situation, Lage. **2.** *v.i.* sich stellen, posieren, figurieren, auftreten. **3.** *v.t.* in Positur setzen, in eine bestimmte Lage stellen (lassen).

postwar ['poustwɔ:], *adj.* Nachkriegs–.

posy ['pouzi], *s.* 1. der Blumenstrauß; 2. (*obs.*) Denkspruch.

pot [pɔt], **1.** *s.* 1. der Topf, die Kanne, (*Tech.*) der Tiegel; ***chimney--,*** die Kaminkappe; ***glue--,*** der Leimtiegel; ***ink--,*** das Tintenfaß; (*sl.*) ***big –,*** hohes Tier; (*Prov.*) ***the – calls the kettle black,*** ein Esel schimpft den andern Langohr; (*sl.*) ***he has –s of money,*** er sitzt im Fett, er hat ein Heidengeld, er hat Geld wie Heu; ***keep the – boiling,*** die S. in Gang halten; (*sl.*) ***go to –,*** auf den Hund kommen, vor die Hunde gehen (*a p.*), zugrunde gehen, zuschanden werden (*a th.*); 2. (*coll.*) der Nachttopf; 3. (*sl.*) großer (Wett)einsatz; 4. (*Spt. sl.*) der (Preis)pokal; 5. (*sl.*) ***take a – at,*** schießen auf (*Acc.*). **2.** *v.t.* 1. in einen Topf tun; eintopfen (*plant*), (*usu. pass.*) einmachen (*meat etc.*); 2. (*sl.*) abknallen; 3. (*Bill.*) ins Loch treiben; *see* **potted. 3.** *v.i.* (*sl.*) losknallen (***at,*** auf (*Acc.*)).

potable ['poutəbl], *adj.* (*coll.*) trinkbar.

potash ['pɔtæʃ], **1.** *s.* die Pottasche, das Kali(umkarbonat); (*Agr.*) der Kalidünger; ***bicarbonate of –,*** doppelkohlensaures Kali; ***caustic –,*** das Ätzkali. **potassium** [pə'tæsiəm], *s.* das Kalium; (*Phot.*) – ***bromide,*** das Bromkali; – ***carbonate,*** das Kali(umkarbonat), die Pottasche; – ***hydroxide,*** das Ätzkali, Kaliumhydroxyd; – ***permanganate,*** übermangansaures Kalium.

potation [pou'teiʃən], *s.* 1. der Trank, das Getränk; 2. (*oft. pl.*) der Trunk, das Zechen.

potato [pə'teitou], *s.* (*pl.* **-es**) die Kartoffel; der Erdapfel; ***fried –es,*** Bratkartoffeln; ***mashed –es,*** der Kartoffelbrei, das Kartoffelpüree. **potato|-blight, --chips,** (*Am.*) *See* **crisps. --disease, --rot,** *s.* die Kartoffelkrankheit, Kartoffelfäule.

pot|-bellied, *adj.* (*sl.*) dickwanstig. **--belly,** *s.* (*sl.*) der Dickbauch. **--boiler,** *s.* (*sl.*) 1. die Brotarbeit, Lohnarbeit; 2. das Schundwerk. **--boy,** *s.* der Bierkellner.

poteen [pɔ'ti:n], *s.* (heimlich gebrannter) irischer Whisky.

potence, potency ['poutəns(i)], *s.* 1. die Macht, Stärke; 2. Wirksamkeit, Kraft; 3. (*Physiol.*) Potenz, Zeugungsfähigkeit; 4. (*fig.*) der Einfluß, die Autorität, Durchschlagskraft, Gewalt. **potent,** *adj.* 1. mächtig, stark, wirksam; 2. (*Physiol.*) potent, zeugungsfähig; 3. (*fig.*) einflußreich, überzeugend, zwingend, durchschlagend.

potentate ['poutənteit], *s.* der Machthaber, Herrscher.

potential [pə'tenʃəl], **1.** *adj.* 1. möglich; 2. (*Phys.*) latent, potentiell; – ***energy,*** latente Kraft, die Energie der Lage. **2.** *s.* 1. die Möglichkeit; 2. (*Elec.*) Spannung, das Potential; – ***difference,*** die Potentialdifferenz, der Spannungsabstand. **potentiality** [–ʃi'æliti], *s.* 1. die Möglichkeit; 2. innere Kraft. **potentially,** *adv.* möglicherweise, unter Umständen.

potentiometer [pətenʃi'ɔmitə], *s.* (*Elec.*) das Potentiometer, der Spannungsteiler.

potheen, *see* **poteen.**

pother ['pʌðə, 'pɔðə], **1.** *s.* 1. der Lärm, Aufruhr, Tumult, die Aufregung; ***be in a – about,*** *see* **2**; 2. der Rauch, Dunst. **2.** *v.i.* viel Aufhebens machen (***about,*** von), sich aufregen (über (*Acc.*)). **3.** *v.t.* verwirren, aufregen.

pot|-herb, *s.* das Küchenkraut, Suppengemüse. **-hole,** *s.* 1. das Schlagloch; 2. (*Geol.*) der Strudelkessel, Gletschertopf; 3. (*coll.*) unterirdische Höhle. **-holing,** *s.* (*coll.*) die Höhlenforschung. **--hook,** *s.* 1. der Kesselhaken; 2. (*coll.*) (*in writing*) die Schlinge. **--house,** *s.* die Kneipe. **--hunter,** *s.* (*coll.*) der Preisjäger.

potion ['pouʃən], *s.* der (Arznei)trank.

pot|-luck, *s.* (*coll.*) ***take –,*** essen, was es gerade gibt; fürliebnehmen mit dem, was es gerade (zum Essen) gibt. **-man,** *s. See* **--boy.**

potpourri [poupu:'ri:], *s.* 1. wohlriechende Kräuter (*pl.*); 2. (*Mus. etc.*) das Potpourri.

pot|-roast, *s.* das Schmorfleisch, der Schmorbraten. **-sherd,** *s.* (*Archaeol.*) die (Topf)scherbe. **--shot,** *s.* der Zufallsschuß.

pottage ['pɔtidʒ], *s.* (*obs.*) (dicke) Suppe.

potted ['pɔtid], *adj.* 1. eingemacht (*meat*); 2. eingetopft, Topf– (*plant*); 3. (*coll.*) konzentriert, gekürzt; 4. (*music*) zur späteren Wiedergabe aufgenommen, auf Band (gespielt).

[1]**potter** ['pɔtə], *s.* der Töpfer; ***–'s clay,*** der Töpferton; ***–'s wheel,*** die Töpferscheibe.

[2]**potter, 1.** *v.i.* (*coll.*) (*oft.* – ***about***) herumbummeln, herumlungern; herumhantieren, herumkramen, herumpfuschen (***at***, an (*Dat.*)). **2.** *v.t.* – ***away,*** vertrödeln, verplempern (*one's time*).

pottery ['pɔtəri], *s.* 1. Töpferwaren, Tonwaren (*pl.*), das Steingut, Steingeschirr, die Keramik; 2. Töpferei.

pottle [pɔtl], *s.* (*obs.*) 1. (ein) Maßkrug (*approx.* $2\frac{1}{4}$ *l.*); 2. das Obstkörbchen.

potty ['pɔti], **1.** *adj.* (*sl.*) 1. verrückt, närrisch (***about***, auf (*Acc.*)), vernarrt (in (*Acc.*)); 2. lächerlich, unbedeutend. **2.** *s.* (*coll.*) (*also* ***baby's*** –) das Töpfchen.

pouch [pautʃ], **1.** *s.* die Tasche, (*also Zool.*) der Beutel; (*Mil.*) die Patronentasche; (*coll.*) der Tabaksbeutel; ***–es under one's eyes,*** Falten unter den Augen. **2.** *v.i.* sich bauschen, sackförmig fallen. **3.** *v.t.* bauschen, sackähnlich formen.

pouf(fe) [pu:f], *s.* 1. das Sitzkissen, Sitzpolster; 2. (*of dress*) die Tournüre.

poulterer ['poultərə], *s.* der Geflügelhändler.

poultice ['poultis], **1.** *s.* der (Brei)umschlag, die Breipackung. **2.** *v.t.* einen Umschlag machen (*Dat.*) *or* auflegen auf (*Acc.*).

poultry ['poultri], *s.* das Geflügel, Federvieh. **poultry|-farm,** *s.* der Geflügelhof, die Geflügelfarm. **--farming,** *s.* die Geflügelzucht. **--yard,** *s.* der Hühnerhof.

[1]**pounce** [pauns], **1.** *v.i.* springen, (sich) stürzen (***at***, auf (*Acc.*)), herfallen (über (*Acc.*)); – ***(up)on,*** herabstoßen *or* (her)niederstoßen auf (*Acc.*); (*fig.*) sich stürzen auf (*Acc.*) (*mistake etc.*), losgehen auf (*Acc.*), losziehen *or* loslegen gegen (*a p.*). **2.** *s.* 1. das Herabstoßen, Herabschießen; 2. der Sprung, Satz; ***on the –,*** sprungbereit, auf dem Sprung; ***make a –,*** einen Sprung tun, einen Satz machen; 3. (*obs.*) der Fang, die Klaue, Kralle (*of predators*).

[2]**pounce, 1.** *s.* 1. das Bimssteinpulver, Glättpulver; 2. Holzkohlenpulver, Pauspulver. **2.** *v.t.* 1. mit Bimsstein abreiben, bimsen, glätten; 2. durchpausen.

[1]**pound** [paund], *s.* das Pfund (*weight and money*); – ***avoirdupois,*** (englisches Handels)pfund (= *456.6 g.*); – ***troy,*** das Apothekerpfund (= *373.25 g.*); – ***sterling,*** das Pfund Sterling; *5* ***–s*** (*£5*), 5 Pfund (Sterling); 5 ***–s*** (***5 lb.***) ***of sugar,*** 5 Pfund Zucker.

[2]**pound, 1.** *s.* 1. die Hürde, der Pferch; 2. Pfandstall. **2.** *v.t.* einpferchen, einsperren.

[3]**pound, 1.** *v.t.* 1. zerstoßen, zerstampfen, zerschlagen, zermalmen; 2. (*coll.*) hämmern, schlagen, klopfen; hämmern *or* trommeln auf (*Dat.*). **2.** *v.i.* 1. (los)schlagen, (los)hämmern (***at, on,*** auf (*Acc.*)); 2. (*of a ship, machine*) stampfen, (*of a p.*) (*usu.* – ***along***) wuchtig einhergehen.

poundage ['paundidʒ], *s.* 1. das Gewicht (in Pfunden); 2. die Bezahlung pro Pfund Gewicht; 3. die Gebühr *or* Provision pro Pfund (Sterling).

pounder ['paundə], *s.* der Stößel; *see* [3]**pound.**

-pounder, *s. suff.* der . . . pfünder (*cannon*).

pounding ['paundiŋ], *s.* 1. das Zerstoßen; Schlagen; Stampfen; 2. (*Mil.*) (*coll.*) schwerer Beschuß.

pour [pɔ:], **1.** *v.t.* gießen, schütten (***out of, from,*** aus; ***in(to),*** in (*Acc.*); ***(up)on,*** auf (*Acc.*)); (*fig.*) – ***cold water on,*** einen Dämpfer aufsetzen (*Dat.*); (*fig.*) – ***oil on the flame(s),*** Öl ins Feuer gießen; (*fig.*) – ***oil on troubled waters,*** Öl auf die Wogen gießen *or* schütten, die Gemüter beruhigen; – ***forth*** or ***out,*** (aus)strömen lassen; vergießen (*blood*), hervorstoßen (*curses*), verschwenden, wegwerfen (*money*), ausschütten (*feelings*); – ***off,*** (vorsichtig) abgießen, dekantieren; – ***out,*** einschenken, eingießen (*drinks*). **2.** *v.i.* strömen, fließen, gießen rinnen; sich ergießen (***from,*** aus); – ***down,*** niederströmen, herabfließen; – ***forth*** or ***out,*** sich ergießen, herausströmen (***from,*** aus); (*usu. fig.*) – ***in,*** hereinströmen; – ***over,*** überfließen; – (***with rain***), (in Strömen) gießen; ***it never rains but it –s,*** ein Unglück kommt selten allein.

pourboire [puə'bwɑ:], *s.* das Trinkgeld.

pouring ['pɔ:riŋ], **1.** *adj.* – ***rain,*** strömender Regen. **2.** *adv.* – ***wet,*** triefend naß, patschnaß.

pourparler ['puəpɑ:'lei], *s.* (vorbereitende) Besprechung.

pout [paut], **1.** *v.i.* schmollen, maulen, die Lippen spitzen *or* verziehen; (her)vorstehen (*of lips*). **2.** *v.t.* aufwerfen, spitzen (*lips*). **3.** *s.* das Schmollen, der Flunsch; ***put on a –,*** einen Flunsch ziehen. **pouter(-pigeon),** *s.* die Kropftaube.

poverty ['pɔvəti], *s.* 1. die Armut; 2. (*fig.*) Dürftigkeit, Armseligkeit, Ärmlichkeit (***of,*** *Gen.*), der Mangel (an (*Dat.*)). **poverty-stricken,** *adj.* 1. verarmt; 2. (*fig.*) armselig, dürftig.

powder ['paudə], **1.** *s.* 1. der Staub, das Pulver; ***grind to –,*** pulverisieren; ***not worth – and shot,*** keinen Schuß Pulver wert; ***the smell of –,*** die Kriegserfahrung; 2. (*cosmetic*) der Puder. **2.** *v.t.* 1. zerreiben, pulverisieren; 2. pudern (*the face*); 3. bestreuen, bepudern (***with,*** mit). **3.** *v.i.* 1. sich pulverisieren lassen, zu Pulver werden; 2. (*cosmetic*) sich pudern. **powdered,** *adj.* 1. pulverisiert, Puder–; – ***milk,*** das Milchpulver, die Trockenmilch; – ***sugar,*** der Puderzucker; 2. bepudert (*face*); 3. bestreut.

powder|-magazine, *s.* das Pulvermagazin, (*fig.*) Pulverfaß. **–mill,** *s.* die Pulverfabrik. **--monkey,** *s.* (*Naut. Hist.*) der Pulverjunge. **--puff,** *s.* die Puderquaste. **--room,** *s.* (*Am.*) die Damentoilette. **--train,** *s.* der Pulversatz, Brandsatz. **powdery,** *adj.* 1. staubig, pulverig, pulverartig; – ***snow,*** der Pulverschnee; 2. zerreibbar.

power ['pauə], **1.** *s.* 1. die Macht, Gewalt, Herrschaft, Autorität (***over,*** über (*Acc.*)), der Einfluß (auf (*Acc.*)); (*Pol.*) ***balance of –,*** das Gleichgewicht der Kräfte; ***have – over,*** Einfluß haben auf (*Acc.*); ***absolute –,*** unbeschränkte Macht; ***in –,*** an der Macht, am Ruder; ***in his –,*** in seiner Gewalt; ***come into –,*** zur Macht gelangen *or* kommen; 2. das Vermögen, die Fähigkeit, Kraft, Energie; ***reasoning –,*** die Urteilskraft; – ***of resistance,*** die Widerstandskraft; ***do all in one's –,*** alles tun, was in seiner Macht steht; ***be out of*** or ***not in his –,*** nicht in seiner Macht stehen; 3. *pl.* Fähigkeiten, Kräfte, Anlagen (*pl.*), das Talent; ***–s of description,*** das Talent zur Beschreibung; ***–s of the mind,*** Geisteskräfte; 4. (*Pol.*) (*oft. pl.*) der Staat, die Regierung, Macht; ***the –s that be,*** die maßgeblichen Stellen, die Obrigkeit; ***belligerent –s,*** kriegführende Mächte; ***great European –s,*** europäische Großmächte; ***military –,*** die Kriegsmacht; ***sea –,*** die Seemacht; 5. *pl.* ***–s of darkness,*** die Mächte der Finsternis; ***the heavenly –s,*** die himmlischen Mächte; 6. (*Math.*) die Potenz; ***raise to the fourth –,*** in die vierte Potenz erheben; 7. (*Elec.*) der Starkstrom; 8. (*Opt.*) die Vergrößerungskraft, (Brenn)stärke; 9. (*Law*) Vollmacht, Ermächtigung, Befugnis; – ***of attorney,*** die Vollmacht; ***discretionary –, plenary –(s),*** die Generalvollmacht, unumschränkte Vollmacht; ***full –s,*** die Vollmacht; ***have full –s,*** Vollmacht haben; 10. (*Tech.*) die Leistung (*of a machine*); ***brake –,*** die Bremsleistung; ***effective –,*** die Nutzkraft; ***horse––,*** die Pferdestärke, Pferdekraft; ***mechanical –,*** mechanische Kraft; ***penetrating –,*** die Durchschlagskraft; ***rated –,*** die Nennleistung; ***steam –,*** die Dampfkraft; ***water –,*** die Wasserkraft; 11. (*Rad.*) die Sendestärke, Sendeleistung; 12. (*coll.*) ***a – of,*** eine Masse *or* große Menge von. **2.** *v.t.* mit Kraft versehen.

power|-amplification, *s.* (*Rad.*) die Leistungsverstärkung. **--amplifier,** *s.* der Endverstärker. **--assisted,** *adj.* – ***steering,*** die Kraftsteuerung. **--boat,** *s.* das Motorboot. **--cable,** *s.* die Starkstromleitung. **--circuit,** *s.* der Kraftstromkreis.

--consumption, *s.* der Energieverbrauch, Stromverbrauch. **--current,** *s.* der Starkstrom. **--drill,** *s.* elektrische Bohrmaschine. **--drive,** *s.* der Kraftantrieb; (*Av.*) der (Vollgas)sturzflug. **--driven,** *adj. See* **--operated.** – **factor,** *s.* der Leistungsfaktor.

powerful ['pauəful], *adj.* stark, kräftig, mächtig, gewaltig; (*fig.*) leistungsfähig, wirksam, eindringlich, nachdrücklich; – ***engine,*** starker Motor; – ***man,*** starker *or* kräftiger Mann (*physical*), (*fig.*) mächtiger *or* einflußreicher *or* bedeutender Mann; – ***argument,*** überzeugendes Argument.

power|-glider, *s.* der Motorsegler. **--house,** *s.* das Maschinenhaus; (*fig.*) die Kraftquelle; *see also* **--station.**

powerless ['pauəlis], *adj.* 1. kraftlos, machtlos, unfähig, ohnmächtig; 2. (*fig.*) (*also* – ***to act***) unvermögend, wirkungslos, einflußlos. **powerlessness,** *s.* 1. die Schwäche Machtlosigkeit, Ohnmacht; 2. Wirkungslosigkeit, Einflußlosigkeit, das Unvermögen.

power|-loading, *s.* (*Av.*) die Leistungsbelastung. **--loom,** *s.* mechanischer Webstuhl. **--loving,** *adj.* machtliebend. **--operated,** *adj.* kraftbetätigt, kraftbetrieben. **--pack,** *s.* (*Rad.*) der Netzteil. **--plant,** *s.* die Kraftanlage. **--point,** *s.* der Starkstromstecker. **--politics,** *pl.* die Machtpolitik. **--shovel,** *s.* die Löffelbagger. **--station,** *s.* das Kraftwerk, Elektrizitätswerk. **--steering,** *s.* die Servolenkung. **--stroke,** *s.* (*Tech.*) der Arbeitshub, Arbeitstakt. **--supply,** *s.* (*Elec.*) die Energieversorgung, Stromversorgung, (*Rad.*) der Netzanschluß. **--tool,** *s.* der Elektro-Handbohrer. **--transformer,** *s.* (*Rad.*) der Netztransformator. **--transmission,** *s.* die Energieübertragung. **--unit,** *s.* das Triebwerk. **--valve,** *s.* (*Rad.*) die Lautsprecherröhre (*receiver*), Senderöhre, Großleistungsröhre (*transmitter*). **--winch,** *s.* die Kraftwinde.

pow-wow ['pauwau], **1.** *s.* 1. indianischer Medizinmann; 2. die Krankheitsbeschwörung; 3. (*coll.*) Besprechung. **2.** *v.i.* (*coll.*) besprechen, debattieren.

pox [pɔks], *pl.* (*sing. constr.*) 1. Pocken, Blattern (*pl.*); 2. (*coll.*) die Syphilis.

practicability [præktikə'biliti], *s.* 1. die Durchführbarkeit, Ausführbarkeit, Tunlichkeit; 2. Brauchbarkeit, Anwendbarkeit, Verwendbarkeit; 3. (*of road etc.*) Wegsamkeit, Befahrbarkeit. **practicable** ['præktikəbl], *adj.* 1. durchführbar, ausführbar, möglich, tunlich; 2. brauchbar, anwendbar, verwendbar; 3. (*of road etc.*) begehbar, befahrbar, wegsam, gangbar, fahrbar.

practical ['præktikl], *adj.* 1. praktisch, angewandt (*opp. theoretical*); – ***chemistry,*** angewandte Chemie; – ***knowledge,*** praktische Kenntnisse; – ***politics,*** das (politisch) Erreichbare; 2. praktisch, tatsächlich, wirklich, faktisch; 3. praktisch *or* in der Praxis tätig, ausübend; – ***man,*** der Mann der Praxis; 4. praktisch veranlagt, aufs Praktische gerichtet, für die Praxis geeignet (*of p.*), praktisch (anwendbar), ausführbar, zweckmäßig, tunlich, nützlich, brauchbar (*of a th.*); ***for all – purposes,*** praktisch, in praktischer Hinsicht; 5. – ***joke,*** der Jux, Streich, handgreiflicher Spaß, grober Scherz; – ***joker,*** der Spaßvogel. **practicality** [–'kæliti], *s.* 1. das Praktische; 2. praktische Veranlagung (*of a p.*), praktische Anwendbarkeit, die Tunlichkeit (*of a th.*). **practically,** *adv.* 1. sachdienlich; 2. (*coll.*) praktisch, faktisch, nahezu, so gut wie.

practice ['præktis], **1.** *s.* 1. die Praxis (*opp. theory*; *also Law, Med.*), Gewohnheit, der Brauch, Usus, übliches Verfahren; ***in –,*** in Wirklichkeit, in der Praxis, tatsächlich; ***make a – of it,*** es sich (*Dat.*) zur Gewohnheit machen; ***put into –,*** in die Tat umsetzen, praktisch anwenden, ausführen, verwirklichen; 2. die (Aus)übung; ***in –,*** in der Übung; ***out of –,*** aus der Übung; (*Prov.*) – ***makes perfect,*** Übung macht den Meister; 3. (*Math.*) Welsche Praktik; 4. *pl.* Umtriebe, Machenschaften, Praktiken, Ränke, Kniffe, Schliche (*pl.*). **2.** *v.t., v.i.* (*esp. Am.*) *see* **practise. 3.** *attrib. adj.* Übungs–.

practise ['præktis], **1.** *v.t.* 1. tätig sein in (*Dat.*), ausüben (*a profession etc.*); – ***what you preach,*** üben selbst was du predigst; 2. ausbilden, schulen, drillen (*a p.*); 3. sich üben in (*Dat.*), (ein)üben (*piece of music etc.*). **2.** *v.i.* 1. (sich) üben, sich einspielen (*esp. Mus.*); 2. praktizieren; – ***at the bar,*** als Rechtsanwalt praktizieren; 3. – ***upon,*** mißbrauchen, sich (*Dat.*) zunutze machen, Kapital schlagen aus; ausnützen, sein Spiel treiben mit (*a p.*). **practised,** *adj.* geübt, geschult (*in,* in (*Dat.*)).

practitioner [præk'tiʃənə], *s.* 1. der Praktiker; 2. Rechtsanwalt; 3. ***general*** or ***medical*** **–,** praktischer Arzt.

praecipe ['pri:sipi], *s.* (*Law*) die Aufforderung, der Befehl. **praemunire** [–mju:'niəri], *s.* (*Law*) die Vorladung wegen Überschreitung der Kirchengewalt. **praeposter** [pri'pɔstə], *s. See* **prefect. praetor** [–tə], *s.* (*Hist.*) der Prätor. **praetorian** [pri'tɔ:riən], *s.* prätori(ani)sch.

pragmatic [præg'mætik], *adj.* 1. pragmatisch; (*fig.*) (*Hist.*) – ***sanction,*** die Staatssanktion; 2. (*fig.*) *see* **pragmatical. pragmatical,** *adj.* 1. pragmatisch, praktisch, sachlich, nüchtern; 2. tätig, geschäftig; 3. (über)eifrig, aufdringlich, zudringlich; 4. eigensinnig, eigenwillig, rechthaberisch, von sich eingenommen. **pragmatism** ['prægmətizm], *s.* 1. der Pragmatismus; 2. die Aufdringlichkeit, Zudringlichkeit; 3. der Übereifer; 4. Eigensinn. **pragmatize** ['prægmətaiz], *v.t.* als real darstellen.

Prague [prɑ:g], *s.* Prag (*m.*).

prairie ['prɛəri], *s.* die Prärie, Steppe, Grasebene. **prairie-dog,** *s.* der Präriehund.

praise [preiz], **1.** *s.* das Lob, die Anerkennung; Lobpreisung, das Preisen; ***in – of,*** zum Lobe *or* zu Ehren (*Gen.*); ***be loud in one's –s,*** des Lobes voll sein; ***unstinted –,*** uneingeschränktes Lob. **2.** *v.t.* loben, rühmen; (*Eccl.*) lobsingen (*Dat.*), (lob)preisen; – ***to the sky*** or ***skies,*** in den Himmel erheben. **praise|worthiness,** *s.* die Preiswürdigkeit, Löblichkeit. **-worthy,** *adj.* löblich, lobenswert.

[1]**pram** [prɑ:m], *s.* (*Naut.*) der Prahm.

[2]**pram** [præm], *s.* (*coll. for*) **perambulator.**

prance [prɑ:ns], *v.i.* 1. tänzeln (*as horse*); (einher)stolzieren, paradieren; 2. (*coll.*) hüpfen, springen.

prandial ['prændiəl], *adj.* Mahl(zeits)–.

[1]**prank** [præŋk], *s.* 1. der Possen, (Schelmen)streich; ***play a – on him,*** ihm einen Streich spielen; 2. (*fig. coll. as of machine*) die Faxe.

[2]**prank, 1.** *v.t.* – ***up,*** – ***out,*** herausputzen, schmücken. **2.** *v.i.* prangen, prunken.

prase [preiz], *s.* (*Min.*) der Pras(em).

prate [preit], **1.** *v.i.* schwatzen, plappern. **2.** *v.t.* (her)ausplappern. **3.** *s.* das Gerede, Geschwätz. **prating, 1.** *s. See* **prate, 3. 2.** *adj.* schwatzhaft, geschwätzig.

prattle ['prætl], **1.** *v.i.* (kindisch) schwatzen, plappern, plaudern, schwafeln. **2.** *s.* das Geschwätz, Geplapper, Geplauder. **prattler,** *s.* der (die) Schwätzer(in).

prawn [prɔ:n], *s.* (*Ichth.*) die Steingarnele.

pray [prei], **1.** *v.i.* 1. (*Eccl.*) beten (*to,* zu; *for,* um); – ***for the dead,*** für die Verstorbenen beten; – ***for rain,*** um Regen beten; 2. bitten, ersuchen, nachsuchen (*for,* um); – ***tell me . . .,*** bitte, sagen Sie mir . . .. **2.** *v.t.* 1. flehen zu (*God*); 2. (inständig) bitten, ersuchen, anflehen (*for,* um) (*a p.*); 3. erbitten, erflehen (*a th.*).

prayer [prɛə], *s.* 1. das Gebet; (*oft. pl.*) der Gottesdienst, die Andacht; ***at –,*** beim Gebet; ***offer a –,*** ein Gebet verrichten; ***say one's –s,*** beten, sein Gebet verrichten; ***Book of Common Prayer,*** *see* **prayer-book**; ***Lord's Prayer,*** das Vaterunser; ***morning –s,*** die Morgenandacht; 2. die Bitte, das Flehen, Ersuchen, Gesuch. **prayer-book,** *s.* das Gebetbuch (der anglikanischen Kirche). **prayerful,** *adj.* 1. andächtig, fromm; 2. (*fig.*) inständig. **prayer|-meeting,** *s.* die Gebetsversammlung. **--rug,** *s.* der Gebetsteppich. **--wheel,** *s.* die Gebetsmühle.

praying ['preiiŋ], **1.** *adj.* betend; (*Zool.*) – ***mantis,*** die Gottesanbeterin. **2.** *s.* das Beten, Gebet.

pre— [pri(:)], *pref.* (*time*) vor(her); (*place*) (da)vor.

preach [pri:tʃ], **1.** *v.i.* 1. predigen, eine Predigt halten (*to*, vor (*Dat.*)); – ***on*** (*or rare* ***to***), predigen über (*Acc.*)) (*a text*); 2. (*fig.*) ermahnen, Moral predigen. **2.** *v.t.* 1. predigen; – ***a sermon,*** eine Predigt halten; 2. (*fig.*) ermahnen zu, verkünden. **preacher,** *s.* 1. der Prediger; 2. (*fig.*) Ermahner (*of*, zu). **preachify** [–ifai], *v.i.* (*coll.*) salbadern. **preaching, 1.** *s.* 1. die Lehre, Predigt; das Predigen; 2. (*coll.*) die Salbaderei, Moralpredigt. **2.** *adj.* Prediger–. **preachment,** *s.* (*coll.*) *see* **preaching, 1,** 2. **preachy,** *adj.* (*coll.*) salbungsvoll, moralisierend.

preamble [pri'æmbl], *s.* 1. die Vorrede, Präambel, das Vorwort; 2. die Einleitung, das Vorspiel, der Auftakt.

prearrange [priə'reindʒ], *v.t.* vorbereiten, vorher anordnen *or* bestimmen. **prearrangement,** *s.* vorherige Bestimmung, die Abmachung.

prebend ['prebənd], *s.* die Pfründe, Präbende. **prebendal** [pri'bendl], *adj.* Pfründen–. **prebendary,** *s.* der Pfründner, Präbendar, Stiftsherr, Domherr.

precarious [pri'kɛəriəs], *adj.* 1. (*Law*) widerruflich; 2. (*fig.*) unsicher, prekär, gefährdet, bedenklich, fragwürdig, anfechtbar; 3. gefährlich, gefahrvoll. **precariousness,** *s.* die Ungewißheit, Unsicherheit.

precatory ['prekətəri], *adj.* eine Bitte enthaltend, Bitt–.

precaution [pri'kɔ:ʃən], *s.* 1. die Vorsicht; 2. Vorsichtsmaßregel, Vorkehrung; ***as a –,*** vorsichtshalber; ***take –s,*** Vorkehrungen *or* Vorsorge treffen. **precautionary,** *adj.* 1. vorbeugend, Vorsichts–; – ***measures,*** Vorkehrungen, Vorsichtsmaßregeln; 2. Warn(ungs)–.

precede [pri'si:d], **1.** *v.t.* 1. vorangehen, vorausgehen, vorgehen (*Dat.*); – ***hostilities by a declaration of war,*** Feindseligkeiten (*Dat.*) eine Kriegserklärung vorausgehen lassen *or* vorausschicken, Feindseligkeiten durch eine Kriegserklärung einleiten *or* einführen; 2. (*of a p.*) den Vortritt *or* Vorrang *or* Vorzug haben vor (*Dat.*). **2.** *v.i.* vorangehen, vorausgehen, vorhergehen.

precedence ['presidəns], *s.* 1. das Vorhergehen, Vorausgehen, Vorangehen, die Priorität; 2. der Vortritt, Vorrang; ***order of –,*** die Rangordnung; ***take –,*** den Vortritt *or* Vorrang haben (***of, over,*** vor (*Dat.*)); ***yield – to,*** den Vorrang einräumen (*Dat.*). **precedency,** *s.* (*obs.*) *see* **precedence. precedent, 1.** [pri'si:dənt], *adj.* (*rare*) vorhergehend. **2.** ['presidənt], *s.* (*Law*) der Präzedenzfall (*also fig.*), (*Law*) die Vorentscheidung; ***create*** or ***set a –,*** einen Präzedenzfall schaffen *or* abgeben; ***without*** (***a***) –, ohne Beispiel, noch nicht dagewesen. **preceding** [pri'si:diŋ], **1.** *adj.* vorhergehend. **2.** *prep.* vor (*Dat.*).

precentor [pri'sentə], *s.* (*Eccl.*) der Vorsänger, Kantor, Chorleiter.

precept ['pri:sept], *s.* 1. die Vorschrift, Regel, Richtlinie, Richtschnur, das Gebot; 2. (*Law*) schriftliche Anordnung, der Gerichtsbefehl; 3. die Lehre, Unterweisung. **preceptive** [pri'septiv], *adj.* 1. befehlend, verordnend; 2. didaktisch, belehrend, ermahnend, lehrhaft. **preceptor** [pri'septə], *s.* der Lehrer, Schulleiter.

precession [pri'seʃən], *s.* (*Astr.*) die Präzession; – (***of the equinoxes***) das Vorrücken (der Tag– und Nachtgleichen).

precinct ['pri:sinkt], *s.* 1. die Umfriedung, der Domplatz; 2. (*Am.*) Wahlbezirk; 3. (*pl. fig.*) Bereich, die Umgebung, Nachbarschaft; ***within the –s of,*** innerhalb (der Grenzen) (*Gen.*).

preciosity [preʃi'ɔsiti], *s.* die Affektiertheit, Geziertheit, Ziererei, Preziosität.

precious ['preʃəs], **1.** *adj.* 1. edel, Edel– (***stones, metals etc.***), kostbar; – ***stone,*** der Edelstein; 2. (*fig.*) wertvoll, unschätzbar (*to*, für); 3. (*fig.*) affektiert, geziert, preziös; 4. (*coll. iron.*) schön, nett, höchst; (*coll.*) ***a – lot he cares!*** es ist ihm total schnuppe! **2.** *s.* ***my –,*** mein Liebling. **3.** *adv.* – ***few,*** verflucht wenige; – ***little,*** verflucht wenig. **preciousness,** *s.* 1. die Kostbarkeit; 2. Affektiertheit.

precipice ['presipis], *s.* die Klippe; (*also fig.*) der Abgrund; ***on the brink of a –,*** am Rande des Abgrunds.

precipitable [pri'sipitəbl], *adj.* (*Chem.*) fällbar, abscheidbar, niederschlagbar.

precipitance, precipitancy [pri'sipitəns(i)], *s.* die Eile, Hast, Übereilung, Überstürzung.

precipitant [pri'sipitənt], **1.** *s.* (*Chem.*) das Abscheidungsmittel, Fäll(ungs)mittel. **2.** *adj.* übereilt, voreilig, vorschnell, hastig.

precipitate, 1. [pri'sipiteit], *v.t.* 1. hinabstürzen; 2. (*fig.*) (hinein)stürzen, versetzen (***into***, in (*Acc.*)); 3. heraufbeschwören, beschleunigen, herbeiführen (*events*); 4. (*Chem.*) niederschlagen, (aus)-fällen; 5. (*Meteor.*) verflüssigen, niederschlagen. **2.** [–teit], *v.i.* 1. hinabstürzen, (hin)stürzen; 2. (*Chem.*) sich ablagern *or* setzen; 3. (*Meteor.*) sich niederschlagen, Niederschlag bilden. **3.** [–tət], *adj.* 1. jäh(lings), steil; 2. (*fig.*) eilig, hastig, voreilig, vorschnell, unüberlegt, übereilt, überstürzt. **4.** [–tət], *s.* der Niederschlag, das Präzipitat.

precipitately [pri'sipitətli], *adv.* hastig, übereilt, überstürzt, kopfüber. **precipitateness,** *s.* die Voreiligkeit, Übereilung, Überstürzung. **precipitation** [–'teiʃən], *s.* 1. das Herabstürzen, jäher Sturz; 2. die Hast, Übereilung, Überstürzung; 3. (*Chem.*) Fällung, Präzipitation; 4. (*Meteor.*) der Niederschlag.

precipitous [pri'sipitəs], *adj.* 1. jäh, steil, abschüssig; 2. (*fig.*) überstürzt, übereilt. **precipitousness,** *s.* die Steilheit.

précis ['preisi:], **1.** *s.* gedrängte Darstellung, die Zusammenfassung, Übersicht. **2.** *v.t.* kurz zusammenfassen.

precise [pri'sais], *adj.* 1. präzis, exakt, genau, richtig; 2. (*of a p.*) korrekt, steif, pedantisch, gewissenhaft, umständlich. **preciseness,** *s.* (peinliche) Genauigkeit, (ängstliche) Gewissenhaftigkeit, die Pedanterie. **precisian** [–'siʒən], *s.* der Rigorist, Pedant. **precision** [–'siʒən], *s.* die Genauigkeit, Exaktheit, Präzision; – ***adjustment,*** die Feinstellung; – ***bombing,*** der Punktzielbombenwurf; – ***engineering,*** die Feinmechanik; – ***instrument,*** das Präzisionsinstrument. **precisionist** [–'siʒənist], *s.* der Sprachreiniger, Purist.

preclude [pri'klu:d], *v.t.* 1. ausschließen (***from,*** von); 2. zuvorkommen (*Dat.*), vorbeugen (*Dat.*), verhindern (*a th.*), hindern (*a p.*) (***from,*** an (*Dat.*); ***from doing,*** zu tun). **preclusion** [–'klu:ʒən], *s.* 1. die Ausschließung, der Ausschluß (***from,*** von); 2. die Verhinderung. **preclusive** [–'klu:siv], *adj.* 1. ausschließend; 2. (ver)hindernd; ***be – of,*** *see* **preclude.**

precocious [pri'kouʃəs], *adj.* frühreif (*also of p.*), vorzeitig, frühzeitig; altklug (*of p.*). **precociousness, precocity** [–'kɔsiti], *s.* die Frühzeitigkeit, Frühreife, (*of a p.*) Frühreife, Altklugheit.

precognition [pri:kəg'niʃən], *s.* 1. die Vorkenntnis; 2. (*Scots Law*) Voruntersuchung.

preconceive [pri:kən'si:v], *v.t.* sich (*Dat.*) vorher ausdenken *or* vorstellen; ***–d opinion*** *or* **preconception** [–'sepʃən], *s.* vorgefaßte Meinung, das Vorurteil.

preconcert [pri:kən'sə:t], *v.t.* vorher verabreden *or* vereinbaren *or* abmachen.

precondition [pri:kən'diʃən], **1.** *s.* die Vorbedingung; ***make it a – of,*** es zur Vorbedingung machen für. **2.** *v.t.* die Vorbedingung sein für.

preconize ['pri:kənaiz], *v.t.* öffentlich verkünden *or* (*R.C.*) bestätigen (*appointment*).

preconsider [pri:kən'sidə], *v.t.* vorher überlegen. **preconsideration** [–'reiʃən], *s.* vorherige Überlegung.

precursor [pri'kə:sə], *s.* 1. der Vorläufer, Vorbote; 2. (Amts)vorgänger. **precursory,** *adj.* vorbereitend, einleitend.

predaceous (*Am.*), **predacious** [pri'deiʃəs], *adj.* vom Raube lebend, Raub(tier)–.

predate ['pri:'deit], *v.t.* 1. zurückdatieren (*cheque etc.*); 2. zurückreichen bis zur Zeit vor (*Dat.*), zeitlich vorangehen (*Dat.*).

predator ['predətə], *s.* 1. das Raubtier; 2. raubgieriger Mensch. **predatory** [–ri], *adj.* plündernd, räuberisch, Raub–; – ***bird,*** der Raubvogel; – ***war,*** der Raubkrieg.

predecease [pri:di'si:s], *v.t.* früher sterben als, sterben vor (*Dat.*).

predecessor ['pri:disesə], *s.* der Vorgänger (*of p. or th.*), *pl.* (*of p. only*) Vorfahren (*pl.*).

predestinate, **1.** [pri:'destineit], *v.t.* (vorher)-bestimmen, auserwählen, ausersehen (***to,*** für *or* zu), (*esp. Eccl.*) prädestinieren. **2.** [–nət], *adj.* auserwählt, prädestiniert. **predestination** [–'neiʃən], *s.* 1. die Vorherbestimmung; 2. (*Eccl.*) Gnadenwahl, Prädestination. **predestine** [pri:'destin], *v.t. See* **predestinate.**

predeterminable [pri:di'tə:minəbl], *adj.* vorherbestimmbar. **predeterminate** [–minət], *adj.* vorherbestimmt. **predetermination** [–'neiʃən], *s.* 1. die Vorherbestimmung; 2. vorgefaßter Entschluß. **predetermine** [–'tə:min], *v.t.* vorher bestimmen *or* beschließen *or* festsetzen.

predial ['pri:diəl], *adj.* (*Law*) Land–, Grund–, Guts–, Prädial–.

predicable ['predikəbl], **1.** *adj.* aussagbar, (*of a p.*) beilegbar (*Dat.*). **2.** *s.* (*Phil.*) ***–s,*** Prädikabilien, Prädikate, Allgemeinbegriffe (*pl.*).

predicament [pri'dikəmənt], *s.* 1. (*Phil.*) die Grundform der Aussage, Kategorie; 2. (*fig.*) schlimme *or* mißliche Lage.

predicate, **1.** ['predikeit], *v.t.* 1. aussagen, behaupten; 2. (*Phil.*) prädizieren; 3. (*coll.*) (be)gründen, basieren (***on,*** auf (*Acc.*)). **2.** [–kət], *s.* 1. (*Gram.*) das Prädikat, die Satzaussage; 2. (*Phil.*) Aussage. **3.** *adj.* (*Gram.*) Prädikat(s)–, prädikativ. **predication** [–'keiʃən], *s.* die Aussage, Behauptung. **predicative** [pri'dikətiv], *adj.* 1. aussagend, Aussage–, behauptend; 2. (*Gram.*) *see* **predicate, 3.**

predict [pri'dikt], *v.t.* voraussagen, vorhersagen, weissagen, prophezeien; (*Artil.*) ***–ed position,*** der Vorhaltepunkt. **predictable,** *adj.* vorherzusagen(d), voraussagbar, berechenbar. **prediction** [–'dikʃən], *s.* die Voraussage, Vorhersage, Weissagung, Prophezeiung. **predictor,** *s.* 1. der Prophet, Weissagende(r); 2. (*Artil.*) das Kommandogerät, Leitgerät.

predilection [pri:di'lekʃən], *s.* die Vorliebe, Voreingenommenheit (***for,*** für).

predispose [pri:dis'pouz], *v.t.* 1. im voraus geneigt machen (***to,*** zu *or* für); 2. (*esp. Med.*) anfällig *or* empfänglich machen, einnehmen, prädisponieren (für). **predisposition** [–pə'ziʃən], *s.* 1. die Geneigtheit, Neigung (***to,*** zu); 2. (*Med., fig.*) Prädisposition, Anfälligkeit, Empfänglichkeit (***to,*** für).

predominance [pri'dəminəns], *s.* 1. das Vorwiegen, Überwiegen, Vorherrschen, Übergewicht (***in,*** in (*Dat.*); ***over,*** über (*Acc.*)); 2. die Vorherrschaft, Überlegenheit. **predominant,** *adj.* vorherrschend, vorwiegend, überwiegend; überlegen; ***be –,*** vorherrschen, vorwiegen, überwiegen. **predominate** [–eit], *v.i.* vorherrschen, vorwiegen, überwiegen, das Übergewicht *or* die Oberhand haben (***over,*** über (*Acc.*)). **predominating,** *adj. See* **predominant.**

pre-eminence [pri:'eminəns], *s.* der Vorrang, Vorzug (***over,*** vor (*Dat.*)), die Überlegenheit (über (*Acc.*)). **pre-eminent,** *adj.* hervorragend; ausgezeichnet, vorzüglich; ***be –,*** hervorragen, sich hervortun (***among,*** unter (*Dat.*); ***in,*** in (*Dat.*); ***for,*** wegen).

pre-empt [pri:'empt], *v.t.* 1. durch Vorkaufsrecht erwerben; 2. (*coll.*) mit Beschlag belegen. **pre-emption** [–'empʃən], *s.* der Vorkauf; das Vorkaufsrecht. **pre-emptive,** *adj.* Vorkaufs–.

preen [pri:n], **1.** *v.t.* putzen (*feather*) (*of birds*); ***– o.s.,*** sich putzen (*of birds*); (*fig.*) sich brüsten (***on,*** mit), sich etwas einbilden (auf (*Acc.*)). **2.** *attrib. adj.* (*Orn.*) – ***gland,*** die Bürzeldrüse.

pre-engage [pri:in'geidʒ], *v.t.* im voraus verpflichten (*a p.*), vorbestellen (*a th.*). **pre-engagement,** *s.* vorher eingegangene Verbindlichkeit, vorhergegangenes Versprechen, vorherige Verpflichtung *or* Bestellung, die Vorbestellung.

pre-exist [pri:ig'zist], *v.i.* vorher vorhanden *or* dasein, früher existieren, präexistieren (*of the soul*). **pre-existence,** *s.* früheres Vorhandensein *or* Dasein, (*Eccl.*) die Präexistenz. **pre-existent,** *adj.* früher vorhanden, vorher existierend.

prefab ['pri:fæb], *s.* (*coll.*) das Fertighaus. **prefabricate** [–'fæbrikeit], *v.t.* vorfabrizieren, vorfertigen, (genormte) Fertigteile herstellen für. **prefabrication** [–'keiʃən], *s.* die Vorfertigung, Fertigbauweise.

preface ['prefəs], **1.** *s.* die Vorrede, das Geleitwort, Vorwort, (*also fig.*) die Einleitung. **2.** *v.t.* mit einer Vorrede versehen, (*also fig.*) einleiten (***with,*** mit; ***by saying,*** indem (er *etc.*) sagt). **prefatory** [–təri], *adj.* einleitend, Einleitungs–; – ***note,*** die Vorbemerkung, das Vorwort.

prefect ['pri:fekt], *s.* 1. (*Pol.*) der Präfekt, Statthalter; – ***of police,*** der Polizeipräsident (*of Paris*); 2. der Aufsichtsschüler, Vertrauensschüler. **prefecture** [–fektʃə], *s.* die Präfektur.

prefer [pri'fə:], *v.t.* 1. (es) vorziehen *or* bevorzugen, lieber haben *or* sehen *or* mögen; – ***to watch rather than to play,*** lieber zusehen als spielen; – ***it done,*** lieber haben *or* sehen, daß es getan wird; – ***coffee to tea,*** (den) Kaffee dem Tee vorziehen; ***preferred stock,*** Vorzugsaktien (*pl.*); 2. vortragen, vorbringen, einreichen (***to,*** bei) (*complaint, request etc.*); – ***a charge,*** eine Klage vorbringen; – ***a claim,*** einen Anspruch erheben; 3. erheben, befördern (***to,*** zu) (*rank etc.*). **preferable** ['prefərəbl], *adj.* (*usu. pred.*) vorzuziehen(d) (***to,*** *Dat.*). **preferably** ['prefərəbli], *adv.* lieber, am liebsten *or* besten, vorzugsweise.

preference ['prefərəns], *s.* 1. der Vorzug, die Bevorzugung, der Vorrang (***of,*** *Gen.*; ***over, above, before,*** vor (*Dat.*)); ***do from –,*** vorziehen zu tun, vorzugsweise tun; ***give – to,*** den Vorzug geben (*Dat.*), vorziehen, bevorzugen; ***in – to,*** lieber als; 2. die Vorliebe (***for,*** für); ***by –,*** mit (besonderer) Vorliebe; ***have a – for,*** eine Vorliebe haben für; 3. (*Comm.*) das Vor(zugs)recht, die Priorität; Vergünstigung, der Vorzugstarif, Begünstigungstarif; – ***stock,*** Vorzugsaktien (*pl.*). **preferential** [–'renʃəl], *adj.* 1. bevorzugt, Vorzugs–; – ***treatment,*** die Vorzugsbehandlung; 2. (*Comm.*) bevorrechtet, Vorzugs–; – ***duty,*** der Begünstigungszoll, Präferenzzoll; – ***tariff,*** der Vorzugstarif. **preferentially,** *adv.* vorzugsweise.

preferment [pri'fə:mənt], *s.* 1. die Ernennung, Beförderung (***to,*** zu); 2. (*Eccl.*) das Ehrenamt.

prefiguration [pri:figə'reiʃən], *s.* 1. die Vorhergestaltung, Vorwegnahme; 2. das Urbild, Vorbild. **prefigure** [–'figə], *v.t.* 1. vorher darstellen, vorbilden; 2. als Vorbild darstellen, sich (*Dat.*) vorher ausmalen.

prefix ['pri:fiks], **1.** *v.t.* 1. vor(an)setzen (***to,*** *Dat.*), vorausgehen lassen; 2. (*Gram.*) vorsetzen. **2.** *s.* (*Gram.*) die Vorsilbe, das Präfix.

pregnancy ['pregnənsi], *s.* die Schwangerschaft (*of women*); Trächtigkeit (*of animals*); 2. (*fig.*) Prägnanz, Gedrängtheit, Bedeutungsschwere, der Bedeutungsgehalt, tiefer Sinn; 3. die Gedankenfülle, Schöpferkraft. **pregnant,** *adj.* 1. schwanger (*of women*); trächtig (*of animals*); 2. (*fig.*) prägnant, vielsagend, bedeutungsvoll, gewichtig, schwerwiegend; 3. ideenreich, gedankenreich; 4. fruchtbar, reich (***with,*** an (*Dat.*)); – ***with meaning,*** bedeutungsvoll; – ***with danger,*** voller Gefahr.

preheat ['pri:'hi:t], *v.t.* vorwärmen, anwärmen.

prehensile [pri'hensail], *adj.* Greif–, zum Greifen geeignet. **prehensility** [pri:hen'siliti], *s.* die Greiffähigkeit, das Greifvermögen. **prehension** [–ʃən], *s.* 1. das Fassen, (Er)greifen; 2. (*fig.*) Erfassen.

prehistoric [pri:his'tɔrik], *adj.* vorgeschichtlich, urgeschichtlich, prähistorisch. **prehistory** [–'histəri], *s.* die Vorgeschichte, Urgeschichte.

pre-ignition [pri:ig'niʃən], *s.* (*Motor.*) die Vorzündung, Frühzündung.

prejudge [pri:'dʒʌdʒ], *v.t.* vorschnell *or* im voraus beurteilen.

prejudice ['predʒudis], **1.** *s.* 1. das Vorurteil, die Voreingenommenheit; (*of a p.*) Befangenheit; ***have a – against*** (***in favour of***), ein Vorurteil haben gegen (für); 2. der Schaden, Nachteil; ***to the – of***, zum Schaden (*Gen.*) *or* Nachteil von; (*Law*) ***without –***, ohne Verzicht auf (mein *etc.*) Recht, unter Vorbehalt; ***without – to***, unbeschadet (*Gen.*), ohne Schaden für. **2.** *v.t.* 1. (*esp. Law*) benachteiligen, beeinträchtigen, schädigen; Abbruch tun (*Dat.*), schaden (*Dat.*); 2. (*a p.*) einnehmen, beeinflussen (***against***, gegen; ***in favour of***, für); mit einem Vorurteil erfüllen. **prejudiced** [–t], *adj.* (vor)eingenommen. **prejudicial** [–'diʃəl], *adj.* schädlich, nachteilig (***to***, für); ***be – to***, schaden (*Dat.*), Abbruch tun (*Dat.*).

prelacy ['preləsi], *s.* die Prälatenwürde, Prälatur; (*collect.*) Prälaten (*pl.*). **prelate** [–it], *s.* der Prälat. **prelatic(al)** [–'lætik(l)], *adj.* Prälaten–, prälatisch.

prelect [pri'lekt], *v.i.* Vorträge halten (***on***, über (*Acc.*); ***to***, vor (*Dat.*)); (*Univ.*) lesen. **prelection** [–kʃən], *s.* (öffentliche) Vorlesung, der Vortrag. **prelector,** *s.* der Dozent.

prelim ['pri:lim, pri'lim], *s.* (*Univ.*) (*coll.*) *see* ***preliminary examination.*** **preliminary** [pri'liminəri], **1.** *adj.* vorläufig, vorübergehend; einleitend, vorbereitend, Vor–; ***– discussion,*** die Vorbesprechung; (*Univ.*) ***– examination***, die Vorprüfung, Aufnahmeprüfung, (*Med.*) das Physikum; (*Law*) ***– inquiry,*** die Voruntersuchung; ***– measures,*** vorbereitende Maßnahmen; ***– remarks,*** die Vorbemerkung(en); (*Spt.*) ***– round,*** die Vorrunde; ***– steps,*** vorbereitende Schritte; ***– treatment,*** die Vorbehandlung; ***– work,*** die Vorarbeit. **2.** *s.* (*usu. pl.*) die Einleitung, Vorbereitung(en), vorbereitende Maßnahmen, Vorverhandlungen, erste Schritte, Präliminarien (*pl.*).

prelude, 1. ['prelju:d], *s.* 1. (*Mus.*) das Präludium; 2. (*fig.*) der Auftakt, das Vorspiel, die Einleitung (***to***, zu). **2.** ['prelju:d, pri'lju:d], *v.t.* (*fig.*) eröffnen, einleiten. **3.** ['prelju:d], *v.i.* (*Mus.*) präludieren; als Einleitung dienen.

premarital [pri:'mæritl], *adj.* vorehelich.

premature ['premətjuə], *adj.* 1. frühzeitig, vorzeitig, verfrüht, unzeitig; ***– birth,*** die Frühgeburt; (*Artil.*) ***– burst,*** der Frühsprenger; ***– death,*** frühzeitiger Tod; (*Motor.*) ***– ignition,*** die Frühzündung; 2. (*fig.*) voreilig, vorschnell, übereilt; 3. frühreif. **prematureness, prematurity** [–'tjuəriti], *s.* 1. die Frühreife; 2. Frühzeitigkeit, Vorzeitigkeit; 3. Voreiligkeit, Übereiltheit.

premedical [pri:'medikl], *adj.* vorklinisch (*studies*).

premeditate [pri(:)'mediteit], *v.t.* vorher überlegen, bedenken. **premeditated,** *adj.* vorsätzlich, mit Vorbedacht. **premeditation** [–'teiʃən], *s.* der Vorbedacht.

premier ['premiə], **1.** *adj.* erst, (rang)ältest, Haupt–. **2.** *s.* der Premierminister, Ministerpräsident, Staatschef.

première ['premiεə], *s.* die Premiere, Erstaufführung, Uraufführung.

premiership ['premiəʃip], *s.* die Ministerpräsidentschaft, das Amt des Staatschefs.

¹**premise** [pri'maiz], *v.t.* 1. vorausschicken, vorher erwähnen; 2. voraussetzen, postulieren.

²**premise** ['premis], *s.* 1. (*Phil.*) die Prämisse, der Vordersatz; die Voraussetzung; 2. *pl.* (*Law*) das Obenerwähnte.

premises ['premisiz], *pl.* (*coll.*) das Haus nebst Zugehör; Grundstück; Lokal; ***business –,*** Geschäftsräume (*pl.*); ***licensed –,*** das Schanklokal; ***on the –,*** im Hause; am Schankort; an Ort und Stelle.

premiss, *s. See* ²**premise,** 1.

premium ['pri:miəm], *s.* 1. die Prämie, der Preis; ***put a – on,*** einen Preis aussetzen für; 2. das Agio, Aufgeld, die Extradividende, Belohnung; (*Comm.*) ***be at a –,*** über Pari stehen; (*fig.*) hoch im Kurse stehen, nur für teures Geld zu haben sein, sehr gesucht *or* geschätzt sein; ***sell at a –,*** mit Gewinn verkaufen; 3. (*coll.*) die Versicherungsprämie; 4. das Lehrgeld (eines Lehrlings).

premonition [pre–, pri:mə'niʃən], *s.* die Warnung, (Vor)ahnung, das Vorgefühl. **premonitory** [pri'mɔnitəri], *adj.* warnend, anzeigend.

prenatal [pri:'neitl], *adj.* vorgeburtlich, vor der Geburt (eintretend).

prentice ['prentis], *s.* (*obs.*) *see* **apprentice.**

prenuptial [pri:'nʌpʃəl], *adj.* vorehelich.

preoccupancy [pri'ɔkjupənsi], *s.* 1. (das Recht der) vorherige(n) Besitznahme; 2. die Inanspruchnahme (***in***, durch), das Vertieftsein (in (*Acc.*)), Beschäftigtsein (mit). **preoccupation** [–'peiʃən], *s.* 1. das Vorurteil, die Voreingenommenheit; 2. Hauptbeschäftigung, Haupttätigkeit; Befangenheit, Zerstreutheit; *see also* **preoccupancy.**

preoccupy [pri'ɔkjupai], *v.t.* 1. vorher *or* vor einem andern in Besitz nehmen, vorwegnehmen; 2. (*a p.*) völlig in Anspruch nehmen, ausschließlich beschäftigen; ***be preoccupied,*** ganz in Anspruch genommen sein; zerstreut *or* geistesabwesend sein.

preordain [pri:ɔ:'dein], *v.t.* vorher bestimmen *or* anordnen.

prep [prep], *s.* (*sl.*) das Vorbereiten (*of lessons*); Hausaufgaben (*pl.*); (*coll.*) ***– school,*** die Vor(bereitungs)schule.

prepaid [pri:'peid], *adj.* vorausbezahlt, vorher bezahlt, (*of post*) (porto)frei, franko, frankiert; *see* **prepay.**

preparation [prepə'reiʃən], *s.* 1. die Vorbereitung; ***in –,*** in Vorbereitung (befindlich); ***in – for,*** als Vorbereitung für *or* auf (*Acc.*); ***make –s,*** Anstalten *or* Vorbereitungen treffen; 2. die Bereitschaft; 3. Bereitstellung, (Zu)bereitung (*of food etc.*), Herstellung, Aufbereitung (*of ores etc.*); 4. (*Chem., Med.*) das Präparat, Arzneimittel; 5. Präparieren, Vorbereiten (*of lessons*), Hausaufgaben (*pl.*). **preparative** [pri'pærətiv], **1.** *adj. See* **preparatory. 2.** *s.* die Vorbereitung (***for***, auf (*Acc.*) *or* für), vorbereitender Schritt (***to***, zu). **preparatory** [pri'pærətəri], *adj.* vorbereitend, Vorbereitungs–, Vor–; ***– department,*** die Vorschule; ***– school,*** die Vor(bereitungs)schule; (*Am.*) *See* ***Public school.*** ***– work,*** Vorarbeiten (*pl.*); ***be – to,*** vorbereiten; ***– to his departure,*** vors einer Abreise; ***– to departing,*** bevor *or* ehe er (*etc.*) abreiste.

prepare [pri'pεə], **1.** *v.t.* 1. vorbereiten; herstellen, (zu)bereiten (*food*); ***– a document,*** eine Schrift aufstellen; ***– one's lessons,*** sich für die Schule vorbereiten; 2. vorbereiten (***for***, für, zu *or* auf (*Acc.*)), geeignet *or* bereit *or* geneigt machen (zu), gefaßt machen (auf (*Acc.*)); ***– the ground for,*** den Boden bereiten für; ***– o.s. for,*** sich rüsten für, sich gefaßt machen auf (*Acc.*); ***– the way,*** Bahn brechen (***for***, *Dat.*); 3. (aus)rüsten, ausbilden, bereitstellen (***for***, für); ***– for action,*** bereitstellen (*troops*); 4. (*Tech.*) zurichten, zurechtmachen, anrichten, beschicken, bestellen, präparieren; 5. (*ore etc.*) aufbereiten. **2.** *v.i.* sich vorbereiten (***for***, auf (*Acc.*)) *or* anschicken (zu), Anstalten *or* Vorbereitungen treffen (für); ***– for war,*** (sich) zum Krieg rüsten; (*Mil.*) ***– to . . . !*** fertig zum . . . ! **prepared,** *adj.* 1. fertig, bereit, vorbereitet; 2. (*as food etc.*) zubereitet, hergestellt; 3. (*Tech.*) präpariert; 4. (*fig.*) gefaßt (***for***, auf (*Acc.*)); 5. bereit, gewillt, willig. **preparedness,** *s.* die Bereitschaft, das Vorbereitetsein, Gefaßtsein (***for***, auf (*Acc.*)).

prepay [pri:'pei], *irr.v.t.* vorausbezahlen, im voraus *or* pränumerando bezahlen; frankieren (*a letter*). **prepayment,** *s.* die Vorausbezahlung, Frankierung. *See* **prepaid.**

prepense [pri'pens], *adj.* (*Law*) vorbedacht, vorsätzlich; ***with*** or ***of malice –,*** in böswilliger Absicht.

preponderance [pri'pɔndərəns], *s.* 1. das Übergewicht (*also fig.*) (***over***, über (*Acc.*)); 2. (*fig.*)

Schwergewicht, überwiegende Zahl, das Überwiegen. **preponderant,** *adj.* vorwiegend, überwiegend; ***be* –,** überwiegen. **preponderate** [–eit], *v.i.* 1. überwiegen, vorwiegen, vorherrschen; 2. das Übergewicht haben (***over,*** über (*Acc.*)), (an Zahl) überlegen sein (*Dat.*), übersteigen (*Acc.*).

preposition [prepə'ziʃən], *s.* die Präposition, das Verhältniswort. **prepositional,** *adj.* präpositional.

prepositive [pri'pɔzitiv], *adj.* vor(an)gesetzt.

prepossess [pri:pə'zes], *v.t.* 1. (*esp. pass.*) (im voraus) einnehmen *or* erfüllen (***with,*** mit; ***in favour of,*** für; ***against,*** gegen); 2. günstig beeindrucken *or* beeinflussen (*a p.*). **prepossessed,** *adj.* voreingenommen; eingenommen (***by,*** durch). **prepossessing,** *adj.* einnehmend, gewinnend, sympathisch, anziehend. **prepossession** [–'zeʃən], *s.* die Voreingenommenheit (***in favour of,*** für), vorgefaßte Meinung (***for,*** von), das Vorurteil (***against,*** gegen).

preposterous [pri'pɔstərəs], *adj.* 1. verkehrt, unsinnig, widersinnig, widernatürlich, unnatürlich; 2. albern, lächerlich, absurd. **preposterousness,** *s.* die Widersinnigkeit, Lächerlichkeit.

prepotence, prepotency [pri'poutəns(i)], *s.* 1. die Vorherrschaft, Überlegenheit, Übermacht; 2. (*Biol.*) stärkere Vererbungskraft. **prepotent,** *adj.* 1. vorherrschend, überlegen, übermächtig; 2. (*Biol.*) sich stärker vererbend.

prepuce ['pri:pju:s], *s.* (*Anat.*) die Vorhaut.

prerequisite [pri:'rekwizit], **1.** *s.* die Vorbedingung, Voraussetzung. **2.** *adj.* vorauszusetzen(d), notwendig (***to,*** für).

prerogative [pri'rɔgətiv], **1.** *s.* das Vorrecht, Privileg(ium), die Prärogative; – ***of mercy,*** das Begnadigungsrecht; ***royal* –,** das Hoheitsrecht. **2.** *adj.* bevorrechtet, Vorzugs–.

presage ['presidʒ], **1.** *s.* 1. die Vorbedeutung, Ahnung, das Vorgefühl; 2. Omen, Warn(ungs)zeichen, Anzeichen, Vorzeichen. **2.** *v.t.* 1. vorhersagen, voraussagen, prophezeien, weissagen; 2. (vorher) anzeigen *or* ankündigen.

presbyopia [prezbi'oupiə], *s.* die Weitsichtigkeit. **presbyopic** [–'ɔpik], *adj.* weitsichtig.

presbyter ['prezbitə], *s.* 1. Kirchenälteste(r), der Kirchenvorsteher; 2. Hilfsgeistliche(r). **Presbyterian** [–'tiəriən], **1.** *adj.* presbyterianisch. **2.** *s.* der Presbyterianer. **Presbyterianism** [–'tiəriənizm], *s.* der Presbyterianismus. **presbytery,** *s.* 1. das Presbyterium, der (Presbyter)sprengel; 2. presbyterianische Kreissynode; 3. (*R.C.*) die Pfarre, das Pfarrhaus; 4. (*Archit.*) der Chorraum.

pre-school ['pri:sku:l], *adj.* vorschulisch (*training*), noch nicht schulpflichtig (*child*); – ***age,*** vorschulpflichtiges Alter.

prescience ['presiəns], *s.* das Vorherwissen, die Voraussicht. **prescient,** *adj.* vorherwissend (***of,*** *Acc.*); ***be* – *of,*** vorherwissen, voraussehen.

prescind [pri'sind], **1.** *v.t.* 1. (*fig.*) entfernen, (ab)trennen, loslösen (***from,*** von); 2. absondern, herausheben. **2.** *v.i.* – ***from,*** Abstand nehmen von, absehen von, beiseitelassen.

prescribe [pris'kraib], **1.** *v.t.* 1. vorschreiben (***a th. to him,*** ihm etwas); 2. (*Med.*) verordnen, verschreiben (***for*** (*a p.*), *Dat.*; ***for*** (*a complaint*), gegen); 3. (*Law*) durch Verjährung ungültig machen, verjähren lassen. **2.** *v.i.* 1. Anordnungen treffen, Vorschriften machen; 2. (*Med.*) ein Rezept ausstellen (***for,*** *Dat.*); 3. (*Law*) hinfällig werden, verjähren; Verjährung(srecht) beanspruchen *or* geltend machen (***for,*** für *or* auf (*Acc.*)).

prescript ['pri:skript], *s.* die Vorschrift, Anordnung. **prescription** [pris'kripʃən], *s.* 1. *See* **prescript**; 2. (*esp. Med.*) das Rezept; 3. (*Law*) die Verjährung; (*fig.*) althergebrachter Brauch; (*Law*) (*also* ***positive* –**) die Erwerbung durch ständigen Genuß, Ersitzung, altbestehendes Recht; ***negative* –,** (der Verlust durch) Verjährung. **prescriptive** [pris'kriptiv], *adj.* 1. verordnend; 2. (*Law*) durch ständigen Genuß erworben, durch Brauch gefestigt, ersessen; (*fig.*) altergebracht, (alt)herkömmlich; – ***debt,*** die Verjährungsschuld; – ***right,*** das Gewohnheitsrecht.

presence ['prezəns], *s.* 1. die Gegenwart, Anwesenheit, das Beisein, Vorhandensein, Auftreten; ***in the* – *of our chairman,*** im Beisein unseres Vorsitzenden; – ***of mind,*** die Geistesgegenwart; ***in the* – *of witnesses,*** vor Zeugen; 2. (unmittelbare) Nähe, (*of royalty etc.*) die Audienz; ***the* –,** die hohen Herrschaften selbst; ***in the* – *of danger,*** angesichts der Gefahr; ***page of the* –,** der Leibpage; 3. Äußere(s), das Aussehen, die Gestalt, äußere *or esp.* stattliche Erscheinung; das Auftreten, Benehmen, die Haltung; 4. (Geister)erscheinung.

presence-chamber, *s.* das Audienzzimmer.

[1]**present** ['preznt], **1.** *adj.* 1. (*time*) gegenwärtig, augenblicklich, jetzig, momentan, heutig (*day*), laufend (*year or month*), Gegenwarts–; ***the* – *day,*** die gegenwärtige Zeit; ***the* – *king,*** der jetzige König; – ***participle,*** das Mittelwort der Gegenwart, Partizip präsens; (*Artil.*) – ***position,*** der Abschußpunkt; (*Gram.*) – ***tense,*** die Gegenwart, das Präsens; – ***time,*** see – ***day***; – ***value,*** der Gegenwartswert, (*St. Exch.*) Tageswert; – ***writer,*** der Verfasser dieser Zeilen; 2. (*space*) anwesend, vorhanden, zugegen; –***!*** hier! ***be* – *at,*** zugegen sein bei, beiwohnen (*Dat.*), teilnehmen an (*Dat.*); – ***company,*** die Anwesenden; – ***company excepted,*** Anwesende *or* die Anwesenden (stets *or* immer) ausgenommen; – ***in a place,*** an einem Ort vorhanden; ***be* – *to my mind,*** mir gegenwärtig sein, mir vor den Augen stehen; 3. (*fig.*) fraglich, vorliegend; – ***case,*** vorliegender Fall. **2.** *s.* die Gegenwart, gegenwärtige Zeit; (*Gram.*) das Präsens, die Gegenwart; ***at* (*the*) –,** gegenwärtig, jetzt, momentan, im Augenblick; (*Comm.*) ***by the* –,** durch Gegenwärtiges; (*Law*) ***by these* –*s,*** hierdurch, hiermit; ***for the* –,** für jetzt, vorläufig, einstweilen, einstweilig.

[2]**present** [preznt], *s.* das Geschenk, die Gabe; ***make him a* – *of it,*** es ihm zum Geschenk machen, es ihm schenken.

[3]**present** [pri'zent], **1.** *v.t.* 1. (dar)bieten, vorbringen, vorlegen, einreichen; (*Mil., Comm.*) präsentieren; – ***an argument,*** ein Argument vorbringen; – ***arms,*** das Gewehr präsentieren; – ***a bill of exchange,*** einen Wechsel präsentieren *or* zum Akzept vorlegen; – ***a petition,*** ein Gesuch einreichen; 2. (*a p.*) vorstellen, vorführen (***to,*** *Dat.*), (bei Hofe) einführen; – ***at court,*** bei Hofe einführen; – ***o.s.,*** sich vorstellen, sich melden (***to,*** bei; ***for,*** zu); sich einfinden, erscheinen; sich bieten (*of a th.*); 3. überreichen, übergeben, schenken (*a gift*) (***to,*** *Dat.*), beschenken, bedenken (*a p.*) (***with,*** mit); – ***one's apologies,*** sich entschuldigen; – ***one's compliments*** or ***respects to him,*** sich ihm empfehlen; 4. (*fig.*) bieten, darstellen, vor Augen führen; vorführen, spielen, bringen (*play, film etc.*); – ***an appearance of,*** erscheinen als; – ***difficulties,*** Schwierigkeiten bieten; – ***a smile,*** ein lächelndes Gesicht zeigen; 5. richten, anlegen (*firearms*) (***at,*** auf (*Acc.*)). **2.** *s.* (*Mil.*) ***at the* –,** in Präsentierhaltung.

presentability [prizentə'biliti], *s.* (*coll.*) die Respektabilität, Stattlichkeit. **presentable** [pri'zentəbl], *adj.* 1. zur Darbietung geeignet, präsentierbar; 2. (*coll.*) annehmbar, ansehnlich, präsentabel.

presentation [prezn'teiʃən], *s.* 1. die Schenkung, (feierliche) Übergabe *or* Überreichung; – ***copy,*** das Freiexemplar, Widmungsexemplar; 2. das Geschenk, die Gabe; 3. (*Theat. etc.*) Vorführung, Aufführung, Darbietung, Vorstellung, Darstellung, Wiedergabe; 4. (*Comm.*) das Vorlegen, Vorzeigen, die Präsentation; ***on* –,** bei Sicht *or* Vorzeigung, gegen Vorlage; 5. (*Med.*) die Lage, Stellung (*of the foetus*); 6. (*Psych.*) Vorstellung; 7. Einführung, (formelle) Vorstellung (*at court*); 8. (*Eccl.*) Ernennung, der Vorschlag; das Vorschlagsrecht.

presentiment [pri'zentimənt], *s.* (böse) (Vor)ahnung, das Vorgefühl, die Vorempfindung.

presently ['prezntli], *adv.* 1. kurz darauf, bald (darauf), alsbald, in *or* binnen kurzer Zeit; 2. (*Scots or obs.*) jetzt, augenblicklich, zur Zeit.

presentment [pri'zentmənt], *s.* 1. das Bild, die Wiedergabe, Schilderung, (*Theat.*) Darstellung, Darbietung, Aufführung, Vorstellung; 2. (*Law*) die von der Anklagejury erhobene Anklage.

preservable [pri'zə:vəbl], *adj.* erhaltbar, zu erhalten(d); konservierbar.

preservation [prezə'veiʃən], *s.* 1. die (Auf)-bewahrung, Erhaltung, (Er)rettung (*from*, vor (*Dat.*)); – *of the countryside*, der Natur- und Heimatschutz; *in (a) good (state of)* –, gut erhalten, in gut erhaltenem Zustande; 2. das Einmachen, die Konservierung (*of fruit*). **preservative** [pri-'zə:vətiv], **1.** *adj.* bewahrend, erhaltend, schützend, Schutz–. **2.** *s.* 1. das Schutzmittel, Vorbeugungsmittel (*against, from*, gegen); 2. Konservierungsmittel.

preserve [pri'zə:v], **1.** *v.t.* 1. bewahren, (be)-schützen, behüten (*from*, vor (*Dat.*)) (*a p.*); *Heaven – me!* der Himmel bewahre mich! 2. erhalten, aufrechthalten, (bei)behalten; (*fig.*) – *one's gravity*, ernst bleiben; – *silence*, still bleiben, Stillschweigen bewahren; 3. aufheben, (auf)-bewahren, in gutem Zustande erhalten, konservieren; *well -d*, gut erhalten; 4. hegen (*game*); 5. einmachen, einlegen, einkochen (*fruit etc.*); *-d meat*, die Fleischkonserve. **2.** *s.* 1. (*also pl.*) Eingemachte(s), die Konserve; 2. (*also pl.*) (*Hunt.*) das Gehege; (*fig.*) Sondergebiet, Sonderinteresse; (*fig.*) *poach on his -s*, ihm ins Gehege kommen.

preserving-jar, *s.* das Einmachglas.

preset [pri:'set], *irr.v.t.* voreinstellen.

pre-shrunk ['pri:'ʃrʌŋk], *adj.* schrumpffest, dekatiert, sanforisiert.

preside [pri'zaid], *v.i.* den Vorsitz führen, das Präsidium haben, präsidieren, die Aufsicht führen (*at*, bei; *over*, über (*Acc.*)), vorstehen (*over, Dat.*); *be -d over by*, geleitet werden von.

presidency ['prezidənsi], *s.* 1. der Vorsitz, das Präsidium, die Oberaufsicht; 2. (*Pol.*) Präsidentschaft, Präsidialperiode. **president**, *s.* Vorsitzende(r), der Präsident (*also Pol.*); (*Comm. esp. Am.*) Direktor; *Lord President of the Council*, der Vorsitzende des Staatsrates. **presidential** [-'denʃəl], *adj.* Präsidenten–; – *address*, die Ansprache des Vorsitzenden; (*Pol.*) – *election*, die Präsidentenwahl; (*Pol.*) – *term*, die Amtsperiode des Präsidenten.

presidium [pri'zidiəm], *s.* das Präsidium.

press [pres], **1.** *v.t.* 1. (zusammen)drücken, (zusammen)pressen; – *the button*, auf den Knopf drücken; *he -ed my hand*, er drückte mir die Hand; 2. bügeln, plätten (*clothes*), keltern (*grapes*), (aus)-pressen (*juice*) (*from*, aus); 3. (*fig.*) (nieder)-drücken *or* lasten auf (*Acc.*), einen Druck ausüben auf (*Acc.*), in die Enge treiben, bedrücken, bedrängen, bestürmen, dringen in (*Acc.*), zusetzen (*Dat.*), hetzen, drängen, antreiben, zwingen; *see also* **pressed**; 4. aufdrängen, aufnötigen, eindringlich empfehlen (*upon, Dat.*); – *him for*, ihn eindringlich bitten um; – *him to go*, ihn dringend bitten zu gehen; 5. – *home an advantage*, einen Vorteil ausnutzen; – *one's point*, auf seiner Meinung nachdrücklich bestehen; 6. (*Mil., Naut.*) pressen, gewaltsam anheuern; – *into service*, zum Dienst pressen, (*fig.*) mißbrauchen als.
2. *v.i.* 1. drücken, (einen) Druck ausüben, schwer liegen; **2.** (sich) drängen (*of p.*); – *for*, drängen auf (*Acc.*), fordern, verlangen, dringend bitten um; – *forward*, vor(wärts)drängen; – *on*, weiterrücken, vorrücken; – *on with*, weitertreiben; 3. drängen, pressieren (*of time*); *the matter is not -ing*, die S. hat keine Eile; *see also* **pressing, 1**, 2.
3. *s.* 1. das Drücken, der Druck; Andrang, das Gedränge (*of people*); Drängen; der Drang, die Dringlichkeit, Eile, Hast; 2. (*Tech.*) Presse; Kelter (*for wine*), der Schrank (*for clothes etc.*); (*Typ.*) die Druckerpresse, Druckerei; das Drucken, der Druck; *pass for* –, das Imprimatur erteilen (*Dat.*); *ready for* –, druckreif, druckfertig; *come from the* –, die Presse verlassen; *get ready for* –, zum Druck fertig machen; *in the* –, unter der Presse, im Druck; *see a th. through the* –, den Druck einer S. überwachen; *go to* –, in Druck gehen; *send to* –, in Druck geben; 3. das Zeitungswesen, die Presse; *have a bad* –, ungünstig beurteilt *or* aufgenommen werden.

press|-agency, *s.* das Nachrichtenbüro, die Nachrichtenagentur. **--agent**, *s.* der Presseagent. **--box**, *s.* die Presseloge. **--button**, **1.** *s.* der Druckknopf. **2.** *adj. See* **push-button**. **--cake**, *s.* der Preßkuchen. **--conference**, *s.* die Pressekonferenz. – **copy**, *s.* 1. der Durchschlag; 2. das Rezensionsexemplar. – **cutting**, *s.* der Zeitungsausschnitt.

pressed [prest], *adj.* 1. (*Tech.*) Preß–; 2. (*fig.*) *be – for*, in Verlegenheit sein um; *be – for money*, in Geldverlegenheit sein; *be – for time*, keine Zeit *or* es eilig haben, unter Zeitdruck stehen; *hard* –, bedrängt. **presser**, *s.* 1. (*Tech.*) der Presser, (*Typ.*) Drucker; 2. (*Tech.*) die Presse, (*Typ.*) Druckwalze.

press|-fastener, *s.* der Druckknopf. **--gallery**, *s.* die Presse(galerie) (*House of Commons*). **-gang**, **1.** *s.* (*Naut. Hist.*) die Preßpatrouille. **2.** *v.t. See* **press, 1**, 6. **--guide**, *s.* der Zeitungskatalog.

pressing ['presiŋ], **1.** *adj.* 1. drückend, pressend; 2. (*fig.*) drängend, dringend, dringlich, angelegentlich, eilig; *be* –, drängen; 3. aufdringlich (*of a p.*). **2.** *s.* 1. das Pressen, Drücken; *--board*, das Preßbrett; *--iron*, das Bügeleisen, Plätteisen; *--roller*, die Druckwalze; 2. (*Tech.*) das Preßstück; 3. (*gramophone record*) der Plattenabdruck, die Preßplatte.

press| item, *s.* die Pressenotiz. **--key**, *s.* die Drucktaste. **-man**, *s.* 1. der Drucker; 2. Journalist, Pressevertreter. **-mark**, *s.* die Standortnummer, Signatur. – **photographer**, *s.* der Bildberichterstatt)er. **--proof**, *s.* letzte Korrektur. **--reader**, *s.* der Korrektor. **--room**, *s.* der Druckereiraum. **--stud**, *s.* der Druckknopf. **--up**, *s.* (*Gymn.*) der Liegestütz.

pressure ['preʃə], *s.* 1. das Drücken; der Druck (*also Meteor.*), (*Tech.*) die Druckkraft; *atmospheric* –, der Luftdruck; *blood* –, der Blutdruck; *high* –, (*Tech.*) der Hochdruck, (*Meteor.*) der Hochdruck, das Hoch; *low* –, (*Tech.*) der Niederdruck, (*Meteor.*) Tiefdruck, das Tief; *under* –, unter Druck (*also fig.*); 2. (*fig.*) der Druck, das Drängen, der Drang, die Dringlichkeit; Bedrückung, Last, der Zwang; *bring – to bear on him*, Druck auf ihn ausüben; – *of business*, der Drang der Geschäfte; *work at high* –, mit Hochdruck arbeiten; *put – on*, Druck *or* Zwang ausüben auf (*Acc.*); 3. die Knappheit, Not, Bedrängnis; *monetary* –, der Geldmangel, die Geldnot, Geldknappheit; – *of space*, der Raummangel.

pressure|-cabin, *s.* die Höhenkabine. **--cooker**, *s.* der Schnellkocher. **--gauge**, *s.* der Druckmesser, das Manometer. **--group**, *s.* die Interessengruppe. **--point**, *s.* (*Med.*) der Druckpunkt. **--pump**, *s.* die Druckpumpe. **--reading**, *s.* der Manometerstand. **--suit**, *s.* der (Über)druckanzug. **--tank**, *s.* der Druckkessel.

pressurize ['preʃəraiz], *v.t.* 1. (*Av.*) druckfest machen; *-d*, mit Druckausgleich; *-d cabin*, die Druckkabine; 2. (*coll.*) drangsalieren. **pressurizer**, *s.* die Druckanlage.

press-work, *s.* die Druck(er)arbeit.

prestidigitation [prestididʒi'teiʃən], *s.* die Taschenspielerkunst. **prestidigitator** [-'didʒiteitə], *s.* der Taschenspieler.

prestige [pres'ti:ʒ], *s.* das Ansehen, der Nimbus, das Prestige.

presto ['prestou], *adv.* (*Mus.*) schnell, geschwind; (*coll.*) *hey –!* im Handumdrehen, wie der Blitz.

pre-stressed concrete ['pri:'strest], *s.* der Spannbeton.

presumable [pri'zju:məbl], *adj.*, **presumably**, *adv.* vermutlich, mutmaßlich; wahrscheinlich, voraussichtlich.

presume [pri'zju:m], **1.** *v.t.* (als gegeben) annehmen, vermuten, voraussetzen; – ***him (to be) dead,*** seinen Tod vermuten; annehmen, daß er tot ist. **2.** *v.i.* sich erkühnen *or* erdreisten, sich (*Dat.*) herausnehmen *or* anmaßen, wagen; – ***(up)on,*** sich (*Dat.*) etwas einbilden auf (*Acc.*), pochen auf (*Acc.*); ausnutzen, mißbrauchen. **presumed** [–d], *adj.*, **presumedly** [–idli], *adv.* vermutlich, mutmaßlich, vermeintlich; ***presumed dead,*** verschollen. **presuming,** *adj.* anmaßend, vermessen.

presumption [pri'zʌmpʃən], *s.* 1. die Vermutung, Mutmaßung, Annahme; ***the – is that,*** es ist anzunehmen daß, es besteht Grund zu der Annahme daß; ***on the – that,*** in der Annahme daß; (*Law*) – ***of fact,*** die Tatsachenvermutung; 2. die Vermessenheit, Anmaßung, der Dünkel. **presumptive** [–'zʌmptiv], *adj.* mutmaßlich, präsumtiv; (*Law*) – ***evidence,*** der Indizienbeweis; (*Law*) – ***proof,*** der Wahrscheinlichkeitsbeweis; (*Law*) – ***title,*** präsumtives Eigentum; ***heir –,*** mutmaßlicher Erbe. **presumptuous** [–'zʌmptʃuəs], *adj.* anmaßend, vermessen. **presumptuousness,** *s.* die Anmaßung, Vermessenheit, der Dünkel.

presuppose [pri:sə'pouz], *v.t.* im voraus annehmen, voraussetzen, zur Voraussetzung haben. **presupposition** [–sʌpə'ziʃən], *s.* die Voraussetzung.

pretence [pri'tens], *s.* 1. die Vorspiegelung, Vortäuschung (***of,*** *Gen.*), der Vorwand (***of doing,*** zu tun *or* daß er (*etc.*) tue), Scheingrund; (*fig.*) Schein, die Verstellung, Maske, Finte; ***abandon the –,*** die Maske fallen lassen; ***under false –s,*** unter Vorspiegelung falscher Tatsachen; ***make a – of,*** sich (*Dat.*) den Anschein geben, als (täte man *etc.*); vortäuschen; ***make no – of being,*** sich (*Dat.*) nicht den Anschein geben zu sein; ***under the –,*** unter dem Vorwand; 2. die Anforderung (***to,*** an (*Acc.*)), der Anspruch (auf (*Acc.*)); ***make no – to,*** keinen Anspruch erheben auf (*Acc.*), keine Anforderung(en) stellen an (*Acc.*).

pretend [pri'tend], **1.** *v.t.* vortäuschen, vorspiegeln, vorschützen, (er)heucheln, simulieren. **2.** *v.i.* 1. sich (ver)stellen, heucheln, vorgeben; ***he is only –ing,*** er tut nur so; – ***to sleep,*** (so) tun, als ob man schliefe; 2. – ***to,*** Anspruch erheben auf (*Acc.*). **pretended,** *adj.* vorgetäuscht, vorgeblich, angeblich, vermeintlich. **pretender,** *s.* 1. der Heuchler, Scharlatan, Simulant; 2. Anspruchmachende(r) (***to,*** auf (*Acc.*)), der Bewerber (um); – ***to the throne,*** der Thronbewerber, Prätendent.

pretense, (*Am.*) *see* **pretence.**

pretension [pri'tenʃən], *s.* 1. der Anspruch (***to,*** auf (*Acc.*); 2. die Anmaßung, der Dünkel. **pretentious** [–ʃəs], *adj.* (*of a p.*) anmaßend, großspurig, protzig, angeberisch, (*of a th.*) anspruchsvoll, hochtrabend, prätentiös, prunkhaft. **pretentiousness,** *s.* die Anmaßung, Großspurigkeit (*of a p.*); Prunkhaftigkeit, Gespreiztheit (*of a th.*).

preterite ['pretərit], **1.** *adj.* Vergangenheits–. **2.** *s.* (*Gram.*) das Präteritum, (erste) Vergangenheit.

preterition [pri:tə'riʃən], **pretermission** [–'miʃən], *s.* 1. die Nichterwähnung, Auslassung, Unterlassung; 2. Übergehung. **pretermit** [–'mit], *v.t.* auslassen, unterlassen, übergehen. **preternatural** [–'nætʃərəl], *adj.* übernatürlich, abnorm, anormal.

pretext ['pri:tekst], *s.* der Vorwand, die Entschuldigung, Ausrede, Ausflucht; ***make a – of,*** vorschützen, vorgeben; ***on*** or ***under the –,*** unter dem Vorwand *or* Schein (***of,*** *Gen.*).

pretonic [pri:'tɔnik], *adj.* (*Phonet.*) vortonig.

prettify ['pritifai], *v.t.* (*coll.*) verschönern. **prettily** [–li], *adv.* schön, hübsch, niedlich, nett. **prettiness,** *s.* 1. die Schönheit, Hübschheit, Niedlichkeit, Nettigkeit, Anmut, der (Lieb)reiz; 2. die Geziertheit, Gespreiztheit (*of style*). **pretty, 1.** *adj.* 1. hübsch, schön, niedlich, nett, anmutig, reizend, anziehend; – ***face,*** das Puppengesicht; ***my – one,*** mein Liebchen; 2. (*coll.*) ganz schön, fein, prächtig, beträchtlich; – ***kettle of fish,*** schöne Bescherung; ***a – penny,*** eine schöne Stange Geld; (*coll.*) ***be sitting –,*** fein 'raus sein. **2.** *adv.* (*coll.*) ziemlich, leidlich, einigermaßen; – ***considerable,*** ganz beträchtlich; – ***good,*** gar nicht schlecht; – ***much the same,*** ziemlich *or* ungefähr *or* nahezu dasselbe; – ***well*** (*before adj. or adv.*), fast, beinahe, nahezu.

prevail [pri'veil], *v.i.* 1. die Oberhand gewinnen, den Sieg davontragen, (ob)siegen (***over,*** über (*Acc.*)), sich durchsetzen *or* behaupten, erfolgreich sein (***against,*** gegen); 2. überhandnehmen, überwiegen, den Ausschlag geben; 3. (vor)herrschen, vorwiegen, häufig vorkommen, (weit) verbreitet sein; 4. – ***(up)on,*** überreden, bewegen (*a p.*); – ***(up)on o.s.,*** es übers Herz bringen. **prevailing,** *adj.* (vor)herrschend, obwaltend, allgemein (geltend).

prevalence ['prevələns], *s.* das (Vor)herrschen, Überhandnehmen, weite Verbreitung. **prevalent,** *adj.* (vor)herrschend, weit *or* allgemein verbreitet; ***be –,*** herrschen, grassieren.

prevaricate [pri'værikeit], *v.i.* Ausflüchte machen *or* gebrauchen. **prevarication** [–'keiʃən], *s.* die Umgehung *or* Verdrehung der Wahrheit, Ausflüchte (*pl.*). **prevaricator,** *s.* der Wortverdreher.

prevent [pri'vent], *v.t.* 1. verhindern, verhüten, zuvorkommen (*Dat.*), vorbeugen (*Dat.*); 2. abhalten (***from,*** von), hindern (an (*Dat.*)); – ***him from coming,*** – ***his*** (*coll.* ***him***) ***coming,*** sein Kommen verhindern, ihn vom Kommen abhalten, ihn am Kommen hindern. **preventable,** *adj.* abwendbar, verhütbar, zu verhüten(d).

prevention [pri'venʃən], *s.* 1. die Verhinderung, Verhütung; – ***of accidents,*** die Unfallverhütung; ***society for the – of cruelty to animals,*** der Tierschutzverein; 2. (*Med.*) die Vorbeugung; – ***is better than cure,*** Vorbeugen ist besser als Heilen. **preventive** [–tiv], **1.** *adj.* verhütend, vorbeugend; – ***custody,*** die Schutzhaft, Sicherungsverwahrung; – ***medicine,*** die Gesundheitspflege, Präventivbehandlung; – ***measure,*** die Vorsichtsmaßnahme; – ***service,*** der Küstenschutzdienst. **2.** *s.* das Vorbeugungsmittel, Schutzmittel, Präventivmittel, Abwehrmittel (***against,*** gegen).

preview ['pri:vju:], *s.* die (Film)vorschau, private Voraufführung (*film*) *or* Vorbesichtigung (*exhibition etc.*).

previous ['pri:viəs], **1.** *adj.* 1. vorhergehend, vorangehend, vorausgehend; – ***conviction,*** die Vorstrafe; ***without – notice,*** ohne vorherige Ankündigung; (*Parl.*) ***move the – question,*** das Übergehen zur Tagesordnung beantragen; 2. (*coll.*) voreilig, übereilt, verfrüht. **2.** *adv.* – ***to,*** vor (*Dat.*), bevor. **previously,** *adv.* vorher. **previousness,** *s.* (*coll.*) die Voreiligkeit, Verfrühtheit.

prevision [pri:'viʒən], *s.* das Vorhersehen, die Voraussicht, (Vor)ahnung, Voraussage, Vorhersage.

pre-war ['pri:'wɔ:], **1.** *adj.* Vorkriegs–. **2.** *adv.* (*coll.*) vor dem Krieg.

prey [prei], **1.** *s.* der Raub, die Beute; (*fig.*) das Opfer; ***beast of –,*** das Raubtier; ***bird of –,*** der Raubvogel; (*fig.*) ***be(come)*** or ***fall a – to,*** zum Opfer fallen (*Dat.*); ***the – of circumstances,*** das Opfer der Verhältnisse; ***be (an) easy – for,*** leicht zum Opfer fallen (*Dat.*). **2.** *v.i.* – ***on,*** Beute *or* Jagd machen auf (*Acc.*), erbeuten; (*fig.*) berauben, ausbeuten; fressen *or* nagen *or* zehren an (*Dat.*); ***it –ed on his mind,*** es bedrückte ihn, es ging ihm die ganze Zeit im Kopf herum; ***–ing anxiety,*** verzehrende Angst.

price [prais], **1.** *s.* der (Kauf)preis (***of,*** für), Kosten (*pl.*) (*Gen.*); (*St. Exch.*) der Kurs(wert); (*St. Exch.*) ***asked –,*** der Briefkurs; ***at any –,*** um jeden Preis; ***not at any –,*** um keinen Preis; ***catalogue*** or ***list –,*** der Listenpreis; (*St. Exch.*) ***closing –,*** der Schlußkurs; (*coll.*) ***he has his –,*** er ist bestechlich; (*fig.*) ***at a heavy –,*** um einen hohen Preis; (*Spt.*) ***long (short) –,*** gewagte (günstige) Wette; (*St. Exch.*) ***offered –,*** der Geldkurs; ***opening –,*** der Eröffnungskurs; ***quote –s,*** Preise nennen, (*St. Exch.*) Kurse notieren; ***set a – on,*** einen Preis (aus)setzen auf (*Acc.*); ***share –,*** der Aktienkurs; ***what is the – of?*** wieviel kostet? ***what – . . . ?*** (*Spt.*) welche Chance für . . . ? (*sl.*) wie steht es mit . . . ?

2. *v.t.* 1. den Preis festsetzen für; – ***goods in the window,*** Waren im Schaufenster auszeichnen; 2. (*fig.*) bewerten, Wert beilegen *or* beimessen (*Dat.*); 3. (*coll.*) nach dem Preis fragen.

price|-ceiling, *s.* die Preisgrenze, der Höchstpreis. **--control,** *s.* die Preisüberwachung, Preisbindung, der Preisstopp; die Zwangswirtschaft. **--current,** *s. See* **--list. --cut,** *s.* die Preissenkung. **--cutting,** *s.* die Preisunterbietung, Preisdrückerei. **priced,** *adj.* mit Preisangaben; (*as suff.*) . . . im Preis, zu . . . Preisen. **price|-fixing,** *s.* die Preisfestsetzung. **--increase,** *s.* die Preiserhöhung, Preissteigerung.

price|less ['praislis], *adj.* unschätzbar, unbezahlbar; (*coll.*) köstlich. **--level,** *s.* das Preisniveau, der Preisstand, die Preishöhe. **--limit,** *s.* die Preisgrenze. **--list,** *s.* die Preisliste, das Preisverzeichnis, (*St. Exch.*) der Kurszettel. **--maintenance,** *s.* die Preisbindung. **--margin,** *s.* die Preisspanne. **--range,** *s.* die Preislage. **--structure,** *s.* das Preisgefüge. **--tag, --ticket,** *s.* der Preiszettel, das Preisschild. **pricey** [–i], *adj.* (*coll.*) teuer, kostspielig.

prick [prik], **1.** *v.t.* 1. (durch)stechen; (*fig.*) – ***the bubble,*** den Schwindel aufdecken; – ***one's finger,*** sich (*Dat.*) in den Finger stechen; ***his conscience –s him,*** sein Gewissen plagt ihn, er bekommt Gewissensbisse; 2. Löcher stechen in (*Acc.*), (durch)lochen, punktieren; ausstechen (*a pattern*); – ***off,*** abstecken (*with dividers*); – ***out,*** ausstechen, ausradeln (*a pattern*), auspflanzen, umpflanzen, verpflanzen (*seedlings*); 3. – ***up,*** aufrichten, spitzen (*ears, as dogs*); (*fig.*) – ***up one's ears,*** die Ohren spitzen. **2.** *v.i.* 1. stechen, prickeln; 2. (*obs.*) die Sporen geben; 3. – ***up,*** sich aufrichten, in die Höhe stehen (*as dog's ears*). **3.** *s.* 1. der Stich; (*B.*) ***kick against the –s,*** wider den Stachel löcken; 2. (*fig.*) stechender Schmerz, das Stechen; –(*s*) ***of conscience,*** Gewissensbisse (*pl.*); 3. (*vulg.*) der Schwanz.

prick-eared, *adj.* 1. spitzohrig (*of dog*); 2. (*fig.*) wachsam, aufmerksam. **pricker,** *s.* der Stecher, Stichel, Pfriem(en), die Pfrieme, Ahle, das Stecheisen, Locheisen, (Loch)rädchen.

pricket ['prikit], *s.* der Spießbock.

prickle [prikl], **1.** *s.* 1. der Stachel, Dorn; 2. das Prickeln, Kribbeln (*of the skin*). **2.** *v.i.* stechen, prickeln, kribbeln. **prickliness,** *s.* die Stach(e)ligkeit. **prickly,** *adj.* 1. stach(e)lig, dornig; (*Bot.*) Stachel–; – ***pear,*** der Feigenkaktus, Indische Feige; 2. (*fig.*) prickelnd, stechend; (*Med.*) – ***heat,*** Hitzblattern (*pl.*), der Schweißfriesel; 3. (*coll.*) kniffIig, heikel.

pricy, *see* **pricey.**

pride [praid], **1.** *s.* 1. der Stolz (*in,* auf (*Acc.*)); ***the – of his family,*** der Stolz seiner Familie; – ***of place,*** der Ehrenplatz, bevorzugte Stellung; (*fig.*) der Standesdünkel; ***give – of place to,*** große Bedeutung einräumen (*Dat.*); ***take – of place,*** den ersten Rang einnehmen; ***take*** (***a***) – ***in,*** stolz sein auf (*Acc.*); 2. das Selbstgefühl; die Überheblichkeit, der Hochmut; (*Prov.*) – ***goes before a fall,*** Hochmut kommt vor dem Fall; 3. (*obs. fig.*) Glanz, die Pracht, Blüte, Zierde; 4. der Federschmuck (*of a peacock*); 5. Trupp, das Rudel, die Schar (*of lions*). **2.** *v.t.* – ***oneself on,*** stolz sein auf (*Acc.*), sich brüsten mit, sich rühmen (*Gen.*).

priest [pri:st], *s.* der Priester, Geistliche(r); (*Jew.*) ***high –,*** der Hohepriester. **priestcraft,** *s.* die Pfaffenpolitik, Pfaffenlist. **priesthood,** *s.* das Priesteramt; (*collect.*) die Priesterschaft, Priester (*pl.*). **priestliness,** *s.* die Priesterlichkeit. **priestly,** *adj.* priesterlich, Priester–. **priest-ridden,** *adj.* unter Pfaffenherrschaft stehend.

¹**prig** [prig], (*sl.*) **1.** *s.* der Langfinger. **2.** *v.t.* mausen, stibitzen, klauen.

²**prig,** *s.* selbstgefälliger Pedant, dünkelhafter Tugendheld, der Tugendbold. **priggish,** *adj.* selbstgefällig, dünkelhaft. **priggishness,** *s.* die Einbildung, Dünkelhaftigkeit, der Dünkel, geistiger Hochmut.

prim [prim], **1.** *adj.* steif, formell, gedrechselt, geziert, affektiert, zimperlich, spröde. **2.** *v.t.* affektiert verziehen (*the mouth*).

primacy ['praiməsi], *s.* der *or* das Primat (*also Eccl.*), der Vorrang, bevorzugte Stellung.

prima donna ['pri:mə'dɔnə], *s.* erste Sängerin, (*also fig.*) die Primadonna.

prima facie ['praimə'feiʃi:], **1.** *adv.* auf den ersten Blick. **2.** *adj.* – ***evidence,*** (scheinbar) glaubhafter Beweis.

¹**primage** ['praimidʒ], *s.* (*Naut.*) das Primgeld, der Frachtzuschlag.

²**primage,** *s.* (*Tech.*) der Wassergehalt (im Dampf).

primal ['praiməl], *adj.* erst, früh(e)st, ursprünglich, grundlegend, wesentlich. **primarily** [–mərili], *adv.* 1. ursprünglich, anfänglich, zuerst; 2. vor allem, in erster Linie, in der Hauptsache, hauptsächlich.

primary ['praiməri], **1.** *adj.* 1. erst, früh(e)st, ursprünglich, anfänglich, Ur–, Anfangs–, Erst–; (*Geog.*) paläozoisch; (*Am.*) – ***election,*** die Vorwahl; – ***instinct,*** der Urinstinkt; (*Am.*) – ***meeting,*** die Parteiversammlung zur Aufstellung der Wahlkandidaten; – ***rocks,*** das Urgestein; 2. elementar, grundlegend, Elementar–, Grund–; – ***colour,*** die Grundfarbe; – ***meaning,*** die Grundbedeutung; – ***instruction,*** der Volksschulunterricht; – ***school*** die Grundschule, Volksschule, Elementarschule; 3. hauptsächlich, Haupt–, wichtigst, primär; (*Elec.*) – ***cell,*** das Primärelement; – ***coil*** or ***winding,*** die Primärspule; – ***concern,*** die Hauptsorge; – ***current,*** der Primärstrom; – ***feather,*** die Schwungfeder; ***of – importance,*** von höchster Wichtigkeit; – ***stress,*** der Hauptakzent. **2.** *s.* 1. (*Elec.*) der Primärkreis; 2. (*Astr.*) der Hauptplanet; 3. *See* – ***election***; 4. *pl. See* – ***feathers.***

primate ['praimeit], *s.* 1. der Primas; ***Primate of England,*** der Erzbischof von York; ***Primate of all England,*** der Erzbischof von Canterbury; 2. (*Zool.*) der Primat, das Herrentier. **primateship,** *s.* der *or* das Primat.

prime [praim], **1.** *adj.* 1. erst; – ***cost,*** der Einkaufspreis, Selbstkostenpreis, Gestehungskosten (*pl.*); – ***vertical*** (***circel***), erster Vertikalkreis; 2. wichtigst, Haupt–; ***of – importance,*** von höchster Wichtigkeit; – ***minister,*** der Premierminister, Ministerpräsident; – ***mover,*** (*Phys.*) bewegende Kraft, die Primärkraft; (*Tech.*) Antriebsmaschine, der Schlepper; (*fig.*) treibende Kraft, die Triebfeder; – ***reason,*** der Hauptgrund; 3. (*Comm., coll.*) vorzüglich, Prima–, erstklassig; – ***bill,*** vorzüglicher Wechsel; – ***quality,*** erst(klassig)e Qualität; 4. (*Math.*) unteilbar, teilerfremd, Prim–; – ***number,*** die Primzahl. **2.** *s.* 1. höchste Vollkommenheit, die Blüte, Vollkraft, der Kern; ***in his –,*** im besten Mannesalter, in der Blüte seiner Jahre; 2. (*Math.*) die Primzahl; 3. (*R.C.*) erste Gebetstunde, die Prim; 4. (*Fenc.*) Prim; 5. (*Mus.*) Prim(e). **3.** *v.t.* 1. mit Zündpulver versehen *or* laden (*guns*); scharf machen (*bombs*); 2. in Tätigkeit setzen (*pumps*); 3. (*Paint.*) grundieren; 4. (*fig.*) vorher informieren, vorbereiten, einweihen, instruieren, präparieren; 5. (*sl.*) betrunken machen.

primer ['praimə], *s.* 1. die Zündpille, Sprengkapsel, das Zündhütchen; (*Min.*) der Zünddraht; (*of gun*) Zündbolzen, die Zündnadel; 2. (*Paint.*) Grundiermasse, Spachtelmasse; 3. das Elementarbuch, die Fibel, Einführung; 4. ['primə], (*Typ.*) ***great –,*** die Tertia; (*Typ.*) ***long –,*** die Korpus(schrift).

primeval [prai'mi:vəl], *adj.* uranfänglich, uralt, urzeitlich, Ur–.

priming ['praimiŋ], *s.* 1. (*Paint.*) die Grundierung; 2. (*fig.*) Vorbereitung; 3. (*Artil.*) das Fertigmachen; die Zündmasse, der Zündsatz; 4. – ***of the tide,*** verfrühtes Eintreten der Flut. **priming|-charge,** *s.* die Beiladung, Zündladung. **--colour,** *s.* die Grundierfarbe. **--pump,** *s.* die Einspritzpumpe. **--wire,** *s.* der Zünddraht.

primitive ['primitiv], **1.** *adj.* 1. erst, früh(e)st, ursprünglich; Ur–, einfach, anfängerhaft; ***Primitive Church,*** die Urkirche; ***Primitive Germanic,*** urgermanisch; (*Eccl.*) ***Primitive Methodists,***

(Original)methodisten (*pl.*); – ***races,*** Naturvölker, Urvölker (*pl.*); 2. primitiv, unzivilisiert, urtümlich, urzuständlich; 3. (*Biol.*) primordial; 4. Grund– (*of colours*); 5. (*Gram.*) Stamm–; – ***verb,*** das Stammzeitwort. **2.** *s.* 1. (*Gram.*) das Stammwort; 2. der Frühmeister, Früher Meister, der Maler *or* das Kunstwerk der Frührenaissance. **primitiveness,** *s.* 1. die Ursprünglichkeit; 2. Einfachheit, Primitivität.

primness ['primnis], *s.* 1. die Steifheit, Korrektheit, Förmlichkeit; 2. Sprödigkeit, Geziertheit, Ziererei, Affektiertheit.

primogenitor [praimə'dʒenitə], *s.* der Ahnherr, Stammvater, (Ur)ahn, frühester Vorfahr. **primogeniture** [–tʃə], *s.* die Erstgeburt; (*Law*) das Erstgeburtsrecht.

primordial [prai'mɔ:diəl], *adj.* ursprünglich, uranfänglich, Ur–, Primordial–, Anfangs–, Jugend–; – ***leaf,*** das Jugendblatt.

primrose ['primrouz], **1.** *s.* 1. (*Bot.*) Gelbe Schlüsselblume, die Primel; ***Primrose League,*** der Primelbund; – ***path,*** der Rosenweg, Weg der Freude *or* des Vergnügens; 2. das Blaßgelb. **2.** *adj.* blaßgelb.

primula ['primjulə], *s.* (*Bot.*) die (Gattung der) Primel(n).

prince [prins], *s.* 1. der Fürst, Landesherr; ***Prince Bismarck,*** Fürst Bismarck; ***Prince Consort,*** der Prinzgemahl; ***poet*** –, fürstlicher Dichter; 2. (*son of royal house*) der Prinz; ***Black Prince,*** Schwarzer Prinz; – ***of the blood,*** der Prinz von (königlichem) Geblüt; ***Prince Regent,*** der Prinzregent; ***Prince of Wales,*** englischer Kronprinz; 3. (*fig.*) der Fürst; – ***of darkness,*** der Höllenfürst; ***merchant*** –, reicher Kaufherr; – ***of poets,*** der Dichterfürst. **princedom** [–dəm], *s.* *See* **principality. princelike,** *adj.* fürstlich. **princely,** *adj.* 1. fürstlich (*also fig.*); 2. prinzlich; 3. (*fig.*) stattlich, prächtig. **princess** [–'ses], **1.** *s.* 1. die Fürstin (*also wife of ruler*); 2. (*daughter of royal house*) Prinzessin; –***royal,*** älteste Tochter des Herrschers. **2.** *attrib. adj.* Prinzeß– (*of dress*).

principal ['prinsipl], **1.** *adj.* erst, führend, vornehmst, hauptsächlich, Haupt–; – ***actor,*** der Hauptdarsteller; – ***axis,*** die Hauptachse; – ***boy,*** die Heldendarstellerin (*pantomime*); (*Mus.*) – ***chord,*** der Stammakkord; – ***clause,*** der Hauptsatz; – ***creditor,*** der Hauptgläubiger; – ***part,*** (*Gram.*) die Stammform (*of verb*), (*Mus.*) Hauptstimme. **2.** *s.* 1. die Hauptperson, das Haupt; 2. der Vorsteher, (Di)rektor (*of a college etc.*); 3. (*Comm.*) Prinzipal, Chef, Auftraggeber, Selbstkontrahent, Kommittent; 4. (*Comm.*) das (Grund)kapital, die Kapitaleinlage; – ***and interest,*** Kapital und Zins(en); 5. (*Law*) der Haupttäter, Hauptschuldige(r); – ***in the first degree,*** der Haupttäter; – ***in the second degree,*** der Mittäter, Helfershelfer; 6. der Duellant (*in a duel*); 7. (*Theat.*) die Hauptfigur; 8. (*Mus.*) Solostimme; 9. (*Build.*) der Hauptbalken, Stützbalken, das Hauptgebälk.

principality [prinsi'pæliti], *s.* das Fürstentum.

principally ['prinsip(ə)li], *adv.* hauptsächlich, besonders, in der Hauptsache.

principle ['prinsipl], *s.* 1. der Grundsatz, die Richtschnur, das (Grund)prinzip; ***in*** –, im Grunde *or* Prinzip; im allgemeinen; ***make (it) a*** –, es sich (*Dat.*) zum Prinzip machen (***of doing,*** zu tun); ***man of*** –, der Mann mit Grundsätzen; ***on*** –, aus Prinzip, grundsätzlich, prinzipiell; ***on the*** –, nach dem Grundsatz; 2. der Leitgedanke, Leitsatz, Grundgedanke, Grundbegriff; 3. Ursprung, (Ur)grund, die Grundlage, Quelle; 4. (*Chem.*) der Grundbestandteil. **–principled,** *adj. suff.* mit . . . Grundsätzen.

print [print], **1.** *v.t.* 1. (*Typ.*) drucken (lassen), in Druck geben; ***be –ing,*** im Druck sein, gedruckt werden; ***have –ed,*** drucken lassen; 2. bedrucken (*cloth etc.*); 3. abdrucken (*a pattern*); 4. (*Phot.*) kopieren, abziehen; 5. drücken (***on,*** auf (*Acc.*)), hinterlassen, aufdrücken (auf (*Dat.*)); – ***a kiss on her cheek,*** ihr einen Kuß auf die Wange drücken; 6. (*fig.*) einprägen (***on his mind,*** ihm); 7. in Druckschrift *or* Blockbuchstaben schreiben. **2.** *s.* 1. der (Ab)druck; ***in*** –, im Druck, erschienen, veröffentlicht; erhältlich, vorrätig, auf Lager (*of book*); (*coll.*) ***in cold*** –, schwarz auf weiß; ***out of*** –, vergriffen; 2. (*Phot.*) der Abzug, die Kopie; 3. Druckstelle, Spur, das Zeichen, Mal, der Eindruck, Aufdruck; 4. die Druckschrift, Gedruckte(s); ***rush into*** –, unüberlegt veröffentlichen; 5. (*Art*) der Stich, Schnitt; ***coloured*** –, farbiger Stich; 6. (*Typ.*) das Modell, der (Druck)stempel, Druckstock, die Druckform; 7. (*Text.*) das Druckzeug, bedruckter Kattun; – ***dress,*** das Kattunkleid.

printable ['printəbl], *adj.* 1. druckfertig, druckreif (*of MS.*); 2. druckfähig. **printed,** *adj.* 1. gedruckt; – ***form,*** das Formular, der Vordruck; – ***matter,*** die Drucksache; 2. (*Text.*) bedruckt, gemustert; – ***fabric,*** das Druckzeug. **printer,** *s.* der (Buch)drucker, Druckereibesitzer; –***'s devil,*** der Setzerjunge; –***'s error,*** der Druckfehler; –***'s ink,*** die Druckerschwärze; –***'s mark,*** das Druckerzeichen; –***'s pie,*** Zwiebelfische (*pl.*).

printing ['printiŋ], *s.* 1. das Drucken, der Druck; 2. (*Phot.*) das Abziehen, Kopieren; 3. die Buchdruckerkunst; 4. der Tuchdruck; 5. die Druckschrift; 6. Auflage(ziffer). **printing|-block,** *s.* das Klischee, die Druckform. **--frame,** *s.* (*Phot.*) der Kopierrahmen. **--ink,** *s.* die Druckerschwärze. **--machine,** *s.* die Schnellpresse. **--office,** *s.* die Druckerei, Offizin. **--paper,** *s.* das Lichtpauspapier (*for blue-prints*); (*Phot.*) Kopierpapier. **--press,** *s.* 1. *See* **--machine**; 2. die Druckerei. **--types,** *pl.* Lettern (*pl.*). **--works,** *pl.* (*sing. constr.*) *see* **--office.**

print|-line, *s.* (*Typ.*) die Druckzeile. **--shop,** *s.* die Graphikhandlung. **-works,** *pl.* (*sing. constr.*) die Kattunfabrik.

[1]**prior** ['praiə], **1.** *adj.* früher, eher, älter (*to,* als); – ***claim,*** älterer Anspruch, das Vor(zugs)recht (*to,* auf (*Acc.*)); – ***condition,*** erste Voraussetzung. **2.** *adv.* – ***to,*** vor (*Dat.*), (noch) bevor.

[2]**prior,** *s.* der Prior. **priorate** [–rət], *s.* das Priorat, Amt eines Priors. **prioress** [–res], *s.* die Priorin.

priori, *see* **a priori.**

priority [prai'ɔriti], *s.* die Priorität, der Vorrang, Vorzug (*over,* vor (*Dat.*)); das Vor(zugs)recht; – ***of birth,*** die Erstgeburt; ***list of priorities,*** die Dringlichkeitsliste; ***get top*** –, vorzugsweise *or* als besonders dringlich behandelt werden; ***give (high)*** – ***to,*** (besonderen) Vorrang geben (*Dat.*), als (besonders) dringlich behandeln; ***take*** – ***over,*** den Vorrang haben vor (*Dat.*); – ***share,*** die Vorzugsaktie.

priorship ['praiəʃip], *s.* *See* **priorate. priory** [–əri], *s.* die Priorei.

prise [praiz], **1.** *s.* 1. der Hebel; 2. die Hebe(l)kraft. **2.** *v.t.* – ***open,*** aufbrechen, erbrechen; (*fig.*) erschließen; – ***up,*** hochstemmen, aufstemmen.

prism [prizm], *s.* das Prisma; – ***binoculars,*** das Prismenglas. **prismatic** [–'mætik], *adj.* prismatisch, Prismen–; – ***colours,*** Regenbogenfarben (*pl.*); – ***compass,*** die Patentbussole.

prison [prizn], *s.* das Gefängnis, Zuchthaus, die Strafanstalt; (***lie***) ***in*** –, im Gefängnis (sitzen); ***put in*** or ***send to*** –, ins Gefängnis werfen. **prison|-break,** *s.* der Ausbruch aus dem Gefängnis. **--breaking,** *s.* das Ausbrechen aus dem Gefängnis. **--camp,** *s.* das (Kriegs)gefangenenlager. **prisoner,** *s.* Gefangene(r), der Häftling; (*Law*) Angeklagte(r), der Sträfling; – ***at the bar,*** Untersuchungsgefangene(r); (*fig.*) ***be a*** – ***to,*** gefesselt sein an (*Acc.*); ***keep*** or ***hold him (a)*** –, ihn gefangenhalten; ***make*** or ***take*** –, gefangennehmen; – ***of war,*** Kriegsgefangene(r); (***game***) –***'s base,*** das Barlaufspiel. **prison-van,** *s.* der Gefangenenwagen.

prissy ['prisi], *adj.* (*coll.*) zimperlich, preziös, etepetete.

pristine ['pristain], *adj.* 1. ursprünglich, vormalig, ehemalig; 2. unverdorben, unverfälscht.

prithee! ['priði], *int.* (*obs.*) bitte!

privacy ['pr(a)ivəsi], *s.* die Heimlichkeit, Geheimhaltung; *in (strict) –*, (streng) vertraulich, unter vier Augen; 2. die Zurückgezogenheit; Abgeschiedenheit.

private ['praivit], **1.** *adj.* 1. heimlich, geheim; *– account,* das Geheimkonto; *– and confidential,* vertraulich; *for your – ear,* Ihnen ganz im Vertrauen; *– information,* vertrauliche Mitteilung; *– parts,* Geschlechtsteile (*pl.*); *– prayer,* stilles Gebet; *keep it –,* es verheimlichen *or* geheimhalten; 2. vertraulich, zurückgezogen; 3. Privat–, privat, Eigen–, eigen, persönlich; *– affair* or *business* or *concern,* die Privatsache, persönliche Angelegenheit; (*Pol.*) *– bill,* der Antrag eines Abgeordneten; *– chapel,* die Hauskapelle; *– citizen,* der Privatmann; *– consumption,* der Eigenverbrauch; (*sl.*) *– eye,* der Privatdetektiv; *– gentleman,* der Rentner, Privatier; *– hand,* die Privathand; *– house,* das Privathaus; *retire (in)to – life,* ins Privatleben zurückziehen; *– means,* das Privatvermögen; *– property,* das Privateigentum; *– reasons,* private Gründe; *– secretary,* der Privatsekretär; (*Railw.*) *– siding,* der Gleisanschluß; *– tutor,* der Hauslehrer; *for – use,* zum eigenen Gebrauch; 4. nicht öffentlich *or* amtlich, außeramtlich; *– arrangement,* gütlicher Vergleich; (*Comm.*) *– company* or *firm,* die Personalgesellschaft; *sell by – contract,* unter der Hand verkaufen; *– hotel,* das Fremdenheim, die Privatpension; *– road,* nicht öffentliche Straße; *– school,* die Privatschule; *– theatre,* das Liebhabertheater; *– view,* geschlossene Besichtigung (*of exhibition*); 5. (*of a p.*) nicht beamtet, ohne Beruf; (*Parl.*) *– member,* nicht beamteter Abgeordneter. **2.** *s.* 1. (*Mil.*) (*also – soldier*) Gemeine(r), einfacher *or* gemeiner Soldat, (*coll.*) der Landser; 2. *pl.* Geschlechtsteile (*pl.*); 3. *in –,* insgeheim, im geheimen *or* Vertrauen, unter vier Augen.

privateer [praivə'tiə], *s.* 1. der Kommandant eines Kaperschiffs, Freibeuter; 2. das Kaperschiff. **privateering,** *s.* die Kaperei.

privately ['praivitli], *adv.* 1. privat; *--owned,* im Privatbesitz; *settle –,* privat *or* intern regeln; 2. heimlich, vertraulich, im stillen, in aller Stille; *marry –,* in aller Stille heiraten.

privation [prai'veiʃən], *s.* 1. die Entziehung, Beraubung, Wegnahme; 2. (*Phil.*) Verneinung, das Fehlen; 3. (*Eccl. etc.*) die Absetzung, Amtsenthebung, Suspendierung; 4. (*coll.*) Entbehrung, Not, der Mangel.

privative ['privətiv], **1.** *adj.* 1. beraubend, ausschließend; 2. (*Gram.*) verneinend, privativ. **2.** *s.* (*Gram.*) die Verneinungspartikel.

privet ['privit], *s.* (*Bot.*) der Liguster, die Rainweide; (*Ent.*) *– hawk(-moth),* der Ligusterschwärmer.

privilege ['privilidʒ], **1.** *s.* das Vorrecht, Sonderrecht, Privileg(ium); die Vergünstigung; (*Law*) Gerechtsame, Freiheit, Immunität, das Nutzungsrecht; *it is my –,* es steht mir frei, es ist mein gutes Recht (*to do,* zu tun); *it is a –,* es ist eine große *or* besondere Ehre (*to do,* tun zu dürfen); *have the –,* den Vorzug *or* die Ehre haben (*of doing,* zu tun); *breach of –,* die Übertretung der Machtbefugnis, Zuständigkeitsüberschreitung; (*Parl.*) *Committee of Privileges,* der Ausschuß zur Regelung von Übergriffen. **2.** *v.t.* (*usu. pass.*) bevorzugen, bevorrechten, privilegieren, das Vorrecht einräumen (*Dat.*); *be –d,* die Ehre haben (*to do,* zu tun); 2. sichern (*from,* vor (*Dat.*)), ausnehmen, befreien (von).

privily ['privili], *adv.* heimlich, insgeheim; vertraulich.

privity ['priviti], *s.* 1. die Mitwisserschaft, das Mitwissen (*to,* um), Eingeweihtsein (in (*Acc.*)); 2. (*Law*) rechtliche Beteiligung, das Rechtsverhältnis, gemeinsame Interessenbeziehung, die Rechtsbeziehung, (Interessen)gemeinschaft.

privy ['privi], **1.** *adj.* 1. mitwissend (*to,* um), eingeweiht (in (*Acc.*)); *be – to,* wissen um, eingeweiht sein in (*Acc.*); *make him – to,* ihn (mit) ins Vertrauen ziehen; 2. (*Law*) (mit)beteiligt, mitinteressiert, (*esp.*) mitschuldig (*to,* an (*Dat.*)); 3. (*obs.*) geheim, heimlich, verborgen; *Privy Council,* der Staatsrat, Geheimer Rat; *Privy Councillor,* Geheimer Staatsrat, der Geheimrat, das Mitglied des Staatsrats; *– parts,* Schamteile, Geschlechtsteile (*pl.*); *– purse,* königliche Privatschatulle; *– seal,* das Geheimsiegel; *Lord Privy Seal,* der Geheimsiegelbewahrer. **2.** *s.* 1. (*Law*) der Mitinteressent, Teilhaber, Beteiligte(r), (*also*) Mitschuldige(r) (*to,* an (*Dat.*)); 2. (*coll.*) der Abtritt, Abort.

[1]**prize** [praiz], **1.** *s.* der (Sieger)preis; Gewinn, die Belohnung; Prämie, das Los (*lottery*); *first –,* großes Los (*in a lottery*); *– for German,* die Prämie für Deutsch; *–s of a profession,* erstrebenswerte Posten eines Berufes. **2.** *v.t.* (hoch)schätzen, würdigen. **3.** *attrib. adj.* preisgekrönt, präm(i)iert; *– poem,* preisgekröntes Gedicht; (*coll.*) *– idiot,* der Vollidiot.

[2]**prize, 1.** *s.* (*Naut.*) die Prise, Beute; (*fig.*) Beute, guter Fang; *make – of,* als Prise aufbringen *or* kapern. **2.** *v.t.* aufbringen, als Prise nehmen.

[3]**prize,** *see* **prise.**

prize|-court, *s.* (*Naut.*) das Prisengericht. **--crew,** *s.* das Prisenkommando. **--fight,** *s.* der Preisboxkampf. **--fighter,** *s.* der Preisboxer, Berufsboxer. **--fighting,** *s.* das Preisboxen, der Preiskampf. **--giving,** *s.* die Preisverteilung. **--list,** *s.* die Gewinnliste. **–man,** *s. See* **--winner. --money,** *s.* der Geldpreis. **--winner,** *s.* der Preisträger. **--winning,** *attrib. adj. See* [1]**prize, 3.**

[1]**pro** [prou], *s.* (*coll.*) (*Spt.*) der Profi.

[2]**pro,** *s.* die Ja-Stimme, Stimme dafür; *the –s and cons,* das Für und Wider.

[3]**pro–,** *pref.* 1. (da)für, an Seiten von; *--German,* deutschfreundlich; 2. an Stelle von; *--rector,* der Prorektor; 3. vor–, vorwärts–.

proa ['prouə], *s.* malaiisches Segelboot.

probabiliorism [prɔbə'biliərizm], *s.* (*R.C.*) der Probabiliorismus. **probabilism** ['prɔbəbilizm], *s.* (*R.C.*) der Probabilismus, Wahrscheinlichkeitsstandpunkt.

probability [prɔbə'biliti], *s.* die Wahrscheinlichkeit, wahrscheinliches Ereignis; *in all –,* höchstwahrscheinlich, aller Wahrscheinlichkeit nach; (*Math.*) *theory of –,* die Wahrscheinlichkeitsrechnung; *there is no –,* es ist sehr unwahrscheinlich *or* es ist nicht anzunehmen (*of his coming,* daß er kommt). **probable** ['prɔbəbl], *adj.* wahrscheinlich, vermutlich, mutmaßlich; *probably not,* schwerlich.

probang ['proubæŋ], *s.* (*Med.*) die Schlundsonde.

probate ['proubeit], *s.* 1. gerichtliche Bestätigung (eines Testaments); *– court,* das Nachlaßgericht, Erbbestätigungsgericht; 2. beglaubigte Abschrift eines Testaments; *– duty,* die Erbschaftssteuer.

probation [prə'beiʃən], *s.* 1. die Probe, (Eignungs)prüfung; Probezeit; *on –,* auf Probe, widerruflich; *– year,* das Probejahr; 2. (*Eccl.*) das Noviziat; 3. (*Law*) die Bewährungsfrist, bedingte Freilassung, bedingter Straferlaß; *place on –,* auf Bewährung freilassen, Bewährungsfrist zubilligen (*Dat.*), unter Aufsicht stellen; *– officer,* der Bewährungshelfer, Schutzaufsichtsbeamte(r). **probational, probationary,** *adj.* Prüfungs–, Probe–; *– period,* die Probezeit, (*Law*) Bewährungsfrist. **probationer,** *s.* 1. (*Eccl.*) der (*or* die) Novize; 2. (Probe)kandidat(in), (*Med.*) die Lernschwester; 3. (*Law*) bedingt freigelassener Sträfling; 4. (*fig.*) der Neuling.

probative ['proubətiv], *adj.* beweisend, als Beweis dienend (*of,* für), Beweis–.

probe [proub], **1.** *s.* 1. (*Surg.*) die Sonde; 2. (*fig.*) Sondierung, (strenge) Untersuchung; 3. (*rocketry*) die Versuchsrakete; *lunar –,* die Mondrakete. **2.** *v.t.* 1. sondieren; 2. (*fig.*) gründlich erforschen *or* prüfen *or* untersuchen. **3.** *v.i.* (*fig.*) eindringen (*into,* in (*Acc.*)), auf den Grund gehen (*Dat.*). **probe-scissors,** *pl.* die Wundschere.

probity ['proubiti], *s.* die Rechtschaffenheit, Redlichkeit.

problem ['prɔbləm], **1.** *s.* die Aufgabe, das Problem (*also Math.*); schwierige Aufgabe *or* Frage, die

Schwierigkeit, das Rätsel; ***it is a – to me,*** es ist mir rätselhaft *or* ein Rätsel; ***be brought up against a –,*** vor ein Problem gestellt werden; ***set a –,*** eine Aufgabe stellen; (*fig.*) ein Problem aufstellen *or* aufwerfen. **2.** *attrib. adj.* – ***child,*** schwieriges Kind; – ***drama,*** das Problemdrama. **problematic(al)** [–'mætik(l)], *adj.* problematisch, fraglich, zweifelhaft; fragwürdig.

proboscis [prə'bɔskis], *s.* der Rüssel; (*sl.*) Zinken, Schnorchel (= *nose*).

procedural [prə'si:dʒərəl], *adj.* verfahrensrechtlich, Verfahrens–. **procedure,** *s.* das Verfahren (*also Law*), Verhalten, Vorgehen, die Arbeitsweise, Handlungsweise; ***legal –,*** das Gerichtsverfahren, der Prozeß; ***rules of –,*** die Verfahrensordnung, Geschäftsordnung.

proceed [prə'si:d], *v.i.* 1. sich begeben; vorwärtsgehen, weitergehen, weiterfahren, seinen Weg fortsetzen, weiterreisen; – ***on one's journey,*** seine Reise fortsetzen, weiterreisen; 2. (*fig.*) weitergehen, fortschreiten; 3. (zu sprechen) fortfahren; 4. vor sich gehen, vonstatten gehen (*of actions*); 5. (*fig.*) – ***from,*** entspringen (*Dat.*), entstehen aus, kommen *or* ausgehen *or* herrühren von; 6. (*Law*) – ***against,*** prozessieren, gerichtlich vorgehen *or* ein Verfahren einleiten *or* einen Prozeß anstrengen gegen; 7. – ***to,*** sich machen an (*Acc.*), schreiten *or* übergehen zu; – ***to the attack,*** zum Angriff übergehen; (*fig.*) – ***to business,*** beginnen, ans Werk gehen; – ***to do,*** sich anschicken zu tun; 8. – ***upon a principle,*** einen Grundsatz befolgen, nach einem Grundsatz verfahren *or* vorgehen; – ***with,*** in Angriff nehmen; fortsetzen, weiterführen, fortfahren mit; 9. – ***to a degree,*** einen (höheren Universitäts)grad erlangen, promovieren.

proceeding [prə'si:diŋ], *s.* das Verfahren, Vorgehen, die Handlung, Maßnahme. **proceedings,** *pl.* 1. (*Law*) das Verfahren, der Prozeß, die Gerichtsverhandlung; – ***at law,*** der Rechtsgang; ***take (legal) – against,*** *see* **proceed,** 6; 2. (Sitzungs)berichte, Akten, Protokolle (*pl.*).

proceeds ['prousi:dz], *pl.* der Ertrag, Erlös, Gewinn, Einnahmen (*pl.*); ***gross –,*** Bruttoeinnahmen (*pl.*), der Bruttoertrag; ***net –,*** der Reinertrag, Nettoertrag.

¹**process** ['prouses], **1.** *s.* das Fortschreiten, der Fortgang, (Ver)lauf; ***in –,*** im Gange; ***in – of time,*** im Laufe *or* mit der Zeit; 2. der Vorgang, Ablauf, Prozeß, die Entwicklung; – ***of decomposition,*** der Verwesungsvorgang; ***in the –,*** dabei, unterdessen; ***in – of construction,*** im Bau (befindlich *or* begriffen); ***mental –,*** der Denkvorgang; 3. die Methode, das Verfahren; – ***of manufacture,*** das Herstellungsverfahren; 4. (*Law*) die Vorladung; der Prozeß, Rechtsgang, das (Gerichts)verfahren; 5. (*Chem.*) der Prozeß, das Verfahren; 6. (*Bot., Zool., Anat.*) die Verlängerung, der Fortsatz, Auswuchs; 7. (*Typ.*) photomechanische Klischeeherstellung; – ***printing,*** der Mehrfarbendruck. **2.** *v.t.* 1. (*Law*) gerichtlich belangen; 2. (*Typ.*) photomechanisch herstellen *or* reproduzieren; 3. (chemisch) behandeln, aufbereiten; –***(ed) cheese,*** der Schmelzkäse; 4. (*Phot.*) verarbeiten, fertigstellen.

²**process** [prə'ses], *v.i.* (*coll.*) in einem Zuge gehen.

processing ['prousesiŋ], *s.* 1. die Verarbeitung; ***data –,*** die Datenverarbeitung; 2. die Vered(e)lung, Aufbereitung; ***food –,*** die Lebensmittelherstellung.

procession [prə'seʃən], *s.* 1. (feierlicher) Umzug *or* Aufzug, die Prozession; ***funeral –,*** der Leichenzug; 2. die Reihe, Reihenfolge, (weiterer) Verlauf *or* Ablauf; 3. (*Eccl.*) das Ausströmen (*of the Holy Ghost*). **processional, 1.** *adj.* Prozessions–; *see also* **processionary. 2.** *s.* 1. das Prozessionsbuch; 2. die Prozessionshymne. **processionary,** *adj.* (*Ent.*) Prozessions–, Wander–.

proclaim [prə'kleim], *v.t.* 1. (öffentlich) ausrufen *or* erklären, kundgeben, verkünden, bekanntmachen, ankündigen, proklamieren; 2. erklären zu (*a p.*); 3. (*fig.*) kennzeichnen, deutlich zeigen; 4. in die Acht erklären (*a district*); 5. verbieten (*a meeting*).

proclamation [prɔklə'meiʃən], *s.* 1. die Ausrufung, Verkündigung, (öffentliche) Bekanntmachung, der Aufruf, die Proklamation (***to,*** an (*Acc.*)); – ***of martial law,*** die Verhängung des Standrechts; 2. die Erklärung, Ausrufung (*of a p.*) (***as,*** zu).

proclitic [pro'klitik], **1.** *adj.* (*Gram.*) proklitisch. **2.** *s.* proklitisches Wort.

proclivity [prə'kliviti], *s.* die Neigung, der Hang, angeborene Veranlagung, natürliche Anlage (***to,*** zu).

proconsul [prou'kɔnsʌl], *s.* stellvertretender Konsul; (*Hist.*) Prokonsul, (Provinzial)statthalter. **proconsular** [–'kɔnsjulə], *adj.* Statthalter–. **proconsulate** [–'kɔnsjulit], *s.* das Amt *or* die Amtsdauer eines Statthalters.

procrastinate [pro'kræstineit], **1.** *v.i.* zögern, zaudern. **2.** *v.t.* (*rare*) aufschieben, verschieben, hinauszögern, verzögern, auf die lange Bank schieben. **procrastination** [–'neiʃən], *s.* der Aufschub, die Verzögerung; das Zaudern, die Saumseligkeit.

procreant ['proukriənt], *adj.* (er)zeugend, hervorbringend. **procreate** [–ieit], *v.t.* (er)zeugen, hervorbringen; (*fig.*) ins Leben rufen. **procreation** [–i'eiʃən], *s.* die (Er)zeugung, Erschaffung, das Hervorbringen. **procreative** [–krieitiv], *adj.* 1. zeugungsfähig, (er)zeugend, Zeugungs–; 2. fruchtbar. **procreator** [–i'eitə], *s.* der Erzeuger, Vater.

proctor ['prɔktə], *s.* 1. (*Law*) der Anwalt, Prokurator; 2. (*Univ.*) Disziplinarbeamte(r), der Proktor; –***'s man,*** der Pedell. **proctorial** [–'tɔ:riəl], *adj.* Proktor–. **proctorize,** *v.t.* (*Univ.*) vor den Proktor laden. **proctorship,** *s.* das Amt eines Proktors *or* Prokurators.

procumbent [pro'kʌmbənt], *adj.* (*Bot.*) am Boden liegend.

procurable [prə'kjuərəbl], *adj.* erlangbar, erhältlich, aufzutreiben(d), zu verschaffen(d). **procurance,** *s.* die Beschaffung, Verschaffung, Besorgung, Erlangung, Erwerbung, Vermittlung.

procuration [prɔkju'reiʃən], *s.* 1. (*Comm.*) die Prokura, Vollmacht; ***by –,*** per Prokura; 2. (*also* – ***money***) die Maklergebühr, Vermittlungsgebühr; 3. (*Law*) Kuppelei; *see also* **procurance. procurator** ['prɔkjureitə], *s.* der Sachwalter, (Stell)vertreter, Bevollmächtigte(r); (*Scots*) – ***fiscal,*** der Staatsanwalt.

procure [prə'kjuə], **1.** *v.t.* 1. (sich (*Dat.*)) beschaffen *or* verschaffen *or* anschaffen *or* besorgen; 2. erlangen, erwerben; 3. (*rare*) zustande bringen, veranlassen, verursachen, bewerkstelligen, bewirken, herbeiführen. **2.** *v.i.* kuppeln, Kuppelei treiben. **procurement,** *s. See* **procurance**; die Veranlassung, Bewerkstelligung. **procurer,** *s.* 1. der Besorger, Verschaffer; 2. Kuppler, Zuhälter. **procuress,** *s.* die Kupplerin.

prod [prɔd], **1.** *v.t.* 1. stechen, stoßen; 2. (*fig. coll.*) anstacheln, antreiben, anspornen (***into,*** zu). **2.** *s.* 1. das Stechen; der Stich, Stoß; 2. (*fig.*) Ansporn; 3. (*Tech.*) Stachelstock, die Ahle.

prodigal ['prɔdigəl], **1.** *adj.* verschwenderisch (***of,*** mit); ***be – of,*** verschwenderisch umgehen mit; (*B.*) – ***son,*** verlorener Sohn. **2.** *s.* der (die) Verschwender(in). **prodigality** [–'gæliti], *s.* 1. die Verschwendung(ssucht); 2. Üppigkeit, Fülle (***of,*** an (*Dat.*)). **prodigalize,** *v.t.* verschwenden, verschwenderisch umgehen mit.

prodigious [prə'didʒəs], *adj.* 1. ungeheuer, gewaltig, riesig; 2. (*coll.*) großartig, erstaunlich, wunderbar. **prodigy** ['prɔdidʒi], *s.* das Wunder (***of,*** *Gen. or* an (*Dat.*)); ***infant –,*** das Wunderkind.

¹**produce** [prə'dju:s], *v.t.* 1. vorlegen, vorbringen, vorzeigen, anführen, aufwarten mit (*evidence etc.*), beibringen (*witness, proof*); 2. hervorholen, hervorziehen (***from,*** aus); 3. zur Folge haben, verursachen, bewirken, erzeugen, hervorbringen, hervorrufen (*results etc.*); 4. (*Comm.*) erzielen, eintragen, einbringen, abwerfen (*profit etc.*); 5. (*Math.*) verlängern (*a line*); 6. verfassen, schaffen, schreiben (*poetry, books*); 7. verfertigen, herstellen,

produzieren, erzeugen (*manufactures*); 8. bauen, ziehen (*crops*); 9. liefern (*minerals*); 10. (*Theat.*) einstudieren, inszenieren (*a play*).

²**produce** ['prɔdju:s], *s.* 1. das Erzeugnis, Produkt (*also* Erzeugnisse, Produkte (*pl.*)); ***home* –**, inländische Bodenprodukte; **– *market*,** der Warenmarkt; 2. der Gewinn, Ertrag, die Ausbeute; ***net* –**, der Reinertrag.

producer [prə'dju:sə], *s.* 1. der Verfertiger, Hersteller, Erzeuger, Produzent; 2. (*Theat.*) Regisseur, Theaterleiter; (*Rad. etc.*) Spielleiter; 3. (*Tech.*) Generator. **producer-gas,** *s.* das Generatorgas. **producible,** *adj.* 1. erzeugbar, herstellbar, produzierbar; 2. vorzeigbar, aufweisbar, beizubringen(d).

product ['prɔdəkt], *s.* 1. das Erzeugnis, Produkt (*also Math.*); 2. Werk, Ergebnis, Resultat, die Wirkung, Frucht.

production [prə'dʌkʃən], *s.* 1. die Hervorbringung, Entstehung; 2. Vorlegung, Vorlage, das Vorführen, Aufweisen, Erbringen; die Beibringung, Vorzeigung; 3. Erzeugung, Herstellung, Bildung, Gewinnung, Fabrikation, Produktion; **– *capacity*,** *see* **productivity**; **– *car*,** der Serienwagen; ***cost of* –, – *costs*,** Gestehungskosten (*pl.*); **– *figures*,** Ausstoßzahlen (*pl.*); **– *line*,** das Fließband, laufendes Band; **– *manager*,** der Betriebsleiter, Produktionsleiter; 4. das Erzeugnis, Produkt, Fabrikat, Werk, die Schöpfung, Frucht; 5. Verlängerung (*of a line*); 6. (*Theat.*) Aufführung, Vorführung, Inszenierung, Regie, (*Rad. etc.*) Spielleitung.

productive [pre'dʌktiv], *adj.* 1. hervorbringend, hervorrufend, schaffend, erzeugend, herstellend, produzierend (*of, Acc.*); ***be* – *of*,** hervorbringen, bereiten, führen zu; 2. produktiv, rentabel, ertragreich, ergiebig; 3. (*fig.*) produktiv, fruchtbar, schöpferisch; 4. **– *capacity*,** die Leistungsfähigkeit, Produktionsleistung, Mengenleistung. **productiveness, productivity** [prɔdək'tiviti], *s.* die Produktivität, Ergiebigkeit, Leistungsfähigkeit, Ertragsfähigkeit, Rentabilität; (*fig.*) Fruchtbarkeit.

proem ['prouim], *s.* die Vorrede, Einleitung, das Proömium. **proemial** [–'i:miəl], *adj.* einleitend, Einleitungs–.

prof [prɔf], *s.* (*coll.*) *see* **professor.**

profanation [prɔfə'neiʃən], *s.* die Entweihung, Entheiligung, Schändung, Profanierung. **profanatory** [–'fænətri], *adj.* 1. entweihend, entheiligend, profanierend; 2. herabwürdigend, herabsetzend.

profane [prə'fein], **1.** *adj.* 1. profan, weltlich; **– *literature*,** weltliche Literatur; 2. nichtkirchlich, ungeweiht; 3. frevelnd, (gottes)lästerlich, gottlos, ruchlos; **– *language*,** das Fluchen, Lästern. **2.** *v.t.* 1. entweihen, entheiligen, profanieren; 2. herabwürdigen, mißbrauchen. **profanity** [–'fæniti], *s.* 1. die Gottlosigkeit, Ruchlosigkeit; 2. (*oft. pl.*) die (Gottes)lästerung, das Fluchen, Flüche (*pl.*).

profess [prə'fes], *v.t.* 1. (öffentlich) erklären, bekennen; 2. sich bekennen zu *or* als; 3. behaupten, versichern, beteuern; 4. angeben, vorgeben, vortäuschen, heucheln, sich hinstellen *or* ausgeben (*to be*, als); 5. ausüben, betreiben (*a profession*). **professed** [–t], *adj.* 1. angeblich, vorgeblich; **– *excuse*,** der Vorwand; 2. erklärt, ausgesprochen; **– *Christian*,** der Bekenntnischrist; 3. (*rare*) Berufs–; **– *monk*,** der Profeß. **professedly** [–idli], *adv.* 1. offenkundig, unleugbar; 2. eingestandenermaßen, erklärtermaßen, nach eigener Angabe, angeblich.

profession [prə'feʃən], *s.* 1. (*Eccl.*) das (Glaubens)-bekenntnis, der Glaube; das (Ordens)gelübde, die Profeß; heiliges Versprechen; **– *of faith*,** das Glaubensbekenntnis; 2. die Erklärung, Behauptung, Versicherung, Beteuerung; **– *of friendship*,** die Freundschaftsbeteuerung; 3. (freier *or* gelehrter) Beruf, der Stand; (*coll.*) ***the* –**, die Gesamtheit der Berufskollegen; ***by* –**, von Beruf; **– *of arms*,** der Soldatenstand.

professional [prə'feʃənl], **1.** *adj.* 1. beruflich, Berufs–, Standes–; (*Med.*) **– *attendance*,** ärztliche Behandlung; **– *classes*,** höhere Berufsstände; **– *duties*,** Berufspflichten (*pl.*); **– *ethics*,** das Berufsethos; **– *jealousy*,** der Konkurrenzneid, Brotneid; **– *player*,** der Berufsspieler; **– *honour*,** die Standesehre; **– *man*,** der Geistesarbeiter, Angehörige(r) eines freien Berufs; **– *politician*,** der Berufspolitiker; 2. berufsmäßig, zünftig, fachlich, Fach–; **– *education*,** berufliche Ausbildung; **– *examination*,** die Fachprüfung; ***in a* – *manner*** or ***way*,** berufsmäßig, als Broterwerb; ***of a* – *nature*,** fachlicher Natur; **– *studies*,** das Fachstudium. **2.** *s.* 1. der Fachmann, Geistesarbeiter; 2. (*Theat., Arts etc.*) Berufskünstler, Berufssänger, Künstler, Sänger *etc.* von Fach, (*Spt.*) Berufsspieler, (*coll.*) Profi. **professionalism,** *s.* 1. die Berufsausübung; 2. (*Spt.*) das Berufsspielertum, der Professionalismus.

professor [prə'fesə], *s.* der (Universitäts)professor; **– *of theology in the University of Oxford*** or ***at Oxford Univ.*,** Professor der Theologie an der Universität Oxford; (*Am.*) ***assistant* –**, außerordentlicher Professor; ***full* –**, ordentlicher Professor, der Ordinarius. **professorial** [prɔfə'sɔ:riəl], *adj.* Professor–, professorenhaft; **– *chair*,** die Professur, der Lehrstuhl. **professoriate** [prɔfə'sɔ:riət], *s.* der Lehrkörper, Professoren (*pl.*). **professorship,** *s.* die Professur, der Lehrstuhl, das Ordinariat.

proffer ['prɔfə], **1.** *v.t.* anbieten. **2.** *s.* das Anerbieten; der Angebot.

proficiency [prə'fiʃənsi], *s.* die Tüchtigkeit, Fertigkeit. **proficient, 1.** *adj.* tüchtig, geübt, bewandert (*in* (*a subject*), *at* (*an activity*), in (*Dat.*)). **2.** *s.* der Meister, Fachmann.

profile ['proufail], **1.** *s.* 1. das Profil, die Seitenansicht, das Seitenbild; ***in* –**, im Profil; 2. (*Archit.*) senkrechter Durchschnitt; der Längsschnitt, Querschnitt; 3. (*fig.*) knappe biographische Skizze. **2.** *v.t.* im Profil darstellen, profilieren.

profit ['prɔfit], **1.** *s.* 1. der Vorteil, Nutzen; (*fig.*) ***derive* – *from*,** Nutzen ziehen aus; ***to his* –**, zu seinem Vorteil; 2. (*Comm.*) (*oft. pl.*) der Gewinn, Profit, (Rein)ertrag; ***clear* –**, der Nettogewinn, Reingewinn; ***leave a* –**, einen Gewinn abwerfen; **– *and loss*,** Gewinn und Verlust; ***make a* – *on*** ((*sale of*) *goods*) or ***by*** or ***out of*** (*selling goods*), (einen) Gewinn ziehen aus; ***sell at a* –**, mit Gewinn verkaufen. **2.** *v.i.* gewinnen, profitieren (***by*** or (*fig.*) ***from***, von) (*of a th.*), (einen) Gewinn *or* Nutzen ziehen (aus), sich (*Dat.*) zu Nutzen machen (*Acc.*) (*of a p.*); **– *by an opportunity*,** eine Gelegenheit benutzen. **3.** *v.t.* von Nutzen sein für, nutzen *or* nützen (*Dat.*), Nutzen bringen (*Dat.*).

profitable ['prɔfitəbl], *adj.* 1. nützlich, vorteilhaft (*to*, für); 2. (*Comm.*) gewinnbringend, einträglich, rentabel; ***be* –**, sich rentieren. **profitableness,** *s.* 1. die Nützlichkeit; 2. Einträglichkeit. **profiteer** [–'tiə], **1.** *s.* der Profitmacher, Gewinnler, Schieber. **2.** *v.i.* schieben, Schiebergeschäfte *or* Wuchergeschäfte machen. **profiteering** [–'tiəriŋ], *s.* die Schiebung, Preistreiberei, Wuchergeschäfte (*pl.*). **profitless,** *adj.* 1. uneinträglich, unrentabel; 2. (*fig.*) nutzlos. **profit|-making,** *adj.* einträglich, gewinnbringend, gewinnreich, profitbringend. **--margin,** *s.* die Gewinnspanne, Gewinnschere. **--sharing, 1.** *s.* die Gewinnbeteiligung. **2.** *adj.* Gewinnbeteiligungs–. **--taking,** *s.* (*St. Exch.*) die Gewinnsicherung.

profligacy ['prɔfligəsi], *s.* 1. die Verworfenheit, Ruchlosigkeit, Zügellosigkeit, Lasterhaftigkeit, Liederlichkeit; 2. Verschwendung(ssucht), Ausschweifung. **profligate** [–it], **1.** *adj.* 1. verworfen, ruchlos, zügellos, lasterhaft, liederlich; 2. verschwenderisch, ausschweifend. **2.** *s.* liederlicher Mensch, Verworfene(r).

pro forma [prou'fɔ:mə], **1.** *adj.* Proforma–, Schein–, fingiert. **2.** *adv.* nur der Form wegen.

profound [prə'faund], *adj.* 1. tief (*usu. fig. or Poet.*); **– *reverence*,** tiefe Verbeugung; **– *sleep*,** tiefer Schlaf; 2. tiefsitzend, tiefschürfend, tiefreichend, tiefgründig; gründlich, in die Tiefe gehend; tiefsinnig, inhaltsschwer; **– *ignorance*,** krasse Unwissenheit; **– *indifference*,** vollkommene Gleichgültigkeit; **– *interest*,** starkes Interesse; **– *respect*,**

größte Hochachtung; 3. dunkel, unergründlich. **profoundly,** *adv.* 1. sehr, höchst; 2. tief, aufrichtig. **profoundness,** *s. See* **profundity.**

profundity [prəˈfʌnditi], *s.* 1. die Tiefe, der Abgrund; 2. (*fig.*) die Gründlichkeit, Tiefgründigkeit, Tiefsinnigkeit.

profuse [prəˈfju:s], *adj.* 1. überreich, übermäßig, ausgiebig, üppig (*in*, an (*Dat.*)), (über)reichlich; 2. (allzu) verschwenderisch *or* großzügig *or* freigebig (*of*, *in*, mit). **profuseness,** *s.* 1. die Übermäßigkeit, der Überfluß, Reichtum; 2. verschwenderische Freigebigkeit. **profusion** [-ˈfju:ʒən], *s.* 1. der Überfluß, Reichtum (*of*, an (*Dat.*)), die (Über)fülle (von); *in* –, überreichlich, in Hülle und Fülle; 2. die Verschwendung, der Luxus.

1**prog** [prɔg], *s.* (*sl.*) Fressalien (*pl.*), der (Reise)-proviant.

2**prog, 1.** *s.* (*Univ. sl.*) der Proktor. **2.** *v.t.* (*Univ. sl.*) *See* **proctorize.**

progenitive [prouˈdʒenitiv], *adj.* Zeugungs–, zeugungsfähig. **progenitor,** *s.* 1. der Vorfahr, Ahn; 2. (*fig.*) Vorläufer, das Original. **progenitress,** *s.* die Ahne. **progeniture** [–tʃə], *s.* 1. die Zeugung; 2. Nachkommenschaft. **progeny** [ˈprɔdʒəni], *s.* 1. die Nachkommenschaft, Nachkommen (*pl.*), Kinder (*pl.*), (*of beasts*) die Brut, Junge (*pl.*); 2. (*fig.*) das Produkt, die Frucht.

proglottis [prouˈglɔtis], *s.* (*Zool.*) die Proglottide.

prognatnic [prɔgˈnæθik], **prognathous** [–ˈneiθəs], *adj.* vorspringend (*of jaws*). **prognathism** [ˈprɔgnəθizm], *s.* vorstehende Kieferbildung, die Prognathie.

prognosis [prɔgˈnousis], *s.* (*pl.* **-ses** [–si:z]) (*esp. Med.*) die Prognose, Vorhersage.

prognostic [prɔgˈnɔstik], **1.** *adj.* voraussagend (*of*, *Acc.*), warnend, vorbedeutend. **2.** *s.* 1. das Vorzeichen, die Voraussage, Prophezeiung; 2. (*Med.*) Prognose. **prognosticate** [–eit], *v.t.* vorhersagen, voraussagen, prophezeien. **prognostication** [–ˈkeiʃən], *s.* 1. die Voraussage; 2. Weissagung, Prophezeiung, (Vor)ahnung, Vorbedeutung; 3. das Vorzeichen. **prognosticator,** *s.* der (die) Wahrsager(in).

program, (*Am.*) *see* **programme.**

programmatic [prougrəˈmætik], *adj.* programmatisch.

programme [ˈprougræm], **1.** *s.* das Programm; (*Rad., T.V.*) die Sendefolge; (*Theat.*) der Theaterzettel (*for a performance*), Spielplan (*for a season*); Arbeitsplan; (*Pol.*) das (Partei)programm; ***draw up a*** – (***of work***), einen Arbeitsplan aufstellen; (*coll.*) ***what is the – for today?*** was steht heute auf dem Programm? was haben wir heute vor? **2.** *v.t.* planen, ansetzen; (*computers*) programmieren. **programme-music,** *s.* die Programmusik. **programmer,** *s.* (*computers*) der Programmierer.

1**progress** [ˈprougres], *s.* 1. der Fortschritt, Fortschritte (*pl.*); die Entwicklung, Verbesserung; ***make*** –, vorwärtskommen, Fortschritte machen, fortschreiten (***in*** (*a field*), in (*Dat.*); ***with*** (*an activity, problem etc.*), mit); ***the – of mankind,*** das Fortschreiten *or* die (Weiter)entwicklung der Menschheit; ***much*** –, große *or* rasche Fortschritte; (*Parl.*) ***report*** –, den Stand der Verhandlungen kurz berichten; 2. das Fortschreiten, Vorrücken; 3. der Fortgang, Verlauf; ***in*** –, im Gange; ***in the – of time,*** im Laufe *or* mit der Zeit; 4. die Zunahme, das Überhandnehmen, Umsichgreifen; 5. (*Hist.*) die Rundreise, offizielle Fahrt; ***Pilgrim's Progress,*** die Pilgerfahrt.

2**progress** [prəˈgres], *v.i.* 1. weitergehen, weiterschreiten; 2. (*fig.*) weiterkommen, vorwärtskommen, seinen Fortgang nehmen; sich fortentwickeln *or* weiterentwickeln; – ***towards,*** entgegengehen, entgegenschreiten (*Dat.*).

progression [prəˈgreʃən], *s.* 1. das Vorwärtsschreiten, die Fortbewegung; 2. Weiterentwicklung, der Verlauf, Fortgang, Fortschritt; 3. (*Math.*) die Reihe, Progression; 4. (*Mus.*) Fortschreitung, Sequenz. **progressional,** *adj.* fortschreitend, Fortschritts–. **progressionist,** *s.* (*Pol.*) der Fortschrittler.

progressive [prəˈgresiv], **1.** *adj.* 1. fortschreitend, fortlaufend, sich weiterentwickelnd, progressiv; (*Phys.*) – ***wave,*** fortschreitende Welle; 2. aufeinanderfolgend, laufend, gestaffelt; 3. (*fig. also Pol.*) fortschrittlich, progessiv; – ***party,*** die Fortschrittspartei; – ***step,*** der Schritt vorwärts, Fortschritt; – ***thinker,*** fortschrittlicher Denker; 4. (*Gram.*) – ***form,*** die Dauerform (*of a verb*). **2.** *s.* (*Pol.*) der Fortschrittler. **progressively,** *adv.* stufenweise, nach und nach, nacheinander, allmählich. **progressiveness,** *s.* die Fortschrittlichkeit.

prohibit [prəˈhibit], *v.t.* verbieten, untersagen; unterbinden, verhindern; – ***him from doing,*** ihm verbieten *or* ihn verhindern *or* ihn daran hindern zu tun; ***smoking –ed,*** Rauchen verboten; ***–ed area,*** das Sperrgebiet. **prohibition** [prouhiˈbiʃən], *s.* 1. das Verbot, die Untersagung; (*Law*) ***writ of*** –, der Sistierungsbefehl; 2. die Prohibition, das Alkoholverbot. **prohibitionist** [prouhiˈbiʃənist], *s.* der Alkoholgegner, Antialkoholiker. **prohibitive,** *adj.* verbietend, verhindernd, Prohibitiv–, Sperr–; – ***duty,*** der Schutzzoll; – ***cost***(***s***), untragbare Kosten; – ***price,*** unerschwinglicher Preis. **prohibitory,** *adj. See* **prohibitive.**

1**project** [ˈprɔdʒikt], *s.* 1. der Entwurf, Plan, Anschlag, das Projekt, Vorhaben, Unternehmen; 2. die (Forschungs)aufgabe, (*at school*) Planaufgabe.

2**project** [prəˈdʒekt], **1.** *v.t.* 1. (vorwärts)werfen, schleudern; 2. werfen, projizieren (*an image*) (***on to,*** auf (*Acc.*)); (*fig.*) – ***one's feelings,*** seine Gefühle übertragen (***into,*** auf (*Acc.*)); – ***one's thoughts,*** sich in Gedanken versetzen (***into,*** in (*Acc.*)); – ***o.s. into,*** sich (heinein)versetzen in (*Acc.*); 3. entwerfen, planen, projektieren (*a plan*). **2.** *v.i.* hervorragen, vorspringen, vorstehen (***over,*** über (*Acc.*)).

projectile [prəˈdʒektail], **1.** *adj.* 1. Wurf– (*weapon*); Stoß–, Trieb– (*force*). **2.** *s.* das Projektil; (*Artil.*) Geschoß; ***theory of –s,*** die Schießlehre.

projecting [prəˈdʒektiŋ], *adj.* 1. vorgelagert, (her)-vorstehend, hinausragend; 2. (*Archit.*) vorspringend, ausladend, auskragend.

projection [prəˈdʒekʃən], *s.* 1. das Werfen, Schleudern, Vor(wärts)stoßen; 2. der Stoß, Wurf; 3. das Vorstehen, (Her)vorspringen, Hervorragen, Hervortreten; 4. (*Archit.*) die Ausladung, Vorkragung, der Vorsprung, Überhang; 5. (*fig., Math.*) die Projektion; 6. (*Phot.*) Projektion, das Projizieren, Vorführen; Projektionsbild, Lichtbild; – ***camera,*** *see* **projector** (*Opt.*); – ***room,*** der Vorführraum (*cinema*); 7. (*fig.*) die Übertragung (*of guilt etc.*), Hinausverlegung, Vergegenständlichung (*of feelings*); 8. das Planen, Entwerfen; der Entwurf, Plan, Vorsatz.

projector [prəˈdʒektə], *s.* 1. der Pläneschmied, Projektemacher; 2. (*Opt.*) Bildwerfer, Projektionsapparat; (*Tech.*) Scheinwerfer.

prolapse [ˈproulæps], **1.** *s.* (*Med.*) der Vorfall, Prolaps. **2.** *v.i.* vorfallen, prolabieren. **prolapsus,** *s. See* **prolapse, 1.**

prolate [ˈprouleit], *adj.* (*Math.*) gestreckt.

prolegomenary [prouliˈgɔminəri], *adj.* einleitend. **prolegomenon,** *s.* (*usu. pl.* **-mena**) die Vorbemerkung, Einleitung. **prolegomenous,** *adj.* 1. einleitend; 2. (*fig.*) langatmig, weitschweifig.

prolepsis [prouˈlepsis], *s.* (*Rhet.*) vorwegnehmende Antwort, die Vorwegnahme, Prolepsis. **proleptic,** *adj.* vorwegnehmend, vorgreifend.

proletarian [proliˈtɛəriən], **1.** *adj.* proletarisch, Proletarier–. **2.** *s.* der (die) Proletarier(in). **proletariat,** *s.* das Proletariat, Proletarier (*pl.*).

proliferate [prəˈlifəreit], *v.i.* sich fortpflanzen, sich stark vermehren, wuchern. **proliferation** [–ˈreiʃən], *s.* (*Bot.*) die (Aus)sprossung, Durchwachsung; üppiges Wachstum, starke Vermehrung, die Wucherung, Prolifikation.

prolific [prəˈlifik], *adj.* 1. (überaus) fruchtbar (*also fig.*); 2. (*fig.*) reich (*of*, *in*, an (*Dat.*)); 3. produktiv.

prolix [ˈprouliks], *adj.* weitschweifig, langatmig, wortreich. **prolixity** [–ˈliksiti], *s.* die Weitschweifigkeit, Langatmigkeit.

prolocutor [prou'lɔkjutə], *s.* (*Eccl.*) der Wortführer, Vorsitzende(r) (der Synode).

prologize ['proulədʒaiz], *v.i. See* **prologuize. prologue** [–lɔg], *s.* 1. der Prolog, die Vorrede, Einleitung, das Vorwort (*to, Gen.*); 2. (*fig.*) Vorspiel, der Auftakt (zu). **prologuize** [–gaiz], *v.i.* einen Prolog sprechen *or* verfassen.

prolong [prə'lɔŋ], *v.t.* 1. verlängern, ausdehnen; 2. (*Phonet.*) dehnen; 3. (*Comm.*) prolongieren. **prolongate** ['proulɔŋgeit], *v.t. See* **prolong. prolongation** [proulɔŋ'geiʃən], *s.* 1. die Verlängerung, (Aus)dehnung; 2. (*Comm.*) Prolongierung, Prolongation. **prolonged,** *adj.* anhaltend. **prolongment,** *s. See* **prolongation.**

prom [prɔm], *s.* (*coll.*) *see* **promenade, 1,** 2; *and* **promenade concert.**

promenade [prɔmə'nɑ:d], **1.** *s.* 1. der Spaziergang; 2. Spazierweg, Strandweg (*on sea-front*); 3. die Wandelhalle, Wandelanlage; 4. (*Danc.*) Promenade. **2.** *v.i.* spazieren(gehen), auf und ab gehen, promenieren. **3.** *v.t.* 1. auf und ab schreiten, umherspazieren in *or* auf (*Dat.*) (*a place*); 2. spazierenführen, umherführen (*a p.*). **promenade| concert,** *s.* das Promenadenkonzert. – **deck,** *s.* das Promenadendeck.

prominence ['prɔminəns], *s.* 1. das (Her)vorragen, (Her)vorstehen, (Her)vorspringen; ***come into –,*** hervortreten, in den Vordergrund treten *or* rücken, in die Augen fallen; ***give – to,*** hervorheben; 2. der Vorsprung, die Protuberanz; 3. (*fig.*) Auffälligkeit, Berühmtheit, Wichtigkeit, Bedeutung; ***bring into –,*** klar herausstellen, berühmt machen. **prominent,** *adj.* 1. vorstehend, vorspringend; 2. (*fig.*) hervorstechend, hervortretend, auffallend, in die Augen fallend; 3. (*of a p.*) prominent, berühmt, führend, hervorragend.

promiscuity [prɔmis'kjuiti], *s.* 1. die Mannigfaltigkeit, Vermischtheit, Vermischung, Verworrenheit, das Durcheinander; 2. die Promiskuität, zwangloser *or* wahlloser Geschlechtsverkehr. **promiscuous** [prə'miskjuəs], *adj.* 1. mannigfaltig, (durcheinander)gemischt, vermischt, verworren, buntgewürfelt; 2. gemeinsam; gemeinschaftlich; 3. unterschiedslos; 4. (*coll.*) gelegentlich, zufällig; ***– sexual relations,*** die Promiskuität. **promiscuously,** *adv.* 1. durcheinander, kunterbunt; 2. wahllos, unterschiedslos, zufällig.

promise ['prɔmis], **1.** *s.* 1. das Versprechen (*to,* gegenüber), die Zusage, Verheißung; ***breach of –,*** der Bruch des Eheversprechens; ***keep a –,*** ein Versprechen halten *or* einlösen; ***make a –,*** ein Versprechen geben; 2. die Hoffnung, Aussicht, Erwartung (*of,* auf (*Acc.*)); ***of great –,*** vielversprechend, verheißungsvoll. **2.** *v.t.* 1. versprechen, verheißen, geloben, zusagen, zusichern, in Aussicht stellen ((*to*) *a p., Dat.*; *a th., Acc.*); (*B.*) ***–d land,*** gelobtes Land; 2. Hoffnungen erwecken auf (*Acc.*), hoffen lassen, erwarten lassen, befürchten lassen; 3. (*coll.*) versichern (*a p., Dat.*); 4. ***be –d,*** (in die Ehe) versprochen sein. **3.** *v.i.* 1. Versprechungen machen, ein Versprechen geben, versprechen; 2. (*fig.*) Erwartungen *or* Hoffnungen erwecken; ***he –s well,*** er läßt sich gut an, er berechtigt zu den besten Hoffnungen; ***it –s (to be) fine,*** das Wetter verspricht gut zu werden.

promisee [prɔmi'si:], *s.* (*Law*) der Empfänger einer Promesse, Promissar.

promising ['prɔmisiŋ], *adj.* vielversprechend, hoffnungsvoll, verheißungsvoll, günstig, aussichtsreich; ***– weather,*** günstiges Wetter; ***– youth,*** vielversprechender Jüngling.

promisor ['prɔmisɔ:], *s.* (*Law*) der Promittent. **promissory** [–əri], *adj.* versprechend; (*Comm.*) ***– note,*** die Promesse, der Schuldschein, eigner *or* trockener Wechsel, der Solawechsel.

promontory ['prɔməntəri], *s.* 1. das Vorgebirge; 2. (*Anat.*) stumpfer Vorsprung.

promote [prə'mout], *v.t.* 1. befördern (*a p.*), (*at school*) versetzen; 2. Vorschub leisten (*Dat.*), unterstützen, fördern, begünstigen, befürworten (*a th.*), gründen (*a company etc.*); Reklame machen für, anpreisen, propagieren (*goods*); 3. unterstützen, einbringen (*a law*). **promoter,** *s.* 1. der Förderer, Befürworter; 2. Anstifter (*of a plot etc.*); 3. Gründer (*of a company*); 4. Veranstalter (*of a contest etc.*).

promotion [prə'mouʃən], *s.* 1. die Förderung, Begünstigung, Befürwortung; 2. Beförderung (*of a p.*) (*to,* zu); 3. (*Comm.*) Gründung; 4. (*also* ***sales –***) Reklame, Werbung. **promotional,** *adj.* Propaganda–, Reklame–, Werbe–. **promotive** [–tiv], *adj.* fördernd, begünstigend (*of, Acc.*); ***be – of,*** fördern.

prompt [prɔmpt], **1.** *adj.* 1. schnell, rasch, pünktlich, prompt, sofortig, unverzüglich, umgehend (*reply*); 2. bereit, (bereit)willig; 3. (*Comm.*) ***– cash,*** die Barzahlung. **2.** *s.* 1. (*Comm.*) der Zahlungstag, die Zahlungsfrist, das Ziel; ***at a – of 3 months,*** gegen Dreimonatsziel; 2. (*Theat.*) das Stichwort (*also fig.*). **3.** *v.i.* (*Theat.*) soufflieren. **4.** *v.t.* 1. (*Theat.*) soufflieren (*Dat.*); 2. (*fig.*) wecken, hervorrufen, einflößen, eingeben (*feelings, ideas, etc.*), (an)treiben, veranlassen, bewegen (*to,* zu).

prompt|-book, *s.* das Souffleurbuch. **–-box,** *s.* der Souffleurkasten. **prompter,** *s.* 1. (*Theat.*) der Souffleur (die Souffleuse); 2. Anreger, Antreiber. **prompting,** *s.* 1. (*Theat.*) das Soufflieren, Vorsagen; 2. (*fig. oft. pl.*) die Eingebung; Veranlassung. **promptitude** [–itju:d], *s. See* **promptness. promptly,** *adv.* unverzüglich, sofort, kurzweg. **promptness,** *s.* 1. die Schnelligkeit, Unverzüglichkeit, Pünktlichkeit, Promptheit; 2. Bereitwilligkeit. **prompt-note,** *s.* (*Comm.*) der Mahnzettel.

promulgate ['prɔməlgeit], *v.t.* bekanntmachen, veröffentlichen, promulgieren, verkünd(ig)en, verbreiten. **promulgation** [–'geiʃən], *s.* die Bekanntgabe, Veröffentlichung, Promulgation, Bekanntmachung, Verkünd(ig)ung, Verbreitung. **promulgator,** *s.* der Verkünd(ig)er, Verbreiter.

pronate ['prouneit], *v.t.* (*v.i.*) (*Anat.*) (sich) nach unten drehen, pronieren. **pronation** [–'neiʃən], *s.* die Einwärtsdrehung. **pronator** [–'neitə], *s.* der Pronator, Pronationsmuskel.

prone [proun], *adj.* 1. hingestreckt, auf dem Gesicht *or* Bauch liegend; 2. vorwärts geneigt; (*ground*) abschüssig; (*fig.*) ***– to,*** geneigt *or* veranlagt zu, empfänglich für. **proneness,** *s.* der Hang, die Neigung (*to,* zu), Empfänglichkeit (für).

prong [prɔŋ], *s.* 1. die Zinke, Zacke, Spitze; 2. (*Agr.*) Forke, Gabel; 3. Sprosse (*of antlers*). **prongbuck,** *s.* die Gabelantilope. **pronged,** *adj.* zackig, gezinkt; (*as suff.*) –zinkig. **prong-horn,** *s. See* **prong-buck.**

pronominal [pro'nɔminl], *adj.* (*Gram.*) pronominal, fürwörtlich.

pronoun ['prounaun], *s.* das Fürwort, Pronomen.

pronounce [prə'nauns], **1.** *v.t.* 1. aussprechen (*words*); ***– o.s. in favour of it,*** sich dafür aussprechen; 2. verkünden, verhängen, fällen (*on,* über (*Acc.*)) (*a verdict*); 3. (bestimmt) erklären (***to be,*** für), bezeichnen (als). **2.** *v.i.* seine Meinung äußern, sich aussprechen *or* erklären (*for,* zugunsten (*Gen.*); ***against,*** gegen; ***on,*** über (*Acc.*)). **pronounceable,** *adj.* aussprechbar, auszusprechen(d). **pronounced,** *adj.* 1. ausgesprochen, bestimmt, entschieden; 2. deutlich, sichtlich, deutlich hervortretend, (scharf) ausgeprägt. **pronouncement,** *s.* der Ausspruch, die Äußerung, Erklärung, Verkünd(ig)ung. **pronouncing,** *adj.* Aussprache–.

pronto ['prɔntou], *adv.* (*sl.*) bald, prompt, fix, dalli.

pronunciation [prənʌnsi'eiʃən], *s.* die Aussprache.

proof [pru:f], **1.** *s.* 1. der Beweis (*of,* für); Nachweis, Beleg (*also pl.* Belege), Beweisgrund (*also pl.* –gründe), das Beweismittel (*also pl.*); (*Law*) die Beweisaussage, Beweisaufnahme; ***burden of –,*** die Beweislast; ***capable of –,*** beweiskräftig; ***give – of,*** unter Beweis stellen, Beweise abgeben von; ***in – of,*** zum Beweise von; ***– positive,*** eindeutiger Beweis; ***– to the contrary,*** der Gegenbeweis; ***by way of –,*** als *or* zum Beweis; 2. die Probe (*also Math.*), Prüfung; ***put to (the) –,*** auf die Probe stellen; 3.

(*Typ.*) der (Probe)abzug, Korrekturbogen, die Korrektur; (*Phot.*) das Probebild; (*Typ.*) – ***before letters,*** Abzug vor der Schrift; ***correct*** (***the***) ***–s,*** Korrekturen lesen; 4. die Normalstärke (*of alcohol*); (*fig.*) Festigkeit; ***of –,*** undurchdringlich; (*Prov.*) ***the – of the pudding is in the eating,*** in der Praxis allein zeigt sich die Bewährung; ***under –,*** unter Normalstärke. **2.** *adj.* 1. undurchdringlich; 2. (*Tech., Chem.*) beständig, probehaltig, normalstark; 3. erprobt, bewährt; sicher (***against,*** vor (*Dat.*)), unzugänglich (*Dat. or* für), gesichert, gefeit, gewappnet (gegen). **3.** *adj. suff. For examples see under* **bomb, fire, fool, water** *etc.* **4.** *v.t.* imprägnieren.

proof|-mark, *s.* der Probestempel. **--reader,** *s.* der Korrekturleser, Korrektor. **--reading,** *s.* das Korrekturlesen; die Korrektur. **--sheet,** *s.* der Korrekturbogen. **--spirit,** *s.* der Normalweingeist.

[1]**prop** [prɔp], **1.** *s.* die Stütze (*also fig.*), der (Stütz)pfahl; (*fig.*) Halt. **2.** *v.t.* (*also – up*) (unter)stützen; abstützen, (aus)pfählen (*vines etc.*).

[2]**prop,** *s.* (*coll.*) *see* **propeller.**

[3]**prop,** *s.* (*usu. pl.*) *see* **props.**

propaedeutic(al) [prɔpə'dju:tik(l)], *adj.* einführend, vorbereitend, propädeutisch. **propaedeutics,** *pl.* (*sing. constr.*) die Propädeutik.

propaganda [prɔpə'gændə], *s.* die Propaganda, Reklame, Werbung; ***carry on*** or ***make – for,*** Propaganda treiben für. **propagandist,** *s.* der Propagandist. **propagandistic** [–'distik], *adj.* propagandistisch. **propagandize, 1.** *v.i.* Propaganda treiben *or* machen. **2.** *v.t.* Propaganda machen für, propagieren.

propagate ['prɔpəgeit], *v.t.* 1. fortpflanzen (*also Phys., waves etc.*); ***be –d,*** sich fortpflanzen; 2. (*fig.*) propagieren, verbreiten, ausbreiten. **propagation** [–'geiʃən], *s.* 1. die Fortpflanzung (*also Phys.*); 2. (*fig.*) Verbreitung, Ausbreitung. **propagator,** *s.* 1. der Fortpflanzer; 2. Verbreiter.

propane ['proupein], *s.* das Propan(gas).

propel [prə'pel], *v.t.* 1. vorwärtstreiben, antreiben; 2. (*fig.*) (fort)treiben. **propellant** [–ənt], *s.* 1. das Treibmittel, der Treibstoff; 2. (*Artil.*) die Treibladung; 3. (*fig.*) treibende Kraft, der Antrieb. **propellent** [–ənt], **1.** *adj.* vorwärtstreibend, antreibend. **2.** *s. See* **propellant.**

propeller [prə'pelə], *s.* der Propeller, (*Av.*) die Luftschraube, (*Naut.*) Schiffsschraube; ***--blade,*** (*Av.*) das Luftschraubenblatt, (*Naut.*) der Schraubenflügel; ***--driven,*** mit Schraubenantrieb; ***--shaft,*** die Schraubenwelle; – ***slipstream,*** der (Luft)schraubenstrahl.

propelling [prə'peliŋ], *adj.* Trieb–, Treib–; (*Artil.*) – ***charge,*** die Treibladung, der Treibsatz; – ***force,*** die Antriebskraft, Triebkraft; – ***pencil,*** der Dreh(blei)stift.

propensity [prə'pensiti], *s.* die Neigung, der Hang (***to***(***wards***), ***for,*** zu).

proper ['prɔpə], *adj.* 1. eigentümlich, eigen (***to,*** *Dat.*), speziell, besonder; (*Astr.*) – ***motion,*** die Eigenbewegung; – ***name*** or ***noun,*** der Eigenname; 2. geeignet, passend (***to,*** für); gebührend, geziemend, angebracht, zweckmäßig, angemessen; ***in the – place,*** am rechten Platz; ***at the – time,*** zur richtigen *or* passenden Zeit; ***all in its – time,*** alles zu seiner Zeit; (*Math.*) – ***fraction,*** echter Bruch; (*Math.*) – ***number,*** spezielle Zahl; 3. (*coll.*) einwandfrei, korrekt, schicklich, anständig; – ***behaviour,*** einwandfreies *or* anständiges Benehmen; 4. zuständig, maßgebend, normal, gewöhnlich, richtig, genau; ***as you think –,*** wie Sie für richtig halten; ***in the – sense of the word,*** strenggenommen, im eigentlichen Sinne des Wortes; ***that's the – thing to do,*** das ist das (einzig) Richtige; 5. (*following noun*) eigentlich, wirklich; ***the garden –,*** der Garten selbst, der eigentliche Garten; 6. (*coll.*) gründlich, tüchtig, ordentlich, gehörig; ***he is a – scoundrel,*** er ist ein richtiger Schuft. **properly,** *adv.* 1. richtig, wie es sich gehört; ***behave –,*** sich (anständig) benehmen; 2. mit (vollem) Recht; – ***speaking,*** strenggenommen, eigentlich; 3. (*coll.*) gehörig, tüchtig, vollkommen, total.

propertied ['prɔpətid], *adj.* besitzend, begütert.

property ['prɔpəti], *s.* 1. (*without art.*) das Eigentum, Besitztum, der Besitz, das Vermögen, Hab und Gut; ***common –,*** das Gemeingut; ***damage to –,*** der Sachschaden; – ***has its duties,*** Eigentum verpflichtet; ***house –,*** der Hausbesitz; ***man of –,*** vermögender Mann; ***lost –,*** Fundsachen (*pl.*); ***lost-- office,*** das Fundbüro; ***personal –,*** bewegliche Habe; ***public –,*** öffentliches Eigentum; 2. (*also with art.*) der Grundbesitz, Landbesitz, die Besitzung, das Grundstück, Landereien (*pl.*), Immobilien (*pl.*); 3. (*Law*) das Eigentumsrecht; ***literary –,*** literarisches Eigentum(srecht); 4. (*Theat.*) (*usu. pl.*) Requisiten (*pl.*); 5. die Eigenschaft, (*esp. Phil.*) das Merkmal, (*Tech. of materials*) Vermögen, die Fähigkeit; Eigenart, Eigenheit.

property|-assets, *pl.* Vermögenswerte (*pl.*). **--insurance,** *s.* die Sachversicherung. **--market,** *s.* der Grundstücksmarkt. **--master,** *s.* (*Theat.*) der Requisitenmeister, Requisiteur. **--room,** *s.* (*Theat.*) die Requisitenkammer. **--tax,** *s.* die Vermögenssteuer.

prophecy ['prɔfisi], *s.* 1. die Prophezeiung, Weissagung; 2. (*fig.*) Voraussage, Vorhersage. **prophesy** [–sai], **1.** *v.t.* prophezeien, voraussagen (***for him,*** ihm). **2.** *v.i.* weissagen, voraussagen. **prophet** [–fit], *s.* der Prophet, Wahrsager, Weissager, Seher; – ***of evil,*** der Unglücksprophet, Schwarzseher; (*B.*) ***major*** (***minor***) –, großer (kleiner) Prophet. **prophetess,** *s.* die Weissagerin, Prophetin. **prophetic(al)** [prə'fetik(l)], *adj.* prophetisch; ***be prophetic of,*** prophezeien, voraussagen.

prophylactic [prɔfi'læktik], **1.** *adj.* vorbeugend, Vorbeugungs–, Schutz–, prophylaktisch. **2.** *s.* 1. das Vorbeugungsmittel; 2. (*fig.*) vorbeugende Maßnahme. **prophylaxis,** *s.* die Präventivbehandlung, Vorbeugung, Prophilaxe.

propinquity [prə'piŋkwiti], *s.* 1. die Nähe (*in place, time*); 2. enge Verwandtschaft.

propitiate [prə'piʃieit], *v.t.* 1. günstig stimmen, geneigt machen; 2. besänftigen, aussöhnen, versöhnen. **propitiation** [–i'eiʃən], *s.* 1. die Versöhnung, Aussöhnung; 2. (*obs.*) Sühne; das Sühnopfer. **propitiatory** [–'piʃiətəri], *adj.* versöhnend, versöhnlich, besänftigend; – ***sacrifice,*** das Sühnopfer,

propitious [prə'piʃəs], *adj.* 1. günstig, vorteilhaft (***to,*** für); 2. wohlgesinnt, geneigt, gnädig. **propitiousness,** *s.* 1. die Vorteilhaftigkeit, Günstigkeit; 2. Geneigtheit, Gnade, Gunst.

proponent [prə'pounənt], *s.* 1. der Verfechter, Befürworter; 2. (*Law*) präsumtiver Testamentserbe.

proportion [prə'pɔ:ʃən], **1.** *s.* 1. das Verhältnis, Maß; ***in – to,*** im Verhältnis zu; ***in – as,*** in dem Maße wie, je nachdem wie; 2. richtiges Verhältnis, das Ebenmaß, Gleichmaß; ***be out of*** (***all***) ***– to,*** in keinem Verhältnis stehen zu; ***in*** (***the right*** or ***correct***) ***–,*** im richtigen Verhältnis; (*fig.*) ***sense of –,*** der Maßstab für die Wirklichkeit; 3. das Ausmaß, die Größe, der Umfang; 4. (verhältnismäßiger) Anteil; 5. (*Math.*) die Proportion, Verhältnisgleichung; (*also* ***rule of*** –) Dreisatzrechnung, Regeldetri. **2.** *v.t.* 1. in ein richtiges Verhältnis bringen (***to,*** mit *or* zu); gehörig anpassen (*Dat.*); ***well –d,*** wohlgestaltet, ebenmäßig; 2. anteilmäßig verteilen.

proportionable [prə'pɔ:ʃənəbl], *adj.* (*rare*) *see* **proportionate, 1. proportional, 1.** *adj.* 1. verhältnismäßig, Verhältnis–; – ***numbers,*** Proportionalzahlen; – ***representation,*** das Verhältniswahlsystem; 2. anteilmäßig, mengenmäßig; 3. im richtigen Verhältnis (stehend) (***to,*** zu); ***be – to,*** entsprechen (*Dat.*). **2.** *s.* (*Math.*) die Proportionale. **proportionality** [–'næliti], *s.* die Verhältnismäßigkeit, Proportionalität. **proportionate, 1.** [–it], *adj.* angemessen, entsprechend (***to,*** *Dat.*), im richtigen Verhältnis (zu), proportioniert. **2.** *v.t.*

[-eit], *v.t.* verhältnismäßig ausmessen *or* abmessen *or* zuteilen.

proposal [prə'pouzl], *s.* 1. der Vorschlag, Antrag, das Angebot; 2. Heiratsangebot, der Heiratsantrag. **propose, 1.** *v.t.* vorschlagen (*for,* zu *or* als; *to him,* ihm), beantragen; – *as candidate,* als Kandidaten aufstellen; – *his health,* auf seine Gesundheit trinken; – *marriage,* einen Heiratsantrag machen; – *a riddle,* ein Rätsel aufgeben; – *the toast of* or *to him,* den Toast auf ihn ausbringen; – *a vote of censure,* ein Mißtrauensvotum stellen *or* beantragen; – *a vote of thanks,* den Antrag stellen, Dank auszusprechen (*to, Dat.*). **2.** *v.i.* 1. sich vornehmen, gedenken, vorhaben, in Aussicht nehmen, beabsichtigen; (*Prov.*) *man –s, God disposes,* der Mensch denkt, Gott lenkt; 2. anhalten (*to,* um), einen Heiratsantrag machen (*Dat.*). **proposer,** *s.* der Antragsteller, Vorschlagende(r).

proposition [prɔpə'ziʃən], *s.* 1. der Antrag, Vorschlag; (*Math., Log.*) (Lehr)satz; 2. die Behauptung, der Hauptsatz; 3. (*coll.*) die Aufgabe, der Plan; das Geschäft, Unternehmen; (*coll.*) *easy –,* eine Kleinigkeit; (*coll.*) *tough –,* schwieriges Problem, (*of a p.*) schwieriger Fall. **propositional,** *adj.* Satz–.

propound [prə'paund], *v.t.* vorschlagen, vortragen, vorbringen, vorlegen (*to, Dat.*); – *a will,* auf Anerkennung eines Testaments klagen.

proprietary [prə'praiətəri], **1.** *adj.* 1. Eigentums–; – *right,* das Eigentumsrecht; 2. Eigentümer–, Besitzer–, Inhaber–; – *classes,* besitzende Klassen; 3. gesetzlich *or* patentamtlich geschützt; – *article,* der Markenartikel; – *sign,* die Hausmarke. **2.** *s.* (*rare*) 1. der Eigentümer, Besitzer (*also pl.*); 2. das Eigentum(srecht). **proprietor,** *s.* der Eigentümer, Besitzer, Inhaber. **proprietorship,** *s.* das Eigentumsrecht (*in,* an (*Dat.*)). **proprietress, proprietrix,** *s.* die Eigentümerin, Besitzerin, Inhaberin.

propriety [prə'praiəti], *s.* 1. der Anstand, die Anständigkeit, Schicklichkeit; – *of conduct,* anständiges Betragen; 2. *pl.* Anstandsformen (*pl.*), die Wohlanständigkeit; 3. Richtigkeit, Angemessenheit.

props [prɔps], *pl.* (*coll.*) (Bühnen)requisiten (*pl.*).

propulsion [prə'pʌlʃən], *s.* der Antrieb; (*Av.*) *jet–,* der Strahlvortrieb. **propulsive** [-siv], **1.** *adj.* antreibend, vorwärtstreibend, Trieb–. **2.** *s.* die Triebkraft.

propylaeum [prɔpi'leiəm], *s.* der Tempeleingang, Torbauten (*pl.*).

pro rata [prou'rɑ:tə], *adv.* verhältnismäßig, anteilmäßig.

prorogation [prourə'geiʃən], *s.* die Vertagung. **prorogue** [pro'roug], **1.** *v.t.* vertagen. **2.** *v.i.* vertagt werden, sich vertagen.

prosaic [prou'zeiik], *adj.* (*fig.*) prosaisch, alltäglich, nüchtern, trocken.

proscenium [pro'si:niəm], *s.* das Proszenium, die Vorbühne.

proscribe [prou'skraib], *v.t.* 1. (*usu. fig.*) ächten, verbannen; 2. verbieten. **proscription** [–'skripʃən], *s.* 1. die Ächtung, Acht; 2. Verbannung, Ausschließung; 3. (*fig.*) das Verbot. **proscriptive** [–'skriptiv], *adj.* ächtend, Ächtungs–.

prose [prouz], **1.** *s.* 1. die Prosa, ungebundene Rede; – *writer,* der Prosaschriftsteller, Prosaiker; 2. (*fig.*) die Alltäglichkeit, das Prosaische, Alltägliche; 3. die Übersetzung in die Fremdsprache. **2.** *attrib. adj.* Prosa–. **3.** *v.i.* langweilig erzählen. **4.** *v.t.* in Prosa schreiben.

prosector [prou'sektə], *s.* (*Anat.*) der Prosektor.

prosecute ['prɔsikju:t], **1.** *v.t.* 1. verfolgen, weiterführen (*plan etc.*), durchführen (*inquiry*), betreiben (*activity*); 2. (*Law*) betreiben, einklagen (*a claim*); 3. (*Law*) gerichtlich verfolgen, belangen, anklagen (*a p.*) (*for,* wegen). **2.** *v.i.* (*Law*) als Kläger auftreten; die Anklage vertreten. **prosecution** [–'kju:ʃən], *s.* 1. die Verfolgung, Durchführung (*of plan etc.*), das Betreiben (*of studies*); 2. (*Law*) Einklagen (*of a claim*); 3. (*Law*) Verklagen, die Strafverfolgung, gerichtliche Verfolgung; *the –,* die Staatsanwaltschaft, Anklage(behörde); *liable to –,* strafbar; *witness for the –,* der Belastungszeuge; *director of public –s,* der Staatsanwalt. **prosecutor,** *s.* 1. der Verfolger (*of plan etc.*); 2. (*Law*) (An)kläger; *public –,* der Staatsanwalt.

proselyte ['prɔsəlait], *s.* 1. der (die) Proselyt(in), Neubekehrte(r); 2. (*B.*) (zum Judentum) Übergetretene(r). **proselytism** [–lətizm], *s.* der Bekehrungseifer, Proselytismus. **proselytize** [–lətaiz], *v.i.* Anhänger werben, Proselyten machen.

prosiness ['prouzinis], *s.* die Langweiligkeit, Eintönigkeit, Weitschweifigkeit.

prosody ['prɔsədi], *s.* die Silbenmessungslehre, Prosodie.

prospect, 1. ['prɔspekt], *s.* 1. die Aussicht (*also fig.*), (Fern)sicht, der Blick (*of,* auf (*Acc.*)); *a – of,* Aussicht auf (*Acc.*); *some – of success,* Erfolgsaussichten (*pl.*); *hold out a – of,* in Aussicht stellen (*to him,* ihm); *what are your –s?* was haben Sie für Aussichten? *pleasures in –,* Freuden in Aussicht; *have in –,* Aussicht haben auf (*Acc.*); 2. die Landschaft; 3. (*Min.*) Schürfstelle, der Schurf; die Schürfprobe; 4. (*fig.*) voraussichtlicher Ertrag; voraussichtlicher Kunde, der Interessent, Reflektant. **2.** [prəs'pekt], *v.i.* 1. (*Min.*) schürfen, graben (*for,* nach); (*fig.*) Umschau *or* Ausschau halten, suchen, forschen, sondieren (*for,* nach); – *for oil,* nach Öl bohren; 2. versprechen, sich eignen (*well or ill*). **3.** [prəs'pekt], *v.t.* (*Min.*) durchforschen, prüfen, untersuchen, erschürfen (*a district*); (*fig.*) überblicken.

prospective [prəs'pektiv], *adj.* 1. vorausblickend, (zu)künftig, in Aussicht genommen, voraussichtlich; – *customer,* angehender Kunde, der Kaufinteressent, Reflektant; 2. (*Law*) nicht rückwirkend. **prospector,** *s.* (*Min.*) der Schürfer.

prospectus [prəs'pektəs], *s.* die Ankündigung, Werbeschrift; Preisliste, der Prospekt; (*Univ.*) das (Unterrichts)programm, Vorlesungsverzeichnis.

prosper ['prɔspə], **1.** *v.t.* begünstigen, segnen; hold *or* gewogen sein (*Dat.*). **2.** *v.i.* gedeihen, vorwärtskommen, gelingen, glücken, Erfolg *or* Glück haben (*in,* bei). **prosperity** [–'periti], *s.* 1. das Gedeihen, Wohlergehen, Glück, die Wohlfahrt, der Wohlstand; 2. (*Comm.*) Aufschwung, die (Hoch)konjunktur. **prosperous,** *adj.* 1. gedeihend, gedeihlich, blühend, erfolgreich; 2. (*coll.*) wohlhabend.

prostate ['prɔsteit], *s.* (*Anat.*) (*also – gland*) die Vorsteherdrüse, Prostata.

prosthesis ['prɔsθəsis], *s.* 1. (*Gram.*) die Prosthesis, Prosthese; 2. (*Surg.*) Prothese. **prosthetic** [–'θetik], *adj.* 1. (*Gram.*) prosthetisch, vorgesetzt; 2. (*Surg.*) prothetisch.

prostitute ['prɔstitju:t], **1.** *v.t.* preisgeben, hergeben; mißbrauchen, wegwerfen, erniedrigen; – *o.s.,* sich prostituieren *or* verkaufen (*to, Dat. or* an (*Acc.*)). **2.** *s.* die (Straßen)dirne, Prostituierte. **prostitution** [–'tju:ʃən], *s.* 1. gewerbsmäßige Unzucht, die Prostitution; 2. (*fig.*) Entehrung, Herabwürdigung.

prostrate, 1. ['prɔstreit], *adj.* 1. hingestreckt, umgestürzt; (*Bot.*) niederliegend; 2. erschöpft (*with,* vor (*Dat.*)); daniederliegend, hinfällig, zugrunde gerichtet, unterworfen, niedergeschlagen, gebrochen; unterwürfig, fußfällig, gedemütigt; *fall – before,* zu Füßen fallen (*Dat.*); – *with grief,* vor Kummer schwer gebeugt. **2.** [–'treit], *v.t.* 1. niederwerfen, hinwerfen, zu Boden werfen; (*fig.*) unterwerfen, demütigen; – *o.s.,* einen Fußfall tun, sich in den Staub werfen, sich demütigen (*before,* vor (*Dat.*)); 2. (*usu. pass.*) zugrunde richten, entkräften, erschöpfen. **prostration** [–'treiʃən], *s.* 1. die Unterwerfung, Demütigung, Niederwerfung; 2. Verbeugung, der Fußfall; 3. die Entkräftung, Erschöpfung; Niedergeschlagenheit; *nervous –,* die Neurasthenie.

prostyle ['proustail], *s.* das Säulentor, die Säulenhalle.

prosy ['prouzi], *adj.* (*fig.*) prosaisch, langweilig, weitschweifig.

protagonist [prou'tægənist], *s.* 1. der Vorkämpfer, Verfechter; 2. (*Theat.*, *fig.*) die Hauptfigur, Hauptperson.

protasis ['prɔtəsis], *s.* der Vordersatz (*also Rhet.*), (*Gram.*) vorgestellter Bedingungsatz.

protean ['proutiən], *adj.* 1. proteusartig, proteisch; 2. (*fig.*) vielgestaltig.

protect [prə'tekt], *v.t.* 1. (be)schützen (***from***, vor (*Dat.*); ***against***, gegen); – ***one's interests***, seine Interessen wahren; ***–ed by copyright***, urheberrechtlich geschützt; 2. (*Mil.*) (be)schirmen; sichern; 3. (*Chess*) decken; 4. (*Pol.*) (durch Schutzzoll) schützen; 5. (*Comm.*) einlösen, akzeptieren, honorieren (*a bill*).

protection [prə'tekʃən], *s.* 1. der Schutz, die Beschützung (***from***, vor (*Dat.*); ***against***, gegen); 2. die Protektion, Deckung, Sicherung; ***live under his –***, von ihm ausgehalten werden (*of prostitutes etc.*); 3. (*Pol.*) die Schutzzollpolitik, der Zollschutz; 4. (*Comm.*) die Honorierung (*of a bill*); 5. (*sl.*) – ***money***, Ausbeutungsgelder, Erpressungsgelder (*pl.*); – ***racket***, (organisiertes) Erpressungsgeschäft. **protectionism,** *s.* das Schutzzollsystem. **protectionist, 1.** *s.* der Schutzzöllner. **2.** *attrib. adj.* Schutzzoll–.

protective [prə'tektiv], *adj.* schützend, Schutz–; – ***clothing***, die Schutz(be)kleidung; – ***custody***, die Schutzhaft; – ***tariff***, der Schutzzoll. **protectiveness,** *s.* die Fürsorge (*of a p.*), Schutzwirkung (*of a th.*).

protector [prə'tektə], *s.* 1. der Beschützer, Gönner, Schutzherr, Schirmherr; 2. (*English Hist.*) Reichsverweser; 2. Schützer, das Schutzmittel, die Schutzvorrichtung. **protectorate** [–'tektərət], *s.* 1. (*English Hist.*) die Schutzherrschaft, das Protektorat; 2. (*Pol.*) Schutzgebiet. **protectorship,** *s.* das Protektorat, die Reichsverweserschaft. **protectory,** *s.* (*R.C.*) die Anstalt für verwahrloste Kinder. **protectress,** *s.* die Beschützerin.

protégé ['prɔtəʒei], *s.* 1. der Schützling, Schutzbefohlene(r); 2. der Protégé, Günstling. **protégée,** *s.* Schutzbefohlene (*f.*).

protein ['prouti:n], *s.* das Protein, Eiweiß, der Eiweißkörper.

pro tem [prou'tem], *adv.* (*coll.*) vorläufig, einstweilen.

protest, 1. ['proutest], *s.* der Einspruch, Protest, Widerspruch, die Verwahrung; ***enter*** or ***lodge*** or ***make a –***, Verwahrung einlegen, Protest erheben (***with***, bei; ***against***, gegen); ***in –, as a –, by way of –***, zum *or* als Protest; ***under –***, unter Protest *or* Vorbehalt; 2. (*Comm.*) der (Wechsel)protest; 3. (*Naut. Law*) Seeprotest, die Verklarung. **2.** [prə'test], *v.t.* 1. beteuern, (feierlich) versichern *or* erklären; 2. Einwände machen *or* Protest erheben gegen; 3. (*Comm.*) protestieren (*a bill*). **3.** [prə'test], *v.i.* Einwände machen, Einspruch erheben, Verwahrung einlegen, protestieren, aufbegehren, sich auflehnen *or* verwahren (***against***, gegen), etwas einzuwenden haben (***about***, gegen).

protestant [prə'testənt], **1.** *adj.* protestierend. **2.** *s.* Protestierende(r).

Protestant ['prɔtistənt], **1.** *adj.* protestantisch. **2.** *s.* der (die) Protestant(in). **Protestantism,** *s.* der Protestantismus.

protestation [prɔtəs'teiʃən], *s.* 1. die Beteuerung, (feierliche) Versicherung *or* Erklärung; 2. (*rare*) der Protest, Einspruch, die Verwahrung (***against***, gegen). **protester** [prə'testə], *s.* der Beteuerer, (*also Comm.*) Protestierende(r).

protest-meeting, *s.* die Protestversammlung.

prothalamium [prouθə'leimiəm], *s.* der Hochzeitsgesang.

proto– ['proutə], *pref.* 1. erst, frühest, Ur–; 2. (*Chem.*) niedrigst.

protoblast ['proutəbla:st], *s.* membranlose Zelle.

protochloride [proutə'klɔ:raid], *s.* das Chlorür.

protocol ['proutəkɔl], **1.** *s.* der Verhandlungsbericht, (*also fig.*) das Protokoll. **2.** *v.t.* zu Protokoll nehmen, protokollieren. **3.** *v.i.* (das) Protokoll führen.

protogenic [proutə'dʒenik], *adj.* (*Geol.*) primär, protogen.

protomorph ['proutəmɔ:f], *s.* (*Biol.*) die Urform. **protomorphic** [–'mɔ:fik], *adj.* (*Biol.*) primär, ursprünglich.

proton ['proutɔn], *s.* das Proton.

protonotary [proutə'noutəri], *s.* 1. erster (Gerichts)-sekretär; 2. (*Eccl.*) der Protonotar.

protoplasm ['proutəplæzm], *s.* das Protoplasma, der Urschleim. **protoplast** [–pla:st], *s.* (*Biol.*) der Zellkörper, Protoplast.

prototype ['proutətaip], *s.* 1. das Urbild, die Urform, der Urtyp; 2. das Vorbild, Muster(bild); 3. (*Tech.*) (Versuchs)modell.

protoxide [prou'tɔksaid], *s.* (*Chem.*) das Oxydul.

protozoa [proutə'zouə], *pl.* Einzeller, Urtierchen, Protozoen (*pl.*). **protozoic,** *adj.* (*Geol.*) protozoisch.

protract [prə'trækt], *v.t.* 1. (*usu. time*) in die Länge ziehen, hinausziehen, hinausschieben, aufschieben, verzögern; 2. (*Surv.*) nach einem Maßtab entwerfen; 3. (*Zool.*) ausstrecken, vorstrecken (*claws*). **protracted,** *adj.* lang, in die Länge gezogen, langwierig; – ***sleep***, der Dauerschlaf. **protractile** [–tail], *adj.* 1. verlängerungsfähig; 2. (*Zool.*) ausstreckbar, vorstreckbar. **protraction** [–ʃən], *s.* 1. die Verlängerung, Hinausziehung, Hinausschiebung, Verzögerung; 2. (*Surv.*) maßstabsgetreue Zeichnung; 3. (*Zool.*) das (Her)vorstrecken. **protractor** [–tə], *s.* 1. der Gradbogen, Winkelmesser, (Richt)zirkel, Transporteur, die Schmiege; 2. (*Anat.*) der Streckmuskel, Vorziehmuskel.

protrude [prə'tru:d], **1.** *v.t.* vorstoßen, herausstoßen, herausstrecken, hervorstrecken, hervortreten lassen. **2.** *v.i.* hervorragen, hervorstehen, hervortreten, heraustreten, überhangen (***beyond***, über (*Acc.*)). **protrudent,** *adj.* (her)vorstehend, (her)vortretend. **protrusile** [–sail], *adj.* ausstreckbar; vorstreckbar, verlängerungsfähig. **protrusion** [–ʒən], *s.* 1. das Vordringen, Vorspringen, Hervorstoßen, Herausragen, Hervorragen, Hervorstehen, Heraustreten, Hervortreten; 2. der Vorsprung, vorspringender Teil, die Ausbuchtung, Vorwölbung. **protrusive** [–siv], *adj.* vorstehend, vordringend, hervortretend, hervorspringend.

protuberance [prə'tju:bərəns], *s.* 1. der Auswuchs, Höcker, die Beule; 2. Erhöhung, (her)vortretende Stelle; 3. (*Astr.*) die Protuberanz. **protuberant,** *adj.* (her)vorstehend, hervortretend, hervorquellend; – ***eyes***, Glotzaugen (*pl.*).

proud [praud], *adj.* 1. stolz (***of***, auf (*Acc.*)); 2. hochmütig, eingebildet, eitel; 3. (*fig.*) prächtig, stattlich, herrlich; (*coll.*) ***do o.s. –***, sich (*Dat.*) gütlich tun, es sich (*Dat.*) gut gehen lassen; ***do him –***, ihn königlich bewirten; 4. (*Med.*) – ***flesh***, wildes Fleisch.

provable ['pru:vəbl], *adj.* erweislich, beweisbar, nachweisbar.

prove [pru:v], **1.** *v.t.* 1. beweisen, unter Beweis stellen (***it to be***, daß es ist), erweisen, nachweisen, bestätigen, belegen; – ***one's case***, beweisen, daß man recht hat; – ***one's identity***, sich legitimieren *or* ausweisen; – ***o.s. (to be) able***, sich als fähig erweisen; – ***a th. (to be) true***, etwas als wahr erweisen *or* nachweisen; 2. erproben; aufgehen lassen (*dough*); – ***o.s.***, sich bewähren; ***–d remedy***, erprobtes *or* bewährtes Mittel; 3. (*Law*) beglaubigen (*a will*); 4. prüfen (*also Math.*). **2.** *v.i.* sich erweisen *or* herausstellen (***to be***, als . . . *or* daß . . . ist), sich bewähren *or* bestätigen (***to be***, als); sich ergeben, ausfallen; – ***(to be) equal to***, sich gewachsen zeigen (*Dat.*); – ***(false) true***, sich (nicht) bestätigen, sich als (falsch) richtig herausstellen; ***he will – a good soldier***, er wird (noch) einen guten Soldat abgeben.

proven ['pru:vən], *adj.* (*Scots*) erwiesen; (*Law*) ***not –***, Schuldbeweis nicht erbracht.

provenance ['prɔvənəns], *s.* der Ursprung, die Herkunft.

Provençal [prɔvã'sɑ:l], **1.** *adj.* provenzalisch. **2.** *s.* der Provenzale (die Provenzalin). **Provence** [prɔ'vãs], *s.* (*Geog.*) Provence (*f.*).

provender ['prɔvəndə], *s.* 1. das (Trocken)futter, Viehfutter; 2. (*coll.*) die Nahrung, der Proviant.

proverb ['prɔvə:b], *s.* das Sprichwort. **proverbial** [prə'və:biəl], *adj.* sprichwörtlich; *be* –, sprichwörtlich sein, zum Sprichwort geworden sein. **Proverbs,** *pl.* (*B.*) die Sprüche Salomonis.

provide [prə'vaid], **1.** *v.t.* 1. anschaffen, beschaffen, verschaffen, besorgen, zur Verfügung stellen, beistellen, liefern (*him with it* or *it for him,* es ihm); versehen, versorgen, ausstatten, beliefern (*a p.*) (*with,* mit); (*fig.*) – *for,* in Rechnung stellen; 2. (*Law etc.*) vorschreiben, vorsehen, bestimmen, festsetzen. **2.** *v.i.* Vorsorge treffen, Maßnahmen ergreifen (*against,* gegen *or* vor (*Dat.*)), sich schützen (vor (*Dat.*)); Sorge tragen, sorgen (*for,* für); Gelder bereitstellen, Deckung anschaffen; *be –d for,* versorgt sein, (*fig.*) in Rechnung gestellt werden; (*fig.*) – *against,* verhindern, unmöglich machen. **provided, 1.** *adj.* vorbereitet, gefaßt (*for,* auf (*Acc.*)); versorgt, versehen, ausgestattet; (*Hist.*) – *school,* die Gemeindeschule. **2.** *conj.* (*also – that*) vorausgesetzt (daß), unter der Bedingung *or* Voraussetzung daß, es sei denn (daß), wofern (nur), wenn (überhaupt).

providence ['prɔvidəns], *s.* 1. (göttliche) Fügung *or* Vorsehung; 2. (*rare*) die Vorsorge, (weise) Voraussicht; 3. die Sparsamkeit. **provident,** *adj.* 1. voraussehend, vorsorglich, fürsorglich; – *care,* die Vorsorge, Fürsorge; – *fund,* die Unterstützungskasse, Hilfskasse; – *society,* der (Arbeiter)-wohlfahrtsverein, Unterstützungsverein; 2. sparsam, haushälterisch. **providential** [–'denʃəl], *adj.* 1. durch (göttliche) Fügung *or* Vorsehung bewirkt *or* bestimmt, schicksalhaft; 2. günstig, gnädig, glücklich. **providentially,** *adv.* 1. durch (göttliche) Fügung *or* Vorsehung, schicksalhaft; 2. glücklicherweise. **providently,** *adv.* vorsorglich.

provider [prə'vaidə], *s.* 1. der (die) Versorger(in), Fürsorger(in); 2. (*Comm.*) der Lieferant; *universal –(s),* die Gemischtwarenhandlung, das Warenhaus. **providing,** *conj.* (*also – that*) *see* **provided, 2.**

province ['prɔvins], *s.* 1. die Provinz; der Bezirk, Distrikt; 2. (*fig.*) das (Arbeits)gebiet, Amt, Fach, die Fachrichtung, Sphäre, Aufgabe, der (Aufgaben)bereich, Wirkungskreis, Zweig; *that is not within my –,* das schlägt nicht in mein Fach; 3. *pl.* die Provinz. **provincial** [prə'vinʃəl], **1.** *adj.* 1. Provinz–, Provinzial–, provinziell; – *town,* die Provinzstadt; 2. kleinstädtisch, provinzlerisch, ländlich; 3. (*fig.*) spießbürgerlich, engstirnig, beschränkt. **2.** *s.* 1. der (die) Provinzbewohner(in), der Provinzler; 2. (*fig.*) Spießbürger, Spießer. **provincialism,** *s.* 1. provinzielle Beschränktheit *or* Abgeschlossenheit, der Provinzialismus; 2. mundartlicher Ausdruck; *see also* **provinciality** [–ʃi'æliti], *s.* 1. das Provinzlertum, Spießbürgertum, beschränkter Gesichtskreis; 2. der Lokalpatriotismus, die Kirchturmpolitik.

provision [prə'viʒən], **1.** *s.* 1. die Beschaffung, Besorgung, Bereitstellung; (*Comm.*) Rimesse, Deckung; – *of funds,* die Kapitalbeschaffung, Deckung; 2. die Vorkehrung, Maßnahme, Anstalt; Vorsorge, Fürsorge, vorsorgliche Maßnahme; (*esp. Law*) Maßregel, Bestimmung, Verordnung, Verfügung; *make – for* (or *against*), Vorkehrungen *or* Anstalten treffen für (*or* gegen), sorgen für (*or* sich schützen gegen); *in accordance with –s,* laut Bestimmungen; – *for old age,* die Altersversicherung; 3. (*Law*) die Bedingung, der Vorbehalt; *under* (*the*) *usual –s,* unter üblichem Vorbehalt; 4. *pl.* Lebensmittel, Nahrungsmittel (*pl.*), der Proviant, (Lebensmittel)vorrat (*also* –vorräte *pl.*), die Verpflegung; – *dealer,* – *merchant, see* **provisioner**; 5. (*oft. pl.*) Reserven, Rücklagen, Rückstellungen (*pl.*). **2.** *v.t.* mit Lebensmitteln *or* Proviant versorgen, verproviantieren.

provisional [prə'viʒənl], *adj.* provisorisch, vorläufig, Vor–, einstweilig, behelfsmäßig; (*Comm.*) Interims–; – *order,* die Ausnahmeverordnung, einstweilige Verfügung; – *receipt,* die Interimsquittung; – *regulation,* die Übergangsbestimmung; – *result,* das Zwischenergebnis. **provisionally,** *adv.* provisorisch, vorläufig, einstweilen, bis auf weiteres.

provisioner [prə'viʒənə], *s.* der Lebensmittellieferant; Lebensmittelhändler, Kolonialwarenhändler, Feinkosthändler.

proviso [prə'vaizou], *s.* die Bedingung, (Bedingungs)klausel, Einschränkung, der Vorbehalt; *with the –,* unter der Bedingung. **provisorily** [–zərili], *adv.* bedingt, mit *or* unter Vorbehalt, bedingungsweise. **provisory** [–zəri], *adj.* bedingt, bedingend; *see also* **provisional.**

provocation [prɔvə'keiʃən], *s.* 1. die Herausforderung, Provokation; 2. Aufreizung, der (An)reiz, Anlaß, die Veranlassung; *without –,* ohne Anlaß; *at the slightest –,* beim geringsten Anlaß; 3. (*coll.*) Verärgerung, Erbostheit; *under –,* in Erbostheit. **provocative** [prə'vɔkətiv], *adj.* (zum Widerspruch) herausfordernd, aufreizend (*of,* zu); provozierend, provokatorisch, anreizend, anregend; *be – of,* erregen, hervorrufen.

provoke [prə'vouk], *v.t.* 1. herausfordern, provozieren, (auf)reizen, anreizen, antreiben (*a p. to do s.th.*), erregen, hervorrufen, heraufbeschwören (*feelings etc.*), veranlassen, verursachen, bewirken; – *him to anger,* ihn zum Zorn reizen; 2. (*coll.*) erzürnen, (ver)ärgern, aufbringen (*a p.*). **provoking,** *adj.* 1. herausfordernd, provozierend, aufreizend; 2. (*coll.*) (ver)ärgernd, empörend, unausstehlich.

[1]**provost** ['prɔvəst], *s.* der Vorsteher, Leiter (*Eton and some colleges*), (*Scots*) Bürgermeister; (*Scots*) *Lord Provost,* der Oberbürgermeister.

[2]**provost** [prə'vou], *s.* (*Mil.*) der Profos; – *court,* das Feldgericht, Kriegsgericht; – *marshall,* (*Hist.*) der Generalprofos, (*Mil.*) Chef der Militärpolizei, (*Naut.*) Marineprofos; – *sergeant,* der Feldwebel der Militärpolizei.

prow [prau], *s.* der Bug, Schiffsschnabel, das Vorschiff, der *or* das Schiffsvorderteil.

prowess ['prauis], *s.* 1. die Tapferkeit, der (Helden)-mut; 2. (*fig.*) die Meisterschaft.

prowl [praul], **1.** *v.i.* 1. pirschen; 2. herumziehen, herumschleichen, herumstreifen, herumstreichen, herumlungern. **2.** *s.* das Herumziehen, Umherziehen *etc.*; *on the –,* auf der Lauer, herumziehend *etc.* **prowler,** *s.* der Herumtreiber, Vagabund, Bummler.

proximal ['prɔksiml], *adj.* (*Anat.*) proximal, körpernah. **proximate** [–mit], *adj.* (aller)nächst (*also time*), benachbart, naheliegend (*place*), nächstfolgend, kurz bevorstehend, sich (unmittelbar) anschließend (*time*); (*fig.*) unmittelbar. **proxime accessit** [–mi æk'sesit], *s.* zweiter Preisträger. **proximity** [–'simiti], *s.* die Nähe, Nachbarschaft; *in close* or *the immediate –,* in unmittelbarer Nähe; – *of blood,* die Blutsverwandtschaft; – *fuse,* der Annäherungszünder. **proximo,** *adv.* (im) nächsten Monat, des nächsten Monats.

proxy ['prɔksi], **1.** *s.* 1. die (Stell)vertretung, (Handlungs)vollmacht; *by –,* in Vertretung *or* Vollmacht; *marriage by –,* die Ferntrauung; *vote by –,* sich bei der Wahl vertreten lassen; – *vote,* stellvertretenderweise abgegebene Stimme; 2. der (Stell)vertreter, Bevollmächtigte(r); (*Law*) der Mandatar; *appoint a –,* sich vertreten lassen, einen Bevollmächtigten bestellen; *stand – for him,* ihn vertreten, seine Stelle einnehmen, als sein Stellvertreter fungieren.

prude [pru:d], *s.* Prüde(r), Spröde(r).

prudence [pru:dns], *s.* 1. die (Welt)klugheit; 2. Vorsicht, Umsicht(igkeit), Besonnenheit. **prudent** *adj.* 1. umsichtig, vorsichtig; 2. (welt)klug, gescheit. **prudential** [–'denʃəl], *adj.* klug, verständig, vernünftig; – *considerations,* Klugheitsrücksichten, Gründe praktischer Überlegung. **prudent(ial)ly,** *adv.* klüglich, wohlweislich, vernünftigerweise.

prudery ['pru:dəri], *s.* die Prüderie, Sprödigkeit, Ziererei. **prudish,** *adj.* prüde, spröde, zimperlich. **prudishness,** *s. See* **prudery.**

pruinose ['pru:inous], *adj.* (*Bot., Zool.*) bereift, bestäubt.

[1]**prune** [pru:n], *v.t.* beschneiden (*also fig.*), ausputzen, auslauben, zu(recht)stutzen, (*fig.*) säubern, befreien (*of,* von).

[2]**prune,** *s.* die Backpflaume.

[1]**prunella** [pru:'nelə], *s.* (*Med.*) (*obs.*) die Halsbräune.

[2]**prunella,** *s.* der Prunell (*fabric*). **prunelle** [–'nel], *s.* die Prünelle.

pruner ['pru:nə], *s.* die Baumschere. **pruning,** *s.* das Beschneiden, Ausputzen. **pruning|-knife,** *s.* das Baummesser, Gartenmesser. **--shears,** *pl.* die Baumschere.

prurience, pruriency ['pruəriəns(i)], *s.* die Lüsternheit, Geilheit, der (Sinnen)kitzel. **prurient,** *adj.* geil, lüstern, unzüchtig.

pruriginous [pruə'ridʒinəs], *adj.* (*Med.*) juckend, krätzig. **prurigo** [–'raigou], *s.* die Juckflechte, Juckkrankheit.

Prussia ['prʌʃə], *s.* Preußen (*n.*). **Prussian, 1.** *adj.* preußisch; – ***blue,*** das Berlinerblau. **2.** *s.* der Preuße (die Preußin).

prussiate ['prʌʃiət], *s.* (*Chem.*) das Zyanid, blausaures Salz; – ***of potash,*** das Zyankalium. **prussic** ['prʌsik], *adj.* blausauer; – ***acid,*** die Blausäure, Zyanwasserstoffsäure.

[1]**pry** [prai], *v.i.* spähen, neugierig sein; – ***into,*** die Nase stecken in (*Acc.*).

[2]**pry,** *v.t.* (– ***open***) (*coll.*) aufbrechen, erbrechen.

prying ['praiiŋ], *adj.* neugierig, naseweis.

psalm [sɑ:m], *s.* der Psalm; ***Psalm book,*** der Psalter; (*B.*) ***Book of Psalms,*** die Psalmen. **psalmist,** *s.* der Psalmist. **psalmody** [–ədi, 'sælmədi], *s.* der Psalmgesang; (*collect.*) das Psalmenbuch, die Psalmensammlung.

Psalter ['sɔ:ltə], *s.* das Psalmenbuch, Buch der Psalmen.

psalterium [sɔ:l'tiəriəm], *s.* (*Zool.*) der Blättermagen.

psaltery ['sɔ:ltəri], *s.* (*Mus.*) das Psalterium.

psephologist [se'fɔlədʒist], *s.* der Wahlstatistiker. **psephology,** *s.* die Wahlstatistik.

pseudo– ['sju:dou], *pref.* Schein–, Irr–, Pseudo–, falsch.

pseudocarp ['sju:doukɑ:p], *s.* die Scheinfrucht.

pseudomorph ['sju:doumɔ:f], *s.* das Afterkristall. **pseudomorphism** [–'mɔ:fizm], *s.* die Pseudomorphose.

pseudonym ['sju:dənim], *s.* der Deckname, fingierter Name, das Pseudonym. **pseudonymity** [–'nimiti], *s.* die Verwendung eines Decknamens. **pseudonymous** [–'dɔniməs], *s.* pseudonym, unter einem Decknamen.

pseudopod ['sju:doupɔd], **pseudopodium** [–'poudiəm], *s.* (*Zool.*) das Scheinfüßchen.

pshaw! [(p)ʃɔ: (*never spoken*)], *int.* (*obs.*) pah!

psittacosis [(p)sitə'kousis], *s.* die Papageienkrankheit.

psoas ['(p)souæs], *s.* (*Anat.*) der Lendenmuskel.

psora ['(p)sɔ:rə], *s.* (*Med.*) die Krätze. **psoriasis** [–'raiəsis], *s.* (*Med.*) die Schuppenflechte.

psyche ['saiki], *s.* die Seele, der Geist, seelisch-geistiges Leben.

psychiatric [saiki'ætrik], *adj.* psychiatrisch. **psychiatrist** [–'kaiətrist], *s.* der Psychiater, Nervenarzt. **psychiatry** [–'kaiətri], *s.* die Psychiatrie.

psychic ['saikik], *adj.* 1. psychisch, seelisch(-geistig); 2. spiritistisch, übersinnlich. **psychical,** *adj. See* **psychic** (*esp. Med.*); – ***research,*** der Spiritismus.

psycho|-analyse [saikou–], *v.t.* psychoanalytisch behandeln. **--analysis,** *s.* die Psychoanalyse. **--analyst,** *s.* der Psychoanalytiker.

psychogenic [saikou'dʒenik], *adj.* psychisch *or* seelisch bedingt.

psychological [saikə'lɔdʒikl], *adj.* psychologisch; ***the – moment,*** der richtige Augenblick; – ***warfare,*** psychologische Kriegführung. **psychologist** [–'kɔlədʒist], *s.* der Psychologe (die Psychologin). **psychology** [–'kɔlədʒi], *s.* die Psychologie.

psychopath ['saikoupæθ], *s.* der (die) Psychopath(in). **psychopathic** [–'pæθik], *adj.* psychopathisch, geistesgestört.

psychosis [sai'kousis], *s.* die Psychose, Geistesstörung.

psychosomatic [saikousə'mætik], *adj.* psychosomatisch.

psycho|therapeutic, *adj.* psychotherapeutisch. **–therapist,** *s.* der Psychotherapeut. **–therapy,** *s.* die Psychotherapie.

psychotic [sai'kɔtik], **1.** *adj.* psychotisch. **2.** *s.* Psychosekranke(r).

ptarmigan ['tɑ:migən], *s.* (*Orn.*) (*Am.* ***rock*** –) das Alpenschneehuhn (*Lagopus mutus*).

ptero– ['terə], *pref.* Flug–, Flügel–. **pterodactyl** [–'dæktil], *s.* der Flugeidechse, Pterosaurier. **pteropod** [–pɔd], *s.* die Flügelschnecke. **pterosaur** [–sɔ:], *s. See* **pterodactyl.**

pterospermus, *adj.* (*Bot.*) mit geflügelten Samen.

ptomaine ['(p)toumein], *s.* das Ptomain.

pub [pʌb], *s.* (*coll.*) *see* ***public house***; (*sl.*) – ***crawl,*** die Bierreise, Sauftour.

puberty ['pju:bəti], *s.* die Mannbarkeit, Geschlechtsreife, Pubertät; ***age of*** –, das Pubertätsalter, Entwicklungsjahre (*pl.*). **pubes** [–bi:z], *s.* (*Anat.*) Schamhaare (*pl.*), die Schamgegend.

pubescence [pju:'besəns], *s.* 1. die Geschlechtsreife, Mannbarkeit; 2. (*Bot., Zool.*) Behaarung, das Flaumhaar. **pubescent,** *adj.* 1. geschlechtsreif; 2. (*Bot., Zool.*) behaart, flaumhaarig.

pubic ['pju:bik], *adj.* Scham–. **pubis,** *s.* das Schambein.

public ['pʌblik], **1.** *adj.* 1. öffentlich, Staats–, national, Volks–; – ***address system,*** die Lautsprecheranlage; – ***appointment,*** die Staatsanstellung; – ***assistance,*** staatliche Wohlfahrt; – ***auction,*** öffentliche Versteigerung; – ***call box,*** öffentlicher Fernsprecher; – ***convenience,*** öffentliche Bedürfnisanstalt; – ***conveyance,*** öffentliches Verkehrsmittel; – ***corporation,*** öffentliche Körperschaft; – ***debt,*** die Staatsschuld; – ***elementary school,*** die Volksschule; – ***enemy,*** der Volksfeind, Staatsfeind; ***at the – expense,*** auf Kosten des Steuerzahlers; ***the – eye,*** das Auge der Öffentlichkeit; ***be in the – eye,*** im Brennpunkt des öffentlichen Lebens stehen; – ***funds,*** Staatsgelder (*pl.*); fundierte Staatsschuld; – ***good,*** das Gemeinwohl; – ***health,*** öffentliche Gesundheit(spflege); – ***health service,*** öffentlicher Gesundheitsdienst; – ***highways,*** see – ***road***; – ***holiday,*** gesetzlicher Feiertag; – ***house,*** das Wirtshaus, die Schankwirtschaft, Gaststätte; – ***institution,*** gemeinnütziges Unternehmen; – ***law,*** das Staatsrecht; – ***lecture,*** öffentliche Vorlesung; – ***library,*** die Volksbibliothek, Volksbücherei; – ***loan,*** öffentliche Anleihe, die Staatsanleihe; – ***meeting,*** öffentliche Versammlung; – ***money,*** see – ***funds***; – ***notary,*** der Notar; – ***nuisance,*** öffentliches Ärgernis; der Störenfried; – ***opinion,*** öffentliche Meinung; – ***opinion poll,*** öffentliche Umfrage; – ***ownership,*** das Gemeineigentum; – ***property,*** das Staatseigentum; – ***prosecutor,*** der Staatsanwalt; – ***relations,*** Beziehungen zur Öffentlichkeit (*pl.*); die Kontaktpflege, Werbe- und Reklametätigkeit; – ***relations officer,*** der Pressechef; Fachmann für Presse, Reklame und Werbung; – ***revenue,*** Staatseinkünfte (*pl.*); – ***road,*** der Verkehrsweg; – ***school,*** exklusive Internatsschule (*Eng.*); die Volksschule (*Scots and Am.*); – ***servant,*** Staatsbeamte(r), Staatsangestellte(r); – ***service,*** der Staatsdienst; – ***spirit,*** der Gemeinsinn; – ***thoroughfare,*** see – ***road***; – ***utility,*** öffentliche Einrichtung, öffentlicher Versorgungsbetrieb; – ***welfare,*** die Fürsorge; – ***works,*** öffentliche Bauten (*pl.*); – ***worship,*** öffentlicher Gottesdienst; 2. allgemein bekannt, offenkundig; ***make*** –, (allgemein) bekanntmachen; – ***character*** or ***figure,***

(in der Öffentlichkeit) bekannte Persönlichkeit. **2.** *s.* 1. die Öffentlichkeit; ***in* –,** in der Öffentlichkeit, vor der Welt, öffentlich; 2. das Publikum, Volk, die Leute (*pl.*); 3. (*fig.*) die Welt.

publican ['pʌblikən], *s.* 1. der (Gast)wirt, Schankwirt; 2. (*B.*) Zöllner.

publication [pʌbli'keiʃən], *s.* 1. (öffentliche) Verkündung, die Bekanntmachung, Bekanntgabe; Publizierung, Veröffentlichung, Herausgabe (*of a work*); 2. Publikation, Veröffentlichung, (*Comm.*) der Verlagsartikel; ***new* –,** die Neuerscheinung; ***monthly* –,** die Monatsschrift.

publicist ['pʌblisist], *s.* der Publizist.

publicity [pʌb'lisiti], *s.* 1. allgemeine Bekanntheit, die Öffentlichkeit, Offenkundigkeit; ***attract* –,** Aufsehen erregen; ***give* – *to*,** (allgemein *or* der Öffentlichkeit) bekanntmachen; ***no* –,** strengste Diskretion; ***seek* –,** Aufsehen erregen, bekannt werden wollen; 2. die Werbung, Reklame, Propaganda; – ***agent*,** der Werbeagent, Pressechef; – ***campaign*,** der Werbefeldzug; – ***department*,** die Werbeabteilung; – ***manager*,** der Werbeleiter; – ***office*,** das Werbebüro.

public-spirited, *adj.* gemeinsinnig, gemeinnützig.

publish ['pʌbliʃ], *v.t.* 1. bekanntmachen, bekanntgeben, (öffentlich) verkünd(ig)en, veröffentlichen, publizieren, verbreiten, in Umlauf setzen; – ***the banns*,** das Aufgebot (von der Kanzel) verkündigen; 2. (*a book etc.*) herausgeben, verlegen; ***just* –*ed*,** (so)eben erschienen; ***not yet* –*ed*,** noch unveröffentlicht; **–*ed by Cassell's*,** im Cassell-Verlag *or* bei Cassell erschienen. **publisher,** *s.* 1. Verbreiter (*of news*); 2. der Verleger, Verlagsbuchhändler; (***firm of***) **–*s*,** der Verlag, die Verlagsanstalt. **publishing, 1.** *adj.* Verlags–; – ***business*,** der Verlagsbuchhandel; – ***house*,** der Verlag, das Verlagshaus, die Verlagsbuchhandlung. **2.** *s.* der Verlag, die Herausgabe.

puce [pju:s], *adj.* braunrot, dunkelbraun.

puck [pʌk], *s.* 1. der Kobold, Hausgeist; 2. (*Spt.*) die (Eishockey)scheibe.

pucka ['pʌkə], *adj.* (*coll.*) echt, wirklich; – ***sahib*,** anständiger Mensch.

pucker ['pʌkə], **1.** *s.* 1. die Falte; Runzel; 2. (*coll.*) Erregung (***about*,** über (*Acc.*)). **2.** *v.t.* 1. fälteln, kräuseln, einhalten (*sewing*); 2. (*also* – *up*) zusammenziehen, kräuseln (*lips*), runzeln (*brow*). **3.** *v.i.* sich falten *or* zusammenziehen *or* kräuseln, Falten werfen, (*fig.*) Runzeln bilden.

puckish ['pʌkiʃ], *adj.* mutwillig, neckisch, naseweis, vorwitzig.

puddening ['pudniŋ], *s.* (*Naut.*) der Taukranz, die Tauwulst, das Schamfilkissen.

pudding ['pudiŋ], *s.* der Pudding, die Süßspeise, Mehlspeise; ***the proof of the* – *is in the eating*,** in der Praxis allein zeigt sich die Bewährung; 2. die Wurst; ***black* –,** die Blutwurst; ***white* –,** (eine Art) Preßsack. **pudding|-faced,** *adj.* mit feistem Gesicht, mit Vollmondsgesicht. **--head,** *s.* der Dummkopf. **--stone,** *s.* (*Geol.*) der Puddingstein.

puddle ['pʌdl], **1.** *s.* 1. die Pfütze, Lache, der Pfuhl; 2. (*Build.*) der Lehmschlag, Lehmestrich. **2.** *v.i.* 1. (herum)planschen, manschen; 2. (*fig.*) herumpfuschen. **3.** *v.t.* trüben (*water*), puddeln (*iron*), mit Estrich ausfüllen *or* anfüllen, zu Lehmestrich verarbeiten (*clay*); **–*d clay*,** der Lehmschlag.

puddle-iron, *s.* das Puddeleisen. **puddler,** *s.* (*Metall.*) der Puddler, Puddelarbeiter. **puddling,** *s.* 1. (*Build.*) der Lehmschlag; 2. (*Metall.*) Puddeln. **puddling-furnace,** *s.* der Puddelofen.

pudency ['pju:dnsi], *s.* die Verschämtheit, Schüchternheit.

pudenda [pju:'dendə], *pl.* äußere (weibliche) Geschlechtsteile (*pl.*), (weibliche) Scham. **pudendal,** *adj.* Scham–.

pudent [pju:dnt], *adj.* schüchtern, verschämt.

pudgy ['pʌdʒi], *adj.* untersetzt, plump.

puerile ['pjuərail], *adj.* knabenhaft, pueril; 2. (*fig.*) kindisch. **puerility** [–'riliti], *s.* 1. die Puerilität; 2. kindische Dummheit, die Kinderei.

puerperal [pju'ə:pərəl], *adj.* Kindbett–, Wochenbett–.

puff [pʌf], **1.** *s.* 1. der Hauch, Luftstoß, leichter Windstoß; der Zug, Paff (*of a pipe*); 2. die Puffe, der Bausch, Wulst (*on clothing*); 3. (*also* ***powder*–**–) die Puderquaste; 4. (*Cul.*) leichtes Backwerk, der Windbeutel; 5. marktschreierische Anpreisung, die Lobhudelei, (Schwindel)reklame; 6. – ***of smoke*,** das Rauchwölkchen. **2.** *v.i.* 1. blasen, pusten; 2. schnaufen, schnauben, keuchen; – ***and blow*,** schnauben, schnaufen, keuchen; 3. puffen, paffen (*as trains*); – ***at a cigar*,** an einer Zigarre paffen; 4. (*rare*) (marktschreierisch) Reklame machen, den Preis in die Höhe treiben. **3.** *v.t.* 1. ausblasen, ausstoßen, auspaffen (*smoke*); – ***out*,** ausblasen, auspusten (*candle*); 2. (*also* – ***out***) aufblasen, aufblähen (*as cheeks*); (*fig.*) **–*ed up*,** aufgebläht, geschwollen (***with*,** vor (*Dat.*)); 3. – ***up*,** hochtreiben, in die Höhe treiben (*prices*); marktschreierisch anpreisen (*wares*), über den Klee loben; 4. (*coll.*) **–*ed*** (***out***), außer Atem.

puff|-adder, *s.* die Puffotter. **–ball,** *s.* der Bovist, Bofist. **--box,** *s.* die Puderdose. **puffed** [pʌft], **1.** *adj.* – ***sleeve*,** der Puffärmel. **2.** *p.p.* *See* **puff, 3. puffer,** *s.* 1. der Marktschreier, der Preistreiber, Scheinbieter (*at auctions*); 2. (*nursery talk*) der Puffpuff.

puffin ['pʌfin], *s.* (*Orn.*) (*Am.* ***common* –**) der Papageitaucher (*Fratercula arctica*).

puffiness ['pʌfinis], *s.* 1. die Aufgeblasenheit, Aufgeblähtheit, (Auf)gedunsenheit; 2. (*of a p.*) Kurzatmigkeit; 3. Aufbauschung, Schwellung. **puffing,** *s.* 1. die Aufbauschung, Aufblähung; 2. marktschreierische Anpreisung, unsaubere Reklame; 3. (*of a p.*) das Keuchen. **puff|-pastry,** *s.* der Blätterteig. **--puff,** *s.* (*nursery talk*) der Puffpuff. **--sleeve,** *s.* der Puffärmel. **puffy,** *adj.* 1. aufgeblasen, aufgedunsen, aufgebläht; 2. (an)geschwollen; 3. (*rare*) aufgebauscht, schwülstig; 4. (*of a p.*) kurzatmig; 5. (*of wind*) böig.

^{1}**pug** [pʌg], *s.* 1. (*also* **--*dog***) der Mops; (*dial.*) Fuchs; 2. (*sl.*) erster Dienstbote; 3. **--*nose*,** die Stupsnase, Stülpnase; **--*nosed*,** stupsnäsig, stupsnasig.

^{2}**pug, 1.** *s.* der Lehm(schlag). **2.** *v.t.* 1. bereiten, schlagen, kneten (*clay*); 2. ausfüllen, abdichten, verschmieren (*with clay*).

^{3}**pug,** *s.* die Fährte, Fußspur.

pugging ['pʌgiŋ], *s.* 1. das Schlagen, Kneten (*of clay*); 2. die Lehmfüllung.

pugilism ['pju:dʒilizm], *s.* der Faustkampf, das Boxen, die Boxkunst. **pugilist,** *s.* der Faustkämpfer, (Berufs)boxer. **pugilistic** [–'listik], *adj.* Box(er)–.

pugnacious [pʌg'neiʃəs], *adj.* kampflustig, kämpferisch, streitsüchtig. **pugnacity** [–'næsiti], *s.* die Kampflust, Streitsucht.

puisne ['pju:ni], **1.** *adj.* (*Law*) (rang)jünger, untergeordnet. **2.** *s.* (*Law*) der Unterrichter.

puissance ['pwi:səns], *s.* (*Poet.*) die Macht, Stärke, Herrschaft. **puissant,** *adj.* mächtig, gewaltig.

puke [pju:k], *v.i.* (*vulg.*) kotzen.

pukka, *see* **pucka.**

pulchritude ['pʌlkritju:d], *s.* die Schönheit. **pulchritudinous** [–'tju:dinəs], *adj.* schön.

pule [pju:l], *v.i.* winseln, wimmern, plärren.

pull [pul], **1.** *s.* 1. das Ziehen, Zerren; 2. der Zug, Ruck; ***give a* – *at*,** ziehen an (*Dat.*); 3. die Zugkraft; (*esp. fig.*) Anziehungskraft; 4. Zugleine, der Zug, (Zug)griff, Schwengel; 5. (*coll.*) die Ruderpartie, Ruderfahrt; ***go for a* –,** eine Ruderfahrt machen; 6. (*coll.*) mühsamer Anstieg; 7. (*fig.*) (*coll.*) der Vorteil (***over*, *on*, *of*,** vor (*Dat.*) *or* gegenüber), Einfluß (auf (*Acc.*)); 8. (*sl.*) Konnex (***with*,** mit), die Protektion (bei), Beziehungen, Konnexionen (*pl.*) (mit).
2. *v.t.* 1. ziehen *or* zerren (an (*Dat.*)); – ***the chestnuts out of the fire*** (***for him***), (ihm) die Kastanien aus dem Feuer holen; (*coll.*) – ***his leg*,** ihn zum besten *or* zum Narren halten; – ***a muscle*,** sich (*Dat.*) eine Muskelzerrung zuziehen; – ***a pistol***

on, anlegen *or* feuern auf (*Acc.*); *– him by the sleeve,* ihn am Ärmel zupfen; (*sl.*) *– one's socks up,* in die Hände spucken, sich hochrappeln; (*coll.*) *– the strings,* die Fäden in der Hand halten, der Drahtzieher sein; *– a tooth,* einen Zahn ziehen; *– the trigger,* das Gewehr abdrücken; (*coll.*) *– one's weight,* sich tüchtig ins Zeug legen; *– the wires,* geheime Beziehungen haben; *– the wool over his eyes,* ihn hinters Licht führen; 2. reißen, (*Scots*) pflücken; *– to pieces,* zerreißen, zerpflücken; (*fig.*) (*coll.*) herunterreißen, gründlich abrechnen mit, einer vernichtenden Kritik unterziehen; 3. (*Typ.*) abziehen (*a proof*); 4. (*sl.*) verhalten, zurückhalten (*a horse*); 5. *– a good oar,* gut rudern (können); *– the boat,* das Boot rudern; 6. *– a face,* (or *faces*), ein Gesicht (*or* Fratzen (*pl.*)) schneiden; *– a long face,* ein langes Gesicht ziehen *or* machen; 7. (*sl.*) *– the job,* das Ding drehen; (*sl.*) *– a fast one,* ein unredliches Spiel treiben (*on, over,* mit); 8. *– one's punches,* nicht mit voller Kraft schlagen. (*with adv.*) **– about,** hin und her ziehen, (*fig.*) unsanft traktieren; **– apart,** zerreißen, auseinanderreißen; *– down,* herunterziehen, herunterreißen; niederreißen, einreißen (*a house etc.*); herunterziehen, herunterlassen (*blinds*); (*usu. p.p.*) schwächen, entkräften (*a p.'s health*); **– in,** (hin)-einziehen; anziehen, anhalten (*reins*), zügeln (*a horse*); (*fig.*) *– in one's belt,* sich einschränken, sich (*Dat.*) den Riemen enger schnallen; (*fig.*) *– in one's horns,* sich mäßigen; **– off,** wegziehen; abziehen (*also Typ.*), abreißen; abnehmen (*a hat*) (*to,* vor (*Dat.*)), ausziehen (*clothes, boots*); (*coll.*) davontragen (*a prize*), Glück haben mit, zuwegebringen, schaffen; **– on,** anziehen (*clothes*); **– out,** (her)-ausziehen, (her)vorziehen; (*coll., fig.*) *– out all the stops,* alle Mittel anwenden; **– round,** wiederherstellen; (*fig.*) **– through,** durchbringen, durchhelfen (*Dat.*); **– together,** zusammenhalten; *– o.s. together,* sich zusammennehmen *or* zusammenreißen, sich aufraffen; **– up,** hochziehen, hissen (*flag etc.*); ausreißen (*flowers etc.*); *– up* (*sharp*), (plötzlich) anhalten *or* aufhalten *or* zum Stehen bringen; *– up* (*sharply*), (schroff *or* barsch *or* unzart) unterbrechen, Einhalt tun (*Dat.*), (*a p.*) in die Rede fallen (*Dat.*); (*a p.*) tadeln, zurechtweisen, zur Rede stellen; aufbessern. **3.** *v.i.* 1. ziehen, zerren, reißen (*at,* an (*Dat.*)); 2. (*fig.*) Zugkraft haben, ziehen; 3. *– apart,* entzweigerissen werden; 4. *– at a pipe,* an einer Pfeife ziehen *or* saugen; 5. *– against the bit,* pullen; 6. (*boats*) rudern; *– in,* hineinrudern; *– together,* zusammenarbeiten, zusammenhalten, am gleichen Strang ziehen; 7. *– back,* (sich) zurückziehen; 8. *– in,* anhalten (*vehicles*); *– into the station,* in den Bahnhof einfahren; *– out,* abgehen, abfahren, abdampfen; (*coll.*) abziehen, das Feld räumen, sich zurückziehen; *– out of the station,* gerade abfahren; 9. (*coll.*) *– round,* sich erholen, wieder gesund werden; *– through,* glücklich bestehen, überstehen, durchkommen durch (*an illness*), sich durchschlagen *or* durchwinden; 10. *– up,* (an)-halten, haltmachen, stehenbleiben, zum Stehen kommen; (*Spt.*) sich nach vorn schieben, aufholen; *– up short,* plötzlich anhalten; (*Spt.*) *– up with,* einholen.

puller ['pulə], *s.* 1. der Ruderer; 2. Zieher (*horse*).

pullet ['pulit], *s.* das Hühnchen.

pulley ['puli], *s.* 1. die Rolle, Flasche; *block and –, set of –s,* der Flaschenzug, Rollenzug; 2. (*Tech.*) die (Transmissions)scheibe; *belt--,* die Riemenscheibe; 3. (*Naut.*) die Talje. **pulley-block,** *s.* der (Roll)kloben.

pull|-in, *s.* (*Motor.*) der Rastplatz, die Raststätte. **--out,** *s.* das Faltblatt. **-over,** *s.* der Pullover, die Überziehjacke, Strickjacke. **--through,** *s.* der Durchzug, Wischstrick (*for rifles*).

pullulate ['pʌljuleit], *v.i.* 1. (Knospen) treiben, knospen, sprießen, sprossen, keimen; 2. (*fig.*) sich vermehren *or* verbreiten, wuchern, aus dem Boden schießen, um sich greifen, grassieren. **pullulation** [–'leiʃən], *s.* 1. das Sprossen, Knospen, Keimen; 2. (*fig.*) massenhafte Vermehrung *or* Verbreitung.

pull|-up, *s.* 1. (*Gymn.*) der Klimmzug; 2. (*Motor.*) *see* **--in.**

pulmonary ['pʌlmənəri], *adj.* (*Anat.*) Lungen–. **pulmonate** [–neit], *adj.* (*Zool.*) Lungen–. **pulmonic** [–'mɔnik], *adj. See* **pulmonary.**

pulp [pʌlp], **1.** *s.* 1. breiige Masse, der Brei; *beat* or *reduce to –,* zu Brei schlagen; (*fig.*) windelweich schlagen; 2. (*Bot.*) das Fruchtfleisch, Pflanzenmark; 3. (*Anat.*) die (Zahn)pulpa, das Zahnmark; 4. (*Tech.*) Ganzzeug, der Papierbrei, Papierstoff; 5. die Maische (*sugar*). **2.** *v.t.* 1. breiig *or* zu Brei machen; 2. zermalmen, zermahlen; 3. einstampfen (*paper stock*). **3.** *v.i.* breiig *or* zu Brei werden. **pulper,** *s.* der Ganzzeugholländer. **pulpify** [–ifai], *v.t.* zu Brei machen. **pulpiness,** *s.* die Breiigkeit, Matschigkeit, Weichheit.

pulpit ['pulpit], *s.* 1. die Kanzel; *in the –,* auf der Kanzel; 2. (*collect.*) die Geistlichkeit.

pulpy ['pʌlpi], *adj.* 1. breiig, matschig; 2. schwammig, quallig, weich.

pulsate [pʌl'seit], *v.i.* 1. (rhythmisch) schlagen *or* pochen *or* klopfen, pulsieren; 2. schwingen, vibrieren. **pulsatile** ['pʌlsətail], *adj.* 1. pulsierend; 2. (*Mus.*) Schlag–. **pulsating,** *adj.* rhythmisch klopfend, pulsierend, vibrierend. **pulsation** [–'seiʃən], *s.* 1. rhythmisches Schlagen *or* Klopfen, das Pulsieren; 2. Schwingen, Vibrieren; 3. der (Puls)schlag; 4. die Schwingung.

[1]**pulse** [pʌls], **1.** *s.* 1. der Puls(schlag); *feel his –,* seinen Puls fühlen; (*fig.*) ihm auf den Zahn fühlen, bei ihm auf den Busch klopfen; (*fig.*) *have one's finger on the –,* an den Puls fühlen (*of, Dat.*); 2. (*Tech.*) der Impuls; die Schwingung. **2.** *v.i. See* **pulsate.**

[2]**pulse,** *s.* die Hülsenfrucht.

pulverization [pʌlvərai'zeiʃən], *s.* 1. der Zerreibung, Zerstäubung, Pulverisierung; 2. (*fig.*) Zermalmung. **pulverize** ['pʌlvəraiz], **1.** *v.t.* 1. zermahlen, zerkleinern, zerstoßen, zerreiben, pulverisieren, levigieren; 2. zerstäuben; 3. (*fig.*) zermalmen, zertrümmern. **2.** *v.i.* zu Staub werden, zerbröckeln. **pulverizer,** *s.* 1. der Zerstäuber; 2. (*Agr.*) die Krümelegge.

pulverulent [pʌl'verjulənt], *adj.* Staub–, pulverig.

pulvinate(d) ['pʌlvineit(id)], *adj.* 1. kissenförmig, polsterförmig, bauchig; 2. (*Archit.*) konvex gewölbt.

puma ['pju:mə], *s.* der Puma, Kuguar, Silberlöwe.

pumice ['pʌmis], **1.** *s.* (*also --stone*) der Bimsstein. **2.** *v.t.* (ab)bimsen, mit Bimsstein abreiben.

pummel [pʌml], *v.t.* schlagen, puffen.

[1]**pump** [pʌmp], **1.** *s.* die Pumpe; *prime the –,* einen Lauf in die Pumpe gießen. **2.** *v.t.* 1. pumpen; (*Naut.*) *– the bilges,* lenzen; *– out* or *dry,* auspumpen, leerpumpen; (*vulg.*) *– ship,* pissen; *– up,* aufpumpen (*tyre*); 2. (*coll.*) ausfragen (*for,* wegen), ausholen (über (*Acc.*)), anhalten (um) (*a p.*); (*fig.*) *– his brains,* seinen Kopf *or* sein Wissen durchforschen. **3.** *v.i.* pumpen.

[2]**pump,** *s.* (*usu. pl.*) der Tanzschuh, Turnschuh.

pump-handle, *s.* der Pumpenschwengel. **pumping,** *s.* das Pumpen; *--station,* die Pumpanlage, das Pumpwerk.

pumpkin ['pʌmpkin], *s.* der Kürbis.

pump|-room, *s.* die Trinkhalle, Kurhalle. **--water,** *s.* das Brunnenwasser.

pun [pʌn], **1.** *s.* das Wortspiel (*on,* über (*Acc.*) *or* mit). **2.** *v.i.* mit Worten spielen; ein Wortspiel machen, witzeln (*on,* über (*Acc.*) *or* mit). *See also* **punster.**

[1]**punch** [pʌntʃ], *s.* der Punsch.

[2]**punch,** **1.** *s.* 1. der (Faust)schlag, (Faust)hieb; (*fig.*) *beat him to the –,* ihm zuvorkommen; *pull one's –es,* nicht mit voller Kraft schlagen; 2. (*fig.*) die Schlagkraft, Energie, das Gewicht, der Nachdruck, Schwung, Schmiß. **2.** *v.t.* 1. (mit der Faust) schlagen, einen Hieb versetzen (*Dat.*); *– his head,* ihn auf den Kopf schlagen; 2. (*Am.*) treiben (*cattle*).

[3]**punch,** *s.* 1. der Stöpsel, kleine dicke Person; 2. kurzbeiniges (Zug)pferd.

[4]**punch, 1.** *s.* 1. die Punze, der Punzen, Dorn, Durchschlag; 2. Locher, das Locheisen, die Lochzange, der Lochstempel; 3. (Stanz)stempel, die Stanze, Patrize. **2.** *v.t.* 1. durchschlagen, durchlöchern, (durch)lochen; 2. punzen, punzieren, (aus)stanzen, lochstanzen, stempeln; *– a hole,* ein Loch durchschlagen; 3. lochen, knipsen (*tickets*); *–ed card,* die Lochkarte.

Punch, *s.* Kasperle (*m. or n.*); *– and Judy show,* das Kasperletheater.

punch|-ball, *s.* der Sandsack. **–-bowl,** *s.* die Punschbowle. **–-drunk,** *adj.* (*coll.*) (wie) von Faustschlägen betäubt.

[1]**puncheon** [ˈpʌntʃən], *s.* 1. der Pfriem; 2. (*Am.*) das Querbrett.

[2]**puncheon,** *s.* (*obs.*) das Faß (*liquid measure = 330–550 l.*).

punchinello [pʌntʃiˈnelou], *s.* der Hanswurst.

punch-line, *s.* (*coll.*) die Pointe, der Knalleffekt.

punctate [ˈpʌŋkteit], *adj.* (*Bot., Zool.*) punktiert.

punctilio [pʌŋkˈtiliou], *s.* 1. kitzliger *or* heikler Punkt; 2. peinliche Genauigkeit; 3. kleine Förmlichkeit. **punctilious** [–iəs], *adj.* 1. förmlich, formell; 2. peinlich genau, spitzfindig. **punctiliousness,** *s.* peinliche Genauigkeit, die Förmlichkeit.

punctual [ˈpʌŋktjuəl], *adj.* (*usu. pred.*) pünktlich; ***be – in doing,*** pünktlich tun. **punctuality** [–ˈæliti], *s.* die Pünktlichkeit. **punctually,** *adv.* pünktlich.

punctuate [ˈpʌŋktjueit], *v.t.* 1. interpunktieren, interpungieren; 2. (*fig.*) unterbrechen (***with,*** durch *or* mit); 3. hervorheben, betonen, unterstreichen. **punctuation** [–ˈeiʃən], *s.* die Zeichensetzung, Interpunktion; *– **mark,*** das Satzzeichen, Interpunktionszeichen.

puncture [ˈpʌŋktʃə], **1.** *s.* 1. der (Ein)stich, die Punktur, kleines Loch, die (Durch)lochung; 2. (*Motor., Cycl.*) Radpanne, Reifenpanne, der Reifenschaden; *– **outfit,*** das Flickzeug; ***we had a –,*** uns platzte der Reifen; 3. (*Elec.*) der Durchschlag; 4. (*Surg.*) die Punktion. **2.** *v.t.* 1. durchstechen; ein Loch machen in (*Acc. or Dat.*); 2. (*Surg.*) punktieren. **3.** *v.i.* ein Loch bekommen, platzen (*tyres etc.*).

pundit [ˈpʌndit], *s.* 1. gelehrter Brahmane; 2. (*coll.*) Fachgelehrte(r), die Autorität; der Vielwisser, gelehrtes Haus.

pungency [ˈpʌndʒənsi], *s.* das Stechende, Beißende, die Schärfe. **pungent,** *adj.* beißend, stechend, scharf (*also fig.*).

Punic [ˈpju:nik], *adj.* punisch, karthagisch.

punish [ˈpʌniʃ], *v.t.* 1. (be)strafen (***for,*** wegen); 2. (*coll.*) (*Boxing*) mit den Fäusten bearbeiten; schinden (*a horse*); übel zurichten, arg mitnehmen; 3. tüchtig zusprechen (*Dat.*), aufräumen mit (*food*). **punishable,** *adj.* strafbar, sträflich, strafwürdig. **punishment,** *s.* 1. die Strafe, Bestrafung; ***as*** (or ***for***) ***a –,*** als *or* zur Strafe; ***capital –,*** die Todesstrafe; ***corporal –,*** körperliche Züchtigung; ***bring to –,*** zur Strafe ziehen; 2. (*coll.*) üble Zurichtung, die Schinderei; (*Boxing*) ***take –,*** (viel) einstecken müssen.

punitive [ˈpju:nitiv], *adj.* strafend, Straf–.

Punjab [pʌnˈdʒɑ:b], *s.* Pandschab (*n.*). **Punjabi,** *s.* 1. der (die) Bewohner(in) des Pandschabs; 2. (*language*) das Pandschabi.

punk [pʌŋk], **1.** *s.* 1. faules Holz, der Zunder, das Zunderholz; 2. (*sl.*) der Quatsch, Mist, Schund, Plunder; 3. (*sl.*) (*of a man*) Knülch, (*of a woman*) die Hure. **2.** *adj.* faul (*of timber*); (*sl.*) schäbig, miserabel.

punner [ˈpʌnə], *s. See* **punster.**

punnet [ˈpʌnit], *s.* (*esp. Scots*) der Spankorb.

punster [ˈpʌnstə], *s.* der Witzbold, Wortspielmacher; *see* **pun.**

[1]**punt** [pʌnt], **1.** *s.* flacher Flußkahn, der Prahm. **2.** *v.t.* mit Staken fortbewegen, staken. **3.** *v.i.* in einem Flußkahn fahren.

[2]**punt, 1.** *s.* (*Footb.*) der Fallstoß. **2.** *v.t.* (*v.i.*) (den fallenden Ball) wuchtig stoßen.

[3]**punt,** *v.i.* (*coll.*) wetten, setzen (***on,*** auf (*Acc.*)) (*a horse etc.*). **punter,** *s.* Wettende(r); der Spekulant.

punty [ˈpʌnti], *s.* (*Glassw.*) das Hefteisen.

puny [ˈpju:ni], *adj.* winzig, schwächlich, kümmerlich.

pup [pʌp], **1.** *s.* 1. junger Hund; ***in –,*** trächtig (*of dogs*); (*sl.*) ***sell him a –,*** ihn übers Ohr hauen, ihm etwas andrehen *or* auf die Nase binden; 2. (*sl.*) der Laffe, Geck. **2.** *v.i.* Junge werfen.

pupa [ˈpju:pə], *s.* (*pl.* **pupae** [–pi:]) (*Ent.*) die Puppe, Larve. **pupal,** *adj.* Puppen–. **pupation** [–ˈpeiʃən], *s.* die Puppenbildung.

[1]**pupil** [pju:pl], *s.* (*Anat.*) die Pupille.

[2]**pupil,** *s.* 1. der (die) Schüler(in), der Zögling; 2. (*Law*) Minderjährige(r), der (*Austr.* das) *and* die Mündel. **pupilage** [–pilidʒ], *s.* 1. (*Law*) die Minderjährigkeit, Unmündigkeit; 2. Schülerjahre, Lehrjahre (*pl.*); 3. (*fig.*) das Anfangsstadium.

pupil(l)ar [ˈpju:pilə], *adj.* (*Anat.*) Pupillar–.

pupil(l)ary [ˈpju:piləri], *adj.* (*Law*) minderjährig, Mündel–, pupillarisch; *see also* **pupil(l)ar.**

puppet [ˈpʌpit], *s.* die Drahtpuppe, Marionette; (*fig.*) das Werkzeug, der Handlanger; *– **government,*** die Marionettenregierung; *– **play*** or ***show,*** das Puppenspiel. **puppeteer** [–ˈtiə], *s.* der Puppenspieler. **puppetry,** *s.* 1. die Puppenspielkunst; 2. (*fig.*) Maskerade, der Mummenschanz.

puppy [ˈpʌpi], *s. See* **pup. puppydog,** *s.* das Hündchen. **puppyhood,** *s.* (*fig.*) Flegeljahre (*pl.*).

purblind [ˈpə:blaind], *adj.* 1. (*rare*) halbblind, schwachsichtig; 2. (*usu. fig.*) kurzsichtig, verblendet, engstirnig, verstockt.

purchasable [ˈpə:tʃəsəbl], *adj.* käuflich.

purchase [ˈpə:tʃəs], **1.** *v.t.* 1. (ein)kaufen, erstehen, (durch Kauf) erwerben; *– **from,*** abkaufen (*Dat.*); 2. (*fig.*) erkaufen, erringen (*victory etc.*); 3. (*Naut.*) aufwinden, hochwinden (*anchor etc.*). **2.** *s.* 1. der Ankauf, Einkauf, die Erwerbung; ***by –,*** käuflich; ***make –s,*** Einkäufe machen; *– **money*** or ***price,*** der Einkaufspreis; *– **tax,*** die Kaufsteuer; 2. (*Law*) der Jahresertrag; ***at two years' –,*** zum Zweifachen des Jahresertrags; ***his life is not worth an hour's –,*** er hat keine Stunde mehr zu leben, ich gebe nichts mehr für sein Leben; 3. der Kauf, das Kaufobjekt; 4. (*Tech.*) die Hebevorrichtung; (*Naut.*) das Takel, Spill, die Talje; 5. (*fig.*) der Halt, Griff; 6. Ansatzpunkt, Anhaltspunkt, Angriffspunkt, Stützpunkt; 7. Einfluß, die Machtstellung. **purchaser,** *s.* der (die) Käufer(in), Abnehmer(in), Kunde (Kundin). **purchasing,** *adj.* (Ein)kauf–; *– **agent,*** der Einkäufer (*for a firm*); *– **order,*** der Kaufauftrag; *– **power,*** die Kaufkraft.

purdah [ˈpə:də], *s.* der Schleier, Vorhang.

pure [ˈpjuə], *adj.* 1. rein (*also fig.*), unvermischt, lauter, echt, gediegen; *– **gold,*** das Feingold; *– **mathematics,*** reine Mathemathik; *– **silk,*** die Glanzseide; 2. (*Biol.*) reinerbig, homozygot; 3. (*Mus.*) (ton)rein; 4. (*fig.*) keusch, unbefleckt, unberührt, unschuldig; 5. (*coll.*) völlig, bloß, pur, nichts als; *– **nonsense,*** reiner *or* heller *or* purer Unsinn.

pure-bred, *adj.* rasserein, reinrassig.

purée [ˈpjuərei], *s.* der Brei, das Püree.

purely [ˈpjuəli], *adv.* 1. (*fig.*) in Reinheit *or* Unschuld; 2. (*coll.*) rein, ganz, gänzlich, völlig, ausschließlich, lediglich, bloß. **pureness,** *s.* (*fig.*) die Reinheit, Unschuld; *see* **purity.**

purfle [ˈpə:fl], **1.** *s.* der Zierrand, die Schmuckborte (*of dress*). **2.** *v.t.* 1. mit Zierrand schmücken, mit Schmuckborte verzieren; 2. (*Archit.*) mit Randschmuck verzieren. **purfling,** *s.* 1. (*Archit.*) der Randschmuck; 2. Flödel (*of violins etc.*).

purgation [pə:ˈgeiʃən], *s.* 1. (*Law, Eccl.*) die Reinigung; 2. (*Med.*) das Abführen, die Stuhlentleerung. **purgative** [ˈpə:gətiv], **1.** *adj.* 1. (*Med.*) abführend, Abführ–, (*Law*) Reinigungs–. **2.** *s.* das Abführmittel.

purgatorial [pə:gəˈtɔriəl], *adj.* 1. Fegefeuer–; 2. Sühne–, Reinigungs–. **purgatory** [ˈpə:gətəri], *s.* das Fegefeuer (*also fig.*).

purge [pə:dʒ], **1.** *v.t.* 1. reinigen, säubern (*also fig.*), befreien (*of*, von); – ***away,*** säubern, entfernen; – ***o.s. of,*** sich reinwaschen von; 2. läutern, klären (*liquids*); 3. (*Med.*) ein Abführmittel geben (*Dat.*). **2.** *v.i.* abführen(d wirken) (*of medicines*). **3.** *s.* 1. (*Pol.*) die Ausleerung, Entleerung; 2. Reinigung, Säuberung; 3. (*Med.*) das Abführmittel; 4. (*fig.*) (*Pol.*) die Säuberung(saktion).

purification [pjuərifi'keiʃən], *s.* 1. die Reinigung, Läuterung; (*R.C.*) ***the Purification,*** Mariä Reinigung; 2. (*Tech.*) Klärung. **purificator** ['pjuərifikeitə], *s.* (*Eccl.*) das Purifikatorium, Reinigungstüchlein. **purificatory** [–'keitəri], *adj.* reinigend, Reinigungs–.

purifier ['pjuərifaiə], *s.* 1. der Reiniger, das Reinigungsmittel; 2. Raffiniergerät, der Reinigungsapparat. **purify,** *v.t.* 1. reinigen, läutern (***from,*** von); 2. (*Tech.*) klären, schlämmen, raffinieren.

purism ['pjuərizm], *s.* der Purismus, die Sprachreinigung(ssucht). **purist,** *s.* der Sprachreiniger, Genauigkeitskrämer, Pedant.

Puritan ['pjuəritən], **1.** *s.* der (die) Puritaner(in). **2.** *adj.* puritanisch. **puritanical** [–'tænikl], *adj.* puritanisch; sittenstreng, frömmelnd. **Puritanism,** *s.* der Puritanismus.

purity ['pjuəriti], *s.* 1. die Reinheit (*also fig.*), Klarheit, Lauterkeit; Feinheit, Echtheit, Gediegenheit; 2. Unberührtheit, Keuschheit, Unschuld; 3. (*Biol.*) Reinerbigkeit.

[1]**purl** [pə:l], **1.** *s.* 1. gewundener Gold– *or* Silberdraht; 2. (*knitting*) das Linksstricken; – ***stitch,*** linke Masche; 3. *pl.* gestickte Borte, die Häkelkante, Zäckchen (*pl.*). **2.** *v.t.* umsäumen, einfassen. **3.** *v.i.* linksstricken.

[2]**purl, 1.** *s.* das Rieseln, Murmeln, Rauschen, Gemurmel (*of a brook*). **2.** *v.i.* rieseln, murmeln, sanft rauschen.

[3]**purl, 1.** *v.i.* 1. sich drehen, (herum)wirbeln; 2. (*coll.*) (*usu.* – ***over***) umfallen, umkippen; vom Pferd stürzen. **2.** *v.t.* (*sl.*) umwerfen; abwerfen (*a rider*). **3.** *s.* (*coll.*) der Fall, Sturz. **purler,** *s.* (*coll.*) schwerer Sturz, schwerer Schlag *or* Stoß; ***come*** or ***go a –,*** stürzen, heftig fallen.

purlieu ['pə:lju:], *s.* der Außenbezirk, Nachbarbereich; (*usu. pl.*) die Umgebung, Nachbarschaft.

purlin ['pe:lin], *s.* (*Archit.*) die Pfette.

purloin [pə:'lɔin], *v.t.* entwenden, stehlen, mausen.

purple ['pə:pl], **1.** *s.* 1. der Purpur; 2. (*fig.*) die Kardinalswürde; Herrscherwürde, fürstliche Würde. **2.** *adj.* purpurrot, purpurfarben, purpurn; (*Ent.*) ***Purple Emperor,*** der Schillerfalter; (*Am.*) ***Purple Heart,*** das Verwundetenabzeichen; (*fig.*) – ***patch,*** die Glanzstelle. **purplish,** *adj.* purpurfarbig.

purport, 1. ['pə:pɔ:t], *s.* der Inhalt, Sinn, die Bedeutung, Tragweite. **2.** [pə'pɔ:t], *v.t.* 1. besagen, bedeuten, zum Inhalt haben; 2. behaupten, vorgeben, es sich (*Dat.*) zur Aufgabe machen; ***it –s to describe,*** es will beschreiben; ***it –s to contain*** . . ., es enthält scheinbar . . .; es will den Eindruck erwecken, als enthielte es . . . .

purpose ['pə:pəs], **1.** *s.* 1. der Vorsatz, Entschluß; Zweck, das Ziel, Vorhaben, die Absicht; ***answer the –,*** dem Zweck entsprechen *or* genügen, zweckentsprechend sein; ***be at cross –s,*** aneinander vorbeireden, sich gegenseitig mißverstehen, einander unbewußt entgegenhandeln; ***for this –,*** in dieser Absicht, zu diesem Zweck; ***for what –?*** wozu? zu welchem Zweck? ***for the – of,*** zwecks (*Gen.*); ***for*** or ***with the – of doing,*** um zu tun; ***fixity of –,*** die Zielstrebigkeit; ***strength of –,*** die Entschlußkraft, Willensstärke, Zielbewußtheit; ***weakness of –,*** die Unentschlossenheit, mangelnde Entschlußkraft; (*Law*) ***of set –,*** absichtlich, vorsätzlich; ***on –,*** absichtlich, vorsätzlich, mit der Absicht, mit Willen, mit Fleiß; ***on – that,*** damit; ***on – to do,*** um zu tun, in der Absicht zu tun; ***serve the –,*** see ***answer the –***; ***suit his –,*** ihm zweckdienlich sein, ihm in den Kram passen; ***for all practical –s, to all intents and –s,*** praktisch genommen *or* gesehen; ***to the –,*** zweckdienlich, zur Sache; ***what is the – of it?*** welchen Zweck hat es? ***novel with a –,*** der Tendenzroman; 2. der Erfolg, die Wirkung; ***to little –,*** mit geringem *or* ohne rechten Erfolg; ***to no –,*** umsonst, vergeblich; ***be (much) to the same –,*** (fast dasselbe *or*) ebendasselbe sein, auf (ungefähr) dasselbe hinauslaufen, (beinahe) dieselbe Wirkung haben; ***to some –,*** mit gutem Erfolg. **2.** *v.t.* beabsichtigen, vorhaben, sich (*Dat.*) vornehmen.

purpose-built, *adj.* für den Zweck gebaut. **purposeful,** *adj.* 1. zielbewußt, entschlossen (*character*); 2. zweckvoll, beabsichtigt, planmäßig (*action*). **purposeless,** *adj.* zwecklos, ziellos, planlos, vergeblich. **purposely,** *adv.* absichtlich, vorsätzlich, mit Fleiß, mit der Absicht. **purposive,** *adj.* 1. zweckvoll, zweckdienlich, zweckbetont; 2. entschlossen, zielbewußt, zielstrebig.

purpura ['pə:pjurə], *s.* 1. (*Med.*) der Purpurausschlag; 2. (*Zool.*) die Gattung der Purpurschnecken. **purpuric** [–'pjuərik], *adj.* 1. (*Chem.*) Purpur–; 2. (*Med.*) Purpura–.

purr [pə:], *v.i.* 1. schnurren (*cats*), summen, surren (*engines*); 2. (*fig.*) sich geschmeichelt fühlen.

purse [pə:s], **1.** *s.* 1. der Geldbeutel, die Geldtasche, (Geld)börse, das Portemonnaie; (*esp. Am.*) der Beutel, die Handtasche; (*Prov.*) ***one cannot make a silk – out of a sow's ear,*** man kann aus einem Kieselstein keinen Diamanten schleifen; 2. der Geldpreis, das Geldgeschenk; ***make up a – for,*** Geld sammeln für; 3. (*fig.*) die Geldsumme, der Schatz, Fonds; ***common –,*** gemeinsame Fonds (*pl.*), gemeinschaftliche Kasse; ***light –,*** der Geldmangel, wenig Geld; ***long –,*** voller Geldbeutel, der Reichtum, viel Geld; ***privy –,*** königliche Privatschatulle; ***public –,*** der Staatsschatz. **2.** *v.t.* (*also* – ***up***) zusammenziehen; – ***one's lips,*** den Mund spitzen.

purse|-bearer, *s.* der Großsiegelträger. **–-net,** *s.* das Beutelnetz. **–-proud,** *adj.* geldstolz, protzig.

purser ['pə:sə], *s.* (*Naut.*) der Zahlmeister, Proviantmeister.

purse|-seine, *s.* der Kescher. **–-strings,** *pl.* Beutelschnüre (*pl.*); (*fig.*) ***hold the –,*** über den Geldbeutel verfügen; ***keep a tight hand on the –,*** die Hand *or* den Daumen auf dem Beutel halten, den Beutel zuhalten.

pursiness ['pə:sinis], *s.* die Kurzatmigkeit.

purslane ['pə:slin], *s.* (*Bot.*) der Portulak.

pursuance [pə'sju:əns], *s.* die Verfolgung, Fortführung (*of, Gen.*); Ausführung, Befolgung; ***in –,*** im Verfolg, bei der Ausführung (*of, Gen.*), laut (*Dat.*), zufolge *or* gemäß (*Dat. usu. precedes*); ***in – of which,*** demzufolge. **pursuant,** *adj.* – ***to,*** zufolge, gemäß (*Dat. usu. precedes*), laut (*Dat.*), in Übereinstimmung mit, in Ausführung (*Gen.*).

pursue [pə'sju:], **1.** *v.t.* 1. verfolgen, nachgehen (*Dat.*), nachsetzen (*Dat.*); 2. (*fig.*) verfolgen, ständig begleiten; 3. folgen (*Dat.*), einschlagen (*a course*); 4. nachgehen (*Dat.*), ausüben, betreiben (*a profession, studies etc.*); 5. anstellen (*inquiries*); 6. weiterführen, weiter fortsetzen, fortfahren in (*Dat.*) (*discussions etc.*). **2.** *v.i.* 1. fortfahren (*esp. in speech*), weitermachen; 2. (*Scots Law*) Klage erheben. **pursuer,** *s.* 1. der (die) Verfolger(in); 2. (*Scots Law*) (An)kläger(in).

pursuit [pə'sju:t], *s.* 1. die Verfolgung (*of, Gen.*), Jagd (auf (*Acc.*)); ***give –,*** nachjagen (*Dat.*), nachsetzen (*Dat.*), verfolgen; ***in hot –,*** hart auf den Fersen (*of, Dat.*); ***in his –,*** hinter ihm her, auf der Jagd nach ihm; 2. (*fig.*) die Jagd, das Streben, Trachten (*of,* nach); – ***of happiness,*** die Jagd nach dem Glück; – ***of knowledge,*** der Wissensdrang, das Streben nach Wissen; 3. der Verfolg, die Betreibung (*of, Gen.*); ***in – of a th.,*** im Verfolg einer S.; ***in – of the plan,*** im Verfolg *or* in Betreibung des Plans; 4. die Ausübung (*of, Gen.*), Beschäftigung (mit); 5. Betätigung, der Beruf; 6. *pl.* Geschäfte, Arbeiten, Studien (*pl.*).

pursuit-plane, *s.* das Jagdflugzeug.

pursuivant ['pə:swivənt], *s.* 1. (*Her.*) der Persevant; 2. (*Poet.*) Gefolgsmann, Begleiter.

[1]**pursy** ['pə:si], *adj.* 1. beleibt, fettleibig; 2. kurzatmig.

[2]**pursy,** *adj.* zusammengezogen, gefaltet (*of cloth*).

purtenance ['pə:tinəns], *s.* (*obs.*) das Geschlinge.

purulence, purulency ['pjurələns(i)], *s.* 1. das Eitern, die Eitrigkeit, Eiterung; 2. der Eiter. **purulent,** *adj.* eiternd, eitrig; – ***discharge,*** der Eiterausfluß; – ***matter,*** der Eiter.

purvey [pə'vei], **1.** *v.t.* liefern (***to,*** an (*Acc.*)) (*usu. foodstuff*). **2.** *v.i.* – ***for,*** beliefern, versorgen, (Nahrungsmittel) liefern an (*Acc.*) *or* für. **purveyance,** *s.* die Beschaffung, Lieferung. **purveyor,** *s.* der Lieferant; – ***to Her Majesty,*** Königlicher Hoflieferant.

purview ['pə:vju:], *s.* 1. der Wirkungskreis, Bereich, das Betätigungsfeld, Gebiet; 2. Blickfeld, der Gesichtskreis; 3. (*Law*) Wirkungsbereich, Geltungsbereich, die Verfügung.

pus [pʌs], *s.* der Eiter.

push [puʃ], **1.** *s.* 1. der Stoß, Schub; (*sl.*) ***get the –,*** entlassen *or* rausgeschmissen werden, fliegen; ***give him a –,*** ihm einen Stoß geben; (*sl.*) ***give him the –,*** ihn rausschmeißen, ihn fliegen lassen; 2. (*Archit., Geol.*) horizontaler Druck; 3. (*fig.*) der Anstoß, Antrieb; (*coll.*) ***at a –,*** im Notfall, wenn es zum Äußersten kommt; ***bring to the last –,*** auf die Spitze *or* bis zum Äußersten treiben; 4. (*Mil.*) der Vorstoß (***for,*** auf (*Acc.*) *or* nach; ***into,*** in (*Acc.*); ***against,*** gegen); 5. (*coll.*) die Energie, Tatkraft, Strebsamkeit, der Schwung, das Draufgängertum.

2. *v.t.* 1. stoßen, schieben, drücken, rücken, drängen (*also fig.*); ***let o.s. be –ed around by him,*** nach seiner Pfeife tanzen; – ***aside,*** beiseiteschieben, beseitigen; – ***back,*** zurückstoßen, zurückdrängen; (*Mil.*) zurückwerfen, aufrollen; – ***forth,*** aussenden (*roots*), hervortreiben (*shoots*); – ***forward,*** vorwärtsschieben, vorwärtsstoßen; (*fig.*) vorantreiben, beschleunigen; – ***o.s. forward,*** sich vordrängen; – ***open,*** aufstoßen (*door*); – ***out,*** hinausstoßen, fortjagen (*a p.*); vorschieben, vorstrecken (*one's arm etc.*); *see also* – ***forth***; – ***the door to,*** die Tür zuschieben *or* zuschlagen; – ***up,*** hinaufschieben, hochschieben; (*fig.*) in die Höhe treiben, hochtreiben (*prices*); – ***one's way,*** sich (*Dat.*) einen Weg bahnen; sich vordrängen *or* durchdrängen; 2. (*fig.*) (an)treiben, betreiben, verfolgen, beschleunigen, vorwärtsbringen, (be)fördern, vorantreiben; – ***an advantage,*** einen Vorteil ausnützen; – ***a claim,*** einen Anspruch durchsetzen wollen; – ***s.th. too far,*** etwas zu weit treiben; – ***through,*** durchdrücken, durchsetzen; 3. (*coll.*) aufdrängen (***on to,*** *Dat.*), Reklame machen für, propagieren (*goods*); – ***money on him,*** ihm Geld aufdrängen; (*coll.*) – ***s.th. down his throat,*** ihm etwas glaubhaft machen wollen; 4. (*coll.*) ***be –ed for,*** in Not *or* Verlegenheit sein wegen *or* um; ***be –ed for money,*** in Geldverlegenheit sein; ***be –ed for time,*** keine Zeit haben.

3. *v.i.* stoßen, schieben, drücken, drängen; (*coll.*) – ***along,*** weggehen, weitergehen; – ***forward,*** sich vordrängen, vorwärtsdrängen, (*Mil.*) vorstoßen; – ***off,*** abstoßen (*of a boat*); (*coll.*) sich auf den Weg machen, verduften; (*coll.*) – ***on,*** vor(wärts)dringen; (*fig.*) weiterarbeiten (***with,*** an (*Dat.*)); – ***out,*** vorstoßen, vordringen (***to,*** nach).

push|-ball, *s.* (*Spt.*) der Stoßball. **–-bike,** *s.* (*coll.*) das (Fahr)rad. **–-button, 1.** *s.* der Druckknopf. **2.** *attrib. adj.* Drucktasten–. **–cart,** *s.* die (der) Schiebkarre(n), Schubkarre(n). **–-chair,** *s.* der (Sport)kinderwagen.

pusher ['puʃə], *s.* 1. (*coll.*) der Streber, Draufgänger, Emporkömmling; 2. (*Tech.*) Schieber; 3. – ***aeroplane,*** das Flugzeug mit Schubschraube; 4. (*sl.*) der Dealer. **pushful, pushing,** *adj.* 1. energisch, unternehmend, strebsam, streberisch, draufgängerisch; 2. aufdringlich, zudringlich.

push|-over, *s.* (*coll.*) 1. (*of a task*) leichte S., das Kinderspiel, die Kleinigkeit; 2. (*of a p.*) der Gimpel, nicht ernst zu nehmender Gegner; ***he's a –,*** er fällt prompt herein (***for,*** auf (*Acc.*)). **–-pull,** *attrib. adj.* (*Rad.*) Gegentakt–. **–-rod,** *s.* (*Tech.*) die Stoßstange, Schubstange.

pusillanimity [pju:silə'nimiti], *s.* der Kleinmut, die Kleinmütigkeit, Verzagtheit. **pusillanimous** [–'læniməs], *adj.* kleinmütig, verzagt, feig(e).

[1]**puss** [pus], *s.* 1. die Katze, Mieze, das Kätzchen; ***Puss in Boots,*** der Gestiefelte Kater; 2. der Hase.

[2]**puss,** *s.* (*sl.*) die Visage, Schnauze.

puss|-in-the-corner, *s.* (*game*) das Kämmerchenvermieten. – **moth,** *s.* (*Ent.*) der Gabelschwanz.

pussy ['pusi], *s.* (*also* ***–cat***) *see* [1]**puss.**

pussy|foot, 1. *s.* (*sl.*) der Abstinenzler. **2.** *v.i.* (*sl. esp. Am.*) sich ausschweigen (***on,*** über (*Acc.*)), nicht ja und nicht nein sagen (zu), herumreden (um), sich nicht festlegen (auf (*Acc.*)), Entscheidungen aus dem Wege gehen. **–footer,** *s.* (*Am.*) der Leisetreter, Schleicher. **–footing,** *adj.* (*Am.*) leisetreterisch.

pussy-willow, *s.* (*Bot.*) Verschiedenfarbige Weide.

pustular ['pʌstjulə], *adj.* pustelartig, Pustel–. **pustulation** [–'leiʃən], *s.* die Pustelbildung. **pustule** [–tju:l], *s.* die Pustel, das Eiterbläschen.

put [put], **1.** *irr.v.t.* 1. legen, stellen, setzen, stecken; 2. (*coll.*) ansetzen, schätzen (***at,*** auf (*Acc.*)); 3. (*fig.*) stellen, vorlegen (*question etc.*); 4. (*Spt.*) stoßen, schleudern, werfen.

(a) (*with noun*) – ***his age at 50,*** sein Alter auf 50 schätzen; (*coll.*) – ***one's back into it,*** sich dranhalten, rangehen; (*coll.*) – ***his back up,*** ihn aufbringen *or* hochbringen; – ***the blame on him,*** ihm die Schuld geben, ihm die Verantwortung beilegen *or* zuschieben; (*fig.*) – ***one's cards on the table,*** seine Karten auf den Tisch legen; – ***the cart before the horse,*** das Pferd hinter den Wagen spannen; – ***the case to him,*** ihm die S. vorlegen *or* vortragen; – ***the clock back,*** die Uhr zurückstellen; (*fig.*) einen Rückfall *or* Rückgang sein (***to,*** auf (*Acc.*)), eine Rückkehr sein (zu), rückständig *or* rückschrittlich sein; – ***a construction on,*** auslegen, deuten; (*coll.*) – ***a damper on,*** entmutigen, einen Dämpfer aufsetzen (*Dat.*); – ***an end to,*** ein Ende machen (*Dat.*); – ***an end to o.s.*** or ***one's life,*** seinem Leben ein Ende setzen, sich (*Dat.*) das Leben nehmen; – ***a good*** (or ***the best***) ***face on it,*** gute Miene zum bösen Spiel machen; – ***one's best face on,*** sich (*Dat.*) Mühe geben (freundlich zu sein); – ***one's finger on,*** genau hinweisen auf (*Acc.*); (*Am. sl.*) – ***the finger on,*** verpetzen, verpfeifen; – ***a foot wrong,*** den geringfügigsten Fehler machen; – ***one's best foot forward,*** so schnell wie möglich gehen; (*fig.*) sein Bestes tun, sich nach Kräften anstrengen; (*sl.*) – ***one's foot in it,*** ins Fettnäpfchen treten; (*coll.*) – ***one's foot down,*** energisch werden *or* auftreten, auftrumpfen; (*coll.*) – ***one's feet up,*** sich ausruhen; – ***one's hand to the plough,*** Hand ans Werk legen, an die Arbeit gehen; – ***an old head on young shoulders,*** der Jugend Weisheit lehren; (*fig.*) – ***one's heads together,*** die Köpfe zusammenstecken; (*coll.*) ***that –s the lid on it,*** das setzt der S. die Krone auf; – ***money on a horse,*** auf ein Pferd wetten *or* setzen; (*coll.*) – ***paid to,*** erledigen, fertig machen, ein Ende machen mit; – ***pen to paper,*** die Feder ergreifen *or* ansetzen; – ***a question to him,*** ihm eine Frage stellen, eine Frage an ihn richten; (*Spt.*) – ***the shot*** or ***weight,*** kugelstoßen; (*coll.*) – ***one's shoulder to the wheel,*** energisch zugreifen, sich tüchtig ins Zeug legen, in die Speichen greifen; – ***your signature to it!*** setzen Sie Ihre Unterschrift darauf *or* darunter! (*coll.*) – ***a spoke in his wheel,*** ihm einen Knüppel zwischen die Beine werfen; – ***a stop to,*** see – ***an end to***; – ***a tax on,*** eine Steuer legen auf (*Acc.*), besteuern; – ***one's trust in,*** sich verlassen auf (*Acc.*), sein Vertrauen setzen auf (*Acc.*); – ***great value on,*** großen Wert legen auf (*Acc.*), große Bedeutung legen (*Dat.*); (*sl.*) – ***the wind up him,*** ihn einschüchtern, ihm Angst einjagen; – ***words into his mouth,*** ihm Worte in den Mund legen.

(b) (*with prep.*) – ***him across the river,*** ihn über den Fluß bringen *or* befördern; (*sl.*) – ***it across him,*** ihn hereinlegen, es ihm aufbinden *or* anhängen *or* auf die Nase binden; – ***him at his ease,*** ihm die Befangenheit nehmen, ihn beruhigen; – ***a***

horse at a fence, ein Pferd über einen Zaun setzen lassen; (*coll.*) – *it* **before** *him,* es ihm verlegen, es in seine Hände legen; – *o.s.* **in** *his care,* sich in seine Obhut begeben; – *him in charge,* ihn beauftragen; – *him in fear of his life,* ihm eine Todesangst einjagen; – *o.s. in his hands,* sich ihm ganz anvertrauen; (*Naut.*) – *in commission,* in Dienst stellen (*a ship*); (*sl.*) – *him in a hole,* ihm eine Grube graben; – *in mind of,* erinnern an (*Acc.*); – *in order,* in Ordnung bringen; (*sl.*) – *him in the picture,* ihn auf dem laufenden halten, ihn ins Bild setzen; – *o.s. in his place,* sich an seine Stelle *or* in seine Lage versetzen; – *in one's pocket,* in die Tasche stecken; – *him in prison,* ihn ins Gefängnis werfen *or* stecken; – *him in the wrong,* ihn ins Unrecht setzen; – **into** *circulation,* in Umlauf setzen; – *into force,* in Kraft setzen; – *into German,* ins Deutsche übersetzen; – *into his head,* ihm in den Kopf setzen; – *into practice,* in die Praxis umsetzen, ausführen, verwirklichen; – *into shape,* formen, gestalten; – *into words,* in Worte fassen; – *him* **off** *his guard,* seine Aufmerksamkeit ablenken; (*coll.*) – *him off his stroke,* ihn aus dem Takt bringen; – **on** *a diet,* auf Diät setzen; – *him on his guard,* ihn warnen; – *on the last,* über den Leisten schlagen; – *on the market,* auf den Markt bringen; – *him on his mettle,* ihn auf die Probe stellen; – *on oath,* vereidigen; – *on the shelf,* an den Nagel hängen; (*sl.*) – *him on the spot,* ihn in äußerste Verlegenheit bringen, ihn in die Enge treiben, ihn aufs Korn nehmen; – *on the stage,* auf die Bühne bringen; (*coll.*) – *him* **on to** *the idea,* ihn auf die Idee bringen; (*sl.*) – *him on to a p.*, ihn einem in Verbindung bringen; (*Mil.*) – **out of** *action,* außer Betrieb setzen, kampfunfähig machen; – *out of countenance,* aus der Fassung bringen; (*Elec.*) – *out of circuit,* ausschalten; – *out of reach,* außer der Reichweite stellen *or* legen; (*fig.*) unerreichbar *or* unerschwinglich machen; – *him out of temper,* ihn erzürnen *or* in üble Laune versetzen; – *it* **through** *a test,* es einer Prüfung unterziehen; (*coll.*) – *him through it* or *through his paces,* ihn auf Herz und Nieren prüfen; – **to** *account,* in Rechnung stellen; – *to bed,* zu Bett bringen; – *to the blush,* beschämen; – *to death,* hinrichten; – *to expense,* Unkosten machen (*Dat.*); – *to flight,* in die Flucht schlagen; – *to inconvenience,* Unannehmlichkeiten bereiten (*Dat.*); – *to rights,* wieder in Ordnung bringen, zurechtsetzen; – *him to shame,* ihn beschämen; – *to sleep,* schmerzlos beseitigen (*animals*); – *to the sword,* über die Klinge springen lassen; – *to the test,* auf die Probe stellen; – *to (good) use,* (gut) verwenden; – *it to him,* ihn darauf hinweisen, ihm nahelegen; es seiner Entscheidung *or* ihm anheimstellen *or* anheimgeben; ihn fragen *or* bitten; – *to a trade,* für ein Gewerbe bestimmen; – *it to the vote,* darüber abstimmen lassen; – *him to work,* ihn arbeiten lassen, ihn an die Arbeit setzen; – *o.s.* **under** *his care,* see – *o.s. in his care.*

(c) (*with adv.*) – *it clearly,* es klar ausdrücken; – *it mildly,* es milde *or* gelinde ausdrücken; – *right,* in Ordnung bringen, richtigstellen (*mistake*), (über ein Irrtum) aufklären (*a p.*); – *o.s. right,* sich rechtfertigen (*with,* vor (*Dat.*)); (*sl.*) – *him wise,* ihn aufklären *or* in Kenntnis setzen (*to,* über (*Acc.*)), ihn aufmerksam machen (auf (*Acc.*)), ihm reinen Wein einschenken; – **about,** verbreiten, in Umlauf setzen (*a rumour*); (*coll.*) in Aufregung versetzen, beunruhigen, ärgern, Unannehmlichkeiten bereiten (*Dat.*) (*a p.*); (*Naut.*) umlegen, wenden; (*coll.*) – *o.s. about,* sich plagen *or* beunruhigen (*for,* wegen); *be – about,* in Aufregung *or* beunruhigt sein; – **across,** (*coll.*) Erfolg haben mit, ankommen mit (*to,* bei); – **aside,** beiseitelegen, weglegen; – **away,** weglegen, beiseitelegen, wegräumen, wegschaffen, wegtun, auf die Seite legen (*a th.*); ablegen, verbannen (*care*); (*coll.*) einlochen (*a p.*), beseitigen, umbringen (*animals*); verzehren, verputzen (*food*); – **back,** nachstellen, zurückstellen (*a clock*); wieder hinstellen; aufhalten verschieben, aufschieben; – **by,** zurücklegen, beiseitelegen, aufsparen (*money etc.*); – **down,** niederlegen, niedersetzen, hinlegen, hinsetzen, hinstellen, aus der Hand legen; anrechnen, zuschreiben (*to, Dat.*); absetzen, aussteigen lassen (*a passenger*); umbringen, beseitigen (*unwanted animals*), abschaffen (*abuses etc.*), unterdücken, niederschlagen (*opposition*); absetzen, abfertigen, kurz abweisen, vor den Kopf stoßen, zum Schweigen bringen (*a p.*); (*coll.*) halten (*as,* für), auslegen, einschätzen (als), schätzen, festlegen (*at,* auf (*Acc.*)); – *one's name* or *o.s. down,* den Namen *or* sich eintragen; – *him down for,* ihn vormerken für; – *down in writing,* niederschreiben, aufschreiben, vormerken, schriftlich niederlegen; – *down to his account,* ihm in Rechnung stellen; – *down the money,* das Geld auf den Tisch legen, bar zahlen; – *it down to ignorance,* es der Unwissenheit zuschreiben, es als Unwissenheit auslegen; – **forth,** hervorbringen, treiben (*buds etc.*); zeigen, aufbieten, aufwenden (*strength etc.*); vorbringen, stellen (*a question*), vortragen, behaupten, ausgeben (*as,* als); – **forward,** vorbringen, aufstellen, zur Debatte stellen; zur Geltung *or* zum Vorschein bringen; – *forward the date,* vordatieren; (*fig.*) – *o.s. forward,* sich hervortun, sich in den Vordergrund schieben; – **in,** (hin)einsetzen, (hin)einstecken, (hin)einlegen, (hin)einstellen; aufstellen, einstellen, anstellen (*a p.*); einreichen (*application*); einrücken (*advertisement etc.*), einschalten, einschieben (*omission*), erheben, stellen, machen (*claim*) (*for,* auf (*Acc.*)); einspannen (*horses*); einsetzen (*bailiff*); anbringen, vorbringen (*evidence etc.*), **verbringen, dransetzen, aufwenden** (*at,* für), widmen (*Dat.*) (*time*); leisten, stellen (*bail*); – *in an appearance,* erscheinen; – *him in for the examination,* ihn für die Prüfung anmelden; – *in one's oar,* sich in eine S. (ein)mischen; – *in a plea,* einen Rechtseinwand erheben; – *in a word,* ein Wort mitsprechen; – *in a word for,* ein Wort einlegen für; – **off,** ausziehen, ablegen, abnehmen (*clothes*); ausschalten, abschalten, ausdrehen, abdrehen (*light, switch, tap etc.*); (*fig.*) abstreifen; daran hindern, davon abraten (*Dat.*) *or* abbringen (*from doing,* zu tun); vertrösten, hinhalten, abfertigen, abspeisen (*a p.*) (*with,* mit); hinauszögern, verschieben, aufschieben, auf die lange Bank schieben; (*coll.*) *that – me off completely,* das brachte mich völlig aus der Fassung; – **on,** anziehen, anlegen (*clothes*); aufsetzen (*spectacles, hat*); ansetzen, annehmen (*appearance*); aufschlagen (*addition*) (*to,* auf (*Acc.*)); anziehen (*brakes*); bestimmen, aufstellen (*a p.*) (*to,* für); einstellen (*a train, men*); andrehen, aufdrehen, anlassen, anschalten, einschalten (*switch, tap*); aufführen (*play*); veranstalten (*performance*); auflegen (*gramophone record*); verstärken, beschleunigen (*speed*); vorstellen (*clock*); vorsetzen (*a meal*); (*coll.*) vorspiegeln, vortäuschen, sich stellen, heucheln, schauspielern; (*fig.*) – *the screw on,* die Schraube anziehen, einen Druck ausüben; (*Spt.*) – *on a spurt,* spurten; – *on one's thinking-cap,* sich (*Dat.*) die S. überlegen; – *on weight,* Fett ansetzen, zunehmen; – **out,** hinaussetzen, hinauslegen, hinausstellen (*a th.*); hinauswerfen (*a p.*), (*Spt.*) fertigmachen, eliminieren, ausmachen; ausstrecken (*hand*); herausstrecken (*tongue*); aushängen (*flag*); aussetzen (*a boat*); veröffentlichen, herausgeben (*a book*); anlegen, ausleihen (*money*); in Pflege *or* außer Haus geben (*child*); in Submission *or* aus dem Haus geben (*work*); löschen (*fire*); auslöschen (*a light*); (*coll.*) verstimmen, ärgern, reizen; verwirren, irremachen, aus der Fassung *or* dem Konzept bringen (*a p.*); ausrenken (*limb*); *be – out,* sich ärgern, verärgert sein (*with him,* über ihn; *about,* über (*Acc.*)); – *o.s. out,* sich bemühen *or* ereifern (*about,* über (*Acc.*)); – *out his eyes,* ihm die Augen ausstechen; – *out to service,* in Dienst geben; – **over,** *see – across*; (*coll.*) – *o.s.* or *it over,* beim Publikum ankommen *or* Erfolg *or* Anklang finden, sich durchsetzen (*with,* bei); – *it over on him,* ihn an der Nase herumführen, ihn hereinlegen *or* anführen; – **through,** ausführen, durchführen, zu Ende führen; (*Tele.*) verbinden (*a p.*) (*to,* mit), herstellen (*call*); – **together,** zusammensetzen, zusammenstellen; (*fig.*) – *two and two together,* seine Schlüsse ziehen, es

sich (*Dat.*) zusammenreimen, die S. zurechtkombinieren; – **up,** hochziehen, hochschieben (*window etc.*); aufhängen (*curtains, picture*); aufstellen, errichten, erbauen (*structure*); aufschlagen (*bed, tent*); aufstecken, hochstecken (*one's hair*); aufspannen (*umbrella*); aufstellen (*candidate*); vorbringen (*proposition*); verpacken (*goods*); hinaufsetzen, erhöhen (*prices*); anschlagen (*placard*); verlesen lassen, verkünden (*the banns*); leisten (*resistance*); aufstöbern (*game*); emporsenden (*prayer*); (*coll.*) unterbringen, beherbergen (*a p.*), einstellen, einpferchen (*a horse*); (ein)setzen (*wager, pledge*); einstecken (*sword*); (*coll.*) antreiben, anstiften, anzetteln, verleiten (*to*, zu); verständigen, aufklären, informieren (*to*, über (*Acc.*)), warnen (vor (*Dat.*)), bekannt machen (mit); – ***up a (good) fight,*** sich (energisch) einsetzen *or* wehren, (zähen) Widerstand leisten, einen (harten) Kampf liefern; – ***up for sale,*** zum Verkauf *or* zur Versteigerung anbieten, feilbieten; – ***up the shutters,*** den Laden *or* die Bude zumachen.
2. *irr.v.i.* (*coll.*) sich begeben *or* machen; – ***for home,*** sich nach Hause machen; (*coll.*) ***stay*** –, festbleiben, halten; (*of a p.*) sich nicht rühren, an Ort und Stelle bleiben; – **about,** (*Naut.*) wenden; (*fig.*) umkehren; (*Naut.*) – **back,** zurückkehren, zurückfahren; (*Av.*) – **down,** landen; (*Naut.*) – **forth,** auslaufen, in See gehen; – **in,** einlaufen (*at a port*); – ***in for,*** sich bewerben um; – **into *a port,*** einen Hafen anlaufen, in einen Hafen einlaufen; – **off,** – (*out*) **to *sea,*** see – **forth**; (*coll.*) ***when he's – to it,*** wenn er muß, wenn er gezwungen ist; ***be hard – to it,*** arg bedrängt werden, stark *or* hart *or* lange *or* heiß *or* scharf zugesetzt werden (*Dat.*) (***to do,*** zu tun), nur mit großer Mühe (tun) können; – **up,** kandidieren, als Kandidat auftreten (*as candidate*); einkehren, sich einquartieren, absteigen (*at*, in (*Dat.*)) (*an inn*); (*coll.*) – ***up with,*** sich abfinden mit, sich zufrieden geben mit, auskommen mit, sich (*Dat.*) gefallen lassen, dulden, (ruhig) hinnehmen, einstecken (*an insult*); (*coll.*) – **(up)on *him,*** ihm (zu)viel zumuten, ihn ausnutzen. **3.** *s.* 1. (*Spt.*) der Kugelstoß; 2. (*Comm.*) die Rückprämie; – ***and call,*** die Rück- und Vorprämie, die Stellage, das Stell(age)geschäft.

putative ['pju:tətiv], *adj.* vermeintlich, mutmaßlich.

putlock ['pʌtlɔk], **putlog** [–lɔg], *s.* (*Archit.*) die Gerüststange, der Rüstbalken.

put-off ['putɔf], *s.* (*coll.*) die Ausrede, Ausflucht.

putrefaction [pju:tri'fækʃən], *s.* 1. die Fäulnis, Verwesung; 2. (*fig.*) Zersetzung. **putrefactive** [–'fæktiv], *adj.* 1. fäulniswirkend, faulig; 2. Fäulnis–. **putrefy** ['pju:trifai], *v.i.* faul werden, (ver)faulen, verwesen, modern.

putrescence [pju:'tresəns], *s.* 1. das Verfaulen, Verwesen; 2. die Fäulnis. **putrescent,** *adj.* 1. (ver)faulend, angefault; 2. faulig, Fäulnis–.

putrid ['pju:trid], *adj.* 1. faul, verfault, verwest, moderig; 2. (*fig.*) verderbt; 3. (*sl.*) ekelhaft, saumäßig, Sau–; 4. miserabel, hundemäßig. **putridity** [–'triditi], **putridness,** *s.* 1. die Verfaultheit, Fäulnis; 2. (*fig.*) Verderbtheit; 3. (*sl.*) Ekelhaftigkeit.

putt [pʌt], **1.** *v.t., v.i.* (*Golf*) einlochen, putten. **2.** *s.* leichter Schlag auf dem Grün.

puttee ['pʌti], *s.* (*oft. pl.*) die Wickelgamasche.

putter ['pʌtə], *s.* (*Golf*) der Einlochschläger, Putter.

putti ['puti], *pl.* (*Art*) Putten, Kindergestalten (*pl.*).

[1]**putting** ['pʌtiŋ], *s.* (*Golf*) das Einlochen, Putten; —***green,*** das Grün; der Kleingolfplatz.

[2]**putting** ['putiŋ], *s.* (*Spt.*) das Stoßen; – ***the shot*** or ***weight,*** das Kugelstoßen.

putty ['pʌti], **1.** *s.* (*also **glazier's** –*) der (Glaser)kitt; ***jeweller's –, see*** **putty-paste**; ***plasterer's –,*** der Kalkkitt. **2.** *v.t.* (*also – up*) (ver)kitten, zukitten. **putty|-knife,** *s.* der (*Austr.* die) Spachtel. **--paste,** *s.* die Zinnasche.

put-up, *adj.* (*sl.*) – ***job,*** die Schiebung, abgekartetes Spiel.

puzzle [pʌzl], **1.** *s.* 1. das Rätsel, Problem, schwierige Frage; 2. die Verlegenheit, Verwirrung; 3. das Geduldspiel, Vexierspiel. **2.** *v.t.* verwirren, erstaunen, verdutzen, stutzig machen, rätselhaft sein (*Dat.*), vor ein Rätsel stellen, verwundern, zu denken geben (*Dat.*); ***be –d,*** in Verlegenheit sein (***for,*** um), nicht wissen; – ***out,*** enträtseln, austüfteln, herausfinden, herausbekommen; – ***one's head*** or ***brains,*** sich (*Dat.*) den Kopf zerbrechen. **3.** *v.i.* sich (*Dat.*) den Kopf zerbrechen (***over,*** über (*Acc.*)).

puzzle|-headed, *adj.* konfus, wirr(köpfig). **--lock,** *s.* das Kombinationsschloß, Vexierschloß. **puzzler,** *s.* das Rätsel, Problem, schwierige Frage. **puzzling,** *adj.* 1. verwirrend, irremachend; 2. rätselhaft, unbegreiflich.

pyaemia [pai'i:miə], *s.* (*Med.*) das Wundfieber, Eiterfieber, die Blutvergiftung.

pyelitis [paiə'laitis], *s.* (*Med.*) die Nierenbeckenentzündung.

pygmaean [pig'mi:ən], *adj.* pygmäisch, Zwerg–, zwerghaft. **pygmy** ['pigmi], **1.** *s.* der Pygmäe, Zwerg. **2.** *attrib. adj.* 1. (*Zool.*) Zwerg–; (*Orn.*) – ***owl,*** der Sperlingskauz (*Glaucidium passerinum*); 2. (*fig.*) zwerg(en)haft, winzig, unbedeutend.

pyjamas [pə'dʒɑ:məz], *pl.* der Schlafanzug, der (*Austr.* das) Pyjama.

pylon ['pailən], *s.* der Turm, freitragender Mast, (*Elec.*) der Leitungsmast, (*Av.*) die Wendemarke, (*Bridgebuilding*) Pylone.

pyloric [pai'lɔ:rik], *adj.* (*Anat.*) Pförtner–, Pylorus–. **pylorus,** *s.* (*Anat.*) der Pförtner.

pyogenesis [paiə'dʒenisis], *s.* die Eiterbildung. **pyogenic,** *adj.* eiterbildend, Eiter–.

pyorrhœa [paiə'riə], *s.* 1. die Paradentose; 2. der Eiterfluß.

pyramid ['pirəmid], *s.* (*Archit., Math.*) die Pyramide. **pyramidal** [–'ræmidl], *adj.* pyramidal, pyramidisch, pyramidenförmig.

pyre ['paiə], *s.* der Scheiterhaufen.

pyrene ['pairi:n], *s.* (*Chem.*) das Pyren.

Pyrenean [pirə'niən], *adj.* pyrenäisch. **Pyrenees** [–'ni:z], *pl.* Pyrenäen (*pl.*).

pyretic [pai'retik], **1.** *s.* das Fiebermittel. **2.** *adj.* 1. fieberhaft; Fieber–; 2. fiebermildernd.

pyrexia [pai'reksiə], *s.* der Fieberanfall, Fieberzustand.

pyridine ['pairidain, 'piridin], *s.* (*Chem.*) das Pyridin.

pyriform ['pirifɔ:m], *adj.* birnenförmig.

pyrites [pai'raiti:z], *s.* der Schwefelkies, Pyrit; ***iron—,*** der Eisenkies.

pyro ['pairou], *s.* (*coll.*) see **pyrogallol.**

pyro–, *pref.* Feuer–, Brand–, Wärme–, Hitze–.

pyrogallic [pairo'gælik], *adj.* – ***acid or*** **pyrogallol,** *s.* die Pyrogallussäure.

pyrogenous [pai'rɔdʒinəs], *adj.* (*Geol.*) pyrogen.

pyrography [pai'rɔgrəfi], *s.* die Brandmalerei.

pyrolatry [pai'rɔlətri], *s.* die Feueranbetung.

pyromania [pairo'meiniə], *s.* der Brandstiftungstrieb.

pyromaniac [pairo'meiniæk], *s.* der Pyromane, die Pyromanin.

pyrometer [pai'rɔmitə], *s.* der Hitzemesser, das Pyrometer.

pyrotechnic [pairo'teknik], *adj.* Feuerwerks–, (*fig.*) glänzend, blendend. **pyrotechnics,** *pl.* (*usu. pl. constr.*) 1. die Feuerwerkerei, Pyrotechnik; 2. (*fig.*) das Feuerwerk, die Glanzentfaltung. **pyrotechnist,** *s.* der Feuerwerker.

pyroxylin [pai'rɔksilin], *s.* die Schießbaumwolle, Kollodiumwolle.

pyrrhic ['pirik], *adj.* (*Metr.*) – ***verse,*** der Pyrrhichius.

Pyrrhic, *adj.* – ***victory,*** der Pyrrhussieg.

Pythagorean [paiθægə'riən], **1.** *s.* der Pythagoreer. **2.** *adj.* pythagoreisch.

python ['paiθən], *s.* 1. die Riesenschlange; 2. (*Antiqu.*) der Python.

pythoness ['paiθənes], *s.* die Orakelpriesterin,

Wahrsagerin. **pythonic** [–'θɔnik], *adj.* orakelhaft, prophetisch.
pyuria [pai'juəriə], *s.* (*Med.*) das Eiterharnen.
pyx [piks], **1.** *s.* 1. (*Eccl.*) die Pyxis, Monstranz; 2. (*also* – ***chest***) Büchse für Münzproben. **2.** *v.t.* auf Gewicht prüfen (*coins*).

Q

Q, q [kju:], *s.* das Q, q. *See Index of Abbreviations.*
Q-boat, *s.* die U-Boot-Falle, das Kriegsschiff als Handelsschiff getarnt.
qua [kwɑ:], *conj.* (in der Eigenschaft) als.
[1]**quack** [kwæk], **1.** *v.i.* quaken, quäken. **2.** *s.* das Quaken, Quäken, Gequake.
[2]**quack, 1.** *v.i.* quacksalbern, herumpfuschen. **2.** *s.* 1. der Quacksalber, Kurpfuscher; 2. Schwindler, Scharlatan, Schaumschläger. **3.** *attrib. adj.* Quacksalber–, Wunder–, Schwindel–, quacksalberisch; – ***doctor,*** *see* **2,** 1.
quackery ['kwækəri], *s.* die Quacksalberei, Kurpfuscherei; der Schwindel. **quacksalver,** *s. See* [2]**quack, 2,** 1.
quad [kwɔd], *s.* (*coll.*) *see* **quadrangle,** 2; **quadrat**; **quadruplet.**
quadrable ['kwɔdrəbl], *adj.* (*Math.*) quadrierbar.
quadragenarian [kwɔdrədʒi'nɛəriən], **1.** *s.* Vierzigjährige(r). **2.** *adj.* vierzigjährig.
Quadragesima [kwɔdrə'dʒesimə], *s.* (*Eccl.*) der Sonntag Quadragesimä, erster Fastensonntag. **quadragesimal,** *adj.* Fasten–.
quadrangle ['kwɔdræŋgl], *s.* 1. (*Math.*) das Viereck; 2. (viereckiger) Hof. **quadrangular** [–'ræŋgjulə], *adj.* viereckig.
quadrant ['kwɔdrənt], *s.* der Quadrant, Viertelkreis; (*Astr.*) – ***elevation,*** der Erhöhungswinkel.
quadrat ['kwɔdræt], *s.* (*Typ.*) das Quadrat, großer Ausschluß; ***em*** –, das Geviert; ***en*** –, das Halbgeviert.
quadrate, 1. ['kwɔdreit], *v.t.* anpassen (***with,*** an (*Acc.*)), in Übereinstimmung bringen (mit). **2.** [–reit], *v.i.* übereinstimmen (***with,*** mit). **3.** [–rit], *adj.* (*Anat.*) quadratisch, Quadrat–. **4.** [–rit], *s.* 1. (*obs.*) (*Anat.*) viereckiger Muskel; 2. (*Zool.*) das Viereckbein.
quadratic [kwɔd'rætik], **1.** *adj.* 1. quadratisch; 2. (*Math.*) zweiten Grades. **2.** *s.* quadratische Gleichung.
quadrature ['kwɔdrətʃə], *s.* (*Math.*) die Quadratur.
quadrennial [kwɔd'reniəl], *adj.* 1. vierjährlich, alle vier Jahre; 2. vierjährig.
quadriga [kwɔd'raigə], *s.* (*Hist.*) die Quadriga, das Viergespann.
quadrilateral [kwɔdri'lætərəl], **1.** *adj.* vierseitig, viereckig; (*Archit.*) – ***beam*** or ***girder,*** der Rahmenträger. **2.** *s.* das Vierseit, Viereck.
quadrille [kwə'dril], *s.* die Quadrille.
quadrillion [kwə'driliən], *s.* 1. (*Eng.*) die Quadrillion (= 10^{24}); 2. (*Am.*) Billiarde (= 10^{15}).
quadri|nomial [kwɔdri'noumiəl], *adj.* (*Math.*) viergliedrig. **–partite,** *adj.* 1. (*Pol.*) Vierer–, Viermächte–; 2. (*Bot.*) vierteilig. **–plegia** [–'pli:dʒiə], *s.* (*Med.*) die Tetraplegie.
quadroon [kwɔ'dru:n], *s.* der (die) Terzeron(in), Viertelneger(in).
quadrumanous [kwɔd'ru:mənəs], *adj.* (*Zool.*) vierhändig.
quadruped ['kwɔdruped], **1.** *s.* der Vierfüß(l)er. **2.** *adj.* vierfüßig.
quadruple ['kwɔdrupl], **1.** *adj.* vierfach; – ***of*** or ***to,*** viermal so groß wie; – ***alliance,*** die Quadrupelallianz; – ***pact,*** das Viermächteabkommen; (*Mus.*) – ***rhythm*** or ***time,*** der Vierteltakt. **2.** *s.* das Vierfache. **3.** *v.t.* (*v.i.* sich) vervierfachen.
quadruplet ['kwɔdruplet], *s.* (*usu. pl.*) der Vierling.
quadruplicate, 1. [kwɔ'dru:plikeit], *v.t.* viermal *or* vierfach ausfertigen, vervierfachen. **2.** [–kit], *adj.* vierfach (ausgefertigt). **3.** [–kit], *s.* vierfache Ausfertigung. **quadruplication** [–'keiʃən], *s.* die Vervierfachung.
quads [kwɔdz], *pl.* (*sing. rare*) (*coll.*) *see* **quadruplet.**
quaestor ['kwi:stə], *s.* der Quästor. **quaestorial** [–'tɔ:riəl], *adj.* Quästor(s)–. **quaestorship,** *s.* die Quästur.
quaff [kwɔf], **1.** *v.i.* tüchtig trinken, zechen. **2.** *v.t.* (*also* – ***off***) hinunterstürzen, in großen Zügen trinken, austrinken, (aus)leeren.
quag [kwæg], *s. See* **quagmire.**
quagga ['kwægə], *s.* (*Zool.*) das Quagga.
quagmire ['kwægmaiə], *s.* der Sumpf, Morast (*also fig.*); Moorboden, das Moor, Sumpfland, **quaggy,** *adj.* sumpfig.
[1]**quail** [kweil], *s.* (*Orn.*) die Wachtel (*Coturnix coturnix*).
[2]**quail,** *v.i.* 1. verzagen, den Mut sinken lassen; ***his spirit –ed,*** ihm sank der Mut; 2. zittern, beben, zurückweichen (***before,*** vor (*Dat.*)).
quaint [kweint], *adj.* 1. altmodisch, anheimelnd; 2. kurios, wunderlich, drollig, putzig; 3. seltsam, merkwürdig. **quaintness,** *s.* 1. das Altmodische, anheimelnde Schlichtheit; 2. die Seltsamkeit, Wunderlichkeit.
quake [kweik], **1.** *v.i.* zittern, beben (***for, with,*** vor (*Dat.*)); – ***in one's shoes,*** vor Angst außer sich (*Dat.*) sein. **2.** *s.* (*coll.*) das (Erd)beben, die Erschütterung.
Quaker ['kweikə], *s.* der Quäker. **Quakeress,** *s.* die Quäkerin. **Quakerish,** *adj.* quäkerhaft. **Quakerism,** *s.* das Quäkertum.
quaking ['kweikiŋ], *adj.* zittrig, zitternd, bebend. **quaking-grass,** *s.* das Zittergras.
qualification [kwɔlifi'keiʃən], *s.* 1. die Befähigung, Tauglichkeit, Eignung, Qualifikation (***for,*** für *or* zu; ***as,*** als); Fähigkeit (***for,*** zu); ***my – for,*** was mich qualifiziert für *or* befähigt zu; 2. das Eignungszeugnis; 3. die Einschränkung, Modifikation; ***without any*** –, ohne jede Einschränkung; 4. die Vorbedingung, Voraussetzung, das Erfordernis.
qualified ['kwɔlifaid], *adj.* 1. geeignet, befähigt, qualifiziert (***as,*** als; ***for,*** für; ***to do,*** zu tun); 2. autorisiert, befugt; 3. modifiziert, bedingt, eingeschränkt; – ***acceptance,*** bedingte Annahme; ***in a – sense,*** mit Einschränkung(en). **qualify** [–fai], **1.** *v.t.* 1. befähigen, qualifizieren (***for,*** für *or* zu; ***to be,*** zu sein); (behördlich) autorisieren, qualifizieren; 2. bezeichnen, charakterisieren (***as,*** als); 3. (*Gram.*) näher bestimmen, modifizieren; 4. modifizieren, einschränken, mildern, mäßigen; 5. verdünnen, vermischen, verschneiden (*drinks*). **2.** *v.i.* 1. sich qualifizieren *or* eignen, die Eignung besitzen *or* nachweisen (***as,*** als; ***for,*** für), sich als tauglich *or* geeignet erweisen (***for,*** für *or* zu); die Vorbedingungen erfüllen (***for,*** für); 3. (*Spt.*) sich qualifizieren; ***–ing heat*** or ***round,*** die Ausscheidungsrunde.
qualitative ['kwɔlitətiv], *adj.* qualitativ.
quality ['kwɔliti], *s.* 1. (*esp. Comm.*) die Qualität; 2. Eigenschaft, Beschaffenheit, charakterische (Eigen)art; 3. (*Mus.*) die Tonfarbe, Klangfarbe; 4. (*Comm.*) gute Qualität, die Güte, Erstklassigkeit, Klasse; – ***goods,*** Qualitätswaren (*pl.*); 5. (*rare*) (gesellschaftlicher) Rang, die Stellung; 6. Vornehmheit, (vornehmer) Stand; ***the*** –, die vornehme Welt; ***person of*** –, die Standesperson.
qualm [kwɑ:m], *s.* (*usu. pl.*) 1. der Skrupel, Gewissensbiß, Bedenken (*pl.*), Zweifel (*pl.*); 2. (*rare*) der

Schwächeanfall, das Übelkeitsgefühl; 3. Angstgefühl, die Angst, Bedrücktheit. **qualmish,** *adj.* 1. unwohl; 2. Übelkeits–; ***I am –,*** mir wird übel (***at,*** bei *or* von).

quandary ['kwɔndəri], *s.* die Schwierigkeit, Verlegenheit, verzwickte Lage.

quant [kwɔnt], *s.* (*Naut.*) die Stake *or* Stakstange mit Tellerkappe.

quanta ['kwɔntə], *pl. of* **quantum.**

quantic ['kwɔntik], *s.* (*Math.*) homogene Funktion.

quantifiable ['kwɔntifaiəbl], *adj.* quantitativ bestimmbar, meßbar. **quantification** [–fi'keiʃən], *s.* 1. die Quantitätsbestimmung, Messung; 2. Quantifizierung. **quantify** [–fai], *v.t.* 1. quantitativ bestimmen, messen; 2. quantifizieren.

quantitative ['kwɔntiteitiv], *adj.* 1. quantitativ, Mengen–; – ***analysis,*** die Mengenbestimmung; 2. (*Gram., Metr.*) quantitativ, quantitierend, Quantitäts–.

quantity ['kwɔntiti], *s.* 1. die Menge, Quantität; – ***production,*** die Massenproduktion; ***quality and –,*** Qualität und Größe; 2. die Anzahl, große Menge; ***in –*** or ***quantities,*** in großer Menge, in großen Mengen; 3. bestimmte Menge, das Quantum; – ***surveyor,*** der Baukostenfachmann; 4. (*Math.*) die Größe; (*coll. fig.*) ***negligible –,*** völlig unwichtige P., wahre *or* reine Null; ***unknown –,*** unbekannte Größe (*also fig.*); 5. (*Gram., Metr.*) die Quantität; 6. (*Mus.*) Länge, (Ton)dauer.

quantum ['kwɔntəm], *s.* (*pl.* **quanta**) 1. die Menge; 2. der (An)teil; Quantum; (*coll.*) ***I've had my –,*** ich habe schon genug; 3. (*Phys.*) das Quanta; – ***theory,*** die Quantentheorie.

quarantine ['kwɔrənti:n], **1.** *s.* die Quarantäne (*of a ship*); Isolierung (*of a p.*); Quarantänemaßnahmen (*pl.*); – ***flag,*** die Quarantäneflagge. **2.** *v.t.* 1. unter Quarantäne stellen, Quarantäne verhängen über (*Acc.*); 2. (*fig.*) völlig isolieren.

¹**quarrel** ['kwɔrəl], *s.* 1. (*Tech.*) der Steinmetzmeißel; 2. Glaserdiamant; 3. (*Hist.*) Bolzen (*for crossbow*); 4. (*obs.*) *see* ³**quarry,** 3.

²**quarrel, 1.** *s.* der Streit, Zank, Zwist, Hader; ***have no – with,*** nichts auszusetzen haben an (*Dat.*); ***pick*** or ***seek a – with,*** Händel suchen mit, Streit vom Zaun brechen mit. **2.** *v.i.* 1. (sich) streiten, (sich) zanken (***with,*** mit; ***for,*** wegen; ***about, over,*** um *or* über (*Acc.*)); ***– with each other,*** miteinander streiten (*two people*); ***they – among themselves,*** sie streiten *or* zanken sich; 2. sich beklagen (***with,*** über (*Acc.*)), etwas auszusetzen haben (an (*Dat.*)) (*a th.*); ***– with one's bread and butter,*** sich (*Dat.*) selbst im Lichte stehen, sich (*Dat.*) ins eigne Fleisch schneiden; 3. sich entzweien; 4. hadern; ***– with one's lot,*** mit seinem Schicksal hadern. **quarrelsome** [–səm], *adj.* zänkisch, streitsüchtig. **quarrelsomeness,** *s.* die Streitsucht, Zanksucht.

quarrier ['kwɔriə], *s.* der Steinbrecher, Steinhauer.

¹**quarry** ['kwɔri], **1.** *s.* 1. der Steinbruch; 2. (*fig.*) die Fundgrube, Quelle. **2.** *v.t.* 1. brechen, hauen, abbauen (*stone*), aushöhlen (*a mountain*); 2. (*fig.*) ausgraben, herausholen, mühsam erarbeiten *or* gewinnen (***from,*** aus).

²**quarry,** *s.* 1. die Jagdbeute, verfolgtes Wild; 2. (*fig.*) die Beute.

³**quarry,** *s.* 1. der Quaderstein; 2. die Kachel; 3. (*also –* ***light***) rautenförmige Fensterscheibe.

quarry|man, *s. See* **quarrier. –stone,** *s.* der Bruchstein.

¹**quart** [kwɔ:t], *s.* das Quart(maß) (= *1.14 l.*; *Am.* = *0.95 l.*); (*Prov.*) ***you can't get a – into a pint pot,*** das Wenige enthält das Größere nicht.

²**quart** [kɑ:t], *s.* 1. (*Mus.*) die Quarte; 2. (*Fenc., Cards*) Quart.

quartan ['kwɔ:tən], *adj.* viertägig, alle vier Tage; Quartan–; ***– fever,*** das Viertagefieber.

¹**quarter** ['kwɔ:tə], **1.** *s.* 1. das Viertel; ***– of a century,*** ein Vierteljahrhundert; ***for a – (of) the price,*** zum viertel Preis; ***divide into –s,*** vierteln, vierteilen, in vier Teile schneiden; (*coll.*) ***not a – as good,*** bei weitem nicht so gut; 2. das Vierteljahr, Quartal; ***by the –,*** quartalsweise; 3. die Viertelstunde, das Viertelstundenzeichen, Viertel; ***– of an hour,*** eine Viertelstunde; (*coll.*) ***it has gone the –,*** es hat ein Viertel geschlagen; ***strike the –s,*** die Viertel schlagen (*of a clock*); ***at (a) – to three,*** (um) Viertel vor drei, dreiviertel vier; ***a – past three,*** (ein) Viertel nach drei, viertel vier; 4. der (Mond)-viertel; 5. die Himmelsrichtung, Himmelsgegend, (Wind)richtung; ***the wind blows from another –,*** der Wind weht aus einer andern Richtung; 6. der Teil, die Gegend, das Viertel; ***close –s,*** (nächste) Nähe; ***come to close –s,*** handgemein werden; ***from all –s,*** von allen Seiten; ***from another –,*** von anderer Seite; ***poor –,*** das Armenviertel; ***residential –,*** der Wohnbezirk; 7. die Stelle; ***from a good –,*** aus zuverlässiger Quelle; ***in the proper –,*** bei der zuständigen Stelle; ***official –,*** amtliche Seite; 8. (*Spt.*) die Viertelmeile; ***win the –,*** die Viertelmeile gewinnen; 9. (*Naut.*) die (Wind)vierung (*of a ship*); ***on the –,*** backstagsweise; ***on the starboard –,*** an Steuerbord achteraus; 10. (*weight*) der Viertelzentner (*Eng. 28 lb.* = *approx. 12.5 kg.*; *Am. 25 lb.* = *approx. 11.5 kg.*); (*measure*) das Quarter (*8 bushels* = *290 l.*); 11. der Vierteldollar, das 25-Cent-Stück; 12. (*Her.*) Feld eines Gevierts, Quartier; 13. (*Vet.*) Hinterviertel, Hinterteil, die Kruppe; ***– of mutton,*** das Viertel Hammel; ***hind –s,*** die Hinterhand (*of a horse*), (*coll.*) das Hinterteil, der Hintere; 14. *pl.* (*Mil.*) das Quartier, (*coll.*) Logis, die Wohnung, Unterkunft; (*coll.*) ***change one's –s,*** umziehen; (*Mil.*) ***take up one's –s,*** Quartier nehmen, sein Quartier aufschlagen; (*coll.*) ***take up one's –s with,*** sich einquartieren bei; ***confined to –s,*** Zimmerarrest haben; ***free –s,*** das Freiquartier.
2. *v.t.* 1. in vier Teile teilen; 2. (*Her.*) vieren, in vier Felder teilen; 3. vierteilen (*a criminal*); 4. (*Mil.*) einquartieren; (*coll.*) (zwangsweise) unterbringen *or* beherbergen (***on,*** bei); ***– o.s. on him,*** sich bei ihm einquartieren; (*Mil.*) ***be –ed at,*** in Quartier liegen in (*Dat.*); ***be –ed on,*** (*Mil.*) in Quartier liegen bei, (*coll.*) untergebracht werden bei; 5. (*Hunt.*) durchstöbern, durchstreifen, durchqueren (*ground*).

²**quarter,** *s.* (*esp. Mil.*) der Pardon, die Gnade; (*fig.*) Schonung, Nachsicht; ***give no –,*** (*Mil.*) Pardon nicht geben; (*coll.*) nichts schonen; ***call*** or ***cry for –,*** um Gnade flehen; ***find no –,*** keine Schonung *or* Nachsicht finden.

quarterage ['kwɔ:təridʒ], *s.* die Vierteljahrs– *or* Quartalszahlung, das Vierteljahrsgehalt. **quarter|-back,** *s.* (*Am. Footb.*) der Abwehrspieler. **–-bend,** *s.* (*Tech.*) der (Rohr)krümmer. **–-binding,** *s.* der Band mit engem Lederrücken. **–-day,** *s.* der Quartalstag. **–deck,** *s.* das Achterdeck. **quartering, 1.** *s.* 1. das Vierteilen; 2. (*Her.*) die Schildteilung; 3. (*Mil.*) Einquartierung; 4. (*Build.*) das Vierblatt, Sparrenholz. **2.** *adj.* (*Naut.*) Backstags–. **quarterly, 1.** *adv.* vierteljährlich, quartalsweise. **2.** *adj.* vierteljährlich, Vierteljahrs–, Quartals–; ***– accounts,*** vierteljährlicher Rechnungsabschluß. **3.** *s.* die Vierteljahrsschrift. **quartermaster,** *s.* 1. (*Mil.*) der Feldzeugmeister, Quartiermeister; ***–-sergeant,*** der Furier; 2. (*Naut.*) der Steuermann(smaat).

quartern ['kwɔ:tən], *s.* (*obs.*) das Viertel (*as measure*); ***– loaf,*** das Vierpfundbrot. **quarter|-plate,** *s.* (*Phot.*) die Plattengröße 9 × 12 cm. **–-sessions,** *pl.* vierteljährliche Gerichtssitzungen, das Grafschaftsgericht. **–staff,** *s.* (*Hist.*) langer, dicker Stab (*as weapon*). **–-tone,** *s.* (*Mus.*) das Vierteltonintervall. **–-wind,** *s.* der Backstagswind.

quartet [kwɔ:'tet], *s.* das Quartett.

quartile ['kwɔ:tail], *s.* 1. (*Astr.*) der Geviertschein, die Quadratur; 2. (*Stat.*) das Quartil.

quarto ['kwɔ:tou], *s.* das Quart(format).

quartz [kwɔ:ts], *s.* der Quarz. **quartzite** [–ait], *s.* der Quarzit, Quarzfels.

quash [kwɔʃ], *v.t.* 1. aufheben, annullieren, zurückweisen, verwerfen; 2. (*fig.*) unterdrücken, zunichte machen.

quasi ['kweisai], **1.** *adj. pref.* Halb–, Schein–, Quasi–; *--crime,* verbrechenähnliches Delikt. **2.** *adv. pref.* halb–, gleichsam, gewissermaßen, sozusagen; *--official,* halbamtlich.
quassia ['kwɔʃ(i)ə], *s.* die Quassie, der Bitterholzbaum.
quater-centenary [kwætəsen'ti:nəri], *s.* die Vierhundertjahrfeier.
quaternary [kwɔ'tə:nəri], **1.** *adj.* 1. aus vier bestehend; *– number,* die Vierzahl; 2. (*Geol.*) Quartär; 3. (*Chem.*) quartär, quaternär. **2.** *s.* 1. die Vierzahl; 2. (*Geol.*) Quartärperiode, das Quartär. **quaternion,** *s.* 1. die Vierergruppe, der Quaternio; 2. (*Math.*) die Quaternione. **quaternity,** *s.* die Gruppe von vier (Personen).
quatrain ['kwɔtrein], *s.* (*Metr.*) der Vierzeiler.
quatrefoil ['kætrəfɔil], *s.* (*Archit., Her.*) das Vierblatt.
quattrocento [kwætro'tʃentou], *s.* (*Art*) der Frührenaissancestil.
quaver ['kweivə], **1.** *v.i.* 1. zittern; 2. trillern, vibrieren, tremolieren, tremulieren. **2.** *v.t.* 1. stammeln, stammelnd äußern; 2. trillernd singen. **3.** *s.* (*Mus.*) 1. das Tremolo, der Triller; 2. die Achtelnote; *– rest,* die Achtelpause. **quavering, quavery,** *adj.* zitternd, schwankend; stammelnd.
quay [ki:], *s.* der Kai, die Kaimauer. **quayage** ['ki:idʒ], *s.* das Kaigeld, die Kaigebühr. **quayside,** *s.* der Hafendamm, die Uferstraße.
queasiness ['kwi:zinis], *s.* 1. die Übelkeit, der Ekel; 2. übertriebene Empfindlichkeit. **queasy,** *adj.* 1. unwohl, übel; 2. zum Erbrechen geneigt; 3. überempfindlich (*stomach, conscience*).
queen [kwi:n], **1.** *s.* 1. die Königin; (*fig.*) Herrscherin; *Queen Anne's Bounty,* der Unterstützungsfond für arme Geistliche; *Queen Anne's dead!* das sind olle Kamellen! *the king and his –,* der König und seine Gemahlin; *– of the May,* die Maienkönigin; 2. (*Chess, Cards*) die Dame; *the – of hearts,* die Herzdame. **2.** *v.t.* 1. (*Chess*) (in eine Dame) verwandeln; 2. *– it,* die Herrin *or* große Dame spielen.
queen| bee, *s.* die Bienenkönigin, der Weisel. **– dowager,** *s.* die Königinwitwe. **queenhood,** *s.* der Rang einer Königin. **queenly,** *adj.* königlich, majestätisch. **queen| mother,** *s.* die Königinmutter. **--post,** *s.* (*Archit.*) (doppelte) Hängesäule. **--regnant,** *s.* regierende Königin.
queen's|-metal, *s.* das Weißmetall, Lagermetall. **– pawn,** *s.* (*Chess*) der Damenbauer.
queer [kwiə], **1.** *adj.* 1. seltsam, wunderlich, sonderbar, eigenartig; 2. (*coll.*) nicht recht wohl, schwummerig; 3. (*sl.*) schwul; 4. (*coll.*) *be in Queer Street,* in die Tinte geraten, in der Tinte sein. **2.** *v.t.* (*coll.*) *– his pitch,* ihm in die Quere kommen, ihm einen Strich durch die Rechnung machen, ihm ins Handwerk pfuschen. **3.** *s.* (*sl.*) Schwule(r), Warme(r). **queerness,** *s.* die Seltsamkeit, Wunderlichkeit.
quell [kwel], *v.t.* bezwingen, niederwerfen, überwältigen, überwinden, unterdrücken, ersticken, beschwichtigen, dämpfen.
quench [kwentʃ], *v.t.* 1. löschen, stillen (*thirst*), auslöschen (*fire*); 2. ersticken, unterdrücken (*feelings*); 3. (*Metall.*) abschrecken, abkühlen; 4. (*Elec.*) *–ed spark,* der Löschfunke.
quenelle [kə'nel], *s.* das Fleischklößchen.
querist ['kwiərist], *s.* der (die) Fragesteller(in), Fragende(r).
quern [kwə:n], *s.* die Handmühle.
querulous ['kwerələs], *adj.* 1. unzufrieden, mürrisch, nörgelnd, verdrossen; 2. klagend, kläglich, murrend, jammernd, jämmerlich (*as a voice*). **querulousness,** *s.* (stetes) Klagen *or* Jammern, die Nörgelei, Verdrossenheit.
query ['kwiəri], **1.** *s.* 1. die Frage, Erkundigung; 2. der Zweifel, die Beanstandung; 3. (*Typ.*) das Fragezeichen. **2.** *v.t.* 1. bezweifeln, in Zweifel ziehen, in Frage stellen, beanstanden; 2. (*Typ.*) mit einem Fragezeichen versehen. **3.** *v.i.* 1. fragen, sich erkundigen; 2. zweifeln (*whether,* ob).
quest [kwest], **1.** *s.* die Suche, das Suchen, Trachten (*for,* nach); *in – of,* auf der Suche nach. **2.** *v.i.* 1. (*Hunt.*) (*of hounds*) Wild suchen; Laut geben; 2. (*of a p.*) (*rare*) (*also – about*) auf der Suche sein (*for, after,* nach). **3.** *v.t.* (*Poet.*) aufsuchen, aussuchen; trachten nach.
question ['kwestʃən], **1.** *s.* 1. die Frage, Fragestellung, (*Gram.*) der Fragesatz; (*Gram.*) *indirect –,* indirekte Frage; *leading –,* die Suggestivfrage; *the – does not arise,* die Frage ist belanglos *or* nicht zutreffend; *ask –s,* Fragen stellen; *beg the –,* dem wahren Sachverhalt ausweichen; (*coll.*) *pop the –,* einen Heiratsantrag machen (*to, Dat.*); *put a – to,* eine Frage richten an (*Acc.*), eine Frage stellen (*Dat.*); *without –,* ohne weiteres (*see also beyond –*); 2. die Streitfrage, der Streitpunkt, Zweifel, zweifelhafte S.; *there is no – of,* es kann nicht die Rede sein von; *there can be no – of,* es kann kein Zweifel sein an (*Dat.*); *make no – of,* nicht bezweifeln; *beyond –,* zweifellos, außer Zweifel; *be in –,* zweifelhaft sein, angezweifelt werden; *call in –,* in Zweifel stellen *or* ziehen, bezweifeln; *open to –,* fraglich; 3. das Problem, die Angelegenheit; *the – is,* es handelt sich darum, die Frage ist die (*whether,* ob); *that is not the –,* das gehört nicht zur S.; *there is no – but* or *that,* es ist keine *or* steht außer Frage, daß; *be a – of,* sich darum handeln (*doing,* zu tun); *what is the –?* worum handelt es sich? *the point in –,* bewußter *or* betreffender *or* fraglicher Punkt; das worum es sich handelt; *beside the –,* belanglos, unerheblich, nicht zur S. gehörig; *out of –,* (*rare*) *see beyond –*; *be out of the –,* außer Frage stehen, nicht in Betracht *or* Frage kommen, ausgeschlossen sein; *vexed –,* strittige Frage; 4. (*Parl.*) die Anfrage, Interpellation; 5. (*Hist.*) Folter. **2.** *v.t.* 1. (*a p.*) (aus)fragen (*about,* nach *or* wegen), befragen (nach, wegen, über (*Acc.*), um), Fragen stellen (*Dat.*) (über (*Acc.*)), (*Law*) vernehmen, verhören (zu); 2. in Frage stellen, bezweifeln, anzweifeln, in Zweifel stellen *or* ziehen (*facts*). **3.** *v.i.* Fragen stellen, sich erkundigen.
questionable ['kwestʃenəbl], *adj.* 1. fraglich, zweifelhaft, ungewiß, nicht sehr wahrscheinlich; 2. fragwürdig, bedenklich, anfechtbar, verdächtig. **questionableness,** *s.* die Zweifelhaftigkeit, Fragwürdigkeit. **questioner,** *s.* Fragende(r), der (die) Fragesteller(in). **questioning, 1.** *adj.* fragend (*look etc.*). **2.** *s.* das Ausfragen, Verhör, Vernehmen. **question-mark,** *s.* das Fragezeichen.
questionnaire [kwestʃə'nɛə], *s.* der Fragebogen.
question|-paper, *s.* Prüfungsaufgaben (*pl.*). **--time,** *s.* (*Parl.*) die Interpellationszeit.
queue [kju:], **1.** *s.* 1. lange Reihe, die (Anstell)reihe, Schlange; *take one's place in* or *wait in a –, see* **3**; 2. (*obs.*) der Zopf. **2.** *v.t.* (*obs.*) in einen Zopf flechten. **3.** *v.i.* (*also – up*) anstehen, sich anstellen, Schlange stehen.
quibble [kwibl], **1.** *s.* 1. die Ausflucht, Spitzfindigkeit, Wortklauberei, Haarspalterei, Sophisterei; 2. (*rare*) das Wortspiel. **2.** *v.i.* Ausflüchte gebrauchen *or* machen, herumreden, spitzfindig sein, Worte klauben, Haare spalten; *– about* or *over,* tüfteln über (*Acc.*), deuteln an (*Dat.*). **quibbler,** *s.* der Wortklauber, Wortverdreher, Haarspalter, Sophist. **quibbling, 1.** *adj.* spitzfindig. **2.** *s. See* **quibble, 1.**
quick [kwik], **1.** *adj.* 1. schnell, geschwind, rasch, eilig, sofortig, schleunig, hurtig, hastig; (*Mil.*) *– fire,* das Schnellfeuer; *– lunch,* eiliges Mittagessen; (*Mil.*) *– march,* der Exerzierschritt; (*coll.*) *– off the mark,* stracks auf und davon; (*Comm.*) *– returns,* schneller Umsatz; *be – about a th.,* sich mit etwas beeilen; (*coll.*) *that was – work,* das ist schnell gegangen; 2. flink; *– child,* aufgewecktes Kind; *– wits,* die Schlagfertigkeit; *– at repartee,* schlagfertig; *– at understanding,* schnell vom Begriff (*customarily*); *be – to understand,* schnell begreifen (*on one occasion*); 3. hitzig; *– temper,* die Reizbarkeit, der Jähzorn; *he has a – temper,* er hat eine aufbrausende Art; 4. scharf; *– ear,* feines Gehör; *– of ear,* feinhörig; *– eye,* scharfes Auge; 5. lebend,

lebendig; – ***hedge,*** lebende Hecke; (*obs.*) – ***with child,*** (hoch)schwanger; 6. (*Comm.*) – ***assets,*** flüssiges Guthaben. **2.** *s.* 1. (*B.*) ***the –,*** die Lebenden (*pl.*); 2. lebendes Fleisch; (*fig.*) das Leben, Innerste; ***to the –,*** bis ins Fleisch; (*fig.*) bis ins Innerste, bis aufs Mark *or* Blut; ***cut*** or ***touch him to the –,*** ihn sehr schmerzlich berühren, ihn schwer *or* tief kränken, ihm nahegehen.

quick|-change artist, *s.* der Verwandlungskünstler. **--eared,** *adj.* feinhörig.

quicken [ˈkwikən], **1.** *v.t.* 1. beschleunigen; 2. (*fig.*) beleben, beseelen, neuen Auftrieb geben (*Dat.*), anregen, anfeuern, kräftigen, schärfen. **2.** *v.i.* 1. schneller werden, sich beschleunigen; 2. angefeuert *or* belebt *or* gekräftigt werden; 3. (*unborn child*) Leben zeigen, sich regen; 4. (*fig.*) lebendig werden; 5. (*pregnant woman*) Leben fühlen.

quick|-firer, *s.* das Schnellfeuergeschütz. **--firing,** *adj.* Schnellfeuer–. **--freeze,** *irr.v.t.* tiefkühlen. **-lime,** *s.* gebrannter *or* ungelöschter Kalk. **quickly,** *adv.* 1. schnell, rasch, geschwind, schleunigst; 2. eilig, bald, gleich. **quick-match,** *s.* die Zündschnur. **quickness,** *s.* 1. die Schnelligkeit, Geschwindigkeit; 2. Aufgewecktheit, Lebhaftigkeit, Beweglichkeit (*of imagination etc.*); 3. Schärfe, Feinheit (*of senses*); – ***of temper,*** die Hitzigkeit, Reizbarkeit, der Jähzorn.

quick|sand, *s.* der Triebsand, Treibsand, Flugsand, Schwimmsand, Schwemmsand, Schluff. **-set,** *s.* 1. der Setzling, Hagedorn; 2. lebende Hecke. **--sightedness,** *s.* die Scharfsichtigkeit. **-silver,** **1.** *s.* das Quecksilber. **2.** *v.t.* mit Quecksilber beziehen *or* belegen (*glass*). **-step,** *s.* 1. (*Danc.*) der Quickstep; 2. (*Mil.*) Gleichschritt. **--tempered,** *adj.* reizbar, hitzig, jähzornig. **--witted,** *adj.* scharfsinning, schlagfertig. **--wittedness,** *s.* die Schlagfertigkeit.

[1]**quid** [kwid], *s.* der Priem, das Stück Kautabak.

[2]**quid,** *s.* (*sl.*) das Pfund (Sterling).

quiddity [ˈkwiditi], *s.* 1. eigentliches Wesen, die Eigenheit; 2. Spitzfindigkeit.

quidnunc [ˈkwidnʌŋk], *s.* der Naseweis, Neuigkeitskrämer; Kannegießer.

quid pro quo [ˈkwidprouˈkwou], *s.* die Gegenleistung, Entschädigung, der Gegenwert, Ersatz, das Entgelt, Äquivalent (***for,*** für); (*rare*) Mißverständnis, der Mißgriff, die Verwechslung.

quiescence [kwaiˈesəns], *s.* 1. die Ruhe, Stille; Regungslosigkeit; 2. (*Gram.*) das Stummsein. **quiescent,** *adj.* ruhend, ruhig, bewungslos; still, (*Gram.*) stumm.

quiet [ˈkwaiət], **1.** *adj.* 1. ruhig, still; ***be –,*** still sein, schweigen; ***keep –,*** schweigen, Stillschweigen bewahren (***about,*** über (*Acc.*) *or* von); ruhig *or* still bleiben, sich ruhig verhalten; ***keep a th. –,*** etwas für sich behalten; ***as – as a mouse,*** mäuschenstill; 2. sanft, friedlich, ausgeglichen, gelassen, behaglich, beschaulich, friedfertig; – ***horse,*** frommes Pferd; 3. (*as a place*) abgeschlossen, ungestört; 4. (*Comm.*) flau; 5. (*colour etc.*) unauffällig; – ***colour,*** ruhige Farbe; – ***dress,*** schlichtes Kleid. **2.** *s.* 1. die Ruhe, Stille; 2. Ungestörtheit, Friedlichkeit; 3. Ausgeglichenheit, Gelassenheit, Gemütsruhe, Seelenruhe; 4. (*coll.*) ***on the –,*** insgeheim, im geheimen; unter der Hand, im Vertrauen. **3.** *v.t.* (*fig.*) beruhigen, stillen, besänftigen.

quieten [ˈkwaiətn], **1.** *v.t.* 1. (*also* – ***down***) zum Schweigen bringen; 2. (*fig.*) *see* **quiet, 3.** **2.** *v.i.* 1. (*usu.* – ***down***) still *or* ruhig werden; (*also fig.*) zur Ruhe kommen, sich beruhigen, ruhiger werden; 2. (*fig.*) nachlassen, sich legen.

quietism [ˈkwaiətizm], *s.* (*Theol.*) der Quietismus. **quietist,** *s.* der Quietist.

quietly [ˈkwaiətli], *adj.* 1. ruhig, still, geräuschlos; 2. unauffällig. **quietness,** *s.* die Ruhe, Stille, Geräuschlosigkeit, Friedlichkeit. **quietude,** *s.* (*fig.*) (innere) Ruhe, die Gemütsruhe, Friedfertigkeit, Gelassenheit, der Gleichmut.

quietus [kwaiˈi:təs], *s.* 1. der Tod, das (Lebens)-ende; ***give the – to,*** ein Ende machen (*Dat.*); 2. der Gnadenstoß; ***give him his –,*** ihm den Gnadenstoß geben *or* den Garaus machen.

quiff [kwif], *s.* die (Stirn)locke.

quill [kwil], **1.** *s.* 1. (*also* – ***feather***) die Schwungfeder; 2. (*stalk of the feather*) Spule; 3. (*also* – ***pen***) der Federkiel, die Pose; 4. der Stachel (*of a porcupine*); 5. (*Mus. Hist.*) die Rohrpfeife, Panflöte, Syrinx; 6. (*Tech.*) (Weber)spule. **2.** *v.t.* 1. (*obs.*) in Falten legen, fälteln, kräuseln (*a ruff*); 2. (*Tech.*) aufspulen (*thread*).

quill|-driver, *s.* (*coll.*) der Federfuchser, Schmierer, Schreiberling. **--driving,** *s.* (*coll.*) die Schreiberei, Schmiererei. **quilling,** *s.* (*obs.*) die Rüsche, Krause.

quilt [kwilt], **1.** *s.* die Steppdecke, gesteppte (Bett)-decke. **2.** *v.t.* 1. steppen, durchnähen; 2. (*rare*) wattieren, auspolstern. **quilting,** *s.* 1. das Steppen, Durchnähen; – ***seam,*** die Steppnaht; Wattieren; 2. das Auspolstern; 3. die Stepperei, gesteppte Arbeit, das Pikee.

quina [ˈkwainə], *s. See* **quinquina.**

quinary [ˈkwainəri], *adj.* aus fünf bestehend, Fünf–.

quince [kwins], *s.* (*Bot.*) die Quitte.

quincentenary [kwinsenˈti:nəri], **1.** *adj.* fünfhundertjährig. **2.** *s.* die Fünfhundertjahrfeier.

quincuncial [kwinˈkʌnʃəl], *adj.* nach Fünfform geordnet. **quincunx** [ˈkwinkʌŋks], *s.* 1. die Quincunxanordnung; 2. (*Hort.*) Pflanzung in Fünfform, Kreuzpflanzung.

quinine [kwiˈni:n], *s.* das Chinin. **quininism** [–izm], **quinism** [ˈkwainizm], *s.* die Chininvergiftung, der Chininrausch.

quinquagenarian [kwiŋkwədʒiˈnɛəriən], **1.** *adj.* fünfzigjährig. **2.** *s.* Fünfzigjährige(r), der (die) Fünfziger(in).

Quinquagesima [kwiŋkwəˈdʒesimə], *s.* der Sonntag Quinquagesimä.

quinquennial [kwiŋˈkweniəl], *adj.* 1. fünfjährig; 2. fünfjährlich, alle fünf Jahre wiederkehrend. **quinquennium,** *s.* das Jahrfünft.

quinquereme [ˈkwiŋkwəri:m], *s.* (*Hist.*) die Galeere mit fünf Ruderbänken.

quinquina [kwinˈkwainə], *s.* die Chinarinde.

quins [kwinz], *pl.* (*coll.*) *see* **quintuplets.**

quinsy [ˈkwinzi], *s.* (*Med.*) die (Hals)bräune, Mandelentzündung.

[1]**quint** [kwint], *s.* (*Mus.*) die Quint(e).

[2]**quint** [kint], *s.* (*Cards*) die Quinte.

quintal [kwintl], *s.* (metrischer) Zentner, der Doppelzentner (= *100 kg.*). **quintan,** *adj.* fünftägig, Fünftage–, Quintan–.

quinte [kɛ̃t], *s.* (*Fenc.*) die Quinte.

quintessence [kwinˈtesəns], *s.* 1. die Quintessenz; 2. (*fig.*) der Kern, Inbegriff; 3. das Beste. **quintessential** [–tiˈsenʃəl], *adj.* Kern–, wesentlich.

quintet [kwinˈtet], *s.* (*Mus.*) das Quintett.

quintillion [kwinˈtiliən], *s.* 1. (*Eng.*) die Quintillion (= 10^{30}); 2. (*Am.*) Trillion (= 10^{18}).

quintuple [ˈkwintjupl], **1.** *adj.* fünffach. **2.** *s.* fünffacher Betrag, das Fünffache. **3.** *v.t.* verfünffachen. **4.** *v.i.* sich verfünffachen, fünfmal so groß werden. **quintuplets** [–plits], *pl.* Fünflinge (*pl.*). **quintuplicate** [–ˈtju:plikit], **1.** *adj.* fünffach. **2.** *s.* fünftes Exemplar. **quintuplication** [–ˈkeiʃən], *s.* die Verfünffachung.

quip [kwip], **1.** *s.* 1. treffender Stich *or* Hieb, geistreiche Bemerkung, witziger Einfall; ***–s and quirks,*** Schnurren und Schnacken; 2. die Spitzfindigkeit, das Wortspiel. **2.** *v.i.* scherzen, witzeln, spötteln.

quire [ˈkwaiə], *s.* 1. das Buch (Papier) (= *24 sheets*); 2. (*Bookb.*) ***in –s,*** in Lagen.

quirk [kwə:k], *s.* 1. plötzliche Wendung, unerwarteter Zug, der Einfall, Kniff, Witz, die Witzelei, Spitzfindigkeit, der Schnörkel; 2. (*Archit.*) die Hohlkehle. *See also* **quip.**

quisling [ˈkwizliŋ], *s.* (*coll.*) der Landesverräter.

quit [kwit], **1.** *irr.v.t.* 1. verlassen; 2. sich zurückziehen von, aufgeben, verzichten auf (*Acc.*); 3.

(*obs.*) – ***o.s.***, sich entledigen (*of, Gen.*), sich befreien *or* freimachen (von); 4. (*coll.*) aufhören (***doing***, zu tun); (*sl.*) – ***hold of***, loslassen, fahrenlassen; (*coll.*) – ***work(ing)***, aufhören zu arbeiten, mit der Arbeit aufhören; 5. (*obs.*) – ***you(rselves) like men!*** benehmt euch tapfer! 6. (*Poet.*) vergelten, ausgleichen. **2.** *irr.v.i.* räumen, ausziehen, fortgehen; ***notice to*** –, die Kündigung; ***give notice to*** –, kündigen; ***have notice to*** –, gekündigt werden. **3.** *pred. adj.* 1. (*coll.*) los, (los und) ledig (***of***, von); ***you're lucky to be – of him***, du kannst froh sein, ihn loszusein; ***get – of it***, es loswerden; 2. (*obs.*) ***go*** –, frei ausgehen.

quitch(-grass) [kwitʃ], *s.* (*Bot.*) die Quecke.

quit-claim, 1. *s.* 1. (*Law*) der Verzicht, die Verzichtleistung; 2. (*Am.*) Abtretungsurkunde. **2.** *v.t.* Verzicht leisten auf (*Acc.*).

quite [kwait], *adv.* 1. ganz, gänzlich, völlig, vollständig; – ***a different matter***, eine ganz *or* völlig andere S.; – ***the reverse***, genau das Gegenteil; – ***spoilt***, schon gänzlich verdorben; 2. (*coll.*) durchaus, wirklich, wahrhaftig, tatsächlich; recht, ziemlich; (*coll.*) – ***a (big) do***, eine regelrechte Festlichkeit; – ***delighted***, wirklich entzückt; (*coll.*) – ***an amount of***, recht viel; (*coll.*) – ***a number of***, etliche; (*coll.*) – ***a few***, recht viele, eine ziemliche Menge; (*coll.*) – ***a while***, schon etliche Zeit; (*coll.*) – ***a wind***, durchaus windig, ein ordentlicher *or* ziemlicher Wind; (*coll.*) ***it was – a joke***, es war wirklich spaßig; – ***so!*** ganz recht! so ist es! jawohl! das stimmt! allerdings! – ***the thing***, genau das Gegebene; große Mode, der letzte Schrei; (*coll.*) ***she's – pretty***, sie ist ja recht hübsch; ***I think we should go, don't you? –!*** ich bin der Meinung, wir sollen gehen, was meinen Sie? Durchaus! *or* Allerdings!

quitrent ['kwitrent], *s.* (*obs.*) (geringes) Pachtgeld (anstatt Dienstleistung).

quits [kwits], *pred. adj.* (*coll.*) quitt; ***be*** –, (miteinander) quitt sein; ***be*** or ***get – with him***, es ihm heimzahlen; ***call*** or ***cry*** –, klein beigeben; ***call it*** –, see ***be*** –; ***double or*** –, alles riskieren *or* aufs Spiel setzen.

quittance ['kwitəns], *s.* 1. (*Poet.*) die Befreiung (***from***, von), Quittung; 2. Erledigung (*of, Gen.*), Vergeltung, das Entgelt, der Ersatz (für); ***omittance is no*** –, aufgeschoben ist nicht aufgehoben. **quitter,** *s.* (*sl.*) der Drückeberger, Kneifer, Angsthase.

[1]**quiver** ['kwivə], *s.* der Köcher; (*fig.*) ***have a shaft left in one's*** –, noch ein Eisen im Feuer haben; ***a – full of children***, eine kinderreiche Familie.

[2]**quiver, 1.** *v.i.* zittern, beben, zucken (***with***, vor (*Dat.*). **2.** *v.t.* schlagen mit (*wings*). **3.** *s.* 1. das Zittern; Zucken (*of eyelids*); 2. bebende Stimme.

qui vive [ki:'vi:v], *s.* ***be on the*** –, aufpassen, auf der Hut *or* dem Quivive sein.

quixotic [kwik'sɔtik], *adj.* donquichottisch, schwärmerisch, überspannt, weltfremd. **quixotism** ['kwiksətizm], **quixotry** ['kwiksətri], *s.* 1. die Donquichotterie, Narretei, aussichtsloses Unternehmen; 2. der Donquichotismus, weltfremde Abenteuersucht.

quiz [kwiz], **1.** *s.* 1. (*coll.*) die Befragung; 2. (*Rad., T.V.*) das Quiz; – ***master***, der Fragesteller; – ***programme***, die Quizsendung; 3. (*obs.*) komischer Kauz; 4. der Spottvogel. **2.** *v.t.* 1. spöttisch ansehen, neugierig anstarren; 2. abfragen, ausfragen; 3. aufziehen, hänseln. **quizzical,** *adj.* 1. komisch, lächerlich; 2. spöttisch, hänselnd. **quizzing-glass,** *s.* (*obs.*) das Monokel, Einglas.

quod [kwɔd], *s.* (*sl.*) das Loch, Kittchen.

quoin [kwɔin], **1.** *s.* 1. (*Archit.*) (vorspringende) Ecke; (*Build.*) der Eckstein; (*Typ.*) (Form)keil; 2. (*Artil.*) Richtkeil; 3. (*Naut.*) Staukeil. **2.** *v.t.* 1. (*Build.*) mit einem Eckstein schließen; 2. (*Typ.*) einkeilen, schließen; 3. (*Tech.*) verkeilen, festkeilen, stützen.

quoit [kwɔit], *s.* 1. der Wurfring, die Wurfscheibe; 2. *pl.* (*sing. constr.*) das Wurfringspiel, Scheibenwerfen.

quondam ['kwɔndæm], *adj.* früher, ehemalig.

quorum ['kwɔ:rəm], *s.* beschlußfähige Anzahl, das Quorum; ***be a*** –, beschlußfähig sein.

quota ['kwoutə], *s.* 1. die Quote, der Anteil; 2. (*Comm.*) das Kontingent, prozentuale Beteiligung (***of***, an (*Dat.*)); – ***goods***, kontingentierte Waren; – ***system***, das Zuteilungssystem.

quotable ['kwoutəbl], *adj.* 1. anführbar, zitierbar; 2. (*Comm.*) notierbar. **quotation** [–'teiʃən], *s.* 1. das Zitat (***from***, aus); die Anführung, das Zitieren; ***familiar –s***, geflügelte Worte; –***-marks***, Anführungsstriche, (*coll.*) Gänsefüßchen (*pl.*); 2. (*St. Exch.*) der Kurs, die (Kurs– *or* Preis)notierung; 3. (*Comm.*) Preisangabe, der Kostenanschlag.

quote [kwout], **1.** *v.t.* 1. zitieren (*a passage*) (***from***, aus); 2. Bezug nehmen *or* sich beziehen auf (*Acc.*), heranziehen, angeben, nennen (*an author*); 3. (als Beweis) anführen (*a fact*); 4. (*Comm.*) angeben, festsetzen, veranschlagen (*price*); 5. (*St. Exch.*) notieren (***at***, zu *or* mit). **2.** *v.i.* zitieren (***from***, aus). **3.** *s.* 1. (*coll.*) das Zitat; 2. *pl.* (*coll.*) *see* ***quotation-marks***.

quoth [kwouθ], *v.t.* (*obs.*) (*1st and 3rd sing. preterite only*; *usu. precedes subject*) sagte.

quotidian [kwə'tidiən], **1.** *adj.* 1. täglich, Quotidian– (*fever etc.*); 2. alltäglich, abgedroschen. **2.** *s.* das Quotidianfieber.

quotient ['kwouʃənt], *s.* (*Math.*) der Quotient.

R

R, r [ɑ:], das R, r; ***the three Rs***, die Grundlagen der Elementarbildung (Lesen, Schreiben, Rechnen); ***the r months***, September bis April (die Austernzeit). *See Index of Abbreviations.*

rabbet ['ræbit], **1.** *s.* 1. der Falz, die Fuge, Nut(e); 2. (*Tech.*) der Stoßstahl. **2.** *v.t.* nuten, (aus)falzen; zusammenfugen, einfugen. **rabbet|-joint,** *s.* überfalzte Verbindung, die Falzverbindung, Einfalzung, Spundung, Nut-und-Feder-Verbindung, Spundverbindung. **–-plane,** *s.* der Falz– *or* Nut– *or* Simshobel.

rabbi ['ræbai], *s.* der Rabbi, Rabbiner. **rabbinical** [rə'binikl], *adj.* rabbinisch.

rabbit ['ræbit], *s.* 1. das Kaninchen; 2. (*sl.*) der Stümper (*at sports*); 3. ***Welsh*** –, geröstetes Käsebrot. **rabbit|-hutch,** *s.* der Kaninchenstall. **–-punch,** *s.* (*Boxing*) der Nackenschlag. **-warren,** *s.* 1. das Kaninchengehege; 2. (*fig.*) der Irrgarten, das Labyrinth.

[1]**rabble** [ræbl], **1.** *s.* 1. lärmender Haufen; 2. der Pöbel(haufen); 3. (*coll.*) das Durcheinander. **2.** *v.t.* (*coll.*) verwirren, durcheinanderbringen.

[2]**rabble, 1.** *s.* (*Metall.*) die Rührstange. **2.** *v.t.* umrühren.

rabble-rouser, *s.* (*coll.*) der Hetzredner, Aufrührer.

rabid ['ræbid], *adj.* 1. wütend, rasend; 2. toll, fanatisch, rabiat; 3. (*Vet.*) tollwütig. **rabidness,** *s.* die Wut, Tollheit, das Rasen.

rabies ['reibi:z], *s.* (*Vet.*) die Tollwut.

raccoon, (*Am.*) *see* **racoon.**

[1]**race** [reis], *s.* 1. das Geschlecht, Volk, der Stamm, die Familie; ***human*** –, das Menschengeschlecht; 2. (*Ethn.*) die Rasse; – ***hatred***, der Rassenhaß; – ***riot***, der Rassenkrawall; 3. (*Biol.*) die Unterart, Varietät; Herkunft, Abkunft, Abstammung.

[2]**race, 1.** *s.* 1. der Lauf, die Strömung, Stromschnelle; das Gerinne, Flußbett; ***mill***–, das Mühlgerinne; 2. (*Tech.*) die Nut, Laufbahn, Laufspur, Laufrille, Gleitbahn, der Laufring; ***ball-***

–, die Laufrille; 3. (*Spt.*) der Wettlauf, das (Wett)-rennen; ***the –s,*** Pferderennen (*pl.*); ***boat –,*** der Ruderwettkampf, das Wettrudern; ***motor –,*** das Autorennen; (*coll.*) ***play the –s,*** beim Pferderennen wetten; 4. (*fig.*) der Lauf; ***his – is run,*** er hat die längste Zeit gelebt, seine Zeit ist um; 5. (*fig.*) das Wettrennen, der Wettlauf, Kampf (***for,*** um); ***armament –,*** der Rüstungswettlauf. **2.** *v.i.* 1. um die Wette laufen *or* fahren; 2. an einem Rennen teilnehmen; 3. (*coll.*) rennen, (dahin)rasen; ***the blood –d to his head,*** das Blut schoß ihm in den Kopf; 4. (*Tech.*) durchgehen. **3.** *v.t.* 1. um die Wette laufen mit; 2. rennen *or* laufen lassen (*horses*); 3. (*coll.*) ankommen *or* fertigwerden vor (*Dat.*) (*a p.*); 4. (durch)hetzen; (*law etc.*) durchpeitschen (***through,*** durch); 5. (*Tech.*) durchdrehen lassen (*an engine*).

race|-card, *s.* das Rennprogramm. **–course,** *s.* die Rennbahn. **–horse,** *s.* das Rennpferd.

raceme [ræ'si:m], *s.* die (Blüten)traube; razemöser Blütenstand.

race-meeting, *s.* das (Pferde)rennen.

racemic [ræ'si:mik], *adj.* (*Chem.*) Trauben–. **racemose** ['ræsimous], *adj.* (*Bot.*) razemös.

racer ['reisə], *s.* 1. das Rennpferd; 2. Rennboot, Rennrad, die Rennmaschine, der Rennwagen; 3. Rennfahrer. **race|-track,** *s. See* **–course.**

Rachel ['reitʃəl], *s.* (*B.*) Rahel (*f.*).

rachis ['reikis], *s.* 1. (*Bot.*) die Spindel, Hauptachse; 2. (*Anat.*) das Rückgrat. **rachitic** [ræ'kitik], *adj.* rachitisch. **rachitis** [ræ'kaitis], *s.* Englische Krankheit, die Rachitis.

racial ['reiʃəl], *adj.* rassisch, völkisch, Rassen–. **racialism,** *s.* das Rassenvorurteil, der Rassenhaß. **racialist,** *s.* Rassenvorurteilte(r), Rassenbewußte(r).

raciness ['reisinis], *s.* 1. das Pikante, die Würze; 2. das Rassige, die Urwüchsigkeit.

racing ['reisiŋ], **1.** *attrib. adj.* Renn–; ***– car,*** der Rennwagen; ***– cyclist,*** der Radrennfahrer; ***– driver,*** der Rennfahrer; ***– man,*** der Freund des Pferderennens. **2.** *attrib. & pred. adj.* reißend. **3.** *s.* 1. das Wettrennen; 2. der (Pferde)rennsport.

racism ['reisizm], *s.* 1. der Rassenkult; 2. die Rassenpolitik, Rassentheorie; *see also* **racialism.**

[1]**rack** [ræk], **1.** *s.* 1. (*Tech.*) die Zahnstange, Sperrstange; ***– and pinion,*** das Zahnstangengetriebe; ***–(-and-pinion) railway,*** die Zahnradbahn; 2. die Folter(bank), Streckfolter; ***on the –,*** auf der Folter; (*fig.*) in Folterqualen, in höchster Spannung, in quälender Ungewißheit; ***put on*** or ***to the –,*** auf die Folter spannen. **2.** *v.t.* 1. recken, strecken; 2. foltern, auf die Folterbank spannen; (*fig.*) quälen, martern; aufs höchste (an)spannen *or* anstrengen, erschüttern; ***–ed with pain,*** schmerzgequält; ***–ing headache,*** quälende Kopfschmerzen (*pl.*); ***– one's brains,*** sich (*Dat.*) den Kopf zerbrechen; 3. ausnützen, aussaugen, hochschrauben (*rent*), erschöpfen (*land*).

[2]**rack, 1.** *s.* das Gestell, Gerüst, Regal, der Ständer; das Futtergestell, die Raufe (*in stables*); ***bomb –,*** das Bombenmagazin; (*Phot.*) ***draining –,*** der Trockenständer; ***hat-and-coat –,*** die Kleiderleiste; (*Railw.*) (***luggage***) –, das (Gepäck)netz; ***newspaper –,*** der Zeitungsständer; ***plate –,*** das Tellerbrett; ***rifle –,*** der Gewehrmicken; (*Motor.*) ***roof –,*** der Dachgepäckträger. **2.** *v.t.* 1. auf ein Gestell legen (*hay, fodder etc.*); 2. (*also – up*) mit Futter versehen, füttern (*animals*) **3.** *v.i.* ***– up,*** die Raufen füllen.

[3]**rack, 1.** *s.* ziehendes *or* fliegendes Gewölk. **2.** *v.i.* dahinziehen, vom Winde getrieben werden (*of clouds*).

[4]**rack, 1.** *s.* der Paß(gang). **2.** *v.i.* im Paßgang gehen.

[5]**rack,** *s.* ***go to – and ruin,*** völlig zugrunde gehen.

[6]**rack,** *v.t.* (*also – off*) abziehen, abfüllen (*wine*).

[7]**rack,** *s. See* **arrack.**

[1]**racket** ['rækit], *s.* 1. (*Spt. usu. tennis*) der Schläger, das Rakett; 2. (*Am.*) der Schneeschuh, Schneereifen; 3. *pl.* das Rakettspiel.

[2]**racket, 1.** *s.* (*coll.*) 1. der Krach, Radau, Spektakel; ***go on the –,*** sumpfen, schwofeln; 2. das Getöse, Geschrei, Getue, der Trubel, Taumel, Betrieb; ***stand the –,*** (*coll.*) den Trubel aushalten, (*sl.*) die Folgen tragen; 3. (*sl.*) der Schwindel, die Schiebung, Erpressung; (*sl.*) ***be in on the –,*** (auch) an dem Schwindel beteiligt sein; (*sl.*) ***what's his –?*** was ist seine Branche? (*sl.*) ***it's a –,*** das ist glatter Betrug. **2.** *v.i.* Krach *or* Radau machen, lärmen.

racketeer [ræki'tiə], *s.* der Geschäftemacher, Schieber, Gangster. **racketeering,** *s.* Gangstermethoden, Schiebungen (*pl.*), das Gangstertum.

rackety ['rækiti], *adj.* (*coll.*) 1. lärmend; 2. ausschweifend, vergnügungssüchtig.

rack|-railway, *s.* die Zahnradbahn. **–-rent, 1.** *s.* wucherische Miete. **2.** *v.t.* wucherische Miete auferlegen (*Dat.*). **–-wheel,** *s.* das Zahnrad.

raconteur [rækɔ̃'tə:], *s.* (guter) Erzähler.

racoon [rə'ku:n], *s.* der Waschbär.

racy ['reisi], *adj.* 1. rassig, urwüchsig; lebhaft, feurig, kraftvoll, kernig, würzig, pikant, markant; ***– of the soil,*** bodenständig, erdrüchig; 2. (*coll.*) schlüpfrig, zotig.

radar ['reidɑ:], *s.* 1. das Radar, Funkmeßverfahren; 2. (*also – set*) Radargerät, die Radaranlage.

raddle [rædl], **1.** *v.t.* mit Rötel bemalen, rot anmalen. **2.** *s.* der Rötel, Rot(eisen)stein.

radial ['reidiəl], *adj.* 1. strahlenförmig, Strahl(en)–, radial, Radial–; ***– engine,*** der Sternmotor; ***– tyre,*** der Gürtelreifen; 2. (*Anat.*) Speichen–; ***– nerve,*** der Speichennerv.

radian ['reidiən], *s.* (*Math.*) der Einheitswinkel; ***– measure,*** das Bogenmaß.

radiance, radiancy ['reidiəns(i)], *s.* das Strahlen, der Glanz. **radiant, 1.** *adj.* strahlend (*also fig.*), glänzend, leuchtend (***with,*** von *or* vor (*Dat.*)); (*fig.*) ***– beauty,*** strahlende Schönheit; ***– energy,*** die Strahlenenergie; ***– heat,*** die Strahlungswärme; ***– with joy,*** freudestrahlend. **2.** *s.* der Strahl(ungs)-punkt.

radiate, 1. ['reidieit], *v.i.* 1. strahlen, leuchten, glänzen; 2. ausstrahlen, Strahl(ung)en aussenden; 3. sich strahlig *or* strahlenförmig ausdehnen. **2.** [–dieit], *v.t.* 1. ausstrahlen (*also fig.*), (*fig.*) ausströmen, verbreiten; ***– health,*** vor Gesundheit strotzen; ***– heat,*** Wärme ausstrahlen; (*fig.*) ***– warmth,*** Wärme ausströmen; 2. (*Elec.*) aussenden; (*Rad.*) senden, ausstrahlen. **3.** [–diit], *adj.* (*Bot.*) strahlig (an)geordnet, strahlenförmig, Strahl(en)–. **radiation** [–i'eiʃən], *s.* 1. das Strahlen, die (Aus)-strahlung; Strahlungsenergie; ***cosmic –,*** die Höhenstrahlung; ***– dose,*** die Strahlungsdosis; ***– sickness,*** der Strahlenschaden; 2. (*Med.*) die Bestrahlung. **radiator** [–ieitə], *s.* der Heizkörper (*central heating*); Strahlensender; (*Motor.*) Kühler.

radical ['rædikl], **1.** *adj.* 1. (*esp. Gram., Math., Bot.*) Wurzel–; (*Math.*) ***– sign,*** das Wurzelzeichen; 2. (*fig.*) eingewurzelt, angeboren, ursprünglich, grundlegend, fundamental; ***– difference,*** die Grundverschiedenheit; ***– error,*** der Grundirrtum; 3. (*Pol.*) Radikal–, radikal; (*fig.*) drastisch, extrem; ***undergo a – change,*** sich von Grund auf ändern; ***– cure,*** die Radikalkur; ***– measures,*** drastische Maßnahmen (*pl.*); 4. (*Mus.*) Grund(ton)–; 5. (*Chem.*) Radikal–. **2.** *s.* 1. (*Pol.*) Radikale(r); 2. (*Math., Gram.*) die Wurzel; 3. (*Chem.*) das Radikal. **radicalism,** *s.* der Radikalismus. **radically,** *adv.* von Grund auf, grundlegend, ursprünglich, durchaus.

radicel ['rædisel], *s.* (*Bot.*) das Würzelchen, Rhizoid.

radices ['reidisi:z], *pl. of* **radix.**

radicle ['rædikl], *s.* 1. (*Bot.*) die Keimwurzel; 2. (*Anat.*) Nervenwurzel.

radii ['reidiai], *pl. of* **radius.**

radio ['reidiou], **1.** *s.* 1. das Radio, der Rundfunk; ***on the –,*** im Rundfunk; 2. der Funk, drahtlose Telegraphie; 3. der Radioapparat, Rundfunkempfänger. **2.** *v.t.* funken, drahtlos senden; (*rare*) durch den Rundfunk übertragen; ***– him a message,*** ihm eine Funkmeldung durchgeben; ***– the message,*** die Funkmeldung durchsagen *or* senden.

3. *adj.* Radio–, (Rund)funk–; – ***advertising,*** die Funkwerbung; – ***amateur,*** der Radioamateur, Funkbastler; – ***beacon,*** die Funkbake, das Funkfeuer; – ***beam,*** der Richtstrahl, Leitstrahl; – ***bearing,*** der Peilwinkel, die Funkpeilung; – ***broadcast,*** die Rundfunksendung; – ***car,*** der Funkwagen; – ***commentator,*** der Rundfunkberichterstatter; – ***communication,*** die Funkverbindung; – ***control,*** die Funk(fern)steuerung, Fernlenkung; – ***direction finding,*** die Funkpeilung; – ***drama,*** das Hörspiel; – ***engineering,*** die Funktechnik; – ***frequency,*** die Hochfrequenz, Trägerfrequenz; (*coll.*) – ***ham,*** see – ***amateur***; – ***message,*** die Funkmeldung; – ***network,*** das Rundfunknetz; – ***patrol car,*** der Funkstreifenwagen; – ***operator,*** der Funker, (*Av.*) Bordfunker; – ***pirate,*** der Schwarzhörer; – ***receiver*** or ***set,*** der Radioempfänger; – ***reception,*** der Funkempfang; – ***signal,*** das Funksignal, der Funkspruch; – ***silence,*** die Funkstille; – ***station*** or ***transmitter,*** der Radiosender, die Funkstation; – ***tracer,*** radioaktiver Spurenfinder; – ***wave,*** die Radiowelle.

radio|active, *adj.* radioaktiv; – ***series,*** die Zerfallsreihe. **–activity,** *s.* die Radioaktivität.

radiogram [ˈreidiougræm], *s.* 1. das Funktelegramm; 2. (*coll.*) der Radioapparat mit Plattenspieler, die Musiktruhe.

radiograph [ˈreidiougrɑ:f], *s.* das Röntgenbild, Röntgenogramm, die Röntgenaufnahme. **radiographer** [–iˈɔgrəfə], *s.* der (die) Röntgentechniker(in). **radiography** [–iˈɔgrəfi], *s.* die Röntgenographie, Röntgenphotographie; ***mass*** –, die Röntgenreihenuntersuchung.

radio-location, *s.* die Funkortung, Funkpeilung.

radiological [reidiəˈlɔdʒikl], *adj.* Röntgen–. **radiologist** [–iˈɔlədʒist], *s.* der Radiologe, Röntgenologe. **radiology** [–iˈɔlədʒi], *s.* die Radiologie, Strahlenkunde, Röntgenlehre.

radiometer [reidiˈɔmitə], *s.* die Lichtmühle, der Strahlungsmesser.

radio|-photograph, *s.* das Funkbild. **--photography,** *s.* der Bildfunk.

radioscopy [reidiˈɔskəpi], *s.* die Röntgendurchleuchtung.

radio|telegram, *s.* das Funktelegramm. **–telegraphy,** *s.* die Funktelegraphie, der Funk(verkehr). **–telephony,** *s.* die Funktelephonie, das Funkfernsprechen. **–therapeutics,** *pl.* (*sing. constr.*), **–therapy,** *s.* die Strahlentherapie, Radiotherapie, Röntgentherapie.

radish [ˈrædiʃ], *s.* der Rettich.

radium [ˈreidiəm], *s.* das Radium; – ***therapy,*** die Radiumbehandlung, Strahlentherapie.

radius [ˈreidiəs], *s.* (*pl.* **radii** [–diai]) 1. der Halbmesser, Radius; ***turning*** –, die Achsenverschränkbarkeit (*of vehicles*); 2. (*Bot.*) der Strahl; 3. (*Anat.*) die Speiche; 4. (*fig.*) der Umkreis (***of,*** von); 5. Wirkungskreis, Wirkungsbereich, die Reichweite; ***cruising*** –, der Fahrbereich, Flugbereich.

radix [ˈreidiks], *s.* (*pl.* **radices** [–disi:z]) (*Math.*) die Grundzahl, Wurzel.

raffia [ˈræfiə], *s.* 1. (*Bot.*) die Raphia, Nadelpalme; 2. der (Raffia)bast. **raffia-work,** *s.* die Bastarbeit.

raffish [ˈræfiʃ], *adj.* 1. liederlich, verkommen; 2. ordinär, pöbelhaft.

[1]**raffle** [ræfl], **1.** *v.t.* (*also* – ***off***) in einer Tombola verlosen. **2.** *v.i.* an einer Tombola teilnehmen, losen (***for,*** um). **3.** *s.* die Tombola.

[2]**raffle,** *s.* (*Naut.*) das Gerümpel, der Kram, Schund.

raft [rɑ:ft], **1.** *s.* 1. das Floß; 2. (*Am.*) zusammengebundes Treibholz. **2.** *v.t.* flößen.

rafter [ˈrɑ:ftə], *s.* der Sparren, Dachbalken; *pl.* das Sparrenwerk.

raftsman [ˈrɑ:ftsmən], *s.* (*Am.*) der Flößer.

[1]**rag** [ræg], *s.* 1. der Lumpen, Fetzen; Lappen, Lumpenleinen; (*sl.*) ***chew the*** –, quatschen; meckern (***over,*** an (*Dat.*)); ***be like a red – to a bull,*** wie ein rotes Tuch wirken (***to,*** auf (*Acc.*)); (*fig.*) ***not a – of,*** keine Spur *or* kein geringstes Stück von, keinerlei; ***not a – to one's back,*** nicht einen Fetzen auf dem Leibe; 2. (*sl.*) das Schundblatt, Schmierblatt, Hetzblatt; 3. *pl.* (*Paperm.*) Lumpen, Hadern (*pl.*); 4. *pl.* (*coll.*) zerlumpte Kleidung; (*coll.*) ***glad –s,*** die Sonntagskluft; ***in –s,*** zerlumpt.

[2]**rag, 1.** *s.* (*sl.*) 1. die Neckerei, das Piesacken; 2. der Radau, Unfug; ***fancy-dress*** –, das Studentenkostümfest. **2.** *v.i.* (*sl.*) sich raufen, Radau machen, wüste Sachen treiben. **3.** *v.t.* (*sl.*) einen Schabernack spielen (*Dat.*), seinen Ulk treiben mit, necken, piesacken.

[3]**rag,** *s. See* **ragstone.**

ragamuffin [ˈrægəmʌfin], *s.* der Straßenbengel, Lumpenkerl, zerlumpter Kerl.

rag|-and-bone man, *s.* der Lumpensammler, Lumpenhändler. **–bag,** *s.* 1. der Lumpensack; 2. (*fig.*) buntes Durcheinander. **--book,** *s.* unzerreißbares Bilderbuch. **--doll,** *s.* die Stoffpuppe.

rage [reidʒ], **1.** *s.* 1. die Wut, Raserei, der Zorn; ***fly into a*** –, in Wut geraten; 2. die Heftigkeit, das Toben, Rasen, Wüten (*of the wind etc.*); 3. (*coll.*) die Sucht, Manie, Wut (***for,*** nach); (*coll.*) ***be (all) the*** –, die große Mode sein; 4. (*Poet.*) die Begeisterung, der Rausch, Taumel. **2.** *v.i.* wüten, rasen, toben (***against,*** gegen), in Wut sein (***at,*** über (*Acc.*)); ***the battle –s,*** die Schlacht tobt; ***the pestilence –s,*** die Pest wütet; (*coll.*) ***raging toothache,*** rasende Zahnschmerzen (*pl.*).

rag-fair, *s.* der Trödelmarkt.

ragged [ˈrægid], *adj.* 1. zerrissen, zerfetzt, zerlumpt, lumpig, schäbig; 2. rauh, struppig, zottig (*as fur, beard etc.*); 3. ausgefranst, schartig, zackig, ausgezackt (*as edges*); 4. (*fig.*) uneben, holp(e)rig (*as rhymes*). **raggedness,** *s.* 1. die Zerlumptheit, Zerrissenheit, Schäbigkeit; 2. Zottigkeit, Zerfetztheit; 3. Unebenheit, Holp(e)rigkeit. **ragged robin,** *s.* (*Bot.*) die Kuckucksblume.

raglan [ˈræglən], *s.* der Raglan.

ragman [ˈrægmæn], *s.* der Lumpensammler.

ragout [ræˈgu:], *s.* das Ragout.

rag|-paper, *s.* das Haderpapier. **--picker,** *s. See* **–man. –stone,** *s.* der Kieselsandstein. **–tag,** *s.* – ***and bobtail,*** Krethi und Plethi. **–time,** *s.* der Ragtime. **–weed, –wort,** *s.* das (Jakobs)kreuzkraut.

raid [reid], **1.** *s.* 1. der Einfall (***into,*** in (*Acc.*)), Überfall, (plötzlicher) Angriff (***on,*** auf (*Acc.*)), Streifzug; ***bank*** –, der Banküberfall; ***bombing*** –, der Bombenangriff; ***naval*** –, der Flottenstreifzug, die Kaperfahrt; 2. (*fig.*) der (An)sturm, Raubzug; 3. die Razzia (*police*). **2.** *v.t.* 1. einfallen in (*Acc.*), überfallen, einen Überfall machen auf (*Acc.*); (*Mil.*) ***–ing party,*** die Streifabteilung; 2. (*also fig.*) stürmen, plündern; 3. (*police*) eine Razzia machen auf (*Acc.*); 4. (*Comm.*) drücken (*the market*). **raider,** *s.* 1. der Angreifer, Überfallende(r); 2. (*Av.*) der Feindflugzeug.

[1]**rail** [reil], *s.* (*Orn.*) die Ralle; *see* **land –, water –.**

[2]**rail,** *v.i.* schimpfen, schmähen; – ***at*** or ***against,*** beschimpfen; schimpfen *or* herziehen über (*Acc.*).

[3]**rail, 1.** *s.* 1. das Querholz, der Riegel; 2. (*Naut.*) die Reling; 3. Leiste (*for pictures*); 4. Brüstung, das Gitter, Geländer (*of balcony etc.*); 5. (*Railw.*) die (Eisenbahn)schiene, das Gleis, Geleise, der Schienenstrang; ***by*** –, mit der Eisenbahn, per Bahn; ***guide*** –, die Führungsschiene; ***live*** –, die Stromschiene; (*usu. fig.*) ***off the –s,*** entgleist, aus dem Gleis; ***go*** or ***run off the –s,*** entgleisen; 6. *pl.* (*Comm.*) Eisenbahnaktien (*pl.*). **2.** *v.t.* 1. (*also* – ***in***) einfriedigen, mit einem Geländer *or* Gitter umgeben (*a space*); – ***off,*** durch ein Geländer abtrennen; 2. mit Schienen auslegen (*railway-route*); 3. mit der Bahn befördern.

rail|car, *s.* das Schienenfahrzeug, der Triebwagen. **--chair,** *s.* (*Railw.*) die Schienenklammer. **–head,** *s.* 1. die Endstation, Kopfstation; 2. (*Mil.*) der Ausladebahnhof, Verteilerbahnhof.

railing ['reiliŋ], *s.* (*oft. pl.*) 1. das Geländer, Gitter; 2. (*Naut.*) die Reling.

raillery ['reiləri], *s.* die Neckerei, Hänselei, Stichelei, das Gespött.

railroad ['reilroud], **1.** *s.* (*Am.*) *see* **railway. 2.** *v.t.* (*Am.*) (rücksichtslos) (voran)treiben, hetzen (*a p.*), durchpeitschen (*a bill, law etc.*).

railway ['reilwei], *s.* die Eisenbahn; – ***accident,*** das Eisenbahnunglück; – ***carriage,*** der Personenwagen; – ***company,*** die Eisenbahngesellschaft; – ***guide,*** das Kursbuch; – ***junction,*** der Eisenbahnknotenpunkt; – ***line,*** die Eisenbahnlinie; – ***porter,*** der Gepäckträger; – ***station,*** der Bahnhof; – ***terminus,*** der Endbahnhof; – ***ticket,*** die (Eisenbahn)-fahrkarte; – ***train,*** der (Eisenbahn)zug. **railwayman,** *s.* der Eisenbahner.

raiment ['reimənt], *s.* (*Poet.*) die Kleidung.

rain [rein], **1.** *s.* der Regen; *pl.* Regenfälle, Regengüsse (*pl.*); ***the –s,*** tropische Regenzeit; – ***of blows,*** der Hagel von Schlägen; – ***of tears,*** der Strom von Tränen; ***be pouring with –,*** in Strömen regnen; (*coll.*) ***as right as –,*** frisch und munter. **2.** *v.i.* 1. regnen (*also fig.*); ***it –s in,*** es regnet herein *or* durch; – ***in torrents,*** in Strömen regnen; (*Prov.*) ***it never –s but it pours,*** ein Unglück kommt selten allein; 2. (*fig.*) (*usu.* – ***down***) herunterströmen (*of tears*), niederprasseln (*of blows*). **3.** *v.t.* fallen lassen, herniedersenden; – ***blows on,*** Schläge hageln lassen auf (*Acc.*); ***it –s cats and dogs,*** es regnet Bindfaden *or* Strippen *or* in Strömen, es gießt wie mit Mollen; – ***kisses on,*** Küsse schütten auf (*Acc.*); – ***stones upon,*** Steine schleudern auf (*Acc.*); ***his eyes – tears,*** aus seinen Augen strömen Tränen.

rain|-belt, *s.* (*Meteor.*) die Regenlinie. **–bow,** *s.* der Regenbogen; ***colours of the –,*** die Regenbogenfarben. **–coat,** *s.* der Regenmantel. **–drop,** *s.* der Regentropfen. **–fall,** *s.* 1. der Regen(fall); 2. (*Meteor.*) Niederschlag, die Niederschlagsmenge. **–-gauge,** *s.* der Regenmesser, Niederschlagsmesser. **–proof, 1.** *adj.* regendicht, wasserdicht. **2.** *s. See* **–coat. –storm,** *s.* heftiger Regenguß. **–water,** *s.* das Regenwasser.

rainy ['reini], *adj.* regnerisch, verregnet, Regen–; – ***day,*** der Regentag; (*fig.*) die Notzeit, schlimme Tage (*pl.*); ***save up for a – day,*** sich (*Dat.*) einen Notpfennig zurücklegen; – ***season,*** die Regenzeit.

raise [reiz], **1.** *v.t.* 1. aufrichten, aufstellen, aufrecht stellen, aufheben; emporheben, (in die Höhe) erheben; (hoch)heben, hochziehen, hochwinden (*by a crane*); – ***a blister,*** eine Blase ziehen; – ***the curtain,*** den Vorhang aufziehen; – ***a dust,*** Staub aufwirbeln (*also fig.*); (*sl.*) – ***the elbow,*** zuviel trinken; – ***one's eyes,*** aufblicken, die Augen erheben *or* aufschlagen; (*fig.*) – ***one's eyebrows,*** entrüstet aufblicken; ***not – a finger,*** keinen Finger krümmen; – ***one's glass to him,*** das Glas auf seine Gesundheit erheben, ihm zutrinken; – ***one's hand,*** die Hand (hoch)heben; – ***one's hat,*** den Hut abnehmen *or* lüften; – ***one's hat to,*** grüßen; – ***the nap of cloth,*** das Tuch aufrauhen; – ***steam,*** Dampf aufmachen; 2. (*fig.*) errichten, (er)bauen, aufstellen, aufrichten, aufführen (*a structure*); – ***a ladder,*** eine Leiter aufstellen; 3. erheben, befördern (*a p.*) (***to,*** zu); – ***to the peerage,*** in den Adelsstand erheben; – ***to the throne,*** auf den Thron erheben; 4. aufziehen, großziehen (*children*); 5. züchten; – ***cattle,*** Vieh züchten; – ***plants,*** Pflanze ziehen; – ***vegetables,*** Gemüse anbauen; 6. stärken, (ver)mehren, vergrößern; 7. erheben; – ***a claim,*** einen Anspruch *or* Einspruch erheben, eine Forderung stellen; – ***claims under guarantee,*** eine Garantie in Anspruch nehmen; – ***difficulties,*** Schwierigkeiten machen; – ***objections,*** Einwendungen *or* Einwände erheben (***to,*** gegen); – ***a question,*** eine Frage anregen *or* aufwerfen; – ***the question of,*** zur Debatte stellen, zur Sprache *or* auf die Tagesordnung bringen, erörtern, anhängig machen (***with,*** bei); 8. beschaffen; – ***an army,*** ein Heer aufstellen *or* auf die Beine bringen; – ***capital,*** Kapital beschaffen; – ***a loan,*** eine Anleihe aufnehmen; – ***money,*** Geld sammeln *or* zusammenbringen *or* auftreiben; – ***taxes,*** Steuern erheben *or* beitreiben; – ***troops,*** Truppen ausheben; (*sl.*) – ***the wind,*** (das nötige) Geld auftreiben; 9. erhöhen (***by,*** um; ***to,*** auf (*Acc.*)); – ***prices,*** Preise erhöhen *or* hinaufsetzen; – ***salary,*** das Gehalt erhöhen; 10. hervorrufen, erwecken; – ***his anger,*** seinen Zorn erregen; – ***expectations,*** Erwartungen erwecken; – ***feelings,*** Gefühle erwecken *or* erregen; – ***hopes,*** Hoffnungen erwecken; – ***a laugh,*** Gelächter hervorrufen; – ***a smile,*** ein Lächeln hervorrufen; 11. antreiben, anfeuern, anregen; – ***his spirits,*** seine Stimmung beleben *or* anfeuern; 12. erheben; – ***a cry,*** ein Geschrei erheben; – ***a shout,*** aufschreien; – ***one's voice,*** die Stimme erheben; (*fig.*) ***voices were –d,*** Stimmen wurden laut; 13. in Aufruhr bringen, aufrühren, aufwiegeln (***against, upon,*** gegen) (*to revolt*); anstiften; – ***Cain*** or ***the devil*** or ***hell,*** Krach *or* einen Höllenspektakel machen; – ***a hornets' nest,*** in ein Wespennest greifen *or* stechen; – ***a hue and cry,*** Lärm schlagen; (*coll.*) – ***a song*** (***and dance***), großen Krach schlagen; – ***a storm*** (***of protest***), auf heftigen Widerspruch stoßen; 14. – ***spirits,*** Geister beschwören *or* zitieren; 15. – ***from the dead,*** vom Tode *or* von den Toten erwecken; 16. – ***a siege,*** eine Belagerung aufheben; 17. (*Naut.*) sichten (*land etc.*).

2. *v.i.* 1. (*Cards*) höher bieten; 2. (*gambling*) den Einsatz erhöhen.

3. *s.* (*coll. or Am.*) die Erhöhung, Gehaltszulage.

raised [reizd], *adj.* 1. erhöht, gehoben; 2. (*fig.*) gesteigert; 3. erhaben (*as lettering*), (*Tech.*) gehämmert, getrieben; 4. ***with*** or ***in a – voice,*** mit erhobener Stimme. **raiser,** *s.* 1. der Erbauer, Pflanzer (*of plants*); Züchter (*of cattle*); 2. (Er)-heber, Errichter, Erbauer (*of a structure*).

raisin [reizn], *s.* die Rosine.

raison| d'état ['rezɔ̃dei'ta:], *s.* die Staatsräson. **– d'être** [–'detr], *s.* die Daseinsberechtigung.

raj [rɑ:dʒ], *s.* die Herrschaft. **rajah** ['rɑ:dʒə], *s.* der Radscha.

[1]**rake** [reik], **1.** *s.* der Rechen, die Harke; (*Tech.*) Scharre, Kratze; Krücke, Rührstange; der Schürhaken; ***as thin as a –,*** klapperdürr, spindeldürr, spillerig. **2.** *v.t.* 1. (*Hort.*) harken, rechen; 2. (*Mil.*) bestreichen; 3. (*fig.*) mit den Augen absuchen, durchstreifen, durchstöbern; (*coll.*) – ***out,*** auskundschaften; 4. (*coll.*) – ***in,*** zusammenkratzen, zusammenscharren (*money etc.*); – ***together*** or ***up,*** zusammenscharren, zusammenharken; (*fig.*) zusammenholen, zusammentragen, zusammenkratzen; (*coll.*) – ***up,*** ans Licht zerren, aufrühren (*an old story etc.*).

[2]**rake, 1.** *s.* 1. das Überhängen, die Neigung, der Neigungswinkel, Fall; 2. (*Tech.*) Schnittwinkel; 3. (*Av.*) die Abschrägung (*of wings*); 4. (*Geol.*) das Einfallen (*of strata*). **2.** *v.i.* überhängen, sich nach hinten neigen, Neigung *or* Fall haben. **3.** *v.t.* nach hinten biegen *or* neigen, in geneigte Lage bringen.

[3]**rake,** *s.* der Wüstling.

rake-off, *s.* (*sl.*) der Profit, Gewinnanteil, die Provision; ***have*** or ***get a – on,*** Profit ziehen aus.

raking ['reikiŋ], *adj.* schief, geneigt; *see* [2]**rake.**

[1]**rakish** ['reikiʃ], *adj.* (*coll.*) schnittig, schmissig, flott.

[2]**rakish,** *adj.* wüst, liederlich, ausschweifend.

[1]**rally** ['ræli], **1.** *v.t.* 1. (*Mil.*) wieder sammeln, zusammentrommeln; 2. (*fig.*) vereinigen, scharen (***to, round,*** um); 3. aufmuntern, aufrütteln, anfeuern, in Schwung bringen (*a p.*); 4. zusammenraffen, sammeln (*energy*). **2.** *v.i.* 1. sich wieder sammeln; 2. sich sammeln *or* scharen (***round,*** um); 3. sich anschließen (***to,*** *Dat. or* an (*Acc.*)); 4. (*also* – ***round***) sich erholen (*also fig. of prices, the market etc.*), neue Kräfte sammeln, wieder **zu** Kräften kommen. **3.** *s.* 1. das Sammeln, die Wiedervereinigung; – ***point,*** der Sammelplatz, Sammelpunkt; 2. (*coll.*) Zusammenkunft, Massenversammlung, das Treffen; 3. (*fig.*) die Sammlung, Kräftigung, (*also Comm.*) Erholung; 4. (*Tenn.*) schneller Ballwechsel; 5. (*Motor. etc.*) die Rallye, Sternfahrt.

[2]**rally,** *v.t.* aufziehen, zum besten haben, hänseln, sich lustig machen über (*Acc.*) (*a p.*) (*on*, wegen).

ram [ræm], **1.** *s.* 1. der Widder, Schafbock; (*Astr.*) ***the Ram,*** der Widder; 2. (*Mil.*) (*also* ***battering*** –) der Sturmbock; 3. (*Naut.*) Rammsporn, Rammbug; 4. (*Tech.*) die Ramme, der Rammbock, Rammklotz, Rammbär, Fallhammer. **2.** *v.t.* 1. rammen; (*coll.*) (mit Gewalt) schieben *or* stoßen; – ***down,*** festrammen, feststampfen (*earth*); fest einrammen, eintreiben (*a post etc.*); (*coll.*) – ***it down his throat,*** es ihm aufdrängen *or* einpauken *or* einbleuen; (*coll.*) – ***in,*** einrammen, (hinein)-stopfen; (*fig.*) – ***one's head against a brick wall,*** mit dem Kopf durch die Wand (rennen) wollen; 2. (*Mil., Naut.*) rammen; 3. (*Artil.*) ansetzen.

ramble [ræmbl], **1.** *v.i.* 1. (umher)wandern, umherstreifen, umherschweifen; 2. (*Bot.*) ranken; 3. (*coll.*) (vom Thema) abschweifen, nicht bei der S. bleiben; drauflos reden, planlos schreiben; 4. unzusammenhängend reden (*delirium*). **2.** *s.* die Wanderung, der Ausflug, Streifzug. **rambler,** *s.* 1. der Wanderer, Umherstreicher; 2. (*Bot.*) die Schlingrose, Kletterrose. **rambling, 1.** *adj.* 1. (umher)wandernd, umherziehend, umherschweifend; 2. (*coll.*) weitschweifig, planlos, unzusammenhängend, abschweifend; 3. (*fig.*) weiträumig, langgestreckt, unregelmäßig gebaut (*as buildings*); 4. (*Bot.*) kletternd, sich rankend, wuchernd. **2.** *s.* das Wandern, Umherstreifen; – ***club,*** der Wanderverein.

ramie ['ræmi], *s.* (*Bot.*) die Ramie.

ramification [ræmifi'keiʃən], *s.* die Verzweigung, Verästelung (*also fig.*); Zweigbildung, Astbildung; *pl.* Zweige (*also fig.*); (*fig.*) ***–s of the plot,*** die Verzweigungen der Fabel *or* Intrige. **ramify** ['ræmifai], **1.** *v.t.* (*usu. pass.*) verzweigen, in Zweige zerteilen, zweigartig anlegen. **2.** *v.i.* sich verzweigen (*also fig.*).

rammer ['ræmə], *s.* 1. der Stampfer, die (Hand)-ramme, Jungfer; 2. (*Artil.*) der Ansetzer, Ladestock.

ramose ['reimous], *adj.* verzweigt, verästelt.

[1]**ramp** [ræmp], *s.* (*coll.*) der Schwindel, die Geldschneiderei, Erpressung, das Erpressungsmanöver.

[2]**ramp, 1.** *v.i.* 1. sich zum Sprunge erheben, zum Sprung ansetzen, sich aufrichten, auf den Hinterbeinen stehen (*of animals*); 2. wuchern, ranken (*of plants*); 3. toben, rasen, wüten; 4. (*Archit.*) eine Rampe bilden, rampenartig ansteigen *or* absteigen. **2.** *v.t.* mit einer Rampe versehen. **3.** *s.* 1. die (Lade)rampe, die Auffahrt; 2. (*Archit.*) Abschrägung, Abdachung; 3. Biegung, der Krümmling (*in a stair-rail*); 4. die Klappe (*of landing barge*).

rampage, 1. [ræm'peidʒ], *v.i.* herumtoben, herumtollen; herumwüten, herumrasen. **2.** ['ræmpeidʒ], *s.* ***be on the –,*** toben. **rampageous** [–'peidʒəs], *adj.* ungestüm, tobend, lärmend, ausgelassen.

rampancy ['ræmpənsi], *s.* das Umsichgreifen, Überhandnehmen, Grassieren, Wuchern. **rampant,** *adj.* 1. überhandnehmend, um sich greifend, grassierend; ***be –,*** um sich greifen, überhandnehmen, grassieren; Unwesen treiben; 2. (*Archit.*) (an)steigend; 3. (*animals*) aufgerichtet, sprungbereit; 4. (*plants*) üppig, wuchernd; 5. (*fig.*) zügellos, ausgelassen; 6. (*Her.*) (*follows noun*) aufsteigend.

rampart ['ræmpɑ:t], **1.** *s.* 1. der (Festungs)wall, Schutzwall, die Wallanlage, Umwallung, Brustwehr; 2. (*fig.*) der Schutz, die Verteidigung, Schutzwehr. **2.** *v.t.* umwallen.

rampion ['ræmpiən], *s.* (*Bot.*) die Rapunzel.

ramrod ['ræmrɔd], *s.* der Ladestock.

ramshackle ['ræmʃækl], *adj.* baufällig, wackelig, klapperig.

ramson ['ræmsən], *s.* (*Bot.*) der Bärenlauch.

ramstam ['ræmstæm], *adv.* (*coll.*) überstürzt, Hals über Kopf.

[1]**ran** [ræn], *imperf. of* **run.**

[2]**ran,** *s.* 1. die Docke Bindfaden; 2. (*Naut.*) aufgerolltes Tau.

ranch [ræntʃ], *s.* (*Am.*) die Ranch, Viehwirtschaft, Viehfarm, Viehweide. **rancher, ranchman,** *s.* 1. der Farmer, Viehzüchter; 2. Rancharbeiter.

rancid ['rænsid], *adj.* ranzig. **rancidity** [–'siditi], **rancidness,** *s.* die Ranzigkeit.

rancor ['ræŋkə], (*Am.*) *see* **rancour. rancorous,** *adj.* erbittert, boshaft, böswillig, giftig. **rancour,** *s.* der Groll, Haß, die Erbitterung, Böswilligkeit.

[1]**randan** [ræn'dæn], *s.* das Boot für drei Ruderer.

[2]**randan,** *s.* (*coll.*) der Radau; ***on the –,*** auf dem Bummel.

randem ['rændəm], *s.* der Wagen mit drei (voreinandergespannten) Pferden.

random ['rændəm], **1.** *s.* ***at –,*** aufs Geratewohl, auf gut Glück, blindlings, wahllos. **2.** *adj.* zufällig, Zufalls–, ziellos, wahllos; (*Stat.*) – ***sampling,*** die Stichprobenerhebung, zufällige Auswahl; – ***shot,*** der Schuß ins Blaue; – ***test,*** die Stichprobe.

randy ['rændi], *adj.* 1. (*Scots*) lärmend, ausgelassen; 2. (*dial.*) bockig, widerspenstig (*of cattle etc.*); 3. (*coll.*) geil, wollüstig.

ranee, *see* **rani.**

rang [ræŋ], *imperf. of* **ring.**

range [reindʒ], **1.** *v.t.* 1. anordnen, aufreihen, (in Reihen) aufstellen; (*fig.*) einordnen, einreihen, einteilen; – ***o.s. with*** or ***on the side of,*** sich stellen zu *or* auf seiten (*Gen.*); – ***a gun on,*** ein Geschütz richten auf (*Acc.*); 2. durchstreifen, durchwandern (*a place*); – ***the coast,*** an der Küste entlangfahren. **2.** *v.i.* 1. sich ausdehnen, sich erstrecken, reichen, verlaufen; in einer Reihe *or* Linie stehen *or* liegen *or* sich bewegen, eine Linie bilden, auf einer Linie *or* Ebene liegen, sich (in einer Linie *or* Reihe) aufstellen; 2. (*fig.*) im gleichen Rang stehen (***with,*** mit), vorkommen, zu finden sein, rangieren (***among, with,*** unter (*Dat.*)), gehören, zählen (zu); 3. sich bewegen, schwanken, variieren (***from . . . to . . .,*** zwischen . . . und . . .); 4. (*Bot., Zool.*) leben, vorkommen, verbreitet sein; 5. streifen, wandern; – ***wide with one's inquiries,*** mit den Erkundigungen weit ausholen. **3.** *s.* 1. die Kette (*of hills*); 2. Reihe; – ***of goods,*** die Warensammlung, das Sortiment; ***have a wide – of goods,*** eine reiche Auswahl von Waren haben; 3. der Raum, die Ausdehnung; (*fig.*) der Umfang, Bereich, das Gebiet; der Spielraum, Grenzen (*pl.*); – ***of action,*** das Arbeitsfeld, der Spielraum, Aktionsradius, die Bewegungsfreiheit; – ***of activities,*** das Betätigungsfeld; – ***of knowledge,*** der Wissensbereich; – ***of prices,*** die Preislage; – ***of thought,*** der Ideenkreis; ***give one's fancy free –,*** seiner Einbildungskraft freien Lauf lassen; ***salary –,*** die Gehaltsspanne; 4. (*Artil.*) die Reichweite, Tragweite, Schußweite; (*Av.*) der Flugbereich; – ***of vision,*** die Sichtweite; ***at close –,*** aus geringer Entfernung; ***at a – of,*** in einer Entfernung von; (*Artil.*) ***get the –,*** sich einschießen; ***have a long –,*** weit tragen; ***long-– gun,*** das Fernkampfgeschütz; (*Artil.*) ***shorten –,*** zurückverlegen; ***out of –,*** außer Schußbereich, (*fig.*) außer Reichweite; ***within –,*** im Schußbereich, in Reichweite; 5. (*Am.*) die Weidefläche; 6. der (Küchen)herd; 7. (*also* ***firing-–*** or ***shooting-–***) Schießplatz, Schießstand; ***rifle –,*** der Schießstand.

range-finder, *s.* der Entfernungsmesser.

ranger ['reindʒə], *s.* 1. (*esp. Am.*) der Förster, Waldaufseher, Forstwart; 2. (*Mil.*) Jäger, leichter Reiter.

Rangoon [ræŋ'gu:n], *s.* Rangun (*n.*).

rani ['rɑ:ni], *s.* die Rani.

[1]**rank** [ræŋk], **1.** *s.* 1. die Reihe, Linie; ***taxi –,*** der Taxistand(platz); 2. (*Mil.*) das Glied; ***the –s, – and file*** (*pl. constr.*), Mannschaften, Gemeinen, gemeine *or* einfache Soldaten (*pl.*); (*fig.*) gewöhnliche Mitglieder (*pl.*), die breite Masse, das Fußvolk; (*Mil.*) ***break –s,*** aus dem Glied treten; ***in – and file,*** in Reih und Glied; ***in the –s,*** als einfacher Soldat; ***join the –s,*** ins Heer eintreten; ***keep –s!*** in Reih und Glied bleiben! ***reduce to the –s,*** degradieren; ***rise from the –s,*** aus dem Mann-

schaftsstand hervorgehen, von der Pike auf dienen; *thin the –s*, die Reihen lichten; 3. (*fig.*) die Klasse, Schicht, (soziale) Stellung, der Rang, Stand, (*Mil. etc.*) Dienstgrad; *– and fashion*, die vornehme Welt; *all –s and classes*, alle Stände und Klassen; *of the first –*, ersten Ranges; *of second –*, zweitrangig; *man of –*, der Mann von Stand; *take – of*, den Vorrang haben vor (*Dat.*); *take – with*, gleichrangig sein mit. **2.** *v.t.* 1. in einer Reihe (auf)stellen, einreihen, (ein)ordnen; 2. (*fig.*) rechnen, zählen (*with*, *among*, zu), stellen (*above*, über (*Acc.*); *below*, *beneath*, unter (*Acc.*)); 3. (*Am.*) den Vortritt haben vor (*Dat.*). **3.** *v.i.* 1. eine Reihe bilden, sich reihen, sich ordnen, sich aufstellen; 2. (*fig.*) gehören, zählen, gerechnet *or* gezählt werden (*with*, *among*, zu); *– above*, rangieren über (*Dat.*); *– equally*, gleichrangig sein; *– first*, den ersten Rang einnehmen; *– high*, hoch stehen, eine hohe Stellung einnehmen; *– next to . . .*, rangieren hinter (*Dat.*) . . ., im Range gleich nach . . . kommen; *high–-ing officer*, hoher Offizier.

²**rank**, *adj.* 1. üppig; 2. fruchtbar, fett (*as soil*); 3. stinkend, ranzig; 4. (*fig.*) kraß, regelrecht, offenkundig; *– nonsense*, reiner *or* blühender Unsinn; *– outsider*, krasser Außenseiter; *– bad taste*, schreiende Geschmacklosigkeit.

rankle [ræŋkl], *v.i.* 1. (*Poet.*) sich entzünden, eitern, schwären; 2. (*usu. fig.*) um sich *or* weiter fressen, nagen, wühlen; *it –s with him*, es wurmt ihn; *it –s in his mind*, es liegt ihm schwer auf der Seele.

rankness [ˈræŋknis], *s.* 1. die Üppigkeit, üppiges Wachstum; 2. die Ranzigkeit.

ransack [ˈrænsæk], *v.t.* durchwühlen, durchstöbern, durchsuchen (*for*, nach); plündern.

ransom [ˈrænsəm], **1.** *s.* 1. das Lösegeld; (*fig.*) *king's –*, gewaltige Summe; *hold to –*, gegen Lösegeld festhalten; 2. der Loskauf, Freikauf; 3. (*B.*) die Erlösung. **2.** *v.t.* 1. loskaufen, freikaufen, auslösen; 2. (*B.*) erlösen.

rant [rænt], **1.** *s.* die Schwulst, der Redeschwall, Wortschwall, leeres Gerede. **2.** *v.i.* 1. hochtrabend *or* schwülstig reden; 2. eifern, toben, lärmen. **3.** *v.t.* schwülstig *or* theatralisch hersagen. **ranter,** *s.* 1. hochtrabender Schwätzer; 2. der Prahler, Großsprecher, Kulissenreißer.

ranunculus [rəˈnʌŋkjuləs], *s.* (*Bot.*) der Hahnenfuß, die Ranunkel.

¹**rap** [ræp], **1.** *s.* leichter Schlag, der Klaps; das Klopfen (*at*, an (*Acc.*)); *there is a – at the door*, es klopft; (*fig.*) *– on* or *over the knuckles*, der Verweis; *– on the nose*, der Nasenstüber; (*coll.*) *take the –*, die Folgen auf sich nehmen, die Suppe auslöffeln müssen. **2.** *v.i.* schlagen, klopfen, pochen (*at*, an (*Acc.*); *on*, auf (*Acc.*)). **3.** *v.t.* schlagen *or* klopfen an *or* auf (*Acc.*); (*usu. fig.*) *– his knuckles* or *fingers*, ihm auf die Finger klopfen; *– out*, ausstoßen, herausplatzen mit; (*Spiritualism*) durch Klopfen mitteilen (*a message*).

²**rap,** *s.* der Heller, Deut; *I don't care* or *give a – (for it)*, das ist mir ganz gleich(gültig) *or* einerlei *or* egal, ich gebe keinen Pfifferling dafür.

rapacious [rəˈpeiʃəs], *adj.* raubgierig, (*fig.*) habsüchtig, (hab)gierig; *– bird*, der Raubvogel. **rapaciousness, rapacity** [–ˈpæsiti], *s.* die Raubgier; (*fig.*) Habgier, Habsucht.

¹**rape** [reip], **1.** *s.* 1. (*Poet.*) der Raub, die Entführung; 2. (*Law*) Notzucht, Vergewaltigung (*also fig.*); *murder and –*, der Lustmord. **2.** *v.t.* 1. (*Poet.*) rauben, entführen; 2. (*Law*) notzüchtigen, vergewaltigen.

²**rape,** *s.* der Raps, Rübsen.

³**rape,** *s.* (*dial.*) der Gau, Bezirk.

⁴**rape,** *s.* 1. (*oft. pl.*) (*from wine*) Trester, Treber (*pl.*); 2. (*for vinegar*) der *or* das Essigfilter.

rape|-oil, *s.* das Rüböl, Rapsöl. **–seed,** *s.* der Rübsamen, Rapssamen. **–-wine,** *s.* der Tresterwein.

rapid [ˈræpid], **1.** *adj.* 1. schnell, geschwind, rasch (*as growth*); (*Mil.*) *– fire*, das Schnellfeuer; 2. reißend (*as water*); 3. (*fig.*) eilig, plötzlich, jäh; 4. (*Phot.*) hochempfindlich (*film*), lichtstark (*lens*). **2.** *s.* (*usu. pl.*) die Stromschnelle. **rapidity** [rəˈpiditi], *s.* die Geschwindigkeit, Schnelligkeit, Eile.

rapier [ˈreipiə], *s.* das Rapier.

rapine [ˈræpin], *s.* (*Poet.*) der Raub, die Plünderung.

rapist [ˈreipist], *s.* der Vergewaltiger, (Frauen)-schänder.

rappee [ræˈpiː], *s.* grober Schnupftabak.

rapport [ræˈpɔː], *s.* (enge) Beziehung *or* Verbindung, (enges) Verhältnis.

rapprochement [ræˈprɔʃmã], *s.* 1. (*esp. Pol.*) die Fühlungnahme, (Wieder)annäherung; 2. (*fig.*) Versöhnung.

rapscallion [ræpˈskæliən], *s.* (*obs.*) der Lump(enkerl), Schuft.

rapt [ræpt], *adj.* 1. hingerissen, entzückt (*in*, von), außer sich (vor (*Dat.*)), verloren, versunken, vertieft (in (*Acc.*)); 2. gespannt (*as attention*).

raptorial [ræpˈtɔːriəl], **1.** *adj.* räuberisch; Raub–. **2.** *s.* der Raubvogel.

rapture [ˈræptʃə], *s.* das Entzücken, die Verzückung, Begeisterung, Ekstase, der Taumel; *in –s*, begeistert, entzückt, außer sich vor Entzücken (*at*, über (*Acc.*)); *go into –s*, in Verzückung geraten (*over*, über (*Acc.*)). **rapturous,** *adj.* 1. leidenschaftlich, stürmisch (*applause etc.*); 2. verzückt, hingerissen, begeistert (*expression*).

rara avis [ˈrɛərəˈeivis], *s.* (*fig.*) seltene Erscheinung.

¹**rare** [rɛə], *adj.* 1. selten, rar; *– earths*, seltene Erden; 2. ungewöhnlich, außergewöhnlich; 3. (*Phys. etc.*) dünn, verdünnt, nicht dicht; *– gas*, das Edelgas; 4. (*coll.*) (vor)trefflich, ausgezeichnet, köstlich.

²**rare,** *adj.* nicht durchgebraten (*of roast*).

rarebit [ˈrɛəbit], *s.* ***Welsh –***, see ***Welsh rabbit.***

raree-show [ˈrɛəri], *s.* der Guckkasten, Raritätenkasten, (*fig.*) das Schauspiel.

rarefaction [rɛəriˈfækʃən], *s.* die Verdünnung. **rarefy** [ˈrɛərifai], **1.** *v.t.* 1. verdünnen; 2. (*fig.*) verfeinern, läutern. **2.** *v.i.* sich verdünnen.

rarely [ˈrɛəli], *adv.* 1. selten; 2. (*coll.*) äußerst, außerordentlich. **rareness,** *s.* 1. die Seltenheit, Ungewöhnlichkeit; 2. Kostbarkeit, Rarität; 3. (*coll.*) Vortrefflichkeit. **rarity** [–riti], *s.* 1. seltene *or* kostbare S., die Seltenheit; 2. (*Phys.*) Dünnheit (*esp. of gas*); *see also* **rareness.**

rascal [rɑːskl], **1.** *s.* 1. der Schuft, Schurke, Lump, Halunke; 2. (*coll.*) Spitzbube, Schelm, Gauner. **2.** *adj.* (*Poet.*) *see* **rascally. rascaldom** [–dəm], *s.* das Lumpenpack. **rascality** [–ˈkæliti], *s.* 1. die Schurkerei, Schuftigkeit; 2. Büberei, der Schurkenstreich. **rascally,** *adj.* schurkisch, Schurken–, schuftig, niederträchtig, gemein.

rase, *see* **raze.**

¹**rash** [ræʃ], *adj.* 1. hastig, übereilt, überstürzt, vorschnell; 2. unvorsichtig, unbesonnen, tollkühn, waghalsig.

²**rash,** *s.* der (Haut)ausschlag.

rasher [ˈræʃə], *s.* die Schinkenschnitte, Speckschnitte.

rashness [ˈræʃnis], *s.* 1. die Hast, Übereiltheit, Überstürztheit; 2. Unvorsichtigkeit, Unbesonnenheit, Tollkühnheit, Waghalsigkeit.

rasorial [reiˈsɔːriəl], *adj.* 1. hühnerartig, Hühner–; 2. scharrend (*of fowl*).

rasp [rɑːsp], **1.** *s.* 1. die Raspel, Grobfeile, das Reibeisen; 2. Raspeln, Kratzen, der Kratzlaut. **2.** *v.t.* 1. abraspeln, abkratzen, abschaben; 2. zerkratzen, reiben (*the skin*), (*fig.*) reizen (*the nerves*), verletzen, beleidigen (*the feelings*). **3.** *v.i.* (*usu. fig.*) kratzen, krächzen, schnarren. **raspatory** [–ətəri], *s.* 1. (*Surg.*) die Knochenfeile; 2. (*Typ.*) das Abstreichmesser.

raspberry [ˈrɑːzbəri], *s.* 1. die Himbeere; *–-cane*, der Himbeerstrauch; 2. (*sl.*) der Rüffel, Verweis, Wischer, Ausputzer.

rasping [ˈrɑːspiŋ], **1.** *adj.* (*fig.*) kratzend, krächzend, schnarrend. **2.** *s.* 1. das Raspeln; 2. *pl.* Raspelspäne (*pl.*).

rat [ræt], **1.** *s.* 1. die Ratte; *–s!* Unsinn! Quatsch! Blech! (*sl.*) – *race,* halsabschneiderische Berufskonkurrenz, die Postenjägerei; *smell a –,* Lunte *or* den Braten riechen, Unrat wittern; *like a drowned –,* pudelnaß; 2. (*coll.*) der Überläufer, Abtrünnige(r); 3. der Lump, Schuft. **2.** *v.i.* 1. Ratten fangen; 2. (*coll.*) überlaufen, abtrünnig werden, die Farbe wechseln, abfallen; 3. (*sl.*) – *on him,* ihn verraten *or* verkaufen.

ratable, *see* **rateable.**

ratafia [rætəˈfiə], *s.* der Fruchtlikör.

rataplan [rætəˈplæn], **1.** *s.* der Trommelwirbel. **2.** *v.t.* (*v.i.*) trommeln (*on,* auf (*Dat.*)).

rat-a-tat, *see* **rat-tat-tat.**

rat-catcher, *s.* der Rattenfänger.

ratch [rætʃ], *s.* gezahnte Sperrstange.

ratchet [ˈrætʃit], *s.* die Sperrklinke, Knarre; – *brace* or *drill,* die Bohrknarre; – *wheel,* das Sperrad.

[1]**rate** [reit], **1.** *s.* 1. der Preis, Tarif, Satz, Kurs, die Taxe, Rate, Quote; *at a cheap –,* zu einem niedrigen Preis; *at the – of,* zum Preise von; – *of the day,* die Tagesnotierung, der Tageskurs; – *of discount,* der Diskont(satz); – *of exchange,* der Wechselkurs, Umrechnungskurs; *current – of exchange,* der Tageskurs; – *of interest,* der Zinsfuß, Zinssatz; – *of wages,* der Lohnsatz; 2. der Grad, das (Aus)maß; *birth–,* die Geburtenziffer; *mortality–,* die Sterblichkeitsziffer; *at the same –,* in demselben Maße; (*coll.*) *at this –,* auf diese Art *or* Weise; (*coll.*) *at that –,* in diesem Fall, unter diesen Umständen; (*coll.*) *at any –,* um jeden Preis, unter allen Umständen, auf jeden Fall, wenigstens; 3. (*usu. pl.*) die Kommunalsteuer, Gemeindesteuer, Gemeindeabgabe, Umlage; *–s and taxes,* Kommunal- und Staatssteuern (*pl.*); 4. die Schnelligkeit, Geschwindigkeit; (*Av.*) – *of climb,* die Aufstiegszeit, Steigzeit; (*Artil.*) – *of fire,* die Feuergeschwindigkeit, Schußfolge; *at a great –,* mit hoher Geschwindigkeit; *at the – of,* mit einer Geschwindigkeit von; 5. *first–,* erstklassig, (*coll.*) vortrefflich; *second–,* zweitklassig; (*coll.*) *third–,* minderwertig. **2.** *v.t.* 1. veranschlagen, bewerten; 2. abschätzen, einschätzen; 3. rechnen (*among,* unter (*Acc.*) *or* zu), zählen (zu), ansehen, betrachten (*as,* als), halten (für). **3.** *v.i.* 1. bewertet *or* angesehen *or* gerechnet werden (*as,* als); 2. (*Naut.*) geklaßt werden (*ship*), rangieren (*seaman*) (*as,* als).

[2]**rate,** **1.** *v.t.* ausschelten (*for,* wegen). **2.** *v.i.* schelten, schimpfen (*at,* über (*Acc.*)).

rateable [ˈreitəbl], *adj.* 1. (ab)schätzbar, abzuschätzen(d) (*at,* auf (*Acc.*)); 2. steuerbar, steuerpflichtig, umlagepflichtig; – *value,* steuerbarer Wert, der Steuertarif, Umlageanschlag (*of real estate*).

rated [ˈreitid], *adj.* 1. (*Tech.*) Nenn–; 2. *be highly –,* hoch besteuert werden (*of property*); 3. (*Naut.*) *be – as,* see [1]**rate, 3,** 2.

ratel [reitl], *s.* (*Zool.*) der Honigdachs, Ratel.

rather [ˈrɑːðə], *adv.* 1. eher, lieber; *I would* or *had – . . .,* ich möchte lieber . . . (*inf.*), mir wäre es lieber, daß . . .; *I – think,* ich glaube fast, ich möchte glauben; 2. vielmehr, eigentlich; *or –,* oder vielmehr; 3. (*coll.*) ziemlich, etwas; – *late,* etwas *or* ziemlich *or* recht spät; *in – a mess,* in einer ziemlichen Patsche; 4. (*coll. as int.*) freilich! und ob!

ratification [rætifiˈkeiʃən], *s.* 1. die Bestätigung, Gutheißung; 2. (*Pol.*) Ratifikation, Ratifizierung. **ratify** [ˈrætifai], *v.t.* 1. bestätigen, gutheißen; 2. ratifizieren.

[1]**rating** [ˈreitiŋ], *s.* 1. die Steuereinschätzung, Veranlagung, der (Kommunal)steuersatz; 2. (*Comm.*) die (Einschätzung der) Kreditfähigkeit; 3. (*Naut.*) die Schiffsklasse; 4. (einfacher) Matrose; 5. (*Tech.*) die Leistung.

[2]**rating,** *s.* der Verweis, die Rüge, Schelte.

ratio [ˈreiʃiou], *s.* das Verhältnis; *be in the inverse –,* im umgekehrten Verhältnis stehen (*to,* zu), (*Math.*) umgekehrt proportional sein.

ratiocinate [rætiˈɔsineit], *v.i.* logisch schließen, folgern. **ratiocination** [–ˈneiʃən], *s.* 1. (vernunftmäßiges) Schließen *or* Folgern; der Vernunftschluß; 2. die (Schluß)folgerung. **ratiocinative,** *adj.* vernunftmäßig, folgernd.

ration [ˈræʃən], **1.** *s.* 1. die Ration, festes Quantum; *off the –,* markenfrei; – *book* or *card,* die Lebensmittelkarte, der Bezugsschein; 2. die Tagesration, der Tagesbedarf, Verpflegungssatz; *pl.* die Verpflegung, Lebensmittel (*pl.*); (*Mil.*) *emergency* or *iron –,* eiserne Ration. **2.** *v.t.* 1. rationieren; 2. (*also – out*) (in Rationen) verteilen *or* zuteilen (*goods*).

rational [ˈræʃənl], *adj.* 1. vernunftgemäß, rational, beweisfähig; vernunftbegabt, vernünftig, verständig; – *horizon,* wahrer Horizont; 2. rationell, zweckmäßig, praktisch; 3. (*Math.*) rational.

rationale [ræʃiəˈnɑːl(i)], *s.* 1. das Grundprinzip, logische Grundlage; 2. (*rare*) wissenschaftlich begründete Erklärung, vernunftmäßige Darlegung.

rationalism [ˈræʃənəlizm], *s.* der Rationalismus. **rationalist,** **1.** *s.* der Rationalist. **2.** *or* **rationalistic** [–ˈlistik], *adj.* rationalistisch, verstandesmäßig, vernunftgemäß. **rationality** [–ˈnæliti], *s.* 1. die Vernünftigkeit, Vernunftmäßigkeit, Verstandesmäßigkeit; 2. Vernunft, das Denkvermögen.

rationalization [ræʃənəlaiˈzeiʃən], *s.* 1. die Rationalisierung, Vereinfachung; 2. vernunftgemäße Erklärung; 3. (*Math.*) die Umrechnung in eine rationale Form. **rationalize** [ˈræʃənəlaiz], **1.** *v.t.* 1. vernunftgemäß erklären; 2. (*Math.*) in eine rationale Form umrechnen; 3. (*Pol. etc.*) wirtschaftlich gestalten, rationalisieren, vereinfachen (*as an industry*). **2.** *v.i.* rationalistisch *or* vernunftgemäß denken, rationell verfahren *or* vorgehen.

rationing [ˈræʃəniŋ], *s.* die Rationierung, (Lebensmittel)bewirtschaftung; (*Mil.*) – *strength,* die Verpflegungsstärke.

Ratisbon [ˈrætisbɔn], *s.* Regensburg (*n.*).

ratline [ˈrætlin], *s.* (*usu. pl.*) (*Naut.*) die Webeleine.

ratoon [ræˈtuːn], **1.** *s.* der (Zuckerrohr)schößling. **2.** *v.i.* Schößlinge treiben.

ratsbane [ˈrætsbein], *s.* das Rattengift.

rat|-tail, *s.* (*Vet.*) der Rattenschwanz, Rattenschweif. **–-tailed,** *adj.* Rattenschwanz–; – *file,* der Rattenschwanz.

rattan [ræˈtæn], *s.* 1. Spanisches Rohr; 2. der Rohrstock.

rat-tat-tat [rætəˈtæt], *s.* lautes Pochen, das Geknatter.

ratten [rætn], *v.t.* an der Arbeit hindern.

ratter [ˈrætə], *s.* der Rattenfänger.

rattle [rætl], **1.** *v.i.* 1. rasseln, klappern, klirren, knattern, prasseln; 2. röcheln (*of breath*); 3. (*coll.*) plappern; (*coll.*) – *away* or *on,* drauflosreden. **2.** *v.t.* 1. rattern an (*Dat.*) (*the door etc.*); klirren mit (*crockery etc.*); (*fig.*) – *the sabre,* mit dem Säbel rasseln; 2. (*sl.*) durcheinanderbringen, verwirren, nervös machen (*a p.*); 3. (*coll.*) – *off,* herunterleiern (*prayers etc.*). **3.** *s.* 1. das Gerassel, Geklapper; 2. (*coll.*) Geplapper; 3. Röcheln; 4. die Klapper (*of rattlesnake*); 5. (*child's toy*) (Kinder)klapper, Rassel, Schnarre; 6. (*Bot.*) der Klappertopf, das Läusekraut.

rattle-brained, *adj.* (*coll.*) hohlköpfig, geschwätzig. **rattled,** *adj.* (*sl.*) verwirrt, außer Fassung, ängstlich. **rattle-plate,** *s.* (*coll.*) der Hohlkopf, Windbeutel, Schwätzer. **rattler,** *s.* (*Am.*), **rattle|snake,** *s.* die Klapperschlange. **–-trap,** *s.* 1. (*sl.*) der Klapperkasten, die Klapperkiste; 2. (*sl.*) der (die) Schwätzer(in); 3. *pl.* (*sl.*) der (Trödel)kram, Tand. **rattling,** *adj.* (*coll.*) famös, großartig, prächtig, schneidig; *at a – pace,* in schneidigem Tempo. **2.** *adv.* äußerst; – *good meal,* großartiges Essen. **rattly,** *adj.* klappernd, klapp(e)rig.

rat-trap, *s.* die Rattenfalle; (*Cycl.*) – (*pedal*), das Zackenpedal.

ratty [ˈræti], *adj.* 1. rattenartig; 2. (*sl.*) ärgerlich, gereizt.

raucous [ˈrɔːkəs], *adj.* heiser, rauh.

ravage [ˈrævidʒ], **1.** *s.* 1. die Verwüstung, Verheerung, Zerstörung; 2. *pl.* verheerende (Aus)-

wirkung; *–s of time,* der Zahn der Zeit. **2.** *v.t.* verwüsten, verheeren, zerstören, plündern, heimsuchen.

rave [reiv], *v.i.* 1. rasen, toben, wüten; 2. irre reden, phantasieren, faseln; 3. (*coll.*) schwärmen (*about,* von), hingerissen sein (über (*Acc.*)).

ravel [rævl], **1.** *v.t.* verwirren, verwickeln; *– out,* auflösen, auftrennen, entwirren, ausfasern. **2.** *v.i.* sich aufdrehen *or* auflösen *or* ausfasern. **3.** *s.* 1. die Verwirrung, Verwick(e)lung; 2. loser Faden.

ravelin ['rævəlin], *s.* (*Fort.*) das Außenwerk, die Vorschanze.

1**raven** ['reivən], **1.** *s.* der (Kolk)rabe (*Corvus corax*); *black as a –,* (kohl)rabenschwarz. **2.** *adj.* rabenschwarz.

2**raven** ['rævin], **1.** *v.i.* 1. rauben, plündern, Beute machen; 2. gierig sein, lechzen, dürsten, Heißhunger haben (*for,* nach). **2.** *v.t.* gierig (fr)essen, verschlingen. **ravening,** *adj.* (*Poet.*) räuberisch, (beute)gierig, plündernd. **ravenous,** *adj.* 1. ausgehungert, gefräßig, heißhungrig; *– appetite,* der Bärenhunger; 2. gierig (*for,* nach). **ravenousness,** *s.* 1. die Beutegier, Raubgier; 2. Gefräßigkeit, der Heißhunger.

ravine [rə'vi:n], *s.* die (Berg)schlucht, Klamm.

raving ['reiviŋ], **1.** *adj.* 1. (*also – mad*) rasend, tobend, wütend; *– madness,* die Tollwut; 2. (*sl.*) toll, phantastisch. **2.** *s.* (*oft. pl.*) das Faseln, die Faselei, Raserei, irres Gerede, der Fieberwahn.

ravish ['ræviʃ], *v.t.* 1. schänden, entehren, vergewaltigen, (*obs.*) entführen (*a woman*); 2. (*fig.*) hinreißen, entzücken, (*Poet.*) entziehen, entreißen, fortraffen. **ravisher,** *s.* der Schänder, Entführer (*of a woman*). **ravishing,** *adj.* (*fig.*) hinreißend, entzückend. **ravishment,** *s.* 1. die Entzückung, Verzückung; 2. (*rare*) Schändung, Vergewaltigung, Entführung.

raw [rɔ:], **1.** *adj.* 1. roh; ungekocht; *– meat,* rohes Fleisch; 2. (*Tech.*) unverarbeitet, Roh–; ungesponnen (*cotton*); ungewalkt (*cloth*); ungemischt, unverdünnt (*spirits*); ungegerbt (*hides*); *– edge,* die Schnittkante (*of cloth*); *– material,* der Rohstoff, Werkstoff; 3. blutig, geschunden; wund(gerieben) (*of the skin*); 4. (*fig.*) unerfahren, ungeübt, unausgebildet (*as a recruit*); 5. unwirtlich, rauh, naßkalt (*as the weather*); 6. (*sl.*) *– deal,* unfaire Behandlung *or* Abfertigung. **2.** *s.* 1. wunde Stelle; *touch him on the –,* ihn an seiner wunden Stelle treffen; 2. (*Comm.*) die Rohware, der Rohstoff; 3. Rohzustand; *in the –,* im Rohzustand; (*sl.*) nackt. **3.** *v.t.* (*rare*) wundreiben.

raw|-boned, *adj.* hager, grobknochig. **–hide,** *s.* die Reitpeitsche. **rawness,** *s.* 1. der Rohzustand; 2. die Rauheit; 3. Wundheit; 4. (*fig.*) Unerfahrenheit.

1**ray** [rei], **1.** *s.* 1. der (Licht)strahl; 2. Strahl (*also Bot.*); (*Med.*) *– treatment,* die Bestrahlung, Strahlenbehandlung; *pencil of –s,* das Strahlenbündel, Strahlenbüschel; *X–-s,* Röntgenstrahlen (*pl.*); 3. (*fig.*) der Strahl, Funke(n), Schimmer, die Spur; *not a – of hope,* kein Fünkchen Hoffnung. **2.** *v.i.* (aus)strahlen. **3.** *v.t.* bestrahlen.

2**ray,** *s.* (*Ichth.*) der Roche(n).

rayed [reid], *adj.* strahlenförmig, –strahlig.

rayon ['reiɔn], **1.** *s.* die Kunstseide. **2.** *adj.* kunstseiden.

raze [reiz], *v.t.* zerstören, schleifen; *– to the ground,* dem Boden gleichmachen; (*fig.*) tilgen, ausmerzen.

razor ['reizə], *s.* das Rasiermesser; *be on a –* or *the –'s edge,* auf des Messers Schneide stehen; *electric –,* der Elektrorasierer; *safety-–,* der Rasierapparat; *set a –,* ein Rasiermesser abziehen; *as sharp as a –,* haarscharf. **razor|-back, 1.** *adj.* scharfkantig. **2.** *s.* (*also –ed whale*) (*Zool.*) der Finnwal. **–bill,** *s.* (*Orn.*) der Tordalk (*Alca torda*). **–-blade,** *s.* die Rasierklinge. **–-edge,** *s.* haarscharfe Kante, (*fig.*) äußerster Rand, kritische Lage. **–-fish,** *s.* (*Ichth.*) der Schermesserfisch. **–-strop,** *s.* der Streichriemen.

razzia ['ræziə], *s.* der Raubzug.

razzle(-dazzle) ['ræzl(dæzl)], *s.* (*sl.*) das Zechgelage; *be* or *go on the –,* auf den Bummel gehen.

1**re** [rei], *s.* (*Mus.*) zweiter Ton der Tonleiter.

2**re** [ri:], *prep.* (*Law*) in Sachen; (*coll., Comm*). wegen, betreffs, bezüglich.

3**re–** [ri:], *pref.* wieder, noch einmal.

reabsorb [ri:əb'zɔ:b], *v.t.* wiedereinsaugen, wiederaufnehmen, resorbieren. **reabsorption** [–'zɔ:pʃən], *s.* die Wiederaufsaugung, Resorbierung.

reach [ri:tʃ], **1.** *v.i.* 1. reichen, langen, greifen, die Hand ausstrecken (*for,* nach); 2. sich erstrecken *or* ausdehnen, reichen (*to,* bis zu); *as far as the eye can –,* so weit das Auge reicht; 3. (*Naut.*) mit raumem Wind segeln. **2.** *v.t.* 1. erreichen, ankommen an *or* in (*Dat.*) (*a place*); *– home,* nach Hause gelangen; *– the bottom,* den Grund finden; *– his ear,* ihm zu Ohren kommen; *– the target,* das Ziel treffen; *your letter –ed me,* ich erhielt Ihren Brief, Ihr Brief traf bei mir ein *or* kam in meine Hände; 2. (über)reichen, (über)geben (*him,* ihm) (*a th.*); *– him a blow,* ihm einen Schlag verabreichen; *– down,* herunternehmen, herunterreichen, herunterlangen; *– forth* or *out,* reichen, ausstrecken; 3. reichen *or* sich erstrecken bis an (*Acc.*) *or* zu; 4. (*fig.*) erreichen, sich belaufen auf (*Acc.*), erzielen, gelangen; *– a third edition,* eine dritte Auflage erleben; *– the age of discretion,* ein gesetztes Alter erzielen *or* erreichen; *– no conclusion,* zu keinem Schluß gelangen; *– an understanding,* zu einer Einigung kommen, sich verständigen. **3.** *s.* 1. das (Er)reichen; 2. die Reichweite, Tragweite; *beyond* or *out of his –,* außer *or* über seiner Reichweite, (*fig.*) für ihn unerreichbar *or* unerschwinglich; *out of –,* unerreichbar; *within his –,* in seiner Reichweite, (*fig.*) für ihn erreichbar *or* erschwinglich; *within easy – of the town,* von der Stadt (aus) leicht zu erreichen; *within the – of all,* allen zugänglich; 3. der Bereich, Umfang, die Ausdehnung; 4. (*fig.*) Fassungskraft, Leistungsfähigkeit; 5. (*of waterway*) der (Kanal)abschnitt, Lauf, die (Strom)strecke; 6. (*Naut.*) (*tacking*) der Schlag, Gang.

reachable ['ri:tʃəbl], *adj.* erreichbar.

reach-me-down, 1. *adj.* (*sl.*) Konfektions–. **2.** *s.* (*usu. pl.*) die Konfektionskleidung, Kleider (*pl.*) von der Stange.

react [ri'ækt], *v.i.* 1. zurückwirken, zurückfallen, Rückwirkungen haben ((*up*)*on,* auf (*Acc.*)); 2. reagieren, antworten, ansprechen, eingehen (*to,* auf (*Acc.*)); 3. (*Chem.*) reagieren, eine Reaktion bewirken; *slow to –,* reaktionsträge; 4. (*Mil.*) einen Gegenangriff machen; 5. (*coll.*) (*of a p.*) reagieren, sich verhalten; *– against,* widerstreben (*Dat.*), entgegenwirken (*Dat.*), auftreten gegen.

reactance [ri'æktəns], *s.* (*Elec.*) die Reaktanz, der Blindwiderstand.

reaction [ri'ækʃən], *s.* 1. die Gegenwirkung, Rückwirkung, der Rückschlag (*from, against,* gegen); 2. die Reaktion (*to,* auf (*Acc.*)) (*also Chem., Med., Pol.*); *– time,* die Reaktionszeit; 3. (*Elec., Rad.*) die Rückwirkung, Rückkopplung; (*Rad.*) *– coupling,* die Rückkopplung; 4. (*Chem.*) die Umwandlung; 5. (*Pol.*) Rückschrittlichkeit, der Rückschritt; 6. (*Mil.*) Gegenstoß; 7. (*fig.*) Rückgang, Umschwung; 8. Einfluß, die (Ein)wirkung (*on,* auf (*Acc.*)); 9. (*coll.*) (*of a p.*) Stellungnahme, das Verhalten, Reagieren. **reactionary, 1.** *adj.* (*Pol.*) rückschrittlich, reaktionär. **2.** *s.* der (die) Reaktionär(in).

reactivate [ri'æktiveit], *v.t.* wieder aktivieren, reaktivieren. **reactive,** *adj.* 1. rückwirkend, gegenwirkend, Reaktions–; 2. empfänglich (*to,* für); 3. (*Elec.*) *– current,* der Blindstrom; *– load,* die Blindbelastung. **reactivity** [–'tiviti], *s.* die Rückwirkung(skraft), Reaktionsfähigkeit.

reactor [ri'æktə], *s.* 1. (*Elec.*) die Drossel(spule); 2. (*Phys.*) Umwandlungsanlage, der (Kern)reaktor.

1**read** [ri:d], **1.** *irr.v.t.* 1. lesen; ablesen (*meter etc.*); *– him like a book,* ihn genau durchschauen; *– his character,* seinen Charakter durchschauen; *– a*

dream, einen Traum deuten; – ***it in his face,*** es in seinem Gesicht lesen; – ***his fortune,*** seine Zukunft vorhersagen; – ***law,*** Jura studieren; – ***music,*** Noten lesen; – ***a paper,*** ein Referat halten; – ***a riddle,*** ein Rätsel lösen; (*coll.*) – ***him the riot act,*** ihm die Leviten lesen, ihm eine Standpauke halten; (*coll.*) – ***the writing on the wall,*** es sich (*Dat.*) zur Warnung dienen lassen; auf Warnungen hören *or* achten; – ***aloud,*** laut (vor)lesen; – ***into,*** hineinlesen in (*Acc.*); ***what do you – into this?*** wie legen Sie dies aus? – ***off,*** ablesen; – ***out,*** vorlesen; verlesen (*a proclamation etc.*); – ***over*** or ***through,*** durchlesen; – ***to,*** vorlesen (*Dat.*); – ***to o.s.,*** für sich lesen; – ***him*** (or ***o.s.***) ***to sleep,*** ihn (*or* sich) in den Schlaf lesen; – ***up,*** sich einarbeiten in (*Acc.*), einstudieren; 2. (an)zeigen (*of meters etc.*). **2.** *irr.v.i.* lesen; ***no time to –,*** keine Zeit zum Lesen; ***it –s as follows,*** es lautet wie folgt; – ***between the lines,*** zwischen den Zeilen lesen; – ***of*** or ***about,*** lesen über (*Acc.*); – ***for an examination,*** sich auf eine Prüfung vorbereiten; – ***for the press,*** Korrekturen lesen; ***it –s well,*** es liest sich gut.

[2]**read** [red], **1.** *adj.* 1. gelesen (*of a book*); 2. belesen (*of a p.*) (*in,* in (*Dat.*)); ***well –,*** sehr belesen. **2.** *imperf., p.p. of* [1]**read.**

readability [ri:də'biliti], *s.* die Leserlichkeit (*of writing*), Lesbarkeit (*of book*). **readable** ['ri:dəbl], *adj.* leserlich (*of writing*), lesenswert, lesbar. **readableness,** *s. See* **readability.**

readdress [ri:ə'dres], *v.t.* 1. neu adressieren, umadressieren (*a letter*); 2. – ***o.s.,*** sich nochmals wenden (*to,* an (*Acc.*)).

reader ['ri:də], *s.* 1. der (die) Leser(in); Vorleser(in) (*also Eccl.*); Buchliebhaber(in); 2. (*Typ.*) der Korrektor; (Verlags)lektor; 3. (*Univ.*) Extraordinarius, außerordentlicher Professor; 4. das Lesebuch. **readership,** *s.* 1. die Leserschaft, der Leserkreis; 2. (*Univ.*) das Extraordinariat.

readily ['redili], *adv.* 1. bereitwillig, gern (*of a p.*); 2. ohne weiteres, leicht, schnell, sogleich. **readiness,** *s.* 1. die Bereitwilligkeit, Geneigtheit (*of a p.*); – ***to help,*** die Hilfsbereitschaft; 2. die Bereitschaft, das Bereitsein; – ***for war,*** die Kriegsbereitschaft; ***in –,*** bereit, in Bereitschaft; ***hold in –,*** bereithalten; ***place in –,*** bereitstellen; 3. die Leichtigkeit, Gewandtheit, Fertigkeit, Promptheit, Schnelligkeit; – ***of mind*** or ***wit,*** die Geistesgegenwart; – ***of speech,*** die Redegewandtheit, Redefertigkeit.

reading ['ri:diŋ], **1.** *adj.* ***the – public,*** das Lesepublikum. **2.** *s.* 1. das Lesen; 2. das Vorlesen, die (Vor)lesung, der Vortrag; ***give a – from a work,*** aus einem Werk vortragen; 3. der Lesestoff, die Lektüre; ***make interesting –,*** interessant zu lesen sein; 4. (*Theat.*) die Leseprobe; 5. (*Parl.*) Lesung; 6. Lesart, der Wortlaut (*of a MS.*); ***variant –s,*** Varianten (*pl.*); 7. (*fig.*) die Auffassung, Auslegung, Interpretation, Deutung; 8. Anzeigung, Ablesung, der Stand (*of a meter*); 9. die Belesenheit; ***a man of wide –,*** ein Mann von umfassender Belesenheit.

reading|-desk, *s.* das Lesepult. **--glass,** *s.* die Lupe, das Vergrößerungsglas. **--lamp,** *s.* die Leselampe. **--matter,** *s.* 1. der Lesestoff; 2. (*of newspaper etc.*) redaktioneller Teil. **--room,** *s.* der Lesesaal.

readjust [ri:ə'dʒʌst], *v.t.* 1. wieder in Ordnung bringen; 2. (*Tech.*) nachstellen. **readjustment,** *s.* die Wiederanpassung.

readmission [ri:əd'miʃən], *s.* die Wiederzulassung. **readmit,** *v.t.* wieder zulassen. **readmittance,** *s. See* **readmission.**

ready ['redi], **1.** *adj.* 1. bereit, fertig (*for,* zu); (*Naut.*) klar (zu); (*Spt.*) –, ***steady, go!*** Achtung-fertig-los! ***be – with,*** bereit haben *or* halten; ***get*** or ***make it –,*** es bereiten *or* fertig machen; ***get*** or ***make –,*** sich vorbereiten, Vorbereitungen treffen (*for,* für *or* auf (*Acc.*)); – ***for sea,*** seeklar; – ***for use,*** gebrauchsfertig; 2. gefaßt (***for,*** auf (*Acc.*)); 3. bereitwillig, willens, geneigt (*to,* zu); 4. (*coll.*) nahe daran, drauf und dran, im Begriff (*to,* zu); 5. greifbar, gebrauchsfertig, verfügbar, bequem, leicht, naheliegend, direkt; – ***at*** or ***to hand,*** bequem *or* leicht zur Hand; – ***money,*** das Bargeld; ***for – money,*** gegen bar; 6. schnell, sofortig, prompt; – ***acceptance,*** sofortige Annahme; – ***market,*** schneller Absatz; 7. schlagfertig, gewandt, geschickt (***at, in,*** in (*Dat.*)); – ***tongue,*** die Redefertigkeit, beredte Zunge; – ***wit,*** die Schlagfertigkeit. **2.** *s.* (*Mil.*) ***at the –,*** schußfertig.

ready|-built, *adj.* fertiggebaut. **--made,** *adj.* (gebrauchs)fertig; (*clothes*) Konfektions–, von der Stange; – ***clothes,*** die Konfektion(sbekleidung); – ***shop,*** das Konfektionsgeschäft. **--money,** *attrib. adj.* Bar–, Kassa–. – **reckoner,** *s.* die Rechentabelle. **--to-wear,** *adj. See* **--made** (*clothes*). **--witted,** *adj.* schlagfertig.

reaffirm [ri:ə'fə:m], *v.t.* nochmals versichern *or* beteuern. **reaffirmation** [riæfə'meiʃən], *s.* erneute Beteuerung *or* Versicherung.

reafforest [ri:ə'fɔrist], *v.t.* aufforsten. **reafforestation** [–'teiʃən], *s.* die Aufforstung.

reagent [ri:'eidʒənt], *s.* (*Chem.*) das Reagens.

[1]**real** [rei'ɑ:l], *s.* (*pl.* **-(e)s**) (*Hist.*) der Real.

[2]**real** [riəl], **1.** *adj.* 1. wahr, echt, wirklich, tatsächlich, faktisch; – ***life,*** das Leben der Wirklichkeit; (*sl.*) ***the – thing,*** das einzig Wahre; 2. (*Law*) dinglich, Real–; (*Comm.*) unbeweglich, Grund–; – ***action,*** dingliche Klage, die Realklage; – ***estate,*** – ***property,*** der Grundbesitz, Grund und Boden, Liegenschaften (*pl.*), Immobilien (*pl.*), unbewegliches Vermögen; – ***wages,*** der Reallohn; 3. (*Phys., Math.*) reell; (*Elec.*) reell, Wirk–, Nutz–; (*Elec.*) – ***power,*** die Wirkleistung; 4. (*Phil.*) absolut, objektiv, real. **2.** *adv.* (*sl.*) sehr, äußerst, im wahrsten *or* tiefsten *or* eigentlichen Sinne des Worts. **3.** *s.* (*Phil.*) das Reale, die Wirklichkeit.

realgar [ri'ælgɑ:], *s.* (*Chem.*) das Realgar, Rauschrot, Schwefelarsenik.

realism ['riəlizm], *s.* 1. (*Phil., Liter.*) der Realismus; 2. Wirklichkeitssinn, Tatsachensinn; 3. die Sachlichkeit, wirklichkeits(ge)treue Darstellung. **realist,** *s.* 1. der (die) Realist(in); 2. Wirklichkeitsmensch, Tatsachenmensch. **realistic** [–'listik], *adj.* 1. realistisch, sachlich; 2. wirklichkeits(ge)treu, wirklichkeitsnah, Wirklichkeits–. **realistically,** *adv. See* **realistic.**

reality [ri'æliti], *s.* 1. (*no pl.*) die Realität, Wirklichkeit, Tatsächlichkeit, tatsächliches Vorhandensein; 2. die Naturtreue, Wirklichskeitstreue; ***in –,*** in Wirklichkeit, in der Tat, wirklich, tatsächlich, wahrhaftig; 3. (*with pl.*) die Tatsache,Gegebenheit, das Faktum.

realizable ['riəlaizəbl], *adj.* 1. realisierbar, ausführbar, durchführbar, zu verwirklichen(d); 2. (*Comm.*) realisierbar, kapitalisierbar, verwertbar. **realization** [–'zeiʃən], *s.* 1. die Verwirklichung, Ausführung, Durchführung, Realisierung; 2. Vergegenwärtigung, Vorstellung (*in the mind*); 3. (*Comm.*) Verwertung, Liquidation, Realisation; Erzielung.

realize ['riəlaiz], *v.t.* 1. verwirklichen, durchführen, ausführen, realisieren; 2. sich (*Dat.*) vergegenwärtigen *or* vor Augen führen *or* vorstellen *or* klarmachen, sich (*Dat.*) im klaren sein über (*Acc.*), klar einsehen, erkennen, erfassen, begreifen, merken; ***I now –,*** es leuchtet mir jetzt ein; 3. (*Comm.*) zu Geld *or* flüssig machen, realisieren, liquidieren, verwerten; erzielen, einbringen (*profit*).

reallocate [ri:'æləkeit], *v.t.* erneut verteilen. **reallocation** [–'keiʃən], *s.* die Neuverteilung.

really ['riəli], *adv.* wirklich, in Wirklichkeit, tatsächlich, in der Tat; (*as inter.*) wahrlich? wahrhaftig?

realm [relm], *s.* 1. das Reich (*also fig.*), Königreich; 2. (*fig.*) das Gebiet, der Bereich, die Sphäre.

realty ['riəlti], *s. See real estate under* [2]real.

[1]**ream** [ri:m], *s.* das Ries; (*fig.*) ***–s and –s of,*** ganze Bände *or* große Mengen von.

[2]**ream,** *v.t.* erweitern, ausbohren, ausräumen (*a hole*). **reamer,** *s.* die Reibahle, Räumahle.

reanimate [ri:'ænimeit], *v.t.* wiederbeleben.

reanimation [–'meiʃən], *s.* die Wiederbelebung, Neubelebung.

reap [ri:p], **1.** *v.i.* schneiden, mähen, ernten. **2.** *v.t.* 1. schneiden, mähen (*corn etc.*); 2. abernten (*a field*); einernten (*a crop*); 3. (*fig.*) ernten; *– advantage,* Nutzen ziehen (*from,* von *or* aus). **reaper,** *s.* 1. der (die) Schnitter(in); 2. die Mähmaschine; *--binder,* die Mäh– und Bindemaschine. **reaping,** *s.* das Ernten, Schneiden, Mähen; *--hook,* der Sichel; *--machine,* die Mähmaschine.

reappear [ri:ə'piə], *v.i.* wieder erscheinen. **reappearance,** *s.* das Wiedererscheinen, die Wiederkehr.

reapplication [ri:æpli'keiʃən], *s.* 1. wiederholte Anwendung; 2. erneutes Gesuch. **reapply** [ri:ə'plai], *v.t.* 1. wiederholt anwenden; 2. sich wiederholt bewerben (*for,* um).

reappoint [ri:ə'pɔint], *v.t.* wieder anstellen *or* einsetzen *or* ernennen. **reappointment,** *s.* die Wiederanstellung, Wiederernennung.

reappraisal [ri:ə'preizl], *s.* die Neubewertung, Neubeurteilung.

[1]**rear** [riə], **1.** *s.* 1. die Hinterseite, Rückseite; der Hintergrund; *at the – of,* hinter (*Dat.*); *in the –,* im Hintergrund; *to the –,* nach hinten; 2. (*Mil.*) der Nachtrab, die Nachhut; *bring up the –,* (*Mil.*) die Nachhut bilden, (*fig.*) zuletzt kommen; *take by the –,* von hinten angreifen; 3. (*coll.*) der Hintere, das Gesäß. **2.** *attrib. adj.* hinter, Hinter–; (*Mil.*) Nach–, rückwärtig; *– axle,* die Hinterachse; *– echelon,* rückwärtiger Stab; *– rank,* hinteres Glied; *– wheel,* das Hinterrad.

[2]**rear,** **1.** *v.t.* 1. (er)heben, aufrichten, aufstellen; 2. (er)bauen, errichten (*an edifice*); 3. aufziehen, großziehen (*children*); 4. ziehen, anbauen (*plants*), züchten (*animals*). **2.** *v.i.* (*also – up*) 1. sich (auf)-bäumen (*as horse*); 2. (*as mountains etc.*) aufragen, hochragen; 3. (*fig.*) *– up,* sich auf die Hinterbeine stellen, sich aufbäumen, auffahren, aufbrausen, hochfahren.

rear|-admiral, *s.* der Konteradmiral. **--arch,** *s.* (*Archit.*) innerer Bogen. **--engined,** *adj.* mit Heckmotor. **--guard,** *s.* (*Mil.*) die Nachhut; *– action,* das Nachhutgefecht. **--gunner,** *s.* (*Av.*) der Heckschütze. **–lamp, –light,** *s.* (*Motor.*) das Schlußlicht, (*Cycl.*) das Katzenauge.

rearm [ri:'ɑ:m], **1.** *v.t.* wiederbewaffnen; neu ausrüsten. **2.** *v.i.* wiederaufrüsten. **rearmament,** *s.* die (Wieder)aufrüstung.

rearmost ['riəmoust], *adj.* hinterst.

rearrange [ri:ə'reindʒ], *v.t.* 1. neu ordnen, umordnen; 2. erneut abmachen; 3. (*Chem.*) umlagern; 4. (*Math.*) umgruppieren, umschreiben. **rearrangement,** *s.* 1. die Neuordnung, Umordnung; 2. neue Anordnung, die Neugestaltung; 3. (*Chem.*) Umlagerung.

rear|-sight, *s.* das Visier. **–(view) mirror,** *s.* (*Motor.*) der Rück(blick)spiegel.

rearward ['riəwəd], **1.** *adj.* hinter, Rückwärts–. **2.** *adv.* nach hinten, rückwärts. **3.** *s.* (*obs.*) der Nachtrab; *at* or *in the – of,* hinter (*Dat.*). **rearwards,** *adv.* nach hinten, rückwärts.

reason ['ri:zən], **1.** *s.* 1. die Ursache (*for, Gen.,* von *or* für *or* zu), der (Beweg)grund, Anlaß (für *or* zu), das Motiv (*Gen. or* für); *by – of,* auf Grund von, infolge, wegen; *for the same –,* aus demselben Grund; *for the* (*simple*) *– that,* (einfach) weil; *for –s of health,* aus Gesundheitsrücksichten; *all the more – for coming,* ein um so triftigerer Grund, daß man kommt; *there is – for supposing,* es ist Grund zur Vermutung vorhanden; *there is a – for everything,* alles hat seinen Grund; *there is every – to believe,* alles spricht dafür; *the – why,* der Grund warum; *an added – why,* um so mehr Grund warum; *have good – to do* or *for doing,* mit gutem Grunde tun; *– of state,* die Staatsräson; 2. die Vernunft, der Verstand, die Einsicht; *Age of Reason,* die (Zeit der) Aufklärung; *there is – in what he says,* was er sagt, hat Hand und Fuß; *bring him to –,* ihn zur Vernunft bringen; *listen to* or *see –,* Vernunft annehmen, sich belehren lassen; *lose one's –,* den Verstand verlieren; *it stands to –,* es versteht sich (von selbst), es ist ein klarer Fall, es ist doch wohl klar, es leuchtet ein; (*with*)*in –,* mit Maß und Ziel, mit Maßen; *out of all –,* maßlos, unverschämt, ohne Maß und Ziel, über alle Maßen; *without rhyme or –,* ohne Sinn und Verstand; 3. die Begründung, Rechtfertigung; *with –,* mit gutem Recht *or* Grund. **2.** *v.i.* 1. logisch denken, vernünftig urteilen (*about,* über (*Acc.*)); 2. folgern, schließen (*from,* aus); 3. *– with him,* ihn zu überzeugen suchen, ihm Vernunft einreden wollen. **3.** *v.t.* 1. (*oft. – out*) (logisch) durchdenken, vernünftig erörtern, ergründen; *–ed,* wohldurchdacht; 2. *– him into a conciliatory attitude,* ihn durch Zureden zu einer versöhnlichen Stellungnahme bringen; *– him out of his obstinacy,* ihm seinen Starrsinn ausreden, ihn von seiner Hartnäckigkeit abbringen.

reasonable ['ri:zənəbl], *adj.* 1. vernünftig, verständig, einsichtig (*a p.*); *be –,* Einsicht haben, maßvoll sein; (*coll.*) *he's quite –,* er läßt mit sich reden; 2. gerecht, angemessen, billig, annehmbar (*offer, demand etc.*); mäßig (*price*); *– doubt,* berechtigter Zweifel, gerechtfertigtes Bedenken. **reasonableness,** *s.* 1. die Vernünftigkeit, Verständigkeit; 2. Mäßigkeit (*of prices*). **reasonably,** *adv.* vernünftigerweise, billigerweise, (*coll.*) leidlich, ziemlich. **reasoning,** *s.* 1. das Urteilen, Schließen, Folgern; 2. der Gedankengang, die Beweisführung, Schlußfolgerung, das Argument.

reassemble [ri:ə'sembl], **1.** *v.t.* 1. wieder zusammenbauen; 2. wieder versammeln. **2.** *v.i.* sich wieder versammeln. **reassembly,** *s.* 1. wiederholter Zusammenbau; 2. die Wiedersammlung.

reassert [ri:ə'sə:t], *v.t.* wieder(holt) behaupten, erneut feststellen, wieder geltend machen. **reassertion** [–'sə:ʃən], *s.* die Wiederbehauptung, erneute Feststellung.

reassess [ri:ə'ses], *v.t.* nochmals abschätzen, neu veranlagen. **reassessment,** *s.* nochmalige Abschätzung *or* Wertung, die Neuveranlagung.

reassume [ri:ə'sju:m], *v.t.* wieder einnehmen (*one's place*) *or* annehmen *or* übernehmen (*a post, shape*) *or* aufnehmen (*activity*). **reassumption** [–'sʌmpʃən], *s.* nochmalige Einnahme, die Wiederannahme, Wiederaufnahme, erneute Übernahme.

reassurance [ri:ə'ʃuərəns], *s.* 1. erneute Versicherung *or* Beteuerung *or* Bestätigung; 2. die Beruhigung. **reassure,** *v.t.* 1. nochmals beteuern *or* versichern; 2. beruhigen. **reassuring,** *adj.* beruhigend, ermutigend.

rebaptism [ri:'bæptizm], *s.* die Wiedertaufe. **rebaptize** [–'taiz], *v.t.* wiedertaufen, umtaufen.

rebate ['ri:beit], *s.* (*Comm.*) der Rabatt, (Preis)-nachlaß, Abzug (*on,* auf (*Acc.*)).

rebel, **1.** [rebl], *s.* der (die) Aufrührer(in), Rebell(in), Aufständige(r), Aufsässige(r). **2.** [rebl], *attrib. adj.* rebellisch, aufrührerisch, Rebellen–; *– troops,* Rebellen, Aufständige. **3.** [ri'bel], *v.i.* sich empören, sich auflehnen, rebellieren (*against,* gegen).

rebellion [ri'beljən], *s.* 1. der Aufruhr, Aufstand, die Empörung, Erhebung, Rebellion; 2. Auflehnung, offener Widerstand. **rebellious,** *adj.* 1. aufrührerisch, aufständisch, rebellisch; 2. (*fig.*) widerspenstig. **rebelliousness,** *s.* die Widerspenstigkeit.

rebind [ri:'baind], *irr.v.t.* neu (ein)binden (*a book*).

rebirth [ri:'bə:θ], *s.* die Wiedergeburt.

rebite [ri:'bait], *v.t.* nachätzen (*an engraving*).

rebore [ri:'bɔ:], *v.t.* 1. nachbohren; 2. (*Motor.*) ausschleifen, ausbohren (*cylinder*).

reborn [ri:'bɔ:n], *adj.* neugeboren, wiedergeboren.

[1]**rebound,** **1.** [ri'baund], *v.i.* 1. zurückprallen, zurückspringen, schnellen; 2. (*fig.*) zurückschlagen, zurückfallen (*on,* auf (*Acc.*)). **2.** ['ri:baund], *s.* 1. der Rückprall, Rückstoß, Rücksprung; 2. Rückschlag; (*fig.*) *take on the –,* den Rückschlag ausnützen.

[2]**rebound** [ri:'baund], *p.p. of* **rebind.**

rebuff [ri'bʌf], **1.** *s.* die Abweisung, Zurückweisung;

Niederlage, Abfuhr; ***meet with a –***, kurz abgewiesen werden, eine Abfuhr erleiden, (*coll.*) abblitzen. **2.** *v.t.* abweisen, zurückweisen; eine Abfuhr erteilen (*Dat.*), (*coll.*) abblitzen lassen.

rebuild [ri:'bild], *irr.v.t.* 1. wieder (auf)bauen; umbauen; 2. (*fig.*) wiederherstellen.

rebuke [ri'bju:k], **1.** *s.* der Tadel, Vorwurf, Verweis. **2.** *v.t.* zurechtweisen, maßregeln, tadeln.

rebus ['ri:bəs], *s.* der *or* das Rebus, das Bilderrätsel.

rebut [ri'bʌt], *v.t.* (*esp. Law*) widerlegen. **rebuttal,** *s.* die Widerlegung. **rebutter,** *s.* (*Law*) die Quadruplik.

recalcitrance [ri'kælsitrəns], *s.* die Widerspenstigkeit, Unbotmäßigkeit. **recalcitrant,** *adj.* widerspenstig, unbotmäßig, ungehorsam, widersetzlich, widerhaarig (***to***, gegen). **recalcitrate** [–eit], *v.i.* (*rare*) widerspenstig sein, sich sträuben (***against***, gegen).

recall [ri'kɔ:l], **1.** *v.t.* 1. zurückrufen, abberufen (*a p.*); 2. widerrufen, zurücknehmen (*a statement*); ***until –ed***, bis auf Widerruf; 3. sich (*Dat.*) (ins Gedächtnis) zurückrufen, sich erinnern an (*Acc.*); 4. aufrühren, wachrufen (*feelings*); 5. (auf)kündigen (*money lent etc.*); – ***it to him*** or ***to his mind***, ihn daran erinnern, es ihm ins Gedächtnis zurückrufen; – ***having seen***, sich erinnern gesehen zu haben. **2.** *s.* 1. die Zurückrufung, Abberufung; 2. der Widerruf; ***beyond*** or ***past –***, unwiderruflich; 3. (*Comm.*) die (Auf)kündigung, der Aufruf; 4. (*Mil.*) das Signal zur Rückkehr; (*Naut.*) die Signalflagge zur Zurückrufung.

recant [ri'kænt], **1.** *v.t.* widerrufen, zurücknehmen, abschwören. **2.** *v.i.* widerrufen, abschwören. **recantation** [ri:kæn'teiʃən], *s.* der Widerruf, die Widerrufung.

1**recap** ['ri:kæp], (*coll.*) *see* **recapitulate, recapitulation.**

2**recap, 1.** [ri:'kæp], *v.t.* (*Tech.*) besohlen (*tyres*). **2.** ['ri:kæp], *s.* besohlter Reifen.

recapitulate [ri:kə'pitjuleit], *v.t.* kurz wiederholen *or* zusammenfassen, rekapitulieren. **recapitulation** [–'leiʃən], *s.* zusammenfassende Wiederholung, die Rekapitulation. **recapitulative** [–lətiv], *adj.* (*esp. Biol.*) Rekapitulations–. **recapitulatory** [–lətəri], *adj.* zusammenfassend.

recaption [ri:'kæpʃən], *s.* (*Law*) die Zurücknahme, Wiederwegnahme.

recapture [ri:'kæptʃə], **1.** *s.* 1. die Wiedernahme; 2. Zurückeroberung (*of a town*). **2.** *v.t.* 1. wieder ergreifen (*a p.*), wieder erlangen, wieder (in Besitz) nehmen (*a th.*); 2. (*Mil.*) zurückerobern.

recast, 1. [ri:'kɑ:st], *v.t.* 1. (*Metall.*) umgießen; 2. (*fig.*) umgestalten, umformen, umarbeiten, ummodeln; 3. (*Theat.*) neu besetzen (*a play*), neu verteilen (*the parts*). **2.** ['ri:kɑ:st], *s.* 1. der Umguß, die Umschmelzung; 2. Umarbeitung, Umformung, Umgestaltung; 3. (*Theat.*) Neubesetzung.

recce ['reki], *s.* (*sl.*) *see* **reconnaissance.**

recede [ri'si:d], *v.i.* 1. zurücktreten (***before***, von), zurückgehen, weichen (***from***, von); ***receding chin***, fliehendes Kinn; ***receding forehead***, zurückweichende *or* fliehende Stirn; 2. (*fig.*) abstehen, Abstand nehmen (***from***, von); 3. verschwinden, entschwinden; – ***into the background***, in den Hintergrund treten; 4. (*Comm.*) abnehmen, an Wert verlieren, im Wert fallen.

receipt [ri'si:t], **1.** *s.* 1. der Empfang (*letter*), Eingang, die Annahme (*goods*), Einnahme (*money*) (***of***, *Gen.*); ***acknowledge – of***, den Eingang bestätigen von; ***be in – of***, in Besitz sein von; ***on – of***, bei *or* nach Empfang (*Gen.*) *or* von; 2. die Quittung, Empfangsbestätigung, Empfangsbescheinigung, der Empfangsschein, Ablieferungsschein (***for***, für *or* über (*Acc.*)); ***give*** or ***make out a –***, eine Quittung ausstellen; ***against –***, gegen Quittung; 3. *pl.* (*Comm.*) Eingänge, Einnahmen (*pl.*); ***gross –s***, Gesamteinnahmen, Bruttoeinnahmen (*pl.*). **2.** *v.t.* quittieren.

receipt|-book, *s.* das Quittungsbuch. **--stamp,** *s.* der Quittungsstempel, die Quittungsmarke.

receivable [ri'si:vəbl], *adj.* 1. annehmbar, zulässig; (*Comm.*) ***be –***, als Zahlungsmittel gelten; 2. (*Comm.*) zu zahlen(d), ausstehend; ***accounts –***, Forderungen, Außenstände (*pl.*); ***bills –***, Rimessen, Wechselforderungen (*pl.*); 3. gesellschaftsfähig.

receive [ri'si:v], **1.** *v.t.* 1. empfangen (*also Rad.*), erhalten, (*coll.*) bekommen; – ***attention***, Aufmerksamkeit *or* Beachtung finden; – ***a blow***, einen Schlag hinnehmen; – ***a black eye***, ein blaues Auge davontragen; – ***an impression***, einen Eindruck empfangen; – ***the sacrament***, das heilige Abendmahl empfangen; – ***a refusal***, abgelehnt werden, eine Ablehnung erfahren; ***–d with thanks***, dankend erhalten; – ***a welcome***, ein Willkommen erfahren *or* erleben; 2. in Empfang nehmen, entgegennehmen; – ***his confession***, ihm die Beichte abnehmen; – ***a petition***, ein Gesuch entgegennehmen; – ***stolen goods***, Diebesgut an sich nehmen, Hehlerei treiben; 3. (*fig.*) annehmen, einnehmen, aufnehmen; – ***into one's house***, in seinem Hause aufnehmen; 4. auffangen; 5. standhalten (*Dat.*); 6. (als gültig) anerkennen. **2.** *v.i.* 1. (Besuch) empfangen; 2. das Abendmahl empfangen; 3. Empfänger sein; (*B.*) ***it is more blessed to give than to –***, Geben ist seliger denn Nehmen. **received,** *adj.* – ***tradition***, allgemein anerkannte Überlieferung; – ***text***, authentischer *or* echter Text; – ***pronunciation***, vorschriftsmäßige Aussprache.

receiver [ri'si:və], *s.* 1. der (die) Empfänger(in); 2. Annehmer, Einnehmer; 3. (*Tech.*) Behälter, Sammelbecher, das Auffanggefäß; 4. (*Chem.*) Sammelgefäß, der Rezipient, die Vorlage; 5. (*Tele.*) der Hörer; 6. (*Rad.*) Empfänger, das Empfangsgerät; 7. (*Law*) der Konkursverwalter, Zwangsverwalter (*in bankruptcy*); 8. Hehler (*of stolen goods*). **receivership,** *s.* (*Law*) die Konkursverwaltung, Zwangsverwaltung; ***under –***, in Konkurs. **receiving,** *s.* 1. der Empfang, die Annahme; – ***hopper***, der Auffangtrichter; – ***office***, die Annahmestelle; (*Law*) – ***order***, die Einsetzung eines Konkursverwalters; (*Rad.*) – ***set***, der Empfänger, das Empfangsgerät; (*Rad.*) – ***station***, die Empfangsstation; 2. (*Law*) die Hehlerei.

recency ['ri:sənsi], *s.* die Neuheit, Frische.

recension [ri'senʃən], *s.* 1. die Revision (*of texts*); 2. revidierte Ausgabe.

recent ['ri:sənt], *adj.* neu, modern, jung, frisch, unlängst *or* neulich *or* vor kurzem *or* kürzlich entstanden *or* geschehen; (*Geol.*) neuzeitlich; ***of – date***, neueren *or* jüngeren Datums; – ***events***, jüngste Ereignisse; – ***news***, neueste *or* letzte Nachricht. **recently,** *adv.* neulich, unlängst, kürzlich, vor kurzem, jüngst, eben erst; ***till –***, bis vor kurzem; ***as – as***, erst noch. **recentness,** *s. See* **recency.**

receptacle [ri'septəkl], *s.* 1. der Behälter, das Behältnis, Gefäß; 2. (*Bot.*) der Fruchtboden.

receptible [ri'septibl], *adj.* (*rare*) empfänglich, aufnahmefähig (***of***, für).

reception [ri'sepʃən], *s.* 1. der Empfang (*also Rad. and of p.*), die Annahme, Zulassung; 2. (*fig.*) Aufnahme (*impressions etc.*); ***meet with a favourable –***, eine günstige Aufnahme finden; 3. der Empfangsabend. **receptionist,** *s.* 1. der Empfangschef, die Empfangsdame; 2. (*Med.*) die Sprechstundenhilfe. **reception-room,** *s.* 1. das Empfangszimmer; 2. (*in description of dwelling*) der Wohnraum.

receptive [ri'septiv], *adj.* 1. aufnahmefähig, empfänglich, rezeptiv (***of, to***, für); (nur) aufnehmend; 2. (*Biol.*) Empfängnis–, rezeptorisch. **receptivity** [ri:sep'tiviti], *s.* die Aufnahmefähigkeit, Empfänglichkeit.

recess [ri'ses], **1.** *s.* 1. (*Parl.*) Ferien (*pl.*); die Pause, Unterbrechung; 2. Nische, Vertiefung, abgeschiedener Ort, der Schlupfwinkel; 2. (*fig.*) (*oft. pl.*) Tiefen (*pl.*), geheime Winkel (*pl.*), geheimes Innere, der Schoß. **2.** *v.t.* 1. mit Vertiefung(en) versehen; 2. vertiefen, einsenken, zurücksetzen. **3.** *v.i.* (*Parl.*) sich vertagen.

recession [ri'seʃən], *s.* 1. das Zurückgehen, Zurückweichen, Zurücktreten, Abtreten, der Rücktritt (*from*, von); 2. Rückgang (*trade etc.*). **recessional, 1.** *adj.* mit dem Zurückgehen verbunden. **2.** *s.* (*also – hymn*) der Schlußchoral. **recessive** [–siv], *adj.* 1. (*Biol.*) rezessiv; 2. (*Metr.*) rückläufig.

recharge, 1. [ri:'tʃɑ:dʒ], *v.t.* 1. wieder (be)laden (*gun*); 2. (*Mil.*) wiederangreifen; 3. (*Law*) erneut anklagen; 4. (*Elec.*) aufladen. **2.** [–'tʃɑ:dʒ], *v.i.* (*Mil.*) von neuem angreifen. **3.** ['ri:tʃɑ:dʒ], *s.* (*Elec.*) die Wiederaufladung, Nachladung.

recherché [rə'ʃɛəʃei], *adj.* 1. sorgfältig ausgewählt; 2. (*fig.*) ausgeklügelt, gesucht.

recidivism [ri'sidivizm], *s.* die Rückfälligkeit, der Rückfall (in die Kriminalität). **recidivist,** *s.* rückfälliger Verbrecher, der Rückfallverbrecher.

recipe ['resipi], *s.* das Rezept (*also fig.*).

recipient [ri'sipiənt], **1.** *s.* der (die) Empfänger(in); ***be the – of,*** empfangen. **2.** *adj.* empfänglich, aufnahmefähig.

reciprocal [ri'siprəkl], **1.** *adj.* 1. wechselseitig, gegenseitig; ***be –,*** auf Gegenseitigkeit beruhen; ***– action,*** die Wechselwirkung; ***– insurance,*** die Versicherung auf Gegenseitigkeit; ***– relation,*** die Wechselbeziehung; 2. entsprechend, Gegen–; (*Surv.*) ***– bearing,*** die Gegenpeilung; 3. (*Gram.*) reflexiv; 4. (*Math.*) reziprok; ***– value,*** der Kehrwert. **2.** *s.* 1. das Gegenstück; 2. (*Math.*) reziproker Wert.

reciprocate [ri'siprəkeit], **1.** *v.i.* 1. in Wechselbeziehung stehen, sich austauschen; 2. (*Tech.*) sich hin– und herbewegen; ***reciprocating engine,*** der Kolbenmotor; 3. (*fig.*) sich erkenntlich zeigen. **2.** *v.t.* 1. erwidern, vergelten; 2. gegenseitig austauschen. **reciprocation** [–'keiʃən], *s.* 1. (*Tech.*) die Hin– und Herbewegung; 2. Wechselwirkung, Erwiderung, der Austausch.

reciprocity [resi'prɔsiti], *s.* gegenseitige Beziehung; die Gegenseitigkeit, Wechselwirkung, Reziprozität.

recital [ri'saitl], *s.* 1. das Vorlesen, Vortragen, Hersagen, Aufzählen; 2. die Erzählung, der Bericht; 3. die Aufzählung; 4. (*Mus.*) der (Solo)vortrag; ***organ–,*** das Orgelkonzert; ***song–,*** der Liederabend; 5. (*Law*) einleitender Teil (*of a deed*); die Darstellung des Sachverhalts.

recitation [resi'teiʃən], *s.* 1. der Vortrag, die Rezitation; 2. das Vortragsstück; 3. *See* **recital, 1.** **recitative** [–tə'ti:v], **1.** *attrib. adj.* Rezitativ–. **2.** *s.* (*Mus.*) das Rezitativ, der Sprechgesang.

recite [ri'sait], **1.** *v.t.* aufsagen, hersagen, vortragen, rezitieren, deklamieren. **2.** *v.i.* vortragen, rezitieren, deklamieren. **reciter,** *s.* der (die) Vortragskünstler(in), Rezitator(in), Vortragende(r).

reck [rek], *v.i.* (*Poet.*) (*inter. and neg. only*) 1. sich kümmern, sich (*Dat.*) Sorgen machen (***of,*** um), acht(geb)en (auf (*Acc.*)); 2. wissen (***of,*** von *or* um).

reckless ['reklis], *adj.* 1. sorglos, rücksichtslos, leichtfertig, unbesonnen; ***– driver,*** rücksichtsloser Fahrer; 2. leichtsinnig, tollkühn; 3. unbesorgt, unbekümmert (***of,*** um); ***be – of,*** sich nicht kümmern um. **recklessness,** *s.* 1. die Rücksichtslosigkeit, Sorglosigkeit, Leichtfertigkeit, Unbesonnenheit; 2. Tollkühnheit, der Leichtsinn; 3. die Unbekümmertheit, Unbesorgtheit

reckon ['rekən], **1.** *v.t.* 1. (be)rechnen, errechnen (*also* ***– up***), zusammenzählen; 2. (*coll.*) zählen, rechnen (***among,*** unter (*Acc.*)), halten (***as, to be,*** für). **2.** *v.i.* 1. (ab)rechnen; ***– on,*** rechnen *or* sich verlassen auf (*Acc.*); ***– with him,*** mit ihm abrechnen; ***– with a th.,*** mit einer S. rechnen; ***– without him,*** nicht auf ihn rechnen; (*fig.*) ***– without one's host,*** die Rechnung ohne den Wirt machen; 2. (*coll.*) (*with noun clause or inf.*) behaupten, meinen, der Meinung sein; (*coll.*) ***he –s that he can come*** or ***he –s to be able to come,*** er meint, daß er kommen kann; 3. (*coll.*) (*with inf.*) damit rechnen; (*coll.*) ***I always – to get up at 7,*** ich rechne immer damit, um 7 aufzustehen.

reckoner ['rekənə], *s.* 1. der (die) Rechner(in); 2. die Rechentabelle. **reckoning,** *s.* 1. das Rechnen; 2. die Berechnung, Schätzung; (*coll.*) ***according to my –,*** meines Erachtens; 3. die Rechnung, Zeche (*hotel etc.*); 4. Abrechnung, Rechenschaft; ***day of –,*** der Abrechnungstag (*also fig.*), (*Eccl.*) Jüngster Tag; 5. (*Naut.*) die Gissung; ***dead –,*** gegißtes Besteck; ***be out in one's –,*** sich verrechnet haben.

reclaim [ri'kleim], **1.** *v.t.* 1. (*fig.*) zurückbringen, zurückleiten, zurückführen, zurücklenken; bekehren, bessern (*an evil doer*); 2. dem Meer abgewinnen, trockenlegen, urbar machen (*land*); 3. gewinnen, regenerieren (*from waste products*); 4. zivilisieren, zähmen (*wild tribes etc.*); 5. beanspruchen, zurückfordern, reklamieren (*one's property*). **2.** *s.* ***past –,*** unverbesserlich. **reclaimable,** *adj.* 1. (ver)besserungsfähig; 2. zähmbar; 3. kulturfähig (*as land*).

reclamation [reklə'meiʃən], *s.* 1. (*fig.*) das Zurückbringen, die Besserung, Bekehrung; 2. Rückforderung, Reklamation, Beschwerde, der Einspruch, Protest; 3. (*of land*) die Urbarmachung, Neugewinnung, Nutzbarmachung; 4. (*Tech.*) Rückgewinnung.

recline [ri'klain], **1.** *v.t.* lehnen, (hin)legen, niederlegen, stützen (***on, against,*** auf (*Acc.*)). **2.** *v.i.* liegen, ruhen (***on,*** an *or* auf (*Dat.*)), sich (an)lehnen *or* zurücklehnen (an (*Acc.*)). **reclining-chair,** *s.* (verstellbarer) Liegestuhl *or* Lehnstuhl.

recluse [ri'klu:s], **1.** *adj.* 1. einsam, abgeschieden, zurückgezogen (***from,*** von); 2. absiedlerisch. **2.** *s.* 1. der (die) Einsiedler(in), Klausner(in); 2. (*Eccl.*) der Eremit.

recoal [ri:'koul], **1.** *v.t.* mit Kohlen versehen (*a ship etc.*). **2.** *v.i.* Kohlen einnehmen, bunkern.

recoat [ri:'kout], *v.t.* neu anstreichen *or* überstreichen.

recognition [rekəg'niʃən], *s.* 1. die (Wieder)erkennung (*of a p. or th.*); ***past (all) –,*** nicht wiederzuerkennen; ***– light,*** das Kennlicht; ***– signal,*** das Kennsignal, die Kennung; 2. die Anerkennung (*of a fact*); ***as a*** or ***in – of,*** als Anerkennung für; ***win –,*** Anerkennung finden, sich durchsetzen; 3. (*fig.*) die Erkenntnis.

recognizable ['rekəgnaizəbl], *adj.* kenntlich, (wieder)erkennbar.

recognizance [ri'kɔgnizəns], *s.* (*Law*) 1. schriftliche Verpflichtung, das Anerkenntnis; ***enter into –s,*** sich gerichtlich binden; 2. die Sicherheitsleistung, Kaution(ssumme). **recognizant,** *adj.* (*rare*) ***be – of,*** anerkennen (***as,*** als).

recognize ['rekəgnaiz], *v.t.* 1. anerkennen (***as,*** als); 2. (wieder)erkennen (***by,*** an (*Dat.*)); 3. Notiz nehmen von, lobend anerkennen; 4. (*fig.*) zugeben, einsehen; ***– defeat,*** sich geschlagen geben.

recoil, 1. [ri'kɔil], *v.i.* 1. zurückspringen, zurückprallen, (*Artil.*) zurücklaufen; 2. (*fig.*) zurückfahren, zurückweichen, zurückschrecken, zurückschaudern (***at, from,*** vor (*Dat.*)) (*of p.*); 3. (*fig.*) zurückfallen (***on,*** auf (*Acc.*)). **2.** ['ri:kɔil], *s.* 1. das Zurückspringen, Zurückprallen; 2. der Rückprall, Rückstoß, Rücklauf (*of a gun*); 3. (*fig.*) das Zurückfahren, Zurückbeben, Zurückschrecken (***from,*** vor (*Dat.*)).

recoin [ri:'kɔin], *v.t.* umprägen. **recoinage,** *s.* die Umprägung.

recollect [rekə'lekt], **1.** *v.t.* sich erinnern an (*Acc.*), sich besinnen auf (*Acc.*), sich (*Dat.*) ins Gedächtnis zurückrufen. **2.** *v.i.* sich erinnern *or* besinnen. **recollection** [–'lekʃən], *s.* die Erinnerung; das Gedächtnis; ***to the best of my –,*** soweit ich mich erinnere; ***beyond my –,*** mir nicht mehr in Erinnerung; ***within my –,*** mir wohl in Erinnerung.

recommence [ri:kə'mens], **1.** *v.i.* wieder *or* von neuem anfangen, wieder beginnen. **2.** *v.t.* wieder beginnen *or* aufnehmen. **recommencement,** *s.* der Neubeginn, Wiederbeginn.

recommend [rekə'mend], *v.t.* 1. empfehlen, befürworten (***to,*** *Dat.*) (*a th.*); vorschlagen, raten, empfehlen (*Dat.*) (*a p.*); ***he was –ed to do,*** ihm wurde (an)empfohlen zu tun; ***he was –ed to me,*** er wurde mir (als geeignet) empfohlen; 2. anempfehlen, anvertrauen (***to,*** *Dat.*). **recommend-**

able, *adj.* zu empfehlen(d), empfehlenswert, ratsam.
recommendation [rekəmen'deiʃən], *s.* 1. die Empfehlung, Befürwortung; empfehlende Eigenschaft, das Empfehlende; ***on the – of,*** auf Empfehlung von; 2. (*also* ***letter of*** –) das Empfehlungsschreiben. **recommendatory** [–'mendətəri], *adj.* empfehlend, Empfehlungs–.
recommission [ri:kə'miʃən], *v.t.* 1. neu beauftragen; 2. wieder einstellen (*officer, ship etc.*).
recommit [ri:kə'mit], *v.t.* 1. wieder übergeben *or* anvertrauen; – ***to prison,*** wieder ins Gefängnis abführen; 2. (*Parl.*) (an eine Kommission) zurückverweisen (*a bill*). **recommitment, recommittal,** *s.* die Rückverweisung.
recompense ['rekəmpens], **1.** *v.t.* 1. belohnen, entschädigen (*a p.*) (***for,*** für); 2. erstatten, ersetzen, wiedergutmachen, vergüten; 3. heimzahlen, vergelten (*to, Dat.*); – ***him for his kindness,*** ihm seine Güte vergelten. **2.** *s.* 1. der Ersatz, die Entschädigung, Vergütung; 2. Vergeltung, Belohnung.
recompose [ri:kəm'pouz], *v.t.* 1. neu anordnen *or* zusammensetzen, umgestalten, umgruppieren; 2. (*Typ.*) neu setzen; 3. wieder beruhigen *or* in Ordnung bringen. **recomposition** [–kɔmpə'ziʃən], *s.* 1. die Umgestaltung, Umgruppierung, Umbildung, Umarbeitung, Neubearbeitung, Wiederzusammensetzung; (*Typ.*) der Neusatz.
reconcilability [rekənsailə'biliti], *s.* die Vereinbarkeit (***with,*** mit). **reconcilable** ['rekənsailəbl], *adj.* 1. versöhnbar; 2. vereinbar, verträglich (***with,*** mit). **reconcile** ['rekənsail], **1.** *v.t.* 1. versöhnen, aussöhnen (*a p.*) (*to* (*a th.*), ***with*** (*a p.*), mit); – ***o.s. to,*** sich aussöhnen *or* abfinden mit, sich fügen in (*Acc.*); 2. beilegen, schlichten, ausgleichen (*a quarrel*); 3. vereinbaren, in Einklang bringen (***with,*** mit). **reconciliation** [–sili'eiʃən], *s.* 1. die Aussöhnung, Versöhnung (***to, with,*** mit); 2. Schlichtung, Beilegung (*of a quarrel*); 3. Ausgleichung, der Ausgleich, Einklang (***between,*** zwischen *or* unter (*Dat.*)).
recondite ['rekəndait, ri'kɔndait], *adj.* 1. wenig bekannt; 2. geheimnisvoll, tiefgründig, schwer verständlich, abstrus.
recondition [ri:kən'diʃən], *v.t.* wieder instandsetzen, überholen. **reconditioning,** *s.* die (Wieder)instandsetzung.
reconnaissance [ri'kɔnisəns], *s.* 1. (*Mil.*) die Aufklärung, Erkundung; – ***party,*** der Spähtrupp; – ***plane,*** das Aufklärungsflugzeug; 2. (*Geol., Geog. etc.*) die Erforschung, Untersuchung, Rekognoszierung.
reconnoiter (*Am.*), **reconnoitre** [rekə'nɔitə], *v.t.* 1. (*Mil.*) auskundschaften (*also fig.*), beobachten, aufklären, erkunden; 2. (*fig.*) erforschen, rekognoszieren.
reconquer [ri:'kɔŋkə], *v.t.* wiedererobern, zurückerobern. **reconquest** [–kwest], *s.* die Wiedereroberung, Zurückeroberung.
reconsider [ri:kən'sidə], *v.t.* von neuem erwägen, nochmals überlegen *or* in Erwägung ziehen; nachprüfen. **reconsideration** [–'reiʃən], *s.* nochmalige Prüfung *or* Überlegung *or* Erwägung; ***on –,*** bei *or* nach nochmaliger Überlegung.
reconstituent [ri:kən'stitjuənt], **1.** *adj.* (*Med.*) neubildend, wiederaufbauend. **2.** *s.* das Wiederaufbaumittel. **reconstitute** [–'kɔnstitju:t], *v.t.* neu aufstellen *or* einsetzen *or* aufbauen *or* bilden, wiederherstellen. **reconstitution** [–kɔnsti'tju:ʃən], *s.* die Wiederherstellung, Wiedereinsetzung.
reconstruct [ri:kən'strʌkt], *v.t.* 1. wiederaufbauen, wiederherstellen, rekonstruieren; 2. umbauen, umbilden, umformen. **reconstruction** [–ʃən], *s.* 1. der Wiederaufbau, die Wiederherstellung, Rekonstruktion, Sanierung; 2. Umformung, der Umbau.
reconversion [ri:kən'və:ʃən], *s.* 1. die Rückumwandlung; 2. (*Eccl.*) Wiederbekehrung. **reconvert** [–'və:t], *v.t.* 1. rückumwandeln, wieder umändern; 2. (*Eccl.*) wieder bekehren.

[1]**record** [ri'kɔ:d], *v.t.* 1. schriftlich niederlegen, aufschreiben, aufzeichnen, eintragen, niederschrei ben; (*Law*) zur Protokoll nehmen, protokollieren, beurkunden; 2. (*Tech., fig.*) verzeichnen, registrieren; ***self–-ing thermometer,*** das Registrierthermometer; 3. bezeigen, bezeugen (*satisfaction etc.*); 4. abgeben (*a vote*); 5. aufnehmen, festhalten (*on tape or disc*); ***–ed broadcast,*** die Übertragung vom Band; ***–ed music,*** die Schallplattenmusik.
[2]**record** ['rekɔ:d], **1.** *s.* 1. (*Law*) das Protokoll, die Urkunde, Niederschrift, Aufzeichnung, schriftlicher Bericht; ***bear – of,*** bezeugen, Zeugnis ablegen von; (*coll.*) ***for the –,*** um es nun einmal klar festzustellen; ***keep a – of,*** Buch führen über (*Acc.*); ***a matter of –,*** verbürgte Tatsache; ***off the –,*** inoffiziell, im Vertrauen, unter uns gesagt; ***on –,*** geschichtlich *or* urkundlich nachgewiesen *or* belegt *or* niedergelegt, niedergeschrieben; nachweisbar; ***the largest poll on –,*** die größte bisher verzeichnete Stimmabgabe; ***place on –,*** zu Protokoll geben; (*coll.*) ***put on –,*** eine maßgebende Äußerung machen über (*Acc.*); (*Mil.*) ***service –,*** das Führungszeugnis; 2. die Liste, das Register, Verzeichnis; *pl.* Akten (*pl.*); ***– of attendance,*** die Anwesenheitsliste; 3. (*Tech., fig.*) die Registrierung, Verzeichnung; 4. (*Spt.*) Höchstleistung, Bestleistung, Spitzenleistung, der Rekord; ***beat*** or ***break the –,*** den Rekord brechen; ***set up a –,*** einen Rekord aufstellen; 5. (*Tech.*) die Grammophonplatte, Schallplatte; 6. (*fig.*) der Ruf, die Vergangenheit; ***a good –,*** ein guter Ruf *or* Leumund; ***a shady –,*** eine dunkle Vergangenheit. **2.** *attrib. adj.* Rekord–, noch nicht überboten.
record|-breaker, *s.* (*Spt.*) der Rekordmann. **--changer,** *s.* der Plattenwechsler.
recorder [ri'kɔ:də], *s.* 1. der Registrator, Schriftführer, Protokollführer; (*Law*) Stadtrichter, Stadtsyndikus; 2. (*Tech.*) Registrierapparat; das Aufnahmegerät; 3. (*Mus.*) die Blockflöte.
record-holder, *s.* (*Spt.*) der (die) Rekordhalter(in).
recording [ri'kɔ:diŋ], *s.* 1. die Protokollierung, Registrierung, Eintragung; 2. (*Tech.*) Aufzeichnung, (Ton)aufnahme; – ***studio,*** der Aufnahmeraum.
record| library, *s.* das Schallplattenarchiv. – **office,** *s.* das Staatsarchiv. – **player,** *s.* der Plattenspieler.
recount [ri'kaunt], *v.t.* eingehend erzählen *or* berichten.
re-count, 1. [ri:'kaunt], *v.t.* nachzählen. **2.** ['ri:-kaunt], *s.* die Nachzählung.
recoup [ri'ku:p], *v.t.* 1. (*Law*) zurückbehalten, einbehalten, abziehen; 2. entschädigen, schadlos halten (*a p.*) (***for,*** für); ***– o.s.,*** sich schadlos halten (***from,*** an (*Dat.*)); 3. ersetzen, wieder einholen *or* einbringen (*a loss*). **recoupment,** *s.* 1. die Zurückbehaltung, Einbehaltung; 2. Ersetzung, Wiedereinbringung; 3. Schadloshaltung, Entschädigung.
recourse [ri'kɔ:s], *s.* 1. die Zuflucht (***to,*** zu); ***have – to,*** greifen zu, seine Zuflucht nehmen zu; ***have – to a dictionary,*** in einem Wörterbuch nachschlagen; ***have – to law,*** den Rechtsweg beschreiten; 2. (*Comm.*) der Regreß, Ersatzanspruch, Rückanspruch; ***without –,*** ohne Regreß.
recover [ri'kʌvə], **1.** *v.t.* 1. wiedererhalten, wiedererlangen, wiederbekommen, wiederfinden; zurückerhalten, zurückbekommen, zurückgewinnen; wiedererobern, zurückerobern (*territory etc.*); – ***one's balance,*** das Gleichgewicht wiedererlangen; – ***consciousness,*** wieder zum Bewußtsein kommen; – ***one's legs,*** wieder auf die Beine kommen; – ***o.s.,*** zu sich kommen; 2. einziehen, beitreiben, eintreiben (*money*); – ***damages,*** Schadenersatz erhalten; 3. nachholen, wieder aufholen *or* einholen (*time*); 4. ersetzen, wiedergutmachen, verschmerzen, verwinden (*a loss*); – ***one's losses,*** seine Verluste ersetzt erhalten; 5. retten, befreien (*a p.*), bergen (*wreck etc.*) (***from,*** von *or* aus); 6. (*Tech.*) regenerieren, wiedergewinnen, zurückgewinnen (*from waste material*); 7. ***be –ed,*** wiederhergestellt sein (***from,*** von). **2.** *v.i.* 1. sich erholen, genesen (***from,*** von); 2. wieder zu sich

kommen, wieder zum Bewußtsein kommen, sich wiederbeleben; 3. (*Law*) Recht bekommen, entschädigt werden, den Prozeß gewinnen; 4. (*Fenc.*) in die Auslage zurückgehen. **3.** *s.* (*Fenc.*) die Auslagestellung.

re-cover [riː'kʌvə], *v.t.* neu beziehen (lassen) (*umbrellas etc.*).

recoverable [ri'kʌvərəbl], *adj.* 1. eintreibbar (*debt*), wiedererlangbar; 2. wiedergutzumachen(d) (*loss*); 3. (*Med.*) heilbar, wiederherstellbar. **recovery,** *s.* 1. die Wiedererlangung, Wiedergewinnung; 2. Beitreibung, Eintreibung (*of debts*); (*Law*) – ***of damages,*** die Erlangung von Schadenersatz; 3. (*Med.*) die Wiederherstellung, Genesung, Besserung, Erholung; ***beyond*** or ***past*** –, unwiederbringlich *or* unrettbar verloren; (*Med.*) ***make a good*** –, genesen, sich völlig erholen.

recreancy ['rekriənsi], *s.* 1. (*Poet.*) schmähliche Feigheit; 2. die Abtrünnigkeit. **recreant, 1.** *adj.* 1. (*Poet.*) abtrünnig; 2. feig(e). **2.** *s.* 1. Abtrünnige(r), der Verräter; 2. Feigling, Ruchlose(r).

recreate ['rekrieit], **1.** *v.t.* 1. erquicken, erfrischen; 2. unterhalten, ergötzen; 3. – ***o.s.,*** *see* **2. 2.** *v.i.* 1. sich erfrischen *or* erholen; 2. sich ergötzen *or* unterhalten.

re-create [riːkri'eit], *v.t.* neu (er)schaffen.

recreation [rekri'eiʃən], *s.* die Unterhaltung, das Spiel, der Sport; die Erholung, Erfrischung, Entspannung, Ausspannung; – ***room,*** der Aufenthaltsraum; – ***ground,*** der Sportplatz, Spielplatz.

re-creation [riːkri'eiʃən], *s.* 1. die Neu(er)schaffung; 2. das Neuerschaffene, die Neuschöpfung.

recreational [rekri'eiʃənl], *adj.* Erholungs–, Entspannungs–. **recreative** ['rekrieitiv], *adj.* erquickend, erfrischend, erheiternd, Unterhaltungs–.

recrement ['rekrimənt], *s.* 1. (*Med.*) das Rekrement, Sekret; 2. (*rare*) der Abfall(stoff), Auswurfstoff, Ausschuß, Abgang.

recriminate [ri'krimineit], *v.i.* Gegenbeschuldigungen vorbringen. **recrimination** [–'neiʃən], *s.* die Gegenanklage, Gegenbeschuldigung. **recriminative** [–nətiv], **recriminatory** [–nətəri], *adj.* Gegenbeschuldigungs–.

recross [riː'krɔs], *v.t.* wieder überschreiten *or* überqueren *or* kreuzen.

recrudesce [riːkruː'des], *v.i.* 1. wieder aufbrechen (*wounds*); 2. wieder ausbrechen. **recrudescence,** *s.* 1. das Wiederaufbrechen (*wound*); 2. Wiederausbrechen; 3. (*fig.*) Wiederaufleben. **recrudescent,** *adj.* wiederausbrechend, wiederauflebend.

recruit [ri'kruːt], **1.** *v.t.* 1. (an)werben, rekrutieren, ausheben, einziehen (*soldiers*); verstärken, ergänzen (*an army etc.*); anziehen, gewinnen (*followers*); ***be –ed from,*** (*Mil.*) sich rekrutieren aus, (*fig.*) sich ergänzen *or* zusammensetzen aus; 2. (*fig.*) wiederherstellen, erneuern, stärken, auffrischen. **2.** *v.i.* 1. (*Mil.*) Rekruten anwerben; 2. (*fig.*) sich erholen. **3.** *s.* (*Mil.*) der Rekrut; (*fig.*) der Anfänger, Neuling, neues Mitglied; (*fig.*) ***raw*** –, blutiger Anfänger. **recruital,** *s.* die Wiederherstellung, Erholung, Stärkung. **recruiting,** *s.* (*Mil.*) das (An)werben, Ausheben, die Rekrutierung; ***––ground,*** das Werbegebiet, (*usu. fig.*) die Versorgungsquelle; ***––office,*** (*Mil.*) das Wehrbezirkskommando, (*also fig.*) die Werbestelle; ***––officer,*** der Werbeoffizier. **recruitment,** *s.* 1. *See* **recruital**; 2. die Auffrischung, Verstärkung; 3. (*Mil.*) *see* **recruiting.**

rectal ['rektəl], *adj.* Mastdarm–, Rektal–; – ***syringe,*** die Klistierspritze.

rectangle ['rektæŋgl], *s.* das Rechteck. **rectangular** [–'tæŋgjulə], *adj.* rechtwink(e)lig, rechteckig.

rectifiable ['rektifaiəbl], *adj.* 1. verbesserungsfähig, korrigierbar, zu verbessern(d), zu berichtigen(d); 2. abzuhelfen(d), zu beseitigen(d); 3. (*Math.*) rektifizierbar. **rectification** [–fi'keiʃən], *s.* 1. die Berichtigung, Richtigstellung, Verbesserung; 2. Abschaffung, Behebung, Beseitigung (*of abuses*); 3. (*Geom.*) Rektifikation; 4. (*Chem.*) Rektifikation, Destillation; 5. (*Rad.*) Gleichrichtung. **rectifier,** *s.* 1. der Verbesserer, Berichtiger; 2. (*Chem.*) Destillierapparat, Rektifizierapparat; 3. (*Elec.*) Gleichrichter; ***half-wave*** –, der Einweggleichrichter; ***full-wave*** –, der Doppelweggleichrichter. **rectify,** *v.t.* 1. berichtigen, richtigstellen, verbessern, korrigieren, in Ordnung bringen; 2. abhelfen (*Dat.*), abschaffen, beseitigen (*abuses etc.*); 3. (*Chem.*) destillieren, rektifizieren; 4. (*Geom.*) rektifizieren; 5. (*Elec.*) gleichrichten.

rectilinear [rekti'liniə], *adj.* geradlinig.

rectitude ['rektitjuːd], *s.* (charakterliche) Geradheit, die Redlichkeit, Rechtschaffenheit, Aufrichtigkeit.

recto ['rektou], *s.* (*Bookb.*) rechte Seite, die Vorderseite.

rector ['rektə], *s.* 1. der (Ober)pfarrer, Pfarrherr; 2. (*Scots Univ.*) gewählter Vertreter der Studentenschaft; 3. der Direktor (*of Scots school*). **rectorial** [–'tɔːriəl], *adj.* 1. Pfarr–; 2. (*Scots Univ.*) – ***election,*** die Abstimmung für den Studentenschaftsvertreter. **rectory** [–təri], *s.* das Pfarrhaus.

rectum ['rektəm], *s.* der Mastdarm.

recumbency [ri'kʌmbənsi], *s.* liegende Stellung, die Ruhelage. **recumbent,** *adj.* 1. liegend, (sich zurück)lehnend, ruhend (*on*, auf (*Dat.*)); 2. (*Bot., Zool.*) zurückliegend.

recuperate [ri'kjuːpəreit], *v.i.* 1. sich erholen, wieder zu Kräften kommen; 2. (*Artil.*) vorholen. **recuperation** [–'reiʃən], *s.* die Erholung, Wiederherstellung. **recuperative** [–pərətiv], *adj.* kräftigend, stärkend; – ***power,*** die Erholungsfähigkeit. **recuperator,** *s.* (*Artil.*) der Vorholer, die Vorholeinrichtung.

recur [ri'kəː], *v.i.* 1. zurückkommen, wiederkehren, sich wiederholen *or* wiedereinstellen, wieder auftreten *or* auftauchen; 2. einfallen, ins Gedächtnis zurückkommen; 3. zurückkehren (***to***, zu), zurückkommen (auf (*Acc.*)); 4. (*Math.*) (periodisch) wiederkehren; ***recurring decimal,*** periodische Dezimalzahl.

recurrence [ri'kʌrəns], *s.* 1. die Wiederkehr, Wiederholung, das Wiederauftreten; 2. Zurückgreifen (***to***, auf (*Acc.*)), die Zuhilfenahme (von *or Gen.*); 3. (*fig.*) das Zurückkommen (***to***, auf (*Acc.*)), Wiederauftauchen (*of a problem etc.*); 4. (*Math.*) die Rekursion. **recurrent,** *adj.* 1. (periodisch) wiederkehrend, sich wiederholend, periodisch auftretend; – ***fever,*** das Rückfallfieber; 2. (*Math.*) periodisch, rekurrent; 3. (*Anat.*) rückläufig.

recurvate [riː'kəːveit], *adj.* zurückgebogen. **recurve, 1.** *v.t.* zurückbiegen. **2.** *v.i.* sich zurückwenden.

recusancy ['rekjuzənsi], *s.* hartnäckige Weigerung *or* Opposition, die Unbotmäßigkeit, Widerspenstigkeit. **recusant, 1.** *adj.* 1. widerspenstig, unbotmäßig; 2. ablehnend (***against***, gegen); 3. (*Eccl.*) dissentierend. **2.** *s.* 1. Widerspenstige(r); 2. (*Eccl.*) der (die) Rekusant(in). **recuse** [ri'kjuːz], *v.t.* (*Law*) ablehnen.

red [red], **1.** *adj.* 1. rot; (*Ent.*) – ***admiral,*** der Admiral; – ***ant,*** rote Waldameise; – ***antimony,*** der Rotspiegelglanz; – ***book,*** der Adelskalender; – ***cabbage,*** der Rotkohl; (*coll.*) ***––carpet treatment,*** großer Bahnhof; – ***clover,*** der Rotklee; ***Red Cross,*** Rotes Kreuz; – ***currant,*** rote Johannisbeere; – ***deal,*** das Kiefernholz; – ***deer,*** der Rothirsch, Edelhirsch; – ***ensign,*** britische Handelsflagge; – ***eyes,*** entzündete Augen; – ***face,*** roter Kopf (*embarrassment*); – ***flag,*** rote Fahne, das Warnungssignal; – ***grouse,*** schottisches Schneehuhn; (*Bot.*) – ***gum,*** der Rieseneukalyptus; – ***hat,*** der Kardinalshut; – ***herring,*** der Bückling; (*fig.*) das Ablenkungsobjekt, Ablenkungsmanöver; ***draw a – herring across the path,*** Ablenkungsmanöver betreiben; ***Red Indian,*** der Indianer; – ***lead,*** die Mennige, das Bleizinnober; (*fig.*) – ***light,*** das Warnlicht; ***see the – light,*** die Gefahr erkennen; (*sl.*) ***––light district,*** das Bordellviertel; – ***man,*** die Rothaut, der Indianer; – ***ochre,*** die Eisenmennige; – ***pepper,*** der Cayennepfeffer; – ***rag,*** rotes Tuch; ***be a – rag to him,*** auf ihn wie ein rotes Tuch wirken; (*Bot.*)

– ***rot***, das Sonnenkraut, der Sonnentau; – ***sanders***, rotes Sandelholz; ***Red Sea***, Rotes Meer; – ***snow***, der Blutschnee; – ***spider***, die Spinnmilbe; (*fig.*) – ***tape***, der Amtsschimmel, die Paragraphenreiterei, das Schema; die Beamtenwirtschaft, der Zopf; – ***with tears***, rotgeweint; (*coll.*) ***paint the town –***, Spektakel *or* Skandal machen; 2. (*coll.*) kommunistisch, bolschewistisch, marxistisch, sowjetisch; anarchistisch. **2.** *s.* 1. das Rot, rote Farbe; ***see –***, rasend werden, die Fassung vollkommen verlieren, alles rot vor Augen sehen; 2. (*Pol. coll.*) Rote(r), der Kommunist, Marxist, Bolschewist, Anarchist, Linksradikale(r); 3. (*Comm. coll.*) die Debitseite, das Defizit, Schulden (*pl.*); (*coll.*) ***be deep in the –***, tief in den roten Zahlen stecken; (*coll.*) ***be out of the –***, aus den Schulden heraus sein.

redact [ri'dækt], *v.t.* 1. abfassen, formulieren; 2. herausgeben, redigieren. **redaction** [–kʃən], *s.* 1. die (Ab)fassung, Formulierung; 2. Herausgabe, Redaktion; 3. Revision, Neubearbeitung. **redactor,** *s.* der Herausgeber, Redakteur.

redan [ri'dæn], *s.* (*Fort.*) der Redan, die Flesche.

red|-blooded, *adj.* lebenskräftig, lebenssprühend; (*coll.*) feurig, kräftig. **–breast,** *s.* (*Orn.*) das Rotkehlchen. **–cap,** *s.* (*coll.*) der Militärpolizist. **–coat,** *s.* der Rotrock, englischer Soldat.

redd [red], *v.t.* (*Scots*) (*also –* ***up***) in Ordnung bringen, aufräumen, reinigen.

redden [redn], **1.** *v.t.* rot färben, röten. **2.** *v.i.* 1. rot werden, sich röten; 2. (*fig.*) erröten. **redder,** *comp. adj.*, **reddest,** *sup. adj. of* **red. reddish,** *adj.* rötlich.

reddle [redl], *s.* der Rötel, Rotstein.

rede [ri:d], **1.** *v.t., v.i.* (*Poet.*) raten (*Dat.*). **2.** *s.* (*Poet.*) 1. der Rat; 2. die Entscheidung, Absicht.

redecorate [ri:'dekəreit], *v.t.* neu streichen *or* dekorieren (*a house*). **redecoration** [–'reiʃən], *s.* der Neuanstrich, die Neudekorierung.

redeem [ri'di:m], *v.t.* 1. zurückkaufen; 2. einlösen (*a pledge*), abzahlen, ablösen, tilgen, amortisieren (*a loan*), loskaufen, freikaufen (*captives*); 3. (*fig.*) zurückgewinnen, wiedererlangen, wiederherstellen (*one's honour, rights etc.*); 4. nachkommen (*Dat.*), erfüllen, (ein)halten (*a promise*); 5. wiedergutmachen, wettmachen, ausgleichen, aufwiegen, entschädigen für; ***–ing feature***, versöhnender Zug; 6. befreien (***from***, von), bewahren (vor (*Dat.*)), (*Theol.*) erlösen (von). **redeemable,** *adj.* 1. zurückkaufbar; 2. einlösbar, abzahlbar, ablösbar, tilgbar; (*Comm.*) – ***bond***, kündbare Obligation; – ***loan***, das Tilgungsdarlehen; 3. (*fig.*) erfüllbar; 4. wiedergutzumachen(d), wiederherstellbar; 5. (*Theol.*) erlösbar. **redeemer,** *s.* 1. der (die) Rückkäufer(in); 2. (*esp. Theol.*) der Erlöser, Heiland.

redeliver [ri:di'livə], *v.t.* 1. wieder austragen *or* aushändigen *or* übermitteln; 2. wieder befreien *or* erlösen.

redemption [ri'dempʃən], *s.* 1. der Rückkauf; – ***value***, der Rückkaufswert, Tilgungswert; 2. die Rückzahlung (*of capital*), Tilgung, Ablösung, Abzahlung (*of debt*), Einlösung (*of pledge*); – ***fund***, der Amortisationsfonds; – ***payment***, die Ablösungszahlung; 3. der Loskauf, Freikauf (*of captive*); 4. (*fig.*) die Zurückgewinnung, Wiedererlangung, Wiederherstellung (*of honour, rights etc.*); 5. Erfüllung, Einhaltung, Einlösung (*of promise*); 6. Wiedergutmachung, das Wettmachen, Aufwiegen; 7. der Ausgleich (***of***, für), die Versöhnung (mit); 8. Befreiung, Erlösung (***from***, von), Rettung, Bewahrung (vor (*Dat.*)); (*Theol.*) Erlösung; ***beyond*** or ***past –***, hoffnungslos *or* rettungslos (verloren *or* verfahren *or* verderbt). **redemptive** [–tiv], *adj.* (*Theol.*) erlösend, Erlösungs–.

redeploy [ri:di'plɔi], *v.t.* verlegen (*troops*), verschieben, umgruppieren, neu aufstellen *or* entfalten. **redeployment,** *s.* die Verlegung, (Truppen)verschiebung; Umgruppierung, Neuaufstellung, Neuentfaltung.

redevelop [ri:di'veləp], *v.t.* 1. neu entwickeln; 2. umbauen, neugestalten (*an area*); 3. (*Phot.*) nachentwickeln. **redevelopment,** *s.* 1. die Neuentwicklung; 2. der Umbau, die Neugestaltung (*of an area*); 3. (*Phot.*) Nachentwicklung.

red|-haired, *adj.* rothaarig. **–-handed,** *adv.* (*fig.*) ***catch –***, auf frischer Tat ertappen. **–head,** *s.* der Rotkopf. **–headed,** *adj.* rotköpfig, rothaarig. **–-heat,** *s.* die Rotglut. **–-hot,** *adj.* 1. rotglühend; (*Bot.*) – ***poker***, die Fackellilie, Kniphopia; 2. (*fig.*) hitzig, feurig, wild; 3. (*coll.*) (*of news*) allerneuest.

redintegrate [re'dintigreit], *v.t.* wiederherstellen, erneuern. **redintegration** [–'greiʃən], *s.* die Wiederherstellung, Erneuerung.

redirect [ri:di'rekt], *v.t.* umadressieren, nachsenden (*letters etc.*); umstellen (*inquiries etc.*) (***to***, auf (*Acc.*)).

rediscover [ri:dis'kʌvə], *v.t.* wiederentdecken, neuentdecken. **rediscovery,** *s.* die Wiederentdeckung, Neuentdeckung.

redistribute [ri:dis'tribju:t], *v.t.* neu verteilen. **redistribution** [–'bju:ʃən], *s.* die Neuverteilung.

red-letter day, *s.* 1. der Heiligentag, Festtag; 2. (*usu. fig.*) Freudentag, Glückstag, denkwürdiger Tag.

redness ['rednis], *s.* die Röte.

re-do [ri:'du:], *irr.v.t.* 1. nochmals tun; 2. (*coll.*) renovieren.

redolence ['redələns], *s.* 1. der Wohlgeruch, Duft; 2. (*fig.*) Anklang. **redolent,** *adj.* 1. wohlriechend, duftend (***of***, nach); 2. (*usu. fig.*) anklingend, gemahnend (***of***, an (*Acc.*)), umwittert (von), atmend (*Acc.*); (*fig.*) ***be – of***, atmen, erinnern an (*Acc.*), einen Anklang *or* Anstrich haben von.

redouble [ri:'dʌbl], **1.** *v.t.* (*fig.*) verdoppeln, verstärken. **2.** *v.i.* 1. (*fig.*) sich verdoppeln *or* verstärken; 2. (*Cards*) Rekontra gehen.

redoubt [ri'daut], *s.* (*Fort.*) die Redoute, Schanze, das Schanzwerk. **redoubtable,** *adj.* gefürchtet, furchtbar, schrecklich; ehrfurchtgebietend.

redound [ri'daund], *v.i.* 1. gereichen, ausschlagen (***to***, zu); – ***to his credit***, ihm zur Ehre gereichen; 2. zuteil werden, zufallen, zufließen, erwachsen, sich ergeben (***from***, aus; ***to***, *Dat.*); 3. zurückfallen, zurückwirken ((***up***)***on***, auf (*Acc.*)).

redpoll ['redpoul], *s.* (*Orn.*) der Birkenzeisig (*Carduelis linaria*).

redraft, 1. [ri:'drɑ:ft], *v.t.* nochmals entwerfen. **2.** ['ri:drɑ:ft], *s.* 1. neuer Entwurf; 2. (*Comm.*) der Rückwechsel.

redraw [ri:'drɔ:], *irr.v.t.* 1. nochmals zeichnen; 2. (*Comm.*) einen Rückwechsel ziehen, zurücktrassieren (***on***, auf (*Acc.*)).

redress [ri'dres], **1.** *s.* 1. die Wiedergutmachung, Abhilfe, Entschädigung (***for***, für); ***legal –***, die Rechtshilfe; 2. die Behebung, Beseitigung, Abschaffung, Abstellung. **2.** *v.t.* 1. wiedergutmachen (*a wrong*), beheben, beseitigen, abschaffen, abstellen (*evils*), abhelfen (*Dat.*) (*suffering etc.*); (*usu. fig.*) – ***the balance***, das Gleichgewicht wiederherstellen; 2. (*Av.*) abfangen.

re-dress [ri:'dres], **1.** *v.t.* 1. nochmals anziehen; 2. neu verbinden (*a wound*). **2.** *v.i.* sich (nochmals) umkleiden.

red|shank, *s.* (*Orn.*) der Rotschenkel (*Tringa totanus*). **–-short,** *adj.* (*Metall.*) rotbrüchig. **–skin,** *s.* die Rothaut, der (die) Indianer(in). **–start,** *s.* (*Orn.*) der (Garten)rotschwanz (*Phoenicurus phoenicurus*); ***black –***, der Hausrotschwanz (*Ph. ochruros*). **–-tapery** [–'teipəri], **–-tapism** [–'teipizm], *s. See* ***red tape***.

reduce [ri'dju:s], **1.** *v.t.* 1. vermindern, verkleinern, verringern (*size, extent*), herabsetzen (*value, price, rank*), ermäßigen (*price*), verdünnen, abschwächen (*intensity*), erniedrigen, degradieren (*rank*); – ***one's expenses***, sich einschränken; (*Mil.*) – ***to the ranks***, degradieren; ***–d scale***, verjüngter *or* verkleinerter Maßstab; ***at –d prices***, zu herabgesetzten *or* ermäßigten Preisen; ***in –d circumstances***, verarmt, heruntergekommen; 2. zerstampfen, zermahlen (***to***, zu), zerlegen (in (*Acc.*)); verwandeln (zu *or* in (*Acc.*)), machen (zu), zurückführen (auf (*Acc.*));

(*fig.*) anpassen (*Dat. or* an (*Acc.*)), umsetzen (in (*Acc.*)), zwingen, bringen (zu), beschränken (auf (*Acc.*)); – ***to absurdity,*** ad absurdum führen; – ***to ashes,*** einäschern, in Asche verwandeln; – ***to beggary,*** an den Bettelstab bringen; – ***to despair,*** zur Verzweiflung bringen; – ***a proposition to its simplest form,*** einen Satz auf seinen einfachsten Ausdruck zurückführen; (*Mil.*) – ***to half-pay,*** verabschieden; – ***to nothing,*** vernichten; – ***to obedience,*** zum Gehorsam zwingen; – ***to powder,*** zu Pulver zerkleinern, pulverisieren; – ***to a pulp,*** zu Brei machen, (*fig.*) windelweich schlagen; – ***to a system,*** in ein System bringen; – ***to tears,*** zu Tränen rühren; ***–d to a skeleton,*** zum Skelett abgemagert; 3. (*Chem., Math.*) reduzieren; – ***by boiling,*** verkochen; – ***by liquidation,*** ausseigern; – ***to a common denominator,*** auf einen gemeinsamen Nennen bringen; – ***whole numbers to fractions,*** ganze Zahlen in Brüche verwandeln; 4. (*Mil. etc.*) erobern, besiegen, unterwerfen, bezwingen; – ***a fortress,*** eine Festung zur Übergabe zwingen; 5. (*Surg.*) (wieder)einrenken. **2.** *v.i.* eine Abmagerungskur machen.

reducer [ri'dju:sə], *s.* 1. das Verdünnungsmittel, Verschnittmittel; 2. (*Phot.*) der Abschwächer; 3. (*Tech.*) verjüngte Muffe, das Reduktionsstück. **reducible,** *adj.* zurückführbar, reduzierbar (*to,* auf (*Acc.*)); verwandelbar (in (*Acc.*)); ***be –,*** sich zurückführen *or* verwandeln lassen. **reducing|-agent,** *s.* 1. das Reduktionsmittel; 2. (*Med.*) Entfettungsmittel. **--scale,** *s.* verjüngter Maßstab. **--valve,** *s.* das Reduzierventil.

reduction [ri'dʌkʃən], *s.* 1. das Zurückführen, Zurückbringen (***to,*** auf (*Acc.*)); die Verwandlung (in (*Acc.*)); 2. (*Chem.*) Reduktion; (*Math.*) Reduktion, Kürzung, Vereinfachung; Verjüngung (*of a scale*); 3. Herabsetzung (*of prices*); Verminderung, Verkleinerung, Verringerung, Reduzierung; (***price***) –, die Ermäßigung, der Abzug, Rabatt; – ***in wages,*** die Lohnkürzung; – ***in*** or ***of staff,*** der Personalabbau; ***make a –,*** den Preis herabsetzen; 4. die Unterwerfung (*of a town etc.*); 5. (*Surg.*) Einrenkung.

reduction|-compasses, *pl.* der Reduktionszirkel. **--gear,** *s.* das Untersetzungsgetriebe, die Untersetzung.

reduit [re'dwi:], *s.* (*Fort.*) das Kernwerk.

redundance, redundancy [ri'dʌndəns(i)], *s.* 1. die Überzahl, Überfülle, der Überfluß, Überschuß, das Übermaß (***of,*** an (*Dat.*)); 2. die Entlassung; Arbeitslosigkeit; 3. (*fig.*) Weitschweifigkeit. **redundant,** *adj.* 1. überzählig, überschüssig, überreichlich, überflüssig, übermäßig; 2. arbeitslos; ***be made –,*** entlassen werden; 3. überladen (***with,*** mit), überfließend (von).

reduplicate [ri:'dju:plikeit], *v.t.* 1. verdoppeln, wiederholen; 2. (*Gram.*) reduplizieren. **reduplication** [–'keiʃən], *s.* 1. die Verdoppelung, Wiederholung; 2. (*Gram.*) Reduplikation.

red|-water, *s.* (*Vet.*) das Blutharnen, die Piroplasmose; – ***fever,*** das Texasfieber. **–wing,** *s.* (*Orn.*) die Rotdrossel (*Turdus iliacus*). **–wood,** *s.* 1. das Rotholz; 2. Brasilholz, Pernambukholz; Brasilettoholz; Sappanholz; Kamholz; 3. (*Am.*) der Mammutbaum, die Eibensequoie.

re-echo [ri:'ekou], **1.** *v.i.* wiederhallen (***with,*** von). **2.** *v.t.* wiederholen.

reed [ri:d], *s.* 1. das Rohr (*also of organ*), Schilfrohr, Ried(gras); (*collect., usu. pl.*) Röhricht, Schilf; ***broken –,*** schwankendes Rohr; 2. (*Poet.*) die Hirtenpfeife, Rohrpfeife; 3. (*Mus.*) das (Rohr)-blatt (*of reed instruments*); die Zunge (*organ*); *pl.* (*collect.*) Zungeninstrumente (*pl.*) (*of orchestra*); 4. (*Tech.*) das Webblatt, Riet, der Weberkamm; 5. (*Archit.*) Rundstab.

reed-bunting, *s.* (*Orn.*) die Rohrammer (*Emberiza schoeniclus*). **reediness,** *s.* die Piepsigkeit (*of voice*). **reed-instrument,** *s.* das Rohrblattinstrument, Zungeninstrument. **reedling,** *s. See under* **titmouse. reed|-mace,** *s.* (*Bot.*) das Rohrkolbenschilf. **--pipe,** *s.* 1. die Rohrpfeife; 2. (*of organ*) Zungenpfeife. **--stop,** *s.* (*of organ*) die Zungenstimme, das Schnarregister.

re-education [ri:edju'keiʃən], *s.* die Umschulung, Umerziehung.

reed-warbler, *s.* (*Orn.*) der Teichrohrsänger (*Acrocephalus scirpaceus*). **reedy,** *adj.* 1. schilfrig, schilfreich; 2. schrill, piepsig (*as a voice*).

[1]**reef** [ri:f], *s.* 1. das Riff, die Felsenklippe; 2. (*Min.*) goldführende Ader.

[2]**reef, 1.** *s.* (*Naut.*) das Reff; ***take in a –,*** einreffen. **2.** *v.t.* (*Naut.*) reffen; ***close –ed,*** dicht gerefft. **reefer,** *s.* 1. der Reffer; 2. Seekadett; 3. die Seemannsjacke; 4. (*sl.*) Marihuana-Zigarette, Haschzigarette, der Joint. **reef-knot,** *s.* der Reffknoten, Kreuzknoten.

reek [ri:k], **1.** *s.* (*Scots*) 1. der Rauch, Dampf, Dunst; 2. Qualm; 3. (*coll.*) Geruch, Gestank. **2.** *v.i.* 1. dampfen, rauchen, dunsten; 2. (*coll.*) stinken, riechen (***of,*** (*fig.*) ***with,*** nach).

[1]**reel** [ri:l], **1.** *s.* 1. die Winde, Haspel; 2. (Garn)-rolle; (*angling*) Rolle; (*typewriter, film etc.*) Spule; (*sl. fig.*) ***off the –,*** hintereinander weg, in einem Gang; 3. ***news–,*** die Wochenschau. **2.** *v.t.* (*also* – ***up***) (*length of line*) (auf)wickeln, aufrollen, aufwinden, aufspulen; – ***in,*** einholen, heranholen (*fish etc.*); – ***off,*** abhaspeln, abwinden, abwickeln; (*fig.*) herunterrasseln, herunterleiern, wie am Schnürchen hersagen.

[2]**reel, 1.** *v.i.* 1. taumeln, (sch)wanken, (*fig.*) ins Wanken geraten, zurückweichen; 2. sich drehen, wirbeln; ***my head –s,*** mir schwindelt. **2.** *s.* das Taumeln, Wirbeln, (Sch)wanken; (*fig.*) der Taumel, Wirbel.

[3]**reel,** *s.* schottischer Volkstanz.

re-elect [ri:i'lekt], *v.t.* wiederwählen. **re-election** [–kʃən], *s.* die Wiederwahl; ***eligible for –,*** *see* **re-eligible.**

re-eligible [ri:'elidʒəbl], *adj.* wiederwählbar.

re-embark [ri:em'bɑ:k], *v.t.* (*v.i.*) (sich) wieder einschiffen. **re-embarkation** [–'keiʃən], *s.* die Wiedereinschiffung.

re-emerge [ri:i'mə:dʒ], *v.i.* wieder auftauchen *or* auftreten. **re-emergence,** *s.* das Wiederauftauchen, Wiederauftreten.

re-enact [ri:i'nækt], *v.t.* 1. neu verordnen; 2. wieder in Kraft setzen; 3. (*Theat.*) neu inszenieren; 4. (*fig.*) wiederholen. **re-enactment,** *s.* 1. die Wiederinkraftsetzung; 2. Wiederholung; 3. Neuinszenierung.

re-engage [ri:in'geidʒ], **1.** *v.t.* wieder anstellen *or* einstellen. **2.** *v.i. See* **re-enlist, 1. re-engagement,** *s.* die Wiederanstellung, Wiedereinstellung.

re-enlist [ri:in'list], **1.** *v.i.* sich wieder anwerben lassen, weiterdienen, kapitulieren. **2.** *v.t.* 1. wieder anwerben; 2. (*fig.*) wieder in Anspruch nehmen. **re-enlistment,** *s.* 1. die Wiederanwerbung; 2. (*fig.*) Wiederverwendung.

re-enter [ri:'entə], **1.** *v.t.* 1. wieder betreten, (*also fig.*) wieder eintreten in (*Acc.*); neu eintragen (*in a book*); 3. eindrucken (*colour on fabric*). **2.** *v.i.* 1. von neuem eintreten; 2. (*Math.*) einspringen. **re-entering,** *s.* das Eindrucken. **re-entrance,** *s.* das Wiedereintreten. **re-entrant, 1.** *adj.* (*Geom.*) einspringend (*angle*). **2.** *s.* einspringender Winkel. **re-entry,** *s.* (*Law*) das Wiedereintreten, der Wiedereintritt.

re-establish [ri:is'tæbliʃ], *v.t.* 1. wiederherstellen; 2. wieder einführen. **re-establishment,** *s.* die Wiederherstellung.

[1]**reeve** [ri:v], *s.* (*Hist.*) der Vogt, Schultheiß, Amtmann.

[2]**reeve,** *s.* (*Orn.*) das Weibchen des Kampfläufers; *see* [1]**ruff.**

[3]**reeve,** *v.t.* (*Naut.*) (ein)scheren (*rope*). **reeving-line,** *s.* das Schertau.

re-examination [ri:igzæmi'neiʃən], *s.* 1. die Nachprüfung, Wiederholungsprüfung; 2. (*Law*) nochmaliges Verhör, nochmalige Vernehmung. **re-examine** [–'zæmin], *v.t.* 1. nachprüfen, nochmals prüfen; 2. (*Law*) neu vernehmen *or* verhören.

re-exchange [ri:iks'tʃeindʒ], *s.* 1. abermaliger Tausch; 2. (*Comm.*) der Rückwechsel, Rikambio, die Ritratte.

re-export, 1. [ri:eks'pɔ:t], *v.t.* wieder ausführen. **2.** [–'ekspɔ:t], *s.* die Wiederausfuhr.

ref [ref], *s.* (*sl.*) *see* **referee** (*Spt.*).

refashion [ri:'fæʃən], *v.t.* neu formen, umgestalten, ummodeln.

refection [ri'fekʃən], *s.* 1. die Erfrischung, Labung; 2. der Imbiß. **refectory** [–təri], *s.* der Speisesaal; das Refektorium (*in convents etc.*); – ***table,*** langer schmaler Eßtisch.

refer [ri'fə:], **1.** *v.t.* 1. aufmerksam machen, verweisen, hinweisen (*to*, auf (*Acc.*)) (*a th.*); 2. verweisen (*to*, auf (*Acc.*)) (*a p.*); 3. überlassen, übergeben, anheimstellen (*to*, *Dat.*), überweisen, zurückstellen (an (*Acc.*)) (*a p.*); (*Comm.*) – ***to drawer,*** an den Aussteller zurück; 4. zuschreiben, zuweisen, zuordnen (*to*, *Dat.*), zurückführen, beziehen (auf (*Acc.*)). **2.** *v.i.* 1. hinweisen, verweisen, sich beziehen, Bezug haben (*to*, auf (*Acc.*)), betreffen (*Acc.*) (*to a th.*); (*coll.*) – ***to,*** anspielen auf (*Acc.*), erwähnen; ***referring to my letter,*** mit *or* unter Bezug auf meinen Brief; 2. sich wenden (*to*, an (*Acc.*)), befragen (*Acc.*); – ***to a book,*** in einem Buch nachschlagen *or* nachsehen, ein Buch heranziehen; 3. sich berufen *or* beziehen, Bezug nehmen (auf (*Acc.*)) (*to a p.*). **referable,** *adj.* zurückzuführen(d) (*to*, auf (*Acc.*)), zuzuschreiben(d) *or* zuzurechnen(d) (*Dat.*).

referee [refə'ri:], **1.** *s.* 1. (*Spt.*) der Schiedsrichter, (*boxing*) Ringrichter; 2. (*fig.*) Referent, Sachverständige(r), Unparteiische(r). **2.** *v.i.* (*v.t.*) als Schiedsrichter fungieren (bei).

reference ['refərəns], **1.** *s.* 1. die Beziehung (*to*, zu), der Zusammenhang (mit); 2. die Bezugnahme, Verweisung, der Bezug, Verweis, Hinweis (*to*, auf (*Acc.*)); die Berücksichtigung (*Gen.*), Rücksicht (auf (*Acc.*)); ***have – to,*** sich beziehen auf (*Acc.*); ***in*** or ***with – to,*** in *or* mit Bezug(nahme) auf (*Acc.*), hinsichtlich (*Gen.*); ***without – to,*** ohne Bezug auf (*Acc.*); ohne Rücksicht auf (*Acc.*); ***terms of –,*** Richtlinien (*pl.*); 3. (*in a book*) die Verweisstelle, der Verweis; ***cross-–,*** der Kreuzverweis; 4. der Beleg; 5. (*coll.*) die Erwähnung (*to*, *Gen.*), Anspielung (auf (*Acc.*)); ***make – to,*** erwähnen, verweisen auf (*Acc.*); anspielen auf (*Acc.*); 6. die Empfehlung, Referenz (*also p. referred to*); 7. das Nachschlagen, Nachsehen (*to*, in (*Dat.*)); ***for –,*** zur Informierung; zum Nachschlagen (*books*); ***work of –,*** das Nachschlagewerk; 8. der Zuständigkeitsbereich. **2.** *v.t.* mit Verweisen versehen (*book*).

reference| book, *s.* das Nachschlagewerk. – **library,** *s.* die Handbibliothek. – **line,** *s.* (*Math.*) die Bezugslinie. – **mark,** *s.* das Verweis(ungs)zeichen. – **number,** *s.* das Aktenzeichen, die Geschäftsnummer. – **point,** *s.* der Anhaltspunkt (*maps*).

referendum [refə'rendəm], *s.* der Volksentscheid (*on*, über (*Acc.*)).

referential [refə'renʃəl], *adj.* hinweisend, Verweis(ungs)–, Vermerk–.

refill, 1. [ri:'fil], *v.t.* wieder füllen, nachfüllen, auffüllen. **2.** [–'fil], *v.i.* sich wieder füllen. **3.** ['ri:fil], *s.* die Neufüllung, Nachfüllung, Ersatzfüllung; das Ersatzblei (*for pencils*), die Ersatzmine (*for ball-points*), Ersatzbatterie (*for electric torch*), Einlage (*for ring-book*).

refine [ri'fain], **1.** *v.t.* 1. reinigen, läutern (*also fig.*), vergüten, raffinieren (*sugar etc.*), frischen, feinen, abtreiben, abscheiden (*metal*); 2. (*fig.*) bilden, verfeinern, veredeln. **2.** *v.i.* 1. sich verfeinern *or* verbessern, klar *or* rein werden; 2. (*fig.*) – ***(up)on,*** verbessern, verfeinern, vervollkommnen, weiter *or* höher entwickeln. **refined,** *adj.* geläutert (*also fig.*), raffiniert (*also fig., oft. iron.*), Fein–; (*fig.*) fein, gebildet, gepflegt, vornehm, kultiviert; – ***lead,*** das Weichblei; – ***steel,*** der Edelstahl; – ***sugar,*** der Feinzucker, die Raffinade. **refinement,** *s.* 1. (*usu. fig.*) die Feinheit, Vornehmheit, Gepflegtheit, Kultiviertheit, Bildung; 2. Raffinesse, Klügelei, Spitzfindigkeit; 3. Verfeinerung, Vervollkommnung, Verbesserung, Weiterentwicklung, Höherentwicklung (*on*, *Gen.*); 4. (*Tech.*) *see* **refining.**

refiner [ri'fainə], *s.* 1. der Raffineur, Raffinierer, (Zucker)sieder; (*Metall.*) Frischer; 2. Raffinierapparat; (*Metall.*) die Frischanlage; (*Paperm.*) Feinmühle; 3. (*fig.*) der Verfeinerer; 4. Haarspalter, Klügler. **refinery,** *s.* die Raffinerie, Siederei, der Frischofen. **refining,** *s.* 1. die Läuterung, Raffinierung; (*Metall.*) das Feinen, Frischen; – ***furnace,*** der Feinofen, Frischofen, Treibofen; 2. (*fig.*) die Verfeinerung, Klärung, Läuterung.

refit, 1. [ri:'fit], *v.t.* 1. renovieren, wieder instandsetzen; 2. neu ausrüsten. **2.** [–'fit], *v.i.* renoviert *or* wieder instandgesetzt werden. **3.** ['ri:fit], *s.* die Wiederinstandsetzung, Renovierung.

reflect [ri'flekt], **1.** *v.t.* 1. zurückwerfen, widerspiegeln (*also fig.*), zurückstrahlen, reflektieren (*light etc.*); ***be –ed,*** zurückfallen, sich (wider)spiegeln; 2. (*fig.*) (wider)spiegeln, wiedergeben; – ***credit (up)on him,*** ihm Ruhm einbringen, ihm Ehre machen; ***be –ed in,*** sich spiegeln in (*Dat.*), seinen Niederschlag finden in (*Dat.*). **2.** *v.i.* 1. nachdenken, nachsinnen (***(up)on,*** über (*Acc.*)), überlegen (*Acc.*); 2. sich (*Dat.*) entsinnen *or* vor Augen halten, es sich (*Dat.*) (wohl) überlegen, sich (*Dat.*) darüber klar werden *or* im klaren sein, bedenken, darauf besinnen (***that,*** daß); 3. (*fig.*) – ***(up)on him,*** ein schiefes *or* schlechtes Licht auf ihn werfen, ihn in ein schiefes *or* schlechtes Licht setzen, ihm nicht gerade zu Ehre gereichen; (*fig.*) – ***(un)favourably on him,*** ihn in (un)günstigem Licht erscheinen lassen. **reflecting,** *adj.* Reflexions–, Spiegel–; – ***power,*** das Reflexionsvermögen; – ***telescope,*** das Spiegelteleskop.

reflection [ri'flekʃən], *s.* 1. die Zurückwerfung, Zurückstrahlung, Reflektierung, Reflexion, (Wider)spiegelung; ***angle of –,*** der Reflexionswinkel; 2. das Spiegelbild; 3. (*fig.*) die Nachwirkung; 4. Überlegung, Erwägung, das Nachdenken; ***on –,*** nach einigem Nachdenken, bei näherer Erwägung; 5. (*oft. pl.*) die Betrachtung, Bemerkung, Reflexion, der Anspruch, Gedanke; 6. (*fig.*) Tadel (***on,*** an (*Dat.*)), tadelnde Bemerkung (über (*Acc.*)); ***be a – on,*** schlechtes Licht werfen auf (*Acc.*); ***cast –s upon,*** herabsetzen, Vorwürfe häufen auf (*Acc.*).

reflective [ri'flektiv], *adj.* 1. zurückstrahlend, reflektierend; 2. nachdenklich, beschaulich; gedanklich. **reflector,** *s.* 1. der Reflektor, Hohlspiegel; 2. Scheinwerfer; 3. (*Cycl.*) Rückstrahler, das Katzenauge.

reflex ['ri:fleks], **1.** *adj.* 1. Reflex–, Rück–, rückwirkend; – ***camera,*** die Spiegelreflexkamera; 2. entgegengesetzt, Gegen–; 3. (*Math.*) einspringend; 4. (*Bot.*) zurückgebogen. **2.** *s.* 1. der (Licht)reflex, Widerschein (*also fig.*); 2. das Spiegelbild; 3. (*fig.*) die (Wider)spiegelung, Nachbildung, Entsprechung; 4. (*Med. etc.*) der Reflex; – ***action,*** die Reflexbewegung.

reflexible [ri'fleksibl], *adj.* reflektierbar. **reflexion,** *s. See* **reflection. reflexive, 1.** *adj.* (*Gram.*) rückbezüglich, Reflexiv–. **2.** *s.* das Reflexivpronomen, rückbezügliches Zeitwort.

refloat [ri:'flout], **1.** *v.t.* wieder flottmachen. **2.** *v.i.* wieder flott werden.

refluence ['refluəns], *s.* das Zurückfließen, Zurückfluten. **refluent,** *adj.* zurückfließend, zurückflutend.

reflux ['ri:flʌks], *s. See* **refluence**; das Ebben, der Rückfluß (*also fig.*); (*fig.*) das Zurückströmen (*of capital etc.*).

refoot [ri:'fut], *v.t.* einen Füßling neu anstricken an (*Acc.*).

reform [ri'fɔ:m], **1.** *v.t.* 1. verbessern, reformieren (*a th.*); 2. bessern (*a p.*). **2.** *v.i.* besser werden, sich bessern. **3.** *s.* 1. die Reform, Verbesserung (*of a th.*); – ***movement,*** die Reformbewegung; 2. die Besserung (*of a p.*); (*obs.*) – ***school,*** *see* **reformatory, 2.**

re-form [riː'fɔːm], **1.** *v.t.* 1. neu gestalten, umformen, umbilden, umgestalten; 2. (*Mil.*) neu gliedern. **2.** *v.i.* sich neu formieren *or* gliedern.
reformable [ri'fɔːməbl], *adj.* besserungsfähig.
reformation [refə'meiʃən], *s.* 1. die Reformierung, Verbesserung (*of a th.*); 2. Besserung (*of a p.*); 3. (*Eccl.*) ***the Reformation,*** die Reformation.
re-formation [riːfɔː'meiʃən], *s.* die Umformung, Umgestaltung, Umbildung, Neugestaltung.
reformative [ri'fɔːmətiv], *adj.* reformatorisch, Reform(ierungs)–. **reformatory** [–ətəri], **1.** *adj.* Besserungs–. **2.** *s.* die Besserungsanstalt. **reformed,** *adj.* 1. verbessert (*of a th.*); 2. gebessert, geheilt, bekehrt (*of a p.*); 3. (*Eccl.*) reformiert. **reformer,** *s.* 1. (*Pol.*) der Reformist, Reformer; 2. (*Eccl.*) Reformator.
refract [ri'frækt], *v.t.* brechen. **refracting,** *adj.* lichtbrechend, Brechungs–; – ***telescope,*** der Refraktor. **refraction** [–kʃən], *s.* die Brechung; ***index of –,*** der Brechungsexponent. **refractive** [–tiv], *adj.* Brechungs–; Refraktions–; – ***power,*** das Brechungsvermögen.
refractoriness [ri'fræktərinis], *s.* 1. die Widersetzlichkeit, Widerspenstigkeit, Störrigkeit, der Eigensinn (*of a p.*); 2. die Widerstandskraft (***to,*** gegen); (*Metall.*) Strengflüssigkeit; (*Tech.*) Feuerfestigkeit. **refractory,** *adj.* 1. widerspenstig, widersetzlich, störrisch, eigensinnig; 2. hartnäckig (*as disease*); 3. widerstandsfähig (***to,*** gegen), (*Metall.*) strengflüssig; (*Tech.*) feuerfest; – ***clay,*** die Schamotte.
[1]**refrain** [ri'frein], *v.i.* sich enthalten (***from,*** *Gen.*), absehen, abstehen, Abstand nehmen (von); – ***from smoking,*** es unterlassen zu rauchen, das Rauchen unterlassen, vom Rauchen abstehen.
[2]**refrain,** *s.* der Kehrreim, Refrain.
refrangible [ri'frændʒibl], *adj.* brechbar.
refresh [ri'freʃ], **1.** *v.t.* 1. erfrischen, erquicken; 2. (*fig.*) auffrischen. **2.** *v.i.* sich erfrischen. **refresher,** *s.* 1. (*coll.*) die Erfrischung 2. (*fig.*) (*also* – ***course***) der Auffrischungskurs, Wiederholungskurs; 3. (*Law*) das Extrahonorar. **refreshing,** *adj.* 1. erfrischend, erquickend, wohltuend; 2. (*fig.*) belebend, anregend. **refreshment,** *s.* 1. die Erfrischung, Erquickung, Erholung (***to,*** für); 2. (*coll.*) der Trunk, das Gläschen; 3. (*usu. pl.*) der Imbiß; (*Railw.*) – ***car,*** der Speisewagen; – ***room,*** der Erfrischungsraum, die Restauration, das Büfett.
refrigerant [ri'fridʒərənt], **1.** *adj.* (ab)kühlend. **2.** *s.* das Kühlmittel. **refrigerate** [–reit], *v.t.* (ab)kühlen, tiefkühlen, gefrieren. **refrigeration** [–'reiʃən], *s.* die (Ab)kühlung; das Kühlen, die Kälteerzeugung. **refrigerator** [–reitə], *s.* der Kühlschrank, Eisschrank, Kühlraum, die Kühlanlage; (*of a still*) Kühlschlange, das Kühlrohr, der Kühler; (*Railw.*) – ***car,*** der Kühlwagen. **refrigeratory** [–rətəri], **1.** *adj.* kühlend, Kühl–. **2.** *s.* der Verdampfer, Kühlkondensator.
reft [reft], *pred. adj.* (*Poet.*) beraubt (***of,*** *Gen.*), leer (an (*Dat.*)).
refuel [riː'fjuəl], **1.** *v.t.* mit Brennstoff versorgen, auftanken. **2.** *v.i.* Brennstoff einnehmen, tanken. **refuelling,** *s.* das Tanken, die Brennstoffaufnahme.
refuge ['refjuːdʒ], **1.** *s.* 1. die Zuflucht, der Schutz (***from,*** vor (*Dat.*)); ***house of –,*** das Obdachlosenasyl; ***seek*** or ***take –,*** Schutz *or* (seine) Zuflucht suchen; 2. die Zufluchtsort, das Asyl, die Schutzstätte; (*Mount.*) – (***hut***), die Schutzhütte; 3. die Verkehrsinsel (*in street*); 4. (*fig.*) Ausflucht, der Ausweg; ***take – in,*** Zuflucht finden zu. **2.** *v.i.* Zuflucht suchen. **3.** *v.t.* (*Poet.*) Zuflucht gewähren (*Dat.*). **refugee** [–'dʒiː], *s.* der Flüchtling.
refulgence [ri'fʌldʒəns], *s.* der Glanz, Schein, das Leuchten, Strahlen. **refulgent,** *adj.* glänzend, leuchtend, strahlend.
refund, 1. [ri'fʌnd], *v.t.* 1. zurückzahlen, rückvergüten, zurückerstatten, ersetzen (*money etc.*) (***to,*** *Dat.*); 2. die Auslagen ersetzen (*Dat.*), schadlos halten (*a p.*). **2.** [–'fʌnd], *v.i.* Geld zurückzahlen, Rückzahlung leisten. **3.** ['riːfʌnd], *s.* die Rückvergütung, Rückerstattung, Rückzahlung, Refundierung.
refundment [ri'fʌndmənt], *s. See* **refund, 3.**
refurbish [riː'fəːbiʃ], *v.t.* wieder auffrischen, renovieren.
refurnish [riː'fəːniʃ], *v.t.* neu möblieren *or* ausstatten.
refusal [ri'fjuːzl], *s.* 1. die (Ver)weigerung; Zurückweisung, Ablehnung, abschlägige Antwort; (*coll.*) die Abweisung (*of a suitor*), Ablehnung, der Korb (*of offer of marriage*); (*Cards*) die Nichtbedienung; ***in case of –,*** im Weigerungsfalle; ***meet with a –,*** eine abschlägige Antwort bekommen, eine Fehlbitte tun; ***take no –,*** sich nicht abweisen lassen; 2. (*Comm.*) die Vorhand, der Vorkauf, das Vorkaufsrecht; ***first – of,*** erstes Anrecht auf (*Acc.*); ***give him the – of,*** ihm an Hand geben; ***have the – of,*** an Hand haben.
[1]**refuse** [ri'fjuːz], **1.** *v.t.* 1. verweigern (*obedience etc.*); – ***him permission,*** ihm die Erlaubnis verweigern; 2. ablehnen, abweisen, zurückweisen; abschlagen (*a request*); ausschlagen (*an offer*); – ***him,*** ihn zurückweisen, ihm eine Bitte abschlagen, ihm eine abschlägige Antwort geben; – ***the suitor,*** seinen Heiratsantrag ablehnen, den Freier abweisen, dem Freier einen Korb geben; – ***the invitation,*** die Einladung ablehnen; – ***the opportunity,*** von der Gelegenheit keinen Gebrauch machen; ***he –d the money,*** er schlug das Geld aus; ***the horse –s the obstacle,*** das Pferd sträubt sich, das Hindernis zu nehmen. **2.** *v.i.* 1. es ablehnen, sich weigern; – ***to help him,*** ihm Hilfe verweigern; ***he –d to accept the money,*** er weigerte sich, das Geld anzunehmen; ***I must accept the invitation, I can't –,*** ich muß der Einladung Folge leisten, ich kann nicht absagen; 2. (*of a horse*) sich sträuben zu springen; 3. (*Cards*) nicht bedienen.
[2]**refuse** ['refjuːs], *s.* der Abfall (*oft. pl.* Abfälle), der *or* das Kehricht, der Müll; *--bin,* der Abfalleimer, die Mülltonne; – ***collector,*** der Müllfahrer, *pl.* Mülleute; ***--consumer, --destructor,*** der Müllverbrennungsofen; – ***disposal,*** die Kehrichtabfuhr.
refutable [ri'fjuːtəbl], *adj.* widerlegbar. **refutal, refutation** [refju'teiʃən], *s.* die Widerlegung. **refute,** *v.t.* widerlegen.
regain [ri'gein], *v.t.* 1. zurückgewinnen, wiedergewinnen, zurückerhalten, wiedererhalten; – ***consciousness,*** das Bewußtsein wiedererlangen; – ***one's footing*** or ***feet,*** wieder festen Fuß fassen; 2. wieder erreichen (*place*).
regal [riːgl], *adj.* 1. königlich, Königs–; 2. (*fig.*) stattlich, prächtig, fürstlich.
regale [ri'geil], **1.** *v.t.* 1. (festlich) bewirten; 2. (*fig.*) erfreuen, ergötzen, erquicken; – ***o.s.,*** sich gütlich tun, sich weiden *or* laben (***with, on,*** an (*Dat.*)). **2.** *v.i.* schmausen (***on,*** von), sich gütlich tun (an (*Dat.*)). **3.** *s.* (*rare*) 1. das Festmahl, der Schmaus; 2. Leckerbissen.
regalia [ri'geiliə], *pl.* 1. (Krönungs)insignien, Regalien (*pl.*); 2. (*fig.*) königliches Hoheitsrecht; 3. (*coll.*) die Festkleidung. **regalism** ['riːgəlizm], *s.* (*Eccl.*) die Oberherrschaft des Königs. **regality** [–'gæliti], *s.* 1. die Königswürde, Königsmacht, Königsherrschaft, Souveränität; 2. das Hoheitsrecht, königliches Privileg.
regard [ri'gɑːd], **1.** *v.t.* 1. ansehen, betrachten; – ***favourably*** or ***with favour,*** mit Wohlgefallen blicken auf (*Acc.*); 2. (*usu. neg.*) (be)achten, Beachtung schenken (*Dat.*), in Betracht ziehen, berücksichtigen, sich kümmern um; 3. (*usu. neg.*) schätzen, (hoch)achten; 4. – ***as,*** ansehen *or* betrachten als, halten für; ***be –ed as,*** gelten für; 5. betreffen, angehen; ***as –s me,*** was mich angeht *or* (an)betrifft. **2.** *s.* 1. der Blick; 2. (*fig.*) Hinblick, Bezug, die Hinsicht, Beziehung (***to,*** auf (*Acc.*)); ***in this –,*** in dieser Hinsicht; ***in*** or ***with – to,*** in Hinsicht *or* Bezug auf (*Acc.*), hinsichtlich, betreffs (*Gen.*), was . . . betrifft; 3. die (Hoch)achtung (***for,*** vor (*Dat.*)), Rücksicht(nahme) (auf (*Acc.*)); Beachtung, Aufmerksamkeit; ***have*** (***no***) – ***for, pay*** (***no***) – ***to,*** (keine) Rücksicht nehmen auf

(*Acc.*), (nicht) berücksichtigen *or* beachten, sich (nicht) kümmern um; ***hold in high –,*** hochachten, hochschätzen; ***stand in high –,*** hoch angeschrieben sein (***with,*** bei); ***with due – to,*** mit gebührender Rücksicht auf (*Acc.*) *or* Berücksichtigung (*Gen.*); ***without – to,*** ohne Rücksicht(nahme) auf (*Acc.*); 4. *pl.* Grüße, Empfehlungen (*pl.*); ***give her my kind –s,*** grüße sie herzlich von mir!

regardant [ri'gɑ:dənt], *adj.* (*Her.*) zurückblickend. **regardful,** *adj.* rücksichtsvoll (*of*, gegen); ***be – of,*** (be)achten, berücksichtigen. **regarding,** *prep.* in Anbetracht, hinsichtlich, betreffs (*Gen.*). **regardless, 1.** *pred. adj.* 1. rücksichtslos (*of*, gegen); 2. unbekümmert, sorglos (*of*, um), ungeachtet (*Gen.*). **2.** *adv.* (*coll.*) ohne Rücksicht auf die Kosten *or* Folgen.

regatta [ri'gætə], *s.* die Regatta.

regency ['ri:dʒənsi], *s.* die Regentschaft(szeit).

regenerate [ri'dʒenəreit], **1.** *v.t.* 1. wiedererzeugen, neu hervorbringen, erneuern; (*Theol.*) ***be –d,*** wiedergeboren werden; 2. (*Tech.*) zurückgewinnen, wiederverwenden, regenerieren. **2.** *v.i.* 1. (*Med.*) sich neu *or* wieder bilden, wieder wachsen, nachwachsen; 2. (*Tech.*) sich regenerieren. **regeneration** [–'reiʃən], *s.* 1. die Wiedererzeugung, Neubildung, Neuschaffung, Neuwerdung; 2. Neubelebung, Erneuerung, Verjüngung; 3. (*Tech.*) Wiedergewinnung, Regenerierung; 4. (*Rad.*) Rückkopplung; 5. (*Theol.*) Wiedergeburt. **regenerative** [–rətiv], *adj.* 1. Erneuerungs–, Verjüngungs–; 2. Verbesserungs–, verbessernd; 3. (*Rad.*) – ***circuit,*** der Rückkopplungskreis; 4. (*Tech.*) – ***furnace,*** der Regenerationsofen, Vorwärmer, die Regenerativfeuerung. **regenerator** [ri'dʒenəreitə], *s. See* ***regenerative furnace.***

regent ['ri:dʒənt], **1.** *s.* 1. der (die) Regent(in), Reichsverweser(in); 2. (*Scots Univ.*) der Studienleiter. **2.** *adj.* herrschend, regierend.

regicidal ['redʒisaidl], *adj.* Königsmord–, königsmörderisch. **regicide,** *s.* 1. der Königsmörder; 2. Königsmord.

régie ['reiʒi:], *s.* das Staatsmonopol, die Regie.

regild [ri:'gild], *v.t.* neu vergolden.

régime [rei'ʒi:m], *s.* 1. die Regierungsform; 2. (*fig.*) herrschendes System, (althergebrachtes) Verfahren.

regimen ['redʒimen], *s.* 1. die Lebensweise, Lebensführung, (*esp.*) Diät, Kost; 2. (*Gram.*) Rektion.

regiment, 1. ['redʒimənt], *s.* 1. (*Mil.*) das Regiment; 2. (*fig.*) die Schar. **2.** [–'ment], *v.t.* 1. in Regimenter einteilen; 2. (*usu. fig.*) organisieren, kontrollieren, disziplinieren, reglementieren. **regimental** [–'mentl], *adj.* Regiments–; – ***aid post,*** der Truppenverbandplatz; – ***hospital,*** das Feldlazarett; – ***officer,*** der Truppenoffizier. **regimentals,** *pl.* die (Regiments)uniform. **regimentation** [–men'teiʃən], *s.* (*fig.*) die Organisierung, Disziplinierung, Kontrolle, Reglementierung.

region ['ri:dʒən], *s.* 1. das Gebiet, die Gegend, Region, der Landstrich; (Körper)teil, die Gegend (*of the body*); ***the upper –s,*** die höheren Regionen; ***the lower –s,*** die Unterwelt, das Totenreich; ***upper –s of the atmosphere,*** obere Luftschichten; ***abdominal –,*** die Bauchgegend; 2. (*fig.*) der Bereich; ***in the – of,*** von ungefähr. **regional,** *adj.* örtlich, regional, Orts–; lokal, räumlich begrenzt; – ***geography,*** spezielle Länderkunde; – ***government,*** die Bezirksregierung. **regionalism,** *s.* der Landschaftspatriotismus.

register ['redʒistə], **1.** *s.* 1. das Verzeichnis, Register; (*Scots Law*) Grundbuch; (*Naut.*) Schiffsregister, der Registerbrief; – ***of births, deaths and marriages,*** das Standesamtregister, Personenstandsregister; – ***of electors,*** die Wählerliste; ***hotel –,*** das Fremdenbuch; ***parish –,*** das Kirchenbuch; ***University Register,*** die Universitätsmatrikel; 2. der Schieber, die Klappe, das Ventil (*of a boiler*); 3. Register (*of an organ*); (*Mus.*) der Stimmumfang, die Tonlage; 4. (*Tech.*) genaue Einstellung, die Deckung, der Rapport; 5. Registrierapparat; ***cash-–,*** die Registrierkasse, Kontrollkasse. **2.** *v.t.* 1. eintragen, einschreiben, buchen, registrieren; 2. einschreiben (lassen) (*letters*), gesetzlich schützen (lassen) (*a patent*), aufgeben (*luggage*); 3. (*Tech.*) registrieren, automatisch anzeigen, verzeichnen; 4. (*fig.*) sich (*Dat.*) einprägen (*in one's memory*), zur Schau tragen, ausdrücken (*feelings etc.*). **3.** *v.i.* 1. sich eintragen (lassen), sich anmelden; 2. (*Tech.*) Register halten, im Register sein; 3. (*fig.*) einen Eindruck machen (*on a p.*); reagieren (*of a p.*).

registered ['redʒistəd], *adj.* eingetragen (*company*), eingeschrieben (*letter*), (*Comm.*) patentiert, gesetzlich geschützt; (*St. Exch.*) Namens–; – ***design,*** das Gebrauchsmuster; (*Hist.*) – ***mark,*** die Registermark (*currency*); – ***nurse,*** staatlich geprüfte Krankenschwester. **registering** [–t(ə)riŋ], *adj.* Registrier–.

registrar ['redʒistrɑ:], *s.* der Registrator, Archivar, Urkundsbeamte(r), (*esp.*) Standesbeamte(r); –***-general,*** der Leiter des Statistischen Amts; ***–'s office,*** das Standesamt, die Registratur.

registration [redʒis'treiʃən], *s.* die Eintragung, Einschreibung, Anmeldung, Registrierung; das Einschreiben (*of a letter*); ***compulsory –,*** die (An)meldepflicht; – ***of luggage,*** die Gepäckaufgabe; – ***fee,*** die Anmeldegebühr, Vormerkungsgebühr, (*of post*) Einschreibegebühr; – ***form,*** das Anmeldeformular, der Meldezettel.

registry ['redʒistri], *s.* 1. die Registrierung, Eintragung; ***port of –,*** der Registerhafen; 2. die Registratur, das Standesamt; – ***office,*** das Standesamt; ***married at a – office,*** standesamtlich getraut; 3. der Arbeitsnachweis, das Stellenvermittlungsbüro.

Regius ['ri:dʒiəs], *adj.* königlich; – ***Professor,*** durch königliches Patent ernannter Professor.

reglet ['reglit], *s.* (*Typ.*) der Zeilendurchschuß, die Reglette.

regnal ['regnəl], *adj.* Regierungs–; – ***day,*** der Regierungsantrittstag. **regnant,** *adj.* regierend; (*fig.*) (vor)herrschend.

regorge [ri:'gɔ:dʒ], **1.** *v.t.* (wieder) ausspeien. **2.** *v.i.* zurückströmen.

regress, 1. [ri'gres], *v.i.* (*Astr.*) zurückkehren (*also fig.*). **2.** ['ri:gres], *s.* 1. das Zurückkommen, Zurückgehen; die Rückkehr; 2. (*fig.*) der Rückschritt, Rückgang, Rückfall, Rückschlag. **regression** [ri'greʃən], *s.* 1. *See* **regress, 2**; 2. (*Math., Psych.*) die Regression; 3. (*Biol.*) Rückbildung, Involution. **regressive** [ri'gresiv], *adj.* 1. rückläufig; 2. rückgängig, rückwirkend, regressiv.

regret [ri'gret], **1.** *s.* das Bedauern, die Reue (*for*, über (*Acc.*)), Trauer, der Schmerz, Kummer (*at doing*, darum daß man tut); ***have no –s,*** keine Reue empfinden; ***to my –,*** zu meinem Bedauern; ***with many –s,*** mit dem Ausdruck tief(st)en Bedauerns. **2.** *v.t.* bereuen, bedauern, beklagen, mit Bedauern denken an (*Acc.*), trauern um; ***I – I cannot come, I – not being able to come,*** ich bedauere nicht kommen zu können; ***I – to say,*** es tut mir leid sagen zu müssen, leider muß ich feststellen; ***it is to be regretted,*** es ist bedauerlich *or* zu beklagen. **regretful,** *adj.* bedauernd, reuevoll. **regretfully,** *adv.* mit Bedauern. **regrettable,** *adj.* bedauerlich, bedauernswert, zu bedauern(d). **regrettably,** *adv.* bedauerlicherweise.

regroup [ri:'gru:p], *v.t.* umgruppieren, neu gruppieren, umschichten.

regulable ['regjuləbl], *adj.* regulierbar, einstellbar.

regular ['regjulə], **1.** *adj.* 1. regelmäßig, gleichmäßig, ebenmäßig; ***at – intervals,*** in regelmäßigen Abständen; – ***service,*** fahrplanmäßiger Verkehr; 2. gewohnheitsmäßig, gewohnt, gewöhnlich, normal, regelmäßig (wiederkehrend), regulär; – ***course of events,*** normaler Verlauf *or* Ablauf der Ereignisse; – ***customer,*** der Stammkunde, (*at inn*) Stammgast; – ***habits,*** geordnete Lebensweise; 3. regelrecht, ordentlich, geordnet, richtig, den Regeln gemäß, der Regel entsprechend, ordnungsgemäß, vorschriftsgemäß, satzungsgemäß, rechtmäßig, rechtsgültig; 4. gelernt; – ***doctor,*** der Hausarzt; 5. (*Mil.*) regulär; – ***army,*** stehendes *or* aktives Heer, das Berufsheer; – ***soldier,*** aktiver Soldat; 6. (*Eccl.*) – ***clergy,*** die Ordensgeistlichkeit; 7. (*Math.*) regulär; 8. (*Gram.*) regelmäßig; 9. genau, pünktlich; (*as*) – ***as clockwork,*** pünktlich wie eine Uhr; 10. (*coll.*) wirklich, ordentlich, richtig(gehend), tüchtig, förmlich. **2.** *s.* 1. Ordensgeistliche(r); 2. aktiver Soldat, der Berufsoldat; *pl.* reguläre Truppen; 3. (*coll.*) *see* – ***customer.***

regularity [regju'læriti], *s.* 1. die Regelmäßigkeit, Gleichmäßigkeit; 2. Richtigkeit, Ordnung, regelmäßige Form; ***for the sake of*** –, ordnungshalber. **regularize** ['regjuləraiz], *v.t.* regeln, gesetzlich festlegen.

regulate ['regjuleit], *v.t.* 1. regeln, ordnen, einrichten; 2. regulieren, (ein)stellen (*clocks etc.*). **regulating,** *adj.* 1. regelnd, regulierend; 2. (*esp. Tech.*) Regulier–, (Ein)stell–; – ***screw,*** die Stellschraube. **regulation** [–'leiʃən], **1.** *s.* 1. die Regulierung, Regelung, Einstellung; 2. Verordnung, Anordnung, Bestimmung, Verfügung, Vorschrift; *pl.* die Ordnung, Satzungen (*pl.*), Statuten (*pl.*); ***according to –s,*** vorschriftsmäßig; ***contrary to –s,*** vorschriftswidrig; (*Mil.*) ***Queen's Regulations,*** die Dienstvorschrift, (*coll.*) Nullacht-fünfzehn. **2.** *attrib. adj.* 1. vorgeschrieben, vorschriftsmäßig; (*Mil.*) Dienst–, Kommiß–. **regulative** [–lətiv], *adj.* ordnend, regulierend, regelnd, regulativ. **regulator,** *s.* 1. der (Selbst)-regler, Regulator, die Reguliervorrichtung, Steuerung, (*of clock*) der Rucker; 2. (*obs.*) Wanduhr.

regulus ['regjuləs], *s.* 1. (*Chem.*) der Regulus, Metallkönig; 2. (*Orn.*) das Goldhähnchen.

regurgitate [ri'gə:dʒiteit], **1.** *v.t.* wieder ausstoßen *or* von sich geben; ***be –d,*** wieder hochkommen (*food*). **2.** *v.i.* zurückfließen. **regurgitation** [–'teiʃən], *s.* das Erbrechen.

rehabilitate [ri:hə'biliteit], *v.t.* 1. (*a p.*) wieder einsetzen, rehabilitieren (***in,*** in (*Acc.*)), wieder zu Ehren bringen; 2. (*a th.*) wiederherstellen. **rehabilitation** [–'teiʃən], *s.* 1. (*of a p.*) die Wiedereinsetzung, Rehabilitierung; Wiederherstellung der Ehre, Ehrenrettung; – ***centre,*** die Umschulungswerkstätte; 2. (*of a th.*) die Wiederherstellung.

rehash, **1.** [ri:'hæʃ], *v.t.* (*fig.*) aufwärmen, wieder aufbringen. **2.** ['ri:hæʃ], *s.* 1. das Wiederaufwärmen (*of old ideas*); 2. aufgewärmter Brei.

rehear [ri:'hiə], *irr.v.t.* (*Law*) erneut untersuchen *or* verhandeln. **rehearing,** *s.* erneute Verhandlung.

rehearsal [ri'hə:sl], *s.* 1. das Hersagen, die Aufzählung, Wiederholung; 2. (*Mus., Theat.*) Probe, Einstudierung, Einübung; ***at*** –, bei der Probe, beim Proben; ***be in*** –, einstudiert werden, in Vorbereitung sein (*of a play*); ***dress*** –, die Hauptprobe; ***full*** –, die Generalprobe. **rehearse,** **1.** *v.t.* 1. wiederholen, hersagen, proben, aufzählen; 2. proben, einstudieren, einüben. **2.** *v.i.* Probe abhalten.

reheat [ri:'hi:t], *v.t.* aufwärmen.

rehouse [ri:'hauz], *v.t.* in einer neuen Wohnung unterbringen. **rehousing,** *s.* die Umsiedlung; – ***programme,*** das Umsiedlungsprogramm.

reign [rein], **1.** *v.i.* 1. herrschen, Herrscher sein (***over,*** über (*Acc.*)); 2. (*fig.*) (vor)herrschen. **2.** *s.* 1. die Herrschaft (*also fig.*), Regierung(szeit); ***in the – of,*** unter der Regierung von; 2. (*fig.*) das Regiment; ***Reign of Terror,*** die Schreckensherrschaft.

reimburse [ri:im'bə:s], *v.t.* 1. zurückerstatten, vergüten, zurückzahlen (*money*); 2. entschädigen (*a p.*); ***be –d for one's expenses,*** seine Auslagen decken; – ***o.s.,*** sich schadlos halten. **reimbursement,** *s.* 1. die (Wieder)erstattung, Vergütung, Zurückzahlung; 2. Entschädigung, Deckung von Auslagen, der Rembours.

reimport, **1.** [ri:im'pɔ:t], *v.t.* wieder einführen. **2.** [–'impɔ:t], *s.* 1. die Wiedereinfuhr; 2. (*usu. pl.*) wieder eingeführte Ware.

rein [rein], **1.** *s.* der Zügel, Zaum (*also fig.*); ***assume the –s of government,*** die Zügel der Regierung ergreifen; ***draw*** –, anhalten; ***give a horse the –(s),*** dem Pferd die Zügel geben; (*fig.*) ***give*** –, die Zügel schießen lassen, freien Lauf lassen (***to,*** *Dat.*); ***keep a tight – on,*** straff im Zügel halten. **2.** *v.t.* (*also* – ***in***) zügeln, im Zaume halten (*also fig.*).

reincarnate, **1.** [ri:in'kɑ:neit], *v.t.* wieder fleischliche Gestalt geben (*Dat.*). **2.** [–eit], *v.i.* wieder Fleisch werden. **3.** [–it], *adj.* wiedergeboren. **reincarnation** [–'neiʃən], *s.* die Wiederverkörperung, Wiedergeburt.

reindeer ['reindiə], *s.* das Renntier.

reinforce [ri:in'fɔ:s], **1.** *v.t.* 1. verstärken; ***–d concrete,*** der Eisenbeton; ***–d seam,*** die Wulstnaht; 2. (*fig.*) stärken, (be)kräftigen. **2.** *s.* (*Tech.*) die Verstärkung. **reinforcement,** *s.* 1. die Verstärkung; 2. (*fig.*) Bekräftigung; 3. *pl.* (*Mil.*) Verstärkungen (*pl.*), der Nachschub.

reins [reinz], *pl.* (*B.*) Nieren (*pl.*).

reinstall [ri:in'stɔ:l], *v.t.* wiedereinsetzen. **reinstalment,** *s.* die Wiedereinsetzung.

reinstate [ri:in'steit], *v.t.* 1. wiedereinsetzen (*a p.*); 2. wiederherstellen (*a th.*). **reinstatement,** *s.* 1. die Wiedereinsetzung; 2. Wiederherstellung.

reinsurance [ri:in'ʃuərəns], *s.* die Rückversicherung. **reinsure,** *v.t.* rückversichern.

reinvest [ri:in'vest], *v.t.* 1. wiedereinsetzen (*a p.*) (*in,* in (*Acc.*)); 2. wieder bekleiden (*a p.*) (***with,*** mit); 3. wieder anlegen (*money*). **reinvestiture** [–itʃə], *s.* die Wiedereinführung, Wiedereinsetzung. **reinvestment,** *s.* die Wiederanlegung, Neuanlage (*of money*).

reinvigorate [ri:in'vigəreit], *v.t.* von neuem stärken *or* kräftigen.

reissue [ri:'iʃu:], **1.** *v.t.* 1. wieder ausgeben; 2. neu herausgeben (*books*). **2.** *s.* 1. die Neuausgabe; 2. (*of book*) unveränderte Neuausgabe, neue Auflage.

reiterate [ri:'itəreit], *v.t.* ständig wiederholen. **reiteration** [–'reiʃən], *s.* ständige Wiederholung. **reiterative** [–rətiv], *adj.* ständig wiederholend.

reject, **1.** [ri'dʒekt], *v.t.* 1. ablehnen, ausschlagen, nicht annehmen; 2. zurückweisen, nicht anerkennen, verwerfen; 3. abweisen (*a p.*); verschmähen (*a suitor*); 4. wieder von sich geben (*of the stomach*). **2.** ['ri:dʒekt], *s.* (*Comm.*) (*oft. pl.*) die Ausschußware. **rejection** [ri'dʒekʃən], *s.* 1. die Ablehnung, Zurückweisung, Verwerfung, Abweisung; 2. (*Med.*) Abstoßung, Abwerfung; 3. *pl.* Exkremente (*pl.*). **rejector circuit,** *s.* der Drosselkreis.

rejoice [ri'dʒɔis], **1.** *v.t.* Freude machen (*Dat.*), erfreuen; ***be –d,*** sich freuen, erfreut sein (***by, at,*** über (*Acc.*)). **2.** *v.i.* sich freuen (***at, in,*** über (*Acc.*)); – ***in,*** sich erfreuen (*Gen.*), zum Glück besitzen (*a th.*). **rejoicing,** **1.** *adj.* erfreut, froh. **2.** *s.* 1. die Freude, das Vergnügen (***over,*** über (*Acc.*)); 2. *pl.* das Frohlocken, die Lustbarkeit(en), Freudenbezeigungen (*pl.*).

[1]**rejoin** [ri:'dʒɔin], **1.** *v.t.* 1. wieder zusammenfügen; 2. sich wieder anschließen (*Dat.*) *or* an (*Acc.*), sich wieder vereinigen mit, wieder zurückkehren zu. **2.** *v.i.* wieder zusammenkommen, sich wieder vereinigen.

[2]**rejoin** [ri'dʒɔin], *v.i.* (*usu. Law*) erwidern, antworten, entgegnen. **rejoinder,** *s.* (*Law*) die Erwiderung; Duplik.

rejuvenate [ri'dʒu:vəneit], *v.t.* (*v.i.*) (sich) verjüngen. **rejuvenation** [–'neiʃən], *s.* die Verjüngung.

rejuvenesce [ridʒu:və'nes], *v.i.* (*esp. Biol.*) *see* **rejuvenate. rejuvenescence,** *s.* (*esp. Biol.*) *see* **rejuvenation. rejuvenescent,** *adj.* (sich) verjüngend.

rejuvenize [ri'dʒu:vənaiz], *v.t.* verjüngen.

rekindle [ri:'kindl], **1.** *v.t.* 1. wieder anzünden; 2. (*fig.*) neu beleben, wieder entzünden *or* entflammen. **2.** *v.i.* 1. sich wieder entzünden; 2. (*fig.*) wieder aufleben.

relapse [ri'læps], **1.** *v.i.* 1. zurückfallen, wieder fallen; (*fig.*) wieder verfallen (***into,*** in (*Acc.*)), rückfällig werden; 2. (*Med.*) einen Rückfall bekommen. **2.** *s.* der Rückfall, das Zurückfallen.

relate [ri'leit], **1.** *v.t.* 1. berichten, erzählen (***to,***

Dat.); 2. in Beziehung *or* Verbindung *or* Zusammenhang bringen, verbinden, verknüpfen (*with, to,* mit); Beziehung herstellen zwischen (*Dat.*). **2.** *v.i.* sich beziehen, Bezug haben (*to,* auf (*Acc.*)); in Bezug *or* Beziehung *or* Verbindung stehen (*to,* zu); *relating to,* mit Beziehung *or* in *or* mit Bezug auf (*Acc.*). **related,** *adj.* 1. erzählt, berichtet; 2. verwandt; – *by blood,* blutsverwandt; – *by marriage,* verschwägert; 3. verknüpft, verbunden (*to,* mit), in Beziehung zueinander stehend.

relation [ri'leiʃən], *s.* 1. die Erzählung, der Bericht; 2. Zusammenhang, die Beziehung, das Verhältnis (*to,* zu), die Verbindung, Verknüpfung, Bezugnahme (*with,* mit); *in – to,* in bezug auf (*Acc.*); *have – to,* in Zusammenhang *or* Beziehung stehen zu, Bezug nehmen *or* sich beziehen auf (*Acc.*); (*Law*) *have –,* rückwirkend gelten *or* gültig sein, rückwirkende Kraft haben (*to,* von); *be out of – to,* in keinem Zusammenhang *or* Verhältnis *or* in keiner Beziehung stehen zu; 3. (Bluts)verwandte(r); *what – is he to you?* wie ist er mit dir verwandt? 4. *pl.* die Verbindung, Beziehungen (*pl.*) (*with,* mit *or* zu). **relationship,** *s.* die Verwandtschaft (*also fig.*), das (Verwandtschafts)verhältnis (*to,* mit), (*fig.*) Verhältnis, die Beziehung (zu); *degree of –,* der Verwandtschaftsgrad.

relative ['relətiv], **1.** *adj.* relativ (*also Gram.*), verhältnismäßig; sich beziehend, bezüglich (*to,* auf (*Acc.*)); im Verhältnis stehend (*to,* zu), abhängig (von), bedingt (durch); (*Gram.*) – *clause,* der Relativsatz; (*Mus.*) – *key,* die Paralleltonart; (*Math.*) – *number,* die Verhältniszahl; – *position,* das Lageverhältnis; – *pronoun,* das Relativpronomen, bezügliches Fürwort. **2.** *s.* Verwandte(r). **3.** *adv.* – *to,* bezüglich, betreffs, wegen (*Gen.*). **relativism,** *s.* der Relativismus. **relativity** [–'tiviti], *s.* 1. die Relativität; *theory of –,* die Relativitätstheorie; 2. die Bedingtheit (*to,* durch), Abhängigkeit (von).

relax [ri'læks], **1.** *v.t.* 1. entspannen; 2. entleeren, öffnen (*bowls*); 3. (*usu. fig.*) lockern, mildern, mäßigen, herabsetzen; – *one's efforts,* in seinen Bemühungen nachlassen. **2.** *v.i.* 1. sich lockern; 2. (*Med.*) erschlaffen; 3. (*usu. fig.*) sich entspannen, auspannen, (aus)ruhen; 4. nachlassen (*in,* in (*Dat.*)), mäßiger *or* milder werden. **relaxation** [ri:læk'seiʃən], *s.* 1. die Lockerung; 2. (*Med.*) Erschlaffung; 3. (*usu. fig.*) Entspannung, Ausspannung, Zerstreuung, Ablenkung, Erholung; 4. das Nachlassen, die Milderung, Erleichterung. **relaxed** [–t], *adj.* 1. entspannt, schlaff; 2. (*fig.*) zwanglos, gelöst. **relaxing,** *adj.* erschlaffend, weich, Schon– (*climate etc.*).

relay, 1. ['ri:lei], *s.* 1. frischer Vorspann, der Pferdewechsel, Ersatzpferde (*pl.*); das Relais, der Umspannort, Ort des Pferdewechsels; 2. die Ablösung(smannschaft); *in –s,* im rollenden Einsatz, von Etappe zu Etappe; 3. (*Spt.*) die Stafette, Staffel, Teilstrecke; – *race,* der Staffellauf, Stafettenlauf; 4. (*Elec.*) das Relais; (*Tech.*) Hilfstriebwerk, der Hilfsmotor; 5. (*Rad.*) die Übertragung. **2.** [ri'lei], *v.t.* 1. ablösen; 2. (*Rad.*) übertragen. **3.** ['ri:lei], *adj.* (*Tech.*) Hilfs–, zwischen–, Relais–.

re-lay [ri:'lei], *irr.v.t.* umlegen, neu legen (*a pavement etc.*).

release [ri'li:s], **1.** *v.t.* 1. loslassen, losgehen lassen, fallen lassen; – *bombs,* Bomben abwerfen; 2. entlassen, freilassen, auf freien Fuß setzen (*prisoner*); 3. (*fig.*) befreien, erlösen (*from,* von); entheben (*from, Gen.*), entbinden (von *or Gen.*); – *him from his promise,* ihm sein Wort zurückgeben; 4. freigeben (*to the public*); 5. (*Law*) aufgeben, verzichten auf (*Acc.*) (*a right*), erlassen, löschen (*a debt*), übertragen, überlassen (*property*) (*to, Dat.*); 6. (*Chem.*) freisetzen; 7. (*Tech.*) auslösen, ausrücken, ausschalten. **2.** *s.* 1. die Entlassung, Freilassung (*from,* aus); 2. Befreiung, Erlösung (*from,* von); Entlastung, Entbindung, Freistellung (von); 3. (*Law*) Aufgabe, Preisgabe (*of, Gen.*), Verzichtleistung, der Verzicht (auf (*Acc.*)); 4. die (Rechts)übertragung, Löschung; 5. Quittung, Verzichturkunde, der Erledigungsschein; 6. die Freigabe (*of films, goods etc.*); 7. (*Tech.*) Auslösung, Ausklinkung; Auslöseklinke, der Auslöser. **releasement,** *s.* (*Law*) die Befreiung, Entbindung, Erlösung (*from,* von).

relegate ['religeit], *v.t.* 1. (*a p.*) verweisen (*to,* an (*Acc.*)), verbannen, relegieren; 2. (*a th.*) verweisen (*to,* in (*Acc.*)), verdrängen, abschieben; 3. überweisen (*to,* an (*Acc.*)), übertragen, zuweisen (*Dat.*). **relegation** [–'geiʃən], *s.* 1. die Verbannung, Verweisung (*to,* nach), Überweisung (an (*Acc.*)); 2. (*Footb.*) der Abstieg.

relent [ri'lent], *v.i.* sich erweichen lassen, nachgiebig *or* weich *or* mitleidig werden, sich erbarmen. **relenting,** *adj.* nachgiebig, mitleidig, mitleidsvoll. **relentless,** *adj.* unnachgiebig, unbarmherzig, unnachsichtig, schonungslos, hart(näckig). **relentlessness,** *s.* die Unnachgiebigkeit, Unbarmherzigkeit.

relevance, relevancy ['relivəns(i)], *s.* 1. die Erheblichkeit, Wichtigkeit, Bedeutung (*to,* für); 2. Angemessenheit. **relevant,** *adj.* erheblich, wichtig (*to,* für), sachdienlich, entsprechend (*Dat.*), anwendbar (auf (*Acc.*)), gehörig (zu), einschlägig; *be – to,* sich beziehen auf (*Acc.*).

reliability [rilaiə'biliti], *s.* die Zuverlässigkeit, Verläßlichkeit; – *trial,* die Erprobungsfahrt. **reliable** [–'laiəbl], *adj.* 1. zuverlässig, verläßlich; 2. glaubwürdig, vertrauenswürdig; – *authority,* der Gewährsmann, zuverlässige Quelle; – *firm,* reelle Firma; – *witness,* glaubwürdiger Zeuge.

reliance [ri'laiəns], *s.* das Vertrauen, die Zuversicht; *in – on,* unter Verlaß auf (*Acc.*); *have – in,* vertrauen auf (*Acc.*), Vertrauen haben zu; *place – on,* Vertrauen setzen in (*Acc.*). **reliant,** *adj.* vertrauensvoll, zuversichtlich; *be – on,* sich verlassen auf (*Acc.*); *self-–,* voll Selbstvertrauen, selbstvertrauend.

relic ['relik], *s.* 1. die Reliquie (*of a saint etc.*); 2. das Andenken, Gedenkstück; 3. letzter Rest, letzte Spur; *pl.* Überreste (*of a p. or th.*), Überbleibsel (*of a th.*); *–s of the past,* Zeugen der Vergangenheit.

relict ['relikt], *s.* (*rare*) die Hinterbliebene, Witwe.

[1]**relief** [ri'li:f], *s.* 1. die Erleichterung, Entlastung, Befreiung (*from,* von), Linderung; – *train,* der Entlastungszug, Hilfszug, außerfahrplanmäßiger Zug; *–-work,* die Notstandsarbeit, das Hilfswerk; *–-worker,* der Ersatzarbeiter, Hilfsarbeiter; *income-tax –,* die Steuerbegünstigung; 2. (*Hist.*) die Armenunterstützung; – *fund,* der Unterstützungsfonds, Hilfsfonds; 3. die Wohltat, der Trost; 4. (*Law*) Erlaß, die Abhilfe; 5. Erholung, Entspannung, angenehme Abwechslung; 6. die Ablösung (*of a sentry*); der Entsatz (*of a town etc.*); – *column,* Hilfstruppen (*pl.*), der Entsatz.

[2]**relief,** *s.* 1. erhabene Arbeit, (*also Geog.*) das Relief; – *map,* die Hochbildkarte, Reliefkarte; *throw into –,* hervortreten lassen, hervorheben; *stand out in bold –,* sich scharf abheben, deutlich hervortreten.

relieve [ri'li:v], *v.t.* 1. erleichtern, mildern, lindern, abschwächen, abhelfen (*Dat.*); – *one's feelings,* seinen Gefühlen Luft machen; – *nature* or *o.s.,* seine Notdurft *or* sein Bedürfnis verrichten; (*Archit.*) *relieving arch,* der Entlastungsbogen; 2. helfen (*Dat.*), unterstützen (*the poor*); *relieving officer,* der Armenpfleger; 3. ablösen (*sentry*); entsetzen (*a town*); 4. entlasten, entbinden, befreien (*of,* von), entheben (*Gen.*), (*coll.*) erleichtern (um); 5. (*fig.*) beleben, angenehm unterbrechen; – *the monotony,* die Eintönigkeit beleben *or* angenehm unterbrechen, Abwechslung bringen (*of,* in (*Acc.*)); 6. beruhigen, trösten; *I am –d to hear,* es beruhigt mich zu hören.

relievo [ri'li:vou], *s.* das Relief, die Reliefarbeit, erhabene Arbeit.

religion [ri'lidʒən], *s.* 1. die Religion; 2. (*fig.*) fromme Pflicht, heiliger Grundsatz. **religionist,** *s.* religiöser Schwärmer *or* Eiferer. **religiosity** [–i'ɔsiti], *s.* die Religiosität, Frömmelei. **religious** [–dʒəs], *adj.* 1. religiös, fromm, gottesfürchtig; – *house,* das Ordenshaus; – *orders,* geistliche Orden; – ***service,*** der Gottesdienst; – ***wars,*** Religionskriege (*pl.*); 2. (*fig.*) gewissenhaft, peinlich, streng; 3. (*fig.*) – ***silence,*** andächtiges Stillschweigen.

relinquish [ri'liŋkwiʃ], *v.t.* 1. loslassen, fahren *or* fallen lassen; 2. abstehen von, verzichten auf (*Acc.*), aufgeben; 3. abtreten, preisgeben, überlassen (***to,*** *Dat.*). **relinquishment,** *s.* die Aufgabe, Preisgabe (***of,*** *Gen.*), der Verzicht (auf (*Acc.*)).

reliquary ['relikwəri], *s.* das Reliquienkästchen.

relish ['reliʃ], **1.** *s.* 1. der (Wohl)geschmack; ***have no –,*** nicht schmecken; (*fig.*) ***lose its –,*** seinen Reiz verlieren; 2. das Gefallen, Vergnügen, der Genuß (***for,*** an (*Dat.*)), die Neigung (zu), Vorliebe (für); ***have no – for,*** keinen Geschmack *or* kein Gefallen finden an (*Dat.*), keine Neigung haben zu; ***eat with –,*** mit Appetit essen, es sich (*Dat.*) schmecken lassen; 3. pikante Beigabe, die Würze, der Appetithappen, Appetitanreger; 4. (*fig.*) Beigeschmack, Anstrich, Anflug (***of,*** von). **2.** *v.t.* (mit Appetit) genießen, Geschmack *or* Gefallen finden an (*Dat.*); gern haben, sich erfreuen an (*Dat.*); ***do you – your dinner?*** schmeckt *or* mundet dir das Mittagessen? (*fig.*) ***I do not – the idea,*** der Gedanke paßt mir gar nicht *or* sagt mir nicht zu.

relive [ri:'liv], *v.t.* noch einmal erleben *or* durchleben.

reload [ri:'loud], *v.t., v.i.* wieder laden (*a gun*), umladen (*goods*).

reluctance [ri'lʌktəns], *s.* 1. die Abneigung, das Widerstreben, der Widerwille (***to,*** gegen); ***with –,*** ungern, widerstrebend; ***show –,*** wenig geneigt sein; 2. (*Elec.*) magnetischer Widerstand. **reluctant** [–ənt], *adj.* widerwillig, widerstrebend, abgeneigt; ***he is – to do it,*** er tut das ungern *or* zögernd; es widerstrebt ihm, das zu tun. **reluctantly,** *adv.* ungern, widerwillig, wider Willen, mit Widerwillen.

rely [ri'lai], *v.i.* sich verlassen, vertrauen, bauen, zählen ((***up***)***on,*** auf (*Acc.*)), rechnen (mit); sich stützen *or* berufen (auf (*Acc.*)), sich anlehnen (an (*Acc.*)); ***have to – on,*** angewiesen sein auf (*Acc.*).

remain [ri'mein], *v.i.* zurückbleiben, (übrig)bleiben, noch vorhanden *or* übrig(geblieben) sein; verbleiben (*in letters*); ***he –s himself,*** er bleibt derselbe; – ***of the opinion,*** (bei) der Meinung bleiben; ***it –s to be proved,*** es bedarf noch des Beweises, es muß noch bewiesen werden; ***little –s to be done,*** es bleibt nur wenig zu tun; ***it –s to be seen,*** es bleibt abzuwarten; ***it –s to be told,*** es muß noch berichtet werden; ***nothing –s to me but,*** nichts bleibt mir übrig als; – ***in existence,*** weiter bestehen, bestehen bleiben; – ***in force,*** in Kraft bleiben; – ***standing,*** stehenbleiben.

remainder [ri'meində], **1.** *s.* 1. der Rest (*also Arith.*); (*coll.*) ***the –,*** das übrige, alles andere, die übrigen *or* anderen; 2. (*Tech.*) der Rückstand; Übriggebliebene, Überreste (*pl.*); 3. (*Comm.*) der Restbetrag; Restbestand, (*books*) Remittenden (*pl.*), die Restauflage; 4. (*Law*) das Anfallsrecht, Nacherbenrecht, die Anwartschaft. **2.** *v.t.* billig abstoßen (*books*).

remaining [ri'meiniŋ], *adj.* übrig(geblieben); Rest–; ***have –,*** übrig haben; – ***stock,*** der Restbestand; ***the –,*** die übrigen. **remains** [–z], *pl.* 1. Überbleibsel, (Über)reste (*pl.*); 2. (*Tech.*) Rückstände (*pl.*); 3. (*of a p.*) irdische Überreste; (*fig.*) letzte Reste (*pl.*); 4. ***literary –,*** hinterlassene Werke (*pl.*), literarischer Nachlaß.

remake, 1. [ri:'meik], *irr.v.t.* wieder machen, erneuern. **2.** ['ri:meik], *s.* (*film*) die Neuverfilmung.

remand [ri'mɑ:nd], **1.** *v.t.* (*also* – ***in custody***) in Untersuchungshaft zurücksenden. **2.** *s.* (die Zurücksendung in) die Untersuchungshaft; ***appear on –,*** aus der Untersuchungshaft vorgeführt werden; ***prisoner on –,*** Untersuchungsgefangene(r). **remand home,** *s.* die Vollzugsanstalt für Jugendarrest.

remanence ['remənəns], *s.* (*Elec.*) die Remanenz.

remark [ri'mɑ:k], **1.** *s.* die Bemerkung, Äußerung; ***excite –,*** Aufmerksamkeit erregen; ***without –,*** kommentarlos, stillschweigend; ***worthy of –,*** beachtenswert, bemerkenswert. **2.** *v.t.* 1. (be)merken, vermerken, gewahr werden (*Gen.*); 2. sagen, bemerken (***that,*** daß). **3.** *v.i.* sich äußern, Bemerkungen machen ((***up***)***on,*** über (*Acc.*) *or* zu); – ***on,*** erwähnen.

remarkable [ri'mɑ:kəbl], *adj.* 1. bemerkenswert, beachtlich, merkwürdig (***for,*** wegen); 2. einzigartig, auffallend, außerordentlich, erstaunlich. **remarkableness,** *s.* die Merkwürdigkeit, Erstaunlichkeit, Ungewöhnlichkeit.

remarriage [ri:'mæridʒ], *s.* die Wiederverheiratung. **remarry, 1.** *v.i.* wieder heiraten, sich wieder verheiraten. **2.** *v.t.* wieder verheiraten (***to,*** mit).

remediable [ri'mi:diəbl], *adj.* abstellbar; heilbar; ***it is –,*** dem ist abzuhelfen. **remedial,** *adj.* 1. heilend, heilsam, Heil–; – ***gymnastics,*** die Heilgymnastik; 2. abhelfend, Abhilfs–; – ***measures,*** Abhilfsmaßnahmen (*pl.*).

remediless ['remidilis], *adj.* 1. unheilbar, unabwendbar; 2. hilflos, machtlos.

remedy ['remidi], **1.** *s.* 1. das (Heil)mittel, die Arznei (***for, against,*** gegen); 2. das Hilfsmittel, Gegenmittel; (*Law*) das Rechtsmittel, der Rechtsbehelf; – ***of abuses,*** das Beheben von Mißbräuchen. **2.** *v.t.* 1. abhelfen (*Dat.*), beheben, abstellen; 2. berichtigen, verbessern (*a mistake*).

remember [ri'membə], **1.** *v.t.* 1. sich erinnern an (*Acc.*), sich besinnen auf (*Acc.*), sich entsinnen (*Gen.*), sich (*Dat.*) ins Gedächtnis zurückrufen; ***I – seeing*** or ***having seen him,*** ich erinnere mich, ihn gesehen zu haben; 2. im Gedächtnis behalten, sich (*Dat.*) merken *or* vor Augen halten; ***I shall always – him for his kindness,*** ich werde ihn wegen seiner Freundlichkeit immer im Gedächtnis behalten; ***history will – him as the man who . . .,*** er wird in die Geschichte als derjenige eingehen, der . . .; – ***to go,*** vergiß nicht zu gehen; 3. denken an (*Acc.*), gedenken (*Gen.*); 4. etwas vermachen (*Dat.*), bedenken (*a p. in one's will*); 5. empfehlen, grüßen; – ***me to your sister,*** mit einer Empfehlung an deine Schwester! empfiehl mich deiner Schwester! grüße deine Schwester von mir! ***she wishes to be –ed to you,*** sie läßt dich grüßen; 6. – ***o.s.,*** sich (auf sich selbst) besinnen. **2.** *v.i.* sich erinnern *or* entsinnen.

remembrance [ri'membrəns], *s.* 1. die Erinnerung (***of,*** an (*Acc.*)); ***call to –,*** in die Erinnerung rufen; ***have in –,*** in Erinnerung haben; 2. das Gedächtnis; ***escape his –,*** seinem Gedächtnis entfallen; ***within my –,*** soweit ich mich erinnere; 3. das Andenken; ***in – of,*** zum Andenken an (*Acc.*); ***Remembrance Day,*** der Waffenstillstandstag, Gedenktag für die Gefallenen; – ***service,*** der Gedächtnisgottesdienst; 4. (*a th.*) das Andenken; 5. *pl.* Empfehlungen, Grüße (*pl.*); ***give my kind –s to him,*** grüßen Sie ihn bestens von mir! empfehlen Sie mich ihm bestens! **remembrancer,** *s.* 1. der Mahner, Erinnerer (***of,*** an (*Acc.*)); 2. die Erinnerungshilfe; 3. (*Hist.*) Schatzkammerbeamte(r).

remind [ri'maind], *v.t.* erinnern (***of,*** an (*Acc.*)), mahnen (***about,*** wegen); – ***him that I am coming,*** ihn daran erinnern, daß ich komme; – ***him to bring it,*** ihn mahnen, es zu bringen; ***you – me of him,*** du rufst die Erinnerung an ihn in mir wach; ***that –s me,*** da(bei) fällt mir (etwas) ein. **reminder,** *s.* 1. der Wink, die Mahnung (***of,*** an (*Acc.*); ***to,*** an (*Acc.*) *or* für); ***be a – of,*** erinnern an (*Acc.*); 2. der Mahnbrief. **remindful,** *adj.* erinnernd, mahnend (***of,*** an (*Acc.*)).

reminisce ['reminis], *v.i.* (*coll.*) Erinnerungen erzählen. **reminiscence** [–'nisəns], *s.* 1. die Erinnerung; 2. der Anklang (***of,*** an (*Acc.*)); 3. *pl.* (Lebens)erinnerungen, Memoiren (*pl.*). **reminiscent** [–'nisənt], *adj.* erinnernd, Erinnerungs–; ***be – of,*** erinnern *or* Erinnerungen wachrufen an (*Acc.*).

[1]**remise** [ri'maiz], **1.** *v.t.* (*Law*) zurückerstatten, übertragen, überlassen. **2.** *s.* die Zurückerstattung, Überlassung.

[2]**remise** [rə'mi:z], **1.** *s.* 1. der Wagenschuppen; 2. (*Fenc.*) Nachstoß, Nachhieb. **2.** *v.i.* nachstoßen, einen Nachhieb versetzen.

remiss [ri'mis], *adj.* (nach)lässig, säumig, träge; ***be – in,*** vernachlässigen.

remissible [ri'misibl], *adj.* erläßlich, verzeihlich. **remission** [–'miʃən], *s.* 1. die Abnahme, das Nachlassen; 2. die Vergebung (*of sins*); 3. Erlassung, der Erlaß (*of debt, penalty*), Nachlaß, die Ermäßigung (*of fees, taxes*).

remissness [ri'misnis], *s.* die (Nach)lässigkeit.

remit [ri'mit], **1.** *v.t.* 1. übersenden, überweisen (***to,*** *Dat.*) (*money*); 2. vergeben (*sins*); 3. erlassen (*debt, penalty*), nachlassen in (*Dat.*), mäßigen; 4. (*Law*) zurückverweisen, verweisen (***to,*** an (*Acc.*)), ausliefern (*Dat.*). **2.** *v.i.* 1. nachlassen, abnehmen; 2. (*Comm.*) Zahlung leisten, remittieren. **remittal,** *s.* 1. die Erlassung, der Erlaß; 2. (*Law*) die Zurückverweisung. **remittance** [–əns], *s.* 1. die Rimesse, Tratte, Geldsendung; 2. Übersendung, Remittierung; ***make a –,*** remittieren. **remittee** [–'ti:], *s.* der Zahlungsempfänger. **remittent, 1.** *adj.* (*Med.*) nachlassend, remittierend. **2.** *s.* remittierendes Fieber. **remitter** [–tə], *s.* 1. (*Comm.*) der Remittent, Übersender; 2. (*Law*) die Wiedereinsetzung (***to,*** in (*Acc.*)), Verweisung an (*Acc.*).

remnant ['remnənt], *s.* 1. der Rest, das Überbleibsel; 2. (*Comm.*) der (Stoff)rest; ***– sale,*** der Resterausverkauf; 3. (*fig.*) letzter Rest, die Spur.

remodel [ri:'mɔdl], *v.t.* umbilden, umformen, umgestalten, ummodeln.

remonetization [ri:mʌnitai'zeiʃən], *s.* die Wiederinkurssetzung. **remonetize** [–'mʌnitaiz], *v.t.* wieder in Kurs *or* Umlauf setzen.

remonstrance [ri'mɔnstrəns], *s.* die (Gegen)vorstellung, Einwendung, Ermahnung, der Einspruch, Protest. **remonstrant, 1.** *adj.* protestierend, remonstrierend, vorstellig. **2.** *s.* (*Hist.*) der Remonstrant. **remonstrate** ['remənstreit], **1.** *v.i.* 1. Vorwürfe *or* Vorstellungen *or* Einwendungen machen (***with,*** *Dat.* (*a p.*); ***on, about,*** wegen), vorhalten, vorwerfen (***with,*** *Dat.*; ***on, about,*** *Acc.*); 2. Einwände erheben, remonstrieren, protestieren, auftreten, aufbegehren (***against,*** gegen). **remonstration** [remən'streiʃən], *s. See* **remonstrance. remonstrative** [ri'mɔnstrətiv], *adj.* protestierend, Protest–, remonstrierend.

remontant [ri'mɔntənt], **1.** *adj.* (*Bot.*) wiederholt blühend, remontierend. **2.** *s.* die Remontante, remontierende Pflanze.

remora ['remərə], *s.* 1. (*rare*) die Stockung, Hemmung, das Hindernis; 2. (*Ichth.*) der Schildfisch.

remorse [ri'mɔ:s], *s.* (*only sing.*) Gewissensbisse (*pl.*), die Reue, Zerknirschung (***at,*** über (*Acc.*); ***for,*** wegen); (*coll.*) ***without –,*** unbarmherzig; ***in – for,*** aus Mitleid für. **remorseful,** *adj.* reuevoll, reumütig, reuig (***for,*** über (*Acc.*)). **remorsefulness,** *s.* die Reumütigkeit. **remorseless,** *adj.* (*fig.*) unbarmherzig, hartherzig, gefühllos, grausam. **remorselessness,** *s.* die Gefühllosigkeit, Unbarmherzigkeit.

remote [ri'mout], *adj.* 1. (weit) entfernt (*also fig.*), fern (***from,*** von); ***– antiquity,*** graues Altertum; ***– relation,*** weitläufige(r) *or* entfernte(r) Verwandte(r); ***– control,*** die Fernlenkung, Fernsteuerung; 2. entlegen, abgelegen, einsam; 3. (*fig.*) (grund)-verschieden (***from,*** von), wenig gemein *or* zu tun habend (mit), wenig ähnlich (*Dat.*); 4. (*coll.*) schwach, vage; ***not the –st idea,*** nicht die geringste *or* leiseste Ahnung. **remoteness,** *s.* die Entlegenheit, Entfernung, Ferne, Abseitigkeit.

remould [ri:'mould], *v.t.* umformen, umgestalten.

remount, 1. [ri:'maunt], *v.i.* 1. wieder aufsitzen (*on a horse*); 2. wieder (hinauf)steigen *or* ersteigen; 3. zurückkehren (***to,*** zu), zurückgehen (auf (*Acc.*)), zurückreichen (***to,*** (bis) in (*Acc.*)). **2.** [–'maunt], *v.t.* 1. wieder besteigen (*a horse*); 2. mit frischen Pferden versehen (*cavalry*); 3. wieder aufstellen (*a machine*); 4. neu aufziehen (*photograph etc.*). **3.** ['ri:maunt], *s.* (*esp. Mil.*) die Remonte, das Remontepferd, Ersatzpferd.

removability [rimu:və'biliti], *s.* 1. die Entfernbarkeit, Abnehmbarkeit; 2. Absetzbarkeit (*of officials*). **removable** [–'mu:vəbl], *adj.* 1. entfernbar, abnehmbar, demontierbar; 2. zu beseitigen(d), absetzbar (*as officials*). **removal** [–'mu:vl], *s.* 1. das Wegräumen, Wegschaffen, Fortschaffen; 2. die Beseitigung, Entfernung; 3. Verlegung, Versetzung; 4. Entlassung, Absetzung (*of a p.*) (***from,*** aus); 5. der Umzug (*from a house etc.*); ***– van,*** der Möbelwagen.

remove [ri'mu:v], **1.** *v.t.* 1. (*a th.*) wegbringen, wegschaffen, fortschaffen, wegräumen, aus dem Weg räumen; ***– one's eyes from,*** seinen Blick abwenden von; ***– furniture,*** Möbeltransport ausführen *or* besorgen *or* unternehmen; ***– mountains,*** Berge versetzen; 2. entfernen, beseitigen; (weg)-nehmen (***from,*** von *or* aus); beheben (*doubts*); ablegen (*one's clothes*), abnehmen (*one's hat, the receiver, a bandage etc.*); tilgen, verwischen (*traces*); ***– the brackets,*** die Klammern beseitigen *or* auflösen; ***– the cloth,*** (den Tisch) abdecken; ***– one's make-up,*** sich abschminken; ***– a stain,*** einen Fleck entfernen; ***– with acid,*** wegätzen; 3. zurückziehen, zurücknehmen (*one's hand*); 4. (*a p.*) entfernen (lassen), abführen, fortnehmen; ***– into hospital,*** ins Krankenhaus schaffen; 5. beseitigen, umbringen, töten (lassen); 6. absetzen, entlassen (*from office*) (***from,*** aus); ***– him from office,*** ihn seines Amts entheben; ***– him*** (or ***his name***) ***from the list,*** ihn (*or* seinen Namen) von der Liste streichen; 7. versetzen (*from school*). **2.** *v.i.* ausziehen, (um)ziehen (*from a house*); sich entfernen *or* wegbegeben (***from,*** von), ziehen (***to,*** nach); ***– into,*** einziehen in (*Acc.*), beziehen. **3.** *s.* 1. die Versetzung (*in school*); Stufe, Klasse (*in some schools*); ***get one's –,*** versetzt werden; 2. die Entfernung, der Abstand; 3. (Verwandschafts)grad; ***but one – from,*** nur einen Schritt entfernt von.

removed [ri'mu:vd], *adj.* entfernt; ***cousin twice –,*** der Vetter (die Kusine) zweiten Grades. **remover,** *s.* 1. der Möbeltransporteur, Möbelspediteur; 2. ***stain –,*** das Fleckenwasser, der Fleckentferner.

remunerate [ri'mju:nəreit], *v.t.* 1. vergelten (*Dat.*), entschädigen, belohnen (*a p.*); 2. vergüten, ersetzen, bezahlt machen, Entschädigung zahlen für (*a th.*). **remuneration** [–'reiʃən], *s.* 1. die Belohnung, Entschädigung, Vergütung; 2. das Honorar, Entgelt, der Lohn. **remunerative** [–rətiv], *adj.* (be)lohnend, einträglich, rentabel.

renaissance [rə'neisəns, rəne'sɑ̃s], *s.* die Renaissance, (*fig.*) Wiedergeburt, das Wiedererwachen.

renal [ri:nl], *adj.* Nieren–.

rename [ri:'neim], *v.t.* umbenennen, anders benennen, umtaufen.

renascence [ri'næsəns], *s.* die Wiedergeburt, Erneuerung, das Wiederaufleben. **renascent,** *adj.* wieder auflebend, sich erneuend, wiedergeboren.

rend [rend], *irr.v.t., v.i.* reißen, aufreißen, (*also* ***– asunder***) zerreißen, in Stücke reißen; ***– in two,*** entzweireißen; (*fig.*) ***– the air,*** durch die Luft gellen, die Luft erschüttern (*of cries*); ***– one's hair,*** sich die Haare raufen.

render ['rendə], **1.** *v.t.* 1. (*with pred. adj.*) machen; (*with noun*) machen zu; ***– possible,*** ermöglichen; 2. wiedergeben, zurückgeben, zurückerstatten; ***– up,*** zurückgeben, wiedergeben; 3. ***– an account,*** (*Comm.*) eine Rechnung legen *or* einsenden, Rechnung (vor)legen; (*fig.*) Bericht erstatten, Rechenschaft ablegen (***of,*** über (*Acc.*)); (*Comm.*) ***account –ed,*** laut Rechnung; 4. (*fig.*) leisten, erstatten (*help etc.*), abstatten (*thanks*), erweisen (*a service, kindness*) (***to,*** *Dat.*); ***– homage,*** huldigen (***to,*** *Dat.*); ***for services –ed,*** für treue Dienste; (*B.*) ***– unto Caesar the things that are Caesar's,*** gebt dem Kaiser, was des Kaisers ist; 5. vergelten (*evil for good etc.*) (***for,*** mit); 6. übersetzen, übertragen, wiedergeben (*foreign language*) (***in,*** in (*Acc.*)); 7. (*Mus.*) wiedergeben, interpretieren, spielen; 8. (*Art*) darstellen; 9. ausschmelzen, auslassen (*fat*); 10. (*Build.*) verputzen, bewerfen. **2.** *s.* 1. die Zahlung, Gegenleistung; 2. (*Build.*) der Rohbewurf.

rendering ['rendəriŋ], *s.* 1. die Rückgabe, Übergabe; – ***of accounts,*** die Rechnungsablegung, Rechnungsaufstellung; – ***of thanks,*** die Danksagung; 2. (*fig.*) die Wiedergabe, Interpretation, Darstellung, Gestaltung, Ausführung, (*esp. Mus.*) der Vortrag; 3. die Übersetzung, Übertragung; 4. (*Build.*) der Rohbewurf.

rendezvous ['rɔndivu:], **1.** *s.* (*pl.* – [–z]) 1. das Stelldichein, Rendezvous, die Zusammenkunft, Verabredung; 2. (*Mil.*) der Treffpunkt, Sammelplatz. **2.** *v.i.* zusammenkommen, sich treffen, (*esp. Mil.*) sich einstellen *or* versammeln.

rendition [ren'diʃən], *s.* 1. (*rare*) die Übergabe, Auslieferung; 2. Übersetzung, Wiedergabe.

renegade ['renigeid], **1.** *s.* Abtrünnige(r), der Renegat, Apostat, Überläufer. **2.** *adj.* abtrünnig, verräterisch. **3.** *v.i.* abtrünnig werden, abfallen. **renegation** [–'geiʃən], *s.* der Abfall, die Apostasie.

renew [ri'nju:], *v.t.* 1. erneuern; 2. wiederherstellen, renovieren, restaurieren; 3. ergänzen, ersetzen; 4. wiederholen; 5. wieder beginnen *or* aufnehmen; – ***one's efforts,*** sich erneut bemühen, erneute Anstrengungen machen; 6. (*Comm.*) verlängern, prolongieren. **renewable,** *adj.* 1. erneuerbar, zu erneuern(d); 2. (*Comm.*) prolongierbar, verlängerbar. **renewal,** *s.* 1. die Erneuerung; 2. (*Comm.*) Verlängerung, Prolongierung, Prolongation.

reniform ['ri:nifɔ:m], *adj.* nierenförmig.

[1]**rennet** ['renit], *s.* das Lab.

[2]**rennet,** *s.* (*Bot.*) die Renette.

renounce [ri'nauns], **1.** *v.t.* 1. (*a th.*) entsagen (*Dat.*), verzichten auf (*Acc.*); sich zurückziehen aus, abstehen von, aufgeben, ablehnen, zurückweisen, von sich weisen, verwerfen; 2. nicht länger anerkennen, abschwören (*beliefs*); 3. (*a p.*) sich lossagen von, von sich weisen, verstoßen, verleugnen; 4. (*Cards*) nicht bedienen. **2.** *v.i.* 1. Verzicht leisten; 2. (*Cards*) nicht bedienen können. **3.** *s.* (*Cards*) die Renonce. **renouncement,** *s.* die Entsagung, der Verzicht.

renovate ['renəveit], *v.t.* erneuern, wiederherstellen, renovieren, restaurieren. **renovation** [–'veiʃən], *s.* die Erneuerung, Wiederherstellung, Renovierung. **renovator,** *s.* der Erneuerer.

renown [ri'naun], *s.* der Ruhm, (guter) Ruf *or* Name, die Berühmtheit, (hohes) Ansehen. **renowned,** *adj.* berühmt, namhaft (*for*, wegen).

[1]**rent** [rent], **1.** *s.* 1. der Riß, Spalt, die Spalte; 2. (*fig.*) Spaltung. **2.** *imperf., p.p. of* **rend.**

[2]**rent, 1.** *s.* die (Wohnungs)miete, der Mietzins (*of house*), die Pacht, das Pachtgeld (*of land*); die Leihgebühr (*of an article*); ***ground*** –, die Grundlast, Reallast. **2.** *v.t.* 1. mieten, pachten (***from,*** von); 2. vermieten, verpachten (***to,*** *Dat.*); ***house to*** –, Haus zu vermieten. **3.** *v.i.* vermietet *or* verpachtet werden (***at,*** zu).

rental [rentl], **1.** *attrib. adj.* Miet–, Pacht–; – ***allowance,*** der Wohnungsgeldzuschuß. **2.** *s.* 1. die Mieteinnahme, Pachteinnahme, Miete, Pachtsumme; 2. der Mietsatz, Pachtsatz.

rent|-charge, *s.* der Erbzins. **--day,** *s.* der Mietzahlungstag. **rented,** *adj.* vermietet, verpachtet; – ***car,*** der Mietwagen; – ***house,*** das Mietshaus, die Mietwohnung. **rent|-free,** *adj.* mietfrei, pachtfrei. **--roll,** *s.* das Zinsbuch.

renunciation [rinʌnsi'eiʃən], *s.* 1. der Verzicht (*of*, auf (*Acc.*)), die Aufgabe (*Gen.*); 2. Ablehnung, Zurückweisung; 3. Entsagung, (Selbst)verleugnung.

reoccupation [ri:ɔkju'peiʃən], *s.* die Wiederbesetzung. **reoccupy** [–'ɔkjupai], *v.t.* wieder besetzen *or* einnehmen.

reopen [ri:'oupən], **1.** *v.t.* 1. wieder öffnen; 2. (*fig.*) wieder eröffnen *or* beginnen *or* aufnehmen *or* in Betrieb setzen. **2.** *v.i.* 1. sich wieder öffnen; 2. wieder aufmachen, wieder geöffnet werden (*as a shop*); 3. wieder beginnen *or* anfangen.

reorder [ri:'ɔ:də], *v.t.* 1. wieder ordnen *or* in Ordnung bringen; 2. (*Comm.*) nachbestellen.

reorganization [ri:ɔ:gənai'zeiʃən], *s.* 1. die Neuordnung, Neugestaltung, Umbildung; 2. (*Comm.*) Sanierung; 3. (*Mil.*) Umgruppierung. **reorganize** [–'ɔ:gənaiz], *v.t.* 1. reorganisieren, neuordnen, neugestalten; 2. (*Comm.*) sanieren; 3. (*Mil.*) umgruppieren.

reorientate [ri:'ɔ:rienteit], *v.t.* neu orientieren. **reorientation** [–'teiʃən], *s.* die Neuorientierung, Umorientierung.

[1]**rep** [rep], *s.* (*coll.*) *see* **reprobate.**

[2]**rep,** *s.* der Rips.

[3]**rep,** *s.* (*coll.*) *see* ***repertory*** (***theatre***).

[4]**rep,** *s.* (*sl.*) *see* **repetition.**

[5]**rep,** *s.* (*coll.*) *see* **representative.**

repack [ri:'pæk], *v.t.* umpacken.

repaint [ri:'peint], *v.t.* neu streichen, übermalen.

[1]**repair** [ri'pɛə], **1.** *s.* die Ausbesserung, Reparatur (*to*, an (*Dat.*)); Instandsetzung, Wiederherstellung; *pl.* Reparaturen, Instandsetzungsarbeiten (*pl.*); ***in good*** –, in gutem Zustande, gut erhalten; ***in need of*** –, reparaturbedürftig; ***out of*** –, baufällig; ***under*** –, in Reparatur. **2.** *v.t.* 1. reparieren, (wieder) instand setzen, (*coll.*) ausbessern, flicken; 2. (*fig.*) wiederherstellen; 3. wiedergutmachen (*a wrong*), ersetzen (*a loss*).

[2]**repair,** *v.i.* sich begeben (***to,*** nach).

repairable [ri'pɛərəbl], *adj.* reparierbar, reparaturfähig. **repairer,** *s.* der Ausbesserer; ***shoe***––, der Schuster; ***watch***––, der Uhrmacher. **repair|-kit, --outfit,** *s.* (*Cycl.*) der Flickkasten, Reparaturkasten. **--shop,** *s.* die Reparaturwerkstatt. **--service,** *s.* der Kundendienst.

repaper [ri:'peipə], *v.t.* neu tapezieren.

reparable ['repərəbl], *adj.* (*fig.*) wiedergutzumachen(d), ersetzbar. **reparation** [–'reiʃən], *s.* die Wiedergutmachung, Entschädigung, Genugtuung (***for,*** für); *pl.* Reparationszahlungen (*pl.*); ***make*** –(*s*), Genugtuung leisten.

repartee [repɑ:'ti:], *s.* schlagfertige Antwort, die Schlagfertigkeit; ***quick at*** –, schlagfertig.

repartition [ri:pɑ:'tiʃən], **1.** *s.* die Aufteilung, (Neu)verteilung. **2.** *v.t.* (neu) aufteilen *or* verteilen.

repass [ri:'pɑ:s], **1.** *v.i.* zurückgehen, zurückkommen, wieder vorbeikommen. **2.** *v.t.* 1. wieder vorbeikommen an (*Dat.*); 2. wieder durchqueren.

repast [ri'pɑ:st], *s.* die Mahlzeit, das Mahl.

repatriate, 1. [ri:'pætrieit], *v.t.* repatriieren. **2.** [–iit], *s.* Repatriierte(r), der (die) Heimkehrer(in). **repatriation** [–'eiʃən], *s.* die Repatriierung.

repay [ri:'pei], **1.** *irr.v.t.* 1. zurückzahlen, zurückerstatten; 2. (*fig.*) (*a p.*) heimzahlen (*Dat.*), vergelten (*Dat.*), entschädigen, belohnen; 3. (*a th.*) erwidern (*greeting etc.*), lohnen (*trouble*), entschädigen für, vergelten; ***it –s reading,*** es lohnt sich gelesen zu werden. **2.** *irr.v.i.* 1. sich lohnen, der Mühe wert sein; 2. zurückzahlen. **repayable,** *adj.* rückzahlbar. **repayment,** *s.* 1. die Rückzahlung; 2. Erwiderung; 3. Vergeltung.

repeal [ri'pi:l], **1.** *v.t.* widerrufen, aufheben, für ungültig erklären, abschaffen (*a law*). **2.** *s.* die Aufhebung, Abschaffung, der Widerruf. **repealable,** *adj.* widerruflich.

repeat [ri'pi:t], **1.** *v.t.* 1. wiederholen (***to,*** gegenüber); – ***it after me!*** spreche es mir nach! (*Comm.*) – ***an order,*** nachbestellen; 2. weitererzählen, weiterverbreiten (*rumours etc.*); 3. aufsagen, hersagen (*a poem etc.*). **2.** *v.i.* 1. sich wiederholen; ***be –ed,*** sich wiederholen, wiederkehren; 2. (*clocks*) repetieren; 3. (*coll.*) (*of food*) einen Nachgeschmack haben, aufstoßen. **3.** *s.* die Wiederholung; (*Mus.*) Wiederholung, das Dakapo; Wiederholungszeichen; (*Comm.*) *see* **repeat-order. repeated,** *adj.* wiederholt, mehrmalig, nochmalig.

repeater [ri'pi:tə], *s.* 1. (*clock*) die Repetieruhr; 2. (*Math.*) periodischer Dezimalbruch; 3. (*gun*) das Mehrladegewehr; 4. (*Tech.*) der Verstärker; 5. (*coll.*) (*at school*) Repetent, Wiederholer, Sitzengebliebene(r); 6. – ***compass,*** der Tochterkompaß. **repeat|-order,** *s.* die Nachbestellung, Neubestellung. **--performance,** *s.* (*Theat.*) die Wiederholung.

repel [ri'pel], *v.t.* 1. abwehren, zurückschlagen (*attack*), zurücktreiben, zurückdrängen (*enemy*), zurückstoßen; 2. (*Phys.*) abstoßen, zurückstoßen; – ***one another,*** einander abstoßen; 3. abschlagen, ausschlagen (*suggestion etc.*), von sich weisen, zurückweisen, abweisen (*a p., also suggestion etc.*); 4. (*fig.*) anwidern, abstoßen, abstoßend wirken auf (*Acc.*), zuwider sein (*Dat.*) (*a p.*). **repellent, 1.** *adj.* 1. abstoßend; 2. (*fig.*) abstoßend, widerlich. **2.** *s.* das Abwehrmittel.

[1]**repent** [ri'pent], **1.** *v.t.* bereuen (*a th.*; ***doing,*** getan zu haben); (*obs.*) ***I – me of,*** ich bereue (*Acc.*). **2.** *v.i.* – ***of,*** Reue empfinden über (*Acc.*), bereuen; ***marry in haste and – at leisure,*** schnell gefreit, lang bereut.

[2]**repent** ['ri:pənt], *adj.* (*Bot., Zool.*) kriechend.

repentance [ri'pentəns], *s.* die Reue, Bußfertigkeit. **repentant,** *adj.* reuig, reumütig, bußfertig.

re-people [ri:'pi:pl], *v.t.* neu bevölkern.

repercussion [ri:pə'kʌʃən], *s.* 1. der Rückstoß, Rückprall, das Rückprallen; 2. (*fig.*) (*usu. pl.*) der Widerhall, die Rückwirkung, Nachwirkung, Auswirkung(en) (*of, Gen.*; *on,* auf (*Acc.*)). **repercussive** [–'kʌsiv], *adj.* widerhallend, rückwirkend.

repertoire ['repətwɑ:], *s.* (*Theat.*) der Spielplan, das Repertoire. **repertory** [–təri], *s.* 1. das Repertorium; 2. (*fig.*) die Fundgrube (*of,* für *or* von); 3. *See also* **repertoire**; – ***theatre,*** das Repertoiretheater, Theater mit stehender Truppe (und wechselndem Spielplan).

repetend [repə'tend], *s.* die Periode (*of a decimal*).

repetition [repi'tiʃən], *s.* 1. die Wiederholung; 2. (*at school*) mündliche Aufgabe, die Gedächtnisaufgabe, das Hersagen, Aufsagen; 3. die Wiederkehr, wiederholtes Vorkommen (*of events etc.*); 4. die Nachbildung, Kopie (*of a pattern*). **repetitious,** *adj.* langweilig, monoton, sich ständig wiederholend. **repetitive** [rə'petitiv], *adj.* sich wiederholend; wiederholt; ***be –,*** sich wiederholen.

repine [ri'pain], *v.i.* klagen, murren, mißvergnügt *or* unzufrieden sein (*at,* über (*Acc.*)). **repining, 1.** *adj.* mißvergnügt, unzufrieden, mürrisch. **2.** *s.* das Murren, die Unzufriedenheit.

replace [ri:'pleis], *v.t.* 1. wieder (hin)stellen *or* (hin)legen; – ***the receiver,*** den Hörer wieder auflegen; 2. zurückgeben, zurückerstatten (*things taken*); 3. an die Stelle treten von *or* (*Gen.*) (*a p. or th.*), verdrängen (*a th.*); 4. ersetzen (*a p. or th.*) (***with*** (*a th.*), ***by*** (*a p.*), durch); vertreten, ablösen, die Stelle einnehmen (*Gen.*) (*a p.*); ***be –d by,*** abgelöst werden von, ersetzt werden durch. **replaceable** [–əbl], *adj.* ersetzbar (***by,*** durch). **replacement,** *s.* 1. die Ersetzung, der Ersatz; – ***value,*** der Ersetzungswert, Wiederbeschaffungskosten (*pl.*); 2. (*Geol.*) die Verdrängung; 3. (*Spt.*) der Ersatzmann; 4. *pl.* (*Mil.*) der Nachschub, Ergänzungsmannschaften (*pl.*).

replant [ri:'plɑ:nt], *v.t.* umpflanzen, wieder einsetzen (*plants*), neu bepflanzen (*soil*).

replay ['ri:plei], *s.* 1. (*Spt.*) das Wiederholungsspiel; 2. (*tape, film*) die Wiedergabe.

replenish [ri'pleniʃ], *v.t.* 1. (wieder) füllen; anfüllen, auffüllen, ergänzen (***with,*** mit); 2. (*Dye.*) nachsetzen, auffrischen. **replenishment,** *s.* 1. das Nachfüllen; 2. die Auffüllung, Ergänzung.

replete [ri'pli:t], *adj.* voll, übersättigt (***with,*** von), vollgestopft, vollgepfropft, (an)gefüllt (mit). **repletion** [–ʃən], *s.* das Vollsein; die Übersättigung, (Über)fülle; ***full to –,*** voll bis zum Rande *or* zum Bersten.

replevin [ri'plevin], *s.* (*obs.*) (*Law*) die Einlösung gegen Kaution. **replevy** [–i], *v.t.* gegen Kaution einlösen.

replica ['replikə], *s.* 1. die Kopie, Nachbildung, Replik; 2. (*fig.*) das Ebenbild. **replicate, 1.** [–it], *adj.* zurückgeschlagen, zurückgebogen. **2.** [–eit], *v.t.* (*rare*) (*Bot.*) zurückbiegen. **replication** [–'keiʃən], *s.* (*rare*) 1. die Antwort, Erwiderung; 2. (*Law*) Replik; 3. Kopie; Nachbildung.

reply [ri'plai], **1.** *v.i.* antworten, erwidern; – ***to,*** antworten (*Dat.*) (*a p.*); antworten *or* erwidern auf (*Acc.*) (*a question*); (*Mil.*) – ***to the fire,*** das Feuer erwidern. **2.** *s.* die Antwort, Erwiderung, Entgegnung; ***in – to,*** in Erwiderung auf (*Acc.*), in Beantwortung (*Gen.*); ***make a –, say in –,*** antworten, erwidern (***to,*** auf (*Acc.*)); – ***paid,*** Rückantwort bezahlt; – ***postcard,*** die Postkarte mit Rückantwort.

report [ri'pɔ:t], **1.** *s.* 1. (*with opinions*) der Bericht (***on,*** über (*Acc.*)); das (Schul)zeugnis; Gutachten, Referat (*of an expert*); ***annual –,*** der Jahresbericht; 2. (*factual*) die Meldung, Nachricht (***of,*** über (*Acc.*)); ***law –s,*** Berichte über Entscheidungen des Obergerichts; ***newspaper –,*** der Zeitungsbericht; ***official –,*** das Protokoll; – ***of proceedings,*** der Verhandlungsbericht; (*Parl.*) – ***stage,*** das Erörterungsstadium; 3. das Gerücht; – ***has it,*** es geht das Gerücht; 4. der Ruf, Name (*good or bad*); 5. Knall, Schall (*of gun etc.*). **2.** *v.t.* 1. berichten *or* Bericht erstatten über (*Acc.*) (*in the press etc.*); berichten, melden, erzählen, darstellen (***to,*** *Dat.*); ***it is –ed,*** man sagt; ***he is –ed to be ill,*** er soll krank sein; ***he is –ed as saying,*** er soll gesagt haben; – ***progress,*** über den Fortgang berichten; 2. (*a p. for wrongdoing*) melden (***to,*** *Dat.*), anzeigen (bei) (***for,*** wegen); – ***o.s.,*** sich melden. **3.** *v.i.* 1. Bericht erstatten *or* geben, berichten (***on,*** über (*Acc.*); ***to,*** *Dat.*); 2. (*of a p.*) sich melden, sich stellen; – ***for duty,*** sich zum Dienst melden; – ***to the police,*** sich bei der Polizei melden, sich der Polizei stellen.

reportage [repɔ:'tɑ:ʒ], *s.* die Reportage, der Zeitungsstil.

reported [ri'pɔ:tid], *adj.* (*Gram.*) indirekt, abhängig. **reportedly,** *adv.* angeblich, wie gemeldet wird. **reporter,** *s.* der Berichterstatter.

repose [ri'pouz], **1.** *s.* 1. die Ruhe, der Schlaf; die Untätigkeit; Erholung, das Ausruhen (***from,*** von); ***in –,*** ruhend, untätig; 2. (*fig.*) die Gemütsruhe, innere Ruhe, Gelassenheit, Stille, der Friede(n); 3. die Ausgewogenheit, Harmonie (*as of a picture*). **2.** *v.i.* 1. (sich) ausruhen, ruhen; 2. (*fig.*) beruhen, gegründet sein (***on,*** auf (*Dat.*)). **3.** *v.t.* setzen (***in,*** auf (*Acc.*) or in (*Acc.*)) (*confidence etc.*). **reposeful,** *adj.* ruhevoll, ruhig.

repository [ri'pɔzitəri], *s.* 1. das Behältnis, der Behälter; 2. Aufbewahrungsort, Speicher, die Vorratskammer, das Magazin, (Waren)lager, die Niederlage; 3. (*fig.*) Fundgrube, Quelle; 4. Vertraute(r).

repossess [ri:pə'zes], *v.t.* (*Law*) wiedereinsetzen (*a p.*) (***in,*** in (*Acc.*)); wieder in Besitz nehmen (*a th.*); – (*o.s.*), (sich) wieder in Besitz setzen (***of,*** *Gen.*). **repossession** [–ʃən], *s.* die Wiedergewinnung.

repoussé [rə'pu:sei], **1.** *adj.* getrieben, gehämmert, erhaben (*metalwork*). **2.** *s.* getriebene Arbeit.

repp, *see* [2]**rep.**

reprehend [repri'hend], *v.t.* tadeln, rügen, verweisen, zurechtweisen. **reprehensible** [–'hensibl], *adj.* tadelnswert, verwerflich. **reprehension** [–'henʃən], *s.* der Tadel, Verweis, die Rüge, Zurechtweisung.

represent [repri'zent], *v.t.* 1. verkörpern, repräsentieren, vertreten; ***be –ed,*** vertreten sein (***at,*** bei); 2. (graphisch *or* bildlich) darstellen, abbilden (*graphically*) (***by,*** durch), (*Theat.*) aufführen (*a play*), darstellen (*character*); 3. (*fig.*) (anschaulich) darstellen, hinstellen (***as, to be,*** als), schildern, klarmachen, vor Augen führen, zu Gemüte führen, nahebringen (***to,*** *Dat.*); – ***to o.s.,*** sich (*Dat.*) vorstellen.

representation [reprizen'teiʃən], *s.* 1. die Verkörperung; 2. Vertretung; – ***allowance,*** die Aufwandsentschädigung; ***no taxation without –,*** ohne Vertretung keine Besteuerung; (*Pol.*) ***proportional –,*** das Verhältniswahlsystem; ***system of –,*** das Repräsentativsystem; 3. die Darstellung, Schilderung; ***false –s,*** falsche Angaben, die Vorspiegelung falscher Tatsachen; 4. (*Theat.*) die Aufführung, Vorstellung (*of a play*), Darstellung (*of a rôle*); 5. (*oft. pl.*) Vorhaltung, Vorstellung, der Protest; ***make –s,*** Vorhaltungen machen (***to,*** *Dat.*), vorstellig werden (bei) (***about a matter,*** in *or* wegen einer S.). **representational,** *adj.* (*Art*) gegenständlich, figürlich, begrifflich.

representative [repri'zentətiv], **1.** *s.* 1. der (Stell)vertreter, Beauftragte(r), Bevollmächtigte(r) (*of*, *Gen.*); (*Law*) ***natural* –**, der Rechtsnachfolger; 2. (*Comm.*) der Handelsvertreter, Agent (***for***, für); 3. (*Pol.*) Volksvertreter, Abgeordnete(r), Deputierte(r); (*Am.*) ***House of Representatives,*** das Unterhaus, die Volksvertretung; 4. (*fig.*) typischer Vertreter, der Repräsentant, die Verkörperung, das (Muster)beispiel (***of***, für). **2.** *adj.* 1. (symbolisch) darstellend, verkörpernd (***of***, *Acc.*); ***be* – *of*,** darstellen, verkörpern; 2. kennzeichnend, charakteristisch, typisch (***of***, für); ***– selection,*** repräsentative Auswahl, der Querschnitt; 3. vertretend (***of***, *Acc.*), stellvertretend (für), als Vertreter (*Gen.*); 4. (*esp. Pol.*) Repräsentativ–; ***– government,*** die Repräsentativverfassung; 5. Vorstellungs–, Begriffs–. **representativeness,** *s.* repräsentativer Charakter, der Symbolcharakter, die Bildlichkeit.

repress [ri'pres], *v.t.* 1. unterdrücken; zurückhalten, bändigen, hemmen, zügeln, im Zaum halten; 2. (*Psych.*) verdrängen. **repression** [–ʃən], *s.* 1. die Unterdrückung, Zügelung, Bändigung, Hemmung; 2. (*Psych.*) Verdrängung. **repressive** [–siv], *adj.* 1. unterdrückend, Unterdrückungs–; 2. hemmend, Repressiv–.

reprieve [ri'pri:v], **1.** *s.* 1. die Begnadigung; der (Straf– *or* Vollstreckungs)aufschub; 2. (*fig.*) die Gnadenfrist, Atempause. **2.** *v.t.* 1. Strafaufschub gewähren (*Dat.*), begnadigen; 2. (*fig.*) Atempause *or* eine kleine Frist gewähren (*Dat.*), vorübergehend retten (***from***, vor (*Dat.*)).

reprimand ['reprimɑ:nd], **1.** *s.* die Rüge, der Verweis (***for***, wegen). **2.** *v.t.* einen Verweis erteilen (*Dat.*), rügen.

reprint, 1. [ri:'print], *v.t.* neu drucken, nachdrucken. **2.** ['ri:print], *s.* der Neudruck, Nachdruck, neue (unveränderte) Auflage.

reprisal [ri'praizl], *s.* die Vergeltungsmaßnahme; *pl.* Repressalien (*pl.*); ***make –s,*** Vergeltungsmaßregeln ergreifen (***on***, gegen); ***in* –,** als Vergeltungsmaßnahme.

reprise, *s.* 1. [ri'pri:z], (*Mus.*) die Wiederholung, Reprise; 2. [–aiz], (*fig.*) Fortsetzung, Wiederaufnahme; 3. *pl.* [–aiz], (*Law*) jährliche Abzüge.

reproach [ri'proutʃ], **1.** *s.* 1. der Vorwurf, Tadel; ***heap –es on him,*** ihn mit Vorwürfen überhäufen; ***incur* –,** sich (*Dat.*) Vorwürfe zuziehen; ***look of* –,** vorwurfsvoller Blick; ***term of* –,** das Scheltwort; ***without* –,** ohne Tadel; 2. die Schande, Schmach (***to***, für); ***bring*** or ***cast – upon him,*** ihm Schande *or* wenig Ehre machen; ***be a – to,*** Abbruch tun (*Dat.*), schaden. **2.** *v.t.* Vorwürfe machen (*Dat.*), tadeln, rügen (***for***, wegen); ***– him with dishonesty,*** ihm seine Unehrlichkeit vorhalten *or* vorwerfen *or* zur Last legen *or* zum Vorwurf machen; ***– o.s.,*** sich (*Dat.*) vorwerfen *or* Vorwürfe machen; ***he has nothing to – himself with,*** er braucht sich keine Vorwürfe zu machen. **reproachful,** *adj.* vorwurfsvoll.

reprobate ['reprəbeit], **1.** *adj.* 1. verworfen, verkommen, verwerflich, lasterhaft, ruchlos; 2. (*Theol.*) verdammt. **2.** *s.* Verworfene(r), der Schurke, Taugenichts, verkommenes Subjekt. **3.** *v.t.* verdammen, verurteilen, mißbilligen, verwerfen. **reprobation** [–'beiʃən], *s.* 1. die Mißbilligung, Verwerfung; 2. (*Theol.*) Verdammnis.

reproduce [ri:prə'dju:s], **1.** *v.t.* 1. (wieder)hervorbringen (*also fig.*); 2. (*Biol.*) (er)zeugen, züchten; 3. vervielfältigen, (wieder)abdrucken, reproduzieren, kopieren; 4. wiederholen, nachbilden, abbilden, wiedergeben (*also Mus.*). **2.** *v.i.* 1. (*Biol.*) sich fortpflanzen *or* vermehren; 2. (*fig.*) sich vervielfältigen. **reproducible,** *adj.* reproduktionsfähig.

reproduction [ri:prə'dʌkʃən], *s.* 1. die Wiedergabe, Nachbildung; 2. Vervielfältigung, Reproduktion; 3. (*Biol.*) Fortpflanzung, Vermehrung; 4. (*Typ.*) der Nachdruck, (*Phot.*) Abzug; 5. (*Art*) die Reproduktion, Kopie; 6. (*Mus.*) Wiedergabe. **reproductive** [–'dʌktiv], *adj.* Fortpflanzungs–, Reproduktions–. **reproductiveness, reproductivity** [–'tiviti], *s.* das Reproduktionsvermögen, die Vermehrungsfähigkeit.

reproof [ri'pru:f], *s.* der Tadel, Verweis, die Rüge.

re-proof [ri:'pru:f], *v.t.* wieder wasserdicht machen, neu imprägnieren.

reproval [ri'pru:vl], *s.* die Mißbilligung, das Tadeln. **reprove,** *v.t.* tadeln, rügen (*a p.*), (*rare*) mißbilligen (*a th.*). **reproving,** *adj.* tadelnd, rügend, mißbilligend.

reps, *see* ²**rep.**

reptant ['reptənt], *adj.* (*Bot., Zool.*) kriechend.

reptile ['reptail], **1.** *s.* 1. das Reptil, Kriechtier; 2. (*fig.*) der Kriecher. **2.** *adj.* 1. kriechend, Kriech–; 2. (*fig.*) gemein, gedungen, kriecherisch. **reptilian** [–'tiliən], **1.** *adj.* Reptil(ien)–, Kriechtier–, reptil(ien)artig. **2.** *s.* das Reptil, Kriechtier.

republic [ri'pʌblik], *s.* die Republik, der Freistaat; ***– of letters,*** die Gelehrtenwelt. **republican, 1.** *adj.* republikanisch. **2.** *s.* der Republikaner. **republicanism,** *s.* republikanische Gesinnung *or* Staatsform.

republication [ri:pʌbli'keiʃən], *s.* 1. die Neuauflage; 2. Wiederveröffentlichung. **republish** [–'pʌbliʃ], *v.t.* wieder veröffentlichen, neu auflegen.

repudiate [ri'pju:dieit], **1.** *v.t.* 1. nicht anerkennen (*debts etc.*); 2. ableugnen, von sich weisen, in Abrede stellen (*thoughts*); 3. abweisen, zurückweisen (*as unwarranted*); 4. verstoßen (*a wife*). **2.** *v.i.* (*Pol.*) Staatsschuld nicht anerkennen. **repudiation** [–'eiʃən], *s.* 1. die Nichtanerkennung; 2. Ableugnung; 3. Zurückweisung; 4. Verstoßung.

repugn [ri'pju:n], **1.** *v.t.* (*rare*) abstoßen, anwidern (*a p.*), sich (*Dat.*) widersetzen (*a th.*). **2.** *v.i.* ***– against,*** kämpfen gegen.

repugnance, repugnancy [ri'pʌgnəns(i)], *s.* 1. die Abneigung, der Widerwille (***against***, ***to*** (*a th.*), ***for*** (*a p.*), gegen); 2. die Unvereinbarkeit, der Widerspruch. **repugnant,** *adj.* 1. widerlich, widerwärtig, widrig, anstößig, zuwider (***to***, *Dat.*); 2. im Widerspruch stehend (***to***, ***with***, zu), unvereinbar, unverträglich (mit), widerstrebend (*Dat.*).

repulse [ri'pʌls], **1.** *s.* das Zurücktreiben, Zurückschlagen; (*fig.*) die Zurückweisung, abschlägige Antwort, (*coll.*) die Abfuhr; ***meet with a* –,** (*Mil.*) zurückgeschlagen werden; (*fig.*) abgewiesen werden, eine abschlägige Antwort bekommen, (*coll.*) sich (*Dat.*) eine Abfuhr holen. **2.** *v.t.* zurückschlagen, zurückwerfen, zurücktreiben (*enemy*), abschlagen, abweisen (*attack*); (*fig.*) abschlagen (*advances*), ausschlagen (*offers*), abweisen (*a p.*). **repulsion** [–ʃən], *s.* 1. das Zurückwerfen, Zurücktreiben; 2. (*Phys.*) die Abstoßung; 3. (*fig.*) Abneigung, der Widerwille(n). **repulsive** [–siv], *adj.* 1. (*Phys.*) abstoßend, Abstoßungs–, Repulsiv–; 2. (*fig.*) abstoßend, anstößig, abscheulich, widerwärtig, widerlich. **repulsiveness,** *s.* die Widerlichkeit, Widerwärtigkeit.

repurchase [ri:'pə:tʃəs], **1.** *v.t.* wiederkaufen, zurückkaufen. **2.** *s.* der Rückkauf.

reputable ['repjutəbl], *adj.* angesehen, ehrbar, geachtet, achtbar. **reputation** [–'teiʃən], *s.* (guter) Ruf *or* Name, (hohes) Ansehen, der Leumund; ***have the* –,** im Rufe stehen (***of being***, zu sein); ***have a – for,*** bekannt sein wegen.

repute [ri'pju:t], **1.** *v.t.* (*only pass.*) ***be –d to be,*** gehalten *or* erachtet werden für, gelten als. **2.** *s.* *See* **reputation**; ***by* –,** dem Rufe nach; ***of*** (***good***) **–,** von (hohem) Rufe; ***in high* –,** in hohem Ansehen; ***be held in high* –,** hohes Ansehen genießen; ***house of ill* –,** das Bordell. **reputed,** *adj.* 1. berühmt; 2. angeblich, vermeintlich. **reputedly,** *adv.* dem Rufe *or* Leumund *or* Vernehmen nach, angeblich.

request [ri'kwest], **1.** *s.* das Gesuch, Ansuchen, Ersuchen, die Bitte, der Wunsch; ***at his* –,** auf seine Bitte *or* sein Ansuchen hin; ***on* –,** auf Wunsch; ***no flowers by* –,** Blumenspenden dankend verbeten; (*Comm.*) ***in* –,** gesucht, begehrt; ***grant a* –,** eine Bitte gewähren; ***make a* –,** eine

Bitte vorbringen (*to, Dat.*) *or* stellen *or* richten (an (*Acc.*)), bitten (*Acc.*) (***for***, um); – ***programme,*** das Wunschkonzert; – ***stop,*** die Bedarfshaltestelle. **2.** *v.t.* 1. bitten, ersuchen (*a p.*); 2. erbitten, bitten um, ersuchen um (*a th.*); ***as –ed,*** auf Ihre Bitte, wie erbeten, wunschgemäß; – ***a favour of him,*** ihn um eine Gefälligkeit ersuchen; – ***permission,*** um (die) Erlaubnis bitten.

requiem ['rekwiəm], *s.* das Requiem, (*also* – ***mass***) die Seelenmesse, Totenmesse.

require [ri'kwaiə], *v.t.* 1. verlangen, fordern (*a p.*); – ***him to do,*** – ***of him that he does,*** von ihm verlangen *or* fordern daß er tut, ihn auffordern zu tun; ***–d subject,*** das Pflichtfach; 2. erfordern; ***be –d,*** notwendig *or* erforderlich sein; (*Geom.*) ***–d angle,*** gesuchter Winkel; ***–d space,*** erforderlicher *or* vorgeschriebener Raum; ***as –d,*** nach Bedarf; ***if –d,*** wenn nötig, auf Wunsch; 3. brauchen, nötig haben; ***it –s to be done,*** (*coll.*) ***it –s doing,*** es muß getan werden, es ist (noch) zu erledigen; ***it doesn't – doing,*** es braucht nicht getan zu werden.

requirement [ri'kwaiəmənt], *s.* 1. die Bedingung, (An)forderung; ***educational –s,*** Bildungsvoraussetzungen (*pl.*); ***meet the –s,*** (*a th.*) den Anforderungen entsprechen, den Ansprüchen genügen, (*a th. or p.*) die Bedingungen erfüllen; 2. (*oft. pl.*) das Erfordernis, Bedürfnis, der Bedarf; ***meet the –s,*** (*of a th.*) den Bedarf decken, (*of a p.*) den Erfordernissen nachkommen.

requisite ['rekwizit], **1.** *adj.* erforderlich, nötig, notwendig (***for***, für). **2.** *s.* 1. das Erfordernis, die (Vor)-bedingung; 2. (*oft. pl.*) der (Bedarfs)artikel.

requisition [rekwi'ziʃən], **1.** *s.* 1. die Forderung, das Ersuchen; 2. (*Mil.*) die Requirierung, Requisition, Beitreibung; ***put in*** or ***call into –,*** einsetzen; ***be in –,*** beansprucht werden, eingesetzt *or* im Einsatz sein; 3. (*Law*) der Auslieferungsantrag; 4. (amtliche) Aufforderung. **2.** *v.t.* requirieren, beschlagnahmen; beanspruchen, in Anspruch nehmen, (an)fordern. **requisitioning,** *s.* (*Mil.*) die Beitreibung, Beschlagnahme.

requital [ri'kwaitl], *s.* 1. die Vergeltung (***of***, für); 2. Belohnung, Vergütung, Entschädigung (***for***, für). **requite,** *v.t.* 1. vergelten (*a th.*); 2. – ***him for it,*** ihn dafür belohnen, es ihm heimzahlen *or* vergelten; 3. aufwiegen, entschädigen für (*a th.*).

re-read [ri:'ri:d], *irr.v.t.* noch einmal (durch)lesen.

reredos ['riədɔs], *s.* der Altaraufsatz, das Retabel.

resale ['ri:seil], *s.* der Wiederverkauf, Weiterverkauf; – ***price maintenance,*** die Preisbindung der zweiten Hand.

rescind [ri'sind], *v.t.* aufheben, umstoßen, kassieren, widerrufen, für nichtig *or* ungültig erklären, rückgängig machen, kündigen. **rescission** [–'siʒən], *s.* die Aufhebung, Umstoßung, Nichtigkeitserklärung, Rückgängigmachung, Annullierung, Kassation.

rescript ['ri:skript], *s.* amtlicher Bescheid *or* Erlaß, die Verfügung, Verordnung, das Reskript.

rescue ['reskju:], **1.** *v.t.* befreien (***from***, von), retten, bergen (aus); bewahren (*a th.*) (vor (*Dat.*)); – ***from oblivion,*** der Vergessenheit entreißen. **2.** *s.* 1. die Rettung; ***come to his –,*** ihm zu Hilfe kommen; 2. (gewaltsame) Befreiung. **rescue-party,** *s.* die Rettungsmannschaft, Bergungsmannschaft. **rescuer** [–ə], *s.* der Befreier, Retter. **rescue-work,** *s.* Rettungsarbeiten (*pl.*), die Bergung.

research [ri'sə:tʃ], **1.** *v.i.* Forschungen anstellen, forschen (***on***, über (*Acc.*)). **2.** *s.* 1. die Nachforschung (***for, after***, nach); 2. (*oft. pl.*) (wissenschaftliche) Untersuchung, die Forschung, Forschungsarbeit (***on, in***, über (*Acc.*)). **3.** *attrib. adj.* Forschungs–; – ***institute*** or ***station,*** die Forschungsstation; – ***professor,*** der Professor mit Forschungsauftrag; – ***student,*** fortgeschrittener Student; – ***work,*** die Forschung(sarbeit). **researcher,** *s.* der Forscher.

reseat [ri:'si:t], *v.t.* 1. mit neuen Sitzen versehen (*church, etc.*); 2. mit neuem Sitz versehen (*a chair*); 3. einen neuen Boden einnähen in (*Acc.*) (*trousers*).

resect [ri'sekt], *v.t.* (*Surg.*) herausschneiden, abschneiden, resezieren. **resection** [–'sekʃən], *s.* die Resektion.

reseda [ri'si:də], *s.* 1. (*Bot.*) der Wau, die Reseda; 2. graugrüne Farbe.

re-seize [ri:'si:z], *v.t.* wieder in Besitz nehmen.

resell [ri:'sel], *irr.v.t.* wiederverkaufen.

resemblance [ri'zembləns], *s.* die Ähnlichkeit (***between***, zwischen (*Dat.*); ***to***, mit); ***bear*** or ***have a – to,*** ähnlich sehen (*Dat.*). **resemble** [–'zembl], *v.t.* gleichen (*Dat.*), ähneln (*Dat.*), ähnlich sein *or* sehen (*Dat.*).

resent [ri'zent], *v.t.* übelnehmen, verübeln, sich stoßen an (*Dat.*). **resentful,** *adj.* aufgebracht (***of, against***, gegen), grollend, ärgerlich (auf (*Acc.*)), empört (über (*Acc.*)). **resentment,** *s.* die Verstimmung, das Befremden, der Verdruß, Unwille, Unmut, Ärger, die Empörung, Entrüstung (***at, against***, über (*Acc.*)), das Ressentiment, der Groll (gegen).

reservation [rezə'veiʃən], *s.* der Vorbehalt, die Vorbehaltsklausel, das Reservat; ***mental –,*** geheimer Vorbehalt; ***with certain –s,*** mit gewissen Einschränkungen; ***without –,*** ohne Vorbehalt, bedingungslos; 2. (*Am.*) das Naturschutzgebiet, Reservat, die Reservation; 3. Vorbestellung (*of seats*); Platzkarte (*for a seat*).

reserve [ri'zə:v], **1.** *s.* 1. der Überschuß, Vorrat, die Reserve (***of***, an (*Dat.*)); (*Mil.*) Reserve; *pl.* (*Mil., Comm.*) Reserven (*pl.*), (*Comm.*) Rücklagen (*pl.*); – ***account,*** das Reservekonto, Rückstellungskonto; – ***fund,*** der Reservefonds, die Reserve, Rücklage; – ***officer,*** der Reserveoffizier; (*Mil.*) – ***position,*** rückwärtige Stellung, die Auffangstellung; ***in –,*** in Bereitschaft *or* Reserve, im Rückhalt; vorrätig; ***place to –,*** dem Reservefonds überweisen; 2. die Reservation, das Reservat, Schutzgebiet (*for game, primitive tribes*), geschützter Bestand (*of game*); 3. der Ersatz; (*Spt.*) Reservespieler, Ersatzmann; 4. Vorbehalt, die Einschränkung; – ***price,*** der Einsatzpreis (*at auctions*); ***with certain –s,*** unter gewissen Einschränkungen; ***without –,*** ohne Vorbehalt; 5. (*fig.*) die Reserve, Zurückhaltung, Verschlossenheit, Diskretion, zurückhaltendes Wesen; 6. (*Tech.*) die Reservage (*textiles*). **2.** *v.t.* 1. (sich (*Dat.*)) aufheben *or* aufsparen *or* aufbewahren; – ***o.s. for,*** seine Kräfte aufsparen für; 2. reservieren, (zurück)behalten, (*esp. Law*) vorbehalten (***to, for***, *Dat.*); – ***to o.s.,*** sich (*Dat.*) vorbehalten, für sich behalten; – ***the right,*** sich (*Dat.*) das Recht vorbehalten; ***all rights –d,*** alle Rechte vorbehalten; 3. (sich) zurückhalten mit, aufschieben, verschieben, aussetzen (*judgement etc.*); 4. belegen *or* reservieren lassen, (vor)bestellen (*a seat*).

reserved [ri'zə:vd], *adj.* 1. vorbehalten, zurückbehalten, reserviert, vorgemerkt; – ***seat,*** numerierter *or* reservierter Platz; **2.** (*Law*) Reservats–; 3. (*fig.*) reserviert, zurückhaltend. **reservist,** *s.* (*Mil.*) der Reservist.

reservoir ['rezəvwɑ:], *s.* 1. das Behältnis, Bassin, der Wasserspeicher, (Wasser)behälter; (*Rad.*) – ***condenser,*** der Speicherkondensator; 2. der Stausee, Staubecken, das Reservoir; 3. der Wasserturm, Hochbehälter; 4. (*fig.*) das Sammelbecken, der (Reserve)vorrat (***of***, an (*Dat.*)).

[1]**reset** [ri:'set], *v.t., v.i.* (*obs. or Scots Law*) hehlen.

[2]**reset, 1.** [ri:'set], *irr.v.t.* 1. neu (ein)fassen (*gems*); 2. (neu) abziehen (*knives*); 3. (*Typ.*) wieder setzen. **2.** ['ri:set], *s.* (*Typ.*) der Neusatz.

[1]**resetting** [ri:'setiŋ], *s.* (*obs. or Scots Law*) die Hehlerei.

[2]**resetting,** *s.* 1. das Wiedereinsetzen; 2. (*Typ.*) *see* [2]**reset, 2.**

resettle [ri:'setl], **1.** *v.t.* 1. wieder ansiedeln (*population*), wieder einsetzen (*a p.*); 2. neu ordnen, wieder in Ordnung bringen, beruhigen. **2.** *v.i.* 1. sich wieder ansiedeln (*population*); 2. sich wieder legen *or* setzen *or* beruhigen. **resettlement,** *s.* 1. die Wiederansiedlung; 2. Wiedereinsetzung; 3. Neuordnung.

reshape [ri:'ʃeip], *v.t.* umformen, umgestalten, umbilden.

reship [riː'ʃip], *v.t.* 1. wieder verschiffen *or* verladen (*to another place*); 2. umladen (*from one ship to another*). **reshipment,** *s.* die Rück(ver)ladung, der Weiterversand.

reshuffle [riː'ʃʌfl], **1.** *v.t.* 1. (*Cards*) neu mischen; 2. (*fig.*) umgruppieren, umstellen, umbilden (*government etc.*). **2.** *s.* die Umgruppierung, Umstellung, Umbildung.

reside [ri'zaid], *v.i.* 1. wohnen, ansässig sein, seinen ständigen Wohnsitz haben (*in, at*, in (*Dat.*)) (*of p.*); 2. (*fig.*) zustehen, zukommen (*with, in, Dat.*), ruhen, liegen (bei), obliegen (*with, Dat.*), innewohnen (*in, Dat.*).

residence ['rezidəns], *s.* 1. der Wohnort, Wohnsitz; ***permanent* –**, fester *or* ständiger Wohnsitz; ***take up (one's)* –**, seinen Wohnsitz nehmen, sich niederlassen (*in, at*, in (*Dat.*)); ***take up – with,*** sich einmieten bei; 2. die Wohnung, das Wohnhaus, (*of a prince*) die Residenz; ***be in* –**, am Amtsort ansässig sein; ***family* –**, das Einfamilienhaus; ***official* –**, die Amtswohnung; 3. der Aufenthalt; **– *permit,*** die Aufenthaltsgenehmigung.

residency ['rezidənsi], *s.* 1. die Amtswohnung, Residenz; 2. (*Hist.*) Residenzschaft (*in India*).

resident ['rezidənt], **1.** *adj.* 1. wohnhaft, (orts)-ansässig; **– *population,*** die Einwohnerschaft; 2. im Hause *or* am Orte·wohnend; **– *physician,*** der Anstaltsarzt; **– *tutor,*** der Hauslehrer; Internatslehrer; 3. (*fig.*) innewohnend, zustehend (*in, Dat.*). **2.** *s.* 1. der (die) Einwohner(in), Ansässige(r); 2. (*Pol.*) der Ministerresident, Regierungsvertreter; 3. (*Orn.*) Standvogel, Jahresvogel. **residential** [–'denʃəl], *adj.* Wohn–; **– *district,*** das Wohnviertel, Villenviertel. **residentiary** [–'denʃəri], **1.** *adj.* seßhaft, ansässig, wohnhaft. **2.** *s.* residenzpflichtiger Geistlicher. **residentship,** *s.* (*Pol.*) die Residentschaft, Residentenstelle.

residual [ri'zidjuəl], **1.** *adj.* 1. (*Math.*) zurückbleibend, übrig(bleibend); 2. übrig(gebleiben), restlich, Rest–; **– *charge,*** die Restladung; **– *oils,*** Rückstandsöle (*pl.*); **– *product,*** das Nebenprodukt. **2.** *s.* der Rest(betrag), Restwert, die Differenz. **residuary** [–uəri], *adj.* übrig(geblieben), rückständig, restlich; **– *legatee,*** der Nachvermächtnisnehmer. **residue** ['rezidjuː], *s.* 1. der Rest(betrag), Rückstand; 2. (*Chem.*) das Residuum, der Filtriersatz, Bodensatz; 3. (*Law*) Reinnachlaß. **residuum** [–'zidjuəm], *s.* 1. (*Chem.*) der Rest, Bodensatz, Rückstand, das Residuum; 2. (*fig.*) der Abschaum, die Hefe.

resign [ri'zain], **1.** *v.t.* 1. aufgeben, verzichten auf (*Acc.*); 2. niederlegen (*an office*), überlassen (*to, Dat.*); 3. **– *o.s.,*** sich hingeben *or* überlassen *or* anvertrauen (*to, Dat.*), sich ergeben (in (*Acc.*)), sich abfinden (mit). **2.** *v.i.* 1. abdanken, zurücktreten (*from*, von), austreten (aus); 2. (*fig.*) verzichten, sich fügen.

re-sign [riː'sain], *v.t., v.i.* 1. nochmals (unter)-zeichnen; 2. sich wieder verpflichten (*for*, für).

resignation [rezig'neiʃən], *s.* 1. der Rücktritt, Abschied, die Abdankung; das Abschiedsgesuch; die Niederlegung (*of office*); ***give*** or ***send in one's* –**, sein Abschiedsgesuch *or* seinen Rücktritt einreichen; 2. die Verzichtleistung, Aufgabe, der Verzicht; 3. die Überlassung (*to*, an (*Acc.*)); (*fig.*) Hingabe (an (*Acc.*)), Ergebung (in (*Acc.*)); 4. Ergebenheit, Entsagung, Resignation.

resigned [ri'zaind], *adj.* (*fig.*) ergeben, resigniert; ***be – to,*** sich fügen in (*Acc.*), sich abgefunden haben mit. **resignedly** [–nidli], *adv.* mit Ergebung, resigniert, ohne zu klagen.

resilience, resiliency [ri'ziliəns(i)], *s.* 1. das Zurückschnellen, Zurückspringen, Abprallen; 2. die Elastizität, (*of a mattress*) Federung; 3. (*fig.*) Spannkraft, Beweglichkeit, der Schwung. **resilient,** *adj.* 1. zurückspringend, zurückschnellend, zurückprallend; 2. elastisch, federnd; 3. (*fig.*) beweglich, geschmeidig, schwunghaft.

resin ['rezin], **1.** *s.* 1. (*Bot.*) das Harz; 2. *See* **rosin, 1. 2.** *v.t.* 1. mit Harz behandeln; 2. *See* **rosin, 2. resinaceous** [–'neiʃəs], *adj.* harzhaltig, harzig. **resinate** [–eit], *s.* das Harzsäuresalz. **resiniferous** [–'nifərəs], *adj.* harzführend, harzhaltig. **resinify** [–'zinifai], *v.t., v.i.* verharzen. **resinous** [–əs], *adj.* 1. harzhaltig, harzig, Harz–; 2. harzähnlich, harzartig.

resist [ri'zist], **1.** *v.t.* 1. Widerstand leisten (*Dat.*) *or* gegen, widerstehen (*Dat.*), standhalten (*Dat.*); 2. sich stellen *or* sträuben gegen, entgegenarbeiten (*Dat.*), sich widersetzen (*Dat.*); ***I cannot – doing,*** ich kann nicht umhin zu tun. **2.** *v.i.* Widerstand leisten, sich widersetzen, opponieren. **3.** *s.* (*Tech.*) der (Ab)decklack, das Deckmittel, die Schutzbeize.

resistance [ri'zistəns], *s.* 1. der Widerstand (*to*, gegen); ***meet with* –**, auf Widerstand stoßen; ***offer* –**, sich wehren, Widerstand leisten; ***passive* –**, passiver Widerstand; (*Pol.*) **– *movement,*** die Widerstandsbewegung; 2. die Festigkeit, Beständigkeit, Widerstandsfähigkeit, Widerstandskraft; **– *to wear and tear,*** die Verschleißfestigkeit; 3. (*Elec.*) der Widerstand; **– *coil,*** die Widerstandsspule. **resistant,** *adj.* 1. widerstehend, widerstrebend; 2. widerstandsfähig, beständig (*to*, gegen), Widerstands–. **resistible,** *adj.* 1. zu widerstehen(d); 2. widerstandsfähig. **resistless,** *adj.* unwiderstehlich. **resistor,** *s.* (*Elec.*) der Widerstand.

resit, 1. [riː'sit], *irr.v.t.* wiederholen (*an examination*). **2.** ['riːsit], *s.* die Wiederholungsprüfung.

resole [riː'soul], *v.t.* neu besohlen.

resolute ['rezəljuːt], *adj.* entschlossen, standhaft, fest. **resoluteness,** *s.* die Entschlossenheit, Entschiedenheit, Festigkeit, Standhaftigkeit. **resolution** [–'ljuːʃən], *s.* 1. *See* **resoluteness**; 2. (*Mus., Opt.*) die Auflösung; 3. (*Chem., Phys.*) Zerlegung, (*Chem.*) Auflösung, Teilung, Trennung; (*Med.*) Zerteilung (*of a tumour etc.*); 4. (*fig.*) Behebung (*of doubt*), Lösung (*of a question*); 5. der Entschluß, Beschluß, Vorsatz, (*Parl.*) die Resolution; ***good –s,*** gute Vorsätze; ***come to*** or ***form a* –**, sich (fest) vornehmen, zu einem Entschluß kommen; (*Parl.*) ***propose a* –**, eine Entschließung beantragen. **resolutive,** *adj.* (*Med.*) zerteilend, auflösend.

resolvable [ri'zɔlvəbl], *adj.* auflösbar (*into*, in (*Acc.*)). **resolve, 1.** *v.t.* 1. (*Chem., Math., Mus.*) auflösen; (*Chem.*) spalten, trennen, zerlegen; 2. (*Med.*) zerteilen; 3. verwandeln, umwandeln (*into*, in (*Acc.*)); (*Parl.*) ***the house –s itself into a committee,*** das Haus tritt als Ausschuß zusammen; 4. entscheiden, beschließen, den Beschluß fassen (*to do*, zu tun); 5. (*fig.*) lösen, aufklären (*problem*), beheben, zerstreuen (*doubt*). **2.** *v.i.* 1. sich auflösen *or* zerfallen (*into*, in (*Acc.*)); 2. beschließen (*on, Acc.*); sich beschließen *or* entschließen, sich (*Dat.*) vornehmen (*on doing*, zu tun). **3.** *s.* 1. der Entschluß, Beschluß, Vorsatz; 2. (*Am.*) *see* **resolution,** 5. (*Parl.*); 3. *See* **resoluteness. resolved,** *adj.* (fest) entschlossen. **resolvent, 1.** *adj.* (*Chem., Med.*) auflösend. **2.** *s.* (*Med.*) das Lösungsmittel, Auflösemittel.

resonance ['rezənəns], *s.* die Klangfülle, Resonanz, das Mitschwingen; (*fig.*) der Widerhall, Nachhall. **resonant** [–ənt], *adj.* 1. widerhallend, nachhallend, nachklingend, mitklingend; 2. (*as voice*) volltönend; 3. (*Phys.*) Resonanz–, mitschwingend; (*Elec.*) **– *circuit,*** der Resonanzkreis, Schwingkreis. **resonate** [–eit], *v.i.* widerhallen, mitschwingen. **resonator,** *s.* der Resonator, Resonanzboden, Resonanzkörper.

resorb [ri'zɔːb], *v.t.* (wieder) aufsaugen, resorbieren. **resorption** [–'zɔːpʃən], *s.* die Resorption.

resort [ri'zɔːt], **1.** *s.* 1. die Anwendung, Zuhilfenahme (*to*, von), Zuflucht(nahme) (zu); ***have – to force,*** Gewaltmaßnahmen ergreifen, Gewalt anwenden; ***without – to force,*** ohne Gewalt anzuwenden, ohne zu Gewalt zu greifen; 2. (letztes) Hilfsmittel, letzte Möglichkeit; ***as a*** or ***in the last* –**, als letzter Ausweg, wenn Not am Mann ist; notfalls, nötigenfalls, letzten Endes, schließlich; 3. der Versammlungsort; ***bathing*** or ***seaside* –**, das Seebad, der Badeort; ***health* –**, der Kurort; ***winter* –**, der Wintersportplatz. **2.** *v.i.* 1. **– *to,*** sich begeben zu *or* nach, oft besuchen; 2. (*fig.*) **– *to,***

seine Zuflucht nehmen zu, Gebrauch machen von, greifen zu.

resound [ri'zaund], **1.** *v.i.* widerhallen (***with***, von), erschallen, ertönen. **2.** *v.t.* widerhallen lassen; – ***his praises,*** sein Lob laut verkünden. **resounding,** *adj.* schallend, klangvoll.

resource [ri'sɔ:s], *s.* 1. die Zuflucht, der Ausweg, Kunstgriff; 2. (*of a p.*) die Findigkeit, Wendigkeit, Erfindungskraft, Geistesgegenwart, das Geschick; 3. (*rare*) die Zerstreuung, der Zeitvertreib; 4. (*usu. pl.*) die Hilfsquelle, das Hilfsmittel; ***as a last –,*** *see* **resort, 1,** 2; 5. *pl.* Geldmittel (*pl.*) (*of a p.*), Reichtümer (*pl.*) (*of a country etc.*), (*Comm.*) Aktiva (*pl.*); ***natural –s,*** Bodenschätze (*pl.*); ***thrown back on one's own –s,*** auf sich selbst gestellt *or* angewiesen. **resourceful,** *adj.* findig, wendig, einfallsreich, erfinderisch.

respect [ri'spekt], **1.** *s.* 1. der Bezug, die Beziehung, Hinsicht; ***have – to,*** sich beziehen auf (*Acc.*); ***in all –s, in every –,*** in jeder Hinsicht; ***in – of, with – to,*** *see* **respecting**; 2. die Rücksicht, der Hinblick; ***without – of persons,*** ohne Ansehen der Person; 3. die (Hoch)achtung, Verehrung, Ehrerbietung; ***have*** or ***show – for,*** (Hoch)achtung haben vor (*Dat.*); ***be held in high –,*** hoch geachtet sein; ***show – to,*** Ehrerbietung erweisen (*Dat.*); ***out of – for,*** aus Achtung vor (*Dat.*); 4. *pl.* Empfehlungen, Grüße (*pl.*); ***give him my –s,*** grüßen Sie ihn von mir! lassen Sie ihn grüßen! ***pay one's –s,*** sich empfehlen, seine Aufwartung machen (***to***, *Dat.*). **2.** *v.t.* 1. berücksichtigen, Rücksicht nehmen auf (*Acc.*); 2. (hoch)achten, schätzen; ***love and –,*** lieben und schätzen; ***– o.s.,*** (etwas) auf sich (*Acc.*) halten.

respectability [rispektə'biliti], *s.* 1. der Anstand, die Anständigkeit, Schicklichkeit; 2. Achtbarkeit, Ehrbarkeit; 3. das Ansehen; 4. die Konventionalität; 5. Respektspersonen (*pl.*). **respectable** [ri'spektəbl], *adj.* 1. anständig, schicklich; 2. angesehen, geachtet, achtbar, ehrbar, konventionell; 3. (*Comm.*) solid, reell; 4. (*coll.*) beträchtlich, ansehnlich, leidlich.

respecter [ri'spektə], *s.* ***be no – of persons,*** ohne Ansehen der Person handeln, keinen Unterschied der Person machen, die Person nicht ansehen. **respectful,** *adj.* ehrerbietig, höflich, ehrfürchtig, respektvoll; ***be – of,*** achten, respektieren; (*in letters*) ***–ly,*** ergebenst, hochachtungsvoll. **respecting,** *prep.* in Bezug auf (*Acc.*), was . . . (*Acc.*) betrifft *or* anbelangt, bezüglich (*Gen.*), hinsichtlich (*Gen.*), betreffs (*Gen.*). **respective,** *adj.* (*usu. unnecessary in German*) jeweilig, betreffend, respektiv; ***to their – homes,*** jeder nach seinem Hause; ***the – amounts of £5 and £10,*** die Beträge von 5 beziehungsweise 10 Pfund. **respectively,** *adv.* (*follows verb, oft. unnecessary in German*) beziehungsweise, respektive; ***he made approving or disparaging comments – as the answers pleased or annoyed him,*** er machte zustimmende oder *or* beziehungsweise ablehnende Bemerkungen, je nachdem die Antworten ihn erfreuten oder ärgerten.

respiration [respi'reiʃən], *s.* 1. das Atmen, Atemholen, die Atmung, Respiration; 2. der Atemzug. **respirator** ['respireitə], *s.* 1. der Respirator, das Atemgerät; 2. (*Mil.*) die Gasmaske. **respiratory** ['respirətəri], *adj.* Atem–, Atmungs–; ***– organs,*** Atmungsorgane (*pl.*); ***– tract,*** Atemwege (*pl.*). **respire** [ri'spaiə], **1.** *v.i.* 1. atmen, Atem holen; 2. (*fig.*) aufatmen. **2.** *v.t.* (ein)atmen.

respite ['resp(a)it], **1.** *s.* 1. die Stundung; (Stundungs)frist, Nachfrist, der (Zahlungs)aufschub; 2. (*fig.*) die (Ruhe)pause, Unterbrechung, der Unterlaß. **2.** *v.t.* 1. Frist *or* Aufschub gewähren, Urteilsvollstreckung aufschieben (*Dat.*) (*a p.*); 2. vertagen, aufschieben, verschieben (*a th.*), einstellen, zurückhalten (*payment*), stunden (*debt*); 3. (*fig.*) Erleichterung verschaffen von (*pain etc.*).

resplendence, resplendency [ri'splendəns(i)], *s.* 1. der Glanz; 2. (*fig.*) die Pracht. **resplendent,** *adj.* 1. glänzend, strahlend, leuchtend; 2. (*fig.*) prangend, prächtig.

respond [ri'spɔnd], **1.** *v.i.* 1. antworten (***to***, auf (*Acc.*)), erwidern (*Dat.*); ***– to a letter,*** einen Brief beantworten; 2. (*fig.*) entgegenkommen (***to***, *Dat.*), ansprechen, eingehen, reagieren (auf (*Acc.*)), empfänglich sein (für); ***– to a call,*** einem Rufe folgen; 3. (*Eccl.*) antworten, respondieren; 4. (*Tech.*) gehorchen (*Dat.*). **2.** *v.t.* (*Law*) Genugtuung leisten (*Dat.*). **3.** *s.* 1. (*Eccl.*) das Responsorium; 2. (*Archit.*) der Wandpfeiler, Strebepfeiler.

respondence, respondency [ri'spɔndəns(i)], *s.* 1. die Entsprechung, Übereinstimmung; 2. Antwort, Reaktion (***to***, auf (*Acc.*)). **respondent, 1.** *adj.* 1. (*Law*) antwortend, reagierend (***to***, auf (*Acc.*)); 2. (*Law*) beklagt. **2.** *s.* (*Law*) (Scheidungs)-beklagte(r).

response [ri'spɔns], *s.* 1. die Antwort, Erwiderung; ***in – to,*** als Antwort auf (*Acc.*); 2. (*Eccl.*) das Responsorium; 3. (*fig.*) die Reaktion, der Widerhall (***to***, auf (*Acc.*)); ***meet with no –,*** keinen Widerhall *or* keine Aufnahme finden (***from***, bei), keinen Eindruck machen (auf (*Acc.*)); ***meet with a good –,*** gut aufgenommen werden (***from***, von), Erfolg haben (bei).

responsibility [rispɔnsi'biliti], *s.* 1. die Verantwortlichkeit (*of a p.*); 2. Verantwortung; ***accept –,*** die Verantwortung auf sich (*Acc.*) nehmen (***for***, für); ***on one's own –,*** auf eigene Verantwortung; 3. die Verpflichtung, Verbindlichkeit; 4. (*Comm.*) Verläßlichkeit, Zahlungsfähigkeit. **responsible** [ri'spɔnsibl], *adj.* 1. verantwortlich (***to***, *Dat. or* gegenüber; ***for***, für); ***be – for,*** haften *or* einstehen für, verantwortlich sein *or* die Verantwortung tragen für; ***make o.s. – for,*** die Verantwortung übernehmen für; (*Comm.*) verantwortlich zeichnen für; (*Comm.*) ***– partner,*** persönlich haftender Teilnehmer; 2. (*of a p.*) verantwortungsvoll, zuverlässig, vertrauenswürdig; 3. (*Comm.*) verläßlich, solide, zahlungsfähig; 4. verantwortungsvoll; ***– position,*** der Vertrauensposten.

responsive [ri'spɔnsiv], *adj.* 1. antwortend, als Antwort (***to***, auf (*Acc.*)); 2. (*usu. fig.*) entgegenkommend (***to***, *Dat.*); 3. reagierend (***to***, auf (*Acc.*)), zugänglich, empfänglich, empfindlich (für). **responsiveness,** *s.* die Empfänglichkeit, Empfindlichkeit, Zugänglichkeit (***to***, für). **responsory** [–əri], *s.* das Responsorium.

respray, 1. [ri:'sprei], *v.t.* umspritzen (*a car etc.*). **2.** ['ri:sprei], *s.* ***have a –,*** umgespritzt werden.

¹rest [rest], **1.** *s.* 1. die (Nacht)ruhe; Rast, der Schlaf; das Ausruhen, die Erholung (***from***, von); (*Poet.*) ewige *or* letzte Ruhe, der Tod; (*Phys.*) die Ruhe(lage), der Ruhepunkt; ***at –,*** ruhig; ***set his mind at –,*** ihn beruhigen; ***set a matter at –,*** eine S. erledigen; ***in –,*** eingelegt (*as a lance*); ***day of –,*** der Ruhetag; ***come to –,*** zur Ruhe kommen; ***lay to –,*** begraben, bestatten; ***retire to –,*** sich zur Ruhe begeben, schlafen gehen; ***take a –,*** sich ausruhen; ***take one's –,*** ruhen; ***give*** (*a p., animal etc.*) ***a –,*** (ihn *etc.*) sich ausruhen lassen; ***give*** (*a machine etc.*) ***a –,*** ruhen lassen; (*coll.*) ***give s.th. a –,*** mit etwas aufhören, etwas auf sich beruhen lassen; ***have a good night's –,*** sich ausruhen *or* ausschlafen; (*Phys.*) ***state of –,*** der Ruhezustand; (*fig.*) ***without –,*** unaufhörlich; 2. die Unterkunft, das Heim (*for sailors etc.*); 3. (*Mus.*) die Pause, (*Metr.*) Zäsur; 4. der Ständer, Halter, Steg, die Stütze, Lehne, Auflage.

2. *v.i.* 1. (*of a p.*) rasten, Rast machen, (aus)-ruhen; schlafen, (sich) ausruhen; Ruhe finden, zur Ruhe kommen, sich erholen; ***the matter cannot – here,*** dabei kann es nicht bleiben; ***let it –,*** es auf sich beruhen lassen, es dabei bewenden lassen; (*Am.*) ***– up,*** sich erholen, ausruhen; 2. (*of a th.*) liegen, ruhen (***upon***, auf (*Dat.*)), (*as a glance*) ruhen, haften, hängen(bleiben) (auf (*Dat.*)); sich stützen *or* lehnen (***against***, gegen); 3. stehenbleiben, stillstehen; 4. (*fig.*) sich stützen, beruhen, begründet sein, (sich) gründen, fußen (***on***, auf (*Dat.*)); 5. sich verlassen ((***up***)***on***, auf (*Acc.*)).

3. *v.t.* 1. ruhen lassen (*a p.*); ***– o.s.,*** sich ausruhen; ***God – his soul!*** Gott hab' ihn selig! 2. schonen (*eyes etc.*); 3. richten (*glance*) (***on***, auf (*Acc.*)); 4. (*a th.*) legen, lagern (***on***, auf (*Acc.*)), stützen, lehnen (*against*, an (*Acc.*)); 5. (*fig.*) stützen, gründen (*on*, auf (*Acc.*)); 6. (*Law*) – *the case*, die Beweisaufnahme schließen.

[2]**rest, 1.** *s.* 1. der Rest(teil), Überrest; das übrige, die übrigen (*pl.*); *and all the – of it*, und das Weitere, und alles Drum und Dran, und was sonst noch, und alles übrige; *the – of us*, wir übrigen; *all the – (of them)*, alle anderen; *for the –*, im übrigen, übrigens; 2. (*Comm.*) der Reservefonds; Saldo; die Bilanzierung. **2.** *v.i.* bleiben, weiterhin sein; – *assured*, sich darauf verlassen, sicher sein; *it –s with him*, es bleibt ihm überlassen, es liegt an *or* bei ihm *or* in seinen Händen, es hängt von ihm ab.

restart [ri:ˈstɑ:t], **1.** *v.t.* wieder in Gang *or* in Betrieb setzen. **2.** *v.i.* wieder beginnen.

restate [ri:ˈsteit], *v.t.* wiederholt feststellen *or* darlegen, neu formulieren. **restatement,** *s.* die Neuformulierung; wiederholte Darlegung.

restaurant [ˈrestərɔnt], *s.* das Restaurant, die Gaststätte; *--car*, der Speisewagen. **restaurateur** [–ræˈtə:], *s.* der Gastwirt.

rest|-cure, *s.* die Liegekur. **--day,** *s.* der Ruhetag. **rested,** *adj.* ausgeruht, erholt. **restful,** *adj.* 1. ruhevoll, ruhig, friedlich; 2. erholsam, beruhigend. **rest-house,** *s.* das Rasthaus, die Herberge.

resting-place, *s.* 1. der Ruheplatz; 2. (*fig.*) (letzte) Ruhestätte *or* Ruhestatt.

restitution [restiˈtju:ʃən], *s.* 1. die Wiederherstellung; (Zu)rückerstattung, Zurückgabe; Entschädigung; *make – for*, Ersatz *or* Genugtuung leisten für; *make – of*, wiederherstellen; 2. (*Phys.*) die Rückstellung (*by elasticity*).

restive [ˈrestiv], *adj.* 1. störrisch, widerspenstig; 2. unruhig, ungeduldig, nervös; 3. bockig (*as horse*). **restiveness,** *s.* 1. die Widerspenstigkeit, der Starrsinn; 2. die Ungeduld, Unruhe, Nervosität; 3. Bockigkeit (*of horse*).

restless [ˈrestlis], *adj.* 1. rastlos, ruhelos; 2. unruhig; – *night*, schlaflose Nacht. **restlessness,** *s.* 1. die Rastlosigkeit, Ruhelosigkeit; 2. Schlaflosigkeit; 3. (nervöse) Unruhe.

restock [ri:ˈstɔk], *v.t.* neu versorgen (*with*, mit), wieder auffüllen (*warehouse*), neu besetzen (*a pond with fish*).

restoration [restəˈreiʃən], *s.* 1. die Wiederherstellung; Wiedereinsetzung (*to*, in (*Acc.*)), Rückerstattung, Rückgabe; 2. (*Hist.*) Restauration; 3. (*Art etc.*) Ausbesserung, Erneuerung, Restaurierung. **restorative** [riˈstɔ:rətiv], **1.** *adj.* (*Med.*) stärkend. **2.** *s.* das Stärkungsmittel, Belebungsmittel.

restore [riˈstɔ:], *v.t.* 1. wiederherstellen; restaurieren, rekonstruieren; 2. (*Pol.*) wiedereinsetzen (*to*, in (*Acc.*)); 3. zurückbringen (*to*, zu); zurückerstatten, wiedergeben, zurückgeben (*Dat.*); – *to health*, wiederherstellen; – *to liberty*, die Freiheit wiedergeben (*Dat.*); – *to life*, ins Leben zurückrufen; – *a th. to its place*, etwas an seinen Ort zurückstellen; – *to the throne*, wieder auf den Thron setzen. **restorer,** *s.* 1. der Wiederhersteller; 2. (*Art etc.*) Restaurator; 3. *hair –*, das Haarwuchsmittel.

restrain [riˈstrein], *v.t.* 1. zurückhalten, abhalten (*from*, von), hindern (an (*Dat.*)), (*from doing*, zu tun); 2. in Schranken *or* Schach halten, Einhalt gebieten (*Dat.*); 3. bändigen, zügeln, im Zaum halten, unterdrücken, bezähmen (*feelings*); 4. beschränken, einschränken (*power*). **restrainable,** *adj.* zurückzuhalten(d), bezähmbar. **restrained,** *adj.* 1. beherrscht, zurückhaltend, verhalten, maßvoll; 2. gehemmt, gedämpft. **restraint,** *s.* 1. die Zurückhaltung, (Selbst)beherrschung, Zucht; 2. Beschränkung (*oft. pl.*), Einschränkung, Hemmung; *place – on*, beschränken; *without –*, frei, ungezwungen, ungehemmt; 3. (*Law*) die Sicherungsverwahrung, Freiheitsbeschränkung, Haft, der Gewahrsam; *place under –*, in Gewahrsam *or* unter Aufsicht stellen (*a p.*).

restrict [riˈstrikt], *v.t.* beschränken, einschränken (*to*, auf (*Acc.*)); *be –ed*, sich darauf beschränken müssen; *–ed*, nur für den Dienstgebrauch; *–ed area*, das Sperrgebiet. **restriction** [–kʃən], *s.* 1. die Beschränkung, Einschränkung (*on*, *Gen.*); *without –s*, uneingeschränkt; – *on payment*, die Zahlungsbeschränkung; 2. der Vorbehalt. **restrictive** [–tiv], *adj.* beschränkend, einschränkend.

re-string [ri:ˈstriŋ], *irr.v.t.* wieder aufreihen (*beads*), neu besaiten (*violin etc.*).

rest-room, *s.* 1. der Aufenthaltsraum, Tagesraum; 2. (*Am.*) die Toilette.

re-stuff [ri:ˈstʌf], *v.t.* nachfüllen, nachpolstern.

re-style [ri:ˈstail], *v.t.* umarbeiten, umformen, umbilden, umändern.

result [riˈzʌlt], **1.** *v.t.* das Ergebnis, Resultat (*also Arith.*); die Folge, (Aus)wirkung, Nachwirkung; *as a – he died*, die Folge war, daß er starb; *in the –*, letzten Endes, wie es sich ergab; (*coll.*) *get –s*, Erfolge erzielen; *without –*, ergebnislos, ohne Folge *or* Wirkung; *yield –s*, gute Ergebnisse zeitigen. **2.** *v.i.* 1. sich ergeben, folgen (*from*, aus), herrühren (von), seinen Ursprung haben (in (*Dat.*)); – *in*, zur Folge haben, enden mit *or* in (*Dat.*), (hin)auslaufen auf (*Acc.*); 2. (*Law*) zurückfallen (*to*, an (*Acc.*)).

resultant [riˈzʌltənt], **1.** *adj.* sich ergebend, entstehend, resultierend (*from*, aus). **2.** *s.* 1. (*Math.*) die Resultante, Resultierende, Mittelkraft; 2. (*fig.*) das (End)ergebnis, Resultat.

resume [riˈzju:m], **1.** *v.t.* 1. wieder beginnen, fortsetzen, wieder aufnehmen (*work etc.*); *be –d*, wieder einsetzen, fortgeführt werden; 2. wieder einnehmen (*a seat*); wieder übernehmen (*an office, command etc.*); 3. zusammenfassen, resümieren. **2.** *v.i.* 1. die Arbeit wieder aufnehmen; 2. (in der Rede) fortfahren.

résumé [ˈrezjumei], *s.* die Zusammenfassung, kurze Übersicht, das Resümee.

resumption [riˈzʌmpʃən], *s.* 1. die Wiederaufnahme, der Wiederbeginn; 2. die Zurücknahme, Wiederübernahme, Wiederinbesitznahme.

resupinate [riˈsju:pinət], *adj.* (*Bot.*) nach oben gebogen, umgedreht, resupiniert. **resupination** [–ˈneiʃən], *s.* (*Bot.*) umgekehrte Lage, die Rückwärtsdrehung.

resurgence [riˈsə:dʒəns], *s.* das Wiederaufleben, Wiederauftauchen, der Wiederaufstieg. **resurgent,** *adj.* wiederauflebend, wiederaufsteigend, sich wiedererhebend.

resurrect [rezəˈrekt], *v.t.* (*coll.*) ausgraben, wieder aufnehmen *or* einführen, wieder aufleben lassen. **resurrection** [–kʃən], *s.* 1. die Auferstehung, das Fest der Auferstehung Christi; 2. (*fig.*) das Wiedererwachen, Wiederaufleben; die Wiederbelebung, Erneuerung. **resurrectionism,** *s.* der Leichenraub. **resurrectionist,** *s.* der Leichenräuber. **resurrection pie,** *s.* (*coll.*) die Restepastete.

resuscitate [riˈsʌsiteit], **1.** *v.t.* 1. wiederbeleben, ins Leben zurückrufen; 2. (*fig.*) wieder aufleben lassen, erneuern. **2.** *v.i.* 1. wieder zum Bewußtsein kommen; 2. (*fig.*) wieder aufleben. **resuscitation** [–ˈteiʃən], *s.* 1. die Wiederbelebung, Wiedererweckung; 2. (*fig.*) Erneuerung. **resuscitative** [–tətiv], *adj.* wiedererweckend, wiederbelebend.

ret [ret], *v.t.* einweichen, rösten, rötten (*flax*).

retable [riˈteibl], *s.* der Altaraufsatz.

retail, 1. [ri:ˈteil], *v.t.* 1. im kleinen *or* en détail verkaufen; 2. (*fig.*) (umständlich) weitererzählen, verbreiten, weitergeben (*news*). **2.** [–ˈteil], *v.i.* im kleinen *or* en détail verkauft werden; – *at*, im Kleinverkauf kosten. **3.** [ˈri:teil], *s.* der Kleinhandel, Kleinverkauf; *at* or *by –*, im kleinen, en détail, einzeln, stückweise; – *business*, das Detailgeschäft, Einzelhandelsgeschäft; – *dealer*, der Einzelhändler, Kleinhändler; – *price*, der Kleinhandelspreis, Einzelpreis, Ladenpreis; – *price fixing*, die Bestimmung des Einzelhandelspreises; – *shop*, see – *business*; – *trade*, der Detailhandel, Kleinhandel, Einzelhandel. **retailer** [ˈri:teilə], *s.* 1. der Kleinhändler, Einzelhändler, Wiederverkäufer; 2. (*fig.*) Verbreiter, Erzähler (*of news*).

retain [ri'tein], *v.t.* (*a th.*) 1. (zurück)behalten, beibehalten, festhalten an (*Dat.*); 2. (im Gedächtnis) behalten; 3. (*a p.*) bei sich behalten; sich (*Dat.*) halten *or* verpflichten (*a lawyer*); 4. bestellen, belegen (*places etc.*); 5. (*Archit., Tech.*) stützen, sichern, festhalten; 6. zurückhalten, stauen (*water*). **retainer** [–ə], *s.* 1. (*Hist.*) der Gefolgsmann, Lehnsmann; *pl.* das Gefolge; 2. (*Law*) der (Honorar)vorschuß; 3. (*Tech.*) (Kugel)käfig. **retaining,** *adj.* – ***dam,*** das Stauwehr; – ***fee,*** ***see*** **retainer,** 2; – ***wall,*** die Stützmauer.

retake, **1.** [ri:'teik], *irr.v.t.* 1. wiedernehmen; 2. (*Mil.*) wieder einnehmen, zurückerobern; 3. (*Films*) nochmals aufnehmen. **2.** ['ri:teik], *s.* (*Films*) die Neuaufnahme.

retaliate [ri'tælieit], **1.** *v.t.* vergelten (***upon,*** an (*Dat.*)), heimzahlen (*Dat.*). **2.** *v.i.* sich rächen, Vergeltung üben (***upon,*** an (*Dat.*)); Vergeltungsmaßnahmen treffen (***against,*** gegen). **retaliation** [–'eiʃən], *s.* die Vergeltung; ***in – for,*** als Vergeltungsmaßnahme für. **retaliatory** [–iətəri], *adj.* Vergeltungs–; – ***measures,*** Vergeltungsmaßnahmen, Repressalien (*pl.*).

retard [ri'tɑ:d], **1.** *v.t.* aufhalten, hindern (*a p.*); verlangsamen, hemmen, zurückhalten, verzögern, hinhalten, hinausschieben (*a th.*); ***be –ed,*** zurückgeblieben sein (*in development*); (*Tech., Elec.*) nacheilen; (*Motor.*) ***–ed ignition,*** die Spätzündung; ***–ed motion,*** verzögerte Bewegung; ***–ed velocity,*** verlangsamte Geschwindigkeit. **2.** *s.* die Verzögerung. **retardation** [ri:tɑ:'deiʃən], **retardment,** *s.* 1. die Verzögerung, Verlangsamung; 2. (*in development*) Unterentwickeltheit, das Zurückbleiben; 3. (*Tech., Elec.*) die Nacheilung; 4. (*Mus.*) der Vorhalt.

retch [retʃ], *v.i.* sich erbrechen *or* übergeben.

retell [ri:'tel], *irr.v.t.* nochmals *or* noch einmal erzählen, wiederholen.

retention [ri'tenʃən], *s.* 1. das (Zurück)behalten; 2. die Bewahrung, Beibehaltung, Einbehaltung, Zurückbehaltung; – ***of shape,*** die Formbeständigkeit; 3. (*Med.*) die Verhaltung. **retentive** [–tiv], *adj.* 1. behaltend, zurückhaltend; ***be – of,*** behalten, bei sich halten, bewahren; 2. (*of a p.*) mit gutem Gedächtnis begabt; – ***memory,*** gutes Gedächtnis. **retentiveness,** *s.* die Gedächtniskraft. **retentivity** [ri:ten'tiviti], *s.* (*Phys.*) die Koerzitivkraft (*of magnet*); *see also* **retentiveness.**

reticence ['retisəns], *s.* 1. die Zurückhaltung, Verschwiegenheit; 2. Verschweigung (*of facts*). **reticent** [–ənt], *adj.* 1. zurückhaltend, schweigsam; 2. verschwiegen (***about, on,*** über (*Acc.*)).

reticle ['retikl], *s.* (*Opt.*) das Fadenkreuz.

reticular [ri'tikjulə], **reticulate, 1.** [–it], *adj.* netzförmig, netzartig. **2.** [–eit], *v.t.* netzförmig zerteilen *or* verzieren. **3.** [–eit], *v.i.* sich netzförmig ausdehnen. **reticulated** [–eitid], *adj.* netzförmig, Netz–. **reticulation** [–'leiʃən], *s.* 1. das Netzwerk; 2. (*Phot.*) die Netzbildung.

reticule ['retikju:l], *s.* 1. der Strickbeutel, der *or* das Retikül; 2. (*Astr.*) das Retikulum; *see also* **reticle. reticulum** [–'tikjuləm], *s.* (*pl.* **-la**) 1. (*Zool.*) der Netzmagen; 2. (*fig.*) das Netz(werk), Geflecht, netzförmiges Gefüge. **retiform** [–fɔ:m], *adj.* Netz–, Maschen–, maschig, netzförmig.

retina ['retinə], *s.* die Netzhaut. **retinal,** *adj.* Netzhaut–. **retinitis** [–'naitis], *s.* die Netzhautentzündung.

retinue ['retinju:], *s.* das Gefolge.

retiral [ri'taiərəl], *s.* (*Scots*) das (Sich)zurückziehen, Ausscheiden.

retire [ri'taiə], **1.** *v.t.* 1. zurückziehen (*troops*); 2. einlösen (*a bill*); 3. verabschieden, pensionieren, in den Ruhestand versetzen (*a p.*). **2.** *v.i.* 1. sich zurückziehen; – ***from business,*** sich zur Ruhe setzen, sich vom Geschäft zurückziehen; – ***from active service,*** seinen Abschied aus dem aktiven Dienst nehmen; – ***into o.s.,*** sich verschließen; – ***into the country,*** sich aufs Land zurückziehen; 2. zurückweichen, zurücktreten (***from,*** von), sich entfernen, austreten, ausscheiden (***from,*** aus); 3. in den Ruhestand treten; sich pensionieren lassen, in Pension gehen, sich zur Ruhe setzen; 4. schlafen *or* zu Bett gehen. **3.** *s.* (*Mil.*) der Rückzug; Zapfenstreich. **retired,** *adj.* 1. zurückgezogen, einsam; – ***life,*** zurückgezogenes Leben; 2. pensioniert, verabschiedet, im Ruhestand; (*Mil.*) außer Dienst; ***place*** or ***put on the – list,*** verabschieden, pensionieren, in den Ruhestand versetzen, den Abschied geben (*Dat.*); – ***pay,*** das Ruhegehalt, die Pension.

retirement [ri'taiəmənt], *s.* 1. das (Sich)zurückziehen, Ausscheiden, der Austritt, Rücktritt (***from,*** von); 2. die Zurückgezogenheit, Abgeschiedenheit; 3. Pensionierung, der Ruhestand; ***go into –,*** ins Privatleben zurücktreten, sich zur Ruhe setzen, in Pension gehen; 4. (*Mil.*) der Rückzug; 5. (*Comm.*) Rückkauf, die Einziehung. **retiring,** *adj.* 1. zurückhaltend, bescheiden, unauffällig, unaufdringlich; 2. Pensions–, Ruhestands–; – ***age,*** das Pensionierungsalter; – ***pension,*** das Ruhegehalt, die Altersrente, Pension; 3. ***--room,*** die Toilette.

[1]**retort** [ri'tɔ:t], **1.** *v.i.* scharf erwidern *or* entgegnen. **2.** *v.t.* zurückgeben (*on, Dat.*), zurückfallen lassen, zurückwerfen (auf (*Acc.*)), sich rächen für, vergelten (an (*Dat.*)). **3.** *s.* scharfe *or* treffende Entgegnung *or* Erwiderung, schlagfertige Antwort, (*coll.*) die Retourkutsche.

[2]**retort,** *s.* die Retorte, Destillierblase, der Destillationskolben.

retortion [ri'tɔ:ʃən], *s.* 1. (*Law*) die Retorsion; 2. Zurückbiegung, das Zurücklegen, Umwenden, Umkehren, die Rückwendung.

retouch [ri:'tʌtʃ], **1.** *v.t.* überarbeiten, nachbessern, retuschieren. **2.** *or* **retouching,** *s.* das Retuschieren, die Retusche, Überarbeitung, Nachbesserung.

retrace [ri'treis], *v.t.* zurückführen (***to,*** auf (*Acc.*)); zurückverfolgen; – ***one's steps,*** denselben Weg zurückgehen, (*fig.*) alles rückgängig machen.

retract [ri'trækt], **1.** *v.t.* 1. zurückziehen; 2. einziehen (*claws etc.*); 3. (*fig.*) widerrufen, zurücknehmen. **2.** *v.i.* sich zurückziehen, zurücktreten (***from,*** von), widerrufen; ***no –ing,*** kein Zurück. **retractable** [–əbl], *adj.* 1. (*Av., Zool.*) einziehbar; – ***undercarriage,*** das Einziehfahrwerk; 2. (*fig.*) zurücknehmbar, zurückziehbar, widerruflich. **retractation** [ri:træk'teiʃən], *s. See* **retraction,** 1. **retractile** [–tail], *adj. See* **retractable,** 1. **retraction** [–ʃən], *s.* 1. die Zurückziehung; 2. Zurücknahme, der Widerruf. **retractor,** *s.* 1. (*Anat.*) der Retraktionsmuskel, Rückzieher; 2. (*Surg.*) Wundrandhalter; 3. (*Mil.*) (Hülsen)-auszieher.

retrain [ri:'trein], *v.t., v.i.* umschulen.

retranslate [ri:trɑ:ns'leit], *v.t.* (zu)rückübersetzen. **retranslation** [–'leiʃən], *s.* die Rückübersetzung.

retread [ri:'tred], *irr.v.t.* wieder betreten.

re-tread [ri:'tred], *v.t.* (*tyres*) (auf)sommern.

retreat [ri'tri:t], **1.** *s.* 1. der Rückzug (*also Mil.*); (*Mil.*) Zapfenstreich; (*Mil.*) ***beat (sound) the –,*** den Zapfenstreich *or* zum Rückzug schlagen (blasen); (*fig.*) ***beat a –,*** sich zurückziehen *or* aus dem Staube machen; 2. die Abgeschiedenheit, Zurückgezogenheit; 3. der Zufluchtort, Unterschlupf, Schlupfwinkel, die Zuflucht; 4. (*Eccl.*) Einkehr; 5. (*Archit.*) Zurücksetzung. **2.** *v.i.* 1. sich zurückziehen; 2. zurückweichen; ***–ing forehead,*** zurücktretende Stirn.

retrench [ri'trentʃ], **1.** *v.t.* 1. kürzen, beschneiden, beschränken, einschränken, abbauen (*expenses*); 2. entfernen, streichen, weglassen; 3. (*Fort.*) verschanzen. **2.** *v.i.* sich einschränken. **retrenchment,** *s.* 1. die Kürzung, Beschränkung, Einschränkung; 2. der Abbau; 3. die Streichung, Abschaffung, Auslassung; 4. (*Fort.*) Verschanzung.

retrial [ri:'traiəl], *s.* (*Law*) das Wiederaufnahmeverfahren.

retribution [retri'bju:ʃən], *s.* die Vergeltung, Strafe. **retributive** [ri'tribjutiv], **retributory**

[-jutəri], *adj.* vergeltend, Vergeltungs-, ausgleichend.

retrievable [ri'tri:vəbl], *adj.* wiederbringlich, wiedergutzumachen(d). **retrieval,** *s.* das Wiederauffinden. **retrieve, 1.** *v.t.* 1. apportieren (*of dogs*); 2. wiedergewinnen, wiedererlangen; 3. wiedereinbringen, wiedergutmachen, wettmachen (*a loss*); 4. retten (*from*, aus). **2.** *v.i.* apportieren. **3.** *s.* die Rettung; ***past*** or ***beyond*** **–**, rettungslos. **retriever,** *s.* der Apportierhund, Stöberhund.

retro ['retrou], *pref.* (zu)rück-, rückwärts-.

retroact [retrou'ækt], *v.i.* (zu)rückwirken. **retroaction** [-'ækʃən], *s.* die Rückwirkung. **retroactive** [-tiv], *adj.* rückwirkend.

retrocede [retrou'si:d], **1.** *v.i.* 1. zurückgehen; 2. (*Med.*) nach innen schlagen. **2.** *v.t.* (*Law*) wiederabtreten (*to*, an (*Acc.*)). **retrocedent,** *adj.* 1. zurückgehend; 2. (*Med.*) nach innen schlagend. **retrocession** [-'seʃən], *s.* 1. das Zurückgehen; 2. (*Law*) die Wiederabtretung, Rückübertragung, Rückgabe. **retrocessive** [-'sesiv], *adj.* 1. zurückgehend; 2. (*Law*) wiederabtretend.

retrochoir ['retrəkwaiə], *s.* der Rückchor, Retrochorus.

retroflected [retrou'flektid], **retroflex(ed)** ['retroufleks(t)], *adj.* zurückgebogen, rückwärts gebeugt. **retroflexion** [-'flekʃən], *s.* die Zurückbiegung, Beugung nach rückwärts.

retrogradation [retrougrə'deiʃən], *s.* 1. das Zurückgehen; 2. der Rückgang; 3. (*Astr.*) (scheinbar) rückläufige Bewegung. **retrograde** ['retrougreid], **1.** *adj.* 1. rückläufig, Rückwärts-, rückwärtsgehend; 2. (*fig.*) rückschrittlich, rückgängig; – ***step,*** der Rückschritt. **2.** *v.i.* rückläufig sein, zurückgehen (*also fig.*), rückwärts gehen.

retrogress [retrou'gres], *v.i.* 1. zurückgehen, rückwärts gehen; 2. (*fig.*) sich verschlechtern, entarten. **retrogression** [-'greʃən], *s.* 1. das Rückwärtsgehen, rückläufige Bewegung; 2. der Rückschritt, rückläufige Bewegung; 3. (*fig.*) die Rückentwicklung, Rückbildung, Verschlechterung, Entartung. **retrogressive** [-siv], 1. rückschreitend, Rück-; 2. (*fig.*) rückschrittlich.

retro-rocket, *s.* die Bremsrakete.

retrospect ['retrouspekt], *s.* der Rückblick, die Rückschau; ***in*** **–**, rückschauend. **retrospection** [-'spekʃən], *s.* der Rückblick, die Rückschau, Erinnerung. **retrospective** [-'spektiv], *adj.* 1. rückblickend, rückschauend, Rück-; – ***view,*** der Rückblick; 2. (*Law*) rückwirkend.

retroussé [rə'tru:sei], *adj.* nach oben gebogen; – ***nose,*** die Stülpnase.

retroversion [retrou'və:ʃən], *s.* die Rückwärtslagerung, Rückwärtsbeugung (*of the uterus*). **retrovert** [-'və:t], *v.t.* rückwärts verlagern. **retroverted,** *adj.* rückwärtsverlagert (*of the uterus*).

re-try [ri:'trai], *v.t.* (*Law*) von neuem verhören (*a p.*) *or* verhandeln (*a case*).

return [ri'tə:n], **1.** *v.i.* 1. zurückkehren, zurückkommen (*to*, auf (*Acc.*)), wiederkehren, wiederauftreten, wiederkommen; – ***to dust,*** wieder zu Staub werden; – ***to health,*** wieder gesund werden, genesen; – ***home,*** nach Hause zurückkehren *or* zurückgehen; – ***to the matter*** or ***subject,*** noch darauf zurückkommen; 2. (*Law*) zurückfallen (***to***, an (*Acc.*)); 3. antworten, entgegnen, erwidern. **2.** *v.t.* 1. zurückbringen, zurückstellen; 2. zurückgeben, zurücksenden, zurückschicken, zurückerstatten, wiedergeben; 3. zurückwerfen (*rays*); 4. zurückschlagen (*a ball*); 5. zurückzahlen (*money*); 6. abstatten (*a visit, thanks*); erwidern (*accusation, greeting*); – ***a compliment,*** ein Kompliment erwidern; – ***good for evil,*** Böses mit Gutem vergelten; – ***like for like,*** Gleiches mit Gleichem vergelten; – ***thanks,*** danken, Dank sagen (***to***, *Dat.*); – ***a visit,*** einen Gegenbesuch machen *or* abstatten; 7. abgeben (*a vote*), fällen, sprechen (*a verdict*); ***be -ed guilty,*** schuldig gesprochen werden; 8. erklären, angeben, melden (*information*); 9. als Abgeordneten wählen (***to***, in (*Acc.*)); 10. einbringen; – ***a profit,*** Gewinn abwerfen *or* einbringen. **3.** *s.* 1. die Rückkehr; Rückreise, Rückfahrt; – ***of health,*** wiederkehrende Gesundheit; ***by – of post,*** postwendend, mit umgehender Post; ***on sale or –***, in Kommission; ***wish him many happy -s of the day,*** ihm herzliche Glückwünsche zum Geburtsag aussprechen; 2. die Wiederkehr, der Rückfall, das Wiederauftreten (*of disease*); 3. der Wechsel, Umlauf (*of the seasons etc.*); 4. die Wiedergabe, Rückgabe; 5. Rückerstattung, Rückzahlung, Gegenleistung, Entschädigung, Vergeltung, der Ersatz; ***in*** **–**, dafür, dagegen; ***in – for,*** (als Entgelt) für; 6. die Erwiderung, Antwort; – ***of affection,*** die Gegenliebe; – ***of a salute,*** der Gegengruß; – ***of thanks,*** die Danksagung; 7. das Zurückschlagen, der Rückschlag (*of a ball*); 8. (*Comm.*) (*oft. pl.*) die Einnahme, der (Kapital)umsatz, Gewinn, Ertrag, Erlös; ***sales -s,*** Verkaufsergebnisse (*pl.*); ***yield a good –***, viel einbringen; ***yield quick -s,*** schnellen Umsatz haben, schnell abgehen; 9. (amtlicher) Bericht, die Aufstellung, Erklärung, (statistischer) Ausweis; ***income-tax –***, die Einkommensteuererklärung; (*Mil.*) ***strength –***, die Stärkemeldung; 10. (*Parl.*) der Wahlbericht; ***election -s,*** das Wahlergebnis; 11. (*Archit.*) Seitenflügel, vorspringender Teil; 12. (*Tech.*) die Krümmung, Biegung; 13. (*coll.*) die Rückfahrkarte; 14. *pl.* (*Comm.*) das Rückgut, die Remittende (*books etc.*); 15. der Feinschnitt (*tobacco*).

returnable [ri'tə:nəbl], *adj.* 1. zurückzugeben(d), zurückzustellen(d); 2. rückzahlbar (*payment*), umtauschbar (*goods*); – ***cargo,*** die Rückfracht. **returning officer,** *s.* der Wahlkommissar. **return| journey,** *s.* die Rückreise. **– line,** *s.* (*Tele.*) die Rückleitung. **– match,** *s.* die Revanchepartie. **– postage,** *s.* das Rückporto. **– ticket,** *s.* die Rückfahrkarte, der Rückfahrschein. **– valve,** *s.* das Rückschlagventil.

reunification [riju:nifi'keiʃən], *s.* die Wiedervereinigung. **reunion** [-'ju:niən], *s.* 1. die Wiedervereinigung, das Wiedersehen; 2. Treffen. **reunite** [-'nait], *v.t.* (*v.i.* sich) wiedervereinigen.

rev [rev], **1.** *s.* (*coll.*) 1. die Umdrehung; (*Motor.*) Drehzahl; – ***counter,*** der Drehzahlmesser. **2.** *v.t.* (*v.i.*) (*oft.* – ***up***) (*coll.*) – ***up the engine,*** den Motor auf Touren bringen.

revaccinate [ri:'væksineit], *v.t.* wieder impfen, nachimpfen. **revaccination** [-'neiʃən], *s.* die Wiederimpfung, Zweitimpfung.

revalorization [ri:vælərai'zeiʃən], *s.* die Aufwertung, Neubewertung. **revalorize** [ri:'væləraiz], *v.t.* aufwerten, neu bewerten.

revaluation [ri:vælju'eiʃən], *s.* die Umwertung. **revalue** [-'vælju:], *v.t.* umwerten.

reveal [ri'vi:l], **1.** *v.t.* 1. aufdecken, enthüllen, verraten; 2. offenbaren (*also Theol.*); 3. zeigen. **2.** *s.* innere Bogenfläche, die Laibung.

réveillé [ri'væli], *s.* (*Mil.*) das Wecken, der Weckruf, die Reveille.

revel [revl], **1.** *s.* das Gelage; die Lustbarkeit. **2.** *v.i.* 1. schmausen; 2. sich weiden *or* ergötzen (***in***, an (*Dat.*)), schwelgen (in (*Dat.*)).

revelation [revi'leiʃən], *s.* 1. die Offenbarung (***to***, für), Entdeckung, Enthüllung; 2. (*Theol.*) Offenbarung; ***the Revelation of St. John,*** die Offenbarung Johannis.

reveler (*Am.*), **reveller** ['revələ], *s.* 1. der Schwelger (***in***, in (*Dat.*)); 2. (Nacht)schwärmer. **revelry** [-ri], *s.* laute Lustbarkeit, das Gelage.

revenant ['revənã], *s.* Wiederaufgestandene(r), der Geist, das Gespenst.

revenge [ri'vendʒ], **1.** *s.* die Rache, Rachgier, Rachsucht; ***take (one's) –***, sich rächen (***on***, an (*Dat.*)); ***in –***, aus Rache; 2. (*Spt. etc.*) die Revanche; ***have one's –***, sich revanchieren. **2.** *v.t.* rächen (***on***, an (*Dat.*)); ***be -d, – o.s.,*** sich rächen (***on***, an (*Dat.*)). **revengeful,** *adj.* rachsüchtig. **revengefulness,** *s.* die Rachgier, Rachsucht.

revenue ['revinju:], *s.* das Einkommen, Einnahmen (*pl.*), Einkünfte (*pl.*); ***inland –***, Staatseinkünfte (*pl.*), Staatseinnahmen (*pl.*); ***inland – office,*** die Staatssteuerkasse. **revenue| cutter,** *s.* das Zollschiff. – **officer,** *s.* Zollbeamte(r). – **stamp,** *s.* die Banderole, Steuermarke.

reverberant [ri'və:bərənt], *adj.* (*Poet.*) widerhallend. **reverberate** [–eit], **1.** *v.i.* 1. widerhallen, nachhallen; 2. zurückstrahlen (*light*); 3. (*fig.*) zurückwirken (*on,* auf (*Acc.*)). **2.** *v.t.* 1. zurücksenden; 2. zurückwerfen (*light*). **reverberation** [–'reiʃən], *s.* 1. der Widerhall; 2. das Widerhallen; 3. Zurückstrahlen, Zurückwerfen (*of light*). **reverberatory** [–rətəri], *adj.* zurückwerfend, zurückstrahlend; – ***furnace,*** der Flammofen, Strahlungsofen, Reverberierofen.

revere [ri'viə], *v.t.* (ver)ehren.

reverence ['revərəns], **1.** *s.* 1. die Verehrung, Ehrerbietung, Ehrfurcht, der Respekt (***for,*** vor (*Dat.*)); 2. die Reverenz, Verbeugung; 3. ***Your Reverence,*** Euer Ehrwürden. **2.** *v.t.* (ver)ehren. **reverend** [–ənd], *adj.* ehrwürdig; ***Most*** or ***Right*** or ***Very Reverend,*** hochwürdig; Hochwürden (*title*); – ***Sir,*** Euer Ehrwürden. **reverent, reverential** [–'renʃəl], *adj.* ehrerbietig, ehrfurchtsvoll.

reverie ['revəri], *s.* die Träumerei.

revers [rə'vɛə, (*coll.*) –'viə], *s.* (*usu. pl.* [–z]) der Aufschlag, Revers.

reversal [ri'və:sl], *s.* 1. die Umkehr(ung), der Umschwung; – ***of fortune,*** die Schicksalswende; 2. (*Law*) die Umstoßung, Aufhebung.

reverse [ri'və:s], **1.** *s.* 1. die Rückseite, Kehrseite (*of coin etc.*); (*Mil.*) ***take in –,*** im Rücken *or* von hinten packen; 2. Umgekehrte(s), das Gegenteil; ***quite the –,*** gerade umgekehrt; 3. der Rückschlag, Umschlag (*of fortune*), (Glücks)wechsel, (Schicksals)schlag, (*Mil.*) die Niederlage, Schlappe; ***meet with a –,*** eine Schlappe erleiden; 4. (*Motor.*) der Rückwärtsgang; ***in –,*** rückwärtsfahrend. **2.** *v.t.* 1. umkehren, auf den Kopf stellen; – ***arms,*** Gewehre mit dem Kolben nach oben halten; – ***the order,*** die Reihenfolge umkehren; – ***the order of things,*** die Weltordnung umstürzen; 2. aufheben, umstoßen, umstürzen (*decree*); 3. umsteuern (*engines*). **3.** *v.i.* 1. (*Motor.*) rückwärtsfahren; 2. linksherum tanzen (*in a waltz*). **4.** *adj.* umgekehrt, entgegengesetzt; – ***current,*** der Gegenstrom; – ***direction,*** entgegengesetzte Richtung; – ***fire,*** das Rückenfeuer; (*Motor.*) – ***gear,*** der Rücklauf, Rückwärtsgang; – ***order,*** umgekehrte Reihenfolge; – ***side,*** die Rückseite, Kehrseite.

reversibility [rivə:si'biliti], *s.* 1. die Umkehrbarkeit; 2. (*fig.*) Umstoßbarkeit. **reversible** [–'və:sibl], *adj.* 1. umkehrbar; 2. (*Law*) umstoßbar; 3. (*Tech.*) umsteuerbar; 4. wendbar, zweiseitig zu tragen (*as cloth*). **reversing** [–'və:siŋ], *adj.* Umsteuerungs–; ***–-gear,*** die Umsteuerung(svorrichtung); ***–-switch,*** der Umkehrschalter, Wendeschalter, Stromwender.

reversion [ri'və:ʃən], *s.* 1. die Umkehrung (*also Math.*); 2. (*Law*) der Rückfall, Heimfall (***to,*** auf (*Acc.*)); ***right of –,*** das Heimfallsrecht; ***in –,*** mit einem Heimfallsrecht belastet; 3. (*Biol. etc.*) der Atavismus, Rückschlag, die Rückverwandlung. **reversional, reversionary,** *adj.* 1. (*Law*) anwartschaftlich, Anwartschafts–; – ***annuity,*** die Rente auf den Überlebensfall; – ***heir,*** der Nacherbe; – ***interest,*** der Erbanspruch; – ***property,*** die Anwartschaft auf späteren Besitz; 2. (*Biol.*) atavistisch. **reversioner,** *s.* (*Law*) der Anwärter, Nacherbe.

revert, 1. [ri'və:t], *v.i.* 1. zurückkehren (***to,*** zu), zurückfallen (in (*Acc.*)), zurückgreifen, zurückkommen (auf (*Acc.*)); 2. (*Law*) heimfallen, zurückfallen (***to,*** an (*Acc.*)); 3. (*Biol.*) zurückschlagen. **2.** [–'və:t], *v.t.* 1. zurückwenden (*the eyes*); 2. umkehren (*a series*). **3.** ['ri:və:t], *s.* Wiederbekehrte(r). **revertible** [ri'və:tibl], *adj.* (*Law*) heimfällig, rückfällig.

revet [ri'vet], *v.t.* verkleiden, bekleiden (*wall etc.*). **revetment, revetting,** *s.* die Verkleidung, Verschalung; Futtermauer.

review [ri'vju:], **1.** *s.* 1. die Durchsicht, Nachprüfung, Überprufung, Revision; 2. (*Mil.*) Parade, Truppenschau, Truppenmusterung; ***naval –,*** die Flottenparade; ***pass in –,*** mustern (*troops*); 3. der Überblick, Rückblick, die Rückschau (***of,*** auf (*Acc.*)); ***pass in –,*** Rückschau halten über (*Acc.*), (rückschauend) überblicken (*events etc.*); 4. die Besprechung, Rezension, Kritik (*of a book*); – ***copy,*** das Rezensionsexemplar; 5. die Rundschau, Zeitschrift, Revue. **2.** *v.t.* 1. nachprüfen, (über)prüfen, revidieren; 2. überblicken, überschauen, zurückblicken auf (*Acc.*); 3. durchgehen, durchsehen, besprechen, rezensieren (*a book etc.*); 4. (*Mil.*) mustern, inspizieren, Parade abhalten über (*Acc.*). **3.** *v.i.* rezensieren. **reviewal** [–əl], *s.* die Revision, Nachprüfung. **reviewer,** *s.* der Rezensent.

revile [ri'vail], *v.t.* schmähen, verleumden, verunglimpfen. **revilement,** *s.* die Schmähung, Verleumdung, Verunglimpfung.

revisal [ri'vaizl], *s.* die Revision, Nachprüfung. **revisary,** *adj.* Revisions–. **revise, 1.** *v.t.* 1. durchsehen, überarbeiten, revidieren; ***–d edition,*** verbesserte Auflage; ***Revised Version,*** die Revision der Bibel; 2. ändern, verbessern; 3. (*Law*) nachprüfen. **2.** *s.* 1. nochmalige Durchsicht, die Revision; 2. (*Typ.*) zweite Korrektur; (*also* ***–-proof***) der Revisionsbogen. **reviser,** *s.* (*Typ.*) der Korrektor, Revisor, Nachleser. **revision** [–'viʒən], *s.* 1. die Revision (*also Law*), Überprüfung, nochmalige Durchsicht; 2. durchgesehene *or* verbesserte Ausgabe.

revisit [ri:'vizit], *v.t.* nochmals besuchen.

revisory [ri'vaizəri], *adj.* Überwachungs–, Überprüfungs–.

revitalize [ri:'vaitəlaiz], *v.t.* neu beleben.

revival [ri'vaivl], *s.* 1. das Wiederaufleben, Wiederaufblühen, die Wiedergeburt, Wiedererweckung, Wiederbelebung, Erneuerung; ***Revival of Learning,*** die Renaissance; 2. (*Eccl.*) die Erweckung(sbewegung); 3. (*Theat.*) Wiederaufführung, Neuaufnahme. **revivalism,** *s.* (*Eccl.*) der Erweckungseifer; die Glaubenserweckung. **revivalist,** *s.* der Erweckungsprediger.

revive [ri'vaiv], **1.** *v.t.* 1. wieder zu Bewußtsein bringen (*a p.*); 2. wiederherstellen, erneuern, wieder auffrischen, wieder *or* neu beleben, wieder erwecken (*feelings*); 3. wieder aufleben lassen, wieder ins Leben rufen, wieder einführen (*customs*); 4. wieder zur Sprache bringen (*a subject*); 5. wieder aufführen *or* aufnehmen *or* auf die Bühne bringen (*a play etc.*); 6. (*Metall.*) frischen. **2.** *v.i.* 1. wieder zu Bewußtsein kommen, das Bewußtsein wiedergewinnen; 2. wieder aufkommen *or* aufleben *or* aufblühen *or* auftreten. **reviver** [–ə], *s.* 1. das Erfrischungsmittel, Renovierungsmittel; 2. (*sl.*) der Erfrischungstrunk.

revivification [ri:vivifi'keiʃən], *s.* das Wiederaufleben, die Wiederbelebung, Erneuerung. **revivify** [ri'vivifai], *v.t.* wiederbeleben, erneuern, auffrischen. **reviviscent** [ri:vi'visənt], *adj.* 1. wiederauflebend; 2. (*fig.*) wiederbelebend.

revocable ['revəkəbl], *adj.* widerruflich. **revocation** [–'keiʃən], *s.* 1. der Widerruf; 2. (*Law*) die Aufhebung, Rücknahme, der Entzug. **revoke** [ri'vouk], **1.** *v.t.* 1. widerrufen, zurücknehmen; 2. rückgängig machen, aufheben. **2.** *v.i.* (*Cards*) nicht bedienen, Farbe nicht bekennen. **3.** *s.* (*Cards*) das Nichtbekennen, die Renonce.

revolt [ri'voult], **1.** *s.* 1. die Empörung, Auflehnung (***against,*** gegen); 2. der Aufruhr, Aufstand. **2.** *v.i.* 1. sich empören *or* auflehnen (***against,*** gegen); 2. sich abwenden, abfallen (***from,*** von); 3. (*fig.*) sich sträuben (***against, from,*** gegen), Widerwillen empfinden (***at,*** über (*Acc.*)). **3.** *v.t.* empören, abstoßen (*a p.*). **revolting,** *adj.* (*fig.*) abstoßend, empörend, ekelhaft.

revolute ['revəl(j)u:t], *adj.* (*Bot.*) zurückgerollt. **revolution** [revə'l(j)u:ʃən], *s.* 1. (*Tech.*) die (Um)drehung, Tour, der Umlauf, Kreislauf; – ***counter,*** der Drehzahlmesser, Tourenzähler; ***–s per minute,*** die Drehzahl *or* Tourenzahl pro Minute; 2. (*fig.*) der Umschwung, die Umwälzung; 3. (*Pol.*)

Revolution, (Staats)umwälzung, der Umsturz. **revolutionary, 1.** *adj.* 1. revolutionär (*also fig.*), umstürzlerisch, Umsturz–, (staats)umwälzend; 2. (*fig.*) epochemachend. **2.** *s.* der Revolutionär, Umstürzler. **revolutionist,** *s. See* **revolutionary, 2. revolutionize,** *v.t.* 1. revolutionieren, in Aufruhr bringen; 2. (*fig.*) umwälzen, gänzlich umgestalten.

revolve [ri'vɔlv], **1.** *v.i.* 1. sich drehen, rotieren, kreisen (*on* (*Tech.*), *round,* um (*Acc.*)); 2. (*fig.*) herumgehen. **2.** *v.t.* 1. drehen; 2. (*fig.*) (hin und her) überlegen, erwägen (*in one's mind*). **revolver** [ri'vɔlvə], *s.* der Revolver. **revolving,** *adj.* sich drehend, drehbar, Dreh–; – ***bookcase,*** drehbarer Bücherständer; – ***chair,*** der Drehstuhl; (*Naut.*) – ***light,*** das Blinkfeuer; – ***pencil,*** der Drehbleistift; – ***shutter,*** der Rolladen; – ***stage,*** die Drehbühne.

revue [ri'vju:], *s.* (*Theat.*) die Revue.

revulsion [ri'vʌlʃən], *s.* 1. der Umschwung, Umschlag (*of feelings etc.*); 2. (*coll.*) der *or* die Abscheu, der Ekel; 3. (*Med.*) das Ableiten, die Ableitung. **revulsive** [–siv], *adj.* (*Med.*) ableitend.

reward [ri'wɔ:d], **1.** *s.* 1. die Belohnung, Vergütung; der Finderlohn; 2. (*fig.*) die Vergeltung, der Lohn, das Entgelt. **2.** *v.t.* 1. belohnen; 2. vergelten (*Dat.*) (***for,*** *Acc.*) (*services etc.*). **rewarding,** *adj.* lohnend.

rewind [ri:'waind], *irr.v.t.* umspulen (*film, tape etc.*), umwickeln (*a reel*), neu wickeln (*electric motor etc.*).

rewire [ri:'waiə], *v.t.* neu verkabeln, wieder verdrahten.

reword [ri:'wə:d], *v.t.* neu formulieren, anders *or* mit anderen Worten ausdrücken.

rewrite, 1. [ri:'rait], *irr.v.t.* neu *or* nochmals schreiben, umarbeiten. **2.** ['ri:rait], *s.* – ***man,*** der Überarbeiter (*press*).

Reynard ['reinɑ:d], *s.* Reineke (Fuchs).

rhapsodic(al) [ræp'sɔdik(l)], *adj.* begeistert, überschwenglich, ekstatisch, rhapsodisch. **rhapsodist** ['ræpsədist], *s.* 1. der Rhapsode (*Greek*); 2. (*fig.*) begeisterter Schwärmer. **rhapsodize** ['ræpsədaiz], *v.i.* schwärmen (***about, over,*** von). **rhapsody** ['ræpsədi], *s.* 1. die Rhapsodie; 2. (*fig.*) der Wortschwall, überschwenglicher Vortrag; ***go into rhapsodies over,*** sich in überschwenglichen Lob ergehen über (*Acc.*).

rhatany ['rætəni], *s.* **1.** (*Bot.*) der Ratanhiastrauch, die Krameria; 2. Ratanhiawurzel.

rhea ['ri:ə], *s.* (*Orn.*) der Nandu.

Rheims [ri:mz], *s.* (*Geog.*) Reims (*n.*).

Rhenish ['reniʃ] **1.**, *adj.* (*Geog.*) rheinisch, Rhein–; – ***Franconia,*** Rheinfranken (*n.*); – ***Palatinate,*** die Rheinpfalz. **2.** *s.* (*obs.*) der Rheinwein.

rheostat ['ri:əstæt], *s.* (*Elec.*) der Rheostat, Regulierwiderstand, Widerstandsregler.

rhesus ['ri:səs], *s.* der Rhesus(affe); ***Rhesus factor,*** der Rhesusfaktor, Rh-Faktor.

rhetoric ['retərik], *s.* 1. die Redekunst, Rhetorik; 2. (*fig.*) leere Phrasen, der Redeschwall. **rhetorical** [ri'tɔrikl], *adj.* 1. rhetorisch, rednerisch, Redner–; – ***question,*** die Scheinfrage, rhetorische Frage; 2. schönrednerisch, phrasenhaft, schwülstig. **rhetorician** [retə'riʃən], *s.* 1. der Redekünstler; 2. Schönredner, Phrasendrescher.

rheum [ru:m], *s.* (*obs.*) 1. die Flüssigkeit, der Schleim; 2. Schnupfen. **rheumatic** [–'mætik], **1.** *adj.* rheumatisch; – ***fever,*** der Gelenkrheumatismus. **2.** *s.* 1. der (die) Rheumatiker(in); 2. *pl.* (*coll.*) das Rheuma. **rheumatism** [–ətizm], *s.* der Rheumatismus, das Rheuma, Gliederreißen. **rheumatoid** [–ətɔid], *adj.* rheumaartig; – ***arthritis,*** die Arthritis deformans. **rheumy** [–i], *adj.* (*obs.*) wässerig (*eye etc.*).

Rhine [rain], *s.* Rhein (*m.*); ***Lower*** –, der Niederrhein; ***Upper*** –, der Oberrhein; – ***Province,*** die Rheinprovinz; ***Confederation of the*** –, der Rheinbund. **Rhineland,** *s.* das Rheinland. **Rhinelander,** *s.* der (die) Rheinländer(in).

rhino ['rainou] (*coll.*), **rhinoceros** [–'nɔsərəs], *s.* das Nashorn, Rhinozeros.

rhizome ['raizoum], *s.* der Wurzelstock, das Rhizom. **rhizophagous** [–'zɔfəgəs], *adj.* wurzelfressend. **rhizopod** [–əpɔd], *s.* (*Zool.*) *s.* der Wurzelfüßer.

rhodium ['roudiem], *s.* 1. (*Chem.*) das Rhodium; 2. (*also* –***wood***) das Rhodiumholz; Rosenholz.

rhododendron [roudə'dendrən], *s.* das Rhododendron, die Alpenrose.

rhomb [rɔm(b)], *s.* die Raute(nfläche), der Rhombus. **rhombic** [–bik], *adj.* rautenförmig, rhombisch. **rhombohedral** [–bə'hi:drəl], *adj.* rhomboedrisch. **rhombohedron** [–bə'hi:drən], *s.* das Rhomboeder, Rautenflach. **rhomboid** [–bɔid], **1.** *s.* das Rhomboid. **2.** *or* **rhomboidal** [–'bɔidl], *adj.* rautenförmig; rautenähnlich, rhomboidisch. **rhombus** [–bəs], *s. See* **rhomb.**

rhubarb ['ru:bɑ:b], *s.* der Rhabarber.

rhumb [rʌm], *s.* der Kompaßstrich. **rhumb-line,** *s.* die Kompaßlinie.

rhyme [raim], **1.** *s.* 1. der Reim; das Reimwort (***to,*** auf (*Acc.*)); – ***scheme,*** das Reimschema; ***without*** – ***or reason,*** ohne Sinn und Zweck *or* Verstand; 2. der (Reim)vers, das (Reim)gedicht; ***in*** –, in Reimversen; ***nursery*** –, der Kinderreim, das Kinderlied. **2.** *v.i.* 1. sich reimen (***with,*** mit *or* auf (*Acc.*)); 2. Verse machen. **3.** *v.t.* 1. reimen (lassen) (***with,*** auf (*Acc.*)); 2. reimen, in Reimen abfassen. **rhymed** [–d], *adj.* gereimt, Reim–; – ***verse,*** der Reimvers. **rhymeless,** *adj.* reimlos. **rhymer, rhymester** [–stə], *s.* der Reimschmied, Versemacher, Dichterling. **rhyming,** *s.* das Reimen; – ***dictionary,*** das Reimwörterbuch.

rhythm [riðm], *s.* 1. (*Mus.*) der Rhythmus, Takt; (*Metr.*) das Versmaß; 2. (*fig.*) der Pulsschlag, das An- und Abschwellen, regelmäßige Wiederkehr. **rhythmic(al)** [–mik(l)], *adj.* 1. rhythmisch, taktmäßig, Rhythmus–; 2. regelmäßig wiederkehrend, an- und abschwellend; 3. harmonisch, abgemessen, ebenmäßig.

rib [rib], **1.** *s.* 1. (*Anat.*) die Rippe; – ***of beef,*** das Rindsrippenstück; ***dig in the*** –***s,*** der Rippenstoß; 2. (*Bot.*) die (Blatt)ader; 3. der Schaft (*of a feather*); 4. die Schirmstange, der Schirmstab (*of an umbrella*); 5. rippenartiger Streifen (*in cloth*); – ***stitch,*** linke Masche (*knitting*); 6. (*Archit.*) die (Gewölbe)-rippe, Strebe, Leiste; 7. (*Shipb.*) Schiffsrippe, das Inholz, Spant; 8. (*coll.*) die Ehehälfte. **2.** *v.t.* 1. rippen, riefen, riffeln; 2. (*sl.*) aufziehen (*a p.*).

ribald ['ribəld], **1.** *adj.* 1. lüstern, schlüpfrig, zotig; 2. ordinär, respektlos. **2.** *s.* 1. der Spötter; 2. Zotenreißer. **ribaldry** [–ri], *s.* Zoten (*pl.*), ordinäre Rede, das Zotenreißen.

riband ['ribənd], *s.* ***Blue Riband,*** Blaues Band.

ribband ['ribənd], *s.* 1. (*Shipb.*) die Sente; 2. (*Bridgeb.*) der Rödelbalken.

ribbed [ribd], *adj.* gerippt, geriffelt, gewellt, Rippen–, Riffel–; (*Archit.*) – ***vault,*** das Kreuzrippengewölbe. **ribbing,** *s.* 1. (*Archit.*) das Rippenwerk; 2. (*knitting*) das Rippenmuster.

ribbon ['ribən], **1.** *s.* 1. das Band, die Borte; 2. das Farbband (*of typewriter*); 3. (*fig.*) Ordensband; 4. der Fetzen; (*coll.*) ***tear to*** –***s,*** in Fetzen reißen; 5. schmaler Streifen; 6. *pl.* (*coll.*) Zügel (*pl.*). **2.** *v.t.* bebändern. **ribbon|-development,** *s.* der Reihenbau (entlang der Landstraße). **–-fish,** *s.* der Bandfisch.

ribwort ['ribwə:t], *s.* (*Bot.*) der Spitzwegerich.

rice [rais], *s.* der Reis. **rice|-flour,** *s.* das Reismehl. **–-paper,** *s.* das Reispapier. **–-pudding,** *s.* der Milchreis.

rich [ritʃ], *adj.* 1. reich (***in,*** an (*Dat.*)), wohlhabend, begütert; ***the*** –, die Reichen (*pl.*); 2. fett, fruchtbar (*as soil*); – ***coal,*** die Fettkohle; 3. reichhaltig, reich(lich), ergiebig; 4. wertvoll, kostbar, prächtig; 5. voll(tönend), füllig, klangvoll (*as voice*); 6. satt, voll, kräftig (*as colour*); 7. nahrhaft (*as food*); 8. kräftig, gehaltvoll (*as wine*); 9. (*coll.*) köstlich, gelungen (*as a joke*); 10. (*sl.*) unsinnig. **riches** [–iz], *pl.* der Reichtum, Reichtümer (*pl.*). **richly,** *adv.* in reichem Maße, reich(lich); – ***deserved,*** reichlich *or* wohl verdient. **richness,** *s.* 1.

der Reichtum, die Reichhaltigkeit, Fülle; 2. Pracht, der Glanz; 3. die Üppigkeit, Fruchtbarkeit, Ergiebigkeit; 4. (Klang)fülle, Fülligkeit (*of sound*); 5. Sattheit (*of colour*); 6. Nahrhaftigkeit (*of food*); 7. Schwere, der (Voll)gehalt (*of wine*).

rick [rik], **1.** *s.* der (Heu)schober. **2.** *v.t.* in Schobern aufschichten.

rickets ['rikits], *pl.* (*sing. constr.*) Englische Krankheit, die Rachitis. **rickety,** *adj.* 1. (*Med.*) rachitisch; 2. (*fig.*) wack(e)lig, klapperig; 3. (*coll.*) gebrechlich, hinfällig.

rickshaw ['rikʃɔ:], *s.* die Rikscha.

ricochet ['rikəʃei], **1.** *s.* 1. das Abprallen; 2. der Prallschuß, Prellschuß, Abpraller. **2.** *v.i.* rikoschettieren, abprallen.

rictal ['riktəl], *adj.* (*Orn.*) Schnabel–. **rictus,** *s.* 1. (*Bot.*) der Schlund; 2. (*Orn.*) die Sperrweite.

rid [rid], *irr.v.t.* befreien, freimachen (*of*, von); ***– o.s.,*** sich (*Dat.*) vom Halse schaffen (*of*, *Acc.*); ***be – of,*** los sein (*Acc.*); ***get – of,*** loswerden (*Acc.*). **riddance** [–əns], *s.* die Befreiung, Errettung, Erlösung (***from***, von); ***a good – to him! he is a good –!*** Gott sei Dank ist *or* wird man ihn endlich los!

ridden [ridn], **1.** *p.p. of* **ride. 2.** *pred. adj.* (*usu. as suff.*) besessen, beherrscht, verfolgt, geplagt (*by*, von); ***bed–,*** bettlägerig, ans Bett gefesselt; ***disease––,*** von Krankheit heimgesucht.

[1]**riddle** [ridl], **1.** *s.* das Rätsel, Geheimnis. **2.** *v.t.* (*rare*) enträtseln, auflösen. **3.** *v.i.* (*rare*) in Rätseln sprechen.

[2]**riddle, 1.** *s.* das (Draht)sieb; (*Min.*) der Rätter, Durchwurf. **2.** *v.t.* 1. (durch)sieben (*also fig.*), (*Min.*) rättern; 2. (*fig.*) durchlöchern.

ride [raid], **1.** *s.* 1. der Ritt (*on horse*), die Fahrt (*in vehicle*); ***give him a –,*** ihn reiten *or* fahren lassen; ***go for*** or ***take a –,*** ausreiten; ausfahren; (*sl.*) ***take him for a –,*** ihn übers Ohr hauen, ihn aufs Glatteis führen; 2. der Reitweg; die Schneise (*in a wood*). **2.** *irr.v.i.* 1. reiten (*on horse*); ***– at a fence,*** ein Pferd auf ein Hindernis zulenken *or* nach einem Hindernis lenken; ***– at a walking pace,*** (im) Schritt reiten; ***– behind him,*** hinter ihm herreiten; hinten aufsitzen (*on the same horse*); (*fig.*) ***– for a fall,*** ein Unglück heraufbeschwören; ***– off,*** wegreiten; ***– roughshod over him,*** sich über ihn hinwegsetzen, ihn rücksichtslos behandeln, ihn schurigeln; ***– to hounds,*** in der Parforcejagd reiten; (*fig.*) ***– up,*** sich hochrutschen (*collar etc.*); 2. fahren (*on bicycle, in vehicle*); ***– (at) full speed,*** mit voller Geschwindigkeit fahren; ***– with one's back to the engine,*** rückwärts fahren; ***– pillion,*** auf dem Soziussitz fahren; ***– in a pram,*** im Kinderwagen ausgefahren werden *or* ausfahren; ***– on a bicycle,*** radeln, radfahren; 3. (*fig.*) getragen werden, treiben, sich (fort)bewegen, dahinziehen; 4. ruhen, schweben (*on*, auf (*Dat.*)) (*of vessels, things*); (*Naut.*) ***the rope –s,*** das Tau läuft unklar; ***– at*** or ***to anchor,*** vor Anker liegen; 5. zum Reiten geeignet sein (*as ground*). **3.** *irr.v.t.* 1. reiten, rittlings sitzen auf (*Dat.*) (*a horse*), fahren (*a bicycle*); ***– a bicycle,*** radfahren, radeln; ***– the country,*** über Land reiten, das Land durchreiten; ***– a horse at a fence,*** ein Pferd auf ein Hindernis zulenken; (*fig.*) ***– one's high horse,*** sich aufs hohe Roß setzen; (*fig.*) ***– one's hobby horse,*** sein Steckenpferd reiten; (*fig.*) ***– to death,*** zu Tode hetzen (*a theory etc.*); ***– a race,*** an einem Rennen teilnehmen; ***– down,*** niederreiten, über den Haufen reiten; (*in vehicle*) überfahren; 2. (*fig.*) (*usu. pass., see* **ridden**) beherrschen, bedrücken, plagen; 3. (*fig.*) ruhen *or* (auf)liegen *or* sitzen *or* schwingen *or* schweben *or* schwimmen auf (*Dat.*); ***– the waves,*** auf den Wellen reiten; ***– out the storm,*** den Sturm gut *or* heil überstehen (*also fig.*).

rider ['raidə], *s.* 1. der (die) Reiter(in), (*cycle etc.*) Fahrer(in); 2. (*Tech.*) das Laufgewicht, Reitergewicht, Reiterchen; 3. (*Law*) der Nachtrag, Zusatz, die Zusatzklausel; 4. (*Math.*) Zusatzaufgabe; 5. (*Comm.*) (Wechsel)allonge.

ridge [ridʒ], **1.** *s.* 1. der Rücken (*also of the nose*); 2. (*Geog.*) (Berg)kamm, Grat (*also Archit.*), die Hügelkette, Kammlinie; ***– of hills,*** die Hügelkette; 3. (*Agr.*) der (Furchen)rain, Balken; (*Build.*) (Dach)first; 4. (*Meteor.*) ***– of high pressure,*** das Zwischenhoch. **2.** *v.t.* furchen. **ridge|-pole,** *s.* 1. der Kopfbalken, Firstbalken; 2. (*of tent*) die Firststange, Querstange. **--tile,** *s.* der Dachreiter, Firstziegel. **–way,** *s.* der Kammlinienweg.

ridicule ['ridikju:l], **1.** *s.* das Lächerliche, der Spott; die Verspottung; ***hold up to –,*** lächerlich machen; ***turn to –,*** ins Lächerliche ziehen. **2.** *v.t.* verspotten, lächerlich machen. **ridiculous** [–'dikjuləs], *adj.* lächerlich, unsinnig. **ridiculousness,** *s.* die Lächerlichkeit.

[1]**riding** ['raidiŋ], *s.* 1. das Reiten (*on horse*), Fahren (*on cycle etc.*); 2. der Reitsport; Reitweg.

[2]**riding,** *s.* der Verwaltungsbezirk (*in Yorkshire*).

riding|-boots, *pl.* Reitstiefel (*pl.*). **--breeches,** *pl.* die Reithose. **--habit,** *s.* das (Damen)reitkleid. **--lesson,** *s.* die Reitstunde. **--light,** *s.* (*Naut.*) das Ankerlicht. **--whip,** *s.* die Reitgerte, Reitpeitsche.

rife [raif], *pred. adj.* 1. häufig, vorherrschend, weitverbreitet; ***be –,*** grassieren; 2. voll, erfüllt (***with,*** von).

riffle [rifl], *v.t.* riffeln, riefe(l)n.

riff-raff ['rifræf], *s.* 1. das Gesindel, Pack, der Pöbel; 2. Ausschuß, Auswurf.

[1]**rifle** [raifl], *v.t.* ausrauben, (aus)plündern.

[2]**rifle, 1.** *s.* 1. das Gewehr, die Büchse; 2. *pl.* Schützen (*pl.*). **2.** *v.t.* ziehen (*gun-barrels*). **rifle|-corps,** *s.* das Schützenkorps. **--green,** *adj.* jägergrün. **--grenade,** *s.* die Gewehrgranate. **–man,** *s.* der (Scharf)schütze. **--pit,** *s.* das Schützenloch. **--practice,** *s.* die Schießübung. **--range,** *s.* 1. der Schießstand; 2. die Schußweite. **--shot,** *s.* 1. der Gewehrschuß; ***within –,*** innerhalb Gewehrschußweite; 2. der Schütze. **rifling,** *s.* 1. Züge (*pl.*), der Drall (*in gun-barrels*); 2. das Riefe(l)n, Ziehen.

rift [rift], **1.** *s.* die Ritze, Spalte, der Riß, Spalt, Sprung; ***– in the lute,*** die Verstimmung. **2.** *v.t.* aufreißen, zerspalten.

[1]**rig** [rig], **1.** *s.* 1. (*Naut.*) die Takelung, Takelage; 2. (*coll.*) Kleidung, Aufmachung; Ausrüstung, Ausstattung, Ausstaffierung; 3. (behelfsmäßige) Vorrichtung; ***oil––,*** die Bohrinsel. **2.** *v.t.* 1. (*Naut.*) auftakeln; 2. (*Av.*) aufrüsten, montieren; 3. (*coll.*) ***– out*** or ***up,*** ausrüsten, ausstatten; aufputzen, ausstaffieren (*a p.*); (*coll.*) ***– up,*** (behelfsmäßig) herrichten *or* einrichten, zusammenbauen, zusammendrechseln, zurechtbasteln.

[2]**rig, 1.** *s.* Possen (*pl.*), der Streich, Schwindel; ***run a –,*** einen Streich spielen. **2.** *v.t.* betrügerisch handhaben; ***– the market,*** die Kurse *or* den Markt (auf unlautere Art) beeinflussen.

[1]**rigged** [rigd], *adj.* (*Naut.*) (auf)getakelt, betakelt; ***full–– ship,*** das Vollschiff; ***lateen –,*** mit lateinischer Besegelung; ***square –,*** mit Rahsegeln getakelt.

[2]**rigged,** *adj.* (*coll.*) unlauter beeinflußt, (*as prices*) heraufgeschraubt (*or* –gedrückt).

[1]**rigger** ['rigə], *s.* 1. (*Naut.*) der Takler; 2. (*Av.*) Monteur.

[2]**rigger,** *s.* (*coll.*) der Kurstreiber.

rigging ['rigiŋ], *s.* 1. (*Naut.*) das Takelwerk, die Takelung, Takelage; ***standing –,*** stehendes Gut; ***running –,*** laufendes Gut; 2. (*Av.*) die Verspannung. **rigging|-loft,** *s.* (*Theat.*) der Schnürboden. **--screw,** *s.* (*Naut.*) der Wantenspanner.

right [rait], **1.** *adj.* 1. recht, richtig, wahr, in Ordnung, ordnungsgemäß, angemessen, geeignet, passend; (*coll.*) ***– oh! – you are!*** in Ordnung! durchaus! schön! gut! ***all –!*** alles in Ordnung! ganz richtig! recht so! gewiß! abgemacht! ***– and proper,*** recht und billig; ***be –,*** (*of a th.*) recht *or* richtig *or* in Ordnung sein, sich gehören; (*of a p.*) recht haben; ***that's –!*** recht so! das stimmt! so ist's! jawohl! ***it is – for you to go,*** Sie tun recht daran, zu gehen; ***it is only –,*** es ist nicht mehr als recht und billig; ***come –,*** in Ordnung kommen; ***get it –,*** es klarlegen, es in Ordnung bringen, richtigstellen (*a th.*), zurechtweisen, aufklären (*a p.*); ***put o.s. – with him,*** sich mit ihm gut stellen, sich vor ihm rechtfertigen; ***the – man in the – place,*** der rechte

Mann am rechten Ort; *know the – people,* Beziehungen haben, die rechten Leute kennen; – *side,* die Vorderseite, Oberseite (*of fabric etc.*); *the error is on the – side,* der Fehler wirkt sich gut aus; – *side up,* mit der rechten Seite nach oben; *keep on the – side of him,* mit ihm in Güte fertig werden; *on the – side of 40,* noch nicht 40 (Jahre alt); *the – thing,* das Richtige; *say the – thing,* das rechte Wort finden; *have you the – time?* haben Sie die genaue Zeit? *is your watch –?* geht Ihre Uhr richtig? *the – way,* richtig, auf die richtige Art (und Weise); *is this the – way to B.?* bin ich auf dem richtigen Weg nach B.? *go the – way to work,* es richtig angreifen; 2. gesund, wohl; (*coll.*) *as – as rain,* in schönster Ordnung; (*coll.*) *not quite – in the head, not in his – mind,* nicht ganz normal, nicht bei Trost *or* Verstand; *feel quite all –,* sich wohl befinden; 3. recht, rechts gelegen; (*Footb.*) – *back,* rechter Verteidiger; – *hand,* rechte Hand; (*fig.*) treuer Beistand, die Hauptstütze; *at* or *on the – hand,* rechts, zur Rechten; – *side,* rechte Seite; – *wing,* (*Pol.*) rechter Flügel; (*Footb.*) der Rechtsaußen; 4. (*Geom.*) recht; *at – angles,* rechtwink(e)lig; (*Astr.*) – *ascension,* die Rektaszension; 5. (*coll.*) wahr, richtig(gehend), regelrecht; – *idiot,* der Vollidiot.

2. *adv.* 1. rechts, zur rechten Hand; – *and left,* von *or* nach rechts und links; (*fig.*) von *or* nach *or* auf allen Seiten; (*Mil.*) *eyes –!* Augen rechts! *turn –,* (sich) nach rechts drehen *or* wenden; – *turn!* rechtsum! 2. völlig, ganz, regelrecht, vollkommen, in hohem Grade, sehr; – *round,* rund herum; (*fig.*) – *through,* durch und durch; *Right Honourable,* Exzellenz (*title*); 3. gerade, genau, unmittelbar; – *in front,* ganz vorn; 4. sofort, (so)gleich; – *ahead,* geradeaus; – *away,* sogleich; 5. recht, richtig, rechtmäßig; *do –,* recht handeln; *turn out –,* gut enden *or* ausgehen; *it serves us –,* es geschieht uns recht.

3. *s.* 1. das Recht; *do him –,* ihm sein Recht werden lassen, ihm Gerechtigkeit widerfahren lassen; *in the –,* im Recht; *be in the –,* recht haben; *of –,* von Rechts wegen, rechtmäßig; 2. rechte Seite *or* Hand, die Rechte; *on the –,* rechts (*of,* von), zur Rechten; *to the –,* rechts (*of,* von); 3. (*Law*) das (An)recht, der (Rechts)anspruch (*to,* auf (*Acc.*)); die Berechtigung, das Vorrecht, Privilegium; *civil –s,* bürgerliche Ehrenrechte; *all –s reserved!* alle Rechte vorbehalten! *divine – of kings,* Königtum von Gottes Gnaden; – *of assembly,* das Versammlungsrecht; – *of disposal,* das Verfügungsrecht; – *of inheritance,* das Erbrecht; – *of movement,* die Freizügigkeit; – *of possession,* das Eigentumsrecht; – *of recourse,* das Rückgriffsrecht, der Regreßanspruch; – *of redemption,* das Rückkaufsrecht; – *of sale,* das Vertriebsrecht; – *of succession,* das Nachfolgerrecht, Erb(folge)recht; – *of way,* das Durchfahrtsrecht; (*Motor.*) die Vorfahrt; (*Am.*) see *permanent way*; *have a –,* ein (An)recht haben (*to,* auf (*Acc.*)), das Recht haben (zu); *stand on one's –s,* auf seinem Recht bestehen; *in – of his mother,* von seiten *or* im Namen seiner Mutter; *in her own –,* durch Geburt, aus eigenem Recht; *be within one's –s,* das Recht auf seiner Seite haben; 4. das Rechte *or* Richtige, (*oft. pl.*) die Wahrheit, wahrer Sachverhalt; *the –s and wrongs of a matter,* die S. von allen Seiten betrachtet; *put* or *set to –s,* in Ordnung bringen; 5. (*Boxing*) Rechte(r); 6. (*Pol.*) die Rechtspartei, rechter Flügel.

4. *v.t.* 1. Recht widerfahren lassen *or* verschaffen (*Dat.*); 2. berichtigen, wiedergutmachen, wettmachen; 3. (wieder)aufrichten; – *o.s.,* (*a p.*) sich wieder aufrichten, wieder hochkommen; (*a th.*) sich wieder ausgleichen (*as a fault*).

5. *v.i.* (*Naut.*) sich (wieder) aufrichten.

right|-about turn, *s.* die Kehrtwendung. **--and-left shot,** *s.* der Doppelschuß, die Dublette. **--angle(d),** *adj.* rechtwinklig; – *bend,* das Kniestück. **--down,** *adj., adv.* (*obs.*) ausgesprochen, richtiggehend, regelrecht, vollkommen.

righteous ['raitʃəs], *adv.* redlich, aufrecht, gerecht, rechtschaffen; – *indignation,* gerechter Zorn. **righteousness,** *s.* die Redlichkeit, Aufrichtigkeit, Rechtschaffenheit.

rightful ['raitful], *adj.* 1. rechtmäßig; 2. gerecht, berechtigt. **rightfulness,** *s.* 1. die Rechtmäßigkeit, Rechtlichkeit; 2. Berechtigung, Richtigkeit.

right|-hand, *adj.* 1. zur Rechten stehend; – *man,* rechter Nebenmann, (*fig.*) rechte Hand, die Vertrauensperson; 2. recht, rechtshändig, rechtsseitig; 3. (*Tech.*) Rechts–, rechtsgängig, rechtswendig, rechtsläufig. **--handed,** *adj.* rechtshändig. **--hander,** *s.* (*Boxing*) Rechte(r). **--lined,** *adj.* geradlinig. **rightly,** *adv.* mit Recht, richtig; *remember –,* sich recht entsinnen. **right|-minded,** *adj.* rechtschaffen. **--mindedness,** *s.* die Rechtschaffenheit. **rightness,** *s.* 1. die Richtigkeit; 2. Rechtmäßigkeit; 3. Angemessenheit; 4. Geradheit (*of a line*). **righto!** [–ou], *int.* (*coll.*) jawohl! richtig!

rigid ['ridʒid], *adj.* 1. steif, starr, unbeugsam (*also fig.*); – *airship,* das Starrluftschiff; 2. (*fig.*) unnachgiebig, streng, hart; – *economy,* streng(st)e Sparsamkeit; – *principles,* strenge *or* unabänderliche Prinzipien. **rigidity** [–'dʒiditi], *s.* 1. die Steifheit, Starrheit; *coefficient of –,* die Steifigkeitszahl; *post-mortem –,* see *rigor mortis*; 2. (*fig.*) die Strenge, Härte.

rigmarole ['rigməroul], *s.* dummes Zeug, leeres Geschwätz, das Gewäsch, die Salbaderei, Faselei.

[1]**rigor** ['rigə], (*Am.*) *see* **rigour.**

[2]**rigor,** *s.* (*Med.*) der Schüttelfrost; – *mortis,* die Totenstarre, Leichenstarre. **rigorism,** *s.* 1. die Sittenstrenge, Glaubensstrenge, der Rigorismus; 2. strenge Genauigkeit, übertriebene Strenge. **rigorist,** *s.* der Rigorist, strenger Sittenlehrer. **rigorous,** *adj.* 1. streng, hart, unerbittlich, genau; 2. rauh (*of climate*).

rigour ['rigə], *s.* 1. die Strenge, Härte, Unnachgiebigkeit, Unerbittlichkeit; 2. Genauigkeit, Schärfe; 3. (*also pl.*) die Rauheit, Unbilden (*pl.*) (*of climate*).

rig-out, *s.* (*coll.*) die Aufmachung, Klamotten (*pl.*).

rile [rail], *v.t.* (*coll.*) wurmen, ärgern, aufbringen.

rill [ril], *s.* das Bächlein, Rinnsal, die Priele.

rim [rim], **1.** *s.* 1. der Rand, die Kante; 2. (*of wheel*) Felge, der (Rad)kranz. **2.** *v.t.* 1. einfassen; 2. (be)-felgen (*a wheel*). **rim-brake,** *s.* die Felgenbremse.

[1]**rime** [raim], *s.* (*Poet.*) der (Rauh)reif, Rauhfrost.

[2]**rime,** *see* **rhyme.**

rimless ['rimlis], *adj.* randlos. **rimmed** [rimd], *adj.* (*usu. as suff.*) mit . . . Rahmen, –randig; *e.g. horn––,* mit Horngestell; *horn–– spectacles,* die Hornbrille.

rimose ['raimous], **rimous** [–əs], *adj.* rissig, spaltig.

rind [raind], *s.* 1. die (Baum)rinde, Borke; 2. (Käse)-rinde (*of cheese*), Schale, Hülse (*of fruit*), Kruste (*of bread*), Schwarte (*of bacon*).

rinderpest ['rindəpest], *s.* die Rinderpest.

[1]**ring** [riŋ], **1.** *s.* 1. der Ring; *napkin* or *serviette –,* die Serviettenring; *wedding––,* der Trauring; 2. (*Tech.*) der Reif(en); das Öhr, die Öse; 3. der Hof (*of the moon*); 4. Kreis, das Rund (*of persons*); *form* or *make a – round,* einen Kreis bilden um; (*coll.*) *make* or *run –s round him,* ihn in die Tasche stecken; 5. (*Comm.*) das Syndikat, Kartell; (*coll.*) die Clique, Bande; *spy –,* der Spionagering; 6. (*Spt.*) der (Box)ring; Buchermacherplatz; (*collect.*) Buchmacher (*pl.*), die Boxerwelt, Boxer (*pl.*); *judging –,* der Schiedsrichterplatz. **2.** *v.t.* 1. einen Ring anlegen (*Dat.*), (be)ringen (*pigeons etc.*); 2. ringeln (*trees etc.*); 3. in Ringe schneiden (*apples*); 4. – *in,* umringen, einkreisen (*cattle*). **3.** *v.i.* (im Kreis) ansteigen (*as hawks*), sich im Kreis bewegen.

[2]**ring,** **1.** *s.* 1. der (Glocken)klang; das Klingen, Läuten, Klingeln; – *of bells,* das Glockenläuten, Geläute; *there is a – at the door,* es klingelt *or* läutet; 2. das Erklingen, Ertönen, der Schall; (*fig.*) *the – of truth,* der echte Klang der Wahrheit; 3. (*coll.*) (*Tele.*) der (Telefon)anruf; *give me a –,* ruf

mich an! **2.** *irr.v.i.* **1.** läuten (*large bell*), schellen, klingeln (*small bell*), klingen (*as coins*); – ***for the maid,*** nach dem Mädchen klingeln; – ***for dinner,*** zum Essen läuten; (*Tele.*) – ***off,*** (den Hörer) abhängen; – ***true,*** echt *or* wahr klingen; 2. (er-) klingen, (er)schallen, widerhallen (***with,*** von); – ***in his ears,*** ihm in den Ohren klingen; ***my ears are –ing,*** mir klingen die Ohren; – ***out,*** laut schellen *or* tönen, ertönen; sich lösen (*as a shot*); ***the town –s with his praise,*** die Stadt ist erfüllt *or* voll von seinem Ruhm. **3.** *irr.v.t.* klingen lassen; läuten; – ***the bell,*** klingeln; (*sl.*) ***that –s a bell,*** das kommt mir vertraut vor; – ***the changes,*** wechselläuten; (*fig.*) immer in verschiedener Weise zurückkehren (***on,*** zu), immer in neuer Fassung wiederholen (*Acc.*); (*fig.*) – ***the knell of,*** zu Grabe tragen *or* läuten; (*fig.*) – ***his praises,*** ein Loblied auf ihn singen; – ***down the curtain,*** den Vorhang niedergehen lassen; (*fig.*) Schluß machen (***on,*** mit); – ***in,*** einläuten; – ***out,*** ausläuten; – ***up,*** hochgehen lassen (*the curtain*); (*coll.*) (*Tele.*) anrufen, anklingeln (*a p.*).

ring|-a-ring-o'-roses, *s.* (*game*) der Ringelreihen. **--bone,** *s.* (*Vet.*) das Überbein, die Schale. **--dove,** *s.* (*Orn.*) die Ringeltaube (*Columba palumbus*). **ringed** [–d], *adj.* **1.** beringt (*as hand, bird etc.*); (*Orn.*) – ***plover,*** der Halsbandregenpfeifer, Sandregenpfeifer (*Charadrius hiaticula*); 2. – ***around,*** umringt, eingeschlossen. **ring|-fence,** *s.* die Umzäunung, Einfriedung. **--finger,** *s.* der Ringfinger.

ringing ['riŋiŋ], **1.** *adj.* klinge(l)nd, schallend, widerhallend; – ***cheers,*** brausende Hochrufe; – ***laugh,*** schallendes Gelächter. **2.** *s.* das Klinge(l)n, Schellen, (Glocken)läuten; – ***in the ears,*** das Ohrenklingen. **ring-leader,** *s.* der Rädelsführer. **ringlet** [–lit], *s.* **1.** das Ringlein; 2. (*hair*) die Haarlocke, das (Ringel)löckchen. **ring|-mail,** *s.* (*Hist.*) der Kettenpanzer. **–master,** *s.* der Zirkusdirektor. **--ouzel,** *s.* (*Orn.*) die Ringdrossel (*Turdus torquatus*). **–side,** *s.* (*Boxing*) Ringplätze (*pl.*); – ***seat,*** der Ringplatz; (*fig.*) guter Platz. **--snake,** *s.* die Ringelnatter. **–worm,** *s.* die Glatzflechte.

rink [riŋk], *s.* **1.** die Rollschuhbahn; 2. (künstliche) Eisbahn.

rinse [rins], **1.** *v.t.* (*also* – *out*) (aus)spülen, abspülen. **2.** *s.* das (Aus)spülen, Abspülen. **rinsing,** *s. See* **rinse, 2**; *pl.* das Spülwasser, Spülicht.

riot ['raiət], **1.** *s.* **1.** der Aufruhr, (Volks)auflauf, Tumult; (*Hist.*) – ***act,*** das Aufruhrgesetz; (*fig.*) ***read the – act to,*** eine Standpauke halten (*Dat.*), die Leviten lesen (*Dat.*), verwarnen; – ***police,*** die Bereitschaftspolizei; 2. die Schwelgerei, Ausschweifung; ***run –,*** wuchern (*plants*); (*fig.*) sich austoben, ausschweifen; 3. (*fig.*) der Ausbruch; 4. (*sl.*) tolle S. **2.** *v.i.* an einem Aufruhr teilnehmen, meutern, sich zusammenrotten; (sich aus)toben, ausschweifen, schwelgen. **rioter,** *s.* der Aufrührer, Meuterer. **riotous,** *adj.* **1.** aufrührerisch; (*Law*) – ***assembly,*** die Zusammenrottung; 2. tobend, lärmend; 3. zügellos, ausschweifend. **riotousness,** *s.* die Ausgelassenheit, Zügellosigkeit.

[1]**rip** [rip], **1.** *v.t.* auftrennen (*a seam etc.*); (*coll.*) (zer)reißen; – ***off,*** abreißen; – ***open,*** aufreißen, aufschlitzen; – ***out,*** ausreißen; – ***up,*** (in Stücke) zerreißen. **2.** *v.i.* **1.** (zer)reißen, (auf)platzen; 2. (*coll.*) drauflosstürmen; (*sl.*) ***let it –!*** laß es laufen! **3.** *s.* der Riß.

[2]**rip,** *s.* **1.** der Taugenichts, Nichtsnutz; 2. alter Klepper (*horse*).

[3]**rip,** *s.* (*Naut.*) die Kabbelung.

riparian [rai'pɛəriən], **1.** *adj.* Ufer–. **2.** *s.* der Uferbewohner, Uferanlieger.

rip-cord, *s.* (*Av.*) die Reißleine.

ripe [raip], *adj.* **1.** reif, (aus)gereift, voll entwickelt, vollendet; – ***age,*** hohes Alter; – ***scholar,*** vollendeter Gelehrter; – ***wine,*** ausgereifter Wein; 2. (*fig.*) (zeitlich) günstig, wie geschaffen, geradezu gemacht (***for,*** für), bereit, fertig (zu); ***when the time is –,*** wenn die rechte Zeit gekommen ist. **ripen** [–ən], **1.** *v.i.* **1.** reif werden, reifen, zur Reife kommen; 2. heranreifen, sich entwickeln (***into,*** zu). **2.** *v.t.* reifen lassen, zum Reifen *or* zur Reife bringen. **ripeness** [–nis], *s.* **1.** die Reife, das Reifsein; 2. (*fig.*) die Vollendung, Gereiftheit.

riposte [ri'poust], **1.** *s.* **1.** (*Fenc.*) der Nachstoß, die Riposte; 2. (*fig.*) der Gegenschlag, schlagfertige Antwort. **2.** *v.i.* **1.** nachstoßen; 2. (*fig.*) schnell erwidern.

ripper ['ripə], *s.* (*sl.*) der Prachtkerl, das Prachtexemplar. **ripping,** *adj.* (*sl.*) famos, kolossal, prima, Mords–; – (***good***) ***time,*** die Mordsgaudi.

[1]**ripple** [ripl], **1.** *v.i.* **1.** kleine Wellen schlagen, sich kräuseln; 2. plätschern, rieseln, murmeln. **2.** *v.t.* kräuseln (*water*). **3.** *s.* **1.** kleine Welle, die Kräuselung; – ***of laughter,*** leises Lachen; 2. das Plätschern, Rieseln, Murmeln, Geplätscher, Geriesel.

[2]**ripple,** **1.** *v.t.* kämmen, riffeln (*flax*). **2.** *s.* die (Flachs)riffel, Reffkamm.

rip-saw, *s.* die Handsäge, Langsäge.

rise [raiz], **1.** *irr.v.i.* **1.** (*of a p.*) aufstehen, sich erheben; – ***to one's feet,*** aufstehen; – ***from one's bed,*** aus dem Bett aufstehen; – ***on one's hind legs,*** sich (auf die Hinterbeine) stellen, sich bäumen; – ***to*** (***a point of***) ***order,*** beantragen, daß zur Geschäftsordnung gesprochen wird; – ***with the lark,*** mit den Hühnern aufstehen; 2. (*of a th.*) emporsteigen, aufsteigen; ***the glass has risen,*** das Barometer ist gestiegen; ***his hair –s,*** ihm stehen die Haare zu Berge; – ***into the air,*** sich in die Luft erheben; – ***into view,*** in Sicht kommen; ***a sigh rose to his lips,*** ein Seufzer kam ihm auf die Lippen; – ***to a height of . . .,*** eine Höhe von . . . erreichen; 3. steigen, anschwellen (*of water*); 4. anziehen, (an)steigen, in die Höhe gehen (*of prices*); 5. aufgehen (*as dough, curtain, sun*), hochgehen (*curtain*); 6. ansteigen, bergan gehen (*as land*); 7. an die Oberfläche kommen, anbeißen (*as fish*); – ***to a bait,*** (*coll.*) – ***to it,*** anbeißen, darauf hereinfallen; 8. (*fig.*) stärker werden, sich verstärken *or* steigern, wachsen, zunehmen; 9. entspringen, entstehen (***from,*** aus); 10. auftreten, hervortreten, aufkommen, erscheinen, sich zeigen, sichtbar werden, emporragen (***above,*** über (*Acc.*)); (*fig.*) – ***above,*** erhaben sein *or* emporragen *or* hinausragen über (*Acc.*); ***a storm rose,*** ein Sturm erhob sich *or* kam auf; 11. vorwärtskommen (*in the world*), befördert werden; – ***to greatness,*** sich zu Größe erheben; 12. die Sitzung aufheben, sich vertagen, aufbrechen (*as an assembly*); 13. sich empören (***against,*** gegen); – ***in rebellion,*** sich erheben, aufstehen; ***my gorge –s at it,*** es ekelt mich an; – (***up***) ***in arms,*** zu den Waffen greifen; 14. auferstehen (*from the dead*). **2.** *irr v.t.* **1.** aufsteigen lassen; an die Oberfläche locken (*fish*); aufjagen (*bird*); 2. (*Naut.*) sichten, in Sicht bekommen (*a ship*). **3.** *s.* **1.** der Anstieg, Aufstieg (***to,*** zu); 2. das Emporkommen (*in life*); 3. Aufgehen, der Aufgang (*of the sun*); 4. das Hochgehen (*of the curtain*); 5. die Steige, Anhöhe, der Anstieg (*of land*), die Steigung, Höhe (*of a step etc.*); 6. Steigerung, das (An)steigen (*of prices etc.*), (*St. Exch.*) die Hausse, der Aufschwung; – ***in price,*** die Preiserhöhung; – ***in prices,*** das Steigen der Preise; ***be on the –,*** steigen; (*Comm.*) ***buy for a –,*** auf Hausse spekulieren; 7. die Lohnerhöhung, Lohnaufbesserung, Lohnzulage; 8. Verstärkung, das Anschwellen, der Zuwachs, die Zunahme, Erhöhung; 9. der Ursprung, die Entstehung; ***give – to,*** hervorrufen, veranlassen, verursachen, aufkommen lassen, bewirken, herbeiführen, Anlaß geben zu; ***have its – in, take its – from,*** entspringen aus; 10. das Anbeißen (*of fish*); (*coll.*) ***take a – out of him,*** ihn in die Wolle bringen.

risen ['rizən], *p.p. of* **rise**; ***the – Christ,*** der Auferstandene; ***the – sun,*** die aufgegangene Sonne. **riser** ['raizə], *s.* **1.** Aufstehende(r); ***early –,*** der Frühaufsteher; 2. die Setzstufe.

risibility [rizi'biliti], *s.* das Lachvermögen; die Lachlust. **risible** ['rizibl], *adj.* **1.** Lach–, lachlustig; 2. (*rare*) lachhaft, lächerlich.

rising ['raiziŋ], **1.** *adj.* **1.** (empor)steigend, ansteigend; – ***ground,*** die Anhöhe; (*Meteor.*) – ***gust,*** die Steigbö; – ***stress,*** steigender Akzent, der Auftakt; – ***sun,*** aufgehende Sonne; 2. emporkommend, aufstrebend (*a p.*); 3. heranwachsend; – ***generation,*** heranwachsendes Geschlecht, der Nachwuchs. **2.** *prep.* (*coll.*) – ***twelve,*** von nahezu *or* von noch nicht ganz zwölf (Jahren). **3.** *s.* 1. das Aufstehen; 2. (Auf)steigen, Emporsteigen; 3. (An)-steigen, Anschwellen (*of water etc.*); 4. Vorwärtskommen; 5. die Steigerung, Erhöhung, Zunahme; 6. das Aufbrechen, der Aufbruch, die Vertagung (*of an assembly*); 7. Empörung, Erhebung, der Aufstand; 8. Aufgang, das Aufgehen (*of the sun etc.*); 9. die Auferstehung (*from the dead*); 10. (*Geog.*) Steigung, Anhöhe, Erhebung; – ***of a vault,*** die Wölbhöhe, Pfeilhöhe; 11. (*Med.*) die Anschwellung, Geschwulst.

risk [risk], **1.** *s.* die Gefahr, das Wagnis; (*Comm.*) Risiko; ***be at –,*** in Gefahr sein; ***at the –,*** auf die Gefahr hin (***of doing,*** zu tun); ***at the – of one's life,*** unter Lebensgefahr; ***at one's own –,*** auf eigene Gefahr *or* Verantwortung; ***run*** or ***take –s*** or ***a –,*** ein Risiko eingehen *or* auf sich nehmen; ***run the –,*** Gefahr *or* Risiko laufen, sich der Gefahr aussetzen (***of doing,*** zu tun). **2.** *v.t.* wagen, aufs Spiel setzen, riskieren, es ankommen lassen auf (*Acc.*). **risky,** *adj.* 1. gewagt, gefahrvoll; 2. heikel, riskant.

risqué ['ri(:)skei], *adj.* heikel, schlüpfrig (*joke etc.*).

rissole ['risoul], *s.* die Frikadelle.

rite [rait], *s.* 1. der Ritus, die Liturgie, das Zeremoniell; die Zeremonie, feierliche Handlung; Brauch; ***funeral –s,*** die Totenfeier; ***last –s,*** Sterbesakramente (*pl.*); 2. die Gepflogenheit, anerkannter Brauch; ***nuptial –s,*** die Hochzeitsbräuche.

ritual ['ritjuəl], **1.** *attrib. adj.* 1. Ritual–, ritual; 2. feierlich, rituell. **2.** *s.* 1. das Ritual, die Gottesdienstordnung; 2. das Zeremoniell, vorgeschriebene Form. **ritualism,** *s.* 1. der Ritualismus; 2. (*pej.*) Anglokatholizismus (*in England*). **ritualist,** *s.* 1. der Ritualist; 2. Anglokatholik, Hochkirchler. **ritualistic** [–'listik], *adj.* ritualistisch, hochkirchlich.

ritzy ['ritsi], *adj.* (*sl.*) feudal.

rival ['raivəl], **1.** *s.* 1. der (die) Nebenbuhler(in), Rivale (Rivalin) (*to, Gen.*); ***without –,*** ohnegleichen; 2. der (die) Mitbewerber(in), Konkurrent(in) (***for,*** um); ***be –s for,*** (miteinander) konkurrieren um, sich zugleich bewerben um. **2.** *attrib. adj.* 1. wetteifernd, rivalisierend, nebenbuhlerisch; 2. (*esp. Comm.*) Konkurrenz–. **3.** *v.t.* 1. wetteifern *or* konkurrieren *or* rivalisieren mit (***in,*** an *or* in (*Dat.*)); 2. (*fig.*) gleichkommen (*Dat.*), nacheifern (*Dat.*), es aufnehmen mit. **rivalry,** *s.* 1. die Nebenbuhlerschaft, Rivalität; 2. der Wetteifer, Wettbewerb, Wettstreit, die Konkurrenz; ***enter into – with,*** Konkurrenz machen (*Dat.*), in Wettbewerb treten mit, konkurrieren mit.

rive [raiv], **1.** *irr.v.t.* 1. (zer)spalten, aufspalten; 2. auseinanderreißen, zerreißen (*also fig.*). **2.** *irr.v.i.* zerreißen, sich spalten. **riven** ['rivən], *p.p. of* **rive.**

river ['rivə], *s.* der Fluß; Strom (*also fig.*); (*fig.*) die Flut; ***the – Thames,*** die Themse; ***down the –,*** stromab(wärts); ***on the –,*** am Flusse; ***up the –,*** stromauf(wärts). **riverain** [–rein], **1.** *adj. See* **riverine. 2.** *s.* der Flußbewohner. **river|-basin,** *s.* das Stromgebiet. **–-bed,** *s.* das Flußbett. **–head,** *s.* die Flußquelle. **–horse,** *s.* (*Zool.*) das Flußpferd. **riverine** [–rain], *adj.* Fluß–, am Fluß gelegen. **river|-police,** *s.* die Wasserpolizei, Stromwache. **–side, 1.** *s.* das Flußufer. **2.** *attrib. adj.* am Fluß *or* Wasser (gelegen); Ufer–. **–-traffic,** *s.* der Flußverkehr. **–-trout,** *s.* die Bachforelle.

rivet ['rivit], **1.** *v.t.* 1. (ver)nieten; 2. (*fig.*) befestigen (***to,*** an (*Acc.*)), verankern (***in,*** in (*Dat.*)), heften (***on,*** auf (*Acc.*)) (*eyes*), fesseln (*attention*); 3. festnageln (*an error*). **2.** *s.* die Niete, (*Tech.*) der Niet. **riveter,** *s.* 1. der Nieter, Nietschläger; 2. die Nietmaschine. **rivet-head,** *s.* der Nietkopf. **riveting,** *s.* 1. das Nieten; ***–-hammer,*** der Niethammer; 2. die Nietung, Nietnaht, Nietverbindung.

rivulet ['rivjulit], *s.* das Flüßchen, Bach, Bächlein.

[1]**roach** [routʃ], *s.* (*Ichth.*) das Rotauge, die Plötze; ***as sound as a –,*** kerngesund.

[2]**roach,** *s.* (*Naut.*) die Gilling, Gillung.

road [roud], *s.* 1. die (Land)straße; der Weg (*also fig.*), (*Min.*) die Förderstrecke; (*Am.*) das G(e)-leis(e), die Bahnstrecke, Eisenbahn(linie); (*coll.*) ***any –,*** jedenfalls; (*coll.*) ***be in his –,*** ihm im Wege stehen, ihm hinderlich sein; ***by –,*** zu Fuß; per Auto; ***the main*** or ***high –,*** die Landstraße; ***in the –,*** auf der Straße; (*coll.*) hinderlich, im Wege; ***on the –,*** auf dem Wege, unterwegs (***to,*** nach); auf der Wanderschaft; (*Comm.*) geschäftlich unterwegs, auf Reisen; (*Theat.*) auf Tournee; (*coll.*) ***get out of the –,*** den Weg freimachen, aus dem Wege gehen; (*coll.*) ***get it out of the –,*** es aus dem Weg räumen, (*fig.*) es erledigen; ***royal –,*** leichter *or* bequemer *or* sicherer Weg (***to,*** zu); ***– to success,*** der Weg zum Erfolg; ***take to the –,*** Landstreicher werden; ***rule of the –,*** die Straßenverkehrsordnung; 2. *pl.* (*Naut.*) die Reede; ***in the –s,*** auf der Reede.

road| accident, *s.* der Verkehrsunfall. **–-bed,** *s.* der Bahnkörper. **–-block,** *s.* die Straßensperre. **–-construction,** *s.* der Straßenbau, Wegebau. **–-haulage,** *s.* der Güterkraftverkehr. **–-hog,** *s.* (*coll.*) der Verkehrsrowdy, Kilometerfresser, rücksichtsloser Fahrer. **–-holding,** *s.* (*Motor.*) die Straßenlage. **–-house,** *s.* die Gaststätte *or* Wirtschaft (an der Landstraße). **– intersection,** *s.* die Wegkreuzung. **– junction,** *s.* der Straßenknotenpunkt. **–man,** *s.* der Straßenarbeiter. **–-map,** *s.* die Autokarte, Straßenkarte. **–mender,** *s. See* **–man. –-metal,** *s.* die Straßenbeschotterung. **–-race,** *s.* das Straßenrennen. **–-roller,** *s.* die Straßenwalze. **–-sense,** *s.* das Gefühl für Verkehrsordnung. **–side, 1.** *s.* der Straßenrand, Wegrand. **2.** *attrib. adj.* – ***inn,*** das Gasthaus an der Landstraße. **–-sign,** *s.* der Wegzeiger, das Straßenschild. **–stead,** *s.* die Reede.

roadster ['roudstə], *s.* 1. (*Cycl.*) das Tourenrad, (*Motor.*) offener Tourenwagen; das Reisepferd; 2. (*Naut.*) das Schiff vor Anker auf der Reede.

road| surface, *s.* die Straßendecke. **– test,** *s.* die Probefahrt. **– user,** *s.* der Verkehrsteilnehmer. **–-warbler,** *s.* (*Orn.*) der Schlagschwirl (*Locustella fluviatalis*). **–way,** *s.* der Fahrweg, Fahrdamm, die Fahrbahn. **–worthy,** *adj.* straßentauglich (*of vehicle*).

roam [roum], **1.** *v.i.* streifen, ziehen, wandern; – ***about,*** umherstreifen, umhertreiben. **2.** *v.t.* durchstreifen, durchwandern, durchziehen.

roan [roun], **1.** *adj.* rötlichgrau. **2.** *s.* 1. der Rotschimmel; 2. (*Bookb.*) weiches Schafleder.

roar [rɔ:], **1.** *s.* das Gebrüll, Brüllen (*of beasts*); Geschrei, Geheul (*of people*); das Brausen, Heulen, Tosen, Toben (*of wind etc.*); Krachen (*of thunder*); der Donner (*of cannon*); das Getöse, Dröhnen (*of engines*); – ***of laughter,*** schallendes Gelächter; ***set the company in a –,*** die Gesellschaft zu lautem Lachen bringen. **2.** *v.i.* 1. brüllen, heulen (*of animals*), laut schreien (*of a p.*); (*also* – ***with laughter***) laut lachen; 2. brausen, tosen, toben (*as water or wind*); krachen (*as thunder*), donnern (*of cannon*), dröhnen, sausen (*as machinery*); 3. (*Vet.*) keuchen (*of a horse*). **3.** *v.t.* (– ***out***) (heraus)brüllen; – ***down,*** niederschreien; – ***o.s. hoarse,*** sich heiser schreien. **roarer** [–rə], *s.* 1. der Schreier; 2. brüllendes Tier; 3. (*Vet.*) der Lungenpfeifer, keuchendes Pferd. **roaring, 1.** *adj.* 1. brüllend, heulend; 2. brausend, tosend, donnernd; – ***fire,*** loderndes Feuer; – ***forties,*** stürmisches Meergebiet (zwischen 40° und 50° nördlicher Breite); 3. (*coll.*) ungeheuer, enorm, kolossal, famos; (*coll.*) – ***business*** or ***trade,*** das Bombengeschäft. **2.** *s.* 1. das Brüllen, Heulen, Brausen *etc.*; 2. Keuchen (*of horses*).

roast [roust], **1.** *v.t.* 1. braten, rösten (*also metal, coffee*), brennen (*metal, coffee*); 2. (*sl.*) aufziehen, necken. **2.** *v.i.* gebraten werden. **3.** *s.* der Braten; ***rule the –,*** das Regiment *or* Wort führen, herrschen. **4.** *adj.* Röst–, Brat–; – ***beef,*** der Rostbraten, Rinderbraten; – ***meat,*** der Braten; – ***pork,*** der

Schweinebraten; – ***veal,*** der Kalbsbraten. **roaster** [–ə], *s.* 1. der (Brat)rost; das Spanferkel (*for roasting*); 2. der Kaffeebrenner; 3. (*Metall.*) Röstofen. **roasting-jack,** *s.* der Bratenwender.

rob [rɔb], *v.t.* berauben (*a p.*) (*of, Gen.*); ausrauben, plündern (*a place*); (*fig.*) – ***him of his inheritance,*** ihn um sein Erbe bringen; – ***him of (his) speech,*** ihm die Sprache rauben *or* nehmen; (*coll.*) – ***Peter to pay Paul,*** hier anpumpen, um dort zu bezahlen; ein Loch aufreißen, um das andere damit zu stopfen. **robber,** *s.* der Räuber, Dieb; ***highway –,*** der Straßenräuber, Wegelagerer; – ***knight,*** der Raubritter, Strauchritter. **robbery,** *s.* 1. der Raub (***from,*** an (*Dat.*)), Diebstahl; 2. (*coll.*) Wucher, die Ausbeutung, Erpressung, Geldschneiderei.

robe [roub], **1.** *s.* 1. der Talar, Umhang; (*usu. pl.*) Amtstracht, Amtskleidung, der Ornat; ***academic –s,*** akademischer Ornat; ***long –s,*** das Tragkleidchen (*of baby*); ***gentlemen of the (long) –,*** Gerichtsherren, Advokaten, Richter (*pl.*); ***master of the –s,*** der Oberkämmerer; ***state –s,*** das Staatskleid; 2. (*Hist.*) das (Fest)gewand; 3. (*obs.*) Damenkleid, die Robe; (*Am.*) der Bademantel; 4. (*fig.*) Mantel, Schutz. **2.** *v.t.* 1. (feierlich an)kleiden; 2. (*fig.*) hüllen. **3.** *v.i.* sich ankleiden *or* schmücken.

robin ['rɔbin], *s.* (*Orn.*) 1. (*coll. also* – ***redbreast***) das Rotkehlchen (*Erithacus rubecula*); 2. (*Am.*) die Wanderdrossel (*Turdus migratorius*).

robing ['roubiŋ], *s.* das Ankleiden, die Einkleidung; – ***room,*** das Ankleidezimmer.

roborant ['roubərənt], **1.** *adj.* stärkend, roborierend. **2.** *s.* das Stärkungsmittel.

robot ['roubɔt], **1.** *s.* 1. der Roboter, Maschinenmensch; 2. automatische Vorrichtung, selbsttätiger Mechanismus. **2.** *attrib. adj.* automatisch, selbsttätig, Maschinen–.

robust [rou'bʌst], *adj.* 1. stark, kräftig, robust; gesund, rüstig; 2. (*fig.*) kernig, derb (*humour*). **robustious** [–'bʌstʃəs], *adj.* (*coll.*) lärmend, laut, heftig, ungestüm. **robustness,** *s.* die Kraft, Stärke, Rüstigkeit.

roc [rɔk], *s.* (*Myth.*) der Vogel Rock.

rocambole ['rɔkəmboul], *s.* (*Bot.*) die Rokambole, Perlzwiebel, der Schlangenlauch.

rochet ['rɔtʃit], *s.* der Chorrock, das Chorhemd, Rochett (*of prelate*).

[1]**rock** [rɔk], *s.* 1. der Fels(en); (*Geol.*) die Felsart, Gesteinsart, das Gestein; (*collect.*) Felsen (*pl.*); ***firm as a –,*** felsenfest; 2. (*Naut.*) die Klippe; (*fig.*) ***see –s ahead,*** mit Schwierigkeiten rechnen müssen; ***on the –s,*** aufgelaufen, festgefahren; (*coll.*) in Geldnot, auf dem trockenen, pleite; (*sl.*) mit Eis (*whisky etc.*); 3. (*sl.*) der Diamant.

[2]**rock, 1.** *v.t.* 1. schaukeln, wiegen (*a cradle*), in den Schlaf wiegen (*a child*); 2. hin– und herbewegen, rütteln, schütteln, ins Wanken *or* zum Schwanken bringen; (*fig.*) – ***the boat,*** die S. ins Wanken bringen; 3. (*Min.*) im Schwingtrog auswaschen (*ore*). **2.** *v.i.* sich hin– und herbewegen, (sich) schaukeln, (sich) wanken, wackeln.

rock|-bed, *s.* der Felsengrund. **--bottom, 1.** *adj.* (*coll.*) allerniedrigst, äußerst (*price*). **2.** *s.* ***at –,*** im Grunde, in Wirklichkeit. **--bound,** *adj.* von Felsen eingeschlossen, felsumgürtet. **--bunting,** *s.* (*Orn.*) die Zippammer (*Emberiza cia*). **--cake,** *s.* hartgebackener Kuchen. **--cork,** *s.* das Bergholz, Bergleder, der Bergkork, Holzasbest. **--crystal,** *s.* der Bergkristall. **--dove,** *s.* (*Orn.*) die Felsentaube (*Columba livia*). **--drill,** *s.* die Gestein(s)bohrmaschine.

rocker ['rɔkə], *s.* 1. die Kufe (*of cradle etc.*); (*sl.*) ***be off one's –,*** einen Klaps, Knacks, Piep, Rappel, Sparren *or* Vogel haben; 2. (*coll.*) der Schaukelstuhl; 3. (*Min.*) Schwingtrog; 4. (*coll.*) Halbstarke(r). **rocker-arm,** *s.* der Kipphebel, Schwenkarm.

rockery ['rɔkəri], *s.* der Steingarten.

[1]**rocket** ['rɔkit], **1.** *s.* 1. die Rakete; ***long-range –,*** die Fernrakete; 2. (*sl.*) der Anpfiff. **2.** *v.i.* 1. (*coll.*) hochschießen, hochschnellen; 2. (*Hunt.*) steil aufsteigen *or* auffliegen (*of birds*).

[2]**rocket,** *s.* 1. (*Bot.*) die Nachtviole; 2. (*Bot.*) Rauke, der Raukenkohl, Senfkohl.

rocket| apparatus, *s.* das Raketengerät (*for life-saving*). **–(-launching) site,** *s.* die Raketen(abschuß)basis. **--propelled,** *adj.* mit Raketenantrieb. **--propulsion,** *s.* der Raketenantrieb. **--range,** *s.* das Raketenversuchsgelände. **rocketry** [–ri], *s.* die Raketentechnik.

rock-garden, *s. See* **rockery.**

Rockies ['rɔkiz], *pl. See* **Rocky Mountains.**

rockiness ['rɔkinis], *s.* 1. die Felsigkeit; 2. (*coll.*) Wack(e)ligkeit.

rocking ['rɔkiŋ], **1.** *s.* 1. das Schaukeln; 2. die Schwingung, Schwankung. **2.** *adj.* schaukelnd, wiegend, schwingend, (sch)wankend. **rocking|-chair,** *s.* der Schaukelstuhl. **--horse,** *s.* das Schaukelpferd. **--screen,** *s.* (*Min.*) das Schüttelsieb, Schwingsieb. **--stone,** *s.* der Wagstein.

rock|-leather, *s. See* **--cork. --oil,** *s.* das Petroleum, Steinöl, Erdöl. **--pipit,** *s.* (*Orn.*) der Strandpieper (*Anthus spinoletta*). **--plant,** *s.* die Steingartenpflanze, Alpenpflanze. **--rose,** *s.* (*Bot.*) die Zistrose. **--salt,** *s.* das Steinsalz. **--thrush,** *s.* (*Orn.*) die Steindrossel, der Steinrötel (*Monticola saxtilus*). **--wood,** *s. See* **--cork. --work,** *s.* das Grottenwerk, künstliche Felsen (*pl.*).

[1]**rocky** ['rɔki], *adj.* 1. felsig; 2. (*Naut.*) Klippen–, klippenreich; 3. (*fig.*) steinhart.

[2]**rocky,** *adj.* 1. (*coll.*) wack(e)lig, wackelnd; 2. (*fig.*) (sch)wankend.

Rocky Mountains, *pl.* das Felsengebirge.

rococo [rə'koukou], **1.** *s.* das Rokoko. **2.** *adj.* 1. Rokoko–; 2. (*fig.*) schnörk(e)lig, Schnörkel–.

rod [rɔd], *s.* 1. der Stab, die Rute, Gerte, das Reis; ***divining*** or ***dowsing –,*** die Wünschelrute; ***fishing –,*** die Angelrute; 2. (*Tech.*) die Stange; ***connecting –,*** die Pleuelstange; 3. (*Anat.*) das Stäbchen (*of retina*); 4. (*fig.*) die Zuchtrute, der Prügel; die Züchtigung, Prügel (*pl.*), Schläge (*pl.*); (*fig.*) ***kiss the –,*** sich unter der Rute beugen; (*coll.*) ***have a – in pickle for him,*** mit ihm noch ein Hühnchen zu rupfen haben, für ihn Rache auf Lager haben; ***make a – for one's own back,*** sich (*Dat.*) (selbst) eine Rute aufbinden; (*Prov.*) ***spare the – and spoil the child,*** allzu große Nachsicht verwöhnt das Kind; (*fig.*) ***with a – of iron,*** mit eiserner Rute; 5. die Knute, Tyrannei; (*Parl.*) ***Black Rod,*** erster Dienstbeamter des Oberhauses; 6. (*obs.*) die Rute (*= 5.1 m.*); 7. (*Am. sl.*) das Schießeisen.

rode [roud], *imperf., p.p. of* **ride.**

rodent ['roudənt], **1.** *s.* das Nagetier. **2.** *adj.* 1. nagend, Nage–; 2. (*Med.*) fressend.

rodeo [rou'deiou], *s.* der Rodeo (*also Motor. etc.*), die Wildwestschau.

rodomontade [rɔdəmɔn'tɑ:d], **1.** *s.* die Prahlerei, Großsprecherei, Aufschneiderei. **2.** *v.i.* prahlen, großsprechen, aufschneiden.

[1]**roe** [rou], *s.* (*Ichth.*) 1. (*also* ***hard –***) der Rogen, Fischlaich; 2. ***soft –,*** die Milch.

[2]**roe,** *s.* 1. (*also* **--deer**) das Reh(wild); 2. die Hirschkuh, Hindin, Ricke. **roebuck** [–bʌk], *s.* der Rehbock.

Roentgen *etc., see* **Röntgen.**

roestone ['roustoun], *s.* (*Min.*) der Oolith, Rogenstein.

Rogation [rou'geiʃən], *s.* (*Eccl.*) die (Für)bitte; (*usu. pl.*) Allerheiligenlitanei, der Bittgang; – ***days,*** Bittage (*pl.*); – ***Sunday,*** der Sonntag Rogate; – ***week,*** die Bittwoche, Himmelfahrtswoche.

Roger ['rɔdʒə], *s.* (*Naut.*) ***Jolly –,*** die Totenkopfflagge, Piratenflagge.

rogue [roug], *s.* 1. der Schurke, Schuft, Gauner; ***–s' gallery,*** das Verbrecheralbum; 2. (*coll.*) der Schlingel, Schelm, Schalk, Strolch, Spitzbube; 3. (*obs.*) Vagabund, Landstreicher; 4. (*Zool.*) (*also* – ***elephant***) bösartiger Einzelgänger. **roguery** [–əri], *s.* 1. die Schurkerei, Gaunerei, der Betrug; 2. (*coll.*) das Schelmenstück, Bubenstück; 3. die Schalkhaftigkeit. **roguish,** *adj.* 1. schurkisch; 2.

schelmisch, schalkhaft, verschmitzt. **roguishness,** *s.* die Schalkhaftigkeit, Verschmitztheit.

roister ['rɔistə], *v.t.* lärmen, krakeelen, Radau machen. **roisterer,** *s.* der Polterer, Krakeeler. **roistering,** *s.* der Radau, Krakeel. **roisterous,** *adj.* tobend, lärmend.

role, rôle [roul], *s.* 1. (*Theat.*) die Rolle; 2. (*fig.*) die Rolle, Funktion.

roll [roul], **1.** *v.t.* rollen (*also one's r's, one's eyes*); (herum)wälzen (*also fig.*); aufrollen, zusammenrollen, aufwickeln, zusammenwickeln; einwickeln, einrollen (*in*, in (*Acc.*)); (*Metall.*) strecken, walzen; – ***a cigarette,*** eine Zigarette drehen; – ***a drum,*** eine Trommel wirbeln *or* im Wirbel schlagen; – ***the lawn,*** den Rasen walzen; – ***back,*** zurückrollen (lassen); (*Am. Comm.*) senken, zurückschrauben (*prices*); – ***out,*** (dahin)rollen lassen; ausrollen, auswellen (*dough*); strecken, auswalzen (*metal*); deklamieren (*list of names etc.*); – ***over,*** umstoßen, umwerfen, über den Haufen rennen; – ***up,*** aufrollen, aufwickeln; hochkrempeln (*sleeves etc.*). **2.** *v.i.* 1. rollen; dahinrollen, sich (dahin)wälzen; kreisen, sich drehen *or* herumrollen; (*coll.*) ***be –ing,*** schwimmen, wühlen; ***be –ing in money,*** Geld wie Heu haben; (*fig.*) ***set the ball –ing,*** die S. in Gang bringen; – ***away,*** sich verziehen *or* fortwälzen (*as mist*); – ***by,*** vorbeirollen; – ***in,*** hereinrollen; (*coll.*) hereinkommen, hereinschneien; – ***on,*** ablaufen, verlaufen, vergehen, dahingehen, dahinziehen; – ***over,*** sich herumdrehen; – ***up,*** sich zusammenrollen; heranrollen, anfahren, vorfahren (*as vehicle*); (*coll.*) auftauchen, aufkreuzen; 2. (*of sound*) donnern, dröhnen, brausen; wallen, wogen (*sea*); 3. sich ausdehnen *or* erstrecken (*land*); 4. schlingern (*ship*); schlenkern (*a p.*). **3.** *s.* 1. die Rolle (*paper etc.*), der Ballen (*cloth*); die Schriftrolle, das Schriftstück, Verzeichnis, die (Namens)liste, Anwesenheitsliste; ***call the –,*** die Namen verlesen, Appell halten; ***Master of the Rolls,*** der Präsident des Reichsarchivs; ***Roll of Honour,*** die Ehrentafel der Gefallenen; ***put on the –,*** in die Liste eintragen; ***strike off the –(s),*** von *or* aus der Liste streichen, (*doctor, lawyer etc.*) disqualifizieren; 2. (*Archit.*) die Rundleiste, Wulst, Volute; 3. (*Tech.*) Rolle, Walze; 4. das Brötchen, Rundstück, die Semmel (*of bread*); ***meat –,*** die (Fleisch)roulade; ***Swiss –,*** die Biskuitroulade; 5. (*Naut.*) das Schlingern, (*Av.*) Rolling, der Überschlag; 6. (*of drums*) Wirbel, das Wirbeln; 7. (*thunder etc.*) Rollen, Dröhnen, Brausen; (*canary*) Rollen, der Triller; 8. (*gait*) wiegender *or* schlingernder Gang, das Schlenkern.

roll|-back, *s.* (*Am. Comm.*) die (Preis)senkung. **--call,** *s.* die Namensverlesung, der Namensaufruf, (*Mil.*) (Anwesenheits)appell. **--collar,** *s.* der Schalkragen. **rolled** [-d], *adj.* 1. gerollt, Roll–; – ***ham,*** der Rollschinken; – ***r,*** das Zungen-r; 2. (*Metall.*) gewalzt, Walz–; – ***gold,*** das Dubleegold; – ***metal,*** das Walzblech.

roller ['roulə], *s.* 1. die Rolle, Walze, Trommel, der Zylinder; Rollklotz (*for moving heavy goods*), Rollstab (*for rolling up maps etc.*); (*Tech.*) die Laufrolle, Gleitrolle, Führungsrolle; *pl.* (*Tech.*) das Walzwerk; ***feed(ing) –,*** die Auftragswalze; ***road –,*** die Straßenwalze; 2. (*Naut.*) die Flutwelle, Sturzwelle, Brandungswelle, Woge; *pl.* die Brandung; 3. (*Orn.*) die Blauracke (*Coracius garrulus*).

roller| bandage, *s.* die Rollbinde. – **bearing,** *s.* das Rollenlager. – **blind,** *s.* der Rollvorhang, das Rouleau; (*Phot.*) – ***shutter,*** der Schlitzverschluß. – **canary,** *s.* (*Orn.*) Harzer Roller (*Serinus canarius*). **--skate,** *s.* der Rollschuh. **--skating,** *s.* das Rollschuhlaufen. – **towel,** *s.* das Rollhandtuch.

roll film, *s.* (*Phot.*) der Rollfilm.

rollick ['rɔlik], *v.i.* herumtollen, ausgelassen *or* übermütig sein. **rollicking,** *adj.* ausgelassen, übermütig.

rolling ['rouliŋ], **1.** *s.* 1. das Rollen; 2. (*Metall.*) Walzen, Strecken; 3. (*Naut.*) Schlingern; – ***and pitching,*** die Schlinger– und Stampfbewegung. **2.** *adj.* rollend, Roll–; wellig, wellenförmig (*land*); (*Artil.*) – ***barrage,*** die Feuerwalze; – ***capital,*** das Betriebskapital; – ***gait,*** wiegender *or* schlingernder Gang; (*fig.*) – ***stone,*** unsteter Mensch; (*Prov.*) ***a – stone gathers no moss,*** ein rollender Stein setzt kein Moos an.

rolling|-hitch, *s.* (*Naut.*) der Rollstich, Rollsteek. **--mill,** *s.* das Walzwerk. **--pin,** *s.* das Rollholz, Nudelholz. **--press,** *s.* 1. die Walzenpresse; (*Typ.*) Rotationsdruckpresse; 2. (*Paperm.*) Satinierpresse. **--stock,** *s.* (*Railw.*) rollendes Material.

roll|-on, *s.* (*coll.*) der Gummischlüpfer. **--top,** *s.* die Rollade (*of desk*); – ***desk,*** das Rollpult.

roly-poly ['rouli'pouli], (*coll.*) **1.** *s.* gerollter Marmeladepudding. **2.** *attrib. adj.* mollig, rundlich und dick.

Roman ['roumən], **1.** *adj.* römisch, Römer–; – ***candle,*** die Leuchtkugel; – ***character*** or ***letter,*** der Antiquabuchstabe; – ***holiday,*** das Vergnügen auf Kosten anderer; – ***nose,*** die Adlernase; – ***numeral,*** römische Ziffer; – ***road,*** die Römerstraße; – ***woman,*** die Römerin. **2.** *s.* der (die) Römer(in); (*B.*) ***Epistle to the –s,*** der Römerbrief.

Roman Catholic, 1. *adj.* (römisch-)katholisch. **2.** *s.* der (die) Katholik(in), Römisch-Katholische(r).

romance [rou'mæns], **1.** *s.* 1. der (Ritter)roman (*of Middle Ages*); ***Arthurian –,*** der Artusroman; 2. die Romanze (*in Spanish literature, also Mus.*); 3. romantische Erzählung, der Abenteuerroman, Liebesroman; 4. (*fig.*) die Romantik, das Romantische, der Zauber; 5. (*coll.*) die Phantasieerzählung, Phantasterei, Übertreibung; 6. (*coll.*) (Liebes)affäre. **2.** *v.i.* (*coll.*) lügen, fabulieren, fabeln, Romane erzählen, aufschneiden.

Romance, *adj.* romanisch; – ***nations,*** Romanen (*pl.*); – ***philologist,*** der Romanist.

romancer [rou'mænsə], *s.* 1. der Verfasser eines Ritterromans; 2. Romanzendichter; 3. (*coll.*) der (die) Fabulant(in), Phantast(in), Lügner(in), Aufschneider(in).

Romanesque [roumə'nesk], **1.** *adj.* 1. (*Archit.*) romanisch; 2. *See* **Romance. 2.** *s.* romanischer (Bau)stil, die Romanik.

Romania [rou'meiniə], *see* **Rumania.**

Romanist ['roumənist], *s. See* **Roman Catholic** *and* ***Romance philologist.***

Romans(c)h [rou'mænʃ], **1.** *s.* das Rätoromanisch(e), Romaunsch, Romontsch, (Grau)bündnerisch(e). **2.** *adj.* rätoromanisch, (grau)bündnerisch.

romantic [rou'mæntik], **1.** *adj.* 1. romantisch (*also Liter. etc.*); – ***movement,*** die Romantik; 2. phantastisch, schwärmerisch (*of a p.*); 3. malerisch, märchenhaft, abenteuerlich. **2.** *s.* 1. der Romantiker; 2. (*fig.*) der (die) Phantast(in), Schwärmer(in). **romanticism** [–tisizm], *s.* 1. (*Liter. etc.*) die Romantik; 2. das Romantische. **romanticist** [–tisist], *s. See* **romantic, 2. romanticize** [–tisaiz], *v.t.* romantisch darstellen, romantisieren; ***with a tendency to –,*** romantisch veranlagt.

Romany ['roumәni], **1.** *s.* 1. der (die) Zigeuner(in); (*also collect.*) Zigeuner (*pl.*); 2. die Zigeunersprache. **2.** *adj.* Zigeuner–.

Rome [roum], *s.* Rom (*n.*); ***do in – as the Romans do,*** mit den Wölfen heulen; – ***was not built in a day,*** Rom ist nicht an einem Tag erbaut worden. **Romish,** *adj.* (*Eccl.*) (römisch-)katholisch, papistisch.

romp [rɔmp], **1.** *s.* 1. die Range, der Wildfang (*usu. of girls*); 2. das Tollen, Balgen. **2.** *v.i.* 1. (sich aus)toben, sich herumbalgen *or* herumtummeln, umhertollen; 2. (*racing*) – ***home,*** leicht gewinnen; – ***through,*** spielend hindurchkommen. **rompers** [–əz], *pl.* das Spielhöschen.

rondeau ['rɔndou], *s.* das Ringelgedicht, Rondeau, Rondel. **rondel** [–l], *s.* 14-zeiliges Rondeau. **rondo** [–ou], *s.* (*Mus.*) das Rondo. **rondure** [–jə], *s.* (*Poet.*) der Kreis, das Rund.

Röntgen ['rə:ntgən, –jən], *attrib. adj.* Röntgen–. **röntgenization** [–gənai'zeiʃən], *s.* die Bestrahlung, Röntgenbehandlung. **röntgenogram** [–gənəgræm], *s.* das Röntgenbild, die Röntgenaufnahme. **röntgenography** [–gəˈnɔgrəfi], *s.* die Röntgenphotographie. **röntgenological** [–gənəˈlɔdʒikl], *adj.* Röntgen–. **röntgenologist** [–ˈgəˈnɔlədʒist], *s.* der Facharzt für Röntgenbehandlung *or* für Strahlenkunde. **röntgenotherapy** [–gənəˈθerəpi], *s.* die Strahlenbehandlung, Röntgenbestrahlung.

[1]**rood** [ru:d], *s.* 1. (*obs.*) der Viertelmorgen (= ¼ *acre, approx.* 1/10 *Ar*); 2. (*obs.*) die Rute (*approx.* 7 *yds* = 6 *m.*).

[2]**rood,** *s.* (*obs.*) (*Eccl.*) das Kruzifix, Kreuz. **rood|-loft,** *s.* die Empore des Lettners, Chorbühne. **--screen,** *s.* der Lettner. **--spire,** *s.* der Vierungsturm.

roof [ru:f], **1.** *s.* das Dach; – ***of heaven,*** das Himmelszelt, Himmelsgewölbe; – ***of the mouth,*** harter Gaumen; ***under my –,*** in meinem Haus. **2.** *v.t.* bedachen; – ***in,*** (ein)decken; – ***over,*** überdachen. **roofage** [–idʒ], *s. See* **roofing, 1. roofer,** *s.* der Dachdecker. **roof-garden,** *s.* der Dachgarten. **roofing, 1.** *s.* 1. die Dachdeckerarbeit; Überdachung, Bedachung; 2. das Deckmaterial; 3. Dachwerk, Sparrenwerk. **2.** *adj.* – ***felt,*** die Dachpappe; – ***tile,*** der Dachziegel. **roofless,** *adj.* 1. ohne Dach; 2. (*fig.*) obdachlos. **roof|-rack,** *s.* (*Motor.*) der Dachgepäckträger. **--tree,** *s.* 1. der Dachbalken, Firstbalken; 2. (*fig.*) das Obdach, die Behausung.

rook [ruk], **1.** *s.* 1. (*Orn.*) die Saatkrähe (*Corvus frugilegus*); 2. (*Chess*) der Turm; 3. (*fig.*) Gauner, Betrüger, Bauernfänger. **2.** *v.t.* (*coll.*) betrügen, übers Ohr hauen. **rookery,** *s.* 1. die Krähenkolonie; 2. (*of other birds*) Brutstätte, der Nistplatz. **rookie,** *s.* (*sl.*) 1. (*Mil.*) der Rekrut; 2. (*fig.*) Neuling, Anfänger.

room [ru:m], **1.** *s.* 1. das Zimmer, die Stube, Kammer, der Raum; ***in the next –,*** im Nebenzimmer; (*coll.*) ***I prefer his – to his company,*** ich wünschte, er wäre nicht da; 2. der Raum, Platz; (*fig.*) Spielraum, Anlaß, die Gelegenheit, Veranlassung; – ***for complaint,*** der Anlaß zur Klage; ***no – for hope,*** keine Hoffnung mehr, nichts zu hoffen; ***there is – for improvement,*** es könnte etwas besser sein; ***make –,*** Platz machen (***for,*** *Dat.*) (*a p.*), Raum schaffen (für) (*a th.*); ***plenty of –,*** viel Platz; ***no – to swing a cat in*** or ***to turn round in,*** sehr wenig Platz, sehr beengter Raum; ***take up a lot of –,*** viel Platz in Anspruch nehmen. **2.** *v.i.* (*esp. Am.*) wohnen, logieren (***at,*** in (*Dat.*); ***with,*** bei); – ***together,*** zusammenwohnen. **-roomed,** *adj. suff.* –zimmerig; ***five-– flat,*** die Fünfzimmerwohnung.

roomer [ˈru:mə], *s.* (*esp. Am.*) der (die) Untermieter(in). **roomful,** *s.* das Zimmer(voll), der Raum(voll); ***a – of people,*** ein Zimmer voll(er) Leute. **room heating,** *s.* die Raumheizung. **roominess,** *s.* die Geräumigkeit. **rooming house,** *s.* (*Am.*) das Logierhaus, die Pension. **room| mate,** *s.* der (die) Stubenkamerad(in), Zimmergenosse (–genossin). – **temperature,** *s.* die Zimmertemperatur. **roomy,** *adj.* geräumig, weit(läufig).

roost [ru:st], **1.** *s.* die Hühnerstange, der Schlafsitz; der Hühnerstall; ***be at –,*** auf der Stange sitzen, schlafen; (*fig.*) ***come home to –,*** auf den Täter zurückfallen (*of evil deeds etc.*); (*coll.*) ***go to –,*** zur Ruhe gehen, schlafen gehen; ***cock of the –,*** der Hahn im Korb; ***rule the –,*** das Regiment *or* Wort führen, herrschen. **2.** *v.i.* 1. auf der Stange sitzen; 2. (*coll.*) hausen, nächtigen. **rooster,** *s.* der Hahn.

[1]**root** [ru:t], **1.** *s.* 1. die Wurzel (*also Gram., Math. & fig.*) (*fig.*) – ***and branch,*** ganz und gar, völlig, mit Stumpf und Stiel; ***pull out*** or ***up by the –s,*** mit der Wurzel ausreißen; ***take*** or ***strike*** (***deep***) –, (tief) Wurzel fassen, (tief) einwurzeln (*also fig.*); – ***of a hair,*** die Haarwurzel; – ***of the tongue,*** die Zungenwurzel; – ***of a tooth,*** die Zahnwurzel; (*Math.*) ***cube –,*** die Kubikwurzel, dritte Wurzel; ***square –,*** die Quadratwurzel, zweite Wurzel; ***–-mean-square,*** quadratischer Mittelwert; 2. (*fig.*) die Grundlage, Ursache, Quelle, der Grund, Ursprung; Kern, Gehalt, das Wesen(tliche), Wichtigste; – ***idea,*** der Grundgedanke, die Grundidee; ***be at the – of,*** der Grund *or* die Ursache *or* Wurzel sein von; ***get at*** or ***go to the – of the matter,*** der S. auf den Grund gehen; ***the – of the matter,*** der Kern der S.; (*fig.*) ***have its –s in,*** seine Grundlage haben in (*Dat.*), seinen Ausgang nehmen von, basieren auf (*Dat.*). **2.** *v.t.* einwurzeln, tief einpflanzen; (*fig.*) ***fear –s him to the spot*** or ***ground,*** er steht vor Furcht wie angewurzelt; (*fig.*) – ***out,*** ausrotten, vertilgen. **3.** *v.i.* 1. Wurzel schlagen *or* fassen, einwurzeln; 2. (*fig.*) – ***in, see*** **rooted.**

[2]**root, 1.** *v.i.* (mit der Schnauze) wühlen (***for,*** nach); – ***about,*** herumwühlen. **2.** *v.t.* aufwühlen, umwühlen (*earth*); (*fig.*) – ***out,*** ausgraben, ausfindig machen; hervorziehen (***from under,*** unter (*Dat.*)).

root| cause, *s.* eigentliche Ursache, die Grundursache. **--crop,** *s.* die Rübenernte, das Wurzelgemüse, Hackfrüchte (*pl.*).

rooted [ˈru:tid], *adj.* eingewurzelt (*also fig.*), verankert, verwurzelt; (*fig.*) ***be – in,*** wurzeln *or* seinen Grund haben in (*Dat.*), beruhen auf (*Dat.*); – ***to the spot,*** wie angewurzelt. **rootedly,** *adv.* von Grund auf. **rootedness,** *s.* die Verwurzelung, Verankerung.

root| form, *s.* die Grundform. **--grafting,** *s.* das Wurzelpfropfen, die Wurzelhalsveredelung. **–hair,** *s.* (*Bot.*) das Wurzelhaar. **rootless,** *adj.* 1. ohne Wurzel; 2. (*fig.*) ohne festen Boden, entwurzelt. **rootlet** [–lit], *s.* die Wurzelfaser. **root|-sign,** *s.* (*Math.*) das Wurzelzeichen. **-stock,** *s.* der Wurzelstock, das Rhizom. **--treatment,** *s.* (*Dentistry*) die Wurzelbehandlung. **rooty,** *adj.* 1. wurzelreich; 2. wurzelartig, Wurzel–.

rope [roup], **1.** *s.* 1. das Seil, der Strick; (*Naut.*) das Tau, (Tau)ende, Reep; *pl.* das Tauwerk; (*coll.*) ***know the –s,*** sich auskennen, den Kniff 'raushaben, den Rummel verstehen; (*coll.*) ***learn the –s,*** sich einarbeiten, hinter die Schliche kommen; (*Mount.*) ***on the –,*** angeseilt; (*fig. coll.*) ***on the high –s,*** hochfahrend, hochmütig, von oben herab; 2. der Strang, das Bund, Bündel (*onions etc.*); 3. die Schnur (*pearls*); 4. (*fig.*) Handelsfreiheit, Bewegungsfreiheit; ***give him –,*** ihn schalten und walten lassen, ihn gewähren lassen; 5. *pl.* (*Boxing*) Seile (*pl.*); ***be on the –s,*** in den Seilen hängen. **2.** *v.t.* mit einem Strick *or* Seil festbinden, zusammenbinden *or* befestigen; anseilen (*climbers*); – ***in,*** durch ein Seil abgrenzen *or* einschließen (*space*); (*sl.*) einfangen, (her)anlocken, herbeilocken (*a p.*); (*sl.*) – ***into,*** hineinziehen in (*Acc.*), verlocken zu (*a p.*); (*sl.*) – ***him into doing,*** ihn dazu verlocken, zu tun; – ***off,*** mit einem Seil absperren (*a space*). **3.** *v.i.* 1. Fäden bilden *or* ziehen, dick werden (*syrup*); 2. (*Mount.*) sich anseilen; – ***down,*** abseilen.

rope|-dancer, *s.* der (die) Seiltänzer(in). **--ladder,** *s.* die Strickleiter. **--maker,** *s.* der Seiler, Reeper, Reepschläger. – **moulding,** *s.* (*Archit.*) die Schiffstauverzierung, Seilleiste. **--railway,** *s.* die Seilbahn. **ropery** [–əri], *s.* die Seilerei. **rope's-end, 1.** *s.* (*Naut.*) das (Tau)ende, der Tamp. **2.** *v.t.* mit dem Tauende verprügeln. **rope|-stitch,** *s.* der Stielstich. **–walk,** *s.* die Seilerbahn, Reeperbahn. **--walker,** *s. See* **--dancer.** – **yard,** *s. See* **ropery. --yarn,** *s.* das Kabelgarn.

ropiness [ˈroupinis], *s.* 1. die Klebrigkeit, Zähigkeit, Dickflüssigkeit; 2. (*of wine*) die Kahmbildung, Kahmdecke. **ropy,** *adj.* 1. klebrig, zäh, dickflüssig, fadenziehend; 2. (*of wine*) kahmig; 3. (*sl.*) kläglich, schäbig, elend, miserabel.

rorqual [ˈrɔ:kwəl], *s.* (*Zool.*) der Finnwal.

rosace [ˈrouzeis], *s.* (*Archit.*) die (Fenster)rosette, das Rosenfenster. **rosaceous** [–ˈzeiʃəs], *adj.* (*Bot.*) Rosen–.

rosarian [roˈzɛəriən], *s.* 1. der Rosenzüchter; 2. (*R.C.*) Rosenkreuzbruder. **rosarium,** *s.* der Rosengarten.

rosary [ˈrouzəri], *s.* 1. (*R.C.*) der Rosenkranz; 2. (*Hort.*) Rosengarten, das Rosenbeet.

[1]**rose** [rouz], *imperf. of* **rise.**

[2]**rose, 1.** *s.* 1. (*Bot.*) die Rose; ***on a bed of –s,*** auf Rosen gebettet; (*coll.*) ***it's no bed of –s,*** es ist kein reines Vergnügen; ***like milk and –s,*** wie Milch und

Blut; *under the –*, im Vertrauen; 2. die Brause (*of watering-can*); 3. das Rosenrot, die Rosafarbe, Röte; 4. (*Archit.*) Rosette, das Röschen; 5. (*Med.*) *the –*, die Wundrose, der Rotlauf. **2.** *adj.* 1. Rosen–; 2. rosenfarbig.

roseate ['rouzieit], *adj.* 1. rosig (*also fig.*); (*Orn.*) – *tern*, die Rosenseeschwalbe (*Sterna dougallii*); 2. (*fig.*) strahlend, goldig, vielversprechend, optimistisch.

rose|-bud, *s.* die Rosenknospe; – *lips*, der Rosenmund. **--burner,** *s.* der Kronenbrenner. **--bush,** *s.* der Rosenstrauch, Rosenstock. **--coloured,** *adj.* 1. rosenrot, rosafarben; 2. (*fig.*) rosig, rosa(rot); *see everything through – spectacles*, alles durch eine rosa(rote) Brille sehen. **--cut,** *adj.* rosettenartig geschliffen (*diamond etc.*). **--gall,** *s.* der Rosenschwamm. **--hip,** *s.* (*Bot.*) die Hagebutte. **--madder,** *s.* das Krapprosa.

rosemary ['rouzməri], *s.* (*Bot.*) der Rosmarin.

roseola [rou'zi:ələ], *s.* (*Med.*) die Rubeola, Röteln (*pl.*).

rose|-pink, 1. *s.* das Rosa. **2.** *adj.* rosa, rosenrot. **--rash,** *s.* *See* **roseola. --red,** *adj.* *See* **--pink, 2. --tree,** *s.* *See* **--bush.**

rosette [rou'zet], *s.* die Rosette, (Zier)rose, das Röschen, Rosenornament. **rose|-water, 1.** *s.* das Rosenwasser. **2.** *attrib. adj.* (*rare*) sanft(mütig), zart, schonend. **--window,** *s.* die Fensterrose, (Fenster)rosette, das Radfenster. **-wood,** *s.* das Rosenholz.

Rosicrucian [rouzi'kru:ʃən], **1.** *s.* der Rosenkreuzer. **2.** *adj.* Rosenkreuzer–, rosenkreuzerisch.

rosin ['rɔzin], **1.** *s.* das (Terpentin)harz, Geigenharz, Kolophonium. **2.** *v.t.* mit Kolophonium einreiben.

rosiness ['rouzinis], *s.* 1. die Rosigkeit, rosige Farbe, das Rosige; 2. rosiges Aussehen.

roster ['roustə, 'rɔstə], *s.* 1. (*Mil.*) die Dienstliste, der Dienstplan; 2. das Namenverzeichnis.

rostral ['rɔstrəl], *adj.* schnabelförmig. **rostrate(d)** [–eit(id)], *adj.* Schnabel–, geschnäbelt.

rostrum ['rɔstrəm], *s.* 1. die Rednerbühne, Kanzel, Tribüne; das Dirigentenpult; 2. (*fig.*) die Plattform; 3. (*Zool., Bot.*) der Schnabel, schnabelförmiger Fortsatz; 4. (*Hist.*) Schiffsschnabel.

rosy ['rouzi], *adj.* 1. rosenfarbig, rosenrot, rosa; 2. (*fig.*) rosig, blühend. **rosy-cheeked,** *adj.* rosenwangig.

rot [rɔt], **1.** *v.i.* 1. (*also – away*) (ver)faulen, abfaulen, verwesen, (ver)modern, morsch werden; 2. (*fig.*) verkommen, verrotten; (*fig.*) *rotting in gaol*, im Kerker (ver)schmachtend. **2.** *v.t.* 1. faulen lassen, zur Fäulnis bringen; 2. (*sl.*) dumm anreden, hänseln, necken. **3.** *s.* 1. die Fäulnis, Verwesung, Vermoderung, (*also Vet.*) Fäule; 2. (*sl.*) (*also tommy-–*) der Blödsinn, Unsinn, Blech, Quatsch; (*sl.*) *talk –*, quasseln; faseln; 3. (*sl.*) (*Spt., fig.*) die Pechsträhne. **4.** *int.* (*sl.*) Blödsinn! Quatsch!

rota ['routə], *s.* 1. die Dienstliste; 2. der Turnus, Verlauf; 3. (*R.C.*) päpstliches Appellationsgericht.

rotary ['routəri], *adj.* sich drehend, kreisend, umlaufend, rotierend, Rotations–, Dreh–, Kreis–, Umlauf–; *Rotary Club*, der Rotaryclub, Rotarier (*pl.*); (*Elec.*) – *converter*, der Drehumformer; – *current*, der Drehstrom; – *engine*, der Umlaufmotor; – *motion*, die Drehbewegung, Kreisbewegung; (*Typ.*) – *machine or press*, die Rotationsmaschine, Schnellpresse; – *printing*, der Rotationsdruck; – *pump*, die Umlaufpumpe; – *switch*, der Drehschalter; – *velocity*, die Umdrehungsgeschwindigkeit.

¹**rotate** [rou'teit], **1.** *v.i.* 1. sich (um eine Achse) drehen, kreisen, umlaufen, rotieren; 2. der Reihe nach *or* turnusmäßig (ab)wechseln. **2.** *v.t.* 1. kreisen *or* rotieren lassen, (um eine Achse) drehen; 2. wechseln (lassen) (*as crops*).

²**rotate** ['routeit], *adj.* (*Bot.*) radförmig.

rotating [rou'teitiŋ], *adj.* sich drehend, drehbar, Dreh–; – *beacon*, das Drehfeuer; – *field*, das Drehfeld. **rotation** [–'teiʃən], *s.* 1. die (Um)drehung, Rotation, der Kreislauf, Umlauf; *direction of –*, der Drehsinn; 2. (*fig.*) der Wechsel, die Abwechslung; – *of crops*, der Fruchtwechsel; *by or in –*, der Reihe nach, abwechselnd, wechselweise. **rotatory** ['routətəri], *adj.* 1. *See* **rotary**; – *storm*, der Wirbelsturm; 2. abwechselnd, turnusmäßig aufeinanderfolgend.

rote [rout], *s.* *by –*, durch bloße Übung, gewohnheitsmäßig, rein mechanisch, auswendig.

rot-gut, *s.* (*sl.*) der Fusel.

rotifer ['routifə], *s.* (*Zool.*) das Rädertierchen.

rotisserie [ro'ti:səri], *s.* 1. die Fleischbraterei; 2. drehbarer Bratspieß, der Drehgrill (*on a cooker*).

rotogravure [routəgrə'vjuə], *s.* der Kupfer(tief)druck.

rotor ['routə], *s.* 1. (*Elec.*) der Rotor, Anker, Läufer; 2. (*of helicopter*) Drehflügel, die Tragschraube.

rotten [rɔtn], *adj.* 1. faul (*also fig.*), verfault, vermodert, verfallen; wurmstichig (*as fruit*); – *eggs*, faule Eier; – *to the core*, kernfaul, (*fig.*) grundschlecht, durch und durch korrupt; 2. morsch (*as soil, also fig.*), mürbe, brüchig (*as ice*); 3. brandig, stockig (*as wood*); 4. (*fig.*) (*of a p.*) verderbt, bestechlich, korrupt; (*Pol. Hist.*) – *borough*, verfallener Wahlkreis; 5. (*sl.*) schlecht, gemein, niederträchtig; kläglich, miserabel; (*sl.*) – *luck*, das Saupech; (*sl.*) – *trick*, gemeiner Streich; – *weather*, das Sauwetter. **rottenness,** *s.* 1. die Fäulnis, Fäule; 2. (*fig.*) Verderbtheit, Korruptheit.

rotter ['rɔtə], *s.* (*sl.*) der Lump, Schuft, Schweinehund.

rotund [rou'tʌnd], *adj.* 1. rund(lich), (ab)gerundet; 2. schwülstig, pompös (*style*); 3. klangvoll, volltönend (*voice*). **rotunda** [–ə], *s.* der Rundbau, die Rundhalle, Rotunde. **rotundate** [–eit], *adj.* (*Bot.*) (ab)gerundet. **rotundifolious** [–i'fouliəs], *adj.* (*Bot.*) rundblättrig. **rotundity** [–iti], *s.* 1. das Runde, die Rundung; 2. Rundheit, Abgerundetheit; 3. (*of a p.*) Rundlichkeit, Fülligkeit; 4. (*fig.*) (*as style*) Ausgewogenheit.

roué ['ru:ei], *s.* der Wüstling, Lebemann.

rouge [ru:ʒ], **1.** *s.* 1. (rote) Schminke; 2. das Englischrot, Polierpulver. **2.** *adj.* (*Her.*) rot. **3.** *v.t., v.i.* (sich) rot schminken. **rouge-royal,** *s.* rötlicher Marmor.

rough [rʌf], **1.** *adj.* 1. rauh, uneben, holperig; 2. (*of skin*) rissig, aufgesprungen; (*of hair*) zottig, struppig; 3. (*of sea*) stürmisch; – *passage*, stürmische Überfahrt, (*fig.*) schwere Zeit; 4. (*fig.*) (*of a p.*) heftig, ungestüm; rauh, barsch, grob, schroff, derb, roh; unmanierlich, unkultiviert, ungeschliffen, ungehobelt, ungebildet; – *customer*, grober Gesell; – *game*, harter Spiel; (*sl.*) – *stuff*, allgemeine Schlägerei, Gewalttätigkeiten (*pl.*); 5. streng, hart (*with*, gegen); 6. (*coll.*) rauh, hart; (*coll.*) – *luck*, (unverdientes) Pech (*on*, für); *it is – (luck) on him*, es ist hart für ihn; (*coll.*) *they had a – time*, sie haben viel durchgemacht, es ist ihnen schlecht gegangen; – *treatment* or *usage*, schlechte Behandlung; 7. (*of material*) unbearbeitet, im Rohzustand, unfertig, Roh–, (*stone*) unbehauen; – *copy* or *draught*, erster Entwurf, das Konzept; – *diamond*, ungeschliffener Diamant; (*fig.*) das Rauhbein; – *sketch*, die Faustzeichnung, flüchtige Skizze, (*fig.*) der Rohentwurf; – *work*, grobe Arbeit; 8. (*accuracy etc.*) flüchtig, annähernd, ungefähr; – *balance*, rohe Bilanz; – *calculation*, der Überschlag; – *circle*, annähernd richtiger Kreis; – *guess*, grobe Schätzung; (*coll.*) *at a – guess*, über den Daumen gepeilt; 9. (*taste*) herb. **2.** *s.* 1. das Rauhe, Grobe; (*fig.*) *the –(s) and the smooth(s)*, das Auf und Ab; *take the – with the smooth*, die Dinge nehmen wie sie sind, das Schlechte mit dem Guten in Kauf nehmen; 2. der Rohzustand; *in –*, als erster Entwurf, im Konzept; *in the –*, im Rohzustand, noch nicht ausgearbeitet, noch unfertig; 3. (*Golf*) unebener Boden; 4. der Grobian, Lümmel, Rüpel, Rowdy. **3.** *v.t.* 1. *See* **roughen, 1**; 2. – *in*, in den Grundzügen skizzieren; – *out*, roh *or* grob bearbeiten, im groben behauen *or* formen, flüchtig skizzieren, in groben Umrissen entwerfen; 3. – *up*, wider den Strich fahren; (*sl.*) (*a p.*) kräftig zusetzen (*Dat.*); 4. (*coll.*)

– *it,* ein hartes Leben führen, sich mühselig durchschlagen.

roughage ['rʌfidʒ], *s.* das Rauhfutter, grobe Nahrung; unverdauliche Nährstoffe (*pl.*).

rough|-and-ready, *attrib. adj.* Not–, Behelfs–; unfertig, im groben bearbeitet; *in a – manner,* behelfsmäßig, mehr schlecht als recht. **--and-tumble, 1.** *s.* das Handgemenge, die Keilerei. **2.** *attrib. adj.* rauh, heftig. **–cast, 1.** *irr.v.t.* 1. im groben entwerfen, flüchtig skizzieren, im Entwurf anfertigen; 2. (*Build.*) (mit Rauhputz) anwerfen, mit Berapp verputzen, berappen. **2.** *s.* (*Build.*) der Berapp, Rauhputz. **3.** *adj.* 1. im rohen entworfen, unfertig; 2. (*Build.*) mit Berapp verputzt, (mit Rauhputz) angeworfen. **--cut,** *adj.* grob geschnitten (*tobacco*) *or* geschliffen (*diamond*). **--dressed,** *adj.* roh behauen (*masonry*). **--drill,** *v.t.* vorbohren. **--dry, 1.** *v.t.* bügelfertig machen (*laundry*). **2.** *attrib. adj.* – *clothes,* die Trockenwäsche.

roughen ['rʌfən], **1.** *v.t.* (*also – up*) rauh machen, aufrauhen, anrauhen. **2.** *v.i.* rauh(er) *or* grob *or* gröber werden. **rough|-grind,** *irr.v.t.* grob mahlen, schroten (*corn*), (grob) zuschleifen (*tools*). **--hew,** *irr.v.t.* im groben formen *or* schnitzen *or* zurechthauen *or* bearbeiten. **--hewn,** *adj.* 1. flüchtig *or* im groben bearbeitet, unfertig; 2. (*fig.*) (*of a p.*) grobschlächtig, ungeschliffen, ungehobelt. **--house,** *s.* (*sl.*) die Keilerei. **--legged buzzard,** *s.* (*Orn.*) der Rauhfußbussard (*Buteo lagopus*). **roughly,** *adv.* 1. roh, grob, rauh, unsanft; 2. im groben; 3. annähernd, ungenau; – *speaking,* etwa, annähernd, ungefähr, im allgemeinen, ganz allgemein (gesagt). **rough-neck,** *s.* (*sl.*) der Grobian, Rowdy.

roughness ['rʌfnis], *s.* 1. die Rauheit, Unebenheit, rauhe Stelle; 2. (*fig.*) die Rohheit, Grobheit, Schroffheit (*of a p.*); 3. Herbheit (*of wine*); 4. Heftigkeit, das Ungestüm. **rough|-plane,** *v.t.* vorhobeln, schruppen. **--rider,** *s.* 1. der Bereiter, Zureiter; 2. (*Mil.*) irregulärer Kavalerist. **–shod,** *adj.* scharf *or* roh beschlagen (*horses*); *ride – over,* rücksichtslos behandeln, schurigeln, zwiebeln. **--spoken,** *adj.* derb (gesagt).

roulade [ru:'lɑ:d], *s.* (*Mus.*) die Roulade, Passage.

roulette [ru:'let], *s.* 1. das Roulett (*gambling*); 2. (*Engr.*) Rollrädchen.

Roumania, *see* **Rumania.**

round [raund], **1.** *adj.* 1. rund, (ab)gerundet; rundlich, voll, dick (*face etc.*); Rund–; – *arch,* der Rundbogen; – *dance,* der Reigen, Rundtanz; – *file,* die Rundfeile; – *game,* das Gesellschaftsspiel; – *hand,* die Rundschrift; – *robin,* der Sammelbrief mit Unterschriften im Kreise; – *shot,* die Kanonenkugel; *Round Table,* die Tafelrunde (*of Arthur*); – *table conference,* die Konferenz am runden Tisch; – *tour* or *trip,* die Rundreise; Hin- und Rückfahrt; (*Naut.*) – *turn,* der Rundschlag, Rundtörn, ganzer Schlag; – *vowel,* gerundeter Vokal; 2. (*fig.*) rund, ganz, vollständig; – *dozen,* volles *or* ganzes Dutzend; – *number,* abgerundete Zahl; – *sum,* runde *or* beträchtliche Summe; 3. (*rare*) unverblümt, ungeschminkt, ohne Umschweife, offen(herzig), aufrichtig; – *answer,* klare Antwort; – *oath,* kräftiger Fluch; *at a – pace,* in flottem Schritt; *in – terms,* rundweg.
2. *adv.* (*stationary*) (*also – about*) im ganzen Umkreis, auf *or* von *or* nach allen Seiten, in der Runde, überall, rundum(her), ringsum(her), rundherum, ringsherum; (*movement*) (*also – and –*) umher, (im Kreis) herum; (*dimension*) im Umfang; *all –,* ringsum, überall; (*fig.*) auf der ganzen Linie, allgemein, allesamt; *the country – (about),* die Umgegend; *for a mile –,* im Umkreis von einer Meile; (*fig. coll.*) – *about,* ungefähr, etwa; *ask him –,* ihn zu sich bitten; *bring him –,* ihn wieder zu sich *or* zum Bewußtsein bringen; (*fig. coll.*) ihn umstimmen *or* herumkriegen (*to,* zu); *come –,* vorbeikommen, vorsprechen (*of a p.*), wiederkehren, wiederkommen (*of an event*), lavieren (*of a ship*); sich drehen (*of wind*); (*fig. of a p.*) wieder zu sich *or* zu Bewußtsein kommen; (*fig.*) sich bekehren (*to,* zu); *go –,* einen Umweg machen; *go – (and –),* (im Kreis) herumgehen; kreisen; *go – to his house,* bei ihm vorsprechen *or* Besuch machen; *hand –,* herumreichen; *look –,* sich umsehen (*at,* nach); *order –,* vorfahren lassen, herbestellen (*a car etc.*); *show –,* herumführen; *sleep the clock –,* zwölf volle Stunden schlafen; *turn –,* (sich) herumdrehen; *a long way –,* ein weiter Umweg; *all the year –,* das ganze Jahr (hin)durch.
3. *prep.* (*stationary*) (rings) um, um (. . . herum); (*movement*) (rund) um, um (. . . herum); (*fig.*) um (. . . herum); *the shop just – the corner,* der Laden gleich um die Ecke; *go – the corner,* um die Ecke herumgehen; – *me,* um mich her; *a trip – the world,* eine Reise (rund) um die Welt; (*sl.*) *get – him,* ihn herumkriegen; *he looked – him,* er sah sich (nach allen Seiten) um.
4. *s.* 1. die Runde, der Umlauf, Kreislauf, Ablauf, Gang; *daily –,* täglicher Ablauf; 2. (*Mil. etc.*) der Rundgang, die (Dienst)runde, Ronde, Patrouille; *go* or *make the –s,* die Runde machen, herumgehen (*also fig.*); 3. der Kreis, Ring, das Rund; – *of beef,* die Rindskeule; 4. die Scheibe, Schnitte (*of bread etc.*); 5. (*coll.*) Runde (*of drinks*); *buy* or *stand a –,* einen ausgeben; 6. die Sprosse (*of a ladder*); 7. (*Mus.*) der Rundgesang, Kanon; 8. Schuß, die Ladung, Salve; – *of applause,* Hurrarufe (*pl.*); – *of ammunition,* die Ladung, der Schuß; *20 –s,* 20 Schuß; 9. (*Boxing etc.*) die Runde; 10. (*Art*) *in the –,* in plastischer Gestalt; (*fig.*) vollkommen.
5. *v.t.* 1. runden, rund machen; *–ed edges,* abgestumpfte Ecken; *–ed figure,* rundliche Gestalt; – *down,* abrunden (*numbers etc.*); – *off,* abrunden; (*numbers etc.*) ab– *or* aufrunden; (*fig.*) abschließen, zu einem Abschluß bringen; – *up,* aufrunden (*numbers etc.*); 2. (*Naut.*) umfahren, umsegeln (*a headland*); (*Motor.*) herumfahren um (*a corner*); 3. fließend gestalten (*style*); zu einem Abschluß bringen; 4. – *up,* (zusammen)treiben (*cattle*); (*coll.*) zusammenlesen, zusammenbringen; ausheben (*culprits etc.*).
6. *v.i.* 1. rund werden, sich runden; 2. drehen, wenden; (*Naut.*) – *to,* beidrehen; – *on one's heels,* sich plötzlich herumdrehen; – *on him,* ihn anfahren.

roundabout ['raundəbaut], **1.** *adj.* 1. weitläufig, weitschweifig, umständlich; (*fig.*) *in a – way,* durch die Blume; 2. abwegig; – *way,* der Umweg. **2.** *s.* 1. das Karussell; (*coll.*) *make up on the swings what you lose on the –s,* den Verlust wettmachen; 2. (*traffic*) das Rondell, der Kreisverkehr.

round-arm, *adj.* (*Boxing, Crick.*) mit dem Arm in Schulterhöhe.

roundel [raundl], *s.* 1. runde Scheibe, rundes Fenster *or* Feld; 2. (*Her.*) das Medaillon.

roundelay ['raundilei], *s.* 1. der Rundgesang; 2. Reigen, Rundtanz.

rounder ['raundə], *s.* der Lauf (im Schlagballspiel); *pl.* (*sing. constr.*) (eine Art) Schlagballspiel (*n.*).

Roundhead ['raundhed], *s.* (*Hist.*) der Rundkopf, Stutzkopf.

round|-headed, *adj.* rundköpfig (*as nail, also Ethn.*). **–house,** *s.* 1. (*Hist.*) das Gefängnis, die Wache; 2. (*Naut. Hist.*) Achterhütte; 3. (*Railw.*) der Lokschuppen. **rounding,** *s.* 1. (*Phonet.*) die Rundung; 2. (*also --off*) (Ab)rundung. **round-iron,** *s.* das Stabeisen, Rundeisen. **roundish,** *adj.* rundlich. **roundly,** *adv.* 1. allen Ernstes, rundweg, rundheraus, unumwunden, rückhaltlos; 2. gehörig, gründlich, tüchtig. **roundness,** *s.* 1. die Rundung, Rundheit; 2. (*fig.*) Bestimmtheit, Geradheit, Offenheit. **round-nose(d),** *adj.* rundnasig; – *pliers,* die Rundzange.

roundsman ['raundzmən], *s.* der Lieferant, Austräger, Laufbursche.

round-up, *s.* 1. das Zusammentreiben (*of cattle, also fig.*); 2. (*coll.*) Zusammenlesen; 3. die Aushebung (*of culprits*).

[1]**roup** [ru:p], *s.* die Darre, der Pips (*in poultry*).

[2]**roup** [raup], (*Scots*) **1.** *s.* die Auktion, Versteigerung. **2.** *v.t.* versteigern.

rouse [rauz], **1.** *v.t.* 1. (auf)wecken, wachrütteln

(*from,* aus); 2. aufjagen, aufscheuchen, aufstöbern (*game*); 3. (*fig.*) ermuntern, anregen, aufreizen, aufrütteln (*a p.*); (*fig.*) – *o.s.,* sich aufraffen *or* aufrappeln; 4. hervorrufen, wachrufen, erregen, anstacheln, entfachen, entflammen, aufpeitschen (*feelings etc.*); – *his anger,* ihn aufbringen; 5. (*coll.*) erregen, aufregen, reizen, erzürnen (*a p.*). **2.** *v.i.* aufwachen, wach werden. **3.** *s.* (*Mil.*) das Wecken.

rouser ['rauzə], *s.* 1. der Rührapparat (*brewing*); 2. (*sl.*) große Überraschung; 3. (*sl.*) unverschämte Lüge. **rousing,** *adj.* 1. anregend, aufregend; 2. (*fig.*) stürmisch, brausend (*cheers etc.*), spannend, mitreißend, zündend (*speech etc.*).

[1]**rout** [raut], **1.** *s.* 1. wilde Flucht, (*Mil.*) fluchtartiger Rückzug; *put to –, see* **2**; 2. (*coll.*) die Niederlage, Schlappe; 3. Zusammenrottung, der Auflauf, Aufruhr; 4. (*obs.*) große Abendgesellschaft. **2.** *v.t.* in die Flucht schlagen.

[2]**rout,** **1.** *v.i. See* [2]**root**; (*fig.*) – *about,* herumwühlen, herumstöbern. **2.** *v.t.* 1. (*Tech.*) ausfräsen, ausnuten; (*Tech.*) *–ing plane,* der Nuthobel; 2. (*coll.*) – *out,* aufstöbern, ausfindig machen, hervorholen; – *out of bed,* aus dem Bett herausholen.

route [ru:t], **1.** *s.* 1. der Weg, Kurs, die Route; *en –,* unterwegs; 2. (*Mil.*) [*also* raut] die Marschroute, der Marschbefehl; (*Mil.*) *column of –,* die Marschkolonne; *–-map,* die Karte mit eingezeichneter Marschroute; *–-march,* der Übungsmarsch. **2.** *v.t.* 1. die Route bestimmen für; 2. befördern, leiten (*goods*); 3. die Strecke kennzeichnen an (*Dat.*) (*a ticket*).

routine [ru:'ti:n], **1.** *s.* 1. gewohnheitsmäßiger Gang *or* Lauf, der Brauch, alltäglicher Geschäftsgang, (geistlose) Kleinarbeit; 2. alter *or* gewohnter Trott, der Schlendrian; 3. (reine) Formsache, (üblicher) Dienstweg, handwerksmäßige Gewandtheit, die Routine, Schablone. **2.** *adj.* alltäglich, gleichbleibend, laufend, gewöhnlich, üblich, vorschriftsmäßig, ordnungsmäßig, gewohnheitsmäßig, Gewohnheits–, Standard–, normal, schablonenhaft; – *inquiries,* vorschriftsmäßige Untersuchung; – *business,* die Geschäftsroutine, alltägliche Beschäftigung; – *order,* der Tagesbefehl. **routinist,** *s.* der Routinier, Gewohnheitsmensch, Schablonenmensch.

[1]**rove** [rouv], **1.** *v.i.* 1. (*also* – *about*) umherschweifen, (ziellos) umherziehen, umherstreifen; 2. wandern, streifen, schweifen (*as eyes*). **2.** *s.* die Wanderschaft.

[2]**rove,** **1.** *v.t.* vorspinnen, zum Gespinst verarbeiten. **2.** *s.* die Strähne, das Vorgespinst.

[1]**rover** ['rouvə], *s.* 1. der Herumstreicher, Wanderer; 2. das Wandertier; 3. (*obs.*) der Freibeuter, Seeräuber; älterer Pfadfinder; 4. (*archery*) *shoot at –s,* auf gelegentliche Ziele *or* aufs Geratewohl *or* (*fig.*) ins Blaue schießen.

[2]**rover,** *s.* die Vorspinnmaschine.

[1]**roving** ['rouviŋ], **1.** *s.* das Umherwandern, Umherziehen. **2.** *adj.* umherwandernd, umherstreifend; – *commission,* der Wanderauftrag.

[2]**roving,** *s.* (*Tech.*) das Vorspinnen; *pl.* das Vorgespinst; – *frame, see* [2]**rover.**

[1]**row** [rou], *s.* 1. die Reihe; (*Theat.*) Sitzreihe; *in –s,* reihenweise; 2. die Straße, Häuserreihe.

[2]**row** [rou], **1.** *v.t., v.i.* rudern, (*Naut.*) pullen; – *a long stroke,* lang ausholen; – *a steady stroke,* gleichmäßig rudern. **2.** *s.* 1. das Rudern; 2. die Ruderfahrt, Ruderpartie.

[3]**row** [rau], **1.** *s.* (*coll.*) der Lärm, Krach, Krawall, Spektakel; (*coll.*) die Rauferei, Keilerei; (*coll.*) *kick up a –,* Krach *or* Krawall machen; (*fig.*) Krach *or* Krawall schlagen; (*coll.*) *have a – with,* Streit *or* Krach haben mit; (*sl.*) *what's the –?* was ist los? (*coll.*) *get into a –,* eins aufs Dach kriegen. **2.** *v.t.* (*coll.*) die Leviten lesen (*Dat.*), abkanzeln, übers Maul fahren. **3.** *v.i.* miteinander Krach kriegen.

rowan ['rouən, 'rauən], *s.* (*also –-tree*) die Eberesche.

row-boat ['rou–], *s. See under* **rowing.**

rowdiness ['raudinis], *s.* die Pöbelhaftigkeit, Rüpelhaftigkeit. **rowdy** ['raudi], **1.** *s.* der Lärmer, Spektakelmacher, Radaubruder, Raufbold, Rohling, Rowdy. **2.** *adj.* lärmend, pöbelhaft, rüpelhaft, rowdyhaft. **rowdyism** [–diizm], *s.* pöbelhaftes Benehmen, das Rowdytum, die Rüpelei, Gewalttätigkeit.

rowel ['rauəl], **1.** *s.* das Spornrädchen. **2.** *v.t.* anspornen, die Sporen geben (*Dat.*).

rowing ['rouiŋ], *s.* das Rudern, der Rudersport; *–-boat,* das Ruderboot.

rowlock ['rʌlək], *s.* die Rudergabel, Dolle.

royal ['rɔiəl], **1.** *adj.* 1. königlich, Königs–; *Royal Academy,* Königliche Akademie der Künste; – *assent,* königliche Einwilligung; *blood –,* die königliche Familie; – *blue,* das Königsblau; (*Scots*) – *burgh,* korporierte Stadt; *Royal Exchange,* die Londoner Börse; *the – and ancient game,* das Golfspiel; *Royal Highness,* Königliche Hoheit; – *prince,* der Prinz von königlichem Geblüt; *Princess Royal,* des Königs älteste Tochter; *Royal Society,* die Königliche Gesellschaft der Naturwissenschaften; – *standard,* die Königsstandarte; 2. (*fig.*) fürstlich, prächtig, herrlich; – *antler,* dritte Sprosse eines Hirschgeweihs; *battle –,* der Hauptkampf; – *paper,* das Royal(format); (*fig.*) – *road,* bequemer *or* müheloser Weg; – *stag,* der Kapitalhirsch, Zwölfender; (*coll.*) (*right*) – *time,* köstliche *or* herrliche Zeit; 3. (*Naut.*) – *mast,* die Oberbramstenge; – *sail,* das Oberbramsegel. **2.** *s.* 1. *See* – *sail*; 2. (*coll.*) das Mitglied der königlichen Familie; (*usu. pl.*) die königliche Familie.

royalism ['rɔiəlizm], *s.* die Königstreue, der Royalismus; Monarchismus. **royalist,** **1.** *s.* der Monarchist, Royalist, Königstreue(r). **2.** *or* **royalistic** [–'listik], *adj.* königstreu, royalistisch. **royalty** [–ti], *s.* 1. das Königtum, Königreich; 2. königliche Abkunft, die Königswürde, (*also fig.*) Majestät; 3. monarchistische Regierung; 4. (*collect.*) das Königshaus, königliche Familie; Fürstlichkeiten, fürstliche Persönlichkeiten (*pl.*); (*oft. pl.*) (*Hist.*) königliches Privileg, das Regal, Hoheitsrecht, die Abgabe an den König; 5. (*Law*) die Lizenz(gebühr); (Autoren)tantieme, das Honorar; der Gewinnanteil, Ertragsanteil.

rub [rʌb], **1.** *s.* 1. das Reiben; die Reibung, der Strich; *give it a –,* es (ein wenig) reiben; 2. (*fig.*) das Hindernis, die Schwierigkeit, Unannehmlichkeit, der Haken; (*coll.*) *there's the –,* da(s) ist der Haken *or* der wunde Punkt! da liegt der Hund begraben! da liegt der Hase im Pfeffer! 3. der Hieb, die Stichelei. **2.** *v.t.* 1. reiben; – *one's hands,* sich (*Dat.*) die Hände reiben (*also fig.*); (*fig.*) – *shoulders with,* nahekommen (*Dat.*), in nähere *or* enge Berührung kommen mit; – *him* (*up*) *the wrong way,* ihn verärgern *or* verschnupfen, ihn vor den Kopf stoßen; *it –s him* (*up*) *the wrong way,* es geht ihm gegen den Strich; 2. reiben an (*Dat.*), streifen; 3. (ab)schleifen, abreiben, schaben, scheuern, frottieren; – *down,* abreiben, frottieren; striegeln (*horses*); anreiben (*colours*); – *in,* einreiben (*liniment*); (*coll.*) – *it in,* es (ihm *etc.*) unter die Nase reiben, auf der S. herumreiten, es breittreten; – *up,* (auf)polieren; (*fig.*) auffrischen (*memory*); 4. (ab)wischen, (ab)putzen; – *away,* wegwischen, wegreiben; – *off,* abreiben, abwischen; abschleifen; – *out,* wegwischen, ausradieren; (*sl.*) umbringen, um die Ecke bringen; 5. (*Engr.*) abklatschen. **3.** *v.i.* reiben, schleifen, streifen (*against, on,* an (*Dat.*)); (*coll.*) – *along,* durchhalten, auskommen, sich durchbringen, sich durchschlagen, sich über Wasser halten; – *off,* sich abreiben *or* abwischen lassen; abfärben, abschmutzen; – *out,* sich ausradieren lassen; (*fig. coll.*) – *up against,* (zufällig) in Berührung kommen *or* in Verbindung stehen mit.

rub-a-dub ['rʌbədʌb], *s.* der Trommelwirbel, das Getrommel, Taramtamtam.

[1]**rubber** ['rʌbə], *s.* 1. (*also india –*) der Kautschuk, das Gummi; 2. der (Radier)gummi; 3. *pl.* (*esp. Am.*) Gummischuhe, Turnschuhe (*pl.*); Überschuhe (*pl.*); 4. der Reiber, Schleifer, Polierer; 5. Reibstein, die Reibfläche, das Reibkissen, Reibzeug; 6. Frottiertuch, der Wischlappen.

[2]**rubber,** *s.* (*Cards*) der Robber.
rubber| band, *s.* der Gummiring, das Gummiband. – **dinghy,** *s.* das Schlauchboot. – **heel,** *s.* der Gummiabsatz. **rubberize,** *v.t.* mit Gummi imprägnieren, gummieren. **rubber|neck, 1.** *s.* (*Am. sl.*) Neugierige(r), Schaulustige(r). **2.** *v.i.* neugierig gaffen, sich neugierig umsehen. **--plant,** *s.* die Kautschukpflanze. – **solution,** *s.* der Gummikitt, die Gummilösung. – **stamp,** *s.* 1. der Gummistempel; 2. (*fig. coll.*) willenloses Werkzeug. – **truncheon,** *s.* der Gummiknüppel. – **tyre,** *s.* der Gummireifen.
rubbing ['rʌbiŋ], *s.* 1. die Reibung, das Reiben; (*Tech.*) die Abreibung, der Abrieb; – ***brush,*** die Scheuerbürste; – ***rag,*** der Scheuerlappen; das Frottiertuch; 2. (*Engr.*) der Reiberdruck.
rubbish ['rʌbiʃ], *s.* 1. der Schutt, Abfall, Müll, der *or* das Kehricht; 2. (*coll.*) der Schund, Plunder, wertloses Zeug; 3. der Ausschuß, die Ausschußware; 4. (*fig.*) der Unsinn, Quatsch. **rubbish|-chute,** *s.* der Müllschlucker. **--heap,** *s.* der Schutthaufen, Kehrichthaufen. **rubbishy,** *adj.* 1. (*coll.*) minderwertig, wertlos, Schund–; 2. (*fig.*) kitschig.
rubble [rʌbl], *s.* 1. (*Build.*) der Bauschutt, Schotter, Bruchstein(e *pl.*); 2. (*Geol.*) (Stein)schutt, das Trümmergestein, Geschiebe, Geröll. **rubble|-floor,** *s.* der Estrich. **--stone,** *s.* der Rollstein, Bruchstein. **--work,** *s.* das Bruchsteinmauerwerk, Füllwerk.
rub-down, *s.* die Abreibung; ***have a –,*** sich abreiben *or* frottieren.
rubefacient [ru:bi'feiʃiənt], **1.** *adj.* (haut)rötend. **2.** *s.* hautrötendes Mittel. **rubefaction** [–'fækʃən], *s.* die Hautrötung. **rubefy** ['ru:bifai], *v.t.* röten, rot färben. **rubescence** [–'besəns], *s.* das Rotwerden, Erröten. **rubescent** [–'besənt], *adj.* errötend.
Rubicon ['ru:bikən], *s.* Rubikon (*m.*); (*fig.*) ***cross the –,*** den Rubikon überschreiten, einen entscheidenden Schritt tun.
rubicund ['ru:bikənd], *adj.* rötlich, rot, rosig.
rubidium [ru:'bidiəm], *s.* (*Chem.*) das Rubidium.
rubify, *see* **rubefy.**
ruble [ru:bl], *s.* der Rubel.
rubric ['ru:brik], **1.** *s.* 1. der Titelbuchstabe (*on MS.*); (*Typ.*) Titelkopf, die Aufschrift, Überschrift, Rubrik; 2. (*Eccl.*) liturgische Anweisung. **2.** *adj.* rot gedruckt. **rubricate** [–keit], *v.t.* 1. rot bezeichnen; 2. mit Rubriken versehen, rubrizieren.
ruby ['ru:bi], **1.** *s.* 1. der Rubin; 2. die Rubinfarbe, das Rubinrot; 3. (*Typ.*) Pariser Schrift, die Parisienne; 4. (*Horol.*) der Stein. **2.** *adj.* (rubin)-rot.
ruche [ru:ʃ], *s.* die Rüsche. **ruching,** *s.* Rüschen (*pl.*), der Rüschenbesatz.
[1]**ruck** [rʌk], **1.** *s.* die Runzel, Falte. **2.** *v.t.* runzeln, zerknittern, zerknüllen, ramponieren. **3.** *v.i.* (*also* ***– up***) 1. sich runzeln, knittern, zerknüllen; 2. hochrutschen, sich hochschieben.
[2]**ruck,** *s.* (großer) Haufe, das Gedränge (*also Racing*); (*fig.*) die Vielzahl, Allgemeinheit, der Durchschnitt; (*fig.*) ***rise out of the –,*** sich über den Durchschnitt erheben.
ruckle, *see* [1]**ruck.**
rucksack ['rʌksæk], *s.* der Rucksack.
ruction ['rʌkʃən], *s.* (*sl.*) (*oft. pl.*) der Spektakel, Krawall, Krach.
rudd [rʌd], *s.* (*Ichth.*) das Rotauge, die Rotfeder.
rudder ['rʌdə], *s.* 1. (*Naut.*) das (Steuer)ruder, Steuer; 2. (*Av.*) Seitensteuer, Seitenruder; – ***controls,*** die Seitensteuerung. **rudderless,** *adj.* 1. ruderlos; 2. (*fig.*) steuerlos, führerlos, hilflos.
ruddiness ['rʌdinis], *s.* die Röte.
ruddle [rʌdl], *s.* der Rötel, roter Ocker.
ruddy ['rʌdi], *adj.* 1. rot, gerötet, rötlich; 2. rotwangig, rotbackig; 3. (*sl.*) verflucht, verflixt. **ruddy duck,** *s.* (*Orn.*) (*Am.*) die Ruderente (*Oxyura jamaicensis*).
rude [ru:d], *adj.* 1. grob, unverschämt, unhöflich, patzig (*to,* gegen); 2. derb, unfein, unmanierlich, ungesittet, plump, ungeschickt, unelegant, ungehobelt, ungeschlacht; unzivilisiert, unkultiviert, ungebildet; 3. unsanft, stürmisch, heftig, wild, ungestüm; 4. hart, rauh, streng, unwirtlich (*as climate*); 5. robust, kräftig, unverwüstlich (*as health*); 6. uneben, holperig; primitiv, unfertig, unvollkommen, kunstlos, einfach. **rudeness,** *s.* 1. die Unhöflichkeit, Unmanierlichkeit, Grobheit; 2. Derbheit, Roheit, Primitivität, Kunstlosigkeit, Unvollendetheit; 3. Rauheit, Wildheit, Heftigkeit, das Ungestüm. **rudery,** *s.* (*coll.*) die Grobheit, Derbheit.
rudiment ['ru:dimənt], *s.* 1. der Anfang, die Grundlage; 2. (*Biol.*) Anlage, der Ansatz, das Rudiment; der Anlagerest, die Rückbildung; 3. *pl.* Grundlagen, Anfangsgründe (*pl.*). **rudimental** [–'mentl], **rudimentary** [–'mentəri], *adj.* 1. rudimentär, grundlegend, Anfangs–; 2. unvollkommen, verkümmert.
[1]**rue** [ru:], *s.* (*Bot.*) die Raute.
[2]**rue,** *v.t.* 1. bereuen, bedauern; 2. verwünschen, rückgängig machen wollen. **rueful,** *adj.* traurig, kläglich, trübselig, wehmütig, reumütig. **ruefulness,** *s.* die Traurigkeit, Trübseligkeit, der Gram, Kummer.
rufescent [ru:'fesənt], *adj.* (*Zool.*) rötlich.
[1]**ruff** [rʌf], *s.* 1. die Krause; 2. (*Zool.*) Halskrause, der Federring, Haarring; 3. (*Orn.*) der Kampfläufer (*male*) (*Philomachus pugnax*).
[2]**ruff, 1.** *s.* (*Cards*) das Stechen, Trumpfen. **2.** *v.t., v.i.* mit Trumpf stechen, trumpfen.
[3]**ruff,** *s.* (*Ichth.*) der Kaulbarsch.
ruffian ['rʌfiən], *s.* der Raufbold, Rohling, Rowdy, roher Bursche. **ruffianism,** *s.* die Roheit, Brutalität, das Rowdytum. **ruffianly,** *adj.* brutal, roh, wild, unbändig, gewalttätig.
ruffle [rʌfl], **1.** *s.* 1. die Krause, Rüsche; 2. Handkrause, Halskrause, der Volant; *see also* [1]**ruff,** 2; 3. das Kräuseln (*of water*); 4. (*coll.*) die Verwirrung, Aufregung. **2.** *v.t.* 1. kräuseln, kraus machen; zerknüllen, zerknittern, zerzausen; sträuben (*feathers*); in Falten ziehen (*brow*); ***– one's feathers,*** sich aufplustern; (*fig.*) sich aufregen; 2. (*fig.*) außer Fassung bringen, durcheinanderbringen, verwirren, aufregen; – ***his temper,*** ihn verärgern *or* verstimmen, seine gute Laune verderben. **2.** *v.i.* 1. sich kräuseln, (kleine) Wellen schlagen; 2. Falten werfen, flattern; 3. (*fig.*) sich aufregen *or* aufplustern, erregt werden; 4. zerknüllt *or* zerzaust werden. **ruffling,** *s.* Rüschen (*pl.*); das Rüschennähen.
rufous ['ru:fəs], *adj.* fuchsrot, rötlichbraun.
rug [rʌg], *s.* kleiner Teppich, der Vorleger, die Brücke; Wolldecke; ***travelling –,*** die Reisedecke; (*coll.*) ***as snug as a bug in a –,*** wie die Made im Speck.
Rugby (football) ['rʌgbi], *s.* das Rugby-Fußballspiel.
rugged ['rʌgid], *adj.* 1. rauh (*also fig.*), uneben, holperig (*as a way*); 2. schroff, zackig, zerklüftet, wild (*as scenery*); 3. durchfurcht, runzelig (*as a face*); 4. (*fig.*) kräftig, ausgeprägt, derb, schroff, unfreundlich. **ruggedness,** *s.* die Rauheit, Schroffheit.
rugger ['rʌgə], *s.* (*coll.*) *see* **Rugby.**
rugose ['ru:gous], *adj.* gerunzelt, runz(e)lig.
ruin ['ru:in], **1.** *s.* 1. der Sturz, Verfall, Zerfall, Untergang, Zusammenbruch (*also financial*), die Vernichtung, Verwüstung, das Verderben, Zugrunderichten, der Ruin; ***it will be his –*** or ***be the – of him,*** es wird ihn zugrunde richten; ***fall into –,*** in Verfall geraten, verfallen; (*fig.*) ***bring to –,*** zugrunde richten, ins Verderben stürzen; (*fig.*) ***go to –,*** zugrunde gehen; ***be on the verge*** or ***brink of –,*** vor dem Ruin *or* Untergang stehen; ***spell – for him,*** sein Untergang sein; 2. die Ruine (*castle etc.*); *pl.* Trümmer (*pl.*), der Trümmerhaufen; ***in –s,*** verfallen; ***lay in –s,*** zertrümmern, in Schutt und Asche legen; ***lie in –s,*** in Trümmern liegen. **2.** *v.t.* 1. vernichten, zerstören; 2. (*fig.*) zunichte machen, vereiteln, verderben (*plans etc.*); 3. zugrunde richten, ruinieren (*a p.*); 4. entehren, verführen (*a girl*).

ruination [ru:i'neiʃən], *s.* 1. die Zerstörung, Verheerung, Verwüstung; 2. (*usu. coll.*) das Verderben.

ruined ['ru:ind], *adj.* 1. verfallen, zerfallen (*building etc.*); 2. ruiniert, zugrunde gerichtet (*a p.*); 3. (*coll.*) verdorben. **ruinous,** *adj.* 1. verfallen, baufällig (*buildings*); 2. (*fig.*) verderblich, schädlich, gefährlich; 3. (*coll.*) übermäßig, enorm, ruinös (*as price*). **ruinously,** *adv.* (*coll.*) enorm (*expensive*). **ruinousness,** *s.* 1. die Baufälligkeit; 2. Verderblichkeit; 3. (*coll.*) Abnormität (*of prices*).

rule [ru:l], **1.** *s.* 1. die Regel (*also fig.*); das Übliche, die Norm, Gewohnheit, der Normalfall; (*Comm.*) Handelsbrauch, die Usance; ***as a (general) –,*** in der Regel, normalerweise; ***as is the –,*** wie es allgemein üblich ist; ***be the –,*** die Regel sein; ***it is a – with me, it is my –,*** ich habe es mir zur Regel gemacht; ***become the –,*** zur Regel *or* allgemein üblich werden; ***make it a –,*** es sich (*Dat.*) zur Regel machen; ***exception to the –,*** der Ausnahmefall; ***the exception proves the –,*** die Ausnahme bestätigt die Regel; 2. (*Eccl.*) die (Ordens)regel; (*Spt.*) Spielregel; Bestimmung, Vorschrift, Verordnung, Verfügung; *pl.* (*collect.*) Ordnung, Satzung(en (*pl.*)); der Grundsatz, Maßstab, die Richtlinie, Richtschnur; ***according to –,*** laut Vorschrift; ***against the –s,*** satzungswidrig, (*Spt.*) regelwidrig; ***break a –,*** gegen eine Regel verstoßen; ***lay down –s,*** Regeln aufstellen; ***serve as a –,*** als Maßstab *or* Richtschnur dienen; ***work to –,*** die Dienstvorschriften genau einhalten; ***–s of conduct,*** Verhaltungsmaßregeln (*pl.*); ***–s of procedure,*** die Geschäftsordnung, Verfahrensordnung; ***– of the road,*** die (Straßen)verkehrsordnung; ***– of thumb,*** die Faustregel, praktische Erfahrungsmethode, die Überschlagsrechnung; ***by – of thumb,*** erfahrensmäßig, auf praktischem Wege, über den Daumen gepeilt; ***golden –,*** (*B.*) das Tun des göttlichen Willens; (*coll.*) Richtschnuren wie es sich gehört; ***hard and fast –,*** ausnahmsloser Grundsatz; (*Law*) ***– nisi,*** vorläufiger Beschluß; ***special –(s),*** die Sonderregelung; ***standing –,*** die Satzung; 3. (*Pol.*) die Herrschaft, Regierung; ***– of force,*** die Gewaltherrschaft; 4. (*Tech.*) das Lineal, Richtscheit, Richtmaß, der Zollstock; ***carpenter's*** or ***folding –,*** die Schmiege; ***foot –,*** der Zollstock; ***parallel –,*** das Parallellineal; ***slide –,*** der Rechenschieber; 5. (*Typ.*) die (Messing)linie; ***em –,*** das Geviert; ***en –,*** das Halbgeviert; 6. (*Math.*) die Regel; ***– of three,*** die Regeldetri.
2. *v.t.* 1. linieren (*paper*), ziehen (*lines*); ***– out,*** durchstreichen; (*fig.*) (*also **– out of order***) nicht zulassen, ausschließen, ausscheiden; (*fig.*) ***– out the possibility,*** mit der Möglichkeit nicht rechnen; 2. (*Pol., fig.*) (*also **– over***) regieren, beherrschen, herrschen *or* Gewalt haben über (*Acc.*); (*fig.*) Macht haben *or* ausüben über (*Acc.*), leiten, lenken, regeln; (*coll.*) ***– the roost*** or ***roast,*** die Oberhand haben, das Wort *or* Regiment führen; (*Parl.*) ***– him out of order,*** ihm zu sprechen verbieten, ihm das Wort entziehen; (*coll.*) ***be –d,*** sich fügen, Vernunft annehmen; (*fig.*) ***be –d by him,*** seinem (guten) Rat folgen, unter seinem Einfluß stehen, sich von ihm führen *or* leiten lassen.
3. *v.i.* 1. (*Pol.*) herrschen, regieren (***over,*** über (*Acc.*)); 2. (*fig.*) vorherrschen, in Kraft sein, gelten; 3. (*Comm.*) stehen, liegen, notieren (*of prices*); 4. festsetzen, entscheiden, zu der Entscheidung kommen, beschließen, den Beschluß fassen, anordnen, regeln, verfügen, verordnen, verkünden (***that,*** daß).

ruled [ru:ld], *adj.* liniert; ***– paper,*** das Linienpapier. **ruler,** *s.* 1. (*Pol.*) der (die) Herrscher(in); 2. das Lineal. **ruling, 1.** *s.* 1. (*Law etc.*) die Regelung, (amtliche *or* gerichtliche) Entscheidung; ***– of the court,*** richterliche Verfügung; 2. (*Pol.*) die Herrschaft, Verwaltung; 3. (*drawing etc.*) das Linieren; die Linie, Linien (*pl.*). **2.** *adj.* 1. (*Pol.*) herrschend; 2. (*fig.*) vorherrschend, (*esp. Comm.*) laufend, bestehend, gegenwärtig; ***– price,*** der Tagespreis, Marktpreis, Durchschnittspreis.

[1]**rum** [rʌm], *s.* der Rum; ***--running,*** der Alkoholschmuggel.

[2]**rum,** *adj.* (*sl.*) wunderlich, seltsam.

Rumania [ru:'meiniə], *s.* Rumänien (*n.*). **Rumanian, 1.** *s.* 1. der Rumäne (die Rumänin); 2. (*language*) das Rumänisch(e). **2.** *adj.* rumänisch.

rumba ['rʌmbə], *s.* die *or* (*coll.*) der Rumba.

rumble [rʌmbl], **1.** *s.* 1. das Rumpeln, Rattern, Poltern, Gepolter, Rollen, Dröhnen; 2. (*obs.*) der Gepäcksitz, Bedientensitz (*of coach*). **2.** *v.i.* rumpeln, rattern, poltern, dröhnen; rollen (*of thunder*); knurren (*of stomach*). **3.** *v.t.* (*sl.*) kapieren, kleinkriegen, spitzkriegen, fressen, schalten. **rumbling, 1.** *s. See* **rumble, 1,** 1. **2.** *adj.* polternd, dröhnend.

rumbustious [rʌm'bʌstʃəs], *adj.* (*coll.*) wild lärmend, ausgelassen, ungestüm.

rumen ['ru:mən], *s.* der Pansen. **ruminant, 1.** *adj.* wiederkäuend. **2.** *s.* der Wiederkäuer. **ruminate** [–eit], **1.** *v.i.* 1. wiederkäuen; 2. (*fig.*) grübeln, (nach)sinnen (***about, upon,*** über (*Acc.*)). **2.** *v.t.* nachdenken über (*Acc.*). **rumination** [–i'neiʃən], *s.* 1. das Wiederkäuen; 2. (*fig.*) Nachsinnen, Grübeln. **ruminative** [–inətiv], *adj.* (*fig.*) grübelnd, sinnend, nachdenklich.

rummage ['rʌmidʒ], **1.** *v.i.* (*also **– about***) (herum)stöbern, (herum)wühlen, (herum)kramen (***in,*** in (*Dat.*)). **2.** *v.t.* durchsuchen, durchstöbern; ***– out,*** hervorholen, auskramen, hervorkramen. **3.** *s.* 1. der Ausschuß, Ramsch, Restwaren (*pl.*); ***--sale,*** der Ramschverkauf, Wohltätigkeitsbasar; 2. das Durchsuchen, Durchstöbern.

rummer ['rʌmə], *s.* der Römer, Humpen, Pokal.

[1]**rummy** ['rʌmi], *adj.* (*sl.*) *see* [2]**rum.**

[2]**rummy,** *s.* (*Cards*) das Rommé.

rumor (*Am.*), **rumour** ['ru:mə], **1.** *s.* das Gerücht (***of,*** über (*Acc.*)); ***– has it, the – is*** or ***runs,*** es geht das Gerücht. **2.** *v.t.* (*usu. pass.*) ***it is –ed that he is, he is –ed to be . . .,*** es geht das Gerücht *or* man sagt, er sei . . .

rump [rʌmp], *s.* 1. das Hinterteil, der Steiß (*of beasts*), Bürzel (*of fowl*); das Schwanzstück (*of meat*); ***– bone,*** das Kreuzbein; 2. (*Hist.*) ***Rump Parliament,*** das Rumpfparlament.

rumple [rʌmpl], **1.** *v.t.* zerknittern, zerknüllen; zerwühlen, zerzausen (*hair*). **2.** *s.* die Falte.

rumpsteak ['rʌmpsteik], *s.* das Rumpsteak.

rumpus ['rʌmpəs], *s.* (*coll.*) der Spektakel, Krawall.

run [rʌn], **1.** *irr.v.i.* 1. rennen, laufen; eilen, (los)stürzen; ***– riot,*** wuchern, verwildern (*plants*), (*fig.*) nicht zu bändigen sein, sich austoben, einen hemmungslosen Lauf nehmen; 2. (dahin)fliehen, weglaufen, Reißaus nehmen; (*sl.*) ***cut and –,*** ausreißen, abhauen, sich aus dem Staub machen; 3. fahren, verkehren (*vehicle*), schwimmen, wandern, ziehen (*fish*), rollen (*ball*), fahren (*steamer, rope through a block*), segeln (*sailing ship*), sich drehen (*wheels*), in Gang *or* Betrieb sein, arbeiten, gehen (*engines*); ***the boat –s on Sundays,*** der Dampfer verkehrt sonntags; ***his taste does not – that way,*** dafür hat er keinen Sinn; 4. kandidieren (*in elections*); 5. verlaufen, verstreichen, vergehen, hingehen (*time*); 6. sich erstrecken, dauern, abgehalten *or* gegeben werden (*as a performance or meeting*), gespielt *or* aufgeführt werden (*as a play*); ***two days running,*** zwei Tage hintereinander, zwei aufeinanderfolgende Tage; 7. fließen, strömen, rinnen, laufen (*as liquids*), eitern (*as a sore*); (*fig.*) ***it makes my mouth –,*** das läuft mir das Wasser im Mund zusammen; ***a heavy sea is running,*** die See geht hoch; 8. tropfen, triefen, strömen (***with,*** von) (*as s.th. wet*); 9. verlaufen, auslaufen (*as colours*); 10. schmelzen (*as metals*); auftauen (*ice etc.*); 11. in Kraft bleiben, Rechtskraft haben, laufen (*as a lease*); Gültigkeit haben, gelten, herrschen, sich stellen, sich belaufen (*as prices*); 12. laufen, den Wortlaut haben (*as text*); sich verbreiten, umlaufen, umgehen (*as rumours*); 13. aufgehen (*as a seam*), Laufmaschen bekommen (*as stockings*).
(a) (*with adj.*) ***my blood –s cold,*** mich gruselt's; ***still waters – deep,*** stille Wasser sind tief; ***– dry,*** versiegen, vertrocknen; (*Naut.*) ***– foul of,*** anfahren, festfahren in (*Dat.*); (*fig.*) zusammenstoßen mit; ***– high,*** hochgehen (*waves*), heftig *or* erregt *or* leb-

haft werden (*feelings*); – ***hot,*** sich warm laufen (*of engines*); – ***low,*** auf die *or* zur Neige gehen, zu Ende gehen, ausgehen, knapp werden; – ***short,*** see – ***low***; – ***short of,*** knapp werden an (*Dat.*); – ***true to form,*** den Erwartungen entsprechen; – ***wild,*** (*Hort.*) ausarten, wild wachsen, ins Kraut schießen; (*fig.*) wild *or* ohne Aufsicht aufwachsen, verwildern; – ***like wildfire,*** sich verbreiten wie ein Lauffeuer (*as news*).
(b) (*with adv.*) – **about,** herumlaufen, umherlaufen; – ***aground,*** auflaufen, stranden; (*coll.*) – ***along!*** pack dich! – ***amuck,*** wie wild herumlaufen; – ***ashore,*** see – ***aground***; – **away,** davonlaufen, fortlaufen (***from,*** von); durchgehen (*as horses*) (*also fig.*); (*fig.*) – ***away from,*** aus dem Weg gehen (*a p., Dat.*), abschweifen von, sich entfernen von (*a subject*); – ***away with,*** entführen (*a p.*), durchgehen *or* durchbrennen mit (*a th.*); (*fig.*) mitreißen (*a p.*), aufbrauchen, aufzehren (*a th.*); ***don't – away with the idea that,*** verrennen Sie sich nicht in die Idee daß, bilden Sie sich nur nicht ein daß, setzen Sie sich (*Dat.*) nur nicht in den Kopf daß; – **by,** vorbeilaufen an (*Dat.*); – ***counter to,*** zuwiderlaufen (*Dat.*); – ***down,*** hinablaufen (*tears etc.*); ablaufen (*clock*); – **in,** hineinlaufen; zulaufen (***upon,*** auf (*Acc.*)); (*fig.*) übereinstimmen (***with,*** mit); – **off,** davonlaufen, sich davonmachen; ablaufen (*as water*); – ***off with,*** durchgehen mit; – **on,** weiterlaufen (*also fig.*); (*fig.*) fortgesetzt werden, weitergehen; (*coll.*) unablässig schwatzen, fortplaudern; (*Typ.*) fortlaufen; – **out,** hinauslaufen, herauslaufen; herauslaufen, herausfließen (*liquid*); auslaufen, lecken (*of a vessel*); (*fig.*) zu Ende gehen, ablaufen (*time*); zu Ende sein, ausverkauft sein, ausgehen (*stock*); ***have – out of . . .,*** kein . . . mehr haben; – **over,** überlaufen, überfließen; – **up,** hinauflaufen; zulaufen (*to,* auf (*Acc.*)); (*fig.*) einlaufen, eingehen (*cloth*); sich belaufen (*to,* auf (*Acc.*)); schnell anwachsen, hochschießen; – ***up against,*** stoßen auf (*Acc.*).
(c) (*with prep.*) – **across,** zufällig treffen, stoßen auf (*Acc.*); – **after,** nachjagen, nachlaufen (*Dat.*) (*a th.*), herlaufen hinter (*Dat.*) (*a p.*); – **against,** laufen *or* fahren gegen, zusammenstoßen mit; (*Spt.*) sich (im Laufen) messen mit; – **at,** losstürzen auf (*Acc.*); – **before,** herlaufen vor (*Dat.*) (*a p.*); – ***before the wind,*** vor dem Winde segeln; – **down,** hinunterlaufen (*a hill*), (*Naut.*) entlangsegeln (*the coast*); – **for,** laufen nach; wettlaufen um (*a prize*); sich bewerben um (*a position*); (*as a contract*) laufen auf (*Acc.*); (*coll.*) – ***for it,*** – ***for one's life,*** ausreißen, abhauen, sich aus dem Staub machen; – ***for your lives!*** rette sich wer kann! – **in *the blood,*** im Blute liegen *or* stecken; – ***in debt with him,*** in seine Schuld fallen; ***it –s in his head,*** es geht ihm im Kopf herum; – **into,** auffahren auf (*Acc.*); (hinein)rennen *or* (hinein)fahren in (*Acc.*); (*coll.*) (*of a vehicle*) überfahren (*a p.*); (*as a river*) sich ergießen in (*Acc.*); (*fig.*) übergehen in (*Acc.*); (*of amounts*) gehen in (*Acc.*), sich belaufen auf (*Acc.*); – ***into debt,*** sich in Schulden stürzen, in Schulden geraten; – ***into four editions,*** vier Auflagen erleben; (*coll.*) – ***into money,*** ins Geld laufen; ***the colours – into one another,*** die Farben laufen *or* fließen ineinander; *see also* – ***across***; – ***into a port,*** einen Hafen ansegeln; – **off *the rails,*** entgleisen (*also fig.*); – **on,** (*Naut.*) auflaufen auf (*Acc.*); (*Motor.*) fahren mit (*petrol etc.*); (*fig.*) (*talk etc.*) handeln von, gehen über (*Acc.*); – **out of,** knapp werden mit, nicht mehr vorrätig haben; – **over,** (*fig.*) durchgehen, überprüfen, überfliegen; ***my eyes ran over it,*** mein Blick überflog es; (*Motor. coll.*) – ***over him,*** ihn überfahren; – **through,** (*fig.*) *see* – *over* (*fig.*); durchsuchen (*one's pockets etc.*); durchlesen; kurz behandeln; durchmachen, erleben; durchbringen (*a fortune*); (*as a theme*) sich hindurchziehen durch; ***the thought ran through my head,*** der Gedanke schoß mir durch den Kopf; ***it keeps running through my head,*** es geht mir nicht aus dem Sinn; – **to,** sich belaufen auf (*Acc.*); ausreichen für; – ***to extremes,*** alles auf die Spitze treiben, ins Extrem fallen; – ***to fat,*** Fett ansetzen; – ***to seed,*** in Samen schießen; – ***to waste,*** abfließen, (*usu. fig.*) vergeudet werden, verlorengehen; – **upon,** losrennen *or* losfahren auf (*Acc.*); (*fig.*) zielen *or* sich beziehen auf (*Acc.*); sich beschäftigen mit (*of the mind*); – **with,** übereinstimmen mit; – ***with the hare and hunt with the hounds,*** zwei Herren dienen; – ***with sweat,*** vom Schweiß triefen; – ***with tears,*** in Tränen schwimmen.
2. *irr.v.t.* 1. laufen, verfolgen, einschlagen (*a course*); 2. durchlaufen, durchfahren, zurücklegen (*a distance*); 3. (wett)rennen *or* laufen lassen; 4. verkehren *or* gehen lassen; 5. in Gang halten, laufen lassen (*machine*); 6. führen, leiten, betreiben (*a business*); 7. aufstellen (*candidate*); 8. schmelzen; gießen (*metal*); 9. verfolgen (*game*); 10. bohren, stechen, stoßen (*a weapon*).
(a) (*with noun*) – ***the blockade,*** die Blockade brechen; – ***brandy,*** Branntwein schmuggeln; ***do you – a car?*** besitzen *or* halten Sie einen Wagen? ***the car is only – at weekends,*** der Wagen wird nur am Wochenende benutzt; – ***cattle,*** Vieh weiden lassen; (*coll.*) – ***a good chance of,*** gute Aussichten haben zu; – ***its course,*** seinen (*etc.*) Verlauf nehmen; ***things must*** or ***one must let things – their course,*** man muß den Dingen ihren Lauf lassen; – ***the danger of,*** Gefahr laufen zu; – ***debts,*** Schulden machen; – ***errands*** (*or Scots messages*), Besorgungen machen, Wege besorgen; – ***the gauntlet,*** Spießruten laufen; – ***a race,*** um die Wette laufen; – ***risks*** or ***the risk,*** sich der Gefahr aussetzen, das Risiko auf sich nehmen, Gefahr laufen; (*coll.*) – ***the show,*** den Laden *or* die S. schmeißen; – ***the streets,*** sich auf der Straße herumtreiben; – ***a temperature,*** Fieber haben.
(b) (*with adj.*) – ***him close,*** ihm dicht auf den Fersen sein; (*fig.*) nahe an ihn herankommen; (*coll.*) – ***it fine,*** es knapp bemessen; – ***the tank dry,*** den Behälter leerlaufen lassen; – ***him hard,*** ihn heftig bedrängen, ihm tüchtig zusetzen, ihn in die Enge treiben.
(c) (*with prep.*) – ***one's head* against,** mit dem Kopf rennen gegen; – ***him* for *president,*** ihn zum Präsidenten aufstellen; – ***water* down** (*pipe, drain etc.*), Wasser hinunterlaufen lassen *or* hinunterspülen; – ***a knife* into *him,*** ihm ein Messer in den Leib jagen *or* stechen; – ***him into debt,*** ihn in Schulden stürzen; – ***a nail into one's foot,*** sich (*Dat.*) einen Nagel in den Fuß treten; – ***one's hand* over,** mit der Hand fahren über (*Acc.*); – ***one's fingers* through,** mit den Fingern fahren durch; – ***one's pen through,*** durchstreichen; – **to *earth,*** zur Strecke bringen; (*fig.*) aufspüren, ausfindig machen; (*coll.*) – ***him to the station,*** ihn zum Bahnhof im Wagen bringen.
(d) (*with adv.*) – ***aground,*** auflaufen lassen, auf den Strand setzen; – **down,** niederrennen, niederfahren (*a p.*), totjagen, zu Tode hetzen, zur Strecke bringen (*a stag*); in den Grund bohren (*a ship*); entladen, erschöpfen (*a battery*); herunterwirtschaften (*a business*); (*coll.*) aufstöbern, ausfindig machen (*a th.*); (*coll.*) heruntermachen, anschwärzen (*a p.*); ***be*** or ***feel – down,*** herunter *or* abgespannt sein; – **in,** einlaufen lassen, einfahren (*an engine*); (*coll.*) einstecken, einlochen (*a p.*); – **off,** ablaufen lassen (*liquid*); herunterrasseln, vom Stapel lassen (*speech*); austragen, entscheiden (*races*); ausrollen (*cable etc.*); – ***o.s.* out,** sich durch Laufen erschöpfen; – **over,** flüchtig durchsehen, überfliegen, überblicken; – **through,** durchbohren, durchstechen; – **up,** hissen (*a flag*), schnell aufbauen *or* errichten (*houses*); in die Höhe treiben (*prices*); auflaufen lassen (*an account*); zusammennähen (*a seam*); – ***up an account with him,*** bei ihm auf Rechnung kaufen.
3. *s.* 1. das Laufen, Rennen, der (Dauer)lauf; ***go for a –,*** einen Dauerlauf machen; (*coll.*) eine Spazierfahrt machen; (*fig.*) ***have a – for one's money,*** etwas nicht umsonst bekommen; ***on the –,*** auf der Flucht; (*coll.*) auf den Beinen, immer tätig; 2. der Anlauf; ***take a –,*** einen Anlauf nehmen; ***come down with a –,*** heftig *or* plötzlich herabstürzen; 3. der Laufschritt; 4. (*fig.*) (Ver)lauf, Ablauf, (Fort)gang, die Richtung; 5. Bahn (*bob-sleigh*); 6. (*Am.*) der Wasserlauf, Bach; 7. (*Comm.*) Andrang, Ansturm, Zulauf, Zustrom (*of*

customers); starke Nachfrage (*on*, nach); 8. (*Mus.*) (schneller) Lauf, die Passage; 9. Fahrt; ***trial –***, die Probefahrt; 10. (längere) Folge, Serie, Reihe, (*Theat.*) Laufzeit, (*Cards*) Sequenz; ***– of luck***, die Glückssträhne; ***– of office***, die Amtsdauer; (*Theat.*) ***have a – of 40 nights***, 40mal hintereinander gegeben werden; ***in the long –***, schließlich, letztlich, im Endergebnis, auf die Dauer; 11. die Arbeitsperiode, Arbeitszeit (*of machines*); 12. Sorte, Qualität (*of goods*); ***the common – of mankind***, die Allgemeinheit, Menschheit im allgemeinen, der Durchschnittsmensch; (*coll.*) ***– of the mill***, die Durchschnittsware; ***the general – of things***, die Allgemeinheit, der Durchschnitt, die Dinge im Durchschnitt; 13. freier Zugang *or* Zutritt, freie Benutzung; ***have the – of***, freien Zutritt haben zu; ***have the – of the house***, im Haus ein- und ausgehen; 14. der Mühlgang, Mahlgang; 15. die Trift, der Weidegrund (*for cattle*), Auslauf (*for fowl*); 16. (*Av.*) die Rollstrecke; 17. (*esp. Am.*) Laufmasche (*in stockings*); 18. (*Tech.*) das Abflußrohr, die Rinne; Laufschiene, Laufplanke; 19. (*Naut.*) Piek.

run|about, *s.* (*coll.*) der Kleinwagen. **--around**, *s.* (*sl.*) ***give him the –***, ihn von Pontius zu Pilatus schicken, ihn schikanieren. **-away**, **1.** *adj.* entlaufen, davongelaufen, entrissen, ausgerissen; durchgegangen (*horse*); (*esp. Comm.*) unaufhaltsam (steigernd); ***– match*** or ***marriage***, die Heirat nach vorheriger Entführung; ***– victory*** or ***win***, überwältigender Sieg. **2.** *s.* der Ausreißer; Durchgänger (*horse*).

runcinate [ˈrʌnsinət], *adj.* sägeförmig.

run-down, **1.** *adj.* 1. verfallen, heruntergekommen; 2. erschöpft, entladen, verbraucht (*as a battery*), abgelaufen, stehengeblieben (*clock*); 3. (*coll.*) (*of a p.*) abgespannt, ausgepumpt. **2.** *s.* (*coll.*) der Abbau, die Verminderung.

rune [ruːn], *s.* die Rune, der Runenspruch.

[1]**rung** [rʌŋ], *s.* die Sprosse (*of a ladder*); (*fig.*) Stufe.

[2]**rung**, *p.p. of* [2]**ring.**

runic [ˈruːnik], *adj.* Runen-.

run-in, *s.* 1. (*Spt.*) der Einlauf, das Einlaufen; 2. (*Av.*) der Anflug.

runnel [rʌnl], *s.* die Rinne, der Kanal.

runner [ˈrʌnə], *s.* 1. der (die) Läufer(in); 2. der Renner, das Rennpferd; 3. (*Comm.*) der Bote, Laufbursche; (*Mil.*) Melder; 4. Schmuggler; 5. (*Naut.*) das Drehreep; 6. (*Tech.*) die Laufschiene, Laufrinne; Gleitrolle, Laufrolle, Rollwalze, Laufwalze; ***edge –***, der Kollergang; 7. Kufe (*sledge*); 8. der Schieber (*of an umbrella*); 9. (*Bot.*) Ausläufer, Ableger; ***scarlet –***, die Feuerbohne; 10. (*Orn.*) die Ralle (*Rallidae*); 11. schmaler Teppich, der (Tisch)läufer, Zimmerläufer.

runner-up, *s.* zweiter Sieger, Zweite(r), Zweitbeste(r).

running [ˈrʌniŋ], **1.** *adj.* 1. laufend; ***– fight***, das Rückzugsgefecht; ***– jump***, der Sprung mit Anlauf; ***– knot***, die Schlinge, Schleife; ***– rigging***, laufendes Gut; ***– speed***, (*Tech.*) die Umlaufgeschwindigkeit; (*Motor.*) Fahrgeschwindigkeit; ***– stone***, der Mahlstein; 2. fließend; ***– water***, das Fließwasser, fließendes Wasser; 3. eiternd (*as sore*); 4. (fort)laufend, ununterbrochen; ***– account***, laufende Rechnung; ***– commentary***, laufender Kommentar, (*Rad.*) der Hörbericht (*on*, über (*Acc.*)); ***– expenses***, Betriebsunkosten (*pl.*); (*Mil.*) ***– fire***, das Trommelfeuer, Schnellfeuer; ***– hand***, die Kurrentschrift; ***– head(line)*** or ***title***, der Kolumnentitel; ***– pattern***, fortlaufendes Muster; ***– stitch***, der Vorderstich; 5. aufeinanderfolgend; ***5 times –***, 5mal hintereinander. **2.** *s.* 1. das Rennen, Laufen; ***be in (out of) the –***, (keine) Aussichten haben; (nicht) in Betracht kommen; ***make the –***, das Rennen machen, gut abschneiden; ***put him out of the –***, ihn verdrängen, ihn aus dem Rennen werfen *or* außer Konkurrenz setzen; 2. (*Tech.*) der Gang, Lauf.

running-board, *s.* (*Motor.*) das Trittbrett.

run|-off, *s.* der Entscheidungslauf, das Entscheidungsrennen. **--on**, *adj.* (*Typ.*) fortlaufend gesetzt.

runt [rʌnt], *s.* 1. der Zwergochse; 2. verbuttetes Tier; 3. (*vulg.*) untersetzte Person.

run|-up, *s.* (*Av.*) der Zielanflug. **-way**, *s.* (*Av.*) die Startbahn, Rollbahn, Landebahn.

rupee [ruːˈpiː], *s.* die Rupie.

rupture [ˈrʌptʃə], **1.** *s.* 1. das Brechen, Sprengen, (Zer)reißen, Zerplatzen; 2. der Bruch (*also Med.*), Riß, Sprung; ***– support***, das Bruchband; 3. (*fig.*) der (Ab)bruch. **2.** *v.t.* 1. brechen, zersprengen, zerreißen (*also Med.*); ***be –d***, ***– o.s.***, *see* **3**; 2. (*fig.*) abbrechen. **3.** *v.i.* einen Bruch bekommen.

rural [ˈruərəl], *adj.* 1. ländlich; Land-; ***– dean***, der Dekan eines Landbezirks; ***– district***, der Landkreis, ländlicher Verwaltungsbezirk; ***– poetry***, die Dorfpoesie; 2. landwirtschaftlich, Ackerbau-. **ruralize**, **1.** *v.t.* ländlichen Charakter geben (*Dat.*). **2.** *v.i.* sich auf das Landleben umstellen, ein ländliches Leben führen.

ruse [ruːz], *s.* die List; der Kniff.

[1]**rush** [rʌʃ], **1.** *s.* 1. das (Dahin)stürmen, (Vorwärts)-stürzen; (*coll.*) ***in a –***, in aller Eile; ***with a –***, plötzlich, ruckartig; 2. der (An)sturm (***for***, auf (*Acc.*)), lebhafte Nachfrage (nach); ***make a – for***, losstürzen auf (*Acc.*), sich drängen um; 3. der Anfall, Andrang, das Gedränge; (*Elec.*) ***– of current***, der Stromstoß; ***– of blood***, der Blutandrang; 4. die Eile, Hetze, Geschäftigkeit; 5. der Drang, Hochbetrieb (*of business*); 6. (*fig.*) Ausbruch, die Anwandlung; 7. (*Footb.*) der Vorstoß. **2.** *v.i.* 1. (dahin)stürmen, (vorwärts)stürzen, eilen, rennen, rasen, sausen, (dahin)jagen; ***– at***, sich stürzen auf (*Acc.*); ***– in***, hineinstürzen, hereinstürzen; ***– into print***, voreilig an die Öffentlichkeit treten; ***– out***, hinausstürzen; ***– (up)on***, losstürzen auf (*Acc.*), herfallen über (*Acc.*); ***the blood –ed to his face***, das Blut flog *or* schoß ihm ins Gesicht; 2. (*of wind, water etc.*) stürmen, rauschen, sausen. **3.** *v.t.* 1. übereilen, überstürzen; ***– matters***, die S. *or* es überstürzen; 2. drängen, hetzen, (an)treiben; ***– up prices***, die Preise in die Höhe treiben; ***be –ed for time***, es sehr eilig haben, keine Zeit haben; 3. schnell hinbringen (*to*, nach); ***– him to hospital***, ihn schnell ins Krankenhaus schaffen; ***– up***, schnellstens herbeischaffen (*reinforcements*); 4. rasch erledigen (*work*); (*Parl.*) ***– a bill through***, ein Gesetz durchpeitschen; 5. hinwegsetzen über (*Acc.*) (*an obstacle*); 6. (*Mil.*) erstürmen, im Sturm nehmen; (*coll.*) losstürmen auf (*Acc.*), anrennen gegen (*a p.*); 7. (*sl.*) in Rechnung stellen (*Dat.*) (*a p.*); ***how much did he – you?*** wieviel hat er verlangt *or* gefordert *or* berechnet?

[2]**rush**, *s.* (*Bot.*) die Binse; ***not worth a –***, keinen Deut *or* Pfifferling wert. **rush-bearing**, *s.* (*Eccl.*) das Kirchweihfest.

rush-hour, *s.* die Hauptverkehrszeit, Hauptgeschäftszeit.

rush|light, *s.* das Binsenlicht. **--mat**, *s.* die Schilfmatte.

rush-order, *s.* der Eilauftrag.

rusk [rʌsk], *s.* der Zwieback.

russet [ˈrʌsit], **1.** *adj.* ro(s)tbraun. **2.** *s.* 1. das Ro(s)tbraun; 2. der Rötling (*apple*); 3. (*Hist.*) die Bauernkleidung.

Russia [ˈrʌʃə], *s.* Rußland (*n.*); ***– leather***, der Juchten, das Juchtenleder. **Russian**, **1.** *s.* 1. der Russe (die Russin); 2. (*language*) das Russisch(e). **2.** *adj.* russisch; ***– boots***, Russenstiefel (*pl.*).

rust [rʌst], **1.** *s.* 1. der Rost (*also fig.*); 2. (*Bot.*) Rost(pilz), Brand. **2.** *v.i.* (ver)rosten, anrosten, rostig werden, (*also fig.*) einrosten. **3.** *v.t.* rostig machen, verrosten lassen.

rustic [ˈrʌstik], **1.** *adj.* 1. ländlich, bäuerlich, Land-; 2. einfach, schlicht; 3. bäuerisch, grob; 4. aus Baumästen hergestellt. **2.** *s.* der Landmann, Bauer. **rusticate** [-eit], **1.** *v.i.* auf dem Land wohnen, sich aufs Land zurückziehen. **2.** *v.t.* 1. aufs Land senden; 2. (*Univ.*) zeitweilig verweisen, relegieren; 3. (*Archit.*) mit Bossenwerk verzieren. **rustication** [-ˈkeiʃən], *s.* 1. ländliche Zurückgezogenheit; 2. (*Univ.*) (zeitweise) Relegierung; 3. (*Archit.*) *see* **rustic-work. rusticity** [-ˈtisiti], *s.*

1. die Ländlichkeit; 2. das Landleben; 3. ländliche Einfachheit; 4. die Plumpheit, bäurisches Wesen. **rustic-work,** *s.* (*Archit.*) das Bossenwerk, die Rustika.

rustiness ['rʌstinis], *s.* 1. die Rostigkeit; 2. (*fig.*) das Eingerostetsein (*of memory*), die Heiserkeit, Rauheit (*of voice*).

[1]**rustle** [rʌsl], **1.** *v.i.* rascheln, rauschen, knistern. **2.** *v.t.* rascheln lassen. **3.** *s.* das Rascheln.

[2]**rustle,** *v.t.* (*Am.*) stehlen (*cattle*); (*sl.*) – ***o.s.,*** sich anstrengen, sich beeilen; (*sl.*) – ***up,*** zusammenbringen, auftreiben, organisieren. **rustler,** *s.* (*Am.*) der Viehdieb.

rustless ['rʌstlis], **rust|proof,** *adj.* nichtrostend, rostfrei. **--stained,** *adj.* rostfleckig. **rusty,** *adj.* 1. rostig, verrostet; 2. rostfarbig; 3. (*fig.*) eingerostet, vernachlässigt, außer Übung; (*coll.*) heiser, rauh.

[1]**rut** [rʌt], **1.** *s.* die Brunft (*of deer*), Brunst (*other animals*). **2.** *v.i.* brunsten, brunften.

[2]**rut, 1.** *s.* 1. das (Wagen)gleis; die (Rad)spur, Furche; 2. (*fig.*) (ausgefahrenes) Geleise, (alltäglicher) Trott, die Routine; ***get out of the –,*** sich zu etwas aufschwingen; ***stay in the –,*** beim alten Schlendrian verbleiben. **2.** *v.t.* furchen.

rutabaga [ru:tə'beigə], *s.* (*Am.*) *see* **swede.**

ruth [ru:θ], *s.* (*obs.*) das Erbarmen, Mitleid. **ruthless,** *adj.* 1. erbarmungslos, unbarmherzig, grausam; 2. rücksichtslos. **ruthlessness,** *s.* 1. die Unbarmherzigkeit; 2. Rücksichtslosigkeit.

rutted ['rʌtid], *adj.* durchfurcht, ausgefahren.

rutting ['rʌtiŋ], **1.** *adj.* Brunft–, Brunst–. **2.** *s. See* [1]**rut, 1. ruttish,** *adj.* brünftig, brünstig.

rye [rai], *s.* der Roggen. **rye-grass,** *s.* der Lolch.

ryot ['raiət], *s.* indischer Bauer.

S

S, s [es], das S, s. *See List of Abbreviations.*

's [z (*after vowel or voiced consonant*); s (*after voiceless consonant*); iz (*after sibilant*)], **1.** *gen. part.*; ***father's,*** (des) Vaters; ***Lyon's,*** die Firma Lyon; ***St. Michael's,*** die Michaelikirche; ***Tass's reports,*** die Tass-Nachrichten. **2.** (*coll.*) *remainder of word after elision*: 1. = **is**; ***he's, she's*** or ***it's here,*** er *or* sie *or* es ist hier; 2. = **has**; ***he's*** *or* ***she's*** or ***it's made,*** er *or* sie *or* es hat gemacht; 3. = **does**; in ***what's he mean?*** was meint er? 4. = **us**; in ***let's go,*** gehen wir! 5. (*obs.*) = **God's** in ***'sblood,*** mein *or* großer Gott!

Saarland ['zɑ:lənd], *s.* das Saargebiet.

Sabaism ['seibəizm], *s.* die Sternenanbetung.

Sabaoth ['sæbeiɔθ], *s.* (*B.*) Zebaoth; ***the Lord God of –,*** der Herr der Heerscharen.

Sabbatarian [sæbə'tɛəriən], *s.* der (die) Sabbatarier(in), Sabbatist(in). **Sabbatarianism,** *s.* der Sabbastismus. **Sabbath** ['sæbəθ], *s.* der Sabbat, Ruhetag; ***break the –,*** den Sabbat entheiligen; ***keep the –,*** den Sabbat heiligen; ***witches' –,*** der Hexensabbat; ***--breaker,*** der Entheiliger des Sabbats, Sabbatschänder; ***--breaking,*** die Sabbatentheiligung. **sabbatical** [sə'bætikl], *adj.* Sabbat–; – ***year,*** (*Jews*) das Sabbatjahr; (*Univ.*) das Urlaubsjahr. **sabbatize** ['sæbətaiz], *v.t.* als Sabbat feiern.

saber, (*Am.*) *see* **sabre.**

Sabine ['sæbain], **1.** *s.* der (die) Sabiner(in). **2.** *adj.* sabinisch.

[1]**sable** [seibl], **1.** *s.* 1. (*Zool.*) der Zobel; 2. Zobelpelz. **2.** *attrib. adj.* Zobel–.

[2]**sable, 1.** *s.* 1. (*Her.*) das Schwarz; 2. (*also* – ***antelope***) die Rappenantilope; 3. *pl.* (*Poet.*) die Trauer(kleidung). **2.** *adj.* (*Her., Poet.*) schwarz, düster; ***his – Majesty,*** der Höllenfürst, Herrscher der Finsternis.

sabot ['sæbou], *s.* der Holzschuh.

sabotage ['sæbətɑ:ʒ], **1.** *s.* die Sabotage. **2.** *v.t.* sabotieren. **3.** *v.i.* Sabotage treiben *or* üben. **saboteur** [–'tə:], *s.* der Saboteur.

sabre ['seibə], **1.** *s.* 1. der Säbel; ***rattle the –,*** mit dem Säbel rasseln; 2. (*fig.*) der Kavallerist. **2.** *v.t.* niedersäbeln. **sabre|-rattling,** *s.* das Säbelrasseln, Säbelgerassel. **--toothed tiger,** *s.* der Säbelzahntiger. **sabreur** [sæ'brə:], *s.* schneidiger Kavallerieoffizier.

sabulous ['sæbjuləs], *adj.* Sand–, sandig; (*Med.*) – ***matter,*** der Harngrieß, Blasengrieß. **saburra** [–'bʌrə], *s.* (*Med.*) bösartige Ablagerung im Magen.

sac [sæk], *s.* (*esp. Med., Anat.*) der Beutel, Sack, die Zyste, Geschwulst. **saccate** [–eit], *adj.* (*Bot.*) sackförmig, taschenförmig.

saccharate ['sækəreit], *adj.* (*Chem.*) zuckersauer. **saccharic** [sæ'kærik], *adj.* (*Chem.*) Zucker–; – ***acid,*** die Zuckersäure. **sacchariferous** [–'rifərəs], *adj.* zuckerhaltig. **saccharification** [–rifi'keiʃən], *s.* die Zuckerbildung, Verzuckerung. **saccharify** [–rifai], *v.t.* verzuckern, in Zucker verwandeln (*starch*). **saccharimeter** [–'rimitə], *s.* das Polarisationssaccharimeter, der Zuckergehaltsmesser. **saccharin(e)** ['sækərin], *s.* das Saccharin, der Süßstoff. **saccharine** ['sækəri:n], *adj.* 1. Zucker–, Süßstoff–; 2. (*fig.*) zuckersuß, süßlich. **saccharization, saccharize,** *see* **saccharification, saccharify. saccharoid** ['sækərɔid], *adj.* (*Geol.*) körnig. **saccharometer** [–'rɔmitə], *s.* das Aräometer, der Zuckergehaltsmesser (durch Messung des spezifischen Gewichts). **saccharose** [–'rous], *s.* der Rohrzucker.

sacciform ['sæksifɔ:m], *adj.* sackförmig, taschenförmig, beutelartig. **saccular** [–kjulə], **sacculate(d)** [–kjuleit(id)], *adj.* abgekapselt, eingekapselt, mit Zystenbildung, zystisch, zystös. **sacculation** [–kju'leiʃən], *s.* die Zystenbildung, Säckchenbildung, Abkapselung, Einkapselung. **saccule** [–kju:l], *s.* (*esp. Med.*) das Säckchen.

sacerdotal [sæsə'doutl], *adj.* priesterlich, Priester–. **sacerdotalism,** *s.* das Priestertum, die Priesterherrschaft.

sachem ['seitʃəm], *s.* (*Am.*) der Indianerhäuptling.

sachet ['sæʃei], *s.* das Parfümtäschchen, der Parfümbeutel.

[1]**sack** [sæk], **1.** *s.* der Sack; ***a – of corn,*** ein Sack Korn; (*coll.*) ***get the –,*** entlassen werden, fliegen; (*coll.*) ***give him the –,*** ihm den Laufpaß geben, ihn 'rausschmeißen *or* ausbooten *or* an die Luft setzen. **2.** *v.t.* 1. einsacken, in Säcke tun; 2. (*coll.*) *see* ***give him the –.***

[2]**sack, 1.** *s.* die Plünderung; ***put to –,*** *see* **2. 2.** *v.t.* plündern.

[3]**sack,** *s.* (*obs.*) der Südwein.

sackbut ['sækbʌt], *s.* (*obs.*) die Posaune.

sackcloth ['sækklɔθ], *s.* die Sackleinwand, das Sacktuch; (*fig.*) ***in – and ashes,*** in Sack und Asche. **sackful,** *s.* der Sackvoll. **sacking,** *s. See* **sackcloth. sack-race,** *s.* das Sackhüpfen.

sacral ['seikrəl], *adj.* (*Anat.*) Kreuzbein–, Sakral–.

sacrament ['sækrəmənt], *s.* das Sakrament, (Heiliges) Abendmahl; ***last –,*** letzte Ölung; ***administer (receive) the –,*** das Abendmahl spenden (empfangen); ***take the –,*** zum Abendmahl gehen, das Abendmahl nehmen. **sacramental** [–'mentl], **1.** *adj.* 1. sakramental(isch), sakramentlich, Sakrament(s)–; 2. (*fig.*) feierlich, heilig. **2.** *s.* 1. (*usu. pl.*) (*R.C.*) heilige Handlung; 2. *pl.* Sakramentalien (*pl.*). **sacramentarian** [–mən'tɛəriən], *s.* (*Eccl.*) der Sakramentarier.

sacrarium [sæ'krɛəriəm], *s.* das Allerheiligste, die Altarstätte.

sacred ['seikrid], *adj.* 1. heilig; – ***building,*** der Sakralbau; – ***duty,*** heilige Pflicht; 2. kirchlich, geistlich, religiös, Kirchen–; – ***history,*** biblische

Geschichte; – *music,* die Kirchenmusik; 3. geheiligt, geweiht, gewidmet (*to, Dat.*); 4. (*fig.*) unverletzlich, unverbrüchlich, unantastbar; (*coll.*) – *cow,* unantastbare *or* sakrosankte S. *or* P.; *Her Most Sacred Majesty,* Ihre Heilige Majestät. **sacredness,** *s.* die Heiligkeit.

sacrifice ['sækrifais], **1.** *s.* 1. das Opfer (*also fig.*), die Opferung; (*fig.*) Aufopferung, Hingabe, Aufgabe, der Verzicht; *fall a – to,* zum Opfer fallen (*Dat.*); *make a – of,* opfern, aufgeben; *make –s,* Opfer bringen; 2. (*Comm.*) der Verlust, die Einbuße; *sell at a –,* unter großem Verlust verkaufen. **2.** *v.t.* 1. opfern (*to, Dat.*); (*fig.*) verzichten auf (*Acc.*), hingeben, aufgeben; – *one's life,* sein Leben opfern *or* hingeben; (*usu. fig.*) – *o.s. for,* sich (auf)-opfern für; 2. (*Comm.*) unter Verlust verkaufen. **3.** *v.i.* opfern, (ein) Opfer (dar)bringen; (*fig.*) Opfer bringen. **sacrificial** [–'fiʃəl], *adj.* Opfer–; – *victim,* das Opfer.

sacrilege ['sækrilidʒ], *s.* 1. die Entweihung, Entheiligung, (Kirchen)schändung, der Kirchenraub; 2. (*fig.*) Frevel. **sacrilegious** [–'lidʒəs], *adj.* 1. kirchenschänderisch, entweihend, entheiligend, gotteslästerlich; 2. ruchlos, frevlerisch, frevelhaft. **sacrilegist** [–'li:dʒist], *s.* der Schänder, Frevler.

sacrist ['seikrist], *s.* (*R.C.*) der Mesner. **sacristan** ['sækristən], *s.* der Kirchendiener, Küster.

sacrosanct ['sækrəsæŋkt], *adj.* unverletzlich, unantastbar, hochheilig, sakrosankt.

sacrum ['seikrəm], *s.* (*Anat.*) das Kreuzbein.

sad [sæd], *adj.* 1. traurig, niedergeschlagen, betrübt, bekümmert (*at,* über (*Acc.*)); 2. betrübend, beklagenswert; 3. klitsch(ig), schliff, sitzengeblieben (*as bread*); 4. trüb, düster, gedeckt (*as colours*); 5. (*fig.*) arg, kläglich, elend. **sadden** [–n], **1.** *v.t.* 1. betrüben, traurig stimmen *or* machen; 2. abmatten, abtrüben, abdunkeln, nachdunkeln (*colours*). **2.** *v.i.* betrübt werden. **sadder,** *comp. adj.*, **saddest,** *sup. adj. of* **sad.**

saddle [sædl], **1.** *s.* 1. der Sattel; (*fig.*) *in the –,* fest im Sattel, an der Macht, im Amt; 2. der (Berg)-sattel; 3. (*Naut., Tech. etc.*) die Unterlage, Stütze, der Schuh, Querschlitten, das Querholz, Lager; 4. – *of mutton,* der Hammelrücken, das Hammellendenstück. **2.** *v.t.* 1. satteln; 2. (*fig.*) (*oft. pass.*) belasten; – *it on him,* es ihm zur Last legen; – *him with it,* es ihm aufbürden *or* aufladen *or* aufhalsen.

saddle|back, *s.* 1. (sattelförmiger) Bergrücken; 2. (*Archit.*) das Turmdach zwischen zwei Giebeln; 3. (*Zool.*) das Männchen der Sattelrobbe; 4. (*Orn.*) die Nebelkrähe. **–backed,** *adj.* hohlrückig. **–-bag,** *s.* die Satteltasche. **–-blanket,** *s. See* **–-cloth.** **–-bow,** *s.* der Sattelbogen. **–-cloth,** *s.* die Satteldecke, Schabracke, der Woilach. **–-horse,** *s.* das Reitpferd.

saddler ['sædlə], *s.* der Sattler; *–'s wax,* das Sattlerpech. **saddlery,** *s.* 1. die Sattlerei; 2. der Sattelraum; 3. Sattelwaren (*pl.*), das Sattelzeug. **saddle-tree,** *s.* (*Cycl.*) der Sattelbock.

Sadducee ['sædjusi:], *s.* (*B.*) der Sadduzäer.

sadism ['seidizm], *s.* der Sadismus. **sadist,** *s.* der (die) Sadist(in). **sadistic** [sə'distik], *adj.* sadistisch.

sadly ['sædli], *adv. See* **sad**; (*coll.*) arg, schmählich. **sadness,** *s.* die Traurigkeit, Betrübtheit, Schwermut.

Sadowa ['sædouvə], *s* (*Hist.*) *battle of –,* die Schlacht bei Königgrätz.

safari [sə'fɑ:ri], *s.* die Safari, Großwildjagd.

safe [seif], **1.** *adj.* 1. sicher, in Sicherheit (*from,* vor (*Dat.*)); 2. unversehrt, heil, wohlbehalten, geschützt (*from,* von); – *and sound,* gesund und munter; 3. nicht mehr gefährlich, in sicherem Gewahrsam, sicher aufgehoben, nicht (länger) gefährdet, außer Gefahr, ungefährlich, gefahrlos; *it is – to say,* man kann getrost *or* ruhig sagen; (*coll.*) *play –, be on the – side,* vorsichtig sein, sicher gehen; *with a – conscience,* mit ruhigem *or* gutem Gewissen; – *custody,* sicherer Gewahrsam; *as – as houses,* absolut sicher, todsicher; – *period,* unfruchtbare Tage (*pl.*); *not –,* gefährlich; 4. verläßlich, zuverlässig, vertrauenswürdig; 5. vorsichtig, bedächtig; – *driver,* vorsichtiger Fahrer; 6. (*coll.*) sicher; *he is – to win,* er wird sicher gewinnen. **2.** *s.* 1. der Geldschrank; 2. (*also meat–-*) Speiseschrank.

safe|-breaker, *s.* der Geldschrankknacker. **–-conduct,** *s.* 1. freies *or* sicheres Geleit; 2. der Geleitsbrief. – **deposit,** *s.* das Bankfach, der Tresor, die Stahlkammer. **–guard,** **1.** *s.* 1. der Schutz, die Sicherung; Sicherheit, Vorsichtsmaßnahme, (*Law*) Sicherheitsklausel; 2. (*obs.*) *see* **–-conduct.** **2.** *v.t.* schützen; verwahren, sichern, sicherstellen. – **keeping,** *s.* sichere Aufbewahrung, sicherer Gewahrsam. **safeness,** *s. See* **safety.**

safety ['seifti], *s.* die Sicherheit; Gefahrlosigkeit, Ungefährlichkeit; *in –,* in Sicherheit; – *first,* jederzeit Sicherheit; *flee for –,* sich flüchten; *play for –,* see *play safe*; *there is – in numbers,* in der Menge geht man unter; *place of –,* der Sicherheitsort; Zufluchtsort; *carry to –,* in Sicherheit bringen; *jump to –,* sich durch einen Sprung in Sicherheit bringen; *with –,* ohne Gefahr.

safety|-belt, *s.* (*Motor., Av.*) der Sicherheitsgurt. **–-catch,** *s.* die Sicherung (*of a rifle*). **–-chain,** *s.* die Sicherungskette. **–-curtain,** *s.* eiserner Vorhang. **–-factor,** *s.* der Sicherheitsfaktor. **–-fuse,** *s.* der Sicherheitszünder. **–-glass,** *s.* das Schutzglas. **–-lamp,** *s.* die Sicherheitslampe. **–-lock,** *s.* das Sicherheitsschloß. **–-match,** *s.* der Sicherheitszünder. **–-pin,** *s.* die Sicherheitsnadel. **–-razor,** *s.* der Rasierapparat. **–-valve,** *s.* 1. das Sicherheitsventil; 2. (*fig.*) der Ausweg, Spielraum.

saffian ['sæfiən], *s.* das Saffianleder.

safflower ['sæflauə], *s.* (*Bot.*) der Saflor, die Färberdistel, wilder Safran.

saffron ['sæfrən], **1.** *s.* 1. (*Bot.*) echter Safran; 2. das Safrangewürz; 3. Safrangelb. **2.** *adj.* Safran–, safrangelb.

sag [sæg], **1.** *v.i.* 1. sich (in der Mitte) senken, niederhängen, durchhängen, durchsacken, (ab)-sacken; 2. (*fig.*) sinken, fallen, nachlassen; 3. (*Naut.*) – *to leeward,* nach Lee abtreiben. **2.** *s.* das (Ab)sacken, die Senkung, Absackung, Durchbiegung, der Durchhang.

saga ['sɑ:gə], *s.* die Saga.

sagacious [sə'geiʃəs], *adj.* klug, scharfsinnig. **sagacity** [–'gæsiti], *s.* der Scharfsinn, die Klugheit.

[1]**sage** [seidʒ], **1.** *adj.* weise, klug, verständig, urteilsfähig. **2.** *s.* Weise(r).

[2]**sage,** *s.* (*Bot.*) der *or* die Salbei.

saggar, sagger ['sægə], *s.* feuerfestes Gefäß, die Brennkapsel.

Sagittarius [sægi'tɛəriəs], *s.* (*Astr.*) der Schütze.

sago ['seigou], *s.* der Sago.

Sahara [sə'hɑ:rə], *s.* die Sahara.

Sahib ['sɑ:ib], *s.* 1. Herr (*as title following name*); 2. der Engländer, Europäer (*in India*).

said [sed], **1.** *imperf., p.p. of* **say**; *he is – to be rich,* es heißt, er sei reich; er soll reich sein. **2.** *attrib. adj.* (*esp. Law*) vorerwähnt, besagt.

sail [seil], **1.** *s.* 1. das Segel; *hoist –,* die Segel hissen; *in full –,* mit vollen Segeln, mit allen Segeln bei; *make –,* die Segel beisetzen; (*fig.*) *set –,* auslaufen, in See gehen; abreisen, abfahren (*for,* nach); *shorten –,* die Segel einziehen *or* reffen; *lower* or *strike –,* die Segel einholen *or* streichen; (*fig., coll.*) *take the wind out of his –s,* ihm den Wind aus den Segeln nehmen; *under –,* unter Segel; *under full –,* alles bei; 2. (*fig.*) (*no pl.*) das Segelschiff; 3. der Flügel (*of a windmill*); 4. die Segelfahrt. **2.** *v.i.* 1. segeln; (*of a ship*) fahren, auslaufen, (*of a p.*) absegeln, abreisen, sich einschiffen (*to,* nach); zu Schiff fahren *or* reisen; – *close* or *near to the wind,* nah am Winde *or* hoch an den Wind segeln ; (*fig.*) Gefahr laufen, sich strafbar zu machen; *ready to –,* seeklar; 2. gleiten, fliegen (*in the air*); (*fig.*) schwimmen, dahinschweben; 3. (*fig.*) – *in,* majestätisch hereinkommen; (*coll.*) sich ins Mittel legen, loslegen, zupacken; (*coll.*) – *into,* tüchtig anpacken, sich heranmachen an (*Acc.*). **3.** *v.t.* 1.

befahren, durchsegeln (*the sea*); 2. durchfliegen, durchschweben (*the air*); 3. führen (*a boat*).
sail|boat, *s.* (*Am.*) *see* **sailing boat. --cloth,** *s.* das Segeltuch. **sailer,** *s.* der Segler.
sailing ['seiliŋ], **1.** *adj.* Segel–. **2.** *s.* 1. das Segeln, der Segelsport; 2. die (Segel)schiffahrt; (*fig.*) *plain –*, einfache *or* leichte S.; 3. die Abfahrt (*for*, nach); *pl.* Abfahrtszeiten (*pl.*). **sailing| boat,** *s.* das Segelboot. **– directions,** *pl.* das Segelhandbuch. **– orders,** *pl.* 1. der Fahrtauftrag, Befehl zum Auslaufen; 2. (*fig., coll.*) Marschbefehl. **– vessel,** *s.* das Segelschiff.
sail|-loft, *s.* der Schnürboden. **–maker,** *s.* der Segelmacher.
sailor ['seilə], *s.* der Matrose, Seemann; *be a good –*, seefest sein, nicht leicht *or* nie seekrank werden; *be a bad –*, nicht seefest sein, leicht seekrank werden; *–'s knot*, der Schifferknoten; *– hat*, der Matrosenhut. **sailoring,** *s.* das Seemannsleben. **sailorman,** *s.* (*coll.*) der Matrose.
sailplane ['seilplein], *s.* das Segelflugzeug.
sainfoin ['seinfɔin], *s.* (*Bot.*) die Esparsette, der Schildklee.
saint [seint], **1.** *s.* 1. Heilige(r); *patron –*, Schutzheilige(r); *–'s day*, der Heiligentag; *All Saints' day*, Allerheiligen (*pl.*); 2. [sənt] (*before names*) (*abbr.* **S.** or *St.*) heilig, Sankt; *St. Peter*, Sankt Petrus, der heilige Petrus; *St. Andrew's Cross*, das Andreaskreuz; (*Med.*) *St. Anthony's fire*, die Rose, das Erysipel; *St. Elmo's fire*, das Elmsfeuer; (*Court of*) *St. James('s)*, der Großbritannische Hof; (*Bot.*) *St.-John's-wort*, das Johanniskraut; *St. Lawrence*, der Sankt-Lorenz-Strom; *St. Leger*, das Septemberrennen zu Doncaster; *St. Martin's summer*, der Altweibersommer; *St. Valentine's day*, der Valentinstag; *St. Vitus's dance*, der Veitstanz. **2.** *v.t.* heiligsprechen. **sainted,** *adj.* 1. heilig(gesprochen); 2. selig; 3. geheiligt, geweiht. **sainthood,** *s.* die Heiligkeit. **saintliness,** *s.* die Heilig(mäßig)keit, Frömmigkeit. **saintly,** *adj.* heilig(mäßig), fromm.
sake [seik], *s. for God's* or *goodness –*, um alles in der Welt, um Gottes willen; *for his –*, um seinetwillen, ihm zuliebe; *for my own –*, um meiner selbst willen; *for both our –s*, um unser beider willen; *for the – of doing*, in der Absicht zu tun; *for the – of peace*, um des (lieben) Friedens willen, im Interesse des Friedens.
saker ['seikə], *s.* (*Orn.*) weiblicher Sakerfalk. **sakeret** [–'ret], *s.* (*Orn.*) männlicher Sakerfalk.
sal [sæl], *s.* (*Chem.*) das Salz; *– ammoniac*, der Salmiak, das Chlorammonium; *– volatile*, das Hirschhornsalz.
salaam [sə'lɑ:m], **1.** *s.* der Selam, Salem. **2.** *v.i.* eine tiefe Verbeugung machen, (mit einem Selam) grüßen.
salable, *see* **saleable.**
salacious [sə'leiʃəs], *adj.* 1. wollüstig, geil; 2. zotig, obszön. **salaciousness, salacity** [–'læsiti], *s.* 1. die Wollust, Geilheit; 2. Zotigkeit, Obszönität.
salad ['sæləd], *s.* (grüner) Salat. **salad|-bowl,** *s.* die Salatschüssel. **– days,** *pl.* Jugendjahre (*pl.*). **– dressing,** *s.* die Salatsoße. **--oil,** *s.* das Olivenöl.
salamander ['sæləmændə], *s.* 1. (*Zool.*) der Salamander, Molch; 2. (*Cook.*) Feuersalamander, Feuergeist; 3. das Schüreisen, die Eisenschaufel.
salaried ['sælərid], *adj.* besoldet, bezahlt; *– employee*, der Gehaltsempfänger. **salary, 1.** *s.* das Gehalt, die Besoldung. **2.** *v.t.* besolden.
sale [seil], *s.* 1. der Verkauf; *forced –*, der Zwangsverkauf; *forward –*, der Terminverkauf; *for –*, zum Verkauf, verkäuflich; *bill of –*, der Kaufvertrag; *on –*, zu verkaufen(d); *on – or return*, in Kommission; *by private –*, unter der Hand; *– of work*, der Verkauf zu Wohltätigkeitszwecken; 2. der Vertrieb, Abgang, Absatz; *meet with a ready –*, schnellen Absatz finden; 3. die Auktion, Versteigerung; *put up for –*, feilbieten; versteigern; 4. (*also pl.*) der Ausverkauf.
saleability [seilə'biliti], *s.* die Gangbarkeit, Verkäuflichkeit, Marktfähigkeit, Absatzfähigkeit.
saleable ['seiləbl], *adj.* verkäuflich, gangbar, marktfähig, absatzfähig.
sale|-goods, *pl.* Ramschwaren (*pl.*). **--price,** *s.* der Verkaufspreis. **--room,** *s.* das Auktionslokal.
sales| account ['seilz–], *s.* das Warenverkaufskonto. **--clerk,** *s.* (*Am.*) der (Laden)verkäufer. **–girl,** *s.* das Ladenmädchen. **–man** [–mən], *s.* 1. der (Laden)verkäufer; 2. Geschäftsreisende(r). **– manager,** *s.* der Verkaufsleiter.
salesmanship ['seilzmənʃip], *s.* die Verkaufstüchtigkeit, Verkaufsgewandtheit.
sales| promotion, *s.* die Absatzförderung. **– resistance,** *s.* die Kaufunlust. **–room,** *s.* der Verkaufsraum. **– talk,** *s.* 1. die Reklame, Werbung; 2. (*coll.*) Maulfertigkeit, der Redefluß. **– tax,** *s.* die Umsatzsteuer. **–woman,** *s.* die Verkäuferin.
Salic ['sælik], *adj.* salisch; *– law*, Salisches Gesetz.
salicin ['sælisin], *s.* (*Chem.*) das Salizin. **salicyl** [–sil], *s.* das Salizyl. **salicylic** [–'silik], *adj.* Salizyl–, salizylsauer.
salient ['seiliənt], **1.** *adj.* 1. hervorspringend, hervorstechend, hervortretend, hervorragend, auffallend, Haupt–; (*fig.*) *– point*, springender Punkt; 2. (*Archit.*) vorspringend; 3. (*Her.*) springend. **2.** *s.* 1. (*Math.*) vorspringender Winkel; 2. (*Mil.*) vorspringende Verteidigungslinie, der Frontvorsprung.
saliferous [sæ'lifərəs], *adj.* salzhaltig. **saline** ['seilain], **1.** *adj.* Salz–, salzig, salzhaltig. **2.** *s.* 1. die Saline, Salzquelle; 2. Salzlösung. **salinity** [sæ'liniti], *s.* der Salzgehalt, die Salzhaltigkeit, Salzigkeit.
saliva [sə'laivə], *s.* der Speichel. **salivary,** *adj.* Speichel–. **salivate** ['sæliveit], **1.** *v.t.* durch den Speichelfluß reinigen. **2.** *v.i.* Speichel absondern. **salivation** [sæli'veiʃən], *s.* der Speichelfluß, die Speichelabsonderung.
[1]**sallow** ['sælou], *s.* (*Bot.*) die Salweide.
[2]**sallow,** *adj.* gelblich, fahl, farblos, bleich, bläßlich. **sallowness,** *s.* fahle *or* gelbliche Farbe, die Fahlheit, Bläßlichkeit, Blässe.
sally ['sæli], **1.** *s.* 1. (*Mil.*) der Ausfall; (*fig.*) Ausbruch; 2. witzige Bemerkung, geistreicher Einfall. **2.** *v.i.* (*usu. – forth*) aufbrechen, sich aufmachen; (*Mil.*) (*also – out*) ausfallen, einen Ausfall machen. **sally-port,** *s.* das Ausfalltor.
salmagundi [sælmə'gʌndi], *s.* 1. das Ragout; 2. (*fig.*) der Mischmasch.
salmon ['sæmən], *s.* 1. der Lachs, Salm; *– leap*, die Lachsleiter; *--trout*, die Lachsforelle; 2. (*also --colour, --pink*) die Lachsfarbe.
salon ['sælɔn], *s.* der Salon.
Salonika [sælo'ni:kə], *s.* Saloniki (*n.*).
saloon [sə'lu:n], *s.* 1. der (Gesellschafts)saal; *dancing –*, das Tanzlokal; *gambling –*, die Spielhölle; 2. die Kneipe. **saloon| bar,** *s.* vornehmerer Ausschank. **– cabin,** *s.* die Kabine erster Klasse (*on ships*). **--car,** *s.* 1. (*Railw.*) der Salonwagen, Luxuswagen; 2. (*Motor.*) die Limousine. **– deck,** *s.* das Salondeck.
salsify ['sælsəfi], *s.* (*Bot.*) der Bocksbart.
salt [sɔ:lt], **1.** *s.* 1. das Salz; *above* (*below*) *the –*, oben (unten) am Tisch; *common –*, das Kochsalz; (*Chem.*) Chlornatrium; (*fig.*) *eat his –, eat – with him*, sein Gast sein; (*B.*) *the – of the earth*, das Salz der Erde; *in –*, eingesalzen, (ein)gepökelt; *grain of –*, das Körnchen Salz; (*coll.*) *with a grain of –*, mit Vorbehalt *or* einiger Vorsicht; *table –*, das Tafelsalz; *be not worth one's –*, nichts taugen; 2. (*fig.*) der Saft, die Würze; 3. (*fig.*) der Seemann; *old –*, alter Seebär; 4. *pl.* (*usu. smelling –s*), Riechsalze (*pl.*); 5. das Abführmittel; *Epsom –*, englisches Salz. **2.** *adj.* salzig, gesalzen; *– beef*, gepökeltes Rindfleisch; *– butter*, gesalzene Butter; *– marsh*, der Salz(wasser)sumpf; *– meat*, das Pökelfleisch; *– tears*, bittere Tränen; *– water*, das Salzwasser. **3.** *v.t.* 1. salzen; 2. (*also – down*) einsalzen, einpökeln, in Salzlake einlegen (*meat etc.*); 3. (*fig.*) würzen; 4. (*Comm. sl.*) frisieren, salzen, pfeffern (*prices*); 5. (*fig.*) *– away* or *down*, auf die hohe Kante legen, beiseite legen.

saltant ['sæltənt], *adj.* (*Her.*) springend. **saltation** [–'teiʃən], *s.* das Springen, der Sprung. **saltatory** [–tətəri], *adj.* 1. springend, Spring–, Sprung–; 2. (*fig.*) sprunghaft.

salt-cellar, *s.* das Salzfaß, Salzfäßchen, Salznäpfchen. **salted** [–id], *adj.* 1. gesalzen; 2. Salz–, Pökel–; 3. (*coll., fig.*) abgebrüht, abgehärtet, ausgepicht, ausgekocht. **saltern** [–ən], *s. See* **salt-mine.**

saltigrade ['sæltigreid], **1.** *s.* (*Zool.*) die Springspinne. **2.** *adj.* (*Zool.*) mit Springbeinen, springend.

saltiness ['sɔ:ltinis], *s.* die Salzigkeit. **salting, 1.** *s.* 1. das Einpökeln; 2. (*Geog.*) (*usu. pl.*) das Watt, salzreiches Schwemmland. **2.** *adj.* Pökel–.

saltire ['sæltaiə], *s.* (*Her.*) das Schrägkreuz.

saltless ['sɔ:ltlis], *adj.* 1. ungesalzen, salzlos; 2. (*fig.*) seicht. **salt|-lick,** *s.* die Salzlecke. **--mine,** *s.* das Salzbergwerk, die Saline.

salto ['sæltou], *s.* (*esp. Mus.*) der Sprung.

saltpetre [sɔ:lt'pi:tə], *s.* (*Chem.*) der (Kali)salpeter, das Kaliumnitrat.

salt|-pit, *s.* die Salzgrube. **–water,** *adj.* Salzwasser–, Meerwasser–. **--works,** *s. See* **--mine. salty,** *adj.* 1. salzig; 2. (*fig.*) gesalzen, gepfeffert.

salubrious [sə'l(j)u:briəs], *adj.* heilsam, gesund, wohltuend, zuträglich, bekömmlich (*climate etc.*). **salubriousness, salubrity** [–briti], *s.* die Heilsamkeit, Zuträglichkeit.

salutariness ['sæljutərinis], *s. See* **salubrity. salutary,** *adj.* (*usu. fig.*) heilsam, gesund, ersprießlich.

salutation [sælju'teiʃən], *s.* der Gruß, die Begrüßung; ***in –,*** zum Gruß, zur Begrüßung. **salutatory,** *adj.* 1. grüßend, Begrüßungs–; Gruß–; 2. (*Am.*) Eröffnungs–.

salute [sə'l(j)u:t], **1.** *s.* der Gruß (*also Mil.*), die Begrüßung; (*obs.*) der Kuß; (*Mil. etc.*) Salut (*of guns*), das Salutieren, die Ehrenbezeigung; ***in –,*** zum Gruß; ***give a –,*** grüßen; ***give the –,*** den Salut leisten; ***return a –,*** einen Gruß erwidern, wiedergrüßen; ***stand at the –,*** salutieren; ***take the –,*** den Salut *or* Gruß entgegennehmen, die Parade abnehmen; ***– of twelve guns,*** der Salut von 12 Schuß. **2.** *v.t.* 1. grüßen (*also Mil.*); (*Mil.*) salutieren; 2. (*fig.*) begegnen (*Dat.*), begrüßen. **3.** *v.i.* grüßen (***to,*** *Acc.*), salutieren (vor (*Dat.*)).

salvable ['sælvəbl], *adj.* 1. rettbar, (*of a wreck*) zu bergen(d); 2. (*fig.*) errettbar, erlösbar.

salvage ['sælvidʒ], **1.** *s.* 1. (*esp. Naut.*) die Bergung, Rettung; 2. das Bergegut, geborgenes Gut; 3. (*also* ***– money***) der Bergelohn, das Bergegeld; 4. (*coll.*) die (Abfall)verwertung, Wiedergewinnung; 5. gerettetes *or* verwertetes Material. **2.** *v.t.* 1. bergen, retten; 2. (*coll.*) verwerten. **salvage-dump,** *s.* die Beutesammelstelle.

salvation [sæl'veiʃən], *s.* 1. (*Eccl.*) die Erlösung, das (Seelen)heil; ***Salvation Army,*** die Heilsarmee; 2. (*fig.*) die Befreiung, (Er)rettung; (*fig.*) ***work out one's own –,*** auf eigenen Beinen stehen, auf eigene Faust selig werden; 3. der Retter; ***be the – of,*** der Retter sein von. **Salvationist,** *s.* das Mitglied der Heilsarmee.

[1]**salve** [sælv], *v.t.* (*Naut.*) retten, bergen (*see* **salvage**).

[2]**salve, 1.** *s.* 1. die Salbe; 2. (*fig.*) der Trost, Balsam, das Trostpflaster, Heilpflaster, Heilmittel, Beruhigungsmittel, Linderungsmittel. **2.** *v.t.* 1. (*obs.*) einsalben; 2. (*usu. fig.*) besänftigen, beschwichtigen, beruhigen, lindern.

salver ['sælvə], *s.* der Präsentierteller, das Servierbrett.

[1]**salvo** ['sælvou], *s.* 1. (*Law*) der Vorbehalt, die Vorbehaltsklausel; 2. Rettungsmöglichkeit, der Rettungsweg.

[2]**salvo,** *s.* (*Mil.*) die Salve; (*Av.*) der Reihenwurf, Massenabwurf.

salvor ['sælvə], *s.* der Berger, das Bergungsschiff.

Samaritan [sə'mæritən], *s.* (*B.*) der (die) Samariter(in); (*B., coll.*) ***good –,*** barmherziger Samariter.

same [seim], *pron., adj.* ***the –,*** derselbe, dieselbe, dasselbe, der (*etc.*) gleiche *or* nämliche, eben der (*etc.*); ***the very –, just*** or ***exactly the –,*** genau dasselbe, ebendasselbe; (*coll.*) ***– here,*** so geht es mir auch; ***it is all the – to me,*** es ist mir einerlei *or* mir ganz gleich; (*coll.*) ***all*** or ***just the –,*** gleichwohl, gleichviel, trotzdem; ***no longer the – man,*** nicht mehr der alte; ***much the –*** (***thing***), (so) ziemlich dasselbe; ***one and the –*** (***thing***), ein und dasselbe; ***it comes to the – thing,*** es kommt *or* läuft auf dasselbe hinaus; ***the – old story,*** die alte Geschichte, das alte Lied; ***at the – time,*** zur gleichen *or* selben Zeit (***as,*** wie); (*fig.*) jedoch, nichtsdestoweniger; (*coll.*) ***– to you,*** gleichfalls.

samelet ['sæmlit], *s.* junger Lachs.

sameness ['seimnis], *s.* 1. die Gleichheit, Identität; 2. Eintönigkeit, Einförmigkeit.

Samnite ['sæmnait], *s.* (*B.*) der (die) Samniter(in).

Samoan [sə'mouən], **1.** *adj.* samoanisch. **2.** *s.* der (die) Samoaner(in).

Samoyed(e) ['sæmɔjed], **1.** *adj.* samojedisch. **2.** *s.* der Samojede (die Samojedin).

sampan ['sæmpæn], *s.* der Sampan.

sample [sɑ:mpl], **1.** *s.* die Probe (*also fig.*), (*Comm.*) das Muster; ***according to*** or ***as per*** or ***up to –,*** mustergemäß, laut Probe; ***– post,*** Muster ohne Wert; ***random –,*** die Stichprobe. **2.** *v.t.* 1. eine Probe nehmen von, nach Proben beurteilen; 2. (*fig.*) probieren, kosten. **sampler,** *s.* das Stick(muster)tuch, Stickmuster.

Samson ['sæmsən], *s.* (*B.*) Simson (*m.*).

sanative ['sænətiv], *adj.* heilend, heilkräftig, Heil–, heilsam. **sanatorium** [–'tɔ:riəm], *s.* (*pl.* **-ria**) die Heilanstalt, das Sanatorium, Erholungsheim, Genesungsheim. **sanatory** [–təri], *adj. See* **sanative.**

sanctification [sæŋktifi'keiʃən], *s.* die Heiligung, Weihung, Heiligsprechung. **sanctify** ['sæŋktifai], *v.t.* 1. heiligen (*also fig.*), weihen; 2. rechtfertigen.

sanctimonious [sæŋkti'mouniəs], *adj.* scheinheilig. **sanctimoniousness, sanctimony** ['sæŋktiməni], *s.* die Scheinheiligkeit.

sanction ['sæŋkʃən], **1.** *s.* 1. die Bestätigung, Genehmigung, Gutheißung; ***give – to,*** genehmigen, gutheißen, billigen; 2. (*Law*) die Sanktion, Strafmaßnahme, Zwangsmaßnahme; *pl.* (*Pol.*) Sanktionen (*pl.*); ***impose –s,*** Sanktionen auferlegen (***on,*** *Dat.*). **2.** *v.t.* 1. billigen, gutheißen, genehmigen; 2. bekräftigen, bestätigen, sanktionieren.

sanctitude ['sæŋktitju:d] (*rare*), **sanctity** [–ti], *s.* die Heiligkeit, Unverletzlichkeit.

sanctuary ['sæŋktjuəri], *s.* 1. (innerstes) Heiligtum, Allerheiligste(s), die Hochaltarstätte; 2. (*fig.*) heiliger Zufluchtsort, das Asyl, die Freistatt; ***seek –,*** Schutz *or* Zuflucht suchen; ***right of –,*** das Asylrecht.

sanctum ['sæŋktəm], *s.* 1. das Heiligtum, Allerheiligste; 2. (*coll.*) das Privatzimmer, Studierzimmer. **sanctus,** *s.* (*R.C.*) der Sanktus.

sand [sænd], **1.** *s.* 1. der Sand; ***build on –,*** auf Sand bauen; ***make ropes of –,*** leeres Stroh dreschen; ***his –s are running out,*** seine Zeit ist bald um, seine Uhr ist abgelaufen, seine Augenblicke *or* Tage sind gezählt; 2. *pl.* das Sandufer, die Sandbank, die Sandwüste. **2.** *v.t.* 1. mit Sand bestreuen; 2. (*Carp.*) (ab)schmirgeln.

[1]**sandal** [sændl], *s.* die Sandale.

[2]**sandal, sandalwood,** *s.* das Sandelholz; ***–*** (***tree***), der Sandelbaum.

sand|bag, 1. *s.* der Sandsack. **2.** *v.t.* 1. mit Sandsäcken befestigen *or* bekleiden *or* bedecken *or* ausbauen; 2. (*coll.*) niederschlagen. **–bank,** *s.* die Sandbank. **–blast, 1.** *s.* das Sandstrahlgebläse. **2.** *v.t.* sandstrahlen. **–boy,** *s.* (*only in*) ***happy as a –,*** kreuzfidel. **--casting,** *s.* der Sandguß. **--castle,** *s.* die Sandburg. **--drift,** *s.* der Flugsand, Treibsand. **sander,** *s.* (*Tech.*) 1. *See* **sandblast, 1**; 2. die Schleifmaschine.

sanderling ['sændəliŋ], *s.* (*Orn.*) der Sanderling (*Calidris alba*).

sand|glass, *s.* die Sanduhr. **--hill,** *s.* die Düne. **-hopper,** *s.* (*Zool.*) der Strandfloh. **sandiness,** *s.* die Sandigkeit; Sandfarbigkeit.

sandiver ['sændivə], *s.* (*Glassw.*) die Glasgalle.

sand|man, *s.* das Sandmännchen. **--martin,** *s.* (*Orn.*) die Uferschwalbe (*Riparia riparia*). **-paper,** **1.** *s.* das Sandpapier. **2.** *v.t.* (ab)schmirgeln. **-piper,** *s.* (*Orn.*) der Strandläufer. **-pit,** *s.* die Sandgrube. **--shoe,** *s.* der Strandschuh. **-stone,** *s.* der Sandstein. **-storm,** *s.* der Sandsturm. **--table,** *s.* der Sandkasten.

sandwich ['sændwidʒ], **1.** *s.* belegtes Butterbrot. **2.** *v.t.* (*fig.*) einlegen, einschieben, dazwischenschieben, einklemmen, einpferchen. **sandwich|-board,** *s.* wandelndes Plakat. **--box,** *s.* die Butterbrotsdose. **--man,** *s.* der Plakatträger. **--spread,** *s.* der Brotaufstrich.

sandwort ['sændwəːt], *s.* (*Bot.*) das Sandkraut. **sandy,** *adj.* 1. sandig, Sand–; 2. sandfarben, rotblond (*hair*). **sand-yacht,** *s.* der Strandsegler.

sane [sein], *adj.* 1. geistig gesund, bei gesundem Verstande; 2. vernünftig.

sang, *imperf. of* **sing.**

sang-froid [sɑ̃'frwaː], *s.* 1. die Kaltblütigkeit; 2. Gelassenheit, Fassung, Geistesgegenwart.

sangrail [sæn'greil], *s.* Heiliger Gral.

sanguification [sæŋgwifi'keiʃən], *s.* die Blutbildung. **sanguinary** ['sæŋgwinəri], *adj.* 1. blutig, mörderisch; 2. blutrünstig, blutdürstig, grausam. **sanguine** ['sæŋgwin], *adj.* 1. (*fig.*) leichtblütig, lebhaft, heiter, optimistisch; zuversichtlich (*of*, auf (*Acc.*)); ***most – expectations,*** kühnste *or* hoffnungsfreudigste Erwartungen; 2. (*Her., Poet.*) blutrot; 3. (*obs. Med.*) blutreich, vollblütig, heißblütig, sanguinisch. **sanguineous** [–'winiəs], *adj.* 1. Blut–; 2. blutreich, vollblütig; 3. blutrot.

Sanhedrin ['sænidrin], *s.* das Synedrium, die Ratsversammlung, Hoher Rat (*of Jews*).

sanitarium [sæni'tɛəriəm], *s. See* **sanatorium.** **sanitary** ['sænitəri], *adj.* Gesundheits–, Sanitär–, hygienisch; – ***arrangements,*** sanitäre Einrichtungen; – ***inspector,*** Beamte(r) der Gesundheitspolizei; – ***towel,*** die (Damen)binde. **sanitation** [–'teiʃən], *s.* 1. sanitäre Einrichtungen (*pl.*); 2. die Hygiene.

sanity ['sæniti], *s.* 1. geistige Gesundheit, die Zurechnungsfähigkeit; 2. gesunder Verstand, die Vernunft.

sank [sæŋk], *imperf. of* **sink.**

sans [sænz], *prep.* (*obs.*) ohne.

sansculotte [sɑ̃kjuː'lɔt], *s.* 1. (*Hist.*) der Sansculotte; 2. extremer Republikaner.

sanserif [sæn'serif], *s.* (*Typ.*) die Schrift ohne Feinstriche.

[1]**sap** [sæp], *s.* 1. (*Bot.*) der Saft; 2. (*fig.*) das (Lebens)mark, die Kraft; 3. (*sl.*) der Einfaltspinsel, Dussel.

[2]**sap,** **1.** *s.* (*Mil.*) bedeckter Laufgraben, die Sappe. **2.** *v.i.* sappieren. **3.** *v.t.* 1. unterminieren, untergraben; 2. (*fig.*) schwächen, erschöpfen, auszehren (*strength*). **saphead,** *s.* der Sappenkopf.

sapid ['sæpid], *adj.* 1. schmackhaft; 2. (*fig.*) angenehm, interessant. **sapidity** [–'piditi], die Schmackhaftigheit.

sapience ['seipiəns], *s.* die Weisheit (*oft. iron.*), Scheinweisheit. **sapient,** *adj.* weise (*iron.*), (über)klug.

sapless ['sæplis], *adj.* 1. saftlos, dürr; 2. (*fig.*) kraftlos, seicht, fad(e).

sapling ['sæpliŋ], *s.* 1. junger Baum, der Schößling; 2. (*fig.*) junger Windhund; 3. der Jüngling, Grünschnabel.

saponaceous [sæpə'neiʃəs], *adj.* seifig, seifenartig, seifenhaltig, Seifen–. **saponification** [–pɔnifi'keiʃən], *s.* die Seifenbildung, Verseifung. **saponify** [–'pɔnifai], *v.t.* (*v.i.*) zur Seife machen (werden), verseifen.

sapper ['sæpə], *s.* (*Mil. coll.*) der Pionier.

Sapphic ['sæfik], **1.** *adj.* sapphisch. **2.** *s.* (*usu. pl.*) sapphische Verse (*pl.*), sapphische Strophe.

sapphire ['sæfaiə], **1.** *s.* 1. der Saphir; 2. das Saphirblau. **2.** *adj.* 1. Saphir–; 2. (*Her.*) blau.

sappy ['sæpi], *adj.* 1. saftig; 2. (*fig.*) kraftvoll, markig; 3. (*sl.*) dämlich, doof, dusselig, albern.

saprolite ['sæprəlait], *s.* (*Geol.*) das Zerfallgestein. **saprophyte** [–fait], *s.* (*Bot.*) die Fäulnispflanze.

sapwood ['sæpwud], *s.* der Splint, das Splintholz, Grünholz.

saraband ['særəbænd], *s.* die Sarabande.

Saracen ['særəsn], **1.** *s.* der Sarazen (die Sarazenin). **2.** *adj.* sarazenisch.

sarcasm ['sɑːkæzm], *s.* bitterer Hohn, beißender Spott, der Sarkasmus. **sarcastic** [–'kæstik], *adj.* sarkastisch, höhnisch, beißend.

sarcenet ['sɑːsənit], *s.* der Seidentaft, Sarsenett.

sarcode ['sɑːkoud], *s.* (*Biol.*) die Sarkode.

sarcoma [sɑː'koumə], *s.* (*pl.* **-ta**) (*Med.*) das Sarkom. **sarcomatoid, sarcomatous,** *adj.* Sarkom–, sarkomartig, sarkomähnlich.

sarcophagous [sɑː'kɔfəgəs], *adj.* fleischfressend. **sarcophagus,** *s.* der Steinsarg, Sarkophag.

sard [sɑːd], *s.* der Sard(er).

sardine [sɑː'diːn], *s.* (*Ichth.*) die Sardine; ***packed like –s,*** zusammengepfercht wie die Heringe.

Sardinia [sɑː'diniə], *s.* Sardinien (*n.*). **Sardinian,** **1.** *s.* 1. der Sarde (die Sardin); 2. (*language*) das Sardisch(e). **2.** *adj.* sardinisch.

sardius ['sɑːdiəs], *s. See* **sard.**

sardonic [sɑː'dɔnik], *adj.* sardonisch, höhnisch, zynisch, hämisch, bitter.

sardonyx ['sɑːdəniks], *s.* der Sardonyx.

sari ['sɑːri], *s.* der Sari.

sark [sɑːk], *s.* (*Scots*) das Hemd.

sarmentose ['sɑːməntous], **sarmentous** [–'mentəs], *adj.* (*Bot.*) rankig, rankend.

sarong [sə'rɔŋ], *s.* der Sarong.

sarsaparilla [sɑːs(ə)pə'rilə], *s.* die Sarsaparilla.

sarsen [sɑːsn], *s.* (*also* **--stone**) (*Geol.*) der Sandsteinfindling.

sartorial [sɑː'tɔːriəl], *adj.* 1. Schneider–; 2. Kleidung(s)–. **sartorius,** *s.* (*Anat.*) der Schneidermuskel.

[1]**sash** [sæʃ], *s.* die Schärpe, Leibbinde.

[2]**sash,** *s.* (schiebbarer) Fensterrahmen. **sash|-cord,** *s.* der Fenstergurt. **--window,** *s.* das Schiebefenster, Aufziehfenster.

sassafras ['sæsəfræs], *s.* (*Bot.*) der Sassafras.

Sassenach ['sæsənæx], *s.* (*Scots*) der Engländer.

sat [sæt], *imperf., p.p. of* **sit.**

Satan ['seitən], *s.* der Teufel, Satan. **satanic(al)** [sə'tænik(l)], *adj.* satanisch, Satans–; (*fig.*) teuflisch.

satchel [sætʃl], *s.* der Ranzen, die Schulmappe, Schultasche.

[1]**sate** [seit], *v.t.* (*usu. pass.*) (über)sättigen.

[2]**sate** [sæt], *obs. imperf. of* **sit.**

sateen [sæ'tiːn], *s.* der Satin, Baumwollatlas, Englisches Leder.

sateless ['seitlis], *adj.* (*Poet.*) unersättlich.

satellite ['sætəlait], *s.* 1. (*Astr.*) der Trabant, Satellit; 2. (*rocketry*) (Erd)satellit; 3. (*fig.*) Anhänger; – ***state,*** der Satellitenstaat; – ***town,*** die Trabantenstadt.

satiate ['seiʃieit], *v.t.* 1. übersättigen, saturieren; 2. (vollauf) befriedigen, sättigen. **satiation** [–'eiʃən], *s.* die (Über)sättigung. **satiety** [sə'taiəti], *s.* die Sattheit, Übersättigung (*of*, mit), der Überdruß (an (*Dat.*)).

satin ['sætin], **1.** *s.* der Atlas, Seidensatin. **2.** *v.t.* satinieren, glätten (*paper*). **3.** *adj.* 1. Atlas–; – ***paper,*** das Atlaspapier; 2. glatt, glänzend; (*Ent.*) – ***beauty,*** der Seidenspanner; – ***finish,*** die Mattierung (*silver etc.*). **satinet** [–'net], *s.* der Baumwollsatin, Halbatlas. **satinwood,** *s.* das Satinholz, Seidenholz. **satiny,** *adj.* atlasartig, seidig, glänzend.

satire ['sætaiə], *s.* 1. die Satire, Spottschrift, das

Spottgedicht; 2. die Ironie, der Hohn (*on*, auf (*Acc.*)). **satiric(al)** [sə'tirik(l)], *adj.* satirisch, spöttisch, höhnisch. **satirist** ['sætirist], *s.* der Satiriker. **satirize** ['sætiraiz], *v.t.* verspotten, bespötteln, geißeln.

satisfaction [sætis'fækʃən], *s.* 1. die Befriedigung, Zufriedenstellung; Zufriedenheit, Genugtuung (*of doing*, zu tun); ***find* –**, Befriedigung finden (*in doing*, zu tun); ***give* –**, befriedigen; sich bewähren; ***to the* – *of***, zur Zufriedenheit von; 2. die Satisfaktion (*duel*); ***demand* (*give*) –**, Satisfaktion verlangen (geben); 3. (*Theol.*) die Sühne, Buße; 4. Tilgung, Erfüllung (*of a debt*). **satisfactoriness** [–'fæktərinis], *s.* das Befriedigende. **satisfactory** [–'fæktəri], *adj.* 1. befriedigend; genügend, zufriedenstellend (*to*, für); ***be* –**, genügen, hinreichen; ***– explanation***, einleuchtende Erklärung; 2. (*Theol.*) sühnend; ***be – for***, sühnen.

satisfy ['sætisfai], **1.** *v.t.* 1. befriedigen (*requirements*); erfüllen (*request*); Genüge leisten (*Dat.*) (*demands*); nachkommen (*Dat.*) (*obligations*); 2. stillen, sättigen (*hunger*); ***be satisfied***, satt sein, genug haben; 3. genügen (*Dat.*), zufriedenstellen (*a p.*); ***– the examiners***, das Examen mit 'genügend' bestehen; ***be satisfied with***, zufrieden sein *or* sich begnügen mit; ***rest satisfied***, sich zufriedengeben; 4. versichern (*Dat.*), überzeugen (*a p.*); ***– o.s.***, sich überzeugen *or* vergewissern; ***be satisfied***, überzeugt sein (*of*, von; *that*, daß). **2.** *v.i.* 1. (*of a p.*) Genüge leisten, Genugtuung geben (*Dat.*); 2. (*of a th.*) zufriedenstellend *or* befriedigend sein, nichts zu wünschen übriglassen. **satisfying** [–faiiŋ], *adj.* 1. befriedigend, ausreichend, genügend, hinlänglich; 2. sättigend.

satrap ['sætrəp], *s.* der Satrap, tyrannischer Statthalter. **satrapy** [–i], *s.* die Satrapie, Statthalterschaft.

saturable ['sætʃərəbl], *adj.* zu sättigen(d), sättigungsfähig. **saturant, 1.** *adj.* sättigend. **2.** *s.* neutralisierendes *or* Säuren absorbierendes Mittel. **saturate** [–eit], *v.t.* 1. (*Chem.*) imprägnieren, sättigen; 2. durchtränken, durchsetzen; (*coll.*) ***be –d***, durchnäßt sein *or* werden, pudelnaß sein; 3. (*fig.*) ***– o.s. in***, sich versenken *or* vertiefen in (*Acc.*). **saturated,** *adj.* 1. durchnäßt, durchtränkt, gesättigt (*with*, von); 2. satt, kräftig (*colour*). **saturation** [–'reiʃən], *s.* 1. (*Chem.*) die Sättigung; ***– point***, der Sättigungspunkt; 2. die Durchtränkung, Durchnässung, Durchsetzung, Durchwässerung; (*Av.*) ***– bombing***, der Bombenteppichwurf.

Saturday ['sætədi], *s.* der Samstag, Sonnabend.

Saturn ['sætə:n], *s.* 1. (*Myth.*) Saturn(us) (*m.*); 2. (*Astr.*) der Saturn; 3. (*Her.*) das Schwarz. **Saturnalia** [–'neiliə], *pl.* Saturnalien (*pl.*). **Saturnalian,** *adj.* saturnalisch. **saturnine** ['sætənain], *adj.* (*fig.*) finster, düster, schwerfällig, verschlossen.

satyr ['sætə], *s.* 1. der Satyr, Waldgott; 2. (*fig.*) lüsterner Mensch. **satyriasis** [–ti'raiəsis], *s.* gesteigerter Geschlechtstrieb des Mannes. **satyric** [sə'tirik], *adj.* satyrartig, Satyr–.

sauce [sɔ:s], **1.** *s.* 1. die Soße, Sauce, Tunke; (*Prov.*) ***what's – for the goose is – for the gander***, was dem einen recht ist, ist dem andern billig; (*Prov.*) ***hunger is the best –***, Hunger ist der beste Koch; 2. (*Tech.*) die Brühe, Beize, Soße; (*fig.*) Würze; 3. (*coll.*) Frechheit, Unverschämtheit. **2.** *v.t.* 1. würzen; 2. unverschämt sein zu, frech reden mit. **sauce|-boat,** *s.* die Sauciere, Soßenschüssel, der Soßennapf. **–pan** [–pən], *s.* der Kochtopf, Schmortopf, die Pfanne.

saucer ['sɔ:sə], *s.* die Untertasse. **saucer|-eyed,** *adj.* glotzäugig. **–-eyes,** *pl.* Glotzaugen (*pl.*).

sauciness ['sɔ:sinis], *s.* (*coll.*) die Frechheit, Dreistigkeit, Unverschämtheit, Keckheit. **saucy** [–i], *adj.* (*coll.*) 1. dreist, unverschämt, frech, keck, naseweis; 2. flott, schmuck.

Saudi| Arabia ['saudi ə'reibiə], *s.* Saudi-Arabien (*n.*). **– Arabian, 1.** *s.* der (die) Saudiaraber(in). **2.** *adj.* saudiarabisch.

sauna ['sɔ:nə], *s.* die Sauna.

saunter ['sɔ:ntə], **1.** *s.* 1. das (Umher)schlendern; 2. gemächlicher Spaziergang. **2.** *v.i.* (umher)-schlendern, bummeln.

saurian ['sɔ:riən], **1.** *s.* der Saurier. **2.** *adj.* Saurier–, Eidechsen–.

sausage ['sɔsidʒ], *s.* die Wurst. **sausage|-balloon,** *s.* der Fesselballon. **–-machine,** *s.* die Hackmaschine. **–-meat,** *s.* die Wurst(fleisch)masse. **–-roll,** *s.* die Wurstpastete.

sauté ['soutei], *adj.* (*Cul.*) geschwenkt.

savable ['seivəbl], *adj.* rettbar, zu erretten(d).

savage ['sævidʒ], **1.** *adj.* 1. wild, ungezähmt (*beasts*), grimmig, grausam, brutal, roh (*behaviour*), primitiv, barbarisch, unzivilisiert (*tribes*); 2. (*coll.*) wütend, rasend, wild; 3. (*Her.*) nackt. **2.** *s.* der Barbar, Wilde(r). **3.** *v.t.* 1. brutal behandeln (*a p.*); 2. (*as a horse*) anfallen (*a p.*). **savageness,** *s.* 1. die Wildheit, Grausamkeit, Roheit; 2. Wut, Heftigkeit. **savagery** [–ri], *s.* die Wildheit, Barbarei, wilder Urzustand.

savanna(h) [sə'vænə], *s.* die Savanne.

savant ['sævã], *s.* Gelehrte(r).

[1]**save** [seiv], **1.** *v.t.* 1. (er)retten, befreien (*from*, aus *or* vor (*Dat.*) *or* von); ***– his life***, ihm das Leben retten; 2. (*Theol.*) erlösen, retten; 3. schützen, bewahren, sichern (*from*, vor (*Dat.*)); ***to – appearances***, (um) den Schein (zu) wahren; ***– one's face***, sich vor Demütigung schützen; (*Spt.*) ***– the game***, das Spiel retten; ***God – the Queen!*** Gott schütze *or* erhalte die Königin! ***– the situation***, die Situation retten; 4. (*Naut.*) bergen; 5. aufbewahren, aufheben, aufsparen; ***save your breath!*** schone deine Lunge! spare dir deine Worte! 6. (ein)sparen, sparsam umgehen mit; ***– money***, Geld sparen; ***to – time***, um Zeit zu gewinnen, um keine Zeit zu verlieren; 7. (ihn mit etwas) verschonen, (ihm etwas) ersparen; schonen; ***– o.s.***, sich schonen; ***– o.s. the trouble***, sich (*Dat.*) die Mühe ersparen; 8. ausnehmen; ***– the expression!*** entschuldigen Sie den Ausdruck! 9. (*Footb. etc.*) ***– a goal***, den Torschuß abwehren. **2.** *v.i.* (*also – up*) (auf)-sparen. **3.** *s.* (*Footb.*) die Abwehr, Verhinderung eines Tors.

[2]**save,** *prep., conj.* außer (*Dat.*), abgesehen von, ausgenommen; ***– and except***, mit alleiniger Ausnahme von; ***– for***, abgesehen von; ***the last – one***, der Vorletzte; ***– only he***, ausgenommen er allein; ***– that***, ausgenommen davon, daß.

save-all, *s.* 1. der Lichtsparer; 2. Tropfenfänger.

saveloy ['sævəlɔi], *s.* die Zervelatwurst.

saver ['seivə], *s.* 1. der Retter; ***life –***, der Lebensretter; 2. der Sparer; 3. das Ersparnis (*of*, an (*Dat.*)); ***labour –***, das Arbeitsersparnis. **saving, 1.** *adj.* 1. sparsam, haushälterisch (*of*, mit); 2. (*as suff.*) –(er)sparend; 3. (*Law*) Vorbehalts–; ***– clause***, der Vorbehalt, die Vorbehaltsklausel; 4. rettend; ***– grace***, (*Theol.*) seligmachende Gnade, (*coll.*) aufwiegender *or* ausgleichender *or* rettender Umstand. **2.** *s.* 1. das Sparen, die (*Austr.* das) Ersparnis (*of*, an (*Dat.*)); 2. (*usu. pl.*) Ersparnisse (*pl.*), das Spargeld, die Rücklage; 3. (*Law*) der Vorbehalt. **3.** *prep., conj.* außer, ausgenommen; ***– you***, ausgenommen du, dich ausgenommen, außer dir; ***– your presence***, mit Verlaub (zu sagen).

savings|-account, *s.* das Sparkonto. **–-bank,** *s.* die Sparkasse; ***post-office –***, die Postsparkasse. **–-certificate,** *s.* der Sparbon.

savior (*Am.*), **saviour** ['seivjə], *s.* 1. der (Er)retter, Erlöser; 2. (*Theol.*) Heiland.

savoir|-faire ['sævwɑ:'fɛə], *s.* die Gewandtheit, das Feingefühl, Takt(gefühl). **–-vivre** [–'vi:vr], *s.* die Lebensart.

savor (*Am.*), **savour** ['seivə], **1.** *s.* 1. (charakteristischer) Geschmack; 2. (*fig*) der Beigeschmack, Anflug. **2.** *v.i.* 1. (*usu. fig.*) schmecken, riechen (*of*, nach); 2. (*fig.*) einen Anstrich haben (*of*, von), aussehen (wie). **3.** *v.t.* würdigen, auskosten, recht genießen. **savouriness** [–rinis], *s.* 1. die Schmackhaftigkeit; 2. der Wohlgeschmack, Wohlgeruch. **savourless,** *adj.* geschmacklos, fad(e). **savoury**

[-ri], **1.** *adj.* schmackhaft, würzig, pikant. **2.** *s.* pikantes Gericht.

savoy [sə'vɔi], *s.* der Wirsing(kohl).

savvy ['sævi], **1.** *s.* (*sl.*) der Verstand, das Köpfchen, die Grütze. **2.** *v.i.* (*sl.*) kapieren.

¹saw [sɔ:], *imperf. of* **see.**

²saw, *s.* der Spruch, das Sprichwort.

³saw, 1. *s.* die Säge; ***musical* –,** singende Säge. **2.** *irr.v.t.* sägen; **– *the tree down,*** den Baum umsägen; **– *all the wood up,*** all das Holz einsägen; (*fig.*) **– *the air,*** in der Luft herumfuchteln. **3.** *v.i.* sich sägen lassen. **saw|bones,** *s.* (*sl.*) der Knochenbrecher. **–dust,** *s.* das Sägemehl. **--fish,** *s.* der Sägefisch. **– fly,** *s.* die Sägewespe. **sawing|-horse, --jack,** *s.* der Sägebock. **sawmill,** *s.* die Sägemühle. **sawn,** *p.p. of* **³saw.**

sawney ['sɔ:ni], *s.* (*coll.*) 1. der Schotte; 2. Einfaltspinsel, Tölpel.

saw|-set, *s.* das Schränkeisen. **–tooth,** *adj.* (*Elec.*) Kipp–. **–toothed,** *adj.* säge(zahn)förmig, gezähnt, zackig.

sawyer ['sɔ:jə], *s.* der (Holz)säger.

saxe [sæks], *s.* das Sächsischblau.

saxifrage ['sæksifr(e)idʒ], *s.* (*Bot.*) der Wiesensteinbrech, Körnersteinbrech.

Saxon ['sæksən], **1.** *s.* 1. der Sachse (die Sächsin); 2. (*language*) das Sächsisch(e). **2.** *adj.* sächsisch. **Saxony,** *s.* Sachsen (*n.*).

saxophone ['sæksəfoun], *s.* das Saxophon. **saxophonist** [-ist, -'sɔfənist], *s.* der Saxophonspieler.

say [sei], **1.** *irr.v.t.* 1. sagen; äußern; erzählen, berichten; ***what have you to – for yourself?*** was können Sie zu Ihrer Rechtfertigung sagen? ***have nothing to – for o.s.,*** nicht viel(e) Worte machen; ***no sooner said than done,*** gesagt, getan; ***to – nothing of,*** ganz zu schweigen von, geschweige (*Nom.*); ***what do you – to it?*** was sagst du dazu? wie denkst du darüber? ***what I – is,*** ich meine; ***sad to –,*** bedauerlicherweise; ***when all is said and done,*** letzten Endes, schließlich und endlich; ***he is said to be,*** er soll sein; ***that is –ing a great deal,*** das besagt sehr viel, das will viel sagen; ***never – die!*** nur nicht verzagt! **– *nay,*** verweigern, abschlagen; **– *the word!*** schlag ein! (***shall we***) **– *20 years,*** zum Beispiel *or* etwa 20 Jahre; 2. aufsagen, hersagen (*one's lessons etc.*); **– *grace,*** das Tischgebet lesen; **– *one's prayers,*** beten, seine Gebete verrichten. **2.** *irr.v.i.* die Meinung äußern; gesagt werden; ***I –!*** hör *or* sag mal! ich muß schon sagen! fürwahr! ***you don't –*** (***so***)***!*** was Sie nicht sagen! ***just as you –,*** genau wie Sie sagen; ***it –s here,*** hier steht (geschrieben), hier wird gesagt, hier heißt es; ***that is to –,*** das heißt, das will sagen; ***that goes without –ing,*** das versteht sich von selbst; ***who –s so?*** wer sagt das? ***they –, it is said,*** man sagt, es heißt. **3.** *s.* ***final –,*** letztes Wort, die Entscheidung; ***have a*** (***no***) ***– in,*** (nicht) mitzusprechen haben bei; ***have one's –,*** seine Meinung äußern *or* sagen (dürfen) (***on,*** über (*Acc.*) *or* zu), zu Worte kommen (dürfen), sich aussprechen (über (*Acc.*)); ***now it is his –,*** jetzt kommt er daran *or* zu Wort.

saying ['seiiŋ], *s.* 1. das Reden; ***that goes without –,*** das versteht sich von selbst; ***there is no –,*** man kann nicht wissen *or* sagen; 2. die Rede, Äußerung, der Ausspruch; 3. die Redensart; das Sprichwort; ***as the – goes*** or ***is,*** wie man zu sagen pflegt.

say-so, *s.* (*coll.*) 1. die Behauptung, Versicherung; ***only on his –,*** nur nach dem, was er sagt; 2. die Anweisung, der Befehl; ***give the –,*** den Befehl erlassen, den Auftrag erteilen, einwilligen, sich zufrieden geben.

scab [skæb], **1.** *s.* 1. der Grind, Schorf, die Kruste (*of wound*); 2. Krätze, Räude (*in sheep etc.*); 3. (*coll.*) der Streikbrecher; 4. (*sl.*) Lump, Schuft. **2.** *v.i.* (*also – over*) Schorf bilden, verschorfen, (sich) verkrusten.

scabbard ['skæbəd], **1.** *s.* die (Degen)scheide. **2.** *v.t.* in die Scheide stecken.

scabbed [skæbd], *adj.* (*esp. Bot.*) schorfig; *see also* **scabby. scabbiness,** *s.* 1. die Grindigkeit; 2. Räudigkeit; 3. (*coll.*) Schäbigkeit, Erbärmlichkeit.

scabby, *adj.* 1. grindig, schorfig; 2. (*of sheep*) räudig; 3. (*coll.*) schäbig, erbärmlich, schuftig, lumpig.

scabies ['skeibiz], *s.* 1. (*Med.*) die Krätze; 2. (*Vet.*) Räude.

¹scabious ['skeibiəs], *adj.* 1. krätzig, skabiös; 2. (*Vet.*) räudig.

²scabious, *s.* (*Bot.*) die Skabiose.

scabrous ['skeibrəs], *adj.* 1. (*Bot.*) rauh, schuppig; 2. (*fig.*) kniff(e)lig, heikel, schlüpfrig, anstößig.

scaffold ['skæfould], *s.* 1. das (Bau)gerüst, Gestell; 2. Schafott, Blutgerüst. **scaffolding,** *s.* 1. *See* **scaffold,** 1; 2. das Material für das Gerüst, Rüstzeug. **scaffold(ing)-pole,** *s.* der Gerüstbaum.

scalable ['skeiləbl], *adj.* ersteigbar.

scalar ['skeilə], **1.** *adj.* 1. (*Math.*) skalar, ungerichtet; 2. (*Bot.*) leiterförmig. **2.** *s.* (*Math.*) der Skalar.

¹scald [skɔ:ld], *s.* der Skalde, Barde.

²scald, 1. *s.* die Verbrühung, Brandwunde. **2.** *v.t.* 1. verbrennen, verbrühen; 2. (*Cul.*) abkochen, abbrühen; 3. **– *out,*** auskochen, sterilisieren. **scalding,** *adj.* brühend; **– *hot,*** brühheiß.

¹scale [skeil], **1.** *s.* 1. die Schale, Hülse; 2. Schuppe (*of fish, also Med., fig.*); ***the –s fell from his eyes,*** ihm gingen die Augen auf *or* fielen die Schuppen von den Augen; 3. (*Tech.*) der Hammerschlag, Zunder, Glühspan; Kesselstein; Zahnstein (*on teeth*). **2.** *v.t.* 1. abschuppen (*fish etc.*); 2. (ab)schälen, abschaben, abkrusten, enthäuten; 3. ausbrennen; 4. Kesselstein entfernen aus, abklopfen, ausklopfen (*a boiler*); den Zahnstein entfernen (*Dat.*). **3.** *v.i.* (*also – off*) sich (ab)schuppen *or* abschälen, abblättern.

²scale, 1. *s.* die Waagschale; (*usu. pl.*) Waage (*also Astr.*); ***pair of –s,*** eine Waage; ***hold the –s even,*** gerecht urteilen; ***throw into the –***(***s***), geltend machen, in die Waagschale werfen; (*fig.*) ***tip*** or ***turn the –s,*** ins Gewicht fallen, den Ausschlag geben. **2.** *v.t.* wiegen. **3.** *v.i.* gewogen werden.

³scale, 1. *s.* 1. die Stufenleiter, Abstufung, Staffelung; Gradeinteilung, Skala; **– *of charges,*** die Gebührenordnung; **– *of salaries,*** die Gehaltsstaffelung; ***social –,*** die Gesellschaftsstufe; ***wage –,*** der Lohntarif, die Lohnskala, Lohngruppe; 2. (*Mus.*) die Tonleiter; ***descending –,*** absteigende Tonleiter; ***play*** or ***practise one's –s,*** Tonleitern üben; 3. der Maßstab, das Größenverhältnis; (***according***) ***to –,*** maßstab(s)getreu, maßstab(s)gerecht, maßstäblich; ***reduced –,*** verjüngter Maßstab; ***to a – of 1:10,*** im Maßstab 1:10; **– *model,*** verkleinertes Modell; 4. (*coll.*) das Maß, der Umfang; ***on a large –,*** in großem Umfang, in weitem Maße; im großen. **2.** *v.t.* 1. ersteigen, erklettern; (*Mil.*) erstürmen; 2. einen Maßstab festlegen für; **– *down,*** maßstäblich verkleinern; (*fig.*) (herunter)drücken, herunterschrauben (*wages etc.*); **– *up,*** maßstäblich vergrößern; (*fig.*) erhöhen, in die Höhe treiben (*wages*).

scale|-armour, *s.* der Schuppenpanzer. **--beam,** *s.* der Waagebalken. **scaled,** *adj.* 1. schuppig; 2. abgeschuppt; 3. mit einer Skala. **scaleless,** *adj.* schuppenlos.

scalene ['skeili:n], **1.** *adj.* (*Geom.*) ungleichseitig, schiefwink(e)lig. **2.** *s.* ungleichseitiges Dreieck.

scale|-paper, *s.* das Millimeterpapier. **--rule,** *s.* der Maßstock.

scaliness ['skeilinis], *s.* die Schuppigkeit.

scaling ['skeiliŋ], *s.* 1. das (Ab)schuppen; Abblättern; 2. (*Tech.*) die Kesselsteinentfernung; (*Dentistry*) Zahnsteinentfernung; 3. Ersteigung, das Erklettern, (*Mil.*) Erstürmen; 4. maßstab(s)getreue Zeichnung; **– *up,*** maßstäbliche Vergrößerung; (*fig.*) das Hochtreiben (*of prices etc.*); **– *down,*** maßstäbliche Verkleinerung; (*fig.*) das (Herunter)drücken (*of wages etc.*).

scaling-ladder, *s.* (*Mil.*) die Sturmleiter.

scall [skɔ:l], *s.* (*obs.*) der (Kopf)grind.

scallawag, *see* **scallywag.**

scallion [skæliən], *s.* (*Bot.*) die Schalotte.

scallop ['skæləp], **1.** *s.* 1. (*Zool.*) die Kammuschel; 2. (*Cul.*) kleine Schüssel, die Muschelform; 2. (*Dressm.*) der Kerbschnitt; die Ausbogung, Langette. **2.** *v.t.* 1. in der Schale zubereiten (*oysters etc.*); 2. bogenförmig ausschneiden, auszacken, ausbogen.

scallywag ['skæliwæg], *s.* (*coll.*) der Nichtsnutz, Lump.

scalp [skælp], **1.** *s.* 1. die Kopfhaut; 2. der Skalp, (*fig.*) die Siegestrophäe. **2.** *v.t.* skalpieren.

scalpel [skælpl], *s.* das Seziermesser.

scaly ['skeili], *adj.* 1. schuppig, geschuppt, Schuppen–; 2. schuppenartig.

scammony ['skæməni], *s.* 1. (*Bot.*) die Purgierwinde, Purgierwurzel; 2. das Skammonium.

[1]**scamp** [skæmp], *s.* 1. der Schurke, Spitzbube, Taugenichts, Lump; 2. (*usu. coll.*) Halunke, Racker.

[2]**scamp,** *v.t.* schluderig *or* schlampig ausführen, verpfuschen.

scamper ['skæmpə], **1.** *v.i.* (*usu.* – *about*) herumtollen, herumjagen, hetzen, umhersausen, sich umhertummeln; – ***off,*** davonlaufen, dahinjagen. **2.** *v.t.* (*coll.*) *see* [2]**scamp. 3.** *s.* der Lauf, Galopp.

scan [skæn], **1.** *v.t.* 1. skandieren (*verses*); 2. (*fig.*) kritisch *or* genau prüfen, scharf *or* forschend ansehen; 3. (*T.V.*) abtasten; 4. (*coll.*) überfliegen, flüchtig überblicken. **2.** *v.i.* sich skandieren (lassen).

scandal [skændl], *s.* 1. der Skandal, Anstoß, das Aufsehen, öffentliches Ärgernis; 2. die Schmach, Schande; Verleumdung, der Klatsch; ***talk*** –, klatschen, Skandalgeschichten verbreiten.

[1]**scandalize** ['skændəlaiz], *v.t.* Ärgernis geben (*Dat.*), Anstoß erregen bei, schockieren; ***be –d at,*** empört sein über (*Acc.*), Anstoß nehmen an (*Dat.*).

[2]**scandalize,** *v.t.* (*Naut.*) – ***a sail,*** das Baumnock hochschlagen.

scandalmonger ['skændlmʌŋgə], *s.* das Lästermaul, die Klatschbase, Klatsche. **scandalous,** *adj.* 1. Ärgernis *or* Anstoß erregend, anstößig, schockierend, skandalös; 2. schimpflich, schändlich, schmählich; 3. Schmäh–, verleumderisch.

Scandinavia [skændi'neiviə], *s.* Skandinavien (*n.*). **Scandinavian, 1.** *s.* der (die) Skandinavier(in). **2.** *adj.* skandinavisch.

scanner ['skænə], *s.* (*Rad.*) die Drehantenne. **scanning,** *s.* (*T.V.*) die Bildzerlegung, Abtastung; – ***frequency,*** die Rasterfrequenz.

scansion ['skænʃən], *s.* (*Metr.*) die Skandierung.

scansorial [skæn'sɔ:riəl], *adj.* (*Orn.*) Kletter–.

scant [skænt], *adj.* knapp (*of,* an (*Dat.*)), spärlich, karg, kärglich, gering; – ***of breath,*** kurzatmig. **scantiness,** *s.* die Knappheit, Kargkeit, Unzulänglichkeit.

scantling ['skæntliŋ], *s.* 1. kleine Menge; 2. kleiner Balken (*unter 13 cm. Querschnitt*); 3. vorgeschriebene Größe (*of timber or stone*); 4. (*Shipb.*) Normalmessungen (*pl.*); 5. das Faßgestell (*for casks*); 6. *pl.* Balken, Sparren, Kanthölzer, Pfosten (*pl.*).

scantness ['skæntnis], *s. See* **scantiness. scanty,** *adj.* 1. *See* **scant**; 2. ungenügend, unzulänglich.

scape [skeip], *s.* 1. (*Archit.*) der Säulenschaft; 2. (*Bot.*) Blütenschaft; 3. Schaft (*of feather*).

scapegoat ['skeipgout], *s.* der Sündenbock.

scapegrace ['skeipgreis], *s.* der Taugenichts.

scaphoid ['skæfɔid], *adj.* (*Anat.*) Kahn–.

scapula ['skæpjulə], *s.* (*Anat.*) das Schulterblatt. **scapular, 1.** *adj.* Schulter(blatt)–. **2.** *or* **scapulary,** *s.* (*Eccl.*) das Skapulier.

[1]**scar** [skɑ:], **1.** *s.* 1. die Narbe, Schramme; 2. (*fig.*) der (Schand)fleck, Makel. **2.** *v.t.* 1. schrammen; 2. (*fig.*) entstellen. **3.** *v.i.* (*also* – ***over***) vernarben.

[2]**scar,** *s.* steiler Abhang, die Klippe.

scarab ['skærəb], *s.* 1. der Skarabäus; 2. der Mistkäfer.

scarce [skɛəs], **1.** *adj.* 1. selten, rar; (*coll.*) ***make o.s.*** –, von der Bildfläche verschwinden, sich rar *or* dünne *or* aus dem Staub machen; 2. spärlich, kärglich, knapp; – ***commodities,*** Mangelwaren (*pl.*). **2.** *adv.* (*Poet.*) *see* **scarcely. scarcely,** *adv.* kaum, gerade erst, eben gerade; – ***anything,*** fast nichts; – ***ever,*** fast nie; 2. schwerlich, nur eben, nur mit Mühe. **scarceness,** *s.* 1. die Seltenheit; 2. Spärlichkeit, Knappheit, der Mangel (***of,*** an (*Dat.*)). **scarcity** [–iti], *s. See* **scarceness,** 1; – ***value,*** der Seltenheitswert; 2. der Lebensmittelmangel, die Lebensmittelnot, Lebensmittelknappheit, Teuerung.

scare [skɛə], **1.** *v.t.* 1. erschrecken, aufschrecken, in Schrecken versetzen; einen Schrecken einjagen (*Dat.*) (*a p.*); (*coll.*) ***–d stiff,*** zu Tode erschrocken; ***be –d of,*** sich fürchten vor (*Dat.*); 2. (*also* – ***away***) (ver)scheuchen, verjagen. **2.** *s.* 1. der Schreck(en), die Panik; 2. blinder Alarm. **scare|crow,** *s.* 1. die Vogelscheuche; 2. (*fig.*) das Schreckbild, der Popanz. **–monger,** *s.* der Bangemacher, Miesmacher, Unruhestifter.

[1]**scarf** [skɑ:f], **1.** *s.* 1. (*Carp.*) schräges Blatt; abgekantetes Eisen; 2. (*also* ***––joint***) die Blattverbindung, Laschung, (*Naut.*) Scherbe, der Lasch. **2.** *v.t.* 1. (*Carp.*) zusammenblatten; 2. (*Shipb.*) verlaschen, verscherben, splissen.

[2]**scarf,** *s.* 1. der Schal, das Halstuch, die Halsbinde; 2. (*Mil.*) Schärpe. **scarf-pin,** *s.* die Krawattennadel.

scarification [skɛərifi'keiʃən], *s.* (*Surg.*) das Skarifizieren, Hautritzen. **scarifier** ['skɛərifaiə], *s.* (*Agr.*) die Messeregge, der Kultivator. **scarify** ['skɛərifai], *v.t.* 1. (*Surg.*) skarifizieren, einreißen, ritzen; 2. (auf)lockern (*the soil*); 3. (*fig.*) scharf kritisieren, heruntermachen; tief verletzen (*feelings*).

scarlatina [skɑ:lə'ti:nə], *s.* das Scharlachfieber.

scarlet ['skɑ:lit], **1.** *s.* das Scharlachrot. **2.** *adj.* scharlachrot; ***flush*** or ***turn*** –, puterrot werden. **scarlet| admiral,** *s.* (*Ent.*) der Admiral. **– fever,** *s.* das Scharlachfieber. **– hat,** *s.* der Kardinalshut. **– runner,** *s.* (*Bot.*) die Feuerbohne, türkische Bohne.

scarp [skɑ:p], **1.** *s.* 1. steile Böschung; 2. (*Mil.*) die Eskarpe. **2.** *v.t.* abböschen, abdachen. **scarped** [–t], *adj.* steil, abschüssig.

scarred [skɑ:d], *adj.* narbig, narbentragend.

scarus ['skɛərəs], *s.* (*Ichth.*) der Seepapagei.

scary ['skɛəri], *adj.* (*coll.*) ängstlich, furchtsam, schreckhaft.

scathe [skeið], **1.** *s.* (*obs.*) der Schaden, Nachteil. **2.** *v.t.* (*obs.*) beschädigen, verletzen. **scatheless,** *adj.* (*obs.*) unbeschädigt, unverletzt, unversehrt, ohne Schaden. **scathing,** *adj.* (*usu. fig.*) verletzend, vernichtend, scharf, beißend (*as criticism*).

scatology [skə'tɔlədʒi], *s.* 1. (*Geol.*) die Untersuchung von Koprolithen; 2. (*fig.*) Pornographie.

scatter ['skætə], **1.** *v.t.* 1. (aus)streuen, verstreuen, ausbreiten, verbreiten, verteilen; 2. versprengen, zerstreuen; ***be –ed to the four winds,*** in alle Winde zerstreut sein; 3. bestreuen (*a place*) (*with,* mit); 4. (*also* – ***about***) umherstreuen. **2.** *v.i.* 1. sich zerstreuen *or* verbreiten *or* verteilen; 2. (*of rays or shot*) streuen. **3.** *s.* die Streuung. **scatter|brain,** *s.* (*coll.*) der Wirrkopf; flatterhafter Mensch. **–brained,** *adj.* flatterhaft, konfus. **scattered** [–d], *adj.* zerstreut liegend, vereinzelt (auftretend). **scatty,** *adj.* (*sl.*) meschugge, plemplem.

scaup [skɔ:p], *s.* (*Orn.*) die Bergente (*Aythya marila*).

scaur [skɔ:], *s. See* [2]**scar.**

scavenge ['skævindʒ], *v.t.* 1. säubern, reinigen, kehren (*streets etc.*); 2. (*Tech.*) ausfegen (*gases from engine*). **scavenger,** *s.* 1. der Straßenkehrer; 2. (*Zool.*) Aasfresser. **scavenging,** *s.* 1. die Straßenreinigung; 2. (*Tech.*) Spülung.

scenario [si'nɑ:riou], *s.* (*Films*) das Drehbuch.

scene [si:n], *s.* 1. (*Theat.*) der Schauplatz, Ort der Handlung (*of dramatic action*), das Bühnenbild, die Bühnenaustattung, Kulisse (*on the stage*), Szene, der Auftritt (*division of play*); ***behind the –s,*** hinter den Kulissen (*also fig.*); ***change of*** –,

(*Theat.*) der Szenenwechsel; (*fig.*) die Ortsveränderung, (*coll.*) der Tapetenwechsel; (*Theat.*) ***the – changes,*** der Schauplatz wird verlegt; ***the – is laid*** or ***set in,*** die Handlung *or* das Stück spielt in (*Dat.*); ***shift the –s,*** Kulissen schieben; (*fig.*) ***quit the –,*** von der Weltbühne abtreten; 2. (*fig.*) die Tatort (*of crime*), Schauplatz, die Stätte (*of accident etc.*); ***arrive on the –,*** auftreten, erscheinen; ***be on the –,*** zur Stelle sein; 3. (*coll.*) die Szene, (heftiger) Auftritt; ***make a – with him,*** ihm eine Szene machen; 4. (*Art*) das Bild; ***sylvan –,*** die Waldlandschaft; 5. (*Am. sl.*) die Scene.

scene|-dock, *s.* der Requisitenraum, das Dekorationsmagazin. **–-painter,** *s.* der Theatermaler.

scenery ['si:nəri], *s.* 1. die Landschaft, das Landschaftsbild; 2. (*Theat.*) die Szenerie, (Bühnen)-dekoration, Bühnenausstattung, Kulissen (*pl.*).

scene-shifter, *s.* der Kulissenschieber.

scenic ['si:nik], *adj.* 1. Landschafts–; 2. landschaftlich (schön), malerisch; ***– railway,*** die Liliputbahn; 3. (*Theat.*) Bühnen–, Theater–, Ausstattungs–, szenisch, bühnenmäßig. **scenically,** *adv.* in bühnentechnischer Hinsicht.

scenographic [si:nə'græfik], *adj.* perspektivisch. **scenography** [si'nɔgrəfi], *s.* perspektivische Zeichnung, die Perspektivmalerei.

scent [sent], **1.** *s.* 1. der (Wohl)geruch, Duft; das Parfüm; 2. (*Hunt.*) die Witterung; Fährte, Spur; ***follow the –,*** der Spur folgen; ***lose the –,*** die Spur verlieren; ***on the –,*** auf der Fährte; ***on the false*** or ***wrong –,*** auf falscher Fährte; ***put*** or ***throw him off the –,*** ihn von der Spur *or* Fährte abbringen; 3. das Witterungsvermögen (*of dogs*), (*coll.*) die Nase. **2.** *v.t.* 1. riechen; 2. durchduften, parfümieren; 3. (*Hunt., fig.*) (*also – out*) wittern. **scented,** *adj.* 1. wohlriechend, duftend; 2. parfümiert. **scentless,** *adj.* geruchlos.

scepsis ['skepsis], *s.* die Skepsis, der Zweifel.

scepter, (*Am.*) *see* **sceptre.**

sceptic ['skeptik], *s.* der (die) Zweifler(in), Ungläubige(r); Skeptiker(in). **sceptical,** *adj.* zweifelnd, mißtrauisch, skeptisch; ***be – about,*** bezweifeln. **scepticism** [–tisizm], *s.* der Skeptizismus, Zweifel, die Zweifelsucht, Skepsis.

sceptre ['septə], *s.* das Zepter; (*fig.*) königliche Macht; ***wield the –,*** herrschen, das Zepter schwingen. **sceptred** [–d], *adj.* zeptertragend; (*fig.*) herrschend.

schedule ['ʃedju:l, (*Am.*) 'skedʒu:l], **1.** *s.* 1. die Aufstellung, Liste, Tabelle, das Verzeichnis; 2. (*esp. Am.*) der Fahrplan; Arbeitsplan; Stundenplan; ***according to –,*** fahrplanmäßig; ***on –,*** pünktlich; ***behind –,*** verspätet; ***before –,*** frühzeitig. **2.** *v.t.* 1. in eine Liste eintragen, tabellarisch zusammenstellen; 2. (*esp. Am.*) festlegen, festsetzen, (vorher)bestimmen, vorsehen, planen; in einem Fahrplan anzeigen; ***be –d to start,*** fahrplanmäßig abfahren sollen; ***–d time,*** fahrplanmäßige Zeit.

schematic [ski'mætik], *adj.* schematisch, zusammenfassend, anschaulich, im Umriß. **schematism** ['ski:mətizm], *s.* anschauliche *or* systematische *or* schematische Anordnung, der Schematismus. **schematization** [ski:mətai'zeiʃən], *s.* die Schematisierung. **schematize** ['ski:mətaiz], *v.t.* anschaulich *or* übersichtlich *or* systematisch *or* schematisch anordnen, in ein System *or* Schema bringen, schematisieren.

scheme [ski:m], **1.** *s.* 1. das Schema, Verzeichnis, systematische Anordnung *or* Zusammenstellung; ***colour –,*** die Farbenzusammenstellung; 2. die Aufstellung, Tabelle, Liste; 3. Methode, der Plan, Entwurf, das Programm, Projekt; ***work to a –,*** nach einem Plan arbeiten; 4. (*coll.*) das Komplott, der Anschlag, die Machenschaft, Intrige; ***some – is afoot,*** etwas ist im Werke. **2.** *v.t.* 1. systematisch anordnen; 2. planen, entwerfen; 3. (*coll.*) anstiften, anzetteln. **3.** *v.i.* Pläne machen, intrigieren, Ränke schmieden. **schemer** [–ə], *s.* der Ränkeschmied, Intrigant, Projektenmacher. **scheming, 1.** *adj.* intrigierend, ränkevoll. **2.** *s.* das Planen, Anstiften, Intrigieren, Ränkeschmieden; die Intrige, Schliche (*pl.*).

scherzo ['skɛətsou], *s.* (*Mus.*) das Scherzo.

schism [sizm], *s.* 1. das Schisma, die Kirchenspaltung; 2. (*fig.*) Lossagung, Spaltung, Trennung (*with,* von). **schismatic** [–'mætik], **1.** *adj.* 1. schismatisch; 2. ketzerisch, abtrünnig. **2.** *s.* der Schismatiker, Abtrünnige(r). **schismatical,** *adj.* *See* **schismatic, 1.**

schist [ʃist], *s.* der Schiefer. **schistose** [–ous], **schistous,** *adj.* schiefrig, Schiefer–, schieferartig.

schizanthus [skai'zænθəs], *s.* (*Bot.*) die Spaltblume.

schizocarpous [skitsou'kɑ:pəs], *adj.* spaltfrüchtig, Spaltfrucht–.

schizogenesis [skitsou'dʒenisis], *s.* die Schizogonie. **schizogenic** [–'dʒenik], **schizogenous** [–'sɔdʒənəs], *adj.* durch Spaltung entstanden, schizogen.

schizoid ['skitsɔid], *adj.* schizoid.

schizomycetes [skitsoumai'si:ti:z], *pl.* Spaltpilze (*pl.*).

schizophrenia [skitsou'fri:niə], *s.* die Schizophrenie. **schizophrenic,** *adj.* schizophren.

schnap(p)s [ʃnæps], *s.* der Schnaps.

scholar ['skɔlə], *s.* 1. Gelehrte(r); 2. (*fig.*) der Schüler, Jünger; ***he is a good German –,*** er ist im Deutschen gut beschlagen; 3. (*Univ.*) der Stipendiat. **scholarly,** *adj.* gelehrt, Gelehrten–. **scholarship,** *s.* 1. die Gelehrsamkeit; 2. (*Univ. etc.*) das Stipendium; ***travelling –,*** das Reisestipendium.

scholastic [skɔ'læstik], **1.** *adj.* 1. Schul–, Schüler–, schulmäßig; ***– agency,*** die Schulagentur; ***– learning,*** die Schulgelehrsamkeit; 2. Lehr(er)–, erzieherisch, pädagogisch; ***– institution,*** die Lehranstalt; ***– profession,*** der Lehrstand, Lehrberuf, das Schulamt; 3. (*Phil.*) scholastisch; ***– philosophy,*** die Scholastik. **2.** *s.* der Scholastiker. **scholasticism** [–tisizm], *s.* die Scholastik.

scholiast ['skouliæst], *s.* der Scholiast, Kommentator. **scholium** [–liəm], *s.* die Scholie, gelehrte Anmerkung.

[1]**school** [sku:l], **1.** *s.* 1. die Schule; ***– of Art,*** die Kunstakademie; ***– of theology,*** theologisches Seminar; ***at –,*** in *or* auf der Schule; ***from –,*** aus der Schule; (*fig.*) ***tell tales out of –,*** aus der Schule schwatzen; ***go to –,*** zur *or* in die Schule gehen; ***send to –,*** in die Schule schicken; (*obs.*) ***board –,*** die Volksschule; ***boarding –,*** das Internat, Pensionat; ***commercial –,*** die Handelsschule; ***continuation –,*** die Fortbildungsschule; ***day –,*** das Externat; ***elementary –,*** die Volksschule; ***endowed –,*** die Stiftsschule; ***grammar –,*** höhere Schule, das Gymnasium; ***high –,*** höhere Schule (*Scots, Am.*); (*in Engl. usu.*) höhere Mädchenschule, das Lyzeum; ***lower –,*** die unteren Klassen, die Unterstufe; ***primary –,*** die Grundschule; ***preparatory –,*** die Vorschule; ***public –,*** vornehme höhere Schule, die Standesschule (*Engl.*), Volksschule (*Scots, Am.*); ***secondary –,*** höhere Schule; ***senior*** or ***upper –,*** die oberen Klassen, die Oberstufe; ***Sunday –,*** die Bibelschule; 2. das Schulhaus, Schulgebäude; 3. der (Schul)unterricht; 4. (*Univ.*) die Fakultät; ***medical –,*** medizinische Fakultät; 5. (*fig.*) die Schule; ***– of thought,*** die Ideenrichtung; 6. *pl.* (*Oxford Univ.*) die (Ab)schlußprüfung. **2.** *v.t.* 1. ausbilden, (ein)schulen, unterrichten, unterweisen; ***– o.s.,*** sich daran gewöhnen (***to do,*** zu tun); sich gewöhnen (***to,*** an (*Acc.*)), sich üben (in (*Dat.*)); 2. dressieren, zureiten (*horses*); 3. (*obs.*) rügen, tadeln, verweisen.

[2]**school,** *s.* der Schwarm, Zug, die Herde, Gruppe, Schar (*of whales etc.*).

school| age, *s.* schulpflichtiges Alter; ***of –,*** schulpflichtig. **– attendance,** *s.* der Schulbesuch. **–book,** *s.* das Schulbuch. **–boy,** *s.* der Schuljunge, Schüler. **– certificate,** *s.* (*obs.*) (= *etwa*) das Einjährige; ***higher –,*** (= *etwa*) das Abitur, die Reifeprüfung, (*Austr.*) Matura; das Abschlußzeugnis. **–days,** *pl.* die Schulzeit, Schuljahre (*pl.*). **– fees,** *pl.* das Schulgeld. **–fellow,** *s.* der (die) Schulkamerad(in), Mitschüler(in). **–girl,** *s.* das Schulmädchen, die Schülerin; ***– complexion,*** jugendlich frisches Aussehen. **–house,** *s.* 1. das Schulgebäude; 2. Wohnhaus des Schulleiters.

schooling [ˈsku:liŋ], *s.* 1. der (Schul)unterricht, die (Schul)ausbildung; 2. das Zureiten, Schulreiten (*of horses*); 3. (*fig.*) die Schulung. **school|ma'am,** *s.* die Schulmeisterin (*iron.*). **–man** [–mən], *s.* der Scholastiker. **–master,** *s.* der Lehrer, (*fig.*) Schulmeister. **–mate,** *s. See* **–fellow. –mistress,** *s.* die Lehrerin. **–room,** *s.* das Klassenzimmer. **–teacher,** *s.* der (die) (Schul)lehrer(in). **–teaching,** *s.* 1. der Schulunterricht; 2. Lehrberuf. **–time,** *s.* die Schulzeit. **–work,** *s.* die Schularbeit.

schooner [ˈsku:nə], *s.* 1. (*Naut.*) der Schoner; 2. Humpen.

schorl [ʃɔ:l], *s.* der Schörl, schwarzer Turmalin.

schottische [ʃɔˈti:ʃ], *s.* der Schottisch(e) (*dance*).

sciagram [ˈsaiəgræm], **sciagraph,** *s.* das Röntgenbild. **sciagraphy** [saiˈægrəfi], *s.* 1. der Schattenriß, die Schattenmalerei; 2. Röntgenphotographie. **sciamachy** [saiˈæməki], *s.* das Scheingefecht, die Spiegelfechterei.

sciatic [saiˈætik], *adj.* Ischias–. **sciatica** [–ə], *s.* die Ischias.

science [ˈsaiəns], *s.* 1. die Wissenschaft; ***Christian –,*** der Szientismus; ***domestic –,*** die Hauswirtschaftslehre; ***man of –,*** der Wissenschaftler; ***– fiction,*** der Zukunftsroman (*also pl.*); 2. (*also* ***natural –***) die Naturwissenschaft(en (*pl.*)); 3. (*obs.*) das Wissen, Kenntnisse (*pl.*); 4. (*Spt.*) (*coll.*) das Geschick, Können. **scientific** [–ˈtifik], *adj.* 1. (natur)-wissenschaftlich; 2. exakt, systematisch. **scientist** [–tist], *s.* der Naturwissenschaftler; ***Christian –,*** der (die) Szientist(in).

scilicet [ˈsailiset], *adv.* das heißt, nämlich.

scimitar [ˈsimitə], *s.* der Krummsäbel.

scintillant [ˈsintilənt], *adj.* schillernd, funkelnd. **scintillate** [–eit], **1.** *v.i.* 1. funkeln, schillern, glitzern, flimmern, Funken sprühen; 2. (*fig.*) glänzen. **2.** *v.t.* (ver)sprühen (*also fig.*). **scintillation** [–ˈleiʃən], *s.* das Funkeln, Flimmern, Glitzern, Schillern.

sciolism [ˈsaiəlizm], *s.* das Halbwissen. **sciolist,** *s.* Halbgebildete(r).

scion [ˈsaiən], *s.* 1. (*Bot.*) der Ableger, das Pfropfreis; 2. (*fig.*) der Sprößling, Sproß.

scirrhous [ˈsirəs], *adj.* (*Med.*) verhärtet. **scirrhus,** *s.* die Krebsgeschwulst.

scissel [sisl], *s.* Metallspäne (*pl.*), der Metallabfall.

scission [ˈsiʒən], *s.* 1. das Spalten, die Spaltung; 2. (*fig.*) der (Ein)schnitt.

scissor [ˈsizə], *v.t.* (*coll.*) mit der Schere (zer)-schneiden. **scissor|-grinder,** *s.* der Scherenschleifer. **--hold,** *s.* (*Wrestling*) die Beinschere. **--kick,** *s.* (*Swimming*) der Scherenschlag. **scissors** [–əz], *pl.* 1. (*also* ***pair of –***) die Schere; 2. (*Gymn.*, *Wrestling*) Schere, der Scherengriff.

scissure [ˈsiʒə], *s.* das Spalt, Riß, Einschnitt.

sciurine [saiˈjuərin], *adj.* Eichhörnchen–.

scleriasis [skliəˈraiəsis], **scleroma** [–ˈroumə], **sclerosis** [–ˈrousis], *s.* (*Med.*) die Verhärtung, Sklerose. **sclerotic** [–ˈrɔtik], **1.** *adj.* hart, verhärtet. **2.** *s.* die Sklera, Lederhaut (*of eye*). **sclerous** [ˈskliərəs], *adj. See* **sclerotic.**

[1]**scoff** [skɔf], **1.** *s.* der Spott, Hohn. **2.** *v.i.* spotten, höhnen; ***– at,*** spotten über (*Acc.*), verspotten, verhöhnen.

[2]**scoff,** *v.t.* (*coll.*) verschlingen, gierig essen.

scoffer [ˈskɔfə], *s.* der (die) Spötter(in). **scoffing,** *adj.* spöttisch, höhnisch.

scold [skould], **1.** *v.i.* schelten, schimpfen. **2.** *v.t.* (aus)schelten, auszanken. **3.** *s.* der Dragoner, zänkisches Weib. **scolding,** *s.* 1. das Schelten; 2. die Schelte; ***get a –,*** gescholten werden; ***give him a good –,*** ihn tüchtig ausschelten.

scollop [ˈskɔləp], *see* **scallop.**

sconce [skɔns], **1.** *s.* 1. die Verschanzung, Schanze, Schutzwehr; das Bollwerk; 2. der (Wand)leuchter, Klavierleuchter, Lichthalter; 3. (*sl.*) Schädel, die Birne. **2.** *v.t.* (*obs.*) befestigen, verschanzen.

scone [skoun, skɔn], *s.* weicher Gersten– *or* Weizenmehlkuchen.

scoop [sku:p], **1.** *s.* 1. die Schippe, Schöpfkelle, Schaufel, der Löffel; 2. (*Surg.*) Spatel; 3. (*coll.*) Schub, Stoß; ***at*** or ***in*** or ***with one –,*** mit einem Schub; 4. (*sl.*) großer Gewinn *or* Fang, der Treffer; (*Press*) die Erstmeldung, Alleinmeldung, der Knüller. **2.** *v.t.* 1. schöpfen, schaufeln; ***– out,*** aushöhlen, ausschöpfen, ausschaufeln, ausgraben; ***– up,*** aufschaufeln, zusammenschaufeln, zusammenscharren; 2. (*sl.*) einheimsen; (*Press*) zuerst berichten *or* melden.

scoot [sku:t], *v.i.* (*sl.*) 1. rasen, schießen, sausen, flitzen; 2. ausreißen, abhauen. **scooter,** *s.* 1. der (Kinder)roller; 2. (Motor)roller.

scope [skoup], *s.* 1. der Gesichtskreis, Wirkungskreis, das Betätigungsfeld; 2. Gebiet, der Bereich, Umfang, das Ausmaß, die Ausdehnung; ***beyond (within) my –,*** außerhalb (innerhalb) meines Bereiches; 3. die Reichweite, der Spielraum; ***free –,*** die Bewegungsfreiheit; ***give full*** or ***free –,*** freien Lauf lassen (*to*, *Dat.*); ***have more –,*** größerer Spielraum *or* mehr Bewegungsfreiheit haben (***for,*** für).

scorbutic [skɔ:ˈbju:tik], **1.** *adj.* skorbutisch, Skorbut–. **2.** *s.* Skorbutkranke(r).

scorch [skɔ:tʃ], **1.** *v.t.* 1. versengen, ansengen, (ver)-brennen; ***–ed earth,*** verbrannte Erde; 2. trocknen, dörren. **2.** *v.i.* 1. versengt werden; 2. (aus)dörren; (*sl.*) (dahin)rasen, rücksichtlos fahren. **scorcher** [–ə], *s.* 1. (*sl.*) etwas sehr Heißes, (*sl.*) sehr heißer Tag; 2. (*sl.*) die Sensation. **scorching,** *adj.* (*coll.*) glühend, brennend (*weather*).

score [skɔ:], **1.** *s.* 1. die Kerbe, der Einschnitt, Riß, die Ritze; 2. (*fig.*) Rechnung, Zeche; ***run up a –,*** Schulden machen, anschreiben lassen; ***settle old –s,*** eine alte Rechnung begleichen (***with,*** mit), sich rächen (an (*Dat.*)), es heimzahlen (*Dat.*); ***on the – of,*** um (*Gen.*) willen, wegen (*Gen.*), in Hinsicht auf (*Acc.*); ***on this –,*** was dies betrifft, diesetwegen, deswegen, infolgedessen; 3. (*Spt.*) der Spielstand, das Spielergebnis; die Punktzahl, Leistung; ***what's the –?*** wie steht das Spiel? ***keep (the) –,*** die Punktzahl anschreiben; (*sl.*) ***know the –,*** Bescheid wissen; 4. (*Mus.*) die Partitur; 5. (der Satz von) 20 Stück; ***three – years and ten,*** siebzig Jahre; 6. *pl.* eine große Anzahl, große Mengen (*pl.*). **2.** *v.t.* 1. einritzen, einkerben, einschneiden; zerkratzen; ***– out,*** ausstreichen, durchstreichen; 2. (*debts etc.*) aufschreiben, auf die Rechnung setzen, anrechnen, ankreiden; ***– up,*** eintragen, anschreiben, aufschreiben; 3. (*Spt.*) zählen, machen (*points, runs*); (*coll.*) buchen, aufzeichnen, zu verzeichnen haben; ***– a goal,*** ein Tor machen *or* schießen; ***– a hit,*** einen Treffer erzielen; (*fig.*) einen Riesenerfolg haben; 4. (*Mus.*) in Partitur setzen, instrumentieren. **3.** *v.i.* 1. Punkte *or* einen Punkt machen; die Punkte anschreiben; ***– off him,*** ihn übertrumpfen *or* ausstechen; 2. zählen, gerechnet *or* gezählt werden; ***that –s for me,*** das zählt zu meinen Gunsten; 3. gewinnen, Glück *or* Erfolg haben; ***he –d heavily,*** er hat großen Erfolg gehabt.

score|-board, *s.* die Anzeigetafel. **--card,** *s.* das Anschreibeblatt. **scorer** [–ə], *s.* der Punktzähler, Punktrichter.

scoria [ˈskɔ:riə], *s.* 1. (*Metall.*) die Schlacke; 2. (*Geol.*) Gesteinschlacke. **scoriaceous** [–riˈeiʃəs], *adj.* 1. schlackig, schlackenartig; 2. schlackenreich, Schlacken–. **scorification** [–rifiˈkeiʃən], *s.* die Schlackenbildung, Verschlackung. **scorify** [–rifai], *v.t.* verschlacken.

scoring [ˈskɔ:riŋ], *s.* 1. das Einritzen, Einkerben; 2. (*Spt.*) die Punktzählung; 3. (*Mus.*) Instrumentierung, Partiturierung.

scorn [skɔ:n], **1.** *s.* die Verachtung, Geringschätzung, Verspottung, der Spott, Hohn; ***hold in –,*** verachten; ***laugh to –,*** verlachen, auslachen, lächerlich machen; ***treat with –,*** verächtlich behandeln. **2.** *v.t.* 1. verachten, verschmähen; 2. von sich weisen. **scornful,** *adj.* 1. verachtungsvoll, verächtlich; ***be – of,*** verachten; 2. spöttisch, höhnisch.

Scorpio [ˈskɔ:piou], *s.* (*Astr.*) der Skorpion. **scorpion** [–piən], *s.* (*Zool.*) der Skorpion.

Scot [skɔt], *s.* der Schotte (die Schottin).

scot, *s.* (*obs.*) die Steuer, Abgabe; ***pay one's –,*** seinen Beitrag leisten; ***pay – and lot,*** auf Heller und Pfennig bezahlen; ***great –!*** großer Gott!

[1]**scotch** [skɔtʃ], **1.** *s.* der Einschnitt, Riß, die Ritze, Kerbe. **2.** *v.i.* 1. einritzen, schrammen; 2. unterdrücken, unschädlich machen, vernichten; ***– one's chances,*** seine Aussichten stark beeinträchtigen.

[2]**scotch, 1.** *v.t.* (durch Unterlage) hemmen (*a wheel*). **2.** *s.* der Hemmkeil, Hemmklotz, Hemmschuh.

Scotch, *adj.* schottisch (*properly used only in certain everyday contexts, of food etc.; coll. for* ***Scottish*** *and* ***Scots***); ***– broth,*** die Graupensuppe; ***– heather,*** die Hochlandsheide; ***– mist,*** der Staubregen; ***– woodcock,*** das Rührei mit Anschovis; ***– terrier, – whisky*** *etc.* **Scotchman** [–mən], *s.* (*coll.*) *see* **Scotsman.**

scot-free, *adj.* (*fig.*) ungestraft, unbestraft, unbeschadet, unversehrt.

scotia [ˈskouʃə], *s.* (*Archit.*) die Hohlkehle.

Scotland [ˈskɔtlənd], *s.* Schottland (*n.*); ***– Yard,*** die Hauptdienststelle der Londoner Polizei; (*fig.*) Kriminalpolizei. **Scots, 1.** *adj.* schottisch (*commonly used by Scots themselves, but rare otherwise except in certain set usages*); *e.g.* ***– law, – language.*** **2.** *s.* das Schottisch(e) (*language*). **Scots|man** [–mən], *s.* der Schotte. **–woman,** *s.* die Schottin. **Scotticism** [–isizm], *s.* schottische Spracheigenheit. **Scottish,** *adj.* schottisch (*normal in Scotland, but dignified in English usage*); *e.g.* ***– history, – literature.***

scoundrel [ˈskaundrəl], *s.* der Schuft, Schurke, Lump, Halunke. **scoundrelly,** *adj.* schurkisch, schuftig, lumpig.

[1]**scour** [ˈskauə], *v.t.* 1. scheuern, abreiben, schrubben, putzen; 2. säubern, reinigen, ausspülen, ausschwemmen; 3. entschweißen (*wool*); 4. (*fig.*) säubern.

[2]**scour, 1.** *v.i.* schnell dahinfahren, eilen, jagen; ***– about,*** umherstreifen. **2.** *v.t.* abstreifen, durchstreifen, durchsuchen (*an area*).

scourge [skəːdʒ], **1.** *v.t.* 1. (aus)peitschen, geißeln; 2. (*fig.*) quälen, bedrücken, plagen. **2.** *s.* 1. die Peitsche, Geißel; 2. (*fig.*) Plage, Geißel.

[1]**scout** [skaut], **1.** *s.* 1. das Spähen, die Erkundung; ***on the –,*** auf der Lauer *or* Suche; 2. (*Mil.*) der Späher, Kundschafter, (*Av.*) das Aufklärungsflugzeug; 3. (*Motor.*) der Patrouillenfahrer; 4. (*Univ. sl.*) der Diener, Aufwärter; 5. (*sl.*) Kerl, Bursch; 6. (*also* ***boy*** –) Pfadfinder. **2.** *v.i.* spähen, kundschaften. **3.** *v.t.* auskundschaften, erkunden, herumsuchen; ***–ing party,*** der Spähtrupp.

[2]**scout,** *v.t.* verächtlich abweisen *or* zurückweisen *or* von sich weisen.

scout|-car, *s.* (*Mil.*) das Aufklärungsfahrzeug, der Spähwagen. **–craft,** *s.* das Pfadfinderwesen. **scouter,** *s.* (älterer) Pfadfinder. **scouting,** *s.* 1. das Kundschaften, Spähen; 2. Pfadfindertum. **scoutmaster,** *s.* der Pfadfinderführer.

scow [skau], *s.* der Leichter, Prahm, die Schute.

scowl [skaul], **1.** *v.i.* finster blicken; ***– at,*** finster anblicken. **2.** *s.* finsterer Blick, der Flunsch.

scrabble [skræbl], *v.i.* (*coll.*) 1. scharren, krabbeln; 2. kritzeln.

scrag [skræg], **1.** *s.* 1. hagere Person; das Gerippe; etwas Mageres; 2. ***–(-end) of mutton,*** das Hammelhalsstück. **2.** *v.t.* (*sl.*) aufknüpfen, erdrosseln, erwürgen. **scragginess,** *s.* die Magerkeit, Hagerkeit. **scraggy,** *adj.* 1. hager, dürr, mager; 2. zottig, ungepflegt, verwahrlost.

scram [skræm], *v.i.* (*sl.*) (*usu. imper.*) verduften, abhauen.

scramble [skræmbl], **1.** *s.* 1. das (Herum)klettern, Krabbeln; 2. die Jagd (***for,*** nach), Balgerei (um); 3. (***motor-cycle***) –, das Moto-Cross. **2.** *v.i.* krabbeln, herumklettern; ***– for,*** grapsen nach, sich reißen *or* balgen um; ***– to one's feet,*** sich aufrappeln. **3.** *v.t.* 1. durcheinanderwerfen; ***– together,*** zusammenscharren, zusammenraffen, aufraffen; 2. verrühren (*eggs*); ***–d eggs,*** das Rührei; 3. verwürfeln (*a message*). **scrambler,** *s.* die Verwürfelungsvorrichtung.

scran [skræn], *s.* (*sl.*) Speisereste (*pl.*), schlechtes Essen; ***bad – to . . .!*** zum Teufel mit . . .!

[1]**scrap** [skræp], **1.** *s.* 1. der Rest, Brocken (*pl.*), das Stückchen, das *or* der Schnitzel, der Fetzen; ***– of paper,*** der Fetzen Papier; ***–s of paper,*** Papierschnitzel (*pl.*); ***not a –,*** kein bißchen; ***I don't care a –,*** es ist mir ganz einerlei; 2. der (Zeitungs)ausschnitt; 3. (*Tech.*) Ausschuß, Abbruch, Abfall, Schrott, altes Eisen, das Altstoff, Abwrackmetall; 4. *pl.* Überreste, Bruchstücke, Brocken (*pl.*); 5. *pl.* (= *coloured cut-outs collected by children*) Oblaten (*pl.*). **2.** *v.t.* 1. (*Tech.*) verschrot(t)en; 2. (*fig.*) zum alten Eisen werfen, über Bord werfen, wegwerfen, ausrangieren.

[2]**scrap, 1.** *s.* (*coll.*) 1. die Schlägerei, Rauferei, Prügelei; 2. der Streit, Zank. **2.** *v.i.* sich streiten *or* raufen *or* balgen.

scrap-book, *s.* das Sammelbuch, Einklebebuch.

scrape [skreip], **1.** *s.* 1. das Kratzen; 2. der Kratzer, die Schramme; 3. der Kratzfuß; 4. (*coll.*) die Not, Klemme, Patsche; 5. (*sl.*) ***bread and –,*** dünn beschmiertes Brot. **2.** *v.t.* schaben, kratzen; ***– acquaintance with,*** sich anbändeln mit, sich anbiedern *or* anvettern bei; (*fig.*) ***– the barrel,*** zum Äußersten gebracht sein; ***– one's feet,*** mit den Füßen scharren; ***– a living,*** sich mühsam durchschlagen; ***– off,*** abschaben, abkratzen; ***– out,*** auskratzen; ***– together, – up,*** zusammenscharren, zusammenkratzen. **3.** *v.i.* 1. sich reiben *or* scheuern (***against,*** an (*Dat.*)); 2. kratzen, schaben, scharren; kratzen (*on the violin*); ***bow and –,*** buckeln und dienern, einen Kratzfuß machen; 3. (*coll.*) sparen, sparsam sein; ***– along,*** sich abquälen *or* abrackern, sich mühsam durchschlagen; ***– through,*** sich durchwinden *or* durchschlagen; mit Ach und Krach durchkommen (***in an exam,*** bei einer Prüfung). **scraper** [–ə], *s.* 1. der (Fuß)abstreicher, die Kratzbürste, das Kratzeisen, Schabeisen; 2. (*fig.*) Knauser.

scrap-heap, *s.* 1. der Abfallhaufen; 2. Schrotthaufen.

scraping [ˈskreipiŋ], *s.* 1. das Kratzen, Scharren; 2. Schabsel, Zusammengekratzte(s); 3. *pl.* Abfälle, Überbleibsel (*pl.*), (*fig.*) der Abschaum, Auswurf; 4. *pl.* mühsam Erspartes.

scrap|-iron, *s.* das Alteisen, der Schrott. **--merchant,** *s.* der Schrotthändler.

scrappy [ˈskræpi], *adj.* 1. bruchstückartig, fragmentarisch; 2. zusammengestoppelt, zusammengewürfelt; 3. unzusammenhängend, sprunghaft.

scratch [skrætʃ], **1.** *s.* 1. das Kratzen; 2. der Riß, Ritz, die Kratzstelle; (*Med.*) Schramme, Kratzwunde; 3. (*Spt.*) die Startlinie (*races*); Normalklasse; ***come up to (the) –,*** seinen Mann stehen, sich nicht drücken, sich stellen; ***keep him up to –,*** ihn bei der Stange halten; (*Spt.*) ***start from –,*** ohne Vorgabe starten, (*fig.*) ganz von vorne *or* ohne Hilfe anfangen; ***up to –,*** in Form, auf Draht, auf der Höhe; 4. *pl.* (*Vet.*) die Mauke. **2.** *v.t.* 1. (zer)kratzen, schrammen, ritzen; ***– my back and I'll – yours,*** eine Hand wäscht die andere; ***– out,*** (aus)streichen, ausradieren; ***– his eyes out,*** ihm die Augen auskratzen; ***– one's head,*** sich (*Dat.*) den Kopf kratzen; (*fig.*) ***– the surface of,*** nur flüchtig berühren; ***– up,*** zusammenkratzen, zusammenscharren; 2. (*Spt.*) von der Liste streichen, zurückziehen (*a horse etc.*). **3.** *v.i.* 1. (*of a p. etc.*) sich kratzen; (*of a th.*) kratzen; 2. (*Spt.*) ausscheiden, die Meldung zurückziehen. **4.** *attrib. adj.* 1. zusammengewürfelt, hastig zusammengestellt, improvisiert; 2. (*Spt.*) ***– race,*** das Rennen ohne Vorgabe. **scratchy,** *adj.* 1. kratzend, kratzig, kritzlig (*writing*); 2. (*Spt.*) unausgeglichen.

scrawl [skrɔːl], **1.** *v.i.* kritzeln, schmieren. **2.** *v.t.* hinschmieren. **3.** *s.* das Gekritzel, Geschmiere.

scrawny [ˈskrɔːni], *adj.* (*coll.*) hager, knochig.

scray [skrei], *s.* (*Orn.*) die Seeschwalbe (*Sterna hirundo*).

scream [skriːm], **1.** *s.* 1. der Schrei, das Gekreisch,

Geschrei; *-s of laughter,* schallendes Gelächter; 2. (*sl.*) der Hauptspaß, das Mordsding, tolle Sache; toller Kerl; (*sl.*) *he's a -,* er ist zum Schreien *or* Totlachen; (*sl.*) *what a -!* wie toll! **2.** *v.i.* 1. schreien; *- out,* laut aufschreien; *- with laughter,* laut auflachen; 2. kreischen; 3. heulen (*as wind*). **3.** *v.t.* (*usu. - out*), ausrufen, laut ausstoßen; *- o.s. hoarse,* sich heiser schreien. **screamer,** *s.* 1. (*Orn.*) das Straußhuhn; 2. (*sl.*) *see* **scream, 1,** 2. **screaming,** *adj.* 1. schreiend, kreischend, schrill; 2. (*sl.*) toll, ulkig; *-ly funny,* zum Totlachen; 3. grell (*as headlines*).

scree [skri:], *s.* das (Stein)geröll, der Gehängeschutt.

screech [skri:tʃ], **1.** *v.i.* kreischen, schrillen. **2.** *s.* das Gekreisch. **screeching,** *adj.* schrill. **screech-owl,** *s.* (*Orn.*) die Schleiereule (*Tyto alba*).

screed [skri:d], *s.* lange Liste *or* Aufzählung, langatmiges Schreiben, langatmige Rede.

screen [skri:n], **1.** *s.* 1. der Schirm, die Blende; der Ofenschirm, Windschutz; *folding -,* spanische Wand; 2. (*Archit. esp. Eccl.*) die Deckung, Schranke, Zwischenwand, der Lettner; 3. (*Phot.*) Filter, Raster; 4. (*Films*) die Projektionswand, Leinwand; (*T.V.*) der Bildschirm; (*collect.*) das Kino, der Film; *on the -,* im Film; *bring to the -,* verfilmen; 5. (*Motor.*) die Windschutzscheibe; 6. (*Tech.*) das Gittersieb; 7. (*fig.*) die Maskierung, Verschleierung, Tarnung; Maske, der Schutz, Schirm; *smoke -,* künstlicher Nebel; (*fig.*) das Täuschungsmanöver. **2.** *v.t.* 1. (be)schirmen, (be)schützen (*from,* vor (*Dat.*)); 2. (ver)decken; 3. (*Mil.*) verschleiern, maskieren; 4. abblenden (*light*); 5. (durch)sieben (*coal etc.*); *-ed coal,* Würfelkohle (*pl.*); 6. verfilmen.

screen| adaptation, *s.* die Filmbearbeitung. **--grid,** *s.* (*Rad.*) das Anodenschutznetz, Anodenschutzgitter; *- valve,* die Schirmgitterröhre, Zweigitterröhre, Vierelektrodenröhre. **screening,** *s.* 1. die Abschirmung (*also Rad.*); 2. (*Motor.*) Verschleierung; 3. das (Durch)sieben; 4. (*fig., Pol.*) die Eignungsauslese; 5. (*Films*) Verfilmung. **screen|play,** *s.* das Drehbuch. **- test,** *s.* die Probeaufnahme, Filmprobe. **--wiper,** *s.* (*Motor.*) der Scheibenwischer. **- writer,** *s.* der Drehbuchautor.

screw [skru:], **1.** *s.* 1. die Schraube; *endless -,* die Schraube ohne Ende; *female -,* die (Schrauben)mutter; *give it a -,* es anziehen; (*coll.*) *he has a - loose,* bei ihm ist eine Schraube los; *male -,* die Schraube(nspindel); *turn the -,* die Schraube anziehen; 2. (*Naut.*) die Schiffsschraube, (*Av.*) (*also air -*) Luftschraube; 3. das Effet; *put a - on a ball,* einem Ball Effet geben; 4. (*fig.*) der Druck; *apply the -,* Druck ausüben; *put the - on,* unter Druck setzen; 5. (*sl.*) der Lohn, das Gehalt; 6. (*sl.*) der Gefängniswärter; 7. (*coll.*) Knicker, Geizhals, Geizkragen. **2.** *v.t.* 1. schrauben; (*sl.*) *- his neck,* ihm den Hals umdrehen; *- down,* zuschrauben, festschrauben; *- in,* einschrauben; (*coll.*) *have one's head -ed on the right way,* den Kopf an der rechten Stelle haben; *- up,* zuschrauben; (*fig.*) hochschrauben (*prices*); *- up one's courage,* Mut fassen; sich (*Dat.*) ein Herz fassen; *- (up) one's eyes,* blinzeln; *- one's face up,* sein Gesicht verziehen; 2. (*fig.*) bedrängen, bedrücken; *- out of s.o.,* herauspressen aus, erpressen von, abbringen (*Dat.*); 3. (*vulg.*) vögeln, ficken. **3.** *v.i.* 1. sich (ein)schrauben lassen; 2. (*of a p.*) sich winden *or* drehen.

screw|ball, *s.* (*esp. Am.*) 1. der Effetball; 2. (*fig.*) Sonderling, Wirrkopf. **--bolt,** *s.* der Schraubenbolzen. **--cap,** *s.* die Schraubkapsel, Überwurfmutter, (*on bottles etc.*) der Schraubverschluß, Schraubdeckel. **--clamp,** *s.* die Schraubzwinge, Festklemmschraube. **--compasses,** *pl.* der Schraubenzirkel. **--coupling,** *s.* die Schraubenkupplung. **--cutter,** *s.* der Gewindeschneider. **--cutting,** *s.* das Gewindeschneiden. **--die,** *s.* der Gewindeschneider, die Schneidbacke, das Schneideisen. **-driver,** *s.* der Schraubenzieher. **--eye,** *s.* die Ösenschraube. **--jack,** *s.* die Schraubenwinde, der Wagenheber. **--propeller,** *s.* die Schiffsschraube. **- steamer,** *s.* der Schraubendampfer. **--stock,** *s.* die Schneidkluppe. **--tap,** *s.* der Gewindebohrer. **--thread,** *s.* das Schraubengewinde, der Schraubengang. **--top,** *attrib. adj.* mit Schraubenverschluß. **--wrench,** *s.* der Schraubenschlüssel, Engländer. **screwy,** *adj.* (*sl.*) 1. benebelt, beschwipst; 2. verdreht, verrückt, närrisch.

[1]**scribble** [skribl], **1.** *v.i.* kritzeln, schmieren. **2.** *v.t.* (*also - down*) hinkritzeln, hinschmieren, flüchtig hinschreiben. **3.** *s.* das Geschmier(e), Geschreibsel, Gekritzel.

[2]**scribble,** *v.t.* krempeln, schrubbeln (*wool*).

scribbler [ˈskriblə], *s.* 1. der Schmierer; Schreiberling, Skribent; 2. die Krempelmaschine. **scribbling,** *s.* 1. die Kritzelei, Schmiererei; *--pad,* der Notizblock; *--paper,* das Konzeptpapier; 2. das Krempeln.

scribe [skraib], *s.* 1. der Schreiber, Kopist; (*B.*) Schriftgelehrte(r); 2. (*Tech.*) (*also* **scriber**) die Reißahle, Reißnadel.

scrim [skrim], *s.* das Polsterfutter.

scrimmage [ˈskrimidʒ], *s.* 1. die Balgerei, das Getümmel, Handgemenge; 2. (*Rugby footb.*) *see* **scrummage.**

scrimp [skrimp], **1.** *v.t.* kurz *or* knapp halten (*a p.*), knapp bemessen, geizen *or* knausern mit (*a th.*). **2.** *v.i.* knausern, geizen (*on,* mit). **scrimpy,** *adj.* knapp, eng (*of a th.*), knauserig (*of a p.*).

scrimshank [ˈskrimʃæŋk], *v.i.* (*sl.*) sich drücken, eine ruhige Kugel schieben. **scrimshanker,** *s.* (*sl.*) der Drückeberger.

scrimshaw [ˈskrimʃɔ:], *s.* die Muschel- *or* Elfenbeinschnitzerei.

[1]**scrip** [skrip], *s.* (*obs.*) das Ränzel, die Tasche.

[2]**scrip,** *s.* der Interimsschein, die Interimsaktie.

script [skript], *s.* 1. die Handschrift, Urschrift, das Manuskript, Original; 2. schriftliche Prüfungsarbeit; 3. Geschriebene(s), (*Typ.*) die Schreibschrift; 4. Schrift(form), Schriftart; *phonetic -,* die Lautschrift; 5. (*Films*) das Drehbuch; (*Rad.*) der Sprechertext; *- writer,* (*Films*) der Drehbuchautor, (*Rad., T.V.*) Hörspielverfasser, Textverfasser. **scriptorium** [-ˈtɔ:riəm], *s.* das Schreibzimmer (*of monastery*).

scriptural [ˈskriptʃərəl], *adj.* schriftmäßig, (*Eccl.*) biblisch. **scripture** [ˈskriptʃə], *s.* 1. (*also the Scriptures, Holy Scripture*) die Bibel, Heilige Schrift; 2. (*also - class, - lesson*) die Religionsstunde.

scrivener [ˈskrivənə], *s.* (*Hist.*) der (Berufs)schreiber.

scrofula [ˈskrɔfjulə], *s.* Skrofeln (*pl.*), die Skrofulose. **scrofulous,** *adj.* skrofulös.

scroll [skroul], *s.* 1. die (Pergament- *or* Schrift)rolle; 2. Liste, Tabelle; 3. (*esp. Archit.*) Spirale, Volute, Schnörkelverzierung; 4. (*of string instrument*) Schnecke; 5. (*Typ.*) der Schnörkel. **scroll-work,** *s.* die Laubsägearbeit, Schnörkelverzierung.

scrotum [ˈskroutəm], *s.* der Hodensack.

scrounge [skraundʒ], **1.** *v.t.* (*sl.*) erbetteln, organisieren. **2.** *v.i.* schnorren, nassauern, schmarotzen. **scrounger,** *s.* der Schnorrer, Nassauer, Schmarotzer.

[1]**scrub** [skrʌb], **1.** *v.t.* 1. scheuern, schrubben, gründlich reinigen, abreiben; 2. (*Chem.*) auswaschen (*gas*); 3. (*sl.*) streichen, tilgen. **2.** *v.i.* scheuern. **3.** *s.* das Scheuern; *give s.th. a -,* etwas (ab)scheuern.

[2]**scrub,** *s.* das Gestrüpp, Buschwerk, Unterholz.

scrubber [ˈskrʌbə], *s.* 1. der Schrubber, die Scheuerbürste; 2. (*sl.*) Hure. **scrubbiness,** *s.* die Schäbigkeit, Kümmerlichkeit. **scrubbing brush,** *s.* *See* **scrubber.**

scrubby [ˈskrʌbi], *adj.* 1. struppig; 2. (*coll.*) verkümmert, kümmerlich, schäbig. **scrub-oak,** *s.* die Zwergeiche.

scruff [skrʌf], *s.* (*also - of the neck*) das Genick; *seize by the - of the neck,* beim Kragen packen.

scruffy [ˈskrʌfi], *adj.* (*sl.*) schäbig, verkommen, verwahrlost.

scrum(mage) ['skrʌm(idʒ)], *s.* (*Rugby footb.*) das Gedränge.

scrumptious ['skrʌmpʃəs], *adj.* (*sl.*) köstlich, famos, prima, großartig, fabelhaft.

scrunch [skrʌntʃ], **1.** *v.t.* zerkauen, zermalmen. **2.** *v.i.* krachen, knirschen. **3.** *s.* das Krachen, Knirschen.

scruple [skru:pl], **1.** *s.* 1. (*Pharm.*) das Skrupel (= 1·3 g.); 2. (*fig.*) der Skrupel, Zweifel, das Bedenken; ***have*** (***no***) ***-s,*** sich (*Dat.*) (k)ein Gewissen machen (***about doing,*** zu tun); ***make no -,*** kein Bedenken haben *or* tragen; ***without -,*** skrupellos, gewissenlos. **2.** *v.i.* (*usu. neg.*) Bedenken haben *or* tragen, sich (*Dat.*) ein Gewissen machen. **scrupulosity** [-pju'lɔsiti], *s.* *See* **scrupulousness. scrupulous** [-pjuləs], *adj.* skrupulös, überbedenklich, überängstlich, (über)gewissenhaft, (über)genau, peinlich; ***be -,*** sich (*Dat.*) ein Gewissen (daraus) machen. **scrupulousness,** *s.* 1. das Bedenken, die Gewissenhaftigkeit; 2. Ängstlichkeit, Genauigkeit.

scrutineer [skru:ti'niə], *s.* der (Wahl)prüfer. **scrutinize** ['skru:tinaiz], *v.t.* untersuchen, genau prüfen. **scrutiny** ['skru:tini], *s.* 1. genaue Untersuchung *or* Prüfung, die Nachforschung; 2. (*Parl.*) Wahlprüfung; 3. (*coll.*) forschender *or* prüfender Blick.

scud [skʌd], **1.** *s.* tieftreibende Wolke, die Windbö. **2.** *v.i.* 1. eilen, rennen, jagen; 2. (*Naut.*) treiben, lenzen.

scuff [skʌf], *v.t.* abnützen, abscheuern.

scuffle [skʌfl], **1.** *s.* 1. die Balgerei, Rauferei, das Handgemenge, Gewühl; 2. Schlurfen, Schlürfen, Scharren (*usu. of feet*). **2.** *v.i.* 1. sich balgen, sich raufen, handgemein werden; 2. scharren, schlurfen, schlürfen.

scull [skʌl], **1.** *s.* 1. das Skull, der Skullriemen; 2. das Skullboot, der Skuller. **2.** *v.t., v.i.* skullen (*with sculls*); wricken, wriggen (*with one oar*).

scullery ['skʌləri], *s.* die Spülküche, Aufwaschküche, Abwaschküche. **scullery-maid,** *s.* die Küchenmagd.

scullion ['skʌliən], *s.* (*Poet.*) der Küchenjunge.

sculpt [skʌlpt], *v.t.* (*coll.*) *see* **sculpture, 2. sculptor** [-ə], *s.* der Bildhauer. **sculptress** [-ris], *s.* die Bildhauerin. **sculptural** [-tʃərəl], *adj.* Bildhauer-, plastisch. **sculpture** [-tʃə], **1.** *s.* 1. die Bildhauerei, Bildhauerkunst; 2. Skulptur, Plastik, das Bildwerk. **2.** *v.t.* plastisch formen, modellieren, schnitzen, aushauen, meißeln. **sculpturesque** [-tʃə'resk], *adj.* 1. plastisch, wie geschnitzt *or* gemeißelt; 2. (*fig.*) statuenhaft.

scum [skʌm], **1.** *s.* 1. (*Metall.*) der Schaum, Schlacken (*pl.*); 2. (*fig.*) der Abschaum, Auswurf. **2.** *v.t.* abschäumen, entschäumen. **scummy,** *adj.* schaumig, Schaum-.

scupper ['skʌpə], **1.** *s.* (*Naut.*) das Speigatt. **2.** *v.t.* (*sl.*) vereiteln, zuschanden machen, einen Strich durch die Rechnung machen (*Dat.*).

scurf [skə:f], *s.* der Schorf, Grind. **scurfiness,** *s.* die Schorfigkeit. **scurfy,** *adj.* schorfig, grindig.

scurrility [skʌ'riliti], *s.* 1. die Gemeinheit; 2. Zotigkeit, Unflätigkeit. **scurrilous** ['skʌriləs], *adj.* 1. gemein, ordinär; 2. unanständig, zotig, unflätig.

scurry ['skʌri], **1.** *v.i.* eilen, hasten, (dahin)trippeln. **2.** *s.* 1. das Hasten, Eilen; das Getrippel, Trippeln; 2. ***- of rain,*** der Regenschauer.

scurvy ['skə:vi], **1.** *adj.* gemein, niederträchtig. **2.** *s.* (*Med.*) der Skorbut. **scurvy-grass,** *s.* (*Bot.*) das Löffelkraut.

scut [skʌt], *s.* 1. der Stutzschwanz; 2. (*Hunt.*) Wedel (*of deer*), die Blume (*of hare*).

scutage ['skju:tidʒ], *s.* (*Hist.*) die Dienstpflichttaxe, der Schildpfennig.

scutch [skʌtʃ], **1.** *v.t.* schwingen (*flax*). **2.** *s.* die (Flachs)schwingmaschine.

scutcheon ['skʌtʃən], *s.* 1. *See* **escutcheon**; 2. das Namenschild; 3. die Schlüssellochklappe.

scutcher ['skʌtʃə], *s.* *See* **scutch, 2.**

scute [skju:t], *s.* (*Zool.*) die Schuppe. **scutellate(d)** [-əleit(id)], *adj.* schuppig, schuppenartig, Hornplatten-. **scutelliform** [-'telifɔ:m], *adj.* schildförmig. **scutellum** [-'teləm], *s.* das Schildchen, Plättchen. **scutiform** [-ifɔ:m], *adj.* *See* **scutelliform.**

[1]**scuttle** [skʌtl], *s.* (*usu. coal--*) der Kohlenkasten, Kohleneimer.

[2]**scuttle,** **1.** *v.t.* anbohren, (selbst) versenken. **2.** *s.* (*Naut.*) die Springluke, Schütte, das Bodenventil.

[3]**scuttle,** **1.** *v.i.* ***- away,*** forteilen, dahintrippeln. **2.** *s.* 1. eilige Flucht *or* Abreise; 2. eiliger Schritt, das Trippeln, Getrippel.

Scylla ['silə], *s.* (*Myth.*) Szylla (*f.*).

scythe [saið], **1.** *s.* die Sense. **2.** *v.t.* (ab)mähen.

Scythian ['siθiən], **1.** *s.* der Skythe (die Skythin). **2.** *adj.* skythisch.

sea [si:], *s.* 1. die See, das Meer, der Ozean; ***at -,*** auf See; (*as a seaman*) zur See; (*fig.*) (*usu.* ***all at -***) im dunkeln *or* ungewissen, hilflos, ratlos; ***beyond the -(s),*** über See, in Übersee, übers Meer; ***by -,*** auf dem Seeweg, zu Wasser; ***by the -,*** an der Küste, an der See; ***follow the -,*** Seemann sein, zur See fahren; ***freedom of the -s,*** die Meeresfreiheit; (*sl.*) ***half -s over,*** benebelt, beschwipst; ***on the -,*** auf *or* zur See (*see also* ***by the -***); ***on the high -s*** or ***open -,*** auf hoher See; ***high -s fleet,*** die Hochseeflotte; ***go to -,*** in See gehen *or* stechen (*as a ship*), zur See gehen, Seemann werden (*as a sailor*); ***put*** (***out***) ***to -,*** in See stechen; 2. der Seegang, Wellen (*pl.*); ***breaking -,*** die Sturzsee; ***heavy -,*** hochgehende See, schwerer Seegang; ***a heavy -,*** große Welle; 3. (*fig.*) das Meer, der Strom, die Flut.

sea| air, *s.* die Seeluft, Meeresluft. **--anchor,** *s.* der Treibanker. **--anemone,** *s.* (*Zool.*) die Seeanemone. **- bathing,** *s.* das Baden im Meer. **-bird,** *s.* der Seevogel. **-board,** **1.** *s.* die Küstenlinie, Seeküste, das Seeufer, Meeresufer. **2.** *adj.* Küsten-. **--born,** *adj.* (*Poet.*) meerentsprungen. **--borne,** *adj.* auf dem Seewege befördert; von der See getragen; ***- aircraft,*** das Trägerflugzeug; ***- goods,*** Seehandelsgüter (*pl.*); ***- trade,*** der Seehandel. **- bottom,** *s.* der Meeresgrund. **-breeze,** *s.* der Seewind. **--calf,** *s.* der Seehund, die Robbe, das Meerkalb. **- captain,** *s.* der Schiffskapitän. **--chest,** *s.* die Seemannskiste. **- coast,** *s.* die Seeküste, Meeresküste. **--cock,** *s.* das Bodenventil, der Seehahn. **--colander,** *s.* der Gittertang. **--cow,** *s.* das Walroß, die Seekuh. **- cucumber,** *s.* die Seegurke, Seewalze. **- current,** *s.* die Meeresströmung. **--dog,** *s.* 1. *See* **- calf**; 2. (*fig.*) alter Matrose, der Seebär. **--elephant,** *s.* (*Zool.*) die Elefantenrobbe.

sea|farer, *s.* der Seefahrer. **-faring,** **1.** *adj.* seemännisch, seefahrend, Seefahrts-; ***- man,*** der Seemann. **2** *s.* die Seefahrt. **--food,** *s.* eßbare Fische und Schalentiere. **- forces,** *pl.* Seekräfte (*pl.*). **--fowl,** *s.* der Seevogel. **- front,** *s.* die Strandpromenade. **--girt,** *adj.* (*Poet.*) meerumschlungen. **--god,** *s.* der Meeresgott. **-going,** *adj.* seetüchtig, Hochsee-. **--green,** **1.** *s.* das Meergrün. **2.** *adj.* meergrün. **-gull,** *s.* die (See)möwe. **--hog,** *s.* (*Zool.*) das Meerschwein, Kleiner Tümmler. **--horse,** *s.* (*Ichth.*) das Seepferdchen, (*Zool.*) Walroß. **- kale,** *s.* der Strandkohl.

[1]**seal** [si:l], *s.* der Seehund, die Robbe.

[2]**seal,** **1.** *s.* 1. das Siegel, Petschaft; ***Great Seal,*** das Großsiegel; (*Hist.*) ***Lord Keeper of the Great Seal,*** der Großsiegelbewahrer; ***Privy Seal,*** das Geheimsiegel; ***Lord Privy Seal,*** Königlicher Geheimsiegelbewahrer; ***set one's - on,*** besiegeln, sein Siegel aufdrücken (*Dat.*); (*fig.*) ***set one's - to,*** bekräftigen, sein Siegel drücken auf (*Acc.*); ***under -,*** besiegelt, versiegelt; ***under my hand and -,*** unter Brief und Siegel; ***under the - of secrecy,*** unter dem Siegel der Verschwiegenheit; 2. der Siegelabdruck, (Siegel)stempel; die Matrize; ***Christmas -,*** der Weihnachtszierstempel; 3. (*fig.*) die Besiegelung, Bekräftigung, Bestätigung, Zusicherung; 4. (*Tech.*) wasserdichter *or* luftdichter Verschluß, die Abdichtung, (Blei)plombe. **2.** *v.t.* 1. (be)siegeln, mit einem Siegel versehen, ein Siegel setzen auf (*Acc.*); ***a -ed book,*** ein Buch mit

sieben Siegeln; (*Naut. etc.*) *-ed orders*, versiegelte Order (*pl.*); 2. versiegeln, mit einem Siegel verschließen; – *up*, versiegeln, dicht verschließen, abdichten; – *with lead*, plombieren; – *his lips*, ihm Stillschweigen auferlegen; 3. (*Mil.*) – *off*, abriegeln; 4. (*fig.*) bekräftigen, bestätigen, beglaubigen, besiegeln, einen Stempel aufdrücken (*Dat.*); *his fate is -ed*, sein Untergang ist besiegelt *or* bestimmt. **sealant,** *s.* das Dichtungsmittel.

sea|-lavender, *s.* (*Bot.*) die Strandnelke. – **lawyer,** *s.* der Querulant. **--legs,** *pl.* (*fig.*) die Seefestigkeit; *find* or *get one's* –, seefest werden.

seal engraver, *s.* der Stempelschneider.

sealer ['si:lə], *s.* der Robbenfänger. **sealery,** *s.* 1. der Robbenfangplatz; 2. die Robbenbrutstätte.

sea-level, *s.* der Meeresspiegel, die Normalnull.

seal|-fishery, --fishing, --hunting, *s.* der Robbenfang.

sea|-lily, *s.* (*Zool.*) der Haarstern. **--line,** *s.* die Kimm.

sealing-wax ['si:liŋ-], *s.* der Siegellack.

sea-lion, *s.* der Seelöwe. **Sea Lord,** *s.* der Chef des Marinestabs.

sealskin ['si:lskin], **1.** *s.* das Seehundsfell, Seehundsleder. **2.** *adj.* Seehunds-.

seam [si:m], **1.** *s.* 1. der Saum, die Naht (*also Anat.*); *flat* –, die Kappnaht; 2. (*Geol.*) das Lager, Flöz, die (Nutz)schicht; 3. (*Tech.*) Fuge, der Riß, Ritz, Spalt; 4. (*Med.*) die Schramme, Narbe. **2.** *v.t.* 1. säumen; 2. (*also – together*) zusammennähen; 3. (*fig., usu. pass.*) durchfurchen, (zer)furchen, (zer)schrammen, ritzen.

seaman ['si:mən], *s.* der Seemann, Matrose; *ordinary* –, der Leichtmatrose, Matrosengefreite(r); *able* –, der Vollmatrose, Matrosenobergefreite(r); *leading* –, Matrosenhauptgefreite(r); *seamen's jargon*, die Schiffersprache. **seamanlike,** *adj.* seemännisch. **seamanship,** *s.* seemännische Leistung, die Seemannskunst.

sea|-mark(er), *s.* das Seezeichen, die Markierungsboje. **--mew,** *s. See* **-gull.** – **mile,** *s.* die Seemeile.

seamless ['si:mlis], *adj.* nahtlos, ohne Naht.

sea-monster, *s.* das Meeresungeheuer.

seamstress ['si:mstris], *s.* die Näherin.

sea mud, *s.* der Meeresschlamm, Schlick.

seamy ['si:mi], *adj.* gesäumt; (*fig.*) – *side*, unerfreuliche *or* unangenehme Seite, die Schattenseite, Kehrseite.

seance ['seiãs], *s.* spiritistische Sitzung, die Séance.

sea|-piece, *s.* (*Art*) das Seestück. **-plane,** *s.* das Wasserflugzeug, Seeflugzeug. **-port,** *s.* der Seehafen, die Hafenstadt. – **power,** *s.* die Seemacht.

sear [siə], **1.** *adj.* (*Poet.*) verwelkt, welk; *the – and yellow leaf*, der Herbst des Lebens. **2.** *v.t.* 1. austrocknen, ausdörren; 2. versengen, verbrennen; 3. ätzen, brandmarken; 4. (*fig.*) verhärten, abhärten, abstumpfen.

search [sə:tʃ], **1.** *v.t.* 1. untersuchen, durchsuchen (*for*, nach); (*sl.*) – *me!* keine Ahnung! was weiß ich! 2. (über)prüfen, ergründen, erforschen (*one's heart*), absuchen (*the horizon etc.*), prüfend ansehen; 3. – *out*, forschen nach, suchen; herausfinden, auskundschaften, ausfindig machen. **2.** *v.i.* 1. eifrig suchen, forschen (*for*, nach), nachsuchen (*Acc.*); – *after*, streben nach, zu ergründen *or* erlangen suchen, sich umsehen nach; – *for*, fahnden nach (*a wanted man etc.*). **3.** *s.* das Suchen, Forschen, Streben (*for*, nach), die Suche, Durchsuchung, Untersuchung, Überprüfung; *in – of*, auf der Suche nach; *go in – of*, suchen (nach), auf der Suche gehen nach; *make a – for*, suchen; *right of* –, das Durchsuchungsrecht. **searching,** *adj.* 1. eingehend, gründlich; – *test*, eingehende *or* gründliche Prüfung; 2. forschend, prüfend, tiefgehend, eindringend, durchdringend; (*Mil.*) – *fire*, das Streufeuer; – *look*, durchdringender *or* forschender Blick; – *wind*, durchdringender *or* scharfer Wind.

search|light, *s.* der Scheinwerfer. **--party,** *s.* die Rettungsmannschaft, der Suchtrupp. **--warrant,** *s.* der Haussuchungsbefehl.

sea|-risk, *s.* die Seegefahr. **--room,** *s.* die Seeräume. **--route,** *s.* der Seeweg, Schiffahrtsweg. – **rover,** *s.* der Seeräuber. **--salt,** *s.* das Meersalz.

seascape ['si:skeip], *s.* der Ausblick auf das Meer; *see also* **sea-piece.**

sea| scout, *s.* der Pfadfinder mit Seemannsausbildung. – **serpent,** *s.* die Seeschlange. **-shell,** *s.* die Muschelschale. **-shore,** *s.* die Seeküste, Meeresküste, das Ufer. **--sick,** *adj.* seekrank. **--sickness,** *s.* die Seekrankheit. **-side, 1.** *s. at the* –, an der See; *to the* –, an die See. **2.** *adj.* See-, Meeres-, Küsten-, Strand-; – *town*, die Küstenstadt; – *resort*, das Seebad. **--slug,** *s. See* **--cucumber.**

season [si:zn], **1.** *s.* 1. die Jahreszeit; 2. (rechte *or* passende *or* günstige) Zeit; (*Hunt.*) *close* –, die Schonzeit; *dry* –, die Trockenzeit; *in* –, (*Comm.*) auf dem Markt (zu haben); (*fig.*) zur rechten Zeit; *everything in its* –, alles zu seiner Zeit; *in* (–) *and out of* –, jederzeit; *mating* –, die Brunstzeit, Paarungszeit; (*Hunt.*) *open* –, die Jagdzeit; *rainy* –, die Regenzeit; *out of* –, (*Comm.*) nicht (auf dem Markt) zu haben; (*fig.*) ungelegen, zur Unzeit; 3. (*Comm.*) die Haupt(betriebs- *or* geschäfts)zeit; *dead* or *dull* –, stille Geschäftszeit; 4. die Saison, Badezeit, Kurzeit; *height of the* –, die Hochsaison; *holiday* –, die Ferienzeit; 5. (*Theat.*) die Theatersaison, Spielzeit; 6. Festzeit; *compliments of the* –, beste Wünsche zum Fest; 7. (*coll. or obs.*) eine Zeitlang, Weile; *for a* –, eine Weile *or* Zeitlang; 8. (*coll.*) *see* **season-ticket. 2.** *v.t.* 1. (aus)reifen lassen, zur Reife bringen; 2. (*timber*) austrocknen lassen, ablagern; 3. (*Cul.*) würzen (*also fig.*); 4. (*fig.*) abhärten, gewöhnen; *be -ed to*, gewöhnt sein an (*Acc.*); *become -ed to*, sich gewöhnen an (*Acc.*); *-ed troops*, kampfgewohnte *or* fronterfahrene Truppen. **3.** *v.i.* 1. reifen, reif werden; 2. (*timber*) austrocknen, auswittern, ablagern; 3. (*fig.*) abgehärtet werden, sich akklimatisieren *or* eingewöhnen.

seasonable ['si:zənəbl], *adj.* 1. zeitgemäß, (der Jahreszeit) angemessen; 2. rechtzeitig, zur rechten Zeit; 3. (*fig.*) angebracht, günstig, passend. **seasonableness,** *s.* rechte *or* günstige *or* passende Zeit, das Zeitgemäße. **seasonal,** *adj.* 1. Jahreszeiten-, jahreszeitlich; 2. (*Comm.*) Saison-, saisongemäß, saisonbedingt; – *work*, die Saisonarbeit. **seasoning,** *s.* 1. das Reifen, Ablagern, Austrocknen; 2. (*Cul.*) die Würze, das Gewürz. **season-ticket,** *s.* die Dauerkarte, Zeitkarte, Abonnementskarte, Wochenkarte, Monatskarte.

sea|-squirt, *s.* (*Zool.*) die Seescheide. **--swallow,** *s. See* **tern.**

seat [si:t], **1.** *s.* 1. der Sitz; Sessel, Stuhl, die Bank; (*Theat.*) der Sitz, (Sitz)platz; – *of judgement*, der Richterstuhl; *keep one's* –, sitzen bleiben; *take a* –, sich setzen, Platz nehmen; (*coll.*) *take a back* –, sich in den Hintergrund zurückziehen; *take one's* –, den angewiesenen Platz einnehmen; *take your -s!* Platz nehmen! (*Railw.*) einsteigen! 2. (*residence*) der Wohnsitz, Familiensitz, Landsitz; 3. (*of events, activities*) Ort, (Schau)platz, die Stätte; (*Med.*) (*of disease*) der Sitz, Herd, die Stelle; – *of war*, der Kriegsschauplatz; 4. (*on horse etc.*) die Sitzart, Sitzhaltung, der Sitz; 5. (*Parl.*) Sitz, das Sitzrecht, die Mitgliederschaft; – *on the council*, der Sitz im Rat; 6. (*of trousers*) die Sitzfläche, das Gesäß, Hinterteil, der Hosenboden; 7. (*Tech.*) das Fundament, (Auf)lager, die Auflage(fläche); 8. (*coll. of a p.*) das Gesäß, der Hintere. **2.** *v.t.* 1. (hin)setzen; einen Platz verschaffen *or* anweisen (*Dat.*); – *o.s.*, sich (hin)setzen; *be -ed*, sitzen (*of a p.*), ihren Wohnsitz haben in (*Dat.*) (*of a family*), liegen, gelegen sein (*of building etc.*); *pray be -ed!* nehmen Sie bitte Platz! – *him on the throne*, ihn auf den Thron erheben; 2. (*of a room etc.*) Sitzplätze haben für; 3. den Sitz erneuern in (*Dat.*) (*a chair*); einen neuen Hosenboden einsetzen in (*Acc.*) (*trousers*); 4. (*Tech.*) lagern, betten.

seat-belt, *s.* der Sicherheitsgurt; (*Av.*) *fasten your*

–s! bitte anschnallen! **seated,** *adj.* 1. sitzend; 2. (*as suff.*) –sitzig; ***deep––,*** tiefsitzend, tiefliegend. **seater,** *s.* (*as suff.*) –sitzer, *e.g.* ***4––,*** der Viersitzer. **seating, 1.** *s.* 1. Sitzgelegenheiten (*pl.*), das Versehen mit Sitzplätzen; 2. das (Sich)setzen; 3. (*for chairs*) Polstermaterial, Stuhlzeug; 4. (*Tech.*) *see* **seat, 1,** 7. **2.** *adj.* Sitz–; – ***accommodation,*** die Sitzgelegenheit.

sea| trade, *s.* der Seehandel, Seeverkehr. **--trout,** *s.* (*Ichth.*) die Lachsforelle, Meerforelle. **--urchin,** *s.* (*Zool.*) der Seeigel. – **voyage,** *s.* die Seereise, Seefahrt. **--wall,** *s.* der (Hafen)damm, Deich, die Kaimauer.

seaward ['si:wəd], **1.** *adj.* nach der See gerichtet, der See zugewandt. **2.** *or* **seawards** [–z], *adv.* seewärts, zum Meere hin.

sea|water, *s.* das Seewasser, Meerwasser. **–way,** *s.* (*Naut.*) (*movement through water*) die Fahrt. **–weed,** *s.* der (See)tang, die Alge, das Seegras. **–worthiness,** *s.* die Seetüchtigkeit. **–worthy,** *adj.* seetüchtig, seefest.

sebaceous [si'beiʃəs], *adj.* (*Med.*) talgig, Talg–; – ***follicle,*** die Haarbalgdrüse; – ***gland,*** die Talgdrüse. **sebacic** [–'bæsik], *adj.* (*Chem.*) Sebacin–. **sebum** ['si:bəm], *s.* (*Med.*) der Hauttalg.

sec [sek], *adj.* trocken, herb (*of wine*).

secant ['si:kənt], **1.** *adj.* schneidend. **2.** *s.* (*Math.*) die Sekante, Schnittlinie.

secateur ['sekətə:], *s.* (*usu.* (***pair of***) ***–s***) die Baumschere.

seccotine ['sekəti:n], **1.** *s.* (*registered trade name*) der Klebstoff. **2.** *v.t.* kleben.

secede [si'si:d], *v.i.* sich lossagen *or* trennen, abfallen (***from,*** von). **seceder,** *s.* Abtrünnige(r).

secern [si'sə:n], *v.i.* (*Med.*) ausscheiden, absondern. **secernent, 1.** *adj.* ausscheidend, absondernd, sekretierend. **2.** *s.* das Absonderungsorgan.

secession [si'seʃən], *s.* der Abfall, die Lossagung; (*Hist.*) (Kirchen)spaltung; ***War of Secession,*** Amerikanischer Bürgerkrieg. **secessionism,** *s.* Abfallsbestrebungen (*pl.*). **secessionist,** *s.* Abtrünnige(r), der Sonderbündler, Sezessionist.

seclude [si'klu:d], *v.t.* abschließen, absondern, fernhalten. **secluded,** *adj.* abgeschlossen, abgeschieden, zurückgezogen, einsam; (*of a place*) abgelegen. **seclusion** [–'klu:ʒən], *s.* **1.** die Abgeschlossenheit, Abgeschiedenheit, Zurückgezogenheit; 2. die Abschließung, Isolierung.

[1]**second** ['sekənd], **1.** *adj.* 1. zweit, ander, nächst, folgend; ***come –,*** als Zweite(r) *or* an zweiter Stelle kommen; – ***Advent,*** die Wiederkunft Christi; – ***ballot,*** die Stichwahl; – ***best,*** Zweitbeste(r); – ***Chamber,*** das Oberhaus; – ***childhood,*** das Greisenalter; – ***coming,*** see – ***Advent;*** – ***fermentation,*** die Nachgärung; – ***floor,*** zweiter (*Am.* erster) Stock; (*Footb.*) – ***half,*** zweite Halbzeit; ***at – hand,*** aus zweiter Hand; ***come as*** or ***be – nature to him,*** ihm in Fleisch und Blut übergegangen sein, ihm zur zweiten Natur geworden sein; ***in the – place,*** zweitens, an zweiter Stelle; (*Math.*) – ***power,*** das Quadrat, zweite Potenz; – ***sight,*** das Hellsehen; ***on – thoughts,*** bei nochmaliger *or* näherer Überlegung; ***a – time,*** noch einmal, zum zweitenmal; – ***wind,*** (*Spt.*) zweite Luft; (*fig.*) frischer *or* neuer Auftrieb; ***every – year,*** alle zwei Jahre, ein Jahr ums andere; 2. nachstehend, untergeordnet (***to,*** *Dat.*); ***be*** or ***stand – to,*** nachstehen (*Dat.*); (*Rad.*) – ***channel interference,*** das Wellenecho; – ***cousin,*** der Vetter *or* die Base zweiten Grades; – ***driver,*** der Beifahrer; (*fig.*) ***play – fiddle,*** die Nebenrolle *or* untergeordnete Rolle spielen; – ***lieutenant,*** der Leutnant; (*Mil.*) – ***line defences,*** Auffangstellungen (*pl.*); – ***mate,*** zweiter Steuermann; – ***to none,*** unerreicht, keinem nachstehend, hinter keinem zurückstehend; – ***quality,*** untergeordnete Qualität. **2.** *adv.* an zweiter Stelle, als zweit(er, –e, –es), zweitens. **3.** *s.* 1. der *etc.* Zweite (*or* Nächste *or* (Nach)folgende); (*Comm.*) – ***of exchange,*** der Sekundawechsel; ***run him a good –,*** ihm sehr nahekommen; 2. (*Mus.*) zweite *or* begleitende Stimme; ***take the –,*** die begleitende Stimme übernehmen; 3. (*Mus.*) die Sekunde; 4. (*Boxing etc.*) der Sekundant; (*fig.*) Beistand, Helfer; ***act as a –,*** sekundieren; 5. (*coll.*) zweite Klasse in einer Universitätsprüfung; 6. *pl.* (*Comm.*) Waren (*pl.*) zweiter Güte. **4.** *v.t.* 1. beistehen (*Dat.*), unterstützen; (*Boxing etc.*) sekundieren (*Dat.*); 2. [si'kɔnd] (*Mil.*) abkommandieren.

[2]**second,** *s.* (*Math., time*) die Sekunde; (*coll.*) der Augenblick, Moment.

secondarily ['sekəndərili], *adv.* in zweiter Linie. **secondariness,** *s.* die Zweitrangigkeit; das Sekundäre, Untergeordnete. **secondary, 1.** *adj.* 1. in zweiter Linie stehend, in zweiter Hinsicht, nebensächlich, untergeordnet, abhängig, entlehnt, abgeleitet, Neben–, Hilfs–; – ***accent,*** der Nebenton; – ***cause,*** die Nebenursache; – ***colour,*** zusammengesetzte Farbe, die Mischfarbe, Mittelfarbe, Zwischenfarbe; (*Meteor.*) – ***depression,*** das Randtief; – ***fever,*** das Nachfieber; ***a matter of – importance,*** eine Nebensache; (*Mil.*) – ***objective,*** das Ausweichziel; – ***proposition,*** der Nebensatz; 2. (*Geol., Elec., Chem., Phil.*) Sekundär–, sekundär; – ***current,*** der Sekundärstrom; 3. – ***education,*** höhere Schulbildung; – ***school,*** höhere Schule, (*Austr.*) die Mittelschule. **2.** *s.* 1. der Stellvertreter, Untergeordnete(r); 2. die Mischfarbe, zusammengesetzte Farbe; 3. (*Elec.*) die Sekundärwicklung; der Sekundärkreis; 4. (*Orn.*) hintere Schwungfeder.

second|-best, 1. *s.* das Zweitbeste. **2.** *adj.* zweitbest; ***come off –,*** unterliegen, den kürzeren ziehen. **--class,** *adj.* 1. zweitrangig, zweitklassig; 2. zweiten Ranges *or* Grades, zweiter Klasse; – ***mail*** or ***matter,*** Postsachen (*pl.*) zweiter Ordnung. **--floor,** *adj.* im zweiten (*Am.* ersten) Stock. **--hand, 1.** *adj.* 1. gebraucht (*car etc.*), getragen, abgelegt (*clothes*), antiquarisch (*books*); – ***dealer,*** der Altwarenhändler; – ***bookshop,*** das Antiquariat; – ***bookseller,*** der Antiquar; 2. (*fig.*) indirekt, entlehnt, übernommen. **2.** *adv.* aus zweiter Hand, antiquarisch. – **hand,** *s.* (*Horol.*) der Sekundenzeiger. **--in-command,** *s.* 1. (*Mil.*) stellvertretender Kommandeur; 2. (*Naut.*) erster Offizier. **secondly,** *adv.* zweitens, an zweiter Stelle. **second|-rate,** *adj.* (nur) zweiten Ranges, zweitklassig, zweitrangig, minderwertig, mittelmäßig. **--rater,** *s.* (*coll.*) mittelmäßige Person.

secrecy ['si:krisi], *s.* 1. die Heimlichkeit, Verborgenheit, Verschlossenheit; ***in –,*** (ins)geheim, heimlich, im Geheimen; 2. die Verschwiegenheit, Geheimhaltung; ***observe –,*** Verschwiegenheit bewahren; ***be sworn to –,*** zur (Amts)verschwiegenheit verpflichtet werden.

secret ['si:krit], **1.** *adj.* geheim, Geheim–, heimlich, verborgen, (*also of a p.*) verschwiegen; – ***ballot,*** geheime Wahl; – ***door,*** die Geheimtür; – ***service,*** der Geheimdienst; – ***society,*** der Geheimbund; – ***treaty,*** der Geheimvertrag; ***keep –,*** geheimhalten, verheimlichen. **2.** *s.* das Geheimnis (***from,*** vor (*Dat.*)); ***dead –,*** tiefes Geheimnis; ***in –,*** im geheimen, insgeheim, heimlich, im Vertrauen; ***be in the –,*** (in das Geheimnis) eingeweiht sein; ***let him into the –,*** ihn in das Geheimnis einweihen; ***keep a –,*** ein Geheimnis bewahren; ***keep it a –,*** es geheimhalten; ***let out a –,*** ein Geheimnis preisgeben; ***make no – of,*** kein Geheimnis *or* Hehl machen aus; ***open –,*** offenes Geheimnis.

secretaire [sekri'tɛə], *s.* der Schreibschrank.

secretarial [sekri'tɛəriəl], *adj.* Schreib–, Büro–, Sekretär–. **secretariat,** *s.* 1. das Sekretariat; 2. die Kanzlei; 3. (*collect.*) Kanzleiangestellte (*pl.*).

secretary ['sekrətəri], *s.* 1. der (die) Sekretär(in) (***to,*** bei); ***private –,*** der (die) Privatsekretär(in); 2. (*of a society etc.*) der Schriftführer, Schriftwart; ***general –,*** der Geschäftsführer; ***honorary –,*** ehrenamtlicher Schriftführer; 3. der (Kabinett)minister; ***Secretary of State,*** der Minister (*U.K.*), Außenminister (*Am.*); ***Secretary of State for Foreign Affairs, Foreign Secretary,*** der Außenminister (*U.K.*); ***Secretary of State for Home Affairs, Home Secretary,*** (***Am. Secretary of the Interior***), der Innenminister; (*Am.*) ***Secretary of***

the Treasury, der Finanzminister; ***Secretary of State for War*** (***Am. Secretary of War***), der Kriegsminister; 4. *See* **secretaire. secretary-bird,** *s.* der Stelzgeier. **secretaryship,** *s.* 1. das Sekretärsamt, Schriftführeramt; 2. (*Pol.*) Ministeramt.

secrete [si'kri:t], *v.t.* 1. verbergen, verstecken (*from*, vor (*Dat.*)); – ***o.s.,*** sich verbergen; 2. absondern, abscheiden, sezernieren. **secretion** [–i:ʃən], *s.* die Absonderung, Sekretion; das Sekret, der Ausfluß. **secretive,** *adj.* 1. ['si:kritiv], verschwiegen, verschlossen, heimlichtuerisch; 2. [si'kri:tiv], Absonderungs–, Sekretions–. **secretiveness** ['si:kritivnis], *s.* die Verschwiegenheit, Verschlossenheit, Heimlichtuerei, Geheimniskrämerei. **secretory** [si'kri:təri], *adj. See* **secretive, 2.**

sect [sekt], *s.* die Sekte, Konfession, Religionsgemeinschaft. **sectarian** [–'tɛəriən], **1.** *adj.* 1. sektierererisch, Sekten–; 2. konfessionell, Konfessions–. **2.** *s.* der (die) Sektierer(in), der Eiferer, Fanatiker. **sectarianism,** *s.* die Sektiererei, das Sektierertum, der Fanatismus.

section ['sekʃən], **1.** *s.* 1. die Durchschneidung, Durchteilung; (*Surg.*) Öffnung, Sektion; 2. der (Bestand)teil, das (Einzel)teil; 3. der Ausschnitt, Teil (*of population etc.*); 4. (*Railw.*) Streckenabschnitt, die Teilstrecke; 5. der Abschnitt, Absatz, Paragraph; 6. (*Bot., Zool.*) die Klasse; Gruppe, (Unter)abteilung; 7. (*Math.*) der Schnitt; ***conic –,*** der Kegelschnitt; ***cross –,*** der Querschnitt (*also fig.*); 8. (*Mil.*) die Abteilung, Gruppe, der Halbzug, (*Av.*) die Halbstaffel. **2.** *v.t.* (*oft.* – ***off***) (ein)teilen, abteilen. **sectional,** *adj.* 1. Teil–; 2. Lokal–; – ***interests,*** Lokalinteressen (*pl.*); 3. (*Tech.*) Schnitt–; – ***drawing,*** der Schnitt; 4. zusammensetzbar, zusammenlegbar; – ***furniture,*** das Anbaumöbel, Aufbaumöbel. **sectionalism,** *s.* der Partikularismus. **sectionalize,** *v.t.* zerlegen, aufteilen.

sector ['sektə], *s.* 1. (*Geom.*) der Sektor, Kreisausschnitt; 2. (*Mil.*) Frontabschnitt; 3. (*fig.*) Sektor, Bereich, Kreis.

secular ['sekjulə], **1.** *adj.* 1. weltlich, nicht kirchlich, profan, säkular, Säkular–, diesseitig; – ***arm,*** weltliche Gerichtsbarkeit; – ***clergy,*** die Weltgeistlichkeit; – ***music,*** weltliche Musik; 2. hundertjährlich, hundertjährig. **2.** *s.* (*R.C.*) Weltgeistliche(r). **secularism,** *s.* 1. die Weltlichkeit, der Säkularismus; 2. (*Pol.*) Antiklerikalismus. **secularist, 1.** *adj.* säkularistisch, antiklerikal. **2.** *s.* der Säkularist, Kirchengegner. **secularity** [–'læriti], *s.* die Weltlichkeit, Diesseitigkeit, weltliche Interessen (*pl.*).

secularization [sekjulərai'zeiʃən], *s.* 1. die Verweltlichung, Säkularisation; 2. Säkularisierung. Verstaatlichung. **secularize** ['sekjuləraiz], *v.t.* 1. säkularisieren; 2. einziehen, verstaatlichen (*church property*); 3. (*fig.*) verweltlichen, entheiligen.

secund [si'kʌnd], *adj.* (*Bot.*) einseitig, einseitswendig.

secundine ['sekəndain], *s.* (*usu. pl.*) die Nachgeburt.

securable [si'kjuərəbl], *adj.* erreichbar, zu erlangen(d).

secure [si'kjuə], **1.** *adj.* 1. sicher, gesichert, in Sicherheit, geschützt (*against, from*, vor (*Dat.*)); 2. sorglos, sorgenfrei, ruhig, gewiß, zuversichtlich. **2.** *v.t.* 1. sichern, schützen (*from, against*, gegen *or* vor (*Dat.*)); 2. befestigen, festmachen (*to*, an (*Dat.*)); 3. fest zumachen *or* (ver)schließen (*as a door*); (*Mil.*) befestigen; 4. festnehmen, einsperren (*a thief etc.*); 5. in Gewahrsam *or* Sicherheit bringen, sicherstellen (*as valuables*); 6. (*esp. Comm.*) Sicherheit bieten *or* geben (*Dat.*); 7. sich (*Dat.*) sichern *or* beschaffen, erlangen; belegen (*a seat etc.*).

security [si'kjuəriti], *s.* 1. die Sicherheit, der Schutz (*from, against*, vor (*Dat.*) *or* gegen); ***Security Council,*** der Sicherheitsrat; – ***pact,*** der Sicherheitspakt; – ***police,*** die Sicherheitspolizei; – ***risk,*** für den Staatsdienst Ungeeignete(r); ***in –,*** in Sicherheit; 2. die Sorglosigkeit, Zuversicht, Gewißheit; 3. (*Comm.*) Garantie, Bürgschaft, Kaution, Sicherheitsleistung, Deckung, das Unterpfand, der Bürge; ***collateral –,*** die Nebenbürgschaft, Nebensicherheit; ***collective –,*** kollektive Sicherheit; ***furnish*** or ***give –,*** Bürgschaft leisten, Kaution stellen; ***in – for,*** als Garantie *or* Sicherheitsleistung für; 4. *pl.* (*Comm.*) Wertpapiere, Effekten (*pl.*); – ***market,*** die Effektenbörse; ***bearer securities,*** Inhaberpapiere; ***gilt-edged securities,*** mündelsichere Wertpapiere; ***public securities,*** Staatspapiere.

sedan [si'dæn], *s.* 1. (*also* ––***chair***) die Sänfte; 2. (*Motor.*) Limousine.

sedate [si'deit], *adj.* gesetzt, gelassen, ruhig. **sedateness,** *s.* die Gesetztheit, Gelassenheit, Ruhe.

sedation [si'deiʃən], *s.* (*Med.*) die (Nerven)beruhigung. **sedative** ['sedətiv], **1.** *adj.* (nerven)-beruhigend, schmerzstillend. **2.** *s.* das Sedativ(um), (Nerven)beruhigungsmittel, schmerzstillendes Mittel.

sedentariness ['sedəntərinis], *s. See* ***sedentary life.*** **sedentary,** *adj.* sitzend; – ***life,*** sitzende Lebensweise.

sederunt [si'diərənt], *s.* (*Scots*) die Sitzung.

sedge [sedʒ], *s.* das Schilfgras, Riedgras. **sedge-warbler,** *s.* (*Orn.*) der Schilfrohrsänger (*Acrocephalus schoenobaenus*). **sedgy,** *adj.* 1. schilfig, Schilf–; 2. mit Riedgras bewachsen.

sediment ['sedimənt], *s.* 1. der (Boden)satz, Niederschlag, die Hefe; 2. (*Geol.*) Ablagerung, das Sediment. **sedimentary** [–'mentəri], *adj.* (*Geol.*) Sediment–, sedimentär.

sedition [si'diʃən], *s.* die Aufwiegelung, Agitation, Meuterei. **seditious,** *adj.* aufwieglerisch, aufrührerisch.

seduce [si'dju:s], *v.t.* verführen (*a girl etc.*); (*fig.*) verführen, verleiten, verlocken (*to*, zu); abbringen, weglocken (*from*, von). **seducer,** *s.* der Verführer. **seducible,** *adj.* (leicht) verführbar. **seduction** [–'dʌkʃən], *s.* die Verführung, Verlockung, Verleitung, Versuchung. **seductive** [–'dʌktiv], *adj.* verführerisch, verlockend. **seductiveness,** *s.* verführerischer Reiz, verlockender Zauber.

sedulity [si'dju:liti], *s. See* **sedulousness. sedulous** ['sedjuləs], *adj.* emsig, fleißig, beharrlich, unverdrossen. **sedulousness,** *s.* die Emsigkeit, Beharrlichkeit, der Fleiß.

[1]**see** [si:], **1.** *irr.v.i.* 1. sehen; – ***into,*** ergründen, untersuchen; – ***over,*** besichtigen, sich (*Dat.*) ansehen; – ***through,*** durchschauen (*insep. when fig.*); 2. (*fig.*) einsehen, verstehen; ***I –!*** ich verstehe (schon)! ach so! ***you –?*** verstehst du? 3. sich (*Dat.*) überlegen, nachsehen; – ***fit,*** es für angebracht *or* zweckmäßig *or* günstig *or* richtig halten *or* erachten; ***let me –!*** warte mal! einen Augenblick! ***we'll –!*** mal abwarten! ***wait and –,*** abwarten; kommt Zeit, kommt Rat; – ***about,*** besorgen, sich kümmern um, Sorge tragen für; (*coll.*) sich (*Dat.*) überlegen; – ***after,*** sich kümmern um, achten auf (*Acc.*), sorgen für; – ***to,*** sorgen für, sich kümmern um; in die Hand nehmen; achten auf (*Acc.*); – ***to it that,*** achten darauf, daß.
2. *irr.v.t.* 1. sehen; ansehen, betrachten, nachsehen; (*coll.*) – ***the back of him,*** ihn los sein *or* loswerden; – ***him come*** or ***coming,*** ihn kommen sehen; ***go and –,*** siehe nach; (*fig.*) ***I – daylight,*** mir geht ein Licht auf; ***what the eye does not –, the heart does not grieve over,*** was ich nicht weiß, macht mich nicht heiß; (*coll.*) – ***the last of,*** endlich nicht mehr sehen, zum letzten Male gesehen haben; – ***the light,*** das Licht der Welt erblicken; – ***the light of day,*** das Tageslicht erblicken; ***now I – the light,*** jetzt geht mir ein Licht auf; (*sl.*) – ***red,*** die Fassung verlieren, wütend werden; (*coll.*) ***be –ing things,*** Gesichte haben; ***I cannot – my way to doing it,*** ich sehe keine Möglichkeit, es zu tun; – ***it out,*** es bis zum Ende sehen *or* mitmachen; – ***him through,*** ihm durchhelfen; – ***it through,*** es durchführen *or* zu Ende führen; es bis zum Ende durchhalten; 2. einsehen, verstehen, merken, gewahr werden (*Gen.*), ersehen, entnehmen; – ***eye to eye with,*** völlig

übereinstimmen mit; – ***a joke,*** einen Spaß verstehen; ***I don't – any use*** or ***good in doing it,*** ich finde, es hat keinen Sinn *or* Zweck, es zu tun; – ***how the land lies,*** wissen, woher der Wind weht *or* wie der Hase läuft; – ***the point,*** den Zweck der S. einsehen; – ***his point,*** seinen Standpunkt verstehen; 3. erkennen, erfahren, erleben; – ***action,*** mitkämpfen (***at,*** bei); ***have seen better days,*** bessere Tage gesehen *or* erlebt haben; – ***life,*** das Leben kennenlernen, Erfahrungen machen; – ***service,*** (Kriegs)dienst tun; ***you've not seen the worst of it yet,*** das Schlimmste steht dir noch bevor; ***live to –,*** erleben; ***it remains to be seen,*** es bleibt abzuwarten; 4. darauf achten, sorgen für; – ***justice done to him,*** dafür sorgen, daß ihm Gerechtigkeit widerfährt; – ***fair play,*** den Schiedsrichter machen; 5. ersehen (***by, from,*** aus); 6. sich (*Dat.*) ansehen, besuchen; aufsuchen, befragen, konsultieren (***about,*** wegen); – ***company,*** in Gesellschaft gehen; – ***a lawyer*** (***doctor*** *etc.*), zu einem Anwalt (Arzt *etc.*) gehen; – ***a play,*** sich (*Dat.*) ein Stück ansehen; ***go*** or ***come to*** or ***and – him,*** ihn besuchen *or* aufsuchen; 7. empfangen; 8. begleiten, bringen; – ***him home*** or ***to the door,*** ihn nach Hause *or* an die Tür bringen *or* begleiten; – ***him off,*** ihn an die Bahn (*etc.*) bringen *or* zur Bahn (*etc.*) begleiten; – ***him out,*** ihn hinausbegleiten *or* zur Tür bringen.

[2]**see,** *s.* (erz)bischöflicher Stuhl, das (Erz)bistum; ***Holy See,*** Päpstlicher Stuhl.

seed [si:d], **1.** *s.* 1. die Saat, der Same(n); ***go*** or ***run to –,*** in Samen schießen; (*fig.*) seine besten Tage hinter sich (*Dat.*) haben; 2. (*B.*) die Nachkommenschaft; 3. *pl.* (*fig.*) der Keim, Ursprung, die Saat, Quelle; ***sow the –s of discord,*** Zwietracht säen *or* stiften. **2.** *v.i.* Samen tragen, in Samen schießen. **3.** *v.t.* 1. besäen (*a field*); 2. entkernen (*fruit*); 3. (*Spt.*) setzen (*a competitor*).

seed|-bearing, *adj.* samentragend. **--bed,** *s.* 1. das Treibbeet; 2. (*fig.*) die Brutstätte. **--cake,** *s.* der Kümmelkuchen. **--drill,** *s.* die (Reihen)sämaschine. **seeder,** *s.* 1. der (Frucht)entkerner; 2. (*Ichth.*) der Laichfisch; 3. *See* **seed-drill.**

seediness ['si:dinis], *s.* (*coll.*) 1. die Unpäßlichkeit; 2. Schäbigkeit. **seed-leaf,** *s.* das Keimblatt. **seedless,** *adj.* kernlos. **seedling,** *s.* der Sämling.

seed|-pearls, *pl.* Samenperlen, Staubperlen (*pl.*). **--plot,** *s. See* **--bed. --potato,** *s.* die Saatkartoffel.

seedsman ['si:dzmən], *s.* der Samenhändler, Saatguthändler.

seed|-time, *s.* der Aussaat, die Bestellzeit. **--vessel,** *s.* die Fruchthülle. **seedy,** *adj.* 1. voller Samen, in Samen schießend; 2. (*coll.*) schäbig, fadenscheinig, heruntergekommen; 3. (*coll.*) mies, elend, katzenjämmerlich.

seeing ['si:iŋ], **1.** *s.* das Sehen; – ***is believing,*** Sehen ist Glauben; ***worth –,*** sehenswert. **2.** *adj.* sehend, sehfähig. **3.** *conj.* – (***that***), in Anbetracht dessen daß, da doch (nun mal). **4.** *prep.* angesichts (*Gen.*), in Anbetracht (*Gen.*).

seek [si:k], **1.** *irr.v.t.* 1. suchen; (*obs.*) ***is to –,*** ermangelt (*Gen.*), fehlt, ist nicht vorhanden, ist nicht zu finden; ***not far to –,*** leicht zu finden; 2. aufsuchen; – ***out,*** aufsuchen; 3. begehren, zu entdecken *or* erlangen *or* bekommen suchen, erstreben, streben *or* trachten nach; – ***fame,*** nach Ruhm trachten; – ***his life,*** ihm nach dem Leben trachten; – ***in marriage,*** anhalten um; 4. erbitten (***from,*** von); – ***his advice,*** seinen Rat erbitten; – ***his aid,*** bei ihm um Hilfe suchen; 5. (*with inf.*) (ver)suchen, trachten. **2.** *irr.v.i.* suchen (***for,*** nach); – ***after*** (*obs. except pass.* ***sought after,*** gesucht, gefragt, begehrt). **seeker,** *s.* der Sucher; – ***after truth,*** Wahrheitssuchende(r).

seel [si:l], *v.t.* (*obs.*) blenden (*a hawk, also fig.*), (*fig.*) täuschen, irreführen.

seem [si:m], *v.i.* (zu sein) scheinen, erscheinen, den Anschein haben (*to, Dat.*); ***I – (to be),*** ich bin anscheinend; ***all –ed pleased,*** allen schien es zu gefallen; ***it –s as if*** or ***though,*** es scheint so *or* es sieht so aus *or* es hat den Anschein, als ob; ***it –s (that),*** es scheint daß, anscheinend ist *or* hat; ***it would – that,*** man sollte glauben daß; ***it –s to me,*** es scheint mir *or* kommt mir vor; ***as –s possible,*** wie es wahrscheinlich ist. **seeming, 1.** *adj.* scheinbar. **2.** *s.* der (An)schein. **seemingly,** *adv.* scheinbar, anscheinend.

seemliness ['si:mlinis], *s.* die Schicklichkeit, der Anstand. **seemly,** *adj.* geziemend, schicklich, anständig.

seen [si:n], *p.p. of* [1]**see.**

seep [si:p], *v.i.* (durch)sickern; – ***away,*** versickern; – ***into,*** einsickern in (*Acc.*); (*fig.*) – ***out,*** durchsickern. **seepage** [-idʒ], *s.* 1. das Durchsickern; 2. das Sickerwasser, (durch)sickernde Feuchtigkeit.

seer [siə], *s.* der (die) Seher(in), Prophet(in), Wahrsager(in).

seersucker ['siəsʌkə], *s.* gestreiftes, kreppartiges Leinen.

seesaw ['si:sɔ:], **1.** *s.* 1. die Wippe, Schaukelbank; 2. das Wippen, Schaukeln; 3. (*fig.*) ständiges Schwanken *or* Auf und Ab *or* Hin und Her. **2.** *v.i.* 1. wippen, (sich) schaukeln; 2. (*fig.*) auf und ab gehen, (hin und her) schwanken, steigen und fallen. **3.** *attrib. adj.* hin- und hergehend, auf- und abgehend, schaukelnd, pendelnd, wechselnd, schwankend.

seethe [si:ð], *v.i.* sieden, kochen, (*esp. fig.*) brodeln, schäumen, (auf)wallen, gären.

segment ['segmənt], *s.* 1. der Abschnitt, das Segment; 2. (*Zool.*) Körpersegment, Glied, der Ring. **segmental** [-'mentl], *adj.* segmental, segmentär. **segmentation** [-'teiʃən], *s.* 1. die Segmentation, Gliederung; 2. (*Zool.*) Zellteilung, Eifurchung.

segregate, 1. ['segrigeit], *v.t.* 1. absondern, trennen, isolieren; 2. (*Tech.*) seigern, ausscheiden. **2.** [-eit], *v.i.* 1. sich absondern; 2. (*Chem.*) sich abscheiden. **3.** [-it], *adj.* abgesondert, getrennt, isoliert. **segregation** [-'geiʃən], *s.* 1. die Absonderung, Ausscheidung, Abtrennung; 2. (*Chem.*) Abscheidung; 3. (*Pol.*) Rassentrennung. **segregationist,** *s.* der (die) Anhänger(in) der Rassentrennung(spolitik). **segregative** ['segrigətiv], *adj.* sich absondernd, trennend.

seigneur [sein'jə:], **seignior** ['si:njə], *s.* der Lehnsherr, Feudalherr, Grundherr. **seigniorage** ['seinjəridʒ], *s.* 1. königliche Münzgebühr; 2. herrschaftliches Vorrecht, das Regal. **seign(i)orial** [-'n(j)ɔ:riəl], *adj.* grundherrlich, herrschaftlich, (*also fig.*) feudal.

Seine [sein], *s.* (*Geog.*) die Seine.

seine, *s.* das Wadenetz, die Wade.

seise [si:z], *v.t.* (*Law*) Besitzerrechte übertragen (*Dat.*) (*of,* an (*Dat.*)), in den Besitz setzen (*of,* von); ***–d of,*** im Besitz von. **seisin** [-in], *s.* (*Law*) der Besitz von Land; die Ergreifung von Grundbesitz, der Grundbesitz.

seismic ['saizmik], *adj.* Erdbeben-, seismisch. **seismograph** [-məgrɑ:f], *s.* der Erdbebenanzeiger, der Seismograph. **seismologist** [-'mɔlədʒist], *s.* der Erdbebenforscher, Seismologe. **seismology** [-'mɔlədʒi], *s.* die Seismik, Erdbebenkunde. **seismometer** [-'mɔmitə], *s.* der Erdbebenmesser. **seismoscope** [-məskoup], *s. See* **seismograph.**

seizable ['si:zəbl], *adj.* (er)greifbar.

seize [si:z], **1.** *v.t.* 1. (*also* – ***hold of***) (er)greifen, fassen, packen; 2. sich bemächtigen (*Gen.*), sich (*Dat.*) aneignen, an sich reißen; 3. beschlagnahmen, in Beschlag *or* Besitz nehmen, mit Beschlag belegen; 4. erobern, (ein)nehmen (*a town etc.*), gefangennehmen, festnehmen (*a p.*); 5. (*fig.*) ergreifen, packen, überkommen, befallen (*as fear etc.*); ***be –d with,*** ergriffen *or* befallen sein von; 6. begreifen, erfassen (*idea etc.*); 7. (*Naut.*) zusammenbinden, zurren, laschen, zeisen, anbändseln; 8. (*Law*) *see* **seise. 2.** *v.i.* 1. (*Tech.*) (*also* – ***up***) festfahren, sich festfressen; (*fig.*) sich festklemmen, stecken bleiben; 2. – (***up***)***on,*** ergreifen, aufgreifen (*an idea*).

seizin, *see* **seisin.**

seizing ['si:ziŋ], *s.* 1. das Ergreifen, die Ergreifung;

2. (*Naut.*) das Bändsel, der Zurring, Lasching, das Seising; die Zurrung, Laschung, Lasche. **seizure** ['si:ʒə], *s.* 1. die Ergreifung; 2. (*Law*) Besitznahme, Beschlagnahme; 3. Verhaftung, (vorläufige) Festnahme; 4. (*Med.*) (plötzlicher) Anfall, der Schlaganfall.

sejant ['si:dʒənt], *adj.* (*Her.*) sitzend.

selachian [si'leikiən], **1.** *s.* der Hai(fisch). **2.** *adj.* Haifisch–.

seldom ['seldəm], *adv.* selten.

select [si'lekt], **1.** *v.t.* auslesen, auswählen. **2.** *adj.* 1. (aus)erlesen, auserwählt; – ***committee***, der Sonderausschuß, engerer Ausschuß; 2. exklusiv, vornehm; 3. wählerisch. **selected,** *adj.* ausgewählt. **selection** [–kʃən], *s.* 1. das (Aus)wählen, die Wahl; ***for*** –, zur Auswahl; ***make a*** –, eine Auswahl treffen; ***make one's own*** –, selbst die Auswahl treffen; 2. die Auslese, Auswahl (*of*, an (*Dat.*); ***from***, aus); 3. (*Biol.*) Zuchtwahl, Selektion. **selective** [–tiv], *adj.* 1. auswählend, Auswahl–; 2. (*Rad.*) selektiv, trennscharf. **selectivity** [selek'tiviti], *s.* (*Rad.*) die Abstimmschärfe, Trennschärfe, Selektivität. **selectness,** *s.* die Auserlesenheit, Exklusivität. **selector,** *s.* 1. der Auswähler; 2. (*Rad.*) Wähler.

selenate ['selineit], *s.* (*Chem.*) selensaures Salz. **selenic** [si'lenik], *adj.* selensauer. **selenium** [si'li:niəm], *s.* das Selen.

selenography [seli'nɔgrəfi], *s.* die Mondbeschreibung. **selenology** [–'nɔlədʒi], *s.* die Mondkunde, Mondforschung.

self [self], **1.** *s.* (*pl.* **selves** [selvz]) das Selbst, Ich; ***his better*** –, sein besseres Selbst; ***love of*** –, die Selbstliebe, Eigenliebe; ***my other*** –, mein zweites Ich; ***one's own*** –, das eigne Ich; ***my poor*** or ***humble*** –, meine Wenigkeit. **2.** *pron.* (*only in compounds*) selbst; ***he him***–, er selbst.

self|-abandonment, *s.* die Selbstvergessenheit, Selbstlosigkeit, Aufopferung, Entsagung, Hingabe. **--abasement,** *s.* die Selbsterniedrigung. **--abhorrence,** *s.* der Abscheu vor sich selbst. **--abnegation,** *s.* die Selbstverleugnung. **--absorbed,** *adj.* in sich selbst vertieft. **--abuse,** *s.* die Selbstbefleckung, Onanie. **--acting,** *adj.* selbsttätig, automatisch. **--addressed envelope,** *s.* der Freiumschlag. **--adjusting,** *adj.* selbstregelnd. **--aggrandizement,** *s.* die Selbstverherrlichung. **--appointed,** *adj.* selbsternannt. **--appreciation,** *s.* die Selbstwürdigung. **--approval,** *s.* die Selbstgefälligkeit. **--assertion,** *s.* das Geltungbedürfnis, die Anmaßung. **--assertive,** *adj.* geltungsbedürftig, anmaßend. **--assurance,** *s.* das Selbstbewußtsein, Selbstvertrauen. **--assured,** *adj.* selbstbewußt, selbstsicher. **--awareness,** *s.* das Selbstbewußtsein.

self|-betrayal, *s.* der Selbstverrat. **--centred,** *adj.* ichbezogen, selbstisch, egozentrisch, egoistisch. **--coloured,** *adj.* 1. naturfarbig; 2. einfarbig. **--complacent,** *adj.* selbstgefällig, selbstzufrieden. **--composed,** *adj.* beherrscht, gefaßt. **--conceit,** *s.* der Eigendünkel. **--conceited,** *adj.* dünkelhaft; eingebildet. **--confidence,** *s.* das Selbstbewußtsein, Selbstvertrauen. **--confident,** *adj.* selbstbewußt, selbstsicher. **--congratulation,** *s.* die Selbstbelobigung. **--conscious,** *adj.* verlegen, befangen, gehemmt, unfrei. **--consciousness,** *s.* die Verlegenheit, Befangenheit. **--consistent,** *adj.* konsequent, folgerichtig. **--constituted,** *adj.* selbsternannt. **--contained,** *adj.* 1. in sich abgeschlossen, eigenständig, unabhängig; (*Tech.*) vollständig, in sich geschlossen; – ***house***, das Einfamilienhaus; 2. (*of a p.*) selbstgenügsam, zurückhaltend, reserviert. **--contempt,** *s.* die Selbstverachtung. **--contented,** *adj.* selbstzufrieden, selbstgefällig. **--contradiction,** *s.* innerer Widerspruch. **--contradictory,** *adj.* sich (*Dat.*) selbst widersprechend, widerspruchsvoll. **--control,** *s.* die Selbstbeherrschung. **--critical,** *adj.* selbstkritisch. **--criticism,** *s.* die Selbstkritik.

self|-deception, *s.* der Selbstbetrug, die Selbsttäuschung. **--deceptive,** *adj.* sich selbst täuschend. **--defence,** *s.* die Selbstverteidigung, (*Law*) Notwehr; ***in*** –, aus Notwehr. **--delusion,** *s.* *See* **--deception. --denial,** *s.* die Selbstverleugnung. **--denying,** *adj.* selbstverleugnend. **--dependent,** *adj.* unabhängig, selbständig, auf sich selbst gestellt. **--depreciation,** *s.* die Selbstunterschätzung. **--determination,** *s.* die Selbstbestimmung. **--discipline,** *s.* die Selbstzucht. **--drive,** *adj.* Selbstfahrer–; – ***cars for hire***, Autovermietung für Selbstfahrer. **--driven,** *adj.* automatisch, selbstgetrieben, mit Selbstantrieb.

self|-educated, *adj.* autodidaktisch; – ***p.***, der Autodidakt. **--employed,** *adj.* selbständig. **--evident,** *adj.* selbstverständlich, offensichtlich, einleuchtend, augenscheinlich. **--feeder,** *s.* der Dauerbrandofen. **--feeding,** *adj.* sich selbst speisend, selbstregulierend. **--forgetful,** *adj.* selbstvergessen. **--glorification,** *s.* die Selbstverherrlichung. **--governing,** *adj.* sich selbst verwaltend, autonom. **--government,** *s.* die Selbstregierung, Selbstverwaltung, Autonomie. **--help,** *s.* die Selbsthilfe.

self|-ignition, *s.* die Selbstentzündung. **--importance,** *s.* der Eigendünkel, die Selbstüberhebung, Wichtigtuerei. **--imposed,** *adj.* selbstauferlegt. **--incrimination,** *s.* die Selbstanklage, Selbstbeschuldigung. **--induction,** *s.* (*Elec.*) die Selbstinduktion. **--indulgence,** *s.* die Genußsucht. **--indulgent,** *adj.* bequem. **--inflation,** *s.* die Aufgeblasenheit. **--inflicted,** *adj.* selbstauferlegt (*punishment*), selbstbeigebracht, selbstzugefügt (*injury*); (*Mil.*) – ***wounds***, die Selbstverstümmelung. **--interest,** *s.* eigener Vorteil, der Eigennutz. **--interested,** *adj.* eigennützig.

selfish ['selfiʃ], *adj.* selbstsüchig, egoistisch, eigennützig. **selfishness,** *s.* die Selbstsucht, der Egoismus, Eigennutz.

self|-justification, *s.* die Selbstrechtfertigung. **--knowledge,** *s.* die Selbsterkenntnis.

selfless ['selflis], *adj.* selbstlos, uneigennützig. **selflessness,** *s.* die Selbstlosigkeit.

self|-loading, *adj.* Selbstlade–. **--locking,** *adj.* selbstsperrend. **--love,** *s.* die Eigenliebe. **--lubricating,** *adj.* selbstschmierend. **--made,** *adj.* selbstgemacht; – ***man***, der Emporkömmling, Selfmademan. **--mastery,** *s.* die Selbstbeherrschung. **--mutilation,** *s.* die Selbstverstümmelung. **--opinion(at)ed,** *adj.* dünkelhaft, eigensinnig, eingebildet. **--pity,** *s.* die Selbstbemitleidung. **--portrait,** *s.* das Selbstbildnis. **--possessed,** *adj.* gefaßt, gelassen, (selbst)beherrscht. **--possession,** *s.* 1. die Selbstbeherrschung; 2. Fassung, Gelassenheit, Ruhe. **--praise,** *s.* das Eigenlob; – ***is no recommendation***, Eigenlob stinkt. **--preservation,** *s.* die Selbsterhaltung; ***instinct of*** –, der Selbsterhaltungstrieb. **--propelled,** *adj.* Selbstfahr–, mit Selbstantrieb; – ***gun***, das Geschütz mit Selbstfahrlafette. **--protection,** *s.* der Selbstschutz; ***in*** –, zum Selbstschutz.

self|-raising flour, *s.* das Mehl mit Backpulver. **--recording,** *adj.* selbstregistrierend. **--regard,** *s.* der Eigennutz, die Selbstachtung. **--regulating,** *adj.* selbstregelnd. **--reliance,** *s.* die Selbstsicherheit, das Selbstvertrauen. **--reliant,** *adj.* selbstvertrauend, selbstsicher. **--reproach,** *s.* der Gewissensvorwurf. **--respect,** *s.* die Selbstachtung. **--restraint,** *s.* die Selbstbeschränkung, Selbstbeherrschung. **--revelation,** *s.* die Selbstenthüllung. **--righteous,** *adj.* selbstgerecht. **--righteousness,** *s.* die Selbstgerechtigkeit.

self|-sacrifice, *s.* die Selbstaufopferung. **--sacrificing,** *adj.* sich selbst aufopfernd, aufopferungsvoll. **–same,** *adj.* ebenderselbe, ein und derselbe. **--satisfaction,** *s.* die Selbstzufriedenheit. **--satisfied,** *adj.* selbstzufrieden. **--sealing,** *adj.* selbstdichtend, schußsicher (*tank*). **--seeker,** *s.* der (die) Egoist(in), Selbstsüchtige(r), Eigennützige(r). **--seeking, 1.** *s.* die Selbstsucht, der Eigennutz. **2.** *adj.* egoistisch, eigennützig. **--service, 1.** *s.* die Selbstbedienung. **2.** *adj.* mit Selbstbedienung, Selbstbedienungs–. **--starter,** *s.* der Anlasser. **--styled,** *adj.* von eigenen Gnaden. **--sufficiency,** *s.* 1. der Hochmut,

Eigendünkel, die Selbstüberhebung; 2. (*Pol.*) Selbstversorgung, Autarkie, wirtschaftliche Unabhängigkeit. **--sufficient,** *adj.* 1. selbstgenügsam, dünkelhaft; 2. (*Pol.*) autark, wirtschaftlich unabhängig. **--suggestion,** *s.* die Autosuggestion. **--supporting,** *adj.* Selbstversorger–. **--surrender,** *s.* die Selbstaufgabe, Selbstpreisgabe.

self|-taught, *adj. See* **--educated. --timer,** *s.* (*Phot.*) der Selbstauslöser. **--will,** *s.* der Eigenwille, Eigensinn. **--willed,** *adj.* eigenwillig, eigensinnig. **--winding,** *adj.* mit Selbstaufzug, automatisch (*clock*).

Seljuk [sel'dʒu:k], **1.** *s.* der Seldschuke. **2.** *adj.* Seldschuken–.

sell [sel], **1.** *irr.v.t.* 1. verkaufen (*to,* an (*Acc.*); *at,* zu), veräußern, absetzen; *– by auction,* versteigern; *to be sold,* zu verkaufen; *– one's life dearly,* sein Leben teuer verkaufen; *– off* or *out,* ausverkaufen, räumen; *sold out,* ausverkauft, nicht mehr auf Lager; *– the pass,* Verrat begehen, treulos sein; *– up,* auspfänden; 2. (*fig.*) verkaufen, verraten; *– one's country,* sein Vaterland verraten; (*sl.*) *– him down the river,* ihn verraten und verkaufen; 3. (*sl.*) anpreisen, andrehen; (*usu. pass. be sold*) anschmieren, beschummeln, bemogeln, hereinlegen (*a p.*); *– him a pup,* ihm etwas aufschwatzen; *sold on,* begeistert von, eingenommen für. **2.** *v.i.* 1. verkaufen, handeln; 2. sich verkaufen (lassen), Absatz finden, abgehen (*as goods*). **3.** *s.* (*sl.*) der Schwindel, Betrug, Reinfall.

seller ['selə], *s.* 1. der (die) Verkäufer(in); *–'s market,* der Verkäufermarkt; 2. (*of goods*) der (Verkaufs)-schlager; *best –,* der Bestseller. **selling,** *s.* der Verkauf; *– cost,* Vertriebskosten (*pl.*); *– price,* der Verkaufspreis, Ladenpreis. **sell-out,** *s.* 1. (*coll.*) (*Theat.*) großer Erfolg, ausverkauftes Theaterstück; 2. (*sl.*) der Verrat.

Seltzer ['seltsə], *s.* das Selterswasser.

selvage ['selvidʒ], *s.* das Salband, die Salleiste, Gewebeleiste, Borte, feste (Webe)kante.

selves [selvz], *pl. of* **self.**

semantics [si'mæntiks], *pl.* (*sing. constr.*) die Wortbedeutungslehre, Semantik.

semaphore ['seməfɔ:], **1.** *s.* 1. (*Railw.*) der Signalapparat, Signalarm, das Flügelsignal; 2. optischer Telegraph; 3. (*Naut.*) das Flaggenwinken. **2.** *v.t.* durch Winkzeichen signalisieren, winken.

semblance ['sembləns], *s.* die Ähnlichkeit (*to,* mit), der Anschein, äußere Form *or* Gestalt, die Erscheinung.

sem(e)iology [si:mi'ɔlədʒi], *s.,* **sem(e)iotics** [–'ɔtiks], *pl.* (*sing. constr.*) (*Med.*) die Semiotik, Symptomatologie.

semen ['si:mən], *s.* (tierischer) Samen, das Sperma.

semi– ['semi], *pref.* Halb–, halb–.

semi|-annual, *adj.* halbjährlich. **--automatic,** *adj.* halbautomatisch. **-breve,** *s.* ganze Note; *– rest,* ganze Pause. **-circle,** *s.* der Halbkreis. **-circular,** *adj.* halbkreisförmig, Halbkreis–. **-colon,** *s.* der Strichpunkt, das Semikolon. **-conductor,** *s.* der Halbleiter. **-conscious,** *adj.* halbbewußt. **--detached,** *adj.* halb freistehend, an einer Seite angebaut; *– house,* die eine Hälfte eines alleinstehenden Doppelhauses. **--durable,** *adj.* beschränkt haltbar. **--final,** *s.* (*Spt.*) die Vorschlußrunde, das Halbfinale. **--fluid, --liquid,** *adj.* halbflüssig, zähflüssig.

seminal ['seminl], *adj.* 1. Samen–, Sperma–; Zeugungs–; 2. (*fig.*) Entwicklungs–, Keim–, schöpferisch, fruchtbar, zukunftsträchtig.

seminar ['seminɑ:], *s.* (*Univ.*) das Seminar. **seminary** [–əri], *s.* 1. die Bildungsanstalt, Akademie; 2. (*R.C.*) das (Priester)seminar; 3. (*fig.*) die Pflanzstätte, (Pflanz)schule.

semination [semi'neiʃən], *s.* (*Bot.*) die Samenbildung.

semi|-official, *adj.* halbamtlich. **--precious,** *adj.* Halbedel–. **--professional,** *adj.* nebenberuflich. **-quaver,** *s.* die Sechzehntelnote; *– rest,* die Sechzehntelpause. **--rigid,** *adj.* halbstarr (*airships*). **--skilled,** *adj.* angelernt. **--solid,** *adj.* halbfest.

Semite ['si:mait], *s.* der Semit (die Semitin). **Semitic** [si'mitik], **1.** *s.* das Semitisch(e) (*language*). **2.** *adj.* semitisch. **Semitism** ['semitizm], *s.* judenfreundliche Politik.

semi|tone, *s.* der Halbton, halber Ton. **--tracked,** *adj.* Halbketten– (*vehicle*). **--transparent,** *adj.* halbdurchsichtig. **--tropical,** *adj.* halbtropisch. **--vowel,** *s.* der Halbvokal.

semolina [semə'li:nə], *s.* der (Weizen)grieß.

sempiternal [sempi'tə:nl], *adj.* immerwährend unendlich, ewig.

sempstress ['sempstris], *s. See* **seamstress.**

senate ['senit], *s.* 1. der Senat (*also Univ.*); (*Univ.*) *Senate house,* das Senatsgebäude; 2. (*Am. Pol.*) *the Senate,* der Senat, das Oberhaus. **senator,** *s.* der Senator, das Senatsmitglied. **senatorial** [–'tɔ:riəl], *adj.* senatorisch, Senats–. **senatus** [sə'neitəs], *s.* (*Scots Univ.*) der Senat.

send [send], **1.** *irr.v.t.* 1. senden, schicken; befördern, verschicken, absenden, übersenden, zuschicken, zukommen lassen; *– one's love to,* herzlich grüßen lassen; *– a message to,* Bescheid schicken (*Dat.*); *– one's regards to,* grüßen lassen; *God – him a speedy release!* Gott gebe ihm baldige Erlösung! *– word,* sagen lassen (*Dat.*), Nachricht geben (*Dat.*), benachrichtigen; 2. (*with verb complement*) *– flying,* hinschleudern; *– packing,* fortjagen, hinauswerfen (*a p.*); *– staggering,* ins Taumeln bringen; 3. (*Rad. etc.*) senden. **(a)** (*with adv.*) *– away,* fortschicken, wegschicken; entlassen; *– down,* (*Univ.*) (zeitweise) relegieren; herabdrücken; *– forth,* hinausschicken; aussenden (*light*); hervorbringen, treiben (*leaves etc.*); hervorbringen, ausstoßen, von sich geben (*a cry*); veröffentlichen, verbreiten; *– in,* hineinschicken; einschicken, einsenden, einreichen; *– in one's name,* sich melden; *– in one's papers,* seinen Abschied einreichen; *– off,* abschicken, absenden (*a th.*); wegschicken, fortschicken, entlassen (*a p.*); *– on,* vorausschicken; nachsenden (*a letter*); *– out,* hinausschicken; aussenden, verbreiten, veröffentlichen; *– round,* herumreichen, umlaufen lassen; *– up,* hinaufschicken; von sich geben, ausstoßen (*a cry*); in die Höhe treiben (*prices*); (*sl.*) einsperren.
(b) (*with prep.*) *– him about his business,* ihn kurz abfertigen; *– him on an errand,* ihm einen Auftrag geben, ihn einen (Boten)gang tun lassen; *– him out of his mind,* ihn rasend machen; *– a stone through the window,* einen Stein durchs Fenster werfen; *– s.th. to him,* ihm etwas schicken; *– him to Coventry,* ihn schneiden; *– coals to Newcastle,* Eulen nach Athen tragen; *– goods to market,* den Markt beschicken; *– to school,* zur Schule schicken; *– him to prison,* ihn einsperren.
2. *irr.v.i.* 1. (*Rad. etc.*) senden; 2. *– for,* senden *or* schicken nach, holen lassen, bestellen (*a th.*), kommen lassen (*a p.*); *– for the doctor,* den Arzt holen *or* rufen.

sender ['sendə], *s.* der (die) Absender(in), (Über)-sender(in). **send|-off,** *s.* (*coll.*) 1. der Abschied, die Verabschiedung; 2. Abschiedsfeier. **--up,** *s.* (*coll.*) die Nachahmung, Karikatur.

senescence [si'nesəns], *s.* das Altwerden, Altern. **senescent,** *adj.* alternd.

seneschal ['senəʃəl], *s.* (*Hist.*) der Hausmeier, Majordomus.

senile ['si:nail], *adj.* greisenhaft, altersschwach, senil; *– decay,* die Altersschwäche; *– dementia,* der Altersblödsinn. **senility** [si'niliti], *s.* die Greisenhaftigkeit, Altersschwäche, Senilität.

senior ['si:niə], **1.** *adj.* 1. älter; 2. dienstälter, rangälter; *– common room,* das Dozentenzimmer; *– partner,* der Seniorchef, älterer Teilhaber. **2.** *s.* 1. Ältere(r); *he is my – by five years* or *five years my –,* er ist fünf Jahre älter als ich; 2. der Senior, Dienstältere(r), Rangältere(r), Vorgesetzte(r); *he is my – in office,* er geht mir im Dienstalter vor. **seniority** [–ni'ɔriti], *s.* höheres (Dienst)alter; *by –,* nach dem Dienstalter.

senna ['senə], *s.* Sennesblätter (*pl.*).
sennight ['senait], *s.* (*obs.*) acht Tage, eine Woche; *this day* –, heute vor *or* in acht Tagen.
sensation [sen'seiʃən], *s.* 1. die (Sinnes)empfindung, (Sinnes)wahrnehmung, der Sinneseindruck, das Gefühl; 2. (*coll.*) der Eindruck, das Aufsehen, die Erregung, Aufregung, Sensation; *make* or *create a* –, Aufsehen erregen; 3. (*coll.*) (*of a th.*) die Sensation. **sensational,** *adj.* 1. (*coll.*) aufsehenerregend, Sensations–, sensationell; 2. (*Psych.*) Sinnes–, Gefühls–, Empfindungs–, sensualistisch. **sensationalism,** *s.* 1. (*coll.*) die Effekthascherei, Sensationssucht; 2. (*Psych.*) der Sensualismus. **sensationalist,** *s.* der Effekthascher.
sense [sens], **1.** *s.* 1. der Sinn; die Sinnesfunktion, das Sinnesvermögen, Sinnesorgan; – *of hearing,* der Gehörsinn; – *of sight,* der Gesichtssinn; – *of smell,* der Geruchssinn; – *of taste,* der Geschmackssinn; – *of touch,* der Tastsinn; *the five* –*s,* die fünf Sinne; *bring him to his* –*s,* ihn zur Vernunft *or* Besinnung bringen; *out of one's* –*s,* von *or* nicht bei Sinnen; *take leave of one's* –*s,* den Verstand verlieren; 2. das Gefühl (*of, Gen.*); – *of dread,* das Gefühl der Furcht; – *of pain,* das Schmerzgefühl; – *of security,* das Gefühl der Sicherheit; – *of shame,* das Schamgefühl; – *of wrong,* das Gefühl erlittenen Unrechts; 3. das Gefühl, Verständnis, die Empfänglichkeit, Empfindung, der Sinn (*of,* für); – *of beauty,* der Sinn für Schönheit; – *of direction,* der Orientierungssinn, Ortssinn, das Ortsgedächtnis; – *of duty,* das Pflichtbewußtsein; – *of honour,* das Ehrgefühl; – *of humour,* der Sinn für Humor; – *of justice,* der Gerechtigkeitssinn; *moral* –, sittliches Empfinden, das Sittlichkeitsgefühl; – *of proportion,* das Gefühl fürs richtige Verhältnis; – *of propriety,* das Gefühl für Anstand; – *of responsibility,* das Verantwortungsgefühl, Verantwortungsbewußtsein; 4. die Vernunft, der Verstand; *common* –, gesunder Menschenverstand; *good* –, die Klugheit; *man of* –, verständiger Mensch; *have the* – *to do it,* gescheit genug sein, es zu tun; *talk* –, vernünftig reden; 5. die Bedeutung, der Sinn (*of a word etc.*); *figurative* –, übertragener *or* bildlicher Sinn; *literal* –, wörtlicher Sinn; *proper* –, eigentliche Bedeutung; *strict* –, engerer Sinn; *in a* or *one* –, in gewissem Sinne *or* gewisser Hinsicht, gewissermaßen; *devoid of all* –, völlig sinnlos; *that makes* –, das hat Hand und Fuß, das klingt plausibel; *make* – *of,* sich (*Dat.*) zusammenreimen, Sinn hereinbringen in (*Acc.*), klug werden aus; *make no* –, keinen Sinn haben; 6. (*Math.*) die Richtung.
2. *v.t.* ahnen, fühlen, empfinden, spüren.
senseless ['senslis], *adj.* 1. sinnlos, unsinnig (*of a th.*); 2. unvernünftig, blödsinnig (*of a p.*); 3. (*rare*) gefühllos, empfindunglos; 4. (*coll.*) bewußtlos, besinnungslos, ohnmächtig. **senselessness,** *s.* 1. die Sinnlosigkeit; 2. Unvernunft; 3. Bewußtlosigkeit.
sensibility [sensi'biliti], *s.* 1. das Empfindungsvermögen, Empfinden, Gefühl; 2. die Empfänglichkeit, Empfindlichkeit (*to,* für); 3. *pl.* das Feingefühl, Zartgefühl, die Sensibilität. **sensible** ['sensibl], *adj.* 1. fühlbar, empfindbar, (be)merkbar, wahrnehmbar, erkennbar, spürbar, merklich; 2. (*of a p.*) verständig, vernünftig, einsichtig; 3. *be* – *of,* empfinden, fühlen, merken; einsehen, würdigen, sich (*Dat.*) bewußt sein (*Gen.*). **sensibleness** ['sensiblnis], *s.* die Klugheit, Einsicht, Vernünftigkeit, Verständigkeit.
sensitive ['sensitiv], *adj.* 1. Empfindungs–, empfindend; 2. (über)empfindlich (*to,* gegen); *be* – *to,* empfindlich sein gegen, empfänglich sein für, (leicht) reagieren auf (*Acc.*); 3. (*Tech.*) empfindlich, (*Phot.*) lichtempfindlich; – *market,* schwankender Markt; – *plant,* die Sinnpflanze, Mimose; 4. (*of a p.*) feinfühlig, feinnervig, sensibel. **sensitiveness, sensitivity** [–i'tiviti], *s.* 1. die Empfindungsfähigkeit; 2. Empfindlichkeit (*to,* gegen) (*also Tech.*); 3. (*of a p.*) Sensibilität, das Feingefühl.
sensitization [sensitai'zeiʃən], *s.* (*Phot.*) das Lichtempfindlichmachen. **sensitize** ['sensitaiz], *v.t.* sensibilisieren; (licht)empfindlich machen. **sensitized,** *adj.* lichtempfindlich. **sensitizer,** *s.* (*Phot.*) der Sensibilisator.
sensorial [sen'sɔ:riəl], *adj.* *See* **sensory. sensorium,** *s.* 1. (*Anat.*) der Sitz der bewußten Sinneswahrnehmungen (im Gehirn); 2. (*Psych.*) Sinnesapparat, das Bewußtsein. **sensory** ['sensəri], *adj.* Sinnes–, Empfindungs–.
sensual ['sensjuəl], *adj.* 1. sinnlich, wollüstig; 2. (*esp. B.*) fleischlich, körperlich; 3. (*Phil.*) sensualistisch. **sensualism,** *s.* 1. (*Phil.*) der Sensualismus; 2. die Sinnlichkeit. **sensualist,** *s.* 1. (*Phil.*) der Sensualist; 2. Sinnenmensch. **sensuality** [–ju'æliti], *s.* die Sinnlichkeit, Lüsternheit. **sensualize,** *v.t.* sinnlich machen.
sensuous ['sensjuəs], *adj.* 1. sinnlich, Sinnes–, Sinnen–; 2. sinnenfreudig, sinnfällig. **sensuousness,** *s.* die Sinnlichkeit, Sinnfälligkeit, Sinnenfreudigkeit.
sent [sent], *imperf., p.p. of* **send**; *heaven*-–, vom Himmel gesandt.
sentence ['sentəns], **1.** *s.* 1. (*Gram.*) der Satz; *compound* –, zusammengesetzter Satz; *complex* –, das Satzgefüge; 2. (*Law*) der Rechtsspruch, Richterspruch, das Urteil; die Strafe; *pass* –, das Urteil fällen (*on,* über (*Acc.*)); (*fig.*) ein Urteil fällen; *serve one's* –, seine Strafe absitzen; – *of death,* das Todesurteil; *pass* – *of death* (*up*)*on,* zum Tode verurteilen; *under* – *of death,* zum Tode verurteilt; – *of imprisonment,* die Gefängnisstrafe, Freiheitsstrafe; *life* –, lebenslängliche Zuchthausstrafe. **2.** *v.t.* (*Law*) das Urteil fällen *or* sprechen über (*Acc.*), verurteilen (*to,* zu).
sententious [sen'tenʃəs], *adj.* 1. spruchreich, sentenzenreich; 2. kurz und bündig, gedrängt, prägnant. **sententiousness,** *s.* die Kürze, Gedrängtheit, Prägnanz, Bündigkeit.
sentience ['senʃəns], *s.* das Gefühl, die Empfindung. **sentient,** *adj.* empfindend, fühlend, empfindungsfähig.
sentiment ['sentimənt], *s.* 1. das Gefühl, die (Gefühls)regung; Empfindung, Empfindsamkeit, Gefühlsseligkeit, Rührseligkeit, Gefühlsduselei; *man of* –, zartfühlender Mensch; 2. (*oft. pl.*) die Meinung, Gesinnung, Haltung; *noble* –*s,* edle Gesinnung.
sentimental [senti'mentl], *adj.* 1. gefühlvoll, empfindsam, rührselig, sentimental; 2. gefühlsmäßig, Gefühls–; – *value,* der Liebhaberwert. **sentimentalism, sentimentality** [–'tæliti], *s.* die Empfindsamkeit, Sentimentalität, Rührseligkeit, Gefühlsduselei. **sentimentalist,** *s.* der Gefühlsmensch. **sentimentalize, 1.** *v.i.* sentimental sein *or* werden *or* reden *or* schreiben (*over, about,* über (*Dat.*) *or* bei). **2.** *v.t.* sentimental gestalten.
sentinel ['sentinəl], *s.* 1. (*fig.*) der Wächter, Wach(t)mann; *stand* –, Wache stehen; 2. (*Mil.*) *see* **sentry,** 1. **sentinel crab,** *s.* die Stielaugenkrabbe.
sentry ['sentri], *s.* (*Mil.*) 1. die (Schild)wache, der (Wacht)posten; 2. der Wachdienst; *on* –, auf Posten *or* Wache; *stand* –, Wache stehen *or* (*coll.*) schieben, (auf) Posten stehen. **sentry|-box,** *s.* das Schilderhaus. **–-go,** *s.* der Wachdienst, Postengang.
sepal [sepl], *s.* (*Bot.*) das Kelchblatt.
separability [sepərə'biliti], *s.* die Trennbarkeit. **separable** ['sepərəbl], *adj.* 1. trennbar, (ab)lösbar; 2. (*Chem.*) scheidbar. **separableness,** *s.* die Trennbarkeit.
separate, 1. ['sepəreit], *v.t.* 1. trennen, (ab)sondern, (aus)scheiden, entfernen; 2. (*Law*) scheiden, (ehelich) trennen; auseinanderbringen (*combatants etc.*); 3. unterscheiden, auseinanderhalten; 4. (*Chem.*) scheiden, (ab)spalten; zentrifugieren (*milk*), absetzen lassen (*cream from milk*). **2.** [–eit], *v.i.* 1. auseinandergehen, scheiden; sich trennen, sich lossagen, sich lösen (*from,* von), ausscheiden (aus); 2. (*Law*) sich (ehelich) trennen; 3. (*Chem.*) sich absondern *or* ausscheiden. **3.** [–it], *adj.* 1. getrennt, losgelöst, abgesondert, isoliert; *keep* –,

auseinanderhalten; 2. gesondert, Sonder–, einzeln, Einzel–, Separat–; verschieden, zu unterscheiden(d); (*Law*) – ***estate,*** eingebrachtes Sondergut (*of the wife*); – ***beds,*** getrennte Betten, Einzelbetten.

separately ['sepəritli], *adv.* besonders, getrennt, für sich. **separateness,** *s.* die Abgeschiedenheit, Isoliertheit. **separates,** *pl.* (*coll.*) zweiteiliges Kleid. **separating** [–eitiŋ], *adj.* Trenn–, Scheide–.

separation [sepə'reiʃən], *s.* 1. die Trennung, Auflösung, Absonderung, das Scheiden; 2. (*Law*) die Aufhebung der ehelichen Gemeinschaft, (Ehe)-trennung; – ***allowance,*** (*Law*) Alimente (*pl.*), (*Mil.*) die Familienunterstützung.

separatism ['sepərətizm], *s.* der Separatismus, das Loslösungsbestreben. **separatist, 1.** *s.* 1. der Separatist, Sonderbündler, Sezessionist; 2. (*Eccl.*) Sektierer. **2.** *adj.* separatistisch. **separative,** *adj.* Trennungs–, trennend. **separator** [–eitə], *s.* 1. (*Weav.*) der Scheidekamm, Schlichtkamm; 2. die Zentrifuge, Trennschleuder (*for milk*).

sepia ['si:piə], *s.* 1. (*Ichth.*) der Kuttelfisch, die Tintenschnecke; 2. Sepia (*colour*).

sepoy ['si:pɔi], *s.* der Sepoy.

sepsis ['sepsis], *s.* die Sepsis, Blutvergiftung.

sept [sept], *s.* die Sippe, Gruppe, der Stamm, das Geschlecht.

sept–, *pref.* sieben–.

septal [septl], *adj.* (*Bot.*) Septum–. **septate** [–teit], *adj.* durch eine Scheidewand abgeteilt, mit Scheidewänden, septiert.

September [sep'tembə], *s.* der September; ***in*** –, im September.

septenary [sep'ti:nəri], **1.** *adj.* 1. Sieben–; 2. *See* **septennial. 2.** *s.* der Satz von sieben Dingen. **septennial** [–'teniəl], *adj.* 1. siebenjährig; 2. siebenjährlich, alle sieben Jahre.

septentrional [sep'tentriənl], *adj.* nördlich, Nord–.

septet [sep'tet], *s.* (*Mus.*) das Septett.

septi– ['septi], *pref. See* **sept–.**

septic ['septik], **1.** *adj.* fäulniserregend; (*Med.*) septisch, infiziert, vereitert. **2.** *s.* (*Tech.*) – ***tank,*** der Faulbehälter. **septicaemia** [–ti'si:miə], *s.* die Sepsis, Blutvergiftung.

septuagenarian [septjuədʒi'nɛəriən], **1.** *adj.* siebzigjährig. **2.** *s.* der (die) Siebziger(in), Siebzigjährige(r). **Septuagesima** [–'dʒesimə], *s.* (der Sonntag) Septuagesima (*f.*). **Septuagint** ['septjuədʒint], *s.* die Septuaginta.

septum ['septəm], *s.* (*Anat., Bot.*) die (Scheide)-wand, das Septum.

septuple ['septju:pl], *adj.* siebenfach.

sepulchral [si'pʌlkrəl], *adj.* 1. Grab–, Begräbnis–, Bestattungs–; 2. (*fig.*) Grabes–, Toten–, düster. **sepulchre** ['sepəlkə], *s.* das Grab(mal), die Gruft, Grabstätte.

sepulture ['sepəltʃə], *s.* das Begräbnis, die Beisetzung, Beerdigung, Bestattung, Grablegung.

sequel ['si:kwəl], *s.* 1. die Folge (*to, Gen.*); ***in the*** –, in der Folge, wie sich herausstellte; 2. die Folgeerscheinung, Wirkung (*of, Gen.*); 3. Fortsetzung (*to a story*).

sequence ['si:kwəns], *s.* 1. die (Reihen)folge, Aufeinanderfolge; – ***of tenses,*** die Zeitenfolge; 2. die Reihe, Serie; (*Cards, Mus.*) Sequenz; ***in*** –, der Reihe nach; 3. (*Films*) die Szene; 4. (*fig.*) Folgerichtigkeit, logische Folge, die Konsequenz. **sequent, 1.** *adj.* (aufeinander)folgend (***to, on,*** auf (*Acc.*)). **2.** *s.* zeitliche *or* logische Folge. **sequential** [si'kwenʃəl], *adj.* 1. folgend (***to,*** auf (*Acc.*)); 2. folgerichtig, konsequent.

sequester [si'kwestə], *v.t.* 1. entfernen, zurückziehen; 2. *See* **sequestrate. sequestered** [–təd], *adj.* abgeschieden, zurückgezogen, einsam. **sequestrate** [–treit, 'si:kwestreit], *v.t.* (*Law*) sequestrieren, mit Beschlag belegen, beschlagnahmen. **sequestration** [si:kwes'treiʃən], *s.* 1. die Absonderung, Entfernung, Ausschließung, der Ausschluß (***from,*** von *or* aus); 2. (*Law*) die Beschlagnahme, Sequestration, Zwangsverwaltung, das Sequester. **sequestrator** ['si:kwestreitə], *s.* der Sequester, Zwangsverwalter.

sequestrum [si'kwestrəm], *s.* (*Med.*) das Sequester, abgestorbenes Knochenstück.

sequin ['si:kwin], *s.* 1. (*Hist.*) die Zechine; 2. die Ziermünze, Spange.

Sequoia [si'kwɔiə], *s.* die Riesentanne, der Mammutbaum.

seraglio [sə'rɑ:liou], *s.* 1. das Serail; 2. der Harem.

serai [se'rai], *s.* die Karawanserei.

seraph ['serəf], *s.* (*pl.* **-s** *or* **-im**) der Seraph. **seraphic** [–'ræfik], *adj.* seraphisch, engelhaft, (*fig.*) ekstatisch, verzückt.

Serb [sə:b], **1.** *s.* der Serbe (die Serbin). **2.** *adj.* serbisch. **Serbia** [–iə], *s.* Serbien (*n.*). **Serbian, 1.** *adj. See* **Serb, 2. 2.** *s.* 1. *See* **Serb, 1**; 2. (*language*) das Serbisch(e). **Serbo-Croatian** [–oukrou'eiʃən], *s.* das Serbokroatisch(e).

[1]**sere** [siə], *see* **sear.**

[2]**sere,** *s.* der Abzugsstollen (*of firearms*).

serenade [serə'neid], **1.** *s.* das Ständchen, die Abendmusik, Nachtmusik, Serenade. **2.** *v.t., v.i.* ein Ständchen bringen (*Dat.*).

serene [si'ri:n], *adj.* 1. klar, hell, heiter (*as weather*); 2. (*of a p.*) friedlich, gelassen, ruhig(-heiter); 3. (*as title*) ***His Serene Highness,*** Seine Durchlaucht, Serenissimus. **serenity** [si'reniti], *s.* 1. die Heiterkeit; 2. Gelassenheit, heitere (Gemüts)ruhe, gelassene Heiterkeit; 3. Durchlaucht (*f.*) (*as title*).

serf [sə:f], *s.* Leibeigene(r). **serfdom** [–dəm], **serfhood,** *s.* die Leibeigenschaft.

serge [sə:dʒ], *s.* die Serge, Sersche, Sarsche.

sergeant ['sɑ:dʒənt], *s.* der Sergeant, Unteroffizier; ***colour–***–, der Feldwebel; ***drill–***–, der Exerzierunteroffizier; ***quartermaster–***–, der Furier; ***staff–***–, der Unterfeldwebel (*infantry*), Unterwachtmeister (*cavalry, artillery*). **sergeant-major,** *s.* der Feldwebel (*infantry*), Wachtmeister (*cavalry, artillery*); ***regimental*** –, der Regiments-Hauptfeldwebel.

serial ['siəriəl], **1.** *adj.* periodisch, serienmäßig, Reihen–, Serien–; – ***number,*** laufende Nummer, die Seriennummer; – ***production,*** die Serienherstellung; – ***story,*** die Fortsetzungsgeschichte. **2.** *s.* das Lieferungswerk, Serienwerk; der Fortsetzungsroman; (*Rad., T.V.*) die Sendereihe. **serialization** [–ai'zeiʃən], *s.* periodische Veröffentlichung. **serialize,** *v.t.* in Fortsetzungen veröffentlichen. **serially,** *adv.* in Lieferungen, reihenweise. **seriate** [–rieit], *adj.* in Reihen geordnet, Reihen–. **seriatim** [–ri'eitim], *adv.* der Reihe nach.

sericeous [se'riʃəs], *adj.* seidig, seidenartig, Seiden–. **sericulture** ['serikʌltʃə], *s.* die Seidenraupenzucht, Seidenproduktion.

series ['siəri:z], *s.* die Reihe (*also Math.*), (Reihen)-folge, Serie, der Satz; – ***of books,*** die Bücherfolge; (*Elec.*) – ***connection,*** die Reihenschaltung.

serif ['serif], *s.* (*Typ.*) der Haarstrich.

serin ['serin], *s.* (*Orn.*) der Girlitz (*Serinus canaria*).

seringa [si'riŋgə], *s.* (*Bot.*) der Pfeifenstrauch.

serio-comic ['siəriou'kɔmik], *adj.* ernst-komisch.

serious ['siəriəs], *adj.* 1. ernst(gemeint), ernsthaft, ernstlich; ***be*** –, es ernst *or* im Ernst meinen (***about,*** mit); – ***attempt,*** ernsthafter Versuch; – ***matter,*** ernsthafte Angelegenheit; 2. ernstzunehmend, bedenklich, kritisch, gefährlich; – ***enemy,*** ernstzunehmender Feind; – ***illness,*** gefährliche *or* schwere Krankheit; 3. bedeutend, (ge)wichtig; 4. seriös, gesetzt, feierlich. **seriously,** *adv.* ernst, im Ernst, ernstlich; – ***now,*** allen Ernstes, ernst gesprochen. **seriousness,** *s.* 1. die Ernsthaftigkeit, der Ernst; 2. die Wichtigkeit; 3. Bedenklichkeit.

serjeant ['sɑ:dʒənt], *s. See* **sergeant. serjeant|-at-arms,** *s.* (*Parl.*) der Stabträger, höchster Ordnungsbeamter. **–-at-law,** *s.* (*obs.*) höherer Rechtsanwalt, der Staatssyndikus.

sermon ['sə:mən], *s.* 1. die Predigt; ***preach a*** –, eine Predigt halten; ***Sermon on the Mount,*** die Bergpredigt; 2. (*coll.*) die Mahnrede, Gardinenpredigt, Strafpredigt. **sermonize, 1.** *v.i.* im Predigerton sprechen; Moral predigen. **2.** *v.t.* vorpredigen (*Dat.*), eine Moralpredigt halten (*Dat.*), abkanzeln.

serology [siə'rɔlədʒi], *s.* die Serumkunde. **serosity** [–siti], *s.* 1. seröser Zustand; 2. seröse Flüssigkeit. **serous** ['siərəs], *adj.* 1. serös, serumartig; 2. serumabsondernd.

serpent ['sə:pənt], *s.* 1. (große) Schlange; 2. (*fig.*) die (Gift)schlange. **serpentine** [–ain], **1.** *adj.* 1. schlangenartig, schlangenförmig, Schlangen–; 2. (*fig.*) sich schlängelnd *or* windend, geschlängelt. **2.** *v.i.* sich schlängeln *or* winden. **3.** *s.* 1. die Serpentine, Schlangenlinie; 2. (*Geol.*) der Serpentin.

serpiginous [sə:'pidʒinəs], *adj.* flechtenartig. **serpigo** [–'paigou], *s.* (*Med.*) fressende Flechte.

serradilla [serə'dilə], *s.* (*Bot.*) die Serradella.

serrate ['sereit], **serrated** [sə'reitid], *adj.* gezähnt, gezackt, zackig. **serration** [sə'reiʃən], *s.* die Auszackung, Auszähnung, Zacke, der Zacken.

serried ['serid], *adj.* dicht(gedrängt), geschlossen (*ranks*).

serum ['siərəm], *s.* 1. das (Blut)serum; 2. Heilserum, Schutzserum.

serval [sə:vl], *s.* der Serval, die Buschkatze.

servant ['sə:vənt], *s.* 1. der Diener (*also fig.*), Dienstbote; (*also* **–girl**) das Dienstmädchen, die Magd, Dienerin; *pl.* Dienstboten (*pl.*), das Hauspersonal; ***domestic* –**, Hausangestellte(r); (*coll.*) ***your humble* –**, meine Wenigkeit; ***your obedient* –**, Ihr sehr ergebener (*in official letters*); ***–'s hall***, die Gesindestube; 2. ***civil* –**, Staatsbeamte(r); ***public* –**, Beamte(r), Angestellte(r).

serve [sə:v], **1.** *v.t.* 1. dienen (*Dat.*), im Dienst stehen bei; ***if my memory –s me right***, wenn ich mich recht erinnere; ***it –s him as*** or ***for a handkerchief***, es dient ihm als Taschentuch; 2. bedienen (*customers*); 3. (*also* – *up*) servieren, reichen, vorlegen, auftragen (*food*); (*fig. coll.*) ***– up***, auftischen; ***first come first –d***, wer zuerst kommt mahlt zuerst; 4. verwalten (*an office*); 5. ableisten; ***– an apprenticeship***, in die Lehre gehen; ***– one's sentence***, seine Strafe verbüßen *or* absitzen; ***– one's time***, amtieren (*in office*), (*Mil.*) seine Zeit abdienen; ***– out***, ausdienen (*time*); 6. erfüllen; ***– my purpose***, meinen Zwecken dienen; ***– the purpose of***, den Zweck erfüllen als; ***– no purpose***, nichts nützen; ***it –s his turn***, es paßt sich gerade für ihn, es nützt ihm gerade; 7. befriedigen, begnügen; ***– his needs***, seine Bedürfnisse befriedigen; 8. (*Law*) zustellen (*Dat.*); ***– a notice*** or ***summons*** or ***warrant*** or ***writ on him***, ***– him with a notice etc.***, ihm eine Vorladung schicken, ihm einen Gerichtsbefehl zustellen, ihn vorladen *or* vor Gericht zitieren; 9. ***– out***, verteilen, austeilen (*supplies*); 10. behandeln; (*coll.*) ***– him out (for it)***, es ihm (mit gleicher Münze) heimzahlen; ***it –s him right***, das geschieht ihm recht; 11. bedienen (*guns*); 12. (*Naut.*) bekleiden (*ropes*); 13. belegen, bespringen, decken (*female animal*); 14. (*Tenn.*) aufschlagen, angeben. **2.** *v.i.* 1. dienen (*also Mil.*), (*Mil.*) (Wehr)dienst tun (***with***, bei); in Dienst sein, (*Mil.*) im Dienst stehen (***under***, *Gen.*); angestellt sein (***with***, bei); 2. amtieren, fungieren (*in an official position*); 3. (*Comm.*) aufwarten, bedienen; servieren (*at table*); 4. passen, geeignet *or* günstig *or* zuträglich sein; ***as occasion –s***, bei passender Gelegenheit; 5. genügen, ausreichen, hinlänglich sein; 6. dienen, nützen; ***it –s to show***, daran kann man sehen *or* erkennen; 7. (*Tenn.*) den Aufschlag machen, angeben. **3.** *s.* (*Tenn.*) der Aufschlag.

server ['sə:və], *s.* 1. (*Eccl.*) der Meßdiener, Ministrant; 2. (*Tenn.*) Aufschläger; 3. Präsentierteller, das Tablett; *pl.* Servierbesteck.

Servian ['sə:viən], *see* **Serbian.**

[1]**service** ['sə:vis], **1.** *s.* 1. der Dienst; die (Dienst)stellung (*of servants*); ***in* –**, in Stellung *or* Dienst; ***go into* –**, in Stellung gehen; ***go out to* –**, in Stellung gehen; ***take – with***, eine Stellung annehmen bei; ***take him into one's* –**, ihn in Stellung nehmen; 2. die Dienstleistung, Unterstützung, Hilfe, Gefälligkeit, der Gefallen; ***be at his* –**, ihm zu Diensten *or* zur Verfügung stehen; ***do*** or ***render him a* –**, ihm einen Gefallen tun; ***offer one's –s***, seine Unterstützung *or* Hilfe *or* seinen Beistand bieten; ***place it at his* –**, es ihm zur Verfügung stellen; 3. der Nutzen, Vorteil; ***be of – to***, nützlich sein (*Dat.*), nützen (*Dat.*), von Nutzen sein für; 4. der Dienst; ***news* –**, der Nachrichtendienst; ***postal* –**, das Postwesen, der Postdienst; ***press* –**, der Pressedienst; ***social* –**, soziale Arbeit; ***telephone* –**, der Telephondienst; 5. öffentlicher Dienst, der Wehrdienst, Militärdienst, Kriegsdienst; ***– abroad***, der Auslandsdienst; ***active* –**, aktiver Dienst; ***on active* –**, im aktiven Dienst; ***armed –s***, Gesamtstreitkräfte (*pl.*); ***civil* –**, der Staatsdienst, die Beamtenschaft; ***consular* –**, der Konsulatsdienst; ***the (fighting) –s***, die Wehrmacht; ***foreign* –**, *see* ***– abroad***; ***on Her Majesty's* –**, frei durch Ablösung (*on letters*); ***merchant* –**, die Handelsmarine; ***military* –**, der Kriegsdienst; Wehrdienst, Militärdienst; ***universal military* –**, allgemeine Wehrpflicht; ***public* –**, öffentlicher Dienst; ***secret* –**, der Geheimdienst; ***see* –**, Kriegsdienst tun; ***senior* –**, die Marine; 6. die Bedienung, das Aufwarten, Servieren; (*Comm.*) der Kundendienst; (*Motor.*) Inspektion; ***after-sale* –**, der Kundendienst; 7. (*also* ***divine* –**) der Gottesdienst, kirchliche Handlung; ***attend* –**, den Gottesdienst besuchen; ***conduct*** or ***take the* –**, den Gottesdienst abhalten; ***divine* –**, der Gottesdienst; ***marriage* –**, die Trauhandlung; Trauungsliturgie; ***morning* –**, die Morgenandacht, der Frühgottesdienst; 8. das Service, Tafelgeschirr, Tafelgerät; ***dinner* –**, das Speiseservice; 9. der Betrieb; ***in* –**, in Betrieb; ***go into* –**, in Betrieb gesetzt *or* genommen werden; ***out of* –**, außer Betrieb; 10. die Versorgung, der (Versorgungs)betrieb (*of gas, water etc.*); ***essential –s***, lebenswichtige Betriebe (*pl.*); 11. der Verkehr, Verkehrsdienst, Transport; ***passenger* –**, der Personenverkehr; ***train* –**, die Bahnverbindung; 12. (*Artil.*) die Bedienung; 13. (*Tenn.*) der Aufschlag, die Angabe; 14. (*Naut.*) das Bekleidungsmaterial; 15. (*Law*) die Zustellung (*of a writ*). **2.** *v.t.* instandsetzen, überholen; instandhalten, warten (*a vehicle etc.*), (*in Germany official & obligatory*) technisch überwachen.

[2]**service,** *s.* **–berry,** der Speierling, die Elzbeere; **–tree,** der Sperberbaum, Zahme Eberesche.

serviceable ['sə:visəbl], *adj.* 1. nützlich, brauchbar; 2. haltbar, dauerhaft, solide, strapazierfähig (*as cloth*). **serviceableness,** *s.* die Nützlichkeit, Brauchbarkeit.

service| area, *s.* (*Rad. etc.*) der Sendebereich. **– charge,** *s.* der Bedienungszuschlag. **–-corps,** *s.* (*Mil.*) Versorgungstruppen, Fahrtruppen (*pl.*). **–-court,** *s.* (*Tenn.*) das Aufschlagsfeld. **– department,** *s.* (*Comm.*) die Kundendienstabteilung. **– depot,** *s.* die Reparaturstelle, Kundendienststelle. **–-dress,** *s.* (*Mil.*) der Dienstanzug. **– flat,** *s.* die Etagenwohnung mit Bedienung. **–-hatch,** *s.* die Durchreiche, das Servierfenster. **–-line,** *s.* (*Tenn.*) die Grundlinie. **–man** [–mən], *s.* Angehörige(r) der Streitkräfte. **–-pipe,** *s.* das Zuleitungsrohr, Anschlußrohr. **–-station,** *s.* (*Motor.*) die Reparaturwerkstatt; (*official*) Technische Überwachungsverein (*abbr.* TÜV).

servicing ['sə:visiŋ], *s.* die Instandhaltung, Wartung, Pflege; (*Motor.*, *official*) technische Überwachung.

serviette [sə:vi'et], *s.* die Serviette, das Mundtuch.

servile ['sə:vail], *adj.* 1. sklavisch, knechtisch; unterwürfig, servil, kriechend; 2. (*fig.*) sklavisch genau, unselbständig, unoriginell; 3. (*obs.*) Sklaven–. **servility** [–'viliti], *s.* 1. (sklavische) Unterwürfigkeit, Hörigkeit; Liebdienerei, Kriecherei; 2. (*fig.*) Unselbständigkeit.

serving ['sə:viŋ], *s.* die Portion. **serving|-girl,** *s.* (*obs.*) das Dienstmädchen. **–-man,** *s.* (*obs.*) der Diener.

servitor ['sə:vitə], *s.* 1. (*Poet.*) der (die) Diener(in); 2. (*fig.*) Anhänger(in), der Gefolgsmann; 3. (*obs.*) (zu Diensten verpflichteter) Stipendiat (*at Oxford Univ.*).

servitude ['sə:vitju:d], *s.* 1. die Knechtschaft,

Sklaverei; ***in – to***, in einem Dienstverhältnis zu; ***penal –***, die Zuchthausstrafe, Zwangsarbeit; 2. (*fig.*) die Unfreiheit, Versklavung; 3. (*Scots Law*) die *or* das Servitut, die Nutznießung, das Nutzungsrecht.

servo ['sə:vou], *s. Abbr. for* **servo|motor. --control,** *s.* die Servosteuerung, Servolenkung. **–motor,** *s.* der Servomotor, Stellmotor.

sesame ['sesəmi], *s.* (*Bot.*) der Sesam; das Sesamöl; ***open –!*** Sesam, tu dich auf!

seseli ['sesəli], *s.* (*Bot.*) der Bergfenchel, Sesel.

sesqui– ['seskwi], *pref.* anderthalb. **sesqui|-alter(al)** [–'æltə(rəl)], *adj.* anderthalbmal soviel, im Verhältnis von 3:2. **–centennial,** *adj.* (*s.*) hundertfünfzigjährig(e Feier). **–ocellus,** *s.* der Augenfleck (*butterfly's wing*). **–pedalian** [–pe-'deiliən], *adj.* vielsilbig, schwerfällig, ungelenk (*of a word*). **–tertial,** *adj.* im Verhältnis von 4:3.

sessile ['sesail], *adj.* (*Bot.*) stiellos.

session ['seʃən], *s.* 1. die Sitzung, Sitzungsperiode; ***be in –***, tagen; ***full –***, die Plenarsitzung; 2. (*Univ.*) akademisches Jahr, das Studienjahr; 3. *pl.* Gerichtssitzungen (*pl.*); ***petty –s***, summarisches Gericht; ***quarter –s***, vierteljährliches Grafschaftsgericht. **sessional,** *adj.* Sitzungs–.

sestet [ses'tet], *s.* 1. (*Mus.*) das Sextet; 2. (*Metr.*) zweite Hälfte eines Sonetts. **sestina** [–'ti:nə], *s.* (*Metr.*) die Sestine.

set [set], **1.** *irr.v.t.* 1. setzen (*also sails, type*), stellen (*also clocks, problems*); 2. (ein)richten, einsetzen, ansetzen, festsetzen, angeben, bestimmen, vorschreiben, aufstellen, niederlegen; 3. versetzen, zurechtsetzen, zurechtstellen, zurechtmachen, herrichten, einstellen, anlegen, anordnen; 4. fassen (*precious stones*); 5. in Musik setzen, vertonen (*a text*); 6. ansetzen (*seeds*), (aus)pflanzen (*trees etc.*); 7. gerinnen lassen (*milk*), hart werden lassen (*cement etc.*); 8. schärfen, schleifen, abziehen (*knives*), richten (*files*), schränken (*saws*); 9. (*Hunt.*) stellen, anzeigen (*game*).

(a) (*with noun*) ***– the alarm,*** den Wecker stellen; (*coll.*) ***– the ball rolling,*** den Stein ins Rollen bringen; ***– bounds to,*** see ***– limits***; (*coll.*) ***she – her cap at him,*** sie war hinter ihm her, sie suchte ihn zu angeln; ***– a date for,*** ein Datum ansetzen *or* das Datum festsetzen für; ***– a dog on*** or ***at,*** einen Hund hetzen auf (*Acc.*); ***– an examination paper,*** Prüfungsaufgaben stellen; ***– an example,*** ein Beispiel geben; ***– (one's) eyes on,*** zu Gesicht bekommen; ***– one's face against,*** sich widersetzen (*Dat.*); ***– the fashion,*** die Mode einführen *or* vorschreiben, (*fig.*) den Ton angeben; ***– fire to,*** anzünden, in Brand stecken, Feuer legen an (*Acc.*); ***– a fracture,*** einen (Knochen)bruch einrichten; ***have one's hair –,*** sich (*Dat.*) die Haare einlegen lassen; ***– one's hand to,*** Hand legen an (*Acc.*), in Angriff nehmen; ***I – my hand and seal to,*** hiermit unterzeichne ich; ***– one's heart on,*** sein Herz hängen an (*Acc.*); ***– one's hopes on,*** Hoffnung setzen auf (*Acc.*); (*fig.*) ***– one's house in order,*** Ordnung schaffen; ***– limits to,*** Grenzen setzen (*Dat.*); ***– one's mind on,*** seinen Sinn richten auf (*Acc.*), versessen sein auf (*Acc.*); ***– one's mind to,*** sich widmen (*Dat.*), sich befleißigen (*Gen.*), sich (*Dat.*) Mühe geben mit; ***– his mind at rest,*** ihn beruhigen; ***– one's mouth*** (or ***lips***), den Mund zusammenziehen; ***– the pace,*** das Tempo angeben; ***– a pattern,*** ein Musterbeispiel geben; ***– pen to paper,*** die Feder ansetzen *or* ergreifen; zur Feder greifen; ***– a price on,*** einen Preis aussetzen auf (*Acc.*); ***– a razor,*** ein Rasiermesser abziehen; ***– sail,*** unter Segel gehen; (*fig.*) ***– sail for,*** abreisen nach; (*fig.*) ***– its seal on,*** besiegeln; ***– one's shoulder to the wheel,*** sich tüchtig ins Zeug legen, sich kräftig anstrengen; ***– spies on,*** bespitzeln; ***– spurs to,*** die Sporen geben (*Dat.*); ***– (great) store by,*** (großen) Wert legen auf (*Acc.*), hoch einschätzen; ***– little store by,*** gering einschätzen; ***– the table,*** den Tisch decken; ***– him a task,*** ihm eine Aufgabe stellen; ***– one's teeth,*** die Zähne zusammenbeißen; ***– a trap,*** eine Falle (auf)stellen; ***– one's trust in,*** sein Vertrauen setzen in (*Acc.*) *or* auf (*Acc.*); ***– a watch,*** eine Wache aufstellen.

(b) (*with adv.*) **– afoot,** *see* ***– on foot***; **– apart,** beiseite legen, auf die Seite legen; **– alight,** *see* ***– fire to***; **– aside,** 1. beiseitelegen, beiseitesetzen; 2. (*fig.*) verwerfen, (*esp. Law*) aufheben, umstoßen, für ungültig *or* nichtig erklären, annullieren; **– back,** zurückstellen; **– by,** zurücklegen, aufsparen; **– down,** 1. absetzen, niedersetzen, hinsetzen (*a th.*); 2. absetzen, aussteigen lassen (*a p.*); 3. niederschreiben, aufschreiben, (schriftlich) niederlegen, aufzeichnen (*in writing*); 4. (*fig.*) zuschreiben (*to, Dat.*), halten (*as,* für), betrachten, einschätzen, auslegen, erklären (als); **– forth,** darlegen, darstellen, dartun, an den Tag legen, zeigen; erklären, auseinandersetzen; (*coll.*) ***– one's best foot*** **forward,** auf dem rechten Wege voranschreiten; **– in,** einsetzen; **– off,** 1. explodieren lassen (*bomb etc.*), in Tätigkeit setzen, betätigen (*mechanism*); 2. (*with pres. part.*) bringen zu; ***it – me off laughing,*** es brachte mich zum Lachen; 3. (*fig.*) hervorheben, hervortreten lassen, zur Geltung bringen; 4. abheben, kontrastieren, herausstreichen; 5. ausgleichen, aufwiegen, wettmachen, beheben (*deficiency*); 6. anrechnen (***against,*** gegen), als Ausgleich nehmen (für); **– on,** 1. anstellen, antreiben (*a p.*), hetzen (*dogs etc.*) (*to,* auf (*Acc.*)); 2. (*coll.*) anstellen, engagieren (*workers*); 3. (*rare*) anspornen, dazu verleiten; **– out,** 1. ausbreiten, anordnen, arrangieren, herrichten; 2. (*fig.*) darlegen, auseinandersetzen; ***– o.s. out,*** es sich (*Dat.*) zum Ziel setzen (*to do,* zu tun); **– up,** 1. errichten, aufrichten, aufstellen, aufschlagen; (*coll.*) ***that will – me up again,*** das bringt mich wieder auf die Beine; 2. (*fig.*) gründen, (er)schaffen, ins Leben rufen (*business etc.*), etablieren (*a p.*) (*with financial help*), versorgen, versehen (*a p.*) (*with goods*); 3. erheben (*a cry etc.*); 4. ***– o.s. up as,*** Anspruch darauf machen, zu sein.

(c) (*with prep.*) **– against,** 1. (*a p.*) aufbringen gegen; ***– o.s. against,*** sich auflehnen gegen, sich zur Wehr setzen gegen; 2. (*a th.*) als Ausgleich nehmen für; 3. entgegensetzen, gegenüberstellen (*Dat.*); **– at *defiance,*** Trotz bieten (*Dat.*); ***– at ease,*** beruhigen; ***– him at his ease,*** ihm die Befangenheit nehmen; ***– at large*** or ***liberty,*** befreien, in Freiheit setzen; ***– at nought*** or ***naught,*** in den Wind schlagen; ***– at rest,*** beruhigen; ***– at variance,*** entzweien; **– before,** vorsetzen, vorlegen, darlegen, ausbreiten (*Dat.*); **– by *the ears,*** see ***– at variance***; (*coll.*) ***be (all)*** **– for,** startklar sein für; **– in *action,*** in Gang *or* zum Funktionieren bringen; ***– in order,*** ordnen, in Ordnung bringen; **– on,** herfallen über (*Acc.*); ***– on edge,*** hochkantig stellen; (*fig.*) ***– his teeth*** or ***nerves on edge,*** ihn kribbelig *or* nervös machen; ***– on fire,*** in Brand stecken; (*fig.*) (*a p.*) entflammen; ***he won't – the Thames on fire,*** er ist kein großes Kirchenlicht, er hat das Pulver nicht erfunden; ***– on foot,*** in Gang *or* zustande bringen, in die Wege leiten; ***– on high,*** erheben; (*coll.*) ***be – on,*** versteift *or* erpicht *or* versessen sein auf (*Acc.*); ***be – on going,*** fest entschlossen sein zu gehen; **– to *music,*** vertonen, in Musik setzen; ***– to rights,*** in Ordnung bringen; ***– him to work,*** ihn beschäftigen *or* zur Arbeit anstellen; **– upon,** *see* ***– on.***

(d) (*with verb*) ***– him to do,*** ihn veranlassen *or* ihm aufgeben zu tun; ***– o.s. to do,*** sich (*Dat.*) vornehmen *or* sich (*Dat.*) angelegen sein lassen, zu tun; ***– going,*** in Gang bringen; ***– him laughing,*** ihn zum Lachen bringen; ***– him thinking,*** ihm zu denken geben.

2. *irr.v.i.* 1. gerinnen (*milk*), hart *or* fest werden (*jelly*), abbinden (*cement*), (*fig.*) starr *or* steif werden, sich zusammenziehen, einen entschlossenen Ausdruck annehmen (*of face*); 2. ausreifen, sich fertig entwickeln, die endgültige Form annehmen; 3. fließen, strömen, laufen (*of tide*), wehen, kommen (*of wind*); 4. (*fig.*) sich richten (*of attitudes*); 5. untergehen (*sun etc.*); 6. (*Hunt.*) vorstehen (*as dogs*).

(a) (*with prep.*) **– about,** 1. in Angriff nehmen, sich machen an (*Acc.*), sich anschicken, anfangen, beginnen (***doing,*** zu tun); 2. (*coll.*) herfallen über (*Acc.*) (*a p.*); **– to *work,*** sich an die Arbeit machen, sich daranmachen *or* darangehen.

(b) (*with adv.*) – **forth,** *see* – *off*; – **in,** eintreten, sich einstellen; einsetzen (*as weather*); – **off,** sich aufmachen, aufbrechen, sich auf den Weg machen (*for*, nach); – ***off on a journey,*** eine Reise antreten; – **out,** 1. *See* – *off*; 2. (*fig.*) es sich (*Dat.*) zum Ziel machen, sich (*Dat.*) vornehmen, sich anschicken; 3. (*fig.*) ausgehen (***from,*** von); – **to,** ernstlich darangehen, sich (energisch) daranmachen, (*coll.*) sich dahinterklemmen; – **up,** sich niederlassen *or* etablieren; – ***up for o.s.,*** sich selbständig machen; – ***up to be,*** Anspruch darauf machen zu sein, sich ausgeben für, sich aufspielen als.

3. *adj.* 1. fest, festgelegt, gefestigt, unbeweglich, starr; – ***face,*** starre Miene; – ***purpose,*** fester Vorsatz; ***with – teeth,*** mit zusammengebissenen Zähnen; 2. festgesetzt, vorherbestimmt, festgelegt, vorgeschrieben; – ***books,*** vorgeschriebene Bücher; ***at – distances,*** in bestimmten Entfernungen; 3. (ein)gefaßt (*jewels*); 4. wohlgesetzt, wohldurchdacht, formell (*speech etc.*); 5. ***be hard –,*** in bedrängter Lage *or* großer Not; 6. ***thick-–,*** untersetzt; ***well-–,*** wohlgestaltet, wohlgebaut.

4. *s.* 1. (*of things*) der Satz, die Garnitur, das Besteck (*of instruments*), Service (*of crockery*); (*Math.*) die Menge, Reihe, Folge, Serie, Sammlung, (*Comm.*) Kollektion; – ***of rooms,*** die Zimmerflucht; – ***of teeth,*** das Gebiß; 2. (*of persons*) der Kreis, Klüngel, die Gruppe, Gesellschaft, Clique, Sippschaft, Bande; (*coll.*) ***the fast*** or ***jet –,*** die Lebewelt; 3. die Haltung, Lage (*of head etc.*); 4. der Sitz, Schnitt (*of dress*); 5. Lauf, die Richtung (*of wind*); (*fig.*) Strömung; 6. Neigung; 7. (*Theat.*) die Dekoration, (Bühnen)ausstattung, das Bühnenbild; 8. (*Rad.*) das Gerät, der Apparat; 9. (*of a dance*) die Tour; 10. (*Hort.*) der Ableger, Setzling; 11. (*Tenn.*) Satz; 12. das Festwerden, Hartwerden (*of liquids*); 13. (*Poet.*) der Untergang (*of sun*); 14. das Lager (*of a badger*); 15. (*Hunt.*) das Vorstehen (*of dogs*); (*sl.*) ***make a dead – at,*** heftig angreifen, nicht loslassen wollen; (*sl.*) ***make a dead – at men,*** nach Männern angeln (*of women*).

setaceous [si'teiʃəs], *adj.* borstig, Borsten–, borstenartig.

set|back, *s.* der Rückschlag, Rückfall. **–down,** *s.* der Dämpfer, die Zurechtweisung. **–-off,** *s.* 1. der Kontrast; 2. Schmuck, die Zierde; 3. (*Comm.*) Entschädigung, Gegenforderung; der Ausgleich. **–-screw,** *s.* (*Tech.*) die Klemmschraube, Stellschraube. **–-square,** *s.* das Zeichendreieck, Winkellineal.

settee [se'ti:], *s.* das Sofa, der Polsterbank, Polstersitz.

setter ['setə], *s.* 1. der Vorstehhund; 2. (*oft. in compounds*) Setzer, *e.g.* ***type-–,*** der Schriftsetzer.

setterwort ['setəwə:t], *s.* (*Bot.*) Stinkende Nieswurz.

setting ['setiŋ], *s.* 1. das Setzen; 2. (Ein)fassen (*of jewels*); die Fassung; ***claw-–,*** die Ajourfassung; ***crown-–,*** die Kastenfassung; 3. (*Tech.*) die Bettung, der Sockel, Untersatz; 4. (*Theat.*) die Ausstattung, das Bühnenbild; (*fig.*) Milieu, die Situation, Lage, Umgebung, der Hintergrund, Rahmen, Schauplatz, Handlungsraum; 5. Untergang (*of sun etc.*); 6. das Hartwerden, Festwerden, die Erstarrung, Gerinnung (*of fluid*); 7. (*Tech.*) Einstellung; 8. (*Mus.*) Vertonung.

setting|-rule, *s.* (*Typ.*) die Setzlinie. **–-stick,** *s.* (*Typ.*) der Winkelhaken.

[1]**settle** [setl], **1.** *v.i.* 1. sich ansiedeln *or* niederlassen (*in territory*), ansässig werden (*in a place*); – ***down,*** sich niederlassen, sich häuslich einrichten, einen Hausstand gründen, (*fig.*) sich ins tägliche Leben zurückfinden, sich zurechtfinden, sich einleben; – (***down***) ***to work,*** sich auf die Arbeit konzentrieren, sich der Arbeit widmen *or* zuwenden; – ***in,*** einziehen (*new dwelling*); 2. sich niederlassen (*as a bird*); 3. sich setzen *or* niederschlagen (*as sediment*); sich abklären (*as a liquid*); sich senken, (ab)sinken (*as a wall*); – ***down,*** sinken, absacken (*as a ship*), sich setzen (*as sediment*); (*fig., as fury*) zur Ruhe kommen, nachlassen, sich legen *or* beruhigen; – ***into shape,*** feste Form annehmen; – ***out,*** ausscheiden, ausfallen (*as sediment*); 4. sich festsetzen (***in, on,*** in (*Dat.*)), sich legen (auf (*Acc.*)) (*as a disease*); 5. (*fig.*) sich einigen *or* abfinden, eine Vereinbarung treffen; (*coll.*) – ***for,*** sich zufrieden geben mit; – (***up***)***on,*** sich entschließen zu, sich entscheiden für; 6. zahlen, abrechnen; (*coll.*) – ***up,*** die Rechnung bezahlen; – ***with him,*** mit ihm abrechnen, zu einem Vergleich mit ihm kommen; 7. sich aufklären, beständig werden (*as weather*). **2.** *v.t.* 1. festsetzen, bestimmen, abmachen, ausmachen, ansprechen, vereinbaren, sich einigen auf (*Acc.*); (*iron.*) ***that –s it!*** das hat noch gefehlt! ***that is –d,*** das ist ausgemacht; 2. erledigen, ordnen, regeln, klären (*a matter*); 3. bezahlen, begleichen (*a debt*); 4. schlichten, beilegen, ausgleichen (*disputes etc.*); 5. besiedeln (*territory*), ansiedeln (*population*); versorgen, unterbringen, etablieren (*one's children*), unter die Haube bringen (*a daughter*); – ***o.s.,*** sich niederlassen, (*fig.*) sich in Ruhe anschicken (***to,*** zu), sich heranmachen (an (*Acc.*)); 6. (*Law*) aussetzen (*sum of money*) (***on,*** *Dat.*), (*property*) vermachen (*Dat.*), überschreiben, übertragen (auf (*Acc.*)); 7. (*coll.*) (*a p.*) zum Schweigen bringen; den Garaus machen (*Dat.*); – ***his hash,*** ihm einen Strich durch die Rechnung machen.

[2]**settle,** *s.* (*obs.*) die Ruhebank, Sitzbank.

settled [setld], *adj.* 1. fest(stehend), gefestigt, bestimmt; entschieden, erwiesen; – ***abode,*** ständiger Wohnort; – ***conviction,*** feste Überzeugung; – ***habit,*** eingewurzelte Gewohnheit; – ***order of things,*** fest begründete Ordnung; – ***weather,*** beständiges Wetter; 2. versorgt, verheiratet; besiedelt (*territory*); ***be –,*** ansässig sein; – ***life,*** ruhiges *or* gesetztes Leben.

settlement ['setlmənt], *s.* 1. die Festsetzung, Regelung; ***Act of Settlement,*** das Gesetz zur Festsetzung der Thronfolge; 2. die Beilegung, Schlichtung, Beseitigung (*of differences*), Lösung, Klärung (*of doubts, queries*); 3. (*Comm.*) Bezahlung, Begleichung (*of debts*), Abmachung, Vereinbarung, der Vergleich, Ausgleich, das Abkommen, Übereinkommen; (*St. Exch.*) die Abrechnung, Kontenabgleichung; ***come to*** or ***reach a –,*** ein Übereinkommen treffen, zu einem Vergleich gelangen; ***compulsory –,*** der Zwangsvergleich; (*fig.*) ***day of –,*** der Tag der Abrechnung; ***marriage –,*** der Ehevertrag; 4. die Versorgung, Unterbringing, Etablierung (*of dependants*); 5. Besiedelung, Ansiedelung (*of territory*); Niederlassung, Siedlung, Kolonie; 6. soziale Arbeitsgemeinschaft (*in Engl.*); ***university –,*** das Universitätshilfwerk (im Armenviertel); 7. (*Law*) die (Eigentums)übertragung, das Vermächtnis; ***make a – upon,*** ein Vermächtnis aussetzen (*Dat.*); 8. (*Build.*) das Absacken, Absinken.

settler ['setlə], *s.* 1. der Ansiedler, Kolonist; 2. (*coll.*) das Ausschlaggebende *or* Entscheidende, der Treffer; 3. (*sl.*) derbe Abfertigung, die Abfuhr. **settling,** *s.* 1. die Ansiedelung, Besiedelung (*of a country*); 2. Senkung (*of ground, buildings*); 3. Beilegung (*of disputes*); 4. (*Comm.*) Abrechnung; (*Tech.*) Ablagerung, der Niederschlag; *pl.* (*Tech.*) der (Boden)satz. **settling-day,** *s.* (*St. Exch.*) der Abrechnungstag.

set|-to, *s.* (*coll.*) heftige Auseinandersetzung, die Rauferei. **–-up,** *s.* (*coll.*) der Aufbau, die Anlage, Organisation.

seven [sevn], **1.** *num. adj.* sieben; (*for clock time see under* **eight**) –***-league boots,*** Siebenmeilenstiefel (*pl.*); ***Seven Years' War,*** Siebenjähriger Krieg. **2.** *s.* die Sieben; ***the – of clubs,*** Treff *or* Kreuz sieben; ***be at sixes and –s,*** auf dem Kopf stehen, in Verwirrung sein; uneinig sein (***about,*** über (*Acc.*)). **sevenfold,** *adj.* siebenfach.

seventeen [sevn'ti:n], *num. adj.* siebzehn; ***sweet –,*** blühende Jugendschönheit. **seventeenth, 1.** *num. adj.* siebzehnt. **2.** *s.* (*fraction*) das Siebzehntel.

seventh [sevnθ], **1.** *num. adj.* sieb(en)t; ***Seventh Day Adventists,*** Sabbatarier, Siebenten-Tags-Adventisten (*pl.*); ***in the – heaven,*** im siebenten Himmel.

2. *s.* **1.** (*fraction*) das Sieb(en)tel; 2. (*Mus.*) die Septime. **seventhly,** *adv.* sieb(en)tens.

seventies ['sevntiz], *pl.* die Siebziger (*of life-span*), die siebziger Jahre (*of century*). **seventieth** [-tiəθ], **1.** *num. adj.* siebzigst. **2.** *s.* (*fraction*) das Siebzigstel. **seventy** [-ti], **1.** *num. adj.* siebzig; *--one,* einundsiebzig. **2.** *s.* die Siebzig.

sever ['sevə], **1.** *v.t.* 1. (ab)trennen, (ab)sondern, scheiden (*from*, von); 2. zerschneiden, zerreißen, durchtrennen, zertrennen (*rope etc.*); 3. (*Law*) teilen; 4. (*fig.*) lösen; *- o.s.,* sich lösen *or* absondern. **2.** *v.i.* sich trennen, (zer)reißen (*as a rope*).

several ['sevərəl], *adj.* 1. (*also sing.*) (*Law, formal*) einzeln, besonder, verschieden; ***three - armies,*** drei verschiedene Heere; (*Law*) ***joint and -,*** Gesamt–; ***each - part,*** jeder einzelne Teil; 2. eigen, persönlich; ***they went their - ways,*** sie gingen jeder seinen (eigenen) Weg; 3. (*usu. pl.*) mehrere, verschiedene; ***- large ships,*** mehrere große Schiffe; ***- times,*** mehrmals. **severally,** *adv.* besonders, gesondert, einzeln; ***jointly and -,*** einzeln und gemeinsam. **severalty** [-ti], *s.* (*Law*) der Eigenbesitz.

severance ['sevərəns], *s.* 1. die Trennung; 2. (*usu. fig.*) Lösung; ***- of relations,*** der Abbruch der Beziehungen; (*Comm.*) ***- pay,*** die Abfindungsentschädigung.

severe [si'viə], *adj.* 1. streng, hart, schonungslos, unnachsichtig ((***up***)*on*, gegen); 2. heftig, stark (*as pain*); 3. ernst, schmucklos, schlicht, einfach (*in style*); 4. rauh, streng (*as weather*); 5. genau, gründlich, schwer, exakt (*as a test*); 6. schlimm, schwer (*accident etc.*); 7. scharf (*criticism*); 8. schwer, hart, mühsam (*exertions*). **severely,** *adv.* streng, strikt; ***- ill,*** ernstlich *or* schwer krank; ***leave - alone,*** streng *or* (*iron.*) ängstlich meiden, einen großen Bogen machen um. **severity** [-'veriti], *s.* 1. die Strenge, Härte, Schärfe, Heftigkeit, Stärke; 2. Rauheit; 3. Schmucklosigkeit, Ernsthaftigkeit, der Ernst, die Einfachheit, Schlichtheit; 4. Genauigkeit, Schwierigkeit, Exaktheit, Gründlichkeit.

Seville [sə'vil], *s.* Sevilla, *n.*; ***- orange,*** die Bitterorange.

sew [sou], **1.** *irr.v.t.* nähen; heften, broschieren (*a book*); ***- in,*** einnähen; ***- on,*** annähen; ***- up,*** zunähen, zusammennähen; ***- up a wound,*** eine Wunde nähen; (*sl.*) (*pass. only*) ***all -n up,*** schon herausklamüsert. **2.** *irr.v.i.* nähen.

sewage ['sju:idʒ], *s.* das Kloakenwasser, Abwasser, Sielwasser; ***- disposal,*** die Abwasserbeseitigung; ***- farm,*** das Rieselfeld.

[1]**sewer** ['souə], *s.* 1. der (die) Näher(in); 2. (*Bookb.*) die Heftmaschine.

[2]**sewer** ['sju:ə], *s.* der Abwasserkanal, Siel, die Kloake. **sewerage** [-ridʒ], *s.* die Kanalisation. **sewer|-gas,** *s.* das Faulschlammgas. **--rat,** *s.* die Wanderratte.

sewing ['souiŋ], *s.* das Nähen, die Näharbeit, Näherei; ***- machine,*** die Nähmaschine.

sex [seks], *s.* 1. (natürliches) Geschlecht; ***of both -es,*** beiderlei Geschlechts; ***the gentle -,*** das zarte Geschlecht; ***the weaker -,*** das schwache Geschlecht; 2. (*coll.*) Geschlechtliche(s), der Sexus, die Erotik; ***- appeal,*** der Sex-Appeal.

sex–, *pref.* sechs–.

sexagenarian [seksədʒi'nɛəriən], **1.** *s.* der (die) Sechziger(in), Sechzigjährige(r). **2.** *adj.* sechzigjährig. **sexagenary** [-'dʒi:nəri], *adj.* 1. sechzigteilig; 2. sechzigjährig. **Sexagesima** [-'dʒesimə], *s.* (der Sonntag) Sexagesima (*f.*). **sexagesimal** [-'dʒesiml], *adj.* sechzigst; Sexagesimal–, mit 60 als Grundzahl, sechzigfach untergeteilt.

sex|angle, *s.* das Sechseck, Hexagon. **–angular,** *adj.* sechseckig, sechswinkelig, hexagonal.

sex-bomb, *s.* (*sl.*) das Sexbömbchen.

sexcentenary [seksen'ti:nəri], **1.** *s.* die Sechshundertjahrfeier. **2.** *adj.* sechshundertjährig.

sex|-crime, *s.* das Sexualverbrechen. **--determination,** *s.* die Geschlechtsbestimmung.

sex|digital, –digitate [-'didʒiteit], *adj.* sechsfingerig, sechszehig.

sex-education, *s.* sexuelle Aufklärung, die Sexualpädagogik.

sexennial [seks'eniəl], *adj.* 1. sechsjährig; 2. sechsjährlich.

sexifid ['seksifid], *adj.* (*Bot.*) sechsspaltig, sechsteilig. **sexifoil,** *s.* (*Archit.*) sechsblätterige Figur.

sexillion [sek'siliən], *s.* *See* **sextillion.**

sexiness ['seksinis], *s.* (*coll.*) die Sinnlichkeit.

sexi|syllabic, *adj.* sechssilbig. **–valence,** *s.* (*Chem.*) die Sechswertigkeit. **–valent,** *adj.* sechswertig.

sexless ['sekslis], *adj.* geschlechtslos, ungeschlechtlich, asexual, agamisch. **sex|-life,** *s.* das Sexualleben, Geschlechtsleben. **--linked,** *adj.* (*Biol.*) gengebunden. **sexology** [-'ɔlədʒi], *s.* die Sexualwissenschaft.

sexpartite [seks'pɑ:tait], *adj.* sechsteilig.

sextain ['sekstein], *s.* sechszeilige Strophe, das Hexastichon.

sextant ['sekstənt], *s.* der Sextant. **sextet** [seks'tet], *s.* das Sextett.

sextillion [seks'tiliən], *s.* die Sextillion (*Brit.* = 1 mit 36 Nullen; *French, Am.* = 1 mit 21 Nullen).

sexto ['sekstou], *s.* das Sexto(format). **sextodecimo** [-'desimou], *s.* das Sedez(format).

sexton ['sekstən], *s.* der Küster, Kirchendiener; Totengräber. **sexton-beetle,** *s.* der Aaskäfer.

sextuple [seks'tju:pl], **1.** *adj.* sechsfach; (*Mus.*) ***- time,*** der Sechsertakt. **2.** *v.t.* versechsfachen. **sextuplet** ['sekstjuplit], *s.* 1. der Sechsling (*child*); 2. die Sechsergruppe; 3. (*Mus.*) Sextole.

sexual ['seksjuəl], *adj.* geschlechtlich, Geschlechts–, sexual, sexuell; ***- desire,*** die Geschlechtslust, der Geschlechtstrieb; ***- intercourse,*** der Geschlechtsverkehr. **sexuality** [-ju'æliti], *s.* die Geschlechtlichkeit, Sexualität. **sexy** ['seksi], *adj.* (*coll.*) geschlechtsbetont, sinnlich; (*of a novel etc.*) schwül.

Seychelles [sei'ʃel(z)], *pl.* die Seschellen (*pl.*).

shabbily ['ʃæbili], *adv.* *See* **shabby. shabbiness,** *s.* 1. die Schäbigkeit; 2. (*coll.*) Gemeinheit. **shabby,** *adj.* 1. schäbig (*also fig.*), abgetragen, abgenutzt, fadenscheinig; 2. (*fig.*) niederträchtig, lumpig, gemein; 3. (*coll.*) filzig, knickerig. **shabby|-genteel,** *adj.* vornehm aber arm. **--gentility,** *s.* vornehme Armut.

shabrack ['ʃæbræk], *s.* (*Mil.*) die Schabracke.

shack [ʃæk], *s.* (*coll.*) die Hütte, Bude, Baracke.

shackle [ʃækl], **1.** *s.* 1. (*Naut.*) der Schäkel; 2. *pl.* Fesseln, Handschellen, Beinschellen (*pl.*); (*fig.*) die Fessel, Ketten (*pl.*). **2.** *v.t.* 1. (*Naut.*) (an)-schäkeln; 2. (*fig.*) fesseln, hemmen.

shad [ʃæd], *s.* (*Ichth.*) die Alse.

shaddock ['ʃædək], *s.* (*obs.*) die Pampelmuse.

shade [ʃeid], **1.** *s.* 1. der Schatten; das Dunkel; schattiger *or* dunkler Ort; ***the -s,*** die Unterwelt, das Schattenreich; ***leave in the -,*** weit hinter sich lassen; ***light and -,*** Licht und Schatten. (*fig.*) die Kontrastwirkung; ***cast*** or ***put*** or ***throw in(to) the -,*** in den Schatten stellen (*also fig.*); 2. (*Paint.*) der Farbton, die Farbstufe, (*also fig.*) Schattierung, Abstufung, Nuance; 3. der Schirm; *pl.* (*sl.*) die Sonnenbrille; 4. (*coll.*) Kleinigkeit, Spur; 5. (*Poet.*) der Geist, das Gespenst. **2.** *v.t.* 1. beschatten, umschatten, überschatten; verdunkeln, in den Schatten stellen; 2. abhalten (*light*) (***from***, von); schützen (*the eyes*) (***from***, vor (*Acc.*)); 3. verhüllen, verdecken (***from***, vor (*Acc.*)); 4. (*Paint.*) schattieren; (*fig.*) nuancieren, abstufen, abtönen. **3.** *v.i.* (*also* ***- away, - off***) unmerklich übergehen (***into***, in (*Acc.*)).

shadiness ['ʃeidinis], *s.* 1. die Schattigkeit, das Schattige; 2. (*coll.*) die Anrüchigkeit, Zweifelhaftigkeit, Fragwürdigkeit. **shading,** *s.* 1. die Schattierung; 2. (*fig.*) Abstufung, Nuancierung.

shadow ['ʃædou], **1.** *s.* 1. der Schatten, das Dunkel; Schattenbild; ***cast a -,*** einen Schatten werfen;

under the – of night, unter dem Schutz der Dunkelheit; ***may your – never grow less,*** ich wünsche dir allen Erfolg; ***land of –s,*** das Schattenreich; 2. (*fig.*) die Verstimmung, Betrübnis; trügerischer *or* leerer Schein; 3. die Kleinigkeit, Spur; ***without a – of doubt,*** ohne den geringsten Zweifel; 4. (*coll.*) ständiger Begleiter; der Detektiv; 5. *See* **shade, 1,** 2. **2.** *v.t.* 1. beschatten, verdunkeln; 2. (*also – forth*) dunkel andeuten, anspielen auf (*Acc.*), undeutlich darstellen, versinnbildlichen; 3. (*coll.*) auf der Ferse folgen (*Dat.*), unbemerkt verfolgen, unter Beobachtung halten.

shadow|-boxing, *s.* das Schattenboxen. **--cabinet,** *s.* das Schattenkabinett. **--factory,** *s.* der Ausweichbetrieb, das Schattenwerk. **shadowless,** *adj.* schattenlos. **shadowy,** *adj.* 1. düster, schattenhaft, dämmerig; 2. (*usu. fig.*) schattenhaft, unbestimmt, vage, verschwommen; 3. wesenlos, unwirklich; *see also* **shady.**

shady [ˈʃeidi], *adj.* 1. beschattet, schattig, geschützt; ***on the – side of 40,*** über die Vierzig hinaus; 2. (*coll. fig.*) fragwürdig, zweifelhaft, anrüchig.

shaft [ʃɑ:ft], *s.* 1. der Schaft (*of spear etc.*), Stiel, Griff (*of axe*); 2. die Deichsel (*of cart*), (*Tech.*) Spindel, Achse, Welle, der Wellbaum; 3. (*Min.*) Schacht; ***elevator*** or ***lift –,*** der Aufzugsschacht; ***light--,*** der Lichtschacht; ***sink a –,*** einen Schacht abteufen; ***ventilation –,*** der Luftschacht; 4. (*Poet.*) der Pfeil (*also fig. of satire etc.*); 5. (*fig.*) Strahl; ***– of light,*** der Lichtstrahl. **shaft-horse,** *s.* das Deichselpferd. **shafting,** *s.* (*Tech.*) die Transmission.

shag [ʃæɡ], *s.* 1. (*rare*) zottiges Haar; 2. (*obs.*) rauhes Tuch; (*Am.*) der Plüsch(stoff); 3. Feinschnitt(tabak), Shag; 4. (*Orn.*) die Krähenscharbe (*Phalacrocorax aristotelis*). **shagginess,** *s.* die Zottigkeit, Struppigkeit. **shaggy,** *adj.* rauhhaarig, zottig, struppig; ***--dog story,*** langwieriger und pointenloser Witz.

shagreen [ʃæˈɡri:n], *s.* das Chagrinleder, Körnerleder.

shah [ʃɑ:], *s.* der Schah.

shake [ʃeik], **1.** *irr.v.t.* 1. schütteln; rütteln, ausschütteln (*carpets etc.*); ***– him by the arm,*** ihn am Arm schütteln; ***– the dust off one's feet,*** den Staub von den Füßen schütteln; ***– hands,*** sich (*Dat.*) die Hand geben; ***– his hand, – him by the hand, – hands with him,*** ihm die Hand geben *or* schütteln; ***– one's head,*** den Kopf schütteln (*also fig.*) (*at, over,* über (*Acc.*)); (*coll.*) ***– a leg,*** das Tanzbein schwingen; sich beeilen; ***– one's sides with laughing,*** sich vor Lachen schütteln; ***to be –n before taken*** or ***use,*** vor dem Gebrauch schütteln; ***– down,*** herunterschütteln (*fruit etc.*), ausbreiten (*straw*); ***– off,*** abschütteln (*also fig. pursuers etc.*); ***– out,*** ausschütteln; ***– to pieces,*** auseinanderrütteln; ***– up,*** zusammenschütteln, durchschütteln, zusammenschütten (*as components*); aufschütteln (*as a cushion*); 2. (*fig.*) (*also* (*coll.*) *of a p.*) erschüttern; ***be –n,*** ergriffen *or* erschüttert sein; ***badly –n,*** arg mitgenommen; ***– up,*** verwirren, bestürzen, durcheinanderbringen (*as with shock*), aufrütteln (*out of lethargy*); 3. (*Am.*) mischen (*cards*). **2.** *irr.v.i.* 1. zittern, beben (***with,*** vor (*Dat.*)); ***– in one's shoes,*** Bammel haben; 2. sich schütteln, wackeln, (sch)wanken; ***– with laughter,*** sich vor Lachen schütteln; 3. (*Mus.*) trillern; 4. (*coll.*) ***– down,*** sich abfinden *or* angewöhnen *or* eingewöhnen *or* einleben; sich (*Dat.*) ein Notlager bereiten. **3.** *s.* 1. das Schütteln, Rütteln; (*coll.*) ***the –s,*** der Schüttelfrost; ***– of the hand,*** der Händedruck; ***– of the head,*** das Kopfschütteln; (*coll.*) ***in three –s of a duck's tail, in a couple of –s,*** im Handumdrehen *or* Nu; 2. (*Mus.*) der Triller; 3. Sprung, Riß, Spalt (*in wood*); 4. (*coll.*) das Erdbeben; 5. (*coll.*) Mischgetränk; 6. (*fig.*) die Erschütterung; (*sl.*) ***no great –s,*** nichts Besonderes *or* Erschütterndes.

shake-down, 1. *s.* (*coll.*) das Notlager, Nachtlager. **2.** *attrib. adj.* Probe– (*flight, cruise etc.*).

shaken [ˈʃeikən], *adj.* 1. erschüttert, (sch)wankend; 2. (*of wood*) (kern)rissig. **shaker,** *s.* der Mixbecher (*for cocktails*).

Shakespearian [ʃeikˈspiəriən], *adj.* shakespearisch.

shake-up, *s.* (*coll.*) die Umwälzung, Aufwühlung, Umgruppierung, der Umschwung.

shakiness [ˈʃeikinis], *s.* 1. die Wackligkeit, Zittrigkeit; 2. (*of a p.*) Hinfälligkeit, Gebrechlichkeit; 3. (*of an undertaking*) Unsicherheit, Unzuverlässigkeit. **shaking, 1.** *adj.* zitternd, schüttelnd; ***– palsy,*** die Schüttellähmung. **2.** *s.* 1. das Schütteln; 2. (*fig.*) die Erschütterung.

shako [ˈʃækou], *s.* der Tschako.

shaky [ˈʃeiki], *adj.* 1. zitternd, zittrig; 2. wankend, unsicher, unzuverlässig; 3. (*coll.*) wackelig, schwach, hinfällig, gebrechlich; 4. rissig (*of wood*).

shale [ʃeil], *s.* der Schieferton, Brandschiefer. **shale-oil,** *s.* das Schieferöl.

shall [ʃæl], *irr.aux.v.* (*only pres.*) 1. (*1st p. sing. and pl.*) werde(n) (*with inf. to form future*); ***– not*** ((*coll.*) ***shan't***), werde(n) nicht; ***I – go,*** ich werde gehen, (*coll.*) ich gehe; 2. (*2nd and 3rd p. sing. and pl.*) soll(st), sollt *or* sollen; ***– not,*** soll(st) *or* darf(st) *or* sollen *or* dürfen nicht; ***he – go,*** er soll gehen; ***you – not go,*** du sollst *or* darfst nicht gehen; 3. (*in questions*) (*1st and 3rd p. sing. and pl.*) soll(en) *or* darf *or* dürfen; (*1st p. only*) werde(n); (*in 2nd p. sing. and pl. rare, usu.* ***will***) wirst *or* werdet; ***– I fetch it?*** soll *or* darf ich es holen? 4. (*in dependent clauses*) (*1st, 2nd and 3rd p. sing. or pl.*) soll(en) *or* sollst *or* sollt. *See also* **should.**

shalloon [ʃəˈlu:n], *s.* der Chalon.

shallop [ˈʃæləp], *s.* die Schaluppe.

shallot [ʃəˈlɔt], *s.* die Schalotte.

shallow [ˈʃælou], **1.** *adj.* flach, seicht (*also fig.*), nicht tief; (*fig.*) oberflächlich. **2.** *s.* die Untiefe, seichte Stelle; *pl.* seichtes Gewässer. **3.** *v.i.* seicht *or* flach werden, (sich) verflachen. **shallow-brained,** *adj.* hohlköpfig, oberflächlich, seicht. **shallowness,** *s.* die Seichtheit (*also fig.*), (*fig.*) Oberflächlichkeit.

shalt [ʃælt], (*obs., Poet.*) *2nd p. sing. of* **shall.**

sham [ʃæm], **1.** *v.t.* vortäuschen, vorspiegeln, vorheucheln; ***– illness,*** sich krank stellen, simulieren. **2.** *v.i.* sich (ver)stellen, heucheln. **3.** *s.* 1. die (Vor)täuschung, der Schwindel, Schein, (Be)trug; 2. (*of a p.*) Schwindler, Heuchler, Scharlatan; (*of a th.*) Ersatz, die Nachahmung. **4.** *adj.* 1. unecht, nachgemacht, falsch; 2. Schein–, fingiert, vorgetäuscht.

shamble [ʃæmbl], **1.** *v.i.* schlenkern, watscheln. **2.** *s.* der Watschelgang.

shambles [ʃæmblz], *pl.* (*sing. constr.*) 1. die Schlachtbank; das Schlachthaus; 2. (*fig.*) Schlachtfeld; (*coll.*) Durcheinander, der Trümmerhaufen, die Schweinerei.

shame [ʃeim], **1.** *s.* 1. die Scham, das Schamgefühl; ***feel – at,*** sich schämen über (*Acc.*); ***blush for*** or ***with –,*** vor Scham erröten; ***for –!*** pfui! schäme dich! 2. die Schmach, Schande; ***bring – upon,*** Schande bereiten (*Dat.*); ***cry – upon,*** sich entrüsten über (*Acc.*); ***more's the –,*** um so schlimmer; ***– on you!*** schäme dich! ***put to –,*** beschämen (*a p.*), in den Schatten stellen (*a th.*); ***what a –!*** wie schade! **2.** *v.t.* 1. beschämen; ***– him into doing,*** ihn durch Beschämung dahin bringen, zu tun; 2. Schande machen (*Dat.*).

shamefaced [ˈʃeimfeist], *adj.*, **shamefacedly** [–idli], *adv.* verschämt, kleinlaut. **shamefacedness** [–idnis], *s.* die Verschämtheit.

shameful [ˈʃeimful], *adj.* schmachtvoll, schmählich, schimpflich, schändlich, unanständig, ungehörlich. **shamefulness,** *s.* die Schändlichkeit, Unanständigkeit. **shameless,** *adj.* 1. schamlos, unverschämt; 2. *See* **shameful. shamelessness,** *s.* 1. die Schamlosigkeit, Unverschämtheit; 2. *See* **shamefulness.**

shammer [ˈʃæmə], *s.* der (die) Heuchler(in), Schwindler(in).

shammy (leather) [ˈʃæmi], *s.* (*coll.*) das Sämischleder.

shampoo [ʃæmˈpu:], **1.** *s.* 1. das Haarwaschmittel, Shampoo; 2. Schampunieren, die Haarwäsche, Kopfwäsche. **2.** *v.t.* 1. schampunieren, waschen

und massieren (*hair*); 2. (*obs.*) massieren, frottieren.
shamrock ['ʃæmrɔk], *s.* (irischer) Klee.
shandy ['ʃændi], *s.* Bier mit Sprudelwasser.
Shanghai [ʃæŋ'hai], *s.* Schanghai (*n.*). **shanghai,** *v.t.* schanghaien (*sailors*); (*fig.*) gewaltsam herumkriegen (*into* (*doing*), zu (tun)).
shank [ʃæŋk], **1.** *s.* (*Anat.*) das Schienbein, der Unterschenkel; (*Bot.*) Stiel; (*Tech.*) Schaft; (*coll.*) das Bein; (*coll.*) ***on –s's pony,*** auf Schusters Rappen. **2.** *v.i.* (*Bot.*) – ***off,*** abfallen. **shanked** [–t], *adj. suff.* –schenkelig.
shanny ['ʃæni], *s.* grüner Schleimfisch.
shan't [ʃɑ:nt] = **shall not.**
shantung [ʃæn'tʌŋ], *s.* der Schantung.
[1]**shanty** ['ʃænti], *s.* die Hütte, Baracke, der Schuppen; – ***town,*** die Barackensiedlung.
[2]**shanty,** *s.* das Matrosenlied, Shanty.
shape [ʃeip], **1.** *s.* 1. (äußere) Form, die Gestalt, der Umriß; ***in the – of,*** in Gestalt von; ***take*** (***definite***) –, feste Form *or* Gestalt annehmen; ***put into –,*** formen, (*fig.*) ordnen; 2. die Form, Figur, Fasson; (*coll.*) ***lick into –,*** zurechtbiegen (*a th.*), gute Manieren beibringen (*Dat.*) (*a p.*); ***out of –,*** außer Fasson; 3. (*Tech., Cook.*) die Form; das Modell (*for hats*). **2.** *v.t.* formen, gestalten, bilden, einrichten, ordnen; (*Naut.*) – ***a course for,*** ansteuern, den Kurs nehmen auf (*Acc.*) (*also fig.*). **3.** *v.i.* 1. sich formen lassen, Form annehmen; 2. (*fig.*) sich gestalten *or* entwickeln.
shaped [ʃeipt], *adj. suff.* –gestaltet. **shapeless,** *adj.* 1. formlos, gestaltlos; 2. mißgestaltet, ungestalt(et), unförmig. **shapelessness,** *s.* 1. die Formlosigkeit, Gestaltlosigkeit; 2. Unförmigkeit. **shapeliness** [–linis], *s.* die Wohlgestalt, Formschönheit, das Ebenmaß. **shapely,** *adj.* wohlgestalt(et), schöngeformt. **shapen,** *adj. suff.* (*obs.*) *see* **shaped.**
shard [ʃɑ:d], *s.* 1. (*obs.*) die Scherbe; 2. (*Ent.*) Flügeldecke.
[1]**share** [ʃɛə], *s.* die Pflugschar; ***—beam,*** der Pflugbaum, Grindel.
[2]**share, 1.** *s.* 1. der (An)teil (*of*, an (*Dat.*)); – ***and – alike,*** zu gleichen Teilen; ***fall to his –,*** ihm zuteil werden, ihm zufallen; ***go –s with him in s.th.,*** etwas mit ihm teilen; 2. die Beteiligung, Teilhaberschaft (*in*, an (*Dat.*)); der Beitrag (*towards*, zu); ***bear one's –,*** seinen Teil tragen von; ***do one's –,*** seinen Teil tun; ***have*** or ***take a –,*** Anteil haben, beteiligt sein, teilhaben, teilnehmen (*in*, an (*Dat.*)); 3. die Quote, der Kontingent; 4. (*Comm.*) die Aktie, der Geschäftsanteil, Gewinnanteil; ***hold –s,*** Aktionär sein (*in*, *Gen.*); ***deferred –,*** die Nachzugsaktie; ***mining –,*** der Kux; ***ordinary –,*** die Stammaktie. **2.** *v.t.* 1. teilen (*a th.*) (***with,*** mit; ***among,*** unter (*Acc.*)); – ***an opinion,*** eine Meinung teilen; ***generally –d opinion,*** allgemein geteilte Meinung; – ***out,*** verteilen, austeilen (***among,*** unter (*Acc.*)), zuteilen (*Dat.*); 2. sich beteiligen an (*Dat.*), teilhaben *or* teilnehmen an (*Dat.*); – ***the cost,*** sich an den Kosten beteiligen; – ***the blame,*** sich in die Schuld teilen. **3.** *v.i.* – ***in,*** sich beteiligen an (*Dat.*), teilhaben *or* teilnehmen an (*Dat.*), sich teilen in (*Acc.*); – ***and – alike,*** gleich teilen, sich gleich daran beteiligen, gleiche Teile bekommen.
share|-broker, *s.* der Aktienmakler. **–holder,** *s.* der Aktionär, Aktieninhaber; Teilhaber, Gesellschafter. **—out,** *s.* (*coll.*) die Verteilung, Austeilung. **—pusher,** *s.* (*coll.*) der Winkelmakler.
shark [ʃɑ:k], *s.* 1. der Hai(fisch); 2. (*coll.*) Gauner, Schwindler, Hochstapler, Preller.
sharp [ʃɑ:p], **1.** *adj.* 1. scharf, spitz; 2. (*fig.*) scharf, herb, sauer (*as taste*), schneidend (*as cold*), schrill (*as sound*), heftig (*as contest, pain*); – ***contrast,*** scharfer *or* starker Gegensatz; – ***distinction,*** scharfe *or* klare Unterscheidung; – ***eyes,*** scharfe *or* gute Augen; – ***struggle,*** heftiger *or* hitziger Streit; – ***temper,*** heftiges Temperament; – ***tongue,*** böse Zunge; – ***words,*** bittere Worte; 3. (*of p.*) klug, scharfsinnig, aufgeweckt, gewitzt, pfiffig; ***keep a – look-out,*** auf der Hut sein (*for*, vor (*Dat.*)); ***look –!*** mach schnell! hurtig! 4. (*coll.*) verschlagen, raffiniert, schlau, gerieben, gerissen; – ***practice,*** skrupellose Praktiken (*pl.*), die Gaunerei, Beutelschneiderei; 5. (*Mus.*) zu hoch, um einen Halbton erhöht; ***C–***(♯), Cis. **2.** *adv.* 1. plötzlich; 2. pünktlich; ***1 o'clock –,*** Punkt 1 Uhr, genau um 1 Uhr; 3. (*Mus.*) zu hoch; ***sing –,*** zu hoch singen. **3.** *s.* (*Mus.*) das Kreuz, Erhöhungszeichen; die Erhöhung, der Halbton (*of*, über (*Dat.*)).
sharp-edged, *adj.* scharfkantig.
sharpen ['ʃɑ:pən], *v.t.* 1. schärfen, wetzen, schleifen (*a blade*), (an)spitzen (*a pencil etc.*); 2. (*fig.*) anregen, verschärfen, zuspitzen. **sharpener,** *s.* ***pencil-–,*** der Bleistiftspitzer.
sharper ['ʃɑ:pə], *s.* der Gauner, Bauernfänger.
sharp-eyed, *adj.* 1. scharfsichtig; 2. (*fig.*) scharfsinnig.
sharply ['ʃɑ:pli], *adv.* 1. scharf; 2. schrill; heftig, barsch. **sharpness,** *s.* 1. die Schärfe, Spitze; 2. (*fig.*) Herbheit, Bitterkeit, Heftigkeit, Deutlichkeit; 3. der Scharfsinn, die Schlauheit.
sharp|-pointed, *adj.* spitz(ig). **–shooter,** *s.* der Scharfschütze, (*Mil.*) Freischärler. **—tongued,** *adj.* spitzzüngig. **—witted,** *adj.* scharfsinnig.
shatter ['ʃætə], **1.** *v.t.* zerschlagen, zerbrechen, zertrümmern, zerschmettern; (*fig.*) vernichten, zunichte machen (*hopes*), zerrütten (*nerves*); (*coll.*) ***I am –ed,*** ich bin erschüttert. **2.** *v.i.* zerbrechen, zersplittern, in Stücke gehen. **shattering,** *adj.* (*fig.*) überwältigend, vernichtend.
shave [ʃeiv], **1.** *v.t.* 1. rasieren (*a p.*), (*also* – ***off***) abrasieren, wegrasieren (*beard etc.*), abschaben, abfalzen (*skins etc.*); – ***o.s.,*** sich rasieren; ***be*** or ***get –d,*** sich rasieren lassen; 2. (*coll.*) streifen; (*coll.*) – ***the corner,*** die Ecke mitnehmen. **2.** *v.i.* sich rasieren. **3.** *s.* das Rasieren, die Rasur; ***have a –,*** sich rasieren (lassen); ***he needs a –,*** er muß sich rasieren; (*coll.*) ***have a close*** or ***narrow –,*** knapp *or* mit knapper Not *or* mit heiler Haut davonkommen; (*coll.*) ***by a narrow –,*** um Haaresbreite, um ein Haar.
shaveling ['ʃeivliŋ], *s.* (*obs.*) der Glatzkopf, (*usu.*) Pfaffe, Priester.
shaven ['ʃeivən], *adj.* rasiert; geschoren (*head*). **shaver,** *s.* 1. (*obs.*) der Barbier; 2. (*usu.*) Rasierapparat; 3. (*coll.*) ***young –,*** der Grünschnabel, Milchbart.
Shavian ['ʃeiviən], *adj.* Shawsch, für G. B. Shaw charakteristisch.
shaving ['ʃeiviŋ], *s.* 1. das Rasieren; 2. (*usu. pl.*) der (Hobel)span, Splitter, der *or* das Schnitzel, das (Ab)schabsel. **shaving|-brush,** *s.* der Rasierpinsel. **– kit,** *s.* das Rasierzeug. **—soap, —stick,** *s.* die Rasierseife.
shawl [ʃɔ:l], *s.* der Schal, das Umschlagtuch, Umhängetuch.
shawm [ʃɔ:m], *s.* (*Mus.*) die Schalmei.
she [ʃi:], **1.** *pers. pron.* sie (*of females*); er *or* sie *or* es (*personified ships, countries etc.*); – ***who,*** diejenige welche. **2.** *s.* die Sie, das Weib(chen). **3.** *pref.* ***—bear,*** die Bärin; ***—devil,*** das Teufelsweib; ***—goat,*** die Geiß; ***—wolf,*** die Wölfin.
shea [ʃiə], *s.* (*Bot.*) (*also* ***—tree***) der (Schi)butterbaum; – ***butter,*** die Bambukbutter, Schibutter.
sheaf [ʃi:f], **1.** *s.* (*pl.* **sheaves** [ʃi:vz]) die Garbe (*of corn*); das Bündel. **2.** *v.t.* in Garben binden (*corn*).
shealing, *see* **shieling.**
shear [ʃiə], **1.** *irr.v.t.* 1. scheren (*sheep*); 2. mähen, schneiden; (*usu.* – ***off***) abschneiden; *see* **shorn. 2.** *irr.v.i.* schneiden. **3.** *s.* 1. (*dial.*) die Schur (*of sheep*); 2. (*Tech. Geol.*) der Schub, die Scherung, Scherkraft. **shearer** [–rə], *s.* 1. der Schafscherer; 2. (*Scots*) Schnitter.
shearing ['ʃiəriŋ], *s.* 1. die Schur; ***wool of the second –,*** zweischürige Wolle; – ***time,*** die Schurzeit; 2. (*dial.*) die Mahd, das Mähen; 3. (*Geol.*) die (Ab)scherung; – ***force,*** die Schubkraft; – ***stress,*** die Scherbeanspruchung; 4. *pl.* die Scherwolle.
shear-legs, *pl.* (*Naut.*) der Scherenkran, Mastenkran.
shearling ['ʃiəliŋ], *s.* das Schaf nach der ersten Schur.

shear-pin, *s.* der Scherbolzen.
shears [ʃiəz], *pl.* große Schere, die Gartenschere, Metallschere, Blechschere.
shear|-stress, *s. See shearing stress.* **-water,** *s.* (*Orn.*) der Sturmtaucher (*Puffinus*).
sheath [ʃi:θ], *s.* (*pl.* **-s** [ʃi:ðz]) 1. die Scheide (*also Bot.*); *– knife,* der Dolch; 2. (*Ent.*) die Flügeldecke. **sheathe** [ʃi:ð], *v.t.* 1. in die Scheide stecken (*sword*); 2. (*Tech.*) umkleiden, umhüllen, überziehen, beschlagen. **sheathing** [–ðiŋ], *s.* 1. das Verschalen, Verkleiden, Überziehen, Beschlagen; 2. die Verschalung, Verkleidung, (Außen)haut, der Überzug, Mantel, Beschlag; (*of cable*) die Bewehrung.
¹**sheave** [ʃi:v], *s.* (*Tech.*) die Rolle, Scheibe.
²**sheave,** *v.t. See* **sheaf, 2. sheaves,** *pl. of* **sheaf.**
Sheba [ˈʃi:bə], *s.* (*B.*) Saba (*n.*).
shebang [ʃiˈbæŋ], *s.* (*sl.*) die Bude, der Laden. **shebeen** [–ˈbi:n], *s.* (*Scots, Irish*) illegale Schnapsbude.
¹**shed** [ʃed], *s.* der Schuppen, die Hütte, das Wetterdach, Schirmdach.
²**shed,** *irr.v.t.* 1. vergießen, verschütten, fließen lassen; 2. abstoßen, abstreifen, abwerfen (*horns, leaves etc.*); verlieren (*teeth*), ablegen (*clothes*); *– feathers,* (sich) mausern; *– skin,* sich häuten; 3. verbreiten, ausströmen, ausstrahlen, aussenden, ausbreiten (*light, heat etc.*); (*fig.*) *– light on,* Licht werfen auf (*Acc.*); 4. (*fig.*) verringern (*load*).
sheen [ʃi:n], *s.* der Schein, Glanz, Schimmer.
¹**sheeny** [ˈʃi:ni], *adj.* glänzend, schimmernd.
²**sheeny,** *s.* (*sl.*) der Itzig.
sheep [ʃi:p], *s.* (*also pl.*) das Schaf (*also fig.*); (*fig.*) *black –,* schwarzes Schaf; *a wolf in –'s clothing,* der Wolf im Schafspelz; *cast –'s eyes at,* schmachtende Blicke zuwerfen (*Dat.*).
sheep|dog, *s.* der Schäferhund. **--farm,** *s.* die Schäferei. **--farmer,** *s.* der Schafzüchter. **--farming,** *s.* die Schafzucht. **--fold,** *s.* (*obs.*) *see* **--pen. --hook,** *s.* der Hirtenstab.
sheepish [ˈʃi:piʃ], *adj.* einfältig, schüchtern, blöde. **sheepishness,** *s.* die Schüchternheit, Einfältigkeit, Blödheit, Blödigkeit.
sheep|-pen, *s.* der Pferch, die Schafhürde. **--run,** *s.* die Schafweide, Schaftrift. **-shank,** *s.* (*Naut.*) der Trompetenstek, Schafschenkel. **--shearing,** *s.* die Schafschur. **-skin,** *s.* das Schaffell, Schafleder. **--walk,** *s. See* **--run.**
¹**sheer** [ʃiə], **1.** *adj,* 1. bloß, rein, gänzlich, absolut, völlig, glatt, bar; 2. senkrecht, steil, jäh (*of slope*); 3. dünn, durchsichtig (*of fabric*); 4. unvermischt, unverfälscht, unverdünnt, pur. **2.** *adv.* direkt, senkrecht, gerade(n)wegs, kerzengerade.
²**sheer, 1.** *v.i.* (*Naut.*) gieren, abweichen, ausweichen; *– from,* aus dem Weg gehen (*Dat.*), meiden; (*Naut.*) *– off,* abscheren, abgieren; (*sl.*) sich scheren. **2.** *s.* 1. das Abgieren, die Abweichung; 2. die Erhöhung, der Sprung (*of deck*), Linien (*pl.*) (*of a ship*). **sheer-legs,** *pl. see* **shear-legs.**
sheerness [ˈʃiənis], *s.* 1. (jähe) Steilheit; 2. (*fig.*) Absolutheit, Gänzlichkeit; 3. Durchsichtigkeit (*of fabric*).
sheer|-plan, *s.* (*Shipb.*) der Seitenriß, Längsriß. **-strake,** *s.* (*Naut.*) der Schergang.
sheet [ʃi:t], **1.** *s.* 1. das Bettuch, (Bett)laken; *as white as a –,* kreideweiß; 2. das Blatt (*of paper or metal*), der Bogen (*of paper*), die Platte (*of metal*), Platte, Tafel, Scheibe (*of glass*); *blank –,* unbeschriebenes Blatt (*also fig.*); (*fig.*) *clean –,* tadellose Führung, reine Weste; (*Bookb.*) *in –s,* nicht gebunden, ungefalzt; 3. (weite) Fläche (*of water*); *come down in –s,* in Strömen regnen; *– of flame,* die Feuermasse, das Flammenmeer; *– of lightning,* der Flächenblitz. **2.** *v.t.* (in Leintücher) einhüllen.
²**sheet, 1.** *s.* (*Naut.*) der Schot, die Schote, Segelleine; (*sl.*) *three –s in the wind,* sternhagelvoll. **2.** *v.t.* (*also – in, – home*) anholen (*sails*).
sheet|-anchor, *s.* der Notanker; (*fig.*) die Stütze, letzte Rettung. **-bend,** *s.* (*Naut.*) der Schotstek, Schotstich. **– copper,** *s.* das Kupferblech. **– glass,** *s.* das Tafelglas, Scheibenglas. **– ice,** *s.* das Glatteis.
sheeting [ˈʃi:tiŋ], *s.* 1. der Stoff für Bettücher; 2. der Beschlag (*of metal*).
sheet| iron, *s.* das Eisenblech. **– lead,** *s.* das Tafelblei. **– lightning,** *s.* der Flächenblitz, das Wetterleuchten. **– metal,** *s.* das Blech. **– music,** *s.* Notenblätter, Noten in Blattform (*pl.*).
sheikh [ʃeik, ʃi:k], *s.* 1. der Scheich, Scheik; 2. (*sl.*) Herzensbrecher. **sheikhdom** [–dəm], *s.* das Scheichtum, arabisches Fürstentum.
shekel [ʃekl], *s.* 1. der Sekel; 2. *pl.* (*sl.*) die Pinkepinke.
sheld duck [ʃeld], *s.* (*Orn.*) die Brandente (*Tadorna tadorna*).
shelf [ʃelf], *s.* (*pl.* **shelves** [ʃelvz]) 1. das Bord, Regal, Gestellbrett, Fach, der Sims; *put on the –,* beiseite legen, beiseite schieben, auf die lange Bank schieben; *on the –,* abgetan, ausrangiert; sitzengeblieben (*of women*); (*Comm.*) *– life,* die Lagerfähigkeit, (zulässige) Lagerfrist; 2. (*Geog.*) das Riff, die Sandbank, Felsplatte; der *or* das Schelf, der Sockel; *continental –,* der Festlandssockel.
shell [ʃel], **1.** *s.* 1. die Muschel(schale); das Schneckenhaus, (Schnecken)gehäuse (*of snails*), die Schale (*egg, nut, also fig.*), Hülse (*also fig.*); der Panzer, Rückenschild (*of tortoise*); (*fig.*) *come out of one's –,* aus seiner Zurückhaltung heraustreten; 2. der Rumpf (*of a ship*); das Gerippe, Gerüst (*of a house etc.*); 3. (*Mil.*) Artilleriegeschoß, die Granate; 4. (*fig.*) äußere Erscheinung *or* Form, die Hülle; 5. Mittelstufe (*at school*). **2.** *v.t.* 1. schälen (*an egg*); ausmachen, entschoten, enthülsen (*nuts, peas etc*); 2. (*Mil.*) beschießen, bombardieren; 3. (*sl.*) *– out,* herausrücken (*money*). **3.** *v.i.* (*sl.*) *– out,* blechen, mit dem Geld herausrücken.
shellac [ʃəˈlæk], *s.* der Schellack.
shell|-bit, *s.* der Löffelbohrer. **--crater,** *s.* der Granattrichter. **--egg,** *s.* das Frischei. **-fire,** *s.* das Granatfeuer. **-fish,** *s.* das Schalentier. **shelling,** *s.* (*Artil.*) der Beschuß, die Beschießung. **shell|-proof,** *adj.* bombenfest, beschußsicher. **-shock,** *s.* die Schützengrabenneurose. **-shocked,** *adj.* an Schützengrabenneurose leidend. **--work,** *s.* die Muschel(einlege)arbeit.
shelter [ˈʃeltə], **1.** *s.* 1. das Obdach, die Unterkunft; *night-–,* das Obdachlosenheim; 2. der Schuppen, das Schutzdach; *air-raid –,* der Schutzraum, Bunker; 3. (*fig.*) der Schutz, die Zuflucht, Sicherheit; *take – from,* Schutz *or* Zuflucht suchen vor (*Dat.*); *give –, see* **2**; *under the – of,* unter dem Schutz von. **2.** *v.t.* 1. (be)schützen, beschirmen (*from,* vor (*Dat.*)); 2. Schutz *or* Zuflucht gewähren (*Dat.*), aufnehmen, beherbergen (*a p.*); (*also –* **o.s.**) Schutz *or* Zuflucht suchen, sich verstecken *or* verbergen. **3.** *v.i.* Obdach *or* Schutz suchen; sich unterstellen.
shelve [ʃelv], **1.** *v.t.* 1. auf ein (Bücher)bord *or* in ein Regal legen *or* stellen (*books*); 2. mit Brettern *or* Fächern *or* Regalen versehen (*a room*); 3. (*fig.*) beiseitelegen, beiseiteschieben, unberücksichtigt lassen, auf die lange Bank schieben, aufschieben; beilegen (*differences*); (*sl.*) ausrangieren (*a p.*). **2.** *v.i.* sich neigen, schräg hinablaufen. **shelves** [–z], *pl. of* **shelf. shelving, 1.** *s.* 1. (Bretter für) Regale *or* Fächer (*pl.*); 2. das Beiseiteschieben. **2.** *adj.* schräg, abschüssig.
Shem [ʃem], *s.* (*B.*) Sem (*m.*).
shenanigan [ʃiˈnænigən], *s.* (*sl.*) der Mumpitz, fauler Zauber.
shepherd [ˈʃepəd], **1.** *s.* der Schäfer, Hirt; *–'s crook,* der Hirtenstab; *–'s dog,* der Schäferhund; *–'s pie,* der Kartoffelauflauf mit Fleisch; *–'s plaid,* schwarzweiß gewürfelter Wollstoff; (*Bot.*) *–'s purse,* das Hirtentäschel; (*Bot.*) *–'s rod* or *staff,* die Kardandistel; (*B.*) *the good –,* der gute Hirt. **2.** *v.t.* 1. hüten; 2. (*usu. fig.*) (wie ein Hirt) (an)führen *or* geleiten. **shepherd-boy,** *s.* der Hirtenjunge. **shepherdess,** *s.* die Schäferin, Hirtin.
sherbet [ˈʃə:bət], *s.* der *or* das Sorbett, das Limonadenpulver.

sherd [ʃəːd], *see* **shard.**

sherif [ʃə'riːf], *s.* arabischer Gouverneur *or* Fürst.

sheriff ['ʃerif], *s.* der Sheriff; (*Am.*) Bezirksrichter; (*Engl.*) ***High Sheriff,*** erster Grafschaftsbeamter; (*also* **--*depute***) (*Scots*) oberster Grafschaftsrichter.

sherry ['ʃeri], *s.* der Sherry, Jerezwein.

shew, *see* **show.**

shewbread ['ʃoubred], *s.* (*B.*) das Schaubrot.

shibboleth ['ʃibəleθ], *s.* das Erkennungszeichen, Losungswort.

shield [ʃiːld], **1.** *s.* 1. (*Her.*) der Schild (*also fig.*), Wappenschild; 2. (*fig.*) Schutz, Schirm, der (die) (Be)schützer(in), (Be)schirmer(in); 3. (*Tech.*) die Schutzplatte, Schutzwand, Schutzvorrichtung, der Schutzschild, Schutzschirm, das Schutzdach; 4. (*Elec.*) die (Ab)schirmung; 5. (*Zool.*) der Panzer, Rückenschild. **2.** *v.t.* (be)schirmen, (be)schützen (***from***, vor (*Dat.*)), decken, verteidigen.

shield|-bearer, *s.* der Schildträger. **--fern,** *s.* (*Bot.*) der Schildfarn. **--hand,** *s.* linke Hand.

shieling ['ʃiːliŋ], *s.* (*Scots*) die Schutzhütte.

shift [ʃift], **1.** *v.t.* (ver)schieben, wegschieben, versetzen, verstellen, umstellen, verändern, verlegen, verlagern, (aus)wechseln; (*fig.*) ***– one's ground,*** den Standpunkt ändern; (*Theat.*) ***– the scenes,*** die Kulissen verschieben; 2. abwälzen, (ab)schieben (*blame*) (***to, on,*** auf (*Acc.*)); 3. (*sl.*) loswerden, beseitigen, (*food*) wegputzen. **2.** *v.i.* 1. sich bewegen, (die Lage) wechseln, sich verändern, sich verlagern, sich verschieben, verschoben *or* verlegt werden; 2. sich ändern *or* wenden, umspringen (*as wind*); 3. ***– for o.s.,*** sich selbst helfen, für sich selbst sorgen, auf sich selbst gestellt sein. **3.** *s.* 1. die Veränderung, Verschiebung, Verstellung, der Wechsel, (*of wind*) das Umspringen; 2. die (Arbeits)schicht, Belegschaft (*of workmen*); ***– work,*** die Schichtarbeit; ***be on –s,*** Schichtarbeit machen; ***day –,*** die Tagschicht; 3. das Hilfsmittel, der (Not)behelf, Ausweg, die Ausflucht; ***make –,*** sich behelfen (***with,*** mit); fertigwerden, sich durchschlagen; es fertigbringen (***to do,*** zu tun); 4. die List, der Kniff; 5. (*Mus.*) das Übergreifen; 6. (*obs.*) Frauenhemd.

shifter ['ʃiftə], *s.* 1. (*Tech.*) die Verstellvorrichtung, Schaltung, der Schalter, Umleger, Ausrücker; 2. (*coll.*) unzuverlässiger Mensch; 3. ***scene-–,*** der Kulissenschieber. **shiftiness,** *s.* die Unzuverlässigkeit, Verschmitztheit. **shifting,** *adj.* sich bewegend *or* verschiebend, veränderlich, beweglich; ***– sand,*** der Treibsand. **shift-key,** *s.* die Umschalttaste (*typewriter*). **shiftless,** *adj.* hilflos, ratlos, ungeschickt, unbeholfen, unfähig. **shiftlessness,** *s.* die Ratlosigkeit, Hilflosigkeit, Unbeholfenheit, Unfähigkeit. **shifty,** *adj.* 1. unzuverlässig, durchtrieben, gerissen, verschmitzt, schuftig; 2. (*rare*) veränderlich, unstet, unbeständig.

shillelagh [ʃi'leilə], *s.* (*Irish*) eichener Knüttel.

shilling ['ʃiliŋ], *s.* (*obs.*) der Schilling; (*Hist.*) ***take the King's*** or ***Queen's –,*** sich anwerben lassen, Rekrut werden; (*obs.*) ***a – in the pound,*** 5 Prozent; ***cut off with a –,*** enterben.

shilly-shally ['ʃili'ʃæli], **1.** *s.* die Unentschlossenheit, das Schwanken, Zögern. **2.** *adj.* unschlüssig, unentschlossen, zögernd, schwankend. **3.** *v.i.* schwanken, zögern, unentschlossen *or* unschlüssig sein.

shim [ʃim], *s.* (*Tech.*) der Ausfüllstreifen, die Ausgleichsscheibe, das Einlegestück, Unterlegstück, Toleranzplättchen.

shimmer ['ʃimə], **1.** *v.i.* schimmern, flimmern. **2.** *s.* der Schimmer, das Schimmern, Flimmern. **shimmery,** *adj.* schimmernd, flimmernd.

shimmy ['ʃimi], *s.* (*coll.*) 1. das (Frauen)hemd; 2. ein Tanz mit Schüttelbewegungen.

shin [ʃin], **1.** *s.* das Schienbein; ***– of beef,*** die Rindshachse. **2.** *v.i.* (*coll.*) ***– up,*** hinaufklettern; ***– down,*** hinunterklettern. **shinbone,** *s.* das Schienbein.

shindig ['ʃindig], *s.* (*Am. sl.*) der Tanz, die Party.

shindy ['ʃindi], *s.* (*coll.*) der Krach, Krawall, Krakeel, Spektakel.

shine [ʃain], **1.** *s.* 1. der Schein, Glanz, das Leuchten; ***in rain or –,*** bei jedem Wetter; (*fig.*) unter allen Umständen; (*coll.*) ***take the – out of,*** ausstechen, in der Schatten stellen (*a p.*), den Glanz nehmen (*Dat.*) (*a th.*); (*Am.*) ***take a – to,*** Gefallen finden an (*Dat.*) (*a p.*); 2. (*coll.*) das Aufheben, der Krach; ***kick up a –,*** Skandal machen. **2.** *irr.v.i.* 1. scheinen, leuchten, strahlen, glänzen; ***– forth, – out,*** hervorleuchten, aufleuchten; 2. (*fig.*) glänzen, sich hervortun (*as*, als; *in*, in (*Dat.*)). **3.** *reg.v.t.* (*coll.*) blank putzen (*shoes etc.*). **shiner,** *s.* 1. (*sl.*) blaues Auge; 2. (*sl.*) das Goldstück.

[1]**shingle** [ʃiŋgl], **1.** *s.* 1. die (Dach)schindel; 2. der Herrenschnitt (*ladies hair*). **2.** *v.t.* 1. mit Schindeln decken; 2. in Herrenschnitt *or* sehr kurz schneiden; ***–d hair,*** der Herrenschnitt.

[2]**shingle,** *s.* 1. der Strandkies, Schotter; 2. steiniger Strand.

shingles [ʃiŋglz], *s.* (*Med.*) die Gürtelrose.

shining ['ʃainiŋ], *adj.* leuchtend, strahlend, glänzend (*also fig.*), schimmernd.

Shinto(ism) ['ʃintou(izm)], *s.* der Schintoismus.

shiny ['ʃaini], *adj.* 1. (*coll.*) *see* **shining**; 2. blank (*of shoes etc.*); 3. fadenscheinig, abgetragen (*of clothes*).

ship [ʃip], **1.** *s.* das Schiff; (*Naut.*) dreimastiges (Segel)schiff, das Vollschiff; ***aboard*** (or ***on board***) ***–,*** an Bord, auf dem Schiff; ***by –,*** mit dem *or* per Schiff; ***when my – comes home,*** wenn ich mein Glück mache, wenn das Geldschiff ankommt; ***capital –,*** das Großkampfschiff; ***– of the desert,*** das Wüstenschiff, Kamel; ***– of the line,*** das Linienschiff; ***– of state,*** das Staatsschiff; ***take –,*** an Bord gehen, sich einschiffen (***for***, nach); ***–'s articles,*** der Heuervertrag; ***–'s company,*** die Besatzung, Schiffsmannschaft; ***–'s husband,*** der Mitreeder, Schiffsbevollmächtigte(r); ***–'s manifest,*** das Ladungsverzeichnis, Manifest; ***–'s papers,*** Schiffspapiere (***pl.***). **2.** *v.t.* 1. (*from shore aboard*) an Bord bringen *or* nehmen, verladen, einschiffen; (*from port to port*) verschiffen, absenden; (*esp. Am. by land or sea*) verladen, verfrachten, transportieren; 2. anmustern, dingen, (an)heuern (*sailors*); 3. ***– the mast,*** den Mast festmachen; ***– the oars,*** die Ruder einlegen *or* klarmachen; 4. ***– a sea,*** eine Sturzwelle übernehmen. **3.** *v.i.* 1. sich (als Matrose) verdingen, sich anheuern (lassen); 2. sich einschiffen.

ship|-biscuit, *s.* der Schiffszwieback. **–board,** *s.* ***on –,*** auf dem Schiff, an Bord. **--breaker,** *s.* der (Schiffs)verschrotter, Schröter. **--broker,** *s.* der Schiffsmakler. **–builder,** *s.* der Schiffbaumeister. **–building,** *s.* der Schiff(s)bau. **– canal,** *s.* der Seekanal. **--chandler,** *s.* der Schiffslieferant. **–load,** *s.* die Schiffsladung. **–mate,** *s.* der Schiffskamerad.

shipment ['ʃipmənt], *s.* 1. die Verladung, Verschiffung; Schiffsladung; 2. (*also by land*) Verfrachtung, der Versand; die Sendung.

ship|-money, *s.* (*Hist.*) die Kriegsschiffsteuer. **–owner,** *s.* der Schiffseigentümer, Reeder.

shippen ['ʃipən], *s.* (*dial.*) der Kuhstall, Viehstall.

shipping ['ʃipiŋ], **1.** *s.* 1. die Verladung, Verschiffung; ***ready for –,*** zur Verladung bereit; 2. (*esp. Am. also by land*) die Verfrachtung, Spedition, der Versand; 3. die Schiffahrt, das Schiffswesen; 4. (*collect.*) (alle) Schiffe, der Schiffsbestand, die Gesamttonnage; ***the harbour is crowded with –,*** es liegen sehr viele Schiffe im Hafen. **2.** *attrib. adj.* Schiffs–, Schiffahrts–.

shipping|-agent, *s.* 1. der Schiffsmakler, Schiffsagent; 2. Hafenspediteur; 3. Reedereivertreter. **--articles,** *pl.* der Heuervertrag. **--clerk,** *s.* der Vorsteher der Versandabteilung. **– company,** *s.* die Schiffahrtsgesellschaft, Reederei. **– intelligence,** *s.* Schiffahrtsberichte (*pl.*). **--note,** *s.* der Schiffszettel. **--office,** *s.* das Speditionsbüro.

ship|-rigged, *adj.* als Vollschiff getakelt. **–shape,** *adj.* (*fig.*) gehörig, richtig, ordentlich, in guter

Ordnung. **–wreck, 1.** *s.* 1. der Schiffbruch; 2. das Wrack, schiffbrüchiges Schiff; 3. (*fig.*) die Zerstörung, völliger Zusammenbruch, der Schiffbruch, Untergang, Ruin, das Scheitern, (endgültiges) Versagen; (*fig.*) ***make a – of,*** vernichten, zerstören. **2.** *v.t.* 1. stranden *or* scheitern lassen, (*also fig.*) zum Scheitern bringen; ***be –ed,*** Schiffbruch erleiden, gestrandet *or* gescheitert *or* schiffbrüchig werden *or* sein; 2. (*fig.*) zugrunde richten, ruinieren, zerstören, vernichten. **3.** *v.i.* 1. Schiffbruch erleiden; 2. (*fig.*) scheitern, vernichtet *or* zerstört werden. **–wright,** *s.* 1. der Schiffbaumeister, Schiffbauer; 2. (*Naut.*) (Schiffs)zimmermann. **–yard,** *s.* die Werft.

shire ['ʃaiə (*as suff.* ʃ(i)ə)], *s.* die Grafschaft. **shire|-horse,** *s.* schweres Zugpferd. **–-mote,** *s.* (*Hist.*) angelsächsisches Grafschaftsgericht.

shirk [ʃə:k], **1.** *v.t.* ausweichen (*Dat.*), sich drücken vor (*Dat.*), sich entziehen (*Dat.*); umgehen. **2.** *v.i.* (*coll.*) sich drücken. **shirker,** *s.* (*coll.*) der Drückeberger.

shir(r) [ʃə:], **1.** *s.* (*Am.*) eingewebtes Gummiband, elastisches Gewebe. **2.** *v.t.* in Falten ziehen, fälteln, kräuseln. **shirred** [–d], *adj.* mit Gummi durchwebt, gekräuselt.

shirt [ʃə:t], *s.* das (Ober)hemd; ***– of mail,*** das Panzerhemd; (*coll.*) ***not have a – to one's back,*** kein Hemd am *or* auf dem Leib haben; (*sl.*) ***keep one's – on,*** ruhig bleiben, ruhig Blut bewahren, sich nicht aufregen; (*sl.*) ***put one's – on a horse,*** alles auf ein Pferd setzen.

shirt|-cuffs, *pl.* Manschetten (*pl.*). **–-front,** *s.* das Vorhemd, der Oberhemdeinsatz. **shirting,** *s.* das Hemdentuch. **shirt|-sleeve,** *s.* der Hemd(s)ärmel; ***in one's –s,*** in Hemd(s)ärmeln. **–-tail,** *s.* der Hemdenschoß. **shirty,** *adj.* (*sl.*) ärgerlich, verdrießlich, kurz angebunden.

shit [ʃit], **1.** *s.* (*vulg.*) 1. die Scheiße; 2. der Scheißkerl. **2.** *irr.v.i.* (*vulg.*) scheißen.

[1]**shiver** ['ʃivə], **1.** *v.t.* zertrümmern, zersplittern, zerschmettern; ***– my timbers!*** Gott strafe mich! **2.** *v.i.* zersplittern, zerbrechen. **3.** *s.* das Bruchstück, der Splitter; (*Min.*) Schiefer.

[2]**shiver, 1.** *s.* der Schauer, das Schauern, Frösteln, Zittern; *pl.* ***the –s,*** der Schüttelfrost, Fieberschauer; (*coll.*) die Gänsehaut; ***it gives me*** (***a fit of***) ***the –s,*** mich überläuft es kalt; ***send a – down his spine,*** ihm eine Gänsehaut über den Rücken kriechen lassen. **2.** *v.i.* 1. schauern, frösteln, zittern, sich schütteln (***with,*** vor (*Dat.*)) (*cold*), zittern, beben (vor (*Dat.*)) (*excitement*); 2. (*Naut.*) flattern, killen. **shivering,** *s.* das Schauern, der Schauer; ***– fit,*** der Schüttelfrost, Fieberschauer. **shivery,** *adj.* zitternd, fröstelnd, fiebrig.

[1]**shoal** [ʃoul], **1.** *s.* 1. der Schwarm, Zug (*of fish*); 2. (*fig. coll.*) (*oft. pl.*) die (Un)menge, Masse. **2.** *v.i.* in Schwärmen auftreten (*of fish*).

[2]**shoal, 1.** *s.* 1. die Untiefe, Sandbank, flache Stelle; 2. (*fig.*) die Falle, Klippe. **2.** *v.i.* flacher *or* seichter werden. **3.** *adj.* flach, seicht, untief (*of water*). **shoaly,** *adj.* durch Untiefen gefährlich, voller Untiefen.

[1]**shock** [ʃɔk], **1.** *s.* die Hocke, (Korn)puppe, Mandel, der Garbenhaufen. **2.** *v.t.* in Hocken aufstellen (*corn*).

[2]**shock,** *s.* ***– of hair,*** der Haarschopf, zottiges Haar.

[3]**shock, 1.** *s.* der Stoß, Schlag, Zusammenstoß (*also Mil.*), Zusammenprall, Anprall, die Erschütterung; 2. (*fig.*) der (Schicksals)schlag, Schreck, das Ärgernis (***to,*** für); (*coll.*) ***get the – of one's life,*** sein blaues Wunder erleben, wie vom Schlag getroffen werden; ***give him quite a –,*** ihn ziemlich erschüttern; ***it was a great –,*** es war ein schwerer *or* harter Schlag; 3. (*Med.*) der Nervenschock, (Wund)schock, (*Scots*) Schlag(anfall); 4. (*Elec.*) Schlag. **2.** *v.t.* 1. entsetzen, empören, entrüsten, abstoßen, mit Entsetzen *or* Abscheu erfüllen, einen Schock versetzen (*Dat.*); ***I was –ed to see,*** zu meinem *or* mit Entsetzen sah ich; 2. schockieren, Anstoß erregen bei, anstößig sein (*Dat.*); ***be –ed,*** entsetzt *or* entrüstet *or* empört *or* schockiert sein (***by,*** durch; ***at,*** über (*Acc.*)).

shock|-absorber, *s.* der Stoßdämpfer. **–-absorption,** *s.* die Federung. **–-cord,** *s.* das Gummiseil, **–-effect,** *s.* die Stoßwirkung.

shocker ['ʃɔkə], *s.* (*coll.*) 1. etwas Aufregendes *or* Sensationelles *or* Abscheuliches; 2. der Schauerroman.

shock-headed, *adj.* struppig, zottig, strubbelig, struw(w)elig.

shocking ['ʃɔkiŋ], *adj.* 1. unerhört, anstößig, ungehörig, schockierend; 2. (*coll.*) entsetzlich, abscheulich, schrecklich, furchtbar, ekelhaft, scheußlich.

shock|-proof, *adj.* stoßsicher. **– tactics,** *pl.* 1. (*Mil.*) die Durchbruchstaktik; 2. (*coll.*) die Überraschungsstrategie. **– therapy, – treatment,** *s.* die Schockbehandlung. **–-troops,** *pl.* Stoßtruppen. **–-wave,** *s.* die Stoßwelle.

shod [ʃɔd], **1.** *imperf., p.p. of* **shoe, 2. 2.** *adj.* beschlagen (*of horse*).

shoddy ['ʃɔdi], **1.** *s.* 1. die Reißwolle, das Shoddy; Shoddytuch; 2. (*fig.*) der Schund; 3. (*Am.*) Protz. **2.** *adj.* 1. Shoddy–; 2. unecht, wertlos, minderwertig, schlecht, kitschig, Schund–; 3. (*Am.*) protzig.

shoe [ʃu:], **1.** *s.* 1. der (Halb)schuh; (*fig.*) ***dead men's –s,*** eine Stelle, die erst durch einen Todesfall frei wird; ***know where the – pinches,*** wissen wo der Schuh drückt; ***be*** or ***stand in his –s,*** in seiner Haut stecken, an seiner Stelle sein; ***now the – is on the other foot,*** nun paßt es ihm (*etc.*) nicht mehr in den Kram; ***shake in one's –s,*** vor Angst zittern, Bammel haben; ***step into his –s,*** seine Stelle einnehmen; 2. das Hufeisen (*of horses*); 3. eiserner Beschlag, der Hemmschuh, Bremsschuh. **2.** *irr.v.t.* 1. beschuhen; 2. beschlagen (*horses, wheels, sticks etc.*).

shoe|black, *s.* der Schuhputzer. **–-brush,** *s.* die Schuhbürste. **–horn,** *s.* der Schuhanzieher.

shoeing ['ʃu:iŋ], *s.* das Beschlagen, Beschuhen; ***–-smith,*** der Hufschmied.

shoe|lace, *s.* das Schuhband, der Schuhriemen, Schnürsenkel. **–-leather,** *s.* das Schuhleder; (*coll.*) ***save –,*** sich (*Dat.*) den Gang ersparen.

shoeless ['ʃu:lis], *adj.* ohne Schuhe, barfuß. **shoe|-lift,** *s. See* **–horn. –maker,** *s.* der Schuhmacher, Schuster; ***–'s thread,*** der Pechdraht. **–-polish,** *s.* die Schuhwichse. **–-scraper,** *s.* der Schuhkratzer, das Schuheisen. **–shine,** *s.* (*Am.*) der Schuhputzer. **–string,** *s.* (*obs.*) *see* **–lace**; (*fig. coll.*) ***on a –,*** mit knappen Mitteln.

shone [ʃɔn], *imperf., p.p. of* **shine.**

shoo [ʃu:], **1.** *v.t.* (*also* ***– away***) (ver)scheuchen. **2.** *int.* husch!

shook [ʃuk], *imperf. of* **shake.**

shoot [ʃu:t], **1.** *irr.v.i.* 1. schießen, feuern (***at,*** auf (*Acc.*) *or* nach); ***go –ing,*** auf die Jagd gehen; 2. (*fig.*) fliegen, flitzen, rasen, sausen, schießen, stürzen; ***– ahead,*** voraneilen, sich an die Spitze schieben; ***– ahead of,*** vorbeischießen an (*Dat.*), überholen, hinter sich (*Dat.*) lassen; 3. (*Bot.*) keimen, sprießen, sprossen, ausschlagen, Knospen treiben; ***– out,*** hervorschießen, sich (plötzlich) ausstrecken; ***– up,*** aufschießen, hochschießen, in die Höhe schießen *or* schnellen; (*fig.*) schnell heranwachsen; 4. stechen (*pain*); 5. (*Footb.*) aufs Tor schießen.

2. *irr.v.t.* 1. schießen, erlegen, jagen (*game etc.*); erschießen, totschießen (*a p.*); ***– down,*** niederschießen, niederknallen, abschießen (*aircraft*); (*coll.*) ***– up,*** zusammenschießen (*a p.*), durch Schießerei terrorisieren (*a town*); 2. (ab)schießen, (ab)feuern (*bullets, arrows*) (***at,*** auf (*Acc.*) *or* nach); 3. jagen in (*Dat.*), bejagen (*hunting-ground*); 4. werfen, schleudern (*glance etc.*), aussenden (*rays*); (*sl.*) ***– a line,*** angeben, übertreiben; ***– questions at,*** mit Fragen bombardieren; 5. auswerfen (*anchor, nets etc.*); ausschütten, abladen, ausleeren (*rubbish etc.*); 6. vorschieben (*a bolt*); 7. ***– a bridge,*** unter einer Brücke durchfahren; ***– rapids,*** über Stromschnellen fahren; 8. ***– forth,*** treiben (*buds etc.*); ***– out,*** vorstrecken (*one's legs*), ausstrecken (*one's tongue*), ausstoßen (*words*); 9. (*coll.*) ***– the moon,***

bei Nacht und Nebel ausrücken; (*Naut.*) – ***the sun,*** die Höhe der Sonne messen; 10. (*Footb.*) schießen (*ball, goal*).
3. *s.* 1. (*Hort.*) der Sprößling, Schößling, Sproß, Schoß, Trieb, das Reis; 2. (*Hunt.*) die Jagd, Jagdgesellschaft; das Jagdrevier; (*sl.*) ***the whole –,*** der ganze Rummel.

shooter ['ʃu:tə], *s.* 1. der Schütze; 2. ***six-–,*** sechsschüssiger Revolver.

shooting ['ʃu:tiŋ], **1.** *s.* 1. das Schießen, die Schießerei; Erschießung, das Erschießen (*of a p.*); 2. Jagen, die Jagd; das Jagdrevier; 3. (*Films*) Drehen. **2.** *adj.* stechend (*as pain*).

shooting|-box, *s.* das Jagdhäuschen. **--brake,** *s.* der Kombiwagen. **--gallery,** *s.* die Schießbude. **--iron,** *s.* (*sl.*) das Schießeisen. **--licence,** *s.* der Jagdschein. **--lodge,** *s. See* **--box. --match,** *s.* 1. das Wettschießen, Preisschießen; 2. (*coll.*) die Schießerei. **--party,** *s.* die Jagdgesellschaft. **--range,** *s.* der Schießstand. **--script,** *s.* (*Films*) der Drehplan. **--season,** *s.* die Jagdzeit. **– star,** *s.* die Sternschnuppe.

shop [ʃɔp], **1.** *s.* 1. der (Kauf)laden, das Geschäft; (*sl.*) ***all over the –,*** überall verstreut, in großer Unordnung; in alle Himmelsrichtungen; ***keep a –,*** einen Laden halten; ***set up –,*** ein Geschäft aufmachen; (*fig. coll.*) ***shut up –,*** das Geschäft aufgeben; (*coll.*) ***come to the wrong –,*** an die falsche Adresse kommen; 2. die Werkstatt; ***talk –,*** fachsimpeln; (*coll.*) ***the Shop,*** die Militärakademie zu Woolwich. **2.** *v.i.* einkaufen, Einkäufe *or* Besorgungen machen. **3.** *v.t.* (*sl.*) petzen gegen, verpfeifen (*a p.*).

shop|-assistant, *s.* Ladenangestellte(r), der (die) Verkäufer(in). **--boy,** *s.* der Ladenjunge. **--breaking,** *s.* der Ladeneinbruch. **--committee,** *s.* der Betriebsausschuß. **--floor,** *s.* (*coll.*) der Betrieb, das Werk. **--front,** *s.* das Schaufenster. **--girl,** *s.* das Ladenmädchen, die Verkäuferin. **--keeper,** *s.* der (die) Ladenbesitzer(in), Ladeninhaber(in), Kleinhändler(in), Krämer(in); ***nation of –s,*** das Krämervolk. **--keeping,** *s.* der Kleinhandel, das Detailgeschäft. **–lifter,** *s.* der (die) Ladendieb(in). **–lifting,** *s.* der Ladendiebstahl. **--man** [–mən], *s.* der Ladengehilfe.

shopper ['ʃɔpə], *s.* der (die) (Ein)käufer(in). **shopping,** *s.* der Einkauf, das Einkaufen; Besorgungen (*pl.*), Einkäufe (*pl.*); ***do one's*** or ***go –,*** Einkäufe machen; – ***bag,*** die Einkaufstasche; – ***centre,*** das Geschäftszentrum; – ***expedition,*** der Einkaufsbummel; – ***street,*** die Geschäftsstraße.

shop|-price, *s.* der Ladenpreis. **--soiled,** *adj.* beschädigt, angestaubt; (*fig.*) verbraucht, abgerissen; – ***goods,*** die Ausschußware. **--steward,** *s.* der Betriebsrat, Vertrauensmann. **–walker,** *s.* der (die) Ladenaufseher(in). **--window,** *s.* das Schaufenster. **--woman,** *s.* die Verkäuferin, das Ladenfräulein. **--worn,** *adj.* (*Am.*) *see* **--soiled.**

[1]**shore** [ʃɔ:], *s.* das Ufer, Gestade, die Küste, der Strand; ***off –,*** in einiger Entfernung von der Küste; ***on –,*** an Land, ans Land *or* Ufer, auf dem Land, am Ufer.

[2]**shore, 1.** *s.* die Stütze, (Stütz)strebe, der Stützbalken, Strebebalken, (*Naut.*) die Schore. **2.** *v.t.* (*usu.* – ***up***) (unter)stützen, abstützen.

shore|-based, *adj.* Küsten–. **--battery,** *s.* die Küstenbatterie. **--leave,** *s.* der Landurlaub. **shoreless,** *adj.* uferlos (*also fig.*), (*fig.*) grenzenlos. **shoreline,** *s.* die Küstenlinie, Uferlinie.

shoreward ['ʃɔ:wəd], *adj.* Küsten–, Ufer–. **shorewards** [–z], *adv.* nach der Küste zu.

shoring ['ʃɔ:riŋ], *s.* 1. das (Ab)stützen; 2. (*collect.*) Stützbalken (*pl.*).

shorn [ʃɔ:n], *p.p. of* **shear**; – ***of,*** beraubt (*Gen.*).

short [ʃɔ:t], **1.** *adj.* 1. kurz (*time and space, also fig.*); (*coll.*) – ***cut,*** die Wegkürzung, der Abkürzungsweg, Durchgang; (*fig.*) das Schnellverfahren; (*Arith.*) – ***division,*** abgekürzte Division; ***on the – list,*** auf der Auswahlliste *or* engen Wahl; – ***memory,*** schwaches *or* schlechtes Gedächtnis; – ***shrift,*** die Galgenfrist; ***give – shrift, make – shrift of,*** kurzen Prozeß machen mit; ***he will get – shrift,*** mit ihm wird kurzer Prozeß gemacht; – ***sight,*** die Kurzsichtigkeit; – ***story,*** die Novelle, Kurzgeschichte; ***to cut a long story –,*** um es kurz zu fassen *or* machen; – ***temper,*** die Reizbarkeit; – ***time,*** die Kurzarbeit, Arbeitsverkürzung; ***a – time ago,*** vor kurzem, kürzlich; ***in a – time,*** in kurzer Zeit, in kurzem; ***make – work of,*** kurzen Prozeß machen mit; – ***and sweet,*** kurz und gut *or* bündig; ***be –, make it –,*** sich kurz fassen; – ***for,*** eine Abkürzung für; 2. klein (*stature*); 3. (*Comm.*) auf kurze Sicht, kurzfristig; – ***bill,*** ungedeckte Wechsel, der Blankowechsel, der Wechsel auf kurze Sicht; ***at – date,*** auf kurze Sicht; – ***loan,*** kurzfristige Anleihe; ***at – notice,*** kurzfristig; (*coll.*) innerhalb kurzer Zeit; 4. kurz angebunden, barsch; – ***answer,*** barsche Antwort; ***be – with,*** kurz abfertigen; 5. knapp, beschränkt, fehlend, mangelhaft, unzulänglich, unzureichend; kurz (*of,* vor (*Dat.*)), weniger (als); ***a – 10 miles,*** knappe 10 Meilen; ***a – 10 minutes,*** knappe 10 Minuten; – ***rations,*** knappe Verpflegung; ***be in – supply,*** knapp sein; – ***weight,*** das Fehlgewicht; ***come*** or ***fall – of,*** nicht erreichen (*also fig.*), (*fig.*) zurückbleiben hinter (*Dat.*); ***little – of,*** beinahe, kaum weniger als; ***nothing – of,*** nichts weniger als, geradezu, überaus; ***stop – of nothing,*** vor nichts zurückschrecken; 6. – ***of,*** knapp an (*Dat.*); – ***of breath,*** kurzatmig; – ***of cash,*** nicht bei Kasse; ***be – of,*** Mangel haben an (*Dat.*); ***go – of,*** Mangel leiden an (*Dat.*); ***run – of,*** knapp werden an (*Dat.*); 7. brüchig, bröckelig, mürbe (*pastry, metal*); – ***pastry,*** der Mürbeteig; 8. – ***drink,*** starkes *or* unvermischtes Getränk.
2. *adv.* 1. kurz(erhand), plötzlich; ***cut –,*** unterbrechen; ***stop –,*** plötzlich innehalten; ***take him up –,*** ihn plötzlich unterbrechen; (*coll.*) ***be taken –,*** plötzlich müssen; 2. – ***of,*** bis auf (*Acc.*); ***he will do anything – of killing,*** er nimmt alles auf sich bis auf töten; ***it is the only thing to do – of starting again,*** es bleibt das Einzige, wenn man nun gerade nicht von vorn anfangen will; 3. (*Comm.*) ***sell –,*** ohne Deckung verkaufen.
3. *s.* 1. die Kurzform, Abkürzung; ***for –,*** der Kürze halber, kurz; ***in –,*** in Kürze, in wenigen Worten, kurz(um); ***the long and the – of it is,*** der Kern der S. ist nämlich; 2. (*Metr.*) kurze Silbe, kurzer Vokal; 3. (*Artil.*) der Kurzschuß; 4. (*Elec.*) Kurzschluß; 5. Kurzfilm; 6. *pl. See* **shorts.**

shortage ['ʃɔ:tidʒ], *s.* 1. der Mangel, die Knappheit (*of,* an (*Dat.*)); 2. der Fehlbetrag.

short|bread, –cake, *s.* der Mürbekuchen. **--change,** *v.t.* (*sl.*) übers Ohr hauen. **--circuit, 1.** *s.* (*Elec.*) der Kurzschluß. **2.** *v.t., v.i.* kurzschließen. **–coming,** *s.* (*usu. pl.*) die Unzulänglichkeit, schwache Seite, der Fehler, Mangel. **--dated,** *adj.* auf kurze Sicht, kurzfristig.

shorten [ʃɔ:tn], **1.** *v.t.* 1. (ver)kürzen, abkürzen; (*Hort.*) stutzen, beschneiden; (*fig.*) vermindern, verkleinern, verringern; 2. (*Naut.*) bergen, einziehen (*sail*). **2.** *v.i.* 1. kürzer werden, abnehmen; 2. sich senken, fallen, zurückgehen (*as price*). **shortening,** *s.* 1. die (Ver)kürzung, das Kürzen; 2. die Verminderung, das Abnehmen; 3. (*Cook.*) Backfett.

short|fall, *s.* der Fehlbetrag. **–hand,** *s.* die Kurzschrift, Stenographie; **––*typist,*** der (die) Stenotypist(in). **--handed,** *adj.* unter Arbeitermangel leidend. **–horn,** *s.* das Kurzhornrind.

shortish ['ʃɔ:tiʃ], *adj.* etwas *or* ziemlich kurz.

short|-list, *v.t.* in die engere (Aus)wahl ziehen. **–lived,** *adj.* kurzlebig, von kurzer Dauer.

shortly ['ʃɔ:tli], *adv.* 1. in kurzem, in kurzer Zeit, (als)bald; – ***after,*** bald *or* kurze Zeit nachher, bald nachdem; – ***before,*** kurz vorher *or* davor; 2. kurz, bündig, schroff. **shortness,** *s.* 1. die Kürze; – ***of memory,*** die Gedächtnisschwäche; 2. die Knappheit, der Mangel (*of,* an (*Dat.*)); – ***of breath,*** die Kurzatmigkeit; – ***of money,*** der Geldmangel.

short-range, *attrib. adj.* Nahkampf–.

shorts [ʃɔ:ts], *pl.* die Kniehose, kurze Hose; (*Am.*) *see* **pants; briefs.**

short|-sighted, *adj.* kurzsichtig. **--sightedness,** *s.* die Kurzsichtigkeit (*also fig.*). **--tempered,** *adj.* reizbar. **--term,** *adj.* kurzfristig. **--time,** *adj.* Kurzzeit–; – *working,* die Kurzarbeit. **--wave,** **1.** *s.* die Kurzwelle. **2.** *attrib. adj.* Kurzwellen–. **--winded,** *adj.* kurzatmig.

shot [ʃɔt], **1.** *s.* 1. der Schuß, das Geschoß, die Kugel; ***long –,*** der Schuß auf weites Ziel, (*fig.*) kühner Versuch; (*sl.*) ***not by a long – !*** wo! (*coll.*) ***like a –,*** wie aus der Pistole geschossen, bereitwillig; fluchtartig, blitzschnell; (*fig.*) ***a – in the dark,*** die Vermutung aufs Geratewohl; (*fig.*) ***make a bad –,*** fehlschießen, danebenhauen, danebenschießen; ***take a – at,*** schießen auf (*Acc.*) *or* nach; 2. der Schrot, Schrotkugeln (*pl.*), Schrotkörner (*pl.*); ***charge of –,*** die Schrotladung; ***small –,*** das Schrotkorn; 3. (*Spt.*) die Stoßkugel; ***put the –,*** Kugel stoßen; ***putting the –,*** das Kugelstoßen; 4. der Schütze; ***crack –,*** der Meisterschütze; ***dead –,*** unfehlbarer Schütze; 5. (*Spt.*) der Stoß, Wurf, Schlag; ***good –!*** gut getroffen! 6. (*Films*) die Aufnahme; (*Phot.*) (*coll.*) (Film)aufnahme; 7. (*coll.*) der Versuch; ***at the third –,*** beim dritten Versuch; ***have a – at,*** (zu bekommen) versuchen; 8. (*Med.*) (*coll.*) die Einspritzung, Spritze; (*fig.*) ***a – in the arm,*** die Belebungsspritze. **2.** *imperf., p.p. of* **shoot. 3.** *adj.* 1. gesprenkelt, schillernd, changierend; – ***silk,*** die Changeant-Seide; 2. – ***through with,*** durchschossen *or* durchsetzt mit.

shot|-effect, *s.* 1. der Changeanteffekt (*fabric*); 2. (*Phys.*) Schroteffekt. **-gun,** *s.* die Schrotflinte; – ***marriage,*** die Mußheirat. **-proof,** *adj.* kugelfest. **--tower,** *s.* der Schrotturm. **--wound,** *s.* die Schußwunde.

should [ʃud], *imperf. of* **shall**; 1. sollte(st), sollten; 2. (*for subjunctive*) (*1st pers. sing. and pl.*) würde(n) (*in principal clause*); ***I – like to,*** ich möchte (gern); ***he – have done it,*** er hätte es tun sollen; 3 (*indic. in subordinate clause with* **that**) ***it is unbelievable that he – be (have been) so stupid,*** es ist unglaublich daß er so dumm (gewesen) ist (***as to,*** zu).

shoulder [ˈʃouldə], **1.** *s.* 1. die Schulter (*also of a horse*), Achsel; der Bug, das Vorder-Schulterblatt (*of quadrupeds*); – ***to –,*** Schulter an Schulter; (*fig.*) ***have broad –s,*** einen breiten Rücken haben; (*coll.*) ***have a chip on one's –,*** der ganzen Welt böse sein, ständiges Ressentiment hegen; ***give him the cold –,*** ihm die kalte Schulter zeigen, ihn geringschätzig behandeln, ihn links liegen lassen; ***put one's – to the wheel,*** sich tüchtig ins Zeug legen, sich kräftig anstrengen; (*fig.*) ***head and –s above,*** haushoch überlegen (*Dat.*); ***you cannot put old heads on young –s,*** Jugend hat keine Tugend; (*coll.*) ***rub –s with,*** nahekommen (*Dat.*), in nähere Berührung kommen mit; 2. das Schulterstück (*of meat*); – ***of mutton,*** die Hammelkeule; 3. (*fig.*) der Vorsprung, die Brüstung (*of building*); 4. das Bankett (*of road*); 5. Schulterteil, die Schulterpartie (*of clothing*). **2.** *v.t.* 1. schultern, auf die Schulter *or* Achsel nehmen, (*fig.*) auf sich nehmen; – ***arms!*** Gewehr über! 2. stoßen, schieben, drängen; – ***one's way,*** sich drängen.

shoulder|-bag, *s.* die Schultertasche, Umhäng(e)-tasche. **--belt,** *s.* das Schultergehenk, Wehrgehenk. **--blade,** *s.* (*Anat.*) das Schulterblatt. **--strap,** *s.* 1. das Achselband, Trägerband, der Träger (*on ladies' underwear*); 2. (*Mil.*) die Achselklappe, das Achselstück.

shout [ʃaut], **1.** *s.* der Ruf, Schrei, das Geschrei; ***give a –,*** aufschreien. **2.** *v.i.* schreien (***with,*** vor (*Dat.*); ***for,*** nach *or* um), rufen; – ***for joy,*** vor Freude jauchzen; – ***at,*** anschreien; – ***out,*** aufschreien; – ***to,*** zurufen (*Dat.*). **3.** *v.t.* laut rufen *or* schreien; – ***him down,*** ihn niederschreien; – ***out,*** ausrufen; – ***o.s. hoarse,*** sich heiser schreien. **shouting,** *s.* das Geschrei, Schreien.

shove [ʃʌv], **1.** *v.t.* schieben, stoßen, (*coll.*) stellen, legen, stecken, stopfen; – ***aside,*** beiseite schieben; – ***away,*** wegschieben; – ***off,*** abstoßen (*boat*). **2.** *v.i.* (sich) drängen; – ***by,*** sich vorbeidrängen; (*Naut.*) – ***off,*** abstoßen; (*sl.*) abdampfen, verduften; (*sl.*) – ***on,*** weitergehen. **3.** *s.* der Stoß, Schub, (*coll.*) Schubs.

shovel [ʃʌvl], **1.** *s.* die Schaufel, die Schippe. **2.** *v.t.* schaufeln, schippen. **shovel-board,** *s.* das Beilkespiel; die Beilketafel. **shoveler,** (*Am.*) *see* **shoveller. shovelful,** *s.* die Schaufelvoll. **shovel-hat,** *s.* (*Eccl.*) breitkrempiger Hut. **shoveller,** *s.* (*Orn.*) die Löffelente (*Spatula clypeata*).

show [ʃou], **1.** *s.* 1. das Erscheinen, die Erscheinung; 2. das Schauspiel, der Anblick; ***for –,*** um zu renommieren, um Eindruck zu schinden; ***make a fine –,*** prächtig aussehen; (*coll.*) ***put on a show,*** sich aufspielen; 3. der Anschein, (leerer) Schein, der Vorwand; ***make a – of anger,*** sich zornig stellen; ***make a – of doing,*** so tun *or* sich stellen, als wenn man tun wollte; ***under a – of,*** unter dem Schein *or* Vorwand von; 4. die Ausstellung, Schau, Zurschaustellung; – ***of force,*** die Demonstration der Macht; ***by – of hands,*** durch Handzeichen; – ***of teeth,*** das Zähnefletschen; ***make a – of,*** zur Schau tragen, sehen lassen; ***on –,*** ausgestellt, zu besichtigen; 5. die Leistung; ***put up a fine –,*** eine schöne Leistung vollbringen; (*sl.*) ***bad –!*** wie schade! ***good –!*** gut gemacht! bravo! 6. (*coll.*) die Vorstellung, Vorführung, Aufführung, Darbietung; ***dumb –,*** die Pantomime; ***put on a fine –,*** eine prachtvolle Darbietung aufführen; ***steal the –,*** den Vogel abschießen; 7. (*sl.*) das Unternehmen, die Sache, Angelegenheit, Einrichtung, der Kram; (*sl.*) ***all over the –,*** überall verstreut; ***give the – away,*** das Geheimnis verraten; ***run the –,*** die S. *or* den Laden schmeißen.

2. *irr.v.t.* 1. zeigen, sehen lassen; vorweisen, (her)-zeigen (*ticket etc.*); – ***o.s.,*** sich zeigen, erscheinen; – ***o.s. to be,*** sich zeigen *or* erweisen als; – ***one's cards,*** see – ***one's hand***; – ***one's true colours,*** sein wahres Gesicht *or* sich im wahren Licht zeigen; – ***dirt,*** leicht schmutzen; – ***him the door,*** ihm die Tür weisen, ihn vor die Tür setzen; – ***him to the door,*** ihn zur Tür begleiten; – ***one's face,*** sich blicken lassen; – ***the white feather,*** sich feige zeigen; – ***fight,*** kampflustig sein, sich zur Wehr setzen; (*fig.*) – ***one's hand,*** seine Karten aufdecken, seine Absichten zu erkennen geben; – ***a clean pair of heels,*** ausreißen, sich aus dem Staub machen; (*coll.*) – ***a leg,*** aufstehen; (*coll.*) – ***him his place,*** ihm zeigen wo er hingehört; – ***one's teeth,*** die Zähne fletschen (***to,*** gegen) *or* (*fig.*) zeigen; (*ellipt. coll.*) ***I'll – you!*** ich werd's dir beibringen! (*threat*); 2. aufführen (*play*), vorführen (*film etc.*); 3. ausstellen (*in exhibition*); 4. zur Schau stellen, an den Tag legen (*knowledge etc.*); 5. enthüllen, bekanntmachen, offenbaren, erkennen lassen (*one's intentions etc.*), aufzeigen, aufweisen, darlegen, beweisen; (*Law*) – ***cause,*** einen triftigen Grund vorbringen; – ***proof,*** einen Beweis nachweisen *or* liefern; 6. erzeigen, erweisen (*kindness etc.*); – ***him a favour,*** ihm eine Gunst erweisen; – ***gratitude,*** sich dankbar erweisen (***to,*** gegenüber); – ***willing,*** sich bereitwillig erklären.

(*with adv. or prep.*) – ***forth,*** aufzeigen, darlegen, bekanntmachen, kundtun, dartun; – ***in,*** (her)-einführen, eintreten lassen; – ***off,*** vorlegen, vorführen, hervorheben; prahlen *or* protzen mit, zur Schau tragen; – ***over*** or ***round,*** führen durch, herumführen in (*Dat.*), zeigen; – ***out,*** hinausbegleiten, hinausbringen, an die Tür bringen (*a p.*); – ***up,*** heraufführen, hinaufführen (*a p.*); deutlich zeigen (*a th.*); (*coll.*) enthüllen, aufdecken (*a th.*), entlarven, bloßstellen (*a p.*).

3. *irr.v.i.* 1. sich zeigen, sichtbar werden, zu sehen sein; ***be –ing,*** gezeigt *or* vorgeführt werden (*as films*); ***time will –,*** die Zeit wird es lehren; 2. erscheinen, aussehen; 3. – ***off,*** sich aufspielen *or* brüsten, großtun, prahlen, protzen, angeben; 4. – ***up,*** sich abheben, hervortreten (***against,*** gegen); (*coll.*) erscheinen, sich sehen lassen, aufkreuzen, auftauchen.

show|-bill, *s.* der Theaterzettel. **-bread,** *s.* das Schaubrot, Opferbrot. **--business,** *s.* (*coll.*) die Unterhaltungsindustrie. **--card,** *s.* das Reklameplakat, Werbeplakat. **--case,** *s.* der Schaukasten, Ausstellungskasten, die Vitrine. **--down,** *s.* (*coll.*) der Entscheidungskampf, entscheidende Kraftprobe, endgültige Auseinandersetzung.

shower ['ʃauə], **1.** *s.* 1. der (Regen)schauer; – *of rain,* der Regenguß; 2. der Regen(fall); Hagel (*of arrows or bullets*); 3. (*fig.*) Erguß, die Fülle, Menge; 4. (*sl.*) das Gesindel; 5. *See* **shower-bath. 2.** *v.t.* 1. (*also* – *down*) regnen *or* herunterströmen lassen; 2. (*fig.*) überschütten, überhäufen (*a p.*), häufen (*things*) (*upon,* auf (*Acc.*)). **3.** *v.i.* 1. leicht regnen; 2. (*fig.*) – *down,* herabströmen, niederprasseln.

shower-bath, *s.* die Brause, Dusche, das Brausebad.

showeriness ['ʃauərinis], *s.* das Regnerische. **showery,** *adj.* regnerisch; – *weather,* das Regenwetter.

show-girl, *s.* das Revuegirl.

showiness ['ʃouinis], *s.* der Prunk, die Pracht, Prunkhaftigkeit, Auffälligkeit. **showing,** *s.* die Darstellung, Vorführung; *on his own* –, nach seiner eigenen Aussage *or* Behauptung *or* Darstellung; *make a poor* –, sich als eine Niete *or* ein Versager ausweisen.

show-jumping, *s.* das Turnierreiten.

showman ['ʃoumən], *s.* 1. der Schausteller, Schaubudenbesitzer; 2. (*coll. fig.*) geschickter Propagandist. **showmanship,** *s.* 1. effektvolle Darbietung; 2. die Effekthascherei.

shown [ʃoun], *p.p. of* **show.**

show|-off, *s.* (*coll.*) der Angeber, das Großmaul. **-piece,** *s.* das Ausstellungsstück, Paradestück. **-place,** *s.* (*coll.*) der Ort mit berühmten Sehenswürdigkeiten. **--pupil,** *s.* der Paradeschüler. **--ring,** *s.* der Vorführplatz (für Tiere). **-room,** *s.* der Ausstellungsraum, Vorführungsraum.

showy ['ʃoui], *adj.* prunkhaft, auffallend, auffällig, prächtig.

shrank [ʃræŋk], *imperf. of* **shrink.**

shrapnel ['ʃræpnəl], *s.* das Schrapnell; *piece of* –, der Granatsplitter.

shred [ʃred], **1.** *s.* 1. der Fetzen, das *or* der Schnitzel, der Brocken, das Bruchstück; *tear to –s,* in Fetzen reißen, zerfetzen; (*fig.*) *tear an argument to –s,* ein Argument gründlich widerlegen; 2. (*fig.*) das Stückchen, der Funken, die Spur; *not a – of,* keine Spur von. **2.** *v.t.* zerfetzen, zerreißen, zerschneiden, schnitzeln (*vegetables*). **3.** *v.i.* zerreißen, in Fetzen gehen. **shredder,** *s.* die Schneidemaschine, der Reißwolf.

shrew [ʃru:], *s.* 1. zänkisches Weib, der Zankteufel; *Taming of the Shrew,* Der Widerspenstigen Zähmung; 2. (*Zool.*) (*also* *--mouse*) die Spitzmaus.

shrewd [ʃru:d], *adj.* 1. scharfsinnig, scharfsichtig, gescheit, klug; *have a – guess,* gut raten; 2. schlau, gerieben, gerissen, gewitzt, pfiffig. **shrewdness,** *s.* der Scharfsinn, die Klugheit, Schlauheit, Geschicklichkeit, das Geschick.

shrewish ['ʃru:iʃ], *adj.* zänkisch, giftig, boshaft.

shriek [ʃri:k], **1.** *s.* der Schrei, das Geschrei, Kreischen, Gekreisch; *–s of laughter,* gellendes Gelächter. **2.** *v.i.* aufschreien (*with,* vor (*Dat.*)), kreischen; (*of wind*) heulen.

shrievalty ['ʃri:vəlti], *s.* die Scheriffswürde, Scheriffsgerichtsbarkeit.

shrift [ʃrift], *s.* (*obs.*) die Beichte; (*only in*) *short* –, die Galgenfrist; *give him short* –, kurzen Prozeß mit ihm machen; *he will get short* –, mit ihm wird kurzer Prozeß gemacht.

shrike [ʃraik], *s.* (*Orn.*) der Würger (*Lanius*); *redbacked* –, der Neuntöter (*L. collurio*).

shrill [ʃril], **1.** *adj.* 1. gellend, schrill (*of sound*); 2. (*fig.*) grell, schreiend (*of colour etc.*); 3. (*fig.*) scharf, schneidend, stechend, durchdringend; verbissen, hartnäckig. **2.** *v.i.* schrillen, gellen. **shrillness,** *s.* das Gellende *or* Schrille. **shrill-voiced,** *adj.* mit gellender Stimme.

shrimp [ʃrimp], **1.** *s.* 1. die Garnele; 2. (*fig.*) der Knirps, Wicht. **2.** *v.i.* Garnelen fangen. **shrimper,** *s.* der Garnelenfischer.

shrine [ʃrain], *s.* 1. der (Heiligen)schrein, das Heiligengrab(mal); der Reliquienschrein; 2. (*fig.*) geweihter Platz, geheiligte Stätte, das Heiligtum.

shrink [ʃriŋk], **1.** *irr.v.i.* 1. (ein– *or* zusammen)-schrumpfen, sich zusammenziehen (*into,* zu), einlaufen, eingehen (*of fabric*), sich werfen (*of wood*); 2. (*fig.*) abnehmen, schwinden, kleiner werden; 3. (*also* – *away* or *back*) zurückschrecken, zurückweichen, zurückschaudern, zurückfahren, sich fürchten *or* scheuen *or* entsetzen (*from,* vor (*Dat.*)), sich zurückziehen (von); – *from doing,* widerwillig *or* ungern tun. **2.** *irr.v.t.* 1. einschrumpfen *or* zusammenschrumpfen *or* einlaufen lassen, krimpen, krump(f)en, schrimpen, schrümpen, dekatieren (*fabric*); 2. (*fig.*) vermindern, verkürzen. **shrinkage** [–idʒ], *s.* 1. das Einschrumpfen, Zusammenschrumpfen, Einlaufen, Dekatieren, die Krimpe, Krümpe (*of fabric*); 2. (*Tech.*) der Schwund, das Schwindmaß, die Schrumpfung; 3. (*fig.*) der Schwund, die Verminderung, Abnahme. **shrinking,** *adj.* (*fig.*) ausweichend, widerwillig, scheu, verschüchtert. **shrink-proof,** *adj.* schrumpffest.

shrive [ʃraiv], *irr.v.t.* (*Eccl. obs.*) beichten lassen, die Beichte abnehmen (*Dat.*), Absolution erteilen (*Dat.*).

shrivel [ʃrivl], **1.** *v.i.* 1. (*also* – *up*) (ein)schrumpfen, zusammenschrumpfen, sich zusammenziehen, runz(e)lig werden; 2. (*of plants*) (ver)welken; 3. (*fig.*) verkümmern. **2.** *v.t.* einschrumpfen lassen, runz(e)lig machen. **shrivelled** [–d], *adj.* 1. runz(e)lig, zusammengeschrumpft; 2. verwelkt, welk.

[1]**shroud** [ʃraud], **1.** *s.* 1. das Leichentuch, Grabtuch, Leichenhemd, Sterbehemd; 2. (*fig.*) die Hülle, Decke, Bedeckung, Umhüllung, der Schleier. **2.** *v.t.* 1. in ein Leichentuch einhüllen; 2. (*usu. fig.*) (ein)hüllen (*in,* in (*Acc.*)), verschleiern, verdecken, (ver)hüllen.

[2]**shroud,** *s.* (*Naut.*) die Want.

shrove [ʃrouv], *imperf. of* **shrive.**

Shrove|-tide, *s.* die Fastenzeit. **--Tuesday,** *s.* die Fastnacht.

[1]**shrub** [ʃrʌb], *s.* die Staude, der Strauch, Busch.

[2]**shrub,** *s.* (eine Art) Punsch (*m.*).

shrubbery ['ʃrʌbəri], *s.* das Gebüsch, Gesträuch; Büsche, Sträuche (*pl.*). **shrubby,** *adj.* strauchig, buschig, Strauch–.

shrug [ʃrʌg], **1.** *s.* das Achselzucken; *give a* –, die Achseln zucken. **2.** *v.i.* (*v.t.*) – (*one's shoulders*), mit den Achseln zucken.

shrunk [ʃrʌŋk], *p.p. of* **shrink. shrunken,** *adj.* eingeschrumpft, eingefallen, verkümmert, abgemagert, abgezehrt.

shuck [ʃʌk], **1.** *s.* (*esp. Am.*) die Hülse, Schale, Schote. **2.** *v.t.* schälen, entschoten, enthülsen, entschalen. **shucks!** *int.* (*coll.*) (*esp. Am.*) Unsinn! Blech!

shudder ['ʃʌdə], **1.** *v.i.* schaudern, (er)zittern, (er)-beben, besorgt sein, befürchten (*lest,* daß); – *at,* – *away from,* schaudern bei, zurückschaudern vor (*Dat.*), Ekel empfinden über (*Acc.*); *I – to think,* es schaudert mich bei dem Gedanken. **2.** *s.* der Schauder, das Zittern, Schaudern; *it gives me the –s,* es macht mich schaudern.

shuffle [ʃʌfl], **1.** *s.* 1. das Schlurfen, Schlurren, schlurfender *or* schleppender Gang; 2. (*Danc.*) der Schleifer; 3. das (Karten)mischen; 4. (*fig.*) die Ausflucht, der Kunstgriff, Schwindel. **2.** *v.t.* 1. hin– und herschieben, (herum)hantieren mit; – *one's feet,* (mit den Füßen) scharren; 2. (*Cards*) mischen; 3. – *off,* (von sich) schieben, abschütteln, abstreifen, abwälzen (*on to,* auf (*Acc.*)); ausweichen (*Dat.*) (*responsibility*). **3.** *v.i.* 1. nachlässig *or* schleppend gehen; mit den Füßen schlurren; (mit den Füßen) scharren *or* schlurfen; unruhig sitzen; – *off,* sich fortschleppen; 2. (die Karten) mischen; 3. (*fig.*) Ausflüchte machen, sich herauszuhelfen suchen; (*fig.*) – *out of,* ausweichen (*Dat.*), sich herausziehen aus. **shuffling, 1.** *adj.* 1. schlurfend, schlurrend, schleppend, schlodderig, schlaksig (*gait*); 2. (*fig.*) ausweichend, unredlich, unaufrichtig; – *excuse,* die Ausflucht, faule Ausrede. **2.** *s.* 1. *See* **shuffle, 1,** 3; 2. (*fig.*) (*collect.*) Winkelzüge, Ausflüchte (*pl.*).

shun [ʃʌn], *v.t.* (ver)meiden; ausweichen (*Dat.*), sich fernhalten von.

shunt [ʃʌnt], **1.** *v.t.* 1. (*Railw.*) auf ein Nebengleis *or* anderes Gleis fahren, verschieben, rangieren; 2. (*Elec.*) parallel schalten, nebenschalten; 3. (*fig.*) (*also* – *off*) abzweigen, ableiten, beiseite schieben (*a th.*), kaltstellen (*a p.*). **2.** *v.i.* (*Railw.*) auf ein Nebengleis fahren, rangieren. **3.** *s.* 1. (*Railw.*) das Nebengleis, die Weiche; 2. (*Elec.*) der Neben(an)-schluß, Nebenwiderstand, die Parallelschaltung; – ***winding,*** die Nebenschlußwicklung; 3. (*fig.*) das Ausweichen. **shunter,** *s.* (*Railw.*) der Rangierer, Weichensteller.

shunting [ˈʃʌntiŋ], *s.* das Rangieren, Verschieben. **shunting|-engine,** *s.* die Rangierlokomotive. **--yard,** *s.* der Rangierbahnhof, Verschiebebahnhof.

shunt-wound [–waund], *adj.* (*Elec.*) Nebenschluß–.

shut [ʃʌt], **1.** *irr.v.t.* (ver)schließen, zumachen; zuschlagen, zuklappen (*a book etc.*), zusammenklappen, zusammenfalten (*folding articles*); (*fig.*) – ***one's eyes to,*** die Augen verschließen vor (*Dat.*), nicht sehen wollen; (*fig.*) – ***the door on,*** unmöglich machen; – ***one's mouth,*** den Mund schließen; – ***his mouth,*** ihn zum Stillschweigen bringen *or* verpflichten, ihm den Mund stopfen; – ***o.s. away,*** sich abschließen (*from,* von); – ***down,*** einstellen, stillegen (*a business etc.*); – ***in,*** einschließen; die Aussicht versperren; – ***off,*** absperren, abdrehen, abstellen (*water, gas etc.*); – ***out,*** keinen Zutritt gewähren (*Dat.*), nicht (her)einlassen (*a p.*), ausschließen, aussperren, versperren (*the view*); – ***to,*** zuschließen; – ***up,*** verschließen, einschließen, abschließen; – ***o.s. up,*** sich einschließen; (*sl.*) – ***him up,*** ihn einsperren; (*sl.*) (*fig.*) ihn zum Schweigen bringen, ihm den Mund stopfen; (*fig.*) (*coll.*) – ***up shop,*** den Laden *or* die Bude zumachen. **2.** *irr.v.i.* sich schließen, zugehen; – ***down,*** die Arbeit einstellen, stillgelegt werden; – ***to,*** sich schließen; (*sl.*) – ***up,*** den Mund *or* das Maul halten. **3.** *s.* (*Tech.*) die Schweißnaht, Schweißstelle.

shut|-down, *s.* (*coll.*) die Stillegung, Betriebseinstellung. **--eye,** *s.* (*sl.*) das Nickerchen.

shutter [ˈʃʌtə], *s.* 1. der Fensterladen; ***put up the –s,*** die Fensterläden schließen; (*fig.*) das Geschäft schließen, den Laden dichtmachen; 2. die (Schließ)klappe, (*Phot.*) der Verschluß; 3. (*lock-gates*) das Schütz(entor), die Schütze.

shuttle [ʃʌtl], *s.* 1. (*Weav.*) das Weberschiff(chen), der Schützen; (*Sew.-mach.*) das Schiffchen; 2. die Schütze, das Schütz, Schleusentor; 3. *See* **shuttle-service. shuttle|cock,** *s.* 1. der Federball; 2. (*fig.*) der Streitgegenstand, Fangball. **--service,** *s.* (*Railw. etc.*) der Pendelverkehr. **--thread,** *s.* der Spulenfaden, Querfaden.

[1]**shy** [ʃai], **1.** *v.t.* (*coll.*) werfen, schleudern. **2.** *s.* der Wurf; (*fig.*) Hieb, Stich, die Stichelei; der Versuch; ***have a – at,*** werfen nach; (*fig.*) es versuchen mit.

[2]**shy, 1.** *adj.* 1. (*of animals*) scheu, (*of a p.*) schüchtern, verschüchtert, verlegen, zurückhaltend, reserviert; 2. behutsam, vorsichtig, zögernd, ängstlich, zaghaft; mißtrauisch, argwöhnisch; (*coll.*) ***fight – of,*** meiden; vorsichtig aus dem Wege gehen (*Dat.*); ***fight – of doing,*** sich scheuen zu tun. **2.** *v.i.* 1. (*of horses*) scheuen (*at,* vor (*Dat.*)); 2. (*fig.*) – ***away from,*** – ***at,*** zurückschrecken vor (*Dat.*). **shyness,** *s.* 1. die Scheu; Schüchternheit, Zurückhaltung; 2. der Argwohn, das Mißtrauen.

shyster [ˈʃaistə], *s.* (*sl.*) der Winkeladvokat, Rechtsverdreher; (*fig.*) Lump, Halunke.

si [si:], *s.* (*Mus.*) siebenter Ton der Tonleiter, das H.

Siam [saiˈæm], *s.* (*obs.*) *see* **Thailand. Siamese** [saiəˈmi:z], **1.** *s.* der Siamese (die Siamesin). **2.** *adj.* siamesisch; – ***cat,*** die Siamkatze; – ***twins,*** siamesische Zwillinge.

Siberia [saiˈbiəriə], *s.* Sibirien (*n.*). **Siberian, 1.** *s.* der (die) Sibirier(in). **2.** *adj.* sibirisch.

sibilance [ˈsibiləns], *s.* (*Phonet.*) das Zischen. **sibilant, 1.** *adj.* zischend, Zisch–. **2.** *s.* der Zischlaut. **sibilate** [–eit], *v.t., v.i.* zischen. **sibilation** [–ˈleiʃən], *s.* das Zischen.

sibling [ˈsibliŋ], *s.* (*usu. pl.*) Geschwister (*pl.*).

sibyl [ˈsibil], *s.* die Sybille; Wahrsagerin, Seherin. **sibylline** [–ain], *adj.* sibyllinisch, prophetisch, dunkel, rätselhaft, geheimnisvoll.

siccative [ˈsikətiv], **1.** *adj.* trocknend. **2.** *s.* das Sikkativ, Trockenmittel.

Sicilian [siˈsiliən], **1.** *s.* der (die) Sizilier(in), Sizilianer(in). **2.** *adj.* sizili(ani)sch. **Sicily** [ˈsisili], *s.* Sizilien (*n.*).

sick [sik], **1.** *adj.* 1. (*usu. only attrib.*) krank, leidend, unwohl; erkrankt (*of,* an (*Dat.*)); – ***at heart,*** tief betrübt; ***fall –,*** krank werden; (*esp. Mil.*) ***go –,*** sich krank melden; (*B., obs.*) – ***of,*** krank *or* erkrankt an (*Dat.*); (*B., obs.*) – ***to death,*** todkrank; 2. (*when pred. usu.*) übel, zum Erbrechen geneigt; ***be –,*** sich erbrechen *or* übergeben; ***as – as a dog,*** hundeelend; ***feel –,*** sich übergeben müssen, Brechreiz fühlen; ***I feel –,*** mir ist schlecht; ***it makes me –,*** es ekelt mich, mir wird übel dabei; – ***headache,*** die Migräne; 3. (*fig. coll.*) angewidert, angeekelt (*of,* von), überdrüssig (*Gen.*); ***be – (and tired) of it,*** es gründlich satt haben; – ***of waiting,*** des Wartens überdrüssig; ***I'm – to death of it,*** es hängt mir schon zum Halse heraus; 4. (*coll.*) faul, flau (*of business*); 5. (*sl.*) grausig (*of humour etc.*). **2.** *s.* (*collect.*) ***the –,*** die Kranken (*pl.*).

sick|-bay, *s.* das (Schiffs)lazarett, (Kranken)revier. **--bed,** *s.* das Krankenbett. **--benefit,** *s.* das Kranken(kassen)geld.

sicken [ˈsikən], **1.** *v.i.* 1. erkranken, krank werden, kränkeln; ***be –ing for s.th.,*** etwas in den Gliedern haben; 2. (*fig.*) sich ekeln, Ekel *or* Abscheu *or* Widerwillen *or* Übelkeit empfinden (*at,* vor (*Dat.*)); 3. (*coll.*) müde *or* überdrüssig werden (*of, Gen.*). **2.** *v.t.* (*usu. fig.*) anwidern, anekeln; ***be –ed,*** Ekel *or* Übelkeit *or* Abscheu *or* Widerwillen empfinden (*at,* bei), überdrüssig werden (*with, Gen.*); ***be –ing,*** widerwärtig *or* widerlich *or* ekelhaft *or* zum Überdruß sein.

sickish [ˈsikiʃ], *adj.* (*coll.*) kränklich, unpäßlich, unwohl.

sickle [sikl], *s.* die Sichel.

sick-leave, *s.* der Krankenurlaub, Erholungsurlaub; ***on –,*** wegen Krankheit beurlaubt.

sickliness [ˈsiklinis], *s.* 1. die Kränklichkeit, Schwächlichkeit; 2. (*of climate*) Unzuträglichkeit.

sick-list, *s.* (*Mil.*) der Krankenstand; (*Mil.*) ***go on the –,*** sich krank melden; (*coll.*) ***be on the –,*** krank sein.

sickly [ˈsikli], *adj.* 1. kränklich, schwächlich, leidend; ***be –,*** kränkeln; 2. krankhaft (aussehend), blaß, bleich; – ***smile,*** schwaches Lächeln; 3. (*of climate*) unzuträglich, ungesund; 4. (*fig.*) Ekel erregend, widerlich; – ***sentiment(ality),*** schwächliche *or* krankhafte Gefühlsduselei; – ***taste,*** ekelhaft süßlicher Geschmack.

sickness [ˈsiknis], *s.* 1. die Krankheit, Erkrankung, das Kranksein; – ***insurance,*** die Krankenversicherung, Krankenkasse; ***sleeping –,*** die Schlafsucht (*morbus dormitivus*); ***sleepy –,*** die Gehirnentzündung (*Encephalitis lethargica*); 2. das Erbrechen, die Übelkeit; 3. (*fig.*) Schwäche, Krankhaftigkeit.

sick|-nurse, *s.* die Krankenschwester. **--pay,** *s.* das Krankengeld. **--report,** *s.* (*Mil.*) der Krankenschein. **-room,** *s.* das Krankenzimmer, die Krankenstube.

side [said], **1.** *s.* 1. die Seite; ***at the –s,*** an der Seite *or* den Seiten; ***at*** or ***by his –,*** an seiner Seite, ihm zur Seite, neben ihm; ***stand by my –,*** neben mir stehen, (*fig.*) mir zur Seite stehen, mir helfen; – ***by –,*** nebeneinander; – ***by – with,*** neben, (*fig.*) im Vergleich mit; ***by*** or ***on the female*** or ***maternal*** or ***mother's –,*** mütterlicherseits; ***from every –*** or ***all –s,*** von allen Seiten; ***on all –s*** or ***every –,*** auf *or* von allen Seiten; (***on***) ***either – of,*** auf beiden Seiten von; ***on every –,*** nach allen Seiten; (*coll.*) ***on the –,*** zusätzlich, nebenbei, unter der Hand, außerdem, dazu; ***err on the – of generosity,*** zu freigebig sein; (*coll.*) ***on the hot –,*** ziemlich heiß;

on my –, meinerseits; *put on one –,* beiseite legen; *the mistake was on the right –,* der Fehler wirkte sich gut aus; (*coll.*) *on the right* (*wrong*) *– of 30,* unter (über) 30; (*fig.*) *get on the right – of him,* sich mit ihm auf guten Fuß stellen; (*fig.*) *keep on the right – of him,* mit ihm gut Freund bleiben; *to be on the safe –,* der Vorsicht halber; (*coll.*) *be rather on the small –,* etwas klein geraten sein; *on this – of,* diesseits (*Gen.*); *on the other – of,* jenseits (*Gen.*); (*coll.*) *get out of bed* (*on*) *the wrong –,* mit dem linken Fuß aufstehen; (*coll.*) *on the wrong – of the blanket,* unehelich, außerehelich; (*Naut.*) *over the –,* über Bord; (*fig.*) *blind –,* schwache Seite; *bright –,* die Sonnenseite, Lichtseite; (*fig.*) *dark* or *shady –,* die Schattenseite; *near* (*off*) *–,* linke (rechte) Seite (*of vehicle*); 2. (*Anat.*) die Seite, Weiche; (*coll.*) *hold* or *split one's –s* (*with laughing*), sich vor Lachen ausschütten, sich (*Dat.*) (vor Lachen) den Bauch halten; *turn over on one's –,* sich auf die Seite legen; 3. (*Geom.*) die Seite(nlinie), Seitenfläche; 4. (*Spt.*) Mannschaft, (*Spt., Law etc.*) Partei; (*Spt.*) *opposing –,* die Gegenpartei, gegnerische Mannschaft; *change –s,* zum Gegner übergehen, sich auf die Seite des Gegners schlagen; (*Spt.*) das Spielfeld wechseln; *choose* or *pick –s,* die Parteien wählen; *take his –, take –s with him,* Partei für ihn ergreifen, sich für ihn bekennen, sich ihm anschließen; *take –s,* Partei ergreifen, Stellung nehmen; *win over to one's –,* für sich gewinnen; 5. die Uferseite (*of river*), (Seiten)wand, der (Ab)hang (*of hill*), (Seiten)rand (*of road etc.*); 6. Studienzweig, die Studienrichtung, Abteilung (*at school*); *classical –,* die Gymnasialabteilung; *modern –,* die Realabteilung (*in schools*); 7. (*fig.*) der Standpunkt, Blickpunkt; *there are two –s to every question,* alles hat (seine) zwei Seiten; 8. (*Bill. etc.*) das Effet; *put – on a ball,* einem Ball Effet geben; 9. (*coll.*) die Batzigkeit; (*coll.*) *put on –,* angeben, sich aufblasen, großtun, vornehm tun, protzen; 10. (*Footb. etc.*) *on –,* nicht abseits; *no –!* Spiel aus! **2.** *v.i. – with,* Partei nehmen *or* ergreifen für, es halten mit.

side|-aisle, *s.* das Seitenschiff. **–-arms,** *pl.* das Seitengewehr. **–band,** *s.* (*Rad.*) das Seitenband. **–board,** *s.* der Anrichtetisch, das Büfett. **–burns,** *pl.* Koteletten (*pl.*), der Backenbart. **–car,** *s.* (*Motor.*) der Beiwagen; *– passenger,* der Beifahrer.

sided ['saidid], *suff.* –seitig.

side|-dish, *s.* das Nebengericht. **–-door,** *s.* die Seitentür. **–-drum,** *s.* die (Wirbel)trommel. **–-effect,** *s.* die Nebenwirkung, Begleiterscheinung. **–-entrance,** *s.* der Seiteneingang. **–face,** *s.* die Seitenansicht, das Profil. **–-glance,** *s.* 1. der Seitenblick; 2. (*fig.*) beiläufige Anspielung. **–-issue,** *s.* 1. der Seitenzweig, Nebenzweig; 2. (*fig.*) die Nebenfrage, Nebensache, Belanglosigkeit; *be only a –,* erst in zweiter Linie in Betracht kommen. **–-kick,** *s.* (*sl.*) der Kumpan, der (die) Helfershelfer(in). **–light,** *s.* 1. das Seitenlicht, Seitenfenster; 2. (*Naut.*) die Seitenlampe; 3. (*fig.*) das Streiflicht. **–line,** *s.* 1. der Nebenerwerb, Nebenberuf, die Nebenbeschäftigung; 2. (*Comm.*) der Nebenartikel; 3. (*Spt.*) die Seitenlinie; 4. *pl.* (*fig.*) Zuschauerplätze (*pl.*). **–long, 1.** *adv.* seitwärts, zur Seite. **2.** *adj.* 1. Seiten–, Seitwärts–, schräg; 2. (*fig.*) versteckt, verhohlen, indirekt. **–-on,** *attrib. adj.* Seiten–.

sidereal [si'diəriəl], *adj.* siderisch, Sternen–, Stern–; *– day,* der Sterntag; *– period* or *revolution,* die Umlaufzeit der Gestirne.

siderite ['sidərait], *s.* das Meteorgestein, (*Chem.*) der Eisenspat.

siderography [sidə'rɔgrəfi], *s.* die Stahlstecherkunst, der Stahlstich.

side|-saddle, *s.* der Damensattel. **–show,** *s.* die Jahrmarktsbude. **–slip,** *v.i.* (*Motor.*) schleudern, seitlich abrutschen.

sidesman ['saidzmən], *s.* (*Eccl.*) das Kirchenratsmitglied.

side|-splitting, *adj.* zwerchfellerschütternd (*laughter*). **–step, 1.** *v.i.* zur Seite *or* beiseite treten; ausweichen (*also fig.*). **2.** *v.t.* (*Boxing*) mittels Seitenschritt ausweichen (*Dat.*) (*a blow*). **3.** *s.* das Seitwärtstreten, der Seitenschritt. **–stroke,** *s.* das Seitenschwimmen. **–-table,** *s.* der Seitentisch. **–-track, 1.** *s.* 1. (*Railw.*) das Seiten– *or* Nebengleis; 2. (*fig.*) die Sackgasse. **2.** *v.t.* 1. auf ein Nebengleis schieben; 2. (*fig.*) ablenken; kaltstellen, beiseite schieben. **–view,** *s.* die Seitenansicht. **–walk,** *s.* (*Am.*) der Gehweg, Bürgersteig.

sideward ['saidwəd], **1.** *adj.* seitlich, Seiten–, seitwärts–. **2.** *or* **sidewards,** *adv.* seitwärts. **sideways, 1.** *adv.* seitwärts, von der Seite. **2.** *adj.* seitlich.

side-whiskers, *pl.* der Backenbart, Koteletten (*pl.*).

sidewise ['saidwaiz], *see* **sideways.**

siding ['saidiŋ], *s.* 1. (*Railw.*) das Nebengleis, Anschlußgleis, Rangiergleis, Ausweichgleis, Abstellgleis; 2. die Stellungnahme, Parteinahme.

sidle [saidl], *v.i.* sich seitwärts bewegen, sich schlängeln; *– up to,* heranschleichen *or* sich heranschlängeln an (*Acc.*).

siege [si:dʒ], *s.* 1. (*Mil.*) die Belagerung, (*fig.*) Bestürmung, Zermürbung; *state of –,* der Belagerungszustand; *lay – to,* (*Mil.*) belagern, (*fig.*) bestürmen; *raise the –,* die Belagerung aufheben; *undergo a –,* belagert werden; 2. (*Tech.*) der Werktisch. **siege-train,** *s.* der Belagerungspark.

sienna [si'enə], *s.* die Sienaerde.

siesta [si'estə], *s.* die Mittagsruhe, Siesta.

sieve [siv], **1.** *s.* das Sieb; *pass* or *put through a –,* durchsieben, durchseihen, (durch ein Sieb) passieren. **2.** *v.t.* 1. durchsieben, aussieben; 2. (*fig.*) sortieren, sichten.

sift [sift], **1.** *v.t.* 1. (durch)sieben, beuteln; sortieren, sondern (*from,* von); *– the chaff from the wheat,* die Spreu von dem Weizen sondern; 2. (*fig.*) sichten, (über)prüfen, untersuchen; *– to the bottom,* bis auf den Grund untersuchen. **2.** *v.i.* (*also – through*) durchrieseln, eindringen (*into,* in (*Acc.*)). **sifter,** *s.* das Sieb. **sifting,** *s.* 1. das (Durch)sieben; 2. *pl.* Durchgesiebte(s), Siebabfälle (*pl.*).

sigh [sai], **1.** *s.* der Seufzer; *with a –,* seufzend; *heave* or *fetch a –,* seufzen, aufatmen; *heave a – of relief,* erleichtert aufatmen. **2.** *v.i.* 1. (auf)seufzen; *– with relief,* erleichtert aufatmen (*with,* vor (*Dat.*)); 2. (*fig.*) schmachten (*for,* nach). **3.** *v.t.* seufzend äußern, aushauchen.

sight [sait], **1.** *s.* 1. das Sehvermögen, Gesicht, Augenlicht, die Sehkraft, (*fig.*) das Auge; *have good –,* gute Augen haben; *long –,* die Weitsichtigkeit, Fernsichtigkeit; *near* or *short –,* die Kurzsichtigkeit; *second –,* zweites Gesicht, das Hellsehen, seherische Gabe; *lose one's –,* erblinden, das Augenlicht verlieren; *loss of –,* die Erblindung; *ruin one's –,* sich (*Dat.*) die Augen verderben; 2. das (An)sehen, der (An)blick, die Sicht; Einsicht, der Einblick; (*Comm.*) *after –,* nach Sicht; *at –,* beim (ersten) Anblick; (*Mus.*) vom Blatt; (*Comm.*) bei Sicht; *shoot at –,* sofort niederschießen; *at first –,* auf den ersten Blick, beim ersten Anblick, im ersten Augenblick; (*Comm.*) *at short –,* auf kurze Sicht; *by –,* vom Ansehen; *play from –,* vom Blatt spielen; *in the – of,* vor den Augen (*Gen.*); (*fig.*) *in one's own –,* seiner eigenen Anschauung nach; *in the – of God,* vor Gott; *on –,* beim ersten Anblick; *catch – of,* erblicken; *get a – of,* zu Gesicht bekommen; *hate the – of,* nicht ausstehen können; *lose – of,* aus den Augen verlieren, (*fig.*) übersehen, vergessen; 3. die Sicht(weite); *vanish from his –,* aus seinem Blickfeld verschwinden; (*with*)*in –,* in Sichtweite, in der Nähe; (*fig.*) in Sicht, absehbar; *come in –,* sichtbar werden, in Sicht *or* zum Vorschein kommen; (*with*)*in – of completion,* kurz vor der Vollendung; *keep in –,* im Auge behalten; *out of –,* außer Sicht; *out of – of,* unsichtbar für; *get out of my –!* geh mir aus den Augen! *put out of –,* aus den Augen legen; *he watched it out of –,* er beobachtete es, bis er es nicht mehr sehen konnte; *out of –, out of mind,* aus den Augen, aus dem Sinn; 4. die Sehenswürdigkeit; Erscheinung, das

Schauspiel, der Anblick; *the -s*, die Sehenswürdigkeiten (*of a town etc.*); *sad -*, trauriger Anblick; (*coll.*) *a - for sore eyes*, die Augenweide, erfreulicher Anblick; *a - for the gods*, ein Anblick für Götter; *look a -*, toll aussehen; *a - to see*, prächtig anzusehen; *what a - he is!* wie sieht er nur aus! 5. (*Astr.*, *Naut.*) die Beobachtung; 6. (*of gun*) das Korn, Visier, die Visiereinrichtung; *line of -*, die Ziellinie; *take -*, visieren; *fire over open -s*, über Kimme und Korn schießen; 7. (*sl.*) der Haufen, die Menge, Masse, Stange (*in comparisons*); (*sl.*) *a damned - harder*, verflucht schwieriger; *a long - better*, bei weitem besser; *not by a long -*, noch lange *or* bei weitem nicht.
2. *v.t.* 1. erblicken, zu Gesicht bekommen, sichten; 2. (*Artil.*) zielen auf (*Acc.*), aufs Korn *or* Visier nehmen, anvisieren (*the target*), richten (*the gun*); 3. (*Comm.*) akzeptieren, präsentieren (*a bill*).

sight|-bill, --draft, *s.* die Sichttratte, der Sichtwechsel.

sighted ['saitid], *adj.* (*usu. suff.*) -sichtig. **sighting,** *s.* 1. das Sichten; 2. (*Artil.*) Zielen, Visieren; *- mechanism*, das Zielgerät, die Visiereinrichtung; *- shot*, der Anschuß, Probeschuß; *- telescope*, das Zielfernrohr. **sightless,** *adj.* blind. **sightlessness,** *s.* die Blindheit. **sightliness,** *s.* die Schönheit, Stattlichkeit, Ansehnlichkeit, Wohlgestalt. **sightly,** *adj.* ansehnlich, stattlich, gut aussehend.

sight|-read, *irr.v.t.*, *v.i.* vom Blatt spielen *or* singen. **--reading,** *s.* das Spielen *or* Singen vom Blatt. **-seeing,** *s.* die Besichtigung *or* der Besuch von Sehenswürdigkeiten; *go -*, die Sehenswürdigkeiten besichtigen; *- tour*, die Rundfahrt. **-seer,** *s.* Schaulustige(r), der (die) Tourist(in).

sigmoid(al) ['sigmɔid, -'mɔidl], *adj.* sigmaförmig, S-förmig.

sign [sain], **1.** *s.* 1. das Zeichen, Abbild, Symbol; *- of the cross*, das Kreuzzeichen; *- of the zodiac*, das Tierkreiszeichen; 2. das (An)zeichen, Signal, Symptom (*of*, von *or* für); *good -*, gute Vorbedeutung, gutes Zeichen; *- of life*, das Lebenszeichen; *make no -*, sich nicht rühren; 3. das Kennzeichen (*of*, von); 4. der Wink, die Handbewegung, Gebärde; *give* or *make a -*, einen Wink *or* ein Zeichen geben; 5. das (Aushänge)schild; (*obs.*) *at the - of the White Horse*, im (Wirtshaus zum) Weißen Rössel; 6. (*Math.*, *Mus.*) das Vorzeichen; *conventional -*, das Kartenzeichen; 7. (*esp. B.*) das Himmelszeichen, Wunderzeichen. **2.** *v.t.* unterzeichnen, unterschreiben (*a document*), schreiben (*one's name*); (*Law*) *-ed, sealed and delivered*, unterschrieben, besiegelt und vollzogen; *- away* or *over*, übertragen, abtreten; *- off*, entlassen (*employee*); *- on* or *up*, anstellen, (vertraglich) verpflichten; (*Mil.*) anwerben, anmustern. **3.** *v.i.* 1. (zu)winken, ein Zeichen geben (*to*, *Dat.*); 2. unterschreiben, unterzeichnen, (*Comm.*) zeichnen; *- for*, quittieren; *- on*, sich (vertraglich) verpflichten (*for*, zu), die Arbeit aufnehmen; (*Mil.*) Soldat werden, sich anwerben lassen; (*Rad. etc.*) den Beginn einer Sendung ansagen; *- off*, die Arbeit niederlegen; (*Rad. etc.*) das Ende einer Sendung ansagen; *- up for*, sich (an)melden *or* eintragen für.

signal ['signəl], **1.** *s.* 1. das Signal, Zeichen (*for*, für *or* zu) (*also fig.*); *all-clear -*, die Entwarnung; *call -*, das Rufzeichen; *distress -*, das Notsignal; (*Rad.*) *--to-noise ratio*, das Signal-Rauschverhältnis; *time -*, das Zeitzeichen; 2. (*fig.*) die Losung, der Anlaß, die Veranlassung (*for*, zu). **2.** *adj.* bemerkenswert, außerordentlich, beachtlich, außergewöhnlich, ungewöhnlich. **3.** *v.i.* Signale geben, Zeichen machen *or* geben. **4.** *v.t.* 1. (ein) Zeichen geben, winken (*Dat.*) (*a p.*), (*fig.*) zu verstehen geben (*Dat.*); 2. signalisieren, durch Signale melden.

signal-box, *s.* (*Railw.*) das Stellwerk.

signaler *etc.*, (*Am.*) *see* **signaller.**

signal|-gun, *s.* der Signalschuß. **--halyard,** *s.* (*Naut.*) die Flaggleine.

signalize ['signəlaiz], *v.t.* auszeichnen, kennzeichnen, besonders betonen, herausstellen, hervorheben, charakterisieren, zu erkennen geben; *- o.s.*, sich auszeichnen *or* hervortun.

signal-lamp, *s.* die Signallampe, Blinklampe, der Blinker.

signaller ['signələ], *s.* (*Mil.*) der Melder, Blinker, (*Naut.*) Signalgast. **signalling, 1.** *s.* der Nachrichtenverkehr, das Signalisieren. **2.** *adj.* Signal-. **signally,** *adv. See* **signal, 2.**

signal|man [-mən], *s.* 1. (*Railw.*) der Bahnwärter; 2. (*Naut.*) Signalgast. **--officer,** *s.* der Fernmeldeoffizier. **--rocket,** *s.* die Leuchtrakete, Leuchtkugel. **--strength,** *s.* (*Rad.*) die Lautstärke, Signalspannung.

signatory ['signətəri], **1.** *adj.* unterzeichnend; *- power*, (*Pol.*) die Signatarmacht; (*Comm.*) die Unterschriftsvollmacht. **2.** *s.* der Unterzeichner, Vertragspartner; (*Pol.*) Signatar, die Signatarmacht.

signature ['signətʃə], *s.* 1. (eigenhändige) Unterschrift, der Namenszug; 2. (*fig. obs.*) charakteristisches Merkmal, das (Kenn)zeichen; 3. (*Mus.*) die Signatur; *key -*, das Vorzeichen, die Tonartvorzeichnung; *time -*, die Taktbezeichnung; 4. (*Typ.*) die Signatur; 5. (*Rad.*) *- tune*, die Kennmusik, Einleitungsmelodie, Devise.

signboard ['sainbɔ:d], *s.* das (Aushänge)schild.

signet ['signit], *s.* das Siegel, Petschaft; (*Scots*) *writer to the -*, der Rechtsanwalt. **signet-ring,** *s.* der Siegelring.

significance, significancy [sig'nifikəns(i)], *s.* 1. die Bedeutung (*to*, für), tieferer Sinn; 2. die Wichtigkeit, Bedeutsamkeit; *of no -*, nicht von *or* ohne Bedeutung; *of deep -*, vielsagend. **significant,** *adj.* 1. bedeutsam, von Bedeutung, wichtig (*for*, für); 2. bezeichnend (*of*, für); *be - of*, bedeuten, beweisen; 3. (*fig.*) bedeutungsvoll, vielsagend; 4. (*Math.*) geltend (*figures of decimal*). **signification** [-'keiʃən], *s.* 1. die Bedeutung, der Sinn; 2. die Bekundung, Bezeichnung. **significative** [-ətiv], *adj.* 1. bezeichnend, kennzeichnend (*of*, für); 2. bedeutungsvoll, bedeutsam, Bedeutungs-.

signify ['signifai], **1.** *v.t.* 1. andeuten, bedeuten; 2. ankündigen, kundtun; 3. zu verstehen *or* erkennen geben. **2.** *v.i.* von Bedeutung sein, zu bedeuten haben; *it doesn't -*, es tut *or* macht nichts, es hat nichts auf sich, es ist von keiner Bedeutung, es hat nichts zu bedeuten.

sign|-language, *s.* die Zeichensprache, Gebärdensprache. **--manual,** *s.* (*obs.*) (eigenhändige) Unterschrift, der Namenszug, das Handzeichen. **--painter,** *s. See* **-writer. -post,** *s.* der Wegweiser. **-writer,** *s.* der Plakatmaler, Schildermaler, Schriftmaler.

silage ['sailidʒ], *s.* das Silofutter.

silence ['sailəns], **1.** *s.* das (Still)schweigen; die Ruhe, Stille; (*Tech.*) Geräuschlosigkeit; *impose -*, Stillschweigen auferlegen (*on*, *Dat.*); *keep* or *preserve -*, Stillschweigen wahren *or* beobachten; *pass over in -*, stillschweigend *or* mit Stillschweigen übergehen; *wrapped in -*, in Schweigen gehüllt; *- gives consent*, wer schweigt, stimmt zu; *- is golden*, Schweigen ist Gold. **2.** *int.* Ruhe! still! Silentium! **3.** *v.t.* 1. zum Schweigen bringen (*also Mil.*); 2. (*fig.*) unterdrücken. **silencer,** *s.* der Schalldämpfer, (*Motor.*) der Auspufftopf.

silent ['sailənt], *adj.* schweigend, stumm, still; ruhig, leise, geräuschlos; schweigsam, verschwiegen; *be -*, schweigen, sich ausschweigen (*on*, *about*, über (*Acc.*)); *- consent*, stillschweigende Zustimmung; *- film*, der Stummfilm; *as - as the grave*, stumm wie das Grab; *- syllable*, stumme Silbe; *- partner*, stiller Teilhaber; *- prayer*, stilles Gebet; *- reading*, stilles Lesen; *the Silent Service*, die Marine.

Silesia [sai'li:ʃə], *s.* Schlesien (*n.*). **Silesian, 1.** *s.* der (die) Schlesier(in). **2.** *adj.* schlesisch.

silhouette [silu'et], **1.** *s.* der Schattenriß, das Schattenbild, die Silhouette. **2.** *v.t.* (*usu. pass.*) *be -d*, sich als Schattenriß abheben.

silica ['silikə], *s.* die Kieselerde, Kieselsäure. **silicate** [-eit], *s.* kieselsaures Salz, das Silikat.

siliceous [–'liʃəs], *adj.* kieselartig, kiesel(erde)-haltig, Kiesel–; – ***earth,*** die Kieselgur. **silicic** [–'lisik], *adj.* – ***acid,*** die Orthokieselsäure. **siliciferous** [–'sifərəs], *adj.* kieselerdehaltig. **silicify** [–'lisifai], **1.** *v.t.* verkieseln. **2.** *v.i.* (sich) in Kieselerde verwandeln. **silicious,** *adj. See* **siliceous.**

silicon ['silikən], *s.* das Silizium. **silicone** [–koun], *s.* (*Chem.*) das Silikon. **silicosis** [–'kousis], *s.* (*Med.*) die Silikose.

silk [silk], **1.** *s.* die Seide, der Seidenstoff, das Seidengewebe; die Seidenfaser, der Seidenfaden, das Seidengespinst; ***in –s and satins,*** in Samt und Seide; ***tussore –,*** die Rohseide; ***take –,*** höherer Anwalt werden; ***watered –,*** die Moiréseide. **2.** *adj.* seiden; (*coll.*) – ***hat,*** der Zylinder(hut); (*coll.*) ***you cannot make a – purse out of a sow's ear,*** aus nichts wird nichts; – ***ribbon,*** das Seidenband; – ***stocking,*** der Seidenstrumpf. **silken,** *adj.* 1. (*Poet.*) seiden; 2. (*fig.*) seidenartig, seidenweich, seidig (glänzend). **silkiness,** *s.* 1. das Seidenartige *or* Seidige, die Weichheit; 2. (*fig.*) Sanftheit, (*of wine*) Lieblichkeit.

silk|-moth, *s.* (*Ent.*) der Seidenspinner. **–worm,** *s.* die Seidenraupe. **silky,** *adj.* 1. seiden(artig), seidenweich; – ***lustre,*** der Seidenglanz; 2. (*fig.*) sanft, zart, lieblich (*also of wine*), einschmeichelnd.

sill [sil], *s.* 1. die Schwelle (*of a door etc.*), das Fensterbrett (*of a window*); 2. die Grundschwelle (*of docks etc.*); 3. (*Min.*) das *or* der Süll, der Lagergang.

sillabub ['siləbʌb], *s.* süßes Getränk aus Wein und Sahne.

silliness ['silinis], *s.* die Albernheit, Dummheit. **silly,** *adj.* einfältig, töricht, dumm, dämlich (*of a p.*), leichtfertig, unklug (*of actions*), dumm, albern, verrückt, absurd, lächerlich (*of a th.*); – ***season,*** die Sauregurkenzeit.

silo ['sailou], *s.* der Silo, Getreidespeicher, die Grünfuttergrube.

silt [silt], *s.* der Schlamm, Schlick, Treibsand, Triebsand. **2.** *v.i., v.t.* (*usu.* – ***up***) verschlammen, versanden.

Silurian [sai'ljuəriən], **1.** *adj.* (*Geol.*) silurisch, Silur–. **2.** *s.* das Silur.

silvan, *see* **sylvan.**

silver ['silvə], **1.** *s.* 1. das Silber; ***German –,*** das Neusilber; 2. das Silbergeld, Silbermünzen (*pl.*); ***loose –,*** das Silberkleingeld; 3. *See* ***– plate.*** **2.** *adj.* Silber–, silbern; (*Bot.*) – ***fir,*** die Weißtanne, Edeltanne; – ***foil,*** die Silberfolie, das Blattsilber; – ***fox,*** der Silberfuchs; – ***leaf,*** das Blattsilber; (*fig.*) – ***lining,*** der Silberstreifen, der Lichtblick; – ***paper,*** das Staniolpapier; – ***plate,*** das Silbergeschirr, Silber(zeug), Tafelsilber; – ***poplar,*** die Silberpappel; – ***wedding,*** silberne Hochzeit; ***be born with a – spoon in one's mouth,*** ein Glückskind sein. **3.** *v.t.* versilbern, mit Silber überziehen, mit Folie belegen (*a mirror etc.*).

silver|-coloured, *adj.* silberfarbig. **--gilt,** *s.* vergoldetes Silber. **--glance,** *s.* das Schwefelsilber. **--grey,** **1.** *adj.* silbergrau. **2.** *s.* silbergraue Farbe. **--haired,** *adj.* silberhaarig.

silveriness ['silvərinis], *s.* der Silberglanz. **silvering,** *s.* 1. das Versilbern, die Versilberung; 2. der Silberbelag.

silver| nitrate, *s.* der Höllenstein. **–plated,** *adj.* silberplattiert. **–plating,** *s.* die Silberplattierung. **–smith,** *s.* der Silberschmied. **–ware,** *s. See* ***silver plate.*** **silvery,** *adj.* 1. silberweiß, silberfarben; 2. (*fig.*) silberhell, silberklar (*as voice*).

silviculture ['silvikʌltʃə], *s.* die Forstkultur, der Waldbau.

simian ['simiən], *adj.* affenartig, Affen–.

similar ['similə], *adj.* 1. ähnlich, (annähernd) gleich (*to, Dat.*); 2. gleichartig, verwandt; 3. (*Elec.*) gleichnamig. **similarity** [–'læriti], *s.* die Ähnlichkeit (*to,* mit), Gleichartigkeit, der Vergleich. **similarly,** *adv.* gleicherweise, gleichermaßen. **simile** [–li:], *s.* das Gleichnis, der Vergleich.

similitude [–'militju:d], *s.* 1. die Ähnlichkeit (*also Math.*); 2. das Ebenbild.

simmer ['simə], *v.i.* **1.** leicht *or* schwach *or* langsam kochen, wallen; 2. (*fig.*) kochen (***with,*** vor (*Dat.*)), aufwallen, gären; (*fig.*) – ***down,*** sich beruhigen *or* abregen, ruhig werden.

simony ['saiməni], *s.* die Simonie, der Ämterkauf, Pfründenschacher.

simoom [sai'mu:m], *s.* der Samum.

simper ['simpə], **1.** *s.* geziertes *or* albernes Lächeln. **2.** *v.i.* geziert *or* albern lächeln.

simple [simpl], **1.** *adj.* 1. einfach, nicht zusammengesetzt *or* verwickelt, unkompliziert, übersichtlich, klar; ungekünstelt, schmucklos, schlicht, anspruchslos; – ***fraction,*** gemeiner Bruch; – ***interest,*** Kapitalzinsen (*pl.*); (*coll.*) ***pure and –,*** schlechthin; (*Mus.*) – ***time,*** 2- oder 4teiliger Takt; 2. (*fig. of a p.*) dumm, töricht, einfältig, leichtgläubig; ***Simple Simon,*** der Dummerjan, Einfaltspinsel. **2.** *s.* das Heilkraut; *pl.* einfache Arzneipflanzen, Heilkräuter (*pl.*).

simple|-hearted, *adj.* arglos, unschuldig. **--heartedness,** *s.* die Arglosigkeit, Harmlosigkeit, Naivität. **--minded,** *adj.* dumm, einfältig. **--mindedness,** *s.* die Einfalt, Dummheit.

simpleton ['simpltən], *s.* der Einfaltspinsel, Dummkopf, Tropf.

simplicity [sim'plisiti], *s.* 1. die Einfachheit, Unkompliziertheit, Klarheit, Übersichtlichkeit, Schmucklosigkeit, Schlichtheit; Einfalt, Einfältigkeit, Arglosigkeit, Naivität; Dummheit.

simplification [simplifi'keiʃən], *s.* die Vereinfachung. **simplify** ['simplifai], *v.t.* vereinfachen, erleichtern.

simplistic [sim'plistik], *adj.* allzu *or* übertrieben vereinfacht.

simply ['simpli], *adv.* 1. einfach, klar, leicht; – ***and solely,*** einzig und allein; 2. schlicht, schmucklos, unauffällig; 3. (*coll.*) geradezu, schlechthin.

simulacrum [simju'leikrəm], *s.* das Abbild, Scheinbild, leerer Schein, hohle Form.

simulate ['simjuleit], *v.t.* vorgeben, vortäuschen, (vor)heucheln, (*esp. Med.*) simulieren, nachahmen. **simulation** [–leiʃən], *s.* 1. die Vorspiegelung, Vortäuschung; 2. Verstellung, Heuchelei, Nachahmung.

simultaneity [siməltə'ni:iti], *s.* die Gleichzeitigkeit. **simultaneous** [–'teiniəs], *adj.* gleichzeitig; (*Math.*) – ***equation,*** die Simultangleichung. **simultaneousness,** *s. See* **simultaneity.**

sin [sin], **1.** *s.* die Sünde, das Vergehen, der Verstoß, die Versündigung (***against,*** gegen *or* an (*Dat.*)); ***besetting –,*** die Gewohnheitssünde; (*sl.*) ***like –,*** wie der Teufel, heftig; ***live in –,*** in wilder Ehe *or* unerlaubtem Umgang leben; ***deadly*** or ***mortal –,*** die Todsünde; ***original –,*** die Erbsünde; – ***of omission,*** die Unterlassungssünde. **2.** *v.i.* 1. sündigen, eine Sünde begehen; 2. sich versündigen (***against,*** an (*Dat.*)), verstoßen, sich vergehen (gegen). **3.** *v.t.* begehen (*a sin*).

sinapism ['sinəpizm], *s.* das Senfpflaster.

since [sins], **1.** *adv.* 1. seitdem, seither; ***ever –,*** von jeher; ***long –,*** seit langem, vor langer Zeit; ***how long –?*** seit wann? seit wie lange? vor wie langer Zeit? ***how long is it –?*** wie lange ist es her? ***a short time –,*** vor kurzem; ***a week –,*** eine Woche her, vor einer Woche; 2. später, mittlerweile, inzwischen. **2.** *prep.* seit. **3.** *conj.* 1. seit(dem); ***how long is it – he was here?*** wie lange ist es her, daß er hier war? 2. weil, da . . . (ja), indem; – ***you are here, I can go,*** da Sie (ja) hier sind, kann ich gehen.

sincere [sin'siə], *adj.* aufrichtig, ehrlich, offen, wahr, treu, echt, lauter, rein, im Ernst; ***yours –ly,*** Ihr ergebener (*in letters*). **sincerity** [–'seriti], *s.* die Aufrichtigkeit, Offenheit, Wahrhaftigkeit, Echtheit, Lauterkeit.

sinciput ['sinsiput], *s.* das Vorderhaupt, Schädeldach.

[1]**sine** [sain], *s.* (*Geom.*) der Sinus; – ***of angle,*** der

Sinuswinkel; (*Rad.*) – ***wave,*** die Sinuswelle, harmonische Schwingungswelle.

[2]**sine** ['saini], *prep.* (*Law*) ohne.

sinecure ['sinəkjuə], *s.* die Sinekure, der Ruheposten, einträgliches Ehrenamt, fette Pfründe. **sinecurist** [–rist], *s.* der Inhaber einer Sinekure.

sine| die ['saini'daii:], *adv.* (*Law*) auf unbestimmte Zeit. – **qua non** [–kwei'nɔn], *s.* (*Law*) unerläßliche Bedingung, notwendige Voraussetzung.

sinew ['sinju:], *s.* 1. die Sehne, Flechse; 2. (*fig.*) die Kraft(reserve), Stärke, Hauptstütze, der Nerv; ***the –s of war,*** Kriegsmittel (*pl.*). **sinewless,** *adj.* (*fig.*) kraftlos, schwach. **sinewy,** *adj.* 1. sehnig, zäh, zaddrig (*as meat*); 2. (*fig.*) nervig, kräftig, kraftvoll.

sinful ['sinful], *adj.* sündhaft, sündig. **sinfulness,** *s.* die Sündhaftigkeit.

sing [siŋ], **1.** *irr.v.i.* 1. singen (*also of birds*), (*Poet.*) dichten; – ***of,*** singen von, besingen; – ***out,*** schreien, laut rufen; – ***out of tune,*** falsch singen; (*coll.*) – ***small,*** kleinlaut werden, klein beigeben; – ***to,*** vorsingen (*Dat.*); – ***up,*** lauter singen; 2. (*coll.*) summen (*as a kettle*); 3. summen, klingen (*as the ears*); 4. heulen, sausen (*of the wind*); 5. (*sl.*) gestehen, singen (*as criminal*). **2.** *irr.v.t.* singen, besingen, vorsingen (***to,*** *Dat.*); (*fig.*) – ***another tune,*** andere Saiten aufziehen, einen anderen Ton anschlagen; – ***a child to sleep,*** ein Kind in den Schlaf singen; – ***his praise(s),*** sein Lob singen, ihn preisen *or* verherrlichen; (*fig.*) – ***the same song,*** in dasselbe Horn blasen. **singable,** *adj.* singbar.

Singapore [siŋə'pɔ:], *s.* Singapur (*n.*).

singe [sindʒ], **1.** *v.t.* (ver)sengen, absengen (*poultry*). **2.** *v.i.* versengen. **3.** *s.* (leichter) Brandschaden. **singeing,** *s.* 1. die Versengung, das Versengen; 2. (An)sengen, Absengen.

singer ['siŋə], *s.* der (die) Sänger(in). **singing, 1.** *adj.* singend. **2.** *s.* 1. das Singen, der Gesang; 2. das Sausen, Heulen, Summen, Tönen, Pfeifen, Klingen; – ***in the ears,*** das Ohrensausen. **singing|-bird,** *s.* der Singvogel. **--lesson,** *s.* die Gesangstunde. **--master,** *s.* der Gesanglehrer. **--voice,** *s.* die Singstimme.

single [siŋgl], **1.** *adj.* 1. einzig, nur ein, alleinig, bloß; ***with the – exception,*** mit der bloßen *or* alleinigen Ausnahme; ***not a – one,*** kein *or* nicht ein einziger; 2. einzeln, Einzel–, Allein–, alleinstehend; – ***bed,*** das Einzelbett; – ***bill,*** der Solawechsel; – ***combat,*** der Zweikampf; – ***file,*** der Gänsemarsch; (*Railw.*) – ***line,*** eingleisige Strecke; – ***room,*** das Einzelzimmer, Einbettzimmer; 3. einmalig, einfach, Ein–; ***book-keeping by – entry,*** einfache Buchhaltung; – ***payment,*** einmalige Zahlung; – ***ticket,*** einfache Fahrkarte; 4. ledig, unverheiratet; (*coll.*) – ***blessedness,*** lediger Stand, der Ledigenstand; – ***man,*** Alleinstehende(r), der Junggeselle; – ***woman,*** Alleinstehende, die Junggesellin; 5. vereint; ***with a – voice,*** mit vereinter Stimme; 6. aufrichtig; ***with a – mind,*** zielbewußt, zielstrebig. **2.** *v.t.* (*usu.* – ***out***) auslesen, auswählen, aussuchen (***from,*** aus), aussondern, absondern (von); es absehen auf (*Acc.*), hervorheben, herausheben (***as, for,*** als), bestimmen (zu). **3.** *s.* 1. einzelnes Stück; 2. einfache Fahrkarte; 3. (*Crick.*) ein (1) Lauf; 4. (*oft. pl.*) (*Tenn.*) das Einzel(spiel).

single|-barrelled, *adj.* einläufig. **--breasted,** *adj.* einreihig (*coat*). **--decker,** *s.* der Eindecker. **--entry,** *adj.* einfach (*book-keeping*). **--eyed,** *adj.* (*fig.*) klar(sehend); aufrichtig, redlich, geradeheraus. **--handed, 1.** *adj.* 1. einhändig; 2. (*fig.*) eigenhändig, alleinig, ohne Hilfe, auf eigene Faust. **2.** *adv.* allein, selbständig. **--hearted,** *adj.* aufrichtig, redlich. **--minded,** *adj.* zielbewußt, zielstrebig. **--mindedness,** *s.* die Zielstrebigkeit.

singleness ['siŋglnis], *s.* 1. die Einmaligkeit; 2. Aufrichtigkeit; – ***of purpose,*** die Zielstrebigkeit; 3. die Ehelosigkeit, der Ledigenstand.

single|-phase, *adj.* (*Elec.*) einphasig, Einphasen–. **--pole,** *adj.* einpolig. **--seater,** *s.* der Einsitzer. **-stick,** *s.* 1. das Stockfechten; 2. der Fechtstock.

singlet ['siŋglit], *s.* das Unterhemd, Trikot(hemd).

single-track, *adj.* eingleisig, einspurig; (*fig.*) ***have a – mind,*** einseitig interessiert sein.

singly ['siŋgli], *adv. See* **single.**

singsong ['siŋsɔŋ], **1.** *s.* 1. der Singsang, das Gesinge; 2. Gemeinschaftssingen. **2.** *adj.* ***in a – voice,*** mit eintöniger Stimme.

singular ['siŋgjulə], **1.** *adj.* 1. einzeln, vereinzelt, gesondert; 2. einmalig, einzigartig, ungewöhnlich, außergewöhnlich, sonderlich, sonderbar, eigentümlich; 3. ausgezeichnet, hervorragend; 4. (*Gram.*) singularisch, Singular–; 5. (*Phil., Math.*) singulär. **2.** *s.* (*Gram.*) die Einzahl, der Singular. **singularity** [–'læriti], *s.* 1. die Einzelheit; 2. Einzigartigkeit, Eigenheit, Besonderheit, Eigentümlichkeit, Seltsamkeit. **singularly,** *adv.* ungewöhnlich, ungemein, besonders, höchst.

sinister ['sinistə], *adj.* 1. böse, schlimm, schlecht, drohend, unheilvoll; 2. unheimlich, düster, finster; 3. (*Her.*) link, zur Linken. **sinistral** [–rəl], *adj.* 1. link, link(s)seitig, linksliegend; 2. linkswendig, links gewunden.

sink [siŋk], **1.** *irr.v.i.* 1. sinken, versinken, niedersinken, herabsinken; einsinken, untersinken, untergehen; – ***back,*** zurücksinken; – ***down,*** niederfallen, sich niederlassen; (*fig.*) – ***or swim,*** auf Biegen oder Brechen; ***his heart*** or ***spirits sank*** (***within him***), ihm schwand der Mut; 2. (ab)fallen, sich senken *or* neigen; 3. (*fig.*) (ein)dringen (***into,*** in (*Acc.*)), sich einprägen (*Dat.*); – ***in,*** sich einprägen (*words etc.*); 4. übergehen, verfallen (***into,*** in (*Acc.*)), erliegen (***under,*** *Dat.*); – ***into oblivion,*** in Vergessenheit geraten; – ***into sleep,*** in Schlaf (ver)sinken; ***he is –ing fast,*** mit ihm geht es zusehends zu Ende; 5. nachlassen, abnehmen. **2.** *irr.v.t.* 1. senken (*a ship*), senken, sinken lassen (*head, voice etc.*), (*sl.*) ***be sunk,*** geliefert *or* erledigt werden; ***be sunk in thought,*** in Gedanken versunken sein; 2. senken, herabsetzen (*prices etc.*); 3. abteufen, ausgraben, ausheben, bohren (*a hole*); eingraben, einsenken, einlassen (*pipes etc. in the ground*); 4. (*fig.*) anlegen (*money*), tilgen, abtragen (*debt*); 5. (*fig.*) beilegen (*a difference*), verheimlichen, verschweigen, schweigend übergehen; – ***differences,*** Uneinigkeiten beiseite lassen, sich über Streitigkeiten hinwegsetzen; 6. (*Tech.*) eingravieren, einsetzen, einlassen, einbetten, einschneiden; schneiden (*a die*). **3.** *s.* 1. der Spülstein, Ausguß, das Ausgußbecken; ***kitchen –,*** der Küchenausguß; 2. das Abzugsrohr, der Ablaufkanal, Abfluß; – ***of iniquity,*** der Sündenpfuhl; 3. (*Theat.*) die Versenkung.

sinkable ['siŋkəbl], *adj.* versenkbar. **sinker,** *s.* 1. das Senkblei, Senkgewicht, der Senkkörper; 2. Stempelschneider. **sinking,** *s.* 1. das (Ver)sinken, Untergehen; 2. die (Ver)senkung, Vertiefung, Aushöhlung, (*Min.*) Abteufung; 3. (*Comm.*) Tilgung; 4. (*also* – ***feeling***) das Schwächegefühl; – ***in the stomach,*** die Beklommenheit, das Angstgefühl. **sinking fund,** *s.* der Tilgungsfonds.

sinless ['sinlis], *adj.* sündenfrei, sündlos, unschuldig. **sinlessness,** *s.* die Sündlosigkeit. **sinner,** *s.* der (die) Sünder(in). **sin-offering,** *s.* das Sühnopfer.

sinter ['sintə], **1.** *s.* (*Geol., Tech.*) der Sinter. **2.** *v.t.* (*Tech.*) sintern, fritten (*ore*).

sinuate ['sinjuit], *adj.* (*esp. Bot.*) (aus)gebuchtet. **sinuation** [–u'eiʃən], **sinuosity** [–'ɔsiti], *s.* 1. die Krümmung, Windung, Biegung, Ausbuchtung; 2. Gekrümmtheit, Gewundenheit. **sinuous** [–uəs], *adj.* 1. wellenförmig, geschlängelt, gewunden, gekrümmt, sich windend, (*fig.*) krumm; 2. geschmeidig, biegsam.

sinus ['sainəs], *s.* 1. die Krümmung, Kurve; 2. (*Bot.*) Ausbuchtung, Höhlung; 2. (*Anat.*) (Knochen)höhle; Tasche, der (Venen)sinus. **sinusitis** [–'saitis], *s.* (*Med.*) die Nebenhöhlenentzündung, Sinu(s)itis. **sinusoidal** [–'sɔidl], *adj.* (*Math., Elec.*) sinusförmig, Sinus–.

sip [sip], **1.** *s.* das Schlückchen, Nippen. **2.** *v.t.* nippen an (*Dat.*), schlürfen.

siphon ['saifən], **1.** *s.* 1. der (Saug)heber; 2. die Druckflasche, Siphonflasche; 3. (*Zool.*) der Sipho. **2.** *v.t.* (*also* – ***out***) aushebern.

sippet ['sipit], *s.* geröstete Brotschnitte.

sir [sə:], *s.* 1. Herr (*in addressing*); *yes, –,* ja mein Herr; *Dear Sir,* sehr geehrter Herr; 2. Sir (*as title*).

sire ['saiə], **1.** *s.* 1. (*obs.*) (Eure) Majestät (*in addressing*); der Herr, Gebieter; 2. (*Poet.*) Vater, Vorfahr; 3. männliches Stammtier (*of horses, dogs etc.*). **2.** *v.t.* 1. zeugen (*of horses*); 2. (*fig.*) hervorbringen.

siren ['saiərən], **1.** *s.* 1. die Sirene (*Myth. also fig.*); (*fig.*) die Verführerin; 2. (*Tech.*) Sirene, das Heulsignal; 3. (*Zool.*) der Armmolch. **2.** *attrib. adj.* Sirenen–, verführerisch. **sirenian** [sai'ri:niən], *s.* (*Zool.*) die Seekuh, Sirene.

sirloin ['sə:lɔin], *s.* das Lendenstück (*of beef*).

sirocco [si'rɔkou], *s.* der Schirokko.

sirup, *see* **syrup.**

sisal [saisl], *s.* (*also* **–-grass, –-hemp**) der Sisal(hanf).

siskin ['siskin], *s.* (*Orn.*) der Zeisig (*Carduelis spinus*).

sissy, *see* **cissy.**

sister ['sistə], **1.** *s.* 1. die Schwester; *they are brother and –,* sie sind Geschwister; *my brothers and –s,* meine Geschwister; *foster –,* die Pflegeschwester; *half–,* die Halbschwester; 2. (*Eccl.*) die Nonne, (Ordens)schwester; *Sister of Mercy,* barmherzige Schwester; 3. die Oberschwester (*in hospital*). **2.** *attrib. adj.* Schwester–; *– language,* die Schwestersprache; *– ship,* das Schwesterschiff.

sisterhood ['sistəhud], *s.* (*Eccl.*) die Schwesternschaft, der Schwesternorden. **sister-in-law,** *s.* die Schwägerin. **sisterless,** *adj.* ohne Schwester. **sisterliness,** *s.* die Schwesterlichkeit. **sisterly,** *adj.* schwesterlich, Schwester–.

Sistine ['sist(a)in], *adj.* sixtinisch.

Sisyphean [sisi'fiən], *adj.* Sisyphus–.

sit [sit], **1.** *irr.v.i.* 1. sitzen; (*sl.*) *be sitting pretty,* es gut haben, gut dran sein; *– still,* ruhig *or* still sitzen; (*coll.*) *– tight,* ruhig sitzen bleiben, (*fig.*) unbeirrt bei der S. bleiben; abwarten; 2. sich (hin)setzen; 3. ruhen, liegen (*of things*); 4. eine Sitzung (ab)halten, zur Sitzung zusammentreten, tagen (*of committee*), Mitglied sein (*on, Gen.*), einen Sitz innehaben (*members of a committee*); 5. Modell sitzen (*for an artist*); 6. die Prüfung machen, sich dem Examen unterziehen (*for a scholarship etc.*); 7. brüten, sitzen (*as hens etc.*); 8. passen, sitzen (*as clothes*); *– close,* eng sitzen *or* anliegen; 9. *the wind –s fair,* der Wind sitzt gut. **(a)** (*with adv.*) – **back,** 1. sich zurücklehnen; 2. (*fig.*) sich ausruhen; 3. sich zurückziehen, nicht mehr mitmachen; – **down,** sich niedersetzen *or* niederlassen *or* (hin)setzen, Platz nehmen; *– down and do nothing,* die Hände in den Schoß legen; *– down under an insult,* sich (*Dat.*) eine Beleidigung gefallen lassen, eine Beleidigung einstecken *or* ruhig hinnehmen; (*coll.*) – **in** *for him,* ihn vertreten, an seine Stelle treten, seine Stelle einnehmen; – **out,** aussetzen (*a dance*), nicht mittanzen; nicht mitspielen (*at cards*); *– out* (*in the open*), draußen *or* im Freien sitzen; – **up,** 1. sich aufrichten, geradesitzen, aufrecht sitzen; *– up!* mach schön! (*to dogs*); (*coll.*) *make him – up,* ihn aufhorchen lassen, ihn rankriegen; (*coll.*) *– up and take notice,* aufhorchen, aufmerksam werden, (plötzlich) Interesse zeigen; 2. aufbleiben, wachen (*with,* bei). **(b)** (*with prep.*) – **at** *his feet,* zu seinen Füßen sitzen; *– at table,* bei Tisch sitzen; *– at work,* über der Arbeit sitzen; – **for** *a constituency,* einen Wahlkreis vertreten; *– for an examination,* sich einer Prüfung unterziehen, eine Prüfung machen; *– for one's portrait,* sich malen lassen; – (*in judgement*) **on,** zu Gericht sitzen über (*Acc.*); *– on a committee,* einem Ausschuß angehören; *– on the bench,* Polizeirichter sein; (*fig.*) *– on the fence,* sich neutral verhalten; unentschlossen sein; *– on a jury,* Geschworene(r) sein; (*fig.*) *– heavy on him,* auf ihm schwer lasten; *– heavy on the stomach,* (schwer) im Magen liegen; (*sl.*) *– on him,* ihm eins draufgeben, ihm aufs Dach steigen, ihm Mores lehren *or* die Flötentöne beibringen; – **through,** ganz anhören (*a lecture*), bis zum Ende (*Gen.*) bleiben; – **upon,** *see* – *on.* **2.** *irr.v.t. – a hen on eggs,* eine Glucke setzen; *– a horse,* zu Pferde sitzen; *– o.s.,* sich setzen; (*coll.*) *– him down,* ihn (hin)setzen; (*sl.*) *– him out,* länger bleiben *or* aushalten als er; *– out a dance,* einen Tanz auslassen; *– out* or *through,* bis zu Ende ansehen *or* anhören (*a play, concert etc.*).

sit-down, 1. *adj. – strike,* der Sitzstreik; *– supper,* das Abendessen zu Tische. **2.** *s.* (*Am.*) *see – strike.*

site [sait], **1.** *s.* 1. die Lage; 2. Stelle, (Fund)stätte; 3. der Sitz; 4. (*also building –*) Bauplatz, das Baugelände. **2.** *v.t.* placieren (*house etc.*).

sitter ['sitə], *s.* 1. Sitzende(r); 2. die Bruthenne, Brüterin, Glucke; 3. (*Art*) das Modell; 4. (*sl.*) leichter Treffer *or* Fang; (*fig.*) eine Leichtigkeit. **sitting, 1.** *adj.* 1. sitzend; (*sl. fig.*) *– duck,* wehrlos ausgeliefertes *or* wehrloses Ziel; *– member,* gegenwärtiger Abgeordneter; 2. brütend (*birds*); *– hen,* die Glucke. **2.** *s.* 1. das Sitzen, Brüten; 2. die Sitzung (*of committee or for artist*); (*coll.*) *at one* or *a –,* auf einen Sitz, in einem Zug; 3. der Satz (*of eggs*). **sitting-room,** *s.* das Wohnzimmer.

situate ['sitjueit], **1.** *v.t.* aufstellen. **2.** *adj.* (*obs. Law*) *see* **situated,** 1. **situated** [–id], *adj.* 1. (*of a th.*) gelegen; *be –,* liegen; 2. (*of a p.*) in einer Lage befindlich; *– as he is,* in seiner Lage; *be awkwardly –,* sich in einer schwierigen Lage befinden; *well –,* gut gestellt. **situation** [–u'eiʃən], *s.* 1. die Lage, Stellung, der Platz; 2. (*fig.*) die (Sach)lage, Situation, der Zustand, Umstände (*pl.*); 3. die Stelle, Stellung, der Posten.

six [siks], **1.** *num. adj.* sechs (*for clock-times see under* **eight**); (*coll.*) *– of one and half a dozen of the other,* das ist Jacke wie Hose; das ist gehupft wie gesprungen. **2.** *s.* die Sechs; *be at –es and sevens,* in völliger Verwirrung sein, auf dem Kopf stehen; uneinig sein (*with,* mit; *about,* über (*Acc.*)).

six|-cylinder, *attrib. adj.* sechszylindrig. **–fold,** *adj.* sechsfach, sechsfältig. **–-footer,** *s.* (*coll.*) zwei Meter großer Mensch, baumlanger Kerl. **–pence** [–pəns], *s.* (*obs.*) das 6-Pence-Stück. **–-pounder,** *s.* der Sechspfünder. **–-shooter,** *s.* (*coll.*) sechsschüssiger Revolver. **–-sided,** *adj.* sechsseitig.

sixteen ['siks'ti:n], **1.** *num. adj.* sechzehn. **2.** *s.* die Sechzehn. **sixteenth** [–θ], **1.** *num. adj.* sechzehnt. **2.** *s.* 1. der *etc.* Sechzehnte; 2. (*fraction*) das Sechzehntel.

sixth [siksθ], **1.** *num. adj.* sechst; *– form,* die Prima; *– form boy* (*girl*), der (die) Primaner(in); *– of March,* der 6. März; (*coll.*) *– sense,* das Ahnungsvermögen. **2.** *s.* 1. der *etc.* Sechste; 2. (*fraction*) das Sechstel; 3. (*Mus.*) die Sexte. **sixthly,** *adv.* sechstens.

sixtieth ['sikstiəθ], **1.** *num. adj.* sechzigst. **2.** *s.* 1. der *etc.* Sechzigste; 2. (*fraction*) das Sechzigstel. **sixty, 1.** *num. adj.* sechzig. **2.** *s.* die Sechzig; *the sixties,* die sechziger Jahre; *in his sixties,* in den Sechzigern.

sizable, *see* **sizeable.**

sizar ['saizə], *s.* der Stipendiat (*Cambridge and Dublin Univ.*).

[1]**size** [saiz], **1.** *s.* 1. der Umfang, die Größe, Länge, Dicke, (*of a book*) das Format; *what – is it?* wie groß ist es? *they are of a –,* sie sind von derselben Größe; *the – of an elephant,* ebenso groß wie ein Elefant; (*coll.*) *that's about the – of it,* da hast du es gerade getroffen; 2. die Größe, Nummer (*of clothes*); *what – (do you take in) shoes?* welche Schuhgröße (haben Sie)? 3. (*fig.*) die Größe, Bedeutung, das Ausmaß, Format. **2.** *v.t.* nach Größe ordnen *or* (*Mil.*) aufstellen; (*coll.*) *– up,* einschätzen, abschätzen, sich ein Urteil bilden über (*Acc.*). **3.** *v.i. – up,* gleichkommen (*with, to, Dat.*). **4.** *adj. suff. See* **–size(d).**

[2]**size, 1.** *s.* 1. der Leim, Kleister; das Planierwasser, Grundierwasser; 2. die Schlichte, Steife, Appretur. **2.** *v.t.* 1. leimen, planieren, grundieren; 2. steifen, schlichten, appretieren.

sizeable ['saizəbl], *adj.* ziemlich groß, beträchtlich, ansehnlich. **size(d),** *adj. suff.* –groß, *e.g. fair–,* ziemlich groß; ***full--***, in voller Größe; ***life--***, in Lebensgröße; ***medium-*** or ***middle--***, von mittlerer Größe; ***small--***, klein; ***standard--***, normalgroß.

[1]**sizing** ['saiziŋ], *s.* die Größenbestimmung, Ordnung *or* Sichtung nach der Größe.

[2]**sizing,** *s.* das Leimen, die Leimung.

sizzle [sizl], *v.i.* zischen, brutzeln. **sizzling,** *adj.* (*coll.*) sehr heiß; – ***weather,*** die Hitzeperiode.

sjambok ['ʃæmbɔk], *s.* die Nilpferdpeitsche.

skald [skɔ:ld], *s.* der Skalde, Barde.

skat [skæt], *s.* (*Cards*) der Skat.

[1]**skate** [skeit], **1.** *s.* der Schlittschuh; ***roller--***, der Rollschuh. **2.** *v.i.* Schlittschuh laufen, eislaufen; Rollschuh laufen; (*fig.*) leicht dahingleiten; (*fig.*) – ***on*** or ***over thin ice,*** sich aufs Glatteis begeben.

[2]**skate,** *s.* (*Ichth.*) der Glattrochen.

skater ['skeitə], *s.* der (die) Eisläufer(in), Schlittschuhläufer(in), Rollschuhläufer(in). **skating,** *s.* das Eislaufen, Schlittschuhlaufen; Rollschuhlaufen. **skating-rink,** *s.* die Eisbahn; Rollschuhbahn.

skean(-dhu) ['ski:n('du:)], *s.* (irischer *or* schottischer) Dolch.

skedaddle [ski'dædl], **1.** *v.i.* (*coll.*) ausreißen, abhauen, türmen, verduften, sich aus dem Staube machen. **2.** *s.* (*coll.*) das Ausreißen, Türmen.

skeg [skeg], *s.* (*Naut.*) die Kielhacke.

skein [skein], *s.* 1. der Strang, die Docke, Strähne (*wool etc.*); 2. die Kette, Schar, der Schwarm, Flug (*wild geese etc.*).

skeletal ['skelitl], *adj.* Skelett–. **skeleton** [–n], **1.** *s.* 1. das Skelett, Gerippe (*also fig.*); – ***in the cupboard,*** das Familiengeheimnis; ***reduced to a*** –, zum Skelett abgemagert; 2. (*coll.*) das Knochengerüst (*thin p.*); 3. (*fig.*) (*Tech.*) Gerüst, Gestell, der Rahmen; 4. (*Mil. etc.*) Kader, Stamm(bestand); 5. der Rohbau, Umriß, Entwurf. **2.** *adj.* Skelett–; Rahmen–; – ***agreement,*** das Rahmenabkommen, Mantelabkommen; – ***army,*** das Rahmenheer; – ***bill,*** das Wechselblankett, unausgefülltes Formular; – ***construction,*** der Skelettbau, Stahlbau; – ***crew,*** die Stammbesatzung; – ***key,*** der Dietrich, Nachschlüssel; – ***staff,*** das Stammpersonal. **skeletonize,** *v.t.* 1. skelettieren (*animals*); 2. (*fig.*) in großen Zügen darstellen, im Rohbau vorbereiten, entwerfen, skizzieren.

skelp [skelp], **1.** *s.* (*Scots*) der Schlag, Klaps. **2.** *v.t.* schlagen.

skene, *see* **skean(-dhu).**

skep [skep], *s.* (*dial.*) der (Bienen)korb.

skeptic *etc.* (*Am.*), *see* **sceptic.**

skerry [skeri], *s.* das (Felsen)riff, die Schäre.

sketch [sketʃ], **1.** *s.* 1. die Skizze, Studie; der Entwurf, Grundriß, das Schema; ***rough*** –, die Faustzeichnung, (*fig.*) flüchtiger Entwurf; 2. (*Theat.*) der Sketch. **2.** *v.t.* (*also* – *in*) skizzieren; (*fig.*) (*also* – *out*) entwerfen, in großen Zügen schildern. **3.** *v.i.* Skizzen machen, zeichnen. **sketch-book,** *s.* das Skizzenbuch. **sketcher,** *s.* der Skizzenzeichner. **sketchiness,** *s.* (*fig.*) die Skizzenhaftigkeit, Unvollkommenheit, das Skizzenhafte, Flüchtige, Oberflächliche. **sketch-map,** *s.* das Kroki. **sketchy,** *adj.* (*fig.*) skizzenhaft, leicht hingeworfen, unvollkommen, oberflächlich, flüchtig, unzureichend.

skew [skju:], *adj.* schräg, schief(winkelig); – ***bridge,*** schräge Brücke; – ***chisel,*** der Schiefmeißel. **skewbald,** *adj.* scheckig (*horse*). **skewed** [–d], *adj.* abgeschrägt.

skewer ['skju:ə], **1.** *s.* der Speil(er), Fleischspieß. **2.** *v.t.* speile(r)n, spießen (*meat*), aufspießen.

ski [ski:], **1.** *s.* der Ski, Schi, Schneeschuh. **2.** *v.i.* skilaufen.

skiagram *etc. See* **sciagram.**

skid [skid], **1.** *s.* 1. der Hemmschuh, Bremsschuh, Bremsklotz (*for carts*); 2. (*Av.*) die (Gleit)kufe, der Sporn; 3. (*Naut.*) Holzfender, das Reibholz; 4. (*Motor.*) das Rutschen, Schleudern. **2.** *v.t.* hemmen, bremsen (*a wheel*). **3.** *v.i.* 1. (aus)rutschen, (aus)gleiten, abgleiten; 2. (*Motor.*) ins Rutschen kommen, schleudern.

skid|-chain, *s.* (*Motor.*) die Schneekette. **--mark,** *s.* die Bremsspur, Schleuderspur. **--proof,** *adj.* rutschfest, gleitsicher.

skier ['ski:ə], *s.* der (die) Skiläufer(in).

skies [skaiz], *pl. of* **sky.**

skiff [skif], *s.* kleines Boot, der Kahn; Renneiner.

skiing ['ski:iŋ], *s.* das Skifahren, Skilaufen, der Skilauf, Skisport. **ski|-jump,** *s.* die Sprungschanze. **--jumping,** *s.* das Skispringen.

skilful ['skilful], *adj.* geschickt, gewandt. **skilfulness,** *s. See* **skill.**

skill [skil], *s.* 1. die Geschicklichkeit, Gewandtheit; das Geschick, Können, die Fähigkeit, (Kunst)fertigkeit; 2. Sachkenntnis, Fachkenntnis (*in, at,* in (*Dat.*)). **skilled** [–d], *adj.* gewandt, geschickt, geübt; erfahren, bewandert (*in, at,* in (*Dat.*)); – ***hands,*** geschickte Hände; (*fig.*) gelernte Arbeiter (*pl.*); – ***labour,*** Facharbeiter (*pl.*); – ***work,*** die Facharbeit; – ***workman*** or ***worker,*** gelernter (Fach)arbeiter.

skillet ['skilit], *s.* 1. (*Tech.*) der (Schmelz)tiegel; 2. (*Cul.*) die Bratpfanne.

skillful, (*Am.*) *see* **skilful.**

skilly ['skili], *s.* 1. der Haferschleim, die Grütze; 2. Armensuppe.

skim [skim], **1.** *v.t.* 1. abschäumen, abschöpfen, abstreichen; 2. entrahmen, abrahmen (*milk etc.*); 3. streifen, hinstreifen über (*Acc.*); 4. überfliegen, flüchtig lesen, durchblättern, rasch durchsehen (*a book*). **2.** *v.i.* 1. streifen, (hinweg)gleiten (*over,* über (*Acc.*)); 2. – ***over,*** hinstreifen über (*Acc.*); 3. – ***through,*** durchblättern, überfliegen (*a book*). **3.** *s.* (*coll.*) dünne Schicht. **skimmer,** *s.* 1. die Schaumkelle, Rahmkelle; 2. (*Orn.*) der Scherenschnabel (*Rhynchops*). **skim-milk,** *s.* entrahmte Milch, die Magermilch. **skimming,** *s.* (*oft. pl.*) 1. das Abgeschäumte; – ***ladle,*** *see* **skimmer;** 2. (*fig.*) die Abschöpfung.

skimp *etc. See* **scrimp.**

skin [skin], **1.** *s.* 1. die Haut; ***dark*** –, dunkle Haut(farbe); ***have a thick*** –, dickfellig sein, ein dickes Fell haben; ***have a thin*** –, feinfühlig *or* zart besaitet sein; ***jump out of one's*** –, aus der Haut fahren; ***mere*** (or ***nothing but***) – ***and bone***(***s***), bloß noch Haut und Knochen; ***save one's*** –, mit heiler Haut davonkommen; ***by*** or ***with the – of one's teeth,*** mit knapper Not, mit Hängen und Würgen; ***be in his*** –, in seiner Haut stecken; ***to the*** –, bis auf die Haut; ***next to one's*** –, auf der bloßen Haut; (*coll.*) ***it gets under my*** –, es regt mich auf, es geht mir auf die Nerven; 2. das Fell, der Pelz, Balg (*of beasts*); 3. (*Bot.*) die Schale, Hülse, Rinde, Pelle; 4. (*Naut.*) Beplattung, Außenhaut; 5. Haut (*on milk etc.*). **2.** *v.t.* 1. (ent)häuten, abhäuten, abbalgen (*animals*); schälen (*fruit*), abrinden (*a tree*); – ***one's finger,*** den Finger abschaben; (*coll.*) – ***a flint,*** geizig sein; ***keep one's eyes –ed,*** auf der Hut sein; 2. (*sl.*) ausrauben, ausplündern, ausnehmen, rupfen (*a p.*). **3.** *v.i.* 1. abblättern, sich häuten; 2. (*usu.* – *over*) neue Haut bekommen, vernarben, verharschen, zuheilen.

skin|-deep, *adj.* nicht tiefgehend, oberflächlich. **–disease,** *s.* die Hautkrankheit. **--diver,** *s.* der Sporttaucher, Schwimmtaucher. **--diving,** *s.* das Schwimmtauchen. **--dresser,** *s.* der Kürschner. **--effect,** *s.* (*Elec.*) die Hautwirkung. **–flint,** *s.* (*coll.*) der Geizhals, Knicker. **--friction,** *s.* die Oberflächenreibung.

skinful ['skinful], *s.* (*vulg.*) der Bauchvoll.

skin|-game, *s.* (*coll. esp. Am.*) die Bauernfängerei, der Betrug. **--graft,** *s.* das Hauttransplantat. **--grafting,** *s.* die Hauttransplantation, Hautübertragung.

skinned [skind], *adj.* 1. enthäutet, gehäutet; 2. (*as suff.*) –häutig, –fellig. **skinner,** *s.* 1. der Kürschner, Pelz(waren)händler, Rauchwarenhändler; 2. Abdecker. **skinniness,** *s.* 1. (*coll.*) die Magerkeit, Hagerkeit; 2. (*fig.*) Knauserigkeit, Filzigkeit, Knickerigkeit. **skinning,** *s.* 1. das Abblättern; 2.

die Hautbildung. **skinny,** *adj.* 1. häutig; 2. (*coll.*) mager, hager, ausgezehrt, abgemagert; 3. (*fig.*) geizig, knauserig, knickerig, filzig.

skin-tight, *adj.* eng anliegend, hautnah.

skint [skint], *adj.* (*sl.*) pleite, abgebrannt.

¹skip [skip], *s.* der Mannschaftsführer (*at bowls, curling*).

²skip, *s.* (*Min.*) der Förderkorb, Eimer, Kübel.

³skip, 1. *v.t.* 1. (*also* – ***over***) springen über (*Acc.*), überspringen; 2. (*fig.*) auslassen, übergehen, überschlagen; (*sl.*) – ***it!*** Schwamm drüber! **2.** *v.i.* 1. seilspringen; 2. springen, hüpfen; 3. (*in reading*) Stellen *or* Seiten überspringen, Sprünge machen. **3.** *s.* der Hupf, Sprung.

skip|-bomb, *s.* (*Av.*) die Abprallerbombe. **--distance,** *s.* (*Rad.*) tote Zone. **-jack,** *s.* 1. (*Ichth.*) der Springer, Blaufisch; 2. (*Ent.*) Schnellkäfer; 3. Springauf, das Stehaufmännchen (*toy*).

¹skipper ['skipə], *s.* 1. der Hüpfer, Springer; 2. (*fig.*) flüchtiger Leser; 3. (*Ent.*) der Schnellkäfer, Dickkopf(falter).

²skipper, *s.* (*Naut.*) der Kapitän; (*Av.*) Flugkapitän; (*Spt. coll.*) Mannschaftsführer.

skippet ['skipit], *s.* (*Hist.*) die Siegelklausel.

skipping ['skipiŋ], *s.* das Hüpfen, (*esp.*) (Seil)-springen. **skipping-rope,** *s.* das Springseil.

skirl [skə:l], *s.* das (Dudelsack)pfeifen.

skirmish ['skə:miʃ], **1.** *s.* 1. das Scharmützel, Geplänkel; 2. (*fig.*) Wortgeplänkel. **2.** *v.i.* scharmützeln, plänkeln. **skirmisher,** *s.* der Plänkler.

skirt [skə:t], **1.** *s.* 1. der (Frauen)rock; 2. Rockschoß (*of a coat*); 3. Saum, Rand, die Grenze (*of a wood etc.*); 4. (*sl.*) das Weibsstück. **2.** *v.t.* 1. grenzen, (um)säumen; herumgehen um, sich entlangziehen an (*Dat.*); 2. (*fig.*) umgehen. **3.** *v.i.* – ***along,*** entlanggehen *or* –fahren, sich am Rande hinziehen. **skirt-dance,** *s.* der Serpentintanz. **skirting,** *s.* 1. der Rand, Saum; 2. Stoff für Damenröcke; 3. (*usu.* ***--board***) die Wandleiste, Fußleiste, Scheuerleiste.

skit [skit], *s.* 1. sarkastische Bemerkung, die Stichelei; 2. Parodie, Satire (***on***, über *or* auf (*Acc.*)).

skitter ['skitə], *v.i.* an der Wasseroberfläche fliegen (*as ducks*).

skittish ['skitiʃ], *adj.* leichtfertig, flatterhaft, launisch, unberechenbar; ausgelassen, ungebärdig; scheu, bockig (*as a horse*).

skittle [skitl], **1.** *s.* der Kegel; *pl.* (*sing. constr.*) das Kegeln, Kegelspiel; ***play at –s,*** kegeln, Kegel schieben; ***life is not all beer and –s,*** das Leben ist nicht eitel Freude. **2.** *v.t.* (*Crick.*) – ***out,*** in rascher Folge abfertigen (*a team*).

skittle|-alley, --ground, *s.* die Kegelbahn.

skive [skaiv], **1.** *s.* das Schleifrad (*for diamonds*). **2.** *v.t.* 1. abschleifen (*precious stones*); 2. spalten, (ab)schaben (*leather*). **3.** *v.i.* (*sl.*) sich drücken; (*sl.*) – ***off,*** abhauen, auskneifen. **skiver, 1.** *s.* 1. das Lederspaltmesser; 2. Spaltleder; 3. (*sl.*) der Drückeberger. **skiving,** *s.* (*sl.*) die Drückebergerei.

skivvy ['skivi], *s.* (*sl.*) die Dienstspritze, der Besen.

skua ['skju:ə], *s.* (*Orn.*) die Raubmöwe (*Stercorariidae*); (*Am.*) Große Raubmöwe (*Stercorarius skua*).

skulduggery [skʌl'dʌgəri], *s.* (*coll.*) die Gaunerei, Schuftigkeit.

skulk [skʌlk], *v.i.* 1. lauern, sich verstecken; 2. (umher)schleichen; – ***away,*** sich fortschleichen; 3. sich drücken. **skulker,** *s.* 1. der Schleicher; 2. Drückeberger. **skulking,** *adj.* hinterhältig, feige.

skull [skʌl], *s.* die Hirnschale, der Schädel; (*fig.*) Kopf; ***fractured –,*** der Schädelbruch; (*fig.*) ***thick –,*** harter Schädel; – ***and crossbones,*** der Totenkopf (*as warning*); (*Naut.*) die Piratenflagge. **skull-cap,** *s.* das Käppchen.

skunk [skʌŋk], *s.* 1. der Skunk, das Stinktier; (*fur*) der Skunk(s)pelz; 2. (*fig. sl.*) Schuft, gemeiner Hund.

sky [skai], **1.** *s.* 1. (sichtbarer) Himmel, der Wolkenhimmel, das Himmelszelt, Himmelsgewölbe, Firmament; ***in the –,*** am Himmel; ***out of a clear –,*** aus heiterem Himmel; ***under the open –,*** im Freien, unter freiem Himmel; ***praise (up) to the skies,*** über alle Maßen loben; (*coll.*) ***the –'s the limit,*** nach oben sind keine Grenzen gesetzt; 2. (*oft. pl.*) die Gegend, der Himmelsstrich; das Klima. **2.** *v.t.* 1. (zu) hoch aufhängen (*a picture*); 2. hoch in die Luft schlagen (*a ball*).

sky|-blue, 1. *adj.* himmelblau. **2.** *s.* das Himmelblau. **--high,** *adj., adv.* himmelhoch. **-lark, 1.** *s.* (*Orn.*) die Feldlerche (*Alauda arvensis*). **2.** *v.i.* Possen *or* Ulk treiben. **-larking,** *s.* das Possenreißen, die Ulkerei; tolle Streiche (*pl.*). **-light,** *s.* das Oberlicht, Dachfenster. **-line,** *s.* der Horizont. **--marker,** *s.* (*Av.*) der Zielbeleuchter. **--pilot,** *s.* (*sl.*) Geistliche(r). **--rocket, 1.** *s.* die (Signal)-rakete. **2.** *v.i.* (*esp. of prices*) hochschnellen, in die Höhe schießen. **-scraper,** *s.* das Hochhaus, der Wolkenkratzer. **--sign,** *s.* hohe Lichtreklame.

skyward ['skaiwəd], **1.** *adj.* himmelwärts gerichtet. **2.** *or* **skywards,** *adv.* himmelwärts, himmelan.

sky|way, *s.* (*Am.*) die Luftroute, der Flugweg. **-writing,** *s.* die Himmelsschrift, Luftwerbung.

slab [slæb], **1.** *s.* 1. die (Stein- *or* Marmor)platte, Tafel, Fliese; 2. das Schalholz, Schwartenbrett, Schalbrett, Schellstück, die Holzschwarte (*of wood*); 3. Bramme, der Rohblock (*of metal*); 4. (*coll.*) dickes Stück, dicke Scheibe. **2.** *v.t.* zurichten, behauen (*tree-trunk*).

slabber ['slæbə], *see* **slobber.**

¹slack [slæk], **1.** *adj.* 1. schlaff (*also fig.*), locker, lose; – ***vowel,*** offener Vokal; – ***water,*** das Stauwasser, totes *or* stilles Wasser; 2. (*fig.*) (nach)lässig, träge, schlapp (*of a p.*); flau, lustlos (*as trade*), geschäftslos (*season*); 3. langsam, gemächlich (*pace*). **2.** *s.* 1. loses *or* herabhängendes Ende, das *or* die Lose (*of rope or sail*); 2. *See* – ***water***; 3. (*Comm.*) flaue *or* geschäftslose Zeit, die Flaute. **3.** *v.t. see* **slacken, 2. 4.** *v.i.* 1. (*coll.*) faulenzen, trödeln; 2. *See* **slacken, 1.**

²slack, *s.* das Kohlenklein, der Kohlengrus.

slacken ['slækən], **1.** *v.i.* 1. (*also* – ***off***) schlaff *or* locker werden, (*fig.*) erschlaffen, nachlassen; 2. (*usu.* – ***off***) (*Comm.*) flau werden, stocken; 3. (*usu.* – ***up***) sich verlangsamen, abnehmen. **2.** *v.t.* 1. (*also* – ***off***) lockern, lösen; 2. (*Naut.*) lose geben, losgeben, fieren (*a rope*); 3. (*fig.*) verlangsamen, vermindern, mäßigen (*speed, efforts*).

slacker ['slækə], *s.* (*coll.*) der Faulenzer, Drückeberger. **slackness,** *s.* 1. die Schlaffheit, Lockerheit; 2. Unbelebtheit, das Stockung, Stille, Flaute, Flauheit, der Stillstand (*of business*); 3. (*Tech.*) das Spiel, die Lockerheit; 4. (*coll.*) (Nach)lässigkeit, Trägheit, Saumseligkeit, Schlappheit. **slacks,** *pl.* lange (weite) Hose.

slag [slæg], **1.** *s.* die Schlacke. **2.** *v.i., v.t.* verschlacken. **slaggy,** *adj.* schlackig. **slag-heap,** *s.* die Halde.

slain [slein], *p.p. of* **slay.**

slake [sleik], *v.t.* löschen (*also lime*), stillen (*thirst*); ***-d lime,*** gelöschter Kalk, der Löschkalk.

slalom ['slɑ:ləm], *s.* (*Spt.*) der Slalom.

slam [slæm], **1.** *v.t.* 1. zuwerfen, zuschlagen, zuschmeißen (*a door etc.*); – ***the door to,*** die Tür zuschlagen; – ***the door in his face,*** ihm die Tür vor der Nase zuschlagen; (*fig.*) ihn endgültig abweisen; 2. (*coll.*) schlagen; (*sl.*) – ***him (down),*** ihn restlos herunterputzen. **2.** *v.i.* 1. (*also* – ***to***) heftig zufallen, zugeschlagen werden; 2. (*Cards*) einen Schlemm machen. **3.** *s.* 1. der Krach, Knall, Schlag; 2. (*Cards*) Schlemm.

slander ['slɑ:ndə], **1.** *s.* die Verleumdung, Ehrabschneidung, üble Nachrede; (*Law*) mündliche Ehrenkränkung. **2.** *v.t.* verleumden, verunglimpfen. **slanderer,** *s.* der (die) Verleumder(in). **slanderous,** *adj.* verleumderisch, ehrenrührig.

slang [slæŋ], **1.** *s.* 1. der Slang, niedere Umgangssprache; 2. die Sondersprache, der Jargon; ***thieves' –,*** die Gaunersprache, das Rotwelsch; ***schoolboy –,*** die Schülersprache. **2.** *v.t.* (*coll.*) beschimpfen, tüchtig ausschimpfen, heruntermachen, herunterreißen (*a p.*); (*coll.*) ***-ing match,*** gegenseitige

Beschimpfung. **slanginess,** *s.* unfeine *or* ordinäre Ausdrucksweise. **slangy,** *adj.* 1. slangartig, Slang–, ordinär, unfein; 2. slangsprechend (*a p.*).

slant [slɑ:nt], **1.** *v.t.* 1. schief *or* schräg legen, kippen; 2. (*fig., coll.*) zurechtstutzen, frisieren (*an account etc.*). **2.** *v.i.* schräg *or* schief liegen *or* sein, sich neigen, kippen. **3.** *s.* 1. die Schräge, schiefe Ebene, schräge Fläche *or* Richtung *or* Linie; ***on the –***, schief, schräg; 2. (*fig., coll.*) die Neigung, der Hang; 3. (*fig., sl.*) Seitenblick; Seitenhieb (***at***, auf (*Acc.*)). **slanting,** *adj.*, **slantwise,** *adv.* schief, schräg, geneigt.

slap [slæp], **1.** *s.* der Klaps, Schlag; ***– in*** or ***on the face,*** die Ohrfeige; (*fig.*) Enttäuschung; Beleidigung, der Schlag ins Gesicht; (*fig.*) ***– on the back,*** die Beglückwünschung; Ermunterung; (*sl.*) ***have a – at,*** sich machen an (*Acc.*), anpacken. **2.** *v.t.* 1. klapsen, klopfen, schlagen, einen Klaps geben (*Dat.*); ***– his face,*** ihm eine Ohrfeige geben; ***– him on the back,*** ihm auf den Rücken klopfen; (*fig.*) ihm gratulieren, ihm Glück wünschen, ihn beglückwünschen; (*sl.*) ***– him around,*** ihn erbarmungslos schurigeln; 2. (*sl.*) werfen, schmeißen. **3.** *v.i.* klatschen, schlagen. **4.** *adv.* (*coll.*) Knall und Fall, (schnur)stracks, plumps, gerade(n)wegs.

slap|-bang, *adv.* (*coll.*) Hals über Kopf, spornstreichs, stracks, blindlings, plumps, knallbums. **–dash, 1.** *adj.* 1. hastig, ungestüm; 2. sorglos, fahrig, zerfahren; 3. oberflächlich (*work*). **2.** *adv.* *See* **–-bang. –-happy,** *adj.* (*coll.*) übermütig, tolldreist. **–stick,** *s.* die Pritsche, der Narrenstock; (*usu. fig.*) – (***comedy***), die Radaukomödie, der Schwank, das Possenstück. **–-up,** *adj.* (*sl.*) mit allen Schikanen, erstklassig, famos.

slash [slæʃ], **1.** *v.t.* 1. (auf)schlitzen, zerfetzen, zerschneiden; ***–ed sleeve,*** der Schlitzärmel; 2. (*fig.*) peitschen, hauen; 3. (*sl.*) erbarmungslos kritisieren, herunterreißen; 4. drastisch zusammenstreichen. **2.** *v.i.* hauen (***at***, nach); ***– out,*** um sich hauen. **3.** *s.* 1. tiefe Schnittwunde, der Schnitt; 2. Schlitz (*in a dress*); 3. Streich, Hieb. **slashing,** *adj.* (*fig.*) heftig, vernichtend, scharf (*of criticism*).

slat [slæt], *s.* dünner Streifen *or* Stab, die Latte, Leiste.

[1]**slate** [sleit], **1.** *s.* 1. (*Geol.*) der Schiefer; 2. (*Build.*) Dachschiefer, die Schieferplatte; 3. Schiefertafel (*for children*); (*fig.*) ***clean –***, reine Weste, reiner Tisch; (*fig.*) ***wipe the – clean,*** reinen Tisch machen; (*coll.*) ***on the –***, auf Borg *or* Pump. **2.** *v.t.* mit Schiefer decken.

[2]**slate,** *v.i.* (*coll.*) heftig tadeln, durch den Kakao ziehen, heruntermachen, abkanzeln,

slate|-blue, *adj.* schieferblau. **–-club,** *s.* private Sparkasse. **–-coloured,** *adj.* schiefergrau. **–-pencil,** *s.* der Griffel, Schieferstift. **–-quarry,** *s.* der Schieferbruch.

slater ['sleitə], *s.* 1. der Schieferdecker; 2. (*Ent.*) die Assel, Holzlaus.

[1]**slating** ['sleitiŋ], *s.* 1. das Schieferdecken; 2. die Schieferbedachung, Schiefer (*pl.*).

[2]**slating,** *s.* (*coll.*) 1. scharfe Kritik, der Verriß; 2. die Strafpredigt.

slatted ['slætid], *adj.* Latten–.

slattern ['slætən], *s.* die Schlampe, Schlumpe. **slatternliness,** *s.* die Schlamperei, Schlampigkeit. **slatternly,** *adj.* schlampig, schlump(e)rig.

slaty ['sleiti], *adj.* 1. schieferartig, schief(e)rig; 2. schiefergrau.

slaughter ['slɔ:tə], **1.** *s.* 1. das Schlachten (*of animals*); 2. (*fig.*) Abschlachten; Gemetzel, Blutbad; ***– of the Innocents,*** der Kindermord zu Bethlehem. **2.** *v.t.* 1. schlachten (*cattle*); 2. (*fig.*) abschlachten, niedermetzeln. **slaughterer,** *s.* 1. der Schlächter; 2. (*fig.*) Mörder. **slaughter-house,** *s.* das Schlachthaus. **slaughterous,** *adj.* mörderisch.

Slav [slɑ:v], **1.** *s.* der Slawe (die Slawin). **2.** *adj.* slawisch, Slawen–.

slave [sleiv], **1.** *s.* der Sklave (die Sklavin); (*fig.*) der Knecht, Packesel, das Arbeitstier; (*fig.*) ***a – to, the – of,*** ein Sklave (*Gen.*). **2.** *v.i.* wie ein Sklave arbeiten, schuften, sich plagen *or* abrackern *or* schinden *or* placken.

slave|-bangle, *s.* der Sklavenreif. **–-born,** *adj.* als Sklave geboren. **–-dealer,** *s.* der Sklavenhändler. **–-driver,** *s.* 1. der Sklavenaufseher; 2. (*fig.*) Menschenschinder. **–-labour,** *s.* die Zwangsarbeit. **–-market,** *s.* der Sklavenmarkt.

[1]**slaver** ['sleivə], *s.* 1. das Sklavenschiff; 2. der Sklavenhändler, Sklavenhalter.

[2]**slaver, 1.** *s.* 1. der Geifer, Sabber, Speichel; 2. (*fig.*) die Speichelleckerei, Lobhudelei. **2.** *v.t.* belecken, begeifern, besabbern. **3.** *v.i.* 1. geifern, sabbern; 2. (*fig.*) schmeicheln, lobhudeln. **slaverer,** *s.* 1. der Geiferer; 2. (*fig.*) Lobhudler, Speichellecker.

slavery ['sleivəri], *s.* 1. die Sklaverei; 2. (*fig.*) Hörigkeit, sklavische Abhängigkeit (***to***, von); 3. die Sklavenarbeit, Schinderei, Plackerei.

slave|-ship, *s.* das Sklavenschiff. **–-trade,** *s.* der Sklavenhandel. **–-trader,** *s.* der Sklavenhändler. **–-traffic,** *s. See* **–-trade**; ***white –***, das Mädchenhandel.

slavey ['sleivi], *s.* (*sl.*) das Mädchen für alles, der Besen.

Slavic ['slævik], *adj.* (*rare*) *see* **Slav, 2.**

slavish ['sleiviʃ], *adj.* (*usu. fig.*) sklavisch, knechtisch. **slavishness,** *s.* sklavisches Wesen, der Knechtsinn.

Slavonia [slə'vouniə], *s.* Slawonien (*n.*). **Slavonian, 1.** *s.* der Slawone (die Slawonin). **2.** *adj.* slawonisch.

slay [slei], *irr.v.t.* erschlagen, töten; ***the slain,*** die Erschlagenen, Toten. **slayer,** *s.* der (die) Totschläger(in).

sleazy ['sli:zi], *adj.* 1. dünn (*of fabric*); 2. elend, schmutzig; gemein.

sled [sled], *s.* kleiner Schlitten.

sledge [sledʒ], **1.** *s.* der Schlitten. **2.** *v.i.* Schlitten fahren, rodeln. **2.** *v.t.* mit einem Schlitten befördern.

sledge-hammer, 1. *s.* der Vorschlaghammer, Schmiedehammer. **2.** *v.t.* (*coll.*) niederschmettern. **3.** *adj.* (*coll.*) Holzhammer–, wuchtig, schonungslos (*attacks etc.*), schwerfällig, klobig.

sleek [sli:k], **1.** *adj.* 1. glatt (*also fig.*); 2. (*fig.*) ölig, schmeichlerisch, geschmeidig. **2.** *v.t.* 1. glatt machen, glätten; 2. glatt kämmen (*hair*). **sleekness,** *s.* 1. die Glätte, Glattheit; 2. (*fig.*) Geschmeidigkeit.

sleep [sli:p], **1.** *irr.v.i.* schlafen; übernachten, die Nacht zubringen; ***the bed has been slept in by him,*** im Bett hat er geschlafen; ***– on a th.***, etwas überschlafen; ***– like a top*** or ***log,*** wie ein Dachs schlafen; ***– out,*** außer Hause schlafen; ***– rough,*** mit einem Notlager vorliebnehmen *or* auskommen; ***– the clock round,*** volle zwölf Stunden schlafen; ***not – a wink,*** kein Auge zutun. **2.** *irr.v.t.* 1. schlafen; ***– one's last sleep,*** seinen letzten Schlaf tun; ***– away*** or ***off,*** verschlafen (*the time, a headache*); (*coll.*) ***– off the effects, – o.s. sober,*** seinen Rausch ausschlafen; 2. (zum Schlafen) unterbringen, Betten haben für (*a number of people*). **3.** *s.* der Schlaf; (*fig.*) die Ruhe, Untätigkeit; ***beauty –***, erster erfrischender Schlaf; ***broken –***, gestörter *or* unruhiger Schlaf; ***the – of the dead,*** der Todeschlaf; ***get to*** or ***go to –***, einschlafen; ***get some –***, ein wenig schlafen; ***have one's – out,*** sich ausschlafen; ***put to –***, einschläfern; ***walk in one's –***, nachtwandeln.

sleeper ['sli:pə], *s.* 1. der (die) Schläfer(in), Schlafende(r); ***be a light –***, unruhig schlafen; ***be a sound –***, gut *or* fest schlafen; 2. (*Railw.*) (*coll.*) der Schlafwagen; 3. (*Tech.*) die Schwelle. **sleepiness,** *s.* die Schläfrigkeit, Verschlafenheit.

sleeping ['sli:piŋ], **1.** *s.* das Schlafen. **2.** *adj.* schlafend; ***let – dogs lie,*** an Vergangenes soll man nicht rühren. **sleeping|-accommodation,** *s.* die Schlafgelegenheit. **–-bag,** *s.* der Schlafsack. **Sleeping Beauty,** *s.* Dornröschen (*n.*). **sleeping|-berth,** *s.* (*Railw.*) das Schafwagenbett, (*Naut.*) die Koje. **–-car, –-compartment,** *s.* (*Railw.*) der Schlafwagen. **–-draught,** *s.* der Schlaftrunk.

– partner, *s.* stiller Teilhaber. **–-sickness,** *s.* die Schlafsucht. **–-suit,** *s.* der Schlafanzug.

sleepless ['sli:plis], *adj.* schlaflos; (*fig.*) ruhelos, rastlos, wachsam. **sleeplessness,** *s.* die Schlaflosigkeit.

sleep|-walker, *s.* der (die) Nachtwandler(in). **–-walking,** *s.* das Nachtwandeln.

sleepy ['sli:pi], *adj.* 1. (*of a p.*) schläfrig, verschlafen, (*fig.*) träge; 2. (*of a place*) verschlafen, verträumt, träumerisch. **sleepy|head,** *s.* (*coll.*) die Schlafmütze, der Dussel. **– sickness,** *s.* die Gehirnentzündung.

sleet [sli:t], **1.** *s.* Schloßen (*pl.*), Graupeln (*pl.*), der Graupelregen. **2.** *v.i.* graupeln. **sleety,** *adj.* Graupel–, graupelig.

sleeve [sli:v], **1.** *s.* 1. der Ärmel; ***laugh in*** or ***up one's –***, sich (*Dat.*) ins Fäustchen lachen; ***wear one's heart on one's –***, das Herz auf der Zunge haben; ***have s.th. up one's –***, etwas bereithalten, etwas bereit *or* in Bereitschaft *or* auf Lager *or* in petto haben; ***roll*** or ***turn up one's –s***, sich (*Dat.*) die Ärmel aufkrempeln; 2. (*Tech.*) die Muffe; Manschette, Buchse, Büchse, Hülse; 3. (*for gramophone records*) Hülle, Tasche; 4. (*Av.*) Schleppscheibe, der Schleppsack. **2.** *v.t.* 1. mit Ärmeln versehen; 2. (*Tech.*) vermuffen, verbuchsen, verbüchsen.

sleeve-coupling, *s.* die Muffenkupplung. **sleeved** [–d], *suff.* –ärmelig. **sleeve-fish,** *s.* (*Ichth.*) der Tintenfisch. **sleeveless,** *adj.* ärmellos, ohne Ärmel. **sleeve|-link,** *s.* der Manschettenknopf. **–-valve,** *s.* das Muffenventil.

sleigh [slei], **1.** *s.* der Schlitten. **2.** *v.i.* (im) Schlitten fahren. **sleigh-bell,** *s.* die Schlittenschelle.

sleight [slait], *s.* der Kunstgriff, die Geschicklichkeit. **sleight-of-hand,** *s.* 1. das (Taschenspieler)-kunststück; 2. die Fingerfertigkeit, Taschenspielerei.

slender ['slendə], *adj.* 1. schlank, schmal; 2. dünn, schmächtig; 3. (*fig.*) karg, mager, schmal, spärlich, dürftig, unzulänglich, unzureichend (*as means*); 4. schwach, gering (*as hopes*). **slenderness,** *s.* 1. die Schlankheit; 2. (*fig.*) Spärlichkeit, Kargheit, Unzulänglichkeit; 3. Geringfügigkeit, Schwachheit.

slept [slept], *imperf., p.p. of* **sleep.**

sleuth [slu:θ], **1.** *s.* (*coll.*) der Detektiv. **2.** *v.t.* nachspüren (*Dat.*), die Spur verfolgen (*Gen.*). **3.** *v.i.* (*coll.*) den Detektiv spielen. **sleuth-hound,** *s.* der Spürhund (*also fig.*), Bluthund.

[1]**slew** [slu:], *imperf. of* **slay.**

[2]**slew, 1.** *v.t.* (*oft.* ***– round***) herumdrehen, herumschleudern. **2.** *v.i.* sich herumdrehen.

slice [slais], **1.** *s.* 1. die Schnitte, Scheibe, das Stück; ***– of bread and butter***, das Butterbrot; ***– of meat***, das Stück Fleisch; 2. (*fig., coll.*) der (An)teil, die Portion; ***– of luck***, die Portion Glück; 3. der *or* die Spa(ch)tel, (*Cul.*) die Kelle, Schaufel, der Heber. **2.** *v.t.* 1. (*oft.* ***– up***) aufschneiden, in Scheiben schneiden; ***– off***, abschneiden; 2. (*Golf*) ***– a ball***, einen Ball nach rechts ausschlagen. **slicer,** *s.* die Schneidemaschine, der Schneider.

slick [slik], **1.** *adj.* 1. (*coll.*) glatt, glitschig; 2. (*fig.*) raffiniert, pfiffig, flott. **2.** *adv.* glattweg, wie geschmiert. **3.** *s.* der Schlick (*of oil etc.*). **slicker,** *s.* (*sl.*) der Gauner, Gaudieb, schlauer Kerl. **slickness,** *s.* (*fig.*) die Pfiffigkeit; Flottheit.

slid [slid], *imperf., p.p. of* **slide.**

slide [slaid], **1.** *irr.v.i.* 1. gleiten, rutschen; ***– down***, hinunterrutschen; (*fig.*) ***– over s.th.***, etwas übergehen, über etwas hinweggehen; ***let things –***, die Dinge laufen lassen, den Dingen ihren Lauf lassen; 2. schlitten, schurren (*on the ice*); 3. ausgleiten, ausglitschen, ausrutschen; 4. (*fig.*) übergehen, hineingleiten (***into***, in (*Acc.*)), verfallen (*Dat.*). **2.** *irr.v.t.* gleiten lassen. **3.** *s.* 1. das Gleiten, Rutschen; 2. (*Geol.*) der Rutsch; 3. die Schurrbahn, Schlitterbahn, Eisbahn, Rutschbahn; 4. die (Haar)spange; 5. (*Tech.*) der Schieber, Läufer, Reiter, Schlitten; 6. Objektträger, Glasstreifen (*of microscope*); 7. (*Phot.*) das Lichtbild, Dia(positiv); 8. (*Mus.*) der Schleifer, Vorschlag; 9. (*of trombone*) Auszug, (*on organ*) die Schleife.

slide-bar, *s.* die Gleitschiene, Gleitbahn, Geradführung. **slider,** *s.* der Schieber. **slide|-rule,** *s.* der Rechenschieber. **–-valve,** *s.* das Schieberventil, der Schieber.

sliding ['slaidiŋ], **1.** *adj.* gleitend, verschiebbar, Schiebe–; ***– contact***, der Schleifkontakt; ***– door***, die Schiebetür; ***– fit***, der Gleitsitz, die Gleitpassung; (*fig.*) ***–-scale***, bewegliche (Lohn– *or* Preis)skala, der Staffeltarif, die Staffelung; ***– seat***, der Rollsitz (*of boat*); ***– surface***, die Gleitfläche. **2.** *s.* das Gleiten, Rutschen.

slight [slait], **1.** *adj.* 1. schwach, mild, oberflächlich, leicht, gering(fügig), unwichtig, unbedeutend; ***– cold***, leichte Erkältung; ***– effort***, geringe Anstrengung; ***not in the –est***, nicht im geringsten; 2. (*of a p.*) dünn, schmächtig. **2.** *v.t.* geringschätzig behandeln, mißachten, vernachlässigen, nicht beachten, ignorieren. **3.** *s.* 1. die Geringschätzung, Mißachtung, Nichtachtung; 2. Beleidigung, Kränkung, Zurücksetzung. **slighting,** *adj.* herabsetzend, abschätzig. **slightness,** *s.* 1. die Schlankheit, Schmächtigkeit, Schwäche; 2. Geringfügigkeit, Bedeutungslosigkeit.

slim [slim], **1.** *adj.* 1. schlank; 2. (*fig., coll.*) gering, dürftig, armselig, schwach; ***– chance***, geringe Aussichten (*pl.*); ***– pretext***, fadenscheiniger Vorwand. **2.** *v.i.* eine Schlankheitskur machen, sich trimmen.

slime [slaim], *s.* der Schleim, Schlamm, Schlick. **sliminess** [–inis], *s.* das Schleimige, Schlammige.

slimmer ['slimə], *comp. adj.*, **slimmest** ['slimist], *sup. adj. See* **slim.**

slimming ['slimiŋ], *s.* 1. das Schlankwerden; 2. die Schlankheitskur, das Trimmen. **slimness,** *s.* 1. die Schlankheit; 2. (*fig.*) Dürftigkeit, Geringfügigkeit, Armseligkeit, Schwäche.

slimy ['slaimi], *adj.* 1. schleimig, schmierig, glitschig; schlammig, schlickig; 2. (*fig.*) schmutzig, ekelhaft, kriecherisch.

[1]**sling** [sliŋ], **1.** *s.* 1. (*Hist.*) die Schleuder, Wurfmaschine; 2. (*coll.*) der Wurf. **2.** *irr.v.t.* schleudern, werfen; (*sl.*) ***– one's hook***, türmen, sich aus dem Staub machen; (*fig.*) ***– mud at***, mit Schmutz bewerfen; (*coll.*) ***– out***, hinauswerfen.

[2]**sling, 1.** *s.* 1. (*Med.*) die (Arm)schlinge, Binde; 2. der Tragriemen, Schulterriemen, Gurt (*of rifle etc.*); 3. (*Naut.*) Stropp. **2.** *irr.v.t.* aufhängen; (*Mil.*) ***– arms!*** Gewehr umhängen! **3.** *irr.v.i.* (*usu. be –ing*) hängen (***from***, an (*Dat.*)).

[1]**slink** [sliŋk], *irr.v.i.* schleichen; ***– away*** or ***off***, fortschleichen, wegschleichen.

[2]**slink, 1.** *irr.v.i.* fehlgebären, vor der Zeit gebären, verwerfen (*of animals*). **2.** *irr.v.t.* vor der Zeit werfen; ***– a calf***, verkalben. **3.** *s.* die Fehlgeburt, Frühgeburt. **4.** *adj.* fehlgeboren, zu früh geboren.

[1]**slip** [slip], **1.** *s.* 1. das (Aus)gleiten, (Aus)rutschen, Abglitschen; 2. (*Geol.*) die Verwerfung, der (Erd)-rutsch; 3. Fehltritt (*also fig.*); (*fig.*) Schnitzer, Flüchtigkeitsfehler, Verstoß, das Versehen; ***– of the pen***, der Schreibfehler; ***it was a – of the tongue***, ich habe mich versprochen; (*coll.*) ***give him the –***, ihm entkommen *or* ausweichen; (*Prov.*) ***there's many a – 'twixt the cup and the lip***, zwischen Lipp' und Kelchesrand schwebt der finstern Mächte Hand; ***make a –***, sich versehen, einen Fehltritt tun; 4. (*Tech.*) die Schlüpfung, der Schlupf; 5. (*Shipb.*) die Helling; 6. (*Hunt.*) (Hunde)leine, Koppel (*for dogs*); 7. (*Crick.*) der Eckmann; 8. (*Theat.*) Schiebekulissen (*pl.*); 9. der (Kissen)bezug; 10. das Unterkleid, der Unterrock; 11. *pl.* die Badehose.

2. *v.t.* 1. gleiten lassen, schieben, stecken, (unbemerkt) hineinschieben *or* hineinstecken; ***– s.th. to him***, (*coll.*) ***– him s.th.***, ihm etwas zustecken; ***– in***, einfließen lassen, dazwischenwerfen (*a word*); 2. loslassen (*dogs*); (*Naut.*) schießen lassen, schlippen (*a cable*); (*Railw.*) (während der Fahrt) abhängen (*a coach*); 3. abstreifen (*fetters*), (*knitting*) überziehen; ***– off***, ausziehen, abstreifen (*clothes*); – **on,** anziehen, überziehen (*clothes*); 4. entgehen (*Dat.*); – **his memory,** ihm entfallen. **3.** *v.i.* 1. (aus)gleiten, (aus)rutschen; sich verschieben, aufgehen, losgehen (*as knots*); **his foot slipped,** er glitt aus; – **down,** hinfallen; hinuntergleiten an (*Dat.*) (*a rope etc.*); – **from** or **out of one's hand,** aus der Hand gleiten, der Hand entgleiten; – **from one's mind,** dem Gedächtnis entfallen; – **off,** hinabgleiten *or* hinunterrutschen von; 2. (*coll.*) schnell (hin)gehen; – **away** or **off,** entschlüpfen, entgehen, sich davonmachen, entkommen, entwischen; – **by,** vergehen, verstreichen (*time*); – **in,** sich einschleichen; – **into,** hineinschlüpfen in (*Acc.*) (*clothes*), sich einschleichen *or* (heimlich) hineinschieben in (*Acc.*) (*a room*), (unmerklich) geraten in (*Acc.*) (*difficulties*); – **out,** hinausschlüpfen; entschlüpfen (*as a remark*); (*coll.*) einen Sprung hinausmachen; (*coll.*) **let it –,** sich verplappern; **let an opportunity –,** sich (*Dat.*) eine Gelegenheit entgehen lassen; 3. (*fig.*) sich irren *or* versehen, einen Fehler machen; – **up,** sich irren, im Irrtum sein, sich vertun.

[2]**slip,** *s.* 1. der Schein, Abschnitt, (*coll.*) Zettel, das Stückchen Papier; 2. (*Hort.*) der Ableger, Setzling, das Pfropfreis; der Schößling; – **of a girl,** schmächtiges *or* unscheinbares junges Mädchen.

[3]**slip,** *s.* (*Pottery*) der Schlicker, geschlemmet Tonmasse.

slip|-carriage, *s.* (*Railw.*) der Abhängewagen. **--cover,** *s.* die Schutzhülle, der Schutzdeckel (*on books*), Schonbezug (*on furniture*). **--knot,** *s.* der Schleifknoten, Laufknoten. **--on,** *s.* (*coll.*) der Pulli, die Schlupfjacke.

slipper ['slipə], *s.* 1. der Pantoffel, Hausschuh; 2. Hemmschuh (*for cart*).

slipperiness ['slipərinis], *s.* 1. die Glattheit; Schlüpfrigkeit; 2. (*fig.*) Unzuverlässigkeit. **slippery,** *adj.* 1. glatt, schlüpfrig, glitschig; 2. (*fig.*) (*of a p.*) geschmeidig, aalglatt, unzuverlässig; (*of circumstances*) unsicher, zweifelhaft, heikel. **slippy,** *adj.* 1. (*coll.*) schlüpfrig, glitschig; 2. (*coll.*) fix, schnell; **look –,** sich beeilen.

slip|-ring, *s.* das Schleifrad. **--road,** *s.* die Umgehungsstraße. **--rope,** *s.* (*Naut.*) das Schlipptau, Springtau. **-shod,** *adj.* (*fig.*) nachlässig, unordentlich, liederlich, schlampig. **-stream,** *s.* (*Av.*) die Propellerbö, der Schraubenstrahl. **--up,** *s.* (*coll.*) der Schnitzer, Flüchtigkeitsfehler. **-way,** *s.* (*Shipb.*) der Stapel, die Helling.

slit [slit], **1.** *irr.v.t.* (auf)schlitzen, aufschneiden, spalten, ritzen. **2.** *irr.v.i.* reißen, einen Riß bekommen. **3.** *s.* der Schlitz, Spalt, die Spalte, Ritze; (*Mil.*) – **trench,** der Deckungsgraben. **slit-eyed,** *adj.* schlitzäugig.

slither ['sliðə], *v.i.* (*coll.*) rutschen, (aus)gleiten.

sliver ['slivə], **1.** *s.* 1. der Splitter, Span; 2. (*Weav.*) Kammzug. **2.** *v.t.* zerspalten, abspalten. **3.** *v.i.* sich spalten.

slob [slɔb], *s.* (*sl.*) grober Flegel, der Grobian, Rüpel.

slobber ['slɔbə], **1.** *v.i.* geifern, sabbern; (*coll.*) – **over her,** sie abknutschen. **2.** *v.t.* begeifern. **3.** *s.* 1. der Geifer, Sabber; 2. (*fig.*) die Salbaderei. **slobbery,** *adj.* 1. geifernd, sabbernd; 2. (*fig.*) salbadernd, gefühlsduselig.

sloe [slou], *s.* die Schlehe, der Schwarzdorn, Schlehdorn.

slog [slɔg], **1.** *v.t.* (*coll.*) heftig schlagen. **2.** *v.i.* (*coll.*) (*oft.* – **away** or **on**) schuften, sich placken; mühsam vorwärtskommen. **3.** *s.* 1. wuchtiger Schlag; 2. (*fig.*) die Plackerei.

slogan ['slougən], *s.* 1. das Schlagwort, der Werbespruch; (*Pol.*) Wahlspruch, die Losung; 2. (*Scots*) der Schlachtruf.

slogger ['slɔgə], *s.* (*coll.*) 1. tüchtiger Schläger; 2. (*fig.*) das Arbeitstier.

sloid [slɔid], *s.* der Handfertigkeitsunterricht.

sloop [slu:p], *s.* die Schaluppe; Korvette, das Geleitschiff.

[1]**slop** [slɔp], *s.* (*sl.*) der Polyp.

[2]**slop, 1.** *s.* 1. (*oft. pl.*) das Spülicht, Spülwasser; *see also* [1]**slops**; **make a –,** Flüssigkeit verschütten, eine Pfütze machen; 2. (*fig., sing. only*) der Kitsch. **2.** *v.t.* verschütten. **3.** *v.i.* 1. (*usu.* – **over**) überfließen, überschwappen; 2. (*fig., coll.*) – **over,** schwärmen für. **slop-basin,** *s.* 1. der Spülnapf; 2. die Schale zum Ausleeren der Teetassen.

slope [sloup], **1.** *s.* der (Ab)hang, das Gefälle, die Steigung, Neigung; (*Fort.*) Böschung; (*Geol.*) Senke; (*Tech.*) Abdachung, Schräge, Gehre; (*Math.*) der Richtungskoeffizient; **on the –,** schräg, schief; abschüssig (*as ground*); (*Mil.*) **at the –,** übergenommen (*of rifle*); **steep –,** der Steilhang; **windward –,** die Luvseite. **2.** *v.i.* sich neigen *or* senken, abfallen (*as ground*); schräg sein *or* abgehen; (*sl.*) – **off,** sich davonmachen *or* aus dem Staub machen, abhauen. **3.** *v.t.* (*Fort.*) (ab)böschen; abdachen, abschrägen; (*Mil.*) – **arms!** Gewehr über! **sloping,** *adj.* schräg, abgeschrägt, geneigt; ansteigend, abfallend, abschüssig.

slop-pail, *s.* der Toiletteneimer.

sloppiness ['slɔpinis], *s.* 1. die Nässe, Matsche, der Matsch; 2. (*coll., fig.*) die Schlampigkeit; 3. Gefühlsduselei, Rührseligkeit. **sloppy,** *adj.* 1. naß, matschig, wässerig, lappig, schwabbelig; 2. (*coll., fig.*) nachlässig, schlampig, unordentlich; 3. rührselig, weichlich, kitschig.

[1]**slops** [slɔps], *pl.* das Schmutzwasser, Abwasser.

[2]**slops,** *pl.* 1. (*sl.*) fertige Kleider (*pl.*), die Konfektionskleidung; (*Naut.*) das Bettzeug; 2. weite Hose.

slosh [slɔʃ], **1.** *s. See* **slush. 2.** *v.i.* (*coll.*) panschen, schwappen. **3.** *v.t.* 1. verschütten; 2. (*sl.*) schlagen, hauen. **sloshed,** *adj.* (*sl.*) sternhagelvoll.

[1]**slot** [slɔt], *s.* die Fährte, Spur (*of deer*).

[2]**slot,** *s.* (*dial.*) der Riegel, das Querholz.

[3]**slot, 1.** *s.* 1. der Schlitz(einwurf) (*of vending machine*); 2. Einschnitt, die Kerbe, Ritze, Spalte, Vertiefung, Nut(e). **2.** *v.t.* auskerben, nuten.

sloth [slouθ], *s.* 1. die Faulheit, Trägheit; 2. (*Zool.*) das Faultier. **slothful,** *adj.* träge, faul. **slothfulness,** *s.* die Trägheit, Faulheit.

slot-machine, *s.* der Spielautomat, (Waren)automat. **slotted wing,** *s.* (*Av.*) der Spaltflügel. **slotting-machine,** *s.* die Nutenstanzmaschine.

slouch [slautʃ], **1.** *s.* 1. latschiger *or* schleppender Gang, schlottrige *or* schlaffe Haltung; 2. (*sl.*) der Schlendrian. **2.** *v.i.* 1. herabhängen (*of hat*); 2. sich schlaff halten, latschen; – **about,** umherschlendern. **slouch-hat,** *s.* der Schlapphut.

[1]**slough** [slau], *s.* die Pfütze, sumpfige Stelle, der Morast; – **of despond,** hoffnungslose Verzweiflung.

[2]**slough** [slʌf], **1.** *s.* abgestreifte *or* abgeworfene Haut (*of animals*); der Schorf (*of a wound*). **2.** *v.i.* sich häuten (*of animals*); – **off,** sich ablösen. **3.** *v.t.* 1. abwerfen (*skin*); 2. (*fig.*) (*also* – **off**) aufgeben, ablegen, abstreifen. **sloughy** [-i], *adj.* schorfig.

Slovak ['slouvæk], **1.** *s.* der Slowake (die Slowakin). **2.** *adj.* slowakisch. **Slovakia** [-'vækiə], *s.* die Slowakei. **Slovakian,** *see* **Slovak.**

sloven ['slʌvən], *s.* die Schlampe, Schlumpe, Schmutzliese; der Schmutzfink, Liederjahn.

Slovene ['slouvi:n], **1.** *s.* der Slowene (die Slowenin). **2.** *adj.* slowenisch. **Slovenia** [-'vi:njə], *s.* Slowenien (*n.*). **Slovenian,** *see* **Slovene.**

slovenliness ['slʌvənlinis], *s.* die Schlampigkeit, Unordentlichkeit, Nachlässigkeit. **slovenly,** *adj.* unordentlich, schlampig, liederlich, nachlässig.

slow [slou], **1.** *adj.* 1. langsam; – **and** or **but sure,** langsam aber sicher; – **train,** der Personenzug, (*coll.*) Bummelzug; **my watch is –,** meine Uhr geht nach; **be – to do** or **in doing,** nur langsam *or* widerwillig tun; **be – to take offence,** es nicht leicht übelnehmen; – **to wrath,** geduldig, (*B.*) langsam zum Zorn; 2. (*Mus.*) getragen; (*Mil.*) – **march,** langsames Marschtempo; 3. (*fig.*) säumig, (nach)lässig; **be – in arriving,** spät *or* unpünktlich ankommen; – **of payment,** nachlässig im Bezahlen; 4. langweilig, langwierig, uninteressant, ermüdend, öde; 5. (*Comm.*) flau, träg(e) (*business*); 6. schleichend (*fever*); 7. allmählich (*growth*); 8. schwerfällig, stumpfsinnig, dumm (*of a p.*); (*coll.*) ***be – on the uptake,*** schwer von Begriff sein, eine lange Leitung haben; – ***of apprehension,*** schwach von Begriff, begriffsstutzig; ***be – of speech,*** eine schwere Zunge haben. **2.** *v.i.* (*usu.* – ***down*** or ***up***) langsamer fahren, sich verlangsamen; langsamer werden, nachlassen. **3.** *v.t.* (*usu.* – ***down***) 1. verlangsamen, langsamer fahren lassen; 2. verringern, verzögern, hinziehen.

slow|coach, *s.* (*coll.*) langsamer Mensch, der Trödelfritz. **--combustion stove,** *s.* der Dauerbrandofen. **--down,** *s.* (*coll.*) die Verlangsamung.

slowly ['slouli], *adv. See* **slow.**

slow|-match, *s.* (*Artil.*) die Lunte. **--motion,** *adj.* Zeitlupen–.

slowness ['slounis], *s.* 1. die Langsamkeit, Trägheit, Schwerfälligkeit, Dummheit, Langwierigkeit, Öde; 2. das Nachgehen (*of a watch etc.*).

slow|-witted, *adj.* schwer von Begriff, begriffsstutzig. **-worm,** *s.* (*Zool.*) die Blindschleiche.

sloyd, *see* **sloid.**

slub [slʌb], **1.** *s.* das Vorgespinst. **2.** *v.t.* grob vorspinnen. **slubber,** *s.* die Vorspinnmaschine.

sludge [slʌdʒ], *s.* der Matsch, Schlamm, Schlick; (*Tech.*) Rückstand, Bodensatz.

slue, *see* **2slew.**

1slug [slʌg], **1.** *s.* die Wegschnecke. **2.** *v.i.* (*obs.*) faulenzen, träge sein.

2slug, *s.* 1. der Metallklumpen, das Metallstück; der Posten, grober *or* grobes Schrot; 2. die Flintenkugel; 3. (*Typ.*) Reglette, der Zeilensatz, Zeilenguß.

3slug, 1. *v.t.* (*sl.*) in die Fresse hauen. **2.** *s.* (*sl.*) der Schlag.

slug-abed ['slʌgəbəd], *s.* (*coll.*) der (die) Langschläfer(in).

sluggard ['slʌgəd], **1.** *s.* der Faulpelz. **2.** *adj.* faul.

sluggish ['slʌgiʃ], *adj.* 1. träge, schwerfällig; 2. langsam fließend; (*Dye.*) – ***vat,*** ermüdete Küpe; 3. (*Comm.*) flau. **sluggishness,** *s.* die Trägheit, Schwerfälligkeit, Langsamkeit.

sluice [slu:s], **1.** *s.* 1. die Schleuse, das Siel, Schütz, (Stau)wehr; 2. der Abflußkanal, Abflußgraben; 3. (*Min.*) die Waschrinne. **2.** *v.t.* 1. ablassen, (durch eine Schleuse) abfließen lassen (*water*), das Wasser ablassen (*Gen.*) (*a pond etc.*); 2. begießen, überschwemmen, (aus)spülen; 3. (*Min.*) waschen (*ore*).

slum [slʌm], **1.** *s.* schmutziges Hintergäßchen *or* Haus; *pl.* das Elendsviertel, Armenviertel. **2.** *v.i.* (*only in*) ***go slumming,*** die Elendsviertel besuchen.

slumber ['slʌmbə], **1.** *s.* (*oft. pl.*) ruhiger Schlaf, der Schlummer. **2.** *v.i.* schlummern. **3.** *v.t.* – ***away,*** verschlummern. **slumb(e)rous,** *adj.* schläfrig; einschläfernd.

slum-clearance, *s.* die Städtesanierung, Umsiedlung der Einwohner aus Elendsvierteln.

slummock ['slʌmək], *v.i.* (*coll.*) sich schlaff *or* schlotterig halten *or* bewegen.

slump [slʌmp], **1.** *v.i.* 1. hinplumpsen, plötzlich umfallen *or* hinfallen; 2. (*Comm.*) plötzlich sinken, stürzen. **2.** *s.* der (Preis)sturz, die Baisse; Wirtschaftskrise, (Geschäfts)stockung, der Tiefstand, schlechte Konjunktur.

slung [slʌŋ], *imperf., p.p. of* **sling.**

slunk [slʌŋk], *imperf., p.p. of* **slink.**

slur [slə:], **1.** *s.* 1. der Schandfleck, Vorwurf, Tadel; ***cast a – on,*** Schande machen (*Dat.*), Abbruch tun (*Dat.*), in ein schlechtes Licht bringen, verunglimpfen; 2. (*Mus.*) die Bindung, der Bindebogen, das Bindungszeichen; 3. (*Typ.*) die Verschmierung, der Schmitz. **2.** *v.t.* 1. undeutlich aussprechen, verschlucken (*words etc.*); – ***one's words,*** undeutlich sprechen, nuscheln; 2. (*Mus.*) binden; 3. (*fig.*) verwischen, verschmelzen; 4. (*fig.*) – ***over,*** (hastig) hinweggehen über (*Acc.*).

slush [slʌʃ], *s.* 1. der Schlamm, Matsch; Schneematsch; (*Geol.*) das Schlammeis; 2. (*Tech.*) die Schmiere; 3. (*fig.*) der Schund, Kitsch; die Salbaderei, gefühlsduseliges Geschwätz. **slushy,** *adj.* 1. schlammig, matschig; 2. (*fig.*) gefühlsduselig.

slut [slʌt], *s.* die Schlumpe, Schlampe. **sluttish,** *adj.* schlampig, liederlich, unordentlich, schmutzig.

sly [slai], *adj.* schlau, listig, verschlagen, hinterhältig; (*coll.*) schelmisch, schalkhaft, verschmitzt; ***on the –,*** verstohlen, insgeheim, im Geheimen. **slyboots,** *pl.* (*sing. constr.*) der Schlauberger, Pfiffikus. **slyness,** *s.* die Schlauheit, Verschlagenheit.

1smack [smæk], **1.** *s.* 1. (leichter) (Bei)geschmack; 2. der Anstrich, Anflug, die Spur. **2.** *v.i.* schmecken (*also fig.*); (*fig.*) klingen, riechen (*of,* nach).

2smack, 1. *s.* 1. der Schlag, Schmatz; Klatsch, Klaps; (*coll.*) – ***in the eye,*** der Schlag ins Gesicht *or* Kontor; (*coll.*) ***have a – at,*** sich versuchen in (*Dat.*) *or* an (*Dat.*); 2. das Schmatzen, Klatschen; 3. (*coll.*) der Schmatz (*a kiss*). **2.** *v.t.* einen Klaps geben (*Dat.*), schlagen, klapsen; – ***one's lips,*** mit den Lippen schmatzen; – ***the whip,*** mit der Peitsche knallen. **3.** *int.* patsch! klatsch! plauz! **4.** *adv.* (*coll.*) direkt, gerade, bums.

3smack, *s.* (*Naut.*) die Schmack(e).

smacker ['smækə], *s.* 1. (*coll.*) der Schmatz, schmatzender Kuß; 2. (*sl.*) das Pfund (*money*), (*Am.*) der Dollar. **smacking, 1.** *adj.* heftig, frisch (*of a breeze*). **2.** *s.* die Tracht Prügel.

small [smɔ:l], **1.** *adj.* (*size*) klein, (*number*) gering, niedrig, (*extent, degree*) gering(fügig), unbedeutend, armselig, dürftig; – ***blame to him,*** er ist wenig zu tadeln, er hat ganz recht; (*Typ.*) – ***cap(ital)s,*** Kapitälchen (*pl.*); – ***change,*** das Kleingeld; (*sl. fig.*) die Lappalie, Kleinigkeit; – ***coal,*** die Schmiedekohle; – ***farmer,*** der Kleinbauer; – ***fry,*** (*coll.*) kleines Volk, Kinder, (die) Kleinen (*pl.*); (*sl.*) unbedeutende Menschen, kleine Fische; – ***hand,*** gewöhnliche Schreibschrift; – ***hours,*** frühe Morgenstunden; ***a – matter,*** eine Kleinigkeit, geringfügige S.; – ***trader*** or ***tradesman,*** der Kleinhändler, Einzelhändler; – ***wares,*** Kurzwaren (*pl.*); ***in a – way,*** bescheiden; (*coll.*) – ***wonder,*** das nimmt kaum wunder; ***feel –,*** sich schämen; zerknirscht sein; ***make him feel –,*** ihn beschämen. **2.** *adv.* ***sing –,*** kleinlaut sein, klein beigeben; ***think – of,*** herabsehen auf (*Acc.*). **3.** *s.* 1. schmaler *or* dünner Teil; – ***of the back,*** das Kreuz; 2. *pl.* (*coll.*) die Leibwäsche, Unterwäsche.

small|-arms, *pl.* Handwaffen (*pl.*). – **beer,** *s.* 1. (*obs.*) das Dünnbier; 2. (*coll.*) Kleinigkeiten (*pl.*), unbedeutende P. *or* S.; ***think no – of o.s.,*** sich nicht wenig einbilden. **--clothes,** *pl.* (*Hist.*) Kniehosen, Beinkleider (*pl.*). **-holder,** *s.* der Kleinbauer. **-holding,** *s.* der Kleinlandbesitz.

smallish ['smɔ:liʃ], *adj.* ziemlich *or* etwas klein.

small|-minded, *adj.* engstirnig, borniert, kleinlich. **--mindedness,** *s.* die Engstirnigkeit, Borniertheit, Kleinlichkeit.

smallness ['smɔ:lnis], *s.* 1. die Kleinheit, Geringfügigkeit; 2. (*fig.*) Kleinlichkeit.

small|pox, *s.* die Pocken, Blattern (*pl.*). **--scale,** *adj.* (*fig.*) in kleinen Rahmen; – ***map,*** die Großraumkarte. **--talk,** *s.* das Geplauder, leichte Plauderei. **--time,** *adj.* (*coll.*) unbedeutend, Schmalspur–.

smalt [smɔ:lt], *s.* 1. die Schmalte, Smalte, das Kobaltglas; 2. Schmelzblau.

smaragd [smæ'rægd], *s.* der Smaragd.

smarmy ['smɑ:mi], *adj.* (*coll.*) kriecherisch; gefühlsduselig.

smart [smɑ:t], **1.** *adj.* 1. (*appearance*) schick, fesch, forsch, schneidig, flott, elegant, gepflegt, modisch; – ***set,*** elegante Welt; 2. (*as a blow*) heftig, kräftig, tüchtig, hart, derb, scharf, (*of pain*) stechend, schneidend, beißend; 3. (*of a p.*) schlagfertig, witzig, naseweis, geschickt, gerissen; 4. (*of manner, movement*) frisch, munter, flink, fix, lebendig, lebhaft, rührig. **2.** *s.* der Schmerz. **3.** *v.i.* 1.

schmerzen, weh(e)tun, brennen (*as a wound*); 2. (Schmerzen) leiden; (*fig.*) – ***for***, büßen.

smart aleck [–'ælik], *s.* (*coll.*) der Naseweis, Schlaumeier, Schlauberger, Besserwisser, Neunmalkluger, Klugschnacker.

smarten [smɑ:tn], **1.** *v.t.* 1. – ***the pace***, der Schritt beschleunigen; 2. (*usu.* – ***up***) herausputzen, zurechtmachen. **2.** *v.i.* – ***up***, sich zurechtmachen *or* aufputzen. **smart-money,** *s.* das Reugeld, Schmerzensgeld. **smartness,** *s.* 1. die Klugheit, Aufgewecktheit; 2. Eleganz, der Schick, Schneid.

smash [smæʃ], **1.** *v.t.* 1. zerschlagen, in Stücke schlagen, zerschmettern, zertrümmern, zerbrechen; 2. vernichten(d schlagen) (*opponent*), (*coll.*) fertigmachen, (*Comm.*) bankrott machen; 3. (*Tenn.*) schmettern (*ball*). **2.** *v.i.* 1. zusammenbrechen, zerbrechen, zersplittern, zerschmettert werden; 2. (*Comm.*) *see* ***go*** –; 3. stürzen (***against***, gegen; ***into***, in (*Acc.*)); – ***into each other***, zusammenstoßen. **3.** *s.* 1. das Zerschmettern, Zertrümmern; (*coll.*) ***all to*** –, in tausend Stücken; 2. der Aufprall, Schlag, Krach (*also fig.*); 3. (*fig.*) (*Comm.*) Bankrott, Zusammenbruch; (*coll.*) ***go*** –, bankrott werden *or* gehen, Bankrott machen; 4. (*Motor. etc.*) der Zusammenstoß; 5. (*Tenn.*) Schmetterschlag, Schmetterball.

smash-and-grab raid, *s.* der Schaufenstereinbruch. **smasher,** *s.* (*sl.*) flotter Käfer (*girl*), (*of a th.*) das Mordsding, die Wucht, tolle S. **smash hit,** *s.* (*sl.*) der Bombenerfolg. **smashing,** *adj.* 1. heftig (*blow*), vernichtend (*defeat*); 2. (*sl.*) überwältigend, hinreißend (*success etc.*), Klasse, prima, enorm, famos.

smattering ['smætəriŋ], *s.* oberflächliche Kenntnis (***of***, von).

smear [smiə], **1.** *v.t.* 1. einschmieren, einfetten, einreiben; 2. beschmutzen, besudeln, beschmieren (*a th.*) (***with***, mit); 3. auftragen, schmieren (*grease etc.*) (***on***, auf (*Acc.*)); 4. verwischen, verschmieren (*as writing*); 5. (*fig.*) beflecken, besudeln. **2.** *v.i.* schmieren, sich verwischen. **3.** *s.* 1. der Schmutzfleck, Fettfleck; – ***of grease***, leichte *or* dünne Fettschicht; 2. (*Med.*) der Abstrich. **smeary** ['smiəri], *adj.* schmierig, beschmiert, verschmiert.

smell [smel], **1.** *s.* 1. der Geruchssinn; 2. Geruch, Duft; ***a – of gas***, der Gasgeruch; 3. (*fig.*) der Anstrich, Anflug (***of***, von). **2.** *irr.v.t.* riechen; riechen an (*Dat.*), beriechen; (*fig.*) – ***out***, herausfinden, auffinden, aufspüren; (*coll.*) – ***a rat***, Lunte riechen. **3.** *irr.v.i.* 1. riechen (***at***, an (*Dat.*); ***of***, nach) (*also fig.*), duften (***of***, nach); – ***of the lamp***, nach Gelehrsamkeit riechen; 2. stinken, muffig *or* übel riechen; ***his breath –s***, er riecht aus dem Mund. **smeller,** *s.* (*sl.*) der Riecher, Riechkolben. **smelling,** *s.* das Riechen; ***--bottle***, das Riechfläschchen; ***--salts***, das Riechsalz. **smelly,** *adj.* übelriechend; muffig.

[1]**smelt** [smelt], *imperf., p.p. of* **smell.**

[2]**smelt,** *s.* (*Ichth.*) der Stint.

[3]**smelt,** *v.t.* (*Tech.*) schmelzen; – ***down***, einschmelzen. **smelter,** *s.* 1. der Schmelzarbeiter; 2. die Schmelzhütte. **smelting,** *s.* die Verhüttung; ***--furnace***, der Schmelzofen.

smilax ['smailæks], *s.* (*Bot.*) die Stechwinde.

smile [smail], **1.** *s.* das Lächeln; ***give a*** –, lächeln; – ***of contempt***, verächtliches Lächeln; ***with a*** –, lächelnd. **2.** *v.i.* lächeln; (*coll.*) ***come up smiling***, den Kopf nicht hängen lassen; – ***at***, zulächeln (*Dat.*), anlächeln (*a p.*); lächeln über (*Acc.*) (*a p. or th.*); (*fig.*) belächeln (*a th.*); – (***up***)***on***, zulächeln (*Dat.*), gnädig *or* hold sein (*Dat.*) (*a p.*); – ***through one's tears***, unter Tränen lächeln. **3.** *v.t.* durch Lächeln ausdrücken; – ***acknowledgement***, lächelnd anerkennen; – ***consent***, zustimmend lächeln; – ***away*** or ***off***, durch Lächeln vertreiben, hinweglächeln. **smiling,** *adj.* 1. lächelnd; 2. (*fig.*) günstig, freundlich, heiter.

smirch [smə:tʃ], **1.** *v.t.* (*usu. fig.*) beschmutzen, beschmieren, besudeln, in den Schmutz ziehen *or* treten. **2.** *s.* 1. der (Schmutz)fleck; 2. (*fig.*) Schandfleck.

smirk [smə:k], **1.** *s.* das Schmunzeln, geziertes Lächeln. **2.** *v.i.* schmunzeln, geziert lächeln.

smite [smait], **1.** *irr.v.t.* 1. (*Poet.*) schlagen; (*obs.*) erschlagen, niederstrecken, hinstrecken; 2. (*usu. pass.*) (*fig.*) ergreifen, packen, quälen, peinigen, plagen, (*B.*) strafen, züchtigen; ***his conscience –s him***, das Gewissen peinigt *or* plagt ihn; ***be smitten with***, befallen *or* gepackt *or* ergriffen *or* getroffen werden von; entflammt *or* hingerissen *or* verzehrt werden von; (*coll.*) verliebt sein in (*Acc.*). **2.** *irr.v.i.* (*Poet.*) – ***upon***, schlagen auf *or* an (*Acc.*), treffen.

smith [smiθ], *s.* der Schmied.

smither(een)s [smiðə'ri:nz, 'smiðəz], *pl.* (*coll.*) (*only in*) ***to*** –, in (tausend) Stücke.

smithery ['smiðəri], *s.* das Schmiedehandwerk, die Schmiedearbeit. **smithy** ['smiði], *s.* die Schmiede.

smitten [smitn], *p.p. of* **smite.**

smock [smɔk], **1.** *s.* (*also* ***--frock***) der Arbeitskittel, Spielkittel, Schmutzkittel. **2.** *v.t.* fälteln, smoken. **smocking,** *s.* der Faltenbesatz, die Smokarbeit.

smog [smɔg], *s.* (*coll.*) der Rauchnebel, die Dunstglocke.

smokable ['smoukəbl], *adj.* rauchbar.

smoke [smouk], **1.** *v.i.* 1. rauchen; qualmen, blaken (*as a fire*); 2. dampfen (***with***, von); 3. (Pfeife *or* Zigarre *or* Zigarette) rauchen; (*coll.*) – ***like a chimney***, wie ein Schlot qualmen. **2.** *v.t.* 1. rauchen (*tobacco, pipe etc.*); 2. räuchern (*hams etc.*); ***be –d***, Rauch annehmen (*as milk etc.*); 3. durch Rauch schwärzen, verrußen; 4. – ***out***, ausräuchern (*a room etc.*), (*fig.*) austreiben (*enemy etc.*). **3.** *s.* 1. der Rauch, Qualm, Dunst; (*coll.*) ***like*** –, im Handumdrehen, wie der Wind; (*Prov.*) ***no – without fire***, wo Rauch ist, muß auch Feuer sein; ***go up*** or ***end in*** –, zu Wasser werden, sich im Sand verlaufen; 2. das Rauchen; etwas Rauchbares; die Zigarettenpause; (*coll.*) ***want a*** –, einen Zug tun wollen.

smoke|-ball, *s. See* **--bomb. --black,** *s.* die Rußschwärze, der Kienruß. **--bomb,** *s.* die Rauchbombe, Rauchgranate, Nebelgranate. **--box,** *s.* der Rauchkasten. **--candle,** *s.* die Rauchkerze, Nebelkerze. **--consumer,** *s.* der Rauchverzehrer.

smoked [smoukt], **smoke-dried,** *adj.* geräuchert. **smokeless,** *adj.* rauchlos. **smoker,** *s.* 1. der Raucher; ***–'s cough***, der Raucherhusten; ***heavy*** –, starker Raucher; 2. der (Fleisch)räucherer; 3. (*Railw.*) (*coll.*) das Raucherabteil.

smoke|-room, *s. See* **smoking-room. --screen,** *s.* (*Mil.*) der Nebelschleier, die Nebelwand, Einnebelung; (*fig.*) das Täuschungsmanöver. **–stack,** *s.* der Schornstein, Rauchfang. **--stained,** *adj.* verräuchert, verrußt.

smokiness ['smoukinis], *s.* die Rauchigkeit, Dunstigkeit.

smoking ['smoukiŋ], *s.* 1. das Rauchen; ***no*** –, Rauchen verboten! 2. das Räuchern. **smoking|-cap,** *s.* das Rauchkäppchen. **--car(riage), --compartment,** *s.* das Raucherabteil. **--concert,** *s.* das Konzert bei dem geraucht werden darf. **--jacket,** *s.* der Hausrock. **--mixture,** *s.* die Tabakmischung. **--room,** *s.* das Herrenzimmer, Rauchzimmer.

smoky ['smouki], *adj.* 1. rauchig, voll Rauch, dunstig; – ***chimney***, qualmender Kamin; – ***city***, rauchige *or* dunstige Stadt; – ***fire***, rauchendes Feuer; 2. rauchartig, rauchgrau.

smolder, (*Am.*) *see* **smoulder.**

smooch [smu:tʃ], *v.i.* (*sl.*) sich abknutschen.

smooth [smu:ð], **1.** *adj.* 1. glatt, eben; ruhig (*as sea*), geglättet (*hair*); (*Cul.*) ***beat to a – consistency***, glattrühren; – ***crossing***, ruhige Überfahrt; 2. (*fig.*) weich, sanft, angenehm, geschmeidig; ***make*** –, glätten, ebnen (***for***, *Dat.*); 3. reibungslos, gleichmäßig, ruhig (*as movement*), fließend, geschliffen (*style etc.*); 4. glattzüngig, gleisnerisch, schmeichlerisch (*of a p.*); 5. lieblich (*of wine*). **2.** *v.t.* glätten, (ein)ebnen; ausglätten, glatt machen, plätten; – ***the way for***, den Weg bahnen *or* ebnen (*Dat.*); – ***away***, entfernen, beseitigen, ausmerzen (*difficulties*); – ***down***, glattstreichen; (*fig.*) beruhigen, schlichten; – ***out***, ausbügeln, ausplätten (*creases* etc.), *see also* – ***away***; (*fig.*) – ***over,*** beschönigen, bemänteln. **3.** *v.i.* (*also* – ***down***) 1. sich glätten; 2. (*fig.*) sich beruhigen.

smooth|-bore, *attrib. adj.* mit glattem Lauf (*firearm*). **-faced,** *adj.* 1. bartlos, glattrasiert; 2. (*fig.*) glattzüngig, katzenfreundlich. **--haired,** *adj.* glatthaarig.

smoothing ['smu:ðiŋ], *s.* das Glätten, Schlichten, (*Carp.*) Glatthobeln; *--iron,* das Plätteisen, Bügeleisen; *--plane,* der Schlichthobel. **smoothness,** *s.* 1. die Glätte, Ebenheit; 2. Geschmeidigkeit, Sanftheit, der Schliff; 3. die Glattzüngigkeit. **smooth-tongued,** *adj.* glattzüngig, schmeichlerisch.

smote [smout], *imperf. of* **smite.**

smother ['smʌðə], **1.** *v.t.* 1. ersticken; 2. (*fig.*) dämpfen; unterdrücken (*rage etc.*); 3. (*coll.*) verbergen, verdecken; bedecken, überhäufen (***in, with,*** mit); 4. (*Footb.*) festhalten. **2.** *v.i.* (*rare*) ersticken.

smoulder ['smouldə], *v.i.* schwelen; glimmen (*also fig.*).

smudge [smʌdʒ], **1.** *s.* der Schmutzfleck, Schmierfleck. **2.** *v.t.* beschmutzen, beschmieren, verschmieren; (*fig.*) beflecken, besudeln (*good name*). **3.** *v.i.* schmieren, klecksen. **smudged, smudgy,** *adj.* verschmiert, beschmutzt, verwischt, klecksig, schmierig.

smug [smʌg], **1.** *adj.* 1. (*obs.*) schmuck, geschniegelt; 2. selbstgefällig, spießig. **2.** *s.* (*Univ. sl.*) der Streber, Büffler.

smuggle [smʌgl], *v.t., v.i.* schmuggeln. **smuggler,** *s.* der Schmuggler, Schleichhändler. **smuggling,** *s.* das Schmuggeln, der Schmuggel, Schleichhandel.

smut [smʌt], **1.** *s.* 1. der Ruß(fleck), Schmutzfleck; 2. (*Bot.*) Brand; 3. (*fig.*) die Zote, Zoten (*pl.*), die Schlüpfrigkeit; ***talk*** –, zoten. **2.** *v.t.* 1. beschmutzen; 2. (*Bot.*) brandig machen. **3.** *v.i.* (*Bot.*) brandig werden.

smutch [smʌtʃ], **1.** *v.t.* beschmutzen, besudeln. **2.** *s.* 1. die Rußflocke, der Schmutz(fleck); 2. (*Bot.*) (Getreide)brand.

smuttiness ['smʌtinis], *s.* 1. die Schmutzigkeit; Rußigkeit; 2. (*fig.*) Schlüpfrigkeit, Zotigkeit. **smutty,** *adj.* 1. schmutzig, rußig; 2. (*Bot.*) brandig; 3. (*fig.*) schmutzig, zotig, schlüpfrig.

snack [snæk], *s.* 1. der Imbiß; 2. (*coll.*) ***go –s,*** teilen. **snack-bar,** *s.* die Imbißstube.

snaffle [snæfl], **1.** *s.* die Trense. **2.** *v.t.* 1. die Trense anlegen (*Dat.*) (*a horse*); 2. (*sl.*) stibitzen, klauen.

snag [snæg], **1.** *s.* 1. der Aststumpf, Baumstumpf, Knorren, Knoten; im Fluß treibender Baumstamm; 2. (*Am.*) der Raffzahn; 3. (*coll.*) unerwartetes Hindernis, der Haken; (*coll.*) ***there is a –*** (***in it***), da ist ein Haken dabei. **2.** *v.t.* 1. (*Am.*) von treibenden Baumstämmen säubern (*a river*); gegen einen Baumstamm treiben (*a boat*); 2. (*coll.*) zuschanden machen, durchkreuzen; zuvorkommen (*Dat.*).

snail [sneil], *s.* die Schnecke; ***at a –'s pace,*** im Schneckentempo. **snail|-shell,** *s.* das Schneckenhaus. **--wheel,** *s.* (*Horol.*) das Schneckenrad.

snake [sneik], **1.** *s.* die Schlange; – ***in the grass,*** geheimer Feind; verborgene Gefahr. **2.** *v.i.* (*or usu. v.t.* – ***one's way***) sich schlängeln.

snake|-bird, *s. See* **wryneck.** **--bite,** *s.* der Schlangenbiß. **--charmer,** *s.* der Schlangenbändiger. **-skin,** *s.* die Schlangenhaut, das Schlangenleder. **-stone,** *s.* der Ammonit, das Ammonshorn.

snaky ['sneiki], *adj.* 1. schlangenartig, Schlangen–; 2. (*fig.*) sich windend *or* schlängelnd, geschlängelt; 3. schlangengleich, hinterlistig, hinterhältig.

snap [snæp], **1.** *s.* 1. das Schnappen, Knallen, Knacken, Klicken; 2. der Biß (*of dog, fish etc.*); ***make a – at,*** schnappen nach; ***not worth a –,*** wertlos; 3. der Knacks, Sprung, Bruch; 4. Knall (*of a whip*); 5. das Schnappschloß, der Schnapper (*of bracelets etc.*); 6. (*coll.*) Schneid, Schwung, die Lebhaftigkeit; 7. plötzlicher Kälteeinbruch; 8. (*coll.*) der Schnappschuß, das Foto, die Momentaufnahme. **2.** *v.t.* 1. haschen, erschnappen, ergreifen; – ***his head*** or ***nose off,*** ihn anschnauzen *or* grob *or* barsch anfahren; – ***to,*** zuschnappen lassen, zuklappen; – ***up,*** aufschnappen, erhaschen; aufkaufen, sich (*Dat.*) sichern *or* sicherstellen; (*coll.*) anschnauzen, grob anfahren (*a p.*); 2. zerbrechen, durchbrechen, entzweibrechen; – ***off,*** abbrechen; 3. – ***one's fingers,*** mit den Fingern schnippen *or* schnalzen; – ***one's fingers at,*** verhöhnen, verächtlich *or* mit einem Achselzucken abtun; ein Schnippchen schlagen (*Dat.*); 4. (*Phot.*) knipsen. **3.** *v.i.* 1. schnappen, beißen (***at,*** nach); zuschnappen (*as a dog*); – ***at,*** anfahren, anschnauzen (*a p.*), gierig erschnappen, hastig greifen nach (*a th.*); – ***at the chance,*** die Gelegenheit beim Schopf packen; 2. abbrechen, zerbrechen, zerspringen; 3. (*of sound*) klicken, knallen, knacken; 4. – ***to,*** ins Schloß fallen, zuschnappen (*as a door*); 5. (*coll.*) – ***to it!*** nun aber los! (*coll.*) – ***out of it!*** hör auf damit! **4.** *attrib. adj.* (*Pol.*) – ***division,*** – ***vote,*** unerwartete Abstimmung; – ***fastening,*** der Schnappverschluß; – ***shot,*** der Schnellschuß; *see also* **snapshot.**

snap|dragon, *s.* (*Bot.*) das Löwenmaul. **--fastener,** *s.* der Druckknopf. **--hook,** *s.* der Karabinerhaken. **--lock,** *s.* das Schnappschloß.

snappish ['snæpiʃ], *adj.* bissig (*as dogs*); (*fig.*) auffahrend, schnippisch, reizbar, barsch. **snappishness,** *s.* die Bissigkeit; Heftigkeit, Barschheit, schnippisches Wesen. **snappy,** *adj.* (*coll.*) lebhaft, lebendig, schwungvoll, energisch, forsch, zackig, flott, schneidig, schick; (*sl.*) ***make it –!*** mach ein bißchen fix!

snapshot ['snæpʃɔt], **1.** *s.* (*Phot.*) der Schnappschuß, die Momentaufnahme. **2.** *v.t., v.i. See* **snap, 2.** 4.

snare [snɛə], **1.** *s.* 1. die Schlinge (*also fig.*), der Fallstrick, (*fig.*) die Falle; (*fig.*) ***lay*** or ***set a – for him,*** ihm eine Falle stellen; 2. die Schnarrsaite, Sangsaite (*of a drum*). **2.** *v.t.* mit einer Schlinge fangen; (*fig.*) eine Falle stellen (*Dat.*), verstricken, umstricken. **snarer,** *s.* der Schlingenleger.

[1]**snarl** [snɑ:l], **1.** *s.* das Knurren. **2.** *v.i.* knurren (*as a dog*) (*also fig.*); (*fig.*) brummen, murren; – ***at,*** anknurren, anfauchen, bissig anfahren.

[2]**snarl,** **1.** *s.* der *or* das Knäuel; (*fig.*) die Verwickelung, das Gewirr. **2.** *v.t.* verwirren, verwickeln, verheddern. **3.** *v.i.* sich verwirren *or* verwickeln. **snarling-iron,** *s.* das Bossiereisen. **snarl-up,** *s.* (*coll.*) die Verkehrsstauung.

snatch [snætʃ], **1.** *s.* 1. das Haschen, Schnappen, Zugreifen; der Griff; (*coll.*) Raubüberfall; 2. das Bruchstück; ***in –es,*** ab und zu, hin und wieder, ruckweise; ***–es of a conversation,*** (unzusammenhängende) Brocken eines Gespräches; ***–es of sunshine,*** sonnige Augenblicke. **2.** *v.t.* 1. hastig ergreifen, erschnappen, erhaschen, erwischen, an sich reißen; entreißen (***from,*** *Dat.*); – ***away,*** wegraffen, entreißen (***from,*** *Dat.*); – ***a kiss,*** einen Kuß rauben; – ***up,*** aufraffen; 2. (*Spt.*) hochreißen (*weight*); 3. (*Am. sl.*) entführen, kidnappen. **3.** *v.i.* schnappen, greifen, haschen (***at,*** nach).

snead [sni:d], *s.* (*dial.*) der Sensengriff.

sneak [sni:k], **1.** *s.* der Schleicher, Kriecher; (*sl.*) die Petze, der (die) Angeber(in). **2.** *v.i.* 1. schleichen, kriechen; – ***about,*** herumschnüffeln; – ***away*** or ***off,*** sich fortschleichen; – ***up on,*** heranschleichen an (*Acc.*); 2. (*sl.*) angeben, petzen. **3.** *v.t.* (*sl.*) klauen, mausen, stibitzen. **sneakers,** *pl.* (*Am. sl.*) Turnschuhe (*pl.*). **sneaking,** *adj.* kriechend, schleichend, gemein; (*coll.*) – ***suspicion,*** heimlicher Verdacht. **sneak|-raid,** *s.* (*Av. coll.*) der Überraschungsangriff. **--thief,** *s.* (*coll.*) der Gelegenheitsdieb, Langfinger. **sneaky,** *adj.* (*coll.*) *see* **sneaking.**

sneer [sniə], **1.** *s.* das Hohnlächeln; der Spott, Hohn. **2.** *v.i.* spötteln, sich lustig machen, höhnisch lächeln, hämisch grinsen (***at,*** über (*Acc.*)); – ***at,*** bespötteln, verhöhnen. **sneering,** *adj.* höhnisch, spöttisch.

sneeze [sni:z], **1.** *s.* das Niesen. **2.** *v.i.* niesen; (*coll.*)

not to be –d at, nich zu verachten. **sneezewort,** *s.* (*Bot.*) die Sumpfgarbe, das Nieskraut.

snib [snib], (*Scots*) **1.** *s.* der Riegel. **2.** *v.t.* verriegeln; (*fig.*) fangen.

snick [snik], **1.** *s.* 1. der Einschnitt, die Kerbe; 2. (*Crick.*) leichter Schlag. **2.** *v.t.* 1. hacken, schneiden; 2. (*Crick.*) leicht anschlagen.

snicker ['snikə], **1.** *s.* das Kichern, Gekicher. **2.** *v.i.* 1. kichern; 2. wiehern (*of horses*).

snide [snaid], *adj.* herabwürdigend, schmälernd, nachteilig.

sniff [snif], **1.** *s.* 1. das Schnüffeln, Schnuppern; 2. schnüffelnder Atemzug; 3. (*fig.*) das Naserümpfen. **2.** *v.t.* 1. (*also* ***– in*** or ***– up***) durch die Nase einziehen; 2. beriechen, beschnuppern; 3. (*fig.*) ausschnüffeln, wittern. **3.** *v.i.* 1. schnüffeln, schnuppern (***at,*** an (*Dat.*)); 2. (*fig.*) die Nase rümpfen (***at,*** über (*Acc.*)). **sniffy,** *adj.* 1. (*coll.*) übelriechend, muffig; 2. (*fig.*) verächtlich, hochfahrend; 3. schnüfflig (*as a cold*).

snigger ['snigə], *see* **snicker.**

snip [snip], **1.** *v.t.* schnippeln, schneiden; ***– off,*** abschneiden. **2.** *s.* 1. der Schnitt; 2. das Stückchen, der *or* das Schnipsel, Schnitzel; 3. (*coll.*) der Schneider; 4. (*sl.*) leichte *or* sichere S.; 5. *pl.* (*Tech.*) die Blechschere.

snipe [snaip], **1.** *s.* (*Orn.*) die Schnepfe (*Gallinago*); ***common*** (*Am.* ***European***) **–,** die Bekassine (*G. gallinago*); ***jack –,*** die Zwergschnepfe (*Lymnocryptes minimus*). **2.** *v.i.* 1. Schnepfen schießen; 2. (*Mil.*) aus dem Hinterhalt schießen. **sniper,** *s.* (*Mil.*) der Heckenschütze, Scharfschütze.

snippet ['snipit], *s.* der *or* das Schnipsel, Schnitzel; (*fig. usu. pl.*) das Bruckstück. **snipping,** *s.* (*usu. pl.*) *see* **snippet.**

snitch [snitʃ], **1.** *v.i.* (*Am.*) (*sl.*) angeben, petzen, pfeifen. **2.** *v.t.* (*sl.*) klauen, mausen, stibitzen. **3.** *s.* 1. (*sl.*) der Riecher, Rüssel; 2. (*Am. sl.*) der (die) Angeber(in), die Petze.

snivel [snivl], **1.** *v.i.* 1. schnüffeln, aus der Nase triefen; 2. (*fig.*) wimmern, schluchzen, heulen, plärren, wehleidig tun; 3. scheinheilig tun, heucheln. **2.** *s.* der Nasenschleim, Rotz. **snivelling, 1.** *s.* 1. das Gejammer, Gewimmer, Geplärr; 2. scheinheiliges Getue. **2.** *adj.* 1. rotznasig, triefnasig; 2. (*fig.*) weinerlich, wehleidig.

snob [snɔb], *s.* der Snob. **snobbery,** *s.* der Snobbismus, das Protzentum, die Vornehmtuerei. **snobbish,** *adj.* snobistisch, vornehmtuend, aufgeblasen, hochnäsig. **snobbishness,** *s. See* **snobbery.**

snood [snu:d], *s.* (*Scots*) das Stirnband, die Haarschleife.

[1]**snook** [snu:k], *s.* (*sl.*) ***cock a –,*** eine lange Nase machen (*at, Dat.*).

[2]**snook,** *s.* (*Ichth.*) der Seehecht.

snooker ['snu:kə], *s.* (eine Art) Billardspiel (*n.*).

snoop [snu:p], (*sl.*) *v.i.* (*also* ***– around***) herumschnüffeln. **snooper,** *s.* der Schnüffler. **snooping,** *s.* die Schnüffelei.

snoot [snu:t], (*sl.*) *s.* die Fresse, Fratze, Schnute. **snooty,** *adj.* (*sl.*) großkotzig, batzig, patzig, schnoddrig.

snooze [snu:z], **1.** *s.* das Schläfchen, Nickerchen. **2.** *v.i.* dösen, ein Schläfchen *or* Nickerchen machen.

snore [snɔ:], **1.** *s.* das Schnarchen. **2.** *v.i.* schnarchen.

snort [snɔ:t], **1.** *v.i.* schnauben, schnaufen. **2.** *s.* das Schnauben, Schnaufen. **snorter,** *s.* 1. Schnaufende(r); 2. (*coll.*) grober Schlag, der Nasenstüber; 3. tolle S., das Mordsding. **snorting,** *adj.* (*coll.*) heftig, ungeheuer.

snot [snɔt], *s.* (*vulg.*) der Rotz; ***– rag,*** die Rotzfahne. **snotty, 1.** *adj.* (*vulg.*) 1. rotzig; 2. (*fig.*) lumpig, gemein. **2.** *s.* (*sl.*) der Seekadett.

snout [snaut], *s.* 1. die Schnauze, der Rüssel; (*sl.*) Schnorchel, Riecher; 2. (*fig.*) die Tülle, das Mundstück, der Schnabel (*of vessel etc.*).

snow [snou], **1.** *s.* 1. der Schnee; Schneefall, Schneefälle (*pl.*); die Schneedecke, Schneemassen (*pl.*); Schneeverhältnisse (*pl.*); 2. (*sl.*) der Koks. **2.** *v. imp.* schneien; (*fig.*) fallen, hageln. **3.** *v.t.* (*usu. pass.*) ***– in*** or ***up,*** einschneien, zuschneien; ***– under,*** mit Schnee bedecken; (*usu. fig. and usu. pass.*) überlasten, überschütten, überhäufen (***with,*** mit), ersticken (in (*Dat.*)).

snow|ball, 1. *s.* der Schneeball. **2.** *v.t.* mit Schneebällen bewerfen. **3.** *v.i.* 1. Schneebälle werfen, schneeballen; 2. (*fig.*) lawinenartig anwachsen. **–balling,** *s.* die Schneeballschlacht. **–berry,** *s.* (*Bot.*) die Schneebeere. **–bird,** *s.* (*Am.*) (*Orn.*) Nordamerikanischer Schneefink (*Junco hyemalis*). **–blind,** *adj.* schneeblind. **–bound,** *adj.* eingeschneit. **–bunting** *s.* (*Orn.*) die Schneeammer (*Plectrophenax nivalis*). **--capped, --clad,** *adj.* schneebedeckt. **–drift,** *s.* die Schneewehe, das Schneetreiben. **–drop,** *s.* (*Bot.*) das Schneeglöckchen. **–fall,** *s.* der Schneefall, die Schneemenge. **–flake,** *s.* die Schneeflocke. **--goggles,** *pl.* die Schneebrille. **--line,** *s.* die Schneegrenze. **–man,** *s.* der Schneemann; (*coll.*) ***abominable –,*** der Schneemensch. **--plough,** *s.* der Schneepflug. **–shoe, 1.** *s.* der Schneeschuh. **2.** *v.i.* Schneeschuh laufen. **–slip,** *s.* die (Schnee)lawine. **–storm,** *s.* der Schneesturm. **--white,** *adj.* schneeweiß. **Snow-White,** *s.* Schneewittchen (*n.*). **snowy,** *adj.* schneebedeckt, Schnee–, schneeweiß; schneeig.

snub [snʌb], **1.** *v.t.* 1. kurz abweisen, derb zurückweisen, herunterputzen, die kalte Schulter zeigen (*Dat.*); 2. (*Naut.*) ruckartig straffziehen *or* stoppen. **2.** *s.* derbe Zurechtweisung *or* Abfertigung, der Verweis; ***meet with a –,*** kurz abgefertigt werden, abblitzen.

snub|-nose, *s.* die Stumpfnase, Stupsnase. **--nosed,** *adj.* stumpfnasig, stupsnasig.

[1]**snuff** [snʌf], **1.** *s.* der Schnupftabak; (*coll.*) ***be up to –,*** schlau *or* pfiffig sein, mit allen Hunden gehetzt sein, die Kniffe kennen; ***take –,*** schnupfen; ***pinch of –,*** die Prise Schnupftabak. **2.** *v.i.* schnüffeln, schnuppern. **3.** *v.t.* 1. (*also* ***– up***) (durch die Nase) einatmen *or* einziehen; 2. beschnüffeln, beschnuppern.

[2]**snuff, 1.** *s.* die Schnuppe (*of a candle*). **2.** *v.t.* putzen, schneuzen (*a candle*); ***– out,*** auslöschen; (*fig.*) ersticken (*opposition etc.*). **3.** *v.i.* (*coll.*) ***– it*** or ***out,*** abkratzen, ins Gras beißen.

snuff|box, *s.* die Schnupftabak(s)dose, Tabatiere. **--coloured,** *adj.* tabakfarben, gelbbraun.

snuffers ['snʌfəz], *pl.* die Lichtputzschere, Schneuze.

snuffle [snʌfl], **1.** *v.i.* 1. schnaufen, schnüffeln, schnuppern; 2. durch die Nase sprechen, näseln. **2.** *s.* 1. das Schnaufen, Schnüffeln; 2. Näseln; 3. *pl.* (*coll.*) chronischer Schnupfen.

snuff|-taker, *s.* der (Tabak)schnupfer. **--taking,** *s.* das Schnupfen. **snuffy,** *adj.* nach Schnupftabak riechend, mit Schnupftabak beschmutzt; (*coll.*) verschnupft, verärgert.

snug [snʌg], **1.** *adj.* 1. eng(anliegend); 2. behaglich, gemütlich, traulich; 3. gut eingerichtet, wohnlich bequem; geschützt, geborgen, intim, verborgen, versteckt; (*coll.*) ***as – as a bug in a rug,*** wie die Made in Speck; 4. (*Naut.*) seetüchtig. **2.** *v.i.* ***– down,*** es sich (*Dat.*) behaglich machen. **3.** *v.t.* (*Naut.*) ***– down,*** auf Sturm vorbereiten. **snuggery,** *s.* (*coll.*) behagliche *or* gemütliche Bude.

snuggle [snʌgl], **1.** *v.i.* sich (an)schmiegen (***up to,*** an (*Acc.*)); ***– up,*** sich einhüllen *or* kuscheln; ***– down,*** sich behaglich niederlegen. **2.** *v.t.* herzen, an sich drücken *or* schmiegen.

snugness ['snʌgnis], *s.* die Behaglichkeit.

so [sou], **1.** *adv.* so, dermaßen, auf diese Art, in der Weise; (*exclamation*) so (sehr), überaus; (*as substitute for preceding clause*) auch; ***she is tired and – is he,*** sie ist müde und er auch; ***be – kind as to come,*** sei so gut und komme; ***– be it,*** so sei es; ***– beautiful a day,*** ein so schöner Tag; ***even –,*** selbst dann, selbst in dem Falle; ***– far – good,*** so weit so gut; ***– far as I know,*** soweit ich weiß; ***– help me God,*** so wahr mir Gott helfe; ***and – forth,*** see ***and – on; just –,*** ganz recht; (*coll.*) ***just – –,*** nichts Besonderes; (*coll.*) ***– long!*** auf Wiedersehen!

not –, nicht doch, nicht; ***not – rich as,*** nicht so reich wie; ***and – on,*** und so weiter; ***quite –,*** see ***just –***; ***is that –?*** wirklich? ***she is – pretty,*** sie ist sehr *or* überaus hübsch. **2.** *conj.* so (*oft. with inversion*) also, daher, deshalb, folglich; (*obs.*) wenn *or* wofern nur; ***as a man thinks, – will he act,*** wie ein Mensch denkt, so handelt er; ***it rained all day, – we stayed indoors,*** es regnete den ganzen Tag, daher blieben wir zuhause; (*coll.*) – ***it is true?*** also ist es doch wahr? (*coll.*) ***I won't, – there,*** ich will es nicht, nun weißt du's *or* da hast du's; (*coll.*) – ***what?*** na und? und wenn schon! ***why –?*** wieso? warum? **3.** *pron., adv.* es; ***I think –,*** ich glaube (es); ***I said –,*** das sagte ich; – ***saying,*** bei diesen Worten; – ***to speak,*** sozusagen; ***I suppose –,*** vermutlich, ich glaube schon. **4.** (*in stock phrases*) – ***as to*** (*inf.*), so daß, damit, um zu; – ***long as,*** wenn nur, vorausgesetzt daß; – ***much,*** lauter, (eben)soviel (*nonsense etc.*); ***not – much as,*** nicht einmal; – ***much for that,*** damit basta; – ***much the better,*** um so besser; (*coll.*) ***ever – much,*** sehr; – ***that,*** so daß; ***if –,*** wenn ja, wenn dies der Fall ist; ***or –,*** etwa, ungefähr; ***the more – as,*** um so mehr als.

soak [souk], **1.** *v.t.* 1. einweichen, durchtränken, durchfeuchten; – ***up,*** aufsaugen, einsaugen; (*fig.*) ***be –ed in,*** durchtränkt werden von; 2. (auf)quellen (*dried fruit etc.*); 3. durchweichen, durchnässen (*with rain*); (*fig.*) – ***o.s. in,*** sich vertiefen in (*Acc.*); 4. (*sl.*) schröpfen (*a p.*). **2.** *v.i.* 1. (durch)sickern; – ***into,*** einsickern in (*Acc.*); (*fig.*) – ***in,*** eingehen, eindringen, einsinken; – ***through,*** (durch)sickern durch; 2. wässern, weich werden, weichen; 3. (*vulg.*) saufen. **3.** *s.* 1. das Einweichen, Durchweichen; die Weiche; ***give a th. a –,*** etwas einweichen; ***lie in –,*** in der Weiche sein; 2. (*sl.*) die Sauferei, der Suff; (*sl.*) ***on the –,*** beim Saufen; 3. (*of a p.*) der Säufer.

soakage ['soukidʒ], *s.* 1. das Durchsickern; 2. Sickerwasser, durchgesickerte Flüssigkeit. **soaker,** *s.* 1. (*coll.*) der Regenguß; 2. (*of a p.*) Säufer. **soaking, 1.** *s.* das Durchnässen, Einweichen; ***get a –,*** durch und durch naß werden. **2.** *adv.* (*only in*) – ***wet,*** triefend *or* durch und durch naß.

so-and-so ['souənsou], *s.* der *or* die Soundso.

soap [soup], **1.** *s.* die Seife; ***soft –,*** die Schmierseife; (*coll.*) die Schmeichelei; ***cake of –,*** das Stück Seife. **2.** *v.t.* (ein)seifen.

soap|-boiler, *s.* der Seifensieder. **–-boiling,** *s.* die Seifensiederei. **–-box, 1.** *s.* 1. die Seifenkiste; 2. (*coll.*) Rednerbühne. **2.** *attrib. adj.* (*coll.*) Seifenkisten–. **–-bubble,** *s.* die Seifenblase. **–-dish,** *s.* der Seifennapf. **–-flakes,** *pl.* Seifenflocken (*pl.*). **– opera,** *s.* (*T.V., Rad.*) rührseliges Hör– *or* Fernsehspiel. **–-powder,** *s.* das Seifenpulver. **–stone,** *s.* der Speckstein, Seifenstein. **–-suds,** *pl.* die Seifenlauge, das Seifenwasser. **–-works,** *pl.* die Seifenseiderei. **–wort,** *s.* (*Bot.*) das Seifenkraut.

soapy ['soupi], *adj.* 1. seifig, Seifen–, seifenartig; 2. (*fig.*) schmeichlerisch, salbungsvoll.

soar [sɔː], *v.i.* 1. hochfliegen, (auf)steigen; 2. (*Av.*) segeln, segelfliegen; 3. (*fig.*) sich aufschwingen *or* emporschwingen; 4. schweben; 5. in die Höhe gehen (*prices*). **soaring, 1.** *adj.* (*oft. fig.*) hochfliegend, emporstrebend, erhaben; – ***flight,*** der Segelflug. **2.** *s.* das Segeln, Segelfliegen.

sob [sɔb], **1.** *v.i.* schluchzen. **2.** *v.t.* (*usu.* – ***out***) schluchzend *or* unter Schluchzen äußern. **3.** *s.* das Schluchzen; (*sl.*) – ***stuff,*** rührselige *or* gefühlsduselige Geschichte, die Schnulze, Geschichte mit 'Wein'-Zwang.

sober ['soubə], **1.** *adj.* 1. nüchtern (*also fig.*); ***as – as a judge,*** stocknüchtern; ***sleep o.s. –,*** seinen Rausch ausschlafen; 2. (*fig.*) mäßig, gesetzt, gelassen, ausgeglichen; 3. feierlich, ernsthaft; ***in – earnest,*** allen Ernstes, in vollem Ernste; 4. schlicht, matt (*as colour*). **2.** *v.t.* 1. (*also coll.* – ***up***) nüchtern machen; 2. (*fig.*) (*also* – ***down***) ernüchtern, beruhigen, dämpfen. **3.** *v.i.* 1. (*also* – ***up***) nüchtern werden; 2. (*fig.*) (*also* – ***down***) sich ernüchtern *or* beruhigen.

sober|-minded, *adj.* gelassen, besonnen, ruhig. **–-mindedness,** *s.* die Gelassenheit, Besonnenheit.

soberness ['soubənis], **sobriety** [–'braiəti], *s.* 1. die Nüchternheit; 2. Mäßigkeit, Gelassenheit, Besonnenheit; 3. Ernsthaftigkeit, Schlichtheit, der Ernst.

sobriquet ['soubrikei], *s.* der Spitzname, Beiname.

soc [sɔk], *s.* (*Hist.*) 1. die Gerichtsbarkeit; 2. der Gerichtsbezirk. **socage** [–idʒ], *s.* (*Hist.*) der Frondienst(besitz), das Bauernlehen.

so-called, *adj.* sogenannt, angeblich.

soccer ['sɔkə], *s.* (*coll.*) das Fußballspiel.

sociability [souʃə'biliti], *s.* die Geselligkeit. **sociable** ['souʃəbl], **1.** *adj.* 1. gesellig, umgänglich; 2. freundschaftlich, gemütlich, ungezwungen. **2.** *s.* 1. (*obs.*) der Phaeton; 2. zweisitziges Dreirad; 3. die Causeuse (*sofa*); 4. (*Am.*) gesellige Zusammenkunft. **sociableness,** *s. See* **sociability.**

social ['souʃəl], **1.** *adj.* 1. gesellig lebend (*of animals*); 2. gesellschaftlich, umgänglich; – ***evening,*** geselliger Abend; – ***gathering,*** geselliges Beisammensein; 3. gesellschaftlich, Gesellschafts–, sozial; – ***class,*** die (Gesellschafts)klasse, Gesellschaftsschicht, der Stand; – ***climber,*** der Streber, Emporkömmling; – ***contract,*** der Gesellschaftsvertrag; – ***environment,*** gesellschaftliche Umwelt, das Milieu; – ***evil,*** die Prostitution; – ***intercourse,*** gesellschaftlicher Verkehr; – ***organization,*** die Gesellschaftsstruktur; – ***problem,*** soziale Frage; – ***science,*** die Sozialwissenschaft; – ***studies,*** die Gesellschaftskunde; 4. Sozial–; – ***insurance,*** see – ***security***; – ***legislation,*** die Sozialgesetzgebung; – ***security,*** die Sozialversicherung; – ***service,*** der Gemeinschaftsdienst, die Wohlfahrt; – ***services,*** soziale Einrichtungen; – ***work,*** die Fürsorge(arbeit); – ***worker,*** der (die) Fürsorger(in); 5. (*Am. Pol.*) – ***democrat,*** der Sozialdemokrat. **2.** *s.* (*coll.*) gesellige Zusammenkunft.

socialism ['souʃəlizm], *s.* der Sozialismus. **socialist, 1.** *s.* der (die) Sozialist(in). **2.** *or* **socialistic** [–'listik], *adj.* sozialistisch. **socialite,** *s.* (*Am. coll.*) Prominente(r). **socialization** [–ai'zeiʃən], *s.* die Sozialisierung, Vergesellschaftung, Verstaatlichung. **socialize,** *v.t.* sozialisieren, vergesellschaften, verstaatlichen.

society [sə'saiiti], *s.* 1. die Gesellschaft, (Volks)gemeinschaft; ***fashionable –,*** die Hautevolee, vornehme *or* elegante Welt; ***in –,*** in der guten Gesellschaft; ***go into –,*** in Gesellschaft gehen; 2. der Verkehr, Umgang (***with,*** mit); 3. (*Comm.*) die Gesellschaft, der Verein, Verband; ***building –,*** die Baugenossenschaft; ***co-operative –,*** die Konsumgenossenschaft, der Konsumverein; ***Society of Friends,*** die Gesellschaft der Freunde, Quäker (*pl.*); ***Society of Jesus,*** die Gesellschaft Jesu, der Jesuitenorden.

sociological [sousiə'lɔdʒikl], *adj.* soziologisch. **sociologist** [–si'ɔlədʒist], *s.* der Soziologe. **sociology** [–si'ɔlədʒi], *s.* die Soziologie, Gesellschaftslehre.

[1]**sock** [sɔk], *s.* die Socke, (kurzer) Strumpf; die Einlegesohle; (*coll.*) ***pull one's –s up,*** sich zusammennehmen; (*sl.*) ***put a – in it!*** halt's Maul!

[2]**sock, 1.** *s.* (*sl.*) der Schlag; (*sl.*) ***give him –s,*** ihn verhauen *or* durchhauen; (*sl.*) ***have a – at it,*** es versuchen *or* probieren. **2.** *v.t.* hauen, prügeln.

socket ['sɔkit], *s.* 1. die (Steck)hülse, Buchse, Muffe, der Flansch, Rohransatz; 2. (*Elec.*) die Fassung (*of lamp*), Steckdose, der Steckkontakt (*in wall*); 3. (*Anat.*) die Höhle (*of eyes*); (Gelenk)pfanne (*of bones*). **socket-joint,** *s.* (*Anat.*) das Kugelgelenk.

socle [sɔkl], *s.* (*Archit.*) der Sockel, Untersatz.

[1]**sod** [sɔd], **1.** *s.* der Rasen, die Rasendecke, das Rasenstück; ***under the –,*** im Grabe, unter dem grünen Rasen. **2.** *v.t.* mit Rasen bedecken.

[2]**sod,** *s.* (*vulg.*) der Luder, Schweinehund, Saukerl.

soda ['soudə], *s.* 1. das Natriumkarbonat, kohlensaures Natrium, das *or* die Soda; ***bicarbonate of –,*** doppeltkohlensaures Natrium, das Natron;

***caustic* –,** das Natriumhydroxyd, Ätznatron; 2. *See* **soda-water.**

soda-fountain, *s.* der Mineralwasserausschank.

sodality [so'dæliti], *s.* (*R.C.*) karitative Bruderschaft.

soda|-lye, *s.* die Natronlauge. **–-water,** *s.* das Sodawasser, Mineralwasser, Selterswasser, der Sprudel.

sodden [sɔdn], *adj.* 1. durchnäßt, durchweicht; 2. unausgebacken, klitschig, schleifig, streifig (*as bread*); 3. (*fig.*) aufgedunsen, aufgeschwemmt; 4. (*sl.*) versoffen.

sodium ['soudiəm], *s.* das Natrium; *– **carbonate,*** see **soda**; *– **hydroxide,*** see ***caustic soda***; *– **nitrate,*** das Chilesalpeter, Natriumnitrat, salpetrigsaures Natron; *– **sulphate,*** das Glaubersalz, schwefelsaures Natron *or* Natrium; *– **sulphide,*** das Schwefelnatrium; *– **sulphite,*** das Natriumsulfit, schwefligsaures Natrium.

sodomite ['sɔdəmait], *s.* der (die) Sodomit(in). **sodomy,** *s.* widernatürliche Unzucht, die Sodomie.

soever [sou'evə], *adv. suff.* auch *or* nur immer.

sofa ['soufə], *s.* das Sofa. **sofa-bed,** *s.* die Bettcouch.

soffit ['sɔfit], *s.* (*Archit.*) die Gewölbedecke, Laibung, innere Gewölbefläche; (*esp. Theat.*) die Soffitte.

soft [sɔft], *adj.* 1. weich, geschmeidig, nachgiebig; *– **coal,*** die Weichkohle, bituminöse Kohle; *– **currency,*** weiche Währung; *– **drink,*** alkoholfreies Getränk; *– **goods,*** Tuchwaren, Webwaren, Textilien (*pl.*); *– **hat,*** schlapper Hut; *– **iron,*** das Weicheisen; *– **palate,*** weicher Gaumen; (*Ichth.*) *– **roe,*** die Milch; *– **soap,*** die Schmierseife; (*coll.*) Schmeichelei; *– **solder,*** das Schnellot, Weichlot, Zinnlot; *– **water,*** kalkfreies *or* weiches Wasser; (*Crick.*) *– **wicket,*** aufgeweichtes Spielfeld; 2. (*fig.*) leise, gedämpft, leicht, sacht, sanft, zart, mild, angenehm, zärtlich, liebenswürdig; *– **answer,*** milde Antwort; *– **colour,*** weiche Farbe; *– **heart,*** mitleidiges *or* mitfühlendes Herz; (*Mus.*) *– **pedal,*** das Pianopedal; (*fig. coll.*) ***apply the – pedal,*** einen Dämpfer aufsetzen; einen sanften Ton anschlagen, kleinlaut werden; 3. (*coll.*) leicht; *– **option,*** leichte Alternative, die leichtere der gebotenen Möglichkeiten; 4. (*coll.*) einfältig; *– **in the head,*** blöde; 5. (*sl.*) verliebt (*on,* in (*Acc.*)).

soften [sɔfn], **1.** *v.t.* 1. weich machen, erweichen; enthärten (*metal, water*); 2. rühren (*the heart*); 3. lindern (*pain*), mildern (*pain, colour etc.*); verschmelzen, abstufen, vertreiben (*colouring*); 4. (ab)schwächen, entkräften, verweichlichen; 5. (*Mil.*) *– **up,*** zermürben, sturmreif machen. **2.** *v.i.* 1. weich(er) *or* sanft(er) werden; 2. sich erweichen, sich mildern, sich verschmelzen (*as colours*); 3. sich erwärmen (*to,* für) (*as a p.*). **softener,** *s.* 1. das Enthärtungsmittel; 2. Linderungsmittel (*of pain*). **softening,** *s.* 1. das Weichwerden, die Erweichung; *– **of the brain,*** die Gehirnerweichung; 2. (*fig.*) die Nachgiebigkeit, Rührung.

soft|-eyed, *adj.* sanftäugig. **–-headed,** *adj.* einfältig, schwachköpfig. **–-hearted,** *adj.* weichherzig. **–-heartedness,** *s.* die Weichherzigkeit.

softly ['sɔftli], *adv.* weich, zart; leise, ruhig, sachte, sanft. **softness,** *s.* die Weichheit, Sanftheit, Sanftmut, Milde, Nachgiebigkeit, Weichlichkeit.

soft|-nosed, *adj.* zersprengend (*bullet*). **–-pedal,** *v.t.* (*coll.*) dämpfen, (ab)mildern. **–-soap,** *v.t.* (*a p.*) schmeicheln, Honig um den Mund schmieren (*Dat.*), beschwatzen. **–-spoken,** *adj.* leise sprechend; (*fig.*) sanft, friedlich. **–-voiced,** *adj.* mit sanfter Stimme.

softy ['sɔfti], *s.* (*coll.*) der Schwachkopf, Einfaltspinsel.

soggy ['sɔgi], *adj.* 1. feucht, naß, durchnäßt; 2. sumpfig (*land*); schleifig, klitschig (*baking*).

soho! [sou'hou], *int.* (*obs.*) holla!

soi-disant [swadi:'zɑ̃], *adj.* angeblich, sogenannt.

[1]**soil** [sɔil], *s.* der (Erd)boden, Grund, Acker, das Ackerland, die Erde; (*fig.*) Scholle; ***native –,*** heimatliche Erde *or* Scholle, das Heimatland; ***racy*** or ***redolent of the –,*** erdrüchig, bodenständig.

[2]**soil, 1.** *s.* 1. der Schmutz(fleck), Dreck; 2. Dünger, Dung; 3. Pfuhl, die Suhle. **2.** *v.t.* 1. beschmutzen, verunreinigen; 2. düngen (*fields*); 3. (*esp. fig.*) beflecken, besudeln; (*fig.*) *– **one's hands with,*** sich (*Dat.*) die Hände schmutzig machen mit. **3.** *v.t.* schmutzig *or* fleckig werden, schmutzen.

[3]**soil,** *v.t.* mit Grünfutter füttern (*cattle*). **soilage,** *s.* das Grünfutter.

soiled [sɔild], *adj.* 1. schmutzig, beschmutzt; 2. (*fig.*) befleckt, besudelt.

soil-pipe, *s.* das Abflußrohr (*of W.C.*).

soirée ['swa'rei], *s.* die Abendgesellschaft, Soiree.

sojourn ['sɔdʒə:n], **1.** *s.* der Aufenthalt, das Verweilen; der Aufenthaltsort. **2.** *v.i.* sich aufhalten, verweilen (***in, at,*** in *or* an (*Dat.*) (*a place*); ***with,*** bei (*a p.*)). **sojourner,** *s.* der Gast, Besucher, Fremde(r), Verweilende(r).

soke [souk], *s.* (*Hist.*) 1. die Gerichtsbarkeit; 2. der Gerichtsbezirk.

sol [sɔl], *s.* (*Mus.*) fünfter Ton der Tonleiter, das G.

solace ['sɔləs], **1.** *s.* der Trost, die Erquickung (***to,*** für; ***in,*** in (*Dat.*)), Erleichterung (***from,*** von). **2.** *v.t.* trösten; *– **o.s. with,*** sich trösten mit, Trost suchen in (*Dat.*).

solanum [so'leinəm], *s.* (*Bot.*) der Nachtschatten.

solar ['soulə], *adj.* Sonnen–; *– **eclipse,*** die Sonnenfinsternis; (*Anat.*) *– **plexus,*** der Solarplexus, das Sonnengeflecht; *– **system,*** das Sonnensystem. **solarize,** *v.t.* (*Phot.*) überbelichten.

solatium [so'leiʃiəm], *s.* (*Law*) das Schmerzensgeld, die Entschädigung, Vergütung.

sold [sould], *imperf., p.p. of* **sell.**

solder ['sɔldə], **1.** *s.* das Lot, Lötmetall, Lötmittel, Lötblei, die Lötmasse; ***hard –,*** das Hartlot, Schlaglot; ***soft –,*** das Schnellot, Weichlot, Zinnlot. **2.** *v.t.* löten. **soldering,** *s.* das Löten, die Lötung; ***–-flux,*** die Lötflüssigkeit; ***–-iron,*** der Lötkolben.

soldier ['souldʒə], **1.** *s.* der Soldat; ***play at –s,*** Soldat(en) spielen; *– **of fortune,*** der Glücksritter. **2.** *v.i.* als Soldat dienen, Soldat werden; (*coll.*) *– **on,*** sich hartnäckig *or* verbissen durchkämpfen, sich durchbeißen. **soldierlike, soldierly,** *adj.* soldatisch. **soldiery,** *s.* 1. das Militär, Soldaten (*pl.*); 2. der Soldatenhaufen, die Soldateska.

[1]**sole** [soul], *adj.* einzig, alleinig, Allein–; *– **agent,*** der Alleinvertreter; (*Comm.*) *– **bill,*** der Solawechsel; (*Law*) ***corporation –,*** der Einzelne als Rechtsträger; (*Law*) ***feme –,*** unverheiratete Frau; *– **heir,*** der Universalerbe; *– **owner,*** der Alleininhaber.

[2]**sole, 1.** *s.* 1. die (Fuß)sohle; 2. (Schuh)sohle; 3. (*Tech.*) Sohle, Grundfläche, Bodenfläche, der Boden. **2.** *v.t.* besohlen.

[3]**sole,** *s.* (*Ichth.*) die Seezunge.

solecism ['sɔlisizm], *s.* der Sprachfehler, Verstoß gegen das Sprachgefühl, Schnitzer; (*fig.*) Verstoß, die Ungehörigkeit, Ungeschicklichkeit. **solecistic** [–'sistik], *adj.* grammatisch falsch, fehlerhaft; ungehörig.

solely ['soulli], *adv.* nur, ausschließlich, (einzig und) allein.

solemn ['sɔləm], *adj.* 1. feierlich, weihevoll, erhaben; *– **declaration,*** feierliche Erklärung, bindende Aussage; 2. ernst, würdevoll, ehrwürdig; 3. (*Law*) formell; 4. gewichtig; *– **warning,*** eindringliche Warnung. **solemnity** [–'lemniti], *s.* 1. die Feierlichkeit; 2. (feierlicher) Ernst, würdevolles Aussehen; 3. (*Law*) die Formalität, Förmlichkeit; 4. (*usu. pl.*) feierliches Zeremoniell. **solemnize** [–mnaiz], *v.t.* feiern, feierlich begehen; *– **a marriage,*** eine Ehe feierlich vollziehen.

solenoid ['soulənɔid], *s.* (*Elec.*) das Solenoid, die Magnetspule.

sol-fa ['sɔl'fɑ:], **1.** *s.* (*Mus.*) die Solmisation. **2.** *v.i.* solfeggieren, solmisieren.

solfatara [sɔlfə'tɑ:rə], *s.* (*Geol.*) die Schwefeldampfquelle, Solfatare.

solfeggio [sɔl'fedʒiou], *s.* (*Mus.*) das Solfeggio, die Gesangsübung ohne Text.

solicit [sə'lisit], *v.t.* 1. bitten, angehen, ersuchen (*a p.*) (***for***, um); 2. (*as a prostitute etc.*) ansprechen, anhalten (*a p.*); 3. erbitten (*a th.*) (***of, from***, von); sich bewerben *or* sich bemühen um (*a th.*). **solicitation** [–'teiʃən], *s.* das Ansuchen, Ersuchen, dringende Bitte, die (Be)werbung, Aufforderung, das Ansprechen.

solicitor [sə'lisitə], *s.* (*Law*) der Anwalt, Rechtsbeistand, Sachwalter; ***Solicitor General***, zweiter Kronanwalt; (*Am.*) stellvertretender Justizminister.

solicitous [sə'lisitəs], *adj.* besorgt, bekümmert (***about, for, of***, um *or* wegen); bestrebt, eifrig bemüht (***to do***, zu tun). **solicitude** [–tju:d], *s.* die Sorge, Besorgtheit, Besorgnis, Beunruhigung (***about, for***, um).

solid ['sɔlid], **1.** *s.* 1. (*Phys.*) fester Körper; (*Geom.*) der Körper; 2. *pl.* feste Speise (*pl.*). **2.** *adj.* 1. fest (*also fig.*); dicht, starr, stark, kräftig, geballt; – ***food***, feste Nahrung; – ***fuel***, der Festkraftstoff; – ***lubricant***, die Starrschmiere; – ***meal***, nahrhafte Mahlzeit; 2. gediegen, stabil, kompakt, massiv; – ***oak***, massiveichen; – ***silver***, gediegenes Silber; (*Phys.*) – ***state***, fester Zustand; –***-state physics***, die Festkörperphysik; – ***tyre***, der Vollreifen; 3. körperlich, räumlich; (*Math.*) Raum–, Kubik–; – ***angle***, der Raumwinkel; – ***capacity***, der Raumgehalt, Kubikgehalt; – ***geometry***, die Raumgeometrie, Stereometrie; – ***measure***, das Raummaß, Kubikmaß; 4. (*Typ.*) – ***matter***, kompresser Satz; 5. voll; ***two – hours***, zwei volle *or* geschlagene Stunden; 6. (*fig.*) gründlich, zuverlässig (*of a p.*), (*Comm.*) kreditfähig, solid(e), reell (*of a p.*); 7. (*fig.*) triftig, gewichtig, handfest, stichhaltig (*of reasons etc.*); 8. (*coll.*) einmütig, einstimmig, geschlossen (*of a p.*); ***be – for***, sich einmütig entscheiden für; ***be –ly behind him***, geschlossen hinter ihm stehen. **3.** *adv.* (*coll.*) einmütig, einstimmig; ***vote –***, einmütig stimmen.

solidarity [sɔli'dæriti], *s.* die Solidarität, der Zusammenhalt, das Zusammengehörigkeitsgefühl.

solid|-drawn, *adj.* (nahtlos) gezogen (*as tubes*). **–-hoofed,** *adj.* einhufig.

solidification [sɔlidifi'keiʃən], *s.* die Erstarrung, Verdichtung, das Festwerden. **solidify** [–'lidifai], **1.** *v.t.* fest werden lassen, verfestigen, verdichten. **2.** *v.i.* fest werden, sich verdichten, erstarren. **solidity** [–'liditi], *s.* 1. die Festigkeit, Dichtheit, Dichtigkeit, Dichte; 2. (*Math.*) Körperlichkeit; 3. (*fig.*) Gründlichkeit; 4. (*Comm.*) Kreditfähigkeit, Zuverlässigkeit, Solidität. **solidness** ['sɔlidnis], *s. See* **solidity,** 3, 4.

solidungulate [sɔli'dʌŋgjuleit], **1.** *adj.* einhufig. **2.** *s.* der Einhufer.

soliloquize [sə'liləkwaiz], *v.i.* Selbstgespräche führen. **soliloquy** [–kwi], *s.* das Selbstgespräch, der Monolog.

soliped ['sɔliped], *s. See* **solidungulate.**

solipsism ['sɔlipsizm], *s.* (*Phil.*) der Solipsismus.

solitaire [sɔli'tɛə], *s.* 1. der Solitär, einzeln gefaßter Edelstein; 2. (*Cards*) das Solitär(spiel), die Patience.

solitariness ['sɔlitərinis], *s.* die Einsamkeit. **solitary** [–təri], **1.** *adj.* 1. einsam; 2. einzeln, Einzel–; – ***confinement***, die Einzelhaft; 3. einzig, alleinstehend, alleinig (*exception etc.*); 4. alleinlebend, einsiedlerisch, zurückgezogen (*of a p.*), einzeln lebend (*of animals*), alleinwachsend (*of plants*), abgelegen, verlassen (*of places*). **2.** *s.* der Einsiedler. **solitude** [–tju:d], *s.* 1. die Einsamkeit, Abgeschiedenheit; 2. (Ein)öde.

solmization [sɔlmi'zeiʃən], *s. See* **sol-fa, 1.**

solo ['soulou], **1.** *s.* (*pl.* **-s**) 1. das Solo(spiel), der Sologesang; 2. (*coll.*) (*also* – ***flight***) der Alleinflug. **2.** *adv.* allein; ***fly –***, einen Alleinflug machen. **soloist,** *s.* der (die) Solist(in).

Solomon ['sɔləmən], *s.* (*B.*) Salomon (*m.*).

solstice ['sɔlstis], *s.* die Sonnenwende. **solstitial** [–'stiʃəl], *adj.* Sonnenwend–.

solubility [sɔlju'biliti], *s.* 1. die Löslichkeit; 2. (*fig.*) Lösbarkeit. **soluble** ['sɔljubl], *adj.* 1. löslich; 2. (*fig.*) (auf)lösbar, erklärbar. **solution** [sə'l(j)u:ʃən], *s.* 1. die Lösung; (*Chem.*) (Auf)lösung; ***rubber –***, die Gummilösung; 2. (*fig.*) die Lösung, Erklärung (***of, to***, *Gen.*).

solvable ['sɔlvəbl], *adj.* (*fig.*) (auf)lösbar, erklärbar. **solve** [sɔlv], *v.t.* (auf)lösen; erklären, eine Lösung *or* Erklärung finden für, beheben.

solvency ['sɔlvənsi], *s.* (*Comm.*) die Zahlungsfähigkeit. **solvent, 1.** *adj.* 1. (*Chem.*) (auf)lösend; 2. (*Comm.*) zahlungsfähig. **2.** *s.* das Lösungsmittel, (*fig.*) Zersetzungsmittel.

somatic [so'mætik], *adj.* körperlich, physisch, leiblich; – ***cell***, die Somazelle. **somatology** [soumə'tɔlədʒi], *s.* die Körperkunde.

sombre ['sɔmbə], *adj.* 1. düster, dunkel; 2. (*fig.*) schwermütig, trüb. **sombreness,** *s.* die Düsterkeit, Trübheit.

sombrero [sɔm'brɛərou], *s.* der Sombrero.

some [sʌm, səm], **1.** *adj.* **(a)** (*before sing.*) 1. irgendein, irgendwelch; – ***day***, see ***at – time***; ***to – extent***, einigermaßen; ***at – time or other***, irgendeinmal, eines Tages; – ***time***, einige *or* eine beträchtliche Zeit; – ***time ago***, vor einiger Zeit; – ***little time***, etliche Zeit; – ***such***, ein solches *or* derartiges; ***in – way or other***, irgendwie; 2. etwas, ein wenig; – ***bread***, etwas Brot; – ***more***, noch etwas; 3. (*sl. emph.*) beträchtlich, bedeutend; – ***ability***, beträchtliche Anlagen. **(b)** (*before pl.*) 1. einige, ein paar, mehrere, (*emph.*) etliche, manche, ziemlich viele; – ***few***, einige wenige; (*sl.*) – ***hope!*** ausgeschlossen! aussichtslos! keinerlei Aussichten! ***for – years***, schon manches Jahr; 2. (*with num.*) etwa, ungefähr, gegen; – ***70 miles***, etwa *or* ungefähr *or* gegen 70 Meilen. **2.** *pron.* (*with sing.*) etwas, ein Teil von; (*with pl.*) einige.

some|body [–bədi], **1.** *pron.* irgendeiner, jemand. **2.** *s.* (*coll. emph.*) (*also pl.*) bedeutende Persönlichkeit. **–how,** *adv.* auf irgendeine Weise, irgendwie; – ***or other***, aus irgendeinem Grund. **–one,** *s. See* **–body.**

somersault ['sʌməsɔ:lt], **1.** *s.* der Purzelbaum, Salto, Luftsprung; ***turn a –***, einen Purzelbaum schlagen, einen Salto machen. **2.** *v.i. See* ***turn a –***; (*fig. of a th.*) sich überschlagen.

some|thing, 1. *s.* (irgend) etwas; – ***of a***, so etwas wie ein(e); ***a certain –***, ein gewisses Etwas; – ***new***, etwas Neues; – ***or other***, irgend etwas; (*coll.*) ***make – of***, sich (*Dat.*) zunutze machen, verwerten; ***or –***, oder so etwas; ***there is – in that***, es ist etwas daran *or* hat etwas für sich. **2.** *adv.* (*coll.*) 1. (*with pred. adj.*) ***the result was – awful***, die Folge war direkt erschreckend; ***he swears – shocking***, er flucht unheimlich; 2. (*coll.*) – ***like***, ungefähr, annähernd, so etwas wie; (*coll.*) ***that is – like a song***, das ist aber *or* wirklich ein (tolles) Lied; (*coll.*) ***that is – like***, das läßt sich hören *or* sehen, das lasse ich mir gefallen. **–time, 1.** *adv.* 1. (*usu. future*) eines Tages, irgendwann, irgendeinmal, zu irgendeinem Zeitpunkt; 2. (*obs.*) früher, ehemals, (der)einst; 3. *See* ***some time***. **2.** *adj.* ehemalig, früher, weiland. **–times,** *adv.* manchmal, zuweilen, bisweilen, dann und wann, gelegentlich; – ***here***, – ***there***, mal hier, mal da *or* dann wieder da. **–what, 1.** *adv.* etwas, ein wenig *or* bißchen, einigermaßen. **2.** *s.* (irgend)etwas; ***she is – about my age***, sie ist so ziemlich in meinem Alter; – ***the same size***, etwa derselben Größe. **–where,** *adv.* irgendwo(hin); – ***else***, anderswo(hin), sonstwo(hin), woanders(hin); (*coll. fig.*) – ***about***, um . . . herum, (so) etwa, annähernd.

somnambulate [sɔm'næmbjuleit], *v.i.* (*rare*) nachtwandeln, schlafwandeln. **somnambulism,** *s.* das Schlafwandeln, Nachtwandeln. **somnambulist,** *s.* der Nachtwandler, Schlafwandler. **somnambulistic** [–'listik], *adj.* nachtwandlerisch, schlafwandlerisch.

somniferous [sɔm'nifərəs], *adj.* schlafbringend, einschläfernd. **somniloquence** [–ləkwəns], *s.* das Schlafreden.

somnolence ['sɔmnələns], *s.* (*Med.*) die Schlafsucht; Schlaftrunkenheit, Schläfrigkeit. **somnolent,** *adj.* schläfrig, schlaftrunken.

son [sʌn], *s.* 1. der Sohn; – *and heir,* der Stammhalter; *every mother's* –, jedermann; – *of God,* der Sohn Gottes; – *of man,* der Menschensohn, Christus; 2. (*coll.*) (*as form of address to boy*) Junge; 3. (*fig.*) der Nachkomme, Abkomme, (*oft. pl.*) die Nachkommenschaft, Nachfolger (*pl.*); (*sl.*) – *of a gun,* der Teufelskerl.

sonancy ['sounənsi], *s.* (*Phonet.*) die Stimmhaftigkeit. **sonant,** 1. *adj.* stimmhaft. 2. *s.* stimmhafter Laut.

sonata [sə'nɑ:tə], *s.* die Sonate. **sonatina** [sɔnə'ti:nə], *s.* die Sonatine.

song [sɔŋ], *s.* 1. das Lied, der Gesang; *be in* (*full*) –, (laut) singen (*of birds*); *burst into* –, zu singen anfangen; *drinking* –, das Trinklied; (*coll.*) *for a* (*mere*) –, um einen Pappenstiel, spottbillig; – *of joy,* der Freudengesang; (*coll.*) *nothing to make a – about,* nicht des Aufhebens wert; (*coll.*) *make a – and dance about,* wunder was erzählen über (*Acc.*); (*coll.*) *plug a* –, ein Lied ewig wiederholen; (*coll.*) *the same old* –, das alte Geleier; 2. (lyrisches) Gedicht; *Song of Solomon* or *of Songs,* das Hohelied (Salomonis).

song|bird, *s.* der Singvogel. **–book,** *s.* das Gesangbuch, Liederbuch.

songster ['sɔŋstə], *s.* der Singvogel; (*rare*) Sänger, Dichter. **songstress** [–tris], *s.* die Sängerin.

song-thrush, *s.* die Singdrossel, Zippe.

sonic ['sɔnik], *adj.* Schall–; – *bang* or *boom,* der Überschall-Knall; – *barrier,* die Schallgrenze, Schallmauer; – *depth-finder,* das Echolot.

son-in-law, *s.* (*pl.* **sons-–**) der Schwiegersohn.

sonnet ['sɔnit], *s.* das Sonett. **sonneteer** [–'tiə], 1. *s.* der Sonettdichter. 2. *v.i.* Sonette dichten.

sonny ['sʌni], *s.* (*only in address*) Junge, Kleiner.

sonometer [sɔ'nɔmitə], *s.* der Schallmesser, Sonometer. **sonority** [–riti], *s.* 1. der (Wohl)klang, die (Ton)stärke; 2. Klangfülle, Schallfülle. **sonorous** ['sɔnərəs], *adj.* (voll)tönend, (wohl)klingend, klangvoll.

sonsy ['sɔnzi], *adj.* (*Scots*) drall, gesundheitstrotzend; (*esp. in*) – *lass,* dralle Dirne.

soon [su:n], *adv.* 1. bald; – *after(wards),* bald darauf; *as – as,* so bald als *or* wie (*as adv.*), sobald (*as conj.*); *as – as possible,* so bald *or* früh wie möglich; *we shall leave as – as he comes,* wir gehen sobald er kommt; 2. früh(zeitig); 3. schnell, unverzüglich, gern; (*just*) *as* – (. . . *as*), ebenso gern (. . . wie). **sooner,** *comp. adv.* 1. eher, früher; – *or later,* früher oder später; *no* – . . . *than,* kaum . . . als; *no – said than done,* gesagt, getan; *the – the better,* je früher desto besser; 2. schneller, lieber; *I would* – . . . *than* . . ., ich möchte lieber *or* ehe . . . als . . .. **soonest,** *sup. adv.* frühestens, schnellstens, nächstens.

soot [sut], 1. *s.* der Ruß, das *or* der Sott. 2. *v.t.* berußen.

sooth [su:θ], *s.* (*obs.*) die Wahrheit; *in* –, – *to say,* um die Wahrheit zu sagen, wahrhaftig, in der Tat, wirklich, wahrlich, fürwahr.

soothe [su:ð], *v.t.* besänftigen, beruhigen, beschwichtigen; mildern, lindern, stillen (*pain*).

soothfast ['su:θfɑ:st], *adj.* (*obs.*) treu, wahrhaft, verläßlich.

soothing ['su:ðiŋ], *adj.* besänftigend, lindernd, wohltuend.

sooth|say, *irr.v.i.* prophezeien, vorhersagen, wahrsagen, weissagen. **–sayer,** *s.* der (die) Wahrsager(in), Prophet(in). **–saying,** *s.* das Wahrsagen, die Prophezeiung, Vorhersagung.

sootiness ['sutinis], *s.* die Rußigkeit, Schwärze. **sooty,** *adj.* rußig, geschwärzt.

sop [sɔp], 1. *s.* 1. eingetunkter Bissen; 2. (*fig.*) das Beruhigungsmittel (*to,* für); (*coll.*) – *to Cerberus,* der Beschwichtigungsversuch, das Schmiergeld; *throw a – to,* (zu) beschwichtigen (suchen). 2. *v.t.* 1. eintunken, eintauchen; 2. durchnässen.

sophism ['sɔfizm], *s.* 1. der Trugschluß, Sophismus, das Scheinargument; 2. die Spitzfindigkeit, Tüftelei. **sophist,** *s.* der Sophist; Klügler, Tüftler. **sophistic(al)** [sə'fistik(l)], *adj.* spitzfindig, tüftelnd, sophistisch.

sophisticate [sə'fistikeit], *v.t.* 1. sophistisch darstellen *or* verdrehen, verfeinern; 2. verdrehen, verderben, verkünsteln, (ver)fälschen. **sophisticated,** *adj.* 1. verfälscht, unecht, unnatürlich, gekünstelt, verfeinert, ausgefallen, hochentwickelt; 2. (*of a p.*) kultiviert, aufgeklärt; anspruchsvoll, weltmännisch, weltklug. **sophistication** [–'keiʃən], *s.* 1. die Sophisterei; Verfälschung, der Trugschluß; 2. Intellektualismus, die Kultiviertheit, Weltklugkeit.

sophistry ['sɔfistri], *s.* 1. die Sophisterei, Spitzfindigkeit; 2. der Trugschluß.

sophomore ['sɔfəmɔ:], *s.* (*Am.*) der Student im zweiten Jahre.

soporiferous [sɔpə'rifərəs], **soporific** [–'rifik], 1. *adj.* schlaffördernd, einschläfernd. 2. *s.* das Schlafmittel.

soppiness ['sɔpinis], *s.* (*coll.*) die Sentimentalität, Rührseligkeit.

sopping ['sɔpiŋ], *adj.* durchnäßt, triefend; – *wet,* patschnaß.

soppy ['sɔpi], *adj.* 1. durchweicht, durchnäßt; 2. (*coll.*) rührselig, gefühlsduselig; (*sl.*) – *on,* vernarrt *or* verknallt in (*Acc.*).

soprano [sə'prɑ:nou], *s.* der Sopran, die Sopranstimme, Sopranpartie; (*of a p.*) der (die) Sopranist(in), Sopransänger(in).

sorb [sɔ:b], *s.* (*Bot.*) der Sperberbaum, Speierling.

sorbet ['sɔ:bit], *s.* der Sorbett.

sorbo rubber ['sɔ:bou], *s.* der Schwammgummi.

sorcerer ['sɔ:sərə], *s.* der Zauberer, Hexenmeister. **sorceress** [–ris], *s.* die Zauberin, Hexe. **sorcery,** *s.* die Zauberei, Hexerei.

sordid ['sɔ:did], *adj.* 1. gemein, niedrig, schmutzig; unlauter, unsauber; 2. geizig, eigennützig. **sordidness,** *s.* die Gemeinheit, Niedrigkeit, Schmutzigkeit; Unlauterkeit, Unsauberkeit.

sordine ['sɔ:di:n], *s.* (*Mus.*) der Dämpfer.

sore [sɔ:], 1. *adj.* 1. wund, schmerzhaft, weh(e), empfindlich, entzündet; *my eyes are* –, meine Augen tun weh; (*coll.*) *sight for – eyes,* erfreulicher Anblick, die Augenweide; – *feet,* wunde Füße; – *finger,* schlimmer Finger; (*coll.*) *like a bear with a – head,* mürrisch, verdrießlich; – *place,* empfindliche *or* wunde Stelle; – *throat,* Halsschmerzen (*pl.*); 2. (*Poet. or obs.*) schlimm, schwer, ernst, groß, heftig; 3. (*coll.*) reizbar, ärgerlich, verärgert, verdrießlich, mürrisch (*about,* über (*Acc.*)); 4. (*fig.*) heikel; – *point,* wunder *or* peinlicher *or* heikler Punkt. 2. *adv.* (*Poet.*) *see* **sorely.** 3. *s.* wunde Stelle; (*fig.*) *open* –, altes Übel, ständiges Ärgernis. **sorely,** *adv.* 1. arg, ernstlich, schlimm; 2. heftig, äußerst, sehr; – *grieved,* tief betrübt; – *tried,* schwer geprüft; – *vexed,* sehr verärgert. **soreness,** *s.* 1. die Empfindlichkeit (*also fig.*); 2. Schmerzhaftkeit; 3. (*fig.*) Reizbarkeit, Entrüstung, der Ärger, Groll (*at,* über (*Acc.*)).

sorites [sə'raiti:z], *s.* (*Log.*) der Kettenschluß.

sorority [sə'rɔriti], *s.* die Schwesternschaft.

sorosis [sə'rousis], *s.* die Sammelfrucht.

1**sorrel** ['sɔrəl], *s.* (*Bot.*) der Sauerampfer.

2**sorrel,** 1. *adj.* rotbraun, fuchsrot (*of horse*). 2. *s.* das Rotbraun, der (Rot)fuchs (*horse*).

sorriness ['sɔrinis], *s.* die Armseligkeit, Kläglichkeit.

sorrow ['sɔrou], 1. *s.* der Kummer, Schmerz, Gram (*for,* um; *at,* über (*Acc.*)), die Klage, der Jammer (*for,* um), die Reue (*for,* wegen), Trauer, Betrübnis, Trübsal, das Leid; *to my* –, zu meinem Bedauern *or* Leidwesen. 2. *v.i.* trauern, klagen, jammern, sich (*Dat.*) Sorgen machen, Kummer haben, sich grämen *or* härmen (*for him,* um ihn; *over, at, for,* über (*Acc.*) *or* wegen (*a th.*)). **sorrowful,** *adj.* sorgenvoll, kummervoll, bekümmert, betrübt, traurig. **sorrowfulness,** *s.* die

Traurigkeit, Betrübtheit, Betrübnis, der Kummer, das Elend.

sorry ['sɔri], *adj.* 1. (*only pred.*) bekümmert, betrübt, traurig (*for*, um); ***I am –!*** Verzeihung! es tut mir leid; ***I am – for you,*** ich bedaure Sie, Sie tun mir leid; (*coll.*) ***be – for o.s.,*** deprimiert sein, sich selbst bedauern; ***be – about,*** bereuen; ***I am – to say,*** leider muß ich sagen; 2. (*only attrib.*) elend, erbärmlich, kläglich, jämmerlich, armselig; ***– excuse,*** faule Ausrede; ***– sight,*** trauriger Anblick.

sort [sɔ:t], **1.** *s.* 1. die Sorte, Art, Gattung, Klasse, der Typ; (*coll.*) ***a good –,*** anständiger *or* guter Kerl;
(*before of*) ***all –s of people,*** allerlei Leute; ***all –s of things,*** alles Mögliche, alle möglichen *or* allerlei Dinge; ***no – of,*** durchaus kein; (*sl.*) ***– of,*** gewissermaßen, gleichsam; ***a strange – of man,*** seltsamer Mensch; ***that – of thing*** (*also coll.* ***those – of things***), so etwas, etwas Derartiges; ***and that – of thing*** or (*coll.*) ***those – of things,*** und dergleichen;
(*after of*) ***s.th. of the –,*** etwas Ähnliches; ***nothing of the –,*** nichts dergleichen; ***have looks of a –,*** nicht gerade häßlich sein; ***of all –s,*** aller Arten; (*coll.*) ***a painter of a –*** or ***of –s,*** so etwas wie ein Maler, ein sogenannter Maler, ein Maler – aber was für einer, ein Maler wenigstens dem Namen nach;
(*after other preps.*) ***after a –,*** gewissermaßen, bis zu einem gewissen Grade; ***in some – of way,*** in gewisser Weise; (*coll.*) ***out of –s,*** unpäßlich, unwohl;
2. *pl.* (*Typ.*) die Schriftart, Schriftgarnitur; ***out of –(s),*** ausgegangen.
2. *v.t.* 1. sortieren, klassifizieren, (ein)ordnen, einteilen; 2. (*Comm.*) assortieren; 3. (*Scots*) reparieren, wiederherstellen, herrichten; 4. ***– out,*** aussortieren, aussuchen, auslesen, aussondern, ausscheiden; (*coll.*) in Ordnung bringen (*ideas etc.*).
3. *v.i.* (*obs.*) passen (***with,*** zu), angemessen sein (*Dat.*), übereinstimmen, harmonieren (mit).

sorter ['sɔ:tə], *s.* der Sortierer.

sortie ['sɔ:ti], *s.* (*Mil.*) der Ausfall; (*Av.*) Einsatz, Feindflug.

sortilege ['sɔ:tilidʒ], *s.* das Wahrsagen durch Lose.

so-so ['sousou], (*coll.*) **1.** *pred. adj.* leidlich, passabel. **2.** *adv.* so lala.

sot [sɔt], **1.** *s.* der Trunkenbold, Säufer. **2.** *v.i.* saufen, sich betrinken. **sottish,** *adj.* 1. versoffen, trunksüchtig; 2. blöde. **sottishness,** *s.* die Versoffenheit, Trunksucht.

sotto voce ['sɔtou'voutʃi], *adv.* mit gedämpfter Stimme.

soubrette [su:'bret], *s.* (*Theat.*) die Soubrette.

souffle [su:fl], *s.* (*Med.*) das Geräusch.

soufflé ['su:flei], *s.* (*Cul.*) der Auflauf.

sough [sau, sʌf], **1.** *s.* das Sausen, Heulen, Pfeifen. **2.** *v.i.* sausen, heulen, pfeifen (*of the wind*).

sought [sɔ:t], *imperf., p.p. of* **seek. sought-after,** *adj.* begehrt, gesucht, umworben.

soul [soul], *s.* 1. die Seele (*also fig.*); (*fig.*) das Innere, Gemüt, Herz, der Geist; (*coll.*) ***he cannot call his – his own,*** er hat nichts zu melden; ***upon my –!*** (bei) meiner Seele! ***with heart and –,*** von ganzem Herz, mit Leib und Seele; 2. das Sinnbild, die Verkörperung, das Wesen, der Kern, Inbegriff; ***the – of honour,*** die Ehrenhaftigkeit selbst; 3. (*oft. without art.*) die Energie, (Saft und) Kraft; ***the life and – of the party,*** der Mittelpunkt *or* die Triebfeder *or* Seele der Gesellschaft; 4. die Person, Menschenseele, der Mensch, Einwohner; ***be a good –!*** sei so gut! ***be kindred –s,*** seelenverwandt sein; ***not a –,*** keine Menschenseele; ***poor –!*** armes Ding! armer Kerl *or* Teufel *or* Wicht! ***simple –,*** einfacher *or* schlichter Mensch.

soul-destroying, *adj.* entmutigend, bedrückend, trostlos. **soulful,** *adj.* seelenvoll; (*fig.*) gefühlvoll. **soulless,** *adj.* seelenlos; (*fig.*) herzlos, gefühllos. **soul-stirring,** *adj.* herzergreifend.

1**sound** [saund], **1.** *adj.* 1. gesund (*in mind and body, also fig.*); unversehrt, unbeschädigt, tadellos, gut erhalten, intakt, fehlerfrei; unverdorben (*as fruit*); (*as*) ***– as a bell,*** kerngesund; ***– health,*** gute Gesundheit; ***– in mind and limb,*** an Geist und Körper gesund; ***safe and –,*** gesund und munter; 2. tief, fest, ungestört (*as sleep*); 3. kräftig, tüchtig, gehörig (*as a blow*); 4. stichhaltig, gültig, begründet, rechtmäßig, vernünftig, folgerichtig (*as arguments*); 5. zuverlässig, einwandfrei (*of a p.*); 6. (*Comm.*) solid, sicher, gut fundiert. **2.** *adv.* ***– asleep,*** fest schlafend.

2**sound,** *s.* der Sund, die Meerenge.

3**sound,** *s.* (*Ichth.*) die Schwimmblase.

4**sound, 1.** *v.i.* 1. (er)tönen, (er)klingen, (er)schallen; (*sl.*) ***– off,*** sich beschweren; 2. (*fig.*) (er)scheinen, sich anhören, klingen, den Eindruck machen. **2.** *v.t.* ertönen *or* erklingen *or* erschallen lassen; ***– abroad,*** verkündigen, ausposaunen; ***– the h,*** das h (aus)sprechen; ***– a note,*** einen Ton anschlagen; ***– the retreat,*** zum Rückzug blasen; ***– his praises,*** sein Lob verkünden *or* singen; ***– the trumpet,*** die Trompete blasen (lassen). **3.** *s.* der Ton, Schall, Laut, Klang; das Geräusch; ***– and fury,*** leerer Schall und Rauch; ***velocity of –,*** die Schallgeschwindigkeit; ***to the – of,*** unter dem Klang von; ***within –,*** in Hörweite; ***without a –,*** lautlos; (*fig.*) ***I don't like the – of it,*** der Ton gefällt mir nicht.

5**sound, 1.** *v.t.* 1. (*Naut.*) (aus)loten, peilen, abmessen, pegeln; 2. (*Surg., also fig.*) sondieren, (*fig.*) (*also* ***– out***) erkunden, erforschen, untersuchen, (*a p.*) abhorchen, auf den Zahn fühlen (*Dat.*). **2.** *v.i.* auf Grund gehen, (weg)tauchen (*as a whale*). **3.** *s.* (*Med.*) die Sonde.

sound|-amplifier, *s.* (*Rad.*) der Lautverstärker. **--barrier,** *s.* die Schallgrenze, Schallmauer. **-board,** *s.* der Resonanzboden (*also fig.*), das Schallbrett. **--box,** *s.* die Schalldose. **--broadcasting,** *s. See* **--radio. --detector,** *s.* (*Av.*) das Horchgerät. **--effects,** *pl.* (*Films, Rad.*) Toneffekte (*pl.*). **--film,** *s.* der Tonfilm.

1**sounding** ['saundiŋ], *adj.* klingend, schallend, tönend.

2**sounding,** *s.* (*Naut.*) das Loten; (*oft. pl.*) die Lotung, Wassertiefe; ***take –s*** or ***a –,*** loten, Lotungen vornehmen.

sounding|-board, *s. See* **sound-board. --lead,** *s.* das Senkblei, (Peil)lot. **--line,** *s.* die Lotleine, Senkschnur. **--rod,** *s.* der Peilstock.

soundless ['saundlis], *adj.* lautlos, klanglos, tonlos.

sound|-locator, *s. See* **--detector.**

soundness ['saundnis], *s.* die Gesundheit, Unversehrtheit, Intaktheit, Tadellosigkeit, Folgerichtigkeit, Echtheit, Rechtmäßigkeit, Rechtgläubigkeit; Gründlichkeit, Tiefe, Festigkeit (*of sleep*), (*Comm.*) Zuverlässigkeit, Sicherheit, Stabilität, Solidität; ***– of health,*** gute Gesundheit; ***– of judgement,*** gesundes Urteil.

sound|-post, *s.* der Stimmstock, die Stimme, Seele (*of violin etc.*). **-proof,** *adj.* schalldicht. **--proofing,** *s.* die Schalldämpfung, Schallisolation. **--radio,** *s.* der Tonrundfunk, Hörfunk. **--ranging,** *s.* das Schallmeßverfahren, die Schallmessung. **--recording,** *s.* die Tonaufnahme. **--shift,** *s.* die Lautverschiebung. **--track,** *s.* der Tonstreifen, die Tonspur. **--wave,** *s.* die Schallwelle.

soup [su:p], **1.** *s.* 1. die Suppe, (Fleisch)brühe; (*coll.*) ***in the –,*** in der Klemme *or* Patsche *or* Tinte; 2. (*sl.*) dicker Nebel; 3. (*sl. Motor.*) die Pferdestärke. **2.** *v.t.* (*sl. Motor.*) ***– up,*** hochzüchten, frisieren (*engines*), (*fig.*) Schwung geben (*Dat.*).

soupçon ['su:psɔ̃], *s.* die Spur (***of,*** von).

soup|-kitchen, *s.* die Volksküche. **--ladle,** *s.* die Suppenkelle. **--spoon,** *s.* der Suppenlöffel. **--tureen,** *s.* die Suppenschüssel, Suppenterrine.

sour ['sauə], **1.** *adj.* 1. sauer; herb, bitter, scharf; ***– cherry,*** die Sauerkirsche; (*Bot.*) ***– gourd,*** der Affenbrotbaum; (*fig.*) ***– grapes,*** sauere Trauben; ***– milk,*** sauere Milch, die Sauermilch; ***turn –,*** sauer werden; 2. (*as soil*) kalkarm; 3. (*fig.*) verdrießlich, griesgrämlich, verbittert, sauertöpfisch, mürrisch (*of a p.*); (*coll.*) ***– puss,*** der Sauertopf, Griesgram, Miesepeter. **2.** *v.t.* 1. sauer machen, (an)säuern; (*fig.*) verbittern. **3.** *v.i.* **1.** sauer werden; 2. (*fig.*) verbittert *or* mürrisch *or* verdrießlich werden.

source [sɔ:s], *s.* die Quelle (*of*, von *or* für), der Ausgang, Ursprung; (*Poet.*) der Quell, Strom; ***draw from a –***, einer Quelle entnehmen, aus einer Quelle schöpfen; ***from a reliable –***, aus sicherer *or* zuverlässiger Quelle; ***take its – from***, herstammen von, entspringen (*Dat.*); ***have its – in***, seinen Ursprung *or* Ausgang haben in (*Dat.*); ***– of supply***, die Bezugsquelle.

sourish ['sauəriʃ], *adj.* angesäuert, säuerlich. **sourness,** *s.* 1. die Säure, Herbheit; 2. (*fig.*) Verdrießlichkeit, Mürrischkeit, Bitterkeit, das Verbittertsein.

souse [saus], **1.** *s.* der Pökel, die Pökelbrühe, Salzbrühe, Lake; Sülze, das Pökelfleisch, Gepökelte(s). **2.** *v.t.* 1. (ein)pökeln, einsalzen; 2. ins Wasser werfen, eintauchen; durchnässen. **soused,** *adj.* 1. (ein)gepökelt, Pökel–; 2. (*sl.*) besoffen. **sousing,** *s.* der Sturz ins Wasser, das Durchnässen; ***get a –***, durchnäßt werden.

soutane [su:'tɑ:n], *s.* (*R.C.*) die Sutane.

souteneur [su:tə'nə:], *s.* der Zuhälter.

south [sauθ], **1.** *s.* der Süden, (*Poet.*) Süd; (*Am.*) ***the South,*** die Südstaaten; ***the – of France,*** Südfrankreich; ***from the –***, aus Süden (*wind*); aus dem Süden (*a p.*); ***in the – of,*** im Süden von; ***to the – of,*** südlich von; ***towards the –***, nach Süden. **2.** *attrib. adj.* südlich, Süd–; ***South Africa,*** Südafrika(nische Republik); ***South America,*** Südamerika (*n.*); ***South Magnetic Pole,*** magnetischer Südpol; ***South Pole,*** der Südpol; ***South Sea,*** die Südsee; (*Hist.*) ***South Sea Bubble,*** der Südseeschwindel; ***South Sea Islands,*** die Südsee-Inseln; ***– wind,*** der Südwind. **3.** *adv.* südwärts, nach Süden; ***– of,*** südlich von.

south|-east, 1. *adj.* südöstlich, Südost–. **2.** *adv.* nach Südosten; ***– of,*** südöstlich von. **3.** *s.* der Südosten; ***to the – of,*** südöstlich von. **--easter,** *s.* der Südostwind. **--easterly, 1.** *adj.* südöstlich, Südost–. **2.** *adv.* nach Südosten. **--eastern,** *attrib. adj.* südöstlich, Südost–. **--eastward, 1.** *adv.* nach Südosten; südostwärts; ***– of,*** südöstlich von. **2.** *s.* der Südosten; ***to the –***, nach Südosten. **--eastwards,** *adv. See* **--eastward, 1.**

southerly ['sʌðəli], *adj.* südlich, Süd–. **southern** ['sʌðən], *attrib. adj.* südlich; (*Astr.*) ***Southern Cross,*** das Kreuz des Südens; ***Southern England,*** Südengland; ***Southern Rhodesia*** (*obs.*), Südrhodesien (*n.*); ***Southern States,*** die Südstaaten. **southerner,** *s.* der Südländer, (*Am.*) Südstaatler. **southernmost,** *adj.* südlichst.

southing ['sauðiŋ], *s.* 1. die Südrichtung, südliche Fahrt; 2. (*Astr.*) die Kulmination (*of moon*), südliche Deklination (*of star*).

south|-south-east, *n., adj., adv.* der Südsüdosten, südsüdöstlich (*for other forms see under* **--east**). **--south-west,** *n., adj., adv.* der Südsüdwesten, südsüdwestlich (*other forms as above*).

southward ['sauθwəd], *adj.* nach Süden, südlich. **southward(s)** [–z], *adv.* nach Süden, südwärts.

south|-west, 1. *adj.* südwestlich, Südwest–. **2.** *adv.* südwestlich, nach Südwesten. **3.** *s.* der Südwesten. **--wester,** *s.* 1. der Südwestwind; 2. *See* **sou'-wester. --westerly, --western, --westward(s),** *for forms see under* **--easterly** *etc.*

souvenir ['su:vəniə], *s.* das Andenken.

sou'wester [sau'westə], *s.* der Südwester (*fisherman's hat*).

sovereign ['sɔvrin], **1.** *adj.* 1. oberst, allerhöchst; 2. königlich, fürstlich; unumschränkt, souverän; ***– emblem,*** das Hoheitszeichen; ***our – lady, Queen Elizabeth,*** Ihre Majestät, die Königin E.; ***– state,*** souveräner Staat; 3. unfehlbar, allerbest, wirksamst (*remedy*); 4. äußerst; ***– contempt,*** tiefste Verachtung. **2.** *s.* 1. der Souverän, (souveräner) Herrscher, der (die) Landesherr(in), Monarch(in); 2. (*obs.*) das Hundertpfennigstück, der Sovereign (*coin*). **sovereignty,** *s.* 1. höchste *or* oberste Staatsgewalt, unumschränkte Gewalt.

soviet ['souvjət, 'sɔvjət], **1.** *s.* der Sowjet. **2.** *attrib. adj.* Sowjet–, sowjetisch. **Soviet Union,** *s.* die Sowjetunion.

[1]**sow** [sau], *s.* (*Zool.*) die Sau; 2. (*Tech.*) Mulde, Massel (*of pig-iron*).

[2]**sow** [sou], **1.** *irr.v.t.* säen (*seed*), besäen (*field*); (*fig.*) ausstreuen, verbreiten; ***– the seeds of hatred,*** Haß säen; ***– one's wild oats,*** sich (*Dat.*) die Hörner ablaufen. **2.** *irr.v.i.* säen.

sow|-bread ['sau–], *s.* (*Bot.*) das Saubrot, Alpenveilchen. **--bug,** *s.* die Kellerassel.

sower ['souə], *s.* 1. der Sämann, Säer; 2. die Sämaschine; 3. (*fig.*) der Verbreiter, Anstifter. **sowing,** *s.* das Säen, die (Aus)saat; ***--corn,*** das Saatkorn; ***--machine,*** die Sämaschine. **sown** [–n], **1.** *p.p. of* [2]**sow. 2.** *adj.* (*oft. fig.*) bestreut, besät.

sow-thistle ['sau–], *s.* die Saudistel, Gänsedistel.

soya ['sɔiə], *s.* (*also* ***--bean***) die Sojabohne.

sozzled [sɔzld], *adj.* (*sl.*) berotzt, besoffen.

spa [spɑ:], *s.* die Mineralquelle, Heilquelle; der Kurort, Badeort, das Bad.

space [speis], **1.** *s.* 1. der Raum; (*in area*) die Weite, Ausdehnung, Fläche; ***disappear into –***, in Nichts verschwinden; ***look into –***, vor sich hinblicken; ***save –***, Raum sparen; 2. der Zwischenraum, Abstand, die Stelle, Lücke; ***leave*** (*some*) ***–***, Platz lassen; ***blank –***, leere Stelle; 3. (*in time*) der Zeitraum, die Weile, Frist; ***after a –***, nach einer Weile; ***for a short –***, ein Weilchen; ***within the – of,*** innerhalb (*Gen.*); 4. (*Astr.*) der (Welt)raum, das Weltall; 5. (*Typ.*) der Durchschuß, Ausschluß, das Spatium, Ausschlußstück; 6. (*Mus.*) der Zwischenraum (*between lines*). **2.** *v.t.* 1. (*also* ***– out***) (*Typ.*) spatiieren, spationieren, ausschließen, durchschießen, sperren; 2. (räumlich *or* zeitlich) einteilen, in Zwischenräumen anordnen.

space|-age, *s.* das Weltraumzeitalter. **--bar,** *s.* die Zwischenraumtaste (*typewriter*). **--charge,** *s.* (*Elec.*) die Raumladung. **--fiction,** *s.* Weltraumromane (*pl.*). **--flight,** *s.* die Raumfahrt, der (Welt)raumflug. **-man,** *s.* 1. der (Welt)raumfahrer, Astronaut; 2. Weltraumbewohner.

spacer ['speisə], *s.* 1. (*Tech.*) das Abstandstück, der Distanzring, die Distanzscheibe; 2. *See* **space-bar.**

space|-research, *s.* die Raumforschung. **--rule,** *s.* (*Typ.*) die Querlinie. **--ship,** *s.* das Raumschiff. **--station,** *s.* die Weltraumstation. **--suit,** *s.* der Raumanzug. **--travel,** *s.* die Raumfahrt.

spacial, *see* **spatial.**

spacing ['speisiŋ], *s.* 1. das Einteilen; Sperren; 2. der Abstand, (*Typ.*) Zwischenraum.

spacious ['speiʃəs], *adj.* 1. geräumig, ausgedehnt; 2. (*fig.*) weit, umfangreich, umfassend. **spaciousness,** *s.* 1. die Geräumigkeit; 2. (*fig.*) Weite, der Umfang, das Ausmaß.

[1]**spade** [speid], **1.** *s.* der Spaten; ***call a – a –***, das Kind *or* Ding beim (rechten) Namen nennen. **2.** *v.t.* (mit dem Spaten) umgraben.

[2]**spade,** *s.* (*Cards*) das Pik, Schippen, die Pikkarte; (*usu. pl.*) Pikfarbe, Pikkarten (*pl.*); ***ace of –s,*** das Pikas.

spadeful ['speidful], *s.* der Spatenvoll. **spadework,** *s.* 1. das Umgraben; 2. (*usu. fig.*) (mühevolle) Kleinarbeit, (unbeachtete) Vorarbeit, die Pionierarbeit.

spadix ['speidiks], *s.* (*pl.* **-dices** [–disi:z]) (*Bot.*) der Kolben.

spado ['speidou], *s.* (*pl.* **-nes** [–'douni:z]) der Eunuch, Kastrat, Entmannte(r); verschnittenes Tier.

spaghetti [spə'geti], *s.* Spaghetti (*pl.*), Fadennudeln (*pl.*).

spahi [spɑ:'hi:], *s.* (*Mil.*) algerischer Kavallerist.

Spain [spein], *s.* Spanien (*n.*).

spall [spɔ:l], **1.** *v.t.* zerkleinern, zerstückeln (*esp. ore*). **2.** *v.i.* sich abspalten, absplittern, zerbröckeln.

spalpeen ['spælpi:n], *s.* (*Irish*) der Schurke, Nichtsnutz.

[1]**span** [spæn], (*obs.*) *imperf. of* **spin.**

[2]**span, 1.** *s.* 1. die Spanne (*also as measure*); gespreizte Hand; die Stützweite (*of a bridge*); (*Archit., Av.*) Spannweite; 2. (*fig.*) (Zeit)spanne, der Umfang (*of time*); 3. (*Am.*) das Gespann. **2.** *v.t.* 1. (um- *or* über)spannen, sich erstrecken über (*Acc.*); – *with a bridge,* überbrücken; 2. (nach Spannen) abmessen; 3. (*Naut.*) zurren.

spandrel ['spændrəl], *s.* (*Archit.*) die Spandrille.

spangle [spæŋgl], **1.** *s.* der Flitter, das Flitterplättchen, die Spange. **2.** *v.t.* 1. mit Flitter(plätzchen) besetzen; 2. (*fig.*) schmücken, übersäen, besprenkeln; *–d heavens,* gestirnter Himmel.

Spaniard ['spænjəd], *s.* der (die) Spanier(in).

spaniel ['spænjəl], *s.* der Wachtelhund.

Spanish ['spæniʃ], **1.** *s.* 1. (*collect.*) Spanier (*pl.*); 2. das Spanisch(e) (*language*). **2.** *adj.* spanisch; *--American,* spanisch-amerikanisch; – *chestnut,* die Edelkastanie; – *Main,* die Nordostküste Südamerikas; – *onion,* der Lauch, Porree.

spank [spæŋk], (*coll.*) **1.** *v.t.* schlagen, (ver)prügeln. **2.** *v.i.* (*also – along*) dahineilen. **3.** *s.* der Klaps, Schlag. **spanker,** *s.* 1. schneller Läufer (*horse*); 2. (*sl.*) der Prachtkerl, das Prachtexemplar; 3. (*Naut.*) der Besan. **spanking, 1.** *adj.* 1. schnell laufend *or* dahinfahrend; 2. (*sl.*) stark, kräftig, tüchtig, fein. **2.** *s.* die Tracht Prügel.

spanner ['spænə], *s.* der Schraubenschlüssel; (*coll.*) *throw a – in(to) the works,* einen Knüppel zwischen die Beine werfen (*Dat.*).

span-roof, *s.* das Satteldach.

[1]**spar** [spɑ:], *s.* (*Min.*) der Spat; *heavy –,* der Schwerspat, das Barium; *light –,* das Lenzin.

[2]**spar,** *s.* 1. (*Naut.*) die Spiere, der Sparren; das Rundholz; 2. (*Av.*) der Tragholm.

[3]**spar,** *v.i.* 1. (*Boxing*) Scheinhiebe machen, sparren; 2. (*fig.*) sich zanken *or* streiten, einander in die Haare liegen.

sparable ['spærəbl], *s.* die (Schuh)zwecke, der Schuhnagel.

spar|-buoy, *s.* die Spierenboje. **--deck,** *s.* das Spardeck.

spare [spɛə], **1.** *adj.* 1. mager, dürr; – *figure,* hagere Gestalt; 2. spärlich, kärglich, dürftig, knapp; – *diet,* schmale Kost; 3. überflüssig, überschüssig, überzählig, übrig; – *moment,* freier Augenblick; – *money,* überschüssiges Geld; – *room,* das Gastzimmer; – *time,* die Mußezeit, Freizeit; *--time activities,* die Freizeitgestaltung; 4. Ersatz–, Reserve–; – *anchor,* der Notanker; – *horse,* das Reservepferd; – *lead,* das Füllblei (*for propelling pencil*); – *part,* der *or* das Ersatzteil; – *tyre,* der Ersatzreifen; (*coll.*) Rettungsring (*abdominal fat*); – *wheel,* das Reserverad. **2.** *s.* (*Tech.*) der *or* das Reserveteil, Ersatzteil. **3.** *v.t.* 1. sparsam sein *or* umgehen mit, kargen *or* knausern mit; – *no expense,* keine Kosten scheuen; – *no pains,* keine Mühe scheuen; – *him the trouble of coming,* ihm die Mühe (er)sparen zu kommen; 2. übrig haben, erübrigen; *can you – me a cigarette?* haben Sie eine Zigarette für mich übrig? *no time to –,* keine Zeit übrig; *enough and to –,* vollauf, reichlich; 3. entbehren, ablassen (*Dat.*); 4. (ver)schonen (*a p.*); – *my blushes!* bringen Sie mich nicht in Verlegenheit! schonen Sie mein Zartgefühl! – *me your excuses!* verschonen Sie mich mit Ihren Ausreden! – *his life,* ihm das Leben schenken; *if I am –d,* wenn ich am Leben bleibe; – *o.s.,* sich schonen. **4.** *v.i.* 1. sparen, sparsam sein; 2. Nachsicht haben, gnädig *or* nachsichtig sein, Gnade walten lassen.

spareness ['spɛənis], *s.* die Spärlichkeit, Magerkeit, Dürftigkeit.

sparerib ['spɛərib], *s.* das Schweinsrippchen, Rippenstückchen, der Rippenspeer.

sparing ['spɛəriŋ], *adj.* sparsam, karg (*of,* mit), dürftig, spärlich, gering, knapp. **sparingness,** *s.* 1. die Sparsamkeit, Kargheit; 2. Spärlichkeit; 3. Seltenheit.

[1]**spark** [spɑ:k], **1.** *s.* der Funke(n); (*fig.*) zündender Funke; (*Motor.*) der Zündfunke, die Zündung; (*fig.*) *not a – of,* keine Spur *or* kein Funke von; *vital –,* der Lebensfunke. **2.** *v.i.* Funken sprühen; (*Motor.*) zünden. **3.** *v.t.* (*fig. coll.*) – *off,* entzünden, auslösen.

[2]**spark,** *s.* (*coll.*) flotter Bursche.

spark|-gap, *s.* (*Elec.*) die Funkenstrecke. **--plug,** *s.* *See under* **sparking.**

sparking ['spɑ:kiŋ], *s.* die Funkenbildung. **sparking|-coil,** *s.* der Funkeninduktor; (*Motor.*) die Zündspule. **--plug,** *s.* (*Motor.*) die Zündkerze.

sparkle [spɑ:kl], **1.** *s.* 1. das Funkeln, Glitzern, Flimmern, Schäumen (*wine etc.*); 2. der Glanz, Schein, Funke(n), Schimmer; 3. die Lebhaftigkeit (*of a p.*). **2.** *v.i.* 1. funkeln, blitzen, strahlen, glänzen (*also fig.*), glitzern, flimmern; 2. perlen, schäumen, moussieren (*as wine*); 3. (*fig.*) sprühen (*as wit*). **sparkler,** *s.* 1. (*firework*) die Wunderkerze; 2. (*sl.*) der Diamant. **sparkling,** *adj.* 1. funkelnd, funkensprühend, glänzend, strahlend, schillernd; (*of wine*) perlend, schäumend, moussierend, Schaum–; 2. (*fig.*) (geist)sprühend.

sparks [spɑ:ks], *s.* (*sl. esp. Naut.*) der Funker.

sparring ['spɑ:riŋ], *s.* 1. (*Boxing*) das Sparring, Übungsboxen; 2. (*fig.*) Geplänkel. **sparring-partner,** *s.* der Sparringpartner, Übungspartner.

sparrow ['spærou], *s.* (*Orn.*) der Sperling, Spatz (*Passer*); *see* *house –, hedge –, tree –.* **sparrow-hawk,** *s.* (*Orn.*) 1. der Sperber (*Accipiter nisus*); 2. (*Am.*) der Buntfalke (*Falco sparverius*).

sparry ['spɑ:ri], *adj.* spatartig; Spat–; – *gypsum,* das Marienglas; – *iron,* der Spateisenstein.

sparse [spɑ:s], *adj.* dünn (gesät), spärlich, zerstreut, selten. **sparseness,** *s.* die Zerstreutheit, Spärlichkeit, Seltenheit.

Spartan ['spɑ:tən], **1.** *s.* der (die) Spartaner(in). **2.** *adj.* spartanisch (*also fig.*).

spasm [spæzm], *s.* 1. der Krampf, die Zuckung; 2. (*fig.*) der Anfall. **spasmodic** [–'mɔdik], *adj.* 1. krampfhaft, krampfartig, spasmodisch; 2. (*fig.*) sprunghaft, unregelmäßig. **spasmodically,** *adv.* sprunghaft, stoßweise.

spastic ['spæstik], **1.** *adj.* (*Med.*) Krampf–, krampfartig, spastisch. **2.** *s.* der (die) Spastiker(in).

[1]**spat** [spæt], *s.* der Laich (*oysters etc.*).

[2]**spat,** *imperf., p.p. of* [2]**spit.**

[3]**spat,** *s.* (*usu. pl.*) die (Schuh)gamasche.

spatchcock ['spætʃkɔk], **1.** *s.* frisch geschlachtetes und zubereitetes Huhn. **2.** *v.t.* (*coll.*) einflicken, einfügen (*words etc.*).

spate [speit], *s.* 1. die Überschwemmung, Überflutung, das Hochwasser; 2. (*fig.*) die Flut, der Erguß; – *of talk,* der Wortschwall.

spathe [speið], *s.* (*Bot.*) die Blütenscheide.

spathic ['spæθik], *adj.* (*Geol.*) spatartig, lamellenartig, blätterig.

spathose ['speiθous], **spathous** [–əs], *adj.* (*Bot.*) Blütenscheiden–.

spatial ['speiʃəl], *adj.* räumlich, Raum–.

spats, *see* [3]**spat.**

spatter ['spætə], **1.** *v.t.* spritzen, sprenkeln (*on,* auf (*Acc.*)), bespritzen (*with,* mit); (*fig.*) besudeln. **2.** *v.i.* spritzen, sprühen, sprudeln. **spatterdash,** *s.* (*usu. pl.*) die (Reit)gamasche.

spatula ['spætjulə], *s.* der *or* die Spachtel, der Spatel. **spatular** [–lə], **spatulate** [–lit], *adj.* spatelförmig.

spavin ['spævin], *s.* (*Vet.*) der Spat. **spavined,** *adj.* 1. (*Vet.*) spatig; 2. (*fig.*) lahm, gelähmt.

spawn [spɔ:n], **1.** *s.* 1. der Laich (*of fishes and frogs*); 2. (*fig.*) die Brut, Ausgeburt, das Gezücht. **2.** *v.i.* 1. laichen; 2. (*fig., vulg.*) in Massen entstehen. **3.** *v.t.* 1. ablegen (*eggs*); 2. (*vulg.*) massenweise in die Welt setzen; 3. (*fig.*) ausbrüten, aushecken, hervorbringen. **spawning, 1.** *adj.* Laich–; (*fig.*) – *ground,* die Brutstätte; – *time,* die Laichzeit. **2.** *s.* das Laichen.

speak [spi:k], **1.** *irr.v.i.* sprechen, reden; (*Tele.*) *who is it –ing? Smith –ing,* wer ist am Apparat? Schmidt am Apparat; – *him fair,* ihm gute *or*

schöne Worte sagen; ***frankly –ing***, offen gesagt; ***generally*** or ***roughly –ing***, im allgemeinen, über dem Daumen gepeilt; ***so to –***, sozusagen; ***strictly –ing***, streng genommen.
(a) (*with prep.*) – ***about***, sprechen über (*Acc.*), besprechen; – ***for***, sprechen für, ein gutes Wort *or* gute Worte einlegen für; ***it –s well for him***, es spricht für ihn; – ***for o.s.***, selbst sprechen, nur die eigene Meinung äußern; – ***for yourself!*** da bin ich anderer Meinung! ***that –s for itself***, das spricht für sich selbst; – ***of***, sprechen von *or* über (*Acc.*); – ***highly*** or ***well of***, loben, gut sprechen von; ***not to – of***, geschweige (denn), ganz zu schweigen von; ***nothing to – of***, nicht der Rede wert, nichts Erwähnenswertes; – ***of the devil and he appears***, wenn man den Teufel an die Wand malt, dann kommt er; – ***on a subject***, über ein Thema sprechen *or* eine Rede halten; – ***to***, sprechen *or* reden mit; anreden, ansprechen; (*fig.*) bezeugen, bestätigen; zurückkommen *or* zu sprechen kommen auf (*Acc.*), behandeln.
(b) (*with adv.*) – ***on***, weiter reden; – ***out***, frei heraussprechen *or* reden, frei von der Leber weg sprechen, mit der Sprache herausrücken, kein Blatt vor den Mund nehmen, sich aussprechen; *see also* – ***up***; – ***up***, laut *or* deutlich sprechen; – ***up for***, sich einsetzen für, eintreten für.
2. *irr.v.t.* (aus)sprechen; äußern, sagen; – ***English***, sich in Englisch ausdrücken, Englisch (sprechen) können; – ***one's mind***, seine Meinung sagen; (*coll.*) – ***one's piece***, sich aussprechen; (*Naut.*) – ***a ship***, ein Schiff anrufen, (an)preien; – ***the truth***, die Wahrheit sagen; ***that –s volumes***, das spricht Bände.

speakeasy [ˈspiːkiːzi], *s.* (*sl.*) verbotener Alkoholausschank, unkonzessionierte Kneipe.

speaker [ˈspiːkə], *s.* 1. der (die) Sprecher(in), Redner(in); ***previous –***, der (Herr) Vorredner; 2. (*Parl.*) ***the Speaker***, der Präsident *or* Vorsitzende(r) des Unterhauses; 3. (*coll. Rad.*) der Lautsprecher.

speaking [ˈspiːkiŋ], *adj.* sprechend, beredt, ausdrucksvoll; sprechend ähnlich (*of likeness*); – ***acquaintance***, flüchtige *or* oberflächliche Bekanntschaft; ***on – terms***, flüchtig *or* oberflächlich bekannt; ***not be on – terms***, sich entzweit *or* gezankt haben, nicht (mehr) miteinander sprechen; – ***voice***, die Sprechstimme. **speaking|-trumpet, –-tube,** *s.* das Sprachrohr.

spear [spiə], **1.** *s.* der Speer, die Lanze. **2.** *v.t.* (auf)spießen, durchbohren.

spear|-grass, *s.* (*Bot.*) Liegende Quecke. **–head,** *s.* 1. die Lanzenspitze; 2. (*fig.*) Spitze(nlinie), vorderste Kampflinie; die Stoßgruppe. **–man,** *s.* der Lanzenträger. **–mint,** *s.* (*Bot.*) grüne Minze. **–-shaped,** *adj.* lanzenförmig. **–-side,** *s.* (*obs.*) männliche Linie, väterlicher Zweig. **–-thistle,** *s.* (*Bot.*) die Speerdistel, Heildistel. **–wort,** *s.* (*Bot.*) das Egelkraut, der Hahnenfuß.

spec [spek], *s. Abbr. of* **speculation**; (*coll.*) ***on –***, auf gut Glück.

special [ˈspeʃəl], **1.** *adj.* 1. besonder, Sonder–, Separat–, Extra–, Ausnahme–; – ***area***, das Notstandsgebiet; – ***bargain***, das Sonderangebot; – ***case***, der Sonderfall; – ***constable***, der Hilfspolizist; – ***correspondent***, der Sonderberichterstatter; – ***delivery***, die Eilzustellung (*post*); – ***dividend***, die Extradividende; – ***edition***, (*book*) die Sonderausgabe, (*newspaper*) das Extrablatt; – ***pass***, der Sonderausweis; – ***pleading***, die Rechtsverdrehung, Sophisterei; – ***train***, der Sonderzug; 2. spezialisiert, speziell, Spezial–, außergewöhnlich; eigen, individuell; – ***knowledge***, die Fachkenntnis; – ***line***, das Spezialfach; – ***subject***, das Spezialgebiet; 3. bestimmt, ausdrücklich (*as orders*). **2.** *s.* (*coll.*) 1. der Sonderzug; 2. das Extrablatt; 3. der Hilfspolizist.

specialism [ˈspeʃəlizm], *s.* das Spezialfach, Sondergebiet; die Spezialisierung. **specialist,** *s.* 1. der Spezialist, Sachverständige(r), der Fachmann; 2. Spezialarzt, Facharzt. **speciality** [–ʃiˈæliti], *s.* 1. die Besonderheit, besonderes Merkmal, besondere Eigenschaft; 2. (*Comm., Cul.*) die Spezialität; *see also* **specialty. specialization** [–laiˈzeiʃən], *s.* die Spezialisierung. **specialize, 1.** *v.i.* sich spezialisieren (*in*, auf (*Acc.*)); – ***in***, als Spezialfach studieren. **2.** *v.t.* einzeln erwähnen, präzisieren, gesondert anführen *or* aufführen; (*Biol.*) zu einem besonderen Zweck entwickeln. **specially,** *adv.* 1. besonders, im besonderen; 2. eigens, extra, ausdrücklich, in der besonderen Absicht. **specialty,** *s.* 1. (*esp. Am.*) *see* **speciality, specialism**; 2. (*Comm.*) der Sonderartikel, die Neuheit; 3. (*Law*) besiegelte Urkunde.

specie [ˈspiːʃi], *s.* 1. das Metallgeld, Hartgeld, die Münze; 2. das Bargeld; ***in –***, in bar.

species [ˈspiːʃiːz], *s.* 1. die Art; (*Zool., Bot.*) Spezies; ***human –***, die Menschheit; ***origin of the –***, die Entstehung der Arten; 2. (*Theol.*) sichtbare Gestalt; 3. (*fig.*) die Art, Sorte; ***a – of***, eine (besondere) Sorte *or* Art von.

specifiable [ˈspesifaiəbl], *adj.* einzeln aufzählbar *or* anführbar, unterscheidbar. **specific** [spəˈsifik], **1.** *adj.* 1. arteigen, spezifisch, Art–, Gattungs–; – ***name***, der Artname; 2. bestimmt, ausdrücklich, definitiv; eigen(tümlich), kennzeichnend, wesentlich; – ***gravity***, spezifisches Gewicht, das Volumengewicht, die Wichte; – ***heat***, spezifische Wärme, die Eigenwärme. **2.** *s.* spezifisches (Heil)mittel. **specification** [–fiˈkeiʃən], *s.* 1. die Spezifizierung; 2. genaues Verzeichnis, ausführliche Aufzählung *or* Beschreibung; 3. die Einzeldarstellung; 4. (*Tech.*) (*usu. pl.*) der Voranschlag; 5. (*Law*) die Patentbeschreibung. **specify,** *v.t.* spezifizieren, besonders *or* einzeln *or* im einzelnen nennen *or* angeben *or* bestimmen *or* aufzählen *or* anführen *or* aufführen *or* bezeichnen.

specimen [ˈspesimin], *s.* das Muster, Beispiel (*of*, für); die Probe, das Exemplar (von); (*fig. coll.*) Individuum, Exemplar (*of a p.*); ***museum –***, das Museumstück; – ***copy***, das Probeexemplar.

specious [ˈspiːʃəs], *adj.* bestechend, blendend, trügerisch, Schein–, scheinbar einleuchtend. **speciousness,** *s.* trügerischer Schein, das Bestechende.

speck [spek], *s.* der Fleck(en), das Fleckchen, Pünktchen; (*fig.*) bißchen, Körnchen. **speckle** [–l], **1.** *s.* das Fleckchen, der Tupfen, Tüpfel, Sprenkel. **2.** *v.t.* 1. flecken, sprenkeln, tüpfeln; 2. (*Paperm.*) masern. **speckled,** *adj.* gefleckt, getüpfelt, gesprenkelt, punktiert, meliert, bunt. **speckless** [–lis], *adj.* (*usu. fig.*) fleckenlos, tadellos, untadelig, sauber.

specs [speks], *pl.* (*coll.*) die Brille.

spectacle [ˈspektəkl], *s.* 1. das Schauspiel, Schaustück, die Schau(stellung), Aufmachung; ***make a – of o.s.***, (unangenehm) auffallen, sich zur Schau stellen; 2. der Anblick; 3. *pl.* (***also pair of –s***) die Brille. **spectacle-case,** *s.* das Brillenfutteral. **spectacled** [–d], *adj.* 1. bebrillt, brillentragend; 2. (*Zool.*) Brillen–. **spectacle–frame,** *s.* das Brillengestell. **spectacular** [–ˈtækjulə], **1.** *adj.* 1. auffallend, in die Augen fallend, sensationell; 2. schauspielerisch, schauspielmäßig, Schau–. **2.** *s.* (*Theat. coll.*) das Ausstattungsstück. **spectator** [–ˈteitə], *s.* der (die) Zuschauer(in).

specter, (*Am.*) *see* **spectre.**

spectral [ˈspektrəl], *adj.* 1. geisterhaft, gespensterhaft, gespenstisch; 2. (*Opt.*) Spektral–. **spectre** [–tə], *s.* 1. die (Geister)erscheinung, das Gespenst, der Geist; 2. (*fig.*) das Schreckgespenst; Phantom, Hirngespinst.

spectrograph [ˈspektrɔgrɑːf], *s.* der Spektrograph; das Spektrogramm. **spectroscope** [–skoup], *s.* das Spektroskop. **spectroscopic** [–ˈskɔpik], *adj.* spektroskopisch, spektralanalytisch.

spectrum [ˈspektrəm], *s.* 1. das Spektrum; ***solar –***, das Sonnenspektrum; – ***analysis***, die Spektralanalyse; 2. (*fig.*) die Skala.

specula [ˈspekjulə], *pl. of* **speculum. specular** [–lə], *adj.* spiegelnd, Spiegel–; – ***gypsum***, das Marienglas; – ***iron***, der Roteisenstein, Eisenglanz, Hämatit.

speculate ['spekjuleit], *v.i.* 1. nachdenken, nachsinnen, grübeln ((*up*)*on, about, as to*, über (*Acc.*)); 2. (*Comm.*) spekulieren. **speculation** [–'leiʃən], *s.* 1. das Nachdenken, Nachsinnen, Grübeln, die Grübelei; 2. Betrachtung, Theorie, Annahme, Vermutung; 3. (*Comm.*) Spekulation. **speculative** [–lətiv], *adj.* 1. nachdenklich, grübelnd (*of a p.*); 2. theoretisch, erdacht, übersinnlich; 3. (*Phil.*) spekulativ; 4. (*Comm.*) spekulativ, Spekulations–. **speculator** [–leitə], *s.* 1. der Denker, Grübler, Theoretiker; 2. (*usu. Comm.*) Spekulant.

speculum ['spekjuləm], *s.* der (Flügel)spiegel, das Spekulum.

sped [sped], *imperf., p.p. of* **speed.**

speech [spi:tʃ], *s.* 1. die Sprache; Sprachfähigkeit, das Sprachvermögen; ***have – of,*** sprechen mit, Rücksprache nehmen mit (*a p.*); 2. das Sprechen, Reden, die Sprachweise, Ausdrucksweise, Aussprache; ***figure of –,*** die Redensart, Redewendung, Redefigur; ***freedom*** or ***liberty of –,*** die Redefreiheit; 3. die Rede, Ansprache, der Vortrag; ***deliver*** or ***make a –,*** eine Rede halten (*on*, über (*Acc.*); *to*, vor (*Dat.*)); (*Parl.*) ***maiden –,*** die Jungfernrede.

speech|-centre, *s.* das Sprachzentrum (*of the brain*). **--day,** *s.* die (Schul)schlußfeier. **--defect,** *s.* der Sprachfehler.

speechifier ['spi:tʃifaiə], *s.* (*coll.*) der Vielredner. **speechify,** *v.i.* (*coll.*) viel(e) Worte machen, unermüdlich reden, schwätzen.

speechless ['spi:tʃlis], *adj.* 1. sprachlos (*with*, vor (*Dat.*)); 2. wortkarg, stumm (*as a p.*); 3. unsagbar, unsäglich (*grief etc.*). **speechlessness,** *s.* die Sprachlosigkeit.

speed [spi:d], **1.** *s.* 1. die Eile, Schnelligkeit, Geschwindigkeit; (*Av.*) ***air –,*** die Eigengeschwindigkeit; ***at a – of 60 m.p.h.,*** in einer Geschwindigkeit von 100 km in der Stunde; ***travel at –,*** schnell fahren; ***at full –,*** mit äußerster *or* größter Geschwindigkeit; (*Naut.*) ***full – ahead,*** volle Kraft voraus; ***gather –,*** an Geschwindigkeit zunehmen; (*Av.*) ***ground –,*** absolute Geschwindigkeit; ***high*** or ***top –,*** die Höchstgeschwindigkeit; (*Naut.*) ***half –,*** halbe Fahrt; (*Naut.*) ***slow –,*** kleine Fahrt; (*Naut.*) ***three-quarter –,*** große Fahrt; ***with all possible –,*** möglichst eilig; (*Prov.*) ***more haste, less –,*** Eile mit Weile; 2. (*Motor.*) der Gang; 3. (*Opt.*) die Belichtungszeit (*of shutter*), Lichtstärke (*of lens*); 4. (*obs.*) der Erfolg. **2.** *irr.v.i.* 1. (sich be)eilen; 2. (*only reg.*) (*Motor. coll.*) die Höchstgeschwindigkeit überschreiten, (zu) schnell fahren, rasen; 3. (*only reg.*) ***– up,*** sich beschleunigen; 4. (*obs.*) Glück haben, gedeihen, vorwärtskommen. **3.** *irr.v.t.* 1. eilig fortschicken, schnell verabschieden (*a p.*); ***– the parting guest,*** sich von dem scheidenden Gast verabschieden; 2. schnell befördern *or* absenden *or* ausführen *or* zu Ende führen *or* abfertigen *or* erledigen; 3. (*only reg.*) (*also* ***– up***) beschleunigen; (*fig.*) erhöhern (*production etc.*); 4. (*obs.*) fördern, beistehen (*Dat.*), Glück wünschen (*Dat.*), gedeihen lassen; (*obs.*) ***God – you!*** Gott geleite dich!

speed|-boat, *s.* das Schnellboot. **--cop,** *s.* (*sl.*) motorisierter Verkehrspolizist.

speeder ['spi:də], *s.* der Schnellfahrer.

speed|-gauge, --indicator, *s.* 1. der Geschwindigkeitsmesser; 2. Drehzahlmesser, Tourenzähler.

speediness ['spi:dinis], *s.* die Eile, Schnelligkeit. **speeding,** *s.* (*Motor.*) die Geschwindigkeitsübertretung, das Schnellfahren.

speed|-limit, *s.* erlaubte Höchstgeschwindigkeit. **--merchant,** *s.* (*Motor. coll.*) der Kilometerfresser.

speedometer [spi:'dɔmitə], *s.* (*Motor.*) der Kilometerzähler. **speedster** ['spi:dstə], *s.* (*coll.*) der Kilometerfresser.

speed|-test, *s.* (*Psych.*) der Geschwindigkeitstest. **--trap,** *s.* (*Motor.*) die Autofalle. **--up,** *s.* die Beschleunigung. **–way,** *s.* die Motorradrennbahn.

speedwell ['spi:dwel], *s.* (*Bot.*) der Ehrenpreis.

speedy ['spi:di], *adj.* schnell, rasch, geschwind; baldig, prompt, unverzüglich, umgehend.

speiss [spais], *s.* (*Metall.*) die Speise.

speleologist [spi:li'ɔlədʒist], *s.* der Höhlenforscher. **speleology,** *s.* die Höhlenforschung.

[1]**spell** [spel], *s.* 1. bestimmte Arbeit(sleistung); die Arbeitszeit, Schicht; ***take a – at,*** sich eine Zeitlang beschäftigen mit; 2. (*coll.*) kurze Zeit, das Weilchen, die Weile, Zeitlang, Zeitspanne, Periode, der Zeitabschnitt; ***for a –,*** eine Weile lang; ***hot –,*** die Hitzeperiode; ***long – of fine weather,*** andauernde Schönwetterperiode.

[2]**spell,** *s.* der Zauber (*also fig.*); Zauberspruch, das Zauberwort, die Zauberformel; (*fig.*) der Bann, Reiz, die Bezauberung, Anziehungskraft; ***under a magic –,*** verzaubert; ***cast a – on*** or ***over,*** verzaubern, behexen.

[3]**spell,** **1.** *irr.v.t.* 1. buchstabieren; (orthographisch) richtig schreiben; ***c, a, t –s cat,*** c, a, t bildet ‚cat'; ***how do you – this word?*** wie schreibt man das Wort? ***be spelt with,*** sich schreiben mit; 2. ***– out,*** Buchstabe für Buchstabe lesen; (*fig.*) ausdrücklich erklären, eindeutig auseinandersetzen; 3. (*fig.*) bedeuten, besagen (*to*, für). **2.** *irr.v.i.* richtig schreiben.

spell|binder, *s.* fesselnder Redner. **–binding,** *adj.* fesselnd. **–bound,** *adj.* gefesselt, fasziniert, festgebannt.

speller ['spelə], *s.* 1. die Fibel; 2. ***be a good (bad) –,*** orthographisch (nicht) richtig schreiben. **spelling,** *s.* das Buchstabieren; die Rechtschreibung, Orthographie. **spelling|-bee,** *s.* das Buchstabierspiel. **--book,** *s.* die Fibel.

[1]**spelt** [spelt], *imperf., p.p. of* [3]**spell.**

[2]**spelt,** *s.* (*Bot.*) der Spelz, Dinkel.

spelter ['speltə], *s.* das Rohzink.

[1]**spencer** ['spensə], *s.* (*Dressm.*) der Spenzer.

[2]**spencer,** *s.* (*Naut.*) das Gaffelsegel.

spend [spend], **1.** *irr.v.t.* 1. ausgeben (*money*) (*on*, (*only with verbal notion*) *in*, für); (*coll.*) ***– a penny,*** austreten, mal verschwinden; 2. aufwenden, verwenden, anlegen (*time*) (auf (*Acc.*), *or* für); 3. zubringen, verbringen (*time*); 4. durchbringen, vergeuden, verschwenden, vertun, unnütz ausgeben, verausgaben (*in*, für) (*a fortune*); 4. aufbrauchen, erschöpfen (*a supply etc.*); ***– itself,*** sich legen (*as anger etc.*); ***– o.s.,*** sich verausgaben *or* erschöpfen. **2.** *v.i.* Aufwand *or* Ausgaben machen, Geld ausgeben. **spending money,** *s.* das Taschengeld. **spendthrift, 1.** *s.* der (die) Verschwender(in). **2.** *adj.* verschwenderisch.

spent [spent], **1.** *imperf., p.p. of* **spend. 2.** *adj.* erschöpft, entkräftet (***with***, von); kraftlos, verbraucht; matt (*as a bullet*); ***– liquor,*** das Abwasser, die Ablauge.

[1]**sperm** [spə:m], *s.* die Samenflüssigkeit, das Sperma; Samenkörperchen.

[2]**sperm,** *s.* (*also* ***--whale***) der Pottwal. **spermaceti** [–ə'seti], *s.* der *or* das Walrat.

spermary ['spə:məri], *s.* die Keimdrüse, (männliche) Samendrüse. **spermatic** [–'mætik], *adj.* Samen–, samenhaltig.

spermatoblast ['spə:mətəblæst], *s.* die Ursamenzelle. **spermatogenesis** [–'dʒenisis], *s.* die Samenbildung. **spermatogenetic** [–dʒi'netik], *adj.* samenfädenerzeugend. **spermatophore** [–fɔ:], *s.* der Samenträger, die Samenkapsel. **spermatorrhoea** [–'riə], *s.* der Samenfluß. **spermatozoon** [–'zouən], *s.* (*usu. pl.* **-zoa** [–'zouə]) das Spermatozoon, die Spermie.

spermo– ['spə:mou], *pref.* Samen–; *for compounds see under* **spermato–.**

spew [spju:], (*coll.*) **1.** *v.t.* (*also* ***– up*** or ***out***) ausspeien, ausspucken, auswerfen. **2.** *v.i.* 1. sich erbrechen, (*vulg.*) kotzen; 2. (*fig.*) (*also* ***– forth***) (heraus)fließen. **3.** *s.* der Auswurf, (*vulg.*) die Kotze.

sphacelate ['sfæsileit], *v.i.* brandig werden. **sphacelation** [–'leiʃən], *s.* die Nekrose; Brandbildung.

sphagnum ['sfægnəm], *s.* das Torfmoos, Sumpfmoos.

sphenoid(al) ['sfi:nɔid (sfi'nɔidl)], *adj.* keilförmig, keilartig, Keil–; – ***bone,*** das Keilbein.

sphere ['sfiə], *s.* 1. (*Math.*) die Kugel; der Himmelskörper; die Erdkugel; das Himmelsgewölbe; ***celestial*** –, das Himmelsgewölbe; ***music of the -s,*** die Sphärenmusik; 2. (*Poet.*) der Himmel; 3. (*fig.*) die Sphäre, der (Wirkungs)kreis, Bereich, das Gebiet, Feld; – ***of activity,*** der Wirkungskreis, Wirkungsbereich; – ***of interest,*** die Interessensphäre; ***in his*** –, auf seinem Gebiet; ***out of*** or ***beyond his*** –, außerhalb seines Bereichs.

spheric ['sferik], *adj.* 1. kugelförmig; 2. (*Poet.*) himmlisch; *see also* **spherical. spherical,** *adj.* kugelförmig, kugelig, kugelrund; (*Math.*) sphärisch; – ***sector,*** der Kugelausschnitt; – ***segment,*** das Kugelsegment; – ***triangle,*** das Kugeldreieck. **sphericity** [–'risiti], *s.* die Rundheit, Kugelgestalt. **spherics,** *pl.* (*sing. constr.*) die Kugellehre, Sphärik.

spheroid ['sfiərɔid], *s.* das Rotationsellipsoid, Sphäroid. **spheroidal** [–'rɔidl], *adj.* kugelig, sphäroidisch.

spherule ['sferju:l], *s.* das Kügelchen. **spherulite** [–julait], *s.* (*Min.*) der Sphärolith, Nierenstein.

sphincter ['sfiŋktə], *s.* (*Anat.*) der Schließmuskel, Ringmuskel.

sphinx [sfiŋks], *s.* (*Myth.*) die Sphinx; die *or* der Sphinx (*in Egypt*). **sphinx|-like,** *adj.* sphinxartig, rätselhaft. **--moth,** *s.* (*Ent.*) der Schwärmer (*Sphingidae*).

sphragistics [sfræ'dʒistiks], *pl.* (*sing. constr.*) die Siegelkunde.

sphygmogram ['sfigmogræm], *s.* die Pulskurve. **sphygmograph,** *s.* der Pulsschreiber, Pulskurvenmesser. **sphygmomanometer** [–mə'nɔmitə], *s.* der Blutdruckmesser.

spica ['spaikə], *s.* (*pl.* **-cae** [–si:]) die Ähre, Granne. **spicate** [–keit], *adj.* ährenförmig.

spice [spais], **1.** *s.* 1. das Gewürz, die Würze; 2. (*fig.*) der Anstrich, Anflug, Beigeschmack. **2.** *v.t.* würzen (*also fig.*). **Spice Islands,** *pl.* die Gewürzinseln, Molukken (*pl.*). **spiciness,** *s.* die Würzigkeit; das Pikante.

spick-and-span ['spikən'spæn], *adj.* geschniegelt (und gebügelt), wie aus dem Ei gepellt; ***make*** –, auf Glanz herrichten.

spicular ['spikjulə], *adj.* ährenförmig, nadelförmig. **spicule** ['spaikju:l], *s.* das Ährchen, die Nadel, nadelförmiger Fortsatz; (*Zool.*) der Stachel.

spicy ['spaisi], *adj.* würzig, gewürzt, pikant.

spider ['spaidə], *s.* 1. die Spinne; ***–'s web,*** das Spinn(en)gewebe, die Spinnwebe; 2. (*Tech.*) der Dreifuß, das Drehkreuz. **spider-like,** *adj.* spinnenartig. **spidery,** *adj.* (*usu. fig.*) Spinnen–, spinnenartig, dünn.

spiffing ['spifiŋ], *adj.* (*obs. coll.*) glänzend, großartig.

spif(f)licate ['spiflikeit], *v.t.* (*sl.*) vernichten, abtun, erledigen, fertigmachen, den Garaus machen (*Dat.*). **spif(f)lication** [–'keiʃən], *s.* die Vernichtung, Erledigung.

spigot ['spigət], *s.* der Zapfen, Hahn.

spike [spaik], **1.** *s.* 1. langer Nagel, der Bolzen, Spieker; 2. Dorn, Stachel, die Spitze; (*Bot.*) Ähre; 3. *pl.* (*Spt.*) Spikes (*pl.*). **2.** *v.t.* 1. mit eisernen Spitzen versehen; 2. vernageln (*a gun etc.*); (*fig.*) – ***his guns,*** seine Pläne vereiteln; 3. (*sl.*) einen Schuß Alkohol geben (*Dat.*) (*a drink*).

spikenard ['spaiknɑ:d], *s.* (*Bot.*) die Narde; das Nardenöl.

spike-oil, *s.* das Lavendelöl. **spiky,** *adj.* spitz(ig), stach(e)lig, zackig.

spile [spail], **1.** *s.* 1. der Spund, Zapfen; 2. Pflock, Pfahl. **2.** *v.t.* 1. spunden, verspünden; 2. (*obs. or dial.*) anzapfen.

[1]**spill** [spil], *s.* der Fidibus.

[2]**spill, 1.** *irr.v.t.* 1. verschütten; ***it's no use crying over spilt milk,*** geschehene Dinge sind nicht zu ändern; (*sl.*) – ***the beans,*** alles ausquatschen; 2. vergießen (*blood*); 3. (*coll.*) abwerfen, herunterschleudern (*a rider etc.*); 4. killen lassen (*a sail*). **2.** *irr.v.i.* verschüttet werden, überlaufen. **3.** *s.* (*coll.*) der Sturz, Fall. **spillage** [–idʒ], *s.* das Verschüttete, Vergossene.

spillikin ['spilikin], *s.* 1. das Stäbchen; 2. *pl.* Federspiel.

spillway ['spilwei], *s.* der Abflußkanal.

spilt, *imperf., p.p. of* [2]**spill.**

spin [spin], **1.** *irr.v.t.* 1. spinnen (*thread*), ausziehen (*glass etc.*); (*coll. fig.*) – ***a yarn,*** Seemannsgarn spinnen; – ***out,*** in die Länge ziehen, ausdehnen; 2. wirbeln, drehen (*a top*); 3. (*Av.*) trudeln lassen. **2.** *irr.v.i.* spinnen, herumwirbeln, kreiseln, sich drehen; (*Av.*) trudeln; ***my head is spinning,*** mir schwindelt, mir dreht sich alles; ***send him spinning,*** ihn hinschleudern; – ***along,*** schnell dahinrollen; – ***out,*** sich ausspinnen *or* in die Länge ziehen; – ***round,*** sich im Kreise drehen. **3.** *s.* 1. das Herumdrehen, Wirbeln, schnelle Drehung; 2. rasche Fahrt, kurze Spazierfahrt; 3. (*Av.*) das Trudeln, die Sturzspirale.

spinach ['spinitʃ], *s.* der Spinat.

spinal [spainl], *adj.* Rückgrat(s)–, Wirbel–, Rückenmarks–; – ***column,*** das Rückgrat, die Wirbelsäule; – ***curvature,*** die Rückgratsverkrümmung; – ***cord*** or ***marrow,*** das Rückenmark.

spindle [spindl], *s.* die Spindel; Welle, Achse, der Achszapfen. **spindle|-shanks,** *pl.* (*coll.*) 1. dünne Beine; 2. (*sing. constr.*) das Langbein, dünnbeiniger Mensch. **--shaped,** *adj.* spindelförmig. **--side,** *s.* (*obs.*) weibliche Linie, mütterlicher Zweig. **spindly,** *adj.* spindeldürr; lang und dünn.

spin|-drier, *s.* der Wäscheschleuder. **-drift,** *s.* der Gischt, (Wellen)schaum.

spine [spain], *s.* (*Anat.*) das Rückgrat, die Wirbelsäule; ***send a shiver down his*** –, ihm eine Gänsehaut über den Rücken kriechen lassen; 2. (*Bot.*) der Dorn, Stachel; 3. (*Bookb.*) (Buch)rücken; 4. Kamm, (Gebirgs)grat. **spineless,** *adj.* 1. rückgratlos; 2. (*fig.*) haltlos, schlaff, schlapp, schwach.

spinel ['spinəl], *s.* (*Min.*) der Spinell.

spinet [spi'net], *s.* das Spinett.

spinnaker ['spinəkə], *s.* (*Naut.*) der Spinnaker, das Dreiecksegel.

spinner ['spinə], *s.* 1. der (die) Spinner(in); 2. die Spinnmaschine; 3. (*Spt. coll.*) der Drehball; 4. (*Angling*) Blinker; 5. (*Ent.*) *see* **spinneret**; 6. (*coll.*) *see* **spin-drier. spinneret,** *s.* die Spinndrüse.

spinney ['spini], *s.* das Gehölz, Gestrüpp, Gebüsch, Dickicht.

spinning ['spiniŋ], **1.** *adj.* rotierend, sich drehend. **2.** *s.* 1. das Drehen, Wirbeln, Trudeln; 2. (*Tech.*) das Spinnen, die Spinnerei. **spinning|-jenny,** *s.* die Feinspinnmaschine, Jennymaschine. **--machine,** *s.* die Spinnmaschine. **--mill,** *s.* die Spinnerei. **--wheel,** *s.* das Spinnrad.

spinose ['spainous], *adj. See* **spinous. spinosity** [–'nɔsiti], *s.* das Dornige, Stach(e)lige, die Dornigkeit, Stach(e)ligkeit. **spinous** [–əs], *adj.* dornig, stach(e)lig; – ***process,*** der Dornfortsatz.

spinster ['spinstə], *s.* 1. unverheiratete Frau; – ***aunt,*** unverheiratete Tante; 2. älteres Fräulein, alte Jungfer. **spinsterhood,** *s.* 1. lediger Stand (*of woman*), der Altjungfernstand; 2. die Altjüngferlichkeit.

spiny ['spaini], *adj.* dornig, stach(e)lig; (*Zool.*) – ***ant-eater,*** der Ameisenigel.

spiracle ['spairəkl], *s.* das Luftloch, Atemloch, die Trachealöffnung; das Nasenloch, Spritzloch (*of a whale*).

spiraea [spaiə'riə], *s.* (*Bot.*) die Spiräe, Spierstaude, der Geißbart.

spiral ['spaiərəl], **1.** *adj.* schraubenförmig, spiral(förmig), schneckenförmig; Spiral–; gewunden; – ***nebula,*** der Spiralnebel; – ***spring,*** die Spiralfeder; – ***staircase,*** die Wendeltreppe. **2.** *s.* 1. die Spirale, Schneckenlinie, Schraubenlinie; 2. (*Av.*) der Spiral(gleit)flug; 3. (*fig., Comm.*) die Spirale. **3.** *v.i.* sich spiralförmig bewegen.

spirant ['spaiərənt], **1.** *s.* (*Phonet.*) der Reibelaut, Spirant, die Spirans. **2.** *adj.* spirantisch.

[1]**spire** ['spaiə], *s.* 1. die Turmspitze, spitzer Kirchturm; 2. spitzer Körper.

[2]**spire,** *s.* 1. die Windung, Spirale; 2. (*Zool.*) das Gewinde (*of shell*).

spirit ['spirit], **1.** *s.* 1. der Geist, die Seele, der Odem; – ***of the age,*** der Zeitgeist; ***in*** (***the***) –, im Geist; 2. der Geist, das Gespenst; ***evil*** –, böser *or* schädlicher Geist; ***Holy Spirit,*** Heiliger Geist; 3. das Feuer, Leben, der Schwung, Elan, Mut, die Energie, Lebhaftigkeit; ***break his*** –, ihn mutlos *or* verzagt machen; ***enter into the*** –, enthusiastisch mitmachen; ***with*** –, mit Feuer *or* Schwung *or* Elan; 4. seelisch-geistige *or* treibende Kraft, das Wesen, eigentlicher Gehalt *or* Sinn; – ***of charity,*** die Nächstenliebe; – ***of mischief,*** böse Absicht; ***public*** –, der Gemeinsinn; ***take it in the wrong*** –, es falsch auffassen; (*coll.*) ***that's the*** –*!* so ist's recht! 5. geistige Haltung *or* Einstellung, die Gesinnung; *pl.* (*usu. with attrib.*) Stimmung; ***great*** or ***good*** or ***high*** –***s,*** die Heiterkeit, Munterkeit, der Frohsinn, fröhliche *or* gehobene Stimmung; ***in*** (***good***) –***s,*** heiter, gut aufgelegt; ***low*** –***s,*** die Niedergeschlagenheit, Deprimiertheit, gedrückte Stimmung; ***in low*** –***s, out of*** –***s,*** niedergeschlagen, bedrückt, deprimiert; (*B.*) ***the poor in*** –, die geistlich Armen; ***revive his*** –***s,*** ihn aufheitern; 6. (*Chem. etc.*) der Alkohol, Spiritus; –***s of wine,*** der Weingeist; ***methylated*** –***s,*** denaturierter Spiritus, der Methylalkohol; 7. *pl.* geistiges Getränk, Spirituosen (*pl.*). **2.** *v.t.* – ***away,*** hinwegzaubern, verschwinden lassen.

spirited ['spiritid], *adj.* 1. lebhaft, lebendig, energisch, mutig, feurig; 2. (*as suff.*) -gesinnt, -gesonnen; ***high***-–, ausgelassen, feurig; ***low***-–, niedergeschlagen; ***public***-–, gemeinsinnig, um das Gemeinwohl besorgt; ***poor***-–, ***tame***-–, verzagt, mutlos. **spiritedness,** *s.* das Feuer, der Mut, die Lebendigkeit, Energie, Lebhaftigkeit.

spiritism ['spiritizm], *s.* der Spiritismus. **spiritist,** *s.* der (die) Spiritist(in). **spiritistic** [–'tistik], *adj.* spiritistisch.

spirit-lamp, *s.* die Spirituslampe.

spiritless ['spiritlis], *adj.* 1. niedergeschlagen, verzagt, mutlos, zaghaft, kleinlaut, kleinmütig; 2. leblos, geistlos, temperamentlos, schwunglos. **spiritlessness,** *s.* 1. die Niedergeschlagenheit, Mutlosigkeit, Verzagtheit, der Kleinmut; 2. die Geistlosigkeit, Temperamentlosigkeit, Schwunglosigkeit.

spirit|-level, *s.* die Libelle, Nivellierwaage. **–-rapping,** *s.* das Tischklopfen, Geisterklopfen. **–-stain,** *s.* die Spritbeize. **–-stove,** *s.* der Spirituskocher.

spiritual ['spiritjuəl], **1.** *adj.* 1. geistig, unkörperlich, seelisch; – ***life,*** das Seelenleben; 2. (*Eccl.*) geistlich, kirchlich; ***Lords Spiritual,*** die Bischöfe im Oberhaus. **2.** *s.* das Spiritual. **spiritualism,** *s.* 1. (*Phil.*) der Spiritualismus; 2. (*Eccl.*) Geisterglaube, Spiritismus. **spiritualist,** *s.* 1. (*Phil.*) der Spiritualist; 2. (*Eccl.*) Spiritist. **spiritualistic** [–'listik], *adj.* 1. (*Phil.*) spiritualistisch; 2. (*Eccl.*) spiritistisch. **spirituality** [–ju'æliti], *s.* 1. die Geistigkeit, Unkörperlichkeit, das Geistige, Seelische; 2. geistige Natur *or* Eigenschaft. **spiritualization** [–ai'zeiʃən], *s.* die Vergeistigung. **spiritualize,** *v.t.* vergeistigen.

spirituous ['spiritjuəs], *adj.* weingeisthaltig, alkoholisch, Alkohol–; – ***liquors,*** Spirituosen (*pl.*).

spirit-varnish, *s.* der Spritlack.

spirketing ['spə:kitiŋ], *s.* (*Naut.*) der Plankengang.

spirt, *see* [1]**spurt.**

[1]**spiry** ['spaiəri], *adj.* 1. spitz zulaufend; 2. viettürmig.

[2]**spiry,** *adj.* spiralförmig.

[1]**spit** [spit], **1.** *s.* 1. der (Brat)spieß; 2. (*Geog.*) die Landzunge. **2.** *v.t.* an den Bratspieß stecken; (*fig.*) aufspießen.

[2]**spit, 1.** *s.* der Speichel, die Spucke; (*coll.*) ***the very*** or ***dead*** – (***and image***) ***of his father,*** seinem Vater wie aus dem Gesicht geschnitten; 2. das Fauchen (*of a cat*); 3. (*coll.*) der Sprühregen. **2.** *irr.v.i.* 1. speien, spucken; – ***at*** or ***upon,*** anspucken, bespucken; (*fig.*) schändlich behandeln; – ***in his face,*** ihm ins Gesicht spucken; 2. fauchen (*as a cat*); 3. (*coll.*) sprühen (*as rain*); 4. spritzen (*as boiling fat*). **3.** *irr.v.t.* – ***out,*** ausspucken; (*fig.*) ausstoßen (*remarks*); (*sl.*) – ***it out!*** heraus damit!

[3]**spit,** *s.* der Spatenstich.

spit-curl, *s.* (*coll.*) die Schmachtlocke.

spite [spait], **1.** *s.* 1. die Boshaftigkeit, Bosheit, Gehässigkeit; 2. der Groll, Ärger; 3. ***in – of,*** trotz (*Gen.*), ungeachtet (*Gen.*); ***in – of that,*** dessenungeachtet; ***in – of you,*** dir zum Trotz. **2.** *v.t.* ärgern, kränken; (*coll.*) ***cut off one's nose to – one's face,*** sich (*Dat.*) ins eigene Fleisch schneiden. **spiteful,** *adj.* boshaft, gehässig. **spitefulness,** *s.* die Boshaftigkeit, Gehässigkeit.

spit|fire, *s.* der Hitzkopf, Brausekopf. **–-roaster,** *s.* *See* **rotisserie.**

spittle ['spitl], *s.* der Speichel, die Spucke. **spittoon** [–'tu:n], *s.* der Spucknapf.

spiv [spiv], *s.* (*sl.*) der Schwarzhändler, Schmarotzer.

splanchnic ['splæŋknik], *adj.* Eingeweide–.

splash [splæʃ], **1.** *v.t.* bespritzen (***with,*** mit), spritzen; (*fig.*) (be)sprenkeln. **2.** *v.i.* 1. (auf)spritzen; 2. planschen, platschen, plätschern. **3.** *s.* 1. das Spritzen, Plätschern; 2. plätscherndes Geräusch; 3. der Klecks, Spritzfleck; – ***of colour,*** der Farbfleck; 4. (*coll.*) das Aufsehen, die Furore. **splashboard,** *s.* 1. das Spritzbrett, Schutzbrett; 2. der Wandschoner. **splasher,** *s.* das Schutzblech, der Kotflügel. **splashy,** *adj.* 1. spritzend, platschend; 2. bespritzt.

splatter ['splætə], *v.i.* platschen, planschen, plätschern. **splatterdash,** *s.* der Lärm, das Getöse.

splay [splei], **1.** *adj.* gespreizt, auswärts gebogen (*as foot*), ausgebreitet, schief, schräg. **2.** *s.* (*Archit.*) die Schräge, Ausschrägung. **3.** *v.t.* 1. ausbreiten; 2. (*Archit.*) ausschrägen; 3. (*Vet.*) verrenken. **4.** *v.i.* ausgeschrägt sein, schräg liegen. **splayed,** *adj.* *See* **splay, 1. splay-foot,** *s.* der Spreizfuß.

spleen [spli:n], *s.* 1. (*Anat.*) die Milz; 2. (*fig.*) schlechte *or* üble Laune, der Ärger, Verdruß; ***give vent to*** or ***vent one's*** –, seiner schlechten Laune Luft machen. **spleenful, spleenish,** *adj.* griesgrämig, übelgelaunt, mürrisch.

splendent ['splendənt], *adj.* glänzend, leuchtend. **splendid** [–did], *adj.* glänzend, prächtig, herrlich, (*coll.*) großartig, ausgezeichnet, famos. **splendiferous** [–'difərəs], *adj.* (*coll.*) prächtig, herrlich. **splendour** [–də], *s.* der Glanz, Prunk, die Pracht, Herrlichkeit.

splenectomy [spli'nektəmi], *s.* (*Surg.*) die Milzentfernung. **splenetic** [–'netik], **1.** *adj.* 1. Milz–; 2. (*Med.*) milzkrank; 3. (*fig.*) verdrießlich, mürrisch; schwermütig, launisch. **2.** *s.* 1. (*Med.*) Milzkranke(r); 2. (*fig.*) der Griesgram, Hypochonder. **splenic** ['splenik], *adj.* Milz–; – ***fever,*** der Milzbrand. **splenitis** [spli'naitis], *s.* die Milzentzündung.

splice [splais], **1.** *s.* 1. (*Naut.*) die Splissung, der Spleiß; ***eye*** –, der Augspleiß; 2. (*Carp.*) die (Ein)falzung, Anscherung; 3. (*Films*) die Klebestelle, Klammerstelle. **2.** *v.t.* 1. (*Naut.*) spleißen, zusammensplissen (*ropes*); (*coll.*) – ***the main brace,*** die Rumration austeilen *or* ausgeteilt bekommen; 2. (*Carp.*) falzen, anscheren; 3. (*Films etc.*) zusammenkleben, zusammenfügen, verbinden; 4. (*sl.*) ehelich verbinden, verheiraten; ***get*** –***d,*** sich verheiraten.

spline [splain], *s.* (*Tech.*) die (Metall– *or* Holz)feder, der Keil.

splint [splint], **1.** *s.* (*Surg.*) die Schiene; ***in*** –***s,*** geschient, in Schienen. **2.** *v.t.* anschienen, einschienen (*a broken limb*). **splint|-bone,** *s.* das Wadenbein. **–-coal,** *s.* die Splitterkohle, Schieferkohle.

splinter ['splintə], **1.** *s.* der Splitter, Span; ***shell*** –, der Granatsplitter; ***break*** or ***fly in***(***to***) –***s,*** zersplittern, in tausend Stücke gehen. **2.** *v.t.* (zer)splittern. **3.** *v.i.* absplittern, zersplittern, zersplittert werden, in Stücke gehen. **splinter|-bar,** *s.*

der Schwengel, das Ortscheit. **--party,** *s.* (*Pol.*) die Splittergruppe. **--proof,** *adj.* splittersicher. **splintery,** *adj.* splitt(e)rig, blätt(e)rig, leichtsplitternd, Splitter–.

split [split], **1.** *s.* 1. der Spalt, Riß, Sprung; 2. (*fig.*) die Zersplitterung, Spaltung (*of a group*), Trennung, Entzweiung, der Bruch, das Zerwürfnis (*between individuals*); 3. *pl.* (*Gymn.*) die Grätsche, Grätschstellung, der Spagat; ***do the –s,*** Spagat machen. **2.** *irr.v.t.* 1. (zer)spalten, (auf)spalten (*also atoms*), zerteilen; – ***hairs,*** Haarspalterei treiben; – ***off,*** abspalten; – ***one's sides*** (***with laughing***), sich totlachen; 2. (*coll.*) (*also* – ***up***) unter sich teilen, aufteilen; – ***the difference,*** sich in die Differenz teilen; (*fig.*) sich auf einen Kompromiß einigen. **3.** *irr.v.i.* 1. sich (auf)spalten, bersten, zerplatzen, zerspringen, zersplittern, zerreißen; ***my head is splitting,*** mir will der Kopf zerspringen; 2. sich teilen *or* spalten (***into,*** in (*Acc.*)); – ***off,*** sich spalten; 3. (*coll.*) sich teilen (***on,*** in (*Acc.*)); 4. (*fig.*) (*also* – ***up***) sich entzweien *or* trennen; 5. (*sl.*) aus der Schule schwatzen; (*sl.*) – ***on him,*** ihn denunzieren *or* verraten *or* angeben. **4.** *adj.* gespalten, Spalt–; – ***infinitive,*** gespaltener Infinitiv; – ***leather,*** das Spaltleder; (*Archit.*) ***--level,*** mit Zwischenstockwerken; – ***peas,*** halbe Erbsen; – ***personality,*** gespaltene Persönlichkeit; (*Elec.*) – ***phase,*** die Hilfsphase; – ***pin,*** der Splint, geschlitzter Stift; – ***ring,*** der Spaltring; (*coll.*) – ***second,*** der Moment, Nu; (*Am. Pol.*) – ***ticket,*** der Wahlzettel mit mehreren Kandidaten.

splitting ['splitiŋ], **1.** *adj.* – ***headache,*** rasende Kopfschmerzen. **2.** *s.* die (Zer)spaltung, der Zerfall; – ***of the atom,*** die Atomspaltung.

splodge [splɔdʒ], *s.* der Klecks, Schmutzfleck. **splodgy,** *adj.* fleckig, schmutzig.

splurge [splə:dʒ], *s.* (*sl.*) offensichtliche Anstrengung, auffällige Bemühung, aufdringliche Zurschaustellung.

splutter ['splʌtə], **1.** *s.* das Sprühen, Verspritzen, Sprudeln. **2.** *v.i.* 1. hastig sprechen, plappern; 2. sprudeln, sprühen, spritzen; 3. klecksen (*as a pen*); 4. kleckern (*as a candle*); 5. kotzen, stottern, spucken (*as an engine*). **3.** *v.t.* – ***out,*** heraussprudeln, herausplappern, hervorstoßen (*words*).

spoil [spɔil], **1.** *irr.v.t.* 1. verderben, ruinieren, vereiteln, beeinträchtigen; (*coll.*) verpatzen, verschandeln; 2. verhätscheln, verziehen, verwöhnen (*child*); 3. (*only reg.*) (*obs.*) berauben, ausrauben, verwüsten, (aus)plündern. **2.** *irr.v.i.* 1. verderben, schlecht werden; 2. ***be –ing for,*** sich heftig sehnen nach, sehnlichst wünschen, schmachten nach, begierig sein auf (*Acc.*); ***–ing for a fight,*** streitsüchtig, rauflustig. **3.** *s.* 1. (*usu. pl.*) die (Sieges)-beute, der Raub, das Diebesgut; ***–s of war,*** die Kriegsbeute; 2. (*usu. pl.*) (*fig.*) die Ausbeute, Einkünfte (*pl.*), der Profit, Gewinn; 3. (*sing. only*) ausgehobene Erde; 4. der Schutt.

spoilage ['spɔilidʒ], *s.* 1. (*Typ.*) die Makulatur, der Fehldruck; 2. (*Comm.*) Verlust, Verderb.

spoil-bank, *s.* die Schutthalde.

spoiler ['spɔilə], *s.* der Plünderer, Verderber, Verwüster.

spoilsman ['spɔilzmən], *s.* (*Am.*) der Postenjäger, Schieber.

spoilsport ['spɔilspɔ:t], *s.* der (die) Spielverderber(in).

spoils system, *s.* (*Am. Pol.*) das Futterkrippensystem.

spoilt [spɔilt], *imperf., p.p. of* **spoil.**

[1]**spoke** [spouk], *imperf. of* **speak.**

[2]**spoke,** *s.* 1. die Speiche (*of a wheel*); 2. Sprosse (*of a ladder*); 3. (*Naut.*) Spake; 4. Bremsvorrichtung, der Hemmschuh; (*coll.*) ***put a – in his wheel,*** ihm ein Bein stellen, ihm den Knüppel zwischen die Beine werfen. **spoke-bone,** *s.* (*Anat.*) die Speiche.

spoken ['spoukən], **1.** *p.p. of* **speak. 2.** *adj.* 1. mündlich; 2. (*as suff.*) –sprechend, –redend.

spokeshave ['spoukʃeiv], *s.* (*Carp.*) der Schabhobel.

spokesman ['spouksmən], *s.* der Wortführer, (Für)sprecher. **spokeswoman,** *s.* die Wortführerin; (Für)sprecherin.

spoliate ['spoulieit], **1.** *v.t.* (aus)plündern, berauben, ausrauben. **2.** *v.i.* plündern. **spoliation** [–i'eiʃən], *s.* die Plünderung, Beraubung.

spondaic [spɔn'deiik], *adj.* spondeisch. **spondee** ['spɔndi:], *s.* der Spondeus.

spondyl(e) ['spɔndil], *s.* (*Anat.*) der Wirbelknochen. **spondylitis** [–'laitis], *s.* die Wirbelentzündung.

sponge [spʌndʒ], **1.** *s.* 1. der Schwamm (*also Zool.*); ***pass the – over,*** für erledigt erklären; aus dem Gedächtnis löschen; ***throw up the –,*** (*Boxing*) das Handtuch werfen; (*fig.*) die Flinte ins Korn werfen, sich geschlagen geben; 2. (*Artil.*) der Wischer; 3. (*fig.*) Schmarotzer, Nassauer, Schnorrer. **2.** *v.i.* 1. sich vollsaugen; 2. (*fig.*) schmarotzen, nassauern (***on,*** bei). **3.** *v.t.* 1. (mit einem Schwamme) abwischen *or* abwaschen; – ***down,*** abwaschen, abwischen; – ***up,*** aufsaugen; 2. (*sl.*) ergattern, schnorren (***from,*** von *or* bei), abknöpfen (*Dat.*). **spongeable,** *adj.* wischfest.

sponge|-bag, *s.* der Schwammbeutel. **–cake,** *s.* die Sandtorte. **--cloth,** *s.* das Frottee. **--down,** *s.* das Abwaschen, Abwischen, Abreiben; ***have a –,*** sich abwaschen *or* abwischen.

sponger ['spʌndʒə], *s.* 1. der Schwammfischer; 2. (*fig.*) Schmarotzer, Nassauer, Schnorrer.

sponge-rubber, *s.* der *or* das Schaumgummi.

sponginess ['spʌndʒinis], *s.* die Schwammigkeit. **sponging,** *s.* 1. das Abwaschen; 2. Schwammsammeln; 3. (*sl.*) Schmarotzen, Nassauern. **sponging-house,** *s.* (*Hist.*) provisorisches Schuldgefängnis. **spongy,** *adj.* **1.** schwamm(art)ig, Schwamm–; 2. (*fig.*) schwammig, porös, elastisch, locker; – ***platinum,*** der Platinschwamm; 3. sumpfig (*as soil*).

sponsal ['spɔnsəl], *adj.* hochzeitlich, Hochzeits–.

sponsion ['spɔnʃən], *s.* die Bürgschaft.

sponson ['spɔnsən], *s.* das Radgehäuse, der Radkasten (*of paddle-steamers*), Stützschwimmer (*of seaplanes*).

sponsor ['spɔnsə], **1.** *s.* 1. der Bürge (die Bürgin); ***stand – for,*** Bürge stehen *or* Bürgschaft leisten *or* (sich ver)bürgen für; 2. der (Tauf)pate (die (Tauf)patin), Taufzeuge (die Taufzeugin) (*to a child*); ***stand – to,*** Pate stehen bei; 3. (*fig.*) der (die) Gönner(in), Schirmherr(in), der Förderer. **2.** *v.t.* 1. unterstützen, fördern; 2. bürgen für, verantwortlich zeichnen für; 3. (*Rad., T.V.*) als Sponsor finanzieren. **sponsorial** [–'sɔ:riəl], *adj.* Paten–. **sponsorship,** *s.* 1. die Bürgschaft; 2. Patenschaft; 3. Verantwortlichkeit; 4. Gönnerschaft.

spontaneity [spɔntə'ni:iti], *s.* 1. die Freiwilligkeit, eigener *or* freier Antrieb; 2. die Ungezwungenheit, Natürlichkeit, Spontaneität. **spontaneous** [–'teiniəs], *adj.* 1. spontan, freiwillig, aus eignem *or* freiem Antrieb; 2. natürlich, ungekünstelt, ungezwungen; 3. automatisch, selbsttätig, instinktiv, unwillkürlich, unvorbereitet, Selbst–; – ***combustion,*** die Selbstverbrennung; – ***generation,*** die Urzeugung, Abiogenese; – ***ignition,*** die Selbstzündung. **spontaneously,** *adv.* von selbst, von innen heraus. **spontaneousness,** *s.* *See* **spontaneity.**

spoof [spu:f], **1.** *s.* (*sl.*) der Schwindel, Betrug, Humbug. **2.** *v.t.* (*sl.*) beschwindeln, verkohlen. **3.** *v.i.* schwindeln, flunkern. **4.** *adj.* vorgetäuscht, Schwindel–.

spook [spu:k], **1.** *s.* (*coll.*) das Gespenst, der Spuk. **2.** *v.i.* (*coll.*) (herum)geistern, spuken. **spooky,** *adj.* (*coll.*) spukhaft, gespenstisch.

spool [spu:l], **1.** *s.* die Spule, Haspel, Rolle. **2.** *v.t.* (auf)spulen, aufrollen, aufwickeln.

spoon [spu:n], **1.** *s.* 1. der Löffel; ***be born with a silver – in one's mouth,*** als Glückskind geboren *or* ein Sonntagskind sein; 2. (*Angling*) *see* **spoonbait**; 3. (*Golf*) der Spoon. **2.** *v.t.* 1. (*also* – ***up,*** – ***out***) auflöffeln, auslöffeln; 2. (*Spt.*) in die Höhe schlagen (*a ball*). **3.** *v.i.* (*sl.*) schmusen, poussieren.

spoon|-bait, *s.* der Blinker, Löffelköder. **–bill,** *s.* (*Orn.*) (*Am. **white** –*) der Löffler (*Platalea* *leucorodia*). **--bit,** *s.* (*Carp.*) der Löffelbohrer. **-drift,** *s.* (*Naut.*) der *or* die Gischt, der Schaum.

spoonerism [ˈspuːnərizm], *s.* der Schüttelreim.

spoon|-fed, *adj.* (*fig.*) verhätschelt, aufgepäppelt. **--feed,** *irr.v.t.* (*fig.*) verhätscheln, hochpäppeln, gängeln, am Gängelband halten *or* führen. **spoonful,** *s.* der Löffelvoll. **spoonwort,** *s.* (*Bot.*) das Löffelkraut. **spoony,** *adj.* (*sl.*) verliebt, vernarrt, verknallt, verschossen (***on***, in (*Acc.*)).

spoor [spuə], **1.** *s.* die Spur, Fährte. **2.** *v.t.* aufspüren, verfolgen. **3.** *v.i.* einer Spur folgen, eine Spur verfolgen.

sporadic(al) [spɔˈrædik(l)], *adj.* vereinzelt (auftretend), zerstreut, sporadisch.

sporange [ˈspɔrəndʒ], **sporangium** [spəˈrændʒiəm], *s.* der Sporenbehälter.

spore [spɔː], *s.* 1. (*Bot., Zool.*) die Spore, das Keimkorn; 2. (*fig.*) der Keim, die Keimzelle. **sporiferous** [–ˈrifərəs], *adj.* sporenbildend. **sporogenesis** [–roˈdʒenisis], *s.* die Sporenbildung. **sporozoon** [–roˈzouən], *s.* (*usu. pl.* **-zoa**) das Sporentierchen.

sporran [ˈspɔrən], *s.* (schottische) Felltasche.

sport [spɔːt], **1.** *s.* 1. der Sport, das Spiel; *pl.* Leichtathletikwettkämpfe (*pl.*), die Sportveranstaltung; ***go in for –,*** Sport treiben; 2. der Scherz, Spaß; ***capital*** or ***great –,*** der Hauptspaß, das Hauptvergnügen; ***make – of,*** zum besten haben, seinen Spaß haben mit, Spaß treiben mit, sich belustigen über (*Acc.*); ***in*** or ***for –,*** im *or* zum Scherz; 3. die Belustigung, Kurzweil, der Zeitvertreib; 4. (*fig.*) Spielball, das Spielzeug, Opfer; ***the – of every wind,*** das Spielzeug der Winde; 5. (*Biol.*) die Abart, Spielart; 6. (*sl.*) anständiger *or* guter Kerl. **2.** *v.i.* spielen, scherzen, sich belustigen, sich tummeln (***with***, mit). **3.** *v.t.* zur Schau tragen, sich sehen lassen mit, paradieren mit; (*Univ. coll.*) ***– one's oak,*** die Tür seiner Bude schließen *or* verschlossen halten.

sporting [ˈspɔːtiŋ], *adj.* 1. sportlich, Sport–; ***– activities,*** sportliche Umtriebe; (*coll.*) ***– chance,*** die Chance, gute Aussicht; ***take a – chance,*** es wagen; ***– news,*** der Sportbericht, (*esp.*) Rennergebnisse (*pl.*); ***– paper,*** das Sportblatt; 2. Jagd–; ***– gun,*** das Jagdgewehr; 3. (*coll.*) sportlich, fair, anständig; ***– conduct,*** sportliches Benehmen, die Fairneß.

sportive [ˈspɔːtiv], *adj.* 1. verspielt, mutwillig; 2. scherzhaft, spaßhaft. **sportiveness,** *s.* 1. die Verspieltheit, Mutwilligkeit; 2. Scherzhaftigkeit, Spaßhaftigkeit.

sports| badge, *s.* das Sportabzeichen. **– car,** *s.* der Sportwagen. **– clothes,** *pl. See* **–wear. – coat,** *s. See* **– jacket. – day,** *s.* das Sportfest. **– field, – ground,** *s.* der Sportplatz. **– jacket,** *s.* das Herrenjackett, der Sportsakko.

sportsman [ˈspɔːtsmən], *s.* 1. der Sportler, Sportsmann, Sportliebhaber; Jäger, Angler, Fischer; 2. (*coll.*) anständiger Kerl. **sportsmanlike,** *adj.* sportlich. **sportsmanship,** *s.* die Sportlichkeit, sportliches Benehmen, die Fairneß.

sports| outfitter, *s.* der Sportwarenhändler. **– page,** *s.* der Sportteil, die Sportbeilage. **–wear,** *s.* die Sportkleidung. **–woman,** *s.* die Sportlerin.

sporty [ˈspɔːti], *adj.* (*coll.*) sportlich.

sporular [ˈspɔrjulə], *adj.* (*Biol.*) Sporen–, sporenartig. **sporule** [ˈspɔrjuːl], *s.* die Spore.

spot [spɔt], **1.** *s.* 1. der Fleck(en), Klecks; 2. Tupfen, Farbfleck; ***a leopard cannot change its –s,*** man kann nicht aus seiner Haut heraus; (*sl.*) ***knock –s off him,*** ihn nach Strich und Faden besiegen; 3. (*Med.*) der Pickel, die (Haut)pustel, das Eiterbläschen; Hautmal, der Leberfleck; 4. die Stelle, der Platz, Ort; ***on the –,*** zur Stelle, an Ort und Stelle; (*coll.*) auf der Stelle, sogleich, sofort, unverzüglich; (*sl.*) (*also* ***in a –***) in der Klemme; (*sl.*) ***put him on the –,*** ihn in die Enge treiben; ***sore –,*** empfindliche *or* wunde Stelle; 5. der Tropfen, (*coll.*) das bißchen, Stückchen; 6. (*Bill.*) der Point; 7. (*fig.*) der Fleck(en), Schandfleck, Makel; 8. *pl.* (*Comm.*) *see* ***– goods***; 9. (*coll.*) (*Theat.*) *see* **spotlight. 2.** *v.t.* 1. beflecken (*also fig.*), fleckig machen; 2. sprenkeln, tüpfeln, betupfen; 3. (*fig.*) besudeln, beschmutzen; 4. (*Mil.*) sichten, beobachten, ausmachen, lokalisieren; (*coll.*) bemerken, erkennen, entdecken, herausfinden, ausfindig machen; 5. (*Bill.*) placieren. **3.** *v.i.* flecken, fleckig werden, Flecke bekommen. **4.** *adj.* (*Comm.*) sofort zahlbar *or* lieferbar; bar, Bar–; ***– business,*** das Lokogeschäft, Platzgeschäft; ***– cash,*** die Barzahlung, sofortige Kasse; ***– goods,*** Lokowaren (*pl.*); ***– market,*** der Barverkehr(smarkt); ***– price,*** der Kassapreis; ***– transaction,*** das Kassageschäft.

spot-check, *s.* die Stichprobe.

spotless [ˈspɔtlis], *adj.* fleckenlos, (*fig.*) unbescholten, unbefleckt, makellos. **spotlessness,** *s.* die Fleckenlosigkeit, (*fig.*) Unbescholtenheit, Unbeflecktheit, Makellosigkeit.

spotlight [ˈspɔtlait], **1.** *s.* 1. das Scheinwerferlicht; 2. (*fig.*) Rampenlicht der Öffentlichkeit. **2.** *v.t.* 1. anstrahlen; 2. (*fig.*) in den Vordergrund (der Aufmerksamkeit) ziehen, die Aufmerksamkeit lenken auf (*Acc.*).

spotted [ˈspɔtid], *adj.* 1. gefleckt, getüpfelt, gesprenkelt; (*coll.*) ***– dick*** or ***dog,*** der Korinthenpudding; ***– fever,*** die Genickstarre; 2. (*fig.*) befleckt, besudelt. **spotter,** *s.* (*Av.*) der Erkundungsflieger, (*Mil.*) Artilleriebeobachter, Anzeiger (*rifle-shooting*), Flugmelder, die Flugwache (*anti-aircraft*).

spot|-test, *s. See* **--check.**

spottiness [ˈspɔtinis], *s.* 1. die Fleckigkeit, Beflecktheit; 2. (*complexion*) Pickeligkeit. **spotting,** *s.* 1. die Fleckenbildung; 2. (*Av., Mil.*) Schußbeobachtung, Erkundung, Aufklärung, (*anti-aircraft*) der Fliegerwarndienst. **spotty,** *adj.* fleckig, gefleckt; befleckt; pickelig (*of complexion*).

spot|-weld, *v.t., v.i.* punktschweißen. **--welding,** *s.* die Punktschweißung.

spousal [spauzl], **1.** *s.* (*usu. pl.*) (*obs.*) die Hochzeit. **2.** *adj.* hochzeitlich, Hochzeits–, ehelich, bräutlich. **spouse** [spaus], *s.* der Gatte (die Gattin), der (die) Gemahl(in).

spout [spaut], **1.** *s.* 1. die Tülle, Schneppe, Schnauze, der Schnabel (*of a vessel*); 2. das Abflußrohr, Speirohr, der Ausguß (*of a gutter*); 3. (*coll.*) die Dachrinne, Traufe; 4. der Wasserstrahl; *see esp.* **waterspout**; (*of whale*) die Fontäne; 5. (*sl.*) ***up the –,*** verpfändet; futsch, hin. **2.** *v.t.* 1. ausspeien, hervorsprudeln, herausspritzen; 2. (*sl.*) deklamieren, hersagen (*verse etc.*). **3.** *v.i.* 1. hervorsprudeln, hervorquellen, spritzen (*also of whales*); 2. (*sl.*) deklamieren, ein gutes Mundwerk haben, große Reden halten. **spouter,** *s.* 1. (*coll.*) spritzender Wal; 2. (*coll.*) die Ölquelle; 3. (*sl.*) der Kannegießer, Schwätzer.

sprag [spræg], *s.* der Hemmschuh, Bremskeil.

sprain [sprein], **1.** *s.* die Verrenkung, Verstauchung. **2.** *v.t.* verrenken, verstauchen.

sprang [spræŋ], *imperf. of* [1]**spring.**

sprat [spræt], **1.** *s.* die Sprotte; (*fig. coll.*) ***throw a – to catch a mackerel,*** mit der Wurst nach der Speckseite werfen. **2.** *v.i.* Sprotten fangen, nach Sprotten fischen.

sprawl [sprɔːl], **1.** *v.i.* 1. sich rekeln, sich hinlümmeln *or* hinfläzen (*of a p.*), ausgestreckt daliegen, sich ausbreiten *or* erstrecken *or* dehnen; 2. (*Bot.*) wuchern. **2.** *s.* das Rekeln, Spreizen, die Ausbreitung; ***urban –,*** ungeregelte Ausbreitung des Stadtgebiets.

[1]**spray** [sprei], **1.** *s.* der Zweig, das Reis, Reisig; ***– of flowers,*** der Blütenzweig.

[2]**spray, 1.** *s.* 1. der Sprühregen, Wasserstaub, das Sprühwasser, Spritzwasser; 2. der (Wellen)schaum, Gischt; 3. (*fig.*) Regen (*of bullets etc.*); 4. die Sprühdose, der Zerstäuber, Spray(apparat). **2.** *v.t.* 1. (be)spritzen, (be)sprengen; 2. zerstäuben. **3.** *v.i.* spritzen, sprühen, zerstieben. **sprayer,** *s.* die Spritze, der Zerstäuber. **spray-gun,** *s.* die Spritzpistole.

spread [spred], **1.** *irr.v.t.* 1. ausbreiten, ausdehnen; ***– the cloth,*** den Tisch decken; ***the peacock –s his tail,*** der Pfau schlägt ein Rad; ***– o.s.,*** sich ausbreiten; (*fig.*) sich wichtig tun, sich mächtig anstrengen; – ***out,*** ausbreiten, ausstrecken, entfalten, entrollen; 2. (zer)streuen, verteilen (*manure etc.*); 3. streichen (*bread, also butter on bread*) (*on*, auf (*Acc.*)); 4. bedecken, bestreichen, überziehen, übersäen (***with,*** mit); 5. (*fig.*) verbreiten, ausstreuen; – ***abroad,*** verbreiten, aussprengen (*rumours*). **2.** *irr.v.i.* 1. (*also* – ***out***) sich ausbreiten *or* erstrecken *or* vertellen *or* ausdehnen; 2. sich auftragen *or* streichen lassen (*as paint, butter etc.*); 3. (*fig.*) sich verbreiten; – ***like wildfire,*** sich wie ein Lauffeuer verbreiten. **3.** *s.* 1. die Verbreitung, Ausbreitung; 2. Ausdehnung, der Umfang, die Weite, Breite, Spanne, Differenz; ***lateral*** –, die Seitenausdehnung; (*coll.*) ***middle-age*** –, die Behäbigkeit, Körperfülle der mittleren Jahre; 3. die Spannweite; (*Av., Orn.*) ***wing*** –, die Geflügelspanne; 4. (*Press*) die Aufschlagseite, Anzeige; 5. (*esp. Am. St. Exch.*) das Stellagegeschäft, die Stellage; 6. (*Math., Stat.*) (Zer)streuung, Verteilung; 7. der (Brot)aufstrich; 8. (*coll.*) Schmaus, das Gelage, Mahl. **4.** *adj.* 1. verstreut; 2. gespreizt.

spread| eagle, *s.* 1. (*Her.*) der Wappenadler; 2. (*coll. Am.*) Hurrapatriot; 3. Angeber, Aufschneider. **--eagle, 1.** *adj.* 1. (*Am. coll.*) hurrapatriotisch; 2. angeberisch, aufschneiderisch, prahlerisch, anmaßend. **2.** *v.t.* ausbreiten, spreizen.

spreader ['spredə], *s.* 1. die Abstandstütze, Spannvorrichtung; 2. Streumaschine, der Verteiler; 3. (*Naut.*) Ausleger, blinde Rahe. **spreading,** *adj.* ausgebreitet, verbreitet, weit verstreut. **spread-over,** *s.* (*coll.*) die Verteilung, Austeilung.

spree [spri:], *s.* (*coll.*) das Zechgelage; lustiger Streich, der Spaß, Feez; ***go on the*** –, auf den Bummel gehen; ***spending*** –, der Einkaufsrummel.

Spree [sprei], *s.* die Spree (*river*).

sprig [sprig], **1.** *v.t.* 1. mit kleinen Zweigen verzieren; 2. mit Zwecken befestigen. **2.** *s.* 1. der Zweig, Sprößling, das Reis; 2. (*Naut., Carp.*) der Stift, die Zwecke.

sprightliness ['spraitlinis], *s.* die Lebendigkeit, Lebhaftigkeit, Behendigkeit, Munterkeit. **sprightly,** *adj.* lebhaft, munter.

[1]**spring** [spriŋ], **1.** *irr.v.i.* 1. springen, hüpfen; schnellen; 2. entspringen, quellen, sprudeln (***from,*** aus); 3. herkommen, herstammen (***from,*** von); 4. sich werfen (*wood*).

(a) (*with prep.*) – ***at,*** losspringen auf (*Acc.*); – ***at his throat,*** ihm an die Kehle springen; – ***from,*** entspringen aus (*or Dat.*), entstehen aus; (*of a p.*) abstammen von; (*coll.*) ***where did you – from?*** wo kommst du her? – ***into existence,*** (plötzlich) entstehen; – ***into fame,*** plötzlich berühmt werden; – (***up***)***on,*** losstürzen *or* springen auf (*Acc.*), anfallen; – ***to arms,*** zu den Waffen greifen; – ***to his assistance,*** ihm beispringen, ihm zu Hilfe eilen; (*Mil.*) – ***to attention,*** stramm stehen; – ***to one's feet,*** aufspringen, auf die Füße springen; – ***to the eyes,*** auffallen, in die Augen springen.

(b) (*with adv.*) – ***back,*** zurückspringen, zurückschnellen; – ***forth,*** herausspringen, herausschießen, (hervor)quellen, sprudeln; – ***open,*** aufspringen; – ***to,*** zuspringen, zuschnappen; – ***up,*** in die Höhe schießen, aufspringen; aufkommen (*wind*); aufschießen, sprießen (*plants*); (*fig.*) plötzlich entstehen; (*fig.*) – ***up like mushrooms,*** wie Pilze aus der Erde schießen.

2. *irr.v.t.* 1. sprengen, springen lassen (*mines etc.*); (*fig.*) – ***a mine,*** mit der Tür ins Haus fallen; – ***a rattle,*** eine Schnarre drehen *or* schwingen; – ***a trap,*** eine Falle zuklappen *or* zuschnappen lassen; 2. – ***a leak,*** leck werden, ein Leck bekommen; 3. aufjagen, aufscheuchen (*game etc.*); 4. unerwartet hervorbringen; (*coll.*) – ***it on him,*** es ihm plötzlich enthüllen *or* eröffnen; – ***a surprise on him,*** ihm eine Überraschung bereiten, ihn mit einer Überraschung überfallen; 5. (*sl.*) vorschießen, springen lassen (*money*); – ***him for £1,*** ihm ein Pfund abknöpfen; 6. (*sl.*) befreien, 'rausholen (*from prison*); 7. federn (*chairs etc.*).

3. *s.* 1. die Quelle (*also fig.*), der Brunnen; ***hot*** –, heiße Quelle; 2. (*fig.*) der Ursprung, die Herkunft; 3. der Sprung, Satz; 4. die Sprungkraft, Schnellkraft, Federkraft, Elastizität; (*fig.*) Spannkraft; 5. (*Tech.*) (Sprung)feder, Federung, Triebfeder (*also fig.*); ***coil*** –, die Bandfeder, Schraubenfeder; ***compression*** –, die Druckfeder; ***impulse*** –, die Antriebsfeder; ***leaf*** –, die Blattfeder; ***main*** –, die Hauptfeder, Schlagfeder; ***retaining*** –, die Sperrfeder; ***spiral*** –, die Spiralfeder; 6. (*Naut.*) die Springleine, das Springtau; 7. (*fig.*) Motiv, der Anlaß, Beweggrund; 8. Sprung, Riß, Spalt (*in timber*); die Krümmung, (Ver)biegung (*of a plank etc.*); 9. (*usu. pl.*) (*Naut.*) Springflut.

[2]**spring,** *s.* der Frühling, das Frühjahr, (*Poet.*) der Lenz; ***early*** –, der Vorfrühling.

spring|-balance, *s.* die Federwaage. **--bed,** *s.* die Sprungfedermatratze. **-board,** *s.* das Sprungbrett (*also fig.*).

springbok ['spriŋbɔk], *s.* der Springbock.

spring|-bolt, *s.* der Federriegel. **--bows** [-bouz], *pl.* der Federzirkel, Nullenzirkel. **--clean,** *v.t., v.i.* gründlich reinmachen. **--cleaning,** *s.* das Gründlichreinmachen, Großreinmachen. **--clip,** *s.* 1. die Federklammer; 2. der Quetschhahn.

springe [sprindʒ], **1.** *s.* die Schlinge, Falle, der Sprenkel; (*fig.*) Fallstrick. **2.** *v.t.* in einer Schlinge fangen; (*fig.*) verstricken.

springer ['spriŋə], *s.* 1. (*Archit.*) der (Bogen)kämpfer, (Gewölbe)anfangstein, Tragstein; 2. Stöberhund.

spring|-gun, *s.* das Selbstgeschoß, der Selbstschuß. **-head,** *s.* (*fig.*) die Quelle, der Ursprung.

springiness ['spriŋinis], *s.* die Sprungkraft, Federkraft, Schnellkraft, Elastizität.

springing ['spriŋiŋ], *s.* die (Ab)federung (*of vehicles etc.*).

spring|-loaded, *adj.* mit Federbetrieb. **--lock,** *s.* das Schnappschloß. **--mattress,** *s.* *See* **--bed. --tide,** *s.* die Springflut. **-tide** (*Poet.*), **-time,** *s.* der Frühling, die Frühlingszeit. **--water,** *s.* das Brunnenwasser.

springy ['spriŋi], *adj.* 1. federnd, elastisch; 2. (*fig.*) schwungvoll, leichtbeschwingt.

sprinkle [spriŋkl], **1.** *v.t.* (ver)streuen, (ver)sprengen, sprenkeln (***on,*** auf (*Acc.*)); bestreuen, besprenkeln, besprengen, bespritzen, übersäen; anfeuchten, befeuchten, benetzen (***with,*** mit); – ***sand on the ice,*** Sand auf das Eis streuen; – ***the ice with sand,*** das Eis mit Sand bestreuen. **2.** *v.i.* spritzen, tröpfeln, sprühen. **3.** *s.* das Gesprenkel, die Sprenkelung; (*coll.*) – ***of rain,*** leichter Regenschauer, der Sprühregen, Spritzer; – ***of salt,*** etwas Salz. **sprinkler,** *s.* 1. die Gießkanne, der Gießkannenkopf; Berieselungsapparat, Sprengwagen, Rasensprenger; 2. automatisches Feuerlöschsystem, die Löschbrause; 3. (*Eccl.*) der Weihwedel. **sprinkling,** *s.* das Sprengen, Spritzen, Sprenkeln; Gesprengsel; dünne Schicht; (*fig.*) ***a – of,*** ein bißchen, etwas, ein paar, einige; eine Spur *or* ein Anstrich *or* Anflug von; (*coll.*) – ***of rain,*** der Spritzer.

sprint [sprint], **1.** *s.* der Kurzstreckenlauf, Sprint. **2.** *v.i.* sprinten, schnell rennen. **sprinter,** *s.* der Kurzstreckenläufer, Sprinter.

sprit [sprit], *s.* das Spriet.

sprite [sprait], *s.* der Geist; Kobold, Schrat.

spritsail ['spritseil], *s.* das Sprietsegel.

sprocket ['sprɔkit], *s.* der Radzahn. **sprocket-wheel,** *s.* das Zahnrad, Kettenrad.

sprout [spraut], **1.** *v.i.* keimen, sprießen, sprossen, aufschießen. **2.** *v.t.* (hervor)treiben, hervorbringen, entwickeln. **3.** *s.* 1. der Sproß, Sprößling, Ableger; 2. *pl.* (*also* ***Brussel***(***s***) –***s***) der Rosenkohl.

[1]**spruce** [spru:s], *s.* 1. die Fichte, Rottanne; 2. das Fichtenholz.

[2]**spruce, 1.** *adj.* sauber, ordentlich, geputzt, adrett, schmuck. **2.** *v.t.* (*also* – ***up***) fein machen, herausputzen. **spruceness,** *s.* die Sauberkeit, Adrettheit.

sprung [sprʌŋ], **1.** *p.p. of* [1]**spring. 2.** *adj.* 1. gefedert; 2. zersprungen, (*of timber*) rissig; 3. (*Metr.*) – ***rhythm,*** die Akzentverschiebung.

spry [sprai], *adj.* flink, hurtig.
spud [spʌd], **1.** *s.* 1. der Reutspaten; 2. (*coll.*) die Kartoffel. **2.** *v.t.* (– *out*) ausgraben, ausjäten.
spue, *see* **spew.**
spume [spju:m], *s.* der Schaum, Gischt. **spumous, spumy,** *adj.* schaumig, schäumend.
spun [spʌn], **1.** *imperf., p.p. of* **spin. 2.** *adj.* – ***glass,*** Glasfasern (*pl.*); – ***gold,*** der Goldfaden; – ***silk,*** das Seidengarn, die Schappseide; – ***sugar,*** die Zuckerwatte; (*Naut.*) – ***yarn,*** das Schiemannsgarn.
spunk [spʌŋk], *s.* 1. die Lunte, der Zunder, Zündschwamm; 2. (*coll.*) Mut, Schwung, (*coll.*) Mumm; die Energie, das Feuer.
spun-out, *adj.* (*coll.*) langatmig, ausgesponnen.
spur [spə:], **1.** *s.* 1. (*Mil.*) der Sporn; ***clap*** or ***put*** or ***set –s to one's horse,*** seinem Pferde die Sporen geben; (*fig.*) ***win one's –s,*** sich (*Dat.*) die Sporen verdienen; 2. (*Bot.*) der Sporn, Dorn, Stachel; 3. (*Zool.*) Sporn; 4. (*Archit.*) die Strebe, Stütze; der Mauervorsprung, Strebebalken; 5. (*Fort.*) das Vorwerk, vorspringender Außenwall; 6. (*Naut.*) die Ramme, der Schiffsschnabel; 7. (Gebirgs)-vorsprung, Ausläufer (*of mountain*); 8. (*fig.*) Antrieb, Auftrieb, Ansporn, Anreiz (*to*, für); ***on the – of the moment,*** ohne Überlegung, unter dem ersten Eindruck, spornstreichs, spontan, einer plötzlichen Eingebung folgend. **2.** *v.t.* 1. mit Sporen versehen (*a boot*); ***booted and spurred,*** gestiefelt und gespornt; 2. die Sporen geben (*Dat.*) (*a horse*); 3. (*fig.*) (*also* – ***on***) anspornen, antreiben, anstacheln, anfeuern, anreizen, aufreizen. **3.** *v.i.* 1. die Sporen geben; 2. (*usu.* – ***on***) sprengen, eilen, sich beeilen; (*fig.*) vorwärtsdrängen.
spurge [spə:dʒ], *s.* (*Bot.*) die Wolfsmilch.
spur|-gear, *s.* das Stirnrad. **–-gearing,** *s.* das Stirnradgetriebe.
spurge-laurel, *s.* (*Bot.*) der Lorbeerseidelbast.
spurious [ˈspjuəriəs], *adj.* 1. unecht, falsch, Schein–; gefälscht, nachgemacht, untergeschoben; 2. unehelich. **spuriousness,** *s.* 1. die Unechtheit, Falschheit; 2. Unehelichkeit.
spurn [spə:n], *v.t.* 1. von sich weisen, abweisen, zurückstoßen (*a p.*); verwerfen, zurückweisen, verschmähen (*an offer etc.*); 2. (*obs.*) einen Fußtritt geben (*Dat.*).
spurred [spə:d], *adj.* sporentragend, gespornt.
spurr(e)y [ˈspʌri], *s.* (*Bot.*) der Spergel, Spörgel.
[1]**spurt** [spə:t], **1.** *v.i.* hervorspritzen, aufspritzen. **2.** *v.t.* ausspritzen. **3.** *s.* der (Wasser)strahl.
[2]**spurt, 1.** *s.* 1. (*Spt.*) plötzliche Anstrengung, der Spurt; ***put on a –,*** *see* **2**; 2. (*Comm.*) das Anziehen, der (Preis)anstieg. **2.** *v.i.* eine kurze Anstrengung machen, spurten.
spur|-wheel, *s. See* **–-gear.**
sputnik [ˈsputnik], *s.* der Sputnik, (Erd)satellit.
sputter [ˈspʌtə], **1.** *v.i.* sprühen, sprudeln, spritzen; klecksen (*as a pen*). **2.** *v.t.* heraussprudeln, verspritzen. **3.** *s.* das Sprudeln, Spritzen, Sprühen.
sputum [ˈspju:təm], *s.* der Speichel, Auswurf.
spy [spai], **1.** *s.* der (die) Spion(in), Kundschafter(in), Späher(in). **2.** *v.t.* erspähen, gewahren, wahrnehmen; – ***out,*** ausfindig machen, auskundschaften. **3.** *v.i.* spionieren, Spionage treiben; (*fig.*) – ***into,*** herumspionieren in (*Acc.*); – ***(up)on,*** nachspionieren (*Dat.*). **spy|glass,** *s.* das Fernglas. **–hole,** *s.* das Guckloch. **spying,** *s.* 1. das Spionieren, Spähen, Aufpassen; 2. (*Mil.*) die Spionage. **spy-ring,** *s.* die Spionageorganisation.
squab [skwɔb], **1.** *s.* 1. junge Taube, ungefiederter Vogel; 2 (*fig*) feiste P., der Dickwanst, Fettkloß (*a p.*); 3. das Polstersofa, Polsterkissen, Sitzkissen. **2.** *adj.* 1. ungefiedert, noch nicht flügge (*of birds*); 2. feist, plump, untersetzt, gedrungen (*of a p.*).
squabble [skwɔbl], **1.** *v.i.* (sich) zanken *or* streiten (***about,*** um). **2.** *v.t.* (*Typ.*) verrücken. **3.** *s.* der Streit, Zank, das Gezänk. **squabbling,** *s.* die Zänkerei, Stänkerei.
squabby [ˈskwɔbi], *adj. See* **squab, 2,** 2.
squad [skwɔd], *s.* (*Mil.*) die Korporalschaft, der Zug, Trupp; (*Gymn.*) die Mannschaft, Abteilung, Gruppe, Riege; (*coll.*) ***awkward –,*** noch nicht ausgebildete Rekruten; ***flying –,*** das Überfallkommando; ***rescue –,*** die Rettungsmannschaft, Bergungsmannschaft. **squad-car,** *s.* der Streifenwagen.
squadron [ˈskwɔdrən], *s.* (*Mil.*) die Eskadron, Schwadron (*cavalry*), das Bataillon (*tanks*); (*Naut.*) Geschwader; (*Av.*) die Staffel. **squadron-leader,** *s.* (*Av.*) der Staffelführer, Major der Luftwaffe.
squalid [ˈskwɔlid], *adj.* 1. schmutzig, unsauber, verwahrlost; 2. (*fig.*) erbärmlich, ärmlich, garstig, eklig. **squalidness,** *s. See* **squalor.**
[1]**squall** [skwɔ:l], *s.* der Stoßwind, Windstoß, die Bö; (*coll.*) ***look out for –s,*** auf der Hut sein, sich vorsehen.
[2]**squall, 1.** *v.i.* laut schreien, aufschreien. **2.** *s.* lauter Schrei, der Aufschrei. **squaller,** *s.* der Schreier, Schreihals.
squally [ˈskwɔ:li], *adj.* böig, stürmisch.
squalor [ˈskwɔlə], *s.* der Schmutz, die Unsauberkeit, Verwahrlosung.
squama [ˈskweimə], *s.* (*pl.* **-ae** [–mi:]) (*Bot., Zool.*) die Schuppe. **squamiferous** [–ˈmifərəs], *adj.* schuppentragend. **squamose** [–mous], **squamous,** *adj.* schuppig, schuppenartig, Schuppen–.
squander [ˈskwɔndə], *v.t.* verschwenden, vergeuden. **squandering, 1.** *s.* die Verschwendung, Vergeudung. **2.** *adj.* verschwenderisch. **squandermania** [–ˈmeiniə], *s.* (*coll.*) die Verschwendungssucht.
square [skwɛə], **1.** *s.* 1. das Viereck, Quadrat (*also Math.*); 2. die Quadratzahl; 3. viereckiges Stück (*of material*), die Scheibe (*of glass*); 4. der Platz (*in a town*); 5. (*Tech.*) das Winkelmaß, Geviert, der (Anschlag)winkel, die Reißschiene; ***on the –,*** im rechten Winkel; (*coll.*) ehrlich, anständig; (*coll.*) ***be on the –,*** es ehrlich meinen; ***out of –,*** nicht rechtwink(e)lig; ***T–-,*** die Reißschiene; 6. (*Mil. Hist.*) das Karree; 7. Feld (*of a chess-board*); 8. (*sl.*) der Spießer, Philister. **2.** *adj.* 1. (*Math.*) quadratisch, Quadrat–, (*following measurement*) im Quadrat; – ***measure,*** das Flächenmaß, Quadratmaß; – ***mile,*** die Quadratmeile; – ***number,*** die Quadratzahl; – ***root,*** die Quadratwurzel; 2. (*esp. Tech.*) viereckig, vierkantig, Vierkant–; – ***file,*** die Vierkantfeile; – ***neck,*** viereckiger Ausschnitt; (*fig.*) – ***peg in a round hole,*** der Mensch am falschen Platz; – ***roof,*** das Winkeldach; 3. rechtwink(e)lig (***to,*** zu), aufrecht, gerade; – ***bracket,*** eckige Klammer; 4. (*fig. coll.*) ehrlich, aufrichtig; – ***deal,*** reeller Handel, anständige Behandlung; 5. vierschrötig, stämmig (*as build*); 6. reichlich, handfest (*as a meal*); 7. quitt, ausgeglichen (*as accounts*); (***all***) –, in Ordnung *or* Einklang; (*Golf*) gleichstehend; ***be – with,*** quitt sein mit (*a p.*); ***get – with,*** sich abfinden mit, quitt werden mit (*a p.*); 8. (*sl.*) philisterhaft, spießbürgerlich, altmodisch. **3.** *adv.* rechtwink(e)lig, direkt gegenüber; ***sit – on one's seat,*** sich gerade setzen. **4.** *v.t.* 1. rechtwink(e)lig machen; im rechten Winkel legen zu; – ***one's shoulders,*** sich nicht unterkriegen lassen, Trotz bieten, frischen Mut fassen; sich zur Wehr setzen (***against,*** gegen), entschlossen vorgehen (*Dat.*), kühn entgegentreten (*Dat.*); (*Naut.*) – ***the yards,*** die Rahen vierkant brassen; 2. auf den rechten Winkel prüfen; 3. in Quadrate einteilen, karieren (*paper etc.*); ***–d paper,*** das Millimeterpapier; 4. vierkantig behauen (*timber*); 5. ausgleichen, abrechnen, abgleichen, saldieren (*an account*); begleichen (*debt*); 6. ins Quadrat erheben, quadrieren (*a number etc.*); – ***the circle,*** den Kreis quadrieren; (*fig.*) Unmögliches unternehmen; 7. anpassen (***to,*** an (*Acc.*)), in Einklang bringen (***with,*** mit); 8. (*sl.*) sich abfinden mit, Schweigegeld bezahlen (*Dat.*), schmieren (*a p.*); – ***one's conscience,*** sich mit seinem schlechten Gewissen abfinden. **5.** *v.i.* 1. passen, stimmen (***with,*** zu); zusammenpassen, übereinstimmen, in Einklang stehen (mit); 2. (*Naut.*) – ***away,*** anbrassen; 3. – ***up,***

abrechnen; 4. (*fig.*) – *up to,* (nicht wanken und) nicht weichen vor (*Dat.*), keinen Zoll zurückweichen vor (*Dat.*).

square|-built, *adj.* 1. viereckig gebaut; 2. (*fig.*) vierschrötig, stämmig, breitschulterig. – **dance,** *s.* 1. die Quadrille; 2. der Kontertanz. –**head,** *s.* (*Am.*) (*coll.*) deutscher *or* skandinavischer Einwanderer. –**-headed,** *adj.* (*Tech.*) Vierkant– (*bolt etc.*).

squareness ['skwεənis], *s.* 1. das Viereckige, Quadratische; 2. Rechteckige, Rechtwinklige.

square|-rigged, *adj.* mit Rahsegeln getakelt, vollgetakelt. –**-rigger,** *s.* das Rahschiff. –**-sail,** *s.* das Rahsegel. –**-shouldered,** *adj.* breitschulterig. –**-toed,** *adj.* 1. vorne breit (*of shoes*); 2. (*fig.*) altmodisch, hausbacken; formell, steif. –**-toes,** *pl.* (*sing. constr.*) der Pedant, Kleinigkeitskrämer.

squaring ['skwεəriŋ], *s.* 1. das Quadrieren, die Quadrierung, Quadratur; 2. – ***of accounts,*** der Kontenausgleich. **squarish,** *adj.* ungefähr quadratisch.

squash [skwɔʃ], **1.** *s.* 1. der Matsch, Brei; das Patschen, der Platsch; Fruchtsaft; 2. (*coll.*) die (Menschen)menge, das Gedränge; 3. (*also* – ***rackets***) (eine Art) Rakettspiel. **2.** *v.t.* 1. (zer)quetschen, zerdrücken, zusammenpressen; 2. (*coll.*) unterdrücken, niederschlagen, (im Keim) ersticken, mundtot machen. **3.** *v.i.* zerquetscht *or* zusammengequetscht werden; sich zusammenquetschen (lassen). **squashy,** *adj.* breiig, matschig.

squat [skwɔt], **1.** *v.i.* 1. kauern, hocken, (*coll.*) sitzen, sich setzen; 2. sich ohne Rechtstitel niederlassen. **2.** *adj.* gedrungen, untersetzt, pummelig. **squatter,** *s.* 1. der Ansiedler ohne Rechtstitel; 2. (*Austral.*) Schafzüchter.

squaw [skwɔ:], *s.* das Indianerweib, die Indianerin.

squawk [skwɔ:k], **1.** *v.i.* 1. quietschen, kreischen, schreien (*esp. birds*); 2. (*sl.*) meckern. **2.** *s.* greller Aufschrei, das Geschrei, Kreischen, Quietschen.

squeak [skwi:k], **1.** *s.* das Gequiek, Gepiepe, Quietschen, Knarren; (*coll.*) ***narrow*** or ***near*** –, knappes Entrinnen; ***have a narrow*** –, mit knapper Not davonkommen. **2.** *v.i.* 1. quieken, piep(s)en (*as mice*), knarren, quietschen (*as boots*), knirschen, knarren (*as a door*); 2. (*sl.*) petzen. **squeaker,** *s.* 1. der Schreier, Schreihals; 2. junger Vogel; 3. (*sl.*) Petzer, Angeber. **squeaky,** *adj.* quiekend, quietschend, knarrend.

squeal [skwi:l], **1.** *s.* lautes Quieken, schriller Schrei. **2.** *v.i.* 1. quieken, schreien; 2. (*sl.*) petzen, pfeifen; (*sl.*) – ***on him,*** ihn verpfeifen. **squealer,** *s.* 1. der Schreiber, Schreihals; 2. junger Vogel; 3. (*sl.*) der Petzer, Angeber.

squeamish ['skwi:miʃ], *adj.* 1. Ekel empfindend, sehr empfindlich, zimperlich; 2. wählerisch, mäkelig, übergewissenhaft. **squeamishness,** *s.* der Ekel, die Übelkeit, Überempfindlichkeit, Zimperlichkeit, übertriebene Gewissenhaftigkeit.

squeegee ['skwi:dʒi:], *s.* der Rollenquetscher, Gummiwischer, die Quetschwalze.

squeezable ['skwi:zəbl], *adj.* zusammendrückbar, zerdrückbar.

squeeze [skwi:z], **1.** *s.* 1. der Druck, das Drücken, Pressen, Quetschen; der Händedruck; innige Umarmung; 2. das Gedränge; (*coll.*) ***be in a tight*** –, in der Klemme sitzen; 3. (*coll.*) (*Comm.*) die Beschränkung, Geldknappheit; ***credit*** –, die Kreditbeschränkung; 4. (*coll.*) die Erpressung; (*sl.*) ***put the – on him,*** ihn erpressen. **2.** *v.t.* 1. drücken, pressen, auspressen, ausquetschen, ausdrücken (*juice etc.*); – ***his hand,*** ihm die Hand drücken; – ***out,*** auspressen, ausquetschen; 2. (hinein– *or* hinaus)drängen *or* –zwängen; – ***one's way,*** sich drängen; – ***in,*** hineinzwängen, einklemmen; 3. (*coll.*) bedrücken, unter Druck setzen, bedrängen, in die Enge treiben, schinden (*a p.*); 4. erpressen (*a th.*) (***from, out of,*** von), herausschinden (aus). **3.** *v.i.* sich zwängen *or* drängen; – ***in,*** sich hineinzwängen; – ***through,*** sich durchdrängen.

squeeze-box, *s.* (*sl.*) die Quetschkommode.

squeezer ['skwi:zə], *s.* die Preßmaschine, Presse, Quetsche; ***lemon*–**–, die Zitronenpresse.

squelch [skwel(t)ʃ], **1.** *v.t.* zerdrücken, zermalmen, zerstampfen, zerquetschen. **2.** *v.i.* p(l)atschen, glucksen. **3.** *s.* das P(l)atschen, Glucksen.

squib [skwib], *s.* 1. der Schwärmer, Frosch, die Knallerbse (*fireworks*); (*fig. coll.*) ***damp*** –, die Pleite, der Blindgänger; 2. (*fig.*) die Stichelei, das Spottgedicht.

squid [skwid], **1.** *s.* 1. (*Zool.*) der Tintenfisch; 2. (*Angling*) künstlicher Köder. **2.** *v.i.* mit künstlichem Köder angeln.

squiffy ['skwifi], *adj.* (*sl.*) beschwipst, angeheitert.

squill [skwil], *s.* 1. (*Bot.*) die Meerzwiebel; 2. (*Zool.*) der Heuschreckenkrebs.

squint [skwint], **1.** *adj.* (*coll.*) schief, schräg. **2.** *s.* 1. das Schielen, schielender Blick; ***have a*** –, schielen; 2. (*sl.*) der Blick; (*sl.*) ***have a – at,*** einen Blick werfen auf (*Acc.*). **3.** *v.i.* 1. schielen (***at,*** nach); 2. (*sl.*) – ***at,*** blicken auf (*Acc.*). **squint-eyed,** *adj.* schielend. **squinting, 1.** *adj.* schielend. **2.** *s.* das Schielen.

squire ['skwaiə], **1.** *s.* 1. der Junker, Rittergutsbesitzer, Landedelmann; 2. (*Hist.*) (Schild)knappe. **2.** *v.t.* 1. geleiten, begleiten; 2. (*Hist.*) Ritterdienste leisten (*Dat.*). **squirearchy** [–rɑ:ki], *s.* die Junkerherrschaft, das Junkertum; (*collect.*) Junker (*pl.*). **squireen** [–'ri:n], *s.* irischer Landjunker, kleiner Gutsbesitzer.

squirm [skwə:m], **1.** *v.i.* sich krümmen *or* winden (*also fig.*). **2.** *s.* 1. das Krümmen; 2. (*Naut.*) die Kink (*in a rope*).

squirrel ['skwirəl], *s.* 1. (*Zool.*) das Eichhörnchen, Eichkätzchen; 2. (*fur*) das Grauwerk, Feh.

squirt [skwə:t], **1.** *s.* 1. die Spritze; 2. der (Wasser)strahl; 3. (*sl.*) der Wichtigtuer. **2.** *v.i.* (hervor)spritzen, (heraus)sprudeln. **3.** *v.t.* bespritzen, anspritzen (*with liquid*); hervorspritzen (*liquid*).

stab [stæb], **1.** *s.* 1. der Stich (*also fig.*); (Dolch)stoß, die Stichwunde; (*fig.*) – ***in the back,*** der Dolchstoß, die Verleumdung; 2. (*sl.*) der Versuch; (*sl.*) ***have*** or ***make a – at,*** sich wagen an (*Acc.*), versuchen, probieren. **2.** *v.t.* 1. erstechen, erdolchen (*a p.*); – ***in the back,*** hinterrücks anfallen, in den Rücken fallen (*Dat.*) (*also fig.*); (*fig.*) verleumden; 2. durchstechen, durchbohren; bohren, jagen, stoßen (*a weapon*); 3. (*Bookb.*) vorstechen; 4. (*fig.*) verwunden, verletzen; (*fig.*) – ***to the heart,*** einen Stich ins Herz geben (*Dat.*). **3.** *v.i.* stechen (***at,*** nach).

stability [stə'biliti], *s.* 1. die Beständigkeit (*also fig.*); (*Phys. etc.*) das Beharrungsvermögen, die Haltbarkeit, Festigkeit, Unveränderlichkeit, Dauerhaftigkeit, Stabilität; (*Chem.*) Resistenz; (*Comm.*) Stabilität; 2. (*Av.*) dynamisches Gleichgewicht; 3. (*fig.*) die Standhaftigkeit, (Charakter)festigkeit.

stabilization [steibilai'zeiʃən], *s.* die Stabiliserung, Festigung. **stabilize** ['steibilaiz], *v.t.* stabilisieren, festigen. **stabilizer,** *s.* 1. (*Av.*) die Dämpfungsflosse, Höhenflosse; 2. (*Naut.*) Schlingerdämpfungsanlage; 3. (*Chem. etc.*) der Stabilisator.

[1]**stable** [steibl], *adj.* 1. stabil, standfest; unveränderlich, haltbar, fest, dauerhaft, beständig (*also fig.*); 2. (*fig.*) standhaft, gefestigt.

[2]**stable, 1.** *s.* 1. der Stall; *pl.* Stallungen (*pl.*); 2. (*Spt.*) der Rennstall(bestand); 3. *pl.* (*Mil.*) Stalldienst. **2.** *v.t.* (ein)stallen. **3.** *v.i.* hausen.

stable|-boy, *s.* der Stalljunge. –**-call,** *s.* (*Mil.*) der Stalldienstsignal. –**-companion,** *s.* das Pferd aus dem gleichen Stall, (*also fig.*) der Stallgefährte. –**-door,** *s.* die Stalltür; ***shut the – when the horse has bolted,*** den Brunnen zudecken, wenn das Kind ertrunken ist. –**man** [–mən], *s.* der Stallknecht.

stableness ['steiblnis], *s. See* **stability.**

stable-yard, *s.* der Stallhof, Viehhof.

stabling ['steibliŋ], *s.* die Stallung, Stallungen (*pl.*), Ställe (*pl.*).

staccato [stə'kɑ:tou], *adv.* (*Mus.*) stakkato; (*fig.*) abgesetzt, abgehackt.

stack [stæk], **1.** *s.* 1. die Miete, der Haufen, Schober, Feim (*of hay etc.*); Haufen, Stoß, Stapel (*of wood, books etc.*); ein Holzmaß (= *108 cu. ft.*); die Pyramide (*of rifles*); 2. (*oft. pl.*) das (Bücher)regal; 3. (*coll.*) (*usu. pl.*) die Masse, große Menge, großer Haufen; 4. (*also* ***smoke--***) der Schornstein; 5. (*Geog. Scots*) die Felssäule. **2.** *v.t.* 1. aufschichten, aufschobern (*hay etc.*); aufhäufen, aufstapeln (*wood etc.*); zusammensetzen (*arms etc.*); 2. (*coll.*) vollstapeln (*floor, room etc.*).

stadium ['steidiəm], *s.* 1. (*Spt.*) das Stadion, Sportfeld, der Sportplatz, die Kampfbahn; 2. (*Med., fig.*) das Stadium, die Phase, der Abschnitt.

stad(t)holder ['stædhouldə], *s.* der Statthalter.

staff [stɑːf], **1.** *s.* 1. (*pl. also rarely* **staves** [steivz]) der Stab, Stock, die Stange (*for flag*); (*fig.*) Stütze; ***flag-,*** die Fahnenstange, (*Naut.*) der Flaggenstock; ***the - of life,*** das Brot, die Nahrung; ***pastoral -,*** der Bischofsstab; 2. (*pl. only* **staves**) (*Mus.*) Notenlinien (*pl.*), das Noten(linien)-system; 3. (*pl.* (*rare*) *only* **staffs**) Angestellte (*pl.*), der (Beamten)stab, das Personal, die Belegschaft; der Lehrkörper, das Lehrerkollegium (*school etc.*); (*Mil.*) der Stab, das Oberkommando; ***editorial -,*** die Schriftleitung, Redaktion, der Redaktionsstab; ***general -,*** der Generalstab; ***medical -,*** das Arztpersonal (*of a hospital*), (*Mil.*) Stabärzte, Militärärzte (*pl.*); ***nursing -,*** das Pflegepersonal; ***trained -,*** das Fachpersonal; ***be on the -,*** (*Mil.*) zum Stabe gehören, (*Comm.*) fest angestellt sein, eine feste Anstellung haben; zum Lehrkörper gehören (*at school etc.*); 4. (*Horol.*) die Unruhewelle. **2.** *v.t.* (mit Personal) besetzen.

staff| college, *s.* die Generalstabsakademie. – **notation,** *s.* (*Mus.*) die Liniennotenschrift. – **officer,** *s.* der Stabsoffizier. – **outing,** *s.* der Betriebsausflug. **--room,** *s.* das Lehrerzimmer. **--sergeant,** *s.* (*Mil.*) der Oberfeldwebel. **--surgeon,** *s.* (*Navy*) der Oberstabsarzt.

stag [stæg], **1.** *s.* 1. der Hirsch; ***warrantable -,*** fünfjähriger Hirsch; 2. das Männchen (*of various animals*); 3. (*Comm.*) (*sl.*) der Aktenspekulant; 4. (*sl.*) Herr ohne Damenbegleitung; (*sl.*) ***go -,*** unbeweibt gehen. **2.** *v.i.* 1. (*Comm.*) (*sl.*) Differenzgeschäfte machen, in Aktien spekulieren; 2. (*sl.*) ohne Damenbegleitung gehen. **3.** *v.t.* (*Comm.*) (*sl.*) hochtreiben, durch Konzertzeichnung beeinflussen (*the market*).

stag-beetle, *s.* der Hirschkäfer.

stage [steidʒ], **1.** *s.* 1. das Gerüst, Gestell; Podium, die Tribüne; (*Theat.*) Bühne; (*fig.*) das Theater, die Theaterwelt, der Schauspielberuf; (*fig.*) Schauplatz (*of happenings*); ***landing--,*** die Landungsbrücke, Landungsstelle; ***be on the -,*** Schauspieler(in) *or* beim Theater *or* an der Bühne sein; ***come on (to) the -,*** auftreten, eintreten (*of actors*); ***go off*** or ***leave the -,*** abtreten; ***go on the -,*** Schauspieler werden, zur Bühne gehen; (*fig.*) ***have a clear -,*** freies Feld haben; ***hold the -,*** sich (auf der Bühne) halten (*of plays*); ***off -,*** hinter der Szene; ***put on the -,*** auf die Bühne bringen, inszenieren; ***quit the -,*** die Theaterlaufbahn aufgeben; 2. (*Hist.*) die Post(station); Postkutsche; 3. Haltestelle; (Weg)strecke, (*bus, tram etc.*) Teilstrecke; (*fig.*) Etappe, der Abschnitt; ***by*** or ***in -s,*** etappenweise; ***by*** or ***in easy -s,*** in kurzen Absätzen, in kleinen Abschnitten, mit häufigen Unterbrechungen; 3. das Stadium, die (Entwicklungs)stufe, der (Entwicklungs)stand; (*Law*) ***-s of appeal,*** der Instanzweg; ***at this -,*** in diesem Stadium; (*Parl.*) ***report -,*** die Erörterung vor der dritten Lesung; 4. (*Geol.*) die Stufe; 5. (*Rocketry*) Stufe; 6. (*of microscope*) der Objekttisch. **2.** *v.t.* 1. auf die Bühne bringen, inszenieren; 2. (*fig.*) in Szene setzen, veranstalten.

stage|-box, *s.* (*Theat.*) die Proszeniumsloge. **-coach,** *s.* die Postkutsche. **-craft,** *s.* die Bühnenkunst, Bühnentechnik, Bühnenerfahrung. – **direction,** *s.* die Regieanweisung, Bühnenanweisung. – **door,** *s.* der Bühneneingang. – **effect,** *s.* die Bühnenwirkung; Bühnenwirksamkeit. – **fright,** *s.* das Lampenfieber. **-hand,** *s.* der Bühnenarbeiter. **--manage,** *v.t.* (*coll. fig.*) inszenieren, arrangieren. – **management,** *s.* die Regie, Spielleitung, Theaterleitung. – **manager,** *s.* der Regisseur, Intendant, Spielleiter, Inspizient. – **name,** *s.* der Künstlername, Bühnenname. – **play,** *s.* das Bühnenstück. – **properties,** *pl.* Theaterrequisiten (*pl.*).

stager ['steidʒə], *s.* (*coll.*) ***old -,*** alter Praktikus.

stage| rights, *pl.* das Aufführungsrecht. – **setting,** *s.* das Bühnenbild. **--struck,** *adj.* theaterbegeistert, theaterbesessen.

stag-evil, *s.* (*Vet.*) die Maulsperre, Hirschkrankheit (*of horses*).

stage| whisper, *s.* weithin hörbares Geflüster. **-worthy,** *adj.* bühnengerecht, bühnengeeignet. **stagey,** *adj. See* **stagy.**

staggard ['stægəd], *s.* vierjähriger Hirsch, der Sechsender.

stagger ['stægə], **1.** *v.i.* 1. (sch)wanken, taumeln, torkeln (***with,*** vor (*Dat.*)); 2. (*fig.*) wankend *or* unsicher werden, stutzen. **2.** *v.t.* 1. ins Wanken *or* Taumeln bringen; 2. (*fig.*) verblüffen, erschüttern, stutzig machen; 3. (*Tech.*) versetzt *or* gestaffelt anordnen; staffeln (*defences*); geteilt nehmen (*holidays*); ***-ed hours,*** gleitende Arbeitszeit. **staggering,** *adj.* 1. (sch)wankend, taumelnd; 2. (*coll.*) erschütternd, verblüffend, überwältigend; phantastisch (*price etc.*), niederschmetternd (*blow*). **staggers,** *pl.* (*sing. constr.*) die Drehkrankheit (*of sheep*), der Koller (*of horses, cattle*), (*coll.*) der Schwindel (*of a p.*).

stag|horn, *s.* 1. das Hirschhorn; 2. (*Bot.*) der Hirschfarn. **-hound,** *s.* der Hirschhund. **--hunt(ing),** *s.* die Hirschjagd.

staginess ['steidʒinis], *s.* die Theatralik, Effekthascherei.

staging ['steidʒiŋ], *s.* 1. das Gerüst; 2. (*Hist.*) Postkutschenwesen; 3. (*Theat.*) die Inszenierung, Bühnenbearbeitung. – **area,** *s.* (*Mil.*) die Durchgangszone, der Bereitstellungsraum. – **post,** *s.* die Zwischenlandestation.

stagnancy ['stægnənsi], *s.* 1. die Stockung, Stagnation, der Stillstand; 2. (*esp. Comm.*) Stille, Flauheit. **stagnant,** *adj.* 1. (still)stehend, stockend, stagnierend, abgestanden; 2. (*Comm.*) flau, träge. **stagnate** [-neit], *v.t.* 1. stillstehen, stocken; stagnieren; (*of water*) versumpfen; 2. träge werden (*of a p.*); (*Comm.*) flau werden *or* sein. **stagnation** [-'neiʃən], *s. See* **stagnancy.**

stag party, *s.* die Herrengesellschaft.

stagy ['steidʒi], *adj.* theatralisch, effekthaschend.

staid [steid], *adj.* gesetzt, ruhig, gelassen. **staidness,** *s.* die Gesetztheit, Gelassenheit, Ruhe.

stain [stein], **1.** *s.* 1. der (Schmutz)fleck(en); 2. Farbstoff, das Färbemittel, die (Holz)beize; Färbung; 3. (*fig.*) der Makel, Schandfleck; ***without a - on his character,*** von untadeligem Ruf. **2.** *v.t.* 1. färben, beizen; ***-ed glass,*** buntes *or* bemaltes Glas, das Buntglas; ***-ed-glass windows,*** bunte Fenster; 2. beflecken (*also fig.*), beschmutzen; (*fig.*) besudeln. **3.** *v.i.* schmutzen, Flecken bekommen; Flecken machen *or* lassen. **staining,** *s.* 1. die Verfärbung, Verschmutzung; 2. das Beizen, Färben; ***- of glass,*** die Glasmalerei. **stainless,** *adj.* 1. unbefleckt, ungefleckt; 2. rostfrei, nichtrostend (*steel*); 3. (*fig.*) fleckenlos, makellos.

stair [stɛə], *s.* die (Treppen)stufe, der (Treppen)tritt; (*usu. pl.*) die Treppe; ***flight of -s,*** die Treppe; ***above -s,*** bei der Herrschaft; ***below -s,*** bei dem Dienstpersonal.

stair|-carpet, *s.* der Treppenläufer. **-case,** *s.* das Treppenhaus, der Treppenaufgang, die Treppe; ***back -,*** die Hintertreppe; ***main -,*** der Hauptaufgang; ***moving -,*** die Rolltreppe; ***spiral*** or ***winding -,*** die Wendeltreppe. **-head,** *s.* oberster Treppenabsatz. **--rail,** *s.* das Treppengeländer. **--rod,** *s.* die (Treppen)läuferstange. **-way,** *s.* (*Am.*) die Treppe, das Treppenhaus. **--well,** *s.* der Treppenschacht.

[1]**stake** [steik], **1.** *s.* 1. die Stange, der Pfahl; 2. (*Hist.*) Brandpfahl, Scheiterhaufen; ***die at the -,***

auf dem Scheiterhaufen sterben. **2.** *v.t.* 1. einpfählen (*ground etc.*); – ***off*** or ***out,*** abpfählen, einpfählen, abstecken; (*fig.*) – ***out a claim,*** eine Forderung umreißen; 2. auf einem Pfahle aufspießen; 3. (*plants*) an einen Pfahl anbinden, mit einem Pfahl stützen.

[2]**stake, 1.** *s.* 1. der (Wett)einsatz; *pl.* die Einlage, der Preis; das Preisrennen; ***be at*** –, auf dem Spiele stehen; ***have at*** –, auf dem Spiel stehen haben; ***sweep the*** *–s,* den ganzen Gewinn einstreichen; (*fig.*) ***play for high*** *–s,* sich (*Dat.*) hohe Ziele setzen; 2. (*fig.*) das Interesse, der Anteil (***in,*** an (*Dat.*)); ***have a – in,*** Anteil nehmen *or* haben an (*Dat.*), ein Interesse haben *or* interessiert sein an (*Dat.*). **2.** *v.t.* aufs Spiel setzen; (als Einsatz) setzen (*money*) (***on,*** auf (*Acc.*)); – ***one's word,*** sein Wort verpfänden (***on,*** für).

stake|-boat, *s.* (*at regattas*) *usu.* das Startboot; *also* Zielboot. – **holder,** *s.* der Verwahrer der Wetteinsätze. **–-net,** *s.* das Staknetz.

stalactic(al) [stə'læktik(l)], **stalactiform** [–fɔ:m], *adj. See* **stalactitic. stalactite** ['stæləktait], *s.* der Tropfstein, Stalaktit. **stalactitic** [stælək'titik], *adj.* tropfsteinartig, stalaktitisch.

stalagmite ['stæləgmait], *s.* der Säulentropfstein, Stalagmit. **stalagmitic** [–'mitik], *adj.* stalagmitisch.

[1]**stale** [steil], *adj.* 1. schal, abgestanden (*beer*), fad(e) (*wine*); trocken, alt(backen) (*bread*); verbraucht, verdorben, schlecht, muffig (*air etc.*); 2. (*fig.*) abgenutzt, abgearbeitet, überanstrengt, verbraucht (*of a p.*), (*Spt.*) übertrainiert, ausgepumpt; 3. alt, veraltet, abgegriffen, abgedroschen (*of th.*); – ***cheque,*** verjährter Scheck.

[2]**stale, 1.** *v.i.* stallen, harnen (*of horses etc.*). **2.** *s.* der Harn (*of horses etc.*).

stalemate ['steilmeit], **1.** *s.* (*Chess*) das Patt; (*fig.*) der Stillstand, die Stockung, Sackgasse, toter Punkt. **2.** *v.t.* patt setzen; (*fig.*) zum Stillstand bringen; matt setzen, ausschalten, in die Enge treiben.

staleness ['steilnis], *s.* 1. die Schalheit, Abgestandenheit; 2. (*fig.*) Abgenutztheit, Abgedroschenheit, Fadheit; (*of a p.*) Überarbeitung, Verbrauchtheit.

[1]**stalk** [stɔ:k], *s.* der Stiel (*also of feather, tumbler, Zool.*), Stengel (*of a flower*); Halm (*of corn*); ***on the*** –, auf dem Halm (*corn*).

[2]**stalk, 1.** *v.i.* 1. pirschen (*game*); 2. (*also* – ***along***) (einher)stolzieren, (einher)schreiten; 3. (*fig.*) um sich greifen, umgehen (***through,*** in (*Dat.*)). **2.** *v.t.* 1. anpirschen (*game*); 2. sich heranschleichen an (*Acc.*). **3.** *s.* 1. die Pirsch(jagd), das Pirschen; 2. stolzer *or* stolzierender Schritt.

stalked [stɔ:kt], *adj.* gestielt; (*as suff.*) –stielig.

stalker ['stɔ:kə], *s.* 1. (*Hunt.*) der Pirschjäger; 2. (*fig.*) Einherstolzierende(r). **stalking,** *s.* das Pirschen, die Pirschjagd. **stalking-horse,** *s.* 1. (*Hunt.*) das Versteckpferd; 2. (*fig.*) der Vorwand, Deckmantel; 3. (*of a p.*) Strohmann, die Marionette(nfigur); ***make him a*** –, ihn vorschieben.

stalkless ['stɔ:klis], *adj.* stiellos, ungestielt. **stalky,** *adj.* 1. stielartig, stengelartig; 2. (*fig.*) langstielig, stakig.

[1]**stall** [stɔ:l], **1.** *s.* 1. der Stand, die Box (*in a stable*); der Pferdestall, Rinderstall; 2. (Verkaufs)stand, die (Markt)bude; 3. (*Eccl.*) der Kirchenstuhl, Chor(herren)stuhl; (*Theat.*) Sperrsitz, Parkettsitz. **2.** *v.t.* einstallen, im Stalle halten (*cattle*).

[2]**stall, 1.** *s.* 1. (*Tech., Motor.*) der Stillstand; 2. (*Av.*) Sackflug, überzogener Flug. **2.** *v.i.* 1. stehenbleiben, zum Stillstand kommen; 2. (*Av.*) abrutschen, durchsacken. **3.** *v.t.* 1. abdrosseln, blockieren, zum Stillstand bringen (*an engine*); 2. (*Av.*) überziehen.

[3]**stall, 1.** *v.i.* (*coll.*) sich sträuben, sich stur stellen, sich herumdrücken, ausweichen, Ausflüchte machen. **2.** *v.t.* (*sl.*) (*usu.* – ***off***) hinhalten, abwimmeln.

stallage ['stɔ:lidʒ], *s.* das Standgeld, Marktgeld.

stall|-fed, *adj.* mit Stallfütterung großgezogen. **–-feed,** *irr.v.t.* im Stalle füttern. **–-feeding,** *s.* die Stallfütterung, Stallmast.

stalling ['stɔ:liŋ], *s.* (*Av.*) das Überziehen; – ***speed,*** kritische Geschwindigkeit.

stallion ['stæliən], *s.* der (Zucht)hengst, Deckhengst.

stalwart ['stɔ:lwət], **1.** *adj.* 1. stark, kräftig, (hand)fest, stramm; 2. tapfer, entschlossen, standhaft, unentwegt, unerschütterlich, treu. **2.** *s.* standhafter Verfechter, treuer Anhänger, (*coll.*) strammer Kerl.

stamen ['steimən], *s.* der Staubfaden, das Staubblatt, Staubgefäß.

stamina ['stæminə], *s.* die Stärke, (Widerstands)kraft, Zähigkeit, Ausdauer; Lebenskraft, Vitalität.

staminal, *adj.* 1. ['stæminl] Widerstands–; 2. ['steiminl] (*Bot.*) Staubgefäß–. **staminate** ['steimineit], **staminiferous** [–'nifərəs], *adj.* Staubgefäße tragend, staubfädentragend; – ***flower,*** männliche Blüte.

stammer ['stæmə], **1.** *v.i.* stammeln, stottern. **2.** *v.t.* (*usu.* – ***out***) stammeln. **3.** *s.* das Gestammel, Gestotter, Stammeln, Stottern. **stammerer,** *s.* der Stammler, Stotterer. **stammering, 1.** *adj.* stammelnd, stotternd. **2.** *s. See* **stammer, 3.**

stamp [stæmp], **1.** *s.* 1. das Stampfen (*with the foot*); 2. (*Tech.*) der (Poch)stempel, Prägestempel, die Stampfe, Stanze, das Stanzeisen; 3. der (Amts)stempel, die Stempelmarke; (*fig.*) ***set one's – on,*** seinen Stempel aufdrücken (*Dat.*); 4. die Marke, das Wertzeichen, (*also* ***postage*** –) die (Brief)marke, das Postwertzeichen; ***affix a*** –, eine Marke aufkleben; ***put a – on,*** eine Marke kleben auf (*Acc.*); ***trading*** –, die Rabattmarke; 5. (*fig.*) der Stempel, das Gepräge, der Schlag, die Art, der Charakter; ***of a different*** –, anders veranlagt; ***a man of that*** –, ein Mann von diesem Schlag. **2.** *v.t.* 1. stampfen, stampfen auf (*Acc.*); stampfen mit (*foot*); – ***down,*** niedertreten; – ***one's foot,*** mit dem Fuße stampfen, aufstampfen; – ***out,*** austreten (*a fire*); (*fig.*) ausrotten, ausmerzen, niederschlagen, unterdrücken; – ***to the ground,*** niedertrampeln, zu Boden trampeln; 2. frankieren, freimachen (*letters etc.*); ***–ed addressed envelope,*** adressierter Freiumschlag; 3. stempeln (*with a rubber stamp*); 4. pochen, stampfen (*ore*); prägen (*coins*); drucken (*cloth*); ausstanzen, ausschneiden (*sheet metal*); (*Tech.*) – ***out,*** ausstanzen, prägen; 5. (*fig.*) stempeln (***as,*** zu), kennzeichnen (als), prägen (***with,*** von); ***that –ed him in my eyes,*** das charakterisierte ihn in meinen Augen; 6. aufprägen (*design*) (***on,*** auf (*Acc.*)), einprägen (***in,*** in (*Acc.*)), (*fig.*) (fest) einprägen (*ideas*) (***on,*** *Dat.*). **3.** *v.i.* stampfen, mit den Füßen treten.

Stamp Act, *s.* (*Hist.*) das Stempelgesetz. **stamp|-album,** *s.* das Briefmarkenalbum. **–-collection,** *s.* die Markensammlung. **–-collector,** *s.* der Markensammler. **–-duty,** *s.* die Stempelgebühr, Stempelsteuer; ***exempt from*** –, stempelfrei; ***subject to*** –, stempelpflichtig.

stampede [stæm'pi:d], **1.** *s.* 1. wilde Flucht, die Massenflucht; 2. (*fig. Pol.*) plötzlicher Meinungsumschwung. **2.** *v.i.* durchgehen (*as horse*); in wilder Flucht davonlaufen, flüchten, im (ersten) Schrecken aufbrechen. **3.** *v.t.* 1. in wilder Flucht jagen *or* treiben; 2. (*fig.*) überrumpeln.

stamper ['stæmpə], *s.* 1. die Ramme, Stampfe, der Stampfer (*for paper*); 2. (Brief)stempler.

stamping ['stæmpiŋ], *s.* 1. das Stampfen; 2. (*Tech.*) Ausstanzen; das Preßstück, Gesenkschmiedestück; die Prägung. **stamping|-die,** *s.* der Stempel. **–-ground,** *s.* (*coll.*) der Lieblingsaufenthalt. **–-machine,** *s.* die Frankiermaschine; *see also* **–-press. –-mill,** *s.* das Pochwerk, die Prägmaschine. **–-press,** *s.* die Stanzmaschine, Stanze, Stempelpresse.

stamp|-mill, *s.* (*Paperm.*) das Stampfwerk, die Stampfmühle. **–-office,** *s.* das Stempelamt. **–-pad,** *s.* das Stempelkissen.

stance [stæns], *s.* die Haltung, Stellung; (*Golf*) Fußstellung.

[1]**stanch** [stɑːntʃ], *v.t.* stillen (*blood, also fig.*), hemmen (*flow of blood*).

[2]**stanch** [stɔːntʃ], *see* [2]**staunch.**

stanchion [ˈstænʃən], **1.** *s.* 1. die Stüzte, Strebe, der Pfosten; 2. die Fensterstange, der Gitterstab; 3. (*Naut.*) Stieper, Steiper. **2.** *v.t.* stützen, an einen Pfosten binden.

stand [stænd], **1.** *s.* 1. das Stehen, der Stillstand; ***bring to a –***, zum Stehen bringen; ***come to a –***, zum Stehen kommen, steckenbleiben; 2. (*fig.*) der Widerstand, (entschlossenes) Eintreten; ***make a –***, Widerstand leisten, sich widersetzen *or* (entgegen)-stellen, standhalten (***against***, *Dat.*); energisch eintreten (***for***, für; ***against***, gegen); 3. der Standort, Stand(platz), (Halte)platz, die Stelle; (*fig.*) der Standpunkt; (*Law*) ***take the –***, den Zeugenstand betreten, (*fig.*) als Zeuge aussagen *or* bekennen; ***take one's –***, sich (hin)stellen *or* aufstellen; ***take a –***, eine Stellung einnehmen, Farbe bekennen; ***take one's – on***, beschwören; 4. (*esp. Theat.*) der Aufenthalt, das Gastspiel, die Gastspieldauer; ***one-night –***, einmaliges Gastspiel; 5. der Ständer, Untersatz, das Gestell, Regal, Stativ (*for camera etc.*); 6. die Bude, der Kiosk, (Verkaufs)stand; 7. (*also* ***grand–***) die Tribüne; 8. ***– of arms***, vollständige (Waffen)ausrüstung; 9. ***– of wheat***, stehendes Korn.

2. *irr.v.i.* 1. stehen, aufstehen, aufrechtstehen, hochstehen; ***– or fall***, siegen oder sterben; 2. (*with inf.*) im Lage sein; (*coll.*) ***he –s to win***, er kann nur gewinnen; 3. stehenbleiben, stillstehen, stocken; ***– and deliver!*** halt! das Geld her! ***leave –ing***, stehenlassen; 4. (*fig.*) sich behaupten, standhalten, Widerstand leisten; 5. dastehen, sein, bleiben, liegen, sich befinden, dauern, sich halten, bestehen, beharren; ***and so it –s***, und dabei bleibt es; ***as things –***, wie die Dinge liegen, nach Lage der Dinge, unter den gegebenen Umständen; ***let –***, abstehen lassen (*liquids*); 6. (*Parl.*) kandidieren; 7. gelten (***as***, als), gültig *or* in Kraft sein; 8. (*Naut.*) steuern, segeln, einen Kurs halten (***for***, nach).

(a) (*with adj., noun*) ***– aghast***, bestürzt sein; ***– alone***, allein stehen, ohne Hilfe sein; (*of a th.*) unerreicht dastehen; ***– condemned***, überführt sein; ***– corrected***, sein Unrecht einsehen *or* zugeben; ***– erect***, gerade stehen; ***– fast*** or ***firm***, feststehen, (*of a p.*) standhalten, nicht weichen; ***– first***, zuerst kommen, obenan stehen; ***– godfather***, Gevatter stehen (***to***, zu); ***– good***, gültig sein; ***– high***, hohes Ansehen genießen; (*Am. coll.*) ***– pat***, am alten feststehen, bei seinem Entschluß bleiben; ***– ready***, bereit sein; ***– security***, sich verbürgen, Bürgschaft *or* Sicherheit leisten; ***– still***, stillstehen; ***– well with***, gutstehen mit; ***– well over 6 ft.***, gut über 6 Fuß messen *or* hoch sein.

(b) (*with adv.*) ***– about***, umherstehen; ***– aloof***, sich fernhalten, abseits stehen, (*fig.*) sich distanzieren; ***– apart***, für sich stehen, (*fig.*) nicht mitmachen, sich ausschließen; ***– aside***, auf die Seite *or* beiseite treten; aus dem Wege gehen (***from***, *Dat.*); (*fig.*) zurücktreten, verzichten; ***– back***, zurücktreten; ***– by***, dabeistehen, dabei sein, (ruhig) zusehen; (*esp. Mil.*) bereitstehen, sich bereit *or* in Bereitschaft halten; (*Naut.*) sich klar halten, klarstehen; (*T.V., Rad.*) sendebereit sein, auf Empfang bleiben; ***– clear***, sich fernhalten *or* freihalten; ***– down***, zurücktreten, abtreten; (*Law, Mil.*) abtreten; (*Spt.*) ausscheiden; (*Mil.*) ***– easy!*** rührt euch! ***– forth***, hervortreten; (*coll.*) ***– in***, (als Ersatz) einspringen (***for***, für); (*Naut.*) ***– in*** (***for the shore***), auf Einlaufkurs liegen; (*coll.*) ***– in with***, in Beziehung stehen zu; ***– off***, abseits stehen, sich abseits halten, sich fernhalten; ***– off*** (***from the shore***), see ***– out to sea***; ***– out***, hervortreten, hervorspringen; (*of ears*) abstehen; (*fig.*) herausragen, sich herausheben (***from***, aus), sich abheben (von *or* gegen), hervorstechen, in die Augen fallen; (*fig. of a p.*) aushalten, durchhalten; nicht mitmachen, sich fernhalten; ***– out against***, widerstehen (*Dat.*), Stellung nehmen gegen, Verwahrung einlegen gegen; ***– out for***, eintreten für; ***– out of my way!*** mach mir Platz! (*Naut.*) ***– out*** (***to sea***), auf Auslaufkurs liegen; ***– over***, liegenbleiben, verschoben *or* aufgeschoben *or* zurückgestellt werden; ***– over towards***, zuhalten auf (*Acc.*); (*Mil.*) ***– to***, sich zum Angriff vorbereiten; ***– up***, aufstehen (*from a seat*), aufrecht stehen, sich aufrecht halten, sich aufrichten; ***– up against***, sich behaupten gegen, sich erheben wider; ***– up for***, rechtfertigen, verteidigen, eintreten *or* sich einsetzen für; ***– up to***, standhalten (*Dat.*), gegenübertreten (*Dat.*), sich gewachsen zeigen (*Dat.*); es aufnehmen mit, entgegentreten (*Dat.*).

(c) (*with prep.*) (*Mil.*) ***– at attention***, stillstehen; ***– at bay***, gestellt sein; (*Mil.*) ***– at ease!*** rührt euch! ***– by***, beistehen (*Dat.*), halten zu (*a p.*), festhalten *or* beharren bei, treubleiben (*Dat.*) (*a th.*); beistimmen (*Dat.*); ***– by one's word***, zu seinem Wort stehen; ***– for***, stehen *or* gelten für, bedeuten, bezeichnen; vertreten; (*Parl.*) kandidieren für; (*coll.*) hinnehmen, dulden, sich (*Dat.*) gefallen *or* bieten lassen; ***– in awe of***, Ehrfurcht haben vor (*Dat.*); ***– in dread of***, Angst haben vor (*Dat.*); ***– in line***, Schlange stehen; ***– in need of***, nötig haben; (*fig.*) ***– in his shoes***, in seiner Haut stecken; ***– him in good stead***, ihm nützlich sein, ihm zustatten kommen; ***– instead of***, dienen als; ***– on***, beruhen auf (*Dat.*); ***– on ceremony***, Umstände machen; ***– on the defensive***, Widerstand leisten; ***– on one's dignity***, sich nichts vergeben; ***– on end***, aufrechtstehen, zu Berge stehen (*as hair*); ***– on one's guard***, auf der Hut sein; (*fig.*) ***– on one's own*** (***two***) ***feet***, unabhängig sein; ***– on one's head***, kopfstehen, Kopfstand machen; (*coll.*) ***– on one's hind legs***, hochgehen; ***– on record***, aufgezeichnet sein; ***– on one's rights***, auf seinem Recht bestehen, auf sein Recht pochen; ***– over***, beaufsichtigen, aufpassen auf (*Acc.*); (*fig.*) ***– to one's guns***, nicht zurückweichen, nicht nachgeben; sich von seiner Meinung nicht abbringen lassen; ***it –s to reason***, es ist selbstverständlich, es versteht sich (von selbst), es leuchtet ein; ***– upon***, see ***– on***.

3. *irr.v.t.* 1. stellen; 2. widerstehen (*Dat.*), standhalten (*Dat.*); ***– one's ground***, sich behaupten *or* durchsetzen, seinen Mann stehen; auf seiner Meinung beharren; (*coll.*) ***– the racket***, gut durchkommen; die Folgen zu tragen wissen, die Suppe auslöffeln; ***– the test***, sich bewähren; 3. leiden, dulden, sich (*Dat.*) gefallen lassen, aushalten, (er)tragen, vertragen, ausstehen; ***– the cold***, die Kälte vertragen; ***I cannot – him***, ich kann ihn nicht ausstehen *or* (*coll.*) riechen; ***I cannot – it***, ich kann es nicht aushalten, es ist mir zuviel, das geht mir über die Hutschnur; ***– the loss***, den Verlust tragen; ***– a lot***, viel vertragen, sich (*Dat.*) viel gefallen lassen; ***– no nonsense***, nicht mit sich spaßen *or* spielen lassen; ***– the pain***, den Schmerz aushalten; ***– the strain***, der Belastung gewachsen sein; 4. (*coll.*) spendieren, zum besten geben; ***– him a drink***, ihm einen spendieren; (*coll.*) ***– treat***, die Zeche bezahlen; 5. ***– a chance***, Aussicht *or* eine Chance haben; (*sl.*) ***not – an earthly***, nicht die geringste Aussicht haben; 6. ***– one's trial***, gerichtlich verhört werden, sich vor Gericht verantworten.

standard [ˈstændəd], **1.** *s.* 1. die Standarte, Fahne (*also fig.*); 2. der Pfosten, Pfeiler, Ständer, die Stütze, das Gestell; ***lamp –***, der Lampenständer; 3. (*Hort.*) freistehender Strauch, der Hochstamm, das Hochstämmchen; 4. Normalmaß, Eichmaß, Richtmaß (*also fig.*), die Normale; 5. der Normalpreis, Münzfuß, die Währung, Valuta; gesetzlicher Feingehalt (*metal*), der Titer (*liquids*); ***gold –***, die Goldwährung; 6. (*fig.*) der Maßstab, das Vorbild, Muster, die Richtlinie; der Durchschnitt, Standard, die Regel, Norm, der Stand, Grad, das Niveau; ***– of value***, der Wertmesser; ***above*** (***below***) ***–***, über (unter) dem Durchschnitt; ***be of high –***, ein hohes Niveau haben; ***– of life*** or ***living***, der Lebensstandard, die Lebenshaltung; ***set a –***, vorbildlich *or* mustergültig sein; ***set a high –***, viel fordern *or* verlangen; ***set the – for***, den Maßstab abgeben für; ***be*** or ***come up to*** (***the***) ***–***, den Anforderungen entsprechen *or* genügen; 7. die Klasse, Stufe (*at school*). **2.** *adj.* 1. maßgebend, führend; mustergültig, Muster–; Standard–,

Normal–, Einheits–, Serien–; – ***author,*** klassischer Schriftsteller; – ***candle,*** die Normalkerze; – ***edition,*** die Standardausgabe; – ***English,*** mustergültiges *or* hochsprachliches Englisch; – ***German,*** deutsche Bühnensprache *or* Schriftsprache, die Hochsprache, Gemeinsprache, Einheitssprache; (*Railw.*) – ***gauge,*** die Normalspurweite; – ***gold,*** das Münzgold; – ***measure,*** das Normalmaß; die Maßeinheit; – ***model,*** das Serienmodell; – ***work,*** das Standardwerk; 2. stehend, aufrecht, Steh–; – ***lamp,*** die Stehlampe; 3. (*Hort.*) hochstämmig.

standard-bearer, *s.* 1. der Fahnenträger, (*Hist.*) Fähnrich; 2. (*fig.*) Bannerträger, (An)führer.

standardization [stændədai'zeiʃən], *s.* die Standardisierung, Normierung, Normalisierung, Normung, Vereinheitlichung; (*Chem. etc.*) Titrierung; (*weights and measures*) Eichung. **standardize** ['stændədaiz], *v.t.* standardisieren, normalisieren, normieren, normen, vereinheitlichen; festlegen, eichen; einstellen, titrieren.

stand|-by, 1. *s.* 1. die Stütze, Hilfe, der Beistand, Helfer; Ersatz, Reserveapparat, das Zusatzgerät; 2. (*Mil. etc.*) die (Alarm)bereitschaft. **2.** *attrib. adj.* 1. Ersatz–, Reserve–; 2. (*Mil. etc.*) Bereitschafts–, Warte–. **--easy,** *s.* die Ruhepause. **--in,** *s.* (*Films etc.*) das Double, der (die) Ersatzspieler(in).

standing ['stændiŋ], **1.** *adj.* 1. stehend; ***all*** –, unvorbereitet, so wie man ist; – ***army,*** stehendes Heer; (*Dye.*) – ***bath,*** die Flotte; – ***corn,*** das Getreide auf dem Haln; – ***headroom,*** die Stehhöhe; – ***jump,*** der Schlußsprung; (*Typ.*) – ***matter,*** der Stehsatz; (*Naut.*) – ***rigging,*** stehendes Gut; – ***rule,*** (fest)stehende Regel; ***sold*** –, auf dem Halm verkauft; – ***stone,*** der Steinblock, Monolith; – ***wave,*** stehende *or* stationäre Welle; 2. dauernd, beständig, fest; – ***charge,*** laufende Unkosten; – ***committee,*** ständiger Ausschuß; – ***joke,*** altbewährter Witz; – ***nuisance,*** dauerndes *or* ständiges Ärgernis; – ***order,*** (*Comm.*) der Dauerauftrag, (*for periodicals*) das Abonnement; – ***orders,*** (*Parl.*) die Geschäftsordnung, (*Mil.*) Dauerbefehle (*pl.*), ständige Dienstanweisung. **2.** *s.* 1. das Stehen; ***no*** –, keine Stehplätze; 2. der Stand, Rang, das Ansehen; ***of good*** –, hochangesehen; 3. die Dauer, der Bestand; ***of long*** –, alt, langjährig; ***be of 10 years*** –, zehnjährigen Bestand haben, schon 10 Jahre bestehen.

standing-room, *s.* 1. der Platz zum Stehen; 2. Stehplatz.

stand|-offish [–'ɔfiʃ], *adj.* (*coll.*) zurückhaltend, reserviert, distanziert; abweisend, unnahbar, überheblich. **-pipe,** *s.* das Standrohr. **-point,** *s.* der Standpunkt, Gesichtspunkt. **-still,** *s.* der Stillstand; – ***agreement,*** das Stillhalteabkommen; ***be at a*** –, stillstehen, stocken; ***bring to a*** –, zum Stillstand *or* Stehen *or* Stocken bringen; ***come to a*** –, ins Stocken *or* zum Stillstand kommen, stehenbleiben; ***fight to a*** –, bis zur Erschöpfung kämpfen. **--up,** *attrib. adj.* (hoch)stehend, Steh–; – ***collar,*** der Stehkragen; – ***fight,*** regelrechter Kampf; – ***supper,*** kaltes Büfett.

stank [stæŋk], *imperf. of* **stink.**

stannary ['stænəri], *s.* das Zinn(berg)werk. **stannate** [–eit], **1.** *adj.* zinnsauer. **2.** *s.* zinnsaures Salz, das Stannat. **stannic,** *adj.* Zinn–; – ***acid,*** die Zinnsäure; – ***oxide,*** das Stannioxyd, Zinndioxyd. **stanniferous** [–'nifərəs], *adj.* zinnhaltig. **stannous** [–əs], *adj.* zinnähnlich; – ***oxide,*** das Zinnmonoxyd, Zinnoxydul; – ***salt,*** das Stannosalz, Zinnoxydulsalz.

stanza ['stænzə], *s.* die Strophe, Stanze. **stanzaic** [–'zeiik], *adj.* Stanzen–, strophisch.

[1]**staple** [steipl], **1.** *s.* 1. das Haupterzeugnis, der Haupthandelsartikel (*of a country*); (*fig.*) Hauptgegenstand, Hauptinhalt, das Hauptthema; 2. (*Tech.*) der Stapel, einzelne Fadenlänge *or* Faser (*of wool etc.*); die Rohwolle; (*fig.*) der Rohstoff; – ***fibre,*** die Zellwolle; 3. (*Hist.*) Stapelplatz, Markt, das Zentrum, Lager. **2.** *attrib. adj.* 1. Stapel–, Haupt–; – ***food,*** das Hauptnahrungsmittel; – ***subject of conversation,*** gängiges Gesprächsthema; 2. (*Comm.*) Haupthandels–, Massen–; 3. (*Hist.*) Monopol–. **3.** *v.t.* (nach der Faser) sortieren (*wool etc.*).

[2]**staple, 1.** *s.* 1. die Krampe, Haspe, Kramme; 2. (*Bookb.*) Heftklammer, der Heftdraht. **2.** *v.t.* 1. festklammern; 2. (*Bookb.*) mit Draht heften.

[1]**stapler** ['steiplə], *s.* 1. der (Baumwoll)sortierer; 2. (*Hist.*) Großkaufmann.

[2]**stapler, stapling machine,** *s.* die Heftmaschine.

star [stɑ:], **1.** *s.* 1. der Stern (*also fig.*); (*Bot.*) – ***of Bethlehem,*** der Milchstern; ***fixed*** –, der Fixstern; (*coll.*) ***I see -s,*** es flimmert mir vor den Augen; ***falling*** or ***shooting*** –, die Sternschnuppe; 2. der Ordensstern; 3. (*Typ.*) das Sternchen; 4. (*fig.*) der (Glücks)stern, das Geschick, Schicksal; ***the -s are against it,*** es steht unter keinem guten Stern; ***my – is in the ascendant,*** mein Stern ist im Aufgehen; ***my – has set,*** mein Stern ist erloschen; ***thank one's (lucky) -s,*** seinem Schicksal verdanken, von Glück sagen können; ***unlucky*** –, der Unstern; 5. der (die) berühmte Künstler(in) *or* Schauspieler(in) *or* Sänger(in), die Größe, Berühmtheit, Filmgröße, der (Film)star. **2.** *v.t.* 1. besternen, mit Sternen besetzen *or* schmücken; 2. (*Typ.*) mit Sternchen versehen; 3. (*Theat.*) (*an actor*) eine Hauptrolle geben (*Dat.*). **3.** *v.i.* (*Theat.*) die Hauptrolle spielen, in der Hauptrolle auftreten.

starblind ['stɑ:blaind], *adj.* halbblind.

starboard ['stɑ:bəd], **1.** *s.* (*also* – ***hand***) das Steuerbord; – ***the helm!*** Ruder am Steuerbord! **2.** *adj.* Steuerbord–; – ***side,*** das Steuerbord.

starch [stɑ:tʃ], **1.** *s.* 1. die (Pflanzen)stärke; 2. (Wäsche)stärke; 3. (*fig.*) die Steifheit, Formalität; 4. (*Chem.*) Kohle(n)hydrate (*pl.*). **2.** *v.t.* stärken, stiefen.

Star Chamber, *s.* (*Hist.*) die Sternkammer; (*fig.*) Willkür(justiz).

starched [stɑ:tʃt], *adj.* 1. gestärkt; 2. (*fig.*) steif, formell, förmlich. **starchiness,** *s.* 1. die Stärkehaltigkeit; 2. (*usu. fig.*) Steifheit, Förmlichkeit. **starchy,** *adj.* 1. stärkehaltig; 2. (*fig.*) steif, formell, förmlich.

star-crossed, *adj.* von einem Unstern verfolgt. **stardom,** *s.* (*Theat.*) die Welt der Stars. **stardrift,** *s.* das Sterntreiben.

stare [stɛə], **1.** *s.* das Starren, Stieren, starrer Blick. **2.** *v.i.* starren, stieren; große Augen machen; – ***at,*** anstarren, anstieren, groß ansehen, den Blick heften auf (*Acc.*); – ***into space,*** vor sich hinstarren; ***make him*** –, ihn in Erstaunen versetzen; – ***back at him,*** seinen starrenden Blick erwidern. **3.** *v.t.* – ***him in the face,*** (*of a p.*) *see* – ***at***; (*of a th.*) ihm in die Augen springen, ihm deutlich vor Augen stehen; – ***out of countenance,*** durch starre Blicke aus der Fassung bringen.

star|finch, *s.* (*Orn.*) das Rotschwänzchen (*Pheonicurus*). **-fish,** *s.* der Seestern. **-gazer,** *s.* der Sterngucker. **-gazing,** *s.* die Sternguckerei, Verträumtheit.

staring ['stɛəriŋ], *adj.* 1. starrend; 2. (*fig.*) auffallend, grell.

stark [stɑ:k], *adj., adv.* 1. steif, starr; 2. kahl, öde; 3. (*coll.*) bar, glatt, völlig, gänzlich, ganz; ***--raving*** or ***-staring mad,*** total verrückt; – ***naked,*** splitternackt. **starkness,** *s.* (*fig.*) die Öde, Kahlheit; reine Sachlichkeit.

starless ['stɑ:lis], *adj.* sternenlos. **starlet,** *s.* 1. das Sternchen; 2. (*usu. Theat.*) Filmsternchen, angehender (Film)star, das Starlet. **star|light, 1.** *s.* das Sternenlicht. **2.** *adj.* sternklar, stern(en)hell. **-like,** *adj.* sternförmig.

[1]**starling** ['stɑ:liŋ], *s.* (*Orn.*) der Star (*Sturnus vulgaris*).

[2]**starling,** *s.* das Pfeilerhaupt, der Eisbrecher, Strombrecher (*of a bridge*).

star|lit, *adj.* (nur) von den Sternen beleuchtet. **-performance,** *s.* die Elitevorstellung.

starred [stɑ:d], *adj.* 1. gestirnt (*sky*); mit Sternen geschmückt *or* besät; 2. (*Typ.*) mit Sternchen versehen; 3. (*Theat.*) (*of an actor*) als Star herausgestellt. **starry** ['stɑ:ri], *adj.* 1. gestirnt, Sternen–

(*sky*), stern(en)hell, sternklar (*night*), sternengeschmückt, besternt; strahlend (*eyes*); 2. sternförmig, Stern–. **starry-eyed,** *adj.* (*coll.*) unpraktisch, unrealistisch, idealistisch; verträumt, romantisch.

star|-shaped, *adj.* sternförmig. **--shell,** *s.* (*Mil.*) die Leuchtkugel. **--spangled,** *adj.* sternbesät; (*Am.*) – ***banner***, das Sternenbanner; amerikanisches Nationallied.

start [stɑːt], **1.** *v.i.* 1. anfangen, beginnen, seinen Anfang nehmen, (*fig.*) ausgehen (***from***, von); aufbrechen, abreisen, sich auf den Weg machen, sich aufmachen (***for***, nach), abgehen, abfahren (*as trains etc.*), (*Naut.*) auslaufen, (*Av.*) abfliegen; anlaufen, anspringen (*as an engine*); (*Spt.*) starten; 2. zusammenfahren, auffahren, in die Höhe fahren, hochschrecken, aufschrecken, aufspringen; 3. sich werfen *or* krümmen, klaffen, gap(p)en (*as planks*); 4. sich lockern *or* lösen (*as nails*).
(a) (*with adv.*) – ***back***, 1. die Rückreise antreten; 2. zurückweichen, zurückspringen, zurückschrecken (***from***, vor (*Dat.*)); (*coll.*) – ***in***, beginnen; (*coll.*) – ***off***, abfahren, aufbrechen, die Reise antreten; – ***out***, die Reise antreten, aufbrechen; (*coll.*) sich daran machen; – ***up***, 1. auffahren, aufschrecken, aufspringen, stutzen (***at***, bei); 2. anspringen (*as a car*); 3. (*coll.*) entstehen, auftauchen.
(b) (*with prep.*) ***his eyes –ed from his head***, ihm traten die Augen aus dem Kopfe; – ***in business***, ein Geschäft eröffnen *or* anfangen; (*coll.*) – ***on***, beginnen mit (*a th.*), Händel suchen mit (*a p.*); ***to – with***, um es vorwegzunehmen, für den Anfang.
2. *v.t.* 1. aufjagen, aufschrecken, aufscheuchen, auftreiben, aufstöbern (*game*); (*fig.*) – ***another hare***, ein neues Thema anschneiden; 2. gründen, einrichten, aufmachen (*a business*); ins Leben rufen, in Gang bringen, in Gang *or* Betrieb *or* Bewegung setzen, anlassen (*an engine*), in die Welt setzen (*a theory etc.*), anregen, aufbringen, aufwerfen, anschneiden (*a question*), verbreiten, in Umlauf bringen (*a rumour*), antreten (*a journey*), (*Spt.*) starten (lassen); – ***the ball rolling***, den Stein *or* die S. ins Rollen bringen; – ***him in business***, ihn auf eigene Füße stellen, ihn etablieren; – ***him coughing***, ihn zum Husten bringen; 3. stürzen (*a cask*), lockern, losmachen (*nails, planks etc.*).
3. *s.* 1. der Anfang, Beginn; Aufbruch, die Abfahrt, Abreise; (*Av.*) der Abflug, Aufstieg; (*Spt.*) Start; die Startlinie; ***at the –***, am Anfang, bei Beginn; ***from the –***, von Anfang an; ***from – to finish***, von Anfang bis (zu) Ende; ***make a –***, anfangen, beginnen; ***make an early –***, zeitig aufbrechen; 2. die Vorgabe, (*also fig.*) der Vorsprung; (*fig.*) ***get*** or ***have the – of him***, ihm zuvorkommen; ***have a – over him***, vor ihm einen Vorsprung haben; ***an hour's –***, eine Vorgabe von einer Stunde; 3. der Ruck, das Auffahren, Zusammenfahren; ***by (fits and) –s***, ruckweise, sprungweise; ***give a –***, auffahren; ***give him a –***, ihn aufschrecken.

starter [ˈstɑːtə], *s.* 1. der Starter (*with the gun*); 2. das Pferd *or* der (die) Läufer(in) am Start, Teilnehmer(in) (*in a race*); 3. (*Motor.*) der Anlasser, Starter; ***—motor***, *see* **starting-motor.**

star-thistle, *s.* (*Bot.*) die Flockenblume.

starting [ˈstɑːtiŋ], *s.* der Aufbruch; (*Spt.*) Starten; ***order of –***, die Startordnung. **starting|-block,** *s.* der Startblock. **--gate,** *s.* die Startmaschine. **--gun,** *s.* die Startpistole. **--handle,** *s.* die Anlaßkurbel. **--line,** *s.* die Startlinie. **--motor,** *s.* der Anlaßmotor; **--place,** *s.* der Ausgangsort. **--point,** *s.* der Ausgangspunkt (***of***, für). **--post,** *s.* die Startlinie, das Startmal. **--price,** *s.* 1. der Startpreis, Kurs vor dem Start (*racing*); 2. Eröffnungspreis, Einsatzpreis (*auction*).

startle [stɑːtl], *v.t.* 1. überraschen, bestürzen; alarmieren, entsetzen, erschrecken; aufschrecken; 2. aufscheuchen. **startling,** *adj.* bestürzend, überraschend, aufsehenerregend, erschreckend, alarmierend.

star-turn, *s.* (*coll. fig.*) die Hauptnummer, Hauptattraktion.

starvation [stɑːˈveiʃən], *s.* das Hungern, Hungerleiden; Verhungern, die Aushungerung, der Hungertod; – ***wages***, der Hungerlohn.

starve [stɑːv], **1.** *v.i.* hungern, Hunger leiden; – (***to death***), verhungern, Hungers *or* vor Hunger sterben; (*coll.*) ***be starving***, vor Hunger fast umkommen; (*fig.*) – ***for***, hungern *or* dürsten nach. **2.** *v.t.* hungern lassen; – (***to death***), verhungern lassen, Hungers *or* vor Hunger sterben lassen; (*fig.*) verkümmern lassen (*plants etc.*); ***be –d***, hungern müssen, Hunger leiden; ***he was –d (to death)***, man ließ ihn verhungern; (*coll.*) ***be –d with cold***, durchfroren sein; – ***into***, durch Hunger zwingen zu; – ***out***, aushungern. **starveling** [–liŋ], **1.** *s.* ausgehungertes Tier; verkümmerte Pflanze; der Hungerleider. **2.** *adj.* hungrig, ausgehungert, abgezehrt.

stasis [ˈsteisis], *s.* (*Med.*) die (Blut)stockung, Stauung.

¹**state** [steit], **1.** *s.* 1. der Zustand; Stand, die Lage, Stellung, Verfassung, Beschaffenheit; das Stadium; – ***of affairs***, die Sachlage; – ***of emergency***, der Notstand, Ausnahmezustand; (*Eccl.*) – ***of grace***, der Stand der Gnade; – ***of health***, der Gesundheitszustand; – ***of mind***, der Geisteszustand; (*coll.*) – ***of nature***, nackt; ***good (poor) – of repair***, gut (schlecht) erhaltener Zustand; – ***of siege***, der Belagerungszustand; – ***of things***, see – ***of affairs***; (*Am.*) – ***of the Union message***, die Rechenschaftsbericht an die Nation; – ***of war***, der Kriegszustand; 2. der Staat; ***affairs of –***, Staatsgeschäfte (*pl.*); ***run by the –***, staatlich, Staats–; ***Secretary of State***, der Staatssekretär, Minister; 3. (*obs.*) die Pracht, der Staat, Pomp, Aufwand; (*coll.*) ***in –***, mit großem Pomp; in Galauniform; ***lie in –***, auf dem Paradebett *or* feierlich aufgebahrt liegen; ***live in (great) –***, großen Staat machen; 4. (*coll.*) die Erregung, Aufgeregtheit; (*coll.*) schlechter *or* unglaublicher Zustand; ***be in a –***, aufgebracht sein; 5. *pl.* (*Hist.*) Stände (*pl.*). **2.** *adj.* 1. staatlich, Staats–; 2. feierlich.

²**state,** *v.t.* 1. angeben, klarlegen, darlegen, erklären; (*esp. Law*) aussagen, vortragen, vorbringen, anführen; behaupten, berichten, melden, erwähnen; ***as –d***, wie angegeben *or* erwähnt; ***he was –d to have said***, er soll gesagt haben; 2. festsetzen, festlegen, feststellen; (*Math.*) (auf)stellen.

state|-aid, *s.* die Staatshilfe, staatliche Unterstützung. **--aided,** *adj.* staatlich unterstützt. **-apartments,** *pl.* Galaräume, Paraderäume (*pl.*). **- cabin,** *s.* die Luxuskabine. **--control,** *s.* staatliche Aufsicht *or* Kontrolle. **--controlled,** *adj.* verstaatlicht, unter staatlicher Aufsicht. **–craft,** *s.* die Staatskunst, Staatsklugheit.

stated [ˈsteitid], *adj.* bestimmt, festgesetzt, festgestellt; ***at – intervals***, in regelmäßigen Abständen; ***at the – time***, zur festgesetzten Zeit.

State Department, *s.* (*Am.*) Auswärtiges Amt, das Außenministerium.

statehood [ˈsteithud], *s.* die Souveränität, Eigenstaatlichkeit. **stateless,** *adj.* staatenlos.

stateliness [ˈsteitlinis], *s.* die Stattlichkeit, Erhabenheit, Würde, Pracht. **stately,** *adj.* stattlich, majestätisch, imposant, erhaben, würdevoll, würdig.

state medicine, *s.* öffentliches *or* staatliches Gesundheitswesen.

statement [ˈsteitmənt], *s.* 1. die Feststellung, Behauptung, Angabe, Erklärung, Aussage, Verlautbarung; (*esp. Law*) Darstellung, Darlegung, Aufzeichnung, Niederschrift; (*Law*) – ***of claim***, die Klageschrift; ***make a –***, eine Behauptung aufstellen; ***prisoner's –***, die Gefangenenaussage; 2. (*Comm.*) die Aufstellung, der Bericht, (*Banking*) (Konto)auszug, die Bilanz; – ***of account***, der Rechnungsauszug; (*Comm.*) ***as per –***, laut Angabe *or* Bericht; – ***of charges***, die Kostenrechnung; – ***of prices***, die Preisliste.

state| occasion, *s.* der Staatsakt. – **papers,** *pl.* Staatsakten (*f. pl.*). – **prison,** *s.* das Staatsgefängnis. – **property,** *s.* das Staatseigentum.

– **room,** *s.* der Prunksaal; (*Naut.*) die Luxuskabine.

States-General, *pl.* 1. Generalstaate (*pl.*) (*Netherlands*); 2. (*Hist.*) Generalstände (*pl.*) (*France*).

statesman ['steitsmən], *s.* der Staatsmann. **statesmanlike,** *adj.* staatsmännisch, (*fig.*) diplomatisch. **statesmanship,** *s.* die Staatskunst, Regierungskunst. **stateswoman,** *s.* (bedeutende) Politikerin.

static ['stætik], **1.** *adj.* 1. statisch, ruhend, Ruhe–; (fest)stehend, ortsfest; – ***warfare,*** die Stellungskrieg; – ***water-tank,*** der Feuerlöschteich; 2. (*Elec.*) elektrostatisch; – ***electricity,*** statische Elektrizität; (*Rad.*) – ***gain,*** die Verstärkung pro Stufe. **2.** *s.* (*Rad.*) atmosphärische Störungen (*pl.*). **statics,** *pl.* (*sing. constr.*) die Statik.

station ['steiʃən], **1.** *s.* 1. (*esp. Mil.*) der Standort; Platz, Posten (*of a sentry etc.*); (amtliche) Stelle; die Station; ***airforce*** –, der Fliegerhorst; (*Mil.*) ***dressing*** –, der Verbandplatz; (*Mil.*) ***duty*** –, die Dienststelle; ***filling*** –, die Tankstelle; ***fire*** –, die Feuer(wehr)wache, das Feuerdepot; ***naval*** –, der Flottenstützpunkt; ***police*** –, das Polizeirevier, die Polizeiwache; ***polling*** –, das Wahllokal; (*Elec.*) ***power*** –, das Kraftwerk, Elektrizitätswerk; ***take up one's*** –, seinen Platz *or* Posten einnehmen; 2. (*Rad.*) die Station; ***jamming*** –, der Störsender; ***radio*** –, der (Rundfunk)sender, die Sendestation; 3. (*Railw.*) die Station, der Bahnhof; ***at the*** –, auf dem Bahnhof; (*Comm.*) ***free*** –, bahnfrei; ***goods*** –, der Güterbahnhof; 4. (*Austral.*) ***cattle*** –, die Viehfarm; 5. (hohe) Stellung, der Stand, (hoher) Rang; ***above one's*** –, über seinem Stand; – ***in life,*** gesellschaftliche Stellung; ***man of*** –, der Mann von hohem Rang; 6. die Haltestelle, Rast, der Rastort (*on a journey*); 7. (*Eccl.*) ***–s of the Cross,*** der Kreuzweg; 8. (*Astr.*) (scheinbarer) Stillstand; 9. (*Surv.*) der Standpunkt. **2.** *v.t.* stationieren, aufstellen, postieren; – ***o.s.,*** sich (auf)stellen, seinen Platz einnehmen.

stationary ['steiʃənəri], *adj.* (still)stehend; feststehend, ortsfest, stationär, gleichbleibend, beständig, unverändert; unveränderlich, unbeweglich, seßhaft, (in sich) ruhend; ***be*** or ***remain*** –, nicht weiterkommen, (still)stehen; sich gleichbleiben, in sich ruhen; – ***engine,*** der Standmotor.

stationer ['steiʃənə], *s.* der Papierhändler, Schreibwarenhändler; ***Stationers' Company,*** Londoner Buchhändlergilde; ***Stationers' Hall,*** Londoner Buchhändlerbörse; ***–'s*** (***shop***), das Papiergeschäft, die Schreibwarenhandlung. **stationery** [–ri], *s.* Schreibwaren, Papierwaren (*pl.*); das Schreibpapier, Briefpaper; ***office*** –, das Büromaterial; (***H.M.***) ***Stationery Office,*** Königlicher Staatsverlag.

station|-house, *s.* (*Am.*) die Polizeiwache. **–master,** *s.* der Bahnhofsvorsteher. **––pointer,** *s.* die Meßrute (*Surv.*). **––wag(g)on,** *s.* (*Motor.*) der Kombi(wagen).

statist ['steitist], *s.* 1. (*obs.*) der Staatsmann; 2. Anhänger einer einheitlich geplanten Volkswirtschaft.

statistic [stə'tistik], *s.* statistische Angabe; *pl.* statistische Angaben, die Statistik, Statistiken (*pl.*); ***prove by –s,*** statistisch nachweisen. **statistical,** *adj.* statistisch; – ***table,*** statistische Aufstellung, die Statistik. **statistician** [stætis'tiʃən], *s.* der (die) Statistiker(in). **statistics** [stə'tistiks], *pl.* 1. (*sing. constr.*) (*branch of Math.*) die Statistik; 2. (*pl. constr.*) *see* **statistic.**

stator ['steitə], *s.* der Stator.

statuary ['stætjuəri], **1.** *s.* 1. Standbilder, Statuen, Skulpturen, Bildhauerarbeiten (*pl.*); 2. die Bildhauerkunst, Bildhauerei. **2.** *adj.* Bildhauer–; – ***marble,*** der Bildsäulenmarmor. **statue** ['stætju:], *s.* das Standbild, die Bildsäule, Statue. **statuesque** [–'esk], *adj.* 1. statuenhaft, statuarisch, standbildhaft; 2. (*fig.*) würdevoll. **statuette** [–'et], *s.* kleine Statue, die Statuette.

stature ['stætʃə], *s.* 1. die (Körper)größe, Gestalt, Statur, der Wuchs; 2. (*fig.*) das Format, Kaliber.

status ['steitəs], *s.* 1. (*Law*) die Rechtsstellung, der Status; ***equality of*** –, politische Gleichberechtigung; ***legal*** –, die Rechtsfähigkeit; ***national*** –, die Staatsangehörigkeit; 2. die Lage; ***financial*** –, die Vermögenslage; 3. die Stellung, der Rang; 4. (*Med. etc.*) Zustand; 5. Stand.

status| quo [–'kwou], *s.* gegenwärtiger Zustand. – **quo ante** [–'ænti], *s.* voriger Zustand. **––symbol,** *s.* das Standeskennzeichen, Statussymbol.

statute ['stætju:t], *s.* 1. (geschriebenes) Gesetz, das Gesetzesrecht; – ***of limitations,*** das Verjährungsgesetz; 2. die Bestimmung, Vorschrift, Verordnung, Satzung, das Statut; 3. die Parlamentsakte. **statute|-book,** *s.* das Reichsgesetzbuch, die Gesetz(es)sammlung; ***be put on the*** –, Gesetz werden. **––labour,** *s.* (*Hist.*) die Fron(de), der Frondienst. **––law,** *s.* geschriebenes Recht, das Gesetzesrecht.

statutory ['stætjutəri], *adj.* gesetzlich, Gesetz–; – ***corporation,*** die Körperschaft des öffentlichen Rechts; – ***declaration,*** eidesstattliche Erklärung; – ***holidays,*** staatliche Feiertage.

[1]staunch, *see* **[1]stanch.**

[2]staunch [stɔ:ntʃ], *adj.* treu, standhaft, zuverlässig, unerschütterlich (*of a p.*); fest, solid(e) (*of a th.*). **staunchness,** *s.* die Treue, Standhaftigkeit; Festigkeit, Solidität.

stave [steiv], **1.** *s.* 1. die (Faß)daube; 2. (Leiter)sprosse; der Steg (*of chair etc.*); 3. (*obs.*) Stock, Knüppel, Knüttel; 4. (*Metr.*) die Strophe; 5. (*Mus.*) das Noten(linien)system. **2.** *irr.v.t.* 1. (*only reg.*) mit Dauben *or* Sprossen versehen; 2. (*usu. irr.*) – ***in,*** einschlagen, ein Loch schlagen in (*Acc.*); 3. (*usu. reg.*) (*fig.*) – ***off,*** abhalten, abwenden, abwehren; aufschieben, aufhalten, verzögern.

stay [stei], **1.** *v.i.* 1. bleiben; – ***at home,*** zu Hause bleiben; – ***away,*** wegbleiben; – ***behind,*** zurückbleiben; – ***down,*** sitzenbleiben (*at school*); – ***for,*** warten auf (*Acc.*) (*a p.*); – ***for*** or ***to dinner,*** zum Mittagessen bleiben; – ***in,*** zu Hause bleiben; – ***on,*** länger bleiben, den Aufenthalt verlängern; (*coll.*) – ***put,*** (an Ort und Stelle) bleiben; (*coll.*) ***it has come to*** –, es wird bleiben, es hat sich fest eingebürgert; – ***out,*** draußenbleiben; – ***up,*** aufbleiben; 2. verweilen, sich aufhalten; zu Besuch sein (***with,*** bei); (*Scots*) wohnen; – ***at a hotel,*** in einem Hotel unterkommen *or* logieren; – ***in London,*** sich in London aufhalten; – ***with,*** bleiben bei; zu Besuch sein ((*Scots*) wohnen) bei; 3. (*Spt.*) aushalten, durchhalten; (*sl.*) – ***with,*** es aufnehmen mit. **2.** *v.t.* 1. zurückhalten, aufhalten, anhalten, hindern, hemmen; (*Law*) einstellen, aussetzen, sistieren; zum Stehen bringen (*an advance*); 2. stillen (*hunger*); befriedigen (*desire*); 3. – ***the course,*** bis zum Ende durchhalten; 4. (*coll.*) – ***dinner,*** see – ***for under*** **1**; (*coll.*) – ***the night,*** übernachten, über Nacht bleiben. **3.** *s.* 1. das Bleiben, Verweilen, der Aufenthalt; ***make a*** –, sich aufhalten; 2. (*Law*) die Einstellung, Aussetzung; ***put a – on,*** behindern, hemmen.

[2]stay, 1. *s.* 1. (*Naut.*) das Stag, Stütztau; ***in –s,*** im Wenden; ***miss –s,*** das Wenden verfehlen; 2. die Strebe, Stütze (*also fig.*); 3. *pl.* das Korsett; ***a pair of –s,*** ein Korsett. **2.** *v.t.* stagen (*a mast*); durch den Wind bringen (*a ship*).

stay-at-home, 1. *s.* der (die) Stubenhocker(in). **2.** *adj.* daheimgeblieben, stubenhockerisch. **stayer,** *s.* (*Spt.*) der Steher, durchhaltender Renner. **staying,** *adj.* aushaltend; – ***power,*** die Widerstandskraft, Ausdauer.

staysail ['steisəl], *s.* das Stagsegel, die Stagfock (*on a cutter*).

stead [sted], *s.* (*fig.*) die Statt, Stelle; ***in his*** –, an seiner Statt *or* Stelle; ***stand him in good*** –, ihm zustatten kommen, ihm nützlich sein.

steadfast ['stedfɑ:st], *adj.* 1. fest, unentwegt, beharrlich, standhaft, unerschütterlich, entschlossen, treu (*of a p.*); 2. unverwandt (*of a glance*), unbeweglich, unveränderlich, unabänderlich. **steadfastness,** *s.* die Festigkeit, Beständigkeit, Standhaftigkeit; – ***of purpose,*** die Zielstrebigkeit.

steadiness ['stedinis], *s.* 1. die Sicherheit, Festigkeit; 2. Beständigkeit, Beharrlichkeit, Standhaftigkeit (*of character*); 3. Stetigkeit, Gleichmäßigkeit. **steady, 1.** *adj.* 1. fest (*also fig.*), sicher, stabil, standfest, unbeweglich; – ***hand,*** sichere Hand; – ***prices,*** stabile Preise; ***remain*** –, sich halten (*as prices*); 2. (*fig.*) standhaft, beständig, beharrlich, unerschütterlich (*as character*); – ***nerves,*** starke Nerven; 3. ständig, stetig, gleichbleibend, gleichmäßig, regelmäßig; – ***work,*** regelmäßige Arbeit; 4. zuverlässig, solid(e), gesetzt; 5. – (***on***)! langsam! vorsichtig! ruhig! **2.** *v.t.* 1. festmachen, festigen, sichern; – ***o.s.,*** sich stützen; 2. zügeln, zurückhalten (*a horse etc.*); 3. verlangsamen (*the pace*); 4. zur Vernunft *or* Ruhe bringen (*a p.*). **3.** *v.i.* 1. fest *or* ruhig *or* sicher werden; 2. – ***down,*** sich beruhigen, zur Vernunft kommen, Vernunft annehmen.

steak [steik], *s.* das Steak, die (Fleisch)schnitte.

steal [sti:l], **1.** *irr.v.t.* stehlen (***from,*** *Dat.*); – ***a march on him,*** ihm zuvorkommen; – ***a glance,*** einen verstohlenen Blick werfen; – ***a kiss,*** einen Kuß rauben; (*fig.*) – ***the limelight,*** im Mittelpunkt des Interesses stehen; – ***his thunder,*** ihm den Wind aus den Segeln nehmen; – ***the show,*** den Vogel abschießen. **2.** *irr.v.i.* 1. stehlen; 2. sich stehlen, schleichen; – ***away,*** sich fortstehlen; – ***into,*** sich einschleichen in (*Acc.*); – ***over,*** beschleichen, sich einschleichen bei (*of feelings etc.*); – ***upon,*** beschleichen, überfallen, sich allmählich bemerkbar machen bei.

stealth [stelθ], *s.* die List, Heimlichkeit; ***by*** –, verstohlen(erweise), heimlich, hinterrücks. **stealthiness** [–inis], *s.* die Heimlichkeit, Verstohlenheit. **stealthy,** *adj.* verstohlen, heimlich.

steam [sti:m], **1.** *s.* 1. der (Wasser)dampf, die Dampfkraft; ***exhaust*** –, der Abdampf; ***at full*** –, mit Volldampf (*also fig.*); ***full – ahead,*** Volldampf voraus; ***get – up,*** Dampf anmachen; (*fig.*) Dampf dahinter machen *or* setzen; ***have – up,*** unter Dampf liegen *or* stehen; ***let off*** –, Dampf ablassen; (*fig.*) sich Luft machen, den Gefühlen freien Lauf lassen; ***saturated*** –, der Sattdampf; ***superheated*** –, der Heißdampf; (*fig.*) ***under one's own*** –, ohne Mithilfe anderer, auf eigene Faust; 2. der Dunst, die Verdunstung, Feuchtigkeit; 3. (*fig.*) Kraft, Energie. **2.** *v.i.* 1. dampfen, dunsten; 2. fahren, laufen (*of a steamer*); (*fig.*) – ***ahead,*** gut vorankommen; 3. – ***over*** or ***up,*** sich beschlagen (*as glass*). **3.** *v.t.* 1. dämpfen, mit Dampf behandeln; (*Cul.*) dünsten; dekatieren (*cloth*); 2. beschlagen (*as glass*); 3. (*sl.*) ***get –ed up,*** in Erregung geraten, in Fahrt kommen.

steam|boat, *s.* das Dampfschiff, der Dampfer. **–-boiler,** *s.* der Dampfkessel. **–-chest,** *s.* der Schieberkasten. **–-coal,** *s.* die Kesselkohle. **–-engine,** *s.* die Dampfmaschine.

steamer [ˈsti:mə], *s.* 1. der Dampfer, das Dampfschiff; 2. (*Cul.*) der Dampfkochtopf.

steam-gauge, *s.* das Manometer, der Dampfdruckmesser.

steaminess [ˈsti:minis], *s.* die Dunstigkeit; (*coll.*) Beschlagenheit (*as windows*).

steam|-iron, *s.* das Dampfbügeleisen. **–-jacket,** *s.* der Dampfmantel. **–-navigation,** *s.* die Dampfschiffahrt. **–-navvy,** *s.* der Trockenbagger. **–-pipe,** *s.* das Dampfrohr. **–-power,** *s.* die Dampfkraft. **–roller, 1.** *s.* die Dampfwalze (*also fig.*), Straßenwalze. **2.** *v.t.* (*fig.*) niederwalzen. **–ship,** *s.* der Dampfer, das Dampfschiff. **–-shovel,** *s. See* **–-navvy. –-vessel,** *s. See* **–ship.**

steamy [ˈsti:mi], *adj.* dampfig, dunstig, dampfend, Dampf–; (*coll.*) beschlagen (*as windows*).

stearate [ˈstiəreit], **1.** *s.* das Stearat, stearinsaures Salz. **2.** *adj.* stearinsauer. **stearic** [stiˈærik], *adj.* Stearin–; – ***acid,*** die Stearinsäure, Talgsäure. **stearin** [–rin], *s.* das Stearin; – ***candle,*** die Stearinkerze.

steatite [ˈstiətait], *s.* der Speckstein.

steatoma [stiəˈtoumə], *s.* (*pl.* **-ta** [–ˈmɑ:tə]) (*Med.*) die Fettgeschwulst. **steatosis** [–ˈtousis], *s.* (*Med.*) die Verfettung.

steed [sti:d], *s.* (*Poet.*) das (Schlacht)roß.

steel [sti:l], **1.** *s.* 1. der Stahl (*also fig.*); Schleifstahl, Wetzstahl; die Stange (*in a corset*); ***cast*** –, der Gußstahl; ***cold*** –, Stahlwaffen (*pl.*); ***forged*** –, das Schmiedeeisen; ***high-speed*** –, der Schnellschnittstahl; ***ingot*** or ***mild*** –, der Flußstahl; ***a heart of*** –, ein Herz von Stein; ***muscles of*** –, stählerne Muskeln; 2. (*Poet.*) das Schwert; ***foe worthy of my*** –, der mir würdige Gegner; 3. (*fig.*) die Stärke, Härte. **2.** *adj.* 1. stählern, Stahl–; 2. (*fig.*) stahlhart, eisern. **3.** *v.t.* 1. (ver)stählen; 2. (*fig.*) (*oft.* – ***o.s.***) (sich) stärken *or* wappnen *or* rüsten.

steel|-clad, *adj.* stahlgepanzert. **– engraving,** *s.* 1. die Stahlstecherkunst; 2. der Stahlstich.

steeliness [ˈsti:linis], *s.* die Stahlhärte; (*usu. fig.*) Härte, Unbeugsamkeit.

steel|-plated, *s. See* **–-clad. –wool,** *s.* Stahlspäne (*pl.*), die Stahlwolle. **–work,** *s.* die Stahlarbeit, Stahlteile (*pl.*). **–works,** *pl.* (*sing. constr.*) das Stahlwerk.

steely [ˈsti:li], *adj.* 1. stählern, Stahl–; stahlfarben; 2. (*usu. fig.*) (stahl)hart, unbeugsam; – ***composure,*** eiserne Ruhe; – ***glance,*** eiskalter Blick.

steelyard [ˈsti:ljɑ:d], *s.* die Laufgewichtswaage, Schnellwaage.

¹**steep** [sti:p], **1.** *adj.* 1. steil, jäh, schroff, abschüssig; – ***coast,*** die Steilküste; – ***slope,*** der Steilhang; (*Av.*) – ***turn,*** die Steilkurve; 2. (*coll.*) unwahrscheinlich, unglaubhaft (*story*), unverschämt, gepfeffert (*prices*). **2.** *s.* der Steilhang, steiler Abhang.

²**steep, 1.** *s.* das Einweichen, Eintauchen; Einweichwasser, die Lauge; ***put the clothes in*** –, die Wäsche einweichen. **2.** *v.t.* 1. eintauchen (***in,*** in (*Acc.*)), einweichen, durchfeuchten, (durch)tränken (in (*Dat.*)); 2. (*fig.*) (*usu. pass.*) ***–ed in,*** versenkt *or* verstrickt in (*Acc.*) *or* versunken *or* befangen in (*Dat.*), durchdrungen von; – ***o.s. in,*** sich versenken in (*Acc.*).

steepen [ˈsti:pən], **1.** *v.t.* 1. steiler machen; 2. (*fig.*) vermehren. **2.** *v.i.* steiler werden.

steeple [sti:pl], *s.* der Kirchturm, Spitzturm. **steeple|chase, –chasing,** *s.* das Hindernisrennen. **–jack,** *s.* der Turmdecker, Schornsteinarbeiter.

steepness [ˈsti:pnis], *s.* die Steilheit, Steile, Abschüssigkeit. **steep-to,** *adj.* (*Naut.*) steil abfallend *or* ansteigend.

¹**steer** [stiə], *s.* junger Ochs.

²**steer, 1.** *v.t.* 1. steuern; 2. (*fig.*) lenken, leiten; führen, dirigieren, lotsen; 3. – ***a course,*** einen Kurs einhalten. **2.** *v.i.* steuern, gesteuert werden, sich steuern lassen; fahren, laufen, segeln, schiffen (***for,*** nach); (*usu. fig.*) – ***clear of,*** meiden, sich fernhalten von, aus dem Wege gehen (*Dat.*). **steerable** [–rəbl], *adj.* lenkbar, steuerbar. **steerage** [ˈstiəridʒ], *s.* 1. die Steuerung, Lenkung; 2. das Zwischendeck. **steerage-way,** *s.* (*Naut.*) die Steuerkraft, Fahrkraft; ***have*** –, steuerfähig sein.

steering [ˈstiəriŋ], *s.* das Steuern, die Steuerung, Lenkung. **steering|-gear,** *s.* die Steuerung, Lenkvorrichtung, das Lenkgetriebe. **–-play,** *s.* (*Motor.*) toter Gang. **–-wheel,** *s.* das Steuerrad, Lenkrad.

steersman [ˈstiəzmən], *s.* der Rudergänger, Steuerer.

steeve [sti:v], *s.* (*Naut.*) der Erhöhungswinkel des Bugspriets.

stele [ˈsti:li], *s.* die Stele, freistehende Pfeilersäule.

stellar [ˈstelə], *adj.* sternförmig, sternartig, Stern(en)–. **stellate** [–eit], *adj.* sternförmig; – ***flower,*** die Strahlenblume. **stellular** [–julə], *adj.* sternchenartig, Sternen–.

¹**stem** [stem], **1.** *s.* 1. der Stamm (*of a tree*), Stiel, Stengel (*of a plant, fruit*), Halm (*of corn etc.*); 2. Stiel (*of pipe, wineglass*), die Röhre (*of a thermometer*); 3. (Aufzieh)krone (*of a watch*); 4. (*Gram.*) der Stamm; 5. (*Mus.*) Notenschwanz; 6. (*Typ.*) Grundstrich. **2.** *v.t.* abstengeln, entstengeln, abstielen, von Stengeln befreien. **3.** *v.i.* (*fig.*) –

from, (ab)stammen *or* herrühren von, zurückgehen auf (*Acc.*).

[2]**stem, 1.** *s.* (*Naut.*) der (Vorder)steven, (*Hist.*) Schiffsschnabel; ***from – to stern,*** von vorn bis achtern, vom Bug zum Heck. **2.** *v.t.* 1. sich entgegenstemmen (*Dat.*), ankämpfen *or* vorankommen gegen (*as a ship*); ***– the tide,*** gegen den Strom *or* die Flut ankämpfen (*also fig.*); 2. eindämmen, hemmen (*also fig.*); stillen (*blood*); abdämmen, abdichten, zustopfen (*a hole*); (*fig.*) Einhalt gebieten (*Dat.*), aufhalten, abwehren.

stemhead ['stemhed], *s.* (*Naut.*) der Stevenlauf. **stemless,** *adj.* ungestielt, stiellos, stengellos.

stemma ['stemə], *s.* (*pl.* **-ta** [–tə]) 1. das Stemma (*also Zool.*), der Stammbaum; 2. (*Zool.*) einfaches Punktauge, die Facette (*of insect's eye*).

stemmed [stemd], *adj. suff.* –stämmig. **stemwinder,** *s.* die Remontoiruhr.

stench [stentʃ], *s.* der Gestank, übler Geruch. **stench-trap,** *s.* die Schließklappe.

stencil [stensl], **1.** *s.* (*also* ***--plate***) die Schablone, Patrone, Matrize; die Schablonenzeichnung, der Matrizenabzug; ***make*** or ***type a –,*** auf einer Matrize tippen *or* schreiben; ***roll off a –,*** eine Matrize abziehen. **2.** *v.t.* 1. schablonieren, mittels Schablone malen (*a design*) *or* bemalen (*a surface*); 2. auf Matrizen tippen *or* schreiben (*a document*).

Sten gun [sten], *s.* die Maschinenpistole.

stenograph ['stenogrɑ:f], **1.** *v.t.* stenographieren. **2.** *s.* das Stenogramm. **stenographer** [–'nɔgrəfə], *s.* der (die) Stenograph(in). **stenographic** [–'græfik], *adj.* stenographisch. **stenographist** [–'nɔgrəfist], *s. See* **stenographer. stenography** [–'nɔgrəfi], *s.* die Kurzschrift, Stenographie.

stenotic [ste'noutik], *adj.* (*Med.*) (krankhaft) verengt; ***– murmur,*** das Durchpreßgeräusch.

stenotype ['stenətaip], *s.* die Stenographiermaschine. **stenotypist,** *s.* der (die) Stenotypist(in).

stenter ['stentə], *s.* der Trockenrahmen.

stentorian [sten'tɔ:riən], *adj.* überlaut, Stentor–.

step [step], **1.** *s.* 1. der Schritt (*also fig.*), (Tanz– *or* Marschier)schritt; Fußstapfen, die Fußspur; ***at every –,*** bei jedem Schritt; (*Mil.*) ***break –,*** aus dem Schritt kommen; ***bend*** or ***direct*** or ***turn one's –s to,*** seine Schritte lenken nach; ***– by –,*** Schritt für Schritt, schrittweise; ***false –,*** der Fehltritt (*also fig.*); (*Spt.*) ***hop, – and jump,*** der Dreisprung; ***in – with,*** im gleichen Schritt mit; (*fig.*) im Einklang *or* in Harmonie mit; ***keep – with,*** Schritt halten *or* im Schritt bleiben mit; ***know him by his –,*** ihn am Schritt kennen; ***make*** or ***take a –,*** einen Schritt machen *or* tun; (*coll.*) ***mind your –!*** see ***watch your –! not move a –,*** keinen Schritt tun (*also fig.*); ***out of – with,*** nicht im Schritt mit; ***retrace one's –s,*** denselben Weg zurückgehen; (*fig.*) seine Maßnahmen rückgängig machen; ***tread*** or ***walk in his –s,*** in seinen Fußstapfen treten; (*fig.*) seinem Beispiel folgen; (*coll.*) ***watch your –!*** sei vorsichtig! paß auf! 2. die Stufe (*of stairs*) (*also fig.*), Sprosse (*of a ladder*); das Trittbrett (*of vehicle*); (*fig.*) ***by –s,*** stufenweise; (*Mil.*) ***fire –,*** der Schützenauftritt, die Feuerstufe; ***mind the –!*** Vorsicht, Stufe! ***stone –s,*** die Steintreppe; 3. *pl.* (*coll.*) (*also* ***pair of –s***) die Trittleiter, Treppenleiter; 4. (*Mus.*) das Intervall, die (Tonleiter)stufe; 5. (*Naut.*) Mastspur; 6. (*fig.*) (*oft. pl.*) Maßnahme; ***take –s,*** Schritte unternehmen; 7. (*coll.*) kurzer Schritt, ein paar Schritte, der Katzensprung; ***within a – of,*** nur eine kurze Entfernung von.

2. *v.i.* schreiten, gehen, treten; ***– this way,*** treten Sie näher! (*sl.*) ***– on the gas,*** (*Motor.*) Gas geben; (*also* ***– on it***) sich beeilen; ***– into the breach,*** einspringen; ***– aside,*** beiseite treten, zur Seite treten; ***– back,*** zurücktreten; ***– down,*** hinuntergehen; (*fig.*) einen Rückzieher machen, nachgeben; ***– in,*** eintreten; (*fig.*) eingreifen, einschreiten, sich ins Mittel legen; ***– out,*** hinaustreten, ausgehen; (*also coll.* ***– it out***) tüchtig ausschreiten; (*coll.*) ***– round*** (*to*), auf einen Sprung besuchen; ***– up to,*** zugehen *or* zutreten *or* zuschreiten auf (*Acc.*).

3. *v.t.* 1. ausführen, machen (*a pace*), (*also* ***– out***) abschreiten (*a distance*); 2. (*Naut.*) einspuren, einsetzen (*a mast*); 3. (*Elec.*) ***– down,*** heruntertransformieren; ***– up,*** (*Elec.*) hochtransformieren; (*coll.*) erhöhen, steigern (*production etc.*).

step|-dance, *s.* der Steptanz. **--down,** *adj.* (*Elec.*) Abwärts–. **--ladder,** *s.* die Trittleiter, Treppenleiter.

stepmother ['stepmʌðə], *s.* die Stiefmutter; ***evil*** or ***wicked –,*** die Rabenmutter.

steppe [step], *s.* die Steppe.

stepped [stept], *adj.* (ab)gestuft, Stufen–; abgesetzt, gestaffelt. **stepper,** *s.* guter Gänger (*horse*).

stepping-stone, *s.* 1. der Schrittstein; 2. (*fig.*) die Stufenleiter, das Sprungbrett (*to,* zu).

step-up, 1. *adj.* (*Elec.*) Aufwärts–. **2.** *s.* 1. (*coll.*) die Beförderung; 2. (*Rad.*) Verstärkung.

stereo ['stiəriou, 'steriou], *s.* (*coll.*) (*Rad. etc.*) die Raumtonwiedergabe. **stereogram,** *s.* das Raumbild, raumbildliche Darstellung. **stereography** [–'ɔgrəfi], *s.* die Stereographie, perspektivische Darstellung. **stereometry** [–'ɔmitri], *s.* die Stereometrie, Raumbildmessung. **stereophonic** [–'fɔnik], *adj.* Stereoton–. **stereophony** [–'ɔfəni], *s.* die Raumtonwiedergabe. **stereoscope** [–skoup], *s.* das Stereoskop. **stereoscopic** [–'skɔpik], *adj.* stereoskopisch; ***– camera,*** die Stereokamera.

stereotype ['stiəriətaip], **1.** *s.* 1. (*Typ.*) die Stereotypie, der Plattendruck; die Druckplatte, Stereotype; 2. (*fig.*) Schablone, das Klischee. **2.** *adj.* 1. (*Typ.*) Stereotyp–; 2. (*fig.*) schablonenhaft, klischeehaft, stereotyp, abgedroschen. **3.** *v.t.* 1. stereotypieren; 2. (*fig.*) unverändert wiederholen, unveränderlich *or* ein für allemal festlegen. **stereotyped,** *adj. See* **stereotype, 2. stereotypography** [–tai'pɔgrəfi], *s.* der Stereotypdruck, das Stereotypdruckverfahren.

sterile ['sterail], *adj.* 1. unfruchtbar (*also fig.*), steril, zeugungsunfähig, (*Bot.*) geschlechtslos, nichtblühend, nicht keimfähig; (*Med.*) keimfrei, steril; 2. (*fig.*) fruchtlos, ergebnislos, öde, hohl, leer. **sterility** [–'riliti], *s.* 1. die Unfruchtbarkeit (*also fig.*), Sterilität; Keimfreiheit; 2. (*fig.*) Hohlheit, Ergebnislosigkeit. **sterilization** [–ilai'zeiʃən], *s.* die Sterilisation. **sterilize** ['sterilaiz], *v.t.* unfruchtbar machen (*animals etc.*), entkeimen, sterilisieren (*milk etc.*). **sterilizer,** *s.* 1. das Sterilisationsmittel; 2. der Sterilisator, Sterilisierapparat.

sterling ['stə:liŋ], **1.** *s.* der Sterling (*engl. Währung*). **2.** *adj.* 1. Sterling–; ***a pound –,*** ein Pfund Sterling; ***– area,*** der Sterlingblock; 2. (*fig.*) wahr, lauter, echt, erprobt, bewährt, gediegen, tadellos, vollwertig.

[1]**stern** [stə:n], *s.* 1. das Heck, Achterschiff, Schiffshinterteil; ***down by the –,*** achterlastig; 2. der Spiegel (*of an animal*); (*coll.*) das Hinterteil.

[2]**stern,** *adj.* hart, starr, unerbittlich, unnachgiebig, streng, strikt, ernst (***with, towards,*** gegen); ***– glance,*** düsterer *or* finsterer *or* abschreckender Blick; ***– necessity,*** harte *or* unbeugsame Notwendigkeit.

sterna ['stə:nə], *pl. of* **sternum. sternal,** *adj.* Brustbein–.

stern|-chaser, *s.* (*Hist.*) das Heckgeschütz. **–fast,** *s.* das Achtertau, Hecktau. **--frame,** *s.* das Spiegelspant. **–most,** *adj.* achter(lich)st, hinterst.

sternness ['stə:nnis], *s.* die Härte, Strenge, der Ernst; die Unnachgiebigkeit, Unbeugsamkeit.

stern|port, *s.* (*Hist.*) die Hinterpforte, Heckpforte. **–post,** *s.* der Achtersteven. **--sheets,** *pl.* Achtersitze (*pl.*).

sternum ['stə:nəm], *s.* (*pl.* **-na**) das Brustbein.

sternutation [stə:nju'teiʃən], *s.* das Niesen. **sternutatory** [–'tcitəri], **1.** *adj.* zum Niesen reizend, Nies–. **2.** *s.* das Nies(reiz)mittel.

sternwards ['stə:nwədz], *adj., adv.* achterlich. **sternway,** *s.* die Heckfahrt, Fahrt nach achtern.

stertorous ['stə:tərəs], *adj.* schnarchend, röchelnd.

stet [stet], *imper.* (*Typ.*) bleibt!

stethoscope ['steθəskoup], **1.** *s.* (*Med.*) das Hörrohr, Horchrohr, Stethoskop. **2.** *v.t.* abhorchen, auskultieren.

stevedore ['sti:vədɔ:], *s.* der Stauer, Hafenarbeiter, Schiffsbelader, Güterpacker, Schauermann.

stew [stju:], **1.** *v.t.* dämpfen, dünsten, schmoren; (*coll.*) ***the tea is –ed,*** der Tee hat zu lange gezogen. **2.** *v.i.* schmoren, gedämpft werden; (*coll.*) ***leave him to*** or ***let him – in his own juice,*** ihn (im eigenen Saft) schmoren lassen. **3.** *s.* 1. (*also* ***Irish*** –) das Schmorgericht, Eintopfgericht; 2. (*fig. coll.*) die Herzensangst, Sorge; ***be in a –,*** in Schwulitäten sein; 3. (*usu. pl.*) (*obs.*) das Bordell.

steward ['stjuəd], *s.* 1. der Verwalter, Aufseher, Inspektor (*of estates*); Haushofmeister, Majordomus (*in princely houses*); 2. Proviantmeister, Steward (*on ships*); Kämmerer, Küchenmeister (*of clubs etc.*); 3. Aufseher, (Fest)ordner (*of races etc.*); 4. ***Lord High Steward,*** der Großhofmeister. **stewardess,** *s.* die Aufwärterin; Stewardeß (*on ships, aircraft etc.*), Flugbegleiterin. **stewarding,** *s.* der Ordnerdienst (*at meetings etc.*). **stewardship,** *s.* das Verwalteramt; die Verwaltung.

stewed [stju:d], **1.** *imperf., p.p. of* **stew. 2.** *adj.* 1. geschmort; – ***apples,*** das Apfelkompott; – ***fruit,*** das Kompott; 2. (*sl.*) besoffen, schief geladen. **stewing** ['stju:iŋ], *s.* – ***apples,*** Kochäpfel (*pl.*). **stew|pan, –pot,** *s.* der Schmortopf.

stibial ['stibiəl], *adj.* Antimon–, Spießglanz–. **stibium,** *s.* das Antimon, der Spießglanz.

stich [stik], *s.* der Vers. **stichic,** *adj.* aus Versen bestehend. **stichomythia** [–o'miθiə], *s.* die Stychomythie, Wechselrede (*in drama*).

[1]**stick** [stik], **1.** *s.* 1. der Stock; (*also* ***walking–***–) Spazierstock; Stab, Stecken, die Stange, Gerte, Rute, das Stück Holz, Scheit; *pl.* Brennholz, Reisig(holz); (*fig.*) ***in a cleft –,*** in der Klemme; ***get hold of the wrong end of the –,*** die Lage völlig mißdeuten; (*coll.*) ***get the –,*** eine Tracht Prügel bekommen; (*coll.*) ***give him the –,*** ihm eine Tracht Prügel geben; ***take the – to him,*** ihn verprügeln; 2. der Stengel, Stiel (*of celery, rhubarb*); 3. (*Mus.*) Taktstock, Dirigentenstab; 3. (*Typ.*) Winkelhaken; 4. (*Naut.*) Mast, Knüppel; 5. (*Av.*) Steuerknüppel; 6. (*Spt. esp. hockey*) Schläger, das Schlagholz; 7. (*Crick.*) der Dreistab; 8. (*fig. coll.*) ***dry –,*** der Stockfisch; ***queer –,*** komischer Kauz; 9. *pl.* (*fig. coll.*) Hinterwälder (*pl.*). **2.** *v.t.* 1. mit einem Stock stützen (*plants etc.*); 2. (*Typ.*) in den Winkelhaken nehmen.

[2]**stick, 1.** *irr.v.t.* 1. stecken, stoßen, treiben (*a pointed th.*) (*in*(*to*), in (*Acc.*); ***through,*** durch), durchstecken, durchbohren, durchstoßen (*s.th. with a pointed th.*), stecken, aufspießen (*s.th. on a pointed th.*), abstechen, schlachten (*a pig etc.*); 2. befestigen, heften, kleben; – ***no bills!*** Plakatankleben verboten! – ***together,*** zusammenkleben; 3. (*coll.*) legen, setzen; 4. (*sl.*) (*usu. neg.*) aushalten, ausstehen, leiden, ertragen; 5. (*coll.*) ***be stuck,*** festsitzen, stecken(bleiben), nicht weiterkönnen; (*sl.*) ***be stuck for,*** in Verlegenheit sein um; (*sl.*) ***be stuck on,*** versessen sein auf (*Acc.*), eingenommen sein für; (*sl.*) ***be stuck with,*** nicht mehr loswerden können; 6. – ***out,*** herausst(r)ecken (*tongue*); – ***out one's chest,*** sich (*Dat.*) in die Brust werfen; (*sl.*) – ***one's neck out,*** es darauf ankommen lassen; – ***up,*** (*coll.*) errichten, aufstellen; (*sl.*) (anhalten und) überfallen (*a p.*), ausrauben (*a bank etc.*).
2. *irr.v.i.* 1. (fest)kleben, haften(bleiben), hängenbleiben), klebenbleiben (*to,* an (*Dat.*)); 2. stecken(bleiben) (*also fig.*), sich festfahren, (*fig.*) nicht weiterkönnen, stocken; 3. (*fig.*) sich heften (*to,* an (*Acc.*)), sich festklammern *or* festhalten (an (*Dat.*)), (*coll.*) bleiben (bei), treu *or* verbunden bleiben (*Dat.*); 4. festsitzen (*as ideas*).
(a) (*with prep.*) (*coll.*) – ***at,*** 1. bleiben *or* beharren bei, aushalten; 2. (*coll.*) sich stoßen an (*Dat.*), Anstoß *or* Anstand nehmen an (*Dat.*), zurückschrecken vor (*Dat.*); – ***at nothing,*** vor nichts zurückschrecken; – ***by,*** bleiben bei, nicht weichen von; treubleiben (*Dat.*); (*coll.*) – ***in his throat,*** ihm im Halse stecken; – ***to one's guns,*** seiner S. treu bleiben; – ***to the point,*** bei der S. bleiben.
(b) (*with adv.*) – ***out,*** hervorstehen, abstehen (***from,*** aus); (*sl.*) – ***it*** or – (***it***) ***out,*** es aushalten, durchhalten, standhalten, nicht nachgeben; (*sl.*) – ***out for,*** bestehen *or* beharren auf (*Dat.*); (*coll.*) ***it –s out a mile,*** es ragt deutlich hervor, es ist klar zu sehen; – ***together,*** zusammenhalten (*people*); zusammenbacken, zusammenkleben (*pages etc.*); – ***up,*** aufrechtstehen, hervorragen, emporragen, aufragen; ***his hair –s up,*** ihm stehen die Haare zu Berge; (*coll.*) – ***up for,*** eintreten *or* Partei nehmen für; (*coll.*) – ***up to,*** Widerstand leisten (*Dat.*), sich nicht beugen vor (*Dat.*); (*sl.*) ***stuck up,*** aufgeblasen, hochnäsig.

sticker ['stikə], *s.* 1. der Klebestreifen, Aufklebezettel; 2. (*coll.*) beharrlicher Arbeiter; 3. (*Comm.*) der Ladenhüter; 4. (*sl.*) verwirrende Bemerkung, schwierige Frage; 5. (*sl.*) langes Messer. **stickiness,** *s.* 1. die Klebrigkeit, Zähigkeit; 2. (*coll.*) Schwierigkeit, Heik(e)ligkeit.

sticking| place, *s.* (*coll.*) der Anschlag, Haltepunkt, Höhepunkt, Wendepunkt. **––plaster,** *s.* das Heftpflaster. **– point,** *s. See* **– place.**

stick| insect, *s.* (*Ent.*) die Gespenstheuschrecke. **––in-the-mud,** *s.* 1. der Schlendrian, die Schlafmütze, schwerfälliger Mensch; 2. der Rückschrittler.

stickle [stikl], *v.i.* Skrupel haben, Bedenken äußern, Einwände erheben; eifern (***for,*** für); zanken, streiten (***about,*** um); – ***for a th.,*** eine S. verfechten.

stickleback ['stiklbæk], *s.* (*Ichth.*) der Stichling.

stickler ['stiklə], *s.* der Eiferer (***for,*** für); (*also* – ***for detail***) der Kleinigkeitskrämer.

stick-up, *s.* (*sl.*) der (Raub)überfall.

sticky ['stiki], *adj.* 1. klebrig, zäh; (*Mil.*) – ***bomb,*** die Haftmine; 2. (*fig. coll.*) zögernd; 3. (*sl.*) schwierig, heikel; (*sl.*) – ***end,*** schlimmes Ende; (*coll.*) ***strike a – patch,*** kein Glück haben; 4. schwül (*as weather*).

stiff [stif], **1.** *adj.* 1. steif (*also fig.*), unbiegsam, starr; – ***collar,*** steifer Kragen; ***keep a – face,*** ernst bleiben; ***my legs are –,*** ich habe Muskelkater in den Beinen; ***keep a – upper lip,*** sich nicht unterkriegen lassen, die Ohren steif halten; – ***neck,*** steifer Hals; 2. dick(flüssig), zäh(e) (*as liquids*); 3. (*fig.*) gezwungen, formell (*of manners*); ungelenk, schwerfällig (*as style*); 4. (fest) entschlossen, hartnäckig, unbeugsam; – ***opposition,*** hartnäckiger Widerstand; 5. stark (*as wind*); 6. scharf (*as drinks*); – ***dose,*** starke Dosis; 7. fest, stabil (*of the market*); 8. übermäßig, hoch (*of prices*); 9. schwierig, mühsam, beschwerlich; – ***climb,*** beschwerlicher Anstieg; – ***examination,*** schwere Prüfung; 10. zu Tode; ***bore him –,*** ihn zu Tode langweilen; ***scared –,*** zu Tode erschrocken. **2.** *s.* 1. (*sl.*) der Tölpel, Stoffel, Stöffel; 2. (*sl.*) Kassiber; 3. (*sl.*) Leichnam, die Leiche.

stiffen ['stifən], **1.** *v.t.* 1. steif machen (*limbs etc.*), verdicken, fest werden lassen (*liquid*), (ver)stärken, (ver)steifen (*cloth etc.*); 2. (*fig.*) (be)stärken (*resolution etc.*), den Nacken *or* Rücken steifen (*Dat.*) (*a p.*). **2.** *v.i.* 1. starr *or* steif(er) *or* stärker *or* fester werden, erstarren, sich verstärken *or* versteifen; 2. (*fig.*) sich verhärten *or* verdichten (***into,*** zu); 3. anziehen (*of prices*). **stiffener,** *s.* 1. steife Einlage; 2. (*coll.*) das Stärkungsmittel, die Stärkung. **stiffening,** *s.* 1. das Steifen, Stärken (*of clothes etc.*); 2. steife Einlage, die Versteifung, das Steifmaterial, Steifleinen. **stiff-necked,** *adj.* halsstarrig, eigensinnig, verstockt, hartnäckig. **stiffness,** *s.* 1. die Steifheit (*also fig.*), Steife, Starrheit, Unbiegsamkeit; 2. Zäheit, Dickflüssigkeit; 3. (*fig.*) Unbeholfenheit, Gezwungenheit.

[1]**stifle** [staifl], *v.t.* 1. ersticken (*also fig.*); 2. (*fig.*) zurückdrängen, unterdrücken.

[2]**stifle,** *s.* 1. (*also* ***––joint***) das Kniegelenk (*of a horse*); 2. (*Vet.*) die Kniegelenkgalle. **stifle-bone,** *s.* die Kniescheibe (*of a horse*).

stifling ['staifliŋ], *adj.* erstickend, drückend; – ***atmosphere,*** die Stickluft.

stigma ['stigmə], *s.* (*pl.* **-ta** [–mətə]) 1. das Stigma (*also Med., Zool., Bot.*); (*Med.*) (Kenn)zeichen, Merkmal, (Wund)mal; *pl.* (*Eccl.*) Wundmale Christi (*pl.*); 2. (*Ent.*) das Luftloch, die Atmungsöffnung; 3. (*Bot.*) die Narbe; 4. (*pl.* **-s**) (*fig.*) das Brandmal, der Schandfleck, Schimpf. **stigmatization** [–tai'zeiʃən], *s.* die Stigmatisierung; Brandmarkung. **stigmatize,** *v.t.* (*esp. fig.*) kennzeichnen, brandmarken, stigmatisieren.

stile [stail], *s.* der Zauntritt, die Steige.

stiletto [sti'letou], *s.* das Stilett, der Dolch; Pfriem, Stecher; (*coll.*) – ***heel,*** der Pfennigabsatz.

[1]**still** [stil], **1.** *adj.* still, ruhig; unbeweglich, bewegungslos, reg(ungs)los; lautlos, geräuschlos; nicht schäumend (*of drinks*); ***sit –,*** stillsitzen; ***stand –,*** stillstehen; (*Art*) – ***life,*** das Stilleben; (*Prov.*) – ***waters run deep,*** stille Wasser sind tief. **2.** *s.* (*Poet.*) 1. *See* **stillness**; 2. (*Art*) das Stilleben; 3. (*Films*) Standphoto. **3.** *v.t.* stillen, beruhigen, beschwichtigen, zur Ruhe bringen.

[2]**still, 1.** *adv.* noch (immer), immer noch, bis jetzt; (*before comp.*) noch; – ***more*** or ***more –,*** noch *or* immer mehr, mehr noch; – ***more so because,*** um so mehr als. **2.** *conj.* dennoch, (je)doch, trotzdem, nichtsdestoweniger.

[3]**still, 1.** *s.* der Destillierapparat, Destillierkolben; die Brennerei (*for spirits*). **2.** *v.t.* (*obs.*) destillieren. **stillage** [–idʒ], *s.* das Faßlager, Faßgestell, die Stellage.

still|-birth, *s.* die Totgeburt. **–born,** *adj.* 1. totgeboren; 2. (*fig.*) wirkungslos.

stilliform ['stilifɔ:m], *adj.* tropfenförmig.

stillness ['stilnis], *s.* die Stille, Ruhe; Lautlosigkeit, das Schweigen; die Bewegungslosigkeit.

still-room, *s.* 1. der Destillationsraum; die Hausbrennerei; 2. Vorratskammer.

stilly ['stili], *adj.* (*Poet.*) still, ruhig.

stilt [stilt], *s.* 1. (*usu. pl.*) die Stelze; (*Orn.*) ***black-winged –,*** der Strandreiter (*Himantopus himantopus*); 2. (*also* **––bird**) der Stelzenläufer, Stelzvogel. **stilted,** *adj.* 1. (*Archit.*) gestelzt, überhöht; 2. (*Orn.*) Stelz–; 3. (*fig.*) geschraubt, gespreizt, hochtrabend. **stiltedness,** *s.* (*fig.*) die Geschraubtheit, Gespreiztheit.

stimulant ['stimjulənt], **1.** *s.* 1. das Reizmittel (*also fig.*), Belebungsmittel, Anregungsmittel, das Stimulans; 2. (*fig.*) der Antrieb (***to,*** zu). **2.** *adj.* (*esp. Med.*) anreizend, belebend, stimulierend. **stimulate** [–eit], **1.** *v.t.* 1. anreizen, anregen, beleben, stimulieren; 2. (*fig.*) anregen, (vor)antreiben, anreizen, anstacheln, anspornen; 3. (*with alcohol*) animieren. **2.** *v.i.* anregen, beleben, stimulieren. **stimulation** [–'leiʃən], *s.* 1. der Reiz, die Reizung, Erregung; 2. (*fig.*) Belebung, Anregung, der Anreiz, Antrieb. **stimulative** [–lətiv], *adj.* (an)reizend, (An)reiz–, anspornend, antreibend. **stimulus** [–ləs], *s.* (*pl.* **-i** [–li:]) 1. (*Med.*) der Reiz, das Reizmittel, Stimulans; 2. der Ansporn, Antrieb, Anreiz, treibende Kraft.

sting [stiŋ], **1.** *irr.v.t.* 1. stechen (*also fig.*); 2. beißen *or* brennen auf (*Dat.*) *or* in (*Dat.*); ***the pepper –s my tongue,*** der Pfeffer brennt *or* beißt mir auf der Zunge; 3. (*fig.*) verwunden, verletzen, plagen, quälen, schmerzen, kränken; ***stung with remorse,*** von Reue geplagt; 4. aufstacheln, anstacheln, aufreizen, antreiben ((***in***)***to,*** zu); 5. (*sl.*) übervorteilen, beschwindeln; ***be stung,*** geneppt werden; – ***him for a pound,*** ein Pfund bei ihm anpumpen. **2.** *irr. v.i.* 1. stechen (*as bees, nettles*), brennen (*as pepper*); 2. weh tun, schmerzen (*as a wound*). **3.** *s.* 1. (*Zool.*) der Stachel (*also fig.*); 2. (*Bot.*) die Brennborste, das Nesselhaar, Brennhaar; 3. Stechen, der Stich, Biß, Schmerz; – ***of conscience,*** der Gewissensbiß; 4. (*fig.*) der Anreiz, Antrieb; 5. (*fig.*) die Spitze, Schärfe, der Schwung. **stinger,** *s.* (*coll.*) schmerzender Schlag; beißende Bemerkung.

stinginess ['stindʒinis], *s.* (*coll.*) der Geiz, die Knauserei, Knick(e)rigkeit.

stinging ['stiŋiŋ], *adj.* stechend, beißend, verletzend, schmerzend, scharf. **stinging-nettle,** *s.* die Brennessel.

sting-ray, *s.* (*Zool.*) der Stechrochen.

stingy ['stindʒi], *adj.* (*coll.*) knaus(e)rig, knick(e)rig, geizig (*of a p.*); dürftig, kärglich, knapp (*of a th.*); ***be – with,*** knausern *or* geizen mit.

stink [stiŋk], **1.** *irr.v.i.* 1. stinken, übel riechen (***of,*** nach); (*sl.*) ***it –s in his nostrils,*** es hängt ihm zum Halse heraus; 2. (*sl.*) in üblem Rufe stehen; 3. nichts wert *or* eine faule S. sein. **2.** *irr.v.t.* – ***out,*** durch Gestank austreiben, ausstänkern. **3.** *s.* 1. der Gestank, übler Geruch; (*sl.*) ***kick up*** or ***make a –,*** viel Aufhebens machen; 2. *pl.* (*coll.*) die Chemie.

stinkard ['stiŋkəd], *s.* (*Zool.*) das Stinktier. **stink-bomb,** *s.* die Stinkbombe. **stinker,** *s.* (*sl.*) 1. ausgesprochener Ekel (*a th. or p.*), widerlicher Kerl, der Schuft; 2. anstößiger Brief. **stinking,** *adj.* 1. stinkend, übelriechend; 2. (*sl.*) widerlich, anstößig, miserabel. **stink-pot,** *s.* 1. (*Hist.*) der Stinktopf; 2. (*sl.*) (*of a p.*) Stinkstiefel.

[1]**stint** [stint], *s.* (*Orn.*) ***little –,*** der Zwergstrandläufer (*Calidris minuta*).

[2]**stint, 1.** *v.t.* einschränken, knausern mit (*a th.*); einschränken, knapp halten (*a p.*) (***of,*** mit); – ***o.s.,*** sich einschränken (***of,*** mit), sich (*Dat.*) nichts vergönnen, sich vom Munde absparen. **2.** *s.* 1. die Einschränkung, Beschränkung; ***without –,*** ohne Einschränkung, unbeschränkt, rückhaltlos; 2. vorgeschriebenes Maß, festgesetzter Anteil; zugewiesene Arbeit, das Pensum; (*esp. Min.*) Tagwerk, die Schicht; ***work by –,*** auf Schicht arbeiten. **stinted,** *adj.* knapp, karg, beschränkt.

stipate ['staipeit], *adj.* (*Bot.*) gedrängt. **stipe** [staip], *s.* (*Bot.*) der Stengel, Stiel, Strunk, (*Zool.*) Stiel. **stipellate** [–əleit], *adj.* (*Bot.*) mit Nebenblättchen.

stipend ['staipend], *s.* die Besoldung, das Gehalt. **stipendiary** [–'pendjəri], **1.** *adj.* 1. besoldet (*a p.*), vergütert, honoriert (*duties*); 2. Gehalts–. **2.** *s.* 1. der Gehaltsempfänger; 2. (*also* – ***magistrate***) Polizeirichter.

stipple [stipl], **1.** *v.t., v.i.* in Punktmanier malen *or* stechen, punktieren, tüpfeln. **2.** *s.* die Punktiermanier, der Pointillismus.

stipular ['stipjulə], *adj.* Nebenblatt–, nebenblattartig.

stipulate ['stipjuleit], **1.** *v.t.* ausmachen, ausbedingen, anberaumen, festsetzen, vereinbaren, verabreden; ***as –d,*** vertragsgemäß. **2.** *v.i.* – ***for,*** ausbedingen, zur Bedingung machen; übereinkommen *or* eine Vereinbarung treffen über (*Acc.*). **stipulation** [–'leiʃən], *s.* 1. die Übereinkunft, Abmachung, Verabredung; 2. Bedingung, Klausel. **stipulator,** *s.* der Kontrahent, die Vertragspartei.

stipule ['stipju:l], *s.* (*Bot.*) das Nebenblatt; (*Zool.*) die Stoppelfeder.

stir [stə:], **1.** *v.t.* 1. rühren, bewegen, in Bewegung setzen; anrühren, (*also* – ***up***) durchrühren, umrühren (*liquids*); 2. schüren (*the fire*); 3. (*fig.*) (*oft.* – ***up***) tüchtig umrühren, (*fig.*) aufrühren, aufrütteln, aufhetzen, aufreizen (*a p.*), erregen, anzetteln, entfachen, hervorrufen (*a th.*); (*fig.*) – ***up mud,*** (immer wieder) den alten Dreck aufrühren. **2.** *v.i.* sich regen *or* bewegen *or* rühren; ***be stirring,*** auf(gestanden) sein; im Gange *or* Umlauf sein; sich ereignen; – ***abroad,*** ausgehen; ***not – from,*** nicht verlassen. **3.** *s.* 1. die Bewegung; ***give it a –,*** es umrühren; ***not a –,*** nicht die geringste Bewegung; 2. der Aufruhr, das Getümmel, Treiben, Aufsehen, die Aufregung.

stirk [stə:k], *s.* einjähriges Rind.

stirps [stə:ps], *s.* 1. (*Law*) der Familienzweig, (Familien)stamm; 2. (*Zool.*) die Abart.

stirring ['stə:riŋ], *adj.* bewegt, aufregend (*times events*); mitreißend, schwungvoll (*speech etc.*); (*rare*) geschäftig, rührig (*a p.*).

stirrup ['stirəp], *s.* 1. der Steigbügel; ***be firm in one's –s,*** fest im Sattel sitzen; 2. der Bügel, die Klampe. **stirrup|-bone,** *s.* (*Anat.*) der Steigbügel (*in ear*). **––cup,** *s.* der Abschiedstrunk. **––iron,** *s.* das Steigbügeleisen. **––leather,** *s.* der Steigbügelriemen. **––pump,** *s.* die Handspritze.

stitch [stitʃ], **1.** *s.* 1. der Stich (*sewing, Surg.*), die

Masche (*knitting*); ***without a – of clothing,*** splitternackt; (*coll.*) ***not do a –,*** keinen Strich tun; ***have not a dry – on,*** keinen trockenen Faden am Leibe haben; ***drop a –,*** eine Masche fallen lassen; ***every – of canvas,*** alle Segel; ***have –es in a wound,*** eine Wunde vernähen lassen; ***pick*** or ***take up a –,*** eine Masche aufnehmen; ***a – in times saves nine,*** was du heute kannst besorgen, das verschiebe nicht auf morgen; 2. die Stichart, Strickart; 3. (*Med.*) stechender Schmerz, der Stich, das Stechen; (*coll.*) ***get the –,*** Stiche bekommen; ***– in the side,*** das Seitenstechen; (*coll.*) ***have him in –es,*** ihn in Lachkrämpfe *or* in ein schnallendes Gelächter versetzen. **2.** *v.t.* (zusammen)nähen; (*Bookb.*) broschieren, (zusammen)heften; (*Surg.*) zusammennähen; – ***up,*** zusammennähen, vernähen, zuflicken. **3.** *v.i.* nähen, Stiche machen; heften. **stitching,** *s.* das Nähen, die Näherei; Stickerei; (*Bookb.*) das Heften. **stitchwort,** *s.* (*Bot.*) die Sternmiere.

stithy ['stiði], *s.* (*obs.*) die Schmiede.

stiver ['staivə], *s.* (*Hist.*) der Stüber; (*coll.*) Heller, Deut, Pfifferling.

stoa ['stouə], *s.* 1. (*Phil.*) stoische Philosophie, die Stoa; 2. (*Archit.*) Stoa, Säulenhalle.

stoat [stout], *s.* das Hermelin.

stock [stɔk], **1.** *s.* 1. der (Baum)stamm; Wurzelstock; Stengel, Strunk; (*fig.*) ***–s and stones,*** unbeseelte Dinge; ***over – and stone,*** über Stock und Stein; 2. (*Tech.*) der Grundstock, Block, Pfosten, das Gerüst, die Stütze, (*Naut.*) der Ankerstock; ***– of an anchor,*** der Ankerstock; ***– of an anvil,*** der Amboßstock; 3. (*fig.*) der Urtyp, Schlag, die Rasse, Zucht; Familie, Herkunft, Abkunft, der Stamm, Ursprung; 4. Schaft, Stiel, Griff (*of a gun*); ***lock, – and barrel,*** ganz und gar, alles zusammen, mit allem Drum und Dran; 5. (*Comm.*) der Vorrat, Bestand, das Lager; der Viehbestand, lebendes Inventar (*of a farm*); ***dead –,*** totes Inventar; ***fat –,*** das Schlachtvieh; ***– in trade,*** der Betriebsvorrat, Warenbestände (*pl.*); (*fig.*) das Arbeitsmaterial; stereotype Züge (*pl.*); ***in –,*** vorrätig, auf Lager; ***– on hand,*** der Warenbestand; ***out of –,*** nicht mehr vorrätig, ausverkauft; (*Railw.*) ***rolling –,*** Betriebsmittel (*pl.*), rollendes Material; ***take –,*** den Bestand aufnehmen; (*fig.*) sich (*Dat.*) Rechenschaft ablegen; ***take – of,*** in Augenschein nehmen, in Betracht ziehen; (*coll.*) aufmerksam beobachten; 6. (*St. Exch.*) das Anleihekapital, Wertpapiere (*pl.*), die Aktie, Aktien (*pl.*), Effekten (*pl.*), das Aktienkapital; Betriebskapital, Geschäftskapital, der Anteil; Staatspapiere (*pl.*), die Staatsanleihe; ***– in bank,*** das Bankkapital; ***joint –,*** das Stammkapital, Aktienkapital; ***–s and shares,*** Börsenpapiere (*pl.*); 7. (*Tech.*) der Grundstoff, das Rohmaterial; (*Cul.*) die (Suppen)brühe; 8. (*Bot.*) Levkoje; 9. steife Halsbinde, der Stehkragen; 10. *pl.* (*Shipb.*) Stapel, die Helling; ***on the –s,*** auf Stapel; (*fig.*) in Vorbereitung, im Bau *or* Werden; 11. *pl.* (*Hist.*) der (Zwang)block, Fußblock.
2. *adj.* 1. (*Comm.*) auf Lager, stets vorrätig; 2. (*fig. coll.*) Standard–, Normal–, stehend, stereotyp, abgegriffen, abgedroschen; 3. (*Theat.*) Repertoire–.
3. *v.t.* 1. versehen, versorgen, beliefern, ausstatten, ausrüsten; 2. schäften (*a gun*); 3. stocken (*an anchor*); 4. (*coll.*) führen, vorrätig haben, auf Lager halten (*goods*).
4. *v.i.* (*usu.* – ***up***) ein Lager einrichten, sich eindecken.

stock-account, *s.* das Kapitalkonto, Effektenkonto, die Effektenrechnung.

stockade [stɔ'keid], **1.** *s.* 1. die Einpfählung, Einfried(ig)ung, das Gehege, Staket; 2. (*Mil.*) die Pfahlsperre, Palisade. **2.** *v.t.* 1. einfried(ig)en, einpfählen, mit einem Staket umgeben; 2. (*Mil.*) verpalisadieren.

stock|-book, *s.* das Lagerbuch, Warenverzeichnis. **--breeder,** *s.* der Viehzüchter. **-broker,** *s.* der Börsenmakler, Effektenhändler. **-broking,** *s.* das Effektengeschäft. **--car,** *s.* 1. der Serienwagen; 2. (*Railw.*) Viehwagen. **--clerk,** *s.* der Lagerverwalter. **-dove,** *s.* (*Orn.*) die Hohltaube (*Columba oenas*). **--exchange,** *s.* die (Effekten)börse, Fondsbörse. **--farming,** *s.* die Viehzucht. **-fish,** *s.* der Stockfisch. **--gilliflower,** *s.* die Winterlevkoje. **-holder,** *s.* der Aktionär, Effekteninhaber. **-holding,** *s.* der Aktienbesitz.

stockiness ['stɔkiness], *s.* die Untersetztheit, Stämmigkeit.

stockinet [stɔki'net], *s.* das Trikot, Stockinett.

stocking ['stɔkiŋ], *s.* der Strumpf; ***elastic –,*** der Gummistrumpf; ***in one's --feet,*** ohne Schuhe. **stocking|-foot,** *s.* der Füßling. **--frame,** *s.* der Strumpfwirkerstuhl.

stockist ['stɔkist], *s.* der Fachhändler, einschlägiger Händler, das Fachgeschäft.

stock|-jobber, *s.* der Agioteur, Börsenspekulant, Effektenhändler. **--jobbing,** *s.* Effektengeschäfte (*pl.*), die Börsenspekulation.

stockless ['stɔklis], *adj.* schaftlos, stocklos.

stock|-list, *s.* der Kurszettel. **-man,** *s.* der Viehhüter. **--market,** *s.* 1. die Effektenbörse, Fondsbörse; 2. der Viehmarkt. **-pile, 1.** *s.* der Vorratsstapel, das Vorratslager. **2.** *v.t.* aufstapeln, anhäufen, lagern. **3.** *v.i.* einen Vorrat anlegen. **-piling,** *s.* die Einlagerung. **-pot,** *s.* der Suppentopf. **-room,** *s.* der Lagerraum, Vorratsraum. **--still,** *adj.* stockstill, mäuschenstill, regungslos. **-taking,** *s.* die Inventur, Bestandsaufnahme (*also fig.*); – ***sale,*** der Inventurausverkauf.

stocky ['stɔki], *adj.* untersetzt, stämmig.

stockyard, *s.* der Viehhof.

stodge [stɔdʒ], **1.** *v.t.* (*sl.*) vollstopfen (*bag etc.*), hineinstopfen (*contents*). **2.** *v.i.* (*sl.*) sich vollstopfen *or* vollfressen *or* vollhauen, sich (*Dat.*) den Magen vollschlagen. **3.** *s.* (*sl.*) 1. der Brei, Matsch; Fraß; 2. das Gedränge. **stodginess,** *s.* die Unverdaulichkeit, Schwerfälligkeit, Fadheit. **stodgy,** *adj.* breiig, klumpig; schwerverdaulich, unverdaulich; schwerfällig, fade.

stoic ['stouik], **1.** *s.* der Stoiker. **2.** *adj.* (*Phil.*) stoisch; (*fig. usu.*) **stoical,** *adj.* unerschütterlich, gleichmütig, gelassen. **stoicism** [–sizm], *s.* der Stoizismus, (*fig.*) Gleichmut, die Gelassenheit.

stoke [stouk], *v.t.* (*also* – ***up***) schüren (*also fig.*), bedienen, beschicken, heizen (*a boiler etc.*). **stoke|hold,** *s.* (*Naut.*) der Heizraum. **-hole,** *s.* 1. das Schürloch; 2. der Heizraum. **stoker,** *s.* der Heizer.

[1]**stole** [stoul], *s.* (*Eccl.*) die Stola; der Pelzkragen, Umhang.

[2]**stole,** *imperf.*, **stolen,** *p.p.* *of* **steal**; ***stolen goods,*** das Diebsgut; ***receiver of stolen goods,*** der Hehler.

stolid ['stɔlid], *adj.* stumpf, schwerfällig, gleichgültig, teilnahmslos, phlegmatisch. **stolidity** [–'liditi], **stolidness,** *s.* die Schwerfälligkeit, Stumpfheit, Gleichgültigkeit, Teilnahmslosigkeit, das Phlegma.

stolon ['stoulən], *s.* (*Bot.*) der Schößling, Ausläufer, Stolo.

stoma ['stoumə], *s.* (*pl.* **-ta** ['stɔmətə]) (*Zool.*) die Öffnung, das Atmungsloch; (*Bot.*) die Spaltöffnung, das Stoma.

stomach ['stʌmək], **1.** *s.* 1. der Magen; ***on an empty –,*** auf leeren *or* mit leerem Magen, nüchtern; ***lie heavy on his –,*** ihm schwer im Magen liegen; ***lining of the –,*** die Magenwand; ***turn his –,*** ihm Ekel *or* Erbrechen verursachen; 2. (*coll.*) der Bauch, Leib; 3. (*fig.*) Hunger, Appetit (*for,* auf (*Acc.*)), die Neigung, Lust (zu). **2.** *v.t.* (*fig.*) sich (*Dat.*) gefallen *or* bieten lassen, sich abfinden mit, verschmerzen, hinnehmen, ertragen, einstecken (*an affront*). **stomach-ache,** *s.* Magenschmerzen, Bauchschmerzen (*pl.*), das Bauchweh. **stomacher,** *s.* (*obs.*) das Brusttuch, Mieder, der Latz. **stomachic** [sto'mækik], **1.** *adj.* 1. magenstärkend, verdauungsfördernd, appetitanregend; 2. gastrisch, Magen–. **2.** *s.* das Magenmittel, die Magenstärkung. **stomach-pump,** *s.* die Magenpumpe.

stomata ['stɔmətə], *pl. of* **stoma. stomatal,** *adj.*

(*Bot.*) Spaltöffnungs–. **stomate** ['stoumət], **1.** *s. See* **stoma. 2.** *adj. See* **stomatic. stomatitis** [–'taitis], *s.* (*Med.*) die Mundfäule, Mundschleimhautentzündung. **stomatology** [–'tɔlədʒi], *s.* die Lehre von Mundkrankheiten.

stone [stoun], **1.** *s.* 1. der Stein; ***kill two birds with one –***, zwei Fliegen mit einer Klappe schlagen; ***break –s***, Steine klopfen; ***leave no – unturned***, nichts unversucht lassen; ***philosopher's –***, der Stein der Weisen; (*fig.*) ***rolling –***, unsteter Mensch; (*Prov.*) ***a rolling – gathers no moss***, ein rollender Stein setzt kein Moos an; ***sermons in –s***, Steine, die uns predigen; (*fig.*) ***–'s throw***, der Katzensprung; ***people in glass houses shouldn't throw –s***, wer im Glashause sitzt, soll nicht mit Steinen werfen; 2. der Steinblock, Felsstein, Felsen; ***heart of –***, steinernes Herz; ***turned to –***, (wie) versteinert; 3. (*Med.*) der Stein, das Steinleiden; 4. der (Obst)-kern; 5. (*also* ***precious*** –) Edelstein; 6. *pl.* (*sl.*) (*Anat.*) Eier (*pl.*), Hoden (*pl.*); 7. (*no pl.*) der Stein (*weight = 14 lb., approx. 6·5 kg.*). **2.** *adj.* Stein–, steinern. **3.** *v.t.* 1. entsteinen, entkernen (*fruit*); 2. (*also* ***– to death***) steinigen.

stone| age, *s.* die Steinzeit. **–-blind,** *adj.* stockblind. **–break,** *s.* (*Bot.*) der Steinbrech. **–-breaker,** *s.* der Steinklopfer (*a p.*); die Steinbrechmaschine. **–chat,** *s.* (*Orn.*) das Schwarzkehlchen (*Saxicola torquata*). **–-coal,** *s.* die Steinkohle. **–-cold,** *adj.* eiskalt. **–-coloured,** *adj.* steinfarben. **–crop,** *s.* (*Bot.*) der Mauerpfeffer, die Fetthenne, das Steinkraut. **– curlew,** *s.* (*Orn.*) der Triel (*Burhinus oedicnemus*). **–-cutter,** *s.* der Steinmetz; Steinschleifer (*gems*).

stoned [stound], *adj.* 1. entkernt, entsteint (*fruit*); 2. (*sl.*) besoffen, sternhagelvoll.

stone|-dead, *adj.* mausetot. **–-deaf,** *adj.* stocktaub. **–-dresser,** *s. See* **–-cutter. –-fruit,** *s.* das Steinobst, Kernobst.

stoneless ['stounlis], *adj.* steinlos, kernlos (*fruit*).

stone|-marten, *s.* (*Zool.*) der Steinmarder. **–mason,** *s.* der Steinmetz, Steinhauer. **–-quarry,** *s.* der Steinbruch. **–wall,** *v.i.* (*coll.*) Obstruktion treiben. **–walling,** *s.* die Obstruktion. **–ware,** *s.* das Steingut. **–work,** *s.* das Mauerwerk.

stoniness ['stouninis], *s.* 1. das Steinige; 2. (*fig.*) die Härte, Starrheit. **stoning,** *s.* die Steinigung.

stony ['stouni], *adj.* 1. voller Steine, steinig; ***– ground***, der Steinboden; 2. steinern, (stein)hart (*also fig.*); 3. (*fig.*) starr (*stare etc.*); 4. (*sl.*) *see* **stony-broke. stony|-broke,** *adj.* (*sl.*) pleite, abgebrannt. **–-hearted,** *adj.* hartherzig, gefühllos, grausam.

stood [stud], *imperf., p.p. of* **stand.**

stooge [stu:dʒ], **1.** *s.* (*sl.*) der Handlanger, Jasager, Helfershelfer; (*Theat.*) Stichwortgeber. **2.** *v.i.* 1. (*usu.* ***– around, – about***) (*sl.*) herumstehen, herumschlendern; 2. ***– for him***, sein Handlanger sein.

stook [stuk], **1.** *s.* der Garbenhaufen, die Hocke, Puppe, die *or* der Mandel. **2.** *v.t.* in Haufen zusammensetzen.

stool [stu:l], *s.* 1. der Hocker, Bock; (*also* ***foot-–***) Schemel; ***camp –***, der Klappstuhl; ***office –***, der Kontorstuhl; ***fall between two –s***, sich zwischen zwei Stühle setzen; ***three-legged –***, dreibeiniger Hocker; 2. (*also* ***night-–, close-–***) der Nachtstuhl; (*Med.*) Stuhl(gang); ***go to –***, Stuhlgang haben; 3. der Baumstumpf, Wurzelstock.

stool-pigeon, *s.* 1. die Locktaube, der Lockvogel; 2. (*sl.*) (Lock)spitzel.

stoop [stu:p], **1.** *v.i.* 1. sich bücken, sich beugen; 2. gebückt *or* gebeugt gehen *or* sein, sich krumm *or* gebeugt halten; 3. (*fig.*) sich herablassen *or* erniedrigen *or* demütigen; 4. (*of a bird*) sich niederlassen, sich herabstürzen (**on**, auf (*Acc.*)). **2.** *s.* 1. gebeugte Haltung, krummer Rücken; ***have a –***, sich krumm halten; ***walk with a –***, gebeugt *or* krumm gehen; 2. das Niederstoßen, der Sturz (*of a bird*). **stooping,** *adj.* gebeugt, gebückt; ***– shoulders***, hängende Schultern (*pl.*).

stop [stɔp], **1.** *v.t.* 1. (damit) aufhören, (davon) ablassen (***doing***, zu tun); ***– it!*** hör auf damit! laß das! ***– doing it***, es bleiben lassen; davon ablassen, es zu tun; 2. ein Ende machen *or* bereiten (*Dat.*), Einhalt gebieten (*Dat.*), unterbinden, anhalten, aufhalten, unterbrechen, stoppen, hemmen (*movement*); abschneiden, einstellen (*proceedings, payment, work etc.*), sperren lassen (*a cheque*), anhalten, zum Halten *or* Stehen bringen (*machines etc.*); ***– thief!*** haltet den Dieb! 3. abwehren, parieren (*a blow*); (*coll.*) ***– a bullet***, eine Kugel abkriegen; 4. stillen (*blood*), abstellen (*steam, water etc.*); (*also* ***– up***) verstopfen, zustopfen, versperren, blockieren; auffüllen, ausfüllen, zumachen, schließen (*a hole*), füllen, plombieren (*a tooth*); ***– one's ears***, sich (*Dat.*) die Ohren zuhalten; ***– a gap***, eine Lücke ausfüllen; ***– a leak***, ein Leck verstopfen; (*sl.*) ***– his mouth***, ihm den Mund stopfen; 5. zurückhalten (*a p.*) (***from***, von), hindern (an (*Dat.*)); 6. (*Mus.*) greifen (*strings*); 7. interpunktieren (*writing*); 8. (*Phot.*) ***– down***, abblenden; 9. ***– out***, abdecken (*etching*).
2. *v.i.* 1. halten, haltmachen, zum Stehen kommen, stillstehen, stehenbleiben (*as clocks*); stoppen, stocken; 2. (*also* ***– dead, – short***) aufhören, einhalten, anhalten, innehalten; ***–!*** halt! ***– at nothing***, vor nichts zurückschrecken; (*coll.*) ***– short of***, nicht erreichen; 3. bleiben, sich aufhalten, zu Besuch sein (***with***, bei); ***– in***, zu Hause bleiben; ***– out***, ausbleiben, nicht nach Hause kommen; (*coll.*) ***– over***, die Fahrt unterbrechen; ***– up***, aufbleiben; 4. ***– for***, warten auf (*Acc.*).
3. *s.* 1. das (An)halten, Aufhalten, Innehalten, der Stillstand, Einhalt; ***come to a (dead) –***, (plötzlich) anhalten *or* aufhören; ***put a – to***, abstellen, einstellen, Einhalt gebieten (*Dat.*), ein Ende machen (*Dat.*); 2. der Aufenthalt; 3. die Haltestelle (*bus etc.*), Station (*train*), Anlegestelle (*ship*); 4. das Aufhören, Ende, die Pause; 5. (*Tech.*) Hemmung, Arretierung, Sperre, Sperrvorrichtung, Hemmvorrichtung; 6. (*Naut.*) das Bändsel; 7. (*Phot.*) die Blende; 8. (*Mus.*) der Zug, das Register, die Stimme (*organ*), Klappe, das Griffloch, Ventil (*wind instruments*), der Griff (*violin etc.*); (*fig.*) Ton, die Saite, das Register; (*coll.*) ***pull out all the –s***, mit allen Mitteln versuchen; 9. (*fig.*) die Sperrung (*of cheque etc.*); ***put a – on***, sperren, anhalten; 10. (*Typ.*) das Satzzeichen, Interpunktionszeichen; (*also* ***full –***) der Punkt; (*fig.*) ***come to a full –***, an einem Endpunkt sein, nicht weiterkommen; 11. (*Phonet.*) der Verschlußlaut; ***glottal –***, der Knacklaut.

stop|cock, *s.* der Absperrhahn. **–gap,** *s.* der Lückenbüßer, Notbehelf. **–-light,** *s.* das Stopplicht, Schlußlicht. **–over,** *s.* (*coll.*) die Fahrtunterbrechung; (*Av.*) Zwischenlandung.

stoppage ['stɔpidʒ], *s.* 1. die Stockung (*traffic etc.*); Sperrung (*supplies etc.*); Hemmung (*activity*); 2. Einstellung (*work, payment*); 3. Verstopfung (*also Med.*), Blockierung (*of a pipe etc.*); 4. das Anhalten, der Stillstand; 5. Aufenthalt; 6. (Gehalts)-abzug. **stopper, 1.** *s.* 1. der Stöpsel, Pfropf(en), Spund, Verschluß; (*coll.*) ***put a – on***, Einhalt tun (*Dat.*), zum Stillstand bringen; 2. (*Naut.*) der Stopper (*on rope etc.*). **2.** *v.t.* zustopfen, zustöpseln, zuspunden. **stopping,** *s.* 1. das Anhalten, Aufhalten; 2. (Ver)stopfen, Verschließen; 3. (*Tech.*) Ausfüllen, Ausstreichen; die Ausstreichmasse; 4. (*Dentistry*) das Plombieren; die Plombe, Zahnfüllung; 5. (*Mus.*) der Griff. **stopping| distance,** *s.* (*Motor.*) der Bremsweg, die Bremsstrecke. **– place,** *s.* die Haltestelle. **– train,** *s.* der Bummelzug.

stopple [stɔpl], **1.** *s.* der Stöpsel, Pfropf, Spund. **2.** *v.t.* zustöpseln.

stop|-press, *s.* letzte Nachrichten. **–-volley,** *s.* (*Tenn.*) der Stoppflugball. **–-watch,** *s.* die Stoppuhr.

storage ['stɔ:ridʒ], *s.* das Lagern, die (Auf)-speicherung, Aufbewahrung, (Ein)lagerung (*of goods*); das Lagergeld; ***– battery*** or ***cell***, der Akku(mulator), Sammler, die Speicherbatterie; ***cold –***, die Kühlraumlagerung, Kaltlagerung; (*fig.*) ***put in(to) cold –***, auf die lange Bank schieben.

store [stɔ:], **1.** *s.* 1. der Vorrat, Bestand, Bestände (*pl.*) (*of*, an (*Dat.*)), das (Vorrats)lager; ***in –***, vorrätig, auf Lager; (*fig.*) ***be in – for him,*** ihm vorbehalten sein *or* bevorstehen; (*fig.*) ***have in –***, bereit halten (*for*, für), bringen werden (*Dat.*); (*fig.*) ***set great*** (***little***) ***– by,*** großen (wenig) Wert legen auf (*Acc.*), hoch (gering) einschätzen; 2. (*fig.*) die Menge, Fülle, der Überfluß, Schatz, Reichtum (*of*, an (*Dat.*)); 3. das Lagerhaus, Magazin, der Speicher; ***for –***, zum Aufbewahren; ***put into –***, einlagern (*furniture etc.*); 4. (*esp. Am.*) das Geschäft, der Laden; (*also pl.*) das Warenhaus, Kaufhaus; 5. *pl.* der Bedarf, die Ausrüstung, Vorräte (*pl.*); (*esp. Naut.*) der Proviant. **2.** *v.t.* 1. (*also* ***– up, – away***) aufbewahren, aufspeichern, auf Lager nehmen, (ein)lagern (*furniture etc.*); ***– furniture,*** Möbel einlagern (*as the owner*), Lagerraum für Möbel bieten; 2. ausstatten, versorgen (***with***, mit); 3. verproviantieren (*a ship*).

store|house, *s.* 1. das Lagerhaus, (Waren)lager, Magazin, der Speicher; 2. (*fig.*) die Schatzkammer, Fundgrube. **–keeper, –man** [–mən], *s.* 1. der Lagermeister, Magazinverwalter; 2. (*Am.*) der Ladenbesitzer. **–room,** *s.* die Vorratskammer, Rumpelkammer.

storey [ˈstɔːri], *s.* (*pl.* **-s**) der Stock, das Stockwerk, Geschoß; ***three-– house,*** dreistöckiges Haus; ***third-– window,*** das Fenster im dritten Stock; (*sl.*) ***upper –***, das Oberstübchen. **storeyed** [–d], *adj.* mit Stockwerken; ***three-– house,*** dreistöckiges Haus.

stork [stɔːk], *s.* (*Orn.*) der Storch (*Ciconia*). **stork's-bill,** *s.* (*Bot.*) der Storchschnabel.

storm [stɔːm], **1.** *s.* der Sturm (*also Mil., fig.*); das Unwetter; (*also* ***thunder–***) Gewitter; ***– of applause,*** der Beifallssturm; ***the calm after the –***, die Ruhe nach dem Sturm; ***after the – comes a calm,*** auf Regen folgt Sonnenschein; ***hail-–***, schwerer Hagelfall; ***rain-–***, der Platzregen; (*fig.*) ***raise a –***, Aufruhr erregen; ***snow-–***, der Schneesturm; ***Storm and Stress Period,*** die Sturm- und Drangperiode; (*Mil.*) ***take by –***, im Sturm nehmen; ***– in a tea-cup,*** der Sturm im Wasserglas. **2.** *v.t.* (*Mil.*) erstürmen, im Sturm nehmen, (*fig.*) bestürmen. **3.** *v.i.* 1. stürmen; 2. toben, wüten (*of wind, rain etc., also fig.*) (*at*, gegen); (*fig.*) wütend sein (auf (*Acc.*)).

storm|-beaten, *adj.* vom Sturm gepeitscht. **–-bird,** *s.* die Sturmschwalbe. **–-bound,** *adj.* vom Sturm festgehalten. **–-canvas,** *s.* die Sturmbesegelung. **–-centre,** *s.* das Sturmzentrum; (*fig.*) der Mittelpunkt *or* Herd der Unruhe. **–-cloud,** *s.* die Gewitterwolke. **–cock,** *s. See* ***missel thrush.*** **–-cone,** *s.* (*Naut.*) der Sturmkegel.

storminess [ˈstɔːminis], *s.* das Stürmische, Ungestüm. **storming, 1.** *s.* (*Mil.*) das Stürmen, Sturmlaufen, die Erstürmung. **2.** *attrib. adj.* Sturm–; ***– party,*** die Sturmkolonne.

storm|-jib, *s.* (*Naut.*) die Sturmfock. **–proof,** *adj.* sturmfest. **–-sail,** *s.* das Sturmsegel. **–-signal,** *s.* das Sturmzeichen, Sturmsignal. **–-tossed,** *adj.* vom Sturm umhergetrieben. **–-trooper,** *s.* (*Hist.*) der SA-Mann. **–troops,** *pl.* Sturmtruppen, Stoßtruppen (*pl.*), (*Hist.*) die Sturmabteilung.

stormy [ˈstɔːmi], *adj.* stürmisch, (*fig.*) ungestüm; ***– weather,*** das Sturmwetter, Unwetter (*also fig.*). **stormy petrel,** *s.* (*Orn.*) die Sturmschwalbe (*Hydrobatus pelagicus*).

[1]**story** [ˈstɔːri], *s.* die Erzählung, Geschichte; ***short –***, die Novelle; 2. die Handlung, Fabel (*of a drama, novel etc.*); ***as the – goes,*** wie man sagt, wie es heißt, wie verlautet; 3. die Darstellung, der Bericht; ***quite another*** or ***a different –***, etwas ganz anderes; ***cut*** or ***make a long – short,*** um es ganz kurz zu sagen, um zum Ende zu kommen; 4. (*coll.*) die Flunkerei, Finte, Lüge, das Lügenmärchen; ***cock-and-bull –***, das Ammenmärchen; ***the same old –***, das alte Lied.

[2]**story,** (*esp. Am.*) *see* **storey.**

story|book, *s.* das Geschichtenbuch, Märchenbuch. **–teller,** *s.* 1. der (Geschichten)erzähler; 2. (*coll.*) Flunkerer, Lügenbold. **–telling,** *s.* 1. das Erzählen; die Erzählkunst; 2. (*coll.*) das Flunkern.

stoup [stuːp], *s.* (*obs.*) der Becher, das Trinkgefäß; (*Eccl.*) Weihwasserbecken; (*Scots.*) der Eimer.

stout [staut], **1.** *adj.* 1. stark, fest, kräftig, dauerhaft (*of a th.*); rüstig, tapfer, kühn, wacker, mannhaft, beherzt, standhaft, standfest (*of p., qualities, resistance etc.*); 2. korpulent, dick, beleibt (*of p.*). **2.** *s.* dunkles Bier. **stout|-hearted,** *adj.* tapfer, mutig, unerschrocken, beherzt, herzhaft. **–-heartedness,** *s.* die Tapferkeit, Unerschrockenheit, Beherztheit. **stoutish,** *adj.* (*of a p.*) etwas korpulent. **stoutness,** *s.* 1. (*of a p.*) die Beleibtheit, Korpulenz; (*of character*) Mannhaftigkeit, Standhaftigkeit, Tapferkeit; 2. (*of a th.*) Stärke, Festigkeit.

[1]**stove** [stouv], **1.** *s.* 1. der Ofen; 2. (Koch)herd; 3. (*Hort.*) das Treibhaus; 4. (*Tech.*) Brennofen; die Trockenkammer; ***slow-combustion –***, der Dauerofen **2.** *v.t.* 1. (*Tech.*) trocknen; 2. schwefeln, (mit Schwefelsäuregas) bleichen; 3. (*Hort.*) im Treibhaus ziehen.

[2]**stove,** *imperf., p.p. of* **stave.**

stove|pipe, *s.* das Ofenrohr; (*coll.*) ***– hat,*** die Angströhre. **–-plant,** *s.* das Treibhausgewächs.

stow [stou], **1.** *v.t.* 1. (*esp. Naut.*) (ver)stauen; (ver)packen, unterbringen (*goods*); volladen, vollpacken, (be)laden, vollfüllen (*a receptacle*) (***with***, mit); (*coll.*) ***– away,*** in Sicherheit bringen, wegräumen, wegschaffen, beiseite legen, beiseite schaffen, wegpacken; 2. (*sl.*) (*usu. imper.*) aufhören mit, sein *or* bleiben lassen, unterlassen; (*sl.*) ***– it!*** hör damit auf! **2.** *v.i.* ***– away,*** als blinder Passagier mitfahren. **stowage** [–idʒ], *s.* 1. (*esp. Naut.*) das Stauen, Packen; 2. (*Naut.*) der Stauraum, Packraum, Lagerraum; 3. das Staugeld, die Staugebühr. **stowaway** [–əwei], *s.* blinder Passagier.

strabismal [strəˈbizməl], **strabismic,** *adj.* Schiel–, schielend. **strabismus,** *s.* das Schielen. **strabotomy** [–ˈbɔtəmi], *s.* die Schieloperation.

straddle [ˈstrædl], **1.** *v.i.* 1. die Beine spreizen, breitbeinig gehen *or* stehen, rittlings sitzen; 2. (*fig.*) sich ausstrecken *or* ausdehnen; 3. (*Am. coll.*) unentschlossen *or* wankelmütig sein. **2.** *v.t.* 1. spreizen (*legs*); 2. breitbeinig stehen auf (*Dat.*), rittlings sitzen auf (*Dat.*); 3. (*Cards*) verdoppeln (*stake*); 4. (*Artil.*) eingabeln, decken. **3.** *s.* 1. das Spreizen, Rittlingssitzen; 2. (*St. Exch., esp. Am.*) die Stellage. **straddle-legged,** *adj.* breitbeinig.

strafe [strɑːf, streif], **1.** *v.t.* strafen; (*Mil.*) (*coll.*) beschießen, bombardieren. **2.** *s.* (*coll.*) der Beschuß, die Beschießung, Bombardierung.

straggle [strægl], *v.i.* umherstreifen, umherschweifen; (*Mil.*) versprengt werden, sich verirren; zerstreut *or* abseits liegen; wuchern (*as plants*); (*fig.*) abweichen, abschweifen, abirren. **straggler,** *s.* der Herumstreicher; (*Mil.*) Versprengte(r), (*also Naut.*) der Nachzügler; (*Hort.*) wilder Schößling. **straggling,** (*coll.*) **straggly,** *adj.* umherschweifend, abschweifend, abweichend, zerstreut; (*as hair*) schütter; (*Hort.*) wuchernd.

straight [streit], **1.** *adj.* 1. gerade (*also fig.*); (*Math.*) ***– angle,*** gestreckter Winkel; ***– as an arrow*** or ***a poker,*** kerzeng(e)rade; (*fig.*) ***– as a die,*** grundehrlich; ***keep a – face,*** ein ernstes Gesicht bewahren; ***– hair,*** glattes Haar; (*Math.*) ***– line,*** die Gerade; (*coll.*) ***keep on the – and narrow*** (***path***), (sich (*Dat.*)) keine Seitensprünge erlauben; 2. unmittelbar, direkt; (*Pol.*) ***– fight,*** der (Wahl)kampf zwischen zwei Kandidaten; 3. (*coll.*) offen, freimütig, aufrecht, ehrlich, redlich, rechtschaffen, verläßlich, zuverlässig; ***– tip,*** zuverlässiger Tip; 4. (*only pred.*) geordnet, in Ordnung; (*sl.*) ***get it*** (or ***him***) ***–***, es (*or* ihn) richtig verstehen; ***make*** or ***put –***, in Ordnung bringen; 5. (*Cards*) ***– flush,*** die Sequenz von fünf Karten; 6. (*coll.*) ***– play,*** konventionelles Drama. **2.** *adv.* geradeaus, gerade(n)wegs, in gerader Linie, stracks, direkt, unmittelbar; (*coll.*) *see also* ***– out***; (*coll.*) ***– from the horse's mouth,*** frisch von der Quelle; (*sl.*) ***go –***, keine krummen Sachen mehr machen; (*coll.*) ***see –***, richtig sehen; (*coll.*) ***think –***, logisch denken; ***– ahead,*** geradeaus; ***– off,*** see **straightaway**; ***– on,*** see ***– ahead***; ***– out,***

rundheraus, glattweg, ohne Umschweife, klipp und klar. **3.** *s.* die Geradheit; Gerade, Ebene; (*Spt.*) (Ziel)gerade; (*coll.*) ***the – and narrow,*** die Lebensführung ohne Ausschweifungen.

straight|away, *adv.* sofort, stracks, auf der Stelle. **--edge,** *s.* das Richtscheit, Lineal.

straighten ['streitən], **1.** *v.t.* 1. (*also – out*) geradmachen, geradebiegen, geraderichten; durchdrücken (*one's legs etc.*); (*fig.*) ***– one's face,*** eine ernste Miene aufsetzen; 2. (*fig.*) (*usu. – out*) in Ordnung bringen, regeln; klarstellen, entwirren. **2.** *v.i.* gerade werden; (*Av.*) ***– out,*** sich fangen; ***– up,*** sich aufrichten.

straight|-faced, *adj.* mit ernstem Gesicht. **-forward,** *adj.* 1. schlicht, einfach, unkompliziert; 2. (*fig.*) direkt, offen, redlich, ehrlich, aufrichtig. **-forwardness,** *s.* die Offenheit, Ehrlichkeit, Redlichkeit, Aufrichtigkeit. **-forwards,** *adv.* geradeaus, gerade(n)wegs. **--line,** *adj.* geradlinig. **straightness,** *s.* 1. die Geradheit, Geradlinigkeit; 2. (*fig.*) Redlichkeit, Offenheit, Ehrlichkeit. **straight|way,** *adv. See* **-away.**

[1]**strain** [strein], **1.** *v.t.* 1. straff anziehen *or* (an)spannen, strecken; (*fig.*) überanstrengen (*one's eyes etc.*); Gewalt antun (*Dat.*), forcieren; (*Tech.*) verbiegen, verzerren, verformen, deformieren; verstauchen, verrenken (*wrist etc.*), zerren (*muscle*); ***– one's eyes towards,*** die Augen (krampfhaft) richten auf (*Acc.*); ***– every nerve,*** sein Äußerstes tun, das Letzte hergeben, alles aufbieten; ***– a point,*** zu weit gehen; 2. (*Poet.*) drücken, pressen (*to one's heart etc.*) (***to,*** an (*Acc.*)); 3. (durch)seihen, (durch)sieben, filtrieren, filtern, passieren, läutern (*a fluid*). **2.** *v.i.* 1. ziehen, zerren (***at,*** an (*Dat.*)); (*fig.*) ***– at a gnat,*** bei Kleinigkeiten Umstände machen; 2. sich anstrengen *or* bemühen *or* abmühen (***to do,*** zu tun; ***for, with,*** um), streben, eifern (nach); 3. durchtropfen, durchsickern. **3.** *s.* 1. die (Über)anstrengung, Anspannung, Bemühung, der Kraftaufwand; ***at full –,*** aufs äußerste angespannt; 2. der Zug, Druck, die Spannung, Belastung, Beanspruchung, Inanspruchnahme; ***– of living in the city,*** der Druck *or* die Last *or* Bürde *or* Anspannung des Stadtlebens; ***be a – on his nerves,*** ihm auf die Nerven gehen *or* fallen; ***– on his pocket,*** starke Belastung für sein Geldbeutel; ***put a great – on,*** große Anforderungen stellen an (*Acc.*); ***be under a –,*** unter Druck stehen; ***suffer under the –*** or ***from –,*** mit den Nerven herunter sein, mitgenommen sein; 3. (*Med.*) die Verstauchung, Verrenkung, Zerrung; 4. (*Tech.*) Verzerrung, Distortion; 5. (*oft. pl.*) Weise, Melodie, Tonfolge, Klänge (*pl.*); ***march to the – of,*** unter den Klängen (*Gen.*) marschieren; 6. (*fig.*) die (Ausdrucks)weise, Manier; der Ton, Stil.

[2]**strain,** *s.* 1. die Linie, Abkunft, Abstammung; Familie, das Geschlecht, (*Biol.*) Rasse, Abart, Spielart; 2. Charaktereigenschaft, (Erb)anlage; 3. Veranlagung, Neigung, der Hang (***of,*** zu); 4. die Beimischung, Spur, der Anflug, Zug (***of,*** von).

strained [streind], *adj.* 1. gespannt (*as relations*), gezwungen, erzwungen, unnatürlich, gekünstelt, forciert (*of manner*); 2. (*Med.*) überanstrengt (*heart, nerves*), gezerrt (*muscles*), verrenkt, verstaucht (*joints*).

strait [streit], **1.** *adj.* (*obs.*) 1. eng, schmal; 2. hart, strikt, streng. **2.** *s.* (*usu. pl.*) 1. die Meerenge, Straße; 2. (*fig.*) Verlegenheit, Klemme, der Engpaß; ***financial –s,*** finanzielle Schwierigkeiten; ***reduce to desperate*** or ***dire –s,*** in eine Zwangslage bringen. **straiten,** *v.t.* (*obs.*) eng(er) machen, verenge(r)n; begrenzen, beschränken, einschränken, einengen; (*only pass.*) in Verlegenheit *or* Schwierigkeiten bringen, bedrängen; ***–ed circumstances,*** beschränkte *or* bedrängte Verhältnisse. **strait|-jacket,** *s.* die Zwangsjacke. **--laced,** *adj.* (*fig.*) prüde, sittenstreng, engherzig. **straitness,** *s.* (*rare*) 1. die Enge, Begrenztheit; 2. Härte, Strenge; 3. Not, Beschwernis.

strake [streik], *s.* (*Naut.*) der Plankengang.

stramash [strə'mæʃ], *s.* (*Scots*) der Spektakel.

stramineous [strə'miniəs], *adj.* Stroh–, strohfarben.

[1]**strand** [strænd], **1.** *s.* (*Poet.*) der Strand, das Ufer. **2.** *v.t.* 1. auf den Strand *or* an Land setzen *or* werfen; ***–ed property,*** das Strandgut; 2. (*fig.*) zum Scheitern bringen, scheitern lassen; ***be left –ed,*** auf dem trocknen sitzen. **3.** *v.i.* stranden, auf Grund laufen.

[2]**strand,** *s.* die Faser, der Faden (*of fabric*), Strang, die Ducht, Litze (*of rope*); Strähne (*of hair*); ***– of wire,*** die Drahtlitze; ***–ed wire,*** der Litzdraht.

stranding ['strændiŋ], *s.* die Strandung, der Schiffbruch.

strange [streindʒ], *adj.* 1. fremd, unbekannt, ungewohnt, neu, nicht geläufig (*to, Dat.*); 2. eigenartig, wunderlich, seltsam, merkwürdig, sonderbar; ***– to say, –ly enough,*** seltsamerweise; 3. ausländisch; 4. (*of a p.*) nicht vertraut (***to,*** mit), nicht gewohnt (an (*Acc.*)), unbewandert, unerfahren (in (*Dat.*)). **strangeness,** *s.* 1. die Merkwürdigkeit, Sonderbarkeit, Eigenartigkeit, Seltsamkeit, Wunderlichkeit; 2. Fremdheit, Fremdartigkeit.

stranger ['streindʒə], *s.* Fremde(r), Unbekannte(r), der Fremdling, Neuling, Unerfahrene(r); (*Law*) Unbeteiligte(r); ***I am a – here,*** ich bin hier fremd; ***be a – to,*** unbekannt sein mit, unerfahren sein in (*Dat.*), nicht vertraut sein mit; (*coll.*) ***you are quite a –,*** ich habe dich ewig nicht gesehen; (*coll.*) ***little –,*** kleiner Neuankömmling; ***be –s to each other,*** sich nicht kennen; ***be no – to,*** gut kennen (*a p.*), wohl vertraut sein mit (*a th.*); (*Parl.*) ***spy –s,*** die Räumung der Galerie beantragen.

strangle ['stræŋgl], *v.t.* 1. erwürgen, erdrosseln; einschnüren (*as a collar*); 2. (*fig.*) unterdrücken, ersticken. **stranglehold,** *s.* 1. der Halsgriff (*wrestling*); 2. (*fig.*) Würgegriff, die Umklammerung. **strangles,** *pl.* (*usu. sing. constr.*) (*Vet.*) die Druse.

strangulate ['stræŋgjuleit], *v.t.* (*Med., Bot.*) abbinden, abschnüren; ***–d hernia,*** eingeklemmter Bruch. **strangulation** [–'leiʃən], *s.* 1. die Erwürgung, Erdrosselung; 2. (*Med.*) Abschnürung; Einklemmung.

strangury ['stræŋgjuri], *s.* 1. (*Med.*) der Harnzwang, Harndrang; 2. (*Bot.*) die Einschnürungswulst.

strap ['stræp], **1.** *s.* der (Leder)riemen; Gurt, das (Schnür)band, die Strippe; (*Tech.*) der Treibriemen; (*Tech.*) Metallbügel, das Gelenkband, Metallband; (*Bot.*) Blatthäutchen, die Ligula; (*Naut.*) der Stropp; Halteriemen, die Schlaufe (*in bus etc.*), der Tragriemen (*of rucksack*), Träger (*of underwear*). **2.** *v.t.* 1. mit Riemen festschnüren *or* festbinden *or* befestigen; festschnallen, anschirren; (*Naut.*) stroppen; (*Med.*) (*also – up*) einen Heftpflasterverband machen (*Dat.*); 2. mit einem Riemen züchtigen.

strap-hanger, *s.* stehender Fahrgast (*in a bus etc.*). **strapless,** *adj.* trägerlos, schulterfrei (*dress*).

strappado [strə'peidou], **1.** *s.* (*Hist.*) der Wippgalgen. **2.** *v.t.* wippen. **strapper** ['stræpə], *s.* (*coll.*) strammer Bursche, strammes Mädchen. **strapping, 1.** *adj.* (*coll.*) stämmig, stramm; drall (*of a girl*). **2.** *s.* 1. Riemen, Bänder (*pl.*); 2. (*Med.*) das Heftpflaster; 3. (*coll.*) die Tracht Prügel.

Strasbourg ['stræzbə:g], *s.* Straßburg (*n.*).

strata ['strɑ:tə], *pl. of* **stratum.**

stratagem ['strætədʒəm], *s.* (*Mil.*) der Kriegsplan, die Kriegslist; (*fig.*) List, der Kunstgriff. **strategic(al)** [strə'ti:dʒik(l)], *adj.* strategisch; ***– position,*** strategisch wichtige Position. **strategist** ['strætidʒist], *s.* der Stratege. **strategy** ['strætidʒi], *s.* die Feldherrnkunst, Kriegskunst; Strategie; (*fig.*) List, Taktik, Berechnung.

strathspey [stræθ'spei], *s.* lebhafter schottischer Tanz.

stratification [strætifi'keiʃən], *s.* die Schichtung, Schichtenbildung. **stratified** ['strætifaid], *adj.* geschichtet, schichtenförmig; ***– rock,*** das Schichtgestein. **stratiform** ['strætifɔ:m], *adj.* 1. (*Geol.*) schichtenförmig; 2. (*Meteor.*) schichtwolkenartig. **stratify** ['strætifai], *v.t.* schichten. **stratigraphic(al)** [–'græfik(l)], *adj.* Formations–, stratigraphisch. **stratigraphy** [–'tigrəfi], *s.* (*Geol.*) die Formationskunde.

stratocirrus ['streitou'sirəs], *s.* (*Meteor.*) dichter Zirrostratus.

stratocracy [strə'tɔkrəsi], *s.* die Militärherrschaft, Militärregierung.

stratocumulus ['streitou'kju:mjuləs], *s.* (*Meteor.*) der Stratokumulus, die Haufenschichtwolke.

stratosphere ['strætəsfiə], *s.* die Stratosphäre.

stratum ['strɑ:təm], *s.* (*pl.* **strata**) die Schicht (*also fig.*); Lage; *social* –, die Gesellschaftsschicht.

stratus ['streitəs], *s.* (*pl.* **strati** [–tai]) (*Meteor.*) die Schichtwolke.

straw [strɔ:], **1.** *s.* der Strohhalm, (*for drinking*) Trinkhalm; (*fig.*) Pappenstiel; (*collect.*) das Stroh; (*fig.*) ***not care a* –**, sich nichts daraus machen; (*fig.*) ***clutch*** or ***grasp at a* –**, sich an einen Strohhalm klammern; (*fig.*) ***last* –**, letzter Schlag, der Rest; (*fig.*) ***that's the last* –**, das fehlte (mir *etc.*) gerade noch; das geht (mir *etc.*) über die Hutschnur; ***the*** (***last***) ***– that breaks the camel's back,*** der Tropfen, der das Faß zum Überlaufen bringt; ***not worth a* –**, keinen Heller *or* Pfifferling wert; ***man of* –**, der Strohmann, vorgeschobene P.; unbedeutende Figur.

strawberry ['strɔ:bəri], *s.* die Erdbeere; – ***jam,*** die Erdbeermarmelade; –***mark,*** (rotes) Muttermal.

straw| bid, *s.* (*Am.*) das Scheingebot. **–board,** *s.* die Strohpappe. **--coloured,** *adj.* strohfarben, strohgelb. **– hat,** *s.* der Strohhut. **--thatched,** *adj.* strohgedeckt. **– vote,** *s.* (*Am.*) die Probeabstimmung.

stray [strei], **1.** *v.i.* 1. sich verirren *or* verlaufen; 2. umherstreifen, herumirren; 3. abgehen, abirren (***from,*** von); weglaufen (von); (*fig.*) abschweifen, wandern (*as attention, eyes*); 4. (*fig.*) irren, in die Irre gehen, vom rechten Weg abkommen; 5. (*Elec.*) streuen, vagabundieren. **2.** *adj.* 1. verirrt, entlaufen, streunend (*animal*); 2. vereinzelt, verstreut; – ***bullet,*** der Ausreißer; – ***thoughts,*** Gedankensplitter (*pl.*); 3. gelegentlich, zufällig, beiläufig; 4. (*Elec.*) – ***current,*** vagabundierender Strom, der Streustrom. **3.** *s.* 1. verirrtes *or* streunendes Tier; 2. Heimatlose(r), Herumirrende(r); 3. *pl.* (*Rad.*) atmosphärische Störungen (*pl.*). **strayed,** *adj.* verirrt, verlaufen.

streak [stri:k], **1.** *s.* 1. der Streifen, Strich; – ***of lightning,*** der Blitz(strahl); (*coll.*) ***like a – of lightning,*** blitzschnell, wie ein geölter Blitz; 2. (*Geol.*) die Schliere; 3. Ader, Maser (*in wood*); 4. (*fig.*) der Anflug, Einschlag, die Spur, Anwandlung; (*coll.*) – ***of luck,*** die Glückssträhne; (*coll.*) – ***of bad luck,*** die Pechsträhne. **2.** *v.t.* streifen. **3.** *v.i.* (*coll.*) rasen, flitzen, wie ein geölter Blitz sausen. **streaked, streaky,** *adj.* streifig, gestreift; geädert, gemasert (*as wood*); durchwachsen (*as bacon*).

stream [stri:m], **1.** *s.* 1. der Bach, Fluß, Strom, (Wasser)lauf, die Strömung (*also fig.*); das Fahrwasser; ***against the* –**, gegen *or* wider den Strom; ***down* –**, stromabwärts; ***up* –**, stromaufwärts; ***with the* –**, mit dem Strom; (*fig.*) ***drift with the* –**, mit dem Strom schwimmen; 2. (*fig.*) (*oft. pl.*) der Strom, Ströme (*pl.*), der Strahl, Schwall (*of words*), Schwung (*of traffic*), Flut (*of light*); – ***of consciousness,*** der Bewußtseinsstrom; 3. (*fig.*) die Strömung, Richtung, der Lauf, Gang; 4. (*in schools*) die Leistungsstufe. **2.** *v.i.* 1. strömen, fließen, rinnen, (*esp. light*) fluten; 2. überlaufen, überfließen, überströmen (***with,*** von), triefen (vor (*Dat.*)); 3. flattern, wehen (*as a flag*). **3.** *v.t.* 1. (*Naut.*) aussetzen, auswerfen, über Bord werfen; 2. fliegen *or* flattern lassen (*a flag*); 3. (*in school*) nach Leistungsstufen einteilen.

stream-anchor, *s.* der Stromanker, Warpanker.

streamer ['stri:mə], *s.* 1. der Wimpel, kleine Fahne, fliegendes Band; 2. die Papierschlange; 3. der Plakatstreifen, das Transparent; 4. der Lichtstrahl, Lichtstrom, Lichtstreifen. **streaming, 1.** *adj.* 1. strömend, fließend, rinnend; 2. überfließend, triefend. **2.** *s.* 1. das Strömen, Fließen, Rinnen; 2. Überströmen, Triefen.

streamlet ['stri:mlit], *s.* das Bächlein.

stream|line, 1. *s.* die Stromlinie. **2.** *adj. See* **–lined. 3.** *v.t.* 1. Stromlinienform geben (*Dat.*); 2. (*fig.*) modernisieren, rationalisieren, wirkungsvoller machen, von allem Ballast befreien. **–lined,** *adj.* 1. stromlinienförmig, Stromlinien–, windschnittig, windschlüpfrig; 2. (*fig.*) zeitgemäß, fortschrittlich; schnittig, rassig.

streamy ['stri:mi], *adj.* (*coll.*) überströmend, überfließend, triefend.

street [stri:t], **1.** *s.* die Straße, (*Austr.*) Gasse; ***in the* –**, auf der Straße; ***the man in the* –**, der Durchschnittsmensch, Mann aus dem Volke, (*collect.*) die große Masse; (*coll.*) **–*s ahead,*** weit überlegen (***of,*** *Dat.*); (*coll.*) ***not in the same – with,*** nicht zu vergleichen mit; (*coll.*) ***not up his* –**, ihm nicht liegen, nicht seine Stärke sein; ***be on the –s,*** auf den Strich gehen, Prostituierte sein; ***walk the –s,*** die Straßen ablaufen; *see also* ***be on the –s.***

street| arab, –boy, *s.* der Straßenjunge, Gassenjunge. **–car,** *s.* (*Am.*) die Straßenbahn. **--cleaner,** *s.* (*Am.*) *see* **--sweeper. --corner,** *s.* die Straßenecke. **--door,** *s.* die Haustür. **--fighting,** *s.* der Straßenkampf. **--lamp,** *s.* die Straßenlaterne. **--lighting,** *s.* die Straßenbeleuchtung. **--market,** *s.* der Freiverkehrsmarkt. **--organ,** *s.* der Leierkasten, die Drehorgel. **--refuge,** *s.* die Verkehrsinsel. **--sweeper,** *s.* 1. der Straßenkehrer; 2. die Straßenkehrmaschine. **--trader, --vendor,** *s.* der (die) Straßenhändler(in). **–walker,** *s.* die Straßendirne, das Strichmädchen. **–walking,** *s.* das Dirnenwesen, (öffentliche) Prostitution.

strength [streŋθ], *s.* 1. die Kraft, Kräfte (*pl.*), die Stärke; ***be*** or ***go beyond his –, be too much for his* –**, über seine Kraft gehen; ***feat of* –**, das Kraftstück; ***in* –**, was die Kraft *or* Stärke betrifft; ***gather* –**, Kräfte sammeln, zu Kräften kommen; (*fig.*) – ***of a horse,*** gewaltige Kraft; ***go from – to* –**, von Erfolg zu Erfolg schreiten; ***measure one's – with him,*** seine Kräfte *or* sich mit ihm messen; ***squander one's* –**, sich verzetteln; 2. die Festigkeit, Härte (*of things*); Wirkungskraft, Intensität (*of influences*); Widerstandskraft (*of a fortress etc.*); 3. Stärke(wirkung), der Gehalt, Titer (*of liquids*); 4. (*Mil.*) die Stärke, Stammrolle, Etatstärke, der (Soll)bestand; ***actual* –**, die Iststärke; ***below* –**, unter Normalstärke, (*coll.*) unvollständig; (*fig.*) ***in*** (***full***) **–**, vollzählig; ***in great* –**, in großer Zahl; ***on the* –**, in der Stammrolle; ***up to* –**, in voller Stärke; 5. die Beweiskraft, Überzeugungskraft (*of argument*); ***on the – of,*** auf Grund (*Gen.*), kraft (*Gen.*), (*Gen.*) zufolge, auf (*Acc.*) hin, unter Berufung auf (*Acc.*); ***on the – of it,*** daraufhin; 6. besondere Stärke (*of a p.*); – ***of purpose,*** die Willensstärke, Charakterstärke.

strengthen ['streŋθən], **1.** *v.t.* 1. stärken, stark machen, kräftigen; (*fig.*) – ***his hand,*** ihn ermutigen, ihm Mut machen, ihm neue Kraft geben; 2. (*Tech. etc.*) verstärken; 3. (*fig.*) vermehren; 4. (*fig.*) bestärken, bestätigen, bekräftigen. **2.** *v.i.* erstarken, stark werden; sich verstärken, stärker werden. **strengthener,** *s.* die Stärkung (*to,* für); (*Med.*) das Stärkungsmittel; (*Tech.*) Verstärkungsteil, die Verstärkung. **strengthening, 1.** *adj.* 1. stärkend, kräftigend; verstärkend, Verstärkungs–; 2. (*fig.*) vermehrend, Vermehrungs–. **2.** *s.* die (Ver)stärkung, (*fig.*) Vermehrung. **strengthless,** *adj.* kraftlos, matt. **strengthlessness,** *s.* die Kraftlosigkeit, Mattigkeit.

strenuous ['strenjuəs], *adj.* 1. tätig, emsig, rührig, rastlos, betriebsam, unentwegt; 2. eifrig, tatkräftig, energisch (*protest etc.*); 3. (*of activity*) mühsam, anstrengend. **strenuously,** *adv. Also* angestrengt. **strenuousness,** *s.* 1. die Tatkraft, Energie, Emsigkeit, Rührigkeit, der Eifer (*of a p.*); 2. das Anstrengende, Mühsame (*of activity*).

streptococcus [streptə'kɔkəs], *s.* der Streptokokkus.

stress [stres], **1.** *s.* 1. der Druck, die Kraft, das Gewicht (*also fig.*); 2. (*fig.*) der Nachdruck, Wert, die Bedeutung, Wichtigkeit; ***lay –*** (***up***)***on,*** betonen, Wert *or* Gewicht *or* Nachdruck legen auf (*Acc.*); 3. die Beanspruchung, Belastung, Last, Spannung;

(*fig.*) Anspannung, Anstrengung; ***Storm and Stress,*** der Sturm und Drang; ***times of –,*** Zeiten der Krise; ***under the – of,*** unter dem Druck von, gezwungen durch; 4. die Heftigkeit, das Ungestüm, Unbilden (*pl.*) (*of weather etc.*); 5. (*Metr.*) die Betonung, der Ton, Akzent. **2.** *v.t.* 1. Nachdruck *or* Gewicht *or* Wert legen auf (*Acc.*), betonen, unterstreichen, hervorheben, in den Vordergrund stellen; (*Metr.*) den Akzent legen auf (*Acc.*); – ***the point,*** unmißverständlich darauf hinweisen; 2. (*Tech.*) beanspruchen.

stretch [stretʃ], **1.** *v.t.* 1. strecken, spannen, ziehen, ausdehnen; 2. (*also* – ***out***) ausbreiten, ausstrecken; – ***one's legs,*** die Beine ausstrecken; (*fig.*) sich (*Dat.*) die Beine vertreten, einen kleinen Spaziergang machen; – ***o.s.,*** sich (aus)strecken *or* recken *or* rekeln; – ***forth*** or ***out one's hand,*** die Hand ausstrecken *or* hinhalten *or* hinstrecken *or* vorstrecken; 3. (*coll.*) niederstrecken, zur Strecke bringen (*a p.*); 4. (*fig.*) auf die Spitze treiben, überspannen, übertreiben (*meaning*); – ***a point,*** ein Übriges tun, fünf gerade sein lassen, ein Auge zudrücken, es nicht allzu genau nehmen, eine Ausnahme machen; 5. überbeanspruchen, überschreiten; (*fig.*) ***fully –ed,*** ausgelastet (*of a p.*); 6. anspannen (*credit*).
2. *v.i.* 1. sich strecken *or* recken *or* rekeln (*of a p.*); 2. sich (aus)dehnen *or* dahinziehen *or* erstrecken, reichen (***to,*** bis zu); 3. sich (aus)weiten (*clothes etc.*); 4. (*usu. neg.*) sich dehnen *or* strecken lassen; 5. (*coll.*) zu weit gehen, flunkern, übertreiben, aufschneiden.
3. *s.* 1. das Strecken, (Aus)dehnen, (Aus)weiten; 2. (Sich-)Strecken, (Sich-)Recken, (Sich-)Rekeln; (*coll.*) ***give a –,*** sich recken; 3. (*fig.*) die (An)spannung, Anstrengung, Überschreitung, Übertreibung, Überspannung; (*sl.*) ***at a –,*** unter Aufgebot *or* Aufbietung *or* Anspannung aller *or* der letzten Kräfte; ***by any*** or ***every – of the imagination,*** unter Aufbietung aller Phantasie, beim besten Willen; ***by no – of the imagination,*** auch nicht unter Aufbietung aller Phantasie, (auch) beim besten Willen nicht; ***on the –,*** unter Spannung (*as a spring*), (*fig.*) angespannt, (über)angestrengt (*as nerves*); 4. der Zeitraum, die (Zeit)spanne (*in time*), Strecke, Fläche, Ausdehnung (*in space*); ***at a –,*** ununterbrochen, ohne Unterbrechung, in einem Zuge, durchlaufend, hintereinander; 5. (*sl.*) die Zuchthausstrafe; ***be doing a –,*** eine Strafe absitzen; ***go up for a –,*** brummen.

stretcher [ˈstretʃə], *s.* 1. der Spanner (*shoes, trousers etc.*), Strecker, die Streckvorrichtung, das Streckwerkzeug; 2. der Spannstab (*of an umbrella*); 3. Fußlatte, das Stemmbrett (*in a boat*); 4. die Tragbahre, Krankentrage, Pritsche (*for the sick etc.*); 5. (*Build.*) der Läufer; 6. (*coll.*) die Übertreibung, Flunkerei. **stretcher-bearer,** *s.* der Krankenträger. **stretchy,** *adj.* (*coll.*) dehnbar, elastisch; (*coll.*) ***be –,*** sich rekeln wollen.

strew [stru:], *irr.v.t.* (be)streuen (*an area*); (*also* – ***about***) ausstreuen (*material*). **strewn, 1.** *p.p. of* **strew. 2.** *adj.* bestreut.

stria [ˈstraiə], *s.* (*pl.* **striae** [ˈstraii:]) 1. der Streifen, die Furche, Riefe (*on shells*); 2. Riffel (*on pillars*); 3. (*Geol.*) (*usu. pl.*) (Gletscher)schramme, Kritze; 4. *pl.* (*Med.*) Striemen, Narben (*pl.*). **striate, 1.** [ˈstraiət], *adj.* gestreift; gerief(el)t, gefurcht. **2.** [straiˈeit], *v.t.* 1. furchen, riefe(l)n; 2. (*Geol.*) kritzen. **striated** [–ˈeitid], *adj. See* **striate, 1. striation** [–ˈeiʃən], *s.* die Riefelung; Furchung, Riefenbildung, Furchenbildung, Streifenbildung; (*collect.*) Furchen, Riefen, (*Geol.*) Schrammen, Kritzen (*pl.*). **striature** [–ˈeitʃə], *s.* (die Anordnung der) Furchen *etc.*

stricken [ˈstrikən], **1.** *adj.* 1. (*esp. Hunt.*) getroffen; (*Poet.*) – ***field,*** (verlassenes) Schlachtfeld; 2. (*of a p.*) ergriffen (***with,*** von) (*fear etc.*), befallen (von) (*sickness*), heimgesucht, schwer betroffen (von) (*mishaps*); 3. (*fig.*) gebeugt, niedergeschlagen; – ***in years,*** hochbetagt, hochbejahrt, von Alter gebeugt. **2.** *p.p. of* **strike.**

strickle [strikl], **1.** *s.* das Streichholz (*for corn*), Modelholz, die Abstreichlatte (*casting*), das Schleifbrett. **2.** *v.t.* glattstreichen, abstreichen.

strict [strikt], *adj.* streng (***with,*** mit *or* gegen); genau, rigoros, exact, peinlich, strikt (***about, in*** (***the matter of***), in (*Dat.*)); ***in – confidence,*** streng vertraulich; – ***seclusion,*** völlige Abgeschiedenheit; ***in the – sense*** (***of the word***), ***–ly speaking,*** genau genommen. **strictness,** *s.* die Strenge, Genauigkeit.

stricture [ˈstriktʃə], *s.* 1. (*Med.*) die Striktur, krankhafte Verengerung; 2 (*fig.*) (*usu. pl.*) tadelnde Bemerkung (***on,*** über (*Acc.*)), scharfe Kritik (an (*Dat.*)).

stridden [ˈstridən], *p.p. of* **stride.**

stride [straid], **1.** *s.* 1. langer *or* großer Schritt; (*coll.*) ***get into one's –,*** in Schwung *or* Fahrt *or* auf Touren kommen; ***take long –s,*** lange Schritte machen; (*coll.*) ***take in one's –,*** ohne Schwierigkeiten *or* mühelos *or* so nebenbei *or* spielend bewältigen; 2. die Schrittlänge; 3. (*fig.*) der Fortschritt; ***make rapid –s,*** schnelle Forschritte machen. **2.** *irr.v.i.* schreiten, große Schritte machen, mit langen Schritten gehen; – ***out,*** tüchtig ausschreiten. **3.** *irr.v.t.* 1. abschreiten, durchschreiten, überschreiten; 2. rittlings sitzen auf (*Dat.*) (*a horse*).

stridence, stridency [ˈstraidəns(i)], *s.* die Schrillheit, das Kreischende, Grelle. **strident,** *adj.* schrill, kreischend, grell, knarrend.

stridulate [ˈstridjuleit], *v.i.* zirpen, schwirren. **stridulation** [–ˈleiʃən], *s.* das Zirpen, Schwirren.

strife [straif], *s.* der Streit, Hader, Zank, Zwist; Krieg, Kampf; (*fig.*) ***at –,*** uneins.

striga [ˈstraigə], *s.* (*pl.* **strigae** [ˈstraidʒi]) 1. die Strichborste, das Striegelhaar; 2. (*Archit.*) die Riefe. **strigillose** [striˈdʒilous], **strigose** [ˈstraigous], *adj.* borstig, striegelig.

strike [straik], **1.** *s.* 1. der Stoß, Schlag, Streich; 2. Glockenschlag (*of clock*); 3. (*Artil.*) Treffer, Aufschlag; 4. (*Mil., esp. Av.*) Angriff; 5. Streik, Ausstand; ***on –,*** ausständig, streikend; ***be on –,*** streiken; ***call off a –,*** einen Streik abbrechen *or* abblasen; ***come out on –, go on –,*** in Streik treten; 6. (*Geol.*) das Streichen, die (Streich)-richtung; 7. der Fund (*of oil, ore etc.*), (*coll.*) Treffer, Glücksfall; (*Angling*) das Anbeißen; (*coll.*) ***make a – with,*** Erfolg haben mit; 8. (*Tech.*) das Abstreichholz.
2. *irr.v.t.* 1. schlagen, einen Schlag geben (*Dat.*) (*a p. or th.*); – ***terror into him,*** ihm einen Schrecken einflößen *or* einjagen; 2. ausführen, versetzen (*a blow*); – ***a blow for,*** eine Lanze brechen für; 3. treffen, stoßen an (*Acc.*) *or* auf (*Acc.*), zusammenstoßen mit; (*Naut.*) – ***bottom,*** auflaufen, auf Grund laufen; (*fig.*) einen Tiefpunkt erreicht haben; – ***his ear,*** sein Ohr treffen; – ***his eye,*** ihm auffallen, ihm in die Augen springen; – ***one's head against,*** mit dem Kopfe stoßen gegen; – ***oil,*** Petroleum entdecken, (*fig.*) Glück haben, es gut treffen; – ***a rock,*** auf einen Felsen auflaufen; – ***his sight,*** see – ***his eye***; 4. ***the clock has struck the hour,*** die Uhr hat voll geschlagen; (*Naut.*) – ***8 bells,*** 8 Glas glasen; (*Mus.*) – ***the key,*** die Taste anschlagen; – ***a note,*** einen Ton anschlagen (*also fig.*); 5. einschlagen in (*Acc.*) (*as lightning*); 6. prägen, münzen (*coins etc.*); 7. streichen, (weg)-fieren, niederholen (*a flag, sails etc.*); abbrechen (*a tent*); – ***camp,*** das Lager abbrechen; 8. anstreichen, anzünden (*a match*); – ***a light,*** Feuer anschlagen; 9. – ***an attitude,*** eine Haltung annehmen *or* einnehmen; – ***an average,*** den Durchschnitt nehmen; – ***a*** or ***the balance,*** den Saldo ziehen, (*fig.*) einen Ausgleich finden; – ***a bargain,*** einen Handel abschließen, handelseinig werden; (*Math.*) – ***a mean,*** einen Mittelwert errechnen; 10. (*fig.*) auffallen (*Dat.*); einfallen (*Dat.*), in den Sinn kommen (*Dat.*); Eindruck machen auf (*Acc.*), vorkommen (*Dat.*), beeindrucken; – ***his fancy,*** ihm gefallen, sein Interesse erwecken; ***it –s me as strange,*** es kommt mir sonderbar vor, es mutet mich fremd an; ***the thought struck me,*** mir kam der Gedanke, mir fiel es ein; 11. – ***root***(***s***), Wurzel schlagen *or* fassen,

einwurzeln (*also fig.*); 12. – ***work,*** die Arbeit niederlegen, in Streik *or* den Ausstand treten, streiken.
(a) (*with adj.*) – ***blind,*** blind machen, erblinden; – ***dead,*** erschlagen; – ***dumb,*** zum Schweigen bringen, betäuben; (*sl.*) – ***me pink!*** Gott strafe mich!
(b) (*with adv.*) – ***down,*** niederschlagen, niederstrecken, zu Boden schlagen, fällen; (*of disease*) (*usu. pass.*) ***be struck down,*** ergriffen sein; – ***off,*** 1. abschlagen, abhauen; 2. (*Typ.*) abziehen; – ***out,*** 1. ausstreichen, tilgen; 2. (*fig.*) einschlagen, bahnen (*a path*); – ***up,*** anstimmen (*tune*), anknüpfen (*friendship*).
(c) (*with prep.*) – ***off,*** streichen von (*list etc.*); – ***him off the roll,*** ihn von der Liste streichen; – ***with,*** erfüllen mit (*awe etc.*); (*fig.*) ***be struck with,*** ergriffen werden von, eingenommen sein von.
3. *irr.v.i.* 1. schlagen (*also of clocks*), losschlagen, zustoßen, ausholen, (hin)zielen (***at,*** nach); (*Prov.*) – ***while the iron is hot,*** das Eisen schmieden, solange es heiß ist; – ***at the root of,*** an der Wurzel treffen; – ***back,*** zurückschlagen, sich zur Wehr setzen; ***the hour has struck,*** es hat voll geschlagen; ***his hour has struck,*** seine Stunde hat geschlagen; – ***inwards,*** (sich) nach innen schlagen (*of disease*); – ***out,*** einen Schlag führen (***at,*** gegen), einschlagen (auf (*Acc.*)); zum Schlag ausholen (nach); ausschreiten, loslegen, (*swimming*) ausgreifen (***for,*** nach); (*fig.*) – ***out for o.s.,*** sich selbst einen Weg bahnen; 2. (an)schlagen, stoßen (***against,*** gegen; ***on,*** an (*Acc.*)), auflaufen, aufstoßen (auf (*Acc.*)) (*on a rock*); – ***home,*** sicher *or* ins Ziel treffen, sitzen (*of blows*), (*fig.*) Eindruck machen, wirken, seine Wirkung tun; 3. – ***up,*** anheben, einsetzen (*of musician, singer*); 4. fallen, auftreffen (***on,*** auf (*Acc.*)) (*of light*); einschlagen (*of lightning*); 5. sich entzünden (*matches*); 6. (*of fish*) anbeißen; 7. (*Hort.*) einwurzeln, Wurzel schlagen; 8. sich ergeben, die Flagge streichen; 9. streiken, die Arbeit einstellen; 10. (*fig.*) auffallen, in die Augen fallen, Eindruck machen.

strike|-bound, *adj.* vom Streik betroffen, bestreikt. **--breaker,** *s.* der Streikbrecher. **--pay,** *s.* das Streikgeld, Streikgelder (*pl.*). **--picket,** *s.* der Streikposten.

striker ['straikə], *s.* 1. (*Spt. etc.*) der (die) Schläger(in); 2. (*in a smithy*) Zuschläger; 3. (*Tech.*) Schläger, das Schlaggerät; der Hammer, Klöppel (*of bell etc.*), Schlagbolzen (*of a gun*); 4. (*in industry*) Streikende(r), Ausständige(r). **striking,** *adj.* 1. schlagend (*also fig.*); 2. Schlag– (*clock etc.*); 3. (*fig.*) auffallend, bemerkenswert, wirkungsvoll, eindrucksvoll, treffend; – ***facts,*** nicht zu übersehende Tatsachen; – ***likeness,*** sprechende *or* verblüffende Ähnlichkeit. **striking|-circle,** *s.* (*Hockey*) der Schußkreis. **--distance,** *s.* die Schlagweite, der Schlagbereich. **--force,** *s.* (*Mil.*) die Eingriffstruppe. **strikingness,** *s.* das Auffallende, Treffende. **striking|-power,** *s.* (*Mil.*) die Schlagkraft. **--velocity,** *s.* die Aufschlagsgeschwindigkeit (*of a shell*).

string [striŋ], **1.** *s.* 1. der Bindfaden, die Schnur, das Band; (*fig.*) Gängelband; (*fig.*) ***be a second –,*** die zweite Geige spielen, zur zweiten Garnitur gehören, zweitrangig sein; (*fig.*) ***have him on a –,*** ihn am Bändchen haben *or* am Gängelband führen; ***hold all the –s,*** alle Fäden in der Hand haben; (*fig.*) ***pull the –s,*** die Fäden in der Hand haben, der Drahtzieher sein; ***be tied to one's mother's apron –s,*** an Mutters Schürzenzipfel hängen; ***with no –s attached,*** ohne Klauseln *or* Haken; 2. die Sehne (*of a bow*); ***have two –s to one's bow,*** zwei Eisen im Feuer haben; 3. (*Mus.*) die Saite; *pl.* Streicher (*pl.*), Streichinstrumente (*pl.*); ***be always harping on the same –,*** immer auf der alten Leier spielen; 4. die Schnur, Kette (*of pearls etc.*); 5. (*Bot.*) Fiber, Faser; 6. (*coll.*) Reihe, Kette, Folge. **2.** *irr.v.t.* 1. (auf)reihen, aufziehen (*beads etc.*); (*coll.*) – ***out,*** auseinanderhalten, auseinanderstellen; (*fig. coll.*) – ***together,*** aneinanderreihen, verknüpfen; (*sl.*) – ***up,*** aufhängen, aufknüpfen (*a p.*); 2. besaiten, mit Saiten beziehen, bespannen (*musical instrument, racket*); spannen (*bow*); (*fig.*) (*usu. p.p.*) anspannen; ***highly strung,*** erregbar, reizbar, nervös, überempfindlich, feinbesaitet; 3. abziehen (*beans*); 4. (*also* – ***up***) zubinden, verschnüren, (zu)schnüren. **3.** *irr.v.i.* 1. Fäden ziehen (*of fluids*); 2. (*coll.*) – ***along with him,*** sich ihm (*or* seinen Ansichten) anschließen, nach seiner Pfeife tanzen.

string|-bag, *s.* das Einkaufsnetz. – **band,** *s.* die Streichkapelle. **--beans,** *pl.* grüne Bohnen (*pl.*). **--course,** *s.* (*Archit.*) der Sims, Fries.

stringed [striŋd], *adj.* (*Mus.*) Saiten–, Streich–.

stringency ['strindʒənsi], *s.* 1. die Strenge, Schärfe, Härte; 2. zwingende Kraft, die Bündigkeit (*of argument*); 3. Knappheit (*money etc.*). **stringent,** *adj.* 1. streng, scharf, hart; 2. bindend, zwingend; 3. kräftig, bündig, eindrucksvoll; nachdrücklich, überzeugend; 4. knapp.

stringer ['striŋə], *s.* der Tragbalken, Streckbalken, Längsbalken. **stringiness,** *s.* die Faserigkeit, Zähigkeit, Zaddrigkeit. **stringing,** *s.* (*Mus.*) die Besaitung, der Bezug (*of violin etc.*).

string| instrument, *s.* das Saiteninstrument. – **quartet,** *s.* das Streichquartett. **stringy** ['striŋi], *adj.* faserig, zäh, zaddrig (*as meat*), zähflüssig, klebrig, Fäden ziehend (*of liquid*).

strip [strip], **1.** *v.t.* 1. abstreifen, abziehen; abkratzen (*paint from walls*); (ab)schälen, abrinden, enthülsen (*fruit etc.*); – ***a bed,*** ein Bett abziehen; – ***a screw*** or ***the thread,*** das Gewinde überdrehen; 2. entkleiden (*also fig.*), ausziehen, entblößen (*a p.*); – ***him naked*** or ***to the skin,*** ihn bis auf die Haut ausziehen; 3. abtakeln (*ships*), auseinandernehmen, abmontieren, demontieren (*machines*); 4. – ***him of a th.,*** ihm etwas entziehen, ihn einer S. (*Gen.*) berauben *or* (*of a post,* des Amtes) entkleiden. **2.** *v.i.* sich ausziehen. **3.** *s.* (schmaler) Streifen; ***air*** or ***landing –,*** der Landestreifen; ***comic –,*** – ***cartoon,*** Comics (*pl.*); – ***cultivation,*** die Dreifelderwirtschaft; – ***iron,*** das Bandeisen; – ***lighting,*** die Neonbeleuchtung; (*sl.*) ***tear a – off him,*** ihm eine Moralpauke halten, ihm den Kopf waschen *or* zurechtsetzen, ihn gehörig herunterputzen.

stripe [straip], **1.** *s.* 1. der Streifen, Strich; (*Am.*) ***stars and –s,*** das Sternenbanner; 2. der Striemen, die Schwiele; 3. der Streich, Hieb, Schlag; 4. (*Mil.*) die Tresse, Litze, der Ärmelstreifen; ***get one's –s,*** die Tressen bekommen, Unteroffizier werden; ***wound –,*** das Verwundetenabzeichen. **2.** *v.t.* streifen. **striped** [–t], *adj.* gestreift, streifig.

stripling ['stripliŋ], *s.* junger Bursche, der Grünschnabel.

stripper ['stripə], *s.* 1. (*Tech.*) die Schälmaschine; 2. (*coll.*) Nackttänzerin, Schönheitstänzerin; 3. ***paint –,*** der Farbentferner. **stripping,** *s.* das Abziehen, Abstreifen; die Entfärbung (*of walls etc.*); – ***agent,*** das Abziehmittel, Entfärbungsmittel; – ***bath,*** die Abziehflotte; – ***knife,*** der Farbabkratzer.

striptease ['stripti:z], **1.** *s.* die Entkleidungsnummer. **2.** *adj.* Nackt–, Entkleidungs–.

stripy ['straipi], *adj. See* **striped.**

strive [straiv], *irr.v.i.* 1. streben (***after, for,*** nach), sich mühen (um); 2. sich anstrengen, sich (*Dat.*) Mühe geben, bestrebt sein (***to do,*** zu tun); 3. streiten, kämpfen, ringen; – ***against,*** ankämpfen *or* sich sträuben gegen.

strode [stroud], *imperf. of* **stride.**

[1]**stroke** [strouk], **1.** *s.* 1. der Strich (*of brush or pen*), Zug (*of pen*); ***down –,*** der Abstrich, Grundstrich; ***up–,*** der Haarstrich; ***at*** or ***with a – of the pen,*** mit einem Federzug; ***put the finishing – to,*** die letzte Hand legen an (*Acc.*), den letzten Schliff geben (*Dat.*); 2. der Schlag, Streich, Hieb (*of an axe etc.*), Stoß (*billiards, swimming*); (Schicksals)-schlag; ***at a*** or ***one –,*** mit einem Schlage; – ***of business,*** ein gutes Geschäft; – ***of (good) luck,*** der Glückstreffer, Glücksfall; ***not do a – of work,*** keinen Finger rühren; 3. (*Spt.*) der Schlag, die Schlagart; ***breast –,*** der Bruststil (*swimming*); 4. der Schlag (*of a clock*); ***on the –,*** pünktlich; ***on the***

– *of three,* Schlag drei; 5. (*Med.*) der Schlag(anfall); *have a –,* einen Schlaganfall bekommen; 6. (*Rowing*) der Schlagmann; *row –,* als Vormann *or* Schlagman rudern; 7. (*Tech.*) der (Kolben)hub; die Hubhöhe; der Takt (*of an engine*); *four-–,* Viertakt– (*engine*); 8. (*fig.*) die Leistung; – *of genius,* geniale Leistung; *masterly –,* das Meisterstück. **2.** *v.t.* – *a boat,* als Schlagmann rudern.

[2]**stroke,** *v.t.* streichen über (*Acc.*); streicheln; – (*up*) *the wrong way,* ärgern, reizen.

stroke-oar, strokesman [-smən], *s.* (*Rowing*) der Schlagmann.

stroll [stroul], **1.** *s.* das Herumziehen, Herumschlendern; kleiner Spaziergang, der Bummel; *go for* or *take a –,* einen Bummel machen. **2.** *v.i.* spazierengehen, bummeln, herumspazieren, (herum)schlendern. **stroller,** *s.* der Bummler, Spaziergänger. **strolling,** *adj.* umherziehend; – *player,* wandernder Schauspieler; – *players,* die Wandertruppe.

stroma [ˈstroumə], *s.* (*pl.* **-ta** [–mətə]) das Bindegewebe, Grundgewebe.

strong [strɔŋ], **1.** *adj.* 1. stark (*of p. or th.*); kräftig, gesund, robust (*of p.*); – *candidate,* aussichtsreicher Kandidat; *of – character,* charakterfest, willensstark; – *constitution,* robuste Gesundheit; *have – feelings about,* sich erregen über (*Acc.*); (*coll.*) – *as a horse* or *an ox,* robust, (kern)gesund, rüstig; (*fig.*) – *in,* stark *or* gut *or* tüchtig in (*Dat.*), begabt für; – *language,* Kraftausdrücke (*pl.*); *use – language,* sich kraftvoll *or* derb ausdrücken, fluchen; – *mind,* kluger Kopf; *1000 –,* 1000 Mann stark; – *will,* die Willensstärke; – *on the wing,* schon gut flügge (*of young birds*); 2. stabil, fest, dauerhaft (*of th.*); *my – point,* meine starke Seite; 3. heftig (*as wind*); (*Naut.*) – *breeze,* starker Wind; (*Naut.*) – *gale,* der Sturm; 4. kräftig, laut (*as voice etc.*); 5. scharf, ranzig (*as a taste, smell etc.*); 6. hell, grell (*as light*); 7. (*fig.*) heftig, entschieden, ausgeprägt (*as attitudes*); energisch, drastisch, gewaltsam (*as methods*); *with a – hand,* mit Gewalt; *a – hold over* or *on,* großen Einfluß auf (*Acc.*), große Macht über (*Acc.*); 8. (*fig.*) zwingend, überzeugend, triftig, gewichtig, nachdrücklich (*as reasons*); – *conviction,* feste Überzeugung; – *impression,* tiefer Eindruck; – *point,* entscheidender Punkt, der Schwerpunkt (*of argument etc.*); 9. (*Comm.*) – *demand,* lebhafte Nachfrage; – *market,* fester Markt; 10. (*Gram.*) stark. **2.** *adv.* (*sl.*) *be going –,* gut in Schuß sein, wohlauf *or* auf der Höhe sein; *come* or *go it –,* (tüchtig) ins Geschirr gehen, sich (tüchtig) ins Geschirr werfen.

strong|-arm, *attrib. adj.* (*coll.*) Gewalt–, Zwangs–. **--bodied,** *adj.* stark, voll (*of wine*). **-box,** *s.* die Geldkassette. **-hold,** *s.* 1. die Festung, Feste; 2. (*fig.*) Hochburg, das Bollwerk.

strongly [ˈstrɔŋli], *adv.* kräftig, heftig; *be – of the opinion,* der festen Meinung sein; *feel – about,* sich erregen über (*Acc.*); – *recommended,* sehr zu empfehlen(d).

strong|-minded, *adj.* willensstark, unerschütterlich. **--mindedness,** *s.* die Willensstärke, Unerschütterlichkeit. **-point,** *s.* (*Mil.*) der Stützpunkt. **-room,** *s.* die Stahlkammer, das Panzergewölbe, der Tresorraum, (Geld)tresor. **--smelling,** *adj.* stark duftend. **--willed,** *adj.* entschlossen, hartnäckig, eigenwillig.

strontia(n) [ˈstrɔnʃiə(n)], *s.* die Strontianerde, das Strontiumoxyd. **strontium** [–ʃiəm, –tiəm], *s.* das Strontium.

strop [strɔp], **1.** *s.* 1. der Streichriemen, Abzieher (*for razors*); 2. (*Naut.*) Stropp. **2.** *v.t.* abziehen.

strophe [ˈstroufi], *s.* die Strophe. **strophic,** *adj.* strophisch.

strove [strouv], *imperf. of* **strive.**

struck [strʌk], *imperf., p.p. of* **strike**; (*fig.*) – *by,* beeindruckt durch; (*sl.*) – *on,* verschossen *or* verknallt in (*Acc.*) (*a girl etc.*); (*oft. neg.*) *not – on,* gar nicht begeistert von.

structural [ˈstrʌktʃərəl], *adj.* 1. strukturell, baulich, Bau–, Konstruktions–, Struktur–; – *analysis,* die Baustatik; – *change,* die Strukturwandlung; – *parts,* Bauteile (*pl.*); – *error,* der Konstruktionsfehler; – *steelwork,* das Stahlfachwerk; – *timber,* das Zimmerholz, Bauholz; (*Av.*) – *weight,* das Rüstgewicht; – *works,* bauliche Anlagen (*pl.*); 2. organisch (*disease*); 3. (*Geol.*) tektonisch.

structure [ˈstrʌktʃə], *s.* 1. das Bauwerk, Gebäude, der Bau; 2. (*Biol.*) Organismus; 3. (*Geol.*) die Tektonik; 4. (*Phys., Chem.*) Struktur, das Gefüge, der Aufbau; 5. (*fig.*) die Struktur, Anordnung, Gliederung, Zusammensetzung; *economic –,* das Wirtschaftssystem; *price –,* die Preisstruktur; *sentence –,* der Satzbau; – *of society,* der Aufbau der Gesellschaft. **structured,** *adj.* 1. (organisch) gegliedert; 2. (*as suff.*) –gebaut, –gefügt. **structureless,** *adj.* unorganisch, strukturlos, ohne Gliederung.

struggle [strʌgl], **1.** *s.* das Ringen, Sträuben, Streben; der Streit, Kampf (*for,* um); *carry on a –,* einen Kampf durchführen; – *for existence,* der Existenzkampf, Kampf ums Dasein; *mental –,* der Seelenkampf. **2.** *v.i.* 1. sich anstrengen, sich (ab)mühen, Anstrengungen machen; (*coll.*) – *along,* sich durchschlagen; – *to one's feet,* mühsam hochkommen *or* auf die Beine kommen; 2. sich winden, sich wehren *or* sträuben, zappeln (*against,* gegen); 3. ringen, kämpfen, streiten (*for,* für; *with,* mit); – *for breath,* nach Atem ringen.

strum [strʌm], **1.** *v.i.* klimpern (*on,* auf (*Dat.*)). **2.** *v.t.* klimpern auf (*Dat.*).

struma [ˈstru:mə], *s.* 1. die Skrofel; 2. der Kropf.

strumming [ˈstrʌmiŋ], *s.* das Geklimper.

strumose [ˈstru:mous], **strumous,** *adj.* 1. Kropf–, kropfartig; 2. skrofulös.

strumpet [ˈstrʌmpit], *s.* (*obs.*) die Dirne, Metze, Hure.

strung [strʌŋ], *imperf., p.p. of* **string.**

[1]**strut** [strʌt], **1.** *v.i.* sich brüsten *or* spreizen, stolzieren. **2.** *s. See* **strutting, 1.**

[2]**strut,** *s.* der Strebebalken, die Strebe, Stütze, Steife, Verstrebung.

struthious [ˈstru:θiəs], *adj.* (*Orn.*) Strauß–.

[1]**strutting** [ˈstrʌtiŋ], *s.* 1. das Einherstolzieren, Sichbrüsten; 2. (*fig.*) die Affektiertheit, Prahlerei.

[2]**strutting,** *s.* (*Tech.*) Strebebalken (*pl.*); die Versteifung, Verstrebung.

strychnine [ˈstriknin], *s.* das Strychnin.

stub [stʌb], **1.** *s.* 1. der Stumpf, Stummel; 2. (*also* –*nail*) Kuppnagel; 3. (*coll.*) (*also* – *end*) die Kippe; 4. (*coll.*) der Talon, Kontrollabschnitt (*of cheque etc.*). **2.** *v.t.* 1. (*usu.* – *up*) roden (*land*), ausroden, entwurzeln (*stumps*); 2. (*coll.*) sich stoßen an (*Dat.*) (*one's toe etc.*); 3. (*coll.*) – *out,* ausdrücken, ausmachen (*cigarette*).

stubble [stʌbl], *s.* 1. die Stoppel; 2. das Stoppelfeld; 3. der Stoppelbart, (Bart)stoppeln (*pl.*). **stubbly,** *adj.* Stoppel–, stopp(e)lig.

stubborn [ˈstʌbən], *adj.* 1. hartnäckig, widerspenstig, störrisch, verstockt, eigensinnig, dickköpfig, starrköpfig, halsstarrig (*of p.*); 2. unnachgiebig, unbeugsam, beharrlich, starr, standhaft (*of th.*); 3. (*Metall.*) strengflüssig, spröde. **stubbornness,** *s.* 1. die Verstocktheit, Hartnäckigkeit, Halsstarrigkeit, der Eigensinn, Starrsinn (*of a p.*); 2. die Unnachgiebigkeit, Unbeugsamkeit, Starrheit, Standhaftigkeit, Beharrlichkeit, Entschlossenheit; 3. (*Metall.*) Spröde, Sprödigkeit, Strengflüssigkeit.

stubby [ˈstʌbi], *adj.* (*coll.*) untersetzt, stämmig.

stub| end, *s. See* **stub, 1,** 3. **– mortise,** *s.* versetztes Zapfenloch. **--nail,** *s. See* **stub, 1,** 2. **– tenon,** *s.* der Fußstapfen.

stucco [ˈstʌkou], **1.** *s.* 1. der Stuck, Verputz; 2. (*also* –*work*) die Stukkatur, Stuckarbeit, Stuckverzierung. **2.** *v.t.* verputzen, mit Stuck verzieren.

stuck [stʌk], *imperf., p.p. of* [2]**stick**; (*coll.*) *be –,* steckenbleiben, festsitzen, nicht weiter(kommen) können; (*coll.*) *be – for,* verlegen sein um. **stuck-up,** *adj.* (*coll.*) aufgeblasen, hochnäsig.

[1]**stud** [stʌd], **1.** *s.* 1. der Knauf, Beschlagnagel; 2. (Vorhemd– *or* Kragen)knopf, (*Am.*) Manschetten-

knopf; 3. (*Tech.*) Steg, die Warze, Stiftschraube; 4. (*Build.*) der Ständer, Pfosten, die (Wand)säule. **2.** *v.t.* 1. beschlagen, verzieren (*with nails etc.*); 2. (*fig.*) besetzen, bestreuen, besäen.

[2]**stud,** *s.* das Gestüt; (*collect.*) Pferde (*pl.*) eines Rennstalls, der Stall; ***at* –,** zur *or* auf Zucht.

stud|-bolt, *s.* der Schraubenbolzen. **--book,** *s.* das Zuchtstammbuch; (*horses*) Gestütbuch, Stutbuch. **--chain,** *s.* die Stegkette.

studding-sail [stænsl], *s.* (*Naut.*) das Leesegel, Beisegel.

student ['stju:dənt], *s.* 1. (*Univ.*) der (die) Student(in), Hörer(in), Studierende(r); *pl.* (*collect.*) die Studentenschaft, Hörer (*pl.*) (*of a professor*); ***– body,*** die Studentenschaft; ***– of law,*** der Student der Rechte; ***medical –,*** der Student der Medizin; ***–s' hostel,*** das Studentenheim; ***–s' union,*** der Studentenausschuß; 2. der (die) Schüler(in); 3. der (die) Forscher(in), Gelehrte(r); ***be a – of,*** studieren. **studentship,** *s.* 1. das Stipendium; ***travelling –,*** das Reisestipendium; 2. die Studentenzeit.

stud|-farm, *s.* das Gestüt. **--horse,** *s.* der Zuchthengst, Beschäler.

studied ['stʌdid], *adj.* 1. durchdacht, wohlüberlegt, vorbedacht, vorsätzlich, geflissentlich; 2. gesucht, gekünstelt, (ein)studiert; 3. gelehrt, belesen, beschlagen, bewandert (*in,* in (*Dat.*)).

studio ['stju:diou], *s.* 1. der (Künstler)atelier; ***– couch,*** die Bettcouch; 2. der (Film)atelier; (*Rad.*) der Senderaum, Aufnahmeraum.

studious ['stju:diəs], *adj.* 1. fleißig, arbeitsam, emsig, lernbegierig; 2. gelehrt(enhaft); 3. bedacht (*of,* auf (*Acc.*)), besorgt, beflissen, bemüht (um); 4. gewissenhaft, geflissentlich, gesucht. **studiousness,** *s.* der Fleiß, Eifer, die Emsigkeit, Beflissenheit, Gewissenhaftigkeit.

stud-mare, *s.* die Zuchtstute.

study ['stʌdi], **1.** *s.* 1. das Studieren, Lernen, (wissenschaftliches) Studium; das Forschen, die Forschung, wissenschaftliche Untersuchung, die Studie (*in, of,* über (*Acc.*) *or* zu); ***brown –,*** die Träumerei, Gedankenverlorenheit; ***make a – of,*** eingehend studieren; (*fig.*) ***make a – of doing,*** es darauf absehen *or* sich (*Dat.*) zum Ziel setzen *or* sich (*Dat.*) Mühe geben, zu tun; 2. (*Mus.*) die Etüde; (*Art, Liter.*) Studie, Skizze, der Entwurf; 3. das (Studien)fach, der Studienzweig; das Studienobjekt; 4. Arbeitszimmer, Herrenzimmer, Studierzimmer; 5. (*fig.*) Streben, Bemühen, der Fleiß, Eifer. **2.** *v.t.* 1. studieren; (er)lernen, einstudieren (*a part etc.*); 2. sorgsam beobachten, betrachten, durchforschen, mustern; 3. sich bemühen um, bedacht sein auf (*Acc.*); ***– his wishes,*** seinen Wünschen entgegenkommen. **3.** *v.i.* studieren (*at a univ.*); Studien betreiben; ***– for*** sich vorbereiten auf (*Acc.*) (*a profession*).

study-group, *s.* die Arbeitsgemeinschaft.

stuff [stʌf], **1.** *s.* 1. der Stoff (*also fig.*), das Material, der Rohstoff; (*sl.*) ***good –!*** ausgezeichnet! trefflich! bravo! (*sl.*) ***do one's –,*** das Seine tun; (*sl.*) ***know one's –,*** Bescheid wissen; (*sl.*) ***that's the –!*** so ist's richtig! ***green –,*** das Gemüse, Grünzeug; ***the – that heroes are made of,*** das Holz, aus dem Helden geschnitzt sind; 2. (*Text.*) der Wollstoff, das Zeug, Gewebe; ***– gown,*** der Wolltalar (*of lawyer*); 3. (*Paperm.*) das Ganzzeug, die Papiermasse; ***– box,*** der Stoffauflauf; 4. (*Build.*) der Baustoff, das Baumaterial; 5. (*coll.*) Zeug, Gerümpel, der Plunder; ***– (and nonsense)!*** dummes Zeug! **2.** *v.t.* 1. vollstopfen, vollpfropfen, vollpacken, (an)füllen; (*vulg.*) ***– o.s.,*** sich vollstopfen *or* überfüllen *or* überessen; ***– up,*** zustopfen, verstopfen (*a hole etc.*); (*coll.*) ***–ed shirt,*** aufgeblasene Null, vornehmer Wichtigtuer; 2. ausstopfen (*dead animals etc.*); 3. polstern (*chair etc.*); 4. (*Cul.*) farcieren, füllen; 5. (*coll.*) stecken, schieben, packen, stopfen (*into,* in (*Acc.*)). **3.** *v.i.* (*vulg.*) sich vollstopfen, fressen.

stuffiness ['stʌfinis], *s.* 1. die Dumpfigkeit, Stickigkeit, Muffigkeit, Schwüle (*air etc.*); 2. (*coll.*) Verstaubtheit, Pedanterie, Beschränktheit; Langweiligkeit, Fadheit (*of p.*).

stuffing ['stʌfiŋ], *s.* das Stopfen, Füllen; Verstopfen; (*furniture*) Ausstopfen, Polstern; das Füllhaar, Polstermaterial; (*Cul.*) Füllsel, die Füllung, Farce; (*fig.*) das Füllmaterial, Füllsel; (*coll.*) ***knock the – out of him,*** ihn kleinkriegen *or* gefügig machen.

stuffy ['stʌfi], *adj.* 1. stickig, dumpf, schwül, muffig, drückend; 2. verstopft (*nose etc.*); 3. (*coll.*) langweilig, fade; verstaubt, verknöchert, pedantisch, beschränkt.

stultification [stʌltifi'keiʃən], *s.* 1. die Blamage, Verdummung, Veralberung; 2. (*Law*) der Beweis der Unzurechnungsfähigkeit. **stultify** ['stʌltifai], *v.t.* 1. lächerlich machen, verdummen, veralbern, zum Narren halten; 2. vereiteln, nutzlos *or* wirkungslos machen, widerlegen; (*Law*) als unzurechnungsfähig erklären; ***– itself,*** sich widersprechen.

stumble [stʌmbl], **1.** *v.i.* 1. stolpern (***over,*** über (*Acc.*)) (*also fig.*), straucheln; ***– into,*** unerwartet geraten in (*Acc.*); ***– across*** or ***(up)on,*** zufällig stoßen auf (*Acc.*), geraten an (*Acc.*), unerwartet finden; 2. (*fig.*) fehlen, einen Fehltritt machen; 3. in der Rede stocken. **2.** *s.* 1. das Straucheln, Stolpern; 2. (*fig.*) der Fehler, Fehltritt. **stumbling,** *s.* das Stolpern, Gestolper. **stumbling-block,** *s.* das Hindernis (*to,* für), der Stein des Anstoßes.

stumer ['stju:mə], *s.* (*sl.*) gefälschte Münze.

stump [stʌmp], **1.** *s.* 1. der Stumpf (*of tree, tooth, limb*), Stummel (*of cigar etc.*), Strunk (*of branch*); ***buy on the –,*** auf dem Stamm kaufen (*timber*); ***go on the –, take the –,*** politische Propagandareise machen; 2. (*Crick.*) der Stab; ***draw (the) –s,*** das Spiel abbrechen; 3. (*Draw.*) der Wischer; 4. (*coll.*) das Holzbein; ***stir one's –s,*** Beine machen, die Beine unter die Arme nehmen. **2.** *v.t.* 1. stoßen (***against,*** an (*Acc.*); ***on,*** auf (*Acc.*)); 2. (*fig.*) (*esp. pass.*) in Verlegenheit setzen, in die Enge treiben, aus der Fassung bringen, verblüffen; (*coll.*) ***be –ed,*** verblüfft *or* ratlos *or* aufgeschmissen sein; 3. (*Crick.*) (*also* ***– out***) den Dreistab eines außerhalb der Schlagmallinie stehenden Schlägers umwerfen; 4. (*Draw.*) abtönen; 5. ***– the country,*** als Wahlredner herumziehen; 6. (*coll.*) ***– up,*** blechen, berappen (*money*). **3.** *v.i.* 1. schwerfällig gehen, stapfen, humpeln; 2. (*sl.*) ***– up,*** mit dem Gelde herausrücken, Kosten bestreiten, bluten *or* herhalten *or* aufkommen müssen (***for,*** für). **stumper,** *s.* 1. (*coll.*) harte Nuß, verblüffende Frage; 2. (*Crick.*) der Torhüter. **stump-orator,** *s.* der Wahlredner, Volksredner. **stumpy,** *adj.* stämmig, untersetzt.

stun [stʌn], *v.t.* 1. betäuben, bewußtlos machen; 2. (*fig.*) niederschmettern, überwältigen; verblüffen, bestürzen, verdutzen.

stung [stʌŋ], *imperf., p.p. of* **sting.**

stunk [stʌŋk], *p.p. of* **stink.**

stunner ['stʌnə], *s.* (*sl.*) 1. etwas Großartiges, famose S., die Pfundsache, Bombensache; 2. der Prachtkerl, das Prachtexemplar; ***she is a –,*** sie ist Klasse. **stunning,** *adj.* 1. betäubend; 2. niederschmetternd; 3. (*sl.*) fabelhaft, sagenhaft, überwältigend, phantastisch, toll, famos.

[1]**stunt** [stʌnt], *v.t.* im Wachstum hindern *or* hemmen, verkümmern lassen, verkrüppeln.

[2]**stunt, 1.** *s.* (*coll.*) die Kraftleistung, Kraftprobe, das Kunststück, Glanzstück; (*Av.*) der Kunstflug; Reklameschlager, das Reklamestück, Schaustück, Bravourstück, die Sensation; großes Tamtam, tolles Ding *or* Stück, der Jux; ***– flying,*** das Kunstfliegen; ***– film,*** der Trickfilm; (*Films*) ***– man,*** das Double; ***– press,*** die Sensationspresse. **2.** *v.i.* (*coll.*) Flugkunststücke machen.

stunted ['stʌntid], *adj.* verkümmert, verkrüppelt. **stuntedness,** *s.* die Verkümmerung, Verkrüppelung.

stunter ['stʌntə], *s.* der Kunstflieger. **stunting,** *s.* das Kunstfliegen.

stupe [stju:p], **1.** *s.* heißer Umschlag, die Bähung.

2. *v.t.* einen heißen Umschlag anlegen *or* auflegen (*Dat.*); bähen.
stupefaction [stju:pi'fækʃən], *s.* 1. die Betäubung, Abstumpfung; 2. (*fig.*) Verblüffung, Bestürzung.
stupendous [stju:'pendəs], *adj.* erstaunlich, gewaltig, enorm, horrend, ungeheuer, riesig. **stupendousness,** *s.* das Ungeheure, Erstaunliche, die Erstaunlichkeit, Gewaltigkeit.
stupified ['stju:pifaid], *adj.* 1. betäubt, abgestumpft; 2. (*fig.*) verblüfft, bestürzt, benommen. **stupify,** *v.t.* 1. betäuben, abstumpfen; 2. verblüffen, bestürzen, verdutzen.
stupid ['stju:pid], *adj.* 1. dumm, töricht, einfältig, albern, blöd, stupid(e), stumpfsinnig; – ***fellow,*** der Dummkopf; 2. (*obs.*) betäubt, benommen (***with,*** von). **stupidity** [stju:'piditi], *s.* die Dummheit, Torheit, Blödheit, Albernheit, Einfalt, Stupidität, der Stumpfsinn. **stupidly,** *adv.* dummerweise.
stupor ['stju:pə], *s.* 1. die Betäubung, Erstarrung; 2. Benommenheit, Stumpfheit, der Stumpfsinn.
sturdiness ['stə:dinis], *s.* die Stärke, Kräftigkeit, Rüstigkeit, Robustheit (*of p.*), Festigkeit, Härte (*of th.*).
[1]**sturdy** ['stə:di], *adj.* stark, kräftig, rüstig, robust, derb, fest, massiv, hart, standhaft.
[2]**sturdy,** *s.* die Drehkrankheit (*of sheep*).
sturgeon ['stə:dʒən], *s.* (*Ichth.*) der Stör.
stutter ['stʌtə], **1.** *v.i.* stottern, stammeln. **2.** *v.t.* (*oft.* – ***out***) hervorstammeln. **3.** *s.* das Stottern, Stammeln; ***have a*** –, stottern. **stutterer,** *s.* der Stotterer, Stammler.
[1]**sty** [stai], **1.** *s.* der (Schweine)stall (*also fig.*). **2.** *v.t.* in einem Schweinestall halten.
[2]**sty(e),** *s.* (*Med.*) das Gerstenkorn (***in,*** an (*Dat.*)).
Stygian ['stidʒiən], *adj.* stygisch; höllisch, teuflisch, düster, finster.
style [stail], **1.** *s.* 1. der Stil, die Ausdruckweise, Schreibweise; (guter) Stil, die Eleganz, Vornehmheit; der (Bau)stil, die Bauart, der (Kunst)stil, die Manier, Technik, das Genre; die Lebensart, der Lebensstil, die Mode; Art (und Weise); Aufmachung, Ausführung, Machart, der Typ; ***in*** –, stilvoll; ***in the*** – ***of,*** im Stil *or* in der Manier von; (*coll.*) ***in fine*** –, fein, nobel; ***latest*** –, letzte *or* neueste Mode; ***in*** (***grand*** or ***great***) –, auf großem Fuße; (*coll.*) ***that*** – ***of behaviour, behaviour of that*** –, derartiges Benehmen; ***in the same*** –, in derselben Ausführung *or* (Mach)art; 2. die Anrede, Benennung, Bezeichnung, der Titel; ***under the*** – ***of,*** unter dem Namen *or* der Firma von; 3. die Zeitrechnung; ***New Style,*** neuer Stil, neue Zeitrechnung; 4. (*Bot.*) der Griffel; 5. (*Surg.*) die Sonde; 6. *See* **stylus. 2.** *v.t.* 1. benennen, betiteln, anreden, bezeichnen; 2. modisch formen *or* entwerfen.
stylet ['stailit], *s.* 1. das Stilett; 2. (*Surg.*) die Sonde; 3. (*Engr.*) der Griffel, Stichel. **styliform** [–ifɔ:m], *adj.* (*Bot.*) griffelförmig.
styling ['stailiŋ], *s.* das Stilisieren, die Formgebung. **stylish,** *adj.* stilvoll, modisch, elegant, fesch. **stylishness,** *s.* die Eleganz.
stylist ['stailist], *s.* der Stilist, Meister des Stils. **stylistic** [–'listik], *adj.* stilistisch, Stil–. **stylistically,** *adv.* dem Stil nach, in stilistischer Hinsicht.
stylite ['stailait], *s.* (*Eccl.*) Säulenheilige(r), der Stilit.
stylization [stailai'zeiʃən], *s.* die Stilisierung. **stylize** ['stailaiz], *v.t.* stilisieren.
stylo ['stailou], *s. See* **stylograph.**
stylobate ['stailəbeit], *s.* (*Archit.*) abgestuftes Fußgestell, die Säulenstufe.
stylograph ['stailəgrɑ:f], *s.* der Füllstift, Stylo.
styloid ['stailɔid], *adj.* griffelförmig; (*Anat.*) – ***process,*** der Griffelfortsatz. **stylus,** *s.* 1. der Schreibgriffel; 2. (*gramophone*) die Schneidnadel (*for making records*), Nadel (*for reproduction*); 3. der Zeiger (*of sundial*).
stymie, stymy ['staimi], **1.** *s.* 1. (*Golf*) die Lage der Bälle in gerader Linie mit dem Loch; 2. (*fig.*) Lahmlegung. **2.** *v.t.* 1. durch die Lage des Balls das Spiel des Gegners hindern; 2. (*fig.*) vereiteln, (ver)hindern, durchkreuzen (*a plan etc.*).
styptic ['stiptik], **1.** *adj.* blutstillend; – ***pencil,*** der Alaunstift. **2.** *s.* blutstillendes Mittel.
styrene ['stairi:n], *s.* (*Chem.*) das Styrol.
Styria ['stiriə], *s.* Steiermark (*f.*). **Styrian, 1.** *adj.* stei(e)risch, steiermärkisch. **2.** *s.* der Stei(e)rer (die Steierin), Steiermärker(in).
Suabian, *see* **Swabian.**
suasion ['sweiʒən], *s.* die Überredung; ***moral*** –, gütliches Zureden. **suasive** [–siv], **suasory,** *adj.* überredend, überzeugend, zuredend.
suave [swɑ:v], *adj.* 1. höflich, verbindlich, zuvorkommend, gewinnend; 2. lieblich (*as wine*). **suavity,** *s.* 1. die Höflichkeit, Verbindlichkeit, Zuvorkommenheit; 2. Lieblichkeit, Annehmlichkeit, Milde.
sub [sʌb, səb], **1.** *prep.* unter; (*Law*) – ***judice,*** noch anhängig, noch nicht entschieden; – ***rosa,*** vertraulich, unter dem Siegel der Verschwiegenheit. **2.** *s. coll. abbr. for* ***subaltern, submarine, subordinate, substitute*** or ***subscription,*** *q.v.* **3.** *v.i.* (*coll.*) – ***for,*** vertreten, einspringen für. **4.** *pref.* 1. Unter–, Grund–; 2. Neben–, Hilfs–, Nach–; 3. annähernd, fast, kaum, teilweise.
sub|acetate, *s.* basisch essigsaures Salz. **–acid, 1.** *s.* säuerliche Substanz, die Säuerlichkeit. **2.** *adj.* säuerlich. **–-acoustic,** *adj.* Unterschall–. **–-acute,** *adj.* (*Med.*) latent. **–alpine,** *adj.* subalpin(isch).
subaltern ['sʌbltən], **1.** *s.* Unterbeamte(r), Untergebene(r), (*Mil.*) der Leutnant. **2.** *adj.* subaltern, untergeordnet, Unter–.
sub|aqueous, *adj.* Unterwasser–. **–arctic,** *adj.* subarktisch. **–-audible,** *adj.* kaum hörbar, nicht mehr hörbar. **–-breed,** *s.* (*Zool.*) die Unterart. **–-calibre,** *adj.* Abkommkaliber–; – ***gun,*** die Abkommkanone. **–caudal,** *adj.* unter dem Schwanz liegend. **–clavian,** *adj.* Unterschlüsselbein–. **–-committee,** *s.* der Unterausschuß. **–conscious, 1.** *s.* das Unterbewußtsein. **2.** *adj.* unterbewußt; (*coll.*) halbbewußt. **–-consciousness,** *s.* das Unterbewußtsein. **–-continent,** *s.* der Landteil. **–-contract, 1.** *s.* der Nebenvertrag. **2.** *v.t.* durch einen Nebenvertrag regeln. **3.** *v.i.* einen Nebenvertrag abschließen. **–-contractor,** *s.* der Nebenlieferant; Unterkontrahent, Akkordant. **–contrary,** *adj.* (*Log.*) subkonträr. **–costal,** *adj.* unter den Rippen liegend. **–cutaneous,** *adj.* subkutan, unter der *or* die Haut. **–-dean,** *s.* der Unterdechant. **–-deity,** *s.* die Nebengottheit. **–divide, 1.** *v.t.* unterteilen, nochmals teilen; aufgliedern, (auf)teilen. **2.** *v.i.* in Unterabteilungen zerfallen. **–division,** *s.* 1. die Unterabteilung; 2. Unterteilung, Aufgliederung. **–-dominant,** *s.* (*Mus.*) die Unterdominante, Quarte.
subdual [səb'djuəl], *s.* die Bändigung, Bezwingung, Unterwerfung.
subduct [səb'dʌkt], *v.t.* 1. (*rare*) entziehen, wegnehmen; 2. (*Math.*) abziehen, subtrahieren.
subdue [səb'dju:], *v.t.* bezwingen, unterwerfen, unterjochen; überwältigen, überwinden; (*fig.*) bändigen, zähmen (*feelings*), unterdrücken, lindern (*pain*), mildern, dämpfen (*sound, light etc.*). **subdued,** *adj.* gemildert, gedämpft, matt (*sound, light, colours*).
sub|-edit, *v.t.* bearbeiten (*MSS. etc.*). **–-editor,** *s.* der Hilfsredakteur, zweiter Redakteur. **–-equal,** *adj.* fast gleich.
suber ['sju:bə], *s.* der Kork, die Korkrinde, das Korkholz. **suberic** [–'berik], *adj.* Kork–. **suberin,** *s.* der Korkstoff. **suberose, suberous,** *adj.* korkig, Kork–; korkartig.
sub|-family, *s.* die Unterfamilie. **–febrile,** *adj.* annähernd fiebernd. **–form,** *s.* die Nebenform. **–-genus,** *s.* die Unterart. **–glacial,** *adj.* 1. teilweise glazial; 2. unter dem Gletscher befindlich. **–heading,** *s.* der Untertitel, Nebentitel, Zwischentitel; die Unterabteilung. **–-human,** *adj.* 1. un(ter)menschlich, menschenunwürdig; 2. annähernd menschlich.
subjacent [sʌb'dʒeisənt], *adj.* darunter *or* tiefer liegend; (*fig.*) zugrundeliegend.

subject, 1. ['sʌbdʒikt], *adj.* 1. untertan, untergeben (*to, Dat.*); 2. abhängig (*to*, von); (*fig.*) ausgesetzt, unterworfen (*Dat.*); – *to this,* unter diesem Vorbehalt; *be – to,* unterliegen (*Dat.*), vorbehalten bleiben (*Dat.*), vorbehaltlich sein (*Gen.*), abhängig sein von; – *to duty,* zollpflichtig; – *to reservations,* unter Vorbehalt; 3. (*coll.*) empfindlich (*to*, gegen), anfällig (für), geneigt (zu); – *to headaches,* leicht Kopfschmerzen bekommen. **2.** [–dʒikt], *s.* 1. (*Pol.*) der (die) Untertan(in), Staatsbürger(in), Staatsangehörige(r); *British –,* britischer Staatsangehöriger; 2. das Thema (*also Mus.*), der Gegenstand, Stoff; *on the – of,* bezüglich, betreffs, hinsichtlich (*Gen.*); – *catalogue,* der Realkatalog, Schlagwortkatalog; – *heading,* die Rubrik im Sachregister; – *index,* das Sachverzeichnis, Sachregister; – *matter,* der Gegenstand, Stoff, Inhalt; – *reference,* der Gegenstandsverweis; 3. der Grund, Anlaß, die Veranlassung, Ursache (*for*, zu); 4. das Fachgebiet, (Studien)fach; *compulsory –,* obligatorisches Fach; *optional –,* wahlfreies *or* fakultatives Fach; 5. (*Gram.*) das Subjekt, der Satzgegenstand; 6. (*Log.*) Grundbegriff, Subjektsbegriff, das Subjekt; 7. (*Phil.*) Ich, die Substanz; 8. (*Anat. etc.*) Leiche, der Kadaver, das (Versuchs)objekt; (*Med.*) die (Versuchs)person. **3.** [səb'dʒekt], *v.t.* 1. unterwerfen, unterjochen (*to, Dat.*), abhängig machen (von); 2. aussetzen (*to, Dat.*); *be –ed to,* ausgesetzt werden (*Dat.*).

subjection [səb'dʒekʃən], *s.* die Unterwerfung, Unterjochung (*to*, unter (*Acc.*)), Abhängigkeit (von); *be in – to,* abhängig sein von, unterstehen (*Dat.*); *bring under –,* unterwerfen.

subjective [səb'dʒektiv], **1.** *s.* (*Gram.*) der Nominativ. **2.** *adj.* 1. subjektiv, persönlich, einseitig; 2. (*Psych.*) introspektiv, ichbezogen; 3. (*Gram.*) Subjekts–. **subjectiveness,** *s. See* **subjectivity. subjectivism,** *s.* der Subjektivismus. **subjectivity** [sʌbdʒek'tiviti], *s.* die Subjektivität.

subjoin [sʌb'dʒɔin], *v.t.* hinzufügen, hinzusetzen; beilegen, beifügen. **subjoinder,** *s.* die Hinzufügung, der Anhang.

subjugate ['sʌbdʒugeit], *v.t.* unterjochen, unterwerfen (*to, Dat.*). **subjugation** [–'geiʃən], *s.* die Unterwerfung, Unterjochung.

subjunctive [səb'dʒʌŋktiv], **1.** *adj.* konjunktivisch. **2.** *s.* der Konjunktiv, die Konjunktivform.

sub|-kingdom, *s.* (*Bot., Zool.*) die Unterabteilung. **–lease,** *s.* die Untervermietung. **–lessee,** *s.* der (die) Untermieter(in), Unterpächter(in). **–let,** *irr. v.t.* weitervermieten, untervermieten. **––lieutenant,** *s.* der Leutnant zur See.

sublimate, 1. ['sʌblimit], *s.* (*Chem.*) das Sublimat; *corrosive –,* das Quecksilberchlorid, Ätzsublimat. **2.** [–mit], *adj.* sublimiert. **3.** [–meit], *v.t.* 1. (*Chem., Psych.*) sublimieren; 2. (*fig.*) veredeln, vergeistigen. **sublimation** [–'meiʃən], *s.* (*Chem., Psych.*) die Sublimation, Sublimierung, (*fig.*) Veredelung, Vergeistigung, Läuterung.

sublime [sə'blaim], **1.** *adj.* 1. erhaben, gehoben, hoch, hehr; *Sublime Porte,* die Hohe Pforte; 2. (*coll.*) hervorragend, großartig, gewaltig, grandios, majestätisch; 3. (*iron.*) vollendet, komplett, hochgradig, kraß. **2.** *s.* das Erhabene.

subliminal [səb'liminl], *adj.* unterbewußt; – *advertising,* unterschwellige Reklame; – *perception,* unterschwellige Wahrnehmung.

sublimity [səb'limiti], *s.* 1. die Erhabenheit, Gehobenheit; 2. (*coll.*) Großartigkeit.

sub|lingual, *adj.* unter der Zunge liegend. **–lunar(y),** *adj.* 1. unter dem Monde befindlich; 2. (*fig.*) irdisch. **––machine-gun,** *s.* die Maschinenpistole. **–marine, 1.** *adj.* unterseeisch, Untersee–; – *cable,* das Tiefseekabel. **2.** *s.* das Unterseeboot, U-Boot. **–mariner,** *s.* der U-Bootmann. **–maxillary,** *adj.* Unterkiefer–.

submerge [səb'mə:dʒ], **1.** *v.t.* 1. unter Wasser setzen, überschwemmen (*land etc.*), untertauchen, eintauchen, versenken; 2. (*fig.*) übertönen, unterdrücken; *–d tenth,* allerärmste Bevölkerungsschicht. **2.** *v.i.* untersinken, untertauchen; tauchen (*as submarines*). **submergence,** *s.* 1. das Versenken, Eintauchen, Untertauchen; 2. die Überschwemmung, Überflutung (*of land etc.*); 3. das Untersinken; 4. (*fig.*) die Versunkenheit. **submersion** [–'mə:ʃən], *s.* das Untertauchen, Versinken.

submission [səb'miʃən], *s.* 1. die Unterwerfung, Unterordnung (*to*, unter (*Acc.*)); Ergebenheit, Ergebung (in (*Acc.*)); Unterwürfigkeit, der Gehorsam; 2. die Vorlage; Überantwortung (*to*, an (*Acc.*)), (*Law*) Unterbreitung, Vorlegung; das Plädoyer. **submissive** [–siv], *adj.* unterwürfig, ergeben, willfährig, gehorsam. **submissiveness,** *s.* die Unterwürfigkeit, Ergebenheit.

submit [səb'mit], **1.** *v.t.* 1. unterwerfen, unterziehen, aussetzen (*to, Dat.*); – *o.s. to,* sich unterwerfen *or* unterziehen (*Dat.*), sich fügen *or* ergeben in (*Acc.*); 2. (*esp. Law*) vortragen, vorlegen, übergeben, einreichen, unterbreiten, beibringen (*testimonial etc.*); – *an application,* ein Gesuch einreichen (*to*, bei); 3. beantragen, zum Vorschlag bringen, anheimstellen (*suggestion etc.*), (*coll.*) zu erwägen *or* bedenken geben. **2.** *v.i.* sich fügen (*to, Dat. or* in (*Acc.*)), sich unterwerfen (*Dat.*); – *to treatment,* sich behandeln lassen.

submittance, *s. See* **submission.**

sub|multiple, *s.* (*Math.*) höhere (als die zweite) Wurzel. **–normal,** *adj.* unternormal; (*Psych.*) geistig minderwertig. **––order,** *s.* (*Zool., Bot.*) die Unterordnung.

subordinate, 1. [sə'bɔ:dinit], *adj.* 1. untergeordnet, nachgeordnet, unterstellt (*to, Dat.*); *be – to,* an Bedeutung nachstehen (*Dat.*); 2. Unter–, nebensächlich, unwichtig; 3. (*Gram.*) abhängig, Neben–; – *clause,* der Nebensatz. **2.** [–it], *s.* 1. Untergebene(r); 2. nebensächliche *or* untergeordnete S. **3.** [–eit], *v.t.* unterordnen (*a th.*) (*to, Dat.*), zurückstellen (*a p.*) (hinter (*Acc.*)). **subordinating,** *adj.* (*Gram.*) unterordnend. **subordination** [–'neiʃən], *s.* 1. die Unterordnung, Unterwerfung (*to*, unter (*Acc.*)); Abhängigkeit (von), Unterlegenheit; 2. Unterwürfigkeit, der (Dienst)gehorsam. **subordinative** [–nətiv], *adj.* unterordnend.

suborn [sə'bɔ:n], *v.t.* (*Law*) anstiften, verleiten; bestechen (*witnesses*), abtrünnig machen. **subornation** [–'neiʃən], *s.* die Anstiftung, Verleitung, Bestechung (*of*, zu).

subplot ['sʌbplɔt], *s.* die Nebenhandlung.

subpoena [səb'pi:nə], **1.** *s.* (*also writ of –*) die Vorladung unter Strafandrohung, der Vorladungsbefehl. **2.** *v.t.* unter Strafandrohung vorladen.

subreption [səb'repʃən], *s.* (*Law*) die Erschleichung.

subrogation [sʌbrə'geiʃən], *s.* die Subrogation, Ersetzung, Unterschiebung.

subscribe [səb'skraib], **1.** *v.t.* 1. unterschreiben (*a document*), (unter)zeichnen mit, daruntersetzen (*one's name*); 2. zeichnen (*sum of money*) (*to*, zu; *for*, für), beitragen, beisteuern (*to, Dat.*). **2.** *v.i.* 1. Geld beisteuern (*to, Dat.*), einen Beitrag leisten *or* zahlen (für); – *for,* vorausbestellen (*a book*); – *to,* abonnieren auf (*Acc.*) (*periodical*); (*fig.*) beipflichten (*Dat.*), gutheißen, billigen, anerkennen, einwilligen in (*Acc.*), zustimmen (*Dat.*) (*a proposal etc.*). **subscriber,** *s.* 1. Unterzeichnete(r), der (die) Unterzeichner(in) (*to, Gen.*); 2. Abonnent(in), Subskribent(in); Zeichner(in) (*to a fund*); 3. (*Tele.*) Fernsprechteilnehmer(in); – *trunk dialling,* der Selbstwähl(er)fernverkehr.

subscription [səb'skripʃən], *s.* 1. das Unterschreiben, die Unterzeichnung, Unterschrift; 2. Einwilligung (*to*, in (*Acc.*)), Zustimmung (zu), Anerkennung (*Gen.*); 3. Zeichnung, Subskription (*to*, auf (*Acc.*)); das Abonnement, die Vorbestellung (*Gen.*); Subskriptionssumme, Gebühr (für), der (Mitglieds)beitrag (für *or* zu) (*club etc.*); – *list,* die Subskriptionsliste, Zeichnungsliste; – *price,* der Subskriptionspreis, Bezugspreis.

sub-section, *s.* der Unterabschnitt, die Unterabteilung.

subsequence ['sʌbsikwəns], *s.* späteres Eintreten. **subsequent,** *adj.* später, (nach)folgend, nachträglich, nachherig, Nach–; – *to*, nach, später als, folgend auf (*Acc.*); – *upon*, infolge (*Gen.*). **subsequently,** *adv.* darauf(hin), später, hernach, nachher, nachträglich.

subserve [səb'sə:v], *v.t.* förderlich *or* dienlich sein (*Dat.*), fördern. **subservience, subserviency,** *s.* 1. die Dienlichkeit, Nützlichkeit (*to*, für); 2. Unterwürfigkeit (*to*, gegenüber); *in – to*, aus Willfährigkeit gegen. **subservient,** *adj.* 1. dienlich, nützlich, förderlich (*to*, *Dat.*), dienstbar, untergeordnet (*to*, *Dat.*); 2. unterwürfig, gehorsam (*to*, *Dat.*).

sub-set, *s.* (*Math.*) die Teilmenge.

subside [səb'said], *v.i.* 1. (*Chem.*) sich (ab)setzen *or* niederschlagen; 2. sich senken, (ein)sinken, absacken (*of th.*), (*coll.*) sinken, sich niederlassen (*of p.*); 3. sich legen, nachlassen, abklingen, abnehmen, abflauen. **subsidence,** *s.* 1. das Absinken, Sichsenken, Sichsetzen; 2. die (Boden)-senkung; 3. (*fig.*) Abnahme, das Nachlassen, Abflauen, Versinken.

subsidiary [səb'sidiəri], 1. *adj.* 1. Hilfs–, Unterstützungs–, Subsidien–; – *treaty*, der Subsidienvertrag; 2. Neben–, untergeordnet (*to*, *Dat.*); – *company*, die Tochtergesellschaft; – *subject*, das Nebenfach; 3. behilflich, ergänzend (*to*, zu); *be – to*, ergänzen, unterstützen, dienen (*Dat.*). 2. *s.* 1. (*usu. pl.*) die Hilfe, Stütze; 2. der Beistand, Gehilfe; 3. (*Comm.*) die Tochtergesellschaft, Filiale; 4. *pl.* Hilfstruppen (*pl.*).

subsidization [sʌbsidai'zeiʃən], *s.* die Subventionierung. **subsidize** ['sʌbsidaiz], *v.t.* Subsidien zahlen für, mit Geld unterstützen, Zuschuß geben (*Dat.*), subventionieren. **subsidy** ['sʌbsidi], *s.* (staatliche) Unterstützung, die Subvention, Beihilfe (aus öffentlichen Geldern); *pl.* Hilfsgelder, Subsidien (*pl.*).

subsist [səb'sist], 1. *v.i.* existieren, (weiter)bestehen, fortdauern, in Gebrauch *or* Kraft sein; – *on*, sein Leben fristen, leben, sich erhalten *or* ernähren von; – *in*, liegen *or* bestehen in (*Dat.*), beruhen auf (*Dat.*). 2. *v.t.* erhalten, unterhalten. **subsistence,** *s.* 1. das Bestehen, Dasein, die Existenz; 2. der (Lebens)unterhalt, das Auskommen; – *allowance*, der Unterhaltszuschuß; – *minimum*, das Existenzminimum.

sub|soil, *s.* der Untergrund. **–sonic,** *adj.* Unterschall–. **–-species,** *s.* die Unterart. **–stage,** *s.* 1. (*Geol.*) die Unterstufe; 2. der Träger (*of microscope*).

substance ['sʌbstəns], *s.* 1. (*Phys.*) die Substanz, der Stoff, Körper, die Masse, Materie; 2. (*Phil.*) Substanz, das Wesen; 3. (*fig.*) der Inhalt, Gehalt, Kern, Gegenstand, das Wesentliche; *in –*, im wesentlichen; *of little –*, wenig stichhaltig (*as argument*); 4. (*coll.*) das Kapital, Vermögen, Mittel (*pl.*); *man of –*, vermögender Mann.

sub-standard, *adj.* unter der (vorgeschriebenen) Norm.

substantial [səb'stænʃəl], *adj.* 1. wesentlich, materiell, wirklich (vorhanden), beträchtlich, ansehnlich; 2. nahrhaft, reichlich, gehaltvoll (*as food*); 3. stark, fest, kräftig, solid(e), dauerhaft; 4. (*Phil.*) substantiell; 5. (*coll.*) wohlhabend, vermögend. **substantiality** [–ʃi'æliti], *s.* 1. (*Phil.*) die Substantialität; 2. Wirklichkeit, Stofflichkeit; 3. Greifbarkeit; 4. Stichhaltigkeit, Maßgeblichkeit; 5. Stärke, Festigkeit, Gediegenheit. **substantially,** *adv.* in der Hauptsache, im wesentlichen. **substantiate** [–ʃieit], *v.t.* 1. bestätigen, begründen, rechtfertigen, erhärten; nachweisen, beweisen; 2. stärken, festigen, kräftigen; Gestalt *or* Wirklichkeit verleihen (*Dat.*), verwirklichen, verkörpern. **substantiation** [–ʃi'eiʃən], *s.* 1. die Erhärtung, Bestätigung, Begründung, der Beweis; *in – of*, zum Beweis *or* zur Erhärtung von *or* (*Gen.*); 2. die Verwirklichung, Gestaltgebung.

substantival [sʌbstən'taivl], *adj.* substantivisch, Substantiv–. **substantive** ['sʌbstəntiv], 1. *s.* das Hauptwort, Substantiv. 2. *adj.* 1. wirklich (vorhanden), tatsächlich, wesentlich, beträchtlich; unabhängig, selbständig; – *law*, materielles Recht; 2. (*Mil.*) mit Patent; 3. (*Gram.*) substantivisch.

sub-station, *s.* die Nebenstelle, Außenstelle, Hilfsstation; (*Elec.*) Transformatorenstation.

substitute ['sʌbstitju:t], 1. *v.t.* ersetzen (*for*, durch), austauschen (gegen); einsetzen (anstelle von), an die Stelle setzen (*Gen. or* von). 2. *v.i.* – *for*, vertreten (*a p.*), als Ersatz dienen (*a th.*). 3. *s.* der (Stell)vertreter, Ersatz(mann); Ersatz(stoff), das Ersatzmittel, Surrogat; *act as a – for*, vertreten (*a p.*), als Ersatz dienen für (*a th.*). **substitution** [–'tju:ʃən], *s.* 1. der Austausch, die Ersetzung, Substitution, Unterschiebung, Einsetzung; 2. (*Math.*) Substitution; 3. (*Biol.*) Ersetzung; 4. (*Chem., Phys.*) Verdrängung; 5. (*Law*) Einsetzung eines Nacherben. **substitutive,** *adj.* Ersatz–, Substitutions–; stellvertretend.

sub|stratum, *s.* 1. (*Geol.*) die Unterschicht; 2. (*Phil.*) Unterlage, Grundlage, das Substrat; 3. (*Biol.*) der Nährboden, Keimboden. **–structure,** *s.* der Unterbau, die Grundlage.

subsume [səb'sju:m], *v.t.* subsumieren, unterordnen, zusammenfassen (*under*, unter (*Dat. or Acc.*)); einbegreifen, einschließen, einordnen, einreihen (*in*, in (*Acc.*)); in sich schließen. **subsumption** [–'sʌmpʃən], *s.* die Zusammenfassung, Einreihung, Einordnung (*under*, unter (*Dat. or Acc.*); *in*, in (*Acc.*)).

sub|-tenancy, *s.* die Untermiete, Unterpacht. **–-tenant,** *s.* der (die) Untermieter(in), Unterpächter(in).

subtend [səb'tend], *v.t.* (*Geom.*) gegenüberliegen (*Dat.*); *–ed by*, einer Seite gegenüberliegend.

subterfuge ['sʌbtəfju:dʒ], *s.* die Ausflucht, Ausrede, der Vorwand.

subterranean [sʌbtə'reiniən], **subterraneous** [–niəs], *adj.* 1. unterirdisch; 2. (*fig.*) heimtückisch, heimlich.

subtile ['sʌbtil], *adj.* (*obs.*) *see* **subtle. subtilization** [–ai'zeiʃən], *s.* 1. die Verfeinerung (*also fig.*), Veredelung; 2. (*Chem.*) Verflüchtigung; 3. (*fig.*) Klügelei, Spitzfindigkeit. **subtilize,** 1. *v.t.* 1. verfeinern, veredeln, sublimieren; 2. (*Chem.*) verdünnen, verflüchtigen; 3. (*fig.*) klügeln, spitzfindig auslegen. 2. *v.i.* spitzfindig argumentieren, sich in Spitzfindigkeiten ergehen.

sub-title, *s.* der Untertitel.

subtle [sʌtl], *adj.* 1. fein (*also fig.*), zart, dünn; 2. (*fig.*) feinsinnig, subtil, raffiniert; – *irony*, leise Ironie; – *point*, heik(e)ler Punkt; 3. spitzfindig. **subtlety** [–ti], *s.* 1. die Feinheit, Zartheit (*also fig.*); 2. (*fig.*) der Scharfsinn, Scharfblick, die Scharfsinnigkeit, Finesse; Spitzfindigkeit; Gerissenheit.

sub-tonic, *s.* (*Mus.*) der Leitton.

subtract [səb'trækt], 1. *v.t.* (*Math.*) abziehen, subtrahieren. 2. *v.i.* (*fig.*) – *from*, schmälern. **subtraction** [–'trækʃən], *s.* 1. die Subtraktion; 2. (*fig.*) der Abzug, Entzug, die Wegnahme.

subtrahend ['sʌbtrəhend], *s.* der Subtrahend.

sub|-tropical, *adj.* subtropisch. **–-tropics,** *pl.* Subtropen (*pl.*). **–-type,** *s.* untergeordneter Typus.

suburb ['sʌbə:b], *s.* die Vorstadt, der Vorort; *pl.* die Vorstadt, Randbezirke (*pl.*). **suburban** [sə'bə:bən], 1. *adj.* 1. vorstädtisch, Vorstadt–, Vororts–; 2. (*fig.*) spießig, kleinstädtisch. 2. *or* **suburbanite,** *s.* der (die) Vorstadtbewohner(in), Vorstädter(in). **suburbia** [–'bə:biə], *s.* die Vorstadt, der Stadtrand.

sub-variety, *s.* untergeordnete Abart.

subvention [səb'venʃən], *s.* der Zuschuß, die Beihilfe, Beisteuer, Subvention, Unterstützung. **subventioned,** *adj.* staatlich unterstützt, subventioniert.

subversion [səb'və:ʃən], *s.* 1. der (Um)sturz, die Zerstörung, Vernichtung; 2. (*fig.*) Zerrüttung, Untergrabung. **subversive** [–siv], *adj.* 1. umstürzlerisch, Umsturz–; 2. zerstörerisch, verderblich, zerrütend; *be – of* or *to*, untergraben, zerrütten, zerstören. **subvert** [–'və:t], *v.t.* 1. stürzen, umstoßen, umwerfen; vernichten, zerstören; 2. (*fig.*) zerrütten, erschüttern, untergraben.

subway ['sʌbwei], *s.* 1. die Unterführung; 2. (*Am.*) Untergrundbahn, U-Bahn.

succeed [sək'si:d], **1.** *v.i.* 1. (*rare*) (nach)folgen; (*of p.*) Nachfolger *or* Erbe werden; – ***to the throne,*** auf den Thron folgen; – ***to the title,*** den Titel erben; 2. (*of th.*) glücken, gelingen, nach Wunsch verlaufen (***with,*** bei); (*of th. or p.*) erfolgreich sein; (*of p.*) Erfolg haben, sein Ziel erreichen, sich durchsetzen (***with,*** bei; ***in,*** mit); ***I -ed in doing,*** es gelang mir zu tun; ***he -s in everything,*** alles gelingt ihm *or* glückt bei ihm; ***nothing -s like success,*** ein Erfolg zieht den andern nach sich. **2.** *v.t.* (*of th. or p.*) folgen auf (*Acc.*), (*of p.*) (nach)-folgen (*Dat.*), Nachfolger werden (*Gen.*); – ***him as heir,*** ihn beerben; – ***him in office,*** sein Amt antreten.

success [sək'ses], *s.* 1. (guter) Erfolg, erfolgreicher Ausgang; Glück, glückliches Ergebnis; – ***story,*** die Handlung mit erfolgreichem Ausgang; ***achieve –,*** erfolgreich sein, zu Erfolg gelangen; ***make a – of,*** Erfolg haben mit; ***wish him –,*** ihm Glück wünschen (***in,*** zu); ***with –,*** erfolgreich; ***without –,*** vergeblich, erfolglos; 2. (*coll.*) erfolgreiche P. *or* S., die Glanzleistung, die *or* das Furore; ***be a –,*** (*of th. or p.*) ein Erfolg sein, Erfolg haben, (*of p.*) erfolgreich sein. **successful,** *adj.* (*of th. or p.*) erfolgreich; (*of th.*) glücklich, gelungen; (*of p.*) ***be – in doing,*** Erfolg haben bei, mit Erfolg tun.

succession [sək'seʃən], *s.* 1. das Folgen; die (Aufeinander)folge, Reihe(nfolge); ***in –,*** aufeinander, nacheinander, hintereinander; ***in quick –,*** in rascher Folge; 2. (*Law*) die Erbfolge, Nachfolge, Übernahme (***to,*** *Gen.*); (*also* ***law of –***) das Erbfolgerecht; (*also* ***order of –***) die Erbfolgeordnung; (*collect.*) Nachkommen (*pl.*), die Nachkommenschaft; ***apostolic –,*** apostolische Nachfolge *or* Sukzession; ***in – to,*** als Nachfolger von; ***be next in – to,*** als nächste(r) folgen auf (*Acc.*); ***right of –,*** das Erbfolgerecht; (*Hist.*) ***– states,*** Nachfolgestaaten (*pl.*); ***– to an office,*** die Übernahme eines Amtes; ***– to the throne,*** die Thronfolge; (*Hist.*) ***war of –,*** der Erbfolgekrieg; 3. die Fruchtfolge (*of crops*); 4. (*Mus.*) Folge, Fortschreitung, der Gang.

successive [sək'sesiv], *adj.* aufeinanderfolgend; ***the third – night,*** die dritte Nacht darauf; ***three – nights,*** drei Nächte hintereinander; ***– development,*** fortlaufende Entwicklung. **successively,** *adv.* nacheinander, hintereinander, der Reihe nach.

successor [sək'sesə], *s.* der (die) Nachfolger(in) (***of, to,*** *Gen. or* ***von***); ***– to the throne,*** der Thronfolger.

succinct [sək'siŋkt], *adj.* kurz(gefaßt), knapp, gedrängt, bündig, prägnant. **succinctness,** *s.* die Kürze, Knappheit, Bündigkeit, Prägnanz.

succory ['sʌkəri], *s.* (*Bot.*) die Zichorie.

succotash ['sʌkətæʃ], *s.* (*Am.*) ein Gericht aus Bohnen und Mais *etc.*

succour ['sʌkə], **1.** *s.* die Hilfe, Unterstützung, der Beistand; (*Mil.*) Entsatz; *pl.* (*rare*) Hilfstruppen (*pl.*). **2.** *v.t.* helfen (*Dat.*), beistehen (*Dat.*), zu Hilfe kommen (*Dat.*), unterstützen.

succulence, succulency ['sʌkjuləns(i)], *s.* die Saftigkeit. **succulent, 1.** *adj.* saftig (*also fig.*), (*fig.*) üppig; (*Bot.*) sukkulent, fleischig. **2.** *s.* (*Bot.*) die Sukkulente, Fettpflanze.

succumb [sə'kʌm], *v.i.* 1. – ***to,*** unterliegen (*Dat.*) (*an adversary*), erliegen (*Dat.*) (*temptation, injuries*), sterben an (*Dat.*) (*injuries*), zusammenbrechen unter (*Dat.*) (*suffering etc.*); 2. – ***to*** or ***under*** or ***before,*** weichen (*Dat.*) *or* vor (*Dat.*), nachgeben (*Dat.*).

succursal [sə'kə:sl], **1.** *adj.* (*Eccl.*) Filial–, Tochter–. **2.** *s.* die Zweigniederlassung (*of a sect*).

succuss [sə'kʌs], *v.t.* schütteln, erschüttern. **succussion** [–'kʌʃən], *s.* das Schütteln, die Erschütterung.

such [sʌtʃ], **1.** *adj.* 1. solch, derartig, so; – ***misery*** solch(es) *or* derartiges Elend; ***I have – pain,*** ich habe solchen Schmerz *or* solche Schmerzen; ***no – thing,*** nichts dergleichen; – ***another,*** auch so einer, eben ein solcher; (*before indef. art.*) – ***a man,*** ein solcher *or* derartiger Mann, so *or* solch ein Mann; ***of – a man,*** so(lch) eines Mannes *or* eines solchen Mannes; ***I never heard – a thing,*** ich habe so etwas nie gehört; – ***a one,*** ein solcher, eine solche *or* ein solches, so einer, so eine *or* so ein(e)s; ***with – a fine house,*** mit so einem *or* einem solch(en) schönen Haus; (*before pl.*) – ***men,*** solche *or* derartige Menschen; – ***good men,*** solch gute *or* solche gute(n) Menschen; ***the lives of – good men,*** das Leben solch(er) guter *or* solcher guten Menschen; ***there are – things,*** es gibt so etwas; ***of many – things,*** vieler solchen *or* solcher Dinge; – ***and –,*** so einer, der und der; 2. – (. . .) ***as,*** (so) wie; – ***a life as*** or ***a life – as he leads,*** ein Leben wie er es führt; – ***as*** (*after pl. noun*), wie (zum Beispiel); – ***as it is,*** (so) wie es auch *or* es nun einmal ist, wenn man es so nennen darf; ***a thing – as this,*** ein derartiges Ding; ***be – as to . . .,*** derart(ig) sein daß . . .; ***at – a time as suits you,*** zu jeder Zeit die Ihnen paßt; 3. (*pred.*) – ***being the case,*** da der Fall so liegt, da es sich so verhält; – ***is life,*** so geht's in der Welt; – ***was the noise,*** so groß war der Lärm, der Lärm war dermaßen groß. **2.** *pron.* ein solcher, eine solche, ein solches, solche (*pl.*); ***and –*** (***like***), und dergleichen; ***all –,*** alle dieser Art; ***another –,*** ein anderer solcher, noch ein solcher; ***cold as –,*** Kälte als solche; – ***as we mentioned above,*** diejenigen *or* solche *or* alle welche *or* die wir oben erwähnten. **suchlike,** *adj.* (*coll.*) derartig, (*pred.*) dergleichen.

suck [sʌk], **1.** *v.t.* 1. saugen, lutschen; – ***his blood,*** ihm das Blut aussaugen; (*coll. fig.*) – ***his brains,*** ihn ausholen; – ***in,*** einsaugen, aufnehmen, (hin)-einziehen; – ***out,*** aussaugen; – ***up,*** aufsaugen, absorbieren; 2. saugen *or* lutschen an (*Dat.*); – ***one's thumb,*** am Daumen lutschen; 3. (*fig.*) holen, ziehen, gewinnen (***from,*** aus). **2.** *v.i.* 1. saugen, lutschen, ziehen (***at,*** an (*Dat.*)) (*a pipe*); 2. einziehen (*as a pump*); 3. (*sl.*) – ***up to,*** ihm Honig um den Bart schmieren, (*vulg.*) ihn am Arsch lecken. **3.** *s.* 1. das Saugen; ***give – to,*** säugen, stillen; ***take a – at,*** saugen *or* lutschen an (*Dat.*); 2. der Strudel, Wirbel; 3. (*sl.*) (kleiner) Schluck.

sucker ['sʌkə], *s.* 1. (*Hort.*) der Sprößling; 2. (*Zool.*) Saugrüssel, das Saugorgan; 3. (*Ichth.*) der Seehase, Lumpfisch; 4. (*Tech.*) die Saugscheibe, das Saugrohr, der Saugkolben; 5. (*coll.*) der *or* das Lutschbonbon; 6. (*sl.*) der Trottel, Einfaltspinsel, melkende Kuh, Gefoppte(r); ***play him for a –,*** ihn für dumm verkaufen, ihn anschmieren.

sucking ['sʌkiŋ], **1.** *adj.* saugend. **2.** *s.* das Saugen. **sucking|-pig,** *s.* das Spanferkel. **–-pump,** *s.* die Saugpumpe.

suckle [sʌkl], *v.t.* säugen, stillen. **suckling,** *s.* 1. das Säugen; 2. der Säugling, das Brustkind; 3. Jungtier.

sucrose ['sju:krous], *s.* der Rohrzucker.

suction ['sʌkʃən], *s.* das (An)saugen, die Einsaugung, Saugfähigkeit; (*Tech.*) der Sog, Unterdruck. **suction|-pipe,** *s.* das Ansaugrohr, Einsaugrohr. **–-pump,** *s.* die Saugpumpe. **suctorial** [sʌk'tɔ:riəl], *adj.* Saug–.

Sudan [su:'dɑ:n], *s.* Sudan (*m.*). **Sudanese** [–də'ni:z], **1.** *adj.* sudan(es)isch. **2.** *s.* der (die) Sudaner(in), Sudanese (Sudanesin).

sudarium [sju'dɛəriəm], *s.* (*pl.* **-ria**) (*Eccl.*) das Schweißtuch (der Heiligen Veronika). **sudation** [–'deiʃən], *s.* der Schweiß, das Schwitzen. **sudatorium** [–də'tɔ:riəm], *s.* das Schwitzbad. **sudatory** ['sju:dətəri], **1.** *s.* 1. schweißtreibendes Mittel; 2. *See* **sudatorium.** **2.** *adj.* schweißtreibend, Schweiß–, Schwitz–.

sudden [sʌdn], *adj.* plötzlich, unvorhergesehen, unerwartet, unvermutet, überraschend; jäh, hastig, vorschnell (*as actions*); (*coll.*) (***all***) ***of a –,*** (ganz) plötzlich. **suddenness,** *s.* die Plötzlichkeit.

sudoriferous [sju:də'rifərəs], *adj.* schweißabsondernd, Schweiß–. **sudorific** [–'rifik], **1.** *adj.* 1. schweißtreibend; 2. *See* **sudoriferous.** **2.** *s.* schweißtreibendes Mittel.

suds [sʌdz], *pl.* (*usu. soap–*) das Seifenwasser, die Seifenlauge.

sue [sjuː], **1.** *v.t.* verklagen (***for***, wegen *or* auf (*Acc.*)), belangen, anhalten (um). **2.** *v.i.* 1. klagen (***for***, auf (*Acc.*)), eine Klage einreichen (***for***, wegen; ***to***, bei); – ***for debt***, eine Schuld einklagen; – ***for divorce***, auf Scheidung klagen; 2. flehen, bitten (***for***, um); – ***for mercy***, um Gnade flehen.

suède [sweid], *s.* das Wildleder.

suet [ˈsjuit], *s.* das Nierenfett; der Talg; – ***pudding***, der Pudding aus Mehl und Talg. **suety,** *adj.* talgig, Talg–.

suffer [ˈsʌfə], **1.** *v.t.* 1. ertragen, erdulden, (er)leiden; 2. (*usu. neg.*) leiden, dulden, ausstehen, aushalten; 3. (*Poet.*, *B.*) (zu)lassen, gestatten, erlauben (*Dat.*). **2.** *v.i.* 1. leiden (***from***, an (*Dat.*); (*fig.*) ***from, under***, unter (*Dat.*)); 2. (*of th.*) zu Schaden kommen, Schaden erleiden; mitgenommen werden; 3. bestraft werden, büßen (***for***, für). **sufferable,** *adj.* erträglich, leidlich; tragbar. **sufferance,** *s.* 1. (stillschweigende) Duldung, die Einwilligung; ***on*** –, unter stillschweigender Duldung, nur *or* stillschweigend geduldet; ***be beyond*** –, alle menschliche Geduld übersteigen; 2. (*obs.*) das Leiden, Erdulden. **sufferer,** *s.* Leidende(r) (***from***, an (*Dat.*)); der (die) Dulder(in), Märtyrer(in), Geschädigte(r); ***fellow*** –, der Leidensgefährte; ***be a – by***, leiden durch, verlieren bei; ***be a – from***, leiden an (*Dat.*). **suffering, 1.** *adj.* leidend. **2.** *s.* das Leiden, Dulden.

suffice [səˈfais], *v.i.* genügen, ausreichen, hinreichen, hinreichend sein (***for***, für); – ***it to say***, es genüge zu sagen.

sufficiency [səˈfiʃənsi], *s.* 1. die Hinlänglichkeit, Zulänglichkeit, Angemessenheit; 2. hinreichendes Auskommen; hinreichende Zahl *or* Menge; 3. (*obs.*) hinreichende Fähigkeit, die Befähigung. **sufficient,** *adj.* 1. genügend, ausreichend, zureichend, hinlänglich, hinreichend (***for***, für), genug; ***be*** –, genügen, (aus)reichen; ***it is – for me***, es genügt mir; – ***reason***, zureichender Grund; (*B.*) – ***unto the day is the evil thereof***, jeder Tag hat seine Plage; 2. (*obs.*) geeignet, tauglich, fähig (***for***, zu). **sufficiently,** *adv.* genügend, zur Genüge, genug.

suffix, 1. [ˈsʌfiks], *s.* die Nachsilbe, das Suffix. **2.** [səˈfiks], *v.t.* (*Gram.*) als Suffix anfügen; (*fig.*) anhängen, anfügen, hinzufügen (***to***, an (*Acc.*)).

suffocate [ˈsʌfəkeit], **1.** *v.t.* ersticken; (*fig.*) ***be –d***, erdrückt *or* benommen werden (***with***, von). **2.** *v.i.* ersticken (***with***, an (*Dat.*)); (*fig.*) umkommen (vor (*Dat.*)). **suffocating,** *adj.* erstickend; stickig (*air*); (*fig.*) erdrückend. **suffocation** [–ˈkeiʃən], *s.* das Ersticken, die Erstickung, (*Med.*) Atembeklemmung; ***death by*** –, der Erstickungstod; (*fig.*) ***to*** –, bis zum Ersticken.

suffragan [ˈsʌfrəgən], *s.* (*also* – ***bishop***) der Suffraganbischof.

suffrage [ˈsʌfridʒ], *s.* 1. das Stimmrecht, Wahlrecht; ***female*** –, das Frauenstimmrecht; ***universal*** –, allgemeines Wahlrecht; 2. die (Wahl)stimme; die Abstimmung. **suffragette** [–rəˈdʒet], *s.* die Frauenrechtlerin. **suffragist** [–rədʒist], *s.* der Stimmrechtler.

suffuse [səˈfjuːz], *v.t.* übergießen, benetzen (*of liquids*); überziehen, bedecken (*of colours*), überfluten, überströmen, durchfluten (*of light*); (*fig.*) erfüllen; ***–d with blushes***, schamrot. **suffusion** [–ˈfjuːʒən], *s.* 1. die Übergießung, Überflutung; 2. (*Med.*) Blutunterlaufung; 3. (*fig.*) Schamröte, Errötung.

sugar [ˈʃugə], **1.** *s.* der Zucker; ***beet*** –, der Rübenzucker; ***brown*** –, der Rohzucker; ***cane*** –, der Rohrzucker; ***castor*** –, der Streuzucker; ***icing*** –, der Staubzucker, Puderzucker; ***lump*** –, der Würfelzucker; ***lump of*** –, das Stück Zucker; – ***of lead***, der Bleizucker; ***maple*** –, der Ahornzucker. **2.** *v.t.* zuckern; (*fig.*) versüßen.

sugar|-basin, *s.* die Zuckerdose. **–-beet,** *s.* die Zuckerrübe. – **candy,** *s.* der Kandis(zucker). **–-cane,** *s.* das Zuckerrohr. **–-coated,** *adj.* verzuckert. **–-daddy,** *s.* (*coll.*) der Goldonkel. – **icing,** *s.* der Zuckerguß.

sugariness [ˈʃugərinis], *s.* die Süße, Süßigkeit, Zuckerhaltigkeit; (*fig.*) Süßlichkeit.

sugar|-loaf, *s.* 1. der Zuckerhut; 2. (*fig.*) Bergkegel. **–-maple,** *s.* der Zuckerahorn. **–-mite,** *s.* die Zuckermilbe. **–-plantation,** *s.* die Zucker(rohr)pflanzung. **–plum,** *s.* das Zuckerplätzchen (*also fig.*). **–-refinery,** *s.* die Zuckerfabrik, Zuckerraffinerie. **–-tongs,** *pl.* die Zuckerzange.

sugary [ˈʃugəri], *adj.* 1. zuck(e)rig, zuckersüß; 2. zuckerhaltig; Zucker–; 3. (*fig.*) süßlich.

suggest [səˈdʒest], *v.t.* 1. vorschlagen, andeuten, anspielen auf (*Acc.*); nahelegen, empfehlen, anregen zu; 2. hinweisen *or* hindeuten auf (*Acc.*), zu verstehen geben, schließen lassen auf (*Acc.*); 3. suggerieren, eingeben, einflüstern, einflößen; – ***itself***, sich aufdrängen (*as an idea*); – ***itself to him***, ihm in den Sinn kommen. **suggestibility** [–iˈbiliti], *s.* die Beeinflußbarkeit. **suggestible,** *adj.* beeinflußbar, zu beeinflussen(d), suggerierbar, suggestibel (*of a p.*). **suggestion** [–tʃən], *s.* 1. der Vorschlag, Hinweis, Wink, die Anregung; ***at the – of***, auf Anregung von; ***make a*** –, einen Vorschlag machen; 2. die Andeutung, Anspielung (***of***, auf (*Acc.*)), Idee, Spur, der Hauch, Anflug; ***no – of***, keine Spur von; 3. die Eingebung, Einflüsterung, Beeinflussung, Suggestion. **suggestive** [–tiv], *adj.* 1. andeutend (***of***, *Acc.*), erinnernd (an (*Acc.*)); ***be – of***, deuten auf (*Acc.*), andeuten; 2. anregend, vielsagend; 3. (*fig.*) anzüglich, zweideutig, schlüpfrig. **suggestiveness,** *s.* 1. das Gedankenanregende, Vielsagende; 2. (*fig.*) die Anzüglichkeit, Zweideutigkeit, Schlüpfrigkeit.

suicidal [s(j)uːiˈsaidl], *adj.* selbstmörderisch, Selbstmord–. **suicide** [ˈs(j)uːisaid], *s.* 1. der Selbstmord, Freitod; ***commit*** –, Selbstmord begehen; 2. der (die) Selbstmörder(in).

suint [swint], *s.* das Schafwollfett, der Wollschweiß.

suit [sjuːt], **1.** *s.* 1. (*Law*) (*also – **at law, law–***) die Klage(sache), der Rechtsstreit, Rechtshandel; ***civil*** –, die Zivilklage; 2. das Gesuch, Anliegen, die Bitte; Werbung, der (Heirats)antrag; 3. (*also – **of clothes***) Anzug (*of a man*), das Kostüm (*of a woman*); ***cut one's – according to one's cloth***, sich nach der Decke strecken; 4. (*rare*) der Satz, die Garnitur; – ***of armour***, vollständige Rüstung; – ***of harness***, die Geschirrgarnitur; – ***of sails***, der Satz Segel; 5. (*Cards*) die Farbe; ***follow*** –, Farbe bekennen, (*fig.*) dem Beispiel folgen, dasselbe tun. **2.** *v.t.* 1. anpassen (***to***, *Dat.*), passend *or* geeignet machen (zu), abstimmen (auf (*Acc.*)), einrichten (nach); – ***the action to the word***, dem Worte die Tat folgen lassen; 2. passen (*Dat.*), gefallen (*Dat.*), recht sein (*Dat.*) (*a p.*); (*coll.*) – ***yourself!*** tu, wie's dir beliebt! ***are you –ed?*** haben Sie etwas Passendes gefunden? 3. angemessen sein (*Dat.*), sich eignen für *or* zu, sich schicken *or* ziemen für, entsprechen (*Dat.*); (*coll.*) – ***his book***, ihm in den Kram passen; – ***the occasion***, sich der Lage anpassen; – ***his purpose***, seinem Zwecke entsprechen; 4. passen zu, (an)stehen (*Dat.*), kleiden (*as clothes*); ***the hat –s her*** (*Scots **she –s the hat***), der Hut steht ihr; 5. bekommen (*Dat.*), zusagen (*Dat.*) (*as climate, food etc.*). **3.** *v.i.* 1. passen (*Dat.*), zufriedenstellen; 2. passen (***to, with***, zu), entsprechen (*Dat.*), übereinstimmen (mit).

suitability [sjuːtəˈbiliti], *s.* die Eignung, Angemessenheit, Gemäßheit, Schicklichkeit. **suitable** [ˈsjuːtəbl], *adj.* passend, geeignet (***to, for***, zu *or* für); angemessen, gemäß (*Dat.*), schicklich, geziemend (für); ***be*** –, sich eignen, passen; sich schicken. **suitableness,** *s. See* **suitability.**

suitcase, *s.* der Handkoffer.

suite [swiːt], *s.* 1. das Gefolge (*of a prince etc.*); 2. die Reihe, Folge (***of***, von); 3. das Appartement; (Zimmer)einrichtung, (Möbel)garnitur; – ***of rooms***, die Zimmerflucht; ***bedroom*** –, die Schlafzimmereinrichtung; 4. (*Mus.*) die Suite.

suited [ˈsjuːtid], *adj.* geeignet, passend (***to, for***, zu *or* für). **suiting,** *s.* der Herrenstoff. **suitor,** *s.*

1. (*Law*) der Kläger, Prozeßführende(r); 2. der Freier; 3. Bewerber (*for*, um), Bittsteller.
sulcate(d) ['sʌlkeit(id)], *adj.* (*Bot., Anat.*) gefurcht, furchig. **sulcus,** *s.* die Furche.
sulfur *etc.*, (*Am.*) *see* **sulphur.**
sulk [sʌlk], **1.** *v.i.* schmollen, trotzen. **2.** *s.* (*usu. pl.*) das Schmollen, Trotzen; ***have the –s,*** schlechte Laune haben. **sulkiness,** *s.* das Schmollen, schlechte *or* üble Laune. **sulky, 1.** *adj.* mürrisch, verdrießlich, schmollend, übelgelaunt. **2.** *s.* (*obs.*) zweirädriger einsitziger Einspänner.
sullen ['sʌlən], *adj.* düster, finster, trübe; mürrisch, verdrießlich, grämlich; trotzig, störrisch, eigensinnig, widerspenstig, verstockt. **sullenness,** *s.* die Düsterkeit, Verdrießlichkeit, Widerspenstigkeit, der Trotz, Eigensinn.
sully ['sʌli], **1.** *v.t.* besudeln, beschmutzen (*usu. fig.*). **2.** *v.i.* schmutzig werden, schmutzen.
sulphate ['sʌlfeit], *s.* das Sulfat, schwefelsaures Salz; – ***of copper,*** das Kupfervitriol; – ***of soda,*** schwefelsaures Natron, das Glaubersalz. **sulphide** [–faid], *s.* das Sulfid; ***hydrogen –,*** der Schwefelwasserstoff; ***mercuric –,*** der Zinnober. **sulphite** [–fait], *s.* das Sulfit, schwefligsaures Salz.
sulphur ['sʌlfə], *s.* der Schwefel; – ***dioxide,*** das Schwefeldioxyd; ***flowers of –,*** die Schwefelblüte, Schwefelblumen (*pl.*); ***milk of –,*** die Schwefelmilch; ***stick –,*** der Stangenschwefel; – ***spring,*** die Schwefelquelle.
sulphurate ['sʌlfjəreit], *v.t.* (ein)schwefeln. **sulphuration** [–'reiʃən], *s.* das Schwefeln, die (Aus)schwefelung. **sulphureous** [–'fjuəriəs], *adj.* schwef(e)lig, schwefelhaltig, Schwefel–. **sulphuret** [–ret], *s.* (*obs.*) die Schwefelverbindung. **sulphuretted,** *adj.* geschwefelt; – ***hydrogen,*** der Schwefelwasserstoff. **sulphuric** [–'fjuərik], *adj.* Schwefel–; – ***acid,*** die Schwefelsäure. **sulphurize** [–raiz], *v.t.* (aus)schwefeln, sulfieren, sulfonieren, sulfurieren, vulkanisieren. **sulphurous** [–rəs], *adj.* Schwefel–, schwef(e)lig; – ***acid,*** schwef(e)lige Säure.
sultan ['sʌltən], *s.* der Sultan. **sultana** [–'tɑ:nə], *s.* 1. die Sultanin; 2. (*also* – ***raisin***) Sultanine. **sultanate** [–tənit], *s.* das Sultanat.
sultriness ['sʌltrinis], *s.* die Schwüle. **sultry,** *adj.* schwül (*also fig.*), drückend.
sum [sʌm], **1.** *s.* 1. die Summe (*also fig.*), Geldsumme, der (Gesamt)betrag, die Endsumme; – ***total,*** die Gesamtsumme, der Gesamtbetrag; 2. (*fig.*) die Gesamtheit, das Ganze; ***in –,*** insgesamt; 3. (*fig.*) das Wesen, der Kern, Inbegriff; 4. (*obs. fig.*) Höhepunkt, Gipfel; 5. (*coll.*) die Rechenaufgabe; *pl.* (*coll.*) das Rechnen; ***do a –,*** (eine Aufgabe) rechnen; ***good at –s,*** gut im Rechnen sein, gut rechnen können. **2.** *v.t.* 1. zusammenrechnen, zusammenzählen, summieren, addieren; – ***up,*** ausmachen; 2. (*fig.*) (*usu.* – ***up***) (kurz) zusammenfassen, resümieren, rekapitulieren; 3. (*fig. coll.*) – ***up,*** zusammennehmen, aufbieten (*resources, strength etc.*); 4. – ***up,*** abschätzen, prüfend messen (*with a glance*). **3.** *v.i.* (*fig.*) – ***up,*** zusammenfassen, eine Übersicht geben.
Sumerian [su'miəriən], **1.** *s.* 1. der (die) Sumerer(in); 2. (*language*) das Sumerisch(e). **2.** *adj.* sumerisch.
summariness ['sʌmərinis], *s.* die Kürze, summarisches Verfahren. **summarize,** *v.t.* zusammenfassen. **summary, 1.** *adj.* (kurz) zusammenfassend, summarisch; – ***court,*** einfaches Militärgericht; – ***jurisdiction,*** die Schnellgerichtsbarkeit; – ***procedure,*** das Schnellverfahren. **2.** *s.* die Zusammenstellung, Zusammenfassung, Übersicht, der Abriß, Hauptinhalt. **summation** [sʌ'meiʃən], *s.* 1. die Summierung, das Zusammenzählen; 2. die (Gesamt)summe.
[1]**summer** ['sʌmə], *s.* (*Archit.*) der Trägerbalken, Tragstein, Kragstein, die Oberschwelle.
[2]**summer, 1.** *s.* der Sommer; ***Indian –,*** der Spätsommer, Nachsommer, Altweibersommer; ***of 18 –s,*** von 18 Jahren. **2.** *adj.* sommerlich, Sommer–; – ***clothes,*** Sommerkleider (*pl.*); ***–('s) day,*** der Sommertag; – ***lightning,*** das Wetterleuchten; – ***solstice,*** die Sommersonnenwende; – ***term,*** das Sommersemester; – ***time,*** die Sommerzeit (*on clocks*); *see also* **summertime**; – ***weather,*** sommerliches Wetter. **3.** *v.i.* den Sommer verbringen *or* zubringen, (*of cattle*) übersommern. **4.** *v.t.* übersommern lassen (*cattle*).
summerhouse, *s.* das Gartenhaus, die Gartenlaube. **summerlike, summerly,** *adj.* sommerlich. **summer|-resort,** *s.* die Sommerfrische. **–time,** *s.* die Sommerszeit, der Sommer. **summery,** *adj. See* **summerlike.**
summing-up ['sʌmiŋ'ʌp], *s.* das Resümee, kurze Zusammenfassung; (*Law*) die (Rechts)beratung.
summit ['sʌmit], *s.* 1. der Gipfel (*also fig.*), die (Berg)spitze; – ***conference,*** die Gipfelkonferenz; – ***level,*** die Scheitelhöhe; 2. (*fig.*) der Höhepunkt, höchstes Ziel.
summon ['sʌmən], *v.t.* 1. (ein)berufen, zusammenrufen (*a meeting*); 2. (*Law*) vorladen, (vor Gericht) laden *or* zitieren; 3. kommen lassen, (zu sich) bestellen, (auf)rufen, auffordern; – ***away,*** wegrufen; 4. (*fig.*) (*also* – ***up***) zusammennehmen, aufbieten (*strength*), fassen (*courage*). **summoner,** *s.* (*Hist.*) der Gerichtsbote. **summons** [–z], **1.** *s.* 1. der Aufruf, die Aufforderung; 2. Berufung, Zusammenrufung; 3. (*Law*) (Vor)ladung; ***take out*** or ***issue a – against,*** vorladen lassen; ***serve a – on,*** vorladen, eine Ladung zustellen (*Dat.*). **2.** *v.t.* (*coll.*) vorladen, (vor Gericht) laden *or* zitieren.
sump [sʌmp], *s.* 1. der Sammelbehälter, die Senkgrube; 2. (*Motor.*) Ölwanne; 3. (*Min.*) das Gesenk, der (Schacht)sumpf.
sumpter ['sʌmptə], **1.** *s.* (*obs.*) das Lasttier, Saumtier. **2.** *attrib. adj.* Pack–, Saum–.
sumption ['sʌmpʃən], *s.* (*Log.*) der Obersatz.
sumptuary ['sʌmptjuəri], *adj.* den Aufwand betreffend, Aufwand(s)–.
sumptuous ['sʌmptjuəs], *adj.* kostbar, kostspielig, herrlich, prächtig. **sumptuousness,** *s.* der (Pracht)aufwand, Luxus, die Pracht.
sun [sʌn], **1.** *s.* 1. die Sonne; der Sonnenschein, das Sonnenlicht, die Sonnenwärme; ***against the –,*** (*Phot.*) gegen die Sonne *or* das Licht; gegen den Uhrzeigersinn; ***have the – in one's eyes,*** die Sonne im Gesicht haben; ***in the –,*** in der Sonne, im Sonnenschein; (*fig.*) ***a place in the –,*** ein Platz an der Sonne; (*Astr.*) ***mock –,*** die Nebensonne; (*Naut.*) ***shoot*** or ***take the –,*** die Höhe der Sonne messen, die Sonne schießen; ***under the –,*** unter der Sonne, auf Erden; ***with the –,*** im Uhrzeigersinn; bei Tagesanbruch; 2. (*Poet.*) der Tag. **2.** *v.i.* sich sonnen, ein Sonnenbad nehmen. **3.** *v.t.* sonnen, der Sonne aussetzen, in die Sonne stellen; – ***o.s.,*** sich sonnen.
sun|-and-planet (gear), *s.* das Planetengetriebe. **–-baked,** *adj.* an der Sonne (aus)getrocknet. **–-bath,** *s.* das Sonnenbad. **–-bathe,** *v.i.* sich sonnen, ein Sonnenbad nehmen. **–beam,** *s.* der Sonnenstrahl. **–blind,** *s.* die Markise, das Sonnendach. **–burn,** *s.* der Sonnenbrand. **–burned, –burnt,** *adj.* sonn(en)verbrannt.
sundae ['sʌndei], *s.* das Fruchteis, der Eisbecher.
Sunday ['sʌndi], **1.** *s.* der Sonntag; ***on –,*** (am) Sonntag; ***on –s,*** sonntags; (*coll.*) ***a month of –s,*** ewig, unendlich lange (Zeit), eine Ewigkeit. **2.** *attrib. adj.* (*coll.*) – ***best,*** der Sonntagsstaat, Sonntagskleider (*pl.*); – ***school,*** die Sonntagsschule. **Sunday-go-to-meeting,** *attrib. adj.* (*coll.*) Feiertags–.
sunder ['sʌndə], **1.** *v.t.* (*Poet.*) sondern, trennen; (*fig.*) entzweien. **2.** *v.i.* zerreißen, sich trennen. **3.** *s.* (*Poet.*) ***in –,*** entzwei, auseinander.
sun|dew, *s.* (*Bot.*) der Sonnentau. **–dial,** *s.* die Sonnenuhr. **–down,** *s.* (*esp. Am.*) der Sonnenuntergang. **–downer,** *s.* (australischer) Landstreicher. **–-dried,** *adj.* an der Sonne getrocknet.
sundries ['sʌndriz], *pl.* 1. Verschiedenes, Diverses; 2. Extraspesen (*pl.*), Nebenkosten (*pl.*). **sundry** [–ri], *adj.* verschiedene, mannigfaltige, allerlei, allerhand, mehrere, etliche, einige; ***all and –,*** all und jeder, alle miteinander.

sun|fish, *s.* der Sonnenfisch, Mondfisch, Klumpfisch. **–flower,** *s.* die Sonnenblume.

sung [sʌŋ], *p.p. of* **sing.**

sun|-god, *s.* der Sonnengott. **--helmet,** *s.* der Tropenhelm.

sunk [sʌŋk], **1.** *p.p. of* **sink. 2.** *adj.* 1. (*Tech.*) versenkt, vertieft, eingelassen; – ***fence,*** das Aha; 2. (*sl.*) ruiniert, (unrettbar) verloren (*of a p.*). **sunken,** *adj.* 1. versunken, (ein)gesunken; – ***road,*** der Hohlweg; – ***rock,*** blinde Klippe; – ***ship,*** gesunkenes Schiff; 2. tiefliegend, tief eingelassen, versenkt; 3. eingefallen (*cheeks*), hohl (*eyes*).

sun-lamp, *s.* künstliche Höhensonne. **sunless,** *adj.* sonnenlos, ohne Sonne, lichtlos. **sun|light,** *s.* der Sonnenschein, das Sonnenlicht. **–like,** *adj.* sonnenähnlich, Sonnen–. **–lit,** *adj.* von der Sonne beleuchtet, sonnenbeschienen. **sunniness,** *s.* 1. die Sonnigkeit; 2. (*fig.*) Heiterkeit. **sunny,** *adj.* sonnig (*also fig.*), sonnenhell, sonnenklar; (*fig.*) heiter; ***the – side,*** die Sonnenseite; (*fig.*) Lichtseite, heitere Seite.

sun|-parlour, *s.* (*Am.*) die Glasveranda. **–proof,** *adj.* für Sonnenstrahlen undurchlässig, lichtfest, sonnenbeständig. **–ray,** *s.* der Sonnenstrahl. **–rise,** *s.* der Sonnenaufgang. **–set,** *s.* der Sonnenuntergang; ***at –,*** bei Sonnenuntergang; – ***sky,*** das Abendrot, der Abendhimmel. **–shade,** *s.* der Sonnenschirm. **–shine,** *s.* 1. der Sonnenschein, das Sonnenlicht; sonniges Wetter; (*Motor.*) – ***roof,*** das Schiebedach; 2. (*fig.*) die Fröhlichkeit, Heiterkeit; das Glück, der Glanz. **–shiny,** *adj.* sonnig (*also fig.*); (*fig.*) heiter. **–spot,** *s.* der Sonnenfleck. **–stroke,** *s.* der Hitzschlag, Sonnenstich. **–tan,** *s.* die Sonnenbräune. **--up,** *s.* (*Am.*) der Sonnenaufgang. **--worship,** *s.* die Sonnenanbetung. **--worshipper,** *s.* der (die) Sonnenanbeter(in).

[1]**sup** [sʌp], **1.** *s.* der Schluck, Mundvoll; ***a bite and a –,*** etwas zu essen und zu trinken; ***neither bite nor –,*** nichts zu nagen und zu beißen. **2.** *v.i.* nippen. **3.** *v.t.* 1. (*esp. Scots*) in kleinen Mengen essen *or* trinken; 2. (*fig. Poet.*) (gründlich) auskosten, erleben.

[2]**sup,** *v.i.* (*Poet., obs.*) zu Abend essen; – ***on*** or ***off,*** zum Abendessen haben.

super [ˈs(j)uːpə], **1.** *s.* (*coll.*) *abbr. for* **superintendent,** (*Theat.*) **supernumerary. 2.** *adj.* (*sl.*) fabelhaft, prima, erstklassig. **3.** *pref.* über–, Über–, ober–.

superable [ˈsjuːpərəbl], *adj.* überwindbar, überwindlich.

super|abound, *v.i.* 1. überreichlich vorhanden sein; 2. Überfluß *or* Überschuß *or* eine Überfülle haben (***in, with,*** an (*Dat.*)). **–abundance,** *s.* der Überfluß, Überschuß, die Überfülle (***of,*** an (*Dat.*)). **–abundant,** *adj.* überreichlich, übergenug, im Überfluß vorhanden. **–add,** *v.t.* noch hinzufügen (***to,*** zu); ***be –ed to,*** noch dazukommen zu. **–addition,** *s.* weitere Hinzufügung, die Zugabe, der Zusatz; ***in –,*** zusätzlich, noch obendrein. **–annuate,** *v.t.* in den Ruhestand versetzen, pensionieren. **–annuated,** *adj.* 1. pensioniert, in den Ruhestand versetzt, entpflichtet, ausgedient; 2. (*coll.*) überaltert, überholt, verjährt, veraltet, unmodern. **–annuation,** *s.* 1. die Pensionierung, Entpflichtung; 2. Pension, Altersrente, das Ruhegehalt; – ***contribution,*** der Altersversicherungsbeitrag.

superb [sjuˈpəːb], *adj.* prächtig, prachtvoll, herrlich; ausgezeichnet, hervorragend, vorzüglich, großartig.

super|cargo, *s.* der Ladungsaufseher, Kargadeur. **–charged,** *adj.* vorverdichtend, Kompressor– (*engine*). **–charger,** *s.* der Überverdichter, Vorverdichter; das Aufladegebläse.

superciliary [sjuːpəˈsiliəri], *adj.* Augenbrauen–. **supercilious,** *adj.* 1. hochmütig, hochnäsig, anmaßend; 2. herablassend, geringschätzig, verächtlich. **superciliousness,** *s.* 1. der Hochmut, die Anmaßung, Hochnäsigkeit; 2. Herablassung, Geringschätzigkeit.

super|dominant, *s.* (*Mus.*) die Oberdominante. **–eminence,** *s.* 1. die Vorzüglichkeit, Vortrefflichkeit, überragende Bedeutung; 2. Vorrangstellung, der Vorrang. **–eminent,** *adj.* vorzüglich, vortrefflich, überragend, hervorragend (***for,*** wegen).

supererogation [sjuːpərerəˈgeiʃən], *s.* die Mehrleistung, überschüssige *or* übergebührliche Leistung; (*fig.*) die Übertreibung, das Übermaß; (*R.C.*) ***works of –,*** über Gebühr getane gute Werke. **supererogatory** [–rəˈrɔgətəri], *adj.* übergebührlich, ungefordert, überschüssig, überflüssig.

super|excellence, *s.* höchste Vortrefflichkeit. **–excellent,** *adj.* höchst vortrefflich, unübertrefflich. **–fecundation,** *s.* 1. (*Biol.*) die Überbefruchtung, Überschwängerung; 2. (*fig.*) Überproduktion, der Überfluß (***of,*** an (*Dat.*)).

superficial [sjuːpəˈfiʃəl], *adj.* 1. Flächen–, Quadrat– (*measure*); 2. Oberflächen–, oberflächlich (*also fig.*), äußer(lich); 3. (*fig.*) flüchtig, seicht. **superficiality** [–iˈæliti], *s.* 1. die (Ober)flächenlage; 2. (*usu. fig.*) Oberflächlichkeit, Seichtheit. **superficies** [–ˈfiʃiiːz], *s.* die Oberfläche, Außenseite, äußeres Erscheinungsbild, äußerer Anschein.

super|fine, *adj.* 1. extrafein, hochfein, superfein; 2. überfeinert, preziös. **–fineness,** *s.* 1. extrafeine Qualität; 2. die Überfeinerung.

superfluity [sjuːpəˈfluiti], *s.* der Überfluß (***of,*** an (*Dat.*)); die Überflüssigkeit. **superfluous** [sjuˈpəːfluəs], *adj.* 1. überflüssig, überschüssig, überzählig, unnötig; 2. (über)reichlich (vorhanden).

super|foetation, *s. See* **–fecundation, 1. –heat,** *v.t.* überhitzen; ***–ed steam,*** der Heißdampf. **–het(erodyne)** [–ˈhet(ərədain)], *s.* (*Rad.*) der Überlagerungsempfänger. **–human,** *adj.* übermenschlich.

super|impose, *v.t.* 1. legen, setzen, schichten, lagern (***on,*** auf (*Acc.*) *or* über (*Acc.*)); 2. überlagern; 3. hinzufügen (***on,*** zu). **–imposed,** *adj.* 1. übereinanderliegend, darübergelegt, übereinandergeschichtet; 2. überlagert (***with,*** von); 3. hinzugefügt. **–incumbent,** *adj.* daraufliegend, darüberliegend. **–induce,** *v.t.* noch hinzufügen, beifügen (***on,*** *Dat.*), zusätzlich herbeiführen *or* einführen (zu).

superintend, *v.t.* vorstehen (*Dat.*), überwachen, beaufsichtigen, verwalten. **superintendence,** *s.* die (Ober)aufsicht (***over,*** über (*Acc.*)), Verwaltung, Leitung (***of,*** *Gen.*). **superintendency,** *s.* 1. der Aufsichtsbereich, Verwaltungsbezirk; 2. (*Eccl.*) die Superintendentur. **superintendent, 1.** *s.* 1. der Inspektor, Vorsteher, Verwalter, Leiter, Direktor; – ***of police,*** der Polizeidirektor; 2. der Oberaufseher, Aufsichtsbeamte(r); 3. (*Eccl.*) der Superintendent. **2.** *adj.* Aufsichts–, Kontroll–, leitend, aufsichtführend.

superior [sjuːˈpiəriə], **1.** *adj.* 1. höher(stehend), ober; 2. (*in rank*) vorgesetzt, Ober–; – ***court,*** das Obergericht, höhere Instanz; – ***officer,*** Vorgesetzte(r); 3. (*in degree*) überlegen (***to,*** *Dat.*), erhaben (über (*Acc.*)), größer, stärker, besser, bedeutender (als); ***be – to,*** übertreffen (***in,*** in *or* an (*Dat.*)); ***be – in number,*** zahlenmäßig überlegen sein (***to,*** *Dat.*), in der Überzahl *or* Übermacht sein; – ***force,*** die Übermacht; 4. (*esp. Comm.*) hervorragend, ausgezeichnet, erlesen, (*as wine*) Edel–; – ***quality,*** erste *or* beste Qualität; 5. (*Typ.*) hochgestellt, hochstehend; 6. (*iron.*) überheblich, herablassend; 7. (*iron.*) vornehm, fein. **2.** *s.* 1. (*usu. with poss. pron.*) Überlegene(r) (***in,*** in *or* an (*Dat.*)); ***he has no –,*** ihn übertrifft keiner, ihm kommt keiner gleich (***in,*** in *or* an (*Dat.*)); ***he is my –,*** er übertrifft mich, er ist mir überlegen (***in,*** in *or* an (*Dat.*)); 2. (*in rank*) Vorgesetzte(r); 3. (*Eccl.*) der Superior, Oberer; ***mother –,*** die Oberin. **superiority** [–iˈɔriti], *s.* 1. die Überlegenheit, Erhabenheit (***to, over,*** über (*Acc.*); ***in,*** in *or* an (*Dat.*)); 2. Übermacht, das Übergewicht, der Vorzug, Vorrang; 3. (*iron.*) die Überheblichkeit.

superlative [sjuːˈpəːlətiv], **1.** *adj.* 1. höchst, größt; überragend, hervorragend, unübertrefflich; 2. (*Gram.*) superlativisch, Superlativ–; – ***degree,*** der Superlativ. **2.** *s.* (*Gram.*) der Superlativ, die Meiststufe; ***speak in –s,*** übertreiben, in den höchsten Tönen sprechen. **superlatively,** *adv.* überaus, im höchsten Grade, über die Maßen. **superlativeness,** *s.* 1. höchster Grad; 2. die Vortrefflichkeit, Unübertrefflichkeit.

super|man, *s.* der Übermensch. **–market,** *s.* der Supermarkt. **–maxilla,** *s.* (*Anat.*) der Oberkiefer. **–maxillary,** *adj.* Oberkiefer–. **–mundane,** *adj.* überweltlich, überirdisch.

supernal [sju:'pə:nl], *adj.* (*Poet.*) erhaben, überirdisch, jenseitig, himmlisch.

super|natural, 1. *adj.* übernatürlich, wunderbar. 2. *s.* das Übernatürliche, Wunderbare. **–naturalism,** *s.* der Supernaturalismus, Wunderglaube, Offenbarungsglaube. **–naturalness,** *s.* die Übernatürlichkeit. **–normal,** *adj.* überdurchschnittlich, übernormal, ungewöhnlich, außergewöhnlich. **–nova,** *s.* (*Astr.*) die Supernova. **–numerary,** 1. *adj.* außerplanmäßig, überzählig, extra. 2. *s.* 1. überzählige P. *or* S., Hilfsangestellte(r), außerplanmäßiger Beamter; 2. (*Theat.*) der (die) Statist(in). **–oxide,** *s.* das (Su)peroxyd. **–phosphate,** *s.* das Superphosphat, überphosphorsaures Salz.

super|pose, *v.t.* (auf)legen, lagern, schichten (*on,* auf *or* über (*Acc.*)), übereinanderlegen, übereinanderstellen. **–position,** *s.* (*Geol.*) die Über(einander)lagerung, Schichtung. **–power,** 1. *adj.* (*Elec.*) Groß–, Hochleistungs–. 2. *s.* (*Pol.*) die Supermacht. **–saturate,** *v.t.* übersättigen. **–saturation,** *s.* die Übersättigung. **–scribe,** *v.t.* beschriften, überschreiben. **–scription** [–'skripʃən], *s.* die Überschrift, Aufschrift.

supersede [sju:pə'si:d], *v.t.* 1. beiseitesetzen, beseitigen, abschaffen, außer Gebrauch setzen, aufheben (*a th.*); 2. ersetzen (*a th. or p.*), verdrängen, überflüssig machen, an die Stelle treten von; ablösen, Nachfolger (*Gen.*) werden (*a p.*); ***be –d by,*** abgelöst werden von. **supersedeas** [–iəs], *s.* (*Law*) der Suspendierungsbefehl, Hemmungsbefehl. **supersedence, supersedure** [–'si:djə], *s.* 1. die Ersetzung, der Ersatz (***by,*** durch); 2. die Verdrängung, Abschaffung, Absetzung, Enthebung.

super|sensitive, *adj.* überempfindlich. **–sensual, –sensuous,** *adj.* übersinnlich.

supersession [sju:pə'seʃən], *s. See* **supersedence.**

supersonic [sju:pə'sɔnik], *adj.* (*Phys.*) Ultraschall–; (*Av.*) Überschall–.

superstition [sju:pə'stiʃən], *s.* der Aberglaube. **superstitious** [–ʃəs], *adj.* abergläubisch. **superstitiousness,** *s.* der Hang zum Aberglauben, Aberglaube.

super|stratum, *s.* obere Schicht, die Oberschicht. **–structure,** *s.* der Oberbau, Überbau, Aufbauten (*pl.*). **–tax,** *s. See* **surtax. –temporal,** *adj.* überzeitlich.

supervene [sju:pə'vi:n], *v.i.* (noch) dazukommen *or* hinzukommen *or* hinzutreten ((***up***)***on,*** zu), unvermutet eintreten, sich plötzlich einstellen. **supervention** [–'venʃən], *s.* das Hinzukommen, Dazwischenkommen, unvermutetes Eintreten.

supervise ['sju:pəvaiz], *v.t.* die Aufsicht haben *or* führen über (*Acc.*), beaufsichtigen, überwachen. **supervision** [–'viʒən], *s.* die Überwachung, Beaufsichtigung, (Ober)aufsicht, Leitung, Kontrolle (***of,*** über (*Acc.*)). **supervisor** [–vaizə], *s.* der Aufseher, Inspektor, Leiter. **supervisory,** *adj.* Aufsichts–, Überwachungs–.

supination [sju:pi'neiʃən], *s.* (*Anat.*) die Aufwärtsdrehung. **supine** ['sju:pain], 1. *adj.* 1. auf dem Rücken liegend, rückwärts gestreckt, zurückgelehnt; – ***position,*** die Rückenlage; 2. (*fig.*) energielos, untätig, träge, nachlässig. 2. *s.* (*Gram.*) das Supinum. **supineness,** *s.* die (Nach)lässigkeit, Gleichgültigkeit, Untätigkeit, Trägheit.

supper ['sʌpə], *s.* das Abendessen, Abendbrot, Nachtmahl; (*Eccl.*) Abendmahl; ***the Last Supper,*** das letzte Abendmahl; ***the Lord's Supper,*** das Heilige Abendmahl. **supperless,** *adj.* ohne Abendessen.

supplant [sə'plɑ:nt], *v.t.* (vom Platz *or* Amt) verdrängen (*a p.*); verdrängen, ersetzen (*a th.*).

supple [sʌpl], 1. *adj.* biegsam, geschmeidig (*also fig.*), elastisch; (*fig.*) nachgiebig, fügsam, anpassungsfähig, lenkbar, willfährig. 2. *v.t.* biegsam machen.

supplement, 1. ['sʌplimənt], *s.* 1. die Ergänzung, der Nachtrag, Anhang, Zusatz (***to,*** zu); 2. die Beilage (*to a newspaper*); 3. der Ergänzungsband, Nachtragsband (*to a book*); 4. (*Geom.*) das Supplement. 2. [–ment], *v.t.* ergänzen (***with,*** durch); ***the work was –ed with some illustrations,*** in dem Werk wurden einige Bilder nachgetragen. **supplemental** [–'mentl], (*usu.*) **supplementary** [–'mentəri], *adj.* ergänzend, Ergänzungs–, Nach(trags)–, Zusatz–; (*Geom.*) Supplementär–; ***be – to,*** ergänzen, einen Nachtrag bilden zu; – ***agreement,*** das Zusatzabkommen; – ***claim,*** die Nachforderung; (*Pol.*) – ***estimates,*** der Nachtragsetat; – ***order,*** die Nachbestellung; – ***engine,*** der Hilfsmotor, Ersatzmotor. **supplementation** [–'teiʃən], *s.* 1. das Ergänzen, Nachtragen; 2. die Ergänzung, der Zusatz, Nachtrag.

suppleness ['sʌplnis], *s.* die Biegsamkeit, Geschmeidigkeit, Nachgiebigkeit, Fügsamkeit, Willfährigkeit.

suppliant ['sʌpliənt], 1. *adj.* demütig bittend, flehend. 2. *s.* der Bittsteller, Flehende(r).

supplicant ['sʌplikənt], *s., adj. See* **suppliant. supplicate** [–keit], 1. *v.t.* 1. demütig bitten, anflehen, ersuchen (*a p.*); 2. erflehen, erbitten, bitten um (*a th.*). 2. *v.i.* demütig bitten, flehen, nachsuchen (***for,*** um). **supplication** [–'keiʃən], *s.* demütige Bitte (***for,*** um); das Flehen, (Bitt)gesuch, die Bittschrift; (Bitt)gebet. **supplicatory** [–kətəri], *adj.* flehend, demütig bittend, Bitt–.

supplier [sə'plaiə], *s.* der Versorger, Lieferant.

[1]**supply** [sə'plai], 1. *v.t.* 1. liefern, beschaffen, bereitstellen, zuführen (***to,*** *Dat.*); 2. beliefern, versorgen, versehen, ausstatten, speisen (***with,*** mit); 3. abhelfen (*Dat.*), ersetzen, ausgleichen (*a lack*), decken, befriedigen (*a need*), ausfüllen, ergänzen (*the background*); – ***the missing word,*** das fehlende Wort ergänzen; – ***the place of,*** vertreten. 2. *s.* 1. die Lieferung, Zufuhr, Beschaffung, Bereitstellung (***to,*** an (*Acc.*)); Versorgung, Belieferung; ***water –,*** die Wasserzufuhr, Wasserversorgung; 2. (*oft. pl.*) das Lager, der Bestand, Vorrat (***of,*** an (*Dat.*)); 3. die Ersetzung, Stellvertretung, Ergänzung; der Stellvertreter, Ersatzmann; ***on –,*** in Vertretung, als Stellvertreter *or* Ersatz; 4. (*Comm.*) das Angebot; – ***and demand,*** Angebot und Nachfrage; ***in short –,*** knapp; 5. (*Mil., usu. pl.*) der Proviant; Nachschub, das Versorgungsmaterial, Verstärkungen (*pl.*), Zufuhren (*pl.*); 6. (*Parl.*) gesondert zu bewilligende Gelder (*pl.*). 3. *attrib. adj.* (*Mil.*) – ***base,*** der Stapelplatz; (*Mil.*) – ***column,*** die Fahrtruppe, Nachschubkolonne; (*Mil.*) – ***lines,*** Nachschubverbindungen (*pl.*); – ***pipe,*** die Zuleitung, das Zuführungsrohr; – ***ship,*** das Troßschiff, Versorgungsschiff; – ***teacher,*** der Hilfslehrer.

support [sə'pɔ:t], 1. *v.t.* 1. (ab)stützen, tragen, (aufrecht)halten; – ***arms!*** Gewehr in Arm! 2. (*fig.*) ertragen, (er)dulden, aushalten; 3. eintreten für, fördern, befürworten, verteidigen (*a cause*), bestätigen, bekräftigen, begründen, rechtfertigen, vertreten (*a theory*), erhärten (*a charge*), unterstützen, (aufrecht)erhalten, behaupten (*an opinion etc.*); 4. erhalten, unterhalten, ernähren, sorgen für (***on,*** von) (*o.s., a family*); – ***o.s. on,*** sich erhalten von; 5. beistehen (*Dat.*), den Rücken decken (*Dat.*), zur Seite stehen (*Dat.*) (*a p.*); 6. (*Comm.*) finanzieren (*a project*), decken (*currency*). 2. *s.* 1. die Stütze, (Rück)halt; 2. Unterstützung, Hilfe, der Beistand; (*Mil.*) – ***trench,*** der Bereitschaftsgraben; ***give – to,*** unterstützen; (*Mil.*) ***in –,*** in Reserve; ***with the – of,*** mit Hilfe *or* dem Beistand von; 3. die Bekräftigung, Bestätigung, Verteidigung, Aufrechterhaltung, Erhärtung; ***in – of,*** zur Unterstützung (*Gen.*), zur Bestätigung von; 4. die Erhaltung, Unterhaltung; der (Lebens)unterhalt; 5. (*Tech.*) Ständer, Halter, Träger, das Gestell, Stativ, die Stütze, Strebe, Unterlage, Absteifung; Einlage (*for shoes*); 6. (*Theat.*) das Zusammenspiel, Ensemble.

supportable [sə'pɔ:təbl], *adj.* 1. tragbar, haltbar, vertretbar; 2. erträglich, zu ertragen(d), leidlich. **supporter,** *s.* 1. der (die) Unterstützer(in), Helfer(in), Gönner(in); Verteidiger(in), Verfechter(in) (*of an opinion etc.*); Anhänger(in), Vertreter(in) (*of a cause*); die Hilfe, der Beistand; 2. (*Tech.*) Träger, die Stütze; 3. (*Her.*) Wappenhalter, Schildhalter. **supporting,** *adj.* Stütz–, Unterstützungs–; – ***cast,*** das Ensemble; – ***film,*** zweiter Film, der Beifilm; (*Artil.*) – ***fire,*** das Unterstützungsfeuer; (*Theat.*) – ***player,*** der (die) Mitspieler(in), Nebendarsteller(in).

suppose [sə'pouz], *v.t.* 1. (als möglich *or* gegeben) annehmen, voraussetzen; – ***he didn't do it,*** angenommen *or* gesetzt, er täte es nicht; wenn er es nun nicht täte; – ***we go*** or ***went?*** wie wäre es, wenn wir gingen? 2. vermuten, mutmaßen, sich (*Dat.*) denken *or* vorstellen, meinen, glauben, (für wahrscheinlich) halten; ***I –,*** ich glaube es, ich nehme es an; ***I don't – so,*** vermutlich *or* wahrscheinlich nicht; ***I don't – he will come,*** ich glaube nicht, daß er kommen wird; (*coll. polite request*) ***I don't – you could . . .?*** könnten Sie doch vielleicht . . .? ***I – you are aware . . .,*** Sie wissen vermutlich . . .; ***they are soldiers, I –,*** es werden wohl Soldaten sein; 3. halten für; ***she is –d to be clever,*** sie gilt *or* man hält sie für klug, sie soll klug sein; 4. sollen; ***he is –d to know,*** man erwartet, daß er im Bilde ist; seine Aufgabe ist es, zu wissen. **supposed,** *adj.* vermutlich, angeblich, mutmaßlich, vermeintlich.

supposition [sʌpə'ziʃən], *s.* die Voraussetzung, Annahme, Vermutung, Mutmaßung; ***on the –,*** unter der Voraussetzung, in der Annahme. **suppositional,** *adj.* angenommen, vorausgesetzt, hypothetisch. **supposititious** [səpɔzi'tiʃəs], *adj.* untergeschoben, vergeblich, erdichtet, unecht, nur angenommen.

suppository [sə'pɔzitəri], *s.* das Darmzäpfchen, Stuhlzäpfchen; Scheidezäpfchen.

suppress [sə'pres], *v.t.* 1. niederschlagen, niederwerfen (*a rising*), unterdrücken (*a rising, publication, feelings*); 2. hemmen, stillen (*haemorrhage*), verhalten, ersticken (*feelings*); 3. streichen, tilgen, beseitigen (*a passage*), verbieten (*book etc.*); 4. abstellen, abschaffen, aufheben (*abuses etc.*); 5. verheimlichen, unterschlagen, verschweigen, vertuschen (*the truth etc.*); 6. (*Psych.*) verdrängen, hemmen. **suppressible,** *adj.* unterdrückbar. **suppression** [–'preʃən], *s.* 1. die Unterdrückung (*of riot, rumour, book, truth etc.*), Aufhebung, Abschaffung; 2. das Ersticken, Zurückhalten; 3. die Verschweigung, Verheimlichung, Vertuschung; 4. Streichung, Tilgung, Auslassung, Weglassung (*of a word*); 5. Hemmung, Verhaltung (*of the urine*). **suppressive** [–siv], *adj.* unterdrückend, Unterdrückungs–. **suppressor,** *s.* (*Tech.*) das Sperrgerät; (*Elec.*) Entstörungselement; (*Rad.*) – ***grid,*** das Fanggitter.

suppurate ['sʌpjureit], *v.i.* eitern. **suppuration** [–'reiʃən], *s.* die Eiterbildung, Eiterung. **suppurative** [–rətiv], *adj.* Eiter–, eiternd.

supra– ['sju:prə], *pref.* über–, ober–; *see* **super–.**

supra-axillary, *adj.* (*Bot.*) oberwinkelständig.

supralapsarian [sju:prəlæp'sɛəriən], *adj.* dem Sündenfall vorhergehend.

supramundane [sju:prəmʌn'dein], *adj.* überweltlich, überirdisch.

supremacy [sju'preməsi], *s.* 1. die Obergewalt, das Supremat (*of the king*); höchste Gewalt, die Oberhoheit, Herrschaft, Souveränität; ***oath of –,*** der Suprematseid; 2. (*fig.*) die Vorherrschaft, Überlegenheit, der Vorrang, das Übergewicht; ***naval –,*** die Vormachtstellung zur See.

supreme [sju:'pri:m], *adj.* oberst, höchst, größt, äußerst, letzt; – ***authority,*** oberste Regierungsgewalt; ***be –,*** herrschen (***over,*** über (*Acc.*)); ***Supreme Being,*** das höchste Wesen; (*Mil.*) – ***command,*** das Oberkommando; (*Am.*) ***Supreme Court,*** Oberstes Bundesgericht; (*Engl.*) ***Supreme Court of Judicature,*** Oberster Gerichtshof, (*Germany*) das Reichsgericht; (*coll.*) ***act of – folly,*** der Gipfel der Torheit; (*Phil.*) ***the – good,*** das höchste Gut; – ***moment,*** entscheidender *or* kritischer Augenblick; (*Comm.*) – ***quality,*** erstklassige Qualität; ***reign –,*** unumschränkte Herrschaft haben; – ***sacrifice,*** die Hingabe *or* Opferung *or* das Opfer des Lebens.

sural ['sjuərəl], *adj.* Waden–.

surbase ['sə:beis], *s.* (*Archit.*) der Kragen *or* Kranz des Postaments.

surcease [sə:'si:s], **1.** *s.* (*obs.*) 1. das Ende, Aufhören; 2. Nachlassen, die Unterbrechung, der Aufschub. **2.** *v.i.* 1. ein Ende nehmen, aufhören; 2. ablassen (***from,*** von).

surcharge, 1. [sə:'tʃɑ:dʒ], *v.t.* 1. (*rare*) überbürden, über(be)lasten, überladen; 2. überfüllen, übersättigen; 3. (*usu. Comm.*) zusätzlich belasten (*an account*); mit Strafgebühr *or* Zuschlag(s)porto belegen; überdrucken (*postage stamps*). **2.** ['sə:tʃɑ:dʒ], *s.* 1. (*rare*) die Überbürdung, Überladung, Über(be)lastung; 2. Überfüllung, Übersättigung; 3. (*usu. Comm.*) der Überpreis, die Mehrbelastung, Überforderung; Zuschlag(s)gebühr, Strafgebühr, das Zuschlag(s)porto, Nachporto, Strafporto; der Überdruck, neuer Aufdruck (*postage stamps*).

surcingle ['sə:siŋgl], *s.* 1. der (Sattel)gurt; 2. (*Eccl.*) Leibgurt.

surcoat ['sə:kout], *s.* (*Hist.*) der Wappenrock (*over armour*), Überrock.

surd [sə:d], **1.** *adj.* 1. (*Phonet.*) stimmlos; 2. (*Math.*) irrational. **2.** *s.* 1. (*Phonet.*) stimmloser Konsonant; 2. (*Math.*) irrationale Größe.

sure [ʃuə], **1.** *adj.* 1. (*pred. only: subjective opinion*) sicher, überzeugt, gewiß; ***be – of*** or ***about it,*** dessen sicher *or* davon überzeugt sein; ***I am –!*** allerdings! wirklich! ***I am not –,*** ich bin nicht sicher; ***are you –?*** wirklich? ***to be –!*** freilich! sicherlich! selbstverständlich! natürlich! 2. (*pred. only: objective reality*) zweifellos, (ganz) sicher *or* bestimmt, gewiß (wahr); ***as – as fate,*** so wahr ich lebe, todsicher; (*coll.*) ***as – as eggs is eggs,*** so sicher wie das Amen in der Kirche; ***be – to come,*** sicher kommen; ***be – and*** or ***to come!*** Sie müssen ja *or* gewiß kommen, Sie dürfen nicht vergessen zu kommen; ***you may be – that . . .,*** du kannst dich darauf verlassen daß . . .; – ***enough,*** tatsächlich, in der Tat, allerdings; (*coll.*) ***for –,*** sicher, gewiß; (*coll.*) ***to make –,*** um sicher zu gehen; ***make –,*** sich überzeugen (***of,*** von), sich versichern *or* vergewissern (*Gen.*) (*a th.*); sich bemächtigen (*Gen.*), sich (*Dat.*) sichern (*Acc.*) (*a fortress, throne etc.*); 3. sicher, gesichert, fest, standhaft; vertrauenswürdig, zuverlässig, verläßlich, unfehlbar; (*sl.*) – ***thing,*** see ***for –;*** – ***sign of,*** unfehlbares Anzeichen für *or* von *or* Kennzeichen *or* Merkmal von. **2.** *adv.* 1. (*coll. esp. Am.*) *see* **surely**; 2. (*Am. sl.*) wirklich, überaus, ungemein; 3. (*in reply*) gewiß, ganz bestimmt, selbstverständlich, klar.

sure|fire, *adj.* (*sl. esp. Am.*) verläßlich, zuverlässig. **–footed,** *adj.* fest auf den Füßen, sicher auf den Beinen, trittsicher; (*fig. coll.*) sicheren Fußes, unbeirrbar.

surely ['ʃuəli], *adv.* sicher(lich), zweifellos, ungezweifelt, wahrhaftig, in der Tat, doch (wohl); ***slowly but –,*** langsam aber sicher; ***he – cannot mean it,*** es kann doch (wohl) nicht sein Ernst sein. **sureness,** *s.* die Sicherheit, Gewißheit; Unbeirrbarkeit, feste Überzeugung. **surety** [–r(i)ti], *s.* 1. die Bürgschaft, Kaution, Garantie; der Bürge, Bürgschaftsgeber, Garant; ***stand –,*** Bürgschaft *or* Sicherheit leisten; 2. ***of a –,*** wahrhaftig, ganz gewiß, sicher(lich), ohne Zweifel.

surf [sə:f], **1.** *s.* die Brandung. **2.** *v.i.* wellenreiten.

surface ['sə:fis], **1.** *s.* 1. die Oberfläche; ***bring to the –,*** an die Oberfläche bringen; ***come to the –,*** an die Oberfläche *or* nach oben kommen; 2. (*fig.*) die Oberfläche; ***on the –,*** so weit man sehen kann *or* man sieht, oberflächlich (betrachtet), bei oberflächlicher Betrachtung; 3. die Außenseite, das Äußere, (*Geom.*) die Fläche; (*Geom.*) ***plane –,*** ebene Fläche, die Ebene; 4. (*Av.*) tragende Fläche, die Tragfläche; 5. (*Min.*) Erdoberfläche, der Tag; ***on the –,*** im Tagebau, über Tag; ***bring to the –,*** zutage fördern; 6. der Spiegel (*of water*).

2. *v.t.* 1. die Oberfläche behandeln; beschottern (*a road*); 2. (*Tech.*) plandrehen, planhobeln (*a material*). **3.** *v.i.* auftauchen (*as submarines*). **4.** *adj.* 1. Oberflächen–; – ***coat,*** der Deckanstrich; – ***crack,*** der Anriß; – ***craft,*** das Überwasserfahrzeug; –***-mail,*** gewöhnliche Post; – ***noise,*** das Störgeräusch (*gramophone*); – ***printing,*** der Reliefwalzendruck (*calico printing*); (*Typ.*) Reliefdruck, Hochdruck; – ***speed,*** die Überwassergeschwindigkeit (*of submarines*); – ***tension,*** die Oberflächenspannung; –***-to-air missile,*** der Fla-Flugkörper; –***-to-– missile,*** der Boden-Boden-Flugkörper; – ***water,*** das Oberflächenwasser; (*Min.*) – ***worker,*** der Tagebauarbeiter; 2. (*fig.*) oberflächlich, äußerlich, Schein–; – ***impression,*** oberflächlicher Eindruck; – ***value,*** der Augenschein, äußerer Eindruck.

surfboard [ˈsəːfbɔːd], *s.* das Gleitbrett.

surfeit [ˈsəːfit], **1.** *v.t.* übersättigen (*also fig.*), überfüttern; (*fig.*) überfüllen, überladen. **2.** *v.i.* sich übersättigen, übersättigt sein *or* werden, sich (*Dat.*) den Magen überladen (*of, with,* mit), bis zum Überdruß essen *or* trinken (von). **3.** *s.* 1. die Übersättigung, Überfüllung (*of,* mit); 2. Überfülle, das Übermaß, der Überfluß (an (*Dat.*)); Überdruß, Ekel; ***to*** (***a***) –, bis zum Überdruß.

surfing [ˈsəːfiŋ], **surf-riding,** *s.* das Wellenreiten.

surge [səːdʒ], **1.** *s.* 1. die Woge, Sturzsee; 2. Wellenbewegung, Brandung; 3. (*fig.*) (Auf)wallung, das Wogen (*of emotion*); 4. (*Elec.*) plötzlicher Anstieg. **2.** *v.i.* 1. branden, hochgehen (*of waves*); – ***forward,*** vorwärtsdrängen (*as a crowd*); 2. (*fig.*) (*oft.* – *up*) wogen, aufwallen, aufbrausen; 3. (*Elec.*) plötzlich ansteigen, heftig schwanken.

surgeon [ˈsəːdʒən], *s.* 1. der Chirurg; ***dental*** –, der Zahnarzt; ***house*** –, der Krankenhauschirurg; 2. (*Hist.*) der Wundarzt; 3. (*Mil.*) Schiffsarzt, Stabsarzt. **surgery** [–əri], *s.* 1. die Chirurgie; chirurgische Behandlung; (*fig.*) einschneidende Behandlung; ***plastic*** –, die Wiederherstellungschirurgie; 2. der Operationssaal; (*coll.*) das Sprechzimmer; (*coll.*) – ***hours,*** die Sprechstunde. **surgical** [–ikl], *adj.* chirurgisch; – ***wool,*** die Verbandwatte.

surging [ˈsəːdʒiŋ], **1.** *adj.* 1. wogend, brandend; 2. (*fig.*) (auf)wallend, (auf)brausend, ungestüm. **2.** *s.* 1. das Wogen, Branden; 2. (*fig.*) (Auf)brausen, (Auf)wallen; 3. (Vorwärts)drängen; 4. (*Elec.*) Pendeln, Schwingen, Schwanken.

surliness [ˈsəːlinis], *s.* die Verdrießlichkeit, Schroffheit, Grobheit. **surly** [–li], *adj.* mürrisch, verdrießlich, mißlaunig, griesgrämig; schroff, grob.

surmise [səːˈmaiz], **1.** *v.t.* 1. vermuten, mutmaßen, sich (*Dat.*) einbilden; 2. argwöhnen. **2.** *s.* 1. die Vermutung, Mutmaßung, Einbildung; 2. der Argwohn, Verdacht.

surmount [səːˈmaunt], *v.t.* 1. übersteigen (*obstacle*), überwinden (*difficulty*); 2. (*fig.*) (*rare*) überragen. **surmountable,** *adj,* übersteigbar, (*fig.*) überwindlich.

surname [ˈsəːneim], **1.** *s.* 1. der Familienname, Zuname; 2. (*obs.*) Beiname. **2.** *v.t.* (*rare*) den Beinamen geben (*Dat.*), (be)nennen.

surpass [səːˈpɑːs], *v.t.* 1. übersteigen (*a th.*); 2. übertreffen (*a p. or th.*); – ***o.s.,*** sich selbst übertreffen; ***not to be –ed,*** unübertrefflich. **surpassing,** *adj.* hervorragend, unübertrefflich, unerreicht, außerordentlich. **surpassingly,** *adv.* überaus, ungemein, außerordentlich.

surplice [ˈsəːplis], *s.* das Chorhemd, der Chorrock, die Stola.

surplus [ˈsəːpləs], **1.** *s.* 1. der Überschuß, Mehrbetrag, Rest; – ***fund,*** der Reservefonds, Überschußfonds, die Rücklage; 2. (*Comm.*) der Mehrertrag, Mehrwert, Wertüberschuß; – ***brought forward,*** der Gewinnvortrag. **2.** *adj.* überschüssig, Über(schuß)–, Mehr–, Reserve–; – ***population,*** die Überbevölkerung, der Bevölkerungsüberschuß; – ***profit,*** der Mehrertrag, überschüssiger Gewinn; – ***value,*** der Mehrwert; – ***weight,*** das Übergewicht, Mehrgewicht. **surplusage** [–idʒ], *s.* 1. der Überschuß, Überfluß (*of,* an (*Dat.*)); 2. (*Law*) unwesentlicher Umstand.

surprisal [səˈpraizl], *s.* (*obs.*) die Überraschung.

surprise [səˈpraiz], **1.** *v.t.* 1. überraschen; in Verwunderung *or* Erstaunen versetzen, verblüffen, befremden; ***be –d at,*** erstaunt sein *or* sich wundern über (*Acc.*); ***be –d by,*** überrascht *or* überfallen werden von; 2. (*Mil., fig.*) überrumpeln, überfallen; – ***him in the act,*** ihn auf frischer Tat ertappen. **2.** *s.* 1. die Überraschung (***to, for,*** für); ***come as a –,*** überraschend *or* unerwartet *or* als Überraschung kommen (*to, Dat.*); ***get the – of one's life,*** sein blaues Wunder erleben; ***give him a –, spring a – on him,*** ihn überraschen; ***stare in –,*** große Augen machen; ***to my –,*** zu meiner Überraschung; 2. (*Mil.*) die Überrumpelung, der Überfall; ***take by –,*** überraschen, (*also fig.*) überrumpeln, überfallen; 3. das Erstaunen, Befremden, die Bestürzung, Verwunderung (*at,* über (*Acc.*)); ***I have heard with – that . . .,*** zu meinem Befremden habe ich gehört daß . . .. **3.** *adj.* überraschend, Überraschungs–. **surprising,** *adj.* überraschend, erstaunlich.

surrealism [səˈriəlizm], *s.* der Surrealismus. **surrealist, 1.** *s.* der (die) Surrealist(in). **2.** *or* **surrealistic** [–ˈlistik], *adj.* surrealistisch.

surrebutter [sʌriˈbʌtə], *s.* (*Law*) die Quintuplik. **surrejoinder** [–ˈdʒɔində], *s.* (*Law*) die Triplik.

surrender [səˈrendə], **1.** *v.t.* übergeben, überlassen, überliefern, aushändigen, ausliefern (*to, Dat.*); – ***the fortress,*** die Festung übergeben; – ***the prisoner,*** den Gefangenen ausliefern; 2. (*Law*) verzichten auf (*Acc.*), preisgeben, (freiwillig) aufgeben *or* abtreten; – ***an insurance policy,*** eine Versicherungspolice abtreten; 3. – ***o.s.,*** kapitulieren, sich ergeben; (*usu. fig.*) sich hingeben *or* überlassen (*to, Dat.*). **2.** *v.i.* 1. (*usu. Mil.*) sich ergeben, die Waffen strecken, kapitulieren, (*usu. Law*) sich stellen (***to, Dat.***); 2. (*fig.*) sich überlassen *or* hingeben (***to, Dat.***) (*grief etc.*), klein beigeben (*in argument etc.*). **3.** *s.* 1. (*Mil.*) die Kapitulation, Übergabe (***to,*** an (*Acc.*)), Überlassung, Auslieferung, Aushändigung (*of prisoners etc.*); 2. (*esp. Law*) Abtretung, Preisgabe, Aufgabe; Herausgabe, Überlieferung (***to,*** an (*Acc.*)); – ***of a right,*** der Verzicht auf ein Recht; (*Insur.*) – ***value,*** der Rückkaufswert.

surreptitious [sʌrəpˈtiʃəs], *adj.* 1. erschlichen, betrügerisch; 2. heimlich (und unerlaubt), verstohlen; – ***edition,*** unerlaubter Nachdruck.

surrogate [ˈsʌrəgit], *s.* 1. der Stellvertreter (*esp. of a bishop*); 2. Ersatz, das Surrogat.

surround [səˈraund], **1.** *v.t.* umgeben (*also fig.*), umringen, einschließen; (*esp. Mil.*) einkreisen, umzingeln, umstellen; herumstehen um. **2.** *s.* 1. die Einfassung, Umrandung, der Fußboden zwischen Teppich und Wand; 2. (*Am.*) die Treibjagd. **surrounding,** *adj.* umgebend, umliegend; – ***country,*** die Umgebung, Umgegend. **surroundings,** *pl.* die Umgegend, Umgebung, das Randgebiet; (*fig.*) die Umwelt, der Umkreis.

surtax [ˈsəːtæks], *s.* der Steuerzuschlag, Steueraufschlag, die Zuschlagsteuer.

surtout [ˈsəːtuː], *s.* (*Hist.*) der Überrock, Überzieher.

surveillance [səːˈveiləns], *s.* die Kontrolle, Aufsicht, Beaufsichtigung, Bewachung, Überwachung.

survey, 1. [səːˈvei], *v.t.* 1. überblicken, überschauen (*a region*), prüfen, mustern, besichtigen (*a thing*); 2. begutachten, (ab)schätzen (*a problem*); 3. ausmessen, vermessen, aufnehmen (*land*); 4. (*coll.*) einen Überblick geben über (*Acc.*). **2.** [ˈsəːvei], *s.* 1. der Überblick, die Übersicht (*of,* über (*Acc.*)); (*coll.*) ***make a – of,*** übersehen, überblicken, einen Überblick geben über (*Acc.*); 2. die Prüfung, Besichtigung, Schätzung, Begutachtung; 3. das Gutachten, der (Prüfungs)bericht; 4. (*Surv.*) die Ausmessung, Vermessung, Aufnahme; ***Ordnance Survey,*** amtliche Landesvermessung; 5. der Plan, Riß; 6. die Umfrage. **surveying** [–ˈveiiŋ], *s.* 1. das Vermessen; 2. die (Land)vermessung, Feldmeßkunde. **surveyor** [–ˈveiə], *s.*

1. (*Surv.*) der Feldmesser, Landmesser; 2. Verwalter, Inspektor; 3. (*Insur.*) Gutachter, Sachverständige(r).

survival [sə'vaivl], *s.* 1. das Überleben; Fortleben, Weiterleben; – ***of the fittest,*** das Überleben *or* der Fortbestand der Tüchtigen; 2. der Überrest, das Überbleibsel. **survive, 1.** *v.t.* 1. überleben, überdauern (*a p. or th.*); 2. überstehen, überleben (*a disaster*). **2.** *v.i.* 1. am Leben bleiben, übriggeblieben sein, noch am Leben sein; 2. weiterbestehen, fortbestehen, weiterleben, fortleben. **surviving,** *adj.* überlebend (*a p.*), übrigbleibend, übriggeblieben (*a th.*). **survivor** [–ə], *s.* Überlebende(r), Hinterbliebene(r).

susceptance [sə'septəns], *s.* (*Elec.*) der Blindleitwert.

susceptibility [səsepti'biliti], *s.* 1. die Empfänglichkeit, Anfälligkeit (*to,* für), Empfindlichkeit (gegen); 2. *pl.* empfindliche Stelle, wunder Punkt. **susceptible** [–'septibl], *adj.* anfällig, empfänglich (*to,* für), zugänglich (*Dat.*), empfindlich (gegen); (*only pred.*) ***be – of,*** zulassen. **susceptive** [–'septiv], *adj.* aufnahmefähig, empfänglich (*of,* für). **susceptivity** [sʌsep'tiviti], *s.* die Aufnahmefähigkeit, Empfänglichkeit.

suspect, 1. [səs'pekt], *v.t.* 1. befürchten, (be)argwöhnen; 2. bezweifeln, anzweifeln, Mißtrauen hegen gegen, mißtrauen (*Dat.*) (*a th.*); 3. verdächtigen (*of, Gen.*), im Verdacht haben (*of,* wegen; ***of doing,*** getan zu haben) (*a p.*); ***be –d of,*** verdächtigt werden (*Gen.*), im Verdacht stehen wegen; 4. vermuten, mutmaßen, annehmen, ahnen, (halb) glauben, für wahrscheinlich *or* möglich halten. **2.** [–'pekt], *v.i.* Argwohn *or* Verdacht hegen, argwöhnisch sein. **3.** ['sʌspekt], *s.* Verdächtigte(r), die Verdachtsperson, (*Law*) mutmaßlicher Täter. **4.** ['sʌspekt], *adj.* (*only pred.*) verdächtig, fragwürdig, zweifelhaft; ***be –,*** irgendwie belastet sein. **suspected** [–'pektid], *adj.* 1. (*attrib.*) verdächtig; 2. (*pred.*) verdächtigt (*of, Gen.*).

suspend [səs'pend], *v.t.* 1. (auf)hängen, herunterhängen lassen (*from,* an (*Dat.*)); 2. (*fig.*) aufschieben, verschieben, in der Schwebe *or* unentschieden *or* offen *or* anstehen lassen, aussetzen, nicht festlegen (*judgement*), (zeitweilig) aufheben *or* außer Kraft setzen (*regulations etc.*), (zeitweilig) einstellen (*payment etc.*), zurückhalten mit; (*Law*) – ***the execution,*** die Urteilsvollstreckung aussetzen *or* einstellen; – ***hostilities,*** die Feindseligkeiten einstellen; 3. (*fig.*) (zeitweilig) vom Dienst *or* des Amtes entheben, suspendieren (*a p.*), (*from membership*) (zeitweilig) ausschließen; 4. (*Chem.*) schwebend halten. **suspended,** *adj.* 1. hängend, Hänge–; ***be –,*** hängen (***from, by,*** an (*Dat.*)); 2. schwebend, Schwebe–; 3. (*fig.*) aufgeschoben, verschoben, ausgesetzt, (zeitweilig) eingestellt; – ***animation,*** der Scheintod; – ***sentence,*** aufgeschobener Strafvollzug. **suspender,** *s.* 1. der Strumpfhalter; – ***belt,*** der Hüfthalter; 2. *pl.* (*Am.*) Hosenträger (*pl.*).

suspense [səs'pens], *s.* die Besorgnis, Spannung, bange Erwartung, die Ungewißheit (*of a p.*), Unentschiedenheit, Schwebe, der Zweifel (*of a matter*); ***in –,*** gespannt, voller Spannung (*of a p.*), in der Schwebe (*of a matter*); ***hold*** or ***keep in –,*** im ungewissen *or* Zweifel lassen, hinhalten; ***tortured with –,*** in peinlicher Ungewißheit; (*Comm.*) – ***account,*** das Interimskonto. **suspension** [–ʃən], *s.* 1. das (Auf)hängen; 2. (*Tech.*) die Aufhängung, Federung; ***be held in –,*** in der Schwebe erhalten werden; (*Motor.*) ***front-wheel –,*** die Vorderrad-Aufhängung; ***points of –,*** Aufhängepunkte (*pl.*); ***––bridge,*** die Hängebrücke, Kettenbrücke; ***––railway,*** die Schwebebahn; (*Motor.*) ***––spring,*** die Tragfeder; 3. (*fig.*) die Aussetzung, Aufhebung, der Aufschub (*of judgement*), die Einstellung (*of payment*), Verschiebung, Unterbrechung; – ***of hostilities,*** die Waffenruhe, Einstellung der Feindseligkeiten; – ***of payment,*** die Zahlungseinstellung; 4. (*of a p.*) die (Amts)enthebung, Suspension, Suspendierung, (*from a group*) der Ausschluß, (*also Spt.*) die Ausschließung, Ausstoßung, Ausschaltung; 5. (*Mus.*) der Vorhalt; 6. (*Chem.*) die Aufschwemmung, Suspension.

suspensive [səs'pensiv], *adj.* (*esp. Law*) *see* **suspensory.**

suspensory [səs'pensəri], *adj.* 1. hängend, Hänge–, schwebend, Schwebe–; 2. (*Med.*) Aufhänge–, Trag–, Stütz–; – ***bandage,*** die Tragbinde, das Bruchband, Suspensorium; 3. (*Law*) Aufschub–, Aussetzungs–, aufschiebend, Suspensiv–; (*Pol.*) – ***veto,*** suspensives Veto.

suspicion [səs'piʃən], *s.* 1. der Argwohn, das Mißtrauen (*of,* gegen), der Verdacht, die Verdächtigung; Ahnung, Vermutung; (*usu. neg.*) Andeutung, Spur, der Anflug; ***have one's –s about,*** in *or* im Verdacht haben; ***entertain*** or ***have a –,*** Verdacht schöpfen *or* hegen, einen Verdacht haben; ***above –,*** über jeden Verdacht erhaben; ***on – of,*** unter dem Verdacht (*Gen.*); ***cast – on,*** den Verdacht lenken auf (*Acc.*), verdächtigen; – ***fell on him,*** der Verdacht richtete sich auf *or* gegen ihn; ***come under –,*** in Verdacht kommen; ***be under –,*** in *or* im Verdacht stehen, verdächtigt werden; 2. die Ahnung, Vermutung; 3. (*usu. neg.*) Andeutung, Spur, der Anflug. **suspicious** [–ʃəs], *adj.* argwöhnisch, mißtrauisch (*of,* gegen); ***be – of,*** in Verdacht haben, mißtrauen (*Dat.*) (*a p.*), befürchten (*a th.*); 2. verdachterregend, verdächtig. **suspiciousness,** *s.* das Mißtrauen, der Argwohn (*of,* gegen).

suspiration [sʌspi'reiʃən], *s.* das Seufzen, Stöhnen; der Seufzer. **suspire** [səs'paiə], *v.i.* (*obs.*) 1. seufzen, stöhnen; 2. (*Poet.*) aufatmen, (*fig.*) schmachten, sich sehnen (***after, for,*** nach).

sustain [səs'tein], *v.t.* 1. halten, tragen, stützen (*also fig.*); 2. (*fig.*) (aufrecht)erhalten, unterhalten, unterstützen (*life etc.*), stärken, Kraft geben (*Dat.*) (*a p.*); 3. standhalten (*Dat.*), aushalten, (er)tragen (*attack, comparison etc.*); 4. in Gang halten, weiterführen (*conversation*), wachhalten (*interest*); 5. erleiden (*a loss*), davontragen (*an injury*); 6. (*Mus.*) (aus)halten; 7. (*Law*) bestätigen, erhärten, bekräftigen, als rechtsgültig anerkennen, stattgeben (*Dat.*). **sustainable,** *adj.* haltbar, tragbar, aufrechtzuerhalten(d). **sustained** [–d], *adj.* 1. ununterbrochen, anhaltend, (an)dauernd, Dauer–; 2. (*Law*) angenommen, aufrechterhalten; 3. (*Mus.*) getragen. **sustainment,** *s.* 1. die Stütze, Erhaltung; 2. der Lebensunterhalt; 3. Beistand.

sustenance ['sʌstinəns], *s.* 1. der (Lebens)unterhalt, das Auskommen; 2. die Nahrung, Ernährung, Versorgung, Lebensmittel (*pl.*); 3. die Nährkraft, der Nährwert. **sustentation** [–'teiʃən], *s.* (*rare*) 1. die Unterstützung, (Aufrecht)erhaltung, Bewahrung; 2. Ernährung, Versorgung, der Unterhalt.

sutler ['sʌtlə], *s.* der Heereslieferant, Marketender. **sutler-woman,** *s.* die Marketenderin.

suttee [sʌ'ti:], *s.* die Suttee, Sati.

sutural ['sju:tʃərəl], *adj.* Naht–. **suture** [–tʃə], **1.** *s.* 1. die (Wund)naht; 2. Nahtstelle; 3. das Nahtmaterial; 4. (Zusammen)nähen. **2.** *v.t.* (*Surg.*) (ver)nähen, zu(sammen)nähen.

suzerain ['su:zərein], **1.** *s.* 1. der Ober(lehns)herr; 2. Suzerän, die Oberhoheit. **2.** *attrib. adj.* oberherrlich, oberhoheitlich. **suzerainty,** *s.* 1. die Oberlehnsherrlichkeit; 2. Oberhoheit, Oberherrschaft, Obergewalt, Suzeränität.

svelte [svelt], *adj.* schlank, graziös, grazil, anmutig.

swab [swɔb], **1.** *s.* 1. der Schrubber, Putzlappen, Scheuerlappen; (*Naut.*) Schwabber; 2. (*Med.*) Abstrich. **2.** *v.t.* 1. aufwischen; (*Med.*) betupfen, abtupfen; 2. (*Naut.*) (*also* – ***down***) schwabbern, schrubben.

Swabia ['sweibiə], *s.* Schwaben (*n.*). **Swabian, 1.** *s.* der Schwabe (die Schwäbin). **2.** *adj.* schwäbisch; – ***emperors,*** Hohenstaufen(kaiser) (*pl.*).

swaddle [swɔdl], **1.** *s.* (*Am.*) die Windel. **2.** *v.t.* 1. in Windeln legen, einwindeln, wickeln (*a child*); 2. (*fig.*) (*also* – ***up***) einwickeln. **swaddling,** *s.* das Einwindeln, Wickeln; Einwickeln; – ***bands,*** – ***clothes,*** Windeln (*pl.*).

swag [swæg], *s.* 1. (*sl.*) die Diebesbeute; 2. (*coll.*) (*Austral.*) der Ranzen, das (Reise)bündel.

swage [sweidʒ], *s.* (*Tech.*) das Gesenk.

swagger [ˈswægə], **1.** *v.i.* 1. prahlen, großtun, aufschneiden, renommieren (*about*, mit); 2. (einher)stolzieren. **2.** *s.* 1. die Großtuerei, Prahlerei; 2. das Stolzieren. **3.** *adj.* (*coll.*) elegant, schick. **swagger|-cane,** *s.* (*Mil.*) das Ausgehstöckchen. **--coat,** *s.* loser Damenmantel.

swagman [ˈswægmæn], *s.* (*Austral.*) reisender Handwerksbursche.

swain [swein], *s.* (*Poet.*) 1. der Bauernbursche; Schäfer; 2. Verehrer, Liebhaber.

[1]**swallow** [ˈswɔlou], *s.* (*Orn.*) (*Am.* ***barn*** –) die (Rauch)schwalbe (*Hirundo rustica*); (*Am.*) ***bank*** –, *see* **sandmartin**; (*Prov.*) ***one – does not make a summer,*** eine Schwalbe macht keinen Sommer.

[2]**swallow, 1.** *s.* 1. die Kehle, Gurgel, der Schlund; 2. Schluck; 3. das Schlucken, (Ver)schlingen. **2.** *v.t.* 1. (ver)schlucken, verschlingen; – ***the bait,*** auf den Leim gehen; – ***the bitter pill,*** in den sauren Apfel beißen; 2. (*fig.*) hinnehmen, schlucken, einstecken, sich (*Dat.*) gefallen lassen (*an insult*); 3. verschlingen, begierig in sich aufnehmen, für bare Münze nehmen (*statements, opinions etc.*); 4. widerrufen, zurücknehmen (*one's words*); 5. (*also* – ***down***) hinunterschlucken, unterdrücken (*anger etc.*); 6. (*also* – ***up***) an sich reißen, sich einverleiben (*defeated territory*); 7. (*fig.*) – ***up,*** verschlingen (*as sea, land*), verbrauchen (*as time*), verzehren (*as money*). **3.** *v.i.* schlucken; – ***the wrong way,*** sich verschlucken.

swallow|-tail, *s.* 1. (*Bot., Ent., Fort., Carp.*) der Schwalbenschwanz; 2. *pl.* (*coll.*) der Frack. **--tailed,** *adj.* schwalbenschwanzartig, Schwalbenschwanz–; – ***coat,*** der Frack.

swam [swæm], *imperf. of* **swim.**

swamp [swɔmp], **1.** *s.* der Sumpf, Morast, das Moor. **2.** *v.t.* 1. überschwemmen, überfluten; versenken (*a boat*); 2. (*fig.*) (*usu. pass.*) überschwemmen, überhäufen, überwältigen, erdrücken; ***be –ed with,*** überschwemmt *or* überhäuft werden mit. **swampland,** *s.* das Moor(land), das *or* der Bruch. **swampy,** *adj.* sumpfig, morastig, Sumpf–, Moor–.

swan [swɔn], *s.* (*Orn.*) der Schwan (*Cygnus*); ***mute*** –, der Höckerschwan (*C. olor*); ***whooper*** –, der Singschwan (*C. cygnus*); ***Swan of Avon,*** Shakespeare; (*Prov.*) ***all his geese are –s,*** er übertreibt alles, er schlägt alles zu hoch an.

swank [swæŋk], **1.** *s.* (*coll.*) 1. die Großtuerei, Prahlerei, Angeberei, Aufschneiderei; Großspurigkeit, Protzerei, das Protzentum; 2. (*a p.*) der Angeber, Aufschneider. **2.** *v.i.* (*coll.*) großtun, angeben, protzen, prahlen, renommieren, flunkern, aufschneiden. **3.** *adj.* (*sl.*) großspurig, protzig. **swank-pot,** *s.* (*sl.*) der Protz, Angeber. **swanky,** *adj.* (*coll.*) 1. *See* **swank, 3**; 2. auffällig elegant, flott, schick, fesch.

swan|like, *adj.* schwanengleich, schwanenhaft. **--maiden,** *s.* die Schwanenjungfrau. **--neck,** *s.* der Schwanenhals.

swannery [ˈswɔnəri], *s.* der Schwanenteich.

swansdown, swan's-down [ˈswɔnzdaun], *s.* 1. die Schwanendaune; 2. *See* **swanskin.**

swan|skin, *s.* weicher Flanell. **–song,** *s.* der Schwanen(ge)sang. **--upping,** *s.* jährliches Zeichnen der Themseschwäne.

swap [swɔp], **1.** *v.t.* (*sl.*) (ver)tauschen, austauschen, wechseln; – ***a th. for,*** etwas eintauschen für *or* vertauschen mit. **2.** *v.i.* tauschen. **3.** *s.* das Tauschen, Tauschgeschäft, der Tausch(handel); Tauschgegenstand; ***do a –,*** einen Tausch machen.

sward [swɔːd], *s.* der Rasen, die Rasenfläche. **sward-cutter,** *s.* der Rasenstecher.

swarf [swɔːf], *s.* der Abdraht, Abdrehspäne (*pl.*).

[1]**swarm** [swɔːm], **1.** *s.* 1. der Schwarm (*of bees etc., also fig.*); 2. (*fig.*) das Gewimmel, der Haufen, die Horde, Schar. **2.** *v.i.* 1. schwärmen (*as bees*); 2. (*fig.*) wimmeln (***with***, von); 3. sich drängen, strömen.

[2]**swarm, 1.** *v.t.* (*also* – ***up***) hochklettern an (*Dat.*), hinaufklettern, erklettern. **2.** *v.i.* klettern.

swarming [ˈswɔːmiŋ], **1.** *s.* das Schwärmen. **2.** *adj.* (*fig.*) wimmelnd, gedrängt voll. **swarm-spore,** *s.* die Schwärmspore.

swart [swɔːt], *adj.* (*Poet.*) *see* **swarthy.**

swarthiness [ˈswɔːðinis], *s.* das Dunkelfarbige, die Schwärze, dunkle Gesichtsfarbe. **swarthy,** *adj.* schwärzlich, dunkelfarbig, dunkelhäutig.

swash [swɔʃ], **1.** *s.* das Schwappen, Planschen, Platschen, Klatschen. **2.** *v.t.* platschen *or* klatschen lassen. **3.** *v.i.* schwappen, planschen, platschen, klatschen (*of liquids*). **swash|buckler** [–bʌklə], *s.* der Säbelraßler, Schwadroneur, Bramarbas; Schaumschläger, Prahlhans. **–buckling,** *adj.* säbelrasselnd, schwadronierend, prahlerisch. **--letter,** *s.* (*Typ.*) der Zierbuchstabe.

swastika [ˈswɔstikə], *s.* das Hakenkreuz.

swat [swɔt], *v.t.* (*coll.*) zerdrücken, zerschlagen, zerquetschen.

swath [swɔːθ], *s.* der Schwaden (*of cut grass*); (*fig.*) Streifen.

swathe [sweið], **1.** *v.t.* einhüllen, umhüllen, einwickeln, umwickeln. **2.** *s.* die Hülle, Binde, Packung, der Umschlag, Verband.

sway [swei], **1.** *v.t.* 1. schwingen, schwenken, schaukeln, (hin-und-her)bewegen, auf-und-abbewegen; – ***the sceptre,*** das Zepter führen; 2. (*fig.*) beeinflussen, bewegen; lenken, regieren, beherrschen, herrschen über (*Acc.*); – ***the audience,*** das Publikum mit sich reißen. **2.** *v.i.* 1. schwanken, sich schwingen; taumeln, torkeln; wippen, sich wiegen; sich hin-und-herbewegen *or* auf-und-abbewegen; 2. sich neigen; herrschen. **3.** *s.* 1. das Schwanken, Schwingen; der Schwung, die Wucht; 2. (*fig.*) das Übergewicht; der Einfluß, Bann, die Herrschaft, Macht, Gewalt; ***hold – over,*** beherrschen, herrschen über (*Acc.*); ***fall under his –,*** unter seinen Einfluß *or* seine Herrschaft *or* in seine Gewalt geraten.

swear [swɛə], **1.** *irr.v.t.* 1. schwören, (feierlich) geloben; – ***an affidavit,*** eine eidesstattliche Erklärung ablegen; – ***an oath,*** einen Eid leisten *or* ablegen; – ***revenge,*** Rache schwören; 2. beschwören, durch Schwur bekräftigen; 3. den Eid abnehmen (*Dat.*), vereidigen, eidlich verpflichten (*a p.*) (*to*, zu); – ***him in,*** ihn vereidigen. **2.** *irr.v.i.* 1. einen Eid leisten; – ***by*** or ***on the Bible,*** auf die Bibel schwören; – ***by God,*** bei Gott schwören; – ***by all that's holy,*** Stein und Bein schwören; (*coll.*) – ***by,*** schwören auf (*Acc.*), sich rückhaltslos verlassen auf (*Acc.*); (*coll.*) – ***for,*** garantieren *or* gutstehen für; – ***off,*** abschwören (*smoking etc.*); (*coll.*) – ***to,*** geloben, (die Wahrheit (*Gen.*)) beschwören; 2. fluchen; – ***at,*** fluchen auf (*Acc.*); – ***like a trooper,*** fluchen wie ein Landsknecht.

swearing [ˈswɛəriŋ], *s.* 1. das Schwören, die Eidesleistung; 2. das Fluchen. **swearing-in,** *s.* die Vereidigung, Beeidigung.

swear-word, *s.* das Fluchwort, der Fluch.

sweat [swet], **1.** *s.* 1. der Schweiß; (*coll.*) ***be in a –,*** in Schweiß gebadet sein, schwitzen; Angst schwitzen; ***bloody –,*** blutiger Schweiß; ***by the – of one's brow,*** im Schweiße seines Angesichts; ***cold –,*** kalter Schweiß; 2. (*sl.*) ***old –,*** der Zwölfender, alter Knochen. **2.** *v.i.* 1. schwitzen; 2. (*of a th.*) ausdünsten; 3. (*coll.*) sich abschinden *or* abplacken *or* abmühen; für einen Hungerlohn arbeiten. **3.** *v.t.* 1. schwitzen (*blood etc.*); – ***out,*** ausschwitzen (*a cold etc.*); 2. (*coll.*) schinden, ausbeuten, aussaugen; 3. (*Tech.*) schweißen, löten.

sweat|band, *s.* das Schweißleder (*in hats*). **–cloth,** *s.* das Schweißtuch. **--duct,** *s.* der Schweißgang, Schweißkanal.

sweated [ˈswetid], *adj.* für einen Hungerlohn hergestellt (*goods*); schlecht bezahlt (*labour*). **sweater** [–ə], *s.* 1. der Sweater, die Strickjacke, wollene Jacke; 2. der Ausbeuter, (Leute)schinder.

sweat-gland, *s.* die Schweißdrüse.

sweatiness [ˈswetinis], *s.* schwitziger Zustand, die Verschwitztheit.

sweating ['swetiŋ], *s.* 1. das Schwitzen, die Schweißabsonderung; 2. (*fig.*) Ausbeutung. **sweating|-bath,** *s.* das Schwitzbad. **--sickness,** *s.* das Schweißfieber, Englischer Schweiß. **--system,** *s.* das Ausbeutungssystem.

sweat|-shirt, *s.* die Trainingsbluse. **-shop,** *s.* der Ausbeuterbetrieb.

sweaty ['sweti], *adj.* schweißig, schwitzig, verschwitzt.

swede [swi:d], *s.* die Streckrübe.

Swede, *s.* der Schwede (die Schwedin). **Sweden,** *s.* Schweden (*n.*). **Swedish,** 1. *s.* das Schwedisch(e) (*language*). 2. *adj.* schwedisch.

sweeny [swi:ni], *s.* (*Vet.*) der Muskelschwund.

sweep [swi:p], 1. *irr.v.t.* 1. kehren, fegen (*rubbish etc.*); auskehren, ausfegen (*a room*); – ***away,*** wegkehren, wegfegen; (*fig.*) – ***the board,*** alles gewinnen, den Sieg davontragen; (*Naut.*) – ***a channel,*** das Fahrwasser ausbaggern *or* räumen; 2. peitschen, schlagen über (*Acc.*) (*as waves*); bestreichen (*as bullets*); – ***the dust,*** den Staub wegnehmen (*as a skirt*); – ***one's hand over,*** mit der Hand streichen *or* (hin)gleiten über (*Acc.*); 3. fortjagen, forttreiben (*the enemy etc.*); – ***aside,*** beseitigen, beiseite schieben, aus dem Weg räumen; – ***away,*** aufräumen mit, beseitigen, beiseite schieben; (*fig.*) fortraffen, wegreißen, mit sich fortreißen; – ***before one,*** vor sich hertreiben; – ***off,*** hinwegraffen, dahinraffen (*as illness etc.*); – ***him off his feet,*** ihn überwältigen *or* überrennen, (*fig.*) ihn hinreißen *or* mitreißen; 4. absuchen; – ***the horizon,*** den Horizont (mit den Augen) absuchen (***for,*** nach).
2. *irr.v.i.* 1. fegen, kehren (*as a broom*); ***a new broom -s clean,*** neue Besen kehren gut; 2. (*fig.*) schießen, sausen, stürmen, rauschen; – ***across his mind,*** ihm durch den Sinn fahren; – ***by,*** vorübersausen; – ***down,*** herfallen, sich stürzen (***on,*** auf (*Acc.*)); 3. sich erstrecken *or* (da)hinziehen; 4. sich ergießen, fluten (*as feelings*); 5. einherschreiten (*as a p.*); 6. gleiten, schweifen (*as the eyes*).
3. *s.* 1. das Fegen, Kehren; ***give the room a –,*** das Zimmer ausfegen; (*fig.*) ***make a clean – of,*** reinen Tisch machen mit, aufräumen mit; 2. der (Schornstein)feger; 3. (*fig.*) das Brausen, Dahinstürmen (*as of wind*), Schleppen, Rauschen (*as of a skirt*), Schwingen, Schwenken (*as of arms*), der Schlag (*of oars*), schwungvolle Bewegung; – ***of the hand,*** schwungvolle Handbewegung; ***a – of his sword,*** ein Schwung mit seinem Schwert; 4. der Bereich, Spielraum, die Reichweite, Ausdehnung, das Ausmaß; 5. (*Mil. etc.*) die Streife; 6. Windung, der Bogen, Schwung (*as of road, river*), fließende Linie (*of drapery*); 7. (*Naut.*) langes Ruder, die Petsche; 8. – ***of the tiller,*** der Leuwagen des Ruders; 9. (*coll.*) *see* **sweepstake.**

sweepback ['swi:pbæk], *adj.* (*Av.*) pfeilförmig, Pfeilform– (*wing*).

sweeper ['swi:pə], *s.* 1. (*also* ***road--, crossing--***) der (Straßen)kehrer; 2. (*also* ***carpet--***) die Kehrmaschine. **sweeping,** 1. *adj.* gründlich, durchgreifend, weittragend, umfassend; mitreißend, fortreißend, schwungvoll, heftig; – ***measures,*** durchgreifende Maßnahmen; – ***statement,*** zu allgemeine Behauptung; – ***victory,*** der Sieg auf der ganzen Linie. 2. *s.* 1. das Kehren, Fegen; 2. *pl.* der Kehricht; (*fig.*) Auswurf, Abgang. **sweepingness,** *s.* (*fig.*) das Durchgreifende, Weittragende, Umfassende, die Gründlichkeit, Heftigkeit.

sweep|-net, *s.* das Schleppnetz. – **(second)-hand,** *s.* (*Horol.*) der Zentralsekundenzeiger. **-stake,** *s.* (*also pl.*) das Toto, Wettspiel; – ***ticket,*** die Totokarte.

sweet [swi:t], 1. *adj.* 1. süß (*also fig.*); süßlich, süß schmeckend; ***have a – tooth,*** ein Leckermaul sein; 2. (*fig.*) duftig, wohlriechend, lieblich (*as smell*), melodisch, wohlklingend, angenehm (*as sound*), köstlich, wohltuend (*as sleep*); 3. frisch (*as soil, butter etc.*); 4. (*of a p.*) lieb (***to,*** zu), liebenswürdig, gütig, hold (gegen); – ***nature,*** sanftes *or* liebliches Gemüt, die Gutmütigkeit; – ***seventeen,*** noch unschuldig (*of a girl*), mädchenhaft; – ***and twenty,*** in strahlender Jugendblüte (*of a girl*); ***at his own – will,*** wie es ihm gefällt, nach seinem Köpfchen; (*sl.*) ***be – on,*** verliebt sein in (*Acc.*); 5. (*coll.*) reizend, entzückend. 2. *s.* 1. das Süße; die Süßigkeit; 2. der *or* das Bonbon; 3. (*oft. pl.*) der Nachtisch, die Süßspeise; 4. ***my –,*** mein Liebes *or* Süßes *or* Liebling *or* Schatz; 5. (*usu. pl.*) die Freude, Annehmlichkeit.

sweet| balsam, *s.* (*Bot.*) das Ruhrkraut. – **basil,** *s.* (*Bot.*) das Basilienkraut. – **bay,** *s.* (*Bot.*) der Lorbeerbaum. – **bent,** *s.* (*Bot.*) die Feldsimse. **-bread,** *s.* das Bröschen, Kalbsbries, die Kalbmilch. – **brier,** *s.* (*Bot.*) die Zaunrose. – **chestnut,** *s.* (*Bot.*) die Edelkastanie. – **cicely,** *s.* (*Bot.*) wohlriechende Süßdolde. – **clover,** *s.* (*Bot.*) der Honigklee. – **corn,** *s.* der Zuckermais.

sweeten ['swi:tən], *v.t.* 1. süßen, süß(er) machen. **sweetener,** *s.* 1. das Versüßungsmittel; 2. (*fig.*) Beschwichtigungsmittel; Schmiergeld.

sweet|heart, *s.* der Schatz, das Liebchen. – **herbs,** *pl.* Küchenkräute (*pl.*).

sweetie ['swi:ti], *s.* 1. (*sl.*) der Schatz; 2. (*coll.*) (*usu. pl.*) der *or* das Bonbon, die Süßigkeit. **sweeting,** *s.* der Johannisapfel, Süßling. **sweetish,** *adj.* süßlich.

sweet| marjoram, *s.* (*Bot.*) das Marienkraut. **-meat,** *s.* das Zuckerkonfekt, Zuckerwerk. **--natured,** *adj.* sanft, lieblich.

sweetness ['swi:tnis], *s.* 1. die Süßigkeit, Süße; Frische; der Wohlgeruch; 2. (*fig.*) die Lieblichkeit, Liebenswürdigkeit, Anmut, Milde, Sanftheit, Annehmlichkeit.

sweet| oil, *s.* das Speiseöl, Olivenöl. – **pea,** *s.* (*Bot.*) die Gartenwicke. – **pepper,** *s.* (*Bot.*) der Ziegenpfeffer. – **potato,** *s.* (*Bot.*) die Batate. **--scented,** *adj.* wohlriechend, duftend. **-shop,** *s.* der Süßwarenladen. **--smelling,** *adj. See* **--scented. --tempered,** *adj.* gutartig, gutmütig, sanftmütig. **--toothed,** *adj.* schleckerhaft. – **william,** *s.* (*Bot.*) die Bartnelke. **sweety,** *s. See* **sweetie.**

swell [swel], 1. *irr.v.i.* 1. (*also* – ***out*** or ***up***) (auf)schwellen, (an)schwellen (***into,*** zu), dick werden; 2. sich (aus)bauschen *or* blähen; 3. aufquellen, ansteigen (*water*); 4. (*fig.*) steigen, (an)wachsen ((***in***)***to,*** zu), (*Archit.*) sich ausbauchen; 5. aufwallen, sich steigern (*as feelings*), sich aufblähen *or* aufplustern (*with pride*), bersten *or* platzen (wollen) (***with,*** vor (*Dat.*)) (*with rage*). 2. *irr.v.t.* 1. anschwellen lassen, dick werden lassen, zum Schwellen bringen; 2. aufblasen, dehnen, ausweiten; 3. steigen lassen, (an)schwellen (*rivers*); 4. (*usu. pass.*) aufblähen (***with,*** vor (*Dat.*)); 5. (*fig.*) steigern, vergrößern, vermehren. 3. *s.* 1. das Anschwellen, Aufschwellen; 2. (*Archit.*) die Wölbung, Ausbuchtung, Ausbauchung; 3. Dünung, der Wellengang, Seegang (*of the sea*); 4. die Steigung, Anhöhe (*of land*); 5. (*fig.*) das (An)steigen, Anwachsen, Anschwellen; 6. (*of organ*) Schwellwerk, der Schweller; 7. (*sl.*) Stutzer, Modeherr; (*rare*) Mordskerl, die Kanone. 4. *adj.* (*sl.*) schick, (hoch)elegant, aufgedonnert; tipptopp, prima, feudal, pfundig, Pfunds–.

swell-box, *s.* das Schwellergehäuse, der Schwellkasten (*of an organ*). **swelled** [sweld], *adj.* (*Med.*) angeschwollen; (*coll.*) – ***head,*** die Aufgeblasenheit. (*coll.*) **swelled|-headed,** *adj.* aufgeblasen, eingebildet. **--headedness,** *s. See* ***swelled head.*** **swell-fish,** *s.* der Kugelfish. **swelling,** 1. *adj.* 1. (an)schwellend, sich aufblähend; 2. aufquellend; 3. (*fig.*) anschwellend, anwachsend, ansteigend; 4. geschwollen, schwülstig, hochtrabend, überschwenglich; – ***heart,*** überladenes Herz. 2. *s.* das Anschwellen, Aufschwellen; Aufquellen; Aufblähen; die Erhöhung, erhöhte Stelle, die Ausbuchtung, Ausbauchung, Wölbung, der Vorsprung; (*Med.*) die Geschwulst, Schwellung. **swell|mob(sman)** [–mɔb(zmən)], *s.* der Hochstapler. **--pedal,** *s.* der Rollschweller (*of an organ*).

swelter ['sweltə], 1. *v.i.* vor Hitze umkommen *or* vergehen, in Schweiß gebadet sein. 2. *s.* drückende Hitze. **sweltering, sweltry,** *adj.* drückend, schwül.

swept [swept], *imperf., p.p. of* **sweep. swept-back wing,** *s.* (*Av.*) der Pfeilflügel.

swerve [swə:v], **1.** *v.i.* 1. seitwärts abbiegen, seitlich abweichen, abschweifen (*also fig.*); 2. (*fig.*) abgehen, abweichen, sich abbringen lassen. **2.** *v.t.* 1. ablenken, zum Abweichen bringen; 2. Effet geben (*Dat.*), schneiden (*a ball*). **3.** *s.* 1. die Abweichung, Seitenbewegung; das Abschweifen; 2. (*Spt.*) seitgeschnittener Ball.

swift [swift], **1.** *adj.* schnell, geschwind, rasch, eilig, hurtig, flink; flüchtig (*moment etc.*); – ***action,*** sofortige Ausführung; – ***reply,*** umgehende Antwort; – ***to anger,*** jähzornig; – ***to do,*** schnell bereit zu tun, eilends *or* eilfertig tun. **2.** *s.* 1. (*Orn.*) der (Mauer)segler, die Turmschwalbe (*Apus apus*); 2. (*Zool.*) der Zaunleguan. **swiftness,** *s.* die Schnelligkeit, Geschwindigkeit; Hast, Eile.

swig [swig], **1.** *v.t.* (*coll.*) hinunterschlucken, austrinken. **2.** *v.i.* einen tüchtigen Zug tun (*at*, aus *or* von). **3.** *s.* (tüchtiger *or* kräftiger) Zug *or* Schluck.

swill [swil], **1.** *v.t.* 1. (ab)spülen, abwaschen; 2. (*sl.*) in sich hineinsaufen, herunterspülen (*a drink*). **2.** *v.i.* (*sl.*) (sich be)saufen. **3.** *s.* 1. die (Ab)spülung, das (Ab)spülen; Spülwasser, Spülicht; 2. der Spültrank (*for pigs*); Speisereste (*pl.*), der Abfall, die Schlempe; 3. (*sl.*) das Gesöff.

swim [swim], **1.** *irr.v.i.* 1. schwimmen (*also fig.*); – ***with the stream*** or ***tide,*** mit dem Strom schwimmen; ***my head –s*** or ***is swimming,*** es schwimmt mir vor den Augen, es schwindelt mir; 2. (*fig.*) überfließen; – ***in*** or ***with blood,*** von Blut überschwemmt sein; 3. treiben, getragen *or* getrieben werden (*of th.*). **2.** *irr.v.t.* 1. durchschwimmen (*a distance*), hinüberschwimmen über (*Acc.*) (*a river*); 2. schwimmen lassen (*horses etc.*). **3.** *s.* 1. das Schwimmen; ***have*** or ***take a –,*** schwimmen, baden; ***go for a –,*** schwimmen gehen; 2. (*coll.*) der Strom des Lebens; ***be in the –,*** auf dem laufenden sein; mit dazu gehören; ***be out of the –,*** nicht mehr dazugehören; 3. (*fig.*) schwindelndes Gefühl.

swimmer ['swimə], *s.* 1. der (die) Schwimmer(in); 2. (*Orn.*) der Schwimmvogel. **swimmeret** [–ret], *s.* (*Zool.*) der Schwimmfuß.

swimming ['swimiŋ], **1.** *adj.* 1. schwimmend, Schwimm–; – ***eyes,*** tränende Augen; 2. (*fig.*) schwindelnd. **2.** *s.* 1. das Schwimmen; ***go –,*** schwimmen gehen; 2. (*fig.*) das Schwindelgefühl, der Schwindel. **swimming|-bath,** *s.* (*oft. pl.*) die Badeanstalt, das Schwimmbad. **--bladder,** *s.* (*Ichth.*) die Schwimmblase. **--lesson,** *s.* die Schwimmstunde; ***take –s,*** Schwimmunterricht haben.

swimmingly ['swimiŋli], *adv.* leicht, mühelos, reibungslos, glatt, von selbst, ohne Schwierigkeit; ***get on –,*** glänzend auskommen *or* vorankommen; ***go –,*** glatt vonstatten gehen.

swimming|-pool, *s.* das Freibad, Schwimmbecken. **--race,** *s.* das Wettschwimmen.

swimsuit ['swimsju:t], *s.* der Badeanzug.

swindle [swindl], **1.** *v.t.* beschwindeln, betrügen (*a p.*) (***out of,*** um); erschwindeln (*a th.*) (***out of,*** von). **2.** *v.i.* schwindeln, mogeln, betrügen. **3.** *s.* der Betrug, Schwindel. **swindler,** *s.* der (die) Schwindler(in), Hochstapler(in), Betrüger(in), Gauner(in). **swindling,** *s.* die Schwindelei, Betrügerei.

swine [swain], *s.* (*pl.* -) 1. (*Poet.*) das Schwein; (*collect.*) Schweine (*pl.*); ***cast pearls before –,*** Perlen vor die Säue werfen; 2. (*fig.*) der Schweinehund. **swine|bread,** *s.* die Trüffel. **--fever,** *s.* (*Vet.*) die Schweineseuche. **-herd,** *s.* der Schweinehirt. **--pox,** *s.* (*Vet.*) Schweinepocken (*pl.*).

swing [swiŋ], **1.** *irr.v.i.* 1. schwingen, pendeln, baumeln, schaukeln; sich schaukeln (*on a swing*); 2. sich drehen (*as a door*); – ***open,*** auffliegen, sich auftun; – ***round,*** sich (in großem Bogen) umdrehen; – ***to,*** zuschlagen; 3. (*Naut.*) schwoien, schwojen; – ***to the tide,*** auf den Strom schwoien; 4. mit Schwung marschieren; – ***along,*** mit Schwung dahinziehen; (*Mil.*) – ***into line,*** einschwenken; – ***past,*** mit Schwung vorbeimarschieren; 5. (*sl.*) baumeln, gehängt werden (***for,*** wegen *or* für). **2.** *irr.v.t.* 1. schwingen, schwenken; schlenkern (*one's arms*); – ***one's legs,*** mit den Beinen baumeln; 2. pendeln *or* baumeln lassen, aufhängen (***from,*** an (*Dat.*)); (*coll.*) ***there's no room to – a cat*** (***in***), man kann sich kaum umdrehen; (*sl.*) – ***the lead, be –ing it,*** sich krank stellen, sich drücken; 3. schaukeln (*a p.*); 4. durchdrehen (*a propeller*); 5. (*Naut.*) – ***ship,*** rundschwoien; 6. (*sl.*) herumkriegen (*opinion etc.*); – ***it,*** es hinkriegen *or* schaukeln *or* schaffen. **3.** *s.* 1. das (Hin– und Her)-schwingen, Pendeln, Schaukeln; die Schwingung, Schwenkung; Schwungweite, Pendelweite, der Ausschlag; ***be on the –,*** hin– und herschaukeln, hin– und herpendeln; – ***of the pendulum,*** die Pendelschwingung; (*fig.*) das Hin– und Herpendeln; 2. die Schaukel; ***what you lose on the –s, you make up*** or ***gain on the roundabouts,*** ein Verlust hier wird aufgewogen durch einen Gewinn dort; du hältst dich schadlos; du machst deine Verluste wett; 3. (*fig.*) der Schwung, schwingender Rhythmus; das Auf-und-Ab, Hin-und-Her, der Spielraum; ***in full –,*** in Schuß *or* Schwung *or* Fluß *or* vollem Gange, im Zuge; ***go with a –,*** in vollem Schwung vorangehen; ***get into the – of,*** sich gewöhnen an (*Acc.*); ***give full – to,*** freien Lauf lassen (*Dat.*); 4. (*Boxing*) der Schwinger; (*sl.*) ***take a – at him,*** nach ihm schlagen; 5. (*Mus.*) der Swing(rhythmus).

swing|-back, *s.* 1. (*Phot.*) die Einstellscheibe; 2. (*fig. coll.*) Umkehr, Rückkehr, der Rückschlag, Umschwung (*to*, zu). **-boat,** *s.* die Schiffsschaukel. **-bridge,** *s.* die Drehbrücke. **--door,** *s.* die Schwingtür.

swinge [swindʒ], *v.t.* (*obs.*) peitschen, prügeln. **swingeing,** *adj.* (*coll.*) wuchtig (*blow*), faustdick (*lie*), gewaltig, riesig.

swinging [swiŋiŋ], **1.** *s.* 1. das Schwingen, Schwenken, Pendeln, Schaukeln; 2. (*Naut.*) Schwojen, Schwoien; ***--berth, --room,*** der Schwoikreis; 3. Schwingungen, Schwankungen (*pl.*). **2.** *adj.* schwingend, Schwing–, schwenkend, Schwenk–, pendelnd, Pendel–, schaukelnd, Schaukel–; – ***door,*** die Schwingtür; (*Tech.*) – ***wheel,*** das Schwungrad.

swingle [swiŋgl], **1.** *v.t.* schwingen (*flax etc.*). **2.** *s.* die Schwinge, Schwingmaschine, das Schwingbrett. **swingletree,** *s.* der Schwengel. **swingling-tow,** *s.* das Werg, die Hede.

swinish ['swainiʃ], *adj.* (*fig.*) schweinisch, säuisch. **swinishness,** *s.* die Schweinerei.

swipe [swaip], **1.** *v.i.* (*coll.*) kräftig zuschlagen (***at,*** nach). **2.** *v.t.* 1. kräftig schlagen; 2. (*sl.*) stibitzen, klauen. **3.** *s.* 1. kräftiger *or* derber Schlag; 2. (*Am.*) das Dünnbier (*pl.*).

swirl [swə:l], **1.** *v.i.* einen Strudel bilden (*as water*), sich drehen, wirbeln. **2.** *v.t.* herumwirbeln. **3.** *s.* der Wirbel, Strudel.

swish [swiʃ], **1.** *v.i.* sausen, schwirren, zischen, flutschen; plätschern, rauschen; rascheln (*as a dress*). **2.** *v.t.* 1. niedersausen lassen; 2. durchprügeln (*a p.*). **3.** *s.* 1. das Sausen, Rauschen, Rascheln; 2. der Peitschenhieb; 3. flüchtiger (Pinsel)strich. **4.** *adj.* (*sl.*) vornehm, elegant, schick.

Swiss [swis], **1.** *s.* der (die) Schweizer(in); (*collect.*) Schweizer (*pl.*). **2.** *adj.* schweizerisch, Schweizer–; – ***cheese,*** der Schweizerkäse; – ***German,*** das Schweizerdeutsch; – ***roll,*** die Biskuitroulade.

switch [switʃ], **1.** *s.* 1. die Gerte, Rute; 2. (*Railw.*) Weiche, das Stellwerk; 3. (*Elec.*) der (Um)schalter; ***two-way –,*** der Wechselschalter; 4. (*fig.*) der Umschwung, Übergang, Wechsel, die Umstellung, das Übergehen; 5. falscher Zopf. **2.** *v.t.* 1. peitschen; 2. (*Railw.*) rangieren (*a train*); 3. (*Elec.*) (um)schalten; – ***off,*** abdrehen, abschalten, ausschalten, ausknipsen (*light etc.*), (*Rad.*) abstellen; – ***on,*** andrehen, anknipsen, einschalten; 4. (*fig.*) wechseln, umstellen, überleiten (***to,*** auf (*Acc.*)). **3.** *v.i.* – ***over,*** überwechseln (***to,*** auf (*Acc.*)); (*fig.*) übergehen, überleiten (zu).

switch|back, *s.* die Achterbahn, Berg– und Talbahn. **-board,** *s.* 1. die Schalttafel, das Schaltbrett; 2. (*Tele.*) der Klappenschrank, die Vermittlung; –

operator, der (die) Telephonist(in). **--box,** *s.* (*Elec.*) der Schaltkasten. **-gear,** *s.* (*Elec.*) die Schaltvorrichtung. **-man,** *s.* (*Railw.*) der Weichensteller. **--point,** *s.* (*Railw.*) die Zungenschiene.

Switzerland ['switsələnd], *s.* die Schweiz; *in* –, in der Schweiz.

swivel [swivl], **1.** *s.* (*Tech.*) der Drehring, Drehzapfen, Wirbel; der Karabinerhaken; *butt--*, der Klammerfuß (*of rifle*). **2.** *v.i.* sich drehen. **3.** *v.t.* drehen, schwenken.

swivel|-bridge, *s.* die Drehbrücke. **--chair,** *s.* der Drehstuhl. **--eyed,** *adj.* (*sl.*) schieläugig. **--gun,** *s.* (*Hist.*) die Drehbasse. **--mounted,** *adj.* (*Artil.*) schwenkbar. **--mounting,** *s.* das Drehgestell. **--plough,** *s.* der Kippflug.

swiz(zle) [swiz(l)], *s.* (*sl.*) der Betrug, Schwindel.

swizzlestick ['swizlstik], *s.* der Sektquirl.

swollen ['swoulən], *p.p. of* **swell.**

swoon [swu:n], **1.** *s.* die Ohnmacht, der Schwächeanfall. **2.** *v.i.* in Ohnmacht fallen, ohnmächtig werden (*with*, vor (*Dat.*)).

swoop [swu:p], **1.** *v.i.* (*also* – *down*) (herab)stoßen, (nieder)schießen, (sich) stürzen ((*up*)*on*, *at*, auf (*Acc.*)); (*fig.*) herfallen ((*up*)*on*, über (*Acc.*)). **2.** *v.t.* (*coll.*) – *up*, wegschnappen, aufraffen. **3.** *s.* der Sturz, Stoß, (*fig.*) Überfall; *at one* (*fell*) –, mit einem (einzigen) Stoß, auf einen Hieb *or* Streich.

swop [swɔp], *see* **swap.**

sword [sɔ:d], *s.* das Schwert, der Säbel, Degen; – *in hand*, mit dem Schwert in der Hand; *at the point of the* –, mit Gewalt; *cross* –*s*, die Klingen kreuzen (*also fig.*); *draw* –*s*, kämpfen; *draw one's* –, zum Schwert greifen; *fall to the* –, durch das Schwert fallen; *put to the* –, über die Klinge springen lassen.

sword|-arm, *s.* rechter Arm. **--bayonet,** *s.* das Säbelbajonett. **-bearer,** *s.* der Schwertträger. **--belt,** *s.* das Degengehenk. **--cane,** *s.* der Stockdegen. **--cut,** *s.* der Säbelhieb. **--dance,** *s.* der Schwertertanz. **-fish,** *s.* der Schwertfisch. **--guard,** *s.* das Stichblatt. **--hilt,** *s.* der Degengriff. **--knot,** *s.* die Degenquaste, der Faustriemen. **-lily,** *s.* (*Bot.*) die Schwertlilie, Siegwurz. **-play,** *s.* die Fechtkunst, das Säbelfechten.

swordsman ['sɔ:dzmən], *s.* der Fechter. **swordsmanship,** *s.* die Fechtkunst.

sword|stick, *s. See* **--cane. --thrust,** *s.* der Schwertstoß.

swore [swɔ:], *imperf. of* **swear. sworn, 1.** *p.p. of* **swear. 2.** *adj.* durch Eid gebunden; Eid–; vereidigt, beeidigt; – *ally*, verschworener Bundesgenosse; – *enemy*, der Todfeind; – *member*, vereidigtes Mitglied; – *statement*, eidliche Aussage.

swot [swɔt], **1.** *v.i.* (*sl.*) büffeln, ochsen, stucken, pauken, bimsen. **2.** *v.t.* (*oft.* – *up*) (sich (*Dat.*)) einpauken. **3.** *or* **swotter,** *s.* der Büffler, Ochser. **swotting,** *s.* die Paukerei, Büffelei.

swum [swʌm], *p.p. of* **swim.**

swung [swʌŋ], *imperf., p.p. of* **swing.**

sybarite ['sibərait], *s.* der Sybarit, Genüßling, Schwelger, Schlemmer, Wollüstling. **sybaritic** [–'ritik], *adj.* sybaritisch, schwelgerisch, verweichlicht, genußsüchtig. **sybaritism** [–ətizm], *s.* die Genußsucht, Schwelgerei.

sycamore ['sikəmɔ:], *s.* die Sykomore, der Bergahorn.

sycophancy ['sikəfənsi], *s.* die Kriecherei, Speichelleckerei. **sycophant,** *s.* der Kriecher, Schmeichler, Speichellecker, Ohrenbläser. **sycophantic** [–'fæntik], *adj.* kriecherisch, schmeichlerisch.

sycosis [sai'kousis], *s.* (*Med.*) die Bartflechte.

syenite ['saiənait], *s.* (*Geol.*) der Syenit.

syllabary ['siləbəri], *s.* die Silbentabelle, Silbenliste. **syllabic** [si'læbik], *adj.* syllabisch, Silben–; silbisch, silbenbildend; (*as suff.*) –silbig.

syllable ['siləbl], **1.** *s.* die Silbe; *one-- word*, einsilbiges Wort; *not breathe a* –, keine Silbe *or* kein Wort *or* Sterbenswörtchen verlauten lassen; *repeat every* –, Wort für Wort wiederholen. **2.** *v.t.* in Silben bringen, syllabieren. **syllabled** [–bld], *adj. suff.* –silbig.

syllabus ['siləbəs], *s.* (*pl.* **-bi** [–bai]) **1.** das Verzeichnis, Programm, der Prospekt; Lehrplan; **2.** (*R.C.*) Syllabus.

syllepsis [si'lepsis], *s.* (*pl.* **-es** [–si:z]) die Syllepsis.

syllogism ['silədʒizm], *s.* der Syllogismus, Vernunftschluß; *false* –, der Trugschluß. **syllogistic** [–'dʒistik], *adj.* syllogistisch. **syllogize** [–dʒaiz], *v.i.* durch Syllogismus schließen, folgern.

sylph [silf], *s.* **1.** (*Myth.*) der & die Sylphe, der Luftgeist; Waldgott; **2.** die Sylphide, zierliches Mädchen. **sylphlike,** *adj.* sylphenhaft, zierlich, anmutig.

sylvan ['silvən], *adj.* (*Poet.*) waldig, bewaldet, waldreich, Wald–.

symbiosis [sim'baiousis], *s.* die Symbiose. **symbiotic** [–bi'ɔtik], *adj.* symbio(n)tisch.

symbol ['simbəl], *s.* das Sinnbild, Symbol, Zeichen. **symbolic(al)** [–'bɔlik(l)], *adj.* sinnbildlich, symbolisch (*of*, für); *be* – *of*, versinnbildlichen. **symbolics** [–'bɔliks], *pl.* (*sing. constr.*) (*Eccl.*) die Symbolik. **symbolism** [–bəlizm], *s.* **1.** sinnbildliche Darstellung, die Symbolik; **2.** (*Art, Liter.*) der Symbolismus; **3.** (*collect.*) Symbole (*pl.*). **symbolist** [–bəlist], *s.* der Symbolist, Anhänger des Symbolismus. **symbolization** [–lai'zeiʃən], *s.* sinnbildliche Darstellung, die Versinnbildlichung, Symbolisierung. **symbolize** [–laiz], *v.t.* versinnbildlichen, sinnbildlich darstellen, symbolisieren.

symmetric(al) [si'metrik(l)], *adj.* **1.** gleichmäßig, ebenmäßig, symmetrisch; **2.** (*Math., usu. symmetrical*) symmetrisch, Symmetrie–. **symmetrize** ['simitraiz], *v.t.* symmetrisch machen, in Symmetrie bringen. **symmetry** ['simitri], *s.* die Symmetrie; (*fig.*) Ausgewogenheit, das Ebenmaß.

sympathetic [simpə'θetik], *adj.* **1.** mitfühlend, einfühlend, verständnisvoll, teilnehmend; **2.** gleichgesinnt, gleichgestimmt, kongenial, sympathisch; **3.** (*coll.*) wohlwollend (*to*(*wards*), gegenüber), günstig gesinnt (*Dat.*); **4.** (*obs.*) geheimwirkend, sympathetisch; – *cure*, die Heilung durch Besprechen; – *ink*, sympathetische Tinte, die Geheimtinte; **5.** (*Physiol.*) – *nerve*, der Sympathikus, sympathischer Nerv; **6.** (*Phys.*) – *resonance*, die Nebenwellenresonanz.

sympathize ['simpəθaiz], *v.i.* **1.** sympathisieren (*with*, mit), gleichgesinnt *or* gleichgestimmt sein (*Dat.*); **2.** mitfühlen, mitleiden, mitempfinden (*with*, mit), sein Mitgefühl *or* Beileid ausdrücken (*Dat.*); **3.** wohlwollend gegenüberstehen (*with*, *Dat.*), übereinstimmen (mit). **sympathizer,** *s.* der (die) Anhänger(in) (*with*, *Gen.*), Sympathisierer(in) (mit).

sympathy ['simpəθi], *s.* **1.** die Sympathie, Zuneigung (*for*, für); *be in* – *with*, wohlwollen (*Dat.*), wohlwollend gegenüberstehen (*Dat.*), günstig gesinnt sein (*Dat.*), sich günstig aussprechen über (*Acc.*), gewogen sein (*Dat.*); *be out of* – *with*, nicht gewogen sein (*Dat.*); *strike in* –, der Sympathiestreik; *go on strike in* –, aus Sympathie streiken; **2.** das Mitgefühl, Mitleid (*for*, für; *with*, mit), Beileid, die (An)teilnahme; *express one's* –, sein Beileid ausdrücken *or* aussprechen *or* bekunden *or* bezeigen (*with*, *Dat.*) (*a p.*); *have* or *feel* – *with*, Mitleid haben mit (*a p.*), Anteil nehmen an (*Dat.*), teilnehmen an (*Dat.*); *offer one's* – or *sympathies*, sein Beileid bezeigen (*to*, *Dat.*); *letter of* –, das Beileidsschreiben; **3.** (*Physiol.*) die Mitleidenschaft, Wechselwirkung, wechselseitige Beeinflussung; **4.** die Harmonie, Übereinstimmung, der Einklang.

sympetalous [sim'petələs], *adj.* (*Bot.*) mit verwachsener Blumenkrone.

symphonic [sim'fɔnik], *adj.* symphonisch, sinfonisch; Symphonie–, Sinfonie–; – *poem*, die Tondichtung. **symphonious** [–'founiəs], *adj.* (*rare*) (harmonisch) zusammenklingend (*to*, mit). **symphonist** ['simfənist], *s.* der Symphonie-Komponist, Symphoniker. **symphony** ['simfəni], *s.* **1.** die Symphonie, Sinfonie; **2.** (*obs. or fig.*) (harmonischer) Zusammenklang, die Harmonie.

symphysis ['simfisis], *s.* (*Anat.*) die Symphyse, Knochenfuge.

sympodium [sim'poudiəm], *s.* (*Bot.*) die Scheinachse.

symposium [sim'pouziəm], *s.* (*pl.* **-a** [–ziə]) 1. (*Hist.*) das Gastmahl, Gelage; 2. die Sammlung von Beiträgen, das Sammelwerk; 3. die Tagung (*of persons*).

symptom ['simptəm], *s.* das Symptom (*of*, für *or* von); Krankheitszeichen; (äußeres) Zeichen, das Anzeichen (*of*, von). **symptomatic** [–'mætik], *adj.* symptomatisch; charakteristisch, bezeichnend (*of*, für); *be – of*, kennzeichnen, andeuten. **symptomatology** [–mə'tɔlədʒi], *s.* (*Med.*) die Symptomatik.

synagogue ['sinəgɔg], *s.* die Synagoge.

synalepha [sinə'li:fə], *s.* die Verschleifung zweier Silben.

synantherous [si'nænθərəs], *adj.* (*Bot.*) synandrisch, mit verwachsenen Staubbeuteln; – *plant*, die Komposite, der Korbblüter.

syncarp ['sinkɑ:p], *s.* (*Bot.*) die Sammelfrucht.

synchromesh ['siŋkromeʃ], *adj.* (*Motor.*) – *gear*, das Synchrongetriebe.

synchronism ['siŋkrənizm], *s.* 1. die Gleichzeitigkeit, der Gleichlauf, Synchronismus; 2. synchronistische Zusammenstellung *or* Tabelle. **synchronization** [–ai'zeiʃən], *s.* die Synchronisierung, zeitliches Zusammenfallen. **synchronize** [–naiz], 1. *v.i.* 1. gleichzeitig sein, (zeitlich) zusammenfallen *or* übereinstimmen; 2. synchron laufen (*as clocks*) (*with*, mit). 2. *v.t.* 1. synchronisieren, auf Gleichlauf bringen; 2. (zeitlich) zusammenfallen lassen, zum Zusammenspiel bringen, (zeitlich) in Übereinstimmung bringen. **synchronous** [–nəs], *adj.* gleichzeitig, (zeitlich) zusammenfallend; gleichlaufend, synchron, gleichgehend (*as clocks*); *be – with*, Schritt halten *or* (*as clocks*) gleichgehen mit.

synclinal [sin'klainl], *adj.* (*Geol.*) muldenförmig. **syncline** ['siŋklain], *s.* die Mulde.

syncopal ['siŋkəpəl], *adj.* (*Med.*) Ohnmachts–. **syncopate** [–peit], *v.t.* 1. kürzen, zusammenziehen (*words*); 2. (*Mus.*) synkopieren. **syncopation** [–'peiʃən], *s.* die Synkope, Synkopierung. **syncope** ['siŋkəpi], *s.* 1. (*Med.*) die Ohnmacht, Bewußtlosigkeit; 2. (*Mus., Metr.*) Synkope. **syncopic, syncoptic** [sin'kɔp(t)ik], *adj.* Ohnmachts–.

syncretic [sin'kretik], *adj.* (*Phil., Gram.*) synkretistisch. **syncretism** ['sinkrətizm], *s.* der Synkretismus. **syncretistic** [–'tistik], *adj. See* **syncretic.**

syndic ['sindik], *s.* der Syndikus, Rechtsberater, Bevollmächtigte(r). **syndicalism** [–əlizm], *s.* der Syndikalismus. **syndicate, 1.** [–it], *s.* das Syndikat, Kartell, Konsortium, die Interessengemeinschaft, der Ring. **2.** [–eit], *v.t.* zu einem Syndikat zusammenschließen. **syndication** [–'keiʃən], *s.* die Syndikatsbildung.

syndrome ['sindroum], *s.* (*Med.*) das Syndrom.

syne [sain], *adv.* (*Scots*) seitdem, lange her; ***auld lang –***, vor langer Zeit.

synecdoche [si'nekdəki], *s.* die Synekdoche.

synergic [si'nə:dʒik], *adj.* (*Anat., Biol., Theol.*) synergetisch, synergistisch, zusammenwirkend.

synod ['sinəd], *s.* 1. die Kirchenversammlung, Synode, das Konzil; 2. (*Astr.*) die Konjunktion. **synodal** [–l], **synodic(al)** [–'nɔdik(l)], *adj.* 1. Synodal–; 2. (*Astr.*) synodisch.

synonym ['sinənim], *s.* sinnverwandtes Wort, das Synonym. **synonymous** [–'nɔniməs], *adj.* sinnverwandt, gleichbedeutend; bedeutungsgleich, synonym(isch).

synopsis [si'nɔpsis], *s.* (*pl.* **-ses** [–si:z]) die Synopse, Übersicht, Zusammenfassung; Zusammenschau, der Abriß. **synoptic** [–tik], **1.** *adj.* 1. (*Eccl.*) synoptisch; 2. zusammenfassend, übersichtlich. **2.** *or* **synoptist,** *s.* (*Eccl.*) der Synoptiker.

synovia [si'nouviə], *s.* (*Anat.*) die Gelenkschmiere.

synovial, *adj.* Gelenkschleim–. **synovitis** [sainə'vaitis], *s.* die Gelenkentzündung.

syntactic(al) [sin'tæktik(l)], *adj.* syntaktisch. **syntax** ['sintæks], *s.* die Satzlehre, Syntax; der Satzbau.

synthesis ['sinθisis], *s.* (*pl.* **-ses** [–si:z]) die Synthese, Zusammensetzung, Zusammenfügung, Verbindung, Verknüpfung, Verschmelzung; (*Chem.*) der Aufbau. **synthesize** [–saiz], 1. *v.t.* verbinden, verschmelzen, zusammenfügen, durch Synthese aufbauen; synthetisch verfahren mit *or* behandeln; 2. (*Tech.*) synthetisieren, künstlich herstellen (*from*, aus). **synthetic** [–'θetik], *adj.* 1. (*Phil., Gram.*) synthetisch, zusammensetzend; 2. (*Tech.*) künstlich (hergestellt), Kunst–; – ***rubber,*** der Kunstgummi. **synthetical,** *adj. See* **synthetic,** 1. **synthetize** [–taiz], *v.t. See* **synthesize.**

syntonic [sin'tɔnik], *adj.* (*Rad.*) auf derselben Wellenlänge abgestimmt. **syntonize** ['sintənaiz], *v.t.* abstimmen, einstellen (*to*, auf (*Acc.*)). **syntony** ['sintəni], *s.* die Resonanz, (Frequenz)abstimmung.

syphilis ['sifilis], *s.* die Syphilis, Lues. **syphilitic** [–'litik], **1.** *adj.* syphilitisch, lu(et)isch. **2.** *s.* der (die) Syphilitiker(in).

syphon, *see* **siphon.**

Syria ['siriə], *s.* Syrien (*n.*). **Syriac** [–iæk], *s.* das (Alt)syrisch(e) (*language*). **Syrian,** 1. *s.* der (die) Syrer(in). **2.** *adj.* syrisch.

syringa [si'riŋgə], *s.* (*Bot.*) der Flieder.

syringe ['sirindʒ], **1.** *s.* die Spritze; ***hypodermic*** –, die Pravaz-Spritze. **2.** *v.t.* ausspritzen (*ears etc.*), bespritzen, abspritzen (*plants etc.*), (ein)spritzen (*a liquid*).

syringitis [sirin'dʒaitis], *s.* (*Med.*) der (Ohr)tubenkatarrh. **syringotomy** [–iŋ'gɔtəmi], *s.* (*Surg.*) der Fistelschnitt. **syrinx** ['siriŋks], *s.* (*pl.* **-nges** [–'rindʒi:z]) 1. (*Hist.*) die Syrinx, Hirtenflöte; 2. (*Anat.*) Eustachische Röhre; 3. (*Surg.*) die Fistel.

syrup ['sirʌp], *s.* der Sirup; (Frucht)saft; (*Am.*) *See* **treacle. syrupy,** *adj.* sirupartig, dickflüssig.

system ['sistim], *s.* das System, die Anordnung; der Plan, die Methode, Ordnung; (*Geol.*) Formation; (*coll.*) der Organismus, Körper; ***electoral*** –, das Wahlsystem, Wahlverfahren; ***legal*** –, das Rechtssystem, die Rechtsordnung; (*Math.*) – ***of lines,*** die Geradenschar; ***nervous*** –, das Nervensystem; ***on the – of,*** nach dem Plan *or* System von; – ***of pulleys,*** der Flaschenzug; ***railway*** –, das Eisenbahnnetz. **systematic(al)** [–'mætik(l)], *adj.* planmäßig, methodisch, systematisch, planvoll, zweckvoll, zweckmäßig, zielbewußt. **systematist** [–mətist], *s.* der Systematiker. **systematization** [–mətai'zeiʃən], *s.* die Systematisierung. **systematize** [–mətaiz], *v.t.* systematisieren, planmäßig *or* systematisch *or* methodisch ordnen, in ein System bringen. **systematology** [–ə'tɔlədʒi], *s.* die Systemlehre.

systole ['sistəli], *s.* die Systole, (*Med.*) die Zusammenziehung (des Herzens), das Herzspannen; (*Metr.*) die Silbenkürzung (vor der Hebung).

systyle ['sistail], *adj.* (*Archit.*) dicht aneinanderstehend (*of pillars*).

T

T, t [ti:], *s.* das T, t; (*coll.*) ***to a*** –, aufs Haar genau; –***girder,*** der T-Träger; –***square,*** die Reißschiene; –***shaped,*** T-förmig. *See List of Abbreviations.*

ta! [tɑ:], *int.* (*nursery talk*) danke!

Taal [tɑ:l], *s.* das Afrikaans(ch).

tab [tæb], *s.* 1. die Lasche, Patte, Klappe, (Schuh)-strippe; der Lappen, Streifen, Zipfel; 2. (*Mil.*) Kragenspiegel; 3. (*Av.*) das Trimmruder; 4. Schildchen, Etikett; der (Kartei)reiter; 5. (*sl.*) das Konto, die Rechnung; (*sl.*) ***keep -s*** or ***a – on,*** kontrollieren, genau beobachten, unter Kontrolle halten.

tabard ['tæbəd], *s.* (*Hist.*) der Heroldsrock, Wappenrock.

tabby ['tæbi], **1.** *s.* 1. das *or* der Moiré; 2. der Kalkmörtel; 3. (*also* ***– cat***) (getigerte) Katze; 4. (*coll.*) alte Jungfer, die Klatschbase. **2.** *adj.* 1. gewässert, geflammt, moiriert, Moiré-gestreift; 2. gescheckt, scheckig. **3.** *v.t.* moirieren, wässern (*fabric*).

tabernacle ['tæbənækl], **1.** *s.* 1. das Zelt, die Hütte, (*B.*) Stiftshütte; ***Feast of Tabernacles,*** das Laubhüttenfest; 2. (*R.C.*) das Tabernakel, Ziborium; die Nische mit Schutzdach; das Bethaus (*of dissenters*); 3. (*Naut.*) der Mastsockel, Mastbock, Mastkoker. **2.** *v.i.* (*fig.*) sich aufhalten, sein Zelt aufschlagen. **3.** *v.t.* beherbergen, schützen, verwahren. **tabernacular** [–'nækjulə], *adj.* (*Archit.*) Tabernakel–.

tabes ['teibi:z], *s.* die Schwindsucht; ***dorsal –,*** Rückenmarksschwindsucht. **tabescence** [tə'besəns], *s.* die Auszehrung. **tabetic** [tə'betik], **1.** *adj.* schwindsüchtig. **2.** *s.* Schwindsüchtige(r).

tablature ['tæblətʃə], *s.* 1. (*Mus.*) die Tabulatur; 2. (*Art*) Deckenmalerei, Wandmalerei; (*fig.*) das Phantasiebild.

table [teibl], **1.** *s.* 1. der Tisch, die Tafel; ***bedside –,*** der Nachttisch; ***clear the –,*** (den Tisch) abdecken; ***dining –,*** der Eßtisch; ***folding –,*** der Klapptisch; ***occasional –,*** der Gartentisch; ***sliding –,*** der Anziehtisch; (*Parl.*) ***lay on the –,*** verschieben, vertagen, zurückstellen; (*Parl.*) ***lie on the –,*** verschoben werden; ***sit at a –,*** an einem Tisch sitzen; ***sit down to –,*** sich zu Tisch setzen; ***take the head of the –,*** bei Tisch obenan sitzen; ***turn the -s,*** den Spieß umdrehen ((***up***)***on,*** gegen); ***the -s are turned,*** das Blatt hat sich gewendet; 2. (*fig.*) die Kost, Mahlzeit, das Essen; ***at –,*** bei Tisch, beim Essen; ***keep a good –,*** eine gute Küche führen; ***lay the –,*** (den Tisch) decken; ***rise from –,*** vom Tisch aufstehen, die Tafel aufheben; ***wait at –,*** bei Tisch aufwarten; 3. die Tischgesellschaft, Spielgesellschaft, Tischrunde, Tafelrunde; ***Round Table,*** die Tafelrunde; 4. die Tabelle, Liste, das Verzeichnis, Register; ***– of contents,*** das Inhaltsverzeichnis; (*B.*) ***Tables of the Law,*** Gesetzestafeln, 10 Gebote (*pl.*); ***– of logarithms,*** die Logarithmentafel; ***learn one's -s,*** rechnen lernen; ***multiplication –,*** das Einmaleins; 5. (*Archit.*) die Tafel, Platte, das Feld; 6. (*Geog.*) Plateau, Tafelland, die Ebene, (Land)fläche. **2.** *v.t.* 1. tabellarisch verzeichnen, in eine Tabelle aufnehmen *or* eintragen; 2. (*Parl.*) einbringen, vorlegen, auf den Tisch legen (*a proposal*).

tableau ['tæblou], *s.* (*pl.* **-s** *or* **-x** [–ou(z)]) das Gemälde, anschauliche Darstellung; das Gruppenbild. **tableau vivant** [–vi:'vɑ̃], *s.* lebendes Bild.

table|-centre, *s.* der Tischläufer. **–cloth,** *s.* das Tischtuch, die Tischdecke.

table d'hôte ['tɑ:bl'dout], *s.* feste Speisefolge.

table|-knife, *s.* das Tafelmesser, Tischmesser. **--lamp,** *s.* die Tischlampe. **–land,** *s.* die Hochebene. **--linen,** *s.* das Tischzeug, die Tischwäsche. **--mat,** *s.* der Untersatz. **Table Mountain,** *s.* (*Geog.*) der Tafelberg. **table|-napkin,** *s.* die Serviette. **--rapping,** *s.* das Tischklopfen. **--runner,** *s. See* **--centre.** **--salt,** *s.* das Speisesalz, Tafelsalz. **–spoon,** *s.* der Eßlöffel.

tablet ['tæblit], *s.* 1. das Täfelchen, die (Inschrift)-tafel, Gedenktafel; (*obs.*) Schreibtafel, der Notizblock; 2. (*Med.*) die Tablette; Tafel (*of chocolate*), das Stück (*of soap etc.*).

table|-talk, *s.* das Tischgespräch. **--tennis,** *s.* das Tischtennis. **--top,** *s.* die Tischplatte. **--turning,** *s.* das Tischrücken. **–ware,** *s.* das Tafelgeschirr. **--water,** *s.* das Mineralwasser, Tafelwasser

tabloid ['tæblɔid], **1.** *s.* 1. (*Med.*) die Pastille, Tablette, das Plätzchen; 2. (*coll.*) die Volkszeitung, Bildzeitung, das Sensationsblatt. **2.** *attrib. adj.* knapp, konzentriert.

taboo [tə'bu:], **1.** *s.* der Tabu, Bann, Verruf, die Acht, Ächtung, das Verbot; ***put under –,*** für tabu erklären. **2.** *pred. adj.* unantastbar, tabu, verboten, verrufen, verpönt, in Verruf. **3.** *v.t.* für tabu erklären, in den Bann tun, ächten, ausstoßen.

tabor ['teibə], *s.* (*Hist.*) die Handtrommel, das Tamburin.

tabo(u)ret ['tæbərit], *s.* 1. der Hocker; 2. Stickrahmen.

tabular ['tæbjulə], *adj.* 1. tafelförmig; Tafel–, flächig, flach; 2. blätterig; 3. (*fig.*) tabellarisch, Tabellen–; ***– form,*** die Tabellenform, tabellarische Anordnung.

tabula rasa ['tæbjulə'reizə], *s.* 1. unbeschriebenes Blatt; reiner Tisch; 2. völlige Leere.

tabulate ['tæbjuleit], **1.** *adj.* tafelförmig. **2.** *v.t.* in Tabellen bringen, tabellarisch ordnen, tabellarisieren. **tabulation** [–'leiʃən], *s.* die Tabellarisierung, tabellarische Darstellung. **tabulator,** *s.* der Tabulator, Kolonnensteller (*typewriters*).

tachometer [tæ'kɔmitə], *s.* der Geschwindigkeitsmesser, Tourenzähler.

tacit ['tæsit], *adj.* (*esp. Law*) stillschweigend. **taciturn** ['tæsitə:n], *adj.* schweigsam, wortkarg. **taciturnity** [–'tə:niti], *s.* die Schweigsamkeit, Verschlossenheit, Wortkargheit.

tack [tæk], **1.** *s.* 1. kleiner Nagel, der Stift, die Zwecke; (*coll.*) ***get down to brass -s,*** zur S. kommen; (*Am.*) ***thumb--,*** die Reißzwecke; 2. der Heftelstich (*sewing*); 3. der Hals (*of a sail*); 4. (*Naut.*) das Lavieren; der Schlag, Gang (beim Lavieren); ***be on the port –,*** auf Backbordhalsen *or* über Backbordbug liegen, mit Backbordhalsen segeln, nach Backbord lavieren; 5. (*coll.*) die Handlungsweise, Richtung, der Weg, Kurs; ***change one's –,*** eine neue Richtung einnehmen; ***on the wrong –,*** auf der falschen Fährte, auf dem Holzwege; ***be on a new –,*** einen neuen Kurs einschlagen; 6. (*Naut.*) die Kost, Nahrung; ***hard –,*** der Schiffszwieback; 7. der Ausschuß, die Ausschußware; (*sl.*) der Bafel, das Brack; 8. die Klebrigkeit. **2.** *v.t.* heften (*sewing*); (*Carp. etc.*) befestigen, anheften; (*coll.*) anschließen, anhängen, anfügen ((*on*)*to,* an (*Acc.*)), hinzufügen (zu); ***– together,*** aneinanderfügen. **3.** *v.i.* (*Naut.*) wenden, kreuzen, lavieren, in die Kreuz fahren.

tack-hammer, *s.* der Zweckenhammer.

tackiness ['tækinis], *s.* die Klebrigkeit.

tackle [tækl], **1.** *s.* 1. (*Naut.*) die Talje, das Takel; Takelwerk, die Takelage; ***ground--,*** das Ankertauwerk; 2. (*also* ***block and –***) der Flaschenzug; ***hoisting--,*** der Flaschenzug, das Hebewerk; 3. (*coll.*) das Gerät, Zeug, Gerätschaften (*pl.*), Werkzeuge (*pl.*), die Ausrüstung; ***fishing--,*** das Angelgerät; (*coll.*) ***shaving--,*** das Rasierzeug; 4. (*Footb.*) das Angreifen. **2.** *v.t.* 1. (*Footb.*) angreifen, (an)packen; 2. (*fig. coll.*) angehen (*a p.*) (*on,* betreffs); 3. in Angriff nehmen, anpacken, sich heranmachen an (*Acc.*) (*a problem etc.*).

tacky ['tæki], *adj.* klebrig.

tact [tækt], *s.* 1. der Takt, Anstand, das Taktgefühl, Feingefühl, Zartgefühl; 2. (*Mus.*) der Takt-(schlag). **tactful,** *adj.* taktvoll. **tactfulness,** *s. See* **tact,** 1.

tactical ['tæktikl], *adj.* (*Mil.*) taktisch; (*fig.*) klug, planvoll. **tactician** [–'tiʃən], *s.* der Taktiker. **tactics,** *pl.* (*sing. constr.*) die Taktik (*also fig. with pl. constr.*).

tactile ['tæktail], *adj.* 1. fühlbar, greifbar, tastbar; 2. taktil, Tast–. **tactility** [–'tiliti], *s.* die Fühlbarkeit, Tastbarkeit.

tactless ['tæktlis], *adj.* taktlos. **tactlessness,** *s.* die Taktlosigkeit.

tactual ['tæktjuəl], *adj. See* **tactile.**

tadpole ['tædpoul], *s.* die Kaulquappe.

taenia ['ti:niə], *s.* (*Anat.*) die Längsfaserschicht des Dickdarms; der Bandwurm.

taffeta ['tæfitə], *s.* der Taft, Taffet.

taffrail ['tæfreil], *s.* (*Naut.*) das Heckgeländer, die Heckreling.

[1]**tag** [tæg], **1.** *s.* 1. das Anhängsel, der Zipfel; 2. (Senkel)stift, die Metallspitze (*of shoelace etc.*); 3. (*Tech.*) Lötöse, der Lötstift; 4. Anhänger, das Etikett, Schildchen; 5. (*fig. coll.*) stehende Redensart, bekannter Ausspruch, feste Wendung; 6. (*coll.*) (*also* – *end*) das Ende, der Rest; ***rag, – and bobtail,*** Krethi und Plethi, das Lumpenpack. **2.** *v.t.* 1. mit einem Stift versehen; 2. (*sl.*) verfolgen (*a p.*). **3.** *v.i.* (*coll.*) – ***along,*** hinterherlaufen; – ***along after,*** – (*o.s.*) ***on to,*** auf den Fersen folgen (*Dat.*), nachlaufen (*Dat.*).

[2]**tag, 1.** *s.* das Letztengeben, Kriegenspielen (*game*). **2.** *v.t.* den Letzten geben (*Dat.*), kriegen, haschen.

Tagus ['teigəs], *s.* (*Geog.*) der Tajo (*river*).

[1]**tail** [teil], *s.* (*Law*) die Beschränkung der Erbfolge; beschränktes Erbrecht; ***estate in – male,*** das Fideikommiß; ***heir in –,*** der Vorerbe; ***issue in –,*** erbberechtigte Nachkommenschaft.

[2]**tail, 1.** *s.* 1. der Schwanz, (*Poet.*) Schweif (*also of comet*); Schoß (*of coat, shirt etc.*), die Schleppe (*of dress*); (*Mus.*) der Hals (*of a note*); *pl.* (*coll.*) Frack; ***the dog wags his –,*** der Hund wedelt mit dem Schwanz; (*fig.*) ***the – wags*** or ***is wagging the dog,*** das Unbedeutendste ist am Ruder; (*fig.*) ***on his –,*** ihm dicht auf den Fersen; ***out of the – of one's eye,*** aus dem Augenwinkel, mit einem Seitenblick; ***turn –,*** Fersengeld geben, ausreißen (***on,*** vor (*Dat.*)); (*coll.*) ***with his – between his legs,*** wie ein begossener Pudel; (*coll.*) ***–s up,*** fidel, guter Laune, in guter Stimmung; 2. die Rückseite, Kehrseite, Wappenseite (*of coins*); 3. (*fig.*) der Schluß, das Ende; 4. der Anhang; *pl.* (*esp. milling*) Rückstand, Abfall, Abfälle (*pl.*). **2.** *v.t.* 1. mit einem Schwanz versehen (*as a kite*); 2. stutzen, beschneiden (*an animal*), putzen, entstielen (*gooseberries*); 3. (*coll.*) dicht auf den Fersen folgen (*Dat.*) (*a p.*); 4. – ***in,*** in die Wand einlassen (*a beam etc.*). **3.** *v.i.* – ***after,*** hergehen hinter, nachlaufen (*Dat.*) (*a p.*); – ***along,*** hinterherlaufen; (*coll.*) – ***away,*** abnehmen, abflauen, sich verziehen *or* verlieren, verebben; (*coll.*) – ***off,*** abfallen, schlechter *or* kleiner werden.

tail|-board, *s.* die Ladeklappe (*of lorry etc.*). **--end,** *s.* (*coll.*) das Ende, der Schluß. **--fin,** *s.* (*Av.*) die Seitenflosse. **--first,** *adv.* rückwärts. **--gate,** *s.* unteres Tor, das Untertor (*of a lock*). **--heavy,** *adj.* (*Av.*) schwanzlastig. **tailless,** *adj.* schwanzlos, ohne Schwanz, ungeschwänzt; – ***airplane,*** das Nurflügelflugzeug. **tail-light,** *s.* das Schlußlicht.

tailor ['teilə], **1.** *s.* der Schneider; ***–'s dummy,*** die Modellierpuppe. **2.** *v.i.* schneidern, nach Maß arbeiten. **3.** *v.t.* schneidern, nach Maß anfertigen; (*fig.*) zuschneiden, abstellen (***to,*** auf (*Acc.*)), zurechtmachen (für). **tailoress,** *s.* die Schneiderin. **tailoring,** *s.* die Schneiderarbeit. **tailor-made, 1.** *adj.* nach Maß angefertigt, Schneider–. **2.** *s.* das Schneiderkostüm.

tail|-piece, *s.* 1. (*Typ.*) die Schlußverzierung, Schlußvignette; 2. der Saitenhalter (*of violin etc.*); 3. (*fig.*) Anhang. **--plane,** *s.* (*Av.*) die Höhenflosse. **--race,** *s.* das Schußwasser. **--skid,** *s.* der (Schwanz)sporn. **--spin,** *s.* (*Av.*) das (Ab)trudeln. **--unit,** *s.* das Leitwerk. **--wind,** *s.* der Rückenwind.

taint [teint], **1.** *v.t.* vergiften, anstecken, verpesten (***with,*** mit), verderben, beeinträchtigen (durch); beflecken, besudeln. **2.** *s.* 1. die Ansteckung (***of,*** von), Belastung (mit), Anlage (zu); ***hereditary –,*** erbliche Belastung; 2. (*fig.*) der Anflug, Zug, die Spur (***of,*** von); 3. (*fig.*) der (Schand)fleck, Makel; die Verderbtheit.

take [teik], **1.** *irr.v.t.* 1. nehmen; annehmen, aufnehmen; wegnehmen, entnehmen, hernehmen (***from,*** *Dat.*); fassen, packen, fangen, (er)greifen; (ein)nehmen (*fortress*), erobern (*territory*), gefangennehmen (*prisoners*), kapern, aufbringen (*ship*); 2. einnehmen, zu sich nehmen (*food*); 3. bekommen, sich (*Dat.*) zuziehen *or* holen (*illness*); 4. (mit)nehmen (*a th.*), (hin)bringen (*a p. or th.*), führen (*a p.*); 5. (*fig.*) verstehen, begreifen, (er)fassen, auffassen, aufnehmen, hinnehmen, annehmen, auslegen, der Meinung sein; 6. (*fig. usu. imp.*) kosten, erfordern, brauchen, bedürfen (*Gen.*), in Anspruch nehmen, beanspruchen.

(a) (*with nouns*) – ***account of,*** beachten, berücksichtigen, in Betracht ziehen, in Rechnung stellen; Rechnung tragen (*Dat.*); – ***action,*** vorgehen, Schritte unternehmen; – ***advantage of,*** Vorteil ziehen aus, ausnützen; – ***his advice,*** seinen Rat befolgen; – (***legal***) ***advice,*** (juristischen) Rat einholen; – ***aim at,*** zielen auf (*Acc.*); – ***the air,*** frische Luft schöpfen; (*Av.*) abfliegen, aufsteigen; – ***alarm at,*** alarmiert sein über (*Acc.*); – ***a bath,*** ein Bad nehmen, sich baden; – ***the bearings of,*** anpeilen; (*coll.*) – ***the bit between one's teeth,*** auf die Stange beißen; – ***a bow,*** sich verbeugen, eine Verbeugung machen; – ***breakfast,*** frühstücken; – ***a breath,*** aufatmen, Atem schöpfen *or* holen; – ***a breather,*** Luft holen, (*fig.*) Ruhepause machen; (*coll.*) – ***the bull by the horns,*** den Stier an *or* bei den Hörnern packen; (*sl.*) – ***the cake,*** den Vogel abschießen, doch die Höhe sein; – ***care,*** vorsichtig sein, aufpassen, sich in acht nehmen; – ***care of,*** achtgeben auf (*Acc.*), sorgen für (*a th.*), aufpassen auf (*Acc.*), betreuen (*a p.*); – ***care to do,*** trachten *or* sich bemühen *or* nicht vergessen zu tun; – ***care not to do,*** sich hüten zu tun; – ***the chair,*** den Vorsitz übernehmen; – ***one's chance,*** die Gelegenheit ausnützen; – ***a chance,*** es darauf ankommen lassen (***on his coming,*** ob er kommt); – ***chances,*** die Gefahr auf sich nehmen, sich der Gefahr aussetzen; – ***charge,*** die Verantwortung, übernehmen (***of,*** für); – ***one's choice,*** nach Belieben auswählen; – ***a class,*** Stunde *or* Unterricht geben; – ***comfort,*** sich trösten (***in,*** mit), Trost finden (in (*Dat.*)); – ***command,*** das Kommando übernehmen (***of,*** über (*Acc.*)); – ***compassion on,*** Mitleid empfinden mit, sich erbarmen über (*Acc.*); – ***counsel,*** sich beraten *or* besprechen (***with,*** mit), sich (*Dat.*) Rat holen (bei); – ***the consequences,*** die Konsequenzen ziehen, die Folgen tragen *or* auf sich nehmen; (*Boxing*) – ***the count,*** ausgezählt werden; – ***courage,*** Mut fassen; – ***one's courage in both one's hands,*** seinen ganzen Mut zusammennehmen; ***let it – its course,*** einer S. freien Lauf lassen; – ***cover,*** Deckung nehmen; (*Theat.*) – ***the curtain,*** vor dem Vorhang erscheinen; (*Univ.*) – ***one's degree,*** einen akademischen Grad erlangen; – ***delight in,*** Vergnügen finden an (*Dat.*), seine Freude haben an (*Dat.*); – ***a delight in doing,*** ein Vergnügen daraus machen, zu tun; – ***one's departure,*** sich verabschieden, Abschied nehmen; – ***a dislike to,*** eine Abneigung haben gegen; – ***a drive,*** ausfahren, eine Spazierfahrt machen; – ***the edge off,*** abstumpfen (*knife*), stillen (*appetite*), (*fig.*) die Spitze abbrechen (*Dat.*); – ***effect,*** in Kraft treten; – ***an examination,*** eine Prüfung ablegen; – ***exception to,*** see – ***offence at***; – ***exercise,*** sich (*Dat.*) Bewegung machen; – ***his fancy,*** seine Phantasie fesseln; – ***a fancy to,*** eine Zuneigung fassen zu, eingenommen sein für, Gefallen finden an (*Dat.*); – ***the field,*** (*Mil.*) ins Feld ziehen, ausrücken, (*Spt.*) das Sportfeld betreten; – ***fire,*** Feuer fangen, aufflammen; – ***flight,*** fliehen, die Flucht ergreifen; – ***the floor,*** tanzen; (*Parl. etc.*) das Wort ergreifen; – ***food,*** Nahrung zu sich nehmen; – ***French leave,*** sich französisch empfehlen; – ***fright,*** einen Schreck bekommen; – ***the good with the bad,*** see – ***the rough with the smooth***; (*Naut.*) – ***the ground,*** auflaufen; – ***a hand in,*** teilnehmen an (*Dat.*); – ***heart,*** sich (*Dat.*) ein Herz fassen, Mut fassen; – ***a hedge,*** über eine Hecke setzen; – ***heed,*** achtgeben, aufpassen; – ***a hint,*** einen Wink verstehen, es sich (*Dat.*) gesagt sein lassen; – (***a***) ***hold of,*** (er)fassen, ergreifen (*a th.*), sich bemächtigen (*Gen.*) (*a p.*); – ***a hold on,*** Eindruck machen auf (*Acc.*), beeindrucken; – ***a holiday,*** Ferien machen, Urlaub nehmen; – ***horse,*** reiten, aufsitzen; – ***an interest in,*** sich interessieren für, Interesse haben an (*Dat.*); – ***an inventory of,*** inventarisieren, Inventur machen von; – ***issue with,*** widersprechen (*Dat.*); – ***a journey,*** eine Reise machen; – ***a knock,*** einen Schlag abkriegen (*also fig.*); – ***the lead,*** vorangehen; die Führung übernehmen; (*fig.*) den Ton angeben; – ***a leaf out of his book,*** sich (*Dat.*) ihn zum Muster nehmen; – ***one's leave,*** fortgehen; – (***one's***) ***leave of,*** Abschied nehmen von; – ***leave of one's senses,*** nicht bei Sinnen sein; – ***leave to do,*** sich (*Dat.*) erlauben zu tun; – ***lessons,*** Unterricht *or* Stunden nehmen; – ***the liberty of doing,*** sich (*Dat.*) die Freiheit nehmen zu tun; – ***liberties,*** sich (*Dat.*) Freiheiten herausnehmen *or* gestatten (***with,*** gegenüber); – ***his life,*** ihn umbringen; – ***one's*** (***own***) ***life,*** sich (*Dat.*) (selbst) das Leben nehmen; – ***one's life in one's own hands,*** sein Leben aufs Spiel setzen; – ***a liking for*** or ***to,*** see – ***a fancy to***; – ***a look at,*** einen Blick werfen auf (*Acc.*); ***that –s a lot of believing*** or (*coll.*) ***swallowing,*** das kann man nicht (ohne weiteres) für bare Münze nehmen; – ***the measurements of,*** ausmessen; – ***his measurements,*** ihm Maß nehmen; – ***measures,*** Maßregeln ergreifen; (*fig.*) – ***one's medicine,*** die Pille schlucken; (*sl.*) – ***the micky out of,*** frotzeln, schikanieren; – ***the minutes,*** das Protokoll aufnehmen; – ***the name from,*** benannt sein nach; – ***a newspaper,*** eine Zeitung halten; – ***note of,*** berücksichtigen; – ***notes*** or ***a note of,*** (sich (*Dat.*)) Notizen machen von, notieren; – ***notice,*** aufpassen, achtgeben; – ***notice of,*** Kenntnis nehmen von (*a th.*), beachten, Notiz nehmen von (*a p.*); – ***no notice of,*** nicht beachten, ignorieren; – ***an oath,*** einen Eid ablegen, sich eidlich verpflichten; – ***offence at,*** Anstoß nehmen an (*Dat.*), gekränkt *or* beleidigt sein *or* sich gekränkt *or* beleidigt fühlen über (*Acc.*), übelnehmen; – ***office,*** ein Amt antreten; – ***the opportunity,*** die Gelegenheit ergreifen (***of doing,*** zu tun); (*Comm.*) – ***an order,*** eine Bestellung annehmen (***for,*** für), einen Auftrag hereinnehmen (auf (*Acc.*)); (*Eccl.*) – (***holy***) ***orders,*** in den geistlichen Stand treten, die heilige Weihe empfangen; – ***pains,*** sich (*Dat.*) Mühe geben, sich anstrengen (***with, over,*** bei); – ***a part,*** (*Theat.*) eine Rolle übernehmen, (*fig.*) teilnehmen (***in,*** an (*Dat.*)); – ***his part,*** seine Partei ergreifen; – ***his photograph,*** eine Aufnahme von ihm machen, ihn aufnehmen; – ***pity on,*** Mitleid haben *or* empfinden mit, bemitleiden; – ***place,*** stattfinden, sich ereignen; – ***the place of,*** ersetzen (*a p. or a th.*), vertreten, die Stelle einnehmen (*Gen.*) (*a p.*); – ***your places!*** nehmen Sie Ihre Plätze ein! – ***pleasure in,*** Vergnügen finden an (*Dat.*); – ***one's pleasure,*** sich amüsieren; – ***poison,*** sich vergiften; – ***a polish,*** Hochglanz bekommen; – ***possession of,*** Besitz ergreifen von, in Besitz nehmen; – ***one's post,*** seinen Posten beziehen; – ***pot-luck,*** vorlieb nehmen müssen; – ***precautions,*** Vorsorge treffen; – ***precedence,*** den Vorrang haben (***over,*** vor (*Dat.*)); – (***a***) ***pride in,*** stolz sein auf (*Acc.*); – ***him prisoner,*** ihn gefangennehmen; – ***refuge,*** see – ***shelter***; – ***a rest,*** sich ausruhen; Pause *or* Rast machen; – ***its rise,*** entspringen (***in,*** in (*Dat.*); ***from,*** *Dat. or* aus); (*coll.*) – ***a rise out of,*** in Harnisch *or* in die Wolle bringen; – ***a risk,*** sich einer Gefahr aussetzen; – ***a room,*** ein Zimmer mieten; – ***the rough with the smooth,*** es hinnehmen wie es gerade kommt *or* es einmal ist; – ***a seat,*** sich setzen, Platz nehmen; (*fig.*) – ***a back seat,*** sich im Hintergrund halten, zurücktreten; – ***shape,*** Gestalt annehmen; – ***shelter,*** sich unterstellen, Schutz suchen, Zuflucht nehmen; – ***ship,*** sich einschiffen (***for,*** nach); – ***sides,*** Partei ergreifen, Stellung nehmen; ***what size does he – in shoes?*** welche Schuhgröße hat er? – ***snuff,*** schnupfen; – ***one's stand,*** sich aufstellen; (*fig.*) eine Stellung einnehmen, Farbe bekennen; (*fig.*) – ***one's stand on,*** sich berufen auf (*Acc.*); – ***steps,*** see – ***measures***; – ***stock,*** (*Comm.*) Inventur machen, den Bestand aufnehmen, (*fig.*) sich (*Dat.*) Rechenschaft ablegen; (*Metr.*) – ***the stress,*** den Ton haben (***on,*** auf (*Dat.*)); – ***his temperature,*** sein Fieber messen; – ***things easy,*** see – ***it easy*** (*under* **(b)**); ***taking one thing with another,*** eins ins andere gerechnet; – ***a ticket,*** eine Karte lösen; ***that –s time,*** das erfordert *or* bedarf *or* braucht *or* kostet Zeit; – ***the time,*** sich Zeit lassen; ***it will – me a long time,*** ich brauche viel Zeit; (*coll.*) ***it –s me all my time,*** es kostet mich unendliche Mühe; – ***time by the forelock,*** die Gelegenheit beim Schopf fassen; – ***trouble,*** sich (*Dat.*) Mühe geben (***over,*** bei); – ***the trouble,*** sich (*Dat.*) die Mühe machen (***to do,*** zu tun); (*coll.*) – ***a turn,*** einen kleinen Spaziergang machen; – ***a turn at,*** sich vorübergehend befassen mit, sich versuchen an (*Dat.*); – ***a turn for the worse,*** sich zum Schlechtern wenden, eine Wendung zum Schlechtern machen; – ***one's turn,*** (ab)warten bis man an die Reihe kommt; – ***turns,*** (sich gegenseitig) abwechseln (***at,*** bei); – ***umbrage,*** see – ***offence***; – ***a view of,*** beurteilen; – ***a different view,*** anderer Ansicht sein; (*coll.*) – ***a dim view of,*** über die Achsel ansehen; – ***a walk,*** einen Spaziergang machen; – ***warning,*** sich warnen lassen (***by,*** von); (*Naut.*) – ***water,*** Wasser machen, leck sein; – ***the water,*** ins Wasser gehen, vom Stapel laufen; – ***the waters,*** Brunnen trinken; – ***a wife,*** heiraten; (*fig.*) – ***the wind out of his sails,*** ihm den Wind aus den Segeln nehmen; – ***wing,*** davonfliegen; ***I – your word for it,*** ich zweifle daran nicht; – ***the words out of his mouth,*** sagen gerade was er sagen wollte.

(b) (*with it*) ***I – it that*** . . ., ich fasse es so auf *or* nehme an, daß . . .; ***as I – it,*** nach meiner Auffassung; – ***it easy,*** es sich (*Dat.*) bequem machen; sich schonen; – ***it ill,*** es übelnehmen; (***you may***) – ***it from me,*** glauben Sie's mir! (*coll.*) ***I can – it,*** ich kann's hinnehmen *or* einstecken; (*coll.*) – ***it or leave it!*** mach was du willst! entweder - oder! (*coll.*) – ***it on the chin,*** die Ohren steif halten; – ***it in good part,*** es gut aufnehmen, sich (dadurch) nicht beleidigt fühlen.

(c) (*with prep.*) – ***him at a disadvantage,*** ihn in einer unvorteilhaften Lage antreffen; – ***him at his word,*** ihn beim Worte nehmen; – ***by the hand,*** bei der Hand nehmen; – ***by storm,*** im Sturm nehmen; – ***by surprise,*** überraschen, überrumpeln; – ***by the throat,*** an der Kehle packen; – ***him for a fool,*** ihn für einen Narren halten; – ***for granted,*** als selbstverständlich *or* erwiesen annehmen, voraussetzen; – ***too much for granted,*** sich (*Dat.*) zuviel herausnehmen; (*sl.*) – ***for a ride,*** um die Ecke bringen; – ***for a walk,*** auf einen Spaziergang mitnehmen; – ***from,*** wegnehmen; (*Math.*) abziehen von; – ***in the act,*** auf frische Tat ertappen; – ***in hand,*** unternehmen (*a th.*), fest in die Hand nehmen (*a p.*); – ***in marriage,*** zur Frau nehmen; (*B.*) – ***in vain,*** mißbrauchen; – ***into account,*** see – ***account of*** (*under* **(a)**); – ***into one's confidence,*** ins Vertrauen ziehen; – ***into consideration,*** see – ***account of***; – ***into one's own hands,*** sich (*Dat.*) selbst annehmen (*Gen.*); – ***the law into one's own hands,*** sich (*Dat.*) selbst Recht verschaffen; – ***into one's head,*** sich (*Dat.*) in den Kopf setzen; – ***him off his feet,*** ihn umwerfen; – ***s.th. off his hands,*** ihm etwas abnehmen; – ***his mind off*** (*his work etc.*), ihn ablenken von; – ***one's mind off*** . . ., sich ablenken lassen von; – ***a load off his mind,*** ihm einen Stein vom Herzen nehmen; – ***on,*** see – ***upon***; – ***out of,*** (ent)nehmen (*Dat.*), herausnehmen *or* entfernen aus; (*coll.*) ***the hot weather –s it out of me,*** die Hitze macht mich fertig; ***be –n out of o.s.,*** sich selbst vergessen; – ***him out of his way,*** ihn einen Umweg machen lassen; – ***to heart,*** sich (*Dat.*) zu Herzen nehmen, beherzigen; – ***to one's heart,*** liebgewinnen; – ***to pieces,*** zerlegen, auseinandernehmen; – ***to task,*** zur Rede stellen; – ***to wife,*** zur Frau nehmen; – (***up***)***on one***(***self***), auf sich nehmen; ***he –s it upon him***(***self***), er fühlt sich berufen (***to do,*** zu tun); – ***with,*** mitnehmen; (*coll.*) ***be –n with,*** entzückt *or* begeistert sein von.

(d) (*with adv. or adj.*) – ***aback,*** (*usu. pass.*) überraschen, verblüffen; – ***along,*** mitnehmen; – ***amiss,*** falsch auffassen; übelnehmen; – ***apart,*** zerlegen, auseinandernehmen; – ***aside,*** beiseitenehmen; – ***away,*** wegnehmen, fortnehmen, entfernen; (*Math.*) see – ***from*** (*under* **(c)**); – ***his breath away,*** ihm den Atem verschlagen; – ***back,*** 1. zurücknehmen, zurückbringen; 2. widerrufen (*a statement*); 3. zurückversetzen, zurückführen (*a p. in spirit*) (***to,*** in (*Acc.*)) (*a time etc.*); – ***down,*** 1. herunternehmen, abnehmen; 2. fällen (*trees*), abbrechen, abreißen, abtragen (*buildings*); 3. aufschreiben, niederschreiben, zu Papier bringen; 4. (*also* – ***down a peg***) demütigen, einen Dämpfer aufsetzen (*Dat.*) (*a p.*); **– *it easy, see under*** **(b)**; **– *forward,*** weiterführen, weiterbringen; **– *hard,*** hart getroffen werden von; ***be –n ill,*** krank werden; *see also under* **(b)**; **– *in,*** 1. einnehmen; 2. annehmen, übernehmen (*work, money etc.*), ankaufen, einkaufen, hereinnehmen, einlegen (*goods*); 3. aufnehmen, beherbergen (*guests*); 4. einführen, zu Tisch führen (*partner*); 5. (*fig.*) einschließen, umfassen, in sich fassen *or* schließen (*expanse*); 6. erfassen, erkennen, aufnehmen, überschauen (*with one's senses*); 7. (*coll.*) anführen, hereinlegen, übers Ohr hauen; 8. (*Dressm.*) enger machen, einnähen, einlassen; 9. einholen (*a sail*); **– *in washing,*** Wäsche ins Haus nehmen; **– *in petrol,*** tanken; (*coll.*) ***it will – me too long,*** es wird mich zu weit führen; (*coll.*) **– *lying down,*** hinnehmen, einstecken (*insult etc.*). **– *off,*** 1. abnehmen, ziehen (*hat*), ablegen, ausziehen (*coat etc.*); 2. (*knitting*) abnehmen, zusammenstricken; 3. einstellen (*train service etc.*); 4. (*Naut.*) von Bord bringen (*passenger*); 5. (*coll.*) nachäffen, karikieren; (*fig.*) **– *off one's hat to,*** den Hut ziehen vor (*Dat.*); **– *a day off,*** sich (*Dat.*) einen Tag freinehmen; **– *o.s. off,*** fortgehen, sich fortmachen *or* entfernen. **– *on,*** 1. anstellen, einstellen (*workers*), annehmen, unternehmen (*work*), annehmen, sich (*Dat.*) geben (*character, appearance etc.*), eingehen (*wager*); (*Naut.*) an Bord nehmen, aufnehmen (*cargo, passengers*); 2. (*coll.*) es aufnehmen mit (*a rival*). **– *out,*** herausnehmen; entfernen, wegnehmen (*of,* von *or* aus); abheben (*money*), lösen, erwerben, erwirken (*licence etc.*), abschließen (*insurance*), entleihen (*book from library*); ausführen (*a p. to dinner etc.*); **– *out for a walk,*** spazierenführen; (*coll.*) ***when he is annoyed he –s it out on the children,*** wenn er verstimmt ist, läßt er seinen Ärger an den Kindern aus. **– *over,*** übernehmen; (*coll.*) ***be –n short,*** Durchfall bekommen; **– *unawares,*** überraschen. **– *up,*** 1. aufnehmen, aufheben; ergreifen, in die Hand nehmen (*weapon, tool etc.*), einsteigen *or* zusteigen lassen (*passengers*); 2. (*fig.*) aufnehmen, beginnen, anfangen mit, sich zuwenden (*Dat.*) (*work, study etc.*), ergreifen (*a career*), antreten, aufnehmen (*duties*), beziehen (*a position*); 3. einnehmen, ausfüllen, beanspruchen, in Anspruch nehmen (*space, time*); 4. (ein)spannen, enger machen; 5. (*fig. coll.*) unterbrechen, zurechtsetzen (*a p.*); **– *up the carpet,*** den Teppich aufheben; **– *up the cudgels for,*** eintreten *or* Partei ergreifen für; **– *him up in the lift,*** ihn im Aufzug nach oben fahren; **– *up the matter,*** die S. aufgreifen, die Klage erheben; **– *up the pavement,*** das Pflaster aufreißen; **– *up residence,*** Wohnung nehmen, unterkommen (***in, at,*** in (*Dat.*); ***with,*** bei); (*Tech.*) **– *up the slack,*** spielfrei einstellen; (*knitting*) **– *up a stitch,*** eine Masche aufnehmen *or* auffangen; **– *up the story,*** in der Geschichte fortfahren, die Geschichte fortführen; (*coll.*) **– *him up on it,*** seine Herausforderung annehmen; (*coll.*) **– *him up short,*** ihn anfahren; ***be –n up with,*** vertieft sein in (*Acc.*), beschäftigt sein mit.

2. *irr.v.i.* 1. wirken, Wirkung haben, Eindruck machen, (*as medicine*) anschlagen, (*of colour*) haften, (*of plants etc.*) Wurzel fassen, anwachsen, (*of fish*) anbeißen; 2. (*Cards*) stechen, (*Chess*) schlagen; 3. (*coll.*) sich photographieren (lassen); 4. (*coll.*) *see also* **– *on*** (*of th.*).

(a) (*with prep.*) **– *after,*** geraten nach, nachschlagen (*Dat.*), ähneln (*Dat.*). **– *from,*** herabsetzen, schmälern, schwächen, Abbruch tun (*Dat.*). **– *to,*** 1. sich begeben *or* flüchten nach *or* zu *or* in (*Acc.*); (*also fig.*) Zuflucht nehmen zu; 2. (*fig.*) sich beschäftigen *or* abgeben mit, sich verlegen auf (*Acc.*), sich widmen *or* hingeben (*Dat.*); 3. Gefallen finden an (*Dat.*), hingezogen werden *or* sich hingezogen fühlen zu, liebgewinnen; **– *to one's bed,*** bettlägerig werden; **– *to the boats,*** in die Boote gehen; **– *to drink,*** das Trinken anfangen, sich (*Dat.*) das Trinken angewöhnen; **– *to one's heels,*** Fersengeld geben, sich aus dem Staub machen; **– *to the water,*** ins Wasser gehen; (*coll.*) ***he –s to it like a duck –s to water,*** sofort ist er Feuer und Flamme dafür; **– *to the woods,*** in die Wälder flüchten; (*usu. neg.*) **– *kindly to,*** sich befreunden mit, sich hingezogen fühlen zu, geneigt sein (*Dat.*); ***he doesn't – kindly to the idea,*** der Vorschlag ist ihm nicht sympathisch.

(b) (*with adv.*) **– *long,*** lange dauern; **– *off,*** (*Av.*) aufsteigen, abfliegen, (*also Spt.*) starten. (*coll.*) **– *on,*** 1. (*of p.*) sich aufregen, großes Getue machen, sich haben; sich aufspielen (***about,*** wegen); 2. (*of th.*) gut *or* allgemein aufgenommen werden, Anklang finden, einschlagen, ankommen. **– *over,*** die Initiative ergreifen, die S. in die Hand nehmen, (*Pol.*) die Regierung übernehmen; (*coll.*) **– *up with,*** sich einlassen mit, anbändeln mit.

3. *s.* 1. der Fang (*of fish*); 2. die Einnahme (*at box office*); 3. Szenenaufnahme (*films*), Probeaufnahme (*recordings*); 4. (*Typ.*) die Schiebung.

take|-home pay, *s.* (*coll.*) der Nettolohn. **--in,** *s.* (*coll.*) der Reinfall, die Prellerei.

taken ['teikən], *p.p. of* **take.**

take|-off, *s.* 1. (*coll.*) die Karikatur; 2. (*Av.*) der Start, Abflug, (*Spt.*) Absprung; (*Av.*) **– *run,*** der Anlauf. **--over,** *s.* (*Comm.*) die Übernahme; **– *bid,*** das Übernahmeangebot.

taker ['teikə], *s.* der (die) Käufer(in), Abnehmer(in). **taking, 1.** *adj.* einnehmend, anziehend, reizend, entzückend, gewinnend, fesselnd. **2.** *s.* 1. das Nehmen, die Einnahme (*of a fortress etc.*); 2. (*usu. pl.*) die Einnahme, der Gewinn.

talc [tælk], **talcum** [-əm], *s.* der Talk, das Talkum; ***talcum powder,*** der Körperpuder.

tale [teil], *s.* die Erzählung, Geschichte, der Bericht; (*also fairy-–*) das Märchen, (*obs.*) die (Auf)zählung; ***thereby hangs a –,*** daran knüpft sich eine Geschichte; ***old wives' –,*** das Ammenmärchen; ***dead men tell no –s,*** tote Hunde beißen nicht; ***tell –s*** (***out of school***), aus der Schule schwatzen *or* plaudern. **tale-bearer,** *s.* der (die) Zuträger(in), Zwischenträger(in), Angeber(in), Ohrenbläser(in), die Klatsche, Klatschbase, das Klatschmaul.

talent ['tælənt], *s.* 1. die Gabe, Anlage, Begabung, Fähigkeit, das Talent; ***man of –,*** talentierter *or* talentvoller *or* begabter Mann; 2. (*Hist.*) das Talent. **talented,** *adj.* begabt, talentiert, talentvoll. **talentless,** *adj.* talentlos, untalentiert, unbegabt.

tales [teilz], *s.* (*Law*) die Liste der Ersatzgeschworenen. **talesman** [-mən], *s.* Ersatzgeschworene(r).

talion ['tæliən], *s.* (*Law*) die Wiedervergeltung.

talisman ['tælizmən], *s.* der Talisman, das Zauberzeichen. **talismanic** [-'mænik], *adj.* zauberisch, magisch.

talk [tɔ:k], **1.** *v.i.* reden, sprechen; plaudern, sich unterhalten (***to, with,*** mit; ***of,*** von; ***about, on,*** über (*Acc.*)); (*coll.*) ***now you are –ing!*** nun hat dein Reden Sinn! so laß ich mir's gefallen! das läßt sich hören! (*coll.*) ***you can –!*** Sie haben gut reden! (*coll.*) **– *back,*** grob antworten; (*coll.*) **– *big,*** aufschneiden, prahlen, großreden; (*coll.*) **– *about your roses, you should see mine,*** wenn deine Rosen gut sein sollen, dann mußt du meine erst sehen; ***he –s of doing it,*** er spricht davon, daß er es tun will; (*coll.*) **– *of the devil . . .,*** (man soll nicht) den Teufel an die Wand malen; ***–ing of,*** bezüglich, da wir gerade sprechen von; **– *over the heads of one's audience,*** über die Köpfe der Zuhörer hinwegreden; **– *round a th.,*** um etwas herumreden *or* herumsprechen; (*sl.*) **– *through one's hat,*** dummes Zeug reden; **– *to,*** sprechen mit; (*coll.*) ernsthaft reden mit, ins Gewissen reden (*Dat.*); **– *to o.s.,*** vor sich hinreden; **– *down to,*** herablassend *or* patronisierend reden zu. **2.** *v.t.* sprechen (*German etc.*); (*coll.*) **– *the hind leg off a donkey,*** ihm *etc.* ein Loch in den Bauch reden; **– *nonsense,*** Unsinn reden; **– *politics,*** über Politik reden *or* sprechen; **– *sense,*** vernünftig reden; **– *shop,*** fachsimpeln; (*sl.*) **– *turkey,*** offen *or* ohne Umschweife reden; **– *down,*** zum Schweigen bringen, unter den Tisch reden; **– *him into*** (or ***out of***) ***it,*** es ihm einreden (*or* ausreden); ihn dazu überreden (*or* davon abreden); **– *o.s. into,*** sich (*Dat.*) einreden; **– *o.s. hoarse,* – *one's head off,*** sich heiser reden; **– *over,*** besprechen, durchsprechen (*a th.*); **– *him over*** or ***round,*** ihn überreden. **3.** *s.* 1. das Gespräch, die

Plauderei, Unterhaltung; 2. Besprechung, Unterredung; der Vortrag, die Ansprache; (*Pol.*) ***have –s***, eine Unterredung *or* Ansprache halten (***about***, über (*Acc.*)); 3. das Reden, Gerede, Geschwätz, der Klatsch, die Rederei; ***it is all –***, es ist nur leeres Gerede; ***it is all the –***, es geht das Gerücht; ***idle –***, leeres Geschwätz; ***small –***, das Geplauder, leichte Plauderei; ***– of the town***, das Stadtgespräch.

talkative ['tɔ:kətiv], *adj.* gesprächig, redselig, geschwätzig. **talkativeness,** *s.* die Gesprächigkeit, Geschwätzigkeit, Redseligkeit.

talker ['tɔ:kə], *s.* der (die) Schwätzer(in). **talkie** [–i], *s.* (*coll.*) der Tonfilm. **talking, 1.** *s.* das Geplauder; ***all the – was on his side***, er führte allein das Wort. **2.** *attrib. adj.* (*fig.*) sprechend, ausdrucksvoll. **talking|-film, --picture,** *s.* der Tonfilm. **--point,** *s.* der Gesprächsstoff. **--to,** *s.* (*coll.*) die Schelte, Standpauke; ***give him a –***, ihm eine Standpauke halten, ihm ins Gewissen reden, ihn ins Gebet nehmen.

tall [tɔ:l], *adj.* groß (*of stature*), hoch (*as trees, houses etc.*); (*coll.*) ***– order***, (starke) Zumutung, starkes Stück, harte Nuß; (*coll.*) ***– story***, unglaubliche *or* übertriebene Geschichte, das Seemannsgarn; (*coll.*) ***– talk***, großspuriges Reden, die Angeberei.

tallboy ['tɔ:lbɔi], *s.* die Kommode.

tallish ['tɔ:liʃ], *adj.* ziemlich groß. **tallness,** *s.* die Länge, Höhe, Größe.

tallow ['tælou], **1.** *s.* der Talg, das Unschlitt; ***– candle***, das Talglicht. **2.** *v.t.* mit Talg einschmieren. **tallow|-chandler,** *s.* der Lichtzieher. **--faced,** *adj.* bleich. **tallowy,** *adj.* talgig, talgartig.

tally ['tæli], **1.** *s.* 1. (*Hist.*) das Kerbholz; 2. (*coll.*) die Rechnung; 3. Etikette, das Etikett, die Marke, der Schein, Kupon; 4. das Seitenstück, Gegenstück, Duplikat (***of***, zu). **2.** *v.t.* buchen, registrieren, kontrollieren; bezeichnen. **3.** *v.i.* ***– with***, passen zu, (überein)stimmen mit; entsprechen (*Dat.*).

tally-ho ['tæli'hou], **1.** *int.* (*Hunt.*) halali! **2.** *s.* das Hallo, der Weidruf, Jagdruf.

tally|-sheet, *s.* der Zählbogen, Rechnungsbogen. **--system,** *s.* das Abzahlungssystem. **--trade,** *s.* das Abzahlungsgeschäft.

talmi-gold ['tælmi–], *s.* das Talmi.

Talmud ['tælmud], *s.* der Talmud. **Talmudic(al)** [–'mudik(l)], *adj.* talmudisch.

talon ['tælən], *s.* 1. die Klaue, Kralle; 2. (*Archit.*) die Kehlleiste; 3. (*Comm.*) der Talon, Erneuerungsschein; 4. (*Cards*) Talon.

talus ['teiləs], *s.* (*pl.* **tali** [–lai]) 1. (*Anat.*) das Sprungbein; 2. (*Fort.*) die Böschung, Abdachung; 3. (*Geol.*) Schutthalde, das Geröll.

tamable, *see* **tameable.**

tamarack ['tæməræk], *s.* (*Bot.*) Amerikanische Lärche.

tamarin ['tæmərin], *s.* (*Zool.*) der Tamarin, Seidenaffe.

tamarind ['tæmərind], *s.* (*Bot.*) die Tamarinde.

tamarisk ['tæmərisk], *s.* (*Bot.*) die Tamariske.

tambour ['tæmbuə], **1.** *s.* 1. die Trommel; der Trommelschläger; 2. *See* **tambour-frame**; 3. (*Archit.*) die Säulentrommel, der Trommelstein. **2.** *v.t.* tamburieren. **tambour-frame,** *s.* der Tambur, Stickrahmen. **tambourine** [–bə'ri:n], *s.* das Tamburin, die Handtrommel, Schellentrommel. **tambour|-stitch,** *s.* der Tamburierstich. **--work,** *s.* die Tamburierstickerei.

tame [teim], **1.** *v.t.* zähmen, bändigen (*an animal*); (*fig.*) bezähmen, gefügig machen, unterwerfen, beugen. **2.** *adj.* 1. zahm, gezähmt; (*fig.*) mutlos, unterwürfig, folgsam, gefügig; 2. (*coll.*) geistlos, fad(e), schal, langweilig. **tameable,** *adj.* (be)zähmbar. **tameness,** *s.* 1. die Zahmheit; Mutlosigkeit; 2. (*fig.*) Langweiligkeit, Fadheit, Geistlosigkeit. **tamer,** *s.* der (die) Bändiger(in) (*of animals*).

Tamil ['tæmil], *s.* das Tamil, Tamulisch.

tam-o'-shanter ['tæmə'ʃæntə], *s.* die Baskenmütze.

tamp [tæmp], **1.** *v.t.* abdämmen, zustopfen (*hole*); (*Artil.*) feststampfen, feststoßen (*the charge*). **2.** *s.* die Handramme.

tamper ['tæmpə], *v.i.* sich (ein)mischen, hineinpfuschen (***with***, in (*Acc.*)), herumpfuschen (an (*Dat.*)); ***– with***, fälschen (*a document*), zu bestechen suchen (*a p.*), unsachgemäße *or* unerlaubte Eingriffe machen in (*Acc.*).

tamping ['tæmpiŋ], *s.* 1. das Abdämmen, Feststampfen; 2. die Stopfmasse, Stampfmasse, der Besatz.

tampion ['tæmpiən], *s.* der Mündungspfropfen (*of a gun*).

tampon ['tæmpən], **1.** *s.* der Pfropfen; (*Med.*) Mullbausch, Wattebausch, Gazestreifen. **2.** *v.t.* tamponieren (*a wound*).

tan [tæn], **1.** *s.* 1. die Lohe; 2. Lohfarbe, braune Farbe; 3. die Sonnenbräunung. **2.** *v.t.* 1. gerben; 2. bräunen (*one's face*); 3. (*coll.*) (durch)prügeln, versohlen, das Fell gerben (*Dat.*) (*a p.*). **3.** *v.i.* 1. sich gerben lassen (*leather*); 2. braun *or* sonnenverbrannt werden, sich bräunen (*skin*). **4.** *adj.* lohfarben, (gelb)braun. **tanbark,** *s.* die Lohe; ***spent –***, ausgelaugte Lohe.

tandem ['tændəm], **1.** *s.* das Tandem (*also Cycl.*); hintereinandergespannte Pferde (*pl.*). **2.** *adv.* ***drive –***, mit hintereinandergespannten Pferden fahren.

[1]**tang** [tæŋ], **1.** *s.* 1. scharfer Ton *or* Klang; 2. scharfer Geschmack *or* Geruch; 3. (*fig.*) der Beigeschmack, Nachgeschmack, Anflug (***of***, von). **2.** *v.i.* laut ertönen. **3.** *v.t.* (laut) ertönen lassen, anschlagen (*a bell*).

[2]**tang, 1.** *s.* der Griffzapfen, Heftzapfen (*of a knife*), Dorn, die Angel(zunge) (*of a buckle*), Schloßhalterung (*of gun*). **2.** *v.t.* mit einer Angel versehen.

[3]**tang,** *s.* (*Bot.*) der Seetang, die Braunalge.

tangency ['tændʒənsi], *s.* die Berührung, Tangenz. **tangent, 1.** *s.* die Tangente; ***– of an angle***, die Winkeltangente; ***– of motion***, die Bahntangente; (*fig.*) ***fly*** or ***go off at a –*** vom Thema abschweifen, plötzlich abschwenken; (*Artil.*) ***– elevation***, der Aufsatzwinkel; ***– plane***, die Berührungsebene. **2.** *adj. See* **tangential,** 1. **tangential** [–'dʒenʃəl], *adj.* 1. Berührungs–, Tangential–; ***be – to***, berühren; ***– coordinates***, Linienkoordinaten; ***– force***, die Tangentialkraft, Zentrifugalkraft; 2. (*fig.*) flüchtig, sprunghaft, abschweifend, abweichend.

tangerine [tændʒə'ri:n], *s.* die Mandarine.

tangibility [tændʒi'biliti], *s.* die Greifbarkeit, Fühlbarkeit, Berührbarkeit. **tangible** ['tændʒibl], *adj.* greifbar (*also fig.*), fühlbar; (*Law*) real, materiell; (*fig.*) handgreiflich; (*Law*) ***– property***, das Sachvermögen; (*Comm.*) ***– assets***, greifbare Aktiven. **tangibles,** *pl. See* ***tangible property.***

Tangier [tæn'dʒiə], *s.* Tanger (*n.*).

[1]**tangle** [tæŋgl], **1.** *s.* das Gewirr, der Knäuel, die Verschlingung, Verwicklung, (*fig.*) Verwirrung, das Durcheinander. **2.** *v.t.* verwirren, verwickeln, durcheinanderbringen; verschlingen, verflechten, verstricken (*also fig.*). **3.** *v.i.* (*also* ***– up***) verwirrt *or* verwickelt werden, sich verheddern; (*sl.*) ***– up with***, sich (in einen Kampf) einlassen mit.

[2]**tangle,** *s.* (*Bot.*) der Riementang.

tango ['tæŋgou], **1.** *s.* der Tango. **2.** *v.i.* Tango tanzen.

tank [tæŋk], **1.** *s.* 1. der Behälter, das Bassin, Becken; die Zisterne; 2. (*Tech.*) der Tank; 3. (*Mil.*) Panzer; 4. (*Railw.*) Wasserkasten; 5. *See* **tank-engine**; 6. (*Phot.*) Wanne, das Bad. **2.** *v.i.* tanken; (*sl.*) ***– up***, sich vollaufen lassen *or* besaufen. **tankage,** *s.* das Fassungsvermögen eines Tanks.

tankard ['tæŋkəd], *s.* der Deckelkrug, die Kanne, das Seidel.

tank|-buster, *s.* (*Mil. sl.*) der Panzerknacker. **--car,** *s.* (*Railw.*) der Kesselwagen. **--carrier,** *s.* Panzertransportwagen. **--engine,** *s.* die Tenderlokomotive.

tanker ['tæŋkə], *s.* 1. *See* **tankship**; 2. der Tankwagen.

tank|ship, *s.* das Tankschiff, der Tankdampfer.

--transporter, *s. See* **--carrier. --trap,** *s.* die Panzerfalle. **--truck,** *s. See* **tanker,** 2.
tan-liquor, *s.* die Lohbrühe, Beizbrühe.
tannable ['tænəbl], *adj.* gerbbar. **tannate,** *s.* gerbsaures Salz, das Tannat. **tanned** [tænd], *adj.* lohgar (*leather*), sonnengebräunt (*skin*).
[1]**tanner** ['tænə], *s.* der (Loh)gerber.
[2]**tanner,** *s.* (*obs. sl.*) das Sechspencestück (= 2½p).
tannery ['tænəri], *s.* die Gerberei. **tannic,** *adj.* Gerb–; – *acid,* die Gerbsäure. **tannin,** *s. See* ***tannic acid.*** **tanning,** *s.* 1. das Gerben; 2. (*sl.*) Prügel (*pl.*). **tan-pit,** *s.* die Lohgrube.
tansy ['tænzi], *s.* (*Bot.*) der Rainfarn, Gänserich.
tantalization [tæntəlai'zeiʃən], *s.* die Tantalusqual, das Quälen, Zappelnlassen. **tantalize** ['tæntəlaiz], *v.t.* quälen, peinigen, zappeln lassen; ***be –d,*** Tantalusqualen leiden. **tantalizing,** *adj.* quälend, quälerisch, peinigend, schmerzlich.
tantalum ['tæntələm], *s.* (*Chem.*) das Tantal.
tantamount ['tæntəmaunt], *adj.* gleichwertig, gleichbedeutend (*to,* mit); ***be – to,*** gleichkommen (*Dat.*), auf dasselbe hinauslaufen wie.
tantivy [tæn'tivi], **1.** *s.* 1. rasender Galopp; 2. das Hussa, der Jagdruf. **2.** *adv.* geradewegs, spornstreichs, mit verhängtem Zügel.
tantrum ['tæntrəm], *s.* (*usu. pl.*) schlechte Laune, der Wutanfall, Koller.
tan-yard, *s. See* **tannery.**
[1]**tap** [tæp], **1.** *v.t.* 1. leicht schlagen, klopfen auf (*Acc.*); 2. flicken (*shoes*). **2.** *v.i.* schlagen, klopfen (*at, on,* gegen *or* an (*Acc.*)). **3.** *s.* 1. leichter Schlag, der Klaps, Taps; 2. (*on shoes*) Flicken; 3. *pl.* (*Mil.*) Zapfenstreich.
[2]**tap, 1.** *v.t.* 1. anzapfen, anstechen (*a cask*); abzapfen, ablassen (*liquid*); 2. (*Tech.*) ein Gewinde bohren in (*Acc.*), mit einem Gewinde versehen; 3. (*Med.*) punktieren; 4. (*Tele.*) abgreifen, anzapfen (*line*), abfangen, abhören (*message*); 5. (*fig. coll.*) angehen, anpumpen (*for,* um) (*a p.*), erschließen, nutzbar machen (*resources*). **2.** *s.* 1. der Zapfen, Spund, (Faß)hahn; ***on –,*** angezapft, angestochen; (*fig.*) auf Lager, verfügbar; 2. der Gashahn, Wasserhahn; 3. (*Tech.*) (*also **screw–***) Schraubenbohrer, Gewindebohrer; 4. (*Elec.*) Abstich, die Abzweigung.
tap|-dance, *s.* der Steptanz. **--dancing,** *s.* das Steppen.
tape [teip], **1.** *s.* das (Zwirn)band; der Papierstreifen, (*teleprinter, computer*) Lochstreifen, (*sound reproduction*) das (Magnetophon)band; (*Spt.*) das Zielband; ***adhesive –,*** das Leukoplast; ***breast the –,*** durchs Ziel gehen (*racing*); ***insulating –,*** das Isolierband; ***masking –,*** das Abdeckband; (*fig.*) ***red –,*** die Pedanterie, Paragraphenreiterei, der Bürokratismus, Amtsschimmel. **2.** *v.t.* 1. mit Band umwickeln; 2. (*coll.*) auf (Ton)band aufnehmen; 3. (*sl.*) ***have*** (*s.o., s.th.*) ***–d,*** im Bilde sein über (*Acc.*).
tape|-deck, *s.* die Spulenanlage. **--machine,** *s.* der Fernschreiber. **--measure,** *s.* das Meßband, Bandmaß, Zentimetermaß.
taper ['teipə], **1.** *s.* 1. die Wachskerze, der Fidibus; 2. die Verjüngung, Konizität. **2.** *adj.* spitz (zulaufend), sich verjüngend; (*Archit.*) verjüngt. **3.** *v.t.* zuspitzen, spitz zulaufen lassen. **4.** *v.i.* (*also **– off*** or ***away***) spitz zulaufen, sich verjüngen; (*fig.*) allmählich aufhören, nachlassen, abnehmen, sich allmählich verlieren; – ***to a point,*** spitz zulaufen.
tape|-recorder, *s.* das Tonbandgerät, Magnetophon. **--recording,** *s.* die Bandaufnahme.
tapered ['teipəd], **tapering,** *adj.* spitz zulaufend, sich verjüngend.
tapestry ['tæpistri], **1.** *s.* gewirkte Tapete, der Wandteppich, die Tapisserie. **2.** *v.t.* mit Wandteppichen behängen.
tapeworm ['teipwə:m], *s.* der Bandwurm.
tapioca [tæpi'oukə], *s.* die Tapioka.
tapir ['teipiə], *s.* (*Zool.*) der Tapir.
tapis ['tæpi:], *s.* (*only in*) ***be on the –,*** erörtert werden, zur Sprache kommen, aufs Tapet gebracht werden; ***come on the –,*** aufs Tapet kommen.
tappet ['tæpit], *s.* der Stößel (*of a valve*); (*Motor.*) Nocken, Hebel, Daumen, die Steuerknagge; – ***gear,*** die Nockensteuerung; – ***rod,*** der Gleitstöpsel.
tapping ['tæpiŋ], *s.* 1. leichtes Schlagen, das (Be)klopfen; 2. Anzapfen (*of cask*), Abzapfen (*of liquid*); (*Med.*) Punktieren, Perkutieren; (*fig.*) die Erschließung; der Abstich, Abgriff; 3. (*Tech.*) das Gewindeschneiden.
tap|room, *s.* die Schankstube, Schenkstube. **–root,** *s.* die Pfahlwurzel.
tapster ['tæpstə], *s.* (*obs.*) der Schenkkellner, Schankkellner.
tap water, *s.* das Leitungswasser.
tar [tɑ:], **1.** *s.* 1. der Teer; 2. (*Naut. coll.*) (*also **Jack Tar***) die Teerjacke. **2.** *v.t.* teeren; – ***and feather,*** teeren und federn; ***tarred with the same brush,*** die nämlichen Mängel aufweisen.
taradiddle, *see* **tarradiddle.**
tarantella [tærən'telə], *s.* die Tarantella (*dance*).
tarantula [tə'ræntjulə], *s.* (*Ent.*) die Tarantel.
tar-board, *s.* die Teerpappe.
tarboosh ['tɑ:buʃ], *s.* der Tarbusch, Fes.
tar-brush, *s.* die Teerquaste; (*pej.*) ***dash of the –,*** Negerblut in den Adern.
tardigrade ['tɑ:digreid], **1.** *adj.* langsam, träge. **2.** *s.* (*Zool.*) das Bärtierchen.
tardiness ['tɑ:dinis], *s.* 1. die Langsamkeit, Saumseligkeit, Säumigkeit, Trägheit; 2. (*Am.*) Verspätung. **tardy,** *adj.* 1. langsam, saumselig, säumig, träge; 2. (*Am.*) verspätet, spät.
[1]**tare** [tɛə], *s.* 1. (*Bot.*) die Wicke; 2. (*B.*) das Unkraut.
[2]**tare, 1.** *s.* (*Comm.*) die Tara; – ***and tret,*** Tara und Gutgewicht. **2.** *v.t.* tarieren.
target ['tɑ:git], *s.* 1. die (Schieß)scheibe; 2. (*fig.*) Zielscheibe; 3. (*obs.*) Tartsche. **target|-area,** *s.* der Zielraum. **--date,** *s.* (*coll.*) der Termin, angesetzter Zeitpunkt. **--figures,** *pl.* Sollzahlen (*pl.*). **--image,** *s.* das Zielbild. **--practice,** *s.* das Übungsschießen, Scheibenschießen, die Schießübung.
tariff ['tærif], *s.* 1. der Tarif; Zolltarif, die Zoll(gebühr); 2. (*Comm.*) das Preisverzeichnis. **tariff| reform,** *s.* die Schutzzollpolitik. **– reformer,** *s.* der Schutzzöllner. **– wall,** *s.* die Zollschranke.
tarlatan ['tɑ:lətən], *s.* der Tarlatan.
tarmac ['tɑ:mæk], *s.* 1. die Macadamisierung, der Teerbeton; 2. (*Av. coll.*) die Rollbahn.
tarn [tɑ:n], *s.* kleiner Bergsee.
tarnish ['tɑ:niʃ], **1.** *v.t.* 1. trüben, matt *or* trübe machen; mattieren; 2. (*fig.*) beschmutzen, beflecken, den Glanz nehmen (*Dat.*) (*reputation*). **2.** *v.i.* trübe *or* matt werden, sich trüben; anlaufen (*metal*). **3.** *s.* 1. der Belag, Überzug; 2. (*fig.*) Makel. **tarnishing,** *s.* die Trübung, das Anlaufen.
taro ['tærou], *s.* (*Bot.*) eßbare Zehrwurzel.
tarpaulin [tɑ:'pɔ:lin], *s.* 1. die Persenning, Zeltbahn; 2. (*also pl.*) das Ölzeug, die Ölkleidung.
tarradiddle ['tærədidl], *s.* (*coll.*) die Flunkerei, Flausen (*pl.*).
tarragon ['tærəgən], *s.* (*Bot.*) der Estragon.
[1]**tarry** ['tɑ:ri], *adj.* geteert; teerartig.
[2]**tarry** ['tæri], **1.** *v.i.* zögern, säumen, zaudern, sich aufhalten. **2.** *v.t.* (*obs.*) abwarten.
tarsal ['tɑ:səl], *adj.* (*Anat.*) Fußwurzel–. **tarsus,** *s.* die Fußwurzel.
[1]**tart** [tɑ:t], *adj.* 1. scharf, sauer, herb; 2. (*fig.*) schroff, beißend, bissig.
[2]**tart,** *s.* die (Obst)torte.
[3]**tart, 1.** *s.* (*sl.*) die Nutte, Fose. **2.** *v.t.* (*sl.*) (*usu.* **– up**) aufputzen, aufdonnen, herausschmücken, verschönern.
tartan ['tɑ:tən], *s.* der Tartan, buntkariertes Muster; das Schottentuch.
Tartar ['tɑ:tə], **1.** *s.* der (die) Tatar(in). **2.** *adj.*

tatarisch; (*coll.*) ***catch a –***, übel ankommen, an den Falschen geraten.

tartar, *s.* 1. (*Chem.*) der Weinstein; ***cream of –***, gereinigter Weinstein, doppelweinsteinsaures Kali; – ***emetic***, der Brechweinstein, das Antimonkaliumtartrat; 2. (*Dentistry*) der Zahnstein. **tartaric** [–'tærik], *adj.* Weinstein–; weinsauer; – ***acid***, die Wein(stein)säure.

tartlet ['tɑ:tlit], *s.* das Törtchen.

tartness ['tɑ:tnis], *s.* 1. die Schärfe, Säure, Herbheit; 2. (*fig.*) Schroffheit, Bissigkeit.

tartrate ['tɑ:treit], *s.* wein(stein)saures Salz, das Tartrat.

task [tɑ:sk], **1.** *s.* 1. die Aufgabe; ***take to –***, zur Rede stellen, ins Gebet nehmen (*for*, wegen); 2. die Schularbeit, Schulaufgabe; 3. das Pensum, schwieriges Problem. **2.** *v.t.* beschäftigen, stark beanspruchen, anstrengen. **task|-force,** *s.* (*Mil.*) die (Sonder)kampfgruppe. **–master,** *s.* der Aufseher, strenger Zuchtmeister (*also fig.*). **--work,** *s.* die Akkordarbeit, Stückarbeit.

tassel [tæsl], **1.** *s.* die Troddel, Quaste. **2.** *v.t.* mit Quasten schmücken.

tassie ['tæsi], *s.* (*Scots*) kleiner Becher.

taste [teist], **1.** *v.t.* 1. schmecken, kosten, probieren; ***I cannot – anything***, ich habe keinen Geschmack; (*fig.*) – ***blood***, Blut lecken, auf den Geschmack kommen; 2. prüfen (*wine, tea etc.*); 3. (*fig.*) erfahren, erleben, genießen; versuchen, essen, trinken; ***I had never –d it before***, ich hatte es noch nie gegessen *or* getrunken. **2.** *v.i.* schmecken (*of*, nach). **3.** *s.* 1. der Geschmack; Nachgeschmack; (*fig.*) ***leave a bad*** or ***nasty – in the mouth***, einen üblen Eindruck *or* Nachgeschmack hinterlassen; 2. der Beigeschmack, Anstrich, Anflug (*of*, von); 3. Vorgeschmack, die Probe (*of*, von); (*fig.*) ***give him a – of***, ihm eine Probe geben von; 4. die (Kost)probe, der Bissen, Happen, das Stückchen, Schlückchen, Tröpfchen; 5. Schmecken, der Geschmackssinn; 6. (*fig.*) die Geschmacksrichtung, Mode; ***in bad –***, geschmacklos, unfein; ***in good –***, geschmackvoll; ***man of –***, der Mann von gutem Geschmack; ***popular –***, allgemeine Geschmacksrichtung, allgemeiner Geschmack; ***there is no accounting for –s***, über Geschmack läßt sich nicht streiten; 7. der Appetit (*for*, auf (*Acc.*)), Geschmack, das Gefallen (an (*Dat.*)), die Neigung (zu), Vorliebe, der Sinn (für); ***matter of –***, die Geschmackssache; ***add spices to –***, nach Belieben würzen!

taste-bud, *s.* (*Anat.*) der Geschmacksbecher.

tasteful ['teistful], *adj.* schmackhaft; (*usu. fig.*) geschmackvoll. **tastefulness,** *s.* (*fig.*) guter Geschmack. **tasteless,** *adj.* unschmackhaft, fad(e); (*fig.*) geschmacklos. **tastelessness,** *s.* (*fig.*) die Geschmacklosigkeit. **taster,** *s.* 1. der Koster, Schmecker (*tea, wine etc.*), Abschmecker, Vorkoster (*before serving*); 2. Probestecher (*for cheese etc.*). **tastiness,** *s.* die Schmackhaftigkeit. **tasty,** *adj.* schmackhaft.

¹**tat** [tæt], *s.* (*only in*) ***tit for –***, mit gleicher Münze (bezahlt).

²**tat,** *v.i.* Frivolitätenarbeit *or* Schiffchenarbeit machen.

tata [tæ'tɑ:], **1.** *s.* (*nursery talk*) der Spaziergang. **2.** *int.* auf Wiedersehen.

Tatar, *see* **Tartar.**

tatter ['tætə], *s.* (*usu. pl.*) der Lumpen, Fetzen; ***in –s***, zerfetzt. **tatterdemalion** [–də'meiliən], **1.** *s.* zerlumpter Kerl. **2.** *attrib. adj.* zerlumpt. **tattered** [–d], *adj.* zerlumpt, zerfetzt.

tatting ['tætiŋ], *s.* die Frivolitätenarbeit, Schiffchenarbeit; (*coll.*) (weibliche) Handarbeit.

tattle [tætl], **1.** *s.* das Geschwätz, Gewäsch, der Tratsch, Klatsch. **2.** *v.i.* schwatzen, klatschen, plaudern. **tattler,** *s.* der (die) Schwätzer(in), die Klatschbase.

¹**tattoo** [tæ'tu:], **1.** *s.* 1. (*Mil.*) der Zapfenstreich; ***beat a devil's –***, ungeduldig mit den Fingern trommeln; 2. militärisches Schaustück, die Parade mit Vorführungen. **2.** *v.i.* (*rare*) den Zapfenstreich schlagen *or* blasen; (*fig.*) *see* ***beat a devil's –***.

²**tattoo,** **1.** *v.t.* tätowieren, tatauieren (*the skin*), eintatauieren (*a design*) (*on*, in (*Acc.*)). **2.** *s.* die Tätowierung, Tatauierung. **tattooing,** *s.* das Tätowieren, Tatauieren.

tatty ['tæti], *adj.* (*coll.*) billig, schäbig.

taught [tɔ:t], *imperf., p.p. of* **teach.**

taunt [tɔ:nt], **1.** *s.* der Spott, Hohn, die Stichelei. **2.** *v.t.* (ver)höhnen, verspotten; – ***him with***, ihm Vorwürfe machen wegen, ihm vorwerfen (*Acc.*). **taunting,** *adj.* höhnisch, spöttisch, spottend, vorwurfsvoll.

taurine ['tɔ:rain], *adj.* Stier–, stierartig. **Taurus** [–rəs], *s.* (*Astr.*) der Stier.

taut [tɔ:t], *adj.* straff, stramm, angespannt; (*Naut.*) dicht. **tauten,** **1.** *v.t.* straff anspannen, strammziehen. **2.** *v.i.* sich straffen, straff werden. **tautness,** *s.* die Straffheit.

tautological [tɔ:tə'lɔdʒikl], **tautologous** [–'tɔlədʒəs], *adj.* tautologisch; dasselbe besagend. **tautology** [–'tɔlədʒi], *s.* die Tautologie, Doppelaussage.

tavern ['tævən], *s.* die Schenke, Kneipe, das Wirtshaus.

¹**taw** [tɔ:], *s.* die Murmel, das Murmelspiel.

²**taw,** *v.t.* weißgerben.

tawdriness ['tɔ:drinis], *s.* die Flitterhaftigkeit; (*fig.*) Wertlosigkeit, Geschmacklosigkeit. **tawdry,** *adj.* flitterhaft; (*fig.*) wertlos, geschmacklos.

tawer ['tɔ:ə], *s.* der Weißgerber. **tawery,** *s.* die Weißgerberei.

tawniness ['tɔ:ninis], *s.* die Lohfarbe, das Gelbbraun. **tawny,** *adj.* lohfarben, gelbbraun, braungelb; (*Orn.*) – ***owl***, der Waldkauz (*Strix aluca*); (*Orn.*) – ***pipit***, der Brachpieper (*Anthus campestris*).

taws(e) [tɔ:z], **1.** *s.* (*Scots*) die Peitsche, Gerte, Fuchtel, der Riemen. **2.** *v.t.* peitschen.

tax [tæks], **1.** *s.* 1. die (Staats)steuer; Abgabe, Gebühr, Taxe; Besteuerung (*on*, *Gen.*); ***corporation –***, die Körperschaftssteuer; ***income –***, die Einkommensteuer; ***land –***, die Grundsteuer; ***property –***, die Vermögen(s)steuer; ***purchase –***, die Warenumsatzsteuer; ***value-added –***, die Wertzuwachssteuer; ***rates and –es***, Kommunal– und Staatssteuern; 2. (*fig.*) die Last, Bürde, Belastung, Beanspruchung, Inanspruchnahme; – ***on his strength***, die Inanspruchnahme seiner Kräfte. **2.** *v.t.* 1. besteuern, eine Steuer auferlegen (*Dat.*) (*a p. or th.*); 2. (*Law*) einschätzen, abschätzen, ansetzen, veranschlagen, taxieren (*costs*) (*at*, auf (*Acc.*)); 3. (*fig.*) belasten, in Anspruch nehmen, anspannen, anstrengen, auf die Probe stellen; (*fig.*) – ***him with***, ihn bezichtigen *or* beschuldigen (*Gen.*), ihm vorwerfen (*Acc.*). **taxable,** *adj.* 1. besteuerbar, steuerpflichtig; 2. (*Law*) gebührenpflichtig (*costs*). **taxation** [–'eiʃən], *s.* 1. die Besteuerung; 2. (*Law*) Abschätzung; 3. (*collect.*) Steuern (*pl.*).

tax| avoidance, *s.* die Steuerabschreibung. **--bracket,** *s.* die Steuerklasse. **--collector,** *s.* Steuerbeamte(r), der Steuereinnehmer. **--evasion,** *s.* die Steuerhinterziehung. **--exemption,** *s.* die Steuerfreiheit. **--free,** *adj.* steuerfrei.

taxi ['tæksi], **1.** *s.* (*also* **--cab**) das Taxi, Mietauto, die (Auto)taxe. **2.** *v.i.* (*Av.*) rollen.

taxidermal [tæksi'də:ml], **taxidermic,** *adj.* Ausstopf–. **taxidermist** ['tæksidə:mist], *s.* der (Tier)ausstopfer, Präparator. **taxidermy** ['tæksidə:mi], *s.* das Ausstopfen *or* Präparieren von Tieren.

taxi|-driver, *s.* der Taxifahrer, Taxichauffeur. **–meter,** *s.* der Taxameter, Fahrpreisanzeiger, Zähler.

tax|payer, *s.* der Steuerzahler. **--reduction,** *s.* die Steuerermäßigung. **--return,** *s.* die Steuererklärung.

tea [ti:], *s.* der Tee; ***after –***, nach dem Tee; ***beef-–***, die Kraftbrühe; ***blend –***, Teesorten mischen; ***five o'clock –***, der Fünfuhrtee; ***high –***, ***meat –***, kaltes Abendessen.

tea|-bread, *s.* das Teegebäck. **--caddy,** *s.* die Teedose, Teebüchse. **--cake,** *s.* der Teekuchen. **--cannister,** *s. See* **--caddy.**

teach [ti:tʃ], **1.** *irr.v.t.* lehren, unterrichten (*a p. or th.*), beibringen (*Dat.*), unterweisen (*a p.*), Unterricht erteilen *or* geben in (*Dat.*) (*a th.*), abrichten, dressieren (*animals*); (*coll.*) ***that will – you!*** das wird dich eines Besseren belehren! (*coll.*) ***I will – you to laugh at me,*** ich werde dir das Lachen vertreiben; (*sl.*) ***go – your grandmother to suck eggs!*** mir kannst du nichts vormachen! (*coll.*) ***you can't – an old dog new tricks,*** was Hänschen nicht lernt, lernt Hans nimmermehr; – ***him manners,*** ihm Manieren beibringen; – ***him to read,*** ihm das Lesen beibringen. **2.** *irr.v.i.* lehren, unterrichten, Unterricht geben. **teachable,** *adj.* belehrbar, gelehrig (*a p.*), lehrbar (*a th.*). **teachableness,** *s.* die Belehrbarkeit, Gelehrigkeit (*of a p.*), Lehrbarkeit (*of a th.*). **teacher,** *s.* der (die) Lehrer(in); –(*s'*) ***training college*** (*Am.* ***–s' college***), die Lehrerbildungsanstalt.

tea-chest, *s.* die Teekiste.

teaching ['ti:tʃiŋ], **1.** *s.* 1. das Unterrichten, Lehren, der Unterricht; 2. Lehrberuf; 3. (*oft. pl.*) die Lehre. **2.** *attrib. adj.* – ***profession,*** der Lehrberuf; – ***staff,*** der Lehrkörper, die Dozentenschaft.

tea|-cloth, *s.* das Geschirrtuch. **--cosy,** *s.* die Teehaube, Teemütze. **–cup,** *s.* die Teetasse; ***storm in a –,*** der Sturm im Wasserglas. **--gown,** *s.* das Nachmittagskleid. **--grower,** *s.* der Teepflanzer.

teak [ti:k], *s.* 1. der Tiekbaum, Teakbaum; 2. das Tiekholz, Teakholz.

teal [ti:l], *s.* (*Orn.*) (*Am.* ***European –***) die Krickente (*Anas crecca*).

tea|-leaf, *s.* das Teeblatt. **--leaves,** *pl.* der Teesatz.

team [ti:m], **1.** *s.* 1. das Gespann (*of horses etc.*); der Zug, Flug (*of birds*); 2. die Gruppe, Abteilung, Schicht (*of workmen etc.*); 3. (*Spt.*) Mannschaft. **2.** *v.t.* zusammenspannen (*horses*). **3.** *v.i.* (*coll.*) (*usu.* – ***up***) sich zusammenschließen *or* zusammentun (***with,*** mit).

team|-game, *s.* das Mannschaftsspiel. **--mate,** *s.* der (die) Mannschaftskamerad(in). **--spirit,** *s.* der Mannschaftsgeist; (*fig.*) Korpsgeist, das Mannschaftsgefühl. **teamster** [–stə], *s.* der Fuhrmann. **teamwork,** *s.* 1. die Zusammenarbeit; 2. (*Spt.*) das Zusammenspiel; 3. (*Theat.*) Ensemblespiel.

tea|-party, *s.* die Teegesellschaft; (*Hist.*) ***Boston Tea-Party,*** der Teesturm von Boston. **–pot,** *s.* die Teekanne.

[1]**tear** [tɛə], **1.** *s.* der Riß; ***wear and –,*** die Abnutzung, der Verschleiß. **2.** *irr.v.t.* 1. zerreißen; – ***apart,*** auseinanderreißen; – ***in*** or ***to pieces,*** in Stücke reißen; – ***in two,*** entzweireißen; – ***one's clothes,*** sich (*Dat.*) die Kleider zerreißen; (*sl.*) ***that's torn it!*** damit ist es ausgeplatzt! das hat einen Strich durch die Rechnung gemacht! – ***up,*** zerreißen, in Stücke reißen; 2. (aus)raufen (*one's hair*); 3. ritzen, aufreißen, zerfleischen (*the skin*); 4. herausreißen (***out of,*** aus), wegreißen, fortreißen (***from,*** von), entreißen (*Dat.*); – ***down,*** umreißen, abreißen, niederreißen, herunterreißen; – ***off,*** wegreißen, abreißen; von sich reißen (*clothes*); – ***out,*** (her)-ausreißen; – ***up,*** aufreißen (*pavement etc.*); – ***up by the roots,*** mit den Wurzeln ausreißen; 5. (*fig.*) ***torn between,*** hin- und hergerissen zwischen; ***torn by,*** zerrissen von (*war etc.*). **3.** *irr.v.i.* 1. reißen, zerren (***at,*** an (*Dat.*)); 2. (zer)reißen; 3. (*coll.*) jagen, stürzen, stürmen, rasen; – ***about*** or ***around,*** hin- und herrennen; – ***ahead,*** vorausstürmen, voranstürmen; – ***along,*** angerannt kommen; – ***off,*** losstürmen, losrennen; – ***round,*** see – ***around***; – ***through,*** fliegen durch (*a book etc.*).

[2]**tear** [tiə], *s.* 1. die Träne; ***burst into –s,*** in Tränen ausbrechen; ***crocodile –s,*** Krokodilstränen (*pl.*); ***in –s,*** weinend, in *or* unter Tränen; ***reduce to –s,*** zu Tränen bringen; ***shed –s,*** Tränen vergießen; 2. (*fig.*) der Tropfen.

tearaway ['tɛərəwei], **1.** *adj.* (*coll.*) ungestüm. **2.** *s.* (*coll.*) der Radaubengel.

tear|drop ['tiə–], *s.* der Tränentropfen. **--duct,** *s.* der Tränenkanal.

tearful ['tiəful], *adj.* tränenvoll; in Tränen, weinerlich, traurig; ***be –,*** weinen. **tearfulness,** *s.* die Weinerlichkeit.

tear|-gas ['tiə–], *s.* das Tränengas. **--gland,** *s.* die Tränendrüse.

tearing ['tɛəriŋ], *adj.* (*coll.*) heftig, rasend, wütend, tobend; – ***rage,*** rasende Wut. **tearing-strength,** *s.* die Zerreißfestigkeit.

tear-jerker ['tiə–], *s.* (*sl.*) die Schnulze, der Schmachtfetzen.

tear-off ['tɛərɔf], *attrib. adj.* Abreiß–.

tea|room, *s.* die Teestube, das Café, Kaffee(haus). **--rose,** *s.* die Teerose.

tear-stained ['tiə–], *adj.* tränenbenetzt; verweint (*eyes*).

tease [ti:z], **1.** *v.t.* 1. kämmen, krempeln, kardätschen (*wool*); hecheln (*flax*), kardieren, (auf)-rauhen (*cloth*), auszupfen (*yarn*); 2. (*fig.*) necken, hänseln, aufziehen, foppen, zum Besten haben; ärgern, plagen, belästigen (***for,*** wegen). **2.** *s.* (*coll.*) der Necker, Quälgeist, Plagegeist.

teasel [ti:zl], **1.** *s.* 1. (*Bot.*) die Kardedistel; 2. (*Tech.*) Karde, Kardätsche, Krempel. **2.** *v.t.* aufrauhen, kardieren, krempeln (*cloth*).

teaser, *s.* 1. *See* **tease, 2**; 2. (*coll.*) schwierige Frage, harte Nuß.

tea|-service, --set, *s.* das Teegeschirr, Teeservice. **–shop,** *s. See* **–room.**

teasing ['ti:ziŋ], *s.* das Necken, Hänseln, die Neckerei. **teasingly,** *adv.* neckend, hänselnd.

teaspoon ['ti:spu:n], *s.* der Teelöffel.

teat [ti:t], *s.* 1. die Brustwarze, (*of animals*) Zitze; 2. (*also* ***rubber –***) der Lutscher.

tea|-things, *pl.* (*coll.*) see **--service. --time,** *s.* die Teestunde. **--towel,** *s. See* **--cloth. --urn,** *s.* die Teemaschine.

teazle, *see* **teasel.**

tec [tek], *s.* (*coll.*) *abbr. for* **detective.**

tech [tek], *s.* (*coll.*) *abbr. for* ***technical school.*** **technic** ['teknik], **1.** *adj. See* **technical. 2.** *s.* 1. *See* **technique**; 2. *pl. See* **technics. technical,** *adj.* 1. technisch; kunstgerecht, fachgemäß; Fach–; – ***college,*** technische Hochschule; – ***language,*** die Fachsprache; – ***school,*** die Gewerbeschule; – ***term,*** der Fachausdruck; 2. (*fig.*) genau genommen, buchstäblich, regelrecht. **technicality** [–'kæliti], *s.* 1. das Technische; technische Eigentümlichkeit; 2. der Fachausdruck; 3. *pl.* technische Einzelheiten (*pl.*). **technically,** *adv.* (*coll.*) eigentlich, genau genommen. **technician** [–'niʃən], *s.* technischer Fachmann, der Techniker.

technicolour ['teknikʌlə], *s.* das Farbfilmverfahren; ***film in –,*** der Farbfilm.

technics ['tekniks], *pl.* (*sing. constr.*) technische Handhabung, die Handfertigkeit, Kunstfertigkeit. **technique** [–'ni:k], *s.* die Technik, Kunstfertigkeit, Methode *or* Art der technischen Ausführung, technisches Geschick.

technocracy [tek'nɔkrəsi], *s.* die Technokratie, Herrschaft der Maschine. **technological** [–nə-'lɔdʒikl], *adj.* technologisch, gewerblich, gewerbekundlich. **technologist** [–'nɔlədʒist], *s.* Gewerbekundige(r), der Technologe. **technology,** *s.* die Technologie; ***school of –,*** technische Hochschule.

techy ['tetʃi], *adj.* (*coll.*) *see* **testy.**

tectology [tek'tɔlədʒi], *s.* (*Biol.*) die Strukturlehre. **tectonic** [–'tɔnik], *adj.* tektonisch, strukturell, Bau–. **tectonics,** *pl.* (*sing. constr.*) die Tektonik, Gliederung, der Aufbau.

tectorial [tek'tɔ:riəl], *adj.* (*Anat.*) bedeckend, Deck–. **tectrices** ['tektrisi:z], *pl.* (*Orn.*) Deckfedern (*pl.*).

Teddy|-bear ['tedi–], *s.* der Teddy(bär). **--boy,** *s.* Halbstarke(r).

Te Deum ['ti:'diəm], *s.* der Dankgottesdienst, Lobgesang.

tedious ['ti:diəs], *adj.* 1. lästig, langwierig, umständlich, weitschweifig; 2. langweilig, ermüdend. **tediousness,** *s.* die Langweiligkeit, Umständlichkeit, Langwierigkeit, Weitschweifigkeit. **tedium,** *s.* die Langeweile, der Überdruß; *see also* **tediousness.**

tee [ti:], **1.** *s.* das Ziel, Mal, (*Golf*) der Erdhaufen, die Abschlagstelle; *--shot,* der Abschlag. **2.** *v.t.* auf den Erdhaufen legen (*the ball*). **3.** *v.i.* *– off,* den Ball abschlagen; (*coll.*) anfangen, starten.

teem [ti:m], *v.i.* 1. wimmeln, strotzen, (über)voll sein (*with,* von); wuchern, überreichlich vorhanden sein; 2. strömen, gießen (*rain*); (*coll.*) *it is –ing with rain,* es gießt in Strömen; 3. (*obs.*) fruchtbar *or* schwanger sein. **teeming,** *adj.* 1. wimmelnd, strotzend, gedrängt voll (*with,* von); 2. überaus fruchtbar; 3. (*coll.*) *– rain,* strömender Regen.

teenage ['ti:neidʒ], *adj.* jugendlich, Jugend–. **teenager,** *s.* (*coll.*) Jugendliche(r), der Teenager. **teens,** *pl.* Jugendjahre (*pl.*); *be in one's –,* ein Teenager sein.

teeny(-weeny) ['ti:ni('wi:ni)], *adj.* (*nursery talk*) winzigklein.

teeter ['ti:tə], *v.i.* (*coll.*) schwanken, wanken.

teeth [ti:θ], *pl. of* **tooth.**

teethe [ti:ð], *v.i.* zahnen, Zähne bekommen. **teething,** *s.* das Zahnen; *--ring,* der Beißring; (*fig.*) *– troubles,* Kinderkrankheiten, Anfangsschwierigkeiten (*pl.*).

teetotal [ti:'toutl], *adj.* abstinent, Abstinenz(ler)–. **teetotal(l)er,** *s.* der (die) Abstinenzler(in), Temperenzler(in). **teetotalism,** *s.* die Abstinenz(bewegung).

teetotum [ti:'toutəm], *s.* der Drehwürfel, Kreisel.

tegument ['tegjumənt], *s.* die Hülle, Decke; (*Bot., Zool., Anat.*) das Integument. **tegumental** [–'mentl], **tegumentary** [–'mentəri], *adj.* Decken–, Hüllen–, Haut–.

telamon ['teləmən], *s.* (*pl.* **-es** [–'mouni:z]) (*Archit.*) das Telamon, die Tragsäule in Männergestalt.

tele– ['teli], *pref.* Tele–, Fern–. **–camera,** *s.* die Fernsehkamera. **–cast, 1.** *pred. adj.* im Fernsehen übertragen. **2.** *s.* die Fernsehübertragung. **3.** *v.t.* im Fernsehen übertragen. **–caster,** *s.* der (die) Fernsehsprecher(in). **–communication,** *s.* (*oft. pl.*) die Fernmeldetechnik. **–film,** *s.* der Fernsehfilm.

telegram ['teligræm], *s.* das Telegramm; *by –,* telegraphisch.

telegraph ['teligrɑ:f], **1.** *v.t.* drahten, telegraphieren (*a message*), telegraphisch benachrichtigen (*a p.*). **2.** *v.i.* telegraphieren, drahten (*to, Dat. or* an (*Acc.*)); (*fig.*) Zeichen geben (*Dat.*), signalisieren. **3.** *s.* 1. der Telegraph; *see also* **telegram**; *– boy,* der Telegraphenbote; *– code,* der Telegrammschlüssel; *– form,* das Telegrammformular; *– key,* die Morsetaste; *– line,* die Telegraphenleitung; *– pole,* die Telegraphenstange, der Telegraphenmast; 2. (*Spt.*) die Anzeigetafel. **telegraphese** [–grə'fi:z], *s.* der Telegrammstil. **telegraphic** [–'græfik], *adj.* telegraphisch; (*fig.*) im Telegrammstil, telegrammartig; *– address,* die Drahtanschrift. **telegraphist** [ti'legrəfist], *s.* der (die) Telegraphist(in). **telegraphy** [ti'legrəfi], *s.* die Telegraphie; *wireless –,* drahtlose Telegraphie.

teleological [teliə'lɔdʒikl], *adj.* teleologisch, zweckbestimmt. **teleology** [–'ɔlədʒi], *s.* die Teleologie, Zweckmäßigkeit, Zielstrebigkeit.

telepathic [teli'pæθik], *adj.* telepathisch. **telepathy** [ti'lepəθi], *s.* die Telepathie, Gedankenübertragung.

telephone ['telifoun], **1.** *s.* der Fernsprecher, das Telephon; *automatic –,* der Selbstandschluß(fernsprecher); *at the –,* am Telephon *or* Apparat; *inquiry by –,* telephonische Anfrage; *on the –,* am Telephon; telephonisch, durch Fernsprecher; *be on the –,* Telephon(anschluß) haben; am Apparat sein; *over the –,* durch (das) Telephon. **2.** *v.i.* telephonieren. **3.** *v.t.* 1. telephonieren (*a th.*); 2. antelephonieren, (telephonisch) anrufen (*a p.*).

telephone|-booth, --box, *s.* die Fernsprechzelle. **--call,** *s.* der Telephonanruf, das Telephongespräch. **--connection,** *s.* der Fernsprechanschluß. – **directory,** *s.* das Fernsprechbuch, Telephonbuch. **--exchange,** *s.* das Fernsprechamt, die (Telephon)zentrale *or* –vermittlung. **--message,** *s.* telephonische Bestellung, das Telephongespräch. **--operator,** *s.* der (die) Telephonist(in). **--receiver,** *s.* der (Telephon)hörer. – **subscriber,** *s.* der Fernsprechteilnehmer.

telephonic [teli'fɔnik], *adj.* telephonisch, Fernsprech–. **telephonist** [ti'lefənist], *s.* der (die) Telephonist(in). **telephony** [ti'lefəni], *s.* die Telephonie, das Fernsprechwesen.

tele|photo, 1. *attrib. adj.* *– lens,* das Teleobjektiv. **2.** *or* **–photograph,** *s.* die Fernaufnahme, das Fernbild. **–photographic,** *adj.* fernphotographisch, bildtelegraphisch. **–photography,** *s.* die Fernphotographie, Bildtelegraphie.

tele|print, *v.t.* durch Fernschreiber übermitteln, fernschreiben. **–printer,** *s.* der Fernschreiber. **--recording,** *s.* die Fernsehaufnahme, Fernsehaufzeichnung.

telescope ['teliskoup], **1.** *s.* das Fernrohr, Teleskop. **2.** *v.t.* (*v.i.*) (sich) ineinanderschieben. **telescopic** [–'skɔpik], *adj.* 1. teleskopisch; *– sight,* das Scharfschützenfernrohr, der Fernrohraufsatz (*for rifle*); 2. ineinanderschiebbar; Auszieh– (*as a table*).

tele|type, *v.t.* *See* **–print. --typesetter,** *s.* die Fernsetzmaschine.

televise ['telivaiz], *v.t.* durch Fernsehen übertragen. **television** [–'viʒən], **1.** *s.* das Fernsehen; *on –,* im Fernsehen. **2.** *attrib. adj.* Fernseh–; *– screen,* die Bildröhre, der Bildschirm.

telex ['teleks], *s.* das Fernschreibnetz.

tell [tel], **1.** *irr.v.t.* 1. erzählen, berichten (*about,* über (*Acc.*)), mitteilen, melden, erklären, versichern, sagen, äußern, offenbaren, enthüllen, bekanntgeben, (mit Worten) ausdrücken (*to, Dat.*) (*a p.*); *– it abroad,* es herumerzählen; *– fortunes,* wahrsagen (*from,* aus); (*sl.*) *– him where he gets off* or *where to get off,* ihm die Leviten lesen; *– lies* or *a lie,* lügen; *– me his name,* nennen Sie mir seinen Namen! (*coll.*) *– a tale,* eine jammervolle Geschichte erzählen; *– tales,* flunkern, aus der Schule plaudern; *– its own tale,* für sich selbst sprechen, sich von selbst erklären; (*coll.*) *– that to the marines!* erzähl' mir doch keine Märchen! mache das einem andern weis! *– a secret,* ein Geheimnis mitteilen; *– the truth,* die Wahrheit sagen; *to – the truth, truth to –,* offen gesagt; *be able to – the time,* die Uhr lesen können; *can you – me the time?* können Sie mir sagen, wieviel Uhr es ist? (*coll.*) *I can – you!* hör mal zu! (*coll.*) *I'm –ing you!* du kannst mir's glauben! (*sl.*) *you're –ing me!* und wie! wem sagt du das? (*coll.*) *– me another!* das machst du mir nicht weis! (*coll.*) *I told you so,* ich hab's dir ja gleich gesagt; (*coll.*) *I'll – you what!* ich will dir was sagen *or* verraten! 2. angeben, anzeigen (*the time: as clocks*); 3. (*with inf.*) heißen, befehlen; *do as you're told!* tu wie dir geheißen! 4. unterscheiden (*from,* von), feststellen, erkennen (*by, from,* an (*Dat.*)); *– apart,* auseinanderhalten; 5. aufzählen, (ab)zählen; *all told,* alles in allem, im ganzen; *– one's beads,* den Rosenkranz beten; 6. *– off,* abzählen; (*Mil.*) abkommandieren (*a p.*); (*coll.*) anschnauzen (*a p.*). **2.** *irr.v.i.* 1. erzählen, berichten, sprechen (*about,* über (*Acc.*); *of,* von); 2. erkennen (*by,* an (*Dat.*)); *you never can –!* man kann (es) nie wissen! 3. sich abheben, hervortreten (*against,* gegen *or* von); 4. Eindruck *or* sich bemerkbar *or* sich geltend machen, sich auswirken, wirksam sein (*on,* bei *or* auf (*Acc.*)); *it –s against him,* es spricht gegen ihn; *every shot told,* jede Kugel traf; *every word –s,* jedes Wort sitzt; 5. Beweis *or* ein Zeichen sein (*of,* für *or* von); 6. (*coll.*) petzen; *– on him,* ihn angeben *or* verpetzen *or* verraten *or* anzeigen.

teller ['telə], *s.* 1. der Zähler; (*Parl.*) Stimmenzähler; 2. Kassier(er), Schalterbeamte(r), Kassenbeamte(r) (*in banks*); 3. (*also story –*) Erzähler; *fortune–-,* der (die) Wahrsager(in). **telling, 1.** *adj.*

wirkungsvoll, wirksam, eindrucksvoll, effektvoll, durchschlagend. **2.** *s.* das Erzählen; ***in the* –,** beim Erzählen; ***there is no* –,** es läßt sich nicht *or* man kann nicht wissen *or* sagen, es ist nicht zu sagen. **telltale, 1.** *s.* der (die) Angeber(in), Ohrenbläser(in), Zuträger(in), Zwischenträger(in). **2.** *attrib. adj.* 1. sprechend, verräterisch; 2. Warnungs–, Erkennungs–.

tellural [teˈluərəl], *adj.* irdisch, Erde–. **tellurate** [ˈteləreit], *s.* tellursaures Salz. **tellurian** [–ˈluəriən], **1.** *adj. See* **tellural. 2.** *s.* der (die) Erdbewohner(in). **telluric** [–ˈluərik], *adj.* tellurisch, tellursauer, Tellur–; – ***acid,*** die Tellursäure. **tellurium** [–ˈluəriəm], *s.* das Tellur. **tellurous** [ˈtelərəs], *adj.* tellurig.

telly [ˈteli], *s.* (*coll.*) *abbr. for* **television.**

telpher [ˈtelfə], *adj.* der elektrischen Beförderung dienend. **telpherage** [–ridʒ], *s.* elektrische Lastenbeförderung. **telpher-line,** *s.* (elektrische) Drahtseilbahn, die Elektrohängebahn.

telstar [ˈtelstɑː], *s.* der Telstar, Nachrichtensatellit.

temerarious [teməˈrɛəriəs], *adj.* verwegen, unbesonnen, tollkühn. **temerity** [tiˈmeriti], *s.* die Verwegenheit, Unbesonnenheit, Tollkühnheit.

temper [ˈtempə], **1.** *v.t.* 1. härten, ablöschen, anlassen (*metals*), glühfrischen, tempern (*steel*); 2. anmachen, mischen (*colours*), anrühren (*clay etc.*); 3. (*Mus.*) temperieren (*piano etc.*); 4. (*fig.*) mäßigen, mildern, abschwächen (***with,*** durch); – ***justice with mercy,*** Gnade für Recht ergehen lassen; ***God –s the wind to the shorn lamb,*** Gott legt niemand mehr auf als er (v)ertragen kann. **2.** *s.* 1. richtige Mischung, gehörige Beschaffenheit; 2. (*Metall.*) die Härte, der Härtegrad; die Festigkeit (*of clay*); 3. (*fig.*) Veranlagung, Gemütsart, das Gemüt, Naturell, Temperament, der Charakter; die Stimmung, Laune; ***in a bad –, out of –,*** schlechtgelaunt, schlechter Laune; ***in a good –,*** gutgelaunt, guter Laune; ***have an evil –,*** jähzornig sein; ***keep one's –,*** die Ruhe bewahren, ruhig bleiben; ***lose one's –,*** wütend werden, in Wut geraten; ***put out of –,*** erzürnen, in üble Laune versetzen, die Laune verderben (*Dat.*); 4. die Gereiztheit, Heftigkeit, Wut, der Zorn, Ärger; ***have a quick –,*** heftig sein; ***be in a –,*** wütend sein; ***get into a –,*** wütend werden; ***try his –,*** ihn reizen *or* aufbringen.

tempera [ˈtempərə], *s.* die Tempera(malerei).

temperament [ˈtempərəmənt], *s.* 1. das Temperament, Naturell, die Gemütsart, Charakteranlage, Veranlagung; 2. (*Mus.*) Temperatur, temperierte Stimmung. **temperamental** [–ˈmentl], *adj.* launenhaft, launisch, reizbar. **temperamentally,** *adv.* von Natur, anlagemäßig, konstitutionell.

temperance [ˈtempərəns], *s.* 1. die Mäßigkeit, (Selbst)beherrschung, Enthaltsamkeit; 2. Abstinenz, Temperenz; – ***hotel,*** alkoholfreies Hotel; – ***movement,*** die Temperenzbewegung. **temperate** [–rit], *adj.* 1. mäßig, enthaltsam; 2. (selbst)beherrscht, zurückhaltend; 3. maßvoll (*language etc.*); 4. gemäßigt (*climate*). **temperateness,** *s.* 1. die Mäßigung, Beherrschtheit, Zurückhaltung; 2. Mäßigkeit, Enthaltsamkeit, das Maß; 3. (*climate*) die Gemäßigtheit, Milde; 4. (*Mus.*) Temperiertheit.

temperature [ˈtempritʃə], *s.* die Temperatur; ***at a – of,*** bei einer Temperatur von; (*coll.*) ***have a –,*** Fieber *or* erhöhte Temperatur haben; ***take the –,*** Temperatur messen; ***take his –,*** ihm die Temperatur messen. **temperature-curve,** *s.* (*Med.*) die Fieberkurve.

tempered [ˈtempəd], *adj.* 1. gehärtet, angelassen, gestählt, Temper–; 2. (*Mus.*) temperiert; 3. (*as suff., fig.*) –gelaunt, –gestimmt; ***even–,*** gleichmütig, gelassen; ***good–,*** gutmütig, gutartig; ***hot–,*** zähzornig; ***ill–,*** übelgelaunt.

tempest [ˈtempist], *s.* der Sturm, das Gewitter. **tempest-tossed,** *adj.* von Sturm getrieben. **tempestuous** [–ˈpestjuəs], *adj.* stürmisch, ungestüm. **tempestuousness,** *s.* das Ungestüm, die Heftigkeit.

Templar [ˈtemplə], *s.* 1. (*Hist.*) der Tempelritter, Tempelherr; 2. Student der Rechte in London.

template, *see* **templet.**

[1]**temple** [ˈtempl], *s.* (*Anat.*) die Schläfe.

[2]**temple,** *s.* 1. der Tempel; 2. eins der beiden Rechtsinstituten in London (***Inner Temple Middle Temple***).

templet [templit], *s.* 1. (*Tech.*) die Schablone, Lehre; 2. (*Archit.*) Pfette.

tempo [ˈtempou], *s.* (*pl.* **-pi** [–piː]) (*Mus.*) das Tempo; (*coll.*) die Geschwindigkeit.

[1]**temporal** [ˈtempərəl], *adj.* Schläfen–. *See* [1]**temple.**

[2]**temporal,** *adj.* 1. zeitlich; (*Gram.*) temporal, Zeit–; ***spatial and –,*** räumlich und zeitlich; 2. weltlich, irdisch, diesseitig; – ***power,*** weltliche Macht; ***spiritual and –,*** geistlich und weltlich. **temporality** [–ˈræliti], *s.* 1. die Weltlichkeit, Diesseitigkeit; 2. Zeitlichkeit, Zeitweiligkeit, Zeitbedingtheit; das Zeitliche, Vorübergehende; 3. *pl.* (*Eccl.*) weltlicher Besitz, Temporalien (*pl.*), (*Law*) zeitliche Güter.

temporarily [ˈtempərərili], *adv.* zeitweise, vorübergehend, zeitweilig, einstweilig. **temporariness,** *s.* die Zeitweiligkeit, Einstweiligkeit. **temporary,** *adj.* 1. einstweilig, zeitweilig, vorübergehend; 2. vorläufig, provisorisch, Gelegenheits–, (Aus)hilfs–, Not–, Interims–, Zwischen–.

temporization [tempəraiˈzeiʃən], *s.* das Warten, Zögern, (Zeit)abwarten, die Zeitgewinnung. **temporize** [ˈtempəraiz], *v.i.* die Zeit abwarten, Zeit zu gewinnen suchen, den Mantel nach dem Wind hängen, mit dem Strom schwimmen, sich nach den Umständen richten, sich nicht festlegen, sich vorläufig anpassen *or* anbequemen, zögern, warten; – ***with,*** hinhalten, verhandeln mit. **temporizer,** *s.* der Achselträger, Opportunist. **temporizing,** *adj.* hinhaltend, abwartend, achselträgerisch, opportunistisch.

tempt [tempt], *v.t.* 1. verführen, verlocken, in Versuchung führen (*to evil*); überreden, dazu bringen (*with promises*); ***be –ed,*** geneigt sein; – ***fate,*** das Schicksal versuchen *or* herausfordern; 2. (*of th.*) locken, reizen. **temptation** [–ˈteiʃən], *s.* 1. die Versuchung, Verlockung, Verführung; ***lead into –,*** in Versuchung führen; 2. der Anreiz, das Lockmittel. **tempter,** *s.* der Versucher, Verführer. **tempting,** *adj.* 1. verführerisch, verlockend; 2. reizvoll; appetitanregend (*of food*). **temptress** [–tris], *s.* die Verführerin.

ten [ten], **1.** *num. adj.* zehn; *for clock-time see under* ***eight.*** **2.** *s.* die Zehn; ***–s of thousands,*** Zehntausende (*pl.*); ***nine out of –,*** neun von zehnen; (*coll.*) – ***to one,*** zehn zu eins, todsicher.

tenability [tenəˈbiliti], *s.* die Haltbarkeit. **tenable** [ˈtenəbl], *adj.* 1. (*Mil.*) haltbar (*also fig.*), verteidigungsfähig; (*fig.*) tragbar, überzeugend; 2. ***be –,*** verliehen *or* vergeben werden (***for,*** auf (*Acc.*) *or* für) (*as a scholarship*).

tenacious [tiˈneiʃəs], *adj.* 1. zusammenhaltend, klebrig, zäh (*also fig.*), fest, festhaltend (*also fig.*); (*fig.*) beharrlich, hartnäckig (*as an enemy*); ***be – of,*** zäh festhalten an (*Dat.*), bestehen auf (*Dat.*); ***be – of life,*** zähe am Leben festhalten; 2. gut, treu, verläßlich (*of memory*). **tenaciousness, tenacity** [–ˈnæsiti], *s.* 1. die Zähigkeit, zähes Festhalten, die Beharrlichkeit, Ausdauer, Hartnäckigkeit; – ***of life,*** zähes Leben; – ***of purpose,*** die Zielstrebigkeit; 2. die Verläßlichkeit, Treue, Stärke.

tenancy [ˈtenənsi], *s.* 1. der Pachtbesitz, Mietbesitz; 2. das Pachtverhältnis, Mietverhältnis, die Pachtung; 3. Pachtdauer, Mietdauer. **tenant, 1.** *s.* der Pächter, Mieter; Einwohner, Bewohner, Insasse; – ***at will,*** jederzeit kündbarer Pächter; – ***farmer,*** der Pachtbauer, (Guts)pächter; – ***right,*** der Pächteranspruch. **2.** *v.t.* (*usu. pass.*) bewohnen **tenantable,** *adj.* 1. pachtbar, mietbar; 2. wohnbar. **tenantless,** *adj.* unvermietet, unbewohnt. **tenantry,** *s.* (*collect.*) Pächter (*pl.*).

tench [tentʃ], *s.* (*Ichth.*) die Schleie.

[1]**tend** [tend], *v.t.* bedienen, hüten (*flocks*), pflegen (*patient*), bedienen, aufwarten (*machine*).

[2]**tend,** *v.i.* 1. sich bewegen *or* richten, streben, seine Richtung nehmen, gerichtet sein (*to(wards)*, nach), (*Math.*) zustreben (*Dat.*); 2. (*fig.*) hinauslaufen, hinarbeiten, abzielen, gerichtet sein (*to*, auf (*Acc.*)), neigen, tendieren, eine Neigung *or* Tendenz haben (*to*, zu), dazu neigen *or* führen *or* beitragen (*to do*, zu tun). **tendency,** *s.* 1. die Richtung, Strömung, Tendenz, Hinwendung, Hinneigung, der Gang, Lauf, das Hinstreben (*to*, nach); 2. der Hang, Zug (*to*, zu), Vorliebe, Neigung (für), die Absicht, der Zweck; ***have a – to do,*** geneigt sein zu tun; 3. die Absicht, der Zweck. **tendentious** [–'denʃəs], *adj.* tendenziös, Tendenz–.

[1]**tender** ['tendə], **1.** *s.* 1. das Anerbieten, (Lieferungs)angebot, Offert, die Ausschreibung, Offerte, der Kostenanschlag; ***by –,*** durch *or* in Submission, auf Submissionsweg, durch Ausschreibung; 2. ***legal –,*** gesetzliches Zahlungsmittel. **2.** *v.t.* anbieten, darbieten, darreichen, einreichen; ***– an oath,*** den Eid abnehmen (*to*, *Dat.*); ***– one's resignation,*** seine Entlassung beantragen; ***– one's thanks,*** seinen Dank aussprechen. **3.** *v.i.* (*Comm.*) offerieren, eine Offerte machen, ein Angebot stellen.

[2]**tender,** *s.* 1. der (die) Wärter(in); 2. (*Naut.*) der Tender, Leichter, das Beiboot, Begleitschiff; 3. (*Railw.*) der Tender, Begleitwagen.

[3]**tender,** *adj.* 1. zart, weich, mürbe (*as food*); 2. zerbrechlich, schwach, schwächlich; ***at a – age,*** im zarten Alter; 3. (*fig.*) schonend, sorgsam, besorgt (*of*, um), liebevoll, zärtlich (*as love*); ***– passion,*** die Liebe; 4. zart, sanft, mitleidig, mitfühlend, gütig (*heart*), empfindlich (*as a wound, conscience*).

tenderer ['tendərə], *s.* (*Comm.*) der Offertsteller, Submittent.

tender|foot, *s.* Unerfahrene(r), der Neuling, Anfänger. **--hearted,** *adj.* weichherzig. **-loin,** *s.* das Lendenstück (*butchery*).

tenderness ['tendənis], *s.* 1. die Zartheit; Weichheit; 2. Zärtlichkeit, Güte, Freundlichkeit (*to*, gegen), Besorgtheit (um); 3. Empfindlichkeit (*of a wound etc.*).

tendinous ['tendinəs], *adj.* sehnig. **tendon** [–ən], *s.* die Sehne, Flechse.

tendril ['tendril], *s.* die (Wickel)ranke.

tenebrous ['tenibrəs], *adj.* (*obs.*) dunkel, finster, düster.

tenement ['tenəmənt], **1.** *s.* 1. das Wohnhaus, die (Miet(s))wohnung; 2. der Wohnsitz; 3. (*Law*) ständiger Besitz; 4. (*also* ***– house***) das Mietshaus, die Mietskaserne. **tenemental** [–'mentl], **tenementary** [–'mentəri], *adj.* Pacht–, Miets–.

tenet ['tenit], *s.* der (Grund)satz, Lehrsatz, die Lehre, das Dogma.

tenfold ['tenfould], *adj., adv.* zehnfach. **tenner** ['tenə], *s.* (*coll.*) die Zehnpfundnote.

tennis ['tenis], *s.* das Tennis(spiel). **tennis|-ball,** *s.* der Tennisball. **--court,** *s.* der Tennisplatz. **--racket,** *s.* der (Tennis)schläger.

tenon ['tenən], **1.** *s.* der Zapfen. **2.** *v.t.* verzapfen. **tenon-saw,** *s.* die Rückensäge, der Fuchsschwanz.

[1]**tenor** ['tenə], *s.* 1. der (Fort)gang, (Ver)lauf; gleichbleibende Beschaffenheit; 2. der Sinn, wesentlicher Inhalt, sachlicher Kern.

[2]**tenor,** *s.* der Tenor, Tenorsänger, die Tenorstimme; ***– clef,*** der Tenorschlüssel.

tenpin (bowling) ['tenpin], *s.* (amerikanisches) Bowling(spiel).

[1]**tense** [tens], *s.* (*Gram.*) die Zeitform, das Tempus.

[2]**tense,** *adj.* 1. (an)gespannt, stramm, straff; 2. (*fig.*) (*of th.*) spannend, voll Spannung, spannungsgeladen, (*of p.*) gespannt (***with***, vor (*Dat.*)). **tenseness,** *s.* die Spannung (*also fig.*), Gespanntheit (*also fig.*); Straffheit.

tensibility [tensi'biliti], *s.* die Dehnbarkeit. **tensible,** *adj. See* **tensile.**

tensile ['tensail], *adj.* 1. dehnbar, streckbar; 2. Dehn(ungs)–, Spannungs–; ***– strength,*** die Zugfestigkeit, Dehnfestigkeit, (Zer)reißfestigkeit.

tension [tenʃən], *s.* 1. die Spannung, Straffheit, Gespanntheit; 2. (*Elec.*) Spannung; ***high –,*** die Hochspannung; 3. (*Med.*) der Druck; 4. die Dehnung, Zugkraft, Spannkraft; 5. (*fig.*) Spannung, Gespanntheit, gespanntes Verhältnis. **tension|-rod,** *s.* die Spannstange. **--roller,** *s.* die Spannrolle.

tensor ['tensɔ:], *s.* der Streckmuskel, Spannmuskel.

[1]**tent** [tent], *s.* das Zelt; ***pitch one's –,*** sein Zelt aufschlagen; (*fig.*) sich häuslich niederlassen.

[2]**tent, 1.** *s.* (*Surg.*) die Mullgaze; der Quellstift. **2.** *v.t.* offen halten (*a wound*).

[3]**tent,** *s.* der Tintowein.

tentacle ['tentəkl], *s.* der Fühler, Fühlarm, Fühlfaden, das Fühlhorn. **tentacular** [–'tækjulə], *adj.* Fühler–.

tentative ['tentətiv], **1.** *adj.* 1. versuchend, Versuchs–, probierend, Probe–; 2. vorläufig, provisorisch; 3. zögernd, zaghaft. **2.** *s.* der Versuch, die Probe. **tentatively,** *adv.* versuchsweise.

tent-cloth, *s.* die Zeltleinwand, Zeltbahn. **tented** [–id], *adj.* Zelt–.

tenter ['tentə], *s.* der Spannrahmen, Trockenrahmen. **tenterhook,** *s.* der Spannhaken; (*fig.*) ***be on –s,*** in größter Spannung *or* Ungewißheit sein, wie auf heißen Kohlen sitzen.

tenth [tenθ], **1.** *num. adj.* zehnt. **2.** *s.* der *or* die *or* das Zehnte; (*fraction*) das Zehntel; (*Mus.*) die Dezime. **tenthly,** *adv.* zehntens.

tent|-peg, *s.* der Zeltpflock, Hering. **--pole,** *s.* die Zeltstange.

tenuis ['tenjuis], *s.* (*pl.* **-ues** [–i:z]) die Tenuis, stimmloser Verschlußlaut.

tenuity [te'nju:iti], *s.* 1. die Dünnheit; Zartheit, Feinheit; 2. (*fig.*) Dürftigkeit, Spärlichkeit. **tenuous** ['tenjuəs], *adj.* 1. dünn, fein, zart; 2. (*fig.*) dürftig, spärlich.

tenure ['tenjə], *s.* 1. der (Land)besitz, das Lehen; ***feudal –,*** der Lehensbesitz; 2. die Besitzart; der Besitzanspruch, Besitztitel; 3. die Bekleidung, das Innehaben; ***– of office,*** die Amtsdauer; 4. (*fig.*) der Genuß, Besitz.

tepee ['ti:pi:], *s.* das Indianerzelt, der Wigwam.

tepefy ['tepifai], **1.** *v.t.* lauwarm machen. **2.** *v.i.* lauwarm werden. **tepid** [–pid], *adj.* lau (*also fig.*), lauwarm. **tepidity** [–'piditi], **tepidness,** *s.* die Lauheit (*also fig.*).

terce [tə:s], *s.* (*R.C.*) die Terz.

tercel [tə:sl], *s.* männlicher Falke.

tercentenary [tə:sen'ti:nəri], **1.** *adj.* dreihundertjährig. **2.** *s.* die Dreihundertjahrfeier.

tercet ['tə:sit], *s.* (*Mus.*) die Triole, (*Metr.*) Terzine.

terebinth ['terəbinθ], *s.* (*Bot.*) die Terebinthe, Terpentinpistazie.

teredo [tə'ri:dou], *s.* der (Schiffs)bohrwurm.

tergiversate ['tə:dʒivə:seit], *v.i.* Ausflüchte *or* Winkelzüge machen; sich widersprechen, hin- und herreden, sich winden, sich wenden und drehen. **tergiversation** [–'seiʃən], *s.* 1. die Ausflucht, Finte; 2. der Wankelmut, die Inkonsequenz, Unbeständigkeit.

term [tə:m], **1.** *s.* 1. (*in time*) bestimmte Zeitdauer, die Frist; der Termin, die Zeitgrenze; (*Comm.*) Laufzeit, das Ziel; (*Univ. etc.*) Semester, Trimester, Quartal; (*Law*) die Sitzungsperiode; der Zahltag, Quartalstermin; ***– of office,*** die Amtsdauer, Amtszeit; ***– of payment,*** der Zahlungstermin; ***for a –,*** eine Zeit lang; ***in –,*** im Semester; ***long-–,*** langfristig; ***end of (the) –,*** der Schulschluß (*schools*), Semesterschluß (*universities*); (*Comm.*) ***on –,*** auf Zeit; ***carry to full –,*** austragen (*pregnancy*); ***keep –s,*** Jura studieren; 2. (*in space*) (*obs.*) die Grenzlinie, Begrenzung, Schranke, Grenze; (*Archit.*) der Terme, Grenzstein; ***set a –,*** eine Grenze setzen, einen Termin festlegen (*to*, *Dat.*); 3. (*Log.*) der Begriff; (Fach)ausdruck, Terminus, das Wort; (*Math.*) Glied; *pl.* Worte (*pl.*), Ausdrücke (*pl.*), die Sprache, Ausdrucksweise, der Wortlaut; ***–s of reference,*** Leitsätze; ***by the –s of the contract,*** nach Wortlaut des Kontrakts; ***exact –s,*** genauer Wortlaut; ***contradiction in –s,*** der Widerspruch in sich, innerer Widerspruch; ***in –s of approval,*** beifällig; ***in –s of praise,*** mit lobenden Worten; ***in the following –s,*** folgendermaßen; ***in plain*** or ***round –s,*** unverblümt, mit deutlichen Worten, rundheraus (gesagt); ***in set –s,*** festgelegt; 4. *pl.* Bedingungen (*pl.*), Bestimmungen (*pl.*), Verfügungen (*pl.*); (*between persons*) Beziehungen (*pl.*), das Verhältnis; (*Comm.*) Zahlungsforderungen (*pl.*), der Preis, das Honorar; ***–s of delivery,*** Liefer(ungs)bedingungen; ***–s of payment,*** Zahlungsbedingungen; ***inclusive –s,*** der Pauschalpreis; ***on any –s,*** unter jeder Bedingung; ***on bad –s,*** verfeindet (*of a p.*); ***on the best of –s,*** auf bestem Fuße; ***on easy –s,*** unter günstigen Bedingungen (*of payment*), auf vertrautem Fuß (*with a p.*); ***on equal –s,*** unter gleichen Bedingungen; ***on –s of equality,*** auf gleichem Fuß (*with a p.*); ***be on good –s,*** auf guten Fuß stehen; ***on reasonable –s,*** zum vernünftigen Preis; ***on speaking –s,*** im Sprechverhältnis; ***not be on speaking –s,*** nicht miteinander sprechen; ***on visiting –s,*** auf Besuchsfuße; ***special –s,*** der Sonderpreis; ***come to –s,*** sich einigen *or* vergleichen, handelseinig werden (***with,*** mit). **2.** *v.t.* (be)nennen, bezeichnen als.

termagant ['tə:məgənt], **1.** *s.* zanksüchtiges Weib, der Zankteufel, (*coll.*) Hausdrache. **2.** *adj.* zänkisch, zanksüchtig.

terminability [tə:minə'biliti], *s.* die Begrenztheit, Begrenzbarkeit, Befristung. **terminable** ['tə:minəbl], *adj.* zeitlich begrenzt, begrenzbar, befristet, auf begrenzter Zeit; lösbar, kündbar (*as contract etc.*).

terminal ['tə:minl], **1.** *adj.* 1. begrenzend, Grenz–, End– (*of place*); ***– velocity,*** die Endgeschwindigkeit; ***– voltage,*** die Klemmenspannung; 2. (Ab)schluß–, Termin–, terminmäßig, letzt (*of time*); (*Univ.*) Semester–, Trimester–; 3. (*Comm.*) Zustell–, Eingangs–; 4. (*Bot.*) gipfelständig; 5. (*Med.*) unheilbar. **2.** *s.* 1. die Spitze, das Endstück, Ende; 2. (*Elec.*) der Pol, die Klemme, Klemmschraube; 3. (*Railw.*) (*coll.*) die Endstation; 4. (*Univ.*) Semesterprüfung.

terminate, **1.** ['tə:mineit], *v.t.* 1. (be)endigen, abschließen, zu Ende führen; 2. begrenzen. **2.** [–neit], *v.i.* end(ig)en, zu Ende gehen (*in,* in (*Dat.*)), aufhören (mit), (*as word etc.*) ausgehen, enden (auf (*Acc.*)). **3.** [–nit], *adj.* 1. begrenzt; 2. (*Math.*) endlich. **termination** [–'neiʃən], *s.* 1. das Aufhören; 2. Ende, die Beendigung, der (Ab)schluß, Ablauf, Ausgang, das Resultat; 3. (*Gram.*) die Endung. **terminative** [–nətiv], *adj.* End–, Schluß–.

terminological [tə:minə'lɔdʒikl], *adj.* terminologisch; (*hum.*) ***– inexactitude,*** die Unwahrheit. **terminology** [–'nɔlədʒi], *s.* die Terminologie, Fachsprache; (*collect.*) Fachausdrücke (*pl.*).

terminus ['tə:minəs], *s.* 1. (*Railw.*) die Endstation; 2. das Ende, Endziel, der Endpunkt; ***– ad quem,*** der Zeitpunkt bis zu dem gerechnet wird; ***– a quo,*** der Zeitpunkt von dem ab gerechnet wird.

termite ['tə:mait], *s.* (*Ent.*) die Termite.

tern [tə:n], *s.* (*Orn.*) die Seeschwalbe (*Sterna hirundo*).

ternary ['tə:nəri], **1.** *adj.* dreifach, drei–; (*Math.*) ternär; (*Chem.*) dreistoffig, Dreistoff–; (*Bot.*) dreizählig. **2.** *s.* die Dreizahl. **ternate** [–neit], *adj.* dreiteilig; (*Bot.*) dreizählig.

terra ['terə], *s.* die Erde; ***– firma,*** festes Land; fester Boden; ***– incognita,*** unbekanntes Land; (*fig.*) unerforschtes Gebiet.

terrace ['terəs], **1.** *s.* 1. die Terrasse; (*Geol.*) Geländestufe, Erderhöhung; 2. (*Archit.*) der Altan, Söller; 3. die Häuserreihe; abseits gelegene Straße. **2.** *v.t.* in Terrassen anlegen. **terraced,** *adj.* terrassenförmig angelegt; flach (*as a roof*). **terrace-house,** *s.* das Reihenhaus.

terrain [tə'rein], *s.* das Terrain, Gelände.

terraneous [tə'reiniəs], *adj.* (*Bot.*) auf dem Land wachsend.

terrapin ['terəpin], *s.* die Dosenschildkröte.

terraqueous [–'rækwiəs], *adj.* aus Land und Wasser bestehend. **terrene** [–ri:n], *adj.* irdisch, weltlich, diesseitig, Erd–. **terrestrial** [–'restriəl], *adj.* irdisch, weltlich; Erd(en)–, Land–; (*Geol.*) Festland–, terrestrisch; ***– globe,*** der Globus, Erdball; ***– magnetism,*** der Erdmagnetismus.

terrible ['teribl], *adj.* schrecklich, entsetzlich, furchtbar, fürchterlich. **terribleness,** *s.* die Schrecklichkeit, Entsetzlichkeit, Furchtbarkeit, Fürchterlichkeit. **terribly,** *adv.* furchtbar, schrecklich (*also coll. fig.*).

[1]**terrier** ['teriə], *s.* 1. der Terrier; 2. (*sl.*) (*abbr. for* **territorial**) der Landwehrmann.

[2]**terrier,** *s.* (*Law*) das Flurbuch, der Kataster.

terrific [tə'rifik], *adj.* 1. furchtbar, fürchterlich; 2. (*usu. coll.*) kolossal, enorm, gewaltig, wuchtig, ungeheuer. **terrified** ['terifaid], *adj.* erschrocken, in Angst, ängstlich; ***be – of,*** Angst haben vor (*Dat.*), sich fürchten vor (*Dat.*). **terrify** ['terifai], *v.t.* erschrecken, Angst *or* einen Schreck(en) einjagen (*Dat.*); ***be terrified by,*** erschrocken werden durch, einen Schrecken bekommen von; ***I am terrified at the prospect,*** die Aussicht erschreckt *or* ängstigt mich.

territorial [teri'tɔ:riəl], **1.** *adj.* 1. Grund–, Boden–; 2. Gebiets–, Landes–, territorial; ***Territorial Army,*** die Landwehr; ***– waters,*** Hoheitsgewässer (*pl.*). **2.** *s.* ***Territorial,*** der Landwehrmann. **territory** ['teritəri], *s.* 1. das (Staats)gebiet, Landesgebiet, Territorium, Hoheitsgebiet; ***on British –,*** auf britischem Staatsgebiet; 2. die Region, Landschaft, Gegend; 3. das Revier (*of birds etc.*); Vertretungsgebiet (*of commercial traveller*); (*fig.*) Gebiet, der Bereich; 4. (*Footb.*) die Spielfeldhälfte.

terror ['terə], *s.* 1. der Schrecken, das Entsetzen, schreckliche Angst; ***strike – into,*** in Schrecken versetzen; 2. (*Pol.*) die Schreckensherrschaft, Gewaltherrschaft, der Terror; ***reign of –,*** die Schreckensherrschaft; 3. die Schrecklichkeit, Entsetzlichkeit, das Schrecknis; (*coll. of a p.*) der Quälgeist, lästige P., (*of a th.*) die Plage, der Schrecken, das Schreckgespenst; ***in – of,*** besorgt *or* in Angst um; (*coll.*) ***he's a – for work,*** er arbeitet wie versessen; (*coll.*) ***he's a young –,*** er ist ein Wildfang *or* Tollkopf *or* Unband. **terrorism,** *s.* die Gewaltherrschaft, Schreckensherrschaft, der Terrorismus; *see also* **terrorization. terrorist,** *s.* der Terrorist. **terrorization** [–rai'zeiʃən], *s.* die Terrorisierung, Einschüchterung (durch Gewaltmaßnahmen). **terrorize,** *v.t.* terrorisieren, einschüchtern, in Schrecken versetzen. **terror|-stricken, --struck,** *adj.* von Schrecken ergriffen, schreckerfüllt.

terry ['teri], *s.* ungeschnittener Samt.

terse [tə:s], *adj.* kurz (und bündig), knapp, gedrängt, präzis. **terseness,** *s.* die Kürze, Knappheit, Gedrängtheit, Bündigkeit, Präzision.

tertian ['tə:ʃən], **1.** *adj.* dreitägig, Tertian–. **2.** *s.* das Tertianfieber. **tertiary,** **1.** *adj.* an dritter Stelle (stehend), tertiär, Tertiär–. **2.** *s.* (*Geol.*) das Tertiär, die Terziärzeit.

terylene ['terili:n], *s.* das Terylene.

terza-rima ['tɛətsə'ri:mə], *s.* die Terzine (mit Reimfolge aba, bcb, cdc, *usw.*). **terzetto** [tɛət'setou], *s.* (*Mus.*) das Terzett, Trio.

tessellar ['tesilə], *adj.* würfelförmig. **tessellate** [–eit], *v.t.* mit Täfelchen auslegen; mosaikartig zusammensetzen, tessellieren; ***–d pavement,*** der Mosaikfußboden. **tessellation** [–'leiʃən], *s.* 1. die Mosaikarbeit; 2. (*Biol.*) Felderung.

test [test], **1.** *s.* 1. die Probe, der Versuch, Test; 2. die Untersuchung, Prüfung, Stichprobe; ***blood –,*** die Blutprobe; (*fig.*) ***acid*** or ***crucial –,*** die Feuerprobe; ***on –,*** unter Probe; ***put to the –,*** auf die Probe stellen, erproben; (*fig.*) ***severe –,*** harte Prüfung; ***stand the –,*** die Probe bestehen, sich bewähren; ***undergo a –,*** sich einer Prüfung unterziehen; 3. der Prüfungsmaßstab, Prüfstein (***of,*** für); 4. (*Psych.*) Test, die Eignungsprüfung, Leistungsprüfung; 5. (*Chem.*) Analyse (***for,*** auf (*Acc.*)), das Reagenz (für); 6. der Prüfbefund, Nachweis; 7. (*Metall.*) Versuchstiegel, die Kapelle; 8. (*Hist.*) der Testeid; ***take the –,*** den Testeid leisten; 9. (*Crick.*) (*coll.*)

see **test-match.** **2.** *v.t.* 1. prüfen (*for*, auf (*Acc.*) (. . hin)); 2. erproben, einer Prüfung unterziehen; (*Psych. etc.*) testen; auf die Probe stellen; (*also coll. – out*) ausprobieren; 3. (*Chem.*) analysieren, untersuchen. **testable,** *adj.* prüfbar, untersuchbar.

testacean [tes'teiʃən], **1.** *adj.* hartschalig, schalentragend, Schaltier–. **2.** *s.* das Schaltier. **testaceous,** *adj.* hartschalig, Schalen–.

Test Act, *s.* (*Hist.*) die Testakte.

testament ['testəmənt], *s.* 1. (*B.*) das Testament; 2. (*Law*) (*only in*) ***last will and –,*** letzter Wille, letztwillige Verfügung. **testamentary** [–'mentəri], *adj.* (*Law*) testamentarisch, Testaments–, letztwillig.

testate ['testeit], *pred. adj.* mit Hinterlassung eines Testaments. **testator** [–'teitə], *s.* der Erblasser, Testator. **testatrix** [–'teitriks], *s.* die Erblasserin, Testatorin.

test| bench, *s.* (*Tech.*) der Prüfstand, Versuchsstand. **– case,** *s.* 1. das Musterbeispiel, Schulbeispiel, typischer Fall; 2. (*Law*) der Präzedenzfall. **– cricketer,** *s.* der Nationalmannschaftsspieler. **tested,** *adj.* geprüft, getestet; erprobt, ausprobiert.

[1]**tester** ['testə], *s.* 1. der Prüfer; 2. Prüfapparat.

[2]**tester,** *s.* der Baldachin, Himmel (*of bed etc.*); ***--bed,*** das Himmelbett.

testes ['testi:z], *pl. of* **testis.**

test flight, *s.* der Probeflug.

testicle ['testikl], *s.* (*Anat.*) der Hoden, Testis.

testification [testifi'keiʃən], *s.* der Beweis, das Zeugnis (*to, of,* für). **testify** ['testifai], **1.** *v.t.* 1. (eidlich) bezeugen, unter Eid aussagen, zeugen von, Zeugnis ablegen von; 2. (*fig.*) bekunden, kundtun, zum Ausdruck bringen. **2.** *v.i.* Zeugnis ablegen, aussagen; (*fig.*) ***– to,*** bezeugen, beweisen.

testimonial [testi'mouniəl], **1.** *s.* 1. das (Führungs)-zeugnis, Attest, Empfehlungsschreiben (*of a p.*), Gutachten, die Beurteilung (*of a th.*); 2. (*fig.*) das Zeichen der Anerkennung. **2.** *adj.* Anerkennungs–, Ehren–.

testimony ['testiməni], *s.* 1. das Zeugnis, der Beweis (*to,* für); (*Law*) (mündliche) Zeugenaussage; ***have his – for,*** ihn zum Zeugen haben für; (*Law*) ***in – whereof,*** zum Zeugnis *or* zu Urkund *or* urkundlich dessen; 2. (*Eccl.*) die Offenbarung; 3. (*fig. collect.*) Zeugnisse (*pl.*).

testiness ['testinis], *s.* die Verdrießlichkeit, Gereiztheit, Reizbarkeit.

testis ['testis], *s.* (*pl.* **-tes** [–ti:z]) *see* **testicle.**

test| match, *s.* (*Crick.*) das Nationalmannschaftsspiel. **--paper,** *s.* 1. das Prüfungsformular, der Prüfungsbogen (*in examination*); 2. (*Chem.*) das Reagenzpapier. **--pilot,** *s.* (*Av.*) der Einflieger. **--run,** *s.* (*Tech.*) der Probelauf. **--tube,** *s.* (*Chem.*) das Reagenzglas, die Probierröhre, Eprouvette; ***– baby,*** das Retortenbaby.

testudo [tes'tju:dou], *s.* (*Zool.*) die Schildkröte.

testy ['testi], *adj.* verdrießlich, mürrisch, reizbar, gereizt.

tetanus ['tetənəs], *s.* (*Med.*) der (Wund)starrkrampf.

tetchiness ['tetʃinis], *s.*, **tetchy,** *adj.* *See* **testiness, testy.**

tete-à-tete ['teitɑ:'teit], **1.** *s.* vertrautes Zwiegespräch, das Gespräch unter vier Augen. **2.** *adv.* unter vier Augen, vertraulich.

tether ['teðə], **1.** *s.* 1. die Leine, der Haltestrick; 2. (*fig.*) Spielraum; (*fig.*) ***be at the end of one's –,*** sich (*Dat.*) nicht mehr zu helfen wissen, mit seiner Kraft *or* Geduld *or* seinem Latein am Ende sein. **2.** *v.t.* 1. anbinden (*cattle etc.*); 2. (*fig.*) binden.

tetrabrach ['tetrəbræk], *s.* (*Metr.*) der Versfuß aus vier Kürzen. **tetrachloride,** *s.* (*Chem.*) das Tetrachlorid. **tetrachord,** *s.* (*Mus.*) das Tetrachord.

tetrad ['tetræd], *s.* die Vierzahl. **tetradic** [–'trædik], *adj.* (*Math.*) vierstellig; (*Chem.*) vierwertig.

tetragon ['tetrəgən], *s.* das Tetragon, Viereck. **tetragonal** [–'trægənl], *adj.* viereckig. **tetragynous** [–'trædʒinəs], *adj.* (*Bot.*) mit vier Griffeln. **tetrahedral** [–'hi:drəl], *adj.* vierflächig. **tetrahedron** [–'hi:drən], *s.* das Tetraeder. **tetralogy** [te'trælədʒi], *s.* die Tetralogie. **tetrameter** [–'træmitə], *s.* der Tetrameter. **tetrandrous** [–'trændrəs], *adj.* (*Bot.*) viermannig.

tetrapod ['tetrəpɔd], *s.* (*Zool.*) der Vierfüßler.

tetrarch ['tetrɑ:k], *s.* der Vierfürst. **tetrarchy,** *s.* das Vierfürstentum.

tetrasyllabic [tetrəsi'læbik], *adj.* viersilbig.

tetrode ['tetroud], *s.* (*Rad.*) die Vierpolröhre.

tetter ['tetə], *s.* die Hautflechte, der Hautausschlag.

Teuton ['tju:tən], *s.* der Germane (die Germanin). **Teutonic** [–'tɔnik], *adj.* germanisch; ***– Knight,*** der Deutschordensritter; ***– Order,*** der Deutschritterorden. **Teutonism,** *s.* das Germanentum, germanische Eigenart; der Germanismus (*in language*).

text [tekst], *s.* der Text, Wortlaut; die Bibelstelle; (*coll.*) ***stick to one's –,*** bei der S. bleiben. **text|-book,** *s.* das Lehrbuch, der Leitfaden. **--hand,** *s.* (*Typ.*) große Schreibschrift.

textile ['tekstail], **1.** *adj.* gewebt, Web–, Gewebe–, Textil–; ***– goods,*** Textilien (*pl.*); ***– industry,*** die Textilindustrie. **2.** *s.* der Webstoff, das Gewebe; *pl.* Textilien (*pl.*).

textual ['tekstjuəl], *adj.* 1. Text–, textlich; 2. wörtlich, wortgetreu.

textural ['tekstjurəl], *adj.* strukturell, Struktur–. **texture** ['tekstʃə], *s.* 1. das Gewebe (*also Anat.*); 2. die Struktur, das Gefüge (*of minerals*); 3. die Zeichnung, Maserung (*of wood*); 4. (*fig.*) Beschaffenheit, Struktur, das Gefüge.

thalamus ['θæləməs], *s.* (*pl.* **-mi** [–mai]) 1. (*Anat.*) der Thalamus; 2. (*Bot.*) Fruchtboden.

thallic ['θælik], *adj.* (*Chem.*) Thallium–. **thallium** [–liəm], *s.* das Thallium.

Thames [temz], *s.* die Themse; ***he won't set the – on fire,*** er hat das Pulver nicht erfunden.

than [ðæn, ðən], *conj.* (*after comp.*) als; ***a man – whom no one . . .,*** ein Mann der wie kein anderer . . ..

thane [θein], *s.* der Lehnsmann; (*Scots*) Than.

thank [θæŋk], **1.** *v.t.* danken (*Dat.*), sich bedanken bei; ***– you,*** bitte (*affirmative*), danke (*neg.*); ***yes, – you,*** wenn ich bitten darf; ***no, – you,*** nein, danke; (*coll.*) ***– goodness! – heavens!*** Gott sei Dank! ***– one's lucky stars,*** von Glück sagen können; ***you have yourself to – for it,*** du hast es dir selbst zuzuschreiben; ***I will – you,*** ich möchte Sie bitten (*to do,* zu tun; *for,* um); ***– you for nothing,*** es geht dann auch ohne Sie. **2.** *s.* (*only pl.*) der Dank, die Danksagung, Dankesbezeigung; (*coll.*) ***–s!*** danke! ***express –s,*** Dank aussprechen *or* sagen; ***in –s for,*** zum Dank für; ***letter of –s,*** das Dankschreiben; ***many –s,*** vielen Dank; ***return –s,*** see ***express –s;*** ***–s (be) to God,*** Gott sei Dank *or* gedankt; ***no*** or ***small –s to you!*** ohne deine Hilfe *or* dein Zutun; ***–s to,*** dank (*Dat.*); ***vote of –s,*** die Dankadresse, Dankesworte (*pl.*); ***with –s,*** mit Dank, dankend.

thankful ['θæŋkful], *adj.* dankbar, erkenntlich (*to, Dat.*). **thankfulness,** *s.* die Dankbarkeit, Erkenntlichkeit. **thankless,** *adj.* undankbar (*of a p. or th.*), wenig erfreulich, unergiebig, unfruchtbar (*of a th.*). **thanklessness,** *s.* die Undankbarkeit.

thank-offering, *s.* das Dankopfer, Sühneopfer. **thanksgiving,** *s.* 1. die Danksagung; 2. das Dankfest.

that, **1.** [ðæt], *dem. pron.* 1. (*absolute, no pl.*) das; ***so –'s –,*** das wäre erledigt, und damit basta; ***and all –,*** und allerlei anderes; ***for all –,*** trotz alledem; ***let it go at –,*** lassen wir es dabei bewenden; ***like –,*** so; ***–'s so*** or ***it*** or ***the way!*** so ist's recht! so ist es! ***(is) – so?*** ist das wirklich so? ***–'s what it is,*** daran *or* so liegt es, das ist es ja gerade; ***talk of this and –,*** von allerlei Dingen reden; ***– is (to say),*** das heißt; ***– was the children,*** das waren die Kinder, das haben die Kinder getan; ***– is my fault,*** das ist meine Schuld; ***– is right*** or ***true,*** das stimmt; ***what's – to me?*** was geht das mich an? (*coll.*) ***–'s a good boy!*** so bist du *or* sei doch ein braver Junge! 2. (*with pl.* **those** [ðouz]) (*of th.*) der, das, die;

jene(r, –s); ***of the two hats I like – better,*** von den beiden Hüten habe ich den lieber; (*of p., only with to be*) das; – ***is his son,*** das ist sein Sohn; ***those are his sons,*** das sind seine Söhne; – ***which,*** das was; ***those which,*** diejenigen welche. **2.** [ðæt], *dem. adj.* (*sing.*) der, das, die, jene(r, –s), diese(r, –s); (*sl.*) – ***there,*** jene(r, –s); *pl. See* **those. 3.** [ðət], *rel. pron.* (*introducing defining clause, nowadays not usu. of a p.*) der, die, das, welche(r, –s), was; ***the best – I have,*** das Beste was ich habe; ***it was you – said so,*** Sie waren es, der (*or* die) es sagte; ***it was no one – I know,*** es war niemand den ich kenne; ***his wife, Miss B. – was,*** seine Frau, geborene B. **4.** [ðət], *conj.* daß; ob; damit, so daß; ***it was here – he died,*** hier starb er; ***in –,*** deshalb weil, insofern als; ***in order –,*** damit; ***I do not know – I am right,*** ich weiß nicht ob ich recht habe; ***not –,*** nicht daß *or* weil; ***now –,*** nun da, jetzt da; ***rather –,*** eher deshalb weil; ***I'm not sure –,*** ich bin nicht sicher daß *or* ob; ***seeing –,*** see ***in –***; ***so (. . .) –,*** so (. . .) daß; ***at the time –,*** zu der Zeit als. **5.** [ðæt], *adv.* (*coll.*) so (sehr), dermaßen, derartig; ***it was – cold,*** es war dermaßen kalt; ***I am not all – old,*** ich bin nicht so (sehr) alt.

thatch [θætʃ], **1.** *s.* 1. das Strohdach; 2. Dachstroh, Deckmaterial. **2.** *v.t.* mit Stroh decken; ***–ed roof,*** das Strohdach; ***–ed cottage,*** strohgedecktes Häuschen. **thatcher,** *s.* der Strohdecker. **thatching,** *s.* 1. das Dachstroh; 2. Dachdecken mit Stroh.

thaumaturgic(al) [θɔ:mə'tə:dʒik(l)], *adj.* wundertätig, zauberhaft, Wunder–. **thaumaturgist** ['θɔ:mətə:dʒist], *s.* der Wundertäter, Zauberer. **thaumaturgy** ['θɔ:mətə:dʒi], *s.* die Zauberei, Wundertätigkeit.

thaw [θɔ:], **1.** *s.* das (Auf)tauen; Tauwetter (*also fig.*). **2.** *v.i.* (auf)tauen, schmelzen; (*fig.*) auftauen. **3.** *v.t.* schmelzen, (*fig.*) (*also* ***– out***) zum Auftauen bringen, auftauen lassen.

the [ðə, ði, ði: *dependent on emphasis*], **1.** *def. art.* der, die, das, *pl.* die (*with corresponding case forms*); ***all – men,*** alle Männer; ***all – world,*** die ganze Welt; ***by – dozen,*** dutzendweise; ***50p. – pound,*** 50 Pence das Pfund; ***– Smiths,*** die Familie Schmidt. **2.** *adv.* (*before comp.*) desto, um so; ***– fewer – better,*** je weniger desto besser; ***so much – worse,*** um so schlimmer; ***not any – worse,*** keineswegs *or* um nichts schlechter; ***– more as,*** um so mehr als.

theater, (*Am.*) *see* **theatre.**

theatre ['θiətə], *s.* 1. das Theater, Schauspielhaus; ***open-air –,*** die Freilichtbühne; ***go to the –,*** ins Theater gehen; ***be good –,*** bühnenwirksam sein (*of a play*); 2. (*fig.*) der Schauplatz (*of war*); 3. die Bühne, das Theaterwesen; ***the world of the –,*** die Bühnenwelt; 4. ***lecture –,*** der Hörsaal; ***operating –,*** der Operationssaal. **theatre|-goer,** *s.* der (die) Theaterbesucher(in). **--going,** *s.* der Theaterbesuch.

theatrical [θi'ætrikl], **1.** *adj.* 1. Bühnen–, Theater–; 2. (*fig.*) theatralisch, prunkend, pomphaft. **2.** *pl.* (*coll.*) Theateraufführungen (*pl.*); ***amateur –s,*** die Liebhaberbühne. **theatricality** [–'kæliti], *s.* theatralisches Wesen.

Thebes [θi:bz], *s.* Theben (*n.*).

thee [ði:], (*Poet., B.*) dich, dir; ***of –,*** deiner.

theft [θeft], *s.* der Diebstahl (***from,*** an (*Dat.*) (*a p.*), aus (*a place*)).

theine ['θi:in], *s.* (*Chem.*) das Tein.

their [ðɛə], *poss. adj.* ihr (*sing.*); ihre (*pl.*); ***they came in – hundreds,*** sie kamen zu Hunderten heran. **theirs** [–z], *poss. pron.* der, die *or* das ihr(ig)e, ihr(e, –es); ***it is –s,*** es gehört ihnen; ***a friend of –,*** ein Freund von ihnen, einer von ihren Freunden.

theism ['θi:izm], *s.* der Theismus. **theist,** *s.* der (die) Theist(in). **theistic(al)** [–'istik(l)], *adj.* theistisch.

them [ðem], **1.** *pers. pron.* sie, ihnen; ***of –,*** ihrer; ***to –,*** ihnen. **2.** *refl. pron.* sich.

thematic [θi'mætik], *adj.* thematisch.

theme [θi:m], *s.* 1. das Thema (*also Mus.*), der Stoff, Gegenstand; 2. Aufsatz, die(Schul)aufgabe. **theme-song,** *s.* der Hauptschlager, die Titelmelodie; Kennmelodie (*film etc.*).

themselves [ðəm'selvz], *pl. pron.* sie selbst; (*used reflexively*) sich (selbst); ***they –,*** sie selbst; ***things in – innocent,*** an (und für) sich unschuldige Dinge.

then [ðen], **1.** *adv.* 1. damals; ***long before –,*** lange vorher; 2. dann, darauf, hierauf; ***now and –,*** dann und wann; ***every now and –,*** alle Augenblicke, von Zeit zu Zeit, immer wieder; ***by –,*** bis dahin, inzwischen; ***from – (on),*** von da ab; (*sl.*) ***and – some,*** und noch viel mehr dazu; ***– and there, there and –,*** auf der Stelle, sofort; ***till –, up to –,*** bis dahin; ***not till –,*** erst von da ab, erst dann; ***what –?*** was dann? was weiter? 3. in dem Falle, denn, also; (*coll.*) ***now –!*** aber bitte! nun also! ***all right –, well –,*** nun gut denn. **2.** *adj.* damalig. **3.** *conj.* 1. dann, ferner, außerdem; ***but –,*** aber andererseits *or* freilich; 2. also, folglich.

thence [ðens], *adv.* 1. von da *or* dort (*place*); 2. von da *or* von der Zeit an, seitdem, seit jener Zeit (*time*); 3. aus diesem Grunde, deshalb, daher, folglich; aus dieser Tatsache, daraus (*causal*); ***– it follows,*** daraus ergibt sich. **thenceforth, thenceforward,** *adv.* in Zukunft, hinfort; *see also* **thence,** 1.

theocentric [θiə'sentrik], *adj.* theozentrisch.

theocracy [θi'ɔkrəsi], *s.* die Theokratie, Gottesherrschaft; Priesterherrschaft. **theocratic** [θiə'krætik], *adj.* theokratisch.

theodicy [θi'ɔdisi], *s.* die Theodizee.

theodolite [θi'ɔdəlait], *s.* (*Surv.*) der Theodolit.

theogony [θi'ɔgəni], *s.* die Theogonie, Götterabstammungslehre.

theologian [θiə'loudʒən], *s.* der Theologe. **theological** [–'lɔdʒikl], *adj.* theologisch. **theology** [θi'ɔlədʒi], *s.* die Theologie, Gottesgelehrtheit.

theomachy [θi'ɔməki], *s.* der Kampf der Götter *or* unter den Göttern. **theomorphic** [θiə'mɔ:fik], *adj.* gottähnlich, in göttlicher Gestalt, theomorph(isch). **theophany** [–'ɔfəni], *s.* die Erscheinung Gottes (in menschlicher Gestalt).

theorem ['θiərəm], *s.* der Lehrsatz, Grundsatz.

theoretical [θiə'retikl], *adj.* theoretisch, spekulativ. **theoretician** [–ri'tiʃən], **theorist** ['θiərist], *s.* der Theoretiker. **theorize** ['θiəraiz], *v.i.* theoretisieren, Theorien aufstellen, spekulieren. **theory** ['θiəri], *s.* die Theorie, Lehre; ***in –,*** theoretisch; (*coll.*) ***pet –,*** die Lieblingsidee; (*coll.*) ***have a – about,*** eine Auffassung haben von.

theosophic(al) [θiə'sɔfik(l)], *adj.* theosophisch. **theosophist** [θi'ɔsəfist], *s.* der Theosoph. **theosophy** [–'ɔsəfi], *s.* die Theosophie.

therapeutic(al) [θerə'pju:tik(l)], *adj.* therapeutisch, Heil–. **therapeutics,** *pl.* (*sing. constr.*) die Therapeutik, Behandlungslehre. **therapist** ['θerəpist], *s.* der (die) Therapeut(in). **therapy** ['θerəpi], *s.* die Therapie, Behandlung, das Heilverfahren; ***occupational –,*** die Beschäftigungstherapie.

there [ðɛə], **1.** *adv.* 1. da, dort, daselbst; (*sl.*) ***be all –,*** aufgeweckt sein; (*sl.*) ***not all –,*** überspannt; ***– he is,*** da ist er; (*fig.*) ***– it is,*** so ist *or* steht es; ***down –,*** da *or* dort unten; ***in –,*** da drinnen; ***out –,*** da draußen; ***over –,*** da drüben; ***up –,*** da oben; ***here and –,*** da und dort; ***– and then, then and –,*** hier und jetzt, auf der Stelle, sofort; ***– you are*** or ***go!*** siehst du! hab' ich es nicht gesagt? da haben Sie es! 2. hin, dahin, dorthin; ***– and back,*** hin und zurück; 3. es (*before v.i.*); ***– is,*** es ist, es gibt; ***– are,*** es sind, es gibt; ***will – be dancing?*** wird getanzt (werden)? ***– is no saying*** or ***telling*** . . ., es läßt sich *or* man kann nicht sagen . . .; ***– is no stopping her,*** bei ihr gibt's kein Zurück; ***–'s a good boy,*** sei doch *or* das ist ein braver Junge, so ist es brav; ***–'s a good chap,*** sei so gut. **2.** *int.* na! ***– –,*** sei ruhig! ***– now!*** nun weißt du's! ***so –!*** damit basta! Punktum!

there|about(s) ['ðɛərəbauts], *adv.* da herum, etwa da, in der Nähe. **–abouts,** *adv.* (*fig.*) so etwa *or* ungefähr; ***then or –,*** ungefähr um diese Zeit. **–after,** *adv.* seither, danach, hernach, nachher. **–at,** *adv.* (*obs.*) dabei, daselbst, bei der Gelegenheit. **–by,** *adv.* daneben; damit, dadurch; ***come –,***

dazu *or* in den Besitz davon kommen; – ***hangs a tale,*** daran knüpft sich eine Geschichte. **-for,** *adv.* (*obs.*) dafür.
therefore ['ðɛəfɔ:], *adv., conj.* deswegen, deshalb, darum, daher, also, folglich, demgemäß, mithin.
there|from, *adv.* daher, daraus. **–in,** *adv.* darin, in dieser Hinsicht. **–inafter,** *adv.* (*Law*) später, (weiter) unten, nachstehend. **–of,** *adv.* (*obs.*) daraus, davon; dessen, deren. **–on,** *adv.* (*obs.*) darauf, daran. **–to,** *adv.* (*obs.*) dazu, dafür, daran; außerdem, darüber hinaus. **–under,** *adv.* (*obs.*) darunter. **–upon,** *adv.* darauf, danach, hierauf; daraufhin, darum, demzufolge, infolgedessen. **–with,** *adv.* damit; *see also* **–upon. –withal,** *adv.* (*obs.*) damit; überdies, außerdem.
therm [θə:m], *s.* 1. die Wärmeeinheit; die Gramm-Kalorie; Kilo(gramm)-Kalorie; 2. (*gas*) 100,000 Wärmeeinheiten. **thermae** [-i:], *pl.* warme Quellen. **thermal, 1.** *adj.* Thermal–; Wärme–, Hitze–, Heiz–; – ***efficiency,*** der Wärmewirkungsgrad; – ***springs,*** Thermen (*pl.*); – ***unit,*** die Wärmeeinheit; – ***value,*** der Heizwert (*of fuel*). **2.** *s.* (*Meteor.*) die Thermik, Warmluftströmung. **thermic,** *adj. See* **thermal, 1.**
thermionic [θə:mi'ɔnik], *adj.* (*Rad.*) Kathoden–, Elektronen–.
thermite ['θə:mait], *s.* (*Chem.*) das Thermit.
thermo- ['θə:mou], *pref.* Wärme–, Thermo–. **thermo|-chemistry,** *s.* die Thermochemie. **--couple,** *s.* das Thermoelement. **-dynamics,** *pl.* (*sing. constr.*) die Wärmekraftlehre, die Thermodynamik. **--electric(al),** *adj.* thermoelektrisch. **--electricity,** *s.* die Thermoelektrizität.
thermometer [θə'mɔmitə], *s.* das Thermometer. **thermometric(al)** [θə:mə'metrik(l)], *adj.* thermometrisch.
thermo|nuclear, *adj.* thermonuklear; – ***bomb,*** die Wasserstoffbombe. **-pile,** *s.* die Thermosäule.
thermos-(flask) ['θə:məs], *s.* die Thermosflasche.
thermostat ['θə:məstæt], *s.* der Thermostat, Temperaturregler.
thesaurus [θi:'sɔ:rəs], *s.* der Wortschatz, das Lexikon.
these [ði:z], (*pl. of* **this**), **1.** *dem. adj.* diese; – ***9 years,*** seit 9 Jahren; ***one of – days,*** eines Tages; ***in – days,*** heutzutage, heutigentags; ***one of – days,*** in den nächsten Tagen, demnächst. **2.** *pron.* diese; (*with verb to be*) dies; – ***are my children,*** dies sind meine Kinder.
thesis ['θi:sis], *s.* 1. der (Streit)satz, die These, Behauptung, das Postulat; 2. (*Univ.*) die Dissertation, Doktorarbeit.
thespian ['θespiən], *adj.* Schauspiel–.
Thessalonians [θesə'louniəns], *pl.* (*sing. constr.*) (*B.*) der Thessalonicherbrief.
thews [θju:z], *pl.* 1. Muskeln (*pl.*), Sehnen (*pl.*); 2. (*fig.*) die (Körper)kraft.
they [ðei], *pers. pron.* sie; – ***who,*** die(jenigen) welche; – ***say,*** man sagt, es heißt.
thick [θik], **1.** *adj.* 1. dick; (*sl.*) – ***ear,*** dicke Backe; 2. dicht (besät), erfüllt (***with,*** mit), voll (*Dat. or* von), voller (*Dat.*), reich (an (*Dat.*)); – ***with dust,*** mit Staub bedeckt; 3. dickflüssig; – ***soup,*** legierte Suppe; 4. dicht, undurchdringlich (*woods, fog etc.*); 5. heiser, belegt (*voice*); 6. (*sl.*) intim, vertraut, dick; (*sl.*) – ***on,*** verknallt in (*Acc.*); (*sl.*) – ***with,*** engbefreundet mit; (*coll.*) ***they are as – as thieves,*** sie halten zusammen wie Pech und Schwefel; 7. (*sl.*) zu viel, stark, dick; (*coll.*) ***a bit –,*** ein starkes Stück, zu arg, happig; 8. (*coll.*) beschränkt, dumm, stumpf(sinnig). **2.** *adv.* 1. dick; (*sl.*) ***lay it on –,*** es dick auftragen; 2. dicht; ***come*** or ***fall – and fast,*** dicht *or* rasch aufeinander kommen. **3.** *s.* 1. schwierigster Teil; 2. (*fig.*) der Brennpunkt, das Gewoge; ***in the – of the fight,*** im dichtesten Kampfgewühl; ***be in the – of,*** mitten stehen in (*Dat.*); ***be in the – of it,*** mittendrin stehen, dastehen wo es am heißesten hergeht; ***through – and thin,*** durch dick und dünn.
thicken ['θikən], **1.** *v.t.* 1. dick(er) machen, verdicken; 2. (*Cul.*) dick werden lassen, eindicken, einkochen; 3. (*distribution*) dicht(er) machen, verdichten; 4. (*fig.*) verstärken, vermehren. **2.** *v.i.* 1. dick(er) werden; 2. dicht(er) werden, sich verdichten; 3. dick(flüssig) werden (*of fluids*); 4. sich trüben; 5. sich verstärken *or* vermehren; ***the fight –s,*** der Kampf wird heftiger; ***the plot –s,*** der Knoten schürzt sich. **thickener,** *s.* (*Cul.*) das Verdickungsmittel. **thickening,** *s.* 1. die Verdickung; 2. verdickte Stelle, (*Med.*) die Anschwellung; 3. Verdichtung, das Dichtermachen; 4. (*Cul.*) die Eindickung, das Eindicken; Verdickungsmittel.
thicket ['θikit], *s.* das Dickicht, Gebüsch.
thick|-headed, *adj.* dickköpfig, begriffsstutzig. **--headedness,** *s.* der Dickköpfigkeit, Begriffsstutzigkeit. **--knee,** *s.* (*Orn.*) (*Am.*) *see* **stone-curlew. --lipped,** *adj.* dicklippig.
thickness ['θiknis], *s.* 1. die Dicke; 2. dicke Stelle, die Verdickung; 3. Dichte, Dichtheit; 4. (*of fluid*) Dickflüssigkeit; Undurchsichtigkeit, Trübe, Trübheit; – ***of speech,*** schwere Zunge; 5. die Lage, Schicht.
thick|set, *adj.* 1. untersetzt (*a p.*); 2. dicht bepflanzt (*plants*); – ***hedge,*** dichte Hecke. **--skinned,** *adj.* 1. dickhäutig, dickschalig; 2. (*fig.*) dickfellig. **--skulled,** *adj.* dickköpfig.
thief [θi:f], *s.* (*pl.* **thieves** [θi:vz]) der Dieb, Räuber; (*Prov.*) ***set a – to catch a –,*** den Bock zum Gärtner machen; ***thieves' Latin,*** die Gaunersprache. **thieve** [θi:v], *v.i., v.t.* stehlen. **thievery,** *s.* die Dieberei. **thievish,** *adj.* diebisch, Diebs–, spitzbübisch (*also fig.*). **thievishness,** *s.* 1. der Hang zum Stehlen; 2. das Diebische, Spitzbübische (*of a look etc.*).
thigh [θai], *s.* der (Ober)schenkel. **thigh|-bone,** *s.* das Schenkelbein. **--boot,** *s.* der Wasserstiefel.
thill [θil], *s.* die (Gabel)deichsel. **thiller, thill-horse,** *s.* das Deichselpferd.
thimble [θimbl], *s.* 1. der Fingerhut; 2. (*Tech.*) Metallring, (*Naut.*) die Kausche. **thimbleful,** *s.* 1. der Fingerhutvoll; 2. (*fig.*) das Schlückchen, die Kleinigkeit. **thimble|rig, 1.** *v.t.* beschwindeln, betrügen. **2.** *v.i.* 1. Taschenspielerkunststücke vorführen; 2. täuschen, schwindeln. **3.** *or* **-rigging,** *s.* das Kunststück; die Taschenspielerei, List.
thin [θin], **1.** *adj.* 1. dünn; – ***clothes,*** leichte Kleidung; (*fig.*) ***on – ice,*** in einer heiklen Lage, auf gefährlichem Boden; ***wear –,*** sich abnutzen *or* verbrauchen; 2. leicht, zart, fein, schwach, zierlich; – ***voice,*** schwache *or* piepsige Stimme; 3. (*of p.*) dünn, mager, hager, dürr; ***as – as a lath*** or ***rake,*** spindeldürr; ***grow –,*** dünn *or* mager werden; 4. (*of hair*) schütter, (*woods etc.*) licht; 5. (*of fluid*) dünn(flüssig), wässerig, verdünnt; 6. (*fig.*) ärmlich, kümmerlich, spärlich, dürftig; seicht, inhaltlos; – ***attendance,*** spärlicher Besuch, geringe Beteiligung; – ***crop,*** magere *or* spärliche Ernte; – ***excuse,*** nichtige *or* fadenscheinige Entschuldigung; (*Theat.*) – ***house,*** schwach besuchte Vorstellung; (*sl.*) ***he has a – time (of it),*** es geht ihm dreckig *or* mies. **2.** *v.t.* 1. dünn(er) machen; (*liquid*) verdünnen; strecken; 2. (*also* – ***out***) weiter auseinander setzen (*seedlings*), lichten (*woods etc.*); 3. (*fig.*) (*also* – ***down***) vermindern, verringern. **3.** *v.i.* 1. sich verdünnen, dünn(er) werden; 2. (*also* – ***out***) sich vermindern *or* verringern, geringer *or* spärlicher werden, sich verlaufen, abnehmen; sich lichten (*woods*), (*Geol.*) sich auskeilen; ***his hair is thinning,*** sein Haar lichtet sich.
thin-bodied, *adj.* dünnflüssig (*liquid*).
thine [ðain], **1.** *poss. pron.* (*Poet., B.*) der *or* die *or* das dein(ig)e, deine(r, –s). **2.** *poss. adj.* (*before vowel or mute* h) *see* **thy.**
thin-faced, *adj.* schmalbackig.
thing [θiŋ], *s.* 1. (*no pl.*) (beliebiges) Ding, die (Tat)sache, Angelegenheit, das Geschäft; (*with pl.*) (beliebiger) Gegenstand; ***above all –s,*** vor allen Dingen, vor allem; ***in all –s,*** in jeder Hinsicht; ***of all –s,*** obendrein noch; und was das Schönste dabei ist; ***for another –,*** andererseits; ***that's another –,*** das ist(et)was anderes; ***not an earthly –,***

(gar) nichts; ***first –*** (***in the morning***), in aller Frühe; ***a lot of good –s,*** viele gute Sachen (zum Essen und Trinken); ***do great –s,*** Großes vollbringen; ***make a good – of,*** profitieren von, seinen Schnitt machen bei; ***the one good – was,*** das einzige Gute war; ***do the handsome –,*** sich großzügig *or* anständig verhalten (***by,*** gegen); (*sl.*) ***have a – about,*** erpicht *or* versessen sein auf (*Acc.*); etwas haben gegen; ***know a – or two,*** Bescheid wissen, im Bilde sein (***about,*** über (*Acc.*)), bewandert sein (in (*Dat.*)), einiges verstehen (von); ***last –*** (***at night***), ganz spät, gleich vorm Schlafengehen; ***a little – of mine,*** eine Kleinigkeit von mir; ***too much of a good –,*** zuviel des Guten; ***it was a near –,*** es ging um Haaresbreite; (*iron.*) ***that's a nice –,*** das ist eine schöne Geschichte; ***for one –,*** erstens einmal, als erstes, einerseits, einesteils, überhaupt, an und für sich; ***tell me one –,*** sagen Sie mir eins; ***one – or the other,*** das eine oder das andere; ***taking one – with another,*** im großen (und) ganzen; ***it's a strange –,*** es ist sonderbar *or* etwas Sonderbares; ***it comes to the same –,*** es läuft auf dasselbe hinaus; ***no small –,*** keine Kleinigkeit; ***it's a strange – that,*** es ist merkwürdig daß; ***no such –,*** nichts dergleichen; 2. (*coll.*) ***the –,*** das Richtige *or* Gegebene *or* Passende *or* Schickliche; das Wichtigste *or* Wesentliche, die Hauptsache; (*coll.*) ***not*** (***quite***) ***the –,*** nicht gerade das Schickliche; ***just the – we need,*** gerade das was wir nötig haben; ***latest –,*** das Allerneueste (***in,*** an (*Dat.*)); 3. (lebendes) Wesen, das Ding, Geschöpf, die Person; (*coll.*) ***old –,*** mein Lieber; (*coll.*) ***poor –!*** du Ärmster! armer Kerl! ***poor little –,*** armes kleines Ding *or* Wesen; 4. (*only pl.*) Dinge (*pl.*), Sachen (*pl.*), Angelegenheiten (*pl.*), der Kram; Verhältnisse (*pl.*), Einrichtungen (*pl.*), die (Sach)-lage; ***how are –s?*** wie geht's? ***as –s are*** or ***go*** or ***stand,*** wie es so geht, wie die Dinge liegen; ***in the nature of –s,*** in der Natur der Verhältnisse; ***it's just one of those –s,*** da kann man nichts machen; ***be out of –s,*** abseits *or* ausgeschlossen bleiben; 5. *pl.* (*coll.*) Sachen (*pl.*), Kleider (*pl.*), die Kleidung, das Zeug, Zubehör, Eigentum, Geräte (*pl.*), Werkzeuge (*pl.*).

thingamy ['θiŋəmi], **thingumabob** [–əbɔb] (*of th. only*), **thingumajig** [–ədʒig] (*of th. only*), **thingummy** [–əmi], *s.* das Dings, der *or* die *or* das Dingsda; ***Mr. Thingamy*** or ***Thingummy,*** Herr Dingsda *or* Soundso.

think [θiŋk], **1.** *irr.v.t.* 1. denken; hegen (*a thought*); ausdenken, sich (*Dat.*) vorstellen, sich (*Dat.*) (in Gedanken) zurechtlegen; ***– out,*** ausdenken, ersinnen; zu Ende denken; ***– over,*** nachdenken über (*Acc.*), sich (*Dat.*) überlegen; (*coll.*) ***– up,*** ausdenken, aushecken; 2. sich (*Dat.*) eine Vorstellung machen von, sich (*Dat.*) vor Augen halten, bedenken, erwägen, nachdenken über (*Acc.*), überlegen; 3. denken an (*Acc.*), im Sinn *or* Kopf haben; 4. meinen, der Meinung sein, glauben, annehmen, halten *or* erachten für, betrachten *or* ansehen als; ***what do you –?*** wie meinen Sie? ***– enough of him to . . .*** (*with inf.*), so viel von ihm halten daß . . .; ***– o.s. clever,*** sich für klug halten; ***– it advisable,*** es für angebracht halten; ***– it best,*** es für das beste halten; ***– it fit*** or ***proper,*** es für richtig halten; 5. gedenken, beabsichtigen. **2.** *irr. v.i.* 1. (sich (*Dat.*)) denken *or* vorstellen; nachdenken, überlegen; ***– about,*** denken an (*Acc.*), (nach)denken über (*Acc.*), überlegen; ***– twice about,*** es zweimal überlegen; 2. ***– of,*** denken an (*Acc.*), gedenken (*Gen.*) (*see also* ***– about***); sich erinnern an (*Acc.*), kommen auf (*Acc.*), sich entsinnen (*Gen.*); (*oft.* ***be –ing of***) daran denken, im Sinn haben; (*usu. neg.*) ***I wouldn't – of going,*** es würde mir nicht (im Traum) einfallen, zu gehen; ***I know his name but cannot – of it,*** ich kenne seinen Namen aber komme nicht darauf; ***I have a wife to – of,*** ich habe eine Frau, an die ich denken muß; (*coll.*) ***to – of his marrying at his age!*** kaum zu glauben, daß er in seinem Alter heiraten will! (*coll.*) ***come to – of it!*** wenn ich mir's richtig überlege; 3. meinen, der Meinung sein, glauben, urteilen; ***– highly*** or ***much*** or ***well of,*** große Stücke *or* viel halten von; ***– nothing of,*** sich (*Dat.*) nichts machen aus; ***– better of it,*** sich eines Besseren besinnen; ***– the world of,*** wunder was halten von; ***'I – so,*** ich glaube (es) auch; ***I '– so*** (*in reply to question*), ich glaube, ja; ***I should – so,*** das will ich meinen; ***I should – not!*** das fehlte noch! (*sl.*) ***I 'don't –!*** (*following iron. statement*) gerade das Gegenteil!

thinkable [θiŋkəbl], *adj.* denkbar. **thinker,** *s.* der Denker, Philosoph. **thinking, 1.** *s.* das Denken, die Meinung; ***way of –,*** die Denkart; ***to my*** (***way of***) ***–,*** meiner Meinung *or* Ansicht nach; ***he is of my way of –,*** er teilt meine Ansicht, er denkt wie ich. **2.** *adj.* denkend; ***all – men,*** jeder vernünftig Denkende.

thinly ['θinli], *adv.* 1. dünn; 2. spärlich. **thinner, 1.** *comp. adj. of* **thin. 2.** *s.* der Verdünner, das Verdünnungsmittel.

thinness ['θinnis], *s.* 1. die Dünne, Dünnheit; 2. Magerkeit (*of p.*); 3. (*distribution*) Spärlichkeit, Seltenheit; 4. (*fig.*) Dürftigkeit, Kümmerlichkeit, Ärmlichkeit, Seichtigkeit.

thinnest ['θinist], *sup. adj. of* **thin. thinning, 1.** *adj.* (sich) verdünnend, dünn *or* spärlich werdend. **2.** *s.* 1. das Verdünnen, die Verdünnung; 2. (*Hort.*) das Lichten, Ausschneiden, Ausputzen (*of plants*), Ausforsten, Ausholzen, der Hieb (*of forest*). **thinnish,** *adj.* ziemlich dünn.

third [θə:d], **1.** *num. adj.* dritt; (*coll.*) ***– degree,*** das Folterverhör, Zwangsmaßnahmen (der Polizei); (*Law*) ***– party,*** dritte Person. **2.** *s.* 1. der *or* die *or* das Dritte; 2. (*fraction*) das Drittel; (*Mus.*) die Terz. **thirdly,** *adv.* drittens. **third|-party insurance,** *s.* die Haftpflichtversicherung. **--party risk,** *s.* die Haftpflicht. **--rail,** *s.* (*Railw.*) die Stromschiene. **--rate,** *adj.* drittklassig, drittrangig; (*coll.*) minderwertig.

thirst [θə:st], **1.** *s.* der Durst (***for,*** nach) (*also fig.*); ***die of –,*** verdursten. **2.** *v.i.* dursten, dürsten (***for, after,*** nach). **thirstiness,** *s.* die Durstigkeit, der Durst. **thirsty,** *adj.* durstig (*also fig.*); dürr, trocken (*as soil*); ***I am –,*** ich habe Durst, mich durstet; (*coll.*) ***– work,*** Arbeit, die Durst macht.

thirteen [θə:'ti:n], **1.** *num. adj.* dreizehn. **2.** *s.* die Dreizehn. **thirteenth, 1.** *num. adj.* dreizehnt. **2.** *s.* 1. der, die *or* das Dreizehnte; 2. (*fraction*) das Dreizehntel. **thirtieth** ['θə:tiəθ], **1.** *num. adj.* dreißigst. **2.** *s.* 1. der, die *or* das Dreißigste; 2. (*fraction*) das Dreißigstel. **thirty** ['θə:ti], **1.** *num. adj.* dreißig; ***Thirty Years' War,*** Dreißigjähriger Krieg. **2.** *s.* 1. die Dreißig; 2 *pl.* die dreißiger Jahre (*of a century*), Dreißiger(jahre) (*of life*).

this [ðis], **1.** *dem. pron.* (*with pl.* **these**); 1. (*of th.*) diese(r, –s); 2. (*of p.*) (*only with verb to be*) dies; ***– is my son,*** dies ist mein Sohn; 3. (*no pl.*) dies, das; ***all –,*** dies alles, all das; ***at –,*** dabei, daraufhin; ***after –,*** danach; ***before –,*** zuvor, schon vorher; ***by –,*** inzwischen, indessen, mittlerweile; ***ere –,*** ehedem; ***like –,*** so, folgendermaßen; ***– above all,*** dies vor allem; ***– that and the other,*** allerhand, allerlei; ***– is what I said,*** ich sagte Folgendes; ***– happened some years ago,*** dies geschah vor einigen Jahren. **2.** *dem. adj.* (*pl.* **these**) diese(r, –s); ***– day week,*** heute in 8 Tagen; ***in – country,*** hierzulande; ***– month,*** dieses Monats; ***– morning,*** heute morgen; ***– much,*** so viel; ***– once,*** dieses eine Mal; ***– one,*** dieser; ***– time,*** diesmal; ***by – time,*** mittlerweile; ***– year,*** dieses *or* in diesem Jahr, (*Austr.*) heuer.

thistle [θisl], *s.* die Distel. **thistledown,** *s.* die Distelwolle, Distelfrucht.

thither ['ðiðə], *adv.* (*obs.*) dorthin, dahin; ***hither and –,*** hin und her.

thole [θoul], *s.* (*also* ***--pin***) die Dolle, der Ruderpflock.

thong [θɔŋ], *s.* der Riemen, Gurt, die Peitschenschnur.

thoracic [θɔ'ræsik], *adj.* Brust–. **thorax** ['θɔ:ræks], *s.* (*Anat.*) der Brustkasten, Brustkorb, (*Ent.*) der Mittelleib, das Bruststück.

thorium ['θɔ:riəm], *s.* (*Chem.*) das Thorium.

thorn [θɔ:n], *s.* der Dorn, Stachel; ***be a – in the*** (or ***his***) ***side*** or ***flesh,*** (ihm) ein Dorn im Auge sein;

be or *sit on –s*, wie auf (glühenden) Kohlen sitzen. **thorn|-apple,** *s.* der Stechapfel. **–bush,** *s.* der Dornbusch, Hagedorn, Weißdorn. **--hedge,** *s.* die Dornenhecke. **thornless,** *adj.* dornenlos. **thorny,** *adj.* 1. dornig, stach(e)lig; 2. (*fig.*) dornenvoll, beschwerlich, mühselig.

thorough ['θʌrə], *adj.* 1. gründlich, durchgreifend, durchdringend; völlig, gänzlich, vollständig, vollendet, vollkommen; 2. (*of a p.*) genau, pedantisch, penibel. **thorough|-bass,** *s.* (*Mus.*) der Generalbaß. **–bred, 1.** *adj.* 1. rasserein, reinrassig, Vollblut–; (*fig.*) gediegen, erstklassig; 2. gründlich, richtiggehend. **2.** *s.* das Vollblut(pferd), der Vollblüter. **–fare,** *s.* 1. der Durchgang, die Durchfahrt; *no –!* keine Durchfahrt! 2. die Durchgangsstraße, Hauptverkehrsstraße. **–going,** *adj.* durchgreifend, gründlich; (*coll.*) extrem, kompromißlos, durch und durch.

thoroughly ['θʌrəli], *adv.* durchaus, gänzlich, völlig, vollkommen. **thoroughness,** *s.* 1. die Gründlichkeit, Genauigkeit; 2. Vollkommenheit, Gediegenheit. **thorough-paced,** *adj.* durch und durch (*following noun*), echt, gediegen, ausgemacht, ausgekocht, abgefeimt, durchtrieben, Erz– (*thief, scoundrel*).

those [ðouz], *dem. pron. and adj.* (*pl. of* **that**).

[1]**thou** [ðau], **1.** *pers. pron.* (*Poet., B.*) du. **2.** *v.t., v.i.* (*also – and thee*) duzen.

[2]**thou** [θau], *s.* (*sl.*) *abbr. of* **thousand(th).**

though [ðou], **1.** *conj.* 1. obgleich, obwohl, obschon; 2. selbst wenn, wenn auch, wenngleich; *even –,* selbst wenn; wenn . . . auch; *important – it is,* so wichtig es auch ist; *what – it rains?* was macht es schon aus, wenn es regnet? wenn es nun auch regnet? (*coll.*) *– I say it* (*myself*), ohne mich zu rühmen; *as –,* als ob, als wenn; *as – he were ill,* als wenn er krank wäre. **2.** *adv.* (*coll.*) (*usu. at end of sentence*) aber, (je)doch, immerhin, allerdings, dennoch, indessen; *you will come, –,* Sie kommen aber doch; *I wish you had told me, –,* hätten Sie es mir immerhin *or* dennoch gesagt!

thought [θɔ:t], **1.** *imperf., p.p. of* **think. 2.** *s.* 1. (*only sing.*) das Denken, Vorstellungsvermögen; 2. Sinnen, Nachdenken, die Überlegung, Erwägung; *give* (*some* or *a*) *– to, spare a – for,* denken an (*Acc.*), Aufmerksamkeit schenken (*Dat.*); *on second –(s), after serious –,* nach ernsthafter Erwägung, bei reiflicher Überlegung; *without –,* ohne zu überlegen; *take –,* sich (*Dat.*) überlegen, mit sich zu Rate gehen; 3. die Denkarbeit, der Denkprozeß; 4. die Denkweise, Gedankenwelt; *modern –,* moderne Gedankenwelt; 5. die Sorge, Rücksicht, Aufmerksamkeit; *no – for others,* keine Rücksicht auf andere; *take – for,* achten auf (*Acc.*), Sorge tragen um; 6. (*also pl.*) der Gedanke, Gedankengang, Einfall; *it never entered my –s, I never gave it a –,* es kam mir nie in den Sinn; *a penny for your –s!* woran denkst du nur? *happy –,* guter Einfall; *lost in –,* in Gedanken vertieft; *quick as –,* blitzschnell; *the – of it frightens me,* der (bloße) Gedanke erschreckt mich; 7. der Plan, die Absicht; *he has no – of going,* er hat nicht die Absicht zu gehen; 8. (*usu. pl.*) der Gedanke, die Meinung, Ansicht; 9. (*coll.*) *a –,* eine Idee *or* Spur, ein wenig, etwas (*with adj.*).

thoughtful ['θɔ:tful], *adj.* 1. gedankenvoll; gedankenreich, gedankenschwer (*as a book*); 2. nachdenklich, beschaulich, besinnlich, bedächtig, in Gedanken versunken; 3. rücksichtsvoll, umsichtig, zuvorkommend; achtsam, bedacht (*of,* auf (*Acc.*)). **thoughtfulness,** *s.* 1. die Nachdenklichkeit, Beschaulichkeit; Gedankentiefe, der Gedankenreichtum; 2. die Rücksichtnahme, Zuvorkommenheit. **thoughtless,** *adj.* 1. gedankenlos; 2. sorglos, unbekümmert (*of,* um); rücksichtslos, unbesonnen, unüberlegt. **thoughtlessness,** *s.* die Gedankenlosigkeit, Unbesonnenheit, Unüberlegtheit, Unbekümmertheit, Sorglosigkeit, Rücksichtslosigkeit.

thought|-reading, *s.* das Gedankenlesen. **--transference,** *s.* die Gedankenübertragung.

thousand ['θauzənd], **1.** *num. adj.* (*a* or *one*) –, tausend; (*fig.*) *a – and one,* zahllos, unzählig; *a – and one things to do,* allerhand zu tun; *– times,* tausendmal. **2.** *s.* das Tausend; *one in a –,* einer unter Tausenden; *ten –,* zehntausend; *in their –s,* zu Tausenden; *hundreds of –s,* hunderttausende; *many –s of,* viele tausend. **thousandfold,** *adj.* tausendfach. **thousandth, 1.** *num. adj.* tausendst. **2.** *s.* 1. der *or* die *or* das Tausendste; 2. (*fraction*) das Tausendstel.

Thrace [θreis], *s.* Thrakien (*n.*).

thraldom ['θrɔ:ldəm], *s.* die Leibeigenschaft, Hörigkeit; (*fig.*) Knechtschaft. **thrall** [θrɔ:l], *s.* Leibeigene(r), Hörige(r); (*fig.*) der Knecht, Sklave; *in –,* in der Gewalt, im Bann (*to, Gen.*).

thrash [θræʃ], **1.** *v.t.* 1. (durch)prügeln, durchhauen, bimsen; (*fig.*) schlagen, besiegen; *– the life out of him,* ihn tüchtig vermöbeln; 2. *– out,* gründlich erörtern (*a problem etc.*). *See also* **thresh. 2.** *v.i.* (*also – about*) hin und her schlagen, um sich schlagen; (*Naut.*) knüppeln. **thrasher (shark),** *s.* (*Ichth.*) der Seefuchs. **thrashing,** *s.* die Dresche, Tracht Prügel; (*fig.*) Niederlage; *give him a –,* ihn tüchtig verdreschen *or* verprügeln.

thread [θred], **1.** *s.* 1. der Faden (*also fig.*); Zwirn, das Garn; (*fig.*) der Zusammenhang; (*fig.*) *gather up the –s,* zusammenfassen; (*fig.*) *resume the – of one's discourse,* den Faden seiner Rede wieder aufnehmen; (*fig.*) *hang by a –,* an einem Faden hängen; 2. (*Tech.*) das (Schrauben)gewinde, der Schraubengang. **2.** *v.t.* 1. einfädeln (*a needle*); aufreihen (*beads*); durchziehen (*with threads*) (*also fig.*); 2. (*fig.*) *– one's way* (*through*), sich winden *or* schlängeln (durch), sich hindurchschlängeln (durch).

threadbare ['θredbɛə], *adj.* 1. fadenscheinig, abgetragen; 2. (*fig.*) dürftig, armselig (*excuses etc.*), abgedroschen, abgenützt (*sayings*). **threadbareness,** *s.* 1. die Fadenscheinigkeit, Schäbigkeit; 2. Dürftigkeit, Armseligkeit; Abgenutztheit, Abgedroschenheit.

threat [θret], *s.* 1. die Drohung (*to, against,* gegen; *of,* mit); 2. Androhung, Bedrohung (*to, Gen.*), Gefahr (für); *under – of,* bei *or* unter Androhung (*Gen.*); *there is a – of snow,* es droht Schnee *or* zu schneien. **threaten** [–n], **1.** *v.t.* 1. *– him,* ihm drohen (*with,* mit), ihm androhen (*Acc.*), ihn bedrohen (mit); 2. (*fig.*) drohend ankündigen (*storm etc.*); 3. gefährden (*safety etc.*). **2.** *v.i.* 1. drohen; 2. (*fig.*) im Anzuge sein, bedrohlich aussehen (*as weather*). **threatening, 1.** *adj.* 1. drohend, Droh–; *– letter,* der Drohbrief; 2. (*fig.*) bedrohlich. **2.** *s.* die Drohung.

three [θri:], **1.** *num. adj.* drei; *for clock-time see under* **eight**; (*coll.*) *– parts finished,* fast *or* beinahe fertig. **2.** *s.* die Drei; *by* or *in –s,* zu dreien.

three|-card trick, *s.* das Kümmelblättchen. **--colour process,** *s.* der Dreifarbendruck. **--cornered,** *adj.* dreieckig; *– hat,* der Dreispitz. **--decker,** *s.* der Dreidecker. **--dimensional,** *adj.* (*also 3-D*) dreidimensional. **–fold,** *adj.* dreiteilig, dreifach. **--foot,** *adj.* drei Fuß lang. **--halfpence,** *s.* (*obs.*) anderthalb Penny. **--handed,** *adj.* dreihändig. **--legged race,** *s.* das Dreibeinwettlaufen. **--master,** *s.* der Dreimaster.

threepence ['θrepəns], *s.* drei Pence. **threepenny** ['θrepəni], *adj.* für drei Pence; drei Pence wert; (*obs.*) *– piece* or *bit,* das Dreipencestück.

three| per cent, *adj.* dreiprozentig. **--phase current,** *s.* der Drehstrom, Dreiphasenstrom. **--phase motor,** *s.* der Drehstrommotor. **--piece,** *adj.* dreiteilig (*suit*). **--pin plug,** *s.* (*Elec.*) dreipoliger Stecker. **--ply,** *adj.* dreischichtig (*wood*), dreifach (*thread*); *– wood,* das Sperrholz. **--point landing,** *s.* (*Av.*) die Dreipunktlandung. **--quarter,** *adj.* dreiviertel; (*Rugby Footb.*) *– backs,* die Dreiviertel-Reihe; *– face,* das Halbprofil; *--length portrait,* das Hüftbild. **–score,** *adj.* sechzig. **--sided,** *adj.* dreiseitig. **–some,** *s.* das Dreierspiel. **--speed gear,** *s.* (*Cycl. etc.*) dreifache Übersetzung. **--storied,** *adj.* dreistöckig. **--way switch,** *s.* der Dreiwegeschalter. **--year-old,** *s.* Dreijährige(r).

threnody ['θri:nədi], *s.* das Klagelied, Trauerlied.
thresh [θreʃ], **1.** *v.t.* dreschen; (*fig.*) – ***out,*** gründlich erörtern (*a problem*); (*fig.*) – ***straw,*** leeres Stroh dreschen. *See also* **thrash. 2.** *v.i.* Korn dreschen. **thresher,** *s.* 1. der Drescher; 2. die Dreschmaschine. **threshing,** *s.* das Dreschen; der Drusch; – ***floor,*** die Tenne.
threshold ['θreʃ(h)ould], *s.* 1. die Schwelle (*also fig. and Psych.*); 2. (*Psych.*) Grenze; 3. (*fig.*) der Anfang (***of,*** *Gen.*), Eingang (zu).
threw [θru:], *imperf. of* **throw.**
thrice [θrais], *adv.* 1. dreimal; 2. (*fig.*) überaus, höchst, sehr.
thrift [θrift], *s.* 1. die Wirtschaftlichkeit, Sparsamkeit; 2. (*Bot.*) Seenelke, Meernelke; Grasnelke. **thriftiness,** *s.* die Wirtschaftlichkeit, Sparsamkeit. **thriftless,** *adj.* verschwenderisch. **thriftlessness,** *s.* die Verschwendung. **thrifty,** *adj.* 1. haushälterisch, sparsam, vorsorglich (***of, with,*** mit); 2. gedeihlich, gedeihend, üppig (wachsend).
thrill [θril], **1.** *s.* 1. der Schauer, das Zittern, (Er)-beben; 2. die Erregung, Erschütterung, das Entzücken; die Sensation, spannendes Erlebnis. **2.** *v.t.* 1. durchlaufen, überlaufen, durchdringen, durchschauern; erbeben *or* erzittern *or* erschauern lassen; 2. begeistern, entzücken, erregen, erschüttern, packen. **3.** *v.i.* 1. erschauern, beben; 2. ergriffen *or* hingerissen *or* erschüttert werden (***with,*** vor (*Dat.*)), durchbebt sein (von). **thriller,** *s.* der Sensationsroman, Schauerroman, Detektivroman, Kriminalroman, Krimi. **thrilling,** *adj.* aufregend, erregend, begeisternd, spannend, packend, hinreißend, sensationell.
thrive [θraiv], *reg. & irr.v.i.* gedeihen (*also fig.*), sich kräftig entwickeln (*as plants*); vorwärtskommen, Glück *or* Erfolg haben; reich werden (*of a p.*); (*fig.*) hochkommen, blühen. **thriving,** *adj.* blühend, gedeihend, emporkommend, gedeihlich; – ***town,*** blühende Stadt; – ***trade,*** gut gehendes Geschäft.
throat [θrout], *s.* 1. die Gurgel, Kehle, der Rachen, Schlund; ***clear one's*** –, sich räuspern; (*coll.*) ***jump down his*** –, ihm an die Gurgel fahren; ***lie in one's*** –, unverschämt lügen; ***sore*** –, Halsschmerzen (*pl.*), der Rachenkatarrh; ***the words stuck in my*** –, die Worte blieben mir im Halse stecken; (*fig.*) ***ram*** or ***thrust it down his*** –, es ihm aufdrängen *or* aufhalsen; 2. der Hals; ***be at one another's –s,*** sich in den Haaren liegen; ***cut one's*** (or ***his***) –, sich (*or* ihm) den Hals abschneiden; (*fig.*) ***cut one's own*** (or ***one another's***) –, sich selbst (*or* einander) zugrunde richten; ***seize*** or ***take him by the*** –, ihn an der Gurgel packen; 3. (*Tech.*) der Eingang, Durchgang, die Öffnung, Gicht, Ausladung; (*Archit.*) Hohlkehle; 4. Zahnlücke (*of a saw*); (*Naut.*) Klau.
throat|-microphone, *s.* das Kehlkopfmikrophon. **--plate,** *s.* (*Sew.-mach.*) die Stichplatte. **throaty,** *adj.* 1. guttural, Kehl–; 2. heiser, rauh (*voice*).
throb [θrɔb], **1.** *s.* das Schlagen, Klopfen, Pochen, Pulsieren; der Pulsschlag (*also fig.*). **2.** *v.i.* schlagen, pochen, klopfen; pulsieren.
throe [θrou], *s.* (*usu. pl.*) Schmerzen (*pl.*); (Geburts)-wehen (*pl.*); (*fig.*) ***in the –s of,*** in der Anstrengung *or* Gärung (*Gen.*); ***death –s,*** der Todeskampf, die Agonie.
thrombosis [θrɔm'bousis], *s.* die Thrombose. **thrombus** ['θrɔmbəs], *s.* der Blutpfropf, das Blutgerinnsel.
throne [θroun], **1.** *s.* der Thron; (*fig.*) königliche Macht; ***come to the*** –, auf den Thron kommen; ***succeed to the*** –, auf den Thron folgen. **2.** *v.t.* auf den Thron setzen. **3.** *v.i.* thronen. **throneless,** *adj.* ohne Thron.
throng [θrɔŋ], **1.** *s.* 1. das Gedränge; der Andrang, Zulauf; 2. die Menschenmenge, Menschenmasse; (*of th.*) Menge, Schar, der Haufen. **2.** *v.i.* sich (zusammen)drängen, sich scharen, herbeiströmen; – ***upon,*** bedrängen, sich aufdrängen (*Dat.*). **3.** *v.t.* bedrängen, umdrängen; sich drängen in (*Dat.*), überschwemmen (*a place*). **thronged** [–d], *adj.* gedrängt voll.
throstle [θrɔstl], *s.* 1. (*Orn.*) *see* **song-thrush**; 2. (*Tech.*) die Spinnmaschine.
throttle [θrɔtl], **1.** *s.* 1. (*coll.*) die Kehle, Luftröhre; 2. (*Tech.*) Drossel(klappe), das Drosselventil; (*Motor.*) ***open the*** –, Gas geben. **2.** *v.t.* 1. (*coll.*) erwürgen, erdrosseln; (*fig.*) unterdrücken, ersticken; 2. (*Tech.*) (*oft.* – ***back,*** – ***down***) (ab)-drosseln (*an engine*).
through [θru:], **1.** *prep.* 1. (*space*) (quer) durch, durch *or* zwischen . . . hindurch; 2. (*time*) während, (*following noun*) lang, hindurch; 3. (*fig.*) (*consequence*) durch, aus, vor, wegen, (*usu. following noun*) zufolge; 4. (*fig.*) (*cause*) durch, mittels(t); 5. (*with many v.i., pref.* ***durch–*** *produces v.t. oft. with meaning of* completely *or* to the end) ***have been*** –, erlebt *or* durchgemacht haben; (*coll.*) ***get*** –, fertig sein mit; bestehen (*an examination*); ***go*** or ***pass*** –, erleben, durchmachen; ***see*** –, durchschauen. **2.** *adv.* 1. (ganz) durch, (mitten) durch (*oft. as pref.* ***durch–*** *with v.t. or v.i.*); (*Tele.*) ***you are*** –, hier ist Ihre Verbindung, der Teilnehmer meldet sich; (*coll.*) ***fall*** –, nicht zustande kommen, ins Wasser fallen; (*fig.*) ***go*** –, angenommen *or* bewilligt werden; ***the whole night*** –, die ganze Nacht hindurch; 2. (*coll.*) völlig, durch und durch; – ***and*** –, durch und durch, ganz und gar; ***wet*** –, völlig durchnäßt; 3. fertig, vollkommen, zu Ende; ***carry*** –, ***go – with,*** ausführen, durchführen, zu Ende bringen; 4. (*coll.*) ***be – with,*** fertig sein mit, hinter sich haben (*a th.*); (*coll.*) ***I am – with him,*** ich bin mit ihm fertig, für mich ist er erledigt; (*coll.*) ***are you –?*** wirst du endlich fertig? **3.** *attrib. adj.* (*Railw.*) – ***coach,*** der Kurswagen; – ***passenger,*** Durchreisende(r), der Passant; – ***ticket,*** direkte *or* durchgehende Fahrkarte; – ***traffic,*** der Durchgangsverkehr; – ***train,*** durchgehender Zug.
throughout [θru:'aut], **1.** *prep.* 1. (*space*) überall in (*Dat.*); 2. (*time*) während, (*following noun*) hindurch. **2.** *adv.* 1. gänzlich, ganz und gar, durch und durch, durchweg, überall, in allen Teilen, durchaus, in jeder Beziehung; 2. die ganze Zeit (hindurch).
throughway ['θru:wei], *s.* (*Am.*) die Durchgangsstraße.
throw [θrou], **1.** *s.* 1. das Werfen, Schleudern; 2. der Wurf (*also wrestling, dice*), die Wurfweite; (*coll.*) ***a stone's*** –, ein Katzensprung; 3. die Hubhöhe, Hublänge, das Hubspiel (*of a piston*), die Kröpfung (*of crankshaft*), der Ausschlag (*needle of measuring instrument*); 4. (*Geol.*) die Sprunghöhe (*of fault*).
2. *irr.v.t.* 1. werfen (*also wrestling, fig.*), schleudern; – ***dice,*** würfeln; 2. zuwerfen (*usu. fig., glance, kiss etc.*) (***to,*** *Dat.*); 3. werfen mit (*stones etc.*); 4. abwerfen (*rider, skin*); verlieren (*horseshoe*); ***be –n from one's horse,*** vom Pferd abgeworfen werden; 5. zwirnen (*silk*); 6. formen, drehen (*pottery*); 7. (*sl.*) mit Absicht verlieren (*a race etc.*); 8. – ***a bridge over,*** eine Brücke schlagen über (*Acc.*); 9. (*coll.*) – ***a fit,*** einen Anfall bekommen *or* erleiden; 10. (*coll.*) – ***a party,*** eine Gesellschaft geben.
(a) (*with adv.*) (*coll.*) – ***one's weight*** **about,** seinen Einfluß geltend machen; – **away,** 1. fortwerfen, wegwerfen; 2. (*fig.*) vergeuden, verschwenden (*time etc.*) (***on,*** an (*Acc.*)), verpassen, in den Wind schlagen (*opportunity*); – **back,** zurückwerfen (*also fig.*); ***be –n back upon,*** angewiesen sein auf (*Acc.*), seine Zuflucht nehmen zu; – **down,** hinwerfen, niederwerfen; umwerfen, umstürzen; – ***down the gauntlet,*** den Fehdehandschuh hinwerfen; – **in,** 1. (hin)einwerfen; – ***in one's hand*** or ***the towel,*** sich geschlagen geben, den Kampf aufgeben; – ***in one's lot with him,*** seine Partei nehmen *or* ergreifen, auf seine Seite treten, sich auf Gedeih und Verderb mit ihm verbinden, das Los mit ihm teilen, mit ihm gemeinsame S. machen; 2. (*fig.*) einwerfen, einflechten, einschieben, einschalten; 3. (*coll.*) (hin)zufügen, gratis (dazu)geben; ***meals –n in,*** Mahlzeiten einbegriffen; – **off,** 1. abwerfen; von sich werfen, loswerden; – ***one's clothes off,*** sich schnell ausziehen; 2. abschütteln (*a p.*); 3. (*fig.*) sich freimachen *or* befreien von; 4. (*Hunt.*)

ablenken; von der Fährte abbringen; (*Typ.*) abziehen; 5. (*coll.*) schnell hinwerfen, von sich geben, aus dem Ärmel schütteln (*a poem etc.*); – *one's clothes* **on,** sich schnell anziehen; – **open,** 1. aufreißen (*door*), eröffnen (*meeting*); 2. ausschreiben (*for competition*), allgemein zugänglich machen (*to*, *Dat.*); – **out,** 1. (hin)auswerfen, hinausschleudern; vertreiben, austreiben; 2. von sich geben, hervorbringen, ausstrahlen, ausbreiten, aussenden (*also troops*), ausstellen (*sentries*), äußern, fallenlassen, zu verstehen geben; – ***out a hint,*** einen Wink geben; 3. verwerfen, ablehnen, abweisen, zurückweisen; 4. (*coll.*) verwirren, aus dem Konzept bringen; 5. (*fig.*) – ***out a feeler,*** auf den Busch klopfen, einen Fühler ausstrecken; – ***out one's chest,*** sich in die Brust werfen; – **over(board),** 1. über Bord werfen, über den Haufen werfen, verwerfen, aufgeben; 2. (*a p.*) im Stich lassen, verlassen; – **together,** zusammenwerfen, zusammenbringen, miteinander in Verbindung bringen; ***be –n together,*** zusammenkommen; – **up,** 1. in die Höhe werfen, hochwerfen; – ***up one's hands,*** die Hände hochheben; 2. aufwerfen, hastig errichten (*defences*); 3. (*coll.*) aufgeben, niederlegen, zurücktreten von (*a post*); 4. – ***up one's food,*** sich übergeben.
(b) (*with prep.*) (*fig.*) – **at** ***his head,*** ihm an den Kopf werfen; (*fig.*) – **in** ***his face*** or ***teeth,*** ihm ins Gesicht schleudern; – **into** ***the bargain,*** (beim Kauf) draufgeben, als Draufgabe hinzufügen; – ***into confusion,*** in Verwirrung versetzen *or* bringen; – ***into prison,*** ins Gefängnis werfen; (*fig.*) – ***into raptures,*** in Entzücken versetzen; – ***into the shade,*** in den Schatten stellen; – ***o.s.*** or ***one's heart and soul into,*** sich (hinein)stürzen *or* versenken in, völlig aufgehen in (*Dat.*); (*coll.*) – ***a spanner in(to) the works,*** querschießen, einen Knüppel zwischen die Beine werfen (*Dat.*); (*Railw.*) ***be –n*** **off** ***the line,*** entgleisen; – ***the blame*** **on** ***him,*** ihm die Schuld in die Schuhe schieben; (*fig.*) – ***light on,*** Licht werfen auf (*Acc.*), aufklären; (*coll.*) – ***cold water on,*** einen Dämpfer aufsetzen (*Dat.*); (*fig.*) – **out of** ***gear,*** stören, aus dem Gleis bringen; ***be –n out of work,*** arbeitslos werden; – ***one's eyes*** **to** ***the ground,*** die Augen niederschlagen; – ***o.s.*** **(up)on,** sich stürzen auf (*Acc.*) (*a th.*); – ***o.s. (up)on one's knees,*** sich auf die Knie werfen; (*fig.*) – ***o.s. (up)on his mercy,*** sich seiner Gnade (an)vertrauen, an seine Gnade appellieren; ***be –n upon o.s.*** or ***one's own resources,*** auf sich selbst angewiesen sein.
3. *irr.v.i.* 1. werfen; würfeln (*with dice*); 2. – ***back,*** zurückkehren (*to*, zu), zurückgreifen (auf (*Acc.*)), nachgeraten (*Dat.*); (*Biol.*) rückarten, Merkmale der Vorfahren aufweisen; 3. – ***up,*** sich übergeben.

throw|away, *adj.* (*coll.*) beiläufig *or* nebenbei hingeworfen *or* eingefügt (*remark etc.*). **–back,** *s.* 1. die Rückkehr (*to*, zu), das Wiederauftreten (*Gen.*), der Atavismus, atavistische Form; 2. (*coll.*) der Rückschlag. **thrower,** *s.* 1. der (die) Werfer(in); 2. (*Tech.*) Seidenzwirner; 3. (*pottery*) Former. **throw-in,** *s.* (*Footb.*) der Einwurf. **throwing,** *s.* das Werfen, Schleudern; (*Spt.*) – ***the hammer,*** das Hammerwerfen; – ***the javelin,*** das Speerwerfen. **thrown, 1.** *p.p. of* **throw. 2.** *adj.* (*Tech.*) gezwirnt; – ***silk,*** der *or* das Organsin, die Kettseide. **throw-out,** *s.* Abgelegte(s), Beschädigte(s). **throwster,** *s.* der Seidenspinner.

[1]**thrum** [θrʌm], **1.** *s.* 1. (*usu. pl.*) der *or* das Trumm, der Saum, die Franse; 2. *pl.* Garnabfälle (*pl.*). **2.** *v.t.* befransen.

[2]**thrum, 1.** *v.i.* klimpern, mit den Fingern trommeln (*on*, auf (*Acc.*)). **2.** *v.t.* klimpern auf (*Dat.*) (*an instrument*), (mit den Fingern) trommeln auf (*Acc.*) (*a table etc.*).

[1]**thrush** [θrʌʃ], *s.* (*Orn.*) die Drossel (*Turdus*); *see* ***song–, mistle–.***

[2]**thrush,** *s.* 1. (*Med.*) der Mundschwamm; 2. (*Vet.*) Hufgrind, die Strahlfäule.

thrust [θrʌst], **1.** *irr.v.t.* 1. stoßen; 2. stecken, schieben (***into***, in (*Acc.*)); – ***s.th. forward,*** etwas vorwärtstreiben *or* –schieben; – ***one's hands into one's pockets,*** die Hände in die Taschen stecken; – ***one's nose into,*** die Nase stecken in (*Acc.*); – ***out one's hand,*** die Hand ausstrecken; 3. drängen, treiben; – ***o.s. forward,*** sich vordrängen; – ***o.s. into,*** eindringen *or* sich drängen in (*Acc.*); – ***aside,*** zur Seite stoßen; – ***home,*** vorantreiben; – ***into prison,*** ins Gefängnis werfen; – ***upon him,*** ihm aufdrängen (*Dat.*). **2.** *irr.v.i.* 1. stoßen (***at***, nach); 2. sich drängen (***at***, gegen). **3.** *s.* 1. der Stoß, Hieb; ***cut and –,*** Hieb und Gegenhieb; (*fig.*) das Hin und Her; ***home –,*** sitzender Hieb; 2. (*Tech.*) der Schub, die Schubkraft; 3. (*Archit.*) der (Seiten)-schub, Druck; 4. (*Mil.*) Vorstoß (***towards***, nach), Angriff (***at***, auf (*Acc.*)). **thrust-bearing,** *s.* das Drucklager. **thruster,** *s.* (*coll.*) der Draufgänger, Streber.

thud [θʌd], **1.** *v.i.* dumpf (auf)schlagen; dröhnen. **2.** *s.* dumpfer Schlag *or* Ton, der Anprall; das Dröhnen (*of engines, hoofs etc.*).

thug [θʌg], *s.* 1. der Raubmörder; 2. (*coll.*) Rowdy, Rohling.

thumb [θʌm], **1.** *s.* der Daumen; ***rule of –,*** die Faustregel, Überschlagsrechnung; ***by rule of –,*** erfahrungsmäßig, auf praktischem Wege, über den Daumen gepeilt; ***under her –,*** unter ihrer Fuchtel, in ihrer Gewalt; (*coll.*) ***his fingers are all –s,*** er hat zwei linke Hände. **2.** *v.t.* 1. abgreifen, beschmutzen (*book etc.*); ***well–-d,*** abgegriffen; 2. (*coll.*) – ***a lift,*** per Anhalter fahren, sich mitnehmen lassen; – ***a vehicle,*** einen vorbeifahrenden Wagen anhalten.

thumb|mark, *s.* der Daumenabdruck. **–nail,** *s.* der Daumennagel; – ***sketch,*** rasch *or* nur in Umrissen angefertigte Zeichnung *or* (*fig.*) Schilderung. **–nut,** *s.* (*Am.*) die Flügelmutter. **–print,** *s.* der Daumenabdruck. **–screw,** *s.* 1. (*Hist.*) die Daumenschraube; 2. (*Tech.*) Flügelschraube. **–stall,** *s.* der Däumling. **–tack,** *s.* (*Am.*) die Heftzwecke, der Reißnagel.

thump [θʌmp], **1.** *s.* 1. dumpfer Schlag, das Bumsen, der Bums; 2. Puff, Knuff. **2.** *v.t.* 1. schlagen *or* plumpsen auf (*Acc.*) *or* gegen; 2. puffen, knuffen. **3.** *v.i.* 1. (auf)schlagen, bumsen, plumpsen (***on***, auf (*Acc.*); ***against,*** gegen); 2. (heftig) klopfen, pochen (*as the heart*). **thumper,** *s.* (*coll.*) 1. (eine) Wucht; 2. faustdicke Lüge. **thumping,** *adj.* (*coll.*) (*also* – ***great***) riesig, gewaltig, ungeheuer, enorm, wuchtig, Mords–; faustdick (*lie*).

thunder [ˈθʌndə], **1.** *s.* der Donner; (*fig.*) das Brausen, Getöse; ***clap*** or ***peal of –,*** der Donnerschlag; – ***of applause,*** tosender *or* brausender Beifall; (*coll.*) ***steal his –,*** ihm den Wind aus den Segeln nehmen, ihm die Trümpfe aus der Hand nehmen. **2.** *v.i.* donnern (*also fig.*); (*fig.*) brausen, tosen; wettern, brüllen (*of a p.*). **3.** *v.t.* (*also* – ***forth,*** – ***out***) herausdonnern, brüllen.

thunder|bolt, *s.* 1. (*Geol., Myth.*) der Donnerkeil; 2. Blitzstrahl, (*fig.*) Strahl, die Geißel, plötzlicher Schlag. **–clap,** *s.* der Donnerschlag. **–cloud,** *s.* die Gewitterwolke.

thundering [ˈθʌndəriŋ], *adj.* 1. donnernd, tosend, brausend; 2. (*sl.*) *see* **thumping. thunderous,** *adj.* donnernd; (*fig.*) donnerartig, brausend, tosend.

thunder|-shower, *s.* der Gewitterregen. **–storm,** *s.* das Gewitter. **–struck,** *adj.* (*fig.*) wie vom Donner gerührt; wie (vom Blitz) erschlagen. **thundery,** *adj.* gewitterhaft, gewitterschwül.

thurible [ˈθjuəribl], *s.* das Weihrauchfaß. **thurifer** [–ifə], *s.* der Rauchfaßträger. **thurification** [–fiˈkeiʃən], *s.* die Räucherung, das Räuchern.

Thuringia [θuˈrindʒiə], *s.* Thüringen (*n.*). **Thuringian, 1.** *adj.* thüringisch. **2.** *s.* der (die) Thüringer(in).

Thursday [ˈθə:zdi], *s.* der Donnerstag; ***Holy –,*** der Himmelfahrtstag; ***Maundy –,*** der Gründonnerstag; ***on –,*** am Donnerstag; ***on –s,*** donnerstags.

thus [ðʌs], *adv.* so, auf die(se) Art *or* Weise, folgendermaßen, wie folgt; demgemäß, dementsprechend, daher, folglich; – ***far,*** soweit; bis jetzt; – ***much,*** so viel.

thwack [θwæk], **1.** *v.t.* schlagen, prügeln, verbleuen, durchwalken. **2.** *s.* der Puff, Schlag.

thwart [θwɔːt], **1.** *v.t.* durchkreuzen, vereiteln (*a plan etc.*); einen Strich durch die Rechnung machen (*Dat.*), in die Quere kommen (*Dat.*), entgegenarbeiten (*Dat.*) (*a p.*). **2.** *s.* (*Naut.*) die Ruderbank, Ducht. **3.** *adj.* (*obs.*) querliegend, schräg. **4.** *prep.* (*obs.*) quer (durch *or* über (*Acc.*)).

thy [ðai], *poss. adj.* (*Poet., B.*) dein(e).

thyme [taim], *s.* (*Bot.*) der Thymian.

thymus [ˈθaiməs], *s.* die Thymusdrüse.

thyroid [ˈθairɔid], *adj.* Schilddrüsen–; – ***gland,*** die Schilddrüse.

thyrsus [ˈθəːsəs], *s.* der Thyrsus, Bacchantenstab.

thyself [ðaiˈself], *pron.* (*Poet., B.*) (*Nom.*) du selbst; (*Acc.*) dich, (dich) selbst; (*Dat.*) dir, (dir) selbst.

tiara [tiˈɑːrə], *s.* 1. die Tiara; (*fig.*) päpstliche Würde; 2. der Stirnreif.

Tibetan [tiˈbetn], **1.** *s.* der (die) Tibeter(in). **2.** *adj.* tibetisch.

tibia [ˈtibiə], *s.* (*pl.* **-e** [–iiː], **-s**) das Schienbein. **tibial,** *adj.* Schienbein–, Unterschenkel–.

tic [tik], *s.* das Gesichtszucken.

[1]**tick** [tik], *s.* (*Ent.*) die Zecke.

[2]**tick,** *s.* der Kissenbezug, Überzug, das (Daunen)-inlett.

[3]**tick,** *s.* (*sl.*) der Pump, Borg, Kredit; ***on –,*** auf Pump.

[4]**tick, 1.** *s.* 1. das Ticken; (*coll.*) ***on*** or ***to the –,*** pünktlich, auf den Glockenschlag; 2. (*coll.*) der Augenblick, Moment; (*coll.*) ***in two –s,*** im Augenblick; 3. das Häkchen, Vermerkzeichen. **2.** *v.i.* ticken (*as a clock*); (*sl.*) ***what makes him –?*** was treibt ihn? (*coll.*) – ***along,*** gerade existieren, nur haperig funktionieren; – ***over,*** leer laufen (*of an engine*). **3.** *v.t.* 1. (*also* – ***off***) abhaken, anzeichnen, anstreichen; 2. – ***away,*** verticken (*the hours etc.*); 3. (*sl.*) – ***off,*** anschnauzen, herunterputzen.

ticker [tikə], *s.* 1. der Börsentelegraph; – ***tape,*** der Papierstreifen (des Börsentelegraphen); 2. (*coll.*) die Uhr; 3. (*coll.*) das Herz.

ticket [ˈtikit], **1.** *s.* 1. der Zettel, das Schildchen, Etikett (*Swiss* die Etikette) (*for labelling*); ***price –,*** der Preiszettel; 2. die Fahrkarte, der Fahrschein (*for travelling*); Gepäcksschein; Pfandschein; die (Eintritts)karte, das Billet (*for admission*); ***lottery –,*** das (Lotterie)los; ***season –,*** die Abonnementskarte; 3. (*Motor. coll.*) der Strafzettel; 4. (*Naut., Av. coll.*) Führerschein, die Lizenz; 5. (*Am. Pol.*) Kandidatenliste, Wahlliste; das Partei– *or* Wahlprogramm; 6. (*sl.*) das Richtige. **2.** *v.t.* etikettieren, auszeichnen, beschriften (*goods*).

ticket|-agent, *s.* die Vorverkaufsstelle (*theatre etc.*), das Reisebüro (*travelling*). **--clerk,** *s.* Schalterbeamte(r). **--collector,** *s.* der (Bahnsteig)-schaffner. **--inspector,** *s.* der (Fahrkarten)-kontrolleur. **--office,** *s.* die Fahrkartenausgabe, der Schalter. **--of-leave,** *s.* ***be on –,*** unter Polizeiaufsicht stehen; auf Bewährung entlassen werden; – ***man,*** auf Bewährung entlassener Sträfling. **--punch,** *s.* die Lochzange. **--window,** *s.* (*Am.*) *see* **--office.**

ticking [ˈtikiŋ], *s.* der Drell, Drillich; *see* [2]**tick.**

ticking-off, *s.* (*coll.*) der Wischer, Ausputzer; *see* [4]**tick, 3,** 3.

tickle [tikl], **1.** *v.t.* 1. kitzeln (*also fig.*); (*fig.*) reizen, angenehm *or* freudig erregen, schmeicheln (*Dat.*); – ***his nose,*** ihn an der Nase kitzeln; – ***the palate,*** den Gaumen kitzeln; 2. (*coll.*) amüsieren, belustigen; (*coll.*) ***–d pink*** or ***to death,*** ganz weg vor Freude. **2.** *v.i.* 1. kitzeln; ***the blanket –s,*** die Wolldecke kitzelt; 2. jucken; ***my nose –s,*** es juckt mich an der Nase, meine Nase juckt. **3.** *s.* das Kitzeln; Jucken; der Juckreiz, Kitzel (*also fig.*). **tickler,** *s.* 1. (*coll.*) kitzlige Frage, schwieriges Problem; 2. (*Am. coll.*) das Notizbuch. **ticklish,** *adj.* 1. kitz(e)lig (*also fig.*); 2. heikel, schwierig. **ticklishness,** *s.* die Kitz(e)ligkeit.

tick|-tack, *s.* (*sl.*) der Buchmachergehilfe. **--tock,** *s.* 1. (*coll.*) das Ticken, Ticktack; 2. (*nursery talk*) die Tick(e)tack(e).

tidal [ˈtaidl], *adj.* Flut–; Gezeiten–; – ***basin,*** das Tidebecken; – ***chart,*** die Gezeitentabelle; – ***harbour,*** der Fluthafen; – ***inlet,*** der Priel; – ***range,*** der Gezeitenhub, Tidenhub; – ***river,*** von Ebbe und Flut abhängiger Fluß; – ***stream,*** der Gezeitenstrom; – ***wave,*** die Sturmflut, Flutwelle; (*fig.*) Woge.

tiddler [ˈtidlə], *s.* (*Ichth. coll.*) der Stichling.

tiddl(e)y [ˈtidli], **1.** *adj.* (*sl.*) beschwipst, beduselt, angeheitert, im Tran. **2.** *s.* (*sl.*) das Gesöff.

tiddlywinks [ˈtidliwiŋks], *s.* das Flohhüpfspiel.

tide [taid], **1.** *s.* 1. die (Ebbe und) Flut, Tide, Tiden (*pl.*), Gezeiten (*pl.*); ***the – is going out,*** die Flut fällt; ***the – is coming in,*** die Flut steigt; ***ebb –,*** die Ebbe; ***flood –,*** see ***high –;*** ***high –,*** die Flut; Fluthöhe, höchster Flutstand, das Hochwasser; (*fig.*) der Höhepunkt; ***the – is in,*** es ist Flut; ***low –,*** die Ebbe, niedrigster Flutstand, das Niedrigwasser; ***neap –,*** die Nippflut; ***the – is out,*** es ist Ebbe; ***spring –,*** die Springflut; ***turn of the –,*** der Gezeitenwechsel; (*fig.*) die Wendung, der Umschwung, Glückswechsel; (*fig.*) ***the – turns,*** das Blatt *or* Glück wendet sich; 2. (*fig.*) der Lauf, Strom; – ***of events,*** die Zeitströmung; (*fig.*) ***swim with the –,*** mit dem Strom schwimmen; 3. (*obs. except in compounds*) die Zeit; ***Christmas–,*** die Weihnachtszeit; ***even–,*** die Abendzeit; ***spring–,*** die Frühlingszeit. **2.** *v.i.* 1. (mit dem Strom) treiben; 2. (*fig.*) – ***over,*** hinwegkommen über (*Acc.*), durchstehen, überstehen, überwinden; (*esp. financially*) sich über Wasser halten, über die Runden kommen. **3.** *v.t.* – ***over,*** hinweghelfen (*Dat.*) *or* hinwegbringen über (*Acc.*), (*esp. financially*) über Wasser halten, unter die Arme greifen (*Dat.*), über die Runden bringen.

tide|-borne, *adj. See* **--rode. --gate,** *s.* das Fluttor, Flutgatter. **--gauge,** *s. See* **--mark,** 1. **–land,** *s.* das Watt(enmeer). **--mark,** *s.* 1. der Gezeitenpegel; 2. die Hochwasserlinie; 3. (*fig. sl.*) der Dreckrand, Speckrand (*on bath, boy's neck etc.*). **--rode,** *adj.* stromgerecht (*of ship at anchor*). **--tables,** *pl.* die Gezeitentafel. **–water,** *s.* das Gezeitenwasser, Flutwasser. **–way,** *s.* der Priel.

tidiness [ˈtaidinis], *s.* die Ordnung; Sauberkeit, Nettigkeit.

tiding [ˈtaidiŋ], *s.* (*usu. pl.*) die Nachricht, Mitteilung, Botschaft.

tidy [ˈtaidi], **1.** *adj.* 1. ordentlich, geordnet, reinlich, sauber; 2. nett, niedlich, (*coll.*) (ganz) ordentlich, beträchtlich. **2.** *s.* 1. das Zierdeckchen, Schutzdeckchen (*for furniture*); 2. Behälter, Arbeitsbeutel. **3.** *v.t.* herrichten, zurechtmachen, in Ordnung bringen, Ordnung bringen in (*Acc.*), ordnen, richten; (*also* – ***up***) aufräumen. **4.** *v.i.* aufräumen, Ordnung schaffen.

tie [tai], **1.** *s.* 1. der Schlips, die Krawatte, Schleife, Binde (*for the neck*); 2. (*Tech., Archit.*) Befestigung, Klammer, das Verbindungsstück, Bindestück; (*Archit.*) der Anker; 3. (*esp. Am.*) die Schwelle; 4. (*Mus.*) Bindung, Ligatur, der Haltebogen; 5. das Schnürband, (*Naut.*) Beschlagzeising; 6. (*fig.*) Band; (*coll.*) die Verpflichtung, (lästige) Fessel, (große) Last; 7. (*Spt. etc.*) unentschiedenes Spiel, das Unentschieden; der Gleichstand, die Punktgleichheit, (*Parl. etc.*) Stimmgleichheit; 8. (*Spt*) das Ausscheidungsspiel. **2.** *v.t.* 1. anbinden, festbinden, befestigen (***to,*** an (*Acc.*)); binden, zuschnüren; (zusammen)knoten (*cord etc.*); (*Med.*) unterbinden (*artery*); – ***in a bow,*** zu einer Schleife binden; (*fig.*) ***my hands were –d,*** mir waren die Hände gebunden; – ***a knot,*** einen Knoten machen; – ***one's tie,*** den Schlips binden; – ***down,*** festbinden, fesseln; ***be –d to one's mother's apron-strings,*** an Mutters Schürzenzipfel hängen; – ***up,*** zusammenbinden; verschnüren, einschnüren, einbinden (*a parcel etc.*); befestigen, festbinden, anbinden (***to,*** an (*Acc.*)); verbinden (*a wound*); (*Naut.*) vertäuen; (*coll.*) ***get o.s. –d up in knots,*** sich verheddern; 2. (*Tech., Build.*) festmachen, verankern; 3. (*Mus.*) aneinanderbinden (*notes*); 4. (*fig.*) verknüpfen, zusammenfügen, verbinden; – ***in,*** einbauen (***with,*** in (*Acc.*)); 5. (*fig.*) verpflichten (*to*, zu), binden (an (*Acc.*)); – ***down,*** festlegen (*to*, auf (*Acc.*)), binden (an (*Acc.*)), verpflichten (zu); (*Law*) – ***up,*** festlegen (*money*), einer Verfügungsbeschränkung unterwerfen (*an estate*); ***be –d for time,*** sehr beschäftigt sein; (*coll.*) ***be –d up,*** vergeben *or* nicht abkömmlich sein. **3.** *v.i.* 1. (*Spt.*) gleichstehen, punktgleich sein; 2. (*Naut.*) – ***up,*** festmachen, sich vermuren, das Schiff vertäuen; 3. (*fig.*) – ***in with,*** übereinstimmen mit; (*fig.*) – ***up with,*** sich verbinden *or* eine Verbindung eingehen mit.

tie|-bar, *s.* (*Tech.*) die Verbindungsstange; (*Typ.*) der Bogen. **--beam,** *s.* (*Archit.*) der Ankerbalken, Spannbalken, Zugbalken, Zugträger.

tied [taid], *adj.* gebunden, gefesselt; – ***house,*** das Wirtshaus im Besitz einer Brauerei.

tie|-in, *s.* 1. (*coll.*) der Zusammenhang; 2. (*Comm.*) die Kopplung. **--on,** *attrib. adj.* zum Festmachen *or* Anbinden, Anhänge–. **-pin,** *s.* die Krawattennadel.

¹tier ['taiə], *s.* 1. der Binder; das Band; 2. (*Am.*) die (Kinder)schürze, der Schürzenlatz, das Lätzchen.

²tier [tiə], *s.* die Reihe, Lage, Linie, Schicht; (*Theat.*) Sitzreihe, der Rang; ***in –s,*** reihenweise *or* schichtenweise *or* in Reihen übereinander (angeordnet).

tierce ['tiəs], *s.* (*Eccl., Fenc., Cards*) die Terz.

tiercel [tə:sl], *s.* das Falkenmännchen.

tie-rod, *s.* (*Tech.*) die Kuppelstange.

tiers état [tjɛərzei'tɑ:], *s.* dritter Stand, das Bürgertum.

tie|-up, *s.* 1. (*coll.*) die Verbindung; 2. das Kartell, die Vereinigung; 3. (*Am.*) Arbeitseinstellung, (*esp.*) der Eisenbahnerstreik, die Lahmlegung des Verkehrs. **--wig,** *s.* die Knotenperücke.

¹tiff [tif], *s.* (*coll.*) die Mißstimmigkeit, Reiberei, Kabbelei, das Theater, der Krach, Stank, Stunk.

²tiff, *s.* (*obs.*) der Schluck.

tiffin ['tifin], *s.* das Gabelfrühstück (*in India*).

tig [tig], *s. See* **²tag.**

tige [ti:ʒ], *s.* 1. (*Archit.*) der (Säulen)schaft; 2. (*Bot.*) Stamm, Stengel, Stiel.

tiger ['taigə], *s.* 1. der Tiger; (*fig.*) das Untier, der Wüterich; ***American –,*** der Jaguar; 2. (*obs.*) (Livree)bediente(r); 3. (*Am.*) letzter Hochruf, der Schlußtusch. **tiger-cat,** *s.* die Wildkatze. **tigerish,** *adj.* tigerisch; (*fig.*) grausam, blutdürstig.

tight [tait], **1.** *adj.* 1. dicht, abgedichtet, undurchlässig; 2. fest(sitzend); (an)gespannt, straff, stramm, prall; ***keep a – rein on,*** fest an die Kandare nehmen; 3. knapp, (zu) eng *or* klein, enganliegend (*as clothes*); ***–fit,*** knapper *or* enganliegender Sitz, (*Tech.*) die Feinpassung; – ***squeeze,*** dichtes Gedränge; 4. (*fig.*) schwierig, heikel, bedenklich, kritisch; – ***corner*** or ***squeeze,*** die Klemme; 5. knapp (*as money*); ***he is – for money,*** ihm ist das Geld knapp; 6. *See* **tight-fisted**; ***he is – with money,*** er ist mit dem Geld knickerig; 7. (*sl.*) besoffen, (sternhagel)voll, blau. **2.** *adv.* ***hold –!*** festhalten! ***sit –,*** sitzenbleiben, sich nicht rühren.

tighten [taitn], **1.** *v.t.* festziehen, spannen; (fest) anziehen, fester machen, festigen, straff *or* enger machen; zusammenziehen, verengen; (*fig.*) – ***one's belt,*** sich (*Dat.*) den Gürtel enger schnallen; (*fig.*) ***make him – his belt,*** ihm den Brotkorb höher hängen; – ***the screw,*** die Schraube anziehen. **2.** *v.i.* sich (fest) zusammenziehen; straff *or* enger werden, sich straffen *or* versteifen.

tight|-fisted, *adj.* geizig, knauserig, knickerig. **--fitting,** *adj.* knapp, enganliegend; (*Tech.*) Paß–, genau eingepaßt. **--laced,** *adj.* 1. fest geschnürt; 2. (*fig.*) engherzig, pedantisch. **--lipped,** *adj.* verkniffen (*smile*); (*fig.*) (*of a p.*) verschlossen, wortkarg.

tightness ['taitnis], *s.* 1. die Dichtheit, Dichtigkeit; 2. Straffheit; Enge, Dichte; 3. (*fig.*) (Geld)knappheit; 4. (*sl.*) Knickerei, Knick(e)rigkeit, der Geiz. **tightrope** ['taitroup], *s.* das Drahtseil; – ***walker,*** der (die) Seiltänzer(in).

tights [taits], *pl.* der Trikotanzug, das Trikot (*of dancers*), die Strumpfhose (*women's wear*).

tightwad ['taitwɔd], *s.* (*Am.*) *see* **miser.**

tigress ['taigris], *s.* die Tigerin.

tike [taik], *s.* der Lümmel, Grobian.

tilbury ['tilbəri], *s.* zweirädriger Wagen.

tilde ['tildə], *s.* die Tilde, das Wiederholungszeichen.

tile [tail], **1.** *s.* 1. der (Dach)ziegel; die Fliese; (Ofen)kachel; ***Dutch –,*** Delfter Kachel; ***floor –,*** die Fußbodenfliese; (*sl.*) ***have a – loose,*** einen Klaps *or* Fimmel *or* Rappel haben, bematscht *or* plemplem sein; (*sl.*) ***be (out) on the –s,*** sumpfen; 2. (*sl.*) der Zylinder(hut), die Angströhre. **2.** *v.t.* mit Ziegeln decken (*a roof*), mit Fliesen *or* Kacheln auslegen (*a wall or floor*); ***–d floor,*** der Fliesenfußboden; ***–d roof,*** das Ziegeldach. **tiler,** *s.* der Ziegeldecker. **tileworks,** *s.* die Ziegelfabrik, Ziegelbrennerei, Ziegelei.

tiliaceous [tili'eiʃəs], *adj.* (*Bot.*) Linden–.

tiling ['tailiŋ], *s.* 1. das Dachdecken; Fliesen– *or* Kachellegen; 2. (*collect.*) die Ziegelbedachung; Fliesen, Kacheln (*pl.*).

¹till [til], **1.** *prep.* bis (in (*Acc.*) *or* zu); ***not . . . –,*** erst; – ***now,*** bis jetzt, bisher; – ***then,*** bis dahin *or* nachher. **2.** *conj.* bis; ***not . . . –,*** erst wenn *or* als; ***to be left – called for,*** postlagernd; (*coll.*) – ***the cows come home,*** bis in alle Ewigkeit, ewig und drei Tage, jahraus jahrein, für Zeit und Ewigkeit.

²till, *s.* die Ladenkasse, Schalterkasse; Geldkassette, das Geldfach.

³till, *v.t.* bebauen, bestellen, bearbeiten, pflügen, (be)ackern; – ***the soil,*** Ackerbau treiben. **tillage** ['tilidʒ], *s.* der Ackerbau, Feldbau, die Bodenbestellung; das Ackerland, bestelltes Land; ***in –,*** bebaut.

¹tiller ['tilə], *s.* der Ackersmann, Pflüger; – ***of the soil,*** der Ackerbauer.

²tiller, *s.* die Ruderpinne.

³tiller, *s.* der Schößling, Wurzelsproß.

¹tilt [tilt], **1.** *s.* die Plane, (Wagen)decke, das Verdeck (*on carts*), Zeltdach, Sonnendach (*on stalls*). **2.** *v.t.* überdecken, bedecken.

²tilt, **1.** *s.* die Neigung, Schräglage, Schrägstellung; ***on a*** or ***the –,*** in schiefer *or* schräger Lage. **2.** *v.t.* neigen, kippen, schief *or* schräg stellen *or* legen; – ***up*** or ***over,*** umkippen. **3.** *v.i.* sich neigen, kippen; – ***up*** or ***over,*** umkippen, umfallen, überkippen.

³tilt, **1.** *s.* (*Hist.*) das Lanzenstechen, (Ritter)turnier; (*coll.*) ***(at) full –,*** mit voller Wucht, mit aller Gewalt. **2.** *v.i.* im Turnier kämpfen, turnieren; – ***at,*** stechen *or* stoßen nach; (*fig.*) kämpfen gegen, anstürmen; – ***at windmills,*** gegen eingebildete Feinde kämpfen.

⁴tilt, *v.t.* (*obs.*) (mit dem Schwanzhammer *or* Stielhammer) schmieden.

tilt-cart, *s.* der Sturzkarren, Kippkarren.

tilth [tilθ], *s.* (*Agr.*) 1. die Oberflächenerde; 2. (*obs.*) Ackerbestellung; bestelltes Land; ***in good –,*** gut bestellt.

tilt-hammer, *s.* (*obs.*) der Schwanzhammer, Stielhammer.

tilting ['tiltiŋ], **1.** *s.* (*Hist.*) das Turnier. **2.** *attrib. adj.* Turnier–.

tilt|-mill, *s.* (*obs.*) das Hammerwerk, die Hammerschmiede. **--yard,** *s.* der Turnierplatz.

timbal [timbl], *s.* (*Hist.*) die (Kessel)pauke.

timber ['timbə], **1.** *s.* das Bauholz, Nutzholz; (*also* ***standing –***) Holz auf dem Stamm; (*Naut.*) der Spant, das Inholz; *pl.* Rippenwerk, Gerippe, Balken (*pl.*), (*Naut.*) das Spantenwerk. **2.** *attrib. adj.* Holz–. **timbered** [–d], *adj.* bewaldet (*ground*), (aus)gezimmert (*building etc.*). **timber-hitch,** *s.* (*Naut.*) der Balkenstek, Zimmermannstek. **timbering,** *s.* 1. die Holzverkleidung, (Ver)zimmerung, Verschalung; 2. das Bauholz, Zimmerholz. **timber|-line,** *s.* die Baumgrenze. **--merchant,** der Holzhändler. **--trade,** *s.* der Holzhandel. **-work,** *s.* das Zimmerwerk, Balkengerüst, Gebälk. **-yard,** *s.* der Zimmerhof, Zimmerplatz.

timbre ['tæmbə, tɛ̃br], *s.* die Klangfarbe.

timbrel ['timbrəl], *s.* die Schellentrommel, das Tamburin.

time [taim], **1.** *s.*
1. die Zeit; *– of day,* die Tageszeit; (*coll.*) *pass the – of day with,* grüßen; *– of life,* das Alter; *ravages of –,* der Zahn der Zeit; *stand the test of –,* sich bewähren, Bestand haben; *astronomical –,* die Sternzeit; *the correct* or *right –,* die genaue *or* richtige Zeit; *have a good –,* sich gut unterhalten; *have a good –!* viel Vergnügen! *have a bad* or *hard – (of it),* Schlimmes durchmachen müssen; *– past, present and to come,* Vergangenheit, Gegenwart und Zukunft; *solar –,* wahre Sonnenzeit; *standard –,* die Ortszeit; *what –?* um welche Zeit? wann? *what is the –? what – is it?* wieviel Uhr ist es? wie spät ist es? *gain –,* vorgehen (*as clock*); *keep (good) –,* richtiggehen (*as clock*); *lose –,* nachgehen (*as clock*); (*coll.*) *what do you make the –?* see *what is the –?* (*Spt.*) *play for –,* auf Zeit spielen; *spend –,* Zeit verbringen; *– will show* or *tell,* die Zeit wird's lehren; *– will tell in our favour,* die Zeit arbeitet für uns; *tell me the –,* see *what is the –? waste –,* Zeit vergeuden; *watch the –,* auf die Uhr achten; *against –,* gegen die Uhr, mit größter Eile; *in –,* rechtzeitig (*to do,* um zu tun), zur rechten Zeit; mit der Zeit; *in – to come,* in Zukunft; *in good –,* (gerade) rechtzeitig; *all in good –,* alles zu seiner Zeit; *in the nick of –,* im richtigen Augenblick, gerade zur rechten Zeit; *with –,* mit der Zeit; *to –,* rechtzeitig, pünktlich;
2. der Zeitpunkt; *– of arrival,* die Ankunftszeit; (*fig.*) *at this – of day,* in diesem späten Stadium; *– of departure,* die Abfahrtszeit; *–s of the trains,* Abfahrts- und Ankunftszeiten der Züge; *some – about,* etwa um; *this – yesterday,* gestern um diese Zeit; *this – twelve months,* heute übers Jahr; *the – is drawing near,* die Zeit wird bald kommen; *at –s,* dann und wann, gelegentlich; *at any –,* jemals, zu irgendeiner Zeit; zu jeder (beliebigen) Zeit; *at all –s,* stets, jederzeit, zu jeder Zeit; *at no –,* nie(mals); *at one –,* seinerzeit, einst, früher (einmal); *at one – or another,* zu verschiedenen Zeiten, gelegentlich, im Lauf der Zeit; *at the present –,* derzeit, gegenwärtig; *at the same –,* zur selben Zeit, zu gleicher Zeit, gleichzeitig; zugleich, ebenfalls, jedoch; *at some – or other,* irgendeinmal, irgendwann; *at such –s,* bei solchen Gelegenheiten; *at the* or *that –,* zu der Zeit, damals; seinerzeit; *at this –,* zu der *or* dieser Zeit; *not before –,* erst im letzten Augenblick, erst als es beinahe zu spät war; *be behind –,* zu spät sein, Verspätung haben; *between –s,* in der Zwischenzeit; *by that* or *this –,* unterdessen, inzwischen, bis dahin; *for that –,* für damals; *for the – being,* vorläufig, vorderhand, für jetzt, für den Augenblick, unter den gegenwärtigen Umständen; *from – to –,* von Zeit zu Zeit, dann und wann, gelegentlich; *near one's –,* der Entbindung nahe (*of pregnant woman*); *on –,* rechtzeitig, pünktlich; *till such – as,* so lange als, bis; *up to the present* or *this –,* bis jetzt; *up to that –,* bis dann *or* dahin;
3. der Zeitabschnitt, die Zeitdauer; Arbeitszeit; (*Comm.*) Frist; *– of delivery,* die Lieferzeit; *length of –,* die Zeitdauer; *in the course* or *length of –,* auf die Dauer; (*coll.*) *have the – of one's life,* sich glänzend amüsieren; (*Phys.*) *– of oscillation,* die Schwingungsdauer; *a work of –,* zeitraubende Arbeit; *all the* or *that –,* die ganze Zeit (hindurch); *broken –,* der Verlust an Arbeitszeit und Stundenlohn; *– enough,* früh *or* Zeit genug; *little –,* wenig Zeit; *a little –,* etwas *or* ein wenig Zeit; *not for a long –,* noch lange nicht; *take a long –,* viel Zeit *or* lange brauchen; *most of the –,* die meiste Zeit; *have no –,* keine Zeit haben; *have no – for,* nichts übrig haben für; *some – longer,* noch einige Zeit; *he had a thin –,* es ging ihm dreckig; *the – is past* or *up,* die Zeit ist abgelaufen *or* um; (*sl.*) *do –,* Knast schieben; *you must give me –,* du mußt mir Zeit lassen; *have – on one's hands,* viel Zeit haben, nichts zu tun haben; *kill –,* die Zeit totschlagen; *there is no – to lose,* es eilt, es ist keine Zeit zu verlieren; *serve one's –,* amtieren (*in office*), seine Strafe verbüßen (*in prison*), (*Mil.*) seine Zeit abdienen; *take –,* sich (*Dat.*) die Zeit nehmen (*to do,* zu tun); *take one's –,* sich (*Dat.*) Zeit nehmen *or* lassen; *after –,* nach Arbeitsschluß; *after a –,* nach etlicher Zeit; *for a* or *some –,* eine Zeitlang, einige Zeit; *for a long – past,* seit langer Zeit, schon seit langem; *be pressed for –,* es eilig haben; *all in good –,* alles zu seiner Zeit; *in your own (good) –,* wenn es dir paßt; *in no –,* im Handumdrehen, im Nu; *be out of one's –,* ausgedient *or* ausgelernt haben;
4. das Zeitalter, Zeiten (*pl.*), die Epoche, Ära; *– out of mind,* seit *or* vor undenklichen Zeiten; *for all –,* für alle Zeiten; *– was when . . .,* es gab eine Zeit in der . . ., die Zeit ist vorüber als . . .; *it will last my –,* es wird dauern solange ich lebe; *ahead of one's –,* seiner Zeit voraus; *before one's –,* vor der Zeit, zu früh; *from – immemorial,* seit un(vor)denklichen Zeiten; *in the – of,* zur Zeit (*Gen.*); *in Goethe's –, in the – of Goethe,* zu Goethes Lebzeiten; *in –s of old, in olden –s,* in alten Zeiten; *once upon a –,* vor Zeiten, einst(mals), einmal;
5. (passende) Gelegenheit; *it is high –,* es ist höchste Zeit; *now is the –,* jetzt ist die passende Gelegenheit; *there is a – for everything,* alles zu seiner Zeit, alles hat seine Zeit; *the – was not yet,* die Zeit war noch nicht gekommen; *bide one's –,* seine Zeit abwarten; *the – is* or *has come,* es ist an der Zeit; *take – by the forelock,* die Gelegenheit beim Schopfe fassen; *watch one's –,* den günstigen Augenblick abpassen;
6. (*Mus.*) der Takt, das Tempo, Zeitmaß; *dance –,* das Tanztempo; (*Mil.*) *quick –,* der Geschwindschritt; *slow –,* langsames Tempo; *beat –,* Takt schlagen; *keep –,* Takt halten; *mark –,* (*Mil.*) auf der Stelle treten; (*fig.*) nicht vom Fleck kommen; abwarten; *in –,* im Takt; *out of –,* nicht im Takt;
7. das Mal; *– and again, – after –,* wiederholt, immer wieder; *at a –,* zusammen, auf einmal, jeweils; *each* or *every –,* jedesmal; *for the last –,* zum letzten Mal; *many a –,* manches Mal; *many –s,* oft, häufig; *the next –,* das nächste Mal; *some other –,* ein anderes Mal; *one at a –,* jeder für sich; einzeln; *two at a –,* paarweise, zu zweit; *for the first –,* zum ersten Male; *for this –,* für diesmal; *–s without number,* unzählige Male;
8. *pl.* (*Math.*) mal, -mal; *12 –s as many* or *as much as,* 12mal soviel wie; *12 –s the size of,* 12mal so groß wie; *12 – the (number of),* 12mal so viele wie; *12 –s 12 is* or *are 144,* 12 mal 12 ist *or* macht 144;
9. *pl.* Zeiten (*pl.*), Zeitverhältnisse (*pl.*); *be abreast of the –s, move with the –s,* mit der Zeit gehen; *hard –s,* schlimme *or* schwere Zeiten; *as –s go,* wie die Zeiten stehen, bei den jetzigen Zeiten; *behind the –s,* rückständig; *the –s are out of joint,* die Zeit ist aus den Fugen.
2. *v.t.* 1. die (richtige) Zeit festsetzen *or* ansetzen *or* wählen für, die Zeit messen *or* bestimmen *or* feststellen (*Gen.*), zur richtigen Zeit tun; *– o.s.,* feststellen wie lange man braucht; *– one's words ill,* seine Worte zur Unzeit anbringen; 2. zeitlich regeln *or* einrichten *or* abstimmen (*to,* nach), im zeitlichen Einklang bringen (mit); 3. (*Mus.*) das Tempo *or* den Takt angeben für.
3. *v.i.* 1. Takt halten; 2. zeitlich übereinstimmen (*with,* mit).

time|-allowance, *s.* die Zeitvorgabe (*yacht racing*). **--and-motion study,** *s.* Zeitstudien (*pl.*). **--bargain,** *s.* (*Comm.*) das Termingeschäft, Zeitgeschäft. **--base voltage,** *s.* die Kippspannung. **--bomb,** *s.* die Zeit(zünder)bombe. **--clock,** *s.* die Stechuhr, Kontrolluhr. **--consuming,** *adj.* zeitraubend.

timed [taimd], *adj.* zeitlich reguliert; *ill--,* ungelegen; *well--,* zeitlich günstig.

time|-exposure, *s.* die Zeitaufnahme, Zeitbelichtung. **--fuse,** *s.* der Zeitzünder. **--honoured,** *adj.* altehrwürdig. **-keeper,** *s.* 1. das Chronometer, der Zeitmesser; *the clock is a good –,* die Uhr geht genau; 2. Aufseher (*in factories etc.*); (*Spt.*) Zeitnehmer. **--lag,** *s.* (*Tech.*) die Verzögerung, Nacheilung; 2. (*coll.*) Zwischenzeit.

timeless ['taimlis], *adj.* zeitlos, ewig, unendlich,

unbegrenzt. **timelessness,** *s.* die Zeitlosigkeit, Ewigkeit, Unendlichkeit, Unbegrenztheit.

time-limit, *s.* die Frist.

timeliness ['taimlinis], *s.* 1. die Rechtzeitigkeit; 2. Zeitgemäßheit, Aktualität, Angebrachtheit; 3. (*rare*) (Früh)zeitigkeit. **timely,** *adj.* 1. rechtzeitig; 2. zeitgemäß, aktuell, angebracht; 3. (*rare*) (früh)-zeitig.

time|piece, *s.* die Uhr, der Zeitmesser, die Stoppuhr, Sekundenuhr. **--saving,** *adj.* zeit(er)sparend. **-server,** *s.* der Konjunkturritter, der (die) Opportunist(in), Achselträger(in). **-serving, 1.** *s.* der Opportunismus, die Achselträgerei, Gesinnungslumperei, Liebedienerei. **2.** *adj.* opportunistisch, achselträgerisch, liebedienerisch. **--sheet,** *s.* die (Arbeitszeit)kontrollkarte, Stempelkarte. **--shutter,** *s.* (*Phot.*) der Zeitverschluß. **--signal,** *s.* (*Rad. etc.*) das Zeitzeichen. **--signature,** *s.* (*Mus.*) die Takt(art)bezeichnung, Taktvorzeichnung. **--switch,** *s.* (*Elec.*) der Zeitschalter. **-table,** *s.* (*Railw.*) das Kursbuch, der Fahrplan, (*Av.*) Flugplan; (*school etc.*) Stundenplan. **--work,** *s.* nach Zeit bezahlte Arbeit. **-worker,** *s.* nach Zeit bezahlter Arbeiter. **-worn,** *adj.* verbraucht, abgenutzt. **--zone,** *s.* (*Geol.*) die Zeitzone.

timid ['timid], *adj.* 1. furchtsam, ängstlich (***of,*** vor (*Dat.*)); 2. zaghaft, schüchtern. **timidity** [–'miditi], **timidness,** *s.* 1. die Furchtsamkeit, Ängstlichkeit; 2. Zaghaftigkeit, Schüchternheit.

timing ['taimiŋ], *s.* 1. die Zeiteinteilung, Zeitplanung, Dispositionen (*pl.*); 2. zeitliche Abstimmung *or* Koordinierung, Synchronisierung; 3. (*Spt.*) Zeitmessung; 4. (*Tech.*) (zeitliche) Regelung *or* Einstellung *or* Steuerung; ***ignition –,*** die Zünd(folge)steuerung.

timpanist ['timpənist], *s.* (*Mus.*) der Kesselpauker. **timpano** [–nou], *s.* (*usu. pl.* **-ni** [–ni]) die Kesselpauke.

tin [tin], **1.** *s.* 1. (*Chem., Metall.*) das Zinn; 2. (*also* ***--plate***) Weißblech; 3. (*coll.*) die (Blech)dose, Konservendose, (Konserven)büchse; (*coll.*) ***a – of peaches,*** eine Dose Pfirsich; 4. (*sl.*) der Kies, Zaster, das Moos, Moneten (*pl.*). **2.** *v.t.* 1. (*Metall.*) (*also* ***--plate***) verzinnen; 2. (*coll.*) konservieren, in Dosen *or* Büchsen einmachen. **3.** *adj.* 1. zinnern, Zinn–; 2. Blech–; ***– box,*** die Blechbüchse, Blechschachtel; ***– can,*** die Blechdose; (*Naut. sl.*) ***– fish,*** der Aal (= ***torpedo***); (*coll.*) ***– god,*** aufgeblasener Mensch, der Bonze, Popanz; (*coll.*) ***– hat,*** der Stahlhelm; (*coll.*) ***– Lizzie,*** alter Fordwagen; (*coll.*) ***– soldier,*** der Bleisoldat.

tincal [tiŋkl], *s.* roher Borax.

tincture ['tiŋktʃə], **1.** *s.* 1. die Tinktur, der Aufguß; 2. (*fig.*) die Färbung, Schattierung, Beimischung, der Beigeschmack, Anstrich. **2.** *v.t.* (*fig.*) (leicht) färben, einen Anstrich geben (*Dat.*) (***with,*** von); ***be –d with,*** einen Anstrich haben von.

tinder ['tində], *s.* der Zunder. **tinderbox,** *s.* 1. (*Hist.*) das Feuerzeug; 2. (*fig.*) das Pulverfaß.

tine [tain], *s.* 1. die Zinke, Zacke; 2. (*Hunt.*) Sprosse, das Ende (*of antlers*).

tinfoil, 1. *s.* das Blattzinn, Stanniol(papier). **2.** *adj.* Stanniol–.

ting [tiŋ], **1.** *v.i.* (hell) erklingen. **2.** *v.t.* läuten, erklingen lassen. **3.** *s.* das Klingeln, (helles) Klingen.

tinge [tindʒ], **1.** *s.* 1. leichter Farbton, der Stich, die Färbung, Tönung, Schattierung; ***– of red,*** der Stich ins Rote; 2. (*fig.*) die Spur, der Anhauch, Anstrich, Anflug, Beigeschmack. **2.** *v.t.* 1. (leicht) färben, tönen, schattieren; 2. (*usu. fig.*) einen Anstrich *or* Beigeschmack geben (*Dat.*) (***with,*** von); ***be –d with,*** einen Anstrich *or* Beigeschmack haben von.

tingle [tiŋgl], **1.** *v.i.* 1. prickeln, stechen, kribbeln (*sensation*); 2. klingen, summen (***with,*** vor (*Dat.*)) (*sound*); ***my ears are tingling,*** mir klingen die Ohren. **2.** *s.* 1. das Prickeln, Stechen, Kribbeln; 2. Klingen, Summen.

tinier ['tainiə], *comp.* **tiniest,** *sup. adj. of* **tiny.**

tinker ['tiŋkə], **1.** *s.* der Kesselflicker; (*coll.*) Schelm, Racker; ***not worth a –'s cuss,*** keinen roten Heller wert. **2.** *v.i.* (*fig.*) herumpfuschen (***with,*** an (*Dat.*)), herumbasteln (***at,*** an (*Dat.*)).

tinkle [tiŋkl], **1.** *v.i.* klingeln, hell klingen. **2.** *v.t.* läuten, erklingen lassen. **3.** *s.* das Geklingel; (*sl.*) ***give him a –,*** ihn anrufen. **tinkling, 1.** *s.* das Läuten, Klinge(l)n, Geklingel. **2.** *adj.* klinge(l)nd, läutend.

tin|man [–mən], *s.* der Blechschmied, Klempner, Spengler. **--mine,** *s.* die Zinngrube, das Zinnbergwerk.

tinned [tind], *adj.* 1. (*Metall.*) verzinnt; 2. (*coll.*) konserviert, Dosen–, Büchsen–, Konserven–; ***– fruit,*** Obstkonserven (*pl.*), eingemachtes Obst; ***– meat,*** das Büchsenfleisch. **tinning,** *s.* 1. (*Metall.*) das Verzinnen; 2. (*coll.*) die Konservierung.

tinnitus [ti'naitəs], *s.* das Ohrenklingen, Ohrensausen.

tinny ['tini], *adj.* 1. zinnhaltig, zinnreich; 2. (*coll.*) blechern, metallen.

tin|-opener, *s.* der Büchsenöffner, Dosenöffner. **-plate, 1.** *s.* das Weißblech. **2.** *v.t.* verzinnen. **-pot,** *adj.* (*sl.*) schäbig, lumpig. **--putty,** *s.* (*Chem.*) die Zinnasche, das Zinndioxyd.

tinsel [tinsl], **1.** *s.* 1. das Rauschgold, Flittergold, Flittersilber, die Lametta; 2. (*fig.*) der Flitter(kram), täuschender Glanz. **2.** *adj.* 1. Flitter–; 2. (*fig.*) flitterhaft, Schein–.

tin|smith, *s. See* **-man.**

tint [tint], **1.** *s.* der Farbton, die Farbnuance, Färbung, Tönung, Schattierung, zarte Farbe; ***reddish –,*** der Stich ins Rote. **2.** *v.t.* leicht färben, abtönen, nuancieren.

tin-tack, *s.* der Tapeziernagel, verzinnter Nagel.

tinted ['tintid], *adj.* leicht gefärbt, getönt, nuanciert; (*as suff.*) –farbig, –farben; ***– glass,*** das Rauchglas; ***– paper,*** das Tonpapier; ***– spectacles,*** farbige Brille.

tintinnabulary [tinti'næbjuləri], *adj.* klingelnd. **tintinnabulation** [–ju'leiʃən], *s.* das Klinge(l)n, Geklingel, Tönen.

tin|ware, *s.* Blechwaren (*pl.*), das Zinngeschirr. **-works,** *pl.* (*usu. sing. constr.*) die Zinngießerei, Zinnhütte.

tiny ['taini], *adj.* sehr klein, winzig.

[1]**tip** [tip], **1.** *s.* die Spitze, der Zipfel, die Zwinge (*of a stick etc.*); das Mundstück (*of cigarette*); ***– of the ear,*** das Ohrläppchen; ***– of the finger,*** die Fingerspitze; ***have at the –(s) of one's fingers,*** im kleinen Finger haben; ***on the –s of one's toes,*** auf den Zehenspitzen; ***I have it on the – of my tongue,*** mir schwebt es auf der Zunge. **2.** *v.t.* mit einer Spitze *or* Zwinge versehen.

[2]**tip, 1.** *v.t.* leicht berühren *or* schlagen, antippen (*ball etc.*); (*coll.*) ***– one's cap,*** an den Hut tippen; ***– one's cap to him,*** ihm einen saloppen Gruß geben. **2.** *s.* leichte Berührung, leichter Schlag, der Klaps.

[3]**tip, 1.** *s.* (*coll.*) das Trinkgeld. **2.** *v.i.* Trinkgeld geben. **3.** *v.t.* ein Trinkgeld geben (*Dat.*).

[4]**tip, 1.** *s.* (*coll.*) der Tip, Wink, Hinweis, Fingerzeig, Ratschlag; ***straight –,*** richtiger Tip; ***take the –,*** den Ratschlag befolgen. **2.** *v.t.* (*usu.* ***– off***) einen Tip *or* Wink geben (*Dat.*), rechtzeitig warnen (*a p.*); (*sl.*) ***– him the wink,*** ihm verstohlen einen Wink geben; (*racing*) ***– the winner,*** auf den Sieger tippen.

[5]**tip, 1.** *v.t.* 1. kippen, neigen; ***– over,*** umkippen, umwerfen, umstürzen; ***– to one side,*** auf die Seite schieben *or* kippen; ***– up,*** hochkippen; (*coll.*) ***– the scale(s) at 10 kg.,*** knapp 10 kg. wiegen; (*fig.*) ***– the scale(s),*** ins Gewicht fallen; 2. abladen (*rubbish*); ***– out,*** ausschütten, ausgießen; (*coll.*) ***– him into the water,*** ihn ins Wasser stoßen. **2.** *v.i.* sich neigen; ***– out,*** herausfallen; ***– over*** or ***up,*** umkippen. **3.** *s.* 1. die Neigung; 2. der Abladeplatz, die Halde.

tip|-and-run raid, *s.* der Überraschungsüberfall, (*usu. Av.*) Einbruchsangriff. **--cart,** *s.* der Kippkarren. **-cat,** *s.* das Spatzeck(spiel). **--off,** *s.* (*sl.*) rechtzeitige Warnung, der Wink, Tip.

tipped [tipt], *adj.* mit einer Spitze *or* Zwinge (versehen), (*cigarette*) mit Mundstück. **tipper,** *s.* (*coll.*) der Kippwagen, Kipper.

tippet ['tipit], *s.* der Pelzkragen, die Pelerine.

tipple [tipl], **1.** *v.i.* gewohnheitsmäßig trinken, picheln, saufen, zechen. **2.** *s.* üblicher Tropfen. **tippler,** *s.* der Schnapsbruder, Zechbruder.

tipstaff ['tipsta:f], *s.* (*pl.* **-staves**) 1. der Amtsstab; 2. Gerichtsdiener.

tipster ['tipstə], *s.* (berufsmäßiger) Tipgeber, Wettberater.

tipsy ['tipsi], *adj.* beschwipst, angeheitert. **tipsy-cake,** *s.* (eine Art) Kuchen mit Weingeschmack.

tiptoe ['tiptou], **1.** *adv.* (*Poet.*) (*coll.* ***on*** –) auf den Zehenspitzen; (*fig.*) ***on*** –, neugierig, gespannt (***with,*** vor (*Dat.*)); ***on – with expectation,*** gespannt, erwartungsvoll, voller Erwartung. **2.** *v.i.* auf den Zehenspitzen gehen.

tiptop ['tip'tɔp], **1.** *s.* (*coll.*) der Gipfel(punkt), Höhepunkt, höchster Grad, das Höchste *or* Beste. **2.** *adj.* (*coll.*) tipptopp, prima, erstklassig, tadellos.

tip-up, *attrib. adj.* aufklappbar, Klapp–.

tirade [tai'reid], *s.* die Tirade, der Wortschwall, Rede(er)guß.

tirailleur [tirai'jə:], *s.* der Tirailleur, (Scharf)-schütze.

¹tire ['taiə], **1.** *v.t.* (*obs.*) schmücken, putzen, bekleiden. **2.** *s.* (*obs.*) der Kopfputz.

²tire, (*Am.*) *see* **tyre.**

³tire, 1. *v.t.* müde machen, ermüden (*also fig.*), erschöpfen; (*fig.*) langweilen; – ***out*** or ***to death,*** vollständig erschöpfen, todmüde machen; (*fig.*) – ***to death,*** zum Sterben langweilen. **2.** *v.i.* ermüden, ermatten, müde werden (***with, by,*** durch); (*fig.*) müde *or* überdrüssig werden (***of,*** *Gen.*; ***of doing,*** zu tun).

tired ['taiəd], *adj.* 1. (*of a p.*) müde, ermüdet, erschöpft (***with, by,*** von); – ***to death,*** todmüde; (*fig.*) ***be -d of,*** satt *or* überdrüssig sein (*Gen.*), (*coll.*) satt haben; ***make*** –, ermüden, (*fig.*) langweilen; – ***out,*** (*of p. only*) todmüde, völlig erschöpft; 2. (*of a th.*) erschöpft, verbraucht, abgenutzt. **tiredness,** *s.* die Ermüdung, Müdigkeit, Mattigkeit; (*fig.*) der Überdruß. **tireless,** *adj.* unermüdlich. **tirelessness,** *s.* die Unermüdlichkeit. **tiresome,** *adj.* 1. (*fig.*) ermüdend, langweilig; 2. lästig, verdrießlich. **tiresomeness,** *s.* 1. die Langweiligkeit; 2. Lästigkeit.

tiring ['taiəriŋ], *adj.* ermüdend, erschöpfend.

tiring|-room, *s.* (*Theat.*) die Garderobe; (*obs.*) der Ankleideraum. **--woman,** *s.* (*obs.*) die Kammerfrau, Kammerzofe.

tiro, *see* **tyro.**

tissue ['tisju:, 'tiʃu:], *s.* 1. (feines) Gewebe; 2. (*Biol.*) das (Zell)gewebe; – ***culture,*** die Gewebekultur; 3. (*fig.*) das Gewebe, Netz (*of lies etc.*); 4. – ***paper,*** das Seidenpapier.

¹tit [tit], *s.* 1. (*rare*) kleines Pferd; 2. (*Orn.*) *see* **titmouse.**

²tit, *s.* (*vulg.*) die Zitze.

³tit, *s.* – ***for tat,*** wie du mir, so ich dir; eine Hand wäscht die andere; Wurst wider Wurst; ***give – for tat,*** Gleiches mit Gleichem vergelten (*Dat.*), mit gleicher Münze heimzahlen (*Dat.*).

titan ['taitən], *s.* der Titan, Gigant, Riese. **titanic** [–'tænik], *adj.* 1. Titanen–, titanenhaft, riesengroß, riesig, gigantisch; 2. (*Chem.*) Titan–. **titanium** [–'teiniəm], *s.* (*Chem.*) das Titan.

titbit ['titbit], *s.* der Leckerbissen.

tithable ['taiðəbl], *adj.* zehntpflichtig. **tithe, 1.** *s.* das Zehntel; (*Eccl.*) (*usu. pl.*) der Zehnte; (*fig.*) ***not a – of,*** nicht der zehnte Teil von. **2.** *v.t.* 1. den Zehnten erheben von, mit dem Zehnten belegen; 2. den Zehnten bezahlen von. **tithing,** *s.* (*Hist.*) die Zehntschaft.

titillate ['titileit], *v.t.* kitzeln, prickeln, angenehm anregen *or* reizen. **titillation** [–'leiʃən], *s.* das Kitzeln, Prickeln; (*fig.*) der Kitzel, das Lustgefühl, angenehmer Reiz.

titivate ['titiveit], **1.** *v.t.* herausputzen, feinmachen, schniegeln. **2.** *v.i.* sich herausputzen *or* feinmachen. **titivation** [–'veiʃən], *s.* das Herausputzen, Schniegeln.

titlark ['titla:k], *s.* (*Orn.*) der (Wiesen)pieper (*Anthus pratensis*).

title [taitl], **1.** *s.* 1. der Titel; die Überschrift, Aufschrift, Benennung, Bezeichnung, der Name; 2. (Adels)titel, Ehrentitel, Amtstitel; ***bear a*** –, einen Titel führen; – ***of earl,*** der Grafentitel; – ***of nobility,*** der Adelsbrief, das Adelsprädikat; 3. (*Spt.*) Titel; 4. (*Law., fig.*) der Rechtstitel, (Rechts)anspruch, das (An)recht (***to,*** auf (*Acc.*)); 5. (*Typ.*) ***bastard*** –, der Schmutztitel. **2.** *v.t.* betiteln, benennen. **titled,** *adj.* 1. betitelt, tituliert; 2. (*people*) adlig.

title|-deed, *s.* die Eigentumsurkunde. **--holder,** *s.* 1. der (Rechts)titelinhaber; 2. (*Spt.*) Titelverteidiger. **--page,** *s.* das Titelblatt. **--role,** *s.* (*Theat.*) die Titelrolle.

¹titling ['titliŋ], *s. See* **titlark.**

²titling ['taitliŋ], *s.* 1. die Benennung, Betitelung; 2. (*Typ.*) das Prägen des Buchtitels; (aufgeprägter) Buchtitel; 3. (*Typ.*) – ***type,*** die Verschalschrift.

titmouse ['titmaus], *s.* (*Orn.*) die Meise (*Paridae*); ***bearded*** –, die Bartmeise (*Panurus biarmicus*); ***great*** –, die Kohlmeise (*Parus major*); ***long-tailed*** –, die Schwanzmeise (*Aegithalos caudatus*). *See also* **blue titmouse, coal-titmouse.**

titrate ['taitreit], *v.t.* titrieren. **titration** [–'treiʃən], *s.* die Titrierung, Titrieranalyse, Maßanalyse.

titter ['titə], **1.** *v.i.* kichern. **2.** *s.* das Kichern, Gekicher.

tittle [titl], *s.* 1. der Tüttel, i-Punkt, das i-Tüpfelchen; 2. (*fig.*) Tüttelchen, Tüpfelchen, Jota, bißchen, die Kleinigkeit; ***not one jot or*** –, nicht ein Jota, nicht das Geringste, nicht die Bohne; ***to a*** –, aufs Haar genau.

tittle|-tattle, 1. *s.* 1. das Geschwätz, Geklatsch, Gerede, der Klatsch, Tratsch; 2. der (die) Schwätzer(in), die Klatschbase, das Klatschmaul. **2.** *v.i.* schwatzen, schwätzen, klatschen, tratschen. **--tattler,** *s. See* **--tattle, 1,** 2.

titty ['titi], *s.* (*nursery talk*) 1. die Zitze, Titte; 2. der Schnuller; 3. die (Mutter)milch; 4. Mutterbrust. **titty-bottle,** *s.* die Saugflasche.

titubation [titju'beiʃən], *s.* (*rare*) das Taumeln, (Sch)wanken.

titular ['titjulə], **1.** *adj.* 1. Titel–; – ***bishop,*** der Titularbischof; – ***honour,*** die Titelehre; 2. Titular–, nominell; – ***aunt,*** die Nenntante. **2.** *s.* der Titular; Titelträger, Titelinhaber. **titulary,** *adj. See* **titular, 1** (*esp. Law*).

tizzy ['tizi], *s.* (*sl.*) tolle Aufregung.

to [tu:, tə *acc. to emphasis*], **1.** *part.* **(a)** (*before inf.*) – ***be or not – be,*** sein oder nicht sein; ***I want – come,*** ich will *or* möchte kommen, ich wünsche zu kommen; ***I want him – come,*** ich will, daß er kommt; ***he was seen – come,*** man sah ihn kommen; ***he was the first – arrive,*** er kam als erster an; ***the best is yet – come,*** das Beste kommt noch; ***in years – come,*** in zukünftigen Jahren; – ***hear him talk, you would think*** . . ., wenn man ihn reden hört, würde man meinen . . .; ***is there no one – help you?*** ist niemand da, der dir hilft? ***what is there – say?*** was soll ich sagen? ***what is – be said?*** was ist zu sagen? **(b)** (*with emphasis on purpose*) um . . . zu; ***he only does it*** (*in order*) ***– annoy me,*** er tut es nur, um mich zu ärgern. **(c)** (*indicating omitted inf. explicit or implicit in foregoing*) ***I certainly meant*** –, ich hatte gewiß die Absicht; ***I was coming but I had no time*** –, ich wollte kommen, hatte aber keine Zeit dazu; ***I couldn't go even if I wanted*** –, ich könnte nicht hingehen, auch wenn ich wollte; ***I want*** –, ich möchte es gern.

2. *part.* (*forming Dat.*) (*coll. oft. omitted*) ***I gave it*** (–) ***him,*** ich gab es ihm; ***I made it clear – him,*** ich erklärte es ihm; ***it seems – me,*** es scheint mir.

3. *prep.* **(a)** (*direction and goal*) zu, nach, an (*Acc.*), in (*Acc.*), auf (*Acc.*), nach (. . . hin); – ***arms!*** zu den Waffen! ***back – back,*** Rücken an *or* gegen

Rücken; *go – bed,* zu Bett gehen; *go – Cologne,* nach Köln fahren; (*coll.*) *have you been – Cologne?* sind Sie in Köln gewesen? *face – face,* Auge in Auge, unter vier Augen; *– his face,* ihm ins Gesicht; *spring – one's feet,* auf die Füße springen, aufspringen; *throw . . . to ground,* auf den *or* zu Boden werfen; *from hand – hand,* von Hand zu Hand; *– the point,* zur Sache; *– the right,* auf der rechten Seite, zur Rechten, rechter Hand, rechts; *go – school* (*on one occasion*), in die Schule gehen; *from north – south,* von Norden nach Süden. **(b)** (*time*) bis (zu), bis gegen, vor (*Dat.*), auf (*Acc.*); *a quarter – one,* (ein) Viertel vor eins; *– the last,* bis zuletzt; *– the present day,* bis zum heutigen Tag; *– the second,* (bis) auf die Sekunde (genau). **(c)** (*aim, purpose, intention*) zu, an (*Acc.*), in (*Acc.*), auf (*Acc.*), für; *that is all there is – it,* das ist alles was drum und dran ist; *as –,* betreffs, was . . . (an)betrifft; *– his cost,* auf seine Kosten, zu seinem Schaden; *– his credit,* zu seinen Gunsten; *– the good,* zum Guten; (*Comm.*) *– (one's) hand,* zur Hand; *when it comes – the point,* wenn es darauf ankommt; (*Theat.*) *play – an empty house,* vor einem leeren Haus spielen; *– the life,* (getreu) nach dem Leben; (*coll.*) *here's – you!* auf dein Wohl! Prosit! *it is nothing – me,* es geht mich nichts an, das macht mir nichts aus, das ist nichts für mich; *– what end* or *purpose?* wozu? *– no end* or *purpose,* zwecklos. **(d)** (*appropriateness*) nach, gemäß, für; *– all appearances,* allem Anschein nach; *– one's heart's desire,* nach Herzenslust; *– my knowledge,* meines Wissens, soviel ich weiß; *– my mind,* meiner Ansicht nach; *– my taste,* nach meinem Geschmack. **(e)** (*degree, extent*) (bis) zu, (bis) an (*Acc.*), (bis) auf (*Acc.*), in (*Dat.*); *– bursting point,* zum Bersten; *– the core,* bis ins Herz *or* Innerste; *– a high degree,* in hohem Grade; *– the end that . . .,* zu dem Zweck daß . . ., damit . . .; *– a certain extent,* gewissermaßen, bis zu einem gewissen Grad; *– the last* or *a man,* bis auf den letzten Mann; *– a nicety,* aufs Haar; *– the point of,* bis zur Höhe *or* zum Betrag von; *– a T,* aufs Haar; *– the tune of,* nach der Melodie von; (*coll.*) *see – the value of*; *– the value of,* im Wert von. **(f)** (*relationship, comparison*) (im Vergleich) zu, gegen(über); *ten – one,* zehn gegen *or* zu eins; *10 is – 5 as 2 is – 1,* 10 verhält sich zu 5 wie 2 zu 1; *nothing –,* nichts im Vergleich zu; (*compared*) *–,* gegen, verglichen mit.

4. *prep. in many idiomatic usages as the appropriate form following* **(a)** *nouns, e.g.* ***answer –, aversion –, duty –, injury –, loss –, secretary –, stranger – etc.*; **(b)** *verbs, e.g.* ***admit –, attend –, belong –, listen –, read –, speak –, subscribe –, swear – etc.*; **(c)** *adjs. e.g.* ***agreeable –, alive –, deaf –, due –, faithful –, familiar –, known –, lost – etc.*** *In all instances refer to the significant word.*

5. *adv.* 1. geschlossen, zu; *pull the door –,* die Tür zuziehen; 2. heran; *buckle –,* sich eifrig an die Arbeit machen; *fall –,* (tüchtig) zulangen, zugreifen; *go –!* weiter! nur zu! geh zu! wohlan! *set –,* sich ans Werk machen, einen Anfang machen; *close –,* gleich bei der Hand; *– and fro,* hin und her, auf und ab; 3. bei *or* zu sich; *bring him –,* ihn wieder zu sich bringen; *come –,* wieder zu sich *or* zu Bewußtsein kommen.

toad [toud], *s.* die Kröte (*also fig. of p.*); (*coll.*) *– in the hole,* die Fleisch- *or* Wurstpastete. **toad|flax,** *s.* (*Bot.*) das Leinkraut. **–stone,** *s.* der Krötenstein. **–stool,** *s.* der Giftpilz.

toady ['toudi], **1.** *s.* der Speichellecker. **2.** *v.i.* in serviler Weise schmeicheln (*to, Dat.*). **toadying, toadyism,** *s.* die Speichelleckerei.

to-and-fro ['tu:ənd'frou], *attrib. adj.* Hin- und Her-.

[1]**toast** [toust], **1.** *s.* geröstetes Brot, der Toast; (*sl.*) *have him on –,* ihn ganz in der Hand haben; *as warm as –,* schön warm; *make –,* Brot rösten. **2.** *v.t.* toasten, rösten; (*fig.*) wärmen; *– one's toes,* sich (*Dat.*) die Füße wärmen.

[2]**toast, 1.** *s.* der Trinkspruch, Toast; *loyal –,* der Trinkspruch auf Herrscher und Herrscherhaus; *propose the – of,* einen Toast ausbringen auf (*Acc.*). **2.** *v.t.* trinken *or* einen Trinkspruch ausbringen auf (*Acc.*).

toaster ['toustə], *s.* der (Brot)röster, Toaster. **toasting,** *attrib. adj.* Röst-.

toast-master, *s.* der Toastmeister.

toast-rack, *s.* der Toastständer.

tobacco [tə'bækou], *s.* der Tabak; (*collect.*) Tabakwaren (*pl.*); *– heart,* das Nikotinherz. **tobacconist** [-kənist], *s.* der Tabakhändler; *–'s* (*shop*), der Tabakladen. **tobacco|-pipe,** *s.* die Tabakspfeife. **--plant,** *s.* die Tabakpflanze. **--pouch,** *s.* der Tabaksbeutel.

toboggan [tə'bɔgən], **1.** *s.* der Rodel(schlitten). **2.** *v.t.* rodeln. **tobogganer,** *s.* der Rodler. **tobogganing,** *s.* das Rodeln. **tobogganist,** *s.* *See* **tobogganer. toboggan-slide,** *s.* die Rodelbahn.

toccata [tə'kɑ:tə], *s.* die Tokkata.

tocsin ['tɔksin], *s.* die Sturmglocke, Alarmglocke; das Alarmsignal, Warnsignal.

tod [tɔd], *s.* (*sl.*) (*only in*) *on one's –,* ganz allein.

today [tə'dai], **1.** *adv.* 1. heute; *– week,* heute in 8 Tagen *or* über 8 Tage; 2. heutzutage, gegenwärtig, heutigentags. **2.** *s.* 1. heutiger Tag; *–'s paper,* heutige Zeitung, die Zeitung von heute; 2. das Heute, heutige Zeit, die Gegenwart; *the politicians of –,* die Politiker der Gegenwart *or* der heutigen Zeit.

toddle [tɔdl], *v.i.* watscheln; (*coll.*) *– off* or *along,* abschieben, sich trollen. **toddler,** *s.* das Kleinkind.

toddy ['tɔdi], *s.* der Eisbrecher, Punsch, Grog.

to-do [tə'du:], *s.* (*coll.*) das Aufheben, der Krach, Lärm; *make a –,* Krach schlagen, viel Aufhebens machen (*about,* über (*Acc.*) *or* von).

toe [tou], **1.** *s.* 1. die Zehe; *from top to –,* von Kopf bis Fuß; (*fig.*) *tread on his –s,* ihm auf die Füße *or* Hühneraugen treten; (*fig.*) *on one's –s,* auf Draht; *turn one's –s in,* einwärts gehen; *turn one's –s out,* auswärts gehen; (*sl.*) *turn up one's –s,* krepieren, ins Gras beißen; 2. die Spitze (*of stocking*), Kappe (*of shoe*). **2.** *v.t.* 1. mit neuen Spitzen versehen (*stockings*), vorschuhen (*shoes*); 2. mit den Zehen berühren; *– the line,* (*Spt.*) in Linie antreten, sich zu einem Rennen aufstellen; (*fig.*) sich der Parteilinie unterwerfen, linientreu sein, sich einfügen, spuren; 3. (*sl.*) einen Fußtritt geben (*Dat.*).

toe-cap, *s.* die (Schuh)kappe. **toed** [toud], *adj. suff.* -zehig.

toe|-dancer, *s.* der (die) Spitzentänzer(in). **--hold,** *s.* 1. (*Mount.*) der Halt mit den Zehenspitzen; 2. (*fig.*) dürftiger Ansatzpunkt. **--nail,** *s.* der Zehennagel.

toff [tɔf], *s.* (*sl.*) der (Patent)fatzke.

toffee ['tɔfi], *s.* der *or* das Rahmbonbon; (*coll.*) *he cannot sing for –,* vom Singen hat er keine Ahnung.

tog [tɔg], **1.** *v.i.* (*sl.*) *– up,* sich feinmachen; sich ausstaffieren. **2.** *v.t.* *– up* or *out,* ausstaffieren.

toga ['tougə], *s.* die Toga.

together [tə'geðə], *adv.* zusammen, beisammen, miteinander, gemeinsam; (*coll.*) *belong –,* zusammengehören, zueinandergehören; (*coll.*) *get –,* zusammenkommen, (*fig.*) sich einigen, übereinkommen; 2. aufeinander, gegeneinander, ineinander (*of movement*); *fight –,* gegeneinander kämpfen; 3. zugleich, zu gleicher Zeit, gleichzeitig (*in time*); 4. hintereinander; *for days –,* tagelang (hintereinander); 5. *– with,* zusammen *or* gemeinsam mit, (mit)samt. **togetherness,** *s.* (*coll.*) das Zusammengehörigkeitsgefühl.

toggery ['tɔgəri], *s.* (*sl.*) *see* **togs.**

toggle [tɔgl], **1.** *s.* (*Naut.*) der Knebel. **2.** *v.t.* festknebeln, mit einem Querholz verbinden *or* befestigen. **toggle|-joint,** *s.* das Kniegelenk, Knebelgelenk. **--switch,** *s.* (*Elec.*) der Kippschalter.

togs [tɔgz], *pl.* Klamotten (*pl.*).

[1]**toil** [tɔil], **1.** *s.* mühselige Arbeit, die Mühe, Plage, Plackerei, Schererei. **2.** *v.i.* mühselig arbeiten (*at,*

an (*Dat.*)), sich abmühen *or* abplacken (mit), schuften (an (*Dat.*) *or* bei); – ***along,*** sich vorwärtsarbeiten *or* weiterschleppen; – ***through,*** sich mühselig durcharbeiten durch; – ***up the hill,*** sich an der Anhöhe mühsam hocharbeiten.

²**toil,** *s.* (*usu. pl.*) das Netz, die Schlinge; ***in the -s of,*** verstrickt in (*Acc.*), in den Schlingen (*Gen.*).

toiler ['tɔilə], *s.* Schwerarbeitende(r), das Arbeitstier.

toilet ['tɔilət], *s.* 1. die Toilette, das Anziehen, Ankleiden; ***make one's –,*** Toilette machen; 2. das Klosett, die Toilette. **toilet|-case,** *s.* das Reisenecessaire. **--paper,** *s.* das Toilettenpapier, Klosettpapier. **--roll,** *s.* die Rolle Toilettenpapier. **--set,** *s.* die Toilettengarnitur. **--soap,** *s.* die Toilettenseife.

toilsome ['tɔilsəm], *adj.* mühevoll, mühsam, mühselig. **toilsomeness,** *s.* die Mühsamkeit, Mühseligkeit. **toilworn,** *adj.* abgearbeitet.

Tokay [tou'kei], *s.* der Tokaier(wein).

token ['toukən], **1.** *s.* 1. das (An)zeichen (*of, Gen. or* von), Merkmal (für), der Beweis (für *or Gen.*), das Andenken (an (*Dat.*)); ***as a*** or (*fig.*) ***in – of,*** zum Zeichen (*Gen.*); ***more by –,*** um so mehr; ***by the same –,*** ebensfalls, ferner, außerdem, überdies, desgleichen; genauso gut, mit demselben Recht, aus demselben Grund; 2. (*Hist.*) die Scheidemünze; 3. (*Comm.*) Marke, der Gutschein, Bon. **2.** *adj.* Schein–; ***–money,*** das Ersatzgeld, Notgeld; die Scheidemünze; – ***payment,*** vorläufige Teilzahlung; – ***raid,*** der Scheinangriff; – ***strike,*** der Warnstreik.

Tokyo ['toukiou], *s.* Tokio (*n.*).

told [tould], *imperf., p.p. of* **tell**; ***all –,*** alles in allem.

tolerable ['tɔlərəbl], *adj.* 1. erträglich (*to,* für); 2. leidlich, mittelmäßig. **tolerableness,** *s.* 1. die Erträglichkeit; 2. Leidlichkeit, Mittelmäßigkeit. **tolerably,** *adv.* leidlich, ziemlich.

tolerance ['tɔlərəns], *s.* 1. die Duldung, Nachsicht (*of,* mit); Duldsamkeit, Toleranz; 2. (*Tech.*) die Fehlergrenze, Toleranz, zugelassene Abweichung, der Spielraum, das Abmaß; 3. (*Med.*) die Toleranz, Widerstandsfähigkeit. **tolerant,** *adj.* 1. duldsam, tolerant (*of,* gegen); nachsichtig, geduldig (***towards,*** gegen); 2. (*Med.*) widerstandsfähig (*of,* gegen).

tolerate ['tɔləreit], *v.t.* 1. dulden, duldsam sein gegen, ertragen; sich abfinden mit, sich (*Dat.*) gefallen lassen, über sich ergehen lassen, gestatten, zulassen; 2. (*Med.*) vertragen. **toleration** [–'reiʃən], *s.* die Duldung, Nachsicht; Duldsamkeit, Toleranz; ***show – for,*** Nachsicht üben mit.

¹**toll** [toul], **1.** *v.t.* (in langsamen Zwischenräumen) läuten (*a bell*); schlagen (*the hours*); – ***him to his grave, – his departure,*** ihn zu Grabe läuten, die Toten– und Sterbeglocke für ihn läuten. **2.** *v.i.* schlagen, läuten. **3.** *s.* (langsames feierliches) Läuten, der Glockenschlag.

²**toll,** *s.* 1. der Zoll (*also fig.*), die Steuer, Abgabe, (*obs.*) Maut; 2. das Wegegeld, Brückengeld; 3. (*fig.*) der Tribut, das Opfer; – ***of the road,*** Verkehrsopfer (*pl.*); (*fig.*) ***take – of,*** fordern; ***take a heavy – of their lives,*** ihnen schwere Menschenverluste zufügen.

toll|-bar, *s.* der Schlagbaum, die Zollschranke. **--bridge,** *s.* die Zollbrücke. **--call,** *s.* (*Tele.*) Vorortsgespräch, Nahverkehrgespräch, (*Am.*) Ferngespräch. **--gate,** *s. See* **--bar. --house,** *s.* das Zollhäuschen. **--keeper,** *s.* der Zolleinnehmer, Zöllner, Mautner. **--line dialling,** *s.* (*Am.*) der Selbstwählerfernverkehr.

toluene ['tɔljui:n] (*Chem.*), **toluol** [–juəl], *s.* das Toluol.

Tom [tɔm], *s.* 1. *abbr. of* **Thomas**; ***–, Dick and Harry,*** Hinz und Kunz; – ***Thumb,*** der Däumling; – ***Tiddler's ground,*** das Niemandsland; (eine Art) Kinderspiel; 2. *See also* **tom-cat.**

tomahawk ['tɔməhɔ:k], **1.** *s.* die Streitaxt, das Kriegsbeil (*of American Indians*); (*fig.*) ***bury the –,*** Frieden schließen. **2.** *v.t.* 1. mit der Streitaxt erschlagen; 2. (*fig.*) schonungslos kritisieren.

tomato [tə'mɑ:tou], *s.* (*pl.* **-es**) die Tomate; ***gooseberry*** or ***strawberry –,*** die Erdkirsche.

tomb [tu:m], *s.* die Gruft, Grabstätte, das Grabgewölbe, Grab(mal).

tombac ['tɔmbək], *s.* der Tombak, Rotguß, das Rotmessing.

tombola ['tɔmbələ], *s.* die Tombola, das Lottospiel.

tombolo ['tɔmbəlou], *s.* (*Geog.*) die Sandbank, Nehrung.

tomboy ['tɔmbɔi], *s.* der Wildfang, die Range. **tomboyish,** *adj.* wild, ausgelassen (*of a girl*). **tomboyishness,** *s.* die Wildheit, Ausgelassenheit.

tombstone ['tu:mstoun], *s.* der Leichenstein, Grabstein; die Grabplatte.

tom-cat, *s.* der Kater.

tome [toum], *s.* (*coll.*) dicker Band, der Wälzer, Schmöker.

tomentose ['toumәntous], *adj.* filzig. **tomentum** [–'mentəm], *s.* 1. (*Bot.*) der Filz; 2. (*Anat.*) die Flocke.

tomfool ['tɔm'fu:l], **1.** *s.* der Einfaltspinsel, (Hans)narr. **2.** *adj.* albern. **tomfoolery,** *s.* 1. die Albernheit, Narretei; 2. der Unsinn, dummes Zeug.

tomium ['toumiəm], *s.* (*Orn.*) der Schneidrand (*of beak*).

Tommy ['tɔmi], *s. abbr. of* **Thomas**; – ***Atkins, tommy,*** (*coll.*) der Tommy (= *British soldier*); Landser. **tommy,** *s.* (*Mil. sl.*) das (Stück) Brot, Futteralien (*pl.*); ***soft –,*** frisches Brot; 2. (*Tech.*) (*also* **--bar**) der Schraubenhebel. **tommy|-gun,** *s.* die Maschinenpistole. **–rot,** *s.* (*sl.*) das Blech, der Quatsch, Blödsinn. **--system,** *s.* das Trucksystem.

tomorrow [tə'mɔrou], **1.** *adv.* morgen; – ***morning,*** morgen früh; ***the day after –,*** übermorgen; – ***week,*** morgen in 8 Tagen. **2.** *s.* das Morgen, morgiger Tag; ***–'s,*** morgig.

tomtit ['tɔmtit], *s.* (*Orn.*) die Blaumeise (*Parus caeruleus*).

tom-tom ['tɔmtɔm], *s.* die (Indianer)trommel; das Tamtam, (chinesischer) Gong.

¹**ton** [tɔ̃], *s.* herrschende Mode, die Modewelt.

²**ton** [tʌn], *s.* 1. die Tonne (= *2,240 lb.*); ***long*** or ***gross –,*** = *2,400 lb.* (*Am. 2240 lb.*); (*Am.*) ***short –,*** = *2,000 lb.*; ***metric –,*** = *2,205 lb.* = *1,000 kg.*; ***displacement –,*** = *35 cu. ft.*; ***freight –,*** = *40 cu. ft.*; ***register –,*** die Registertonne = *100 cu. ft.*; (*coll.*) ***weigh a –,*** einen (halben) Zentner wiegen; 2. (*sl.*) (*esp. motor-cycling*) 100 Stundenmeilen; 3. *pl.* (*coll.*) eine große Menge, Unmenge; (*coll.*) ***–s of,*** sehr viel(e), Unmassen von; ***–s of money,*** Geld wie Heu.

tonal [tounl], *adj.* Ton–, Klang(farben)–. **tonality** [–'næliti], *s.* (*Mus.*) die Tonalität, Klangfarbe; der Toncharakter (*of an instrument*); (*Art*) Farbton, die Färbung, Tönung.

tone [toun], **1.** *s.* 1. der Ton, Klang, Laut; 2. (*Mus.*) (Ganz)ton; 3. (*Mus.*) Klangcharakter, die Klangfarbe (*of an instrument*); 4. (*Phonet.*) Tonhöhe, Betonung; (*in Chinese*) das Tonhöhenzeichen; (*of speech*) der Ton(fall), die Sprechweise, Intonation; (*fig.*) ***in an angry –,*** mit zorniger Stimme; 5. (*Art*) das Kolorit, der Farbton, die Farbgebung, Tönung, Färbung, Schattierung; 6. (*fig.*) Neigung, Stimmung, Haltung, das Verhalten, der Stil, Charakter; (*St. Exch.*) – ***of the market,*** die Haltung *or* das Verhalten der Preise; ***moral –,*** moralisches Niveau; ***set the –,*** den Ton angeben (***for,*** für), tonangebend sein (in (*Dat.*)); bezeichnend sein (für); 7. (*Med.*) der Tonus (*of a muscle*); (*fig.*) Schwung, die (Spann)kraft. **2.** *v.t.* 1. Ton *or* Färbung geben (*Dat.*), abtönen; (*fig.*) – ***down,*** herabstimmen, mildern, dämpfen; – ***in with,*** abstimmen auf (*Acc.*); (*fig.*) – ***up,*** (ver)stärken, kräftigen; 2. (*Phot.*) tonen. **3.** *v.i.* – ***down,*** milder werden; (*fig.*) – (***in***) ***with,*** stimmen *or* passen zu, übereinstimmen *or* harmonieren *or* sich verschmelzen mit.

tone|-arm, *s.* der Tonarm (*of gramophone*). **--control,** *s.* die Klangfarbenregelung. **--colour,** *s.* die

Klangfarbe, der Klang. **--deaf,** *adj.* ohne musikalisches Gehör.

toneless ['tounlis], *adj.* 1. tonlos; 2. (*Phonet.*) unbetont; 3. (*fig.*) farblos, ausdruckslos.

tone|-picture, *s.* (*Mus.*) das Tongemälde. **--poem,** *s.* die Tondichtung.

tongs [tɔŋz], *pl.* die Zange; ***pair of –,*** eine Zange; ***curling –,*** die Brennschere; (*coll.*) ***go at it hammer and –,*** mit aller Kraft *or* wie der Teufel drauflosgehen; (*coll.*) ***I wouldn't touch it with a pair of –,*** ich würde es nicht einmal mit einer Zange anfassen.

tongue [tʌŋ], **1.** *s.* 1. die Zunge; (*Med.*) ***coated*** or ***furred –,*** belegte Zunge; ***my – cleaves to the roof of my mouth,*** die Zunge klebt mir am Gaumen; ***find one's –,*** die Sprache wiederfinden; ***give –,*** anschlagen, bellen (*as dogs*); ***have a – in one's head,*** gut reden können; ***have a long –,*** geschwätzig sein; ***hold one's –,*** den Mund halten; ***keep a civil – in one's head,*** (schön) höflich bleiben; ***keep one's – in check, keep a rein on one's –,*** die Zunge hüten *or* wahren *or* zügeln *or* im Zaum halten; ***malicious –,*** böse Zunge; ***put out one's –,*** die Zunge herausstrecken; ***slip of the –,*** unvorsichtiges *or* entschlüpftes Wort; ***it was a slip of the –,*** ich habe mich versprochen; (*Cul.*) ***smoked –,*** die Räucherzunge; ***I had the word on the tip of my –,*** das Wort schwebte *or* lag mir auf der Zunge; ***with his – in his cheek, – in cheek,*** ironisch; (*coll.*) ***wag one's –,*** tratschen; ***set –s wagging,*** ein Gerede aufbringen; 2. (*fig.*) die Sprache; ***mother –,*** die Muttersprache; 3. (*fig.*) die Zunge; ***– of flame,*** die Flammenzunge; ***– of land,*** die Landzunge; 4. der Klöppel (*of a bell*); 5. Zeiger (*of a balance*), Dorn (*of a buckle*); 6. (*Carp.*) Spund, Zapfen, die Feder; 7. Latsche (*of a shoe*). **2.** *v.t., v.i.* (*Mus.*) mit Flatterzunge blasen.

tongue-and-groove joint, *s.* (*Carp.*) die Spundung.

tongued [tʌŋd], *adj.* 1. (*Carp.*) gezapft, gefedert; 2. (*as suff.*) -züngig. **tongueless** ['tʌŋlis], *adj.* 1. ohne Zunge; 2. (*fig.*) sprachlos.

tongue|-shaped, *adj.* zungenförmig. **--tied,** *adj.* stumm, sprachlos, maulfaul, (*pred.*) auf den Mund gefallen. **--twister,** *s.* der Zungen(zer)brecher; ***this is a –,*** daran kann man sich die Zunge abbrechen.

tonguing ['tʌŋiŋ], *s.* 1. (*Carp.*) die Zapfung, Federung; 2. (*Mus.*) der Zungenstoß, die Zunge.

tonic ['tɔnik], **1.** *adj.* 1. (*Med.*) tonisch; ***– spasm,*** der Starrkrampf; 2. (*Med.*) stärkend, kräftigend; ***– water,*** der Sprudel, das Selterswasser; 3. (*Mus.*) tonisch, (Grund)ton-, grundtonartlich, tonlich; ***– chord,*** der Grundakkord; ***– sol-fa,*** die Tonika-Do-Methode; 3. (*Phonet.*) ***– accent,*** der Hochton. **2.** *s.* 1. (*Med.*) das Stärkungsmittel, Tonikum, tonisches *or* stärkendes Mittel; 2. (*Mus.*) die Tonika, der Grundton. **tonicity** [-'nisiti], *s.* 1. (*Med.*) die Spannkraft, Elastizität; 2. (*Mus.*) musikalischer Ton.

tonight [tə'nait], **1.** *adv.* heute abend, heute nacht. **2.** *s.* heutiger Abend, die kommende *or* diese Nacht.

tonnage ['tʌnidʒ], *s.* 1. die Tragfähigkeit, der Tonnengehalt, Frachtraum (*of a ship*); 2. die Gesamttonnage, der Gesamtschiffsraum (*of a country*); 3. die Gesamtproduktion (*of an industry*).

tonneau ['tɔnou], *s.* (*Motor.*) der Wagenfond, hinterer Innenraum.

-tonner ['tʌnə], *suff.* (*coll.*) das Schiff von . . . Tonnen.

tonometer [to'nɔmitə], *s.* der Ton(höhen)messer.

tonsil [tɔnsl], *s.* (*Anat.*) die Mandel(drüse). **tonsil(l)ar,** *adj.* Mandel-, Tonsillen-. **tonsillectomy** [-si'lektəmi], *s.* die Mandelentfernung. **tonsillitis** [-si'laitis], *s.* die Mandelentzündung.

tonsorial [tɔn'sɔ:riəl], *adj.* Barbier-. **tonsure** ['tɔnʃə], **1.** *s.* (*Eccl.*) die Tonsur; das Haarschneiden, die Haarschur. **2.** *v.t.* eine Tonsur schneiden (*Dat.*), die Haare scheren (*Dat.*), tonsurieren. **tonsured** ['tɔnʃəd], *adj.* tonsuriert, geschoren, kahl(köpfig).

too [tu:], *adv* 1. (*before adv. or adj.*) (all)zu; (*coll.*) ***he is – big for his boots,*** er ist dummstolz; er meint, er hat die Weisheit mit Löffeln gegessen *or* die Weisheit (für sich) gepachtet; ***all – familiar,*** nur zu vertraut; ***none – good,*** nicht gerade *or* allzu gut, ziemlich schlecht; ***– much of a good thing,*** zu viel des Guten; 2. (*coll.*) (zu)sehr, höchst, außerordentlich, ungemein; ***it's not – easy,*** es ist gar nicht so leicht; ***you are – kind,*** das ist sehr nett von Ihnen; ***I'm only – glad to help,*** es ist mir ein reines Vergnügen, Ihnen zu helfen; 3. (*never at beginning of clause, except Am.*) auch, außerdem, noch dazu, ebenfalls, obendrein, überdies.

toodle-oo! ['tu:dl'u:], *int.* (*coll.*) tjüs! auf Wiedersehen!

took [tuk], *imperf. of* **take.**

tool [tu:l], **1.** *s.* 1. das Werkzeug, Instrument, Gerät; *pl.* das Handwerkzeug; 2. (*Bookb.*) der (Präge)stempel; 3. (*Tech.*) Drehstahl, das Drehwerkzeug, Arbeitsstück (*for lathes*); 4. (*fig.*) (Hilfs)mittel; (*fig. coll.*) (*a p.*) Werkzeug, der Handlanger; *pl.* das Rüstzeug. **2.** *v.t.* 1. (*also* ***– up***) mit den nötigen Maschinen ausstatten; 2. (mit einem Werkzeug) bearbeiten (*esp. stone*); 3. (*Bookb.*) prägen, punzen. **3.** *v.i.* ***– up,*** die nötigen Maschinen aufstellen; (*sl.*) ***– along,*** gemütlich dahingondeln, kutschieren.

tool|bag, *s.* die Werkzeugtasche. **-chest,** *s.* der Werkzeugkasten. **tooler,** *s.* das Breiteisen (*stone-masonry*). **tool|house,** *s.* *See* **-shed.**

tooling ['tu:liŋ], *s.* 1. die Bearbeitung; 2. (*Bookb.*) Prägung, Punzarbeit, der Prägedruck; ***blind –,*** die Blindprägung; 3. (*masonry*) das Bearbeiten, Behauen; 4. (*also* ***– up***) die Werkzeugausstattung.

tool|kit, *s.* *See* **-bag. -maker,** *s.* der Werkzeugschlosser. **-shed,** *s.* der Geräteschuppen.

toot [tu:t], **1.** *v.t., v.i.* tuten, blasen, (*Motor.*) hupen. **2.** *v.t.* blasen. **3.** *s.* das Blasen, Tuten, der (Trompeten)stoß.

tooth [tu:θ], **1.** *s.* (*pl.* **teeth** [ti:θ]) 1. der Zahn; ***artificial*** or ***false teeth,*** künstliches Gebiß; ***brush*** or ***clean one's teeth,*** sich (*Dat.*) die Zähne putzen; ***clench one's teeth,*** see ***set one's teeth***; ***cut one's teeth,*** zahnen, die ersten Zähne bekommen; (*fig.*) ***draw his teeth,*** ihn unschädlich machen; ***have a – drawn*** or ***extracted,*** sich (*Dat.*) einen Zahn ziehen lassen; (*coll.*) ***fed up to the teeth,*** es mehr als satt haben; (*fig.*) ***get one's teeth into,*** sich hineinknien in (*Acc.*); ***in the teeth of,*** trotz (*Dat. or Gen.*), zum Trotz (*Dat.*), angesichts (*Gen.*), direkt entgegen (*Dat.*); ***cast it in his teeth,*** es ihm vorwerfen *or* ins Gesicht schleudern; ***long in the –,*** alt; ***– and nail,*** mit aller Kraft *or* Wucht, unerbittlich; ***pick one's teeth,*** (sich (*Dat.*)) in den Zähnen herumstochern; ***show one's teeth,*** fletschen, die Zähne zeigen; ***set one's teeth,*** die Zähne zusammenbeißen; ***set his teeth on edge,*** ihn nervös *or* kribbelig machen; ***by the skin of one's teeth,*** mit Hängen und Würgen, mit knapper Not; ***have a sweet –,*** ein Leckermaul *or* genäschig *or* naschhaft sein; ***have a – filled*** or ***stopped,*** sich (*Dat.*) einen Zahn plombieren lassen; ***take the bit between one's teeth,*** auf die Stange beißen; ***armed to the teeth,*** bis an die Zähne bewaffnet; 2. der Zahn (*of saw, comb, rake*); 3. Zahn, Zacken (*of gear*); 4. das Zähnchen (*of leaf*); 5. die Zinke, Zacke (*of fork*). **2.** *v.t.* verzahnen (*a wheel*). **3.** *v.i.* ineinandergreifen (*wheels*).

tooth|-ache, *s,* das Zahnweh, Zahnschmerzen (*pl.*). **-brush,** *s.* die Zahnbürste. **-comb,** *s.* der Staubkamm.

toothed [tu:θt], *adj.* 1. gezahnt; 2. (*Bot.*) gezähnt, gezähnelt, gezackt; 3. (*Tech.*) verzahnt; ***– wheel,*** das Zahnrad. **toothing,** *s.* die Verzahnung (*of a wheel*), Zahnung (*of a saw*). **toothless,** *adj.* zahnlos.

tooth|paste, *s.* die Zahnpaste. **-pick,** *s.* der Zahnstocher. **--powder,** *s.* das Zahnpulver.

toothsome ['tu:θsəm], *adj.* schmackhaft.

tooth-wheel, *s.* *See* ***toothed wheel.***

tootle [tu:tl], **1.** *v.t., v.i.* leise tuten, blasen. **2.** *s.* leises Tuten.

[1]**top** [tɔp], **1.** *s.* oberes Ende, das Kopfende, obere Seite *or* Fläche, oberster Teil, der Oberteil; Kopf (*of tree, page*), Wipfel, die Krone (*of tree*), Oberfläche (*of water*), Spitze, der Gipfel (*of hill, also fig.*), Scheitel (*of head*), das Verdeck (*of vehicle*); (*Naut.*) der Topp, Mars, Mastkorb; die Stulpe, das Oberleder (*of boot*); die Blume (*of beer*), (*Bot.*) (*oft. pl.*) Blätter (*pl.*), das Kraut (*of root crops*); (*fig.*) die Höhe, der Höchststand, höchste Stufe, höchster Punkt *or* Rang *or* Grad; ***at the* –,** obenan, an der Spitze; ***be (at) the – of the class,*** Primus sein; ***at the – of one's form,*** in allerbester Form; (*fig.*) ***at the – of the ladder*** or ***tree,*** an oberster Stelle, in höchster Stellung; ***page 1 at the –,*** Seite 1 oben; ***at the – of one's speed,*** mit höchster Geschwindigkeit; ***at the – of the table,*** am oberen Ende des Tisches; ***at the – of one's voice,*** aus voller Kehle *or* vollem Halse; (*sl.*) ***the –s,*** eine Klasse für sich, ganz große Klasse, (einfach) Klasse; (*coll.*) ***the big –,*** das Zirkuszelt; (*sl.*) ***blow one's –,*** aus der Haut fahren, aus dem Häuschen geraten; ***from – to bottom,*** von oben bis unten, vom Scheitel bis zur Sohle; ***from – to toe,*** von (*or* vom) Kopf bis (zum) Fuß; (*Motor.*) ***in –,*** im höchsten Gang; (*sl.*) ***off one's –,*** übergeschnappt; ***on (the) – of,*** oben auf (*Dat.*), (*fig.*) über (*Acc.*) . . . hinaus; ***on – of everything else,*** noch dazu, darüber hinaus, obendrein, zu allem anderen; ***be on –,*** obenauf liegen; (*coll.*) ***be on – of the world,*** immer obendrauf sein; ***come out on –,*** als Erste(r) *or* Beste(r) *or* Sieger(in) hervorgehen; ***come out –,*** am besten abschneiden; ***come to the –,*** nach oben *or* an die Oberfläche kommen, (*fig.*) sich durchsetzen, an die Spitze kommen; (*Mil. coll.*) ***go over the –,*** über die Deckung springen, (*fig.*) den Sprung wagen; ***to the – of one's bent,*** nach besten Kräften, nach Herzenslust, bis zum äußersten.
2. *adj.* oberst, höchst, Haupt–; ***– boy,*** der Primus; (*sl.*) ***– brass,*** Stabsoffiziere (*pl.*), Hochgestellte (*pl.*), Bonzen (*pl.*); ***– coat,*** der Deckanstrich (*of paint*) (*see also* **topcoat**); (*Tech.*) ***– dead-centre,*** oberer Totpunkt; (*sl.*) ***– dog,*** Überlegene(r), Erste(r), der (die) Sieger(in); ***– drawer,*** oberste Schublade; (*coll.*) die Oberschicht, eine der ersten Familien; (*coll.*) ***– efficiency,*** die Spitzenleistung; ***– fermentation,*** die Obergärung; ***be in the – flight,*** erstklassig *or* unter den Ersten *or* an der Spitze sein; ***– gear,*** höchster *or* letzter Gang; (*Mil. sl.*) (*esp. Am.*) ***– kick,*** der Spieß; ***– price,*** der Höchstpreis; ***– score,*** beste Leistung; ***– secret,*** strenges Geheimnis; ***– speed,*** größte Geschwindigkeit; ***– table,*** der Ehrentisch.
3. *v.t.* 1. bedecken, bekränzen, krönen; 2. die erste Stelle einnehmen in (*Dat.*), die Spitze bilden *or* an der Spitze stehen von; 3. größer sein als, (an Größe) übertreffen, überragen, überschreiten, überbieten; 4. hinausgehen *or* steigen über (*Acc.*); 5. beschneiden, stutzen, kappen (*plants*); 6. die Spitze *or* den Gipfel erreichen von (*a hill*); 7. zu hoch treffen (*golf ball etc.*); 8. ***– up,*** (auf)füllen, vollfüllen.

[2]**top,** *s.* der Kreisel; ***humming –,*** der Brummkreisel; (*sl.*) ***old –,*** alter Knabe; ***spin a –,*** den Kreisel schlagen; ***sleep like a –,*** wie ein Murmeltier schlafen.

topaz ['toupæz], *s.* der Topas; ***smoky –,*** der Rauchtopas.

top|-beam, *s.* der Hahnbalken. **–boots,** *pl.* Stulpenstiefel (*pl.*), Langschäfter (*pl.*). **–coat,** *s.* der Überrock, Mantel. **––dressing,** *s.* 1. (*Agr.*) der Kopfdünger; 2. (*on roads*) die Oberflächenbeschotterung.

[1]**tope** [toup], *v.i.* (*sl.*) saufen.

[2]**tope,** *s.* (*Ichth.*) der Glatthai.

topee ['toupi:], *s.* der Tropenhelm.

top|gallant, 1. *adj.* Bram–. **2.** *s.* das Bramsegel. **––hamper,** *s.* (*Naut.*) obere Takelung, (*fig.*) (überflüssige) Belastung. **––hat,** *s.* der Zylinder(hut). **––heaviness,** *s.* 1. die Topplastigkeit, Oberlastigkeit, Kopflastigkeit; 2. (*fig. Comm.*) Überbewertung; Überkapitalisierung; Überbelastung durch den Verwaltungsapparat. **––heavy,** *adj.* 1. (*Naut.*) topplastig; 2. kopflastig, oberlastig; 2. (*fig.*) durch den Verwaltungsapparat überbelastet, an der Spitze überorganisiert (*organization*); überkapitalisiert (*economy*); überbewertet (*securities*). **––hole,** *pred. adj.* (*obs. coll.*) erstklassig, tipptopp, prima.

topiary ['toupiəri], *s.* 1. die Kunst des Baumschneidens; 2. der Formbaum, Formstrauch.

topic ['tɔpik], *s.* 1. der Gegenstand, das Thema; 2. (*Phil.*) die Beweisquelle, Topik. **topical,** *adj.* 1. aktuell; ***– news,*** Tagesneuigkeiten (*pl.*); 2. (*Med.*) örtlich, lokal. **topicality** [–'kæliti], *s.* die Aktualität, lokale *or* aktuelle Bedeutung.

topknot ['tɔpnɔt], *s.* 1. das Haarbüschel, der Haarknoten; Schopf, das Federbüschel (*of birds*); 2. (*sl.*) der Kopf.

topless ['tɔplis], *adj.* 1. (*Poet.*) unermeßlich hoch; 2. (*coll. of dress*) oben ohne.

top|-level, *attrib. adj.* auf höchster Ebene. **–light,** *s.* (*Naut.*) die Topplaterne. **––liner,** *s.* (*sl.*) Prominente(r), der Haupthahn. **–mast,** *s.* die Marsstenge (*on square-rigger*). **–most,** *adj.* höchst, oberst. **––notch,** *adj. See* **––hole. ––notcher,** *s.* (*sl.*) (*Spt. etc.*) die Kanone, Spitzenklasse.

topographical [tɔpə'græfikl], *adj.* topographisch; ***– features,*** die Bodengestaltung. **topography** [–'pɔgrəfi], *s.* (*Geog., Med.*) die Topographie, (*Mil.*) Geländekunde.

topological [tɔpə'lɔdʒikl], *adj.* topologisch, Orts–, Lage–. **topology** [–'pɔlədʒi], *s.* 1. (*Med.*) topographische Anatomie; 2. (*Math.*) die Topologie, Geometrie der Lage; Ortsbeziehung (*of sets*); 3. (*Geog.*) Ortskunde.

toponymy [tɔ'pɔnimi], *s.* 1. (*Med.*) anatomische Nomenklatur; 2. (*Geog.*) die Ortsnamenkunde.

topped [tɔpt], *adj.* 1. gestutzt, gekappt; 2. übertroffen, überragt (***by,*** von); 3. bedeckt, bekränzt, gekrönt (***with,*** mit); 4. (*fig.*) vervollständigt. **topper** ['tɔpə], *s.* 1. (*Build.*) oberer Stein; 2. (*coll.*) der Zylinder(hut), die Angströhre; 3. (*sl.*) das Mordsding, tolle S.; der Mordskerl. **topping, 1.** *adj.* (*coll.*) fabelhaft, großartig, famos, erstklassig, tipptopp, knorke. **2.** *s.* (*Cul.*) der Überguß. **topping|-lift,** *s.* (*Naut.*) der Hänger. **––out (ceremony),** *s.* (*Build.*) das Richtfest.

topple [tɔpl], **1.** *v.i.* wackeln, kippen, stürzen; ***– down*** or ***over,*** umfallen, umkippen, niederstürzen. **2.** *v.t.* stürzen; ***– down*** or ***over,*** umstürzen, niederwerfen.

top|sail [tɔpsl], *s.* das Marssegel (*on square-rigger*), Toppsegel (*on schooner*). **––secret,** *adj.* streng geheim. **––sergeant,** *s.* (*Am.*) der Hauptfeldwebel. **–sides,** *pl.* (*Naut.*) obere Seitenteile (*pl.*). **–soil,** *s.* die Bödenfläche, Ackerkrume, der Mutterboden.

topsy-turvy ['tɔpsi'tɔ:vi], **1.** *adj.* durcheinanderliegend, auf den Kopf gestellt. **2.** *adv.* 1. das Oberste zuunterst, das Unterste zuoberst, kopfüber; 2. in Unordnung, durcheinander, auf den Kopf, drunter und drüber; ***turn –,*** auf den Kopf stellen. **3.** *s.* völlige Unordnung, das Durcheinander, Chaos, der Wirrwarr, der *or* das Kuddelmuddel.

toque [touk], *s.* 1. runder Frauenhut, die Toque; (*Hist.*) das Barett; 2. (*Zool.*) der Hutaffe.

torch [tɔ:tʃ], *s.* 1. die Fackel (*also fig.*); (***electric***) ***–,*** die Taschenlampe; 2. (*fig.*) die Flamme, das Feuer. **torch|-battery,** *s.* die Stabbatterie. **––bearer,** *s.* der Fackelträger (*also fig.*). **–light,** *s.* die Fackelbeleuchtung, der Fackelschein; ***– procession,*** der Fackelzug.

tore [tɔ:], *imperf. of* [1]**tear.**

toreador ['tɔriədɔ:], *s.* (berittener) Stierkämpfer.

toric ['tɔrik], *adj.* 1. (*Archit.*) wulstförmig; 2. (*Med.*) knotenförmig; 3. (*Geom., Opt.*) torisch.

torment, 1. ['tɔ:mənt], *s.* 1. die Pein, Qual, der Schmerz; 2. (*Hist.*) die Folter(ung); 3. (*coll.*) der Plagegeist, Quälgeist. **2.** [–'ment], *v.t.* quälen, peinigen, plagen, belästigen (***with,*** mit); ***–ed with*** or ***by,*** gequält *or* gepeinigt von, geplagt von *or* mit, belästigt durch. **tormentor** [–'mentə], *s.* 1. der Peiniger; (*coll.*) Quälgeist; 2. (*Theat.*) vordere Kulisse; 3. (*Cul.*) lange Fleischgabel.

tormina [ˈtɔːminə], *s.* das Bauchgrimmen, die Kolik, Leibschmerzen (*pl.*).

torn [tɔːn], *p.p. of* ¹**tear.**

tornado [tɔːˈneidou], *s.* (*pl.* **-es**) der Wirbelsturm, Tornado; (*fig.*) Ausbruch, Sturm (*of abuse etc.*).

torose [tɔˈrous], **torous** [ˈtɔːrəs], *adj.* knorrig, wulstig.

torpedo [tɔːˈpiːdou], **1.** *s.* 1. der Torpedo; 2. (*Ichth.*) (*also* **--fish**) Zitterrochen. **2.** *v.t.* 1. torpedieren (*also fig.*); 2. (*fig.*) vereiteln, vernichten, zunichte machen. **torpedo-boat,** *s.* das Torpedoboot; – ***destroyer,*** der (Torpedoboot)zerstörer.

torpid [ˈtɔːpid], *adj.* schwerfällig, träge, stumpf, apathisch. **torpidity** [–ˈpiditi], **torpidness,** *s.* die Starrheit, Trägheit, Stumpfheit, Schwerfälligkeit, Apathie. **torpor** [ˈtɔːpə], *s.* die Erstarrung, Betäubung, Lethargie, Trägheit, Stumpfheit.

torque [tɔːk], *s.* das Drehmoment, die Drehkraft, der Drall. **torque|-arm,** *s.* (*Motor.*) die Schubstange. **--reaction,** *s.* das Gegendrehmoment. **--rod,** *s.* (*Motor.*) die Kardanwelle. **--wrench,** *s.* der Drehmomentschlüssel.

torrefaction [tɔriˈfækʃən], *s.* das Dörren, Darren, Rösten. **torrefy** [ˈtɔrifai], *v.t.* dörren, darren, rösten.

torrent [ˈtɔrənt], *s.* 1. der Gießbach, Sturzbach, Wildbach, Gebirgsstrom, (reißender) Strom; 2. (*coll.*) der Wolkenbruch, schwerer Regenguß; ***rain in –s,*** in Strömen gießen; 3. (*fig.*) der Strom, Schwall, Ausbruch, die Flut. **torrential** [–ˈrenʃəl], *adj.* gießbachartig, wolkenbruchartig, strömend, reißend; (*fig.*) überwältigend, ungestüm; – ***rain,*** der Wolkenbruch.

torrid [ˈtɔrid], *adj.* brennend, glühend, sengend, Glut– (*heat*); dürr, verbrannt, ausgedörrt; (*Geol.*) – ***zone,*** heiße Zone, Tropen (*pl.*).

torsion [ˈtɔːʃn], *s.* 1. die Drehung, Windung; 2. (*Phys.*) Verdrillung, Torsion; 3. (*Med.*) Abschnürung (*of an artery*). **torsional,** *adj.* (Ver)dreh(ungs)–, Torsions–. **torsion-balance,** *s.* die Drehwaage, Torsionsfadenwaage.

torso [ˈtɔːsou], *s.* (*pl.* **-s**) der Torso (*also fig.*), Rumpf, (*fig.*) das Bruchstück, unvollendetes Werk.

tort [tɔːt], *s.* das Zivilunrecht, Delikt; ***law of –s,*** das Schadenersatzrecht.

tortile [ˈtɔːtail], *adj.* gedreht, gewunden.

tortious [ˈtɔːʃəs], *adj.* rechtswidrig; – ***act,*** rechtswidrige Handlung, die Straftat.

tortoise [ˈtɔːtəs], *s.* die Schildkröte; (***as***) ***slow as a –,*** langsam wie eine Schnecke. **tortoise-shell, 1.** *s.* das Schildpatt; --(***butterfly***), Großer *or* Kleiner Fuchs; – ***cat,*** die Schildpattkatze. **2.** *adj.* Schildpatt–.

tortuosity [tɔːtjuˈɔsiti], *s.* 1. die Windung, Krümmung; 2. Gewundenheit; 3. (*fig.*) Umständlichkeit; 4. (*fig.*) Unaufrichtigkeit, Unehrlichkeit. **tortuous** [ˈtɔːtjuəs], *adj.* 1. gewunden, geschlängelt, verschlungen; 2. (*fig.*) umständlich; 3. (*fig.*) unaufrichtig, unehrlich. **tortuousness,** *s.* (*usu. fig.*) *see* **tortuosity.**

torture [ˈtɔːtʃə], **1.** *s.* 1. die Folter(ung), Tortur (*also fig.*); ***put to the –,*** auf die Folter spannen; ***instrument of –,*** das Folterwerkzeug; 2. (*fig.*) (*oft. pl.*) die Marter, Qual, Pein, der Schmerz. **2.** *v.t.* 1. auf die Folter spannen, foltern (*also fig.*); 2. (*fig.*) quälen, peinigen; 3. pressen, verdrehen, entstellen (*text etc.*). **torture-chamber,** *s.* die Folterkammer. **torturer** [–rə], *s.* 1. der Folterknecht; 2. (*fig.*) Peiniger, Quäler.

torus [ˈtɔːrəs], *s.* (*Archit., Anat.*) der Wulst; (*Bot.*) Blütenboden; (*Math.*) die Ringfläche.

Tory [ˈtɔːri], **1.** *s.* Konservative(r), der Tory. **2.** *adj.* konservativ, Tory–. **Toryism,** *s.* der Konservatismus.

tosh [tɔʃ], *s.* (*coll.*) der Quatsch, das Blech.

toss [tɔs], **1.** *v.t.* 1. (hoch)werfen, in die Höhe werfen; – ***a coin,*** eine Münze hochwerfen; – ***him for,*** mit ihm losen um; – ***hay,*** Heu wenden; 2. schleudern, schmeißen; hin– und herwerfen (*by the sea*); – ***about,*** herumwerfen, hin– und herschleudern; 3. zurückwerfen (*the head*); 4. (*Naut.*) – ***oars,*** die Riemen pieken; 5. – ***off,*** hinunterstürzen (*a drink*). **2.** *v.i.* 1. (*also* – ***about***) sich hin– und herwälzen, sich herumwerfen (*in sleep*); 2. hin– und hergeworfen werden, umhergeworfen werden; rollen, stoßen (*as ships*); auf– und abgehen (*as waves*); 3. – (***up***) ***for,*** eine Münze hochwerfen um, losen um. **3.** *s.* 1. das Werfen, Schleudern; Zurückwerfen, Hochwerfen (*of the head*); 2. der Wurf; (Los)wurf (*of coin*); ***argue the –,*** sich (hartnäckig) streiten um; ***win the –,*** das Los gewinnen; 3. ***take a –,*** (vom Pferde) abgeworfen werden. **toss-up,** *s.* (*fig.*) ungewisse Sache; ***it's a – whether*** . . ., es ist reiner Zufall *or* völlig ungewiß, ob . . . .

¹**tot** [tɔt], **1.** *v.t.* (*coll.*) – ***up,*** zusammenzählen, addieren. **2.** *v.i.* (*coll.*) – ***up to,*** sich belaufen auf (*Acc.*).

²**tot,** *s.* (*coll.*) der Knirps, das Wurm; (*coll.*) das Gläschen, Schlückchen.

total [toutl], **1.** *adj.* 1. gänzlich, total, Total–, vollständig, völlig; – ***eclipse,*** totale Finsternis; 2. (*only attrib.*) ganz, gesamt, Gesamt–. **2.** *s.* das Ganze, die Ganzheit; (*also* ***grand*** or ***sum*** –) der Gesamtbetrag; die (Gesamt)summe, Gesamtmenge; ***in –,*** als Ganzes. **3.** *v.t.* 1. sich (im ganzen) belaufen auf (*Acc.*), ausmachen, betragen; 2. (*of a p.*) zusammenrechnen, zusammenzählen. **4.** *v.i.* – ***up to,*** sich (im ganzen) belaufen auf (*Acc.*).

totalitarian [toutæliˈtɛəriən], *adj.* totalitär. **totality** [–ˈtæliti], *s.* das Ganze, die Gesamtheit, Vollständigkeit. **totalizator** [ˈtoutəlaizeitə], *s. See* **totalizer. totalize** [ˈtoutəlaiz], *v.t.* zusammenzählen, (zu einem Ganzen) zusammenfassen, summieren. **totalizer,** *s.* der Totalisator.

¹**tote** [tout], **1.** *v.t.* (*sl. esp. Am.*) tragen, schleppen, mit sich führen. **2.** *s.* (*sl.*) die Last.

²**tote,** *s.* (*coll.*) der Toto.

totem [ˈtoutəm], *s.* das Totem, Stammwappen (*of Indians*). **totemism,** *s.* der Totemismus. **totem-pole,** *s.* der Totempfahl.

totter [ˈtɔtə], *v.i.* wanken, taumeln, torkeln (*of a p.*); wackeln, (sch)wanken (*of a th.*); – ***to one's grave,*** nicht mehr lange mitmachen; – ***to its fall,*** zusammenbrechen, niederstürzen. **tottering,** *adj.* (sch)wankend, wack(e)lig.

toucan [ˈtuːkən], *s.* (*Orn.*) der Tukan, Toko, Pfefferfresser.

touch [tʌtʃ], **1.** *s.* 1. die Berührung, das Berühren, Anrühren, Anfühlen; leichte Berührung, leichter Druck *or* Schlag *or* Stoß; ***at a –,*** beim Anrühren; ***be rough to the –,*** sich rauh anfühlen; ***on the slightest –,*** bei der leisesten Berührung; 2. leichter Anfall (*of illness*); 3. der Anschlag (*of pianist*), Strich (*of violinist*), (Pinsel)strich (*of artist*); ***give*** or ***put the final*** or ***finishing –***(***es***) ***to,*** die letzte Feile *or* Hand legen an (*Acc.*), den letzten Schliff geben (*Dat.*); ***sure –,*** sichere Hand, sicherer Griff; 4. (*also* ***sense of –***) der Tastsinn, das Tastgefühl, Tastempfinden; 5. (*fig.*) die Fühlung(nahme), Verbindung, der Kontakt; ***be in – with,*** in Verbindung stehen mit; ***get in***(***to***) ***– with,*** Verbindung aufnehmen mit, in Verbindung treten mit, sich in Verbindung setzen mit; ***keep in – with,*** in Verbindung bleiben mit; ***put in***(***to***) ***– with,*** verbinden mit; ***lose – with,*** die Verbindung verlieren mit; ***out of – with,*** nicht mehr in Verbindung mit; 6. der Anschlag, (An)strich, (An)hauch, Beigeschmack, Zug, die Spur; ***fine –,*** schöner Zug; ***personal –,*** persönliche Note; 7. die Probe; ***put to the –,*** auf die Probe stellen; 8. (*Footb. etc.*) *see* **touch-line.**

2. *v.t.* 1. (*of a p.*) berühren, angreifen, anfassen, antasten, anfühlen, betasten, befühlen; (*fig.*) (*usu. neg.*) sich befassen mit, etwas (*or usu.* nichts) zu tun haben wollen mit; anfassen, anrühren (*also food etc.*); (*coll.*) ***I wouldn't – it with a barge-pole!*** ich werde mich hüten! – ***the bell,*** klingeln; – ***one's hat to him,*** ihn grüßen; – ***him on the raw,*** ihn an seinem empfindlichen *or* wunden Punkt treffen; (*coll.*) ***I never –ed him,*** ich habe ihm nichts getan; (*Prov.*) ***they that***

– *pitch will be defiled*, wer Pech angreift, besudelt sich; (*coll.*) *it –es my pocket*, das reißt in meinem Beutel; – *him to the quick*, ihn bis ins Mark treffen; (*coll.*) – *wood!* unberufen! 2. (*sl.*) anpumpen, anhauen (*a p.*) (*for*, um); 3. (*of th.*) in Berührung stehen *or* kommen mit, grenzen *or* stoßen an (*Acc.*); (*Naut.*) – *bottom*, auf Grund geraten; *our gardens – each other*, unsere Gärten grenzen *or* stoßen aneinander; *the chairs are –ing each other*, die Stühle berühren sich; – *glasses*, anstoßen; 4. betreffen, angehen, sich beziehen auf (*Acc.*); 5. (*fig.*) (*of p. or th.*) beeindrucken, beeinflussen, bewegen, rühren, eine Wirkung haben auf (*Acc.*); – *him to the heart*, ihm zu Herzen gehen; (*coll.*) *nothing will – these spots*, nichts richtet bei diesen Flecken was aus; 6. erreichen, reichen an (*Acc.*); (*coll.*) erreichen, nahekommen (*Dat.*), gleichkommen (*Dat.*); (*coll.*) *no-one can – him*, niemand reicht an ihn heran *or* kommt ihm gleich; 7. (*Naut.*) anlaufen, anlegen an (*Dat.*), haltmachen in (*Dat.*); 8. – *off*, zur Explosion bringen, (*fig.*) auslösen, zur Auslösung bringen, in Bewegung setzen; 9. – *up*, aufbessern, auffrischen, aufpolieren; retuschieren, restaurieren (*a picture etc.*).
3. *v.i.* sich berühren, aneinanderstoßen, in Berührung *or* Kontakt kommen; (*Naut.*) – *at*, anlegen in (*Dat.*), anlegen; – *down*, (*Av.*) landen; (*Rugby*) die Hand auflegen; (*fig.*) – *on*, grenzen an (*Acc.*), fast gleichkommen (*Dat.*); (*fig.*) – (*up*)*on*, Bezug haben *or* sich auswirken auf (*Acc.*), berühren; kurz zu sprechen kommen auf (*Acc.*), kurz erwähnen *or* berühren (*a question*).

touch|-and-go, 1. *pred. adj.* (*or s.*) prekäre Situation, gewagte S.; *it was* (*a matter of*) – *whether*, es fehlte nicht viel daß, es stand auf des Messers Schneide ob; *it was – with him*, es stand sehr kritisch mit ihm, sein Leben (*etc.*) hing an einem Haar. **2.** *attrib. adj.* riskant, gewagt, höchst gefährlich. **--down,** *s.* 1. (*Rugby*) das Handauf; 2. (*Av.*) die (Zwischen)landung.

touched [tʌtʃt], *adj.* 1. gerührt, ergriffen, bewegt (*by, with*, von); 2. (*coll.*) verdreht, klapsig, bekloppt.

touch-hole, *s.* (*Hist.*) das Zündloch.

touchily [ˈtʌtʃili], *adv See* **touchy. touchiness,** *s.* die Überempfindlichkeit, Reizbarkeit. **touching, 1.** *adj.* rührend, ergreifend. **2.** *prep.* in bezug auf (*Acc.*).

touch|-judge, *s.* (*Rugby*) der Linienrichter, Seitenrichter. **--line,** *s.* (*Footb. etc.*) die Seitenlinie, Grenzlinie, Seitengrenze, Mark(linie). **--me-not,** *s.* (*Bot.*) das Rührmichnichtan, Nolimetangere, (Großblütiges) Springkraut. **--paper,** *s.* das Zündpapier. **–stone,** *s.* 1. der Probierstein; 2. (*fig.*) Prüfstein, das Kriterium. **--type,** *v.i.* blindschreiben. **--typist,** *s.* der (die) Zehnfingersystemtypist(in). **–wood,** *s.* das Zunderholz, der Zunder.

touchy [ˈtʌtʃi], *adj.* 1. (*of a p.*) überempfindlich, reizbar (*on*, in bezug auf (*Acc.*)); 2. (*of a th.*, heikel, kitz(e)lig.

tough [tʌf], **1.** *adj.* 1. zäh, hart, (bruch)fest; 2. (*coll.*) (*of a p.*) zäh, ausdauernd, kräftig, robust (*physically*), zäh, unnachgiebig, hartnäckig (*mentally*); (*esp. Am.*) – *guy*, der Draufgänger, Kraftmeier, Kraftbold; 3. (*coll.*) (*of a th.*) schwierig, schwer, hart, sauer, unangenehm; *it was – going*, es war ein saures Stück Arbeit; – *job*, schwierige Arbeit; (*sl.*) – *luck*, das Pech; *he's in a – spot*, bei ihm ist dicke Luft; *when things get –*, wenn es mulmig wird; 4. (*sl.*) (*of a p. or th.*) übel, verrufen, rowdyhaft; – *customer*, übler Kunde; – *neighbourhood*, verrufene Gegend. **2.** *s.* (*coll.*) der Raufbold, Rowdy, Rabauke, übler Kunde, schwerer Junge. **toughen** [–ən], **1.** *v.t.* zäh(er) *or* fest(er) machen, kräftigen, abhärten. **2.** *v.i.* zäh(er) *or* fest(er) werden. **tough-minded,** *adj.* realistisch, praktisch, unsentimental. **toughness,** *s.* 1. die Zähigkeit, Festigkeit, Härte; 2. (*of a p.*) Zäh(leb)igkeit, Stärke, Robustheit (*physical*), Hartnäckigkeit, Unnachgiebigkeit (*mental*).

toupee, toupet [ˈtuːpei], *s.* das Toupet, falsche Locken (*pl.*).

tour [tuə], **1.** *s.* 1. die (Rund)reise, (Rund)fahrt, Tour, der Ausflug; *circular –*, die Rundreise; (*Hist.*) *grand –*, die Europareise, Kavalierstour; *foreign –*, die Reise ins Ausland; *walking –*, die (Fuß)wanderung, Fußreise; 2. der Rundgang; – *of inspection*, der Besichtigungsrundgang; 3. (*Theat.*) die Gastspielreise, Tournee; *on –*, auf Tournee; 4. (*Mil.*) (*also – of duty*) die Dienstzeit. **2.** *v.t.* 1. bereisen, durchreisen, eine Rundreise machen durch; 2. einen Rundgang machen um *or* durch; (*Theat.*) auf Tournee gehen mit. **3.** *v.i.* reisen; (*Theat.*) auf Tournee gehen, eine Gastspielreise machen.

tour de force [ˈtuədəˈfɔːs], *s.* der Gewaltsstreich, (*usu. fig.*) die Glanzleistung.

tourer [ˈtuərə], *s. See* ***touring car***. **touring,** *s.* das Reisen; – *car*, der Tourenwagen; – *exhibition*, die Wanderausstellung. **tourism,** *s.* der Reiseverkehr, Fremdenverkehr. **tourist,** *s.* (Vergnügungs)reisende(r), der (die) Tourist(in), Ausflügler(in); – *agency*, das Reisebüro; – *class*, die Touristenklasse; – *guide*, der Fremdenführer; – *industry*, *see* **tourism**; – *season*, die Reisezeit; – *ticket*, das Rundreisebillet.

tourmaline [ˈtuəməlin], *s.* der Tourmalin.

tournament [ˈtuənəmənt], *s.* (*Spt.*) das Turnier, der Wettkampf; (*Hist.*) *see* **tourney**; *chess –*, das Schachturnier. **tourney** [ˈtuəni], **1.** *s.* (*Hist.*) das (Ritter)turnier ,(Ritter)kampfspiel. **2.** *v.i.* turnieren.

tourniquet [ˈtuənikei], *s.* die Aderpresse.

tousle [tauzl], *v.t.* (zer)zausen (*hair etc.*).

tout [taut], **1.** *v.i.* Kunden werben, Werbung treiben (*for*, für); – *for custom*, nach Kundschaft suchen. **2.** *v.t.* (*coll.*) Reklame machen für, an die große Glocke hängen, über den grünen Klee loben. **3.** *s.* 1. der Kundenwerber; 2. (*also racing –*) der Tip(p)geber.

[1]**tow** [tou], *s.* das Werg, die Hede.

[2]**tow, 1.** *v.t.* (am Seil *or* Strick) schleppen, (*Naut.*) treideln, bugsieren, ins Schlepptau nehmen; abschleppen (*a car*); (*coll.*) mit sich ziehen, hinter sich herziehen, mitschleppen, bugsieren. **2.** *s.* 1. das Schleppen; (*Naut.*) (*also –rope, –line*) das Schlepptau; *take in –*, (*usu. fig.*) ins Schlepptau nehmen; *have in –*, schleppen, im Schlepptau haben (*also fig.*); *on –*, im Schlepptau; 2. der Schleppzug (*of boats*); geschleppter Wagen. **towage** [–idʒ], *s.* 1. das Schleppen, Bugsieren; 2. der Bugsierlohn, die Schleppgebühr.

toward, 1. [ˈtouəd], *adj.* (*obs.*) (*only pred.*) 1. gelehrig, fügsam, geneigt, (bereit)willig; 2. im Gange, am Werk; 3. nahe, bevorstehend. **2.** [təˈwɔːd, tɔːd], (*Poet.*), **towards** [təˈwɔːdz, tɔːdz], *prep.* 1. (*place*) zu . . . hin, nach . . .hin, nach . . . zu, auf (*Acc.*) . . . zu, gegen (. . . hin); 2. (*time*) gegen; – *midday*, gegen Mittag; 3. (*purpose*) zum Zwecke von (*or Gen.*), zwecks, zu, um, für; – *his expenses*, zur Deckung seiner Ausgaben; 4. (*relation*) gegen(über), betreffend; *attitude –*, die Einstellung gegen.

towel [ˈtauəl], **1.** *s.* das Handtuch; *roller –*, das Rollhandtuch; (*coll.*) *throw in the –*, sich geschlagen geben. **2.** *v.t.* 1. abtrocknen, abreiben; 2. (*sl.*) verdreschen, verhauen. **towel-horse,** *s.* der Handtuchständer. **towelling,** *s.* 1. der Handtuchdrell; 2. die Abreibung; 3. (*sl.*) Tracht Prügel. **towel-rail,** *s.* der Handtuchhalter.

tower [ˈtauə], **1.** *s.* der Turm; (*Hist.*) die Feste, Burg, der Zwinger, das Bollwerk, Kastell; (*fig.*) – *of strength*, starker Hort, mächtige Stütze. **2.** *v.i.* (hoch)ragen, sich emportürmen *or* erheben; – *above* or *over*, überragen (*also fig.*). **towering,** *adj.* 1. turmhoch (aufragend), sich auftürmend, hoch emporsteigend; 2. (*fig.*) aufbrausend, maßlos (*rage etc.*), hochfliegend, hochstrebend (*ambition*).

towing [ˈtouiŋ], *s.* das Schleppen, Treideln. **towing-path,** *s. See* **towpath.**

tow|line, *s. See* **–rope.**

town [taun], *s.* 1. die Stadt; *all over the –*, in der ganzen Stadt; (*coll.*) *paint the – red*, Spektakel machen, auf die Pauke hauen; *talk of the –*, das

Stadtgespräch; 2. (*without art.*) Stadtinnere(s), das Stadtzentrum; ***man about –***, der Lebemann; ***in –***, in der Stadt; ***out of –***, verreist, auf dem Lande; ***go up to –***, in die Stadt (*oft.* nach London) fahren; (*sl.*) ***go to –***, sich mit Haut und Haar verschreiben (***over***, *Dat.*); 3. (*Univ.*) Bürger (*pl.*), die Bürgerschaft; ***– and gown***, Bürgerschaft und Studentenschaft.

town|-clerk, *s.* der Stadtsyndikus. **--council,** *s.* der Gemeinderat, Stadtrat. **--councillor,** *s.* Stadtverordnete(r), der Stadtrat. **--crier,** *s.* (*Hist.*) der Ausrufer. **--dweller,** *s.* der Stadtbewohner, Städter.

townee [tau'ni:], *s.* (*sl.*) 1. *See* **town-dweller**; 2. (*Univ.*) Bürger.

town|hall, *s.* das Rathaus. **--house,** *s.* die Stadtwohnung. **--major,** *s.* (*Mil.*) der Ortskommandant. **--planning,** *s.* die Stadtplanung, Städteplanung, der Städtebau.

townsfolk ['taunzfouk], *pl.* Stadtbewohner (*pl.*), Städter (*pl.*).

township ['taunʃip], *s.* 1. die Stadtgemeinde, das Stadtgebiet; 2. (*Am.*) der Grafschaftsbezirk; 3. (*Am. Surv.*) das Gebiet von 36 Quadratmeilen; 4. (*Austral.*) die Siedlung. **towns|man,** *s.* der Bürger, Städter; ***fellow –***, der Mitbürger. **–people,** *pl. See* **–folk. –woman,** *s.* die Stadtbewohnerin, Städterin.

tow|path, *s.* der Leinpfad, Treidelweg. **--plane,** *s.* das Schleppflugzeug. **–rope,** *s.* das Schlepptau, Zugtau, Bugsiertau, der Treidel, die Treidelleine. **--take-off,** *s.* der Schleppstart (*gliders*).

toxaemia [tɔk'si:miə], *s.* die Blutvergiftung. **toxic** ['tɔksik], *adj.* giftig, gifthaltig, Gift–. **toxicant** ['tɔksikənt], **1.** *s.* der Giftstoff, das Gift. **2.** *adj.* toxisch, giftig. **toxicological** [–kə'lɔdʒikl], *adj.* giftkundlich, toxokologisch. **toxicology** [–'kɔlədʒi], *s.* die Toxokologie, Giftkunde, Giftlehre. **toxin** ['tɔksin], *s.* das Toxin, der Giftstoff.

toxophilite [tɔk'sɔfilait], *s.* der Bogenschütze, Armbrustschütze.

toy [tɔi], **1.** *s.* 1. das (Kinder)spielzeug; *pl.* Spielsachen (*pl.*), Spielwaren (*pl.*); 2. (*fig.*) der Tand, die Lappalie. **2.** *adj.* ***– dog***, der Schoßhund; ***– railway***, die Spielzeugeisenbahn; ***– soldier***, der Bleisoldat. **3.** *v.i.* spielen, tändeln, liebäugeln. **toyshop,** *s.* das Spielwarengeschäft.

[1]**trace** [treis], *s.* 1. der Strang, Zugriemen; ***in the –s***, angespannt; (*fig.*) ***kick over the –s***, über die Stränge schlagen; 2. (*Angling*) das Vorfach.

[2]**trace, 1.** *s.* 1. die Spur (*also fig.*), Fährte; (*fig.*) der (Über)rest, das (An)zeichen; ***be hot on the –s of***, dicht auf den Fersen sein (*Dat.*); ***leave no –*** (***behind***), keine Spur hinterlassen; (*Chem.*) ***– element***, das Spurenelement; 2. die Kleinigkeit, geringe Menge, (ein) bißchen; ***not a – of***, keine Spur von; 3. die Skizze, Zeichnung, (*usu.*) Pauszeichnung, Pause, (*Archit.*) der Grundriß; (*Tech.*) die Aufzeichnung, Kurve (*of visual instrument*). **2.** *v.t.* 1. der Spur nachgehen (*Gen.*), nachspüren (*Dat.*); aufspüren, ausfindig machen, erforschen, verfolgen; erkennen, feststellen; nachweisen, herleiten (***from***, von); ***– back***, zurückverfolgen (***to***, bis zu), zurückführen auf (*Acc.*); 2. durchzeichnen, (durch)pausen, kopieren; abstecken, (nach)zeichnen; (*of instruments*) verzeichnen, aufzeichnen.

traceable ['treisəbl], *adj.* aufspürbar, auffindbar, nachweisbar, nachweislich; zurückverfolgen(d) (***to***, auf (*Acc.*)), zuzuschreiben(d) (*Dat.*). **tracer,** *s.* 1. (*Biol.*) der (Radio)indikator, Tracer; 2. (*also* ***– bullet***) das Lichtspurgeschoß, Rauchspurgeschoß.

tracery ['treisəri], *s.* (*Archit.*) das Maßwerk; (*fig.*) Flechtwerk, Netzwerk.

trachea [trə'kiə], *s.* (*pl.* **-cheae** [–'kii:]) (*Anat.*) die Luftröhre; (*Zool.*) Trachee; (*Bot.*) das Spiralgefäß. **tracheal,** *adj.* Luftröhren–; Tracheen–; Gefäß–. **tracheitis** [træki'aitis], *s.* die Luftröhrenentzündung. **tracheotomy** [træki'ɔtəmi], *s.* der Luftröhrenschnitt.

tracing ['treisiŋ], *s.* 1. das Suchen, die Nachforschung; 2. (*Tech.*) Durchpausen, (Auf)zeichnen; die Pause, Kopie, Pauszeichnung; der (Auf)riß, Plan; (*on an instrument*) die Aufzeichnung; ***make a – of***, (durch)pausen. **tracing-paper,** *s.* das Pauspapier.

track [træk], **1.** *s.* 1. (*Hunt.*) die Spur (*also fig.*), Fährte; Fahrrinne, Wagenspur, (Wagen)furche; (*usu. pl.*) Fußspur; ***be on his –***(*s*), ihm auf der Spur sein; ***cover one's –s***, seine Spuren verwischen; (*fig.*) ***follow in his –s***, seinem Beispiel folgen; ***keep – of***, laufend verfolgen, sich auf dem laufenden halten über (*Acc.*); ***lose – of***, aus dem Auge verlieren (*a p.*), nicht mehr verfolgen (*a th.*); (*sl.*) ***make –s***, ausreißen, durchbrennen; sich begeben (***for***, nach); ***stop in one's –s***, auf der Stelle stehenbleiben, (*fig.*) plötzlich innehalten; ***off the –***, auf falscher Fährte, auf dem Holzweg; ***on the – of***, auf der Spur (*Gen.*); 2. das Fahrwasser, Kielwasser (*of a ship*); 3. der Pfad, Weg; ***beaten –***, der Trampelweg, altes *or* ausgetretenes Gleis; 4. die Bahn (*of a comet etc.*); 5. (*Spt.*) (Renn)bahn; ***– events***, Laufdisziplinen (*pl.*); ***cinder –***, die Aschenbahn; 6. (*Railw.*) Schienen (*pl.*), die Trasse, das Gleis; 7. (*Elec.*) die Kriechspur, Kriechstrecke; 8. Raupenkette, Laufkette, Gliederkette (*of tanks etc.*); 9. das (Reifen)profil (*tyres*). **2.** *v.t.* 1. aufspüren; nachspüren (*Dat.*), verfolgen; ***– down***, aufspüren, ausfindig machen; 2. ***–ed vehicle***, das Kettenfahrzeug. **3.** *v.i.* 1. Spur verfolgen; 2. in der Wagenspur *or* auf der Schiene bleiben (*of wheels*); 3. (*Tech.*) gleichlaufen.

trackage ['trækidʒ], *s.* (*Railw. coll.*) der Schienenstrang, Schienen (*pl.*). **tracker,** *s.* 1. fährtengerechter Jäger, der Fährtenfinder; 2. (*also* **--dog**) Spürhund. **tracking,** *s.* 1. (*Hunt.*) das Fährtensuchen; 2. (*Tech.*) der Gleichlauf (*of gears etc.*); 3. (*Elec.*) das Kriechen. **tracking-station,** *s.* die Beobachtungsstation. **track-layer,** *s.* (*Railw.*) der Schienenleger. **trackless,** *adj.* spurlos, pfadlos, unbetreten. **track-suit,** *s.* (*Spt.*) der Trainingsanzug.

[1]**tract** [trækt], *s.* die Strecke, Gegend, der (Land)strich, das Gebiet, ausgedehnte Fläche; ***digestive –***, das Verdauungssystem; ***respiratory –***, Atemwege (*pl.*).

[2]**tract,** *s.* die Abhandlung; der Traktat, das Traktätchen, (religiöse) Flugschrift.

tractability [træktə'biliti], *s.* die Lenksamkeit, Gefügigkeit. **tractable** ['træktəbl], *adj.* lenksam, fügsam, folgsam (*of a p.*), gefügig, leicht zu bearbeiten(d), handlich (*of material*).

Tractarian [træk'tɛəriən], *s.* der Traktarianer. **tractate** ['trækteit], *s. See* [2]**tract.**

tractile ['træktail], *adj.* dehnbar, streckbar.

traction ['trækʃən], *s.* 1. das Ziehen, der Zug; das Dehnen; (*Tech.*) die Zugkraft, Zugleistung; (*Anat.*) Zusammenziehung; 2. der Transport, die Beförderung. **tractional,** *adj.* Zug–. **traction-engine,** *s.* die Zugmaschine, Straßenlokomotive, der Trecker, Traktor.

tractor ['træktə], *s.* 1. der (Raupen)schlepper; ***--plough***, der Motorpflug; 2. (*Av.*) (*also* ***--propeller***) die Zugschraube; ***--airplane***, das Flugzeug mit Zugschraube; 3. (*Med.*) der Streckapparat; 4. *See* **traction-engine.**

trade [treid], **1.** *s.* 1. der Handel, (Handels)verkehr; ***Board of Trade***, das Handelsministerium, (*Am.*) die Handelskammer; ***coasting –***, die Küstenfahrt; ***domestic –***, der Binnenhandel; ***foreign –***, der Außenhandel; ***free –***, der Freihandel; ***do – with***, Handel treiben mit; 2. das Geschäft, Gewerbe, Handwerk, Metier, der Beruf, die Branche; ***be in –***, Geschäftsmann sein; ***carry on a –***, ein Geschäft betreiben; ***carrying –***, das Transportgeschäft, die Spedition; ***do a good –***, gute Geschäfte machen; ***Jack of all –s***, Hans Dampf in allen Gassen; ***sell to the –***, an Wiederverkäufer abgeben; ***trick of the –***, der Geschäftskniff; 3. (*coll.*) ***the –s***, *see* **trade winds. 2.** *v.i.* 1. handeln, Handel treiben (***in***, mit (*a th.*); ***with***, mit (*a p.*)); 2. (*coll.*) ***–*** (***up***)***on***, ausnützen, mißbrauchen; spekulieren auf (*Acc.*).

3. *v.t.* (*coll.*) vertauschen, (ein)tauschen (*for*, gegen), austauschen; – *s.th. in,* etwas in Zahlung *or* Kauf geben.

trade|-allowance, *s.* der Rabatt für Wiederverkäufer, Warenskonto. **--balance,** *s.* die Handelsbilanz. **--board,** *s.* das Lohnamt, die Arbeitgeber- und -nehmerbehörde. **--cycle,** *s.* der Konjunkturzyklus. **--directory,** *s.* das Firmenverzeichnis, Handelsadreßbuch. **--discount,** *s. See* **--allowance. --disputes,** *pl.* Arbeitsstreitigkeiten (*pl.*). **--fair,** *s.* die Handelsmesse. **--in,** *s.* (*coll.*) (der Gegenstand als) Teilzahlung. – **journal,** *s.* die Fachzeitschrift. **-mark,** *s.* die Schutzmarke, das Warenzeichen. **--name,** *s.* 1. der Markenname, die Handelsbezeichnung (*of article*); 2. der Firmenname. **--price,** *s.* der Großeinkaufspreis, Wiederverkäuferpreis, Handelspreis, Engrospreis.

trader ['treidə], *s.* 1. der Händler, Handelsmann, Kaufmann; 2. das Handelsschiff, Kauffahrteischiff.

trade|-route, *s.* der Handelsweg, die Handelsstraße. **--school,** *s.* die Gewerbeschule. **--secret,** *s.* das Betriebsgeheimnis. **--show,** *s.* (geschlossene) Filmvorführung für Abnehmer.

trades|man [-mən], *s.* 1. Gewerbetreibende(r); der Geschäftsmann, (Klein)händler; 2. (*esp. Scots*) Handwerker; *-'s entrance,* der Eingang für Lieferanten; 3. (*Mil.*) der Spezialist. **-people,** *pl.* Geschäftsleute, Handelsleute, Gewerbetreibende (*pl.*).

trade|-union, *s.* die Gewerkschaft. **--unionism,** *s.* die Gewerkschaftsbewegung; das Gewerkschaftswesen. **--unionist,** *s.* der (die) Gewerkschaftler(in). – **winds,** *pl.* Passatwinde (*pl.*).

trading ['treidiŋ], *s.* das Handeln, der Handel. **trading| capital,** *s.* das Betriebskapital. – **company,** *s.* die Handelsgesellschaft. – **estate,** *s.* die Industriesiedlung. **--post,** *s.* die Handelsniederlassung. **--stamp,** *s.* der Gutschein, die Rabattmarke. – **vessel,** *s.* das Handelsschiff.

tradition [trə'diʃən], *s.* 1. die Überlieferung, Tradition, alter Brauch, das Herkommen, Brauchtum; (*coll.*) *be in the* –, sich im Rahmen der Tradition halten; 2. (*Law*) die Übergabe, Auslieferung. **traditional,** *adj.* traditionell, Traditions-, überliefert; herkömmlich, hergebracht, üblich, von alters her gewohnt. **traditionalism,** *s.* der Traditionalismus, das Festhalten an der Überlieferung.

traduce [trə'dju:s], *v.t.* verleumden. **traducement,** *s.* die Verleumdung. **traducer,** *s.* der Verleumder.

traffic ['træfik], **1.** *s.* 1. der Handel, (Handels)verkehr (*in*, in (*Dat.*) *or* mit); (*coll.*) *have no – with,* nichts zu tun haben mit, keine Beziehung haben zu; *white-slave* –, der Mädchenhandel; 2. (öffentlicher) Verkehr, der Straßenverkehr; *freight* or *goods* –, der Güterverkehr; *heavy* –, der Andrang, starker Verkehr; *one-way* –, die Einbahnstraße; *passenger* –, der Personenverkehr. **2.** *v.i.* 1. handeln, Handel treiben (*in*, in (*Dat.*); *with*, mit); 2. schachern (*for*, um). **3.** *v.t.* (*also – away*) verschachern.

trafficator ['træfikeitə], *s.* (*Motor.*) der Winker, Blinker.

traffic|-control, *s.* die Verkehrsregelung. **--jam,** *s.* die Verkehrsstockung.

trafficker ['træfikə], *s.* 1. der Händler; 2. Schacherer, Intrigant.

traffic|-light, *s.* das Verkehrssignal, die Verkehrsampel. **--manager,** *s.* (*Railw.*) der Betriebsinspektor. **--offence,** *s.* der Verstoß gegen die Verkehrsregeln. – **regulations,** *pl.* Verkehrsvorschriften (*pl.*), Verkehrsregeln (*pl.*), die (Straßen)verkehrsordnung. **--returns,** *pl.* die Betriebsstatistik. **--sign,** *s.* das Verkehrszeichen, die Verkehrstafel.

tragacanth ['trægəkænθ], *s.* der Tragant(gummi).

tragedian [trə'dʒi:diən], *s.* 1. der Tragödiendichter, Tragiker; 2. tragischer Schauspieler, der Tragöde. **tragedienne** [-i'en], *s.* tragische Schauspielerin, die Tragödin. **tragedy** ['trædʒidi], *s.* 1. das Trauerspiel, die Tragödie; 2. (*fig.*) tragischer Vorfall, das Unglück; der Unglücksfall; das Tragische. **tragic** ['trædʒik], *adj.* tragisch (*also fig.*); (*fig.*) unheilvoll, unselig; – *actor* (*actress*), *see* **tragedian (tragedienne). tragical,** *adj.* (*rare*) *see* **tragic. tragicomedy** [trædʒi'kɔmidi], *s.* die Tragikomödie. **tragicomic,** *adj.* tragikomisch.

trail [treil], **1.** *s.* 1. (*Hunt.*) die Witterung, Fährte, Spur (*also fig.*); *on the* –, auf der Fährte *or* (*fig.*) Spur; *off the* –, von der Fährte abgekommen, (*fig.*) auf der falschen Spur; 2. (ausgetretener) Weg *or* Pfad; (*fig.*) *blaze a* –, einen Weg bahnen; 3. der Schweif (*of meteor*), Streifen, die Fahne (*of smoke*), (*Av.*) Kondensfahne; 4. (*Artil.*) der (Lafetten)schwanz. **2.** *v.t.* 1. (nach)schleppen, (nach)schleifen, hinter sich herziehen; (*coll.*) – *along,* mit sich schleppen; (*Mil.*) – *arms!* Gewehr rechts! (*fig.*) – *one's coat,* einen Streit vom Zaun brechen; 2. nachgehen (*Dat.*), nachspüren (*Dat.*), auf der Spur *or* den Fersen sein (*Dat.*); 3. (*Motor.*) trailern (*caravan etc.*). **3.** *v.i.* 1. schleifen, sich (hin)schleppen *or* hinziehen; – *along,* sich dahinschleppen; 2. kriechen (*as plants*); 3. (*coll.*) nachhinken, zurückbleiben; 4. – *off,* verklingen, verhallen.

trailer ['treilə], *s.* 1. der Anhänger (*of vehicles*); 2. (*Bot.*) die Kriechpflanze, rankender Ausläufer; 3. (*Films*) die Vorschau, Voranzeige. **trailing,** *adj.* (*Bot.*) kriechend; (*Av.*) – *aerial,* die Hängeantenne; (*Motor.*) – *axle,* die Hinterachse; (*Av.*) – *edge,* die Hinterkante. **trail-net,** *s.* das Schleppnetz.

train [trein], **1.** *s.* 1. die Schleppe (*of a dress*); 2. Serie, Reihe, Kette, Folge; – *of thought,* die Gedankenfolge, der Gedankengang; *in* –, in Gang, im Zuge, im Entstehen; *put in* –, in Gang setzen; 3. (*Mil.*) die Kolonne, Fahrtruppe, der Train, Troß; 4. (*also railway-*–) (Eisenbahn)zug; *by* –, mit dem Zuge, mit der Bahn; *change -s,* umsteigen; *be on the* –, mitfahren, im Zuge sein; *slow* –, der Personenzug, Bummelzug; *special* –, der Sonderzug; 5. das Gefolge, die Begleitung; *bring in its* –, nach sich ziehen, mit sich bringen; 6. der Schweif (*of comet*); 7. (*Horol.*) das Räderwerk; 8. (*for explosives*) die Zündlinie, das Leitfeuer. **2.** *v.t.* 1. abrichten, dressieren (*animals*), zureiten (*horses*), trainieren (*athletes*); erziehen, aufziehen, bilden, schulen (*children etc.*), ausbilden, (ein)üben, (ein)exerzieren, drillen (*recruits*); 2. (auf)ziehen (*plants*); 3. zielen, richten (*a gun*) (*on*, auf (*Acc.*)). **3.** *v.i.* 1. (*Spt.*) (sich) üben, (sich) trainieren (*for*, für); 2. sich ausbilden *or* vorbereiten *or* schulen (*as, for*, als *or* zu); 3. (*sl.*) – (*it*), mit der Eisenbahn fahren.

train|-band, *s.* (*Hist.*) die Bürgerwehr. **--bearer,** *s.* der Schleppenträger.

trained [treind], *adj.* 1. geschult, ausgebildet, gelernt; 2. vorgebildet, (ein)geübt. **trainee** [-'ni:], *s.* der Kursteilnehmer, Anlernling (*in industry*); (*Mil.*) (*esp. Am.*) Rekrut. **trainer** ['treinə], *s.* 1. der Trainer, Sportlehrer; Lehrmeister, Exerziermeister; Zureiter (*of horses*); Abrichter, Dresseur (*of dogs etc.*); 2. (*Av.*) das Schulflugzeug.

train-ferry, *s.* der *or* das (Eisenbahn)trajekt.

training ['treiniŋ], *s.* 1. die Erziehung, Ausbildung, Schulung, Schule, Übung, Vorbereitung; *further* –, die Weiterbildung; 2. (*Spt.*) die Trainierung, das Training; *in good* –, gut im Training; 3. das Einüben, Einexerzieren, Abrichten, Zureiten; 4. (*Hort.*) Ziehen.

training|-camp, *s.* das Schulungslager. **--college,** *s.* das Lehrerseminar. **--film,** *s.* der Lehrfilm. **--ground,** *s.* der Exerzierplatz, Übungsplatz. **--ship,** *s.* das Schulschiff.

train| journey, *s.* die Bahnfahrt. **--oil,** *s.* das Fischöl, der Tran. – **service,** *s.* die Eisenbahnverbindung, der Eisenbahnverkehr. **--staff,** *s.* das Zugpersonal.

traipse, *see* **trapse.**

trait [trei(t)], *s.* der (Charakter)zug, das Merkmal, die Eigenart.

traitor ['treitə], *s.* der Verräter (*to*, an (*Dat.*)).

traitorous, *adj.* verräterisch, treulos. **traitress** [-tris], *s.* die Verräterin.
traject, 1. [trəˈdʒekt], *v.t.* (*rare*) übertragen (*thoughts etc.*). **2.** [ˈtrædʒekt], *s.* (*rare*) die Fähre, der *or* das Trajekt. **trajectory** [trəˈdʒektəri], *s.* 1. (*Math.*) die Bahn(kurve); 2. (*Artil. etc.*) Schußbahn, Wurfbahn, Flugbahn; ***flat-- fire,*** das Flachfeuer.
[1]**tram** [træm], *s.* 1. (*Min.*) der Laufkarren, Förderwagen, Hund, die Lore; *see also* **tramway** (*Min.*); 2. *See* **tramcar**; ***by* –,** mit der Straßenbahn.
[2]**tram,** *s.* (*Tech.*) der Ellipsenzirkel.
tram|car, *s.* die Straßenbahn, der Straßenbahnwagen. **--conductor,** *s.* der Straßenbahnschaffner. **--driver,** *s.* der Straßenbahnführer. **-line,** *s.* 1. die Straßenbahnschiene; 2. *pl.* (*Tenn. coll.*) Seitenlinien (*pl.*).
trammel [træml], **1.** *s.* 1. der Spannriemen, Fesselriemen (*for horses*); 2. (*also* – ***net***) das Schleppnetz; 3. der Kesselhaken (*on a hearth*); 4. *See* [2]**tram**; 5. (*fig.*) (*usu. pl.*) die Fessel, Fesseln (*pl.*), der Zwang, Hemmschuh. **2.** *v.t.* (*usu. fig.*) hindern, hemmen, fesseln.
tramontane [trəˈmɔntein], *adj.* 1. jenseits der Alpen, transalpin(isch); 2. (*fig.*) fremd.
tramp [træmp], **1.** *v.i.* 1. derb auftreten, mit schwerem Schritt gehen; trampeln, treten (***on,*** auf (*Acc.*)); 2. (*oft.* – ***it***) (zu Fuß) reisen, wandern, trampen. **2.** *v.t.* 1. durchstreifen, durchwandern; 2. – ***down,*** niedertreten, festtreten, niedertrampeln. **3.** *s.* 1. das Getrampel, Trampeln; 2. die Fußwanderung, Fußreise; ***on the* –,** auf der Wanderschaft; 3. der Landstreicher, Vagabund; 4. (*sl.*) das Flittchen, der Berber; 5. Tramp(dampfer).
trample [træmpl], **1.** *v.t.* (*also* – ***down***) (zer)trampeln, niedertreten (*grass etc.*); – ***out,*** austreten (*a fire*); (*fig.*) – ***under foot,*** niedertreten, mit Füßen treten, herumtrampeln auf (*Dat.*); – ***to death,*** zu Tode trampeln. **2.** *v.i.* (herum)trampeln, (herum)treten (***on,*** auf (*Dat.*)), treten (auf (*Acc.*)); (*fig.*) – ***(up)on,*** mit Füßen treten. **3.** *s.* das Getrampel, Trampeln.
trampoline [ˈtræmpəli:n], *s.* das (die) Trampolin(e), das Federbrett.
tram|road, *s. See* **-way** (*Min.*). **--stop,** *s.* die Straßenbahnhaltestelle. **--ticket,** *s.* der Straßenbahnfahrschein. **-way,** *s.* 1. die Straßenbahn(linie); 2. (*Min.*) die Grubenbahn, Förderbahn.
trance [trɑ:ns], *s.* 1. die Verzückung, Ekstase; 2. Hypnose, hypnotischer Schlaf, der Entrückungszustand, die Trance; (*coll.*) Verwirrung, Benommenheit.
tranquil [ˈtrænkwil], *adj.* 1. ruhig, ruhevoll, friedlich, ungestört; 2. unbewegt, gelassen. **tranquillity** [-ˈkwiliti], *s.* 1. die Ruhe, Stille; 2. Gelassenheit, Gemütsruhe. **tranquillization** [-laiˈzeiʃən], *s.* die Beruhigung. **tranquillize,** *v.t.* beruhigen. **tranquillizer,** *s.* das Sedativum, Beruhigungsmittel.
transact [trænˈzækt], *v.t.* verrichten, (ab)machen, abwickeln, abschließen, zustande bringen, (durch)führen, erledigen; – ***business,*** Geschäfte machen, ein Geschäft abmachen *or* abwickeln. **transaction** [-ˈzækʃən], *s.* 1. die Verrichtung, Durchführung, Abwicklung, Erledigung; Unterhaltung, Verhandlung, (*Law*) Abmachung, Übereinkunft, der Vergleich, das Rechtsgeschäft; 2. (*Comm.*) Geschäft, geschäftliches Unternehmen, der Geschäftsvorgang, Geschäftsabschluß, die Transaktion; *pl.* der Geschäftsumsatz, Umsätze (*pl.*); 3. *pl.* (*of a society etc.*) das Protokoll, Verhandlungen (*pl.*), der Verhandlungsbericht, (Sitzungs)bericht. **transactor,** *s.* der Unterhändler.
trans|alpine [trænzˈælpain], *adj.* jenseits der Alpen, transalpin(isch). **-atlantic,** *adj.* transatlantisch, Übersee–; – ***flight,*** der Ozeanflug; – ***liner,*** der Überseedampfer.
transceiver [trænˈsi:və], *s.* (*Rad.*) der Senderempfänger.
transcend [trænˈsend], *v.t.* 1. übersteigen, überschreiten; 2. übertreffen. **transcendence, transcendency,** *s.* 1. die Überlegenheit, Vortrefflichkeit, Erhabenheit; 2. (*Phil., Theol.*) Transzendenz. **transcendent,** *adj.* 1. vortrefflich, vorzüglich, überragend, hervorragend; 2. (*Phil., Theol.*) transzendent. **transcendental** [-sənˈdentl], **1.** *adj.* 1. übernatürlich, außergewöhnlich, übersinnlich, phantastisch; 2. spekulativ, abstrakt; dunkel, verworren, unklar, abstrus; 3. (*Phil.*) transzendental, metaphysisch, apriorisch; 4. (*Math.*) transzendent. **2.** *s.* 1. (*Phil.*) transzendentaler Begriff, die Grundvoraussetzung, das Transzendentale; 2. (*Math.*) die Transzendente. **transcendentalism** [-ˈdentəlizm], *s.* die Transzendentalphilosophie.
transcontinental [trænskɔntiˈnentl], *adj.* transkontinental.
transcribe [trænˈskraib], *v.t.* 1. abschreiben, kopieren; ausschreiben (*notes*); 2. umschreiben, übertragen (*shorthand etc.*); 3. (*Mus.*) transkribieren, umsetzen.
transcript [ˈtrænskript], *s.* die Abschrift, Kopie. **transcription** [-ˈskripʃən], *s.* 1. das Abschreiben, Umschreiben; 2. Abschrift, Umschrift; 3. (*Mus.*) Übertragung, Transkription; 4. (*Rad.*) Tonaufnahme.
transducer [trænsˈdju:sə], *s.* (*Elec.*) der (Energie)umwandler, Umsetzer.
transept [ˈtrænsept], *s.* das Querschiff, Kreuzschiff.
transfer, 1. [ˈtrænsfə:], *s.* 1. die Versetzung, Verlegung (***to,*** nach); 2. Übertragung (***to,*** auf (*Acc.*)), Überführung (in *or* an *or* auf (*Acc.*) *or* nach); 3. (Geld)überweisung (***to,*** an (*Acc.*) (*a p.*), auf (*Acc.*) (*an account*)), (Geld)anweisung (***of £50,*** auf £50); 4. (*Law*) Übertragung, Abtretung, Zession (***to,*** an (*Acc.*)); Übertragungsurkunde; 5. (*Comm.*) Umbuchung, der Übertrag; 6. (*Art*) das Abziehen, Umdrucken; der Abzug, Umdruck, das Abziehbild. **2.** [-ˈfə:], *v.t.* 1. hinübertragen, hinüberbringen (***to,*** nach); 2. (*fig.*) übergeben, übermitteln (***to,*** *Dat.*), übertragen (auf (*Acc.*)); 3. versetzen (*also a p.*), verlegen (***to,*** nach); 4. überweisen (*money*) (***to,*** *Dat.* (*a p.*), an (*Acc.*) (*an account*)); 5. (*Law*) übertragen, überlassen, abtreten, zedieren (*Dat.*); 6. (*Comm.*) übertragen, vortragen, umbuchen ((***in***)***to,*** in (*Acc.*)); 7. (*Art*) übertragen, abziehen, umdrucken (*designs*) (***on to,*** auf (*Acc.*)). **3.** [-ˈfə:], *v.i.* 1. verlegt *or* (*of a p.*) versetzt werden (***to,*** zu *or* nach), (*of a p.*) übertreten (zu); 2. (*Am.*) umsteigen (*trains etc.*).
transferability [trænsfərəˈbiliti], *s.* die Übertragbarkeit. **transferable** [-ˈfə:rəbl], *adj.* übertragbar (***to,*** auf (*Acc.*)), abtretbar (an (*Acc.*)).
transfer|-book, *s.* das Umschreibungsbuch. **--deed,** *s.* die Übertragungsurkunde.
transferee [trænsfə:ˈri:], *s.* 1. (*Law*) der Zessionar; 2. (*Comm.*) Indossatar. **transference** [ˈtrænsfərəns], *s.* 1. die Übertragung, Umschreibung; 2. Versetzung, Verlegung. **transferential** [-fəˈrenʃəl], *adj.* Übertragungs–.
transfer-ink, *s.* die Umdrucktinte.
transferor [ˈtrænsfərə], *s.* 1. (*Law*) Abtretende(r), der Zedent; 2. (*Comm.*) Übertragende(r), der Indossant.
transfer|-paper, *s.* das Umdruckpapier. **--printing,** *s.* der Abziehbilderdruck (*on pottery etc.*).
transferrer [trænsˈfə:rə], *s.* 1. der Übertrager; 2. (*Law, Comm.*) see **transferor.**
transfer-ticket, *s.* 1. (*Railw.*) das Umsteigebillett; 2. (*Comm.*) der Überweisungsscheck; Übertragungsschein.
transfiguration [trænsfigjuˈreiʃən], *s.* 1. die Umgestaltung; 2. (*Eccl.*) Verklärung. **transfigure** [-ˈfigə], *v.t.* 1. umgestalten, verwandeln (***into,*** in (*Acc.*)); 2. (*Eccl.*) verklären.
transfix [trænsˈfiks], *v.t.* durchstechen, durchbohren; (*fig.*) ***be -ed with pain,*** vor Schmerz starr sein; (*fig.*) ***be -ed to the spot,*** wie gelähmt *or* angewurzelt dastehen. **transfixion** [-kʃən], *s.* 1. die Durchbohrung; 2. (*fig.*) das Erstarrtsein.
transform [trænsˈfɔ:m], **1.** *v.t.* 1. umgestalten, umbilden, umformen, verwandeln, umwandeln (***into,*** in (*Acc.*) *or* zu); (*Elec.*) transformieren, um-

spannen, umformen; 3. (*Math.*) umgestalten, umformen. **2.** *v.i.* sich verwandeln *or* umbilden (*into*, zu). **transformable,** *adj.* umwandelbar, verwandelbar. **transformation** [–fə'meiʃən], *s.* 1. die Umbildung, Umformung, Umgestaltung, Umwandlung, Verwandlung; (*Zool. etc.*) Metamorphose; (*Chem. etc.*) Umsetzung, Umwandlung; (*Math.*) Umgestaltung, Umformung; (*fig.*) Wandlung, Änderung; – ***of energy,*** die Energieumsetzung; – ***scene,*** die Verwandlungsszene; 2. (*Elec.*) die Transformation, Umspannung. **transformational** [–fə'meiʃənl], **transformative** [–'fɔ:mətiv], *adj.* umgestaltend, umbildend, umwandelnd. **transformer** [–'fɔ:mə], *s.* (*Elec.*) der Umformer, Umspanner, Transformator.

transfuse [træns'fju:z], *v.t.* 1. übergießen, umgießen; 2. transfundieren, übertragen (*blood*); 3. (*fig.*) durchtränken, durchfluten, erfüllen (***with,*** mit *or* von), einflößen, einprägen (*into*, *Dat.*). **transfusion** [–'fju:ʒən], *s.* 1. das Umgießen; 2. (*fig.*) die Übertragung; 3. (*Med.*) Blutübertragung, Transfusion.

transgress [trænz'gres], **1.** *v.t.* überschreiten, übertreten, verletzen, verstoßen gegen, nicht innehalten. **2.** *v.i.* sich vergehen, fehlen, sündigen. **transgression** [–'greʃən], *s.* 1. die Überschreitung, Übertretung, (Gesetz)verletzung, das Vergehen; 2. (*Geol.*) übergreifende Auflagerung. **transgressive** [–'gresiv], *adj.* verstoßend (***of,*** gegen). **transgressor,** *s.* der (die) Übertreter(in), Missetäter(in).

tranship [træn'ʃip], *v.t.* umladen, umschlagen. **transhipment,** *s.* die Umladung, der Umschlag; – ***port,*** der Umladehafen, Umschlag(e)platz.

transience, transiency ['trænziəns(i)], *s.* die Flüchtigkeit, Vergänglichkeit. **transient,** *adj.* 1. vorübergehend; 2. vergänglich, flüchtig; 3. (*esp. Am.*) Durchgangs– (*of passengers*); – ***guest*** or ***visitor,*** Durchreisende(r), der (die) Passant(in); – ***hotel,*** das Passantenhotel, Durchgangshotel; 4. (*Mus.*) Übergangs–; – ***shake,*** der Pralltriller; 5. (*Elec.*) – ***current,*** der Ausgleichsstrom; (*Phys.*) – ***wave,*** die Wanderwelle.

transilient [træn'siliənt], *adj.* (*esp. Geol.*) überspringend, ineinander übergehend.

transire [træn'zaiərə], *s.* der Passierschein, (Zoll)-begleitschein.

transistor [træn'zistə], *s.* der Transistor. **transistorize,** *v.t.* transistorisieren.

transit ['trænzit], **1.** *s.* 1. das Durchfahren, Durchschreiten; 2. (*Comm.*) die Durchfuhr, der Transport; Durchgang (*also Astr.*); Durchgangsverkehr; ***in –,*** beim Transport, auf der Fahrt, unterwegs; 3. (*fig.*) der Übergang (***to,*** zu).

transit|-camp, *s.* das Durchgangslager. **--circle,** *s.* (*Astr.*) der Durchgangskreis. **--duty,** *s.* der Durchfuhrzoll, Durchgangszoll. **--hotel,** *s.* das Passantenhotel.

transition [træn'ziʃən], *s.* der Übergang (*also Mus.*); – ***period,*** die Übergangsperiode; – ***stage,*** das Übergangsstadium. **transitional,** *adj.* Übergangs–.

transitive ['trænzitiv], *adj.* 1. Zwischen–, übergehend (*also fig.*); 2. (*Gram.*) transitiv.

transitoriness ['trænzitərinis], *s.* die Vergänglichkeit, Flüchtigkeit. **transitory,** *adj.* vergänglich, flüchtig, vorübergehend.

transit|-permit, *s.* die Durchfuhrgenehmigung. **--trade,** *s.* der Durchgangshandel. **--traffic,** *s.* der Durchgangsverkehr. **--visa,** *s.* das Durchreisevisum.

translatable [trænz'leitəbl], *adj.* übertragbar, übersetzbar. **translate** [trænz'leit], *v.t.* 1. übersetzen, übertragen (*also fig.*) (***from,*** von *or* aus; ***into,*** in (*Acc.*)); 2. (*fig.*) umsetzen (***into,*** in (*Acc.*)) (*also Math.*), umwandeln (in (*Acc.*) *or* zu), (*Tech.*) ummodeln, aufarbeiten; 3. (*Eccl.*) versetzen (*a bishop etc.*) (***to,*** nach); 4. (*obs.*) entrücken, verzücken, hinreißen; 5. (*of God*) (aus dem irdischen Leben) abberufen, zu sich rufen; 6. (*Tech.*) automatisch weiterbefördern (*telegram*). **translation** [–'leiʃən], *s.* 1. die Übersetzung, Übertragung (*also fig.*); ***in –,*** in der *or* einer Übersetzung; 2. (*Eccl.*) die Versetzung; 3. (*Tech.*) Umsetzung; 4. (*obs.*) Entrückung. **translator,** *s.* der (die) Übersetzer(in), Dolmetscher(in).

transliterate [trænz'litəreit], *v.t.* transkribieren, umschreiben. **transliteration** [–'reiʃən], *s.* die Transkription, Umschreibung.

translucence, translucency [trænz'lu:səns(i)], *s.* das Durchscheinen; die Halbdurchsichtigkeit. **translucent,** *adj.* durchscheinend; halbdurchsichtig, lichtdurchlässig.

transmarine [trænzmə'ri:n], *adj.* überseeisch, Übersee–.

transmigrate [trænzmai'greit], *v.i.* 1. auswandern, übersiedeln, wegziehen; 2. übergehen, wandern (*as souls*). **transmigration** [–'greiʃən], *s.* 1. die Auswanderung, Übersiedelung; 2. – ***of souls,*** die Seelenwanderung. **transmigratory** [–'maigrətəri], *adj.* übersiedelnd, wegziehend, wandernd, Wander–.

transmissibility [trænzmisi'biliti], *s.* die Übertragbarkeit. **transmissible** [–'misibl], *adj.* übertragbar, übersendbar (***to,*** auf (*Acc.*)).

transmission [trænz'miʃən], *s.* 1. die Verschickung, Übersendung, Übermittlung, Mitteilung, Weitergabe; 2. (*Comm.*) der Versand, die Spedition, Beförderung; 3. (*Law*) Überlassung, Übertragung; 4. (*Tech.*) Übertragung, Übersetzung, Transmission; das Getriebe, Triebwerk, die Triebwelle; – ***belt,*** der Treibriemen; – ***gear(ing),*** das Übersetzungsgetriebe; – ***ratio,*** das Übersetzungsverhältnis; – ***shaft,*** die Getriebewelle; 5. (*Rad.*) die Sendung; (*Phys.*) Übertragung, Fortpflanzung (*of waves etc.*); 6. (*Biol.*) Vererbung; (*Med.*) Ansteckung, Verschleppung (*of disease*); 7. Überlieferung (*of texts etc.*).

transmit [trænz'mit], *v.t.* 1. überschicken, übersenden, (ver)schicken, (ver)senden, befördern; übermitteln, überliefern, weitergeben (***to,*** *Dat.*); 2. (*Law*) überlassen, hinterlassen (***to,*** *Dat.*), übertragen (auf (*Acc.*)); 3. vermitteln, mitteilen (*impressions*) (***to,*** *Dat.*); 4. (*Biol.*) vererben, weitergeben (***to,*** *Dat.*); 5. (*Phys.*) weiterleiten, fortleiten (*waves etc.*), durchlassen (*light, heat*); 6. (*Med.*) übertragen (*disease*); 7. (*Rad.*) senden. **transmittable,** *adj. See* **transmissible. transmitter,** *s.* 1. der Übersender, Überlieferer, Übermittler; 2. (*Rad.*) Sender, das Sendegerät, die Sendestelle. **transmitting, 1.** *s.* (*Rad.*) das Senden. **2.** *adj.* Sende–; – ***station,*** der Sender, die Sendestelle.

transmogrify [trænz'mɔgrifai], *v.t.* gänzlich umgestalten.

transmutability [trænzmju:tə'biliti], *s.* die Umwandelbarkeit, Verwandelbarkeit. **transmutable** [–'mju:təbl], *adj.* umwandelbar, verwandelbar. **transmutation** [–'teiʃən], *s.* 1. die Verwandlung, Umwandlung (*also alchemy*); 2. (*Biol.*) Umbildung, Transmutation. **transmute** [–'mju:t], *v.t.* verwandeln, umwandeln; umbilden, umgestalten (***into,*** in (*Acc.*)).

transoceanic [trænzouʃi'ænik], *adj.* überseeisch, Übersee–; – ***flight,*** der Ozeanflug (*of aircraft*), die Ozeanüberfliegung (*of birds*).

transom ['trænsəm], *s.* 1. (*Build.*) das Querholz, der Querbalken; 2. (*Naut.*) das Heckwerk, der Heckspiegel; 3. (*Am.*) das Oberlicht.

transparency [træns'pɛərənsi], *s.* 1. die Durchsichtigkeit, Lichtdurchlässigkeit, Transparenz; 2. das Transparent(bild), Leuchtbild; 3. (*Phot.*) Dia(positiv). **transparent,** *adj.* 1. durchsichtig (*also fig.*), transparent, lichtdurchlässig; – ***colour,*** die Lasurfarbe; 2. (*fig.*) klar, offensichtlich, offenkundig; offen, ehrlich.

transpierce [trænz'piəs], *v.t.* durchbohren; (*fig.*) durchdringen.

transpiration [trænspi'reiʃən], *s.* die Absonderung, Ausdünstung; Schweißabsonderung, (*Zool.*) Hautatmung, (*Bot.*) Verdunstung. **transpire** [–'paiə], **1.** *v.t.* ausdünsten, ausschwitzen, (*Bot.*) verdunsten. **2.** *v.i.* 1. ausgedünstet werden, ausdünsten, ausdunsten; 2. (*fig.*) durchsickern,

bekannt *or* ruchbar werden, verlauten, verlautbaren; 3. (*sl.*) sich ereignen *or* zutragen, vorfallen.
transplant, 1. [træns'plɑ:nt], *v.t.* 1. versetzen, umpflanzen, verpflanzen (*also fig.*); 2. (*fig.*) umsiedeln (*population*); 3. (*Surg.*) transplantieren. **2.** [-'plɑ:nt], *v.i.* sich versetzen *or* verpflanzen *or* umpflanzen lassen. **3.** ['trænsplɑ:nt], *s.* 1. (*Surg.*) verpflanztes Organ *or* Gewebe; 2. *See* **transplantation. transplantation** [-'teiʃən], *s.* 1. die Umpflanzung; 2. (*fig.*) Verpflanzung, Versetzung; 3. (*Surg.*) Transplantation, Verpflanzung, Übertragung.
transport, 1. [træns'pɔ:t], *v.t.* 1. transportieren, befördern, versenden, fortschaffen, fortbringen; ***it -s me back to my youth,*** es versetzt mich in meine Jugend zurück; 2. deportieren (*criminals etc.*); 3. (*fig.*) ***be -ed with,*** außer sich *or* entzückt *or* hingerissen sein von *or* vor (*Dat.*). **2.** ['trænspɔ:t], *s.* 1. der Transport, die Beförderung, Überführung, Fortschaffung, Spedition, der Versand; – ***café,*** die Raststätte für Lastautofahrer; – ***charges,*** Versandkosten (*pl.*), Transportkosten (*pl.*), Speditionskosten; ***Minister of Transport,*** der Verkehrsminister; 2. (*Mil.*) der Truppentransporter, das Transportschiff, Truppenschiff; (*usu.* – ***plane***) Transportflugzeug; 3. (*fig.*) Entzücken, der Ausbruch, (heftiger) Anfall; ***go into -s*** (*of joy*), vor Freude außer sich *or* in Entzücken geraten; – ***of rage,*** rasende Wut.
transportability [trænspɔ:tə'biliti], *s.* die Transportfähigkeit, Versandfähigkeit. **transportable** [-'pɔ:təbl], *adj.* versendbar, transportierbar. **transportation** [-'teiʃən], *s.* 1. die Beförderung, Fortschaffung, Versendung, Verschickung, Überführung, der Transport; 2. Deportierung, Landesverweisung (*of criminals*). **transporter** [-'pɔ:tə], *s.* 1. der Beförderer; 2. die Transportvorrichtung.
transposable [træns'pouzəbl], *adj.* 1. versetzbar, auswechselbar; 2. (*Mus.*) transponierbar. **transposal,** *s.* die Umsetzung, Umstellung, Versetzung, Auswechselung. **transpose,** *v.t.* 1. umstellen, umsetzen, auswechseln, verstellen, versetzen (*also Typ.*); 2. (*Math.*) umstellen, transponieren; 3. (*Mus.*) transponieren, übertragen (*key*), versetzen (*register*). **transposition** [-pə'ziʃən], *s.* 1. das Umstellen, Verstellen; 2. die Umstellung, Verstellung, Versetzung; 3. (*Mus.*) das Transponieren, Versetzen; die Transposition, Versetzung, transponierte Fassung.
transship, *see* **tranship.**
transubstantiate [trænsəb'stænʃieit], *v.t.* verwandeln (*also Eccl.*), umwandeln. **transubstantiation** [-'eiʃən], *s.* die (Substanz- *or* Stoff)-umwandlung, (*Eccl.*) Transubstantiation.
transudation [trænsju'deiʃən], *s.* die Aussonderung, Absonderung. **transude** [-'sju:d], **1.** *v.i.* durchsickern, (durch)dringen. **2.** *v.t.* absondern, aussondern.
transversal [trænz'və:sl], **1.** *adj.* quer hindurchlaufend, schräg (ver)laufend, Quer-. **2.** *s.* (*Math.*) die Transversale. **transverse** ['trænzvə:s], **1.** *adj.* (*esp. Math.*) schräg, quer(laufend), Quer-, diagonal; – ***section,*** der Querschnitt. **2.** *s.* 1. das Querstück; 2. die Querachse, große Achse (*of ellipse*).
Transylvania [trænsil'veiniə], *s.* Siebenbürgen (*n.*).
[1]**trap** [træp], **1.** *s.* 1. die (Tier)falle, Fußangel; (*fig.*) Falle, Schlinge; (*Mil.*) der Hinterhalt; ***fall*** or ***walk into the*** –, in die Falle gehen; ***lay*** or ***set a*** –, eine Falle stellen (*for, Dat.*); 2. (*Tech.*) der Gasverschluß, Wasserverschluß (*for drains etc.*); 3. die Klappe, Lüftungstür; 4. (*obs.*) leichter zweirädiger Wagen; 5. (*Theat.*) (*also* –***door***) die Falltür, Versenkung; 6. (*sl.*) Klappe, Schnauze. **2.** *v.t.* 1. fangen; (*fig.*) ertappen; (*Mil.*) einschließen, (ein)fangen; 2. (*Tech.*) mit einem Verschluß *or* einer Klappe versehen (*pipe etc.*), abfangen (*gas etc.*); 3. (*Spt.*) auffangen (*ball*). **3.** *v.i.* Fallen setzen (*for, Dat.*).
[2]**trap,** *s.* (*coll.*) (*usu. pl.*) das Gepäck, die Habe, Habseligkeiten (*pl.*), Siebensachen (*pl.*).
[3]**trap,** *s.* (*Geol.*) der Trapp.
trap|-ball, *s.* (*obs.*) (eine Art) Schlagballspiel; der Schlagball. **–-door,** *s.* die Falltür; (*Min.*) Wettertür; (*Ent.*) – ***spider,*** die Minierspinne.
trapes, *see* **trapse.**
trapeze [trə'pi:z], *s.* das Trapez, Schwebereck. **trapeziform** [-ifɔ:m], *adj.* trapezförmig. **trapezium** [-iəm], *s.* 1. (*Math.*) das (Parallel)trapez, (*obs., Am.*) Trapezoid; 2. (*Anat.*) großes Vieleckbein. **trapezoid** ['træpizɔid], *s.* 1. (*Math.*) das Trapezoid, (*obs., Am.*) Paralleltrapez; 2. (*Anat.*) kleines Vieleckbein. **trapezoidal** [træpi'zɔidl], *adj. See* **trapeziform.**
trapper [træpə], *s.* 1. der Fallensteller; 2. Trapper, Pelztierjäger.
trappings ['træpiŋz], *pl.* das Staatsgeschirr, der Pferdeschmuck; (*fig.*) der Putz, Schmuck, Staat.
trapse [treips], *v.i.* (*v.t.*) (*coll.*) umherschlendern, umherziehen, bummeln (***about, around,*** in (*Dat.*) *or* auf (*Dat.*)).
trash [træʃ], **1.** *s.* 1. abgebrochene Zweige (*pl.*), das Reisig (*of trees*), die Bagasse (*sugar canes*); 2. (*coll.*) wertloses Zeug, der Schund, Abfall, Auswurf, Ausschuß, Plunder, Schofel; (*fig.*) Kitsch, Schund (*as books*); der Unsinn, das Blech (*as statements*); 3. Gesindel, der Pöbel (*as people*); (*Am. sl.*) ***white*** –, arme(r) Weiße(r). **2.** *v.t.* beschneiden, entblättern (*trees etc.*). **trash-can,** *s.* (*Am.*) der Abfalleimer. **trashiness,** *s.* die Wertlosigkeit, Minderwertigkeit. **trashy,** *adj.* wertlos, minderwertig, kitschig, Kitsch-, Schund-, schofel, schoflig.
trass [træs], *s.* (*Geol.*) der Traß, Tuffstein, Duckstein.
trauma ['trɔ:mə], *s.* (*Med.*) die Wunde, Verletzung, (*psychiatry*) seelische Erschütterung, das Trauma, der Nervenschock. **traumatic** [-'mætik], *adj.* (*Med.*) Wund-; traumatisch; – ***neurosis,*** traumatische Neurose.
travail ['træveil], **1.** *v.i.* 1. (*rare*) kreißen, in den Wehen liegen; 2. (*obs.*) sich (ab)mühen *or* plagen, schwer arbeiten. **2.** *s.* 1. (Geburts)wehen (*pl.*), das Kreißen; (*usu. fig.*) ***be in – with,*** schwer zu ringen haben mit; 2. (*obs.*) mühevolle Arbeit, die Plackerei.
travel [trævl], **1.** *v.i.* 1. reisen, eine Reise machen; fahren; – ***to and fro to work,*** zur Arbeit (hin und her) pendeln; – ***for a firm of publishers,*** Geschäftsreisende(r) für ein Verlagshaus sein; – ***in ladies' underwear,*** Geschäftsreisende(r) in Damenwäsche sein; 2. (*fig.*) sich ausdehnen, schweifen, wandern (*as eyes, a glance*); 3. (*Phys.*) sich (fort)bewegen, sich fortpflanzen (*as light, sound*); 4. (*Tech.*) laufen, sich hin- und herbewegen (*as a piston*); 5. (*coll.*) sich schnell bewegen, sausen. **2.** *v.t.* bereisen (*also Comm.*), durchreisen, durchwandern (*an area*), durchlaufen, zurücklegen (*a distance*). **3.** *s.* 1. das Reisen; *pl.* Reisen, Wanderungen (*pl.*); ***book of -s,*** die Reisebeschreibung; ***in*** or ***on your -s,*** auf Ihren Reisen; ***in*** –, auf Reisen; 2. (*Tech*). die Bewegung, der Lauf, Hub.
travel|-agency, *s.* das Reisebüro. **–-allowance,** *s.* der Reise(kosten)zuschuß, Reisespesen (*pl.*).
travelled ['trævəld], *adj.* 1. weitgereist, vielgereist; 2. (*of a track*) (viel)befahren. **traveller,** *s.* 1. Reisende(r); (***commercial***) –, Geschäftsreisende(r), Handlungsreisende(r); (*coll.*) ***fellow*** –, (politischer) Mitläufer; ***-'s cheque,*** der Reisescheck; (*Bot.*) ***-'s joy,*** Deutsche Waldrebe; ***-'s tale,*** die Münchhausiade, das Lügenmärchen; 2. (*Tech.*) die Laufkatze (*of crane*), das Laufstück, der Schieber (*of balance etc.*); 3. (*Naut.*) der Leiter(ring). **travelling, 1.** *s.* das Reisen. **2.** *adj.* Reise-, Wander-; – ***bag,*** der Reisekoffer; – ***circus,*** der Wanderzirkus; – ***clock,*** der Reisewecker; – ***crane,*** der Laufkran; – ***companion,*** Mitfahrende(r), der Reisegefährte; – ***expenses,*** Reisekosten (*pl.*), Reisespesen (*pl.*); ***--rug,*** die Reisedecke; – ***salesman,*** see (***commercial***) ***traveller***; ***--scholarship,*** das Reisestipendium; (*Elec.*) – ***wave,*** fortschreitende Welle. **travelogue** [-lɔg], *s.* die Reisebeschreibung, der Reisebericht; Reisefilm.
traversable ['trævəsəbl], *adj,* 1. überschreitbar; durchquerbar; passierbar, befahrbar; **2.** (*Tech.*)

drehbar, schwenkbar; 3. (*Law*) anfechtbar, Rechtseinwand zuzulassen(d). **traverse, 1.** *adj.* quer(liegend), querlaufend. **2.** *s.* 1. das Überqueren, die Überquerung, Durchquerung; das Querstück, Querholz, der Querriegel, Querbalken, die Querschwelle; (*Archit.*) Quergalerie, der Quergang; die Traverse (*also Fort., Mount.*); (*Fort.*) Schulterwehr, der Querwall, Querdamm; 2. (*Naut.*) Koppelkurs, die Querfahrt; 3. (*Surv.*) der Polygonzug; 4. (*Tech., Artil.*) die Schwenkung, Seitwärtsdrehung; 5. (*Law*) Leugnung, der Rechtseinwand, Einspruch; 6. (*fig., rare*) Querstrich, das Hindernis, die Widerwärtigkeit. **3.** *v.t.* 1. quer liegen über (*Dat.*); quer gehen über (*Acc.*), durchwandern, durchreiten, durchfahren, durchziehen, durchqueren, überqueren, durchkreuzen; (*Mount.*) queren; 2. (*Tech., Artil.*) seitwärts drehen, schwenken; 3. (*fig.*) durchkreuzen, hintertreiben, zuwiderhandeln (*Dat.*); 4. ableugnen, bestreiten, widersprechen (*Dat.*); (*Law*) Einspruch erheben gegen, anfechten. **4.** *v.i.* 1. (*Equest.*) querspringen, traversieren; 2. (*Fenc.*) seitwärts ausfallen; 3. (*Mount.*) queren; 4. (*Fort.*) Traverse machen; 5. (*Tech.*) sich drehen, sich seitwärts richten lassen. **traverser,** *s.* 1. (*Law*) der Leugner; 2. (*Railw.*) die Drehscheibe.

traverse|-sailing, *s.* der Koppelkurs. **--survey,** *s.* polygoniometrische Vermessung; ***make a* –**, polygonisieren. **--table,** *s.* (*Naut.*) 1. die Koppeltafel; 2. (*Railw.*) *see* **traverser,** 2.

travesty [ˈtrævisti], **1.** *s.* die Travestie; (*fig.*) Karikatur, das Zerrbild; ***it is a – of justice,*** es spottet jeder Gerechtigkeit. **2.** *v.t.* travestieren, karikieren, verzerren.

trawl [trɔːl], **1.** *s.* (*also* ***--net***) das (Grund)schleppnetz, die Kurre. **2.** *v.i.* mit dem Schleppnetz fischen. **3.** *v.t.* schleppen (*the net*), mit dem Schleppnetz fangen (*fish*). **trawler,** *s.* der Schleppnetzfischer, Trawler.

tray [trei], *s.* das Servierbrett, Tablett; der (Ablege)-kasten (*in an office*); (Koffer)einsatz (*in a trunk*); (*Phot.*) ***developing--,*** die Entwicklerschale; ***loading--,*** die Ladeschale (*of a gun*). **tray-cloth,** *s.* die Tablettdecke.

treacherous [ˈtretʃərəs], *adj.* 1. verräterisch, treulos, falsch (*to*, gegen); 2. trügerisch, unsicher (*as ice*), unzuverlässig (*as memory*), tückisch (*as a dog*). **treacherousness,** *s.* 1. die Treulosigkeit; 2. Tücke, Unzuverlässigkeit. **treachery,** *s.* der Verrat (*to*, an (*Dat.*)), Treubruch, die Falschheit, Tücke, Treulosigkeit (gegen).

treacle [triːkl], *s.* der Sirup, die Melasse. **treacly,** *adj.* sirupartig; (*fig.*) süßlich, salbungsvoll.

tread [tred], **1.** *irr.v.i.* 1. treten, trampeln ((*up*)*on*, auf (*Acc.*)); schreiten; – ***lightly,*** leise auftreten, (*fig.*) vorsichtig zu Werke gehen; – ***on,*** zertrampeln, zertreten; – ***on air,*** wie auf Wolken gehen; – ***on his corns*** or ***toes,*** ihm auf die Hühneraugen treten; – ***in his footsteps,*** in seinen Fußstapfen treten; – ***on his heels,*** ihm auf dem Fuße *or* den Fersen folgen; 2. sich paaren (*of birds*). **2.** *v.t.* 1. betreten, beschreiten; – ***the boards,*** als Schauspieler auftreten; – ***grapes,*** Trauben keltern; – ***the ground,*** gehen; – ***a measure,*** tanzen; – ***a path,*** einen Weg gehen; sich (*Dat.*) einen Weg bahnen; – ***water,*** Wasser treten; – ***down,*** niedertreten, niedertrampeln; – ***out,*** austreten (*fire*); – ***under foot,*** niedertreten, mit Füßen treten; 2. treten, begatten (*a hen*). **3.** *s.* 1. der Tritt, Schritt, Gang, die Gangart; 2. Schuhsohle, Trittfläche (*of a shoe*); Lauffläche (*of a wheel or rail*); das Profil (*of a tyre*); 3. Trittbrett (*of step-ladder*), der Auftritt (*of a step*); 4. Hahnentritt (*in eggs*); 5. die Begattung, das Treten (*of fowls*).

treadle [tredl], **1.** *s.* das Trittbrett, der Fußhebel, die Tretkurbel; das Pedal. **2.** *v.i.* treten.

treadmill [ˈtredmil], *s.* die Tretmühle (*also fig.*).

treason [triːzn], *s.* der (Landes)verrat (***against, to,*** an (*Dat.*) *or* gegen); ***high* –**, der Hochverrat. **treasonable** [–zənəbl], *adj.* verräterisch, Hochverrats–. **treasonableness,** *s.* (hoch)verräterisches Treiben.

treasure [ˈtreʒə], **1.** *s.* der Schatz (*also fig.*), Schätze (*pl.*), Reichtümer (*pl.*), (*fig.*) die Kostbarkeit, Seltenheit; (*coll.*) ***a perfect* –**, eine wahre Perle (*of a p.*). **2.** *v.t.* 1. (hoch)schätzen, hegen, werthalten; 2. (*usu.* – ***up***) (auf)bewahren, (an)sammeln, aufhäufen, anhäufen, horten. **treasure-house,** *s.* die Schatzkammer; (*fig.*) Fundgrube, Goldgrube. **treasurer,** *s.* 1. der Schatzmeister; (***Lord***) ***High Treasurer,*** Lord Oberschatzmeister; 2. der Kassier(er), Kassenwart; 3. Finanzbeamte(r), Fiskalbeamte(r). **treasurership,** *s.* das Schatzmeisteramt, Kassieramt. **treasure-trove,** *s.* 1. herrenloser Schatzfund; 2. (*fig.*) wertvoller Fund.

treasury [ˈtreʒəri], *s.* 1. die Schatzkammer; der Staatsschatz; das Schatzamt, Finanzministerium (*in England*); ***First Lord of the Treasury,*** der Präsident des Schatzamtes; ***Treasury bench,*** die Ministerbank (*in House of Commons*); – ***bill,*** kurzfristiger Schatzwechsel; – ***bond,*** die Schatzanweisung; (*Am.*) ***Treasury Department,*** das Finanzministerium; – ***note,*** die Banknote; (*Am.*) der Staatskassenschein; 2. (*fig.*) die Anthologie, Blumenlese.

treat [triːt], **1.** *v.t.* 1. behandeln, umgehen mit (*a p.*); 2. (*Med.*) behandeln (*disease, patient*) (***for,*** wegen *or* gegen); 3. (*Chem. etc.*) behandeln, bearbeiten (***with,*** mit); (*a subject etc.*) behandeln, (*also in speech*) besprechen, (*also in graphic arts*) darstellen; (*coll.*) – ***it as a joke,*** es als Scherz betrachten *or* ansehen; 4. (*coll.*) – ***him to s.th.,*** ihn mit etwas bewirten *or* freihalten *or* traktieren, ihm etwas spendieren, ihm mit etwas einen Genuß bereiten; – ***o.s. to s.th.,*** sich mit etwas leisten. **2.** *v.i.* – ***of,*** handeln von, behandeln, erörtern; – ***with,*** verhandeln, unterhandeln *or* Verhandlungen führen mit. **3.** *s.* 1. die Bewirtung, das Freihalten; ***it is my* –**, es geht auf meine Rechnung; ***stand*** (***a***) **–**, zum besten geben, traktieren, bewirten; 2. das Fest, der Schmaus; (Schüler)ausflug; 3. Hochgenuß, die Freude.

treatise [ˈtriːtiz], *s.* die Abhandlung, Monographie.

treatment [ˈtriːtmənt], *s.* 1. die Behandlung (*also Med., Chem. etc.*); (*Med.*) ***under* –**, in Behandlung; 2. das Verfahren, die Handhabung; 3. (*Tech.*) Bearbeitung.

treaty [ˈtriːti], *s.* 1. der Vertrag; ***commercial* –**, der Handelsvertrag; ***peace* –**, der Friedensvertrag; 2. (*rare*) die Verhandlung, Unterhandlung; ***be in* – *with him for a th.,*** mit ihm über etwas verhandeln.

treaty|-port, *s.* der Vertragshafen. **--powers,** *pl.* Vertragsmächte (*pl.*).

treble [trebl], **1.** *adj.* 1. dreifach; – ***figures,*** dreistellige Zahlen; 2. (*Mus.*) Diskant–, Sopran–; – ***clef,*** der Violinschlüssel; 3. hoch, schrill. **2.** *s.* 1. das Dreifache; 2. (*Mus.*) der Diskant, Sopran; die Sopranstimme; Diskantlage; der (die) Diskantsänger(in). **3.** *v.t.* (*v.i.* sich) verdreifachen.

trecento [triˈtʃentou], **1.** *s.* (*Art*) das 14. Jahrhundert. **2.** *adj.* des 14. Jahrhunderts.

tree [triː], **1.** *s.* 1. der Baum; ***fruit--,*** der Obstbaum; ***as the – is, so is the fruit,*** der Apfel fällt nicht weit vom Baum; (*B.*) ***Tree of Knowledge,*** der Baum der Erkenntnis; – ***of life,*** (*Bot.*) der Lebensbaum; (*B.*) Baum des Lebens; (*coll.*) ***at the top of the* –**, in höchster Stellung, auf dem Gipfel (*esp. of one's profession*); ***not see the wood for the –s,*** den Wald nicht vor Bäumen sehen; (*coll.*) ***be up a* –**, in der Klemme *or* Patsche sitzen; 2. (*Tech., esp. in compounds*) der Stamm, Schaft, Balken, die Welle; ***axle--,*** die Kronenwelle; (***boot***)**--**, der Stiefelleisten; 3. ***family*** or ***genealogical* –**, der Stammbaum. **2.** *v.t.* 1. auf einen Baum treiben (*an animal*); (*fig.*) in die Ecke treiben; 2. auf den Leisten schlagen (*shoes*).

tree|-creeper, *s.* (*Am.* ***brown* –**) (*Orn.*) der (Wald)-baumläufer (*Certhia familiaris*). **--frog,** *s.* der Laubfrosch.

treeless [ˈtriːlis], *adj.* baumlos.

tree|-line, *s.* die Baumgrenze. **--louse,** *s.* die Blattlaus. **-nail,** *s.* (*esp. Naut.*) der Döbel, Dübel, langer Holzstift. **--pipit,** *s.* (*Orn.*) der Baumpieper

(*Anthus trivialis*). **--sparrow,** *s.* (*Am. European* –) (*Orn.*) der Feldsperling (*Passer montanus*). **–top,** *s.* der Wipfel. **--trunk,** *s.* der Baumstamm.

trefoil ['trefɔil], *s.* 1. (*Bot.*) der Klee; ***bird's-foot* –**, Gemeiner Hornklee; 2. (*Archit., Her.*) das Dreiblatt, Kleeblatt.

trek [trek], **1.** *v.i.* (mit *or* im Ochsenwagen) ziehen, trekken, trecken, reisen, wandern. **2.** *s.* der Auszug, Treck, die Reise, Wanderung.

trellis ['trelis], **1.** *s.* 1. das Gitter, Gatter; 2. Spalier (*for plants*). **2.** *v.t.* 1. vergittern; ***–ed window,*** das Gitterfenster; 2. am Spalier ziehen (*plants*). **trellis-work,** *s.* das Gitterwerk, Lattenwerk.

trema ['tremə], *s.* (*Phonet.*) das Trema.

tremble [trembl], **1.** *v.i.* zittern, beben (*also of the earth*) (***with,*** vor (*Dat.*)); flattern (*as leaves*); (*fig.*) erzittern, erschaudern (***at,*** bei), zittern, bangen, fürchten (***for,*** um *or* für); ***– all over,*** am ganzen Leibe zittern; (*fig.*) ***– in the balance,*** an einem Faden hängen, in der Schwebe sein; ***– to think*** or ***at the thought,*** bei dem Gedanken zittern. **2.** *s.* das Zittern; (*coll.*) ***be all of a –,*** am ganzen Leibe zittern; ***in a –,*** zitternd. **trembler,** *s.* (*Elec.*) der Selbstunterbrecher, Schwingungshammer. **trembling,** *adj.* zitternd; ***– grass,*** das Zittergras; ***– poplar,*** die Zitterpappel, Espe. **trembly,** *adj.* (*coll.*) *see* **trembling.**

tremendous [tri'mendəs], *adj.* 1. furchtbar, fürchterlich, entsetzlich, schrecklich; 2. (*usu. coll.*) gewaltig, außerordentlich, enorm, ungeheuer, riesig, kolossal; (*sl.*) ausgezeichnet.

tremolo ['treməlou], *s.* 1. (*Mus.*) das Tremolo; 2. (*of organ*) der Tremulant.

tremor ['tremə], *s.* 1. das Zittern, Beben (*also of earth*), Zucken; 2. (*coll.*) (Er)beben, die Erregung. **tremulous** [–mjələs], *adj.* 1. zitternd, bebend; 2. nervös, zitt(e)rig; ängstlich, furchtsam. **tremulousness,** *s.* das Zittern, Bangen.

trenail [trenl], *s. See* **treenail.**

trench [trentʃ], **1.** *v.t.* 1. mit Gräben durchziehen, tief umgraben, rigolen (*land*); 2. (*Mil.*) durch Gräben befestigen, verschanzen. **2.** *v.i.* 1. Gräben ziehen *or* ausheben; (*Mil.*) Schützengräben anlegen *or* ausheben; 2. – (***up***)***on,*** beeinträchtigen, übergreifen auf (*Acc.*), eingreifen in (*Acc.*). **3.** *s.* 1. der Graben (*also Geol.*), Einschnitt, tiefe Rinne *or* Furche; ***cut –es,*** Gräben ziehen *or* ausheben; 2. (*Mil.*) der Schützengraben, Laufgraben; ***mount the –es,*** die Schützengräben beziehen.

trenchancy ['trentʃənsi], *s.* die Schärfe, das Schneidende. **trenchant,** *adj.* (ein)schneidend, scharf, entschieden, durchdringend, wirksam, energisch.

trench-coat, *s.* der Wettermantel, Trenchcoat.

trencher ['trentʃə], *s.* das Tranchierbrett, Schneidebrett. **trencher|-cap,** *s.* viereckige Studentenmütze. **–man** [–mən], *s.* starker Esser.

trench|-fever, *s.* das (Schützen)grabenfieber. **-foot,** *s.* (*Med.*) der Fußbrand. **--mortar,** *s.* der Granatwerfer. **--warfare,** *s.* der Stellungskrieg.

trend [trend], **1.** *s.* 1. (allgemeine) Neigung *or* Richtung, die Bestrebung, Entwicklung, Grundbewegung, Tendenz, der Trend, (Ver)lauf, Gang, Zug; (*Comm.*) ***– analysis,*** die Konjunkturanalyse; ***upward*** (***downward***) –, steigende (fallende) Tendenz; 2. (*Geol.*) die Streichrichtung. **2.** *v.i.* 1. sich neigen, in die Richtung laufen *or* abgehen, eine Richtung haben *or* nehmen (***towards,*** nach); 2. (*Geol.*) streichen. **trend-setter,** *s.* (*coll.*) der (die) Tonangeber(in). **trendy,** *adj.* (*coll.*) neumodisch.

[1]**trepan** [tri'pæn], *v.t.* in einer Falle fangen, betrügen, überlisten.

[2]**trepan, 1.** *s.* 1. (*Surg.*) der Schädelbohrer; 2. (*Min.*) die Bohrmaschine. **2.** *v.t.* trepanieren.

trepidation [trepi'deiʃən], *s.* 1. (*Med.*) das (Glieder)-zittern, Zucken; 2. (*usu. fig.*) die Angst, Ängstlichkeit, Besorgtheit, das Hangen und Bangen.

trespass ['trespəs], **1.** *v.i.* 1. (*Law*) ***– on,*** widerrechtlich betreten; (*fig.*) mißbrauchen, ausnützen, zu sehr beanspruchen *or* in Anspruch nehmen; übergreifen auf (*Acc.*), eingreifen in (*Acc.*); ***– against,*** schuldig werden *or* sich vergehen *or* versündigen an (*Dat.*). **2.** *s.* (*Law*) unbefugtes Betreten, die Besitzstörung; Übergriff (***on,*** auf (*Acc.*)), unbefugter Eingriff (in (*Acc.*)), die Beeinträchtigung, der Mißbrauch (*Gen.*); das Vergehen, die Übertretung, Sünde. **trespasser,** *s.* Unbefugte(r), der Besitzstörer, Rechtsverletzer; ***–s will be prosecuted,*** Durchgang *or* Eintritt *or* unbefugtes Betreten bei Strafe verboten.

tress [tres], **1.** *s.* 1. die (Haar)flechte, Locke; 2. (*oft. pl.*) langes (lockiges) Haar. **2.** *v.t.* (*rare*) flechten, binden (*hair*). **tressure** ['treʃə], *s.* 1. (*Her.*) der Saum; 2. (*obs.*) das Haarband.

trestle [tresl], *s.* das Gestell, Gerüst, der Bock, Schragen.

tret [tret], *s.* die Gewichtsvergütung, Refaktie, das Gutgewicht.

Treves [tri:vz], *s.* Trier (*n.*).

trews [tru:z], *pl.* (*Scots*) die Hose; ***a pair of –,*** eine Hose.

triable ['traiəbl], *adj.* (*Law*) verhörbar, verhandlungsreif (*a case*), belangbar, verfolgbar (*a p.*).

triad ['traiæd], *s.* 1. die Dreiheit, Dreizahl; 2. (*Math.*) Dreiergruppe, Trias; 3. (*Chem.*) Dreiwertigkeit, dreiwertiges Element; 4. (*Mus.*) der Dreiklang. **triadic** [–'ædik], *adj.* 1. (*Math.*) dreistellig, dreiglied(e)rig; 2. (*Chem.*) dreiwertig; 3. (*Mus.*) Dreiklangs–.

trial ['traiəl], **1.** *s.* 1. der Versuch, die Probe (***of,*** mit), Prüfung; ***– and error,*** (*Math.*) die Regula Falsi; (*coll.*) das Herumprobieren; ***give him a –,*** einen Versuch machen mit ihm; ***give it a –,*** es auf die Probe stellen, es ausprobieren *or* erproben; ***make a –,*** eine Probe anstellen; ***make a – of,*** erproben, ausprobieren; ***– of strength,*** die Kraftprobe; ***by way of –,*** versuchsweise; (*Comm.*) ***on –,*** zur *or* auf Probe; 2. (*Law*) das Verhör, der Prozeß, gerichtliche Untersuchung, das Gerichtsverfahren, die Gerichtsverhandlung; ***commit*** or ***send for –,*** dem Schwurgericht überweisen *or* übergeben; ***– by jury,*** das Schwurgerichtsverfahren; ***on –,*** vor Gericht; ***be on*** or ***stand –,*** unter Anklage stehen (***for,*** wegen); ***put on*** or ***bring to –,*** vor Gericht stellen; 3. (*Motor.*) die Probefahrt, (*Av.*) der Probeflug; 4. (*fig.*) die (Schicksals)-prüfung, Anfechtung, Heimsuchung; 5. (*coll.*) Plage, Belästigung; ***he is a great – to us,*** er ist unsere große Sorge. **2.** *attrib. adj.* (*Comm.*) ***– balance,*** die Rohbilanz; ***– flight,*** der Probeflug, das Einfliegen; ***– marriage,*** die Probeehe; ***– run,*** (*Motor. etc.*) die Probefahrt, (*Tech. etc.*) der Probelauf, (*Theat.*) die Probeaufführung.

triangle ['traiæŋgl], *s.* 1. (*Geom.*) das Dreieck; (*coll.*) ***eternal –,*** das Dreiecksverhältnis; 2. (*Mus.*) der Triangel. **triangular** [–'æŋgjulə], *adj.* dreieckig, dreiwinklig. **triangularity** [–'læriti], *s.* die Dreiecksform. **triangulate** [–'æŋgjuleit], *v.t.* triangulieren, trigonometrisch vermessen (*land*). **triangulation** [–'leiʃən], *s.* 1. (*Surv.*) die Triangulation, Dreiecksaufnahme; 2. (*Artil.*) das Dreieckzielen.

Trias ['traiəs], *s.* (*Geol.*) die Trias(formation). **Triassic** [–'æsik], *adj.* Trias–.

tribade ['tribəd], *s.* die Lesbierin. **tribadism,** *s.* lesbische Liebe.

tribal [traibl], *adj.* Stammes–. **tribalism** [–bəlizm], *s.* die Stammesorganisation, das Stammessystem; Stammesgefühl.

tribasic [trai'beisik], *adj.* (*Chem.*) dreibasisch.

tribe [traib], *s.* 1. der (Volks)stamm, das Geschlecht; 2. (*Bot., Zool.*) die Tribus; 3. (*coll.*) Horde, Zunft, Clique, Sippe, Sippschaft. **tribesman** [–zmən], *s.* Stammesangehörige(r).

tribrach ['tr(a)ibræk], *s.* (*Metr.*) der Tribrachys.

tribulation [tribju'leiʃən], *s.* die Trübsal, Drangsal, das Leiden.

tribunal [trai'bju:nl], *s.* der Richterstuhl (*also fig.*), Gerichtshof, das Gericht, Tribunal. **tribunate** ['tribjunət], *s.* (*Hist.*) das Tribunat. **tribune** ['tribju:n], *s.* 1. (*Hist.*) der (Volks)tribun; (*fig.*)

öffentlicher Verteidiger *or* Beschützer; 2. die Rednerbühne, Tribüne; (*Eccl.*) der Bischofsthron. **tribuneship,** *s. See* **tribunate.**

tributary ['tribjutəri], **1.** *adj.* 1. tributpflichtig, abgabepflichtig, zinspflichtig (*to, Dat.*); 2. beisteuernd (*to*, zu); 3. Neben– (*as a river*); ***be – to,*** sich ergießen in (*Acc.*) (*of a river*). **2.** *s.* 1. Tributpflichtige(r), Zinspflichtige(r); 2. (*Geog.*) der Nebenfluß.

tribute ['tribju:t], *s.* 1. der Tribut (*also fig.*); Zins, Zoll, die Abgabe, Steuer; ***hold him to –,*** sich (*Dat.*) ihn tributpflichtig halten; ***lay him under –,*** sich (*Dat.*) ihn tributpflichtig machen; ***pay one's*** or ***a –,*** seinen Tribut zollen (*to, Dat.*); 2. (*fig.*) die Ehrung, Huldigung, Hochachtung; ***– of respect,*** die Achtungsbezeigung. **tribute-money,** *s.* der Zinsgroschen.

tricar ['traikɑ:], *s.* dreirädriger Kraftwagen.

trice [trais], **1.** *v.t.* (*Naut.*) aufholen, aufheißen. **2.** *s.* (*coll.*) ***in a –,*** im Nu *or* Handumdrehen.

triceps ['traiseps], *s.* (*Anat.*) dreiköpfiger Muskel.

trichina ['trikinə], *s.* die Trichine, der Fadenwurm. **trichinosis** [–'nousis], *s.* die Trichinose, Trichinenkrankheit.

trichome ['traikoum], *s.* (*Bot.*) das Pflanzenhaar.

trichord ['traikɔ:d], **1.** *adj.* Dreisaiten–. **2.** *s.* (*Mus.*) das Dreisaiteninstrument.

trichotomy [tri'kɔtəmi], *s.* die Dreiteilung, Dreiheit.

trick [trik], **1.** *s.* 1. der Kniff, Schlich, Dreh, Trick, die List; *pl.* Schliche (*pl.*), Ränke (*pl.*), Winkelzüge (*pl.*); ***be up to his –s,*** seine Schliche durchschauen; ***know the –s,*** den Kniff kennen; ***know a – worth two of that,*** noch gerissener sein; ***–s of the trade,*** besondere Kunstgriffe; (*coll.*) ***the whole bag of –s,*** der ganze Kram; 2. die Täuschung, Illusion, das Blendwerk; ***–s of fortune,*** die Tücken des Schicksals; 3. der Scherz, Spaß, dummer Streich, die Posse; ***be up to one's –s,*** Unfug *or* dumme Streiche machen; ***dirty*** or ***mean –,*** gemeiner Streich; ***play him a –, play a – on him,*** ihm einen Streich spielen; ***play –s,*** Unfug *or* Mätzchen machen; 4. der Kunstgriff, das Kunststück; ***card –,*** das Kartenkunststück; (*coll.*) ***do the –,*** den Zweck erreichen; 5. die Eigenart, Eigenheit, Besonderheit, Eigentümlichkeit, üble Gewohnheit; 6. (*Cards*) der Stich; 7. (*Naut.*) Dienst (am Steuer). **2.** *attrib. adj.* (*sl., esp. Mil.*) ***– cyclist,*** der Psychiater; ***– flying,*** das Kunstfliegen, der Kunstflug; ***– rider,*** der (die) Kunstreiter(in). **3.** *v.t.* 1. betrügen, täuschen, hintergehen, überlisten, prellen (***out of,*** um), verführen, verleiten (***into doing,*** zu tun); 2. – (*o.s.*) ***out,*** aufputzen, schmücken, (sich) zieren; ***–ed out in,*** herausgeputzt mit.

trickery ['trikəri], *s.* die Gaunerei, der Betrug. **trickiness,** *s.* 1. die Durchtriebenheit, Verschlagenheit, Verschmitztheit, List (*of a p.*), (*coll.*) Unzuverlässigkeit; 2. Kompliziertheit, Verwickeltheit, Schwierigkeit (*of a th.*). **trickish,** *adj.* (*rare*) *see* **tricky.**

trickle [trikl], **1.** *v.i.* sickern, rieseln, rinnen, tröpfeln, träufeln; (*coll.*) langsam rollen (*of a ball*). **2.** *s.* 1. das Tröpfeln, Rieseln; 2. der Tropfen. **trickle-charger,** *s.* (*Elec.*) der Kleinlader.

trickster ['trikstə], *s.* der Schwindler, Gauner. **tricksy,** *adj.* (*coll.*) listig, schlau; schelmisch, mutwillig. **tricky,** *adj.* 1. (*of p.*) listig, schlau; raffiniert, gerieben; 2. (*of th.*) kompliziert, verzwickt; heikel.

triclinic [trai'klinik], *adj.* triklin (*of crystals*).

tricolour ['trikʌlə], *s.* die Trikolore.

tricorn(e) ['traikɔ:n], *s.* der Dreispitz (*hat*).

tricot ['trikou], *s.* der Trikot (*fabric*), das Trikot (*garment*).

tricuspid [trai'kʌspid], *adj.* (*Anat.*) dreizipf(e)lig, Dreikuspidal–.

tricycle ['traisikl], *s.* das Dreirad.

trident ['traidənt], *s.* der Dreizack, dreizackiger Speer. **tridental,** *adj.* dreizackig.

tried [traid], **1.** *imperf., p.p. of* **try. 2.** *adj.* erprobt, bewährt, zuverlässig.

triennial [trai'eniəl], *adj.* dreijährig, dreijährlich.

trier ['traiə], *s.* (*coll.*) strebsamer Mensch; ***he's a –,*** er läßt nichts unversucht.

trierarchy ['traiərɑ:ki], *s.* (*Hist.*) die Dreiherrschaft, Trierarchie.

Trieste [tri'est], *s.* Triest (*n.*).

trifid ['traifid], *adj.* (*Bot.*) dreispaltig.

trifle [traifl], **1.** *s.* 1. die Kleinigkeit, Lappalie, Bagatelle, das bißchen; Kinderspiel; ***mere –,*** (nur) ein Kinderspiel; ***a – odd,*** etwas *or* ein wenig merkwürdig; ***not stick at –s,*** sich nicht mit Kleinigkeiten abgeben; 2. (*Cul.*) süßer Auflauf. **2.** *v.i.* 1. tändeln, spielen (***with,*** mit) (*a th.*); 2. spaßen; sein Spiel treiben (***with,*** mit) (*a p.*); ***he is not to be –d with,*** er läßt nicht mit sich spaßen, mit ihm ist nicht zu spaßen *or* fackeln. **3.** *v.t.* (*usu.* ***– away***) vertändeln, vertrödeln. **trifler,** *s.* der Tändler, Müßiggänger, frivoler Mensch. **trifling,** *adj.* belanglos, geringfügig, unbedeutend, oberflächlich, läppisch.

trifoliate [trai'fouliət], *adj.* dreiblätt(e)rig. **trifolium,** *s.* (*Bot.*) (eine Gattung der) Kleegewächse (*pl.*).

trifurcate ['traifə:keit], **1.** *adj.* dreizackig, dreigab(e)lig, dreifach gegabelt. **2.** *v.t.* (*v.i.*) (sich) dreifach *or* in drei Teile gabeln.

¹**trig** [trig], **1.** *v.t.* hemmen (*wheels*); ***– up,*** stützen. **2.** *s.* der Hemmschuh, Hemmkeil, Hemmklotz.

²**trig, 1.** *adj.* nett, hübsch, schmuck, adrett. **2.** *v.t.* (*usu. pass.*) herausputzen.

³**trig,** *s.* (*coll.*) *abbr. for* **trigonometry.**

trigger [trigə], **1.** *s.* der Abzug, Drücker (*of a gun*); (*Phot.*) Auslöser; ***pull the –,*** abdrücken; (*fig. coll.*) ***quick on the –,*** schlagfertig, reaktionsschnell. **2.** *v.t.* (*oft.* ***– off***) (*fig.*) auslösen, zur Folge haben. **trigger|-finger,** *s.* der Zeigefinger. **--guard,** *s.* der Abzugsbügel. **--happy,** *adj.* (*coll.*) schießlustig.

triglyph ['traiglif], *s.* (*Archit.*) die Triglyphe, der Triglyph, Dreischlitz.

trigonometric(al) [trigənə'metrik(l)], *adj.* trigonometrisch. **trigonometry** [–'nɔmitri], *s.* die Trigonometrie.

trihedral [trai'hi:drəl], *adj.* dreiflächig, dreiseitig.

trilateral [trai'lætərəl], *adj.* dreiseitig.

trilby ['trilbi], *s.* (*also* ***– hat***) weicher (Filz)hut.

trilinear [trai'liniə], *adj.* (*Math.*) dreilinig.

trilingual [trai'liŋgwəl], *adj.* dreisprachig.

trill [tril], **1.** *s.* der Triller. **2.** *v.t., v.i.* 1. (*Mus.*) trillern; 2. (*Phonet.*) rollen; ***–ed r,*** das Zungen–r, gerolltes r.

trillion ['triliən], *s.* (*Engl.*) die Trillion (= 10^{18}), (*Am.*) die Billion (= 10^{12}).

trilobate [trai'loubeit], *adj.* (*Bot.*) dreilappig.

trilogy ['trilədʒi], *s.* die Trilogie.

trim [trim], **1.** *s.* 1. die Ordnung, Bereitschaft, richtiger *or* ausgerüsteter Zustand, richtige Verfassung; ***in fighting –,*** gefechtsbereit; ***in fine*** or ***good –,*** in bester Verfassung; 2. richtige Stellung (*of sails*), richtige Verfassung (*of cargo*), (*Naut., Av.*) die Schwimmlage, Gleichgewichtslage, der Trimm; ***in sailing –,*** segelfertig; 3. der (Auf)putz, Staat; 4. das Ausputzen, Zurechtschneiden (*of hair etc.*); 5. (*Am.*) die Schaufensterdekoration; 6. (*Motor. etc.*) der Blendring, die Wandblende. **2.** *adj.* gut in Ordnung, gepflegt, sauber, niedlich, nett, schmuck. **3.** *v.t.* 1. ordnen, in Ordnung bringen, zurechtmachen; 2. schmücken, aufputzen, (her)ausputzen; 3. putzen (*lamp*); 4. garnieren, besetzen (*hats etc.*); 5. ausputzen, stutzen, beschneiden, zurechtschneiden (*hair, hedges etc.*); 6. behauen, zurichten (*timber, stone*); 7. schüren (*the fire*); 8. stellen, brassen (*sails*), trimmen (*sails or boat*); in Trimmlage bringen, seemäßig (ver)stauen (*cargo*); (*fig.*) ***– one's sails to every wind,*** den Mantel nach dem Winde hängen. **4.** *v.i.* 1. (*Naut.*) trimmen, Trimmlage einnehmen; 2. (*fig.*) einen Mittelkurs steuern, die Mitte halten; schwanken, lavieren, sich anpassen; ***– with the times,*** Opportunistenpolitik treiben, mit den Zeiten gehen, sich den Zeiten anpassen.

trimaran ['traimərӕn], *s.* das Dreirumpfboot.

trimester [tri'mestə], *s.* (*Univ.*) das Trimester.

trimeter ['trimitə], *s.* (*Metr.*) der Trimeter.

trimmer ['trimə], *s.* 1. Besatznäherin, Putzmacherin; 2. (*Build.*) der Wechselbalken; 3. (*Naut.*) (Kohlen)trimmer, Stauer; 4. (*fig. coll.*) der (die) Opportunist(in), Achselträger(in), Schwankende(r), die Wetterfahne.

trimming ['trimiŋ], *s.* 1. das (Auf)putzen, Ausputzen, Zurichten; 2. Zu(recht)schneiden, Ausputzen, Beschneiden; 3. der Besatz, die Garnitur, Einfassung, Borte; (*usu. pl.*) Besatzartikel (*pl.*), Borten (*pl.*), Posamenten (*pl.*) (*for dress*); 4. *pl.* die Garnierung, Beilagen (*pl.*), Zutaten (*pl.*) (*for food*); *pl.* (*coll.*) das Beiwerk, Zubehör; 5. *pl.* Abfälle (*pl.*) (*from cutting*); 6. (*Naut.*) das Trimmen, (Ver)stauen; die Staulage, richtige *or* seemäßige Verteilung *or* Verstauung; (*Av.*) – ***flap***, die Trimmklappe; – ***tank***, die Trimmzelle (*of submarine*); 7. (*fig.*) die Achselträgerei, Gesinnungslumperei, der Opportunismus.

trimness ['trimnis], *s.* gute Ordnung; die Gepflegtheit, Sauberkeit, Nettigkeit, Niedlichkeit, gutes Aussehen.

trinal [trainl], *adj.* dreifach. **trine,** 1. *adj. See* **trinal.** 2. *s.* (*Astr.*) der Gedrittschein, Trigonalschein, Trigonalaspekt.

Trinitarian [trini'tɛəriən], 1. *adj.* Dreieinigkeits–. 2. *s.* der Trinitarier. **Trinitarianism,** *s.* die Dreieinigkeitslehre.

trinitrotoluene [trainaitrou'tɔlui:n], **trinitrotoluol** [–uɔl], *s.* (*Chem.*) das Trinitrotoluol.

trinity ['triniti], *s.* 1. die Dreiheit; 2. (*Eccl.*) ***the Trinity,*** die Dreieinigkeit; ***Trinity (law) sittings,*** die Sommersitzungen; ***Trinity Sunday,*** der Sonntag Trinitatis; ***Trinity term,*** das Sommersemester.

trinket ['triŋkit], *s.* 1. das Schmuckstück; *pl.* Schmucksachen (*pl.*), der Schmuck, das Geschmeide; 2. (*fig.*) der Tand, Flitterkram.

trinomial [trai'noumiəl], 1. *adj.* dreigliedrig, dreinamig. 2. *s.* dreigliedrige Größe; das Trinom.

trio ['triou], *s.* 1. (*Mus.*) das Trio (*also fig.*); 2. (*fig.*) das Kleeblatt (*of persons etc.*). **triode** ['traioud], *s.* (*Rad.*) die Dreielektrodenröhre. **triolet** ['triəlet], *s.* das Triolett, achtzeiliges Ringelgedicht.

trip [trip], 1. *s.* 1. der Ausflug, die Tour, (Vergnügungs)reise, (See)fahrt; (*sl.*) (*of drug addicts*) Reise; ***go on*** or ***make*** or ***take a*** –, einen Ausflug machen; ***round*** –, die Reise hin und zurück, Rundreise; 2. das Straucheln, Stolpern; Vergehen, (*esp. fig.*) der Fehltritt; das Beinstellen; 3. (*Tech.*) die Auslösevorrichtung. 2. *v.t.* 1. (*also* – ***up***) ein Bein stellen (*Dat.*), zu Fall bringen (*also fig.*), (*fig.*) aufs Glatteis führen; 2. (*fig.*) ertappen, erwischen (***in***, bei) (*a p.*); 3. vereiteln, zunichte machen (*a plan*); 4. (*Tech.*) auslösen; 5. (*Naut.*) lichten (*anchor*), anlüften (*spar*). 3. *v.i.* 1. trippeln, hüpfen, tänzeln; 2. (*also* – ***up***) straucheln, stolpern (***over***, über (*Acc.*)), fehltreten, ausgleiten, (*fig.*) sich vergehen *or* irren, fehlgehen, straucheln, einen Fehltritt tun.

tripartite [trai'pɑ:tait], *adj.* 1. (*esp. Bot.*) dreiteilig, dreigeteilt; 2. (*Law etc.*) dreifach (ausgefertigt); dreiseitig, Dreier–; – ***treaty,*** der Dreimächtevertrag.

tripe [traip], *s.* 1. Kaldaunen (*pl.*), Flecke (*pl.*), Kutteln (*pl.*); 2. (*sl.*) der Mist, Quatsch, Kitsch, Schund.

trip-hammer, *s.* der Aufwerfhammer.

triphthong ['trifθɔŋ], *s.* (*Phonet.*) der Dreilaut, Triphthong.

triplane ['traiplein], *s.* (*Av.*) der Dreidecker.

triple [tripl], 1. *adj.* 1. dreifach; Drei–, drei–, dreimalig; ***Triple Alliance,*** der Dreibund; – ***crown,*** (*Eccl.*) die Tiara; (*Rugby*) dreifacher Sieg in den Nationalspielen; 2. (*Mus.*) Tripel–, dreiteilig; – ***time,*** der Tripeltakt. 2. *v.t.* verdreifachen. **triplet** ['triplit], *s.* 1. der Drilling (*child*); *pl.* Drillinge (*pl.*); 2. die Dreiergruppe, das Kleeblatt, Trio; 3. (*Mus.*) die Triole; 4. (*Metr.*) dreizeilig reimende Strophe.

trip-lever, *s.* der Auslösehebel.

triplex ['tripleks], 1. *adj.* dreifach. 2. *s.* (*also* – ***glass***) das Dreischichtenglas, splitterfreies Glas.

triplicate, 1. ['triplikit], *adj.* dreifach ausgefertigt. 2. [–kit], *s.* dritte Ausfertigung, das Triplikat; ***in*** –, in dreifacher Ausfertigung *or* Ausführung. 3. [–keit], *v.t.* dreifach ausfertigen *or* anfertigen, verdreifachen. **triplication** [–'keiʃən], *s.* die Verdreifachung.

tripod ['traipɔd], *s.* der Dreifuß, das Dreibein; (*Phot.*) Stativ.

tripoli ['tripəli], *s.* (*Geol.*) der Tripel, Polierschiefer.

Tripoli, *s.* (*Geog.*) Tripolis (*n.*).

tripos ['traipɔs], *s.* (*Cambridge Univ.*) das Schlußexamen.

tripper ['tripə], *s.* (*coll.*) der (die) Ausflügler(in), Tourist(in). **tripperish,** *adj.* (*coll.*) auf Ausflügler eingestellt (*of a resort*).

tripping ['tripiŋ], 1. *adj.* trippelnd, hüpfend, leicht(füßig), flott, flink, munter. 2. *s.* 1. das Hüpfen; 2. Beinstellen.

triptych ['triptik], *s.* das Triptychon.

triptyque ['triptik], *s.* (*Motor.*) das Triptyk.

trip-wire, *s.* der Stolperdraht, Trampelfaden.

trireme ['traiəri:m], *s.* die Trireme, Triere, der Dreiruderer.

trisect [trai'sekt], *v.t.* in drei gleiche Teile teilen, dreiteilen. **trisection** [–'sekʃən], *s.* die Dreiteilung.

trismus ['trizməs], *s.* (*Med.*) der Kaumuskelkrampf, die Kieferklemme.

trisyllabic [traisi'lӕbik], *adj.* dreisilbig. **trisyllable** [–'siləbl], *s.* dreisilbiges Wort.

trite [trait], *adj.* abgedroschen, abgegriffen, abgenützt, alltäglich, seicht, platt. **triteness,** *s.* die Abgedroschenheit, Alltäglichkeit, das Alltägliche.

Triton ['traitɔn], *s.* das Triton, Meergott.

triturate ['tritjureit], *v.t.* zerreiben, zermahlen, zerstoßen, pulverisieren. **trituration** [–'reiʃən], *s.* die Zerreibung, Zerstoßung, Pulverisierung.

triumph ['traiəmf], 1. *s.* 1. der Triumph, Sieg (***over***, über (*Acc.*)); 2. die Siegesfreude (***at***, über (*Acc.*)); (*Hist.*) der Siegeszug; ***in*** –, triumphierend; 3. (*fig.*) glänzender Erfolg, die Errungenschaft. 2. *v.i.* 1. den Sieg davontragen *or* erringen, die Oberhand gewinnen, Sieger bleiben, siegen; 2. frohlocken, jubeln, triumphieren (***over***, über (*Acc.*)). **triumphal** [trai'ʌmfəl], *adj.* Triumph–, Sieges–; – ***arch,*** der Triumphbogen; – ***procession,*** der Siegeszug. **triumphant** [–'ʌmfənt], *adj.* 1. triumphierend; siegreich, glorreich, erfolgreich; 2. jubelnd, frohlockend.

triumvir [trai'ʌmviə], *s.* der Triumvir. **triumvirate** [–'ʌmvirət], *s.* das Triumvirat; (*fig.*) das Dreigestirn.

triune ['traiu:n], *adj.* dreieinig.

trivet ['trivit], *s.* der Dreifuß; (*coll.*) ***as right as a*** –, ganz in Ordnung, sauwohl.

trivial ['triviəl], *adj.* 1. gering(fügig), nichtig, unbedeutend, unerheblich, belanglos, nichtssagend; 2. trivial, banal, alltäglich, gewöhnlich; oberflächlich, seicht, flach. **triviality** [–'ӕliti], *s.* die Trivialität, Plattheit, Geringfügigkeit, Unerheblichkeit; *pl.* Nebensächlichkeiten (*pl.*), nichtssagende Bemerkungen.

trochaic [tro'keiik], *adj.* trochäisch. **trochee** ['trouki:], *s.* der Trochäus.

trod [trɔd], *imperf., p.p.,* **trodden** [trɔdn], *p.p. of* **tread.**

troglodyte ['trɔglədait], *s.* der Höhlenbewohner, Troglodyt, (*fig.*) Einsiedler. **troglodytic** [–'ditik], *adj.* troglodytisch.

troika ['trɔikə], *s.* die Troika, (russisches) Dreigespann.

Trojan ['troudʒən], 1. *adj.* trojanisch. 2. *s.* der (die) Trojaner(in); (*coll.*) ***work like a*** –, arbeiten wie ein Pferd.

[1]**troll** [troul], *s.* der Kobold, Troll, Unhold.
[2]**troll, 1.** *v.t.* 1. (*obs.*) rollen, trudeln (*a ball etc.*); 2. trällern, im Rundgesang anstimmen (*a song*); 3. herumgehen lassen, herumreichen (*at table*). **2.** *v.i.* 1. rollen, (sich) drehen, trudeln; 2. trällern, einen Rundgesang anstimmen; 3. mit der Schleppangel fischen (*for*, *Acc.*). **3.** *s.* 1. der Rundgesang; 2. die Schleppangel.
trolley ['trɔli], *s.* 1. der Karren; 2. (*Min.*) Förderwagen, Hund, die Laufkatze; 3. (*Railw.*) Draisine; 4. der Rolltisch, Teewagen; 5. die Kontaktrolle (*of tramcar*); 6. (*Am.*) Straßenbahn. **trolley|-bus,** *s.* der Oberleitungsomnibus, Obus. **--car,** *s.* (*Am.*) der Straßenbahnwagen. **--pole,** *s.* die Kontaktstange. **--wire,** *s.* der Fahrdraht, die Oberleitung.
trollop ['trɔləp], **1.** *v.i.* (*Scots*) schlampen, schlumpen, schlunzen. **2.** *s.* die Schlampe, Schlumpe, Schlunze.
trombone [trɔm'boun], *s.* die Posaune. **trombonist,** *s.* der Posaunist.
Trondheim ['trɔnheim], **Trondhjem** ['trɔnjem], *s.* Trondheim (*n.*).
troop [tru:p], **1.** *s.* der Trupp, Haufe(n), die Schar; (*cavalry*) die Schwadron, Reiterabteilung, der Beritt; *pl.* (*Mil.*) Truppen (*pl.*). **2.** *v.i.* 1. sich scharen, sich sammeln; 2. (in Scharen) ziehen, strömen; – ***away*** or ***off,*** sich davonmachen, abziehen. **3.** *v.t.* – ***the colours,*** die Fahnenparade abnehmen; ***–ing the colours,*** die Fahnenparade. **troop-carrier,** *s.* das Truppentransportflugzeug. **trooper** ['tru:pə], *s.* 1. der Reiter, Kavallerist; ***swear like a –,*** fluchen wie ein Landsknecht; 2. das Kavalleriepferd; 3. (*coll.*) *see* **troopship. troop|-horse,** *s.* das Kavalleriepferd. **–ship,** *s.* das Truppentransportschiff.
trope [troup], *s.* bildlicher Ausdruck, der Tropus (*also Mus.*), die Trope.
trophied ['troufid], *adj.* mit Trophäen geschmückt. **trophy** [–fi], *s.* 1. die Trophäe, Siegesbeute, das Siegeszeichen; 2. (*Spt.*) der Preis.
tropic ['trɔpik], **1.** *s.* 1. der Wendekreis; 2. *pl.* die Tropen. **2.** *adj. See* [1]**tropical.**
[1]**tropical** ['trɔpikl], *adj.* tropisch, Tropen–; – ***disease,*** die Tropenkrankheit; – ***fruit,*** Südfrüchte (*pl.*); – ***heat,*** tropische Hitze.
[2]**tropical, tropological** [–ə'lɔdʒikl], *adj.* figürlich, bildlich, metaphorisch, übertragen. **tropology** [–'pɔlədʒi], *s.* bildliche Ausdrucksweise; (*Eccl.*) die Figuralinterpretation.
troposphere ['troupəsfiə], *s.* die Troposphäre.
trot [trɔt], **1.** *s.* 1. der Trott, Trab (*also fig.*); ***at a –,*** im Trabe; (*coll.*) ***be always on the –,*** dauernd auf den Beinen sein; 2. (*Am. sl.*) die Eselsbrücke, Klatsche. **2.** *v.i.* trotten, traben (*of horses*), im Trab reiten (*of riders*); (*coll.*) – ***along*** or ***off,*** davongehen, fortgehen. **3.** *v.t.* 1. trotten *or* traben lassen, in Trab bringen *or* setzen (*a horse*); (*coll.*) – ***him round the museums,*** ihn in den Museen herumführen; 2. (*sl.*) – ***out,*** vorführen, anführen, vorbringen, auftischen, angeben mit.
troth [trouθ], *s.* (*obs.*) die Treue, das Treuegelöbnis; ***by*** or ***upon my –!*** meiner Treu! wahrlich! ***pledge one's –,*** sein Wort geben (*to*, *Dat.*), ewige Treue schwören; ***plight one's –,*** sich verloben; ***plighted –,*** die gelobte Treue.
trotter [trɔtə], *s.* 1. der Traber (*horse*); 2. (*of pigs, sheep*) Fuß. **trotting (race),** *s.* das Trabrennen.
troubadour ['tru:bədɔ:], *s.* der Troubadour.
trouble [trʌbl], **1.** *v.t.* 1. stören, belästigen, behelligen, Mühe machen (*Dat.*), beschwerlich fallen (*Dat.*), Unannehmlichkeiten bereiten (*Dat.*); 2. bemühen (*for*, um); ***may I – you to pass me the salt,*** darf ich Sie um das Salz bitten; ***I will – you to keep your mouth shut,*** ich werde dich noch lange bitten, den Mund zu halten; 3. Sorge(n) *or* Kummer *or* Verdruß machen *or* bereiten (*Dat.*), betrüben, beunruhigen, ängstigen, verwirren, plagen, quälen, heimsuchen; ***be –d,*** sehr beunruhigt sein; ***be –d about,*** sich (*Dat.*) Sorgen machen über (*Acc.*); – ***one's head about,*** sich (*Dat.*) den Kopf zerbrechen über (*Acc.*); ***–d with gout,*** von der Gicht geplagt; 4. (*rare*) trüben (*waters*); (*fig.*) ***–d waters,*** getrübte Verhältnisse; ***pour oil on –d waters,*** Frieden stiften. **2.** *v.i.* 1. sich (*Dat.*) die Mühe machen, sich (*Dat.*) Umstände machen; ***don't –,*** mach dir keine Umstände! bemüh dich nicht! ***don't – to write*** or ***about writing,*** Sie brauchen nicht zu schreiben; 2. sich beunruhigen; ***I shan't – if . . .,*** ich werde ganz beruhigt wenn . . . .
3. *s.* 1. die Sorge, Not, der Kummer, Verdruß, das Leid, Unglück, Mißgeschick; ***ask*** or ***look for –,*** sich (*Dat.*) selbst Schwierigkeiten bereiten, das Unglück herausfordern; ***be in –,*** in Not *or* Gefahr sein, in der Patsche *or* Tinte sein, (*coll. of a girl*) schwanger sein; ***bring – upon,*** Unheil bringen über (*Acc.*); ***get into –,*** sich (*Dat.*) Unannehmlichkeit zuziehen, sich in die Nesseln setzen; ***get him into –,*** ihm Unannehmlichkeit bereiten; 2. die Mühe, Beschwerde, Unannehmlichkeit, Belästigung, Last, Schwierigkeit, Schererei, Mißhelligkeiten (*pl.*); ***be a – to him,*** für ihn eine Belastung sein, ihm zur Last fallen; ***give him –,*** ihm Mühe verursachen; ***go to the –,*** sich (*Dat.*) besondere Mühe machen *or* geben; ***make –,*** Schwierigkeiten machen (*for*, *Dat.*); ***put him to the –,*** ihm die Mühe machen; ***save o.s. the –,*** sich (*Dat.*) die Mühe ersparen (***of doing***, zu tun); ***to spare him the –,*** um ihm Unannehmlichkeiten zu ersparen; ***take –,*** sich (*Dat.*) Mühe geben (***with***, ***over***, mit); ***take the –,*** sich (*Dat.*) die Mühe nehmen *or* machen; 3. der Fehler, Haken, das Problem, (*Tech.*) der Defekt, die Störung, Panne, (*Med.*) Krankheit, das Leiden, Beschwerden (*pl.*); 4. (*Pol.*) (*oft. pl.*) der Konflikt, Aufruhr, Krawall, Krach, (öffentliche) Unruhe(n), Wirren (*pl.*); ***stir up –,*** Unruhe *or* Verwirrung stiften.
troubled [trʌbld], *adj.* 1. beunruhigt, bekümmert, sorgenvoll; 2. besorgt (***about***, um); 3. geplagt, heimgesucht (***by***, ***with***, von).
trouble|maker, *s.* der Störenfried, der (die) Unruhestifter(in), **–shooter,** *s.* (*esp. Am.*) (*Tech., fig.*) der Störungssucher.
troublesome ['trʌblsəm], *adj.* 1. störend, beschwerlich, lästig; 2. mühsam, peinlich, unbequem, unangenehm. **troublous** ['trʌbləs], *adj.* (*obs.*) unruhig, ruhelos, aufgeregt; – ***times,*** bewegte Zeiten.
trough [trɔf], *s.* 1. der Trog, Bottich, die Wanne; 2. Mulde, Rinne, Furche (*on land*), das Wellental (*on sea*); 3. (*Meteor.*) Tief, die (Tiefdruck)rinne.
trounce [trauns], *v.t.* 1. prügeln, züchtigen, durchhauen, verwichsen; 2. (*fig. of critics*) heruntermachen, fertigmachen.
troupe [tru:p], *s.* die (Schauspieler)truppe.
trouser|-button ['trauzə], *s.* der Hosenknopf. **--clip,** *s.* (*Cycl.*) die Hosenklammer. **trousering,** *s.* der Hosenstoff. **trouser|-leg,** *s.* das Hosenbein. **--pocket,** *s.* die Hosentasche. **--press,** *s.* der Hosenstrecker. **trousers,** *pl.* (*also* ***pair of –***) die Hose; (*coll.*) ***she wears the –,*** sie führt das Regiment, sie hat die Hosen an. **trouser-suit,** *s.* der Hosenanzug.
trousseau ['tru:sou], *s.* die Aussteuer, Brautausstattung.
trout [traut], *s.* die Forelle; ***river –,*** die Bachforelle, Steinforelle; ***sea –,*** die Lachsforelle, Meerforelle.
trover ['trouvə], *s.* (*Law*) rechtswidrige Inbesitznahme; ***action of –,*** die Fundklage.
trow [trau], *v.i.* (*obs.*) glauben (*Dat.*), meinen; (*foll. a question*) ***I –,*** möchte ich wissen! frage ich!
trowel ['trauəl], **1.** *s.* die (Maurer)kelle; (*Hort.*) Blumenkelle, der Hohlspatel, Pflanzenheber; (*coll.*) ***lay it on with a –,*** übertreiben, dick auftragen. **2.** *v.t.* mit der Kelle glätten.
troy [trɔi], *s.* (*also* – ***weight***) das Troygewicht (*1 lb. = 12 oz. = 372.25 gr.*).
Troy, *s.* Troja (*n.*).
truancy ['truənsi], *s.* das Ausbleiben, Wegbleiben, (Schul)schwänzen. **truant, 1.** *adj.* 1. (schul)schwänzend; 2. (*fig.*) (ab)schweifend, zerstreut (*as thoughts*). **2.** *s.* der (Schul)schwänzer; ***play –,*** (die Schule) schwänzen.

truce [tru:s], *s.* der Waffenstillstand, die Waffenruhe; (*fig.*) Ruhepause; ***flag of* –**, die Parlamentärflagge; **– *of God,*** der Gottesfriede; ***a – to . . .!*** hör auf *or* Schluß mit . . .!

Trucial States [ˈtru:ʃəl], *pl.* Befriedetes Oman.

[1]**truck** [trʌk], **1.** *v.i.* Tauschhandel treiben; handeln, schachern (***for,*** um), tauschen (gegen). **2.** *v.t.* (aus)-tauschen, vertauschen, eintauschen (***for,*** gegen). **3.** *s.* 1. der Tausch(handel), Tauschverkehr, Warenaustausch; ***have no – with,*** nichts zu tun haben mit; (*coll.*) ***stand no –,*** sich (*Dat.*) nichts gefallen lassen; 2. der Kleinkram, Hausbedarf, Trödel, Plunder; 3. (*Am.*) das Gemüse.

[2]**truck,** *s.* 1. der Blockwagen, Rollwagen, Handwagen, Handkarren; (*Min.*) Förderwagen, Hund, die Lore; (*Railw.*) offener Güterwagen; (*esp. Am.*) der Lastkraftwagen, das Lastauto; 2. Blockrad, die Rolle; (*Railw.*) das Untergestell, Radgestell, Drehgestell; 3. (*Naut.*) der Flaggenknopf.

truckage [ˈtrʌkidʒ], *s.* 1. das Rollgeld, Wagengeld; 2. der Wagentransport. **truck-driver,** *s.* der Wagenführer. **trucker,** *s.* (*Am.*) 1. *See* **truck-farmer**; 2. *See* **truck-driver. truck-farmer,** *s.* der Gemüsegärtner. **trucking,** *s.* 1. der Tauschhandel; 2. (*Am.*) der Wagentransport, die Autospedition; 3. (*Am.*) der Gartenbau, Gemüsebau. **truck-system,** *s.* das Trucksystem, die Bezahlung in Naturalien.

truckle [trʌkl], *v.i.* sich unterwerfen *or* fügen *or* demütigen (***to,*** *Dat.*), (zu Kreuze) kriechen (vor (*Dat.*)). **truckle-bed,** *s.* das Rollbett, Schiebebett.

truck|man, *s.* (*Am.*) *see* **--driver.**

truculence, truculency [ˈtrʌkjələns(i)], *s.* die Streitsucht, Händelsucht, Unversöhnlichkeit, Widerspenstigkeit, Roheit, Gehässigkeit. **truculent,** *adj.* streitsüchtig, ausfällig, widerspenstig, unversöhnlich, gehässig, bramarbasierend.

trudge [trʌdʒ], **1.** *v.i.* mühsam zu Fuß gehen; ***– along,*** sich mühsam weiterschleppen. **2.** *v.t.* mühsam durchwandern. **3.** *s.* langer mühsamer *or* mühseliger Weg.

true [tru:], **1.** *adj.* 1. (*of a p.*) wahr(haft), redlich, aufrichtig, zuverlässig; treu (***to,*** *Dat.*); ***– as steel,*** treu wie Gold; ***– friend,*** treuer Freund; ***– to myself,*** mir selbst treu; ***– to one's word,*** seinem Worte treu; 2. (*of a th.*) richtig, genau, echt; ***be –,*** zutreffen (***of,*** (in bezug) auf (*Acc.*)); ***it is – I did it,*** es stimmt *or* ich gebe zu, ich habe es getan; ich habe es zwar *or* freilich *or* allerdings getan; ***is it – that . . .?*** stimmt es, daß . . .? ***prove to be –,*** sich als wahr *or* richtig herausstellen; ***– bill,*** vom Schwurgericht bestätigte *or* für begründet erklärte Anklage; ***– love,*** echte Liebe; ***– weight,*** richtiges *or* genaues Gewicht; 3. (*of a th.*) getreu; ***– copy,*** getreue Abschrift; ***– to,*** in Einklang mit; ***– to life,*** lebenswahr; ***– to nature,*** naturgetreu; ***– to size,*** maßgerecht; ***– to type,*** typisch, artgemäß; 4. wahr(haftig), wirklich, (regel)recht, rechtmäßig; ***– heir,*** rechtmäßiger Erbe; ***– story,*** wahre Geschichte; ***come –,*** sich bewahrheiten *or* bestätigen, sich erfüllen (*as dreams*); 5. (*Naut.*) rechtweisend; ***– bearing,*** rechtweisende Peilung; ***– course,*** rechtweisender Kurs; ***– north,*** geographisch Nord. **2.** *adv.* 1. wahrheitsgemäß, wahrhaftig; ***speak –,*** die Wahrheit sagen; 2. richtig, genau; 3. (*Biol.*) ***breed –,*** sichˈreinrassigˈvermehren. **3.** *v.t.* (*usu.* ***– up***) zentrieren (*wheels*), ausrichten (*bearings*). **4.** *s.* (*Tech.*) ***out of –,*** unrund.

true|-blue, 1. *adj.* waschecht; standhaft, treu. **2.** *s.* standhafter Anhänger. **--born,** *adj.* echt (von Geburt). **--bred,** *adj.* rasserein, reinrassig. **--hearted,** *adj.* redlich, treuherzig, treugesinnt. **--heartedness,** *s.* die Redlichkeit, Treuherzigkeit, treue Gesinnung. **--love,** *s.* das Liebchen, Geliebte(r). **--love(r's) knot,** *s.* der Liebesknoten.

trueness [ˈtru:nis], *s.* 1. die Wahrheit, Treue, Echtheit, Redlichkeit; 2. (*Tech.*) Exaktheit, Richtigkeit, Genauigkeit.

truffle [trʌfl], *s.* die Trüffel.

truism [ˈtru:izm], *s.* die Binsenwahrheit, der Gemeinplatz.

trull [trʌl], *s.* (*obs.*) die Dirne, Hure.

truly [ˈtru:li], *adv.* 1. aufrichtig, ehrlich; ***yours –,*** Ihr ergebener, hochachtungsvoll (*in letters*), (*hum.*) meine Wenigkeit; 2. wahrheitsgemäß, wahrhaftig, offen (gesagt), wirklich, in der Tat.

[1]**trump** [trʌmp], **1.** *s.* 1. (*Cards*) (*usu. pl.*) der Trumpf; *see also* **trump-card**; ***no –s,*** kein Trumpf; (*fig.*) ***turn up –s,*** sich als das beste erweisen (*a th.*), immer Glück haben (*a p.*); 2. (*fig. coll.*) guter Kerl, der Prachtmensch. **2.** *v.t.* (über)-trumpfen, stechen; (*fig.*) übertrumpfen, ausstechen. **3.** *v.i.* Trumpf spielen, trumpfen, stechen.

[2]**trump,** *v.t.* (*usu.* ***– up***) erdichten, sich (*Dat.*) aus den Fingern saugen, abkarten, zurechtschwindeln.

[3]**trump,** *s.* (*Poet.*) der Trompetenstoß; (*obs.*) die Trompete; ***– of doom,*** die Posaune des Jüngsten Gerichts.

trump-card, *s.* die Trumpfkarte; (*fig.*) ***play one's –,*** alle Trümpfe *or* den höchsten Trumpf ausspielen.

trumped-up [ˈtrʌmptˈʌp], *adj.* erdichtet, erfunden, falsch, aus den Fingern gesogen.

trumpery [ˈtrʌmpəri], **1.** *s.* 1. der Trödel(kram), Plunder, Ramsch, die Ramschware, wertloses Zeug; 2. das Geschwätz, Gewäsch, der Quatsch. **2.** *adj.* 1. wertlos, Schund–; 2. belanglos, nichtig, nichtssagend.

trumpet [ˈtrʌmpit], **1.** *s.* die Trompete; (*B.*) Posaune; (*fig.*) ***blow one's own –,*** sein eigenes Lob ausposaunen *or* singen; ***ear--,*** das Hörrohr; ***the last –,*** die Posaune des Jüngsten Gerichts; ***speaking--,*** das Sprachrohr, der Schalltrichter. **2.** *v.i.* trompeten (*also of elephants*), Trompete blasen. **3.** *v.t.* (*fig.*) (*usu.* ***– forth***) ausposaunen, laut verkünden. **trumpet-call,** *s.* das Trompetensignal; (*fig.*) der Trompetenruf. **trumpeter,** *s.* 1. Trompeter; (*fig.*) Ausposauner; 2. (*Orn.*) die Trompetertaube.

trumpet|-major, *s.* (*Mil.*) der Stabstrompeter. **--shaped,** *adj.* trompetenförmig, trichterförmig. **--tongued,** *adj.* mit Posaunenstimme.

truncate [ˈtrʌnkeit], **1.** *v.t.* stutzen, beschneiden; (*Geom.*) abstumpfen; (*fig.*) verstümmeln. **2.** *adj.* abgestumpft, abgestutzt. **truncated,** *adj.* verstümmelt, abgekürzt, verkürzt; ***– cone,*** der Kegelstumpf. **truncation** [–ˈkeiʃən], *s.* die Abstumpfung; Stutzung, Verstümmelung.

truncheon [ˈtrʌntʃən], *s.* 1. der (Polizei)knüppel; 2. (*Her.*) Kommandostab.

trundle [trʌndl], **1.** *v.t.* rollen, wälzen, trudeln; schlagen (*a hoop*). **2.** *v.i.* rollen, trudeln, sich wälzen. **3.** *s.* die Rolle, Walze. **trundle-bed,** *s.* das Rollbett.

trunk [trʌŋk], *s.* 1. der (Baum)stamm; 2. Rumpf, Leib (*of men etc.*); (*Sculp.*) Torso; 3. (*Archit.*) Schaft (*of a column*); 4. Rüssel (*of an elephant*); 5. (Reise)koffer, die Kiste; 6. (*Tech.*) Rohrleitung, der Schacht; 7. (*Tele.*) (*usu. pl.*) die Fernleitung, Fernverbindung; ***–s please!*** Fernamt bitte! 8. (*Am.*) (*Motor.*) der Kofferraum; 9. *pl.* (*Hist.*) die Pluderhose, (*Theat.*) Kniehose, (*Spt.*) Badehose.

trunk|-bending, *s.* (*Gymn.*) das Rumpfbeugen. **--call,** *s.* das Ferngespräch. **--dialling,** *s.* (*Tele.*) der Selbstwählfernanschluß. **--exchange,** *s.* das Fernamt. **-fish,** *s.* der Kofferfisch. **--hose,** *pl.* (*Hist.*) die Pluderhose. **--line,** *s.* 1. (*Railw.*) die Hauptstrecke, Hauptlinie; 2. (*Tele.*) die Fernleitung, Fernverbindung. **--road,** *s.* die Hauptstraße, Landstraße, Autostraße.

trunnion [ˈtrʌnjən], *s.* der (Dreh)zapfen; (*Mil.*) Schildzapfen.

truss [trʌs], **1.** *s.* 1. das Bund, Bündel (*of hay = 60 lb. = 27 kg.; of straw = 37 lb. = 16.2 kg.*); 2. (*Surg.*) Bruchband; 3. (*Naut.*) Rack; 4. (*Build.*) Hängewerk, Gitterwerk, Gerüst; 5. (*Bot.*) die Dolde. **2.** *v.t.* 1. dressieren (*poultry*); 2. (*Build.*) absteifen, stützen; 3. (*also* ***– up***) zusammenbinden, (auf)bündeln; (fest)schnüren, (an)binden; (*obs.*) aufstecken, hochschürzen (*clothes*); 4. (*coll.*) aufknüpfen, aufhängen (*criminal*). **truss|-beam,** *s.*

der Eisenbalken. **--bridge,** *s.* die Gitterbrücke, Fachwerkbrücke. **--frame,** *s.* das Hängewerk.

trust [trʌst], **1.** *s.* 1. das Vertrauen (*in*, auf (*Acc.*) *or* zu), Zutrauen (zu); die Zuversicht, zuversichtliche Hoffnung *or* Erwartung; ***position of –***, der Vertrauensposten; ***place*** or ***put one's – in,*** sein Vertrauen setzen auf (*Acc.*); ***take on –***, auf Treu und Glauben hinnehmen; 2. die Pflicht; ***fulfil one's –***, seine Verpflichtung erfüllen; 3. (*Law*) das Treuhandverhältnis, die Treuhand, Pflegschaft; Verwahrung, Obhut; anvertrautes Gut, das Treuhandvermögen; ***hold in –***, (zu treuen Händen) verwahren, (treuhänderisch *or* als Treuhänder) verwalten; ***breach of –***, der Treubruch, Vertrauensbruch; 4. (*Comm.*) der Trust, Ring, das Kartell; 5. der Kredit; ***on –***, auf Kredit *or* Borg. **2.** *v.t.* 1. anvertrauen, in Verwahrung geben (*a th.*) (*to*, *Dat.*); 2. (ver)trauen (*Dat.*), glauben (*Dat.*), sich verlassen auf (*Acc.*) (*a p.*); ***I don't – him,*** ich traue ihm nicht; ***– me for that!*** verlaß dich nur auf mich! (*coll.*) ***– him to lose his way,*** es sieht ihm ähnlich, sich zu verirren; 3. in Verwahrung geben (*Dat.*), anvertrauen (*Dat.*) (*a p.*) (***with***, *Acc.*); ***– o.s. to him,*** sich ihm anvertrauen; 4. zuversichtlich hoffen *or* erwarten, überzeugt sein. **3.** *v.i.* 1. Vertrauen haben (***to***, ***in***, zu), sein Vertrauen setzen, vertrauen, sich verlassen (auf (*Acc.*)); ***– in God,*** sein Vertrauen auf Gott setzen; 2. zuversichtlich hoffen *or* erwarten.

trust|-company, *s.* die Treuhandgesellschaft. **--deed,** *s.* die Übertragungsurkunde eines Treuhandvermögens.

trustee [trʌs'tiː], *s.* Bevollmächtigte(r), Beauftragte(r), der Treuhänder, Sachwalter, Verwalter, Kurator, Vertrauensmann; ***– in bankruptcy, official –***, der Konkursverwalter; ***board of –s,*** das Kuratorium; ***– stock,*** mündelsichere Papiere (*pl.*). **trusteeship,** *s.* (*Pol.*) die Treuhandverwaltung; (*Law, Comm.*) Treuhänderschaft, Sachwalterschaft, das Kuratorium.

trustful ['trʌstful], *adj.* vertrauensvoll, zutraulich. **trustfulness,** *s.* die Zutraulichkeit, das Vertrauen.

trust|-fund, *s.* der Treuhandfonds, Treuhandgelder (*pl.*), Mündelgelder (*pl.*). **--house,** *s.* von einem Kartell verwaltetes Hotel.

trustification [trʌstifi'keiʃən], *s.* die Trustbildung, Vertrustung.

trustiness ['trʌstinis], *s.* die Treue, Zuverlässigkeit. **trusting,** *adj. See* **trustful**; ***too –***, vertrauensselig. **trust|worthiness,** *s.* die Zuverlässigkeit, Vertrauenswürdigkeit. **--worthy, trusty,** *adj.* treu, zuverlässig, vertrauenswürdig.

truth [truːθ], *s.* 1. die Wahrheit; ***in*** (***very***) ***–***, wahrhaftig; ***home –s,*** eindrückliche Wahrheiten; ***tell him some home –s,*** ihm gehörig die Meinung *or* Wahrheit sagen; ***there is no – in it,*** daran ist nichts Wahres; ***that's the – of it,*** das ist die volle Wahrheit; (*coll.*) ***the moment of –***, entscheidender Augenblick; ***tell the –***, die Wahrheit sagen; ***to tell the –, – to tell,*** um die Wahrheit zu sagen, ehrlich gesagt; 2. die Wirklichkeit, Echtheit, Treue, Genauigkeit, Richtigkeit; ***be out of –***, nicht genau passen *or* stimmen; ***– to life,*** die Lebenstreue; 3. (*rare, of a p.*) die Wahrhaftigkeit, Aufrichtigkeit, Ehrlichkeit.

truthful ['truːθful], *adj.* 1. (*of a p.*) ehrlich, wahrheitsliebend; 2. (*of statement etc.*) wahr(heitsgemäß), echt, getreu, genau. **truthfulness,** *s.* 1. die Wahrhaftigkeit, Wahrheitsliebe; 2. Echtheit, Genauigkeit, Wahrheit. **truth-loving,** *adj.* wahrheitsliebend.

try [trai], **1.** *v.t.* 1. (aus)probieren, versuchen, in Angriff nehmen; ***– one's best,*** sein Bestes tun; ***– one's hand,*** seinen (ersten) Versuch machen (***at***, mit); ***– one's hardest,*** sich (*Dat.*) die größte Mühe geben, sein Äußerstes tun; 2. es versuchen mit, experimentieren mit, einen Versuch *or* ein Experiment anstellen *or* machen mit, (durch)probieren, prüfen, erproben, testen; kosten (*food*); ***– conclusions with,*** sich messen mit, es versuchen mit; ***– the door,*** die Tür zu öffnen suchen; ***– one's luck,*** sein Glück versuchen (***with***, bei); ***– on,*** anprobieren (*a coat etc.*); (*sl.*) ***– it on,*** zu übervorteilen *or* übertölpen suchen; (*sl.*) ***– it on with him,*** ihn zu nasführen *or* einzuseifen versuchen, ihn auf den Leim zu locken suchen; (*sl.*) ***– it on with her,*** sehen, wie weit man bei ihr gehen kann; (*sl.*) ***don't – that on*** (***with***) ***me!*** machen Sie mir nichts vor! ***– over,*** durchprobieren, durchgehen (*music etc.*); 3. auf die Probe *or* auf eine Probe stellen (*patience*), stark beanspruchen, (über)anstrengen, angreifen (*eyes etc.*), plagen, quälen, arg mitnehmen (*a p.*); 4. (*Law*) verhören, verhandeln gegen, einen Prozeß führen gegen, vor Gericht bringen *or* stellen (*a p.*) (***for***, wegen); verhandeln, (gerichtlich) untersuchen (*a case*); 5. scheiden, reinigen, raffinieren (*metals*), rektifizieren (*spirit*), eichen (*standards*). **2.** *v.i.* 1. (es) versuchen, einen Versuch machen; (*coll.*) ***– and do it,*** es versuchen; sich bemühen, es zu tun; (*coll.*) ***– and come,*** zu kommen versuchen; ***come and –!*** mach mal den Versuch! 2. sich bemühen (***for***, um), trachten (nach). **3.** *s.* 1. der Versuch, die Probe; ***have a –***, versuchen, (aus)probieren (***at***, *Acc.*), einen Versuch machen (mit); 2. (*Rugby*) der Versuch, 4 Punkte.

trying ['traiiŋ], *adj.* unangenehm, peinlich, mißlich (*a th.*), belästigend, quälend (*a p.*); anstrengend, mühsam, beschwerlich (***to***, für); ***be –***, auf die Nerven gehen (***to***, *Dat.*).

try|-on, *s.* 1. die Anprobe (*of clothes*); 2. (*sl.*) freche Zumutung, der Täuschungsversuch. **--out,** *s.* die Erprobung, Probe, der Vorversuch; (*Theat.*) die Probevorstellung. **–sail** [traisl], *s.* das Gaffelsegel. **--square,** *s.* der Anschlagwinkel.

tryst [trist, traist], **1.** *s.* 1. die Verabredung, das Stelldichein; 2. (*Scots*) der Viehmarkt. **2.** *v.i.* sich verabreden. **3.** *v.t.* hinbestellen (*a p.*), verabreden (*time*). **trysting-place,** *s.* der Zusammenkunftsort, Treffpunkt, Ort des Stelldicheins.

tsar [zɑː], *s.* der Zar. **tsarevitch** [–rəvitʃ], *s.* der Zarewitsch. **tsarina** [–'riːnə], *s.* die Zarin.

tsetse(-fly) ['tsetsi], *s.* die Tsetsefliege.

T|-shirt, *s.* das Sporthemd. **--square,** *s. See* **try-square.**

tub [tʌb], **1.** *s.* 1. das Faß, der Kübel, Zuber, Bottich, die Wanne, Bütte, Balge, Kufe; 2. (*Min.*) der Förderkarren, Förderkorb; 3. (*Rowing*) das Übungsboot, (*coll.*) plumpes Schiff; 4. (*Am. or coll.*) die Badewanne; das (Wannen)bad; (*Am. or coll.*) ***take a –***, baden. **2.** *v.t.* 1. in Kübel setzen (*plants*); 2. (*coll.*) baden (*children*); 3. (*sl.*) Ruderunterricht geben (*Dat.*). **3.** *v.i.* (sich) baden.

tuba ['tjuːbə], *s.* die Baßtuba.

tubby ['tʌbi], *adj.* 1. tonnenförmig, (*coll. of p.*) rundlich, untersetzt, dickbäuchig; 2. (*coll. of sound*) hölzern, dumpf, hohl.

tube [tjuːb], *s.* 1. die Röhre (*also Bot., Anat.*), das Rohr; ***feeding –***, die Magensonde; ***glass –***, die Glasröhre; ***speaking-–***, das Sprachrohr; 2. (*Cycl. etc.*) (*usu.* ***inner –***) der Schlauch; ***rubber –***, der Gummischlauch; 3. die Tube (*of paint etc.*); 4. (*coll.*) (Londoner) Untergrundbahn, die U-Bahn; ***by –***, mit der U-Bahn; ***--station,*** die U-Bahn-Haltestelle; 5. (*Am.*) die (Radio)röhre. **tubeless,** *adj.* (*of tyres*) schlauchlos.

tuber ['tjuːbə], *s.* 1. (*Bot.*) der Knollen, die Knolle; 2. (*Anat.*) das Knollengewächs, der Knoten, Knorren, Höcker. **tubercle** ['tjuːbəkl], *s.* 1. (*Bot.*) kleine Knolle; 2. (*Anat.*) die Schwellung, kleine Geschwulst, das Knötchen; der (*Austr.* die) (Lungen)tuberkel; ***– bacillus,*** der Tuberkuloseerreger. **tubercular** [–'bəːkjulə], *adj.* 1. (*Bot.*) warzig, höckerig, knotig; 2. (*Med.*) tuberkulös, Tuberkel–. **tuberculin** [–'bəːkjulin], *s.* das Tuberkulin; ***– test,*** die Tuberkulinprobe. **tuberculosis** [–'lousis], *s.* die (Lungen)schwindsucht, Tuberkulose. **tuberculous** [–'bəːkjuləs], *adj.* 1. tuberkulös, schwindsüchtig, Tuberkel–; 2. (*Bot.*) (*rare*) *see* **tubercular.**

tuberose ['tjuːbərous], **1.** *s.* (*Bot.*) die Tuberrose, Nachthyazinthe. **2.** *adj. See* **tuberous. tuberosity** [–'rɔsiti], *s. See* **tuber,** 2. **tuberous,** *adj.* knotig,

knollig, höckerig; (*Bot.*) knollenähnlich; knollentragend.
tubing ['tju:biŋ], *s.* 1. das Röhrenmaterial; (*collect.*) Röhrenwerk, die Röhrenanlage, Rohrleitung, Röhren (*pl.*); (*coll.*) das Stück Röhre; 2. ***rubber –***, der Gummischlauch.
tub|-thumper, *s.* (*coll.*) der Hetzredner, Kanzelpauker. **--thumping, 1.** *s.* Hetzreden (*pl.*). **2.** *adj.* Hetz–.
tubular ['tju:bjələ], *adj.* rohrförmig, röhrenförmig, Röhren–; – ***furniture,*** das Stahlrohrmöbel. **tubule** [–ju:l], *s.* 1. das Röhrchen; 2. (*Anat.*) Kanälchen.
tuck ['tʌk], **1.** *s.* 1. (*Dressm. etc.*) der Saum, Umschlag, Einschlag, die Biese; ***make*** or ***take a – in,*** einen Einschlag *or* eine Biese nähen in (*Acc.*); 2. (*Naut.*) die Gillung, Gilling; 3. (*sl.*) Fressalien (*pl.*), (*esp.*) Leckereien (*pl.*). **2.** *v.t.* 1. in Falten legen, Biesen nähen in (*Acc.*) (*material*); einschlagen (*a tuck*); – ***in,*** einschlagen, einnähen (*cloth etc.*); – ***up,*** hochschürzen, hochstecken (*skirt*), aufkrempeln, hochstreifen (*sleeves*); 2. (*coll.*) verstauen, (weg)stecken, klemmen; (*coll.*) – ***away,*** verstauen, verstecken, verbergen; (*coll.*) – ***in,*** einstecken; (*coll.*) – ***him into bed,*** ihn ins Bett packen; (*coll.*) – ***him up*** (***in bed***), ihn im Bett behaglich einpacken *or* einwickeln. **3.** *v.i.* 1. (sich in) Falten legen, sich zusammenziehen; 2. (*sl.*) – ***in,*** tüchtig zugreifen, einhauen (*with food*); (*sl.*) – ***into,*** tüchtig zusprechen (*Dat.*), wegputzen, verdrücken (*food*).
tuck-box, *s.* (*school sl.*) der Eßkorb.
tucker ['tʌkə], **1.** *s.* 1. (*Sew.-mach.*) der Faltenleger; 2. (*Hist.*) das Brusttuch; (*coll.*) (***best***) ***bib and –,*** der Sonntagsstaat. **2.** *v.t.* (*Am. sl.*) (*oft.* – ***out***) (*usu. pass.*) völlig erschöpfen, fertigmachen.
tucket ['tʌkit], *s.* (*obs.*) der Trompetenstoß, Tusch.
tuck|-in, *s.* (*sl.*) die Fresserei. **--shop,** *s.* (*sl.*) die Konditorei, das Süßwarengeschäft.
Tuesday ['tju:zdi], *s.* der Dienstag; ***on –,*** am Dienstag; ***on –s,*** dienstags.
tufa ['tju:fə], *s.* (*Geol.*) (*oft.* ***calcareous –***) der Kalktuff. **tufaceous** [–'feiʃəs], *adj.* Kalktuff–. **tuff** [tʌf], *s.* (*Geol.*) der Tuff(stein). **tuffaceous,** *adj.* Tuff–.
tuft [tʌft], *s.* 1. das Büschel, der Busch, Schopf; – ***of feathers,*** der Federbusch; – ***of grass,*** das Grasbüschel; – ***of hair,*** das Haarbüschel, der Haarschopf; 2. die Quaste, Troddel. **tufted,** *adj.* 1. büschelig; 2. mit Quasten verziert; 3. (*Orn.*) Hauben–. **tufter,** *s.* (*Hunt.*) der Stöberhund. **tuft-hunter,** *s.* (*coll.*) der Streber, Snob, Speichellecker. **tufty,** *adj.* büschelig.
tug [tʌg], **1.** *s.* 1. heftiger Zug *or* Ruck, das Zerren, Reißen, Ziehen; (*fig.*) große Anstrengung, erbitterter Kampf (***for,*** um); ***give a – at,*** zerren, reißen, heftig ziehen an (*Dat.*); 2. (*Naut.*) *see* **tugboat. 2.** *v.t.* 1. heftig ziehen, reißen, zerren (an (*Dat.*)); 2. (*Naut.*) schleppen. **3.** *v.i.* heftig ziehen, zerren, reißen (***at,*** an (*Dat.*)).
tug|boat, *s.* der Schlepper, Schleppdampfer, Bugsierdampfer. **--of-war,** *s.* (*Spt.*) das Tauziehen; (*fig.*) wogender Kampf (***for,*** um).
tuition [tju:'iʃən], *s.* der Unterricht; die Belehrung, Unterweisung; ***private –,*** der Privatunterricht, Privatstunden (*pl.*). **tuitional, tuitionary,** *adj.* Unterrichts–.
tulip ['tju:lip], *s.* die Tulpe. **tulip-tree,** *s.* der Tulpenbaum, die Magnolie.
tulle [tyl, t(j)ʊl], *s.* der Tüll.
tumble [tʌmbl], **1.** *v.i.* 1. (*oft.* – ***over*** or ***down***) (hin)fallen, umfallen, (um)stürzen, purzeln (***over,*** über (*Acc.*)); – ***down,*** (*of a th.*) einstürzen, einfallen, niederfallen; – ***down the stairs,*** die Treppe hinunterfallen; – ***in,*** einstürzen; (*coll.*) – ***in(to bed)***, in die Federn kriechen; – ***out of bed,*** aus dem Bett herausfallen; (*coll.*) eilig aufstehen; – ***to pieces,*** in Stücke fallen; 2. (*Poet.*) sich herumwerfen *or* hin– und herwälzen, hin– und herrollen (*as waves etc.*); 3. (*coll.*) stürzen, stolpern; – ***over the chair,*** über den Stuhl stolpern; – ***over each other,*** sich überschlagen; 4. (*obs.*) Purzelbäume schlagen; 5. (*coll.*) – ***on,*** stoßen auf (*Acc.*); (*sl.*) – ***to,*** plötzlich begreifen, spitzkriegen. **2.** *v.t.* 1. zu Fall bringen, umwerfen, niederwerfen, (um)stürzen; durcheinanderwerfen, durchwühlen, in Unordnung bringen; (*coll.*) – ***him out of,*** ihn schmeißen *or* schleudern *or* (hinaus)werfen aus; 2. (*Tech.*) schleudern. **3.** *s.* 1. der Sturz, Fall; (*fig.*) die Unordnung, das Durcheinander; (*coll.*) ***rough and –,*** die Rauferei; 2. (*Poet.*) das Hin– und Herrollen (*as of waves*); 3. (*obs.*) der Purzelbaum.
tumble|-bug, *s.* (*Am.*) (*Ent.*) der Pillendreher. **-down,** *adj.* baufällig. **--drier,** *s.* der Trommeltrockner.
tumbler [tʌmblə], *s.* 1. das (Trink)glas, Wasserglas; 2. (*obs.*) Akrobat, Gaukler; 3. (*Orn.*) der Tümmler, die Purzeltaube; 4. (*Tech.*) das Rollfaß, die Poliertrommel; 5. *See* **tumble-drier**; 6. die Nuß (*on guns*); 7. Zuhaltung (*of locks*). **tumbler|-spring,** *s.* die Zuhaltungsfeder. **--switch,** *s.* der Kippschalter.
tumbrel, tumbril ['tʌmbril], *s.* 1. der Schuttkarren; 2. (*Hist., Fr. Rev.*) Schinderkarren; 3. (*Artil.*) Munitionskarren.
tumefacient [tju:mi'feiʃiənt], *adj.* aufschwellend, anschwellend. **tumefaction** [–'fækʃən], *s.* die (An)schwellung; Geschwulst. **tumefy** ['tju:mifai], **1.** *v.t.* (an)schwellen lassen. **2.** *v.i.* anschwellen, aufschwellen. **tumescence** [–'mesəns], *s. See* **tumefaction. tumescent,** *adj.* (an)geschwollen, aufgeschwollen.
tumid ['tju:mid], *adj.* 1. (an)geschwollen, aufgeschwollen; 2. (*fig.*) schwülstig, hochtrabend. **tumidity** [–'miditi], *s.* 1. die Geschwollenheit; 2. (*fig.*) Schwülstigkeit.
tummy ['tʌmi], *s.* (*coll.*) das Bäuchlein. **tummy-ache,** *s.* (*coll.*) das Bauchweh.
tumor, (*Am.*) *see* **tumour.**
tumour ['tju:mə], *s.* die Geschwulst, der Tumor.
tum-tum ['tʌmtʌm], *s.* (*coll.*) *see* **tummy.**
tumular ['tju:mjulə], *adj.* hügelförmig; (*Archaeol.*) Grabhügel–.
tumult ['tju:mʌlt], *s.* der Lärm, Tumult, das Getöse, Getümmel; der Auflauf, Aufruhr (*also fig.*); (*fig.*) Sturm, die (Auf)wallung, Erregung. **tumultuary** [–'mʌltjuəri], *adj.* undiszipliniert, unordentlich, verworren; aufrührerisch, tumultartig. **tumultuous** [–'mʌltjuəs], *adj.* (*usu. fig.*) tumultuarisch, turbulent, erregt, ungestüm, stürmisch, heftig, lärmend. **tumultuousness,** *s.* (*fig.*) das Ungestüm, die Heftigkeit, Verwirrung; lärmendes Treiben.
tumulus ['tju:mjələs], *s.* (*pl.* **-li**) der Grabhügel, das Hügelgrab.
tun [tʌn], *s.* 1. (*obs. measure*) die Tonne (= *252 gallons* = *1,145 l.*); 2. das Faß.
tuna ['tju:nə], *s. See* **tunny.**
tundish ['tʌndiʃ], *s.* (*dial.*) der Trichter.
tundra ['tʌndrə], *s.* (*Geog.*) die Tundra.
tune [tju:n], **1.** *s.* 1. die Melodie, Weise; (*fig.*) ***call the –,*** zu bestimmen haben; ***he who pays the piper calls the –,*** wer bezahlt, hat zu bestimmen; ***catchy –,*** einnehmende Melodie; (*fig.*) ***change one's –,*** einen anderen Ton anschlagen, andere Saiten aufziehen, ein anderes Lied singen; ***give us a –,*** sing *or* spiel uns eine Melodie! ***sing another –,*** auf ein anderes Loch pfeifen; ***to the – of,*** nach der Melodie von; (*coll.*) in der Höhe *or* im Ausmaß *or* im *or* zum Betrage von; 2. (richtige) (Ein)stimmung (*of a piano etc.*; *also fig.*); (*fig.*) der Einklang; ***in –,*** (richtig) gestimmt (*of instrument*), tonrein (*of performer*); (*Rad.*) genau *or* scharf eingestellt; (*fig.*) ***be in – with,*** in Einklang stehen mit; (*fig.*) ***be in – with one another,*** aufeinander abgestimmt sein; ***not in –, out of –,*** verstimmt (*of instrument*); (*fig.*) ***be out of – with,*** nicht harmonieren mit, im Widerspruch *or* in einem Mißverhältnis stehen zu; ***keep*** or ***stay in –,*** Stimmung halten (*of instrument*); ***keep –,*** Ton halten (*of performer*); ***sing in –,*** tonrein *or* sauber *or* richtig singen; ***sing out of –,*** unrichtig *or* unrein singen. **2.** *v.t.* 1. (*Mus.*) (*also* – ***up***) (ab)stimmen (***to,*** auf (*Acc.*)); 2. (*Rad.*) abstimmen,

einstellen (*to*, auf (*Acc.*)); – *in*, einstellen (*on*, *to*, *Acc.*); – *out*, ausschalten, abstellen; *–d circuit*, abgestimmter Kreis; 3. (*fig.*) anpassen (*to*, an (*Acc.*)), in Einklang bringen (mit); 4. (*Motor.*, *Av.*) – *up*, einsatzbereit *or* startbereit machen; einfahren (*an engine*); (*fig.*) hinaufschrauben (*expectations etc.*). **3.** *v.i.* (*Mus.*) – *up*, stimmen.

tuneful [ˈtju:nful], *adj.* melodisch, wohlklingend, klangvoll. **tunefulness,** *s.* der Wohlklang. **tuneless,** *adj.* 1. unmelodisch, mißtönend; 2. klanglos, stumm. **tuner,** *s.* 1. der (Klavier)stimmer; 2. (*on organs*) die Stimmvorrichtung; 3. (*Rad.*) Abstimmvorrichtung, der Abstimmknopf.

tungstate [ˈtʌŋsteit], *s.* das Wolframsäuresalz, Wolframat, wolframsaures Salz; – *of*, wolframsauer. **tungsten** [–stən], *s.* der Wolfram. **tungstic,** *adj.* Wolfram–. **tungstite,** *s.* der Wolframocker.

tunic [ˈtju:nik], *s.* 1. die Tunika; Jacke, der Rock, Kittel; (*Mil.*) Waffenrock; 2. (*Anat.*) der Mantel, die Hülle, Haut, das Häutchen. **tunica,** *s.* *See* **tunic,** 2. **tunicate,** *adj.* (*Bot.*) häutig, (*Zool.*) Mantel–. **tunicle,** *s.* (*R.C.*) das Meßgewand.

tuning [ˈtju:niŋ], *s.* 1. (*Mus.*) das (Ein)stimmen; 2. (*Rad.*) Abstimmen, Einstellen, die Abstimmung; Abstimmschärfe. **tuning| circuit,** *s.* (*Rad.*) der Abstimmkreis. – **coil,** *s.* (*Rad.*) die Abstimmspule. – **condenser,** *s.* (*Rad.*) der Abstimmkondensator. – **eye,** *s.* (*Rad.*) magisches Auge. **--fork,** *s.* (*Mus.*) die Stimmgabel.

tunnel [tʌnl], **1.** *s.* der Tunnel, die Unterführung; unterirdischer Gang (*also of animals*); (*Min.*) der Stollen, Schachtgang. **2.** *v.i.* einen Tunnel anlegen *or* bauen *or* stechen *or* hindurchführen (*through*, durch). **3.** *v.t.* untertunneln, durchtunneln, einen Tunnel bohren durch. **tunnelling,** *s.* 1. der Tunnelbau; 2. die Tunnelanlage.

tunny [ˈtʌni], *s.* (*also* *--fish*) (*Ichth.*) der Thunfisch.

tup [tʌp], **1.** *s.* 1. (*Zool.*) der Widder; 2. (*Tech.*) Rammklotz, Rammbär, Hammerkopf. **2.** *v.t.* bespringen, belegen (*of rams*).

tuppence [ˈtʌpəns], *s.* (*sl.*) *see* **twopence.**

turban [ˈtə:bən], *s.* der Turban.

turbary [ˈtə:bəri], *s.* 1. das Torfmoor; 2. (*Law*) das Recht, Torf zu stechen.

turbid [ˈtə:bid], *adj.* 1. trüb, getrübt, dick(flüssig), schlammig; 2. (*fig.*) verworren, verschwommen, unklar. **turbidity** [–ˈbiditi], **turbidness,** *s.* 1. die Trübung, Trübheit; 2. (*fig.*) Verworrenheit, Verschwommenheit, Unklarheit.

turbine [ˈtə:bain], *s.* die (Dampf– *or* Wasser)-turbine. **turbo|jet** [ˈtə:bou–], *s.* (*Av.*) die Strahlvortriebturbine. **–prop,** *s.* (*Av.*) die Propellerturbine. **--ram-jet,** *s.* (*Av.*) die Staustrahlturbine.

turbot [ˈtə:bət], *s.* (*Ichth.*) der Steinbutt.

turbulence, turbulency [ˈtə:bjuləns(i)], *s.* 1. die Unruhe, der Sturm, Aufruhr, das Ungestüm; 2. (*Phys.*) die Turbulenz. **turbulent,** *adj.* 1. unruhig, heftig, aufbrausend, stürmisch, ungestüm; 2. (*Phys.*) turbulent.

turd [tə:d], *s.* (*vulg.*) das Stück Kot.

tureen [tjuˈri:n], *s.* die Terrine, Suppenschüssel.

turf [tə:f], **1.** *s.* 1. der Rasen(platz); 2. (*with pl.*) das Rasenstück, die Grasnarbe; (*dial.*) der Torf; *a –*, ein Stück Torf; 3. *the –*, die Rennbahn; (*fig.*) das Pferderennen, der Rennsport. **2.** *v.t.* 1. mit Rasen belegen; 2. (*sl.*) – *out*, hinausschmeißen.

turf|-accountant, *s.* der Buchmacher. **--clad,** *adj.* rasenbedeckt. **--cutter,** *s.* (*dial.*) der Torfstecher.

turgescence [tə:ˈdʒesəns], *s.* die Anschwellung, Aufschwellung, Aufgedunsenheit. **turgescent,** *adj.* (an)schwellend. **turgid** [ˈtə:dʒid], *adj.* 1. (an)-geschwollen, aufgeschwollen; (auf)gedunsen; 2. (*fig.*) schwülstig, pompös, bombastisch. **turgidity** [–ˈdʒiditi], **turgidness,** *s.* 1. die Geschwollenheit; 2. (*fig.*) Schwülstigkeit. **turgor** [ˈtə:dʒə], *s.* (*Med.*, *Bot.*) der Turgor.

turion [ˈtjuriən], *s.* (*Bot.*) die Überwinterungsknospe, der Sprößling.

Turk [tə:k], *s.* 1. der Türke (die Türkin); 2. (*coll.*) der Wildfang, Schelm.

Turkey [ˈtə:ki], *s.* die Türkei; – *carpet*, der Orientteppich; – *red*, das Türkischrot.

turkey, *s.* 1. (*also* *--cock*) der Puter, Truthahn; *as red as a --cock*, puterrot; 2. (*also* *--hen*) die Pute, Truthenne; 3. (*Am. coll.*) *talk –*, kein Blatt vor den Mund nehmen, frisch von der Leber weg reden, offen *or* unverblümt reden, mit der Sprache herausrücken.

Turkish [ˈtə:kiʃ], **1.** *adj.* türkisch; – *bath*, das Schwitzbad, Dampfbad, die Sauna; – *delight*, der (*Austr.* das) Fondant; – *tobacco*, der Orienttabak; – *towel*, das Frottier(hand)tuch. **2.** *s.* das Türkisch(e) (*language*).

Turkistan [tə:kisˈtɑ:n], *s.* Turkestan (*n.*).

Turkoman [ˈtə:kəmən], *s.* 1. (*pl.* **-s**) der Turkmane; 2. (*language*) das Turkmenisch(e).

Turk's|-cap, *s.* (*Bot.*) der Türkenbund. **--head,** *s.* der Türkenbund (*knot*).

turmeric [ˈtə:mərik], *s.* 1. (*Bot.*) die Gelbwurz, Gilbwurz; 2. Turmerikwurzel, Kurkuma; 3. das Kurkumagelb; (*Chem.*) – *paper*, das Kurkumapapier.

turmoil [ˈtə:mɔil], *s.* der Aufruhr. Tumult, die Unruhe.

turn [tə:n], **1.** *v.t.* 1. (um eine Achse) drehen, (her)-umdrehen; 2. wenden, lenken, kehren, richten (*to*, auf (*Acc.*)); abwenden, ablenken, abwehren, abbringen (*from*, von); 3. wenden (*a coat etc.*); 4. drechseln (*on a lathe*); 5. formen; 6. bilden, (ab)-runden (*a sentence*); 7. hinaus sein über (*Acc.*); *be –ed fifty*, gerade fünfzig sein.

(a) (*with noun*) – *one's attention to*, seine Aufmerksamkeit zuwenden (*Dat.*); – *his attention to*, seine Aufmerksamkeit lenken auf (*Acc.*); – *one's back*, sich umdrehen; – *one's back on*, den Rücken kehren (*Dat.*), (*fig.*) sich abwenden von, im Stich lassen; – *the balance*, see – *the scale*; – *his blood cold*, ihm das Blut in den Adern gefrieren *or* gerinnen *or* erstarren *or* stocken lassen; (*B.*) – *the other cheek*, den andern Backen auch darbieten (*to*, *Dat.*); (*coll.*) – *one's coat*, den Mantel nach dem Winde hängen; – *colour*, die Farbe wechseln; – *a compliment*, ein Kompliment drechseln; – *the conversation*, die Unterhaltung ändern *or* wechseln; – *the corner*, um die Ecke biegen; (*fig.*) über das Schlimmste hinweg sein, über den Berg hinwegkommen, die Krise überstehen *or* überwinden; – *a deaf ear*, sich taub stellen (*to*, gegen); – *the edge of*, abstumpfen (*a knife*); (*fig.*) die Spitze abbrechen (*Gen.*); – *a blind eye*, ein Auge zudrücken (*to*, bei); – *one's face*, sein Gesicht wenden; – *the enemy('s flank)*, den Feind umgehen *or* umfassen; – *the ground*, das Land umgraben *or* umbrechen; *not – a hair*, nicht mit der Wimper zucken; – *one's hand to*, Hand anlegen bei, in Angriff nehmen; *be able to – one's hand to anything*, praktisch veranlagt *or* sehr geschickt sein; – *his head*, ihm den Kopf verdrehen; *her head is –ed with success*, der Erfolg ist ihr zu Kopf gestiegen, ihr ist der Kopf vom Erfolg verdreht; – *head over heels*, einen Purzelbaum schlagen; (*coll.*) – *on the heat*, Druck *or* Zwang ausüben; – *the key*, zuschließen; – *the page*, die Seite umdrehen; – *the pages*, umblättern; (*coll.*) – *an honest penny*, sich ehrlich durchschlagen (*by*, mit); (*Railw.*) – *the points*, die Weichen stellen; (*fig.*) – *the scale*, ausschlaggebend sein, den Ausschlag geben, in die Waagschale *or* ins Gewicht fallen; – *a cold shoulder on*, die kalte Schulter zeigen (*Dat.*); – *one's steps*, die Schritte wenden *or* lenken (*towards*, nach); *it –s my stomach*, dabei dreht sich mir der Magen um, mir wird davon schlecht *or* übel, es verdirbt mir den Appetit; – *the tables*, den Spieß umdrehen (*on*, gegen), der S. eine andere Wendung geben; *the tables are –ed*, das Blatt hat sich gewendet; – *tail*, davonlaufen, Fersengeld geben (*on*, vor (*Dat.*)); – *one's thoughts*, seine Gedanken richten (*to*, auf (*Acc.*)); (*Naut.*) – *turtle*, kentern; sich überschlagen, umkippen.

(b) (*with prep.*) – *against*, aufbringen *or* aufhetzen gegen (*a p.*), richten gegen, abzielen auf (*Acc.*) (*remarks*); – *in one's mind*, überlegen; (*Chem. etc.*) – *into*, verwandeln, umwandeln *or* umsetzen in

(*Acc.*); **– *into money,*** zu Geld machen; **– *into ridicule,*** lächerlich machen; **– *into German,*** ins Deutsche übertragen *or* übersetzen; **– *to (good) account*** or ***to good use,*** Nutzen *or* Vorteil ziehen aus.
(c) (*with adv.*) **– *about,*** herumdrehen; **– *adrift,*** (*Naut.*) Wind und Wellen preisgeben, (*fig.*) dem Schicksal überlassen; hinaussetzen, vertreiben; **– *aside,*** abwenden; **– *away,*** wegwenden, abwenden (*one's eyes etc.*), abweisen, fortschicken (*others*); ***be –ed away,*** keinen Eintritt finden; (*Theat.*) **– *away money,*** die Türe schließen müssen; **– *back,*** zurückschicken, umkehren lassen, zur Umkehr veranlassen (*others*); umdrehen, umwenden (*a th.*); **– *down,*** 1. umbiegen, umlegen, herunterklappen, einschlagen (*a page*), verdeckt halten (*cards*), kleinstellen (*gas etc.*), leise(r) stellen (*radio*), abschwächen (*light*), aufdecken (*a bed*); 2. abweisen, ablehnen (*offer etc.*), zurückweisen (*applicant*), einen Korb geben (*Dat.*) (*suitor*); **– *in,*** 1. einschlagen, einwärts *or* nach innen biegen; einackern, eingraben (*weeds etc.*); einwärts stellen (*one's feet*); 2. (*coll.*) einhändigen, einreichen, einsenden (*application etc.*); (*sl.*) **– *him in,*** ihn anzeigen *or* übergeben; (*sl.*) **– *it in,*** aufgeben, damit aufhören; **– *inside out,*** umstülpen, das Innere nach außen kehren; **– *loose,*** losmachen, losbinden; loslassen, freilassen, befreien, auf freien Fuß setzen; **– *off,*** 1. abdrehen, absperren (*water, gas etc.*), abstellen (*radio etc.*), ausmachen, abschalten (*light*), zudrehen (*a tap*); 2. ablenken, abhalten, abwenden (*a blow etc.*); 3. fortschicken, entlassen (*a p.*); **– *off with a laugh,*** mit einem Scherz hinweggehen über (*Acc.*); **– *on,*** andrehen, aufdrehen (*a tap*), anstellen (*water, radio etc.*), anmachen, einschalten (*light*); (*sl.*) hinreißen (*a p.*); (*coll.*) **– *on the waterworks,*** zu heulen anfangen; **– *out,*** 1. auswärts *or* nach außen stellen *or* setzen (*one's feet*); 2. hinauswerfen, vertreiben, verjagen (*a p.*), (*from home or country*) ausweisen, (*from post*) entfernen (*of,* aus); 3. herstellen, produzieren, liefern, hervorbringen (*goods*); 4. hinaustreiben, auf die Weide treiben (*cattle*); 5. ausräumen, gründlich reinmachen (*a room*); ausleeren (*one's pockets*); 6. stürzen (*government*); 7. ausdrehen, auslöschen, ausmachen (*light*); abstellen (*gas*); 8. antreten lassen (*the guard*); 9. ausstatten, ausrüsten; (*coll.*) ***be well –ed out,*** gut angezogen sein, eine gute Erscheinung sein; **– *over,*** 1. umwenden, umdrehen (*a page etc.*); 2. übertragen, überlassen (*a th.*), ausliefern (*a p.*) (*to, Dat.*); 3. (*Comm.*) Umsatz haben von, umsetzen (*money*); ***please – over,*** bitte wenden! **– *over a new leaf,*** ein neues Leben anfangen, sich bessern; **– *over the pages,*** die Seiten umblättern *or* umschlagen; ein Buch durchblättern; **– *over in one's mind,*** sich (*Dat.*) überlegen, sich durch den Kopf gehen lassen; **– *round,*** (herum)drehen, umkehren; **– *him round one's little finger,*** ihn um den Finger wickeln; **– *topsy-turvy,*** durcheinanderbringen; **– *up,*** 1. nach oben wenden *or* drehen, hochschlagen, aufschlagen (*one's collar*), umschlagen, einschlagen, aufstecken (*a dress etc.*); aufdecken (*a card*); 2. (weiter) aufdrehen (*gas*), lauter stellen (*radio*); 3. aufstöben, ans Licht bringen, zutage fördern, ausgraben; 4. (*sl.*) bleibenlassen, aufstecken, hinschmeißen (*a job etc.*); 5. (*sl.*) anekeln; **– *up one's nose at,*** die Nase rümpfen über (*Acc.*); (*coll.*) **– *up one's toes,*** abkratzen, hops gehen; **– *upside down,*** auf den Kopf stellen, das Oberste zuunterst kehren; (*fig.*) durcheinanderwerfen.
2. *v.i.* 1. sich (um die Achse *or* im Kreis) (herum)drehen; sich umdrehen *or* umwenden, (sich) umkehren; 2. sich wenden; ***my stomach –s,*** mir wird übel; ***the tide has –ed,*** die Flut (ist ge)kentert; (*fig.*) das Blatt hat sich gewendet; 3. gehen, sich begeben, seinen Weg nehmen, sich richten; **– *homewards,*** nach Hause zurückkehren; 4. sich abwenden, abbiegen, umbiegen; **– *left!*** links abbiegen! ***not know which way*** or ***where to –,*** nicht wissen, was zu tun; ***even a worm will –,*** selbst ein Wurm krümmt sich; 5. umschlagen (*weather*); 6. (*with adj. or noun*) werden (zu); **– *Christian,*** zum Christentum übertreten, Christ werden; **– *grey,*** grau werden; **– *Queen's (King's)*** (*or Am. state's*) ***evidence,*** Kronzeuge werden; **– *pale,*** erbleichen, blaß werden; **– *nasty,*** unangenehm werden; **– *soldier,*** Soldat werden; **– *traitor,*** zum Verräter werden; 7. (*coll.*) gerinnen, sauer werden (*as milk*); ***the milk has –ed (sour),*** die Milch ist sauer geworden; 8. sich drechseln lassen (*on a lathe*).
(a) (*with adv.*) **– *about,*** umdrehen; **– *aside,*** sich abwenden; **– *away,*** sich abwenden; fortgehen, weggehen; **– *back,*** zurückgehen, zurückkehren, umkehren; **– *down,*** herunterhängen, sich herunterziehen, nach unten gebogen sein; **– *in,*** 1. sich einwärts wenden, nach innen gebogen sein; 2. (*coll.*) eintreten, einkehren, hineingehen; (*coll.*) sich schlafen legen, zu Bett gehen; **– *inside out,*** sich umstülpen; **– *off,*** abbiegen, abzweigen, sich seitwärts wenden; **– *out,*** 1. hinausgehen, hinausziehen; herauskommen (*of,* aus); (*Mil.*) ausrücken, ausziehen; antreten, sich versammeln; 2. sich auswärts wenden, auswärts gerichtet sein; 3. (*fig.*) werden, ausfallen; 4. sich erweisen *or* herausstellen *or* entpuppen als; ablaufen, ausgehen, enden, sich gestalten; **– *out well,*** einen guten Ausgang nehmen; **– *over,*** sich (her)umdrehen (*in bed*); umschlagen, umkippen; **– *round,*** sich (herum)drehen; (*fig.*) umschwenken, sich anders besinnen; (*coll.*) **– *to,*** sich anstrengen *or* befleißigen, sich an die Arbeit machen, darangehen; **– *up,*** 1. sich nach oben drehen *or* wenden, nach oben gerichtet sein, hochgeschlagen sein; 2. (*coll.*) zum Vorschein *or* ans Licht kommen, auftreten (*th.*), auftauchen (*th. or p.*), aufkreuzen, sich anfinden (*a p.*), eintreten, dazwischenkommen (*events*); (*coll.*) **– *up trumps,*** sich als das Beste erweisen *or* herausstellen; ***wait for s.th. to – up,*** sich abwartend verhalten.
(b) (*with prep.*) **– *against,*** sich wenden gegen; **– *from,*** sich wenden von; **– *(in)to,*** (*of th. or substance*) werden zu, sich verändern *or* (ver)wandeln in (*Acc.*); übergehen *or* ausarten *or* umschlagen in (*Acc.*); **– *on,*** 1. sich drehen um *or* in (*Dat.*); 2. (*fig.*) *see* **– *upon***; **– *on one's heel(s),*** kehrtmachen, sich kurz umdrehen; **– *to,*** 1. sich wenden *or* schwenken nach, abbiegen nach; (*fig.*) sich zuwenden (*Dat.*), sich beschäftigen *or* befassen mit (*a th.*); sich anschicken (***doing,*** zu tun); 2. sich (hin)wenden *or* richten an (*Acc.*), seine Zuflucht nehmen zu, sich (*Dat.*) Rat holen bei, zu Rate ziehen (*Acc.*) (*a p.*); 3. *See also* **– *into*** (*esp. for state or condition*); **– *to the left,*** sich nach links wenden (*of p.*), nach links abbiegen (*of road, vehicle*); **– *to p. 20,*** siehe S.20! **– *(up)on,*** 1. herfallen über (*Acc.*), angreifen (*a p.*); 2. abhängen von (*circumstances*); sich drehen um, handeln von, zum Gegenstand haben (*subject matter*).
3. *s.* 1. (*motion*) die (Um)drehung, der Umschwung; 2. (*change of direction*) die Wendung (*also Av., fig.*); (*Mil.*) (Kehrt)wendung, Schwenkung; der Lauf, Weg; die Krümmung, Windung, Biegung, Kehre, Kurve; der Wechsel, die Veränderung; (*fig.*) Wende, der Wendepunkt, die Krise, Krisis; **– *of the century,*** die Jahrhundertwende; **– *of the scale,*** der Ausschlag; **– *of the tide,*** der Gezeitenwechsel; (*fig.*) Umschlag, die Wendung der Lage; ***be on the –,*** sich umwenden, umschlagen; ***the tide is on the –,*** (*Naut.*) die Flut wendet sich *or* kentert; (*fig.*) die Lage bessert sich; ***give a certain –,*** eine gewisse Wendung geben (*to, Dat.*); ***take an interesting –,*** eine interessante Wendung nehmen; ***take a – for the worse,*** sich zum Schlechtern wenden; ***right –!*** rechtsum! ***right about –!*** rechtsum kehrt! 3. (*Comm.*) der Umschlag; **– *of the market,*** der Marktumschlag; 4. kurzer (Spazier)gang; ***take a –,*** einen (Spazier)gang machen; 5. die Reihenfolge, der Turnus, die (Arbeits)schicht, der Dienst, die Gelegenheit (*for,* für *or* zu); ***await one's –,*** warten, bis man an die Reihe kommt; ***it is my –,*** ich bin an der Reihe, die Reihe ist an mir; ***give him a –,*** ihn an der Reihe nehmen; ***take a – at,*** sich versuchen an (*Dat.*), sich befassen *or* beschäftigen mit; ***take one's –,*** an die Reihe kommen; ***take –s,*** sich gegenseitig abwechseln (***at,*** bei); ***at every –,*** auf allen Seiten, bei jeder Gelegenheit, auf Schritt

und Tritt; ***by –s, – (and –) about,*** nacheinander, abwechselnd, reihum, wechselweise; ***in –,*** der Reihe nach; ***he in his –,*** er seinerseits; ***out of –,*** außer der Reihe; (*fig.*) fehl am Platz; ***when it comes to my –,*** wenn die Reihe an mich kommt, wenn ich daran *or* an die Reihe komme; 6. herrschende Richtung, die Eignung, Veranlagung (***for,*** für), Neigung, der Hang, das Talent (zu); 7. der Dienst, Gefallen; ***do him a good –,*** ihm einen Dienst *or* eine Gefälligkeit erweisen, ihm einen Gefallen tun; (*Prov.*) ***one good – deserves another,*** eine Liebe ist der andern wert, eine Hand wäscht die andere; 8. der Zweck; ***serve his –,*** seinem Zweck dienen, ihm nützen; 9. die Form, Art, Beschaffenheit, Gestalt, der Zuschnitt; ***– of expression,*** die Formulierung; ***– of mind,*** die Denkart, Denkweise, geistiger Zuschnitt; (*coll.*) ***have a good – of speed,*** was leisten *or* hergeben (*of a car*); 10. (*coll.*) der Schreck, Nervenschock; (*coll.*) ***give him a –,*** ihn erschrecken, ihm einen Schrecken einjagen; 11. (*Mus.*) der Doppelschlag; 12. (*Theat.*) die Nummer; 13. (*Cul.*) ***done to a –,*** durchgebraten; (*fig.*) ***to a –,*** aufs Haar, ausgezeichnet, vorzüglich, tadellos.

turn|-buckle, *s.* die Spannschraube, Spannvorrichtung, der Wirbel, Spanner. **–coat,** *s.* Abtrünnige(r), der Überläufer. **–cock,** *s.* der Drehhahn. **–-down,** *attrib. adj.* Umlege–.

turned [tə:nd], *adj.* 1. gedreht, gedrechselt; (*fig.*) gestaltet, geformt; 2. (*Typ.*) auf dem Kopf stehend, umgedreht; ***– letter,*** der Fliegenkopf; 3. (*coll.*) sauer, ranzig, schlecht geworden; 4. ***–-down,*** *see* **turn-down**; ***–-up collar,*** hochgeschlagener Kragen; ***–-up nose,*** die Stülpnase. **turner,** *s.* der Dreher, Drechsler. **turnery,** *s.* die Drechslerei. **turning,** *s.* 1. das Drehen, Drechseln; *pl.* Drehspäne (*pl.*); ***– chisel,*** der (Ab)drehstahl; ***–-lathe,*** die Drehbank; 2. die Drehung, Wendung, Windung, Biegung, Krümmung; Abzweigung, Querstrasse; (*Mil.*) ***– movement,*** die Umgehung; ***–-point,*** die Wendemarke (*in races etc.*), (*fig.*) der Wendepunkt.

turnip ['tə:nip], *s.* 1. (weiße) Rübe; 2. (*sl.*) die Zwiebel (*a watch*). **turnip-tops,** *pl.* das Rübenkraut.

turn|key, *s.* 1. der Schließer, Gefangenenwärter; 2. *See* **–cock.** **–-off,** *s.* (*coll.*) die Abzweigung, Querstraße. **–-out,** *s.* 1. (*coll.*) die Aufmachung, Ausstattung, Ausstaffierung, äußere Erscheinung; 2. (*Comm.*) die Gesamtproduktion, Gesamtherstellung; 3. Versammlung, Zuschauer (*pl.*), Besucher (*pl.*). **–over,** *s.* 1. (*Comm.*) der Umschlag, Umsatz; ***– tax,*** die Umsatzsteuer; 2. (*Comm.*) die Umgruppierung, Umwandlung, Umorganisierung, Umänderung, Veränderung, Verschiebung; 3. der Zu- und Abgang (*of new and old*); 4. Umschwung, das Umschlagen (*of opinion*); 5. (*Cul.*) ***apple –,*** der Apfel im Schlafrock, die Apfeltasche. **–pike,** *s.* 1. (*Hist.*) die Zollschranke; 2. der Schlagbaum; 3. ***–-road,*** die Landstraße, Chaussee. **–-round,** *s.* der Umschlag (*of ship in port*). **–screw,** *s.* der Schraubenzieher. **–spit,** *s.* der Bratenwender. **–stile,** *s.* das Drehkreuz. **–table,** *s.* (*Railw. etc.*) die Drehscheibe; (*gramophone*) der Plattenteller. **–-up,** *s.* 1. der Umschlag (*on trousers etc.*); 2. (*sl.*) (*also* ***– for the book***(*s*)) die Überraschung, unerwartete Wendung.

turpentine ['tə:pəntain], *s.* das Terpentin; (*also* ***oil of –***) das Terpentinöl.

turpitude ['tə:pitju:d], *s.* die Schlechtigkeit, Niederträchtigkeit, Schändlichkeit, Verworfenheit.

turps [tə:ps], *s.* (*coll.*) *abbr. for* ***oil of turpentine.***

turquoise ['tə:kwɔiz], **1.** *s.* 1. der Türkis; 2. das Türkisblau. **2.** *adj.* türkisblau, blaugrün.

turret ['tʌrit], *s.* 1. das Türmchen; 2. (*Mil.*) der Geschützturm, Panzerturm, (*Av.*) die Kanzel. **turreted,** *adj.* betürmt. **turret|-gun,** *s.* das Turmgeschütz. **–-lathe,** *s.* die Revolverdrehbank.

turtle [tə:tl], *s.* die (Meer)schildkröte; ***turn –,*** (*Naut.*) kentern; (*fig.*) umschlagen; umkippen, sich überschlagen. **turtle|-dove,** *s.* (*Orn.*) die Turteltaube (*Streptopelia turtur*). **–-neck,** *s.* der Rollkragen. **–-soup,** *s.* die Schildkrötensuppe.

Tuscan ['tʌskən], **1.** *adj.* toskanisch. **2.** *s.* 1. der (die) Toskaner(in); 2. das Toskanisch(e) (*language*). **Tuscany,** *s.* die Toskana.

tush! [tʌʃ], *int.* pah!

tusk [tʌsk], *s.* der Stoßzahn (*of elephant, walrus*), Hauer (*of boar*); (*coll.*) (vorstehender) Eckzahn. **tusked** [–t], *adj.* mit Hauern. **tusker,** *s.* der Elefant *or* das Wildschwein mit ausgebildeten Stoßzähnen. **tusky,** *adj.* (*coll.*) mit vorstehenden Zähnen.

tussle [tʌsl], **1.** *s.* das Ringen, der Kampf, Streit, die Rauferei, Balgerei. **2.** *v.i.* kämpfen, ringen, raufen, sich streiten *or* balgen (***with,*** mit; ***for,*** um).

tussock ['tʌsək], *s.* das Büschel (*of grass etc.*).

tussore ['tʌsə], *s.* (*also* ***– silk***) die Rohseide, Tussahseide.

tut! [tʌt], *int.* (*also* ***–-tut***) Unsinn! dummes Zeug! ach was! na na!

tutelage ['tju:tilidʒ], *s.* 1. die Vormundschaft, Bevormundung, der Schutz; 2. die Unmündigkeit; 3. Belehrung, (An)leitung. **tutelar(y)** [–lə(ri)], *adj.* schützend, Schutz–, Vormunds–, Vormundschafts–, vormundschaftlich.

tutor ['tju:tə], **1.** *s.* 1. der (Haus)lehrer, Privatlehrer, Hofmeister; (*Univ.*) (***college***) –, Studienleiter, Universitätslehrer; ***private –,*** Hauslehrer, (*coll.*) Einpauker; 2. (*Scots Law*) der Vormund. **2.** *v.t.* 1. Privatunterricht erteilen (*Dat.*), unterrichten; 2. (*fig.*) – (***o.s.***), (sich) schulen. **tutorial** [–'tɔ:riəl], **1.** *adj.* Lehrer–; ***– college,*** die Presse. **2.** *s.* (*Univ.*) (*coll.*) die Arbeitsgemeinschaft, Studiengruppe.

tuxedo [tʌk'si:dou], *s.* (*Am.*) der Smoking.

TV ['ti:'vi:], (*coll.*) *abbr. for* **television.**

twaddle [twɔdl], **1.** *s.* albernes Geschwätz *or* Gewäsch, der Unsinn, Quatsch. **2.** *v.i.* schwatzen, quatschen.

twain [twein], **1.** *adj.* (*obs.*) zwei; ***in –,*** entzwei. **2.** *s.* Zwei (*pl.*).

twang [twæŋ], **1.** *s.* 1. gellender *or* scharfer Ton, das Schwirren; 2. (*also* ***nasal –***) näselnde Aussprache. **2.** *v.i.* gellend klingen, schwirren (*of an arrow etc.*). **3.** *v.t.* zupfen (*violin string etc.*).

tweak [twi:k], *v.t.* zwicken, kneifen.

tweed [twi:d], *s.* der Tweed; (*usu. pl.*) das Tweedkostüm, der Tweedanzug.

tweeny ['twi:ni], *s.* (*coll.*) (*also* ***–-maid***) das Aushilfsmädchen.

tweet [twi:t], *v.i.* piepsen, zwitschern.

tweezers ['twi:zəz], *pl.* (*also* ***pair of –***) die Pinzette.

twelfth [twelfθ], **1.** *num. adj.* zwölft. **2.** *s.* 1. der *or* die *or* das Zwölfte; ***Twelfth-night,*** der Dreikönigsabend, das Dreikönigsfest; 2. (*fraction*) das Zwölftel. **twelve** [–lv], **1.** *num. adj.* zwölf. **2.** *s.* die Zwölf; *for clock-time see under* **eight**; (*Typ.*) ***in –s,*** in Duodez(format). **twelvemo** [–vmou], *s.* das Duodez(format). **twelve|month,** *s.* das Jahr, die Jahresfrist; ***this day –,*** heute in *or* vor einem Jahr. **–-tone,** *adj.* (*Mus.*) Zwölfton–.

twentieth ['twentiəθ], **1.** *num. adj.* zwanzigst. **2.** *s.* 1. der *or* die *or* das Zwanzigste; 2. (*fraction*) das Zwanzigstel. **twenty,** **1.** *num. adj.* zwanzig; ***–one,*** einundzwanzig. **2.** *s.* 1. die Zwanzig; 2. ***the twenties,*** die zwanziger Jahre (*of a century*), die zwanziger Zahlen (*20 to 29*); ***in his twenties,*** in den Zwanzigern. **twentyfold,** *adj.* zwanzigfach.

twerp [twə:p], *s.* (*sl.*) jämmerlicher Alltagsmensch.

twice [twais], *adv.* zweimal; doppelt, zweifach; ***– the amount,*** doppelter Betrag; ***– as much,*** zweimal, noch einmal *or* doppelt soviel; ***think –,*** sich zweimal überlegen; ***not think – about,*** nicht lange überlegen (***doing,*** zu tun), ohne Bedenken (tun). **twice-told,** *adj.* wiederholt *or* oft erzählt, abgedroschen.

twiddle [twidl], **1.** *v.t.* müßig herumdrehen, spielen mit; ***– one's thumbs,*** Daumen drehen, (*fig.*) die Hände in den Schoß legen. **2.** *s.* 1. das Drehen; 2. der Schnörkel.

[1]**twig** [twig], *s.* der Zweig, die Rute; Wünschelrute;

(*sl.*) ***hop the* –**, hops gehen, von der Bühne verschwinden.

²**twig**, *v.t., v.i.* (*sl.*) kapieren.

twilight ['twailait], **1.** *s.* das Zwielicht, Halbdunkel, die (Abend)dämmerung; (*fig.*) der Dämmerzustand; ***by* –**, in der Dämmerung; **– *sleep***, der Dämmerschlaf; **– *of the gods***, die Götterdämmerung. **2.** *adj.* dämmernd, Dämmer(ungs)–; zwielichtig, dämmerig, schattenhaft.

twill [twil], **1.** *s.* der Köper. **2.** *v.t.* köpern.

twin [twin], **1.** *s.* der Zwilling; (*fig.*) das Gegenstück; ***identical* –*s***, eineiige Zwillinge. **2.** *adj.* Zwillings–; (*Bot. etc.*) doppelt, Doppel–, gepaart; (*fig.*) eng verwandt; **– *beds***, zwei Einzelbetten; **– *brother***, der Zwillingsbruder; **– *souls***, verwandte Seelen. **twin-cylinder,** *attrib. adj.* Zweizylinder–.

twine [twain], **1.** *s.* 1. starker Bindfaden, die Schnur, der Strick; (*Text.*) Zwirn, gezwirntes Garn; 2. (*fig.*) die Wick(e)lung, Verschlingung; 3. Windung, das Geflecht. **2.** *v.t.* 1. zwirnen, zusammendrehen (*threads etc.*); 2. binden (*a wreath*); 3. schlingen, winden ((***a)round***, um); (*fig.*) verflechten, verweben, ineinanderschlingen; **– *o.s. round***, sich schlingen um. **3.** *v.i.* sich verschlingen *or* verflechten; sich ranken *or* schlingen (*as plants*); sich winden *or* schlängeln (*as a path*).

twin-engined, *adj.* Zweimotoren–, zweimotorig.

twiner ['twainə], *s.* 1. (*Tech.*) die Zwirnmaschine 2. (*Bot.*) Schlingpflanze, Kletterpflanze.

twinge [twindʒ], **1.** *s.* der Stich (*also fig.*), stechender Schmerz, das Stechen, Reißen, Zwicken; **– *of conscience***, der Gewissensbiß. **2.** *v.t., v.i.* stechen, zwicken, kneifen.

twinkle [twiŋkl], **1.** *v.i.* funkeln, blitze(l)n, aufblitzen, glitzern, flimmern (*of the eyes*), funkeln, blitzeln, zwinkern. **2.** *s.* das Funkeln, Blinze(l)n, Glitzern, Flimmern; Zwinkern; ***merry* –**, lustiges Zwinkern (mit den Augen). **twinkling,** *s. See* **twinkle, 2**; (*fig.*) ***in the* – *of an eye, in a* –**, im Augenblick, im Nu, im Handumdrehen.

twinned [twind], *adj.* gepaart, gekoppelt; (*as crystals*) verzwillingt; (*fig.*) verein(ig)t. **twinning,** *s.* die Zwillingsgeburt; (*of crystals*) Verzwillingung; (*fig.*) Vereinigung, Verknüpfung.

twin|-screw, *adj.* Doppelschrauben–. **–set,** *s.* der *or* das Twinset.

twirl [twə:l], **1.** *s.* 1. schnelle Umdrehung, der Wirbel; 2. Schnörkel. **2.** *v.t.* drehen, wirbeln; zwirbeln (*the moustache etc.*), schwingen (*a stick*). **3.** *v.i.* wirbeln, sich schnell drehen.

twist [twist], **1.** *v.t.* 1. (zusammen)drehen; zwirnen (*threads*), winden, flechten, wickeln, schlingen; (*fig.*) **– *him round one's little finger***, ihn um den Finger wickeln; 2. biegen, krümmen; verzerren, verziehen (*features*); **– *one's ankle***, sich (*Dat.*) den Fuß verrenken *or* verstauchen; 3. (*fig.*) verflechten, verschlingen, verwickeln; verdrehen, entstellen (*meaning*); 4. (*Tech.*) ziehen; **–*ed barrel***, gezogener Lauf (*of a gun*); 5. (*sl.*) prellen, beschummeln (*a p.*) (***out of***, um). **2.** *v.i.* 1. sich drehen; **– *round***, sich umdrehen; 2. sich winden (*also fig.*) *or* schlängeln (*as roads, rivers*). **3.** *s.* 1. die Drehung, Windung (*also fig.*), Biegung, Krümmung; ***give it a* –**, es (um)drehen; 2. (*Tech.*) der Drall (*of barrel, rope etc.*); 3. das Effet (*on a ball*); 4. Geflecht, die Spirale; 5. (*Sewing*) der Twist, das Maschinengarn; 6. der Rollentabak; 7. (*dance*) Twist; 8. (*fig.*) die Wendung, der Dreh; die Verdrehung, Verzerrung, Entstellung; Schlinge, Verschlingung; 9. (*coll.*) Unehrlichkeit, Schikane.

twist-drill, *s.* der Spiralbohrer.

twisted ['twistid], *adj.* (*also sl. of a p.*) verschroben; unehrlich. **twister,** *s.* 1. der Seiler, Flechter, Zwirner, die Zwirnmaschine; 2. (*Spt.*) der Schnittball; 3. (*coll.*) harte Nuß, schwierige Frage; 4. (*coll.*) der Schurke, Gauner, Halunke; 5. (*coll.*) die Wasserhose, der Wirbelwind, Tornado. **twisting, twisty,** *adj.* sich windend.

¹**twit** [twit], *v.t.* (*coll.*) aufziehen, verhöhnen; **– *him with s.th.***, ihm etwas vorwerfen.

²**twit,** *s.* (*sl.*) der Trottel.

twitch [twitʃ], **1.** *v.t.* zerren *or* zupfen an (*Dat.*); zucken mit. **2.** *v.i.* zerren, zupfen (***at***, an (*Dat.*)); zucken (***with***, vor (*Dat.*)). **3.** *s.* 1. das Zerren, Zupfen, der Ruck; das Zucken, die Zuckung, der Krampf; 2. das Stechen, Zwicken, Kneifen, der Stich (*of pain*). **twitch-grass,** *s. See* **couch-grass.**

twite [twait], *s.* (*Orn.*) der Berghänfling (*Carduelis flavirostris*).

twitter ['twitə], **1.** *s.* 1. das Gezwitscher, Zwitschern; 2. (*coll.*) Zittern, Beben, die Angst, Aufregung; ***in a* –**, ängstlich, aufgeregt. **2.** *v.i.* 1. zwitschern (*of birds*); zirpen (*of insects*); piepsen (*of a p.*); 2. (*coll.*) beben, zittern, aufgeregt sein. **3.** *v.t.* zwitschern.

two [tu:], **1.** *num. adj.* zwei, beide; *for clock-time see under* **eight**; ***one or* –**, einige, ein paar; ***in a day or* –, *in* – *or three days***, in ein paar *or* in einigen Tagen; (*fig.*) ***be in* – *minds***, unschlüssig sein; (*sl.*) ***in* – *ticks***, im Nu *or* Handumdrehen. **2.** *s.* die Zwei; **– *and* –**, paarweise; (*fig.*) ***put* – *and* – *together***, seine Schlüsse ziehen, es sich (*Dat.*) zusammenreimen; **– *is company***, zwei machen ein Paar; ***in* –*s***, zu zweien, zu zweit, paarweise; ***in* –**, enrzwei; ***into* –**, in zwei Teile *or* Stücke; **– *can play at that game***, so grob kann ich auch sein, das kann ein anderer auch; ***the* –**, beide, die beiden; ***the* – *of them***, sie beide.

two|-edged, *adj.* zweischneidig (*also fig.*). **–-faced,** *adj.* (*fig.*) heuchlerisch, falsch, doppelzüngig. **–fold,** *adj.* zweifach, doppelt. **–-foot,** *attrib. adj.* zwei Fuß lang. **–-four time,** *s.* (*Mus.*) der Zweivierteltakt. **–-handed,** *adj.* 1. zweihändig; **– *sword***, der Zweihänder; 2. (*Cards etc.*) für zwei Personen. **–-horse,** *attrib. adj.* zweispännig. **–-legged,** *adj.* zweibeinig. **–pence** ['tʌpəns], *s.* zwei Pence; (*coll.*) ***I don't care* –**, es ist mir ganz schnuppe *or* einerlei; **– *halfpenny***, zwei(und)einhalb Pence. **–penny** ['tʌpni], *adj.* zwei Pence wert *or* kostend, (*fig.*) wertlos, armselig; (*coll.*) **–-*halfpenny***, erbärmlich, minderwertig, elend. **–-phase,** *attrib. adj.* Zweiphasen–, zweiphasig. **–-piece, 1.** *attrib. adj.* zweiteilig. **2.** *s.* das Komplet. **–-ply,** *attrib. adj.* zweischäftig (*ropes*), zweisträhnig (*wool*). **–-seater,** *s.* der Zweisitzer. **–-sided,** *attrib. adj.* zweiseitig.

twosome ['tu:səm], *s.* 1. das Spiel für zwei Spieler; 2. (*coll.*) das (Liebes)pärchen.

two|-speed gear, *s.* doppelte Übersetzung. **–-step,** *s.* der Twostep (*dance*). **–-stor(e)y,** *attrib. adj.* zweistöckig. **–-stroke,** *attrib. adj.* Zweitakt– (*engine*). **–-time,** *v.t.* (*sl.*) betrügen. **–-tone,** *attrib. adj.* zweifarbig. **–-way,** *attrib. adj.* Doppel–, Zweiwege–; (*road*) Zweibahn–. **–-year-old, 1.** *attrib. adj.* zweijährig. **2.** *s.* zweijähriges Kind *or* Tier.

tycoon [tai'ku:n], *s.* (*sl.*) der Industriemagnat, Großkapitalist.

tying ['taiiŋ], *see* **tie.**

tyke [taik], *s.* (*sl.*) der Lümmel, Grobian.

tylosis [tai'lousis], *s.* (*Med.*) die Schwielenbildung, Gewebeverhärtung.

tympan ['timpən], *s.* 1. (*Typ.*) der Preßdeckel; 2. *See* **tympanum, 2. tympanic** [tim'pænik], *adj.* (*Anat.*) Mittelohr–, Trommelfell–; **– *membrane***, das Trommelfell. **tympanist** ['timpənist], *s.* (*Mus.*) der Schlagzeuger. **tympanum** ['timpənəm], *s.* 1. (*Anat.*) das Trommelfell, Mittelohr; 2. Giebelfeld; 3. *See* **timpano.**

type [taip], **1.** *s.* 1. der Typ, Schlag, die Art, Sorte, Kategorie, das Kaliber; 2. der Typus, die Grundform, Urform, das Urbild, Vorbild, Muster, Modell; 3. (*Typ.*) die Type, (Druck)letter, (*collect.*) der Druckbuchstabe, die Schrift, Lettern (*pl.*); ***bold* –**, der Fettdruck; ***in* –**, gedruckt, gesetzt; ***set up in* –**, setzen; ***German* –**, die Fraktur; ***italic* –**, der Kursivdruck; ***roman* –**, lateinischer Druck; ***set of* –**, der Satz Schrift; ***spaced* –**, der Sperrdruck; ***specimen of* –**, die Satzprobe, Schriftprobe. **2.** *v.t., v.i.* 1. auf *or* mit der (Schreib)maschine schreiben, tippen; –***d***, maschinegeschreiben; 2. (*Med.*) die Blutgruppe feststellen.

type|-bar, *s.* der Typenhebel (*typewriter*). **–-cast,** *irr.v.t.* auf bestimmte Rollen festlegen (*actors*).

--caster, *s. See* **-founder. --face,** *s.* das Schriftbild. **--founder,** *s.* der Schriftgießer. **--foundry,** *s.* die Schriftgießerei. **--metal,** *s.* das Schriftmetall, Letternmetall. **--page,** *s.* der Satzspiegel. **-script,** *s.* die Maschinenschrift. **-setter,** *s.* der (Schrift)setzer. **-setting,** *s.* das Setzen; – ***machine,*** die Setzmaschine. **-write,** *irr.v.t., v.i.* auf *or* mit der Maschine schreiben, tippen. **-writer,** *s.* die Schreibmaschine; – ***ribbon,*** das Farbband. **-writing,** *s.* das Maschineschreiben, Tippen; – ***paper,*** das Maschinenpapier. **-written,** *adj.* auf *or* mit der Maschine geschrieben, maschinegeschrieben, in Maschinenschrift; – ***copy,*** das Maschinenschriftexemplar.

typhoid ['taifɔid], **1.** *adj.* Typhus–. **2.** *s.* (*also* – ***fever***) der (Unterleibs)typhus.

typhoon [tai'fu:n], *s.* der Taifun, Wirbelsturm.

typhus ['taifəs], *s.* der Flecktyphus, das Fleckfieber.

typical ['tipikl], *adj.* typisch, repräsentativ, bezeichnend, kennzeichnend, charakteristisch (***of,*** für); sinnbildlich, symbolisch; vorbildlich, urbildlich; ***be – of,*** kennzeichnen, charakterisieren; verkörpern, sinnbildlich darstellen. **typicalness,** *s.* das Typische, die Sinnbildlichkeit. **typify** [–fai], *v.t.* versinnbildlichen, symbolisieren; repräsentieren, verkörpern, typisch *or* ein typisches Beispiel sein für.

typing ['taipiŋ], *s.* das Maschinenschreiben; (*collect.*) die Maschinenschrift; – ***error,*** der Tippfehler. **typist** ['taipist], *s.* der (die) Maschinenschreiber(in), Typist(in); ***shorthand –,*** der (die) Stenotypist(in).

typographer [tai'pɔgrəfə], *s.* der Druckberater. **typographic(al)** [–pə'græfik(l)], *adj.* drucktechnisch, typographisch, Buchdruck(er)–; – ***error,*** der Druckfehler, Setzfehler; – ***layout,*** die Satzanordnung. **typography** [–'pɔgrəfi], *s.* die Buchdruckerkunst, Typographie.

typological [taipə'lɔdʒikl], *adj.* Typen–, typologisch. **typology** [–'pɔlədʒi], *s.* (*Theol.*) die Typologie, Typik; Typenlehre.

tyrannical [t(a)i'rænikl], *adj.* tyrannisch, despotisch. **tyrannicidal** [–'saidl], *adj.* Tyrannenmord–. **tyrannicide** [–'rænisaid], *s.* 1. der Tyrannenmord; 2. Tyrannenmörder. **tyrannize** ['tirənaiz], **1.** *v.i.* despotisch *or* tyrannisch herrschen; – ***over,*** tyrannisieren. **2.** *v.t.* tyrannisieren, tyrannisch beherrschen. **tyrannous** ['tirənəs], *adj.* 1. *See* **tyrannical**; 2. (*fig.*) grausam, unerbittlich. **tyranny** ['tirəni], *s.* 1. die Tyrannei, Gewaltherrschaft, Willkürherrschaft, Diktatur, der Despotismus; 2. (*fig.*) die Grausamkeit, grausame Härte. **tyrant** ['tairənt], *s.* der Tyrann, Despot; (*fig.*) Menschenschinder.

Tyre ['taiə], *s.* (*Geog.*) Tyrus (*n.*).

tyre, *s.* der Reifen; *pl.* die Bereifung; – ***gauge,*** der Reifendruckmesser; – ***lever,*** der Montierhebel; – ***marks,*** die Reifenspur, Bremsspur.

tyro ['tairou], *s.* der Anfänger, Neuling.

Tyrol [ti'roul], *s.* Tirol (*n.*). **Tyrolean** [tirə'liən], **Tyrolese** [–'li:z], **1.** *s.* der (die) Tiroler(in). **2.** *adj.* tirolisch, Tiroler–.

tzar, *see* **tsar.**

U

U, u [ju:], **1.** *s.* das U, u. **2.** *adj.* (*coll.*) vornehm, fein (*of language, behaviour etc.*); ***non-U,*** nicht vornehm, unfein. *See Index of Abbreviations.*

uberous ['ju:bərəs], *adj.* viel Milch gebend; (*fig.*) im Überfluß vorhanden, voll, reichlich.

ubiquitous [ju:'bikwitəs], *adj.* überall zu finden(d), allgegenwärtig. **ubiquity** [–ti], *s.* die Allgegenwart, das Überallsein.

U|-boat, *s.* (deutsches) Unterseeboot, das U-Boot. **--bolt,** *s.* der U-Bolzen.

udal ['ju:dəl], *s.* das Freigut (*in Orkney and Shetland*); (*Hist.*) Allod(ium).

udder ['ʌdə], *s.* das Euter. **udderless,** *adj.* (*fig.*) mutterlos (*of a lamb*).

udometer [ju:'dɔmitə], *s.* der Regenmesser. **udometry,** *s.* die Regenmessung.

ugh! [u:], *int.* hu!

uglify ['ʌglifai], *v.t.* entstellen, verunzieren. **ugliness,** *s.* die Häßlichkeit, Garstigkeit; (*fig.*) Widerlichkeit, Widerwärtigkeit. **ugly,** *adj.* 1. häßlich, garstig, abstoßend, unschön; (*fig.*) – ***duckling,*** häßliches Entlein; 2. widerlich, widerwärtig; 3. gemein, schändlich; 3. bedrohlich, gefährlich (*as weather*), bösartig, unangenehm; (*coll.*) – ***customer,*** gefährlicher Bursche, übler Kunde.

uhlan [u:'lɑ:n], *s.* (*Hist.*) der Ulan.

ukase [ju:'keis], *s.* (*Hist.*) der Ukas.

ukelele [ju:kə'leili], *s.* das Ukelele.

Ukraine [ju:'krein], *s.* Ukraine (*f.*). **Ukrainian, 1.** *s.* der (die) Ukrainer(in). **2.** *adj.* ukrainisch.

ulcer ['ʌlsə], *s.* (*Path.*) das Geschwür, (*fig.*) die Beule; 2. (*fig.*) der Schandfleck. **ulcerate** [–reit], *v.i.* schwären, eitern. **ulcerated,** *adj.* vereitert, eitrig. **ulceration** [–'reiʃən], *s.* das Schwären, die (Ver)eiterung, Geschwürbildung; das Geschwür. **ulcerous,** *adj.* geschwürig, eiternd, Geschwür(s)–, Eiter–, (*fig.*) schädlich, giftig.

ullage ['ʌlidʒ], *s.* die Leckage, der Schwund, das (Flüssigkeits– *or* Gewichts)manko.

ulmic ['ʌlmik], *adj.* – ***acid,*** die Humussäure, Ulminsäure.

ulna ['ʌlnə], *s.* (*pl.* **-nae** [–ni:]) (*Anat.*) die Elle. **ulnar,** *adj.* Ellen–.

ulster ['ʌlstə], *s.* der Ulstermantel.

ulterior [ʌl'tiəriə], *adj.* 1. (*space*) jenseitig, darüber hinausliegend; 2. (*time*) weiter, später, ferner, zukünftig, (später) folgend; 3. (*fig.*) anderweitig, sonstig; 4. tieferliegend, verdeckt, verheimlicht; – ***motives,*** Hintergedanken (*pl.*).

ultimate ['ʌltimət], *adj.* 1. (*time*) (aller)letzt, endlich, schließlich; 2. (*space*) entferntest, entlegenst, äußerst; 3. (*fig.*) endgültig, entscheidend, End–; – ***goal,*** höchstes Ziel; – ***result,*** das Endergebnis; 4. (*fig.*) elementar, grundlegend, Grund–; 5. (*Tech.*) Höchst–, Grenz–, maximal. **ultimately,** *adv.* schließlich, endlich, letzten Endes, im Grunde.

ultimatum [ʌlti'meitəm], *s.* das Ultimatum, letzte Forderung, letzter Vorschlag, letztes Wort.

ultimo ['ʌltimou], *adv.* (*Comm.*) (*abbr.* ***ult.***) vorigen *or* letzten Monats.

ultra ['ʌltrə], **1.** *attrib. adj.* extrem, Ultra–, Erz–. **2.** *attrib. & pred. adj.* übertrieben, übermäßig. **3.** *s.* der Extremist, Radikale(r). **4.** *pref.* 1. jenseits (liegend); 2. übersteigend, überschreitend; 3. übermäßig, übertrieben.

ultra|-fashionable, *adj.* übermodern. – **high frequency,** *s.* die Ultrahochfrequenz(welle), Dezimeterwelle. **-marine, 1.** *adj.* ultramarin(blau). **2.** *s.* das Ultramarin(blau). **--modern,** *adj.* übermodern. **-montane** [–'mɔntein], **1.** *adj.* 1. jenseits der Berge *or* südlich der Alpen liegend; 2. (*fig.*) ultramontan, streng päpstlich. **2.** *or* **-montanist** [–'mɔntənist], *s.* Ultramontane(r), der Erzkatholik. **--short wave,** *s.* die Ultrakurzwelle. **--violet,** *adj.* ultraviolett; (*Med.*) – ***light*** or ***rays,*** das UV-Licht. – **vires** [–'vaiəri:z], *pred. adj., adv.* (*Law*) vollmachtsüberschreitend.

ululate ['ju:ljuleit], *v.i.* heulen. **ululation** [–'leiʃən], *s.* das Heulen, Geheul.

umbel [ʌmbl], *s.* die Dolde. **umbellate** [–bəleit], *adj.* doldenblütig, Dolden–. **umbellifer** [–'belifə], *s.* das Doldengewächs. **umbelliferous** [–bə'lifərəs], *adj.* doldentragend, Dolden–.

umber ['ʌmbə], *s.* die Umbra, Umber(erde).
umbilical [ʌm'bilikl], *adj.* Nabel–; – *cord,* die Nabelschnur. **umbilicate** [–'bilikeit], *adj.* nabelförmig. **umbilicus** [–'laikəs], *s.* 1. (*Anat.*) der Nabel; 2. (*Math.*) Nabelpunkt.
umbo ['ʌmbou], *s.* 1. der Buckel (*on a shield*); 2. (*Bot., Zool.*) Vorsprung, Höcker, die Wölbung.
umbra ['ʌmbrə], *s.* (*pl.* **-rae** [–bri:]) (*Astr.*) der Kernschatten.
umbrage ['ʌmbridʒ], *s.* 1. der Anstoß, das Ärgernis; ***give* – *to,*** Anstoß erregen bei, beleidigen; ***take* – *at,*** Anstoß nehmen an (*Dat.*), übelnehmen; 2. (*obs. or Poet.*) der Schatten (*of trees*).
umbrageous [ʌm'breidʒəs], *adj.* (*Poet.*) schattig, schattenreich, schattenspendend. **umbrageousness,** *s.* (*Poet.*) der Schattenreichtum. **umbral** ['ʌmbrəl], *adj.* (*Astr.*) Schatten–.
umbrella [ʌm'brelə], **1.** *s.* der (Regen)schirm; (*fig.*) ***aerial* –,** der Jagdschutz, die Deckung durch Jagdverbände; ***put an* – *up,*** einen Schirm aufspannen. **2.** *attrib. adj.* Dach– (*organization etc.*). **umbrella-stand,** *s.* der Schirmständer.
umpire ['ʌmpaiə], **1.** *s.* (*Spt.*) Unparteiische(r), der Schiedsrichter. **2.** *v.i.* Schiedsrichter sein. **3.** *v.t.* als Schiedsrichter leiten (*a game*).
umpteen ['ʌmpti:n], *adj.* (*sl.*) viele, zig. **umpteenth,** *attrib. adj.* soundsovielt, zigst.
un– [ʌn], *negating pref. With noun, adj. and adv.* (= Un–, un–, nicht), *but over and above mere negation the resultant word frequently has positive force, e.g.* ***unkind*** *suggests cruelty rather than just lack of kindness. With vb.* (= ver–, los–, ent–, auf–) *the pref. indicates reversal or removal, e.g.* ***untie, undress,*** *though occ. it does no more than emphasize the reversal or removal already expressed by the simplex, e.g.* ***unloosen.*** *The stress is variable; with noun, adj. and adv., usu. stressed or with secondary stress, though with common adjs. oft. unstressed; with vb. usu. double stress.*
The use of the pref. is virtually unlimited, the only limitation being those words derived from Latin which form negatives with in– or im–, e.g. ***intolerable, impartial.*** *The selection below is restricted to words which include less obvious equivalents.*
unabashed ['ʌnə'bæʃt], *adj.* 1. unverschämt, unverfroren, schamlos; 2. unerschrocken, furchtlos.
unabating ['ʌnə'beitiŋ], *adj.* unablässig, anhaltend, nicht nachlassend.
unable [ʌn'eibl], *adj.* unfähig; ***be* –,** nicht können; nicht imstande *or* in der Lage sein, außerstande sein; – ***to pay,*** zahlungsunfähig.
unabridged ['ʌnə'bridʒd], *adj.* unverkürzt, ungekürzt, vollständig.
unaccompanied ['ʌnə'kʌmpənid], *adj.* unbegleitet, allein, (*also Mus.*) ohne Begleitung.
unaccountable ['ʌnə'kauntəbl], *adj.* 1. unerklärlich, seltsam, eigenartig, sonderbar; 2. nicht haftbar *or* verantwortlich. **unaccountably,** *adv.* auf unerklärliche Weise. **unaccounted-for,** *adj.* unerklärt (geblieben).
unaccredited ['ʌnə'kreditid], *adj.* nicht akkreditiert *or* anerkannt, unbeglaubigt.
unaccustomed ['ʌnə'kʌstəmd], *adj.* 1. nicht gewöhnt (*to, Dat. or* an (*Acc.*)); 2. ungewöhnlich, ungewohnt, fremd.
unacknowledged ['ʌnək'nɔlidʒd], *adj.* 1. nicht anerkannt; 2. uneingestanden, nicht eingestanden *or* zugegeben; 3. nicht bestätigt, unbeantwortet (*letter*).
unacquainted ['ʌnə'kweintid], *adj.* unbekannt, nicht vertraut (***with,*** mit), unkundig (*Gen.*), unerfahren (in (*Dat.*)); ***be* – *with,*** nicht vertraut sein mit, nicht kennen.
unactable [ʌn'æktəbl], *adj.* nicht bühnengerecht, unaufführbar. **unacted,** *adj.* nicht aufgeführt.
unadaptable ['ʌnə'dæptəbl], *adj.* (*of a p.*) nicht anpassungsfähig (***to,*** an (*Acc.*)); (*of a th.*) nicht anwendbar (***to,*** auf (*Acc.*)), ungeeignet (für *or* zu).
unadapted, *adj.* ungeeignet, nicht eingerichtet (***to,*** für); nicht angepaßt (*Dat. or* an (*Acc.*)).
unaddressed ['ʌnə'drest], *adj.* ohne Anschrift.
unadopted ['ʌnə'dɔptid], *adj.* 1. nicht adoptiert (*child*); 2. (von der Gemeinde) nicht unterhalten (*road*).
unadorned ['ʌnə'dɔ:nd], *adj.* ungeschmückt, schmucklos, schlicht, einfach.
unadulterated ['ʌnə'dʌltəreitid], *adj.* unverfälscht, unvermischt, unverschnitten, rein; echt.
unadventurous ['ʌnəd'ventʃərəs], *adj.* 1. ereignislos (*as a journey*); 2. ohne Unternehmungsgeist (*as a p.*).
unadvisable ['ʌnəd'vaizəbl], *adj.* unratsam, nicht ratsam, nicht empfehlenswert *or* zu empfehlen(d). **unadvised,** *adj.* 1. unüberlegt, unbedacht, unbesonnen, unklug, unvorsichtig, vorschnell; 2. unberaten.
unaffected ['ʌnə'fektid], *adj.* 1. unberührt, ungerührt, unbeeindruckt, unbeeinflußt (***by,*** von), unverändert (durch); 2. (*of a p.*) ungekünstelt, unbefangen, nicht affektiert, natürlich; 3. aufrichtig, echt (*pleasure*). **unaffectedness,** *s.* die Natürlichkeit, Unbefangenheit.
unafraid ['ʌnə'freid], *adj.* unerschrocken, furchtlos; nicht bange (***of,*** vor (*Dat.*)).
unaggressive ['ʌnə'gresiv], *adj.* nicht angriffslustig, friedfertig.
unaided [ʌn'eidid], *adj.* ohne Hilfe (***by,*** von); bloß, unbewaffnet (*of eye*).
unalleviated ['ʌnə'li:vieitid], *adj.* unvermindert, ungemildert, ohne Erleichterung.
unallotted ['ʌnə'lɔtid], *adj.* nicht vergeben *or* zugeteilt.
unalloyed ['ʌnə'lɔid], *adj.* unvermischt, unversetzt, ohne Beimischung, unlegiert (*metals*); (*fig.*) ungemischt, ungetrübt, echt, rein, lauter.
unamazed ['ʌnə'meizd], *adj.* nicht verwundert; ***be* – *at,*** sich nicht wundern über (*Acc.*).
unambiguous ['ʌnæm'bigjuəs], *adj.* eindeutig, unzweideutig. **unambiguousness,** *s.* die Eindeutigkeit.
unambitious ['ʌnæm'biʃəs], *adj.* 1. nicht ehrgeizig (*of a p.*); 2. schlicht, anspruchslos (*of a th.*).
unamenable ['ʌnə'mi:nəbl], *adj.* unzugänglich (***to,*** für); – ***to law,*** strafunmündig.
unamended ['ʌnə'mendid], *adj.* nicht ergänzt *or* abgeändert, unverbessert.
unamusing ['ʌnə'mju:ziŋ], *adj.* nicht unterhaltend, langweilig.
unanimity [ju:nə'nimiti], *s.* die Einmütigkeit, Einstimmigkeit; ***with* –,** einmütig, einstimmig. **unanimous** [–'næniməs], *adj.* einmütig, einstimmig; ***be* –,** sich einig sein (***on,*** über (*Acc.*)).
unanswerable [ʌn'ɑ:nsərəbl], *adj.* 1. nicht zu beantworten(d), unbeantwortbar; 2. unlösbar (*riddle*); 3. unwiderlegbar, unbestreitbar (*charge*); 4. nicht verantwortlich *or* haftbar (*of a p.*). **unanswered,** *adj.* 1. unbeantwortet (*letter*); 2. unwiderlegt (*charge*).
unapparent ['ʌnə'pærənt], *adj.* nicht sichtbar.
unappeasable ['ʌnə'pi:zəbl], *adj.* unversöhnlich, nicht zu befriedigen(d) *or* besänftigen(d), nicht zufriedenzustellen(d); unersättlich (*hunger*). **unappeased,** *adj.* unversöhnt, unbesänftigt; ungestillt.
unapplied ['ʌnə'plaid], *adj.* nicht gebraucht *or* angewandt; – ***funds,*** totes Kapital.
unappreciated ['ʌnə'pri:ʃieitid], *adj.* nicht gehörig *or* entsprechend beachtet *or* geschätzt *or* gewürdigt. **unappreciative** [–iətiv], *adj.* unempfänglich (***of,*** für), verständnislos.
unapprehended ['ʌnæpri'hendid], *adj.* 1. nicht gefaßt *or* ergriffen (*fugitive*); 2. (*fig.*) nicht begriffen, unverstanden. **unapprehensive,** *adj.* furchtlos, unbekümmert.
unapproachable ['ʌnə'proutʃəbl], *adj.* 1. unzu-

For negatives with **un–** not listed see the simple word.

gänglich, unerreichbar, nicht betretbar (*places*), unnahbar (*of a p.*); 2. (*fig.*) unvergleichbar, unvergleichlich.

unappropriated ['ʌnə'prouprieitid], *adj.* 1. nicht verbraucht *or* verwendet; – ***funds***, unausgeschüttete *or* nicht zugeteilte Gelder; 2. nicht angeeignet, herrenlos.

unarm [ʌn'ɑ:m], **1.** *v.t.* entwaffnen. **2.** *v.i.* die Waffen niederlegen, (*Hist.*) die Rüstung ablegen. **unarmed,** *adj.* unbewaffnet, wehrlos; (*Zool., Bot.*) unbewehrt. **unarmoured** [–əd], *adj.* (*Mil.*) ungepanzert, ohne Panzerung.

unascertainable ['ʌnæsə'teinəbl], *adj.* nicht zu ermitteln(d), nicht feststellbar. **unascertained,** *adj.* unermittelt, nicht festgestellt.

unashamed ['ʌnə'ʃeimd], *adj.* 1. nicht beschämt; 2. schamlos, unverschämt.

unaspiring ['ʌnə'spaiəriŋ], *adj.* nicht strebsam, ohne Ehrgeiz, anspruchslos, bescheiden.

unassailable ['ʌnə'seiləbl], *adj.* unangreifbar, (*fig.*) unwiderleglich, unbestreitbar, unanfechtbar, unantastbar, unerschütterlich.

unassimilated ['ʌnə'simileitid], *adj.* nicht assimiliert; (*fig.*) nicht angeglichen.

unassisted ['ʌnə'sistid], *adj.* ohne Unterstützung *or* Beistand *or* Stütze *or* Hilfe; unbewaffnet (*as eye*).

unassuming ['ʌnə'sju:miŋ], *adj.* bescheiden, anspruchslos.

unattached ['ʌnə'tætʃt], *adj.* 1. nicht verbunden (***to***, mit) *or* befestigt (an (*Dat.*)); 2. (*fig.*) unabhängig, nicht organisiert; 3. frei, ungebunden, ledig, (*coll.*) ohne Anhang; 4. (*Mil.*) zur Disposition gestellt; 5. (*Univ.*) keinem College angehörend, extern.

unattended ['ʌnə'tendid], *adj.* 1. unbegleitet, ohne Begleitung; 2. (*also* –***to***) unbeaufsichtigt, vernachlässigt.

unattractive ['ʌnə'træktiv], *adj.* reizlos, unansehnlich, nicht einnehmend *or* anziehend.

unauthorized [ʌn'ɔ:θəraizd], *adj.* nicht autorisiert *or* bevollmächtigt, eigenmächtig, unberechtigt, vorschriftswidrig, unrechtmäßig, unbefugt, unerlaubt.

unavailable ['ʌnə'veiləbl], *adj.* 1. nicht erreichbar *or* verfügbar *or* erhältlich *or* vorhanden; 2. nicht nutzbar, unbrauchbar. **unavailing,** *adj.* vergeblich, unnütz, nutzlos, fruchtlos.

unaware ['ʌnə'wɛə], *pred. adj.* in Unkenntnis, nicht gewahr (***of***, *Gen.*); ***be – of***, nicht wissen *or* ahnen, sich (*Dat.*) nicht bewußt sein (*Gen.*). **unawares** [–z], *adv.* 1. unversehens, versehentlich, aus Versehen, unwissentlich, unbeabsichtigt; 2. unerwartet, unvermutet; ***catch*** or ***take*** –, überraschen.

unbalance [ʌn'bæləns], *v.t.* aus dem Gleichgewicht bringen. **unbalanced,** *adj.* 1. aus dem *or* nicht im Gleichgewicht, (*fig.*) unausgeglichen, unstet, ungefestigt; ***mentally*** –, geistesgestört; 2. (*Comm.*) nicht ausgeglichen *or* saldiert.

unbar [ʌn'bɑ:], *v.t.* aufriegeln, öffnen.

unbefriended ['ʌnbi'frendid], *adj.* freundlos, ohne Freunde.

unbeknown ['ʌnbi'noun], *pred. adj.* unbekannt (***to***, *Dat.*); – ***to me***, ohne mein Wissen.

unbelief ['ʌnbi'li:f], *s.* 1. der Unglaube; 2. das Mißtrauen, der Zweifel. **unbeliever** [–'li:və], *s.* Ungläubige(r), Glaubenslose(r). **unbelieving,** *adj.* 1. ungläubig, glaubenslos; 2. mißtrauisch, skeptisch.

unbend [ʌn'bend], **1.** *irr.v.t.* 1. entspannen (*a bow*); 2. abschlagen (*sails*); losmachen (*a rope*). **2.** *irr.v.i.* 1. sich herablassen, freundlich *or* mitteilsam werden, sich gehen lassen, auftauen; 2. sich entspannen. **unbending,** *adj.* (*fig.*) unbeugsam, unnachgiebig, hartnäckig; resolut, entschlossen.

unbiased [ʌn'baiəst], *adj.* unvoreingenommen, ohne Vorurteil, vorurteilslos, sachlich, unbefangen, unbeeinflußt, unparteiisch.

unbind [ʌn'baind], *irr.v.t.* losbinden, aufbinden, lösen.

unblemished [ʌn'blemiʃt], *adj.* fleckenlos; (*fig.*) unbefleckt, makellos, rein.

unblushing [ʌn'blʌʃiŋ], *adj.* schamlos.

unbolt [ʌn'boult], *v.t.* aufriegeln, öffnen.

unborn [ʌn'bɔ:n], *adj.* (noch) ungeboren; (zu)künftig.

unbosom [ʌn'buzm], *v.t.* – ***o.s.***, sein Herz ausschütten, sich anvertrauen *or* eröffnen *or* offenbaren (***to***, *Dat.*).

unbound [ʌn'baund], *adj.* 1. ungebunden, geheftet, broschiert (*as books*); 2. (*fig.*) nicht gebunden, frei. **unbounded,** *adj.* 1. unbegrenzt, unbeschränkt; 2. (*fig.*) grenzenlos, schrankenlos.

unbreakable [ʌn'breikəbl], *adj.* unzerbrechlich.

unbreeched [ʌn'britʃt], *adj.* noch keine Hosen tragend (*of a boy*).

unbridgeable [ʌn'bridʒəbl], *adj.* unüberbrückbar.

unbridled [ʌn'braidld], *adj.* 1. abgezäumt; 2. (*usu. fig.*) zügellos, hemmungslos; – ***tongue,*** loses Mundwerk.

unbroken [ʌn'broukən], *adj.* 1. ungebrochen, unverletzt, ganz, heil; 2. ununterbrochen; – ***sleep***, ungestörter Schlaf; 3. nicht zugeritten (*of horses*); 4. ungepflügt (*land*); 5. unübertroffen (*record*); 6. (*fig.*) unvermindert, ungeschwächt.

unbuckle [ʌn'bʌkl], *v.t.* losschnallen, aufschnallen.

unburden [ʌn'bə:dn], *v.t.* (*fig.*) entlasten, erleichtern; – ***o.s.***, sich erleichtern, sein Herz ausschütten; sich befreien (***of***, von), sich entledigen (*Gen.*); – ***o.s. of***, loswerden, abladen; – ***one's mind of***, sein Herz befreien *or* erleichtern von; – ***one's heart***, sein Herz ausschütten (***to***, *Dat.*).

unburned [ʌn'bə:nd], **unburnt,** *adj.* nicht verbrannt; ungebrannt (*as bricks*).

unbusinesslike [ʌn'biznislaik], *adj.* unkaufmännisch, nicht geschäftsmäßig; (*fig.*) nachlässig, unpünktlich.

unbutton [ʌn'bʌtn], *v.t.* aufknöpfen, losknöpfen. **unbuttoned,** *adj.* (*fig.*) ungehemmt, gelöst, zwanglos.

uncalled-for [ʌn'kɔ:ldfɔ:], *adj.* (*fig.*) unangebracht, unerwünscht, unnötig, überflüssig; ungerechtfertigt, unberechtigt, ungehörig.

uncanny [ʌn'kæni], *adj.* unheimlich, nicht geheuer.

uncared-for [ʌn'kɛədfɔ:], *adj.* unversorgt, vernachlässigt.

uncarpeted [ʌn'kɑ:pitid], *adj.* ohne Teppich.

unceasing [ʌn'si:siŋ], *adj.* andauernd, unaufhörlich, unablässig.

unceremonious ['ʌnseri'mouniəs], *adj.* zwanglos, ungezwungen. **unceremoniously,** *adv.* kurzweg, ohne Umstände.

uncertain [ʌn'sə:tn], *adj.* unsicher, ungewiß, unbestimmt, zweifelhaft (*of a th.*); unzuverlässig, unstet, veränderlich, unberechenbar, launenhaft (*of a p.*); unbeständig (*weather*); ***be – of***, nicht gewiß *or* sicher sein (*Gen.*). **uncertainty,** *s.* die Unsicherheit, Ungewißheit, Unbestimmtheit; Zweifelhaftigkeit; Unzuverlässigkeit, Unberechenbarkeit, Unbeständigkeit.

uncertificated ['ʌnsə'tifikeitid], *adj.* ohne Zeugnis. **uncertified** [ʌn'sə:tifaid], *adj.* unbeglaubigt, nicht bescheinigt.

unchain [ʌn'tʃein], *v.t.* losketten.

unchallengeable [ʌn'tʃælindʒəbl], *adj.* unanfechtbar, unbestreitbar, nicht anzuzweifeln(d).

unchanging [ʌn'tʃeindʒiŋ], *adj.* gleichbleibend, unveränderlich.

uncharitable [ʌn'tʃæritəbl], *adj.* hartherzig, lieblos.

uncharted [ʌn'tʃɑ:tid], *adj.* auf keiner Karte verzeichnet; (*fig.*) unbekannt.

unchartered [ʌn'tʃɑ:təd], *adj.* ohne Freibrief, nicht privilegiert, unverbrieft, unberechtigt.

For negatives with **un-** not listed see the simple word.

uncial [ˈʌnʃəl], **1.** *adj.* Unzial–. **2.** *s.* der Unzialbuchstabe, die Unziale.

unciform [ˈʌnsifɔ:m], *adj.* (*Anat.*) hakenförmig. **uncinate** [–neit], *adj.* 1. hakenförmig; 2. (*Bot., Zool.*) stacheltragend.

uncircumcised [ʌnˈsə:kəmsaizd], *adj.* unbeschnitten. **uncircumcision** [–ˈsiʒən], *s.* die Unbeschnittenheit; (*B.*) ***the –***, Heiden (*pl.*).

uncivil [ʌnˈsivil], *adj.* unhöflich, grob, schroff, barsch (***to***, gegen).

unclaimed [ʌnˈkleimd], *adj.* 1. nicht beansprucht *or* angesprochen; 2. nicht abgenommen *or* abgeholt (*as goods*); nicht abgehoben (*as money*), unbestellbar (*as letters*).

unclasp [ʌnˈklɑ:sp], *v.t.* loshaken, lösen, öffnen.

unclassified [ʌnˈklæsifaid], *adj.* 1. nicht eingeordnet *or* klassifiziert; 2. (*Pol.*) nicht (mehr) geheim.

uncle [ʌnkl], *s.* 1. der Onkel, Oheim; 2. (*sl.*) Pfandverleiher.

unclean [ʌnˈkli:n], *adj.* 1. unrein, unsauber, schmutzig; 2. (*fig.*) unkeusch. **uncleanliness** [–ˈklenlinis], *s.* die Unreinlichkeit, Ungepflegtheit. **uncleanly** [–ˈklenli], *adj.* unreinlich, ungepflegt. **uncleanness,** *s.* 1. die Unsauberkeit, der Schmutz; 2. (*fig.*) Unreinheit, Unkeuschheit.

unclench [ʌnˈklentʃ], **1.** *v.t.* lockern, öffnen. **2.** *v.i.* sich lockern *or* öffnen.

uncloak [ʌnˈklouk], *v.t.* 1. den Mantel abnehmen (*Dat.*); 2. (*fig.*) enthüllen, entlarven, bloßstellen.

unclothe [ʌnˈklouð], *v.t.* entkleiden, auskleiden, entblößen. **unclothed,** *adj.* unbekleidet, entblößt, nackt.

unclouded [ʌnˈklaudid], *adj.* 1. wolkenlos, unbewölkt; 2. (*fig.*) heiter, klar, unbetrübt.

unco' [ˈʌnkə], **1.** *adj.* (*Scots*) ungewöhnlich, beachtenswert. **2.** *adv.* äußerst, höchst; ***the – guid,*** die Selbstgerechten.

uncock [ʌnˈkɔk], *adj.* entspannen (*a gun*).

uncoil [ʌnˈkɔil], *v.t.* (*v.i.* sich) abwickeln, abrollen, abspulen.

uncollected [ˈʌnkəˈlektid], *adj.* 1. nicht eingesammelt; 2. (*Comm.*) nicht eingefordert *or* erhoben.

uncoloured [ʌnˈkʌləd], *adj.* ungefärbt; (*fig.*) ungeschminkt.

uncomeliness [ʌnˈkʌmlinis], *s.* die Unansehnlichkeit, Reizlosigkeit. **uncomely,** *adj.* 1. unansehnlich, reizlos, ohne Anmut; 2. (*rare*) ungebührlich, ungeziemend.

uncomfortable [ʌnˈkʌmfətəbl], *adj.* 1. unbequem, unbehaglich, ungemütlich; 2. (*fig.*) unangenehm, unerfreulich, beunruhigend; – ***feeling,*** ungutes Gefühl.

uncommitted [ˈʌnkəˈmitid], *adj.* nicht gebunden (***to***, an (*Acc.*) *or* verpflichtet (zu)); – ***funds,*** nicht zweckgebundene Gelder; – ***nations,*** die Neutralen.

uncommon [ʌnˈkɔmən], *adj.* ungewöhnlich, selten, außergewöhnlich, außerordentlich. **uncommonly,** *adv.* ungemein, äußerst.

uncommunicable [ˈʌnkəˈmju:nikəbl], *adj.* nicht mitteilbar. **uncommunicative,** *adj.* nicht mitteilsam, reserviert, verschlossen. **uncommunicativeness,** *s.* die Verschlossenheit, Reserviertheit.

uncompanionable [ˈʌnkəmˈpænjənəbl], *adj.* ungesellig, nicht umgänglich.

uncomplaining [ˈʌnkəmˈpleiniŋ], *adj.* ohne Murren *or* Klagen, klaglos, geduldig, ergeben.

uncomplicated [ʌnˈkɔmplikeitid], *adj.* nicht kompliziert, einfach.

uncomplimentary [ˈʌnkɔmpliˈmentəri], *adj.* nicht schmeichelhaft, unhöflich.

uncomprehending [ˈʌnkɔmpriˈhendiŋ], *adj.* verständnislos.

uncompromising [ʌnˈkɔmprəmaiziŋ], *adj.* 1. zu keinem Vergleich bereit, nicht entgegenkommend; 2. unbeugsam, unnachgiebig, unversöhnlich; 3. eindeutig, entschieden, unmißverständlich (*as a reply*).

unconcern [ˈʌnkənˈsə:n], *s.* die Gleichgültigkeit, Interesselosigkeit, Sorglosigkeit; ***with –***, gleichgültig, gelassen. **unconcerned,** *adj.* 1. gleichgültig (***about***, gegen), unbesorgt, unbekümmert (um); 2. unbeteiligt (***in***, an (*Dat.*)), nicht verwickelt (in (*Acc.*)), nicht betroffen (von); 3. uninteressiert (***with***, an (*Dat.*)).

unconditional [ˈʌnkənˈdiʃənl], *adj.* unbedingt, bedingungslos, vorbehaltlos, uneingeschränkt. **unconditioned,** *adj.* 1. ohne (Vor)bedingung, nicht bedingt; (*Phil.*) unbedingt, absolut, unendlich; 2. (*Psych.*) angeboren, unwillkürlich.

uncongenial [ˈʌnkənˈdʒi:niəl], *adj.* 1. ungleichartig, nicht kongenial; 2. unsympathisch, nicht zusagend (***to***, *Dat.*), nicht passend (zu), ungeeignet, ungünstig.

unconnected [ˈʌnkəˈnektid], *adj.* 1. unverbunden, getrennt, isoliert; 2. unzusammenhängend, nicht folgerichtig.

unconquerable [ʌnˈkɔŋkərəbl], *adj.* unbesiegbar, unüberwindlich.

unconscientious [ˈʌnkɔnʃiˈenʃəs], *adj.* nicht gewissenhaft.

unconscionable [ʌnˈkɔnʃənəbl], *adj.* 1. skrupellos, gewissenlos, unverantwortlich; 2. (*coll.*) unglaublich, enorm, ungeheuer, übermäßig.

unconscious [ʌnˈkɔnʃəs], **1.** *adj.* 1. unbewußt; ***be – of s.th.,*** sich (*Dat.*) einer S. (*Gen.*) nicht bewußt sein, etwas nicht wissen *or* ahnen; 2. unbeabsichtigt, unabsichtlich, unfreiwillig, unwillkürlich; 3. (*Med.*) bewußtlos, ohnmächtig. **2.** *s.* (*Psych.*) das Unbewußte. **unconsciousness,** *s.* 1. die Unbewußtheit, Unkenntnis; 2. (*Med.*) Bewußtlosigkeit, Ohnmacht.

unconstitutional [ˈʌnkɔnstiˈtju:ʃənl], *adj.* verfassungswidrig.

unconstrained [ˈʌnkənˈstreind], *adj.* ungezwungen, frei; zwanglos, natürlich. **unconstraint,** *s.* die Ungezwungenheit, Zwanglosigkeit.

uncontaminated [ˈʌnkənˈtæmineitid], *adj.* nicht angesteckt, unbefleckt, unberührt, rein.

uncontested [ˈʌnkənˈtestid], *adj.* unbestritten, unumstritten; – ***election,*** die Wahl ohne Gegenkandidat.

uncontrollable [ˈʌnkənˈtrouləbl], *adj.* unbändig, unbeherrscht, zügellos, unkontrollierbar. **uncontrolled,** *adj.* 1. ohne Aufsicht, unbeaufsichtigt; 2. ungehindert, unbeherrscht, zügellos.

unconventional [ˈʌnkənˈvenʃənl], *adj.* 1. unkonventionell, nicht herkömmlich; 2. ungezwungen, zwanglos, natürlich. **unconventionality** [–ˈnæliti], *s.* die Zwanglosigkeit, Ungezwungenheit.

unconversant [ˈʌnkənˈvə:sənt], *adj.* unbewandert (***in***, in (*Dat.*)), nicht vertraut (***with***, mit).

unconvinced [ˈʌnkənˈvinst], *adj.* nicht überzeugt. **unconvincing,** *adj.* nicht überzeugend, fadenscheinig.

uncooked [ʌnˈkukt], *adj.* roh, ungekocht.

uncork [ʌnˈkɔ:k], *v.t.* entkorken.

uncounted [ʌnˈkauntid], *adj.* ungezählt; unzählig, zahllos.

uncouple [ʌnˈkʌpl], *v.t.* loskoppeln; trennen, loslösen; (*Tech.*) abhängen, abkuppeln, auskuppeln, loskuppeln.

uncouth [ʌnˈku:θ], *adj.* unbeholfen, ungehobelt, ungeschlacht, ungelenk, linkisch, plump, schwerfällig; rauh, roh, grob, unfein, ungebildet.

uncovenanted [ʌnˈkʌvənəntid], *adj.* nicht (vertraglich *or* kontraktlich) verpflichtet *or* gebunden *or* vereinbart *or* abgemacht *or* gesichert.

uncover [ʌnˈkʌvə], **1.** *v.t.* 1. aufdecken (*also fig.*), bloßlegen, freilegen; entblößen (*one's head*); 2. (*Mil.*) ohne Deckung lassen; 3. (*fig.*) enthüllen, offenbaren (*feelings etc.*). **2.** *v.i.* den Hut abnehmen. **uncovered,** *adj.* 1. unbedeckt, ungedeckt;

For negatives with **un-** not listed see the simple word.

unbekleidet, nackt; barhäuptig; 2. (*Mil., Comm.*) ungedeckt, ohne Deckung.

uncreasable [ʌn'kri:səbl], *adj.* knitterfrei, knitterfest.

uncritical [ʌn'kritikl], *adj.* unkritisch, ohne Urteilsvermögen, kritiklos.

uncross [ʌn'krɔs], *v.t.* geradelegen. **uncrossed,** *adj.* 1. nicht gekreuzt; – ***cheque,*** nicht gekreuzter Scheck, offener Scheck, der Barscheck; 2. (*fig.*) unbehindert, nicht gehindert (***by,*** von *or* durch).

uncrowned ['ʌn'kraund], *adj.* nicht gekrönt.

uncrushable [ʌn'krʌʃəbl], *adj.* 1. knitterfrei (*stuffs*); 2. (*fig.*) nicht einzuschüchtern(d).

unction ['ʌŋkʃən], *s.* 1. (*Eccl.*) die Salbung (*also fig.*), Ölung, Einreibung; (*Med.*) das Einreibemittel, Öl, die Salbe; ***extreme*** –, letzte Ölung; 2. (*fig.*) das Pathos, die Rührung, Wärme, Inbrunst; ***with*** –, salbungsvoll. **unctuous** ['ʌnktjuəs], *adj.* ölig, fettig; (*usu. fig.*) salbungsvoll.

uncultivated [ʌn'kʌltiveitid], *adj.* 1. unbebaut, unangebaut, (*also fig.*) unkultiviert (*as land*); 2. (*fig.*) ungebildet, roh, verwildert, ungepflegt, vernachlässigt.

uncumbered [ʌn'kʌmbəd] (*rare*), *adj.* unbeschwert, unbelastet.

uncurbed [ʌn'kə:bd], *adj.* ohne Kinnkette (*horses*), (*fig.*) ungehemmt, ungezähmt, entfesselt, zügellos.

uncurl [ʌn'kə:l], **1.** *v.t.* entkräuseln, glätten. **2.** *v.i.* glatt *or* gerade werden, sich glätten *or* entkräuseln.

uncushioned ['ʌn'kuʃənd], *adj.* ohne Kissen.

undamped ['ʌn'dæmpt], *adj.* ungedämpft (*oscillations*), nicht niedergeschlagen *or* entmutigt (*courage*).

undate(d) ['ʌndeit(id)], *adj.* (*Bot., Her.*) wellenförmig, wellig, gewellt.

undated [ʌn'deitid], *adj.* undatiert, ohne Datum.

undaunted [ʌn'dɔ:ntid], *adj.* unerschrocken, unverzagt, furchtlos.

undebated ['ʌndi'beitid], *adj.* ohne Debatte.

undeceive ['ʌndi'si:v], *v.t.* (über Irrtum) aufklären (*of,* über (*Acc.*)), die Augen öffnen (*Dat.*), die Illusion zerstören (*Dat.*), eines Besseren belehren. **undeceived,** *adj.* nicht getäuscht *or* irregeführt (***by,*** durch).

undecided ['ʌndi'saidid], *adj.* 1. unentschieden; ***leave a question*** –, eine Frage offen lassen; 2. schwankend, unentschlossen, unschlüssig (*of a p.*), (*fig.*) unbestimmt, unausgesprochen (*as appearance*).

undecipherable ['ʌndi'saifərəbl], *adj.* nicht entzifferbar *or* zu entziffern(d), unerklärlich.

undeclared ['ʌndi'klɛəd], *adj.* 1. nicht erklärt, nicht bekanntgemacht; – ***war,*** der Krieg ohne Kriegserklärung; 2. (*Comm.*) nicht deklariert, ohne Angabe.

undefiled ['ʌndi'faild], *adj.* unbefleckt, makellos; nicht entweiht.

undemonstrative ['ʌndi'mɔnstrətiv], *adj.* reserviert, zurückhaltend, gemessen, unaufdringlich.

undeniable ['ʌndi'naiəbl], *adj.* unleugbar; unbestreitbar, nicht abzuleugnen(d). **undeniably,** *adv.* unleugbar, unstreitig, gewiß, sicher(lich).

undenominational ['ʌndinɔmi'neiʃənl], *adj.* interkonfessionell; – ***school,*** die Simultanschule.

under ['ʌndə], **1.** *adv.* unten; unterhalb; ***as*** –, wie unten *or* hierunter; ***go*** –, zugrunde gehen, zusammenbrechen, eingehen, unterliegen, erliegen; ***keep*** –, niederhalten, im Zaume halten; ***knuckle*** –, nachgeben, klein beigeben, sich unterwerfen (***to,*** *Dat.*); (*fig.*) ***be snowed*** –, überhäuft sein (***with,*** von). **2.** *adj.* 1. unter, Unter–, untergeordnet; 2. ungenügend. **3.** *prep.* 1. (*position*) unter (*Dat.*), unterhalb (*Gen. or* von); (*direction*) unter (*Acc.*); – ***arms,*** unter (den) Waffen; (*fig.*) – ***one's belt,*** im Magen; – ***one's breath,*** leise, flüsternd; – ***the burden,*** unter dem Last; – ***these circumstances,*** unter diesen Umständen; (*fig.*) ***be – a cloud,*** übel beleumdet sein, unter dem Verdacht stehen; – ***cover of,*** im Schutz (*Gen.*); (*Comm.*) – ***this cover,*** beiliegend; – ***separate cover,*** mit getrennter Post; – ***fire,*** unter Feuer; – ***foot,*** unter dem Fuße, auf dem Boden; (*fig.*) unter die Füße; ***from*** – . . ., unter (*Dat.*) . . . hervor; – ***ground,*** unter dem (Erd)boden, unter der Erde; – ***his hand and seal,*** von ihm unterschrieben und gesiegelt; – ***King George,*** während der Zeit König Georgs; – ***lock and key,*** hinter Schloß und Riegel; ***be*** or ***labour – a misapprehension,*** sich in einem Irrtum befinden; ***be – the necessity of,*** genötigt sein zu; (*fig.*) – ***his nose,*** ihm vor der Nase; – ***oath,*** unter Eid; – ***an obligation,*** verpflichtet; – ***pain of death,*** bei Todesstrafe; – ***protest,*** unter Protest; – ***the rose,*** im Vertrauen; – ***sail,*** unter Segel; – ***sentence of*** . . ., zu . . . verurteilt; 2. (*fig.*) in (*Dat.*); ***be – consideration,*** noch erwogen *or* erörtert werden; – ***chloroform,*** in der Narkose; – ***construction,*** im Bau; ***be – discussion,*** zur Diskussion stehen; – ***repair,*** in Reparatur; – ***restraint,*** in Gewahrsam (*of mental patient*), (*fig.*) im Zaume; – ***suspicion,*** im Verdacht; – ***treatment,*** in Behandlung; (*Naut., also fig.*) – ***way,*** in Fahrt, in vollem Lauf; 3. (*fig.*) gemäß, nach, laut, auf Grund von; ***I speak – correction,*** nach meiner unmaßgeblichen Meinung; – ***the treaty,*** laut Vertrag; 4. weniger *or* niedriger *or* geringer als; – ***age,*** minderjährig, unmündig; – ***2 miles,*** weniger als 2 Meilen. **4.** *pref.* Unter– (*before noun: stressed*), unter– (*before vb.: secondary stress*).

under|act, 1. *v.t.* ungenügend darstellen (*a play*), nicht gerecht werden (*a part*). **2.** *v.i.* verhalten spielen. **–-age,** *adj.* minderjährig, unmündig. **–arm, 1.** *adv.* mit dem Unterarm. **2.** *attrib. adj.* Unterarm–. **–belly,** *s.* 1. der Bauch; 2. (*fig.*) schwache Stelle. **–bid,** *irr.v.t.* unterbieten. **–bred,** *adj.* nicht rasserein *or* reinrassig; (*fig.*) unfein, ungebildet. **–carriage,** *s.* (*Av.*) das Fahrgestell; ***float*** –, das Schwimmergestell; ***retractable*** –, das Verschwindfahrgestell. **–charge,** *v.t.* 1. zu gering berechnen *or* belasten (*a p.*) (***for,*** für); 2. ungenügend laden (*a gun etc.*). **–clothes,** *pl.*, **–clothing,** *s.* die Unterwäsche, Leibwäsche. **–coat,** *s.* der Grundanstrich, Untergrund (*of paint*). **–cover,** *attrib. adj.* Geheim–, Spitzel–. **–croft,** *s.* (*Archit.*) unterirdisches Gewölbe, die Krypta. **–current,** *s.* 1. die Unterströmung; 2. (*fig.*) verborgene (Gegen)strömung *or* Tendenz. **–cut, 1.** [–'kʌt], *irr.v.t.* 1. aushöhlen, unterhöhlen; 2. (*Comm.*) unterbieten. **2.** ['ʌndəkʌt], *s.* (*Cul.*) das Filet(stück).

under|develop, *v.t.* (*Phot.*) unterentwickeln; ***–ed country,*** das Entwicklungsland. **–do,** *irr.v.t.* 1. (*Cul.*) nicht genug kochen *or* braten; 2. unvollkommen *or* mangelhaft tun. **–dog,** *s.* Benachteiligte(r), Unterlegene(r), Getretene(r), Schwächere(r), das Stiefkind des Glücks. **–done,** *adj.* nicht gar gekocht *or* durchgebraten. **–employed,** *adj.* unterbeschäftigt. **–estimate, 1.** [–'estimeit], *v.t.* unterbewerten, unterschätzen. **2.** [–mit] *or* **–estimation,** *s.* die Unterbewertung, Unterschätzung. **–expose,** *v.t.* (*Phot.*) unterbelichten. **–exposure,** *s.* (*Phot.*) die Unterbelichtung. **–fed,** *adj.* unterernährt. **–feed, 1.** *irr.v.t.* unterernähren, nicht genügend ernähren *or* füttern. **2.** *irr.v.i.* sich ungenügend ernähren. **–feeding,** *s.* die Unterernährung. **–felt,** *s.* die (Filz)unterlage. **–foot,** *adv.* unter den Füßen, unten, darunter, am Boden; ***tread*** –, mit (den) Füßen niedertreten. **–frame,** *s.* (*Motor.*) das Untergestell. **–garment,** *s.* das Unterkleid; *pl.* die Unterwäsche, Leibwäsche. **–go,** *irr.v.t.* 1. durchmachen, erfahren, erleben, ausgesetzt sein (*Dat.*); 2. ertragen, erleiden, erdulden; 3. sich unterziehen (*Dat.*) (*an operation*). **–graduate,** *s.* der (die) Student(in).

underground, 1. ['ʌndəgraund], *adj.* 1. unterirdisch; (*Railw.*) Untergrund–; Erd– (*cable*), Tiefbau– (*workings*); (*Min.*) unter Tage; – ***engineering,*** der Tiefbau; – ***mining,*** der Untertagebau; – ***railway,*** die Untergrundbahn; – ***water,*** das

For negatives with **un-** not listed see the simple word.

Grundwasser; 2. (*fig.*) geheim, Geheim–, verborgen; (*Pol.*) Untergrund–; (*Pol.*) – ***movement,*** die Untergrundbewegung. **2.** ['ʌndə–], *s.* 1. die Untergrundbahn; 2. (*Pol.*) Untergrundbewegung. **3.** [–'graund], *adv.* 1. unterirdisch, unter der Erde 2. (*fig.*) im geheimen *or* verborgenen; ***go –,*** ins Verborgene *or* (*esp. Pol.*) zur Untergrundbewegung gehen.

under|growth, *s.* das Unterholz, Gebüsch, Gestrüpp. **–hand,** *adj., adv.* 1. heimlich, verstohlen, heimtückisch, hinterhältig, hinterlistig; 2. (*Crick. etc.*) mit dem Handrücken nach unten. **–handed,** *adj. See* **–hand. –handedness,** *s.* die Hinterlist, Heimlichkeit, Hinterhältigkeit. **–hung,** *adj.* 1. über den Oberkiefer vorstehend (*as a jaw*), mit vorstehendem Unterkiefer (*of a p.*); 2. (*of sliding door*) auf einer Unterschiene laufend. **–insure,** *v.t.* unter dem Wert versichern. **–lay, 1.** [–'lei], *irr.v.t.* unterlegen, stützen. **2.** [–'lei], *irr.v.i.* (*Min.*) sich neigen, einfallen. **3.** ['ʌndəlei], *s.* 1. die Unterlage; 2. (*Typ.*) der Zurichtebogen. **–lie,** *irr.v.t.* 1. liegen *or* sich befinden unter (*Dat.*); 2. unterworfen sein (*Dat.*), unterliegen (*Dat.*); 3. (*fig.*) zugrunde liegen (*Dat.*). **–line,** *v.t.* unterstreichen (*also fig.*), (*fig.*) betonen, hervorheben. **–linen,** *s.* die Leibwäsche, Unterwäsche.

underling ['ʌndəliŋ], *s.* Untergebene(r), der Gehilfe, Handlanger.

under|lip, *s.* die Unterlippe. **–lying,** *adj.* zugrundeliegend, eigentlich; – ***idea,*** der Grundgedanke. **–manned** [–'mænd], *adj.* nicht genügend bemannt. **–mentioned,** *adj.* unten erwähnt. **–mine,** *v.t.* 1. unterminieren; 2. (*fig.*) untergraben, aushöhlen, unterhöhlen; zerstören, zugrunde richten.

undermost ['ʌndəmoust], **1.** *adv.* zuunterst. **2.** *adj.* unterst.

underneath [ʌndə'ni:θ], **1.** *adv.* unten, unterhalb; unterwärts, darunter (liegend); ***from –,*** von unten her. **2.** *prep.* unter, unterhalb; ***from – . . .,*** von unter (*Dat.*) . . . her.

under|noted, *adj.* unten erwähnt. **–nourished,** *adj.* unterernährt. **–paid,** *adj.* ungenügend *or* schlecht bezahlt. **–pants,** *s.* die Unterhose. **–pass,** *s.* die Unterführung. **–pay,** *irr.v.t., v.i.* schlecht bezahlen. **–payment,** *s.* unzureichende Bezahlung. **–pin,** *v.t.* 1. unterbauen, untermauern (*also fig.*), abstützen; 2. (*fig.*) (unter)stützen, erhärten, bekräftigen. **–pinning,** *s.* 1. die Untermauerung, der Unterbau, das Stützwerk; das Abstützen, Untermauern; 2. (*fig.*) die Unterstützung, Stütze, der Halt. **–play,** *v.t., v.i. See* **–act. ––populated,** *adj.* unterbevölkert. **––privileged,** *adj.* benachteiligt, schlecht gestellt, zu kurz gekommen; ***the –,*** die (gesellschaftlich) Schlechtgestellten. **––production,** *s.* die Unterproduktion. **–quote,** *v.t.* niedriger berechnen *or* (*St. Exch.*) notieren. **–rate,** *v.t.* unterschätzen, unterbewerten. **–score,** *v.t. See* **–line. –sealing,** *s.* (*Motor.*) der Unterbodenschutz. **––secretary,** *s.* der Unterstaatssekretär. **–sell,** *irr.v.t.* unterbieten, billiger verkaufen als (*another person*); unter dem Wert verkaufen, verschleudern (*goods*). **–shot,** *adj.* 1. unterschlächtig (*of waterwheels*); 2. mit vorstehendem Unterkiefer. **–signed,** *s.* Unterzeichnete(r). **–size(d),** *adj.* unter Normalgröße. **–skirt,** *s.* der Unterrock. **–slung,** *adj.* Hänge–; (*Motor.*) Unterzug–. **––staffed,** *adj.* zu schwach besetzt.

understand [ʌndə'stænd], **1.** *irr.v.t.* 1. verstehen; begreifen; einsehen, erkennen, erfahren, hören, vernehmen, schließen (***from,*** aus), entnehmen (*Dat. or* aus); ***as I – it,*** wie ich es auffasse; ***give him to –,*** ihm zu verstehen geben, ihn erkennen lassen; ***– by,*** verstehen unter (*Dat.*); ***be it understood,*** wohlverstanden; ***he was understood to say,*** man hat seine Worte so aufgefaßt, daß . . .; dem Vernehmen nach soll er gesagt haben; ***make o.s. understood,*** sich verständlich machen; 2. (als gegeben) annehmen, meinen, (stillschweigend) voraussetzen; ***an understood thing,*** eine selbstverständliche *or* ausgemachte S.; das versteht sich von selbst; 3. sich erkennen in (*Dat.*), sich verstehen auf (*Acc.*); ***he –s horses,*** er versteht sich auf Pferde. **2.** *irr.v.i.* begreifen, Verstand haben; volles Verständnis aufbringen; – ***about,*** Bescheid wissen *or* informiert sein über (*Acc.*). **understandable,** *adj.* verständlich, begreiflich, faßbar.

understanding [ʌndə'stændiŋ], **1.** *s.* 1. der Verstand, die Intelligenz, Urteilskraft; der Intellekt, das Denkvermögen, das Begriffsvermögen; 2. das Verständnis, die Einsicht (***of,*** für); 3. Verständigung, Vereinbarung, Abmachung, Übereinkunft, Einigung, das Einvernehmen, Übereinkommen; ***come to*** or ***have an – with,*** zu einer Einigung kommen *or* sich verständigen mit; ***have a good – with,*** in gutem Einvernehmen stehen mit; ***on the – that,*** unter der Voraussetzung *or* Bedingung daß. **2.** *adj.* 1. verständig, urteilsfähig; 2. einsichtsvoll, verständnisvoll.

under|state, *v.t.* 1. gering angeben; 2. zurückhaltend darstellen, mit Vorbehalt aussagen, bewußt mildern *or* abschwächen. **–statement,** *s.* 1. ungenügende Angabe, die Unterschätzung, Unterbewertung; 2. zurückhaltende *or* maßvolle Aussage *or* Darstellung. **–stocked,** *adj.* ungenügend versorgt *or* beliefert. **–stood, 1.** *imperf., p.p. of* **–stand. 2.** *adj.* abgemacht, vereinbart. **–stratum,** *s.* (*Geol.*) Liegende(s). **–strength,** *adj.* (*Mil.*) nicht auf der Sollstärke. **–study, 1.** *s.* der (die) Ersatzschauspieler(in). **2.** *v.t.* als Ersatzspieler einstudieren (*a part*), als Ersatzspieler *or* Vertreter stehen für (*an actor*). **–take, 1.** *irr.v.t.* 1. auf sich *or* in die Hand nehmen, sich befassen mit, übernehmen (*a task*), unternehmen (*a journey etc.*); 2. sich verpflichten *or* verbürgen, garantieren (***to do,*** zu tun). **2.** *irr.v.i.* (*rare*) einstehen, bürgen. **–taker,** *s.* der Leichenbestatter. **–taking,** *s.* 1. das Unternehmen, Unterfangen, die Unternehmung; 2. Garantie, Gewähr, bindendes Versprechen; ***give an –,*** sich verpflichten; ***on the –,*** mit der Zusicherung, unter der Bedingung. **–tone,** *s.* 1. gedämpfte Stimme; (*fig.*) der Unterton, die Unterströmung; ***in an –*** or ***–s,*** mit gedämpfter Stimme; 2. (*St. Exch.*) die Grundstimmung, Tendenz. **–tow,** *s.* (*Naut.*) der Sog, die Unterströmung.

under|-valuation, *s.* die Unterschätzung, Unterbewertung. **–value,** *v.t.* zu niedrig ansetzen *or* einschätzen, unterschätzen, unterbewerten; (*fig.*) gering bewerten, geringschätzen. **–vest,** *s.* das Unterhemd. **–water,** *adj.* Unterwasser–; (*Naut.*) unter der Wasserlinie. **–wear,** *s. See* **–clothes. –weight, 1.** ['ʌndə–], *s.* das Untergewicht, Fehlgewicht, der Gewichtsausfall. **2.** [–'weit], *adj.* untergewichtig. **–went,** *imperf. of* **–go. –wood,** *s. See* **–growth. –world,** *s.* die Unterwelt; (*fig.*) Verbrecherwelt. **–write,** *irr.v.t., v.i.* versichern, assekurieren, unterzeichnen; (*fig.*) garantieren *or* bürgen für. **–writer,** *s.* der Versicherer, Versicherungsträger; Garant, Assekurant. **–writing,** *s.* 1. die (See)versicherung, Assekuration; 2. das Versicherungsgeschäft.

undeserving ['ʌndi'zə:viŋ], *adj.* unwert, unwürdig (***of,*** *Gen.*); ***be – of,*** nicht verdienen.

undesigned ['ʌndi'zaind], *adj.* nicht beabsichtigt, unabsichtlich. **undesigning,** *adj.* harmlos, ehrlich, aufrichtig.

undesirable ['ʌndi'zaiərəbl], **1.** *adj.* unerwünscht, lästig; nicht wünschenswert. **2.** *s.* lästige *or* unerwünschte P.; *pl.* unbequeme Elemente. **undesirous,** *adj.* nicht begierig (***of,*** nach); ***be – of,*** nicht wünschen.

undetachable ['ʌndi'tætʃəbl], *adj.* nicht abnehmbar *or* abtrennbar.

undetermined ['ʌndi'tə:mind], *adj.* (noch) nicht entschieden, unentschieden, in der Schwebe, schwebend, offen (*of a th.*), unentschlossen, unschlüssig, schwankend (*of a p.*).

undeterred ['ʌndi'tə:d], *adj.* nicht abgeschreckt (***by,*** durch).

For negatives with **un-** not listed see the simple word.

undeviating [ʌn'di:vieitiŋ], *adj.* nicht abweichend; unbeirrbar, unentwegt, stetig, beständig.
undid ['ʌn'did], *imperf. of* **undo.**
undies ['ʌndiz], *pl.* (*coll.*) die (Damen)unterwäsche.
undifferentiated ['ʌndifə'renʃieitid], *adj.* homogen.
undigested ['ʌndi'dʒestid], *adj.* unverdaut; (*fig.*) verworren, chaotisch.
undirected ['ʌndi'rektid], *adj.* 1. ungeleitet, führungslos; 2. ohne Adresse, unadressiert (*as letters*).
undiscerning ['ʌndi'sə:niŋ], *adj.* einsichtslos, urteilslos, kurzsichtig.
undisciplined [ʌn'disiplind], *adj.* zuchtlos, undiszipliniert.
undisclosed ['ʌndis'klouzd], *adj.* nicht bekanntgegeben, geheimgehalten.
undiscriminating ['ʌndis'krimineitiŋ], *adj.* 1. unterschiedslos, ohne Unterschied; 2. unkritisch.
undisposed ['ʌndispouzd], *adj.* 1. abgeneigt, nicht aufgelegt, unwillig; 2. *—of,* nicht vergeben *or* verteilt, unverkauft.
undistinguished ['ʌndis'tiŋgwiʃt], *adj.* (*fig.*) unbekannt, nicht bekannt *or* ausgezeichnet.
undistracted ['ʌndis'træktid], *adj.* nicht gestört *or* abgelenkt *or* zerstreut.
undistributed ['ʌndis'tribjutid], *adj.* nicht aufgeteilt; (*Log.*) – ***middle term,*** falsch angewandter Mittelwert.
undivided ['ʌndi'vaidid], *adj.* 1. nicht getrennt, ungeteilt; 2. ganz, alleinig; – ***attention,*** volle Aufmerksamkeit.
undo ['ʌn'du:], *irr.v.t.* 1. aufmachen, auspacken, öffnen (*a parcel etc.*), aufknüpfen, lösen (*a knot*); aufknöpfen (*coat etc.*), abnehmen, losbinden (*collar etc.*); auftrennen (*a seam*); 2. aufheben, ungeschehen *or* rückgängig machen (*s.th. done*); 3. (*coll.*) vernichten, zerstören, zugrunde richten, unglücklich machen. **undoing** [ʌn'du:iŋ], *s.* 1. das Aufmachen *etc.*; 2. Rückgängigmachen; 3. (*usu. fig.*) Verderben, der Untergang, Ruin, die Zerstörung, Vernichtung, das Unglück. **undone** ['ʌn'dʌn], *adj.* 1. ungetan, unausgeführt, unerledigt, unvollendet; ***leave –,*** ungetan lassen, nicht vollenden, unterlassen; ***leave nothing –,*** nichts unterlassen, nichts unversucht lassen, alles tun; 2. aufgemacht, unbefestigt; ***come –,*** aufgehen; 3. (*coll.*) verloren, vernichtet, ruiniert, hin, aus; ***I am –,*** es ist aus mit mir.
undoubted [ʌn'dautid], *adj.* unbezweifelt, unbestritten, unzweifelhaft, nicht in Frage gestellt. **undoubtedly,** *adv.* unstreitig, gewiß, zweifelsohne, ohne Zweifel, zweifellos. **undoubting,** *adj.* zuversichtlich.
undreamed [ʌn'dri:md], **undreamt** [–'dremt], *adj.* *—of,* völlig unerwartet, ungeahnt, unerhört.
undress [ʌn'dres], **1.** *v.t.* (*v.i.*) (sich) ausziehen, (sich) entkleiden. **2.** *s.* 1. das Hauskleid, Negligé; 2. (*Mil.*) die Interimsuniform. **undressed,** *adj.* 1. unbekleidet, nicht angezogen, nackt; 2. ungarniert, unzubereitet (*salad*); 3. unverbunden (*wounds*); 4. ungegerbt (*leather*).
undrinkable [ʌn'driŋkəbl], *adj.* nicht trinkbar.
undue [ʌn'dju:], *adj.* 1. unpassend, unangemessen, nicht gemäß, unschicklich, ungebührlich, ungehörig; – ***influence,*** unzulässige Beeinflussung; 2. unnötig, übermäßig, übertrieben.
undulate ['ʌndjuleit], *v.i.* sich wellenförmig bewegen, Wellen werfen, wallen, wogen. **undulating,** *adj.* 1. wallend, wogend; 2. Wellen–, wellenförmig, wellig, gewellt. **undulation** [–'leiʃən], *s.* die Wellenbewegung, Wellenschwingung, (Schwingungs)welle. **undulatory** [–leitəri], *adj.* wellenförmig, Wellen–.
unduly [ʌn'dju:li], *adv.* 1. übertrieben, übermäßig; 2. ungerechtfertigt(erweise), unzulässigerweise.
undutiful [ʌn'dju:tiful], *adj.* pflichtvergessen, ungehorsam, unehrerbietig. **undutifulness,** *s.* die Pflichtwidrigkeit, Pflichtvergessenheit; der Ungehorsam, die Unehrerbietigkeit.
undying [ʌn'daiiŋ], *adj.* 1. unsterblich, unvergänglich; 2. unaufhörlich, unendlich.
unearned ['ʌnə:nd], *adj.* unverdient; nicht erarbeitet; – ***income,*** das Kapitalvermögenseinkommen; – ***increment,*** unverdienter Wertzuwachs *or* Mehrertrag.
unearth [ʌn'ə:θ], *v.t.* ausgraben (*beasts*), (*fig.*) ans (Tages)licht bringen, ausfindig machen, entdecken, aufdecken, aufstöbern. **unearthly,** *adj.* überirdisch, übernatürlich, geisterhaft, unheimlich; (*coll.*) ***at an – hour,*** unmenschlich früh, in aller Herrgottsfrühe, zu einer nachtschlafenden Zeit.
uneasiness [ʌn'i:zinis], *s.* innere Unruhe, die Besorgnis, Unbehaglichkeit, das Unbehagen. **uneasy,** *adj.* 1. unbehaglich, bedrückend, beunruhigend, beklemmend, ungemütlich (*feeling, suspicion etc.*); 2. (innerlich) unruhig, beunruhigt, beklommen, besorgt, ängstlich, verlegen.
uneatable [ʌn'i:təbl], *adj.* ungenießbar, nicht eßbar.
unemotional ['ʌni'mouʃənəl], *adj.* leidenschaftslos, teilnahmslos, nüchtern.
unemployable ['ʌnim'plɔiəbl], **1.** *adj.* arbeitsunfähig (*of a p.*), verwendungsunfähig, nicht verwendbar (*of a th.*). **2.** *s.* Nichtarbeitsfähige(r), Arbeitsunfähige(r). **unemployed, 1.** *adj.* arbeitslos, erwerbslos, unbeschäftigt (*of a p.*), brachliegend, ungebraucht, unbenutzt (*of a th.*); – ***capital,*** totes Kapital. **2.** *s.* ***the –,*** die Arbeitslosen (*pl.*). **unemployment,** *s.* die Arbeitslosigkeit, Erwerbslosigkeit; – ***benefit*** or ***relief,*** die Arbeitslosenunterstützung; – ***insurance,*** die Arbeitslosenversicherung.
unending [ʌn'endiŋ], *adj.* endlos, nicht endend, unaufhörlich, ständig.
unendowed ['ʌnin'daud], *adj.* nicht dotiert *or* ausgestattet, ohne Zuschuß.
unenforceable ['ʌnin'fɔ:səbl], *adj.* nicht erzwingbar.
unenterprising [ʌn'entəpraiziŋ], *adj.* nicht unternehmend *or* unternehmungslustig, ohne Unternehmungsgeist.
unenviable [ʌn'enviəbl], *adj.* nicht beneidenswert *or* zu beneiden(d).
unequal [ʌn'i:kwəl], *adj.* 1. ungleich(artig), unterschiedlich; 2. (*of a p.*) ***be – to,*** nicht gewachsen sein (*Dat.*). **unequalled,** *adj.* unvergleichlich (***for,*** wegen), unübertroffen, unerreicht (***by,*** von); beispiellos, (*pred. only*) ohnegleichen.
unequivocal ['ʌni'kwivəkl], *adj.* unzweideutig, eindeutig, unmißverständlich.
unerring [ʌn'ə:riŋ], *adj.* nicht irregehend, unfehlbar, sicher, untrüglich. **unerringly,** *adv.* ohne irrezugehen.
unessential ['ʌni'senʃəl], **1.** *adj.* unwesentlich, unwichtig, nebensächlich, entbehrlich. **2.** *s.* (*usu. pl.*) die Nebensache, Unwesentliche(s).
uneventful ['ʌni'ventful], *adj.* ereignislos, ereignisleer, ruhig, still.
unexampled ['ʌnig'zɑ:mpəld], *adj.* beispiellos, unvergleichlich; (*pred. only*) ohnegleichen; ***not –,*** nicht ohne Beispiel.
unexceptionable ['ʌnik'sepʃənəbl], *adj.* tadellos, einwandfrei, nicht zu beanstanden(d). **unexceptional,** *adj.* nicht außergewöhnlich.
unexciting ['ʌnik'saitiŋ], *adj.* ruhig, spannungslos, nicht aufregend.
unexpired ['ʌnik'spaiəd], *adj.* noch nicht abgelaufen *or* verfallen, (*pred. only*) noch in Kraft.
unexpressive ['ʌnik'spresiv], *adj.* ausdruckslos.
unfading [ʌn'feidiŋ], *adj.* unverwelklich, nicht verblassend, (*fig.*) unvergänglich.
unfailing [ʌn'feiliŋ], *adj.* 1. unfehlbar, sicher; 2. unversiegbar, unerschöpflich, nie versagend.
unfair [ʌn'fɛə], *adj.* unbillig, unfair, unsportlich (***to,*** gegenüber), parteiisch, ungerecht, unrechtmäßig; – ***competition,*** unlauterer Wettbewerb; – ***means,***

For negatives with **un-** not listed see the simple word.

ungerechte *or* unlautere Mittel (*pl.*). **unfairly,** *adv.* zu Unrecht. **unfairness,** *s.* die Unbilligkeit, Unehrlichkeit; unsportliches Verhalten.

unfaithful [ʌn'feiθful], *adj.* 1. un(ge)treu, treulos; 2. nicht (wort)getreu, ungenau (*translation*). **unfaithfulness,** *s.* die Treulosigkeit, Untreue.

unfaltering [ʌn'fɔ:ltəriŋ], *adj.* nicht (sch)wankend, ohne Zaudern; unbeugsam, fest, entschlossen, mutig.

unfamiliar ['ʌnfə'miliə], *adj.* unbekannt, ungewohnt, fremd (*to, Dat.*); nicht vertraut (***with***, mit). **unfamiliarity** [–mili'æriti], *s.* die Unbekanntheit, Unvertrautheit, Fremdheit.

unfashionable [ʌn'fæʃənəbl], *adj.* altmodisch, unmodern, (*pred. only*) aus der Mode.

unfasten [ʌn'fɑ:sn], **1.** *v.t.* aufmachen, aufbinden, losbinden, lösen. **2.** *v.i.* aufgehen, sich lösen. **unfastened,** *adj.* unbefestigt, lose.

unfathomable [ʌn'fæðəməbl], *adj.* unergründlich (tief); unermeßlich; (*fig.*) unfaßbar, unerklärlich, unbegreiflich.

unfavourable [ʌn'feivərəbl], *adj.* ungünstig, unvorteilhaft (***to, for***, für), widrig; **– *balance of trade,*** passive Handelsbilanz. **unfavourableness,** *s.* die Unvorteilhaftigkeit, Ungunst.

unfeeling [ʌn'fi:liŋ], *adj.* gefühllos, herzlos; unempfindlich.

unfeigned [ʌn'feind], *adj.* unverstellt, nicht geheuchelt, echt, wahr, aufrichtig, ehrlich.

unfeminine [ʌn'feminin], *adj.* unweiblich, unfraulich.

unfenced [ʌn'fenst], *adj.* nicht umzäunt *or* eingehegt; nicht verschanzt, unbefestigt.

unfettered [ʌn'fetəd], *adj.* (*usu. fig.*) entfesselt, unbeschränkt, ungezwungen, unbehindert.

unfilial [ʌn'filiəl], *adj.* pflichtvergessen, nicht anhänglich.

unfilled [ʌn'fild], *adj.* 1. un(aus)gefüllt, leer; 2. unbesetzt (*post*).

unfit ['ʌnfit], **1.** *adj.* untauglich (*also Mil.*), unfähig, ungeeignet (***for***, zu); (*Mil.*) ***medically –***, dienstuntauglich. **2.** *v.t.* ungeeignet *or* untauglich *or* unfähig machen. **unfitness,** *s.* die Untauglichkeit, Unbrauchbarkeit (***for***, zu). **unfitted,** *adj.* 1. untauglich, ungeeignet; 2. nicht ausgestattet *or* ausgerüstet (***with***, mit).

unfix ['ʌn'fiks], *v.t.* losmachen, lösen; **– *bayonets!*** Seitengewehr ab! **unfixed,** *adj.* lose, locker, unbefestigt, beweglich.

unflagging [ʌn'flægiŋ], *adj.* (*fig.*) nicht erschlaffend *or* erlahmend, unermüdlich, unentwegt.

unflattering [ʌn'flætəriŋ], *adj.* wenig schmeichelnd *or* schmeichelhaft (***to***, für).

unfledged [ʌn'fledʒd], *adj.* 1. nicht flügge, ungefiedert; 2. (*fig.*) unreif, unentwickelt.

unfleshed [ʌn'fleʃt], *adj.* 1. ungeatzt (*as hounds*); 2. (*fig.*) nicht erprobt.

unflinching [ʌn'flintʃiŋ], *adj.* nicht zurückschreckend *or* (zurück)weichend (***from***, vor (*Dat.*)); (*fig.*) entschlossen, unentwegt, unerschütterlich.

unfold [ʌn'fould], **1.** *v.t.* 1. entfalten, ausbreiten; 2. (*fig.*) enthüllen, offenbaren, darlegen, vorlegen, unterbreiten. **2.** *v.i.* 1. sich entfalten *or* öffnen; 2. (*fig.*) sich entwickeln *or* ausbreiten.

unforced ['ʌn'fɔ:st], *adj.* ungezwungen; (*fig.*) natürlich.

unforgiving ['ʌnfə'giviŋ], *adj.* unversöhnlich, nachtragend.

unformed ['ʌn'fɔ:md], *adj.* ungeformt, formlos, (*fig.*) unentwickelt, unfertig, nicht ausgeformt.

unfortunate [ʌn'fɔ:tʃənit], **1.** *adj.* unglücklich, Unglücks–, verhängnisvoll; unglückselig, bedauerlich, bedauernswert. **2.** *s.* Unglückliche(r). **unfortunately,** *adv.* unglücklicherweise, leider, bedauerlicherweise.

unfounded [ʌn'faundid], *adj.* unbegründet, grundlos, gegenstandslos.

unframed [ʌn'freimd], *adj.* ungerahmt, (noch) nicht eingerahmt.

unfrequented ['ʌnfri'kwentid], *adj.* nicht *or* wenig besucht, einsam, verlassen, abgelegen.

unfrock ['ʌn'frɔk], *v.t.* das Priesteramt entziehen (*Dat.*).

unfruitful [ʌn'fru:tful], *adj.* unfruchtbar; (*usu. fig.*) fruchtlos, ergebnislos. **unfruitfulness,** *s.* die Unfruchtbarkeit, Fruchtlosigkeit.

unfulfilled ['ʌnful'fild], *adj.* unerfüllt, nicht verwirklicht.

unfunded [ʌn'fʌndid], *adj.* nicht fundiert, schwebend.

unfurl [ʌn'fə:l], **1.** *v.t.* entfalten, entrollen, ausbreiten, auseinanderbreiten; losmachen (*sails*); aufspannen (*a fan*). **2.** *v.i.* sich ausbreiten *or* entfalten.

unfurnished [ʌn'fə:niʃt], *adj.* nicht ausgerüstet; unmöbliert (*as houses*); **– *room,*** das Leerzimmer.

ungainliness [ʌn'geinlinis], *s.* die Plumpheit, Ungeschicklichkeit. **ungainly,** *adj.* plump, ungeschickt, ungelenk, linkisch.

ungenerous [ʌn'dʒenərəs], *adj.* 1. nicht freigiebig, knauserig, knickerig; 2. kleinlich, nicht großmütig, unedel(mütig).

ungentle [ʌn'dʒentl], *adj.* unsanft, unhöflich, grob, schroff, rauh, hart. **ungentlemanlike** [ʌn'dʒentlmənlaik], *adj.* *See* **ungentlemanly**; unfein, unvornehm, unedel. **ungentlemanliness,** *s.* unedles *or* unvornehmes *or* unwürdiges Benehmen. **ungentlemanly,** *adj.* ohne Lebensart, unfein, unvornehm, unedel.

un-get-at-able [ʌnget'ætəbl], *adj.* (*coll.*) unzugänglich, unnahbar, schwer erreichbar.

ungird [ʌn'gə:d], *v.t.* losgürten, lockern. **ungirded, ungirt,** *adj.* nicht gegürtet, gelockert.

unglazed [ʌn'gleizd], *adj.* 1. unglasiert, ohne Glasur (*as paper*); **– *paper,*** das Fließpapier; 2. unverglast, ohne Scheiben (*as window*).

ungodliness [ʌn'gɔdlinis], *s.* die Gottlosigkeit, Verruchtheit. **ungodly,** *adj.* 1. gottlos, verrucht; 2. (*coll.*) unmenschlich, abscheulich, unerhört.

ungovernable [ʌn'gʌvənəbl], *adj.* 1. unlenksam, unbeherrschbar, un(be)zähmbar; 2. zügellos, unbändig, heftig, wild.

ungraceful [ʌn'greisful], *adj.* 1. ungraziös, ohne Anmut; 2. plump, schwerfällig, ungelenk.

ungrounded [ʌn'graundid], *adj.* unbegründet, grundlos.

ungrudging [ʌn'grʌdʒiŋ], *adj.* (bereit)willig, ohne Murren; großzügig, freimütig; ***be – in,*** reichlich *or* neidlos spenden.

ungual ['ʌŋgwəl], *adj.* (*Zool.*) Huf–, Klauen–, Nagel–.

unguent ['ʌŋgwənt], *s.* die Salbe.

ungulate ['ʌŋgjulət], **1.** *adj.* hufförmig, Huf(tier)–. **2.** *s.* das Huftier.

unhallowed [ʌn'hæloud], *adj.* 1. ungeweiht, nicht geheiligt; 2. unheilig, profan, gottlos.

unhampered [ʌn'hæmpəd], *adj.* ungehindert, frei.

unhand ['ʌn'hænd], *v.t.* loslassen.

unhandiness [ʌn'hændinis], *s.* 1. die Ungeschicklichkeit, das Ungeschick (*of a p.*); 2. die Unhandlichkeit (*of a th.*). **unhandy,** *adj.* unhandlich, unbequem (*of a th.*), ungeschickt, ungelenk, unbeholfen, linkisch (*of a p.*).

unhappily [ʌn'hæpili], *adv.* unglücklich(erweise), leider. **unhappiness,** *s.* das Unglück, die Unglückseligkeit, Traurigkeit, das Elend. **unhappy,** *adj.* 1. unglücklich, traurig, elend; 2. un(glück)selig, unheilvoll.

unharmonious ['ʌnhɑ:'mouniəs], *adj.* unharmonisch (*also fig.*), mißtönend.

unharness [ʌn'hɑ:nis], *v.t.* abschirren, ausspannen.

unhasp [ʌn'hɑ:sp], *v.t.* loshäkeln.

unhealthiness [ʌn'helθinis], *s.* die Ungesundheit, Kränklichkeit. **unhealthy,** *adj.* 1. ungesund (*also*

For negatives with **un-** not listed see the simple word.

of th. and place), kränklich; 2. gesundheitsschädlich; (*fig.*) krankhaft; (*coll.*) gefährlich.

unheard-of [ʌn'hə:dɔv], *adj.* unerhört, beispiellos, noch nicht dagewesen.

unheeded [ʌn'hi:did], *adj.* unbeachtet; ***go –,*** nicht beachtet werden. **unheedful,** *adj.* sorglos, unachtsam; nicht achtend (***of,*** auf (*Acc.*)). **unheeding,** *adj.* unachtsam, sorglos, nachlässig.

unhelpful [ʌn'helpful], *adj.* 1. nicht hilfreich (*a p.*); 2. (*pred. only*) nutzlos, ohne Nutzen (***to,*** für).

unhesitating [ʌn'heziteitiŋ], *adj.* 1. nicht zögernd, ohne Zögern, unverzüglich; 2. bereitwillig, unbedenklich, anstandslos. **unhesitatingly,** *adv.* ohne weiteres.

unhinge [ʌn'hindʒ], *v.t.* 1. aus den Angeln heben; 2. (*fig.*) verwirren, zerrütten, aus der Fassung *or* dem Gleichgewicht bringen.

unhitch [ʌn'hitʃ], *v.t.* loshaken, losmachen; ausspannen (*horses*).

unholy [ʌn'houli], *adj.* 1. unheilig, ungeheiligt, nicht geweiht, profan; gottlos, ruchlos; 2. (*coll.*) heillos, furchtbar, gräßlich, schrecklich, scheußlich, abscheulich; skandalös, schockierend.

unhonoured [ʌn'ɔnəd], *adj.* nicht verehrt *or* geehrt.

unhook [ʌn'huk], *v.t.* aufhaken, loshaken; aushängen.

unhoped-for [ʌn'houptfɔ:], *adj.* unerhofft, unverhofft, ungeahnt, unerwartet, unwahrscheinlich.

unhorse [ʌn'hɔ:s], *v.t.* aus dem Sattel heben *or* werfen, abwerfen.

unhoused [ʌn'hauzd], *adj.* obdachlos.

unhouselled [ʌn'hauzəld], *adj.* ohne das Heilige Abendmahl.

unhung [ʌn'hʌŋ], *adj.* nicht gehenkt, noch nicht aufgehängt.

unhurried [ʌn'hʌrid], *adj.* gemächlich, gemütlich, ohne Hast.

unicellular ['ju:ni'seljulə], *adj.* (*Biol.*) einzellig; ***– animals,*** Urtiere, Protozoen.

unicorn ['ju:nikɔ:n], *s.* das Einhorn.

unidentified ['ʌnai'dentifaid], *adj.* unerkannt; ***– flying object,*** unbekanntes Flugobjekt, das Ufo.

uni|dimensional ['ju:ni–], *adj.* eindimensional. **-directional,** *adj.* in einer Richtung verlaufend.

unification [ju:nifi'keiʃən], *s.* die (Ver)einigung, Vereinheitlichung. **unified** ['ju:nifaid], *adj.* 1. einheitlich, vereinheitlicht; 2. (*Comm.*) konsolidiert.

uniform ['ju:nifɔ:m], **1.** *adj.* 1. gleichbleibend, unveränderlich, konstant, gleichmäßig; 2. gleich(förmig), übereinstimmend, einheitlich, einförmig, Einheits–. **2.** *s.* die Uniform, Dienstkleidung. **uniformed,** *adj.* uniformiert, in Uniform. **uniformity** [–'fɔ:miti], *s.* die Gleichförmigkeit, Übereinstimmung, Einheitlichkeit, Gleichmäßigkeit, Regelmäßigkeit, Einförmigkeit; Eintönigkeit.

unify ['ju:nifai], *v.t.* verein(ig)en, vereinheitlichen.

unilateral ['ju:ni'lætərəl], *adj.* einseitig; ***– contract,*** einseitig bindender Vertrag.

unimaginative [ʌni'mædʒinətiv], *adj.* phantasielos, phantasiearm.

unimpassioned ['ʌnim'pæʃənd], *adj.* leidenschaftslos.

unimpeachable ['ʌnim'pi:tʃəbl], *adj.* unanfechtbar, unantastbar; vorwurfsfrei, untadelig, tadellos.

unimportant ['ʌnim'pɔ:tənt], *adj.* unwichtig, unbedeutend, unwesentlich, bedeutungslos, nebensächlich.

unimposing ['ʌnim'pouziŋ], *adj.* eindruckslos, nicht imponierend *or* imposant.

unimpressionable ['ʌnim'preʃənəbl], *adj.* (für Eindrücke) unempfänglich, nicht zu beeindrucken(d). **unimpressive** [–'presiv], *adj.* eindruckslos, ausdruckslos, unscheinbar.

uninflected ['ʌnin'flektid], *adj.* unflektiert, flexionslos.

uninfluenced [ʌn'influənst], *adj.* 1. unbeeinflußt (***by,*** durch); 2. unbefangen, unvoreingenommen. **uninfluential** ['ʌninflu'enʃəl], *adj.* nicht einflußreich, ohne Einfluß; ***be –,*** keinen Einfluß haben; ***remain –,*** ohne Einfluß bleiben.

uninformed ['ʌninfɔ:md], *adj.* 1. nicht unterrichtet *or* informiert (***on, about,*** über (*Acc.*)), nicht eingeweiht (in (*Acc.*)); 2. unwissend, ungebildet.

uninhibited ['ʌnin'hibitid], *adj.* ungehemmt, hemmungslos, zügellos, maßlos, unbändig, ungestüm, überstürzt.

uninspired ['ʌnin'spaiəd], *adj.* nicht begeistert, schwunglos. **uninspiring,** *adj.* nicht anregend.

uninstructed ['ʌnin'strʌktid], *adj.* 1. nicht unterrichtet; 2. (*pred. only*) ohne Verhaltungsmaßregeln. **uninstructive,** *adj.* nicht belehrend *or* lehrreich.

unintelligent ['ʌnin'telidʒənt], *adj.* unintelligent, geistlos, dumm, beschränkt.

unintended ['ʌnin'tendid], **unintentional** [–'tenʃənl], *adj.* unbeabsichtigt, unabsichtlich, nicht vorsätzlich.

uninterested [ʌn'intəristid], *adj.* uninteressiert, interesselos (***in,*** an (*Dat.*)); gleichgültig, unbeteiligt. **uninteresting,** *adj.* uninteressant, reizlos, langweilig.

uninterrupted ['ʌnintə'rʌptid], *adj.* ununterbrochen, ungestört (***by,*** von); durchgehend, fortlaufend, kontinuierlich, anhaltend, andauernd.

uninventive ['ʌnin'ventiv], *adj.* nicht erfinderisch, phantasielos.

uninvested ['ʌnin'vestid], *adj.* nicht investiert, unangelegt, brachliegend, tot (*capital*).

uninviting ['ʌnin'vaitiŋ], *adj.* nicht verlockend *or* anziehend *or* einladend, ohne Reiz, reizlos; unappetitlich (*food etc.*).

union ['ju:niən], *s.* 1. die Vereinigung, Verbindung, (*esp. Pol.*) der Zusammenschluß, Anschluß; 2. eheliche Verbindung, die Ehe; 3. Eintracht, Harmonie, Übereinstimmung; 4. der Verein, (Zweck)verband, (*Pol.*) Staatenbund, die Union; (*Am. Hist.*) ***the Union,*** die Nordstaaten; 5. (*also* ***trade–***–) die Gewerkschaft; ***– card,*** der Gewerkschaftsausweis; ***– dues,*** der Gewerkschaftsbeitrag; 6. (*Hist.*) der Kirchspielverband (*for the care of the poor*), das Armenhaus; 7. (*Tech.*) (*also* ***––joint***) die Röhrenkupplung, Schraubverbindung; 8. (*Text.*) (*also* ***––flannel***) ein Mischgewebe; 9. (*Naut.*) die Gösch; ***Union Jack,*** Großbritannische Nationalflagge. **unionism,** *s.* 1. die Gewerkschaftspolitik; 2. (*Hist.*) konservative Politik. **unionist,** *s.* 1. Konservative(r), der Unionist; 2. (*rare*) der Gewerkschaftler. **unionize,** *v.t.* gewerkschaftlich organisieren.

uniparous [ju:'nipərəs], *adj.* nur ein Junges (bei einem Wurf) gebärend *or* werfend, nur ein Ei legend.

unipartite ['ju:ni'pɑ:tait], *adj.* einteilig, aus einem Teil bestehend, nicht in Teile zerlegt.

unipolar ['ju:ni'poulə], *adj.* einpolig, Einpol–.

unique [ju:'ni:k], **1.** *adj.* 1. einzig(artig), einmalig, alleinig; unerreicht, (*pred. only*) ohnegleichen; ***– of its kind,*** einzig in seiner Art; 2. (*coll.*) außerordentlich, außergewöhnlich. **2.** *s.* das Unikum, die Seltenheit. **uniquely,** *adv.* 1. allein, ausschließlich; 2. in einzigartiger Weise. **uniqueness,** *s.* 1. die Einzigartigkeit, Einmaligkeit; 2. (*Math.*) Eindeutigkeit.

unisexual ['ju:ni'seksjuəl], *adj.* 1. eingeschlechtig; 2. (*Bot.*) getrenntgeschlechtig.

unison ['ju:nisən], *s.* der Einklang (*also fig.*), Gleichklang; (*fig.*) die Harmonie, Übereinstimmung; ***in –,*** (*Mus.*) einstimmig, unisono; (*fig.*) in Einklang. **unisonous** [ju:'nisənəs], *adj.* einstimmig, gleichtönend; (*fig.*) übereinstimmend, gleichgestimmt.

unit ['ju:nit], *s.* 1. die Einheit; (*Phys. etc.*) der Grundmaßstab; ***– (of) force,*** die Krafteinheit; ***– (of) power,*** die Leistungseinheit; 2. (*Math.*) ganze Zahl, einzelne Größe, der Einer; 3. (*Mil.*) Ver-

For negatives with **un-** not listed see the simple word.

band, die Einheit; 4. (Bau)einheit; – ***furniture,*** Anbaumöbel (*pl.*); ***power* –,** (*Tech.*) das Triebwerk, (*Rad.*) Netzteil; 5. (*fig.*) die Grundeinheit, Basis.

Unitarian ['ju:ni'tɛəriən], **1.** *s.* 1. (*Eccl.*) der Unitarier; 2. (*Pol.*) Verfechter des Zentralismus. **2.** *adj.* 1. (*Eccl.*) unitarisch; 2. (*Pol.*) zentralistisch. **Unitarianism,** *s.* 1. (*Eccl.*) der Unitarismus; 2. (*Pol.*) Zentralismus.

unitary ['ju:nitəri], *adj.* 1. Einheits–; einheitlich; 2. (*Pol.*) zentralistisch.

unite [ju:'nait], **1.** *v.t.* 1. vereinigen, verbinden (*also Chem.*), zusammenbringen; 2. (ehelich) verbinden, verheiraten; 3. in sich vereinigen, gemeinsam haben (*qualities*). **2.** *v.i.* 1. sich vereinigen *or* zusammenschließen (***with,*** mit) (*a p.*); 2. (*Chem.*) sich verbinden; 3. (*of a group*) sich zusammentun, sich geschlossen einsetzen; 4. (*rare*) sich verheiraten *or* ehelich verbinden (***with,*** mit). **united,** *adj.* verein(ig)t, verbunden; gemeinsam, Einheits–; – ***front,*** die Einheitsfront; ***United Kingdom,*** Großbritannien und Nordirland; ***United Nations,*** Vereinte Nationen; ***United Provinces,*** die Vereinigten Niederlande; ***United States*** (***of America***), die Vereinigten Staaten (von Amerika).

unity ['ju:niti], *s.* 1. die Einheit (*also Math. etc.*); ***the three unities,*** die drei Einheiten (des Dramas); 2. die Einheitlichkeit; ***give – to a th.,*** einer S. Einheitlichkeit verleihen; 3. die Einigkeit, Eintracht, Einmütigkeit, Solidarität, Übereinstimmung; ***be at* –,** übereinstimmen, in Eintracht *or* Einklang sein, einträchtig beisammen sein; (*Prov.*) – ***is strength,*** Einigkeit macht stark.

univalent [ju:ni'veilənt], *adj.* (*Chem.*) einwertig.

univalve ['ju:nivælv], **1.** *adj.* (*Zool.*) einschalig. **2.** *s.* das Einschaltier.

universal [ju:ni'və:sl], **1.** *adj.* allgemein(gültig), universell, generell; universal, Universal–, allumfassend, weltumfassend, Welt–; ganz, gesamt; – ***heir,*** der Alleinerbe; – ***joint,*** das Universalgelenk; – ***language,*** die Weltsprache; – ***legacy,*** das Universalvermächtnis; – ***mind,*** allumfassender Geist; ***Universal Postal Union,*** der Weltpostverein; – ***remedy,*** das Universalmittel; – ***screw-wrench,*** der Engländer; – ***suffrage,*** allgemeines Wahlrecht. **2.** *s.* das Allgemeine, allgemeiner Begriff; *pl.* Allgemeinbegriffe (*pl.*). **universalism,** *s.* der Universalismus. **universality** [–'sæliti], *s.* 1. die Universalität, Allgemeingültigkeit; 2. Vielseitigkeit; 3. (*rare*) Allgemeinheit. **universalize,** *v.t.* allgemein verbreiten *or* verwenden *or* bindend machen, Allgemeingültigkeit verleihen (*Dat.*). **universally,** *adv.* universell, generell, allgemein.

universe ['ju:nivə:s], *s.* das (Welt)all, Universum, der Kosmos.

university [ju:ni'və:siti], *s.* die Hochschule, Universität; – ***of the air, open* –,** das Telekolleg; ***go*** (***up***) ***to the* –,** die Universität besuchen *or* beziehen; ***go down from the* –,** die Universität verlassen; ***at the* –,** an *or* auf der Universität; ***the University of Berlin,*** die Universität Berlin, Berliner Universität; – ***chair,*** der Lehrstuhl; – ***education,*** die Hochschulbildung; – ***extension,*** die Volkshochschule; – ***lecturer,*** der Universitätsdozent; – ***man,*** der Akademiker, akademisch Gebildete(r); – ***professor,*** der Ordinarius, ordentlicher Professor; – ***register,*** die Universitätsmatrikel.

univocal [ju:ni'voukl], *adj.* eindeutig, unzweideutig.

unjaundiced [ʌn'dʒɔ:ndist], *adj.* neidlos, nicht mißgünstig *or* eifersüchtig, unvoreingenommen.

unjustifiable [ʌn'dʒʌstifaiəbl], *adj.* nicht zu rechtfertigen(d), unverantwortlich.

unkempt [ʌn'kempt], *adj.* ungekämmt, ungepflegt; unordentlich, vernachlässigt, schlampig, liederlich.

unkind [ʌn'kaind], *adj.* unfreundlich, ungefällig, lieblos, rücksichtslos (***to,*** gegen). **unkindness,** *s.* die Unfreundlichkeit, Lieblosigkeit, Ungefälligkeit.

unknot ['ʌn'nɔt], *v.t.* aufknoten, aufmachen.

unknowable [ʌn'nouəbl], *adj.* un(er)kennbar, jenseits menschlicher Erkenntnis. **unknowing,** *adj.* unwissend; (*pred. only*) ohne zu wissen. **unknowingly,** *adv.* ahnungslos, unwissentlich. **unknown, 1.** *adj.* unbekannt (***to,*** *Dat.*); – ***to him,*** ohne sein Wissen. **2.** *s.* das Unbekannte; (*Math.*) die Unbekannte.

unlabelled [ʌn'leibəld], *adj.* nicht etikettiert *or* beschriftet, ohne Zettel *or* Marke.

unlaboured [ʌn'leibəd], *adj.* (*fig.*) ungezwungen, leicht, fließend, natürlich (*of style*).

unlace ['ʌnleis], *v.t.* aufschnüren.

unladen [ʌn'leidn], *adj.* unbeladen, (*fig.*) unbelastet.

unladylike [ʌn'leidilaik], *adj.* nicht damenhaft, unschicklich.

unlatch ['ʌn'lætʃ], *v.t.* aufklinken.

unlawful [ʌn'lɔ:ful], *adj.* ungesetzlich, gesetzwidrig, rechtswidrig, widerrechtlich, unzulässig, illegal; unerlaubt, unrechtmäßig. **unlawfulness,** *s.* die Ungesetzlichkeit, Gesetzwidrigkeit, Widerrechtlichkeit.

unlay ['ʌn'lei], *irr.v.t.* aufflechten (*a rope*).

unleaded [ʌn'ledid], *adj.* 1. ohne Blei, unverbleit; 2. (*Typ.*) ohne Durchschuß.

unleash ['ʌn'li:ʃ], *v.t.* loskoppeln (*hounds*), (*fig.*) loslassen, befreien.

unlearn ['ʌn'lə:n], *v.t.* verlernen, vergessen. **unlearned,** *adj.* 1. [–id] unwissend, ungelehrt; 2. [(*also* **unlearnt**) –t], nicht gelernt *or* erlernt.

unless [ʌn'les], *conj.* wenn *or* wofern *or* falls nicht, vorausgesetzt daß nicht, außer *or* ausgenommen wenn, es sei denn daß.

unlettered [ʌn'letəd], *adj.* (*fig.*) ungelehrt, ungebildet, unbelesen.

unlicensed [ʌn'laisənst], *adj.* nicht konzessioniert, ohne Lizenz *or* Genehmigung, unerlaubt, unberechtigt.

unlicked ['ʌn'likt], *adj.* (*usu. fig.*) ungeleckt, unbeleckt, ungeschliffen, ungehobelt, unreif; – ***cub,*** ungeleckter Bär, grüner Junge.

unlike [ʌn'laik], **1.** *adj.* unähnlich, ungleich, verschieden. **2.** *prep.* anders als, verschieden von; ***it is – him,*** das ist gar nicht seine Art, das sieht ihm gar nicht ähnlich.

unlikelihood [ʌn'laiklihud], **unlikeliness,** *s.* die Unwahrscheinlichkeit. **unlikely,** *adj., adv.* unwahrscheinlich.

unlimber [ʌn'limbə], *v.t.* (*Mil.*) abprotzen.

unlimited [ʌn'limitid], *adj.* unbegrenzt, uneingeschränkt, unbeschränkt, (*fig.*) grenzenlos, uferlos; (*Comm.*) – ***liability,*** unbeschränkte Haftung *or* Haftpflicht.

unlined [ʌn'laind], *adj.* 1. ungefüttert, ohne Futter (*clothes*); 2. unliniert, ohne Linien (*paper*); 3. faltenlos, ohne Falten (*face*).

unliquidated [ʌn'likwideitid], *adj.* 1. unbezahlt, unbeglichen; 2. nicht festgestellt, offenstehend, unbestimmt.

unload [ʌn'loud], *v.t.* 1. entladen (*vehicle, gun*), abladen, ausladen (*goods*), (*Naut.*) löschen; 2. (*fig.*) entlasten, erleichtern, befreien; 3. (*Comm.*) auf den Markt werfen, abstoßen, verschleudern.

unlock [ʌn'lɔk], *v.t.* aufschließen, aufsperren, öffnen. **unlocked,** *adj.* nicht zugeschlossen *or* verschlossen.

unlooked-for [ʌn'luktfɔ:], *adj.* unerwartet, überraschend, unvorhergesehen.

unloose [ʌn'lu:s], *v.t.* losmachen, loslassen. **unloosen,** *v.t.* aufmachen, lösen.

unlovable [ʌn'lʌvəbl], *adj.* nicht liebenswert, unliebenswürdig. **unlovely,** *adj.* unschön, unansehnlich, reizlos. **unloving,** *adj.* lieblos, unfreundlich.

unluckily [ʌn'lʌkili], *adv.* unglücklicherweise. **unlucky,** *adj.* unglücklich, erfolglos; ungünstig, verhängnisvoll, unheilbringend, unheilvoll; ***be* –,** Unglück *or* Pech haben.

For negatives with **un-** not listed see the simple word.

unmaidenly [ʌn'meidənli], *adj.* nicht mädchenhaft, unschicklich.

unmake ['ʌn'meik], *irr.v.t.* aufheben, umstoßen, widerrufen, rückgängig machen, für nichtig erklären (*decisions*); von Grund auf ändern, vernichten, zerstören; absetzen (*king*).

unman ['ʌn'mæn], *v.t.* 1. entmannen, der Manneskraft berauben; (*fig.*) entkräftigen, entmutigen; 2. (*Naut.*) der Mannschaft berauben.

unmanageable [ʌn'mænidʒəbl], *adj.* unlenksam, unkontrollierbar, widerspenstig; schwer zu bewältigen(d) *or* handhaben(d), schwierig, unhandlich.

unmannerliness [ʌn'mænəlinis], *s.* die Unart, Ungezogenheit. **unmannerly,** *adj.* ungezogen, unmanierlich.

unmarketable [ʌn'mɑ:kitəbl], *adj.* unverkäuflich, nicht marktfähig *or* marktgängig.

unmarriageable [ʌn'mæridʒəbl], *adj.* 1. nicht heiratsfähig; 2. (*fig.*) unvereinbar, nicht zu vereinbaren(d). **unmarried,** *adj.* unverheiratet, ledig.

unmask [ʌn'mɑ:sk], **1.** *v.t.* die Maske abnehmen (*Dat.*), demaskieren; (*fig.*) entlarven. **2.** *v.i.* sich demaskieren, die Maske abnehmen; (*fig.*) die Maske fallenlassen, sein wahres Gesicht zeigen. **unmasking,** *s.* die Entlarvung, Demaskierung.

unmatched [ʌn'mætʃt], *adj.* unvergleichlich, unübertroffen, unerreicht; ***be –***, nicht seinesgleichen haben.

unmeaning [ʌn'mi:niŋ], *adj.* nichtssagend, bedeutungslos, sinnlos.

unmeasured [ʌn'meʒəd], *adj.* (*fig.*) unermeßlich, unbegrenzt, grenzenlos; übermäßig, unmäßig.

unmelodious ['ʌnmə'loudiəs], *adj.* unmelodisch, mißtönend.

unmentionable [ʌn'menʃənəbl], *adj.* nicht zu erwähnen(d), unnennbar, unaussprechlich. **unmentioned,** *adj.* nicht erwähnt (*by*, von).

unmethodical ['ʌnmi'θɔdikl], *adj.* unmethodisch, planlos.

unmindful [ʌn'maindful], *adj.* uneingedenk (*of*, *Gen.*), ohne Rücksicht (auf (*Acc.*)); ***be – of***, vergessen, nicht beachten, nicht achten auf (*Acc.*), sich nicht abhalten lassen durch.

unmistakable ['ʌnmis'teikəbl], *adj.* unmißverständlich, unverkennbar, deutlich.

unmitigated [ʌn'mitigeitid], *adj.* 1. ungemildert, ungeschwächt; 2. (*fig.*) unbedingt, durch und durch, völlig, ausgesprochen, Erz–.

unmixed ['ʌnmikst], *adj.* ungemischt (*also fig.*), nicht gemischt, unvermischt, (*fig.*) rein, ungetrübt.

unmodified [ʌn'mɔdifaid], *adj.* nicht (ab)geändert, unverändert.

unmolested ['ʌnmo'lestid], *adj.* unbelästigt, ungestört, (*pred. only*) in Frieden.

unmoor ['ʌn'muə], **1.** *v.t.* (von der Vertäuung) losmachen (*a ship*). **2.** *v.i.* die Anker lichten, abankern.

unmortgaged ['ʌn'mɔ:gidʒd], *adj.* unverpfändet; hypothekenfrei, nicht belastet.

unmounted [ʌn'mauntid], *adj.* unberitten (*troops*), nicht montiert (*gun*), nicht aufgezogen (*print*), nicht eingefaßt (*gem*).

unmoved [ʌn'mu:vd], *adj.* unbewegt, ungerührt, unerschüttert, unverändert, fest, standhaft, ruhig, gefaßt, gelassen. **unmoving,** *adj.* bewegungslos, regungslos.

unmurmuring [ʌn'mə:məriŋ], *adj.* ohne Murren, nicht murrend, klaglos.

unmusical [ʌn'mju:zikl], *adj.* unmusikalisch (*a p.*), unharmonisch, unmelodisch, mißtönend (*sounds*).

unmuzzle [ʌn'mʌzl], *v.t.* den Maulkorb abnehmen (*Dat.*), (*fig.*) freie Meinungsäußerung gewähren (*Dat.*).

unnameable [ʌn'neiməbl], *adj.* unnennbar, unsagbar, unbeschreiblich. **unnamed,** *adj.* 1. ungenannt, nicht (namentlich) erwähnt; 2. unbenannt, namenlos, ohne Namen.

unnatural [ʌn'nætʃərəl], *adj.* 1. unnatürlich, widernatürlich, naturwidrig; übernatürlich, außergewöhnlich, ungewöhnlich; 2. abscheulich, ungeheuerlich.

unnavigable [ʌn'nævigəbl], *adj.* nicht befahrbar, nicht schiffbar.

unnecessarily [ʌn'nesisərəli], *adv.* unnötigerweise. **unnecessary,** *adj.* nicht notwendig, unnötig, überflüssig.

unneeded [ʌn'ni:did], *adj.* nicht benötigt (*by*, von). **unneedful,** *adj.* unnötig, nicht erforderlich.

unneighbourly [ʌn'neibəli], *adj.* nicht nachbarlich, unfreundlich.

unnerve ['ʌn'nə:v], *v.t.* entnerven, erschüttern, entkräften, schwächen; entmutigen, mürbe machen, zermürben. **unnerving,** *adj.* erschütternd, niederschmetternd; entmutigend, zermürbend.

unnoted ['ʌn'noutid], *adj.* unbemerkt, unbeachtet, nicht geachtet *or* bedacht. **unnoticed** [–ist], *adj.* 1. *See* **unnoted**; 2. vernachlässigt.

unnumbered [ʌn'nʌmbəd], *adj.* 1. ungezählt, zahllos, unzählig; 2. unnumeriert (*seats etc.*), ohne Seitenzahl(en) (*as books*).

unobjectionable ['ʌnəb'dʒekʃənəbl], *adj.* untadelhaft, tadellos, einwandfrei, unanfechtbar.

unobliging ['ʌnə'blaidʒiŋ], *adj.* nicht hilfsbereit *or* zuvorkommend, ungefällig.

unobscured ['ʌnəb'skjuəd], *adj.* nicht verdeckt *or* verdunkelt (*by*, durch).

unobtainable ['ʌnəb'teinəbl], *adj.* unerreichbar, nicht erhältlich, nicht zu haben; (*Tele.*) ***the number is –***, der Teilnehmer meldet sich nicht.

unobtrusive ['ʌnəb'tru:siv], *adj.* (*of p.*) unaufdringlich, nicht zudringlich, zurückhaltend, bescheiden; (*of th.*) unauffällig. **unobtrusiveness,** *s.* die Zurückhaltung, Bescheidenheit, Unaufdringlichkeit; Unauffälligkeit.

unoccupied [ʌn'ɔkjupaid], *adj.* 1. nicht besetzt, unbesetzt (*seat*), leer(stehend), unbewohnt (*house*); 2. (*fig.*) unbeschäftigt, frei.

unoffending ['ʌnə'fendiŋ], *adj.* nicht anstößig; harmlos, unschädlich.

unofficial ['ʌnə'fiʃəl], *adj.* inoffiziell, nicht amtlich.

unopened [ʌn'oupənd], *adj.* ungeöffnet, verschlossen, (*letter*) unerbrochen.

unopposed ['ʌnə'pouzd], *adj.* unbehindert, unbeanstandet (*by*, durch); ***– by***, ohne Gegnerschaft *or* Widerstand *or* Einspruch seitens (*Gen.*).

unorganized [ʌn'ɔ:gənaizd], *adj.* unorganisch, unorganisiert, ohne Organisation *or* organischen Aufbau.

unoriginal ['ʌnə'ridʒinl], *adj.* nicht originell *or* original *or* ursprünglich; aus zweiter Hand, entlehnt.

unostentatious ['ʌnɔstin'teiʃəs], *adj.* nicht prunkend *or* bombastisch; nicht grell *or* schreiend *or* auffallend, unaufdringlich, dezent (*as colours*); unauffällig, anspruchslos, einfach, bescheiden.

unpack ['ʌn'pæk], *v.t.* auspacken.

unpaid ['ʌnpeid], *adj.* unbezahlt (*debt*), unbesoldet, ehrenamtlich (*a p.*), unfrankiert (*letter*), rückständig (*wages etc.*).

unpalatable [ʌn'pælətəbl], *adj.* nicht schmackhaft, fad(e) (*as food*), ungenießbar, unangenehm, widrig, widerwärtig.

unparalleled [ʌn'pærəleld], *adj.* unvergleichlich, beispiellos, einmalig.

unpeg ['ʌn'peg], *v.t.* 1. lospflöcken; 2. (*Comm.*) (*coll.*) nicht (fest)halten (*the market*), von Einschränkungen befreien, nicht mehr stützen (*currency*).

unperforated [ʌn'pə:fəreitid], *adj.* nicht perforiert (*stamps*).

For negatives with **un-** not listed see the simple word.

unperformed ['ʌnpə'fɔ:md], *adj.* nicht ausgeführt, unverrichtet, ungetan; (*Theat.*) nicht aufgeführt.
unperturbed ['ʌnpə'tə:bd], *adj.* nicht beunruhigt, unbeirrt, gelassen.
unpick ['ʌn'pik], *v.t.* auftrennen (*a seam*). **unpicked,** *adj.* 1. ungepflückt (*flowers etc.*); 2. unsortiert, nicht ausgelesen *or* ausgesucht.
unpin ['ʌn'pin], *v.t.* die Nadeln herausnehmen aus; losmachen, abmachen.
unpitying ['ʌn'pitiiŋ], *adj.* unbarmherzig, erbarmungslos, mitleid(s)los.
unplaced [ʌn'pleist], *adj.* 1. nicht untergebracht *or* angestellt, unversorgt, ohne Stellung; 2. (*Racing*) unplaciert.
unplait ['ʌn'plæt], *v.t.* aufflechten, glätten (*hair etc.*).
unplayable ['ʌn'pleiəbl], *adj.* 1. nicht spielbar (*music*), zum Spielen untauglich, unbespielbar (*pitch*); 2. nicht zu spielen(d) (*ball*).
unpleasant [ʌn'plezənt], *adj.* unangenehm, unerfreulich, mißfällig, widerlich, eklig, (*of a p.*) unfreundlich, unwirsch. **unpleasantness,** *s.* 1. Unannehmlichkeit, Widerlichkeit; 2. Mißhelligkeit, Unstimmigkeit, Reibung, das Mißverständnis.
unpolitical ['ʌnpə'litikl], *adj.* 1. unpolitisch, politisch unfähig *or* unklug; 2. an Politik uninteressiert.
unpolluted ['ʌnpə'l(j)u:tid], *adj.* nicht verseucht; (*fig.*) unverdorben, unbefleckt.
unposted [ʌn'poustid], *adj.* 1. nicht aufgegeben *or* zur Post gebracht; 2. nicht informiert.
unprecedented [ʌn'presidentid], *adj.* unerhört, beispiellos, noch nie dagewesen; (*Law*) ohne Präzedenzfall.
unprejudiced [ʌn'predʒədist], *adj.* vorurteilslos, vorurteilsfrei, unbefangen, unvoreingenommen, unparteiisch.
unpremeditated ['ʌnpri'mediteitid], *adj.* unüberlegt, unvorbereitet, unbeabsichtigt, nicht vorbedacht; improvisiert, aus dem Stegreif.
unprepared ['ʌnpri'pɛəd], *adj.* unvorbereitet; – *for,* nicht vorbereitet auf (*Acc.*), nicht gerüstet für.
unprepossessing ['ʌnpri:pə'zesiŋ], *adj.* nicht einnehmend *or* anziehend, reizlos.
unpresentable ['ʌnpri'zentəbl], *adj.* nicht präsentabel, nicht gesellschaftsfähig.
unpresuming ['ʌnpri'zju:miŋ], *adj.* bescheiden, anspruchslos.
unpresumptious ['ʌnpri'zʌmpʃəs], *adj.* nicht überheblich *or* anmaßend *or* arrogant.
unpretending ['ʌnpri'tendiŋ], *adj.* unauffällig, schlicht, anspruchslos. **unpretentious** [–'tenʃəs], *adj. See* **unpresuming.**
unpriced ['ʌn'praist], *adj.* ohne Preisangabe.
unprincipled [ʌn'prinsipəld], *adj.* ohne (feste) Grundsätze, charakterlos, haltlos, gewissenlos.
unprintable [ʌn'printəbl], *adj.* zur Veröffentlichung ungeeignet.
unprivileged [ʌn'privilidʒd], *adj.* nicht bevorrechtet *or* bevorrechtigt *or* privilegiert.
unproclaimed ['ʌnprə'kleimd], *adj.* nicht verkündet *or* bekanntgegeben.
unprocurable ['ʌnprə'kjuərəbl], *adj.* nicht erhältlich *or* zu haben(d) *or* zu beschaffen(d).
unproductive ['ʌnprə'dʌktiv], *adj.* unproduktiv, unfruchtbar, unergiebig; nicht einträglich *or* ertragreich, nichts eintragend. **unproductiveness,** *s.* die Unfruchtbarkeit, Unergiebigkeit, Unproduktivität.
unprofessional ['ʌnprə'feʃənl], *adj.* nicht standesgemäß *or* berufsmäßig; unfachmännisch, laienhaft; Laien–.
unprofitable [ʌn'prɔfitəbl], *adj.* 1. unrentabel, nicht einträglich *or* gewinnbringend; 2. (*fig.*) unvorteilhaft, nutzlos, unnütz, zwecklos. **unprofitableness,** *s.* 1. die Uneinträglichkeit; 2. Nutzlosigkeit, Zwecklosigkeit.
unprogressive ['ʌnprə'gresiv], *adj.* nicht fortschrittlich, rückständig, reaktionär. **unprogressiveness,** *s.* die Rückständigkeit, reaktionäre *or* rückschrittliche Einstellung.
unpromising [ʌn'prɔmisiŋ], *adj.* wenig (viel)versprechend, aussichtslos.
unprompted [ʌn'prɔmptid], *adj.* unbeeinflußt (*by,* von), aus eignem Antrieb, freiwillig, spontan.
unprotected ['ʌnprə'tektid], *adj.* ungeschützt, unbeschützt, ungedeckt, schutzlos.
unprotested ['ʌnprə'testid], *adj.* (*Comm.*) nicht protestiert (*bill*).
unprovided ['ʌnprə'vaidid], *adj.* nicht versorgt *or* ausgestaltet *or* versehen (*with,* mit); – *for,* nicht vorgesehen; *be left – for,* unversorgt *or* mittellos *or* ohne Mittel dastehen (*as family*).
unprovoked ['ʌnprə'voukt], *adj.* nicht herausgefordert *or* provoziert *or* veranlaßt, ohne Veranlassung *or* Grund.
unpunctuated [ʌn'pʌŋktjueitid], *adj.* ohne Interpunktion.
unpunished [ʌn'pʌniʃt], *adj.* ungestraft, unbestraft, straffrei; *go –,* straflos ausgehen.
unqualified [ʌn'kwɔlifaid], *adj.* 1. ungeeignet, unbefähigt; unqualifiziert, nicht approbiert *or* kompetent; 2. uneingeschränkt, unbedingt.
unquenchable [ʌn'kwentʃəbl], *adj.* 1. unlöschbar, unstillbar; 2. (*fig.*) unauslöschlich, unersättlich.
unquestionable [ʌn'kwestʃənəbl], *adj.* unzweifelhaft, unbestreitbar, unstreitig. **unquestionably,** *adv.* unstreitig, zweifellos. **unquestioned,** *adj.* unbestritten, unbezweifelt. **unquestioning,** *adj.* 1. blind, bedingungslos; 2. (*pred. only*) ohne zu fragen *or* zu zweifeln, ohne Neugier. **unquestioningly,** *adv.* ohne Zögern *or* zu fragen; bedingungslos.
unquiet ['ʌn'kwaiət], *adj.* (*fig.*) unruhig, ruhelos, turbulent.
unquote ['ʌn'kwout], *v.i.* Ende des Zitats, (ich) beende das Zitat.
unratified ['ʌn'rætifaid], *adj.* nicht ratifiziert.
unrationed ['ʌn'ræʃənd], *adj.* nicht rationiert.
unravel ['ʌn'rævl], **1.** *v.t.* ausfasern, auffasern; auftrennen (*knitting etc.*); (*fig.*) entwirren, enträtseln, (auf)lösen. **2.** *v.i.* sich auffasern *or* auflösen.
unread ['ʌn'red], *adj.* 1. ungelesen; 2. (*of a p.*) unbelesen, unbewandert (*in,* in (*Dat.*)). **unreadable** [ʌn'ri:dəbl], *adj.* 1. unlesbar, unleserlich, undeutlich (*handwriting*); 2. nicht lesbar *or* lesenswert (*book*).
unreadiness [ʌn'redinis], *s.* 1. fehlende Einsatzbereitschaft, das Nichtgerüstetsein; 2. die Unbereitwilligkeit. **unready,** *adj.* 1. nicht bereit (*for,* zu), nicht einsatzbereit, ungerüstet; 2. zaudernd, zögernd, unentschlossen.
unreal [ʌn'riəl], *adj.* unwirklich, wesenlos, nur eingebildet, phantastisch, ohne Substanz. **unreality** ['ʌnri'æliti], *s.* die Unwirklichkeit, Wesenlosigkeit, Substanzlosigkeit.
unrealizable ['ʌn'riəlaizəbl], *adj.* 1. nicht realisierbar *or* zu verwirklichen(d); 2. (*Comm.*) unrealisierbar, nicht verwertbar *or* verkäuflich. **unrealized,** *adj.* 1. nicht verwirklicht *or* erfüllt; 2. nicht begriffen *or* bedacht *or* vergegenwärtigt *or* erkannt (*by,* von).
unreason [ʌn'ri:zn], *s.* die Unvernunft. **unreasonable,** *adj.* unvernünftig, unsinnig; vernunftwidrig, unbillig, ungerechtfertigt; übertrieben, übermäßig, unmäßig, (*coll.*) unverschämt. **unreasonableness,** *s.* die Unsinnigkeit, Unbilligkeit, Unmäßigkeit, Unverschämtheit. **unreasoning,** *adj.* 1. vernunftlos, vernunftwidrig, unlogisch; 2. blind, panisch.
unreceipted ['ʌnri'si:tid], *adj.* unquittiert, ohne Quittung.

For negatives with **un-** not listed see the simple word.

unreceptive [ˈʌnriˈseptiv], *adj.* unempfänglich, nicht aufnahmefähig.
unreclaimed [ˈʌnriˈkleimd], *adj.* 1. nicht zurückgefordert; 2. nicht gebessert; 3. ungezähmt (*as a hawk*); 4. nicht kultiviert, unbebaut (*as land*).
unrecognizable [ʌnˈrekəgnaizəbl], *adj.* nicht wiederzuerkennen(d), unerkennbar. **unrecognized,** *adj.* nicht (an)erkannt.
unrecompensed [ʌnˈrekəmpenst], *adj.* unbelohnt, nicht entschädigt.
unreconciled [ʌnˈrekənsaild], *adj.* unversöhnt, nicht ausgesöhnt (*to*, mit).
unrecorded [ˈʌnriˈkɔːdid], *adj.* nicht aufgezeichnet *or* belegt *or* überliefert *or* (*Law*) eingetragen.
unrectified [ʌnˈrektifaid], *adj.* 1. nicht richtiggestellt, unberichtigt; 2. (*spirits*) nicht destilliert, ungereinigt.
unredeemed [ˈʌnriˈdiːmd], *adj.* 1. (*Theol.*) nicht erlöst; 2. nicht zurückgezahlt, ungetilgt (*debt*), nicht eingelöst (*promise*); 3. (*fig.*) nicht gemildert (*by*, durch); (*coll.*) Erz–.
unredressed [ˈʌnriˈdrest], *adj.* ungesühnt, nicht wiedergutgemacht.
unreel [ˈʌnˈriːl], **1.** *v.t.* abhaspeln, abspulen, abwickeln, abrollen. **2.** *v.i.* sich abwickeln *or* abspulen, ablaufen, abrollen.
unrefined [ˈʌnriˈfaind], *adj.* nicht raffiniert, ungereinigt, ungeläutert, Roh–, (*fig.*) unfein, ungebildet, ohne Lebensart.
unreflecting [ˈʌnriˈflektiŋ], *adj.* 1. (*Phys.*) nicht reflektierend; 2. (*fig.*) unüberlegt, gedankenlos.
unregarded [ˈʌnriˈgɑːdid], *adj.* unberücksichtigt, unbeachtet, vernachlässigt. **unregardful,** *adj.* ohne Rücksicht (*of*, auf (*Acc.*)), unachtsam, rücksichtslos; ***be* – *of*,** nicht beachten *or* berücksichtigen.
unregeneracy [ˈʌnriˈdʒenərəsi], *s.* die Sündhaftigkeit, Verderbtheit, Unverbesserlichkeit. **unregenerate** [–rət], *adj.* 1. sündhaft, sündig, verderbt, unverbesserlich; 2. (*Theol.*) nicht wiedergeboren.
unregistered [ʌnˈredʒistəd], *adj.* 1. nicht eingetragen *or* approbiert; 2. nicht eingeschrieben (*letter*).
unregulated [ʌnˈregjuleitid], *adj.* (*Tech.*) nicht geregelt; (*fig.*) ungeregelt, ungeordnet.
unrehearsed [ˈʌnriˈhəːst], *adj.* (*Theat.*) nicht einstudiert *or* geprobt; (*fig.*) überraschend, unvorhergesehen.
unrelated [ˈʌnriˈleitid], *adj.* 1. in keiner Beziehung stehend (*to*, mit), ohne Beziehung *or* Bezug (auf (*Acc.*)); 2. nicht verwandt; 3. nicht erzählt.
unrelaxed [ˈʌnriˈlækst], *adj.* nicht entspannt *or* ausgeruht. **unrelaxing,** *adj.* nicht nachlassend.
unrelenting [ˈʌnriˈlentiŋ], *adj.* unerbittlich, unnachgiebig, unbeugsam, hart, rigoros; (*fig.*) unvermindert, nicht nachlassend.
unrelieved [ˈʌnriliːvd], *adj.* unvermindert; nicht erleichtert *or* gelindert *or* gemildert (*by*, durch); ununterbrochen, nicht unterbrochen, ohne Abwechslung (*by*, von).
unremitting [ˈʌnriˈmitiŋ], *adj.* unablässig, unermüdlich, unaufhörlich, beharrlich, ausdauernd; (*coll.*) erbarmungslos.
unremunerative [ˈʌnriˈmjuːnərətiv], *adj.* nicht einträglich *or* lohnend, unrentabel, unwirtschaftlich.
unrenewed [ˈʌnriˈnjuːd], *adj.* nicht erneuert.
unrepair [ˈʌnriˈpɛə], *s.* die Schadhaftigkeit, Reparaturbedürftigkeit, Baufälligkeit, der Verfall.
unrepealed [ˈʌnriˈpiːld], *adj.* nicht widerrufen *or* aufgehoben.
unrepentant [ˈʌnriˈpentənt], *adj.* unbußfertig, verstockt, reuelos. **unrepented,** *adj.* unbereut, (*pred. only*) ohne Reue.
unrepining [ˈʌnriˈpainiŋ], *adj.* gelassen, zufrieden, nicht murrend *or* klagend; (*pred. only*) ohne Klage *or* Murren.
unrepresentative [ˈʌnrepriˈzentətiv], *adj.* nicht typisch (*of*, für). **unrepresented,** *adj.* nicht vertreten, ohne Vertreter.
unrequited [ˈʌnriˈkwaitid], *adj.* unerwidert (*love*), unbelohnt (*work*), unvergolten (*crime*).
unreserved [ˈʌnriˈzəːvd], *adj.* 1. nicht reserviert *or* im voraus bestellt (*seats*); 2. offen(herzig), freimütig; 3. vorbehaltlos, rückhaltlos, uneingeschränkt, völlig, voll. **unreservedly** [–idli], *adv.* rückhaltlos, ohne Einschränkung. **unreservedness** [–idnis], *s.* die Offenheit, Offenherzigkeit, Freimütigkeit.
unresisted [ˈʌnriˈzistid], *adj.* ohne Widerstand; ***be* –,** keinen Widerstand finden. **unresisting,** *adj.* widerstandlos, nachgiebig.
unresponsive [ˈʌnriˈspɔnsiv], *adj.* unempfänglich (*to*, für), teilnahm(s)los (gegen), nicht reagierend *or* ansprechend (auf (*Acc.*)).
unrest [ˈʌnˈrest], *s.* 1. die Unruhe, Ruhelosigkeit; 2. (*Pol.*) Unruhen (*pl.*), der Aufruhr. **unrestful,** *adj.* rastlos, ruhelos, unruhig. **unresting,** *adj.* unermüdlich, unaufhörlich.
unrestrained [ˈʌnriˈstreind], *adj.* 1. ungehemmt, unbehindert, uneingeschränkt; 2. zügellos, hemmungslos, unbeherrscht. **unrestraint,** *s.* 1. die Ungehemmtheit, Ungebundenheit; 2. Zügellosigkeit, Hemmungslosigkeit, Ungezwungenheit, Zwanglosigkeit.
unrestricted [ˈʌnriˈstriktid], *adj.* unbeschränkt, uneingeschränkt, schrankenlos.
unreturned [ˈʌnriˈtəːnd], *adj.* 1. nicht zurückgegeben; 2. unerwidert; 3. (*Parl.*) nicht gewählt.
unrevealed [ˈʌnriˈviːld], *adj.* nicht enthüllt *or* entdeckt, nicht offenbar.
unrevised [ˈʌnriˈvaizd], *adj.* nicht revidiert *or* durchgesehen.
unrhymed [ʌnˈraimd], *adj.* ungereimt, reimlos.
unrighteous [ʌnˈraitʃəs], *adj.* (*Theol.*) ungerecht, sündhaft, sündig, gottlos. **unrighteousness,** *s.* die Ungerechtigkeit, Gottlosigkeit.
unrip [ˈʌnˈrip], *v.t.* auftrennen, aufreißen.
unrivalled [ʌnˈraivəld], *adj.* ohne Nebenbuhler, ohnegleichen; konkurrenzlos, unvergleichlich, unerreicht, beispiellos.
unroadworthy [ˈʌnˈroudwəːði], *adj.* verkehrsuntüchtig.
unroll [ʌnˈroul], **1.** *v.t.* 1. aufrollen, entrollen, abrollen; 2. (*fig.*) darlegen, entwickeln, entfalten, ausbreiten. **2.** *v.i.* 1. sich auseinanderrollen *or* aufrollen; 2. (*fig.*) sich entfalten *or* ausbreiten.
unromantic [ˈʌnroˈmæntik], *adj.* unromantisch, prosaisch.
unround [ˈʌnˈraund], *v.t.* (*Phonet.*) entrunden.
unruffled [ʌnˈrʌfəld], *adj.* 1. ungekräuselt, glatt; 2. (*fig.*) ruhig, unbewegt, gelassen.
unruliness [ʌnˈruːlinis], *s.* die Unbändigkeit, Widerspenstigkeit, Aufsässigkeit; Wildheit, Ausgelassenheit. **unruly,** *adj.* unfolgsam, aufsässig, widerspenstig, störrisch; unbändig, ausgelassen, wild.
unsaddle [ʌnˈsædl], *v.t.* 1. absatteln (*horse*); 2. aus dem Sattel heben *or* werfen (*rider*).
unsafe [ʌnˈseif], *adj.* unsicher, gefährlich. **unsafeness,** *s.* die Unsicherheit, Gefährlichkeit.
unsalaried [ʌnˈsælərid], *adj.* unbesoldet, ehrenamtlich.
unsanctioned [ʌnˈsæŋkʃənd], *adj.* unbestätigt, nicht bekräftigt.
unsatisfied [ʌnˈsætisfaid], *adj.* unzufrieden, unbefriedigt, nicht zufriedengestellt; (*Comm.*) nicht befriedigt.
unsavouriness [ʌnˈseivərinis], *s.* 1. die Unschmackhaftigkeit; 2. Widerlichkeit, Anstößigkeit. **unsavoury,** *adj.* 1. unschmackhaft; 2. widerlich, anstößig.

For negatives with **un-** not listed see the simple word.

unsay ['ʌn'sei], *irr.v.t.* zurücknehmen, widerrufen, sich distanzieren von.
unscathed [ʌn'skeiðd], *adj.* unbeschädigt, unversehrt.
unscramble ['ʌn'skræmbl], *v.t.* dechiffrieren, entschlüsseln (*code*).
unscreened [ʌn'skri:nd], *adj.* 1. nicht abgeschirmt, ungeschützt; (*Elec., Rad.*) ungeschirmt; 2. (*Tech.*) ungesiebt; 3. (*Pol.*) nicht überprüft.
unscrew [ʌn'skru:], **1.** *v.t.* aufschrauben, abschrauben, losschrauben. **2.** *v.i.* sich abschrauben *or* herausschrauben (lassen).
unscriptural [ʌn'skriptʃərəl], *adj.* unbiblisch, schriftwidrig.
unscrupulous [ʌn'skru:pjuləs], *adj.* skrupellos, gewissenlos, bedenkenlos. **unscrupulously,** *adv.* ohne Skrupel *or* Bedenken. **unscrupulousness,** *s.* die Skrupellosigkeit, Gewissenlosigkeit.
unseal [ʌn'si:l], *v.t.* entsiegeln, das Siegel abnehmen; (*fig.*) öffnen (*s.o.'s lips*), enthüllen (*a mystery*).
unseasoned [ʌn'si:zənd], *adj.* 1. nicht abgelagert *or* ausgetrocknet (*as wood*); 2. (*fig.*) nicht gewöhnt (*to*, an (*Acc.*)), nicht abgehärtet; 3. (*Cul.*) ungewürzt.
unseat ['ʌn'si:t], *v.t.* aus dem Sattel heben *or* werfen, abwerfen (*a rider*); das Mandat entziehen (*Dat.*), stürzen, absetzen (*politician*).
unseaworthiness ['ʌn'si:wə:ðinis], *s.* die Seeuntüchtigkeit. **unseaworthy,** *adj.* seeuntüchtig, nicht seetüchtig.
unsectarian ['ʌnsek'tɛəriən], *adj.* nicht sektiererisch, frei von Sektiererei.
unsecured ['ʌnsi'kjuəd], *adj.* 1. ungesichert, unbefestigt; 2. (*Comm.*) nicht sichergestellt *or* abgesichert.
unseeing ['ʌn'si:iŋ], *adj.* ***with – eye,*** mit leerem Blick. **unseen, 1.** *adj.* 1. ungesehen, unbemerkt, nicht wahrgenommen; (*Mil.*) uneingesehen, tot (*ground*); unsichtbar; 2. unvorbereitet (*translation*). **2.** *s.* 1. das Unsichtbare; 2. die Klausur(arbeit).
unselfish [ʌn'selfiʃ], *adj.* uneigennützig, selbstlos, altruistisch. **unselfishness,** *s.* die Uneigennützigkeit, Selbstlosigkeit.
unsensational ['ʌnsen'seiʃənl], *adj.* nicht sensationell *or* aufregend.
unsentimental ['ʌnsenti'mentl], *adj.* unsentimental, frei von Sentimentalität.
unsettle [ʌn'setl], *v.t.* aus der Lage bringen; (*fig.*) verwirren, in Verwirrung bringen, durcheinanderbringen; aus dem (gewohnten) Gleis werfen, aus den Angeln heben, beunruhigen, aufregen; ins Wanken bringen, erschüttern (*beliefs*). **unsettled** [–təld], *adj.* 1. nicht gefestigt, unsicher (*conditions*), nicht festgesetzt, unbestimmt, ungewiß, in der Schwebe, unentschieden (*decisions*), unentschlossen, wankelmütig, unstet, schwankend (*a p.*), unbeständig, veränderlich (*weather*); unruhig, bewegt (*times*); 2. unerledigt, unbezahlt, unbeglichen (*an account*); 3. unbesiedelt (*territory*).
unsew ['ʌn'sou], *irr.v.t.* auftrennen (*a seam*).
unsex ['ʌn'seks], *v.t.* der Eigenschaften als Frau berauben; (*coll.*) – ***o.s.,*** sich emanzipieren (*of women*).
unshackle [ʌn'ʃækl], *v.t.* die Fesseln abnehmen (*Dat.*), (*Naut.*) ausschäkeln; (*fig.*) entfesseln, befreien. **unshackled,** *adj.* (*fig.*) nicht gebunden *or* gehemmt, unbehindert.
unshaded [ʌn'ʃeidid], *adj.* nicht beschattet, schattenlos, unverdunkelt.
unshakable [ʌn'ʃeikəbl], *adj.* (*fig.*) unerschütterlich. **unshaken,** *adj.* (*fig.*) unerschüttert, fest, beharrlich, standhaft.
unshaped ['ʌn'ʃeipt], *adj.* formlos, gestaltlos, ungeformt. **unshapely,** *adj.* ungestalt, unförmig, mißgestaltet.
unsheathe [ʌn'ʃi:θ], *v.t.* aus der Scheide ziehen (*sword*), herausstrecken (*claws*); (*fig.*) – ***the sword,*** den Krieg erklären *or* beginnen.
unsheltered [ʌn'ʃeltəd], *adj.* ungeschützt, schutzlos, obdachlos.
unship [ʌn'ʃip], *v.t.* ausschiffen (*passengers*), ausladen, löschen (*cargo*), herausheben, abbauen, abtakeln (*mast*), aushängen (*oars*).
unshod ['ʌn'ʃɔd], *adj.* unbeschuht, barfuß; unbeschlagen (*horse*).
unshrinkable [ʌn'ʃriŋkəbl], *adj.* nicht einlaufend. **unshrinking,** *adj.* nicht zurückweichend *or* nachgebend; furchtlos, unverzagt.
unsighted [ʌn'saitid], *adj.* (*esp. Naut.*) (noch) nicht gesichtet *or* in Sicht. **unsightliness** [ʌn'saitlinis], *s.* die Unansehnlichkeit, Häßlichkeit. **unsightly,** *adj.* unansehnlich, häßlich.
unsigned [ʌn'saind], *adj.* nicht unterzeichnet.
unsinkable [ʌn'siŋkəbl], *adj.* unversenkbar.
unskimmed ['ʌn'skimd], *adj.* nicht entrahmt; – ***milk,*** die Vollmilch.
unsmiling ['ʌn'smailiŋ], *adj.* ernst.
unsmoked ['ʌn'smoukt], *adj.* 1. ungeräuchert (*bacon*); 2. nicht (zu Ende) geraucht (*cigarette*).
unsociability ['ʌnsouʃə'biliti], *s.* die Ungeselligkeit, Reserviertheit, Zurückgezogenheit. **unsociable** [–'souʃəbl], *adj.* ungesellig, reserviert, zurückgezogen, nicht umgänglich (*a p.*), ungastlich, unwirtlich (*surroundings*). **unsociableness,** *s. See* **unsociability. unsocial** [–'souʃəl], *adj.* unsozial, asozial, gesellschaftsfeindlich.
unsold ['ʌn'sould], *adj.* unverkauft; ***subject to being*** –, Zwischenverkauf vorbehalten.
unsolder [ʌn'souldə], *v.t.* ablöten.
unsolicited ['ʌnsə'lisitid], *adj.* 1. unverlangt, unaufgefordert, ungebeten; 2. nicht begehrt, freiwillig.
unsophisticated ['ʌnsə'fistikeitid], *adj.* naiv, natürlich, einfach, ungekünstelt, arglos, unverfälscht, lauter, echt, rein, unverdorben.
unsought ['ʌn'sɔ:t], *adj.* (*also coll.* *–-for*) nicht erstrebt *or* gesucht, ungebeten, unvermutet.
unsound ['ʌn'saund], *adj.* 1. ungesund (*also fig.*); – ***of*** or ***of – mind,*** geisteskrank, geistesgestört, unzurechnungsfähig; 2. (*as fruit*) angegangen, verdorben, verfault, wurmstichig; (*as a tree*) morsch, astfaul; 3. (*fig.*) nicht stichhaltig, unzuverlässig, anfechtbar; – ***argument,*** unbegründeter *or* nicht stichhaltiger Beweisgrund; (*Theol.*) – ***doctrine,*** die Irrlehre; 4. – ***ice,*** unzuverlässiges *or* unsicheres *or* brüchiges Eis. **unsoundness,** *s.* 1. die Ungesundheit; – ***of mind,*** die Unzurechnungsfähigkeit; 2. die Verderbtheit, Verdorbenheit; 3. Unrichtigkeit, Anfechtbarkeit, Fehlerhaftigkeit, Unzuverlässigkeit.
unsparing [ʌn'spɛəriŋ], *adj.* 1. schonungslos (***to, with,*** gegen); 2. freigebig, verschwenderisch (***in, of,*** mit); ***be – in,*** nicht kargen *or* zurückhalten mit; ***be – in one's efforts,*** keine Mühe scheuen.
unspeakable [ʌn'spi:kəbl], *adj.* 1. unsagbar, unbeschreiblich, unaussprechlich, unsäglich; 2. (*fig.*) entsetzlich, scheußlich, greulich.
unspecialized ['ʌn'speʃəlaizd], *adj.* nicht spezialisiert.
unspecified ['ʌn'spesifaid], *adj.* nicht besonders *or* einzeln angegeben *or* vorgeschrieben, nicht spezifiziert.
unspent ['ʌn'spent], *adj.* nicht verbraucht *or* verausgabt *or* ausgegeben, unerschöpft, unverbraucht.
unspiritual [ʌn'spiritjuəl], *adj.* geistlos, ungeistig.
unspoiled [ʌn'spɔild], **unspoilt,** *adj.* 1. unverdorben, unbeschädigt; 2. (*as a child*) nicht verzogen.
unspoken [ʌn'spoukən], *adj.* ungesagt, nicht geäußert, un(aus)gesprochen; – ***of,*** unerwähnt; – ***to,*** unangeredet, unangesprochen.
unsporting [ʌn'spɔ:tiŋ], **unsportsmanlike,** *adj.* 1. unsportlich, unfair, unritterlich; 2. nicht sportlerisch *or* sportmäßig; (*Hunt.*) unweidmännisch.

For negatives with **un-** not listed see the simple word.

unspotted [ʌn'spɔtid], *adj.* 1. fleckenlos; (*fig.*) unbefleckt, makellos; 2. (*coll.*) unentdeckt.
unstable [ʌn'steibl], *adj.* 1. nicht fest, unsicher, schwankend, labil (*also fig.*); 2. (*Chem.*) unbeständig (*also fig.*), instabil; 3. (*fig.*) unstet.
unstained [ʌn'steind], *adj.* ungefärbt, ungebeizt; *see also* **unspotted,** 1.
unsteadfast [ʌn'stedfɑ:st], *adj.* nicht standhaft, wankelmütig.
unsteadiness [ʌn'stedinis], *s.* 1. das Schwanken, die Unsicherheit, Unfestigkeit; 2. Veränderlichkeit, Unregelmäßigkeit. **unsteady,** *adj.* 1. unsicher, wack(e)lig (*on*, auf (*Dat.*)); 2. ungleichmäßig, veränderlich, unregelmäßig; 3. (*fig.*) unstet, unbeständig, schwankend, unzuverlässig (*in*, in (*Dat.*)).
unstep ['ʌn'step], *v.t.* ausnehmen (*mast etc.*).
unstinted [ʌn'stintid], *adj.* uneingeschränkt, unbegrenzt, unbeschränkt. **unstinting,** *adj.* nicht geizend *or* kargend, freigebig, reichlich, großzügig.
unstitch ['ʌn'stitʃ], *v.t.* auftrennen (*sewing*); ***come -ed,*** aufgehen.
unstrained [ʌn'streind], *adj.* 1. nicht angestrengt *or* angespannt; 2. unfiltriert, ungefiltert; 3. (*fig.*) ungezwungen, mühelos, zwanglos, natürlich.
unstrap ['ʌn'stræp], *v.t.* losschnallen, aufschnallen, abschnallen.
unstressed ['ʌn'strest], *adj.* unbetont, tonlos.
unstrung ['ʌn'strʌŋ], *adj.* 1. ungespannt (*bow*), saitenlos (*musical instrument*), abgereiht (*pearls*); 2. (*fig.*) abgespannt, überanstrengt, nervös.
unstudied [ʌn'stʌdid], *adj.* (*fig.*) ungekünstelt, zwanglos, ungezwungen, natürlich.
unsubdued [ʌnsəb'dju:d], *adj.* unbesiegt, unbezwungen, nicht unterjocht *or* unterworfen.
unsubmissive ['ʌnsəb'misiv], *adj.* nicht unterwürfig, widerspenstig.
unsubstantial ['ʌnsəb'stænʃəl], *adj.* 1. wesenlos, substanzlos, nicht stofflich, unkörperlich; 2. gehaltlos (*a meal etc.*); 3. (*fig.*) unwirklich, unwesentlich, inhalt(s)los, unbegründet, haltlos.
unsuccessful ['ʌnsək'sesful], *adj.* erfolglos, ohne Erfolg, fruchtlos, Fehl-; durchgefallen (*in an examination*); zurückgewiesen (*candidate*). **unsuccessfulness,** *s.* die Erfolglosigkeit, das Mißlingen.
unsullied [ʌn'sʌlid], *adj.* (*usu. fig.*) unbefleckt, makellos.
unsung ['ʌn'sʌŋ], *adj.* 1. ungesungen; 2. (*fig.*) unbesungen, nicht besungen.
unsupported ['ʌnsə'pɔ:tid], *adj.* 1. ungestützt; 2. (*fig.*) nicht unterstützt *or* bekräftigt, unbestätigt.
unsure [ʌn'ʃuə], *adj.* ungewiß, unsicher, zweifelhaft, schwankend.
unsuspected ['ʌnsəs'pektid], *adj.* 1. nicht verdächtigt, unverdächtig; 2. ungeahnt, nicht vermutet. **unsuspecting,** *adj.* 1. arglos, nicht argwöhnisch *or* mißtrauisch; 2. ahnungslos, nichtsahnend. **unsuspectingly,** *adv.* unvermutet. **unsuspicious** [-'piʃəs], *adj.* 1. unverdächtig, harmlos; 2. ohne Mißtrauen, nicht mißtrauisch, arglos.
unswerving [ʌn'swə:viŋ], *adj.* nicht wankend, fest, standhaft, unentwegt, unerschütterlich, unwandelbar.
unsympathetic ['ʌnsimpə'θetik], *adj.* 1. teilnahm(s)los, nicht mitempfindend, ohne Mitgefühl (*of a p.*); 2. unsympathisch.
unsystematic ['ʌnsisti'mætik], *adj.* unsystematisch, ungeordnet, planlos.
untamable [ʌn'teiməbl], *adj.* unbezähmbar, nicht zu bändigen(d), unbezwingbar.
untangle [ʌn'tæŋgl], *v.t.* entwirren, (auf)lösen.
untarnished [ʌn'tɑ:niʃt], *adj.* ungetrübt; (*fig.*) unbefleckt, makellos.
untaught [ʌn'tɔ:t], *adj.* 1. ungebildet, unwissend, nicht unterrichtet *or* unterwiesen (*of a p.*); 2. nicht beigebracht (*of th.*).
untaxed [ʌn'tækst], *adj.* unbesteuert, steuerfrei.
unteachable [ʌn'ti:tʃəbl], *adj.* 1. unbelehrbar, unlehrig (*a p.*); 2. nicht lehrbar *or* beizubringen(d) (*a th.*).
untempered [ʌn'tempəd], *adj.* 1. (*Tech.*) ungehärtet; 2. (*fig.*) nicht gemildert *or* gemäßigt (***by, with***, durch), unerbittlich.
untempted [ʌn'temptid], *adj.* nicht in Versuchung geführt.
untended [ʌn'tendid], *adj.* 1. unbehütet, unbewacht, unbeaufsichtigt; 2. ungepflegt, vernachlässigt.
untested [ʌn'testid], *adj.* ungeprüft, nicht überprüft; nicht erprobt *or* ausprobiert.
unthinking [ʌn'θiŋkiŋ], *adj.* 1. gedankenlos; 2. achtlos, unbesonnen.
unthought [ʌn'θɔ:t], *adj.* ungedacht; – ***of,*** unvermutet, unerwartet.
unthread [ʌn'θred], *v.t.* ausfädeln (*a needle*); (*fig.*) auflösen, entwirren.
unthrifty [ʌn'θrifti], *adj.* unsparsam, unwirtschaftlich, nicht haushälterisch, verschwenderisch.
unthrone [ʌn'θroun], *v.t.* entthronen.
untidiness [ʌn'taidinis], *s.* die Unordnung (*of th.*), Unordentlichkeit (*a p.*). **untidy,** *adj.* unordentlich (*th. or p.*), schlampig (*a p.*).
untie [ʌn'tai], **1.** *v.t.* aufbinden, losbinden, aufmachen, aufknoten; (*fig.*) lösen. **2.** *v.i.* sich (auf)lösen.
until [ən'til], **1.** *prep.* bis (zu *or* auf (*Acc.*)); ***not –,*** erst. **2.** *conj.* bis; ***not –,*** erst als, erst wenn, nicht eher als.
untimeliness [ʌn'taimlinis], *s.* die Unzeit(igkeit), Frühzeitigkeit. **untimely,** *adj.* 1. unzeitig; frühzeitig, vorzeitig, verfrüht; 2. unpassend, ungünstig, ungelegen. **untimeous** [-məs], *adj.* (*Scots*) *see* **untimely.**
untitled ['ʌn'taitld], *adj.* ohne Adelsrang *or* Titel.
unto ['ʌntu(:)], *prep.* (*obs. or Poet.*) *see* **to.**
untold [ʌn'tould], *adj.* 1. nicht berichtet *or* erzählt; 2. (*fig.*) ungezählt, unzählig, zahllos (*before pl.*); unsäglich, unsagbar, unausprechlich, unermeßlich (*before sing.*).
untouchable [ʌn'tʌtʃəbl], **1.** *adj.* unberührbar, unantastbar, unnahbar, unerreichbar. **2.** *s.* Unberührbare(r). **untouched,** *adj.* 1. unberührt, unangetastet; nicht gekostet (*food*); 2. nicht zurechtgemacht; 3. (*Phot.*) unretuschiert; 4. (*fig.*) ungerührt (***by***, durch), nicht beeinflußt *or* beeindruckt (von).
untoward [ʌn'touwəd, -'tɔ:d], *adj.* widrig, widerwärtig, ungünstig; widerspenstig, widerhaarig, eigensinnig; steif, starr, schwer zu bearbeiten(d) *or* zu behandeln(d). **untowardness,** *s.* 1. die Widerwärtigkeit, Widerspenstigkeit, Ungunst; 2. Widerspenstigkeit, der Eigensinn.
untraceable [ʌn'treisəbl], *adj.* 1. unaufspürbar; 2. nicht zurückführbar (***to***, auf (*Acc.*)).
untravelled [ʌn'trævəld], *adj.* ungereist (*as a p.*); unbereist (*as a land*).
untrimmed ['ʌntrimd], *adj.* 1. ungeschmückt, ohne Besatz (*as dress*); 2. unbeschnitten (*as hair etc.*).
untrue ['ʌn'tru:], *adj.* 1. unwahr, falsch, irrig; 2. treulos, untreu (***to***, *Dat.*); 3. nicht in Übereinstimmung (mit), abweichend (von). **untruly,** *adv.* irrtümlich(erweise), fälschlich(erweise), falsch.
untrustworthiness [ʌn'trʌstwə:ðinis], *s.* die Unzuverlässigkeit. **untrustworthy,** *adj.* nicht vertrauenswürdig, unzuverlässig.
untruth ['ʌn'tru:θ], *s.* 1. die Unwahrheit, Falschheit; 2. Lüge, Unaufrichtigkeit. **untruthful,** *adj.* 1. falsch, irrig (*of a th.*); 2. unwahr (*of a p. or th.*), lügenhaft, unaufrichtig (*of a p.*). **untruthfulness,** *s.* 1. die Lügenhaftigkeit, Unaufrichtigkeit; 2. Unwahrheit, Falschheit.
unturned [ʌn'tə:nd], *adj.* ungewendet, nicht umgewendet; ***leave no stone –,*** nichts unversucht lassen.

For negatives with **un-** not listed see the simple word.

untutored [ʌn'tju:təd], *adj.* ungebildet, ungeschult, ungelehrt; einfach, natürlich, naturhaft, roh (*as instincts*).

untwine [ʌn'twain], **untwist** [–'twist], **1.** *v.t.* entflechten, aufflechten. **2.** *v.i.* sich aufdrehen, aufgehen.

unused, *adj.* 1. [ʌn'ju:zd], unbenutzt, ungebraucht, brachliegend; 2. [–'ju:st], nicht gewöhnt (*to*, an (*Acc.*)), nicht gewohnt (***to doing***, zu tun). **unusual** [–'ju:ʒuəl], *adj.* ungewöhnlich, ungewohnt, außergewöhnlich, ungebräuchlich, selten. **unusualness,** *s.* die Außergewöhnlichkeit, Ungewöhnlichkeit, Seltenheit.

unutterable [ʌn'ʌtərəbl], *adj.* unaussprechlich, unbeschreibbar, unsagbar; ausgefeimt (*scoundrel etc.*).

unvalued [ʌn'vælju:d], *adj.* nicht geschätzt *or* geachtet, untaxiert, nicht abgeschätzt; – ***shares,*** Quotenaktien, Aktien ohne Nennwert.

unvaried [ʌn'vɛərid], *adj.* unverändert, einförmig.

unvarnished [ʌn'vɑ:niʃt], *adj.* 1. unlackiert, ungefirnißt; unpoliert (*nails*); 2. (*fig.*) ungeschminkt, ungeschmückt, schmucklos, schlicht.

unvarying, *adj.* unveränderlich, unwandelbar, andauernd, eintönig.

unveil [ʌn'veil], **1.** *v.t.* entschleiern (*face*), enthüllen (*statue etc., also fig.*), (*fig.*) aufdecken. **2.** *v.i.* den Schleier fallen lassen, sich entschleiern *or* enthüllen.

unversed [ʌn'və:st], *adj.* (*fig.*) unerfahren, unbewandert (*in*, in (*Dat.*)).

unvisited [ʌn'visitid], *adj.* nicht besucht; (*fig.*) nicht aufgesucht *or* heimgesucht.

unvoiced [ʌn'vɔist], *adj.* 1. unausgesprochen, nicht geäußert; 2. (*Phonet.*) stimmlos.

unwalled [ʌn'wɔ:ld], *adj.* unbefestigt, nicht ummauert, ohne Mauer.

unwanted [ʌn'wɔntid], *adj.* nicht begehrt, ungewünscht, unerwünscht.

unwarranted [ʌn'wɔrəntid], *adj.* ungerechtfertigt, unbefugt.

unwashed [ʌn'wɔʃt], *adj.* ungewaschen, unbespült (*by sea etc.*); (*coll.*) ***the great –***, der Pöbel.

unwavering [ʌn'weivəriŋ], *adj.* nicht wankend, unerschütterlich, standhaft, beharrlich, fest.

unweaned [ʌn'wi:nd], *adj.* nicht entwöhnt.

unwearable [ʌn'wɛərəbl], *adj.* nicht zu tragen(d).

unwearied [ʌn'wiərid], *adj.* nicht ermüdet, unermüdlich. **unwearying,** *adj.* unermüdlich, nicht ermüdend.

unwed(ded) [ʌn'wed(id)], *adj.* unverheiratet, unvermählt, ledig.

unwell [ʌn'wel], *pred. adj.* unwohl, nicht wohl, unpäßlich, übel; ***I am –,*** ich fühle mich nicht wohl, mir ist übel.

unwholesome [ʌn'houlsəm], *adj.* ungesund; (gesundheits)schädlich; (*fig.*) verderbt, verderblich. **unwholesomeness,** *s.* die Ungesundheit, Schädlichkeit; (*fig.*) Verderbtheit, Verderblichkeit.

unwieldiness [ʌn'wi:ldinis], *s.* 1. die Schwerfälligkeit, Unbeholfenheit; 2. Unhandlichkeit. **unwieldy,** *adj.* 1. schwerfällig, unbeholfen (*of a p.*); 2. unhandlich, schwer zu handhaben(d), massig, sperrig (*of th.*).

unwilling [ʌn'wiliŋ], *adj.* nicht gewillt, unwillig, widerwillig, abgeneigt; ***be –,*** nicht wollen, abgeneigt sein, keine Lust haben; ***I am – to admit,*** ich gebe ungern zu; ***I am – for my name to appear,*** ich will nicht *or* bin nicht gewillt, daß mein Name erscheint; ***willing or –,*** man mag wollen oder nicht. **unwillingly,** *adv.* ungern, widerwillig, wider Willen. **unwillingness,** *s.* die Abneigung, der Widerwille.

unwind [ʌn'waind], **1.** *irr.v.t.* loswickeln, abwickeln, abwinden, abrollen, abspulen, abhaspeln. **2.** *irr.v.i.* sich abwickeln *or* loswickeln *or* abwinden.

unwise [ʌn'waiz], *adj.* unklug, unvernünftig, töricht.

unwished [ʌn'wiʃt], *adj.* ungewünscht; ***--for,*** unerwünscht.

unwitnessed [ʌn'witnist], *adj.* (*Law*) ohne Zeugenunterschrift.

unwitting [ʌn'witiŋ], *adj.* unwissentlich, unbewußt, unbeabsichtigt, unabsichtlich; ***– of,*** unbewußt (*Gen.*), nichtsahnend (*Acc.*).

unwonted [ʌn'wountid], *adj.* (*Poet.*) 1. nicht gewohnt (***to***, an (*Acc.*)); 2. selten, ungewöhnlich.

unworkable [ʌn'wə:kəbl], *adj.* 1. unausführbar, undurchführbar (*plan*); 2. nicht zu handhaben(d) *or* behandeln(d) *or* bearbeiten(d) (*material*), nicht betriebsfähig *or* bauwürdig. **unworked,** *adj.* unbearbeitet (*ground*), (*Min.*) unverritzt; ***– coal,*** anstehende Kohle. **unworkmanlike,** *adj.* unfachmännisch, unsauber *or* nicht fachgemäß ausgeführt, stümperhaft.

unworldliness [ʌn'wə:ldlinis], *s.* 1. die Unweltlichkeit, Weltfremdheit; Geistigkeit, nicht weltliche Gesinnung; 2. die Uneigennützigkeit. **unworldly,** *adj.* 1. unweltlich, nicht weltlich; weltfremd; 2. uneigennützig.

unworn [ʌn'wɔ:n], *adj.* 1. ungetragen (*clothes*); 2. nicht abgenutzt *or* abgetragen.

unworthy [ʌn'wə:ði], *adj.* 1. unwürdig, verabscheuungswürdig, verächtlich (*of a p.*); 2. unverdient (*treatment*); 3. (*pred.*) ***be – of,*** unwürdig sein (*Gen.*), nicht verdienen, nicht wert sein.

unwound [ʌn'waund], *adj.* abgewickelt, losgewunden; abgelaufen, nicht aufgezogen (*as a watch*); ***come –,*** sich loswinden.

unwrap [ʌn'ræp], *v.t.* aufmachen, auswickeln, auspacken; ***come unwrapped,*** sich aufwickeln, aufgehen.

unwrinkled [ʌn'riŋkəld], *adj.* nicht gerunzelt, faltenlos.

unwritten [ʌn'ritn], *adj.* ungeschrieben, nicht schriftlich niedergelegt; ***– agreement,*** mündliche Abmachung; ***– law,*** das Gewohnheitsrecht.

unwrought [ʌn'rɔ:t], *adj.* unbearbeitet, unverarbeitet, roh, Roh–.

unyielding [ʌn'ji:ldiŋ], *adj.* unbiegsam, fest, steif; (*fig.*) unnachgiebig, unbeugsam, starrsinnig, hart(näckig); unzugänglich (***to***, für).

unyoke [ʌn'jouk], *v.t.* losspannen, ausspannen, (*fig.*) lösen, lostrennen.

unzip [ʌn'zip], *v.t.* (*coll.*) den Reißverschluß aufmachen von.

up [ʌp], **1.** *adv.* auf, hoch, oben; aufrecht; in die *or* der Höhe, empor, aufwärts; herauf, hinauf; auf (*Acc.*) . . . zu, her(an), hin(an); auf(gestanden); aufgegangen (*sun, plants etc.*); (*coll.*) abgelaufen, vorüber, vorbei, aus (*time*); ***– and –,*** höher und höher, immer höher; ***– and down,*** auf und ab, hin und her; ***– there,*** dort oben.
(a) (*before preps.*) ***be – against,*** stehen vor (*Dat.*), gegenüberstehen (*Dat.*); (*coll.*) ***be – against it,*** in Not *or* Schwierigkeiten sein, in der Klemme sein *or* sitzen; ***run – against,*** anrennen gegen; (*fig.*) stoßen auf (*Acc.*); ***be*** (*or sl. of p. only* ***be had***) ***– before the court,*** vorgeladen *or* verhört (*of a p.*) *or* verhandelt (*of a case*) werden; ***– from the country,*** vom Lande; ***from his youth –,*** seit seiner Jugend, von Jugend auf; ***be – for discussion,*** zur Diskussion stehen, erörtert werden; ***be – for election,*** auf der Wahlliste stehen; ***be – for examination,*** sich einer Prüfung unterziehen; ***be – for sale,*** zum Kauf stehen; ***be – for trial,*** vor Gericht stehen (*a p.*), verhandelt werden (*a case*); (*coll.*) ***be – in,*** bewandert sein in (*Dat.*); (*coll.*) ***be well – in,*** beherrschen; ***be – in arms,*** unter Waffen stehen, (*coll.*) sich auf die Hinterbeine stellen; ***– into the sky,*** hinauf in den Himmel; (*coll.*) ***be – on,*** höher *or* mehr sein als; ***– till,*** bis; ***– to*** (*see also* **(c)** *below*), hinauf zu, bis zu *or* an (*Acc.*); ***– to town,*** nach London; ***– to date,*** bis heute; (*coll.*) ***– to par*** or ***scratch,*** auf der Höhe; ***– to standard,*** vollwertig; ***– to strength,*** in voller Stärke; ***come – to,*** reichen bis an (*Acc.*), entsprechen (*Dat.*); ***count – to 10,***

For negatives with **un-** not listed see the simple word.

bis (auf) 10 zählen; ***draw – to,*** vorfahren vor (*Acc.*); (*coll.*) ***dressed – to the nines,*** aufgedonnert; (*coll.*) ***feel – to doing,*** sich in der Lage *or* sich (*Dat.*) gewachsen fühlen *or* in Stimmung *or* bereit sein zu tun; ***go – to,*** gehen auf (*Acc.*) *or* (bis) zu; ***live – to,*** entsprechend handeln (*Dat.*) (*promises etc.*); ***– to now*** or ***the present,*** bis auf den heutigen Tag; (*coll.*) ***it's all – with him,*** es ist aus mit ihm; ***keep – with,*** Schritt halten mit.
(b) (*with to be*) (*usu. coll.*) ***his blood is –,*** sein Blut ist in Wallung; ***be – all night,*** die ganze Nacht auf sein *or* aufbleiben; ***he is not – yet,*** er ist noch nicht auf(gestanden); (*sl.*) ***what's –?*** was gibt's *or* ist los? ***be – and about,*** (wieder) auf den Beinen sein; ***be – and coming,*** flink, rührig, auf Draht *or* tüchtig sein; ***be – and doing,*** aktiv *or* rege *or* tätig sein; ***the game is –,*** es ist aus *or* erledigt *or* verloren; ***be hard –,*** in schlechten Umständen *or* in der Klemme *or* böse dran sein; ***prices are –,*** die Preise stehen hoch *or* sind im Steigen *or* gestiegen *or* in die Höhe gegangen; ***the sun is –,*** die Sonne ist aufgegangen; ***be 10 –,*** 10 Punkte voraus sein; ***be – a whole tone,*** einen ganzen Ton zu hoch sein.
(c) (*usu. coll.*) ***be – to,*** 1. gefaßt *or* vorbereitet sein auf (*Acc.*), fähig *or* bereit sein zu, gewachsen sein (*Dat.*); ***be – to his tricks,*** ihm auf die Schliche kommen; ***what have you been – to?*** was hast du angestellt? ***be – to mischief,*** Unfug im Schilde führen; ***be – to the mark,*** auf der Höhe sein; ***it is not – to much,*** es taugt nicht viel; ***he is not – to much,*** mit ihm ist nicht viel los; ***be – to no good,*** Böses im Schilde führen; ***be – to a thing or two,*** gerissen sein; 2. liegen an (*Dat.*); abhängen von, entsprechen (*Dat.*); ***it is – to you,*** es liegt an dir, es hängt von dir ab, es ist deine S.
(d) (*with other vbs.*) 1. *with virtually any vb. of movement the pref.* ***auf–*** *can supply the upward direction*; 2. *with many other vbs. emphasis on the completion of the action is rendered by various prefs.,* ***auf–, aus–, ver–, zusammen–.*** *Here only a representative cross-section is given*; *see under the separate vbs.*): ***add –,*** zusammenzählen; ***bind –,*** verbinden; ***be bound – with,*** verbunden sein mit; ***bring –,*** aufziehen, erziehen; ***burn –,*** aufflammen, gänzlich verbrennen; ***clean –,*** gänzlich reinigen, (*sl.*) einheimsen; ***coil –,*** aufrollen, sich zusammenrollen; ***come –,*** herankommen; (*coll.*) ***crop –,*** zum Vorschein kommen, auftauchen; ***drink –,*** austrinken; ***dry –,*** austrocknen, eintrocknen, vertrocknen; (*sl.*) zu reden aufhören; ***eat –,*** aufessen; ***finish –,*** (endgültig) beendigen; ***fold –,*** (zusammen)falten, zusammenlegen; ***follow –,*** (eifrig) verfolgen, ausnutzen; ***gather –,*** aufsammeln, zusammennehmen; ***get –,*** aufstehen; ***give o.s. –,*** sich stellen (*to, Dat.*); (*fig.*) sich widmen (*to, Dat.*); ***go –,*** steigen, in die Höhe gehen, hochgehen; ***grow –,*** aufwachsen, groß werden; ***heal –,*** verheilen, zuheilen; ***hurry –,*** sich beeilen; ***jump –,*** aufspringen; ***lay –,*** sammeln, aufhäufen (*riches etc.*); ***lock –,*** einsperren (*a p.*), zuschließen (*a door*); ***look –,*** hinaufblicken; ***move – in the world,*** in der Welt vorankommen; ***own –,*** offen gestehen; ***pluck – courage,*** Mut fassen; ***polish –,*** aufpolieren; ***pull the blinds –,*** die Jalousien hochziehen *or* aufziehen; (*coll.*) ***put –,*** beherbergen, unterbringen; (*Naut.*) ***put the helm –,*** die Pinne nach Luv drehen, abfallen; ***put one's collar –,*** den Kragen hochschlagen; ***put one's sleeves –,*** die Ärmel hochkrempeln; ***put a tent –,*** ein Zelt aufschlagen; ***put one's umbrella –,*** den Schirm aufspannen; ***settle –,*** abmachen, abschließen; ***sit –,*** sich aufrichten, gerade *or* aufrecht sitzen; ***speak –,*** lauter sprechen; ***spring –,*** aufspringen, aufschießen; aufkommen (*wind*); (*fig.*) auftauchen; ***stand –,*** aufstehen, sich erheben; ***stay –,*** aufbleiben; ***tear –,*** zerreißen; ***use –,*** verbrauchen, aufbrauchen; ***work one's way –,*** sich hocharbeiten.
2. *int.* (*elliptical for* ***get –, hold –, put –*** *etc.*) auf! ***– and away!*** auf und davon! ***hands –!*** Hände hoch!
3. *prep.* hinauf, auf (*Acc.*) . . . (hinauf); ***– country,*** landeinwärts; (*sl.*) ***– a gum-tree,*** in der Klemme; ***– the hill,*** den Berg hinauf, bergauf, bergan; ***– hill and down dale,*** über Berg und Tal; (*sl.*) ***– the pole,*** in der Klemme; überschnappt; ***– the river,*** flußaufwärts; (*sl.*) ***– the spout,*** als Pfand gelassen; dahin; kaputt; ***– five flights of stairs,*** fünf Treppen hoch; ***– the street,*** die Straße *or* auf der Straße entlang; ***further – the street,*** weiter oben an der Straße; (*coll.*) ***that's (right) – my street,*** das paßt mir gerade in den Kram; ***– there,*** dort oben, droben.
4. *s.* ***the –s and downs,*** das Auf und Ab, Steigen und Fallen, die Höhen und Tiefen, Wechselfälle (*pl.*).
5. *v.i.* (*Poet.*) ***then – and spake,*** dann erhob sich und sprach; (*sl.*) ***he –s and says,*** er sagte plötzlich.
6. *v.t.* (*coll.*) erhöhen (*prices etc.*).

up|-and-coming, *attrib. adj.* (*coll.*) rührig, vielversprechend. **--and-up,** *s.* (*coll.*) ***on the –,*** im ständigen Fortschritt, immer besser; (*sl.*) tadellos.

upas ['ju:pəs], *s.* (*also* ***--tree***) der Giftbaum, Upasbaum.

up|-beat, *s.* der Auftakt. **--bow,** *s.* der Aufstrich (*string instruments*).

upbraid [ʌp'breid], *v.t.* ***– him with*** or ***for s.th.,*** ihn tadeln *or* (aus)schelten *or* ihm Vorwürfe machen wegen einer S., ihm etwas vorwerfen *or* vorhalten *or* zum Vorwurf machen *or* zur Last legen. **upbraiding, 1.** *adj.* vorwurfsvoll. **2.** *s.* der Tadel, Vorwurf.

upbringing ['ʌpbriŋiŋ], *s.* die Erziehung; das Aufziehen, Großziehen.

upcast ['ʌpkɑ:st], **1.** *adj.* aufgeschlagen (*eyes*), nach oben gerichtet (*glance*). **2.** *s.* 1. (*Geol.*) die Überschiebung, der Sprung; 2. (*Min.*) (*also* ***– shaft***) Ausflußschacht, Luftschacht, Wetterschacht.

up|-country, 1. *s.* das Binnenland, Land(es)innere. **2.** *adj.* binnenländisch, Binnen–. **--current,** *s.* der Aufwind. **--date,** *v.t.* aufs laufende bringen, modernisieren. **--end, 1.** *v.t.* hochkant stellen. **2.** *v.i.* hochkant stehen. **--grade, 1.** *s.* der Aufstieg, die Steigung; ***on the –,*** im (Auf)steigen. **2.** *v.t.* höher einstufen, auf eine höhere Stufe stellen *or* heben.

upheaval [ʌp'hi:vl], *s.* 1. der Umbruch, die Umwälzung; 2. (*Geol.*) Bodenerhebung. **upheave,** *v.t., v.i.* (*rare*) emporheben.

uphill, 1. ['ʌphil], *adj.* (an)steigend, den Berg hinaufführend; (*fig.*) mühsam, mühselig, beschwerlich. **2.** [ʌp'hil], *adv.* bergauf(wärts), bergan; aufwärts, nach oben.

uphold [ʌp'hould], *irr.v.t.* hochhalten, (aufrecht)halten, stützen, tragen; (*usu. fig.*) aufrechterhalten, unterstützen, billigen; (*rare*) instandhalten. **upholder,** *s.* der Erhalter, Verteidiger, Hüter, die Stütze.

upholster [ʌp'houlstə], *v.t.* (aus)polstern (*furniture*), tapezieren (*a room*); ***–ed chair,*** der Polsterstuhl; (*sl.*) ***well--ed,*** gut gepolstert (*a p.*). **upholsterer,** *s.* der Tapezier(er), Dekorateur. **upholstery,** *s.* die Polsterung; der Möbelbezug(stoff), das Polstermaterial; (*collect.*) Polsterwaren (*pl.*).

upkeep ['ʌpki:p], *s.* 1. die Instandhaltung; Aufrechterhaltung, der Unterhalt; 2. Unterhaltskosten (*pl.*), Instandhaltungskosten (*pl.*).

upland ['ʌplənd], **1.** *s.* (*usu. pl.*) das Hochland, Oberland, die Hochebene. **2.** *adj.* Hochlands–.

uplift, 1. [ʌp'lift], *v.t.* 1. hochheben, emporheben; erheben (*voice*), heben (*mood*); 2. (*usu. fig.*) erbauen, aufrichten; 3. (*Scots*) abholen (*parcel etc.*), abheben (*money*). **2.** ['ʌplift], *s.* 1. (*Geol.*) die Erhebung; 2. (*fig.*) der Aufschwung, die Besserung; 3. Erbauung, Aufbauarbeit, soziale Reform. **3.** ['ʌplift], *adj.* ***– brassière,*** der Büstenheber. **uplifting** [–'liftiŋ], *adj.* (*usu. fig.*) erbauend.

up-line, *s.* die Bahnlinie nach der Stadt (*usu.* nach London).

upmost ['ʌpmoust], *see* **uppermost.**

upon [ə'pɔn], *prep.* (= **on,** *which is generally commoner, esp. in coll. usage; its use is particularly fig. at the end of phrases for emphasis, in cumulative expressions, and in stock phases, viz.*) ***he is not to be depended*** or ***relied –,*** man kann sich nicht auf ihn verlassen; ***loss – loss,*** Verlust auf Verlust, wiederholte Verluste; – *inquiry*, nach Erkundigung; ***my blood be – your head***, mein Blut komme über euer Haupt; ***rush –***, sich werfen *or* stürzen auf (*Acc.*); ***– this***, hierauf; ***once – a time***, es war einmal; ***– my word!*** auf mein Wort!

upper ['ʌpə], **1.** *adj.* ober, höher, Ober–; – ***arm***, der Oberarm; (*Min.*) – ***beds***, das Hangende; (*Typ.*) – ***case***, oberer Schriftkasten, der Oberkasten; Versalien (*pl.*), Großbuchstaben (*pl.*); (*Theat.*) – ***circle***, zweiter Rang; ***the – class(es)*** or (*sl.*) ***crust***, obere Gesellschaftsschicht; – ***deck***, das Oberdeck; (*fig.*) ***get*** or ***gain the – hand***, die Oberhand *or* den Vorteil gewinnen; (*Parl.*) – ***house***, das Oberhaus; – ***jaw***, der Oberkiefer; – ***leather***, das Oberleder; – ***limit***, obere Grenze, die Höchstgrenze; – ***lip***, die Oberlippe; (*coll.*) ***keep a stiff – lip***, die Ohren steif halten; – ***storey***, oberes Stockwerk; (*coll.*) das Oberstübchen. **2.** *s.* (*usu. pl.*) das Oberleder; (***down***) ***on one's –s***, mit zerlumpten Schuhen, (*usu. fig.*) heruntergekommen, ganz auf dem Hund.

upper|-case, *adj.* (*Typ.*) Versal–. **--class**, *adj.* . . . der Oberschicht(en). **–cut**, *s.* (*Boxing*) der Kinnhaken.

uppermost ['ʌpəmoust], **1.** *adj.* 1. höchst, oberst; 2. erst, wichtigst. **2.** *adv.* 1. zuoberst, ganz oben; 2. an erster Stelle, am wichtigsten; vorherrschend; ***say whatever comes –***, sagen, was einem auf die Zunge kommt *or* gerade einfällt.

uppish ['ʌpiʃ], **uppity**, *adj.* (*coll.*) anmaßend, hochnäsig.

up-platform, *s.* der Bahnsteig für Städtezüge (*or* für Züge nach London).

upraise [ʌp'reiz], *v.t.* (*obs.*) erheben, erhöhen.

uprear [ʌp'riə], *v.t.* aufrichten.

upright ['ʌprait], **1.** *adj.* 1. (*pred.*) aufrecht, gerade; 2. (*attrib.*) aufrecht, senkrecht, geradestehend, aufgerichtet; – ***piano***, das (Wand)klavier, Pianino; 3. (*attrib.*) (*fig.*) aufrecht, aufrichtig, ehrlich, redlich, bieder, rechtschaffen. **2.** *s. s.* 1. die Senkrechte, senkrechte Stellung; 2. (*Tech.*) der Ständer, Stutzbalken, Pfeiler, Pfosten; 3. *pl.* (*Footb.*) Torpfosten (*pl.*). **uprightness**, *s.* 1. die Geradheit, aufrechte Stellung *or* (*of posture*) Haltung; 2. (*fig.*) die Aufrichtigkeit, Ehrlichkeit, Biederkeit, Redlichkeit, Rechtschaffenheit.

uprise [ʌp'raiz], *irr.v.i.* (*Poet.*) sich erheben, aufstehen. **uprising**, *s.* 1. das Aufstehen; Aufsteigen, Ansteigen; Aufgehen, der Aufgang (*of the sun*); (*fig.*) Aufstieg, Anstieg; 2. (*Pol.*) Aufstand, Aufruhr, die Erhebung.

up-river, *adv. See* **upstream.**

uproar ['ʌprɔ:], *s.* das Geschrei, der Lärm, Tumult, Aufruhr. **uproarious** [ʌp'rɔ:riəs], *adj.* lärmend, laut, schallend, tosend, tobend, stürmisch. **uproariousness**, *s.* das Lärmen, Toben.

uproot [ʌp'ru:t], *v.t.* entwurzeln, ausreißen, (*fig.*) entreißen (*from, Dat.*), herausreißen (aus) (*a p.*); ausrotten, ausmerzen (*a th.*).

upset, **1.** [ʌp'set], *irr.v.t.* 1. umwerfen, zu Boden werfen, umstürzen, umstoßen; stürzen (*government*), über den Haufen werfen, zu Fall bringen, vereiteln (*plans*), kentern, zum Kentern bringen (*boat*); (*coll.*) – ***the apple-cart***, die Pläne zunichte machen *or* über den Haufen werfen; 2. (*fig.*) bestürzen, aus der Fassung bringen, stören, beunruhigen, verwirren, aufregen; ***he has eaten s.th. that – him*** or ***his stomach***, er hat sich (*Dat.*) den Magen verdorben; ***the sausage has – me***, die Wurst ist mir nicht bekommen; 3. stauchen (*metals*). **2.** [–'set], *irr.v.i.* umschlagen, umfallen, umkippen; (*Naut.*) kentern. **3.** ['ʌpset], *s.* 1. das Umstoßen, Umwerfen, Umstürzen, der (Um)sturz; das Umfallen, Umschlagen, Umkippen, der Fall; 2. (*fig.*) das Zunichtemachen (*of plans*), die Bestürzung, Verwirrung, Erregung, Verstimmung (*also of stomach*), der Ärger; 3. das Durcheinander, die Unordnung. **4.** ['ʌpset], *adj.* 1. umgeworfen, umgestürzt; durcheinandergeworfen, durcheinandergeraten; 2. (*fig.*) bestürzt, außer Fassung, verwirrt, aufgeregt; aufgebracht, (*of stomach*) verstimmt; 3. – ***price***, der Anschlagpreis, Einsatzpreis (*at auctions*).

upshot ['ʌpʃɔt], *s.* das Ende, (End)resultat, (End)ergebnis, der Ausgang, Schluß(effekt); ***in the –***, am Ende, schließlich, letzten Endes; ***what will be the –?*** was wird dabei herauskommen?

upside-down ['ʌpsaid'daun], *adv.* das Oberste zuunterst, mit dem Kopf nach unten; (*fig.*) drunter und drüber, vollkommen durcheinander; ***turn –***, (sich) auf den Kopf stellen (*also fig.*).

upstage [ʌp'steidʒ], **1.** *adv.* in den *or* im Hintergrund der Bühne. **2.** *adj.* (*fig. coll.*) hochnäsig, von oben herab.

upstairs, **1.** [ʌp'stɛəz], *adv.* (nach) oben, die Treppe hinauf; (*fig. sl.*) ***be kicked –***, weggelobt werden. **2.** ['ʌpstɛəz], *adj.* oben gelegen, im oberen Stockwerk. **3.** [ʌp'stɛəz], *s.* das Obergeschoß, oberes Stockwerk.

upstanding [ʌp'stændiŋ], *adj.* 1. großgewachsen; 2. (*fig.*) ehrlich, aufrichtig; 3. (*esp. Scots*) stehend, aufrecht.

upstart ['ʌpstɑ:t], **1.** *s.* der Emporkömmling, Parvenü. **2.** *attrib. adj.* emporgekommen.

upstream [ʌp'stri:m], **1.** *adv.* stromauf(wärts); gegen den Strom. **2.** *adj.* stromaufwärts gelegen.

upstroke ['ʌpstrouk], *s.* 1. der Aufstrich, Haarstrich (*in writing*); 2. (*Tech.*) Hub, Kolbenaufgang; 3. die Aufwärtsbewegung.

upsurge(nce) ['ʌpsə:dʒ (–'sə:dʒəns)], *s.* die Aufwallung, das Ansteigen.

upswing ['ʌpswiŋ], *s.* (*usu. fig.*) der Aufschwung, Aufstieg.

uptake ['ʌpteik], *s.* (*coll.*) ***quick on the –***, rasch begreifen; ***be slow on the –***, eine lange Leitung haben, begriffsstützig *or* schwer von Begriff sein.

upthrow ['ʌpθrou], *s.* (*Geol.*) die Verwerfung.

upthrust ['ʌpθrʌst], *s.* 1. das Emporschleudern; 2. (*Geol.*) die Horstbildung.

up-to-date ['ʌptə'deit], *adj.* 1. bis in die Gegenwart reichend, modern, neuzeitlich, zeitgemäß, zeitnah, aktuell, den neuesten Erkenntnissen entsprechend; 2. modisch, auf der Höhe *or* dem laufenden.

up-train, *s.* in die Stadt (*or* nach London) fahrender Zug.

upturn ['ʌp'tə:n], **1.** *v.t.* umstülpen, umdrehen, umkippen. **2.** *s.* das (An)steigen, der Aufschwung, die Besserung. **upturned**, *adj.* 1. nach oben gebogen *or* gerichtet; – ***nose***, die Stupsnase; 2. umgeworfen, umgekippt; (*Naut.*) gekentert.

upward ['ʌpwəd], *adj.* nach oben *or* aufwärts gerichtet; (*Comm.*) (an)steigend; – ***glance***, der Blick nach oben; – ***movement***, das Steigen, die Aufwärtsbewegung. **upward(s)**, *adv.* aufwärts, nach oben, in die Höhe, höher (hinauf), (*fig.*) darüber (hinaus); – ***of***, mehr als, über (*with numbers*); ***from*** (***his etc.***) ***youth –***, von Jugend auf.

uraemia [juə'ri:miə], *s.* (*Med.*) die Urämie, Harnvergiftung.

uranite ['juərənait], *s.* der Uranglimmer. **uranitite** [ju'rænitait], *s.* der Uranpecherz, die Pechblende. **uranium** [ju'reiniəm], *s.* das Uran. **uranography** [–'nɔgrəfi], *s.* die Himmelsbeschreibung. **uranous** ['juərənəs], *adj.* Uran–.

urban ['ə:bən], *adj.* Stadt–, städtisch; – ***district***, der Stadtbezirk.

urbane [ə:'bein], *adj.* höflich, verbindlich, weltmännisch, weltgewandt. **urbanity** [–'bæniti], *s.* die Höflichkeit, Verbindlichkeit, Weltgewandtheit, feine Umgangsformen (*pl.*).

urbanization [ə:bənai'zeiʃən], *s.* 1. die Verstädterung; 2. Verfeinerung. **urbanize** ['ə:bənaiz], *v.t.* 1. verstädtern; 2. verfeinern.

urchin ['ə:tʃin], *s.* der Schelm, Bengel, Balg; 2. ***sea-–***, der Seeigel.

urea ['juəriə], *s.* der Harnstoff, das Karbamid. **ureal**, *adj.* Harnstoff–. **uremia**, *see* **uraemia.** **ureter** [juə'ri:tə], *s.* der Harnleiter. **urethra** [–'ri:θrə], *s.* die Harnröhre. **uretic** [–'retik], *adj.* harntreibend, diuretisch.

urge [əːdʒ], **1.** *v.t.* 1. (*also* – *on*) (an)treiben, anhalten, drängen, nötigen, dringend ersuchen *or* auffordern, dringen in (*Acc.*); 2. zusetzen (*Dat.*), bedrängen, bestürmen (*a p.*); betreiben, vor(wärts)treiben, vorantreiben, vorwärtsdrängen (*a th.*); 3. vorbringen, anführen, Nachdruck legen auf (*Acc.*), nahelegen, einschärfen, bestehen auf (*Dat.*), ans Herz legen, vor Augen führen, hervorheben, eindringlich vorstellen, nachdrücklich betonen *or* empfehlen (*a point of view*) (*upon*, *Dat.*). **2.** *s.* der Drang, (An)trieb, Impuls, das Verlangen, die Inbrunst; ***creative* –,** der Schaffensdrang.

urgency [ˈəːdʒənsi], *s.* die Dringlichkeit, dringende Eile *or* Not(wendigkeit), der Zeitdruck; die Eindringlichkeit, dringende Aufforderung; ***with the utmost* –,** äußerst dringend. **urgent,** *adj.* dringend, ernstlich; drängend, dringlich, eilig; ***be* –,** darauf drängen, drängend *or* begierig sein (*of a p.*); drängen, eilen (*of a th.*).

uric [ˈjuərik], *adj.* Harn(säure)–; – ***acid,*** die Harnsäure. **urinal** [ˈjuərinl], *s.* 1. die Bedürfnisanstalt, das Pissoir; 2. die Urinflasche. **urinary, 1.** *adj.* Harn–, Urin–; – ***calculus,*** der Blasenstein. **2.** *s.* das Pissoir. **urinate** [–eit], *v.i.* harnen, urinieren, Harn lassen. **urine** [ˈjuərin], *s.* der Urin, Harn. **urinometer** [–ˈnɔmitə], *s.* der Urinmesser.

urn [əːn], *s.* die Urne, der (Wasser)krug; ***funeral* –,** die Graburne; ***tea* –,** die Teemaschine.

uroscopy [juəˈrɔskəpi], *s.* die Harnuntersuchung.

ursine [ˈəːsain], *adj.* bärenartig, Bären–.

urtica [ˈəːtikə], *s.* (eine Gattung der) Nesselgewächse (*pl.*). **urticaria** [–ˈkɛəriə], *s.* (*Med.*) die Nesselsucht.

urus [ˈjuərəs], *s.* der Auerochse, Ur.

us [ʌs], *pers. pron.* uns; ***to* –,** (zu) uns; ***all of* –,** wir alle; ***both of* –,** wir beide.

usable [ˈjuːzəbl], *adj.* brauchbar, verwendbar. **usage** [ˈjuːzidʒ, –sidʒ], *s.* 1. der Brauch, Usus, die Gewohnheit, Gepflogenheit, Sitte, übliches *or* herkömmliches Verfahren; 2. der Gebrauch, die Verwendung, Benutzung; Behandlung(sweise); 3. der Sprachgebrauch; 4. (*Comm.*) Handelsbrauch, Geschäftsbrauch, die Usance; 5. (*Law*) das Gewohnheitsrecht. **usance,** *s.* 1. (*obs.*) *see* **usage**; 2. (*usu. Comm.*) der Handelsbrauch, Geschäftsbrauch, die Usance, der Uso; ***at* –,** nach Uso; ***bill at* –,** der Usowechsel.

use, 1. [juːs], *s.* 1. der Gebrauch; die Benutzung, Benützung, Anwendung, Verwendung; ***for* –,** zum Gebrauch; ***directions for* –,** die Gebrauchsanweisung; ***fit for* –,** brauchbar; ***ready for* –,** gebrauchsfertig; ***in* –,** gebräuchlich, in Gebrauch; ***come into* –,** in Gebrauch kommen, gebräuchlich werden; ***in daily* –,** täglich gebraucht; ***in common* –,** allgemein üblich *or* gebräuchlich; ***bring into* –,** gebrauchen, verwenden; ***out of* –,** nicht mehr gebräuchlich, nicht in Gebrauch; ***fall*** or ***go*** or ***pass out of* –,** ungebräuchlich werden, außer Gebrauch kommen; ***have no* – *for,*** nichts übrig haben für, nichts anfangen können mit, nicht brauchen können; ***have the* – *of,*** benutzen können; ***make (good)* – *of,*** (gut) anwenden *or* benutzen *or* gebrauchen, (guten) Gebrauch machen von; ***with* –,** beim *or* im *or* durch *or* nach Gebrauch; 2. die Nützlichkeit, Verwendbarkeit, Brauchbarkeit; der Nutzen, Zweck, Vorteil; ***for the* – *of,*** zum Nutzen von; ***be of* –,** brauchbar *or* nützlich *or* dienlich *or* von Nutzen sein (*to*, für); ***can I be of any* –?** kann ich helfen? ***is it of any* – *to you?*** können Sie es (ge)brauchen? ***of no* –,** nutzlos, unnütz, unbrauchbar, ohne Nutzen; ***it is (of) no* –,** es ist zwecklos, es hat keinen Zweck, es hilft nichts; ***what* – *is it? what is the* – *of it?*** was nützt *or* hilft es? was hat es für einen Zweck *or* Sinn? ***everything here has its* –,** hier hat alles seinen Sinn und Zweck; ***lose the* – *of an eye,*** auf einem Auge nicht mehr sehen können; ***lose the* – *of one's right arm,*** den rechten Arm nicht mehr bewegen können; (*coll.*) ***make* – *of,*** ausnutzen (*a p.*); ***put to* –,** verwenden, nutzbar *or* mit Nutzen anwenden; 3. der Brauch, die Gewohnheit; Praxis; – ***and wont,*** Sitte und Gewohnheit; 4. (*Law*) der Genuß, die Nutznießung.

2. [juːz], *v.t.* 1. gebrauchen, benutzen, benützen, verwenden, anwenden, sich bedienen (*Gen.*), sich (*Dat.*) zunutze machen, zur Anwendung bringen, ausüben; handhaben (*a th.*); – ***care,*** sorgfältig verfahren; – ***discretion,*** nach Gutdünken handeln; – ***force,*** Gewalt anwenden; – ***strong language,*** fluchen, schimpfen; – ***threatening language,*** mündlich bedrohen; (*sl.*) – ***your loaf!*** sei gescheit! (*coll.*) ***may I* – *your name?*** darf ich mich auf Sie berufen? 2. behandeln, verfahren mit, begegnen (*Dat.*) (*a p.*); ***how has the world* –*d you?*** wie ist es dir ergangen? 3. verbrauchen, verausgaben; – ***up,*** verbrauchen, aufbrauchen.

3. *v.i.* (*only past tense* [juːst]) war gewohnt, pflegte; ***we* –*d to live here,*** wir wohnten früher hier; ***he* –*d to say,*** er pflegte zu sagen; ***I* –*d to smoke very little,*** ich rauchte sonst sehr wenig; ***now I smoke more than I* –*d to,*** jetzt rauche ich mehr als früher; ***I* –*d not* (*sl. didn't* –) *to smoke at all,*** früher *or* sonst pflegte ich gar nicht zu rauchen.

used, 1. [juːzd], *attrib. adj.* – ***car,*** der Gebrauchtwagen; – ***clothes*** or ***clothing,*** gebrauchte *or* getragene Kleider; (*coll.*) – ***up,*** erschöpft, erledigt, fertig. **2.** [juːst], *pred. adj.* gewohnt (*to*, *Acc.*), gewöhnt (an (*Acc.*)); ***get* – *to,*** sich gewöhnen an (*Acc.*).

useful [ˈjuːsful], *adj.* 1. nützlich, brauchbar; (zweck)dienlich, (gut) verwendbar, von Wert, vorteilhaft, zweckmäßig (*to*, *Dat.* (*a p.*); ***for,*** zu, bei *or* in (*Dat.*) (*a purpose*)); (*esp. Tech.*) nutzbar, Nutz–; ***make o.s.* –,** sich nützlich machen; – ***current,*** der Wirkstrom; – ***effect,*** der Nutzeffekt; – ***load,*** das Zuladegewicht, die Nutzlast. **usefulness,** *s.* die Nützlichkeit, Brauchbarkeit; Zweckmäßigkeit, Verwendungsfähigkeit. **useless** [ˈjuːslis], *adj.* 1. nutzlos, nicht zu verwenden(d), unbrauchbar; 2. unnütz, sinnlos, zwecklos, fruchtlos, vergeblich; ***be* –,** sich erübrigen. **uselessness,** *s.* die Nutzlosigkeit, Zwecklosigkeit, Unbrauchbarkeit.

user [ˈjuːzə], *s.* 1. der (die) Benutzer(in); 2. (*Law*) der Genuß, Nießbrauch, die Nutznießung, das Benutzungsrecht; der (die) Nutznießer(in), Benützer(in), Nießbraucher(in).

usher [ˈʌʃə], **1.** *s.* 1. der Gerichtsdiener; 2. Platzanweiser; Pförtner, Türsteher; 3. ***Gentleman* –,** Zeremonienmeister (*in Parliament etc.*); 4. (*obs.*) der Unterlehrer, Hilfslehrer. **2.** *v.t.* (*usu.* – *in*) (her- *or* hin)einführen, anmelden; (*fig.*) ankündigen, einleiten. **usherette** [–ˈret], *s.* die Platzanweiserin.

usual [ˈjuːʒuəl], *adj.* gewöhnlich, gebräuchlich, üblich; Stamm–; ***business as* –,** der Verkauf geht weiter; ***it is* – *for me to be here,*** ich bin gewöhnlich hier; ***the rudeness* – *with him,*** seine übliche Grobheit; ***as* –,** wie gewöhnlich *or* üblich *or* sonst; ***more than* –,** mehr als gewöhnlich; ***our* – *table,*** unser Stammtisch; ***the* – *thing,*** das Übliche; ***it is (the)* – *(thing) with him,*** es ist bei ihm gang und gebe; (*sl.*) ***the* –,** die Regel (*of women*). **usually,** *adv.* gewöhnlich, meist(ens), in der Regel.

usucapion [juːzjuˈkeipiən], **usucaption** [–ˈkæpʃən], *s.* (*Law*) die Ersitzung. **usufruct** [ˈjuːzjufrʌkt], *s.* der Nießbrauch, die Nutznießung. **usufructuary** [juːzjuˈfrʌktjuəri], *s.* der (die) Nutznießer(in), Nießbraucher(in).

usurer [ˈjuːʒərə], *s.* der Wucherer. **usurious** [juːˈzjuəriəs], *adj.* wucherisch, wucherhaft, Wucher–. **usuriousness,** *s.* die Wucherei.

usurp [juːˈzəːp], *v.t.* 1. an sich reißen, sich (*Dat.*) widerrechtlich aneignen, sich bemächtigen (*Gen.*); 2. sich (*Dat.*) anmaßen, unrechtmäßig beanspruchen. **usurpation** [–ˈpeiʃən], *s.* 1. rechtswidrige *or* widerrechtliche Besitzergreifung *or* Besitznahme *or* Aneignung (*of*, *Gen.*); 2. unberechtigter Eingriff (*on*, in (*Acc.*)). **usurper,** *s.* 1. der Usurpator, unrechtmäßiger *or* unberechtigter Besitzergreifer; 2. rechtswidrige Throninhaber, der Thronräuber; 3. (*fig.*) der Eindringling (*on*, in (*Acc.*)). **usurping,** *adj.* widerrechtlich (sich aneignend), alles an sich reißend.

usury ['ju:ʒəri], *s.* 1. der Wucher; ***practise* –,** Wucher treiben, wuchern; 2. Wucherzinsen (*pl.*) (***at***, auf (*Acc.*)).

utensil [ju:'tensl], *s.* das Gerät, (Hand)werkszeug, der Gebrauchsgegenstand; Haushaltsgegenstand, *pl.* Utensilien (*pl.*), Gerätschaften (*pl.*), das (Küchen)geschirr.

uterine ['ju:tərin], *adj.* 1. Gebärmutter–; 2. (*Law*) von derselben Mutter stammend; – ***brother,*** der Halbbruder mütterlicherseits. **uterus** [–rəs], *s.* die Gebärmutter.

utilitarian [ju:tili'tεəriən], **1.** *adj.* utilitaristisch, Nützlichkeits–. **2.** *s.* der Utilitarier, Anhänger des Nützlichkeitsprinzips; Nützlichkeitsmensch, Utilitarist. **utilitarianism,** *s.* die Nützlichkeitslehre, der Utilitarismus. **utility** [ju:'tiliti], **1.** *s.* die Nützlichkeit, der Nutzen (***to***, für); ***public* –,** öffentlicher Betrieb, öffentliche Einrichtung. **2.** *attrib. adj.* Gebrauchs–; – ***actor*** or ***man,*** der Schauspieler für kleine Rollen; – ***goods,*** Gebrauchswaren, Einheitswaren (*pl.*).

utilizable ['ju:tilaizəbl], *adj.* nutzbar, verwendbar, verwertbar. **utilization** [–'zeiʃən], *s.* die Nutzbarmachung, Verwendung, Verwertung, (Nutz)anwendung, (Aus)nutzung. **utilize,** *v.t.* benutzen, verwenden, verwerten, (aus)nutzen, sich (*Dat.*) zunutze machen.

utmost ['ʌtmoust], **1.** *adj.* äußerst, fernst, weitest, entlegenst; (*fig.*) höchst, größt. **2.** *s.* das Äußerste, Höchste; ***do one's* –,** sein möglichstes *or* äußerstes tun; ***at the* –,** höchstens; ***to the* –,** aufs äußerste; ***to the – of my power,*** nach besten Kräften.

utopia [ju:'toupiə], *s.* das Luftschloß, Idealland, der Idealzustand, Zukunftstraum, die Utopie. **utopian, 1.** *adj.* utopisch, ideal, visionär, erträumt, phantastisch. **2.** *s.* der Utopist, Idealist, Phantast, Schwärmer. **utopianism,** *s.* der Utopismus, (politische) Schwärmerei.

utricle ['ju:trikl], *s.* (*Bot.*) der Schlauch, kleines Bläschen, (*Anat.*) blasenartiges Gefäß. **utricular** [–'trikjulə], *adj.* schlauchartig, blasenartig.

[1]**utter** ['ʌtə], *adj.* äußerst, gänzlich, völlig; endgültig; (*coll.*) regelrecht, ausgekocht, abgefeimt, Erz–.

[2]**utter,** *v.t,* 1. ausstoßen, hervorbringen, von sich geben (*sounds*); äußern, ausdrücken, aussprechen (*thoughts*); 2. in Umlauf setzen (*coins etc.*). **utterance,** *s.* 1. der Ausdruck, die Äußerung; (*also pl.*) Äußerung, der Ausspruch; ***give – to,*** Ausdruck geben (*Dat.*), Luft geben (*Dat.*), äußern; 2. der Vortrag, die Sprechweise; 3. Ausgabe (*of coin etc.*).

utterly ['ʌtəli], *adv.* völlig, ganz, gänzlich, durchaus. **uttermost,** *see* **utmost. utterness,** *s.* (*coll.*) das Höchstmaß, die Vollständigkeit.

uvula ['ju:vjulə], *s.* das Zäpfchen. **uvular,** *adj.* Zäpfchen–.

uxorial [ʌk'sɔ:riəl], *adj.* einer (Ehe)frau geziemend. **uxorious,** *adj.* der Ehefrau blind ergeben, unter dem Pantoffel stehend. **uxoriousness,** *s.* die Ergebenheit *or* Unterwürfigkeit (gegenüber seiner Frau).

Uzbek ['ʌzbek], **1.** *s.* der Usbeke (die Usbekin). **2.** *adj.* usbekisch.

V

V, v [vi:], *s.* das V, v; *see Index of Abbreviations.*

vac [væk], *abbr. for* **vacation.**

vacancy ['veikənsi], *s.* 1. die Leere, Lücke, leerer Raum; ***stare into* –,** ins Leere blicken; 2. freie Stelle, die Vakanz; 3. (*fig.*) Gedankenlosigkeit, Geistesabwesenheit, Leerheit. **vacant,** *adj.* 1. leer(geworden); frei, unbesetzt (*seat, post etc.*), leerstehend, unbewohnt, unvermietet (*house*), offen, vakant (*post*); – ***lot,*** unbebautes Grundstück; – ***possession,*** sofort zu beziehen; ***fall* –,** frei *or* vakant werden; 2. (*fig.*) gedankenleer, geistesabwesend, ausdruckslos (*appearance*); – ***look,*** leerer Blick.

vacate [və'keit, 'veikeit], *v.t.* räumen, verlassen (*place*), freimachen (*seat*), aufgeben, niederlegen (*post*).

vacation [və'keiʃən, vei'keiʃən], *s.* 1. Ferien (*pl.*), die Ferienzeit, der Urlaub; ***long* –,** große Ferien, Sommerferien (*pl.*); ***be on* –,** Urlaub machen, auf Urlaub sein; 2. die Niederlegung, Aufgabe (*of a post*): Räumung (*of a house etc.*).

vaccinate ['væksineit], *v.t.* impfen. **vaccination** [–'neiʃən], *s.* die (Schutzpocken)impfung. **vaccinator,** *s.* der Impfarzt. **vaccine** ['væksin], **1.** *adj.* Impf–, Kuhpocken–. **2.** *s.* der Impfstoff, die Lymphe, Vakzine, das Vakzin. **vaccinia** [–'siniə], *pl.* Kuhpocken (*pl.*).

vacillate ['væsileit], *v.i.* schwanken (*also fig.*), torkeln, wackeln, unsicher sein; (*usu. fig.*) zaudern, unentschlossen *or* unschlüssig sein. **vacillating,** *adj.* schwankend, unschlüssig. **vacillation** [–'leiʃən], *s.* das Schwanken; die Unschlüssigkeit, Unentschlossenheit, der Wankelmut, Schwankungen (*pl.*).

vacuity [væ'kjuiti], *s.* die Leere, (*usu. fig.*) geistige Leere, die Ausdruckslosigkeit, Gedankenlosigkeit; (*also pl.*) Nichtigkeit, Belanglosigkeit. **vacuous** ['vækjuəs], *adj.* leer; (*usu. fig.*) gedankenlos, ausdruckslos, inhaltlos, nichtssagend.

vacuum ['vækjuəm], *s.* 1. (luft)leerer Raum, das Vakuum; (*fig.*) die Lücke, Leere; 2. (*coll.*) *abbr. for* **vacuum-cleaner.**

vacuum|-brake, *s.* die Unterdruckbremse. **--cleaner,** *s.* der Staubsauger. **--flask,** *s.* die Thermosflasche. **--packed,** *adj.* luftdicht gepackt. **--pump,** *s.* die Absaugepumpe. **--seal,** *s.* die Vakuumdichtung. **--tube,** *s.* die Elektronenröhre.

vade-mecum ['veidi'mi:kəm], *s.* der Leitfaden, das Handbuch, Vademekum.

vagabond ['vægəbɔnd], **1.** *s.* der Landstreicher, Vagabund; (*coll.*) Halunke, Spitzbube, Taugenichts. **2.** *adj.* herumstreichend, vagabundierend; herumwandernd, Wander–. **vagabondage** [–idʒ], **vagabondism,** *s.* die Landstreicherei, das Vagabundieren, Vagabundentum, Vagabundenleben. **vagabondize,** *v.i.* vagabundieren, umherschweifen, umherstreichen.

vagarious [və'gεəriəs], *adj.* unberechenbar, launisch. **vagary** [və'gεəri, 'veigəri], *s.* (*usu. pl.*) die Laune, Grille, Schrulle, wunderlicher Einfall.

vagina [və'dʒainə], *s.* die Scheide. **vaginal,** *adj.* Scheiden–. **vaginitis** [vædʒi'naitis], *s.* die Scheidenentzündung.

vagrancy ['veigrənsi], *s.* die Landstreicherei, das Vagabundentum; Umherstreifen, Vagabundieren. **vagrant** [–ənt], **1.** *adj.* wandernd, umherziehend, vagabundierend. **2.** *s.* der Landstreicher, Vagabund.

vague [veig], *adj.* unbestimmt, undeutlich, unklar, undefinierbar, unbestimmbar, verschwommen, nebelhaft, vag(e) (*of a th.*); (*coll.*) zerstreut (*of a p.*); – ***answer,*** zweideutige Antwort; ***not the –st notion,*** nicht die leiseste Ahnung; – ***promise,*** nichtssagendes Versprechen; – ***rumour,*** dunkles Gerücht; – ***suspicion,*** unklarer Verdacht; ***–ly familiar,*** irgendwie bekannt. **vagueness,** *s.* die Unbestimmtheit, Unklarheit, Verschwommenheit; (*coll. of a p.*) Zerstreutheit.

vain [vein], *adj.* 1. eitel, eingebildet, großspurig (*of a p.*); 2. vergeblich, fruchtlos, ergebnislos, nutzlos, unnütz (*as effort etc.*); leer, hohl, unwesentlich, wertlos, nichtig, eitel (*of a th.*); ***in* –,** umsonst, vergeblich, vergebens; – ***effort,*** vergebliche Mühe; – ***hope,*** leere Hoffnung; – ***pleasure,*** nichtige Freude; – ***show,*** hohle Prahlerei; – ***threat,*** inhaltlose Drohung; – ***wish,*** eitler Wunsch; (*B.*) ***take God's name in –,*** den Namen Gottes mißbrauchen. **vain|glorious,** *adj.* großsprecherisch, prahlerisch, aufgeblasen, großspurig, hoffärtig, ruhmredig. **-glory,** *s.* die Großtuerei, Prahlerei, Angeberei, Aufgeblasenheit, Hoffart. **vainly,** *adv. See* ***in vain.*** **vainness,** *s.* die Vergeblichkeit, Fruchtlosigkeit, Nichtigkeit.

Valais [væ'le], *s.* (*Geog.*) Wallis (*n.*).

valance ['væləns], *s.* der Bettbehang, Volant.

[1]**vale** [veil], *s.* (*Poet.*) das Tal; – ***of tears*** or ***woe,*** das Jammertal.

[2]**vale** [veili], **1.** *int.* lebewohl! **2.** *s.* das Lebewohl.

valediction [væli'dikʃən], *s.* der Abschied, Abschiedsworte (*pl.*); das Abschiednehmen, Lebewohl. **valedictory** [–'diktəri], **1.** *adj.* Abschieds–. **2.** *s.* die Abschiedsansprache, Abschiedsrede.

valence, valency ['veiləns(i)], *s.* (*Chem.*) die Wertigkeit, Valenz.

valentine ['væləntain], *s.* 1. der Valentingruß; 2. (*a p.*) Schatz, Erwählte(r).

valerian [və'liəriən], *s.* (*Bot.*) der Baldrian.

valet ['væle, 'vælit], **1.** *s.* der (Kammer)diener. **2.** *v.t.* Diener sein bei, bedienen, versorgen.

valetudinarian [vælitju:di'nɛəriən], **1.** *adj.* kränkelnd, kränklich, schwächlich. **2.** *s.* Kränkelnde(r). **valetudinarianism,** *s.* die Kränklichkeit. **valetudinary** [–'tju:dinəri], *adj. See* **valetudinarian.**

valiance, valiancy ['væliəns(i)], *s. See* **valour.** **valiant,** *adj.* tapfer, mutig, kühn, heldenhaft; Helden–, heroisch.

valid ['vælid], *adj.* (*Law*) rechtskräftig, (rechts)gültig; (wohl)begründet, unbestreitbar, triftig, stichhaltig (*as arguments*); ***be –,*** gelten. **validate** [–eit], *v.t.* für rechtskräftig *or* gültig erklären, bestätigen. **validation** [–'deiʃən], *s.* die Gültigkeitserklärung, Inkraftsetzung. **validity** [və'liditi], *s.* 1. die (Rechts)gültigkeit, Rechtswirksamkeit; Stichhaltigkeit; Triftigkeit; 2. Gültigkeit(sdauer) (*of a ticket*).

valise [və'li:s], *s.* 1. der Handkoffer, die Reisetasche; 2. (*Mil.*) der Tornister.

valkyrie ['vælkiri], *s.* (*Myth.*) die Walküre.

valley ['væli], *s.* 1. das Tal, Flußgebiet; – ***bottom,*** die Talsohle; 2. (*Build.*) die Dachrinne, (Dach)kehle.

vallum ['væləm], *s.* (*Hist.*) der Verteidigungswall, die Schanze, Verschanzung.

valor, (*Am.*) *see* **valour.**

valorization [vælərai'zeiʃən], *s.* die Aufwertung, Preisregelung. **valorize** ['væləraiz], *v.t.* aufwerten, den Preis stützen (*Gen.*).

valorous ['vælərəs], *adj. See* **valiant.** **valour** ['vælə], *s.* die Tapferkeit, Furchtlosigkeit, der (Helden)mut; ***discretion is the better part of –,*** Vorsicht ist der bessere Teil der Tapferkeit (*Shakesp.*), (*Prov.*) Vorsicht ist besser als Nachsicht.

valuable ['væljuəbl], **1.** *adj.* 1. wertvoll (***to, for,*** für (*a p.*), zu (*a th.*)); kostbar, teuer; – ***belongings,*** Wertsachen (*pl.*); 2. abzuschätzen(d), (ab)schätzbar. **2.** *s.* (*usu. pl.*) der Wertgegenstand, die Wertsache, Kostbarkeit. **valuation** [–ju'eiʃən], *s.* 1. die (Ein)schätzung, Wertbestimmung, Veranschlagung; Bewertung, Taxierung; 2. Taxe, der Schätzungswert, eingeschätzter Preis *or* Wert; 3. (*fig.*) die Wertschätzung, Würdigung; ***take him at his own –,*** ihn so beurteilen wie er sich selbst beurteilt. **valuator** ['væljueitə], *s.* der Taxator, Abschätzer.

value ['vælju:], **1.** *s.* 1. der Wert, Nutzen (***to,*** für); ***be of – to,*** wertvoll *or* nützlich sein (*Dat.*); ***standard of –,*** der Wertmesser; 2. (*Comm.*) die Kaufkraft, der Preis, Betrag, Geldwert, Materialwert, Tauschwert, Gegenwert; ***at –,*** zum Tageskurs; ***cash*** (or ***surrender***) –, der Rückkaufswert; ***estimated –,*** der Schätzungswert; ***exchange –,*** der Marktpreis; – ***in exchange,*** der Tauschwert; ***face –,*** der Nennwert, Nominalwert; (*fig.*) ***at its face –,*** für bare Münze; ***get good – for one's money,*** reell bedient werden, preiswert kaufen; ***give good –,*** reell bedienen; ***of good –,*** vollwertig; ***in –,*** an Wert; – ***as per invoice,*** Wert in Faktura; ***of –,*** von Wert; – ***received,*** Gegenwert *or* Gegenleistung erhalten; ***to the – of,*** im Betrag von; im *or* bis zum Werte von; 3. (*fig.*) die Bewertung, Wertschätzung; ***place*** or ***set much*** or ***great*** or ***a high –*** (***up***)***on,*** hoch einschätzen, (großen *or* hohen) Wert legen auf (*Acc.*), großen Wert *or* große Bedeutung beilegen (*Dat.*); 4. das Gewicht, die Bedeutung, Geltung, der Gehalt; ***intrinsic –,*** innerer Gehalt; ***sentimental –,*** der Liebhaberwert; 5. (*Mus.*) der Notenwert, Zeitwert; (*Phonet.*) Lautwert, die Qualität; (*Math.*) ***approximate –,*** der Näherungswert; (*Math.*) ***range of –s,*** der Wertebereich; 6. *pl.* Werte (*pl.*) (*of a p. etc.*). **2.** *v.t.* 1. einschätzen, abschätzen, veranschlagen, taxieren (*at,* auf (*Acc.*)); 2. (*fig.*) bewerten, Wert legen auf (*Acc.*), (hoch)schätzen, achten (*for,* wegen).

value-added tax, *s.* die Wertzuwachssteuer.

valued ['vælju:d], *adj.* (*usu. fig.*) geschätzt, (hoch)geachtet. **valueless,** *adj.* wertlos, nutzlos. **valuer** ['væljuə], *s. See* **valuator.**

valve [vælv], *s.* 1. die Klappe (*also Anat., Bot.*); (*Tech.*) das Ventil; ***safety –,*** das Sicherheitsventil; 2. (*Rad.*) die Röhre; (*Rad.*) ***output –,*** die Endröhre; ***thermionic –,*** die Elektrodenröhre. **valve|-gear,** *s.* die Ventilsteuerung. **--set,** *s.* der Röhrenapparat.

valvular ['vælvjulə], *adj.* klappenförmig, Klappen–. **valvule** [–ju:l], *s.* kleine Klappe. **valvulitis** [–ju'laitis], *s.* (*Med.*) die Herzklappenentzündung.

vamoose [və'mu:s], *v.i.* (*sl.*) ausreißen, abhauen, durchbrennen.

[1]**vamp** [væmp], **1.** *s.* 1. das Oberleder (*on shoes*), (*fig.*) das Flickwerk; 2. (*Mus.*) (*coll.*) improvisierte Begleitung. **2.** *v.t.* 1. vorschuhen; (*fig.*) ausbessern, flicken; zurechtschustern; 2. (*Mus.*) aus dem Stegreif begleiten. **3.** *v.i.* (*Mus.*) Begleitung improvisieren.

[2]**vamp,** **1.** *s.* (*coll.*) der Vamp, die Verführerin. **2.** *v.t.* behexen, neppen, verführen.

vampire ['væmpaiə], *s.* 1. der Vampir (*also fig.*); 2. (*also* – ***bat***) Vampir; 3. (*fig.*) Ausbeuter, Blutsauger. **vampirism,** *s.* 1. der Vampirglaube; 2. das Blutsaugen; 3. (*fig.*) die Ausbeutung, Blutsaugerei.

[1]**van** [væn], *s.* (*Mil.*) die Vorhut, der Vortrab; (*fig.*) die Spitze, vorderste Reihe.

[2]**van,** **1.** *s.* die (Getreide)schwinge; (*Min.*) Schwingschaufel; Schwingprobe. **2.** *v.t.* sieben, worfeln, schwingen (*corn*), schwingen, waschen (*ore*).

[3]**van,** *s.* der Lastwagen, Frachtwagen, Rollwagen, Lieferwagen, Transportwagen; ***delivery –,*** Lieferwagen; ***furniture –,*** Möbelwagen; (*Railw.*) ***luggage –,*** Gepäckwagen, Güterwagen, Dienstwagen.

vanadic [və'nædik], *adj.* vanadiumhaltig, Vanadin–. **vanadium** [və'neidiəm], *s.* das Vanadium.

Vandal [vændl], *s.* 1. (*Hist.*) der Vandale (die Vandalin); 2. (*fig.*) ***vandal,*** (mutwilliger) Zerstörer. **vandalism** ['vændəlizm], *s.* der Vandalismus, die Zerstörungswut; (Natur)verschandelung, der (Kunst)frevel.

vandyke [væn'daik], *s.* das Zackenmuster, die Zackenspitze; der Spitzenkragen; – ***beard,*** der Knebelbart; – ***brown,*** das Van-Dyck-Braun; – ***collar,*** ausgezackter Halskragen.

vane [vein], *s.* 1. die Wetterfahne, der Wetterhahn; 2. (*Surv.*) Diopter, das Nivelliergerät; 3. (*Tech.*) Blatt, die Schaufel, der Flügel (*of turbine, fan etc.*); 4. die Fahne (*of feather*), Fiederung (*of arrow*), Platte (*of variable condenser*).

vang [væŋ], *s.* (*Naut.*) die Geer(de), Gei.

vanguard ['vængɑ:d], *s. See* [1]**van.**

vanilla [və'nilə], *s.* die Vanille.

vanish ['væniʃ], *v.i.* verschwinden (*also Math.*), entschwinden, dahinschwinden, sich verlieren (***from,*** von *or* aus), unsichtbar werden; sich auflösen, zergehen, vergehen (***into,*** in (*Acc.*)); (*Math.*) Null werden; – ***from*** (***his***) ***sight,*** seinen

Blicken entschwinden; – *into nothing* or *into thin air*, sich in nichts auflösen. **vanishing,** *s.* das Verschwinden; – *cream*, die Hautcreme, Tagescreme; – *fraction*, der Infinitesimalbruch; – *line*, die Fluchtlinie; – *point*, der Fluchtpunkt, (*fig.*) Nullpunkt.

vanity ['væniti], *s.* 1. die Eitelkeit, Selbstgefälligkeit (*of a p.*); – *bag*, die Kosmetiktasche; – *fair*, der Jahrmarkt der Eitelkeit; 2. die Nichtigkeit, Leerheit, Hohlheit, Nutzlosigkeit (*of a th.*).

van|load, *s.* die Wagenladung. **–man** [–mən], *s.* der Rollwagenführer, Fahrer (eines Lieferwagens).

vanquish ['væŋkwiʃ], **1.** *v.t.* besiegen, erobern; unterwerfen, überwältigen; (*fig. Poet.*) bezwingen, überwinden. **2.** *v.i.* Sieger *or* siegreich sein, siegen. **vanquisher,** *s.* der Eroberer, Sieger.

vantage ['væntidʒ], *s.* (*rare*) *see* **advantage. vantage|-ground, --point,** *s.* (*usu. fig.*) vorteilhafte Stellung, günstige Lage.

vapid ['væpid], *adj.* schal (*also fig.*), geschmacklos, abgestanden; (*fig.*) leblos, geistlos, fad(e), flach, stumpf, eintönig, langweilig, trocken. **vapidity** [və'piditi], **vapidness,** *s.* die Schalheit, Flachheit, Leblosigkeit, Geistlosigkeit, Fadheit, Langweiligkeit, Trockenheit.

vapor, (*Am.*) *see* **vapour.**

vaporization [veipərai'zeiʃən], *s.* die Verdunstung, Verdampfung. **vaporize** ['veipəraiz], **1.** *v.i.* verdunsten, verdampfen. **2.** *v.t.* 1. verdunsten *or* verdampfen lassen, verdünsten, eindampfen; 2. zerstäuben. **vaporizer,** *s.* der Verdampf(ungs)-apparat, Zerstäuber. **vaporous,** *adj.* 1. dampfig, dunstig, Dampf–; dampferfüllt, dunsterfüllt; 2. (*fig.*) nebelhaft, verschwommen, substanzlos, phantastisch; 3. duftig, gazeartig (*of fabric*).

vapour ['veipə], **1.** *s.* 1. der Dampf, Dunst, Nebel; (*Phys.*) Dampf, das Gas; (*Meteor.*) die (Luft)-feuchtigkeit; *water* –, der Wasserdampf; – *bath*, das Dampfbad; (*Av.*) – *trail*, der Kondensstreifen; 2. (*fig.*) der Dunst, Wahn, Phantom, das Hirngespinst; 3. *pl.* (*obs. Med.*) die Blähung; (*obs. fig.*) *the –s*, die Hypochondrie, Melancholie. **2.** *v.i.* 1. (*rare*) *see* **vaporize**; 2. (*fig., rare*) prahlen, sich aufblähen. **vapoured** [–d], *adj.* (*obs. fig.*) hypochondrisch, melancholisch. **vapourer,** *s.* 1. (*rare*) der Großmaul, Prahlhaus, Windmacher, Schaumschläger, Aufschneider; 2. (*Ent.*) Bürstenspinner. **vapouring,** *s.* (*usu. pl.*) die Prahlerei. **vapourish,** *adj. See* **vapoured. vapoury,** *adj.* dunstig, Dunst–, (*fig.*) verschwommen, nebelhaft.

Varangian [væ'rændʒiən], **1.** *s.* (*Hist.*) der Waräger. **2.** *adj.* Waräger–.

variability [vεəriə'biliti], *s.* die Veränderlichkeit, das Schwanken; (*Biol.*) die Variabilität. **variable** ['vεəriəbl], **1.** *adj.* veränderlich, wechselnd, schwankend; (*Biol., Math.*) variabel; unbeständig, wandelbar; (*Rad.*) – *condenser*, der Drehkondensator; – *pitch*, ungleicher Ton; (*Av.*) – *pitch propeller*, die Verstelluftschraube; – *winds*, Winde aus wechselnden Richtungen. **2.** *s.* 1. (*Math.*) die Variable, Veränderliche; 2. (*Meteor.*) veränderlicher Wind; 3. (*Astr.*) variabler Stern. **variable-geometry,** *attrib. adj.* (*Av.*) mit verstellbaren Tragflächen. **variableness,** *s. See* **variability.**

variance ['vεəriəns], *s.* 1. die Veränderung, der Wechsel; 2. Unterschied, die Abweichung, Verschiedenheit; Unstimmigkeit, Uneinigkeit, der Zwist, (Wider)streit; (*Law*) Widerspruch; *be at* –, uneinig sein, sich streiten (*of persons*), unvereinbar *or* in Widerspruch sein (***with***, mit), im Gegensatz *or* Widerspruch stehen (zu); *set at* –, entzweien. **variant, 1.** *adj.* abweichend. **2.** *s.* 1. die Variante, Lesart; 2. (*Biol.*) Spielart, der Abweicher; 3. (*Math.*) variabler Wert.

variation [vεəri'eiʃən], *s.* 1. die Veränderung, Abänderung, Abwechs(e)lung; 2. der Wechsel, Unterschied, die Verschiedenheit, Schwankung, Abweichung; 3. Mißweisung, Deklination (*of compass needle*); 4. (*Stat.*) Variationsbreite, der Schwankungsbereich; 5. (*Mus., Astr., Math., Biol.*) die Variation.

varicocele ['værikəsi:l], *s.* der Krampfaderbruch. **varicose** ['værikous], *adj.* krampfadrig; Krampfader–; – *vein*, die Krampfader.

varied ['vεərid], *adj.* verschieden(artig), mannigfaltig, abwechselnd, abwechslungsreich, abwechslungsvoll, bunt.

variegate [vεəriəgeit], *v.t.* 1. farbig *or* bunt machen; 2. (*fig.*) durch Abwechslung beleben, variieren, Abwechslung hineinbringen in (*Acc.*). **variegated,** *adj.* 1. bunt(gefleckt), buntscheckig, vielfarbig; 2. wechselvoll, wechselnd, gemischt. **variegation** [–'geiʃən], *s.* die Vielfarbigkeit, Buntfarbigkeit, Buntheit.

variety [və'raiəti], *s.* 1. die Mannigfaltigkeit, Verschiedenheit, Verschiedenartigkeit, Vielfalt; Abwechs(e)lung, Buntheit, Vielseitigkeit; 2. (*Bot., Zool.*) (Ab)art, Spielart, Varietät; 3. Anzahl, Auswahl, Reihe, Menge (*of*, von); *a – of things*, allerlei *or* verschiedenartige Dinge; 4. (*Theat.*) das Varieté; – *show*, die Varietévorstellung.

variola [və'riələ], *s.* Blattern, Pocken (*pl.*). **variolar,** *adj.* Pocken–. **variolite** ['vεəriəlait], *s.* (*Geol.*) der Blatterstein.

variorum-edition [væri'ɔ:rəm–], *s.* die Ausgabe mit Anmerkungen verschiedener Ausleger; Ausgabe mit verschiedenen Lesarten.

various ['vεəriəs], *adj.* verschieden(artig); (*before pl.*) verschiedene, mehrere, viele.

varix ['vεəriks], *s.* (*pl.* **varices** ['vεərisi:z]) der Krampfaderknoten.

varlet ['vɑ:lit], *s.* (*Hist.*) der Knappe; (*obs. or hum.*) Schuft, Halunke.

varmint ['vɑ:mint], *s.* (*sl.*) der Taugenichts, Racker.

varnish ['vɑ:niʃ], **1.** *s.* der Firnis, Lack; (*fig.*) die Politur, Glasur, der Anstrich. **2.** *v.t.* firnissen, lackieren; polieren; glasieren; (*fig.*) (*also* – *over*) einen Anstrich geben (*Dat.*), übertünchen, verschönern, beschönigen.

varsity ['vɑ:siti], *s.* (*coll.*) die Uni.

vary ['vεəri], **1.** *v.t.* (ab)ändern, verändern, abwandeln, variieren. **2.** *v.i.* 1. (ab)wechseln, sich ändern, variieren; 2. sich unterscheiden, voneinander verschieden sein; abweichen (***from***, von), nicht übereinstimmen (mit); 3. veränderlich sein (*as wind*). **varying,** *adj.* wechselnd, veränderlich; unterschiedlich.

vascular ['væskjulə], *adj.* Gefäß–; (*Anat.*) – *system*, das Gefäßsystem; (*Bot.*) – *tissue*, das Stranggewebe. **vasculum,** *s.* die Botanisierbüchse.

vas deferens ['væsdefə'renz], *s.* (*Anat.*) der Samenleiter.

vase [vɑ:z], *s.* die Vase.

vasectomy [væ'sektəmi], *s.* die Samenstrangexstirpation.

vaseline ['væsəli:n], *s.* (*registered trade mark*) das Vaselin, die Vaseline.

vassal [væsl], *s.* der Lehnsmann, Untertan, Vasall; (*fig.*) Sklave, Knecht. **vassalage,** *s.* der Lehndienst, das Lehnsverhältnis, Vasallentum; (*fig.*) die Unterwerfung, Knechtschaft, Abhängigkeit.

vast [vɑ:st], *adj.* unermeßlich, weit (ausgedehnt) (*in extent*); (*fig.*) ungeheuer (groß), riesig; ungeheuer (viel), zahllos, zahlreich; (*coll.*) gewaltig, beträchtlich; *a – crowd*, eine Unmenge; – *majority*, überwiegende Mehrzahl; – *quantities*, Unmengen; – *sum*, die Unzahl. **vastly,** *adv.* in hohem Grade *or* Maße, unermeßlich, weit. **vastness,** *s.* die Unermeßlichkeit, Weite; ungeheure Größe; die Unmenge, Unzahl.

vat [væt], *s.* großes Faß, der Bottich, Trog, die Bütte, Kufe; (*Dye.*) (Färber)küpe; (*Tan.*) (Loh)-grube.

Vatican ['vætikən], *s.* der Vatikan.

vaticinal [væ'tisinl], *adj.* prophetisch, seherisch. **vaticinate** [–neit], *v.t.* prophezeien, weissagen. **vaticination** [–'neiʃən], *s.* die Weissagung, Prophezeiung.

Vaud [vou], *s.* (*Geog.*) Waadt (*n.*).

vaudeville ['voudəvil], *s.* das Varieté.

Vaudois [vou'dwɑ:], **1.** *s.* der (die) Waadtländer(in). **2.** *adj.* waadtländisch.

[1]**vault** [vɔ:lt], **1.** *s.* 1. das Gewölbe; – ***of heaven,*** das Himmelsgewölbe; 2. das Grabgewölbe, die Gruft; 3. die Stahlkammer, Schatzkammer, der Tresor (*of a bank etc.*); 4. die Wölbung; (*Anat.*) Höhlung, der Bogen; 5. (*oft. pl.*) das Kellergewölbe, der Keller; ***wine –s,*** der Weinkeller. **2.** *v.t.* überwölben.

[2]**vault, 1.** *v.i.* springen, sich schwingen; Kunstsprünge machen. **2.** *v.t.* springen *or* hinwegsetzen über (*Acc.*), überspringen. **3.** *s.* der Sprung, Satz; (*Equest.*) die Kurbette; (*Gymn.*) ***flank*** –, die Flanke; (*Gymn.*) ***front –,*** die Wende; (*Spt.*) ***pole –,*** der Stabhochsprung; ***rear*** –, die Kehre.

vaulted ['vɔ:ltid], *adj.* (*Archit.*) gewölbt, Gewölbe–.

vaulter ['vɔ:ltə], *s.* der (die) Springer(in).

[1]**vaulting** ['vɔ:ltiŋ], *s.* die Wölbung, das Gewölbe; der Gewölbebau.

[2]**vaulting,** *s.* (*Spt.*) das Springen; (*Gymn.*) ***—horse,*** das (Sprung)pferd.

vaunt [vɔ:nt], **1.** *v.t.* 1. rühmen, (an)preisen; 2. sich rühmen (*Gen.*), angeben, protzen *or* sich brüsten mit. **2.** *v.i.* prahlen (*of,* mit), sich rühmen (*Gen.*), sich (*Dat.*) in die Brust werfen. **vaunter,** *s.* der (die) Prahler(in), Angeber(in), Aufschneider(in). **vaunting,** *adj.* prahlerisch.

veal [vi:l], *s.* das Kalbfleisch; ***roast*** –, der Kalbsbraten; – ***cutlet,*** das Kalbskotelett.

vector ['vektə], *s.* (*Math.*) der Vektor. **vectorial** [–'tɔ:riəl], *adj.* Vektor(en)–; – ***angle,*** der Polarwinkel.

Veda ['veidə], *s.* der Weda. **Vedaic** [vi'deiik], *adj.* wedisch; – ***Sankrit,*** das Sankrit des Weda.

vedette [vi'det], *s.* die Vedette, der Kavallerie(wacht)posten.

Vedic ['veidik], *adj. See* **Vedaic.**

veer [viə], **1.** *v.i.* sich drehen, lavieren (*as ship*), umspringen, fieren (*as wind*); (*fig.*) sein Verhalten ändern; – ***about,*** umspringen (*as wind*); (*fig.*) – ***round,*** umschwenken (*to,* nach), hinüberschwenken (zu), umschlagen (*as fortune etc.*). **2.** *v.t.* vor dem Winde wenden, halsen (*a ship*); (*Naut.*) (*also* – ***away*** or ***out***) loslassen, abschießen, laufen lassen, fieren (*a cable*).

vegetable ['vedʒitəbl], **1.** *s.* die Pflanze; das Gemüse (*for cooking*); *pl.* das Gemüse, Gemüsearten (*pl.*); (*fig.*) ***be a –,*** *see* **vegetate**; ***green –s,*** grünes Gemüse. **2.** *attrib. adj.* vegetabilisch, pflanzlich, Pflanzen–, Gemüse–; – ***diet,*** vegetarische Kost; – ***dye,*** der Pflanzenfarbstoff; – ***garden,*** der Gemüsegarten; – ***ivory,*** vegetabilisches Elfenbein; – ***kingdom,*** das Pflanzenreich; – ***marrow,*** der Kürbis; – ***oil,*** das Pflanzenöl.

vegetal ['vedʒitl], *adj.* pflanzlich, vegetativ, Vegetations–; vegetabilisch, Pflanzen–. **vegetarian** [–i'tɛəriən], **1.** *adj.* vegetarisch, Vegetarier–. **2.** *s.* der (die) Vegetarier(in). **vegetarianism,** *s.* der Vegetarismus.

vegetate ['vedʒiteit], *v.i.* (wie eine Pflanze) wachsen; (*usu. fig.*) vegetieren, stumpf dahinleben, ein Pflanzenleben führen. **vegetation** [–'teiʃən], *s.* 1. der Pflanzenwuchs, die Vegetation; Pflanzenwelt, Pflanzen (*pl.*); 2. (*Med.*) die Wucherung; (*fig.*) das Dahinvegetieren. **vegetative** ['vedʒitətiv], *adj.* 1. pflanzlich, vegetativ (*also fig.*), wie Pflanzen wachsend; (*fig.*) passiv; 2. Vegetations–, Wachstums–.

vehemence, vehemency ['vi:iməns(i)], *s.* die Heftigkeit, Vehemenz, Wucht, Gewalt; (*fig.*) Hitze, Leidenschaft, Inbrunst, das Ungestüm, Feuer. **vehement,** *adj.* heftig, gewaltig, ungestüm, lebhaft, heiß (*as desires*); hitzig, leidenschaftlich (*as a p.*).

vehicle ['vi:ikl], *s.* 1. das Fuhrwerk, Fahrzeug, Gefährt, Beförderungsmittel; 2. (*fig.*) Medium, Vehikel, Ausdrucksmittel, der Träger, Vermittler. **vehicular** [vi:'hikjulə], *adj.* Wagen–, Fahrzeug–.

veil [veil], **1.** *s.* der Schleier (*also fig.*); (*Eccl., Bot.*) das Velum; die Hülle, Maske, Verschleierung, der Deckmantel; (*fig.*) ***draw a – over,*** *see* **2.** (*fig.*); ***take the –,*** den Schleier nehmen, Nonne werden. **2.** *v.t.* verschleiern, verhüllen (*one's face*), (*fig.*) verschleiern, verhüllen, verbergen, bemänteln, tarnen. **veiling,** *s.* 1. die Verschleierung; 2. der Schleierstoff.

vein [vein], *s.* 1. (*Anat.*) die Vene; 2. (*Geol.*) (Erz)-ader, der Gang, Flöz; 3. (*Bot.*) die Rippe; 4. Maser (*in wood*), Ader (*in marble etc.*); 5. (*fig.*) (Wesens)zug (*in a p.*), Beigeschmack (*in a th.*), Hang, die Neigung, Anlage; Art, der Stil; die Stimmung, Laune; ***be in the – for,*** aufgelegt *or* in Stimmung sein zu; ***satirical –,*** satirische Ader. **veined,** *adj.* geädert, äd(e)rig, gerippt, marmoriert, gemasert. **veining,** *s.* die Äderung, Maserung.

velar ['vi:lə], **1.** *adj.* Gaumen–, velar. **2.** *s.* der Gaumenlaut, Velarlaut.

veld(t) [velt, felt], *s.* das Grasland, Weideland.

velleity [və'li:iti], *s.* (*obs.*) kraftloser Wille.

vellum ['veləm], *s.* das Schreibpergament; ***--paper,*** das Velin(papier).

velocipede [vi'lɔsipi:d], *s.* (*obs.*) das Fahrrad.

velocity [vi'lɔsiti], *s.* die Geschwindigkeit, Schnelle, Schnelligkeit; – ***of sound,*** die Schallgeschwindigkeit.

velour(s) [və'luə], *s.* der Velours.

velum ['vi:ləm], *s.* (*Anat.*) weicher Gaumen, das Gaumensegel, (*Bot.*) Segel, die Membran.

velvet ['velvit], **1.** *s.* 1. der Samt; (*coll.*) ***be on –,*** glänzend dastehen; 2. der Bast (*on antlers*). **2.** *adj.* Samt–; samtweich, samtartig; (*fig.*) ***handle him with – gloves,*** ihn mit Samthandschuhen anfassen. **velveteen** [–'ti:n], *s.* der Baumwollsamt, Man(s)chester. **velvety,** *adj.* samtartig, samtweich; lieblich (*as wine*).

venal [vi:nl], *adj.* käuflich, feil, bestechlich; (*fig.*) korrupt. **venality** [vi'næliti], *s.* die Käuflichkeit, Feilheit, Bestechlichkeit.

venation [vi'neiʃən], *s.* (*Bot.*) die Äderung, das Geäder.

vend [vend], *v.t.* (*Law*) verkaufen, feilbieten. **vendee** [–di:], *s.* der Käufer. **vender,** *s.* der Verkäufer, Händler. **vendible,** *adj.* verkäuflich, gängig, gangbar. **vending-machine,** *s.* der (Verkaufs)automat. **vendition** [–'diʃən], *s.* der Verkauf.

vendetta [ven'detə], *s.* die Blutrache.

vendor [–dɔ:], *s.* (*Law*) *see* **vender.**

veneer [və'niə], **1.** *s.* 1. das Furnier(holz), Furnierblatt; 2. (*fig.*) äußerer Anstrich, der Schein, falscher Glanz, die Tünche. **2.** *v.t.* 1. furnieren; 2. (*fig.*) einen äußeren Anstrich geben (*Dat.*), verdecken (***with,*** durch), verschönern, umkleiden (mit). **veneering,** *s.* das Furnieren, die Furnierarbeit.

venerability [venərə'biliti], *s. See* **venerableness. venerable** ['venərəbl], *adj.* ehrwürdig, verehrungswürdig; (*as title*) hochwürdig; (*fig.*) alt(ehrwürdig) (*of building*); (*Eccl.*) ***Venerable Sir,*** Hochwürden. **venerableness,** *s.* die Verehrungswürdigkeit, Ehrwürdigkeit. **venerate** ['venəreit], *v.t.* (ver)ehren, hochachten. **veneration** [–'reiʃən], *s.* die Verehrung (***for,*** für), Ehrfurcht, Hochachtung (vor (*Dat.*)); ***hold in –,*** verehren.

venereal [vi'niəriəl], *adj.* geschlechtlich, sexuell, Sexual–, Geschlechts–; geschlechtskrank, venerisch; – ***disease,*** die Geschlechtskrankheit.

[1]**venery** ['venəri], *s.* (*obs.*) der Geschlechtsgenuß, Geschlechtsverkehr.

[2]**venery,** *s.* (*obs.*) die Jagd, das Weidwerk.

venesection [veni'sekʃən], *s.* der Aderlaß.

Venetian [vi'ni:ʃən], **1.** *s.* der (die) Venezianer(in). **2.** *adj.* venezianisch; – ***blind,*** der Rolladen, die Jalousie.

Venezuela [venə'zweilə], *s.* Venezuela (*n.*). **Venezuelan, 1.** *s.* der (die) Venezolaner(in). **2.** *adj.* venezolanisch.

vengeance ['vendʒəns], *s.* die Rache; ***take – on,*** sich rächen an (*Dat.*); (*coll.*) ***with a –,*** tüchtig, ganz gehörig, gewaltig, erst recht; und wie; daß es eine Art hat. **vengeful,** *adj.* rachsüchtig, rachedurstig, nachtragend.

venial ['vi:niəl], *adj.* verzeihlich, entschuldbar, nicht schwerwiegend; (*Eccl.*) läßlich; – ***sin,*** erläßliche Sünde. **veniality** [–i'æliti], *s.* die Verzeihlichkeit.

Venice ['venis], *s.* Venedig (*n.*).

venison ['venizn], *s.* das Wildbret.

venom ['venəm], *s.* 1. das Tiergift; (*less accurately*) Gift, der Giftstoff; 2. (*fig.*) die Gehässigkeit, Bosheit, Tücke. **venomed** [–d], *adj.* (*usu. fig.*) giftig, boshaft, gehässig. **venomous,** *adj.* giftig (*also fig.*), Gift–; (*fig.*) boshaft, gehässig. **venomousness,** *s.* die Giftigkeit, (*fig.*) Boshaftigkeit, Gehässigkeit.

venose ['vi:nous], *adj.* (*Bot.*) geädert. **venosity** [vi'nɔsiti], *s.* (*Med.*) venöse Beschaffenheit (*of blood*). **venous,** *adj.* (*Anat.*) venös, Venen–; (*Bot.*) geädert.

vent [vent], **1.** *s.* 1. die Öffnung; das Spundloch (*of a cask*); Zündloch (*of guns*); der After (*of birds and fishes*); 2. Vulkanschlot; 3. (*fig.*) Ausbruch, Erguß; (*fig.*) ***give –,*** Luft machen, freien Lauf lassen (***to,*** *Dat.*). **2.** *v.t.* (*usu. fig.*) lüften, auslassen (***on,*** an (*Dat.*)), Luft machen (*Dat.*), freien Lauf lassen (*Dat.*); äußern, verbreiten. **ventage** [–idʒ], *s.* das Fingerloch (*of wind instruments*).

venter ['ventə], *s.* der Bauch, Unterleib, die Magenhöhle (*of insects*).

ventilate ['ventileit], *v.t.* 1. ventilieren (*also fig.*), belüften, entlüften, auslüften, (durch)lüften (*a room etc.*), Luftlöcher anbringen in (*Dat.*) (*a box etc.*); 2. schwingen (*corn*); 3. (*fig.*) zum Ausdruck bringen, äußern (*opinion*), diskutieren, erörtern, erwägen, anschneiden (*a question*). **ventilation** [–'leiʃən], *s.* 1. das Ventilieren, (Be)lüften; (*Min.*) die Bewetterung; 2. Lüftung, der Luftzufuhr, Luftwechsel (*in a room*); (*Min.*) die Wetterführung; 3. (*fig.*) Erörterung, Äußerung; Diskussion, Aussprache. **ventilator** [–leitə], *s.* der Ventilator, die Luftklappe, Lüftungsvorrichtung, Lüftungsanlage; (*Min.*) der Wetterschacht.

ventral ['ventrəl], *adj.* Bauch–, abdominal.

ventricle ['ventrikl], *s.* (*Anat.*) der Ventrikel, die Höhlung, Höhle (*in brain*), Kammer (*in the heart*). **ventricular** [–'trikjulə], *adj.* Höhlen–, (Herz)kammer–.

ventriloquial [–tri'loukwiəl], *adj.* bauchrednerisch, Bauchrede–. **ventriloquism** [–'triləkwizm], *s.* die Bauchredekunst, das Bauchreden. **ventriloquist** [–'triləkwist], *s.* der Bauchredner. **ventriloquize** [–'triləkwaiz], *v.i.* bauchreden. **ventriloquous** [–'triləkwəs], *adj. See* **ventriloquial.**

venture ['ventʃə], **1.** *s.* 1. das Wagnis, Risiko; (*Comm.*) Unternehmen, die Spekulation; ***put to the –,*** versuchen, riskieren, es versuchen mit; 2. das Geratewohl; ***at a –,*** aufs Geratewohl, auf gut Glück. **2.** *v.t.* 1. wagen, riskieren, aufs Spiel setzen; (*Prov.*) ***nothing –, nothing have,*** frisch gewagt ist halb gewonnen; 2. zu äußern wagen (*an opinion*). **3.** *v.i.* sich (*Dat.*) erlauben *or* unterstehen, sich wagen; ***– on a th.,*** sich in eine S. einlassen, sich an eine S. wagen; ***I – to ask,*** ich erlaube *or* gestatte mir zu fragen. **venturesome** [–səm], *adj.* kühn, verwegen, waghalsig, wagemütig (*of a p.*); riskant, gefährlich, gewagt (*of a th.*). **venturesomeness,** *s.* die Kühnheit, Verwegenheit, Unternehmungslust, Waghalsigkeit; Gefährlichkeit, Gewagtheit. **venturous,** *adj. See* **venturesome** (*of a p.*).

venue ['venju:], *s.* 1. (*Law*) zuständiger Gerichtsort; 2. (*coll.*) der Schauplatz, Zusammenkunftsort, Treffpunkt.

veracious [və'reiʃəs], *adj.* wahrhaft, wahrheitsliebend, vertrauenswürdig (*of a p.*), glaubwürdig, wahr(heitsgetreu) (*of a statement*). **veracity** [–'ræsiti], *s.* die Wahrhaftigkeit, Wahrheitsliebe (*of a p.*), Glaubwürdigkeit, Richtigkeit, Wahrheit (*of a statement*).

veranda [və'rændə], *s.* die Veranda.

verb [və:b], *s.* das Zeitwort, Verb(um). **verbal,** *adj.* 1. wortgetreu, (wort)wörtlich, buchstäblich; – ***changes,*** Änderungen im Wortlaut; 2. Verbal–, Wort–; (*Eccl.*) – ***inspiration,*** die Verbalinspiration; – ***memory,*** das Wortgedächtnis; (*Pol.*) – ***note,*** die Verbalnote; 3. mündlich; – ***agreement,*** mündliches Abkommen; – ***tradition,*** mündliche Überlieferung; 4. (*Gram.*) verbal, Zeitwort–; – ***noun,*** das Verbalsubstantiv.

verbalism ['və:bəlizm], *s.* der Verbalismus, das Wortwissen, die Wortklauberei. **verbalist,** *s.* der Wortklauber. **verbalization** [–ai'zeiʃən], *s.* 1. die Formulierung; 2. (*Gram.*) Verwandlung in ein Verb. **verbalize, 1.** *v.t.* 1. in Worte fassen, formulieren; 2. (*Gram.*) in ein Zeitwort verwandeln. **2.** *v.i.* wortreich sein, viele Worte machen. **verbally,** *adj.* mündlich, auf mündlichem Wege.

verbatim [və:'beitim], *adj., adv.* (wort)wörtlich, wortgetreu, Wort für Wort.

verbiage ['və:biidʒ], *s.* der Wortschwall.

verbose [və:'bous], *adj.* wortreich, überladen (*of language*), weitschweifig, geschwätzig (*of a p.*). **verbosity** [–'bɔsiti], *s.* die Wortfülle, der Wortschwall; die Weitschweifigkeit.

verdancy ['və:dənsi], *s.* 1. das Grün(e), frisches Grün, grüne Frische; 2. (*fig.*) die Unreife. **verdant,** *adj.* 1. grün (*also fig.*), grünend, frisch; 2. (*fig.*) unerfahren, naiv.

verderer ['və:dərə], *s.* (*Hist.*) königlicher Förster.

verdict ['və:dikt], *s.* der Urteilsspruch, Rechtsspruch, Wahrspruch, (*fig.*) das Urteil, die Entscheidung, Meinung, Ansicht; – ***of not guilty,*** der Freispruch; (*Law*) ***open –,*** die Feststellung einer Straftat ohne Nennung des Täters; (*fig.*) ***pass a – upon,*** ein Gutachten abgeben über (*Acc.*); ***return a – of murder,*** auf Mord erkennen.

verdigris ['və:digri:s], *s.* der Grünspan.

verdure ['və:djə], *s.* 1. das Grün, grüne Vegetation, üppiger Pflanzenwuchs; 2. (*fig.*) das Gedeihen, die Frische, Kraft, Blüte.

verge [və:dʒ], **1.** *s.* 1. der Rand, die Grenze; ***on the –,*** an der Grenze *or* am Rande (***of,*** *Gen.*), nahe (*Dat.*), nahe daran, im Begriff (***of doing,*** zu tun); 2. die Raseneinfassung, der Grasstreifen; 3. (*Hist.*) Amtsstab; 4. (*Horol.*) die Spindel. **2.** *v.i.* streifen, grenzen, stoßen, liegen (***on,*** an (*Acc.*)) (*also fig.*).

verger ['və:dʒə], *s.* 1. (*Hist.*) der Stabträger; 2. Kirchendiener, Küster.

verier ['veriə], *comp. adj.* (*obs.*) noch echter. **veriest,** *sup. adj.* (*rare*) reinst, schierst, pur(e)st; – ***chance,*** reinster Zufall; – ***nonsense,*** schierster *or* ausgemachtester Unsinn; – ***limit,*** äußerste Grenze.

verifiable ['verifaiəbl], *adj.* erweislich, nachweislich, nachweisbar, beweisbar, nachprüfbar. **verification** [–fi'keiʃən], *s.* die Überprüfung, Feststellung der Richtigkeit; der Wahrheitsnachweis, Beleg, die Beglaubigung, Bestätigung, Beurkundung; (*Law*) ***in – of which,*** urkundlich dessen. **verify,** *v.t.* 1. (*Law*) durch Beweis erhärten, bestätigen, beurkunden, belegen, beglaubigen; als wahr nachweisen *or* beweisen, auf die Wahrheit *or* Echtheit (nach)prüfen *or* überprüfen, die Richtigkeit feststellen (*Gen.*); 2. wahrmachen, erfüllen, verwirklichen.

verily ['verili], *adv.* (*B., obs.*) wahrlich, fürwahr. **verisimilitude** [–si'militju:d], *s.* die Wahrscheinlichkeit. **veritable** [–təbl], *adj.* wahr(haft), wirklich, echt, authentisch. **verity** [–iti], *s.* die Wahrheit, Wirklichkeit; (*also pl.*) wahre Tatsache, die Grundwahrheit; (*obs.*) ***of a –!*** wahrhaftig! wirklich! fürwahr!

verjuice ['və:dʒu:s], *s.* unreifer Obstsaft; (*fig.*) die Säure.

vermeil ['və:mil], *adj.* (*Poet.*) purpurrot, scharlachrot, hochrot.

vermicelli [və:mi'seli], *s.* Fadennudeln (*pl.*).

vermicide ['və:misaid], *s.* das Wurm(tötungs)mittel. **vermicular** [–'mikjulə], *adj.* 1. Wurm–; wurmartig, wurmförmig; 2. gewunden. **vermiculate** [–'mikjulit], *adj.* (*usu. fig.*) wurmförmig, gewunden, geschlängelt. **vermiculated** [–'mikjuleitid], *adj.* 1. wurmstichig; 2. mit gewundenen Verzierungen. **vermiculation** [–'leiʃən], *s.* 1. der Wurmfraß; 2. (*Med.*) die Peristaltik; 3. (*Archit. etc.*) wurmlinige Verzierung. **vermiform** ['və:mifɔ:m], *adj.* wurmförmig; (*Anat.*) – ***appendix,*** der Wurmfortsatz. **vermifuge** [–fju:dʒ], *s. See* **vermicide.**

vermilion [və:'miliən], **1.** *s.* 1. das Zinnober, die Mennige; 2. das Zinnoberrot. **2.** *adj.* zinnoberrot, scharlachrot.

vermin ['və:min], *s.* (*usu. pl. constr.*) (*collect.*) 1. Schädlinge (*pl.*), das Ungeziefer; 2. (*fig.*) Gesindel, Geschmeiß. **verminate** [–eit], *v.i.* Ungeziefer erzeugen. **verminous,** *adj.* 1. verlaust, verseucht; Ungeziefer–; 2. (*fig.*) gemein, parasitisch.

vermouth ['və:məθ], *s.* der Wermut(wein).

vernacular [və'nækjulə], **1.** *adj.* einheimisch, landeseigen, Landes–, Volks–, Heimat– (*of language*). **2.** *s.* die Muttersprache, Landessprache, Volkssprache; der Dialekt, Jargon, die Lokalsprache, Fachsprache.

vernal [və:nl], *adj.* Frühlings–, frühlingsartig; (*fig.*) jugendlich, frisch; – ***equinox,*** die Frühlings-Tagundnachtgleiche; (*Bot.*) – ***grass,*** das Ruchgras.

vernier ['və:niə], *s.* der Nonius, Vernier, Feinsteller.

veronal ['verənəl], *s.* das Veronal.

veronica [və'rɔnikə], *s.* (*Bot.*) der Ehrenpreis.

verruca [və'ru:kə], *s.* (*pl.* **-cae** [–si:]) die Warze.

versatile ['və:sətail], *adj.* 1. wendig, geschmeidig, wandlungsfähig, anpassungsfähig, beweglich, gewandt, vielseitig (begabt); 2. wandelbar, veränderlich, unbeständig; 3. (*Bot., Zool.*) drehbar, sich drehend. **versatility** [–'tiliti], *s.* 1. die Vielseitigkeit, Gewandtheit, (geistige) Beweglichkeit, Anpassungsfähigkeit, Wandlungfähigkeit; 2. Wandelbarkeit, Veränderlichkeit, Unbeständigkeit.

[1]**verse** [və:s], *s.* 1. die Verszeile, Gedichtzeile; die Strophe; 2. (*coll.*) (*no art.*) Verse (*pl.*), Gedichte (*pl.*), die Poesie, Dichtkunst, der Vers (*also B.*), (Vers)dichtung; 3. das Versmaß, metrische Form; ***in –,*** in Versen.

[2]**verse,** *v.t.* – ***o.s.,*** sich vertraut machen (***in,*** mit), sich einlesen (in (*Acc.*)).

[1]**versed** [və:st], *adj.* erfahren, bewandert, geschlagen, versiert (***in,*** in (*Dat.*)).

[2]**versed,** *adj.* (*Math.*) ungekehrt; – ***sine,*** der Sinusversus.

verse-monger, *s. See* **versifier.**

versicle ['və:sikl], *s.* (*Eccl.*) der Versikel. **versicular** [–'sikjulə], *adj.* Vers–.

versification [və:sifi'keiʃən], *s.* 1. das Versemachen, die Verskunst; 2. der Versbau, das Metrum. **versifier** ['və:sifaiə], *s.* der Reimschmied, Verseschmied, Dichterling. **versify, 1.** *v.i.* Verse machen *or* schmieden, reimen, dichten. **2.** *v.t.* in Verse bringen, in Versen besingen, versifizieren.

[1]**version** ['və:ʃən], *s.* 1. die Übersetzung; 2. Lesart; Darstellung, Fassung, Version.

[2]**version,** *s.* (*esp. Med.*) die Wendung (*obstetrics*).

verso ['və:sou], *s.* die Rückseite (*of a page or coin*), (*Typ.*) das Verso; der Revers (*of coin*).

verst [və:st], *s.* die Werst.

versus ['və:səs], *prep.* (*Law., Spt.*) gegen.

[1]**vert** [və:t], *s.* (*coll.*) Übertretene(r), der Konvertit.

[2]**vert,** *s.* 1. (*Hist.*) das Unterholz, Dickicht; Holzungsrecht; 2. (*Her.*) Grün.

vertebra ['və:tibrə], *s.* (*pl.* **-ae** [–bri:]) der Rückenwirbel; *pl.* die Wirbelsäule. **vertebral,** *adj.* Wirbel–; – ***column,*** die Wirbelsäule. **vertebrate** [–it], **1.** *adj.* mit Rückenwirbeln versehen, Wirbel–; (*fig.*) mit Rückgrat, gediegen. **2.** *s.* das Wirbeltier. **vertebrated** [–breitid], *adj. See* **vertebrate, 1. vertebration** [–'breiʃən], *s.* die Wirbelbildung.

vertex ['və:teks], *s.* (*pl.* **vertices** [–tisi:z]) 1. (*Geom.*) der Scheitel(punkt), die Spitze; 2. (*Anat.*) der Scheitel, Vorderkopf; 3. (*Astr.*) Zenit; 4. (*fig.*) die Krone, der Gipfel.

vertical ['və:tikl], **1.** *adj.* 1. senkrecht, lotrecht, vertikal; – ***engine,*** (senkrecht) stehende Maschine; – ***ray,*** senkrecht fallender Lichtstrahl; (*Av.*) – ***take-off,*** der Senkrechtstart; – ***take-off plane,*** der Senkrechtstarter; 2. Scheitel–, Höhen–, Vertikal–; – ***angle,*** der Scheitelwinkel; (*Astr.*) – ***circle,*** der Höhenkreis, Vertikalkreis. **2.** *s.* senkrechte Linie, die Senkrechte, Vertikale.

verticil ['və:tisil], *s.* (*Bot.*) der Quirl, Wirtel; quirlige Blattstellung. **verticilate** [–'tisilit], *adj.* quirlig, quirlständig.

vertiginous [və:'tidʒinəs], *adj.* 1. wirbelnd, kreiselnd; 2. schwindlig, Schwindel–; schwindelerregend, schwindelnd (*height*). **vertigo** ['və:tigou], *s.* der Schwindel(anfall), das Schwindelgefühl.

vertu, *see* **virtu.**

vervain ['və:vein], *s.* das Eisenkraut.

verve [və:v], *s.* der Schwung, die Begeisterung, das Feuer.

very ['veri], **1.** *adv.* 1. sehr, äußerst, in hohem Grade; – ***good,*** sehr gut; (*as response*) sehr wohl, in Ordnung, einverstanden; – ***well,*** sehr gut; (*in response*) meinetwegen, freilich, nun gut, wenn es sein muß; ***not –,*** nicht gerade; – ***much fatigued,*** sehr *or* außerordentlich ermüdet; 2. (*before sup.*) aller–; ***to the – last piece,*** bis auf das (aller)letzte Stück; 3. (*with poss. pron. and own*) ganz; ***for his – own,*** für sich (allein), ganz für sich. **2.** *adj.* 1. (*after the*) allein, bloß; gerade, genau; ***in the – act,*** auf frischer Tat; ***at the – beginning,*** gerade *or* gleich am Anfang; ***the – air you breathe,*** selbst die Luft, die man einatmet; ***to the – bone,*** bis auf den Knochen; ***the – day,*** gerade an dem Tag; (*coll.*) ***the – devil,*** das ist rein *or* direkt zum Totärgern; ***the – fact,*** die bloße Tatsache, allein die Tatsache; ***the – one,*** genau *or* gerade derjenige *etc.*; ***the – opposite,*** gerade das Gegenteil; ***from the – outset,*** schon von Anfang an; ***the – same,*** genau dasselbe *etc.*; ***the – thing,*** gerade das Richtige; ***the – idea*** or ***thought,*** schon der (bloße) Gedanke; ***the – truth,*** die reine *or* lautere Wahrheit; 2. (*after* **this** or **that**) derselbe *etc.*; ***that – day,*** an ebendemselben Tag; ***this – day,*** noch heute; 3. (*obs.*) (*after poss. pron.*) schon, selbst; ***his – children,*** schon *or* selbst seine Kinder; 4. (*obs.*) (*after indef. art.*) wirklich, echt; ***a – present help,*** sofortige Hilfe.

vesica ['vesikə], *s.* (*Anat., Zool.*) die Blase, Zyste, (*Bot.*) das Säckchen. **vesical,** *adj.* Blasen–. **vesicant, 1.** *adj.* blasenziehend. **2.** *s.* blasenziehendes Mittel, das Zugpflaster. **vesicate** [–eit], **1.** *v.t.* Bläschen ziehen auf (*Dat.*). **2.** *v.i.* Blasen ziehen. **vesication** [–'keiʃən], *s.* die Blasenbildung. **vesicatory** [–kətri], *s., adj. See* **vesicant.**

vesicle ['vesikl], *s.* die Blase, das Bläschen. **vesicular** [və'sikjulə], *adj.* blasig, blasenförmig, Bläschen–, Blasen–. **vesiculate** [və'sikjuleit], **1.** *v.t.* (*esp. Geol.*) Bläschen bilden in (*Dat.*). **2.** *v.i.* Bläschen bilden. **vesiculation** [–'leiʃən], *s.* (*Geol.*) die Bläschenbildung.

vesper ['vespə], *s.* 1. (*Poet.*) der Abend; Abendstern; 2. *pl.* (*Eccl.*) die Vesper, Abendandacht, der Abendgottesdienst; die Abendglocke, das Abendläuten. **vespertine** [–t(a)in], *adj.* abendlich, Abend–.

vessel [vesl], *s.* 1. das Gefäß (*also fig.*), der Behälter; 2. (*Naut.*) das Schiff; 3. (*fig. esp. B.*) Werkzeug.

vest [vest], **1.** *s.* 1. das Unterhemd (*for men*), Hemdchen (*for women*); 2. (*Comm. or Am.*) die Weste, Unterjacke. **2.** *v.t.* 1. (*Poet. or Eccl., except when fig.*) bekleiden, ausstatten; 2. (*Law*) verleihen, übertragen (***in,*** *Dat.*); (*fig.*) (*usu. pass.*) ***be –ed in him,*** ihm zustehen, bei ihm *or* in seinen Händen liegen. **3.** *v.i.* 1. (*Eccl.*) sich ankleiden; 2. (*Law*) zufallen, anheimfallen, übertragen werden (***in,*** *Dat.*), übergehen (auf (*Acc.*)); 3. (*fig.*) (*rare*) *see under* **2** (*fig.*).

vesta ['vestə], *s.* (*obs.*) (*also* ***wax*** –) das Wachsstreichholz.

vestal ['vestəl], **1.** *adj.* vestalisch; (*fig.*) keusch, jungfräulich; – ***virgin,*** die Vestalin. **2.** *s.* die Vestalin.

vested ['vestid], *adj.* unabdingbar, (rechtmäßig) erworben; (*fig.*) althergebracht.

vestibule ['vestibju:l], *s.* 1. der Vorhof (*also Anat.*), Vorplatz, Vorsaal, Flur, das Vorzimmer, Vestibül, die Vorhalle; 2. (*Am.*) (*Railw.*) der Durchgang. **vestibule-train,** *s* (*Am.*) der D-Zug, Durchgangszug.

vestige ['vestidʒ], *s.* 1. die Spur (*also fig.*), das Zeichen, Zeugnis, sichtbares Merkmal; 2. (*fig.*) der (Über)rest, das Überbleibsel, bißchen; 3. (*Biol.*) Rudiment, verkümmertes Glied. **vestigial** [–'tidʒiəl], *adj.* (*Biol.*) rudimentär, verkümmert; restlich, Spuren–.

vestment ['vestmənt], *s.* (*Eccl.*) das Meßgewand; Gewand, die Amtskleidung, Amtstracht.

vestry ['vestri], *s.* 1. die Sakristei; 2. (*also* ***common*** –) der Kirchenvorstand, die Gemeindeversammlung. **vestry|-clerk,** *s.* der Kirchenbuchführer. **–man** [–mən], *s.* das Kirchenvorstandsmitglied, der Gemeindevertreter.

vesture ['vestʃə], *s.* (*Poet.*) Kleider (*pl.*), die Kleidung, das Kleid, Gewand.

Vesuvius [və'su:viəs], *s.* Vesuv (*m.*).

vet [vet], **1.** *s. abbr. of* ***veterinary surgeon.*** **2.** *v.t.* (*coll.*) genau prüfen, überholen.

vetch [vetʃ], *s.* (*Bot.*) die Wicke. **vetchling,** *s.* (*Bot.*) die Platterbse.

veteran ['vetərən], **1.** *adj.* altgedient, ausgedient; (*fig.*) erprobt, erfahren; – ***troops,*** kampferprobte Truppen. **2.** *s.* ausgedienter Soldat, der Veteran, (*esp. Am.*) Kriegsteilnehmer; (*fig.*) alter Haudegen.

veterinary ['vetərinri], *adj.* tierärztlich; – ***science,*** die Tierheilkunde; – ***surgeon,*** der Tierarzt, Veterinär.

veto ['vi:tou], **1.** *s.* (*pl.* **vetoes**) das Einspruchsrecht, Veto (*also fig.*), (*fig.*) der Einspruch (*on*, gegen). **2.** *v.t.* Veto einlegen gegen; (*fig.*) Einspruch erheben gegen, ablehnen, die Zustimmung verweigern (*Gen.*), untersagen, verbieten.

vex [veks], *v.t.* ärgern; plagen, quälen, belästigen, schikanieren; beunruhigen, ängstigen; ***be –ed with,*** sich ärgern über (*Acc.*), böse sein auf (*Acc.*). **vexation** [–'eiʃən], *s.* die Plage, Belästigung, Plackerei, Schikane; das Ärgernis, der Ärger, Verdruß, Scherereien (*pl.*); die Beunruhigung, Sorge, der Kummer. **vexatious** [–'eiʃəs], *adj.* ärgerlich, verdrießlich, lästig, leidig; (*Law*) schikanös. **vexatiousness,** *s.* die Verdrießlichkeit, Ärgerlichkeit, Lästigkeit, Schikane. **vexed** [–t], *adj.* 1. ärgerlich, verärgert (*at* (*an action*), ***about*** (*a th.*), ***with*** (*a p.*), über (*Acc.*)); 2. umstritten, strittig; ***–d question,*** (viel)umstrittene Frage. **vexing,** *adj.* belästigend, beängstigend, quälend, beunruhigend.

via ['vaiə], **1.** *s.* (*Astr.*) ***Via Lactea,*** die Milchstraße; – ***media,*** der Mittelweg. **2.** *prep.* über (*Acc.*) (*place*); mit Hilfe von.

viability [vaiə'biliti], *s.* die Lebensfähigkeit, Entwicklungsfähigkeit. **viable** ['vaiəbl], *adj.* lebensfähig, entwicklungsfähig, wachstumsfähig.

viaduct ['vaiədʌkt], *s.* der Viadukt, die (Tal)überführung.

vial ['vaiəl], *s.* die Phiole, das Fläschchen; ***pour out the –s of wrath,*** die Schalen des Zorns ausgießen.

viands ['vaiəndz], *pl.* Lebensmittel (*pl.*).

viaticum [vai'ætikəm], *s.* 1. das Reisegeld, die Reiseentschädigung, Wegzehrung, der Zehrpfennig; 2. (*Eccl.*) das Sterbesakrament, letztes Abendmahl.

vibrancy ['vaibrənsi], *s.* die Resonanz, Schwingung. **vibrant,** *adj.* 1. vibrierend, schwingend; hallend, schallend (*sound*); 2. (*fig.*) pulsierend, belebt (***with,*** von), bebend, zitternd (vor (*Dat.*)); lebensprühend (*of personality*). **vibrate** [–'breit], **1.** *v.i.* 1. vibrieren, schwingen, pulsieren, zittern; (*fig.*) (nach)klingen, nachschwingen (*of sounds*); 2. zittern, beben, erschauern (***with,*** vor (*Dat.*)). **2.** *v.t.* in Schwingung versetzen, vibrieren *or* schwingen lassen. **vibration** [–'breiʃən], *s.* 1. das Schwingen, Vibrieren, Zittern; die Schwingung, Oszillation; 2. (*coll.*) Erschütterung. **vibrator** [–'breitə], *s.* (*Tech.*) der Summer. **vibratory** ['vaibrətri], *adj.* vibrierend, schwingend, pulsierend; schwingungsfähig, Schwingungs–.

vicar ['vikə], *s.* 1. (*C. of E.*) der Pfarrer; 2. (*R.C.*) Vikar, stellvertretender Bischof, der Stellvertreter des Papstes; ***Vicar of Christ,*** der Statthalter Christi. **vicarage** [–ridʒ], *s.* das Pfarrhaus. **vicar-general,** *s.* der Generalvikar. **vicarious** [vi'kɛəriəs], *adj.* 1. stellvertretend (*also Med.*), beauftragt; 2. (*coll.*) nachempfunden, Ersatz–.

[1]**vice** [vais], *s.* 1. das Laster, die Untugend; Lasterhaftigkeit, Verderbtheit; – ***squad,*** die Sittenpolizei; 2. der Mangel, Irrtum, Fehler, das Gebrechen; 3. die Unart (***in a horse,*** eines Pferdes).

[2]**vice,** *s.* der Schraubstock, Klemmer, die Zwinge.

[3]**vice–,** *pref.* Vize–, stellvertretend. **vice|-admiral,** *s.* der Vizeadmiral. **–-chairman,** *s.* stellvertretender Vorsitzender, der Vizepräsident. **–-chancellor,** *s.* (*Univ.*) (geschäftsführender) Rektor. **–-consul,** *s.* der Vizekonsul. **–gerent** [–'dʒerənt], *s.* der Statthalter, Verweser. **–-presidency,** *s.* die Vizepräsidentschaft. **–-president,** *s.* der Vizepräsident. **–-presidential,** *adj.* Vizepräsidenten–. **–regal,** *adj.* vizeköniglich, Vizekönigs–. **–roy** ['vaisrɔi], *s.* der Vizekönig. **–royal,** *adj. See* **–regal.**

vice-versa ['vais(i)'və:sə], *adv.* umgekehrt.

vicinage ['visinidʒ], *s.* die Nachbarschaft, Nähe. **vicinal** [–nl], *adj.* benachbart, nah(e), umliegend. **vicinity** [vi'siniti], *s.* (nähere) Umgebung, die Nähe, Nachbarschaft; ***close –,*** unmittelbare Nähe (***to,*** von).

vicious ['viʃəs], *adj.* 1. lasterhaft, verderbt, verworfen (*of p.*); sündhaft, unmoralisch, tadelnswert, verwerflich (*of behaviour*); 2. bösartig, boshaft; – ***circle,*** der Zirkelschluß, die Schraube ohne Ende; 3. störrisch, bösartig (*as a horse*). **viciousness,** *s.* 1. die Lasterhaftigkeit, Verderbtheit, Verwerflichkeit; 2. Bosheit, Bösartigkeit; 3. Unarten (*pl.*) (*of a horse*).

vicissitude [vi'sisitju:d], *s.* der Wechsel, Wandel, die Veränderung; *pl.* Wechselfälle (*pl.*), Schicksalsschläge (*pl.*), das Auf und Ab. **vicissitudinous** [–'tju:dinəs], *adj.* wechselvoll.

victim ['viktim], *s.* das Opfer (*also fig.*); (*fig.*) Leidtragende(r), Betrogene(r); das Schlachtopfer, Opfer(tier) (*of a sacrifice*); ***fall a –,*** erliegen, zum Opfer fallen (***to,*** *Dat.*), überwältigt werden (von); – ***of circumstance,*** das Opfer der Verhältnisse; ***war –,*** das Kriegsopfer. **victimize,** *v.t.* 1. (auf)opfern, preisgeben; 2. prellen, peinigen, quälen, belästigen, schikanieren.

victor ['viktə], *s.* der (die) Sieger(in).

victoria [vik'tɔ:riə], *s.* zweisitziger Einspänner. **Victorian,** **1.** *adj.* viktorianisch. **2.** *s.* der (die) Viktorianer(in).

victorious [vik'tɔ:riəs], *adj.* siegreich (***over,*** über (*Acc.*)), Sieges–; ***be –,*** Sieger sein, als Sieger hervorgehen, den Sieg davontragen, siegen. **victory** ['viktəri], *s.* der Sieg; Erfolg, Triumph.

victual [vitl], **1.** *v.t.* (*v.i.* sich) verproviantieren *or* verpflegen, (sich) mit Lebensmitteln versehen. **2.** *s.* (*usu. pl.*) Lebensmittel (*pl.*), Eßwaren (*pl.*), der Proviant. **victualler** ['vitələ], *s.* 1. der Lebensmittellieferant; ***licensed –,*** der Schankwirt, Schenkwirt; 2. (*Naut.*) das Proviantschiff. **victualling,** *s.* die Verproviantierung; (*Naut.*) – ***ship,*** das Proviantschiff.

vide ['vaidi], *int.* siehe. **videlicet** [vi'di:liset], *adv.* (*usu. abbr. viz.*; *to be read*: ***namely*** or ***that is***) nämlich, das heißt (*abbr.* ***d.h.***).

video– ['vidiou], *adj. pref.* Fernseh–, Bild–; – ***channel,*** der Bildfrequenzkanal; – ***frequency,*** die Bildfrequenz; ***–tape,*** das Magnetbildband.

vie [vai], *v.i.* wetteifern, es aufnehmen (***with,*** mit; ***for,*** um; ***in,*** in (*Dat.*)).

Vienna [vi'enə], *s.* Wien (*n.*). **Viennese** [viə'ni:z],

1. *s.* der (die) Wiener(in). **2.** *adj.* wienerisch, Wiener–.

view [vjuː], **1.** *v.t.* 1. besehen, besichtigen, überblicken, überschauen, in Augenschein nehmen; 2. (*fig.*) (an)sehen, betrachten, beurteilen, auffassen; 3. prüfen, mustern. **2.** *s.* 1. das Zusehen, Hinsehen, Erblicken; die Sicht, der Blick; ***at first*** *–*, auf den ersten Blick; ***disappear from*** *–*, verschwinden; ***be in*** *–*, sichtbar *or* in Sicht sein, vor Augen liegen; ***in*** (***full***) *–* ***of all the people***, (direkt) vor den Augen aller Menschen; ***come into*** *–*, sichtbar werden; ***on*** *–*, ausgestellt, zu besichtigen, zur Besichtigung, zu sehen, zur Ansicht; ***on nearer*** *–*, bei näherer Betrachtung; ***lost to*** *–*, aus dem Auge verloren; (*fig.*) ***take the long*** *–*, auf weite Sicht denken; ***to outward*** *–*, dem äußeren Ansehen nach; ***private*** *–*, private Vorführung (*of a film*); 2. der Ausblick, die Aussicht (*of*, auf (*Acc.*)), der Anblick (von); 3. (*esp. Phot.*) die Ansicht, Aufnahme, das Bild; ***aerial*** *–*, das Luftbild, die Luftaufnahme; ***back*** *–*, die Rückansicht; ***front*** *–*, die Vorderansicht; 4. (*fig.*) die Aussicht, Ansicht, Anschauung, Meinung, Auffassung, der Gesichtspunkt, Standpunkt, das Urteil; ***in my*** *–*, nach meiner Ansicht; ***in*** *–* ***of***, angesichts (*Gen.*), in Anbetracht (*Gen.*), im Hinblick *or* in Hinsicht *or* mit Rücksicht auf (*Acc.*); *–* ***of life***, die Lebensanschauung; ***point of*** *–*, der Standpunkt, Gesichtspunkt; ***form a*** *–* ***of***, sich (*Dat.*) eine Ansicht *or* Auffassung bilden über (*Acc.*); ***take a*** *–* ***of***, einen Standpunkt einnehmen von, eine Auffassung haben von; ***hold*** or ***take the*** *–*, die Ansicht *or* den Standpunkt vertreten; ***take a bright*** or ***rosy*** *–* ***of***, in rosigem Licht betrachten; ***take a grave*** *–* ***of***, ernst beurteilen *or* auffassen; ***–s on a matter***, die Ansicht über eine S.; 5. (*fig.*) (*oft. pl.*) das Ziel, der Plan, Zweck; ***the end in*** *–*, beabsichtigter Zweck; ***have in*** *–*, im Auge *or* in Aussicht haben, beabsichtigen, bezwecken; ***keep in*** *–*, im Auge behalten, berücksichtigen; ***with a*** or ***the*** *–* ***to***, mit dem Ziel *or* Zweck, mit *or* in der Absicht (***doing***, zu tun), in der Hoffnung auf (*Acc.*).

viewable [ˈvjuːəbl], *adj.* zu besichtigen(d). **viewer,** *s.* der Beschauer; (*coll.*) Fernsehteilnehmer. **view|finder,** *s.* (*Phot.*) der Sucher. **--hallo,** *s.* (*Hunt.*) das Hallo, der Halloruf. **–point,** *s.* der Standpunkt, Gesichtspunkt.

vigil [ˈvidʒil], *s.* 1. das Wachen, die Nachtwache; 2. der Vorabend (*of a festival*); 3. (*R.C.*) *pl.* Vigilien (*pl.*). **vigilance** [–əns], *s.* 1. die Wachsamkeit, (*fig.*) Sorgfalt, Umsicht; *–* ***committee***, der Überwachungsausschuß, Sicherheitsausschuß; 2. (*Med.*) die Schlaflosigkeit. **vigilant,** *adj.* wachsam; (*fig.*) aufmerksam, umsichtig. **vigilante** [–ˈlænti], *s.* (*Am.*) das Mitglied eines Selbstschutzverbandes.

vignette [viːˈnjet], *s.* die Vignette; das Zierbild, Titelbildchen.

vigor, (*Am.*) *see* **vigour. vigorous** [ˈvigərəs], *adj.* (tat)kräftig, kraftvoll, lebhaft, tätig (*of a p.*); nachdrücklich, nachhaltig, energisch, eindringlich (*of a th.*). **vigour** [ˈvigə], *s.* die Kraft, Energie, Vitalität, Lebhaftigkeit, Lebenskraft, Tatkraft (*of a p.*); der Nachdruck, die Eindringlichkeit, Durchschlagskraft, Wirksamkeit (*of a th.*).

viking [ˈvaikiŋ], *s.* der Wiking(er).

vile [vail], *adj.* gemein, niederträchtig, schändlich, niedrig, nichtswürdig; (*coll.*) abscheulich, scheußlich, ekelhaft, widerwärtig, widerlich. **vileness,** *s.* die Gemeinheit, Niederträchtigkeit, Schlechtigkeit; Widerwärtigkeit, Scheußlichkeit.

vilification [vilifiˈkeiʃən], *s.* die Verleumdung, Schmähung, Herabsetzung. **vilifier** [ˈvilifaiə], *s.* der Verleumder, Schmäher. **vilify** [ˈvilifai], *v.t.* verleumden, schmähen, herabsetzen.

villa [ˈvilə], *s.* das Einfamilienhaus (*in the town*), Landhaus, die Villa (*in the country*).

village [ˈvilidʒ], **1.** *s.* das Dorf, die Ortschaft, der Ort. **2.** *attrib. adj.* dörflich, Dorf–. **villager,** *s.* der (die) Dorfbewohner(in).

villain [ˈvilən], *s.* der Schuft, Schurke, (*also Theat.*) Bösewicht (*also coll.*), (*coll.*) Schelm, Schlingel.

villainous, *adj.* 1. schändlich, schurkisch; 2. (*coll.*) scheußlich, gräßlich, abscheulich. **villainy,** *s.* die Schurkerei, Niederträchtigkeit, Schändlichkeit; der Schurkenstreich.

villein [ˈvilən], *s.* (*Hist.*) Leibeigene(r), der Hintersaß, Hintersasse. **villeinage** [–idʒ], *s.* 1. die Leibeigenschaft, der Frondienst; 2. das Hintersassengut.

villiform [ˈvilifɔːm], *adj.* (*Zool.*) faserig, zottig. **villous,** *adj.* rauh, haarig, behaart, zottig. **villus,** *s.* (*pl.* **villi** [ˈvilai]) (*Anat.*) die Darmzotte, (*Bot.*) das Zottenhaar.

vim [vim], *s.* (*coll.*) die Kraft, der Schwung, Schneid, Mumm.

vinaceous [viˈneiʃəs], *adj.* Wein–, Trauben–; weinrot.

vinaigrette [viniˈgret], *s.* das Riechfläschen.

vincible [ˈvinsibl], *adj.* besiegbar, überwindlich.

vinculum [ˈviŋkjuləm], *s.* (*pl.* **-la**) 1. (*Math.*) der (Verbindungs)strich, die Überstreichung; 2. (*fig.*) das Band.

vindicable [ˈvindikəbl], *adj.* zu verteidigen(d) *or* rechtfertigen(d). **vindicate** [–keit], *v.t.* 1. rechtfertigen, bestätigen; 2. schützen, in Schutz nehmen, verteidigen (***from***, vor (*Dat*) *or* gegen); 3. rechtgeben (*Dat.*), behaupten, aufrechterhalten; 4. (*Law*) Anspruch erheben auf (*Acc.*), beanspruchen. **vindication** [–ˈkeiʃən], *s.* 1. die Rechtfertigung, Verteidigung; 2. Aufrechterhaltung, Beanspruchung, Behauptung; 3. Ehrenrettung. **vindicatory** [–keitəri], *adj.* 1. verteidigend, Rechtfertigungs–, rechtfertigend; 2. rächend, ahndend, Straf–.

vindictive [vinˈdiktiv], *adj.* rachsüchtig, nachtragend. **vindictiveness,** *s.* die Rachsucht.

vine [vain], *s.* der Weinstock, Rebstock, die Rebe. **vine|-clad,** *adj.* rebenbekränzt. **--disease,** *s.* die Reblauskrankheit. **--dresser,** *s. See* **--grower.**

vinegar [ˈvinigə], **1.** *s.* der (Wein)essig; ***mother of*** *–*, die Essigmutter. **2.** *v.t.* Essig tun an (*Acc.*), säuern, marinieren.

vine|-grower, *s.* der Weinbauer, Winzer. **--growing,** *s.* der Weinbau. **--leaf,** *s.* das Rebenblatt. **--louse, --pest,** *s.* die Reblaus.

vinery [ˈvainəri], *s.* das Treibhaus für Weinstöcke. **vineyard** [ˈvinjəd], *s.* der Weinberg, Weingarten.

viniculture [ˈvinikʌltʃə], *s.* der Weinbau, **vinification** [–fiˈkeiʃən], *s.* die Weinkelterung. **vinosity** [–ˈnɔsiti], *s.* der Weingeistgehalt, die Weinartigkeit. **vinous** [ˈvainəs], *adj.* weinartig, Wein–.

vintage [ˈvintidʒ], *s.* 1. die Weinlese, Traubenernte, Weinernte; der Weinertrag; 2. (Wein)jahrgang; (*fig.*) Jahrgang; *–* ***wine***, der Qualitätswein, Spitzenwein. **vintager,** *s.* der (die) Winzer(in), Weinleser(in). **vintner** [ˈvintnə], *s.* der Weinhändler.

viol [ˈvaiəl], *s.* (*Hist.*) *see* **¹viola.**

¹viola [viˈoulə], *s.* die Viola, Bratsche.

²viola [ˈvaiələ], *s.* (*Bot.*) die Viole, das Veilchen, Stiefmütterchen.

violability [vaiələˈbiliti], *s.* die Verletzbarkeit. **violable** [ˈvaiələbl], *adj.* verletzbar. **violate** [–leit], *v.t.* verletzen (*as oath*), entweihen, entheiligen, schänden (*a sacred place etc.*), zuwiderhandeln (*Dat.*), übertreten (*a law*), brechen (*a promise*), vergewaltigen, schänden, notzüchtigen (*a woman*). **violation** [–ˈleiʃən], *s.* die Verletzung, Übertretung, Zuwiderhandlung (*of laws*), der Bruch (*of an oath etc.*), die Entweihung, Entheiligung, Schändung (*of holy place*), Vergewaltigung, Entehrung, Schändung (*of a woman*); ***in*** *–* ***of***, bei *or* unter Verletzung von. **violator** [ˈvaiəleitə], *s.* der Verletzer, Übertreter; Schänder.

violence [ˈvaiələns], *s.* die Gewalt(tätigkeit), Gewaltsamkeit (*oft. pl.*); (*fig.*) Heftigkeit, das Ungestüm; ***by*** *–*, gewaltsam; (*fig.*) ***do*** *–* ***to***, entstellen, Gewalt antun (*Dat.*); ***offer*** *–* ***to***, gewalttätig behandeln; schänden, notzüchtigen (*a woman*); ***with*** *–*, mit Gewalt, heftig, ungestüm; ***robbery with*** *–*, der Raub mit unmittelbarer

Anwendung von Gewalt. **violent,** *adj.* 1. gewaltig, heftig, stark, kräftig (*as a blow*); – ***pain,*** heftiger Schmerz; 2. gewaltsam, gewalttätig (*as an action*); – ***death,*** gewaltsamer *or* unnatürlicher Tod; -***lay – hands on,*** Gewalt antun (*Dat.*); – ***measures,*** Gewaltmaßnahmen (*pl.*); 3. ungestüm, hitzig, leidenschaftlich (*as a p.*); – ***temper,*** unbändige, ungehemmte *or* hemmungslose *or* besinnungslose *or* sinnlose *or* blinde *or* rasende Wut; 4. grell (*as colour*).

violet ['vaiəlit], **1.** *s.* 1. (*Bot.*) das Veilchen; 2. Violett (*colour*). **2.** *adj.* violett, veilchenblau.

violin [vaiə'lin], *s.* die Geige, Violine; ***play the –,*** Geige spielen; ***play first –,*** die erste Geige spielen. **violinist,** *s.* der Geiger; ***first –,*** der Konzertmeister.

violist ['vaiəlist], *s.* (*rare*) der Bratschist.

violoncellist [viələn'tʃelist], *s.* der Cellist. **violoncello** [–'tʃelou], *s.* das (Violon)cello.

viper ['vaipə], *s.* die Viper, Natter, (Kreuz)otter; (*fig.*) (Gift)schlange. **viperine** [–rain], *adj.* vipernartig, Vipern–, viperisch. **viperous** [–rəs], *adj.* (*fig.*) schlangenähnlich, giftig.

virago [vi'rɑːgou], *s.* das Mannweib; (*fig.*) der Zankteufel.

virgin ['vəːdʒin], **1.** *s.* die Jungfrau (*also Astr.*); ***blessed – Mary,*** die Heilige Jungfrau, die Jungfrau Maria. **2.** *adj.* 1. jungfräulich (*also fig.*), Jungfern–; unberührt; (*fig.*) rein, keusch; – ***birth,*** jungfräuliche Geburt; 2. ungebraucht; gediegen (*metal*); – ***forest,*** der Urwald; – ***honey,*** der Jungfernscheibenhonig; ***Virgin Islands,*** Jungferninseln, Virginische Inseln (*pl.*); – ***snow,*** unbefleckter Schnee; – ***soil,*** unbebauter Boden, (*fig.*) unerforschtes *or* noch nicht bearbeitetes Gebiet.

[1]**virginal** ['vəːdʒinl], *adj.* 1. jungfräulich, Jungfrauen–, Jungfern–; – ***membrane,*** die Jungfernhaut; 2. (*fig.*) züchtig, keusch, rein, mädchenhaft.

[2]**virginal,** *s.* (*also pl.*) (*Mus.*) das Cembalo, Spinett.

virginhood ['vəːdʒinhud], *s.* die Jungfräulichkeit, Jungfernschaft.

Virginia [və'dʒiniə], *s.* 1. (*also – tobacco*) der Virginiatabak; 2. (*Bot.*) – ***creeper,*** Wilder Wein.

virginity [və'dʒiniti], *s.* 1. *See* **virginhood**; 2. (*fig.*) die Unberührtheit, Keuschheit, Unbeflecktheit, Reinheit.

Virgo ['vəːgou], *s.* (*Astr.*) die Jungfrau.

virgule ['vəːgjuːl], *s.* (*Typ.*) der Schrägstrich.

viridescence [viri'desəns], *s.* das Grün(werden). **viridescent,** *adj.* grün(lich). **viridity** [vi'riditi], *s.* (frisches) Grün, (*fig.*) die Frische.

virile ['virail], *adj.* 1. männlich, mannhaft, stark, kräftig, Mannes– (*courage*), Männer– (*voice*); 2. (*Med.*) zeugungskräftig. **virility** [vi'riliti], *s.* 1. die Männlichkeit; Manneskraft; 2. (*Med.*) Zeugungskraft; 3. (*fig.*) Stärke, Kraft.

virologist [vi'rɔlədʒist], *s.* der (die) Virusforscher(in). **virology,** *s.* die Virusforschung.

virtu [vəː'tuː], *s.* 1. die Kunstliebhaberei, der Kunstgeschmack; der Liebhaberwert, Sammlerwert, Kunstwert; 2. (*coll.*) Kunstgegenstände (*pl.*); ***article of –,*** der Kunstgegenstand.

virtual ['vəːtjuəl], *adj.* 1. eigentlich, tatsächlich, faktisch; 2. (*Tech. etc.*) virtuell. **virtually,** *adv.* im Grunde genommen, im wesentlichen.

virtue ['vəːtjuː], *s.* 1. die Tugend(haftigkeit), Unbescholtenheit (*of a p.*); ***make a – of necessity,*** aus der Not eine Tugend machen; 2. die Sittsamkeit, Keuschheit, Reinheit, Unberührtheit (*of women*); 3. Vorzüglichkeit, Wirkung, der Vorzug, Wert (*of a th.*); ***by – of,*** durch, mittels (*Gen.*), kraft (*Gen.*), vermöge (*Gen.*); ***in – of,*** wegen (*Gen.*), um . . . willen.

virtuosity [vəːtju'ɔsiti], *s.* 1. die Virtuosität, Kunstfertigkeit; 2. (*rare*) der Kunstsinn. **virtuoso** [–'ouzou], *s.* (*pl.* **-sos** *or* **-si**) 1. der Virtuose; 2. (*rare*) Kunstkenner.

virtuous ['vəːtjuəs], *adj.* 1. tugendhaft, sittlich; 2. tugendsam, züchtig, sittsam, keusch (*of women*); 3. (*rare*) vorzüglich, wirksam (*of a th.*).

virulence, virulency ['vir(j)uləns(i)], *s.* die Virulenz, Giftkraft, (*fig.*) Giftigkeit, Schärfe, Boshaftigkeit, Bosheit. **virulent** [–ənt], *adj.* virulent, giftig (*also fig.*), (*fig.*) bösartig, boshaft.

virus ['vaiərəs], *s.* das Virus, Gift (*also fig.*), der Giftstoff.

vis [vis], *s.* die Kraft; – ***inertiae,*** (*Phys.*) die Trägheitskraft; (*fig.*) Trägheit; (*Law*) – ***major,*** höhere Gewalt.

visa ['viːzə], *s.* das Visum, der Sichtvermerk; die Einreisegenehmigung.

visage ['vizidʒ], *s.* (*Poet.*) das Antlitz, (An)gesicht.

vis-à-vis ['viːzɑː'viː], **1.** *adv* gegenüber (*to, **with,*** von). **2.** *prep.* gegenüber (*Dat.*). **3.** *s.* das Gegenüber.

viscera ['visərə], *pl.* Eingeweide, (innere) Organe (*pl.*). **visceral,** *adj.* Eingeweide–.

viscid ['viskid], *adj.* klebrig, viskos, Fäden ziehend, seimig, dickflüssig, zähflüssig. **viscidity** [–'kiditi], *s.* die Klebrigkeit, Viskosität, Dickflüssigkeit, Zähflüssigkeit. **viscose** [–kous], *s.* die Zellwolle, Viskose, Zellulose. **viscosity** [–'kɔsiti], *s. See* **viscidity.**

viscount ['vaikaunt], *s.* der Vicomte. **viscountess,** *s.* die Vicomtesse.

vise, *see* [2]**vice.**

visé ['viːze], *s. See* **visa.**

visibility [vizi'biliti], *s.* 1. die Sichtbarkeit; 2. (*Meteor.*) Sicht(igkeit), Sichtweite. **visible** ['vizibl], *adj.* 1. sichtbar; 2. (*fig.*) erkennbar, offensichtlich, offenbar, augenscheinlich. **visibly,** *adv.* (offen)sichtlich, offenbar, merklich.

Visigoth ['vizigɔθ], *s.* (*Hist.*) der Westgote (die Westgotin).

vision ['viʒən], *s.* 1. das Sehen, Sehvermögen, Gesicht, der Gesichtssinn; ***field of –,*** der Blickfeld; 2. der Blick, die Einsicht, Einbildungskraft, das Vorstellungsvermögen; 3. Bild (*also T.V.*), der Anblick; (*T.V.*) – ***frequency,*** die Bildfrequenz; 4. die Vision, Erscheinung, das Phantasiebild, Wunschbild, Traumbild, Gesicht.

visionary ['viʒənəri], **1.** *adj.* 1. eingebildet, unwirklich, phantastisch, verstiegen, überspannt; 2. visionär, (hell)seherisch, Geister–, geisterhaft. **2.** *s.* 1. der Geisterseher, Hellseher; 2. Phantast, Träumer, Schwärmer, Idealist.

visit ['vizit], **1.** *v.t.* 1. besuchen, zu Besuch *or* Gast sein bei (*a p.*), aufsuchen (*an invalid*), besichtigen (*a place, or as a doctor his patient*), visitieren, inspizieren, in Augenschein nehmen (*in an official capacity*); 2. (*fig.*) heimsuchen, befallen; ***be –ed with,*** heimgesucht werden von, bestraft *or* geahndet werden mit; – ***one's indignation upon,*** seinen Zorn auslassen an (*Dat.*); – ***the sins of the parents on the children,*** die Sünden der Eltern an den Kindern vergelten. **2.** *v.i.* Besuche machen; ***go*** (***out***) ***–ing,*** Besuche machen; ***we don't –,*** wir verkehren nicht miteinander. **3.** *s.* der Besuch; ***pay a –,*** einen Besuch abstatten *or* machen (***to,*** bei) (*a p.*), besuchen (*a place*), (*sl.*) mal verschwinden *or* austreten; ***flying –,*** kurzer Besuch; – ***to the doctor,*** der Arztbesuch, die Konsultation beim Arzt; ***on a –,*** auf *or* zu Besuch (***to,*** bei).

visitant ['vizitənt], **1.** *s.* 1. (*Poet.*) der (die) Besucher(in); 2. (*Orn.*) der Strichvogel. **2.** *adj.* (*Poet.*) besuchend. **visitation** [–'teiʃən], *s.* 1. offizieller Besuch, die Visitation, Besichtigung, Durchsuchung (*of an official*); 2. (*Eccl.*) Heimsuchung; 3. (*coll.*) langer Besuch, der Dauerbesuch. **visitatorial** [–ə'tɔːriəl], *adj.* Visitations–, Durchsuchungs–, Aufsichts–, Überwachungs–. **visiting,** **1.** *s.* das Besuchen. **2.** *adj.* Besuchs–; – ***card,*** die Visitenkarte; – ***day,*** der Besuchertag; – ***officer,*** visitierender Offizier; ***be on – terms with,*** auf Besuchsfuß stehen mit, verkehren mit. **visitor** [–ə], *s.* 1. der (die) Besucher(in), (*oft. pl.*) der Besuch (***to,*** bei); (Kur)gast, Tourist; ***I am a – here,*** ich bin hier zu Besuch; ***–s' book,*** das Fremdenbuch; 2. der Inspektor, Visitator. **visitorial** [–'tɔːriəl], *adj. See* **visitatorial.**

visor ['vaizə], *s.* das (Helm)visier; der (Mützen)-schirm.

vista ['vistə], *s.* 1. weite Aussicht, die Fernsicht, der Ausblick (*also fig.*); (*fig.*) lange Reihe, weite Strecke, die Perspektive; 2. (Baum)allee; 3. (*Archit.*) der Gang, Korridor.

Vistula ['vistjulə], *s.* (*Geog.*) Weichsel (*f.*).

visual ['vizjuəl], *adj.* 1. visuell, Seh–, Gesichts–; – ***acuity,*** die Sehschärfe; – ***aids,*** das Anschauungsmaterial; – ***angle,*** der Gesichtswinkel; – ***arts,*** bildende Künste; – ***image,*** anschauliches Bild; – ***field,*** das Gesichtsfeld; – ***memory,*** visuelles Gedächtnis; – ***nerve,*** der Sehnerv; (*Mil.*) – ***reconnaissance,*** die Augenerkundung; – ***signal,*** das Sichtzeichen; 2. sichtbar, wahrnehmbar. **visualization** [–ai'zeiʃən], *s.* die Veranschaulichung, geistige Vergegenwärtigung. **visualize,** *v.t.* sich (*Dat.*) vorstellen *or* veranschaulichen *or* vergegenwärtigen, sich (*Dat.*) ein Bild machen von.

vital [vaitl], **1.** *adj.* Lebens–; lebenswichtig, lebensnotwendig; – ***energy,*** die Lebenskraft; – ***functions,*** Lebensfunktionen (*pl.*); – ***interests,*** lebenswichtige Interessen; – ***part,*** edler Teil (*of the body*), (*fig.*) notwendiger Bestandteil; – ***spark,*** der Lebensfunken; – ***statistics,*** die Bevölkerungsstatistik, (*coll.*) Büsten–, Hüft– und Taillenweite, Körpermaße (*pl.*); 2. (*fig.*) wesentlich, entscheidend, grundlegend, hochwichtig (***to,*** für); ***of – importance,*** lebenswichtig, höchst wichtig; – ***question,*** entscheidende Frage; 3. (*Poet.*) vital, lebenskräftig, lebensprühend, lebenspendend.

vitality [vai'tæliti], *s.* 1. die Lebenskraft, Vitalität; 2. Lebensdauer, Lebensfähigkeit.

vitalization [vaitəlai'zeiʃən], *s.* die Belebung, Kräftigung, Aktivierung; (*fig.*) Verlebendigung, lebendige Gestaltung. **vitalize** [vaitəlaiz], *v.t.* beleben, kräftigen; (*usu. fig.*) verlebendigen, lebendig gestalten.

vitamin(e) ['vitəmin], *s.* das Vitamin, der Wirkstoff, Ergänzungsstoff; – ***deficiency,*** die Mangelkrankheit.

vitiate ['viʃieit], *v.t.* 1. verderben, beeinträchtigen, untauglich machen; 2. (*Law*) ungültig machen, umstoßen, aufheben, entkräften; 3. verunreinigen, verpesten, verseuchen (*air etc.*). **vitiation** [–i'eiʃən], *s.* 1. die Verderbnis, Beeinträchtigung; 2. Verunreinigung, Verpestung; 3. (*Law*) Aufhebung, das Ungültigmachen.

viticulture ['vitikʌltʃə], *s.* der Weinbau.

vitreous ['vitriəs], *adj.* 1. gläsern, Glas–; – ***electricity,*** die Glaselektrizität, positive Elektrizität; – ***body*** or ***humour,*** der Glaskörper (*of the eye*); 2. glasartig, glasig (*lustre*); 3. (*Geol.*) vitrophyrisch. **vitrescence** [–'tresəns], *s.* die Verglasung. **vitrescent** [–'tresənt], *adj.* verglasend. **vitrescible** [–'tresibl], *adj. See* **vitrifiable. vitrifaction** [–i'fækʃən], *s. See* **vitrescence. vitrifiable** [–faiəbl], *adj.* verglasbar. **vitrify** [–ifai], *v.t.* (*v.i.* sich) verglasen.

vitriol ['vitriəl], *s.* das Vitriol; – ***of lead,*** schwefelsaures Bleivitriol; ***oil of –,*** rauchende Schwefelsäure, das Vitriolöl. **vitriolic** [–'ɔlik], *adj.* 1. vitriolisch, Vitriol–; 2. (*fig.*) bissig, sarkastisch.

vituperate [vi'tju:pəreit], *v.t.* schmähen, tadeln, schelten. **vituperation** [–'reiʃən], *s.* die Schmähung, Rüge, Beschimpfung, der Tadel; (*collect.*) Scheltworte (*pl.*), Schimpfworte (*pl.*). **vituperative** [–pərətiv], *adj.* tadelnd, scheltend, schmähend, Schmäh–.

[1]**viva** ['vi:və], **1.** *s.* der Hochruf, das Hoch, Vivat. **2.** *int.* (er *etc.* lebe) hoch!

[2]**viva** ['vaivə], *s.* (*coll.*) *see* **viva-voce, 2.**

vivacious [vi'veiʃes], *adj.* lebhaft, munter. **vivacity** [–'væsiti], *s.* die Lebhaftigkeit, Munterkeit.

viva-voce ['vaivə'vousi], **1.** *adj., adv.* mündlich. **2.** *s.* mündliche Prüfung.

vivid ['vivid], *adj.* lebhaft, intensiv (*imagination etc.*), lebendig, anschaulich (*description etc.*), kräftig, glänzend, leuchtend (*colour*). **vividness,** *s.* die Lebhaftigkeit, Intensität; Lebendigkeit, Anschaulichkeit; Leuchtkraft. **vivify** [–fai], *v.t.* beleben, Leben geben (*Dat.*), lebendig *or* lebensvoll machen, intensivieren.

viviparous [vai'vipərəs], *adj.* lebendgebärend, vivipar.

vivisect ['vivisekt], *v.t., v.i.* vivisezieren, lebend sezieren. **vivisection** [–'sekʃən], *s.* die Vivisektion.

vixen [viksn], *s.* 1. (*Zool.*) die Füchsin, Fähe; 2. (*fig.*) Zänkerin, Keiferin, böse Sieben. **vixenish,** *adj.* zänkisch, keifend.

vizier [vi'ziə], *s.* der Wesir.

Vladivostok [vlædi'vɔstɔk], *s.* Wladiwostok (*n.*).

vocable ['voukəbl], *s.* das Wort, die Vokabel. **vocabulary** [və'kæbjuləri], *s.* 1. das Wörterverzeichnis, Wörterbuch; 2. der Wortschatz, das Vokabular (*of a p.*).

vocal [voukl], *adj.* 1. (*Anat.*) Stimm–; – ***c(h)ords,*** Stimmbänder (*pl.*); – ***power,*** der Stimmaufwand; 2. (*Mus.*) Vokal–, Gesang–, gesungen, gesanglich; – ***music,*** die Vokalmusik, der Gesang; – ***part,*** die Singstimme; – ***recital,*** der Liederabend; 3. (*Phonet.*) tönend, stimmhaft; (*Gram.*) vokalisch; – ***sound,*** der Vokal; 4. gesprochen, mündlich, Sprech–, (*fig.*) widerhallend, tönend, klingend (***with,*** von), lärmend, laut, vernehmbar; ***become –,*** sich hören lassen, sich äußern. **vocalic** [vo'kælik], *adj.* vokalisch, Vokal–.

vocalism ['voukəlizm], *s.* (*Phonet.*) die Stimmgebung, Vokalisation; (*Gram.*) das Vokalsystem. **vocalist,** *s.* der (die) Sänger(in), Gesangkünstler(in). **vocalization** [–ai'zeiʃən], *s.* 1. (*Phonet.*) die Vokalisierung, Vokalisation, Stimmgebung; 2. stimmhafte Aussprache. **vocalize, 1.** *v.t.* 1. (*Phonet.*) stimmhaft aussprechen, vokalisieren; 2. aussprechen, äußern, singen. **2.** *v.i.* sprechen, singen. **vocally,** *adv.* 1. mit der *or* durch die Stimme; 2. gesanglich, in gesanglicher Hinsicht.

vocation [vo'keiʃən], *s.* (*Theol.*) die Berufung; Anlage, Eignung (***for,*** für), Neigung (zu); der Beruf. **vocational,** *adj.* beruflich, berufsmäßig, Berufs–; – ***guidance,*** die Berufsberatung; – ***testing,*** die Eignungsprüfung; – ***training,*** die Berufsausbildung.

vocative ['vɔkətiv], **1.** vokativisch, Anrede–. **2.** *s.* (*also – case*) der Vokativ, Anredefall.

vociferate [vo'sifəreit], *v.i., v.t.* schreien, laut (aus)-rufen, brüllen. **vociferation** [–'reiʃən], *s.* das Schreien, Geschrei, Gebrüll. **vociferous** [–'sifərəs], *adj.* schreiend, brüllend, lärmend, laut.

vodka ['vɔdkə], *s.* der Wodka.

vogue [voug], *s.* die Beliebtheit, der Anklang, hohes Ansehen, guter Ruf; die Mode; ***be in –,*** große Mode sein, sich großer Beliebtheit erfreuen; großen Zulauf haben (*as a play*); ***be the –,*** (die herrschende) Mode sein; ***all the –,*** die neueste Mode; ***come into –,*** Anklang finden, modern werden. **vogue-word,** *s.* das Modewort.

voice [vɔis], **1.** *s.* 1. die Stimme; ***in –,*** bei Stimme; ***at the top of one's –,*** aus vollem Halse; 2. (*fig.*) die Äußerung, der Ausdruck; ***give – to,*** Ausdruck verleihen *or* geben (*Dat.*); 3. die Stimme, Entscheidung, Meinung; ***have a – in,*** mitzusprechen *or* ein Wort mitzureden haben *or* eine Stimme *or* einen Einfluß haben in (*Dat.*) *or* bei; ***with one –,*** einstimmig; 4. (*Phonet.*) die Stimmhaftigkeit, der Stimmton; 5. (*Gram.*) das Genus (*of verbs*); ***active –,*** die Tätigkeitsform, das Aktiv(um); ***passive –,*** die Leideform, das Passiv(um). **2.** *v.t.* 1. äußern, aussprechen, ausdrücken, Ausdruck verleihen *or* geben (*Dat.*), zum Ausdruck bringen, in Worte fassen; 2. regulieren, abstimmen (*organ pipes*); 3. (*Phonet.*) stimmhaft aussprechen. **voiced,** *adj.* 1. (*as suff.*) mit . . . Stimme; 2. (*Phonet.*) stimmhaft. **voiceless,** *adj.* 1. ohne Stimme; sprachlos, stumm; 2. (*Parl.*) nicht stimmberechtigt; 3. (*Phonet.*) stimmlos. **voice-production,** *s.* die Stimmausbildung.

void [vɔid], **1.** *adj.* 1. leer, unbesetzt; – ***of,*** arm *or* leer an (*Dat.*), ohne, frei *or* entblößt von, ermangelnd (*Gen.*); ***be – of,*** keine(n, –s) . . . haben, ermangeln (*Gen.*); ***fall* –,** frei werden; 2. (*fig.*) (*Poet.*) nutzlos, wertlos, sinnlos; zwecklos; 3. (*Law*) unwirksam, nichtig, ungültig; ***null and* –,** null und nichtig. **2.** *s.* leerer Raum, die Leere, Lücke (*also fig.*); ***fill the* –,** die Lücke ausfüllen. **3.** *v.t.* 1. (*Law*) aufheben, für nichtig erklären, unwirksam *or* ungültig machen; 2. ausleeren (*bowels*); 3. (*obs.*) räumen, verlassen. **voidable,** *adj.* (*Law*) anfechtbar, aufhebbar. **voidance,** *s.* 1. die Ausleerung (*of the bowels*); 2. (*esp. Eccl.*) das Freiwerden (*of a benefice*). **voiding,** *s.* (*esp. Law*) das Annullieren, die Nichtigkeitserklärung. **voidness,** *s.* 1. die Leere; 2. (*esp. Law*) Nichtigkeit, Ungültigkeit.

voile [vɔil], *s.* der Schleierstoff.

volant ['vouləntl], *adj.* 1. fliegend, flugfähig; 2. (*Her.*) fliegend, im Flug; 3. (*Poet.*) flüchtig.

volatile ['vɔlətail], *adj.* 1. (*Chem.*) flüchtig (*also fig.*), sich verflüchtigend, verfliegend, verdunstend, ätherisch; – ***oil,*** ätherisches Öl; – ***salt,*** das Riechsalz; 2. (*fig.*) flatterhaft, leichtfertig, unbeständig, wankelmütig, sprunghaft. **volatileness, volatility** [–'tiliti], *s.* 1. die Flüchtigkeit, Verdampfbarkeit; 2. Flatterhaftigkeit, Unbeständigkeit, Wankelmütigkeit. **volatilization** [–lætilai'zeiʃən], *s.* die Verflüchtigung,Verdampfung, Verdunstung. **volatilize** [–'lætilaiz], **1.** *v.t.* verflüchtigen, verdampfen, verdunsten. **2.** *v.i.* sich verflüchtigen, verdampfen, verdunsten, verfliegen, sich auflösen.

vol-au-vent ['vɔlovã], *s.* die Blätterteigpastete mit Fleischfüllung.

volcanic [vɔl'kænik], *adj.* 1. vulkanisch (*also fig.*), Vulkan–; – ***eruption,*** der Vulkanausbruch; – ***glass,*** das Obsidian; – ***rock,*** das Eruptivgestein; 2. feurig, ungestüm, aufbrausend. **volcano** [–'keinou], *s.* (*pl.* **-oes**) der Vulkan; ***sit on the top of a* –,** auf einem Pulverfaß sitzen.

[1]**vole** [voul], *s.* (*Cards*) die Vola, Vole.

[2]**vole,** *s.* (*Zool.*) die Wühlmaus.

Volga ['vɔlgə], *s.* (*Geog.*) Wolga (*f.*).

volition [vo'liʃən], *s.* der Wille, das Wollen, die Willenskraft; der (Willens)entschluß; die Willensentscheidung, Willensäußerung, Willensübung; ***of one's own* –,** willentlich. **volitional,** *adj.* willensmäßig, Willens–.

volley ['vɔli], **1.** *s.* 1. die Salve; (*fig.*) der Hagel (*of stones etc.*), Ausbruch, Schwall, Strom, die Flut (*of words etc.*); 2. (*Spt.*) der Flugball, Flugschlag; (*Spt.*) ***half* –,** der Halbflugschlag. **2.** *v.t.* 1. in einer Salve abschießen; 2. (*Spt.*) als Flugball nehmen *or* spielen. **3.** *v.i.* 1. eine Salve abschießen *or* abfeuern *or* abgeben; 2. einen Flugball spielen *or* nehmen; 3. (*fig.*) (*usu.* – ***forth***) sich entladen *or* ergießen; toben, brüllen. **volleyball,** *s.* das Volleyballspiel.

volplane ['vɔlplein], **1.** *v.i.* im Gleitflug niedergehen. **2.** *s.* der Gleitflug.

[1]**volt** [vɔlt, voult], **1.** *s.* (*Fenc., Equest.*) die Volte, (*Fenc.*) Wendung. **2.** *v.i.* (*Fenc.*) eine Volte *or* Wendung machen, voltieren.

[2]**volt** [voult], *s.* (*Elec.*) das Volt. **voltage** [–idʒ], *s.* die (Strom)spannung. **voltaic** [–teiik], *adj.* voltaisch, galvanisch, Volta(isch)–.

volte-face [vɔlt'fa:s], *s.* (*Fenc.*) die Umdrehung, Kehre; (*fig.*) Wendung um 180 Grad, der Frontwechsel.

voltmeter ['voultmi:tə], *s.* der Spannungsmesser, Voltmesser.

volubility [vɔlju'biliti], *s.* 1. der Redefluß, die Zungenfertigkeit; 2. (*rare*) Beweglichkeit, Drehbarkeit. **voluble** ['vɔljubl], *adj.* 1. zungenfertig, redegewandt, redselig (*of a p.*); 2. fließend, flüssig, geläufig (*of language*); 3. (*Bot.*) sich windend *or* rankend.

volume ['vɔlju:m], *s.* 1. der Band (*of a book*); ***that speaks* -*s*,** das ist höchst bezeichnend, das spricht Bände; 2. (*Phys. etc.*) das Volumen, der (Kubik)inhalt, Rauminhalt; 3. (*fig.*) große Menge, die Flut, Masse; 4. der (Stimm)umfang, das Ausmaß (*of the voice*), (*Mus.*) die Klangfülle, Tonfülle, (*Rad.*) Lautstärke; (*Rad.*) –-***control,*** der Lautstärkenregler. **volumetric** [vɔlju'metrik], *adj.* Raum–, Volumenmaß–; – ***analysis,*** die Maßanalyse; – ***content,*** der Raumgehalt. **voluminous** [və'lju:minəs], *adj.* umfangreich, ausgedehnt; (*coll.*) massenhaft, massig, gewaltig, mächtig, (*as wrappings etc.*) bauschig; (*of literary production*) vielbändig (*works*), vielschreibend (*writer*).

voluntarily ['vɔləntərili], *adv.* aus freiem Entschluß *or* eigenem Antrieb. **voluntariness,** *s.* die Freiwilligkeit; Selbstbestimmung, Willensfreiheit. **voluntary, 1.** *adj.* 1. freiwillig, spontan, willentlich; – ***hospital,*** durch Spenden unterhaltenes Krankenhaus; ***do* – *work,*** unbezahlte Arbeit tun, als Volontär arbeiten; 2. (*Law*) vorsätzlich, absichtlich; 3. (*Psych.*) voluntaristisch, willensmäßig; 4. (*Anat.*) willkürlich. **2.** *s.* (*Mus.*) freies Orgelstück *or* Orgelspiel.

volunteer [vɔlən'tiə], **1.** *s.* 1. Freiwillige(r); 2. (*Comm.*) der Volontär; 3. *pl.* (*Mil.*) das Freiwilligenkorps. **2.** *adj.* Freiwilligen–. **3.** *v.i.* (*Mil.*) als Freiwilliger dienen; sich freiwillig melden (***for,*** zu); freiwillig tätig sein. **4.** *v.t.* freiwillig übernehmen *or* anbieten (*services*), unaufgefordert geben (*information*), zum besten geben (*a song etc.*).

voluptuary [və'lʌptjuəri], *s.* der (Wol)lüstling. **voluptuous,** *adj.* wollüstig, lüstern, geil, sinnlich, Sinnen–. **voluptuousness,** *s.* die Wollust, Sinnenlust, Sinnlichkeit, Geilheit, Lüsternheit, Üppigkeit.

volute [və'lju:t], *s.* 1. (*Archit.*) die Schnecke, Volute; Spirale, der Schnörkel; 2. (*Zool.*) die Rollschnecke. **voluted,** *adj.* schneckenförmig, spiralförmig, gewunden; (*Archit.*) mit Schneckenverzierung; (*Bot.*) eingerollt. **volution** [–'lju:ʃən], *s.* (*Anat.*) die Windung; (*Tech.*) Drehung; das Gewinde (*of a shell*).

vomit ['vɔmit], **1.** *v.t.* (*also* – ***up*** or ***out*** or ***forth***) (aus)brechen, auswerfen, (aus)speien, ausstoßen; ausladen. **2.** *v.i.* sich übergeben *or* erbrechen, (*vulg.*) kotzen. **3.** *s.* 1. das Ausgespie(e)ne, Erbrochene, der Auswurf, (*vulg.*) die Kotze; 2. das Brechmittel; 3. (*fig.*) der Unflat. **vomiting,** *s.* das Erbrechen. **vomitory** [–əri], **1.** *s.* 1. das Brechmittel; 2. Vomitorium, die Hauptausgang (*of Classical theatre*). **2.** *adj.* Erbrechen erregend, Brech–.

voodoo ['vu:du:], *s.* der (Wudu- *or* Wodu)zauber; (*coll.*) Fetisch, die Hexerei, Zauberei. **voodooism,** *s.* der Wodukult.

voracious [vɔ'reiʃəs], *adj.* gefräßig, gierig, (*fig.*) unersättlich. **voracity** [–'ræsiti], *s.* die Gefräßigkeit, Unersättlichkeit, Gier.

vortex ['vɔ:teks], *s.* (*pl.* **-xes** *or* **-tices** [–tisi:z]) der Wirbel, Strudel (*also fig.*). **vortical** [–tikl], *adj.* wirbelnd, Wirbel–, kreiselnd; strudelartig, wirbelartig.

Vosges [vouʒ], *pl.* (*Geog.*) Vogesen (*pl.*).

votary ['voutəri], *s.* 1. Geweihte(r), der (die) Verehrer(in), Anbeter(in); 2. (*fig.*) der Jünger, Anhänger, Verfechter, Vorkämpfer; 3. Enthusiast, Freund (*of music etc.*).

vote [vout], **1.** *s.* 1. die (Wahl)stimme; ***cast one's* –,** seine Stimme abgeben; ***casting* –,** ausschlaggebende Stimme; ***dissentient* –,** die Gegenstimme; ***floating* –,** nichtparteigebundene Wählerschaft; ***give one's* – *to*** (*a p.*) or ***for*** (*a th.*), stimmen für; –***s polled,*** abgegebene Stimmen (*pl.*), die Gesamtstimmenzahl; ***transferable* –,** übertragbare Wahlstimme; 2. das Stimmrecht, Wahlrecht; ***have the* –,** wahlberechtigt *or* stimmberechtigt sein, Stimmrecht haben; 3. die Abstimmung, Stimmabgabe, Wahl; ***by* –,** durch Abstimmung; ***put it to the* –,** darüber abstimmen lassen, es zur Abstimmung bringen; ***take a* –,** abstimmen (***on,*** über (*Acc.*)); 4. das Votum, Wahlergebnis, der Beschluß; – ***of censure,*** – ***of no confidence,*** das Mißtrauensvotum; – ***of confidence,*** das Vertrauensvotum; ***unanimous* –,** einstimmiger Beschluß. **2.** *v.i.* abstimmen, seine Stimme abgeben (***on,*** über (*Acc.*)); – ***for*** (***against***), stimmen für (gegen). **3.** *v.t.* 1. stimmen für, wählen (*a p.*); – ***down,*** ablehnen, niederstimmen, überstimmen; – *in*, (durch Abstimmung) wählen; 2. annehmen, genehmigen, beschließen (*a measure*), bewilligen (*money etc.*); 3. erklären *or* halten für, hinstellen als; 4. (*coll.*) vorschlagen (***that***, daß).

voter ['voutə], *s.* Stimmberechtigte(r), Wahlberechtigte(r); der (die) Wähler(in). **voting, 1.** *adj.* Wahl–, Stimm–. **2.** *s.* das (Ab)stimmen, die Wahl, Abstimmung, Stimmabgabe. **voting-paper,** *s.* der Stimmzettel, Wahlzettel.

votive ['voutiv], *adj.* geweiht, gelobt, Weih(e)–, Denk–, Votiv–.

vouch [vautʃ], **1.** *v.i.* (sich ver)bürgen, zeugen, einstehen (***for***, für). **2.** *v.t.* (*rare*) bezeugen, belegen, bestätigen, verbürgen. **voucher,** *s.* 1. der Zeuge, Gewährsmann, Bürge (***for***, *Gen.*); 2. (*usu.*) das Zeugnis, der Beleg(zettel), (Rechnungs)beleg, Belegschein, Kassenzettel; (*also* ***gift*** –) (Geschenk)-gutschein, Bon; 3. die Unterlage, Quittung, das Zahlungsattest; 4. der Bezugsschein, die Eintrittskarte.

vouchsafe [vautʃ'seif], **1.** *v.t.* gewähren, bewilligen (*to*, *Dat.*); ***not – a word to him,*** ihn nicht eines Wortes würdigen. **2.** *v.i.* geruhen, sich herablassen.

voussoir ['vu:swɑ:], *s.* der Wölbstein, Schlußstein.

vow [vau], **1.** *v.t.* geloben, feierlich versprechen, schwören, beteuern. **2.** *s.* das Gelübde; Gelöbnis, der Schwur, feierliches Versprechen; ***be under a –***, ein Gelübde abgelegt haben; ***make*** or ***take a –***, ein Gelübde tun *or* ablegen; ***take*** (***the***) ***–s***, das Ordensgelübde ablegen, Profeß tun (*of a monk*), den Schleier nehmen, Nonne werden (*of a nun*).

vowel ['vauəl], **1.** *s.* der Vokal, Selbstlaut. **2.** *attrib. adj.* Vokal–, vokalisch. **vowel|-gradation,** *s.* der Ablaut. **--modification, --mutation,** *s.* der Umlaut.

voyage ['vɔiidʒ], **1.** *s.* die (See)reise; ***homeward –*** or ***– home,*** die Rückreise, Heimreise; ***– out*** or ***outward –***, Ausreise, Hinreise; ***return –***, die Rückreise; ***– of discovery,*** die Forschungsreise. **2.** *v.i.* eine (See)-reise machen, (zur See) reisen. **3.** *v.t.* bereisen, befahren. **voyager,** *s.* (See)reisende(r).

vraisemblance ['vreisãblãs], *s.* die Wahrscheinlichkeit.

vulcanite ['vʌlkənait], *s.* der Hartgummi, das Ebonit, die Vulkanfiber. **vulcanization** [–ai'zeiʃən], *s.* das Vulkanisieren. **vulcanize,** *v.t.* vulkanisieren, härten (*rubber*).

vulgar ['vʌlgə], *adj.* 1. gemein, niedrig, ungebildet, ungesittet, unfein, vulgär, ordinär, pöbelhaft, rüpelhaft; 2. gewöhnlich, üblich, gebräuchlich, allgemein (verbreitet), landesüblich, volkstümlich; – ***era,*** christliche Zeitrechnung; – ***fraction,*** gemeiner *or* gewöhnlicher Bruch; – ***herd,*** der Pöbel; – ***Latin,*** das Vulgärlatein; – ***tongue,*** die Volkssprache, Landessprache.

vulgarian [vʌl'gɛəriən], *s.* der Plebejer, Protz, gemeiner Mensch. **vulgarism** ['vʌlgərizm], *s.* die Grobheit, Unfeinheit; (*usu.*) derber *or* vulgärer *or* gemeiner Ausdruck. **vulgarity** [–'gæriti], *s.* die Gewöhnlichkeit, Gemeinheit, Roheit, Pöbelhaftigkeit. **vulgarization** [–rai'zeiʃən], *s.* die Erniedrigung, Herabwürdigung, Popularisierung, Vulgarisierung, allgemeine Verbreitung. **vulgarize** ['vʌlgəraiz], *v.t.* 1. erniedrigen, herabwürdigen, vulgarisieren; 2. popularisieren, allgemein verbreiten, unter das Volk bringen. **vulgarly** ['vʌlgəli], *adv.* 1. allgemein, gewöhnlich, gemeinhin; 2. gemein, vulgär, ordinär, pöbelhaft.

Vulgate ['vʌlgit], *s.* die Vulgata.

vulnerability [vʌlnərə'biliti], *s.* die Verwundbarkeit, Anfechtbarkeit. **vulnerable** ['vʌlnərəbl], *adj.* verwundbar (*also Cards*), verletzbar; (*fig.*) angreifbar, anfechtbar; ungeschützt (*as places*); (*fig.*) – ***to,*** offen (*Dat.*), zugänglich (*Dat.*), anfällig für. **vulnerableness,** *s. See* **vulnerability. vulnerary** ['vʌlnərəri], **1.** *adj.* Wunden heilend, Wund–, Heil–. **2.** *s.* das Wundmittel.

vulpine ['vʌlpain], *adj.* 1. Fuchs–, fuchsartig; 2. (*fig.*) fuchsig, schlau, listig, verschlagen, durchtrieben.

vulture ['vʌltʃə], *s.* der Geier, (*fig.*) Blutsauger, Aasgeier; *see* ***Egyptian –***, ***Griffon –***. **vulturine** [–rain], **vulturish, vulturous,** *adj.* geierartig, (*fig.*) raubgierig.

vulva ['vʌlvə], *s.* (*Anat.*) die Vulva, der Cunnus, weibliche Scham. **vulval, vulvar,** *adj.* Scham-(lippen)–. **vulvitis** [–'vaitis], *s.* die Entzündung der Schamteile.

vying ['vaiiŋ], *adj.* wetteifernd.

W

W, w ['dʌblju:], *s.* das W, w. *See Index of Abbreviations.*

wacky ['wæki], *adj.* (*sl.*) meschugge.

wad [wɔd], **1.** *s.* 1. das Bündel, der Pfropf(en), Bausch (*of cotton wool etc.*), (*Artil.*) Ladepfropf; 2. (*coll.*) Stoß, die Rolle, das Päckchen (*of banknotes etc.*). **2.** *v.t.* verstopfen, zustopfen; wattieren (*a coat etc.*).

wadable ['weidəbl], *adj.* durchwatbar.

wadding ['wɔdiŋ], *s.* das Füllmaterial, die Einlage, Füllung, Polsterung, Wattierung, Watte.

waddle [wɔdl], **1.** *v.i.* watscheln, wackeln. **2.** *s.* watschelnder Gang.

wade [weid], **1.** *v.i.* 1. waten; 2. (*fig.*) sich mühsam durcharbeiten (***through***, durch); (*sl.*) – ***in,*** sich einmischen, dazwischentreten; (*sl.*) – ***into,*** tüchtig zugreifen (*food*). **2.** *v.t.* durchwaten. **wadeable,** *see* **wadable. wader,** *s.* 1. (*Orn.*) der Watvogel; 2. *pl.* Wasserstiefel (*pl.*).

wafer ['weifə], *s.* 1. die Waffel; 2. Siegelmarke, Oblate (*for letters, also Eccl.*); 3. (*Eccl.*) Hostie. **wafer-thin,** *adj.* hauchdünn. **wafery,** *adj.* waffelähnlich.

[1]**waffle** [wɔfl], *v.i.* (*sl.*) schwafeln, quasseln.

[2]**waffle,** *s.* die Waffel. **waffle-iron,** *s.* das Waffeleisen.

waft [wɑ:ft], **1.** *v.t.* (fort)wehen, hauchen, (heran)-tragen. **2.** *v.i.* wehen, schweben. **3.** *s.* 1. der Hauch, Luftzug; Duft; (*fig.*) Anflug; 2. (*Naut.*) das Notsignal, die Flagge im Schau.

[1]**wag** [wæg], **1.** *v.i.* wedeln (*of the tail*), sich hin und her bewegen; (*coll.*) immer in Bewegung sein (*of the tongue*); ***set tongues wagging,*** ein Gerede aufbringen. **2.** *v.t.* hin und her bewegen, wackeln mit; – ***its tail,*** mit dem Schwanz wedeln; – ***one's head,*** mit dem Kopfe wackeln, den Kopf schütteln, nicken; – ***one's finger,*** mit dem Finger drohen (***at***, *Dat.*). **3.** *s.* ***give a – of one's head,*** see ***– one's head***; ***with a – of his*** (*etc.*) ***head,*** mit einem Kopfnicken; ***give a – of the tail,*** see ***– its tail.***

[2]**wag,** *s.* (*coll.*) der Spaßvogel, Possenreißer, Witzbold.

[1]**wage** [weidʒ], *v.t.* unternehmen, führen (*war etc.*) (***on***, gegen).

[2]**wage,** *s.* 1. (*also pl.*) der (Arbeits)lohn; ***earn a good –*** or ***good –s,*** gut verdienen; ***living –***, das Existenzminimum; 2. (*Eccl.*) die Vergeltung; 3. *pl.* (*sing. constr.*) (*fig.*) der Lohn, Entgelt; (*B.*) ***the –s of sin is death,*** der Tod ist der Sünde Sold.

wage|-claim, *s.* die Lohnforderung. **--earner,** *s.* der Lohnempfänger. **--freeze,** *s.* (*coll.*) der Lohnstopp. **--group,** *s.* die Tarifgruppe. **--packet,** *s.* die Lohntüte.

wager ['weidʒə], **1.** *s.* die Wette; der Einsatz, Wettpreis; ***lay a –***, eine Wette machen, wetten. **2.** *v.t.* 1. (als Einsatz) setzen (***on***, auf (*Acc.*)) (*money*); (*fig.*) aufs Spiel setzen (*one's reputation etc.*); 2.

wetten mit (*a p.*) (***that,*** daß). **3.** *v.i.* wetten, eine Wette eingehen.

wage|-scale, *s.* die Lohnskala. **--sheet,** *s.* die Lohnliste. **--slip,** *s.* der Lohnstreifen.

waggery ['wægəri], *s.* der Spaß, die Schelmerei. **waggish,** *adj.* schelmisch, schalkhaft, spaßig. **waggishness,** *s.* die Schalkhaftigkeit.

waggle [wægl], **1.** *v.i.* wackeln, schwanken, wippen. **2.** *v.t.* wackeln *or* wippen mit. **waggly,** *adj.* (*coll.*) wack(e)lig, schwankend.

wag(g)on ['wægən], *s.* der Lastwagen, Gepäckwagen, Frachtwagen, Rollwagen; (*Railw.*) Güterwagen, Waggon; ***by –,*** per Achse; (*sl.*) ***be on the –,*** Abstinenzler sein. **wag(g)onage** [–idʒ], *s.* Frachtgeld, der Fuhrlohn. **wag(g)on-ceiling,** *s.* (*Archit.*) die Tonnendecke. **wag(g)oner,** *s.* der Fuhrmann (*also Astr.*). **wag(g)onette** [–gə'net], *s.* das *or* der Break. **wag(g)on|-load,** *s.* die Fuhre, Wagenladung; (*coll.*) ***by the –,*** waggonweise. **--roof,** *s. See* **--ceiling. --vault,** *s.* das Tonnengewölbe.

wagon-lit ['vægɔ̃'li:], *s.* (*Railw.*) der Schlafwagen.

wagtail ['wægteil], *s.* (*Orn.*) die (Bach)stelze (*Motacilla*); ***pied –,*** die Trauerbachstelze (*M. alba yarelli*); ***white –,*** die Bachstelze (*M. alba alba*); ***yellow –,*** Englische Schafstelze (*M. flava flavissima*); ***blue-headed*** (***Am. yellow***) ***–,*** die Schafstelze (*M. flava flava*).

waif [weif], *s.* 1. heimatloser Mensch; 2. (*usu.*) verwahrlostes Kind; ***–s and strays,*** Obdachlose (*pl.*), verwahrloste Kinder (*pl.*); 3. verlaufenes *or* streunendes Vieh; 4. (*Law*) herrenloses Gut, das Strandgut.

wail [weil], **1.** *s.* die (Weh)klage, das (Weh)klagen, Jammern, (Weh)geschrei; das Weinen, Wimmern. **2.** *v.i.* jammern, (weh)klagen, sich beklagen; weinen, wimmern. **wailing, 1.** *adj.* (weh)klagend, jammernd, Klage–, Jammer–; weinend, wimmernd; ***– wall,*** die Klagemauer. **2.** *s.* das (Weh)klagen, Jammern; Weinen, Wimmern.

wain [wein], *s.* (*Poet.*) der (Ernte)wagen; (*Astr.*) ***Charles's Wain,*** Großer Bär.

wainscot ['weinskət], **1.** *s.* die Täfelung, Wandverkleidung, (Holz)verkleidung, das Getäfel, Tafelwerk. **2.** *v.t.* täfeln, verschalen, verkleiden. **wainscot(t)ing,** *s.* Verkleidungsbretter (*pl.*).

waist [weist], *s.* 1. die Taille; 2. Schweifung (*of bells*); 3. Kuhl (*of a ship*). **waist|band,** *s.* der Bund (*of skirt or trousers*). **–coat,** *s.* die (Herren)weste. **—-deep,** *adv.* (*adj.*) bis an die Taille (reichend), hüfthoch. **waisted,** *adj. suff.* mit . . . Taille. **waist|-high,** *adv., adj. See* **--deep. –line,** *s.* die Taille, Gürtellinie; (*coll.*) ***watch one's –,*** auf die schlanke Linie achten.

wait [weit], **1.** *v.i.* 1. warten; ***keep him –ing, make him –,*** ihn warten lassen; ***– and see,*** abwarten; ***– for,*** warten auf (*Acc.*); ***– for him to come,*** warten bis *or* daß er kommt; ***– for it,*** wart's ab! ***– for dead men's shoes,*** auf eine Erbschaft lauern; ***– up for him,*** aufbleiben bis er kommt; 2. ***–*** (***up***)***on,*** bedienen, aufwarten (*Dat.*); seine Aufwartung machen (*Dat.*); (*rare*) begleiten; ***– at table,*** bei Tisch bedienen *or* aufwarten. **2.** *v.t.* warten auf (*Acc.*), abwarten; ***– his convenience,*** warten bis es ihm paßt; ***– dinner for him,*** mit dem Essen auf ihn warten; ***– one's opportunity,*** die Gelegenheit abwarten. **3.** *s.* 1. das Warten; ***lie in – for,*** auflauern (*Dat.*); 2. die Wartezeit, Verzögerung, der Aufenthalt; 3. *pl.* Straßenmusikanten (*pl.*), Weihnachtssänger (*pl.*)

waiter ['weitə], *s.* 1. der Kellner, (*when addressing him*) (Herr) Ober; 2. Servierteller, Präsentierteller; ***dumb –,*** stummer Diener, drehbares Präsentierbrett. **waiting, 1.** *s.* 1. das (Ab)warten; ***no –!*** Parken verboten! 2. die Bedienung, Aufwartung; der Dienst (*at court etc.*); ***lady-in-–,*** königliche Hofdame; ***lord-in-–,*** diensttuender Kammerherr. **2.** *adj.* 1. (ab)wartend; (*coll.*) ***play a – game,*** sich abwartend verhalten, das Ergebnis abwarten; 2. Warte–; ***—list,*** die Warteliste, Vormerkliste; ***—maid,*** das Kammermädchen; ***—room,*** das Wartezimmer, Vorzimmer; (*Railw.*) der Wartesaal, Warteraum. **waitress** [–ris], *s.* die Kellnerin.

waive [weiv], *v.t.* verzichten auf (*Acc.*), aufgeben, fahrenlassen; ***– an advantage,*** sich eines Vorteils begeben; ***– a claim,*** auf einen Anspruch verzichten. **waiver,** *s.* (*Law*) der Verzicht, die Verzichtleistung (***of,*** auf (*Acc.*)); Verzichterklärung.

[1]**wake** [weik], *s.* das Kielwasser (*of ship*), (*Av.*) der Luftwirbel, Nachstrom; (*fig.*) die Spur; ***– of a torpedo,*** die Blasenbahn, Torpedolaufbahn; ***in the – of,*** im Kielwasser (*Gen.*); (*fig.*) in den Fußstapfen (*Gen.*), auf der Spur (*Gen.*), unmittelbar hinter (*Dat.*); nach dem Vorbild von, in Nachahmung (*Gen.*); ***bring in its –,*** zur Folge haben, nach sich ziehen; ***follow in the – of,*** unmittelbar folgen hinter (*Dat.*), auf dem Fuße folgen (*Dat.*).

[2]**wake, 1.** (*irr.*) *v.i.* wachen, wach sein *or* bleiben; (*also* ***– up***) aufwachen, erwachen (***from, out of,*** aus), wach werden; (*fig.*) sich bewußt werden (***to,*** *Gen.*). **2.** *irr.v.t.* 1. (*also* ***– up***) wecken (*also fig.*), aufwecken, erwecken (*also fig.*), auferwecken (*from the dead*); (*fig.*) wachrufen; aufrütteln, anspornen, anstacheln (***into,*** zu); 2. (*Irish*) ***– a corpse,*** bei einer Leiche wachen, Totenwache halten; einen Leichenschmaus halten. **3.** *s.* 1. (*esp. Irish*) die Leichenfeier, Totenwache; 2. (*usu. pl.*) das Kirchweihfest, Dorffest, die Kirchweih, Kirmes.

wakeful ['weikful], *adj.* 1. wachend; 2. schlaflos, ruhelos; 3. (*fig.*) wachsam. **wakefulness,** *s.* 1. die Schlaflosigkeit; 2. (*fig.*) Wachsamkeit.

waken ['weikən], **1.** *v.i.* 1. erwachen, aufwachen, wach werden (*also fig.*); 2. (*fig.*) (*usu.* ***– up***) sich bewußt werden (***to,*** *Gen.*). **2.** *v.t.* 1. (auf)wecken (***from, out of,*** aus); 2. (*fig.*) erwecken, erregen, wachrufen. **wakening,** *s.* das (Er)wachen, Aufwachen; (Er)wecken, Aufwecken; Wachrufen. **waking, 1.** *adj.* ***– hours,*** wache Stunden. **2.** *s.* das (Er)wachen; ***– or sleeping,*** schlafend oder wachend.

Walachia [wə'leikiə], *s.* (*Geog.*) Walachei (*f.*). **Walachian,** *adj.* walachisch.

wale [weil], *s.* 1. der Striemen, die Strieme, Schwiele; Salleiste, das Salband (*of cloth*); 2. (*Naut.*) Bergholz, Krummholz, Gurtholz, Dollbord.

walk [wɔ:k], **1.** *v.i.* (zu Fuß) gehen; spazierengehen; umgehen, spuken (*as ghosts*); im Schritt gehen (*as a horse*); ***– about,*** umhergehen; ***– along,*** weitergehen; ***– away,*** fortgehen; (*coll.*) ***– away from,*** einfach davonlaufen (*Dat.*), weit hinter sich lassen (*in a race*); (*coll.*) ***– away with,*** spielend leicht gewinnen; ***– back,*** (zu Fuß) zurückgehen; ***– backwards,*** rückwärtsgehen; ***– by,*** vorübergehen; ***– down,*** hinuntergehen; ***– in,*** hineingehen, hereinkommen, eintreten; ***– in one's sleep,*** schlafwandeln, nachtwandeln; ***– off,*** davongehen; (*coll.*) ***– off with,*** klauen, klemmen; *see also* ***– away with;*** (*Theat.*) ***– on,*** als Statist(in) auftreten; ***– on air,*** im siebenten Himmel sein; ***– out,*** hinausgehen; (*coll.*) die Arbeit einstellen, streiken; (*coll.*) ***be –ing out,*** einen Freund haben (*of a girl*); (*coll.*) ***– out with,*** verkehren *or* (aus)gehen mit (*one's sweetheart*); (*coll.*) ***– out on,*** sitzen *or* im Stich lassen; ***– over,*** hinüber– *or* herübergehen *or* –kommen; (*coll.*) ohne Konkurrenz *or* leicht gewinnen; (*coll.*) ***– over one's opponent,*** den Gegner spielend leicht schlagen; (*coll.*) ***– over him,*** ihn unverschämt *or* rücksichtslos behandeln, ihn schurigeln; ***– up,*** hinaufgehen, heraufkommen; ***– up to,*** hingehen zu, zukommen *or* zutreten *or* zugehen auf (*Acc.*).

2. *v.t.* im Schritt gehen lassen (*a horse*); (spazieren)führen (*a person*); (zu Fuß) gehen, zurücklegen (*distance or time*); durchschreiten, (auf und ab) gehen in (*Dat.*) *or* auf (*Dat.*) *or* durch *or* über (*Acc.*) (*a room*), durchwandern (*a district*); ***– the boards,*** auf den Brettern stehen; ***– the earth,*** auf Erden wandeln; ***– the hospitals,*** die klinischen Semester durchmachen; ***– the rounds,*** die Runde machen; ***– the streets,*** auf der Straße auf und ab gehen; ***– off,*** durch einen Spaziergang

vertreiben (*a headache etc.*), abführen, fortführen (*a p.*); – *one's legs off,* sich (*Dat.*) die Beine ablaufen; – *him off his legs,* ihn (durch Wandern) todmüde machen; – *out,* ausführen (*a p.*).
3. *s.* 1. das Gehen; Schrittgehen (*of horse*); der Schritt, Gang, die Gangart; *know him by his –,* ihn an seinem Gang kennen; 2. der Spaziergang; *go for* or *take a –,* einen Spaziergang machen, spazierengehen; *take him for a –,* ihn spazierenführen, mit ihm spazierengehen *or* einen Spaziergang machen; *two-hours' –,* zweistündiger Spaziergang; 3. der (Spazier)weg, die Strecke (zu Fuß); *a good* or *quite a –,* ein gutes Stück zu gehen, eine ordentliche Strecke; 4. die Promenade, der Spazierweg, Fußweg, Fußsteig; 5. (*fig.*) die Laufbahn, der Lebensweg, Lebensgang; – *of life,* der Beruf, Lebensbezirk, die Lebensstellung; *higher –s of society,* höhere Kreise *or* Schichten der Gesellschaft; 6. die Weide (*for sheep etc.*).

walkable ['wɔ:kəbl], *adj.* begehbar, gangbar (*track*), (zu Fuß) zurücklegbar (*distance*).

walk|about, *s.* (*Austral. sl.*) das Herumreisen, die Wanderung; *go –,* unterwegs sein. **--away,** *s.* (*coll.*) *see* **--over.**

walker ['wɔ:kə], *s.* der (die) Fußgänger(in), Spaziergänger(in); (*Spt.*) Geher; *be a good –,* gut zu Fuß sein; (*Theat.*) *--on,* der (die) Statist(in).

walkie-talkie ['wɔ:ki'tɔ:ki], *s.* (*coll.*) tragbares Sprechfunkgerät.

walk-in, *adj.* begehbar (*cupboard etc.*).

walking ['wɔ:kiŋ], **1.** *adj.* gehend; – *corpse,* wandelnde Leiche; – *encyclopædia,* wandelndes Lexikon; (*Theat.*) – *gentleman,* der Statist; (*Theat.*) – *lady,* die Statistin; *–(-on) part,* die Statistenrolle. **2.** *s.* das Gehen, Wandern; *I like –,* ich gehe gern zu Fuß *or* gern spazieren; *within – distance,* zu Fuß zu erreichen.

walking|-boots, *pl.* Marschstiefel (*pl.*). **--dress,** *s.* das Straßenkleid. **--orders,** *pl.* (*coll.*) der Laufpaß. **--stick,** *s.* der Spazierstock. **--tour,** *s.* die Fußwanderung, Fußreise.

walk|-out, *s.* (*coll.*) der Ausstand, Streik. **--over,** *s.* (*coll.*) leichter Sieg, der Spaziergang. **-way,** *s.* der Gehweg, die Promenade.

wall [wɔ:l], **1.** *s.* 1. die Wand (*inside*); Mauer (*outside*); *abdominal –,* die Bauchdecke; (*fig.*) *come up against a blank* or *brick –,* kein Verständnis *or* taube Ohren finden; (*coll.*) *it's enough to drive you up the –,* es ist um die Wände *or* um an den Wänden hochzugehen *or* hinaufzuklettern; *put him up against the –,* ihn an die Wand stellen; *be up against a brick –,* nicht weiter können; *–s have ears,* die Wände haben Ohren; *run one's head against a –,* mit dem Kopf durch die Wand (rennen) wollen; *partition* or *party –,* die Trennungswand; *come up against a – of prejudice,* vergeblich gegen eine Wand von Vorurteilen anlaufen *or* anrennen *or* angehen; *retaining –,* die Stützmauer; *with one's back to the –,* in die Enge getrieben; *have one's back to the –,* verzweifelt Widerstand leisten, sich verzweifelt zur Wehr setzen; *go to the –,* unterliegen, untergehen, zugrunde gehen, an die Wand *or* beiseite gedrückt werden, (*Comm.*) Konkurs machen; 2. (*Fort.*) der (Festungs)wall; *within the –s,* innerhalb der Stadt *or* Festung. **2.** *v.t.* (*also – in*) mit einer Mauer umgeben; umwallen, ummauern; (*fig.*) umschließen, einschließen; – *up,* zumauern, vermauern.

wallaby ['wɔləbi], *s.* kleines Känguruh.

wallah ['wɔlə], *s.* (*sl.*) der Bursche; (*Mil.*) *base –,* das Etappenschwein.

wall|-bars, *pl.* (*Gymn.*) die Sprossenwand. **--bracket,** *s.* der Wandarm, die Wandstütze, Wandkonsole. **--creeper,** *s.* (*Orn.*) der Mauerläufer (*Tichodroma muraria*).

walled [wɔ:ld], *adj.* 1. ummauert, mit Mauerwerk umgeben; 2. (*Fort.*) befestigt; 3. (*as suff.*) -gemauert.

wallet ['wɔlit], *s.* 1. die Brieftasche, Geldtasche; kleine Werkzeugtasche; 2. (*obs.*) der Ranzen, Tornister, das Felleisen.

wall|-eyed, *adj.* glasäugig (*of horses*). **--fern,** *s.* (*Bot.*) die Korallenwurzel. **-flower,** *s.* 1. (*Bot.*) der Goldlack; 2. (*coll.*) das Mauerblümchen. **--fruit,** *s.* das Spalierobst. **--map,** *s.* die Wandkarte.

wallop ['wɔləp], **1.** *s.* 1. (*coll.*) heftiger Schlag; die Wucht, Schlagkraft; 2. (*sl.*) das Bier. **2.** *v.i.* 1. (*coll.*) poltern; 2. (*Scots*) brodeln, wallen. **3.** *v.t.* (*coll.*) (ver)prügeln, verdreschen, vermöbeln, durchhauen (*a p.*), kräftig schlagen (*a th.*). **walloping, 1.** *adj.* (*sl.*) plump, riesig, mächtig. **2.** *s.* (*coll.*) die Dresche, Tracht Prügel.

wallow ['wɔlou], **1.** *v.i.* sich wälzen *or* suhlen; (*fig.*) schwimmen, schwelgen; *be -ing in money,* in Geld schwimmen. **2.** *s.* 1. das Sich-Wälzen, Schwelgen; 2. die Suhle, Suhllache.

wall|paper, *s.* die Tapete. **--plug,** *s.* der Stecker. **--socket,** *s.* die Steckdose, der Steckkontakt. **--space,** *s.* die Wandfläche.

walnut ['wɔ:lnʌt], *s.* 1. die Walnuß; 2. der Walnußbaum; das Nußbaumholz.

walrus ['wɔ:lrəs], *s.* das Walroß.

waltz [wɔ:ls], **1.** *s.* der Walzer. **2.** *v.i.* Walzer tanzen, walzen; (*sl.*) tänzeln; wälzen, rollen. **waltz-time,** *s.* der Dreivierteltakt.

wampum ['wɔmpəm], *s.* das Muschelgeld, der Muschelschmuck (*of Indians*).

wan [wɔn], *adj.* bleich, blaß (*as face*), fahl, matt, trüb(e), farblos, glanzlos (*light*), gezwungen (*smile*).

wand [wɔnd], *s.* die Rute, der (Amts)stab; (*Mil.*) Feldherrnstab, Kommandostab; (*Mus.*) Taktstock; Zauberstab.

wander ['wɔndə], **1.** *v.i.* 1. wandern, wandeln, streifen; (*also – about*) umherwandern, (umher)ziehen, (umher)schweifen, umherstreifen, umherirren; schweifen, irren (*of the eye*); sich schlängeln *or* winden (*as a river*); 2. sich entfernen, abweichen, abirren, abschweifen (*from,* von); sich verirren, irregehen; *be -ing,* phantasieren, faseln, irrereden; zerstreut *or* geistesabwesend sein; – *from the point* or *subject,* vom Gegenstand abschweifen *or* abkommen; – *off course,* vom Kurs abkommen, (*sl.*) franzen. **2.** *v.t.* durchwandern (*the streets etc.*), durchstreifen. **wanderer,** *s.* der Wanderer.

wandering ['wɔndəriŋ], **1.** *adj.* 1. wandernd, Wander–; Nomaden–, umherschweifend; – *bullet,* der Ausreißer; (*Anat.*) – *cell,* die Wanderzelle; – *Jew,* der ewige Jude; 2. (*Bot.*) Kriech–, Schling–; 3. (*fig.*) unstet, ruhelos; abschweifend, konfus, zerstreut (*thoughts*). **2.** *s.* 1. das Wandern, Umherstreifen, Umherschweifen, Umherirren; (*usu. pl.*) die Wanderschaft, weite Wanderung; 2. (*fig.*) (*usu. pl.*) das Irrereden, Faseln, Phantasieren, die Fieberwahn.

wander|lust, *s.* die Wanderlust, der Wandertrieb. **--plug,** *s.* (*Elec.*) der Wanderstecker.

wane [wein], **1.** *v.i.* abnehmen (*moon, also fig.*), verblassen, (v)erbleichen, schwächer werden; (*fig.*) sinken, nachlassen, zurückgehen, vergehen, verfallen, abflauen, schwinden, zu Ende gehen. **2.** *s.* das Abnehmen; (*fig.*) Nachlassen, Schwinden, Zurückgehen, Abflauen, die Abnahme, der Verfall; *at the – of the moon,* bei abnehmendem Mond; *be in* or *on the –,* abnehmen (*of the moon*); (*fig.*) im Abnehmen sein, schwinden, verfallen.

wangle ['wæŋgl], **1.** *v.t.* (*sl.*) sich unter der Hand *or* hintenherum beschaffen, deichseln, organisieren; durch List zustandebringen *or* erreichen, drehen, frisieren (*accounts etc.*); – *s.th. out of him,* ihm etwas ablotsen. **2.** *v.i.* mogeln; – *out of it* or – *through,* sich herauswinden. **3.** *s.* 1. der Kniff, die Machenschaft; 2. Schiebung, Mogelei. **wangler,** *s.* der Mogler, Schieber.

waning ['weiniŋ], *adj.* abnehmend; abflauend, schwindend, zurückgehend, zu Ende gehend, nachlassend.

wanness ['wɔnnis], *s.* die Blässe, Bleichheit.

want [wɔnt], **1.** *s.* 1. der Mangel (*of,* an (*Dat.*)), das Fehlen, die Ermangelung (*Gen.*); *for – of,* aus

Mangel an (*Dat.*), mangels (*Gen.*), in Ermangelung (*Gen.*); ***be in – of,*** bedürfen (*Gen.*), benötigen, brauchen, nötig haben; ***he is in – of money,*** es ermangelt ihm an Geld, er leidet an Geldmangel; ***be in – of repair,*** reparaturbedürftig sein; ***– of spirit,*** die Mutlosigkeit; ***a long-felt –,*** ein seit langem vorhandenes Bedürfnis, ein längst spürbarer Mangel; 2. der Bedarf, die Bedürftigkeit, Armut, Not; ***be in –,*** Not leiden; 3. (*usu. pl.*) das Bedürfnis, Bedürfnisse (*pl.*); ***a man of few –s,*** ein Mann mit geringen Ansprüchen *or* Bedürfnissen. **2.** *v.t.* 1. haben mögen *or* wollen, wollen, wünschen, (*before inf.*) wollen; ***what do you –?*** was wünschen *or* wollen Sie? ***– none of him,*** nicht mit ihm zu tun haben wollen; ***– nothing more of him,*** nichts mehr von ihm haben wollen; ***what do you – with me?*** was wollen Sie mit mir? ***I – to go,*** ich möchte gehen *or* wünsche zu gehen; ***I – him to go,*** ich will *or* möchte *or* wünsche, daß er geht; ***I – it done,*** ich wünsche *or* möchte, daß es getan wird; mir liegt daran, daß es geschieht; ***he is –ed,*** er wird gewünscht *or* gesucht, man will ihn sprechen; ***she is not –ed here,*** man kann sie hier nicht brauchen, man will sie hier nicht haben; ***–ed by the police,*** von der Polizei gesucht; ***situations –ed,*** Stellungsgesuche (*pl.*); 2. bedürfen (*Gen.*), benötigen, nötig haben, brauchen; (*coll.*) (*before inf.*) sollen, müssen; ***– badly,*** dringend benötigen; ***badly –ed,*** dringend erforderlich *or* gesucht; ***the piano –s tuning,*** das Klavier müßte *or* sollte gestimmt werden; (*coll.*) ***you – to see a doctor,*** du mußt einen Arzt aufsuchen; (*coll.*) ***you don't – to be in such a hurry,*** du sollst es nicht so eilig haben; ***what does he – with three cars?*** wozu braucht er drei Autos? 3. Mangel haben an (*Dat.*), es fehlt (mir *etc.*) an (*Dat.*), ermangeln (*Gen.*), entbehren (*Gen. or Acc.*); ***the story –s confirmation,*** die Geschichte bedarf der Bestätigung; ***it –s 10 minutes to 9,*** es fehlen 10 Minuten bis neun. **3.** *v.i.* 1. Not leiden; 2. (*obs.*) ***– for,*** Mangel haben an (*Dat.*), ermangeln (*Gen.*); 3. ***be –ing,*** es fehlen lassen (***in,*** an (*Dat.*)); (*coll.*) geistesschwach sein; ***he is –ing in energy,*** er läßt es an Tatkraft fehlen, es fehlt ihm an Tatkraft; ***he was found –ing,*** er entsprach den Erwartungen nicht, er wurde den Erwartungen nicht gerecht, auf ihn war kein Verlaß.

wantage [ˈwɔntidʒ], *s.* (*Am.*) (*Comm.*) das Defizit, Fehlende, der Fehlbetrag.

wanton [ˈwɔntən], **1.** *adj.* 1. mutwillig, übermütig, ausgelassen; 2. ungerechtfertigt, verantwortungslos, willkürlich, leichtfertig; ***– cruelty,*** rücksichtslose Grausamkeit; 3. (*Poet.*) üppig, wild, schwelgerisch (*as growth*); 4. lüstern, wollüstig, geil, liederlich, ausschweifend (*usu. of a woman*). **2.** *s.* der Wollüstling, Wüstling (*man*), (*usu.*) die Trulle (*woman*). **3.** *v.i.* 1. Mutwillen treiben, ausgelassen sein, umhertollen; buhlen; 2. üppig wachsen, wuchern (*plants*). **wantonness,** *s.* 1. der Mutwille, Übermut, Leichtfertigkeit, Ausgelassenheit, Ausschweifung; 2. Üppigkeit; 3. Lüsternheit, Geilheit.

wapentake [ˈwɔpnteik], *s.* (*Hist.*) der Gau, die Hundertschaft.

war [wɔ:], **1.** *s.* der Krieg; ***be at –,*** Krieg führen (***with,*** mit *or* gegen); (*fig.*) auf Kriegsfuß stehen, im Kampf liegen (mit); ***carry the – into the enemy's camp,*** den Krieg ins feindliche Land *or* Lager tragen; (*fig.*) zum Gegenangriff übergehen; ***civil –,*** der Bürgerkrieg; ***declare –,*** den Krieg erklären (***on,*** *Dat.*); (*fig.*) den Kampf ansagen (*Dat.*); ***drift into –,*** in den Krieg (hinein)gezogen *or* (hinein)getrieben werden; ***fight a –,*** einen Krieg führen, (*fig.*) einen Kampf ausfechten; ***the Great War,*** der 1. Weltkrieg; ***holy –,*** der Religionskrieg; ***in the –,*** im Kriege, während des Krieges; am Kriege beteiligt; (*coll.*) ***have been in the –s,*** arg mitgenommen sein; ***council of –,*** der Kriegsrat; ***declaration of –,*** die Kriegserklärung; ***prisoner of –,*** Kriegsgefangene(r); ***seat*** or ***theatre of –,*** der Kriegsschauplatz; ***Secretary of State for War,*** (*Am.*) ***Secretary of War,*** der Kriegsminister; ***state of –,*** der Kriegszustand; ***– of attrition,*** der Zermürbungskrieg; ***– of liberation,*** der Befreiungskrieg; ***make – on,*** Krieg führen *or* im Kriege sein gegen; ***– to the knife,*** der Krieg *or* Kampf bis aufs Messer, Vernichtungskrieg; ***go to –,*** Krieg beginnen (***with,*** mit), sich bekriegen; ***wage – against,*** see ***make – on***; ***– of words,*** der Wortstreit, das Wortgefecht. **2.** *v.i.* (*usu. fig.*) kämpfen, streiten, im Streit liegen (***against, with,*** mit *or* gegen); sich bekriegen *or* bekämpfen.

warble [wɔ:bl], **1.** *v.i.* trillern, trällern; singen, schmettern, schlagen (*as birds*). **2.** *v.t.* trillern; singen. **3.** *s.* das Trillern. **warbler,** *s.* 1. der Singvogel; 2. (*Orn.*) die Grasmücke (*Sylviidae*). **warbling,** *s.* das Trillern; der Triller.

war|-bond, *s.* die Kriegsschuldverschreibung. **--bride,** *s.* die Soldatenbraut. **--cloud,** *s.* die Kriegsgefahr, Kriegsdrohung. **--correspondent,** *s.* der Kriegsberichterstatter. **--criminal,** *s.* der Kriegsverbrecher. **--cry,** *s.* das Kriegsgeschrei, der Schlachtruf.

ward [wɔ:d], **1.** *v.t.* 1. (*usu.* ***– off***) abwehren, abwenden, parieren (*a blow etc.*); 2. (*obs.*) schützen, verteiden, bewahren (***from,*** vor (*Dat.*)). **2.** *s.* 1. (*Law*) der *or* das Mündel, die Mündel (*of a girl*); (*fig.*) der Schützling; Zögling, Pflegling; 2. (*rare*) die Aufsicht, Vormundschaft, Verwahrung, der Schutz; ***in –,*** unter Vormundschaft; 3. (*obs.*) die Wache; ***keep watch and –,*** Wache halten; 4. (*Fenc.*) die Parade, Abwehr(stellung); 5. (*Tech.*) Besatzung, das Eingerichte, Gewirr(e) (*of a lock*); der (Schlüssel)bart (*of a key*); 6. die Abteilung (*in a prison*); ***casual –,*** das Obdachlosenasyl; 7. Station (*in a hospital*); ***private –,*** das Privatzimmer; 8. der Bezirk, Wahlkreis, das Viertel (*of a town*).

-ward [wəd], *adj. suff. See* **-wards.**

war|-damage, *s.* Kriegsschäden (*pl.*). **--dance,** *s.* der Kriegstanz. **--debt,** *s.* die Kriegsschuld.

warden [wɔ:dn], *s.* der Vorsteher, Aufseher, (*Hist.*) Gouverneur; Rektor (*of a college*); Herbergsvater (*of a youth hostel*); (*also* ***church –***) Kirchenvorsteher; (*Poet.*) Wärter, Wächter, Hüter; ***game –,*** der Jagdaufseher; ***Warden of the Mint,*** der Münzwardein. **wardenship,** *s.* das Amt eines Vorstehers, Aufsehers, Rektors *etc.*

War Department, *s.* (*Am.*) das Kriegsministerium (*Hist. in Britain, though still used of property and stores owned by Ministry of Defence*).

warder [ˈwɔ:də], *s.* 1. der Gefängniswärter, Gefängnisaufseher; 2. (*obs.*) Wärter, Wächter. **wardress** [-ris], *s.* die Gefängniswärterin.

wardrobe [ˈwɔ:droub], *s.* 1. der Kleiderschrank; ***–trunk,*** der Schrankkoffer; 2. der Kleiderbestand, die Garderobe (*of a p.*); 3. (*Theat.*) Garderobe, Requisitenkammer; ***–master,*** der Gewandmeister.

wardroom [ˈwɔ:drum], *s.* (*Naut.*) die Offiziersmesse.

-wards [wədz], *adj. & adv. suff.* -wärts.

wardship [ˈwɔ:dʃip], *s.* die Vormundschaft (*also fig.*) (***over,*** über (*Acc.*)), Minderjährigkeit; (*fig.*) der Schutz, die Aufsicht, Bevormundung.

¹**ware** [wɛə], *v.t.* (*coll.*) (*usu. imper.*) Achtung! Vorsicht!

²**ware,** *s.* 1. (*only sing. collect., usu. in compounds*) die Ware, Waren (*pl.*); ***china–,*** das Geschirr, Porzellan; ***earthen–,*** das Steingut, Töpferwaren (*pl.*); 2. (*only pl.*) Waren (*pl.*), Artikel (*pl.*), Erzeugnisse (*pl.*); ***praise one's own –s,*** sich selbst loben.

warehouse [wɛəˈhous], **1.** *s.* 1. das (Waren)lager, Niederlage der Speicher, das Lagerhaus; 2. Engrosgeschäft, Großhandelsgeschäft, die Großhandlung; ***– account,*** das Lagerkonto. **2.** *v.t.* auf Lager bringen *or* nehmen, (ein)lagern, (ein)speichern, aufspeichern; zur Aufbewahrung geben *or* nehmen (*furniture etc.*). **warehouseman,** *s.* 1. der Lageraufseher, Lagerverwalter, Magazinverwalter, Lagerist; 2. Speicherarbeiter, Lagerarbeiter; 3. Engroshändler, Großkaufmann.

war|fare, *s.* der Kampf (*also fig.*), Kriegszustand; die Kriegführung; (*fig.*) Fehde, der Hader, Streit;

economic –, der Wirtschaftskrieg; ***global*** –, weltweiter Krieg; ***psychological*** –, psychologische Kriegführung; ***static*** –, der Stellungskrieg. **–-footing,** *s.* der Kriegsstand, die Kriegsbereitschaft; ***place on a*** –, kriegsbereit machen; auf Kriegsfuß bringen. **–-game,** *s.* das Kriegsspiel, Planspiel. **–-god,** *s.* der Kriegsgott. **–-grave,** *s.* das Kriegsgrab, Soldatengrab. **–-guilt,** *s.* die Kriegsschuld. **–head,** *s.* der Sprengkopf, Gefechtskopf (*of bomb, torpedo*). **–-horse,** *s.* das Streitroß, (*fig.*) der Haudegen. **–-industry,** *s.* die Kriegsindustrie, Rüstungsindustrie.

wariness ['wɛərinis], *s.* die Vorsicht, Sorgfalt, Behutsamkeit.

war|like, *adj.* 1. kriegerisch, Kriegs–; – ***preparations,*** Kriegsvorbereitungen (*pl.*); 2. kriegsliebend, kampflustig. **–-loan,** *s.* die Kriegsanleihe.

warlock ['wɔ:lɔk], *s.* der Hexenmeister, Zauberer.

war-lord, *s.* der Kriegsherr.

warm [wɔ:m], **1.** *adj.* 1. warm (*also fig.*), heiß, erhitzt, glühend; (*fig.*) freundlich, warmherzig (*as thanks*), herzlich, innig, eifrig, begeistert, enthusiastisch, lebhaft, heftig, feurig, hitzig, erregt, inbrünstig, leidenschaftlich (*of a p.*); ***they are – friends,*** sie sind intime *or* vertraute Freunde; (*Meteor.*) – ***front,*** die Warmluftfront; – ***heart,*** warmes Herz; – ***interest,*** reges Interesse; (*coll.*) – ***reception,*** herzlicher Empfang; (*coll.*) erbitterte Widerstand, feindselige Entgegnung; (*coll.*) – ***work,*** schwere Arbeit; 2. (*Hunt.*) frisch (*scent*); 3. (*coll.*) nahe (*to a goal*). **2.** *v.t.* 1. wärmen, warm machen, aufwärmen, vorwärmen, anwärmen; heizen (*a room*); – ***o.s.,*** sich wärmen; – ***up,*** aufwärmen; 2. (*fig.*) erwärmen; 3. (*sl.*) verprügeln, verdreschen, versohlen. **3.** *v.i.* 1. warm *or* wärmer werden; – ***up,*** warmlaufen (*of an engine*); 2. sich erwärmen (*also fig.*) (***to,*** für); 3. (*fig. also* – ***up***) Interesse zeigen (***to,*** für), interessiert werden (***to,*** an (*Dat.*)); 4. (*Spt., fig.*) – ***up,*** sich bereitmachen (***for,*** zu). **4.** *s.* das Warme, die Wärme; das Wärmen; ***come into the*** –, ins warme Haus *or* Zimmer *etc.* eintreten; (*coll.*) ***have a*** –, sich wärmen. **warm-blooded,** *adj.* 1. warmblütig; – ***animal,*** der Warmblüter; 2. (*fig.*) hitzig.

war-memorial, *s.* das Kriegerdenkmal.

warm|-hearted, *adj.* warmherzig, herzlich. **–-heartedness,** *s.* die Warmherzigkeit, Herzlichkeit. **warming, 1.** *adj.* wärmend. **2.** *s.* 1. das Wärmen, die Erwärmung; 2. (*coll.*) Tracht Prügel.

war|-minded, *adj.* kriegerisch gesinnt. **–monger,** *s.* der Kriegshetzer.

warmth [wɔ:mθ], *s.* 1. die Wärme (*also fig.*); (*fig.*) Warmherzigkeit, Herzlichkeit, Innigkeit; Begeisterung, Hitze, der Eifer; 2. die Erregtheit, Heftigkeit; 3. (*as colour*) Wärme, Lebhaftigkeit.

warn [wɔ:n], *v.t.* 1. warnen (***of*** (*a th.*), ***against*** (*a p.*), vor (*Dat.*)); 2. ermahnen, nahelegen (*Dat.*), (dringend) raten (*Dat.*) (***to do,*** zu tun); 3. verwarnen (***of,*** vor (*Dat.*)); 4. ankündigen (*Dat.*) (***of,*** *Acc.*), im voraus verständigen *or* benachrichtigen *or* in Kenntnis setzen (von), frühzeitig aufmerksam machen (***of,*** auf (*Acc.*)); 5. – ***off,*** abhalten, abweisen, zurückweisen (***from,*** von); hinausweisen, mit einer Mahnung fortschicken (aus). **warning,** *s.* 1. die Warnung (***of,*** vor (*Dat.*)); ***give fair*** –, rechtzeitig ankündigen *or* warnen (***of,*** vor (*Dat.*)); ***take*** –, sich (*Dat.*) zur Warnung dienen lassen (***by,*** *Acc.*), sich warnen *or* belehren lassen (durch); 2. die (Er)mahnung, warnendes *or* mahnendes Beispiel; 3. das Warnsignal, (warnendes) Anzeichen; 4. die Benachrichtigung, (Vor)anzeige, der Wink, Bescheid; die Kündigung; ***at a minute's*** –, sofort, fristlos; ***a month's*** –, die Kündigung nach Monatsfrist; ***without*** –, unerwartet.

warning|-bell, *s.* die Signalglocke. **–-colours,** *pl.* Warnfarben (*pl.*), Trutzfarben (*pl.*) (*of insects etc.*). **–-notice,** *s.* die Warnungstafel. **–-order,** *s.* (*Mil.*) der Vorbefehl.

War Office, *s.* das Kriegsministerium.

warp [wɔ:p], **1.** *s.* 1. (*Weav.*) die Kette, der Aufzug, Zettel, Schweif, Kett(en)fäden (*pl.*), Längsfäden (*pl.*); – ***and woof,*** Zettel und Einschlag; 2. (*Naut.*) der Warp, die Warpleine, (Bugsier)trosse, das Verholtau; 3. Werfen, Ziehen, die Verkrümmung, Verwerfung (*of wood*); 4. (*Agr.*) der Schlamm, Schlick, die Schlammschicht, Schlammablagerung, das Schwemmland; 5. (*fig.*) die Entstellung, Verdrehung, Verzerrung. **2.** *v.t.* 1. krumm machen, krümmen, verziehen, aufwerfen (*wood etc.*); 2. verschlammen (*land*); 3. (*Weav.*) (an)scheren, schären, anzetteln, schweifen, die Kett(en)fäden ausspannen (*Gen.*); 4. (*Naut.*) bugsieren, verholen; 5. (*fig.*) entstellen, verzerren, nachteilig beeinflussen, verdrehen; verleiten (***into,*** zu), abbringen, ablenken (***from,*** von). **3.** *v.i.* 1. sich werfen *or* (ver)ziehen, sich verbiegen *or* krümmen, krumm werden (*as wood*); 2. (*fig.*) entstellt *or* verdreht werden, abweichen.

war|-paint, *s.* 1. die Kriegsbemalung; 2. (*coll.*) voller Wichs, große Gala, der Staat. **–-path,** *s.* der Kriegspfad; (*fig.*) ***on the*** –, kampflustig.

warped ['wɔ:pt], *adj.* 1. geworfen, verzogen, windschief; 2. (*fig.*) verzerrt, verschroben, einseitig.

war|-plane, *s.* das Kampfflugzeug, Militärflugzeug. **–-profiteer,** *s.* der Kriegsgewinnler.

warrant ['wɔrənt], **1.** *s.* 1. die Ermächtigung, Befugnis, Vollmacht (***for,*** zu); – ***of attorney,*** die Prozeßvollmacht; 2. der Vollziehungsbefehl; – ***of apprehension,*** der Steckbrief; – ***of arrest,*** der Haftbefehl; – ***of attachment*** or ***distress,*** der Zwangsvollstreckungsbefehl, Pfändungsbefehl; ***a – is out against him,*** er wird steckbrieflich verfolgt; 3. der Berechtigungsschein, Ausweis, Beleg, die Bescheinigung; das Patent, die Bestallungsurkunde; (*Comm.*) der Lagerschein; 4. (*fig.*) die Berechtigung, Rechtfertigung, der Grund; ***not without*** –, nicht unberechtigt. **2.** *v.t.* 1. Bürgschaft *or* Gewähr leisten für, bürgen, einstehen *or* haften für, garantieren, verbürgen, gewährleisten; 2. (*Law*) ermächtigen, bevollmächtigen, berechtigen, autorisieren, befugen; 3. (*fig.*) begründen, beweisen, erweisen, bezeugen, bestätigen; (*coll.*) ***I('ll)*** – (***you***), ich kann's Ihnen versichern, ich könnte schwören, ich möchte wetten, mein Wort darauf. **warrantable,** *adj.* 1. zu rechtfertigen(d), berechtigt, gerechtfertigt; 2. jagdbar (*of stags*). **warranted,** *adj.* (*Comm.*) garantiert. **warranter,** *s.* der Gewährsmann, Bürge, Garant. **warrant-officer,** *s.* (*Mil.*) der Oberfeldwebel, Feldwebelleutnant; (*Naut.*) Deckoffizier. **warrantor,** *see* **warranter.**

warranty ['wɔrənti], *s.* 1. die (Mängel)garantie, Gewähr(leistung), Bürgschaft; 2. Vollmacht, Ermächtigung, Berechtigung (***for,*** zu); (*fig.*) Rechtfertigung, Begründung (für); 3. der Bürgschaftsschein.

warren ['wɔrən], *s.* das (Kaninchen)gehege, der Kaninchenbau.

warring ['wɔ:riŋ], *adj.* sich bekriegend *or* bekämpfend *or* streitend, (*fig.*) widerstreitend, einander widerstrebend, entgegengesetzt.

warrior ['wɔriə], *s.* der Krieger, Kriegsmann; (*fig.*) Kämpfer.

Warsaw ['wɔ:sɔ:], *s.* Warschau (*n.*).

war|ship, *s.* das Kriegsschiff. **–-strength,** *s.* die Kriegsstärke.

wart [wɔ:t], *s.* die Warze; (*Vet.*) Mauke, (*Bot.*) der Auswuchs. **wart-hog,** *s.* das Warzenschwein.

wartime ['wɔ:taim], *s.* die Kriegszeit.

warty ['wɔ:ti], *adj.* warzig, voller Warzen; warzenartig.

war|-weariness, *s.* die Kriegsmüdigkeit. **–-weary,** *adj.* kriegsmüde. **–-whoop,** *s.* das Kriegsgeheul. **–-worker,** *s.* der (die) Rüstungsarbeiter(in).

wary ['wɛəri], *adj.* vorsichtig, umsichtig, bedächtig, bedacht(sam), behutsam, achtsam, wachsam; ***be*** –, sich hüten (***of doing,*** zu tun); ***be – of,*** sich hüten vor (*Dat.*), auf der Hut sein vor (*Dat.*), achthaben auf (*Acc.*).

was [wɔz], *1st & 3rd pers. sing. imperf. of* **be.**

wash [wɔʃ], **1.** *v.t.* 1. waschen (*also Min., Paint.*),

abwaschen (*crockery*); (aus)spülen (*glasses etc.*); abspülen (*a deck etc.*); – *o.s.,* sich waschen; – *one's hands,* sich (*Dat.*) die Hände waschen; (*fig.*) – *one's hands of,* die Hände in Unschuld waschen in (*Dat.*), die Hände lassen von, nicht verantwortlich sein für, keine Verantwortung übernehmen für, unschuldig sein an (*Dat.*) (*a th.*), nichts mehr zu tun haben wollen mit (*a p.*); – *one's dirty linen in public,* die schmutzige Wäsche vor allen Leuten waschen; 2. schlämmen (*ore*); 3. bespülen (*the shore*); – *ashore,* ans Land schwemmen *or* spülen; – *overboard,* über Bord spülen; 4. (*Paint.*) tuschen; 5. (*Metall.*) dünn überziehen, plattieren.
(*with adv.*) – *away,* wegwaschen, abwaschen; wegspülen, wegschwemmen; – *down,* gründlich abwaschen (*walls etc.*); hinunterspülen (*food*); – *off,* abwaschen, wegwaschen; – *out,* auswaschen, ausspülen, (*coll.*) tilgen, ausmerzen; *be –ed out,* ausgewaschen sein, die Farbe verloren haben; (*fig.*) blaß sein; fertig(gemacht) *or* verbraucht *or* abgespannt sein; – *up,* abspülen, abwaschen (*crockery etc.*); an den Strand werfen, anspülen, ans Ufer spülen; (*sl.*) *–ed up,* erledigt, ausgeschieden.
2. *v.i.* 1. (*of p.*) sich waschen; 2. (*of th.*) sich (gut) waschen (lassen), gewaschen werden können, waschecht sein (*of fabrics*); – *off* or *out,* sich auswaschen lassen, weggewaschen werden, sich durch Waschen entfernen lassen; 3. fließen, fluten, strömen (*of water*) (*over,* über (*Acc.*)); – *ashore,* ans Land geschwemmt werden; 4. (*sl.*) (*usu. neg.*) standhalten, stichhaltig sein, die Probe bestehen, taugen, Annahme finden; (*sl.*) *that won't – with me,* das taugt *or* verfängt *or* zählt bei mir nicht; 5. – *up,* aufwaschen, abwaschen; (*Am.*) sich waschen.
3. *s.* 1. das Waschen; die Wäsche; *be at the –,* auf der Wäscherei sein; *give a th. a –,* etwas waschen; (*coll.*) *have a –,* sich waschen; *in the –,* in der Wäsche; *come out in the –,* sich auswaschen (lassen); (*sl.*) sich befriedigend herausstellen; *send to the –,* zum Waschen *or* in die Wäsche geben; 2. der Wellenschlag, die Brandung; das Branden, Strömen, Anspülen, Anschlagen, Plätschern (*of waves*); 3. (*Naut.*) Fahrwasser, Kielwasser; 4. (*Geog.*) Schwemmland; 5. Gesichtswasser, Haarwasser *etc.*; 6. Spülwasser, Spülicht; 7. (*Paint.*) leicht aufgetragene Farbe, die Tusche, Tünche; 8. (*Metall.*) der Metallüberzug, die Plattierung.

washable [ˈwɔʃəbl], *adj.* waschbar; waschecht.

wash|-basin, *s.* das Waschbecken, die Waschschüssel. **–board,** *s.* 1. (*Naut.*) das Setzbord; 2. Waschbrett. **--bottle,** *s.* (*Chem.*) der Reinigungsapparat (*for gases*). **–day,** *s.* der Waschtag.

washed|-out, *adj.* 1. verwaschen, verblaßt (*of colour*); 2. (*coll.*) erschöpft, ermüdet. **--up,** *adj.* (*sl.*) ruiniert, erledigt, fertig.

washer [ˈwɔʃə], *s.* 1. der (die) Wäscher(in); 2. die Waschmaschine; *dish–,* die Geschirrspülmaschine; 3. (*Tech.*) die (Unterlegs)scheibe, Dichtungsscheibe, der Dichtungsring; *spring –,* der Federring. **washerwoman,** *s.* die Waschfrau, Wäscherin.

wash|hand-basin, *s. See* **--basin. –hand-stand,** *s. See* **–stand. --house,** *s.* der Waschraum, das Waschhaus, die Waschküche. **--in,** *s.* (*Av.*) negative Flügelschränkung.

washiness [ˈwɔʃinis], *s.* 1. die Wässerigkeit; 2. (*fig.*) Verwaschenheit, Schlappheit, Kraftlosigkeit, Saftlosigkeit, Seichtheit (*of style*).

washing [ˈwɔʃiŋ], *s.* 1. das Waschen, Spülen, Reinigen, die Waschung; 2. Erzwäsche, (*Min.*) das Auswaschen, Schlämmen; 3. Fließen, Branden, Strömen (*of water*); 4. (*Paint.*) der (Farb)überzug; 5. (schmutzige) Wäsche; (gewaschene) Wäsche; (*coll.*) *take in one another's –,* sich gegenseitig helfen *or* unterstützen; 6. *pl.* das (Ab)waschwasser, Spülicht, Spülwasser. **washing|-day,** *s.* der Waschtag. **--machine,** *s.* die Waschmaschine. **--powder,** *s.* das Waschpulver, Waschmittel. **--soda,** *s.* die Bleichsoda. **--up,** *s.* das Abwaschen.

wash|-leather, *s.* das Waschleder, Putzleder. **--out,** *s.* 1. (*Geol.*) das Ausspülen, die Unterspülung; 2. Aushöhlung; 3. (*sl.*) der Mißgriff, Mißerfolg, Durchfall, Fehlschlag, das Fiasko, die Pleite; (*of a p.*) Niete, der Versager; 4. (*Av.*) positive Flügelschränkung. **–room,** *s.* der Waschraum. **--stand,** *s.* der Waschtisch, Waschständer. **--tub,** *s.* der Waschkübel, Waschzuber, die Waschwanne.

washy [ˈwɔʃi], *adj.* 1. wässerig, dünn, schwach, (*fig.*) verwaschen, blaß (*as colour*); 2. verwässert, seicht, schlapp, lappig, kraftlos.

wasn't [wɔznt], (*coll.*) = ***was not.***

wasp [wɔsp], *s.* die Wespe. **waspish,** *adj.* wespenartig, (*usu. fig.*) reizbar; gereizt, gehässig, bissig. **waspishness,** *s.* die Reizbarkeit; Gereiztheit, Gehässigkeit. **wasp-waisted,** *adj.* mit einer schmalen Taille.

wassail [ˈwɔseil], *s.* (*Poet.*) 1. süßes Getränk, das Würzbier; 2. Trinkgelage. **wassail-cup,** *s.* der Humpen.

wastage [ˈweistidʒ], *s.* 1. der Verlust (im Gebrauch), Wegfall, Abfall, Schwund; Verschleiß, die Abnützung; 2. Verschwendung, Vergeudung, (*fig.*) der Leerlauf.

waste [weist], **1.** *v.t.* 1. verschwenden, vergeuden, vertrödeln, verschleudern, (*opportunity*) versäumen; – *one's breath,* tauben Ohren predigen, vergeblich reden; 2. (*fig.*) ungenutzt *or* verkommen lassen; *be –d,* ohne Wirkung bleiben (*on,* auf (*Acc.*)), nutzlos sein, am falschen Platz stehen; *it is –d on him,* er macht sich (*Dat.*) nichts daraus. **2.** *v.i.* (*also – away*) abnehmen, verfallen, herunterkommen, dahinschwinden, vergehen; verlorengehen, brachliegen, vergeudet *or* verschwendet werden; dahinsiechen (*of a p.*). **3.** *adj.* 1. wüst, verödet, öde, brach, unbebaut (*of land*); *lay –,* verwüsten, verheeren; *lie –,* brachliegen; 2. ungenutzt, unbenützt, verloren, abgängig, überschüssig, überflüssig, unbrauchbar, unnütz, Ab(fall)–; – *heat,* abgängige Wärme, die Abwärme; – *material,* das Abfallmaterial, Abgänge (*pl.*); (*Biol.*) – *products,* das Abbauprodukt, der Ausscheidungsstoff; – *paper,* das Abfallpapier, Ausschußpapier, die Makulatur. **4.** *s.* 1. die Vergeudung, Verschwendung (*of money etc.*); – *of time,* die Zeitverschwendung; *go* or *run to –,* brachliegen; verwildern (*land*), abfließen (*water*), verlottern, zugrunde gehen, ungenutzt daliegen, vergeudet werden; 2. der Verfall, Verlust, Abgang, Schwund, Verschleiß, die Abnutzung, Abnahme, das Hinschwinden (*of strength etc.*); 3. (*Law*) die Wertminderung; 4. Wüste, Einöde; 5. der Abfall, Schutt, Müll; (*Tech.*) Ausschuß, Abgänge (*pl.*); (*Min.*) der Abraum, taubes Gestein; das Gekrätz, die Krätze (*metal*), Ausschußwolle, Kämmlingswolle, Wollabfälle (*pl.*) (*wool*); (*Comm.*) die Spillage; *cotton –,* das Putzwerg.

wasteful [ˈweistful], *adj.* verschwenderisch (*of,* mit); unrentabel (*methods*); *be – of,* verschwenden. **wastefulness,** *s.* die Verschwendung(ssucht); Unrentabilität.

waste|(paper) basket, *s.* der Papierkorb. **--pipe,** *s.* das Abflußrohr, Abzugsrohr.

waster [ˈweistə], *s.* 1. der Verschwender; *see also* **wastrel, 1**; 2. (*Tech.*) der Fehlguß, das Schrottstück. **wasting, 1.** *s.* 1. die Verschwendung, Vergeudung; 2. der Verlust, Schwund, das (Dahin)schwinden; 3. (*Med.*) die Auszehrung. **2.** *adj.* 1. abnehmend, schwindend; 2. (*Med.*) zehrend; – *disease,* die Abzehrung, zehrende Krankheit. **wastrel** [–rəl], **1.** *s.* 1. der Tunichtgut, Taugenichts; verwahrlostes Kind, der Straßenbengel; 2. (*Comm.*) minderwertige Ware, der Ausschuß, fehlerhaftes Exemplar. **2.** *adj.* 1. verschwenderisch; 2. Abfall–, Ausschuß–; 3. (*of an animal*) schwächlich, verkümmert.

watch [ˈwɔtʃ], **1.** *v.i.* 1. wach sein, wachen (*with,* bei); 2. Ausschau halten (*for,* nach), lauern, aufpassen, achthaben, achtgeben (auf (*Acc.*)); 3. wachsam sein, auf der Hut sein; (*coll.*) – *out,* auf der Hut sein, achtgeben, aufpassen; – *over,* Aufsicht führen über (*Acc.*), wachen über (*Acc.*), bewachen; 4. (*Mil.*) Wache halten, Posten stehen. **2.** *v.t.* 1. bewachen, hüten (*sheep etc.*); 2. (sorgsam) beobachten *or* betrachten, ein wachsames Auge haben auf (*Acc.*); – ***him working,*** zusehen, wie er arbeitet; ihm beim Arbeiten zusehen; (*Prov.*) ***a –ed pot never boils,*** beim Warten wird die Zeit lang; 3. achthaben auf (*Acc.*); – ***one's step,*** vorsichtig gehen, (*fig.*) auf der Hut sein, sich vorsehen; (*sl.*) – ***it!*** paß auf! 4. (*fig.*) im Auge behalten; 5. wahrnehmen, abpassen, abwarten (*an opportunity*), (mit Interesse) verfolgen (*course of events*); (*Law*) im Interesse eines Klienten verfolgen (*a case*). **3.** *s.* 1. die Wachsamkeit, Achtsamkeit, Wache, Wacht; ***keep –,*** Wache halten; ***keep (a) – on him,*** ihn bewachen *or* sorgsam beobachten; (*fig.*) ***keep a close – on,*** sehr bedacht sein auf (*Acc.*); ***be on the – for,*** Ausschau halten *or* auf der Hut *or* Lauer sein nach, lauern *or* achthaben auf (*Acc.*), auflauern (*Dat.*); ***set a – on him,*** ihn beobachten lassen; 2. die (Schild)wache, der (Wacht)posten; (*Naut.*) die Wachmannschaft, Schiffswache; (*obs.*) (*usu. pl.*) (Nacht)wache; ***morning –,*** die Morgenwache; 3. die Taschenuhr, Armbanduhr; ***put a – on*** (or ***back***), eine Uhr vorstellen (*or* nachstellen); ***set a –,*** eine Uhr stellen.

watch|-box, *s.* das Schilderhaus. **--case,** *s.* das Uhrgehäuse. **--chain,** *s.* die Uhrkette. **--committee,** *s.* städtischer Ordnungsdienst. **-dog,** *s.* der Wachhund (*also fig.*), Kettenhund, Hofhund. **watcher,** *s.* der Wächter; Beobachter. **watch-fire,** *s.* das Signalfeuer, Wachtfeuer.

watchful [ˈwɔtʃful], *adj.* wachsam, achtsam, aufmerksam (***of,*** auf (*Acc.*)), auf der Hut (***against,*** vor (*Dat.*)). **watchfulness,** *s.* die Wachsamkeit, Achtsamkeit, Aufmerksamkeit; das Wachen (***over,*** über (*Dat.*)).

watch|-glass, *s.* das Uhrglas. **--guard,** *s.* das Uhrband, die Uhrkette. **--house,** *s.* das Wachthaus, die Wachtstube, Wache.

watching brief, *s.* (*Law*) der Auftrag zur Verfolgung eines Prozesses.

watch|maker, *s.* der Uhrmacher. **-making,** *s.* die Uhrmacherei. **-man** [–mən], *s.* der Wächter, (*also night–-*) Nachtwächter. **--night,** *s.* die Neujahrsnacht. **--pocket,** *s.* die Uhrtasche. **--spring,** *s.* die Uhrfeder. **--stand,** *s.* der Uhrständer. **-tower,** *s.* der Wachtturm, die Warte. **-word,** *s.* die Losung, Parole; das Schlagwort, Kennwort.

water [ˈwɔːtə], **1.** *s.* das Wasser; die Wasserfläche; *pl.* Wasser (*pl.*), Gewässer (*pl.*); (*usu. pl.*) das Wasser, der Brunnen (*at a spa*); ***fresh –,*** das Süßwasser; ***salt –,*** das Salzwasser; ***tap –,*** das Leitungswasser; ***holy –,*** das Weihwasser; ***subsoil –,*** das Grundwasser; ***surface –,*** das Tagwasser; ***mineral –,*** das Mineralwasser; (*Med.*) – ***on the brain,*** der Wasserkopf; (*Med.*) – ***on the knee,*** der Kniegelenkerguß.

(a) (*with adj.*) (*fig.*) ***throw cold – on,*** die Freude an (*Dat.*) . . . *or* die Begeisterung für . . . dämpfen, wie eine kalte Dusche auf (*Acc.*) . . . wirken; ***in deep –(s),*** in der Klemme, in Schwierigkeiten; ***of the first –,*** von reinstem Wasser (*as a diamond etc.*), (*fig.*) bester Art, erster Güte *or* Qualität; ***high –,*** die Flut; (*coll.*) ***be in hot –,*** sich in die Nesseln gesetzt haben (***with,*** bei); ***get into hot –,*** sich in die Nesseln setzen, in Teufels Küche kommen (***for,*** wegen); ***low –,*** die Ebbe; (*fig.*) ***be in low –,*** auf dem trocknen sitzen; ***still –s run deep,*** stille Wasser sind tief; ***fish in troubled –s,*** im trüben fischen; ***pour oil on troubled –s,*** Frieden stiften.

(b) (*with vb.*) ***drink the –s,*** Brunnen trinken; ***much – has flowed under the bridge,*** viel Wasser ist den Fluß hinabgelaufen; ***hold –,*** wasserdicht sein, (*fig.*) stichhaltig sein; (*Naut.*) ***make –,*** Wasser machen, leck sein; ***pass*** or ***make –,*** Wasser abschlagen *or* lassen, harnen, urinieren; ***take the –,*** ins Wasser gehen, vom Stapel laufen; ***take the –s,*** Brunnen trinken.

(c) (*with prep.*) (*fig.*) ***keep one's head above –,*** sich eben über Wasser halten; ***by –,*** zu Wasser, auf dem Wasserwege; (*Av.*) ***take off from the –,*** abwassern; ***on the –,*** auf dem Wasser, zur See; (*Av.*) ***alight*** or ***land on the –,*** wassern; ***like a fish out of –,*** nicht in seinem (*etc.*) Element; ***through fire and –,*** durchs Feuer; ***take to the –,*** ins Wasser gehen; das Wasser lieben; ***under –,*** unter Wasser; ***cast one's bread upon the –s,*** sich ohne Bedenken ausgeben.

2. *v.t.* 1. bewässern, besprengen (*land*), begießen (*flowers*), tränken, zur Tränke führen (*horses etc.*); 2. wässern, flammen, moirieren (*silk etc.*); 3. (*also* – ***down***) verdünnen, strecken, panschen (*wine etc.*); (*coll. fig.*) – ***down,*** verwässern, abschwächern, mildern, populär *or* mundgerecht machen.

3. *v.i.* wässern; tränen (*as the eyes*); wässerig werden; ***make his eyes –,*** ihm die Tränen in die Augen treiben; ***his mouth –s,*** ihm wird der Mund wässerig, das Wasser lief ihm im Mund zusammen (***for, after,*** nach); ***make his mouth –,*** ihm den Mund wässerig machen.

water|-bailiff, *s.* der Fischereiaufseher. **--bed,** *s.* 1. (*Med.*) das Wasserbett, Wasserpolster, Wasserkissen; 2. (*Geol.*) die Grundwasserschicht. **--beetle,** *s.* der Wasserkäfer. **--bird,** *s.* der Wasservogel. **--blister,** *s.* die Wasserblase. **--borne,** *adj.* zu Wasser befördert (*goods*), Wasser– (*traffic*), vom Wasser getragen, durch Wasser übertragen (*infection*), auf dem Wasser schwimmend. **--bottle,** *s.* 1. die Wasserflasche, Karaffe, (*Mil. etc.*) Feldflasche; 2. ***hot–-,*** die Wärmflasche. **--bus,** *s.* der Flußdampfer. **--butt,** *s.* die Regentonne, das Regenfaß. **--cannon,** *s.* der Wasserwerfer. **--carriage,** *s.* der Wassertransport. **--carrier,** *s.* 1. der Wasserträger (*also Astr.*); 2. Wassertankwagen (*vehicle*). **--cart,** *s.* der Sprengwagen. **--chute,** *s.* die Wasserrutschbahn. **--clock,** *s.* die Wasseruhr. **--closet,** *s.* das (Wasser)klosett, die Toilette. **--colour,** *s.* 1. das Aquarell (*picture*); 2. *pl.* Wasserfarben (*pl.*), Aquarellfarben (*pl.*); (***painting in***) ***–s,*** die Aquarellmalerei. **--colourist,** *s.* der (die) Aquarellmaler(in). **--cooled,** *adj.* wassergekühlt. **--cooling,** *s.* die Wasserkühlung. **-course,** *s.* 1. der Wasserlauf, die Wasserrinne; 2. das Flußbett, Strombett. **-cress,** *s.* die Brunnenkresse. **--cure,** *s.* die Wasserkur. **--diviner,** *s.* der Rutengänger.

watered [ˈwɔːtəd], *adj.* 1. gewässert, besprengt; begossen; 2. (*fig.*) verwässert, verdünnt, gemildert, geschwächt; 3. (*Tech.*) moiriert, geflammt, gewässert (*fabric*).

water|fall, *s.* der Wasserfall. **--flag,** *s.* die Wasserschwertlilie. **--flea,** *s.* der Wasserfloh. **-fowl,** *s.* (*collect.*) Schwimmvögel (*pl.*), Wasservögel (*pl.*). **--front,** *s.* das Hafenviertel; der Uferbezirk, die Ufergegend. **--gate,** *s.* die Schleuse, das Schott. **--gauge,** *s.* der Wasserstandsmesser, Pegel. **--glass,** *s.* das Wasserglas. **-glass,** *s.* (*Chem.*) das Wasserglas. **--gruel,** *s.* der Haferschleim. **--heater,** *s.* der Warmwasserbereiter. **-hen,** *s.* *See* **moorhen. --ice,** *s.* Gefrorene(s).

wateriness [ˈwɔːtərinis], *s.* die Wässerigkeit, Wäßrigkeit, Feuchtigkeit, (*fig.*) Verwässerung, Seichtheit. **watering,** *s.* 1. das Bewässern, Berieseln, Besprengen, Begießen; 2. Wässern, Tränken, Schwemmen; 3. (*Tech.*) Flammen, die Moirierung; 4. das Panschen, Verdünnen, Verwässern. **watering|-can,** *s.* die Gießkanne. **--cart,** *s.* der Sprengwagen. **--place,** *s.* 1. die Tränke, Schwemme (*for animals*); 2. der Badeort, Kurort, das (See)bad.

water|-jacket, *s.* der Kühlwassermantel. **--jump,** *s.* der Wassergraben.

waterless [ˈwɔːtəlis], *adj.* wasserlos.

water|-level, *s.* 1. der Wasserstand, Wasserspiegel (*also Geol.*), Pegelstand, die Wasserstandslinie; 2. (*Tech.*) Libelle, Wasserwaage. **--lily,** *s.* die Wasserlilie, Seerose. **-line,** *s.* die Wasser(stands)-linie, Wasserhöhe. **-logged,** *adj.* voll Wasser (*of ships*), voll Wasser gesogen, vollgesogen (*of wood*). **--main,** *s.* das Hauptwasserrohr.

waterman [ˈwɔːtəmən], *s.* der Jollenführer. **watermanship,** *s.* die Wassertüchtigkeit, Ruderfertigkeit.

water|mark, 1. *s.* 1. das Wasserzeichen (*on paper*);

2. (*also high* –) das Flutzeichen, Hochwasserstandszeichen; (*fig.*) *high* –, der Hochstand, Höhepunkt; *low* –, das Tiefwasserstandszeichen, (*fig.*) der Tiefstand. **2.** *v.t.* mit einem Wasserzeichen versehen. **–-melon,** *s.* die Wassermelone. **–-mill,** *s.* die Wassermühle. **–-nymph,** *s.* die Najade. **–-pipe,** *s.* das Wasser(leitungs)rohr. **–-plant,** *s.* die Wasserpflanze. **–-pollution,** *s.* die Wasserverunreinigung. **–-polo,** *s.* der Wasserball. **–-power,** *s.* die Wasserkraft. **–proof, 1.** *adj.* wasserdicht. **2.** *s.* der Regenmantel, Gummimantel. **3.** *v.t.* wasserdicht machen, imprägnieren. **–-proofing,** *s.* 1. die Imprägnierung; 2. wasserdichter Stoff. **–-rail,** *s.* (*Orn.*) die Wasserralle (*Rallus aquaticus*). **–-rat,** *s.* die Wasserratte. **–-rate,** *s.* das Wassergeld. **–-repellent,** *adj.* wasserabstoßend. **–-ret, –-rot,** *v.t.* rösten (*flax*). **–shed,** *s.* die Wasserscheide. **–-shoot,** *s.* die Traufe, Wasserrinne (*of a roof*). **–-shortage,** *s.* der Wassermangel. **–side,** *s.* das Meeresufer, die Wasserkante, Küste. **–-ski, 1.** *s.* der Wasserschi, Wasserski. **2.** *v.i.* Wasserski fahren. **–-softener,** *s.* der (Wasser)enthärter. **–-soluble,** *adj.* wasserlöslich. **–spout,** *s.* 1. die Traufröhre, Dachrinne; 2. (*Meteor.*) Wasserhose. **–-sprite,** *s.* der Wassergeist, die Nixe. **–-supply,** *s.* die Wasserversorgung. **–-system,** *s.* 1. das Wasserleitungsnetz; 2. (*Geog.*) Stromgebiet. **–-table,** *s.* 1. (*Geol.*) der Grundwasserspiegel; 2. (*Archit.*) Wasserschlag, die Wasserabflußleiste. **–-tank,** *s.* der Wasserbehälter. **–tight,** *adj.* 1. wasserdicht; (*fig.*) *in – compartments,* isoliert, für sich; 2. (*fig.*) sicher, zuverlässig; stichhaltig, unanfechtbar, unangreifbar. **–-tower,** *s.* der Wasserturm. **–-vapour,** *s.* der Wasserdampf, Wasserdunst. **–-vole,** *s.* die Wasserratte. **–-wagon,** *s.* der Wasserversorgungswagen; (*coll.*) *be on the* –, Abstinenzler sein. **–-wagtail,** *s.* (*Orn.*) die Bachstelze (*Motacilla*). **–-wave,** *s.* die Wasserwelle. **–way,** *s.* 1. die Wasserstraße, der Schiffahrtsweg; 2. (*Shipb.*) Wassergang. **–-wheel,** *s.* das Wasserrad. **–-wings,** *pl.* der Schwimmgürtel. **–works,** *pl.* (*oft. sing. constr.*) das Wasserwerk; (*coll.*) die Wasserleitung; (*coll.*) *turn on the* –, Tränen vergießen.

watery ['wɔ:təri], *adj.* 1. wässerig, wäßrig (*also fig.*); feucht, naß; tränend (*of eyes*); regnerisch; – *sky,* der Regenhimmel; 2. (*fig.*) verwässert, blaß, dünn (*as colour*); fad(e), geschmacklos (*of food*), schal, seicht, lappig; 3. (*Poet.*) Wasser–; – *grave,* nasses Grab; – *waste,* die Wasserwüste.

watt [wɔt], *s.* (*Elec.*) das Watt. **wattage** [–idʒ], *s.* der Stromverbrauch, die Wattleistung.

wattle [wɔtl], **1.** *s.* 1. das Geflecht, Flechtwerk, Gitterwerk; die Hürde, Umzäunung; – *and daub,* das Fachwerk; 2. *pl.* der Bart, Bartfäden (*pl.*) (*of fishes*), Kehllappen (*pl.*) (*of a cock*); 3. (*Bot.*) – *bark,* die Akazienrinde. **2.** *v.t.* mit Ruten zusammenbinden *or* flechten; aus Flechtwerk herstellen; in Fachwerk bauen.

wattless ['wɔtlis], *adj.* (*Elec.*) leistungslos; – *current,* der Blindstrom; – *power,* die Blindleistung.

wattling ['wɔtliŋ], *s.* das Flechtwerk.

wave [weiv], **1.** *s.* 1. die Welle (*also Phys., fig.*), Woge, (*Naut.*) See; *pl.* (*Poet.*) das Meer; *crest of the* –, der Wellenberg; *trough of the* –, das Wellental; *heat* –, die Hitzewelle; *permanent* –, die Dauerwelle (*in hair*); 2. die Flamme (*in fabric*), Guilloche (*on paintwork*); 3. der Wink, das Winken; – *of the hand,* der Wink mit der Hand. **2.** *v.i.* 1. wehen, flattern (*in the wind etc.*); sich auf– und abbewegen *or* hin– und herbewegen, wogen; 2. winken, (ein) Zeichen geben; – *to him,* ihm zuwinken; 3. sich wellen, wellig sein (*hair*). **3.** *v.t.* 1. schwingen, schwenken; auf– und abbewegen, hin– und herbewegen; – *one's arms,* mit den Armen fuchteln; – *aside,* mit einer Handbewegung abtun; – *goodbye,* ein Lebewohl zuwinken (*to, Dat.*); – *one's hand,* mit der Hand winken; 2. wellen, wellig machen, ondulieren (*hair*); 3. flammen, moirieren (*fabric*), guillochieren (*paintwork etc.*).

wave|-band, *s.* (*Rad.*) das Wellenband. **–-front,** *s.* die Wellenfront. **–-length,** *s.* (*Rad.*) die Wellenlänge; (*fig. coll.*) *be on the same* –, einander verstehen.

wavelet ['weivlit], *s.* kleine Welle.

wave|-like, *adj.* wellenartig, wellenförmig. **–meter,** *s.* der Frequenzmesser. **–-motion,** *s.* die Wellenbewegung.

waver ['weivə], *v.i.* (sch)wanken (*also fig.*); (*fig.*) zaudern, unschlüssig sein; zittern, flimmern, flackern (*as light*); – *from,* abweichen von. **waverer,** *s.* Unentschlossene(r), unschlüssiger Mensch. **wavering, 1.** *adj.* (sch)wankend, unentschlossen, unschlüssig, unstet. **2.** *s.* das (Sch)wanken, die Unentschlossenheit, Unschlüssigkeit.

wave|-train, *s.* der Wellenzug. **–-trap,** *s.* (*Rad.*) der Fangkreis, Sperrkreis.

waviness ['weivinis], *s.* das Wellige, die Welligkeit, Wellenbewegung. **wavy,** *adj.* 1. wallend, wogend, Wellen schlagend; 2. Wellen–, wellenförmig; wellig, gewellt (*of hair, also Her.*); – *lines,* die Wellenlinien.

[1]**wax** [wæks], *v.i.* 1. (*obs., Poet.*) wachsen (*also fig.*), zunehmen (*of the moon, also fig.*); 2. (*with adj.*) werden.

[2]**wax, 1.** *s.* das (Bienen)wachs; (*also ear–*) das Ohrenschmalz; *cobbler's* or *shoemaker's* –, das Schusterpech; *sealing–*, der Siegellack. **2.** *v.t.* wachsen, mit Wachs überziehen, wichsen (*boots*), bohnern (*floors*). **3.** *adj.* wächsern, Wachs–; – *candle,* das Wachslicht, die Wachskerze; – *figure,* die Wachsfigur; – *vestas,* Wachsstreichhölzer (*pl.*). **wax-chandler,** *s.* der Wachszieher.

waxen ['wæksən], *adj.* 1. Wachs–, (*fig.*) wachsähnlich, wachsfarbig; 2. weich.

wax|-end, *s.* der Pechdraht. **–-light,** *s. See* **–-candle. –-paper,** *s.* das Pergamentpapier. **–wing,** *s.* (*Am. Bohemian* –) (*Orn.*) der Seidenschwanz (*Bombycilla garrulus*). **–work,** *s.* die Wachsfigur; *pl.* (*sing. constr.*) das Wachsfigurenkabinett. **waxy,** *adj.* 1. Wachs–, wächsern, wachsähnlich, wachsartig; wachsfarbig, bleich; 2. weich; 3. (*sl.*) ärgerlich, übelgelaunt.

way [wei], **1.** *s.* 1. der Weg; Pfad, die Straße; Bahn; – *in* (*out*), der Eingang (Ausgang); – *back,* der Rückweg; – *home,* der Heimweg; *be in a fair* – *to,* voraussichtlich Erfolg haben mit, auf dem Wege sein (*Gen.*); *go a long* – *round,* einen weiten Umweg machen; *they go their different* –*s,* jeder geht einen anderen Weg; (*Railw.*) *permanent* –, der Bahnkörper, das Geleise; *the right* –, der richtige Weg; (*fig.*) richtig; *round about* –, der Umweg; *this* –*!* hierher! hierdurch! (*fig.*) so, auf diese Art und Weise; *which* – *did he go?* wohin ging er? *the wrong* –, der falsche Weg; (*fig.*) falsch; (*coll.*) *go down the wrong* –, in die falsche Kehle kommen; *how is the weather down your* –? wie ist das Wetter bei euch *or* in eurer Gegend? –*s and means,* Mittel und Wege; (*Parl.*) *Committee of Ways and Means,* der Steuerbewilligungsausschuß; (*fig.*) *parting of the* –*s,* der Scheideweg, entscheidender Augenblick; *right of* –, das Wegerecht, Durchfahrtsrecht; (*Motor.*) Vorfahrt(s)-recht, die Vorfahrt; *ask one's* –, sich nach dem Wege erkundigen; *ask him the* –, ihn nach dem Wege fragen (*to,* nach); (*fig.*) *come his* –, (zufällig) in seinen Besitz *or* in seine Hände kommen; *find one's* –, sich zurechtfinden; *find a* –, einen Ausweg finden; *force one's* –, sich (*Dat.*) einen Weg bahnen; *go one's* –, seines Weges gehen; *go one's* (*own*) –, in allen Stücken seinen Kopf durchsetzen, seinen eigenen Weg gehen; *are you going my* –? gehst du den gleichen Weg wie ich? *know one's* – *about,* den Weg kennen, (*fig.*) Bescheid wissen; *lead the* –, vorangehen; *lose one's* –, vom Weg abkommen, sich verirren; *make one's* –, sich begeben (*to,* nach), (*fig.*) sich (*Dat.*) Bahn brechen, sich durchsetzen, vorankommen; *make the best of one's* – (*to*), so schnell wie möglich gehen (nach); *pave the* –, den Weg ebnen (*for, Dat.*); *point out the* –, den Weg zeigen (*to, Dat.*); *see one's* – *clear,* den Weg vor sich sehen; (*fig.*) eine Möglichkeit (vor sich) sehen, sich in der Lage sehen, sich berechtigt fühlen; *see a* – *out,* einen

Ausweg wissen *or* sehen; ***across the –,*** see ***over the –***; ***by the –,*** im Vorbeigehen, auf dem *or* am Wege, unterwegs; (*fig.*) nebenbei, beiläufig, übrigens; ***not by a long –,*** noch lange nicht, bei weitem nicht; ***return by the same –,*** denselben Weg zurückgehen; ***once in a –,*** ausnahmsweise, ab und zu einmal; ***on one's*** or ***the –,*** auf dem Wege, unterwegs; ***on the – out,*** auf der Hinreise; ***on the – through,*** auf der Durchreise; ***bring him on his –,*** ihn eine Strecke Weges begleiten; ***well on one's*** or ***the –,*** schon weit vorangekommen, (*fig.*) im Gange; (*fig.*) ***go out of one's –,*** ein übriges tun, keine Mühe scheuen, sich (*Dat.*) besondere Mühe geben; ***take him out of his –,*** ihn einen Umweg machen lassen; (*coll.*) ***over the –,*** über die Straße, gegenüber;
2. (*fig.*) der Gang, Lauf; ***– of the world,*** der Gang *or* Lauf der Welt; ***go the – of all flesh,*** den Gang alles Irdischen gehen; ***in the – of business,*** auf dem üblichen Geschäftswege;
3. die Strecke, Weite, Entfernung; (*coll.*) ***a good*** or ***long –,*** eine weite Strecke; ***a little –,*** eine kurze Strecke; ***a long – from,*** weit entfernt von; ***a long – off,*** weit entfernt; (*fig.*) ***go a long – towards,*** viel *or* wesentlich beitragen zu; (*fig.*) ***go a long – with him,*** sehr bei ihm wirken; ***not by a long –,*** noch lange nicht, bei weitem nicht;
4. die Richtung; ***one-– street,*** die Einbahnstraße; ***both –s,*** hin und zurück; ***the other – round,*** in umgekehrter Richtung, umgekehrt; ***I don't know which – to turn,*** ich weiß nicht, wohin ich mich wenden soll; ***which –?*** in welcher Richtung? ***look his –,*** zu ihm hinsehen; ***look the other –,*** wegschauen;
5. (*Naut.*) die Fahrt(geschwindigkeit); (*fig.*) der Fortgang, Fortschritt, das Vorwärtskommen; (*Naut.*) ***gather*** (***lose***) ***–,*** Fahrt vergrößern (verlieren); (*Naut.*) ***make –,*** vorwärtskommen; ***pay one's –,*** für seinen Unterhalt aufkommen, (*fig.*) auf seine Kosten kommen (*of a p.*), sich rentieren (*of a th.*); ***work one's –,*** Werkstudent sein; ***work one's – up,*** sich hocharbeiten; ***under –,*** (*Naut.*) in Fahrt; (*fig.*) in Vorbereitung, in *or* im Gang; ***get under –,*** (*Naut.*) in Fahrt gehen; (*fig.*) in *or* im Gang *or* in Bewegung kommen;
6. (*fig.*) die Art (und Weise), Methode, das Mittel, Verfahren; ***any –,*** auf jede *or* irgendeine Art; ***any – you please,*** ganz wie Sie wollen; ***every –,*** in jeder Hinsicht; ***one – or the other*** or ***another,*** so oder so, irgendwie, auf irgendeine Weise; ***neither one – nor the other,*** weder so noch so; (***in***) ***the same –,*** ebenso, genauso, ebenfalls, gleichfalls, auf gleiche *or* in gleicher Art *or* Weise; ***feel the same – about a th. as,*** genauso über etwas denken wie; ***some – or*** (***an***)***other,*** irgendwie, auf irgendeine Weise, auf die eine oder andere Art; ***there are no two –s about it,*** es verhält sich so und nicht anders; ***you go about it the wrong –,*** Sie packen die S. verkehrt an; ***– of thinking,*** die Denkweise; ***that's the –,*** so ist es richtig; ***have one's*** (***own***) ***–,*** seinen Willen durchsetzen; ***have it all one's own –,*** nur seinen eigenen Willen kennen, nach Gutdünken verfahren; ***if I had my own –,*** wenn es nach mir ginge; ***have a – with,*** zurechtkommen *or* gut auskommen mit; glänzend umzugehen wissen mit; ***in a –,*** gewissermaßen, sozusagen, in gewisser Hinsicht; ***in the – of,*** hinsichtlich, betreffs, in bezug auf (*Acc.*); ***in more –s than one,*** in mehr als einer Beziehung; ***in the ordinary –,*** normalerweise; ***in no –,*** keineswegs, in keiner Hinsicht; ***in her own –,*** in ihrer *or* auf ihre Art; ***in some –,*** irgendwie; ***in some –s,*** in mancher Hinsicht; ***in this –,*** auf diese *or* in dieser Weise; ***be of his – of thinking,*** seine Ansicht *or* Meinung teilen; ***to my – of thinking,*** nach meiner Meinung;
7. die Beschaffenheit, Gewohnheit, Sitte, der Brauch; ***silly –s,*** alberne Manieren (*of a p.*); ***that is always the – with her,*** so macht sie es immer, so ist es immer mit ihr, so geht es ihr immer; ***get into the – of,*** sich einarbeiten in (*Acc.*); ***mend one's –s,*** sich bessern;
8. die Möglichkeit, Gelegenheit, freie Bahn, der Raum, Platz; ***out of harm's –,*** in Sicherheit; ***give –,*** (*of a p.*) Platz machen, nachgeben, (zurück)weichen (*to, Dat.*), (*of a th.*) einbrechen, zusammenbrechen; ***make –,*** Platz schaffen *or* (*fig.*) machen (***for***, *Dat.*), (*fig.*) zurücktreten (vor (*Dat.*)); ***put him in the –,*** ihm verhelfen *or* die Möglichkeit geben, ihn in die Lage versetzen (***of doing***, zu tun); ***put s.th. in his –,*** ihm etwas zukommen lassen; ***stand*** or ***be in his –,*** ihm im Wege stehen, ihm hinderlich sein; ***out of the –,*** abseits, abgeschieden, abgelegen, entlegen, (*fig.*) abwegig, ausgefallen, ungewöhnlich; ***nothing out of the –,*** nicht Besonderes; ***be out of the –,*** aus dem Weg *or* nicht hinderlich sein; ***get out of his –,*** ihm aus dem Wege gehen; ***out of the –!*** Platz da! ***keep out of the –,*** sich abseits halten *or* fernhalten; ***put out of the –,*** aus dem Weg räumen, wegstellen (*a th.*), (*sl.*) abmurksen, um die Ecke bringen (*a p.*);
9. der Zustand, die Lage; ***in a bad –,*** in schlimmer Lage; ***in a small –,*** in kleinem Ausmaße, auf kleinem Fuße; bescheiden; ***in the family –,*** in anderen Umständen, schwanger;
10. ***by – of,*** (auf dem Wege) über (*Acc.*); (*fig.*) an Stelle von, anstatt (*Gen.*); in der Absicht zu, angeblich, zum Zweck (*Gen.*); ***he is by – of being an artist,*** er ist angeblich Künstler, man spricht von ihm als einem Künstler; ***by – of a change,*** zur Abwechslung; ***by – of excuse,*** als Entschuldigung; ***by – of jest,*** im Scherz.
2. *adv.* (*sl.*) weit; ***– up*** (***down***), weit oben (unten).

way|bill, *s.* 1. die Passagierliste; 2. der Frachtbrief. **–farer** [–fɛərə], *s.* der (Fuß)wanderer. **–faring, 1.** *adj.* wanderend, reisend; ***– man,*** Reisende(r). **2.** (*usu. pl.*) die (Fuß)reise. **–lay** [–ˈlei], *irr.v.t.* 1. auflauern (*Dat.*), nachstellen (*Dat.*), abpassen; 2. ansprechen, angehen. **–-leave,** *s.* das Wegerecht. **–side, 1.** *s.* der Straßenrand, die Straßenseite; ***by the –,*** am Wege, an der Straße; (*fig.*) ***fall by the –,*** scheitern, nicht vorankommen. **2.** *adj.* am Wege (stehend *or* wachsend); ***– inn,*** der Gasthof auf offener Straße. **–-station,** *s.* (*Am.*) der Zwischenbahnhof. **–-traffic,** *s.* (*Am.*) der Nahverkehr. **–-train,** *s.* (*Am.*) der Lokalzug, Bummelzug.

wayward [ˈweiwəd], *adj.* launisch, eigensinnig, unberechenbar, widerspenstig; ***– child,*** ungeratenes Kind. **waywardness,** *s.* der Eigensinn, die Launenhaftigkeit, Unberechenbarkeit, Widerspenstigkeit.

way-worn, *adj.* wegmüde, reisemüde.

we [wi:], *pers. pron.* wir; (*royalty, editors and sl.*) = ***I.***

weak [wi:k], *adj.* schwach (*also Comm., Gram., fig.*); schwächlich, kränklich, anfällig, gebrechlich (*health*), haltlos, schwankend, labil (*character*), (*fig.*) kraftlos, schlaff, matt; nicht überzeugend, angreifbar (*argument*), flau; dünn (*liquid*); (*Cards*) ***– hand,*** schlechte Karten; ***– player,*** schlechter Spieler; ***– stomach,*** empfindlicher Magen; ***– point*** or ***side,*** wunder Punkt, schwache Seite, die Blöße, Schwäche; ***the –er sex,*** das schwache Geschlecht.

weaken [ˈwi:kən], **1.** *v.t.* schwächen (*also fig.*), schwächer machen, (*fig.*) entkräften; verdünnen (*liquid*). **2.** *v.i.* schwach *or* schwächer werden; nachlassen, abnehmen, nachgeben, erschlaffen. **weakening,** *s.* die (Ab)schwächung.

weak-kneed, *adj.* (*fig.*) charakterschwach, schlapp, unentschlossen, nachgiebig (*of a p.*), auf schwachen Füßen stehend (*argument*).

weakling [ˈwi:kliŋ], *s.* der Schwächling. **weakly, 1.** *adj.* schwächlich, kränklich. **2.** *adv.* schwach.

weak|-minded, *adj.* schwachsinnig; charakterschwach. **–-mindedness,** *s.* der Schwachsinn; die Charakterschwäche.

weakness [ˈwi:knis], *s.* 1. die Schwäche, Schwachheit; Schwächlichkeit, Kränklichkeit, Anfälligkeit, Gebrechlichkeit; Charakterschwäche, schwache Seite, schwacher Punkt; der Mangel, Nachteil, die Unvollkommenheit; 2. (*coll.*) ***have a – for,*** eine Schwäche *or* Vorliebe haben für.

weak-spirited, *adj.* kleinmütig, mutlos, verzagt.

[1]**weal** [wi:l], *s.* (*obs.*) das Wohl(ergehen), der Wohlstand, die Wohlfahrt; ***the general*** or ***public –,*** das (All)gemeinwohl; ***in – and woe,*** auf Gedeih und

Verderb, in Wohl und Wehe, in guten und bösen Tagen.

[2]**weal, 1.** *s.* die Schwiele, der Striemen. **2.** *v.t.* schwielig schlagen.

weald [wi:ld], *s.* die Hügellandschaft (*in S. England*).

wealth [welθ], *s.* 1. der Reichtum (*also fig.*), Wohlstand, das Vermögen; (*coll.*) Reichtümer (*pl.*), das Geld und Gut; 2. (*fig.*) die Fülle (***of***, an (*Dat.*) *or* von). **wealthy,** *adj.* reich, wohlhabend, vermögend, begütert.

wean [wi:n], *v.t.* 1. entwöhnen (*a child*); 2. (*fig.*) *also* – ***away***) entfremden (***from***, *Dat.*), abbringen (von), abgewöhnen (*Dat.*) (***from***, *Acc.*).

weapon ['wepən], *s.* die Waffe (*also fig.*). **weaponless,** *adj.* wehrlos, unbewaffnet.

[1]**wear** [wɛə], **1.** *irr.v.t.* 1. tragen, anhaben (*a dress etc.*); aufhaben (*a hat*); zeigen, zur Schau tragen, an den Tag legen, annehmen (*a look etc.*); ***what shall I –?*** was soll ich anziehen? – ***one's heart on one's sleeve,*** das Herz auf der Zunge haben; (*coll.*) – ***the trousers,*** die Hosen anhaben; 2. (*also* – ***away,*** – ***down***) abtragen, abnutzen; aushöhlen, eingraben (*a furrow etc.*); (*fig.*) (*usu.* – ***out***) erschöpfen, ermüden, zermürben, ausmergeln; – ***one's clothes into holes,*** die Kleider so lange tragen, bis sie abgenutzt sind; – ***one's fingers to the bone,*** sich abplacken; – ***away,*** abtragen, abnützen, abnutzen, aushöhlen, zerstören; – ***down,*** abnützen, abnutzen, ablaufen (*heels*), austreten (*a step*), (*fig.*) zermürben (*a p.*), brechen, überwinden (*opposition*); – ***off,*** abnutzen, abnützen; – ***out,*** abtragen, abnutzen, abnützen, verschleißen; (*fig., usu. pass.*) aufzehren, verzehren, zerrütten; ermüden, erschöpfen (*a p.'s patience etc.*); – ***o.s. out,*** müde werden. **2.** *irr.v.i.* 1. sich tragen, sich halten, haltbar sein; – ***well,*** strapazierfähig sein, lange halten, sich gut tragen (*as clothes*); (*coll. of a p.*) sich jung halten; (*coll.*) Kritik standhalten; 2. sich abtragen *or* verbrauchen, abgenützt *or* verbraucht werden; – ***away,*** verschleißen, verbraucht werden, abnehmen, vergehen; – ***off,*** sich abtragen *or* abnutzen, (*fig.*) vergehen, sich verlieren, erlöschen; ***their chatter begins to – on me,*** ihr Geschwätz geht mir allmählich auf die Nerven; – ***out,*** sich abnützen *or* abnutzen, sich abtragen; verschleißen; – ***thin,*** fadenscheinig werden (*as clothes*); (*fig.*) die Wirkung verlieren, schwächer werden; 3. (*Poet.*) (*usu.* – ***on,*** – ***to the end***) langsam verrinnen *or* vorrücken, sich dahinschleppen *or* dahinziehen, sich in die Länge ziehen.
3. *s.* 1. das Tragen; die Kleidung; ***for everyday –,*** zum Tragen am Alltag; ***for hard –,*** strapazierfähig; ***be in –,*** Mode sein, getragen werden; ***have in –,*** tragen; ***town –,*** Stadtkleider (*pl.*); 2. die Dauerhaftigkeit, Haltbarkeit; ***still have a good deal of – in it,*** sich noch gut tragen lassen; 3. die Abnützung, Abnutzung, der Verschleiß; – ***and tear,*** natürliche Abnutzung *or* Abnützung, der Verschleiß; (*Comm.*) die Abschreibung für Wertverminderung; ***the worse for –,*** abgetragen, (*fig.*) mitgenommen.

[2]**wear, 1.** *v.t.* (*Naut.*) halsen. **2.** *v.i.* sich drehen, vor dem Winde wenden.

wearable ['wɛərəbl], *adj.* tragbar, zu tragen(d).

weariness ['wiərinis], *s.* die Müdigkeit, Ermüdung.

wearing ['wɛəriŋ], **1.** *s.* 1. das Tragen; 2. (*Tech.*) der Verschleiß, die Abnutzung. **2.** *adj.* (*fig.*) ermüdend, anstrengend, aufreibend, zermürbend, lästig. **wearing apparel,** *s.* die Kleidung, Kleidungsstücke (*pl.*).

wearisome ['wiərisəm], *adj.* ermüdend; mühsam, beschwerlich, lästig, langweilig; ***be –,*** ermüden. **wearisomeness,** *s.* die Mühsal, Mühsamkeit, Lästigkeit. **weary, 1.** *adj.* 1. müde (*also fig.*), ermüdet, erschöpft (***with***, von *or* vor (*Dat.*)); (*fig.*) überdrüssig (***of***, *Gen.*); 2. beschwerlich, ermüdend, lästig; (*coll.*) – ***Willie,*** der Schwächling, Schwachmatikus. **2.** *v.t.* 1. ermüden, müde machen; 2. langweilen (***with***, mit *or* durch), belästigen, aufreiben, Geduld erschöpfen. **3.** *v.i.* müde werden (*also fig.*), (*fig.*) satt *or* überdrüssig werden (***of***, *Gen.*).

weasel [wi:zl], *s.* das Wiesel.

weather ['weðə], **1.** *s.* 1. das Wetter; die Witterung; (*Naut.*) ***make good –,*** auf gutes Wetter stoßen; (*fig.*) ***make heavy –,*** viel Aufhebens *or* Umstände machen (***about***, wegen); – ***permitting,*** bei günstigem *or* gutem Wetter, wenn es das Wetter erlaubt; ***in all –s,*** bei jedem Wetter; ***under stress of –,*** durch das Wetter gezwungen; (*coll.*) ***under the –,*** nicht wohl, unpäßlich; niedergedrückt; 2. (*Naut.*) die Luv(seite). **2.** *v.t.* 1. trotzen (*Dat.*), aushalten, überstehen (*a storm, also fig.*), abwettern (*a storm*), (*fig.*) widerstehen (*Dat.*), überwinden; 2. luvwärts umschiffen (*a cape*), luvwärts vorüberfahren an (*Dat.*), den Wind abgewinnen (*Dat.*) (*a ship*); 3. der Luft *or* dem Wetter aussetzen, auswittern, austrocknen lassen. **3.** *v.i.* (*Geol.*) verwittern.

weather|-beaten, *adj.* 1. wetterhart, abgehärtet; 2. vom Wetter mitgenommen. **--board, 1.** *s.* 1. (*Naut.*) die Windseite, Luv(seite); 2. (*Build.*) das Schutzbrett, Schindelbrett, Schalbrett. **2.** *v.t.* mit Schutzbrettern versehen, verschalen (*a wall*). **--boarding,** *s.* die Verschalung; Schutzbretter (*pl.*). **--bound,** *adj.* vom Wetter zurückgehalten, durch ungünstiges Wetter festgehalten. **--bureau,** *s.* der Wetterdienst. **--chart,** *s.* die Wetterkarte. **-cock,** *s.* die Wetterfahne, der Wetterhahn; (*fig.*) wetterwendischer Mensch.

weathered ['wɛðəd], *adj.* 1. (*Geol.*) verwittert; 2. (*Archit.*) abgeschrägt.

weather|-eye, *s.* ***keep one's – open,*** auf Wind und Wetter achten, (*fig.*) gut aufpassen. **--forecast,** *s.* der Wetterbericht, die Wettermeldung, Wettervorhersage. **--gauge,** *s.* die Luv(seite), Windseite; (*fig.*) der Vorteil. **--glass,** *s.* das Barometer. **--helm,** *s.* (*Naut.*) ***carry –,*** luvgierig sein.

weathering ['wɛðəriŋ], *s.* (*Geol.*) die Verwitterung. **weatherly,** *adj.* (*Naut.*) luvgierig.

weather|man, *s.* (*coll.*) der Meteorologe. **--proof, 1.** *adj.* wetterfest, wetterdicht. **2.** *v.t.* wetterfest machen. **--prophet,** *s.* der Wetterprophet. **--report,** *s.* *See* **--forecast. --ship,** *s.* das Schiff des Wetterdienstes. **--side,** *s.* (*Naut.*) die Luv(seite), Windseite. **--station,** *s.* die Wetterwarte. **--strip,** *s.* die Wetterleiste. **--tight,** *adj.* *See* **--proof. --vane,** *s.* *See* **-cock. --wise,** *adj.* wetterkundig. **--worn,** *adj.* verwittert.

weave [wi:v], **1.** *irr.v.t.* 1. weben; wirken (*fabric*), flechten (*a wreath etc.*); (*fig.*) einflechten (***into***, in (*Acc.*)), verweben, verflechten (zu); 2. erfinden, erdichten, ersinnen; 3. (*fig.*) – ***one's way,*** hin- und hergehen, sich schlängeln. **2.** *irr.v.i.* 1. weben; 2. hin- und herwenden, winden, sich schlängeln *or* hin- und herbewegen; (*sl.*) ***get weaving!*** los! schnell! **3.** *s.* die Webart, das Gewebe. **weaver,** *s.* 1. der (die) Weber(in), Wirker(in); 2. (*also* ***--bird***) der Webervogel. **weaving,** *s.* das Weben, Wirken, die Weberei; – ***loom,*** der Webstuhl; – ***mill,*** die Weberei.

web [web], **1.** *s.* 1. das Gewebe (*also fig.*), Gespinst; 2. (*Zool.*) die Schwimmhaut; 3. Fahne, der Bart (*of a feather*); 4. (*also* ***spider's –***) das Spinn(en)gewebe, die Spinnwebe; 5. das Blatt (*of a saw*); 6. der Stiel, Stag (*of a rail*); 7. die Papierbahn, Papierrolle. **2.** *v.t.* mit Netzwerk überziehen. **webbed** [-d], *adj.* mit Schwimmhäuten versehen; – ***foot,*** der Schwimmfuß. **webbing,** *s.* das Gurtband, der Gurt. **web|-foot,** *s.* der Schwimmfuß. **--footed,** *adj.* schwimmfüßig.

we'd [wi:d], = ***we had*** or ***would*** or ***should.***

wed [wed], **1.** *v.t.* 1. (*Poet.*) heiraten, sich verheiraten mit; verheiraten (***to***, an (*Acc.*)); 2. (*fig.*) verbinden, vereinigen (***to***, ***with***, mit); ***be wedded to a th.,*** einer S. sehr zugetan sein, an einer S. hängen, an eine S. gefesselt *or* gekettet sein, mit einer S. eng verbunden sein, von einer S. nicht zu trennen sein. **2.** *v.i.* (sich ver)heiraten. **wedded** [-id], *adj.* 1. verheiratet (***to***, mit), angetraut (*Dat.*); 2. Ehe-, ehelich. **wedding,** *s.* die Hochzeit, Trauung; ***--breakfast,*** das Hochzeitsessen, Hochzeitsmahl; ***--cake,*** der Hochzeitskuchen; ***--card,*** die Vermählungsanzeige; ***--day,*** der Hochzeitstag; ***--dress,*** das Brautkleid; ***--march,*** der Hochzeitsmarsch; ***--night,*** die Brautnacht; ***--present,*** das Hochzeitsgeschenk; ***--ring,*** der Trauring.

wedge [wedʒ], **1.** *s.* 1. der Keil; ***the thin end of the –,*** erster Anfang *or* Schritt; 2. (*coll.*) die Ecke (*of bread etc.*). **2.** *v.t.* (ver)keilen; einkeilen, eindrängen, einzwängen; – ***o.s. in,*** sich hineinzwängen. **wedge-shaped,** *adj.* keilförmig.

wedlock [ˈwedlɔk], *s.* die Ehe; ***in –,*** ehelich; ***out of –,*** unehelich.

Wednesday [ˈwensdi], *s.* der Mittwoch; ***on –s,*** mittwochs.

[1]**wee** [wiː], *adj.* (*Scots*) klein, winzig, –chen, –lein.

[2]**wee,** *see* **wee-wee.**

weed [wiːd], **1.** *s.* 1. das Unkraut (*also fig.*), (*Poet.*) Kraut, die Pflanze; (*coll.*) der Tabak, die Zigarre, Zigarette; (*Prov.*) ***ill –s grow apace,*** Unkraut verdirbt *or* vergeht nicht; 2. (*sl.*) schmächtiger Mensch. **2.** *v.t.* jäten; (*fig.*) säubern, reinigen (***of,*** von); (*fig.*) – ***out,*** ausmerzen. **3.** *v.i.* (Unkraut) jäten. **weed|-grown,** *adj.* voll Unkraut. **–killer,** *s.* das Unkrautvertilgungsmittel.

weeds [wiːdz], *pl.* (*obs.*) (*only in*) ***widow's –,*** die Witwenkleidung.

weedy [ˈwiːdi], *adj.* 1. voll Unkraut; 2. (*usu. fig.*) klapperdürr, schlaksig; schmächtig, verkümmert.

week [wiːk], *s.* die Woche; ***Holy Week,*** die Karwoche; ***last Monday –,*** Montag vor 8 Tagen; ***today*** or ***this day –,*** heute in acht Tagen *or* über acht Tage; ***a – or two,*** einige Wochen; ***twice a –,*** zweimal wöchentlich; ***by the –,*** wochenweise; ***– by –,*** Woche für *or* um Woche; ***for –s,*** wochenlang; ***– in, – out,*** Woche für Woche.

week|day, 1. *s.* der Wochentag, Alltag. **2.** *attrib. adj.* Wochentags–, Werktags–, Alltags–. **–end, 1.** *s.* das Wochenende. **2.** *attrib. adj.* Wochenend–; ***– ticket,*** die Sonntags(fahr)karte. **3.** *v.i.* das Wochenende verbringen. **–ender,** *s.* der Wochenendausflügler.

weekly [ˈwiːkli], **1.** *adj.* wöchentlich, Wochen–. **2.** *adv.* wöchentlich. **3.** *s.* das Wochenblatt, die Wochenschrift.

ween [wiːn], *v.i.* (*obs.*) wähnen, glauben, meinen, vermuten.

weeny [ˈwiːni], *adj.* (*coll.*) winzig.

weep [wiːp], **1.** *v.i.* 1. weinen, Tränen vergießen (***at, over,*** über (*Acc.*)); – ***for,*** weinen um, beweinen; – ***for joy,*** vor Freude weinen; – ***with pain,*** vor Schmerz weinen; 2. (*fig.*) triefen, tröpfeln, träufeln; 3. feucht sein, schwitzen. **2.** *v.t.* weinen, vergießen (*tears*); – ***one's heart*** or ***eyes out,*** sich (*Dat.*) die Augen ausweinen. **3.** *s.* ***have a good –,*** sich ausweinen. **weeper,** *s.* 1. Weinende(r), Klagende(r); 2. der Trauerschleier, Trauerflor; *pl.* weiße Trauermanschetten (*pl.*) (*of widows*). **weeping, 1.** *s.* das Weinen. **2.** *adj.* 1. weinend, trauernd; tränenvoll (*eyes*); 2. triefend, tropfend, (*Med.*) nässend; 3. (*Bot.*) Trauer–; – ***willow,*** die Trauerweide. **weepy,** *adj.* (*coll.*) weinerlich, rührselig.

weevil [wiːvl], *s.* 1. (*coll.*) der Kornwurm, Getreidekäfer, Wiebel; 2. (*Ent.*) Rüsselkäfer.

wee-wee [ˈwiːwiː], **1.** *s.* (*nursery talk*) der Pipi. **2.** *v.i.* Pipi machen.

weft [weft], *s.* der Einschlag, (Ein)schuß, Querfäden (*pl.*).

weigh [wei], **1.** *v.t.* 1. (ab)wiegen; – ***in,*** nach dem Rennen *or* vor dem Kampf wiegen (*jockeys, boxers*); (*Cul.*) dazugeben; – ***out,*** abwiegen, auswiegen (***to, for,*** *Dat.*); 2. (*fig.*) (ab)wägen, erwägen, abmessen, abschätzen, prüfen; – ***one's words,*** seine Worte abwägen; (*coll.*) – ***up,*** sich (*Dat.*) überlegen, sorgsam prüfen, abschätzen; 3. – ***down,*** niederdrücken, niederbeugen; ***be –ed down,*** niedergebeugt sein; 4. (*Naut.*) – ***anchor,*** den Anker lichten. **2.** *v.i.* 1. wiegen, schwer sein; – ***heavy,*** schwer wiegen, (*fig.*) schwer lasten; 2. (*fig.*) Gewicht haben, gelten, ausschlaggebend *or* von Bedeutung sein (***with,*** bei); 3. (*fig.*) lasten, lastend liegen, drücken (***on,*** auf (*Dat.*)); 4. – ***in,*** sich nach dem Rennen *or* vor dem Kampf wiegen lassen (*jockeys, boxers*); (*coll.*) – ***in with,*** energisch eintreten mit *or* einwerfen *or* vorbringen. **3.** *s.* das Wiegen.

weighable [ˈweiəbl], *adj.* wägbar. **weighage** [–idʒ], *s.* die Wägegebühr, das Wägegeld. **weigh|-bridge,** *s.* die Brückenwaage. **–-house,** *s.* öffentliche Waage. **weighing,** *s.* 1. das Wiegen; ***–-machine,*** die Waage; 2. (*fig.*) das Überlegen, Abwägen, Erwägen, Prüfen.

weight [weit], **1.** *s.* 1. das Gewicht (*also fig.*), die Schwere; Gewichtseinheit, das Gewichtsmaß; ***atomic –,*** das Atomgewicht; ***by –,*** nach Gewicht; ***dead –,*** das Eigengewicht, (*fig.*) drückende Last; ***decrease in –,*** die Gewichtsabnahme; ***gross –,*** das Bruttogewicht; ***2 lb. in –,*** 2 Pfd. schwer; ***live –,*** das Lebendgewicht; ***lose –,*** an Gewicht verlieren, abnehmen; ***–s and measures,*** Maße und Gewichte; ***nett –,*** das Nettogewicht; (*coll.*) ***pull one's –,*** das Seinige tun; (*Spt.*) ***put the –,*** die Kugel stoßen; ***putting the –,*** das Kugelstoßen; ***put on –,*** (an Körpergewicht) zunehmen, Fett ansetzen; ***set of –s,*** der Satz Gewichte; (*coll.*) ***throw one's – about,*** seinen Einfluß zur Geltung bringen, auf seinen Einfluß pochen; ***under –,*** zu leicht, untergewichtig; ***what is your –?*** wieviel wiegen Sie? 2. das Ansehen, der Einfluß, Wert, die Wichtigkeit, Bedeutung, Geltung; ***add – to,*** die Bedeutung erhöhen (*Gen.*), verstärken; ***carry – with,*** schwer wiegen *or* viel gelten bei, (großen) Einfluß haben auf (*Acc.*), ins Gewicht fallen bei; ***give due – to,*** gebührend würdigen, volle Beachtung schenken (*Dat.*), große Bedeutung beimessen (*Dat.*); ***of –,*** schwerwiegend, gewichtig; ***of great –,*** von großer Bedeutung; 3. die Last, Wucht; – ***of evidence,*** die Last des Beweismaterials; 4. die Last, Belastung, Bürde, der Druck; ***the – of years,*** die Last *or* Bürde des Alters; 5. (*Phys., Astr.*) die (Massen)-anziehung(skraft); 6. (*Spt.*) Gewichtsklasse; ***make the –,*** das richtige Gewicht haben (*boxers etc.*); 7. (*Stat.*) statistisches Gewicht, relative Bedeutung. **2.** *v.t.* 1. belasten, beschweren; – ***the scales in favour of,*** etwas in die Waagschale werfen für; 2. (*Stat.*) relative Bedeutung geben (*Dat.*).

weightiness [ˈweitinis], *s.* 1. die Schwere; 2. (*fig.*) das Gewicht, die Wichtigkeit, Bedeutung, Bedeutsamkeit. **weightless,** *adj.* (*Phys.*) schwerelos. **weightlessness,** *s.* die Schwerelosigkeit. **weightlifting,** *s.* (*Spt.*) das Gewichtheben. **weighty,** *adj.* 1. schwer; 2. (*fig.*) lastend, drückend (*cares etc.*), (*fig.*) (ge)wichtig, erheblich, schwerwiegend, bedeutsam.

weir [wiə], *s.* das Wehr; die Reuse (*for fish*).

weird [wiəd], **1.** *adj.* geisterhaft, unheimlich; (*coll.*) seltsam, eigenartig, merkwürdig; ***the – sisters,*** die Schicksalsschwestern. **2.** *s.* (*obs., Scots*) das Schicksal, Verhängnis; (*Scots*) ***dree one's –,*** sein Schicksal ertragen. **weirdness,** *s.* das Unheimliche.

welcome [ˈwelkəm], **1.** *adj.* willkommen (*of a p. or th.*), erfreulich, angenehm (*of a th.*); (*pred. only*) herzlich eingeladen (*of a p.*), gern zugelassen (*of a th.*); ***make him –,*** ihn willkommen heißen; (*coll., oft. iron.*) ***take it and –,*** nehmen Sie es meinetwegen *or* von mir aus *or* liebend gern! (*coll.*) ***you're –,*** nichts zu danken, gern geschehen, keine Ursache; ***you are – to do,*** es steht Ihnen frei zu tun; ***you are – (to it),*** es steht Ihnen zur Verfügung, bitte behalten Sie es! (*coll.*) ***you're – to your own opinion,*** meinetwegen kannst du dir denken was du willst. **2.** *s.* der *or* (*Austr.*) das Willkommen; der Willkomm; Willkommensgruß (***to,*** an (*Acc.*)); die Bewillkommnung, freundliche Aufnahme; ***bid him –,*** ihn willkommen heißen; ***find a ready –,*** gern gesehen *or* freundlich aufgenommen werden; ***give a warm – to him,*** ihn freundlich aufnehmen; ***outstay one's –,*** länger bleiben als man gern gesehen ist; ***words of –,*** Willkommensworte (*pl.*). **3.** *v.t.* bewillkommnen (*also fig.*), willkommen heißen, (*fig.*) begrüßen, gern annehmen. **4.** *int.* willkommen! – ***home!*** willkommen in der Heimat!

weld [weld], **1.** *v.t.* (zusammen)schweißen, anschweißen; (*fig.*) zusammenfügen, zusammenschmieden, verschmelzen, vereinigen. **2.** *v.i.* sich schweißen (lassen). **3.** *s.* die Schweißstelle, Schweißnaht. **weldable,** *adj.* schweißbar. **welded,** *adj.* geschweißt, Schweiß–. **welder,** *s.* der

Schweißer. **welding,** *s.* das Schweißen; – *furnace,* der Schweißofen.

welfare ['welfɛə], *s.* die Wohlfahrt, der Wohlstand, das Wohlergehen; die Fürsorge; *public* –, öffentliche Wohlfahrt; *social* –, soziale Fürsorge. **welfare|-centre,** *s.* das Fürsorgeamt, die Betreuungsstelle. **--department,** *s.* die Sozialabteilung. – **state,** *s.* der Wohlfahrtsstaat. **--work,** *s.* sozial Fürsorge. **--worker,** *s.* der (die) Fürsorger(in).

welkin ['welkin], *s.* (*Poet.*) der Himmel, das Himmelszelt.

[1]**well** [wel], **1.** *s.* 1. der (Zieh)brunnen, die Quelle (*also fig.*); *sink a* –, einen Brunnen bohren *or* graben; 2. der (Öl)schacht, das Bohrloch, die Bohrung; 3. der Pumpensod (*in a ship*); 4. das Treppenhaus (*of stairs*); 5. der Luftschacht, Lichtschacht, Fahrstuhlschacht; 6. Gepäckraum (*in cars*); 7. das Tintenfaß; 8. der Fischbehälter, die Buhne (*in fishing boats*); 9. (*fig.*) der (Ur)quell, Ursprung. **2.** *v.i.* (*also* – *out,* – *up,* – *forth*) hervorquellen (*also fig.*), hervorsprudeln, hervorströmen (*from,* aus); – *over,* überfließen.

[2]**well, 1.** *adv.* 1. gut, wohl, richtig, recht, passend, günstig, vorteilhaft, befriedigend; *behave* –, sich richtig benehmen; *do* –, gut *or* recht daran tun; *he is doing* –, es geht ihm gut; *do o.s.* –, sich gütlich tun; – *done!* bravo! – *met!* du kommst wie gerufen! *only too* –, nur zu gut; *speak* – *of,* Gutes reden von, loben; *it speaks* – *for him,* es spricht sehr für ihn; *stand* – *with him,* gut mit ihm stehen, bei ihm gut angeschrieben sein; *take a th.* –, etwas gut aufnehmen; – *off,* wohlhabend; *be* – *out of,* glücklich hinter sich (*Dat.*) haben; *be* – *rid of,* endgültig los sein; (*coll.*) – *up in,* gut beschlagen in (*Dat.*); 2. tüchtig, ordentlich, eigentlich, reichlich, ziemlich, beträchtlich, in hohem Grade, gründlich; – *and truly,* gründlich, einwandfrei; – *after midnight,* lange nach Mitternacht; – *ahead,* ein gutes Stück voraus; – *away,* weit weg, (*coll.*) gut im Zuge *or* Schwung; – *on in years,* schon bejahrt, in fortgeschrittenem Alter; – *into,* bis spät *or* mitten in (*Acc.*); – *out of sight,* völlig außer Sicht; – *over 60,* weit über 60; – *past,* see – *after*; 3. mit gutem Grund, mit Recht, ja, vielleicht; *as* – (*at end of clause*), ebenso(gut), noch dazu, außerdem, desgleichen; *you may just as* – *come,* du kannst ebensogut kommen; *that is just as* –, das ist ebensogut so; *as* – *as,* so gut wie, sowohl als auch; *you as* – *as I,* sowohl du wie ich, du sowohl wie ich; *I can* – *believe it,* ich kann es leicht glauben; *I don't* – *know,* ich weiß nicht recht; *you may* – *ask,* du kannst wohl *or* mit gutem Grund fragen; *you cannot very* – *ask,* du kannst wohl nicht *or* nicht gut fragen; 4. (*before adj.*) (sehr) wohl, durchaus; – *able,* wohl *or* durchaus imstande; – *done,* durchgebraten, gar (*of food*). **2.** *pred. adj.* 1. wohl, gesund; *be* or *feel* –, sich wohl fühlen; *he is not* –, ihm ist nicht wohl; 2. in Ordnung; (*Prov.*) *all's* – *that ends* –, Ende gut, alles gut; *all being* –, wenn alles gut geht; – *and good,* schön und gut; – *enough,* ziemlich gut, ganz leidlich; *it is* – *for us that,* es ist gut *or* günstig daß; *that's all very* –, *but . . .,* das ist ja alles schön und gut, aber . . .; 3. richtig, ratsam, empfehlenswert; *it would be* –, es würde sich empfehlen (*to do,* daß man tut). **3.** *s. let* – *alone,* die Hände davon lassen, sich nicht einmischen; *wish him* –, ihm Erfolg wünschen. **4.** *int.* –*!* nun! schön! nun wohl! unerhört! –*?* nun? na? und nachher? – *then!* nun also! – *then?* nun also?

we'll [wi:l], = *we shall* or *will.*

well|-acquainted, *adj.* wohlbekannt. **--advised,** *adj.* gut beraten (*a p.*), wohlüberlegt (*action*). **--aimed,** *adj.* gutgezielt. **--appointed,** *adj.* wohl ausgestattet *or* ausgerüstet. **--balanced,** *adj.* im Gleichgewicht, (*fig.*) ausgeglichen, gesetzt, ruhig (*a p.*), abgewogen (*reasons etc.*). **--behaved,** *adj.* wohlerzogen, artig, manierlich. **--being,** *s.* die Wohlfahrt, das Wohl; Wohlergehen, Wohlgefühl, Wohlbehagen. **--beloved,** *adj.* innig geliebt, vielgeliebt. **--born,** *adj.* aus guter Familie. **--bred,** *adj.* wohlerzogen. **--built,** *adj.* wohlgebaut, (*of a p.*) *see* **--knit. --chosen,** *adj.* (gut) gewählt, passend, treffend. **--conditioned,** *adj.* in gutem Zustand. **--connected,** *adj.* mit guten Beziehungen; *see also* **--born. --content(ed),** *adj.* befriedigt, ganz zufrieden. **--defined,** *adj.* gut umrissen. **--deserved,** *adj.* wohlverdient. **--deserving,** *adj.* verdienstvoll. **--directed,** *adj.* gut gezielt (*blow*). **--disposed,** *adj.* wohlgesinnt (*towards, Dat.*), wohlwollend, wohlmeinend (gegen). **--doing,** *s.* gute Werke, die Wohltätigkeit. **--dressed,** *adj.* gut angezogen. **--earned,** *adj.* wohlverdient. **--educated,** *adj.* gebildet. **--established,** *adj.* 1. wohlbegründet, gut fundiert; 2. lange bestehend, feststehend. **--favoured,** *adj.* gutaussehend, hübsch, schön. **--fed,** *adj.* wohlgenährt, gutgenährt. **--found,** *adj.* gut versorgt. **--founded,** *adj.* wohlbegründet. **--groomed,** *adj.* gepflegt (*a p.*), gut gepflegt (*horse*). **--grounded,** *adj. See* **--founded**; mit guten Grundlagen (*knowledge*).

well-head, *s.* 1. die (Ur)quelle; (*fig.*) Hauptquelle; 2. Brunneneinfassung, das Brunnenhäuschen.

well|-heeled, *adj.* (*coll.*) wohlhabend, gut bei Kasse. **--informed,** *adj.* wohlunterrichtet.

wellington boots ['weliŋtən], *s.* (*usu. wellingtons*) Schaftstiefel (*pl.*), Stulpenstiefel (*pl.*); (*usu.*) Gummistiefel (*pl.*), Wasserstiefel (*pl.*).

well|-intentioned, *adj.* 1. gut gemeint, wohlgemeint (*rebuke etc.*); 2. wohlmeinend (*a p.*). **--judged,** *adj.* wohlberechnet, angebracht. **--kept,** *adj.* wohlgepflegt. **--knit,** *adj.* kräftig(gebaut) (*a p.*). **--known,** *adj.* (wohl)bekannt; allgemein *or* weithin bekannt. **--loved,** *adj.* vielgeliebt, teuer. **--made,** *adj.* kräftig gebaut (*as a man*), gut gemacht (*as clothes etc.*). **--mannered,** *adj.* wohlerzogen, manierlich. **--marked,** *adj.* ausgeprägt. **--matched,** *adj.* gut zusammenpassend. **--meaning,** *adj.* wohlwollend, wohlmeinend; *she is* –, sie meint es gut. **--meant,** *adj.* gutgemeint. **--nigh,** *adv.* so gut wie, fast, beinahe. **--off,** *adj.* (*coll.*) in guten Verhältnissen, gut situiert, wohlhabend; – *for,* gut versehen mit. **--oiled,** *adj.* (*sl.*) beschwipst. **--ordered,** *adj.* wohlgeordnet. **--pleasing,** *adj.* wohlgefällig. **--preserved,** *adj.* gut erhalten. **--proportioned,** *adj.* wohlproportioniert. **--read,** *adj.* belesen, bewandert (*in,* in (*Dat.*)). **--regulated,** *adj.* wohlgeordnet. **--rounded,** *adj.* 1. formvollendet, abgerundet, elegant (*style*), vielseitig (*education etc.*); 2. (*coll.*) füllig (*appearance*). **--set,** *adj.* festgefügt. **--set-up,** *adj.* (*coll.*) (*of a p.*) *see* **--proportioned**; muskulös, sehnig. **--spoken,** *adj.* höflich im Ausdruck. **--tempered,** *adj.* (*Tech.*) gut getempert (*steel*), richtig gemischt (*mortar*); (*Mus.*) wohltemperiert. **--thought-of,** *adj.* angesehen. **--thought-out,** *adj.* wohlerwogen, gründlich durchdacht. **--thumbed,** *adj.* abgegriffen. **--timed,** *adj.* angebracht, rechtzeitig. **--to-do,** *adj.* wohlhabend. **--tried,** *adj.* erprobt, bewährt. **--trodden,** *adj.* gebahnt, ausgetreten, (*fig.*) abgedroschen, breitgetreten. **--turned,** *adj.* geschickt formuliert, wohlgeformt (*speech*). **--wisher,** *s.* der (die) Gönner(in), wohlwollender Freund. **--worn,** *adj.* abgenutzt, abgetragen; ausgetreten (*shoes*), (*fig.*) abgedroschen, abgegriffen.

wels [wels], *s.* (*Ichth.*) der Wels.

Welsh [welʃ], **1.** *adj.* walisisch; – *rabbit,* geröstete Käseschnitte (*pl.*). **2.** *s.* 1. (*collect.*) Waliser (*pl.*); 2. (*language*) das Walisisch(e).

welsh, 1. *v.t.* (um sein Geld) betrügen. **2.** *v.i.* mit dem Gewinn durchgehen (*of bookmaker*), (*coll.*) die Schulden nicht begleichen. **welsher,** *s.* betrügerischer Buchmacher; (*sl.*) Betrüger.

Welsh|man [–mən], *s.* der Waliser. **–woman,** *s.* die Waliserin.

welt [welt], **1.** *s.* 1. die Einfassung, (Zier)borte, (Stoß)kante, der Rollsaum, Rand; Rahmen (*of a shoe*); 2. (*coll.*) Striemen, Schmiß, die Strieme, Schmarre; (*sl.*) der Hieb, Schlag. **2.** *v.t.* 1. einfassen, säumen (*soles*); 2. (*sl.*) verhauen.

[1]**welter** ['weltə], **1.** *v.i.* sich wälzen, rollen. **2.** *s.* das Gewirr, Durcheinander, Chaos, wirre Masse.

[2]**welter, 1.** *s.* (*rare*) schwerer Reiter. **2.** *adj.* (*also* **–weight**) Weltergewichts– (*boxer*). **welterweight,** *s.* (*Boxing*) das Weltergewicht (= *bis 147 lb.*).

wen [wen], *s.* die Geschwulst.

wench [wentʃ], **1.** *s.* 1. (*obs. or vulg.*) das Frauenzimmer, Mädchen; 2. (*obs.*) die (Straßen)dirne. **2.** *v.i.* (*vulg.*) huren.

wend [wend], *v.t.* (*only in*) – *one's way,* sich begeben, seinen Weg nehmen, seine Schritte lenken (*to,* nach *or* zu).

went [went], *imperf. of* **go.**

wept [wept], *imperf., p.p. of* **weep.**

were [wɛə], *see* **be**; (*2nd pers. imperf.*) warst, waren; (*1st, 2nd or 3rd pers. pl. imperf.*) waren, waret; (*sing. and pl. imperf. subj.*) wäre(n); ***there* –,** es gab, es waren; ***we – to do it,*** wir sollten es tun; ***as it* –,** gleichsam, sozusagen; (*Mil., coll.*) ***as you –!*** (Griff) zurück!

we're [wiə], = ***we are.*** **weren't** [wə:nt], = ***were not.***

werewolf ['wɛəwulf], *s.* der Werwolf.

west [wɛst], **1.** *s.* 1. der Westen; (*Poet.,Naut.*) West; ***the* –,** das Abendland, der Okzident; (*Am.*) westliche Staaten; – ***by north,*** West zum Nord; ***in the – of,*** im westlichen Teil von; ***the wind is in the* –,** der Wind kommt von Westen; ***to the – of,*** westlich von; 2. (*Poet.*) der Westwind. **2.** *adv.* nach Westen, westwärts; (*sl.*) ***go* –,** untergehen, verlorengehen; krepieren, abkratzen; – ***of,*** westlich von. **3.** *adj.* westlich, West–; ***the – country,*** der Südwesten (Englands); ***West End,*** der Westend; ***West Indiaman,*** der Westindienfahrer; ***West Indian,*** der (die) Westindier(in); ***West Indies,*** Westindien (*n.*).

westbound ['westbaund], *adj.* nach Westen fahrend. **wester** ['westə], **1.** *adj.* (*Scots*) westlich gelegen. **2.** *v.i.* (*Poet.*) nach Westen ziehen *or* neigen. **westerly, 1.** *adj.* im Westen gelegen; aus dem *or* vom Westen kommend, westlich, West– (*wind*). **2.** *s.* (*usu. pl.*) westlicher Wind. **western, 1.** *attrib. adj.* westlich, West–; abendländisch; ***Western Australia,*** Westaustralien (*n.*); – ***empire,*** weströmisches Reich; ***the – world,*** das Abendland. **2.** *s.* 1. (*Am.*) der Weststaatler; 2. Wildwestfilm; Wildwestroman. **westerner,** *s.* der Abendländer; (*Am.*) Weststaatler. **westernize,** *v.t.* abendländischen Charakter geben (*Dat.*). **westernmost,** *adj.* westlichst.

westing ['westiŋ], *s.* (*Naut.*) die Entfernung nach Westen, westliche Richtung.

Westphalia [west'feiliə], *s.* Westfalen (*n.*); (*Hist.*) ***peace of* –,** der westfälische Friede. **Westphalian, 1.** *adj.* westfälisch. **2.** *s.* der Westfale (die Westfälin).

westward ['westwəd], **1.** *adj.* westlich. **2.** *adv.* im Westen, westwärts. **3.** *s.* westliche Richtung; ***to the – of,*** westlich von. **westwards,** *adv. See* **westward, 2.**

wet [wet], **1.** *adj.* 1. naß, durchnäßt, feucht (***with,*** von); – ***blanket,*** der Dämpfer, kalte Dusche; der Spielverderber; – ***and cold,*** naßkalt; – ***paint!*** frisch gestrichen! – ***pack*** or ***poultice,*** feuchte Packung; (*coll.*) – ***behind the ears,*** noch nicht trocken hinter den Ohren; – ***through,*** durchnäßt; – ***to the skin,*** bis auf die Haut naß; – ***with tears,*** tränenbenetzt; 2. regnerisch (*as weather*); – ***season,*** die Regenzeit; – ***weather,*** das Regenwetter; 3. (*Tech.*) Naß–; 4. (*coll.*) nicht unter Alkoholverbot stehend; 5. (*sl.*) trottelhaft. **2.** *s.* 1. die Nässe, Feuchtigkeit; 2. das Regenwetter; ***out in the* –,** draußen im Regen; 3. (*sl.*) der Trottel, Schlappschwanz. **3.** *v.t.* 1. naß machen, (durch)nässen, anfeuchten, benetzen; (*sl.*) – ***one's whistle,*** sich (*Dat.*) die Kehle anfeuchten; 2. (*sl.*) begießen.

wet|-bulb thermometer, *s.* das Verdunstungsthermometer. – **dock,** *s.* das Flutbecken, der Dockhafen.

wether ['weðə], *s.* der Hammel, Schöps.

wetness ['wetnis], *s.* die Nässe, Feuchtigkeit.

wet-nurse, *s.* die (Säug)amme.

wetter ['wetə], *comp.,* **wettest,** *sup. adj. of* **wet. wetting,** *s.* die Durchnässung, das Naßwerden; (*Tech.*) die Anfeuchtung, Befeuchtung; ***get a* –,** durchnäßt *or* naß werden. **wettish,** *adj.* ziemlich *or* etwas feucht.

we've [wi:v], = ***we have.***

wey [wei], *s.* (*obs.*) ein Trockengewicht (40 Scheffel (*salt*), 182 Pfund (*wool*), 48 Scheffel (*corn, coal etc.*)).

whack [wæk], **1.** *s.* 1. (*coll.*) derber Schlag *or* Hieb; 2. (*sl.*) der (An)teil; ***get one's* –,** seinen (An)teil bekommen; 3. (*sl.*) der Versuch; ***have*** or ***take a – at,*** sich wagen *or* versuchen an (*Dat.*), probieren, anpacken. **2.** *v.t.* (*coll.*) schlagen, besiegen; verhauen, verprügeln. **whacker,** *s.* (*sl.*) 1. das Mordsding, etwas Großartiges; 2. plumper Schwindel, faustdicke Lüge. **whacking, 1.** *s.* (*sl.*) Schläge (*pl.*), die Tracht Prügel. **2.** *adj., adv.* (*sl.*) gewaltig, enorm.

whale [weil], **1.** *s.* der Wal(fisch); ***bull* –,** der Walbulle; ***cow* –,** die Walkuh; – ***calf,*** junger Wal; (*sl.*) ***a – of a time,*** der Mordsspaß; (*sl.*) ***be a – on,*** versessen sein auf (*Acc.*). **2.** *v.i.* Walfang treiben, Wale fangen. **whale|bone,** *s.* 1. die Barte (*of whales*); 2. der Fischbeinstab (*of corset*). **–-fishery,** *s.* der Walfang. **–-oil,** *s.* der Walfischtran. **whaler,** *s.* 1. das Walfangboot; 2. der Walfänger. **whaling, 1.** *s.* der Walfang. **2.** *adj.* Walfang–; – ***harpoon,*** das Harpunengeschütz.

wharf [wɔ:f], *s.* (*pl.* **wharves** [–vz]) der Kai, Landungssteg, Landeplatz, Ladeplatz. **wharfage** [–idʒ], *s.* 1. die Ladegelegenheit, Löschgelegenheit; 2. das Kaigeld, die Löschgebühr, Umschlagegebühr. **wharfinger** [–indʒə], *s.* der Kaimeister, Kaiaufseher.

what [wɔt], **1.** *rel. pron.* (das) was; was (auch immer); ***come – may,*** komme was da wolle, es mag kommen was da will; (*coll.*) ***but* –** (*after neg.*), außer dem, der (*or* das); außer der (*or* denen), die; ***not a day but – it rains,*** kein Tag an dem es nicht regnet; ***nothing*** (***compared***) ***to – . . .,*** nichts im Vergleich zu dem, was . . .; ***being – it is,*** wie es nun mal ist; ***with – appeared*** (***to be***) or ***was apparently a serious attempt,*** mit einem scheinbar ernsten Versuch; ***my opinion for – it is worth,*** meine unmaßgebliche Meinung; ***he spent – he had,*** er gab alles aus, was er bei sich hatte; – ***is more,*** außerdem, darüber hinaus; (*sl.*) ***she's got – it takes,*** sie hat *or* besitzt ein gewisses *or* jenes gewisse Etwas. **2.** *inter. pron.* was? – ***about?*** wie steht es mit? was sagst du zu? wie denkst du über (*Acc.*)? – ***for?*** warum? zu welchem Zweck? wofür? wozu? (*coll.*) (***and***) – ***have you,*** und allerlei anderes, was Ähnliches; – ***if?*** was geschieht wenn? wie wenn? – ***next?*** was nun? sonst noch was? was denn noch alles? was sonst noch? – ***is his name?*** wie heißt er? wie ist sein Name? ***and – not,*** und was weiß ich noch alles; – ***of?*** see – ***about?*** – ***of it?*** wenn schon? na und? was tut's? – ***of that?*** was ist denn da schon dabei? was liegt daran? (*coll.*) ***Mr. –'s his name, Mr. –-do-you-call-him,*** Herr Dingsda; – ***is the price of . . .?*** was kostet . . .? (*sl.*) – ***price . . .?*** wie steht es mit . . .? – ***time is it?*** wie spät ist es? wieviel Uhr ist es? (*coll.*) ***I'll tell you* –,** ich will dir was sagen; ***know –'s* –,** im Bilde sein, Bescheid wissen, wissen was los ist; ***tell him –'s* –,** ihm sagen was eine Harke ist; (*coll.*) ***–'s up?*** was ist los? ***so –?*** see – ***of it?*** **3.** *adj.* was für (eine(r, –s)), welche(–r, –s); ***he spent – money he had,*** er gab aus was er an Geld hatte; ***we took – things were left,*** wir nahmen alles was geblieben war; ***come – time you like,*** kommen Sie, wann Sie wollen; (*as int.*) – ***a man!*** was für ein Mann! – ***virtue!*** welche Tugend! – ***haven't we suffered!*** wie sehr haben wir gelitten! **4.** *adv.* – ***though,*** was tut es wenn, und wenn auch *or* schon; – ***with . . .,*** – ***with . . .,*** or – ***with . . . and . . .,*** teils durch . . . teils durch . . .; – ***with one thing and another,*** wenn eins zum andern kommt.

what|ever, 1. *rel. pron.* was auch (immer), alles was; – ***you do,*** was Sie auch tun. **2.** *inter. pron.* (*coll.*) was . . . nur *or* eigentlich *or* überhaupt *or* in aller Welt? **3.** *adj.* einerlei welche(r, –s, –n), ungeachtet all(en, –er) . . . den (die), was für . . . auch immer; (*after noun, emph.*) ***any person –***, irgendeine P., jede beliebige P.; ***nothing –***, überhaupt *or* gar nichts; ***no sense –***, nicht der geringste Verstand. **–-for,** *s.* (*coll.*) eins aufs Dach. **– ho!** *int.* (*coll.*) hallo! holla! heda! **–not,** *s.* 1. der Nipptisch, die Etagere; 2. (*coll.*) (*usu. pl.*) Kleinigkeit(en), alles Mögliche. **–soever** (*emph.*) = **–ever.**

whaup [wɔ:p], *s. See* **curlew.**

wheat [wi:t], *s.* der Weizen. **wheatear** [–iə], *s.* (*Orn.*) der Steinschmätzer (*Oenanthe œnanthe*). **wheaten,** *adj.* Weizen–.

wheedle [wi:dl], **1.** *v.t.* beschwatzen; **– *him into,*** ihn durch glatte Worte *or* Schmeichelei überreden *or* beschwatzen zu; **– *him out of a th.,*** ihm etwas abschwatzen *or* abschmeicheln. **2.** *v.i.* schmeicheln. **wheedling, 1.** *s.* die Schmeichelei. **2.** *adj.* schmeichlerisch, schmeichelnd.

wheel [wi:l], **1.** *s.* 1. das Rad; (*Naut.*) Ruderrad; (*Motor.*) Lenkrad, Steuer(rad); ***at the –***, am Steuer, (*fig.*) am Ruder; ***break on the –***, aufs Rad flechten, rädern; ***break a fly on the –***, mit Kanonen nach Spatzen schießen; ***– of fortune***, das Glückrad; ***the – has come full circle***, das Rad hat sich einmal gedreht; ***put a spoke in his –***, ihm ein Bein stellen, ihm einen Knüppel zwischen die Beine werfen; ***put one's shoulder to the –***, sich ins Zeug legen, tüchtig ins Zeug gehen, sich anstrengen; ***potter's –***, die Töpferscheibe; ***spinning –***, das Spinnrad; ***steering –***, das Steuerrad; (*fig.*) ***turn of the –***, die Schicksalswende; (*fig.*) ***–s within –s***, verwickelte Verhältnisse, Verwicklungen; 2. die Umdrehung; ***free –***, der Freilauf; 3. (*Mil.*) die Schwenkung. **2.** *v.i.* sich (im Kreise) drehen; (*Mil.*) schwenken; ***left –!*** links schwenkt! **– *round***, sich herumdrehen. **3.** *v.t.* 1. rollen, schieben, (auf Rädern) befördern; 2. (*Mil.*) schwenken lassen.

wheel|barrow, *s.* der Schubkarren, der Schiebkarren. **–-base,** *s.* (*Motor.*) der Achs(ab)stand, Radstand. **–chair,** *s.* der Rollstuhl.

wheeled [wi:ld], *adj.* Roll–, fahrbar; (*as suff.*) –räd(e)rig; **– *chair, see* wheelchair**; **– *traffic,*** der Wagenverkehr. **wheeler, 1.** *s. See* **wheel-horse. 2.** *suff.* –rädriger Wagen.

wheel|-horse, *s.* das Stangenpferd, das Deichselpferd. **–house,** *s.* (*Naut.*) das Ruderhaus, Steuerhaus.

wheelless ['wi:llis], *adj.* räderlos, ohne Räder.

wheel|man [–mən], *s.* (*coll.*) der Radfahrer, Radler. **–-rim,** *s.* der Radkranz, die Felge. **–wright,** *s.* der Stellmacher, Wagner.

wheeze [wi:z], **1.** *v.i.* keuchen, schnaufen. **2.** *s.* 1. das Keuchen; 2. (*sl.*) der Scherz, Ulk, Jux. **wheezy,** *adj.* keuchend, schnaufend.

[1]**whelk** [welk], *s.* (*Zool.*) die Wellhornschnecke.

[2]**whelk,** *s.* (*Med.*) der Pickel, die Pustel, Finne.

whelm [welm], *v.t.* (*Poet.*) verschütten, versenken; (*fig.*) überschütten, überdecken (***with, in***, mit).

whelp [welp], **1.** *s.* 1. Junge(s), junger Hund, der Welpe; 2. (*fig.*) der *or* das Balg. **2.** *v.i.* Junge werfen.

when [wen], **1.** *adv.* 1. (*inter.*) wann? ***since –?*** seit wann? ***till –?*** bis wann? (*coll.*) ***say –!*** sag halt! 2. (*rel.*) als, da, wo; ***since –***, seit jener Zeit, und seitdem; ***till –***, und bis dahin; ***the time –***, die Zeit zu *or* in der; ***times –***, Zeiten in denen. **2.** *conj.* (*with past tense*) (damals *or* zu der Zeit) als, nachdem; (*with present tense*) (immer) wenn, jedesmal wenn, so oft, sobald; während, obwohl, wo . . . (doch); (*with past or present*) und dann, woraufhin; ***I only eat – I am hungry,*** ich esse nur, wenn ich Hunger habe; ***why do you stay – you know you ought to go?*** warum bleibst du, wo du doch weißt, daß du gehen sollst? ***we rang the bell, – the door opened immediately,*** wir klingelten, woraufhin die Tür gleich aufgemacht wurde; ***– asleep,*** im Schlaf; ***– a child,*** als Kind; ***– due,*** bei Verfall, zur Verfallzeit; ***even –***, selbst dann wenn; ***– received,*** nach Empfang; ***just –***, gerade *or* eben als.

whence [wens], (*Poet.*) **1.** *adv.* woher (*also fig.*), woraus, von wo, (*fig.*) wie, wodurch, weshalb. **2.** *conj.* woher; (*fig.*) weshalb, und deshalb, und daher.

whenever [wen'evə], **1.** *conj.* immer *or* allemal wenn, einerlei wann, so oft als, wann auch (immer). **2.** *adv.* (*inter.*) wann denn (eigentlich). **whensoever** [–sou'evə] (*emph.*) = **whenever.**

where [wɛə], **1.** *adv.* 1. (*inter.*) wo? wohin? (*rel.*) (dort *or* da) wo, (dahin) wo, wohin; (*fig.*) inwiefern; (*sl.*) ***tell him – to get off,*** ihm zeigen was eine Harke ist. **2.** *pron.* 1. (*inter.*) **– . . . *from?*** woher? wo . . . her? von wo? **– . . . *to?*** wohin? wo . . . hin? 2. (*rel.*) da *or* dort wo; ***from –***, wo, von daher; ***near –***, nahe an der Stelle wo; ***the place –***, der Ort wo *or* an dem; ***before they know – they are,*** ehe sie wissen woran sie sind.

where|abouts, 1. *adv.* wo ungefähr *or* etwa, in welcher Gegend. **2.** *s.* zeitweiliger Aufenthalt(sort) *or* Wohnort. **–as,** *conj.* 1. wohingegen, während *or* wo . . . (doch), da . . . jedoch *or* nun; 2. (*Law*) (all)dieweil, in Anbetracht dessen *or* mit Rücksicht darauf daß. **–at,** *adv.* 1. (*inter.*) worüber? 2. (*rel.*) wobei, und dabei; worüber, und darüber; worauf, und darauf. **–by,** *adv.* 1. (*inter.*) wodurch? wovon? womit? wie? 2. (*rel.*) wodurch, womit. **–fore** [–fɔ:], **1.** *adv.* 1. (*inter.*) weshalb? wofür? warum? wozu? 2. (*rel.*) weswegen, und deshalb. **2.** *s.* das Warum. **–from,** *adv.* (*obs.*) von wo, woher. **–in,** *adv.* 1. (*inter.*) worin? 2. (*rel.*) worin, in dem *or* der *or* denen; und hierein, worin. **–of,** *adv.* (*rel.*) von dem *or* der *or* denen; wovon; dessen *or* deren. **–on,** *adv.* 1. (*inter.*) worauf? 2. (*rel.*) worauf, auf der *or* dem *or* denen. **–soever,** *adv.* (*emph.*) = **wherever. –(un)to,** *adv.* (*rare*) wohin, wozu, woran, worauf, wonach, zu dem (der *or* denen), an den (die *or* das). **–upon,** *adv.* worauf, wonach; daraufhin.

wherever [wɛər'evə], *adv.* wo(hin) denn *or* auch (nur), wo(hin) auch immer, überall wo.

where|with, 1. *adv.* womit. **2.** *prep.* (*rare*) etwas womit. **–withal,** *s.* ***the –***, das Nötige, das (nötige) Geld, die (Geld)mittel (*pl.*).

wherry ['weri], *s.* die Jolle. **wherryman,** *s.* der Fährmann, Jollenführer.

whet [wet], **1.** *v.t.* 1. wetzen, schärfen, schleifen; 2. (*fig.*) reizen, anspornen (*curiosity, desire etc.*), anregen (*appetite*). **2.** *s.* 1. *See* **whetting**; 2. der Appetitanreger; das Reizmittel.

whether ['weðə], *conj.* ob; **– . . . *or not,*** ob . . . oder nicht; ***– or no,*** so oder so, sowieso, auf jeden Fall.

whetstone ['wetstoun], *s.* 1. der Schleifstein, Wetzstein; 2. (*fig.*) Anreiz, Ansporn. **whetting,** *s.* das Wetzen, Schleifen, Schärfen.

whew! [hwu:], *int.* huh! hui!

whey [wei], *s.* die Molke, der Molken, das Käsewasser. **wheyey** [–i], *adj.* 1. molkenartig, molkig; 2. molkenhaltig. **whey-faced,** *adj.* blaß, bläßlich, (käse)bleich.

which [witʃ], **1.** *rel. pron.* der, die, das, welche(r, –s) (*referring to things*), was (*referring to preceding clause or indef. pron.*); ***all of –***, die alle, von denen alle; (*B.*) ***our Father, – art in Heaven,*** unser Vater, der du bist im Himmel; ***I told him to go, – he did,*** ich sagte, er sollte gehen, und das tat er; ***everything –***, alles was; ***take – you will,*** nehmen Sie welche(n, –s) Sie wollen; ***two sons of – I am the younger,*** zwei Söhne von denen ich der jüngere bin; ***the crime of – you accuse him,*** das Verbrechen, dessen Sie ihn beschuldigen. **2.** *inter. pron.* welche(r, –s) (*of p. or th.*); **– *of you?*** wer *or* welcher von Ihnen? ***I don't know – is –***, ich kann sie nicht unterscheiden. **3.** *inter. & rel. adj.* welche(r, –s); ***during – time,*** und während dieser Zeit; ***– things always happen,*** und solche Dinge kommen immer vor.

which|ever (*emph.* **–soever**), *rel. pron.* welche(r, –s) *or* was (auch) immer, ganz gleich welche(r, –s).

whiff [wif], *s.* 1. der Hauch (*also fig.*), (Luft)zug; **– *of grapeshot,*** das Kartäschengeschoß; 2. (*fig.*) der Anflug; 3. Zug (*of a pipe etc.*); ***take a – at one's pipe,*** einen Zug an der Pfeife tun; 4. (*coll.*) (*usu.* übler) Geruch; 5. (*coll.*) das Zigarillo. **whiffle,** *v.i.* böig wehen (*of the wind*).

Whig [wig], *s.* (*Hist.*) (englischer) Liberaler; (*Am.*) National(republikan)er (*in Am. War of Independence*).

while [wail], **1.** *s.* die Weile, (Zeit)spanne, der Zeitraum; ***a little*** or ***short –***, eine (kleine) Weile; ***in a little –***, in kurzer Zeit, binnen kurzem, bald; ***a little – ago*** or ***since***, vor kurzem, kürzlich, unlängst, (erst) kurze Zeit her; ***a long –***, eine ganze Weile, eine Zeitlang; ***a long – ago***, vor einer langen Weile, vor langer Zeit, (schon) lange her; ***between –s***, zwischendurch; ***quite a –***, eine ganze Weile; ***for a –***, eine Zeitlang; ***worth*** (***one's***) ***–***, der Mühe wert; ***be worth –***, sich lohnen; ***make it worth his –***, es ihm vergelten, ihn belohnen; ***once in a –***, gelegentlich, zuweilen, von Zeit zu Zeit, hin und wieder, dann und wann; (*Poet.*) ***the –***, derweil, inzwischen, währenddessen, während (der Zeit wo); ***all the*** or ***this –***, die ganze Zeit über. **2.** *v.t.* (*usu.*) ***– away*** (*time*), (die Zeit) verbringen *or* vertreiben (*for*, *Dat.*; ***with***, mit). **3.** *conj.* 1. (*time*) während, solang(e), indem; 2. (*antithesis*) während ... (hingegen), wo(hin)gegen.

whilom [ˈwailəm], (*obs.*) **1.** *adj.* vormalig, ehemalig, früher, einstig. **2.** *adv.* vormals, ehemals, einst, weiland.

whilst [wailst], *conj. See* **while, 3.**

[1]**whim** [wim], *s.* wunderlicher Einfall, die Marotte, Laune, Grille.

[2]**whim,** *s.* (*Min.*) der Göpel.

whimbrel [ˈwimbrəl], *s.* (*Orn.*) der Regenbrachvogel (*Numenius phæopus*).

whimper [ˈwimpə], **1.** *v.i.* wimmern, winseln. **2.** *s.* das Wimmern, Winseln. **whimpering, 1.** *s.* das Gewimmer, Gewinsel. **2.** *adj.* wimmernd, winselnd.

whimsical [ˈwimzikl], *adj.* grillenhaft, launenhaft, schrullig, absonderlich, seltsam, wunderlich. **whimsicality** [–ˈkæliti], *s.* die Launenhaftigkeit, Grillenhaftigkeit, Absonderlichkeit, Wunderlichkeit. **whimsy, 1.** *s.* die Laune, Grille, Schrulle, wunderlicher Einfall. **2.** *adj. See* **whimsical.**

[1]**whin** [win], *s.* (*Bot.*) der Stechginster, Gaspeldorn.

[2]**whin,** *s.* (*Geol.*) der Basalt(tuff), Dolerit, Trapp.

whin|berry, *s.* die Heidelbeere. **–chat,** *s.* (*Orn.*) das Braunkehlchen (*Saxicola rubetra*).

whine [wain], **1.** *v.i.* 1. winseln, wimmern, jaulen; 2. greinen, quengeln, jammern. **2.** *s.* 1. das Winseln *etc.*; 2. Greinen *etc.* **whining, 1.** *adj.* 1. wimmernd *etc.*; 2. greinend *etc.* **2.** *s.* 1. das Gewinsel, Gewimmer; 2. Gejammer, Gequengel, die Quengelei.

whinny [ˈwini], **1.** *v.i.* wiehern. **2.** *s.* das Wiehern.

whinstone [ˈwinstoun], *s. See* [2]**whin.**

whip [wip], **1.** *s.* 1. die Peitsche, (*fig.*) Zuchtrute, Geißel; ***--and-top***, der Kreisel; 2. der (die) Kutschierer(in); ***be a good –***, gut kutschieren; 3. (*Parl.*) der Einpeitscher; ***one-line –***, die Aufforderung, (bei der Abstimmung) zu erscheinen; ***two-line –***, dringende Aufforderung zu erscheinen; ***three-line –***, die Aufforderung, unbedingt zu erscheinen; (*coll.*) ***– round***, (unvorbereitete) Geldsammlung; 4. (*Hunt.*) der Pikör; 5. (*Tech.*) die Schnellkraft, Federkraft, Biegsamkeit. **2.** *v.t.* 1. peitschen, mit der Peitsche schlagen *or* antreiben; treiben (*a top*); geißeln, auspeitschen, züchtigen (*a p.*); ***– in***, (*Hunt.*) zusammentreiben (*hounds*), (*Parl.*) zusammenbringen, zusammentrommeln (*members*); ***– up***, antreiben (*a horse*), (*coll.*) schnell aufnehmen, aufraffen (*a th.*), zusammentrommeln (*persons*), aufpeitschen (*enthusiasm etc.*); 2. (*Semp.*) überschlagen, übernähen (*a seam*), überwendlich nähen (*a garment etc.*); 3. (*Naut.*) betakeln, umwickeln (*a rope*); 4. schlagen (*cream, eggs*); 5. (*coll.*) schlagen, besiegen, ausstechen, übertreffen (*a p.*); 6. (*coll.*) raffen, reißen, (ruckartig) zerren *or* ziehen, schnellen (*a th.*); ***– off***, schnell wegnehmen (*a th.*), fortreißen, mit sich nehmen (*a p.*); ***– on***, schnell überwerfen *or* anziehen (*a garment*); ***– out***, schnell (aus der Tasche) ziehen; 7. ***– the stream***, den Fluß abangeln. **3.** *v.i.* sausen, flitzen, stürzen, schnellen.

whip|cord, *s.* 1. die Peitschenschnur, die Schmicke; 2. der Kord, geripptes Kammgarn (*fabric*). **--hand,** *s.* rechte Hand; (*fig.*) ***get*** (***have***) ***the –***, die Oberhand gewinnen (haben) (***of***, über (*Acc.*)). **--lash,** *s.* der Peitschenriemen, die Peitschenschnur, Schmicke.

whipped [wipt], *adj.* gepeitscht; ***– cream***, die Schlagsahne; ***– seam***, überwendliche Naht; ***– white of egg***, der Eiweißschnee.

whipper [ˈwipə], *s.* 1. Peitschende(r); 2. (*Hist.*) der Flagellant, Geißelbruder. **whipper|-in,** *s.* (*Hunt.*) der Pikör. **–snapper,** *s.* (*coll.*) freches Bürschchen, der Gernegroß, Naseweis.

whippet [ˈwipit], *s.* 1. der Whippet, die Kreuzung von Windhund und Terrier; 2. (*Mil.*) (*also* ***– tank***) der Panzerkampfwagen.

whippiness [ˈwipinis], *s.* die Biegsamkeit, Geschmeidigkeit. **whipping,** *s.* 1. das Peitschen, Züchtigen; die Tracht Prügel, Schläge (*pl.*), Hiebe (*pl.*); 2. (*Semp.*) überwendliches Nähen; 3. (*Naut.*) die Tautakelung, Garnumwick(e)lung. **whipping|-boy,** *s.* der Prügeljunge. **--post,** *s.* (*Hist.*) der Schandpfahl. **--top,** *s. See* ***whip-and-top.***

whippletree [ˈwipltriː], *s.* das Ortscheit, der Schwengel.

whip-poor-will [ˈwipəwil], *s.* (*Orn.*) (*Am.*) Schreiender Ziegenmelker (*Caprimulgus vociferus*).

whippy [ˈwipi], *adj.* biegsam, federnd, geschmeidig.

whip|saw, 1. *s.* die Schrotsäge, der Fuchsschwanz. **2.** *v.i.* (*Am.*) (*sl.*) Bestechung von zwei Seiten annehmen. **--stitch, 1.** *s.* überwendlicher Stich. **2.** *v.t.* überwendlich nähen.

whir, *see* **whirr.**

whirl [wəːl], **1.** *v.i.* wirbeln, (sich) drehen; ***–*** (***a***)***round***, sich plötzlich umdrehen; (*fig.*) ***my head –s***, mir schwindelt, es wirbelt mir im Kopf. **2.** *v.t.* (herum)drehen, schwingen; ***– up the dust***, den Staub aufwirbeln. **3.** *s.* der Wirbel (*also fig.*), Strudel; (*fig.*) wirres Treiben, das Gewirr, der Sog; ***in a –***, in wilder Eile; ***his head was in a –***, ihm schwindelte der Kopf. **whirlbone,** *s.* das Kugelgelenk.

whirligig [ˈwəːligig], *s.* 1. das Karussell; 2. (*fig.*) der Taumel, Wirbel, Strudel.

whirl|pool, *s.* der Strudel; (*fig.*) der Sog, Wirbel, das Gewirr. **–wind,** *s.* der Wirbelwind, die Windhose, (*fig.*) der Wirbel, Sturm, das Gewirr.

whirr [wəː], **1.** *v.i.* schwirren, surren. **2.** *s.* das Schwirren, Surren.

whisht! [wiʃt], *see* [1]**whist!**

whisk [wisk], **1.** *s.* 1. der (Staub– *or* Fliegen)wedel, (Stroh– *or* Feder)wisch, Wischer; 2. Eierschläger, Schaumschläger, Schneebesen; 3. plötzliche Bewegung (*of the tail etc.*). **2.** *v.t.* 1. (weg)fegen, (weg)wischen; ***– away*** or ***off***, hastig wegnehmen (*a th.*) *or* fortnehmen (*a p.*); 2. schlagen (*eggs*). **3.** *v.i.* flitzen, huschen.

whisker [ˈwiskə], *s.* (*usu. pl.*) 1. der Backenbart; (*coll.*) Bart; ***side--s***, der Kotelettenbart, Koteletten (*pl.*); 2. Schnurrhaare (*pl.*); Schnauzhaare (*of cats etc.*). **whiskered,** *adj.* bärtig.

whisky [ˈwiski], *s.* der Whisky, Kornbranntwein.

whisper [ˈwispə], **1.** *s.* das Flüstern, Geflüster; Raunen, Rascheln; (*usu. pl.*) die Zuflüsterung, das Getuschel, Gemunkel; der Flüsterton, die Flüsterstimme; ***in –s*** or ***a –***, im Flüsterton. **2.** *v.i.* flüstern, wispern; raunen, munkeln, tuscheln; wispeln, rauschen, rascheln (*as leaves*); ***– to***, flüstern mit, zuflüstern (*Dat.*); ***– against***, tuscheln über (*Acc.*). **3.** *v.t.* (ins Ohr) flüstern, zuflüstern (***to***, *Dat.*); ***it is –ed***, es geht das Gerücht, man munkelt. **whisperer,** *s.* Flüsternde(r); der Zuflüsterer, Zuträger, Ohrenbläser. **whispering, 1.** *adj.* flüsternd. **2.** *s.* das Flüstern, Geflüster; ***– campaign***, die Flüsterpropaganda; ***– gallery***, das Flüstergewölbe.

[1]**whist!** [wist], *int.* still! pst!

[2]**whist,** *s.* das Whist(spiel). **whist-drive,** *s.* das Whistturnier.

whistle [wisl], **1.** *v.i.* pfeifen (*also of birds and fig.*), flöten; (*fig.*) heulen (*of wind*), sausen, schwirren (*of bullets*); (*coll.*) ***he can – for it,*** darauf kann er lange warten; ***– for one's money,*** sich (*Dat.*) das Geld in den Kamin *or* Schornstein schreiben. **2.** *v.t.* pfeifen, flöten (*a tune*); (*coll.*) ***– the dog,*** dem Hund pfeifen. **3.** *s.* 1. das Pfeifen, der Pfiff, Pfeifton; 2. (*instrument*) die Pfeife, Flöte; ***blow a –,*** pfeifen, das Pfeifsignal geben; (*sl.*) ***wet one's –,*** sich (*Dat.*) die Kehle anfeuchten.

whistle-stop, *s.* (*Am.*) (*Railw.*) der Nebenbahnhof, die Haltestelle; (*Pol.*) der Zwischenaufenthalt (zwecks Wahlpropaganda); ***– tour,*** die Wahlreise (von Kleinstadt zu Kleinstadt); ***– speech,*** die Wahlrede (vom Sonderzug) an einer Kleinstadt-bahnhof.

whistling ['wisliŋ], **1.** *adj.* pfeifend; ***– buoy,*** die Heulboje; ***– kettle,*** der Pfeifkessel. **2.** *s.* das Pfeifen.

whit [wit], *s.* die Kleinigkeit, der Deut, das Jota, bißchen; ***every – as bad,*** in jeder Hinsicht ebenso schlecht; ***not*** or ***never a –,*** nicht im geringsten, keineswegs, durchaus nicht.

Whit, *adj.* Pfingst–; ***– Monday,*** der Pfingstmontag; ***– Sunday,*** der Pfingstsonntag; ***on – Sunday,*** am Pfingstsonntag; ***– week,*** die Pfingstwoche.

white [wait], **1.** *adj.* 1. weiß; ***– as a lily,*** lilienweiß; ***– as snow,*** schneeweiß; 2. farblos, bleich, blaß; ***– as a sheet,*** leichenblaß, kreideweiß; ***bleed –,*** ausbluten lassen, (*fig.*) aussaugen, schröpfen; 3. (*fig.*) unschuldig, rein, harmlos; 4. (*Am. coll.*) anständig, redlich, rechtschaffen. **2.** *s.* 1. weiße Farbe, das Weiß; ***dressed in –,*** in Weiß gekleidet; ***– of egg,*** das Eiweiß; ***– of the eye,*** das Weiße des Auges; 2. Weiße(r) (*member of white race*); 3. *pl.* (*Med.*) weißer Fluß, die Leukorrhö(e).

white| ant, *s.* die Termite. – **arsenic,** *s.* das Arsentrioxyd. –**bait,** *s.* (*Ichth.*) die Sprotte, der Breitling. – **bear,** *s.* der Eisbär. – **boy,** *s.* (*Hist.*) das Mitglied einer irischen Geheimverbindung. – **bread,** *s.* das Weißbrot. – **caps,** *pl.* Schaumwellen (*pl.*). – **cell,** *s.* weißes Blutkörperchen. – **coffee,** *s.* der Milchkaffee. –-**collar,** *attrib. adj.* (*coll.*) Büro–, Gesites–, Kopf–; ***– job,*** geistiger Beruf; ***– worker,*** (Büro)-angestellte(r). – **corpuscle,** *s. See–* **cell.** – **currant,** *s.* weiße Johannisbeere. – **damp,** *s.* (*Min.*) das Grubengas. – **elephant,** *s.* (*coll.*) lästiger Besitz. – **ensign,** *s.* englische Marineflagge. –-**faced,** *adj.* blaß; ***– horse,*** der Bleß; ***– cow,*** die Blesse. – **feather,** *s.* ***show the –,*** sich feige zeigen. –**fish,** *s.* der Weißfisch. – **flag,** *s.* die Parlamentärflagge; ***hoist*** or ***show the –,*** sich ergeben, kapitulieren (*also fig.*). – **friar,** *s.* der Karmeliter. –-**haired,** *adj.* weißhaarig. –-**heart (cherry),** *s.* Weiße Herzkirsche. – **heat,** *s.* die Weißglut(hitze); (*fig.*) ***at*** (***a***) ***–,*** in fieberhafter Eile, mit fieberhaftem Eifer, bis zur Weißglut. – **horse,** *s.* 1. der Schimmel; 2. *pl.* (*coll.*) die Schaumkrone (*on waves*). –-**hot,** *adj.* weißglühend; (*fig.*) fieberhaft. – **lead,** *s.* das Bleiweiß. – **lie,** *s.* die Notlüge. –-**lipped,** *adj.* angstbleich. –-**livered,** *adj.* (*coll.*) feige, ängstlich. – **magic,** *s.* weiße Magie. – **man,** *s.* 1. Weiße(r); ***–'s burden,*** die Bürde des weißen Mannes; 2. (*fig.*) anständiger Mensch. – **metal,** *s.* das Weißmetall, Lagermetall.

whiten ['waitən], **1.** *v.t.* weißen, weiß machen; bleichen, weißwaschen (*also fig.*). **2.** *v.i.* weiß werden (*of a th.*), bleich *or* blaß werden, erblassen, erbleichen (*of a p.*). **whiteness** ['waitnis], *s.* die Weiße; Blässe, Bleichheit.

White Nile, *s.* Weißer Nil.

whitening ['waitniŋ], *s.* 1. das Weißen, Weißmachen, Weißwaschen; 2. Weißwerden, Bleichwerden; 3. *See* ²**whiting.**

white| paper, *s.* (*Parl.*) der Informationsbericht. – **pepper,** *s.* weißer Pfeffer. – **poplar,** *s.* die Silberpappel. – **race,** *s.* weiße Rasse.

White Russian, 1. *s.* der Weißrusse (die Weißrussin). **2.** *adj.* weißrussisch.

white| sale, *s.* Weiße Woche. – **sauce,** *s.* (*Cul.*) helle Soße. – **sheet,** *s.* (*fig.*) das Sündergewand, Büßerhemd; ***stand in a –,*** seine Sünden bekennen, beichten. –-**skinned,** *adj.* weißhäutig. –-**slave traffic,** *s.* der Mädchenhandel. –**smith,** *s.* der Blechschmied, Feinschmied, Klempner. – **spirit,** *s.* das Terpentinsurrogat. –**thorn,** *s.* (*Bot.*) der Weißdorn. –**throat,** *s.* (*Orn.*) die Dorngrasmücke (*Sylvia communis*). – **trash,** *s.* (*Am.*) armer Weißer, (*collect.*) arme weiße Bevölkerung. –**wash, 1.** *s.* 1. die Tünche (*also fig.*); 2. Beschönigung; Rehabilitation, Ehrenrettung. **2.** *v.t.* 1. tünchen, weißen, kalken; 2. (*fig.*) übertünchen, beschönigen; rehabilitieren, reinwaschen. – **whale,** *s.* der Weißwal. – **wine,** *s.* der Weißwein.

whither ['wiðə], (*Poet.*) **1.** *inter. adv.* wohin? **2.** *rel. adv.* zu welch(em, –er, –en), in welch(en, –e, –es), dahin wo. **whithersoever,** *rel. adv.* wohin auch immer, einerlei wohin.

¹**whiting** ['waitiŋ], *s.* (*Ichth.*) der Weißfisch, Wittling.

²**whiting,** *s.* die Schlämmkreide.

whitlow ['witlou], *s.* das Nagelgeschwür. **whitlow-grass,** *s.* (*Bot.*) der Dreifingersteinbrech.

Whitsun ['witsən], *adj.* Pfingst–; pfingstlich. **Whitsuntide,** *s.* das Pfingstfest, Pfingsten; ***at –,*** zu Pfingsten; ***– recess,*** die Pfingstferien.

whittle [witl], *v.t.* schnitzen; (*fig.*) ***– away*** or ***down,*** beschneiden, herabsetzen.

whiz(z) [wiz], **1.** *v.i.* zischen, schwirren, surren, sausen. **2.** *s.* das Zischen, Schwirren, Surren, Sausen; (*sl*) ***it's a –,*** feine Sache! (*coll.*) ***gee –!*** oh je! **whizzer,** *s.* 1. die Knarre, Rassel; 2. (*Tech.*) (Trocken)zentrifuge. **whizz-kid,** *s.* (*coll.*) hochbegabte, junge P.

who [hu:], **1.** *rel. pron.* der *or* die *or* das welche(r, –s) (*agreeing with antecedent*), wer (*independent of antecedent*); ***I – am your father,*** ich, der ich dein Vater bin; ***he –,*** derjenige, der; ***I know – you are,*** ich weiß, wer du bist. **2.** *inter. pron.* wer? ***– goes there?*** wer da? ***– the deuce*** or ***devil . . .?*** wer zum Kuckuck . . .?

whoa! [wou], *int.* brr! halt!

whodunit [hu:'dʌnit], *s.* (*sl.*) der Krimi.

whoever [hu:'evə], *rel. pron.* wer (auch) immer; jeder(mann) der; gleich *or* einerlei wer.

whole [houl], **1.** *adj.* 1. ganz, gesamt, voll; (*sl.*) ***go the – hog,*** aufs Ganze gehen, alles dransetzen; ***– number,*** ganze Zahl; 2. heil, intakt, unverletzt, unversehrt; ***with a – skin,*** mit heiler Haut; 3. (*fig.*) vollständig, ungeteilt, vollkommen; 4. (*obs.*) gesund. **2.** *s.* ***the –,*** das Ganze (*as a unity*), die Gesamtheit (*collect.*); ***a –,*** ein Ganzes; ***the – of,*** ganz; ***as a –,*** als Ganzes (gesehen); ***in – or in part,*** ganz oder teilweise; ***on the –,*** im (großen und) ganzen, insgesamt, alles in allem.

whole|-coloured, *adj.* einfarbig. –-**hearted,** *adj.* aufrichtig, ernsthaft, ernst gemeint, (*of a p.*) warmherzig, rückhaltlos. –-**heartedly,** *adv.* von ganzem Herzen, aufrichtig, ernstlich. –-**heartedness,** *s.* die Aufrichtigkeit, Ernsthaftigkeit. –-**hogger** [–hɔgə], *s.* (*sl.*) konsequenter Anhänger. –-**length,** *adj.* Ganz–, Voll–, (*of portrait*) in Lebensgröße. –-**life,** *adj.* Erlebensfall– (*insurance*). –**meal,** *s.* das Vollmehl; ***– bread,*** das Vollkornbrot.

wholeness ['houlnis], *s.* die Ganzheit, Vollständigkeit.

wholesale ['houlseil], **1.** *adj.* 1. (*Comm.*) Engros–, Großhandels–; ***– business,*** das Großhandelsgeschäft, Engrosgeschäft; der Großhandel; ***– dealer*** or ***merchant,*** der Großkaufmann, Großhändler, Grossist; ***– firm,*** die Engrosfirma; ***– price,*** der Engrospreis, Großhandelspreis, Partiepreis; ***– trade,*** der Großhandel; 2. (*fig.*) unterschiedslos, unbegrenzt, Pauschal–, Groß–, Massen–; ***– slaughter,*** das Massenschlachten; ***in his – way,*** auf seine überschwengliche Weise. **2.** *adv.* 1. (*Comm.*) en gros; 2. (*fig.*) in Massen, massenweise, ohne Unterschied, unterschiedslos, in Bausch und Bogen. **3.** *s.* der Großhandel, Engroshandel. **wholesaler,** *s. See* ***wholesale dealer.***

wholesome ['houlsəm], *adj.* 1. zuträglich, bekömmlich, gesund(heitsfördernd), heilsam, wohltuend;

2. förderlich, nützlich, dienlich, zweckmäßig. **wholesomeness,** *s.* 1. die Zuträglichkeit, Gesundheit, Heilsamkeit; 2. Nützlichkeit, Dienlichkeit, Zweckmäßigkeit.

who'll [hu:l], = *who will* or *shall*.

wholly ['houli], *adv.* ganz, gänzlich, völlig, vollkommen, durchaus, ausschließlich.

whom ['hu:m], **1.** *rel. pron.* (*Acc. of* **who, 1**) 1. (*agreeing with antecedent*) den *or* die welche(n); *to* –, dem (der, denen); *of* –, dessen (deren), von welch(em, –er, –en); 2. (*independent of antecedent*) wen; den(jenigen) welchen, die(jenige(n)) welche; *all of – were present,* welche alle anwesend waren; *– the gods love die young,* wen die Götter lieben, der stirbt jung. **2.** *inter. pron.* (*Acc. of* **who, 2**) wen? *by* –, durch wen? *of* or *from* –, von wem? *to* –, wem? **whom(so)ever** [–(sou)'evə], *rel. pron.* wen auch (immer); jeden, den (jede, die).

whoop [hu:p], **1.** *s.* 1. lauter Schrei; das Kriegsgeschrei; 2. (*Med.*) Keuchen. **2.** *v.i.* 1. laut aufschreien; 2. (*Med.*) keuchen.

whoopee ['wu:pi:], **1.** *s.* (*sl.*) der Budenzauber, (Freuden)rummel; *make* –, sich austoben, es hoch hergehen lassen. **2.** *int.* juchhe! **whooper** ['hu:pə], *s.* (*also – swan*) der Singschwan. **whooping cough** ['hu:piŋ], *s.* der Keuchhusten.

whop [wɔp], *v.t.* (*sl.*) schlagen, verdreschen, (ver)prügeln. **whopper,** *s.* (*sl.*) 1. das Mordsding, die Pfundssache; 2. faustdicke Lüge. **whopping,** *adj.*, *adv.* (*sl.*) ungeheuer, enorm, kolossal, gewaltig, Riesen–.

whore [hɔ:], **1.** *s.* die Hure, Dirne, Prostituierte. **2.** *v.i.* huren. **whore|monger,** *s.* der Dirnenjäger. **–mongering,** *s.* die Hurerei.

whorl [wɔ:l], *s.* 1. (*Tech.*) der Wirtel; 2. (*Bot.*) Quirl, Wirbel; 3. die Windung (*of a snail*). **whorled,** *adj.* 1. wirtelförmig, spiralförmig, spiralig; 2. (*Bot.*) quirlständig.

whortleberry ['wə:tlberi], *s.* die Heidelbeere; *red* –, die Preiselbeere, Kronsbeere.

who's [hu:z], = *who is* or *has*.

whose [hu:z], **1.** *rel. pron.* (*poss. of* **who, 1**) dessen, deren. **2.** *inter. pron.* (*poss. of* **who, 2**) wessen? *– is it?* wem gehört es? **whose(soe)ver** [–(sou)-'evə], *rel. pron.* wessen auch immer.

whosoever ['hu:sou'evə], *pron. See* **whoever.**

why [wai], **1.** *rel. adv.* warum, weshalb, wozu, weswegen; *the reason* –, der Grund weshalb; *that is* –, darum, deshalb, das ist der Grund weshalb. **2.** *inter. adv.* warum? weshalb? weswegen? wozu? *– so?* warum das? wieso? **3.** *int.* nun, wahrhaftig, (ja) natürlich, doch; –, *to be sure,* aber gewiß, ja freilich. **4.** *s.* das Warum; *the – and the wherefore,* das Wie und Warum, Warum und Weshalb.

wick [wik], *s.* der Docht.

wicked ['wikid], *adj.* schlecht, böse, niederträchtig; sündhaft, gottlos, verrucht; (*coll.*) boshaft, ungezogen, unartig; (*coll.*) *a – shame,* eine Gemeinheit. **wickedness,** *s.* die Schlechtigkeit, Niederträchtigkeit, Niedertracht, Verruchtheit, Sündhaftigkeit, Gottlosigkeit, Bosheit.

wicker ['wikə], *adj.* geflochten, Flecht–, Weiden–, Korb–; *– basket,* der Weidenkorb; *– chair,* der Korbstuhl. **wickerwork,** *s.* das Flechtwerk; Korbwaren (*pl.*).

wicket ['wikit], *s.* 1. (*also* *–gate*) das Pförtchen; die Halbtür; Seitentür, Nebentür; 2. (*Crick.*) das Tor, der Dreistab; die Bahn zwischen beiden Toren; *keep* –, Torwart sein; *take a* –, den Schläger ausmachen; *by 3 –s, with 3 –s in hand,* ohne daß 3 Spieler geschlagen haben; *3 –s down,* 3 Schläger ausgemacht; (*fig.*) *on a good* (*sticky*) –, in einer günstigen (heiklen) Lage. **wicket-keeper,** *s.* der Torwart, Torhüter.

wide [waid], **1.** *adj.* 1. breit; *3 inches* –, 3 Zoll breit; *– skirt,* loser *or* weiter Rock; *– street,* breite Straße; 2. (*fig.*) weit(reichend), umfangreich, umfassend, ausgedehnt; (*sl.*) *– boy,* gerissener Kunde; *– culture,* umfassende Bildung; *– difference,* großer *or* beträchtlicher Unterschied; *– distribution,* weite Verbreitung; *– experience,* reiche Erfahrung; *– public,* breiteres Publikum; *– range,* ausgedehnter Bereich; *– reading,* große Belesenheit; *take a – view,* großzügig *or* weitherzig sein; *– world,* weite Welt; 3. (*usu. pred.*) weit entfernt *or* abirrend (*of*, von); (*Crick.*) *– ball,* der Ball außerhalb der Reichweite des Schlägers; (*Naut.*) *give the rocks a – berth,* weit von den Felsen abhalten; (*fig.*) *give him a – berth,* um ihn einen großen Bogen machen, ihm weit aus dem Wege gehen; *be – of the mark,* weit vom Ziel sein, (*fig.*) ganz und gar nicht zur S. gehören, völlig verkehrt sein. **2.** *adv.* weit; *far and* –, weit und breit; *– apart,* weit auseinander; *– awake,* hellwach, völlig wach, (*fig.*) wachsam, aufmerksam, achtsam (*to*, auf (*Acc.*)); (*coll.*) schlau, gewitzt; *go* or *fall* –, weitab fallen (*of*, von), (weit) danebengehen; *– open,* weit offen; *open* –, weit öffnen; *have one's eyes – open,* die Augen weit aufhalten, auf der Hut sein. **3.** *s.* 1. *See – ball*; 2. (*sl.*) *be broke to the* –, auf dem trockenen sitzen, völlig pleite sein; (*sl.*) *lost to the* –, völlig weg sein.

wide|-angle, *adj.* Weitwinkel–. **–-eyed,** *adj.* mit aufgerissenen Augen; *in – amazement,* ganz verwundert *or* entgeistert.

widely ['waidli], *adv.* weit; *– distributed,* weitverbreitet; *differ* –, sehr verschieden *or* unterschiedlich sein; (*coll.*) sehr unterschiedlicher Meinung sein; *– known,* weit und breit *or* in weiten Kreisen *or* allgemein bekannt; *– scattered,* weit verstreut; *most – used,* am meisten benutzt. **widen, 1.** *v.t.* breiter machen; (*fig.*) erweitern, ausdehnen; *– the gap,* die Kluft vertiefen. **2.** *v.i.* breiter werden; (*fig.*) sich erweitern *or* (aus)weiten *or* ausdehnen *or* vertiefen. **wideness,** *s.* die Weite, Breite, Ausdehnung; *– of range,* die Reichweite. **widening,** *s.* die Erweiterung.

wide|-screen, *adj.* Breitwand–, Raumbild–. **–spread,** *adj.* weit ausgebreitet, ausgedehnt; (*fig.*) weitverbreitet.

widgeon ['widʒən], *s.* (*Am. European* –) (*Orn.*) die Pfeifente (*Anas penelope*).

widow ['widou], *s.* die Witwe; *grass* –, die Strohwitwe; *–'s allowance,* das Witwengeld; *–'s pension,* die Witwenrente; (*Poet.*) *–'s weeds,* die Witwentracht. **widow-bird,** *s.* der Witwenvogel. **widowed** [–d], *adj.* 1. verwitwet; *be* –, verwitwet sein; Witwe werden; 2. (*Poet.*) verlassen, verwaist; beraubt (*of*, *Gen.*). **widower,** *s.* der Witwer. **widowhood,** *s.* die Witwenschaft, der Witwenstand.

width [widθ], *s.* die Weite, Breite.

wield [wi:ld], *v.t.* handhaben, schwingen, führen; (*fig.*) geltend machen, ausüben (*influence etc.*) (*over*, über (*Acc.*)); *– the pen,* schreiben, die Feder führen; *– the sceptre,* das Zepter führen, regieren, herrschen; *– a weapon,* eine Waffe handhaben.

wife [waif], *s.* (*pl.* **wives** [–vz]) die (Ehe)frau, Gattin, Gemahlin, (*obs.*) das Weib; *wedded* –, angetraute Gattin; *old wives' tale,* die Altweibergeschichte, das Ammenmärchen; *take to* –, zur Ehefrau nehmen. **wifehood,** *s.* der Ehestand. **wifelike,** *adj.* frauenhaft, fraulich.

wig [wig], *s.* die Perücke.

wigging ['wigiŋ], *s.* (*coll.*) die Standpauke, Schelte, Rüge; *give him a good* –, ihm gehörig den Kopf waschen, ihn tüchtig abkanzeln.

wigeon, *see* **widgeon.**

wiggle [wigl], **1.** *v.i.* (*coll.*) wackeln. **2.** *v.t.* wackeln mit. **wiggly,** *adj.* (*coll.*) wackelig; *– line,* die Schlangenlinie.

wight [wait], *s.* (*obs.*) der Wicht, Kerl.

wigwam ['wigwæm], *s.* das Indianerzelt, der Wigwam.

wild [waild], **1.** *adj.* 1. wild (wachsend) (*plants*), wild, ungezähmt (*animals*), wild, unzivilisiert, barbarisch (*tribes*); *– flower,* die Feldblume; *– horses will not make me do it,* keine vier Pferde bringen mich dazu; *– man of the woods,* wilder Mann; *sow one's – oats,* sich austoben, sich die Hörner ablaufen; 2. (*fig.*) ungezügelt, unbändig, ungestüm, stürmisch, heftig, ausgelassen; (*coll.*)

wahnsinnig, verrückt, unsinnig, unbesonnen, unvernünftig, hirnverbrannt (*ideas, behaviour etc.*); – ***fancies***, ausschweifende *or* schwärmerische *or* (*coll.*) tolle Einfälle; – ***shot***, der Schuß ins Blaue; – ***talk***, leeres Gerede; 3. wüst, unbebaut (*of land*), wild(romantisch), abenteuerlich (*as scenery*); wirr, unordentlich; – ***hair***, wirres Haar; – ***look***, wirres *or* verstörtes Aussehen; 4. (*coll.*) wütend, rasend, zornig, entzürnt (***about***, über (*Acc.*)); 5. (*coll.*) wild, (be)gierig, versessen (***about***, auf (*Acc.*)). **2.** *adv.* unkontrolliert; ***run*** –, wild wachsen, ins Kraut schießen (*of plants*), (*fig.*) verwildern, wild aufwachsen; ***shoot*** –, ins Blaue schießen, drauflosschießen; ***talk*** –, sinnlos reden. **3.** *s.* (*also pl.*) die Wildnis, Wüste, Wüstenei, Einöde, das Ödland.

wild|-boar, *s.* das Wildschwein. **–cat, 1.** *s.* 1. die Wildkatze; 2. (*fig.*) der Hitzkopf; 3. (*Am.*) (*Min.*) die Probebohrung; 4. (*Am.*) (*Comm.*) das Schwindelunternehmen, unsolide Spekulation. **2.** *attrib. adj.* (*fig.*) unsolid, unreell, Schwindel–; abenteuerlich, wild; – ***company***, die Schwindelgesellschaft; – ***strike***, wilder Streik. **3.** *v.t.* (*v.t.*) (*Am.*) Versuchsbohrungen machen (in (*Dat.*)). **--duck,** *s.* die Wildente, Stockente.

wildebeest ['wildibi:st], *s.* (*Zool.*) das Gnu.

wilderness ['wildənis], *s.* die Wildnis, Wüste; (*B.*) ***voice in the*** –, die Stimme des Predigers in der Wüste; (*Parl.*) ***in the*** –, außer Amt.

wild|-eyed, *adj.* mit wildem Blick. **–fire,** *s.* 1. (*Hist.*) griechisches Feuer; 2. verheerender Brand; (*fig.*) ***spread like*** –, sich wie ein Lauffeuer verbreiten. **–fowl,** *s.* Wildhühner (*pl.*). **--goose,** *s.* die Wildgans; (*fig.*) – ***chase***, vergebliche Mühe, fruchtloses Unternehmen *or* Unterfangen.

wilding ['waildiŋ], *s.* der Wildling, unveredelte Pflanze; der Holzapfel(baum). **wildness,** *s.* die Wildheit, Verwilderung; Ausgelassenheit, Zügellosigkeit.

wile [wail], **1.** *s.* die List, Tücke, Schlauheit, Schläue; (*usu. pl.*) Kniffe, Ränke, Tücken, Schliche (*pl.*). **2.** *v.t.* 1. anlocken, verlocken; 2. – ***away***, *see* **while, 2.**

wilful ['wilful], *adj.* absichtlich, willentlich, bewußt, vorsätzlich; eigenwillig, eigensinnig, halsstarrig. **wilfulness,** *s.* der Eigensinn, Eigenwille; die Absichtlichkeit, Vorsätzlichkeit.

wiliness ['wailinis], *s.* die List, Schläue, Gerissenheit, Verschlagenheit.

[1]**will** [wil], *s.* 1. der Wille; die Willenskraft, das Willensvermögen; Wollen, Verlangen, Belieben, (Be)streben, der Wunsch, Entschluß, die Willensäußerung; ***against his*** –, gegen seinen Wunsch (*s.o. else's action*); ***against his*** (***own***) –, gegen seinen Willen (*one's own action*); ***at*** –, nach Wunsch *or* Belieben; (*B.*) ***Thy – be done***, Dein Wille geschehe; ***free*** –, ***freedom of*** (***the***) –, die Willensfreiheit; ***of one's own*** (***free***) –, freiwillig, aus freien Stücken, aus eigenem Willen; (*coll.*) ***at his own sweet*** –, nach seinem Köpfchen; ***good*** –, das Wohlwollen, die Geneigtheit, Gunst; ***have one's*** –, auf seinem Willen bestehen *or* beharren; ***have a – of one's own***, seinen eigenen Willen haben; ***ill*** –, das Übelwollen, die Feindschaft; ***bear him ill*** –, ihm grollen; – ***to live***, der Lebenswille; – ***power***, die Willenskraft, Willensstärke; ***what is your –?*** was wollen Sie? (*Prov.*) ***where there's a – there's a way***, wo ein Wille ist, ist auch ein Weg; ***with a*** –, eifrig, energisch, mit Energie; ***with the best – in the world***, mit dem denkbar besten Willen; ***work one's*** –, seinen Willen durchsetzen, sein Ziel erreichen (***on, with***, bei); 2. (*Law*) letzter Wille, das Testament, letztwillige Verfügung; ***by*** –, letztwillig, testamentarisch; ***under his*** –, nach *or* gemäß *or* laut seiner letztwilligen Verfügung; ***make one's*** –, sein Testament machen.

[2]**will, 1.** *irr. v. aux.* (*only pres. and imperf.*) **(a)** *subjective volition* (*1st, 2nd and 3rd pers.*) will, willst *etc.*; willens *or* geneigt zu; ***I – do it***, ich will es tun; ***call it what you*** –, man mag es nennen wie man will; ***the door – not shut***, die Tür läßt sich nicht schließen; ***it – not burn***, es brennt einfach nicht, es will nicht brennen; **(b)** *future tense* (*2nd and 3rd pers.*) wird, wirst, werdet, (*Scots and Am. also 1st pers.*) werde(n); ***I – do it***, ich werde es tun; ***you – do it***, – ***you?*** Sie werden *or* wollen es tun, nicht wahr? ***boys – be boys***, Jungens sind nun mal Jungens. **2.** *reg. v.t.* 1. (*Law*) (letztwillig *or* testamentarisch *or* durch Testament) bestimmen *or* verfügen; vermachen, hinterlassen (***to***, *Dat.*); 2. (*of or as God*) bestimmen, entscheiden; (*as hypnotist*) seinen Willen aufzwingen (*Dat.*), zwingen, beeinflussen; – ***o.s. to do***, sich zwingen zu tun. **3.** *reg. v.i.* (es haben) wollen, begehren, verlangen; ***as you*** –, wie sie (es) wollen.

–willed [wild], *adj. suff.* –willig.

willful *etc.*, (*Am.*) *see* **wilful.**

willies ['wiliz], *pl.* (*sl.*) ***the*** –, die Beklemmung, der Bammel.

willing ['wiliŋ], *adj.* 1. (bereit)willig, willfährig, hilfreich; (*pred. only*) gewillt, willens, bereit, geneigt, einverstanden; ***God*** –, so Gott will; 2. gern geschehen *or* geleistet (*action*). **willingly,** *adv.* gern, bereitwillig, mit Vergnügen. **willingness,** *s.* die Bereitschaft, (Bereit)willigkeit, Geneigtheit; das Entgegenkommen.

will-o'-the-wisp ['wiləðə'wisp], *s.* das Irrlicht (*also fig.*).

[1]**willow** ['wilou], *s.* 1. die Weide; ***weeping*** –, die Trauerweide; ***wear the*** –, um die (den) Geliebte(n) trauern; 2. (*Crick. coll.*) das Schlagholz.

[2]**willow, 1.** *s.* die Krempel(maschine), der Krempelwolf, Reißwolf. **2.** *v.t.* krempeln, wolfen.

willow|-herb, *s.* (*Bot.*) der Weiderich, das Weidenröschen, Antonskraut. **--pattern,** *s.* blaues chinesisches Muster mit Weidenlandschaft (*porcelain*). **--warbler, --wren,** *s.* (*Orn.*) der Fitis, Weidenlaubsänger (*Phylloscopus trochilus*).

willowy ['wiloui], *adj.* biegsam, geschmeidig; graziös, schlank.

willy-nilly ['wili'nili], *adv.* wohl oder übel, gezwungen(ermaßen).

[1]**wilt** [wilt], (*obs.*) *2nd pers. sing. pres. of* **will.**

[2]**wilt,** *v.i.* (ver)welken, verblühen; (*fig.*) dahinwelken, schlapp *or* schwach werden, erschlaffen.

wily ['waili], *adj.* listig, schlau, gerissen, verschlagen, verschmitzt.

wimple [wimpl], **1.** *s.* (*Hist.*) das Kopftuch; (*B.*) der Schleier. **2.** *v.t.* (den Kopf *etc.*) verschleiern *or* verhüllen.

win [win], **1.** *irr.v.t.* 1. gewinnen (*battle, contest, prize, s.o.'s hand etc.*), erringen (*victory*); (*fig.*) erhalten, erlangen (*fame, honour, praise etc.*); – ***the day***, den Sieg davontragen, das Feld behaupten (*also fig.*); – ***it from*** or (*coll.*) ***off him***, es ihm abgewinnen; – ***him over***, ihn freundlich stimmen, ihn einnehmen, seine Sympathie erobern, ihn *or* seine Zuneigung gewinnen (***to***, für); ***it will – him much praise***, es bringt ihm viel Lob ein; – ***one's spurs***, die Sporen gewinnen; (*fig.*) sich (*Dat.*) die Sporen verdienen, sich auszeichnen; – ***the toss***, (das Los) gewinnen; 2. (*rare*) erreichen, gelangen zu; – ***the shore***, die Küste erreichen; – ***one's way into***, gelangen zu, seinen Weg machen in (*Acc.*). **2.** *irr.v.i.* siegen, Sieger sein, den Sieg davontragen; gewinnen (*at play etc*); – ***by a head***, um eine Kopflänge gewinnen; – ***easily***, (*coll.*) – ***hands down***, spielend gewinnen; (*coll.*) – ***on*** (*usu.* ***be winning on***), überholen; – ***through***, sich durchkämpfen *or* durchschlagen *or* durchsetzen, ans Ziel gelangen; – ***free*** or ***clear***, sich (endlich) freimachen. **3.** *s.* (*coll.*) 1. der Sieg, Erfolg; 2. Profit, Gewinn.

wince [wins], **1.** *v.i.* zurückschrecken, zurückfahren, zusammenfahren, (zusammen)zucken (***under***, unter (*Dat.*); ***at***, bei); ***without wincing***, ohne mit der Wimper zu zucken. **2.** *s.* das Zusammenfahren, Zurückschrecken, (Zusammen)zucken.

winch [wintʃ], *s.* der Haspel, die Winde; (*Naut.*) Winsch; Kurbel (*of a wheel etc.*).

[1]**wind** [wind], **1.** *s.* der Wind (*also Hunt., Med., fig.*), (*Med.*) die Blähung, (*Hunt.*) Witterung; (*fig.*) Lunge, der Atem; (*Mus.*) ***the*** –, die Blasinstru-

mente (*pl.*), Bläser (*pl.*); ***against the –,*** gegen den Wind; ***before the –,*** vor *or* mit dem Winde; ***between – and water,*** (*Naut.*) zwischen Wind und Wasser, (*fig.*) an einer empfindlichen *or* gefährlichen Stelle; ***break –,*** einen Wind abgehen *or* (*coll.*) fahren lassen; (*Naut.*) ***by the –,*** am *or* beim Winde; ***cast to the –s,*** see ***throw to the –s***; ***the – has changed,*** der Wind ist umgesprungen; ***down –,*** see ***before the –***; ***in the –'s eye,*** see ***in the teeth of the –***; ***break a horse's –,*** ein Pferd überreiten; ***fair –,*** günstiger Wind; ***the four –s,*** die vier Windrichtungen; ***from the four –s,*** aus allen (Himmels)richtungen; (*fig.*) ***be in the –,*** in der Luft *or* im Anzug *or* in Vorbereitung sein; (*Prov.*) ***it's an ill – that blows nobody any good,*** des einen Unglück ist des andern Glück; (*fig.*) ***get – of,*** auf die Spur kommen (*Dat.*), wittern, Wind bekommen von, kommen hinter (*Acc.*), hören von; ***get*** (or ***take*** or ***have***) ***the – of,*** (*Naut.*) die Luv *or* den Wind abgewinnen (*Dat.*), (*fig.*) einen Vorteil haben vor (*Dat.*); ***get one's – (back),*** see ***recover one's –***; (*sl.*) ***get*** (or ***have***) ***the – up,*** Bammel *or* Dampf kriegen (*or* haben); ***knock the – out of him,*** ihm den Atem verschlagen; (*fig.*) ***know which way*** or ***how the – blows*** or ***lies,*** wissen, woher der Wind weht; wissen wie der Hase läuft *or* die Dinge liegen; ***like the –,*** mit Windeseile, wie der Wind; (*Naut.*) ***off the –,*** aus dem Wind; (*Naut.*) ***on the –,*** hart am Wind; ***– and weather permitting,*** bei günstigem Wetter; (*sl.*) ***put the – up him,*** ihn ins Bockshorn jagen; (*sl.*) ***raise the –,*** Geld auftreiben; ***recover one's –,*** (wieder) zu Atem kommen, verschnaufen; ***the – is rising,*** der Wind nimmt zu; ***sail close to the –,*** (*Naut.*) hart am Wind segeln, (*fig.*) sich hart an der Grenze des Erlaubten bewegen; ***get one's second –,*** frischen Atem holen; (*fig.*) ***take the – out of his sails,*** ihm den Wind aus den Segeln nehmen; ***in the teeth of the –,*** gegen den Wind, dem Winde entgegen; (*fig.*) ***throw to the –s,*** in den Wind schlagen, über den Haufen werfen; außer acht lassen (*caution etc.*), ablegen (*one's fears*); (*Naut.*) ***under the –,*** in Lee(seite); ***variable –s,*** wechselnde Winde. **2.** *v.t.* 1. (*Hunt.*) wittern, aufspüren; 2. überreiten (*a horse*); (*usu. pass.*) erschöpfen, außer Atem bringen.

[2]**wind** [waind], **1.** *irr.v.t.* (herum)winden, (herum)wickeln, (herum)schlingen, (herum)schlagen (***round,*** um); drehen, kurbeln (*a handle*); aufwickeln, aufspulen (*thread*); ***– on,*** wickeln auf (*Acc.*); ***– off,*** abwickeln von; ***– him round one's little finger,*** ihn um den kleinen Finger wickeln; ***– itself round,*** umschlingen, (*plants*) umranken, sich ranken um; ***– one's way,*** (sich) schlängeln; (*fig.*) sich einschmeicheln (*into,* bei *or* in (*Acc.*)); ***– up,*** hochziehen, hochwinden, aufwinden; (*Min.*) fördern; aufwickeln, aufhaspeln, aufspulen (*thread etc.*); aufziehen (*clock*); (*fig.*) anspannen, hochspannen, ankurbeln; (*fig.*) (*Comm.*) erledigen, abwickeln (*transaction*), liquidieren, auflösen (*company*); (*coll.*) zu Ende bringen, beenden, (ab)schließen (*speech etc.*). **2.** *irr.v.i.* sich winden, sich schlängeln; sich wickeln, sich schlingen, sich legen, (*plants*) sich ranken (***round,*** um); ***– along*** or ***on,*** sich dahinschlängeln; (*fig.*) ***– up,*** (*Comm.*) aufgelöst *or* liquidiert werden, bank(e)rott machen; (*coll.*) (die Rede) schließen, Schluß machen; (*coll.*) (*of a p.*) enden.

windage ['windidʒ], *s.* 1. (*Artil.*) der Spielraum (*of gun barrel*); Einfluß des Windes (*on shell*); Luftwiderstand, die Luftdruckwelle; 2. (*Naut.*) Windfläche, der Windfang (*of ship above waterline*).

wind|bag ['wind–], *s.* (*coll.*) der Windbeutel, Schwätzer. **--blown,** *adj.* vom Winde verweht *or* zerzaust. **--borne,** *adj.* vom Winde getragen. **--bound,** *adj.* von widrigem Wind aufgehalten. **--break,** *s.* der Windschutz. **--broken,** *adj.* kurzatmig (*of horses*). **--cheater,** *s.* die Windjacke, der Anorak. **--chest,** *s.* die Windlade, der Windkasten (*organ*). **--cone,** *s. See* **--sleeve.**

winded ['windid], *adj.* 1. außer Atem; 2. (*as suff.*) –atmig.

wind-egg ['wind–], *s.* das Windei.

winder ['waində], *s.* 1. der (die) Aufwinder(in), Haspler(in); 2. die Winde, die *or* der Haspel; die Kurbel, der Schlüssel (*clocks etc.*).

wind|fall ['wind–], *s.* das Fallobst; (*fig.*) unerwarteter Gewinn. **–fallen,** *adj.* windbrüchig; ***– tree*** der Windwurf; ***– wood,*** der Windbruch. **--flower,** *s.* das Windröschen. **--gall,** *s.* (*Vet.*) die Windgalle, Fesselgalle. **--gauge,** *s.* der Windmesser, das Anemometer.

windily ['windili], *adv.* 1. windig; 2. (*fig.*) geschwätzig, hochtrabend. **windiness,** *s.* 1. Windige(s), Stürmische(s); 2. (*fig.*) die Aufgedunsenheit, Aufblähung; Aufgeblasenheit.

winding ['waindiŋ], **1.** *adj.* 1. gewunden, sich windend *or* schlängelnd, Wellen–, Schlangen–; ***– curve,*** die Wellenlinie; ***– stairs,*** die Wendeltreppe; 2. schief, krumm; 3. (*attrib. only*) (*Tech.*) Winde–, Haspel–; (*Min.*) Förder–. **2.** *s.* 1. (*Tech. etc.*) das Winden, Spulen, Haspeln, Einwickeln, Aufwickeln; 2. Schlängeln, (Sich-)Winden; 3. die Windung, Biegung, Krümmung; 4. (*Elec.*) Wickelung.

winding|-engine, *s.* die Förderwelle, Dampfwinde. **--frame,** *s.* die Wickelmaschine, Spulmaschine. **--rope,** *s.* das Förderseil. **--sheet,** *s.* das Grabtuch, Leichentuch. **--tackle,** *s.* (*Naut.*) das Gien. **--tower,** *s.* (*Min.*) der Förderturm. **--up,** *s.* 1. das Aufziehen (*of clock*), Aufwinden; 2. (*fig.*) der Abschluß, die Abwicklung, (*Comm.*) Auflösung, Liquidierung; ***– sale,*** der Totalausverkauf.

wind|-instrument ['wind–], *s.* (*Mus.*) das Blasinstrument. **–jammer,** *s.* (*coll.*) der Rahsegler.

windlass ['windləs], *s.* (*Tech.*) die (Montage)winde; (*Min.*) die *or* der Förderhaspel; (*Naut.*) die Ankerwinde, das (Anker)spill.

windless ['windlis], *adj.* windlos, windstill, ohne Wind.

windmill ['windmil], *s.* die Windmühle; ***throw one's cap over the –,*** alle Vorsicht außer acht lassen, sich über alle Bedenken hinwegsetzen; ***tilt at –s,*** einen Kampf gegen Windmühlen führen.

window ['windou], *s.* das Fenster; ***at the –,*** am Fenster; ***climb in at the –,*** zum Fenster hineinklettern; ***bay-–,*** das Erkerfenster; ***casement –,*** das Flügelfenster; ***dress the –,*** das Schaufenster dekorieren; ***French –,*** die Verandatür; (*Motor.*) ***rear –,*** das Rückfenster; ***sash –,*** das Schiebefenster; ***shop-–,*** das Schaufenster; ***look out of the –,*** zum Fenster hinaussehen; ***ticket –,*** der Fahrkartenschalter.

window|-blind, *s.* der Rollvorhang, die Jalousie, das Fensterrouleau. **--box,** *s.* der Blumenkasten. **--cleaner,** *s.* der Fensterputzer. **--display,** *s.* die Schaufensterauslage. **--dresser,** *s.* der Schaufensterdekorateur. **--dressing,** *s.* 1. die Schaufensterdekoration; 2. (*fig.*) die Mache, Aufmachung, Schönfärberei; das Frisieren, die Bilanzverschleierung. **--envelope,** *s.* der Fensterbriefumschlag. **--frame,** *s.* der Fensterrahmen. **--ledge,** *s.* die Fensterbrüstung, das Fensterbrett, der *or* das Fenstersims.

windowless ['windoulis], *adj.* fensterlos.

window|-pane, *s.* die Fensterscheibe. **--sash,** *s.* verschiebbarer Rahmen, der Schiebeflügel. **--seat,** *s.* der Fenstersitz, die Fensterbank. **--shopping,** *s.* (*coll.*) der Schaufensterbummel. **--shutters,** *pl.* Fensterläden (*pl.*). **--sill,** *s. See* **--ledge.**

wind|pipe ['wind–], *s.* (*Anat.*) die Luftröhre. **--rode,** *adj.* (*Naut.*) windgerecht. **–row,** *s.* der Schwaden (*of hay*). **--screen,** (*Am.*) **--shield,** *s.* (*Motor.*) die Windschutzscheibe; ***– wiper,*** der Scheibenwischer. **--sleeve, --sock,** *s.* (*Av.*) der Luftsack. **--swept,** *adj.* sturmgepeitscht. **--tunnel,** *s.* der Windkanal.

wind-up ['waindʌp], *s. See* **winding-up.**

wind-vane ['wind–], *s.* die Windfahne, Wetterfahne.

windward ['windwəd], **1.** *adj.* Wind–, windwärts liegend; (*Geog.*) ***Windward Islands,*** Inseln vor dem Wind. **2.** *adv.* windwärts, in *or* zu Luv, luvwärts. **3.** *s.* die Windseite, Luv(seite); ***sail to –***, anluven, gegen den Wind segeln.

windy ['windi], *adj.* **1.** windig, stürmisch; 2. (*Med.*) blähend, Bläh–; 3. (*fig.*) geschwätzig, schwatzhaft (*a p.*); hochtrabend, wortreich, langatmig; eitel, leer, hohl; 4. (*sl.*) bangbüxig, benaut.

wine [wain], **1.** *s.* der Wein; (*Prov.*) ***good – needs no bush,*** das Gute empfiehlt sich selbst; ***red –,*** der Rotwein; ***white –,*** der Weißwein; ***sparkling –,*** der Schaumwein. **2.** *v.t.* mit Wein traktieren (*a p.*). **3.** *v.i.* Wein trinken.

wine|-bibber, *s.* der Weinsüffler. **--bin,** *s.* das Weinflaschengestell. **--bottle,** *s.* die Weinflasche. **--cask,** *s.* das Weinfaß. **--cellar,** *s.* der Weinkeller. **--cooler,** *s.* der Weinkühler. **-glass,** *s.* das Weinglas. **--grower,** *s.* der Weinbauer. **--list,** *s.* die Weinkarte. **--merchant,** *s.* der Weinhändler. **--press,** *s.* die Weinkelter. **--skin,** *s.* der Weinschlauch. **--stone,** *s.* der Weinstein. **--taster,** *s.* der Weinprober. **--trade,** *s.* der Weinhandel. **--vault,** *s.* der Weinkeller; die Weinstube, Weinschenke.

wing [wiŋ], **1.** *s.* **1.** der Flügel (*also Archit., Pol., Spt.*); (*Poet.*) Fittich, die Schwinge (*of bird*); (*fig.*) ***clip his –s,*** die Flügel stutzen; (*fig.*) ***lend –s to,*** beschleunigen, beflügeln; ***on the –,*** im Fluge; (*Poet.*) ***on the –s of love,*** auf Fittichen der Liebe; ***on the –s of the wind,*** mit Windeseile; ***take –,*** aufsteigen, davonfliegen; (*fig.*) ***take under one's –,*** unter seine Fittiche *or* seinen Schutz nehmen; 2. die Federfahne (*of an arrow*); 3. (*Av.*) (Flieger)gruppe, (*Am.*) das Geschwader; *pl.* das Fliegerabzeichen (*Air Force*); 4. (*Footb. etc.*) (*coll.*) der Außenstürmer; ***left –,*** das Linksaußen (*position*), der Linksaußen (*player*); 5. (*Motor.*) Kotflügel; 6. (*Av.*) die Tragfläche; 7. (*Theat.*) (*usu. pl.*) die Kulisse; ***in the –s,*** an der Bühnenseite; (*fig.*) in Reserve. **2.** *v.t.* **1.** mit Federn versehen, befiedern (*an arrow*); 2. durchfliegen, im Flug zurücklegen (*one's way*); 3. (*fig.*) (*Poet.*) beflügeln, beschwingen, beschleunigen; 4. (*Hunt.*) flügeln, flügellahm schießen; (*coll.*) leicht *or* am Arm *or* an der Schulter) verwunden, treffen.

wing|-area, *s.* (*Av.*) tragende Fläche. **--beat,** *s.* der Flügelschlag. **--case,** *s.* (*Ent.*) der Deckflügel. **--chair,** *s.* der Ohrensessel. **--collar,** *s.* der Eckenkragen. **--commander,** *s.* der Oberstleutnant (der Luftwaffe); (*Am.*) Geschwaderkommodore. **--covert,** *s.* (*Orn.*) die Deckfeder.

winged [wiŋd], *adj.* **1.** geflügelt (*also Bot.*); (*Bot.*) gefiedert; (*as suff.*) –flügelig; ***– creatures,*** das Geflügel; ***– horse,*** das Flügelroß; ***– screw,*** die Flugelschraube; ***– words,*** geflügelte Worte; 2. (*fig.*) (*Poet.*) beflügelt, beschwingt, fliegend; 3. (*Hunt.*) flügellahm, (*coll.*) leicht verwundet. **winger,** *s.* (*Footb.*) (*coll.*) der Flügel(mann), Außenstürmer.

wing|feather, *s.* (*Orn.*) die Schwungfeder. **--footed,** *adj.* (*Poet.*) beflügelt, beschwingt. **-nut,** *s.* die Flügelmutter. **--sheath,** *s.* *See* **--case. --span, -spread,** *s.* (*Orn.*) die Flügelspanne; (*Av.*) (Tragflächen)spannweite. **-tip,** *s.* das Flügelende.

wink [wiŋk], **1.** *s.* das Zwinkern, Blinzeln; (*coll.*) der Wink; (*coll.*) kurzer Augenblick; (*coll.*) ***not get a – of sleep,*** kein Auge zutun; (*coll.*) ***forty –s,*** das Schläfchen, Nickerchen; (*coll.*) ***in a –,*** im Nu; (*coll.*) ***tip him the –,*** ihm einen Wink geben. **2.** *v.i.* zwinkern, blinzeln; (*fig.*) blinken; blitzen, leuchten, flimmern (*of light*); ***– at him,*** ihm zuzwinkern; (*fig.*) ***– at,*** ein Auge zudrücken bei, stillschweigend dulden, gewähren lassen. **winking,** *s.* das Zwinkern, Blinzeln; Blinken, Flimmern; ***as easy as –,*** spielend leicht.

winkle [wiŋkl], **1.** *s.* die Uferschnecke. **2.** *v.t.* (*coll.*) ***– out,*** herausziehen, herausholen. **winklepickers,** *pl.* (*sl.*) Spitzschuhe (*pl.*).

winner ['winə], *s.* der (die) Sieger(in), Gewinner(in); ***he is the –,*** er hat gewonnen. **winning, 1.** *adj.* **1.** gewinnend (*also fig.*), siegreich, Sieger–; ***– move,*** entscheidender Zug (*chess*) *or* (*fig.*) Schritt; ***– name,*** der Name des Siegers; ***– streak,*** die Glückssträhne; 2. (*fig.*) einnehmend; ***– way,*** gewinnendes *or* einnehmendes Wesen. **2.** *s.* **1.** das Gewinnen, der Sieg, siegreicher Ausgang; 2. (*Min.*) der Abbau, die Förderung, Ausbeute; 3. *pl.* der (Wett)gewinn. **winning-post,** *s.* (*Spt.*) das Ziel.

winnow ['winou], **1.** *v.t.* worfeln, schwingen, wannen, (aus)sieben, reinigen (*corn*); (*fig.*) (*also* ***– out***) trennen, sondern, scheiden (*the good from the bad*), aussondern, ausscheiden, ausmerzen (*the bad from the good*). **2.** *s.* die Getreideschwinge, Wanne. **winnower,** *s.* **1.** der (die) Worfler(in); 2. die Worfelmaschine. **winnowing,** *s.* das Worfeln, Schwingen, Wannen. **winnowing-machine,** *s.* *See* **winnower,** 2.

winsome ['winsəm], *adj.* anziehend, (lieb)reizend, einnehmend, gefällig, lieblich.

winter ['wintə], **1.** *s.* der Winter; ***in –,*** im Winter; ***hard*** or ***severe –,*** strenger Winter. **2.** *attrib. adj.* winterlich, Winter–; ***– crop,*** die Winterfrucht; ***–('s) day,*** der Wintertag; ***– garden,*** der Wintergarten; ***– quarters,*** das Winterquartier; ***– sleep,*** der Winterschlaf; ***– sports,*** der Wintersport. **3.** *v.i.* überwintern, den Winter verbringen *or* zubringen. **4.** *v.t.* für den Winter unterbringen, durch den Winter bringen. **wintergreen,** *s.* (*Bot.*) das Wintergrün. **wintering,** *s.* **1.** die Überwinterung (*of cattle etc.*); 2. der Winteraufenthalt.

wintriness ['wintrinis], *s.* die Kälte, Winterlichkeit. **wintry,** *adj.* winterlich, kalt, frostig.

wipe [waip], **1.** *v.t.* **1.** (ab)wischen; abtrocknen; abreiben, reinigen; ***– one's boots,*** sich (*Dat.*) die Schuhe putzen; ***– one's eyes,*** sich (*Dat.*) die Tränen abwischen; (*sl.*) ***– him in the eye,*** ihn ausstechen; (*sl.*) ***– the floor with him,*** mit ihm Schlitten fahren; ***– one's lips,*** sich (*Dat.*) den Mund abwischen; ***– one's nose,*** sich (*Dat.*) die Nase putzen; ***– away,*** wegwischen, abwischen; (*fig.*) ***– off,*** tilgen (*a debt*); (*fig.*) ***– off an old score,*** eine alte Rechnung begleichen, sich für ein Unrecht rächen; ***– out,*** auswischen (*a jug etc.*); (*fig.*) wegwischen, auslöschen, tilgen (*an insult etc.*), zerstören, vernichten (*an army*), ausrotten (*a race etc.*); 2. (*Tech.*) (weich)löten; 3. (*sl.*) hauen. **2.** *s.* **1.** das (Ab)wischen, Reinigen; (*sl.*) ***– in the eye,*** der Ausputzer, Wischer; (*sl.*) ***give him a – in the eye,*** ihm eins auswischen; ***give it a –,*** es abwischen. **wiper,** *s.* **1.** der Wischer, das Wischtuch; 2. (*Motor.*) der Scheibenwischer; 3. (*Elec.*) Schleifarm, Kontaktarm, Schaltarm.

wire ['waiə], **1.** *s.* **1.** der Draht; (*Elec.*) Leitungsdraht; *pl.* das Gestänge (*of a cage*); ***barbed –,*** der Stacheldraht; (*Mil.*) ***barbed – entanglement,*** der Drahtverhau; ***– fence,*** der Drahtzaun, das Drahtgitter; ***live –,*** stromführender Draht, der Hochspannungsdraht, (*fig.*) der Quirl (*of a p.*); (*fig.*) ***pull the –s,*** der Drahtzieher *or* Urheber sein; 2. (*coll.*) das Telegramm, die Drahtnachricht; ***by –,*** telegraphisch; ***send a –,*** telegraphieren, drahten. **2.** *v.t.* **1.** mit Draht befestigen *or* heften *or* steifen *or* stützen; 2. mit Draht(geflecht) *or* Drahtzaun umgeben; 3. (elektrische) Leitung legen in (*Dat.*) (*a room etc.*); 4. (*coll.*) telegraphieren (*message*), telegraphieren, drahten (*Dat.*), telegraphisch benachrichten (*a p.*). **3.** *v.i.* (*coll.*) telegraphieren, drahten.

wire-cutter, *s.* (*also pl.*) die Drahtzange.

wired ['waiəd], *adj.* **1.** mit Draht verstärkt *or* befestigt *or* geheftet *or* (zusammen)gebunden; 2. mit Drahtzaun *or* Drahtgeflecht umgeben; 3. elektrisch installiert, mit Leitungen versehen.

wire|draw, *irr.v.t.* **1.** drahtziehen; 2. (*fig.*) in die Länge ziehen, hinziehen. **-drawer,** *s.* der Drahtzieher. **-drawn,** *adj.* langgezogen, (*fig.*) überspitzt, ausgeklügelt. **--edge,** *s.* der Grat (*of a blade*). **--gauge,** *s.* die Drahtlehre. **--gauze,** *s.* das Drahtgewebe, Drahtnetz. **-haired,** *adj.* Drahthaar– (*dog*).

wireless ['waiəlis], **1.** *adj.* drahtlos, Funk–; ***– listener,*** der Rundfunkhörer; ***– message,*** der Funkspruch; ***– operator,*** der Funktelegraphist, Funker; ***– programme,*** das Rundfunkprogramm; ***– set,*** das Radio, der Radioapparat, Empfänger;

– station, die (Rund)funkstation; *– telegraphy,* die Funktelegraphie, drahtlose Telegraphie; *– transmitter,* der (Rundfunk)sender. **2.** *s.* 1. der Rundfunk, das Radio; *by –,* durch Rundfunk; *on the –,* im Rundfunk *or* Radio; 2. *See also – set, – telegraphy.*

wire|man [–mən], *s.* der Telephonarbeiter, Telegraphenarbeiter. **--nail,** *s.* der Drahtstift. **--netting,** *s.* das Drahtgeflecht, der Maschendraht. **-puller,** *s.* (*fig.*) der Intrigant, Drahtzieher. **-pulling,** *s.* (*fig.*) Manipulationen (*pl.*), Machenschaften (*pl.*), Intrigen (*pl.*). **--rope,** *s.* das Drahtseil. **--tapping,** *s.* das Abhören. **--walker,** *s.* der (die) Drahtseilakrobat(in), Seiltänzer(in). **-worm,** *s.* der Drahtwurm. **--wove,** *adj.* Velin– (*paper*); *–(n) mattress,* die Sprungfedermatratze.

wiring [ˈwaiəriŋ], *s.* 1. das Befestigen *or* Versteifen mit Draht; 2. (*Elec.*) Leitungen (*pl.*), das Leitungsnetz; (*Rad.*) die Schaltung; *– diagram,* das Schaltschema; 3. (*Av.*) Verspannung. **wiry,** *adj.* 1. sehnig, zäh (*of a p.*); 2. drahtig, borstig (*as hair*); 3. surrend, vibrierend (*of sound*).

wisdom [ˈwizdəm], *s.* die Weisheit, Klugheit, Einsicht, der Verstand. **wisdom-tooth,** *s.* der Weisheitszahn.

¹**wise** [waiz], *adj.* weise, klug, einsichtig; vernünftig, verständig, gescheit; (*coll.*) *be* or *get – to,* sich (*Dat.*) klar werden über (*Acc.*); (*sl.*) *– guy,* der Schlaumeier, Besserwisser; *be – after the event,* um eine Erfahrung reicher sein; *none the –r,* genau so schlau wie zuvor; (*coll.*) *put him – to,* ihn aufklären über (*Acc.*) *or* einweihen in (*Acc.*) *or* aufmerksam machen auf (*Acc.*); *– man,* Weise(r); (*obs.*) *– woman,* die Hebamme, weise Frau; Wahrsagerin, Hellseherin; Hexe.

²**wise,** *s.* (*obs.*) die Weise, Art; (*only in*) *in any –,* auf irgendeine Weise, irgendwie; *in no –,* in keiner Weise, keineswegs; *in such – as,* derartig daß; *in this –,* auf diese (Art und) Weise.

wise, *suff.* (*forming adv.*) –weise.

wise|acre, *s.* Überkluge(r), Neunmalkluge(r), der Naseweis, Besserwisser, Klugredner, Klugtuer, Gescheittuer. **-crack, 1.** *s.* das Bonmot, witzige Bemerkung. **2.** *v.i.* witzige Bemerkungen machen. **-cracker,** *s.* der Witzbold, Spaßmacher.

wisely [ˈwaizli], *adv.* vernünftigerweise, klugerweise, klug.

wish [wiʃ], **1.** *v.t.* (sich (*Dat.*)) wünschen, sich sehnen nach, ersehnen, verlangen; *I – he would come,* ich wollte, er würde kommen; *I – to speak with you,* ich möchte mit dir reden; *I – you to come,* ich bitte *or* ersuche dich zu kommen; *– it on him,* es ihm wünschen; *I –ed him dead,* ich wollte, er wäre tot; *– him luck,* ihm Glück wünschen. **2.** *v.i.* wünschen; einen Wunsch äußern; *as heart could –,* nach Herzenswunsch; *– him well,* ihm wohl gesinnt sein, ihm Gutes wünschen; *– for,* haben wollen, sich (*Dat.*) wünschen, sich sehnen nach; *– for nothing better,* sich (*Dat.*) nichts Besseres wünschen. **3.** *s.* 1. der Wille, Wunsch, das Verlangen, Begehren (*for,* nach), die Bitte (um); *he has got his –,* er hat seinen Willen, sein Wunsch ist erfüllt; 2. *pl.* Grüße (*pl.*), (Glück)-wünsche (*pl.*). **wishbone** [ˈwiʃboun], *s.* das Gabelbein.

wished-for [ˈwiʃtfɔ:], *attrib. adj.* ersehnt, erwünscht.

wishful [ˈwiʃful], *adj.* begierig, sehnsüchtig; *– thinking,* das Wunschdenken, die Illusion, Illusionen (*pl.*); *it is merely – thinking,* dabei ist der Wunsch der Vater des Gedankens. **wishfulness,** *s.* die Sehnsucht, das Verlangen, Wunschdenken.

wishing|-bone [ˈwiʃiŋ], *s. See* **wishbone. --cap,** *s.* die Zauberkappe, Wunschkappe, Zaubermütze. **--well,** *s.* der Zauberbrunnen.

wish-wash [ˈwiʃwɔʃ], *s.* 1. (*coll.*) wäßriges Getränk; 2. (*fig.*) (seichtes) Geschwätz. **wishy-washy** [ˈwiʃiˈwɔʃi], *adj.* 1. (*coll.*) wässerig, wäßrig, labb(e)rig; 2. (*fig.*) saft– und kraftlos, farblos, fad(e), seicht.

wisp [wisp], *s.* 1. der Wisch; das Büschel, Bündel; die Strähne (*of hair*); *– of smoke,* die Rauchfahne; 2. das Rudel (*of snipe*).

wistaria [wisˈtɛəriə], *s.* (*Bot.*) die Glyzine.

wistful [ˈwistful], *adj.* 1. sehnsuchtsvoll, sehnsüchtig, schmachtend, wehmütig; 2. sinnend, nachdenklich, gedankenvoll. **wistfulness,** *s.* 1. die Sehnsucht, Wehmut; 2. Nachdenklichkeit.

¹**wit** [wit], *s.* 1. der Witz, Geist; (*usu. pl.*) Verstand, die Intelligenz, Urteilskraft, das Denkvermögen, geistige Fähigkeiten (*pl.*); *mother –,* der Mutterwitz; *have one's –s about one,* seine fünf Sinne beisammen haben; *have the – to do,* Verstand genug haben, zu tun; *be at one's –s' end,* mit seinem Verstand *or* Latein zu Ende sein, sich (*Dat.*) nicht mehr zu helfen wissen; *he hasn't the –(s) to see,* er hat nicht den Kopf, um einzusehen; *be out of one's –s,* den Kopf *or* Verstand verloren haben; *drive him out of his –s,* ihn verrückt machen; *frighten him out of his –s,* ihm einen Todesschreck einjagen; *keep one's –s about one,* auf der Hut sein; *live by one's –s,* von andrer Leute Dummheit leben, sich mehr oder weniger ehrlich durchs Leben schlagen; 2. witziger Mensch, der Witzbold; (*obs.*) geistreicher Mensch, kluger Kopf.

²**wit,** *irr.v.i.* wissen; (*only in*) *to –,* nämlich, das heißt.

witch [witʃ], **1.** *s.* die Hexe; (*coll.*) bezaubernde Frau. **2.** *v.t.* behexen, bezaubern. **witch|-burning,** *s.* die Hexenverbrennung. **-craft,** *s.* die Hexerei; (*fig.*) der Zauber, die Zauberkraft; *– trial,* der Hexenprozeß. **--doctor,** *s.* der Medizinmann, Zauberer.

witchery [ˈwitʃəri], *s. See* **witchcraft.**

witch|-hazel, *s. See* **wych-hazel. --hunt,** *s.* (*fig.*) die Hexenjagd, Verfolgung.

witching [ˈwitʃiŋ], *adj.* Hexen–, Gespenster–, (*fig.*) bezaubernd; *– hour,* die Gespensterstunde, Geisterstunde.

witenagemot [ˈwitənəgəˈmout], *s.* (*Hist.*) der Rat der Weisen, die Ratsversammlung der Angelsachsen.

with [wið], *prep.* 1. (*accompaniment*) mit, nebst, samt, zusammen mit, bei; 2. (*causal*) durch, (ver)-mittels, an (*Dat.*), vor (*Dat.*); 3. (*antithesis*) bei, trotz.

(a) (*with adj.*) *angry –,* böse auf (*Acc.*); *blue – cold,* blau vor Kälte; *patient –,* geduldig mit; *pleased –,* erfreut über (*Acc.*), zufrieden mit; *popular – children,* bei Kindern beliebt; *be successful –,* Erfolg haben bei.

(b) (*with noun or pron.*) *– age,* durch Alter; *– one another,* miteinander; *one – another,* zusammengerechnet, eins ins andere gerechnet; *– child,* schwanger; (*sl.*) *– it,* auf Draht; *I have difficulty – it,* es macht mir Schwierigkeiten; *– each other,* see *– one another*; *– everyone looking on,* während alle zuschauten; *– all his experience,* trotz aller seiner Erfahrung; *– a grin,* grinsend; *that is usual – him,* das ist die Regel bei ihm; *he has a way – him,* er hat etwas an sich; *be down – influenza,* an der Grippe daniederliegen; *it is the same – me,* es geht mir genau so; *– pleasure,* mit Vergnügen, sehr gern; *– all speed,* in aller Eile; *– the stream,* mit dem Strom; *– that,* damit, darauf; *– this,* hiermit, hierauf; *– time,* mit der Zeit; *he is one – us,* er ist mit uns einig; *you are either against us or – us,* entweder sind Sie gegen uns oder für uns; (*coll.*) *I am – you there,* ich bin ganz Ihrer Meinung, ich mache mit; *– young,* trächtig (*of animals*).

(c) (*with vb.*) *be attended –,* begleitet sein von; *break – him,* mit ihm brechen; *she came – him,* sie kam mit ihm; *she took him – her,* sie nahm ihn mit; *be concerned –,* betreffen, behandeln, sich befassen *or* beschäftigen mit; *cure – fasting,* durch Fasten heilen; *differ –,* anderer Meinung sein als; *fight –,* kämpfen mit *or* gegen; (*fig.*) *go –,* passen zu; *have – one,* bei sich haben; (*fig.*) *I leave it – you,* ich überlasse es Ihnen; *part –,* scheiden *or* sich trennen von; *resound – applause,* vom Beifall ertönen; *it rests – you,* es steht *or* liegt bei Ihnen; *stay –,* bleiben mit *or* bei, (*Scots*)

wohnen bei; ***nothing succeeds* – *him,*** nichts gelingt ihm; ***tremble* – *fear,*** vor Angst zittern; ***trust him* –,** ihm anvertrauen; ***what do you want* – *me?*** was wollen Sie von mir? ***weep* – *joy,*** vor Freude weinen.
(d) (*introducing subord. clause*) – ***everyone against him, he had to withdraw,*** da alle gegen ihn waren, mußte er sich zurückziehen.

withal [wið'ɔ:l], *adv.* (*obs.*) außerdem, überdies, obendrein, übrigens.

withdraw [wið'drɔ:], **1.** *irr.v.t.* 1. zurückziehen (*also Mil.*), wegnehmen, entfernen (***from,*** von), entziehen (*Dat.*); widerrufen, zurücknehmen (*statement*); – ***one's assistance from,*** seine Hand abziehen von; – ***from circulation,*** aus dem Verkehr ziehen, außer Kur setzen; – ***o.s.,*** sich zurückziehen (***from,*** von); – ***a child from school,*** ein Kind von der Schule wegnehmen; 2. (*Comm.*) abheben (*money*). **2.** *irr.v.i.* sich zurückziehen (*also Mil., fig.*) (***to,*** auf (*Acc.*); ***from,*** von *or* aus); (*esp. Mil.*) zurückgehen, zurückweichen; abziehen, zurücktreten, sich entfernen (***from,*** von); – ***within o.s.,*** sich in sich zurückziehen. **withdrawal** [–əl], *s.* 1. das Zurückziehen, Einziehen; die Zurückziehung, Entfernung (***from,*** von); das Zurücknehmen, die Zurücknahme, Widerrufung; 2. (*esp. Mil.*) das Zurückgehen, Zurücktreten, der Rückzug, Rücktritt; 3. (*Comm.*) die Abhebung (*of money*); – ***form,*** das Abhebungsformular; 4. (*Med.*) die Entziehung; – ***symptoms,*** Entziehungserscheinungen (*pl.*). **withdrawn,** *adj.* 1. zurückgezogen, isoliert; 2. (*Psych.*) in sich gekehrt *or* versunken, introvertiert.

withe [wiθ, wið, waið], *s.* die Weidenrute.

wither ['wiðə], **1.** *v.t.* welken lassen, austrocknen, ausdörren, (*fig.*) vernichten, zugrunde richten. **2.** *v.i.* (ver)welken, verdorren, vertrocknen, (*fig.*) vergehen, eingehen, verfallen. **withered** [–d], *adj.* 1. welk, verwelkt; dürr, verdorrt, ausgetrocknet; 2. (*fig.*) gelähmt, lahm, eingeschrumpft. **withering,** *adj.* (*usu. fig.*) lähmend, niederschmetternd, vernichtend (*as a glance*).

withers ['wiðəz], *pl.* der Widerrist (*of horse*); (*fig.*) ***my* – *are unwrung,*** das läßt mich kalt, das trifft mich nicht.

withershins ['wiðəʃinz], *adv.* (*Scots*) gegen den (scheinbaren) Lauf der Sonne *or* den Uhrzeigersinn; in entgegengesetzter Richtung, verkehrt.

withhold [wið'hould], *irr.v.t.* 1. abhalten, zurückhalten (***from,*** von), hindern (an (*Dat.*)); – ***o.s. from,*** sich entziehen (*Dat.*); 2. versagen (*Dat.*), vorenthalten (*Dat.*), zurückhalten mit (*a th.*); – ***one's consent,*** seine Zustimmung versagen; – ***one's hand,*** sich zurückhalten.

within [wið'in], **1.** *adv.* 1. im Innern, innerlich; darin, d(a)rinnen, innen; ***from* –,** von innen; 2. (*Poet.*) zuhause; ins Haus, herein. **2.** *prep.* innerhalb (*also of time, distance*), im Innern (*Gen.*), binnen, nicht mehr als (*of time*), nicht weiter als (*of distance*); – ***an ace of,*** beinahe, nahezu; ***be* – *an ace of being killed,*** nahe daran sein, getötet zu werden; dem Tod mit knapper Not entgehen; ***agree* – *an inch,*** bis auf einen Zoll übereinstimmen; – ***call,*** in Ruf(weite); – ***three days,*** binnen drei Tagen, innerhalb drei(er) Tage; – ***doors,*** im Hause; – ***hearing,*** in Hörweite; ***keep*** or ***live* – *one's income,*** nicht über seine Verhältnisse leben; – ***the law,*** nicht illegal; – ***the meaning of the act,*** innerhalb des Gesetzes; – ***memory,*** soweit man zurückdenken kann; – ***my powers,*** innerhalb meiner Machtbefugnis; – ***reach,*** in Reichweite; – ***a short time,*** binnen kurzem; – ***sight,*** in Sehweite; – ***a few steps of,*** nur einige Schritte entfernt von.

without [wið'aut], **1.** *adv.* 1. außen, draußen, außerhalb, äußerlich; ***from* –,** von außen; 2. (*coll.*) ***go* –,** nicht(s) bekommen, leer ausgehen. **2.** *prep.* 1. ohne (***doing,*** zu tun); – ***more ado,*** ohne weitere Umstände; ***be* – *a th.,*** etwas entbehren *or* vermissen; – ***delay,*** ohne Verzug; – ***distinction,*** ohne Unterschied, unterschiedslos, wahllos; – ***distinction of persons,*** ohne Unterschied der Person; ***do* – *a th.,*** etwas entbehren, ohne etwas auskommen *or* fertigwerden; – ***doubt,*** zweifellos, ohne Zweifel; – ***end,*** fortwährend, in Ewigkeit, endlos; ***do* –,** fertig werden ohne; ***go* – *a th.,*** etwas entbehren, sich ohne etwas behelfen; – ***number,*** zahllos; – ***prejudice to,*** unbeschadet (*Gen.*); ***that goes* – *saying,*** das versteht sich von selbst; – ***their*** *or* (*coll.*) ***them seeing me,*** ohne daß sie mich sehen *or* sahen; 2. (*obs.*) außerhalb (*Gen.*).

withstand [wið'stænd], **1.** *irr.v.t.* widerstehen (*Dat.*), sich widersetzen (*Dat.*), Widerstand leisten (*Dat.*). **2.** *irr.v.i.* Widerstand leisten.

withy ['wiði], *s. See* **withe.**

witless ['witlis], *adj.* unvernünftig, geistlos (*remark etc.*), (*of a p.*) dumm, einfältig.

witness ['witnis], **1.** *s.* 1. der Zeuge (die Zeugin), Gewährsmann; ***call to* –,** zum Zeugen aufrufen; – ***for the defence,*** der Entlastungszeuge; – ***for the crown*** or ***prosecution,*** der Belastungszeuge; 2. das Zeugnis, die Bezeugung, Bekräftigung, Bestätigung; ***bear* –,** Zeugnis ablegen (***to,*** von), bezeugen, bestätigen; (*Law*) ***in* – *hereof*** or ***whereof,*** urkundlich *or* zu Urkund dessen. **2.** *v.t.* 1. bezeugen, bestätigen, erweisen; – ***his brother,*** als Beweis dient sein Bruder; 2. Zeuge unterschreiben, (unterschriftlich) beglaubigen (*a document, signature*); 3. (Augen)zeuge sein von, zugegen sein bei; (*coll.*) erleben, sehen; 4. (*fig.*) Zeugnis ablegen von, zeugen von, ein Zeichen sein von, ein Beweis sein für. **3.** *v.i.* zeugen, Zeuge sein, Zeugnis ablegen (***to,*** für); (*fig.*) – ***to,*** bezeugen, Zeuge sein von. **witness|-box,** (*Am.*) **--stand,** *s.* der Zeugenstand, die Zeugenbank.

witted ['witid], *adj. suff.* ***half--,*** blöde, blödsinnig, einfältig, albern; ***quick--,*** scharfsinnig, geistreich, geweckt. **witticism** [–isizm], *s.* der Witz, Scherz, witzige *or* geistreiche Bemerkung. **wittiness,** *s.* die Witzigkeit, (*of a p.*) Schlagfertigkeit. **wittingly,** *adv.* bewußt, absichtlich, wissentlich, geflissentlich, vorsätzlich, gewollt. **witty,** *adj.* witzig, amüsant (*of a p. or story etc.*); geistreich, witzelnd (*of a p.*).

wive [waiv], (*obs.*) **1.** *v.i.* (sich ver)heiraten. **2.** *v.t.* heiraten.

wivern ['waivən], *s.* (*Her.*) geflügelter Drache.

wives [waivz], *pl. of* **wife.**

wizard ['wizəd], **1.** *s.* der Zauberer, Magier, Hexenmeister. **2.** *adj.* (*sl.*) erstklassig, prima.

wizen(ed) ['wizən(d)], *adj.* dürr (*also fig.*), verwelkt, (*fig.*) eingeschrumpft, zusammengeschrumpft, runz(e)lig.

woad [woud], *s.* der (Färber)waid.

wobble [wɔbl], **1.** *v.i.* wackeln, wanken, torkeln, schwanken (*also fig.*), schlottern (*as knees*). **2.** *s.* das Wackeln, Wanken, (*fig.*) Schwanken. **wobbly,** *adj.* wackelig, wankend, unsicher; (*fig.*) schwankend, wankelmütig.

woe [wou], **1.** *s.* (*usu. Poet.*) das Weh, Leid, Elend; (*obs.*) der Kummer, Sorgen (*pl.*), Leiden (*pl.*); ***face of* –,** kummervolles Antlitz; ***the weal and* –,** das Wohl und Wehe; (*coll.*) ***tale of* –,** die Leidensgeschichte. **2.** *int.* wehe! ach! – ***is me!*** wehe mir! ach, ich Unglückliche(r)! – ***betide (you)!*** wehe dir! **woebegone** [–bigɔn], *adj.* niedergebeugt, betrübt, trauervoll, jammervoll, vergrämt. **woeful,** *adj.* 1. elend, jammervoll; traurig, kummervoll, sorgenvoll; 2. betrüblich, beklagenswert, jämmerlich, kläglich, erbärmlich.

woke [wouk], *imperf. of* [2]**wake.**

wold [would], *s.* das Hügelland, Moorland, Heideland.

wolf [wulf], **1.** *s.* (*pl.* **wolves** [wulvz]) der Wolf; (*sl.*) Weiberheld; ***she--,*** die Wölfin; – ***in sheep's clothing,*** der Wolf im Schafspelz; ***cry* –,** blinden Alarm *or* Lärm schlagen; ***keep the* – *from the door,*** sich über Wasser halten, sich recht und schlecht durchschlagen; (*fig.*) ***lone* –,** der Einzelgänger. **2.** *v.t.* (*coll.*) (*also* – ***down***) herunterschlingen, gierig verschlingen.

wolf|-cub, *s.* 1. junger Wolf; 2. (*fig.*) der Jungpfadpfinder, Pimpf. **–hound,** *s.* der Wolfshund.

wolfish ['wulfiʃ], *adj.* wölfisch, Wolfs–, (*fig.*) gefrässig, gierig; – ***appetite,*** der Wolfshunger.

wolf|-note, *s.* (*Mus.*) die Dissonanz, der Mißklang. **--pack,** *s.* (*fig.*) die U-Boot-Flotille.

wolfram ['wulfrəm], *s.* das Wolfram.

wolf's|-bane, *s.* (*Bot.*) Gelber Eisenhut. **--claw, --foot,** *s.* (*Bot.*) der Bärlapp.

wolf-whistle, *s.* (*coll.*) bewundernder *or* beifälliger Pfiff.

wolverine ['wulvəri:n], *s.* (*Zool.*) der Vielfraß.

wolves [wulvz], *pl. of* **wolf.**

woman ['wumən], *s.* (*pl.* **women** ['wimin]) die Frau, das Weib; (*contemptuous*) Weibsbild; (*coll.*) die Mätresse, Geliebte; (*without art.*) Frauen (*pl.*), weibliches Geschlecht; ***born of*** –, vom Weib geboren; ***single*** –, alleinstehende Frau, die Junggesellin; ***kept*** –, die Mätresse; – ***of the world,*** die Weltdame; – ***doctor,*** die Ärztin; – ***student,*** die Studentin; – ***suffrage,*** das Frauenstimmrecht; ***–'s logic,*** weibliche Logik; ***–'s man,*** der Weiberheld. **woman-hater,** *s.* der Weiberfeind.

womanhood ['wumənhud], *s.* 1. das Frauentum, der Frauenstand, die Weiblichkeit, Fraulichkeit; ***grow to*** or ***reach*** –, Frau werden; 2. (*collect.*) die Frauenwelt. **womanish,** *adj.* weibisch. **womanize,** *v.i.* hinter Frauen (*esp.* Dirnen) her sein. **womanizer,** *s.* der Schürzenjäger, Weiberheld. **womankind,** *s.* weibliches Geschlecht, die Frauenwelt, Frauen (*pl.*). **womanliness,** *s.* die Weiblichkeit, Fraulichkeit. **womanly,** *adj.* weiblich, fraulich.

womb [wu:m], *s.* (*Anat.*) die Gebärmutter; der (Mutter)leib, Schoß (*also fig.*).

wombat ['wɔmbæt], *s.* der Wombat, die Beutelmaus.

women ['wimin], *pl. of* **woman**; ***–'s disease,*** die Frauenkrankheit; ***–'s lib(eration),*** die Frauenbefreiungsbewegung; ***–'s rights,*** Frauenrechte (*pl.*); ***–'s team,*** die Damenmannschaft. **womenfolk,** *s.* Frauen (*pl.*) *or* Damen (*pl.*) (einer Gruppe *or* Familie).

won [wʌn], *imperf., p.p. of* **win.**

wonder ['wʌndə], **1.** *s.* 1. das Wunder, Wunderwerk, die Wundertat, Wunderbare(s); ***the – is that,*** man muß sich wundern daß; ***he is a –,*** er ist ein wahres Wunder; ***do*** or ***work –s,*** Wunder tun *or* wirken; ***in the name of –!*** um (des) Himmels willen! ***a nine days' –,*** kurzlebige Sensation, sensationelles Tagesgespräch; ***no –,*** kein Wunder! ***little*** or ***small – that,*** es kann nicht (im mindesten) wundernehmen daß; ***promise –s,*** goldene Berge versprechen; ***the 7 –s of the world,*** die 7 Weltwunder; 2. das (Er)staunen, die Verwunderung; ***excite –,*** Staunen erregen; ***in –,*** erstaunt, verwundert; (*oft. iron.*) ***for a –,*** wunderbarerweise. **2.** *v.i.* 1. sich wundern, erstaunt sein (***at, about,*** über (*Acc.*)); ***it is not to be –ed at,*** es ist nicht erstaunlich *or* zu verwundern (***that,*** wenn); ***I – he came,*** ich bin erstaunt, daß er gekommen ist; ***I shouldn't – that,*** es sollte mich nicht wundern *or* überraschen wenn; 2. sich überlegen *or* fragen, gern wissen möchten, gespannt *or* neugierig sein auf (***about,*** auf (*Acc.*)); ***I –!*** das möchte ich gern wissen! ich weiß nicht recht! ***I was –ing whether,*** ich überlegte mir ob.

wonderful ['wʌndəful], *adj.* wundervoll, wunderbar, bewundernswert, wunderschön; (*coll.*) herrlich, glänzend, prächtig, großartig. **wondering,** *adj.* (*rare*), **wonderingly,** *adv.* erstaunt, staunend, verwundert.

wonderland ['wʌndəlænd], *s.* das Wunderland, Märchenland.

wonderment ['wʌndəmənt], *s.* das (Er)staunen, die Verwunderung. **wonder|-struck,** *adj.* von Staunen ergriffen, vor Staunen platt, erstaunt, verwundert, verblüfft (*at,* über (*Acc.*)). **--working,** *adj.* wunderwirkend, wundertätig.

wondrous ['wʌndrəs], **1.** *adj.* (*Poet.*) wunderbar, herrlich, erstaunlich. **2.** *or* **wondrously,** *adv.* außerordentlich, erstaunlich(erweise).

wonky ['wɔŋki], *adj.* (*sl.*) wacklig, locker; schwankend, unsicher, unzuverlässig, schief.

won't [wount], = ***will not.***

wont [wount], **1.** *s.* die Gewohnheit, der Brauch; ***use and –,*** fester Brauch. **2.** *pred. adj.* gewohnt; ***be – to do,*** zu tun pflegen, gewohnt sein zu tun. **wonted,** *attrib. adj.* 1. gewohnt; 2. gewöhnlich, üblich.

woo [wu:], *v.t.* 1. den Hof machen (*Dat.*), anhalten *or* werben *or* freien um; 2. (*fig.*) trachten nach, buhlen um, zu gewinnen *or* erreichen suchen; 3. locken (***to,*** zu).

wood [wud], *s.* 1. der Wald, Forst, die Waldung, das Gehölz; (*fig.*) ***be out of the –,*** über den Berg sein; ***he cannot see the – for the trees,*** er sieht den Wald vor lauter Bäumen nicht; 2. das Holz; ***dead –,*** dürres Holz, (*fig.*) Veraltete(s), Überholtes, Nutzlose(s), die Spreu; ***touch –!*** unberufen! ***touch –,*** unter den Tisch klopfen; ***wine from the –,*** Wein (direkt) vom Faß.

wood|-agate, *s.* versteinertes Holz. **--alcohol,** *s.* der Holzgeist. **--anemone,** *s.* (*Bot.*) das Windröschen. **–bine** [–bain], *s.* (*Bot.*) das Geißblatt. **–block,** *s.* 1. der Pflasterklotz (*flooring*); 2. (*Typ.*) der Holzstock, Druckstock. **–carver,** *s.* der Holzschnitzer. **--carving,** *s.* die Holzschneidekunst; Holzschnitzerei, das Schnitzwerk. **–chat,** *s.* (*Orn.*) der Rotkopfwürger (*Lanius senator*). **–chuck,** *s.* (*Am.*) das Murmeltier. **--coal,** *s.* die Braunkohle. **–cock,** *s.* (*Am.* ***European*** –) (*Orn.*) die Waldschnepfe. **–craft,** *s.* die Waidmannskunst. **–cut,** *s.* der Holzschnitt. **–cutter,** *s.* der Holzfäller, Holzhacker.

wooded ['wudid], *adj.* waldig, bewaldet, Wald–.

wooden [wudn], *adj.* 1. hölzern (*also fig.*), Holz–; – ***leg,*** das Holzbein, der Stelzfuß; – ***spoon,*** der Holzlöffel; (*fig.*) der Trostpreis; – ***shoes,*** Holzschuhe; (*fig.*) – ***walls,*** Kriegsschiffe (*pl.*); 2. (*fig.*) ledern, steif, plump, unbeholfen; ausdruckslos, langweilig (*expression*).

wood|-engraver, *s.* der Holzschneider. **--engraving,** *s.* die Holzschneidekunst; der Holzschnitt, Holzstich.

wooden|-headed, *adj.* dickköpfig, blöd(e), dumm. **--headedness,** *s.* die Dummheit, Blödheit.

woodenly ['wudnli], *adv.* (*fig.*) steif, plump, unbeholfen, hölzern. **woodenness,** *s.* (*fig.*) die Steifheit, Ausdruckslosigkeit.

woodiness ['wudinis], *s.* 1. der Waldreichtum, die Waldigkeit; 2. Holzigkeit, holzige Beschaffenheit.

wood|land [–lənd], **1.** *s.* das Waldland, die Waldung. **2.** *attrib. adj.* waldig, Wald–. **–lark,** *s.* (*Orn.*) die Heidelerche (*Lullula arbora*). **--louse,** *s.* (*Ent.*) die Bohrassel. **–man** [–mən], *s.* der Holzfäller, Förster, Forstaufseher. **--notes,** *pl.* (*fig.*) die Naturdichtung. **--nymph,** *s.* die Waldnymphe. **–pecker,** *s.* (*Orn.*) der Specht (*Picidae*); ***green –,*** der Grünspecht (*Picus viridis*); ***greater spotted –,*** der Buntspecht (*Dendrocopus major*); ***grey-headed –,*** der Grauspecht (*Picus canus*). **--pigeon,** *s.* die Ringeltaube (*Columba palumbus*). **–pile,** *s.* der Holzhaufen. **--pulp,** *s.* der Holzschliff; Holzzellstoff, die Holzfasermasse. **–ruff,** *s.* (*Bot.*) der Waldmeister. **--screw,** *s.* die Holzschraube. **--shavings,** *pl.* Hobelspäne (*pl.*). **–shed,** *s.* der Holzschuppen; (*coll.*) ***s.th. nasty in the –,*** eine ekelhafte Erfahrung, die man nicht vergessen kann.

woodsman ['wudzmən], *s. See* **woodman.**

wood|-sorrel, *s.* (*Bot.*) der Sauerklee. **--spirit,** *s.* *See* **--alcohol.** **--tar,** *s.* der Holzteer. **--warbler,** *s.* (*Orn.*) der Waldlaubsänger (*Phylloscopus sibilatrix*). **–wind,** *s.* Holzblasinstrumente (*pl.*). **--wool,** *s.* die Holzwolle, Zellstoffwatte. **–work,** *s.* 1. das Holzwerk, der Holzbau; 2. die Holzarbeit, Tischlerei. **–working,** *attrib. adj.* Holzbearbeitungs–.

woody ['wudi], *adj.* 1. holzig, Holz–; 2. waldig, Wald–.

woodyard ['wudjɑ:d], *s.* der Holzlagerplatz.

wooer ['wu:ə], *s.* der Freier, Bewerber.

woof [wu:f], *s.* der Einschlag, (Ein)schuß; das Schußgarn.

wooing ['wu:iŋ], *s.* das Freien, Werben, die Werbung (*of*, um); *go a--*, auf Freiersfüßen gehen.

wool [wul], *s.* 1. die Wolle (*also Bot.*); *dyed in the –*, in der Wolle gefärbt, (*fig.*) ausgepicht, ausgekocht, waschecht; (*sl.*) *lose one's –*, sich auskollern; *pull the – over his eyes*, ihn hinters Licht führen; 2. das Wollgarn, der Wollfaden; das Wolltuch, der Wollstoff; 3. Faserstoff, die Zellwolle, Pflanzenwolle.

wool|-card(er), *s.* die Wollkrempel, Wollkratze. **--comb,** *s.* der Wollkamm. **--dyed,** *adj.* in der Wolle gefärbt.

woolen, (*Am.*) *see* **woollen.**

wool|-gathering, 1. *s.* die Zerstreutheit. **2.** *pred. adj.* zerstreut; *be –*, nicht bei der S. sein. **--grower,** *s.* der Schafzüchter. **--hall,** *s.* die Wollbörse.

woollen ['wulən], *adj.* wollen, Woll–; *– cloth*, wollenes Tuch, das Wollzeug; der Wollstoff; *--draper*, der Wollwarenhändler; *– goods*, Wollwaren (*pl.*). **woollens,** *pl.* Wollwaren (*pl.*), die Wollkleidung, wollene Unterwäsche.

woolliness ['wulinis], *s.* 1. wollige *or* flaumige Beschaffenheit; 2. (*fig.*) die Unklarheit, Verschwommenheit. **woolly, 1.** *adj.* 1. wollig, Woll–; wollartig, weich, flaumig; (*coll.*) *– bear*, die Bärenraupe; 2. (*fig.*) unklar, unbestimmt, verschwommen, verworren. **2.** *s.* (*coll.*) 1. der Sweater, die Wolljacke; 2. *pl.* wollene Unterwäsche.

wool|-pack, *s.* der Wollballen (= *240 lb.*). **-sack,** *s.* der Wollsack (*seat of the Lord Chancellor*). **--sorter,** (*s. p.* or *machine*) der wollsortierer. **--staple,** *s.* der Wollmarkt. **--stapler,** *s.* der Wollgroßhändler. **--trade,** *s.* der Wollhandel. **-work,** *s.* die Wollstickerei.

woozy ['wu:zi], *adj.* (*sl.*) benebelt, beduselt.

word [wə:d], **1.** *s.* 1. das Wort; *a – in his ear*, ein Wort unter vier Augen *or* im Vertrauen; *a – in* (or *out of*) *season*, ein (un)angebrachter Rat; *bandy* or *have –s with*, sich zanken *or* streiten mit, Worte wechseln mit; *eat one's –s*, seine Worte zurücknehmen müssen, zu Kreuze kriechen; *not able to get a – in edgeways*, kaum ein Wort anbringen können; *hang on his –s*, an seinen Worten hängen; *have a – with*, kurz sprechen *or* ein paar Worte reden mit; *have a – to say*, etwas Wichtiges mitzuteilen haben; *lead to –s*, zu Streitigkeiten führen; *play on –s*, das Wortspiel; Wortspiel machen; *put into –s*, in Worte kleiden *or* fassen; *put in* or *say* or *speak a* (*good*) *– for*, ein (gutes) Wort einlegen für; *say the –*, den Wunsch aussprechen; *suit the action to the –*, das Wort in die Tat umsetzen; *waste –s*, in den Wind *or* unnütz reden; *at these –s*, bei diesen Worten; *by – of mouth*, mündlich; *– for –*, Wort für Wort, wörtlich; *too funny for –s*, unsagbar komisch; *in a* or *one –*, mit einem Worte, kurzum, kurz und gut; *in the –s of*, mit den Worten (*Gen.*); *in so many –s*, ausdrücklich, unverblümt; *in other –s*, mit anderen Worten; *man of few –s*, schweigsamer *or* wortkarger Mensch; *man of many –s*, geschwätziger *or* weitschweifiger Mensch; *big –s*, hochtrabende Worte, große Töne; *fair –s*, schmeichelnde Worte; (*Prov.*) *hard –s break no bones*, Schimpfe tut nicht so weh wie Prügel; *hot –s*, zornige Worte; *have the last –*, das letzte Wort haben; (*fig.*) *the last* or *latest –*, die letzte Neuheit; das Vollkommenste; (*Prov.*) *fine –s butter no parsnips*, mit Worten allein ist nicht geholfen; 2. (*without art.*) der Bescheid, die Nachricht, Meldung, Botschaft, Mitteilung; *bring –*, Nachricht bringen; *have* or *receive –*, Nachricht erhalten; *leave – with*, Bescheid hinterlassen bei; *send – to*, ausrichten *or* sagen lassen (*Dat.*), Nachricht geben (*Dat.*); 3. die Parole, Losung, das Losungswort; *money's the –!* Geld ist die Losung! (*coll.*) *mum's the –!* nicht ein Wort! *sharp's the –!* schnell gemacht! flugs! 4. das (Ehren)wort, Versprechen, die Zusage, Versicherung; *– of honour*, das Ehrenwort; *break one's –*, sein Wort brechen, wortbrüchig werden; *give one's –*, sein (Ehren)wort geben; *you have my – for it*, auf mein Wort, ich gebe mein Wort darauf; *keep one's –*, Wort halten; *I take your – for it*, daran zweifle ich nicht, ich glaube es dir; *take him at his –*, ihn beim Worte nehmen; *a man of his –*, ein Mann von Wort; (*upon*) *my –!* bei Gott! *he is as good as his –*, er ist ein Mann von Wort; 5. die Anweisung, der Befehl, das Kommando; *– of command*, das Kommandowort; *give the –*, das Zeichen geben; *at a –*, aufs Wort, sofort, unverzüglich; *at a – from*, auf Anweisung von; *on the –*, bei dem Wort; 6. (*Theol.*) *the Word* (*of God*), das Wort Gottes, Evangelium, die Heilige Schrift; 7. *pl.* der Text. **2.** *v.t.* in Worte fassen *or* kleiden, ausdrücken; *be –ed*, wörtlich lauten.

word|-blindness, *s.* die Wortblindheit. **-book,** *s.* das Wörterbuch, Vokabular. **--building, --formation,** *s.* die Wortbildung.

wordiness ['wə:dinis], *s.* 1. der Wortreichtum, die Wortfülle; 2. Weitschweifigkeit. **wording,** *s.* die Fassung, Formulierung, der Wortlaut. **wordless,** *adj.* wortlos, sprachlos; unausgesprochen.

word|-order, *s.* die Wortstellung. **--painting,** *s.* die Wortmalerei. **--perfect,** *adj.* rollenfest, rollensicher (*actor*); *be –*, die Rolle beherrschen. **--picture,** *s.* bildhafte *or* lebendige Schilderung, das Wortgemälde.

wordy ['wə:di], *adj.* wortreich, weitschweifig, langatmig.

wore [wɔ:], *imperf. of* **wear.**

work [wə:k], **1.** *v.i.* 1. (*of a p.*) arbeiten (*at*, an (*Dat.*)), sich beschäftigen (mit) *or* bemühen (um); beschäftigt *or* tätig sein, Arbeit haben; (*coll.*) *– like a horse*, schuften; 2. (*of machine*) funktionieren, laufen, gehen; (*usu. be –ing*) in Betrieb sein (*factories*); (*coll.*) *it won't –*, es geht nicht; *– loose*, sich lockern; *refuse to –*, versagen (*of an engine*); 3. wirken, wirksam sein, eine Wirkung haben, Wirkung tun, sich auswirken (*on*, auf (*Acc.*)), (*coll.*) glücken, klappen, gelingen (*with*, bei); 4. gären (*as wine*); 5. sich krampfhaft bewegen, sich verziehen, zucken (*of the features*), herumfuchteln (*with the arms*); 6. sich bearbeiten lassen; *this wood –s easily*, dieses Holz läßt sich leicht bearbeiten.

(*with adv. and prep.*) *– against time*, mit der Zeit um die Wette arbeiten; sich anstrengen, um rechtzeitig fertig zu werden; *– away*, drauflosarbeiten (*at*, an (*Dat.*)); *– in*, sich einarbeiten, eindringen; (*fig.*) zusammengehen, harmonieren (*with*, mit); *– on the assumption*, dabei von der Annahme *or* Voraussetzung ausgehen; (*sl.*) *– on him*, ihn bearbeiten, sich (*Dat.*) ihn vorknöpfen; *– out*, zum Vorschein kommen, sich herausarbeiten (*from*, aus); (*fig.*) sich auswirken *or* ergeben; *– out at*, ergeben, sich belaufen auf (*Acc.*); *– round*, sich hindurcharbeiten (*to*, nach), zurückfinden (zu); sich wenden (*of wind*); *– to rule*, die (Dienst)vorschriften genau einhalten; *– to windward*, anluven; *– together*, zusammenarbeiten (*persons*), ineinandergreifen (*wheels*); *– through*, (hin)durcharbeiten (*a book etc.*), sich durcharbeiten *or* durchringen (*as through difficulties*); durchdringen, durchbrechen (*as through a hole*); *– up*, sich emporarbeiten *or* hocharbeiten; hochrutschen (*as a shirt*).

2. *v.t.* 1. verarbeiten, formen, gestalten (*into*, zu), bebauen, kultivieren (*land*), zurichten (*timber*), hämmern, schmieden (*metal*), kneten (*dough*); 2. bewirtschaften (*a farm*), abbauen, ausbeuten (*a mine*); betätigen, bedienen (*a machine*); 3. besticken (*a pattern*); 4. arbeiten lassen (*a p. etc.*); zur Arbeit verwenden (*an animal*); *– o.s. to the bone* or *to death* or *to a shadow*, sich abarbeiten; *– one's jaws*, mit den Kiefern arbeiten; 5. (*Comm.*) (geschäftlich) bereisen (*a district*); 6. (*Math.*) ausarbeiten, lösen; 7. (*coll.*) zustande *or* zuwege bringen, fertigbringen, hervorrufen, bewirken, deichseln; (*sl.*) herausschlagen, ergattern; (*coll.*) *– the oracle*, (auf krummen Wegen) zum Ziel kommen, hinter den Kulissen arbeiten, es schieben; *– a change*, eine Veränderung bewirken; *– wonders*, Wunder tun; 8. *– o.s. into*, sich auf-

schwingen *or* begeistern in (*Acc.*) *or* zu; – ***o.s. up*** (*also* ***get –ed up***), sich aufregen; 9. – ***one's passage,*** die Überfahrt durch Arbeit an Bord verdienen; – ***one's way,*** sich (*Dat.*) einen Weg bahnen, sich durcharbeiten; 10. – ***itself loose,*** sich lockern *or* lösen; – ***itself right,*** sich in die richtige Bahn kommen.
(*with adv. prep.*) – ***in,*** einschalten, einflechten, einfügen, einarbeiten; – ***off,*** 1. (*Typ.*) abziehen, abdrucken; 2. loswerden, abstoßen (***on,*** *Dat.*), abarbeiten (*a debt*), abreagieren, auslassen (*feelings*) (***on,*** an (*Dat.*)); – ***out,*** 1. (*Math.*) ausrechnen, errechnen; lösen; ausarbeiten, entwickeln (*a plan*); 2. ausbeuten, abbauen, erschöpfen (*a mine*); – ***itself out,*** sich auswirken; – ***over,*** revidieren, überarbeiten; – ***up,*** 1. entwickeln, aufarbeiten, ausarbeiten, ausgestalten, erweitern, verarbeiten (***into,*** zu); 2. erregen, aufregen, aufwiegeln, aufpeitschen, schüren (*feelings*); 3. durcharbeiten, (gründlich) studieren (*a subject etc.*); – ***up a business,*** ein Geschäft hocharbeiten *or* hochbringen *or* in die Höhe bringen.
3. *s.* 1. die Arbeit, Beschäftigung, Tätigkeit; der Arbeitsprozeß; (*coll.*) die Handarbeit, Stickerei, Näherei; ***have one's – cut out*** (***for one***), schwer arbeiten müssen, viel zu schaffen haben; ***do –,*** Arbeit leisten; ***make –,*** Arbeit *or* Mühe verursachen; (*iron.*) ***make sad – of,*** etwas Nettes *or* Schönes anrichten bei, arg wirtschaften mit; ***make short – of,*** kurzen Prozeß machen mit; ***at –,*** bei der Arbeit; tätig; ***be at – on,*** arbeiten an (*Dat.*), beschäftigt sein mit; ***be out at –,*** auf Arbeit sein; ***be looking for –,*** Arbeit suchen, auf Arbeitssuche sein; ***be in –,*** Arbeit haben; (*coll.*) ***it's all in a day's –,*** das gehört alles dazu; ***out of –,*** arbeitslos; ***not do a stroke of –,*** keinen Finger rühren, keinen Strich tun; ***be off –,*** (wegen Krankheit) nicht arbeiten; ***set to –,*** an die Arbeit *or* ans Werk gehen, sich an die Arbeit machen; ***set him to –,*** ihn an die *or* eine Arbeit setzen; 2. das Werk, Resultat, Erzeugnis, Produkt; das Arbeitsstück, Werkstück; (*coll.*) ***good –!*** gute Leistung! (*Theol.*) ***good –s,*** gute Werke; ***a good piece of –,*** eine gute Arbeit; – ***of art,*** das Kunstwerk; – ***of the devil,*** das Teufelswerk; – ***of God,*** Gottes Werke; ***the – of time,*** die Schöpfung *or* Früchte der Zeit; ***the –s of Shakespeare,*** die Werke Shakespeares (*N.B.* ***a – by Sh.,*** ein Werk von Sh.; ***a – on Sh.,*** ein Werk über Sh.); 3. (*Phys.*) die Arbeit; ***convert heat into –,*** Wärme in Arbeit verwandeln; 4. *pl.* Bauten (*pl.*), Anlagen (*pl.*), (*Mil.*) das Festungswerk; ***defensive –s,*** Verteidigungswerke (*pl.*); ***Ministry of Works,*** das Ministerium für öffentliche Bauten; ***public –s,*** öffentliche Arbeiten *or* Bauten; 5. *pl.* (*Tech.*) das Triebwerk, Räderwerk, (Uhr)werk, Getriebe; ***–s of a clock,*** das Uhrwerk; 6. *pl.* (*oft. sing. constr.*) das Werk, die Fabrik(anlage), der Betrieb; 7. (*sl.*) ***the –s,*** die ganze Krempel *or* Chose; (*sl.*) ***give him the –s,*** mit ihm Schlitten fahren, ihm sein Fett geben.

workable ['wə:kəbl], *adj.* zu bearbeiten(d) (*soil*), (ab)baufähig (*mine*), bearbeitungsfähig (*materials*), durchführbar, ausführbar (*plans*). **workaday** [-ədei], *adj.* Werktags–, Alltags–, alltäglich.

work|bag, *s.* der Arbeitsbeutel. **–basket,** *s.* der Handarbeitskorb. **--camp,** *s.* das Arbeitslager. **–day,** *s.* der Werktag, Alltag, Wochentag.

worked [wə:kt], *pred. adj.* betrieben, betätigt (*as by hand, electricity etc.*); in Betrieb (*as a mine etc.*); bearbeitet (*as the product*). **worked-up,** *adj.* (*fig.*) (*coll.*) aufgeregt, erregt, aufgebracht.

worker ['wə:kə], *s.* 1. der (die) Arbeiter(in); *pl.* die Arbeiterschaft; Proletarier (*pl.*); ***hard –,*** tüchtiger Arbeiter; ***heavy –,*** der Schwerarbeiter; ***office –s,*** das Büropersonal; ***skilled –,*** gelernter Arbeiter; 2. (*fig.*) der Urheber; (*B.*) ***–s of iniquity,*** Übeltäter (*pl.*); 3. – (***bee***), – (***ant***), der (die) Arbeiter(in).

work|fellow, *s.* der Arbeitskamerad. **--force,** *s.* die Belegschaft. **–house,** *s.* (*Hist.*) das Armenhaus.

working [wə:kiŋ], **1.** *s.* 1. das Arbeiten; (*fig.*) Schaffen, Wirken; Gären (*of yeast*); (*Math.*) Lösen; Funktionieren; (*also pl.*) die Tätigkeit (*of mind*); 2. der Gang, die Bewegung (*of machines*); 3. Bearbeitung, Verarbeitung (*of materials*); 4. Ausbeutung, der Abbau (*of mines etc.*); 5. die (Aus)wirkung; Handlung, Tat; 6. (*oft. pl.*) die Grubenanlage, Bergwerksanlage, Grube, der Bau (*mines*). **2.** *adj.* arbeitend, Arbeits–; – ***assets,*** das Betriebsvermögen; – ***basis,*** die Arbeitsbasis; – ***capacity,*** die Arbeitsleistung; – ***capital,*** das Betriebskapital; – ***class(es),*** die Arbeiterklasse, Arbeiterbevölkerung, der Arbeiterstand; – ***committee,*** der Arbeitsausschuß; – ***day,*** der Arbeitstag; – ***drawing,*** der Bauplan, die Konstruktionszeichnung, Werkstattzeichnung; (*Carp. etc.*) – ***edge,*** die Arbeitskante; – ***expenses,*** die Betriebskosten; (*Carp. etc.*) – ***face,*** die Arbeitsfläche; – ***hours,*** die Arbeitsstunden (*pl.*); – ***instructions,*** Gebrauchsanweisungen (*pl.*); – ***knowledge,*** ausreichende Kenntnisse; – ***life,*** nützliche Lebensdauer (*of machine*), werktätiges Leben (*of worker*); – ***load,*** die Nutzlast; – ***lunch,*** das Arbeitsessen; – ***majority,*** arbeitsfähige Mehrheit; – ***man,*** der Arbeiter; – ***method,*** das Arbeitsverfahren; – ***model,*** das Versuchsmodel; ***in – order,*** in Ordnung, betriebsfähig, funktionierend; ***out of*** or ***not in – order,*** betriebsunfähig, nicht funktionierend *or* in Ordnung; – ***parts,*** Verschleißteile (*pl.*); – ***partner,*** aktiver Teilhaber; – ***party,*** (*esp. Mil.*) der Arbeitstrupp, die Arbeitsabteilung; (*Pol.*) Arbeitsgruppe; – ***population,*** werktätige Bevölkerung; – ***theory,*** eine Theorie mit der sich arbeiten läßt; – ***vocabulary,*** genügender Wortschatz; – ***voltage,*** die Betriebsspannung; – ***woman,*** berufstätige Frau.

working|-class, *attrib. adj.* Arbeiter–. **--day,** *adj.* Alltags–, werktäglich. **--out,** *s.* (*Math.*) die Lösung (*of a problem*); (*coll.*) Entwicklung, Ausarbeitung.

workless ['wə:klis], *adj.* arbeitslos.

workman ['wə:kmən], *s.* der Arbeiter (*esp.* Handarbeiter), Handwerker; ***–'s compensation,*** die Arbeitsunfallversicherung, Betriebsunfallversicherung. **workmanlike,** *adj.* fachmännisch, kunstgerecht, geschickt. **workmanship,** *s.* 1. die Geschicklichkeit, Kunstfertigkeit; 2. (Art der) Ausführung; ***this is his –,*** dies ist von ihm geschaffen, dies ist sein Werk.

work|mate, *s. See* **–fellow. –people,** *pl.* die Arbeitsleute, Arbeiter (*pl.*). **–room,** *s.* der Arbeitsraum.

works council, *s.* der Betriebsrat.

work|shop, *s.* die Werkstatt, Werkstätte. **--shy,** *adj.* arbeitsscheu.

works outing, *s.* der Betriebsausflug.

work|-study, *s.* Zeitstudien (*pl.*). **–table,** *s.* der Nähtisch, Arbeitstisch. **--to-rule,** *s.* der Dienst nach Vorschrift, Bummelstreik. **–woman,** *s.* die Arbeiterin.

world [wə:ld], *s.* die Welt; ***animal –,*** das Tierreich; – ***champion,*** der (die) Weltmeister(in); ***a – of care,*** eine Welt voll Sorgen; – ***of letters,*** gelehrte Welt; ***a – of trouble,*** eine Unmenge Kummer; ***vegetable –,*** das Pflanzenreich; ***be all the – to him*** (***her***), sein (ihr) ein und alles sein; ***all the – over,*** über die ganze *or* auf der ganzen Welt; ***all the – and his wife,*** jedermann; ***fashionable –,*** feine Welt; ***medi(a)eval –,*** die Welt des Mittelalters; ***the next –,*** das Jenseits, zukünftige Welt; ***scientific –,*** die Welt der Wissenschaften; ***sporting –,*** die Sportwelt; ***carry the – before one,*** über alle Hindernisse hinwegsetzen; ***the – to come,*** das Jenseits; ***forsake the –,*** der Welt entsagen; (*coll.*) ***give the –,*** wer weiß nicht was geben; ***as the – goes,*** wie es in der Welt geht; ***see the –,*** Land und Leute kennenlernen; ***think the – of,*** wunder was *or* sehr viel halten von; ***for all the –,*** um alles in der Welt, in jeder Hinsicht; ***not for –s*** or ***for all the –,*** nicht um alles in der Welt, um keinen Preis; ***from all over the –,*** aus aller Welt, aus aller Herren Ländern; ***in the –,*** auf der Welt; ***nothing in the –,*** überhaupt nichts, rein gar nichts; ***what in the –?*** was in aller Welt? ***bring into the –,*** auf die *or* zur Welt bringen; ***come into the –,*** auf die Welt kommen; ***knowledge of the* –**, die Weltkenntnis, Welterfahrung; ***man of the* –**, der Weltmann; (*coll.*) ***on top of the* –**, obenauf sein; ***woman of the* –**, die Weltdame; ***that*** or ***such is the way of the* –**, das ist der Lauf der Welt, es ist nun einmal so, so geht es in der Welt; (*coll.*) ***out of this* –**, phantastisch, himmlisch; (*sl.*) ***blind to the* –**, hilflos betrunken; (*sl.*) ***dead to the* –**, völlig weg; **–** ***without end,*** von Ewigkeit zu Ewigkeit.

world|-famous, *adj.* weltberühmt. **--language,** *s.* die Weltsprache.

worldliness [ˈwəːldlinis], *s.* die Weltlichkeit, der Weltsinn, weltlicher *or* materieller Sinn. **worldling,** *s.* das Weltkind, der Weltmann. **worldly,** *adj.* weltlich, zeitlich, irdisch; **–** ***goods,*** irdische Güter; **–** ***pleasure(s),*** irdisches Vergnügen; **–** ***wisdom,*** die Weltklugheit. **worldly|-minded,** *adj.* weltlich gesinnt. **--mindedness,** *s.* weltliche Gesinnung. **--wise,** *adj.* weltklug, welterfahren.

world|-politics, *s.* die Weltpolitik. **--power,** *s.* die Weltmacht. **--renowned,** *adj.* weltberühmt (***for,*** wegen). **--view,** *s.* die Weltanschauung. **–weariness,** *s.* die Lebensmüdigkeit, der Lebensüberdruß. **--weary,** *adj.* weltmüde, lebensmüde, der Welt *or* des Lebens überdrüssig. **--wide,** *adj.* weitverbreitet, weltumfassend, weltumspannend; ***of – fame,*** weltberühmt; **–** ***reputation,*** der Weltruf.

worm [wəːm], **1.** *s.* 1. der Wurm; (*fig. coll.*) elender Wurm (*a p.*); ***even a – will turn,*** auch der Wurm krümmt sich, wenn er getreten wird; ***–'s eye view,*** die Froschperspektive; 2. (*Tech.*) das Schneckengewinde, die Schnecke; 3. (*Chem.*) (Kühl)-schlange. **2.** *v.t.* 1. von Würmern befreien (*animals*); **–** ***a secret out of him,*** ihm die Würmer aus der Nase ziehen; 2. reinigen, putzen (*a gun*); 3. **–** ***o.s.*** or ***one's way,*** sich winden *or* schlängeln *or* einschleichen. **3.** *v.i.* sich winden *or* schlängeln *or* einschleichen.

worm|-cast, *s.* von Regenwürmern aufgeworfene Erde. **--drive,** *s.* (*Tech.*) der Schneckenantrieb. **--eaten,** *adj.* wurmstichig. **--gear,** *s.* das Schneckengetriebe. **--hole,** *s.* der Wurmstich.

worminess [ˈwəːminis], *s.* die Wurmstichigkeit.

worm|-like, *adj.* wurmartig. **--seed,** *s.* (*Bot.*) der Wurmsame. **--thread,** *s.* das Schneckengewinde. **--wheel,** *s.* das Schneckenrad. **–wood,** *s.* der Wermut, (*fig.*) die Bitterkeit; ***it is (gall and) – to him,*** es wurmt ihn.

wormy [ˈwəːmi], *adj.* wurmig; wurmstichig.

worn [wɔːn], **1.** *p.p. of* **wear. 2.** *adj.* 1. getragen (*of clothes*); 2. (*also* **–** ***out***) abgenutzt, abgetragen (*clothes*); 3. abgehärmt, verhärmt (*features*); (*coll.*) **–** ***to a frazzle,*** völlig erledigt, wie zerschlagen; ***he is – to a shadow,*** er ist nur mehr ein Schatten seines einstigen Selbst; (*fig.*) **–** ***out,*** todmüde, erschöpft, zermürbt, abgespannt (*of a p.*); veraltet, überlebt, abgedroschen (*of a th.*).

worried [ˈwʌrid], *adj.* besorgt, geängstigt, beunruhigt. **worrier,** *s.* der Schwarzseher. **worrisome,** *adj.* (*coll.*) lästig, störend; beunruhigend.

worry [ˈwʌri], **1.** *v.t.* 1. plagen, belästigen; zusetzen (*Dat.*) (***with,*** mit); **–** ***him into,*** ihn durch ständiges Quälen bringen *or* treiben zu; **–** ***s.th. out of him,*** ihm etwas durch Quälereien abpressen, ihn durch Quälereien um etwas bringen; 2. ängstigen, beunruhigen, Sorgen bereiten *or* machen (*Dat.*); **–** ***o.s., be worried,*** sich ängstigen, besorgt sein (***about, over,*** um), sich ärgern (über (*Acc.*)); 3. (*as a dog*) würgen, totbeißen (*sheep, cattle etc.*); 4. **–** ***out a problem,*** ein Problem nicht loslassen bis es gelöst wird. **2.** *v.i.* 1. sich (*Dat.*) Gedanken *or* Sorgen machen, besorgt sein, sich sorgen *or* ängstigen (***about, over,*** um), sich beunruhigen *or* aufregen (über (*Acc.*)); (*coll.*) ***I should –!*** mir ist das schnuppe *or* egal! 2. (*as a dog*) zerren, zerreißen, zausen (***at,*** an (*Dat.*)) (*a bone*). **3.** *s.* 1. die Sorge, Besorgnis; der Ärger, Verdruß, Kummer; 2. (*coll.*) der Quälgeist. **worrying,** *adj.* beängstigend, beunruhigend.

worse [wəːs], **1.** *adj.* schlechter, schlimmer, übler; (*fig.*) ärger; ***to make it –,*** um das Unglück vollzumachen; ***be the – for,*** Schaden gelitten haben durch, schlechter gestellt sein wegen; ***he is none the – for it,*** es hat ihm nichts geschadet; ***be the – for drink,*** einen (Affen) sitzen haben; (*coll.*) **–** ***luck!*** unglücklicherweise! leider! um so schlimmer! ***only make matters –,*** es nur noch schlimmer machen; ***so much the –,*** um so schlimmer; (*coll.*) ***your hands would be none the – for a wash,*** waschen würde deinen Händen wahrhaftig nicht schaden; ***he is – today,*** ihm geht es heute schlechter (*as of health*); (*coll.*) ***the – for wear,*** abgetragen, abgenutzt, (*fig.*) arg mitgenommen; **–** ***and –,*** immer schlechter *or* schlimmer. **2.** *adv.* schlimmer, schlechter; ***no –*** or ***none the –,*** nicht schlechter; ***think none the – of,*** nicht geringer denken von; **–** ***off,*** schlechter daran, (*coll.*) ärmer; ***go farther and fare –,*** aus dem Regen in die Traufe kommen. **3.** *s.* Schlimmere(s); ***for better or for –,*** was auch kommen mag, was auch dabei herauskommt, wohl oder übel, wie man es auch nimmt; ***from bad to –,*** aus dem Regen in die Traufe; ***change for the –,*** die Wendung zum Schlechten, die Verschlechterung; ***take a turn for the –,*** sich verschlechtern; **–** ***followed,*** Schlimmeres folgte.

worsen [wəːsn], **1.** *v.t.* verschlechtern, schlechter machen, verschlimmern; schädigen. **2.** *v.i.* schlechter *or* schlimmer werden, sich verschlechtern *or* verschlimmern. **worsening,** *s.* die Verschlechterung.

worship [ˈwəːʃip], **1.** *s.* 1. die Verehrung, Anbetung, (*Eccl.*) der Gottesdienst; Ritus, Kult(us); ***at –,*** in (frommer) Andacht; ***place of –,*** die Kirche, das Gotteshaus; 2. ***your Worship,*** Euer Gnaden *or* Hochwürden. **2.** *v.t.* 1. anbeten, verehren; 2. huldigen (*Dat.*); (*fig.*) vergöttern. **3.** *v.i.* seine Andacht verrichten, am Gottesdienst teilnehmen. **worshipful,** *adj.* 1. (*in titles*) ehrenwert, wohlangesehen, wohllöblich; 2. (*obs.*) ehrwürdig, angesehen, achtbar. **worshipper,** *s.* Andächtige(r); (*fig.*) Anbeter(in), Verehrer(in); **–** ***of idols,*** der (die) Götzendiener(in).

worst [wəːst], **1.** *adj.* schlimmst, schlechtest, ärgst, übelst. **2.** *adv.* am schlimmsten *or* schlechtesten *or* ärgsten. **3.** *s.* der *or* die *or* das Schlimmste *or* Ärgste; ***at (the) –,*** im schlimmsten Falle; ***see it at its –,*** es von der schlechtesten *or* schwächsten Seite sehen; ***do one's –,*** es so arg machen, wie man nur kann; ***do your –!*** mach' was du willst! ***get the – of it,*** am schlechtesten wegkommen, den kürzeren ziehen; ***the – of it,*** das Schlimmste daran; ***the – is yet to come,*** das Schlimmste kommt noch; ***if the –*** or ***if it comes to the –,*** schlimmstenfalls, wenn es zum Schlimmsten kommt, wenn alle Stricke reißen; ***be prepared for the –,*** aufs Schlimmste gefaßt sein. **4.** *v.t.* (*coll.*) unterkriegen, überwältigen, besiegen.

worsted [ˈwustid], *s.* das Kammgarn; der Kammgarnstoff; **–** ***stockings,*** wollene Strümpfe, Wollstrümpfe (*pl.*).

wort [wəːt], *s.* die (Bier)würze.

-wort, *s.* (*suff.*) die . . .-wurz, das . . . -kraut.

worth [wəːθ], **1.** *pred. adj.* 1. wert (*Acc.*) (***to,*** *Dat.* or für); (*coll. of a p.*) ***be – . . .,*** . . . verdienen, ein Einkommen haben von . . .; . . . (an Vermögen) besitzen; ***it is – little to him,*** es ist ihm *or* für ihn wenig wert; ***be – a great deal,*** viel wert sein; ***not – a penny,*** keinen Pfifferling *or* roten Heller wert; (*coll.*) ***he is – a million,*** er besitzt eine Million, er ist seine Million wert; (*coll.*) ***he is – £10,000 a year,*** er hat ein jährliches Einkommen von *or* er verdient jährlich £10,000; (*coll.*) ***for all one is –,*** so gut man kann, nach besten Kräften; ***for what it is –,*** unter Vorbehalt; ***my opinion for what it is –,*** meine unmaßgebliche Meinung; **–** ***the money*** or ***price,*** preiswert; (*Prov.*) ***a bird in the hand is – two in the bush,*** ein Sperling in der Hand ist besser als eine Taube auf dem Dach; ***it is – its weight in gold,*** das kann nicht mit Gold aufgewogen werden; (*coll.*) **–** ***his salt,*** was taugen; (*coll.*) ***not – his salt,*** nichts taugen; 2. (*fig.*) wert (*Gen.*), würdig; ***be not – the trouble,*** nicht der Mühe wert sein, sich nicht lohnen; ***not – powder and shot,*** keinen Schuß Pulver wert; ***not – bothering about,*** (*coll.*) ***not – the candle,*** nicht der Mühe wert; ***it is – doing,*** es lohnt sich, es zu tun; es ist wert getan zu werden; ***– mentioning,*** erwähnenswert; ***– reading,*** lesenswert; ***– seeing,*** sehenswert; ***– speaking of,*** der Rede wert; ***a tale – telling,*** erzählenswerte Geschichte; ***be – (one's) while,*** (*coll.*) ***be – it,*** sich lohnen, der Mühe wert sein; ***make it – his while,*** es ihm vergelten. **2.** *s.* 1. der (Geld)wert; (*fig.*) Wert, die Wichtigkeit, Bedeutung; ***ten pence – of sweets,*** für zehn Pence Bonbons, Bonbons im Wert von zehn Pence; ***of great –,*** teuer, sehr wertvoll; ***of little*** or ***of no (great) –,*** wertlos; ***nothing of –,*** nichts Wertvolles; ***men of –,*** verdienstvolle *or* verdiente Leute; ***get one's money's –,*** für sein Geld Entsprechendes erhalten; 2. (*obs.*) die Würde, das Ansehen.

worthily ['wə:ðili], *adv.* 1. würdig, in Ehren; 2. mit Recht *or* gutem Grund; 3. angemessen, nach Verdienst. **worthiness,** *s.* die Würdigkeit, der Verdienst, Wert.

worthless ['wə:θlis], *adj.* 1. wertlos, nichts wert, ohne Bedeutung; 2. (*fig.*) nichtswürdig, verächtlich. **worthlessness,** *s.* (*usu. fig.*) die Wertlosigkeit, Nichtswürdigkeit, Unwürdigkeit. **worthwhile,** *attrib. adj.* lohnend.

worthy ['wə:ði], **1.** *adj.* 1. (*pred.*) würdig, wert (***of,*** *Gen.*); ***– of the occasion,*** dem Anlaß angemessen *or* entsprechend; ***– of death,*** todeswürdig; ***he is not – of her,*** er ist ihrer nicht wert *or* würdig; ***be – of praise,*** Lob verdienen; ***– of being*** or ***to be done,*** wert sein *or* verdienen getan zu werden; 2. (*attrib.*) würdig, angesehen, ehrenwert, schätzbar (*of a p.*), angemessen, ausreichend (*of a th.*). **2.** *s.* (*oft. iron.*) die Notabilität; (*usu. pl.*) die Person von Verdienst, große *or* führende Persönlichkeit, der Held, die Größe.

wot [wɔt], *pres. indic. of* [2]**wit**; (*obs.*) ***God –!*** weiß Gott!

would [wud], *imperf. of* [2]**will, 1**; 1. wollte(st), wollten *etc.*; pflegte(st), pflegten *etc.*; ***he – not come,*** er wollte durchaus nicht kommen; ***he – walk for hours,*** er pflegte stundenlang zu gehen; ***it – be about a week ago,*** es mochte wohl eine Woche her sein; ***it – seem,*** es scheint fast; 2. (*in principal clauses 1st pers. sing. and pl.*) möchte(n), wünschte(n); (*2nd pers. in questions*) möchtest, möchten; ***– to God!*** wollte Gott! ***I – rather not,*** ich möchte lieber nicht; ***I – have you know,*** ich muß Ihnen sagen; Sie sollen wissen; 3. (*with conditional clauses*) *2nd or 3rd pers. imperf. subj. or* würde(st), würden, würdet (*with inf.*); ***he – do it if . . .,*** er würde es tun *or* täte es, wenn . . .; ***do what I –,*** was ich auch täte; ***one – think he was ill,*** man sollte denken er sei krank.

would-be ['wudbi:], *attrib. adj.* vorgeblich, angeblich, Schein–; ***– assassin,*** einer der sich als Attentäter ausgibt; ***– important person,*** der Gernegroß, Möchtegern; ***– painter,*** der Farbenkleckser; ***– poet,*** der Dichterling; ***– politician,*** der Biertischpolitiker; ***– sportsman,*** der Sonntagsjäger; ***– wit,*** Möchtegernwitzbold.

wouldn't [wudnt], = ***would not.***

[1]**wound** [wu:nd], **1.** *s.* die Wunde, Verwundung, Verletzung (***in,*** an (*Dat.*)), (*fig.*) Kränkung, Verletzung; ***dress a –,*** eine Wunde verbinden; ***inflict a –,*** eine Wunde beibringen (***on,*** *Dat.*); ***receive a –,*** verwundet werden. **2.** *v.t.* verwunden (***in,*** an (*Dat.*)), verletzen; (*fig.*) verletzen, kränken, beleidigen.

[2]**wound** [waund], *imperf., p.p. of* **wind.**

wounded ['wu:ndid], *adj.* verwundet; ***war-–,*** Kriegsversehrte, Kriegsbeschädigte (*pl.*). **wound-stripe,** *s.* das Verwundetenabzeichen.

wove [wouv], **1.** *imperf. of* **weave. 2.** *adj.* ***– paper,*** das Velinpapier. **woven, 1.** *p.p. of* **weave. 2.** *adj.* ***– fabrics,*** Wirkwaren, Webwaren (*pl.*).

[1]**wow** [wau], *s.* (*Rad. coll.*) das Wimmern.

[2]**wow,** *s.* (*sl.*) die Pfundsache; der Bombenerfolg; Mordskerl, Prachtkerl.

wowser ['wauzə], *s.* (*sl.*) der Moralinonkel.

[1]**wrack** [ræk], *s.* 1. angeschwemmter Seetang; 2. ziehendes Gewölk, windgetriebene Wolken.

[2]**wrack,** *s.* (*obs.*) der Untergang, das Verderben; (*only in*) ***go to – and ruin,*** zugrunde gehen.

wraith [reiθ], *s.* die (Geister)erscheinung, der Geist, das Gespenst.

wrangle ['ræŋgl], **1.** *v.i.* zanken, streiten, hadern, sich in den Haaren liegen, sich katzbalgen (***about, over,*** über (*Acc.*)). **2.** *s.* der Zank, Streit, Hader, die Stänkerei, Katzbalgerei. **wrangler,** *s.* streitsüchtige P., der Zänker; ***senior –,*** der Student, der die mathematische Schlußprüfung am besten besteht (*Cambridge Univ.*).

wrap [ræp], **1.** *v.t.* 1. (*also* ***– up***) (ein)wickeln, (ein)hüllen, (ein)schlagen, (ein)packen (***in,*** in (*Acc.*)); wickeln (*paper*), hüllen (*a cloak etc.*); ***– round o.s.,*** sich einwickeln in (*Acc.*) (*a blanket etc.*); ***– round one's finger,*** sich (*Dat.*) um den Finger wickeln; (*coll.*) ***– up,*** endgültig abwickeln, (zu seiner Zufriedenheit) erledigen; ***he has (got) everything wrapped up,*** es liegt alles in seiner Hand; ***– o.s. up (warm),*** sich warm anziehen; 2. (*fig.*) (ver)hüllen, verdecken, bedecken; verwickeln, verstricken; ***wrapped in allegory,*** allegorisch verkleidet; ***wrapped (up) in mystery,*** rätselhaft verstrickt; ***wrapped up in o.s.,*** von sich selbst allzu eingenommen; ***be wrapped up in,*** gänzlich aufgehen in (*Dat.*), versunken sein in (*Acc.*), völlig in Anspruch *or* eingenommen werden von; ***wrapped in mist*** (or ***silence***), in Nebel (*or* Schweigen) gehüllt. **2.** *v.i.* sich wickeln *or* winden *or* schlingen *or* legen (***round,*** um); ***– up,*** sich einhüllen, sich warm anziehen. **3.** *s.* die Hülle, Decke; der Überwurf, Schal, Umhang. **wrapper,** *s.* 1. der Umschlag, die Hülle, Decke, Verpackung; (*of book*) Schutzhülle, der Buch(umschlag); (*of cigar*) das Deckblatt; (***postal***) –, das Kreuzband, Streifband; 2. der (die) (Ein)packer(in). **wrapping,** *s.* das Einpacken, Verpacken, Einwickeln; (*also pl.*) die Hülle, Umhüllung, Verpackung; ***– paper,*** das Packpapier, Einschlagpapier.

wrasse [ræs], *s.* (*Ichth.*) der Lippfisch.

wrath [rɔ(:)θ], *s.* der Zorn, (In)grimm, die Wut. **wrathful,** *adj.* zornig, grimmig, wütig, wütend (***with,*** auf (*Acc.*)), ergrimmt, wutentbrannt.

wreak [ri:k], *v.t.* (*Poet.*) ausüben, auslassen (*anger, vengeance etc.*) (***on,*** an (*Dat.*)).

wreath [ri:θ], *s.* der Kranz, das Gewinde, die Girlande; ***– of flowers,*** der Blumenkranz, das Blumengewinde; ***– of smoke,*** das Rauchwölkchen; ***– of snow,*** die Schneewehe.

wreathe [ri:ð], **1.** *v.t.* 1. winden, drehen, wickeln (***round,*** um); einhüllen (***in,*** in (*Acc.*)), umgeben (***with,*** mit); 2. flechten, binden (*a garland*), bekränzen, schmücken (*a p.*). **2.** *v.i.* sich drehen *or* winden, sich kräuseln *or* ringeln.

wreck [rek], **1.** *s.* 1. (*Naut.*) das Wrack; der Schiffbruch (*also fig.*); die Ruine, der Trümmerhaufen; ***nervous –,*** das Nervenbündel; 2. (*fig.*) die Zerstörung, Verwüstung, der Ruin, Untergang, das Verderben; 3. (*Law*) Strandgut. **2.** *v.t.* zerschellen lassen, zum Scheitern bringen (*a ship, also fig.*), zugrunde richten, zu Fall bringen, zerstören, vernichten (*plans etc.*); ***– a train,*** einen Zug entgleisen; ***be –ed,*** scheitern, stranden, Schiffbruch erleiden, zerschellen (*a ship*); entgleisen (*a train*), zerstört *or* vernichtet werden. **wreckage,** *s.* (Schiffs)trümmer (*pl.*), das Wrack; (*fig.*) der Schiffbruch, Untergang, das Scheitern, die Vernichtung. **wrecked** [–t], *adj.* 1. gescheitert (*also fig.*), gestrandet (*ship*), schiffbrüchig (*sailors*), Strand– (*goods*); 2. (*fig.*) zerstört, zerrüttet, vernichtet. **wrecker,** *s.* 1. (*Hist.*) der Stranddieb, Strandräuber; Eisenbahnattentäter; 2. Abbrucharbeiter; 3. (*fig.*) Zerstörer, Vernichter.

wren [ren], *s.* (*Orn.*) (***Am. winter –***) der Zaunkönig (*Troglodytes troglodytes*).

wrench [rentʃ], **1.** *s.* 1. heftiger Ruck, heftige Drehung; 2. (*Med.*) die Verrenkung, Verstauchung; 3. (*Tech.*) der Schraubenschlüssel; 4. (*fig.*) (Trennungs)schmerz, schmerzliche Trennung; ***it was a – to me,*** es war für mich sehr schmerzlich;

5. (*fig.*) die Verzerrung, Verdrehung (*of meaning*). **2.** *v.t.* **1.** mit einem Ruck ziehen *or* reißen; entwinden, entreißen (*from, Dat.*); – ***o.s. from,*** sich losreißen von; – ***open,*** mit Gewalt öffnen, aufreißen; 2. verrenken, verstauchen (*a limb*); 3. verzerren, verdrehen (*meaning*).

wrest [rest], **1.** *v.t.* **1.** (gewaltsam) ziehen *or* reißen *or* zerren; – ***from,*** entreißen (*Dat.*), entwinden (*Dat.*), (*fig.*) abringen (*as a living*) (*Dat.*); 2. verdrehen, verzerren, entstellen (*meanings*). **2.** *s.* der Stimmhammer (*for pianos etc.*); **--*pin,*** der Stimmnagel (*on pianos etc.*).

wrestle [resl], **1.** *v.i.* **1.** (*Spt.*) ringen (*also fig.*), sich ringen; 2. (*fig.*) (schwer) kämpfen (***for***, um), sich abmühen *or* abquälen (***with***, mit *or* bei). **2.** *v.t.* ringen mit (*a p.*). **3.** *s.* **1.** der Ringkampf; 2. (*fig.*) das Ringen, schwerer Kampf (***for***, um). **wrestler,** *s.* der Ringer. **wrestling,** *s.* (*also* – ***match***) das Ringen, der Ringkampf.

wretch [retʃ], *s.* der Lump, Schuft; armes Wesen, Elende(r); ***poor*** –, armer Teufel. **wretched** [-id], *adj.* **1.** elend, unglücklich, unglückselig, traurig (*of a p.*); ***feel*** –, sich elend *or* schlecht fühlen; 2. armselig, jämmerlich, erbärmlich, miserabel, kläglich, dürftig, ärmlich, lumpig. **wretchedness,** *s.* **1.** das Elend, Unglück; 2. die Erbärmlichkeit, Armseligkeit, Dürftigkeit.

wriggle [rigl], **1.** *v.i.* sich winden *or* schlängeln, sich hin- und herbewegen; (*as worms etc.*) sich ringeln, (*fig.*) schleichen, krumme Wege gehen; (*fig.*) – ***into,*** sich einschleichen in (*Acc.*); (*fig.*) – ***out of,*** sich herauswinden aus. **2.** *v.t.* – ***one's way,*** sich dahinschlängeln; – ***o.s. into*** (or ***out of***), see – ***into*** (or ***out of***). **3.** *s.* **1.** das Ringeln; 2. die Windung, Krümmung, der Schlängelweg.

-wright [rait], *s. suff.* der . . . –anfertiger, –macher, –bauer; *e.g.* ***play–,*** der Schauspieldichter, Dramatiker; ***wheel–,*** der Stellmacher.

wring [riŋ], **1.** *irr.v.t.* **1.** ringen (*one's hands*), abdrehen (*fowl's neck*); (*fig.*) – ***his neck,*** ihm den Hals umdrehen; – ***his hand*** or ***him by the hand,*** ihm die Hand drücken; 2. herauspressen, herausquetschen, herausdrücken (*liquid*) (***out of,*** aus); (*also* – ***out***) auswinden, aus(w)ringen (*clothes*); 3. (*fig.*) beklemmen, bedrücken, martern, quälen (*the heart*); ***it –s my heart,*** es schmerzt *or* bedrückt mich zutiefst; 4. (*fig.*) – ***from,*** entreißen, entwinden, abringen (*Dat.*) (*confession etc.*), erpressen von (*taxes etc.*). **2.** *s.* ***give a th. a*** –, es auswringen *or* auspressen *or* ausdrücken; ***give his hand a*** –, ihm die Hand drücken. **wringer,** *s.* die Wringmaschine (*for clothes*). **wringing, 1.** *adv.* – ***wet,*** zum Auswringen naß, triefend naß, klitschnaß. **2.** *s.* das Auswringen, Auswinden; **--*machine,*** *see* **wringer.**

wrinkle [riŋkl], **1.** *s.* **1.** die Runzel, Falte (*of features*), der Knitter, Kniff (*cloth, paper etc.*), die Unebenheit, Vertiefung; 2. (*coll.*) der Kniff, Handgriff; 3. (*coll.*) Wink, Tip. **2.** *v.t.* falten, kniffen, zerknittern; (*also* – ***up***) runzeln, zusammenziehen, in Falten legen (*brow*), zusammenkneifen (*eyes*); rümpfen (*nose*). **3.** *v.i.* Falten ziehen *or* werfen Runzeln bekommen, sich runzeln; knittern; ***her face –d into a smile,*** ihr Gesicht verzog sich zu einem Lächeln. **wrinkled,** *adj.* runzlig, faltig; kraus, gekräuselt, zerknittert.

wrist [rist], *s.* **1.** das Handgelenk; 2. (*Tech.*) (*also* **--*pin***) der Kolbenbolzen. **wrist|band,** *s.* das Bündchen, die Prise (*of shirt sleeves*), Hemdmanschette. **--drop,** *s.* die Handgelenkslähmung.

wristlet ['ristlit], *s.* **1.** der Pulswärmer; 2. das Armband; (*sl.*) die Handschelle; – ***watch,*** *see* **wristwatch.**

wrist|-pin, *s. See* **wrist, 2.** **–watch,** *s.* die Armbanduhr.

writ [rit], **1.** *s.* **1.** (*Theol.*) die Schrift; ***Holy*** or ***Sacred Writ,*** die Heilige Schrift; 2. (*Law*) behördlicher Erlaß, die Verfügung, gerichtliche Urkunde, das Schriftstück; schriftliche Aufforderung, die Vorladung; (*coll.*) ***where his – does not run,*** wo er nichts zu sagen hat; ***serve a – upon him, serve him with a*** –, ihn vorladen; ***take out a – against,*** eine Vorladung erwirken gegen; – ***of attachment,*** der Haftbefehl, Verhaftungsbefehl, Vorführungsbefehl, Arrest; – ***of execution,*** der Vollstreckungsbefehl; – ***of subpœna,*** die Vorladung unter Strafandrohung. **2.** *p.p.* (*obs.*) *see* **written**; (*fig.*) – ***large,*** deutlich erkennbar.

write [rait], **1.** *irr.v.t.* schreiben; (*also* – ***down***) aufschreiben, niederschreiben, aufzeichnen, schriftlich niederlegen; brieflich *or* schriftlich mitteilen (***to***, *Dat.*); – ***a cheque,*** einen Scheck ausfüllen *or* ausstellen *or* ausschreiben; (*sl.*) ***nothing to – home about,*** nichts Besonderes; – ***music,*** komponieren; – ***shorthand,*** stenographieren; – ***poetry,*** dichten; – ***against time,*** in der größtmöglichen Eile schreiben; – ***in ink,*** mit Tinte schreiben; – ***to him,*** ihm *or* an ihn schreiben; – ***one's will,*** sein Testament aufsetzen; – ***down,*** niederschreiben, aufschreiben, aufzeichnen, notieren; (*fig.*) schlechtmachen, herabsetzen, herunterreißen; darstellen *or* beschreiben *or* hinstellen als; (*Comm.*) abbuchen, (vom Wert) abschreiben; – ***in,*** eintragen; – ***off,*** herunterschreiben, schnell abfassen; (*fig.*) abbuchen, abschreiben (*a debt*); (*fig. sl.*) für einen Totalverlust halten, als Totalverlust betrachten; (*of a p.*) nicht mehr rechnen mit *or* zählen *or* sich verlassen auf (*Acc.*); – ***out,*** ganz ausschreiben, ungekürzt niederschreiben *or* abschreiben; – ***out a fair copy,*** ins reine abschreiben; – ***o.s. out,*** sich ausschreiben; – ***up,*** ausführlich darstellen; (*fig.*) schriftlich anpreisen, herausstreichen, lobend erwähnen *or* hervorheben; (*Comm.*) aufwerten; eintragen, nachtragen. **2.** *irr.v.i.* schreiben (***about, on,*** über (*Acc.*); ***to,*** *Dat. or* an (*Acc.*)); schriftstellern; Briefe schreiben; – ***to ask,*** schriftlich anfragen; – ***back,*** wiederschreiben, (schriftlich) antworten; – ***for,*** schriftlich bestellen, kommen lassen.

write-off, *s.* **1.** (*Comm.*) die Abschreibung; 2. (*coll.*) der Totalverlust; abgeschmiertes Flugzeug; nicht wieder instandzusetzendes Auto; (nicht wiedergutzumachender) Fehlschlag; (*of a p.*) hoffnungsloser Fall.

writer ['raitə], *s.* der (die) Schreiber(in) (*of a letter*); Schriftsteller(in), Verfasser(in), Autor(in); –***'s cramp,*** der Schreibkrampf; (*Scots*) – ***to the signet,*** der Rechtsanwalt.

write-up, *s.* (*coll.*) (*usu.* anerkennende) Notiz *or* Kritik *or* Besprechung *or* Rezension, (überschwenglicher) Pressebericht, schriftliche Anpreisung.

writhe [raið], *v.i.* sich winden *or* krümmen (***with,*** vor (*Dat.*)); (*fig.*) ***under,*** unter (*Dat.*)).

writing [raitiŋ], **1.** *adj.* schreibend, schriftstellernd, Schriftsteller–. **2.** *s.* **1.** das Schreiben; Schriftstellern, die Schriftstellerei; 2. schriftliche Ausfertigung *or* Abfassung; ***in*** –, schriftlich; ***be in*** –, schriftlich abgefaßt *or* niedergelegt *or* aufgezeichnet sein; ***take down*** or ***put in(to)*** –, schriftlich aufsetzen *or* niederlegen, niederschreiben, aufschreiben; 3. das Schriftstück, Dokument, die Urkunde, Schrift; literarisches Werk, das Schrifttum; Geschriebenes, die Inschrift; der Stil, die Schreibart, Schreibweise; Handschrift; (*fig.*) – ***on the wall,*** der Warnungsruf, das Menetekel.

writing|-book, *s.* das Schreibheft. **--case,** *s.* die Schreibmappe. **--desk,** *s.* das Schreibpult. **--pad,** *s.* **1.** die Schreibunterlage; 2. der Schreibblock. **--paper,** *s.* das Schreibpapier. **--table,** *s.* der Schreibtisch.

written [ritn], **1.** *p.p. of* **write**; ***it is*** –, es steht geschrieben. **2.** *adj.* schriftlich, beschrieben; – ***document,*** das Schriftstück; – ***evidence,*** der Urkundenbeweis; – ***examination,*** schriftliche Prüfung; – ***language,*** die Schriftsprache; – ***law,*** geschriebenes Recht; – ***record,*** die Niederschrift.

wrong [rɔŋ], **1.** *adj.* **1.** unrichtig, irrig; nicht in Ordnung, in Unordnung; unrecht, unbillig; ***be*** –, nicht in Ordnung sein, nicht stimmen (*of a th.*), unrecht haben, sich irren (*of a p.*); ***the clock is*** –, die Uhr geht falsch; ***what is – with?*** was ist los mit? (*a th.*), was fehlt (*Dat.*)? (*a p.*); ***that was – of you,*** das war unrecht von Ihnen; 2. verkehrt, falsch; (*coll.*) ***get hold of the – end of the stick,*** es falsch auffassen *or* völlig mißverstehen; ***hit upon the – person,*** an den Unrechten kommen; ***– side,*** verkehrte Seite (*of the street etc.*), linke Seite (*of cloth*); ***on the – side of 30,*** über 30 Jahre alt; ***– side out,*** das Innere nach außen, verkehrt herum; (*coll.*) ***get out of bed (on) the – side,*** mit dem linken Fuß (*or* Bein) zuerst *or* mit dem falschen Bein aufstehen; (*coll.*) ***on the – side of the blanket,*** außerehelich; ***he will laugh on the – side of his face,*** ihm wird das Lachen noch vergehen; (*coll.*) ***on the – tack,*** auf dem Holzwege; ***he took it the – way,*** er hat es übelgenommen *or* in die falsche Kehle bekommen, es ist ihm in die falsche *or* unrechte Kehle gekommen; ***that mouthful went down the – way,*** ich habe den Bissen verschluckt *or* mich an dem Bissen verschluckt. **2.** *adv.* unrecht, unrichtig, falsch; ***get it –,*** es falsch anrechnen (*a sum*), (*fig. coll.*) es völlig mißverstehen *or* ganz falsch verstehen, sich irren; ***go –,*** nicht richtig funktionieren (*of a th.*), vom rechten Wege abkommen, auf die schiefe Bahn *or* auf Abwege geraten (*usu. of woman*), fehlgehen, (sich) irren (*of a p.*); (*sl.*) ***get in – with him,*** es mit ihm verderben. **3.** *v.t.* 1. Unrecht *or* Schaden tun (*Dat.*), Schaden zufügen (*Dat.*), schaden (*Dat.*); 2. ungerecht behandeln, ungerecht sein gegen, benachteiligen; ***I have been –ed,*** mir ist Unrecht geschehen; 3. eine falsche Meinung haben von. **4.** *s.* 1. das Unrecht, die Ungerechtigkeit, Unbill; ***be in the –,*** im Unrecht *or* Irrtum sein, unrecht haben; ***do –,*** Unrecht tun, ein Unrecht begehen, sündigen; ***do him a –,*** ihm ein Unrecht zufügen; (*coll.*) ***get him in the –,*** ihn in Mißkredit bringen (***with,*** bei); ***put o.s. in the –,*** sich ins Unrecht setzen; 2. (*rare*) die Kränkung, Beleidigung, der Schaden; 3. (*Law*) die Rechtsverletzung, das Delikt, Vergehen, unerlaubte Handlung.

wrong|doer, *s.* der Missetäter, Übeltäter, Sünder. **–doing,** *s.* die Sünde, Missetat; das Vergehen, Verbrechen.

wrongful ['rɔŋful], *adj.* 1. ungerecht, unbillig; 2. unrechtmäßig, widerrechtlich, ungesetzlich; 3. beleidigend, kränkend. **wrongfully,** *adv.* 1. ungerechterweise, irrtümlicherweise; 2. widerrechtlich. **wrongfulness,** *s.* 1. die Unrichtigkeit; 2. Ungerechtigkeit; 3. Unrechtmäßigkeit, Ungesetzlichkeit.

wrong|-headed, *adj.* querköpfig, starrköpfig, verbohrt (*a p.*), verkehrt, verdreht, verschroben (*ideas*). **--headedness,** *s.* die Querköpfigkeit, Starrköpfigkeit, Verbohrtheit.

wrongly ['rɔŋli], *adv.* 1. irrtümlich(erweise), fälschlicherweise; verkehrt, unrichtig, falsch; 2. mit Unrecht, ungerecht(erweise); ungehörig, ungeziemend; ***rightly or –,*** mit Recht oder Unrecht. **wrongness,** *s.* 1. die Unrichtigkeit, Verkehrtheit, Fehlerhaftigkeit; 2. Unrechtmäßigkeit, Ungesetzlichkeit; 3. der Irrtum, das Unrecht.

wrote [rout], *imperf. of* **write.**

wroth [rɔ(:)θ], *pred. adj.* (*Poet.*) ergrimmt, erzürnt, zornig (***with,*** auf (*Acc.*)).

wrought [rɔ:t], (*obs.*) *imperf., p.p. of* **work**; (*still used in*) 1. *imperf.* brachte hervor, bewirkte (*change etc.*); 2. *p.p. as adj.* hervorgebracht, bewirkt; (*esp. Tech.*) bearbeitet, gearbeitet, verarbeitet; gehämmert, geschmiedet (*metal*); ***– into shape,*** geformt; ***– iron,*** das Schmiedeeisen. **wrought|-iron,** *adj.* schmiedeeisern, Schmiedeeisen–. **--up,** *adj.* erregt, aufgeregt, aufgebracht, erhitzt.

wrung [rʌŋ], *imperf., p.p. of* **wring.**

wry [rai], *adj.* schief, krumm, verdreht, verzerrt; ***make*** or ***pull a – face,*** eine Grimasse schneiden, ein schiefes Gesicht ziehen *or* machen. **wry|-mouthed,** *adj.* schiefmäulig. **–neck,** *s.* (*Orn.*) der Wendehals (*Jynx torquilla*).

wych|-elm ['witʃ–], *s.* die Bergrüster, Bergulme. **--hazel,** *s.* virginischer Zauberstrauch.

wyvern, *see* **wivern.**

X

X, x [eks], *s.* das X, x; (*Math.*) (erste) unbekannte Größe. *See Index of Abbreviations.*

X|-certificate, *s.* (*Films*) für Jugendliche verboten! **--chromosome,** *s.* (*Biol.*) das X-Chromosom.

xebec ['zi:bek], *s.* (*Naut.*) die Schebecke.

xenium ['zi:niəm], *s.* (*pl.* **xenia**) (*Hist.*) das Gastgeschenk.

xenogamous [ze'nɔgəməs], *adj.* (*Bot.*) xenogam. **xenogamy,** *s.* die Xenogamie, Fremdbestäubung.

xenophobia [zeno'foubiə], *s.* der Haß gegen Fremde, die Fremdenfeindlichkeit.

xeransis [ziə'rænsis], *s.* die Austrocknung. **xerasia** [–'reiziə], *s.* die Trockenheit des Haares. **xerophagy** [–'rɔfəgi], *s.* (*Eccl.*) trockene Kost. **xerophilous** [–'rɔfiləs], *adj.* (*Bot.*) xerophil; ***– plant,*** *see* **xerophyte. xerophyte** ['ziərofait], *s.* die Xerophyt, Trockenheitspflanze. **xerosis** [ziə'rousis], *s.* (*Med.*) krankhafte Trockenheit.

xiphoid ['zifɔid], *adj.* (*Anat.*) schwertförmig, Schwert–; ***– cartilage*** or ***process,*** der Schwertfortsatz (*of breastbone*).

Xmas ['eksməs], *s.* (*coll.*) *abbr. of* **Christmas.**

X-ray ['eksrei], **1.** *s.* 1. (*usu. pl.*) der Röntgenstrahl, X-strahl; 2. (*coll.*) die Röntgenaufnahme, das Röntgenbild. **2.** *v.t.* röntgen; ein Röntgenbild machen von; (*Med.*) bestrahlen, mit Röntgenstrahlen behandeln; durchleuchten. **3.** *adj.* Röntgen–; ***– examination,*** die Röntgenuntersuchung; ***– photograph,*** das Röntgenbild, die Röntgenaufnahme; ***– therapy,*** die Strahlenbehandlung, Röntgentherapie; ***– tube,*** die Röntgenröhre.

xylene ['zaili:n], *s.* (*Chem.*) das Xylol.

xylograph ['zailəgra:f], *s.* der Holzschnitt. **xylographer** [–'lɔgrəfə], *s.* der Xylograph, Holzschneider. **xylographic** [–lə'græfik], *adj.* xylographisch, Holzschneide–. **xylography** [–'lɔgrəfi], *s.* die Holzschneidekunst.

xylol ['zailɔl], *s. See* **xylene.**

xylophone ['zailəfoun], *s.* das Xylophon.

xylose ['zailous], *s.* der Holzzucker.

xyster ['zistə], *s.* (*Med.*) das Schabemesser, der Knochenschaber.

xystus ['zistəs], *s.* (*pl.* **xysti** [–tai]) (*Hist.*) gedeckter Säulengang.

Y

Y, y [wai], **1.** *s.* das Y, y; (*Math.*) (zweite) unbekannte Größe. **2.** *attrib. adj.* Gabel–, gabelförmig; ***Y-level,*** die Wasserwaage, Libelle. *See Index of Abbreviations.*

y– [i], *pref.* (*obs.*) ge–, *see* **yclept.**

yacht [jɔt], **1.** *s.* die Jacht, das Segelboot; ***– club,*** der Jachtklub. **2.** *v.i.* segeln. **yachting,** *s.* der Segelsport, das Segeln. **yacht-racing,** *s.* das Wettsegeln. **yachtsman** [–smən], *s.* der Segler, Segelsportler. **yachtsmanship,** *s.* die Segelkunst.

yahoo [jə'hu:], *s.* der Rohling, Bestie, brutaler Mensch.

yak [jæk], *s.* der Jak, Grunzochs.

Yale lock ['jeil'lɔk], *s.* das Patentschloß.

yam [jæm], *s.* die Jam(s)wurzel.

yammer ['jæmə], *v.i.* (*Scots*) jammern.
Yangtze ['jæŋtsi], *s.* der Jangtse(kiang).
yank [jæŋk], **1.** *v.t.* (*coll.*) reißen, heftig ziehen. **2.** *v.i.* heftig ziehen (*at*, an (*Dat.*)). **3.** *s.* der Ruck.
Yank, (*sl.*) *abbr. of* **Yankee,** *s.* (*sl.*) der (die) (Nord)amerikaner(in); (*Am.*) Nordstaatler(in), Neuengländer(in).
yap [jæp], **1.** *v.i.* 1. kläffen; 2. (*sl.*) schwätzen, schwatzen. **2.** *s.* das Kläffen, Gekläff.
[1]**yard** [jɑ:d], *s.* 1. das Yard (= 0.914 Meter), die Elle; 2. (*Naut.*) die Rah(e).
[2]**yard,** *s.* der Hof; eingefriedeter Platz; (*oft. in compounds*) *e.g. brick–,* die Ziegelei; *court–,* der Hof(raum); *dock–,* die (Marine)werft; *farm–,* der Viehhof, Wirtschaftshof; *poultry––,* das Geflügelgehege; *railway––,* der Verschiebebahnhof, Rangierbahnhof; *school––,* der Schulhof, das Schulgelände; *ship–,* die (Schiffs)werft.
yardage ['jɑ:didʒ], *s.* die Länge in Yards (*esp. of fabric*).
yard|-arm, *s.* (*Naut.*) die *or* das Rahnock. **–man** [–mən], *s.* 1. der Viehhofarbeiter, Stallarbeiter; 2. Werftarbeiter; 3. Rangierbahnhofsarbeiter. **–master,** *s.* der Rangiermeister.
yarn [jɑ:n], **1.** *s.* 1. das Garn; 2. (*coll.*) Seemannsgarn, die Geschichte; *spin a –,* eine Geschichte erzählen, Seemannsgarn spinnen. **2.** *v.i.* (*fig.*) Garn spinnen, Geschichten erzählen.
yarrow ['jærou], *s.* (*Bot.*) die Schafgarbe.
yashmak ['jæʃmæk], *s.* (mohammedanischer) Gesichtsschleier.
yataghan ['jætəgæn], *s.* der Yatagan, Jatagan, (türkisches) Krummschwert.
yaw [jɔ:], **1.** *v.i.* (*Naut.*) gieren; (*Av.*) scheren; (*fig.*) schwanken, abweichen. **2.** *s.* (*Naut.*) das Gieren, die Gierung; (*Av.*) das Scheren, die Scherung.
yawl [jɔ:l], *s.* (*Naut.*) die Yawl, der Ewer.
yawn [jɔ:n], **1.** *s.* das Gähnen; *give a –,* gähnen. **2.** *v.i.* 1. gähnen; 2. gähnen, klaffen, sich weit auftun *or* öffnen, weit offen stehen. **yawning, 1.** *adj.* gähnend (*also fig.*). **2.** *s.* das Gähnen.
yaws [jɔ:z], *pl.* (*sing. constr.*) (*Med.*) die Himbeerseuche, Frambösie.
yclept [i'klept], (*obs.*) *s.* genannt.
Y-connection, *s.* (*Elec.*) die Dreieckschaltung.
[1]**ye** [ði:], *def. art.* (*pseudo-archaic*) der, die, das.
[2]**ye** [ji:], *pers. pron.* (*obs. or B.*) Ihr, Sie; (*coll.*) *how d'ye do?* wie geht's dir? (*coll. iron.*) (*nice*) *how-d'ye-do,* schöne *or* nette Bescherung.
yea [jei], **1.** *adj.* (*obs.*) ja; gewiß, fürwahr, wahrhaftig. **2.** *s.* das Ja; *pl.* (*Parl.*) die Ja-Stimmen; *the –s and nays,* die Stimmen für und wider.
yean [ji:n], **1.** *v.i.* lammen, werfen (*of sheep*). **2.** *v.t.* werfen (*a lamb*). **yeanling,** *s.* das Lämmchen.
year [jiə], *s.* das Jahr; *for a – and a day,* auf Jahr und Tag; *£500 a –,* £500 jährlich *or* das Jahr; *– after –,* Jahr für Jahr; *a – ago,* vor einem Jahr; *–s before,* vor Jahren; *– by –,* Jahr für Jahr; *every –,* jedes Jahr, jährlich; *every other –,* alle zwei Jahre, ein Jahr ums andre; *for –s,* jahrelang, seit Jahren; *for –s (to come),* auf Jahre hinaus; *from – to –,* Jahr für Jahr; *– in – out,* jahrein jahraus; *in a –'s time,* innerhalb *or* binnen Jahresfrist, in einem Jahr; (*coll.*) *in –s,* see *for –s*; *of late –s,* in den letzten Jahren; *many –s' experience,* langjährige Erfahrung; *New Year,* das Neujahr, neues Jahr; *New Year's Eve,* der *or* das Silvester, der Silvesterabend, die Silvesternacht; *best wishes for the New Year,* fröhliche Wünsche zum Jahreswechsel; *the – of grace* or *of our Lord,* das Jahr des Heils; *three-–-old child,* drei Jahre altes Kind; *once a –,* einmal im Jahr; *of recent –s,* see *of late –s*; *at this time of –,* zu dieser Jahreszeit; *this –'s,* diesjährig; *a – or two,* einige Jahre; *the – under review,* das Berichtsjahr; 2. *pl.* das Alter; (*coll.*) *for donkey's –s,* lange Zeit, eine Ewigkeit; *for his –s,* für sein Alter; *well on in –s,* hochbetagt; *–s of discretion,* gesetztes *or* mündiges Alter. **yearbook,** *s.* das Jahrbuch.
yearling ['jiəliŋ], *s.* der Jährling, einjähriges Tier *– heifer,* einjährige Färse. **yearlong** [–'lɔŋ], *adj.* jahrelang. **yearly, 1.** *adj.* jährlich, Jahres–. **2.** *adv.* jährlich, jedes Jahr *or* alle Jahre (einmal).
yearn [jə:n], *v.i.* 1. sich sehnen, schmachten, verlangen (*for, after,* nach); 2. (*obs.*) sich hingezogen fühlen (*to(wards),* zu), Mitleid empfinden (für *or* mit). **yearning, 1.** *adj.* schmachtend, sehnend, verlangend, sehnsüchtig. **2.** *s.* das Verlangen, die Sehnsucht (*for, after,* nach).
yeast [ji:st], *s.* 1. die Hefe, Bärme; 2. (*fig.*) der Sauerteig. **yeast-powder,** *s.* das Backpulver. **yeasty,** *adj.* 1. heftig; 2. (*fig.*) gärend, schäumend, gischtig; gehaltlos, nichtig.
yell [jel], **1.** *s.* der Aufschrei, gellender Schrei. **2.** *v.i.* 1. gellend *or* laut (auf)schreien (*with,* vor (*Dat.*)); 2. (*coll.*) weinen, heulen. **3.** *v.t.* schreien, gellend hervorstoßen *or* ausstoßen.
yellow ['jelou], **1.** *adj.* 1. gelb; *– peril,* die gelbe Gefahr; *– race,* gelbe Rasse; *Yellow Sea,* Gelbes Meer; 2. (*sl.*) feige; *– streak,* die Neigung zur Feigheit, feiger Zug; 3. (*coll.*) *– press,* die Sensationspresse, Asphaltpresse, Hetzpresse, gelbe Presse. **2.** *s.* 1. das Gelb; gelbe Farbe; gelber Farbstoff; 2. das Eigelb, der *or* das (Ei)dotter. **3.** *v.i.* gelb werden. **4.** *v.t.* gelb färben.
yellow|back, *s.* der Schundroman, Hintertreppenroman, Schmöker. **––earth,** *s. See* **––ochre. ––fever,** *s.* gelbes Fieber, das Gelbfieber. **–hammer,** *s.* (*Orn.*) die Goldammer (*Emberiza citrinella*).
yellowing ['jelouiŋ], *s.* das Gelbwerden. **yellowish,** *adj.* gelblich.
yellow| Jack, *s. See* **––fever.**
yellowness ['jelounis], *s.* gelbe Farbe.
yellow-ochre, *s.* die Gelberde, gelber Ocker.
yelp [jelp], **1.** *v.i.* kläffen (*of dogs*), (*coll.*) schreien. **2.** *s.* das Gekläff, (*coll.*) der Schrei.
Yemen ['jemən], *s.* der Jemen. **Yemeni** [–i], **1.** *s.* der Jemenit(e) (die Jemenitin). **2.** *adj.* jemenitisch.
[1]**yen** [jen], *s.* der Yen, Jen.
[2]**yen, 1.** *s.* (*sl.*) *see* **yearning. 2.** *v.i.* (*sl.*) *see* **yearn.**
yeoman ['joumən], *s.* (*pl.* **–men**) 1. (*Hist.*) der Freibauer, Freisasse; 2. (*Mil.*) berittener Freiwilliger; *– of the guard,* der Leibgardist. **yeomanly,** *adj.* (*fig.*) schlicht, treu, zuverlässig. **yeomanry,** *s.* Freisassen (*pl.*); (*Mil.*) berittene Miliz. **yeoman('s) service,** *s.* (*fig.*) großer Dienst, kräftige Hilfe.
yes [jes], *adv.* ja (*agreement*), jawohl, ja gewiß (*affirmation*), ja doch (*contradiction*); *say – to,* bejahen, sein Jawort geben (*Dat.*). **yes-man,** *s.* (*coll.*) der Jasager.
yester- [jestə], *pref.* (*Poet.*) gestrig, vergangen, letzt. **yester|day, 1.** *s.* gestriger Tag, (*fig.*) das Gestern; *pl.* vergangene Zeiten *or* Tage (*pl.*); *–'s,* gestrig; *the day before –,* vorgestern. **2.** *adv.* gestern; (*coll.*) *I was not born –,* ich bin nicht von gestern. **–eve,** *s.* (*Poet.*) gestriger Abend, gestern abend. **–year,** *s.* (*Poet.*) letztes *or* voriges *or* vergangenes Jahr.
yet [jet], **1.** *adv.* 1. (*with reference to pres. time*) noch immer, (immer) noch; *never –,* noch nie; *not –* (*coll. not – awhile*), noch nicht; *nothing –,* noch nichts; 2. (*in questions*) schon (jetzt), bis jetzt; *as –,* bis jetzt, bisher; *is he here –?* ist er schon hier? 3. (*with reference to future time*) (doch) noch, (der)einst, am Ende; *he'll do it –,* er wird es doch noch tun; 4. (*additional, with reference to past time*) (immer) noch, außerdem, (noch) dazu; *– again,* nochmals; *another and – another,* noch einer und noch einer dazu; *more and (ever) – more,* mehr und immer noch mehr; 5. (*before comp.*) noch, sogar noch; *– more important,* sogar noch wichtiger; 6. (*antithesis*) jedoch, trotzdem, dennoch, aber; *but – he stays,* trotzdem bleibt er; *strange (and* or *but) – true,* seltsam aber wahr *or* und dennoch wahr. **2.** *conj.* (je)doch, dennoch, gleichwohl, nichtsdestoweniger.
yeti ['jeti], *s.* der Schneemensch.
yew [ju:], *s.* 1. (*also –tree*) die Eibe, der Eibenbaum; 2. das Eibenholz.

Yid [jid], *s.* (*pej.*) der Itzig. **Yiddish, 1.** *s.* das Jiddisch, Judendeutsch. **2.** *adj.* 1. (*language*) jiddisch; 2. (*pej.*) jüdisch.

yield [ji:ld], **1.** *v.t.* 1. einbringen, eintragen, abwerfen (*profit*) (*to, Dat.*); hervorbringen, als Ertrag geben, ergeben, liefern (*result*); (*Comm.*) bringen, tragen, abwerfen (*interest*); 2. (*fig.*) zugestehen, gewähren, einräumen (*to, Dat.*); (*also* – *up*) hingeben, hergeben, aufgeben, übergeben, überlassen, abtreten, ausliefern; – ***up the ghost,*** den Geist aufgeben; – ***o.s. to,*** sich überlassen (*Dat.*); – ***the palm to,*** die Siegespalme zugestehen (*Dat.*); – ***place to,*** Platz machen (*Dat.*); – ***the point,*** sich in der Einzelheit geschlagen geben; – ***precedence to,*** den Vorrang einräumen (*Dat.*). **2.** *v.i.* 1. Ertrag geben *or* liefern (*as crops*); 2. (*of a p.*) sich ergeben *or* unterwerfen *or* fügen (*to, Dat.*), einwilligen (in (*Acc.*)); klein beigeben, den Widerstand aufgeben; nachgeben, weichen (***before,*** vor (*Dat.*)), erliegen, unterliegen, sich hingeben (*to, Dat.*); ***he –s to none in determination,*** an Entschlossenheit steht er keinem nach; – ***to despair,*** sich der Verzweiflung hingeben; 3. (*of a th.*) nachgeben, sinken, zusammenbrechen, sich lockern; 4. – ***to,*** beeinflußt werden durch, reagieren *or* eingehen auf (*Acc.*), Rechnung tragen (*Dat.*). **3.** *s.* der Ertrag; die Ernte; Ausbeute, der Gewinn; Zinsertrag (*of capital*); Metallgehalt (*of ore*). **yielding,** *adj.* 1. willfährig, nachgiebig (*of a p.*); 2. nachgebend, biegsam, dehnbar (*of a th.*).

yob [jɔb], *s.* (*sl.*) der Lümmel, Flegel.

yodel [joudl], **1.** *v.i., v.t.* jodeln. **2.** *s.* der Jodelruf. **yodeller,** *s.* Jodler.

yoga ['jougə], *s.* der Joga. **yogi** [–i], *s.* (*pl.* **-s**) der Jogi.

yo-(heave-)ho! ['jou(hi:v)'hou], *int.* (*Naut.*) hauruck!

yoicks! [jɔiks], *int.* (*Hunt.*) hussa! hallo!

yoke [jouk], **1.** *s.* 1. das Joch (*of oxen, also fig.*); 2. die (Schulter)trage, das Tragholz (*for buckets*), Ruderjoch, der Kreuzkopf (*of a boat*), Sattel (*on a skirt*), die Passe (*on a bodice*), das Schulterstück (*on a shirt*); 3. (*fig.*) die Unterwerfung, Knechtschaft. **2.** *v.t.* 1. ins Joch spannen, anjochen, anschirren, anspannen (*oxen*); (*fig.*) paaren, verbinden (***to, with,*** mit); 2. (*fig.*) unterwerfen, unterjochen (***to,*** *Dat.*).

yoke|-bone, *s.* das Jochbein. **--fellow,** *s.* der Arbeitsgenosse, Mitarbeiter, Kollege; der (die) (Lebens)gefährte; Leidensgefährte (–gefährtin).

yokel [joukl], *s.* der Bauer(nlümmel), Bauerntölpel.

yoke|-lines, *s.* (*Naut.*) das Steuerreep, die Jochleine. **-mate,** *s. See* **--fellow.**

Yokohama [joukə'ha:mə], *s.* Jokohama (*n.*).

yolk [jouk], *s.* das *or* der (Ei)dotter, das Eigelb. **yolk-sac,** *s.* die Dotterhaut, der Dottersack.

yon [jɔn], *dem. adj.* (*Poet.*) jene(r, –s) *or* der *or* die *or* das dort (drüben). **yonder, 1.** *dem. adj. See* **yon. 2.** *adv.* da *or* dort drüben.

yore [jɔ:], *adv.* (*only in*) ***of –,*** ehemals, ehedem, vormals; ***in days of –,*** einst, vor alters.

you [ju:, ju *according to emphasis*], *pers. pron.* (*Nom.*) du, ihr, Sie; (*Acc.*) dich, euch, Sie; (*Dat.*) (*also* ***to*** –) dir, euch, Ihnen; (*impers.*) (*Nom.*) man, (*Acc.*) einen, (*Dat.*) (*also* ***to*** –) einem; (*refl. object, rare except after prep.*) dich, dir, euch, Sich; ***is it –?*** bist du es? ***shut the door behind –!*** mach die Tür hinter dir zu! ***get – gone!*** sieh daß du fortkommst! **you'd,** (*coll.*) = ***you had*** or ***would.*** **you'll,** (*coll.*) = ***you shall*** or ***will.***

young [jʌŋ], **1.** *adj.* jung; Jung–, Jugend–, jugendlich; unentwickelt; unreif, unerfahren, neu; – ***animal,*** das Jungtier; (*fig.*) – ***blood,*** junges Blut, die Jugendkraft, jugendliche Frische; (*collect.*) die Jugend, junge Leute *or* Menschen; – ***children,*** kleine Kinder; ***in my – days,*** in meiner Jugend; ***have a – family,*** eine Familie mit kleinen Kindern haben; – ***hopeful,*** hoffnungsvoller Sprößling; – ***in years,*** jung an Jahren; (*coll.*) ***his – lady,*** sein Schatz, seine Freundin; – ***love,*** junge Liebe; ***her – man,*** ihr Schatz *or* Freund; (*coll.*) – ***man in a hurry,*** junger Draufgänger; ***Young Men's*** (or ***Women's***) ***Christian Association,*** Christlicher Verein Junger Männer (*or* Mädchen); ***a – one,*** ein Junger (eine Junge), (*animal*) ein Junges; ***the – ones,*** die Jungen; – ***and old,*** Alt und Jung; – ***people,*** junge Leute, die Jugend; (*Law*) – ***person,*** Jugendliche(r); – ***shoot,*** der Schößling; (*coll.*) ***have an old head on – shoulders,*** altklug sein; ***the day is still –,*** der Tag hat eben begonnen. **2.** *s.* Junge(n) (*pl.*) (*of animals*); ***with –,*** trächtig.

younger ['jʌŋə], *comp. adj.* jünger, neuer, weniger fortgeschritten; – ***hand,*** die Hinterhand (*cards*). **youngest,** *sup. adj.* jüngste(r, –s). **youngish,** *adj.* etwas *or* ziemlich jung. **youngster,** *s.* der Jüngling, Bursche, Knabe, Junge; *pl.* (*coll.*) Kinder (*pl.*).

your [juə, jɔ:, jə:, jə *according to emphasis*], *poss. adj.* Ihr, dein, euer.

you're [juə], (*coll.*) = ***you are.***

yours [juez, jɔ:z (*according to emphasis*)], *poss. pron.* 1. der *or* die *or* das Ihrige, deinige *or* eurige, deine, eure *or* Ihre; ***a friend of –,*** ein Freund von dir, einer deiner Freunde; ***give me –,*** gib mir das deine; ***to you and –s,*** an die Deinen, an deine Angehörigen; ***this is –,*** dies gehört Ihnen; (*coll.*) – ***truly,*** meine Wenigkeit; (*in letters*) – ***faithfully,*** Ihr sehr ergebener; – ***obediently*** or ***respectfully*** or ***truly,*** hochachtungsvoll, mit vorzüglicher Hochachtung; – ***sincerely,*** mit freundlichen Grüssen; 2. (*Comm.*) Ihr Schreiben.

yourself [jɔ:'self], *pron.* (*pl.* **-selves** [–'selvz]) 1. (*emph.*) Sie, du, ihr *etc.* selbst; (*coll.*) ***you are not –,*** Sie sind nicht auf der Höhe; ***by –,*** allein, einsam; allein, selber, selbst(ändig), ohne Hilfe; ***are you by –?*** sind Sie allein? ***do it –!*** mach es selber! ***do it by –!*** tu es ohne Hilfe! ***you always sit by –,*** du sitzt immer allein; ***you are always sitting by –,*** du sitzt immer so einsam; ***get one for –,*** verschaff' dir eins! ***what will you do with –?*** was fangen Sie an? (*coll.*) ***can't you read to –?*** kannst du nicht für dich lesen? 2. (*reflexive object of* **you**) dich, euch, Sich; ***you must wash –,*** du mußt dich waschen; ***pull – together!*** nimm dich zusammen!

youth [ju:θ], *s.* 1. die Jugend; das Jungsein, die Jugendlichkeit, jugendliche Frische; die Jugendzeit; (*fig.*) das Frühstadium, Anfangsstadium, die Frühzeit, Jugendperiode; (*collect.*) junge Leute *or* Menschen, die Jugend; ***in –,*** in der Jugend; 2. (*pl.* **-s** [–ðz]) der Jüngling, junger Mann. **youthful,** *adj.* jung, jugendlich, Jugend–; jugendfrisch; – ***indiscretion,*** die Jugendtorheit. **youthfulness,** *s.* die Jugend(lichkeit), Jugendfrische.

youth| hostel, *s.* die Jugendherberge; ***go youth-hostelling,*** in Jugendherbergen unterkommen. – **hosteller,** *s.* der Jugendherbergsbenutzer. – **movement,** *s.* die Jugendbewegung.

you've [ju:v], (*coll.*) = ***you have.***

yo-yo ['joujou], *s.* das Jo-Jo.

ytterbia [i'tə:biə], *s.* das Ytterbiumoxyd, die Ytterbinerde. **ytterbium,** *s.* (*Chem.*) das Ytterbium.

Yugoslav ['ju:gosla:v], **1.** *s.* der Jugoslawe (die Jugoslawin). **2.** *adj.* jugoslawisch. **Yugoslavia** [–'sla:viə], *s.* Jugoslawien, Südslawien (*n.*).

yttria ['itriə], das Yttriumoxyd, die Yttererde. **yttric,** *adj.* ytterhaltig, Yttrium–. **yttrium,** *s.* (*Chem.*) das Yttrium.

Yule [ju:l], *s.* das Julfest, Weihnachtsfest. **Yule|-log,** *s.* der Weihnachtsklotz, das Weihnachtsscheit. **-tide,** *s.* die Weihnacht(szeit), das Weihnachten.

Z

Z, z [zɛd (*Am.* zi:)], *s.* das Z, z; (*Math.*) dritte unbekannte Größe.

Zagreb ['zɑ:greb], *s.* Agram (*n.*).

Zambesi [zæm'bi:zi], *s.* der Sambesi.

zany ['zeini], **1.** *s.* (*Hist.*) der Hanswurst; (*fig.*) Possenreißer, Trottel. **2.** *adj.* närrisch.

Zanzibar ['zænzibɑ:], *s.* Sansibar (*n.*).

zare(e)ba, zariba [zæ'ri:bə], *s.* befestigtes Lager, die Einzäunung (*Sudan*).

zeal [zi:l], *s.* der (Dienst)eifer; ***full of* –**, (dienst)eifrig; **– *for truth,*** die Begeisterung für die Wahrheit.

zealot ['zelət], *s.* der (Glaubens)eiferer, Zelot; der (die) Fanatiker(in). **zealotry,** *s.* blinder (Glaubens)eifer.

zealous ['zeləs], *adj.* 1. eifrig (***for***, nach), eifernd, eifrig bedacht (auf (*Acc.*)); 2. diensteifrig, begeistert, innig. **zealousness,** *s.* der Eifer, die Begeisterung, Hitze.

zebra ['zi:brə, 'zebrə], *s.* das Zebra; **– *crossing,*** der Zebrastreifen, Fußgängerübergang.

zebu ['zi:bu:], *s.* indischer Buckelochse.

zedoary ['zedouəri], *s.* (*Bot.*) die Zitwerwurzel.

Zealand ['zi:lənd], *s.* Seeland (*n.*).

zenana [zə'nɑ:nə], *s.* das Frauengemach.

zenith ['zeniθ], *s.* (*Astr.*) der Zenit, Scheitelpunkt; (*fig.*) der Höhepunkt, Gipfelpunkt; **– *distance,*** der Zenitabstand.

zephyr ['zefə], *s.* 1. der Westwind; sanfter Wind; 2. (*Text.*) der Zephir, Zephyr (*cloth*), das Zephirgarn (*yarn*).

zeppelin ['zepəlin], *s.* der Zeppelin.

zero ['ziərou], *s.* (*pl.* **-s**) die Null (*also fig.*), das Nichts; der Nullpunkt, Ausgangspunkt (*of a scale*), *esp.* Gefrierpunkt (*thermometer*); (*fig.*) Tiefpunkt, Tiefstand; ***at* –**, auf Null; (*Av. sl.*) unter 1000 Fuß; ***below* –**, unter Null; (*Meteor.*) **– *cloud,*** Wolken unter 50 Fuß hoch; (*Math.*) ***equate to* –**, gleich Null setzen; **– *hour,*** (*Mil.*) Stunde Null; (*fig.*) entscheidender *or* genau festgesetzter Zeitpunkt; **– *visibility,*** sehr begrenzte Sicht (= weniger als 50 m.).

zest [zest], *s.* die Würze, würzender Zusatz; (*usu. fig.*) die Begeisterung (***for***, für), Lust, Freude, der Genuß, Gefallen, Geschmack, das Behagen (an (*Dat.*)); **– *for life*** or ***living,*** die Lebensfreude, der Lebensgenuß; ***give a*** or ***add* – *to,*** Reiz *or* Würze verleihen (*Dat.*), schmackhaft machen; ***with* –** mit Wohlbehagen, voller Freude.

zeugma ['zju:gmə], *s.* (*Gram.*) das Zeugma.

zigzag ['zigzæg], **1.** *s.* der Zickzack; Zickzackkurs, die Zickzacklinie, Zickzackbewegung. **2.** *adj.* zickzackförmig, zickzacklaufend, Zickzack–. **3.** *adv.* im Zickzack. **4.** *v.i.* (im) Zickzack (ver)laufen, Zickzackkurs fahren.

zinc [ziŋk], **1.** *s.* das Zink; **– *bloom,*** die Zinkblüte; **– *ointment,*** die Zinksalbe; **– *white,*** das Zinkoxyd, Zinkweiß. **2.** *v.t.* (*imperf., p.p.* ***zinced*** or ***zin(c)ked***; *pres. part.* ***zincing*** or ***zin(c)king***) zinken. **zinciferous, zinkiferous** [–'kifərəs], *adj.* zinkhaltig. **zincification, zin(c)kification** [–ifi'keiʃən], *s.* die Verzinkung. **zincograph** [–əgrɑ:f], *s.* die Zinkogravüre, Zinkätzung, der Zinkdruck. **zincography** [–'kɔgrəfi], *s.* die Zinkographie.

zinnia ['ziniə], *s.* (*Bot.*) die Zinnie.

Zion ['zaiən], *s.* (*B.*) der Zion, Sion. **Zionism,** *s.* der Zionismus. **Zionist, 1.** *s.* der (die) Zionist(in). **2.** *adj.* zionistisch, Zionisten–.

[1]**zip** [zip], **1.** *s.* 1. das Surren, Schwirren; 2. (*fig. coll.*) der Schneid, Schmiß, Schwung; 3. (*coll.*) *see* **zip-fastener. 2.** *v.i.* 1. surren, schwirren; 2. (*coll.*) Schneid *or* Schmiß *or* Schwung zeigen. **3.** *v.t.* (*usu.* **– *up***) (*coll.*) den Reißverschluß zumachen. **zip-fastener,** *s.* der Reißverschluß. **zipper,** *s.* (*coll. esp. Am.*) *see* **zip-fastener.**

[2]**zip,** *adj.* (*Am.*) die Postleitzahl.

zircon [zə:kn], *s.* (*Chem.*) der Zirkon. **zirconium** [–'kouniəm], *s.* das Zirkonium.

zither ['ziθə], *s.* die Zither.

zodiac ['zoudiæk], *s.* der Tierkreis, Zodiakus; ***signs of the* –**, die Tierkreiszeichen (*pl.*). **zodiacal** [zo'daiəkl], *adj.* Tierkreis–, Zodiakal–.

zombie ['zɔmbi], *s.* (*sl.*) wandelnde Leiche, der Trottel.

zonal ['zounl], *adj.* 1. Zonen–; 2. ringförmig, gürtelartig. **zone** [zoun], **1.** *s.* 1. (*Geog.*) die Zone, der (Erd)gürtel; Landstrich, Bezirk, die Gegend, das Gebiet; (*Poet.*) der Gürtel; ***temperate*** (***frigid***) (***torrid***) **–**, gemäßigte (kalte) (heiße) Zone; 2. (*Poet.*) **– *of chastity,*** der Keuschheitsgürtel. **2.** *v.t.* in Zonen *or* Bezirke aufteilen. **zoning,** *s.* die Zonenabgrenzung.

[1]**zoo** [zu:], *s.* (*coll.*) der Zoo.

[2]**zoo-** [zouə], *pref.* tierisch, Tier–, Zoo–.

zooblast ['zouəblɑ:st], *s.* tierische Zelle.

zoochemistry [zouə'kemistri], *s.* die Zoochemie.

zoography [zou'ɔgrefi], *s.* beschreibende Zoologie.

zoolatry [zou'ɔlətri], *s.* die Tieranbetung.

zoolite ['zouəlait], *s.* der Zoolith, fossiles Tier.

zoological [zouə'lɔdʒikl], *adj.* zoologisch; **– *garden,*** zoologischer Garten, der Tiergarten. **zoologist** [–'ɔlədʒist], *s.* der Zoologe (die Zoologin).

zoom [zu:m], **1.** *v.i.* 1. laut summen *or* brummen; 2. hochschnellen; (*Av.*) in steilem Winkel hochfliegen, steil hochziehen, schnell (an)steigen. **2.** *v.t.* (*Av.*) hochreißen. **zoom-lens,** *s.* die Varioptik, (*coll.*) Gummilinse.

zoomorphic [zouə'mɔ:fik], *adj.* tiersymbolisch.

zoophyte ['zouəfait], *s.* das Pflanzentier, Hohltier, der *or* das Zoophyt.

zoosperm ['zouəspə:m], *s.* die Saumenzelle.

zootomy [zou'ɔtəmi], *s.* die Zootomie, Tieranatomie.

Zouave ['zu:ɑ:v], *s.* der Zuave.

zounds! [zaundz], *int.* (*obs.*) potztausend! Sakerment!

Zuider Zee ['zaidə'zi:], *s.* die Zuidersee, das Ijsselmeer.

Zurich ['zjuərik], *s.* Zürich (*n.*); ***Lake of* –**, der Zürichsee.

zygoma [zai'goumə], *s.* (*pl.* **-mata** [–'gɔmətə]) (*Anat.*) der Jochbogen. **zygomatic** [–gə'mætik], *adj.* Joch(bein)–; **– *arch, see* zygoma**; **– *bone,*** das Jochbein, Wangenbein. **zygote** ['zaigout], *s.* (*Biol.*) die Zygote.

zymosis [zai'mousis], *s.* die Gärung. **zymotic** [–'mɔtik], *adj.* 1. Gärungs–, gärend; 2. (*Med.*) ansteckend, Infektions–.